S0-BKV-068

California
1870
Census Index

Volume I

A - K

Western
Amer.
F
860
.C354
2001
v.1

University of the Pacific Library

If you are interested in any other genealogical products you may contact us at
www.heritagequest.com or
1-800-760-2455.

California 1870 Census Index

Volume I

A - K

Heritage Quest
North Salt Lake, Utah
2001

Heritage Quest, PO Box 540670, North Salt Lake, Utah 84054-0670

©2001, Heritage Quest. All rights reserved

Printed in the United States of America
05 04 03 02 01 5 4 3 2

ISBN 0-945433-98-0

Contents

Foreword

The Census Act of 1790 provided a mandate for counting the United States population at ten-year intervals. The purpose of the census was to insure proper citizen representation at the national level of government, the House of Representatives. Early census data is sparse and shows only the names of heads of household. Statistics of other family members are given by age group, sex, and race (either white or Negro).[1]

The Census Act was amended frequently over the years, however, and by 1850 the schedules reveal much more about individuals within each household. They include each person's name, age, sex, race, place of birth, and for those over 15 years of age, occupation. From 1850 to 1870, the Bureau of the Census collected data according to two designated units, district and subdivision. Districts usually corresponded to a State or part of a State and subdivision to a county or part thereof. Descriptions of these units, delineating boundaries, are available in microfilm as "Descriptions of Census Enumeration Districts, 1830-1890, and, 1910-1950 in National Archives Series T1224, available in 146 rolls. National Archives Series T1210 contains 10 rolls for 1900.[2]

This index volume has been greatly anticipated and promises to fill in many genealogical gaps. As for the census itself, it is not entirely accurate. Each census taker took to the road the first day of June 1870 with the task of completing the count within the subsequent five month period. One notable feature of this particular census is that events were to be recorded as though the census takers had performed their duties on June 1, 1870 regardless of when they actually visited a home. Adherence to the rule made for some awkward notations. Generally, all those who normally lived under the same roof as of June 1st were to be counted as members of that household, even if they were not home on the actual day the census takers dropped by. If a family member had died after June 1st but before the day the census taker visited, that individual was listed as still living. Conversely, infants born after June 1, 1870 were omitted from the listing even if they crawled up to the census taker and bit his leg.[3]

Forms for recording the 1870 schedules contained 20 columns with the following headings (punctuation and capitalization as found in the original):

1. Dwelling houses numbered in the order of visitation.
2. Families numbered in the order of visitation.
3. The name of every person whose place of abode on the first day of June, 1870 was in the family.

Description

4. Age at last birthday. If under 1 year, give months in fractions, thus 3/12.
5. Sex - Males (M), Females (F).
6. Color - White (W), Black (B), Mulatto (M), Chinese (C), Indian (I).
7. Profession, Occupation, or Trade of each person, male or female.

Real Estate Owned

8. Value of Real Estate.
9. Personal Property.
10. Place of Birth, State or Territory of the U.S., Country if foreign born.

Parentage

11. Father of foreign birth.
12. Mother of foreign birth.
13. If born within the year, state month (Jan., Feb., etc.).
14. If married within the year, state month (Jan., etc.).
15 Attended school within the year.

Education

16. Cannot read.
17. Cannot write.
18. Whether deaf and dumb, blind, insane or idiotic.

Constitutional Relations

19. Male Citizen of the U.S. of 21 years of age and upwards.
20. Male Citizen of U.S. 21 years of age and upwards whose right to vote is denied or abridged on other grounds than rebellion or other crime.

When using this index to find your ancestors, keep the following caveat in mind:

1. **Misspellings.** Census enumerators were not necessarily well educated, spelling was not standardized, and there was a high rate of illiteracy among the population. Thus, names were typically spelled as they sounded to the enumerators. In short, the art of transcribing unfamiliar surnames could have been as challenging as transliterating German to Chinese.

2. **Name changes.** Through the years, many people anglicized their names. For example: Schwartz became Black; Weiss became White; Zimmerman became Carpenter; and Schneider became Taylor. The list goes on.

3. **Variant Spellings.** If you know an ancestor was in a specific township or county, don't be discouraged if the name doesn't appear in the census index. Instead search for him

page by page in the last or the next census. His name might appear as a variant spelling you may have missed in the index.

4. **County boundary changes.** As states developed, the boundaries of their various townships and counties changed quite often. Hence, though a family may have remained in the same location, they may have been enumerated in a different township or county from year to year. To determine the correct county in which to search, refer to the map on page xxi.[5]

5. **Errors!** Two copies of the 1870 schedules were made. The intent was to keep the original copy in the courthouse of the County. A copy, transcribed from the original, was to be sent to the Federal courthouse for that jurisdiction, and a second copy was to be sent to Washington, D.C. The generation of handwritten copies made for many errors. In addition to errors made in recopying, many microfilm copies are difficult to read, and handwriting varies ... some good, some bad. Even the best indexer may make an error![6]

6. **Enumeration mistakes.** The enumerator might not have read his instructions. He could have listed a child born after 1 June when he visited the house on 20 August, or not listed a person still alive on 1 June who died between 2 June and 20 August. Or, Dad might have been helping a neighbor build a barn and would have been enumerated in the neighbor's household.

Finally, use your imagination and common sense in census research! Those of us who know how painstaking it is to read census page after census page applaud the publication of this computer generated index.

Good Hunting!

Jane Adams Clarke

Introduction

Format of the Index

The index is alphabetized by surname, given name, middle name or initial, occupation or title, age, and county. All entries that cannot be alphabetized, for whatever reason, are put at the beginning of the index.

Only Heads-of-Household are extracted with the following exceptions:

1. Someone residing within the home who has a different surname, regardless of age.
2. Any male 50 years of age or older.
3. Any female 70 years of age or older.
4. Any color or race change (where the surname stays the same). In this case the oldest person listed is extracted.
5. All individuals living in an institution such as an orphanage, hospital, or poor house.

Special Symbols and Markings

* Interpretation of the name is in doubt.

+ Spelling of the name while “unusual” is correct, as the census taker listed it.

? Portions of the name were illegible, due to a torn, smeared, or ink blotted page.

— The information was not given.

[ ] Brackets have been used to include additional information about the person listed. Such information might be occupation, title, malady, or miscellaneous information useful to the user.

Race Codes

W White
B Black
M Mulatto
I Indian
H Hispanic
O Oriental
C Chinese
J Japanese
X Mixed
— Not Given

In cities, the following designations are used to identify wards. A ward number precedes the designator -WD, for example:

1-WD 1st Ward
2-WD 2nd Ward
S-WD South Ward
N-WD North Ward

General Indexing Rules

When abbreviations appear in the entries on the microfilm they are spelled as-is. Since it is not always possible to tell exactly what an abbreviation stands for, they are normally not spelled out. For example:

Jas Brown would be entered as BROWN, Jas

One major exception to this rule occurs when the surname has been abbreviated. The name is extracted once, "as is," and then a second time "spelled out," if a highly probable name can be derived from the abbreviation. For example, if the census taker listed the name as Thadeus Wmwell it is extracted once as it is shown and then it is spelled out in a second (double) entry, Thadeus Williamwell, because it is unlikely that anyone would search for this individual under the abreviated spelling.

There is no space entered between compound names in the index. Apostrophes and hyphens are the only special punctuation marks used, and they are only used when the entry looks like a mistake without them. When the apostrophes are added it becomes clear that the D' is a contraction for De. When a surname has been hyphenated it is entered, as is, with the hyphen. For example:

SMITH-BARNEY, Juliet.

There are three special groups of names that do not neatly fit into any single category. They are: Nuns, Brothers (Ecclesiastical), and Indians.

After a woman has taken her final vows and begins her life as a nun, she is no longer addressed by her surname. She instead becomes Sister Mary, Sister Margaret, Sister Victoria, etc. Because of this, most nuns are listed simply as Sister "_____." In order to keep all the nuns who have not been listed with a surname in one area in the index, they are entered:

SISTER, Catherine
SISTER, Mary Beth
SISTER, Victoria

By entering them in this way, it is possible to make one quick search to see if any of the nuns is the person being sought. Should any of the nuns happen to be listed with a surname, they are entered as usual.

The same rules that apply to nuns apply to ecclesiastical brothers and to Indians, except that the word "BROTHER" or "INDIAN" is substituted for "SISTER." The terms "Brother" and "Indian" are used here as the surname and it is entered as above. If, however, they happen to be listed with a surname they are entered as usual.

There are some entries with no surname or given name listed on the census record. For entries with no name, three dashes have been used.

A bracketed area is used to include additional or miscellaneous information which might help conclusively identify the person. This includes, but is not limited to, occupations, titles, and maladies. They, however, are only entered when the given name is missing or when such information has been included in the name field on the microfilmed record. Examples are:

KILLAM, [Seamtress]
WOLSON, [Blacksmith]
FARNSWORTH, [Blind]
ADAMS, [Deceased-Estate]
BROOKS, [Insane-In Jail]
KONRAD, Wilhelm [Dr]
PATRIDGE, John [Barrister]
GRANT, U S [President]
PIPER, Jas [General]

In all cases, only important titles are placed in brackets. Brackets are not put around Mr., Ms., Mrs., Sir, Jr., or Sr.

Standard Abbreviations

Locality names such as Creek, River, Ward, etc. have been abbreviated. These abbreviations have been standardized and will be used consistently in all census indexes:

Ms	Miss	P O	Post Office
Mrs	Mistress	-WD	Ward
Mr	Mister	J-PCT	Justice Precinct
Jr	Junior	TWP	Township
Sr	Senior	CO	County
Wid	Widow	PAR	Parish
Rev	Reverend	DIST	District
Dr	Doctor	TERR	Territory
M D	Medical Doctor	BLVD	Boulevard
J P	Justice of the Peace	LN	Lane
Agt	Agent	RD	Road
BT	Beat	CRK	Creek
BORO	Borough	RVR	River

Occasionally, names have been entered twice. The reason for this is that if the name were extracted only as it is listed, it could be placed in a position in the index where most users would never think to look. In such cases, when appropriate, the name has been "double entered", once as it was listed and a second time as it should be listed. This is done only for "gross" errors in spelling or for highly likely different interpretations. For example, the census taker listed the name as Whosay Pelassquez when it should have been Jose Velassquez. It has been extracted this way:

PELASSQUEZ, Whosay (First time)
VELASSQUEZ, Jose (Second time)

When the interpretation of an entry is in doubt, an asterisk (*) is used to show this. If more than one interpretation is highly possible, it will be double-entered.

If part of the name is illegible due to a smeared, torn, or ink-blotted page; question marks are used to show this. Although the number of question marks has been designed to "roughly" show the number of letters perceived to be missing, after three, the value of adding additional question marks is dubious at best. Questions marks, however, are not used for difficult interpretations and never more than three question marks are used per entry. Therefore, if it appears that this entry could be the person bei ng sought, a check of the original microfilm is recommended. In all cases, it is important to remember that the person extracting the information has been trained to do what would be deemed the most helpful.

Occasionally, entries have been encountered that were plainly written and spelled but, appear to be errors. In these cases, a plus sign (+) has been entered after the entry to show that while it looks like an error, it is spelled as the census taker listed it. The plus sign has been used sparingly and only for “really strange” looking names. Example:

ZBREWSKI, Stanislaus+
SQAKAWSKI, William+

Page Numbers

Although most pages of the original census records show several different page numbers, this index uses the National Archives' numbers which were hand stamped in the upper right corner of the page when the records were bound into volumes. There are quite a few page numbering errors. Because of this, it is not unusual to find several pages listed with identical numbers. In addition, pages may even be listed as 491, 491a, 491b, or 491c. When a letter is included on the end of a page number, that page number is listed minus that letter.

Another problem is page numbers which were omitted. For example, if the page numbers were listed on the microfilm as 491, 492, 493, no number, 496, 497, the number 494 is used after page 493. It has been done this way because 494 would be the most logical choice. Page 495 would be omitted and the numbering would then commence with page 496 and continue in its regular fashion.

Although great care has been taken in reading and editing this index, errors may have occurred. In a continuous effort to improve the index the editors would appreciate being informed should any be found. Please send all corrections to:

Heritage Quest
PO Box 540670
North Salt Lake, UT 84054-0670

Table of Common Interpretations

The following table may be useful in looking for names in the census index. The letter the census taker intended to write is in the first column. The second column gives the most common alternative interpretations. These are given in a very rough order of probability. When unable to locate an entry as you expected to find it these other intrepretations should be routinely checked. For example, if you fail to find the name "Aaron," it might have been indexed as ADRAN, HARON, or even HOSAU. "Warren" might appear as WARNER or "Warner" as WARREN.

Letter	Possible Interpretation
A	H, C, O
a	o, u, ei
B	R, P, S
b	li, le, t, h, l
C	G, E, O, Ce
c	e, i, o, u
D	G, S, I, T
d	u, a, n, ie, ct, o
e	i, c
ee	u, n, ll, w
F	T, S, G
f	s, j, g, q, t
G	S, Q, Z, Ci
g	y, z, q
H	N, W, He, F
h	k, li, lc, le
I	J, L, S, T
i	e, c, l
ie	ei, u, ee, w
J	I, L, S
j	y, g, f
Jno	Mr, Mo
K	H, R, B
k	h, le lr, te
L	S, T, F
l	e, i, t
ll	tt, ee, u
M	W, H, N
m	w, rr, ni

Letter	Possible Interpretation
N	H, W, V, Ne
n	u, a, o, w, m
O	C, U, V, D
o	a, u, n, ei, tt
P	R, B, I
p	ss, g, js
Q	Z, D, I
q	g, y, z
R	Pi, B, S
r	e, s, i
S	L, I, J
s	r, i, e
sc	x
ss	fs, p, rr
T	F, S, L
t	l, f, ir, i
te	k
tt	ll
U	V, A, O
u	ee, a, o, n, w
V	N, W, li, Jr, B
v	u, n, b, rr
W	M, N, U
w	m, rr, ur
X	H, Z, N
x	sc, c, r
Y	F, Z, Q
y	g, q, j
Z	g, Q

Birthplace Codes

USA

AK Alaska
AL Alabama
AZ Arizona
CA California
CO Colorado
CT Connecticut
DC District of Columbia
DE Delaware
DTER Dakota Territory
FL Florida
GA Georgia
HI Hawaii
IA Iowa
ID Idaho
IL Illinois
IN Indiana
ITER Indian Territory
KS Kansas
KY Kentucky
LA Louisiana
MA Massachusetts
MD Maryland
ME Maine
MI Michigan
MN Minnesota
MO Missouri
MS Mississippi
MT Montana
NC North Carolina
ND North Dakota
NE Nebraska
NH New Hampshire
NJ New Jersey
NM New Mexico
NV Nevada
NY New York
OH Ohio
OK Oklahoma
OR Oregon
PA Pennsylvania
RI Rhode Island
SC South Carolina
SD South Dakota
TN Tennessee
TX Texas
UNKN Unknown
US United States
UT Utah
VA Virginia
VT Vermont
WA Washington
WI Wisconsin
WV West Virginia
WY Wyoming

FOREIGN

ABER Anhalt Bernburg
ADES Anhalt Dessau
AFRI Africa
ALGE Algeria
ALOR Alsace Lorraine (Elsass Lothringen)
ALSA Alsace
ANHA Anhalt
ANTI Antigua
ARAB Arabia
ARGE Argentina
ARME Armenia
ASEA At Sea
ASIA Asia
AUSL Australia
AUST Austria
AZOR Azores
BADE Baden
BAHA Bahamas
BARB Barbados
BAVA Bavaria (Bayern)
BELG Belguim
BENG Bengal
BERM Bermuda
BOHE Bohemia
BOSN Bosnia
BRAN Brandenburg
BRAZ Brazil
BREM Bremen
BRUN Brunswick (Braunschweig)
BUCH Buchau
BULG Bulgaria
BURM Burma
CAME Central America
CANA Canada
CAPE Cape of Good Hope
CEYL Ceylon
CHIL Chile
CHIN China
CISL Canary Islands
COLO Colombia
CROA Croatia
CUBA Cuba
CZEC Czechoslovakia
DALM Dalmatia
DENM Denmark
ECUA Ecuador
EGYP Egypt
EIND East Indies
ENGL England
EPRU Prussia (East) (Ostpreussen)
EURO Europe
FINL Finland
FLOW Lower Franconia (Unterfranken
FMID Middle Franconia (Mittelfranken)
FRAN France
FRNC Franconia
FRNH Frankenhausen
FRNK Frankfurt
FUPP Upper Franconia
GALI Galicia
GBRI Great Britain
GENO Genoa
GERM Germany
GIBR Gibraltar
GREE Greece
GREN Grenada
GUAD Guadaloupe
GUAM Guam
GUAT Guatemala
GUYA Guyana
HAIT Haiti

HAMB	Hamburg
HANO	Hanover
HCAS	Hesse Cassel (Kurhessen)
HDAR	Hesse Darmstadt
HESS	Hesse
HHEC	Hohenzollern (Hechingen)
HHOM	Hesse Homberg
HOHE	Hohenzollern
HOLD	Hesse Olddorf
HOLL	Holland
HOND	Honduras
HSIG	Hohenzollern (Sigmaringen)
HUNG	Hungary
ICEL	Iceland
INDI	India
IOFC	Isle of Corsica
IOFG	Isle of Guernsey
IOFM	Isle of Man
IOFW	Isle of Wight
IREL	Ireland
ITAL	Italy
ITER	Indian Territory
JAMA	Jamaica
JAPA	Japan
JERU	Jerusalem
JUTL	Jutland
LAUE	Lauenburg
LDET	Lipp Detmold
LIEC	Liechtenstein
LITH	Lithuania
LOMB	Lombardy
LSCH	Lippe Schaumberg
LUEB	Luebeck
LUXE	Luxemburg
MADE	Madera
MALT	Malta
MECK	Mecklenburg
MEXI	Mexico
MONT	Montenegro
MORA	Moravia
MORO	Morrocco
MSCH	Mecklenburg (Schwerin)
MSTR	Mecklenburg (Strelitz)
NCOD	No Code
NETH	Netherlands
NGRA	New Granada
NICA	Nicaragua
NISL	Nevis Island
NORW	Norway
NZEA	New Zealand
OEMP	Ottoman Empire
OLDE	Oldenburg
PALA	Palatinate
PALE	Palestine
PARA	Paraguay
PERS	Persia
PERU	Peru
PFAL	Pfalz
PHIL	Philippines
PIED	Piedmont
PLOW	Palatinate, Lower
POLA	Poland
POME	Pomerania (Pommern)
PORT	Portugal
POSE	Posen
PPFA	Palatinate, Pfalz
PRHE	Palatinate, Rhenish
PRIC	Puerto Rico
PRUS	Prussia
PSAX	Saxony-Province of
PUPP	Palatinate, Upper
RALL	Reuss Altere Linie
REUS	Reuss
RGRE	Reuss Griez
RHIN	Rhineland (Rheinprovinz)
RJUL	Reuss Jungere Linie
ROMA	Romania
ROST	Rostock
RSCG	Reuss Schleiz Gera
RSCH	Reuss Schleiz
RUSS	Russia
SALT	Saxony, Altenburg
SAME	South America
SARD	Sardinia
SAXO	Saxony-Kingdom of
SCAN	Scandinavia
SCHW	Schwarzburg
SCOG	Saxony (Coburg Gotha)
SCOT	Scotland
SCRO	St. Croix
SCRU	Santa Cruz
SDOM	Santo Domingo
SERB	Serbia
SHAN	Shanghai, China
SHOL	Schleswig Holstein (Rudolstadt)
SIAM	Siam
SICI	Sicily
SILE	Silesia (Schlesien)
SKIT	St. Kitts
SMAR	St. Martins
SMEI	Saxony, Meiningen
SPAI	Spain
SSON	Schwarzburg (Sondershausen)
STHO	St. Thomas
STUT	Stuttgart
SURI	Surinam
SVIN	St. Vincent
SWAB	Swabia
SWED	Sweden
SWEE	Saxony (Weimar Eisenach)
SWIT	Switzeralnd
SYRI	Syria
THUR	Thuringia
TRIN	Trinidad
TRIP	Tripoli
TURK	Turkey
TUSC	Tuscany
UKRA	Ukraine
UNKN	Unknown
URUG	Uruguay
VENE	Venezuela
VISL	Virgin Islands
WALD	Waldeck Hesse (Nassau)
WALE	Wales
WEST	Westphalia (Westfalen)
WIND	West Indies
WPRU	Prussia (West) (Westpreussen)
WURT	Württemberg
YUGO	Yugoslavia

California 1870 Census

Series M593

Name	Age	S	R	B-PL	County	Locale	Roll	Pg

---	45	m	w	UNKN	San Joaquin	2-Wd Stockton	86	171
---	40	m	c	CHIN	San Joaquin	Elliott Twp	86	73
---	38	m	c	CHIN	San Joaquin	Elliott Twp	86	72
---	37	m	c	CHIN	San Joaquin	Elliott Twp	86	73
---	34	m	c	CHIN	San Joaquin	2-Wd Stockton	86	161
---	30	m	c	CHIN	San Joaquin	Elliott Twp	86	74
---	30	m	c	CHIN	Sonoma	Petaluma Twp	91	342
---	30	m	c	CHIN	Sonoma	Petaluma Twp	91	342
---	30	m	c	CHIN	Sonoma	Petaluma Twp	91	342
---	30	m	c	CHIN	San Joaquin	Elliott Twp	86	73
---	3	m	c	CHIN	Sonoma	Petaluma Twp	91	342
---	28	m	c	CHIN	Sonoma	Petaluma Twp	91	342
---	28	m	c	CHIN	Sonoma	Petaluma Twp	91	342
---	27	m	c	CHIN	Sonoma	Petaluma Twp	91	342
---	27	m	c	CHIN	Sonoma	Petaluma Twp	91	342
---	24	m	c	CHIN	Sonoma	Petaluma Twp	91	342
---	24	m	c	CHIN	San Joaquin	Elliott Twp	86	75
---	23	m	c	CHIN	Sonoma	Petaluma Twp	91	342
---	22	m	c	CHIN	Sonoma	Petaluma Twp	91	342
---	21	m	c	CHIN	San Joaquin	2-Wd Stockton	86	161
---	21	m	c	CHIN	San Joaquin	Elliott Twp	86	73
---	20	m	c	CHIN	Sonoma	Petaluma Twp	91	342
---	20	m	c	CHIN	Sonoma	Petaluma Twp	91	342
---	19	m	c	CHIN	San Joaquin	Elliott Twp	86	73
---	18	m	c	CHIN	Sonoma	Petaluma Twp	91	342
---	16	m	c	CHIN	San Joaquin	Elliott Twp	86	73
---	15	f	b	US	San Francisco	11-Wd San Francisc	84	611
---	15	m	c	CHIN	Sonoma	Petaluma Twp	91	342
---	12	m	c	CHIN	Sonoma	Petaluma Twp	91	342
---	10	m	c	CHIN	Sonoma	Petaluma Twp	91	342
--- [Chinaman]	52	m	c	CHIN	Siskiyou	Yreka Twp	89	671
--- [Chinaman]	52	m	c	CHIN	Siskiyou	Yreka Twp	89	670
--- [Chinaman]	50	m	c	CHIN	Siskiyou	Scott Valley Twp	89	623
--- [Chinaman]	50	m	c	CHIN	Siskiyou	Yreka Twp	89	670
--- [Chinaman]	48	m	c	CHIN	Siskiyou	Cottonwood Twp	89	594
--- [Chinaman]	48	m	c	CHIN	Siskiyou	Yreka Twp	89	670
--- [Chinaman]	47	m	c	CHIN	Siskiyou	Yreka Twp	89	670
--- [Chinaman]	46	m	c	CHIN	Siskiyou	Cottonwood Twp	89	593
--- [Chinaman]	46	m	c	CHIN	Siskiyou	Butte Twp	89	586
--- [Chinaman]	46	m	c	CHIN	Siskiyou	Scott Valley Twp	89	622
--- [Chinaman]	46	m	c	CHIN	Siskiyou	Callahan P O	89	634
--- [Chinaman]	46	m	c	CHIN	Siskiyou	Scott Valley Twp	89	623
--- [Chinaman]	46	m	c	CHIN	Siskiyou	Yreka Twp	89	670
--- [Chinaman]	46	m	c	CHIN	Siskiyou	Yreka Twp	89	671
--- [Chinaman]	44	m	c	CHIN	Siskiyou	Hamburg Twp	89	598
--- [Chinaman]	44	m	c	CHIN	Siskiyou	Cottonwood Twp	89	593
--- [Chinaman]	44	m	c	CHIN	Siskiyou	Yreka	89	654
--- [Chinaman]	44	m	c	CHIN	Siskiyou	Yreka Twp	89	671
--- [Chinaman]	44	m	c	CHIN	Siskiyou	Yreka Twp	89	670
--- [Chinaman]	44	m	c	CHIN	Siskiyou	Yreka Twp	89	670
--- [Chinaman]	43	m	c	CHIN	Siskiyou	Scott Rvr Twp	89	607
--- [Chinaman]	43	m	c	CHIN	Siskiyou	Cottonwood Twp	89	592
--- [Chinaman]	42	m	c	CHIN	Siskiyou	Butte Twp	89	589
--- [Chinaman]	42	m	c	CHIN	Siskiyou	Scott Rvr Twp	89	605
--- [Chinaman]	42	m	c	CHIN	Siskiyou	Scott Rvr Twp	89	607
--- [Chinaman]	42	m	c	CHIN	Siskiyou	Scott Valley Twp	89	616
--- [Chinaman]	42	m	c	CHIN	Siskiyou	Callahan P O	89	635
--- [Chinaman]	42	m	c	CHIN	Siskiyou	Callahan P O	89	635
--- [Chinaman]	42	m	c	CHIN	Siskiyou	Scott Rvr Twp	89	606
--- [Chinaman]	42	m	c	CHIN	Siskiyou	Scott Rvr Twp	89	606
--- [Chinaman]	42	m	c	CHIN	Siskiyou	Scott Valley Twp	89	622
--- [Chinaman]	41	m	c	CHIN	Siskiyou	Scott Rvr Twp	89	607
--- [Chinaman]	41	m	c	CHIN	Siskiyou	Scott Valley Twp	89	622
--- [Chinaman]	41	m	c	CHIN	Siskiyou	Scott Valley Twp	89	623
--- [Chinaman]	41	m	c	CHIN	Siskiyou	Callahan P O	89	634
--- [Chinaman]	41	m	c	CHIN	Siskiyou	Callahan P O	89	635
--- [Chinaman]	41	m	c	CHIN	Siskiyou	Yreka Twp	89	671
--- [Chinaman]	41	m	c	CHIN	Siskiyou	Yreka Twp	89	671
--- [Chinaman]	41	m	c	CHIN	Siskiyou	Scott Rvr Twp	89	607
--- [Chinaman]	41	m	c	CHIN	Siskiyou	Scott Rvr Twp	89	607
--- [Chinaman]	41	m	c	CHIN	Siskiyou	Scott Valley Twp	89	623
--- [Chinaman]	41	m	c	CHIN	Siskiyou	Scott Valley Twp	89	620
--- [Chinaman]	41	m	c	CHIN	Siskiyou	Scott Valley Twp	89	623
--- [Chinaman]	41	m	c	CHIN	Siskiyou	Scott Valley Twp	89	623
--- [Chinaman]	41	m	c	CHIN	Siskiyou	Scott Valley Twp	89	623
--- [Chinaman]	41	m	c	CHIN	Siskiyou	Scott Valley Twp	89	616
--- [Chinaman]	41	m	c	CHIN	Siskiyou	Scott Valley Twp	89	622
--- [Chinaman]	41	m	c	CHIN	Siskiyou	Yreka Twp	89	670
--- [Chinaman]	40	m	c	CHIN	Siskiyou	Cottonwood Twp	89	592
--- [Chinaman]	40	m	c	CHIN	Siskiyou	Cottonwood Twp	89	593
--- [Chinaman]	40	m	c	CHIN	Siskiyou	Cottonwood Twp	89	593
--- [Chinaman]	40	m	c	CHIN	Siskiyou	Klamath Twp	89	600
--- [Chinaman]	40	m	c	CHIN	Siskiyou	Butte Twp	89	586
--- [Chinaman]	40	m	c	CHIN	Siskiyou	Cottonwood Twp	89	593
--- [Chinaman]	40	m	c	CHIN	Siskiyou	Cottonwood Twp	89	593
--- [Chinaman]	40	m	c	CHIN	Siskiyou	Cottonwood Twp	89	592
--- [Chinaman]	40	m	c	CHIN	Siskiyou	Klamath Twp	89	600
--- [Chinaman]	40	m	c	CHIN	Siskiyou	Cottonwood Twp	89	592
--- [Chinaman]	40	m	c	CHIN	Siskiyou	Cottonwood Twp	89	593
--- [Chinaman]	40	m	c	CHIN	Siskiyou	Cottonwood Twp	89	594
--- [Chinaman]	40	m	c	CHIN	Siskiyou	Scott Rvr Twp	89	607
--- [Chinaman]	40	m	c	CHIN	Siskiyou	Scott Rvr Twp	89	606
--- [Chinaman]	40	m	c	CHIN	Siskiyou	Scott Rvr Twp	89	605
--- [Chinaman]	40	m	c	CHIN	Siskiyou	Scott Valley Twp	89	617
--- [Chinaman]	40	m	c	CHIN	Siskiyou	Yreka	89	650
--- [Chinaman]	40	m	c	CHIN	Siskiyou	Scott Valley Twp	89	622

Series M593

Name	Age	S	R	B-PL	County	Locale	Roll	Pg
--- [Chinaman]	40	m	c	CHIN	Siskiyou	Scott Valley Twp	89	623
--- [Chinaman]	40	m	c	CHIN	Siskiyou	Callahan P O	89	634
--- [Chinaman]	40	m	c	CHIN	Siskiyou	Callahan P O	89	626
--- [Chinaman]	40	m	c	CHIN	Siskiyou	Callahan P O	89	633
--- [Chinaman]	40	m	c	CHIN	Siskiyou	Callahan P O	89	635
--- [Chinaman]	40	m	c	CHIN	Siskiyou	Callahan P O	89	635
--- [Chinaman]	40	m	c	CHIN	Siskiyou	Callahan P O	89	634
--- [Chinaman]	40	m	c	CHIN	Siskiyou	Callahan P O	89	634
--- [Chinaman]	40	m	c	CHIN	Siskiyou	Yreka Twp	89	670
--- [Chinaman]	40	m	c	CHIN	Siskiyou	Scott Rvr Twp	89	607
--- [Chinaman]	40	m	c	CHIN	Siskiyou	Scott Rvr Twp	89	607
--- [Chinaman]	40	m	c	CHIN	Siskiyou	Scott Valley Twp	89	616
--- [Chinaman]	40	m	c	CHIN	Siskiyou	Scott Rvr Twp	89	606
--- [Chinaman]	40	m	c	CHIN	Siskiyou	Scott Rvr Twp	89	605
--- [Chinaman]	40	m	c	CHIN	Siskiyou	Scott Valley Twp	89	620
--- [Chinaman]	40	m	c	CHIN	Siskiyou	Scott Rvr Twp	89	607
--- [Chinaman]	40	m	c	CHIN	Siskiyou	Scott Valley Twp	89	623
--- [Chinaman]	40	m	c	CHIN	Siskiyou	Scott Rvr Twp	89	606
--- [Chinaman]	40	m	c	CHIN	Siskiyou	Scott Rvr Twp	89	606
--- [Chinaman]	40	m	c	CHIN	Siskiyou	Scott Valley Twp	89	622
--- [Chinaman]	40	m	c	CHIN	Siskiyou	Scott Valley Twp	89	623
--- [Chinaman]	40	m	c	CHIN	Siskiyou	Scott Valley Twp	89	623
--- [Chinaman]	40	m	c	CHIN	Siskiyou	Scott Valley Twp	89	623
--- [Chinaman]	40	m	c	CHIN	Siskiyou	Yreka	89	654
--- [Chinaman]	40	m	c	CHIN	Siskiyou	Yreka Twp	89	671
--- [Chinaman]	40	m	c	CHIN	Siskiyou	Yreka Twp	89	671
--- [Chinaman]	39	m	c	CHIN	Siskiyou	Klamath Twp	89	600
--- [Chinaman]	39	m	c	CHIN	Siskiyou	Callahan P O	89	634
--- [Chinaman]	39	m	c	CHIN	Siskiyou	Scott Valley Twp	89	623
--- [Chinaman]	39	m	c	CHIN	Siskiyou	Callahan P O	89	635
--- [Chinaman]	39	m	c	CHIN	Siskiyou	Scott Valley Twp	89	617
--- [Chinaman]	38	m	c	CHIN	Siskiyou	Butte Twp	89	586
--- [Chinaman]	38	m	c	CHIN	Siskiyou	Scott Valley Twp	89	622
--- [Chinaman]	38	m	c	CHIN	Siskiyou	Callahan P O	89	633
--- [Chinaman]	38	m	c	CHIN	Siskiyou	Scott Valley Twp	89	620
--- [Chinaman]	38	m	c	CHIN	Siskiyou	Scott Valley Twp	89	617
--- [Chinaman]	38	m	c	CHIN	Siskiyou	Scott Valley Twp	89	620
--- [Chinaman]	38	m	c	CHIN	Siskiyou	Scott Valley Twp	89	616
--- [Chinaman]	37	m	c	CHIN	Siskiyou	Scott Rvr Twp	89	605
--- [Chinaman]	37	m	c	CHIN	Siskiyou	Scott Valley Twp	89	622
--- [Chinaman]	37	m	c	CHIN	Siskiyou	Scott Valley Twp	89	623
--- [Chinaman]	37	m	c	CHIN	Siskiyou	Scott Valley Twp	89	623
--- [Chinaman]	37	m	c	CHIN	Siskiyou	Callahan P O	89	634
--- [Chinaman]	37	m	c	CHIN	Siskiyou	Callahan P O	89	626
--- [Chinaman]	37	m	c	CHIN	Siskiyou	Callahan P O	89	635
--- [Chinaman]	37	m	c	CHIN	Siskiyou	Callahan P O	89	635
--- [Chinaman]	37	m	c	CHIN	Siskiyou	Callahan P O	89	635
--- [Chinaman]	37	m	c	CHIN	Siskiyou	Callahan P O	89	635
--- [Chinaman]	37	m	c	CHIN	Siskiyou	Callahan P O	89	634
--- [Chinaman]	37	m	c	CHIN	Siskiyou	Callahan P O	89	635
--- [Chinaman]	37	m	c	CHIN	Siskiyou	Callahan P O	89	635
--- [Chinaman]	37	m	c	CHIN	Siskiyou	Callahan P O	89	634
--- [Chinaman]	37	m	c	CHIN	Siskiyou	Scott Rvr Twp	89	607
--- [Chinaman]	37	m	c	CHIN	Siskiyou	Scott Valley Twp	89	622
--- [Chinaman]	37	m	c	CHIN	Siskiyou	Scott Rvr Twp	89	606
--- [Chinaman]	37	m	c	CHIN	Siskiyou	Scott Valley Twp	89	616
--- [Chinaman]	37	m	c	CHIN	Siskiyou	Scott Valley Twp	89	616
--- [Chinaman]	37	m	c	CHIN	Siskiyou	Callahan P O	89	626
--- [Chinaman]	37	m	c	CHIN	Siskiyou	Scott Valley Twp	89	623
--- [Chinaman]	37	m	c	CHIN	Siskiyou	Scott Valley Twp	89	617
--- [Chinaman]	37	m	c	CHIN	Siskiyou	Scott Valley Twp	89	623
--- [Chinaman]	37	m	c	CHIN	Siskiyou	Callahan P O	89	626
--- [Chinaman]	37	m	c	CHIN	Siskiyou	Callahan P O	89	633
--- [Chinaman]	37	m	c	CHIN	Siskiyou	Scott Valley Twp	89	622
--- [Chinaman]	36	m	c	CHIN	Siskiyou	Butte Twp	89	589
--- [Chinaman]	36	m	c	CHIN	Siskiyou	Klamath Twp	89	600
--- [Chinaman]	36	m	c	CHIN	Siskiyou	Klamath Twp	89	600
--- [Chinaman]	36	m	c	CHIN	Siskiyou	Klamath Twp	89	600
--- [Chinaman]	36	m	c	CHIN	Siskiyou	Klamath Twp	89	600
--- [Chinaman]	36	m	c	CHIN	Siskiyou	Klamath Twp	89	600
--- [Chinaman]	36	m	c	CHIN	Siskiyou	Klamath Twp	89	600
--- [Chinaman]	36	m	c	CHIN	Siskiyou	Scott Rvr Twp	89	602
--- [Chinaman]	36	m	c	CHIN	Siskiyou	Scott Rvr Twp	89	605
--- [Chinaman]	36	m	c	CHIN	Siskiyou	Scott Rvr Twp	89	607
--- [Chinaman]	36	m	c	CHIN	Siskiyou	Scott Rvr Twp	89	607
--- [Chinaman]	36	m	c	CHIN	Siskiyou	Scott Rvr Twp	89	606
--- [Chinaman]	36	m	c	CHIN	Siskiyou	Scott Valley Twp	89	617
--- [Chinaman]	36	m	c	CHIN	Siskiyou	Scott Valley Twp	89	620
--- [Chinaman]	36	m	c	CHIN	Siskiyou	Scott Valley Twp	89	621
--- [Chinaman]	36	m	c	CHIN	Siskiyou	Scott Valley Twp	89	622
--- [Chinaman]	36	m	c	CHIN	Siskiyou	Scott Valley Twp	89	622
--- [Chinaman]	36	m	c	CHIN	Siskiyou	Callahan P O	89	626
--- [Chinaman]	36	m	c	CHIN	Siskiyou	Scott Valley Twp	89	622
--- [Chinaman]	36	m	c	CHIN	Siskiyou	Callahan P O	89	635
--- [Chinaman]	36	m	c	CHIN	Siskiyou	Callahan P O	89	635
--- [Chinaman]	36	m	c	CHIN	Siskiyou	Scott Valley Twp	89	623
--- [Chinaman]	36	m	c	CHIN	Siskiyou	Scott Valley Twp	89	623
--- [Chinaman]	36	m	c	CHIN	Siskiyou	Callahan P O	89	633
--- [Chinaman]	36	m	c	CHIN	Siskiyou	Callahan P O	89	635
--- [Chinaman]	36	m	c	CHIN	Siskiyou	Callahan P O	89	634
--- [Chinaman]	36	m	c	CHIN	Siskiyou	Callahan P O	89	634
--- [Chinaman]	36	m	c	CHIN	Siskiyou	Yreka Twp	89	670
--- [Chinaman]	36	m	c	CHIN	Siskiyou	Cottonwood Twp	89	592
--- [Chinaman]	36	m	c	CHIN	Siskiyou	Scott Valley Twp	89	617
--- [Chinaman]	36	m	c	CHIN	Siskiyou	Scott Rvr Twp	89	603
--- [Chinaman]	36	m	c	CHIN	Siskiyou	Scott Valley Twp	89	622
--- [Chinaman]	36	m	c	CHIN	Siskiyou	Scott Rvr Twp	89	606

© 2001 by Heritage Quest. All rights reserved.

Name	Age	S	R	B-PL	County	Series M593 Locale	Roll	Pg
--- [Chinaman]	36	m	c	CHIN	Siskiyou	Scott Valley Twp	89	620
--- [Chinaman]	36	m	c	CHIN	Siskiyou	Scott Rvr Twp	89	605
--- [Chinaman]	36	m	c	CHIN	Siskiyou	Scott Valley Twp	89	621
--- [Chinaman]	36	m	c	CHIN	Siskiyou	Scott Rvr Twp	89	605
--- [Chinaman]	36	m	c	CHIN	Siskiyou	Scott Valley Twp	89	616
--- [Chinaman]	36	m	c	CHIN	Siskiyou	Scott Valley Twp	89	616
--- [Chinaman]	36	m	c	CHIN	Siskiyou	Scott Valley Twp	89	622
--- [Chinaman]	36	m	c	CHIN	Siskiyou	Scott Valley Twp	89	621
--- [Chinaman]	36	m	c	CHIN	Siskiyou	Scott Valley Twp	89	622
--- [Chinaman]	36	m	c	CHIN	Siskiyou	Scott Valley Twp	89	622
--- [Chinaman]	36	m	c	CHIN	Siskiyou	Callahan P O	89	633
--- [Chinaman]	36	m	c	CHIN	Siskiyou	Scott Valley Twp	89	622
--- [Chinaman]	36	m	c	CHIN	Siskiyou	Yreka Twp	89	670
--- [Chinaman]	36	m	c	CHIN	Siskiyou	Yreka Twp	89	671
--- [Chinaman]	36	m	c	CHIN	Siskiyou	Yreka Twp	89	670
--- [Chinaman]	36	m	c	CHIN	Siskiyou	Yreka Twp	89	671
--- [Chinaman]	35	m	c	CHIN	Siskiyou	Klamath Twp	89	600
--- [Chinaman]	35	m	c	CHIN	Siskiyou	Cottonwood Twp	89	593
--- [Chinaman]	35	m	c	CHIN	Siskiyou	Scott Rvr Twp	89	605
--- [Chinaman]	35	m	c	CHIN	Siskiyou	Scott Rvr Twp	89	606
--- [Chinaman]	35	m	c	CHIN	Siskiyou	Scott Rvr Twp	89	605
--- [Chinaman]	35	m	c	CHIN	Siskiyou	Scott Rvr Twp	89	605
--- [Chinaman]	35	m	c	CHIN	Siskiyou	Scott Rvr Twp	89	605
--- [Chinaman]	35	m	c	CHIN	Siskiyou	Scott Rvr Twp	89	606
--- [Chinaman]	35	m	c	CHIN	Siskiyou	Scott Rvr Twp	89	606
--- [Chinaman]	35	m	c	CHIN	Siskiyou	Scott Valley Twp	89	616
--- [Chinaman]	35	m	c	CHIN	Siskiyou	Callahan P O	89	634
--- [Chinaman]	35	m	c	CHIN	Siskiyou	Callahan P O	89	634
--- [Chinaman]	35	m	c	CHIN	Siskiyou	Scott Valley Twp	89	622
--- [Chinaman]	35	m	c	CHIN	Siskiyou	Callahan P O	89	634
--- [Chinaman]	35	m	c	CHIN	Siskiyou	Callahan P O	89	634
--- [Chinaman]	35	m	c	CHIN	Siskiyou	Callahan P O	89	634
--- [Chinaman]	35	m	c	CHIN	Siskiyou	Callahan P O	89	634
--- [Chinaman]	35	m	c	CHIN	Siskiyou	Scott Valley Twp	89	623
--- [Chinaman]	35	m	c	CHIN	Siskiyou	Callahan P O	89	634
--- [Chinaman]	35	m	c	CHIN	Siskiyou	Callahan P O	89	635
--- [Chinaman]	35	m	c	CHIN	Siskiyou	Callahan P O	89	635
--- [Chinaman]	35	m	c	CHIN	Siskiyou	Callahan P O	89	635
--- [Chinaman]	35	m	c	CHIN	Siskiyou	Callahan P O	89	633
--- [Chinaman]	35	m	c	CHIN	Siskiyou	Callahan P O	89	635
--- [Chinaman]	35	m	c	CHIN	Siskiyou	Callahan P O	89	634
--- [Chinaman]	35	m	c	CHIN	Siskiyou	Yreka	89	654
--- [Chinaman]	35	m	c	CHIN	Siskiyou	Callahan P O	89	634
--- [Chinaman]	35	m	c	CHIN	Siskiyou	Yreka	89	650
--- [Chinaman]	35	m	c	CHIN	Siskiyou	Callahan P O	89	634
--- [Chinaman]	35	m	c	CHIN	Siskiyou	Cottonwood Twp	89	593
--- [Chinaman]	35	m	c	CHIN	Siskiyou	Scott Valley Twp	89	616
--- [Chinaman]	35	m	c	CHIN	Siskiyou	Scott Rvr Twp	89	606
--- [Chinaman]	35	m	c	CHIN	Siskiyou	Scott Valley Twp	89	622
--- [Chinaman]	35	m	c	CHIN	Siskiyou	Scott Valley Twp	89	623
--- [Chinaman]	35	m	c	CHIN	Siskiyou	Scott Valley Twp	89	622
--- [Chinaman]	35	m	c	CHIN	Siskiyou	Scott Rvr Twp	89	605
--- [Chinaman]	35	m	c	CHIN	Siskiyou	Scott Valley Twp	89	616
--- [Chinaman]	35	m	c	CHIN	Siskiyou	Scott Rvr Twp	89	607
--- [Chinaman]	35	m	c	CHIN	Siskiyou	Scott Rvr Twp	89	607
--- [Chinaman]	35	m	c	CHIN	Siskiyou	Scott Valley Twp	89	620
--- [Chinaman]	35	m	c	CHIN	Siskiyou	Scott Valley Twp	89	622
--- [Chinaman]	35	m	c	CHIN	Siskiyou	Scott Valley Twp	89	620
--- [Chinaman]	35	m	c	CHIN	Siskiyou	Scott Rvr Twp	89	606
--- [Chinaman]	35	m	c	CHIN	Siskiyou	Scott Valley Twp	89	616
--- [Chinaman]	35	m	c	CHIN	Siskiyou	Scott Rvr Twp	89	607
--- [Chinaman]	35	m	c	CHIN	Siskiyou	Scott Valley Twp	89	616
--- [Chinaman]	35	m	c	CHIN	Siskiyou	Scott Valley Twp	89	616
--- [Chinaman]	35	m	c	CHIN	Siskiyou	Scott Valley Twp	89	620
--- [Chinaman]	35	m	c	CHIN	Siskiyou	Scott Valley Twp	89	623
--- [Chinaman]	35	m	c	CHIN	Siskiyou	Yreka	89	650
--- [Chinaman]	35	m	c	CHIN	Siskiyou	Yreka	89	650
--- [Chinaman]	35	m	c	CHIN	Siskiyou	Yreka Twp	89	670
--- [Chinaman]	34	m	c	CHIN	Siskiyou	Butte Twp	89	586
--- [Chinaman]	34	m	c	CHIN	Siskiyou	Scott Rvr Twp	89	605
--- [Chinaman]	34	m	c	CHIN	Siskiyou	Scott Rvr Twp	89	607
--- [Chinaman]	34	m	c	CHIN	Siskiyou	Callahan P O	89	634
--- [Chinaman]	34	m	c	CHIN	Siskiyou	Yreka Twp	89	670
--- [Chinaman]	34	m	c	CHIN	Siskiyou	Scott Rvr Twp	89	605
--- [Chinaman]	34	m	c	CHIN	Siskiyou	Scott Rvr Twp	89	605
--- [Chinaman]	34	m	c	CHIN	Siskiyou	Scott Rvr Twp	89	606
--- [Chinaman]	34	m	c	CHIN	Siskiyou	Scott Valley Twp	89	615
--- [Chinaman]	34	m	c	CHIN	Siskiyou	Scott Valley Twp	89	623
--- [Chinaman]	34	m	c	CHIN	Siskiyou	Yreka Twp	89	671
--- [Chinaman]	34	m	c	CHIN	Siskiyou	Yreka Twp	89	671
--- [Chinaman]	33	m	c	CHIN	Siskiyou	Hamburg Twp	89	598
--- [Chinaman]	33	m	c	CHIN	Siskiyou	Cottonwood Twp	89	593
--- [Chinaman]	33	m	c	CHIN	Siskiyou	Cottonwood Twp	89	592
--- [Chinaman]	33	m	c	CHIN	Siskiyou	Hamburg Twp	89	598
--- [Chinaman]	33	m	c	CHIN	Siskiyou	Scott Rvr Twp	89	607
--- [Chinaman]	33	m	c	CHIN	Siskiyou	Klamath Twp	89	600
--- [Chinaman]	33	m	c	CHIN	Siskiyou	Scott Valley Twp	89	621
--- [Chinaman]	33	m	c	CHIN	Siskiyou	Callahan P O	89	635
--- [Chinaman]	33	m	c	CHIN	Siskiyou	Callahan P O	89	635
--- [Chinaman]	33	m	c	CHIN	Siskiyou	Scott Valley Twp	89	622
--- [Chinaman]	33	m	c	CHIN	Siskiyou	Callahan P O	89	634
--- [Chinaman]	33	m	c	CHIN	Siskiyou	Butte Twp	89	586
--- [Chinaman]	33	m	c	CHIN	Siskiyou	Scott Rvr Twp	89	605
--- [Chinaman]	33	m	c	CHIN	Siskiyou	Scott Rvr Twp	89	607
--- [Chinaman]	33	m	c	CHIN	Siskiyou	Scott Rvr Twp	89	605
--- [Chinaman]	33	m	c	CHIN	Siskiyou	Scott Valley Twp	89	622
--- [Chinaman]	33	m	c	CHIN	Siskiyou	Scott Valley Twp	89	621
--- [Chinaman]	33	m	c	CHIN	Siskiyou	Scott Rvr Twp	89	605
--- [Chinaman]	33	m	c	CHIN	Siskiyou	Scott Valley Twp	89	623
--- [Chinaman]	33	m	c	CHIN	Siskiyou	Yreka Twp	89	670
--- [Chinaman]	33	m	c	CHIN	Siskiyou	Yreka Twp	89	670
--- [Chinaman]	33	m	c	CHIN	Siskiyou	Yreka Twp	89	671
--- [Chinaman]	33	m	c	CHIN	Siskiyou	Yreka Twp	89	671
--- [Chinaman]	32	m	c	CHIN	Siskiyou	Scott Rvr Twp	89	605
--- [Chinaman]	32	m	c	CHIN	Siskiyou	Scott Rvr Twp	89	602
--- [Chinaman]	32	m	c	CHIN	Siskiyou	Scott Rvr Twp	89	606
--- [Chinaman]	32	m	c	CHIN	Siskiyou	Scott Rvr Twp	89	605
--- [Chinaman]	32	m	c	CHIN	Siskiyou	Scott Rvr Twp	89	606
--- [Chinaman]	32	m	c	CHIN	Siskiyou	Scott Rvr Twp	89	606
--- [Chinaman]	32	m	c	CHIN	Siskiyou	Callahan P O	89	633
--- [Chinaman]	32	m	c	CHIN	Siskiyou	Scott Valley Twp	89	623
--- [Chinaman]	32	m	c	CHIN	Siskiyou	Callahan P O	89	635
--- [Chinaman]	32	m	c	CHIN	Siskiyou	Callahan P O	89	634
--- [Chinaman]	32	m	c	CHIN	Siskiyou	Callahan P O	89	635
--- [Chinaman]	32	m	c	CHIN	Siskiyou	Callahan P O	89	635
--- [Chinaman]	32	m	c	CHIN	Siskiyou	Callahan P O	89	634
--- [Chinaman]	32	m	c	CHIN	Siskiyou	Callahan P O	89	634
--- [Chinaman]	32	m	c	CHIN	Siskiyou	Callahan P O	89	634
--- [Chinaman]	32	m	c	CHIN	Siskiyou	Callahan P O	89	634
--- [Chinaman]	32	m	c	CHIN	Siskiyou	Scott Rvr Twp	89	606
--- [Chinaman]	32	m	c	CHIN	Siskiyou	Scott Rvr Twp	89	606
--- [Chinaman]	32	m	c	CHIN	Siskiyou	Scott Rvr Twp	89	607
--- [Chinaman]	32	m	c	CHIN	Siskiyou	Scott Valley Twp	89	621
--- [Chinaman]	32	m	c	CHIN	Siskiyou	Scott Valley Twp	89	623
--- [Chinaman]	32	m	c	CHIN	Siskiyou	Scott Valley Twp	89	623
--- [Chinaman]	32	m	c	CHIN	Siskiyou	Scott Valley Twp	89	616
--- [Chinaman]	32	m	c	CHIN	Siskiyou	Scott Valley Twp	89	623
--- [Chinaman]	32	m	c	CHIN	Siskiyou	Scott Valley Twp	89	620
--- [Chinaman]	32	m	c	CHIN	Siskiyou	Scott Valley Twp	89	622
--- [Chinaman]	32	m	c	CHIN	Siskiyou	Scott Valley Twp	89	623
--- [Chinaman]	32	m	c	CHIN	Siskiyou	Yreka Twp	89	670
--- [Chinaman]	32	m	c	CHIN	Siskiyou	Yreka Twp	89	670
--- [Chinaman]	31	m	c	CHIN	Siskiyou	Cottonwood Twp	89	592
--- [Chinaman]	31	m	c	CHIN	Siskiyou	Scott Rvr Twp	89	602
--- [Chinaman]	31	m	c	CHIN	Siskiyou	Scott Rvr Twp	89	605
--- [Chinaman]	31	m	c	CHIN	Siskiyou	Scott Rvr Twp	89	605
--- [Chinaman]	31	m	c	CHIN	Siskiyou	Klamath Twp	89	600
--- [Chinaman]	31	m	c	CHIN	Siskiyou	Scott Rvr Twp	89	606
--- [Chinaman]	31	m	c	CHIN	Siskiyou	Scott Rvr Twp	89	606
--- [Chinaman]	31	m	c	CHIN	Siskiyou	Scott Rvr Twp	89	606
--- [Chinaman]	31	m	c	CHIN	Siskiyou	Scott Rvr Twp	89	605
--- [Chinaman]	31	m	c	CHIN	Siskiyou	Callahan P O	89	635
--- [Chinaman]	31	m	c	CHIN	Siskiyou	Scott Valley Twp	89	622
--- [Chinaman]	31	m	c	CHIN	Siskiyou	Callahan P O	89	635
--- [Chinaman]	31	m	c	CHIN	Siskiyou	Callahan P O	89	635
--- [Chinaman]	31	m	c	CHIN	Siskiyou	Callahan P O	89	633
--- [Chinaman]	31	m	c	CHIN	Siskiyou	Callahan P O	89	635
--- [Chinaman]	31	m	c	CHIN	Siskiyou	Yreka Twp	89	671
--- [Chinaman]	31	m	c	CHIN	Siskiyou	Yreka Twp	89	670
--- [Chinaman]	31	m	c	CHIN	Siskiyou	Butte Twp	89	586
--- [Chinaman]	31	m	c	CHIN	Siskiyou	Scott Rvr Twp	89	605
--- [Chinaman]	31	m	c	CHIN	Siskiyou	Scott Rvr Twp	89	606
--- [Chinaman]	31	m	c	CHIN	Siskiyou	Scott Rvr Twp	89	606
--- [Chinaman]	31	m	c	CHIN	Siskiyou	Scott Rvr Twp	89	606
--- [Chinaman]	31	m	c	CHIN	Siskiyou	Scott Rvr Twp	89	606
--- [Chinaman]	31	m	c	CHIN	Siskiyou	Scott Rvr Twp	89	607
--- [Chinaman]	31	m	c	CHIN	Siskiyou	Scott Rvr Twp	89	607
--- [Chinaman]	31	m	c	CHIN	Siskiyou	Scott Valley Twp	89	616
--- [Chinaman]	31	m	c	CHIN	Siskiyou	Callahan P O	89	626
--- [Chinaman]	31	m	c	CHIN	Siskiyou	Scott Rvr Twp	89	606
--- [Chinaman]	31	m	c	CHIN	Siskiyou	Scott Rvr Twp	89	606
--- [Chinaman]	31	m	c	CHIN	Siskiyou	Scott Valley Twp	89	623
--- [Chinaman]	31	m	c	CHIN	Siskiyou	Callahan P O	89	626
--- [Chinaman]	31	m	c	CHIN	Siskiyou	Scott Valley Twp	89	622
--- [Chinaman]	31	m	c	CHIN	Siskiyou	Scott Valley Twp	89	622
--- [Chinaman]	31	m	c	CHIN	Siskiyou	Scott Valley Twp	89	620
--- [Chinaman]	31	m	c	CHIN	Siskiyou	Callahan P O	89	626
--- [Chinaman]	31	m	c	CHIN	Siskiyou	Scott Valley Twp	89	622
--- [Chinaman]	31	m	c	CHIN	Siskiyou	Scott Valley Twp	89	623
--- [Chinaman]	31	m	c	CHIN	Siskiyou	Scott Valley Twp	89	616
--- [Chinaman]	31	m	c	CHIN	Siskiyou	Scott Valley Twp	89	621
--- [Chinaman]	31	m	c	CHIN	Siskiyou	Scott Valley Twp	89	616
--- [Chinaman]	31	m	c	CHIN	Siskiyou	Scott Valley Twp	89	622
--- [Chinaman]	31	m	c	CHIN	Siskiyou	Scott Valley Twp	89	622
--- [Chinaman]	31	m	c	CHIN	Siskiyou	Scott Valley Twp	89	623
--- [Chinaman]	31	m	c	CHIN	Siskiyou	Yreka Twp	89	670
--- [Chinaman]	31	m	c	CHIN	Siskiyou	Yreka Twp	89	671
--- [Chinaman]	30	m	c	CHIN	Siskiyou	Klamath Twp	89	601
--- [Chinaman]	30	m	c	CHIN	Siskiyou	Klamath Twp	89	600
--- [Chinaman]	30	m	c	CHIN	Siskiyou	Hamburg Twp	89	598
--- [Chinaman]	30	m	c	CHIN	Siskiyou	Cottonwood Twp	89	593
--- [Chinaman]	30	m	c	CHIN	Siskiyou	Klamath Twp	89	600
--- [Chinaman]	30	m	c	CHIN	Siskiyou	Scott Rvr Twp	89	605
--- [Chinaman]	30	m	c	CHIN	Siskiyou	Scott Rvr Twp	89	606
--- [Chinaman]	30	m	c	CHIN	Siskiyou	Cottonwood Twp	89	593
--- [Chinaman]	30	m	c	CHIN	Siskiyou	Cottonwood Twp	89	594
--- [Chinaman]	30	m	c	CHIN	Siskiyou	Scott Rvr Twp	89	606
--- [Chinaman]	30	m	c	CHIN	Siskiyou	Scott Rvr Twp	89	607
--- [Chinaman]	30	m	c	CHIN	Siskiyou	Scott Rvr Twp	89	607
--- [Chinaman]	30	m	c	CHIN	Siskiyou	Klamath Twp	89	600
--- [Chinaman]	30	m	c	CHIN	Siskiyou	Scott Rvr Twp	89	606
--- [Chinaman]	30	m	c	CHIN	Siskiyou	Scott Rvr Twp	89	606
--- [Chinaman]	30	m	c	CHIN	Siskiyou	Cottonwood Twp	89	594
--- [Chinaman]	30	m	c	CHIN	Siskiyou	Scott Rvr Twp	89	606

© 2001 by Heritage Quest. All rights reserved.

Name	Age	S	R	B-PL	County	Locale	Roll	Pg
--- [Chinaman]	30	m	c	CHIN	Siskiyou	Scott Rvr Twp	89	606
--- [Chinaman]	30	m	c	CHIN	Siskiyou	Scott Rvr Twp	89	606
--- [Chinaman]	30	m	c	CHIN	Siskiyou	Klamath Twp	89	601
--- [Chinaman]	30	m	c	CHIN	Siskiyou	Scott Rvr Twp	89	605
--- [Chinaman]	30	m	c	CHIN	Siskiyou	Scott Rvr Twp	89	606
--- [Chinaman]	30	m	c	CHIN	Siskiyou	Scott Valley Twp	89	617
--- [Chinaman]	30	m	c	CHIN	Siskiyou	Callahan P O	89	626
--- [Chinaman]	30	m	c	CHIN	Siskiyou	Yreka	89	650
--- [Chinaman]	30	m	c	CHIN	Siskiyou	Scott Valley Twp	89	623
--- [Chinaman]	30	m	c	CHIN	Siskiyou	Scott Valley Twp	89	623
--- [Chinaman]	30	m	c	CHIN	Siskiyou	Callahan P O	89	634
--- [Chinaman]	30	m	c	CHIN	Siskiyou	Callahan P O	89	634
--- [Chinaman]	30	m	c	CHIN	Siskiyou	Scott Valley Twp	89	622
--- [Chinaman]	30	m	c	CHIN	Siskiyou	Callahan P O	89	626
--- [Chinaman]	30	m	c	CHIN	Siskiyou	Callahan P O	89	628
--- [Chinaman]	30	m	c	CHIN	Siskiyou	Callahan P O	89	634
--- [Chinaman]	30	m	c	CHIN	Siskiyou	Callahan P O	89	635
--- [Chinaman]	30	m	c	CHIN	Siskiyou	Callahan P O	89	635
--- [Chinaman]	30	m	c	CHIN	Siskiyou	Callahan P O	89	634
--- [Chinaman]	30	m	c	CHIN	Siskiyou	Callahan P O	89	634
--- [Chinaman]	30	m	c	CHIN	Siskiyou	Callahan P O	89	634
--- [Chinaman]	30	m	c	CHIN	Siskiyou	Callahan P O	89	634
--- [Chinaman]	30	m	c	CHIN	Siskiyou	Yreka Twp	89	671
--- [Chinaman]	30	m	c	CHIN	Siskiyou	Yreka Twp	89	671
--- [Chinaman]	30	m	c	CHIN	Siskiyou	Yreka Twp	89	670
--- [Chinaman]	30	m	c	CHIN	Siskiyou	Yreka Twp	89	670
--- [Chinaman]	30	m	c	CHIN	Siskiyou	Yreka Twp	89	670
--- [Chinaman]	30	m	c	CHIN	Sacramento	4-Wd Sacramento	77	349
--- [Chinaman]	30	m	c	CHIN	Siskiyou	Butte Twp	89	586
--- [Chinaman]	30	m	c	CHIN	Siskiyou	Scott Rvr Twp	89	607
--- [Chinaman]	30	m	c	CHIN	Siskiyou	Scott Rvr Twp	89	606
--- [Chinaman]	30	m	c	CHIN	Siskiyou	Scott Valley Twp	89	616
--- [Chinaman]	30	m	c	CHIN	Siskiyou	Scott Rvr Twp	89	605
--- [Chinaman]	30	m	c	CHIN	Siskiyou	Scott Valley Twp	89	616
--- [Chinaman]	30	m	c	CHIN	Siskiyou	Scott Rvr Twp	89	603
--- [Chinaman]	30	m	c	CHIN	Siskiyou	Scott Rvr Twp	89	605
--- [Chinaman]	30	m	c	CHIN	Siskiyou	Scott Rvr Twp	89	606
--- [Chinaman]	30	m	c	CHIN	Siskiyou	Scott Rvr Twp	89	607
--- [Chinaman]	30	m	c	CHIN	Siskiyou	Scott Valley Twp	89	616
--- [Chinaman]	30	m	c	CHIN	Siskiyou	Scott Rvr Twp	89	607
--- [Chinaman]	30	m	c	CHIN	Siskiyou	Scott Rvr Twp	89	605
--- [Chinaman]	30	m	c	CHIN	Siskiyou	Scott Valley Twp	89	621
--- [Chinaman]	30	m	c	CHIN	Siskiyou	Scott Valley Twp	89	623
--- [Chinaman]	30	m	c	CHIN	Siskiyou	Scott Valley Twp	89	620
--- [Chinaman]	30	m	c	CHIN	Siskiyou	Scott Rvr Twp	89	605
--- [Chinaman]	30	m	c	CHIN	Siskiyou	Scott Rvr Twp	89	606
--- [Chinaman]	30	m	c	CHIN	Siskiyou	Scott Rvr Twp	89	606
--- [Chinaman]	30	m	c	CHIN	Siskiyou	Scott Valley Twp	89	616
--- [Chinaman]	30	m	c	CHIN	Siskiyou	Scott Valley Twp	89	617
--- [Chinaman]	30	m	c	CHIN	Siskiyou	Scott Valley Twp	89	623
--- [Chinaman]	30	m	c	CHIN	Siskiyou	Callahan P O	89	626
--- [Chinaman]	30	m	c	CHIN	Siskiyou	Scott Valley Twp	89	620
--- [Chinaman]	30	m	c	CHIN	Siskiyou	Scott Valley Twp	89	623
--- [Chinaman]	30	m	c	CHIN	Siskiyou	Scott Valley Twp	89	620
--- [Chinaman]	30	m	c	CHIN	Siskiyou	Scott Valley Twp	89	622
--- [Chinaman]	30	m	c	CHIN	Siskiyou	Callahan P O	89	626
--- [Chinaman]	30	m	c	CHIN	Siskiyou	Callahan P O	89	633
--- [Chinaman]	30	m	c	CHIN	Siskiyou	Scott Valley Twp	89	622
--- [Chinaman]	30	m	c	CHIN	Siskiyou	Callahan P O	89	634
--- [Chinaman]	30	m	c	CHIN	Siskiyou	Scott Valley Twp	89	622
--- [Chinaman]	30	m	c	CHIN	Siskiyou	Scott Valley Twp	89	622
--- [Chinaman]	30	m	c	CHIN	Siskiyou	Callahan P O	89	626
--- [Chinaman]	30	m	c	CHIN	Siskiyou	Yreka	89	650
--- [Chinaman]	30	m	c	CHIN	Siskiyou	Yreka	89	650
--- [Chinaman]	30	m	c	CHIN	Siskiyou	Yreka Twp	89	670
--- [Chinaman]	30	m	c	CHIN	Siskiyou	Yreka Twp	89	671
--- [Chinaman]	30	m	c	CHIN	Siskiyou	Yreka Twp	89	671
--- [Chinaman]	30	m	c	CHIN	Siskiyou	Yreka Twp	89	670
--- [Chinaman]	30	m	c	CHIN	Siskiyou	Yreka Twp	89	671
--- [Chinaman]	30	m	c	CHIN	Siskiyou	Yreka Twp	89	671
--- [Chinaman]	29	m	c	CHIN	Siskiyou	Klamath Twp	89	600
--- [Chinaman]	29	m	c	CHIN	Siskiyou	Klamath Twp	89	601
--- [Chinaman]	29	m	c	CHIN	Siskiyou	Scott Rvr Twp	89	605
--- [Chinaman]	29	m	c	CHIN	Siskiyou	Scott Rvr Twp	89	607
--- [Chinaman]	29	m	c	CHIN	Siskiyou	Scott Rvr Twp	89	607
--- [Chinaman]	29	m	c	CHIN	Siskiyou	Callahan P O	89	633
--- [Chinaman]	29	m	c	CHIN	Siskiyou	Callahan P O	89	633
--- [Chinaman]	29	m	c	CHIN	Siskiyou	Callahan P O	89	634
--- [Chinaman]	29	m	c	CHIN	Siskiyou	Callahan P O	89	635
--- [Chinaman]	29	m	c	CHIN	Siskiyou	Callahan P O	89	635
--- [Chinaman]	29	m	c	CHIN	Siskiyou	Callahan P O	89	634
--- [Chinaman]	29	m	c	CHIN	Siskiyou	Scott Valley Twp	89	622
--- [Chinaman]	29	m	c	CHIN	Siskiyou	Scott Valley Twp	89	622
--- [Chinaman]	29	m	c	CHIN	Siskiyou	Scott Valley Twp	89	623
--- [Chinaman]	29	m	c	CHIN	Siskiyou	Scott Valley Twp	89	623
--- [Chinaman]	29	m	c	CHIN	Siskiyou	Callahan P O	89	633
--- [Chinaman]	29	m	c	CHIN	Siskiyou	Callahan P O	89	634
--- [Chinaman]	29	m	c	CHIN	Siskiyou	Scott Valley Twp	89	623
--- [Chinaman]	29	m	c	CHIN	Siskiyou	Callahan P O	89	635
--- [Chinaman]	29	m	c	CHIN	Siskiyou	Callahan P O	89	634
--- [Chinaman]	29	m	c	CHIN	Siskiyou	Callahan P O	89	634
--- [Chinaman]	29	m	c	CHIN	Siskiyou	Callahan P O	89	635
--- [Chinaman]	29	m	c	CHIN	Siskiyou	Callahan P O	89	635
--- [Chinaman]	29	m	c	CHIN	Siskiyou	Scott Valley Twp	89	622
--- [Chinaman]	29	m	c	CHIN	Siskiyou	Scott Rvr Twp	89	606
--- [Chinaman]	29	m	c	CHIN	Siskiyou	Scott Rvr Twp	89	605
--- [Chinaman]	29	m	c	CHIN	Siskiyou	Scott Rvr Twp	89	607
--- [Chinaman]	29	m	c	CHIN	Siskiyou	Scott Valley Twp	89	623
--- [Chinaman]	29	m	c	CHIN	Siskiyou	Scott Rvr Twp	89	605
--- [Chinaman]	29	m	c	CHIN	Siskiyou	Scott Valley Twp	89	620
--- [Chinaman]	29	m	c	CHIN	Siskiyou	Scott Valley Twp	89	617
--- [Chinaman]	29	m	c	CHIN	Siskiyou	Callahan P O	89	626
--- [Chinaman]	29	m	c	CHIN	Siskiyou	Scott Valley Twp	89	620
--- [Chinaman]	29	m	c	CHIN	Siskiyou	Scott Valley Twp	89	622
--- [Chinaman]	29	m	c	CHIN	Siskiyou	Scott Valley Twp	89	622
--- [Chinaman]	29	m	c	CHIN	Siskiyou	Callahan P O	89	629
--- [Chinaman]	28	m	c	CHIN	Siskiyou	Cottonwood Twp	89	592
--- [Chinaman]	28	m	c	CHIN	Siskiyou	Klamath Twp	89	600
--- [Chinaman]	28	m	c	CHIN	Siskiyou	Butte Twp	89	585
--- [Chinaman]	28	m	c	CHIN	Siskiyou	Scott Rvr Twp	89	605
--- [Chinaman]	28	m	c	CHIN	Siskiyou	Scott Rvr Twp	89	605
--- [Chinaman]	28	m	c	CHIN	Siskiyou	Scott Rvr Twp	89	607
--- [Chinaman]	28	m	c	CHIN	Siskiyou	Callahan P O	89	635
--- [Chinaman]	28	m	c	CHIN	Siskiyou	Callahan P O	89	634
--- [Chinaman]	28	m	c	CHIN	Siskiyou	Callahan P O	89	634
--- [Chinaman]	28	m	c	CHIN	Siskiyou	Callahan P O	89	635
--- [Chinaman]	28	m	c	CHIN	Siskiyou	Callahan P O	89	634
--- [Chinaman]	28	m	c	CHIN	Siskiyou	Callahan P O	89	634
--- [Chinaman]	28	m	c	CHIN	Siskiyou	Yreka Twp	89	670
--- [Chinaman]	28	m	c	CHIN	Siskiyou	Yreka Twp	89	670
--- [Chinaman]	28	m	c	CHIN	Siskiyou	Scott Valley Twp	89	616
--- [Chinaman]	28	m	c	CHIN	Siskiyou	Scott Rvr Twp	89	607
--- [Chinaman]	28	m	c	CHIN	Siskiyou	Scott Rvr Twp	89	607
--- [Chinaman]	28	m	c	CHIN	Siskiyou	Scott Valley Twp	89	622
--- [Chinaman]	28	m	c	CHIN	Siskiyou	Scott Valley Twp	89	617
--- [Chinaman]	28	m	c	CHIN	Siskiyou	Scott Valley Twp	89	622
--- [Chinaman]	28	m	c	CHIN	Siskiyou	Scott Valley Twp	89	622
--- [Chinaman]	28	m	c	CHIN	Siskiyou	Scott Valley Twp	89	621
--- [Chinaman]	28	m	c	CHIN	Siskiyou	Scott Valley Twp	89	622
--- [Chinaman]	28	m	c	CHIN	Siskiyou	Scott Valley Twp	89	623
--- [Chinaman]	28	m	c	CHIN	Siskiyou	Scott Valley Twp	89	622
--- [Chinaman]	28	m	c	CHIN	Siskiyou	Scott Valley Twp	89	622
--- [Chinaman]	28	m	c	CHIN	Siskiyou	Yreka Twp	89	670
--- [Chinaman]	28	m	c	CHIN	Siskiyou	Yreka Twp	89	671
--- [Chinaman]	28	m	c	CHIN	Siskiyou	Yreka Twp	89	671
--- [Chinaman]	28	m	c	CHIN	Siskiyou	Yreka Twp	89	670
--- [Chinaman]	28	m	c	CHIN	Siskiyou	Yreka Twp	89	670
--- [Chinaman]	28	m	c	CHIN	Siskiyou	Yreka Twp	89	671
--- [Chinaman]	27	m	c	CHIN	Siskiyou	Klamath Twp	89	600
--- [Chinaman]	27	m	c	CHIN	Siskiyou	Klamath Twp	89	600
--- [Chinaman]	27	m	c	CHIN	Siskiyou	Scott Rvr Twp	89	606
--- [Chinaman]	27	m	c	CHIN	Siskiyou	Scott Rvr Twp	89	605
--- [Chinaman]	27	m	c	CHIN	Siskiyou	Scott Rvr Twp	89	605
--- [Chinaman]	27	m	c	CHIN	Siskiyou	Scott Rvr Twp	89	605
--- [Chinaman]	27	m	c	CHIN	Siskiyou	Scott Rvr Twp	89	605
--- [Chinaman]	27	m	c	CHIN	Siskiyou	Scott Rvr Twp	89	606
--- [Chinaman]	27	m	c	CHIN	Siskiyou	Scott Valley Twp	89	622
--- [Chinaman]	27	m	c	CHIN	Siskiyou	Callahan P O	89	626
--- [Chinaman]	27	m	c	CHIN	Siskiyou	Scott Valley Twp	89	623
--- [Chinaman]	27	m	c	CHIN	Siskiyou	Scott Valley Twp	89	623
--- [Chinaman]	27	m	c	CHIN	Siskiyou	Scott Valley Twp	89	623
--- [Chinaman]	27	m	c	CHIN	Siskiyou	Callahan P O	89	633
--- [Chinaman]	27	m	c	CHIN	Siskiyou	Scott Valley Twp	89	623
--- [Chinaman]	27	m	c	CHIN	Siskiyou	Scott Valley Twp	89	622
--- [Chinaman]	27	m	c	CHIN	Siskiyou	Callahan P O	89	634
--- [Chinaman]	27	m	c	CHIN	Siskiyou	Callahan P O	89	626
--- [Chinaman]	27	m	c	CHIN	Siskiyou	Callahan P O	89	626
--- [Chinaman]	27	m	c	CHIN	Siskiyou	Callahan P O	89	634
--- [Chinaman]	27	m	c	CHIN	Siskiyou	Callahan P O	89	635
--- [Chinaman]	27	m	c	CHIN	Siskiyou	Callahan P O	89	635
--- [Chinaman]	27	m	c	CHIN	Siskiyou	Callahan P O	89	635
--- [Chinaman]	27	m	c	CHIN	Siskiyou	Callahan P O	89	635
--- [Chinaman]	27	m	c	CHIN	Siskiyou	Callahan P O	89	634
--- [Chinaman]	27	m	c	CHIN	Siskiyou	Callahan P O	89	634
--- [Chinaman]	27	m	c	CHIN	Siskiyou	Callahan P O	89	634
--- [Chinaman]	27	m	c	CHIN	Siskiyou	Callahan P O	89	635
--- [Chinaman]	27	m	c	CHIN	Siskiyou	Callahan P O	89	634
--- [Chinaman]	27	m	c	CHIN	Siskiyou	Scott Rvr Twp	89	606
--- [Chinaman]	27	m	c	CHIN	Siskiyou	Scott Rvr Twp	89	606
--- [Chinaman]	27	m	c	CHIN	Siskiyou	Scott Rvr Twp	89	607
--- [Chinaman]	27	m	c	CHIN	Siskiyou	Scott Rvr Twp	89	606
--- [Chinaman]	27	m	c	CHIN	Siskiyou	Scott Valley Twp	89	622
--- [Chinaman]	27	m	c	CHIN	Siskiyou	Scott Valley Twp	89	622
--- [Chinaman]	27	m	c	CHIN	Siskiyou	Klamath Twp	89	601
--- [Chinaman]	27	m	c	CHIN	Siskiyou	Scott Rvr Twp	89	605
--- [Chinaman]	27	m	c	CHIN	Siskiyou	Scott Valley Twp	89	616
--- [Chinaman]	27	m	c	CHIN	Siskiyou	Scott Valley Twp	89	617
--- [Chinaman]	27	m	c	CHIN	Siskiyou	Scott Rvr Twp	89	605
--- [Chinaman]	27	m	c	CHIN	Siskiyou	Scott Valley Twp	89	623
--- [Chinaman]	27	m	c	CHIN	Siskiyou	Scott Rvr Twp	89	607
--- [Chinaman]	27	m	c	CHIN	Siskiyou	Scott Rvr Twp	89	607
--- [Chinaman]	27	m	c	CHIN	Siskiyou	Scott Valley Twp	89	616
--- [Chinaman]	27	m	c	CHIN	Siskiyou	Scott Valley Twp	89	616
--- [Chinaman]	27	m	c	CHIN	Siskiyou	Scott Rvr Twp	89	605
--- [Chinaman]	27	m	c	CHIN	Siskiyou	Scott Valley Twp	89	617
--- [Chinaman]	27	m	c	CHIN	Siskiyou	Scott Valley Twp	89	622
--- [Chinaman]	27	m	c	CHIN	Siskiyou	Scott Valley Twp	89	622
--- [Chinaman]	27	m	c	CHIN	Siskiyou	Scott Valley Twp	89	623
--- [Chinaman]	27	m	c	CHIN	Siskiyou	Scott Valley Twp	89	621
--- [Chinaman]	27	m	c	CHIN	Siskiyou	Scott Valley Twp	89	620
--- [Chinaman]	27	m	c	CHIN	Siskiyou	Scott Valley Twp	89	622
--- [Chinaman]	27	m	c	CHIN	Siskiyou	Scott Valley Twp	89	623
--- [Chinaman]	27	m	c	CHIN	Siskiyou	Scott Valley Twp	89	622
--- [Chinaman]	27	m	c	CHIN	Siskiyou	Scott Valley Twp	89	620

© 2001 by Heritage Quest. All rights reserved.

Name	Age	S	R	B-PL	County	Locale	Roll	Pg
						Series M593		
--- [Chinaman]	27	m	c	CHIN	Siskiyou	Callahan P O	89	626
--- [Chinaman]	26	m	c	CHIN	Siskiyou	Butte Twp	89	586
--- [Chinaman]	26	m	c	CHIN	Siskiyou	Hamburg Twp	89	598
--- [Chinaman]	26	m	c	CHIN	Siskiyou	Klamath Twp	89	600
--- [Chinaman]	26	m	c	CHIN	Siskiyou	Klamath Twp	89	600
--- [Chinaman]	26	m	c	CHIN	Siskiyou	Scott Rvr Twp	89	606
--- [Chinaman]	26	m	c	CHIN	Siskiyou	Scott Rvr Twp	89	605
--- [Chinaman]	26	m	c	CHIN	Siskiyou	Scott Rvr Twp	89	606
--- [Chinaman]	26	m	c	CHIN	Siskiyou	Callahan P O	89	625
--- [Chinaman]	26	m	c	CHIN	Siskiyou	Callahan P O	89	634
--- [Chinaman]	26	m	c	CHIN	Siskiyou	Callahan P O	89	635
--- [Chinaman]	26	m	c	CHIN	Siskiyou	Yreka	89	650
--- [Chinaman]	26	m	c	CHIN	Siskiyou	Butte Twp	89	584
--- [Chinaman]	26	m	c	CHIN	Siskiyou	Cottonwood Twp	89	592
--- [Chinaman]	26	m	c	CHIN	Siskiyou	Cottonwood Twp	89	592
--- [Chinaman]	26	m	c	CHIN	Siskiyou	Butte Twp	89	587
--- [Chinaman]	26	m	c	CHIN	Siskiyou	Scott Valley Twp	89	621
--- [Chinaman]	26	m	c	CHIN	Siskiyou	Scott Valley Twp	89	617
--- [Chinaman]	26	m	c	CHIN	Siskiyou	Scott Valley Twp	89	617
--- [Chinaman]	26	m	c	CHIN	Siskiyou	Scott Valley Twp	89	616
--- [Chinaman]	26	m	c	CHIN	Siskiyou	Callahan P O	89	626
--- [Chinaman]	26	m	c	CHIN	Siskiyou	Scott Valley Twp	89	616
--- [Chinaman]	26	m	c	CHIN	Siskiyou	Scott Valley Twp	89	621
--- [Chinaman]	26	m	c	CHIN	Siskiyou	Scott Rvr Twp	89	605
--- [Chinaman]	26	m	c	CHIN	Siskiyou	Scott Rvr Twp	89	607
--- [Chinaman]	26	m	c	CHIN	Siskiyou	Yreka	89	650
--- [Chinaman]	26	m	c	CHIN	Siskiyou	Yreka	89	650
--- [Chinaman]	26	m	c	CHIN	Siskiyou	Yreka Twp	89	671
--- [Chinaman]	26	m	c	CHIN	Siskiyou	Yreka Twp	89	669
--- [Chinaman]	26	m	c	CHIN	Siskiyou	Yreka Twp	89	671
--- [Chinaman]	26	m	c	CHIN	Siskiyou	Yreka Twp	89	670
--- [Chinaman]	26	m	c	CHIN	Siskiyou	Yreka Twp	89	670
--- [Chinaman]	26	m	c	CHIN	Siskiyou	Yreka Twp	89	670
--- [Chinaman]	25	m	c	CHIN	Siskiyou	Cottonwood Twp	89	592
--- [Chinaman]	25	m	c	CHIN	Siskiyou	Hamburg Twp	89	598
--- [Chinaman]	25	m	c	CHIN	Siskiyou	Klamath Twp	89	600
--- [Chinaman]	25	m	c	CHIN	Siskiyou	Butte Twp	89	586
--- [Chinaman]	25	m	c	CHIN	Siskiyou	Klamath Twp	89	600
--- [Chinaman]	25	m	c	CHIN	Siskiyou	Scott Rvr Twp	89	607
--- [Chinaman]	25	m	c	CHIN	Siskiyou	Scott Rvr Twp	89	607
--- [Chinaman]	25	m	c	CHIN	Siskiyou	Scott Rvr Twp	89	606
--- [Chinaman]	25	m	c	CHIN	Siskiyou	Klamath Twp	89	600
--- [Chinaman]	25	m	c	CHIN	Siskiyou	Scott Rvr Twp	89	605
--- [Chinaman]	25	m	c	CHIN	Siskiyou	Scott Rvr Twp	89	605
--- [Chinaman]	25	m	c	CHIN	Siskiyou	Scott Rvr Twp	89	605
--- [Chinaman]	25	m	c	CHIN	Siskiyou	Scott Rvr Twp	89	606
--- [Chinaman]	25	m	c	CHIN	Siskiyou	Klamath Twp	89	600
--- [Chinaman]	25	m	c	CHIN	Siskiyou	Klamath Twp	89	600
--- [Chinaman]	25	m	c	CHIN	Siskiyou	Scott Rvr Twp	89	606
--- [Chinaman]	25	m	c	CHIN	Siskiyou	Scott Rvr Twp	89	607
--- [Chinaman]	25	m	c	CHIN	Siskiyou	Scott Valley Twp	89	622
--- [Chinaman]	25	m	c	CHIN	Siskiyou	Scott Valley Twp	89	622
--- [Chinaman]	25	m	c	CHIN	Siskiyou	Callahan P O	89	626
--- [Chinaman]	25	m	c	CHIN	Siskiyou	Callahan P O	89	634
--- [Chinaman]	25	m	c	CHIN	Siskiyou	Scott Valley Twp	89	623
--- [Chinaman]	25	m	c	CHIN	Siskiyou	Callahan P O	89	634
--- [Chinaman]	25	m	c	CHIN	Siskiyou	Callahan P O	89	634
--- [Chinaman]	25	m	c	CHIN	Siskiyou	Callahan P O	89	626
--- [Chinaman]	25	m	c	CHIN	Siskiyou	Callahan P O	89	626
--- [Chinaman]	25	m	c	CHIN	Siskiyou	Callahan P O	89	634
--- [Chinaman]	25	m	c	CHIN	Siskiyou	Callahan P O	89	634
--- [Chinaman]	25	m	c	CHIN	Siskiyou	Callahan P O	89	634
--- [Chinaman]	25	m	c	CHIN	Siskiyou	Callahan P O	89	634
--- [Chinaman]	25	m	c	CHIN	Siskiyou	Callahan P O	89	635
--- [Chinaman]	25	m	c	CHIN	Siskiyou	Callahan P O	89	626
--- [Chinaman]	25	m	c	CHIN	Siskiyou	Callahan P O	89	634
--- [Chinaman]	25	m	c	CHIN	Siskiyou	Callahan P O	89	635
--- [Chinaman]	25	m	c	CHIN	Siskiyou	Callahan P O	89	634
--- [Chinaman]	25	m	c	CHIN	Siskiyou	Butte Twp	89	586
--- [Chinaman]	25	m	c	CHIN	Siskiyou	Scott Rvr Twp	89	605
--- [Chinaman]	25	m	c	CHIN	Siskiyou	Scott Rvr Twp	89	605
--- [Chinaman]	25	m	c	CHIN	Siskiyou	Scott Rvr Twp	89	606
--- [Chinaman]	25	m	c	CHIN	Siskiyou	Scott Rvr Twp	89	606
--- [Chinaman]	25	m	c	CHIN	Siskiyou	Scott Valley Twp	89	621
--- [Chinaman]	25	m	c	CHIN	Siskiyou	Scott Valley Twp	89	621
--- [Chinaman]	25	m	c	CHIN	Siskiyou	Scott Valley Twp	89	622
--- [Chinaman]	25	m	c	CHIN	Siskiyou	Klamath Twp	89	600
--- [Chinaman]	25	m	c	CHIN	Siskiyou	Scott Rvr Twp	89	606
--- [Chinaman]	25	m	c	CHIN	Siskiyou	Scott Rvr Twp	89	606
--- [Chinaman]	25	m	c	CHIN	Siskiyou	Callahan P O	89	624
--- [Chinaman]	25	m	c	CHIN	Siskiyou	Scott Valley Twp	89	616
--- [Chinaman]	25	m	c	CHIN	Siskiyou	Scott Valley Twp	89	622
--- [Chinaman]	25	m	c	CHIN	Siskiyou	Scott Rvr Twp	89	605
--- [Chinaman]	25	m	c	CHIN	Siskiyou	Scott Rvr Twp	89	607
--- [Chinaman]	25	m	c	CHIN	Siskiyou	Scott Valley Twp	89	617
--- [Chinaman]	25	m	c	CHIN	Siskiyou	Scott Valley Twp	89	622
--- [Chinaman]	25	m	c	CHIN	Siskiyou	Callahan P O	89	625
--- [Chinaman]	25	m	c	CHIN	Siskiyou	Callahan P O	89	625
--- [Chinaman]	25	m	c	CHIN	Siskiyou	Scott Valley Twp	89	617
--- [Chinaman]	25	m	c	CHIN	Siskiyou	Scott Valley Twp	89	620
--- [Chinaman]	25	m	c	CHIN	Siskiyou	Scott Valley Twp	89	617
--- [Chinaman]	25	m	c	CHIN	Siskiyou	Scott Valley Twp	89	620
--- [Chinaman]	25	m	c	CHIN	Siskiyou	Scott Valley Twp	89	622
--- [Chinaman]	25	m	c	CHIN	Siskiyou	Scott Valley Twp	89	623
--- [Chinaman]	25	m	c	CHIN	Siskiyou	Callahan P O	89	633
--- [Chinaman]	25	m	c	CHIN	Siskiyou	Scott Valley Twp	89	614
--- [Chinaman]	25	m	c	CHIN	Siskiyou	Scott Valley Twp	89	616
--- [Chinaman]	25	m	c	CHIN	Siskiyou	Scott Valley Twp	89	617
--- [Chinaman]	25	m	c	CHIN	Siskiyou	Scott Valley Twp	89	622
--- [Chinaman]	25	m	c	CHIN	Siskiyou	Scott Valley Twp	89	622
--- [Chinaman]	25	m	c	CHIN	Siskiyou	Scott Valley Twp	89	622
--- [Chinaman]	25	m	c	CHIN	Siskiyou	Scott Valley Twp	89	622
--- [Chinaman]	25	m	c	CHIN	Siskiyou	Scott Valley Twp	89	623
--- [Chinaman]	25	m	c	CHIN	Siskiyou	Callahan P O	89	624
--- [Chinaman]	25	m	c	CHIN	Siskiyou	Callahan P O	89	626
--- [Chinaman]	25	m	c	CHIN	Siskiyou	Yreka Twp	89	671
--- [Chinaman]	25	m	c	CHIN	Siskiyou	Yreka Twp	89	671
--- [Chinaman]	24	m	c	CHIN	Siskiyou	Butte Twp	89	585
--- [Chinaman]	24	m	c	CHIN	Siskiyou	Cottonwood Twp	89	594
--- [Chinaman]	24	m	c	CHIN	Siskiyou	Butte Twp	89	585
--- [Chinaman]	24	m	c	CHIN	Siskiyou	Cottonwood Twp	89	593
--- [Chinaman]	24	m	c	CHIN	Siskiyou	Cottonwood Twp	89	592
--- [Chinaman]	24	m	c	CHIN	Siskiyou	Scott Rvr Twp	89	605
--- [Chinaman]	24	m	c	CHIN	Siskiyou	Scott Rvr Twp	89	606
--- [Chinaman]	24	m	c	CHIN	Siskiyou	Klamath Twp	89	600
--- [Chinaman]	24	m	c	CHIN	Siskiyou	Klamath Twp	89	600
--- [Chinaman]	24	m	c	CHIN	Siskiyou	Scott Rvr Twp	89	606
--- [Chinaman]	24	m	c	CHIN	Siskiyou	Scott Valley Twp	89	620
--- [Chinaman]	24	m	c	CHIN	Siskiyou	Scott Valley Twp	89	622
--- [Chinaman]	24	m	c	CHIN	Siskiyou	Callahan P O	89	635
--- [Chinaman]	24	m	c	CHIN	Siskiyou	Callahan P O	89	635
--- [Chinaman]	24	m	c	CHIN	Siskiyou	Callahan P O	89	635
--- [Chinaman]	24	m	c	CHIN	Siskiyou	Callahan P O	89	635
--- [Chinaman]	24	m	c	CHIN	Siskiyou	Callahan P O	89	635
--- [Chinaman]	24	m	c	CHIN	Siskiyou	Callahan P O	89	635
--- [Chinaman]	24	m	c	CHIN	Siskiyou	Callahan P O	89	634
--- [Chinaman]	24	m	c	CHIN	Siskiyou	Callahan P O	89	635
--- [Chinaman]	24	m	c	CHIN	Siskiyou	Yreka	89	650
--- [Chinaman]	24	m	c	CHIN	Siskiyou	Yreka	89	650
--- [Chinaman]	24	m	c	CHIN	Siskiyou	Yreka Twp	89	671
--- [Chinaman]	24	m	c	CHIN	Siskiyou	Yreka Twp	89	670
--- [Chinaman]	24	m	c	CHIN	Siskiyou	Yreka Twp	89	670
--- [Chinaman]	24	m	c	CHIN	Siskiyou	Yreka Twp	89	671
--- [Chinaman]	24	m	c	CHIN	Siskiyou	Butte Twp	89	586
--- [Chinaman]	24	m	c	CHIN	Siskiyou	Hamburg Twp	89	598
--- [Chinaman]	24	m	c	CHIN	Siskiyou	Scott Rvr Twp	89	605
--- [Chinaman]	24	m	c	CHIN	Siskiyou	Scott Rvr Twp	89	605
--- [Chinaman]	24	m	c	CHIN	Siskiyou	Scott Rvr Twp	89	605
--- [Chinaman]	24	m	c	CHIN	Siskiyou	Scott Valley Twp	89	622
--- [Chinaman]	24	m	c	CHIN	Siskiyou	Scott Valley Twp	89	616
--- [Chinaman]	24	m	c	CHIN	Siskiyou	Scott Valley Twp	89	617
--- [Chinaman]	24	m	c	CHIN	Siskiyou	Scott Valley Twp	89	617
--- [Chinaman]	24	m	c	CHIN	Siskiyou	Scott Valley Twp	89	617
--- [Chinaman]	24	m	c	CHIN	Siskiyou	Scott Valley Twp	89	617
--- [Chinaman]	24	m	c	CHIN	Siskiyou	Scott Valley Twp	89	617
--- [Chinaman]	24	m	c	CHIN	Siskiyou	Yreka	89	650
--- [Chinaman]	24	m	c	CHIN	Siskiyou	Yreka Twp	89	671
--- [Chinaman]	24	m	c	CHIN	Siskiyou	Yreka Twp	89	670
--- [Chinaman]	23	m	c	CHIN	Siskiyou	Scott Rvr Twp	89	602
--- [Chinaman]	23	m	c	CHIN	Siskiyou	Klamath Twp	89	600
--- [Chinaman]	23	m	c	CHIN	Siskiyou	Klamath Twp	89	600
--- [Chinaman]	23	m	c	CHIN	Siskiyou	Scott Rvr Twp	89	606
--- [Chinaman]	23	m	c	CHIN	Siskiyou	Klamath Twp	89	600
--- [Chinaman]	23	m	c	CHIN	Siskiyou	Scott Valley Twp	89	623
--- [Chinaman]	23	m	c	CHIN	Siskiyou	Scott Valley Twp	89	622
--- [Chinaman]	23	m	c	CHIN	Siskiyou	Callahan P O	89	634
--- [Chinaman]	23	m	c	CHIN	Siskiyou	Callahan P O	89	635
--- [Chinaman]	23	m	c	CHIN	Siskiyou	Callahan P O	89	634
--- [Chinaman]	23	m	c	CHIN	Siskiyou	Yreka Twp	89	671
--- [Chinaman]	23	m	c	CHIN	Siskiyou	Butte Twp	89	585
--- [Chinaman]	23	m	c	CHIN	Siskiyou	Scott Rvr Twp	89	607
--- [Chinaman]	23	m	c	CHIN	Siskiyou	Scott Rvr Twp	89	602
--- [Chinaman]	23	m	c	CHIN	Siskiyou	Scott Valley Twp	89	621
--- [Chinaman]	23	m	c	CHIN	Siskiyou	Scott Rvr Twp	89	606
--- [Chinaman]	23	m	c	CHIN	Siskiyou	Scott Rvr Twp	89	605
--- [Chinaman]	23	m	c	CHIN	Siskiyou	Scott Rvr Twp	89	606
--- [Chinaman]	23	m	c	CHIN	Siskiyou	Scott Valley Twp	89	616
--- [Chinaman]	23	m	c	CHIN	Siskiyou	Callahan P O	89	626
--- [Chinaman]	23	m	c	CHIN	Siskiyou	Scott Valley Twp	89	616
--- [Chinaman]	23	m	c	CHIN	Siskiyou	Yreka Twp	89	669
--- [Chinaman]	22	m	c	CHIN	Siskiyou	Butte Twp	89	586
--- [Chinaman]	22	m	c	CHIN	Siskiyou	Scott Rvr Twp	89	605
--- [Chinaman]	22	m	c	CHIN	Siskiyou	Cottonwood Twp	89	592
--- [Chinaman]	22	m	c	CHIN	Siskiyou	Scott Rvr Twp	89	605
--- [Chinaman]	22	m	c	CHIN	Siskiyou	Scott Rvr Twp	89	606
--- [Chinaman]	22	m	c	CHIN	Siskiyou	Callahan P O	89	634
--- [Chinaman]	22	m	c	CHIN	Siskiyou	Callahan P O	89	634
--- [Chinaman]	22	m	c	CHIN	Siskiyou	Callahan P O	89	635
--- [Chinaman]	22	m	c	CHIN	Siskiyou	Callahan P O	89	635
--- [Chinaman]	22	m	c	CHIN	Siskiyou	Callahan P O	89	633
--- [Chinaman]	22	m	c	CHIN	Siskiyou	Callahan P O	89	634
--- [Chinaman]	22	m	c	CHIN	Siskiyou	Callahan P O	89	634
--- [Chinaman]	22	m	c	CHIN	Siskiyou	Callahan P O	89	634
--- [Chinaman]	22	m	c	CHIN	Siskiyou	Callahan P O	89	635
--- [Chinaman]	22	m	c	CHIN	Siskiyou	Klamath Twp	89	600
--- [Chinaman]	22	m	c	CHIN	Siskiyou	Scott Rvr Twp	89	605
--- [Chinaman]	22	m	c	CHIN	Siskiyou	Scott Valley Twp	89	616
--- [Chinaman]	22	m	c	CHIN	Siskiyou	Scott Valley Twp	89	616
--- [Chinaman]	22	m	c	CHIN	Siskiyou	Scott Rvr Twp	89	607
--- [Chinaman]	22	m	c	CHIN	Siskiyou	Scott Valley Twp	89	621
--- [Chinaman]	22	m	c	CHIN	Siskiyou	Scott Rvr Twp	89	606
--- [Chinaman]	22	m	c	CHIN	Siskiyou	Scott Valley Twp	89	622
--- [Chinaman]	22	m	c	CHIN	Siskiyou	Scott Valley Twp	89	623
--- [Chinaman]	22	m	c	CHIN	Siskiyou	Scott Valley Twp	89	616

© 2001 by Heritage Quest. All rights reserved.

California 1870 Census

Series M593

Name	Age	S	R	B-PL	County	Locale	Roll	Pg
--- [Chinaman]	22	m	c	CHIN	Siskiyou	Scott Valley Twp	89	616
--- [Chinaman]	22	m	c	CHIN	Siskiyou	Scott Valley Twp	89	621
--- [Chinaman]	22	m	c	CHIN	Siskiyou	Scott Valley Twp	89	617
--- [Chinaman]	22	m	c	CHIN	Siskiyou	Yreka	89	650
--- [Chinaman]	22	m	c	CHIN	Siskiyou	Yreka Twp	89	669
--- [Chinaman]	22	m	c	CHIN	Siskiyou	Yreka Twp	89	671
--- [Chinaman]	22	m	c	CHIN	Siskiyou	Yreka Twp	89	671
--- [Chinaman]	21	m	c	CHIN	Siskiyou	Klamath Twp	89	600
--- [Chinaman]	21	m	c	CHIN	Siskiyou	Scott Rvr Twp	89	606
--- [Chinaman]	21	m	c	CHIN	Siskiyou	Scott Rvr Twp	89	606
--- [Chinaman]	21	m	c	CHIN	Siskiyou	Scott Rvr Twp	89	606
--- [Chinaman]	21	m	c	CHIN	Siskiyou	Scott Rvr Twp	89	606
--- [Chinaman]	21	m	c	CHIN	Siskiyou	Scott Rvr Twp	89	605
--- [Chinaman]	21	m	c	CHIN	Siskiyou	Scott Rvr Twp	89	605
--- [Chinaman]	21	m	c	CHIN	Siskiyou	Scott Rvr Twp	89	606
--- [Chinaman]	21	m	c	CHIN	Siskiyou	Scott Rvr Twp	89	606
--- [Chinaman]	21	m	c	CHIN	Siskiyou	Callahan P O	89	626
--- [Chinaman]	21	m	c	CHIN	Siskiyou	Callahan P O	89	626
--- [Chinaman]	21	m	c	CHIN	Siskiyou	Callahan P O	89	633
--- [Chinaman]	21	m	c	CHIN	Siskiyou	Callahan P O	89	634
--- [Chinaman]	21	m	c	CHIN	Siskiyou	Callahan P O	89	635
--- [Chinaman]	21	m	c	CHIN	Siskiyou	Yreka	89	650
--- [Chinaman]	21	m	c	CHIN	Siskiyou	Yreka Twp	89	671
--- [Chinaman]	21	m	c	CHIN	Siskiyou	Klamath Twp	89	601
--- [Chinaman]	21	m	c	CHIN	Siskiyou	Scott Rvr Twp	89	606
--- [Chinaman]	21	m	c	CHIN	Siskiyou	Scott Rvr Twp	89	605
--- [Chinaman]	21	m	c	CHIN	Siskiyou	Scott Rvr Twp	89	605
--- [Chinaman]	21	m	c	CHIN	Siskiyou	Scott Rvr Twp	89	606
--- [Chinaman]	21	m	c	CHIN	Siskiyou	Scott Rvr Twp	89	605
--- [Chinaman]	21	m	c	CHIN	Siskiyou	Scott Rvr Twp	89	606
--- [Chinaman]	21	m	c	CHIN	Siskiyou	Scott Rvr Twp	89	606
--- [Chinaman]	21	m	c	CHIN	Siskiyou	Scott Rvr Twp	89	605
--- [Chinaman]	21	m	c	CHIN	Siskiyou	Scott Valley Twp	89	620
--- [Chinaman]	21	m	c	CHIN	Siskiyou	Scott Valley Twp	89	622
--- [Chinaman]	21	m	c	CHIN	Siskiyou	Scott Valley Twp	89	617
--- [Chinaman]	21	m	c	CHIN	Siskiyou	Scott Valley Twp	89	623
--- [Chinaman]	21	m	c	CHIN	Siskiyou	Callahan P O	89	625
--- [Chinaman]	21	m	c	CHIN	Siskiyou	Scott Rvr Twp	89	605
--- [Chinaman]	21	m	c	CHIN	Siskiyou	Scott Valley Twp	89	622
--- [Chinaman]	21	m	c	CHIN	Siskiyou	Scott Rvr Twp	89	606
--- [Chinaman]	21	m	c	CHIN	Siskiyou	Scott Valley Twp	89	622
--- [Chinaman]	21	m	c	CHIN	Siskiyou	Callahan P O	89	626
--- [Chinaman]	21	m	c	CHIN	Siskiyou	Callahan P O	89	626
--- [Chinaman]	21	m	c	CHIN	Siskiyou	Scott Valley Twp	89	623
--- [Chinaman]	21	m	c	CHIN	Siskiyou	Callahan P O	89	626
--- [Chinaman]	21	m	c	CHIN	Siskiyou	Scott Valley Twp	89	621
--- [Chinaman]	21	m	c	CHIN	Siskiyou	Yreka Twp	89	671
--- [Chinaman]	21	m	c	CHIN	Siskiyou	Yreka Twp	89	671
--- [Chinaman]	21	m	c	CHIN	Siskiyou	Yreka Twp	89	671
--- [Chinaman]	21	m	c	CHIN	Siskiyou	Yreka Twp	89	671
--- [Chinaman]	20	m	c	CHIN	Siskiyou	Cottonwood Twp	89	592
--- [Chinaman]	20	m	c	CHIN	Siskiyou	Cottonwood Twp	89	593
--- [Chinaman]	20	m	c	CHIN	Siskiyou	Hamburg Twp	89	598
--- [Chinaman]	20	m	c	CHIN	Siskiyou	Cottonwood Twp	89	593
--- [Chinaman]	20	m	c	CHIN	Siskiyou	Scott Rvr Twp	89	606
--- [Chinaman]	20	m	c	CHIN	Siskiyou	Scott Rvr Twp	89	605
--- [Chinaman]	20	m	c	CHIN	Siskiyou	Scott Rvr Twp	89	605
--- [Chinaman]	20	m	c	CHIN	Siskiyou	Cottonwood Twp	89	593
--- [Chinaman]	20	m	c	CHIN	Siskiyou	Cottonwood Twp	89	593
--- [Chinaman]	20	m	c	CHIN	Siskiyou	Scott Rvr Twp	89	602
--- [Chinaman]	20	m	c	CHIN	Siskiyou	Scott Rvr Twp	89	603
--- [Chinaman]	20	m	c	CHIN	Siskiyou	Callahan P O	89	624
--- [Chinaman]	20	m	c	CHIN	Siskiyou	Scott Valley Twp	89	623
--- [Chinaman]	20	m	c	CHIN	Siskiyou	Callahan P O	89	626
--- [Chinaman]	20	m	c	CHIN	Siskiyou	Callahan P O	89	634
--- [Chinaman]	20	m	c	CHIN	Siskiyou	Callahan P O	89	634
--- [Chinaman]	20	m	c	CHIN	Siskiyou	Callahan P O	89	626
--- [Chinaman]	20	m	c	CHIN	Siskiyou	Callahan P O	89	634
--- [Chinaman]	20	m	c	CHIN	Siskiyou	Callahan P O	89	634
--- [Chinaman]	20	m	c	CHIN	Siskiyou	Yreka	89	650
--- [Chinaman]	20	m	c	CHIN	Siskiyou	Callahan P O	89	634
--- [Chinaman]	20	m	c	CHIN	Siskiyou	Yreka Twp	89	671
--- [Chinaman]	20	m	c	CHIN	Siskiyou	Butte Twp	89	586
--- [Chinaman]	20	m	c	CHIN	Siskiyou	Scott Rvr Twp	89	605
--- [Chinaman]	20	m	c	CHIN	Siskiyou	Scott Valley Twp	89	622
--- [Chinaman]	20	m	c	CHIN	Siskiyou	Scott Valley Twp	89	616
--- [Chinaman]	20	m	c	CHIN	Siskiyou	Scott Rvr Twp	89	605
--- [Chinaman]	20	m	c	CHIN	Siskiyou	Scott Rvr Twp	89	605
--- [Chinaman]	20	m	c	CHIN	Siskiyou	Scott Valley Twp	89	617
--- [Chinaman]	20	m	c	CHIN	Siskiyou	Scott Valley Twp	89	621
--- [Chinaman]	20	m	c	CHIN	Siskiyou	Scott Valley Twp	89	623
--- [Chinaman]	20	m	c	CHIN	Siskiyou	Scott Rvr Twp	89	605
--- [Chinaman]	20	m	c	CHIN	Siskiyou	Scott Rvr Twp	89	605
--- [Chinaman]	20	m	c	CHIN	Siskiyou	Scott Valley Twp	89	622
--- [Chinaman]	20	m	c	CHIN	Siskiyou	Callahan P O	89	626
--- [Chinaman]	20	m	c	CHIN	Siskiyou	Scott Valley Twp	89	616
--- [Chinaman]	20	m	c	CHIN	Siskiyou	Callahan P O	89	626
--- [Chinaman]	20	m	c	CHIN	Siskiyou	Scott Valley Twp	89	622
--- [Chinaman]	20	m	c	CHIN	Siskiyou	Yreka Twp	89	670
--- [Chinaman]	20	m	c	CHIN	Siskiyou	Yreka Twp	89	670
--- [Chinaman]	20	m	c	CHIN	Siskiyou	Yreka Twp	89	671
--- [Chinaman]	20	m	c	CHIN	Siskiyou	Yreka Twp	89	671
--- [Chinaman]	20	m	c	CHIN	Siskiyou	Yreka Twp	89	671
--- [Chinaman]	19	m	c	CHIN	Siskiyou	Klamath Twp	89	600
--- [Chinaman]	19	m	c	CHIN	Siskiyou	Scott Rvr Twp	89	603
--- [Chinaman]	19	m	c	CHIN	Siskiyou	Scott Rvr Twp	89	606
--- [Chinaman]	19	m	c	CHIN	Siskiyou	Scott Rvr Twp	89	606
--- [Chinaman]	19	m	c	CHIN	Siskiyou	Scott Rvr Twp	89	606
--- [Chinaman]	19	m	c	CHIN	Siskiyou	Callahan P O	89	635
--- [Chinaman]	19	m	c	CHIN	Siskiyou	Callahan P O	89	635
--- [Chinaman]	19	m	c	CHIN	Siskiyou	Callahan P O	89	633
--- [Chinaman]	19	m	c	CHIN	Siskiyou	Callahan P O	89	634
--- [Chinaman]	19	m	c	CHIN	Siskiyou	Callahan P O	89	634
--- [Chinaman]	19	m	c	CHIN	Siskiyou	Callahan P O	89	634
--- [Chinaman]	19	m	c	CHIN	Siskiyou	Klamath Twp	89	600
--- [Chinaman]	19	m	c	CHIN	Siskiyou	Scott Rvr Twp	89	607
--- [Chinaman]	19	m	c	CHIN	Siskiyou	Klamath Twp	89	600
--- [Chinaman]	19	m	c	CHIN	Siskiyou	Scott Rvr Twp	89	605
--- [Chinaman]	19	m	c	CHIN	Siskiyou	Scott Valley Twp	89	616
--- [Chinaman]	19	m	c	CHIN	Siskiyou	Scott Rvr Twp	89	605
--- [Chinaman]	19	m	c	CHIN	Siskiyou	Scott Rvr Twp	89	607
--- [Chinaman]	19	m	c	CHIN	Siskiyou	Scott Valley Twp	89	617
--- [Chinaman]	19	m	c	CHIN	Siskiyou	Scott Valley Twp	89	623
--- [Chinaman]	19	m	c	CHIN	Siskiyou	Scott Valley Twp	89	621
--- [Chinaman]	19	m	c	CHIN	Siskiyou	Scott Valley Twp	89	622
--- [Chinaman]	19	m	c	CHIN	Siskiyou	Scott Valley Twp	89	622
--- [Chinaman]	19	m	c	CHIN	Siskiyou	Callahan P O	89	626
--- [Chinaman]	19	m	c	CHIN	Siskiyou	Scott Valley Twp	89	623
--- [Chinaman]	19	m	c	CHIN	Siskiyou	Callahan P O	89	626
--- [Chinaman]	18	m	c	CHIN	Siskiyou	Cottonwood Twp	89	593
--- [Chinaman]	18	m	c	CHIN	Siskiyou	Scott Rvr Twp	89	605
--- [Chinaman]	18	m	c	CHIN	Siskiyou	Scott Rvr Twp	89	605
--- [Chinaman]	18	m	c	CHIN	Siskiyou	Scott Rvr Twp	89	606
--- [Chinaman]	18	m	c	CHIN	Siskiyou	Scott Valley Twp	89	622
--- [Chinaman]	18	m	c	CHIN	Siskiyou	Scott Valley Twp	89	622
--- [Chinaman]	18	m	c	CHIN	Siskiyou	Callahan P O	89	634
--- [Chinaman]	18	m	c	CHIN	Siskiyou	Yreka Twp	89	671
--- [Chinaman]	18	m	c	CHIN	Siskiyou	Yreka Twp	89	670
--- [Chinaman]	18	m	c	CHIN	Siskiyou	Cottonwood Twp	89	592
--- [Chinaman]	18	m	c	CHIN	Siskiyou	Butte Twp	89	586
--- [Chinaman]	18	m	c	CHIN	Siskiyou	Scott Rvr Twp	89	602
--- [Chinaman]	18	m	c	CHIN	Siskiyou	Scott Rvr Twp	89	607
--- [Chinaman]	18	m	c	CHIN	Siskiyou	Scott Valley Twp	89	617
--- [Chinaman]	18	m	c	CHIN	Siskiyou	Scott Rvr Twp	89	603
--- [Chinaman]	18	m	c	CHIN	Siskiyou	Scott Rvr Twp	89	605
--- [Chinaman]	18	m	c	CHIN	Siskiyou	Scott Valley Twp	89	616
--- [Chinaman]	18	m	c	CHIN	Siskiyou	Callahan P O	89	626
--- [Chinaman]	18	m	c	CHIN	Siskiyou	Scott Valley Twp	89	622
--- [Chinaman]	18	m	c	CHIN	Siskiyou	Yreka Twp	89	671
--- [Chinaman]	17	m	c	CHIN	Siskiyou	Scott Valley Twp	89	617
--- [Chinaman]	17	m	c	CHIN	Siskiyou	Scott Rvr Twp	89	605
--- [Chinaman]	16	m	c	CHIN	Siskiyou	Yreka Twp	89	670
--- [Chinaman]	16	m	c	CHIN	Siskiyou	Yreka Twp	89	670
--- [Chinaman]	16	m	c	CHIN	Siskiyou	Yreka Twp	89	671
--- [Chinaman]	15	m	c	CHIN	Siskiyou	Scott Rvr Twp	89	606
--- [Chinaman]	15	m	c	CHIN	Siskiyou	Callahan P O	89	634
--- [Chinaman]	14	m	c	CHIN	San Francisco	8-Wd San Francisco	82	291
--- [Chinaman]	13	m	c	CHIN	Siskiyou	Yreka Twp	89	670
--- [Chinawoman]	26	f	c	CHIN	Siskiyou	Yreka	89	650
--- [Chinawoman]	21	f	c	CHIN	Siskiyou	Yreka	89	650
--- [Chinawoman]	20	f	c	CHIN	Siskiyou	Yreka	89	650
--- [Chinawoman]	20	f	c	CHIN	Siskiyou	Yreka	89	650
--- [Chinawoman]	20	f	c	CHIN	Siskiyou	Yreka	89	650
--- [Chinawoman]	20	f	c	CHIN	Siskiyou	Yreka	89	650
--- [Chinawoman]	20	f	c	CHIN	Siskiyou	Yreka	89	650
--- [Chinawoman]	18	f	c	CHIN	Siskiyou	Yreka	89	650
--- [Chinawoman]	18	f	c	CHIN	Siskiyou	Scott Rvr Twp	89	607
--- [Chinawoman]	18	f	c	CHIN	Siskiyou	Yreka	89	650
--- [Chinawoman]	17	f	c	CHIN	Siskiyou	Scott Rvr Twp	89	607
--- [Chinawoman]	16	f	c	CHIN	Siskiyou	Scott Rvr Twp	89	607
--- [Chinawoman]	15	f	c	CHIN	Siskiyou	Scott Rvr Twp	89	607
--- [Chinawoman]	15	f	c	CHIN	Siskiyou	Scott Rvr Twp	89	607
--- [Chinawoman]	15	f	c	CHIN	Siskiyou	Scott Rvr Twp	89	607
--- [Cook]	28	m	c	CHIN	Calaveras	San Andreas P O	70	151
A??hen	24	m	c	CHIN	Klamath	Klamath Twp	73	370
Abalay	18	m	c	CHIN	Klamath	South Fork Twp	73	383
Abrara	20	f	w	CA	Alameda	Murray Twp	68	106
Ach	38	m	c	CHIN	Placer	Bath P O	76	453
Ach	22	m	c	CHIN	Klamath	South Fork Twp	73	385
Ach K	28	m	c	CHIN	Klamath	Liberty Twp	73	374
Achk	29	m	c	CHIN	Klamath	Salmon Twp	73	388
Achtoun	45	m	c	CHIN	Calaveras	San Andreas P O	70	155
Ack	45	m	c	CHIN	Klamath	Salmon Twp	73	388
Ack	43	m	c	CHIN	Klamath	Salmon Twp	73	387
Ack	35	m	c	CHIN	Klamath	South Fork Twp	73	383
Ack	30	m	c	CHIN	Klamath	Dillon Twp	73	369
Ack	20	m	c	CHIN	Placer	Bath P O	76	444
Addison	30	m	w	US	Santa Cruz	Watsonville	89	374
Agoo	45	m	c	CHIN	Alameda	Murray Twp	68	111
Agoo	45	m	c	CHIN	Alameda	Murray Twp	68	114
Ah	77	m	c	CHIN	Sonoma	Santa Rosa	91	401
Ah	34	m	c	CHIN	Klamath	South Fork Twp	73	383
Ah	32	m	c	CHIN	Stanislaus	Branch Twp	92	1
Ah	31	m	c	CHIN	Santa Clara	1-Wd San Jose	88	233
Ah	29	m	c	CHIN	Yuba	Marysville	93	576
Ah	28	m	c	CHIN	Sacramento	1-Wd Sacramento	77	201
Ah	26	m	c	CHIN	Yuba	Marysville	93	620
Ah	18	m	c	CHIN	Sacramento	1-Wd Sacramento	77	200
Aher	50	m	c	CHIN	Yuba	Slate Range Bar Tw	93	669
Ahmy	34	m	c	CHIN	Klamath	Salmon Twp	73	387
Ai	37	m	c	CHIN	Del Norte	Happy Camp Twp	71	471
Aik	23	m	c	CHIN	Yuba	North East Twp	93	645
Ain	3	m	c	CA	Sacramento	1-Wd Sacramento	77	194
Aken	30	m	c	CHIN	Colusa	Colusa	71	299

© 2001 by Heritage Quest. All rights reserved.

Name	Age	S	R	B-PL	County	Locale	Roll	Pg
Aking	32	m	c	CHIN	Butte	Wyandotte Twp	70	141
Akoy	18	m	c	CHIN	Yuba	Marysville	93	599
Alany	26	m	c	CHIN	Sacramento	1-Wd Sacramento	77	180
Alequn	35	m	c	CHIN	Trinity	Junction City Pct	92	209
Allan	45	m	c	CHIN	Sonoma	Sonoma Twp	91	432
Allex	15	m	c	CHIN	Yuba	Bullards Bar P O	93	553
Amesulra	23	m	j	JAPA	El Dorado	Coloma Twp	72	5
Amie	45	m	c	CHIN	Yuba	Slate Range Bar Tw	93	678
Amilia	1	f	w	CA	Alameda	Murray Twp	68	106
Aminy	31	m	c	CHIN	Yuba	North East Twp	93	647
Anddy	40	m	c	CHIN	Del Norte	Happy Camp Twp	71	468
Andy	35	m	c	CHIN	Sutter	Nicolaus Twp	92	109
Ang	50	m	c	CHIN	Butte	Wyandotte Twp	70	143
Anging	30	m	c	CHIN	Placer	Bath P O	76	446
Angom	25	m	c	CHIN	Yuba	Slate Range Bar Tw	93	672
Angone	23	m	c	CHIN	Placer	Bath P O	76	451
Anguia	25	m	c	CHIN	Placer	Bath P O	76	425
Anna	40	f	c	CHIN	Amador	Drytown P O	69	419
Anna	28	f	c	CHIN	Sierra	Downieville Twp	89	521
Annah	20	m	c	CHIN	Alameda	Brooklyn	68	24
Antee	26	m	c	CHIN	Placer	Bath P O	76	429
Antoine	35	m	w	CA	Colusa	Grand Island Twp	71	306
Antone	18	m	w	PORT	Alameda	Murray Twp	68	115
Antonia	45	f	w	MEXI	Yuba	Marysville	93	588
Antonio	25	m	w	CA	Alameda	Murray Twp	68	106
Aran	40	m	c	CHIN	Sutter	Sutter Twp	92	127
Archer	29	m	c	CHIN	Yuba	North East Twp	93	646
Ark	38	m	c	CHIN	Yuba	North East Twp	93	646
Ark	30	m	c	CHIN	Del Norte	Happy Camp Twp	71	468
Ark	30	m	c	CHIN	Yuba	Long Bar Twp	93	560
Ark	27	m	c	CHIN	Yuba	North East Twp	93	646
Ark	25	m	c	CHIN	Yuba	North East Twp	93	646
Ark	20	m	c	CHIN	Yuba	Slate Range Bar Tw	93	668
Arknay	40	m	c	CHIN	Merced	Snelling P O	74	249
Art	32	m	c	CHIN	Yuba	Marysville	93	629
Asinge	20	m	c	CHIN	San Francisco	8-Wd San Francisco	82	467
Assewas	21	m	c	CHIN	Placer	Bath P O	76	423
At Tau	25	m	c	CHIN	Colusa	Colusa	71	293
Atcha	38	m	c	CHIN	Klamath	Orleans Twp	73	381
Atchee	25	m	c	CHIN	Yuba	New York Twp	93	639
Athony	15	m	c	CHIN	Colusa	Butte Twp	71	266
Au	42	f	c	CHIN	Alameda	Alameda	68	18
Auck	22	m	c	CHIN	Placer	Bath P O	76	445
Aung	25	m	c	CHIN	Klamath	Salmon Twp	73	387
Avon	28	m	c	CHIN	Placer	Bath P O	76	451
Awe	25	m	c	CHIN	Klamath	South Fork Twp	73	383
Azoo	30	m	c	CHIN	Alameda	Murray Twp	68	114
Bah	22	m	c	CHIN	Marin	San Rafael	74	51
Bahk	24	m	c	CHIN	Marin	San Rafael	74	58
Baik	18	m	c	CHIN	Yuba	Parks Bar Twp	93	650
Bailey	32	m	c	CHIN	Trinity	Junction City Pct	92	208
Baly	28	m	c	CHIN	Colusa	Colusa	71	299
Band	45	m	c	CHIN	Yuba	Marysville	93	621
Bang	27	m	c	CHIN	Sutter	Yuba Twp	92	142
Bat	34	m	c	CHIN	Klamath	Klamath Twp	73	370
Batt	25	m	c	CHIN	Klamath	South Fork Twp	73	384
Baug	27	m	c	CHIN	Colusa	Monroe Twp	71	316
Bee	28	m	c	CHIN	Sonoma	Salt Point	91	389
Ben	22	m	c	CHIN	Alameda	Brooklyn Twp	68	49
Ben	20	m	c	CHIN	Sutter	Sutter Twp	92	121
Ben [Chinaman]	50	m	c	CHIN	Calaveras	San Andreas P O	70	156
Beng	18	m	c	CHIN	Yuba	Marysville	93	628
Berin	30	m	c	CHIN	Colusa	Monroe Twp	71	311
Bete	40	m	c	CHIN	Klamath	Klamath Twp	73	371
Bill	45	m	c	CHIN	Yuba	Marysville	93	621
Bill	26	m	c	CHIN	Siskiyou	Yreka	89	652
Bing	31	m	c	CHIN	Klamath	Liberty Twp	73	374
Bipilio	34	m	w	MEXI	Fresno	Millerton P O	72	165
Bis	18	f	c	CHIN	Sacramento	1-Wd Sacramento	77	191
Blen	30	m	c	CHIN	Colusa	Monroe Twp	71	316
Bock	29	m	c	CHIN	Klamath	South Fork Twp	73	382
Boid	25	m	c	CHIN	San Francisco	11-Wd San Francisc	84	708
Boley	16	m	c	CHIN	Klamath	Liberty Twp	73	374
Bong	5	m	c	CA	Alameda	Alvarado	68	304
Bong	36	m	c	CHIN	Marin	Tomales Twp	74	80
Bong	26	m	c	CHIN	Del Norte	Happy Camp Twp	71	469
Boo	28	m	c	CHIN	Alameda	Murray Twp	68	111
Booktatny	45	m	c	CHIN	Yuba	Slate Range Bar Tw	93	678
Boon	21	m	c	CHIN	Alameda	Brooklyn Twp	68	41
Bott	37	m	c	CHIN	Klamath	Salmon Twp	73	387
Bow	40	m	c	CHIN	Del Norte	Happy Camp Twp	71	469
Bow	25	m	c	CHIN	Del Norte	Mountain Twp	71	475
Bow	16	m	c	CHIN	Yuba	Marysville	93	593
Bow	16	m	c	CHIN	Marin	Tomales Twp	74	82
Bowe	51	m	c	CHIN	Klamath	Dillon Twp	73	369
Bowey	49	m	c	CHIN	Placer	Bath P O	76	444
Boya	48	m	c	CHIN	Placer	Bath P O	76	444
Brown	38	m	w	IREL	Lake	Knoxville Mines	73	404
Bu	29	m	c	CHIN	Yuba	North East Twp	93	646
Buastista	40	f	i	CA	Monterey	Monterey	74	363
Bue	30	m	c	CHIN	Alameda	Brooklyn Twp	68	49
Bum	32	m	c	CHIN	Alameda	Brooklyn Twp	68	41
Bun	15	m	c	CHIN	Alameda	Brooklyn Twp	68	45
Cage	50	m	c	CHIN	Yuba	North East Twp	93	647
Caion	34	m	c	CHIN	Placer	Bath P O	76	444
Cam	39	m	c	CHIN	Yuba	Linda Twp	93	558
Cam	30	m	c	CHIN	Alameda	Brooklyn Twp	68	42
Cam	18	m	c	CHIN	Alameda	Brooklyn	68	21
Campi	40	m	c	CHIN	Del Norte	Happy Camp Twp	71	469
Can	40	m	c	CHIN	Sacramento	Granite Twp	77	141
Can	27	m	c	CHIN	Alameda	Brooklyn	68	21
Can	24	m	c	CHIN	Sonoma	Salt Point	91	389
Can	18	m	c	CHIN	Alameda	Brooklyn Twp	68	41
Cang	24	m	c	CHIN	Colusa	Colusa	71	299
Cann	18	m	c	CHIN	Sonoma	Sonoma Twp	91	435
Carl	30	m	c	CHIN	Alameda	Eden Twp	68	64
Carricock	26	m	c	CHIN	Napa	Yountville Twp	75	79
Cather	41	f	w	FRAN	Alameda	Oakland	68	239
Cee	31	m	c	CHIN	Yuba	Marysville	93	601
Cha	15	m	c	CHIN	Alameda	Oakland	68	181
Chack	34	m	c	CHIN	Alameda	Brooklyn Twp	68	41
Chah	36	m	c	CHIN	Marin	San Rafael Twp	74	59
Chake	47	m	c	CHIN	Placer	Bath P O	76	442
Chalee	20	m	c	CHIN	Del Norte	Crescent	71	464
Chalk	29	m	c	CHIN	Yuba	Slate Range Bar Tw	93	668
Champ	40	m	w	CANA	Yolo	Grafton Twp	93	499
Chan	15	m	c	CHIN	San Francisco	8-Wd San Francisco	82	435
Chang	42	m	c	CHIN	Butte	Wyandotte Twp	70	148
Chang	42	m	c	CHIN	Marin	Tomales Twp	74	84
Chang	26	m	c	CHIN	Sutter	Nicolaus Twp	92	114
Chang	20	m	c	CHIN	Sonoma	Santa Rosa	91	416
Chang	19	m	c	CHIN	Santa Clara	1-Wd San Jose	88	232
Chaps	28	m	c	CHIN	Sutter	Yuba Twp	92	144
Charles	50	m	w	NY	Sonoma	Sonoma Twp	91	431
Charles	24	m	c	CHIN	Yuba	Long Bar Twp	93	562
Charles	18	m	c	CHIN	Colusa	Monroe Twp	71	316
Charles	15	m	c	CHIN	Yuba	Slate Range Bar Tw	93	678
Charles	10	m	i	ID	Yolo	Buckeye Twp	93	415
Charley	38	m	c	CHIN	Klamath	South Fork Twp	73	382
Charley	33	m	c	CHIN	San Francisco	6-Wd San Francisco	81	65
Charley	30	m	c	CHIN	Klamath	South Fork Twp	73	383
Charley	29	m	c	CHIN	San Francisco	6-Wd San Francisco	81	131
Charley	28	m	c	CHIN	Alameda	Eden Twp	68	93
Charley	27	m	c	CHIN	Colusa	Colusa	71	299
Charley	27	m	c	CHIN	Colusa	Colusa	71	299
Charley	27	m	c	CHIN	Butte	Hamilton Twp	70	68
Charley	25	m	c	CHIN	Butte	Wyandotte Twp	70	147
Charley	25	m	c	CHIN	Siskiyou	Yreka	89	651
Charley	24	m	c	CHIN	Yuba	Marysville	93	596
Charley	22	m	c	CHIN	Sonoma	Sonoma Twp	91	436
Charley	22	m	c	CHIN	Colusa	Grand Island Twp	71	302
Charley	22	m	c	CHIN	Yuba	East Bear Rvr Twp	93	540
Charley	21	m	c	CHIN	Monterey	San Juan Twp	74	397
Charley	20	m	c	CHIN	Siskiyou	Butte Twp	89	588
Charley	18	m	c	CHIN	Sonoma	Salt Point	91	388
Charley	18	m	c	CHIN	Santa Clara	2-Wd San Jose	88	306
Charley	18	m	c	CHIN	Sutter	Nicolaus Twp	92	109
Charley	18	m	c	CHIN	San Francisco	6-Wd San Francisco	81	88
Charley	15	m	c	CHIN	Klamath	Liberty Twp	73	375
Charley [Chinaman]	35	m	c	CHIN	Trinity	North Fork Twp	92	219
Charley [Chinaman]	28	m	c	CHIN	Calaveras	San Andreas P O	70	183
Charley [Chinaman]	24	m	c	CHIN	Tehama	Deer Crk Twp	92	172
Charley [Chinaman]	18	m	c	CHIN	Trinity	Weaverville Pct	92	224
Charley [Chinaman]	16	m	c	CHIN	Butte	Oroville Twp	70	137
Charlie	40	m	c	CHIN	Yuba	Bullards Bar P O	93	548
Charlie	18	m	c	CHIN	Yuba	Long Bar Twp	93	563
Charlie	17	m	c	CHIN	Del Norte	Crescent Twp	71	455
Charlo	7	f	c	CA	Alameda	Alvarado	68	303
Charlrs	40	m	w	UNKN	San Joaquin	2-Wd Stockton	86	167
Charly	37	m	c	CHIN	Colusa	Colusa	71	299
Charly	25	m	c	CHIN	Colusa	Colusa	71	299
Charly [Chinaman]	30	m	c	CHIN	Calaveras	San Andreas P O	70	199
Chaw	50	m	c	CHIN	Yuba	Long Bar Twp	93	565
Chaw	35	m	c	CHIN	Yuba	Marysville	93	601
Chaw	18	m	c	CHIN	Klamath	Orleans Twp	73	380
Chay	39	m	c	CHIN	Butte	Hamilton Twp	70	68
Chay	30	m	c	CHIN	Yuba	New York Twp	93	638
Chay	21	m	c	CHIN	Yuba	Long Bar Twp	93	560
Check	36	m	c	CHIN	Alameda	Brooklyn Twp	68	41
Check	23	m	c	CHIN	Alameda	Brooklyn	68	21
Chee	40	m	c	CHIN	Yuba	Marysville	93	602
Chee	33	m	c	CHIN	Klamath	Salmon Twp	73	387
Chee	30	m	c	CHIN	Alameda	Brooklyn	68	25
Chee	28	m	c	CHIN	Alameda	Brooklyn Twp	68	46
Chee	21	m	c	CHIN	Placer	Bath P O	76	445
Chee	20	m	c	CHIN	Klamath	Liberty Twp	73	374
Chee	13	m	c	CHIN	Yuba	Marysville	93	594
Chen	21	m	c	CHIN	Alameda	Brooklyn	68	21
Chen	16	m	c	CHIN	Yuba	Marysville	93	592
Cheney	36	m	c	CHIN	Yuba	Slate Range Bar Tw	93	678
Cheo	18	m	c	CHIN	Monterey	San Juan Twp	74	397
Cheon	50	m	c	CHIN	Yuba	Bullards Bar P O	93	548
Cheon	31	m	c	CHIN	Yuba	North East Twp	93	647
Cheon	30	m	c	CHIN	Butte	Kimshew Tpw	70	85
Cheon	18	m	c	CHIN	Yuba	Marysville	93	594
Cheon	15	m	c	CHIN	Alameda	Brooklyn	68	21
Cheong	50	m	c	CHIN	Yuba	Slate Range Bar Tw	93	668
Cheong	44	m	c	CHIN	Del Norte	Happy Camp Twp	71	469
Cheong	43	m	c	CHIN	Yuba	Slate Range Bar Tw	93	678
Cheong	41	m	c	CHIN	Del Norte	Crescent	71	464
Cheong	35	m	c	CHIN	Del Norte	Happy Camp Twp	71	470
Cheong	32	m	c	CHIN	Yuba	Slate Range Bar Tw	93	676
Cheong	32	m	c	CHIN	Yuba	Marysville	93	576
Cheong	30	m	c	CHIN	Calaveras	San Andreas P O	70	182

Series M593

© 2001 by Heritage Quest. All rights reserved.

Name	Age	S	R	B-PL	County	Series M593 Locale	Roll	Pg
Cheong	24	m	c	CHIN	Yuba	Slate Range Bar Tw	93	669
Cheong	20	m	c	CHIN	Yuba	Slate Range Bar Tw	93	677
Cheong	11	m	c	CHIN	Yuba	Marysville	93	602
Cheow	25	m	c	CHIN	Del Norte	Happy Camp Twp	71	469
Cherly	16	m	c	CHIN	Yuba	Long Bar Twp	93	562
Chet	22	m	c	CHIN	Alameda	Brooklyn Twp	68	41
Chet	20	m	c	CHIN	Alameda	Brooklyn	68	21
Cheung	60	m	c	CHIN	Calaveras	Copperopolis P O	70	233
Cheung	40	m	c	CHIN	Del Norte	Crescent	71	464
Chew	50	m	c	CHIN	Yuba	Slate Range Bar Tw	93	671
Chew	42	m	c	CHIN	Yuba	Bullards Bar P O	93	552
Chew	40	m	c	CHIN	Yuba	Bullards Bar P O	93	552
Chew	26	m	c	CHIN	Del Norte	Happy Camp Twp	71	468
Chew	23	m	c	CHIN	Klamath	Liberty Twp	73	374
Chew	19	m	c	CHIN	Yuba	Slate Range Bar Tw	93	669
Chew	13	m	c	CHIN	Yuba	New York Twp	93	639
Chick	30	m	c	CHIN	Del Norte	Happy Camp Twp	71	468
Chick	27	m	c	CHIN	Alameda	Brooklyn Twp	68	46
Chick	25	m	c	CHIN	Alameda	Brooklyn Twp	68	41
Chien	29	m	c	CHIN	San Francisco	11-Wd San Francisc	84	688
Chim	38	m	c	CHIN	Alameda	Washington Twp	68	297
Chim	31	m	c	CHIN	Alameda	Brooklyn Twp	68	41
Chim	30	m	c	CHIN	Alameda	Brooklyn Twp	68	52
Chim	29	m	c	CHIN	Alameda	Washington Twp	68	297
Chim	28	m	c	CHIN	Alameda	Brooklyn	68	35
Chim	25	f	c	CHIN	Alameda	Alvarado	68	303
Chim	23	m	c	CHIN	Alameda	Washington Twp	68	301
Chim	22	m	c	CHIN	Placer	Bath P O	76	459
Chim	21	m	c	CHIN	Colusa	Monroe Twp	71	313
Chim	19	m	c	CHIN	Alameda	Brooklyn Twp	68	46
Chim	18	m	c	CHIN	Alameda	Brooklyn Twp	68	46
Chin	42	m	c	CHIN	Klamath	Orleans Twp	73	380
Chin	41	m	c	CHIN	Marin	Tomales Twp	74	86
Chin	39	m	c	CHIN	Butte	Wyandotte Twp	70	142
Chin	32	m	c	CHIN	Placer	Bath P O	76	452
Chin	28	m	c	CHIN	Sutter	Butte Twp	92	89
Chin	19	m	c	CHIN	Alameda	Washington Twp	68	295
Chin	18	m	c	CHIN	Alameda	Washington Twp	68	293
Chin	18	m	c	CHIN	Marin	Novato Twp	74	11
Chin	14	m	c	CHIN	Yuba	Marysville	93	594
Ching	39	m	c	CHIN	Marin	Tomales Twp	74	77
Ching	37	m	c	CHIN	Alameda	Brooklyn Twp	68	41
Ching	31	m	c	CHIN	Yuba	East Bear Rvr Twp	93	545
Ching	31	m	c	CHIN	Placer	Bath P O	76	453
Ching	30	m	c	CHIN	Marin	Novato Twp	74	11
Ching	28	m	c	CHIN	Colusa	Colusa	71	300
Ching	27	m	c	CHIN	Placer	Bath P O	76	444
Ching	26	m	c	CHIN	Alameda	Brooklyn	68	23
Ching	25	m	c	CHIN	Colusa	Colusa	71	299
Ching	25	m	c	CHIN	Alameda	Brooklyn	68	21
Ching	25	m	c	CHIN	Colusa	Spring Valley Twp	71	341
Ching	23	m	c	CHIN	San Francisco	11-Wd San Francisc	84	708
Ching	22	m	c	CHIN	Butte	Hamilton Twp	70	66
Ching	22	m	c	CHIN	Klamath	Liberty Twp	73	374
Ching	20	m	c	CHIN	Yuba	Bullards Bar P O	93	548
Ching	20	m	c	CHIN	Colusa	Colusa	71	298
Ching	13	m	c	CHIN	Sonoma	Sonoma Twp	91	449
Ching	12	m	c	CHIN	Yuba	Marysville	93	602
Ching	11	m	c	CHIN	Sonoma	Santa Rosa	91	421
Chinn	60	m	c	CHIN	Yuba	Slate Range Bar Tw	93	674
Chinn	31	m	c	CHIN	Yuba	North East Twp	93	646
Chinn	30	m	c	CHIN	Yuba	Bullards Bar P O	93	549
Chinn	29	m	c	CHIN	Yuba	Marysville	93	621
Chinn	28	m	c	CHIN	Yuba	Bullards Bar P O	93	548
Chinn	24	m	c	CHIN	Yuba	North East Twp	93	646
Chinn	21	m	c	CHIN	Yuba	Parks Bar Twp	93	650
Chinn	14	m	c	CHIN	Yuba	North East Twp	93	645
Cho	27	m	c	CHIN	Butte	Oregon Twp	70	133
Chock	45	m	c	CHIN	Yuba	Bullards Bar P O	93	552
Chock	40	m	c	CHIN	Yuba	Marysville	93	601
Chock	27	m	c	CHIN	Yuba	Slate Range Bar Tw	93	679
Choe	48	m	c	CHIN	Sacramento	Granite Twp	77	140
Cholan	46	m	c	CHIN	Marin	Tomales Twp	74	88
Chom	20	m	c	CHIN	Alameda	Brooklyn Twp	68	46
Chom	19	m	c	CHIN	Alameda	Brooklyn Twp	68	42
Chom	18	m	c	CHIN	Alameda	Brooklyn	68	22
Chon	55	m	c	CHIN	Yuba	Bullards Bar P O	93	552
Chon	40	m	c	CHIN	Klamath	South Fork Twp	73	382
Chon	35	m	c	CHIN	Yuba	Parks Bar Twp	93	650
Chon	34	m	c	CHIN	Yuba	Bullards Bar P O	93	553
Chon	21	m	c	CHIN	Alameda	Brooklyn Twp	68	42
Chon	13	m	c	CHIN	Yuba	North East Twp	93	645
Chone	24	m	c	CHIN	Klamath	South Fork Twp	73	384
Chong	50	m	c	CHIN	Butte	Ophir Twp	70	103
Chong	42	m	c	CHIN	Yuba	Slate Range Bar Tw	93	677
Chong	40	m	c	CHIN	Klamath	Liberty Twp	73	375
Chong	35	m	c	CHIN	Butte	Kimshew Tpw	70	84
Chong	31	m	c	CHIN	Yuba	Marysville	93	621
Chong	30	m	c	CHIN	Merced	Snelling P O	74	278
Chong	30	m	c	CHIN	San Francisco	5-Wd San Francisco	81	5
Chong	30	m	c	CHIN	Butte	Kimshew Tpw	70	85
Chong	29	m	c	CHIN	Placer	Bath P O	76	443
Chong	25	m	c	CHIN	Alameda	Eden Twp	68	93
Chong	24	m	c	CHIN	Placer	Bath P O	76	442
Chong	23	m	c	CHIN	Alameda	Brooklyn Twp	68	46
Chong	22	m	c	CHIN	Yuba	Bullards Bar P O	93	548
Chong	22	m	c	CHIN	Placer	Bath P O	76	451
Chong	20	m	c	CHIN	Klamath	Salmon Twp	73	387
Chong	17	m	c	CHIN	Yuba	Marysville	93	575
Chonglee	17	m	c	CHIN	Placer	Bath P O	76	456
Chonn	26	m	c	CHIN	Yuba	Slate Range Bar Tw	93	679
Choo	31	m	c	CHIN	Marin	Tomales Twp	74	84
Choo	30	m	c	CHIN	Marin	Tomales Twp	74	85
Choo	24	m	c	CHIN	Marin	Novato Twp	74	10
Choo	22	m	c	CHIN	Yuba	Marysville	93	592
Chooak	20	m	c	CHIN	Marin	San Rafael Twp	74	59
Choong	22	m	c	CHIN	Yuba	Slate Range Bar Tw	93	668
Chounge	42	m	c	CHIN	Placer	Bath P O	76	445
Chow	51	m	c	CHIN	Yuba	Bullards Bar P O	93	552
Chow	45	m	c	CHIN	Yuba	Slate Range Bar Tw	93	669
Chow	44	m	c	CHIN	Marin	Novato Twp	74	11
Chow	40	m	c	CHIN	Yuba	Slate Range Bar Tw	93	676
Chow	38	m	c	CHIN	Alameda	Eden Twp	68	81
Chow	35	m	c	CHIN	Yuba	Slate Range Bar Tw	93	672
Chow	35	m	c	CHIN	Yuba	Slate Range Bar Tw	93	669
Chow	33	m	c	CHIN	Marin	Tomales Twp	74	83
Chow	32	m	c	CHIN	Merced	Snelling P O	74	278
Chow	32	m	c	CHIN	Yuba	Marysville	93	601
Chow	30	m	c	CHIN	Alameda	Hayward	68	74
Chow	30	m	c	CHIN	Yuba	Slate Range Bar Tw	93	678
Chow	29	m	c	CHIN	Butte	Wyandotte Twp	70	148
Chow	28	m	c	CHIN	Alameda	Hayward	68	77
Chow	28	m	c	CHIN	Yuba	Bullards Bar P O	93	548
Chow	23	m	c	CHIN	Butte	Concow Twp	70	9
Chow	23	m	c	CHIN	Yuba	Marysville	93	592
Chow	22	m	c	CHIN	Placer	Bath P O	76	444
Chow	22	m	c	CHIN	Alameda	San Leandro	68	96
Chow	21	m	c	CHIN	Alameda	Brooklyn Twp	68	41
Chow	20	m	c	CHIN	Placer	Bath P O	76	442
Chow	20	m	c	CHIN	Colusa	Colusa	71	299
Chow	19	m	c	CHIN	Butte	Kimshew Tpw	70	85
Chowah	19	m	c	CHIN	Alameda	Eden Twp	68	60
Choy	43	m	c	CHIN	Yuba	W Bear Rvr Twp	93	684
Choy	40	m	c	CHIN	Yuba	East Bear Rvr Twp	93	545
Choy	34	m	c	CHIN	Butte	Bidwell Twp	70	3
Choy	20	m	c	CHIN	Sonoma	Santa Rosa	91	405
Choy	16	m	c	CHIN	San Francisco	8-Wd San Francisco	82	407
Choy	13	f	c	CHIN	Butte	Chico Twp	70	27
Choy	1	m	c	CA	Butte	Ophir Twp	70	103
Chs	42	m	c	CHIN	Yuba	Marysville	93	592
Chu	35	m	c	CHIN	Alameda	Oakland	68	152
Chu	21	m	c	CHIN	Alameda	Brooklyn Twp	68	41
Chu	21	m	c	CHIN	Alameda	Oakland	68	202
Chu	18	m	c	CHIN	Yuba	North East Twp	93	645
Chuck	45	m	c	CHIN	Sacramento	Granite Twp	77	141
Chuck	35	m	c	CHIN	Yuba	Slate Range Bar Tw	93	677
Chuck	35	m	c	CHIN	Alameda	Oakland	68	223
Chuck	28	m	c	CHIN	Alameda	Murray Twp	68	114
Chue	29	m	c	CHIN	Alameda	Washington Twp	68	299
Chuge	40	m	c	CHIN	Alameda	Oakland	68	223
Chum	38	m	c	CHIN	Alameda	Brooklyn Twp	68	46
Chum	33	m	c	CHIN	Alameda	Brooklyn Twp	68	41
Chun	38	m	c	CHIN	Alameda	Oakland	68	224
Chun	32	m	c	CHIN	Marin	Nicasio Twp	74	16
Chun	28	m	c	CHIN	Klamath	Salmon Twp	73	387
Chun	22	m	c	CHIN	Marin	Tomales Twp	74	80
Chun	22	m	c	CHIN	Fresno	Millerton P O	72	184
Chung	56	m	c	CHIN	Klamath	South Fork Twp	73	382
Chung	50	m	c	CHIN	Alameda	Hayward	68	74
Chung	45	m	c	CHIN	Alameda	Oakland	68	266
Chung	45	m	c	CHIN	Alameda	Alameda	68	18
Chung	41	m	c	CHIN	Alameda	Alameda	68	17
Chung	40	m	c	CHIN	Marin	San Rafael Twp	74	59
Chung	40	m	c	CHIN	Alameda	Murray Twp	68	114
Chung	40	m	c	CHIN	Alameda	Oakland	68	224
Chung	40	m	c	CHIN	Alameda	Oakland	68	238
Chung	40	m	c	CHIN	Alameda	Oakland	68	224
Chung	40	m	c	CHIN	Alameda	Oakland	68	224
Chung	40	m	c	CHIN	Alameda	Oakland	68	223
Chung	40	m	c	CHIN	Klamath	Klamath Twp	73	370
Chung	38	m	c	CHIN	Merced	Snelling P O	74	249
Chung	38	m	c	CHIN	Alameda	Oakland	68	223
Chung	38	m	c	CHIN	Alameda	Oakland	68	260
Chung	38	m	c	CHIN	Yuba	Marysville	93	601
Chung	38	m	c	CHIN	Alameda	Oakland	68	223
Chung	37	m	c	CHIN	Alameda	Murray Twp	68	102
Chung	35	m	c	CHIN	Alameda	Murray Twp	68	111
Chung	35	m	c	CHIN	Alameda	Murray Twp	68	102
Chung	35	m	c	CHIN	Alameda	Oakland	68	223
Chung	35	m	c	CHIN	Alameda	Oakland	68	266
Chung	35	m	c	CHIN	Alameda	Oakland	68	157
Chung	34	m	c	CHIN	Yuba	Marysville	93	580
Chung	33	m	c	CHIN	Alameda	Murray Twp	68	102
Chung	30	m	c	CHIN	Alameda	Alameda	68	16
Chung	30	m	c	CHIN	Alameda	Oakland	68	224
Chung	29	m	c	CHIN	Amador	Fiddletown P O	69	429
Chung	29	m	c	CHIN	Alameda	Oakland	68	158
Chung	29	m	c	CHIN	Marin	Tomales Twp	74	88
Chung	28	m	c	CHIN	Alameda	Oakland	68	216
Chung	28	m	c	CHIN	Alameda	Oakland	68	158
Chung	28	m	c	CHIN	Alameda	Oakland	68	224
Chung	28	m	c	CHIN	Alameda	Oakland	68	223
Chung	28	m	c	CHIN	Alameda	Oakland	68	224
Chung	28	m	c	CHIN	Alameda	Oakland	68	267

© 2001 by Heritage Quest. All rights reserved.

Name	Age	S	R	B-PL	County	Locale	Roll	Pg
						Series M593		
Chung	28	m	c	CHIN	Alameda	Oakland	68	152
Chung	27	m	c	CHIN	Alameda	Murray Twp	68	102
Chung	27	m	c	CHIN	Placer	Bath P O	76	444
Chung	26	m	c	CHIN	Alameda	Oakland	68	158
Chung	25	m	c	CHIN	Alameda	Murray Twp	68	111
Chung	25	f	c	CHIN	Placer	Bath P O	76	429
Chung	25	m	c	CHIN	Alameda	Oakland	68	222
Chung	25	m	c	CHIN	Sonoma	Sonoma Twp	91	435
Chung	22	m	c	CHIN	Alameda	Oakland	68	138
Chung	22	m	c	CHIN	Sonoma	Petaluma Twp	91	363
Chung	20	m	c	CHIN	Yuba	Rose Bar Twp	93	666
Chung	14	m	c	CHIN	San Francisco	8-Wd San Francisco	82	289
Chung	13	m	c	CHIN	Alameda	Hayward	68	78
Chuoney	20	m	c	CHIN	Yuba	Slate Range Bar Tw	93	677
Churley	14	m	c	CHIN	Yuba	Marysville	93	611
Churly	38	m	c	CHIN	Yuba	North East Twp	93	647
Chute	40	m	c	CHIN	Yuba	Slate Range Bar Tw	93	668
Cim	39	m	c	CHIN	Alameda	Brooklyn Twp	68	41
Clayo	30	m	c	CHIN	Placer	Bath P O	76	442
Cling	32	m	c	CHIN	Colusa	Monroe Twp	71	324
Clong	37	m	c	CHIN	Yuba	North East Twp	93	647
Cocy	28	m	c	CHIN	Colusa	Colusa	71	296
Coe	18	m	c	CHIN	Alameda	San Leandro	68	96
Coey	28	m	c	CHIN	Yuba	Marysville Twp	93	570
Coey	20	m	c	CHIN	Alameda	Brooklyn Twp	68	43
Columbus	30	m	w	GERM	Yuba	Linda Twp	93	558
Coly	27	m	c	CHIN	Yuba	Marysville Twp	93	567
Con	39	m	c	CHIN	Klamath	South Fork Twp	73	384
Con	39	m	c	CHIN	Alameda	Brooklyn Twp	68	42
Con	27	m	c	CHIN	Alameda	Brooklyn Twp	68	41
Con	26	m	c	CHIN	Alameda	Washington Twp	68	299
Con	20	m	c	CHIN	Klamath	South Fork Twp	73	382
Con	18	m	c	CHIN	Alameda	Brooklyn	68	21
Cong	38	m	c	CHIN	Placer	Bath P O	76	443
Cong	16	m	c	CHIN	Sonoma	Salt Point Twp	91	384
Conn	50	m	c	CHIN	Klamath	South Fork Twp	73	384
Conver	20	m	c	CHIN	Placer	Bath P O	76	444
Cook	35	m	c	CHIN	Merced	Snelling P O	74	249
Cookoo	20	m	c	CHIN	Colusa	Colusa	71	299
Coon	60	m	c	CHIN	Yuba	North East Twp	93	645
Coon	52	m	c	CHIN	Yuba	Bullards Bar P O	93	548
Coon	45	m	c	CHIN	Yuba	Bullards Bar P O	93	548
Coon	43	m	c	CHIN	Yuba	Bullards Bar P O	93	553
Coon	30	m	c	CHIN	Yuba	North East Twp	93	646
Coon	30	m	c	CHIN	Yuba	Slate Range Bar Tw	93	677
Coon	30	m	c	CHIN	Yuba	Bullards Bar P O	93	548
Coon	27	m	c	CHIN	Yuba	Slate Range Bar Tw	93	669
Coon	27	m	c	CHIN	Klamath	South Fork Twp	73	383
Coon	24	m	c	CHIN	Yuba	New York Twp	93	640
Coon	24	m	c	CHIN	Yuba	Slate Range Bar Tw	93	675
Coon	24	m	c	CHIN	Yuba	New York Twp	93	638
Coon	22	m	c	CHIN	Alameda	Brooklyn Twp	68	42
Coon	22	m	c	CHIN	Klamath	Salmon Twp	73	388
Coon	20	m	c	CHIN	Yuba	Slate Range Bar Tw	93	669
Coon	1	m	c	CA	Alameda	Alvarado	68	304
Coung	30	m	c	CHIN	Marin	Novato Twp	74	11
Cow	32	m	c	CHIN	Yuba	North East Twp	93	647
Cow	28	m	c	CHIN	Alameda	Brooklyn Twp	68	41
Cow	26	m	c	CHIN	Alameda	Eden Twp	68	60
Cow	22	m	c	CHIN	Alameda	Brooklyn	68	21
Cow	14	m	c	CHIN	Sutter	Sutter Twp	92	121
Cow	12	m	c	CHIN	Yuba	Marysville	93	580
Cowey	28	m	c	CHIN	Placer	Bath P O	76	453
Coy	28	m	c	CHIN	Yuba	Marysville Twp	93	568
Coy	24	m	c	CHIN	Colusa	Colusa	71	300
Cuck	30	m	c	CHIN	Alameda	Oakland	68	223
Cue	38	m	c	CHIN	Yuba	Bullards Bar P O	93	553
Cue	21	m	c	CHIN	Alameda	Brooklyn Twp	68	46
Cuey	38	m	c	CHIN	Yuba	Slate Range Bar Tw	93	674
Cum	42	m	c	CHIN	Yuba	Marysville	93	600
Cum	18	m	c	CHIN	Alameda	Brooklyn Twp	68	41
Cun	34	m	c	CHIN	Alameda	Brooklyn Twp	68	46
Cune	48	f	c	CHIN	Sacramento	1-Wd Sacramento	77	199
Cung	38	m	c	CHIN	Alameda	Oakland	68	223
Cung	30	m	c	CHIN	Sacramento	Franklin Twp	77	115
Cung	28	m	c	CHIN	Del Norte	Happy Camp Twp	71	469
Dah	21	m	c	CHIN	Alameda	Oakland	68	169
Dan	38	m	c	CHIN	Yuba	East Bear Rvr Twp	93	545
Dan	28	m	c	CHIN	Yuba	W Bear Rvr Twp	93	684
Dan	23	m	c	CHIN	Del Norte	Happy Camp Twp	71	468
Dan	19	m	c	CHIN	Yuba	New York Twp	93	640
Dany	42	m	c	CHIN	Sacramento	Granite Twp	77	140
Dast	32	m	c	CHIN	El Dorado	Georgetown Twp	72	43
Deck	19	m	c	CHIN	Sonoma	Salt Point	91	389
Deck	17	m	c	CHIN	San Francisco	8-Wd San Francisco	82	434
Dick	22	m	c	CHIN	Sacramento	Granite Twp	77	140
Dick [Chinaman]	35	m	c	CHIN	Calaveras	San Andreas P O	70	156
Die	39	m	c	CHIN	Yuba	Marysville	93	594
Doey	32	m	c	CHIN	Klamath	Liberty Twp	73	376
Dominga	50	f	w	CA	Monterey	San Antonio Twp	74	316
Don	18	m	c	CHIN	Del Norte	Mountain Twp	71	475
Don	15	m	c	CHIN	Del Norte	Smith Rvr Twp	71	479
Doong	28	m	c	CHIN	San Francisco	8-Wd San Francisco	82	458
Dought	29	m	c	CHIN	Klamath	Salmon Twp	73	387
Dow	19	m	c	CHIN	Sonoma	Salt Point	91	388
Dowey	15	m	c	CHIN	Klamath	South Fork Twp	73	384
Doy	30	m	c	CHIN	Yuba	Marysville	93	621

Name	Age	S	R	B-PL	County	Locale	Roll	Pg
						Series M593		
Dya	44	m	c	CHIN	Calaveras	Copperopolis P O	70	260
Eaugh	35	m	c	CHIN	Yuba	North East Twp	93	647
Echoy	30	f	c	CHIN	Calaveras	San Andreas P O	70	161
Edwarto	28	m	b	MEXI	San Luis Obispo	Salinas Twp	87	295
Ehh	20	m	c	CHIN	Sonoma	Sonoma Twp	91	433
Eigh	42	m	c	CHIN	Yuba	Slate Range Bar Tw	93	668
Emm	22	m	c	CHIN	Yuba	Marysville	93	620
Ene	17	f	c	CHIN	Sacramento	1-Wd Sacramento	77	192
Eng	41	m	c	CHIN	Butte	Wyandotte Twp	70	148
Eng	23	m	c	CHIN	Yuba	Slate Range Bar Tw	93	669
Eng	18	m	c	CHIN	Yuba	Long Bar Twp	93	562
Engue	29	m	c	CHIN	Yuba	Slate Range Bar Tw	93	671
Eugonk	44	m	c	CHIN	Merced	Snelling P O	74	269
Eulin	27	m	c	CHIN	Klamath	Liberty Twp	73	374
Eye	28	m	c	CHIN	Klamath	South Fork Twp	73	382
Eye	26	m	c	CHIN	Klamath	South Fork Twp	73	382
Fah	32	m	c	CHIN	Placer	Bath P O	76	454
Fah	20	m	c	CHIN	Alameda	Hayward	68	78
Faht	44	m	c	CHIN	Marin	San Rafael	74	58
Fake	23	m	c	CHIN	Del Norte	Happy Camp Twp	71	468
Falk	40	m	c	CHIN	Yuba	Slate Range Bar Tw	93	669
Falk	22	m	c	CHIN	Yuba	North East Twp	93	646
Fam	20	f	c	CHIN	Placer	Bath P O	76	429
Fan	42	m	c	CHIN	Sacramento	Granite Twp	77	141
Fan	3	f	c	CA	Butte	Hamilton Twp	70	73
Fan	25	f	c	CHIN	Sacramento	1-Wd Sacramento	77	196
Fanew	31	m	c	CHIN	Placer	Bath P O	76	444
Fang	37	m	c	CHIN	Placer	Bath P O	76	444
Fang	21	m	c	CHIN	San Francisco	8-Wd San Francisco	82	459
Fang	14	m	c	CHIN	Sonoma	Santa Rosa	91	413
Fank	30	m	c	CHIN	Placer	Bath P O	76	444
Fann	50	m	c	CHIN	Placer	Bath P O	76	444
Fanny	14	f	i	CA	San Francisco	San Francisco P O	83	336
Fat	35	m	c	CHIN	Alameda	Brooklyn Twp	68	55
Fatt	25	m	c	CHIN	Yuba	Slate Range Bar Tw	93	670
Faulk	35	m	c	CHIN	Placer	Bath P O	76	453
Faw	30	m	c	CHIN	Del Norte	Happy Camp Twp	71	471
Fay	28	m	c	CHIN	Alameda	Oakland	68	157
Fay	27	m	c	CHIN	Butte	Hamilton Twp	70	68
Fay	20	m	c	CHIN	Sonoma	Sonoma Twp	91	434
Fay	14	f	c	CHIN	San Francisco	8-Wd San Francisco	82	462
Fee	26	m	c	CHIN	Klamath	South Fork Twp	73	384
Feoo	15	m	c	CHIN	Yuba	Marysville	93	602
Few	29	m	c	CHIN	Del Norte	Happy Camp Twp	71	469
Few	25	m	c	CHIN	Del Norte	Happy Camp Twp	71	469
Fick	15	m	c	CHIN	Yuba	Slate Range Bar Tw	93	676
Fie	70	m	c	CHIN	Sacramento	Granite Twp	77	149
Fie	30	m	c	CHIN	Alameda	Brooklyn Twp	68	46
Fie	24	m	c	CHIN	Alameda	Brooklyn Twp	68	41
Fie	19	m	c	CHIN	Yuba	Marysville	93	575
Fii	32	m	c	CHIN	Yuba	Marysville	93	601
Fim	28	m	c	CHIN	Alameda	Oakland	68	224
Fing	30	m	c	CHIN	Monterey	San Juan Twp	74	397
Flack	19	m	c	CHIN	Alameda	Hayward	68	74
Flinn	20	m	c	CHIN	Yuba	Bullards Bar P O	93	548
Flon	16	m	c	CHIN	Yuba	Bullards Bar P O	93	549
Floney	27	m	c	CHIN	Colusa	Grand Island Twp	71	303
Foe	28	m	c	CHIN	Sacramento	Granite Twp	77	140
Foek	24	m	c	CHIN	Colusa	Grand Island Twp	71	303
Foey	17	m	c	CHIN	Klamath	Salmon Twp	73	387
Fog	30	m	c	CHIN	Alameda	Oakland	68	224
Foge	23	m	c	CHIN	Yuba	Slate Range Bar Tw	93	669
Foke	25	m	c	CHIN	Del Norte	Crescent	71	464
Folk	42	m	c	CHIN	Butte	Wyandotte Twp	70	144
Folk	40	m	c	CHIN	Yuba	Bullards Bar P O	93	548
Folk	29	m	c	CHIN	Yuba	Slate Range Bar Tw	93	676
Folk	22	m	c	IREL	Placer	Bath P O	76	444
Fon	38	m	c	CHIN	Alameda	Oakland	68	224
Fon	20	m	c	CHIN	Klamath	Liberty Twp	73	375
Fon	15	m	c	CHIN	Yuba	Marysville	93	580
Fond	24	m	c	CHIN	Del Norte	Happy Camp Twp	71	469
Fone	56	m	c	CHIN	Yuba	Slate Range Bar Tw	93	668
Foney	20	m	c	CHIN	Yuba	Slate Range Bar Tw	93	668
Fong	45	m	c	CHIN	Yuba	Bullards Bar P O	93	552
Fong	42	m	c	CHIN	Placer	Bath P O	76	444
Fong	42	m	c	CHIN	Yuba	Long Bar Twp	93	560
Fong	40	m	c	CHIN	Yuba	Slate Range Bar Tw	93	672
Fong	40	m	c	CHIN	Yuba	Bullards Bar P O	93	548
Fong	38	m	c	CHIN	Yuba	Bullards Bar P O	93	548
Fong	35	m	c	CHIN	Colusa	Grand Island Twp	71	303
Fong	35	m	c	CHIN	Alameda	Brooklyn Twp	68	41
Fong	32	m	c	CHIN	Alameda	Alvarado	68	305
Fong	30	m	c	CHIN	Del Norte	Crescent	71	464
Fong	30	m	c	CHIN	Yuba	Slate Range Bar Tw	93	669
Fong	29	m	c	CHIN	Placer	Bath P O	76	444
Fong	28	m	c	CHIN	Yuba	North East Twp	93	647
Fong	27	m	c	CHIN	Del Norte	Happy Camp Twp	71	468
Fong	27	m	c	CHIN	Klamath	Liberty Twp	73	374
Fong	27	m	c	CHIN	Yuba	Marysville	93	620
Fong	27	m	c	CHIN	Yuba	Linda Twp	93	558
Fong	25	m	c	CHIN	Yuba	Parks Bar Twp	93	649
Fong	25	m	c	CHIN	Yuba	North East Twp	93	645
Fong	21	m	c	CHIN	Napa	Napa Twp	75	28
Fong	20	m	c	CHIN	Klamath	Liberty Twp	73	375
Fong	20	m	c	CHIN	Yuba	Slate Range Bar Tw	93	676
Fong	18	m	c	CHIN	Alameda	Hayward	68	74
Fong	16	m	c	CHIN	Yuba	North East Twp	93	646

© 2001 by Heritage Quest. All rights reserved.

Series M593

Name	Age	S	R	B-PL	County	Locale	Roll	Pg
Fong	15	m	c	CHIN	Yuba	Long Bar Twp	93	562
Fong	13	m	c	CHIN	San Francisco	8-Wd San Francisco	82	456
Fonk	20	m	c	CHIN	Placer	Bath P O	76	444
Font	14	m	c	CHIN	Merced	Snelling P O	74	278
Foo	40	m	c	CHIN	Butte	Bidwell Twp	70	3
Foo	40	m	c	CHIN	Yuba	Long Bar Twp	93	562
Foo	37	m	c	CHIN	Alameda	Murray Twp	68	114
Foo	37	m	c	CHIN	Yuba	Slate Range Bar Tw	93	669
Foo	36	m	c	CHIN	Alameda	Oakland	68	260
Foo	33	m	c	CHIN	Yuba	North East Twp	93	646
Foo	32	m	c	CHIN	Merced	Snelling P O	74	278
Foo	32	m	c	CHIN	Yuba	Long Bar Twp	93	560
Foo	32	m	c	CHIN	Alameda	Brooklyn Twp	68	41
Foo	32	m	c	CHIN	Alameda	Alvarado	68	305
Foo	32	m	c	CHIN	Yuba	Slate Range Bar Tw	93	674
Foo	29	m	c	CHIN	Alameda	Oakland	68	224
Foo	27	m	c	CHIN	Alameda	Brooklyn	68	21
Foo	25	m	c	CHIN	Alameda	Brooklyn Twp	68	46
Foo	25	m	c	CHIN	Yuba	Slate Range Bar Tw	93	669
Foo	23	m	c	CHIN	Yuba	W Bear Rvr Twp	93	684
Foo	19	m	c	CHIN	Alameda	Brooklyn Twp	68	41
Foo	19	m	c	CHIN	Alameda	Eden Twp	68	81
Foo	18	m	c	CHIN	Alameda	Brooklyn Twp	68	41
Foo	17	m	c	CHIN	Alameda	Brooklyn	68	22
Fooh	25	m	c	CHIN	Yuba	Long Bar Twp	93	566
Fook	37	m	c	CHIN	Butte	Wyandotte Twp	70	144
Fook	31	m	c	CHIN	Yuba	Marysville	93	601
Fook	26	m	c	CHIN	Alameda	Brooklyn Twp	68	42
Fook	22	m	c	CHIN	Yuba	North East Twp	93	645
Fook	21	m	c	CHIN	Alameda	Hayward	68	74
Fooke	24	m	c	CHIN	Placer	Bath P O	76	428
Foon	35	m	c	CHIN	Yuba	Long Bar Twp	93	560
Foon	31	m	c	CHIN	Butte	Bidwell Twp	70	3
Foot	22	m	c	CHIN	Yuba	Slate Range Bar Tw	93	678
Footie	44	m	c	CHIN	Placer	Bath P O	76	445
Fordep	47	m	c	CHIN	Yuba	Long Bar Twp	93	564
Fork	40	m	c	CHIN	Yuba	Slate Range Bar Tw	93	675
Fork	36	m	c	CHIN	Alameda	Oakland	68	254
Fot	25	m	c	CHIN	Del Norte	Happy Camp Twp	71	469
Fou	35	m	c	CHIN	Alameda	Oakland	68	224
Fou	35	m	c	CHIN	Alameda	Oakland	68	224
Fou	30	m	c	CHIN	Alameda	Oakland	68	254
Fou	16	m	c	CHIN	San Francisco	8-Wd San Francisco	82	472
Fouk	37	m	c	CHIN	Yuba	Marysville	93	592
Foulk	32	m	c	CHIN	Yuba	Long Bar Twp	93	562
Foulk	22	m	c	CHIN	Yuba	Slate Range Bar Tw	93	669
Fow	30	m	c	CHIN	Yuba	Bullards Bar P O	93	552
Fow	24	m	c	CHIN	Alameda	Brooklyn Twp	68	41
Fowe	20	m	c	CHIN	Yuba	Slate Range Bar Tw	93	669
Fox	30	m	c	CHIN	Sutter	Sutter Twp	92	127
Foy	41	m	c	CHIN	Klamath	Salmon Twp	73	387
Foy	40	m	c	CHIN	Marin	San Rafael Twp	74	59
Foy	34	m	c	CHIN	Yuba	Marysville	93	592
Foy	32	m	c	CHIN	Yuba	East Bear Rvr Twp	93	545
Foy	31	m	c	CHIN	Placer	Bath P O	76	442
Foy	30	m	c	CHIN	Sacramento	American Twp	77	64
Foy	27	m	c	CHIN	Butte	Hamilton Twp	70	68
Foy	16	m	c	CHIN	Yuba	Marysville	93	592
Francisco	1	m	w	CA	San Diego	San Luis Rey	78	513
Frank	8	m	c	CHIN	Sacramento	1-Wd Sacramento	77	197
Freman	13	m	c	CHIN	Colusa	Colusa	71	293
Fung	40	m	c	CHIN	Placer	Bath P O	76	444
Fung	32	m	c	CHIN	Butte	Hamilton Twp	70	68
Fung	28	m	c	CHIN	Klamath	South Fork Twp	73	384
Fung	28	m	c	CHIN	Yuba	Slate Range Bar Tw	93	672
Fung	23	m	c	CHIN	Colusa	Monroe Twp	71	316
Fut	29	m	c	CHIN	Yuba	Marysville	93	594
Gadn	29	m	c	CHIN	Butte	Bidwell Twp	70	3
Gah	40	m	c	CHIN	Yuba	Rose Bar Twp	93	666
Gah	29	m	c	CHIN	Yuba	Marysville	93	576
Galenda	41	m	w	MEXI	Yuba	Marysville	93	588
Galm	24	m	c	CHIN	Klamath	South Fork Twp	73	382
Gam	20	m	c	CHIN	Merced	Snelling P O	74	279
Gan	30	m	c	CHIN	Sutter	Sutter Twp	92	116
Gan	19	m	c	CHIN	Yuba	North East Twp	93	645
Gan	15	m	c	CHIN	San Francisco	8-Wd San Francisco	82	481
Gang	40	m	c	CHIN	Klamath	South Fork Twp	73	383
Gang	40	m	c	CHIN	Placer	Bath P O	76	454
Gange	19	m	c	CHIN	Yuba	Slate Range Bar Tw	93	668
Gann	25	m	c	CHIN	Klamath	Salmon Twp	73	387
Gann	23	m	c	CHIN	Yuba	East Bear Rvr Twp	93	540
Gat	50	m	c	CHIN	Del Norte	Happy Camp Twp	71	469
Gat	30	m	c	CHIN	Colusa	Grand Island Twp	71	303
Gat	28	m	c	CHIN	Colusa	Monroe Twp	71	313
Gata	21	m	c	CHIN	Klamath	Salmon Twp	73	387
Gay	52	m	c	CHIN	Yuba	Long Bar Twp	93	560
Gay	30	m	c	CHIN	Yuba	North East Twp	93	646
Gay	26	m	c	CHIN	Del Norte	Happy Camp Twp	71	468
Gay	24	m	c	CHIN	Klamath	Salmon Twp	73	388
Gee	50	m	c	CHIN	Sacramento	Granite Twp	77	149
Gee	50	m	c	CHIN	Sacramento	Granite Twp	77	141
Gee	43	m	c	CHIN	Klamath	Sawyers Bar	73	378
Gee	41	m	c	CHIN	Yuba	Slate Range Bar Tw	93	669
Gee	40	m	c	CHIN	Sacramento	Granite Twp	77	140
Gee	35	m	c	CHIN	Yuba	Bullards Bar P O	93	553
Gee	30	m	c	CHIN	Sacramento	Georgianna Twp	77	130
Gee	30	m	c	CHIN	Merced	Snelling P O	74	279
Gee	30	m	c	CHIN	Merced	Snelling P O	74	279
Gee	30	m	c	CHIN	Colusa	Monroe Twp	71	316
Gee	29	m	c	CHIN	Klamath	Liberty Twp	73	374
Gee	29	m	c	CHIN	Yuba	Marysville	93	600
Gee	28	m	c	CHIN	Klamath	Liberty Twp	73	375
Gee	24	m	c	CHIN	Yuba	Bullards Bar P O	93	548
Gee	21	m	c	CHIN	Butte	Wyandotte Twp	70	148
Gee	18	m	c	CHIN	Yuba	Marysville	93	592
Gee	17	m	c	CHIN	San Francisco	8-Wd San Francisco	82	489
Gee	14	m	c	CHIN	San Francisco	8-Wd San Francisco	82	438
Gee	12	m	c	CHIN	San Francisco	8-Wd San Francisco	82	443
Gen	51	m	c	CHIN	Yuba	Marysville	93	594
Gene	27	m	c	CHIN	Del Norte	Happy Camp Twp	71	469
Genn	30	m	c	CHIN	Klamath	Sawyers Bar	73	378
Geo	20	m	c	CHIN	Siskiyou	Hamburg Twp	89	597
Geok	35	m	c	CHIN	Alameda	Brooklyn	68	21
George	40	m	c	CHIN	Klamath	South Fork Twp	73	383
George	38	m	c	CHIN	Klamath	Liberty Twp	73	375
George	36	m	c	CHIN	Monterey	Castroville Twp	74	327
George	30	m	c	CHIN	Yuba	Slate Range Bar Tw	93	673
George	28	m	c	CHIN	Marin	San Rafael Twp	74	30
Gertrudes	30	f	w	CA	San Diego	San Luis Rey	78	513
Geung	34	m	c	CHIN	Yuba	Linda Twp	93	558
Gew	40	m	c	CHIN	Yuba	North East Twp	93	645
Gew	17	m	c	CHIN	Alameda	Brooklyn Twp	68	39
Gim	32	m	c	CHIN	Yuba	New York Twp	93	638
Gim	29	m	c	CHIN	Sacramento	Granite Twp	77	149
Gim	26	m	c	CHIN	Klamath	Liberty Twp	73	374
Gim	25	m	c	CHIN	Yolo	Cache Crk Twp	93	424
Gim	20	m	c	CHIN	Yuba	East Bear Rvr Twp	93	545
Gin	44	m	c	CHIN	Placer	Bath P O	76	443
Gin	30	m	c	CHIN	Merced	Snelling P O	74	279
Gin	25	m	c	CHIN	Colusa	Monroe Twp	71	313
Gin	22	m	c	CHIN	Merced	Snelling P O	74	279
Gin	15	m	c	CHIN	Del Norte	Mountain Twp	71	475
Ging	29	m	c	CHIN	Yuba	Bullards Bar P O	93	547
Ging	25	m	c	CHIN	Yuba	New York Twp	93	638
Ging	18	m	c	CHIN	Klamath	Liberty Twp	73	375
Ging	17	m	c	CHIN	San Francisco	8-Wd San Francisco	82	497
Ginn	46	m	c	CHIN	Yuba	North East Twp	93	647
Ginn	30	m	c	CHIN	Yuba	Slate Range Bar Tw	93	668
Ginn	14	m	c	CHIN	Yuba	W Bear Rvr Twp	93	685
Glan	23	m	c	CHIN	Colusa	Monroe Twp	71	313
Gluck	24	m	c	CHIN	Marin	Tomales Twp	74	84
Go	45	m	c	CHIN	Sacramento	Granite Twp	77	140
Go	45	m	c	CHIN	Sacramento	Granite Twp	77	141
Go	43	m	c	CHIN	Sacramento	Granite Twp	77	140
Go	30	m	c	CHIN	Sacramento	Granite Twp	77	140
Go	29	m	c	CHIN	Sacramento	Granite Twp	77	140
Go	29	m	c	CHIN	Sacramento	Granite Twp	77	149
Go	18	m	c	CHIN	Alameda	Brooklyn	68	24
Goey	26	m	c	CHIN	Klamath	Liberty Twp	73	375
Golle	40	m	c	CHIN	Yuba	New York Twp	93	638
Gom	24	m	c	CHIN	Alameda	Washington Twp	68	295
Gomez	30	m	c	CHIN	Placer	Bath P O	76	442
Gon	24	m	c	CHIN	Del Norte	Happy Camp Twp	71	468
Gon	20	m	c	CHIN	Del Norte	Happy Camp Twp	71	469
Gon	17	m	c	CHIN	Alameda	Washington Twp	68	293
Gon	14	f	c	CHIN	Colusa	Colusa	71	295
Gone	40	m	c	CHIN	Yuba	Bullards Bar P O	93	552
Gong	50	m	c	CHIN	Yuba	Slate Range Bar Tw	93	674
Gong	49	m	c	CHIN	Placer	Bath P O	76	429
Gong	42	m	c	CHIN	Klamath	Salmon Twp	73	388
Gong	38	m	c	CHIN	Alameda	Oakland	68	224
Gong	24	m	c	CHIN	Marin	Tomales Twp	74	77
Gong	22	m	c	CHIN	Del Norte	Happy Camp Twp	71	469
Gong	22	m	c	CHIN	Alameda	Eden Twp	68	60
Gong	18	m	c	CHIN	Yuba	Bullards Bar P O	93	549
Gong	16	m	c	CHIN	Del Norte	Mountain Twp	71	475
Gong	15	m	c	CHIN	Del Norte	Happy Camp Twp	71	468
Gony	35	m	c	CHIN	Yuba	Bullards Bar P O	93	549
Goo	40	m	c	CHIN	Alameda	Murray Twp	68	102
Goo	40	m	c	CHIN	Alameda	Oakland	68	260
Goo	37	m	c	CHIN	Alameda	Oakland	68	267
Goo	35	m	c	CHIN	Alameda	Murray Twp	68	102
Goo	35	m	c	CHIN	Alameda	Oakland	68	266
Goo	34	m	c	CHIN	Alameda	Oakland	68	152
Goo	28	m	c	CHIN	Alameda	Oakland	68	232
Goo	27	m	c	CHIN	Alameda	Murray Twp	68	102
Goo	27	m	c	CHIN	Alameda	Murray Twp	68	111
Gooay	29	m	c	CHIN	Yuba	Marysville	93	592
Gooey	51	m	c	CHIN	Klamath	Salmon Twp	73	387
Gooey	32	m	c	CHIN	Klamath	South Fork Twp	73	384
Gook	20	m	c	CHIN	Alameda	Brooklyn Twp	68	41
Goon	27	m	c	CHIN	Colusa	Colusa	71	299
Goon	25	m	c	CHIN	Placer	Clipper Gap P O	76	376
Goon	23	f	c	CHIN	Butte	Chico Twp	70	27
Goon	18	m	c	CHIN	Alameda	Hayward	68	74
Goone	40	m	c	CHIN	Yuba	North East Twp	93	647
Goone	20	m	c	CHIN	Yuba	North East Twp	93	647
Gore	40	m	c	CHIN	Yuba	Bullards Bar P O	93	553
Gorey	26	m	c	CHIN	Klamath	South Fork Twp	73	384
Gou	40	m	c	CHIN	Yuba	Slate Range Bar Tw	93	677
Gough	45	m	c	CHIN	Klamath	South Fork Twp	73	382
Gough	25	m	c	CHIN	Yuba	Slate Range Bar Tw	93	669
Govey	35	m	c	CHIN	Klamath	Liberty Twp	73	376
Govey	30	m	c	CHIN	Klamath	South Fork Twp	73	383

© 2001 by Heritage Quest. All rights reserved.

Name	Age	S	R	B-PL	County	Series M593 Locale	Roll	Pg
Gow	52	m	c	CHIN	Yuba	Bullards Bar P O	93	552
Gow	36	m	c	CHIN	Alameda	Washington Twp	68	270
Gow	28	m	c	CHIN	Alameda	San Leandro	68	96
Gow	28	m	c	CHIN	Calaveras	San Andreas P O	70	160
Gow	25	m	c	CHIN	Yuba	East Bear Rvr Twp	93	545
Gow	21	m	c	CHIN	Colusa	Colusa	71	299
Gow	20	m	c	CHIN	Alameda	Brooklyn Twp	68	46
Gow	20	m	c	CHIN	San Francisco	8-Wd San Francisco	82	384
Gow	20	m	c	CHIN	Klamath	South Fork Twp	73	384
Gow	19	m	c	CHIN	Alameda	Brooklyn Twp	68	41
Gow	18	m	c	CHIN	Sonoma	Petaluma Twp	91	363
Grecee	30	m	c	CHIN	Colusa	Monroe Twp	71	316
Guadalupa	30	f	w	MEXI	San Diego	San Pasqual Valley	78	524
Guan	38	m	c	CHIN	Butte	Wyandotte Twp	70	144
Gue	40	m	c	CHIN	Yuba	North East Twp	93	647
Gue	38	m	c	CHIN	Alameda	Oakland	68	223
Gue	19	m	c	CHIN	Yuba	North East Twp	93	645
Guen	30	m	c	CHIN	Alameda	Washington Twp	68	295
Guet	30	m	c	CHIN	Klamath	South Fork Twp	73	382
Guin	21	m	c	CHIN	Merced	Snelling P O	74	279
Gum	45	m	c	CHIN	Del Norte	Happy Camp Twp	71	469
Gum	38	m	c	CHIN	Marin	Tomales Twp	74	86
Gum	21	m	c	CHIN	Colusa	Colusa	71	299
Gune	40	m	c	CHIN	Merced	Snelling P O	74	249
Gung	45	m	c	CHIN	Yuba	Slate Range Bar Tw	93	668
Gung	32	m	c	CHIN	Klamath	South Fork Twp	73	384
Gung	31	m	c	CHIN	Placer	Bath P O	76	429
Guon	48	m	c	CHIN	Placer	Bath P O	76	444
Gut	60	m	c	CHIN	Del Norte	Happy Camp Twp	71	468
Hack	40	m	c	CHIN	Yuba	North East Twp	93	646
Hage	44	m	c	CHIN	Yuba	Slate Range Bar Tw	93	678
Hagn	35	m	c	CHIN	Butte	Bidwell Twp	70	3
Haley	24	m	c	CHIN	Alameda	Brooklyn	68	34
Halone	22	m	c	CHIN	Placer	Bath P O	76	451
Halp	30	m	c	CHIN	Yuba	Slate Range Bar Tw	93	672
Ham	20	m	c	CHIN	Yuba	Marysville	93	602
Ham	14	m	c	CHIN	Klamath	South Fork Twp	73	382
Ham	14	m	c	CHIN	Yuba	Marysville	93	578
Han	18	m	c	CHIN	Del Norte	Crescent Twp	71	455
Hand	42	m	c	CHIN	Del Norte	Happy Camp Twp	71	468
Handy	30	m	c	CHIN	Merced	Snelling P O	74	278
Hane	25	m	c	CHIN	Colusa	Colusa	71	299
Hang	60	m	c	CHIN	Klamath	Sawyers Bar	73	378
Hang	48	m	c	CHIN	Alameda	Oakland	68	267
Hang	30	m	c	CHIN	Colusa	Monroe Twp	71	311
Hang	28	m	c	CHIN	Yuba	Marysville	93	620
Hang	28	m	c	CHIN	Colusa	Monroe Twp	71	315
Hang	28	m	c	CHIN	Yuba	Marysville	93	601
Hang	27	m	c	CHIN	San Francisco	11-Wd San Francisc	84	477
Hang	26	m	c	CHIN	Klamath	Salmon Twp	73	388
Hang	26	m	c	CHIN	Del Norte	Happy Camp Twp	71	468
Hang	23	m	c	CHIN	Klamath	Liberty Twp	73	374
Hang	15	m	c	CHIN	Placer	Bath P O	76	454
Hanh	46	m	c	CHIN	Klamath	South Fork Twp	73	385
Hank	50	m	c	CHIN	Placer	Bath P O	76	424
Hank	17	m	c	CHIN	Placer	Bath P O	76	444
Hann	42	m	c	CHIN	Placer	Bath P O	76	444
Hannar	38	m	c	CHIN	Yuba	W Bear Rvr Twp	93	685
Hany	45	m	c	CHIN	Klamath	South Fork Twp	73	382
Happ	42	m	c	CHIN	Yuba	Slate Range Bar Tw	93	668
Harp	25	m	c	CHIN	Yuba	Slate Range Bar Tw	93	678
Harr	24	m	c	CHIN	Yuba	W Bear Rvr Twp	93	684
Hauck	37	m	c	CHIN	Yuba	Slate Range Bar Tw	93	668
Hauk	26	m	c	CHIN	Placer	Bath P O	76	445
Haw	55	m	c	CHIN	Yuba	Bullards Bar P O	93	548
Haw	35	m	c	CHIN	Yuba	North East Twp	93	647
Haw	32	m	c	CHIN	Yuba	North East Twp	93	645
Haw	22	m	c	CHIN	Yuba	Slate Range Bar Tw	93	672
Hawe	20	m	c	CHIN	Yuba	Slate Range Bar Tw	93	668
Hawk	49	m	c	CHIN	Klamath	Salmon Twp	73	387
Hay	50	m	c	CHIN	Sacramento	Granite Twp	77	140
Hay	40	m	c	CHIN	Klamath	South Fork Twp	73	382
Hay	40	m	c	CHIN	Sacramento	Granite Twp	77	141
Hay	36	m	c	CHIN	Alameda	Brooklyn Twp	68	41
Hay	35	m	c	CHIN	Yuba	Long Bar Twp	93	566
Hay	32	m	c	CHIN	Yuba	Bullards Bar P O	93	552
Hay	30	m	c	CHIN	Yuba	New York Twp	93	640
Hay	28	m	c	CHIN	Klamath	Liberty Twp	73	374
Hay	20	m	c	CHIN	Yuba	Slate Range Bar Tw	93	677
Hay	18	m	c	CHIN	Klamath	Liberty Twp	73	376
Hee	60	m	c	CHIN	Sacramento	Granite Twp	77	140
Hee	30	m	c	CHIN	Sonoma	Salt Point	91	389
Hee	24	m	c	CHIN	Yuba	Slate Range Bar Tw	93	677
Hee	22	m	c	CHIN	San Francisco	5-Wd San Francisco	81	17
Hee	22	m	c	CHIN	Yuba	Bullards Bar P O	93	553
Hee	19	m	c	CHIN	Marin	Point Reyes Twp	74	22
Heeh	38	m	c	CHIN	Colusa	Monroe Twp	71	315
Heft	50	m	c	CHIN	Yuba	North East Twp	93	645
Heim	16	m	c	CHIN	Alameda	Eden Twp	68	91
Hein	27	m	c	CHIN	Alameda	Brooklyn Twp	68	41
Hein	19	m	c	CHIN	Alameda	Brooklyn	68	21
Hein	19	m	c	CHIN	San Francisco	8-Wd San Francisco	82	465
Hell	28	m	c	CHIN	Yuba	Bullards Bar P O	93	548
Hem	60	m	c	CHIN	Klamath	Klamath Twp	73	371
Hem	60	m	c	CHIN	Klamath	Klamath Twp	73	371
Hem	48	m	c	CHIN	Yuba	East Bear Rvr Twp	93	545
Hem	40	m	c	CHIN	Yuba	Slate Range Bar Tw	93	674
Hemm	32	m	c	CHIN	Yuba	Slate Range Bar Tw	93	673
Hemn	34	m	c	CHIN	Yuba	North East Twp	93	646
Hemn	23	m	c	CHIN	Yuba	Slate Range Bar Tw	93	669
Hen	45	m	c	CHIN	Klamath	Salmon Twp	73	387
Hen	30	m	c	CHIN	Colusa	Monroe Twp	71	312
Henak	30	m	c	CHIN	Placer	Bath P O	76	424
Heng	26	m	c	CHIN	Yuba	Slate Range Bar Tw	93	668
Hengee	47	m	c	CHIN	Yuba	Slate Range Bar Tw	93	677
Henm	40	m	c	CHIN	Yuba	Slate Range Bar Tw	93	670
Henm	34	m	c	CHIN	Yuba	North East Twp	93	645
Henm	20	m	c	CHIN	Yuba	Slate Range Bar Tw	93	676
Henn	40	m	c	CHIN	Yuba	North East Twp	93	646
Henn	26	m	c	CHIN	Yuba	North East Twp	93	646
Henne	41	m	c	CHIN	Butte	Mountain Spring Tw	70	90
Heny	37	m	c	CHIN	Yuba	Slate Range Bar Tw	93	668
Heom	22	m	c	CHIN	Yuba	North East Twp	93	647
Heong	22	m	c	CHIN	Klamath	Sawyers Bar	73	378
Heong	17	m	c	CHIN	Yuba	Marysville	93	602
Hetty	16	f	w	CA	Sonoma	Mendocino Twp	91	287
Heung	34	m	c	CHIN	Yuba	Marysville	93	576
Heup	34	m	c	CHIN	Klamath	Salmon Twp	73	387
Hew	60	m	c	CHIN	Klamath	South Fork Twp	73	383
Hew	40	m	c	CHIN	Yuba	North East Twp	93	645
Hew	35	m	c	CHIN	Yuba	Slate Range Bar Tw	93	668
Hew	31	m	c	CHIN	Yuba	Slate Range Bar Tw	93	668
Hey	38	m	c	CHIN	Del Norte	Mountain Twp	71	475
Heye	35	m	c	CHIN	Klamath	South Fork Twp	73	384
Hie	50	m	c	CHIN	Sacramento	Granite Twp	77	141
Hie	3	f	c	CA	Alameda	Alvarado	68	304
Hie	23	f	c	CHIN	Sacramento	1-Wd Sacramento	77	199
Hie	22	m	c	CHIN	Alameda	Eden Twp	68	60
Hie	20	m	c	CHIN	Del Norte	Happy Camp Twp	71	468
Him	18	m	c	CHIN	Placer	Bath P O	76	444
Hin	32	m	c	CHIN	Yuba	Linda Twp	93	558
Hin	22	m	c	CHIN	Marin	Tomales Twp	74	81
Hing	60	m	c	CHIN	Sacramento	Granite Twp	77	149
Hing	44	m	c	CHIN	Sacramento	Granite Twp	77	140
Hing	42	m	c	CHIN	Marin	Tomales Twp	74	84
Hing	40	m	c	CHIN	Yuba	North East Twp	93	645
Hing	40	m	c	CHIN	Yuba	Bullards Bar P O	93	548
Hing	40	m	c	CHIN	Marin	San Rafael	74	58
Hing	32	m	c	CHIN	Sacramento	Granite Twp	77	140
Hing	32	m	c	CHIN	Lassen	Susanville Twp	73	441
Hing	30	m	c	CHIN	Colusa	Monroe Twp	71	311
Hing	26	m	c	CHIN	Yuba	North East Twp	93	646
Hing	22	m	c	CHIN	Yuba	New York Twp	93	640
Hing	18	m	c	CHIN	Alameda	Brooklyn Twp	68	39
Hing	18	m	c	CHIN	San Francisco	8-Wd San Francisco	82	434
Hing	15	m	c	CHIN	San Francisco	8-Wd San Francisco	82	441
Hing	12	m	c	CHIN	San Francisco	8-Wd San Francisco	82	461
Ho	41	m	c	CHIN	Sacramento	American Twp	77	64
Ho	32	m	c	CHIN	Sacramento	Granite Twp	77	149
Ho	32	m	c	CHIN	Sacramento	American Twp	77	64
Ho	22	m	c	CHIN	Yuba	Marysville	93	621
Hoa	28	m	c	CHIN	Sacramento	Granite Twp	77	141
Hock	21	m	c	CHIN	Alameda	Brooklyn Twp	68	41
Hocy	60	m	c	CHIN	Klamath	Dillon Twp	73	369
Hoe	40	m	c	CHIN	Sacramento	Granite Twp	77	149
Hoe	35	m	c	CHIN	Sacramento	Granite Twp	77	149
Hoe	24	m	c	CHIN	Alameda	Eden Twp	68	60
Hoey	34	m	c	CHIN	Yuba	Linda Twp	93	558
Hoey	20	m	c	CHIN	Yuba	Marysville	93	601
Hog	40	m	c	CHIN	Klamath	South Fork Twp	73	382
Hogin	24	f	c	CHIN	El Dorado	Placerville Twp	72	97
Hon	24	m	c	CHIN	Alameda	Brooklyn Twp	68	42
Hone	55	m	c	CHIN	Yuba	Slate Range Bar Tw	93	673
Hone	50	m	c	CHIN	Yuba	Slate Range Bar Tw	93	674
Hone	32	m	c	CHIN	Yuba	Slate Range Bar Tw	93	678
Hone	30	m	c	CHIN	Yuba	Slate Range Bar Tw	93	678
Hone	27	m	c	CHIN	Alameda	Alvarado	68	305
Honey	35	m	c	CHIN	Yuba	Slate Range Bar Tw	93	668
Hong	50	m	c	CHIN	Yuba	Slate Range Bar Tw	93	674
Hong	50	m	c	CHIN	Klamath	Salmon Twp	73	387
Hong	47	m	c	CHIN	Marin	Tomales Twp	74	88
Hong	45	m	c	CHIN	Alameda	Murray Twp	68	114
Hong	45	m	c	CHIN	Shasta	Horsetown P O	89	504
Hong	40	m	c	CHIN	Merced	Snelling P O	74	278
Hong	40	m	c	CHIN	Alameda	Murray Twp	68	111
Hong	39	m	c	CHIN	Alameda	Murray Twp	68	111
Hong	38	m	c	CHIN	Alameda	Murray Twp	68	114
Hong	38	m	c	CHIN	Yuba	Bullards Bar P O	93	553
Hong	37	m	c	CHIN	Alameda	Murray Twp	68	102
Hong	36	m	c	CHIN	Klamath	Liberty Twp	73	374
Hong	35	m	c	CHIN	Klamath	Klamath Twp	73	370
Hong	33	m	c	CHIN	Alameda	Brooklyn Twp	68	46
Hong	33	m	c	CHIN	Marin	San Rafael Twp	74	37
Hong	30	m	c	CHIN	Yuba	Slate Range Bar Tw	93	668
Hong	30	m	c	CHIN	Klamath	Salmon Twp	73	388
Hong	29	m	c	CHIN	Alameda	Washington Twp	68	299
Hong	29	m	c	CHIN	Alameda	Murray Twp	68	114
Hong	28	m	c	CHIN	Yuba	Slate Range Bar Tw	93	669
Hong	28	m	c	CHIN	Alameda	Murray Twp	68	102
Hong	27	m	c	CHIN	Yuba	North East Twp	93	646
Hong	25	m	c	CHIN	Alameda	Washington Twp	68	299
Hong	25	m	c	CHIN	Alameda	Brooklyn	68	22
Hong	25	m	c	CHIN	Colusa	Monroe Twp	71	315
Hong	25	m	c	CHIN	Placer	Bath P O	76	453

© 2001 by Heritage Quest. All rights reserved.

Name	Age	S	R	B-PL	County	Locale	Series M593 Roll	Pg
Hong	25	m	c	CHIN	Sonoma	Salt Point	91	380
Hong	24	m	c	CHIN	Yuba	Slate Range Bar Tw	93	669
Hong	22	m	c	CHIN	Yuba	W Bear Rvr Twp	93	684
Hong	22	m	c	CHIN	Klamath	South Fork Twp	73	383
Hong	21	m	c	CHIN	Alameda	Murray Twp	68	120
Hong	20	m	c	CHIN	Sonoma	Santa Rosa	91	401
Hong	18	m	c	CHIN	Alameda	Eden Twp	68	60
Hong	18	m	c	CHIN	Klamath	Liberty Twp	73	376
Hong	18	m	c	CHIN	Sonoma	Vallejo Twp	91	452
Hong	16	m	c	CHIN	Alameda	Oakland	68	181
Hong	12	m	c	CHIN	Alameda	Brooklyn	68	22
Honge	62	m	c	CHIN	Yuba	Slate Range Bar Tw	93	668
Hony	30	m	c	CHIN	Yuba	Bullards Bar P O	93	552
Hoo	26	m	c	CHIN	Alameda	Brooklyn Twp	68	42
Hook	25	m	c	CHIN	Colusa	Monroe Twp	71	311
Hoon	23	m	c	CHIN	Alameda	Washington Twp	68	293
Hoong	25	m	c	CHIN	Sonoma	Salt Point	91	387
Hoore	40	m	c	CHIN	Yuba	Slate Range Bar Tw	93	668
Hop	6	m	c	CHIN	Butte	Chico Twp	70	27
Hop	44	m	c	CHIN	Sacramento	Granite Twp	77	140
Hop	37	m	c	CHIN	Sacramento	American Twp	77	64
Hop	31	m	c	CHIN	Yuba	Marysville	93	601
Hop	30	m	c	CHIN	Sacramento	American Twp	77	64
Hop	28	m	c	CHIN	Sacramento	Granite Twp	77	140
Hop	28	m	c	CHIN	Sacramento	Granite Twp	77	149
Hop	26	m	c	CHIN	Sacramento	Georgianna Twp	77	130
Hop	25	m	c	CHIN	Sacramento	American Twp	77	64
Hop	20	m	c	CHIN	Klamath	South Fork Twp	73	383
Hop	17	m	c	CHIN	Merced	Snelling P O	74	278
Horm	40	m	c	CHIN	Yuba	Slate Range Bar Tw	93	674
Horng	30	m	c	CHIN	Calaveras	Copperopolis P O	70	260
Hortensia	4	f	w	CHIL	Marin	Sausalito Twp	74	67
How	44	m	c	CHIN	Klamath	Klamath Twp	73	370
How	42	m	c	CHIN	Klamath	Orleans Twp	73	381
How	33	m	c	CHIN	Yuba	Marysville	93	592
How	30	m	c	CHIN	Klamath	Liberty Twp	73	374
How	28	m	c	CHIN	Alameda	Murray Twp	68	114
How	20	m	c	CHIN	San Francisco	8-Wd San Francisco	82	422
How	16	m	c	CHIN	San Francisco	8-Wd San Francisco	82	434
How	15	m	c	CHIN	Butte	Bidwell Twp	70	3
Howe	36	m	c	CHIN	Yuba	North East Twp	93	647
Howe	28	m	c	CHIN	Klamath	Orleans Twp	73	380
Howe	21	m	c	CHIN	Alameda	Murray Twp	68	120
Hoy	33	m	c	CHIN	Alameda	Brooklyn Twp	68	41
Hoy	32	m	c	CHIN	Colusa	Spring Valley Twp	71	336
Hoy	28	m	c	CHIN	Marin	Novato Twp	74	11
Hoy	27	m	c	CHIN	Butte	Mountain Spring Tw	70	89
Hoy	25	m	c	CHIN	Merced	Snelling P O	74	250
Hoy	25	m	c	CHIN	Colusa	Monroe Twp	71	324
Hoy	22	m	c	CHIN	Yuba	Marysville	93	595
Hoy	19	m	c	CHIN	Alameda	Brooklyn	68	21
Hoy	11	m	c	CHIN	Sacramento	4-Wd Sacramento	77	326
Huck	23	m	c	CHIN	Yuba	Rose Bar Twp	93	666
Huey	35	m	c	CHIN	Yuba	Slate Range Bar Tw	93	674
Hugh	39	m	c	CHIN	Merced	Snelling P O	74	279
Hugl	25	m	c	CHIN	San Francisco	8-Wd San Francisco	82	420
Humn	45	m	c	CHIN	Yuba	Long Bar Twp	93	560
Hun	34	m	c	CHIN	Yuba	Marysville	93	621
Hun	14	m	c	CHIN	Yuba	Marysville	93	621
Hunee	38	m	c	CHIN	Placer	Bath P O	76	430
Hung	41	m	c	CHIN	Yuba	Marysville	93	601
Hung	40	m	c	CHIN	Del Norte	Crescent	71	463
Hung	38	m	c	CHIN	Klamath	South Fork Twp	73	384
Hung	36	m	c	CHIN	Marin	Tomales Twp	74	88
Hung	27	m	c	CHIN	Marin	Tomales Twp	74	77
Hung	25	m	c	CHIN	Yuba	Marysville	93	601
Hung	21	m	c	CHIN	Yuba	Marysville	93	601
Hung	17	m	c	CHIN	Yuba	Marysville	93	602
Hurdy	25	m	c	CHIN	Klamath	South Fork Twp	73	382
Hy	37	m	c	CHIN	Del Norte	Happy Camp Twp	71	471
Hy	30	f	c	CHIN	Alameda	Alvarado	68	304
Hye	33	m	c	CHIN	Yuba	Slate Range Bar Tw	93	676
I Yew	40	m	c	CHIN	Klamath	Klamath Twp	73	370
Iean	25	m	c	CHIN	Yuba	Slate Range Bar Tw	93	678
Ieni	30	m	c	CHIN	Yuba	Parks Bar Twp	93	650
Igen	27	m	c	CHIN	Klamath	South Fork Twp	73	382
Ione	22	m	c	CHIN	Colusa	Grand Island Twp	71	302
Ione	19	m	c	CHIN	Sacramento	1-Wd Sacramento	77	172
Iumi	18	m	c	CHIN	Yuba	Slate Range Bar Tw	93	678
Ive	41	m	c	CHIN	Calaveras	Copperopolis P O	70	260
Ivey	22	m	c	CHIN	Colusa	Monroe Twp	71	324
Jacinta	20	f	w	CA	San Diego	San Luis Rey	78	513
Jack	43	m	c	CHIN	Yuba	Bullards Bar P O	93	552
Jack	34	m	c	CHIN	Yuba	East Bear Rvr Twp	93	545
Jack	33	m	c	CHIN	Calaveras	Copperopolis P O	70	260
Jack	32	m	c	CHIN	Yuba	Slate Range Bar Tw	93	668
Jack	31	m	c	CHIN	Yuba	W Bear Rvr Twp	93	684
Jack	29	m	c	CHIN	Yuba	Marysville	93	597
Jack	26	m	c	CHIN	Siskiyou	Yreka Twp	89	666
Jack	26	m	c	CHIN	Siskiyou	Cottonwood Twp	89	594
Jack	25	m	c	CHIN	Sacramento	Granite Twp	77	141
Jack	24	m	c	CHIN	Yuba	Marysville Twp	93	568
Jack	20	m	c	CHIN	Lassen	Long Valley Twp	73	437
Jack	20	m	c	CHIN	Siskiyou	Cottonwood Twp	89	595
Jack [Chinaman]	38	m	c	CHIN	Calaveras	San Andreas P O	70	156
Jae	20	m	c	CHIN	Yuba	Bullards Bar P O	93	548
Jake	55	m	c	CHIN	Klamath	Salmon Twp	73	388

Name	Age	S	R	B-PL	County	Locale	Series M593 Roll	Pg
Jake	40	m	c	CHIN	Klamath	Salmon Twp	73	387
Jake	40	m	c	CHIN	Klamath	South Fork Twp	73	382
Jake	35	m	c	CHIN	Yuba	East Bear Rvr Twp	93	546
Jake	35	m	c	CHIN	Klamath	Liberty Twp	73	376
Jake	35	m	c	CHIN	Siskiyou	Scott Valley Twp	89	610
Jake	30	m	c	CHIN	Colusa	Colusa	71	299
Jake	30	m	c	CHIN	Marin	Tomales Twp	74	88
Jake	25	m	c	CHIN	Yuba	Bullards Bar P O	93	548
Jake	25	m	c	CHIN	Colusa	Colusa	71	300
Jam	32	m	c	CHIN	Alameda	Alameda	68	18
Jam	25	m	c	CHIN	Del Norte	Happy Camp Twp	71	468
Jam	18	m	c	CHIN	Del Norte	Happy Camp Twp	71	468
Jan	19	m	c	CHIN	Alameda	Brooklyn Twp	68	53
Jane	17	f	c	CHIN	Alameda	Alameda	68	18
Jaril	28	m	c	CHIN	Klamath	Salmon Twp	73	387
Jarl	40	m	c	CHIN	Sonoma	Sonoma Twp	91	432
Jas	35	m	w	VT	San Francisco	11-Wd San Francisc	84	612
Jay	48	m	c	CHIN	Klamath	Liberty Twp	73	374
Jay	31	m	c	CHIN	Del Norte	Happy Camp Twp	71	469
Jean	38	m	c	CHIN	Placer	Bath P O	76	444
Jean	26	m	c	CHIN	Alameda	Brooklyn Twp	68	41
Jean	20	m	c	CHIN	Alameda	Brooklyn	68	21
Jene	35	m	c	CHIN	Sonoma	Salt Point	91	389
Jenne	19	m	c	CHIN	Yuba	Slate Range Bar Tw	93	669
Jennie [Chinawmn.]	20	f	c	CHIN	Calaveras	San Andreas P O	70	180
Jeon	35	m	c	CHIN	Yuba	North East Twp	93	645
Jeroneme	40	f	w	CA	Monterey	Alisal Twp	74	289
Jew	30	m	c	CHIN	Yuba	Bullards Bar P O	93	552
Jim	50	m	c	CHIN	Yuba	Bullards Bar P O	93	548
Jim	48	m	c	CHIN	Yuba	Bullards Bar P O	93	552
Jim	43	m	c	CHIN	Del Norte	Happy Camp Twp	71	472
Jim	41	m	c	CHIN	Alameda	Murray Twp	68	114
Jim	40	m	c	CHIN	Del Norte	Happy Camp Twp	71	468
Jim	40	m	c	CHIN	Napa	Napa Twp	75	58
Jim	40	m	c	CHIN	Alameda	Oakland	68	224
Jim	40	m	c	CHIN	Del Norte	Happy Camp Twp	71	469
Jim	40	m	c	CHIN	Colusa	Monroe Twp	71	311
Jim	37	m	c	CHIN	Sacramento	American Twp	77	64
Jim	36	m	c	CHIN	Alameda	Murray Twp	68	114
Jim	36	m	c	CHIN	Alameda	Oakland	68	254
Jim	36	m	c	CHIN	Yuba	North East Twp	93	645
Jim	35	m	c	CHIN	Alameda	Oakland	68	158
Jim	35	m	c	CHIN	Alameda	Oakland	68	224
Jim	35	m	c	CHIN	Yuba	North East Twp	93	647
Jim	34	m	c	CHIN	Yuba	Linda Twp	93	558
Jim	34	m	c	CHIN	Sutter	Yuba Twp	92	144
Jim	32	m	c	CHIN	Klamath	South Fork Twp	73	385
Jim	32	m	c	CHIN	Alameda	Oakland	68	245
Jim	30	m	c	CHIN	Klamath	Salmon Twp	73	388
Jim	30	m	c	CHIN	Colusa	Spring Valley Twp	71	339
Jim	30	m	c	CHIN	Sonoma	Salt Point	91	390
Jim	30	m	c	CHIN	Sonoma	Salt Point	91	388
Jim	29	m	c	CHIN	Butte	Wyandotte Twp	70	144
Jim	28	m	c	CHIN	Yuba	East Bear Rvr Twp	93	544
Jim	28	m	c	CHIN	Del Norte	Happy Camp Twp	71	469
Jim	28	m	c	CHIN	Napa	Napa Twp	75	28
Jim	28	m	c	CHIN	Alameda	Oakland	68	232
Jim	28	m	c	CHIN	Colusa	Colusa	71	299
Jim	26	m	c	CHIN	Siskiyou	Hamburg Twp	89	598
Jim	25	m	c	CHIN	Merced	Snelling P O	74	278
Jim	25	m	c	CHIN	Colusa	Monroe Twp	71	312
Jim	25	m	c	CHIN	Del Norte	Happy Camp Twp	71	468
Jim	25	m	c	CHIN	Sacramento	American Twp	77	64
Jim	24	m	c	CHIN	Klamath	Salmon Twp	73	387
Jim	24	m	c	CHIN	Alameda	Eden Twp	68	93
Jim	24	m	c	CHIN	Yuba	North East Twp	93	645
Jim	23	m	c	CHIN	Sutter	Butte Twp	92	89
Jim	23	m	c	CHIN	Alameda	Washington Twp	68	295
Jim	22	m	c	CHIN	Yuba	Marysville	93	580
Jim	21	m	c	CHIN	Colusa	Monroe Twp	71	313
Jim	20	m	c	CHIN	San Francisco	8-Wd San Francisco	82	456
Jim	20	m	c	CHIN	Colusa	Colusa	71	289
Jim	20	m	c	CHIN	Colusa	Colusa	71	299
Jim	20	m	c	CHIN	Yuba	New York Twp	93	638
Jim	19	m	c	CHIN	Sacramento	1-Wd Sacramento	77	179
Jim	18	m	c	CHIN	Napa	Napa Twp	75	32
Jim	17	m	c	CHIN	Alameda	Hayward	68	74
Jim	17	m	c	CHIN	Santa Clara	Gilroy Twp	88	89
Jim	16	m	c	CHIN	Yuba	North East Twp	93	645
Jim	15	m	c	CHIN	San Francisco	11-Wd San Francisc	84	710
Jim	14	m	c	CHIN	Sacramento	4-Wd Sacramento	77	363
Jim	12	m	c	CHIN	Alameda	San Leandro	68	95
Jim	10	m	c	CHIN	Yuba	Long Bar Twp	93	562
Jim [Chinaman]	50	m	c	CHIN	Calaveras	San Andreas P O	70	156
Jim [Chinaman]	21	m	c	CHIN	Trinity	Weaverville Pct	92	224
Jim [Chinaman]	19	m	c	CHIN	Trinity	North Fork Twp	92	217
Jim [Chinaman]	18	m	c	CHIN	Sonoma	Sonoma Twp	91	449
Jim [Chinaman]	16	m	c	CHIN	Monterey	San Juan Twp	74	394
Jime	30	m	c	CHIN	San Francisco	8-Wd San Francisco	82	442
Jime	20	m	c	CHIN	San Francisco	8-Wd San Francisco	82	492
Jimn	20	m	c	CHIN	Yuba	North East Twp	93	646
Jin	35	m	c	CHIN	Yuba	Bullards Bar P O	93	548
Jine	25	m	c	CHIN	San Francisco	8-Wd San Francisco	82	458
Jno [Chinaman]	30	m	c	CHIN	Sacramento	3-Wd Sacramento	77	310
Jo	7	m	c	CHIN	Sacramento	1-Wd Sacramento	77	198
Jo	30	m	c	CHIN	Alameda	Hayward	68	74
Jo	30	m	c	CHIN	Del Norte	Happy Camp Twp	71	469

© 2001 by Heritage Quest. All rights reserved.

Name	Age	S	R	B-PL	County	Locale	Roll	Pg
Jo	30	m	c	CHIN	Sutter	Butte Twp	92	97
Jo	30	m	c	CHIN	Sutter	Sutter Twp	92	127
Jo	30	m	c	CHIN	Sutter	Sutter Twp	92	127
Jo	30	m	c	CHIN	Sutter	Sutter Twp	92	119
Jo	27	m	c	CHIN	Sacramento	Granite Twp	77	141
Joe	46	m	c	CHIN	Klamath	Dillon Twp	73	369
Joe	32	m	c	CHIN	Siskiyou	Hamburg Twp	89	597
Joe	30	m	c	CHIN	Siskiyou	Callahan P O	89	632
Joe	30	m	c	CHIN	Yuba	North East Twp	93	646
Joe	28	m	c	CHIN	Siskiyou	Hamburg Twp	89	598
Joe	26	m	c	CHIN	Siskiyou	Cottonwood Twp	89	593
Joe	26	m	c	CHIN	Colusa	Monroe Twp	71	319
Joe	26	m	c	CHIN	Merced	Snelling P O	74	259
Joe	25	m	c	CHIN	Yuba	East Bear Rvr Twp	93	539
Joe	25	m	c	CHIN	Yolo	Cache Crk Twp	93	428
Joe	25	m	c	CHIN	Del Norte	Happy Camp Twp	71	468
Joe	25	m	c	CHIN	Colusa	Colusa	71	299
Joe	24	m	c	CHIN	Colusa	Colusa	71	299
Joe	24	m	c	CHIN	Klamath	South Fork Twp	73	382
Joe	21	m	c	CHIN	Alameda	Murray Twp	68	120
Joe [Chinaman]	35	m	c	CHIN	Trinity	Hayfork Valley	92	240
Joe [Chinaman]	30	m	c	CHIN	Calaveras	San Andreas P O	70	187
Joe [Chinaman]	30	m	c	CHIN	Siskiyou	Butte Twp	89	584
Joeng	18	m	c	CHIN	Klamath	South Fork Twp	73	384
John	40	m	c	CHIN	Yuba	Slate Range Bar Tw	93	669
John	32	m	c	CHIN	Sutter	Vernon Twp	92	135
John	29	m	c	CHIN	Sacramento	Granite Twp	77	140
John	28	m	c	CHIN	Sacramento	1-Wd Sacramento	77	180
John	28	m	c	CHIN	Siskiyou	Yreka	89	655
John	27	m	c	CHIN	Napa	Napa Twp	75	32
John	25	m	c	CHIN	Sacramento	1-Wd Sacramento	77	179
John	25	m	c	CHIN	Del Norte	Happy Camp Twp	71	468
John	24	m	c	CHIN	Colusa	Colusa	71	299
John	23	m	c	CHIN	Sacramento	1-Wd Sacramento	77	177
John	23	m	c	CHIN	Yuba	Marysville	93	586
John	23	m	c	CHIN	Sutter	Sutter Twp	92	121
John	22	m	c	CHIN	Siskiyou	Scott Valley Twp	89	619
John	21	m	c	CHIN	Colusa	Colusa	71	299
John	21	m	c	CHIN	Del Norte	Crescent	71	463
John	2	m	w	CA	San Francisco	San Francisco P O	85	799
John	19	m	c	CHIN	Yuba	Marysville Twp	93	569
John	19	m	c	CHIN	Sacramento	3-Wd Sacramento	77	275
John	17	m	c	CHIN	Colusa	Grand Island Twp	71	303
John	14	m	c	CHIN	Sacramento	1-Wd Sacramento	77	192
John	14	m	c	CHIN	Sacramento	1-Wd Sacramento	77	181
John	12	m	c	CHIN	Sacramento	1-Wd Sacramento	77	182
John	12	m	c	CHIN	Sutter	Vernon Twp	92	138
John [Chinaman]	30	m	c	CHIN	Sonoma	Petaluma Twp	91	359
John [Chinaman]	23	m	c	CHIN	Sonoma	Sonoma Twp	91	449
John [Chinaman]	18	m	c	CHIN	Sacramento	4-Wd Sacramento	77	353
John [Chinaman]	16	m	c	CHIN	Sonoma	Petaluma Twp	91	334
John [Chinaman]	16	m	c	CHIN	San Francisco	7-Wd San Francisco	81	235
John [Chinaman]	14	m	c	CHIN	San Francisco	7-Wd San Francisco	81	236
John [Chinaman]	14	m	c	CHIN	San Francisco	7-Wd San Francisco	81	235
Johnson	28	m	w	ENGL	Lake	Knoxville Mines	73	405
Jon	40	m	c	CHIN	Del Norte	Happy Camp Twp	71	469
Jone	28	m	c	CHIN	Placer	Bath P O	76	453
Jong	34	m	c	CHIN	Alameda	Brooklyn Twp	68	41
Jong	29	m	c	CHIN	Yuba	Marysville	93	620
Jong	25	m	c	CHIN	Klamath	Liberty Twp	73	375
Jong	22	m	c	CHIN	Klamath	Dillon Twp	73	369
Jong	22	m	c	CHIN	Klamath	South Fork Twp	73	384
Jonsing	40	m	c	CHIN	Klamath	South Fork Twp	73	383
Jose	29	m	w	CA	Monterey	Alisal Twp	74	298
Joses	30	m	c	CHIN	Placer	Bath P O	76	444
Joung	56	m	c	CHIN	Klamath	Salmon Twp	73	387
Jovt	40	m	c	CHIN	Yuba	North East Twp	93	645
Jow	25	m	c	CHIN	Alameda	Brooklyn Twp	68	46
Juan	40	m	c	CHIN	Klamath	South Fork Twp	73	383
Juay	34	m	c	CHIN	Klamath	South Fork Twp	73	383
Jueng	34	m	c	CHIN	Klamath	South Fork Twp	73	383
Jum	35	m	c	CHIN	Yuba	Marysville	93	594
June	52	m	c	CHIN	Klamath	Salmon Twp	73	387
Junes	27	m	c	CHIN	Merced	Snelling P O	74	262
Jung	40	m	c	CHIN	Klamath	Liberty Twp	73	375
Jung	33	m	c	CHIN	Klamath	Salmon Twp	73	388
Jung	30	m	c	CHIN	Klamath	South Fork Twp	73	384
Jung	28	m	c	CHIN	Klamath	South Fork Twp	73	383
Jung	18	m	c	CHIN	Klamath	Liberty Twp	73	375
Jung	15	m	c	CHIN	Marin	Sausalito Twp	74	70
Jyen	26	m	c	CHIN	Klamath	South Fork Twp	73	384
Kahn	37	m	c	CHIN	Marin	Tomales Twp	74	84
Kame	34	m	c	CHIN	Yuba	Slate Range Bar Tw	93	678
Kan	34	m	c	CHIN	Klamath	Liberty Twp	73	374
Kan	18	m	c	CHIN	Marin	Point Reyes Twp	74	22
Kate	55	m	c	CHIN	Yuba	Slate Range Bar Tw	93	669
Kate	20	m	c	CHIN	Colusa	Colusa	71	299
Katsky	35	m	c	CHIN	Del Norte	Happy Camp Twp	71	468
Kay	60	m	c	CHIN	Klamath	Orleans Twp	73	380
Kay	35	m	c	CHIN	Yuba	Marysville	93	601
Kay	34	m	c	CHIN	Klamath	Salmon Twp	73	387
Kay	31	m	c	CHIN	Alameda	Brooklyn Twp	68	41
Kay	26	m	c	CHIN	Yuba	North East Twp	93	646
Kay	24	m	c	CHIN	Yuba	Slate Range Bar Tw	93	678
Kay	24	m	c	CHIN	Klamath	South Fork Twp	73	382
Kay	23	m	c	CHIN	Alameda	Brooklyn	68	21
Kay	22	m	c	CHIN	Yuba	New York Twp	93	638

Name	Age	S	R	B-PL	County	Locale	Roll	Pg
Kee	31	m	c	CHIN	Merced	Snelling P O	74	279
Kee	30	m	c	CHIN	Yuba	Marysville Twp	93	568
Kee	30	m	c	CHIN	Alameda	Oakland	68	224
Kee	30	m	c	CHIN	Alameda	Oakland	68	224
Kee	30	m	c	CHIN	Alameda	Murray Twp	68	120
Kee	29	m	c	CHIN	Alameda	Murray Twp	68	114
Kee	28	m	c	CHIN	Yuba	East Bear Rvr Twp	93	545
Kee	24	m	c	CHIN	Yuba	Marysville	93	594
Kee	24	m	c	CHIN	Sacramento	Granite Twp	77	141
Kee	22	m	c	CHIN	Alameda	Washington Twp	68	293
Kee	21	m	c	CHIN	Alameda	Brooklyn Twp	68	46
Keen	26	m	c	CHIN	Alameda	Brooklyn Twp	68	41
Keene	27	m	c	CHIN	Alameda	Brooklyn	68	21
Keet	19	m	c	CHIN	Yuba	Slate Range Bar Tw	93	669
Kem	30	m	c	CHIN	Yuba	Marysville	93	621
Keme	30	m	c	CHIN	Butte	Mountain Spring Tw	70	89
Ken	30	m	c	CHIN	Alameda	Oakland	68	254
Ken	28	m	c	CHIN	Klamath	South Fork Twp	73	383
Ken	23	m	c	CHIN	Yuba	Rose Bar Twp	93	667
Keon	33	m	c	CHIN	Yuba	Slate Range Bar Tw	93	676
Keoy	30	m	c	CHIN	Colusa	Spring Valley Twp	71	336
Keoy	28	m	c	CHIN	Colusa	Colusa	71	300
Kewen	30	m	c	CHIN	Placer	Bath P O	76	444
Key	26	m	c	CHIN	Marin	Nicasio Twp	74	16
Kie	28	m	c	CHIN	Alameda	Eden Twp	68	60
Kie	25	m	c	CHIN	Del Norte	Happy Camp Twp	71	469
Kim	57	m	c	CHIN	Yuba	Long Bar Twp	93	562
Kim	35	m	c	CHIN	Alameda	Oakland	68	260
Kim	34	m	c	CHIN	Lassen	Susanville Twp	73	441
Kin	32	m	c	CHIN	Colusa	Monroe Twp	71	324
Kin	26	m	c	CHIN	Alameda	Brooklyn Twp	68	46
Kin	25	m	c	CHIN	Del Norte	Happy Camp Twp	71	469
Kin	18	m	c	CHIN	Alameda	Brooklyn Twp	68	46
Kin	14	m	c	CHIN	Yuba	Bullards Bar P O	93	552
King	62	m	c	CHIN	Sonoma	Petaluma Twp	91	363
King	60	m	c	CHIN	Yuba	North East Twp	93	646
King	44	m	c	CHIN	Yuba	Slate Range Bar Tw	93	674
King	37	m	c	CHIN	Yuba	Marysville	93	601
King	36	m	c	CHIN	Merced	Snelling P O	74	279
King	32	m	c	CHIN	Klamath	South Fork Twp	73	383
King	30	m	c	CHIN	Alameda	Washington Twp	68	297
King	27	m	c	CHIN	Klamath	Salmon Twp	73	387
King	21	m	c	CHIN	Yuba	Bullards Bar P O	93	548
Kinn	28	m	c	CHIN	Yuba	Slate Range Bar Tw	93	677
Kip	24	m	c	CHIN	Colusa	Colusa	71	299
Kit	50	m	c	CHIN	Yuba	Marysville	93	601
Know	30	m	c	CHIN	Yuba	North East Twp	93	647
Know	30	m	c	CHIN	Yuba	North East Twp	93	647
Knumb	31	m	c	CHIN	Yuba	North East Twp	93	647
Kobing	28	m	c	CHIN	Calaveras	San Andreas P O	70	202
Kone	31	m	c	CHIN	Butte	Mountain Spring Tw	70	89
Kong	42	m	c	CHIN	Sonoma	Petaluma Twp	91	363
Kong	40	m	c	CHIN	Alameda	Murray Twp	68	114
Kong	37	m	c	CHIN	Alameda	Murray Twp	68	102
Kong	32	m	c	CHIN	Colusa	Monroe Twp	71	313
Kong	30	m	c	CHIN	Colusa	Colusa	71	299
Kong	30	m	c	CHIN	Del Norte	Happy Camp Twp	71	468
Kong	26	m	c	CHIN	Marin	Tomales Twp	74	80
Kong	25	m	c	CHIN	Marin	San Rafael	74	51
Kou	40	m	c	CHIN	Alameda	Oakland	68	260
Kow	36	m	c	CHIN	Alameda	Oakland	68	260
Kow	34	m	c	CHIN	Yuba	Marysville	93	580
Kow	28	m	c	CHIN	Yuba	Marysville	93	600
Kowe	25	m	c	CHIN	Yuba	Slate Range Bar Tw	93	668
Koy	28	m	c	CHIN	Marin	Tomales Twp	74	80
Ku	24	f	c	CHIN	Calaveras	Copperopolis P O	70	260
Kue	31	m	c	CHIN	Alameda	Oakland	68	260
Kuhn	28	m	c	CHIN	Marin	San Rafael	74	58
Kung	42	m	c	CHIN	Yuba	W Bear Rvr Twp	93	684
Kung	35	m	c	CHIN	Alameda	Oakland	68	254
Kung	35	m	c	CHIN	Alameda	Murray Twp	68	102
Kung	29	m	c	CHIN	Yuba	Marysville	93	592
Kuny	68	m	c	CHIN	Yuba	East Bear Rvr Twp	93	545
Kwiy	31	m	c	CHIN	Yuba	Slate Range Bar Tw	93	677
Kye	44	m	c	CHIN	Klamath	South Fork Twp	73	384
Kye	40	m	c	CHIN	Yuba	Slate Range Bar Tw	93	674
Kye	31	m	c	CHIN	Klamath	Liberty Twp	73	374
Kyong	18	m	c	CHIN	Del Norte	Happy Camp Twp	71	469
Lack	30	m	c	CHIN	Sacramento	Granite Twp	77	140
Lage	25	m	c	CHIN	Yuba	North East Twp	93	646
Lake	17	m	c	CHIN	Del Norte	Crescent Twp	71	455
Lala	29	m	c	CHIN	San Joaquin	1-Wd Stockton	86	151
Lamn	20	m	c	CHIN	Yuba	Slate Range Bar Tw	93	668
Lan	45	m	c	CHIN	Klamath	Klamath Twp	73	370
Lan	22	m	c	CHIN	Alameda	Oakland	68	223
Lance	18	m	c	CHIN	Del Norte	Happy Camp Twp	71	471
Lane	30	f	c	CHIN	Trinity	Weaverville Pct	92	229
Lane	28	m	c	CHIN	Alameda	Oakland	68	267
Lang	38	m	c	CHIN	Butte	Wyandotte Twp	70	148
Lang	37	m	c	CHIN	Alameda	Murray Twp	68	114
Lang	34	m	c	CHIN	Klamath	Orleans Twp	73	379
Lang	25	m	c	CHIN	Klamath	South Fork Twp	73	384
Lao	31	m	c	CHIN	Yuba	Marysville	93	575
Lap	48	m	c	CHIN	Klamath	Salmon Twp	73	387
Lap	35	m	c	CHIN	Del Norte	Happy Camp Twp	71	470
Lape	38	m	c	CHIN	Del Norte	Happy Camp Twp	71	469
Lath	35	m	c	CHIN	Del Norte	Happy Camp Twp	71	469

© 2001 by Heritage Quest. All rights reserved.

Name	Age	S	R	B-PL	County	Locale	Roll	Pg
						Series M593		
Laue	30	m	c	CHIN	Yuba	Slate Range Bar Tw	93	678
Lawrence	45	m	w	SWIT	Monterey	Alisal Twp	74	288
Lay	45	m	c	CHIN	Shasta	Horsetown P O	89	504
Lay	34	m	c	CHIN	Alameda	Washington Twp	68	299
Layor	28	m	c	CHIN	Yuba	Bullards Bar P O	93	549
Lea	30	m	c	CHIN	Alameda	Oakland	68	223
Lea	21	f	c	CHIN	Siskiyou	Yreka	89	650
Lead	32	m	c	CHIN	Klamath	Sawyers Bar	73	378
Lee	40	m	c	CHIN	Yuba	Long Bar Twp	93	560
Lee	38	m	c	CHIN	Del Norte	Crescent	71	463
Lee	38	m	c	CHIN	Alameda	Oakland	68	223
Lee	38	m	c	CHIN	Alameda	Oakland	68	169
Lee	36	m	c	CHIN	Sonoma	Salt Point	91	389
Lee	35	m	c	CHIN	Alameda	Oakland	68	223
Lee	32	m	c	CHIN	Del Norte	Happy Camp Twp	71	469
Lee	30	m	c	CHIN	Alameda	Alvarado	68	305
Lee	30	m	c	CHIN	Marin	Tomales Twp	74	88
Lee	30	m	c	CHIN	Yuba	Slate Range Bar Tw	93	669
Lee	28	m	c	CHIN	Alameda	Oakland	68	224
Lee	28	m	c	CHIN	Alameda	Oakland	68	224
Lee	28	m	c	CHIN	Alameda	Oakland	68	224
Lee	27	m	c	CHIN	Alameda	Oakland	68	223
Lee	27	m	c	CHIN	Alameda	Brooklyn Twp	68	41
Lee	26	m	c	CHIN	Alameda	Oakland	68	223
Lee	26	m	c	CHIN	Alameda	Oakland	68	223
Lee	25	m	c	CHIN	Alameda	Oakland	68	224
Lee	25	m	c	CHIN	Colusa	Monroe Twp	71	324
Lee	24	m	c	CHIN	Sutter	Butte Twp	92	94
Lee	21	m	c	CHIN	Yuba	Slate Range Bar Tw	93	678
Lee	19	m	c	CHIN	Alameda	Brooklyn	68	21
Lee	18	m	c	CHIN	Sonoma	Analy Twp	91	233
Leen	30	m	c	CHIN	Alameda	Oakland	68	224
Leff	45	m	c	CHIN	Yuba	Bullards Bar P O	93	552
Leing	32	m	c	CHIN	Merced	Snelling P O	74	249
Leinn	20	m	c	CHIN	Alameda	Eden Twp	68	60
Lem	29	m	c	CHIN	Sonoma	Sonoma Twp	91	433
Lem	17	m	c	CHIN	Yuba	New York Twp	93	637
Lemen	48	m	c	CHIN	Klamath	Salmon Twp	73	387
Lemm	26	m	c	CHIN	Yuba	North East Twp	93	645
Lemmon	50	m	c	CHIN	Klamath	South Fork Twp	73	383
Lemn	30	m	c	CHIN	Yuba	Slate Range Bar Tw	93	669
Lemn	26	m	c	CHIN	Yuba	Long Bar Twp	93	562
Lemn	22	m	c	CHIN	Yuba	Long Bar Twp	93	560
Len	42	m	c	CHIN	Alameda	Murray Twp	68	102
Len	25	m	c	CHIN	Butte	Concow Twp	70	11
Len	25	m	c	CHIN	Yuba	Long Bar Twp	93	560
Len	23	m	c	CHIN	Yuba	W Bear Rvr Twp	93	684
Len	19	m	c	CHIN	Sonoma	Salt Point	91	387
Leng	20	m	c	CHIN	Sacramento	Granite Twp	77	149
Lenie	29	f	c	CHIN	Trinity	Lewiston Pct	92	214
Lenin	40	m	c	CHIN	Merced	Snelling P O	74	249
Lenm	45	m	c	CHIN	Yuba	North East Twp	93	646
Lenm	36	m	c	CHIN	Yuba	Slate Range Bar Tw	93	668
Lenn	44	m	c	CHIN	Placer	Bath P O	76	442
Lenn	35	m	c	CHIN	Klamath	South Fork Twp	73	382
Lenn	32	m	c	CHIN	Yuba	North East Twp	93	646
Lenn	31	m	c	CHIN	Klamath	Sawyers Bar	73	378
Leny	18	m	c	CHIN	Yuba	Slate Range Bar Tw	93	668
Leon	27	m	c	CHIN	Butte	Bidwell Twp	70	3
Leon	13	m	c	CHIN	Napa	Napa Twp	75	75
Leon	13	m	c	CHIN	Napa	Napa	75	27
Leong	42	m	c	CHIN	Yuba	North East Twp	93	645
Leong	32	m	c	CHIN	Sonoma	Salt Point Twp	91	384
Leong	22	m	c	CHIN	Marin	San Rafael Twp	74	59
Leong	22	m	c	CHIN	Alameda	Brooklyn	68	21
Leont	61	m	c	CHIN	Del Norte	Crescent	71	463
Leont	22	m	c	CHIN	Del Norte	Happy Camp Twp	71	472
Leony	30	m	c	CHIN	Yuba	Bullards Bar P O	93	552
Leren	21	m	c	CHIN	Colusa	Colusa	71	295
Less	22	m	c	CHIN	Yuba	North East Twp	93	647
Let	30	m	c	CHIN	Yuba	Long Bar Twp	93	560
Lett	46	m	c	CHIN	Yuba	North East Twp	93	645
Leung	38	m	c	CHIN	Marin	Tomales Twp	74	88
Leung	35	m	c	CHIN	Yuba	Marysville	93	601
Leung	28	m	c	CHIN	Marin	Tomales Twp	74	81
Leung	16	m	c	CHIN	Yuba	Linda Twp	93	558
Lew	26	m	c	CHIN	Alameda	Murray Twp	68	120
Lew	24	m	c	CHIN	Yuba	East Bear Rvr Twp	93	546
Lew	19	m	c	CHIN	Alameda	Brooklyn Twp	68	51
Lewey	29	m	c	CHIN	Yuba	North East Twp	93	646
Lewey [Chinaman]	16	m	c	CHIN	Trinity	Trinity Center Pct	92	204
Lewis	20	m	c	CHIN	Siskiyou	Hamburg Twp	89	596
Lewis	17	m	c	CHIN	Sonoma	Sonoma Twp	91	444
Lewis	16	m	c	CHIN	Yuba	North East Twp	93	645
Lewis	15	m	w	OR	Sonoma	Salt Point	91	389
Ley	38	m	c	CHIN	Alameda	Oakland	68	241
Ley	34	m	c	CHIN	Klamath	Klamath Twp	73	370
Lick	60	m	c	CHIN	Sacramento	Granite Twp	77	140
Lick	25	m	c	CHIN	Yuba	Slate Range Bar Tw	93	677
Liene	13	m	c	CHIN	San Francisco	8-Wd San Francisco	82	437
Like	25	m	c	CHIN	Yuba	Bullards Bar P O	93	548
Lim	50	m	c	CHIN	Alameda	Oakland	68	254
Lim	45	m	c	CHIN	Alameda	Oakland	68	260
Lim	40	m	c	CHIN	Alameda	Oakland	68	224
Lim	38	m	c	CHIN	Alameda	Oakland	68	224
Lim	36	m	c	CHIN	Alameda	Murray Twp	68	120
Lim	35	m	c	CHIN	Alameda	Oakland	68	250
Lim	34	m	c	CHIN	Alameda	Murray Twp	68	111
Lim	30	m	c	CHIN	Yuba	Marysville	93	586
Lim	30	m	c	CHIN	Alameda	Oakland	68	260
Lim	30	m	c	CHIN	Alameda	Murray Twp	68	114
Lim	28	m	c	CHIN	Alameda	Oakland	68	254
Lim	28	m	c	CHIN	Alameda	Murray Twp	68	114
Lim	27	m	c	CHIN	Alameda	Murray Twp	68	120
Lim	25	m	c	CHIN	Placer	Clipper Gap P O	76	376
Lim	22	m	c	CHIN	Alameda	Oakland	68	223
Lim	16	m	c	CHIN	Yuba	East Bear Rvr Twp	93	539
Limb	43	m	c	CHIN	Yuba	New York Twp	93	640
Limb	41	m	c	CHIN	Alameda	Oakland	68	223
Limb	28	m	c	CHIN	Alameda	Oakland	68	223
Limb	18	m	c	CHIN	Yuba	Marysville	93	602
Limepot	38	m	c	CHIN	Klamath	Sawyers Bar	73	378
Lin	41	m	c	CHIN	Del Norte	Crescent	71	464
Lin	40	m	c	CHIN	Alameda	Oakland	68	266
Lin	38	m	c	CHIN	Alameda	Murray Twp	68	111
Lin	30	m	c	CHIN	Alameda	Alameda	68	17
Lin	29	m	c	CHIN	Sacramento	Granite Twp	77	149
Lin	18	m	c	CHIN	Sacramento	4-Wd Sacramento	77	364
Line	30	m	c	CHIN	Alameda	Oakland	68	266
Line	24	f	c	CHIN	Sacramento	1-Wd Sacramento	77	193
Ling	45	m	c	CHIN	Placer	Bath P O	76	459
Ling	40	m	c	CHIN	Sacramento	Granite Twp	77	140
Ling	38	m	c	CHIN	Alameda	Oakland	68	224
Ling	30	m	c	CHIN	Alameda	Alvarado	68	305
Ling	30	m	c	CHIN	Yuba	Marysville	93	620
Ling	28	m	c	CHIN	Sacramento	Granite Twp	77	140
Ling	25	m	c	CHIN	Sacramento	American Twp	77	64
Ling	25	m	c	CHIN	Alameda	Oakland	68	232
Ling	24	m	c	CHIN	Butte	Hamilton Twp	70	68
Ling	23	m	c	CHIN	Butte	Wyandotte Twp	70	143
Ling	23	m	c	CHIN	Yuba	Marysville	93	602
Ling	22	m	c	CHIN	Sacramento	Georgianna Twp	77	130
Ling	19	m	c	CHIN	Sonoma	Petaluma Twp	91	364
Ling	19	m	c	CHIN	Yuba	Marysville	93	592
Ling	18	m	c	CHIN	Marin	Nicasio Twp	74	16
Ling	14	m	c	CHIN	San Francisco	8-Wd San Francisco	82	365
Lingk	16	m	c	CHIN	Merced	Snelling P O	74	278
Lini	12	f	c	CHIN	Sacramento	1-Wd Sacramento	77	195
Linm	45	m	c	CHIN	Yuba	Slate Range Bar Tw	93	668
Linn	46	m	c	CHIN	Klamath	South Fork Twp	73	383
Linn	18	m	c	CHIN	Yuba	Slate Range Bar Tw	93	677
Lip	45	m	c	CHIN	Yuba	Long Bar Twp	93	560
Lip	35	m	c	CHIN	Yuba	Slate Range Bar Tw	93	668
Lip	32	m	c	CHIN	Yuba	Marysville	93	601
Lip	18	m	c	CHIN	Yuba	Slate Range Bar Tw	93	676
Lipskin	43	m	c	CHIN	Trinity	Junction City Pct	92	209
Lisand	30	m	c	CHIN	Napa	Napa	75	14
Lite	22	m	c	CHIN	Sonoma	Salt Point	91	389
Liun	40	m	c	CHIN	Placer	Clipper Gap P O	76	376
Lizzie	37	f	c	CHIN	Merced	Snelling P O	74	279
Lock	40	m	c	CHIN	Yuba	North East Twp	93	646
Lock	34	m	c	CHIN	Yuba	Bullards Bar P O	93	548
Lock	32	m	c	CHIN	Sonoma	Salt Point	91	388
Lock	30	m	c	CHIN	Yuba	Slate Range Bar Tw	93	675
Lock	24	m	c	CHIN	Yuba	Slate Range Bar Tw	93	668
Lock	22	m	c	CHIN	Yuba	Slate Range Bar Tw	93	668
Loe	30	m	c	CHIN	Alameda	Brooklyn Twp	68	46
Logan	26	m	c	CHIN	Colusa	Monroe Twp	71	315
Lon	48	m	c	CHIN	Alameda	Oakland	68	223
Lon	37	m	c	CHIN	Alameda	Oakland	68	152
Lon	27	m	c	CHIN	Klamath	Salmon Twp	73	387
Lone	20	m	c	CHIN	Napa	Napa Twp	75	58
Lone	19	m	c	CHIN	Yuba	Slate Range Bar Tw	93	669
Long	37	m	c	CHIN	Alameda	Oakland	68	152
Long	27	m	c	CHIN	Colusa	Monroe Twp	71	317
Long	26	m	c	CHIN	Alameda	Brooklyn Twp	68	41
Long	25	m	c	CHIN	Del Norte	Happy Camp Twp	71	470
Long	25	m	c	CHIN	Yuba	Slate Range Bar Tw	93	668
Long	20	m	c	CHIN	Yuba	Slate Range Bar Tw	93	669
Longhi	35	m	c	CHIN	Del Norte	Happy Camp Twp	71	469
Loo	34	m	c	CHIN	Yuba	Slate Range Bar Tw	93	678
Loo	19	m	c	CHIN	San Francisco	7-Wd San Francisco	81	174
Loo	19	m	c	CHIN	San Francisco	11-Wd San Francisc	84	687
Loock	25	m	c	CHIN	Yuba	Slate Range Bar Tw	93	669
Look	32	m	c	CHIN	Yuba	Slate Range Bar Tw	93	669
Look	24	m	c	CHIN	Yuba	East Bear Rvr Twp	93	545
Look	21	m	c	CHIN	Alameda	Brooklyn Twp	68	42
Look	19	m	c	CHIN	Yuba	Marysville	93	601
Look	17	f	c	CHIN	Yuba	Slate Range Bar Tw	93	678
Loom	22	m	c	CHIN	Yuba	Bullards Bar P O	93	552
Loon	22	m	c	CHIN	Yuba	Bullards Bar P O	93	548
Loone	28	m	c	CHIN	Yuba	North East Twp	93	645
Lorry	18	m	c	CHIN	Yuba	Marysville	93	594
Lou	25	m	c	CHIN	Del Norte	Mountain Twp	71	475
Louis	33	m	c	CHIN	Yuba	Bullards Bar P O	93	552
Louis	20	m	c	CHIN	Napa	Yountville Twp	75	90
Louke	26	m	c	CHIN	Placer	Bath P O	76	445
Lounk	28	m	c	CHIN	Placer	Bath P O	76	444
Low	48	m	c	CHIN	Alameda	Brooklyn Twp	68	46
Low	26	m	c	CHIN	Del Norte	Happy Camp Twp	71	469
Low	18	m	c	CHIN	Marin	Tomales Twp	74	86
Lowe	24	m	c	CHIN	Klamath	Salmon Twp	73	388
Loy	40	f	c	CHIN	Colusa	Colusa	71	299
Loy	35	m	c	CHIN	Colusa	Colusa	71	299

© 2001 by Heritage Quest. All rights reserved.

Series M593

Name	Age	S	R	B-PL	County	Locale	Roll	Pg
Loy	30	m	c	CHIN	Butte	Chico Twp	70	30
Loy	26	m	c	CHIN	Colusa	Colusa	71	299
Loy	26	m	c	CHIN	Colusa	Colusa	71	299
Loy	25	m	c	CHIN	Alameda	Oakland	68	238
Loy	25	m	c	CHIN	Del Norte	Happy Camp Twp	71	469
Loy	24	m	c	CHIN	Colusa	Colusa	71	299
Loy	20	m	c	CHIN	Colusa	Colusa	71	299
Loy	17	m	c	CHIN	Yuba	Parks Bar Twp	93	649
Loye	32	m	c	CHIN	Yuba	Bullards Bar P O	93	553
Luck	30	m	c	CHIN	Placer	Auburn P O	76	375
Luck	27	m	c	CHIN	Marin	Tomales Twp	74	85
Lucye	40	m	c	CHIN	Placer	Bath P O	76	445
Lue	35	m	c	CHIN	Alameda	Oakland	68	267
Lue	28	m	c	CHIN	Alameda	Oakland	68	202
Lue	22	m	c	CHIN	Yuba	Marysville	93	594
Lue	20	f	c	CHIN	Sacramento	1-Wd Sacramento	77	195
Lugh	56	m	c	CHIN	Klamath	Klamath Twp	73	370
Luhn	45	m	c	CHIN	Marin	San Rafael Twp	74	59
Luk	60	m	c	CHIN	Sacramento	Granite Twp	77	141
Luke	27	m	c	CHIN	Del Norte	Happy Camp Twp	71	470
Luke	24	m	c	CHIN	Sonoma	Salt Point	91	389
Luke La	19	m	c	CHIN	Sutter	Sutter Twp	92	121
Lum	35	m	c	CHIN	Alameda	Oakland	68	245
Lum	30	m	c	CHIN	Marin	Tomales Twp	74	86
Lum	28	m	c	CHIN	Calaveras	Copperopolis P O	70	260
Lum	22	m	c	CHIN	Del Norte	Happy Camp Twp	71	469
Lum	21	m	c	CHIN	Sonoma	Sonoma Twp	91	446
Lun	16	f	c	CHIN	Sacramento	1-Wd Sacramento	77	192
Luna	22	f	c	CHIN	Sacramento	1-Wd Sacramento	77	202
Lune	38	m	c	CHIN	Yuba	Slate Range Bar Tw	93	677
Lung	45	m	c	CHIN	Klamath	Dillon Twp	73	369
Lung	42	m	c	CHIN	Alameda	Oakland	68	232
Lung	40	m	c	CHIN	Alameda	Oakland	68	260
Lung	40	m	c	CHIN	Alameda	Oakland	68	267
Lung	40	m	c	CHIN	Alameda	Oakland	68	266
Lung	40	m	c	CHIN	Alameda	Oakland	68	224
Lung	40	m	c	CHIN	Alameda	Oakland	68	254
Lung	40	m	c	CHIN	Alameda	Oakland	68	223
Lung	40	m	c	CHIN	Sonoma	Sonoma Twp	91	449
Lung	39	m	c	CHIN	Alameda	Alameda	68	17
Lung	38	m	c	CHIN	Alameda	Oakland	68	254
Lung	38	m	c	CHIN	Alameda	Oakland	68	224
Lung	38	m	c	CHIN	Alameda	Oakland	68	224
Lung	38	m	c	CHIN	Alameda	Oakland	68	260
Lung	38	m	c	CHIN	Alameda	Oakland	68	247
Lung	37	m	c	CHIN	Alameda	Oakland	68	254
Lung	37	m	c	CHIN	Alameda	Oakland	68	152
Lung	36	m	c	CHIN	Alameda	Oakland	68	205
Lung	36	m	c	CHIN	Alameda	Murray Twp	68	102
Lung	36	m	c	CHIN	Alameda	Murray Twp	68	102
Lung	35	m	c	CHIN	Alameda	Oakland	68	254
Lung	35	m	c	CHIN	Alameda	Oakland	68	224
Lung	35	m	c	CHIN	Alameda	Oakland	68	158
Lung	33	m	c	CHIN	Alameda	Oakland	68	224
Lung	32	m	c	CHIN	Alameda	Oakland	68	266
Lung	31	m	c	CHIN	Alameda	Oakland	68	158
Lung	30	m	c	CHIN	Alameda	Oakland	68	223
Lung	30	m	c	CHIN	Alameda	Murray Twp	68	111
Lung	29	m	c	CHIN	Alameda	Oakland	68	158
Lung	29	m	c	CHIN	Alameda	Oakland	68	232
Lung	29	m	c	CHIN	Merced	Snelling P O	74	279
Lung	28	m	c	CHIN	Alameda	Oakland	68	224
Lung	28	m	c	CHIN	Alameda	Oakland	68	232
Lung	28	m	c	CHIN	Alameda	Oakland	68	238
Lung	28	m	c	CHIN	Alameda	Oakland	68	152
Lung	27	m	c	CHIN	Alameda	Oakland	68	158
Lung	27	m	c	CHIN	Alameda	Murray Twp	68	111
Lung	26	m	c	CHIN	Sacramento	4-Wd Sacramento	77	341
Lung	24	m	c	CHIN	Sonoma	Petaluma Twp	91	363
Lung	22	m	c	CHIN	Del Norte	Happy Camp Twp	71	469
Lung	20	m	c	CHIN	Alameda	Murray Twp	68	120
Lung	20	m	c	CHIN	Alameda	Oakland	68	223
Lung	18	m	c	CHIN	Alameda	Oakland	68	152
Lung	18	m	c	CHIN	Yuba	Marysville	93	575
Luni	26	f	c	CHIN	Sacramento	1-Wd Sacramento	77	197
Lunn	30	m	c	CHIN	Alameda	Oakland	68	202
Lurie	38	f	c	CHIN	Sierra	Downieville Twp	89	521
Lye	25	m	c	CHIN	Yuba	Long Bar Twp	93	562
Lye	21	m	c	CHIN	Klamath	Salmon Twp	73	388
Mactan	25	m	c	CHIN	Placer	Bath P O	76	453
Mage	32	m	c	CHIN	Yuba	North East Twp	93	645
Mage	20	m	c	CHIN	Yuba	North East Twp	93	645
Mah	46	m	c	CHIN	Klamath	Orleans Twp	73	381
Makoo	32	m	c	CHIN	Colusa	Colusa	71	299
Malon	17	m	c	CHIN	Del Norte	Crescent	71	464
Malop	50	m	c	CHIN	Klamath	Sawyers Bar	73	378
Man	43	m	c	CHIN	Yuba	Linda Twp	93	558
Man	40	m	c	CHIN	Merced	Snelling P O	74	278
Man	38	m	c	CHIN	Alameda	Oakland	68	266
Man	35	m	c	CHIN	Del Norte	Happy Camp Twp	71	469
Man	35	m	c	CHIN	Del Norte	Happy Camp Twp	71	469
Man	33	m	c	CHIN	Del Norte	Happy Camp Twp	71	469
Man	33	m	c	CHIN	Alameda	Brooklyn	68	21
Man	32	m	c	CHIN	Alameda	Brooklyn Twp	68	42
Man	28	m	c	CHIN	Del Norte	Happy Camp Twp	71	468
Man	18	m	c	CHIN	Del Norte	Happy Camp Twp	71	469
Mang	43	m	c	CHIN	Yuba	New York Twp	93	640
Mang	40	m	c	CHIN	Klamath	Dillon Twp	73	369
Mang	18	m	c	CHIN	Alameda	Brooklyn Twp	68	46
Mann	42	m	w	KY	Placer	Auburn P O	76	369
Manwell	30	m	w	MEXI	Yuba	Linda Twp	93	558
Martinez	46	m	w	CA	San Diego	San Luis Rey	78	513
Mary	29	f	c	CHIN	Klamath	Sawyers Bar	73	378
Mary	25	f	c	CHIN	Colusa	Colusa	71	299
Mary	24	f	c	CHIN	San Francisco	6-Wd San Francisco	81	131
Mary	23	f	c	CHIN	Siskiyou	Cottonwood Twp	89	593
Mary	20	f	c	CHIN	Del Norte	Happy Camp Twp	71	469
Mary Ann	45	f	w	IN	Yuba	Rose Bar Twp	93	657
Mattay	20	f	c	CHIN	Placer	Bath P O	76	429
Maw	30	m	c	CHIN	Alameda	San Leandro	68	96
May	39	m	c	CHIN	Alameda	Oakland	68	266
May	30	m	c	CHIN	Alameda	Alameda	68	4
May	22	m	c	CHIN	Alameda	Washington Twp	68	299
Mayah	28	m	c	CHIN	Yuba	W Bear Rvr Twp	93	684
Maye	32	m	c	CHIN	Yuba	North East Twp	93	647
Mee	39	m	c	CHIN	Alameda	Oakland	68	254
Mele	12	m	c	CHIN	Sacramento	1-Wd Sacramento	77	181
Meng	29	m	c	CHIN	Yuba	East Bear Rvr Twp	93	545
Meng	29	m	c	CHIN	Yuba	Linda Twp	93	558
Mewey	28	m	c	CHIN	Klamath	South Fork Twp	73	383
Mikak	32	m	c	CHIN	Del Norte	Happy Camp Twp	71	468
Mill	24	m	c	CHIN	Yuba	Slate Range Bar Tw	93	678
Min	41	m	c	CHIN	Alameda	Oakland	68	223
Min	23	m	c	CHIN	Alameda	Brooklyn Twp	68	41
Ming	39	m	c	CHIN	Klamath	South Fork Twp	73	383
Ming	38	m	c	CHIN	Butte	Wyandotte Twp	70	148
Ming	38	m	c	CHIN	Yuba	Marysville	93	601
Ming	36	m	c	CHIN	Alameda	Brooklyn Twp	68	41
Ming	35	m	c	CHIN	Yuba	Slate Range Bar Tw	93	678
Ming	32	m	c	CHIN	Santa Clara	1-Wd San Jose	88	272
Ming	31	m	c	CHIN	Yuba	Marysville	93	602
Ming	30	m	c	CHIN	Yuba	Bullards Bar P O	93	548
Ming	28	m	c	CHIN	Butte	Wyandotte Twp	70	142
Ming	27	m	c	CHIN	Yuba	East Bear Rvr Twp	93	545
Ming	25	m	c	CHIN	Yuba	New York Twp	93	638
Ming	24	m	c	CHIN	Yuba	East Bear Rvr Twp	93	546
Ming	20	m	c	CHIN	Alameda	Brooklyn	68	21
Ming	2	m	c	CHIN	Butte	Hamilton Twp	70	74
Ming	15	m	c	CHIN	Yuba	North East Twp	93	643
Ming	14	m	c	CHIN	Yuba	Marysville	93	592
Mintung	42	m	c	CHIN	Placer	Bath P O	76	422
Mo	15	m	c	CHIN	Yuba	Marysville	93	594
Moi	18	f	c	CHIN	Sacramento	1-Wd Sacramento	77	177
Moisen	37	m	c	CHIN	Yuba	North East Twp	93	643
Mok	39	m	c	CHIN	Butte	Hamilton Twp	70	68
Moke	49	m	c	CHIN	Placer	Bath P O	76	459
Molly	12	f	i	CA	Siskiyou	Callahan P O	89	625
Mon	50	m	c	CHIN	Yuba	Slate Range Bar Tw	93	677
Mon	41	m	c	CHIN	Butte	Hamilton Twp	70	68
Mon	40	m	c	CHIN	Alameda	Oakland	68	223
Mon	32	m	c	CHIN	Alameda	Oakland	68	220
Mong	45	m	c	CHIN	Yuba	North East Twp	93	646
Mong	40	m	c	CHIN	Alameda	Oakland	68	245
Mong	40	m	c	CHIN	Marin	Tomales Twp	74	86
Mong	37	m	c	CHIN	Yuba	Linda Twp	93	558
Mong	35	m	c	CHIN	Alameda	Brooklyn Twp	68	42
Mong	30	m	c	CHIN	Yuba	W Bear Rvr Twp	93	684
Mong	24	m	c	CHIN	Klamath	Salmon Twp	73	387
Mong	19	m	c	CHIN	Yuba	Marysville	93	575
Monjim	35	m	c	CHIN	Del Norte	Happy Camp Twp	71	469
Monk	45	m	c	CHIN	Sutter	Yuba Twp	92	144
Monn	49	m	c	CHIN	Yuba	Bullards Bar P O	93	552
Moo	27	m	c	CHIN	Yuba	Slate Range Bar Tw	93	669
Mook	30	m	c	CHIN	Alameda	Washington Twp	68	299
Moon	8	m	c	CHIN	Alameda	Oakland	68	157
Moon	48	m	c	CHIN	Yuba	Slate Range Bar Tw	93	674
Moon	40	m	c	CHIN	Klamath	Klamath Twp	73	371
Moon	35	m	c	CHIN	Alameda	Oakland	68	223
Moon	30	m	c	CHIN	Alameda	Oakland	68	260
Moon	28	m	c	CHIN	Alameda	Oakland	68	260
Moon	28	m	c	CHIN	Yuba	New York Twp	93	638
Moon	20	m	c	CHIN	Klamath	South Fork Twp	73	383
Moore	25	m	c	CHIN	Yuba	North East Twp	93	645
Mory	44	m	c	CHIN	Klamath	Klamath Twp	73	370
Mou	35	m	c	CHIN	Alameda	Oakland	68	232
Moung	28	m	c	CHIN	Alameda	Oakland	68	223
Mow	34	m	c	CHIN	Yuba	Marysville	93	594
Mow	32	m	c	CHIN	Yuba	Slate Range Bar Tw	93	678
Mow	32	m	c	CHIN	Butte	Hamilton Twp	70	67
Mow	30	m	c	CHIN	Yuba	Slate Range Bar Tw	93	678
Mow	29	m	c	CHIN	Yuba	Marysville	93	592
Mow	27	m	c	CHIN	Klamath	South Fork Twp	73	383
Mow	25	m	c	CHIN	Yuba	W Bear Rvr Twp	93	682
Mow	23	m	c	CHIN	Yuba	Marysville	93	620
Mow	20	m	c	CHIN	Yuba	Marysville Twp	93	569
Mow	19	m	c	CHIN	Yuba	Marysville	93	592
Mow	16	m	c	CHIN	Yuba	East Bear Rvr Twp	93	545
Mowe	55	m	c	CHIN	Yuba	Slate Range Bar Tw	93	669
Mowe	35	m	c	CHIN	Yuba	Marysville	93	601
Mowe	30	m	c	CHIN	Yuba	Slate Range Bar Tw	93	677
Mowe	26	m	c	CHIN	Yuba	Slate Range Bar Tw	93	678
Moy	30	m	c	CHIN	Alameda	Oakland	68	202
Moy	26	m	c	CHIN	Yuba	East Bear Rvr Twp	93	545
Moy	25	m	c	CHIN	Alameda	Oakland	68	238

© 2001 by Heritage Quest. All rights reserved.

Series M593

Name	Age	S	R	B-PL	County	Locale	Roll	Pg
Mu	37	m	c	CHIN	Yuba	East Bear Rvr Twp	93	545
Muhn	60	m	c	CHIN	Yuba	East Bear Rvr Twp	93	545
Mum	45	m	c	CHIN	Alameda	Oakland	68	241
Mun	27	m	c	CHIN	Alameda	Eden Twp	68	60
Mun	26	m	c	CHIN	Alameda	Brooklyn Twp	68	46
Mun	25	m	c	CHIN	Alameda	Brooklyn Twp	68	41
Mune	30	m	c	CHIN	Alameda	Oakland	68	223
Mung	48	m	c	CHIN	Butte	Wyandotte Twp	70	143
Mung	44	m	c	CHIN	Alameda	Oakland	68	254
Mung	41	m	c	CHIN	Alameda	Murray Twp	68	102
Mung	40	m	c	CHIN	Alameda	Alameda	68	17
Mung	40	m	c	CHIN	Alameda	Alameda	68	16
Mung	40	m	c	CHIN	Alameda	Oakland	68	223
Mung	40	m	c	CHIN	Alameda	Oakland	68	224
Mung	40	m	c	CHIN	Alameda	Oakland	68	224
Mung	40	m	c	CHIN	Alameda	Oakland	68	224
Mung	40	m	c	CHIN	Alameda	Oakland	68	260
Mung	40	m	c	CHIN	Alameda	Oakland	68	254
Mung	40	m	c	CHIN	Del Norte	Happy Camp Twp	71	469
Mung	38	m	c	CHIN	Alameda	Oakland	68	224
Mung	38	m	c	CHIN	Alameda	Oakland	68	254
Mung	38	m	c	CHIN	Alameda	Oakland	68	210
Mung	38	m	c	CHIN	Alameda	Oakland	68	260
Mung	38	m	c	CHIN	Alameda	Oakland	68	266
Mung	38	m	c	CHIN	Alameda	Oakland	68	254
Mung	37	m	c	CHIN	Alameda	Oakland	68	158
Mung	37	m	c	CHIN	Alameda	Oakland	68	224
Mung	36	m	c	CHIN	Alameda	Oakland	68	223
Mung	35	m	c	CHIN	Alameda	Oakland	68	206
Mung	35	m	c	CHIN	Alameda	Alameda	68	6
Mung	35	m	c	CHIN	Alameda	Murray Twp	68	111
Mung	35	m	c	CHIN	Alameda	Oakland	68	224
Mung	35	m	c	CHIN	Alameda	Oakland	68	250
Mung	33	m	c	CHIN	Alameda	Oakland	68	254
Mung	32	m	c	CHIN	Alameda	Alameda	68	17
Mung	32	m	c	CHIN	Alameda	Oakland	68	254
Mung	31	m	c	CHIN	Alameda	Oakland	68	138
Mung	30	m	c	CHIN	Alameda	Oakland	68	202
Mung	30	m	c	CHIN	Alameda	Oakland	68	205
Mung	30	m	c	CHIN	Alameda	Murray Twp	68	102
Mung	30	m	c	CHIN	Alameda	Murray Twp	68	114
Mung	30	m	c	CHIN	Alameda	Oakland	68	223
Mung	30	m	c	CHIN	Alameda	Murray Twp	68	120
Mung	30	m	c	CHIN	Alameda	Oakland	68	224
Mung	30	m	c	CHIN	Alameda	Oakland	68	232
Mung	30	m	c	CHIN	Alameda	Oakland	68	224
Mung	30	m	c	CHIN	Alameda	Oakland	68	223
Mung	29	m	c	CHIN	Alameda	Oakland	68	238
Mung	29	m	c	CHIN	Alameda	Oakland	68	158
Mung	28	m	c	CHIN	Alameda	Oakland	68	232
Mung	28	m	c	CHIN	Alameda	Murray Twp	68	102
Mung	28	m	c	CHIN	Alameda	Oakland	68	224
Mung	28	m	c	CHIN	Alameda	Alameda	68	16
Mung	28	m	c	CHIN	Alameda	Alameda	68	17
Mung	28	m	c	CHIN	Alameda	Oakland	68	223
Mung	28	m	c	CHIN	Alameda	Oakland	68	267
Mung	28	m	c	CHIN	Alameda	Oakland	68	266
Mung	27	m	c	CHIN	Alameda	Murray Twp	68	111
Mung	27	m	c	CHIN	Marin	Tomales Twp	74	84
Mung	26	m	c	CHIN	Marin	Tomales Twp	74	84
Mung	25	m	c	CHIN	Alameda	Murray Twp	68	114
Mung	21	m	c	CHIN	Alameda	Oakland	68	157
Mung	20	m	c	CHIN	Alameda	Murray Twp	68	120
Mung	10	m	c	CHIN	Alameda	Oakland	68	172
Muny	30	m	c	CHIN	Alameda	Alameda	68	6
Muy	30	m	c	CHIN	Alameda	Alameda	68	6
N [Chinaman]	20	m	c	CHIN	San Joaquin	2-Wd Stockton	86	158
Nahm	42	m	c	CHIN	Klamath	Salmon Twp	73	387
Neck	32	m	c	CHIN	Yuba	Marysville	93	601
Neck	30	m	c	CHIN	Klamath	Liberty Twp	73	375
Newey	35	m	c	CHIN	Klamath	Sawyers Bar	73	378
Newey	35	m	c	CHIN	Klamath	South Fork Twp	73	383
Newey	24	m	c	CHIN	Klamath	South Fork Twp	73	385
Niel	50	m	w	IREL	Yuba	Marysville Twp	93	567
Ning	20	m	c	CHIN	Klamath	Salmon Twp	73	388
Nom	40	m	c	CHIN	Yuba	Marysville	93	621
None	28	m	c	CHIN	Del Norte	Happy Camp Twp	71	469
Noon	40	m	c	CHIN	Sacramento	Granite Twp	77	149
Nu	30	m	c	CHIN	Merced	Snelling P O	74	278
Nuae	6M	f	c	CA	Calaveras	San Andreas P O	70	155
Numb	21	m	c	CHIN	Yuba	Marysville	93	620
Numb	17	m	c	CHIN	Yuba	Marysville	93	601
Nung	34	f	c	CHIN	Calaveras	San Andreas P O	70	159
Nung	32	m	c	CHIN	Yuba	Marysville	93	594
O Ah	30	m	c	CHIN	San Joaquin	1-Wd Stockton	86	145
Oblo	29	m	c	CHIN	Alameda	Eden Twp	68	60
Oh	25	m	c	CHIN	Colusa	Colusa	71	300
Ohn	18	m	c	CHIN	Sonoma	Salt Point	91	388
Oin	28	f	c	CHIN	Sacramento	1-Wd Sacramento	77	195
Ok	21	m	c	CHIN	Yuba	Marysville	93	601
Olie	10	f	c	CHIN	Sacramento	1-Wd Sacramento	77	199
On	25	m	c	CHIN	Del Norte	Happy Camp Twp	71	471
On	18	m	c	CHIN	Del Norte	Happy Camp Twp	71	470
Onai	23	m	c	CHIN	Del Norte	Happy Camp Twp	71	471
One	48	m	c	CHIN	Yuba	Slate Range Bar Tw	93	674
One	40	m	c	CHIN	Yuba	North East Twp	93	646
One	37	m	c	CHIN	Yuba	North East Twp	93	647
One	34	m	c	CHIN	Yuba	Marysville Twp	93	568
One	24	m	c	CHIN	Yuba	New York Twp	93	638
One	20	m	c	CHIN	Yuba	Slate Range Bar Tw	93	674
Ong	31	m	c	CHIN	Yuba	Marysville	93	623
Ong	25	m	c	CHIN	Merced	Snelling P O	74	278
Ong	18	m	c	CHIN	Alameda	Eden Twp	68	88
Oon	32	m	c	CHIN	Del Norte	Happy Camp Twp	71	468
Oon	18	m	c	CHIN	Del Norte	Mountain Twp	71	475
Opley	35	m	c	CHIN	Alameda	Alameda	68	18
Opoy	40	m	c	CHIN	Butte	Wyandotte Twp	70	141
Orme	34	m	c	CHIN	Placer	Bath P O	76	445
Orro	7M	-	c	CA	Sacramento	1-Wd Sacramento	77	194
Otin	43	m	c	CHIN	Placer	Newcastle Twp	76	473
Otorano	38	m	w	MEXI	Fresno	Millerton P O	72	155
Ouang	30	m	c	CHIN	Placer	Bath P O	76	428
Ouen	25	m	c	CHIN	Yuba	Slate Range Bar Tw	93	677
Ovey	35	m	c	CHIN	Merced	Snelling P O	74	278
Ovey	18	m	c	CHIN	Klamath	South Fork Twp	73	384
Owe	18	m	c	CHIN	Sutter	Sutter Twp	92	127
Owee	21	m	c	CHIN	Fresno	Millerton P O	72	188
Owen	33	m	c	CHIN	Yuba	Slate Range Bar Tw	93	677
Owen	30	m	c	CHIN	Klamath	Liberty Twp	73	374
Owen	30	m	c	CHIN	Siskiyou	Scott Valley Twp	89	610
Owen	22	m	c	CHIN	Klamath	Liberty Twp	73	374
Own	25	m	c	CHIN	Colusa	Colusa	71	299
Owne	25	m	c	CHIN	Klamath	South Fork Twp	73	384
Oy	25	m	c	CHIN	Marin	Novato Twp	74	11
Pah	28	m	c	CHIN	Yuba	Slate Range Bar Tw	93	671
Paing	3	m	c	CHIN	Sonoma	Petaluma Twp	91	362
Palk	30	m	c	CHIN	Yuba	Slate Range Bar Tw	93	668
Pan	36	m	c	CHIN	Butte	Mountain Spring Tw	70	89
Pan	22	m	c	CHIN	Butte	Oroville Twp	70	139
Pan	15	m	c	CHIN	Colusa	Colusa	71	299
Pang	24	m	c	CHIN	Yuba	Slate Range Bar Tw	93	669
Pang	22	m	c	CHIN	Alameda	Brooklyn	68	21
Pang	18	m	c	CHIN	Merced	Snelling P O	74	266
Park	35	m	c	CHIN	Del Norte	Happy Camp Twp	71	468
Park	20	m	c	CHIN	Del Norte	Happy Camp Twp	71	468
Paul	34	m	c	CHIN	Klamath	Orleans Twp	73	381
Paw	30	m	c	CHIN	Yuba	W Bear Rvr Twp	93	685
Pay	50	m	c	CHIN	Del Norte	Happy Camp Twp	71	468
Pay	40	m	c	CHIN	Yuba	Long Bar Twp	93	560
Pay	29	m	c	CHIN	Yuba	Slate Range Bar Tw	93	674
Paze	28	m	c	CHIN	Colusa	Monroe Twp	71	324
Peck	26	m	c	CHIN	Colusa	Monroe Twp	71	324
Pedro	40	m	w	FRAN	Monterey	San Antonio Twp	74	321
Pekin	28	m	c	CHIN	Del Norte	Happy Camp Twp	71	468
Perig	22	m	c	CHIN	Marin	San Rafael	74	58
Pete	35	m	c	CHIN	Siskiyou	Hamburg Twp	89	599
Pete	27	m	c	CHIN	Colusa	Monroe Twp	71	313
Peu	22	m	c	CHIN	Yuba	Marysville	93	601
Phil	20	m	c	CHIN	Alameda	San Leandro	68	96
Pin	22	m	c	CHIN	Marin	Tomales Twp	74	79
Ping	50	m	c	CHIN	Yuba	Bullards Bar P O	93	553
Ping	38	m	c	CHIN	Yuba	New York Twp	93	640
Ping	28	m	c	CHIN	Yuba	Slate Range Bar Tw	93	675
Ping	28	m	c	CHIN	Yuba	Slate Range Bar Tw	93	668
Plom	21	m	c	CHIN	Alameda	Brooklyn Twp	68	43
Ploy	31	m	c	CHIN	Yuba	Marysville	93	621
Pock	27	m	c	CHIN	Placer	Bath P O	76	429
Pome	40	m	c	CHIN	Yuba	North East Twp	93	645
Pomy	45	m	c	CHIN	Yuba	Slate Range Bar Tw	93	678
Pon	26	m	c	CHIN	Alameda	Eden Twp	68	93
Pon	19	m	c	CHIN	Alameda	Brooklyn Twp	68	46
Pon	19	m	c	CHIN	Alameda	Brooklyn Twp	68	41
Pong	50	m	c	CHIN	San Francisco	11-Wd San Francisc	84	695
Pong	38	m	c	CHIN	Yuba	North East Twp	93	645
Pong	35	m	c	CHIN	Marin	Tomales Twp	74	77
Pong	33	m	c	CHIN	Alameda	Brooklyn Twp	68	42
Pong	32	m	c	CHIN	Yuba	Bullards Bar P O	93	553
Pong	31	m	c	CHIN	Yuba	North East Twp	93	646
Pong	28	m	c	CHIN	Yuba	Bullards Bar P O	93	552
Pong	26	m	c	CHIN	Alameda	Brooklyn Twp	68	41
Pong	19	m	c	CHIN	Alameda	Brooklyn Twp	68	41
Pong	14	m	c	CHIN	San Francisco	8-Wd San Francisco	82	457
Ponga	20	m	c	CHIN	Yuba	North East Twp	93	646
Poo	32	m	c	CHIN	Alameda	Brooklyn Twp	68	46
Poo	30	m	c	CHIN	Alameda	Brooklyn Twp	68	41
Poo	30	m	c	CHIN	Alameda	Oakland	68	224
Poo	29	m	c	CHIN	Yuba	Slate Range Bar Tw	93	671
Poon	45	m	c	CHIN	Alameda	Brooklyn Twp	68	41
Poon	31	m	c	CHIN	Alameda	Brooklyn Twp	68	41
Poon	30	m	c	CHIN	Alameda	Brooklyn Twp	68	41
Poone	24	m	c	CHIN	Alameda	Brooklyn	68	21
Porcho	50	m	w	SPAI	Yolo	Grafton Twp	93	498
Pow	55	m	c	CHIN	Del Norte	Happy Camp Twp	71	469
Pow	46	m	c	CHIN	Butte	Wyandotte Twp	70	148
Pow	31	m	c	CHIN	Alameda	Brooklyn Twp	68	42
Pow	27	m	c	CHIN	Butte	Mountain Spring Tw	70	89
Pow	25	m	c	CHIN	Del Norte	Happy Camp Twp	71	468
Poy	29	m	c	CHIN	Butte	Chico Twp	70	27
Poy	20	m	c	CHIN	Colusa	Colusa	71	299
Poy	20	f	c	CHIN	Colusa	Colusa	71	300
Psi	19	m	c	CHIN	Yuba	Marysville	93	620
Puck	44	m	c	CHIN	Yuba	Bullards Bar P O	93	549
Pun	40	m	c	CHIN	Alameda	Brooklyn Twp	68	46
Pung	43	m	c	CHIN	Marin	Tomales Twp	74	86

© 2001 by Heritage Quest. All rights reserved.

Name	Age	S	R	B-PL	County	Series M593 Locale	Roll	Pg
Pung	40	m	c	CHIN	Alameda	Brooklyn Twp	68	46
Pung	25	m	c	CHIN	Alameda	Washington Twp	68	293
Pung	20	m	c	CHIN	Alameda	Brooklyn Twp	68	41
Pung	16	m	c	CHIN	Yuba	North East Twp	93	645
Puoah	12	m	c	CHIN	Marin	San Rafael Twp	74	59
Put	25	m	c	CHIN	Alameda	Brooklyn	68	21
Putt	25	m	c	CHIN	Yuba	North East Twp	93	646
Puy	33	m	c	CHIN	Yuba	Slate Range Bar Tw	93	674
Qeong	41	m	c	CHIN	Klamath	Salmon Twp	73	387
Qep	26	m	c	CHIN	Klamath	South Fork Twp	73	384
Qua	30	m	c	CHIN	Placer	Bath P O	76	444
Quack	43	m	c	CHIN	Yuba	East Bear Rvr Twp	93	545
Quage	30	m	c	CHIN	Yuba	Slate Range Bar Tw	93	678
Quah	25	m	c	CHIN	Merced	Snelling P O	74	278
Quan	40	m	c	CHIN	Alameda	Brooklyn Twp	68	41
Quan	20	m	c	CHIN	Alameda	Brooklyn	68	21
Quang	45	m	c	CHIN	Klamath	South Fork Twp	73	382
Quang	38	m	c	CHIN	Sierra	Table Rock Twp	89	579
Quang	32	m	c	CHIN	Yuba	Linda Twp	93	558
Quang	27	f	c	CHIN	Yuba	Marysville	93	601
Quang	24	m	c	CHIN	Klamath	Liberty Twp	73	375
Quang	17	m	c	CHIN	Alameda	Washington Twp	68	287
Quank	35	m	c	CHIN	Yuba	East Bear Rvr Twp	93	546
Quay	35	m	c	CHIN	Yuba	Marysville	93	601
Quay	35	m	c	CHIN	Yuba	Slate Range Bar Tw	93	675
Que	44	m	c	CHIN	Klamath	South Fork Twp	73	382
Que	40	m	c	CHIN	Klamath	South Fork Twp	73	383
Que	30	m	c	CHIN	Yuba	Marysville	93	621
Que	29	m	c	CHIN	Klamath	Orleans Twp	73	380
Que	28	m	c	CHIN	Klamath	Liberty Twp	73	375
Que	26	m	c	CHIN	Klamath	Klamath Twp	73	370
Que	15	m	c	CHIN	Sutter	Yuba Twp	92	140
Queany	21	m	c	CHIN	Klamath	South Fork Twp	73	384
Quen	36	m	c	CHIN	Marin	Tomales Twp	74	86
Quen	22	m	c	CHIN	Marin	Tomales Twp	74	77
Quey	30	m	c	CHIN	Klamath	South Fork Twp	73	384
Qui	40	m	c	CHIN	Yuba	North East Twp	93	647
Qui	30	m	c	CHIN	Marin	Tomales Twp	74	83
Quier	35	m	c	CHIN	Yuba	Slate Range Bar Tw	93	668
Quing	52	m	c	CHIN	Placer	Bath P O	76	444
Quing	42	m	c	CHIN	Klamath	Salmon Twp	73	387
Quing	28	m	c	CHIN	Klamath	South Fork Twp	73	384
Quog	25	m	c	CHIN	Alameda	Brooklyn Twp	68	46
Quon	35	m	c	CHIN	Yuba	Bullards Bar P O	93	548
Quon	32	m	c	CHIN	Marin	Tomales Twp	74	80
Quon	32	m	c	CHIN	Yuba	Bullards Bar P O	93	548
Quon	26	m	c	CHIN	Alameda	Brooklyn Twp	68	46
Quon	18	m	c	CHIN	Alameda	Eden Twp	68	60
Quong	45	m	c	CHIN	Yuba	Bullards Bar P O	93	549
Quong	37	m	c	CHIN	Placer	Bath P O	76	442
Quong	34	m	c	CHIN	Alameda	Brooklyn Twp	68	41
Quong	30	m	c	CHIN	Sutter	Sutter Twp	92	121
Quong	29	m	c	CHIN	Yuba	East Bear Rvr Twp	93	546
Quong	26	m	c	CHIN	Alameda	Brooklyn	68	21
Quong	25	m	c	CHIN	Yuba	Marysville Twp	93	569
Quong	24	m	c	CHIN	Yuba	Marysville	93	592
Quong	24	m	c	CHIN	Yuba	Marysville	93	594
Quong	22	m	c	CHIN	Yuba	Slate Range Bar Tw	93	674
Quong	21	m	c	CHIN	Yuba	W Bear Rvr Twp	93	684
Quong	20	m	c	CHIN	Alameda	Washington Twp	68	272
R Doe	34	m	c	CHIN	Lake	Little Borax	73	419
R Eck	25	m	c	CHIN	Lake	Little Borax	73	419
R Gem	25	m	c	CHIN	Lake	Little Borax	73	419
R George	20	m	c	CHIN	Lake	Little Borax	73	419
R Hump	34	m	c	CHIN	Lake	Little Borax	73	419
R John	23	m	c	CHIN	Lake	Little Borax	73	419
R Lier	25	m	c	CHIN	Lake	Little Borax	73	419
R Look	26	m	c	CHIN	Lake	Little Borax	73	419
R Row	35	m	c	CHIN	Lake	Little Borax	73	419
R Sam	28	m	c	CHIN	Lake	Little Borax	73	419
R Sam	22	m	c	CHIN	Lake	Little Borax	73	419
R Tong	45	m	c	CHIN	Lake	Little Borax	73	419
R Tong	22	m	c	CHIN	Lake	Little Borax	73	419
R Took	32	m	c	CHIN	Lake	Little Borax	73	419
R Unyee	48	m	c	CHIN	Lake	Little Borax	73	419
R Yuen	29	m	c	CHIN	Lake	Little Borax	73	419
Ramon	25	m	w	MEXI	San Diego	San Pasqual Valley	78	524
Rancho	40	m	w	ITAL	San Joaquin	2-Wd Stockton	86	163
Rang	25	m	c	CHIN	Alameda	Brooklyn Twp	68	46
Riley [Chinaman]	40	m	c	CHIN	Trinity	Hayfork Valley	92	240
Rim	23	m	c	CHIN	Klamath	South Fork Twp	73	383
Rim	19	m	c	CHIN	Yuba	Marysville Twp	93	567
Rock	40	m	c	CHIN	Yuba	Slate Range Bar Tw	93	668
Rock	25	m	c	CHIN	Colusa	Colusa	71	299
Romanos	25	m	c	CHIN	San Francisco	6-Wd San Francisco	81	66
Rong	17	m	c	CHIN	Colusa	Stony Crk Twp	71	331
Rose	6M	f	w	CA	Siskiyou	Yreka	89	654
Roy	25	m	c	CHIN	San Francisco	11-Wd San Francisc	84	708
Rye	6	f	b	KY	Colusa	Colusa	71	292
Rye	30	m	c	CHIN	Klamath	South Fork Twp	73	382
Rye	26	m	c	CHIN	Klamath	South Fork Twp	73	382
Saad	24	m	c	CHIN	Klamath	Salmon Twp	73	387
Sack	40	m	c	CHIN	Sacramento	Granite Twp	77	140
Sadi	25	f	c	CHIN	Sacramento	1-Wd Sacramento	77	194
Saey	24	m	c	CHIN	Yuba	New York Twp	93	640
Sag	26	m	c	CHIN	Yuba	North East Twp	93	647
Sag	25	m	c	CHIN	Yuba	North East Twp	93	647

Name	Age	S	R	B-PL	County	Series M593 Locale	Roll	Pg
Sag	14	m	c	CHIN	Yuba	North East Twp	93	645
Sago	14	m	c	CHIN	Alameda	Oakland	68	189
Sahm	29	m	c	CHIN	Marin	Novato Twp	74	11
Said	24	m	c	CHIN	Klamath	Salmon Twp	73	387
Sam	60	m	c	CHIN	Colusa	Colusa	71	300
Sam	6	m	w	NV	Sacramento	1-Wd Sacramento	77	193
Sam	47	m	c	CHIN	Klamath	Dillon Twp	73	369
Sam	45	m	c	CHIN	Alameda	Brooklyn	68	23
Sam	43	m	c	CHIN	Yuba	Slate Range Bar Tw	93	677
Sam	41	m	c	CHIN	Sutter	Yuba Twp	92	147
Sam	40	m	c	CHIN	Klamath	South Fork Twp	73	384
Sam	40	m	c	CHIN	Colusa	Colusa Twp	71	274
Sam	40	m	c	CHIN	Del Norte	Happy Camp Twp	71	468
Sam	40	m	c	CHIN	Colusa	Monroe Twp	71	314
Sam	40	m	c	CHIN	Alameda	Oakland	68	224
Sam	39	m	c	CHIN	Alameda	Eden Twp	68	87
Sam	35	m	c	CHIN	Sutter	Nicolaus Twp	92	115
Sam	35	m	c	CHIN	Yuba	Marysville	93	624
Sam	34	m	c	CHIN	Yuba	Marysville	93	592
Sam	34	m	c	CHIN	Siskiyou	Yreka Twp	89	666
Sam	32	m	c	CHIN	Yuba	Marysville Twp	93	568
Sam	32	m	c	CHIN	Yuba	Slate Range Bar Tw	93	670
Sam	32	m	c	CHIN	Yuba	Slate Range Bar Tw	93	668
Sam	31	m	c	CHIN	Sutter	Sutter Twp	92	123
Sam	31	m	c	CHIN	Sonoma	Bodega Twp	91	264
Sam	30	m	c	CHIN	Alameda	Brooklyn	68	21
Sam	30	m	c	CHIN	Sacramento	1-Wd Sacramento	77	177
Sam	30	m	c	CHIN	Siskiyou	Cottonwood Twp	89	594
Sam	30	m	c	CHIN	Sacramento	Granite Twp	77	140
Sam	30	m	c	CHIN	Napa	Napa	75	18
Sam	30	m	c	CHIN	Colusa	Colusa	71	299
Sam	30	m	c	CHIN	Alameda	Brooklyn Twp	68	46
Sam	29	m	c	CHIN	Sutter	Yuba Twp	92	145
Sam	28	m	c	CHIN	Alameda	Murray Twp	68	120
Sam	28	m	c	CHIN	Yuba	Marysville	93	586
Sam	28	m	c	CHIN	Sutter	Butte Twp	92	95
Sam	28	m	c	CHIN	Yuba	Marysville	93	586
Sam	28	m	c	CHIN	Alameda	Oakland	68	266
Sam	28	m	c	CHIN	Sutter	Vernon Twp	92	135
Sam	28	m	c	CHIN	Siskiyou	Scott Valley Twp	89	617
Sam	27	m	c	CHIN	Klamath	South Fork Twp	73	385
Sam	27	m	c	CHIN	Sacramento	1-Wd Sacramento	77	180
Sam	25	m	c	CHIN	Alameda	Oakland	68	152
Sam	25	m	c	CHIN	Alameda	Murray Twp	68	111
Sam	25	m	c	CHIN	Siskiyou	Hamburg Twp	89	598
Sam	24	m	c	CHIN	Alameda	Brooklyn	68	21
Sam	24	m	c	CHIN	Sacramento	1-Wd Sacramento	77	191
Sam	24	m	c	CHIN	Alameda	Brooklyn Twp	68	50
Sam	24	m	c	CHIN	Sutter	Vernon Twp	92	139
Sam	24	m	c	CHIN	Sutter	Vernon Twp	92	135
Sam	23	m	c	CHIN	Sutter	Sutter Twp	92	127
Sam	22	m	c	CHIN	Siskiyou	Callahan P O	89	633
Sam	21	m	c	CHIN	Colusa	Colusa	71	300
Sam	21	m	c	CHIN	Sutter	Sutter Twp	92	124
Sam	21	m	c	CHIN	Sutter	Vernon Twp	92	132
Sam	20	m	c	CHIN	Lake	Kelsey Crk	73	402
Sam	20	m	c	CHIN	Alameda	Eden Twp	68	58
Sam	20	m	c	CHIN	Alameda	Brooklyn Twp	68	41
Sam	20	m	c	CHIN	San Francisco	5-Wd San Francisco	81	36
Sam	20	m	c	CHIN	Yuba	North East Twp	93	647
Sam	20	m	c	CHIN	Yuba	Slate Range Bar Tw	93	678
Sam	19	m	c	CHIN	Alameda	Brooklyn Twp	68	53
Sam	19	m	c	CHIN	Sutter	Yuba Twp	92	148
Sam	19	m	c	CHIN	Yuba	W Bear Rvr Twp	93	684
Sam	18	m	c	CHIN	Colusa	Monroe Twp	71	324
Sam	17	m	c	CHIN	Alameda	Brooklyn Twp	68	46
Sam	16	m	c	CHIN	Sacramento	1-Wd Sacramento	77	181
Sam	16	m	c	CHIN	Alameda	Eden Twp	68	58
Sam	16	m	c	CHIN	San Francisco	5-Wd San Francisco	81	17
Sam	16	m	c	CHIN	Yuba	North East Twp	93	645
Sam	14	m	c	CHIN	Butte	Bidwell Twp	70	3
Sam [Chinaman]	23	m	c	CHIN	Butte	Oroville Twp	70	137
Samm	22	m	c	CHIN	Yuba	North East Twp	93	645
Samn	41	m	c	CHIN	Yuba	North East Twp	93	646
San	29	m	c	CHIN	Alameda	Brooklyn Twp	68	41
San	12	m	c	CHIN	Yuba	New York Twp	93	638
Sane	25	m	c	CHIN	Placer	Bath P O	76	442
Sang	44	m	c	CHIN	Butte	Wyandotte Twp	70	143
Sang	40	m	c	CHIN	Yuba	Slate Range Bar Tw	93	677
Sang	35	m	c	CHIN	Placer	Bath P O	76	454
Sang	25	m	c	CHIN	Del Norte	Happy Camp Twp	71	468
Sang	19	m	c	CHIN	Yuba	Linda Twp	93	558
Sani	19	f	c	CHIN	Sacramento	1-Wd Sacramento	77	199
Sau	28	m	c	CHIN	Del Norte	Happy Camp Twp	71	469
Sau	27	m	c	CHIN	Del Norte	Happy Camp Twp	71	469
Saur	26	m	c	CHIN	Sonoma	Vallejo Twp	91	452
Saurie	22	m	c	CHIN	Yuba	New York Twp	93	638
Saw	20	m	c	CHIN	Yuba	Bullards Bar P O	93	548
Say	37	m	c	CHIN	Alameda	Brooklyn Twp	68	41
Say	35	m	c	CHIN	Yuba	Bullards Bar P O	93	552
Say	30	m	c	CHIN	Sacramento	Granite Twp	77	141
Say	30	m	c	CHIN	Sacramento	Granite Twp	77	141
Say	27	m	c	CHIN	Yuba	North East Twp	93	646
Say	24	m	c	CHIN	Butte	Kimshew Tpw	70	85
Say	20	m	c	CHIN	Alameda	Brooklyn	68	21
Say	17	m	c	CHIN	Sonoma	Santa Rosa	91	424
Saye	42	m	c	CHIN	Colusa	Monroe Twp	71	316

© 2001 by Heritage Quest. All rights reserved.

Series M593

Name	Age	S	R	B-PL	County	Locale	Roll	Pg
Seah	44	m	c	CHIN	Klamath	Salmon Twp	73	387
Seam	19	m	c	CHIN	Monterey	San Juan Twp	74	397
Seang	50	m	c	CHIN	Del Norte	Happy Camp Twp	71	468
See	30	m	c	CHIN	Marin	Point Reyes Twp	74	22
See	24	m	c	CHIN	Yuba	Slate Range Bar Tw	93	669
See	19	m	c	CHIN	Alameda	Brooklyn Twp	68	41
See	18	m	c	CHIN	Alameda	Brooklyn	68	21
Sei	28	m	c	CHIN	Sutter	Yuba Twp	92	144
Sen	25	m	c	CHIN	Alameda	San Leandro	68	95
Sen	24	m	c	CHIN	Klamath	South Fork Twp	73	384
Seney	30	m	c	CHIN	Yuba	Slate Range Bar Tw	93	668
Seng	22	f	c	CHIN	Calaveras	Copperopolis P O	70	260
Seon	17	m	c	CHIN	Yuba	Bullards Bar P O	93	553
Sep	27	f	c	CHIN	Butte	Chico Twp	70	27
Set	27	m	c	CHIN	Yuba	Marysville	93	592
Sett	23	m	c	CHIN	Yuba	Bullards Bar P O	93	549
Seung	20	m	c	CHIN	Yuba	East Bear Rvr Twp	93	545
Seung	20	m	c	CHIN	Trinity	North Fork Twp	92	216
Seuy	38	m	c	CHIN	Klamath	South Fork Twp	73	383
Sew	30	m	c	CHIN	Yuba	Bullards Bar P O	93	548
Sew	30	m	c	CHIN	Yuba	North East Twp	93	646
Sew	25	m	c	CHIN	Yuba	Slate Range Bar Tw	93	678
Sewey	31	m	c	CHIN	Yuba	Slate Range Bar Tw	93	674
Sewey	30	m	c	CHIN	Klamath	Sawyers Bar	73	378
Shack	50	m	c	CHIN	Del Norte	Happy Camp Twp	71	469
Shacke	24	m	c	CHIN	Klamath	Liberty Twp	73	375
Shang	42	m	c	CHIN	Placer	Bath P O	76	459
Shang	34	m	c	CHIN	Klamath	Salmon Twp	73	387
Shang	32	m	c	CHIN	Merced	Snelling P O	74	249
Shang	30	m	c	CHIN	Sutter	Sutter Twp	92	121
Shaw	31	m	c	CHIN	Merced	Snelling P O	74	279
Shay	28	m	c	CHIN	Placer	Bath P O	76	442
She??	15	m	c	CHIN	Klamath	Liberty Twp	73	374
Shew	65	m	c	CHIN	Sonoma	Salt Point	91	388
Shew	36	m	c	CHIN	Klamath	Klamath Twp	73	371
Shew	30	m	c	CHIN	Yuba	North East Twp	93	645
Shew	28	m	c	CHIN	Klamath	South Fork Twp	73	382
Shew	27	m	c	CHIN	Klamath	South Fork Twp	73	384
Shew	14	m	c	CHIN	Alameda	Brooklyn Twp	68	54
Shin	42	m	c	CHIN	Klamath	Salmon Twp	73	387
Shing	37	m	c	CHIN	Klamath	Liberty Twp	73	375
Shing	30	m	c	CHIN	Klamath	Salmon Twp	73	388
Shing	30	m	c	CHIN	Klamath	Liberty Twp	73	374
Shing	28	m	c	CHIN	Klamath	South Fork Twp	73	383
Shing	14	m	c	CHIN	Klamath	Liberty Twp	73	374
Ship	32	m	c	CHIN	Colusa	Monroe Twp	71	324
Shoe	37	m	c	CHIN	Yuba	Marysville	93	601
Shon	20	m	c	CHIN	Klamath	South Fork Twp	73	384
Shong	30	m	c	CHIN	Yuba	North East Twp	93	646
Shoong	27	m	c	CHIN	Placer	Bath P O	76	442
Short	30	m	c	CHIN	Alameda	Alvarado	68	305
Shot	34	m	c	CHIN	Yuba	Bullards Bar P O	93	552
Show	32	m	c	CHIN	Fresno	Millerton P O	72	184
Show	19	m	c	CHIN	Sonoma	Salt Point	91	389
Shrung	31	m	c	CHIN	Alameda	Oakland	68	152
Shu	16	f	c	CHIN	Sacramento	1-Wd Sacramento	77	191
Shuey	30	m	c	CHIN	Yuba	Marysville Twp	93	569
Shum	30	m	c	CHIN	Klamath	Liberty Twp	73	375
Shung	18	m	c	CHIN	Klamath	Liberty Twp	73	375
Siack	18	m	c	CHIN	Klamath	Liberty Twp	73	374
Sick	37	m	c	CHIN	Yuba	Bullards Bar P O	93	549
Sick	36	m	c	CHIN	Alameda	Brooklyn	68	21
Sick	30	m	c	CHIN	Alameda	Brooklyn Twp	68	41
Sick	27	m	c	CHIN	Yuba	Slate Range Bar Tw	93	669
Sick	23	m	c	CHIN	Yuba	East Bear Rvr Twp	93	545
Sick	20	m	c	CHIN	Alameda	Brooklyn Twp	68	46
Sie	20	m	c	CHIN	Yuba	Marysville	93	601
Sien	19	f	c	CHIN	Yuba	Marysville	93	626
Sim	45	m	c	CHIN	Alameda	Murray Twp	68	114
Sim	40	m	c	CHIN	Alameda	Oakland	68	224
Sim	40	m	c	CHIN	Alameda	Oakland	68	260
Sim	38	m	c	CHIN	Alameda	Murray Twp	68	114
Sim	38	m	c	CHIN	Alameda	Oakland	68	224
Sim	38	m	c	CHIN	Alameda	Oakland	68	224
Sim	36	m	c	CHIN	Alameda	Oakland	68	254
Sim	36	m	c	CHIN	Alameda	Murray Twp	68	111
Sim	36	m	c	CHIN	Alameda	Murray Twp	68	102
Sim	34	m	c	CHIN	Alameda	Murray Twp	68	102
Sim	33	m	c	CHIN	Alameda	Murray Twp	68	111
Sim	32	m	c	CHIN	Alameda	Oakland	68	224
Sim	30	m	c	CHIN	Alameda	Oakland	68	266
Sim	30	m	c	CHIN	Alameda	Oakland	68	260
Sim	30	m	c	CHIN	Alameda	Murray Twp	68	102
Sim	30	m	c	CHIN	Alameda	Murray Twp	68	102
Sim	28	m	c	CHIN	Alameda	Oakland	68	174
Sim	28	m	c	CHIN	Alameda	Oakland	68	223
Sim	26	m	c	CHIN	Yuba	North East Twp	93	645
Sim	22	m	c	CHIN	Alameda	Washington Twp	68	299
Sim	15	m	c	CHIN	Alameda	Brooklyn Twp	68	39
Sin	32	m	c	CHIN	Yuba	Long Bar Twp	93	566
Sin	30	m	c	CHIN	Del Norte	Happy Camp Twp	71	469
Sin	25	m	c	CHIN	Alameda	Brooklyn Twp	68	46
Sin	24	m	c	CHIN	Marin	Tomales Twp	74	85
Sin	20	m	c	CHIN	Sutter	Vernon Twp	92	135
Sin	18	m	c	CHIN	Yuba	Marysville	93	594
Siney	40	m	c	CHIN	Yuba	Slate Range Bar Tw	93	678
Sing	55	m	c	CHIN	Sacramento	Granite Twp	77	140
Sing	50	m	c	CHIN	Yuba	Bullards Bar P O	93	552
Sing	48	m	c	CHIN	Sacramento	Granite Twp	77	141
Sing	44	m	c	CHIN	San Francisco	11-Wd San Francisc	84	695
Sing	42	m	c	CHIN	Yuba	Bullards Bar P O	93	548
Sing	41	m	c	CHIN	Klamath	Orleans Twp	73	381
Sing	41	m	c	CHIN	Yuba	Marysville	93	594
Sing	40	m	c	CHIN	Marin	Tomales Twp	74	77
Sing	40	m	c	CHIN	Sacramento	Granite Twp	77	141
Sing	40	m	c	CHIN	Sacramento	Granite Twp	77	140
Sing	40	m	c	CHIN	Yuba	North East Twp	93	645
Sing	40	m	c	CHIN	Yuba	North East Twp	93	646
Sing	40	m	c	CHIN	Yuba	Bullards Bar P O	93	548
Sing	40	m	c	CHIN	Sacramento	American Twp	77	64
Sing	39	m	c	CHIN	Alameda	Brooklyn Twp	68	46
Sing	37	m	c	CHIN	Yuba	W Bear Rvr Twp	93	684
Sing	36	m	c	CHIN	Yuba	Bullards Bar P O	93	552
Sing	35	m	c	CHIN	Placer	Bath P O	76	443
Sing	35	m	c	CHIN	Yuba	Marysville	93	580
Sing	35	m	c	CHIN	San Francisco	11-Wd San Francisc	84	695
Sing	34	m	c	CHIN	Plumas	Mineral Twp	77	23
Sing	33	m	c	CHIN	Alameda	Hayward	68	74
Sing	33	m	c	CHIN	Yuba	North East Twp	93	645
Sing	33	m	c	CHIN	Lassen	Susanville Twp	73	441
Sing	32	m	c	CHIN	Placer	Bath P O	76	429
Sing	31	m	c	CHIN	Yuba	Marysville Twp	93	568
Sing	30	m	c	CHIN	Sacramento	Granite Twp	77	140
Sing	30	m	c	CHIN	Sacramento	Granite Twp	77	149
Sing	30	m	c	CHIN	Placer	Bath P O	76	454
Sing	30	m	c	CHIN	Sacramento	Granite Twp	77	140
Sing	30	m	c	CHIN	Sacramento	Granite Twp	77	149
Sing	30	m	c	CHIN	Yuba	North East Twp	93	646
Sing	30	m	c	CHIN	Yuba	North East Twp	93	647
Sing	30	m	c	CHIN	Yuba	Marysville	93	576
Sing	30	m	c	CHIN	Yuba	Bullards Bar P O	93	548
Sing	30	m	c	CHIN	San Francisco	8-Wd San Francisco	82	458
Sing	30	m	c	CHIN	Klamath	South Fork Twp	73	382
Sing	30	m	c	CHIN	Lassen	Milford Twp	73	438
Sing	30	m	c	CHIN	Lassen	Susanville Twp	73	441
Sing	29	m	c	CHIN	Yuba	East Bear Rvr Twp	93	546
Sing	29	m	c	CHIN	Klamath	South Fork Twp	73	384
Sing	29	m	c	CHIN	Yuba	Marysville	93	592
Sing	28	m	c	CHIN	Colusa	Butte Twp	71	269
Sing	28	m	c	CHIN	Klamath	Dillon Twp	73	369
Sing	28	m	c	CHIN	Yuba	Slate Range Bar Tw	93	669
Sing	28	m	c	CHIN	Yuba	Slate Range Bar Tw	93	668
Sing	28	m	c	CHIN	Klamath	South Fork Twp	73	383
Sing	27	m	c	CHIN	Yuba	East Bear Rvr Twp	93	545
Sing	27	m	c	CHIN	Colusa	Colusa Twp	71	281
Sing	26	m	c	CHIN	Del Norte	Happy Camp Twp	71	468
Sing	26	m	c	CHIN	San Francisco	8-Wd San Francisco	82	471
Sing	25	m	c	CHIN	Lassen	Long Valley Twp	73	437
Sing	25	m	c	CHIN	Alameda	Brooklyn Twp	68	43
Sing	25	m	c	CHIN	Alameda	Brooklyn Twp	68	53
Sing	25	m	c	CHIN	Yuba	North East Twp	93	646
Sing	25	m	c	CHIN	Yuba	North East Twp	93	647
Sing	25	m	c	CHIN	Yuba	Bullards Bar P O	93	553
Sing	25	m	c	CHIN	Merced	Snelling P O	74	278
Sing	25	m	c	CHIN	Placer	Bath P O	76	454
Sing	24	m	c	CHIN	Sacramento	Granite Twp	77	140
Sing	24	m	c	CHIN	Klamath	South Fork Twp	73	384
Sing	24	m	c	CHIN	Marin	Tomales Twp	74	84
Sing	23	m	c	CHIN	Yuba	Slate Range Bar Tw	93	670
Sing	23	m	c	CHIN	Yuba	Marysville Twp	93	569
Sing	23	m	c	CHIN	Klamath	Liberty Twp	73	374
Sing	22	m	c	CHIN	Sutter	Butte Twp	92	89
Sing	21	m	c	CHIN	San Francisco	5-Wd San Francisco	81	10
Sing	21	m	c	CHIN	Sutter	Sutter Twp	92	121
Sing	20	m	c	CHIN	Alameda	Brooklyn	68	21
Sing	20	m	c	CHIN	Placer	Bath P O	76	453
Sing	19	m	c	CHIN	Alameda	Eden Twp	68	60
Sing	18	m	c	CHIN	Alameda	Brooklyn	68	24
Sing	18	m	c	CHIN	Alameda	Brooklyn	68	23
Sing	18	m	c	CHIN	Yuba	Linda Twp	93	558
Sing	18	m	c	CHIN	Sutter	Sutter Twp	92	118
Sing	17	m	c	CHIN	Alameda	Hayward	68	74
Sing	16	m	c	CHIN	San Francisco	8-Wd San Francisco	82	486
Sing	16	m	c	CHIN	San Francisco	11-Wd San Francisc	84	435
Sing	15	m	c	CHIN	Sonoma	Petaluma Twp	91	363
Sing	14	m	c	CHIN	Sonoma	Santa Rosa	91	413
Sing	14	m	c	CHIN	Alameda	Alvarado	68	303
Sing	12	m	c	CHIN	Alameda	Brooklyn Twp	68	39
Sinn	40	m	c	CHIN	Yuba	North East Twp	93	645
Sinn	30	m	c	CHIN	Yuba	North East Twp	93	647
Sinn	19	m	c	CHIN	Yuba	Bullards Bar P O	93	548
Siny	40	m	c	CHIN	Yuba	Slate Range Bar Tw	93	677
Sip	22	m	c	CHIN	Alameda	Brooklyn Twp	68	46
Slam	20	m	c	CHIN	Sutter	Sutter Twp	92	123
Slang	42	m	c	CHIN	Klamath	Dillon Twp	73	369
Sley	44	m	c	CHIN	Klamath	Salmon Twp	73	388
Slick	22	m	c	CHIN	Yuba	East Bear Rvr Twp	93	545
Slim	20	m	c	CHIN	Alameda	Eden Twp	68	92
Slin	24	m	c	CHIN	Alameda	Eden Twp	68	93
Sling	24	m	c	CHIN	Placer	Bath P O	76	459
Slo	21	m	c	CHIN	Sutter	Vernon Twp	92	139
Sluey	33	m	c	CHIN	Klamath	South Fork Twp	73	385
Slung	20	m	c	CHIN	San Francisco	8-Wd San Francisco	82	420
Soe	26	m	c	CHIN	Alameda	Brooklyn	68	21

© 2001 by Heritage Quest. All rights reserved.

Name	Age	S	R	B-PL	County	Locale (Series M593)	Roll	Pg
Soey	41	m	c	CHIN	Klamath	Dillon Twp	73	369
Som	25	m	c	CHIN	Monterey	Castroville Twp	74	327
Somb	50	m	c	CHIN	Del Norte	Happy Camp Twp	71	469
Some	22	m	c	CHIN	Yuba	North East Twp	93	646
Son	45	m	c	CHIN	Alameda	Oakland	68	223
Son	44	m	c	CHIN	Klamath	South Fork Twp	73	383
Son	21	m	c	CHIN	Alameda	Washington Twp	68	295
Sone	27	m	c	CHIN	Sutter	Sutter Twp	92	121
Song	65	m	c	CHIN	Yuba	Long Bar Twp	93	560
Song	45	m	c	CHIN	Yuba	Slate Range Bar Tw	93	670
Song	44	m	c	CHIN	Sacramento	Granite Twp	77	141
Song	39	m	c	CHIN	Placer	Bath P O	76	444
Song	37	m	c	CHIN	Alameda	Murray Twp	68	102
Song	36	m	c	CHIN	Klamath	Klamath Twp	73	370
Song	35	m	c	CHIN	Alameda	Oakland	68	223
Song	35	m	c	CHIN	Yuba	North East Twp	93	646
Song	30	m	c	CHIN	Alameda	Eden Twp	68	60
Song	30	m	c	CHIN	Klamath	South Fork Twp	73	383
Song	26	m	c	CHIN	Yuba	Slate Range Bar Tw	93	669
Song	24	m	c	CHIN	Klamath	Salmon Twp	73	387
Song	21	m	c	CHIN	Alameda	Eden Twp	68	60
Song	14	m	c	CHIN	Yuba	North East Twp	93	647
Soni	32	m	c	CHIN	Klamath	South Fork Twp	73	383
Soni	20	m	c	CHIN	Klamath	South Fork Twp	73	384
Sony	40	m	c	CHIN	Yuba	Bullards Bar P O	93	548
Sook	20	m	c	CHIN	Colusa	Colusa	71	299
Soon	20	m	c	CHIN	Colusa	Grand Island Twp	71	310
Soon	20	m	c	CHIN	Yuba	Bullards Bar P O	93	549
Soot	20	m	c	CHIN	Yuba	Marysville	93	580
Soote	30	m	c	CHIN	Colusa	Colusa	71	299
Sou	28	m	c	CHIN	Del Norte	Happy Camp Twp	71	470
Souname	40	m	c	CHIN	Klamath	Liberty Twp	73	375
Soung	30	m	c	CHIN	Alameda	Oakland	68	232
Soy	4	m	c	CA	Butte	Hamilton Twp	70	73
Stand	39	m	c	CHIN	Yuba	Marysville	93	631
Stanley	39	m	w	ENGL	Marin	San Rafael Twp	74	45
Stege	27	m	c	CHIN	Yuba	Slate Range Bar Tw	93	670
Suah	46	m	c	CHIN	Marin	San Rafael Twp	74	59
Suan	23	m	c	CHIN	Yuba	Slate Range Bar Tw	93	678
Sue	58	m	c	CHIN	Yuba	North East Twp	93	645
Sue	45	m	c	CHIN	Del Norte	Happy Camp Twp	71	469
Sue	38	f	c	CHIN	Sacramento	1-Wd Sacramento	77	199
Sue	37	m	c	CHIN	Yuba	Marysville	93	594
Sue	35	m	c	CHIN	Yuba	Marysville	93	601
Sue	31	m	c	CHIN	Placer	Bath P O	76	453
Sue	30	m	c	CHIN	Yuba	Marysville	93	602
Sue	27	m	c	CHIN	Yuba	New York Twp	93	638
Sue	26	f	c	CHIN	Sacramento	1-Wd Sacramento	77	194
Sue	25	f	c	CHIN	Sacramento	1-Wd Sacramento	77	195
Sue	24	f	c	CHIN	Sacramento	1-Wd Sacramento	77	197
Sue	22	f	c	CHIN	Sacramento	1-Wd Sacramento	77	196
Sue	21	f	c	CHIN	Sacramento	1-Wd Sacramento	77	193
Sue	20	f	c	CHIN	Sacramento	1-Wd Sacramento	77	194
Sue	20	f	c	CHIN	Sacramento	1-Wd Sacramento	77	194
Sue	19	m	c	CHIN	Marin	Sausalito Twp	74	70
Sue	18	f	c	CHIN	Sacramento	1-Wd Sacramento	77	177
Sue	18	f	c	CHIN	Siskiyou	Cottonwood Twp	89	593
Sue	14	m	c	CA	Sacramento	1-Wd Sacramento	77	194
Sue	14	f	c	CHIN	Sacramento	1-Wd Sacramento	77	192
Suey	35	m	c	CHIN	Yuba	Marysville	93	629
Suey	31	m	c	CHIN	Klamath	Salmon Twp	73	387
Suey	24	m	c	CHIN	Yuba	Linda Twp	93	558
Suey	21	m	c	CHIN	Klamath	Liberty Twp	73	375
Suge	28	m	c	CHIN	Yuba	North East Twp	93	647
Sui	25	f	c	CHIN	Sacramento	1-Wd Sacramento	77	199
Sui	18	f	c	CHIN	Sacramento	1-Wd Sacramento	77	192
Sui	16	f	c	CHIN	Sacramento	1-Wd Sacramento	77	192
Suisey	30	f	c	CHIN	Trinity	Weaverville Pct	92	228
Sum	45	m	c	CHIN	Placer	Bath P O	76	443
Sum	31	m	c	CHIN	Yuba	East Bear Rvr Twp	93	546
Sum	28	m	c	CHIN	Alameda	Brooklyn Twp	68	46
Sum	28	m	c	CHIN	Alameda	Brooklyn Twp	68	41
Sum	16	m	c	CHIN	Alameda	Brooklyn	68	21
Sun	55	m	c	CHIN	Del Norte	Happy Camp Twp	71	469
Sun	35	m	c	CHIN	Klamath	South Fork Twp	73	383
Sun	35	m	c	CHIN	Del Norte	Happy Camp Twp	71	468
Sun	32	m	c	CHIN	Alameda	Brooklyn Twp	68	46
Sun	22	m	c	CHIN	Alameda	Oakland	68	254
Sun	22	m	c	CHIN	Del Norte	Happy Camp Twp	71	469
Sun	16	m	c	CHIN	Napa	Napa Twp	75	32
Sun	15	m	c	CHIN	San Francisco	8-Wd San Francisco	82	415
Sung	40	m	c	CHIN	Alameda	Murray Twp	68	102
Sung	37	m	c	CHIN	Marin	Novato Twp	74	11
Sung	34	m	c	CHIN	Klamath	Klamath Twp	73	370
Sung	33	m	c	CHIN	Yuba	Linda Twp	93	558
Sung	31	m	c	CHIN	Klamath	Klamath Twp	73	370
Sung	30	m	c	CHIN	Yuba	New York Twp	93	640
Sung	19	m	c	CHIN	San Francisco	11-Wd San Francisc	84	681
Sung	13	m	c	CHIN	Sacramento	4-Wd Sacramento	77	329
Sung	12	m	c	CHIN	San Francisco	8-Wd San Francisco	82	466
Suni	36	f	c	CHIN	Sacramento	1-Wd Sacramento	77	195
Suni	16	f	c	CHIN	Sacramento	1-Wd Sacramento	77	194
Susan	32	f	c	CHIN	Alameda	Alameda	68	18
Susan	25	f	c	CHIN	San Francisco	6-Wd San Francisco	81	65
Sut	14	m	c	CHIN	Sutter	Vernon Twp	92	136
Sy	40	m	c	CHIN	Sacramento	Granite Twp	77	140
Syen	30	m	c	CHIN	Klamath	South Fork Twp	73	384

Name	Age	S	R	B-PL	County	Locale (Series M593)	Roll	Pg
Tack	24	m	c	CHIN	Yuba	New York Twp	93	640
Tack	20	m	c	CHIN	Yuba	Bullards Bar P O	93	552
Taen	26	m	c	CHIN	Calaveras	Copperopolis P O	70	260
Tage	20	m	c	CHIN	Yuba	Parks Bar Twp	93	650
Tage	18	m	c	CHIN	Yuba	Slate Range Bar Tw	93	669
Tah	27	m	c	CHIN	Klamath	Orleans Twp	73	380
Tahn	42	m	c	CHIN	Marin	San Rafael Twp	74	59
Talk	40	m	c	CHIN	Yuba	Slate Range Bar Tw	93	677
Talk	28	m	c	CHIN	Yuba	Bullards Bar P O	93	552
Tam	20	m	c	CHIN	Del Norte	Happy Camp Twp	71	468
Tan	18	m	c	CHIN	San Francisco	8-Wd San Francisco	82	412
Tang	40	m	c	CHIN	Sonoma	Santa Rosa	91	424
Tang	39	m	c	CHIN	Yuba	Marysville	93	592
Tang	29	m	c	CHIN	Sonoma	Santa Rosa	91	424
Tang	25	m	c	CHIN	Yuba	Slate Range Bar Tw	93	674
Tang	24	m	c	CHIN	Yuba	Slate Range Bar Tw	93	668
Tang	21	m	c	CHIN	Alameda	Brooklyn Twp	68	41
Tango	30	m	c	CHIN	Sutter	Yuba Twp	92	140
Tao	38	m	c	CHIN	Butte	Bidwell Twp	70	3
Tau	14	m	c	CHIN	Yuba	Marysville	93	601
Taw	45	m	c	CHIN	Yuba	New York Twp	93	638
Tay	49	m	c	CHIN	Sacramento	Granite Twp	77	149
Tay	45	m	c	CHIN	Sacramento	Granite Twp	77	149
Tay	36	m	c	CHIN	Sacramento	Granite Twp	77	149
Tay	30	m	c	CHIN	Sacramento	Granite Twp	77	141
Tay	28	m	c	CHIN	Sonoma	Salt Point	91	389
Tay	27	m	c	CHIN	Sacramento	Granite Twp	77	140
Tay	20	m	c	CHIN	Yuba	Bullards Bar P O	93	552
Tay	17	m	c	CHIN	Yuba	North East Twp	93	646
Taye	35	m	c	CHIN	Yuba	Slate Range Bar Tw	93	674
Taye	30	m	c	CHIN	Yuba	Slate Range Bar Tw	93	678
Tchee	34	m	c	CHIN	Klamath	Liberty Twp	73	375
Teek	23	m	c	CHIN	Yuba	Slate Range Bar Tw	93	679
Tein	21	m	c	CHIN	Alameda	Brooklyn	68	21
Tem	30	m	c	CHIN	Del Norte	Happy Camp Twp	71	468
Ten	21	m	c	CHIN	Yuba	East Bear Rvr Twp	93	545
Ten	17	m	c	CHIN	Placer	Bath P O	76	453
Tenn	49	m	c	CHIN	Fresno	Millerton P O	72	184
Tenn	30	m	c	CHIN	Yuba	Bullards Bar P O	93	548
Teo	28	m	c	CHIN	Yuba	Slate Range Bar Tw	93	678
Teo	25	m	c	CHIN	Klamath	Klamath Twp	73	370
Teon	28	m	c	CHIN	Yuba	Slate Range Bar Tw	93	669
Teong	50	m	c	CHIN	Yuba	Slate Range Bar Tw	93	676
Teong	25	m	c	CHIN	Yuba	Slate Range Bar Tw	93	668
Tepp	42	m	c	CHIN	Yuba	Bullards Bar P O	93	548
Teu	30	m	c	CHIN	Yuba	Marysville	93	602
Teung	32	m	c	CHIN	Yuba	East Bear Rvr Twp	93	545
Tew	30	m	c	CHIN	Klamath	Sawyers Bar	73	378
Tew	20	m	c	CHIN	Yuba	Bullards Bar P O	93	552
Thin	16	m	c	CHIN	Sutter	Sutter Twp	92	121
Thing	25	m	c	CHIN	Sonoma	Sonoma Twp	91	435
Thing	18	m	c	CHIN	Marin	Tomales Twp	74	76
Thom	28	m	c	CHIN	Alameda	Brooklyn	68	28
Thomas [Chinaman]	35	m	c	CHIN	Trinity	Douglas	92	234
Thop	22	m	c	CHIN	Sonoma	Salt Point	91	388
Thung	29	m	c	CHIN	Marin	Tomales Twp	74	83
Ti	27	m	c	CHIN	Yuba	W Bear Rvr Twp	93	684
Ti	15	m	c	CHIN	Monterey	San Juan Twp	74	397
Tick	30	m	c	CHIN	Yuba	Slate Range Bar Tw	93	675
Tie	60	m	c	CHIN	Placer	Bath P O	76	444
Tie	35	m	c	CHIN	El Dorado	Georgetown Twp	72	43
Tie	30	m	c	CHIN	Merced	Snelling P O	74	279
Tie	26	m	c	CHIN	Alameda	Brooklyn	68	21
Tien	40	m	c	CHIN	San Francisco	11-Wd San Francisc	84	695
Tike	45	m	c	CHIN	Placer	Bath P O	76	443
Tim	31	m	c	CHIN	Alameda	Brooklyn Twp	68	41
Tim	21	m	c	CHIN	Alameda	Washington Twp	68	295
Tim	21	m	c	CHIN	Yuba	W Bear Rvr Twp	93	684
Tin	36	m	c	CHIN	Alameda	Brooklyn Twp	68	46
Tin	20	m	c	CHIN	Klamath	South Fork Twp	73	384
Tin	18	m	c	CHIN	Del Norte	Mountain Twp	71	475
Ting	37	m	c	CHIN	Yuba	East Bear Rvr Twp	93	545
Ting	28	m	c	CHIN	Sacramento	Granite Twp	77	149
Ting	26	m	c	CHIN	Yuba	Marysville	93	629
Ting	22	m	c	CHIN	Marin	Tomales Twp	74	86
Ting	20	m	c	CHIN	Yuba	W Bear Rvr Twp	93	684
Tinn	20	m	c	CHIN	San Joaquin	2-Wd Stockton	86	164
Tock	27	m	c	CHIN	Yuba	Linda Twp	93	558
Toge	33	m	c	CHIN	Yuba	North East Twp	93	647
Toge	20	m	c	CHIN	Yuba	Long Bar Twp	93	560
Tom	47	m	c	CHIN	Colusa	Monroe Twp	71	324
Tom	42	m	c	CHIN	Klamath	South Fork Twp	73	384
Tom	34	m	c	CHIN	Klamath	Klamath Twp	73	370
Tom	31	m	c	CHIN	Siskiyou	Yreka Twp	89	666
Tom	30	m	c	CHIN	Klamath	South Fork Twp	73	382
Tom	26	m	c	CHIN	Yuba	Rose Bar Twp	93	655
Tom	25	m	c	CHIN	Yuba	Bullards Bar P O	93	548
Tom	21	m	c	CHIN	Yuba	North East Twp	93	646
Tom	17	m	c	CHIN	Yuba	East Bear Rvr Twp	93	546
Tom	16	m	c	CHIN	Alameda	Brooklyn Twp	68	55
Tom	16	m	c	CHIN	Yuba	Slate Range Bar Tw	93	678
Tom [Chinaman]	48	m	c	CHIN	Butte	Oroville Twp	70	137
Tom [Chinaman]	26	m	c	CHIN	Calaveras	San Andreas P O	70	156
Tomson	28	m	c	CHIN	Placer	Bath P O	76	456
Ton	60	m	c	CHIN	Del Norte	Happy Camp Twp	71	468
Tone	40	m	c	CHIN	Klamath	Liberty Twp	73	375
Tone	32	m	c	CHIN	Alameda	Brooklyn Twp	68	41

© 2001 by Heritage Quest. All rights reserved.

Name	Age	S	R	B-PL	County	Locale	Roll	Pg
Tone	25	m	c	CHIN	Alameda	Brooklyn	68	21
Tong	50	m	c	CHIN	Placer	Bath P O	76	459
Tong	45	m	c	CHIN	Placer	Bath P O	76	452
Tong	44	m	c	CHIN	Yuba	East Bear Rvr Twp	93	545
Tong	40	m	c	CHIN	Yuba	Bullards Bar P O	93	552
Tong	40	m	c	CHIN	Fresno	Millerton P O	72	188
Tong	35	m	c	CHIN	Yuba	North East Twp	93	646
Tong	33	m	c	CHIN	Alameda	Brooklyn	68	21
Tong	32	m	c	CHIN	Yuba	New York Twp	93	638
Tong	31	m	c	CHIN	Placer	Bath P O	76	459
Tong	30	m	c	CHIN	Klamath	Liberty Twp	73	376
Tong	30	m	c	CHIN	Placer	Bath P O	76	442
Tong	29	m	c	CHIN	Klamath	Liberty Twp	73	374
Tong	29	m	c	CHIN	Alameda	Brooklyn	68	21
Tong	28	m	c	CHIN	Placer	Bath P O	76	429
Tong	28	m	c	CHIN	Yuba	North East Twp	93	645
Tong	28	m	c	CHIN	Yuba	W Bear Rvr Twp	93	682
Tong	26	m	c	CHIN	Alameda	Brooklyn	68	21
Tong	26	m	c	CHIN	Yuba	Slate Range Bar Tw	93	672
Tong	24	m	c	CHIN	Alameda	Hayward	68	74
Tong	24	m	c	CHIN	Del Norte	Happy Camp Twp	71	469
Tong	24	m	c	CHIN	Klamath	Dillon Twp	73	369
Tong	24	m	c	CHIN	Yuba	North East Twp	93	646
Tong	23	m	c	CHIN	Alameda	Brooklyn	68	21
Tong	22	m	c	CHIN	Alameda	Brooklyn Twp	68	41
Tong	22	m	c	CHIN	Alameda	Brooklyn Twp	68	41
Tong	20	m	c	CHIN	Klamath	South Fork Twp	73	384
Tong	18	m	c	CHIN	Sonoma	Salt Point	91	389
Tong	16	m	c	CHIN	Alameda	Brooklyn	68	27
Tong	15	m	c	CHIN	Yuba	Long Bar Twp	93	560
Tong	14	m	c	CHIN	Yuba	North East Twp	93	646
Too	38	m	c	CHIN	Yuba	North East Twp	93	646
Too	30	m	c	CHIN	Yuba	North East Twp	93	646
Too	30	m	c	CHIN	Colusa	Colusa	71	299
Too	28	m	c	CHIN	Yuba	Slate Range Bar Tw	93	677
Too	27	m	c	CHIN	Yuba	North East Twp	93	646
Too	24	m	c	CHIN	Yuba	Bullards Bar P O	93	548
Too	24	m	c	CHIN	Yuba	Long Bar Twp	93	562
Too	18	m	c	CHIN	Yuba	North East Twp	93	646
Too	18	m	c	CHIN	Yuba	Bullards Bar P O	93	552
Took	19	m	c	CHIN	Alameda	Brooklyn	68	21
Toon	47	m	c	CHIN	Calaveras	San Andreas P O	70	155
Toon	39	m	c	CHIN	Butte	Hamilton Twp	70	73
Toon	35	m	c	CHIN	Yuba	Slate Range Bar Tw	93	677
Toon	30	m	c	CHIN	Yuba	Bullards Bar P O	93	552
Toon	25	m	c	CHIN	Yuba	Slate Range Bar Tw	93	676
Toone	22	m	c	CHIN	Yuba	Slate Range Bar Tw	93	670
Toqui	20	m	c	CHIN	Fresno	Millerton P O	72	184
Toung	27	m	c	CHIN	Placer	Bath P O	76	444
Tow	51	m	c	CHIN	Butte	Bidwell Twp	70	3
Tow	23	m	c	CHIN	Yuba	Bullards Bar P O	93	548
Tow	20	m	c	CHIN	Yuba	Long Bar Twp	93	560
Towe	35	m	c	CHIN	Butte	Wyandotte Twp	70	146
Toy	41	m	c	CHIN	Butte	Hamilton Twp	70	67
Toy	38	m	c	CHIN	Sacramento	American Twp	77	64
Toy	36	m	c	CHIN	Del Norte	Happy Camp Twp	71	469
Toy	32	m	c	CHIN	Placer	Bath P O	76	442
Toy	30	m	c	CHIN	Klamath	South Fork Twp	73	382
Toy	30	m	c	CHIN	Klamath	South Fork Twp	73	383
Toy	28	m	c	CHIN	Klamath	South Fork Twp	73	383
Toy	27	m	c	CHIN	Klamath	Salmon Twp	73	387
Toy	22	m	c	CHIN	Yuba	Marysville	93	580
Toy	20	m	c	CHIN	Klamath	South Fork Twp	73	382
Toz	39	m	c	CHIN	Colusa	Monroe Twp	71	324
Trankilino	50	m	w	MEXI	Yuba	Linda Twp	93	558
Tromon	48	m	w	MEXI	Yuba	Linda Twp	93	558
Tuck	45	m	c	CHIN	Yuba	New York Twp	93	640
Tuck	32	m	c	CHIN	Yuba	Bullards Bar P O	93	553
Tuck	28	m	c	CHIN	Yuba	Marysville	93	600
Tue	22	m	c	CHIN	Yuba	Marysville Twp	93	569
Tuee	16	m	c	CHIN	Yuba	Bullards Bar P O	93	553
Tuhn	22	m	c	CHIN	Marin	San Rafael	74	51
Tum	15	m	c	CHIN	Alameda	Brooklyn	68	25
Tun	26	m	c	CHIN	Sacramento	Granite Twp	77	149
Tung	40	m	c	CHIN	Alameda	Oakland	68	224
Tung	38	m	c	CHIN	Placer	Bath P O	76	444
Tung	34	m	c	CHIN	Klamath	Dillon Twp	73	369
Tung	33	m	c	CHIN	Alameda	Brooklyn Twp	68	46
Tung	31	m	c	CHIN	Yuba	Marysville	93	602
Tung	23	m	c	CHIN	Yuba	Marysville	93	601
Twoo	29	m	c	CHIN	Placer	Bath P O	76	444
Ty	29	m	c	CHIN	Del Norte	Happy Camp Twp	71	468
Ty	20	m	c	CHIN	Del Norte	Crescent	71	464
Tye	20	m	c	CHIN	Marin	Sausalito Twp	74	71
Tyew	40	m	c	CHIN	Yuba	New York Twp	93	637
Une	20	m	c	CHIN	Alameda	Brooklyn	68	21
Une	17	m	c	CHIN	Alameda	Brooklyn	68	21
Ung	25	m	c	CHIN	Del Norte	Happy Camp Twp	71	471
Unggew	44	m	c	CHIN	Klamath	Salmon Twp	73	387
Ungue	28	m	c	CHIN	Yuba	Slate Range Bar Tw	93	668
Varr	41	m	c	CHIN	Yuba	North East Twp	93	645
Ven	20	m	c	CHIN	Sonoma	Sonoma Twp	91	442
Vinsco	35	m	c	CHIN	Placer	Bath P O	76	459
Vong	45	m	c	CHIN	Placer	Bath P O	76	442
Wagin	29	m	c	CHIN	Fresno	Millerton P O	72	184
Wah	60	m	c	CHIN	Klamath	Dillon Twp	73	369
Wah	50	m	c	CHIN	Yuba	Slate Range Bar Tw	93	668
Wah	48	m	c	CHIN	Klamath	Orleans Twp	73	380
Wah	46	m	c	CHIN	Yuba	Slate Range Bar Tw	93	668
Wah	45	m	c	CHIN	Del Norte	Happy Camp Twp	71	470
Wah	45	m	c	CHIN	Klamath	Klamath Twp	73	370
Wah	42	m	c	CHIN	Klamath	South Fork Twp	73	382
Wah	35	m	c	CHIN	Merced	Snelling P O	74	249
Wah	35	m	c	CHIN	Klamath	Sawyers Bar	73	378
Wah	35	m	c	CHIN	Yuba	Slate Range Bar Tw	93	678
Wah	32	m	c	CHIN	Klamath	Klamath Twp	73	370
Wah	30	m	c	CHIN	Marin	Point Reyes Twp	74	21
Wah	29	m	c	CHIN	Klamath	Liberty Twp	73	374
Wah	23	m	c	CHIN	Yuba	Slate Range Bar Tw	93	677
Wah	22	m	c	CHIN	Yuba	Slate Range Bar Tw	93	672
Wah	20	m	c	CHIN	San Francisco	5-Wd San Francisco	81	17
Wah	20	m	c	CHIN	Yuba	North East Twp	93	645
Wah	18	m	c	CHIN	Sacramento	4-Wd Sacramento	77	331
Wah	11	m	c	CHIN	Yuba	Marysville	93	594
Wahow	29	m	c	CHIN	Yuba	Slate Range Bar Tw	93	674
Wam	42	m	c	CHIN	Alameda	Brooklyn	68	21
Wam	41	m	c	CHIN	Alameda	Murray Twp	68	111
Wam	29	m	c	CHIN	Alameda	Oakland	68	254
Wam	25	m	c	CHIN	Alameda	Murray Twp	68	111
Wam	22	m	c	CHIN	Yuba	North East Twp	93	645
Wan	47	m	c	CHIN	Butte	Wyandotte Twp	70	142
Wan	38	m	c	CHIN	Alameda	Murray Twp	68	102
Wan	37	m	c	CHIN	Alameda	Murray Twp	68	102
Wan	34	m	c	CHIN	Del Norte	Happy Camp Twp	71	468
Wan	29	m	c	CHIN	Alameda	Murray Twp	68	102
Wan	29	m	c	CHIN	Alameda	Murray Twp	68	102
Wan	25	m	c	CHIN	Alameda	Murray Twp	68	120
Wan	25	m	c	CHIN	Alameda	Brooklyn Twp	68	41
Wan	25	m	c	CHIN	Placer	Bath P O	76	452
Wan	21	m	c	CHIN	Alameda	Brooklyn Twp	68	46
Wan	18	m	c	CHIN	Butte	Wyandotte Twp	70	148
Wan	16	m	c	CHIN	Yuba	Marysville	93	594
Wan	16	m	c	CHIN	Colusa	Grand Island Twp	71	303
Wand	37	m	c	CHIN	Alameda	Oakland	68	260
Wane	22	m	c	CHIN	Sonoma	Salt Point	91	389
Wang	45	m	c	CHIN	Placer	Bath P O	76	429
Wang	36	m	c	CHIN	Klamath	Liberty Twp	73	375
Wang	32	m	c	CHIN	Yuba	Slate Range Bar Tw	93	668
Wang	31	m	c	CHIN	Yuba	Linda Twp	93	558
Wang	30	m	c	CHIN	Placer	Bath P O	76	444
Wang	28	m	c	CHIN	Klamath	Liberty Twp	73	375
Wang	28	m	c	CHIN	Butte	Oroville Twp	70	139
Wang	19	m	c	CHIN	Alameda	Brooklyn Twp	68	46
Wang	18	m	c	CHIN	Sonoma	Bodega Twp	91	261
Wang	18	m	c	CHIN	San Francisco	8-Wd San Francisco	82	488
Wang	13	m	c	CHIN	Klamath	Sawyers Bar	73	378
Wang	12	m	c	CHIN	San Francisco	8-Wd San Francisco	82	465
Wantie	37	m	c	CHIN	Fresno	Millerton P O	72	184
Watt	34	m	c	CHIN	Klamath	Salmon Twp	73	387
Watt	26	m	c	CHIN	Klamath	South Fork Twp	73	384
Waugh	44	m	c	CHIN	Yuba	Marysville	93	621
Waugh	28	m	c	CHIN	Yuba	Marysville	93	600
Way	55	m	c	CHIN	Yuba	Long Bar Twp	93	560
Way	52	m	c	CHIN	Klamath	South Fork Twp	73	384
Way	34	m	c	CHIN	Klamath	South Fork Twp	73	384
Wayne	43	m	c	CHIN	Yuba	North East Twp	93	646
Wee	30	m	c	CHIN	Sonoma	Salt Point	91	387
Wee	16	m	c	CHIN	Alameda	Brooklyn	68	25
Wee	11	m	c	CHIN	Sonoma	Sonoma Twp	91	442
Whack	27	m	c	CHIN	Sacramento	Granite Twp	77	140
Whack	25	m	c	CHIN	Marin	San Rafael	74	58
Whe	18	m	c	CHIN	San Francisco	8-Wd San Francisco	82	465
Whey	38	m	c	CHIN	Yuba	North East Twp	93	646
Whey	14	m	c	CHIN	San Francisco	8-Wd San Francisco	82	401
Whip	40	m	c	CHIN	Yuba	Slate Range Bar Tw	93	678
Why	40	m	c	CHIN	Marin	Tomales Twp	74	88
Why	23	m	c	CHIN	Yuba	North East Twp	93	645
Why	15	m	c	CHIN	San Francisco	8-Wd San Francisco	82	471
Whye	42	m	c	CHIN	Yuba	Slate Range Bar Tw	93	674
Williams	60	m	w	KY	Kern	Bakersfield P O	73	357
Wim	24	m	c	CHIN	Alameda	Brooklyn Twp	68	46
Win	37	m	c	CHIN	Alameda	Alameda	68	17
Win	30	m	c	CHIN	Alameda	Murray Twp	68	111
Winecleo	35	m	c	CHIN	Sonoma	Petaluma Twp	91	342
Wing	50	m	c	CHIN	Klamath	Liberty Twp	73	376
Wing	40	m	c	CHIN	Yuba	Slate Range Bar Tw	93	668
Wing	35	m	c	CHIN	Yuba	North East Twp	93	647
Wing	35	m	c	CHIN	Yuba	New York Twp	93	638
Wing	32	m	c	CHIN	Butte	Chico Twp	70	52
Wing	30	m	c	CHIN	Sonoma	Sonoma Twp	91	434
Wing	30	m	c	CHIN	Klamath	Salmon Twp	73	387
Wing	29	m	c	CHIN	Yuba	Slate Range Bar Tw	93	676
Wing	26	m	c	CHIN	Colusa	Monroe Twp	71	315
Wing	26	m	c	CHIN	Klamath	Salmon Twp	73	387
Wing	24	m	c	CHIN	Yuba	Linda Twp	93	558
Wing	23	m	c	CHIN	Alameda	Washington Twp	68	299
Wing	22	m	c	CHIN	Placer	Bath P O	76	444
Wing	21	m	c	CHIN	Klamath	Liberty Twp	73	374
Wing	20	m	c	CHIN	Sonoma	Santa Rosa	91	420
Wing	20	m	c	CHIN	Klamath	Liberty Twp	73	374
Wing	19	m	c	CHIN	Alameda	Washington Twp	68	299
Wing	18	m	c	CHIN	Sacramento	4-Wd Sacramento	77	325
Wing	16	m	c	CHIN	Sacramento	1-Wd Sacramento	77	175
Wing	15	m	c	CHIN	Alameda	Brooklyn Twp	68	43

Series M593

© 2001 by Heritage Quest. All rights reserved.

Series M593

Name	Age	S	R	B-PL	County	Locale	Roll	Pg
Wing	15	m	c	CHIN	Yuba	Slate Range Bar Tw	93	669
Winy	40	m	c	CHIN	Yuba	Bullards Bar P O	93	548
Wo	36	m	c	CHIN	Sacramento	Granite Twp	77	140
Wo	35	m	c	CHIN	Sacramento	American Twp	77	64
Wo	34	m	c	CHIN	Sacramento	Granite Twp	77	141
Wo	24	m	c	CHIN	Alameda	Brooklyn Twp	68	46
Won	38	m	c	CHIN	Del Norte	Happy Camp Twp	71	471
Won	34	m	c	CHIN	Alameda	Eden Twp	68	60
Won	31	m	c	CHIN	Alameda	Brooklyn Twp	68	41
Won	30	m	c	CHIN	Del Norte	Mountain Twp	71	475
Won	30	m	c	CHIN	Yuba	Marysville	93	621
Won	29	m	c	CHIN	Butte	Chico Twp	70	27
Won	20	m	c	CHIN	Yuba	Marysville	93	620
Wong	58	m	c	CHIN	Yuba	Long Bar Twp	93	560
Wong	46	m	c	CHIN	Klamath	Salmon Twp	73	387
Wong	36	m	c	CHIN	Placer	Auburn P O	76	375
Wong	35	m	c	CHIN	Del Norte	Happy Camp Twp	71	470
Wong	30	m	c	CHIN	Alameda	Brooklyn Twp	68	55
Wong	27	m	c	CHIN	Alameda	Brooklyn Twp	68	41
Wong	27	m	c	CHIN	Yuba	W Bear Rvr Twp	93	684
Wong	25	m	c	CHIN	Yuba	Bullards Bar P O	93	553
Wong	25	m	c	CHIN	Del Norte	Happy Camp Twp	71	468
Wong	25	m	c	CHIN	Butte	Kimshew Tpw	70	84
Wong	24	m	c	CHIN	Butte	Hamilton Twp	70	74
Wong	24	m	c	CHIN	Klamath	Liberty Twp	73	376
Wong	22	m	c	CHIN	Klamath	Sawyers Bar	73	378
Wong	22	m	c	CHIN	Marin	Tomales Twp	74	84
Wong	22	m	c	CHIN	Yuba	W Bear Rvr Twp	93	682
Wong	21	m	c	CHIN	Yuba	Linda Twp	93	558
Wong	19	m	c	CHIN	Alameda	Brooklyn Twp	68	41
Wong	18	m	c	CHIN	Yuba	Marysville	93	594
Wong	14	m	c	CHIN	Klamath	Liberty Twp	73	374
Woo	40	m	c	CHIN	Alameda	Murray Twp	68	111
Woo	35	m	c	CHIN	Yuba	Marysville	93	621
Woo	32	m	c	CHIN	Alameda	Oakland	68	260
Woo	32	m	c	CHIN	Klamath	South Fork Twp	73	382
Woo	27	m	c	CHIN	Alameda	Brooklyn Twp	68	41
Woo	27	m	c	CHIN	Yuba	Bullards Bar P O	93	553
Woon	30	m	c	CHIN	Yuba	East Bear Rvr Twp	93	545
Wuhaw	20	m	c	CHIN	Sonoma	Salt Point	91	389
Wum	40	m	c	CHIN	Alameda	Brooklyn Twp	68	46
Wung	27	m	c	CHIN	Alameda	Brooklyn Twp	68	42
Wy	34	m	c	CHIN	Alameda	Brooklyn Twp	68	41
Wy	22	m	c	CHIN	Alameda	Brooklyn	68	21
Wy	19	m	c	CHIN	Alameda	Brooklyn	68	21
Y L	18	m	c	CHIN	Marin	San Antonio Twp	74	64
Yack	55	m	c	CHIN	Klamath	Salmon Twp	73	387
Yack	29	m	c	CHIN	Klamath	Dillon Twp	73	369
Yack	25	m	c	CHIN	Klamath	Salmon Twp	73	387
Yae	28	m	c	CHIN	Sacramento	Granite Twp	77	141
Yaht	25	m	c	CHIN	Marin	Tomales Twp	74	77
Yak	25	m	c	CHIN	Del Norte	Happy Camp Twp	71	469
Yake	49	m	c	CHIN	Klamath	South Fork Twp	73	383
Yake	44	m	c	CHIN	Klamath	Orleans Twp	73	380
Yake	24	m	c	CHIN	Klamath	Klamath Twp	73	370
Yake	24	m	c	CHIN	Klamath	Liberty Twp	73	375
Yam	30	m	c	CHIN	Napa	Napa Twp	75	32
Yan	48	m	c	CHIN	Del Norte	Happy Camp Twp	71	468
Yan	35	m	c	CHIN	Del Norte	Happy Camp Twp	71	469
Yan	30	m	c	CHIN	Klamath	Liberty Twp	73	375
Yan	29	m	c	CHIN	Sacramento	Granite Twp	77	141
Yang	30	m	c	CHIN	Klamath	Sawyers Bar	73	378
Yang	27	m	c	CHIN	Yuba	Marysville	93	592
Yang	25	m	c	CHIN	Klamath	Salmon Twp	73	387
Yank	21	m	c	CHIN	Placer	Bath P O	76	451
Yap	40	m	c	CHIN	Placer	Bath P O	76	453
Yap	38	m	c	CHIN	Klamath	South Fork Twp	73	384
Yat	34	m	c	CHIN	Alameda	Alvarado	68	305
Yauk	30	m	c	CHIN	Del Norte	Happy Camp Twp	71	469
Ye	19	m	c	CHIN	Alameda	Brooklyn	68	21
Yea	33	m	c	CHIN	Monterey	Castroville Twp	74	327
Yea	28	m	c	CHIN	Alameda	Brooklyn	68	21
Yea	26	m	c	CHIN	Alameda	Brooklyn Twp	68	41
Yea	25	m	c	CHIN	Alameda	Brooklyn Twp	68	41
Yea	24	m	c	CHIN	Alameda	Brooklyn	68	21
Yea	22	m	c	CHIN	Alameda	Brooklyn	68	21
Yeang	40	m	c	CHIN	Klamath	South Fork Twp	73	382
Yeck	45	m	c	CHIN	Yuba	Rose Bar Twp	93	666
Yee	52	m	c	CHIN	Klamath	South Fork Twp	73	382
Yee	40	m	c	CHIN	Klamath	Salmon Twp	73	388
Yee	34	m	c	CHIN	Yuba	Slate Range Bar Tw	93	674
Yee	32	m	c	CHIN	Klamath	South Fork Twp	73	384
Yeen	36	m	c	CHIN	Butte	Bidwell Twp	70	3
Yeen	28	m	c	CHIN	Klamath	South Fork Twp	73	383
Yeep	32	m	c	CHIN	Klamath	South Fork Twp	73	382
Yeet	40	m	c	CHIN	Klamath	South Fork Twp	73	382
Yek	14	m	c	CHIN	Yuba	Slate Range Bar Tw	93	670
Yelphk	43	m	c	CHIN	Klamath	South Fork Twp	73	382
Yem	14	m	c	CHIN	San Francisco	8-Wd San Francisco	82	459
Yen	60	m	c	CHIN	Klamath	South Fork Twp	73	384
Yen	50	m	c	CHIN	Klamath	Salmon Twp	73	387
Yen	48	m	c	CHIN	Klamath	Salmon Twp	73	388
Yen	46	m	c	CHIN	Klamath	Salmon Twp	73	387
Yen	35	m	c	CHIN	Yuba	Marysville	93	602
Yen	34	m	c	CHIN	Klamath	South Fork Twp	73	383
Yen	34	m	c	CHIN	Klamath	Liberty Twp	73	374
Yen	31	m	c	CHIN	Butte	Wyandotte Twp	70	144
Yen	30	m	c	CHIN	Klamath	Salmon Twp	73	388
Yen	30	m	c	CHIN	Alameda	Eden Twp	68	60
Yen	26	m	c	CHIN	Klamath	Salmon Twp	73	387
Yen	25	m	c	CHIN	Yuba	East Bear Rvr Twp	93	545
Yen	20	m	c	CHIN	Sacramento	4-Wd Sacramento	77	326
Yen	17	m	c	CHIN	Sacramento	4-Wd Sacramento	77	352
Yeng	27	m	c	CHIN	Yuba	Marysville	93	602
Yeng	27	m	c	CHIN	Yuba	Marysville	93	601
Yeng	25	m	c	CHIN	Yuba	Bullards Bar P O	93	549
Yeng	24	m	c	CHIN	Yuba	Slate Range Bar Tw	93	674
Yenge	37	m	c	CHIN	Yuba	North East Twp	93	646
Yenge	25	m	c	CHIN	Yuba	Slate Range Bar Tw	93	668
Yenge	25	m	c	CHIN	Yuba	North East Twp	93	646
Yenn	25	m	c	CHIN	Yuba	Slate Range Bar Tw	93	668
Yeon	40	m	c	CHIN	Yuba	North East Twp	93	645
Yeon	25	m	c	CHIN	Colusa	Monroe Twp	71	324
Yeonge	22	m	c	CHIN	Yuba	Slate Range Bar Tw	93	668
Yeow	27	m	c	CHIN	Del Norte	Happy Camp Twp	71	469
Yep	31	m	c	CHIN	Alameda	Brooklyn Twp	68	46
Yep	29	m	c	CHIN	Yuba	Bullards Bar P O	93	548
Yep	22	m	c	CHIN	Klamath	Salmon Twp	73	387
Yet	65	m	c	CHIN	Klamath	South Fork Twp	73	382
Yet	20	m	c	CHIN	Sacramento	Georgianna Twp	77	130
Yew	50	m	c	CHIN	Yuba	Slate Range Bar Tw	93	678
Yew	35	m	c	CHIN	Del Norte	Happy Camp Twp	71	469
Yew	31	m	c	CHIN	Yuba	Bullards Bar P O	93	548
Yew	24	m	c	CHIN	Yuba	Slate Range Bar Tw	93	672
Yew	23	m	c	CHIN	Del Norte	Happy Camp Twp	71	468
Yin	50	m	c	CHIN	Butte	Kimshew Tpw	70	84
Yin	4	m	c	CA	Alameda	Alvarado	68	304
Ying	43	m	c	CHIN	Yuba	North East Twp	93	647
Ying	40	m	c	CHIN	Yuba	Marysville	93	601
Ying	30	m	c	CHIN	Butte	Kimshew Tpw	70	84
Ying	21	m	c	CHIN	Placer	Bath P O	76	451
Yipchi	30	m	c	CHIN	Del Norte	Happy Camp Twp	71	469
Yo	26	m	c	CHIN	Alameda	Eden Twp	68	81
Yoach	56	m	c	CHIN	Klamath	Orleans Twp	73	380
Yock	50	m	c	CHIN	Klamath	Salmon Twp	73	388
Yoeng	55	m	c	CHIN	Yuba	North East Twp	93	646
Yoke	30	m	c	CHIN	Del Norte	Happy Camp Twp	71	469
Yoke	24	m	c	CHIN	Alameda	Brooklyn	68	21
Yoke	22	m	c	CHIN	Del Norte	Happy Camp Twp	71	469
Yoke	21	m	c	CHIN	Alameda	Brooklyn Twp	68	41
Yolk	50	m	c	CHIN	Yuba	North East Twp	93	647
Yolk	45	m	c	CHIN	Yuba	Slate Range Bar Tw	93	668
Yon	51	m	c	CHIN	Klamath	South Fork Twp	73	382
Yon	48	m	c	CHIN	Klamath	South Fork Twp	73	383
Yon	44	m	c	CHIN	Klamath	South Fork Twp	73	382
Yon	41	m	c	CHIN	Klamath	South Fork Twp	73	382
Yon	35	m	c	CHIN	Del Norte	Mountain Twp	71	475
Yon	34	m	c	CHIN	Alameda	Brooklyn Twp	68	46
Yon	34	m	c	CHIN	Yuba	W Bear Rvr Twp	93	684
Yon	33	m	c	CHIN	Alameda	Brooklyn Twp	68	41
Yon	33	m	c	CHIN	Alameda	Hayward	68	74
Yon	31	m	c	CHIN	Klamath	Klamath Twp	73	370
Yon	30	m	c	CHIN	Sacramento	Granite Twp	77	141
Yon	25	m	c	CHIN	Klamath	South Fork Twp	73	384
Yon	25	m	c	CHIN	Yuba	Marysville	93	601
Yon	19	m	c	CHIN	Alameda	Brooklyn Twp	68	43
Yon	18	m	c	CHIN	Placer	Bath P O	76	453
Yon	17	m	c	CHIN	Alameda	Brooklyn Twp	68	54
Yonbe	30	m	c	CHIN	Sutter	Sutter Twp	92	121
Yond	26	m	c	CHIN	Klamath	South Fork Twp	73	385
Yone	45	m	c	CHIN	Klamath	Salmon Twp	73	388
Yone	34	m	c	CHIN	Klamath	Salmon Twp	73	387
Yone	26	m	c	CHIN	Klamath	Salmon Twp	73	387
Yone	26	m	c	CHIN	Placer	Bath P O	76	442
Yong	47	f	c	CHIN	Calaveras	San Andreas P O	70	161
Yong	40	m	c	CHIN	Yuba	New York Twp	93	638
Yong	38	m	c	CHIN	Butte	Wyandotte Twp	70	144
Yong	34	m	c	CHIN	Klamath	Salmon Twp	73	387
Yong	30	m	c	CHIN	Yuba	Slate Range Bar Tw	93	669
Yong	28	m	c	CHIN	Klamath	Klamath Twp	73	370
Yong	26	m	c	CHIN	Placer	Bath P O	76	442
Yong	25	m	c	CHIN	Yuba	Slate Range Bar Tw	93	669
Yong	22	m	c	CHIN	Colusa	Colusa	71	300
Yong	20	m	c	CHIN	Placer	Bath P O	76	459
Yong	20	m	c	CHIN	Colusa	Grand Island Twp	71	303
Yong	18	m	c	CHIN	Klamath	Klamath Twp	73	370
Yong	15	m	c	CHIN	Klamath	Salmon Twp	73	387
Yong	15	m	c	CHIN	Colusa	Colusa	71	299
Yot	44	m	c	CHIN	Del Norte	Happy Camp Twp	71	469
Yot	21	m	c	CHIN	Colusa	Colusa	71	299
Yot	20	m	c	CHIN	Yuba	Bullards Bar P O	93	553
Yott	25	m	c	CHIN	Placer	Bath P O	76	444
You	45	m	c	CHIN	Yuba	Bullards Bar P O	93	548
You	41	m	c	CHIN	Yuba	Slate Range Bar Tw	93	668
You	40	m	c	CHIN	Del Norte	Happy Camp Twp	71	469
You	40	m	c	CHIN	Yuba	East Bear Rvr Twp	93	545
You	40	m	c	CHIN	Colusa	Monroe Twp	71	324
You	39	m	c	CHIN	Yuba	Marysville Twp	93	568
You	36	m	c	CHIN	Yuba	New York Twp	93	640
You	35	m	c	CHIN	Yuba	East Bear Rvr Twp	93	545
You	32	m	c	CHIN	Yuba	Marysville Twp	93	569
You	30	m	c	CHIN	Yuba	Slate Range Bar Tw	93	671
You	28	m	c	CHIN	Yuba	Slate Range Bar Tw	93	674
You	28	m	c	CHIN	Yuba	Slate Range Bar Tw	93	674

© 2001 by Heritage Quest. All rights reserved.

Name	Age	S	R	B-PL	County	Locale	Series M593 Roll	Pg
You	28	m	c	CHIN	Yuba	Marysville	93	600
You	23	m	c	CHIN	Yuba	Marysville	93	595
You	22	m	c	CHIN	Yuba	Linda Twp	93	558
Youan	23	m	c	CHIN	Placer	Bath P O	76	444
Yough	48	m	c	CHIN	Yuba	Bullards Bar P O	93	552
Yough	35	m	c	CHIN	Yuba	Slate Range Bar Tw	93	669
Youhan	17	m	c	CHIN	Yuba	Marysville	93	589
Youn	40	m	c	CHIN	Marin	Tomales Twp	74	80
Youne	46	m	c	CHIN	Yuba	Slate Range Bar Tw	93	675
Young	42	m	c	CHIN	Yuba	Slate Range Bar Tw	93	675
Young	32	m	c	CHIN	Alameda	Oakland	68	223
Young	31	m	c	CHIN	Del Norte	Happy Camp Twp	71	469
Young	30	m	c	CHIN	Alameda	Oakland	68	223
Young	30	m	c	CHIN	Yuba	Slate Range Bar Tw	93	668
Young	28	m	c	CHIN	Yuba	Slate Range Bar Tw	93	676
Young	28	m	c	CHIN	Yuba	East Bear Rvr Twp	93	545
Young	25	m	c	CHIN	Alameda	Oakland	68	223
Young	23	m	c	CHIN	Yuba	Bullards Bar P O	93	553
Young	21	m	c	CHIN	Marin	San Rafael	74	58
Young	20	m	c	CHIN	Santa Clara	San Jose Twp	88	198
Yow	27	m	c	CHIN	Yuba	Marysville	93	621
Yow	21	m	c	CHIN	Yuba	W Bear Rvr Twp	93	684
Yow	20	m	c	CHIN	Yuba	East Bear Rvr Twp	93	545
Yowe	30	m	c	CHIN	Klamath	South Fork Twp	73	383
Yoy	22	m	c	CHIN	Del Norte	Happy Camp Twp	71	468
Yu	38	m	c	CHIN	Yuba	Slate Range Bar Tw	93	674
Yu	21	m	c	CHIN	Yuba	North East Twp	93	646
Yuen	40	m	c	CHIN	Yuba	Marysville	93	601
Yuen	25	m	c	CHIN	Butte	Kimshew Tpw	70	84
Yuhn	23	m	c	CHIN	Marin	Tomales Twp	74	86
Yum	30	m	c	CHIN	Alameda	Hayward	68	78
Yumm	25	m	c	CHIN	Yuba	Slate Range Bar Tw	93	668
Yun	38	m	c	CHIN	Yuba	Slate Range Bar Tw	93	678
Yun	30	f	c	CHIN	Yuba	Slate Range Bar Tw	93	678
Yun	30	m	c	CHIN	Yuba	Slate Range Bar Tw	93	678
Yun	27	m	c	CHIN	Alameda	Brooklyn Twp	68	46
Yun	27	m	c	CHIN	Alameda	Brooklyn Twp	68	46
Yun	18	m	c	CHIN	Alameda	Brooklyn Twp	68	46
Yune	33	m	c	CHIN	Yuba	Slate Range Bar Tw	93	677
Yung	45	m	c	CHIN	Klamath	Klamath Twp	73	370
Yung	32	m	c	CHIN	Klamath	South Fork Twp	73	383
Yung	32	m	c	CHIN	Klamath	South Fork Twp	73	382
Yung	30	m	c	CHIN	Klamath	Salmon Twp	73	387
Yung	28	m	c	CHIN	Klamath	South Fork Twp	73	382
Yung	25	m	c	CHIN	Klamath	Orleans Twp	73	380
Yung	20	m	c	CHIN	Yuba	Marysville	93	593
Yung	19	m	c	CHIN	Klamath	Dillon Twp	73	369
Yung	19	m	c	CHIN	Yuba	Marysville	93	594
Yunger	26	m	c	CHIN	San Francisco	8-Wd San Francisco	82	459
Yut	28	m	c	CHIN	Yuba	East Bear Rvr Twp	93	545
Yut	22	m	c	CHIN	Yuba	W Bear Rvr Twp	93	684
Zam	33	m	c	CHIN	Yuba	North East Twp	93	647
Zen	42	m	c	CHIN	Klamath	South Fork Twp	73	382
Zenk	18	m	c	CHIN	Yuba	Bullards Bar P O	93	552
Zepp	30	m	c	CHIN	Yuba	North East Twp	93	647
Zick	28	m	c	CHIN	Colusa	Colusa	71	299
Zimm	50	m	c	CHIN	Yuba	North East Twp	93	646
Zoa	26	m	c	CHIN	Yuba	North East Twp	93	645
Zung	36	m	c	CHIN	Alameda	Oakland	68	223
???								
???	50	m	w	PA	San Francisco	2-Wd San Francisco	79	286
???	45	m	w	ENGL	San Francisco	2-Wd San Francisco	79	286
???	32	m	w	NY	San Francisco	San Francisco P O	85	875
George	29	m	w	IREL	San Francisco	San Francisco P O	83	2
Jackson	43	m	w	MA	San Francisco	San Francisco P O	85	877
Nellie	27	f	w	MA	San Francisco	San Francisco P O	85	829
W	3	m	w	CA	San Francisco	San Francisco P O	85	829
William H	54	m	w	VA	Monterey	San Benito Twp	74	382
???AM								
Charles	10	m	w	NY	San Francisco	San Francisco P O	85	828
???ANN								
F G	23	m	w	FRAN	San Francisco	San Francisco P O	85	829
???CH								
Alexder	12	m	w	CA	San Francisco	San Francisco P O	85	828
???D								
James	36	m	w	IREL	San Francisco	San Francisco P O	83	3
???LL								
Isaac [Dr]	51	m	w	NH	San Francisco	San Francisco P O	85	876
???NELL								
Sarah	28	f	w	IREL	San Francisco	San Francisco P O	83	3
??AHAN								
Bernard	35	m	w	IREL	San Francisco	San Francisco P O	83	3
??DDINGTON								
Joseph	37	m	w	IREL	San Francisco	San Francisco P O	83	5
??EEN								
Mary L	16	f	w	CA	San Francisco	San Francisco P O	85	875
??GHRAN								
James	37	m	w	IREL	San Francisco	San Francisco P O	83	3
??ILEY								
Henry	40	m	w	IREL	San Francisco	San Francisco P O	83	4
??LLINGER								
Patrick	51	m	w	IREL	San Francisco	San Francisco P O	83	3
??SON								
Robt F	35	m	w	MA	San Francisco	San Francisco P O	83	3
?AENA								
Peter	45	m	w	FRAN	Shasta	Shasta P O	89	457
?EL??								
Henry	40	m	w	PRUS	San Francisco	11-Wd San Francisc	84	685
?ELL								
Thomas	31	m	w	IREL	San Francisco	San Francisco P O	83	2
?TKEN								
Hugh	40	m	w	IREL	San Francisco	San Francisco P O	83	8
AAMER								
Trinidad	30	m	w	MEXI	San Diego	San Diego	78	484
AAMON								
Isidore	50	m	w	AUST	San Francisco	7-Wd San Francisco	81	243
AANES								
Simon	41	m	w	NORW	San Francisco	3-Wd San Francisco	79	310
AAROE								
Augustus	19	m	w	NORW	Siskiyou	Yreka	89	654
Christian	43	m	w	NORW	Siskiyou	Cottonwood Twp	89	593
AARON								
B	46	m	w	PRUS	San Joaquin	2-Wd Stockton	86	204
Chas H	37	m	w	ENGL	Mono	Bridgeport P O	74	284
David	42	m	w	PRUS	San Francisco	2-Wd San Francisco	79	144
Frank W H	32	m	w	ENGL	Yuba	Marysville	93	616
Hannah	47	f	w	POLA	San Francisco	San Francisco P O	83	52
Henry	40	m	w	PA	Calaveras	San Andreas P O	70	154
Jno	45	m	w	PRUS	San Joaquin	2-Wd Stockton	86	187
Joseph	32	m	w	FRAN	San Francisco	San Francisco P O	85	791
S	46	m	w	PRUS	San Joaquin	2-Wd Stockton	86	194
AARONS								
Herman	26	m	w	MECK	San Francisco	1-Wd San Francisco	79	131
Louis	42	m	w	AUST	San Francisco	1-Wd San Francisco	79	131
AARONSTEIN								
Adolph	37	m	w	BAVA	San Francisco	San Francisco P O	80	538
Clara	30	f	w	BAVA	San Francisco	San Francisco P O	80	405
AAZIE								
Antonio	35	m	w	ITAL	Calaveras	San Andreas P O	70	175
ABACUS								
Carlos	30	m	w	MEXI	Stanislaus	Empire Twp	92	65
ABADANA								
Antoine	14	m	w	CA	Santa Cruz	Pajaro Twp	89	340
ABADIE								
Mary	45	f	w	FRAN	San Francisco	San Francisco P O	80	354
Referzio	26	f	w	CA	Santa Barbara	Santa Barbara P O	87	456
ABADIT								
Fabier	38	m	w	FRAN	San Bernardino	San Bernardino Twp	78	447
ABAGAET								
John	23	m	w	NY	Monterey	Alisal Twp	74	291
ABALENA								
Maria	78	f	w	MEXI	Santa Clara	Milpitas Twp	88	110
ABALIA								
Estephen	25	m	w	MEXI	San Luis Obispo	San Luis Obispo Tw	87	299
ABALLARD								
Joseph	47	m	w	ENGL	San Bernardino	San Bernardino Twp	78	445
ABARAH								
Phelix	40	m	w	MEXI	Alameda	Alameda	68	5
ABARD								
Marcellous	30	m	b	CA	Mariposa	Mariposa P O	74	104
Sarah	36	f	i	CA	Mariposa	Mariposa P O	74	104
ABARDO								
Jose	24	m	w	MEXI	Los Angeles	Los Angeles	73	552
ABARR								
John B	49	m	w	IL	Placer	Bath P O	76	433
ABARTA								
Pedro	56	m	w	FRAN	Los Angeles	Los Angeles	73	504
ABATA								
Luis	55	m	w	CA	Los Angeles	Los Nietos Twp	73	589
Nicola	14	m	w	PA	Sacramento	2-Wd Sacramento	77	234
ABBE								
Andrew	40	m	w	NY	Monterey	San Juan Twp	74	413
Sanford K	40	m	w	CT	Colusa	Butte Twp	71	272
ABBEE								
Henry C W	60	m	w	BADE	Fresno	Millerton P O	72	145
Steven	35	m	w	ME	Amador	Volcano P O	69	379
Theordore	30	m	w	SWED	San Francisco	7-Wd San Francisco	81	220
ABBENS								
Auguste	30	m	w	HAMB	San Francisco	San Francisco P O	83	163
ABBEY								
A	48	m	w	NY	San Joaquin	3-Wd Stockton	86	240
Andrea	24	m	w	OH	Tulare	Tule Rvr Twp	92	261
Dane	56	m	w	CANA	Butte	Ophir Twp	70	112
J	28	f	w	NY	Lassen	Milford Twp	73	438
John J	45	m	w	KY	Yolo	Buckeye Twp	93	411
Richd	53	m	w	ENGL	Sonoma	Russian Rvr	91	375
William	44	m	w	SCOT	Alameda	Washington Twp	68	279
ABBISS								
Wilson J	30	m	w	ENGL	San Luis Obispo	Morro Twp	87	280
ABBITS								
William	49	m	w	BADE	Colusa	Colusa Twp	71	273
ABBOT								
Alexander	42	m	w	MI	Inyo	Lone Pine Twp	73	332
Austin	29	m	w	OH	Inyo	Bishop Crk Twp	73	315
C M	14	m	w	CA	Solano	Benicia	90	21
Charles	30	m	w	ME	Calaveras	Copperopolis P O	70	224
Daniel F	34	m	w	ME	Calaveras	Copperopolis P O	70	227
Elizabeth	70	f	w	TN	Stanislaus	North Twp	92	68
Elizabeth	29	f	w	IN	Sonoma	Sonoma Twp	91	444
Frank	34	m	w	IREL	San Francisco	San Francisco P O	83	44
George	52	m	w	CANA	San Mateo	Pescadero P O	87	415
Henry Burch	48	m	w	PA	Santa Clara	Fremont Twp	88	57
Jane	46	f	w	IREL	Alameda	Oakland	68	179

© 2001 by Heritage Quest. All rights reserved.

Name	Age	S	R	B-PL	County	Locale	Roll	Pg
John	60	m	w	ME	Monterey	San Juan Twp	74	394
John	50	m	w	ME	Sonoma	Sonoma Twp	91	444
John	45	m	w	ENGL	Solano	Benicia	90	18
John M	43	m	w	ME	Santa Clara	San Jose Twp	88	180
Joshua	69	m	w	OH	Stanislaus	North Twp	92	68
L G	30	m	w	NY	Calaveras	Copperopolis P O	70	237
N B	35	m	w	KY	Sierra	Sears Twp	89	558
N B	34	m	w	KY	Sierra	Sears Twp	89	558
R F	34	m	w	NC	Trinity	Indian Crk	92	200
Richardson	37	m	w	AR	Stanislaus	North Twp	92	67
Thomas G	41	m	w	ME	San Francisco	San Francisco P O	85	749
W K	25	f	w	ME	Alameda	Oakland	68	182
ABBOTT								
A J	38	m	w	NH	San Francisco	San Francisco P O	85	791
A R	44	m	w	NY	Sacramento	3-Wd Sacramento	77	316
Alfonzo	21	m	w	WI	Sonoma	Bodega Twp	91	256
Alvin B	43	m	w	CANA	Monterey	Alisal Twp	74	304
Andrew J	43	m	w	ME	Placer	Auburn P O	76	363
Annie	31	f	w	IREL	San Francisco	San Francisco P O	85	818
Arthur	25	m	w	CANA	Monterey	Alisal Twp	74	304
Arthur	25	m	w	CANA	Monterey	Alisal Twp	74	304
Augustus	55	m	w	ME	Butte	Oroville Twp	70	138
Augustus M	32	m	w	ME	Plumas	Goodwin Twp	77	2
Austin	47	m	w	NY	Tuolumne	Sonora P O	93	319
Austin	36	m	w	MI	Mendocino	Ukiah Twp	74	243
Charles	41	m	w	VT	Siskiyou	Yreka Twp	89	670
Charles	34	m	w	MA	Alameda	Brooklyn Twp	68	52
Charles	28	m	w	MA	Colusa	Colusa	71	294
Clara	12	f	w	VA	San Francisco	11-Wd San Francisc	84	496
Corr	44	m	w	CANA	Monterey	Alisal Twp	74	303
D M	15	f	w	CA	Alameda	Oakland	68	236
Daniel C	34	m	w	NJ	Santa Clara	Santa Clara Twp	88	146
Elisha	38	m	w	SC	Colusa	Spring Valley Twp	71	338
Elizabeth	76	f	w	ME	San Francisco	San Francisco P O	83	356
Elizabeth	26	f	w	ME	San Francisco	San Francisco P O	83	169
Eunis	70	f	w	NY	Mendocino	Ukiah Twp	74	243
Francis	33	m	w	IREL	San Francisco	San Francisco P O	83	231
Francis M	7	m	i	CA	Butte	Wyandotte Twp	70	150
Frank	40	m	w	NY	Sutter	Sutter Twp	92	121
Franklin	32	m	w	ENGL	Los Angeles	El Monte Twp	73	457
G F	44	m	w	NY	Napa	Napa	75	17
George	41	m	w	ENGL	Amador	Ione City P O	69	370
Henry	36	m	w	RI	Sutter	Vernon Twp	92	131
Hiram B	45	m	w	OH	Plumas	Seneca Twp	77	49
J C	49	m	w	VT	Nevada	Nevada Twp	75	281
J E	35	m	w	NH	Solano	Vallejo	90	141
James	61	m	w	VA	Placer	Colfax P O	76	389
James	42	m	w	LA	Marin	San Rafael Twp	74	37
James	40	m	w	VA	Placer	Bath P O	76	428
John	57	m	w	CANA	Monterey	Alisal Twp	74	301
John	30	m	w	ME	Contra Costa	Martinez P O	71	424
John N	58	m	w	OH	Yuba	Parks Bar Twp	93	649
Joseph	50	m	w	FRAN	Monterey	Salinas Twp	74	308
Joseph	33	m	w	NH	San Francisco	San Francisco P O	83	258
Joseph P	28	m	w	NH	San Diego	San Diego	78	496
Joshua T	67	m	w	MA	Plumas	Seneca Twp	77	50
Lillie	9	f	w	MA	San Francisco	8-Wd San Francisco	82	386
Louis	43	m	w	MA	San Francisco	San Francisco P O	83	230
M	35	m	w	IREL	Sacramento	3-Wd Sacramento	77	296
M R	26	m	w	CANA	Monterey	San Antonio Twp	74	323
Mary	19	f	w	ME	Napa	Napa Twp	75	34
Mary M	68	f	w	NH	Alameda	Oakland	68	207
Michael	51	m	w	PA	Placer	Colfax P O	76	390
Orrin L	36	m	w	IN	Santa Barbara	Santa Barbara P O	87	472
Orson	52	m	w	NH	Merced	Snelling P O	74	256
Osborne	54	m	w	WIND	San Francisco	11-Wd San Francisc	84	550
Ruth	55	f	w	MA	San Francisco	San Francisco P O	83	178
S J	35	m	w	CANA	Sutter	Vernon Twp	92	133
S Z	26	m	w	MO	Humboldt	Eel Rvr Twp	72	252
Saml	25	m	w	TX	Humboldt	Eel Rvr Twp	72	251
Samuel	47	m	w	NY	San Francisco	11-Wd San Francisc	84	542
Sarah	38	f	w	VA	San Francisco	San Francisco P O	83	172
Stephen	65	m	w	NH	Contra Costa	Martinez P O	71	371
Sterling	5	m	w	CA	Stanislaus	North Twp	92	67
Thomas J	61	m	w	OH	Colusa	Stony Crk Twp	71	332
W S	23	m	w	MO	Humboldt	Eel Rvr Twp	72	252
Warren	32	m	w	NH	Napa	Napa	75	3
Washington	28	m	w	IA	Humboldt	South Fork Twp	72	301
Will	30	m	w	NH	Merced	Snelling P O	74	256
William	40	m	w	NY	Los Angeles	Los Angeles	73	566
William	36	m	w	PA	Sutter	Sutter Twp	92	121
William	28	m	w	CANA	San Francisco	San Francisco P O	83	319
William	21	m	w	OH	Placer	Auburn P O	76	373
William	2	m	w	CA	Nevada	Bloomfield Twp	75	95
Willis	19	m	w	ME	San Joaquin	Oneal Twp	86	99
Wm A	53	m	w	ME	San Diego	San Diego	78	489
ABBS								
G N	40	m	w	MA	Sierra	Butte Twp	89	512
ABBY								
Albert	47	m	w	NY	El Dorado	Georgetown Twp	72	39
F J	42	f	w	ENGL	Alameda	Oakland	68	141
H	9	f	w	CA	Sierra	Downieville Twp	89	517
Hiram	31	m	w	NY	Solano	Silveyville Twp	90	80
Isadora	30	f	w	MO	San Francisco	2-Wd San Francisco	79	147
J W	39	m	w	IN	San Joaquin	3-Wd Stockton	86	246
Matilda	31	f	w	ENGL	Trinity	Weaverville Pct	92	226
Richard	50	m	w	GA	San Francisco	5-Wd San Francisco	81	18

Name	Age	S	R	B-PL	County	Locale	Roll	Pg
Sharlott	9	f	w	CA	Sonoma	Petaluma Twp	91	348
ABECCO								
Antonio	13	m	w	NY	San Francisco	11-Wd San Francisc	84	586
ABEEL								
John H	43	m	w	NY	Placer	Dutch Flat P O	76	405
ABEGGLEN								
Louis	31	m	w	SWIT	Plumas	Indian Twp	77	17
ABEL								
Alexander G	52	m	w	NY	San Francisco	6-Wd San Francisco	81	123
Charles	45	m	w	PRUS	San Francisco	7-Wd San Francisco	81	215
Charles	20	m	w	NY	Santa Clara	2-Wd San Jose	88	312
Christian	53	m	w	NORW	San Francisco	San Francisco P O	83	114
Ezra B	66	m	w	MA	El Dorado	Mud Springs Twp	72	73
George	50	m	w	ENGL	San Joaquin	1-Wd Stockton	86	125
George	27	m	w	GERM	Yolo	Putah Twp	93	513
George A	27	m	w	NORW	San Francisco	San Francisco P O	83	30
Kate	21	f	w	PRUS	San Francisco	San Francisco P O	80	473
Katie	19	f	w	ENGL	San Francisco	San Francisco P O	80	532
Louis	13	m	w	CA	San Francisco	8-Wd San Francisco	82	490
Louis J	25	m	w	NY	Santa Clara	2-Wd San Jose	88	329
Maria	28	f	w	CA	San Diego	San Pasqual	78	519
Martin	42	m	w	NORW	Contra Costa	Martinez P O	71	415
Mary	26	f	w	PRUS	San Francisco	6-Wd San Francisco	81	152
Mary	21	f	w	ENGL	San Francisco	San Francisco P O	80	532
Peter	45	m	w	OH	San Diego	San Pasqual	78	519
Peter	44	m	w	OH	San Diego	San Pasqual Valley	78	524
William	45	m	w	KY	Santa Clara	2-Wd San Jose	88	303
William	26	m	w	VA	Kern	Havilah P O	73	341
ABELA								
A	16	f	w	CA	Los Angeles	Los Angeles	73	570
Antonio	24	m	w	CA	Los Angeles	Santa Ana Twp	73	612
Ignacia	36	f	w	MEXI	Los Angeles	Los Angeles	73	555
Jose	51	m	w	CHIL	Santa Clara	Alviso Twp	88	27
ABELAR								
Marie	11	f	w	CA	Santa Clara	Fremont Twp	88	62
Peter	17	m	w	CA	Santa Clara	Fremont Twp	88	65
ABELARDES								
Jose	42	m	w	MEXI	Monterey	San Juan Twp	74	404
ABELBECK								
F D	43	m	w	HAMB	Sonoma	Santa Rosa	91	400
ABELING								
George G	34	m	w	NY	Los Angeles	Los Nietos Twp	73	591
ABELL								
A E	17	m	w	CA	Alameda	Oakland	68	159
Frank	25	m	w	IL	San Francisco	San Francisco P O	83	74
John M	45	m	w	NC	Tehama	Antelope Twp	92	154
Lewis	12	m	w	CANA	Yolo	Cottonwood Twp	93	464
Nattie	17	f	w	WI	San Joaquin	1-Wd Stockton	86	141
Stockman	25	m	w	CT	San Diego	San Diego	78	501
ABELLA								
Abram	40	m	w	OH	Klamath	Klamath Twp	73	370
ABELLO								
Dolores	40	f	w	MEXI	San Francisco	San Francisco P O	80	465
ABELS								
James	25	m	w	IL	Siskiyou	Callahan P O	89	631
ABENG								
John	34	m	w	SWED	San Francisco	1-Wd San Francisco	79	127
ABENIAS								
John	19	m	w	NORW	San Francisco	11-Wd San Francisc	84	694
ABENSIO								
Pedro	45	m	i	CA	San Mateo	San Mateo P O	87	348
ABER								
Thomas T	37	m	w	NY	Klamath	Orleans Twp	73	379
ABERLY								
Lewis	40	m	w	GERM	Yolo	Cache Crk Twp	93	451
ABERNATA								
George	31	m	w	IL	Colusa	Colusa Twp	71	280
ABERNATHA								
William	35	m	w	MO	Colusa	Colusa	71	298
ABERNATHEY								
J	30	m	w	MO	Humboldt	Eureka Twp	72	269
ABERNATHIE								
Bolin	40	m	w	IL	Solano	Suisun Twp	90	103
ABERNATHY								
A	29	m	w	VT	Sacramento	1-Wd Sacramento	77	190
Archd	47	m	w	NC	Butte	Wyandotte Twp	70	141
Edward	21	m	w	IREL	Monterey	Salinas Twp	74	310
J B	41	m	w	MO	Tuolumne	Sonora P O	93	310
Paschald	34	m	w	MO	Yolo	Cache Crk Twp	93	434
ABERNETHY								
J E	18	f	w	ME	Sacramento	3-Wd Sacramento	77	291
Robert	22	m	w	PRUS	Santa Clara	2-Wd San Jose	88	328
Walter	48	m	w	ENGL	San Francisco	5-Wd San Francisco	81	12
ABERRIGGI								
Demetin	33	m	w	ITAL	Sonoma	Analy Twp	91	236
ABERS								
Gielke	48	m	w	HANO	Calaveras	San Andreas P O	70	206
Peter	45	m	w	HANO	Calaveras	San Andreas P O	70	206
ABERT								
Vincent	30	m	w	FRAN	Los Angeles	Los Angeles Twp	73	497
ABERTO								
Jerel	18	m	w	ITAL	San Mateo	Schoolhouse Statio	87	334
ABERTON								
Wm	32	m	w	IREL	San Francisco	11-Wd San Francisc	84	435
ABES								
Joseph	22	m	w	AZOR	Monterey	Monterey	74	364

© 2001 by Heritage Quest. All rights reserved.

California 1870 Census

Series M593

Name	Age	S	R	B-PL	County	Locale	Roll	Pg
ABESS								
Eliza	57	f	w	FRAN	San Francisco	8-Wd San Francisco	82	361
ABGILE								
Jenlem	26	m	w	ITAL	San Mateo	Schoolhouse Statio	87	346
ABGILO								
Jerelin	19	m	w	ITAL	San Mateo	Schoolhouse Statio	87	334
ABICO								
George M	27	m	w	NY	Monterey	Castroville Twp	74	339
ABIGO								
J	29	f	w	MEXI	Sacramento	4-Wd Sacramento	77	356
ABILA								
Adriena	15	f	w	CA	Los Angeles	Wilmington Twp	73	639
Danvario	47	m	w	CA	Los Angeles	Los Angeles	73	520
F	15	f	w	CA	Los Angeles	Los Angeles	73	570
Felipo	38	m	w	CA	Los Angeles	Wilmington Twp	73	634
Francisca	13	f	w	CA	Los Angeles	Los Angeles	73	519
Henrique	58	m	w	CA	Los Angeles	Wilmington Twp	73	643
Henriquez	14	m	w	CA	Los Angeles	Los Angeles Twp	73	490
Jose C	36	m	w	CA	Los Angeles	San Juan Twp	73	626
Jose Ma	45	m	w	CA	Los Angeles	Wilmington Twp	73	644
Juan	57	m	w	CA	Los Angeles	San Juan Twp	73	624
Juan	34	m	w	CA	Los Angeles	Los Angeles Twp	73	470
Manuel L	32	m	w	CA	Los Angeles	San Juan Twp	73	627
Melvena	59	m	w	CA	Los Angeles	Los Angeles	73	506
Merced	18	f	w	CA	Los Angeles	San Jose Twp	73	623
Milton	40	m	w	MEXI	Santa Barbara	Arroyo Burro P O	87	509
Pedro A	42	m	w	CA	Los Angeles	Los Angeles Twp	73	492
R Quinto	46	m	w	SAME	Los Angeles	Los Angeles	73	551
Ramon	40	m	w	MEXI	Los Angeles	Los Angeles Twp	73	468
Santos	25	m	w	CA	Los Angeles	Soledad Twp	73	632
Tadeo A	17	m	w	CA	Los Angeles	Los Angeles	73	563
Trinidad	40	f	w	CA	Los Angeles	San Jose Twp	73	622
ABILES								
Victorio	38	f	w	MEXI	Mariposa	Mariposa P O	74	120
ABINDER								
Adolphe	33	m	w	HANO	San Francisco	11-Wd San Francisc	84	491
ABIT								
Mary	24	f	w	IREL	Santa Clara	Gilroy Twp	88	73
ABLANG								
Jerry	22	m	w	CANA	Sacramento	4-Wd Sacramento	77	370
ABLAR								
Thomas	27	m	w	CA	Santa Clara	1-Wd San Jose	88	276
ABLE								
Frederick	55	m	w	LUEB	Plumas	Washington Twp	77	53
H S	40	m	w	MA	Amador	Ione City P O	69	351
Henry	20	m	w	ENGL	Alameda	Washington Twp	68	287
James	42	m	w	IL	Stanislaus	San Joaquin Twp	92	82
John F	42	m	w	WURT	Colusa	Colusa Twp	71	276
Joseph	38	m	w	KY	Placer	Auburn P O	76	361
Solomon	29	m	w	BOHE	San Diego	San Diego	78	483
ABLES								
Benjamin	39	m	w	OH	Sonoma	Petaluma Twp	91	351
James B	29	m	w	OH	Marin	Tomales Twp	74	80
Thomas B	36	m	w	OH	Marin	Tomales Twp	74	83
Thomas J	35	m	w	OH	Marin	Tomales Twp	74	80
William C	53	m	w	OH	Santa Clara	San Jose Twp	88	201
ABLESON								
Charles	25	m	w	ENGL	San Francisco	7-Wd San Francisco	81	218
ABLET								
Chas E	27	m	w	ENGL	Santa Barbara	Santa Barbara P O	87	472
ABLEY								
Frederick	42	m	w	CHIL	Kern	Bakersfield P O	73	363
ABLIS								
Louis	13	m	w	CA	San Francisco	7-Wd San Francisco	81	184
ABNER								
Peter	28	m	w	MS	Solano	Vacaville Twp	90	123
ABNEY								
Sarah E	15	f	w	CA	Yuba	New York Twp	93	642
ABODIE								
William	48	m	w	FRAN	Santa Clara	2-Wd San Jose	88	303
ABODOE								
Idina	55	m	w	MEXI	Plumas	Mineral Twp	77	22
ABOIM								
Ah	28	m	c	CHIN	Klamath	Orleans Twp	73	380
ABOLOS								
Remonde	33	m	w	CHIL	Calaveras	San Andreas P O	70	182
ABON								
Elias S	31	m	w	PA	San Francisco	5-Wd San Francisco	81	2
ABONELL								
Vincent	44	m	w	FRAN	Butte	Bidwell Twp	70	3
ABOR								
Charles	22	m	w	MEXI	Solano	Silveyville Twp	90	78
ABORN								
Clement	42	m	w	OH	Sonoma	Russian Rvr	91	378
John	41	m	w	MD	Santa Clara	San Jose Twp	88	213
Samuel	40	m	w	VA	San Francisco	6-Wd San Francisco	81	70
ABOTH								
J R	34	m	w	ME	Klamath	Salmon Twp	73	388
ABOTT								
Henry	50	m	w	NY	San Francisco	5-Wd San Francisco	81	19
Henry	32	m	w	CANA	Mendocino	Point Arena Twp	74	208
ABOUT								
Adolph	18	m	w	KY	Amador	Ione City P O	69	351
Jack C	60	m	w	FRAN	Amador	Volcano P O	69	377
ABRAHAM								
Casper	44	m	w	POLA	Sonoma	Cloverdale Twp	91	268
David	41	m	w	IA	San Francisco	5-Wd San Francisco	81	23
George	40	m	w	ENGL	Nevada	Grass Valley Twp	75	169
Jacob	50	m	w	PRUS	Calaveras	Copperopolis P O	70	255
Jas	40	m	w	POLA	San Francisco	8-Wd San Francisco	82	362
Kate	24	f	w	IREL	San Francisco	5-Wd San Francisco	81	29
L	21	m	w	POLA	Sacramento	3-Wd Sacramento	77	288
Lipman	19	m	w	POSE	Santa Cruz	Watsonville	89	365
Louis	50	m	w	POLA	San Francisco	7-Wd San Francisco	81	204
Louis	40	m	w	PRUS	San Francisco	San Francisco P O	83	49
Louis	37	m	w	WALE	Contra Costa	Martinez P O	71	425
M	45	m	w	PRUS	San Francisco	San Francisco P O	83	294
M	25	f	w	PRUS	San Francisco	San Francisco P O	83	283
Maggy	20	f	w	IREL	San Mateo	Belmont P O	87	372
Marcus	42	m	w	PRUS	San Francisco	7-Wd San Francisco	81	192
Michael	27	m	w	PRUS	Santa Cruz	Watsonville	89	369
Nettie	17	f	w	MA	San Francisco	8-Wd San Francisco	82	364
Peter	41	m	w	PRUS	San Francisco	8-Wd San Francisco	82	359
Peter	28	m	w	SHOL	Sonoma	Petaluma Twp	91	316
Phillip	44	m	w	PRUS	San Francisco	San Francisco P O	83	337
Robt	29	m	w	NY	Solano	Vallejo	90	168
S	24	m	w	POLA	San Francisco	7-Wd San Francisco	81	162
Stephen	32	m	w	MEXI	Nevada	Grass Valley Twp	75	203
ABRAHAMS								
David	49	m	w	PRUS	San Francisco	San Francisco P O	85	802
Gabriel	30	m	w	PRUS	San Francisco	San Francisco P O	83	359
Gustav	19	m	w	PRUS	San Francisco	8-Wd San Francisco	82	413
Henry	48	m	w	PRUS	San Francisco	11-Wd San Francisc	84	586
J	45	m	w	POLA	San Francisco	San Francisco P O	85	790
John	30	m	w	WURT	Solano	Suisun Twp	90	98
Louis	45	m	w	PRUS	San Francisco	2-Wd San Francisco	79	238
Mary	30	f	w	POLA	San Francisco	6-Wd San Francisco	81	78
Moses	30	m	w	PRUS	Solano	Suisun Twp	90	104
ABRAHAMSON								
Annetta	20	f	w	POLA	San Francisco	1-Wd San Francisco	79	135
C	60	m	w	DENM	Siskiyou	Callahan P O	89	631
Edward	25	m	w	PRUS	San Francisco	6-Wd San Francisco	81	41
John	36	m	w	DENM	Inyo	Independence Twp	73	326
Julius	28	m	w	PRUS	San Francisco	3-Wd San Francisco	79	317
S K	11	m	w	CA	Alameda	Oakland	68	159
Susan	32	f	w	NORW	San Francisco	2-Wd San Francisco	79	253
ABRAHMSON								
Peter	41	m	w	PRUS	San Francisco	6-Wd San Francisco	81	152
ABRAIMSON								
Susan	32	f	w	NORW	San Francisco	11-Wd San Francisc	84	685
ABRAM								
Adolph	18	m	w	PA	San Francisco	San Francisco P O	80	472
Joseph	45	m	w	POLA	San Francisco	1-Wd San Francisco	79	56
Joseph	38	m	w	NY	San Francisco	1-Wd San Francisco	79	57
Simon	19	m	w	POLA	San Francisco	1-Wd San Francisco	79	93
Wm	18	m	w	WI	Sacramento	Cosumnes Twp	77	93
ABRAMS								
Anna	55	f	w	POLA	San Francisco	8-Wd San Francisco	82	305
Annie	25	f	w	PRUS	San Francisco	11-Wd San Francisc	84	493
Edward	36	m	w	WIND	San Francisco	San Francisco P O	83	403
Francis J	34	m	w	NY	Klamath	South Fork Twp	73	383
G	39	m	w	SWED	Sacramento	1-Wd Sacramento	77	185
Henny	40	m	w	PRUS	San Francisco	San Francisco P O	80	475
Henry	28	m	w	ENGL	Solano	Vacaville Twp	90	126
Henry	25	m	w	POLA	San Francisco	1-Wd San Francisco	79	104
Isaac	33	m	w	RUSS	San Francisco	1-Wd San Francisco	79	58
Isaac	32	m	w	PRUS	Trinity	Weaverville Pct	92	226
James	39	m	w	PRUS	San Francisco	7-Wd San Francisco	81	284
James	39	m	w	WALE	Placer	Bath P O	76	438
James	37	m	w	ENGL	Klamath	South Fork Twp	73	383
John	30	m	w	NY	Nevada	Nevada Twp	75	274
Marks	16	m	w	POLA	San Francisco	1-Wd San Francisco	79	93
Phil	48	m	w	MA	Sacramento	4-Wd Sacramento	77	325
Samuel	45	m	w	PRUS	San Francisco	San Francisco P O	83	373
Sarah	52	f	m	MS	Sacramento	1-Wd Sacramento	77	187
Thos J	43	m	w	ENGL	Shasta	American Ranch P O	89	500
William	39	m	w	NY	Calaveras	San Andreas P O	70	211
ABRAMSON								
Nelson	27	m	w	NORW	San Francisco	7-Wd San Francisco	81	269
ABRAVES								
Domingoes	70	f	w	MEXI	Amador	Jackson P O	69	326
ABREDE								
Gudson	48	m	w	FRAN	Monterey	San Antonio Twp	74	321
ABRENISK								
M L	40	m	w	POLA	San Joaquin	2-Wd Stockton	86	210
ABRIGO								
Juan	30	m	w	CA	Monterey	Castroville Twp	74	331
Martin	28	m	w	CA	San Francisco	5-Wd San Francisco	81	14
R	28	m	w	CA	Santa Clara	Gilroy Twp	88	78
ABRIL								
Manuel	50	m	w	MEXI	Los Angeles	Los Angeles Twp	73	467
Manuel	50	m	w	MEXI	Los Angeles	Los Angeles	73	508
ABROGO								
Abedel	23	m	w	CA	San Francisco	2-Wd San Francisco	79	190
ABROSO								
M	30	m	w	CA	Alameda	Murray Twp	68	127
ABROTT								
Carsten	35	m	w	SHOL	Contra Costa	Martinez P O	71	393
ABSHAW								
Elza	30	m	w	VA	Yolo	Cache Crk Twp	93	438
ABSHIER								
James	31	m	w	VA	Sonoma	Santa Rosa	91	404
John	41	m	w	VA	Sonoma	Analy Twp	91	238

© 2001 by Heritage Quest. All rights reserved.

Name	Age	S	R	B-PL	County	Locale	Roll	Pg
						Series M593		
ABSHIRE								
Andrew	22	m	w	VA	Yolo	Grafton Twp	93	478
Uriah T	21	m	w	IL	Colusa	Grand Island Twp	71	308
ABSTEVE								
Phillip	21	m	w	PRUS	Sacramento	4-Wd Sacramento	77	340
ABWAY								
Jas	18	m	w	IL	Sierra	Gibson Twp	89	541
ABY								
Mang	21	m	c	CHIN	Plumas	Quartz Twp	77	39
AC								
Ah	45	m	c	CHIN	Sacramento	Georgianna Twp	77	127
Que	21	m	c	CHIN	San Francisco	8-Wd San Francisco	82	421
ACANDA								
Catherine	30	f	w	PORT	Alameda	Washington Twp	68	274
ACANSIO								
Jose	23	m	w	CA	Marin	San Rafael Twp	74	39
ACAPITA								
C	11	f	w	CA	Santa Clara	Gilroy Twp	88	74
ACCOSTA								
John	1	m	i	CA	Del Norte	Crescent	71	467
O	40	m	w	MEXI	Del Norte	Mountain Twp	71	474
ACCUNEO								
Jesus	30	m	w	MEXI	Calaveras	San Andreas P O	70	170
ACCUNIO								
Manuel	25	m	w	MEXI	Los Angeles	Los Angeles	73	554
ACEBEDO								
Claudio	40	m	w	MEXI	Los Angeles	Santa Ana Twp	73	607
Miguel	60	m	w	MEXI	Los Angeles	Santa Ana Twp	73	607
ACEBES								
Antone	40	m	w	MEXI	San Luis Obispo	Santa Rosa Twp	87	327
ACELUS								
Hosea	44	f	w	MEXI	Tehama	Red Bluff	92	181
ACEOM								
Lan	33	m	c	CHIN	Tulare	White Rvr Twp	92	301
Lee	30	m	c	CHIN	Tulare	White Rvr Twp	92	301
ACEPTIN								
Hugh	30	m	w	ENGL	Los Angeles	Los Angeles	73	551
ACEVEDO								
Jacoba D	47	f	w	CA	Monterey	Monterey	74	359
ACH								
Chang	23	m	c	CHIN	Placer	Bath P O	76	451
ACHA								
Joseph	23	m	w	CANA	Alpine	Markleeville P O	69	316
ACHARD								
Charles	48	m	w	CANA	Inyo	Lone Pine Twp	73	330
ACHE								
See	24	m	c	CHIN	San Francisco	3-Wd San Francisco	79	304
ACHEELINE								
Nathan	43	m	w	BAVA	San Francisco	2-Wd San Francisco	79	242
ACHENG								
Meng	34	m	c	CHIN	Tulare	White Rvr Twp	92	301
ACHER								
A M	30	m	w	NY	Monterey	Alisal Twp	74	291
ACHERS								
Jessee	36	m	w	AR	Placer	Roseville P O	76	354
ACHERSON								
Robert	54	m	w	IREL	San Mateo	Redwood Twp	87	367
ACHET								
Frederick	16	m	w	LA	Placer	Bath P O	76	452
ACHIN								
Lema	48	m	w	FRAN	Calaveras	San Andreas P O	70	190
ACHK								
Ah	25	m	c	CHIN	Sonoma	Salt Point	91	386
ACHOA								
Abrem	35	m	w	MEXI	Los Angeles	Los Angeles Twp	73	479
ACHORN								
Hector	42	m	w	ME	Yuba	North East Twp	93	643
John A	31	m	w	ME	Santa Cruz	Santa Cruz Twp	89	394
ACHRON								
Enos C	17	m	w	OH	Yuba	Slate Range Bar Tw	93	672
ACHURE								
Vicente	36	m	w	CHIL	Santa Clara	Fremont Twp	88	50
ACK								
Ah	51	m	c	CHIN	Mariposa	Maxwell Crk P O	74	142
Ah	45	m	c	CHIN	Placer	Dutch Flat P O	76	414
Ah	43	m	c	CHIN	Placer	Dutch Flat P O	76	409
Ah	40	m	c	CHIN	Butte	Kimshew Tpw	70	85
Ah	36	m	c	CHIN	Trinity	Douglas	92	235
Ah	35	m	c	CHIN	El Dorado	Placerville Twp	72	98
Ah	31	m	c	CHIN	Placer	Lincoln P O	76	483
Ah	27	m	c	CHIN	Shasta	French Gulch P O	89	469
Ah	27	m	c	CHIN	Placer	Bath P O	76	445
Ah	22	m	c	CHIN	Sierra	Lincoln Twp	89	552
Ah	19	m	c	CHIN	Trinity	Douglas	92	234
Ah	18	m	c	CHIN	Shasta	French Gulch P O	89	467
Ah	17	m	c	CHIN	Shasta	French Gulch P O	89	469
Chon	24	m	c	CHIN	Marin	Tomales Twp	74	83
Gee	18	m	c	CHIN	Shasta	French Gulch P O	89	464
Hung	40	m	c	CHIN	Marin	San Rafael	74	58
Lah	29	m	c	CHIN	Marin	San Rafael	74	58
Lung	34	m	c	CHIN	Klamath	Liberty Twp	73	374
Sim	40	m	c	CHIN	Siskiyou	Yreka	89	650
Sooey	20	m	c	CHIN	Shasta	French Gulch P O	89	464
Tom	25	m	c	CHIN	Placer	Auburn P O	76	377
Tye	29	m	c	CHIN	Marin	San Rafael Twp	74	59
Woa	45	m	c	CHIN	Marin	San Rafael Twp	74	59
Woa	29	m	c	CHIN	Marin	San Rafael	74	54
ACKELS								
Henry	37	m	w	TN	Yolo	Putah Twp	93	521
ACKER								
George	17	m	w	IN	San Francisco	7-Wd San Francisco	81	227
John	36	m	w	NY	Marin	San Rafael Twp	74	42
R W	48	m	w	NY	Sonoma	Bodega Twp	91	254
S S	25	m	w	MI	Alameda	Murray Twp	68	118
Valentine	37	m	w	HDAR	San Francisco	8-Wd San Francisco	82	309
ACKERLY								
B	56	m	w	NY	Alameda	Oakland	68	210
Charles	38	m	w	IL	Alameda	Murray Twp	68	119
Fredrick	19	m	w	BADE	San Francisco	San Francisco P O	80	478
ACKERMAN								
A	39	m	w	PRUS	Napa	Napa	75	3
A	24	m	w	VT	Sacramento	3-Wd Sacramento	77	309
Abner	32	m	w	MA	Napa	Napa Twp	75	32
C	58	m	w	NY	Yuba	East Bear Rvr Twp	93	544
C	44	m	w	BADE	Sierra	Butte Twp	89	508
C	34	m	w	NY	Sierra	Butte Twp	89	509
Caroline	47	f	w	BAVA	San Francisco	8-Wd San Francisco	82	468
Chas	39	m	w	MA	Mendocino	Ukiah Twp	74	235
Cyrus	39	m	w	NY	Sacramento	3-Wd Sacramento	77	274
D	45	m	w	WURT	Sacramento	3-Wd Sacramento	77	285
David	57	m	w	NY	Tuolumne	Big Oak Flat P O	93	397
David	42	m	w	PRUS	Kern	Havilah P O	73	336
David	40	m	w	OH	Santa Clara	2-Wd San Jose	88	307
Fredrick	40	m	w	WURT	San Francisco	San Francisco P O	80	480
H	16	f	w	MEXI	San Joaquin	2-Wd Stockton	86	174
Hart	32	m	w	GERM	San Francisco	8-Wd San Francisco	82	317
Helon	29	m	w	NY	Sacramento	2-Wd Sacramento	77	239
Henry	50	m	w	BAVA	Sonoma	Vallejo Twp	91	451
Isaac	50	m	w	NY	Tuolumne	Chinese Camp P O	93	365
J H	40	m	w	NY	Yuba	East Bear Rvr Twp	93	544
Jno	44	m	w	WURT	Sonoma	Santa Rosa	91	424
John	46	m	w	ME	San Francisco	7-Wd San Francisco	81	156
John	44	m	w	MA	Sonoma	Petaluma Twp	91	314
John Q	46	m	w	NH	Placer	Bath P O	76	437
Julia	17	f	w	NY	San Francisco	San Francisco P O	83	52
Mary	76	f	w	NH	Alameda	Oakland	68	155
Nathaniel	37	m	w	OH	Sonoma	Analy Twp	91	224
Saml	42	m	w	MA	Mendocino	Ukiah Twp	74	238
Saml	42	m	w	GERM	San Francisco	8-Wd San Francisco	82	317
William	19	m	w	CANA	Santa Clara	Fremont Twp	88	47
Wm	42	m	w	MA	Mendocino	Ukiah Twp	74	235
Wm	39	m	w	PRUS	San Francisco	1-Wd San Francisco	79	83
ACKERS								
Julius	27	m	w	BADE	San Francisco	8-Wd San Francisco	82	351
R	34	m	w	AUST	San Francisco	8-Wd San Francisco	82	358
ACKERSON								
Chs H	34	m	w	NY	San Francisco	8-Wd San Francisco	82	344
J T	43	m	w	NY	Tuolumne	Big Oak Flat P O	93	394
J W	41	m	w	NY	San Francisco	8-Wd San Francisco	82	308
James	50	m	w	NY	Mendocino	Navarro & Big Rvr	74	177
T	50	m	w	NY	Alameda	Oakland	68	130
ACKHAM								
Jas	40	m	w	VA	San Francisco	8-Wd San Francisco	82	306
ACKINS								
Jno	29	m	w	NY	Butte	Kimshew Tpw	70	78
ACKLAN								
John	22	m	w	SWED	Mendocino	Gualala Twp	74	226
ACKLEMAN								
John	30	m	w	PRUS	San Francisco	San Francisco P O	80	391
ACKLER								
Robert	35	m	w	MO	San Francisco	San Francisco P O	80	378
ACKLEY								
C	50	f	w	PA	Yuba	Marysville	93	584
David	25	m	w	ENGL	Santa Clara	1-Wd San Jose	88	254
Edward	35	m	w	MI	San Francisco	11-Wd San Francisc	84	658
Ezra	39	m	w	ME	San Francisco	San Francisco P O	83	417
Ezra	38	m	w	ME	San Francisco	San Francisco P O	83	350
H	40	m	w	ME	Siskiyou	Callahan P O	89	629
Helen	32	f	w	MA	San Francisco	San Francisco P O	83	227
Lyman	62	m	w	NJ	Yuba	Rose Bar Twp	93	667
Maggie	13	f	w	CA	Monterey	Alisal Twp	74	297
Samuel	55	m	w	OH	Monterey	San Juan Twp	74	386
Wm	38	m	w	NY	San Francisco	11-Wd San Francisc	84	671
ACKLIN								
C B	51	m	w	AL	Mariposa	Maxwell Crk P O	74	145
David	24	m	w	PA	Santa Clara	2-Wd San Jose	88	335
ACKLY								
O F	38	m	w	NY	Sierra	Lincoln Twp	89	546
ACKNY								
Charles	33	m	w	IN	Yolo	Cache Crk Twp	93	451
ACKS								
Matilda	17	f	w	PA	San Joaquin	Douglas Twp	86	37
ACKTON								
Robert	28	m	w	IREL	San Francisco	7-Wd San Francisco	81	227
ACLATA								
Maria	35	m	w	MEXI	Santa Clara	1-Wd San Jose	88	257
ACOA								
Susan	28	f	c	CHIN	Tulare	White Rvr Twp	92	301
ACOCK								
James C	21	m	w	MO	Placer	Rocklin P O	76	462
Robt	28	m	w	GERM	San Francisco	8-Wd San Francisco	82	375
Thos L	41	m	w	KY	Sacramento	Lee Twp	77	157
ACONIA								
Angela	29	m	w	MEXI	San Luis Obispo	Salinas Twp	87	290

© 2001 by Heritage Quest. All rights reserved.

Name	Age	S	R	B-PL	County	Locale	Roll	Pg
Antonio	50	m	w	CA	San Luis Obispo	Morro Twp	87	286
Jesus	31	m	w	MEXI	San Luis Obispo	Salinas Twp	87	291
Manuel	34	m	w	CA	San Luis Obispo	Salinas Twp	87	290
ACONIO								
Juan	29	m	w	MEXI	Santa Cruz	Pajaro Twp	89	343
Ventura	36	m	w	MEXI	Santa Cruz	Soquel Twp	89	436
ACORA								
Francis	23	m	w	FRAN	Fresno	Millerton P O	72	164
ACORNIA								
Jesus	32	m	w	MEXI	Fresno	Millerton P O	72	166
ACORS								
Jacob	35	m	w	IREL	Humboldt	Eureka Twp	72	271
ACORY								
Oliver	35	m	w	ME	Santa Cruz	Santa Cruz Twp	89	401
ACOSTA								
Chenclo	50	m	w	MEXI	Sonoma	Petaluma Twp	91	326
F	30	m	w	MEXI	San Joaquin	2-Wd Stockton	86	174
Francisco	37	m	w	AL	Los Angeles	Los Nietos Twp	73	588
Francisco	21	m	i	CA	Los Angeles	Los Angeles Twp	73	498
Herman	16	m	w	CA	San Francisco	San Francisco P O	85	796
Ignacio	40	m	w	MEXI	Los Angeles	Los Angeles Twp	73	473
Jesus	36	m	w	MEXI	Kern	Tehachapi P O	73	356
Jesus	33	m	w	MEXI	Los Angeles	Los Nietos Twp	73	584
Jose	42	m	w	MEXI	Marin	Tomales Twp	74	85
Jose	28	m	w	CA	Santa Cruz	Pajaro Twp	89	349
Jose M	54	m	w	MEXI	Santa Cruz	Soquel Twp	89	449
Juan	32	m	w	CA	Los Angeles	San Jose Twp	73	618
Leonita	21	f	w	MEXI	San Francisco	2-Wd San Francisco	79	249
Ramon	73	m	w	MEXI	Santa Clara	1-Wd San Jose	88	260
Romaldo	25	f	w	MEXI	Los Angeles	Santa Ana Twp	73	612
Thomas	50	m	w	MEXI	Mariposa	Mariposa P O	74	105
Thomas	49	m	w	MEXI	Monterey	Monterey Twp	74	345
Trinidad	30	m	w	MEXI	Los Angeles	Los Nietos Twp	73	588
ACOSTI								
Michl	32	m	w	ITAL	San Francisco	1-Wd San Francisco	79	67
ACOTA								
Palona	29	m	w	MEXI	Alameda	Eden Twp	68	65
ACQUADRE								
John	27	m	w	ITAL	San Francisco	San Francisco P O	85	851
ACQUOM								
Francis	38	m	w	MEXI	El Dorado	Mud Springs Twp	72	81
ACREN								
Josephine	49	f	w	FRAN	San Francisco	San Francisco P O	80	406
ACRES								
Austin	45	m	w	TN	Lake	Big Valley	73	396
John	33	m	w	IA	Santa Barbara	San Buenaventura P	87	431
John	21	m	w	NY	San Bernardino	San Bernardino Twp	78	427
Thomas	26	m	w	PA	Santa Clara	2-Wd San Jose	88	313
ACTON								
Abel	40	m	w	SWED	San Francisco	San Francisco P O	80	429
Martha	45	f	w	ENGL	Sonoma	Petaluma Twp	91	315
Richard	28	m	w	IREL	San Francisco	2-Wd San Francisco	79	155
ACTOR								
William	28	m	b	WIND	San Francisco	San Francisco P O	80	417
ACTSTROM								
Erick	27	m	w	FINL	Placer	Bath P O	76	457
ACUA								
Jose	27	m	w	CA	San Diego	San Luis Rey	78	514
ACUFF								
Joseph C	32	m	w	KY	Siskiyou	Butte Twp	89	585
Marshall	35	m	w	TN	Sonoma	Petaluma Twp	91	364
ACUIRIKO								
Jose	39	m	w	CHIL	Fresno	Millerton P O	72	153
ACULPA								
Juan	33	m	w	CHIL	Santa Clara	2-Wd San Jose	88	335
ACUNA								
Francois	50	m	w	MEXI	Kern	Tehachapi P O	73	356
Jose	22	m	w	MEXI	San Joaquin	1-Wd Stockton	86	133
Rafael	25	m	w	MEXI	Kern	Tehachapi P O	73	356
ACUNIA								
Francois	54	m	w	MEXI	Kern	Tehachapi P O	73	355
Maria	110	f	w	MEXI	Los Angeles	Los Angeles	73	559
Vicente	35	m	w	MEXI	Los Angeles	Los Angeles	73	521
AD								
Ah	33	m	c	CHIN	Siskiyou	Cottonwood Twp	89	594
ADAH								
Wan	13	m	c	CHIN	Solano	Vallejo	90	211
ADAIR								
Geo	40	m	w	OH	Santa Barbara	San Buenaventura P	87	431
H B	28	m	w	IN	Sacramento	3-Wd Sacramento	77	272
H F	20	m	w	PA	Solano	Vallejo	90	200
Henry	61	m	w	NJ	Placer	Auburn P O	76	360
Isaac	40	m	w	OH	Nevada	Nevada Twp	75	294
James	37	m	w	IREL	Mariposa	Mariposa P O	74	109
Jas A	55	m	w	NY	Sacramento	4-Wd Sacramento	77	376
Samuel F	31	m	w	PA	Napa	Napa	75	39
William H	11	m	w	NY	Calaveras	San Andreas P O	70	216
ADALADE								
Jim	33	m	c	CHIN	Tuolumne	Sonora P O	93	316
ADAM								
A	20	m	w	BADE	Alameda	Oakland	68	222
Alexander	30	m	w	CA	Santa Barbara	Arroyo Grande P O	87	508
J H N	49	m	w	NY	San Francisco	San Francisco P O	83	280
Jake	46	m	w	AR	San Joaquin	3-Wd Stockton	86	236
Joachim [Rev]	32	m	w	SPAI	Santa Cruz	Santa Cruz	89	414
John	62	m	w	SWED	San Francisco	2-Wd San Francisco	79	203
Peter	31	m	w	HDAR	San Francisco	San Francisco P O	80	346
Pierre	33	m	w	FRAN	San Francisco	San Francisco P O	83	89
Stephen	21	m	w	CANA	Sierra	Gibson Twp	89	540
Terence	28	m	w	CANA	Contra Costa	Martinez Twp	71	352
William	77	m	w	SCOT	Santa Cruz	Pajaro Twp	89	343
William H	40	m	w	ME	Calaveras	San Andreas P O	70	191
Wm L	33	m	w	SCOT	Santa Barbara	Arroyo Grande P O	87	508
ADAMA								
Francisco	27	m	w	MEXI	San Diego	San Diego	78	506
ADAMI								
Giuseppi	20	m	w	SWIT	Marin	Bolinas Twp	74	6
ADAMS								
A	47	m	w	VT	Lake	Lower Lake	73	416
A J	28	m	w	OH	Nevada	Meadow Lake Twp	75	246
A W	24	m	w	OH	Nevada	Meadow Lake Twp	75	247
Abel	32	m	w	ENGL	Contra Costa	Martinez P O	71	420
Abner	58	m	w	OH	Santa Cruz	Watsonville	89	365
Adam	30	m	w	US	Sacramento	Sutter Twp	77	390
Adde T	12	f	w	PA	Klamath	Camp Gaston	73	372
Albert	35	m	w	KY	El Dorado	Placerville Twp	72	99
Albert F	32	m	w	OR	Sonoma	Salt Point	91	388
Alexander	63	m	w	SCOT	Butte	Oroville Twp	70	138
Alexr P	38	m	w	CANA	San Francisco	San Francisco P O	83	129
Alfred	40	m	w	MA	San Francisco	11-Wd San Francisc	84	435
Amos	52	m	w	NY	Sacramento	Franklin Twp	77	111
Amos C	46	m	w	IL	Calaveras	San Andreas P O	70	196
Amos P	38	m	w	ME	Tuolumne	Sonora P O	93	321
Andrew	43	m	w	NY	Kern	Tehachapi P O	73	353
Andrew J	45	m	w	NC	Santa Barbara	San Buenaventura P	87	439
Andrew J	34	m	w	PA	El Dorado	Mud Springs Twp	72	71
Anne	52	f	w	MS	Tehama	Red Bluff	92	180
Arthur	28	m	w	MA	Tuolumne	Sonora P O	93	317
Asa	34	m	w	NY	Santa Barbara	Santa Barbara P O	87	454
Aurrilla	45	f	w	PA	Calaveras	San Andreas P O	70	194
B	16	f	w	ENGL	Yuba	Marysville	93	602
Barry	43	m	w	IREL	Humboldt	Arcata Twp	72	233
C A	23	m	w	WI	Solano	Vallejo	90	200
C J	40	m	w	NY	Amador	Sutter Crk P O	69	407
C S	40	m	w	MO	Santa Clara	Gilroy Twp	88	71
C W	42	m	w	NH	Alameda	Oakland	68	170
Calvin T	38	m	w	OH	Plumas	Quartz Twp	77	41
Charles	45	m	w	DENM	San Francisco	3-Wd San Francisco	79	297
Charles	43	m	w	OH	Sonoma	Petaluma Twp	91	335
Charles	40	m	w	SCOT	San Francisco	7-Wd San Francisco	81	198
Charles	38	m	w	MA	San Mateo	Woodside P O	87	386
Charles	28	m	w	MO	Lake	Lower Lake	73	420
Charles	27	m	w	NY	Contra Costa	Martinez P O	71	377
Charles	25	m	w	ENGL	Placer	Newcastle Twp	76	475
Charles	23	m	w	MO	Solano	Green Valley Twp	90	39
Charles	22	m	w	NJ	Plumas	Indian Twp	77	13
Charles	21	m	w	MI	Stanislaus	Empire Twp	92	43
Chas	46	m	w	NORW	San Francisco	11-Wd San Francisc	84	519
Chas	28	m	w	NY	Monterey	Alisal Twp	74	298
Chas B	23	m	w	KY	Tehama	Tehama Twp	92	194
Chas W	40	m	w	NC	Sacramento	3-Wd Sacramento	77	294
Clara	18	f	w	KY	San Joaquin	3-Wd Stockton	86	241
Clarisa	64	f	w	MA	Solano	Benicia	90	14
Conrad	42	m	w	HDAR	Sacramento	3-Wd Sacramento	77	285
Cyrus	39	m	w	OH	San Francisco	8-Wd San Francisco	82	374
D	40	m	w	IL	Lake	Lower Lake	73	429
D H	49	f	w	NY	Santa Clara	Gilroy Twp	88	99
D H	32	m	w	ME	Alameda	Eden Twp	68	81
Daniel	36	m	w	ENGL	San Francisco	8-Wd San Francisco	82	375
Daniel T	48	m	w	ME	Santa Clara	1-Wd San Jose	88	252
David	60	m	w	TN	Kern	Tehachapi P O	73	352
David	49	m	w	OH	Stanislaus	Empire Twp	92	39
David	47	m	w	KY	Santa Cruz	Pajaro Twp	89	352
David	40	m	w	IREL	San Francisco	7-Wd San Francisco	81	279
David	28	m	w	PA	San Francisco	San Francisco P O	80	533
David L	34	m	w	IN	Santa Cruz	Santa Cruz Twp	89	393
David M	22	m	w	AR	Santa Clara	2-Wd San Jose	88	336
David Q	42	m	w	MO	Yolo	Cottonwood Twp	93	467
Dio	37	m	w	IREL	San Joaquin	2-Wd Stockton	86	191
Dura	48	f	w	OH	Santa Clara	1-Wd San Jose	88	253
E C	17	m	w	CA	Alameda	Oakland	68	159
Ebenezer	74	m	w	VT	Santa Clara	1-Wd San Jose	88	253
Eber	68	m	w	NY	Santa Barbara	Santa Barbara P O	87	454
Edson	45	m	w	CT	Alameda	Oakland	68	235
Edward	39	m	w	AL	Los Angeles	El Monte Twp	73	451
Edward	32	m	w	NY	San Francisco	7-Wd San Francisco	81	166
Edward	30	m	w	MA	San Francisco	San Francisco P O	80	416
Edward	11	m	w	CA	San Francisco	11-Wd San Francisc	84	586
Edwin	47	m	w	NY	Butte	Oroville Twp	70	139
Eli	42	m	w	PA	Butte	Chico Twp	70	24
Elizabeth G	44	f	w	MA	Sonoma	Petaluma Twp	91	337
Elizebeth	72	f	w	KY	Lake	Zim Zim	73	417
Elmer	22	m	w	ME	Alameda	Hayward	68	73
Elom J	24	m	w	NC	Sonoma	Analy Twp	91	224
Emma	16	f	w	TN	San Francisco	6-Wd San Francisco	81	117
Evelyn A	21	m	w	ME	Santa Cruz	Watsonville	89	371
F J	32	m	w	FRAN	San Joaquin	3-Wd Stockton	86	222
Fitch	43	m	w	NY	San Francisco	San Francisco P O	83	77
Flora	12	f	w	MEXI	Napa	Napa	75	42
Francis	22	m	w	IREL	Humboldt	Pacific Twp	72	297
Francis E	37	m	w	MO	Los Angeles	El Monte Twp	73	456
Frank	35	m	w	NY	San Bernardino	San Bernardino Twp	78	431
Frank	28	m	w	IREL	San Francisco	8-Wd San Francisco	82	356
Frank D	15	m	w	CA	Santa Clara	Fremont Twp	88	57

Series M593

© 2001 by Heritage Quest. All rights reserved.

Series M593

Name	Age	S	R	B-PL	County	Locale	Roll	Pg
Franklin	35	m	w	IL	Santa Clara	Redwood Twp	88	133
Frederick	35	m	w	PA	Santa Cruz	Santa Cruz	89	414
Freeman	35	m	w	IL	Solano	Tremont Twp	90	35
G M	14	m	w	CA	Alameda	Oakland	68	159
G W	40	m	w	MO	Tehama	Antelope Twp	92	154
Garland	36	m	w	KY	Sacramento	Georgianna Twp	77	122
Geo	27	m	w	IL	Monterey	Monterey	74	355
Geo	20	m	w	MO	Sacramento	3-Wd Sacramento	77	310
Geo G	32	m	w	MA	Napa	Napa	75	18
Geo P	40	m	w	IL	San Francisco	5-Wd San Francisco	81	21
Geo W	55	m	w	TN	Shasta	Millville P O	89	489
George	59	m	w	NH	Alameda	Brooklyn Twp	68	52
George	50	m	w	WALE	Santa Cruz	Watsonville	89	374
George	36	m	w	NY	Sacramento	4-Wd Sacramento	77	342
George	36	m	w	GERM	Los Angeles	Los Angeles	73	571
George M	44	m	w	NJ	El Dorado	Diamond Springs Tw	72	23
George M	14	m	w	NY	San Francisco	San Francisco P O	83	159
George N	45	m	w	MA	Santa Clara	Redwood Twp	88	131
Georgiana	27	f	b	AR	Mariposa	Mariposa P O	74	120
Grove	45	m	w	MI	San Francisco	6-Wd San Francisco	81	117
H	44	m	w	PRUS	San Francisco	8-Wd San Francisco	82	345
H E	38	m	w	NY	San Francisco	3-Wd San Francisco	79	319
Hannah	69	f	w	ENGL	San Mateo	Belmont P O	87	373
Harrison	26	m	w	VT	Placer	Bath P O	76	425
Henry	50	m	w	NY	Kern	Bakersfield P O	73	366
Henry	44	m	w	NH	San Joaquin	3-Wd Stockton	86	233
Henry	40	m	w	ME	San Francisco	7-Wd San Francisco	81	222
Henry	38	m	w	HDAR	San Francisco	San Francisco P O	80	462
Henry	37	m	w	MI	Sonoma	Analy Twp	91	237
Henry	31	m	w	ENGL	Nevada	Grass Valley Twp	75	224
Henry	28	m	w	IREL	San Joaquin	Elliott Twp	86	74
Henry	25	m	w	ENGL	Placer	Clipper Gap P O	76	376
Henry	21	m	w	ENGL	Nevada	Grass Valley Twp	75	198
Henry S	44	m	w	AR	Tulare	Venice Twp	92	275
Heny	23	m	w	NY	San Joaquin	1-Wd Stockton	86	126
Hiram	27	m	w	CANA	Sonoma	Bodega Twp	91	258
Horace	45	m	w	NH	San Francisco	6-Wd San Francisco	81	134
Hubert N	24	m	w	MO	Monterey	Monterey Twp	74	346
Hugh	30	m	w	LA	San Francisco	7-Wd San Francisco	81	260
I B	27	m	w	MD	San Francisco	3-Wd San Francisco	79	323
Increase	33	m	w	ME	Santa Barbara	Santa Barbara P O	87	497
Ira W	38	m	w	MA	Santa Barbara	Santa Barbara P O	87	481
J	34	m	w	ENGL	Sierra	Lincoln Twp	89	545
J	28	m	w	IN	Lassen	Susanville Twp	73	439
J B	50	m	w	KY	Lake	Zim Zim	73	417
J D	25	m	w	MO	Lake	Lower Lake	73	429
J F	40	m	w	FRAN	San Joaquin	2-Wd Stockton	86	199
J O	26	m	w	WI	Humboldt	Bald Hills	72	237
J O	1	m	w	CA	Lassen	Susanville Twp	73	439
J P	23	m	w	ME	Sierra	Table Rock Twp	89	576
J Q	33	m	w	NH	Solano	Vallejo	90	169
J S	30	m	w	NY	Alameda	Oakland	68	262
J W	31	m	w	SCOT	San Francisco	1-Wd San Francisco	79	71
James	73	m	w	GA	Sonoma	Mendocino Twp	91	294
James	46	m	w	IREL	San Francisco	8-Wd San Francisco	82	494
James	45	m	w	MA	Nevada	Rough & Ready Twp	75	326
James	40	m	w	IREL	San Francisco	San Francisco P O	83	302
James	39	m	w	IREL	Alameda	Eden Twp	68	85
James	38	m	w	CANA	Sonoma	Salt Point	91	380
James	37	m	w	SC	Sonoma	Analy Twp	91	228
James	37	m	w	OH	Amador	Volcano P O	69	375
James	35	m	w	IREL	Colusa	Colusa Twp	71	274
James	34	m	w	MA	Mendocino	Big Rvr Twp	74	171
James	33	m	w	ENGL	Alameda	Murray Twp	68	126
James	24	m	w	VA	Stanislaus	Empire Twp	92	48
James H	60	m	w	VA	Mendocino	Point Arena Twp	74	206
James H	32	m	w	VT	Nevada	Washington Twp	75	341
James S	52	m	w	IL	Tuolumne	Sonora P O	93	323
Jane	33	f	w	NY	San Francisco	San Francisco P O	83	66
Jannette	26	f	w	ENGL	Butte	Oregon Twp	70	127
Jas	63	m	w	IREL	Solano	Vallejo	90	214
Jim	14	m	i	CA	Lake	Lower Lake	73	429
Jno	38	m	w	IREL	Butte	Kimshew Tpw	70	83
Joan	30	f	w	IREL	Alameda	Oakland	68	138
Joe	44	m	w	MA	San Joaquin	2-Wd Stockton	86	202
Joe	40	m	w	MO	San Joaquin	Douglas Twp	86	50
John	74	m	w	CA	San Francisco	11-Wd San Francisc	84	662
John	60	m	w	PA	Del Norte	Smith Rvr Twp	71	477
John	56	m	b	MD	Calaveras	San Andreas P O	70	197
John	55	m	w	IA	Stanislaus	Empire Twp	92	43
John	50	m	w	GREE	Calaveras	Copperopolis P O	70	255
John	41	m	w	MO	Sonoma	Santa Rosa	91	429
John	41	m	w	NY	Nevada	Nevada Twp	75	296
John	40	m	w	NY	Nevada	Little York Twp	75	244
John	39	m	w	SCOT	Yolo	Cache Crk Twp	93	454
John	39	m	w	AR	San Diego	San Luis Rey	78	513
John	38	m	w	NY	Siskiyou	Surprise Valley Tw	89	641
John	38	m	w	BELG	Mendocino	Little Rvr Twp	74	165
John	38	m	w	IL	Colusa	Grand Island Twp	71	309
John	37	m	w	IA	Butte	Hamilton Twp	70	61
John	36	m	b	IL	Nevada	Nevada Twp	75	290
John	34	m	w	PRUS	San Francisco	San Francisco P O	83	87
John	34	m	b	HI	Tuolumne	Big Oak Flat P O	93	399
John	34	m	w	NY	Los Angeles	Los Angeles Twp	73	476
John	30	m	w	MO	Yolo	Cottonwood Twp	93	475
John	28	m	w	VT	Solano	Vacaville Twp	90	122
John	25	m	w	IREL	Nevada	Meadow Lake Twp	75	246
John	25	m	w	ENGL	Nevada	Grass Valley Twp	75	203
John	25	m	w	ENGL	Nevada	Grass Valley Twp	75	204
John	24	m	w	HANO	Nevada	Meadow Lake Twp	75	265
John	24	m	w	PRUS	San Francisco	5-Wd San Francisco	81	32
John	23	m	w	IN	Yolo	Putah Twp	93	523
John	22	m	w	NY	Alameda	Washington Twp	68	296
John	21	m	w	OH	Stanislaus	Empire Twp	92	38
John	21	m	w	IREL	Butte	Ophir Twp	70	99
John	21	m	w	NY	Yuba	Marysville	93	591
John	21	m	w	BAVA	San Francisco	7-Wd San Francisco	81	279
John	15	m	w	IREL	Santa Barbara	Santa Barbara P O	87	467
John C	61	m	w	NC	Mendocino	Calpella Twp	74	183
John C	34	m	w	ME	Tuolumne	Sonora P O	93	325
John F	53	m	w	IREL	San Diego	San Pasqual	78	520
John F	35	m	w	NY	San Francisco	6-Wd San Francisco	81	104
John H	50	m	w	IL	Santa Clara	San Jose Twp	88	201
John J	40	m	w	GA	San Mateo	Half Moon Bay P O	87	396
John Q	24	m	w	PA	Sacramento	4-Wd Sacramento	77	337
John S	39	m	w	VT	Napa	Napa	75	4
Jonathan	40	m	w	NH	Calaveras	San Andreas P O	70	170
Jos	35	m	w	IREL	San Francisco	8-Wd San Francisco	82	360
Jos W	57	m	w	NY	Shasta	Millville P O	89	483
Joseph	56	m	w	NY	Calaveras	Copperopolis P O	70	257
Joseph	38	m	w	AZOR	San Francisco	1-Wd San Francisco	79	133
Joseph E	41	m	w	NY	Santa Clara	1-Wd San Jose	88	235
Joseph H	52	m	w	NY	San Francisco	2-Wd San Francisco	79	258
Josephine	25	f	w	ENGL	San Francisco	San Francisco P O	83	199
Jule	41	m	w	FRAN	Siskiyou	Callahan P O	89	628
Kate	40	f	w	NY	San Francisco	6-Wd San Francisco	81	108
L C	52	m	w	VT	Sonoma	Russian Rvr	91	373
L E	29	f	w	MA	San Francisco	San Francisco P O	85	826
Laura	53	f	w	CT	Stanislaus	Empire Twp	92	43
Laura A	50	f	w	NY	San Francisco	6-Wd San Francisco	81	121
Lawson S	46	m	w	MA	San Francisco	8-Wd San Francisco	82	378
Levi	35	m	w	IA	Yolo	Cottonwood Twp	93	466
Levi	31	m	w	OH	Yolo	Grafton Twp	93	485
Lilla	25	f	w	NY	San Francisco	San Francisco P O	83	22
Lorenzo	22	m	w	US	El Dorado	Placerville Twp	72	105
Louis	39	m	w	PRUS	Shasta	Dog Crk P O	89	471
Louis	39	m	w	PA	San Joaquin	3-Wd Stockton	86	234
Louis	34	m	w	FRAN	San Joaquin	2-Wd Stockton	86	191
Lowman B	32	m	w	VT	Placer	Lincoln P O	76	488
Lozenzo D	25	m	w	MI	Nevada	Grass Valley Twp	75	157
Margaret	22	f	w	IREL	San Francisco	San Francisco P O	85	853
Maria L	16	f	w	CA	Monterey	San Antonio Twp	74	316
Mary	33	f	w	WALE	San Joaquin	2-Wd Stockton	86	209
Mary	18	f	w	MA	San Francisco	11-Wd San Francisc	84	437
Mat	37	m	w	NY	Sacramento	1-Wd Sacramento	77	172
Mathew	42	m	w	DENM	Nevada	Rough & Ready Twp	75	329
Michl	26	m	w	OH	San Francisco	5-Wd San Francisco	81	27
Minerva	16	f	w	WI	Santa Clara	Milpitas Twp	88	113
Nancy	42	f	w	NY	Santa Clara	Fremont Twp	88	57
Nathaniel	31	m	w	ENGL	San Francisco	San Francisco P O	80	473
Nelson	34	m	w	OH	Monterey	San Antonio Twp	74	319
Nelson B	25	m	w	MA	San Francisco	San Francisco P O	83	170
Nicholas	35	m	w	ENGL	Plumas	Rich Bar Twp	77	8
O	20	m	w	OH	Alameda	Alameda	68	5
O M	40	m	w	NY	Alameda	Oakland	68	162
Orson	41	m	w	NY	San Francisco	San Francisco P O	83	420
Otis	35	m	w	VT	San Francisco	11-Wd San Francisc	84	706
Paul	27	m	w	POLA	San Francisco	7-Wd San Francisco	81	162
Paul A	2	m	w	WI	Nevada	Nevada Twp	75	305
Quincy	43	m	w	NY	San Francisco	San Francisco P O	80	377
R	27	f	w	IN	Lassen	Susanville Twp	73	439
R H	37	m	w	ME	Merced	Snelling P O	74	247
Ranald	40	m	w	LA	San Francisco	8-Wd San Francisco	82	398
Rebecca E	28	f	w	ME	San Francisco	8-Wd San Francisco	82	377
Richard	36	m	w	NY	San Francisco	11-Wd San Francisc	84	477
Richard	25	m	w	PRUS	San Francisco	7-Wd San Francisco	81	226
Robert	20	m	w	CANA	Nevada	Nevada Twp	75	295
Robert	20	m	w	CANA	Nevada	Nevada Twp	75	316
Robert	19	m	w	IL	San Francisco	7-Wd San Francisco	81	279
Robert B	32	m	w	TN	Napa	Yountville Twp	75	90
Robt	45	m	w	IREL	San Francisco	2-Wd San Francisco	79	193
Rodey	54	f	b	VA	San Francisco	San Francisco P O	80	359
Rosalia	10	f	w	IA	Yolo	Grafton Twp	93	486
Rosania	58	f	w	NY	San Francisco	11-Wd San Francisc	84	562
Ross M	35	m	w	PA	San Francisco	1-Wd San Francisco	79	26
S	40	f	w	OR	Humboldt	Eureka Twp	72	277
S	37	m	w	BADE	San Joaquin	2-Wd Stockton	86	193
S C	28	m	w	ME	Nevada	Eureka Twp	75	135
S M	45	f	w	OH	Sacramento	3-Wd Sacramento	77	272
Sally	40	f	w	PA	San Francisco	8-Wd San Francisco	82	336
Saml	62	m	w	US	Sacramento	1-Wd Sacramento	77	184
Saml	55	m	w	IREL	Sacramento	1-Wd Sacramento	77	178
Saml	25	m	w	KY	Humboldt	Pacific Twp	72	296
Saml W	44	m	w	ME	San Francisco	San Francisco P O	83	72
Samuel	61	m	w	PA	Placer	Newcastle Twp	76	474
Samuel	56	m	w	CT	Contra Costa	Martinez P O	71	413
Samuel	46	m	w	MA	Placer	Bath P O	76	438
Samuel	38	m	w	VT	Calaveras	Copperopolis P O	70	246
Samuel	32	m	w	IREL	Contra Costa	Martinez P O	71	369
Samuel	20	m	w	IA	Humboldt	Mattole Twp	72	283
Samuel K	30	m	w	NY	San Francisco	11-Wd San Francisc	84	707
Samuel L	34	m	w	IN	San Francisco	3-Wd San Francisco	79	314
Samuel M	42	m	w	AL	Los Angeles	El Monte Twp	73	451
Samul	59	m	w	MS	San Francisco	8-Wd San Francisco	82	330

© 2001 by Heritage Quest. All rights reserved.

California 1870 Census

Name	Age	S	R	B-PL	County	Locale	Series M593 Roll	Pg
Sarah	59	f	w	NY	San Francisco	2-Wd San Francisco	79	223
Susan	30	f	w	MA	San Francisco	San Francisco P O	85	854
T	82	m	w	KY	Lake	Zim Zim	73	417
Thomas	73	m	w	KY	Yolo	Cottonwood Twp	93	475
Thomas	45	m	w	KY	San Diego	San Luis Rey	78	515
Thomas	42	m	w	ENGL	Placer	Colfax P O	76	392
Thomas	40	m	w	ENGL	Amador	Sutter Crk P O	69	396
Thomas	36	m	w	MO	Yolo	Cache Crk Twp	93	451
Thomas	36	m	w	NY	Tuolumne	Columbia P O	93	356
Thomas	34	m	w	IA	Mendocino	Bourns Landing Twp	74	223
Thomas	24	m	w	TX	Solano	Silveyville Twp	90	84
Thos	46	m	w	MA	San Joaquin	Douglas Twp	86	50
Thos	43	m	w	SCOT	San Francisco	8-Wd San Francisco	82	309
Thos	21	m	w	ME	San Joaquin	Tulare Twp	86	261
Thos G	35	m	w	CANA	San Luis Obispo	Santa Rosa Twp	87	329
Thos H	45	m	w	MA	Klamath	Salmon Twp	73	388
Virginia	18	f	m	MD	San Francisco	San Francisco P O	80	388
W	50	m	w	MA	San Francisco	8-Wd San Francisco	82	367
W	24	m	w	CT	Nevada	Meadow Lake Twp	75	252
W E	36	m	w	OH	Butte	Chico Twp	70	56
Walker W	56	m	w	KY	Inyo	Bishop Crk Twp	73	315
Warren	39	m	w	MO	Yolo	Cache Crk Twp	93	426
William	63	m	w	OH	Yolo	Grafton Twp	93	478
William	57	m	w	MD	Kern	Bakersfield P O	73	360
William	53	m	b	OH	Sacramento	2-Wd Sacramento	77	217
William	44	m	w	OH	Stanislaus	Empire Twp	92	39
William	40	m	w	SCOT	San Francisco	1-Wd San Francisco	79	27
William	39	m	w	ENGL	Mariposa	Mariposa P O	74	100
William	37	m	w	NY	Marin	Sausalito Twp	74	72
William	35	m	w	NY	Napa	Napa Twp	75	46
William	32	m	w	ENGL	Placer	Colfax P O	76	392
William	27	m	w	ENGL	Amador	Ione City P O	69	363
William	26	m	w	MI	Stanislaus	Empire Twp	92	43
William	20	m	w	CANA	Marin	Point Reyes Twp	74	23
William	17	m	w	IN	Lassen	Susanville Twp	73	439
William C	37	m	w	KY	Contra Costa	Martinez P O	71	390
William H	6	m	w	CA	Yolo	Cottonwood Twp	93	466
William J	40	m	w	ME	San Mateo	Menlo Park P O	87	377
William M	53	m	w	NY	Nevada	Rough & Ready Twp	75	325
Williams H	23	m	w	MD	Yolo	Washington Twp	93	530
Willie	7	f	w	NV	San Francisco	5-Wd San Francisco	81	6
Wilson	39	m	w	KY	Sonoma	Cloverdale Twp	91	270
Wm	24	m	w	NY	Yuba	Marysville	93	608
Wm	22	m	w	MA	San Francisco	7-Wd San Francisco	81	279
Wm G	31	m	w	NY	Santa Barbara	San Buenaventura P	87	432
Wm H	43	m	w	NY	San Francisco	8-Wd San Francisco	82	351
Wm H	26	m	w	NY	San Francisco	San Francisco P O	83	79
Wm Henry	39	m	w	IREL	Nevada	Grass Valley Twp	75	207
Wm M	63	m	m	TN	Sacramento	4-Wd Sacramento	77	366
Y	29	m	w	MO	Lake	Lower Lake	73	414
Z B	35	m	w	MA	San Francisco	San Francisco P O	85	857
ADAMSON								
Appolona	30	f	w	CA	Yolo	Putah Twp	93	510
C P	37	m	w	SHOL	Napa	Yountville Twp	75	87
Edwd	24	m	w	IA	Sonoma	Petaluma Twp	91	343
Jacob	52	m	w	TN	Sonoma	Vallejo Twp	91	459
John	36	m	w	DENM	San Francisco	11-Wd San Francisc	84	585
John	28	m	w	ENGL	Solano	Tremont Twp	90	28
Richard	29	m	w	IREL	Napa	Napa	75	43
Sylvester	37	m	w	MO	Tulare	Farmersville Twp	92	245
W	35	m	w	SCOT	San Francisco	1-Wd San Francisco	79	71
Wm	42	m	w	ENGL	San Francisco	5-Wd San Francisco	81	27
ADARE								
Abbie O	36	f	w	MA	San Francisco	San Francisco P O	83	268
George	23	m	w	NY	San Francisco	San Francisco P O	83	220
ADARGA								
Ramon	17	m	w	MEXI	Santa Clara	Santa Clara Twp	88	157
ADARGO								
Jose	15	m	w	CA	Los Angeles	Los Angeles Twp	73	482
ADARO								
Santos	37	m	w	CHIL	Tuolumne	Big Oak Flat P O	93	394
ADATA								
John	34	m	w	ITAL	Calaveras	Copperopolis P O	70	246
ADCOCK								
Wm	13	m	w	CA	San Francisco	San Francisco P O	85	828
ADCRAFT								
W C	50	m	w	ENGL	San Joaquin	2-Wd Stockton	86	158
ADDAM								
John	66	m	w	MA	Trinity	Weaverville Pct	92	226
ADDAMS								
John	50	m	w	IREL	Los Angeles	Los Angeles	73	535
Mary E	30	f	w	MO	Los Angeles	Los Angeles	73	541
P	60	m	w	BAVA	Trinity	Weaverville Pct	92	231
ADDCOCK								
Wm	50	m	w	NY	San Francisco	7-Wd San Francisco	81	233
ADDELSON								
Jane	21	m	w	ENGL	Napa	Napa	75	7
ADDIN								
Anna	35	f	w	CANA	Alameda	Oakland	68	161
ADDINGTON								
A M	47	m	w	IN	Sacramento	Cosumnes Twp	77	96
Charles	16	m	w	CA	Sacramento	Granite Twp	77	144
Stephen	30	m	w	NJ	Colusa	Colusa	71	295
ADDIS								
Katie A	17	f	w	CA	Tuolumne	Sonora P O	93	316
ADDISON								
Christiana	18	f	w	DENM	Sonoma	Bodega Twp	91	251
Frances	45	f	w	FRAN	San Francisco	2-Wd San Francisco	79	142
J K	37	m	w	ENGL	San Joaquin	Liberty Twp	86	87
Jas C	20	m	w	ENGL	Butte	Chico Twp	70	60
John	42	m	w	LA	San Francisco	5-Wd San Francisco	81	14
John E	50	m	w	MD	San Francisco	8-Wd San Francisco	82	479
Martin	42	m	w	ME	San Francisco	San Francisco P O	83	64
Thos	45	m	w	NY	Alameda	Eden Twp	68	83
ADDISSON								
Sarah	38	f	w	MA	San Francisco	San Francisco P O	83	191
ADDLEMAN								
Francis R	21	m	w	PA	Klamath	Camp Gaston	73	372
ADDLER								
Adolph	37	m	w	BAVA	Calaveras	San Andreas P O	70	197
ADDLEY								
John	35	m	w	ENGL	Fresno	Millerton P O	72	168
ADDY								
Sarah	27	f	w	NY	San Joaquin	2-Wd Stockton	86	175
ADEE								
Mary	62	f	w	VA	San Francisco	11-Wd San Francisc	84	544
Mary	32	f	w	ENGL	San Francisco	11-Wd San Francisc	84	544
ADEL								
William T	38	m	w	IL	Santa Clara	2-Wd San Jose	88	298
ADELL								
Frank	35	m	w	PA	Sonoma	Petaluma Twp	91	324
ADELLA								
Pablo	41	m	w	MEXI	Santa Cruz	Soquel Twp	89	438
ADELSDORFER								
Henry	19	m	w	POLA	San Francisco	1-Wd San Francisco	79	104
Isaac	60	m	w	BAVA	San Francisco	San Francisco P O	83	354
ADEMA								
Wm	38	m	w	NY	San Francisco	7-Wd San Francisco	81	250
ADEN								
Jeremiah G	46	m	w	TN	El Dorado	Mud Springs Twp	72	74
ADERHOLD								
Henrietta	13	f	w	PA	San Francisco	11-Wd San Francisc	84	503
ADERSON								
James	35	m	w	OH	El Dorado	Kelsey Twp	72	60
Peter	34	m	w	ENGL	Sacramento	Franklin Twp	77	116
ADERTON								
Nellie	28	f	w	ME	Nevada	Nevada Twp	75	291
ADESTS								
C E	15	m	w	CA	Alameda	Oakland	68	159
ADGATE								
Azure	44	m	w	NY	Yuba	Marysville	93	633
ADGEN								
Keng	40	m	c	CHIN	Tulare	White Rvr Twp	92	301
ADGINS								
I	50	m	w	MO	San Joaquin	Elliott Twp	86	75
ADIE								
E	21	m	w	VA	Sonoma	Vallejo Twp	91	454
ADIN								
John	21	m	w	VT	San Francisco	11-Wd San Francisc	84	708
M	24	m	w	HANO	Solano	Vallejo	90	217
ADIO								
Pedro	41	m	w	CA	Los Angeles	Los Angeles	73	555
ADIS								
Benjamin	46	m	w	HOLL	Placer	Auburn P O	76	382
ADISE								
S J	37	f	w	MEXI	Tuolumne	Sonora P O	93	310
ADISON								
L	28	m	w	NY	Alameda	Oakland	68	264
Richard	37	m	w	TN	Siskiyou	Scott Valley Twp	89	618
ADKIN								
Grace	12	f	w	CA	Santa Cruz	Pajaro Twp	89	340
Henry	32	m	w	KY	Kern	Bakersfield P O	73	361
ADKINS								
Alfred	50	m	w	NC	Siskiyou	Scott Valley Twp	89	615
Andrey	22	m	w	KY	Inyo	Cerro Gordo Twp	73	320
Henry	35	m	w	OH	Kern	Bakersfield P O	73	359
Henry	23	m	w	KY	Butte	Chico Twp	70	20
Henry W	52	m	w	ENGL	Shasta	Horsetown P O	89	503
J C	36	m	w	OH	Monterey	San Juan Twp	74	416
Jessie	40	m	w	TN	Sutter	Nicolaus Twp	92	108
John	68	m	w	ENGL	Solano	Vacaville Twp	90	130
Marcus	33	m	w	GA	Mariposa	Mariposa P O	74	125
Oliver	44	m	w	KY	Yuba	East Bear Rvr Twp	93	545
Tho	45	m	w	MD	Butte	Chico Twp	70	22
ADKINSON								
Charles	55	m	w	VA	Mariposa	Mariposa P O	74	126
ADLAM								
Benj	46	m	w	ENGL	San Francisco	1-Wd San Francisco	79	37
ADLER								
Adelaide	23	f	w	WURT	San Francisco	2-Wd San Francisco	79	240
Bar	48	m	w	WALD	San Francisco	San Francisco P O	83	176
Bernard	51	m	w	POLA	San Francisco	San Francisco P O	80	362
Celia	23	f	w	AUST	San Francisco	San Francisco P O	83	182
Charles	32	m	w	GERM	San Francisco	8-Wd San Francisco	82	374
Charles	32	m	w	BAVA	Alameda	Washington Twp	68	291
Charles	29	m	w	NY	San Francisco	8-Wd San Francisco	82	402
Gottlieb	28	m	w	SWIT	San Francisco	3-Wd San Francisco	79	324
Henrietta	27	f	w	NY	San Francisco	San Francisco P O	83	413
Julius	25	m	w	DENM	San Francisco	1-Wd San Francisco	79	70
Leopold	50	m	w	PRUS	San Francisco	8-Wd San Francisco	82	397
Lewis	50	m	w	PRUS	Sonoma	Sonoma Twp	91	439
Mary J	18	f	w	MO	Sierra	Gibson Twp	89	541
Morris	45	m	w	BAVA	San Francisco	11-Wd San Francisc	84	502
Moses	36	m	w	PRUS	El Dorado	Placerville	72	111

© 2001 by Heritage Quest. All rights reserved.

Name	Age	S	R	B-PL	County	Locale	Roll	Pg
						Series M593		
R	32	m	w	GERM	San Francisco	8-Wd San Francisco	82	374
Simon	40	m	w	PRUS	El Dorado	Placerville	72	117
Solomon	49	m	w	PRUS	San Francisco	8-Wd San Francisco	82	490
ADLEY								
Jas	20	m	w	NY	Humboldt	Eureka Twp	72	258
ADLINGTON								
Daniel	46	m	w	MA	San Francisco	San Francisco P O	80	331
ADMANISK								
Stephen	26	m	w	ITAL	Sacramento	Sutter Twp	77	393
ADNOT								
August	43	m	w	FRAN	Nevada	Grass Valley Twp	75	179
ADOCK								
Robt J	39	m	w	VA	Monterey	Castroville Twp	74	336
ADOLINE								
Herrman	37	m	w	SWED	San Francisco	7-Wd San Francisco	81	228
ADOLP								
Obary	39	m	w	FRAN	Alameda	San Leandro	68	96
ADOLPH								
---	22	m	w	PRUS	Yuba	Marysville	93	591
Conrad	54	m	w	PRUS	Mariposa	Mariposa P O	74	105
J J	44	m	w	PRUS	Monterey	San Juan Twp	74	408
Johnson	30	m	w	SWED	Sonoma	Petaluma Twp	91	334
Taz	50	m	w	FRAN	Los Angeles	Los Angeles	73	537
ADOLPHUS								
Henry	45	m	w	PRUS	San Francisco	1-Wd San Francisco	79	109
ADOMEY								
Christ	17	f	w	MA	Sierra	Table Rock Twp	89	573
ADON								
Leon	40	m	w	FRAN	San Francisco	3-Wd San Francisco	79	319
ADONIS								
Byron	30	m	w	TN	San Francisco	3-Wd San Francisco	79	327
ADRAD								
Joseph J	27	m	w	MA	Colusa	Butte Twp	71	266
ADRAIN								
Edward	49	m	w	FRAN	San Francisco	2-Wd San Francisco	79	233
ADRAL								
Cinto	27	m	w	MEXI	Santa Clara	Almaden Twp	88	11
ADRANCE								
Sarah	18	f	w	WI	Butte	Chico Twp	70	21
ADRIAN								
Anton	44	m	w	BAVA	Placer	Auburn P O	76	369
Fredyanin	50	m	w	ITAL	Placer	Bath P O	76	438
Ygnacio	40	m	w	CHIL	Santa Barbara	Santa Barbara P O	87	477
ADRIANCE								
Edward	12	m	w	CA	San Francisco	San Francisco P O	85	827
Elizabeth	7	f	w	CA	San Francisco	San Francisco P O	85	827
Francis	5	m	w	CA	San Francisco	San Francisco P O	85	827
Mary	41	f	w	IREL	Yuba	Marysville	93	634
Wm	10	m	w	CA	San Francisco	San Francisco P O	85	827
ADRIEN								
Henry S	49	m	w	FRAN	San Francisco	1-Wd San Francisco	79	49
ADRIN								
V	45	m	w	HOLL	Alameda	Oakland	68	136
ADRION								
Adolph	34	m	w	FRAN	San Francisco	1-Wd San Francisco	79	50
ADROIS								
Pedro	30	m	i	MEXI	Inyo	Cerro Gordo Twp	73	320
ADSHEAD								
Wm	41	m	w	ENGL	Fresno	Millerton P O	72	186
ADSID								
Elizabeth	40	f	w	ENGL	San Francisco	8-Wd San Francisco	82	328
ADSIT								
S	42	m	w	NY	Solano	Vallejo	90	197
ADSITT								
Hyman	52	m	w	NY	Nevada	Nevada Twp	75	319
AEH								
Regina	18	f	w	PRUS	San Francisco	San Francisco P O	83	268
AEILKAMA								
Benj D	47	m	w	HOLL	Mariposa	Mariposa P O	74	127
AELSTROM								
Frank	38	m	w	PRUS	San Francisco	1-Wd San Francisco	79	77
AERHART								
Adam	40	m	w	PRUS	San Francisco	San Francisco P O	83	227
AERICKSON								
Peter	40	m	w	SWED	Sonoma	Sonoma Twp	91	434
AERLY								
Washington	26	m	w	MO	Sutter	Vernon Twp	92	135
AFFIDY								
Philip	35	m	w	AUSL	Santa Clara	Santa Clara Twp	88	176
AFFLECK								
Thomas B	72	m	w	PA	El Dorado	Mud Springs Twp	72	73
AFFLERBACH								
Christian H	43	m	w	PRUS	Santa Clara	2-Wd San Jose	88	328
AFFLICK								
Edward	37	m	w	IL	Placer	Auburn P O	76	372
AFFONSO								
D M	33	m	w	SCOT	Siskiyou	Scott Valley Twp	89	612
AFFRAYER								
John	38	m	w	PA	Tehama	Antelope Twp	92	155
AFFREY								
Henry	34	m	w	PRUS	Solano	Montezuma Twp	90	66
AFILL								
Theodore	26	m	w	SWED	San Francisco	1-Wd San Francisco	79	3
AFONG								
---	25	m	c	CHIN	San Francisco	11-Wd San Francisc	84	706
AFORMADO								
Madalina	63	f	w	CA	Los Angeles	San Juan Twp	73	626

Name	Age	S	R	B-PL	County	Locale	Roll	Pg
						Series M593		
AFRAIEGO								
Candido	45	m	w	SPAI	Los Angeles	Los Nietos Twp	73	584
AFSHER								
Chas	26	m	w	PRUS	San Francisco	1-Wd San Francisco	79	40
AFSTAD								
Newton	41	m	w	ENGL	Colusa	Monroe Twp	71	314
AGAIN								
T Milton	36	m	w	MO	Mariposa	Mariposa P O	74	123
AGAN								
Hugh	44	m	w	PA	Placer	Auburn P O	76	380
Luke	42	m	w	IREL	San Joaquin	2-Wd Stockton	86	167
Pat	50	m	w	IREL	Alameda	Oakland	68	266
Patrick	31	m	w	IREL	Butte	Chico Twp	70	47
AGANA								
Ramon	30	m	w	MEXI	Los Angeles	Los Angeles	73	551
AGANTES								
Anton	38	m	w	MEXI	Placer	Auburn P O	76	358
AGAR								
Anna	25	f	w	CHIL	Sacramento	2-Wd Sacramento	77	243
Barney	24	m	w	CANA	Solano	Maine Prairie Twp	90	52
AGARA								
Jesus	38	m	w	CA	Alameda	Washington Twp	68	288
AGARD								
Geo	30	m	w	ENGL	San Francisco	1-Wd San Francisco	79	131
J J	34	m	w	NY	Sacramento	3-Wd Sacramento	77	280
Wm Boulton	54	m	w	ENGL	San Francisco	1-Wd San Francisco	79	131
AGARDINO								
Bernard	39	m	w	AUST	San Francisco	1-Wd San Francisco	79	131
AGARIA								
Ramon	41	m	w	MEXI	Tulare	Farmersville Twp	92	241
Teresa	43	f	w	MEXI	Los Angeles	Los Angeles	73	552
AGARO								
Salveo	30	m	w	CA	Alameda	Washington Twp	68	286
AGARRO								
Thomas	46	m	w	CA	Alameda	Washington Twp	68	285
AGASSIA								
Francisco	48	m	w	ITAL	Marin	Nicasio Twp	74	14
AGATE								
Lovet	35	m	w	FRAN	Solano	Denverton Twp	90	26
Peter	40	m	w	FRAN	Solano	Denverton Twp	90	26
AGEE								
Mary	37	f	w	OH	Solano	Silveyville Twp	90	74
Robert	42	m	w	OH	Solano	Silveyville Twp	90	74
AGELA								
Manuel	36	m	w	MEXI	Los Angeles	Los Angeles Twp	73	473
AGELAIN								
Antone	43	m	w	MEXI	Amador	Jackson P O	69	348
AGELO								
Gastrode	19	m	w	CHIL	San Francisco	San Francisco P O	83	44
AGEN								
Chow	40	m	c	CHIN	Tulare	White Rvr Twp	92	301
John	30	m	w	IREL	San Mateo	Woodside P O	87	386
P	29	m	w	IREL	Lake	Lower Lake	73	418
Thomas	50	m	w	IREL	El Dorado	Salmon Falls Twp	72	130
AGENIA								
Govain	36	m	w	MEXI	Tuolumne	Columbia P O	93	344
AGEPATH								
John	38	m	w	SC	San Francisco	San Francisco P O	80	338
AGER								
Cephus	31	m	w	ME	El Dorado	Mud Springs Twp	72	84
George	39	m	w	NY	Mendocino	Little Lake Twp	74	195
George	27	m	w	ENGL	San Francisco	8-Wd San Francisco	82	493
Jerome B	41	m	w	NY	Siskiyou	Yreka Twp	89	664
John	47	m	w	DC	San Francisco	11-Wd San Francisc	84	555
Joseph	42	m	w	ME	San Francisco	11-Wd San Francisc	84	619
Justina	36	f	w	FRAN	San Francisco	8-Wd San Francisco	82	289
Marcus K	64	m	w	VT	Sonoma	Sonoma Twp	91	434
AGERO								
Juan	45	m	w	CA	Monterey	Monterey Twp	74	344
M	58	m	w	CA	Alameda	Murray Twp	68	108
Segundo	30	m	w	CA	Fresno	Kingston P O	72	219
AGERS								
Wm	45	m	w	ME	San Joaquin	2-Wd Stockton	86	172
AGEY								
Ellsworth	37	m	w	PA	Nevada	Washington Twp	75	343
AGGERT								
Hans	40	m	w	GERM	Yolo	Putah Twp	93	517
AGGIE								
Herman	35	m	w	PRUS	Sacramento	Granite Twp	77	147
AGH								
See Hong	25	f	c	CHIN	Calaveras	San Andreas P O	70	169
AGIDE								
Leonardo	32	m	w	MEXI	Los Angeles	Los Nietos Twp	73	586
AGIER								
Benena	35	m	w	MEXI	Inyo	Bishop Crk Twp	73	310
AGILA								
Antonio	35	m	w	MEXI	Solano	Vacaville Twp	90	138
AGILAR								
L	40	f	w	MEXI	Amador	Jackson P O	69	322
Refugia	25	f	w	MEXI	Santa Clara	2-Wd San Jose	88	315
AGILARRA								
Harriet	42	f	w	MEXI	Mariposa	Mariposa P O	74	100
AGILLON								
Jose	60	m	w	MEXI	Santa Barbara	Santa Barbara P O	87	500
AGMAR								
Benjamin	39	m	w	NY	Placer	Dutch Flat P O	76	401

© 2001 by Heritage Quest. All rights reserved.

California 1870 Census

Name	Age	S	R	B-PL	County	Locale	Series M593 Roll	Pg
AGNA								
Antonio	45	m	w	CHIL	San Francisco	San Francisco P O	80	538
AGNAN								
James	45	m	w	SWIT	Kern	Havilah P O	73	337
AGNEAU								
William	19	m	w	MS	Contra Costa	Martinez Twp	71	350
AGNELINO								
Pedro	32	m	w	ITAL	San Luis Obispo	Arroyo Grande Twp	87	276
AGNES								
A	23	f	w	NH	Sacramento	3-Wd Sacramento	77	277
AGNEW								
Alice	27	f	w	CA	Sacramento	1-Wd Sacramento	77	174
Eliza	28	f	w	ENGL	Santa Clara	1-Wd San Jose	88	238
Gilmore	48	m	w	EIND	San Francisco	San Francisco P O	83	375
James	39	m	w	IREL	Sonoma	Salt Point	91	392
James	25	m	w	IREL	San Francisco	7-Wd San Francisco	81	164
John	48	m	w	IREL	San Francisco	San Francisco P O	83	327
John	35	m	w	ME	San Francisco	7-Wd San Francisco	81	218
John	35	m	w	ME	San Francisco	11-Wd San Francisc	84	519
Luke	32	m	w	NJ	San Francisco	San Francisco P O	83	343
Mary A	14	f	w	NY	Alameda	Oakland	68	230
Patrick	33	m	w	IREL	San Francisco	7-Wd San Francisco	81	170
Samuel	40	m	w	VA	Sonoma	Sonoma Twp	91	438
Theo	38	m	w	KY	Merced	Snelling P O	74	265
Thomas	35	m	w	IREL	Solano	Rio Vista Twp	90	62
Thomas	30	m	w	NJ	San Francisco	San Francisco P O	83	206
Thomas H	39	m	w	PA	Placer	Auburn P O	76	368
AGNO								
Randolph A	37	m	w	NJ	Alameda	Oakland	68	249
AGO								
Celestino	26	m	w	ITAL	Calaveras	Copperopolis P O	70	259
AGOSTINO								
Piti	30	m	w	ITAL	San Francisco	11-Wd San Francisc	84	617
AGOTE								
Wm	50	m	w	KY	Butte	Chico Twp	70	20
AGOUNT								
Harvey	36	m	w	CANA	Nevada	Meadow Lake Twp	75	268
AGREELLA								
Michael	57	m	w	SPAI	San Francisco	8-Wd San Francisco	82	311
AGRELL								
Fertcinet	30	m	w	BADE	Yolo	Cache Crk Twp	93	423
John	39	m	w	SWED	San Francisco	San Francisco P O	83	324
AGRES								
Thos	45	m	w	TN	Sacramento	Lee Twp	77	158
AGRIMA								
Pedro	34	m	w	MEXI	Mariposa	Mariposa P O	74	93
AGUALAR								
Harmon	47	m	w	MEXI	San Bernardino	San Salvador Twp	78	458
AGUAS								
Nicolas	11	m	w	CA	Monterey	San Antonio Twp	74	321
AGUAYO								
Jose Ma	60	m	w	MEXI	Los Angeles	Santa Ana Twp	73	615
Joseph	12	m	w	CA	San Bernardino	San Bernardino Twp	78	418
Loreto	50	m	w	MEXI	San Bernardino	San Salvador Twp	78	456
AGUERA								
Santos	27	m	w	CA	Monterey	Castroville Twp	74	334
AGUERE								
Thomas	40	m	w	PA	San Francisco	San Francisco P O	80	461
AGUERISE								
Manuel	24	m	w	MEXI	San Diego	Temecula Dist	78	526
AGUERRA								
Joaquin	31	m	w	MEXI	Santa Cruz	Soquel Twp	89	439
AGUIERA								
Lazzairo	30	m	w	MEXI	Santa Barbara	San Buenaventura P	87	428
AGUILAR								
Antonio	40	m	w	CA	Los Angeles	San Juan Twp	73	628
Blas	60	m	w	CA	Los Angeles	San Juan Twp	73	624
Cristoval	56	m	w	CA	Los Angeles	Los Angeles	73	551
Fredrick	26	m	w	MEXI	San Francisco	San Francisco P O	80	476
Isadora	36	f	w	CA	Los Angeles	Los Angeles	73	543
Jesus	64	m	w	MEXI	San Luis Obispo	Arroyo Grande Twp	87	278
Jose	43	m	w	CA	Los Angeles	San Juan Twp	73	628
Juan	30	m	w	CA	San Diego	Warners Rancho Dis	78	529
Macedonio	52	m	w	CA	Los Angeles	Los Angeles Twp	73	486
Merejildo	32	m	w	MEXI	Los Angeles	Los Angeles	73	542
Mocincro	28	m	w	CA	San Diego	San Luis Rey	78	514
Rosario	18	m	w	CA	Los Angeles	San Juan Twp	73	627
Salvadora	25	f	w	CA	Los Angeles	San Juan Twp	73	624
AGUILLAR								
Jose	60	m	w	MEXI	Fresno	Millerton P O	72	167
Julian	27	m	w	CA	Santa Barbara	Santa Barbara P O	87	493
AGUILLON								
Camille	42	m	w	FRAN	Sonoma	Sonoma Twp	91	440
AGUIRA								
Blass	50	m	w	CA	Monterey	Castroville Twp	74	334
John	25	m	w	AZOR	San Francisco	1-Wd San Francisco	79	118
Jose	22	m	w	CHIL	Santa Clara	Almaden Twp	88	11
AGUIRE								
Jose	15	m	w	CA	Los Angeles	Los Angeles	73	570
Martin	14	m	w	CA	Los Angeles	Los Angeles	73	570
AGUIRRE								
Jose M	50	m	w	MEXI	Los Angeles	Los Nietos Twp	73	583
Juan	48	m	w	MEXI	Los Angeles	San Gabriel Twp	73	593
Manuel	40	m	w	MEXI	Los Angeles	Los Nietos Twp	73	583
Mercedes	35	m	w	MEXI	Sierra	Sears Twp	89	560
Miguel	21	m	w	CA	Santa Clara	Santa Clara Twp	88	176
Miguel	21	m	w	CA	San Diego	San Diego	78	493

Name	Age	S	R	B-PL	County	Locale	Series M593 Roll	Pg
AGULA								
Pedro	40	m	i	MEXI	Monterey	Monterey	74	361
AGULAR								
Zenobia	16	f	w	CA	Los Angeles	Santa Ana Twp	73	611
AGULO								
Gabriel	16	m	w	MEXI	Los Angeles	Los Angeles	73	513
AGUSIAR								
Frank	49	m	w	CA	Alameda	Oakland	68	251
AGUSTA								
Dolores	38	m	w	MEXI	Santa Clara	Redwood Twp	88	119
AGUSTIN								
Jesus	30	m	w	CHIL	Sacramento	2-Wd Sacramento	77	215
AGUSTUS								
Pedro	45	m	w	SPAI	Monterey	San Juan Twp	74	401
AH								
Ah	6	m	c	CHIN	San Francisco	San Francisco P O	80	449
Ah	57	m	c	CHIN	San Francisco	San Francisco P O	80	522
Ah	56	f	c	CHIN	San Francisco	San Francisco P O	80	508
Ah	51	m	c	CHIN	San Francisco	San Francisco P O	80	499
Ah	45	m	c	CHIN	San Francisco	3-Wd San Francisco	79	304
Ah	44	m	c	CHIN	San Francisco	San Francisco P O	80	527
Ah	42	m	c	CHIN	San Francisco	San Francisco P O	80	442
Ah	41	m	c	CHIN	San Francisco	San Francisco P O	80	439
Ah	41	m	c	CHIN	San Francisco	San Francisco P O	80	513
Ah	40	m	c	CHIN	San Francisco	San Francisco P O	80	442
Ah	40	m	c	CHIN	San Francisco	San Francisco P O	80	517
Ah	38	m	c	CHIN	San Francisco	San Francisco P O	80	446
Ah	38	m	c	CHIN	San Francisco	San Francisco P O	80	501
Ah	37	m	c	CHIN	San Francisco	San Francisco P O	80	454
Ah	37	m	c	CHIN	San Francisco	San Francisco P O	80	516
Ah	37	m	c	CHIN	San Francisco	San Francisco P O	80	530
Ah	36	m	c	CHIN	San Francisco	San Francisco P O	80	440
Ah	36	m	c	CHIN	San Francisco	San Francisco P O	80	436
Ah	36	m	c	CHIN	San Francisco	San Francisco P O	80	452
Ah	36	m	c	CHIN	San Francisco	San Francisco P O	80	511
Ah	36	m	c	CHIN	San Francisco	San Francisco P O	80	513
Ah	36	m	c	CHIN	San Francisco	San Francisco P O	80	525
Ah	34	f	c	CHIN	San Francisco	San Francisco P O	80	526
Ah	31	m	c	CHIN	San Francisco	San Francisco P O	80	446
Ah	30	f	c	CHIN	San Francisco	San Francisco P O	80	440
Ah	30	f	c	CHIN	San Francisco	San Francisco P O	80	508
Ah	30	m	c	CHIN	San Francisco	San Francisco P O	80	524
Ah	29	m	c	CHIN	San Francisco	San Francisco P O	80	437
Ah	28	m	c	CHIN	San Francisco	San Francisco P O	80	436
Ah	28	m	c	CHIN	San Francisco	San Francisco P O	80	502
Ah	28	m	c	CHIN	San Francisco	San Francisco P O	80	514
Ah	28	m	c	CHIN	San Francisco	San Francisco P O	80	520
Ah	28	m	c	CHIN	San Francisco	San Francisco P O	80	512
Ah	27	m	c	CHIN	San Francisco	San Francisco P O	80	444
Ah	27	m	c	CHIN	San Francisco	San Francisco P O	80	515
Ah	26	m	c	CHIN	San Francisco	San Francisco P O	80	496
Ah	26	m	c	CHIN	San Francisco	San Francisco P O	80	510
Ah	26	m	c	CHIN	San Francisco	San Francisco P O	80	510
Ah	26	m	c	CHIN	San Francisco	San Francisco P O	80	522
Ah	25	m	c	CHIN	San Francisco	San Francisco P O	80	431
Ah	25	m	c	CHIN	San Francisco	San Francisco P O	80	493
Ah	24	f	c	CHIN	San Francisco	San Francisco P O	80	433
Ah	24	f	c	CHIN	San Francisco	San Francisco P O	80	445
Ah	23	f	c	CHIN	San Francisco	San Francisco P O	80	432
Ah	23	f	c	CHIN	San Francisco	San Francisco P O	80	507
Ah	23	f	c	CHIN	San Francisco	San Francisco P O	80	521
Ah	22	m	c	CHIN	San Francisco	San Francisco P O	80	335
Ah	22	f	c	CHIN	San Francisco	San Francisco P O	80	433
Ah	22	f	c	CHIN	San Francisco	San Francisco P O	80	448
Ah	22	f	c	CHIN	San Francisco	San Francisco P O	80	449
Ah	22	m	c	CHIN	San Francisco	San Francisco P O	80	502
Ah	21	m	c	CHIN	San Francisco	3-Wd San Francisco	79	307
Ah	21	f	c	CHIN	San Francisco	San Francisco P O	80	435
Ah	21	m	c	CHIN	San Francisco	San Francisco P O	80	501
Ah	21	f	c	CHIN	San Francisco	San Francisco P O	80	529
Ah	20	f	c	CHIN	San Francisco	San Francisco P O	80	434
Ah	20	f	c	CHIN	San Francisco	San Francisco P O	80	438
Ah	20	f	c	CHIN	San Francisco	San Francisco P O	80	437
Ah	20	f	c	CHIN	San Francisco	San Francisco P O	80	493
Ah	20	m	c	CHIN	San Francisco	San Francisco P O	80	491
Ah	19	m	c	CHIN	San Francisco	San Francisco P O	80	451
Ah	19	m	c	CHIN	San Francisco	San Francisco P O	80	520
Ah	19	f	c	CHIN	San Francisco	San Francisco P O	80	523
Ah	18	f	c	CHIN	San Francisco	San Francisco P O	80	432
Ah	18	m	c	CHIN	San Francisco	San Francisco P O	80	453
Ah	17	f	c	CHIN	San Francisco	San Francisco P O	80	528
Ah	15	m	c	CHIN	San Francisco	San Francisco P O	80	506
Ah	15	m	c	CHIN	San Francisco	San Francisco P O	85	725
Ah	12	m	c	CHIN	San Francisco	San Francisco P O	80	424
Ah	1	m	c	CA	San Francisco	San Francisco P O	80	441
Ah	1	m	c	CA	San Francisco	San Francisco P O	80	454
Cehurby	35	m	c	CHIN	Napa	Napa Twp	75	58
Cherm	40	m	c	CHIN	Napa	Napa Twp	75	58
Coon	29	m	c	CHIN	Santa Clara	Santa Clara Twp	88	161
Crong	20	f	c	CHIN	Nevada	Bridgeport Twp	75	110
Die	36	m	c	CHIN	Fresno	Millerton P O	72	199
Fung	19	m	c	CHIN	Santa Clara	1-Wd San Jose	88	272
Geyow	19	f	c	CHIN	Nevada	Bridgeport Twp	75	110
J O	26	m	c	CHIN	El Dorado	Coloma Twp	72	7
Keet	34	m	c	CHIN	Marin	San Rafael Twp	74	41
Kenn	27	f	c	CHIN	Marin	San Rafael Twp	74	43
Louisa	37	f	c	CHIN	Placer	Roseville P O	76	348

© 2001 by Heritage Quest. All rights reserved.

Name	Age	S	R	B-PL	County	Locale	Series M593 Roll	Pg
Loy	37	m	c	CHIN	Santa Clara	1-Wd San Jose	88	272
Man	24	m	c	CA	Santa Clara	Fremont Twp	88	56
Oh	15	m	c	CHIN	Yuba	Marysville	93	602
P	34	m	c	CHIN	El Dorado	Placerville Twp	72	93
Si	24	m	c	CHIN	Mariposa	Maxwell Crk P O	74	145
Sing	19	m	c	CHIN	Shasta	American Ranch P O	89	500
Singhop	36	m	c	CHIN	Monterey	Alisal Twp	74	298
Soine	19	f	c	CHIN	Nevada	Bloomfield Twp	75	94
Ting	30	m	c	CHIN	Del Norte	Happy Camp Twp	71	468
Toie	47	m	c	CHIN	Marin	San Rafael Twp	74	42
Toy	24	m	c	CHIN	Santa Clara	1-Wd San Jose	88	272
W	37	m	c	CHIN	El Dorado	Coloma Twp	72	12
War	12	m	c	CHIN	San Joaquin	1-Wd Stockton	86	151
Wong	29	m	c	CHIN	Trinity	Douglas	92	237
AHA								
Ah	24	m	c	CHIN	San Francisco	San Francisco P O	80	515
Ah	20	m	c	CHIN	San Francisco	San Francisco P O	80	516
Jim	23	m	c	CHIN	Placer	Bath P O	76	451
Joseph	73	m	w	FRAN	San Francisco	8-Wd San Francisco	82	404
Win	30	m	c	CHIN	Alameda	Murray Twp	68	107
AHALA								
Joaquin	66	m	w	CA	Santa Barbara	Las Cruces P O	87	516
AHALT								
Isaac	47	m	w	MD	Napa	Napa Twp	75	28
AHAN								
W J	24	m	w	IREL	Alameda	Oakland	68	158
AHANG								
Thos	39	m	w	NY	Butte	Kimshew Tpw	70	82
AHARAN								
Mary	43	f	w	IREL	Alameda	Brooklyn Twp	68	51
AHART								
James W	37	m	w	TN	El Dorado	Diamond Springs Tw	72	29
Peter	38	m	w	BADE	Placer	Lincoln P O	76	481
Peter	37	m	w	ME	Sutter	Nicolaus Twp	92	110
Spencer	31	m	w	TN	Sonoma	Mendocino Twp	91	294
AHE								
Ham	24	m	c	CHIN	Calaveras	San Andreas P O	70	195
Lew	34	m	c	CHIN	Placer	Bath P O	76	423
She	35	m	c	CHIN	Butte	Hamilton Twp	70	71
AHEARN								
Cornelius	21	m	w	MA	Nevada	Grass Valley Twp	75	220
James	45	m	w	IREL	Nevada	Grass Valley Twp	75	214
Margaret	35	f	w	IREL	Marin	Sausalito Twp	74	69
Michael	27	m	w	IREL	San Mateo	San Mateo P O	87	360
Thomas	28	m	w	IREL	Santa Barbara	San Buenaventura P	87	448
William	36	m	w	IREL	Nevada	Grass Valley Twp	75	212
AHEE								
Yon	21	m	c	CHIN	San Francisco	11-Wd San Francisc	84	528
AHEN								
Aaron	39	m	w	PRUS	San Francisco	San Francisco P O	83	199
AHENS								
G	45	m	w	PRUS	Lake	Lower Lake	73	415
AHERN								
A	35	m	w	IA	Sacramento	4-Wd Sacramento	77	373
Ann	35	f	w	IREL	San Francisco	San Francisco P O	83	220
Catherine	27	f	w	IREL	San Francisco	San Francisco P O	83	253
Cornelius	37	m	w	IREL	San Francisco	San Francisco P O	83	354
Dennis	43	m	w	IREL	Kern	Havilah P O	73	339
Dennis	36	m	w	IREL	Klamath	Trinidad Twp	73	392
Eugene	20	m	w	IREL	San Francisco	San Francisco P O	83	251
H C	50	m	w	PRUS	Tuolumne	Big Oak Flat P O	93	399
James	30	m	w	IREL	San Francisco	San Francisco P O	83	394
Jeremiah	45	m	w	IREL	San Francisco	11-Wd San Francisc	84	483
John M	42	m	w	IREL	San Francisco	San Francisco P O	85	784
Julia	45	f	w	IREL	San Francisco	1-Wd San Francisco	79	105
Kate	30	f	w	IREL	Alameda	San Leandro	68	95
Katie	6	f	w	NY	San Francisco	San Francisco P O	83	329
Margaret	54	f	w	IREL	Yuba	Marysville	93	574
Mary	9	f	w	WI	San Francisco	San Francisco P O	83	304
Michael	33	m	w	IREL	San Francisco	8-Wd San Francisco	82	482
Michael	28	m	w	IREL	Yuba	Long Bar Twp	93	563
Patk	34	m	w	IREL	Tehama	Red Bluff	92	181
Patrick	43	m	w	IREL	San Francisco	San Francisco P O	85	727
Patrick	42	m	w	IREL	San Francisco	San Francisco P O	83	231
Peter	31	m	w	VT	San Francisco	6-Wd San Francisco	81	105
Phillip	46	m	w	GERM	Yuba	Marysville	93	613
Samuel J	21	m	w	RI	Yolo	Cache Crk Twp	93	445
Will C	30	m	w	AUSL	San Francisco	6-Wd San Francisco	81	92
William	29	m	w	IREL	San Francisco	1-Wd San Francisco	79	67
William	27	m	w	IREL	San Francisco	San Francisco P O	83	224
AHERNS								
Julius	38	m	w	PRUS	Del Norte	Crescent	71	464
AHERRING								
A	40	m	w	IREL	Alameda	Oakland	68	266
AHFAT								
Gee	21	m	c	CHIN	Los Angeles	Los Angeles	73	542
AHFELDT								
Morris	42	m	w	PRUS	San Francisco	1-Wd San Francisco	79	135
AHFUT								
Wat	28	m	c	CHIN	Los Angeles	Los Angeles	73	542
AHGIV								
Kivah	16	m	c	CHIN	San Francisco	8-Wd San Francisco	82	384
AHI								
Me	37	m	c	CHIN	San Joaquin	1-Wd Stockton	86	147
Sing	27	m	c	CHIN	Sutter	Sutter Twp	92	123
So	16	f	c	CHIN	Sacramento	1-Wd Sacramento	77	201
Wong	21	m	c	CHIN	Los Angeles	Los Angeles	73	516

Name	Age	S	R	B-PL	County	Locale	Series M593 Roll	Pg
AHINIO								
Frank	28	m	w	FRAN	Los Angeles	Soledad Twp	73	632
AHKMAN								
Thomas	25	m	w	RUSS	Sonoma	Petaluma Twp	91	316
AHL								
William	28	m	w	IL	Shasta	Millville P O	89	488
AHLBOAM								
Henry	36	m	w	PRUS	San Francisco	San Francisco P O	83	14
AHLBOM								
Minnie	39	f	w	WI	San Francisco	7-Wd San Francisco	81	207
AHLERS								
Charles	25	m	w	HAMB	San Francisco	San Francisco P O	85	758
Thomas	29	m	w	HOLL	San Francisco	San Francisco P O	80	535
William	43	m	w	PRUS	San Francisco	San Francisco P O	80	333
AHLERT								
Frederick	50	m	w	PRUS	San Luis Obispo	Arroyo Grande Twp	87	275
AHLEY								
Louis	32	m	w	CANA	Calaveras	San Andreas P O	70	162
AHLF								
Aung	50	m	c	CHIN	Colusa	Butte Twp	71	272
Claus	34	m	w	HANO	Colusa	Colusa Twp	71	275
Henry	45	m	w	HANO	Colusa	Butte Twp	71	272
Jacob	27	m	w	HANO	Colusa	Butte Twp	71	272
AHLGREN								
Charles	24	m	w	FINL	Placer	Bath P O	76	441
AHLMAN								
Peter	35	m	w	SWED	Tulare	Farmersville Twp	92	249
AHLSTRROM								
Fred	40	m	w	FINL	San Francisco	1-Wd San Francisco	79	117
AHMAN								
--- Jr	24	m	c	CHIN	San Francisco	11-Wd San Francisc	84	702
--- Sr	50	m	c	CHIN	San Francisco	11-Wd San Francisc	84	702
AHN								
Ah	32	m	c	CHIN	San Joaquin	1-Wd Stockton	86	145
Get	13	m	c	CHIN	Plumas	Goodwin Twp	77	3
Gong	34	m	c	CHIN	Plumas	Goodwin Twp	77	3
Hang	25	m	c	CHIN	Plumas	Goodwin Twp	77	3
How	29	m	c	CHIN	Plumas	Goodwin Twp	77	3
Lee	35	f	c	CHIN	Sacramento	1-Wd Sacramento	77	192
Shang	31	m	c	CHIN	Plumas	Goodwin Twp	77	3
Wo	28	f	c	CHIN	Sacramento	1-Wd Sacramento	77	192
Yon	32	m	c	CHIN	Plumas	Goodwin Twp	77	3
AHNEN								
Nicolas	29	m	w	HAMB	San Francisco	3-Wd San Francisco	79	294
AHNEW								
Robt	55	m	w	SCOT	Butte	Kimshew Tpw	70	82
AHNG								
---	13	m	c	CHIN	Shasta	French Gulch P O	89	465
H	21	m	c	CHIN	San Diego	San Diego	78	511
AHNIK								
Hank	17	m	c	CHIN	San Francisco	8-Wd San Francisco	82	384
AHNIN								
Joseph	32	m	c	CHIN	Alameda	Eden Twp	68	90
AHPEL								
Carl	34	m	w	HAMB	Sacramento	4-Wd Sacramento	77	323
AHREN								
Conrad	32	m	w	PRUS	San Francisco	1-Wd San Francisco	79	116
David	38	m	w	IREL	Tuolumne	Columbia P O	93	350
AHRENS								
Charles	26	m	w	PRUS	San Francisco	6-Wd San Francisco	81	99
Chas	46	m	w	SHOL	San Francisco	1-Wd San Francisco	79	85
Henry	34	m	w	HANO	San Francisco	San Francisco P O	83	84
Henry	28	m	w	PRUS	San Francisco	San Francisco P O	80	340
John	26	m	w	PRUS	San Francisco	San Francisco P O	80	342
Nellie A	13	f	w	MA	San Francisco	3-Wd San Francisco	79	294
William	21	m	w	HANO	San Francisco	2-Wd San Francisco	79	211
Wm H	30	m	w	HANO	Santa Cruz	Santa Cruz	89	410
AHRON								
Patrick	20	m	w	IREL	San Francisco	7-Wd San Francisco	81	202
AHRT								
Ah	34	m	c	CHIN	Calaveras	San Andreas P O	70	155
AHSBY								
Wm	54	m	w	MA	Alameda	Oakland	68	226
AHT								
Seu	31	m	c	CHIN	Shasta	French Gulch P O	89	470
Sung	40	m	c	CHIN	Calaveras	San Andreas P O	70	155
AHTON								
Hob	18	m	c	CHIN	San Francisco	San Francisco P O	85	806
AHU								
Ah	36	m	c	CHIN	Sierra	Lincoln Twp	89	550
AHUMADA								
Jose	28	m	w	MEXI	San Francisco	1-Wd San Francisco	79	108
AHVENS								
George	36	m	w	PRUS	Placer	Newcastle Twp	76	473
AI								
Ah	32	m	c	CHIN	Sacramento	1-Wd Sacramento	77	194
Ah	22	m	c	CHIN	Solano	Benicia	90	14
Sing	21	m	c	CHIN	Santa Clara	Fremont Twp	88	52
Tah	14	m	c	CHIN	San Francisco	2-Wd San Francisco	79	220
AIBISCHER								
Bruns	52	m	w	SWIT	San Francisco	2-Wd San Francisco	79	147
AICHER								
Wilhelmina	57	f	w	HDAR	San Francisco	San Francisco P O	80	456
AIGGINS								
M	34	m	w	NY	Sacramento	1-Wd Sacramento	77	190
AIGNER								
Geo	33	m	w	BAVA	Butte	Kimshew Tpw	70	83

© 2001 by Heritage Quest. All rights reserved.

California 1870 Census

Name	Age	S	R	B-PL	County	Locale	Roll	Pg
AIK								
Ah	29	m	c	CHIN	Sacramento	1-Wd Sacramento	77	205
AIKE								
Lee	19	m	c	CHIN	San Francisco	San Francisco P O	83	213
AIKEN								
A E	30	f	w	NY	Alameda	Oakland	68	259
Andrew	36	m	w	SWED	San Francisco	1-Wd San Francisco	79	4
George	48	m	w	IREL	San Bernardino	San Salvador Twp	78	459
Jas	47	m	w	SCOT	San Francisco	11-Wd San Francisc	84	424
John	52	m	w	MA	San Francisco	San Francisco P O	85	857
John	31	m	w	NY	Butte	Kimshew Tpw	70	79
John M	50	m	w	NH	Mariposa	Maxwell Crk P O	74	139
John S	19	m	w	PA	Tehama	Tehama Twp	92	194
Peter	27	m	w	PA	Sacramento	1-Wd Sacramento	77	186
Phebe	10	f	w	CA	Santa Clara	2-Wd San Jose	88	285
Robert	22	m	w	SCOT	San Francisco	San Francisco P O	83	168
S D	49	m	w	NY	Sierra	Downieville Twp	89	522
William	48	m	w	NH	San Francisco	5-Wd San Francisco	81	6
AIKENS								
Albert	37	m	w	IREL	San Francisco	5-Wd San Francisco	81	5
AIKER								
Isaac	39	m	w	KY	Sacramento	American Twp	77	66
Jesse	35	m	w	KY	Sacramento	American Twp	77	66
AIKERS								
Montgomery	31	m	w	ME	Sonoma	Sonoma Twp	91	443
AIKIN								
Laura	10	f	w	CA	Los Angeles	Los Angeles Twp	73	479
Mary	5	f	w	NY	Los Angeles	San Gabriel Twp	73	597
Porter	50	m	w	MA	Alameda	Oakland	68	190
William D	45	m	w	TX	Los Angeles	Soledad Twp	73	630
Wm	40	m	w	OH	Sacramento	Lee Twp	77	157
AIKINS								
James	59	m	w	US	Sacramento	Cosumnes Twp	77	93
Joshua	9	m	w	CA	Los Angeles	Los Angeles Twp	73	487
AILKIN								
Elizabeth	55	f	w	SCOT	Nevada	Nevada Twp	75	289
AILLET								
Felix	35	m	w	FRAN	Nevada	Nevada Twp	75	289
AILLGEN								
Hermann	22	m	w	HANO	San Francisco	11-Wd San Francisc	84	510
AILSE								
W	47	m	w	HANO	Alameda	Oakland	68	178
AIMAN								
Wm C	45	m	w	NY	San Francisco	5-Wd San Francisco	81	17
AIMSBAUGH								
Eli	40	m	w	PA	San Joaquin	3-Wd Stockton	86	237
AIMSBERY								
Robert	34	m	w	AUSL	San Francisco	7-Wd San Francisco	81	185
AIMSLEY								
Thomas	20	m	w	MA	San Francisco	7-Wd San Francisco	81	173
AIN								
Ah	43	m	c	CHIN	Sacramento	Natomas Twp	77	167
Long	21	f	c	CHIN	Sacramento	1-Wd Sacramento	77	194
AING								
Ah	25	f	c	CHIN	Sacramento	1-Wd Sacramento	77	195
AINSA								
Augustus	12	m	w	CA	San Francisco	11-Wd San Francisc	84	592
Sola	20	f	w	MEXI	San Francisco	2-Wd San Francisco	79	197
AINSBURY								
Wm	29	m	w	ENGL	Lake	Lower Lake	73	414
AINSLEE								
David G	32	m	w	CANA	Mendocino	Gualala Twp	74	226
AINSLEY								
G D	61	m	w	KY	Mendocino	Calpella Twp	74	182
Thomas	49	m	w	IREL	San Francisco	San Francisco P O	83	337
Thomas	45	m	w	IREL	Tuolumne	Sonora P O	93	325
AINSLIE								
Joseph	34	m	w	CANA	Mendocino	Gualala Twp	74	226
AINSLONE								
Simon	37	m	w	PA	Stanislaus	Buena Vista Twp	92	15
AINSLVEZ								
Jose	26	m	w	MEXI	Stanislaus	Emory Twp	92	25
AINSLY								
Robert	28	m	w	WALE	Santa Clara	2-Wd San Jose	88	308
AINSWORTH								
A	47	m	w	MS	San Joaquin	2-Wd Stockton	86	203
A S	36	m	w	MO	Lake	Lower Lake	73	419
Danl	26	m	w	OH	San Francisco	San Francisco P O	83	61
John	32	m	w	ENGL	Marin	Sausalito Twp	74	73
Mary	17	f	w	NY	Sacramento	4-Wd Sacramento	77	331
Peter	40	m	w	IREL	San Francisco	San Francisco P O	83	313
W H	57	m	w	ENGL	Solano	Benicia	90	10
AINWRIGHT								
John	32	m	w	IREL	San Francisco	7-Wd San Francisco	81	241
AIOLA								
Calitano	26	m	w	MEXI	San Francisco	San Francisco P O	80	465
AIRHEART								
Ebiga	25	m	w	IA	San Joaquin	Elkhorn Twp	86	64
AIRTHWORTH								
Brock	26	m	w	CANA	Sonoma	Vallejo Twp	91	454
AIRY								
Thomas I	35	m	w	ENGL	Santa Clara	Redwood Twp	88	132
AISTON								
John	44	m	w	ENGL	Sacramento	Center Twp	77	84
AITKEN								
Agnes	19	f	w	MA	Santa Clara	1-Wd San Jose	88	263
Andrew	40	m	w	SCOT	El Dorado	Cosumnes Twp	72	14
David	31	m	w	ENGL	Sacramento	4-Wd Sacramento	77	376
Geo	34	m	w	SCOT	Solano	Benicia	90	12
Jeanette	46	f	w	SCOT	San Francisco	11-Wd San Francisc	84	625
John	16	m	w	CA	San Francisco	3-Wd San Francisco	79	287
May	12	f	w	MI	Alameda	Oakland	68	258
Robert	43	m	w	SCOT	Amador	Jackson P O	69	324
Wm H	26	m	w	VT	San Francisco	3-Wd San Francisco	79	318
AITKIN								
Geo	32	m	w	SCOT	Solano	Benicia	90	14
William	53	m	w	NY	Yuba	North East Twp	93	644
AITKINS								
Amos	20	m	w	NY	San Francisco	5-Wd San Francisco	81	15
James	43	m	w	NY	San Francisco	5-Wd San Francisco	81	12
AIVIN								
John	66	m	w	PA	San Joaquin	Elkhorn Twp	86	56
AIVO								
Antonin	40	m	w	WIND	Alameda	Alameda	68	10
AK								
Ah	41	m	c	CHIN	Nevada	Rough & Ready Twp	75	338
Ah	39	m	c	CHIN	San Francisco	11-Wd San Francisc	84	503
Ah	35	m	c	CHIN	Sacramento	1-Wd Sacramento	77	205
Ah	30	m	c	CHIN	Contra Costa	Martinez P O	71	430
Ah	19	m	c	CHIN	San Francisco	3-Wd San Francisco	79	329
Kee	17	m	c	CHIN	Siskiyou	Yreka Twp	89	669
Kune	16	m	c	CHIN	Tehama	Tehama Twp	92	189
Kut	31	m	c	CHIN	Siskiyou	Hamburg Twp	89	598
AKAR								
Charles	17	m	w	WURT	Sacramento	2-Wd Sacramento	77	245
AKARD								
Henry	28	m	w	IREL	San Francisco	San Francisco P O	83	372
AKE								
Ah	39	m	c	CHIN	Sierra	Table Rock Twp	89	579
Ah	33	m	c	CHIN	Mendocino	Gualala Twp	74	223
Ah	18	m	c	CHIN	Mendocino	Gualala Twp	74	223
Ah	13	m	c	CHIN	San Mateo	Half Moon Bay P O	87	408
AKEKE								
Martha	50	f	w	NC	Colusa	Colusa Twp	71	285
AKEM								
Almon M	37	m	w	NY	Sierra	Gibson Twp	89	543
AKEMAN								
William	32	m	w	HANO	San Francisco	7-Wd San Francisco	81	217
AKEN								
Edward	43	m	w	ME	Sacramento	Sutter Twp	77	391
James	30	m	w	IREL	San Francisco	San Francisco P O	83	413
AKER								
Nicholas	50	m	w	NY	Nevada	Nevada Twp	75	292
AKERLY								
C	45	m	w	PRUS	Alameda	Murray Twp	68	123
Thomas	25	m	w	CANA	Sacramento	4-Wd Sacramento	77	319
AKERMAN								
Carlotta	38	f	w	CHIL	Calaveras	Copperopolis P O	70	246
David	32	m	w	WI	Butte	Chico Twp	70	29
Margaret	77	f	w	NH	Alameda	Alvarado	68	305
AKERS								
Albertis	26	m	w	TX	Fresno	Kings Rvr P O	72	204
Ana M	30	m	w	IA	Tehama	Tehama Twp	92	192
Anderson	40	m	w	KY	Fresno	Kings Rvr P O	72	204
Hanry	25	m	w	MA	San Francisco	6-Wd San Francisco	81	146
Harvey	42	m	w	KY	Fresno	Kings Rvr P O	72	204
Henry	30	m	w	TX	Fresno	Kings Rvr P O	72	204
John S	57	m	w	KY	Fresno	Kings Rvr P O	72	204
John W	31	m	w	KY	Tehama	Tehama Twp	92	192
Larkin B	50	m	w	KY	Los Angeles	Los Angeles Twp	73	474
Mary	40	f	w	NJ	San Francisco	San Francisco P O	80	419
Nancy	78	f	w	VA	Trinity	Trinity Center Pct	92	204
Stephen	55	m	w	VA	Sonoma	Sonoma Twp	91	442
T M	36	m	w	IN	San Bernardino	San Bernardino Twp	78	434
AKI								
Ah	24	m	c	CHIN	Mendocino	Point Arena Twp	74	215
AKIN								
Joswaks	29	m	w	PORT	Placer	Bath P O	76	423
William	25	m	w	SCOT	Marin	Novato Twp	74	11
Wm	36	m	w	OH	El Dorado	Coloma Twp	72	6
AKINE								
Mathew	37	m	w	IREL	Sonoma	Bodega Twp	91	251
AKINS								
Francisko	25	f	w	WURT	El Dorado	Placerville	72	107
James	45	m	w	IREL	Trinity	Trinity Center Pct	92	204
Robt	41	m	w	IREL	Shasta	Horsetown P O	89	505
AKOM								
Wm	36	m	w	LA	Merced	Snelling P O	74	261
AKON								
Sy	18	m	c	CHIN	San Francisco	1-Wd San Francisco	79	98
AKOSTAN								
Thomas	24	m	w	CA	Marin	San Rafael Twp	74	39
AKRICH								
George	35	m	w	AR	Los Angeles	El Monte Twp	73	463
AKUN								
Mary	70	f	w	IREL	Contra Costa	San Pablo Twp	71	357
AL								
San	35	m	c	CHIN	Sacramento	1-Wd Sacramento	77	197
ALA								
Chop	21	m	c	CHIN	San Joaquin	1-Wd Stockton	86	143
ALADDI								
William	26	m	w	ITAL	San Francisco	San Francisco P O	80	426
ALAIR								
Juan Jesus	52	m	w	MEXI	Los Angeles	San Jose Twp	73	620

Series M593

© 2001 by Heritage Quest. All rights reserved.

Name	Age	S	R	B-PL	County	Locale	Roll	Pg
						Series M593		
ALALIJA								
Ragosa	25	f	w	MEXI	Yuba	Marysville	93	574
ALAM								
James	34	m	w	MO	Stanislaus	Empire Twp	92	31
ALAMANY								
James P	57	m	w	FRAN	San Francisco	6-Wd San Francisco	81	82
ALAMERON								
Juana	16	f	w	CA	Santa Clara	1-Wd San Jose	88	263
ALAMIRAND								
Santiago	41	m	w	CHIL	Fresno	Millerton P O	72	159
ALAMON								
Peaphilla	38	f	w	MEXI	San Diego	Julian Dist	78	474
ALANEZ								
Brigeda	18	f	w	CA	Los Angeles	Los Angeles	73	526
ALANG								
Ah	20	m	c	CHIN	Sacramento	1-Wd Sacramento	77	200
ALANTES								
Jesus	64	m	w	MEXI	Contra Costa	Martinez Twp	71	350
ALARDE								
Juan	56	m	w	CHIL	Calaveras	San Andreas P O	70	180
ALARI								
Henry	29	m	w	NY	San Francisco	San Francisco P O	85	850
ALARIS								
Louisa	17	f	w	CA	Los Angeles	Los Angeles	73	549
ALASKA								
Catalina	22	f	w	MEXI	San Francisco	8-Wd San Francisco	82	309
Levi	40	m	w	PRUS	Inyo	Lone Pine Twp	73	332
ALASKAS								
Eman	35	m	w	MEXI	San Bernardino	San Bernardino Twp	78	420
ALASON								
Alfred	22	m	w	MEXI	Santa Clara	1-Wd San Jose	88	225
ALASTER								
Nicolasta	34	f	w	CHIL	Calaveras	San Andreas P O	70	197
ALATORN								
Parfisco	24	m	w	MEXI	Monterey	San Juan Twp	74	401
ALATORRE								
Antonio	40	m	w	MEXI	Santa Cruz	Pajaro Twp	89	357
ALATORRI								
Theophilus	30	m	w	MEXI	San Francisco	1-Wd San Francisco	79	134
ALAVADA								
Lewis	40	m	w	PORT	Alameda	Brooklyn Twp	68	55
ALAXANDERSON								
A	35	m	w	PRUS	Sierra	Lincoln Twp	89	551
ALBACK								
A J W	43	m	w	DENM	Merced	Snelling P O	74	256
ALBAN								
Anthony	42	m	w	HAMB	San Francisco	San Francisco P O	83	309
W G	49	m	w	OH	Mendocino	Ukiah Twp	74	237
ALBAUGH								
Sol	32	m	w	OH	Stanislaus	Empire Twp	92	38
Timothy	20	m	w	OH	San Francisco	1-Wd San Francisco	79	64
ALBECHTSSON								
Axel	24	m	w	SWED	San Francisco	1-Wd San Francisco	79	122
ALBEE								
Andrew R	38	m	w	ME	Placer	Pino Twp	76	470
Edward C	23	m	w	ME	Mendocino	Point Arena Twp	74	204
Henry	27	m	w	VA	Yolo	Putah Twp	93	515
Henry A	29	m	w	CANA	Placer	Newcastle Twp	76	477
Mary	34	f	w	CANA	Placer	Newcastle Twp	76	475
ALBERADO								
Antonio	24	m	w	CA	San Diego	Warners Rancho Dis	78	529
ALBERDING								
C H	61	m	w	GERM	Tuolumne	Columbia P O	93	336
ALBERG								
Frank	27	m	w	SWED	San Francisco	3-Wd San Francisco	79	293
P	21	m	w	SWED	Sierra	Table Rock Twp	89	576
ALBERGER								
Jacob	47	m	w	PRUS	Nevada	Little York Twp	75	239
ALBERIGI								
Telice	24	m	w	ITAL	Sonoma	Analy Twp	91	241
ALBERLIGE								
B	42	m	w	FRAN	Calaveras	Copperopolis P O	70	225
ALBERNE								
Louis	51	m	w	ITAL	Santa Barbara	Santa Barbara P O	87	488
ALBERRY								
Richard M	28	m	w	OH	Colusa	Monroe Twp	71	311
ALBERS								
Adolph	38	m	w	NY	Santa Clara	San Jose Twp	88	216
Anthony	43	m	w	PRUS	San Francisco	San Francisco P O	83	398
Charles	36	m	w	MD	San Francisco	San Francisco P O	83	36
Claus H	37	m	w	HANO	Klamath	Dillon Twp	73	369
Marcus	43	m	w	PRUS	San Francisco	San Francisco P O	83	40
Paul	40	m	w	BADE	Butte	Hamilton Twp	70	70
Salassatus	35	f	i	CA	Klamath	Dillon Twp	73	369
ALBERSON								
John	32	m	w	DENM	Alameda	Eden Twp	68	84
ALBERT								
Adonia	77	f	w	BAVA	San Francisco	San Francisco P O	83	22
Caroline	25	f	w	BAVA	San Francisco	San Francisco P O	80	354
Charles	30	m	w	PORT	Sacramento	Georgianna Twp	77	124
Charles	25	m	w	PRUS	San Francisco	San Francisco P O	80	416
David	67	m	w	PA	Yuba	New York Twp	93	638
David W	36	m	w	OH	Yuba	New York Twp	93	639
E	7	m	w	CA	San Francisco	San Francisco P O	85	828
Edward	42	m	w	PRUS	San Luis Obispo	San Luis Obispo Tw	87	299
Edward	30	m	w	SAXO	San Mateo	Half Moon Bay P O	87	392
Emma	45	f	w	ENGL	Contra Costa	Martinez P O	71	419
Ex	48	m	w	FRAN	Sierra	Sears Twp	89	561
Frank	44	m	w	ENGL	San Francisco	2-Wd San Francisco	79	156
Franz	56	m	w	FRAN	Calaveras	San Andreas P O	70	218
Fred	58	m	w	FRAN	Sierra	Table Rock Twp	89	573
George	40	m	w	WURT	Santa Clara	Gilroy Twp	88	81
George	34	m	w	PRUS	Calaveras	Copperopolis P O	70	259
Henry	31	m	w	HCAS	Santa Clara	2-Wd San Jose	88	327
James	25	m	w	PRUS	San Francisco	San Francisco P O	83	281
James W	34	m	w	OH	Yuba	New York Twp	93	638
John	49	m	w	TN	Sutter	Yuba Twp	92	140
John	44	m	w	PRUS	Butte	Mountain Spring Tw	70	87
John	36	m	w	MO	San Francisco	1-Wd San Francisco	79	57
John	20	m	w	IREL	San Francisco	1-Wd San Francisco	79	113
Joseph	40	m	w	PORT	Sacramento	Georgianna Twp	77	123
Joseph	40	m	w	FRAN	Kern	Tehachapi P O	73	356
Jules	30	m	w	AFRI	San Francisco	11-Wd San Francisc	84	631
S	5	m	w	CA	San Francisco	San Francisco P O	85	828
Wm	11	m	w	CA	San Francisco	San Francisco P O	85	828
ALBERTI								
Francis	45	m	w	ITAL	San Francisco	San Francisco P O	80	461
Francis	24	m	w	ITAL	San Francisco	San Francisco P O	80	463
Giuseppe	21	m	w	ITAL	San Francisco	11-Wd San Francisc	84	594
ALBERTO								
Chas	27	m	w	ITAL	San Joaquin	3-Wd Stockton	86	245
Dio	30	m	w	MEXI	Sacramento	2-Wd Sacramento	77	215
ALBERTOLA								
Bernard	36	m	w	SWIT	Santa Clara	2-Wd San Jose	88	320
Mary A	29	f	w	SWIT	Santa Clara	2-Wd San Jose	88	320
ALBERTS								
Cornelius	44	m	w	HANO	Santa Barbara	San Buenaventura P	87	448
Rudolph	48	m	w	PRUS	San Francisco	San Francisco P O	83	175
ALBERTSON								
Jos	49	m	w	IN	Sonoma	Healdsburg & Mendo	91	282
Joseph R	40	m	w	NY	San Francisco	8-Wd San Francisco	82	433
Lauritz	29	m	w	DENM	Monterey	Pajaro Twp	74	370
Wm A	30	m	w	OH	Shasta	Millville P O	89	491
Wm J	20	m	w	MI	San Francisco	San Francisco P O	83	199
ALBERTY								
A J	33	m	w	AR	Tehama	Paynes Crk Twp	92	160
ALBES								
Juan	68	m	w	CA	Monterey	Monterey	74	359
ALBIGHT								
Joshua	40	m	w	CANA	Calaveras	San Andreas P O	70	192
ALBINO								
Trugillo	24	m	w	MEXI	San Diego	San Luis Rey	78	514
ALBION								
Paul	19	m	w	IL	San Francisco	11-Wd San Francisc	84	679
ALBISA								
M Josefa	24	f	w	CA	Monterey	Alisal Twp	74	296
ALBISCO								
Juan	16	m	w	MEXI	Sierra	Sears Twp	89	560
ALBISO								
Carlos	17	m	w	CA	Monterey	Alisal Twp	74	296
Jose A	55	m	w	CA	Monterey	Alisal Twp	74	296
Maria	27	f	w	CA	Monterey	Alisal Twp	74	294
Nicolas	17	m	w	CA	Monterey	Alisal Twp	74	296
ALBITRO								
Petra	18	f	w	CA	Monterey	Salinas Twp	74	313
ALBON								
Edward	69	m	w	ENGL	Santa Clara	1-Wd San Jose	88	254
ALBONO								
John	24	m	w	FRAN	Amador	Sutter Crk P O	69	407
ALBONOS								
Jose	55	m	w	SPAI	Marin	San Rafael	74	48
Pedro	19	m	w	MEXI	Marin	Tomales Twp	74	85
ALBORELLI								
Antone	27	m	w	ITAL	San Francisco	8-Wd San Francisco	82	353
ALBORN								
John	30	m	w	MI	Amador	Sutter Crk P O	69	400
Thos	30	m	w	ENGL	Tehama	Merrill	92	197
ALBORO								
John	24	m	w	PA	San Joaquin	2-Wd Stockton	86	164
ALBRECH								
John	23	m	w	HANO	San Francisco	11-Wd San Francisc	84	567
ALBRECHT								
Athenia	29	f	w	HAMB	San Francisco	8-Wd San Francisco	82	361
Chas	35	m	w	HDAR	Placer	Bath P O	76	426
Chas	20	m	w	GERM	San Francisco	8-Wd San Francisco	82	375
George	33	m	w	BADE	Contra Costa	Martinez P O	71	380
J	19	m	w	ENGL	Sacramento	1-Wd Sacramento	77	184
John	43	m	w	HANO	San Francisco	8-Wd San Francisco	82	359
John	30	m	w	SWIT	San Francisco	8-Wd San Francisco	82	438
Joseph	40	m	w	BADE	San Francisco	San Francisco P O	80	462
Joseph	28	m	w	BADE	San Francisco	San Francisco P O	80	467
Richard	41	m	w	SAXO	San Francisco	8-Wd San Francisco	82	479
Richard	26	m	w	GERM	Klamath	Camp Gaston	73	372
ALBRET								
B	48	m	w	PRUS	Sierra	Lincoln Twp	89	551
ALBRIGHT								
Fred	35	m	w	PRUS	Sutter	Yuba Twp	92	146
Fredrick	49	m	w	PORT	San Francisco	San Francisco P O	80	333
Harrison	25	m	w	NY	Santa Clara	Redwood Twp	88	127
Henry D	50	m	w	PA	Napa	Napa	75	44
James	29	m	w	NY	Santa Clara	San Jose Twp	88	180
Joseph	29	m	w	OH	Santa Cruz	Soquel Twp	89	439
ALBRO								
David	41	m	w	NY	Butte	Hamilton Twp	70	70

© 2001 by Heritage Quest. All rights reserved.

Name	Age	S	R	B-PL	County	Locale	Series M593 Roll	Pg
David	41	m	w	NY	Butte	Chico Twp	70	50
Stephen	37	m	w	NY	Shasta	Buckeye P O	89	482
ALBROUGH								
Edwd	30	f	w	MI	Butte	Chico Twp	70	23
ALBY								
E R	46	m	w	NH	Sierra	Sierra Twp	89	564
G H	44	m	w	NH	Sierra	Sierra Twp	89	564
Joseph	29	m	w	NY	Solano	Montezuma Twp	90	68
Stephen	40	m	w	ME	Amador	Fiddletown P O	69	441
Uriah	42	m	w	ME	Humboldt	Eureka Twp	72	257
ALBYN								
Cyrus	54	m	w	CT	Humboldt	Mattole Twp	72	288
ALCALDA								
Meriquita	4	f	w	MEXI	Santa Clara	2-Wd San Jose	88	310
ALCANTRA								
Francisco	32	m	w	MEXI	Marin	Nicasio Twp	74	15
ALCERMAN								
John	43	m	w	HANO	Trinity	Douglas	92	234
ALCIDO								
Narciso	22	m	w	MEXI	Los Angeles	Los Angeles	73	507
ALCOCK								
Clarence	16	m	w	NY	Fresno	Millerton P O	72	155
ALCON								
A	31	m	w	PRUS	San Joaquin	2-Wd Stockton	86	195
ALCONE								
Mary	14	f	i	AK	San Francisco	7-Wd San Francisco	81	157
ALCORAGE								
Joseph	20	m	i	MEXI	Inyo	Cerro Gordo Twp	73	319
ALCORD								
A R	36	m	w	MA	San Joaquin	3-Wd Stockton	86	229
ALCORN								
Banceford	33	m	w	MO	Nevada	Grass Valley Twp	75	227
Branceford	58	m	w	KY	Santa Cruz	Santa Cruz Twp	89	396
George S	28	m	w	IL	Colusa	Colusa Twp	71	285
John H	32	m	w	KY	Santa Cruz	Santa Cruz Twp	89	395
William	36	m	w	ME	Stanislaus	San Joaquin Twp	92	82
ALCOTT								
James	38	m	w	NY	Sacramento	American Twp	77	68
ALDA								
Lewis	36	m	w	HANO	Siskiyou	Hamburg Twp	89	597
ALDACO								
Doloros	50	m	w	MEXI	Monterey	San Antonio Twp	74	316
ALDAE								
Celandonia	40	m	w	MEXI	Santa Barbara	Santa Maria P O	87	514
ALDEALDER								
J	29	m	w	ITAL	Sierra	Butte Twp	89	508
ALDEIZ								
Ramon	37	m	w	MEXI	Fresno	Millerton P O	72	159
ALDELL								
David	54	m	w	DE	Sutter	Vernon Twp	92	133
ALDEMAN								
Joseph	38	m	w	PA	Stanislaus	Empire Twp	92	44
ALDEN								
Benj F	58	m	w	NY	Sonoma	Analy Twp	91	238
E B	32	m	w	ME	Solano	Vallejo	90	142
Hiram	18	m	w	MI	Alameda	Brooklyn Twp	68	49
S E	55	m	w	CT	Alameda	Oakland	68	219
Saml B	44	m	w	MA	San Francisco	San Francisco P O	85	736
Saml J	39	m	w	IN	El Dorado	Georgetown Twp	72	45
Thomas H	45	m	w	VT	Mendocino	Point Arena Twp	74	215
ALDENFER								
John	28	m	w	MO	Solano	Silveyville Twp	90	74
ALDER								
Charles	20	m	w	PA	Alpine	Silver Mtn P O	69	306
Frank	32	m	w	FRAN	Calaveras	San Andreas P O	70	158
Henry	45	m	w	PRUS	Santa Clara	San Jose Twp	88	199
Joseph	26	m	w	HANO	San Francisco	1-Wd San Francisco	79	56
ALDERMAN								
Alvira	40	f	w	NY	Sacramento	Brighton Twp	77	79
Chas	13	m	w	CA	Sacramento	4-Wd Sacramento	77	363
E M	31	m	w	OH	Monterey	Castroville Twp	74	325
Gilbert	24	m	w	OH	Monterey	San Antonio Twp	74	320
Richard S	45	m	w	ENGL	Nevada	Grass Valley Twp	75	208
ALDERSEY								
Ellen	45	f	w	ENGL	Nevada	Grass Valley Twp	75	159
ALDERSLEY								
John	62	m	w	ENGL	Butte	Wyandotte Twp	70	146
W	35	m	w	ENGL	Lake	Morgan Valley	73	425
ALDERSON								
F B	26	m	w	MA	Sacramento	4-Wd Sacramento	77	373
George	36	m	w	ENGL	El Dorado	Placerville Twp	72	92
Henry	55	m	w	TX	Sacramento	Cosumnes Twp	77	93
J	40	m	w	ENGL	Sierra	Butte Twp	89	512
Richard	56	m	w	ENGL	El Dorado	Placerville	72	112
Robert	26	m	w	ENGL	Marin	San Rafael Twp	74	38
Thomas	39	m	w	ENGL	El Dorado	Placerville Twp	72	92
Wm	12	m	w	CA	Butte	Ophir Twp	70	97
ALDERVERDE								
Henriette	30	f	w	FRAN	San Francisco	5-Wd San Francisco	81	30
Julia	20	f	w	FRAN	San Francisco	5-Wd San Francisco	81	30
ALDIN								
A C	36	m	w	PA	Alameda	Oakland	68	138
ALDINGER								
John J	32	m	w	OH	Sacramento	Franklin Twp	77	108
ALDONNA								
Colchita	25	f	w	CAME	Sacramento	2-Wd Sacramento	77	244
ALDRIANO								
J	15	m	w	CA	Santa Clara	Almaden Twp	88	20
ALDRICH								
B C	34	f	w	MS	Alameda	Oakland	68	181
Brace	40	m	w	SCOT	Del Norte	Happy Camp Twp	71	472
Doughlas	34	m	w	MA	Nevada	Rough & Ready Twp	75	335
Edgar B	24	m	w	MI	Yolo	Cottonwood Twp	93	470
F	10	f	w	AZ	Los Angeles	Los Angeles	73	570
Frank	45	m	w	KY	Santa Cruz	Pajaro Twp	89	353
Fred	45	m	w	PORT	San Francisco	11-Wd San Francisc	84	614
George D	41	m	w	NH	Placer	Lincoln P O	76	484
Henry	60	m	w	NH	Mariposa	Mariposa P O	74	122
J	38	m	w	NY	Yuba	Marysville	93	604
Jesse W	51	m	w	MA	Yolo	Cottonwood Twp	93	470
John	23	m	w	OH	San Francisco	San Francisco P O	80	479
John H	37	m	w	HANO	Calaveras	Copperopolis P O	70	224
John W	42	m	w	IN	Santa Cruz	Pajaro Twp	89	358
Julius	45	m	w	MA	Siskiyou	Callahan P O	89	624
Lucius B	50	m	w	RI	Santa Cruz	Santa Cruz Twp	89	391
Max	33	m	w	PA	Butte	Ophir Twp	70	119
Milton	72	m	w	NH	Sacramento	Brighton Twp	77	78
Ruben	45	m	w	VT	Marin	Novato Twp	74	9
William	46	m	w	NH	San Francisco	San Francisco P O	80	429
William	43	m	w	RI	Alameda	Oakland	68	206
William	41	m	w	KY	Kern	Havilah P O	73	351
ALDRICK								
David	34	m	w	MO	San Bernardino	San Bernardino Twp	78	433
Wm	13	m	w	ME	Napa	Napa Twp	75	73
ALDRID								
Laura	19	f	w	FRAN	San Joaquin	1-Wd Stockton	86	121
Robert	52	m	w	ENGL	San Francisco	7-Wd San Francisco	81	196
ALDRIDG								
Theadore	37	m	w	OH	Humboldt	Mattole Twp	72	287
ALDRIDGE								
Chas	50	m	w	MA	Butte	Ophir Twp	70	117
Chester	25	m	w	CANA	Monterey	Pajaro Twp	74	377
Fred	35	m	w	MA	Butte	Ophir Twp	70	100
Henry	29	m	w	OH	San Francisco	San Francisco P O	83	232
Jonathan	47	m	w	PA	San Joaquin	Union Twp	86	268
Joseph	40	m	w	TN	Tuolumne	Chinese Camp P O	93	381
Saml	20	m	w	ENGL	Sierra	Sears Twp	89	560
Susan	49	f	w	ME	San Francisco	6-Wd San Francisco	81	81
Wm	52	m	w	KY	Shasta	Millville P O	89	488
ALDRIGE								
Thos	20	m	w	MA	San Joaquin	Douglas Twp	86	50
ALDRO								
Antonio	50	m	w	ITAL	San Francisco	2-Wd San Francisco	79	165
ALEAQEEZ								
Jesus	44	m	w	MEXI	Tulare	Visalia	92	299
ALECK								
John	70	m	w	NY	San Francisco	5-Wd San Francisco	81	6
ALEGERA								
Antonio	30	m	w	MEXI	San Diego	Coronado	78	466
ALEGRA								
Blisario	30	m	w	MEXI	Los Angeles	Los Angeles Twp	73	465
ALEGREA								
Jesus	49	m	i	MEXI	San Luis Obispo	Salinas Twp	87	295
ALEGRIA								
Conus	30	m	i	MEXI	Inyo	Cerro Gordo Twp	73	323
ALEIN								
Clorrock	45	m	w	FRAN	Calaveras	San Andreas P O	70	190
ALEJO								
Angelo	32	m	w	ITAL	Mariposa	Mariposa P O	74	98
ALEM								
John	30	m	w	SHOL	San Francisco	2-Wd San Francisco	79	211
ALEMAN								
Bernardo	30	m	w	SPAI	San Francisco	1-Wd San Francisco	79	123
ALENA								
Frank	36	m	m	MEXI	Trinity	Weaverville Pct	92	227
Justo	45	m	w	CA	Santa Barbara	Santa Barbara P O	87	494
ALENEL								
Peter	59	m	w	ITAL	San Joaquin	1-Wd Stockton	86	155
ALENIA								
Manuel	43	m	i	CHIL	Inyo	Cerro Gordo Twp	73	320
ALENSTEIN								
Charles	37	m	w	SAXO	Merced	Snelling P O	74	268
ALERMAN								
Dominico	60	m	w	MEXI	Calaveras	San Andreas P O	70	171
ALERS								
August	45	m	w	OLDE	San Francisco	1-Wd San Francisco	79	110
Wm	45	m	w	PRUS	Mendocino	Sanel Twp	74	228
ALERT								
August	35	m	w	AUST	Colusa	Spring Valley Twp	71	342
ALESKA								
W E	38	m	w	PRUS	San Joaquin	3-Wd Stockton	86	243
ALEX								
H	34	m	w	PRUS	Alameda	Oakland	68	181
Joseph	40	m	w	PORT	San Francisco	San Francisco P O	80	533
Joseph	38	m	w	PORT	San Francisco	2-Wd San Francisco	79	138
L	40	m	w	MA	Alameda	Oakland	68	182
M	30	f	w	HI	Alameda	Oakland	68	185
ALEXANDER								
A C	33	m	w	VA	Sierra	Eureka Twp	89	526
A M	46	m	w	ME	Alameda	Oakland	68	157
A P	28	m	w	ME	Solano	Vallejo	90	141
Abraham	51	m	w	POLA	Santa Cruz	Watsonville	89	365
Abram	40	m	w	POLA	Sacramento	Granite Twp	77	143

© 2001 by Heritage Quest. All rights reserved.

Name	Age	S	R	B-PL	County	Locale	Roll	Pg
						Series M593		
Albert	36	m	w	PRUS	San Francisco	5-Wd San Francisco	81	4
Allen	37	m	w	IL	Colusa	California Twp	71	279
Ambrose	45	m	w	RI	San Bernardino	San Bernardino Twp	78	422
Analia M	22	f	w	IN	Santa Cruz	Santa Cruz	89	421
Andres	13	m	w	CA	San Diego	San Luis Rey	78	514
Andrew	57	m	w	FRAN	Solano	Denverton Twp	90	27
Andrew	45	m	w	FRAN	Solano	Maine Prairie Twp	90	47
Andrew	22	m	w	PA	Butte	Chico Twp	70	20
Andrew R	25	m	w	OH	Santa Clara	1-Wd San Jose	88	247
B B	43	m	w	KY	Klamath	Klamath Twp	73	370
B F	58	m	w	TN	Sacramento	3-Wd Sacramento	77	297
Barton S	47	m	w	RI	San Francisco	San Francisco P O	83	99
Bernard	40	m	w	PRUS	Sacramento	2-Wd Sacramento	77	218
C	47	f	w	MA	Sacramento	3-Wd Sacramento	77	297
Caroline	79	f	w	FRAN	San Francisco	8-Wd San Francisco	82	469
Caroline	70	f	w	FRAN	San Francisco	2-Wd San Francisco	79	246
Caroline	21	f	b	NY	San Francisco	6-Wd San Francisco	81	110
Carrie	26	f	w	IREL	San Francisco	11-Wd San Francisc	84	689
Castain	41	m	w	FRAN	Butte	Chico Twp	70	19
Catharine	25	f	w	SCOT	San Mateo	Menlo Park P O	87	377
Catherine	40	f	w	ENGL	San Francisco	7-Wd San Francisco	81	257
Charles	33	m	w	MA	San Francisco	11-Wd San Francisc	84	703
Charles M	34	m	w	OH	San Mateo	Redwood Twp	87	364
Chas	50	m	w	IL	Sonoma	Healdsburg	91	274
Chas	35	m	w	ME	San Francisco	8-Wd San Francisco	82	322
Chas G	25	m	w	AL	Fresno	Millerton P O	72	152
Cyrus	65	m	w	PA	Sonoma	Mendocino Twp	91	289
D	36	m	w	ME	Siskiyou	Scott Valley Twp	89	614
D	34	m	w	PRUS	Sierra	Sierra Twp	89	562
Daniel	58	m	w	SCOT	San Francisco	11-Wd San Francisc	84	700
David	64	m	w	PRUS	San Francisco	San Francisco P O	83	322
David	42	m	w	SCOT	Tuolumne	Big Oak Flat P O	93	394
David	40	m	w	PA	Nevada	Bridgeport Twp	75	117
David W	60	m	w	IREL	Los Angeles	Wilmington Twp	73	639
Driden	31	m	w	VA	Sierra	Eureka Twp	89	526
Edward	30	m	w	PRUS	San Francisco	San Francisco P O	83	371
Edwd L	32	m	w	NY	San Francisco	1-Wd San Francisco	79	103
Edwin	40	m	w	PRUS	San Francisco	San Francisco P O	83	409
Edwin B	56	m	w	TN	Calaveras	Copperopolis P O	70	250
Eli	84	m	w	PRUS	San Francisco	8-Wd San Francisco	82	469
Eli	84	m	w	FRAN	San Francisco	2-Wd San Francisco	79	246
Elijah	67	m	b	KY	Calaveras	Copperopolis P O	70	249
Elizabeth	14	f	w	CA	San Francisco	San Francisco P O	85	872
Elizabeth	14	f	w	CA	San Francisco	8-Wd San Francisco	82	494
F	33	m	w	KY	Solano	Vallejo	90	203
Frank	40	m	w	KY	Los Angeles	Los Angeles	73	556
Fred	25	m	w	ENGL	San Francisco	San Francisco P O	83	305
Geo	26	m	w	AL	Fresno	Millerton P O	72	193
Geo W	21	m	w	ME	San Francisco	San Francisco P O	85	730
George	37	m	w	FRAN	San Francisco	San Francisco P O	83	249
George	24	m	w	WI	Plumas	Quartz Twp	77	40
George C	54	m	w	NY	Los Angeles	Wilmington Twp	73	639
Granville	38	m	w	NC	Santa Clara	Fremont Twp	88	57
Hannah	78	f	w	PRUS	San Francisco	1-Wd San Francisco	79	114
Henry	51	m	w	KY	Del Norte	Crescent Twp	71	457
Henry	28	m	w	NY	San Francisco	11-Wd San Francisc	84	700
Henry N	38	m	w	OH	Los Angeles	Wilmington Twp	73	638
Henry W	50	m	w	AR	Los Angeles	Los Nietos Twp	73	582
Horatio	37	m	w	ME	El Dorado	Placerville	72	123
Hoyt W	24	m	w	KY	Santa Cruz	Pajaro Twp	89	352
I H	40	m	w	IN	Sierra	Sierra Twp	89	568
Isaac	26	m	b	NC	San Bernardino	San Bernardino Twp	78	445
Israel	31	m	w	POLA	San Francisco	San Francisco P O	80	415
J	43	m	w	PRUS	Alameda	Oakland	68	147
J	36	m	w	VA	Sierra	Downieville Twp	89	514
J F	17	m	w	CA	Alameda	Oakland	68	242
J K	30	m	w	MS	Sacramento	1-Wd Sacramento	77	174
J L	28	m	w	MO	Sonoma	Bodega Twp	91	253
J S	44	m	w	SCOT	Tuolumne	Columbia P O	93	342
James	69	m	w	KY	Yolo	Cottonwood Twp	93	472
James	54	m	w	LA	Humboldt	South Fork Twp	72	302
James	50	m	w	IREL	Calaveras	San Andreas P O	70	189
James	49	m	w	SCOT	San Francisco	11-Wd San Francisc	84	672
James	44	m	w	LA	Yolo	Washington Twp	93	533
James	44	m	w	KY	Sacramento	2-Wd Sacramento	77	213
James	40	m	w	IREL	Alameda	Murray Twp	68	123
James	36	m	w	IREL	San Francisco	San Francisco P O	83	23
James	30	m	w	NY	Los Angeles	Los Nietos Twp	73	585
James S	44	m	w	KY	Sacramento	2-Wd Sacramento	77	251
Jane	50	f	w	SCOT	San Francisco	7-Wd San Francisco	81	201
Jane	49	f	w	SCOT	San Francisco	San Francisco P O	83	187
Jo	42	m	w	NY	San Francisco	5-Wd San Francisco	81	24
John	56	m	w	KY	Colusa	Colusa Twp	71	286
John	41	m	w	TN	Inyo	Lone Pine Twp	73	331
John	38	m	w	KY	Stanislaus	Branch Twp	92	1
John	32	m	w	PA	Stanislaus	Empire Twp	92	60
John	30	m	w	IREL	San Francisco	7-Wd San Francisco	81	257
John	30	m	w	AZOR	Monterey	Castroville Twp	74	333
John	24	m	b	NC	Yolo	Grafton Twp	93	492
John	24	m	w	IREL	Sonoma	Petaluma Twp	91	352
John H	39	m	w	SC	Calaveras	San Andreas P O	70	187
John S	54	m	w	TN	Mariposa	Mariposa P O	74	130
John W	22	m	w	MO	Yolo	Cottonwood Twp	93	472
Joseph	50	m	w	PA	San Francisco	2-Wd San Francisco	79	248
Joseph	42	m	w	FRAN	San Francisco	8-Wd San Francisco	82	469
Joseph	31	m	w	AR	Stanislaus	Branch Twp	92	3
Joseph	26	m	w	IL	Sacramento	4-Wd Sacramento	77	321

Name	Age	S	R	B-PL	County	Locale	Roll	Pg
						Series M593		
Joseph	25	m	w	ITAL	Mendocino	Point Arena Twp	74	204
L L	49	m	w	NH	Alameda	Oakland	68	236
Leon	32	m	w	FRAN	Santa Clara	Almaden Twp	88	14
Levi	41	m	w	OH	Monterey	San Benito Twp	74	381
Louis	52	m	w	PRUS	San Francisco	San Francisco P O	85	818
Lyman	33	m	w	PRUS	San Francisco	San Francisco P O	83	9
Lysander	41	m	w	MO	Santa Clara	Santa Clara Twp	88	167
Manuel	43	m	w	AZOR	Monterey	Monterey	74	360
Manuel	14	m	i	CA	Monterey	Castroville Twp	74	336
Mary	34	f	w	MEXI	Calaveras	San Andreas P O	70	187
Mendal	30	m	w	BAVA	San Francisco	11-Wd San Francisc	84	534
Michal	27	m	w	AZOR	Monterey	Monterey	74	360
Mitchell	44	m	w	PRUS	San Francisco	San Francisco P O	83	377
Nathan	23	m	w	ME	Placer	Roseville P O	76	351
Philip	40	m	w	PRUS	San Francisco	San Francisco P O	80	534
Preston	30	m	b	DC	Nevada	Nevada Twp	75	290
R	50	m	w	SCOT	Solano	Vallejo	90	161
Rachel	28	f	w	NY	San Francisco	1-Wd San Francisco	79	5
Ragena	45	f	w	FRAN	Calaveras	San Andreas P O	70	198
Ralph	24	m	w	CANA	San Francisco	San Francisco P O	83	179
Reuben	20	m	w	WURT	Yolo	Putah Twp	93	516
Robert	43	m	w	SCOT	San Francisco	San Francisco P O	83	59
Robert	25	m	w	IREL	Los Angeles	Los Angeles	73	546
Robt	34	m	w	IREL	Fresno	Millerton P O	72	187
Robt	30	m	w	SCOT	Siskiyou	Surprise Valley Tw	89	636
S	56	m	w	PRUS	Sutter	Sutter Twp	92	126
S	38	m	w	KY	Lassen	Susanville Twp	73	442
S	38	m	w	POLA	Sacramento	3-Wd Sacramento	77	286
Salmon	47	m	w	PRUS	Placer	Gold Run Twp	76	394
Samuel	32	m	w	NC	Yolo	Grafton Twp	93	483
Samuel H	36	m	w	VA	Los Angeles	Los Angeles	73	534
Samuel O	35	m	w	PRUS	San Francisco	8-Wd San Francisco	82	439
Samul	45	m	w	PRUS	San Francisco	7-Wd San Francisco	81	215
Simon	34	m	w	PRUS	San Francisco	San Francisco P O	80	466
Susan	31	f	w	IL	Sacramento	2-Wd Sacramento	77	243
T	34	m	w	FRAN	San Joaquin	2-Wd Stockton	86	159
T C	42	m	w	KY	Sierra	Table Rock Twp	89	572
T R	27	m	w	IL	Sacramento	4-Wd Sacramento	77	345
Theodore	34	m	w	FRAN	San Francisco	San Francisco P O	80	412
Thomas	50	m	w	OH	Nevada	Rough & Ready Twp	75	325
Thomas D	43	m	w	MO	Santa Cruz	Watsonville	89	364
Vincent	45	m	w	KY	Yolo	Cottonwood Twp	93	472
W G	52	m	w	ME	Solano	Vallejo	90	181
W G	46	m	w	SCOT	Tuolumne	Big Oak Flat P O	93	403
W S	43	m	w	IREL	Alameda	Murray Twp	68	106
William	38	m	w	MO	Nevada	Little York Twp	75	243
William	38	m	w	PA	Santa Clara	1-Wd San Jose	88	269
William	33	m	w	PRUS	Santa Cruz	Watsonville	89	369
William	30	m	b	NY	San Francisco	2-Wd San Francisco	79	171
William	28	m	w	CANA	Alameda	Alvarado	68	304
Wm	42	m	w	CANA	Humboldt	Eureka Twp	72	273
Wm	27	m	w	US	Santa Barbara	San Buenaventura P	87	445
Wm F	34	m	w	MA	San Francisco	San Francisco P O	85	755
ALEXANDRIE								
Alf	43	m	w	OH	San Joaquin	Oneal Twp	86	118
ALEXDER								
Richard	40	m	w	US	Nevada	Little York Twp	75	239
ALF								
Ah	50	m	c	CHIN	Sacramento	1-Wd Sacramento	77	201
ALFAGO								
Manwell	22	m	w	MEXI	Yuba	Marysville	93	617
ALFANO								
Pedro	50	m	w	CHIL	Butte	Kimshew Tpw	70	82
ALFERD								
Bernett	34	m	w	NY	Alameda	Murray Twp	68	104
Matthew	50	m	w	NC	Colusa	Colusa	71	296
ALFERS								
John	40	m	w	PRUS	San Francisco	5-Wd San Francisco	81	15
John Mrs	30	f	w	PRUS	San Francisco	5-Wd San Francisco	81	15
ALFINO								
Peter	48	m	b	CAME	San Mateo	Half Moon Bay P O	87	389
ALFONE								
Antone	27	m	w	ITAL	Mendocino	Big Rvr Twp	74	171
ALFONSE								
Gerold	43	m	w	FRAN	Los Angeles	Los Angeles	73	526
ALFONSO								
Mathew	33	m	w	FRAN	Butte	Ophir Twp	70	101
ALFONTZ								
Wm	35	m	w	SWIT	San Francisco	8-Wd San Francisco	82	349
ALFORD								
Daniel	65	m	w	NJ	Plumas	Indian Twp	77	15
Edwin	33	m	w	TX	Tulare	White Rvr Twp	92	301
George	48	m	w	VT	San Luis Obispo	Morro Twp	87	286
John	32	m	w	ENGL	San Joaquin	Douglas Twp	86	47
John	32	m	w	IREL	Alameda	Oakland	68	176
Martha	42	f	w	TN	Alameda	Eden Twp	68	68
Mary C	48	f	w	GA	Solano	Tremont Twp	90	36
Phillip	25	m	w	CA	Colusa	Colusa	71	292
Richard	55	m	w	ENGL	San Francisco	San Francisco P O	83	357
Ruben	38	m	w	GA	Solano	Tremont Twp	90	34
Sarah	58	f	w	NC	Solano	Suisun Twp	90	109
William	70	m	w	VA	Placer	Lincoln P O	76	482
William	19	m	w	TN	Alameda	Eden Twp	68	67
ALFORDS								
James	43	m	w	CA	Fresno	Millerton P O	72	160
ALFRED								
Charles	26	m	w	MO	Contra Costa	Martinez P O	71	410

© 2001 by Heritage Quest. All rights reserved.

California 1870 Census

Name	Age	S	R	B-PL	County	Locale	Series M593 Roll	Pg
John	48	m	w	ENGL	Calaveras	San Andreas P O	70	166
John	27	m	w	SWED	Sacramento	Franklin Twp	77	113
ALFREY								
Frank	30	f	w	NY	San Francisco	8-Wd San Francisco	82	394
ALFRITZ								
Peter	32	m	w	FRAN	San Francisco	2-Wd San Francisco	79	147
ALGAM								
John	26	m	w	SWED	San Francisco	San Francisco P O	83	302
ALGAN								
Miguel	36	m	w	CHIL	Placer	Auburn P O	76	382
ALGER								
Arthur	25	m	w	VT	Monterey	Pajaro Twp	74	371
Chas	26	m	w	PA	Sacramento	3-Wd Sacramento	77	278
Elizabeth	26	f	w	NY	San Francisco	7-Wd San Francisco	81	246
James	36	m	w	MA	San Francisco	2-Wd San Francisco	79	242
Jas L	72	m	w	PA	Sacramento	3-Wd Sacramento	77	278
Rebecca A	52	f	w	MA	Santa Cruz	Santa Cruz	89	425
William	41	m	w	ENGL	Siskiyou	Callahan P O	89	625
ALGES								
James	38	m	w	IREL	Napa	Napa	75	56
Thomas	38	m	w	IREL	Napa	Napa	75	53
ALGIERS								
Adelia	17	f	w	CA	San Francisco	San Francisco P O	85	804
ALGO								
Ann	64	f	w	IREL	San Joaquin	Douglas Twp	86	40
R S	23	m	w	VA	San Joaquin	Douglas Twp	86	40
ALGOCHE								
John	43	m	w	FRAN	Sutter	Vernon Twp	92	134
ALGRAIN								
John	27	m	w	SWED	Klamath	Trinidad Twp	73	392
ALGRAVA								
Jesus	19	m	w	MEXI	Los Angeles	Los Angeles	73	524
ALGRAVE								
Julius	36	m	w	SHOL	San Francisco	1-Wd San Francisco	79	108
ALGREEN								
Jacob	30	m	w	SWED	Calaveras	Copperopolis P O	70	257
ALGREN								
Theodore	42	m	w	BELG	San Francisco	2-Wd San Francisco	79	213
ALGRO								
Stephens	32	m	w	RI	San Joaquin	2-Wd Stockton	86	168
William	34	m	w	OH	San Diego	Julian Dist	78	470
ALGUES								
John	40	m	w	AUST	Monterey	San Juan Twp	74	394
ALHEARN								
J H	30	m	w	MA	San Francisco	San Francisco P O	85	790
ALHOFF								
Joseph	13	m	w	CA	El Dorado	Coloma Twp	72	7
ALI								
Henry	48	m	m	EIND	Sonoma	Bodega Twp	91	248
Yun	35	m	c	CHIN	Mariposa	Maxwell Crk P O	74	147
ALIATTY								
Antonio	30	m	w	FRAN	Santa Clara	San Jose Twp	88	217
ALICE								
Eugene	30	m	w	PRUS	Sacramento	4-Wd Sacramento	77	372
Mary	9	f	w	CA	San Francisco	11-Wd San Francisc	84	710
ALICK								
Malinda	17	f	w	MO	San Joaquin	Elkhorn Twp	86	62
ALIE								
H	18	m	w	CANA	Sierra	Sierra Twp	89	569
Lang	30	f	c	CHIN	Sacramento	1-Wd Sacramento	77	199
ALIF								
Henry	25	m	w	GERM	Alameda	Eden Twp	68	85
ALIN								
L G	26	m	w	NY	Tuolumne	Chinese Camp P O	93	366
ALINAM								
Frederick	28	m	w	GERM	Marin	San Rafael Twp	74	26
ALINGER								
Chris	40	m	w	PRUS	Sacramento	Center Twp	77	82
ALIRE								
H	29	m	w	MO	Nevada	Eureka Twp	75	139
ALIRIE								
Jesus	31	m	w	MEXI	Santa Clara	Almaden Twp	88	15
ALISALDA								
Dolores	17	f	w	CA	Los Angeles	Los Angeles	73	521
Lucien	21	f	w	CA	Los Angeles	Los Angeles	73	560
ALISALDE								
Peter	33	m	w	FRAN	Los Angeles	Los Angeles	73	523
ALISE								
Anna	18	f	w	PRUS	San Francisco	8-Wd San Francisco	82	374
ALISKO								
Chas	19	m	w	FRAN	San Joaquin	Tulare Twp	86	261
ALISKY								
Dora	68	f	w	GERM	Tuolumne	Columbia P O	93	357
ALISON								
Allen	38	m	w	ME	Mendocino	Big Rvr Twp	74	170
Annie Mrs	30	f	w	VT	Monterey	Alisal Twp	74	292
Jane	37	f	w	NY	San Joaquin	1-Wd Stockton	86	132
Joseph	37	m	w	IL	Inyo	Bishop Crk Twp	73	312
Saml B	45	m	w	SC	Fresno	Millerton P O	72	156
ALITORE								
Silberis	25	m	w	MEXI	Monterey	San Antonio Twp	74	317
ALIUS								
Horn	25	m	i	CA	Alameda	Murray Twp	68	103
ALIVERA								
Augustina	52	f	w	CA	San Luis Obispo	San Luis Obispo Tw	87	315
ALIXES								
Hermann	46	m	w	FRAN	San Francisco	8-Wd San Francisco	82	305
ALJIO								
James L	73	m	w	PA	Sutter	Nicolaus Twp	92	114
John M	46	m	w	OH	Sutter	Nicolaus Twp	92	114
ALKEN								
Albert	19	m	w	FRAN	San Francisco	8-Wd San Francisco	82	289
ALKESS								
Wm	26	m	w	MA	Napa	Napa Twp	75	73
ALKIRK								
Almer L	29	m	w	OH	San Diego	San Diego	78	491
ALKOR								
Thomas	72	m	w	MA	Napa	Napa	75	57
ALKY								
John	31	m	w	MO	Solano	Rio Vista Twp	90	62
ALL								
Chung	27	m	c	CHIN	San Francisco	11-Wd San Francisc	84	681
Samuel	26	m	w	IL	Colusa	Spring Valley Twp	71	344
Yen	30	m	c	CHIN	Placer	Bath P O	76	439
ALLA								
Chimma	18	m	c	CHIN	Sonoma	Vallejo Twp	91	462
ALLAGRETTE								
G	30	m	w	ITAL	San Joaquin	1-Wd Stockton	86	140
ALLAMAN								
Mercedes	16	f	w	CA	Placer	Auburn P O	76	358
ALLAN								
Eugene	19	m	w	NY	San Francisco	5-Wd San Francisco	81	10
George G	43	m	w	SCOT	Nevada	Nevada Twp	75	272
James	25	m	w	ENGL	Sonoma	Sonoma Twp	91	436
John	55	m	w	ENGL	Napa	Napa	75	46
Layton	33	m	w	SCOT	Sonoma	Salt Point	91	392
ALLANGER								
William	35	m	w	PRUS	Solano	Green Valley Twp	90	41
ALLANICE								
Adelaida	18	f	w	CA	Los Angeles	Los Angeles	73	532
ALLANSON								
Horace S	42	m	w	SC	Los Angeles	Wilmington Twp	73	643
ALLARD								
Ellen	29	f	w	MO	Sonoma	Russian Rvr	91	368
Frank	50	m	w	CANA	Amador	Volcano P O	69	386
Patrick	36	f	w	NH	San Joaquin	2-Wd Stockton	86	168
Richard	36	m	w	NH	Humboldt	Bucksport Twp	72	243
William	30	m	w	IREL	San Francisco	San Francisco P O	83	414
ALLARE								
C	5	f	w	CA	Los Angeles	Los Angeles	73	569
F	9	f	w	CA	Los Angeles	Los Angeles	73	569
ALLARHEST								
Christopher	30	m	w	HANO	Stanislaus	San Joaquin Twp	92	76
ALLASON								
Peter	25	m	w	ITAL	San Mateo	Menlo Park P O	87	377
ALLAWAY								
John	39	m	w	CANA	Alameda	Brooklyn	68	32
ALLAY								
Charles W	9	m	w	CA	Sonoma	Analy Twp	91	239
ALLBRIGHT								
Albrict	41	m	w	HAMB	Placer	Bath P O	76	420
Andrew	35	m	w	BADE	San Francisco	11-Wd San Francisc	84	649
Charles	42	m	w	HANO	El Dorado	Placerville Twp	72	93
H M	36	m	w	VA	Tehama	Red Bluff	92	174
Henry	21	m	w	OH	Solano	Vacaville Twp	90	127
John	38	m	w	PRUS	San Francisco	San Francisco P O	80	456
John	26	m	w	IREL	Solano	Rio Vista Twp	90	64
John	24	m	w	IREL	Solano	Silveyville Twp	90	74
William	43	m	w	ENGL	El Dorado	Placerville Twp	72	93
ALLBRIGHTON								
C	34	m	w	ENGL	Sierra	Alleghany & Forest	89	535
ALLCOCK								
Robt W	48	m	w	OH	Shasta	Portugese Flat P O	89	471
William	35	m	w	WALE	Contra Costa	Martinez P O	71	428
ALLCORN								
Andrew	56	m	w	IREL	Santa Clara	San Jose Twp	88	195
ALLCOT								
Henry	37	m	w	OH	Butte	Chico Twp	70	41
ALLEFO								
Rosa	38	m	w	PERU	Marin	Sausalito Twp	74	68
ALLEGRETH								
John	33	m	w	FRAN	San Joaquin	1-Wd Stockton	86	155
ALLEL								
Peter	32	m	w	NY	San Francisco	11-Wd San Francisc	84	552
ALLEN								
---	40	m	w	VT	Santa Cruz	Santa Cruz	89	425
A	37	m	w	OH	San Joaquin	Elkhorn Twp	86	56
A G	43	m	w	CANA	Tuolumne	Big Oak Flat P O	93	406
A H	26	m	w	IL	Humboldt	Eureka Twp	72	275
A W	42	m	w	NY	San Joaquin	1-Wd Stockton	86	150
Abina	52	f	w	VA	Santa Clara	Santa Clara Twp	88	144
Achilles	19	m	w	MO	Colusa	Monroe Twp	71	325
Addison	23	m	w	KY	San Francisco	San Francisco P O	83	227
Ah	40	m	c	CHIN	El Dorado	Mud Springs Twp	72	91
Ah	40	m	c	CHIN	Sacramento	3-Wd Sacramento	77	298
Ah	35	m	c	CHIN	El Dorado	Placerville	72	115
Albert	40	m	w	MO	Stanislaus	Branch Twp	92	6
Albert	37	m	w	NY	Butte	Chico Twp	70	24
Albert	35	m	w	CANA	Tehama	Hunters Twp	92	187
Albert	33	m	w	MO	Los Angeles	Los Nietos Twp	73	575
Alborne	58	m	w	MA	Solano	Benicia	90	17
Alexander	52	m	w	IREL	San Francisco	11-Wd San Francisc	84	621
Alexander	40	m	w	AL	Alameda	Hayward	68	76
Alfred	49	m	w	MA	Amador	Jackson P O	69	328

© 2001 by Heritage Quest. All rights reserved.

Name	Age	S	R	B-PL	County	Locale (Series M593)	Roll	Pg
Alfred	38	m	w	NY	San Francisco	11-Wd San Francisc	84	564
Alice	25	f	w	IREL	San Francisco	8-Wd San Francisco	82	468
Alonzo	24	m	w	CA	Monterey	Castroville Twp	74	328
Amelia	70	f	w	KY	Sonoma	Santa Rosa	91	402
Anderson	49	m	w	MO	Mendocino	Little Lake Twp	74	202
Andrew	48	m	w	MO	Contra Costa	Martinez P O	71	387
Andrew	43	m	w	ME	Butte	Chico Twp	70	46
Andrew	42	m	w	ME	Butte	Chico Twp	70	15
Andrew H	43	m	w	IREL	Mono	Bridgeport P O	74	282
Angeline	56	f	w	NY	Tehama	Red Bluff	92	183
Ann	76	f	w	CT	Butte	Wyandotte Twp	70	143
Ann	38	f	w	IREL	Alameda	Eden Twp	68	90
Anna	25	f	w	ENGL	Colusa	Colusa	71	295
Anna F	32	f	w	MA	San Francisco	5-Wd San Francisco	81	6
Asa	55	m	w	VT	San Francisco	8-Wd San Francisco	82	461
August	45	m	w	FINL	Mendocino	Point Arena Twp	74	213
B B	30	m	w	NY	Alameda	Alameda	68	12
B T	47	m	w	NJ	Nevada	Nevada Twp	75	282
Barney K	26	m	w	MA	Napa	Napa	75	35
Bedford B	55	m	w	IL	Yolo	Cache Crk Twp	93	447
Benj	45	m	w	KY	Sacramento	4-Wd Sacramento	77	376
Benj B	49	m	w	SC	Sonoma	Analy Twp	91	233
Benj F	33	m	w	NH	Butte	Chico Twp	70	18
Benj F	22	m	w	IL	Shasta	French Gulch P O	89	469
Benjamin	34	m	w	ENGL	San Francisco	San Francisco P O	83	319
Benjamin	26	m	w	RI	San Francisco	1-Wd San Francisco	79	118
Benjamin	26	m	w	ME	San Mateo	Redwood Twp	87	362
Benjamin B	58	m	w	PA	Yolo	Putah Twp	93	523
Bill	24	m	w	OH	San Joaquin	Dent Twp	86	23
C	42	m	w	ENGL	Calaveras	Copperopolis P O	70	235
C H	40	m	w	NH	Tuolumne	Chinese Camp P O	93	382
Caleb G	38	m	w	NC	Shasta	Millville P O	89	491
Calvin	38	m	b	AL	Siskiyou	Yreka	89	654
Caroline	39	f	b	KY	Nevada	Nevada Twp	75	280
Charles	47	m	w	OH	Yolo	Cache Crk Twp	93	429
Charles	40	m	w	NY	San Francisco	San Francisco P O	83	322
Charles	40	m	b	VA	Mariposa	Mariposa P O	74	112
Charles	32	m	w	NY	Alameda	Washington Twp	68	299
Charles	30	m	w	ENGL	San Francisco	7-Wd San Francisco	81	223
Charles	26	m	w	IA	Tulare	Visalia	92	296
Charles	25	m	w	ENGL	San Francisco	8-Wd San Francisco	82	389
Charles	21	m	w	IREL	Santa Clara	2-Wd San Jose	88	313
Charles	21	m	w	IA	Solano	Silveyville Twp	90	87
Charles	21	m	w	NY	Klamath	Camp Gaston	73	372
Charles	17	m	w	ENGL	Contra Costa	Martinez P O	71	444
Charles E	48	m	w	NY	Santa Clara	2-Wd San Jose	88	318
Charles R	36	m	w	NY	Placer	Rocklin Twp	76	465
Charles S	25	m	w	MO	Colusa	Colusa	71	292
Charlotta	49	f	w	MA	San Francisco	11-Wd San Francisc	84	505
Charlotte Ann	49	f	w	MA	San Joaquin	Douglas Twp	86	30
Chas	38	m	w	CT	Sacramento	4-Wd Sacramento	77	349
Chas	36	m	w	NY	San Francisco	11-Wd San Francisc	84	564
Chas H	57	m	w	KY	Colusa	Colusa	71	291
Chas H	53	m	w	RI	Napa	Napa	75	50
Chas H	35	m	w	CANA	San Joaquin	Oneal Twp	86	102
Chas K	38	m	w	VA	San Francisco	San Francisco P O	83	323
Chas M	33	m	w	MI	Butte	Ophir Twp	70	93
Chas R	24	m	w	MA	San Francisco	San Francisco P O	83	85
Chinn	30	m	w	MO	Colusa	Colusa	71	293
Christian	30	m	w	MA	Alameda	Brooklyn	68	32
Chs E	33	m	w	MA	Monterey	San Antonio Twp	74	315
Cyrus	36	m	w	VT	Alameda	Washington Twp	68	277
D W	33	m	w	NY	Nevada	Nevada Twp	75	306
Daniel G	43	m	w	AL	Tulare	Visalia	92	291
Darwin L	38	m	w	VT	Placer	Roseville P O	76	352
David	65	m	w	NY	Sonoma	Sonoma Twp	91	433
David	48	m	w	AL	Kern	Linns Valley P O	73	346
David	31	m	w	IL	Sacramento	2-Wd Sacramento	77	252
David	28	m	w	NY	Butte	Chico Twp	70	24
David H	61	m	w	NJ	Colusa	Grand Island Twp	71	306
David H	29	m	w	NY	Butte	Chico Twp	70	26
E	52	m	w	MA	Alameda	Oakland	68	154
E C	27	m	w	ME	Sacramento	1-Wd Sacramento	77	181
E G	38	m	w	VT	Yuba	Marysville	93	592
E H	49	m	w	CT	San Joaquin	Elkhorn Twp	86	53
E N	37	f	w	ME	San Joaquin	2-Wd Stockton	86	197
E S	45	m	w	WI	Alameda	Murray Twp	68	117
Ed	20	m	w	IL	Alameda	Oakland	68	149
Edward	54	m	w	ENGL	San Francisco	7-Wd San Francisco	81	206
Edward	50	m	w	MA	Sacramento	Cosumnes Twp	77	90
Edward	50	m	w	MA	Alpine	Woodfords P O	69	309
Edward	38	m	m	MD	San Francisco	2-Wd San Francisco	79	154
Edward	27	m	w	MD	San Francisco	San Francisco P O	80	537
Edward	22	m	w	PA	Colusa	Monroe Twp	71	325
Edward	22	m	w	IREL	Alameda	Washington Twp	68	280
Edward	20	m	w	ENGL	Santa Clara	Alviso Twp	88	26
Edward	10	m	w	CA	Marin	San Rafael Twp	74	28
Edwd	37	m	w	SWIT	Alameda	Oakland	68	176
Edwin T	32	m	w	ME	Sacramento	Brighton Twp	77	74
Egbert	71	m	w	NY	Placer	Bath P O	76	437
Egbert F	33	m	w	NY	Trinity	Weaverville Pct	92	227
Eliza	55	f	w	IREL	San Francisco	San Francisco P O	85	727
Elizabeth	9	f	w	CA	Nevada	Nevada Twp	75	290
Elizabeth	64	f	w	MA	San Francisco	11-Wd San Francisc	84	620
Elizabeth	48	f	w	IREL	San Francisco	San Francisco P O	83	327
Elizabeth	45	f	w	IREL	Santa Clara	2-Wd San Jose	88	293
Elizabeth	39	f	w	NY	Sacramento	1-Wd Sacramento	77	179
Ella	47	m	w	SWIT	Nevada	Meadow Lake Twp	75	262
Ella	26	f	w	MA	San Francisco	6-Wd San Francisco	81	96
Ellen	16	f	w	ENGL	San Francisco	2-Wd San Francisco	79	254
Emma	24	f	w	IL	Trinity	Douglas	92	234
Ephraim	56	m	w	MA	Marin	Bolinas Twp	74	1
Eskin	24	m	w	SWIT	Alameda	Oakland	68	176
Esther	64	f	w	ENGL	Los Angeles	Los Angeles Twp	73	484
Esther	54	f	w	ENGL	San Francisco	San Francisco P O	83	198
Ethan	63	m	w	NY	Los Angeles	Wilmington Twp	73	645
Ethar	29	m	w	IL	Trinity	Hayfork Valley	92	239
Eugene A	21	m	w	ME	San Francisco	San Francisco P O	83	155
Felix	35	m	w	MO	Yolo	Cache Crk Twp	93	444
Francis	32	m	w	GREE	San Francisco	San Francisco P O	80	345
Francis W	49	m	w	SCOT	Placer	Bath P O	76	431
Francisca	36	f	w	SAME	Butte	Oroville Twp	70	139
Frank	40	m	w	MA	Stanislaus	Empire Twp	92	45
Frank	4	m	w	UT	Sutter	Yuba Twp	92	149
Frank	22	m	w	NY	Sacramento	Brighton Twp	77	79
Frank A	20	m	w	IL	Marin	San Rafael Twp	74	40
Fredk	45	m	w	ENGL	San Francisco	5-Wd San Francisco	81	23
Fredk	39	m	w	MA	San Francisco	5-Wd San Francisco	81	23
G D	28	m	w	NY	Sutter	Vernon Twp	92	138
Gabriel	52	m	w	NY	Los Angeles	Wilmington Twp	73	642
Gabriel	34	m	w	AL	Santa Barbara	San Buenaventura P	87	430
Geo	44	m	w	MA	San Francisco	11-Wd San Francisc	84	607
Geo	41	m	w	SWED	San Francisco	7-Wd San Francisco	81	258
Geo	30	m	w	OH	Santa Clara	Gilroy Twp	88	97
Geo	14	m	w	ME	San Francisco	1-Wd San Francisco	79	94
Geo E	30	m	w	PA	Yuba	Marysville	93	611
Geo F	50	m	w	ME	San Francisco	1-Wd San Francisco	79	94
George	54	m	w	IREL	Yolo	Cache Crk Twp	93	426
George	47	m	w	DENM	Placer	Auburn P O	76	361
George	45	m	w	ENGL	Sonoma	Cloverdale Twp	91	273
George	40	m	w	ENGL	Stanislaus	Empire Twp	92	53
George	40	m	w	WALE	Siskiyou	Scott Valley Twp	89	612
George	4	m	w	CA	Los Angeles	Los Angeles Twp	73	483
George	38	m	w	AL	Kern	Havilah P O	73	338
George	37	m	w	NY	Amador	Sutter Crk P O	69	400
George	36	m	w	MO	Tulare	Farmersville Twp	92	243
George	36	m	w	DC	Napa	Napa	75	42
George	24	m	w	MA	San Francisco	San Francisco P O	83	419
George	22	m	w	ME	Trinity	Hayfork Valley	92	238
George A	45	m	w	MO	Tulare	Kings Rvr Twp	92	252
Gregory	68	m	b	VA	Tulare	Farmersville Twp	92	242
Guideon P	27	m	w	NC	Shasta	Millville P O	89	490
H C	38	m	w	IL	Trinity	North Fork Twp	92	220
H W	42	m	w	MA	Amador	Jackson P O	69	328
Hanah	34	f	w	IREL	San Francisco	7-Wd San Francisco	81	191
Harlow	34	m	w	CT	Butte	Bidwell Twp	70	3
Harvey S	54	m	w	MA	El Dorado	Placerville	72	111
Henery	28	m	w	ME	San Francisco	7-Wd San Francisco	81	218
Henry	56	m	w	MD	Los Angeles	Los Angeles	73	507
Henry	39	m	w	ENGL	Sonoma	Santa Rosa	91	399
Henry	38	m	w	MA	San Francisco	11-Wd San Francisc	84	434
Henry	33	m	w	ENGL	Marin	San Rafael Twp	74	42
Henry	32	m	w	MA	San Francisco	8-Wd San Francisco	82	346
Henry	29	m	w	VT	Sacramento	1-Wd Sacramento	77	173
Henry	19	m	w	NY	San Francisco	1-Wd San Francisco	79	85
Henry	12	m	w	CA	Sonoma	Santa Rosa	91	396
Henry M	37	m	w	RI	San Francisco	8-Wd San Francisco	82	476
Henry W	46	m	w	MS	Santa Barbara	Santa Barbara P O	87	487
Henry W	40	m	w	NY	Contra Costa	Martinez P O	71	374
Hiram	49	m	w	AL	Kern	Linns Valley P O	73	348
Hiram	47	m	w	OH	Lake	Big Valley	73	395
Hiram B	41	m	w	NH	Placer	Roseville P O	76	352
Horace	44	m	w	NY	Contra Costa	Martinez Twp	71	349
Hugh	38	m	w	IREL	San Francisco	San Francisco P O	85	848
Ira	50	m	w	NJ	Santa Cruz	Watsonville	89	364
Isaac	60	m	w	IL	Los Angeles	Los Angeles	73	543
Isaac	58	m	w	NJ	Tulare	Farmersville Twp	92	248
Isaac	40	m	w	MA	Santa Clara	San Jose Twp	88	212
Isaac A	50	m	w	VT	San Francisco	6-Wd San Francisco	81	140
Isaac S	53	m	w	NH	Yuba	Long Bar Twp	93	565
J	36	m	w	MO	Alameda	Murray Twp	68	110
J	15	f	w	CA	Alameda	Oakland	68	237
J Bunce	46	m	w	NY	Calaveras	Copperopolis P O	70	228
J C	60	m	w	NY	San Joaquin	Tulare Twp	86	261
J E	70	m	w	KY	Lake	Big Valley	73	395
J E	36	m	w	OH	Butte	Oroville Twp	70	138
J R	29	m	w	NY	Santa Clara	Gilroy Twp	88	68
Jacob	50	m	b	ME	San Joaquin	1-Wd Stockton	86	133
Jacob	45	m	w	MA	El Dorado	Salmon Falls Twp	72	129
Jacob	30	m	w	ME	Solano	Vallejo	90	139
James	62	m	w	MA	Alameda	Brooklyn	68	22
James	54	m	w	MA	Stanislaus	Emory Twp	92	20
James	53	m	w	SCOT	Butte	Wyandotte Twp	70	143
James	51	m	w	NC	Fresno	Millerton P O	72	193
James	50	m	b	HI	Siskiyou	Cottonwood Twp	89	590
James	45	m	w	ENGL	Butte	Kimshew Tpw	70	82
James	44	m	w	SCOT	San Luis Obispo	Morro Twp	87	283
James	40	m	w	IREL	Yolo	Grafton Twp	93	497
James	40	m	w	SCOT	Butte	Chico Twp	70	16
James	40	m	w	IL	Santa Barbara	Arroyo Grande P O	87	508
James	37	m	w	SCOT	Alameda	Washington Twp	68	287
James	36	m	w	VA	Inyo	Lone Pine Twp	73	330
James	35	m	w	ENGL	Los Angeles	Los Angeles	73	542
James	35	m	w	SCOT	Nevada	Nevada Twp	75	304

© 2001 by Heritage Quest. All rights reserved.

California 1870 Census

Name	Age	S	R	B-PL	County	Locale	Series M593 Roll	Pg
James	35	m	w	IREL	San Francisco	San Francisco P O	85	715
James	33	m	w	ENGL	Butte	Kimshew Tpw	70	76
James	33	m	w	CANA	Marin	Novato Twp	74	12
James	32	m	w	TN	Stanislaus	Empire Twp	92	46
James	30	m	w	IREL	San Francisco	San Francisco P O	80	401
James	30	m	w	NJ	Monterey	Pajaro Twp	74	371
James	26	m	w	CANA	Yolo	Washington Twp	93	528
James	24	m	w	NY	Marin	San Rafael Twp	74	38
James D	28	m	w	ENGL	Los Angeles	Los Angeles	73	526
James G	52	m	w	PA	Yolo	Buckeye Twp	93	410
James H	33	m	w	TN	Los Angeles	Santa Ana Twp	73	599
James M	46	m	w	NY	San Francisco	San Francisco P O	83	172
James M	41	m	w	MO	San Francisco	San Francisco P O	83	321
James M	32	m	w	MO	Placer	Dutch Flat P O	76	403
James N	35	m	w	VA	Napa	Napa	75	14
James W	63	m	w	ENGL	Los Angeles	Wilmington Twp	73	639
Jane	40	f	w	IREL	San Francisco	7-Wd San Francisco	81	285
Jane	22	f	i	CA	Siskiyou	Yreka	89	651
Jeremiah	36	m	w	FINL	San Francisco	3-Wd San Francisco	79	288
Jerry [Dr]	61	m	w	NY	San Diego	San Diego	78	491
Jesse	46	m	w	MO	Kern	Linns Valley P O	73	344
Jesse H	53	m	w	NJ	Colusa	Grand Island Twp	71	306
Jessie	42	m	w	NY	Los Angeles	Los Angeles	73	565
Jessie P	55	m	w	BAVA	Mariposa	Maxwell Crk P O	74	145
Jno S	24	m	w	CANA	Sacramento	1-Wd Sacramento	77	181
John	54	m	w	ENGL	Mariposa	Mariposa P O	74	134
John	52	m	w	ENGL	San Francisco	1-Wd San Francisco	79	26
John	49	m	w	CT	Napa	Napa	75	3
John	44	m	w	CANA	San Francisco	11-Wd San Francisc	84	514
John	43	m	w	ENGL	San Francisco	San Francisco P O	83	361
John	40	m	w	HANO	Amador	Fiddletown P O	69	429
John	40	m	w	NY	Yolo	Putah Twp	93	520
John	39	m	w	IREL	San Francisco	San Francisco P O	80	366
John	39	m	w	VA	Solano	Suisun Twp	90	100
John	38	m	w	OH	San Joaquin	Tulare Twp	86	251
John	38	m	w	IREL	San Francisco	San Francisco P O	83	387
John	36	m	w	NY	San Francisco	San Francisco P O	80	459
John	36	m	w	SCOT	San Luis Obispo	Salinas Twp	87	296
John	35	m	w	IREL	San Francisco	San Francisco P O	80	380
John	35	m	w	FRAN	San Francisco	San Francisco P O	83	44
John	35	m	m	MO	Nevada	Grass Valley Twp	75	189
John	35	m	w	IREL	San Francisco	San Francisco P O	83	159
John	34	m	w	AR	Santa Barbara	San Buenaventura P	87	430
John	33	m	w	IREL	San Francisco	7-Wd San Francisco	81	254
John	32	m	w	AL	San Joaquin	Tulare Twp	86	257
John	32	m	w	ME	Sacramento	Georgianna Twp	77	128
John	30	m	w	ENGL	San Francisco	7-Wd San Francisco	81	218
John	29	m	w	KY	Siskiyou	Yreka	89	658
John	28	m	w	MO	Colusa	Colusa	71	296
John	27	m	w	MA	San Joaquin	2-Wd Stockton	86	184
John	26	m	w	SCOT	Colusa	Spring Valley Twp	71	344
John	26	m	w	SC	Santa Clara	Gilroy Twp	88	88
John	24	m	w	ENGL	San Francisco	1-Wd San Francisco	79	127
John	23	m	w	MO	Solano	Silveyville Twp	90	74
John	22	m	w	IREL	San Francisco	11-Wd San Francisc	84	586
John	15	m	w	MA	San Francisco	7-Wd San Francisco	81	190
John	13	m	w	CA	Los Angeles	Los Angeles	73	570
John D	43	m	w	SCOT	Santa Cruz	Santa Cruz Twp	89	402
John H	34	m	w	NC	Monterey	Salinas Twp	74	309
John L	36	m	w	FRAN	San Francisco	San Francisco P O	83	16
John M	41	m	w	IREL	San Mateo	Redwood Twp	87	364
John M	40	m	w	AL	Merced	Snelling P O	74	258
John P	44	m	w	ME	El Dorado	Placerville Twp	72	100
John W	37	m	w	KY	Amador	Volcano P O	69	384
John W	35	m	w	IREL	San Francisco	San Francisco P O	83	239
John W	23	m	w	GA	San Diego	Julian Dist	78	472
Jonathan M	48	m	w	OH	Shasta	French Gulch P O	89	464
Joseph	55	m	w	IL	Nevada	Bridgeport Twp	75	116
Joseph	41	m	w	CANA	Humboldt	Eureka Twp	72	263
Joseph	32	m	w	MA	Placer	Roseville P O	76	351
Joseph	25	m	w	MO	Tulare	Venice Twp	92	275
Joseph	21	m	w	OR	Fresno	Kingston P O	72	222
Joseph C	7	m	w	CA	San Francisco	San Francisco P O	85	799
Josephin	17	f	w	CA	Calaveras	Copperopolis P O	70	245
Josiah A	45	m	w	TN	Mendocino	Calpella Twp	74	184
Judith	61	f	w	OH	San Francisco	San Francisco P O	85	718
Julia	52	f	w	VA	Sacramento	3-Wd Sacramento	77	294
Justin	28	m	w	MA	Contra Costa	Martinez P O	71	447
L	38	m	w	ME	Alameda	Oakland	68	211
Leonard S	23	m	w	MA	San Joaquin	Liberty Twp	86	92
Lewis C	29	m	w	PA	Mendocino	Little Lake Twp	74	200
Lewis D	22	m	w	ME	El Dorado	Diamond Springs Tw	72	34
Logan	26	m	w	MI	San Diego	San Diego	78	491
Lorain	15	f	w	AR	San Joaquin	Castoria Twp	86	8
Lorenzo D	29	m	w	VT	San Francisco	San Francisco P O	85	766
Loring	40	m	w	MI	Santa Clara	Almaden Twp	88	17
Louis T	43	m	w	MA	Placer	Colfax P O	76	391
Louisa	39	f	w	PA	Amador	Volcano P O	69	383
Louisa	34	f	w	NY	San Francisco	5-Wd San Francisco	81	11
Lovett	40	m	w	NY	San Francisco	San Francisco P O	83	87
Lucius H	54	m	w	NY	San Francisco	San Francisco P O	83	203
Lulie	11	f	w	MA	Sacramento	2-Wd Sacramento	77	223
Lyman	63	m	w	VT	Sacramento	Franklin Twp	77	109
Maggie	5	f	w	CA	San Joaquin	Oneal Twp	86	99
Major	54	m	w	GA	Santa Clara	San Jose Twp	88	191
Marcus	35	m	w	MA	San Diego	San Diego	78	495
Margaret	34	f	w	IREL	Yuba	W Bear Rvr Twp	93	684
Margaret	28	f	w	IREL	San Francisco	11-Wd San Francisc	84	634
Margaret	26	f	w	IREL	San Francisco	8-Wd San Francisco	82	389
Margaret	25	f	w	AR	Tulare	Venice Twp	92	278
Maria F	50	f	w	ME	San Francisco	1-Wd San Francisco	79	94
Mary	60	f	w	WALE	Placer	Bath P O	76	452
Mary	29	f	w	IREL	San Francisco	San Francisco P O	83	395
Mary	23	f	w	ME	Merced	Snelling P O	74	261
Mary	11	f	w	CA	San Francisco	San Francisco P O	85	798
Mary A	17	f	w	CA	San Luis Obispo	Arroyo Grande Twp	87	272
Mary F	13	f	w	CA	Santa Clara	Santa Clara Twp	88	152
Mary H	56	f	w	NY	Santa Clara	San Jose Twp	88	199
Matthew	19	m	w	ME	San Francisco	1-Wd San Francisco	79	94
Michael	37	m	w	MI	Solano	Suisun Twp	90	107
Michael	36	m	w	IREL	San Francisco	San Francisco P O	83	292
Michael	35	m	w	IREL	Solano	Suisun Twp	90	110
Michael	35	m	w	IREL	San Francisco	11-Wd San Francisc	84	488
Morgan	44	m	w	NY	Solano	Vacaville Twp	90	138
Mortimer	48	m	w	NY	Trinity	Lewiston Pct	92	211
Moses	44	m	w	MA	Placer	Pino Twp	76	470
Myron W	45	m	w	VT	San Francisco	San Francisco P O	83	58
Nathan	10	m	w	KY	Siskiyou	Scott Valley Twp	89	621
Nathaniel	47	m	w	NY	Humboldt	Pacific Twp	72	296
Nathaniel	42	m	w	NY	Marin	Tomales Twp	74	80
Nathaniel B	25	m	w	RI	San Francisco	1-Wd San Francisco	79	123
Nathl	37	m	w	ME	San Francisco	San Francisco P O	83	123
Neoma	58	f	w	VT	Yuba	Slate Range Bar Tw	93	677
Noah	47	m	w	NY	Napa	Napa Twp	75	32
O H	30	m	w	MA	San Joaquin	2-Wd Stockton	86	201
O S	42	m	w	KY	Sonoma	Santa Rosa	91	402
Oliver	65	m	w	CT	Marin	Nicasio Twp	74	15
Oliver H	65	m	w	KY	Los Angeles	Los Angeles	73	568
Otis	41	m	w	ME	Sonoma	Analy Twp	91	236
Patk	23	m	w	IREL	Sacramento	1-Wd Sacramento	77	204
Patrick	35	m	w	IREL	San Mateo	Half Moon Bay P O	87	407
Peleg C	35	m	w	MA	San Francisco	San Francisco P O	83	142
Peter	35	m	w	NY	San Francisco	San Francisco P O	83	78
Peter	30	m	w	NY	San Francisco	San Francisco P O	83	130
Peter A	25	m	w	KY	Monterey	San Juan Twp	74	390
Petra B	58	f	w	CA	Monterey	Monterey	74	366
Polly	65	f	w	NC	Shasta	Millville P O	89	493
Porter	40	m	w	GA	Stanislaus	Emory Twp	92	22
R B	23	m	w	WI	San Francisco	San Francisco P O	83	281
Reese B	50	m	w	VA	Fresno	Millerton P O	72	152
Reuben H	46	m	w	PA	Butte	Chico Twp	70	13
Richard	57	m	w	IREL	San Bernardino	San Bernardino Twp	78	426
Richard	42	m	w	ENGL	Sacramento	San Joaquin Twp	77	395
Richd	30	m	w	MA	San Joaquin	Douglas Twp	86	50
Richd	19	m	w	NY	Solano	Vallejo	90	210
Robert	44	m	w	OH	Contra Costa	Martinez P O	71	434
Robert	40	m	b	MO	Nevada	Grass Valley Twp	75	221
Robert	26	m	w	NY	San Francisco	11-Wd San Francisc	84	465
Robert	23	m	w	NORW	San Francisco	11-Wd San Francisc	84	694
Robert	23	m	w	SC	Marin	Novato Twp	74	9
Robert M	36	m	w	MO	Tulare	Tule Rvr Twp	92	258
Robt	44	m	w	OH	Sacramento	3-Wd Sacramento	77	280
Robt G	6	m	w	CA	Shasta	Millville P O	89	492
Rosa	11	f	w	CA	Santa Clara	Santa Clara Twp	88	144
Rowena	9	f	w	MO	Stanislaus	San Joaquin Twp	92	81
S A	34	m	w	OH	Marin	San Rafael Twp	74	46
S N	39	m	w	NY	Tuolumne	Chinese Camp P O	93	368
Salvadore	37	m	w	MEXI	Sierra	Table Rock Twp	89	572
Saml B	39	m	w	ME	Tuolumne	Sonora P O	93	320
Samuel H	59	m	w	NJ	Colusa	Grand Island Twp	71	306
Samuel L	40	m	w	VT	San Francisco	6-Wd San Francisco	81	92
Sheldon	33	m	w	MI	Los Angeles	Wilmington Twp	73	645
Sientia	81	f	w	CT	San Joaquin	Castoria Twp	86	12
Spotswood	39	m	w	MO	Stanislaus	Emory Twp	92	24
Stephen	51	m	w	CT	Colusa	Colusa	71	300
Stephen	39	m	w	WALE	Sierra	Sears Twp	89	555
Stephen H	48	m	w	GA	Santa Clara	1-Wd San Jose	88	235
Stephen H	38	m	w	NJ	Colusa	Colusa	71	288
Susan	8	f	w	CA	Alameda	Washington Twp	68	276
Syl S	52	m	w	MA	Sonoma	Washington Twp	91	465
Theodore	24	m	w	IL	Tulare	Tule Rvr Twp	92	266
Theodore H	50	m	w	CT	San Francisco	6-Wd San Francisco	81	110
Tho	50	m	w	IREL	El Dorado	Kelsey Twp	72	58
Thoma H	45	m	w	KY	Tulare	Tule Rvr Twp	92	268
Thomas	58	m	w	IREL	Amador	Drytown P O	69	421
Thomas	55	m	w	IREL	El Dorado	Placerville Twp	72	99
Thomas	44	m	w	NY	Amador	Drytown P O	69	417
Thomas	40	m	w	IREL	Tulare	Tule Rvr Twp	92	265
Thomas	40	m	w	NY	Calaveras	San Andreas P O	70	170
Thomas	40	m	w	RI	Merced	Snelling P O	74	255
Thomas	38	m	w	CANA	Nevada	Nevada Twp	75	297
Thomas	36	m	w	KY	San Diego	Julian Dist	78	473
Thomas	35	m	w	IREL	Tulare	Tule Rvr Twp	92	269
Thomas	32	m	w	IREL	Tuolumne	Columbia P O	93	345
Thomas	32	m	w	IREL	Nevada	Meadow Lake Twp	75	252
Thomas	24	m	w	NY	San Francisco	San Francisco P O	83	154
Thomas	24	m	w	NY	San Francisco	San Francisco P O	83	168
Thomas	22	m	w	CANA	Yolo	Putah Twp	93	516
Thomas	21	m	w	ME	San Francisco	1-Wd San Francisco	79	94
Thomas	18	m	w	CA	Monterey	Monterey	74	363
Thomas J	36	m	w	VA	El Dorado	Diamond Springs Tw	72	30
Thos	7	m	w	CA	Siskiyou	Scott Valley Twp	89	618
Thos	42	m	w	MO	Lake	Lakeport	73	407
Thos	35	m	w	NJ	Butte	Ophir Twp	70	102

© 2001 by Heritage Quest. All rights reserved.

Name	Age	S	R	B-PL	County	Locale	Roll	Pg
						Series M593		
Thos	35	m	w	IREL	Sacramento	Granite Twp	77	150
Thos B	22	m	w	MO	Shasta	Millville P O	89	486
Thos J	41	m	w	PA	Fresno	Millerton P O	72	145
Victor C	20	m	w	NY	San Luis Obispo	Arroyo Grande Twp	87	279
W	5	m	w	CA	San Francisco	San Francisco P O	85	800
W	47	m	w	NJ	Sierra	Downieville Twp	89	522
W H	46	m	w	IN	Humboldt	Bald Hills	72	237
Washington	26	m	w	MO	Fresno	Millerton P O	72	155
William	9	m	w	ME	San Francisco	1-Wd San Francisco	79	94
William	9	m	w	CA	Santa Cruz	Pajaro Twp	89	343
William	54	m	w	ME	San Francisco	San Francisco P O	80	381
William	50	m	w	IREL	Alameda	Oakland	68	183
William	43	m	w	MA	Alameda	Hayward	68	75
William	38	m	w	OH	Trinity	Canyon City Pct	92	201
William	36	m	w	SCOT	San Francisco	3-Wd San Francisco	79	319
William	36	m	w	ME	Nevada	Meadow Lake Twp	75	268
William	36	m	w	SCOT	Butte	Oregon Twp	70	122
William	32	m	c	CHIN	Tuolumne	Sonora P O	93	326
William	30	m	w	SWED	San Francisco	7-Wd San Francisco	81	220
William	27	m	w	PA	Los Angeles	Los Angeles Twp	73	471
William	27	m	w	CA	San Francisco	7-Wd San Francisco	81	156
William	26	m	w	DENM	San Francisco	7-Wd San Francisco	81	218
William B	35	m	w	ENGL	San Francisco	6-Wd San Francisco	81	103
William F	51	m	w	VA	Colusa	Spring Valley Twp	71	335
William H	46	m	w	KY	San Francisco	San Francisco P O	83	355
William H	45	m	w	ENGL	Trinity	Weaverville Pct	92	231
Wm	65	m	w	PRUS	San Joaquin	Castoria Twp	86	7
Wm	51	m	w	SCOT	San Francisco	7-Wd San Francisco	81	267
Wm	49	m	w	IREL	San Joaquin	1-Wd Stockton	86	131
Wm	46	m	w	IREL	San Joaquin	Oneal Twp	86	107
Wm	31	m	w	VT	Sacramento	1-Wd Sacramento	77	173
Wm F	23	m	w	IREL	San Francisco	San Francisco P O	85	875
Wm H	39	m	w	CANA	San Francisco	1-Wd San Francisco	79	56
Wm H	32	m	w	NJ	Monterey	Alisal Twp	74	292
Wm P	60	m	w	OH	Sonoma	Healdsburg	91	274
Wm P	20	m	w	OH	Butte	Hamilton Twp	70	69
Wm R	47	m	w	KY	San Francisco	8-Wd San Francisco	82	317
Wm Y	51	m	w	IL	Sonoma	Mendocino Twp	91	296
ALLENBACK								
A	28	m	w	AUST	Yuba	Marysville	93	583
ALLENBAK								
A	21	m	w	NY	Yuba	Marysville	93	586
ALLENBERG								
Chas	23	m	w	PRUS	Nevada	Eureka Twp	75	126
Lewis E	19	m	w	OH	Nevada	Eureka Twp	75	126
ALLENDER								
Minerva	53	f	w	OH	Solano	Rio Vista Twp	90	63
ALLENERT								
Chas	38	m	w	BRUN	Merced	Snelling P O	74	272
ALLENICE								
Concepciona	44	f	w	CA	Los Angeles	Los Angeles	73	534
ALLENSON								
S	49	m	w	SWIT	Sierra	Downieville Twp	89	520
ALLENT								
Joseph	45	m	w	FRAN	Calaveras	San Andreas P O	70	216
Joseph D	45	m	w	FRAN	Calaveras	San Andreas P O	70	216
ALLENTINE								
Kate	23	f	w	PRUS	San Francisco	San Francisco P O	83	380
ALLENTON								
Joseph	40	m	w	MO	Monterey	San Antonio Twp	74	323
ALLENWOOD								
F	47	m	w	ME	Yuba	Rose Bar Twp	93	664
ALLENY								
Chas	25	m	w	MA	San Francisco	San Francisco P O	85	807
ALLER								
James	55	m	w	IREL	San Francisco	3-Wd San Francisco	79	318
ALLERD								
Mary A	25	f	w	WI	San Joaquin	2-Wd Stockton	86	159
ALLERMAN								
H W	43	m	w	HANO	Solano	Benicia	90	12
ALLERS								
J G	60	m	w	OLDE	Sierra	Alleghany & Forest	89	534
ALLERTON								
Orson	45	m	w	OH	Mono	Bridgeport P O	74	283
ALLERY								
Joseph	49	m	w	SWIT	San Francisco	5-Wd San Francisco	81	3
ALLES								
Christopher	35	m	w	HANO	Tulare	Tule Rvr Twp	92	261
ALLESCEO								
Augustine	27	m	w	SWIT	Plumas	Indian Twp	77	13
ALLESON								
Albert	14	m	w	CA	San Joaquin	Douglas Twp	86	43
ALLESTERO								
Horrozo	28	m	w	MEXI	Fresno	Millerton P O	72	153
ALLEY								
Charles	24	m	w	MA	San Francisco	11-Wd San Francisc	84	556
Dan N	27	m	w	TX	San Diego	San Diego	78	500
Dodge	40	m	w	IA	Yuba	Marysville	93	603
Geo H	28	m	w	IN	Sonoma	Analy Twp	91	240
J A	58	m	w	TN	Lake	Upper Lake	73	411
John	45	m	w	TX	Butte	Oregon Twp	70	128
John	23	m	w	MO	Lake	Upper Lake	73	411
Jonathan	44	m	w	PA	Inyo	Cerro Gordo Twp	73	319
Marshal	35	m	w	IN	Sonoma	Analy Twp	91	246
Maud	70	f	w	IN	Sonoma	Analy Twp	91	246
Obed	46	m	w	MA	Contra Costa	Martinez P O	71	453
P I	42	m	w	MA	Sierra	Sears Twp	89	527

Name	Age	S	R	B-PL	County	Locale	Roll	Pg
						Series M593		
S H	28	m	w	MO	Lake	Upper Lake	73	411
Thos J	38	m	w	IN	Sonoma	Analy Twp	91	246
William	45	m	w	ME	San Francisco	1-Wd San Francisco	79	4
ALLGAUER								
John A	40	m	w	SWIT	San Francisco	San Francisco P O	83	135
ALLGYER								
William	21	m	w	HAMB	San Francisco	San Francisco P O	80	347
ALLICK								
Peter	43	m	w	AUST	Butte	Ophir Twp	70	102
Sam	18	m	c	CHIN	Yuba	Bullards Bar P O	93	553
ALLIERE								
Victor	42	m	w	FRAN	Calaveras	Copperopolis P O	70	244
ALLIGERO								
Narcisso	35	m	w	MEXI	Santa Barbara	Santa Barbara P O	87	472
ALLIGRETTI								
Pietro	26	m	w	ITAL	San Joaquin	1-Wd Stockton	86	155
ALLIN								
James	27	m	w	IREL	San Francisco	11-Wd San Francisc	84	702
Serug	38	m	w	ENGL	Sutter	Butte Twp	92	95
ALLINA								
Joe	47	m	w	SPAI	San Joaquin	1-Wd Stockton	86	140
ALLINDER								
E E	49	f	w	VA	Santa Clara	Gilroy Twp	88	74
ALLINGER								
Frederick	51	m	w	SWIT	Santa Cruz	Santa Cruz	89	409
ALLINGHAM								
Wm	26	m	w	ENGL	San Francisco	1-Wd San Francisco	79	70
ALLINGTON								
Joseph B	44	m	w	IN	Placer	Rocklin Twp	76	463
Stephen	40	m	w	VT	Sacramento	4-Wd Sacramento	77	325
ALLINSON								
Mark	61	m	w	ENGL	Shasta	Horsetown P O	89	502
ALLIPI								
James	36	m	b	HI	Siskiyou	Cottonwood Twp	89	590
ALLIS								
Philander	36	m	w	IREL	San Francisco	11-Wd San Francisc	84	429
Philip	35	m	w	IREL	San Francisco	San Francisco P O	85	860
ALLISON								
A C	47	m	w	PA	San Joaquin	Tulare Twp	86	259
Alzada	23	f	w	RI	Calaveras	San Andreas P O	70	184
Chas	55	m	w	SCOT	San Francisco	7-Wd San Francisco	81	273
Chas	35	m	w	MA	San Joaquin	Elkhorn Twp	86	58
D C	29	m	w	IA	San Francisco	3-Wd San Francisco	79	299
Edward	61	m	w	KY	Nevada	Bridgeport Twp	75	124
Edward	38	m	w	VA	Amador	Fiddletown P O	69	437
Eliza	52	f	w	MA	Santa Clara	2-Wd San Jose	88	296
Eugene	20	m	w	MO	Santa Cruz	Pajaro Twp	89	339
Francis	22	m	w	IA	San Diego	San Diego	78	505
Frank K	30	m	w	NY	San Francisco	8-Wd San Francisco	82	331
Geo	42	m	w	IREL	Sonoma	Mendocino Twp	91	294
George	43	m	w	OH	Solano	Silveyville Twp	90	83
George	33	m	w	PA	Trinity	Lewiston Pct	92	214
Hester	74	f	w	NY	San Diego	Julian Dist	78	473
Hiram	48	m	w	IL	El Dorado	Coloma Twp	72	5
James	60	m	w	PA	Marin	San Rafael	74	55
James	21	m	w	MO	Colusa	Butte Twp	71	270
James G	47	m	w	IL	Yolo	Cache Crk Twp	93	420
Jane	28	f	w	PA	Santa Cruz	Santa Cruz	89	413
John	54	m	w	DC	Santa Cruz	Santa Cruz Twp	89	391
John	40	m	w	SWED	Humboldt	Eureka Twp	72	279
John	38	m	w	IL	Nevada	Grass Valley Twp	75	232
John	30	m	w	US	Santa Cruz	Santa Cruz Twp	89	391
John	27	m	w	ENGL	Humboldt	Table Bluff Twp	72	306
John	27	m	w	IN	Nevada	Washington Twp	75	340
John H	42	m	w	VA	Napa	Napa	75	4
Joseph	24	m	w	NY	Solano	Maine Prairie Twp	90	53
Josiah	54	m	w	OH	Solano	Vacaville Twp	90	124
Marion	16	m	w	CA	Santa Clara	San Jose Twp	88	208
Mary	11	f	w	CA	Los Angeles	Los Angeles	73	506
Milton S	45	f	w	OH	Placer	Dutch Flat P O	76	402
Napoleon	49	m	w	OH	San Diego	Julian Dist	78	474
Napoleon B	49	m	w	OH	Santa Cruz	Watsonville	89	374
Peter	30	m	w	HAMB	San Francisco	1-Wd San Francisco	79	78
R M	46	m	w	DC	Monterey	Monterey	74	362
Richard	46	m	w	ENGL	Nevada	Nevada Twp	75	305
Robert	57	m	w	OH	San Diego	Julian Dist	78	473
Robert	46	m	w	ENGL	Contra Costa	Martinez P O	71	423
Robert	40	m	w	NC	Stanislaus	Washington Twp	92	86
Samuel	50	m	w	OH	Nevada	Nevada Twp	75	297
Thomas	30	m	w	CANA	Solano	Rio Vista Twp	90	63
Thos	55	m	w	PA	Lake	Big Valley	73	397
Thos R	28	m	w	ENGL	San Francisco	1-Wd San Francisco	79	87
William	40	m	w	ENGL	Santa Clara	2-Wd San Jose	88	318
Wm	62	m	w	PA	Tuolumne	Chinese Camp P O	93	379
Wm	37	m	w	SCOT	Sonoma	Salt Point	91	384
Wm	24	m	w	PA	San Joaquin	Douglas Twp	86	35
Wm M	53	m	w	PA	Santa Cruz	Soquel Twp	89	437
ALLISS								
Merbuldie	47	m	w	MEXI	Calaveras	Copperopolis P O	70	263
ALLISTER								
Thomas	41	m	w	NY	Nevada	Meadow Lake Twp	75	249
ALLIVER								
Andrew W	36	m	w	ME	San Diego	San Diego	78	501
ALLKEN								
Saml	26	m	w	PA	Amador	Volcano P O	69	388
ALLKIRE								
Samuel	24	m	w	PA	Amador	Jackson P O	69	322

© 2001 by Heritage Quest. All rights reserved.

California 1870 Census

Name	Age	S	R	B-PL	County	Locale	Series M593 Roll	Pg
ALLMAN								
Frederick	45	m	w	PRUS	Plumas	Seneca Twp	77	50
John	40	m	w	PA	Mendocino	Round Valley Twp	74	218
Miles	36	m	w	IREL	San Francisco	San Francisco P O	85	773
ALLMAND								
Julia	22	f	w	FRAN	San Francisco	San Francisco P O	80	537
ALLN								
J A	50	m	w	NH	San Joaquin	Oneal Twp	86	110
ALLOMINOS								
Paulo	40	m	w	MEXI	Tuolumne	Sonora P O	93	330
ALLON								
Henry	51	m	w	WIND	San Joaquin	Elkhorn Twp	86	59
John	30	m	w	IREL	Solano	Benicia	90	21
ALLPETER								
Henry	30	m	w	PRUS	Amador	Sutter Crk P O	69	398
ALLPORT								
Thomas	26	m	w	NY	San Francisco	San Francisco P O	80	456
W J	38	m	w	VA	Solano	Vallejo	90	190
Wm	69	m	w	NY	San Joaquin	Liberty Twp	86	82
ALLRIGHT								
And	30	m	w	IL	Mono	Bridgeport P O	74	286
ALLS								
Edmond	14	m	w	CA	Sacramento	Franklin Twp	77	111
ALLSON								
Sophia	49	f	w	GERM	San Joaquin	2-Wd Stockton	86	167
ALLSTON								
W V	56	m	w	NY	Tuolumne	Big Oak Flat P O	93	399
ALLSUP								
Jefferson	35	m	w	TN	Stanislaus	Empire Twp	92	36
ALLWELL								
A J	23	m	w	WI	San Joaquin	Dent Twp	86	28
ALLY								
Catherine	54	f	w	OH	Humboldt	Arcata Twp	72	234
Mey	50	m	c	CHIN	Yuba	Bullards Bar P O	93	552
ALLYN								
G W	48	m	w	CT	Nevada	Nevada Twp	75	286
Jas	25	m	w	NY	San Francisco	8-Wd San Francisco	82	359
John	29	m	w	MO	Solano	Suisun Twp	90	102
Sophia H	44	f	w	IL	Santa Barbara	San Buenaventura P	87	440
ALLYNE								
John	32	m	w	MA	San Francisco	San Francisco P O	80	424
ALLYO								
Ochoy	29	m	w	CHIL	Butte	Kimshew Tpw	70	82
ALM								
John	46	m	w	SWED	Butte	Mountain Spring Tw	70	89
Shing	18	m	c	CHIN	San Diego	San Diego	78	488
ALMA								
George	50	m	w	MD	San Francisco	8-Wd San Francisco	82	370
Peter G	44	m	w	SWED	Monterey	San Antonio Twp	74	317
Phillip	50	m	w	PORT	San Mateo	Half Moon Bay P O	87	396
ALMADO								
F	20	m	w	CA	Alameda	Oakland	68	159
ALMAN								
Calvin	47	m	w	US	San Joaquin	2-Wd Stockton	86	168
ALMANDEZ								
Remon	45	m	w	MEXI	Merced	Snelling P O	74	249
ALMANGA								
Renaldo	44	m	w	MEXI	Plumas	Mineral Twp	77	22
ALMASON								
Esperito	40	m	w	MEXI	Contra Costa	Martinez P O	71	449
ALMATAN								
Fernando	38	m	w	MEXI	Los Angeles	Los Angeles	73	552
ALMEDA								
Jesus	35	m	w	MEXI	Fresno	Millerton P O	72	162
ALMERS								
Nicholas	35	m	w	HANO	San Francisco	2-Wd San Francisco	79	234
ALMIJO								
Jesus	41	m	w	MEXI	Plumas	Goodwin Twp	77	1
ALMNOREZ								
Frute	35	m	w	CA	Los Angeles	Los Angeles Twp	73	474
ALMON								
Bark	32	m	w	IREL	Merced	Snelling P O	74	247
David	32	m	w	IREL	San Francisco	San Francisco P O	83	34
Francisco	25	m	w	MEXI	Marin	San Rafael Twp	74	41
Henry	37	m	w	CANA	Santa Clara	Gilroy Twp	88	100
Henry	25	m	w	CANA	Sacramento	San Joaquin Twp	77	399
ALMOND								
Mathew H	42	m	w	IN	Mariposa	Mariposa P O	74	134
ALMORCE								
Francisco	34	m	w	MEXI	Los Angeles	Los Angeles	73	563
ALMORO								
Jesus	16	f	i	MEXI	Los Angeles	Los Angeles Twp	73	498
ALMQUIST								
John	47	m	w	SWED	San Francisco	San Francisco P O	83	220
ALMS								
E	19	m	w	CA	Alameda	Oakland	68	182
ALMSON								
Peter	42	m	w	SWED	San Francisco	7-Wd San Francisco	81	274
ALMSTEAD								
Leonard	33	m	w	NY	Marin	Point Reyes Twp	74	22
Lewis	50	m	w	ME	San Diego	San Diego	78	492
ALMY								
George	27	m	w	MI	San Francisco	San Francisco P O	83	225
Joseph	50	m	w	RI	Marin	San Rafael	74	53
ALNEY								
Cyntha	43	f	w	MO	Sonoma	Healdsburg & Mendo	91	276
ALNUT								
Joseph W	38	m	w	MO	Plumas	Quartz Twp	77	37
ALO								
---	22	f	c	CHIN	Sacramento	1-Wd Sacramento	77	199
ALOK								
Tong	20	m	c	CHIN	Solano	Vacaville Twp	90	120
ALON								
D F	55	m	w	NY	San Joaquin	Douglas Twp	86	33
ALONA								
Edward	19	m	i	CA	Inyo	Cerro Gordo Twp	73	321
ALONG								
Ah	26	m	c	CHIN	Sacramento	1-Wd Sacramento	77	197
ALONZ								
Goon	21	m	c	CHIN	Sierra	Eureka Twp	89	526
ALONZA								
Jose	33	m	w	SPAI	San Francisco	1-Wd San Francisco	79	47
ALONZO								
Charles	58	m	b	NJ	Sacramento	4-Wd Sacramento	77	324
Jesus	42	m	w	MEXI	Monterey	Alisal Twp	74	292
ALORES								
A J	25	m	w	AZOR	Alameda	Murray Twp	68	127
ALOWD								
Edam S	28	m	w	MA	Placer	Cisco P O	76	494
ALPA								
Joseph	57	m	w	ITAL	Amador	Jackson P O	69	343
Laura	6	f	w	CA	Amador	Jackson P O	69	343
ALPAUGH								
James L	33	m	w	NY	Sonoma	Salt Point	91	391
N A	25	f	w	IL	Sonoma	Bodega Twp	91	252
Sylvester	40	m	w	NY	Sonoma	Salt Point	91	384
Sylvester	30	m	w	NY	Shasta	Fort Crook P O	89	476
Thos	41	m	w	NY	Butte	Chico Twp	70	17
Thos	28	m	w	NY	Butte	Chico Twp	70	32
ALPEN								
Harmann	37	m	w	DENM	San Francisco	2-Wd San Francisco	79	174
ALPENS								
Anna	14	f	w	NY	San Francisco	2-Wd San Francisco	79	218
ALPHERTS								
Robert	42	m	w	IREL	San Francisco	San Francisco P O	83	148
ALPHONSO								
Fortail	23	m	w	FRAN	Sacramento	4-Wd Sacramento	77	369
Julius	60	m	w	FRAN	San Francisco	San Francisco P O	80	348
ALPHUS								
Edward	40	m	w	HANO	Nevada	Bridgeport Twp	75	122
ALPIAN								
Jose	50	m	w	MEXI	Merced	Snelling P O	74	250
ALPIN								
Wm D	43	m	w	ENGL	Nevada	Little York Twp	75	240
ALPINE								
John	24	m	w	SWIT	Marin	Point Reyes Twp	74	22
William	35	m	w	ENGL	San Francisco	7-Wd San Francisco	81	212
ALPITE								
Michael	36	m	w	ME	Monterey	Alisal Twp	74	296
ALPOUGH								
P	48	m	w	NY	Sierra	Lincoln Twp	89	547
Wm	46	m	w	NY	Sierra	Lincoln Twp	89	547
ALRANZ								
Francisco	29	m	w	MEXI	Monterey	San Benito Twp	74	379
ALREAM								
Mary	70	f	w	IREL	Marin	San Rafael	74	56
ALROAD								
Antone	42	m	w	FINL	Placer	Bath P O	76	440
ALROOT								
Antone	56	m	w	FINL	Placer	Bath P O	76	457
ALSANDRA								
Fredk	40	m	w	CANA	Sutter	Sutter Twp	92	125
ALSAP								
David	22	m	w	IL	Merced	Snelling P O	74	262
ALSARO								
Lemand	19	m	w	CA	Fresno	Millerton P O	72	167
ALSBERG								
Sigmund	42	m	w	HCAS	El Dorado	Placerville	72	113
ALSEAM								
Thomas	21	m	w	VT	Marin	Sausalito Twp	74	72
ALSEN								
Charles	54	m	w	NJ	Tuolumne	Big Oak Flat P O	93	394
George	28	m	w	SWED	Placer	Gold Run Twp	76	398
ALSENGE								
Jacob	36	m	w	HDAR	San Francisco	San Francisco P O	85	843
ALSHIN								
Elias	37	m	w	VA	Sutter	Sutter Twp	92	126
ALSIP								
Ed K	26	m	w	IN	Sacramento	4-Wd Sacramento	77	337
ALSO								
Thomas	35	m	w	ENGL	Nevada	Grass Valley Twp	75	169
ALSON								
Harris	39	m	w	NORW	Los Angeles	Los Angeles	73	542
John	35	m	w	NORW	San Francisco	11-Wd San Francisc	84	691
Nicholas	36	m	w	WALD	San Francisco	2-Wd San Francisco	79	212
Samuel	44	m	w	NORW	Colusa	Grand Island Twp	71	305
ALSOP								
Azariah	51	m	w	VA	Solano	Rio Vista Twp	90	57
Daniel	31	m	w	VA	Sutter	Vernon Twp	92	134
Elizabeth	24	f	w	CANA	San Mateo	Woodside P O	87	380
I P C	44	m	w	LA	Monterey	San Juan Twp	74	410
May	40	f	w	NY	San Bernardino	San Salvador Twp	78	459
Samuel	29	m	w	ENGL	Monterey	Salinas Twp	74	306

© 2001 by Heritage Quest. All rights reserved.

Name	Age	S	R	B-PL	County	Locale	Series M593 Roll	Pg
Thomas	34	m	w	TN	Yolo	Buckeye Twp	93	415
William	20	m	w	CANA	San Mateo	Woodside P O	87	386
ALSOPE								
James	19	m	w	CANA	San Mateo	Woodside P O	87	386
ALSTEIN								
Henry	45	m	w	DENM	Calaveras	San Andreas P O	70	197
ALSTEN								
George	32	m	w	NORW	Solano	Maine Prairie Twp	90	53
ALSTON								
Swanton	20	m	w	SWED	Tehama	Red Bluff	92	175
Wm	25	m	w	SCOT	San Francisco	2-Wd San Francisco	79	209
ALSTREN								
Arick	27	m	w	FINL	San Francisco	3-Wd San Francisco	79	291
ALSTROM								
Fredrick	27	m	w	FINL	San Francisco	7-Wd San Francisco	81	217
Henry	40	m	w	IREL	Solano	Silveyville Twp	90	73
John	40	m	w	SWED	San Francisco	2-Wd San Francisco	79	149
Swen	44	m	w	SWED	Napa	Napa	75	6
ALSUILA								
Sylvaria	16	m	w	CA	Santa Cruz	Pajaro Twp	89	349
ALT								
Ah	27	m	c	CHIN	San Joaquin	2-Wd Stockton	86	212
Ah	22	m	c	CHIN	San Mateo	San Mateo P O	87	351
Chas	32	m	w	CANA	Sacramento	3-Wd Sacramento	77	271
George W	69	m	w	OH	Mono	Bridgeport P O	74	282
ALTA								
John	37	m	w	ME	San Joaquin	2-Wd Stockton	86	205
ALTAFFER								
George	42	m	w	OH	El Dorado	White Oak Twp	72	141
ALTAGRACIAS								
Juan	28	m	w	MEXI	San Francisco	1-Wd San Francisco	79	91
ALTAMARAN								
Tehunior	28	m	w	CHIL	Fresno	Millerton P O	72	166
ALTAMARANO								
Evelin	46	m	w	CA	Contra Costa	Martinez Twp	71	349
Jose	21	m	w	CA	San Francisco	1-Wd San Francisco	79	111
ALTAMEDAN								
Juan J	65	m	w	MEXI	Santa Cruz	Santa Cruz Twp	89	380
ALTARANA								
Dolores	45	f	w	CA	Fresno	Millerton P O	72	157
ALTEMARANO								
Jose	33	m	w	CA	San Diego	San Diego	78	487
ALTEMUS								
John	31	m	w	BAVA	San Francisco	San Francisco P O	85	831
ALTEN								
James H	28	m	w	OH	Sutter	Vernon Twp	92	137
ALTENBERG								
Chas	47	m	w	PRUS	San Francisco	5-Wd San Francisco	81	3
William	46	m	w	SHOL	Plumas	Goodwin Twp	77	8
ALTENBERGH								
Max	16	m	w	GERM	Marin	San Rafael Twp	74	46
ALTENBURG								
Henry	18	m	w	HDAR	Santa Clara	Fremont Twp	88	58
P F	38	m	w	PRUS	San Francisco	3-Wd San Francisco	79	328
ALTER								
Simon	59	m	w	PA	El Dorado	Placerville	72	118
ALTHENSON								
David	26	m	w	ENGL	San Francisco	5-Wd San Francisco	81	27
ALTHOF								
Ernest	40	m	w	PRUS	San Francisco	8-Wd San Francisco	82	430
ALTHOFF								
Eliza	26	f	w	PRUS	San Francisco	San Francisco P O	83	300
Herman	39	m	w	PRUS	San Francisco	San Francisco P O	83	300
ALTHOUS								
William	24	m	w	PRUS	Santa Clara	2-Wd San Jose	88	323
ALTHOUSE								
Annie	21	f	w	PRUS	San Francisco	San Francisco P O	83	352
Josiah	40	m	w	PA	Mariposa	Mariposa P O	74	125
Murray	27	m	w	CANA	Sonoma	Analy Twp	91	218
Taylor	31	m	w	IL	San Francisco	1-Wd San Francisco	79	100
ALTIMARANO								
Andreas	30	m	w	MEXI	Los Angeles	Santa Ana Twp	73	616
ALTINI								
Joseph	41	m	w	SARD	Tuolumne	Columbia P O	93	350
ALTMAN								
Hannah	12	f	w	NY	San Francisco	San Francisco P O	83	271
Mary K	37	f	w	IREL	San Francisco	San Francisco P O	83	153
Tobias	47	m	w	PRUS	San Francisco	1-Wd San Francisco	79	49
ALTMARK								
Solomon	46	m	w	POLA	Sonoma	Analy Twp	91	220
ALTMAYER								
Aaron	34	m	w	BAVA	San Francisco	8-Wd San Francisco	82	481
ALTON								
Charles	32	m	w	MA	San Francisco	6-Wd San Francisco	81	88
Daniel	35	m	w	OH	Solano	Silveyville Twp	90	73
George M	36	m	w	OH	Sutter	Vernon Twp	92	134
Jane	48	f	w	NY	San Francisco	San Francisco P O	80	411
Wendall	43	m	w	PRUS	Sonoma	Analy Twp	91	232
ALTORO								
Antonio	27	m	w	ITAL	San Francisco	San Francisco P O	85	819
ALTSCHUL								
Emile	24	m	w	BADE	San Francisco	2-Wd San Francisco	79	151
ALTSHULE								
Levi	37	m	w	POLA	San Francisco	11-Wd San Francisc	84	559
ALTY								
Mathew	45	m	w	ENGL	Nevada	Nevada Twp	75	290

Name	Age	S	R	B-PL	County	Locale	Series M593 Roll	Pg
ALUANES								
John	33	m	w	AZOR	Monterey	Monterey Twp	74	344
ALUM								
Ah	25	m	c	CHIN	Stanislaus	Empire Twp	92	62
ALURICH								
W H	13	m	w	CA	Alameda	Oakland	68	159
ALVA								
Antone	50	m	i	CA	San Luis Obispo	San Luis Obispo Tw	87	315
Edward	27	m	w	ENGL	Sonoma	Mendocino Twp	91	299
G	26	m	w	SCOT	Siskiyou	Scott Valley Twp	89	611
Jesus	12	m	w	CA	Santa Clara	1-Wd San Jose	88	266
Manuel S	22	m	w	AZOR	Contra Costa	Martinez P O	71	392
Miguel	29	m	w	MEXI	San Francisco	3-Wd San Francisco	79	320
Miguil	32	m	w	CA	San Luis Obispo	Santa Rosa Twp	87	324
ALVAN								
Carlo	29	m	w	ECUA	Contra Costa	Martinez P O	71	375
ALVAND								
H	46	m	w	PRUS	Yuba	Marysville	93	582
ALVANSAVAN								
B	31	m	w	PRUS	Contra Costa	Martinez P O	71	443
ALVARADO								
A	9	f	w	CA	Alameda	Oakland	68	242
A	20	f	w	CA	Los Angeles	Los Angeles	73	569
Anackle	47	m	w	CHIL	Marin	San Rafael Twp	74	34
Antonio	42	m	w	PORT	Marin	Bolinas Twp	74	4
Arcadia	60	f	w	CA	Los Angeles	Los Angeles	73	527
Arcadia	16	f	w	CA	Los Angeles	San Jose Twp	73	622
Balario	60	m	w	CHIL	El Dorado	Diamond Springs Tw	72	34
Diego	30	m	w	CA	San Diego	Warners Rancho Dis	78	528
Estefan	31	m	w	CA	Los Angeles	Los Angeles	73	525
Felipe	43	m	w	CA	Santa Cruz	Watsonville	89	373
Florentino	25	m	w	MEXI	Santa Clara	1-Wd San Jose	88	258
Francis	54	m	w	CA	San Bernardino	San Salvador Twp	78	459
Francisca	38	m	w	CA	Los Angeles	Los Angeles	73	528
Francisco	34	m	w	CA	Los Angeles	Los Angeles Twp	73	466
Gabrael	20	m	w	MEXI	Los Angeles	Wilmington Twp	73	645
Guadalupa	48	f	w	CA	San Diego	San Pasqual Valley	78	524
Guadalupe	38	m	w	CA	San Diego	San Pasqual	78	519
Guadelupe	33	m	w	CA	Marin	San Rafael Twp	74	41
Ignacio	63	m	w	CA	Los Angeles	San Jose Twp	73	622
Isidro	45	m	w	CA	Los Angeles	San Jose Twp	73	621
J	35	m	w	MEXI	Alameda	Alameda	68	10
J C	26	m	w	CA	Alameda	Oakland	68	142
Jesus	15	m	w	CA	Los Angeles	El Monte Twp	73	453
Jo	30	m	w	MEXI	Alameda	Alameda	68	11
Joaquin	35	m	w	CA	Santa Cruz	Watsonville	89	370
John	61	m	w	CA	Contra Costa	San Pablo Twp	71	355
Jose	42	m	w	CA	San Bernardino	Chino Twp	78	409
Jose M	22	m	w	CA	Los Angeles	San Jose Twp	73	622
Juan	50	m	w	CA	Monterey	San Juan Twp	74	418
Juan D	29	m	w	CA	Los Angeles	San Jose Twp	73	622
Manuel	14	m	w	CA	Los Angeles	Los Angeles Twp	73	469
Marianciana	45	m	w	CA	Los Angeles	Los Angeles	73	548
R	24	f	w	CA	San Bernardino	San Salvador Twp	78	455
Soledad	28	f	w	CA	Los Angeles	San Jose Twp	73	622
Sylvesa	21	m	w	CA	Yuba	Marysville	93	574
Tomas	30	m	w	CA	San Diego	San Pasqual	78	523
ALVARAS								
Pedro	36	m	i	MEXI	Merced	Snelling P O	74	263
ALVARAZ								
Andres	40	m	w	CA	Los Angeles	Los Angeles	73	548
Frances	35	f	w	TN	Marin	San Rafael	74	49
ALVARES								
Angel	45	f	w	CHIL	San Francisco	11-Wd San Francisc	84	520
Antonio	50	m	w	MEXI	Santa Barbara	San Buenaventura P	87	427
Maggie	35	f	w	MEXI	San Bernardino	San Bernardino Twp	78	426
Manuel J	40	m	w	SPAI	Santa Clara	Fremont Twp	88	54
ALVAREZ								
Angel	33	m	w	MEXI	Los Angeles	Los Angeles Twp	73	464
Antonio	30	m	w	PORT	Marin	Bolinas Twp	74	4
Florentine	38	m	w	MEXI	Kern	Havilah P O	73	337
Francisco	8	f	i	CA	Los Angeles	Los Angeles Twp	73	498
Francisco	34	m	w	MEXI	Los Angeles	Santa Ana Twp	73	607
Francisco	23	m	w	CA	Los Angeles	Santa Ana Twp	73	601
Gaefoina	40	m	w	MEXI	San Diego	San Pasqual	78	520
Greggory	49	m	w	MO	Nevada	Little York Twp	75	235
Gregorio	40	m	w	MEXI	San Diego	San Pasqual Valley	78	524
Guillermo	17	f	w	CA	Mariposa	Mariposa P O	74	110
Ignacio	30	m	w	MEXI	Santa Cruz	Pajaro Twp	89	340
Jesus	36	m	w	MEXI	Santa Cruz	Pajaro Twp	89	346
John	43	m	w	PORT	Contra Costa	Martinez P O	71	366
Jose	39	m	w	PORT	Los Angeles	Los Angeles	73	510
Jose M	45	m	w	MEXI	Los Angeles	Wilmington Twp	73	637
Juan	41	m	w	MEXI	San Francisco	1-Wd San Francisco	79	57
Juan	29	m	w	CA	Marin	San Rafael Twp	74	40
Luce	10	f	w	CA	Los Angeles	Los Angeles	73	514
Luisa	27	f	w	CA	Santa Cruz	Pajaro Twp	89	359
M	50	m	w	MEXI	Yuba	Marysville	93	588
Manuel	42	m	w	MEXI	Mariposa	Mariposa P O	74	110
Manuel	30	m	w	MEXI	Santa Cruz	Soquel Twp	89	444
Manuel	21	m	w	MEXI	Los Angeles	Los Angeles Twp	73	466
Maria	15	f	w	CA	San Diego	San Pasqual	78	520
Miguel	49	m	w	CHIL	Monterey	San Juan Twp	74	407
Miquel	42	m	w	MEXI	Fresno	Millerton P O	72	167
Simeon	50	m	w	MEXI	Plumas	Mineral Twp	77	23
Trinidad	50	m	w	MEXI	Plumas	Goodwin Twp	77	5
Trinidad	43	m	w	MEXI	San Luis Obispo	San Luis Obispo Tw	87	306

© 2001 by Heritage Quest. All rights reserved.

Series M593

Name	Age	S	R	B-PL	County	Locale	Roll	Pg
Vincenta	40	f	w	MEXI	San Francisco	San Francisco P O	80	339
Zechariah	43	m	w	MEXI	Santa Clara	Fremont Twp	88	62
ALVARILLO								
Francis	58	m	w	CA	San Bernardino	San Bernardino Twp	78	442
ALVAS								
Henry	63	m	w	SHOL	San Francisco	1-Wd San Francisco	79	74
ALVATER								
Francis	21	m	w	NY	San Francisco	1-Wd San Francisco	79	63
Philip	38	m	w	SAXO	Santa Clara	2-Wd San Jose	88	333
ALVENLY								
Lemark	32	m	w	LA	Siskiyou	Butte Twp	89	586
ALVERA								
Augustin	50	m	w	MEXI	Los Angeles	Los Angeles	73	522
ALVERADO								
Michael	40	m	w	CA	San Bernardino	San Salvador Twp	78	461
Pasquella	38	f	w	MEXI	San Francisco	6-Wd San Francisco	81	106
ALVERAS								
Juan	50	m	w	CHIL	Calaveras	San Andreas P O	70	177
Pasquel	39	m	i	CHIL	Merced	Snelling P O	74	272
ALVERDA								
Bertha	35	f	w	FRAN	San Joaquin	2-Wd Stockton	86	169
ALVERES								
Francis	53	m	w	MEXI	Santa Barbara	Santa Barbara P O	87	492
ALVEREZ								
Carnation	40	m	w	MEXI	Mariposa	Mariposa P O	74	105
Eugene	48	m	w	MO	Colusa	Stony Crk Twp	71	332
ALVERS								
Henry H	16	m	w	CA	San Francisco	6-Wd San Francisco	81	109
ALVERSON								
Frank	54	m	w	VT	Nevada	Rough & Ready Twp	75	331
William	49	m	w	NY	Santa Clara	2-Wd San Jose	88	332
ALVERZ								
Antonio	46	m	w	MEXI	Calaveras	Copperopolis P O	70	242
ALVES								
Antone	30	m	w	PORT	Alameda	Eden Twp	68	69
Frank	20	m	w	PORT	San Mateo	Half Moon Bay P O	87	389
Jesse	47	m	w	PORT	San Francisco	1-Wd San Francisco	79	130
ALVETRO								
Petronella	15	f	w	CA	Monterey	Salinas Twp	74	309
ALVEY								
Chs M	35	m	w	VA	San Francisco	2-Wd San Francisco	79	193
ALVIDO								
M	40	m	w	MEXI	Alameda	Alameda	68	10
ALVIN								
Concepcion	65	f	w	CA	Santa Clara	Santa Clara Twp	88	175
ALVINGTON								
Jo	37	m	w	ENGL	San Francisco	5-Wd San Francisco	81	33
ALVINO								
Juan	30	m	w	MEXI	Santa Clara	Almaden Twp	88	4
ALVIRO								
Manuel	50	m	w	MEXI	San Luis Obispo	San Luis Obispo Tw	87	311
ALVIS								
Angela	36	f	w	CA	Los Angeles	Los Angeles Twp	73	479
Anna	9	f	w	CA	Alameda	Oakland	68	166
John	24	m	w	SCOT	Alameda	Brooklyn Twp	68	56
Manuel	45	m	w	SCOT	Alameda	Brooklyn Twp	68	56
ALVISA								
Jose	40	m	w	MEXI	San Luis Obispo	San Luis Obispo Tw	87	305
Louis	97	m	w	MEXI	Tuolumne	Big Oak Flat P O	93	392
ALVISE								
Carlos	30	m	w	MEXI	San Francisco	2-Wd San Francisco	79	154
H	13	m	w	CA	Alameda	Murray Twp	68	111
ALVISO								
A	40	m	w	IL	San Joaquin	1-Wd Stockton	86	155
Angelo	30	m	w	MEXI	Santa Clara	1-Wd San Jose	88	262
Angelo M	52	m	w	MEXI	Santa Clara	Alviso Twp	88	26
Antonio	35	m	i	CA	San Luis Obispo	Salinas Twp	87	289
Augustin	60	m	w	CA	Alameda	Washington Twp	68	272
Augustine	22	m	w	CA	Santa Clara	Alviso Twp	88	22
Avael	36	m	w	CA	Santa Clara	Milpitas Twp	88	112
Berhenia	2	f	w	CA	Santa Clara	Alviso Twp	88	27
Catravias	36	f	w	CHIL	Santa Clara	Alviso Twp	88	23
F	50	m	w	CA	Alameda	Murray Twp	68	101
Francis	41	m	w	CA	Marin	San Rafael Twp	74	41
Francisco	40	f	w	CA	Fresno	Millerton P O	72	162
Gabriel	12	m	w	CA	Santa Clara	Milpitas Twp	88	112
Jesus	60	f	w	CA	Santa Clara	Gilroy Twp	88	87
Jesus	28	f	w	FRAN	San Francisco	San Francisco P O	80	462
Jesus	25	m	w	MEXI	San Bernardino	Belleville Twp	78	408
Jesus Maria	25	m	w	CA	Alameda	Washington Twp	68	272
Joaquin	26	m	w	MEXI	Stanislaus	Empire Twp	92	58
John	43	m	w	MEXI	Mendocino	Ten Mile Rvr Twp	74	172
Jos	27	m	w	ITAL	San Joaquin	1-Wd Stockton	86	154
Jose	21	m	w	MEXI	San Luis Obispo	San Luis Obispo Tw	87	310
Jose Antonio	70	m	w	CA	Santa Clara	Alviso Twp	88	23
Juan	50	m	w	MEXI	Calaveras	Copperopolis P O	70	262
Juan J	26	m	w	CA	Santa Clara	Alviso Twp	88	26
Juan Jose	34	m	w	CA	Santa Clara	Milpitas Twp	88	112
Leon	30	m	w	MEXI	San Joaquin	Douglas Twp	86	38
Lucio	32	m	w	MEXI	Marin	San Rafael Twp	74	42
Madelana	56	f	w	CA	Santa Clara	2-Wd San Jose	88	300
Pedro	25	m	w	CA	Santa Clara	Fremont Twp	88	50
Pedro	13	m	w	CA	Santa Clara	Milpitas Twp	88	112
Raphael	40	m	w	MEXI	San Joaquin	Douglas Twp	86	38
Romero	28	m	w	CA	Marin	San Rafael Twp	74	46
Rosaria	40	f	w	CA	Santa Clara	Alviso Twp	88	27
Thos	38	m	w	MEXI	Sacramento	Cosumnes Twp	77	92

Series M593

Name	Age	S	R	B-PL	County	Locale	Roll	Pg
ALVISON								
B F	36	m	w	NY	Tuolumne	Sonora P O	93	312
L M	39	m	w	NY	Tuolumne	Sonora P O	93	312
ALVITRA								
Ramon	30	m	w	CA	Marin	San Rafael Twp	74	36
ALVITRE								
Juliana	12	f	w	CA	Los Angeles	El Monte Twp	73	453
Ramona	7	f	w	CA	Los Angeles	El Monte Twp	73	453
Tomas	50	m	w	CA	Los Angeles	El Monte Twp	73	453
ALVITRO								
Andes	45	m	w	CA	San Bernardino	San Salvador Twp	78	461
ALVORADO								
John	20	m	w	PORT	Alameda	Alameda	68	6
ALVORD								
Chas E	43	m	w	NY	Santa Barbara	Santa Barbara P O	87	493
Henry	51	m	w	NY	San Francisco	1-Wd San Francisco	79	108
L	57	m	w	NY	Solano	Vallejo	90	206
Lorenzo	35	m	w	MI	Mariposa	Mariposa P O	74	98
Wm	37	m	w	NY	San Francisco	7-Wd San Francisco	81	250
ALVORNA								
Aniceta	36	m	w	CHIL	Placer	Bath P O	76	461
ALVUERO								
Jesus	28	m	w	CA	Santa Clara	Gilroy Twp	88	90
ALWALT								
Susan	36	f	w	SC	San Joaquin	2-Wd Stockton	86	170
ALWARD								
John	27	m	w	PA	Klamath	Camp Gaston	73	372
ALWAYS								
Antone	42	m	w	MEXI	Yolo	Washington Twp	93	533
ALWELL								
Samuel	29	m	w	ENGL	San Francisco	2-Wd San Francisco	79	169
ALWOOD								
Jno	65	m	w	VT	Alameda	Oakland	68	240
ALYALA								
Chico	52	m	w	MEXI	San Luis Obispo	Salinas Twp	87	291
ALYRSAS								
George	30	m	w	MEXI	Santa Clara	Almaden Twp	88	8
ALZINO								
Francisco	46	m	w	SPAI	Santa Cruz	Santa Cruz	89	406
AM								
Ah	28	m	c	CHIN	Tuolumne	Chinese Camp P O	93	378
Ah	22	m	c	CHIN	San Joaquin	1-Wd Stockton	86	151
Ah	15	m	c	CHIN	San Francisco	8-Wd San Francisco	82	461
Ah Lee	18	m	c	CHIN	Alameda	Hayward	68	74
Bay	36	m	c	CHIN	Shasta	French Gulch P O	89	469
Boy	30	f	c	CHIN	San Francisco	6-Wd San Francisco	81	74
By	34	m	c	CHIN	San Francisco	11-Wd San Francisc	84	521
Hing	38	m	c	CHIN	Calaveras	San Andreas P O	70	190
Hing	30	m	c	CHIN	Calaveras	San Andreas P O	70	164
I	21	f	c	CHIN	Stanislaus	Emory Twp	92	17
Ock	40	m	c	CHIN	Yuba	Marysville	93	622
Woon	10	m	c	CA	San Francisco	6-Wd San Francisco	81	59
AMADON								
O	60	m	w	NY	Sutter	Butte Twp	92	90
Paul	37	m	w	MEXI	Calaveras	Copperopolis P O	70	260
AMADOR								
Antonio	48	m	w	CA	Alameda	Washington Twp	68	288
J M	90	m	w	CA	Alameda	Murray Twp	68	101
Jose	18	m	w	CA	Fresno	Millerton P O	72	164
Kiatano	31	m	w	CA	San Luis Obispo	Santa Rosa Twp	87	328
M	20	f	w	CA	Alameda	Murray Twp	68	101
Maria	20	f	w	CA	Contra Costa	Martinez P O	71	440
Mary	23	f	w	MEXI	San Francisco	2-Wd San Francisco	79	147
Parrian	30	m	w	MEXI	Fresno	Millerton P O	72	164
Trinidad	29	m	w	CA	Marin	Sausalito Twp	74	66
AMAGER								
Leonardo	38	m	w	MEXI	Santa Clara	2-Wd San Jose	88	300
AMALLA								
Benito	46	m	w	CA	Santa Cruz	Santa Cruz Twp	89	384
Davis	35	m	w	CA	Santa Cruz	Santa Cruz	89	430
Edowardo	30	m	w	CA	Santa Cruz	Santa Cruz Twp	89	382
Joseph	25	m	w	CA	Santa Cruz	Santa Cruz	89	430
Rafael	28	m	w	CA	Santa Cruz	Santa Cruz Twp	89	387
AMALOI								
Antone	26	m	w	IREL	Marin	San Rafael Twp	74	25
AMAN								
Frank	59	m	w	FRAN	San Francisco	1-Wd San Francisco	79	133
Peter	40	m	w	GERM	Los Angeles	Los Angeles	73	528
Viclor	44	m	w	FRAN	Mariposa	Mariposa P O	74	128
AMANDA								
Jose	40	m	w	SPAI	San Francisco	1-Wd San Francisco	79	48
AMANDEY								
Julia	40	f	w	SAME	Marin	Sausalito Twp	74	70
AMANO								
Don	25	m	w	CA	San Diego	Warners Rancho Dis	78	528
AMANT								
Prosper	28	m	w	IREL	Solano	Denverton Twp	90	22
AMARAL								
Joseph	30	m	w	ITAL	Calaveras	San Andreas P O	70	204
AMARANTA								
Bartole	48	m	w	MEXI	Los Angeles	Los Angeles Twp	73	480
AMARIQUE								
Jose J	40	m	w	CHIL	Santa Clara	Fremont Twp	88	57
AMARIS								
Bernis	31	m	w	FRAN	San Francisco	2-Wd San Francisco	79	255
AMAT								
Joaquin	37	m	w	SPAI	Santa Barbara	Las Cruces P O	87	515

© 2001 by Heritage Quest. All rights reserved.

Series M593

Name	Age	S	R	B-PL	County	Locale	Roll	Pg
AMAY								
Louisa	5M	f	w	CA	San Francisco	San Francisco P O	83	23
AMBEL								
Conrad	30	m	w	PRUS	San Mateo	Half Moon Bay P O	87	401
AMBERG								
Jacob	58	m	w	SWIT	Nevada	Grass Valley Twp	75	222
Joseph	27	m	w	PA	San Francisco	11-Wd San Francisc	84	523
Solomon	20	m	w	WURT	Nevada	Washington Twp	75	341
AMBERSON								
William	38	m	w	PA	Placer	Alta P O	76	412
AMBERTON								
George	30	m	w	BADE	San Joaquin	Oneal Twp	86	111
AMBLER								
Benj	22	m	w	ENGL	San Francisco	San Francisco P O	83	304
Benj	21	m	w	ENGL	San Francisco	San Francisco P O	83	274
Dilforn	50	m	w	FRAN	Amador	Fiddletown P O	69	435
George	22	m	w	NY	Mariposa	Maxwell Crk P O	74	145
Nathan	40	m	w	OH	San Diego	Julian Dist	78	472
Stephen F	47	m	w	CT	Amador	Sutter Crk P O	69	414
AMBOE								
Gow	36	m	c	CHIN	El Dorado	Coloma Twp	72	1
AMBRESTER								
Mary	50	f	w	BADE	San Francisco	8-Wd San Francisco	82	346
AMBRIS								
Dorotio	53	m	w	MEXI	Monterey	San Antonio Twp	74	317
AMBROM								
Ed	37	m	w	CANA	San Joaquin	1-Wd Stockton	86	155
AMBRONSON								
Laus	40	m	w	SWED	San Francisco	2-Wd San Francisco	79	238
AMBROSE								
Catherine	2	f	w	CA	San Francisco	11-Wd San Francisc	84	711
Charles D	29	m	w	MI	Santa Clara	2-Wd San Jose	88	299
Francis	2M	m	w	CA	San Francisco	11-Wd San Francisc	84	637
George	35	m	w	PA	Colusa	Monroe Twp	71	316
Grief	57	m	b	IN	San Bernardino	San Bernardino Twp	78	419
Hannah	45	f	w	IREL	San Francisco	11-Wd San Francisc	84	483
Henry	25	m	w	WURT	San Francisco	11-Wd San Francisc	84	529
J M	51	m	w	MD	San Francisco	3-Wd San Francisco	79	314
James	32	m	w	IREL	San Francisco	San Francisco P O	85	832
Joe	17	m	w	PORT	Alameda	Murray Twp	68	114
John	36	m	w	KY	Tehama	Battle Crk Twp	92	158
Samuel	52	m	w	NY	Del Norte	Happy Camp Twp	71	471
Thos	25	m	w	IREL	Tehama	Merrill	92	197
AMBROSIO								
F	25	m	w	ITAL	Mariposa	Maxwell Crk P O	74	141
Giovani	27	m	w	SWIT	Santa Cruz	Santa Cruz Twp	89	398
Juan	45	m	i	CA	Santa Barbara	Las Cruces P O	87	506
L	35	m	w	ITAL	Mariposa	Maxwell Crk P O	74	144
AMBROSO								
Carlos	40	m	w	CHIL	El Dorado	Georgetown Twp	72	40
AMBROSS								
C	38	m	w	BAVA	Sacramento	1-Wd Sacramento	77	175
AMBRUSTER								
Andrew	34	m	w	BADE	Placer	Clipper Gap P O	76	376
Danil	47	m	w	BAVA	San Joaquin	Douglas Twp	86	31
Steven	41	m	w	BADE	Placer	Auburn P O	76	381
AMDESOL								
Sandal	40	m	w	MEXI	Santa Clara	Almaden Twp	88	11
AME								
Paul	29	m	w	FRAN	San Francisco	San Francisco P O	80	413
AMEDA								
Henrico	21	m	w	ITAL	San Mateo	Schoolhouse Statio	87	346
AMEDE								
Henrico	77	m	w	ITAL	San Mateo	Schoolhouse Statio	87	345
John	15	m	w	ITAL	San Mateo	Schoolhouse Statio	87	345
Louis	21	m	w	ITAL	San Mateo	Schoolhouse Statio	87	345
Tesso	45	m	w	FRAN	Siskiyou	Yreka	89	656
AMEDIE								
Jules	41	m	m	FRAN	San Francisco	8-Wd San Francisco	82	389
Mary	36	f	w	FRAN	San Francisco	8-Wd San Francisco	82	389
AMEDIER								
Honora	40	m	w	FRAN	Calaveras	San Andreas P O	70	218
AMEDO								
Florez	30	m	w	ITAL	San Mateo	Schoolhouse Statio	87	345
Henrico	22	m	w	ITAL	San Mateo	Schoolhouse Statio	87	346
John	40	m	w	ITAL	San Mateo	Schoolhouse Statio	87	345
John	40	m	w	ITAL	San Mateo	Schoolhouse Statio	87	346
John	26	m	w	ITAL	San Mateo	Schoolhouse Statio	87	345
John	18	m	w	ITAL	San Mateo	Schoolhouse Statio	87	344
AMEDON								
Reuben	38	m	w	NY	Santa Clara	Santa Clara Twp	88	136
AMEDOS								
Jose	29	m	w	CA	Marin	San Rafael Twp	74	38
AMEGO								
Manuel	40	m	w	ITAL	Sonoma	Petaluma Twp	91	363
AMELIA								
A Cowan	26	f	w	NY	Klamath	Hoopa Valley India	73	386
Ann	35	f	w	MEXI	San Joaquin	2-Wd Stockton	86	166
Antone	40	m	w	FRAN	El Dorado	Greenwood Twp	72	51
Jose	37	m	w	ITAL	Marin	Nicasio Twp	74	14
Josephine	1	f	w	CA	Monterey	Castroville Twp	74	339
AMELIUS								
J P	35	m	w	SWED	Sonoma	Mendocino Twp	91	307
AMEN								
Mathias	51	m	w	OH	Sonoma	Cloverdale Twp	91	266
AMENACHER								
Frank	31	m	w	SWIT	Yolo	Putah Twp	93	511
AMEND								
Charles	39	m	w	HDAR	San Francisco	3-Wd San Francisco	79	305
AMENESA								
Antonio	30	m	w	MEXI	Los Angeles	Wilmington Twp	73	639
AMENKA								
Minnie	45	f	w	PRUS	San Francisco	8-Wd San Francisco	82	408
AMER								
Frances	22	f	w	ENGL	San Joaquin	3-Wd Stockton	86	237
Juan	30	m	w	AFRI	Los Angeles	Los Angeles Twp	73	497
AMERIA								
Jesus	19	f	w	MEXI	Los Angeles	Los Angeles	73	561
AMERICA								
Charles	26	m	w	NY	Sacramento	Lee Twp	77	157
Henry	24	m	w	NY	Sacramento	San Joaquin Twp	77	398
John	33	m	w	NY	Sacramento	Lee Twp	77	159
John	25	m	w	OH	Sacramento	Lee Twp	77	158
AMERICAN								
Charles	25	m	w	OH	Sacramento	Lee Twp	77	159
J C	22	m	w	ENGL	Sutter	Vernon Twp	92	130
AMERICUS								
Jacob	35	m	w	US	Sacramento	San Joaquin Twp	77	402
AMERIGE								
George	64	m	w	MA	San Francisco	8-Wd San Francisco	82	439
AMERMAN								
H J	40	m	w	NY	Sonoma	Russian Rvr	91	369
Isaac	40	m	w	NY	Alameda	Eden Twp	68	92
AMERO								
John	45	m	w	ITAL	San Mateo	Schoolhouse Statio	87	332
AMERY								
Suirance	54	m	w	ITAL	Calaveras	San Andreas P O	70	174
AMES								
A D	41	m	w	MA	Alameda	Oakland	68	185
B	18	f	w	MA	Alameda	Oakland	68	138
Benj F	34	m	w	ME	San Francisco	San Francisco P O	83	330
Charles C	37	m	w	ME	Plumas	Indian Twp	77	12
Charles G	40	m	w	MA	Santa Clara	Santa Clara Twp	88	150
Charles P	33	m	w	ME	Sacramento	2-Wd Sacramento	77	238
Chas	25	m	w	MA	Sacramento	4-Wd Sacramento	77	330
Chas G	41	m	w	NY	Sonoma	Santa Rosa	91	413
D J	50	m	w	ME	Tuolumne	Sonora P O	93	308
Daniel	21	m	w	CA	San Diego	San Diego	78	507
David	31	m	w	NY	Sonoma	Vallejo Twp	91	459
E L	57	f	w	ME	San Francisco	San Francisco P O	85	826
Edwin E	31	m	w	MI	San Francisco	San Francisco P O	83	409
Ellis	58	m	w	OH	San Bernardino	San Bernardino Twp	78	423
Ellis	26	m	w	IA	San Bernardino	San Bernardino Twp	78	426
Emma	18	f	w	MA	San Francisco	8-Wd San Francisco	82	458
Everitt	28	m	w	IL	Sacramento	Cosumnes Twp	77	89
Francis	27	m	w	MA	San Joaquin	2-Wd Stockton	86	168
Francisco	28	m	w	MEXI	San Diego	San Diego	78	507
Frank	40	m	w	ENGL	Santa Clara	Fremont Twp	88	58
Frank	28	m	w	ME	San Francisco	11-Wd San Francisc	84	505
Frederick	26	m	w	ME	San Francisco	San Francisco P O	83	341
George	35	m	w	ARGE	Contra Costa	San Pablo Twp	71	364
Harvey	16	m	w	CA	San Francisco	11-Wd San Francisc	84	592
Henry	50	m	w	ME	Sacramento	1-Wd Sacramento	77	175
Henry	34	m	w	MA	San Francisco	11-Wd San Francisc	84	623
Jacob L	19	m	w	ME	Stanislaus	Empire Twp	92	52
Jane	77	f	w	ME	Sacramento	3-Wd Sacramento	77	293
John	45	m	w	ME	Amador	Volcano P O	69	388
John	42	m	w	ENGL	Sacramento	2-Wd Sacramento	77	212
John F	40	m	w	OH	San Bernardino	San Bernardino Twp	78	418
John P	21	m	w	ME	Stanislaus	Emory Twp	92	20
Joseph P	44	m	w	ENGL	San Mateo	Half Moon Bay P O	87	401
Josiah	57	m	w	ME	Sacramento	3-Wd Sacramento	77	293
Louis	43	m	w	NORW	Placer	Newcastle Twp	76	474
Lucy	72	f	w	CT	Sonoma	Bodega Twp	91	248
M	18	f	w	CA	Los Angeles	Los Angeles	73	569
Manley	60	m	w	ME	San Francisco	8-Wd San Francisco	82	487
N	16	f	w	CA	Los Angeles	Los Angeles	73	569
Nicolas	41	m	w	NM	Monterey	Salinas Twp	74	307
Oliver	35	m	w	NY	Alameda	Hayward	68	79
Ordelle T	38	m	w	VT	San Francisco	San Francisco P O	83	52
Otho N	39	m	w	NY	Santa Barbara	Santa Barbara P O	87	460
Perfectro	44	m	w	MEXI	San Diego	San Diego	78	507
Samuel	42	m	w	VT	Amador	Fiddletown P O	69	434
Thaddeus M	47	m	w	NY	Sonoma	Analy Twp	91	242
W	35	m	w	CANA	Sierra	Sierra Twp	89	569
Walter	11	m	w	CA	San Francisco	11-Wd San Francisc	84	592
William H	42	m	w	NY	Mariposa	Mariposa P O	74	111
William Z	35	m	w	MO	Siskiyou	Big Valley Twp	89	580
AMESBURY								
H W	56	m	w	CT	Napa	Napa Twp	75	67
James	43	m	w	ENGL	Yolo	Cache Crk Twp	93	429
James	43	m	w	ENGL	Yolo	Cache Crk Twp	93	430
AMESTE								
Prudenciana	65	f	w	CA	Monterey	Monterey	74	356
AMEY								
Chas W	27	m	w	MD	San Diego	Julian Dist	78	472
Ira	24	m	w	CANA	Santa Cruz	Santa Cruz Twp	89	391
Jacob	52	m	w	WURT	Calaveras	San Andreas P O	70	201
AMICK								
A J	41	m	w	MO	Amador	Ione City P O	69	358
James	14	m	w	CA	Amador	Ione City P O	69	357
AMIDON								
Ellen F	36	f	w	IREL	El Dorado	Diamond Springs Tw	72	21
John	37	m	w	NY	Alameda	Oakland	68	155

© 2001 by Heritage Quest. All rights reserved.

Name	Age	S	R	B-PL	County	Locale	Series M593 Roll	Pg
AMIGLAN								
Sophy	23	f	w	SWED	San Francisco	San Francisco P O	80	400
AMIGO								
Sarius	28	m	w	CHIL	Placer	Rocklin Twp	76	463
AMILLO								
Joseph	34	m	w	ITAL	Los Angeles	Los Angeles	73	551
AMIOT								
Louis	35	m	w	CANA	Nevada	Grass Valley Twp	75	154
AMIOTT								
E	38	m	w	ENGL	Sierra	Lincoln Twp	89	550
J	42	m	w	ENGL	Sierra	Lincoln Twp	89	550
AMIRAS								
W C	11	m	w	GA	Alameda	Oakland	68	155
AMIRDEN								
John	40	m	w	BAVA	Placer	Gold Run Twp	76	395
AMIS								
Everett	29	m	w	NY	Sacramento	Lee Twp	77	159
AMITIE								
Rosana	24	m	w	AZOR	Monterey	Monterey Twp	74	343
AMITO								
Gutierrez	20	m	w	CA	San Luis Obispo	Salinas Twp	87	291
AMMER								
Arther	35	m	w	IREL	San Joaquin	2-Wd Stockton	86	170
AMMERMAN								
Josh	41	m	w	PRUS	San Francisco	1-Wd San Francisco	79	109
AMMIE								
Henry	30	m	w	MD	San Francisco	8-Wd San Francisco	82	381
AMMON								
Charles	53	m	w	MEXI	El Dorado	Mud Springs Twp	72	90
Gaspar	48	m	w	CA	San Diego	Warners Rancho Dis	78	528
K	28	m	w	PA	Alameda	Oakland	68	262
AMMONDS								
Jane	45	f	w	NORW	San Francisco	San Francisco P O	80	403
AMMONS								
David R	38	m	w	IL	Nevada	Little York Twp	75	237
Henry B	49	m	w	KY	Solano	Vacaville Twp	90	118
John J	37	m	w	NC	Yolo	Cache Crk Twp	93	420
Nora	28	f	w	MS	Sacramento	3-Wd Sacramento	77	297
Samuel P	45	m	w	MO	Placer	Clipper Gap P O	76	376
AMNATHY								
Emma	6	f	i	CA	Humboldt	Eureka Twp	72	266
AMNER								
Thomas	29	m	w	ENGL	San Francisco	San Francisco P O	83	72
AMON								
Ah	44	m	c	CHIN	Placer	Auburn P O	76	358
Frank	29	m	w	NY	Sierra	Gibson Twp	89	539
Louis Francis	45	m	w	FRAN	Humboldt	Table Bluff Twp	72	305
AMOND								
John	31	m	w	IREL	Solano	Vallejo	90	201
AMONI								
Franco	31	m	w	ITAL	San Francisco	1-Wd San Francisco	79	122
AMOON								
---	18	m	c	CHIN	Sonoma	Santa Rosa	91	424
AMOR								
Max	40	m	w	PRUS	San Francisco	8-Wd San Francisco	82	452
AMORS								
F R	37	m	w	OH	Alameda	Oakland	68	231
AMOS								
Amariah	53	m	w	MA	Sacramento	Cosumnes Twp	77	89
Antonio	46	m	w	CHIL	San Mateo	Searsville P O	87	383
Geo A	46	m	w	ME	San Francisco	San Francisco P O	83	281
Harvy	55	m	w	VA	San Luis Obispo	Morro Twp	87	284
Isaac	32	m	w	PA	Santa Cruz	Santa Cruz Twp	89	393
John	36	m	w	MD	San Francisco	San Francisco P O	80	385
John	30	m	w	PORT	Alameda	Eden Twp	68	61
Wm C	29	m	w	MD	San Francisco	1-Wd San Francisco	79	15
AMOZ								
Jose	48	m	w	SPAI	Santa Barbara	San Buenaventura P	87	443
AMPARO								
Enedia	15	f	w	MEXI	San Bernardino	San Bernardino Twp	78	430
AMPHLETT								
William	35	m	w	NY	Stanislaus	Empire Twp	92	29
AMSBURY								
Thos	40	m	w	ME	San Francisco	11-Wd San Francisc	84	657
AMSDEN								
E F	20	m	w	NY	Sacramento	1-Wd Sacramento	77	176
Isaac	45	m	w	NY	Mariposa	Mariposa P O	74	120
O Re	26	m	w	CA	Sacramento	1-Wd Sacramento	77	172
AMSKAT								
D	46	m	w	SWIT	San Joaquin	1-Wd Stockton	86	131
AMSLEY								
Wm	37	m	w	MA	San Francisco	San Francisco P O	83	264
AMSTALDEN								
Frank	42	m	w	SWIT	El Dorado	Placerville Twp	72	93
AMSTUTZ								
Henry S	35	m	w	SWIT	Napa	Napa	75	48
AMTON								
E	33	m	w	SCOT	Alameda	Oakland	68	265
AMY								
Alford	19	m	w	CANA	Colusa	Spring Valley Twp	71	337
Clord B	56	m	w	FRAN	Tuolumne	Sonora P O	93	326
Gustav	30	m	w	LA	San Francisco	6-Wd San Francisco	81	95
Lavina	56	f	w	NY	San Francisco	San Francisco P O	80	404
Oscar M	33	m	w	LA	Santa Clara	1-Wd San Jose	88	264
Victor	37	m	w	FRAN	Mariposa	Mariposa P O	74	118
AMYX								
A	12	m	w	CA	Solano	Benicia	90	21
AN								
Ah	33	m	c	CHIN	El Dorado	Diamond Springs Tw	72	25
Ah	31	m	c	CHIN	Sacramento	1-Wd Sacramento	77	204
Ah	25	m	c	CHIN	Sacramento	Georgianna Twp	77	133
Ah	16	m	c	CHIN	Tuolumne	Chinese Camp P O	93	377
Arn	22	m	c	CHIN	Contra Costa	Martinez P O	71	397
Cow	19	m	c	CHIN	Tuolumne	Big Oak Flat P O	93	400
Gee	20	m	c	CHIN	San Francisco	8-Wd San Francisco	82	438
Gow	23	m	c	CHIN	Calaveras	San Andreas P O	70	173
Ha	22	m	c	CHIN	Los Angeles	Los Angeles	73	507
Lan	21	m	c	CHIN	Solano	Green Valley Twp	90	43
Pee	45	m	c	CHIN	Yuba	Marysville	93	625
Up	40	m	c	CHIN	San Joaquin	Liberty Twp	86	95
ANABLE								
John	45	m	w	KY	El Dorado	Coloma Twp	72	4
ANAIN								
Faustina	27	m	w	CA	Santa Cruz	Santa Cruz Twp	89	382
ANANAS								
Juan	27	m	w	CA	Los Angeles	Los Angeles	73	550
ANANDES								
Patricia	39	m	w	MEXI	Yuba	Marysville	93	594
ANANDO								
Ygnacio	30	m	w	CHIL	Mariposa	Mariposa P O	74	129
ANARTA								
Alicia	28	f	w	MEXI	San Francisco	San Francisco P O	80	466
ANASTETTA								
J	40	m	w	MEXI	El Dorado	Greenwood Twp	72	55
ANATEMA								
Emanuel	34	m	w	CHIL	Fresno	Millerton P O	72	159
ANAYA								
Ignacio	37	m	w	MEXI	Mariposa	Mariposa P O	74	123
ANCEELL								
Felix	43	m	w	FRAN	Nevada	Bridgeport Twp	75	124
ANCHO								
Rolen	22	m	w	ITAL	San Francisco	11-Wd San Francisc	84	709
ANCIHERMAN								
Jacob	28	m	w	NY	San Francisco	5-Wd San Francisco	81	13
ANCOSTA								
Miguel	31	m	w	MEXI	Santa Clara	Fremont Twp	88	57
ANCROVA								
Wm	33	m	w	ENGL	Sacramento	Dry Crk Twp	77	103
AND								
Joseph	42	m	w	MO	Kern	Havilah P O	73	338
Joseph	15	m	w	NV	San Francisco	11-Wd San Francisc	84	592
William	29	m	w	IREL	Solano	Silveyville Twp	90	87
ANDALIS								
Manuel	50	m	w	MEXI	Santa Clara	Almaden Twp	88	13
ANDAM								
G A	40	m	w	MEXI	Tuolumne	Sonora P O	93	315
ANDARA								
Patricio	24	m	w	MEXI	Santa Clara	Burnett Twp	88	34
ANDARES								
Joseph	38	m	w	WURT	Placer	Bath P O	76	432
ANDATASA								
Joseph	20	m	i	MEXI	Inyo	Cerro Gordo Twp	73	322
ANDAWORK								
Joseph	50	m	w	SWIT	Tulare	Visalia	92	300
ANDEFFRED								
H	41	m	w	FRAN	San Francisco	San Francisco P O	85	788
ANDENNETTE								
John	45	m	w	ITAL	San Francisco	8-Wd San Francisco	82	429
ANDERLAND								
Frank	42	m	w	FRAN	Marin	San Rafael Twp	74	32
ANDERLIES								
Andrew	24	m	w	FRAN	San Francisco	2-Wd San Francisco	79	278
ANDERLION								
Peter	26	m	w	ITAL	Sonoma	Vallejo Twp	91	454
ANDERS								
Ellen	25	f	w	NC	San Joaquin	Douglas Twp	86	47
ANDERSEN								
Chrisr	24	m	w	DENM	San Francisco	1-Wd San Francisco	79	85
Hans	33	m	w	DENM	Placer	Lincoln P O	76	488
Jas E	31	m	w	NORW	San Francisco	1-Wd San Francisco	79	109
Peter	38	m	w	HAMB	San Francisco	6-Wd San Francisco	81	82
Peter	34	m	w	SWED	San Francisco	6-Wd San Francisco	81	96
Peter	27	m	w	DENM	San Francisco	1-Wd San Francisco	79	120
Peter	25	m	w	SWED	San Francisco	1-Wd San Francisco	79	120
ANDERSON								
--- Mrs	43	f	w	IA	Sacramento	1-Wd Sacramento	77	190
A	45	m	w	SWED	Trinity	Douglas	92	235
A	45	m	w	PRUS	San Joaquin	2-Wd Stockton	86	205
A	40	m	w	SWED	San Francisco	7-Wd San Francisco	81	218
A	35	m	w	DENM	Sierra	Butte Twp	89	510
A	31	m	w	SWED	Del Norte	Crescent Twp	71	454
A	25	m	w	IL	Yuba	Rose Bar Twp	93	666
A B	48	m	w	KY	Merced	Snelling P O	74	253
A G	43	m	w	KY	Los Angeles	Los Angeles Twp	73	472
A H	32	m	w	AL	Sacramento	4-Wd Sacramento	77	345
A J	28	m	w	NY	Alameda	Oakland	68	262
A J	26	m	w	SCOT	Alameda	Oakland	68	247
A P	27	m	w	IA	Merced	Snelling P O	74	262
A R	50	m	w	TN	Calaveras	Copperopolis P O	70	225
Abiara	37	m	w	OH	Sutter	Butte Twp	92	90
Abraham	40	m	w	ENGL	San Francisco	San Francisco P O	83	187
Abraham	35	m	w	SWED	San Francisco	San Francisco P O	83	187
Adam	33	m	w	PA	Placer	Dutch Flat P O	76	415
Addie	18	f	w	DE	San Francisco	San Francisco P O	83	228

© 2001 by Heritage Quest. All rights reserved.

Name	Age	S	R	B-PL	County	Series M593 Locale	Roll	Pg
Adin	23	m	w	NORW	Placer	Summit P O	76	496
Agust	28	m	w	MA	San Francisco	7-Wd San Francisco	81	218
Albert	21	m	w	IA	Santa Clara	1-Wd San Jose	88	278
Alex	19	m	w	CA	Amador	Jackson P O	69	340
Alex E	24	m	w	NY	Butte	Ophir Twp	70	117
Alexander	38	m	w	SCOT	Santa Clara	Milpitas Twp	88	112
Alexr	30	m	w	NY	San Francisco	5-Wd San Francisco	81	3
Alfred	25	m	w	SWED	Santa Cruz	Santa Cruz	89	405
Alx	42	m	w	MS	Napa	Yountville Twp	75	85
Anderson	44	m	w	NORW	San Francisco	7-Wd San Francisco	81	259
Anderson	36	m	w	NORW	Santa Clara	Fremont Twp	88	51
Andrew	59	m	w	SCOT	Alameda	Washington Twp	68	287
Andrew	55	m	w	NY	Santa Clara	Almaden Twp	88	19
Andrew	55	m	w	DENM	Marin	Novato Twp	74	11
Andrew	40	m	w	NY	Plumas	Plumas Twp	77	31
Andrew	40	m	w	FINL	San Francisco	3-Wd San Francisco	79	291
Andrew	39	m	w	PRUS	Mendocino	Anderson Twp	74	157
Andrew	38	m	w	NORW	Monterey	Alisal Twp	74	298
Andrew	36	m	w	DENM	Alameda	Eden Twp	68	86
Andrew	35	m	w	NORW	San Diego	San Diego	78	488
Andrew	34	m	w	SWED	San Mateo	Pescadero P O	87	410
Andrew	33	m	w	SWED	Mendocino	Point Arena Twp	74	214
Andrew	33	m	w	DENM	Stanislaus	Emory Twp	92	26
Andrew	32	m	w	SWED	Mendocino	Point Arena Twp	74	215
Andrew	32	m	w	FINL	Mendocino	Anderson Twp	74	155
Andrew	30	m	w	SCOT	San Francisco	1-Wd San Francisco	79	122
Andrew	28	m	w	SWED	San Mateo	Woodside P O	87	384
Andrew	28	m	w	SWED	Mendocino	Bourns Landing Twp	74	223
Andrew	22	m	w	SWED	San Francisco	1-Wd San Francisco	79	73
Andrew	20	m	w	NORW	Placer	Cisco P O	76	494
Andrew F	24	m	w	SWED	Sonoma	Bodega Twp	91	264
Andrew J	47	m	w	OH	Mendocino	Anderson Twp	74	157
Andw	23	m	w	DENM	San Francisco	1-Wd San Francisco	79	116
Andy	38	m	w	SWIT	Solano	Vallejo	90	170
Anna	48	f	w	DENM	Alameda	Eden Twp	68	92
Anthony	37	m	w	NORW	Calaveras	San Andreas P O	70	157
Augustus	46	m	w	MA	Alameda	Hayward	68	79
Augustus	37	m	w	SWED	Yolo	Grafton Twp	93	493
Augustus	35	m	w	SWED	Tulare	Venice Twp	92	273
Augustus P	44	m	w	VA	Nevada	Grass Valley Twp	75	161
Austin	22	m	w	CANA	Santa Clara	Fremont Twp	88	47
Aw	31	m	w	SWED	Humboldt	Eureka Twp	72	258
Azer R	41	m	w	KY	Tulare	Venice Twp	92	274
B D	48	m	w	NY	Yuba	East Bear Rvr Twp	93	544
B T	35	m	w	AL	Alameda	Murray Twp	68	116
Benj	36	m	w	MO	Nevada	Bridgeport Twp	75	117
Benjamin	26	m	w	RI	San Francisco	7-Wd San Francisco	81	173
Bente	24	m	w	SWED	Mendocino	Casper & Big Rvr	74	164
Bernard	33	m	w	SCOT	San Francisco	1-Wd San Francisco	79	79
C	33	f	w	ENGL	Alameda	Oakland	68	132
C	22	m	w	SWED	Sacramento	3-Wd Sacramento	77	297
Carl M	58	m	w	NY	Sonoma	Mendocino Twp	91	298
Carmelita	40	f	m	NGRA	San Francisco	1-Wd San Francisco	79	128
Catherine	33	f	w	IREL	San Francisco	3-Wd San Francisco	79	294
Charles	50	m	w	PRUS	Solano	Tremont Twp	90	35
Charles	48	m	w	ENGL	Placer	Gold Run Twp	76	400
Charles	48	m	w	NORW	Mendocino	Point Arena Twp	74	215
Charles	46	m	w	DENM	Tuolumne	Chinese Camp P O	93	378
Charles	45	m	w	SCOT	Santa Clara	2-Wd San Jose	88	312
Charles	40	m	w	NORW	El Dorado	Georgetown Twp	72	41
Charles	39	m	w	CANA	El Dorado	Placerville Twp	72	103
Charles	38	m	w	NORW	Placer	Auburn P O	76	358
Charles	37	m	w	SWED	Mendocino	Little Rvr Twp	74	165
Charles	36	m	w	HDAR	Solano	Rio Vista Twp	90	64
Charles	35	m	w	SWED	San Francisco	San Francisco P O	83	364
Charles	34	m	w	SCOT	Tuolumne	Big Oak Flat P O	93	400
Charles	34	m	w	SWED	El Dorado	Salmon Falls Twp	72	131
Charles	32	m	w	IN	Stanislaus	Branch Twp	92	5
Charles	31	m	w	DENM	Mendocino	Navarro & Big Rvr	74	177
Charles	30	m	w	FRAN	San Francisco	San Francisco P O	80	350
Charles	3	m	w	CA	Marin	San Rafael	74	50
Charles	29	m	w	DENM	Sutter	Nicolaus Twp	92	110
Charles	28	m	w	IREL	Placer	Rocklin Twp	76	464
Charles	26	m	w	SWED	Contra Costa	Martinez P O	71	392
Charles Albert	57	m	w	VA	Plumas	Quartz Twp	77	36
Charles L	43	m	w	VA	Santa Cruz	Santa Cruz Twp	89	383
Charlotte	35	f	w	SWED	Alameda	Eden Twp	68	72
Charls S	37	m	w	MO	Inyo	Cerro Gordo Twp	73	318
Chas	46	m	w	VA	San Francisco	11-Wd San Francisc	84	684
Chas	45	m	w	SCOT	San Francisco	San Francisco P O	83	106
Chas	39	m	m	PA	Amador	Volcano P O	69	374
Chas	33	m	w	SWED	San Francisco	7-Wd San Francisco	81	259
Chas	31	m	w	SWED	Shasta	Shasta P O	89	457
Chas	31	m	w	DENM	San Francisco	1-Wd San Francisco	79	86
Chas	28	m	w	NY	San Francisco	1-Wd San Francisco	79	127
Chas	26	m	w	DENM	Napa	Yountville Twp	75	90
Chas	24	m	w	PRUS	Alameda	Murray Twp	68	102
Chas	22	m	b	VA	Marin	San Rafael Twp	74	39
Chas E	30	m	w	PA	San Francisco	6-Wd San Francisco	81	93
Chirestian	25	m	w	FINL	San Francisco	3-Wd San Francisco	79	291
Chis	18	m	w	NORW	Napa	Napa	75	40
Chist	30	m	w	SWED	San Francisco	2-Wd San Francisco	79	194
Christ	36	m	w	DENM	Sonoma	Santa Rosa	91	409
Christ	33	m	w	HANO	Alameda	Eden Twp	68	58
Christ	33	m	w	DENM	Alameda	Eden Twp	68	57
Christ	32	m	w	DENM	Alameda	Eden Twp	68	57
Christ	22	m	w	DENM	Alameda	Hayward	68	76
Christ	21	m	w	DENM	Mendocino	Noyo & Big Rvr Twp	74	173
Christian	40	m	w	DENM	El Dorado	Cosumnes Twp	72	13
Christian	32	m	w	DENM	Mendocino	Little Rvr Twp	74	165
Christine	28	f	w	SWED	San Francisco	1-Wd San Francisco	79	48
Chs	42	m	w	CANA	San Francisco	2-Wd San Francisco	79	248
Clara	11	f	w	CA	Siskiyou	Scott Valley Twp	89	609
Critz	25	m	w	PRUS	Alameda	Murray Twp	68	109
Crs	20	f	w	SWED	Merced	Snelling P O	74	254
Cyntha	52	f	b	NC	Shasta	Shasta P O	89	463
D	28	m	w	IN	Santa Clara	Almaden Twp	88	19
D A	33	m	w	SCOT	Tuolumne	Columbia P O	93	339
D G	58	m	w	KY	Tehama	Paynes Crk Twp	92	167
Daniel	45	m	w	SWED	Mariposa	Mariposa P O	74	101
David	61	m	w	PA	Los Angeles	Los Angeles	73	505
David	51	m	w	SCOT	San Francisco	San Francisco P O	80	337
David	40	m	w	IN	Solano	Denverton Twp	90	26
David	39	m	w	OH	Nevada	Nevada Twp	75	296
David	38	m	w	IN	San Luis Obispo	Arroyo Grande Twp	87	271
David	27	m	w	VA	Tulare	Farmersville Twp	92	243
David	23	m	w	NORW	Placer	Cisco P O	76	494
Delia	40	f	w	NY	Sacramento	2-Wd Sacramento	77	243
Dora	22	f	w	NY	San Francisco	San Francisco P O	83	240
E	44	f	b	VA	Sacramento	3-Wd Sacramento	77	262
E	31	m	w	NY	Alameda	Oakland	68	263
E A	12	m	w	ME	Solano	Vallejo	90	181
E J	28	m	w	NY	Solano	Vallejo	90	162
E M	45	m	w	SWED	San Francisco	3-Wd San Francisco	79	311
Ed	38	m	w	SWED	Sacramento	1-Wd Sacramento	77	189
Edd	25	m	w	MO	Placer	Colfax P O	76	386
Edward	30	m	w	DENM	San Francisco	7-Wd San Francisco	81	218
Edward	24	m	w	NY	Alameda	Washington Twp	68	271
Edwd	23	m	w	ENGL	San Francisco	1-Wd San Francisco	79	82
Elias	53	m	w	KY	Shasta	American Ranch P O	89	499
Elias	34	m	w	NORW	Sierra	Sears Twp	89	560
Elijah	63	m	w	NY	Santa Clara	2-Wd San Jose	88	291
Elijah D	44	m	w	VA	Butte	Oregon Twp	70	127
Elijah M	33	m	w	ME	Plumas	Quartz Twp	77	37
Eliza	30	f	w	SCOT	Sacramento	1-Wd Sacramento	77	200
Eliza	14	f	w	CA	Monterey	Pajaro Twp	74	374
Elizabeth	52	f	w	ENGL	Santa Clara	Fremont Twp	88	44
Elizabeth	47	f	w	IN	Solano	Denverton Twp	90	26
Elizabeth	42	f	w	TN	Fresno	Millerton P O	72	156
Elizabeth	26	f	w	AUST	San Francisco	San Francisco P O	80	483
Elizabeth	18	f	w	MO	Napa	Napa	75	10
Ellen	25	f	w	SWED	Santa Clara	San Jose Twp	88	193
Ellen	22	f	w	AL	San Diego	San Diego	78	501
Erasmus	25	m	w	DENM	San Francisco	3-Wd San Francisco	79	298
F	48	m	w	KY	Amador	Fiddletown P O	69	434
F	44	m	w	PA	Sierra	Downieville Twp	89	518
F G	34	m	w	IL	Merced	Snelling P O	74	256
Florence	13	f	w	CA	Colusa	Colusa	71	297
Frances	30	f	b	GA	San Francisco	6-Wd San Francisco	81	72
Frank	44	m	w	ENGL	San Francisco	11-Wd San Francisc	84	478
Frank	43	m	w	NY	San Francisco	2-Wd San Francisco	79	194
Frank	33	m	w	DENM	Mendocino	Casper & Big Rvr	74	162
Frank	32	m	w	DENM	San Francisco	1-Wd San Francisco	79	79
Frank	32	m	w	WURT	Alameda	Alvarado	68	304
Fred	24	m	w	DENM	San Francisco	11-Wd San Francisc	84	613
Frederick	47	m	w	SWED	San Francisco	1-Wd San Francisco	79	122
Frederick	39	m	w	PRUS	Placer	Bath P O	76	428
Frederick	28	m	w	RUSS	Calaveras	Copperopolis P O	70	262
Fredk	44	m	w	DENM	San Francisco	San Francisco P O	83	34
Fredrick	30	m	w	SWED	Plumas	Washington Twp	77	55
Fritz	49	m	w	PRUS	Solano	Tremont Twp	90	32
G	37	m	w	IA	Nevada	Washington Twp	75	343
G D	40	m	w	VA	Monterey	Alisal Twp	74	301
Garlon	39	m	w	KY	Tulare	Farmersville Twp	92	245
Geo	41	m	w	NORW	San Francisco	1-Wd San Francisco	79	129
Geo	40	m	w	SWED	San Francisco	San Francisco P O	85	825
Geo	38	m	w	SCOT	Tuolumne	Big Oak Flat P O	93	400
Geo	32	m	w	NY	Alameda	Murray Twp	68	99
Geo B	55	m	w	SCOT	Sacramento	4-Wd Sacramento	77	321
George	73	m	w	KY	Sonoma	Mendocino Twp	91	297
George	50	m	w	NH	San Francisco	3-Wd San Francisco	79	287
George	42	m	w	KY	Placer	Blue Canyon P O	76	418
George	40	m	w	IREL	Placer	Pino Twp	76	470
George	40	m	w	CANA	Solano	Suisun Twp	90	108
George	40	m	w	PRUS	San Francisco	San Francisco P O	83	251
George	37	m	w	ENGL	Contra Costa	Martinez P O	71	418
George	35	m	w	SCOT	Amador	Drytown P O	69	422
George	35	m	w	KY	Placer	Emigrant Gap P O	76	417
George	34	m	w	IREL	San Francisco	San Francisco P O	80	336
George	33	m	w	NY	San Francisco	11-Wd San Francisc	84	465
George	33	m	w	FINL	Placer	Summit P O	76	496
George	31	m	w	NORW	San Francisco	2-Wd San Francisco	79	145
George	26	m	w	ENGL	Sacramento	2-Wd Sacramento	77	244
George	23	m	w	VA	Placer	Dutch Flat P O	76	414
George	17	m	w	IL	Siskiyou	Cottonwood Twp	89	590
George W	34	m	w	ENGL	Nevada	Grass Valley Twp	75	150
Gilbert L	32	m	w	SCOT	Santa Cruz	Pajaro Twp	89	340
Gustave	25	m	w	DENM	San Francisco	2-Wd San Francisco	79	194
H	61	m	w	SWED	Amador	Sutter Crk P O	69	413
H C	40	m	w	OH	Nevada	Bloomfield Twp	75	99
Hans C	25	m	w	SWED	San Francisco	1-Wd San Francisco	79	65
Harriett A	52	f	w	NY	Santa Clara	1-Wd San Jose	88	278
Harry	37	m	w	FINL	Placer	Bath P O	76	457
Hartford	52	m	w	PA	Sacramento	Granite Twp	77	146

© 2001 by Heritage Quest. All rights reserved.

California 1870 Census

							Series M593	
Name	Age	S	R	B-PL	County	Locale	Roll	Pg
Harvey	28	m	w	PRUS	San Diego	Julian Dist	78	472
Harvey A	35	m	w	VA	Stanislaus	Branch Twp	92	4
Henery	30	m	w	ENGL	San Francisco	7-Wd San Francisco	81	218
Henry	55	m	w	POLA	San Francisco	1-Wd San Francisco	79	37
Henry	48	m	w	DENM	San Francisco	1-Wd San Francisco	79	52
Henry	46	m	w	OH	Nevada	Bridgeport Twp	75	120
Henry	42	m	w	SWED	San Francisco	2-Wd San Francisco	79	273
Henry	41	m	w	NORW	Nevada	Bloomfield Twp	75	92
Henry	40	m	w	NY	Nevada	Bloomfield Twp	75	95
Henry	40	m	w	HOLL	Fresno	Millerton P O	72	150
Henry	37	m	w	SWIT	San Francisco	3-Wd San Francisco	79	318
Henry	35	m	w	NORW	Yolo	Putah Twp	93	515
Henry	35	m	w	BAVA	San Francisco	8-Wd San Francisco	82	458
Henry	32	m	b	VA	Sacramento	2-Wd Sacramento	77	238
Henry	30	m	w	AR	Colusa	Colusa	71	291
Henry	25	m	w	DENM	Mendocino	Point Arena Twp	74	215
Henry C	42	m	w	KY	Sonoma	Petaluma Twp	91	325
Hilda	38	f	w	SWED	San Francisco	San Francisco P O	83	24
Hong	41	m	w	PRUS	Placer	Dutch Flat P O	76	403
Hugh	42	m	w	SCOT	San Francisco	San Francisco P O	83	336
Hy	30	m	w	SWED	San Francisco	11-Wd San Francisc	84	625
Iredell	36	m	w	IL	Sacramento	Center Twp	77	82
Isaac	43	m	w	NORW	Alameda	Brooklyn	68	36
J	50	m	w	NY	Solano	Vallejo	90	162
J	46	m	w	HANO	Alameda	Oakland	68	194
J	42	m	w	TN	Sierra	Forest Twp	89	531
J	40	m	w	ME	Alameda	Oakland	68	221
J	38	m	w	VT	Alameda	Oakland	68	222
J	37	m	w	CANA	Sierra	Butte Twp	89	511
J	35	m	w	ME	Alameda	Oakland	68	210
J	28	m	w	NY	Sierra	Sierra Twp	89	568
J A	46	m	w	SWED	Tuolumne	Chinese Camp P O	93	369
J A	43	m	w	KY	San Joaquin	Elliott Twp	86	75
J G	48	m	w	VT	Santa Clara	Gilroy Twp	88	85
J R	30	m	w	TX	San Joaquin	Liberty Twp	86	96
J S	49	m	w	CANA	El Dorado	Georgetown Twp	72	40
J S	38	m	w	SWED	Tuolumne	Big Oak Flat P O	93	405
Jackson	41	m	m	MO	Shasta	Shasta P O	89	462
Jacob	44	m	w	OH	Sutter	Yuba Twp	92	146
Jacob	30	m	w	HANO	Alameda	Eden Twp	68	63
Jacob P	24	m	w	SWED	Sonoma	Bodega Twp	91	252
James	51	m	w	MO	Santa Barbara	San Buenaventura P	87	431
James	50	m	w	SCOT	El Dorado	Mud Springs Twp	72	81
James	49	m	b	EIND	San Joaquin	1-Wd Stockton	86	127
James	47	m	w	IREL	San Diego	Poway Dist	78	481
James	46	m	w	MO	Sutter	Sutter Twp	92	120
James	45	m	w	SCOT	Amador	Fiddletown P O	69	437
James	43	m	w	SCOT	San Francisco	San Francisco P O	83	162
James	42	m	w	ENGL	San Luis Obispo	Arroyo Grande Twp	87	275
James	42	m	w	IN	Siskiyou	Butte Twp	89	586
James	42	m	w	MO	Sacramento	Franklin Twp	77	111
James	41	m	w	IN	Contra Costa	Martinez P O	71	403
James	36	m	w	CANA	San Mateo	Half Moon Bay P O	87	398
James	36	m	w	SCOT	San Francisco	1-Wd San Francisco	79	125
James	35	m	w	TN	Trinity	Junction City Pct	92	206
James	32	m	w	DENM	San Francisco	San Francisco P O	83	76
James	30	m	w	SWED	San Francisco	7-Wd San Francisco	81	218
James	29	m	w	NY	Marin	San Rafael Twp	74	40
James	28	m	w	SWED	El Dorado	Georgetown Twp	72	48
James	28	m	w	IREL	Fresno	Millerton P O	72	167
James	24	m	w	DENM	Alameda	Oakland	68	250
James	24	m	w	DENM	Humboldt	Arcata Twp	72	232
James	22	m	w	MO	Colusa	Butte Twp	71	265
James	21	m	w	MD	Alameda	Oakland	68	252
James	21	m	w	CANA	San Francisco	11-Wd San Francisc	84	693
James	20	m	w	DENM	Napa	Napa	75	6
James	13	m	w	MA	San Francisco	11-Wd San Francisc	84	586
James G	47	m	w	IN	Sonoma	Bodega Twp	91	258
James L	36	m	w	MO	Los Angeles	Los Nietos Twp	73	584
James M	43	m	w	SCOT	Monterey	San Juan Twp	74	400
James M	40	m	w	PA	El Dorado	Placerville	72	121
James W	39	m	w	PA	Sonoma	Petaluma Twp	91	328
Jane	48	f	w	IREL	Alameda	Hayward	68	79
Jane	30	f	w	NY	San Francisco	San Francisco P O	85	839
Jas	40	m	w	SCOT	Butte	Kimshew Tpw	70	80
Jas	37	m	w	NY	San Joaquin	Douglas Twp	86	51
Jas	37	m	w	IREL	Calaveras	Copperopolis P O	70	237
Jas	34	m	b	MD	Solano	Vallejo	90	203
Jas	24	m	w	IN	Sacramento	1-Wd Sacramento	77	178
Jas B	23	m	w	DENM	Humboldt	Arcata Twp	72	228
Jasper	22	m	w	SHOL	Placer	Lincoln P O	76	488
Jennie	38	f	w	SCOT	Nevada	Nevada Twp	75	274
Jessie	74	f	w	CA	Tehama	Paynes Crk Twp	92	167
Jim	32	m	w	IREL	Sacramento	4-Wd Sacramento	77	371
Jno	32	m	w	SWED	Sonoma	Santa Rosa	91	424
Jno	22	m	w	SWED	Santa Clara	Gilroy Twp	88	88
Jno B	17	m	w	CA	Butte	Chico Twp	70	22
John	77	m	w	SCOT	Santa Clara	Santa Clara Twp	88	149
John	53	m	w	PA	Siskiyou	Yreka Twp	89	664
John	49	m	w	VA	Nevada	Nevada Twp	75	275
John	48	m	w	FINL	Marin	Sausalito Twp	74	68
John	48	m	w	ENGL	Solano	Vallejo	90	192
John	48	m	w	FINL	Placer	Bath P O	76	457
John	46	m	w	DENM	Stanislaus	Empire Twp	92	27
John	46	m	w	SCOT	San Francisco	11-Wd San Francisc	84	684
John	46	m	w	MA	San Francisco	San Francisco P O	83	123
John	45	m	w	MO	San Joaquin	Elkhorn Twp	86	63
John	45	m	w	NORW	San Francisco	1-Wd San Francisco	79	129
John	44	m	w	SWED	Klamath	Sawyers Bar	73	377
John	44	m	w	FINL	Plumas	Indian Twp	77	12
John	44	m	w	MO	San Joaquin	Liberty Twp	86	93
John	44	m	w	SCOT	San Francisco	1-Wd San Francisco	79	25
John	42	m	w	GA	Shasta	Horsetown P O	89	503
John	41	m	w	SWED	San Francisco	1-Wd San Francisco	79	121
John	40	m	w	CT	Los Angeles	Los Angeles	73	571
John	40	m	w	DENM	San Francisco	6-Wd San Francisco	81	108
John	40	m	w	NY	San Francisco	2-Wd San Francisco	79	215
John	38	m	w	SWED	Tuolumne	Chinese Camp P O	93	369
John	36	m	w	SWED	San Francisco	11-Wd San Francisc	84	518
John	35	m	w	CANA	Humboldt	Bucksport Twp	72	243
John	35	m	w	HANO	Los Angeles	Los Nietos Twp	73	581
John	35	m	w	SWED	Stanislaus	Buena Vista Twp	92	11
John	34	m	w	SWED	San Francisco	7-Wd San Francisco	81	257
John	34	m	w	SWED	San Francisco	11-Wd San Francisc	84	519
John	33	m	w	SWED	San Francisco	2-Wd San Francisco	79	149
John	33	m	w	CANA	Sacramento	2-Wd Sacramento	77	226
John	32	m	w	MA	San Francisco	7-Wd San Francisco	81	220
John	32	m	w	NORW	San Francisco	11-Wd San Francisc	84	615
John	32	m	w	NORW	San Francisco	1-Wd San Francisco	79	126
John	31	m	w	SWED	San Francisco	3-Wd San Francisco	79	295
John	31	m	w	OH	San Francisco	San Francisco P O	80	360
John	30	m	w	RUSS	Contra Costa	Martinez P O	71	368
John	30	m	w	DENM	Stanislaus	Empire Twp	92	54
John	30	m	w	NY	Santa Clara	Fremont Twp	88	42
John	29	m	w	ENGL	Butte	Ophir Twp	70	97
John	28	m	w	DENM	Merced	Snelling P O	74	252
John	28	m	w	SCOT	San Francisco	1-Wd San Francisco	79	88
John	28	m	w	HANO	Merced	Snelling P O	74	260
John	26	m	w	SWED	San Francisco	1-Wd San Francisco	79	126
John	25	m	w	PRUS	Sacramento	Dry Crk Twp	77	101
John	25	m	w	SWED	San Francisco	3-Wd San Francisco	79	292
John	25	m	w	SWED	San Bernardino	San Bernardino Twp	78	448
John	24	m	w	MA	Contra Costa	Martinez P O	71	396
John	24	m	w	DENM	Alameda	Eden Twp	68	59
John	23	m	w	AUSL	Alameda	Murray Twp	68	106
John	22	m	w	IREL	San Francisco	1-Wd San Francisco	79	136
John	22	m	w	SWED	San Francisco	1-Wd San Francisco	79	128
John	22	m	w	ME	Mendocino	Point Arena Twp	74	208
John	21	m	w	ME	Mendocino	Point Arena Twp	74	210
John	20	m	w	IREL	Sacramento	Dry Crk Twp	77	99
John F	44	m	w	TN	San Luis Obispo	San Luis Obispo Tw	87	302
John M	34	m	w	PA	San Francisco	6-Wd San Francisco	81	104
John V	41	m	w	PA	Santa Clara	San Jose Twp	88	219
John W	29	m	w	IA	Humboldt	Eel Rvr Twp	72	247
Jos	28	m	w	HAMB	Solano	Vallejo	90	198
Jos M	44	m	w	OH	San Francisco	8-Wd San Francisco	82	335
Joseph	45	m	w	SCOT	San Mateo	Schoolhouse Statio	87	331
Joseph	40	m	w	SWIT	Calaveras	San Andreas P O	70	156
Joseph A	40	m	w	TN	Los Angeles	San Jose Twp	73	620
Josh	37	m	w	SCOT	San Francisco	1-Wd San Francisco	79	93
Josiah	65	m	w	KY	Butte	Hamilton Twp	70	64
Josiah	62	m	w	KY	San Joaquin	3-Wd Stockton	86	237
Josph	40	m	w	TN	San Joaquin	1-Wd Stockton	86	123
Julius	28	m	w	DENM	San Francisco	8-Wd San Francisco	82	310
K Cam [Dr]	44	m	w	NY	San Diego	San Diego	78	495
L	30	m	w	IL	Yuba	Rose Bar Twp	93	666
L	27	f	w	PRUS	Alameda	Alameda	68	15
Larkin	40	m	w	GA	Nevada	Grass Valley Twp	75	219
Lars	35	m	w	SWED	San Francisco	3-Wd San Francisco	79	295
Laura	9	f	w	PA	Colusa	Colusa Twp	71	277
Lawrence	40	m	w	DENM	Stanislaus	San Joaquin Twp	92	71
Laxis	48	m	w	DENM	San Francisco	San Francisco P O	80	376
Leroy	26	m	w	MI	Sonoma	Petaluma Twp	91	358
Levy H	21	m	w	US	Nevada	Grass Valley Twp	75	232
Lewis	26	m	w	PRUS	Alameda	Brooklyn	68	38
Lizzie	31	f	w	IN	Monterey	Castroville Twp	74	337
Lloyd	23	m	w	VA	Solano	Vacaville Twp	90	133
Louis	35	m	w	DENM	San Francisco	1-Wd San Francisco	79	133
Louisa	41	f	w	IL	Stanislaus	Empire Twp	92	56
Lucius	27	m	w	MI	Nevada	Grass Valley Twp	75	172
Ludick	45	m	w	DENM	Contra Costa	Martinez P O	71	432
Luther	28	m	w	MI	Santa Clara	San Jose Twp	88	202
Lydia	25	f	w	IN	Solano	Vacaville Twp	90	127
M	39	m	w	IN	Santa Clara	Gilroy Twp	88	86
M	26	m	w	PRUS	Nevada	Eureka Twp	75	135
Machin	61	m	w	DENM	San Francisco	11-Wd San Francisc	84	612
Margaret	24	f	w	IREL	San Francisco	San Francisco P O	85	728
Margt	39	f	w	ME	San Francisco	1-Wd San Francisco	79	26
Maria	48	f	w	NJ	San Francisco	San Francisco P O	83	186
Marion	35	m	w	VA	Sonoma	Mendocino Twp	91	292
Martha	33	m	w	TN	San Bernardino	San Bernardino Twp	78	420
Martin	38	m	w	IREL	Mariposa	Mariposa P O	74	133
Martin	37	m	w	DENM	Solano	Green Valley Twp	90	44
Martin	35	m	w	NORW	Mendocino	Casper & Big Rvr	74	163
Martin	35	m	w	SWED	Plumas	Washington Twp	77	54
Martin	18	m	w	OH	Sacramento	2-Wd Sacramento	77	236
Mary	51	f	w	MO	Sonoma	Santa Rosa	91	395
Mary	45	f	w	PA	Butte	Chico Twp	70	22
Mary	43	f	w	IREL	Placer	Rocklin Twp	76	465
Mary	37	f	w	IREL	San Francisco	San Francisco P O	83	36
Mary	36	f	w	CANA	San Francisco	8-Wd San Francisco	82	451
Mary	21	f	w	AR	Stanislaus	Empire Twp	92	52
Mary	15	f	w	MO	San Bernardino	San Bernardino Twp	78	438
Mary A	26	f	w	ENGL	Shasta	Shasta P O	89	462

© 2001 by Heritage Quest. All rights reserved.

Name	Age	S	R	B-PL	County	Locale	Series M593 Roll	Pg
Mary J	14	f	w	OH	Sonoma	Mendocino Twp	91	299
Mat	46	m	w	ENGL	San Diego	San Diego	78	488
Mathew A	44	m	w	SCOT	San Francisco	8-Wd San Francisco	82	327
Matilda	24	f	w	SWED	San Mateo	Pescadero P O	87	412
Michael	43	m	w	IREL	Santa Clara	Alviso Twp	88	24
Michael	35	m	w	CANA	San Mateo	San Mateo P O	87	360
Michl	25	m	w	PRUS	San Francisco	San Francisco P O	83	49
Miles	28	m	w	HDAR	Solano	Suisun Twp	90	97
Milton	58	m	w	KY	Santa Cruz	Pajaro Twp	89	360
Milton	45	m	w	MD	San Francisco	1-Wd San Francisco	79	116
Milton	32	m	w	NY	San Francisco	1-Wd San Francisco	79	100
Miner W	39	m	w	AL	Plumas	Quartz Twp	77	43
Minetta	10	f	w	CA	San Francisco	8-Wd San Francisco	82	494
Minnie	3	f	w	CA	Lake	Lower Lake	73	423
Mitton M	55	m	w	SC	Yuba	Slate Range Bar Tw	93	673
N C	46	m	w	DENM	El Dorado	Greenwood Twp	72	54
N E	29	m	w	IN	San Joaquin	Tulare Twp	86	264
Nancy	75	f	w	NC	Mendocino	Point Arena Twp	74	211
Nancy	40	f	b	VA	Placer	Bath P O	76	455
Nathan	45	m	w	MA	Colusa	Colusa Twp	71	280
Neal	40	m	w	SWED	El Dorado	White Oak Twp	72	143
Neal	25	m	w	SHOL	San Francisco	3-Wd San Francisco	79	294
Neil	40	m	w	WURT	San Francisco	1-Wd San Francisco	79	134
Neils	29	m	w	SWED	Marin	Bolinas Twp	74	6
Neils E	37	m	w	SWED	San Francisco	San Francisco P O	83	33
Nelson	26	m	w	NORW	San Francisco	11-Wd San Francisc	84	662
Nelson	22	m	w	NORW	Solano	Denverton Twp	90	26
Nely	40	m	w	DENM	Sacramento	Franklin Twp	77	116
Neuel	25	m	w	DENM	Sonoma	Petaluma Twp	91	349
Nicholas	41	m	w	NORW	Nevada	Washington Twp	75	339
Nicholas	38	m	w	SWED	Placer	Rocklin P O	76	462
Nichols	50	m	w	SWED	San Francisco	7-Wd San Francisco	81	160
Nicola	43	m	w	SILE	Placer	Bath P O	76	458
O B	35	m	w	NY	Solano	Vallejo	90	217
O I	30	m	w	IN	Sierra	Table Rock Twp	89	575
O N	45	m	w	NORW	Tuolumne	Big Oak Flat P O	93	394
Ole	35	m	w	NORW	Siskiyou	Scott Valley Twp	89	614
Ole	31	m	w	NORW	Alpine	Silver Mtn P O	69	308
Ole	27	m	w	SWED	Sonoma	Mendocino Twp	91	307
Oliver	32	m	w	NORW	San Francisco	7-Wd San Francisco	81	160
Otto	50	m	w	DENM	Santa Cruz	Santa Cruz Twp	89	393
Otto	32	m	w	SWED	Santa Clara	1-Wd San Jose	88	261
P	30	m	w	NY	Sacramento	1-Wd Sacramento	77	186
Patk F	52	m	w	IA	San Francisco	San Francisco P O	85	743
Patrick	24	m	w	IREL	San Francisco	San Francisco P O	83	146
Paul	28	m	w	SWED	San Francisco	6-Wd San Francisco	81	114
Peter	72	m	c	CHIN	Siskiyou	Yreka	89	650
Peter	55	m	b	PA	San Francisco	3-Wd San Francisco	79	317
Peter	50	m	w	SWED	Colusa	Colusa Twp	71	274
Peter	46	m	b	PA	San Francisco	San Francisco P O	80	333
Peter	43	m	w	SWED	Fresno	Kingston P O	72	220
Peter	42	m	w	SWED	Mono	Bridgeport P O	74	283
Peter	36	m	w	DENM	Fresno	Kings Rvr P O	72	212
Peter	35	m	w	SCOT	San Francisco	8-Wd San Francisco	82	334
Peter	34	m	w	SWED	Plumas	Washington Twp	77	55
Peter	33	m	w	IREL	Contra Costa	Martinez P O	71	415
Peter	32	m	w	SWED	San Francisco	1-Wd San Francisco	79	67
Peter	31	m	w	SWED	Plumas	Quartz Twp	77	42
Peter	28	m	w	DENM	San Francisco	2-Wd San Francisco	79	271
Peter	27	m	w	DENM	Humboldt	Arcata Twp	72	226
Peter	25	m	w	NORW	San Francisco	11-Wd San Francisc	84	637
Peter	25	m	w	DENM	Marin	Tomales Twp	74	84
Peter	25	m	w	SWED	Humboldt	Bucksport Twp	72	242
Peter	22	m	w	DENM	Sutter	Nicolaus Twp	92	115
Peter	19	m	w	DENM	Sonoma	Petaluma Twp	91	318
Philip	30	m	w	SCOT	Santa Clara	San Jose Twp	88	201
Phillip	36	m	w	NORW	San Francisco	11-Wd San Francisc	84	645
Phillip	23	m	w	ENGL	Colusa	Monroe Twp	71	313
Phoebe	42	f	w	NY	Sacramento	2-Wd Sacramento	77	210
Poor	27	m	w	NORW	El Dorado	Georgetown Twp	72	40
R	28	m	w	SWED	San Francisco	7-Wd San Francisco	81	220
R	23	m	w	ENGL	Yuba	Rose Bar Twp	93	661
R H	46	m	w	IN	Mendocino	Calpella Twp	74	182
Ralph	29	m	w	MA	San Joaquin	Tulare Twp	86	258
Richard	37	m	w	PRUS	San Francisco	7-Wd San Francisco	81	218
Richard	24	m	w	PA	Santa Clara	1-Wd San Jose	88	225
Richd	33	m	w	ME	Humboldt	Bucksport Twp	72	243
Robert	52	m	w	PA	Santa Clara	1-Wd San Jose	88	254
Robert	52	m	w	IREL	Sacramento	2-Wd Sacramento	77	225
Robert	50	m	w	NORW	Nevada	Little York Twp	75	244
Robert	50	m	w	SWED	Nevada	Grass Valley Twp	75	228
Robert	47	m	w	SCOT	Alameda	Washington Twp	68	284
Robert	45	m	w	SWED	Nevada	Little York Twp	75	239
Robert	45	m	w	VA	Monterey	San Benito Twp	74	382
Robert	40	m	w	MO	Yolo	Cottonwood Twp	93	474
Robert	39	m	w	IREL	Santa Cruz	Santa Cruz Twp	89	386
Robert	30	m	w	AL	Kern	Bakersfield P O	73	365
Robert	26	m	w	IREL	Colusa	Grand Island Twp	71	307
Robert	22	m	w	PA	San Francisco	San Francisco P O	85	757
Robt	66	m	w	NY	San Joaquin	3-Wd Stockton	86	217
Robt	39	m	w	PA	San Francisco	San Francisco P O	83	122
Robt	36	m	w	SCOT	Sutter	Yuba Twp	92	140
Robt	30	m	w	WI	Butte	Chico Twp	70	59
Robt A	42	m	w	SWED	Plumas	Washington Twp	77	55
Ross B	49	m	w	TN	Sonoma	Mendocino Twp	91	295
Ruben	37	m	w	NY	San Bernardino	San Bernardino Twp	78	429
S	48	m	w	SWED	Yuba	Marysville	93	611

Name	Age	S	R	B-PL	County	Locale	Series M593 Roll	Pg
S	28	m	w	SWED	Sacramento	3-Wd Sacramento	77	276
S L	43	m	w	KY	Merced	Snelling P O	74	253
Saml	38	m	w	IREL	San Francisco	2-Wd San Francisco	79	153
Saml	36	m	w	KY	San Diego	San Diego	78	486
Samuel	40	m	w	VA	Santa Barbara	Santa Barbara P O	87	477
Samuel	39	m	w	SWED	San Mateo	Pescadero P O	87	410
Samuel	27	m	w	SWED	San Mateo	Pescadero P O	87	410
Sarah	25	f	w	IL	Butte	Chico Twp	70	55
Sarah	11	f	w	AR	Colusa	Stony Crk Twp	71	329
Simon	50	m	w	CANA	San Francisco	San Francisco P O	80	354
Siver	51	m	w	NORW	Placer	Auburn P O	76	375
Sol	34	m	w	SWED	El Dorado	Placerville Twp	72	95
Theodore	31	m	w	NORW	Nevada	Rough & Ready Twp	75	330
Tho	43	m	w	SWED	El Dorado	Salmon Falls Twp	72	132
Thomas	59	m	w	VA	Trinity	Junction City Pct	92	206
Thomas	55	m	w	VA	Placer	Alta P O	76	419
Thomas	50	m	w	SCOT	Amador	Volcano P O	69	381
Thomas	42	m	w	TN	Sonoma	Sonoma Twp	91	445
Thomas	42	m	w	CANA	San Francisco	8-Wd San Francisco	82	469
Thomas	40	m	w	ENGL	San Francisco	San Francisco P O	83	223
Thomas	38	m	w	OH	Sacramento	2-Wd Sacramento	77	208
Thomas	36	m	w	IREL	San Bernardino	San Bernardino Twp	78	448
Thomas	36	m	w	CANA	Sacramento	2-Wd Sacramento	77	252
Thomas	35	m	w	NY	Sonoma	Petaluma Twp	91	358
Thomas	30	m	w	NORW	San Francisco	1-Wd San Francisco	79	40
Thomas	28	m	w	CANA	Sonoma	Petaluma Twp	91	324
Thomas H B	28	m	w	MO	Solano	Suisun Twp	90	93
Thos	50	m	w	ENGL	San Joaquin	2-Wd Stockton	86	166
Thos	41	m	w	ENGL	Sacramento	Franklin Twp	77	112
Thos N	39	m	w	SCOT	San Francisco	1-Wd San Francisco	79	19
Turner	35	m	w	VA	Colusa	Stony Crk Twp	71	326
W	40	m	w	IREL	Sierra	Sierra Twp	89	569
W	26	m	w	MA	Alameda	Oakland	68	264
W A	18	m	w	CA	Monterey	Castroville Twp	74	325
W B	42	m	w	MO	Sacramento	Cosumnes Twp	77	88
W D	30	m	w	CANA	Solano	Vallejo	90	164
W H	27	m	w	NY	Nevada	Bloomfield Twp	75	96
W H	14	m	m	MA	Sacramento	3-Wd Sacramento	77	262
Warren	44	m	w	NY	San Francisco	6-Wd San Francisco	81	94
William	52	m	w	MO	Los Angeles	Los Angeles Twp	73	494
William	50	m	w	SCOT	Los Angeles	Los Angeles	73	519
William	43	m	w	SWED	Calaveras	San Andreas P O	70	154
William	41	m	w	NY	Marin	San Rafael	74	55
William	38	m	w	SWED	San Francisco	7-Wd San Francisco	81	190
William	35	m	w	NY	San Francisco	7-Wd San Francisco	81	220
William	35	m	w	TX	Kern	Linns Valley P O	73	343
William	33	m	w	FINL	Mendocino	Navarro & Big Rvr	74	177
William	32	m	w	CANA	San Mateo	Half Moon Bay P O	87	401
William	31	m	w	SWED	Mendocino	Little Rvr Twp	74	171
William	31	m	w	IL	Placer	Gold Run Twp	76	396
William	30	m	w	TN	Sonoma	Vallejo Twp	91	463
William	28	m	w	CANA	Nevada	Meadow Lake Twp	75	261
William	27	m	w	SCOT	Los Angeles	Los Angeles	73	519
William	27	m	w	VA	Colusa	Stony Crk Twp	71	326
William	26	m	w	DENM	Contra Costa	San Pablo Twp	71	365
William	26	m	w	MO	Stanislaus	Empire Twp	92	66
William	25	m	w	MEXI	Solano	Vacaville Twp	90	134
William	24	m	w	MA	Marin	San Rafael Twp	74	43
William	23	m	w	ME	Mendocino	Navarro & Big Rvr	74	177
William	20	m	w	CANA	Sonoma	Sonoma Twp	91	431
William	16	m	w	AR	Colusa	Stony Crk Twp	71	328
William B	41	m	w	SHOL	Placer	Bath P O	76	437
William B	18	m	w	CANA	Yolo	Grafton Twp	93	487
Wilson	51	m	b	VA	Amador	Ione City P O	69	357
Wm	46	m	w	SCOT	San Francisco	7-Wd San Francisco	81	244
Wm	43	m	w	ME	San Francisco	San Francisco P O	83	116
Wm	41	m	w	CANA	Yuba	W Bear Rvr Twp	93	684
Wm	40	m	w	CANA	San Joaquin	3-Wd Stockton	86	218
Wm	40	m	w	CANA	San Francisco	11-Wd San Francisc	84	690
Wm	38	m	w	NH	San Francisco	11-Wd San Francisc	84	693
Wm	30	m	w	MO	San Joaquin	Liberty Twp	86	94
Wm	27	m	w	RI	San Joaquin	Liberty Twp	86	96
Wm	25	m	w	ME	Nevada	Meadow Lake Twp	75	261
Wm	23	m	w	MO	Napa	Napa	75	3
Wm	23	m	w	SWED	Yuba	Marysville	93	610
Wm	11	m	w	CANA	San Joaquin	3-Wd Stockton	86	218
Wm A	79	m	w	ENGL	Nevada	Grass Valley Twp	75	218
Wm C	38	m	w	CA	El Dorado	Kelsey Twp	72	59
Wm F	31	m	w	IL	San Francisco	1-Wd San Francisco	79	102
Wm G M	49	m	w	SCOT	El Dorado	Coloma Twp	72	3
Wm H	35	m	w	MO	Butte	Chico Twp	70	50
Wm H	26	m	w	IA	Sonoma	Healdsburg & Mendo	91	280
Wm J	62	m	w	ENGL	Monterey	Castroville Twp	74	327
Wm L	46	m	w	TN	Sonoma	Analy Twp	91	237
Wm N	31	m	w	SCOT	San Francisco	1-Wd San Francisco	79	79
Wm P	69	m	w	SCOT	Yuba	Long Bar Twp	93	561
Wm R	50	m	b	PA	San Francisco	1-Wd San Francisco	79	128
ANDERSSON								
Anw	25	m	w	NORW	Humboldt	Pacific Twp	72	299
ANDERWERD								
Jos	36	m	w	NH	Sacramento	1-Wd Sacramento	77	190
ANDES								
Ascencion	18	f	w	CA	San Francisco	11-Wd San Francisc	84	516
Louis H	40	m	w	HESS	Shasta	Fort Crook P O	89	473
Seledoro G	29	f	w	CA	Los Angeles	Los Angeles	73	526
Ser	36	m	w	FRAN	Los Angeles	Los Angeles	73	526

© 2001 by Heritage Quest. All rights reserved.

California 1870 Census

Name	Age	S	R	B-PL	County	Locale	Roll	Pg
						Series M593		
ANDESOLLA								
Jose A	40	m	w	MEXI	Santa Cruz	Pajaro Twp	89	363
ANDIE								
August	30	m	w	FRAN	San Francisco	2-Wd San Francisco	79	158
Jean Bapd	41	m	w	FRAN	San Francisco	San Francisco P O	83	136
ANDLADO								
Jesus	28	m	w	MEXI	Merced	Snelling P O	74	251
ANDLER								
Jacob	41	m	w	FRAN	San Francisco	San Francisco P O	83	107
ANDLEY								
James	28	m	w	IREL	Colusa	Monroe Twp	71	313
ANDMUS								
G W	24	m	w	LA	Sierra	Lincoln Twp	89	545
ANDONAGUI								
Jose M	44	m	w	SPAI	Santa Barbara	Santa Barbara P O	87	453
ANDONGIE								
A	42	m	w	PORT	Alameda	Alameda	68	10
ANDOREN								
---	40	m	c	CHIN	Sonoma	Sonoma Twp	91	447
ANDRADA								
Albino	28	m	w	CA	Monterey	Castroville Twp	74	331
Domingo	50	m	w	MEXI	Los Angeles	El Monte Twp	73	454
Felipa	40	f	w	CA	Los Angeles	Wilmington Twp	73	637
Jose	42	m	w	MEXI	Santa Barbara	Santa Barbara P O	87	486
Jose	41	m	w	MEXI	Santa Barbara	Santa Barbara P O	87	483
Jose	30	m	w	MEXI	Nevada	Meadow Lake Twp	75	269
Lucia	23	f	w	MEXI	San Diego	San Pasqual	78	519
Luis	50	m	w	MEXI	Los Angeles	San Juan Twp	73	627
Madalena	38	f	w	CA	Monterey	Salinas Twp	74	312
Manuel	25	m	w	MEXI	Los Angeles	San Juan Twp	73	628
Reyes	36	m	w	MEXI	Los Angeles	El Monte Twp	73	461
Secondme	48	m	w	MEXI	Los Angeles	El Monte Twp	73	454
ANDRADE								
Antone	40	m	w	AZOR	Yuba	New York Twp	93	637
Carmen	16	f	w	MEXI	Santa Clara	2-Wd San Jose	88	338
Wm	40	m	w	MEXI	San Francisco	San Francisco P O	83	101
ANDRADEE								
Mateo	31	m	w	MEXI	Marin	San Rafael Twp	74	38
ANDRADO								
Evarista	26	m	w	MEXI	San Francisco	San Francisco P O	80	402
ANDRAS								
Mary E	11	f	w	OR	Santa Cruz	Soquel Twp	89	441
ANDRATA								
Guadalupe	27	f	w	CA	Santa Barbara	Las Cruces P O	87	515
ANDRATH								
Emanuel	39	m	w	MEXI	Fresno	Millerton P O	72	154
ANDRE								
Francis M	44	m	w	CANA	Nevada	Grass Valley Twp	75	163
Manuel	33	m	w	PORT	Santa Clara	Milpitas Twp	88	111
Theopile	36	m	w	FRAN	San Francisco	San Francisco P O	80	342
ANDREADO								
Pedro	35	m	w	MEXI	Los Angeles	Soledad Twp	73	632
ANDREANO								
Peter	15	m	w	AK	San Francisco	2-Wd San Francisco	79	219
ANDREAS								
Chris	23	m	w	WURT	San Francisco	1-Wd San Francisco	79	57
James	45	m	w	IREL	Contra Costa	Martinez P O	71	401
Severana	50	m	w	MEXI	San Francisco	San Francisco P O	80	342
ANDREDA								
Tomas	28	m	w	MEXI	Los Angeles	Los Angeles Twp	73	468
ANDREE								
Emma	12	f	w	WI	Yolo	Cache Crk Twp	93	452
ANDREGA								
Joseph	19	m	w	CHIL	Sacramento	2-Wd Sacramento	77	216
ANDREGAS								
Mary	25	f	w	MEXI	Sacramento	2-Wd Sacramento	77	239
ANDREI								
Anthony	30	m	w	ITAL	San Francisco	6-Wd San Francisco	81	123
Henry	26	m	w	ENGL	San Francisco	2-Wd San Francisco	79	215
ANDRELA								
Alexandro	60	m	w	MEXI	Santa Barbara	San Buenaventura P	87	428
ANDRELE								
Andrew	30	m	w	FRAN	San Francisco	San Francisco P O	80	348
Andrew	30	m	w	FRAN	San Francisco	San Francisco P O	80	347
ANDRELO								
Manuelo J	20	m	w	SPAI	Los Angeles	Santa Ana Twp	73	601
ANDREOS								
P B	30	m	w	NY	San Mateo	San Mateo P O	87	360
ANDRES								
Charles	41	m	w	PRUS	Siskiyou	Yreka	89	655
Chas	40	m	w	FRAN	Yuba	Marysville	93	616
Christ	36	m	w	SWED	San Francisco	8-Wd San Francisco	82	307
Henry	23	m	w	DENM	Monterey	Alisal Twp	74	293
J	30	m	w	IA	San Joaquin	Elliott Twp	86	73
James	35	m	w	IREL	Yuba	Rose Bar Twp	93	664
Jennie	25	f	w	PRUS	San Francisco	8-Wd San Francisco	82	361
Johanna	50	f	w	MECK	Santa Clara	1-Wd San Jose	88	229
Jose	23	m	w	MEXI	Monterey	San Juan Twp	74	385
ANDRESON								
H	36	m	w	CA	Monterey	Salinas Twp	74	307
John G	45	m	w	PRUS	San Francisco	1-Wd San Francisco	79	108
Theo	37	m	w	DC	San Diego	Warners Rancho Dis	78	528
ANDRETH								
Francisco	25	m	w	MEXI	Fresno	Millerton P O	72	154
ANDRETTA								
John	40	m	w	SWIT	Amador	Jackson P O	69	338

Name	Age	S	R	B-PL	County	Locale	Roll	Pg
						Series M593		
ANDRETTI								
Antonio	36	m	w	MEXI	Fresno	Millerton P O	72	156
ANDREUS								
Henry A	21	m	w	NY	Nevada	Nevada Twp	75	275
Hy	28	m	w	WURT	San Francisco	11-Wd San Francisc	84	617
Jesse B	42	m	w	NY	San Francisco	San Francisco P O	83	202
John	51	m	w	ENGL	San Diego	San Diego	78	507
John	40	m	w	ITAL	Tuolumne	Sonora P O	93	308
Oliver	40	m	w	ME	San Francisco	11-Wd San Francisc	84	457
Wm C	42	m	w	IN	Sonoma	Analy Twp	91	229
ANDREW								
---	25	m	w	SWED	San Mateo	Pescadero P O	87	411
A B	36	m	w	VA	San Bernardino	San Bernardino Twp	78	435
Alfred	32	m	w	ENGL	Nevada	Nevada Twp	75	300
Amelia	50	f	w	IL	Sacramento	Georgianna Twp	77	124
Antone	38	m	w	CHIL	Calaveras	San Andreas P O	70	201
Chatera	55	f	w	NY	San Francisco	11-Wd San Francisc	84	634
Deitry	65	m	w	PRUS	San Francisco	San Francisco P O	83	382
E	54	m	w	ENGL	Sonoma	Sonoma Twp	91	442
Edmond	19	m	w	OH	Colusa	Colusa Twp	71	283
Edwin	19	m	w	OH	Colusa	Monroe Twp	71	312
Elisha	48	m	w	ENGL	Nevada	Grass Valley Twp	75	144
Elizabeth	40	f	w	CT	San Diego	San Diego	78	492
Hans	20	m	w	ME	Sacramento	Georgianna Twp	77	130
Henry	39	m	w	PRUS	Mendocino	Point Arena Twp	74	214
Henry	29	m	w	OH	Solano	Montezuma Twp	90	67
J Markham	30	m	w	VT	Klamath	Hoopa Valley India	73	386
Jackson	1	m	w	CA	Monterey	Salinas Twp	74	311
Jalious	33	m	w	NY	Trinity	Weaverville Pct	92	227
John	28	m	w	GREE	Placer	Bath P O	76	442
Joseph	49	m	w	SCOT	Alameda	Brooklyn	68	30
Joseph	24	m	w	IREL	San Francisco	1-Wd San Francisco	79	64
Louis	24	m	w	VA	Solano	Rio Vista Twp	90	61
Pasqual	38	m	w	MEXI	Calaveras	San Andreas P O	70	208
Peter	35	m	w	GREE	San Francisco	3-Wd San Francisco	79	287
Richard	21	m	w	ENGL	Nevada	Grass Valley Twp	75	198
Stephen	32	m	w	ENGL	Plumas	Indian Twp	77	17
Thomas	37	m	w	ENGL	Mariposa	Mariposa P O	74	111
Vincent	41	m	w	SCOT	Inyo	Independence Twp	73	328
William	45	m	w	OH	Nevada	Eureka Twp	75	132
William	43	m	w	PRUS	Calaveras	Copperopolis P O	70	263
William	30	m	w	AZOR	Nevada	Washington Twp	75	339
Wm	44	m	w	MO	Shasta	Shasta P O	89	456
Wm H	52	m	w	NY	Sacramento	Franklin Twp	77	111
ANDREWS								
A	42	m	w	NH	San Joaquin	Dent Twp	86	17
A	41	m	w	NORW	El Dorado	Greenwood Twp	72	55
Abraham	43	m	w	ENGL	San Francisco	San Francisco P O	83	201
Ada	26	f	w	ENGL	San Francisco	San Francisco P O	83	339
Albert A	36	m	m	MO	Mendocino	Point Arena Twp	74	224
Alexander	60	m	w	SCOT	San Francisco	11-Wd San Francisc	84	611
Alexander	41	m	w	KY	Shasta	Shasta P O	89	459
Alexander	22	m	w	IREL	San Francisco	San Francisco P O	85	876
Alfred	8	m	m	CA	San Francisco	6-Wd San Francisco	81	76
Andrew	47	m	m	OH	Mendocino	Anderson Twp	74	150
Anna	40	f	w	ENGL	San Francisco	San Francisco P O	80	381
Anne	48	f	w	MA	San Francisco	San Francisco P O	83	319
Antone	16	m	w	PORT	San Francisco	1-Wd San Francisco	79	116
Asa P	49	m	w	NY	Sacramento	2-Wd Sacramento	77	243
Ash	35	m	w	TN	San Joaquin	Elkhorn Twp	86	66
Benj A	41	m	w	KY	Fresno	Kings Rvr P O	72	205
Benjamin H	33	m	w	MA	Placer	Bath P O	76	461
C D	40	m	w	NY	Del Norte	Crescent Twp	71	454
Carrie E	10	f	w	CA	Yuba	Long Bar Twp	93	566
Charles	38	m	w	MA	San Francisco	San Francisco P O	80	414
Charles	38	m	m	NY	San Francisco	San Francisco P O	80	420
Charles	32	m	w	ENGL	San Mateo	Menlo Park P O	87	378
Charlotte	40	f	w	NORW	San Francisco	San Francisco P O	83	199
Chas	26	m	w	GERM	San Joaquin	2-Wd Stockton	86	213
Chester	39	m	w	CT	San Francisco	1-Wd San Francisco	79	63
Clark W	26	m	w	OH	Sonoma	Petaluma Twp	91	320
D C	40	m	w	IL	San Joaquin	Dent Twp	86	22
David F	30	m	w	CT	Sacramento	2-Wd Sacramento	77	224
E H	32	m	w	NY	Sierra	Eureka Twp	89	523
Edmund	43	m	w	ENGL	Amador	Jackson P O	69	321
Edwd	18	m	w	NY	San Francisco	1-Wd San Francisco	79	108
Elizabeth	65	f	w	IREL	San Francisco	San Francisco P O	85	795
Ellen	44	f	w	IREL	San Francisco	San Francisco P O	80	385
Flora	24	f	w	FL	Placer	Lincoln P O	76	492
Fred	30	m	w	ENGL	San Francisco	11-Wd San Francisc	84	664
Fred	21	m	w	ME	Placer	Dutch Flat P O	76	415
G B	37	m	w	ME	San Francisco	San Francisco P O	85	787
G S	40	m	w	NY	Amador	Jackson P O	69	319
Geo	45	m	w	ENGL	San Francisco	1-Wd San Francisco	79	34
Geo	29	m	w	ENGL	San Francisco	San Francisco P O	83	116
Geo W	43	m	w	MA	Yolo	Cache Crk Twp	93	436
Geo W	32	m	w	NC	San Joaquin	Douglas Twp	86	47
George	52	m	w	CT	Placer	Bath P O	76	460
George	28	m	w	NY	San Francisco	San Francisco P O	80	488
George W	19	m	w	NY	San Bernardino	San Bernardino Twp	78	450
Gustavus	24	m	w	NY	San Francisco	6-Wd San Francisco	81	81
H L	32	m	w	MO	Monterey	Castroville Twp	74	337
H T	29	m	w	NY	Napa	Yountville Twp	75	89
Hanah	40	f	w	IREL	San Francisco	7-Wd San Francisco	81	204
Harry	28	m	w	SWED	Yolo	Grafton Twp	93	496
Harry	26	m	w	IA	San Francisco	11-Wd San Francisc	84	512
Henny	25	m	w	IN	San Francisco	6-Wd San Francisco	81	81

© 2001 by Heritage Quest. All rights reserved.

Name	Age	S	R	B-PL	County	Locale	Roll	Pg
Henry	33	m	w	TN	Solano	Silveyville Twp	90	78
Henry W	65	m	w	VT	Yuba	Long Bar Twp	93	565
Hugh	41	m	w	PA	Siskiyou	Callahan P O	89	628
Isaac H	50	m	w	NY	Marin	San Rafael	74	53
J	54	m	w	NH	San Joaquin	Liberty Twp	86	95
J	54	m	w	OH	San Joaquin	Tulare Twp	86	261
J	30	m	w	NORW	Alameda	Murray Twp	68	109
J H	45	m	w	MA	Solano	Benicia	90	1
J N	40	m	w	MA	Sacramento	3-Wd Sacramento	77	275
J P	46	m	w	MEXI	Tuolumne	Columbia P O	93	355
Jacob	31	m	w	HANO	San Francisco	1-Wd San Francisco	79	52
James	60	m	w	SCOT	Butte	Ophir Twp	70	105
James	49	m	w	ENGL	San Joaquin	1-Wd Stockton	86	120
James	38	m	w	PA	Fresno	Kings Rvr P O	72	216
James	35	m	w	PA	Marin	Tomales Twp	74	78
James	30	m	w	MA	Sacramento	Franklin Twp	77	109
James	30	m	w	ENGL	Nevada	Nevada Twp	75	301
James	25	m	w	IREL	San Francisco	11-Wd San Francisc	84	694
James	17	m	w	CA	San Francisco	7-Wd San Francisco	81	204
Jane	39	f	w	CA	Mendocino	Sanel Twp	74	227
Jerry	33	m	w	GREE	San Francisco	1-Wd San Francisco	79	134
Joel	34	m	w	ENGL	Nevada	Grass Valley Twp	75	199
John	62	m	w	VA	Sonoma	Sonoma Twp	91	447
John	51	m	w	IREL	Butte	Wyandotte Twp	70	149
John	40	m	w	MI	Sacramento	Alabama Twp	77	61
John	40	m	w	VT	San Francisco	6-Wd San Francisco	81	83
John	28	m	w	SWED	San Francisco	11-Wd San Francisc	84	519
John	26	m	w	NY	Marin	Nicasio Twp	74	16
John P	46	m	w	SC	San Luis Obispo	San Luis Obispo Tw	87	312
John R	30	m	w	ENGL	San Francisco	6-Wd San Francisco	81	138
Joseph	45	m	w	SWIT	Sonoma	Sonoma Twp	91	444
Joseph	40	m	w	MA	Calaveras	San Andreas P O	70	204
Joseph	32	m	w	HDAR	San Francisco	8-Wd San Francisco	82	433
Joseph	29	m	w	PORT	Alameda	Washington Twp	68	293
Joseph	23	m	w	OH	Solano	Denverton Twp	90	25
L C	35	m	w	NY	Sutter	Nicolaus Twp	92	106
Levi G	36	m	w	OH	Shasta	Portugese Flat P O	89	472
Lewis	41	m	w	MO	Contra Costa	Martinez P O	71	406
Lewis	20	m	w	MO	Butte	Chico Twp	70	60
Lucy	20	f	w	NY	San Francisco	6-Wd San Francisco	81	84
Luki	17	m	w	CA	Alameda	Oakland	68	258
Lyman	41	m	w	RI	Fresno	Millerton P O	72	149
Margaret	30	f	w	IREL	San Francisco	7-Wd San Francisco	81	204
Maria B	35	f	w	KY	Tulare	Visalia	92	294
Martin	35	m	w	ENGL	Siskiyou	Scott Rvr Twp	89	604
Mary	39	f	w	IREL	Siskiyou	Yreka	89	662
Mary	21	f	w	WURT	San Francisco	San Francisco P O	85	790
Moses	48	m	w	MA	Placer	Auburn P O	76	369
N H	50	f	w	ME	San Francisco	San Francisco P O	85	844
Noah P	39	m	w	ME	Placer	Bath P O	76	447
O B	31	m	w	NH	Sierra	Lincoln Twp	89	549
Peter	40	m	w	ENGL	Solano	Tremont Twp	90	33
Phillip	31	m	w	OH	Stanislaus	Empire Twp	92	53
Richard	40	m	w	ME	San Francisco	San Francisco P O	83	304
Richd	38	m	w	ENGL	San Francisco	1-Wd San Francisco	79	13
Robert	57	m	w	PA	Sonoma	Petaluma Twp	91	351
Robert D	29	m	w	NJ	Yuba	New York Twp	93	637
Robt	45	m	w	VA	El Dorado	Mountain Twp	72	69
Rosanna	39	f	w	CT	San Francisco	San Francisco P O	83	71
S	42	m	w	NY	Yuba	Marysville	93	610
Saml	40	m	w	IREL	Tuolumne	Columbia P O	93	351
Saml	38	m	w	SCOT	Shasta	Millville P O	89	484
Samuel	36	m	w	IL	Stanislaus	Empire Twp	92	48
Shepard	43	m	w	KY	San Diego	San Pasqual	78	523
Simon	44	m	w	ME	Santa Clara	2-Wd San Jose	88	320
Snell	40	m	w	MA	Santa Clara	Santa Clara Twp	88	167
Susan	34	f	w	NY	San Francisco	San Francisco P O	83	182
Tho	52	m	w	KY	El Dorado	Georgetown Twp	72	40
Thomas	9	m	w	CA	San Francisco	7-Wd San Francisco	81	204
Thomas	30	m	w	SCOT	San Francisco	San Francisco P O	83	238
Thos J	38	m	w	NY	San Francisco	8-Wd San Francisco	82	303
Thos Jeff	35	m	w	ENGL	San Francisco	San Francisco P O	83	77
Tophia	33	f	w	IN	San Joaquin	Elliott Twp	86	76
Truman	48	m	w	NY	Santa Clara	San Jose Twp	88	207
Tyre	35	m	w	MO	San Francisco	11-Wd San Francisc	84	450
W	26	m	w	MA	Alameda	Oakland	68	265
W J	50	m	w	NC	Napa	Yountville Twp	75	88
William	56	m	w	MA	San Francisco	11-Wd San Francisc	84	514
William	50	m	w	ME	Kern	Havilah P O	73	341
William	48	m	w	SWIT	Los Angeles	Los Angeles Twp	73	488
William	45	m	w	NY	Placer	Dutch Flat P O	76	409
William	40	m	w	MO	Nevada	Eureka Twp	75	133
William	40	m	w	ENGL	Tuolumne	Columbia P O	93	345
William	24	m	w	ENGL	Nevada	Grass Valley Twp	75	227
William	24	m	w	PRUS	Solano	Tremont Twp	90	34
William H	25	m	w	OH	Yolo	Washington Twp	93	535
William H	25	m	w	OH	Yolo	Washington Twp	93	535
Wm	48	m	w	NY	San Francisco	San Francisco P O	85	767
Wm	45	m	w	ENGL	San Francisco	1-Wd San Francisco	79	95
Wm	28	m	w	ENGL	Napa	Napa Twp	75	46
Wm	21	m	w	CA	San Francisco	11-Wd San Francisc	84	568
Wm H	38	m	w	MA	Mendocino	Round Valley India	74	180
Wm Sherman	28	m	w	CT	Nevada	Grass Valley Twp	75	188
Wood M	56	m	w	MD	Los Angeles	Los Nietos Twp	73	574
Zachariah	21	m	w	MO	Colusa	Grand Island Twp	71	308
ANDREY								
George H	33	m	w	CANA	Inyo	Cerro Gordo Twp	73	318
ANDREZIFONSKI								
Jn	38	m	w	POLA	San Francisco	8-Wd San Francisco	82	337
ANDRIAN								
Jos	43	m	w	ITAL	Solano	Vallejo	90	170
Jos	42	m	w	ITAL	Solano	Vallejo	90	161
ANDRICK								
Charles	64	m	w	FRAN	El Dorado	Placerville	72	125
ANDRICUS								
Jesus	30	m	w	CHIL	Stanislaus	San Joaquin Twp	92	80
Jose	20	m	w	CHIL	Stanislaus	San Joaquin Twp	92	80
ANDRIE								
John	37	m	w	FRAN	Contra Costa	Martinez Twp	71	352
Lewis	40	m	w	GERM	Yolo	Cottonwood Twp	93	463
ANDRIERTA								
Joseph	31	m	w	SWIT	Monterey	Monterey	74	361
ANDRIS								
Petrus B	52	m	w	FRAN	Sacramento	2-Wd Sacramento	77	222
ANDRO								
Angelo	34	m	w	FRAN	San Francisco	San Francisco P O	83	135
Cedon	28	m	w	ITAL	San Francisco	11-Wd San Francisc	84	701
Jose Mona	25	m	w	MEXI	San Diego	San Diego	78	508
ANDRONICA								
Barella	16	m	w	CHIL	San Francisco	2-Wd San Francisco	79	188
ANDROS								
Milton	44	m	w	NY	San Francisco	San Francisco P O	83	188
Spaniard	50	m	w	SPAI	El Dorado	Mud Springs Twp	72	76
ANDROSS								
M C	33	m	w	VT	Tuolumne	Columbia P O	93	335
ANDRUCHI								
Parli	37	m	w	ITAL	Sonoma	Analy Twp	91	240
ANDRUS								
W H	49	m	w	OH	Sacramento	4-Wd Sacramento	77	375
ANDUCKES								
Dumond	30	m	w	FRAN	San Bernardino	San Bernardino Twp	78	431
ANDWIN								
A	29	m	w	IREL	Alameda	Oakland	68	208
ANDY								
Ah	22	m	c	CHIN	Klamath	Orleans Twp	73	380
John R	41	m	w	TN	El Dorado	Coloma Twp	72	4
ANE								
How	30	m	c	CHIN	Calaveras	San Andreas P O	70	175
ANEA								
Anselma	28	m	w	MEXI	Fresno	Millerton P O	72	154
ANEAR								
Fours	61	m	w	MEXI	Fresno	Millerton P O	72	167
ANEBLINA								
Jesus	25	f	w	MEXI	San Diego	Coronado	78	465
ANEL								
Peter	24	m	w	BELG	San Francisco	5-Wd San Francisco	81	10
ANELY								
Lorsea	31	f	w	ITAL	Los Angeles	Los Angeles	73	527
ANEMTO								
Don Jose	17	m	w	CHIL	Yolo	Grafton Twp	93	498
ANEN								
Louis	46	m	w	PRUS	Tuolumne	Chinese Camp P O	93	368
ANER								
Joseph	45	m	w	FRAN	San Francisco	8-Wd San Francisco	82	321
Mary	35	f	w	PRUS	Yuba	Marysville	93	616
ANERED								
Lewis	38	m	w	SWIT	Colusa	Colusa Twp	71	278
ANERY								
Edwin	44	m	w	NC	San Diego	Julian Dist	78	471
ANESSETTA								
J	50	m	w	MEXI	Amador	Jackson P O	69	328
ANESUSBERE								
Francisco	27	m	w	FRAN	Monterey	San Antonio Twp	74	315
ANEVELA								
Lugardo	76	m	w	CA	Monterey	Alisal Twp	74	295
ANEWRIGHT								
Mike	26	m	w	IREL	Sonoma	Santa Rosa	91	405
ANFINER								
Daniel	22	m	w	NY	Solano	Denverton Twp	90	22
ANG								
Ah	45	m	c	CHIN	Sacramento	Granite Twp	77	137
Ah	43	m	c	CHIN	Sacramento	Granite Twp	77	138
Ah	32	m	c	CHIN	Tuolumne	Chinese Camp P O	93	370
Ah	31	m	c	CHIN	Tuolumne	Chinese Camp P O	93	384
Ah	30	m	c	CHIN	Santa Clara	1-Wd San Jose	88	273
Ah	29	m	c	CHIN	Sacramento	Franklin Twp	77	108
Ah	28	m	c	CHIN	Tuolumne	Chinese Camp P O	93	388
Ah	25	m	c	CHIN	Mariposa	Maxwell Crk P O	74	147
Ah	21	m	c	CHIN	Butte	Wyandotte Twp	70	147
Ah	19	m	c	CHIN	Santa Clara	San Jose Twp	88	203
Ah	17	m	c	CHIN	San Francisco	1-Wd San Francisco	79	58
Ah	14	m	c	CHIN	Nevada	Eureka Twp	75	127
Chee	43	m	c	CHIN	Tuolumne	Sonora P O	93	331
Chee	42	m	c	CHIN	Tuolumne	Chinese Camp P O	93	380
Chew	28	m	c	CHIN	Tuolumne	Chinese Camp P O	93	382
Chung	70	m	c	CHIN	Tuolumne	Sonora P O	93	327
Ga	25	m	c	CHIN	Calaveras	Copperopolis P O	70	260
Gee	38	m	c	CHIN	Plumas	Washington Twp	77	57
Gee	34	m	c	CHIN	Tuolumne	Sonora P O	93	321
Gee	22	m	c	CHIN	Butte	Wyandotte Twp	70	147
Gee	20	f	c	CHIN	Santa Clara	1-Wd San Jose	88	269
Gemp	40	m	c	CHIN	Nevada	Bridgeport Twp	75	110
Gen	25	m	c	CHIN	San Francisco	11-Wd San Francisc	84	574
Get	42	m	c	CHIN	Plumas	Goodwin Twp	77	3

Series M593

© 2001 by Heritage Quest. All rights reserved.

Name	Age	S	R	B-PL	County	Locale	Roll	Pg
						Series M593		
Ghe	19	m	c	CHIN	Plumas	Mineral Twp	77	25
Gin	42	m	c	CHIN	Tuolumne	Sonora P O	93	321
Ging	25	m	c	CHIN	Plumas	Goodwin Twp	77	6
Gon	50	m	c	CHIN	Tuolumne	Sonora P O	93	322
Gon	47	m	c	CHIN	Tuolumne	Columbia P O	93	335
Gon	30	m	c	CHIN	Nevada	Little York Twp	75	235
Goot	45	m	c	CHIN	Plumas	Goodwin Twp	77	4
Goot	42	m	c	CHIN	Plumas	Washington Twp	77	58
Goot	13	m	c	CHIN	Plumas	Goodwin Twp	77	4
Gorey	42	m	c	CHIN	Plumas	Goodwin Twp	77	5
Gorey	19	m	c	CHIN	Plumas	Goodwin Twp	77	2
Gow	29	m	c	CHIN	San Francisco	2-Wd San Francisco	79	177
Grey	43	m	c	CHIN	Plumas	Plumas Twp	77	33
Gun	43	m	c	CHIN	Tuolumne	Big Oak Flat P O	93	394
Ho	24	m	c	CHIN	Santa Clara	2-Wd San Jose	88	325
Hoy	22	m	c	CHIN	Santa Clara	Alviso Twp	88	25
Jong	41	m	c	CHIN	Tuolumne	Big Oak Flat P O	93	401
Kee	30	m	c	CHIN	Santa Clara	1-Wd San Jose	88	274
Le	45	m	c	CHIN	Santa Clara	1-Wd San Jose	88	272
Lee	24	m	c	CHIN	Santa Clara	San Jose Twp	88	189
Lee	20	m	c	CHIN	Tuolumne	Big Oak Flat P O	93	393
Lee	18	m	c	CHIN	Tuolumne	Chinese Camp P O	93	367
Ong	22	f	c	CHIN	Santa Clara	1-Wd San Jose	88	270
See	29	m	c	CHIN	Santa Clara	1-Wd San Jose	88	269
Tum	25	m	c	CHIN	Tuolumne	Chinese Camp P O	93	364
Woo	24	m	c	CHIN	San Francisco	11-Wd San Francisc	84	629
Woo	16	m	c	CHIN	Tuolumne	Chinese Camp P O	93	364
Wough	30	m	c	CHIN	Yuba	Marysville	93	622
Yan	20	m	c	CHIN	Placer	Bath P O	76	444
Yon	34	m	c	CHIN	Tuolumne	Sonora P O	93	322
ANGAIS								
Mary	38	f	w	CA	Tuolumne	Sonora P O	93	306
ANGALO								
Nabon	29	m	w	MEXI	Santa Clara	Almaden Twp	88	8
ANGALUS								
Richard	43	m	w	PRUS	San Francisco	San Francisco P O	83	411
ANGE								
Seigneur	35	m	w	FRAN	San Francisco	8-Wd San Francisco	82	354
ANGEL								
---	60	m	w	CA	Santa Barbara	Las Cruces P O	87	516
B	32	m	w	IA	San Joaquin	2-Wd Stockton	86	186
Barbara	56	f	w	CA	Santa Barbara	Las Cruces P O	87	516
Bernhard	48	m	w	PRUS	San Francisco	San Francisco P O	80	333
Henry	52	m	w	HANO	San Francisco	2-Wd San Francisco	79	258
Henry	22	m	w	NY	San Francisco	11-Wd San Francisc	84	533
Horace B	40	m	w	RI	San Francisco	7-Wd San Francisco	81	247
J M	49	m	w	NC	Amador	Drytown P O	69	425
Jas	36	m	w	SCOT	Solano	Vallejo	90	181
Joseph	42	m	w	MEXI	Sacramento	2-Wd Sacramento	77	221
Moses	30	m	w	POLA	San Francisco	2-Wd San Francisco	79	240
Perida	28	m	w	MEXI	San Diego	Coronado	78	465
Philip	44	m	w	FRAN	San Francisco	2-Wd San Francisco	79	226
Smith	19	m	w	CA	Los Angeles	Los Angeles	73	570
Wm	30	m	w	RI	San Francisco	7-Wd San Francisco	81	249
Wooddon	52	m	w	KY	Santa Clara	Gilroy Twp	88	86
ANGELA								
Ahela	16	f	w	CA	San Mateo	Redwood City P O	87	376
Lambarina	30	m	w	ITAL	Sacramento	2-Wd Sacramento	77	239
ANGELAPULO								
P H	40	m	w	GREE	Alameda	Murray Twp	68	126
ANGELAT								
Refundo	48	m	i	MEXI	Inyo	Lone Pine Twp	73	335
ANGELEN								
Thomas	30	m	w	IREL	San Francisco	11-Wd San Francisc	84	450
ANGELES								
Deonicio	44	m	w	FRAN	Los Angeles	Los Angeles Twp	73	492
Maria	40	f	w	FRAN	Los Angeles	Los Angeles Twp	73	492
ANGELI								
Julius	35	m	w	GERM	San Francisco	8-Wd San Francisco	82	370
ANGELKE								
Luis A	40	m	w	PRUS	Tuolumne	Sonora P O	93	321
ANGELL								
Andrew J	39	m	w	RI	Placer	Bath P O	76	433
ANGELLO								
Manly	37	m	w	FRAN	Butte	Ophir Twp	70	115
ANGELLOTTI								
Joseph	49	m	w	ITAL	Marin	San Rafael	74	55
ANGELO								
Barbaro	27	m	w	ITAL	San Francisco	1-Wd San Francisco	79	107
Charles A	60	m	w	ASEA	San Francisco	San Francisco P O	83	345
De Augustino	24	m	w	SWIT	Plumas	Seneca Twp	77	50
Diego	40	m	w	MEXI	San Francisco	San Francisco P O	80	347
Diego	40	m	w	MEXI	San Francisco	San Francisco P O	80	348
Gurdello	26	m	w	ITAL	El Dorado	Diamond Springs Tw	72	29
John	15	m	w	MEXI	Sonoma	Sonoma Twp	91	441
Louisa	32	m	w	ITAL	Sacramento	1-Wd Sacramento	77	173
Masher	28	m	w	ITAL	San Mateo	Redwood City P O	87	375
Naciro	42	m	w	ITAL	Yuba	Marysville	93	616
P	20	m	c	SWIT	Santa Clara	Gilroy Twp	88	93
Pauli	38	m	w	ITAL	San Francisco	1-Wd San Francisco	79	105
Pietro	30	m	w	ITAL	San Francisco	11-Wd San Francisc	84	642
Rame	19	m	w	CA	San Francisco	2-Wd San Francisco	79	259
Scoy	42	m	w	GA	San Joaquin	Douglas Twp	86	46
ANGELOS								
John	30	m	w	FRAN	San Francisco	11-Wd San Francisc	84	679
ANGELS								
Augt	34	m	w	HAMB	San Francisco	8-Wd San Francisco	82	354
						Series M593		
ANGENNO								
Trundad	30	m	w	MEXI	Santa Clara	Alviso Twp	88	24
ANGER								
Eugene	40	m	w	FRAN	San Francisco	San Francisco P O	83	345
James	37	m	w	OH	Nevada	Meadow Lake Twp	75	267
John	36	m	w	SPAI	San Francisco	San Francisco P O	80	415
Louis A	51	m	w	FRAN	Solano	Suisun Twp	90	104
ANGERO								
Domingo	24	m	w	CA	Santa Clara	Burnett Twp	88	30
Jose	38	m	w	CA	Santa Clara	Burnett Twp	88	30
ANGEST								
John	45	m	w	FRAN	San Francisco	7-Wd San Francisco	81	209
ANGEVIN								
Edwin	29	m	w	ENGL	Nevada	Meadow Lake Twp	75	250
ANGGING								
Ah	24	m	c	CHIN	Sonoma	Salt Point	91	380
ANGIER								
Perrin J	40	m	w	NY	Nevada	Bridgeport Twp	75	104
Peter M	52	m	w	WIND	Santa Clara	Alviso Twp	88	23
Thoms	35	m	w	IREL	San Francisco	2-Wd San Francisco	79	214
ANGILO								
Crisano	41	m	w	ITAL	San Mateo	Menlo Park P O	87	378
ANGING								
Ah	21	m	c	CHIN	Santa Cruz	Santa Cruz Twp	89	400
ANGIO								
Joseph	45	m	w	MEXI	San Joaquin	Douglas Twp	86	39
ANGISCHUK								
Phillip	31	m	w	ENGL	Siskiyou	Scott Valley Twp	89	615
ANGLAIS								
Peter	45	m	w	FRAN	Plumas	Rich Bar Twp	77	45
ANGLE								
C	50	m	w	SWIT	Sierra	Butte Twp	89	511
C C	40	m	w	NY	Tuolumne	Chinese Camp P O	93	379
Charles	32	m	w	US	Stanislaus	Empire Twp	92	60
John D	35	m	w	NY	Placer	Colfax P O	76	385
Rench	39	m	w	IL	Mendocino	Calpella Twp	74	182
William	8	m	w	CA	San Francisco	San Francisco P O	83	243
ANGLEBACK								
George Henry	9	m	w	CA	Plumas	Plumas Twp	77	28
George Henry	44	m	w	DENM	Plumas	Mineral Twp	77	22
ANGLER								
Christian	45	m	w	SWIT	Calaveras	San Andreas P O	70	189
ANGLING								
Wm	40	m	w	IREL	San Francisco	1-Wd San Francisco	79	74
ANGLOW								
Jno	48	m	w	IREL	Sacramento	3-Wd Sacramento	77	271
ANGLUND								
Andrew P	50	m	w	SWED	Nevada	Grass Valley Twp	75	203
ANGN								
Lowellaby	20	m	w	IL	Humboldt	Arcata Twp	72	230
ANGNES								
Sarah	75	f	w	VA	Monterey	San Benito Twp	74	381
ANGNEY								
W Z	50	m	w	PA	Santa Clara	Gilroy Twp	88	98
ANGOLA								
A	28	m	w	MEXI	Alameda	Oakland	68	229
ANGOLO								
Miguel	51	m	w	CA	Santa Cruz	Pajaro Twp	89	346
ANGON								
Mariano	35	m	w	CHIL	Fresno	Millerton P O	72	165
ANGONA								
Jose	45	m	w	MEXI	San Joaquin	2-Wd Stockton	86	173
ANGONETTE								
Francis	47	m	w	FRAN	Marin	Sausalito Twp	74	69
ANGOVE								
Ann	70	f	w	ENGL	Nevada	Grass Valley Twp	75	159
Henry	69	m	w	ENGL	Nevada	Grass Valley Twp	75	159
Henry	28	m	w	ENGL	Santa Clara	Burnett Twp	88	31
James	44	m	w	ENGL	El Dorado	Placerville	72	110
John	29	m	w	ENGL	Nevada	Grass Valley Twp	75	142
Thomas	34	m	w	ENGL	Nevada	Grass Valley Twp	75	163
W	42	m	w	ENGL	Sierra	Forest Twp	89	531
ANGUESOLA								
Concepcia	48	f	w	ME	Santa Barbara	San Buenaventura P	87	432
Manuel	25	m	w	ME	Santa Barbara	San Buenaventura P	87	432
ANGUILAR								
Joralda	35	m	w	MEXI	Santa Barbara	Las Cruces P O	87	505
ANGULA								
Francisco	40	m	w	MEXI	Los Angeles	Los Nietos Twp	73	582
ANGULAR								
Garvina	50	m	w	CA	San Diego	Julian Dist	78	474
Jesus	29	m	w	MEXI	San Diego	Coronado	78	465
ANGULO								
Miguel	44	m	w	MEXI	Santa Barbara	Santa Barbara P O	87	470
Tavorcio	47	m	w	MEXI	Santa Barbara	Santa Barbara P O	87	488
ANGUN								
Segundino	28	m	w	MEXI	Santa Barbara	Santa Barbara P O	87	479
ANGUS								
Edward B	30	m	w	MA	Los Angeles	Los Angeles	73	505
James	37	m	w	SCOT	Colusa	Butte Twp	71	267
John	55	m	w	SCOT	El Dorado	Kelsey Twp	72	61
John	30	m	w	NY	Alameda	Washington Twp	68	298
John A	59	m	w	CANA	San Francisco	San Francisco P O	85	746
William O	23	m	w	MA	San Francisco	San Francisco P O	85	749
ANGWIN								
William	27	m	w	ENGL	Santa Clara	Santa Clara Twp	88	151

© 2001 by Heritage Quest. All rights reserved.

Series M593

Name	Age	S	R	B-PL	County	Locale	Roll	Pg
ANHALP								
Herman	24	m	w	BAVA	Napa	Napa	75	18
ANHEIM								
Julius	23	m	w	PRUS	San Francisco	San Francisco P O	83	282
ANHERT								
August	36	m	w	SAXO	Calaveras	San Andreas P O	70	195
ANHOLEM								
Michael	29	m	w	DENM	Mendocino	Noyo & Big Rvr Twp	74	173
ANHOMBOLT								
J	36	m	w	CANA	Sierra	Lincoln Twp	89	545
ANIBLE								
Lucen	38	m	w	FRAN	Calaveras	San Andreas P O	70	193
ANICE								
Mary	14	f	w	NY	Alameda	Oakland	68	148
ANIDO								
Constantine	30	m	w	ITAL	San Mateo	Schoolhouse Statio	87	346
ANIE								
Annie	21	f	w	NY	San Francisco	San Francisco P O	80	473
ANIEB								
Jesus	40	m	w	MEXI	Inyo	Lone Pine Twp	73	334
ANILLA								
Juan	50	m	w	MEXI	Los Angeles	Los Angeles Twp	73	479
Pasqual	50	m	b	PHIL	Mariposa	Mariposa P O	74	104
ANINO								
Merced	37	m	w	MEXI	Fresno	Millerton P O	72	153
ANIO								
Frank	37	m	w	MEXI	San Joaquin	3-Wd Stockton	86	220
ANIOT								
Jesus	35	m	w	MEXI	Inyo	Cerro Gordo Twp	73	319
ANISER								
Xaver	52	m	w	BAVA	Napa	Yountville Twp	75	84
ANJAL								
R	27	m	w	MEXI	Santa Clara	Almaden Twp	88	7
ANJEL								
Jose	28	m	w	MEXI	San Diego	Fort Yuma Dist	78	463
ANK								
Goo	35	m	c	CHIN	Klamath	Sawyers Bar	73	378
ANKENER								
W	23	m	w	WURT	Sacramento	3-Wd Sacramento	77	315
ANKER								
Louis	33	m	w	PRUS	San Bernardino	San Bernardino Twp	78	417
ANKES								
Levi	41	m	w	PA	Sacramento	Sutter Twp	77	380
ANKLIN								
Henry	35	m	w	OH	Shasta	Millville P O	89	491
ANKNER								
Jacob	54	m	w	BADE	Sacramento	American Twp	77	66
ANKNEY								
A B	47	m	w	PA	Alameda	Oakland	68	178
Joseph	37	m	w	PA	Butte	Ophir Twp	70	92
Joseph	32	m	w	PA	San Francisco	1-Wd San Francisco	79	124
Peter	42	m	w	PRUS	Butte	Concow Twp	70	12
ANKROM								
Elizabeth	72	f	w	MD	San Francisco	6-Wd San Francisco	81	154
ANKS								
Jacob	40	m	w	PA	Butte	Wyandotte Twp	70	142
Wm	36	m	w	PA	Yuba	Marysville Twp	93	567
Wm	32	m	w	PA	Butte	Wyandotte Twp	70	148
ANLEY								
Alexr	31	m	w	NY	San Francisco	5-Wd San Francisco	81	12
ANLIPPI								
Barnet	48	m	w	GREE	San Francisco	11-Wd San Francisc	84	650
ANN								
Ah	21	m	c	CHIN	Placer	Colfax P O	76	386
Ho	30	m	c	CHIN	San Joaquin	1-Wd Stockton	86	147
Ling	21	m	c	CHIN	Amador	Lancha Plana P O	69	369
ANNA								
---	29	f	c	CHIN	Amador	Fiddletown P O	69	427
Peter	60	m	w	FRAN	San Mateo	Woodside P O	87	380
ANNAUD								
Herbert	48	m	w	FRAN	Amador	Fiddletown P O	69	429
M S	50	m	w	FRAN	Tuolumne	Chinese Camp P O	93	369
ANNEK								
R	29	m	w	ENGL	Sierra	Butte Twp	89	508
ANNER								
Richd	69	m	w	ENGL	San Joaquin	3-Wd Stockton	86	238
ANNERO								
John	34	m	w	ITAL	San Mateo	Menlo Park P O	87	378
ANNERTEO								
John	54	m	w	GERM	Yolo	Cache Crk Twp	93	451
ANNES								
C W	41	m	w	MI	Alameda	Oakland	68	199
ANNESSINE								
Anthony	38	m	w	AUST	Santa Clara	Santa Clara Twp	88	176
ANNFIELD								
Louis R	26	m	w	MO	San Luis Obispo	Arroyo Grande Twp	87	278
ANNI								
Ah	35	m	c	CHIN	Santa Clara	Santa Clara Twp	88	165
ANNIAS								
B	75	m	w	MEXI	Santa Clara	Almaden Twp	88	3
ANNICK								
Jno R	36	m	w	MO	Santa Barbara	San Buenaventura P	87	447
ANNINGTON								
Patrick	31	m	w	IREL	Inyo	Cerro Gordo Twp	73	320
ANNIS								
A G	37	m	w	ME	Monterey	San Juan Twp	74	405
Abe	44	m	w	PRUS	San Francisco	San Francisco P O	83	156
Caroline	64	f	w	ENGL	San Francisco	San Francisco P O	83	123
James	4	m	w	CA	Sonoma	Petaluma Twp	91	353
James	37	m	w	MO	Calaveras	San Andreas P O	70	181
James	31	m	w	NY	Alameda	Oakland	68	151
Mason	22	m	w	NY	Marin	Point Reyes Twp	74	23
Saml	43	m	w	ME	San Francisco	1-Wd San Francisco	79	2
Thomas	56	m	w	MO	Sacramento	2-Wd Sacramento	77	247
Thomas	39	m	w	NH	Siskiyou	Surprise Valley Tw	89	641
William	43	m	w	NY	Sonoma	Petaluma Twp	91	353
ANNISON								
Carrie	27	f	w	NORW	San Francisco	8-Wd San Francisco	82	347
ANNOD								
Jno Mrs	53	f	w	FRAN	San Francisco	8-Wd San Francisco	82	340
ANNONA								
John	40	m	w	FRAN	Napa	Napa Twp	75	73
ANNSTEY								
Domingo	46	m	w	FRAN	Los Angeles	Los Angeles Twp	73	476
ANO								
J A	40	f	w	CHIL	Tuolumne	Chinese Camp P O	93	377
ANODYNE								
Neils	27	m	w	SWED	Marin	Bolinas Twp	74	8
ANOO								
Louis	51	m	w	FRAN	San Joaquin	1-Wd Stockton	86	125
ANOYO								
Frank	29	m	w	PORT	San Mateo	Half Moon Bay P O	87	394
ANRALDA								
Bridget	35	f	w	IREL	San Francisco	2-Wd San Francisco	79	175
ANSAR								
Guadalupe	18	m	w	CA	Santa Clara	Santa Clara Twp	88	176
ANSBRO								
Thos	33	m	w	IREL	San Francisco	2-Wd San Francisco	79	170
ANSCHEL								
Levi	71	m	w	PRUS	San Francisco	3-Wd San Francisco	79	302
ANSCHER								
Albert	24	m	w	PRUS	Solano	Benicia	90	13
ANSEL								
G	40	m	w	FRAN	Santa Clara	Gilroy Twp	88	85
Gustave	40	m	w	FRAN	Santa Clara	Gilroy Twp	88	79
ANSELICI								
Petrule	27	m	w	SWIT	Santa Clara	2-Wd San Jose	88	320
ANSELL								
G	21	m	w	GERM	Santa Clara	Burnett Twp	88	33
John	28	m	w	NY	San Francisco	11-Wd San Francisc	84	560
Richrd	37	m	w	FRAN	San Joaquin	2-Wd Stockton	86	163
ANSELMA								
Benita	15	m	w	SWIT	Marin	Sausalito Twp	74	66
ANSELMAN								
Joseph	25	m	w	SWIT	Alameda	Oakland	68	147
ANSELMO								
---	45	m	w	CA	Santa Barbara	Santa Maria P O	87	514
ANSERMOZ								
Frank	28	m	w	SWIT	San Francisco	1-Wd San Francisco	79	105
ANSGAST								
John	43	m	w	PRUS	San Francisco	3-Wd San Francisco	79	297
ANSIER								
William	28	m	w	BRUN	Sonoma	Petaluma Twp	91	365
ANSIGLION								
H	64	m	w	FRAN	San Francisco	8-Wd San Francisco	82	367
ANSLER								
Saml	30	m	w	SWIT	Sierra	Sears Twp	89	553
ANSO								
Manuel	58	m	w	CHIL	Amador	Jackson P O	69	339
ANSON								
B D	24	m	w	OH	Sutter	Butte Twp	92	89
F	54	m	w	KY	Santa Clara	Gilroy Twp	88	100
H T	37	m	w	MO	Monterey	San Juan Twp	74	396
Hoe	40	m	w	NORW	San Francisco	1-Wd San Francisco	79	126
John	32	m	w	NORW	San Francisco	San Francisco P O	85	823
Richard	40	m	w	IREL	San Francisco	San Francisco P O	85	777
Wm	75	m	w	SWIT	Sacramento	3-Wd Sacramento	77	273
Wm	21	m	w	DENM	San Francisco	1-Wd San Francisco	79	116
ANSPACHER								
Abraham	50	m	w	BAVA	San Francisco	8-Wd San Francisco	82	407
ANSTEAD								
Joseph	39	m	w	PA	Trinity	Canyon City Pct	92	201
ANSTELL								
Anna	50	f	w	IREL	Alameda	Oakland	68	141
ANSTIS								
Saraposa	8	f	w	CA	Napa	Napa	75	54
ANSWELD								
Fredk H	46	m	w	PRUS	San Francisco	San Francisco P O	85	728
ANT								
---	48	m	c	CHIN	Shasta	Horsetown P O	89	506
---	16	m	c	CHIN	Sierra	Eureka Twp	89	526
Thang	47	m	c	CHIN	Humboldt	Eureka Twp	72	266
ANTARIS								
Ed	36	m	w	MEXI	San Joaquin	3-Wd Stockton	86	228
ANTEERIS								
Miguel	21	m	w	CA	Los Angeles	Los Angeles	73	567
ANTELINS								
R	29	m	w	CA	Santa Clara	Gilroy Twp	88	95
ANTELL								
Geo	10	m	w	CA	San Francisco	11-Wd San Francisc	84	592
Job	35	m	w	ENGL	San Bernardino	San Bernardino Twp	78	435
ANTENI								
Jose	40	m	w	CA	Stanislaus	Washington Twp	92	87

© 2001 by Heritage Quest. All rights reserved.

Name	Age	S	R	B-PL	County	Locale	Roll	Pg
						Series M593		
ANTEREA								
Benfanti	40	m	w	ITAL	Fresno	Millerton P O	72	164
ANTES								
John	32	m	w	PA	San Diego	San Pasqual	78	522
ANTHES								
Frederick	43	m	w	HAMB	San Francisco	8-Wd San Francisco	82	383
John	47	m	w	HHOM	Santa Clara	1-Wd San Jose	88	268
Peter	40	m	w	BAVA	San Francisco	6-Wd San Francisco	81	93
ANTHON								
Frank	28	m	w	AZOR	San Francisco	1-Wd San Francisco	79	102
John	31	m	w	AZOR	San Francisco	1-Wd San Francisco	79	102
ANTHONEY								
Geo J	21	m	w	IN	Monterey	San Antonio Twp	74	315
Lewis H	25	m	w	IN	Monterey	San Antonio Twp	74	315
ANTHONY								
Abraham	34	m	w	PRUS	San Francisco	11-Wd San Francisc	84	447
Albert	35	m	w	MA	San Francisco	8-Wd San Francisco	82	462
Benjamin	32	m	w	MA	Calaveras	Copperopolis P O	70	262
C W	27	m	w	NY	Alameda	Oakland	68	138
Chas V	39	m	w	NY	Nevada	Grass Valley Twp	75	160
D R	24	m	w	PA	Sierra	Sears Twp	89	559
Dorrance	23	m	w	SPAI	Contra Costa	Martinez P O	71	411
E M	38	m	w	VA	Siskiyou	Scott Valley Twp	89	608
E T	38	m	w	NY	San Francisco	San Francisco P O	85	810
Elihu	51	m	w	NY	Santa Cruz	Santa Cruz	89	416
F	29	m	w	AUST	Humboldt	Eureka Twp	72	264
Florence	14	f	w	CA	San Francisco	San Francisco P O	83	130
Francis	10	m	w	CA	Santa Clara	Fremont Twp	88	63
Geo	10	m	w	CA	San Francisco	11-Wd San Francisc	84	592
George	49	m	w	NY	Santa Cruz	Santa Cruz	89	431
Henry	27	m	w	CANA	Sonoma	Analy Twp	91	234
Horace	23	m	w	NY	Mariposa	Mariposa P O	74	134
Hy J	26	m	w	PRUS	San Francisco	San Francisco P O	83	33
I M	11	m	w	CA	Sacramento	3-Wd Sacramento	77	306
J	27	m	w	IN	Santa Clara	Almaden Twp	88	20
J G	40	m	w	MD	Del Norte	Smith Rvr Twp	71	477
James M	67	m	w	CT	San Francisco	San Francisco P O	83	158
Jas	46	m	w	PA	Sacramento	3-Wd Sacramento	77	304
John	40	m	w	PA	Napa	Napa	75	1
John	40	m	w	PA	Napa	Napa	75	1
John	39	m	w	IREL	San Francisco	1-Wd San Francisco	79	11
John	28	m	w	MA	San Francisco	6-Wd San Francisco	81	81
John A	46	m	w	NY	Sacramento	2-Wd Sacramento	77	249
Jos	58	m	w	WALD	Solano	Benicia	90	19
Josiah	45	m	w	MO	Mendocino	Round Valley Twp	74	220
M A	19	f	b	NY	Alameda	Oakland	68	187
M E M	60	f	w	NY	San Francisco	6-Wd San Francisco	81	117
Mark	55	m	w	SCOT	Alameda	Brooklyn	68	30
Mark	33	m	w	IN	San Mateo	Schoolhouse Statio	87	336
Mary	38	f	w	BAVA	San Francisco	7-Wd San Francisco	81	207
Michael	20	m	w	PORT	San Mateo	Schoolhouse Statio	87	341
Robert	35	m	b	MO	Colusa	Monroe Twp	71	324
Samuel	70	m	w	MD	Del Norte	Smith Rvr Twp	71	477
Samuel	45	m	w	MO	Yuba	Long Bar Twp	93	562
Sarah	43	f	w	IREL	San Francisco	San Francisco P O	83	140
Simon H	52	m	w	MA	Stanislaus	Emory Twp	92	18
William	29	m	w	ME	Santa Clara	Fremont Twp	88	43
ANTINELLO								
Abram	35	m	w	ITAL	Calaveras	San Andreas P O	70	179
Stephen	34	m	w	ITAL	Calaveras	San Andreas P O	70	179
ANTIPA								
Nicholas	30	m	w	GREE	Placer	Bath P O	76	440
ANTIS								
Samuel	40	m	w	PA	Santa Clara	Santa Clara Twp	88	139
ANTMAN								
Isaac	46	m	w	AUSL	San Francisco	2-Wd San Francisco	79	178
ANTOAN								
B C	25	m	w	ITAL	Sonoma	Vallejo Twp	91	463
ANTOIN								
Phil	30	m	w	FRAN	Del Norte	Mountain Twp	71	474
ANTOINE								
Carlos	34	m	w	MEXI	Sacramento	2-Wd Sacramento	77	215
Clarcence	19	f	w	FRAN	San Francisco	San Francisco P O	85	752
Frank	36	m	w	AZOR	Shasta	American Ranch P O	89	496
Gaudoloupe	31	m	w	MEXI	Stanislaus	San Joaquin Twp	92	82
Hosa	17	m	w	CA	Colusa	Monroe Twp	71	321
James	36	m	w	CANA	San Francisco	San Francisco P O	80	477
John	22	m	w	SCOT	Siskiyou	Yreka Twp	89	669
John	20	m	w	SCOT	Siskiyou	Yreka Twp	89	668
Joseph	44	m	w	FRAN	Marin	San Rafael	74	50
Manuel	29	m	w	SCOT	Siskiyou	Yreka Twp	89	668
Van	25	m	w	CA	Colusa	Colusa	71	289
ANTOINETTE								
Mary	35	f	w	FRAN	Sacramento	2-Wd Sacramento	77	234
ANTOLA								
John	44	m	w	FRAN	San Francisco	8-Wd San Francisco	82	311
ANTON								
Forge	20	m	w	FRAN	San Joaquin	Elkhorn Twp	86	56
Joce	33	m	w	PRUS	Butte	Kimshew Tpw	70	76
John	29	m	w	PORT	Trinity	North Fork Twp	92	218
Joseph	31	m	w	PORT	Tuolumne	Columbia P O	93	359
ANTONA								
---	35	m	w	ITAL	Sacramento	1-Wd Sacramento	77	201
ANTONE								
---	57	m	w	MEXI	Yuba	Marysville	93	588
F J	37	m	w	ITAL	Sierra	Lincoln Twp	89	551
Francis	30	m	w	PORT	Alameda	Eden Twp	68	90
Frank	50	m	w	PORT	Sacramento	Granite Twp	77	149
Frank	39	m	w	PORT	Alameda	Eden Twp	68	88
Frank	18	m	w	PORT	Trinity	Douglas	92	236
Henry	55	m	w	GERM	El Dorado	White Oak Twp	72	141
John	39	m	w	PRUS	Sacramento	4-Wd Sacramento	77	341
John	31	m	w	PORT	San Mateo	Schoolhouse Statio	87	337
John	30	m	w	PORT	Alameda	Washington Twp	68	274
Joseph	40	m	w	PORT	San Francisco	11-Wd San Francisc	84	658
Joseph	38	m	w	PORT	Santa Cruz	Santa Cruz Twp	89	380
Joseph	36	m	w	PORT	Nevada	Eureka Twp	75	136
Joseph	22	m	w	PORT	Alameda	Washington Twp	68	275
M	28	m	w	PORT	Alameda	Alameda	68	10
Manuel	39	m	w	PORT	Mariposa	Mariposa P O	74	133
Manuel	38	m	w	PORT	Marin	Point Reyes Twp	74	22
Manuel	36	m	w	AZOR	Monterey	San Juan Twp	74	397
Manuel	35	m	w	SCOT	San Luis Obispo	Santa Rosa Twp	87	323
Manuel	25	m	w	PORT	Marin	Bolinas Twp	74	8
Michael	25	m	w	AZOR	Marin	Sausalito Twp	74	70
Peter	30	m	w	SWIT	Humboldt	Mattole Twp	72	283
Philip	40	m	w	FRAN	Marin	Nicasio Twp	74	19
Thomas	40	m	w	SCOT	Alameda	Brooklyn Twp	68	47
Thomas	38	m	w	CHIL	Yolo	Putah Twp	93	515
Victory	25	m	w	PORT	San Mateo	Schoolhouse Statio	87	337
ANTONEL								
Dan	28	m	w	SWIT	Alameda	Oakland	68	250
ANTONELLI								
Avata	18	m	w	ITAL	San Francisco	San Francisco P O	80	426
Domink	16	m	w	ITAL	Tuolumne	Sonora P O	93	330
ANTONI								
Andrews	35	m	w	BAVA	San Francisco	San Francisco P O	83	352
Charles	21	m	w	HI	Yolo	Merritt Twp	93	505
Frank	31	m	w	HI	Yolo	Merritt Twp	93	505
Soleda	20	f	i	CA	Yolo	Cache Crk Twp	93	428
ANTONIA								
Frank	28	m	w	PORT	San Francisco	3-Wd San Francisco	79	291
John	20	m	w	SWIT	San Francisco	11-Wd San Francisc	84	680
Jose	40	m	w	SPAI	San Luis Obispo	Salinas Twp	87	295
Jose	40	m	w	CA	Stanislaus	Buena Vista Twp	92	13
Jose	22	m	w	SDOM	Placer	Auburn P O	76	358
Juan	31	m	w	CA	San Diego	Warners Rancho Dis	78	530
Remone	30	m	i	MEXI	Inyo	Lone Pine Twp	73	335
Victorin	47	m	w	PORT	San Francisco	8-Wd San Francisco	82	373
ANTONIE								
Chinia	26	m	w	SWIT	Napa	Napa Twp	75	69
Eugene	52	m	w	FRAN	San Francisco	8-Wd San Francisco	82	381
Jose	45	m	i	CA	San Luis Obispo	Morro Twp	87	281
Jose	25	m	i	CA	Yolo	Cache Crk Twp	93	427
Large	45	m	w	TX	San Joaquin	Castoria Twp	86	8
ANTONINO								
John	54	m	w	ITAL	Tuolumne	Sonora P O	93	327
ANTONIO								
---	30	m	b	BRAZ	Sacramento	4-Wd Sacramento	77	324
A	28	m	w	MEXI	Alameda	Oakland	68	135
Antone	18	m	w	SWIT	Sonoma	Petaluma Twp	91	348
Apelicar	28	m	w	ITAL	San Francisco	San Francisco P O	80	400
Chapo Jesus	35	m	i	CA	Los Angeles	Los Angeles	73	501
Chas	34	m	w	ITAL	Solano	Vallejo	90	213
Frank	22	m	w	PORT	Solano	Vallejo	90	204
Ignavius	28	m	w	AZOR	San Francisco	1-Wd San Francisco	79	130
Jesus	67	m	w	ITAL	Santa Clara	Gilroy Twp	88	100
John	45	m	w	AZOR	San Francisco	1-Wd San Francisco	79	133
John	40	m	w	PORT	Tuolumne	Sonora P O	93	328
Jose	33	m	w	CA	Santa Clara	Gilroy Twp	88	96
Jose	30	m	i	CA	San Diego	San Luis Rey	78	512
Jose	28	m	w	CA	San Diego	San Jacinto Dist	78	517
Jose	25	m	i	CA	Monterey	San Juan Twp	74	412
Joseph	22	m	w	CA	San Mateo	Half Moon Bay P O	87	396
Josie	39	m	w	CA	San Joaquin	2-Wd Stockton	86	163
L A	34	m	w	MEXI	Solano	Vallejo	90	212
Lewis	27	m	w	ITAL	Tuolumne	Sonora P O	93	327
Lobino	25	m	w	FRAN	Monterey	Monterey	74	361
Louis	53	m	w	IOFC	Marin	San Rafael Twp	74	36
Louis	45	m	w	FRAN	Mariposa	Mariposa P O	74	90
Louis	24	m	w	PORT	Tuolumne	Sonora P O	93	328
Manuel	36	m	w	ITAL	Tuolumne	Chinese Camp P O	93	382
Manuel	31	m	w	CA	San Diego	Warners Rancho Dis	78	530
Manuel	17	m	w	AZOR	San Francisco	1-Wd San Francisco	79	102
Manul	26	m	w	FRAN	Monterey	Monterey	74	366
Marcellus	36	m	w	SCOT	Siskiyou	Yreka Twp	89	669
Marie	24	f	i	CA	Santa Barbara	Las Cruces P O	87	506
Mary	35	f	i	CA	Sonoma	Salt Point Twp	91	382
Matace	40	m	w	SCOT	Alameda	Eden Twp	68	91
Mauricio	30	m	i	CA	Los Angeles	Los Angeles	73	500
ANTONIOVICH								
Florentine	44	m	w	AUST	San Francisco	2-Wd San Francisco	79	241
ANTONITTE								
V	40	m	w	ITAL	El Dorado	Greenwood Twp	72	55
ANTONN								
J	50	m	b	WIND	Alameda	Alameda	68	14
ANTONO								
Frank	32	m	w	AZOR	Monterey	Alisal Twp	74	290
Joseph	20	m	w	AZOR	Monterey	Alisal Twp	74	294
Manuel	21	m	w	AZOR	Monterey	Alisal Twp	74	290
Vallajo	22	m	w	ITAL	San Francisco	11-Wd San Francisc	84	701
ANTONS								
Edward	34	m	w	MEXI	Placer	Emigrant Gap P O	76	416

© 2001 by Heritage Quest. All rights reserved.

Name	Age	S	R	B-PL	County	Locale	Roll	Pg
						Series M593		
ANTONY								
Frank	14	m	w	CA	San Francisco	11-Wd San Francisc	84	592
Henry	21	m	w	HDAR	San Francisco	2-Wd San Francisco	79	187
Mills	47	m	w	RI	Sacramento	1-Wd Sacramento	77	205
Silas	37	m	w	NY	San Joaquin	Oneal Twp	86	109
Walter	16	m	w	CA	San Francisco	11-Wd San Francisc	84	592
William	35	m	w	FL	Sonoma	Petaluma Twp	91	311
Willm	57	m	w	NY	Alameda	Murray Twp	68	126
ANTRIM								
Edward	28	m	w	FRAN	Santa Clara	Fremont Twp	88	66
John	32	m	w	CANA	Solano	Vallejo	90	145
John A	27	m	w	MO	Mendocino	Big Rvr Twp	74	171
Sarah A	35	f	w	NY	San Francisco	6-Wd San Francisco	81	95
ANTROBUS								
John D	39	m	w	IL	Monterey	San Juan Twp	74	399
ANTRON								
Aden	54	m	w	OH	Mendocino	Point Arena Twp	74	205
Rosa	28	m	w	PORT	Stanislaus	Emory Twp	92	26
ANTUREOVICH								
N	33	m	w	AUST	San Francisco	3-Wd San Francisco	79	293
ANTWINE								
G	46	f	w	FRAN	Alameda	Oakland	68	130
ANXIER								
George	34	m	w	PRUS	Kern	Bakersfield P O	73	357
ANZAR								
Ramon	50	m	w	MEXI	Monterey	San Juan Twp	74	417
ANZER								
John	40	m	w	ITAL	San Francisco	San Francisco P O	80	341
ANZINI								
Battiste	20	m	w	SWIT	Marin	San Antonio Twp	74	61
Jose	40	m	w	CA	Marin	Tomales Twp	74	88
Peter	35	m	w	SWIT	Marin	Nicasio Twp	74	15
ANZUERO								
Manuel	18	m	i	MEXI	Inyo	Cerro Gordo Twp	73	319
AO								
Cal	21	m	c	CHIN	San Joaquin	1-Wd Stockton	86	151
AOK								
Ah	35	m	c	CHIN	Napa	Napa Twp	75	68
AON								
Ah	11	m	c	CHIN	San Francisco	11-Wd San Francisc	84	515
AOROZO								
Neb	49	m	w	MEXI	San Joaquin	3-Wd Stockton	86	224
AOW								
Ah	39	m	c	CHIN	Solano	Suisun Twp	90	104
AP								
---	30	m	c	CHIN	Siskiyou	Cottonwood Twp	89	592
Ah	14	m	c	CHIN	Stanislaus	Emory Twp	92	24
Bing	40	m	c	CHIN	San Francisco	6-Wd San Francisco	81	65
Hoy	31	m	c	CHIN	Santa Clara	1-Wd San Jose	88	271
APABLASO								
Cayetano	22	m	w	CA	Los Angeles	Wilmington Twp	73	637
APALESTEL								
Charles	39	m	w	FRAN	Santa Clara	1-Wd San Jose	88	258
APAVACCA								
Thomas	36	m	w	MEXI	Alameda	Alvarado	68	303
APE								
Hee	25	m	c	CHIN	Sonoma	Sonoma Twp	91	432
APEL								
John	57	m	w	PRUS	San Francisco	San Francisco P O	83	360
APELGATE								
A H	22	m	w	OH	San Joaquin	Douglas Twp	86	32
APENA								
Jesus	18	m	w	MEXI	Los Angeles	Los Nietos Twp	73	589
APES								
William	31	m	w	NY	San Francisco	6-Wd San Francisco	81	91
APESARENO								
Manuel	34	m	w	SPAI	Monterey	San Antonio Twp	74	322
APFELBECK								
Jos	28	m	w	DENM	Butte	Kimshew Tpw	70	82
APFORD								
John	35	m	w	ENGL	Marin	San Rafael Twp	74	37
APGAR								
Richard M	33	m	w	OH	Solano	Suisun Twp	90	94
APHOLDT								
August	31	m	w	PRUS	San Francisco	1-Wd San Francisco	79	135
APJOHN								
Anne	20	f	w	NY	San Francisco	6-Wd San Francisco	81	112
APLEGATE								
Joseph	37	m	w	PA	Siskiyou	Scott Valley Twp	89	620
APLEY								
John	38	m	w	SWIT	Sacramento	Natomas Twp	77	168
APO								
Ah	5	m	c	CA	Monterey	Monterey Twp	74	343
APODACO								
Gabriel	54	m	w	MEXI	San Luis Obispo	Salinas Twp	87	295
APODON								
Juan	36	m	w	MEXI	Fresno	Millerton P O	72	164
APOLACO								
Jesus	45	m	w	MEXI	Los Angeles	Los Angeles	73	564
APONE								
Alexr	36	m	w	PA	San Francisco	5-Wd San Francisco	81	34
APOTA								
A	35	m	w	MEXI	Alameda	Murray Twp	68	109
APP								
Augusta	38	f	w	PRUS	Los Angeles	Los Angeles	73	503
John	48	m	w	PA	Tuolumne	Chinese Camp P O	93	374
APPEL								
Frank	35	m	w	PRUS	San Francisco	San Francisco P O	80	339
Frank	34	m	w	PRUS	San Francisco	5-Wd San Francisco	81	15
Henry	40	m	w	OH	Nevada	Meadow Lake Twp	75	268
Louis	33	m	w	HANO	San Francisco	6-Wd San Francisco	81	62
Phillip	31	m	w	HDAR	San Francisco	6-Wd San Francisco	81	71
APPELL								
J C	34	m	w	PA	San Francisco	San Francisco P O	85	812
Samuel	42	m	w	PRUS	San Francisco	San Francisco P O	83	330
APPERCOM								
W	48	m	w	GERM	Sacramento	1-Wd Sacramento	77	174
APPERLEY								
George	43	m	w	ENGL	Fresno	Millerton P O	72	147
APPERSON								
D H	45	m	w	VA	Santa Clara	Gilroy Twp	88	85
Elbert C	19	m	w	MO	Santa Clara	Santa Clara Twp	88	167
James E	35	m	w	VA	Placer	Lincoln P O	76	485
John	30	m	w	VA	Shasta	Horsetown P O	89	506
Randolph	61	m	w	VA	Santa Clara	Santa Clara Twp	88	167
W L	37	m	w	ME	Solano	Vallejo	90	181
APPERTON								
John	28	m	w	ENGL	Calaveras	Copperopolis P O	70	240
APPIARNS								
Wm	30	m	w	WURT	San Francisco	2-Wd San Francisco	79	227
APPIERANS								
Henry	21	m	w	PRUS	San Francisco	San Francisco P O	83	242
APPLE								
Frederick	44	m	w	FRNK	Sacramento	Sutter Twp	77	389
Frederick	18	m	w	MO	Contra Costa	Martinez P O	71	375
Marie	19	f	w	PRUS	San Francisco	6-Wd San Francisco	81	113
Michael	36	m	w	HCAS	Mariposa	Mariposa P O	74	118
Newton L	38	m	w	TN	Inyo	Cerro Gordo Twp	73	321
Simon	23	m	w	PRUS	San Francisco	San Francisco P O	83	253
William	45	m	w	POLA	San Francisco	San Francisco P O	83	213
APPLEBEE								
Holly	52	m	w	MA	San Francisco	San Francisco P O	85	862
John	51	m	w	ENGL	San Francisco	2-Wd San Francisco	79	148
APPLEBY								
Augustine	38	m	w	NJ	Solano	Suisun Twp	90	114
B P	37	m	w	SC	Tuolumne	Columbia P O	93	349
Thomas D	48	m	w	ENGL	Santa Clara	1-Wd San Jose	88	228
William	22	m	w	ENGL	Solano	Vacaville Twp	90	136
Wm	23	m	w	ENGL	San Francisco	11-Wd San Francisc	84	668
APPLEGARTH								
J	41	m	w	CANA	Merced	Snelling P O	74	258
Mabel	37	f	w	CANA	San Francisco	San Francisco P O	85	722
APPLEGATE								
David	33	m	w	OH	Calaveras	San Andreas P O	70	209
G W	42	m	w	MO	Placer	Colfax P O	76	384
Henry	26	m	w	NY	San Francisco	2-Wd San Francisco	79	204
J P	28	m	w	IN	Mendocino	Calpella Twp	74	188
John J	27	m	w	OH	San Francisco	San Francisco P O	83	52
Josiah H	53	m	w	NY	San Francisco	San Francisco P O	83	203
APPLEGATH								
Wm	28	m	w	CANA	San Joaquin	Elkhorn Twp	86	66
APPLELY								
Mary	46	f	w	MEXI	San Francisco	San Francisco P O	80	475
APPLETON								
Abraham	40	m	w	PRUS	San Francisco	San Francisco P O	83	192
D E	38	m	w	NY	Alameda	Oakland	68	174
Edward E	34	m	w	MA	Nevada	Grass Valley Twp	75	232
Ephraim	23	m	w	ME	Alpine	Silver Mtn P O	69	307
George	30	m	w	MA	San Francisco	San Francisco P O	83	228
Henry	41	m	w	CA	Santa Clara	1-Wd San Jose	88	253
Horatio	39	m	w	MD	Sonoma	Sonoma Twp	91	435
Jennie	23	f	w	PRUS	San Francisco	San Francisco P O	83	405
John	72	m	w	IREL	San Francisco	1-Wd San Francisco	79	128
John	35	m	w	HANO	San Francisco	7-Wd San Francisco	81	212
John N	60	m	w	ENGL	Fresno	Millerton P O	72	182
Michael	65	m	w	IREL	Placer	Cisco P O	76	494
Samuel B	54	m	w	ME	Calaveras	Copperopolis P O	70	257
Thomas	38	m	w	ENGL	San Francisco	11-Wd San Francisc	84	620
Wellington	13	m	w	MI	San Francisco	8-Wd San Francisco	82	472
William	24	m	w	NY	Alameda	Brooklyn	68	34
APPLEY								
Peter W	46	m	w	NY	Sonoma	Analy Twp	91	230
APPLING								
C W	36	m	w	GA	Merced	Snelling P O	74	255
E R	46	m	w	GA	Merced	Snelling P O	74	256
John H	41	m	w	GA	Merced	Snelling P O	74	255
Peter C	48	m	w	GA	Fresno	Millerton P O	72	151
Robt A	51	m	w	TN	Fresno	Millerton P O	72	151
William	70	m	w	GA	Merced	Snelling P O	74	255
APPO								
James B	39	m	m	PA	San Francisco	11-Wd San Francisc	84	707
APTED								
Walter	25	m	w	ENGL	San Francisco	San Francisco P O	80	399
AQUIERRE								
Isabel	65	f	w	MEXI	San Francisco	San Francisco P O	80	428
AQUILLA								
Jesus	30	m	w	MEXI	Santa Clara	Almaden Twp	88	18
AR								
Archie	43	m	w	IREL	Butte	Kimshew Tpw	70	81
Cha	10	m	c	CHIN	Calaveras	San Andreas P O	70	171
Chai	22	m	c	CHIN	Calaveras	San Andreas P O	70	171
Chen	34	f	c	CHIN	Calaveras	San Andreas P O	70	169
Cheo	43	m	c	CHIN	Calaveras	San Andreas P O	70	172

© 2001 by Heritage Quest. All rights reserved.

California 1870 Census

Name	Age	S	R	B-PL	County	Locale	Roll	Pg
						Series M593		
Cheon	39	m	c	CHIN	Calaveras	San Andreas P O	70	175
Cheon	35	m	c	CHIN	Calaveras	San Andreas P O	70	180
Cheong	26	m	c	CHIN	Calaveras	San Andreas P O	70	171
Chew	50	m	c	CHIN	Calaveras	San Andreas P O	70	166
Chi	29	f	c	CHIN	Calaveras	San Andreas P O	70	181
Choi	58	m	c	CHIN	Calaveras	San Andreas P O	70	172
Chon	45	m	c	CHIN	Calaveras	San Andreas P O	70	172
Chon	23	m	c	CHIN	Calaveras	San Andreas P O	70	169
Chong	44	m	c	CHIN	Calaveras	San Andreas P O	70	183
Chow	50	m	c	CHIN	Calaveras	San Andreas P O	70	172
Chow	45	m	c	CHIN	Calaveras	San Andreas P O	70	172
Choy	50	m	c	CHIN	Calaveras	San Andreas P O	70	169
Choy	30	m	c	CHIN	Calaveras	San Andreas P O	70	171
Chung	24	m	c	CHIN	Calaveras	San Andreas P O	70	165
Con	4	m	c	CA	Calaveras	San Andreas P O	70	181
Cum	30	m	c	CHIN	Calaveras	San Andreas P O	70	172
Cum	28	f	c	CHIN	Calaveras	San Andreas P O	70	169
Fat	30	m	c	CHIN	Calaveras	San Andreas P O	70	178
Foh	25	f	c	CHIN	Calaveras	San Andreas P O	70	167
Fonk	42	m	c	CHIN	Calaveras	San Andreas P O	70	167
Foo	22	m	c	CHIN	Calaveras	San Andreas P O	70	172
Foo	19	m	c	CHIN	Calaveras	San Andreas P O	70	178
Fook	41	m	c	CHIN	Calaveras	San Andreas P O	70	166
Fung	45	m	c	CHIN	Calaveras	San Andreas P O	70	175
Geen	19	f	c	CHIN	Calaveras	San Andreas P O	70	169
Get	22	f	c	CHIN	Calaveras	San Andreas P O	70	169
Gin	32	m	c	CHIN	Calaveras	San Andreas P O	70	181
Gon	60	m	c	CHIN	Calaveras	San Andreas P O	70	201
Hoon	24	m	c	CHIN	Calaveras	San Andreas P O	70	176
John	38	m	c	CHIN	Calaveras	San Andreas P O	70	169
Kee	54	m	c	CHIN	Calaveras	San Andreas P O	70	167
Ki	52	m	c	CHIN	Calaveras	San Andreas P O	70	202
Ky	62	m	c	CHIN	Calaveras	San Andreas P O	70	181
Ky	35	m	c	CHIN	Calaveras	San Andreas P O	70	165
Lee	28	m	c	CHIN	Calaveras	San Andreas P O	70	166
Lee On	36	m	c	CHIN	Calaveras	San Andreas P O	70	167
Len	22	m	c	CHIN	Calaveras	San Andreas P O	70	178
Lon	30	m	c	CHIN	Calaveras	San Andreas P O	70	166
Long	31	m	c	CHIN	Calaveras	San Andreas P O	70	178
Low	30	m	c	CHIN	Calaveras	San Andreas P O	70	167
Lung	30	m	c	CHIN	Calaveras	San Andreas P O	70	167
Ming Lu	43	m	c	CHIN	Calaveras	San Andreas P O	70	201
Mon	43	m	c	CHIN	Calaveras	San Andreas P O	70	172
Pan	49	m	c	CHIN	Calaveras	San Andreas P O	70	171
Pin	48	m	c	CHIN	Calaveras	San Andreas P O	70	171
Ping	45	m	c	CHIN	Calaveras	San Andreas P O	70	167
Poi	30	m	c	CHIN	Calaveras	San Andreas P O	70	169
Pon	38	m	c	CHIN	Calaveras	San Andreas P O	70	168
Pon	37	m	c	CHIN	Calaveras	San Andreas P O	70	167
Quen	20	f	c	CHIN	Calaveras	San Andreas P O	70	169
Quy	50	m	c	CHIN	Calaveras	San Andreas P O	70	171
Sam	52	m	c	CHIN	Calaveras	San Andreas P O	70	184
Sam	40	m	c	CHIN	Calaveras	San Andreas P O	70	165
Sang	52	m	c	CHIN	Calaveras	San Andreas P O	70	167
Sang	34	m	c	CHIN	Calaveras	San Andreas P O	70	182
See	40	m	c	CHIN	Calaveras	San Andreas P O	70	182
See	39	m	c	CHIN	Calaveras	San Andreas P O	70	172
See	37	m	c	CHIN	Calaveras	San Andreas P O	70	184
See	32	m	c	CHIN	Calaveras	San Andreas P O	70	175
See	30	m	c	CHIN	Calaveras	San Andreas P O	70	169
See	30	m	c	CHIN	Calaveras	San Andreas P O	70	171
Sen	34	m	c	CHIN	Calaveras	San Andreas P O	70	199
Son	41	m	c	CHIN	Calaveras	San Andreas P O	70	175
Son	30	m	c	CHIN	Calaveras	San Andreas P O	70	167
Son	29	m	c	CHIN	Calaveras	San Andreas P O	70	178
Su	30	m	c	CHIN	Calaveras	San Andreas P O	70	171
Suig	38	m	c	CHIN	Calaveras	San Andreas P O	70	199
Sung	38	m	c	CHIN	Calaveras	San Andreas P O	70	171
Sung	35	m	c	CHIN	Calaveras	San Andreas P O	70	167
Sung	31	m	c	CHIN	Calaveras	San Andreas P O	70	169
Sung	30	m	c	CHIN	Calaveras	San Andreas P O	70	176
Tin	60	m	c	CHIN	Calaveras	San Andreas P O	70	165
Tye	30	m	c	CA	Calaveras	San Andreas P O	70	171
Tye	20	m	c	CHIN	Calaveras	San Andreas P O	70	165
Way	30	m	c	CHIN	Calaveras	San Andreas P O	70	167
Yeon	24	m	c	CHIN	Calaveras	San Andreas P O	70	171
Yo	9	f	c	CA	Calaveras	San Andreas P O	70	181
Yon	52	m	c	CHIN	Calaveras	San Andreas P O	70	169
Yong	22	f	c	CHIN	Calaveras	San Andreas P O	70	169
ARABELLA								
Petra	53	f	w	MEXI	San Francisco	2-Wd San Francisco	79	177
ARABULLA								
Louis	40	m	w	FRAN	El Dorado	Cosumnes Twp	72	18
ARACATA								
Maria	40	f	w	MEXI	San Diego	San Diego	78	507
ARACHEO								
Porac	35	m	i	MEXI	Inyo	Lone Pine Twp	73	333
ARACKA								
Rufus	31	m	w	CA	Fresno	Kings Rvr P O	72	214
ARACO								
Jesus	31	m	w	CA	Fresno	Kingston P O	72	219
ARADA								
Alberto	20	m	i	CA	Santa Barbara	Las Cruces P O	87	505
Clemente	20	m	w	CA	Santa Barbara	Las Cruces P O	87	505
Francisco	16	m	m	CA	Santa Barbara	Las Cruces P O	87	505
Jose	28	m	i	MEXI	Santa Barbara	Las Cruces P O	87	505
Marcelino	45	m	w	CHIL	Santa Barbara	Las Cruces P O	87	505
Santos	44	m	w	CHIL	El Dorado	Mud Springs Twp	72	76
ARADELLA								
Seramio	30	m	w	MEXI	Los Angeles	Los Angeles Twp	73	468
ARADO								
Francisco	34	m	w	MEXI	Napa	Napa	75	55
ARAES								
Bernardino	26	m	w	CA	Santa Clara	2-Wd San Jose	88	291
ARAGA								
Jose	28	m	w	CHIL	Fresno	Millerton P O	72	153
ARAGARDO								
A	18	f	w	CA	Los Angeles	Los Angeles	73	569
ARAGO								
C	26	m	w	ITAL	Calaveras	Copperopolis P O	70	233
J	60	m	w	ITAL	Calaveras	Copperopolis P O	70	233
ARAGON								
Juan	32	m	w	MEXI	Monterey	San Juan Twp	74	407
ARAHO								
Hoostenio	16	m	w	CA	Fresno	Millerton P O	72	146
ARAIN								
Santiago	36	m	w	CHIL	El Dorado	Placerville	72	125
ARAISA								
Leocadia	60	m	w	MEXI	Los Angeles	Santa Ana Twp	73	609
ARAJA								
Lefamia	55	m	w	MEXI	Santa Cruz	Pajaro Twp	89	358
ARAJO								
Francisco	36	m	w	MEXI	Los Angeles	Los Angeles	73	513
ARALITE								
Vicente	26	m	w	MEXI	Los Angeles	Los Angeles	73	516
ARALLANES								
Candalaria	43	f	w	CA	Santa Barbara	Las Cruces P O	87	505
Luis	58	m	w	CA	Santa Barbara	Arroyo Grande P O	87	508
Luis	29	m	w	CA	Santa Barbara	San Buenaventura P	87	432
ARALLO								
Senfain	33	m	w	MEXI	Fresno	Millerton P O	72	154
ARAM								
Joseph	61	m	w	NY	Santa Clara	San Jose Twp	88	193
William	50	m	w	NY	Santa Clara	San Jose Twp	88	193
William	22	m	w	CA	Santa Clara	1-Wd San Jose	88	239
ARAMBE								
J	42	m	w	FRAN	Calaveras	Copperopolis P O	70	231
ARAMENTO								
Chico	50	m	w	MEXI	Fresno	Millerton P O	72	150
ARAN								
Pedro	55	m	w	CHIL	Calaveras	San Andreas P O	70	219
ARANA								
F L	44	m	w	MEXI	Tuolumne	Columbia P O	93	344
Sabriana	43	m	i	MEXI	Inyo	Cerro Gordo Twp	73	323
ARANAS								
Rosalie	12	f	w	CA	Napa	Napa	75	55
Santa A	12	m	w	CA	Santa Cruz	Pajaro Twp	89	343
ARANCE								
L	54	m	w	FRAN	Alameda	Alameda	68	19
ARANDO								
Rosaryo	50	m	w	CHIL	Amador	Drytown P O	69	415
ARANE								
Jacob	37	m	w	PRUS	El Dorado	White Oak Twp	72	138
ARANIS								
Augustine	80	m	w	PHIL	Napa	Napa	75	54
ARANO								
Frances	15	f	w	CA	Santa Cruz	Santa Cruz	89	417
Francisco	43	m	w	SPAI	Santa Cruz	Pajaro Twp	89	346
Gavina	14	m	w	CA	Santa Cruz	Santa Cruz Twp	89	381
Genobibo	23	m	w	CA	Santa Cruz	Soquel Twp	89	447
John	30	m	w	CA	Santa Cruz	Soquel Twp	89	450
Joseph	33	m	w	SPAI	Santa Cruz	Soquel Twp	89	438
Manuel	19	m	w	CA	Santa Cruz	Watsonville	89	371
ARANOT								
Joseph	28	m	w	CANA	Mendocino	Gualala Twp	74	225
ARAPETA								
Craza	40	f	w	MEXI	San Bernardino	San Salvador Twp	78	458
ARAS								
Francallius	32	m	w	MEXI	Kern	Bakersfield P O	73	363
ARATA								
Andrew	40	m	w	ITAL	Amador	Jackson P O	69	338
Anglo	25	m	w	SWIT	San Joaquin	2-Wd Stockton	86	170
Antonio	50	m	w	ITAL	Amador	Jackson P O	69	335
Antonio	23	m	w	ITAL	Amador	Jackson P O	69	329
Benjamin	36	m	w	ITAL	Amador	Jackson P O	69	337
G B	21	m	w	ITAL	Amador	Jackson P O	69	335
Giovanni	27	m	w	ITAL	San Francisco	11-Wd San Francisc	84	587
Gioveni	57	m	w	ITAL	Amador	Jackson P O	69	338
Gregorio	44	m	w	ITAL	Santa Barbara	Santa Barbara P O	87	480
Jennette	19	f	w	ITAL	Amador	Jackson P O	69	338
John	58	m	w	ITAL	Calaveras	Copperopolis P O	70	252
John	50	m	w	ITAL	Calaveras	San Andreas P O	70	175
John	26	m	w	ITAL	Amador	Jackson P O	69	338
Juan	44	m	w	SPAI	Santa Barbara	Las Cruces P O	87	505
Mary	50	f	b	ITAL	Sacramento	2-Wd Sacramento	77	234
Stephen	27	m	w	ITAL	Amador	Jackson P O	69	335
ARATON								
Rotania	25	f	w	ITAL	San Joaquin	1-Wd Stockton	86	126
ARATTA								
A	40	m	w	ITAL	Amador	Jackson P O	69	335
Francis	46	m	w	MEXI	Calaveras	San Andreas P O	70	204
John	27	m	w	ITAL	Amador	Jackson P O	69	330
ARATTI								
Rosa	16	f	w	ITAL	San Francisco	2-Wd San Francisco	79	235

© 2001 by Heritage Quest. All rights reserved.

Series M593

Name	Age	S	R	B-PL	County	Locale	Roll	Pg
ARAUYO								
Jose	70	m	w	MEXI	Monterey	San Juan Twp	74	410
ARAVENNA								
Georges	37	m	w	CHIL	Amador	Volcano P O	69	384
ARAYO								
Martina	35	f	w	CHIL	Amador	Jackson P O	69	326
ARAZA								
Horta	73	f	w	CHIL	El Dorado	Placerville	72	117
ARAZAN								
Juan	45	m	w	MEXI	Santa Clara	Almaden Twp	88	14
ARBACK								
Rosa	25	f	w	AUST	San Francisco	8-Wd San Francisco	82	324
ARBALLO								
Anisetto	40	m	w	MEXI	Santa Clara	Fremont Twp	88	50
ARBANKO								
Jno	52	m	w	VT	Butte	Concow Twp	70	9
ARBAREZ								
Juan	30	m	c	CHIN	Kern	Tehachapi P O	73	356
ARBAUGH								
Geo W	48	m	w	AL	Siskiyou	Butte Twp	89	584
ARBAYO								
Anastasio	60	m	w	MEXI	Santa Clara	Milpitas Twp	88	113
ARBEGAST								
Jacob	43	m	w	PA	Nevada	Nevada Twp	75	307
Jacob	26	m	w	PA	Nevada	Nevada Twp	75	308
ARBELOYA								
Aristarcio	40	m	w	MEXI	Santa Clara	Milpitas Twp	88	112
ARBISON								
William D	34	m	w	IL	Calaveras	San Andreas P O	70	197
ARBOGAST								
Ella	21	f	w	MA	San Francisco	8-Wd San Francisco	82	469
Geo	24	m	w	MA	San Francisco	8-Wd San Francisco	82	293
H W	34	m	w	IN	Humboldt	Arcata Twp	72	229
ARBOSCIS								
Beaumor	36	m	w	FRAN	San Mateo	Pescadero P O	87	410
ARBUCKLE								
Elizabeth	35	f	w	GA	Los Angeles	Los Angeles	73	524
Henry	36	m	w	PA	San Francisco	11-Wd San Francisc	84	510
Hugh	64	m	w	SCOT	Sacramento	Dry Crk Twp	77	98
James	28	m	w	ENGL	Alameda	Oakland	68	264
Jas	50	m	w	VT	Butte	Ophir Twp	70	97
Joseph	38	m	w	CANA	Humboldt	Bucksport Twp	72	242
Robert	21	m	w	NY	Marin	San Antonio Twp	74	65
Tacitus	35	m	w	MO	Colusa	Spring Valley Twp	71	342
Wm B	41	m	w	NY	San Luis Obispo	Santa Rosa Twp	87	322
ARBURN								
Ann	42	f	w	PRUS	Alameda	Oakland	68	250
ARCAGIOTA								
Tardelli	23	m	w	ITAL	San Francisco	8-Wd San Francisco	82	490
ARCAN								
Charles E	22	m	w	IL	Santa Cruz	Santa Cruz	89	419
ARCATA								
Rosa	36	f	w	CHIL	Marin	San Rafael Twp	74	33
ARCE								
Joaquin	55	m	w	MEXI	Los Angeles	San Juan Twp	73	626
Jose R	35	m	w	CA	Santa Clara	Gilroy Twp	88	87
Manuela	15	f	w	CA	Los Angeles	Los Angeles	73	522
ARCEANO								
Poseo	30	m	w	MEXI	Contra Costa	Martinez P O	71	385
ARCEO								
Jose M	29	m	w	CA	Marin	San Rafael Twp	74	42
ARCEY								
Mariano	55	m	w	CA	Santa Cruz	Pajaro Twp	89	359
ARCHAMBEAU								
P T	50	m	w	MO	Sonoma	Washington Twp	91	470
ARCHE								
George	48	m	w	IL	Monterey	Alisal Twp	74	302
ARCHEBALD								
Jas	39	m	w	PA	Butte	Ophir Twp	70	117
Sylvester	45	m	w	OH	Butte	Ophir Twp	70	117
ARCHER								
Carlton	33	m	w	NY	Santa Cruz	Santa Cruz	89	407
Catherine	50	f	w	ENGL	San Francisco	San Francisco P O	83	252
Charles	15	m	w	CA	Yuba	North East Twp	93	644
Denis T	40	m	w	IL	San Luis Obispo	San Luis Obispo Tw	87	311
Edward	40	m	b	LA	San Francisco	San Francisco P O	80	412
Edwd	41	m	w	IREL	San Francisco	1-Wd San Francisco	79	111
Frank	34	m	w	WURT	San Francisco	2-Wd San Francisco	79	175
George	39	m	w	NY	Amador	Jackson P O	69	327
George	37	m	w	ITAL	Calaveras	San Andreas P O	70	187
Horace	47	m	w	CT	Siskiyou	Scott Valley Twp	89	609
Jas	30	m	w	IL	Sonoma	Santa Rosa	91	395
Jay	37	m	w	NY	Plumas	Plumas Twp	77	27
Jno	44	m	w	IL	San Joaquin	Douglas Twp	86	40
Jno H	34	m	w	IL	Sonoma	Santa Rosa	91	396
Joel Bird	37	m	w	NC	Plumas	Goodwin Twp	77	1
Lawrence	49	m	w	SC	Santa Clara	1-Wd San Jose	88	276
Rebecca	58	f	w	TN	Tulare	Venice Twp	92	276
Samuel	38	m	w	NY	Amador	Ione City P O	69	359
Sml M	26	m	w	VA	Monterey	Monterey Twp	74	347
W A	42	m	w	IL	Klamath	Trinidad Twp	73	392
William	55	m	w	NY	San Diego	Julian Dist	78	472
William	36	m	w	IREL	San Francisco	San Francisco P O	83	35
William A	42	m	w	US	Klamath	Dillon Twp	73	369
Wm C	50	m	w	IL	San Luis Obispo	San Luis Obispo Tw	87	312
Wm H	25	m	w	IA	San Luis Obispo	Santa Rosa Twp	87	329

Series M593

Name	Age	S	R	B-PL	County	Locale	Roll	Pg
ARCHIBALD								
Andw	40	m	w	SCOT	San Francisco	1-Wd San Francisco	79	136
Charles	30	m	w	CANA	Plumas	Quartz Twp	77	35
J P	28	m	w	CANA	Mendocino	Ukiah Twp	74	237
James	46	m	w	SCOT	Santa Cruz	Santa Cruz Twp	89	399
James	36	m	w	NY	San Francisco	5-Wd San Francisco	81	24
Jas	65	m	w	NY	Mendocino	Round Valley Twp	74	217
Jas	35	m	w	NY	Butte	Kimshew Tpw	70	80
Jessie	28	m	w	CANA	San Francisco	San Francisco P O	83	362
John	60	m	w	SCOT	San Francisco	San Francisco P O	80	426
John	27	m	w	CANA	Stanislaus	Branch Twp	92	3
L	33	m	w	CANA	Monterey	San Juan Twp	74	394
Nelson	28	m	w	CANA	Sonoma	Bodega Twp	91	262
Prescot L	27	m	w	CANA	San Francisco	San Francisco P O	83	10
Putnam	30	m	w	CANA	Placer	Bath P O	76	440
Thomas	35	m	w	PRUS	Kern	Bakersfield P O	73	357
Zac	45	m	w	VA	Tehama	Red Bluff	92	175
ARCHIBALL								
Wm	37	m	w	SCOT	San Francisco	7-Wd San Francisco	81	199
ARCHIE								
Geo	20	m	w	PA	Yuba	Marysville Twp	93	569
Thomas	32	m	w	ENGL	Humboldt	Bucksport Twp	72	243
ARCHON								
Joseph	42	m	w	FRAN	Calaveras	San Andreas P O	70	200
ARCHULETA								
Francisco	15	m	w	CA	San Bernardino	San Bernardino Twp	78	415
Miguel	50	m	w	CA	Santa Clara	2-Wd San Jose	88	301
Pedro	38	m	w	MEXI	Los Angeles	El Monte Twp	73	452
ARCHY								
Israel	28	m	w	CANA	San Joaquin	Douglas Twp	86	41
Lewis	28	m	w	PA	Los Angeles	Los Angeles	73	571
M C	63	m	w	NY	Lake	Upper Lake	73	410
ARCI								
Mateo	50	m	w	MEXI	Los Angeles	Los Angeles Twp	73	480
ARCIA								
Ramon	50	m	w	NM	San Luis Obispo	San Luis Obispo Tw	87	299
Ujenia	12	f	w	CA	Los Angeles	Los Angeles	73	538
ARCINIA								
Baptiste	61	m	w	ITAL	Tuolumne	Big Oak Flat P O	93	404
ARCK								
Ah	35	m	c	CHIN	Shasta	French Gulch P O	89	470
ARCOOR								
---	11	m	c	CHIN	San Francisco	11-Wd San Francisc	84	706
ARD								
Poy	22	m	c	CHIN	Yuba	Marysville	93	629
ARDARY								
James	65	m	w	ENGL	El Dorado	Placerville Twp	72	96
ARDESTY								
Jno	39	m	w	KY	Santa Clara	Almaden Twp	88	12
ARDIFFI								
Beneditto	30	m	w	SWIT	Mariposa	Mariposa P O	74	118
ARDILLO								
Juliana	18	f	w	CA	San Diego	San Luis Rey	78	514
Louis	40	m	w	ITAL	Los Angeles	Los Angeles	73	531
ARDIS								
John C	47	m	w	GA	Los Angeles	Los Nietos Twp	73	580
ARDITTA								
James	34	m	w	ITAL	Amador	Amador City P O	69	394
ARDIZZI								
Ceasar	24	m	w	SWIT	San Francisco	8-Wd San Francisco	82	381
ARDLE								
James M	38	m	w	IREL	Fresno	Millerton P O	72	149
ARDLER								
L	42	m	w	BOHE	San Francisco	San Francisco P O	83	296
Louis	35	m	w	PRUS	San Francisco	3-Wd San Francisco	79	288
ARDO								
Louis	14	m	w	CA	Los Angeles	Los Angeles	73	510
ARDON								
Francisco	45	m	w	MEXI	Santa Clara	Almaden Twp	88	1
James H	50	m	w	BELG	San Francisco	2-Wd San Francisco	79	142
ARDONDE								
Avalina	33	m	w	MEXI	Fresno	Millerton P O	72	167
ARDUC								
John	60	m	w	FRAN	Calaveras	San Andreas P O	70	218
ARDWAN								
Hile	46	m	w	FRAN	Butte	Oregon Twp	70	133
ARDWELL								
Joseph	39	m	w	ENGL	San Francisco	1-Wd San Francisco	79	75
ARDWINN								
Henry	46	m	w	FRAN	Butte	Ophir Twp	70	117
AREA								
Francisco	30	m	w	MEXI	Los Angeles	Los Nietos Twp	73	587
AREAS								
Jesse	35	m	w	CHIL	Calaveras	San Andreas P O	70	157
ARECHE								
Frank	45	m	w	SPAI	Los Angeles	Los Angeles	73	518
ARECTOS								
Eunice	24	f	w	MEXI	San Francisco	6-Wd San Francisco	81	40
AREDA								
Jesus	60	m	w	MEXI	Santa Clara	Burnett Twp	88	34
AREGA								
Jacob	40	m	w	ITAL	San Mateo	Searsville P O	87	382
AREGON								
Antonio	38	m	w	MEXI	San Mateo	Half Moon Bay P O	87	400
Jose M	24	m	w	MEXI	Marin	San Rafael Twp	74	39
ARELARE								
Janacie	53	m	w	MEXI	Inyo	Lone Pine Twp	73	334

© 2001 by Heritage Quest. All rights reserved.

California 1870 Census

Name	Age	S	R	B-PL	County	Locale	Series M593 Roll	Pg
ARELLANES								
Antonio	51	m	w	CA	Santa Barbara	Las Cruces P O	87	505
Barbara	9	f	w	CA	Santa Barbara	Santa Barbara P O	87	463
Felipe	51	m	w	CA	Santa Barbara	Santa Barbara P O	87	479
Francisco	33	m	w	CA	Santa Barbara	Santa Barbara P O	87	468
Guillermo	22	m	w	CA	Santa Barbara	Arroyo Burro P O	87	509
Jose	30	m	w	CA	Santa Barbara	Arroyo Grande P O	87	508
Jose	26	m	w	CA	Santa Barbara	San Buenaventura P	87	427
Juan	31	m	w	CA	Santa Barbara	Las Cruces P O	87	507
Maria	40	f	w	CA	Santa Barbara	Santa Barbara P O	87	464
Refugia	13	f	w	CA	Santa Barbara	Santa Barbara P O	87	476
Valentine	51	m	w	CA	Santa Barbara	Santa Barbara P O	87	462
ARENAS								
Jesus	45	m	w	MEXI	Santa Clara	2-Wd San Jose	88	300
ARENCIMI								
John B	30	m	w	ITAL	San Francisco	2-Wd San Francisco	79	180
ARENDT								
Edward	43	m	w	PRUS	Mariposa	Mariposa P O	74	97
Gottleib	49	m	w	PRUS	San Francisco	San Francisco P O	80	461
ARENS								
Albert	24	m	w	PRUS	San Francisco	San Francisco P O	83	134
Almuth	32	f	w	BREM	Sutter	Nicolaus Twp	92	106
Charlotte	50	f	w	HOLL	San Francisco	San Francisco P O	80	463
Henry	17	m	w	CA	Santa Clara	Santa Clara Twp	88	176
ARENSEVI								
Pepe	40	m	w	CHIL	Calaveras	San Andreas P O	70	208
ARENT								
James	17	m	w	CA	Marin	San Rafael Twp	74	26
ARENTS								
Adolph	23	m	w	SAXO	Marin	San Rafael Twp	74	26
Fred	47	m	w	PRUS	Tehama	Tehama Twp	92	194
Hiram	46	m	w	OH	Butte	Chico Twp	70	17
AREPAS								
Manuel	25	m	w	CA	Los Angeles	Los Angeles Twp	73	482
ARESKOG								
Gustave	35	m	w	SWED	Santa Clara	1-Wd San Jose	88	267
ARESMENDEZ								
Chris	49	f	w	MEXI	Amador	Sutter Crk P O	69	413
AREVA								
Antonio	55	m	w	ITAL	San Mateo	Schoolhouse Statio	87	340
AREVALL								
John W	28	m	w	IREL	San Francisco	San Francisco P O	83	200
ARFF								
Frederick	48	m	w	SHOL	Alameda	Eden Twp	68	58
ARFIN								
Juan	25	m	w	CA	Santa Clara	Almaden Twp	88	3
ARFMAN								
Martin	35	m	w	HANO	Nevada	Bloomfield Twp	75	92
ARFORT								
John	51	m	w	FRAN	San Francisco	San Francisco P O	85	833
ARFSTEN								
Wm	22	m	w	SHOL	Sonoma	Analy Twp	91	225
ARFTEN								
Christ	41	m	w	SHOL	Sonoma	Petaluma Twp	91	349
ARG								
Tov	21	m	c	CHIN	Sonoma	Petaluma Twp	91	357
ARGAD								
Conception	45	m	w	MEXI	Napa	Napa	75	54
ARGARGO								
Josantos	46	m	w	PORT	San Francisco	3-Wd San Francisco	79	301
ARGEN								
Gan	24	f	c	CHIN	Tulare	Farmersville Twp	92	243
ARGENTE								
Tulio	39	m	w	ITAL	San Francisco	11-Wd San Francisc	84	628
ARGENTI								
Jos	39	m	w	ITAL	Alameda	Murray Twp	68	104
ARGENTIN								
Benoit	31	m	w	FRAN	San Francisco	San Francisco P O	83	135
ARGERAS								
Philip	30	m	w	CHIL	Amador	Drytown P O	69	415
ARGILE								
Ramon	50	m	w	CA	San Mateo	San Mateo P O	87	348
ARGILLET								
Jos R	40	m	w	FRAN	San Francisco	8-Wd San Francisco	82	364
ARGO								
John	45	m	w	ENGL	San Francisco	San Francisco P O	83	395
Manuel	35	m	w	SPAI	San Francisco	San Francisco P O	80	376
ARGON								
Thos	35	m	w	NM	San Luis Obispo	Salinas Twp	87	289
ARGOTE								
Sosora	52	m	w	SPAI	Butte	Hamilton Twp	70	64
ARGUELANTE								
Angelo	27	m	w	ITAL	Santa Clara	Alviso Twp	88	23
ARGUELES								
Francisco	70	m	w	CA	San Diego	San Diego	78	503
Francisco	30	m	w	CA	San Diego	San Diego	78	503
Gertrude	28	f	w	CA	San Diego	San Diego	78	503
Guada	52	f	w	CA	San Diego	San Diego	78	503
ARGUELLO								
Alfred	16	m	w	CA	Santa Clara	Santa Clara Twp	88	176
Carlos	13	m	w	CA	Santa Clara	Santa Clara Twp	88	176
Francisco	58	m	w	SPAI	Los Angeles	Los Angeles Twp	73	464
Isabel	14	f	w	CA	Santa Clara	2-Wd San Jose	88	337
Jose R	15	m	w	CA	Santa Clara	Santa Clara Twp	88	176
Joseph R	41	m	w	CA	Santa Clara	Santa Clara Twp	88	162
Louis	40	m	w	CA	Santa Clara	Santa Clara Twp	88	163
Ramon	16	m	w	CA	Los Angeles	Los Angeles	73	570
Soledad	73	f	w	CA	Santa Clara	Santa Clara Twp	88	162
Solita	11	f	w	CA	Santa Clara	2-Wd San Jose	88	338
ARGUGA								
Louis	36	m	w	MEXI	Los Angeles	Los Angeles	73	571
ARGUIS								
Jose	22	m	i	CA	Los Angeles	Los Angeles	73	501
ARGULAS								
Fanny	8	f	w	CA	Los Angeles	Los Angeles	73	509
ARGUS								
Henry	24	m	w	VA	Yuba	Marysville Twp	93	567
Joaquin	26	m	w	CHIL	Santa Clara	Santa Clara Twp	88	147
Ramon	24	m	w	MEXI	San Bernardino	Belleville Twp	78	408
ARGYLE								
James	24	m	i	TN	Contra Costa	Martinez P O	71	452
John F	39	m	w	VA	Yolo	Grafton Twp	93	481
ARGYRAS								
Mary	46	f	w	NY	Monterey	San Antonio Twp	74	320
ARI								
Marie	16	f	w	CA	Los Angeles	Los Angeles	73	522
ARIA								
Arozetta	39	m	w	CHIL	San Francisco	1-Wd San Francisco	79	84
Julien	56	m	w	CHIL	Calaveras	Copperopolis P O	70	251
ARIAGADO								
Bernardo	49	m	w	MEXI	Fresno	Millerton P O	72	167
ARIANES								
Ramon	40	m	w	CA	Santa Clara	Almaden Twp	88	6
ARIANNA								
Francis	21	f	w	CA	Santa Cruz	Santa Cruz	89	415
Jesus	30	m	w	CA	Santa Cruz	Santa Cruz	89	412
ARIANO								
Ramon	17	m	w	CA	Santa Cruz	Santa Cruz Twp	89	382
ARIAS								
Venacio	35	m	w	PERU	San Francisco	3-Wd San Francisco	79	290
ARIAZA								
Jesus O	42	m	w	MEXI	Marin	San Rafael Twp	74	40
ARID								
Rod	28	m	w	MI	El Dorado	Lake Valley Twp	72	64
ARIDA								
Augustine	33	m	w	SPAI	Contra Costa	Martinez P O	71	385
Juan	50	m	w	MEXI	Santa Barbara	Santa Barbara P O	87	492
ARIES								
Nicholas	35	m	w	MEXI	Tulare	Farmersville Twp	92	241
Pedro	27	m	w	CA	Fresno	Kings Rvr P O	72	214
Wm	43	m	w	NJ	Humboldt	Eel Rvr Twp	72	249
ARIGENCI								
Ramon	50	m	w	SPAI	Monterey	San Juan Twp	74	401
ARILA								
Francisco	40	m	w	CA	Santa Clara	Gilroy Twp	88	96
ARILO								
John F	25	m	w	PORT	Stanislaus	Emory Twp	92	25
ARIMO								
Jose	22	m	w	CA	Monterey	Monterey Twp	74	348
ARIN								
Ah	22	m	c	CHIN	San Francisco	1-Wd San Francisco	79	45
ARINS								
Phillip	34	m	i	MEXI	Inyo	Cerro Gordo Twp	73	320
ARIOLO								
Lazzaro	37	m	w	MEXI	Santa Barbara	Santa Barbara P O	87	480
ARIONES								
Refugio	33	m	w	MEXI	Los Angeles	Los Angeles Twp	73	467
ARIS								
Gertrude	21	f	w	PERU	San Francisco	San Francisco P O	83	263
ARISA								
Carmen	30	f	w	MEXI	Calaveras	San Andreas P O	70	207
Rosa	40	f	w	MEXI	Los Angeles	Los Angeles	73	523
ARIZAGA								
Ramon	48	m	w	MEXI	Plumas	Rich Bar Twp	77	8
ARK								
---	24	m	c	CHIN	Shasta	American Ranch P O	89	496
---	23	m	c	CHIN	San Francisco	San Francisco P O	83	63
---	15	m	c	CHIN	Shasta	Horsetown P O	89	507
Ah	14	m	c	CHIN	Shasta	American Ranch P O	89	497
Ah	14	m	c	CHIN	Napa	Napa	75	43
H H	41	m	w	GERM	San Joaquin	2-Wd Stockton	86	164
Lee	22	m	c	CHIN	San Francisco	San Francisco P O	83	259
Wan	28	m	c	CHIN	Colusa	Colusa	71	295
ARKE								
Lue	18	m	c	CHIN	San Francisco	San Francisco P O	83	232
ARKELLS								
S J	39	m	w	NY	Sonoma	Santa Rosa	91	396
ARKIN								
M	62	m	w	GA	Lake	Lakeport	73	403
Robert	39	m	w	IREL	Sonoma	Bodega Twp	91	251
Robinson	49	m	w	SC	El Dorado	Georgetown Twp	72	36
ARKINS								
A M	25	f	w	GA	Lake	Coyote Valley	73	401
ARKLEY								
William	34	m	w	CANA	Santa Clara	Redwood Twp	88	120
ARKLIN								
James	21	m	w	MO	Monterey	San Juan Twp	74	386
ARKTEL								
John	26	m	w	ENGL	Merced	Snelling P O	74	254
ARLARD								
John	35	m	w	CANA	Santa Clara	Fremont Twp	88	65
ARLE								
David	53	m	w	OH	Solano	Tremont Twp	90	30
Joseph	20	m	w	PRUS	San Francisco	San Francisco P O	85	863

© 2001 by Heritage Quest. All rights reserved.

Name	Age	S	R	B-PL	County	Locale	Series M593 Roll	Pg
ARLES								
John	18	m	w	PORT	Alameda	Alameda	68	11
ARLINGTON								
Geo	32	m	w	FRAN	Mariposa	Mariposa P O	74	98
Henry	41	m	w	NY	Kern	Havilah P O	73	336
ARLOTA								
Canbio	26	m	w	ITAL	San Francisco	San Francisco P O	80	464
ARM								
Back	24	m	c	CHIN	Sacramento	1-Wd Sacramento	77	193
ARMAGNAC								
Henry	40	m	w	FRAN	Siskiyou	Scott Valley Twp	89	614
ARMAN								
Mary	14	f	w	MEXI	San Francisco	San Francisco P O	80	385
ARMAND								
Arthur	50	m	w	MA	San Francisco	San Francisco P O	83	373
August	48	m	w	FRAN	El Dorado	White Oak Twp	72	143
Louis	50	m	w	FRAN	San Francisco	5-Wd San Francisco	81	6
S J	36	m	w	MEXI	Tuolumne	Sonora P O	93	306
ARMAS								
Francisco	38	m	w	SCOT	San Francisco	3-Wd San Francisco	79	291
Phillip	59	m	w	CA	San Mateo	Pescadero P O	87	412
ARMATAGE								
Ch	22	m	w	NY	Merced	Snelling P O	74	264
ARMBRUST								
L	35	m	w	PRUS	San Joaquin	2-Wd Stockton	86	200
ARMEDA								
Emanuel	35	m	w	SCOT	Siskiyou	Callahan P O	89	630
ARMENTA								
Josefa	25	f	w	CA	Los Angeles	Los Angeles Twp	73	484
ARMENTER								
Antonio	45	m	w	MEXI	Los Angeles	Santa Ana Twp	73	609
Domingo	38	m	w	MEXI	Los Angeles	Santa Ana Twp	73	609
Jesus	17	f	w	MEXI	Los Angeles	Santa Ana Twp	73	610
ARMENTROUT								
H	36	m	w	VA	Lake	Upper Lake	73	412
J W	37	m	w	VA	Trinity	Weaverville Pct	92	224
ARMER								
Lizzie	19	f	w	AUSL	San Francisco	8-Wd San Francisco	82	336
Wm	37	m	w	IREL	San Francisco	1-Wd San Francisco	79	93
ARMERO								
John	60	m	w	IREL	Los Angeles	Los Angeles Twp	73	479
ARMES								
G W	25	m	w	MA	Alameda	Oakland	68	198
John	50	m	w	NY	Santa Clara	1-Wd San Jose	88	262
Moses	40	m	w	MA	San Francisco	8-Wd San Francisco	82	455
Susan	83	f	w	VT	Santa Clara	2-Wd San Jose	88	282
ARMESQUITA								
Vicente	40	f	w	CA	Santa Cruz	Pajaro Twp	89	347
ARMESTA								
Antonio	50	m	w	NM	Santa Cruz	Soquel Twp	89	438
Bautista	46	m	w	FRAN	Los Angeles	Los Angeles Twp	73	484
ARMFIELD								
A J	49	m	w	VA	Amador	Fiddletown P O	69	429
Jackson	22	m	w	MO	Yolo	Cottonwood Twp	93	463
ARMIA								
Jose	42	m	w	CHIL	Los Angeles	Los Angeles Twp	73	486
ARMIGER								
Charles	28	m	w	MD	San Francisco	San Francisco P O	80	410
John	25	m	w	MD	San Francisco	7-Wd San Francisco	81	287
William	23	m	w	MD	Santa Clara	2-Wd San Jose	88	336
ARMIGO								
Moriana	22	m	w	CA	Santa Clara	Fremont Twp	88	46
ARMIJO								
Agassuito	42	m	w	MEXI	Plumas	Quartz Twp	77	35
Antonio	39	m	w	CA	Santa Clara	Fremont Twp	88	47
ARMILLA								
Astro	36	m	w	MEXI	San Luis Obispo	Salinas Twp	87	289
ARMINGTON								
B N	59	m	w	MA	San Joaquin	2-Wd Stockton	86	186
J F	59	m	w	PA	Del Norte	Smith Rvr Twp	71	478
ARMINTA								
Jesus	25	m	w	CA	Santa Cruz	Pajaro Twp	89	363
Jose	53	m	w	CA	Santa Cruz	Pajaro Twp	89	363
Jose Ant	37	m	w	CA	Santa Cruz	Pajaro Twp	89	363
ARMINTO								
Estanislao	24	m	w	CA	Marin	San Rafael Twp	74	40
ARMISTED								
William	24	m	w	NY	Solano	Silveyville Twp	90	73
ARMITAGE								
Horace	13	m	w	WI	Kern	Bakersfield P O	73	360
John	53	m	w	MA	Solano	Vallejo	90	211
Jos	39	m	w	MA	Solano	Vallejo	90	146
Joseph G	21	m	w	CANA	Sonoma	Petaluma Twp	91	321
Wm	52	m	w	ENGL	Tuolumne	Sonora P O	93	315
ARMON								
Francisco	26	m	w	MEXI	Fresno	Millerton P O	72	165
Frederick	29	m	w	GA	Nevada	Nevada Twp	75	309
ARMOND								
Laura	25	f	w	PRUS	San Joaquin	2-Wd Stockton	86	171
Tirel	55	m	w	FRAN	Calaveras	San Andreas P O	70	200
ARMOR								
Amil	40	m	w	FRAN	Shasta	Shasta P O	89	456
William	36	m	w	IREL	Santa Clara	1-Wd San Jose	88	268
ARMORAL								
Antone	26	m	w	SCOT	Siskiyou	Scott Valley Twp	89	611
ARMORY								
Mary	54	f	w	FRAN	San Francisco	San Francisco P O	80	429
ARMOS								
Robt	16	m	w	CA	San Francisco	2-Wd San Francisco	79	187
ARMPRIEST								
William	65	m	w	VA	Santa Cruz	Pajaro Twp	89	349
ARMSBAUGH								
Hiran	32	m	w	PA	Tuolumne	Sonora P O	93	325
ARMSBRATER								
D	45	m	w	PRUS	San Joaquin	2-Wd Stockton	86	212
ARMSBY								
Henry	22	m	w	CANA	Yolo	Cache Crk Twp	93	430
ARMSONE								
Moses	8	m	w	PRUS	Alameda	Oakland	68	257
ARMSPIKER								
Jim	40	m	w	KY	Butte	Kimshew Tpw	70	80
ARMSRONG								
Almira	46	f	w	NY	Yuba	Long Bar Twp	93	560
ARMSTEAD								
George	26	m	w	VT	San Francisco	6-Wd San Francisco	81	140
Oakley	43	m	w	NY	Yuba	East Bear Rvr Twp	93	542
William	55	m	w	ENGL	Tulare	Farmersville Twp	92	247
Wm	68	m	w	VT	Yuba	East Bear Rvr Twp	93	542
ARMSTED								
David	37	m	w	ME	Los Angeles	Los Angeles Twp	73	488
ARMSTER								
Jacob	39	m	w	PA	Humboldt	Bald Hills	72	238
ARMSTON								
T	47	m	w	NY	Lake	Kelsey Crk	73	402
ARMSTONG								
J W	36	m	w	OH	Sacramento	1-Wd Sacramento	77	186
ARMSTRONG								
Adam	41	m	w	MO	Placer	Bath P O	76	429
Adam	29	m	w	NY	San Francisco	5-Wd San Francisco	81	35
Albert	34	m	w	PA	Sonoma	Salt Point	91	392
Alexander S	34	m	w	PA	Yolo	Cache Crk Twp	93	431
Alexander S	34	m	w	PA	Yolo	Cache Crk Twp	93	421
Alfred	35	m	w	TN	Siskiyou	Table Rock Twp	89	645
Allen R	58	m	w	TN	Shasta	Stillwater P O	89	479
Alonzo	32	m	c	HOLL	Placer	Dutch Flat P O	76	415
Amelia	42	f	m	VA	Sacramento	2-Wd Sacramento	77	218
Amelia	24	f	w	DC	San Francisco	San Francisco P O	83	113
Amos	39	m	w	ME	San Francisco	11-Wd San Francisc	84	519
Amos	16	m	w	CA	Stanislaus	Branch Twp	92	2
Annie	16	f	w	IREL	San Francisco	San Francisco P O	83	253
Arthur E	22	m	w	ENGL	Santa Barbara	Santa Barbara P O	87	491
B	29	f	w	IREL	Sacramento	1-Wd Sacramento	77	177
B F	22	m	w	IA	Monterey	San Juan Twp	74	387
C W	26	m	w	NY	Merced	Snelling P O	74	272
Charles	37	m	w	NY	San Francisco	6-Wd San Francisco	81	41
Charles	35	m	w	NY	San Francisco	7-Wd San Francisco	81	157
Charles B	33	m	w	OH	Alpine	Woodfords P O	69	315
Charles H	26	m	w	NY	Sacramento	2-Wd Sacramento	77	207
Christopher	21	m	w	NY	San Francisco	San Francisco P O	83	349
Crayton	55	m	w	MO	Yolo	Cottonwood Twp	93	474
D B	35	m	w	IL	Lake	Morgan Valley	73	424
D G	29	m	w	IL	Sacramento	4-Wd Sacramento	77	373
David	36	m	w	PA	San Luis Obispo	Santa Rosa Twp	87	320
David	30	m	w	ENGL	Alameda	Washington Twp	68	296
Dennis	39	m	w	IREL	San Francisco	San Francisco P O	83	382
E	24	m	w	MI	Sutter	Nicolaus Twp	92	112
E T	30	m	w	NJ	Solano	Vallejo	90	148
Edd	38	m	w	IREL	San Francisco	6-Wd San Francisco	81	129
Edward R	53	m	w	NY	Los Angeles	Los Angeles	73	536
Eliza	22	f	w	IREL	Sacramento	4-Wd Sacramento	77	345
Elizabeth	23	f	w	OH	Yolo	Cache Crk Twp	93	421
Ellen	25	f	b	DC	Mendocino	Round Valley Twp	74	217
Felix R	35	m	w	AR	Mendocino	Big Rvr Twp	74	175
Francis M	25	m	w	MO	Yolo	Cottonwood Twp	93	471
Francis R	40	m	w	TN	Mendocino	Point Arena Twp	74	209
Frank	38	m	w	IREL	San Francisco	11-Wd San Francisc	84	452
Frank	23	m	w	NY	Butte	Chico Twp	70	34
Frank	23	m	w	MA	San Francisco	3-Wd San Francisco	79	297
G C	45	m	w	NV	Humboldt	Bald Hills	72	239
Geo	50	m	w	SWED	San Francisco	San Francisco P O	85	866
George	54	m	w	IREL	Amador	Volcano P O	69	372
George	42	m	w	CANA	Santa Barbara	Santa Barbara P O	87	484
George	42	m	w	NY	San Francisco	11-Wd San Francisc	84	548
George	32	m	w	MO	Stanislaus	Empire Twp	92	37
George	30	m	w	CANA	San Francisco	7-Wd San Francisco	81	157
George W	59	m	w	DE	San Luis Obispo	Santa Rosa Twp	87	320
H J	59	m	w	KY	Amador	Ione City P O	69	349
Hannibal H	40	m	w	OH	Nevada	Rough & Ready Twp	75	323
Henry	42	m	w	SCOT	Butte	Oregon Twp	70	135
Henry	35	m	w	MD	San Francisco	11-Wd San Francisc	84	462
Henry	24	m	w	ME	San Francisco	7-Wd San Francisco	81	218
Isabella	64	f	w	IREL	Santa Clara	1-Wd San Jose	88	232
Isaiah J	41	m	w	OH	Placer	Bath P O	76	450
J	38	m	w	CANA	Alameda	Oakland	68	221
J	38	m	w	IREL	Humboldt	Eureka Twp	72	269
J	35	m	w	MI	Alameda	Oakland	68	263
J G	36	m	w	NY	Monterey	Alisal Twp	74	300
J L	66	m	w	OH	Monterey	Alisal Twp	74	296
J W	36	m	w	LA	Tuolumne	Big Oak Flat P O	93	394
Jackson	32	m	w	MO	Yolo	Cottonwood Twp	93	474
James	49	m	w	IREL	San Francisco	San Francisco P O	80	540
James	46	m	w	IREL	Mariposa	Mariposa P O	74	128
James	41	m	w	MD	Sonoma	Petaluma Twp	91	310
James	40	m	w	VA	San Francisco	San Francisco P O	83	249

© 2001 by Heritage Quest. All rights reserved.

California 1870 Census

Name	Age	S	R	B-PL	County	Locale	Series M593 Roll	Pg
James	39	m	w	KY	Colusa	Stony Crk Twp	71	327
James	38	m	w	NY	Contra Costa	Martinez P O	71	435
James	38	m	w	CT	San Francisco	San Francisco P O	83	355
James	31	m	w	NY	San Francisco	5-Wd San Francisco	81	35
James	29	m	w	IREL	San Diego	San Diego	78	503
James	28	m	w	IREL	Siskiyou	Table Rock Twp	89	648
James	27	m	w	ENGL	San Francisco	San Francisco P O	83	40
James	26	m	w	CANA	Contra Costa	Martinez P O	71	447
James	26	m	w	ENGL	San Francisco	San Francisco P O	80	531
James A	32	m	w	TN	Yolo	Cache Crk Twp	93	444
James W	19	m	w	MO	Colusa	Spring Valley Twp	71	339
Jane	55	f	w	IREL	Sacramento	Dry Crk Twp	77	102
Jane	13	f	w	TX	Los Angeles	El Monte Twp	73	455
Janie	21	f	w	CANA	San Francisco	2-Wd San Francisco	79	207
Jas	40	m	w	WI	San Francisco	1-Wd San Francisco	79	79
Jas	27	m	w	SCOT	San Francisco	1-Wd San Francisco	79	112
Jas	24	m	w	OH	Sutter	Sutter Twp	92	126
Jean	54	m	w	IREL	San Francisco	11-Wd San Francisc	84	656
Jerome F	28	m	w	IL	Sacramento	4-Wd Sacramento	77	340
Jesse	50	m	w	KY	Santa Clara	Santa Clara Twp	88	169
Jno	26	m	w	VA	Sonoma	Mendocino Twp	91	301
Johanna	45	f	w	NJ	San Francisco	11-Wd San Francisc	84	486
John	51	m	w	NY	Placer	Gold Run Twp	76	400
John	50	m	w	IREL	Santa Barbara	San Buenaventura P	87	426
John	45	m	w	IREL	San Francisco	San Francisco P O	83	188
John	44	m	w	OH	Sutter	Yuba Twp	92	149
John	40	m	w	OH	San Francisco	San Francisco P O	83	212
John	38	m	w	SCOT	Nevada	Bridgeport Twp	75	112
John	36	m	w	SCOT	Humboldt	Eureka Twp	72	262
John	35	m	w	IREL	San Francisco	8-Wd San Francisco	82	491
John	35	m	w	MA	San Francisco	6-Wd San Francisco	81	100
John	26	m	w	IREL	Alpine	Markleeville P O	69	312
John	25	m	w	IREL	Santa Clara	San Jose Twp	88	219
John	19	m	w	CA	Yolo	Cache Crk Twp	93	448
John	19	m	w	CANA	Mendocino	Little Rvr Twp	74	170
John N	50	m	w	DE	El Dorado	Kelsey Twp	72	59
John S	25	m	w	IREL	San Francisco	San Francisco P O	83	187
John W	37	m	w	TN	Mendocino	Big Rvr Twp	74	175
Jos	39	m	w	NH	Sonoma	Mendocino Twp	91	303
Joseph	49	m	w	IREL	Nevada	Grass Valley Twp	75	185
Joseph	43	m	w	IL	Sacramento	Franklin Twp	77	108
K	25	f	w	IREL	Alameda	Oakland	68	148
Kate	34	f	w	MA	San Francisco	San Francisco P O	83	263
Kate	22	f	w	POLY	San Francisco	San Francisco P O	83	139
L	51	m	w	NY	Sacramento	1-Wd Sacramento	77	185
Lissie	28	f	w	IREL	San Francisco	11-Wd San Francisc	84	500
M	23	m	w	WI	Alameda	Oakland	68	192
M	20	m	b	MS	Lassen	Long Valley Twp	73	437
Margaret	15	f	w	IL	Yolo	Cache Crk Twp	93	435
Marietta	45	f	w	NY	San Francisco	8-Wd San Francisco	82	460
Martin	35	m	w	CT	Sonoma	Petaluma Twp	91	330
Mary	70	f	w	IREL	San Francisco	11-Wd San Francisc	84	601
Mary C	23	f	w	IL	San Bernardino	San Bernardino Twp	78	449
Merser	40	m	w	OH	Placer	Colfax P O	76	391
Michael	21	m	w	IREL	San Francisco	San Francisco P O	80	348
Nova	87	f	w	IREL	Sacramento	Cosumnes Twp	77	88
O	46	m	w	KY	Lake	Coyote Valley	73	400
P	40	m	w	IREL	Lake	Lakeport	73	407
P	18	m	w	BADE	Alameda	Oakland	68	202
Pat	30	m	w	IREL	Alameda	Murray Twp	68	117
R	25	m	w	SWED	Sonoma	Sonoma Twp	91	447
R B	32	m	w	ME	Napa	Napa Twp	75	73
R Barter	35	m	w	IREL	San Francisco	San Francisco P O	83	181
Rebbeca	58	f	w	IREL	Alameda	Brooklyn Twp	68	50
Rebecca	41	f	w	IREL	San Francisco	8-Wd San Francisco	82	330
Robert	32	m	w	TN	Yolo	Cache Crk Twp	93	444
Robert	31	m	w	NY	Solano	Tremont Twp	90	28
Robert	23	m	w	MO	Yolo	Cottonwood Twp	93	474
Robert	22	m	w	MO	Yolo	Cottonwood Twp	93	474
Robert	20	m	w	OH	Placer	Bath P O	76	443
Robt	32	m	w	IOFM	Alameda	Oakland	68	139
Robt	21	m	w	CANA	Napa	Napa Twp	75	65
Saml	23	m	w	TN	San Francisco	11-Wd San Francisc	84	516
Samuel	56	m	w	OH	San Diego	Julian Dist	78	471
Samuel	25	m	w	IREL	San Francisco	San Francisco P O	83	412
T Z	38	m	w	IREL	El Dorado	Georgetown Twp	72	38
Thomas	70	m	w	KY	Humboldt	Arcata Twp	72	233
Thomas	45	m	w	KY	San Francisco	San Francisco P O	83	350
Thos	67	m	w	PA	Tuolumne	Columbia P O	93	336
Thos	40	m	w	IREL	Butte	Hamilton Twp	70	63
Thos	34	m	w	NY	Alameda	Hayward	68	79
Thos	30	m	w	MO	Shasta	Millville P O	89	487
Thos	30	m	w	NY	Santa Cruz	Santa Cruz Twp	89	390
Timothy	26	m	w	PA	San Francisco	5-Wd San Francisco	81	24
W J	10	f	w	IL	Mendocino	Round Valley Twp	74	220
W T	35	m	w	NY	Monterey	Salinas Twp	74	307
William	6	m	w	CA	Los Angeles	El Monte Twp	73	462
William	48	m	w	SCOT	Yolo	Buckeye Twp	93	411
William	40	m	w	MA	San Francisco	7-Wd San Francisco	81	220
William	40	m	w	IREL	Stanislaus	Branch Twp	92	6
William	38	m	w	OH	Calaveras	San Andreas P O	70	218
William	35	m	w	MA	San Francisco	San Francisco P O	83	230
William	30	m	w	CANA	Los Angeles	Soledad Twp	73	631
William	28	m	w	NY	Solano	Suisun Twp	90	99
William B	36	m	w	VA	El Dorado	Diamond Springs Tw	72	21
Wm	45	m	w	IREL	Sacramento	Cosumnes Twp	77	88
Wm	42	m	w	PA	Alameda	Brooklyn Twp	68	42

Name	Age	S	R	B-PL	County	Locale	Series M593 Roll	Pg
Wm	40	m	w	IREL	Sonoma	Vallejo Twp	91	452
Wm	40	m	w	IREL	San Francisco	11-Wd San Francisc	84	602
Wm	35	m	w	IL	Butte	Chico Twp	70	34
Wm	35	m	w	IREL	Tuolumne	Sonora P O	93	327
Wm	35	m	w	IREL	Tuolumne	Sonora P O	93	320
Wm	31	m	w	MO	Lake	Coyote Valley	73	400
Wm	30	m	w	SCOT	San Francisco	8-Wd San Francisco	82	369
Wm	26	m	w	OH	Monterey	Alisal Twp	74	296
Wm L	50	m	w	SCOT	Butte	Wyandotte Twp	70	149
Wm P	44	m	w	ENGL	San Mateo	Pescadero P O	87	409
ARMULLER								
August	24	m	w	SWED	Marin	Sausalito Twp	74	73
ARMUSSEN								
Hans	44	m	w	SHOL	San Francisco	1-Wd San Francisco	79	128
ARN								
Boke	38	m	c	CHIN	Amador	Jackson P O	69	343
Goon	22	m	c	CHIN	San Francisco	6-Wd San Francisco	81	44
John	45	m	w	SWIT	Trinity	Lewiston Pct	92	214
Yow	40	m	c	CHIN	Los Angeles	Wilmington Twp	73	640
ARNAIL								
John P	59	m	w	FRAN	Amador	Volcano P O	69	386
ARNALI								
Louis	28	m	w	CHIL	Tuolumne	Sonora P O	93	313
ARNAND								
Jacques	29	m	w	FRAN	San Francisco	11-Wd San Francisc	84	643
Pierre	35	m	w	FRAN	San Francisco	11-Wd San Francisc	84	570
ARNATHO								
Lorenzo	21	m	w	MEXI	Mariposa	Mariposa P O	74	131
ARNBERG								
E	45	m	w	AR	Alameda	Murray Twp	68	128
ARNDS								
Frank	20	m	w	MEXI	Napa	Napa Twp	75	34
ARNE								
Catharine	50	f	w	SWIT	San Francisco	San Francisco P O	83	66
Edward	38	m	w	NY	Santa Clara	San Jose Twp	88	179
ARNEDO								
John	30	m	w	ITAL	San Mateo	Schoolhouse Statio	87	345
John	28	m	w	ITAL	San Mateo	Schoolhouse Statio	87	344
ARNEGGER								
John	22	m	w	MA	San Francisco	San Francisco P O	83	132
ARNEL								
Thomas	31	m	w	IREL	Santa Clara	1-Wd San Jose	88	231
ARNELAIS								
Rosa	25	f	w	ECUA	Sacramento	2-Wd Sacramento	77	249
ARNELL								
William I	35	m	w	PA	Santa Clara	San Jose Twp	88	210
ARNEMAN								
John	55	m	w	BAVA	Butte	Wyandotte Twp	70	142
ARNER								
Lewis	55	m	w	PA	Nevada	Grass Valley Twp	75	200
ARNES								
August	55	m	w	PRUS	Santa Clara	2-Wd San Jose	88	309
Charles B	40	m	w	MA	Calaveras	Copperopolis P O	70	221
Hermann	45	m	w	BREM	San Francisco	San Francisco P O	83	185
John	45	m	w	ENGL	San Mateo	Redwood Twp	87	367
John	24	m	w	ME	San Joaquin	1-Wd Stockton	86	130
Martha	47	f	w	NY	San Mateo	Redwood Twp	87	366
Nathanl O	45	m	w	ME	El Dorado	Placerville Twp	72	93
ARNEST								
J M	56	m	w	MD	San Joaquin	Dent Twp	86	17
John	27	m	w	IL	San Francisco	San Francisco P O	83	199
John Jr	25	m	w	MO	San Francisco	7-Wd San Francisco	81	163
Wm Henry	39	m	w	TN	San Francisco	8-Wd San Francisco	82	321
ARNETT								
Elizabeth	55	f	w	TN	Alameda	Murray Twp	68	107
John	44	m	w	OH	Colusa	Spring Valley Twp	71	341
Robert S	52	m	w	TN	Los Angeles	San Jose Twp	73	622
ARNETTE								
Aleck	30	m	w	FRAN	Solano	Benicia	90	20
David	38	m	w	IA	Shasta	Shasta P O	89	455
Wm C	30	m	w	MO	Shasta	Fort Crook P O	89	476
ARNHEIM								
S S	53	m	w	PRUS	San Francisco	7-Wd San Francisco	81	222
Solomon	41	m	w	PRUS	San Francisco	1-Wd San Francisco	79	79
ARNHOLDT								
Augusta	28	f	w	SAXO	San Francisco	6-Wd San Francisco	81	72
ARNHOOD								
Michael	53	m	w	SWIT	Siskiyou	Yreka Twp	89	672
ARNI								
Nicholas	45	m	w	SWIT	Mariposa	Maxwell Crk P O	74	144
ARNICK								
Henry	37	m	w	BREM	San Francisco	11-Wd San Francisc	84	646
ARNIGH								
Thomas	30	m	w	NY	Solano	Rio Vista Twp	90	59
ARNIJUS								
Jose	20	m	w	MEXI	San Diego	Milquaty Dist	78	475
ARNILL								
D D	42	m	w	ME	Humboldt	Arcata Twp	72	232
ARNIO								
Rebie	25	m	w	MEXI	Tulare	Tule Rvr Twp	92	258
ARNO								
Susan	21	f	w	ME	San Francisco	3-Wd San Francisco	79	320
ARNOLD								
A T	37	m	w	OH	Lassen	Susanville Twp	73	441
Aaron	22	m	w	PRUS	Los Angeles	Los Angeles	73	525
Abner	64	m	w	OH	Nevada	Nevada Twp	75	292
Albert	23	m	w	NY	San Francisco	11-Wd San Francisc	84	509

© 2001 by Heritage Quest. All rights reserved.

California 1870 Census

Series M593

Name	Age	S	R	B-PL	County	Locale	Roll	Pg
Alexander	14	m	w	CA	Santa Cruz	Pajaro Twp	89	347
Amelia	50	f	w	SHOL	San Francisco	1-Wd San Francisco	79	81
Amelia	50	f	w	ENGL	San Francisco	1-Wd San Francisco	79	61
Ames	64	m	w	ME	San Francisco	11-Wd San Francisc	84	637
Amos	40	m	w	PA	San Francisco	5-Wd San Francisco	81	33
Andrew I	33	m	w	RI	Placer	Colfax P O	76	385
Augustus	38	m	w	OH	Colusa	Colusa	71	291
Baylis W	47	m	w	MA	Napa	Yountville Twp	75	91
Benj F	42	m	w	KY	Fresno	Millerton P O	72	149
Benjam	40	m	w	ME	San Francisco	11-Wd San Francisc	84	452
Caleb	64	m	w	VT	Sacramento	San Joaquin Twp	77	401
Charles	33	m	w	WURT	Colusa	Colusa Twp	71	275
Charles H	31	m	w	WI	Santa Clara	1-Wd San Jose	88	252
Chas B	23	m	w	RI	Napa	Napa	75	17
Cutler	51	m	w	OH	Santa Barbara	San Buenaventura P	87	419
Cyrus	28	m	w	IL	San Diego	San Diego	78	498
D E	45	m	w	NY	Solano	Vallejo	90	209
Danl	44	m	w	ME	Butte	Chico Twp	70	47
Danl	35	m	w	MO	Butte	Chico Twp	70	46
David	23	m	w	NY	Santa Clara	Milpitas Twp	88	115
E	33	m	w	IREL	Sierra	Lincoln Twp	89	549
Edward N	38	m	w	IN	Los Angeles	Santa Ana Twp	73	610
Edwd	38	m	w	FRAN	San Francisco	1-Wd San Francisco	79	46
Edwd	38	m	w	IREL	San Francisco	1-Wd San Francisco	79	128
Elbridge	41	m	w	MA	San Francisco	2-Wd San Francisco	79	279
Emily	45	f	w	CT	San Francisco	11-Wd San Francisc	84	471
F W	40	m	w	IREL	San Francisco	San Francisco P O	85	832
Francis	26	m	w	NY	San Francisco	San Francisco P O	83	214
Frank P	31	m	w	MA	San Francisco	6-Wd San Francisco	81	84
Fred	37	m	w	MA	San Joaquin	2-Wd Stockton	86	181
G N	43	m	w	PA	San Joaquin	Liberty Twp	86	94
G W	52	m	w	RI	Sierra	Sierra Twp	89	567
Geo	12	m	w	IA	Sonoma	Russian Rvr	91	376
Geo W	45	m	w	VA	Sonoma	Santa Rosa	91	409
George	33	m	w	AL	Colusa	Grand Island Twp	71	306
George	26	m	w	ME	San Francisco	11-Wd San Francisc	84	637
George	25	m	w	MA	Marin	Novato Twp	74	11
George H	39	m	w	RI	San Francisco	8-Wd San Francisco	82	445
George W	41	m	w	CT	Stanislaus	Emory Twp	92	24
H B	44	m	w	NC	Klamath	Liberty Twp	73	376
Hardman D	32	m	w	KY	Colusa	Grand Island Twp	71	307
Hattie	10	f	w	CA	Yuba	Marysville	93	617
Henry C	41	m	w	RI	Yuba	New York Twp	93	638
Hiram	23	m	w	NY	Butte	Chico Twp	70	46
Jacob	40	m	w	WURT	Sacramento	2-Wd Sacramento	77	224
James	47	m	w	IREL	Tuolumne	Chinese Camp P O	93	375
James	47	m	w	IN	Yolo	Washington Twp	93	529
James	30	m	w	KY	Stanislaus	Empire Twp	92	36
James	29	m	w	MN	Tulare	Venice Twp	92	278
James	24	m	w	VA	Solano	Vacaville Twp	90	117
James C	34	m	w	IL	Fresno	Millerton P O	72	149
James M	44	m	w	KY	Santa Clara	Santa Clara Twp	88	167
Jno	32	m	w	IA	Butte	Oregon Twp	70	129
Johanna	32	f	w	IREL	San Francisco	2-Wd San Francisco	79	152
John	70	m	w	ME	San Francisco	11-Wd San Francisc	84	447
John	68	m	w	KY	Solano	Silveyville Twp	90	76
John	36	m	w	GA	Kern	Linns Valley P O	73	345
John F	42	m	w	MA	San Francisco	6-Wd San Francisco	81	145
John M	63	m	w	NY	Sacramento	Granite Twp	77	147
John T	22	m	w	KY	Colusa	Colusa	71	293
Joseph	30	m	w	PRUS	Nevada	Meadow Lake Twp	75	249
Joseph	28	m	w	FRAN	San Francisco	1-Wd San Francisco	79	28
Joseph H	30	m	w	GERM	Yolo	Cache Crk Twp	93	432
Julia M	37	f	w	NY	San Joaquin	2-Wd Stockton	86	169
L	29	m	w	ENGL	Nevada	Eureka Twp	75	131
L Benton	53	m	w	RI	Placer	Dutch Flat P O	76	407
Leonard	52	m	w	NY	San Diego	San Diego	78	505
Louis	38	m	w	PRUS	San Francisco	San Francisco P O	80	353
Louis	27	m	w	BADE	San Francisco	1-Wd San Francisco	79	69
Louis L	52	m	w	HUNG	San Francisco	6-Wd San Francisco	81	151
Lucy	30	f	w	AL	Sacramento	Sutter Twp	77	392
Margret	24	f	w	IA	Trinity	Douglas	92	235
Martin	28	m	w	CANA	Sacramento	3-Wd Sacramento	77	286
Mary	12	f	w	IA	San Francisco	1-Wd San Francisco	79	59
Mary A	23	f	m	MEXI	Sacramento	2-Wd Sacramento	77	233
Matthew	26	m	w	IL	Santa Barbara	San Buenaventura P	87	419
Michl	40	m	w	ME	San Francisco	5-Wd San Francisco	81	22
N	30	m	w	IA	Santa Clara	Burnett Twp	88	31
N D	25	m	w	MA	San Francisco	San Francisco P O	83	187
Oscar	21	m	w	BAVA	Marin	San Rafael	74	57
Philander	61	m	w	VT	Solano	Denverton Twp	90	24
Philip	40	m	w	KY	San Francisco	8-Wd San Francisco	82	493
Richd	40	m	w	IREL	Solano	Vallejo	90	184
Richd	40	m	w	IA	San Francisco	1-Wd San Francisco	79	59
Richd	30	m	w	ME	Marin	San Rafael	74	49
Robert	42	m	w	IREL	Inyo	Bishop Crk Twp	73	314
Robert A	43	m	w	CANA	Santa Cruz	Soquel Twp	89	447
Robt	45	m	w	ENGL	San Francisco	2-Wd San Francisco	79	244
Rufus	16	m	w	CA	Sacramento	2-Wd Sacramento	77	249
S S	27	m	w	KY	Lake	Big Valley	73	395
Sanford	40	m	w	MA	San Francisco	11-Wd San Francisc	84	626
T J	37	m	w	SC	Alameda	Oakland	68	178
Thomas	45	m	w	ENGL	Mendocino	Point Arena Twp	74	209
Thos C	27	m	w	NY	San Francisco	San Francisco P O	83	282
Volney	23	m	w	IL	Solano	Denverton Twp	90	23
W	28	m	w	IL	San Joaquin	Douglas Twp	86	30
W A	38	m	w	RI	Tuolumne	Columbia P O	93	345
W B	62	m	w	VA	San Joaquin	Elkhorn Twp	86	65
Whipple	60	m	w	RI	Alameda	Alvarado	68	304
William	67	m	w	GA	Kern	Linns Valley P O	73	345
William	40	m	w	WALE	El Dorado	Placerville	72	117
William A	33	m	w	ME	San Francisco	11-Wd San Francisc	84	706
William H	43	m	w	AL	Los Angeles	San Jose Twp	73	621
William S	35	m	w	OH	Los Angeles	Los Angeles Twp	73	469
William S	32	m	w	CANA	Los Angeles	Los Angeles	73	505
Wm	40	m	w	IREL	San Francisco	2-Wd San Francisco	79	257
Wm J	47	m	w	OH	Sonoma	Russian Rvr	91	377
ARNOLDS								
Mathew	22	m	w	DE	San Francisco	7-Wd San Francisco	81	188
ARNOP								
Frank	26	m	w	FRAN	San Francisco	San Francisco P O	80	467
ARNOS								
Elbena	18	f	w	ME	Santa Barbara	San Buenaventura P	87	432
Hariel	25	m	w	MEXI	Fresno	Millerton P O	72	157
Luis	17	m	w	CA	Santa Barbara	San Buenaventura P	87	433
ARNOT								
James	52	m	w	TN	Siskiyou	Big Valley Twp	89	582
Nathaniel	53	m	w	NY	San Francisco	7-Wd San Francisco	81	280
ARNS								
Henry	48	m	w	SHOL	Trinity	North Fork Twp	92	217
ARNSON								
Geo	23	m	w	MO	Yuba	Marysville	93	594
ARNST								
Henry	54	m	w	RUSS	Santa Cruz	Santa Cruz Twp	89	388
P	42	m	w	IREL	Sacramento	4-Wd Sacramento	77	369
ARNSTEIN								
Ernest	34	m	w	PRUS	San Francisco	1-Wd San Francisco	79	116
Eugene	29	m	w	BAVA	San Francisco	2-Wd San Francisco	79	193
ARNT								
George	25	m	w	ME	Stanislaus	Buena Vista Twp	92	13
ARNWAY								
Lorin	41	m	w	OH	Alameda	Eden Twp	68	66
ARO								
Ah	26	m	c	CHIN	Sacramento	1-Wd Sacramento	77	197
AROAYO								
Kuis	33	m	w	MEXI	San Luis Obispo	San Luis Obispo Tw	87	305
AROGAN								
Jesus	24	m	w	MEXI	Monterey	San Antonio Twp	74	323
AROLA								
Manuel	34	m	w	ITAL	Calaveras	Copperopolis P O	70	231
AROLLIA								
Cruz	40	m	w	MEXI	San Luis Obispo	Salinas Twp	87	288
ARON								
A	49	m	w	OH	San Francisco	San Francisco P O	83	265
Abraham	32	m	w	PRUS	San Francisco	San Francisco P O	83	238
Simon	45	m	w	PRUS	San Francisco	San Francisco P O	83	234
ARONALALO								
Barnard	48	m	i	MEXI	Inyo	Lone Pine Twp	73	333
ARONS								
Antonio	62	m	w	CA	San Bernardino	Chino Twp	78	409
ARONSOHN								
Martin	8	m	w	CA	Alameda	Oakland	68	257
Simon	42	m	w	PRUS	San Francisco	8-Wd San Francisco	82	339
ARONSON								
C	10	f	w	CA	Alameda	Oakland	68	257
D	50	m	w	PRUS	San Francisco	San Francisco P O	83	297
Henry	38	m	w	PRUS	Yolo	Cache Crk Twp	93	419
Leon	40	m	w	RUSS	Sacramento	3-Wd Sacramento	77	283
Pauline	21	f	w	PRUS	San Francisco	San Francisco P O	83	344
AROOSE								
R	50	m	w	MEXI	Sierra	Butte Twp	89	508
AROP								
Ramon	35	m	w	MEXI	Kern	Bakersfield P O	73	358
AROQUIA								
Juan	29	m	w	FRAN	Los Angeles	Los Angeles Twp	73	497
AROS								
Magill	34	m	w	CHIL	Amador	Drytown P O	69	425
AROSS								
Selicia	26	f	w	DENM	San Francisco	San Francisco P O	83	160
AROVANA								
Marcus	27	m	w	CHIL	El Dorado	Placerville	72	112
AROYO								
Carlos	58	m	w	CHIL	Santa Barbara	Las Cruces P O	87	516
ARP								
Ar	22	m	c	CHIN	Sonoma	Petaluma Twp	91	342
Henry	28	m	w	SHOL	Yuba	Marysville	93	605
Jochim	21	m	w	PRUS	Sacramento	Alabama Twp	77	59
ARPANAQUA								
Pasqual	29	m	w	ITAL	Calaveras	San Andreas P O	70	183
ARPER								
Thomas	45	m	w	CANA	El Dorado	Placerville Twp	72	100
Walter	17	m	w	ME	Santa Clara	2-Wd San Jose	88	305
ARPINA								
Lacrea	60	m	w	MEXI	Santa Clara	Almaden Twp	88	7
ARPS								
John	40	m	w	PRUS	Alameda	Oakland	68	204
ARR								
Wm	28	m	w	IA	Santa Clara	Gilroy Twp	88	100
ARRADIN								
Jesus	45	m	w	MEXI	Calaveras	San Andreas P O	70	182
ARRAM								
Marcus	40	m	w	CA	Santa Cruz	Santa Cruz	89	424
ARRAMBID								
John	40	m	w	FRAN	San Francisco	8-Wd San Francisco	82	400

© 2001 by Heritage Quest. All rights reserved.

California 1870 Census

Series M593

Name	Age	S	R	B-PL	County	Locale	Roll	Pg
ARRANDT								
James	45	m	w	IREL	Los Angeles	Wilmington Twp	73	643
ARRAS								
Jose	45	m	w	CHIL	San Bernardino	Chino Twp	78	410
Joseph	23	m	w	MEXI	San Francisco	3-Wd San Francisco	79	291
ARRASCO								
Ramon	43	m	w	MEXI	Fresno	Millerton P O	72	151
ARRASIA								
Casuons	28	m	w	CA	Stanislaus	San Joaquin Twp	92	82
ARRAT								
John	39	m	w	MO	Alameda	Murray Twp	68	108
ARRATA								
Jean	49	m	w	ITAL	Calaveras	San Andreas P O	70	186
ARRATI								
David	27	m	w	ITAL	San Francisco	1-Wd San Francisco	79	36
ARRATT								
Batisti	23	m	w	ITAL	San Francisco	11-Wd San Francisc	84	614
ARRATTA								
Antonio	35	m	w	ITAL	Amador	Jackson P O	69	319
ARRATTO								
Angelo	26	m	w	ITAL	Tuolumne	Sonora P O	93	330
Angus	30	m	w	ITAL	Tuolumne	Sonora P O	93	330
Paul	50	m	w	ITAL	Tuolumne	Sonora P O	93	330
ARRAZ								
Santos	60	m	w	CA	Santa Cruz	Soquel Twp	89	449
ARRCA								
Hosepi	49	m	i	MEXI	Inyo	Cerro Gordo Twp	73	320
ARREA								
C	50	m	w	CHIL	Calaveras	Copperopolis P O	70	222
Jose	60	m	w	CHIL	Calaveras	San Andreas P O	70	196
ARREAS								
Joseph	22	m	i	CA	Santa Barbara	San Buenaventura P	87	439
ARREASE								
Marcus	54	m	w	MEXI	Monterey	Monterey	74	364
ARREDO								
Dolores	31	f	w	MEXI	San Francisco	San Francisco P O	80	340
ARREDONDO								
Salvador	35	m	w	MEXI	Santa Cruz	Pajaro Twp	89	362
ARREGA								
Bartolo	50	m	w	CHIL	Calaveras	San Andreas P O	70	214
ARRELANO								
Ramon	30	m	w	CHIL	Contra Costa	Martinez P O	71	369
ARREMONDO								
Prader	47	m	w	MEXI	Calaveras	San Andreas P O	70	203
ARRENDALE								
Bernat	45	m	w	MA	San Francisco	5-Wd San Francisco	81	12
ARRENDALL								
Benj W	54	m	w	TN	Santa Cruz	Santa Cruz	89	421
ARRENT								
Peter	36	m	w	FRAN	San Francisco	San Francisco P O	83	227
ARRENTS								
Hiram Y	24	m	w	NY	Sacramento	Lee Twp	77	160
ARRERO								
Amado	22	m	w	CA	Monterey	Monterey	74	357
Esteven	21	m	w	CA	Monterey	Castroville Twp	74	329
ARREROS								
Richard	38	m	w	CHIL	Contra Costa	Martinez P O	71	367
ARRERRAS								
Antonio	50	m	w	MEXI	Fresno	Millerton P O	72	155
ARRETA								
Juan	30	m	w	CHIL	Contra Costa	Martinez P O	71	439
ARRIEGADA								
Francisco	42	m	w	CHIL	Contra Costa	Martinez P O	71	374
ARRIETO								
Juan	50	m	w	MEXI	Calaveras	Copperopolis P O	70	260
ARRIGO								
Gehernia	35	m	w	MEXI	Kern	Bakersfield P O	73	364
ARRILL								
Wm	37	m	w	ME	San Francisco	7-Wd San Francisco	81	270
ARRINGTON								
Hanna	19	f	w	IREL	San Francisco	7-Wd San Francisco	81	277
Johana	74	f	w	NC	San Francisco	San Francisco P O	80	404
John	45	m	w	IREL	Placer	Colfax P O	76	390
Nicholas O	45	m	w	NC	San Francisco	8-Wd San Francisco	82	333
Thomas	32	m	w	IREL	Humboldt	Eureka Twp	72	258
ARRIOLA								
Antonio	43	m	w	MEXI	Los Angeles	Soledad Twp	73	631
Espirito	17	m	w	MEXI	San Francisco	6-Wd San Francisco	81	123
Ferdinand	42	m	w	MEXI	San Francisco	2-Wd San Francisco	79	155
ARRIS								
Geo	25	m	w	CANA	Solano	Vallejo	90	144
William	32	m	w	ENGL	San Francisco	3-Wd San Francisco	79	298
ARRISE								
Pierre	62	m	w	FRAN	San Francisco	11-Wd San Francisc	84	521
ARRIVALO								
Domingo	56	m	w	CHIL	Contra Costa	Martinez P O	71	447
ARRNOLD								
Cherlofa	30	m	w	CANA	Contra Costa	Martinez P O	71	432
ARRON								
Hans	83	m	w	PRUS	Sonoma	Petaluma Twp	91	365
ARRONGE								
Eugene	16	m	w	FRAN	San Francisco	San Francisco P O	85	831
ARRONT								
Wm	27	m	w	IREL	San Joaquin	1-Wd Stockton	86	121
ARROQUAS								
Joa	28	m	w	CHIL	Fresno	Millerton P O	72	153
ARROS								
Jose	16	m	w	MEXI	Los Angeles	Los Angeles Twp	73	485
Lola	36	f	w	MEXI	Amador	Jackson P O	69	322
ARROSE								
Andre A	64	m	w	ITAL	Santa Cruz	Santa Cruz	89	433
ARROSMITH								
Sylvester	27	m	w	IA	Siskiyou	Yreka Twp	89	666
ARROTTO								
S	19	m	w	ITAL	Amador	Jackson P O	69	327
ARROW								
Ah	19	m	c	CHIN	Monterey	Castroville Twp	74	342
ARROWSMITH								
David	42	m	w	NY	San Francisco	8-Wd San Francisco	82	363
John	40	m	w	ENGL	San Francisco	7-Wd San Francisco	81	270
M	29	f	w	OH	Lassen	Long Valley Twp	73	436
ARROYO								
Cyrilo	30	m	w	CA	Monterey	San Juan Twp	74	402
ARROZAC								
Corse	40	m	w	CHIL	El Dorado	Mountain Twp	72	67
ARSEA								
Maria	11	f	w	CA	San Bernardino	Chino Twp	78	412
ARSENA								
Jean	55	m	w	FRAN	Calaveras	San Andreas P O	70	205
ARSEO								
Felipe	65	m	w	CA	Monterey	San Juan Twp	74	401
ARSHEAR								
---	28	m	c	CHIN	San Francisco	11-Wd San Francisc	84	702
ARSTEE								
Henry	38	m	w	OLDE	Mendocino	Gualala Twp	74	226
ART								
Ah	22	m	c	CHIN	Shasta	American Ranch P O	89	497
Ah	20	m	c	CHIN	San Francisco	8-Wd San Francisco	82	316
Ah	17	m	c	CHIN	San Francisco	8-Wd San Francisco	82	310
Peter	54	m	w	HESS	El Dorado	Diamond Springs Tw	72	33
ARTAGAN								
Anne	19	f	w	PRUS	San Francisco	11-Wd San Francisc	84	689
ARTAMERO								
Antonio	40	m	w	CA	Monterey	Alisal Twp	74	295
ARTEGO								
Antonio	28	m	w	MEXI	Kern	Tehachapi P O	73	354
Francois	28	m	w	CA	Kern	Bakersfield P O	73	357
ARTELLON								
Francisco	6	m	w	CA	Monterey	Monterey	74	364
Pedro	55	m	w	FRAN	Monterey	Monterey	74	364
ARTENAFEN								
Rosalio	23	m	w	MEXI	San Diego	San Pasqual	78	520
ARTENAY								
Thos	45	m	w	GERM	Yuba	Marysville	93	616
ARTENTIO								
Antonio	28	m	w	MEXI	San Bernardino	San Salvador Twp	78	455
ARTETO								
Vicenta	65	f	w	MEXI	Los Angeles	Santa Ana Twp	73	616
ARTEZ								
Gabriel	30	m	w	MEXI	Los Angeles	Los Angeles	73	509
ARTH								
Bernard	25	m	w	IREL	San Francisco	5-Wd San Francisco	81	32
ARTHUR								
Andrew A	28	m	w	PA	Santa Clara	Redwood Twp	88	131
Benj	37	m	w	OH	Mendocino	Round Valley Twp	74	221
Charles	40	m	w	OH	Sonoma	Analy Twp	91	220
Edward	20	m	w	IREL	Santa Cruz	Pajaro Twp	89	345
Francis	34	m	w	ENGL	Nevada	Grass Valley Twp	75	165
James	39	m	w	CANA	Mendocino	Gualala Twp	74	226
James	30	m	w	IREL	San Francisco	1-Wd San Francisco	79	100
John	47	m	w	ENGL	Amador	Sutter Crk P O	69	400
John	45	m	w	ENGL	Tuolumne	Chinese Camp P O	93	370
John	40	m	w	ENGL	Calaveras	Copperopolis P O	70	239
John D	65	m	w	NY	San Francisco	8-Wd San Francisco	82	327
Maria	26	f	w	IREL	San Francisco	San Francisco P O	83	190
Marian	26	f	w	IREL	San Francisco	San Francisco P O	83	201
Mary	36	f	w	IREL	San Francisco	1-Wd San Francisco	79	21
R	40	m	w	ENGL	San Joaquin	2-Wd Stockton	86	200
Richard	47	m	w	ENGL	Nevada	Grass Valley Twp	75	201
Robert	40	m	w	OH	Mariposa	Mariposa P O	74	96
T Geo	50	m	w	NC	Santa Clara	Gilroy Twp	88	102
T W	46	m	w	IN	Amador	Drytown P O	69	420
Thomas	31	m	w	ENGL	Nevada	Grass Valley Twp	75	147
Thos	55	m	w	KY	Shasta	Fort Crook P O	89	477
Thos	53	m	w	SCOT	San Francisco	1-Wd San Francisco	79	97
W	40	m	w	IREL	Sierra	Eureka Twp	89	526
W	14	m	w	CA	Sacramento	1-Wd Sacramento	77	181
William	45	m	w	ENGL	Placer	Bath P O	76	427
William	27	m	w	ENGL	Nevada	Grass Valley Twp	75	148
Wm	29	m	w	KY	Mariposa	Mariposa P O	74	93
Wm J	23	m	w	PA	Sacramento	3-Wd Sacramento	77	271
ARTI								
Ah	25	m	c	CHIN	Napa	Napa	75	50
ARTIGALAS								
Edward	37	m	w	AUST	Calaveras	San Andreas P O	70	181
ARTMAN								
John E	46	m	w	KY	Amador	Jackson P O	69	343
ARTON								
P	38	m	w	GERM	Lake	Morgan Valley	73	425
ARTS								
Mathew P	38	m	w	PRUS	Amador	Sutter Crk P O	69	412
ARTULETTA								
Thomas	36	m	w	NM	San Bernardino	San Salvador Twp	78	461

© 2001 by Heritage Quest. All rights reserved.

Name	Age	S	R	B-PL	County	Locale	Series M593 Roll	Pg
ARTY								
Andrew	33	m	w	IREL	Solano	Vallejo	90	215
ARUMEL								
Paul	20	m	w	CANA	Nevada	Grass Valley Twp	75	223
ARUNDELL								
Thos	49	m	w	ENGL	Santa Barbara	San Buenaventura P	87	448
Wm H	28	m	w	NY	Santa Barbara	San Buenaventura P	87	448
ARUP								
Antonio	50	m	w	MEXI	Kern	Bakersfield P O	73	358
Ramon	47	m	w	MEXI	Kern	Bakersfield P O	73	362
ARUS								
John	44	m	w	FRAN	San Francisco	11-Wd San Francisc	84	449
ARUSO								
Timatao	28	m	w	MEXI	Kern	Bakersfield P O	73	361
ARVALLO								
Terafin	41	m	w	MEXI	Fresno	Millerton P O	72	167
ARVEA								
Santiago	20	m	w	MEXI	Los Angeles	Los Angeles Twp	73	475
ARVENA								
Jesus	27	m	w	MEXI	San Luis Obispo	Arroyo Grande Twp	87	271
ARVESTRA								
Joseph	42	m	w	SPAI	Yuba	Marysville	93	616
ARVIDSSON								
Charles D	11	m	w	CA	El Dorado	Placerville	72	110
Charles J	52	m	w	SWED	El Dorado	Placerville	72	110
ARVILLA								
Alfred	23	m	w	CA	Kern	Linns Valley P O	73	343
Jose	26	m	w	CA	Kern	Linns Valley P O	73	343
ARVIN								
N D	33	m	w	OH	San Joaquin	Elkhorn Twp	86	59
ARVISA								
Eugenio	50	m	w	SPAI	Santa Cruz	Pajaro Twp	89	346
ARYALIA								
Sarciona	29	f	w	CA	Los Angeles	Los Angeles	73	511
ARZAGA								
Francisco	41	m	w	CA	Los Angeles	Wilmington Twp	73	636
AS								
Sam	31	m	c	CHIN	Alameda	Alvarado	68	305
ASA								
Pratt	50	m	w	ME	Klamath	Hoopa Valley India	73	386
ASALINA								
Catherine	20	f	w	ITAL	San Mateo	Schoolhouse Statio	87	333
ASAMA								
P N	50	m	w	MEXI	Tuolumne	Chinese Camp P O	93	367
ASANE								
Christina	80	f	w	CA	Monterey	San Antonio Twp	74	317
ASANO								
Morono	25	m	w	CA	Santa Cruz	Santa Cruz	89	415
ASAVEDO								
Aldo	35	m	w	MEXI	San Bernardino	Chino Twp	78	409
Cludio	64	m	w	CA	San Bernardino	Chino Twp	78	409
ASAY								
Jacob	34	m	w	PA	Yuba	Rose Bar Twp	93	658
ASBECK								
Frederick	37	m	w	PRUS	San Luis Obispo	Salinas Twp	87	288
ASBELL								
Jos M	40	m	w	KY	Shasta	Millville P O	89	494
Pearce	34	m	w	MO	Mendocino	Round Valley Twp	74	218
Wm	65	m	w	KY	Lake	Lower Lake	73	422
Wm Jr	21	m	w	MO	Lake	Lower Lake	73	422
ASBERRY								
Henry B	44	m	w	KY	Calaveras	San Andreas P O	70	192
James	37	m	w	VA	Yolo	Cache Crk Twp	93	436
John	38	m	w	KY	Calaveras	San Andreas P O	70	201
ASBRANT								
August	49	m	w	BADE	Los Angeles	Los Angeles	73	524
ASBURY								
Amy	87	f	w	NJ	Sonoma	Vallejo Twp	91	451
George W	14	m	w	CA	Sonoma	Vallejo Twp	91	451
Henry E	47	m	w	KY	Placer	Auburn P O	76	382
Jacob J	56	m	w	WV	Calaveras	San Andreas P O	70	217
Presley B	36	m	w	KY	Shasta	Millville P O	89	487
Thomas	16	m	w	CA	Sonoma	Vallejo Twp	91	450
Thos	35	m	w	MO	Tehama	Antelope Twp	92	156
Thos	30	m	w	KY	Tehama	Red Bluff	92	183
Volney W	25	m	w	MO	Santa Barbara	Santa Maria P O	87	510
Wm W	36	m	w	KY	Shasta	Millville P O	89	483
ASCCENAUR								
Frank	45	m	w	BAVA	Sacramento	Sutter Twp	77	385
ASCEDO								
Tomas	45	m	w	MEXI	Santa Barbara	San Buenaventura P	87	427
ASCHER								
Moons	19	m	w	PRUS	Butte	Ophir Twp	70	91
ASCHHEIM								
Mayer Samuel	42	m	w	PRUS	Plumas	Indian Twp	77	13
Saml J	28	m	w	PRUS	Plumas	Indian Twp	77	9
ASCHIM								
Chas	29	m	w	PRUS	San Francisco	1-Wd San Francisco	79	54
ASEBES								
Alejo	60	m	w	MEXI	San Luis Obispo	Morro Twp	87	283
ASEL								
Charles	36	m	w	PRUS	San Francisco	6-Wd San Francisco	81	101
ASEVEDO								
Paulina	48	f	w	MEXI	Los Angeles	Los Angeles	73	538
ASEVES								
Jesusa	37	f	w	MEXI	Santa Clara	Burnett Twp	88	35
ASEVILS								
Maria	29	f	w	MEXI	Santa Clara	Almaden Twp	88	1
ASFALT								
J	40	m	w	WURT	Sierra	Butte Twp	89	510
ASH								
Alexander	44	m	w	MI	Yolo	Fremont Twp	93	476
Amelia P	33	f	w	SC	Stanislaus	Empire Twp	92	31
Anna	78	f	w	NC	Merced	Snelling P O	74	266
Anna	30	f	w	SWED	San Francisco	8-Wd San Francisco	82	371
Annie	20	f	w	SHOL	Sonoma	Analy Twp	91	218
Bertha B	6	f	w	NV	Mono	Bridgeport P O	74	286
Chas	68	m	w	CANA	Mono	Bridgeport P O	74	286
Chas J	33	m	w	BADE	Sacramento	4-Wd Sacramento	77	364
Craft D	14	m	w	CA	Alameda	Oakland	68	173
David	51	m	w	IREL	San Francisco	San Francisco P O	83	323
Elizabeth F	37	f	w	IREL	Sacramento	4-Wd Sacramento	77	364
Ferdinand	21	m	w	PA	Sacramento	2-Wd Sacramento	77	244
Geo O	29	m	w	OH	Santa Barbara	San Buenaventura P	87	444
Gilbert	40	m	b	LA	San Joaquin	1-Wd Stockton	86	150
Hannah	29	f	w	NY	Placer	Lincoln P O	76	486
Henry	40	m	w	PRUS	Alameda	Oakland	68	140
Jas M	38	m	w	IL	Humboldt	Arcata Twp	72	231
John	36	m	w	PA	Contra Costa	Martinez P O	71	402
John	26	m	w	IREL	San Francisco	1-Wd San Francisco	79	132
Joseph	41	m	w	OH	Solano	Montezuma Twp	90	68
Lee	40	m	w	PRUS	San Francisco	8-Wd San Francisco	82	455
M	25	m	w	PRUS	Sierra	Downieville Twp	89	517
Mary	33	f	w	IREL	San Francisco	San Francisco P O	83	286
Oscar	46	m	w	OH	Mono	Bridgeport P O	74	286
Peter	40	m	w	IREL	San Francisco	San Francisco P O	83	318
R J	48	m	w	NC	Merced	Snelling P O	74	266
Rob	43	m	w	ENGL	Alameda	Oakland	68	173
Robert	28	m	w	NY	San Francisco	1-Wd San Francisco	79	131
Samuel	40	m	m	NC	Tuolumne	Sonora P O	93	309
Simeon	35	m	w	PRUS	Sacramento	4-Wd Sacramento	77	349
Thomas	37	m	w	TN	Los Angeles	El Monte Twp	73	455
Thomas	26	m	w	NY	San Francisco	8-Wd San Francisco	82	329
Thomas	24	m	w	IREL	Napa	Napa	75	37
William	37	m	w	MO	Solano	Montezuma Twp	90	68
William	27	m	w	NY	Solano	Silveyville Twp	90	87
Wm	58	m	w	TN	San Joaquin	3-Wd Stockton	86	235
ASHALMAN								
George	40	m	w	PA	Placer	Bath P O	76	450
ASHAMAN								
Charles	35	m	w	PA	Santa Clara	2-Wd San Jose	88	320
ASHBAUGH								
Henry	45	m	w	SWIT	San Joaquin	2-Wd Stockton	86	174
ASHBON								
E J	32	m	w	VT	Alameda	Oakland	68	247
ASHBROOK								
A	45	m	w	OH	Napa	Yountville Twp	75	84
Hiram	31	m	w	OH	Contra Costa	Martinez P O	71	436
M V	30	m	w	OH	Del Norte	Crescent Twp	71	454
M V	29	m	w	OH	Solano	Vallejo	90	217
Thos	76	m	w	VA	Napa	Yountville Twp	75	84
ASHBURN								
H A	49	m	w	NORW	Nevada	Nevada Twp	75	283
Wm	34	m	w	PRUS	San Francisco	5-Wd San Francisco	81	9
ASHBURNER								
William	35	m	w	MA	San Francisco	6-Wd San Francisco	81	140
ASHBURY								
Mark	36	m	w	MA	San Francisco	2-Wd San Francisco	79	195
ASHBY								
Faithful D	64	f	w	VA	Yolo	Grafton Twp	93	483
I T	40	m	w	MA	Alameda	Oakland	68	181
Wm	57	m	w	CANA	Butte	Ophir Twp	70	115
ASHCRAFT								
Jas	35	m	w	KY	Sonoma	Santa Rosa	91	420
Jno	30	m	w	MO	Sonoma	Santa Rosa	91	420
Louise	9	f	w	CO	Sonoma	Santa Rosa	91	425
ASHCROFT								
Isiah	44	m	w	NJ	Yuba	New York Twp	93	639
John	55	m	w	ENGL	San Bernardino	Chino Twp	78	411
Mary	34	f	w	PA	El Dorado	Placerville Twp	72	97
S	52	m	w	OH	Yuba	Marysville	93	586
William	48	m	w	MA	San Francisco	San Francisco P O	80	387
ASHDON								
Henry	15	m	w	CA	Klamath	Dillon Twp	73	369
ASHE								
Charles	51	m	w	MA	San Francisco	San Francisco P O	83	30
Richd P	45	m	w	NC	San Francisco	San Francisco P O	83	94
Sala	75	f	b	NC	San Francisco	San Francisco P O	83	94
ASHER								
A B	49	m	w	VA	Sierra	Downieville Twp	89	518
Albert F	21	m	w	IA	San Diego	San Diego	78	511
Edward	23	m	w	ENGL	San Francisco	5-Wd San Francisco	81	32
Emil	17	f	w	FRAN	San Francisco	11-Wd San Francisc	84	507
James	43	m	w	IN	Yolo	Cache Crk Twp	93	437
Joral	33	m	w	PRUS	San Francisco	San Francisco P O	83	378
Joseph M	37	m	w	IL	San Diego	San Diego	78	495
R	46	m	w	ENGL	Sierra	Butte Twp	89	510
Rosa	60	f	w	PRUS	San Francisco	8-Wd San Francisco	82	382
S F	27	m	w	PRUS	Yuba	Marysville	93	602
Samuel	35	m	w	PRUS	San Francisco	San Francisco P O	83	305
Simon	45	m	w	POLA	San Francisco	3-Wd San Francisco	79	295
Simon	18	m	w	RUSS	Yuba	Marysville	93	593
T C	42	m	w	FRAN	Sierra	Butte Twp	89	511

© 2001 by Heritage Quest. All rights reserved.

California 1870 Census

Name	Age	S	R	B-PL	County	Locale	Series M593 Roll	Pg
W C	54	m	w	KY	Monterey	San Juan Twp	74	399
William	36	m	w	SWIT	Napa	Napa	75	26
William	24	m	w	IREL	Yolo	Cache Crk Twp	93	432
ASHERMAN								
Cecelia	52	f	w	PRUS	San Francisco	8-Wd San Francisco	82	385
ASHERTIN								
Thomas	36	m	w	ME	Tuolumne	Chinese Camp P O	93	376
ASHFIELD								
Adam	34	m	w	IREL	Contra Costa	Martinez P O	71	415
Jas	38	m	w	CANA	Shasta	Shasta P O	89	453
Wm	24	m	w	CANA	Humboldt	Bucksport Twp	72	243
ASHFORD								
G W	37	m	w	VA	Tehama	Antelope Twp	92	158
James	42	m	w	ENGL	Los Angeles	Wilmington Twp	73	642
William	44	m	w	CANA	Siskiyou	Scott Valley Twp	89	614
ASHIA								
Benj	50	m	w	ENGL	San Francisco	1-Wd San Francisco	79	76
ASHKANNER								
Robert	35	m	w	ENGL	San Mateo	Schoolhouse Statio	87	340
ASHLEY								
Asoph	52	m	w	NY	Yolo	Buckeye Twp	93	408
Augustus	33	m	w	MA	Santa Clara	1-Wd San Jose	88	228
Caernarvon	40	m	w	KY	Mendocino	Ukiah Twp	74	244
Calvin	38	m	w	OH	San Mateo	Woodside P O	87	385
Chas	27	m	w	WI	San Joaquin	2-Wd Stockton	86	184
D R	45	m	w	NY	San Francisco	8-Wd San Francisco	82	342
Daniel L	28	m	w	MO	Monterey	Salinas Twp	74	310
Delos	15	m	w	CA	San Francisco	11-Wd San Francisc	84	592
Edwd	5	m	w	CA	Santa Clara	Gilroy Twp	88	94
Edwin	29	m	w	PA	San Joaquin	1-Wd Stockton	86	136
Ella	19	f	w	OH	Contra Costa	Martinez P O	71	410
Geo	43	m	w	MA	San Joaquin	Liberty Twp	86	92
Geo	40	m	w	IL	San Joaquin	Union Twp	86	268
George	33	m	w	NJ	Marin	Novato Twp	74	9
George	23	m	b	KY	Napa	Napa	75	56
Henry	51	m	w	CANA	Solano	Denverton Twp	90	27
Henry	30	m	w	GERM	Yolo	Buckeye Twp	93	413
J G	38	m	w	PA	Lake	Lower Lake	73	416
J P	39	m	w	MA	San Joaquin	Douglas Twp	86	40
J R	65	m	w	OH	Sacramento	American Twp	77	68
James	30	m	w	MO	Sutter	Vernon Twp	92	138
James	25	m	w	ENGL	Colusa	Monroe Twp	71	319
James B	64	m	w	VT	Santa Barbara	Santa Barbara P O	87	481
James H	46	m	w	MO	Monterey	Castroville Twp	74	340
John	50	m	w	IREL	Trinity	Minersville Pct	92	203
John	50	m	w	CANA	Santa Clara	2-Wd San Jose	88	327
John T	45	m	w	VT	Placer	Bath P O	76	454
M E	38	m	w	MA	El Dorado	Greenwood Twp	72	54
Mary	85	f	w	IN	Sacramento	American Twp	77	68
Otis Jr	50	m	w	NY	Santa Cruz	Santa Cruz Twp	89	392
Robert A	24	m	w	WI	Merced	Snelling P O	74	252
Samuel	21	m	w	FL	Santa Clara	Santa Clara Twp	88	147
Sidney J	59	m	w	NJ	San Francisco	San Francisco P O	85	715
Smith	47	m	w	OH	Contra Costa	Martinez P O	71	436
Thos	30	m	w	NY	San Francisco	1-Wd San Francisco	79	91
W D	33	m	w	TN	San Joaquin	Union Twp	86	267
William	31	m	w	MO	Sonoma	Bodega Twp	91	256
ASHLIN								
George	47	m	w	ENGL	San Francisco	11-Wd San Francisc	84	525
ASHMAN								
Jas S	43	m	w	PA	Fresno	Millerton P O	72	181
ASHMANN								
Phil	22	m	w	SC	Sacramento	3-Wd Sacramento	77	283
ASHMEAD								
Gus	43	m	w	MA	San Francisco	11-Wd San Francisc	84	666
Richard	39	m	w	NY	San Francisco	11-Wd San Francisc	84	692
ASHMORE								
Fred	28	m	w	GERM	Santa Clara	Gilroy Twp	88	100
Henry	43	m	w	HANO	Yuba	Marysville Twp	93	568
James Y	36	m	w	IL	Inyo	Bishop Crk Twp	73	316
Mat J	42	m	w	SCOT	Santa Barbara	San Buenaventura P	87	435
Nelson	64	m	w	KY	Merced	Snelling P O	74	246
Thos E	19	m	w	CA	Nevada	Bridgeport Twp	75	101
ASHOLD								
Pierce	20	m	w	NY	Solano	Vallejo	90	200
ASHTON								
Charles	27	m	w	DC	San Francisco	San Francisco P O	85	810
J C	30	m	w	IN	Santa Clara	Gilroy Twp	88	79
James	26	m	w	IL	Santa Clara	Gilroy Twp	88	84
John	53	m	w	ENGL	San Francisco	7-Wd San Francisco	81	231
John	46	m	w	PA	El Dorado	Georgetown Twp	72	46
John	30	m	w	PA	Solano	Vallejo	90	183
John W	40	m	w	VA	El Dorado	Diamond Springs Tw	72	34
Morris	36	m	w	OH	Tulare	Visalia	92	294
P C	35	m	w	IN	Santa Clara	Gilroy Twp	88	78
Ruben	71	m	w	VA	Amador	Volcano P O	69	384
Thos	37	m	w	ENGL	Sacramento	1-Wd Sacramento	77	201
Thos	24	m	w	NJ	San Joaquin	Elliott Twp	86	72
William	21	m	w	ENGL	Solano	Vacaville Twp	90	122
Wm	30	m	w	ENGL	San Francisco	7-Wd San Francisco	81	249
ASHURST								
C B	27	m	w	MO	Tehama	Merrill	92	197
Franis	63	m	w	KY	Fresno	Millerton P O	72	162
John M	34	m	w	WALE	Sacramento	Natomas Twp	77	166
W H	25	m	w	MO	Tehama	Merrill	92	197
ASHWORTH								
David C	55	m	w	KY	Mariposa	Mariposa P O	74	124
H	23	m	w	ENGL	Humboldt	Eureka Twp	72	280
James	61	m	w	KY	Santa Clara	San Jose Twp	88	215
John	36	m	w	KY	Santa Clara	1-Wd San Jose	88	249
Melisa	38	f	m	IREL	San Joaquin	1-Wd Stockton	86	136
Sarah	14	f	w	CA	Santa Clara	Fremont Twp	88	45
William	43	m	w	ENGL	Trinity	North Fork Twp	92	219
William	30	m	w	ENGL	Stanislaus	Empire Twp	92	59
ASI								
Carlotta	33	f	w	MEXI	Santa Clara	Almaden Twp	88	7
ASILA								
Case	37	m	w	MEXI	San Joaquin	3-Wd Stockton	86	224
ASK								
Hin	17	m	c	CHIN	San Francisco	2-Wd San Francisco	79	173
ASKEL								
John	46	m	w	FRAN	Sonoma	Sonoma Twp	91	437
ASKERSOM								
Emil	26	m	w	PRUS	San Francisco	San Francisco P O	83	368
ASKEW								
Daniel	51	m	w	ENGL	San Francisco	San Francisco P O	83	298
James	39	m	w	ENGL	El Dorado	Mud Springs Twp	72	90
Wm M	40	m	w	GA	Butte	Chico Twp	70	21
ASKEY								
Armstrong	42	m	w	PA	San Francisco	San Francisco P O	83	277
ASKINS								
Joseph	29	m	w	BAVA	Nevada	Meadow Lake Twp	75	265
Phillip	30	m	w	IL	Stanislaus	Branch Twp	92	1
Thomas	53	m	w	PA	Santa Clara	Redwood Twp	88	119
ASKWITH								
Wm	32	m	w	JAMA	San Francisco	San Francisco P O	83	42
ASLEY								
Robert	45	m	w	MA	Colusa	Colusa	71	295
ASMAN								
Ebasinio	15	m	w	CA	Los Angeles	Los Angeles	73	567
ASMASENE								
Isaac	28	m	w	ME	Mendocino	Albion & Big Rvr T	74	166
ASMUS								
John	46	m	w	SHOL	San Francisco	11-Wd San Francisc	84	617
ASMUSSEN								
Wm	37	m	w	DENM	San Francisco	11-Wd San Francisc	84	455
ASON								
Ah	30	m	c	CHIN	San Luis Obispo	San Luis Obispo Tw	87	297
ASPE								
Charles	40	m	w	SWED	Amador	Jackson P O	69	345
ASPENALL								
Wm	46	m	w	LA	Solano	Vallejo	90	141
ASPER								
Albert	19	m	w	NY	San Francisco	San Francisco P O	83	200
Jacob	45	m	w	FRAN	Kern	Havilah P O	73	336
Wm	35	m	w	NY	San Francisco	7-Wd San Francisco	81	256
ASPERI								
Antonio	21	m	w	SPAI	Santa Clara	Santa Clara Twp	88	147
ASPINWALL								
Able	46	m	w	CANA	Stanislaus	Empire Twp	92	57
Abr	50	m	w	CANA	Stanislaus	Empire Twp	92	61
ASSA								
Yong	40	m	c	CHIN	Alameda	Washington Twp	68	271
ASSAM								
---	21	m	c	CHIN	San Francisco	11-Wd San Francisc	84	702
ASSAREO								
Fales	35	m	w	MEXI	Los Angeles	Soledad Twp	73	632
ASSAYER								
Juan	49	m	w	CHIL	Amador	Jackson P O	69	343
ASSE								
Jose	17	m	i	CA	San Luis Obispo	San Luis Obispo Tw	87	298
ASSELIN								
Susan	50	f	w	FRAN	San Francisco	8-Wd San Francisco	82	312
ASSENHEIMER								
Frederick	21	m	w	WURT	Santa Clara	2-Wd San Jose	88	320
ASSING								
---	32	m	c	CHIN	San Francisco	6-Wd San Francisco	81	54
ASSION								
Henry	42	m	w	PRUS	San Francisco	8-Wd San Francisco	82	321
Jean	19	m	w	FRAN	San Francisco	11-Wd San Francisc	84	595
Joseph	13	m	w	CA	San Francisco	8-Wd San Francisco	82	321
Simon	40	m	w	NORW	San Francisco	8-Wd San Francisco	82	355
ASSMAN								
Adolph	38	m	w	PRUS	San Francisco	8-Wd San Francisco	82	395
ASSOLINO								
Nicholas	30	m	w	ITAL	Santa Clara	2-Wd San Jose	88	323
ASSOP								
John	45	m	w	ENGL	Solano	Vallejo	90	157
ASSURYRE								
Peter	30	m	w	DENM	Alameda	Washington Twp	68	298
AST								
Thomas	22	m	w	OH	San Francisco	2-Wd San Francisco	79	163
ASTA								
Fortunali	52	m	w	ITAL	San Francisco	3-Wd San Francisco	79	288
ASTBURY								
John	34	m	w	ENGL	Sacramento	2-Wd Sacramento	77	238
ASTE								
Charles	45	m	w	ITAL	Santa Clara	Santa Clara Twp	88	176
ASTEL								
James	28	m	w	ENGL	Sacramento	Center Twp	77	83
ASTELL								
Benjamin	31	m	w	IREL	San Francisco	San Francisco P O	83	140
Richard	30	m	w	ENGL	Sacramento	Center Twp	77	83
Zacariah	60	m	w	ENGL	Placer	Roseville P O	76	351

© 2001 by Heritage Quest. All rights reserved.

Series M593

Name	Age	S	R	B-PL	County	Locale	Roll	Pg
ASTIAZARAN								
Fernando	18	m	w	MEXI	San Francisco	San Francisco P O	83	136
ASTLEY								
James	63	m	w	ENGL	Placer	Bath P O	76	435
ASTO								
Guadalupo	35	m	w	CHIL	Santa Clara	Almaden Twp	88	1
ASTON								
James	42	m	w	IREL	San Francisco	San Francisco P O	83	303
John	35	m	w	MD	Monterey	Pajaro Twp	74	374
John	30	m	h	MEXI	Alameda	Alameda	68	14
ASTORGA								
Manuel	48	m	w	CHIL	El Dorado	Placerville	72	117
Maria	35	f	w	MEXI	San Francisco	2-Wd San Francisco	79	141
ASTORIA								
Manuel	48	m	w	CHIL	El Dorado	Diamond Springs Tw	72	34
ASTRA								
John	38	m	w	MEXI	Alameda	Oakland	68	150
ASTRADA								
Margana	36	m	w	CA	San Francisco	1-Wd San Francisco	79	108
Mariana	19	m	w	CHIL	San Francisco	1-Wd San Francisco	79	111
ASTRADO								
Emil	43	m	w	ITAL	San Francisco	San Francisco P O	80	426
James	35	m	w	MEXI	Amador	Jackson P O	69	322
Joaquin	36	m	w	MEXI	San Francisco	San Francisco P O	80	470
Victor	29	m	w	ITAL	San Francisco	San Francisco P O	80	471
ASTREDO								
Anthony	41	m	w	ITAL	San Francisco	2-Wd San Francisco	79	247
Manuel	34	m	w	MEXI	San Francisco	San Francisco P O	80	468
ASTWALL								
Newton	28	m	w	MO	Monterey	San Antonio Twp	74	320
ASU								
Sam	36	m	c	CHIN	Stanislaus	Empire Twp	92	33
ASUNA								
Francico	14	f	i	CA	Contra Costa	Martinez P O	71	452
ASVADO								
Joseph	30	m	w	PORT	San Mateo	Half Moon Bay P O	87	394
ASVIT								
John	26	m	w	PORT	Alameda	Washington Twp	68	275
ASVUAL								
Antone	32	m	w	FRAN	Calaveras	San Andreas P O	70	176
ASWEDA								
Thomas	33	m	w	CA	Monterey	Alisal Twp	74	289
ASWETH								
Joquin	37	m	w	HI	Yolo	Merritt Twp	93	505
Manuel	34	m	w	HI	Yolo	Merritt Twp	93	505
Thomas	24	m	w	CANA	San Francisco	7-Wd San Francisco	81	168
AT								
Cheum	32	m	c	CHIN	Calaveras	San Andreas P O	70	171
Guan	26	m	c	CHIN	Butte	Oregon Twp	70	133
I	18	m	c	CHIN	San Francisco	San Francisco P O	85	806
Son	30	m	c	CHIN	Calaveras	San Andreas P O	70	164
Tin	22	m	c	CHIN	Placer	Blue Canyon P O	76	417
To	15	m	c	CHIN	Los Angeles	El Monte Twp	73	460
Tong	23	m	c	CHIN	Los Angeles	El Monte Twp	73	460
ATARAN								
Ramund	21	m	w	CA	Solano	Denverton Twp	90	24
ATCHENSON								
Wm	40	m	w	ME	Klamath	Klamath Twp	73	370
ATCHERSON								
James	30	m	w	ENGL	Kern	Havilah P O	73	350
ATCHESON								
Anna	30	f	w	PA	Butte	Wyandotte Twp	70	146
J	28	m	w	IREL	Alameda	Oakland	68	154
ATCHICON								
E Hens	40	f	w	MD	Santa Clara	Gilroy Twp	88	92
ATCHINSON								
Alex	23	m	w	CANA	Humboldt	Eureka Twp	72	281
B M	40	m	w	NY	Alameda	Brooklyn	68	31
Geo	49	m	w	VA	San Francisco	5-Wd San Francisco	81	12
Lewis F	18	m	b	CA	San Joaquin	Douglas Twp	86	38
Wm A	33	m	w	NY	Monterey	Alisal Twp	74	290
ATCHISON								
David	40	m	w	IREL	Solano	Vallejo	90	170
Eliza	50	f	w	TX	Nevada	Meadow Lake Twp	75	269
Henry J	60	m	w	OH	Yuba	Slate Range Bar Tw	93	670
J	39	m	w	IL	Sacramento	1-Wd Sacramento	77	179
Jefferson	50	m	w	KY	Sacramento	Lee Twp	77	157
John	50	m	w	TX	Nevada	Meadow Lake Twp	75	269
John	33	m	w	IL	Marin	Tomales Twp	74	77
John	15	m	w	CA	Santa Clara	Santa Clara Twp	88	176
Lizzie	14	f	w	CA	Yuba	Marysville	93	587
Mack	65	m	w	OH	Colusa	Spring Valley Twp	71	335
Mary	16	f	w	CA	Santa Clara	2-Wd San Jose	88	336
S	3	m	w	CA	Yuba	Marysville	93	591
Silas M	46	m	w	OH	Yuba	Long Bar Twp	93	560
Tom	38	m	w	NY	Yuba	Marysville	93	613
Wm H	28	m	w	IL	Sonoma	Analy Twp	91	239
ATELERIA								
Elijah	40	m	w	MEXI	Los Angeles	Los Angeles	73	551
ATEMIRANIS								
Alphonso	38	m	w	MEXI	Santa Barbara	San Buenaventura P	87	427
ATENTIA								
Antonio	34	m	w	NM	San Bernardino	San Salvador Twp	78	462
Jose	53	m	w	NM	San Bernardino	San Salvador Twp	78	462
ATER								
J	30	m	w	MA	Alameda	Oakland	68	265
ATH								
Ah	29	m	c	CHIN	Napa	Napa	75	7
ATHEAM								
C G	44	m	w	MA	San Francisco	San Francisco P O	85	835
ATHEARN								
Chas M	31	m	w	MA	San Francisco	San Francisco P O	85	717
ATHEM								
Robert	33	m	w	WURT	Yolo	Putah Twp	93	510
ATHENON								
Joseph	62	m	w	FRAN	San Francisco	2-Wd San Francisco	79	148
ATHENS								
Anne	23	f	w	NY	San Francisco	6-Wd San Francisco	81	114
ATHERMAN								
William	36	m	w	MO	Colusa	Butte Twp	71	265
ATHERN								
Frank W	27	m	w	MA	Los Angeles	San Juan Twp	73	628
L	28	m	w	IN	San Joaquin	Elliott Twp	86	76
Louisa	57	f	w	MA	San Joaquin	Elliott Twp	86	76
Wm	30	m	w	IN	San Joaquin	Elliott Twp	86	76
ATHERS								
James	41	m	w	ENGL	San Francisco	8-Wd San Francisco	82	375
ATHERTON								
Abner J	65	m	w	MA	Shasta	Buckeye P O	89	482
Frank	20	m	w	CHIL	Monterey	Pajaro Twp	74	376
George	53	m	w	NY	Sacramento	Brighton Twp	77	78
H S	28	m	w	IA	San Joaquin	Tulare Twp	86	256
Jno	55	m	w	ENGL	Sacramento	3-Wd Sacramento	77	309
John	35	m	w	ME	Marin	Novato Twp	74	13
John	34	m	w	MO	Contra Costa	Martinez P O	71	408
Rianza K	28	m	w	OH	Plumas	Indian Twp	77	18
Robt	45	m	w	MA	Butte	Ophir Twp	70	96
Sarah	13	f	w	CA	San Joaquin	Douglas Twp	86	38
Taxon D	55	m	w	MA	San Mateo	Menlo Park P O	87	377
William	55	m	w	ENGL	Yolo	Fremont Twp	93	476
William	36	m	w	OH	Colusa	Grand Island Twp	71	303
William	29	m	w	VT	Contra Costa	Martinez P O	71	405
William	19	m	w	MA	Colusa	Colusa	71	290
ATHESON								
J	43	m	w	NY	Alameda	Oakland	68	253
ATHISON								
I	36	m	w	CANA	Alameda	Oakland	68	214
ATHMAN								
Nathan	40	m	w	SWED	San Francisco	2-Wd San Francisco	79	214
ATHRIDGE								
Thomas	30	m	w	IREL	San Francisco	San Francisco P O	80	371
ATHURAS								
Saml	70	m	w	FRAN	San Francisco	2-Wd San Francisco	79	173
ATIMIRANO								
Jose	26	m	w	CA	Santa Barbara	Arroyo Burro P O	87	509
ATIN								
Ah	32	m	c	CHIN	El Dorado	Placerville Twp	72	97
ATKEN								
Agnes	19	f	w	MA	San Francisco	San Francisco P O	83	417
ATKIN								
James	50	m	w	SCOT	Amador	Sutter Crk P O	69	400
ATKINS								
Alonzo	24	m	w	ME	Mendocino	Anderson Twp	74	154
D L	49	m	w	NY	San Joaquin	Oneal Twp	86	109
George	30	m	w	IREL	San Francisco	7-Wd San Francisco	81	214
George H	42	m	w	VT	Nevada	Little York Twp	75	239
Harriet	14	f	w	IA	Stanislaus	Empire Twp	92	51
Henry B	35	m	w	NY	San Francisco	8-Wd San Francisco	82	448
Hugh	38	m	w	MO	Sutter	Sutter Twp	92	118
Jesse	38	m	w	CA	Santa Clara	San Jose Twp	88	198
John	35	m	w	KY	San Joaquin	Elliott Twp	86	78
John	34	m	w	IL	Sacramento	San Joaquin Twp	77	406
John R	43	m	w	NY	Sacramento	2-Wd Sacramento	77	254
Lemuel	30	m	w	ME	Nevada	Nevada Twp	75	300
P	23	m	w	ENGL	Sonoma	Petaluma Twp	91	322
Quintus N	38	m	w	OH	Shasta	Millville P O	89	483
Richd	35	m	w	ENGL	Santa Clara	Almaden Twp	88	19
Robert C	37	m	w	ME	San Francisco	8-Wd San Francisco	82	402
Russell	25	m	w	IL	Contra Costa	Martinez P O	71	388
S B	36	m	w	OH	Lake	Scotts Crk	73	426
Wm	60	m	w	IREL	Sacramento	4-Wd Sacramento	77	323
Wm	25	m	w	IREL	Sonoma	Salt Point	91	387
Wm G	41	m	w	ENGL	Sonoma	Santa Rosa	91	417
ATKINSON								
A	36	m	w	SWED	Mendocino	Little Lake Twp	74	194
Alfred	9	m	w	CA	Sacramento	4-Wd Sacramento	77	378
Ashly J	46	m	w	OH	Placer	Rocklin P O	76	462
C E	35	f	w	PA	Alameda	Oakland	68	162
Elijah	36	m	w	MA	San Francisco	11-Wd San Francisc	84	430
Elisab	46	f	w	ENGL	Alameda	Oakland	68	165
Emily	46	f	w	CANA	San Joaquin	2-Wd Stockton	86	171
Forrest	6	m	w	CA	Sacramento	4-Wd Sacramento	77	378
Francis	37	m	w	KY	San Francisco	San Francisco P O	83	399
G	55	m	w	ENGL	Lassen	Susanville Twp	73	443
G F	25	m	w	ENGL	Solano	Vallejo	90	142
George	55	m	w	ENGL	San Francisco	11-Wd San Francisc	84	637
George	55	m	w	OH	Yuba	New York Twp	93	641
George	32	m	w	ENGL	San Francisco	San Francisco P O	83	52
Henry	28	m	w	TX	Tulare	Farmersville Twp	92	245
Henry	23	m	w	CANA	Alameda	Eden Twp	68	65
Horatio	21	m	w	CANA	San Francisco	San Francisco P O	83	202
Horatio N	21	m	w	CANA	San Francisco	San Francisco P O	83	160
James	35	m	w	IL	San Francisco	6-Wd San Francisco	81	109

© 2001 by Heritage Quest. All rights reserved.

California 1870 Census

Name	Age	S	R	B-PL	County	Locale	Series M593 Roll	Pg
James	34	m	w	IREL	San Francisco	7-Wd San Francisco	81	250
Jesse	30	m	w	TX	Tulare	Farmersville Twp	92	244
John	46	m	w	ENGL	Placer	Bath P O	76	422
John	42	m	w	CANA	Colusa	Monroe Twp	71	320
John	35	m	w	VA	San Bernardino	San Bernardino Twp	78	425
John	16	m	w	MA	San Francisco	7-Wd San Francisco	81	156
John C	40	m	w	PA	San Diego	San Diego	78	491
John J	33	m	w	ENGL	San Bernardino	San Bernardino Twp	78	452
Joseph	55	m	w	PA	San Francisco	San Francisco P O	80	364
K	20	f	w	MA	Alameda	Oakland	68	237
Lizzie	6	f	w	CA	Sacramento	4-Wd Sacramento	77	378
Nathan	42	m	w	CANA	San Francisco	San Francisco P O	83	189
Nathan	40	m	w	CANA	San Francisco	San Francisco P O	83	275
Robert	59	m	w	NY	Mendocino	Round Valley Twp	74	217
Robert	58	m	w	NY	Mendocino	Round Valley India	74	180
Rose	39	f	w	ME	San Francisco	San Francisco P O	83	268
Saml F	28	m	w	VA	Plumas	Seneca Twp	77	48
Samuel	50	m	w	MD	San Francisco	11-Wd San Francisc	84	563
T B	45	m	w	KY	Yuba	Linda Twp	93	557
Thomas	45	m	w	ENGL	Yolo	Washington Twp	93	534
Thos	67	m	w	IREL	San Francisco	11-Wd San Francisc	84	587
Thos T	29	m	w	ENGL	San Francisco	7-Wd San Francisco	81	248
W A	35	m	w	MO	Amador	Jackson P O	69	345
W W	38	m	w	OH	Amador	Ione City P O	69	358
William	45	m	w	CANA	San Francisco	San Francisco P O	83	360
William	45	m	w	CANA	Marin	San Rafael	74	48
William	31	m	w	ENGL	Contra Costa	Martinez P O	71	429
William H	32	m	w	CANA	Stanislaus	Empire Twp	92	46
Wm	55	m	w	IREL	San Francisco	8-Wd San Francisco	82	324
Wm	42	m	w	TN	San Bernardino	Chino Twp	78	409
Wm	36	m	w	ENGL	Alameda	Brooklyn	68	28
Wm	22	m	w	ENGL	San Bernardino	San Bernardino Twp	78	417
Wm B	21	m	w	ME	Sierra	Gibson Twp	89	540
Wm E	42	m	w	ME	Sierra	Sears Twp	89	553
Wm H	37	m	w	NY	San Francisco	1-Wd San Francisco	79	67
Wm H	26	m	w	MO	Sacramento	Cosumnes Twp	77	90
ATLARM								
Adolph	27	m	w	PRUS	Santa Clara	2-Wd San Jose	88	288
ATLERS								
John	43	m	w	ENGL	San Francisco	8-Wd San Francisco	82	375
ATLING								
Henrietta	9	f	w	NY	San Francisco	San Francisco P O	83	84
ATMORE								
John	39	m	w	ENGL	El Dorado	Mud Springs Twp	72	91
Richard	39	m	w	ENGL	El Dorado	Mud Springs Twp	72	79
Sarah	37	f	w	MI	El Dorado	Mud Springs Twp	72	91
ATNER								
Jno	30	m	w	PRUS	Butte	Hamilton Twp	70	64
ATONDO								
Fernando	33	m	w	MEXI	Los Angeles	Los Angeles Twp	73	464
Refujio	22	m	w	MEXI	Los Angeles	Los Angeles	73	513
ATOY								
John	24	m	c	CHIN	Solano	Green Valley Twp	90	44
ATRADA								
Salvador	35	m	w	MEXI	Santa Barbara	Las Cruces P O	87	505
ATRIDGE								
Hannah	27	f	w	IREL	Alameda	Eden Twp	68	89
Jas	36	m	w	IREL	San Francisco	1-Wd San Francisco	79	18
ATT								
Ah	19	m	c	CHIN	San Francisco	11-Wd San Francisc	84	528
Ludwig	31	m	w	HDAR	San Francisco	San Francisco P O	83	288
ATTAL								
Peter	30	m	w	FRAN	Los Angeles	Los Angeles	73	513
ATTARDT								
George	36	m	w	PRUS	Alameda	Oakland	68	210
ATTELLIE								
Andre	58	m	w	FRAN	Mariposa	Maxwell Crk P O	74	146
ATTEN								
Hosea G	33	m	w	NY	Calaveras	San Andreas P O	70	163
ATTENELLI								
Joseph	38	m	w	NY	Siskiyou	Table Rock Twp	89	647
ATTER								
H	27	m	w	OH	Lake	Little Borax	73	419
Isaac	49	m	w	PA	Lake	Lower Lake	73	419
John	70	m	w	MD	Tuolumne	Big Oak Flat P O	93	399
ATTERBURY								
Alexander	30	m	w	VA	San Francisco	11-Wd San Francisc	84	480
Wm B	44	m	w	KY	Sonoma	Santa Rosa	91	401
ATTERMAN								
Larrian	26	m	w	MEXI	Fresno	Millerton P O	72	163
ATTERSON								
Edward	41	m	w	PRUS	Placer	Gold Run Twp	76	398
Mary	30	f	w	MEXI	San Francisco	San Francisco P O	80	465
William	34	m	b	NY	San Francisco	San Francisco P O	80	465
ATTHEN								
James	49	m	w	SCOT	Amador	Sutter Crk P O	69	403
ATTO								
Richard	29	m	w	SAXO	San Francisco	San Francisco P O	83	199
ATTRIDGE								
Alfred	22	m	w	CUBA	San Francisco	San Francisco P O	83	195
ATTWATER								
David	36	m	w	BAVA	San Francisco	San Francisco P O	80	350
ATTWOOD								
Sarah	13	f	w	CA	Yuba	Rose Bar Twp	93	666
ATWATER								
Edwd	39	m	w	ENGL	Solano	Vallejo	90	162
Gr	35	m	w	OH	Sierra	Lincoln Twp	89	545
Henry	44	m	w	NY	Nevada	Eureka Twp	75	132
Henry H	33	m	w	PA	Sonoma	Petaluma Twp	91	312
Louis	24	m	w	IL	Yolo	Cache Crk Twp	93	430
M D	44	m	w	CT	Merced	Snelling P O	74	264
ATWELL								
A B	39	m	w	NY	Amador	Volcano P O	69	376
A J	28	m	w	NY	Merced	Snelling P O	74	248
Aaron J	36	m	w	NY	Tulare	Visalia	92	294
Benjamin	40	m	w	KY	Tulare	Kings Rvr Twp	92	253
Daniel	66	m	w	CT	Tulare	Visalia	92	294
Horace	40	m	w	NY	Nevada	Meadow Lake Twp	75	248
Hosea W	36	m	w	VT	Yolo	Cache Crk Twp	93	430
John	44	m	w	NY	Alameda	Washington Twp	68	289
Thomas	37	m	w	OH	Placer	Colfax P O	76	385
ATWILL								
Joseph F	59	m	w	MA	San Francisco	San Francisco P O	83	60
ATWOOD								
A	52	m	w	VT	Sierra	Sierra Twp	89	562
A	45	m	w	ME	Yuba	Marysville	93	608
Adam	30	m	w	PA	San Francisco	6-Wd San Francisco	81	129
Banford	45	m	w	CT	San Bernardino	San Bernardino Twp	78	435
Benj J	38	m	w	ME	Nevada	Nevada Twp	75	284
Benjamin	44	m	w	NH	Colusa	Stony Crk Twp	71	330
C	43	m	w	ME	Sierra	Butte Twp	89	510
E W	55	m	w	CT	San Joaquin	Castoria Twp	86	1
Ephrahim	42	m	w	ME	San Francisco	2-Wd San Francisco	79	237
Geo	35	m	w	MA	Merced	Snelling P O	74	247
George	28	m	w	MA	San Francisco	3-Wd San Francisco	79	297
George	25	m	w	ME	San Francisco	11-Wd San Francisc	84	620
Gus	20	m	w	OH	Butte	Hamilton Twp	70	71
Horace	40	m	w	ME	Placer	Summit P O	76	496
James M	42	m	w	MO	Amador	Fiddletown P O	69	433
John	38	m	w	SWED	Stanislaus	Empire Twp	92	40
John	35	m	b	MD	Nevada	Bridgeport Twp	75	100
John B	38	m	w	MA	Sacramento	Center Twp	77	82
L C	2	m	w	MA	Solano	Benicia	90	4
Lucy	45	f	w	ME	San Francisco	11-Wd San Francisc	84	619
Melville	50	m	w	ENGL	San Francisco	8-Wd San Francisco	82	337
Nathan	34	m	w	NY	Placer	Auburn P O	76	373
Peter B	48	m	w	KY	Plumas	Mineral Twp	77	21
Real	56	m	w	NY	Santa Clara	Gilroy Twp	88	97
Stone	21	m	w	ME	Sutter	Yuba Twp	92	140
William	46	m	w	SWED	Stanislaus	Empire Twp	92	59
Wm	24	m	w	MA	Napa	Napa	75	7
AU								
Ah	61	m	c	CHIN	Tuolumne	Big Oak Flat P O	93	397
Jin	19	m	c	CHIN	San Joaquin	Elkhorn Twp	86	66
Shong	30	f	c	CHIN	San Joaquin	2-Wd Stockton	86	167
AUBAYLL								
Julien	47	m	w	FRAN	San Joaquin	1-Wd Stockton	86	141
AUBERECK								
Jacob	59	m	w	OH	Santa Clara	Redwood Twp	88	129
AUBERY								
Chas A	35	m	w	NY	San Francisco	5-Wd San Francisco	81	9
J F	29	m	w	NY	Sacramento	1-Wd Sacramento	77	200
Rollin	36	m	w	OH	Klamath	Dillon Twp	73	369
William	25	m	w	ENGL	San Francisco	7-Wd San Francisco	81	172
AUBI								
Joseph	33	m	w	CANA	Del Norte	Happy Camp Twp	71	472
AUBIER								
David	32	m	w	CANA	Contra Costa	Martinez P O	71	367
AUBLE								
Charles	23	m	w	NY	Siskiyou	Table Rock Twp	89	645
Frank	13	m	w	OH	Siskiyou	Butte Twp	89	588
AUBRAI								
John	50	m	w	FRAN	Santa Clara	Redwood Twp	88	119
AUBRASIA								
John	36	m	w	FRAN	Stanislaus	Branch Twp	92	7
AUBREY								
Alvis E	32	m	w	MO	Colusa	Colusa	71	296
Chas W	41	m	w	ENGL	Nevada	Little York Twp	75	244
Edwd	26	m	w	FRAN	San Francisco	1-Wd San Francisco	79	108
Francis	49	m	w	CANA	San Francisco	11-Wd San Francisc	84	600
Joseph	40	m	w	MO	Santa Clara	San Jose Twp	88	212
Peter F	32	m	w	ITAL	Santa Barbara	Santa Barbara P O	87	451
William	40	m	w	CANA	San Francisco	San Francisco P O	83	186
AUBRY								
Emily	33	f	w	MA	Sacramento	4-Wd Sacramento	77	329
Henry	26	m	w	SWED	San Francisco	1-Wd San Francisco	79	126
AUBURTUS								
J C	43	m	w	NORW	Placer	Roseville P O	76	349
AUBURY								
Ican	35	m	w	FRAN	Santa Clara	Redwood Twp	88	132
Victor	35	m	w	NY	Yolo	Grafton Twp	93	500
AUBUSHON								
Lebon	33	m	w	MO	Shasta	Millville P O	89	489
AUCKER								
Robert	39	m	w	MO	Yolo	Cottonwood Twp	93	468
Robert	34	m	w	IL	Yolo	Cache Crk Twp	93	456
AUCLEBAR								
E	49	m	w	FRAN	Alameda	Oakland	68	135
AUCT								
Sally	33	f	c	CHIN	Amador	Ione City P O	69	364
AUD								
Frances L	47	m	w	KY	Nevada	Meadow Lake Twp	75	250
Maggie	16	f	w	SCOT	San Francisco	2-Wd San Francisco	79	245

© 2001 by Heritage Quest. All rights reserved.

Name	Age	S	R	B-PL	County	Locale	Series M593 Roll	Pg
AUDILET								
M	40	m	w	HDAR	Sacramento	1-Wd Sacramento	77	185
AUDINOT								
John	34	m	w	FRAN	San Francisco	San Francisco P O	80	537
AUER								
Charles	28	m	w	WURT	Sacramento	2-Wd Sacramento	77	245
John	50	m	w	FRAN	San Francisco	2-Wd San Francisco	79	215
AUERBACH								
Louis	38	m	w	PRUS	San Francisco	8-Wd San Francisco	82	497
AUFSCHNIDER								
Chas	39	m	w	BAVA	Shasta	Shasta P O	89	453
AUG								
Ah	55	m	c	CHIN	Plumas	Mineral Twp	77	25
Ah	13	m	c	CHIN	Yuba	Marysville	93	618
Arm	44	f	c	CHIN	Yuba	Marysville	93	577
Gang	32	f	w	CHIN	Plumas	Mineral Twp	77	24
Gen	28	m	c	CHIN	Plumas	Mineral Twp	77	25
Get	22	m	c	CHIN	Plumas	Goodwin Twp	77	3
Gin	14	m	c	CHIN	San Francisco	11-Wd San Francisc	84	477
Goon	46	m	c	CHIN	San Mateo	San Mateo P O	87	351
Goon	22	m	c	CHIN	Plumas	Goodwin Twp	77	2
Gow	14	m	c	CHIN	Plumas	Mineral Twp	77	25
Grey	35	m	c	CHIN	Plumas	Washington Twp	77	57
James	30	m	w	ME	Alameda	Oakland	68	164
Koo	43	m	c	CHIN	Tuolumne	Big Oak Flat P O	93	397
Leo	27	m	c	CHIN	Sonoma	Salt Point	91	386
Long	19	m	c	CHIN	San Francisco	San Francisco P O	85	866
Minor	24	m	w	MI	Marin	San Rafael Twp	74	41
Yu	28	m	c	CHIN	Solano	Suisun Twp	90	106
AUGARDE								
Peter	40	m	w	FRAN	Sonoma	Sonoma Twp	91	439
AUGH								
Ah	33	m	c	CHIN	Calaveras	San Andreas P O	70	205
Ah	17	m	c	CHIN	San Francisco	6-Wd San Francisco	81	48
Joseph	29	m	w	CANA	Sacramento	4-Wd Sacramento	77	363
AUGNER								
Chas	61	m	w	PRUS	San Francisco	11-Wd San Francisc	84	422
AUGNTIX								
E	11	f	w	WI	Alameda	Oakland	68	141
AUGRAVIN								
H	18	m	w	MEXI	San Joaquin	1-Wd Stockton	86	133
AUGTHERSEN								
George	44	m	w	SCOT	San Francisco	3-Wd San Francisco	79	288
AUGUIN								
Elvin	28	m	w	ENGL	Nevada	Meadow Lake Twp	75	266
AUGUST								
A N	49	m	w	FRAN	Tuolumne	Big Oak Flat P O	93	394
Edward	25	m	w	CANA	San Francisco	San Francisco P O	85	805
John	50	m	w	GREE	Plumas	Quartz Twp	77	35
Joseph	35	m	w	SCOT	Alameda	Brooklyn Twp	68	45
Josephine	43	f	w	FRAN	San Francisco	2-Wd San Francisco	79	145
Manuel	35	m	w	PORT	Sacramento	Sutter Twp	77	386
Santignet	39	m	w	FRAN	El Dorado	Salmon Falls Twp	72	131
AUGUSTIN								
Mary	7	f	w	PORT	Alameda	Hayward	68	74
AUGUSTINA								
Antonio	26	m	w	SWIT	San Francisco	2-Wd San Francisco	79	159
AUGUSTINE								
Francisco	36	m	w	FRAN	Calaveras	Copperopolis P O	70	242
Henry	29	m	w	PRUS	San Francisco	San Francisco P O	83	309
J	40	m	w	ITAL	San Joaquin	1-Wd Stockton	86	154
John	40	m	w	PORT	Tuolumne	Columbia P O	93	355
Jos	30	m	w	FRAN	Calaveras	Copperopolis P O	70	239
R	40	m	w	ITAL	Sonoma	Sonoma Twp	91	441
AUGUSTIVE								
Frank	34	m	w	PORT	Alameda	Washington Twp	68	291
AUGUSTO								
---	22	m	w	HAMB	Contra Costa	San Pablo Twp	71	366
Antone	26	m	w	PORT	Marin	Nicasio Twp	74	19
AUGUSTUS								
Charles	28	m	b	KY	Tuolumne	Sonora P O	93	333
Domingo	38	m	w	PORT	Alameda	Brooklyn	68	38
James	28	m	w	FRAN	San Francisco	6-Wd San Francisco	81	101
Jos	30	m	w	CAME	Sacramento	1-Wd Sacramento	77	198
Joseph	37	m	w	NY	San Francisco	1-Wd San Francisco	79	106
AUK								
Yon	41	m	c	CHIN	Nevada	Bridgeport Twp	75	106
AUKING								
William	38	m	w	NY	Colusa	Monroe Twp	71	325
AUL								
Georg	35	m	w	GERM	Humboldt	South Fork Twp	72	303
Samuel	38	m	w	IREL	Mariposa	Mariposa P O	74	98
AULAGA								
Euhania	30	m	w	MEXI	Santa Clara	1-Wd San Jose	88	255
AULD								
Celia	37	f	w	LA	Santa Clara	1-Wd San Jose	88	250
James	62	m	w	ME	Alameda	Oakland	68	163
James	26	m	w	SCOT	San Francisco	2-Wd San Francisco	79	209
John	37	m	w	VA	San Joaquin	2-Wd Stockton	86	185
Martha	43	f	w	NY	San Francisco	6-Wd San Francisco	81	91
Ossian G	40	m	w	NJ	Santa Cruz	Santa Cruz	89	423
William	15	m	w	CA	Santa Clara	Redwood Twp	88	118
AULDER								
John	22	m	w	IL	Yolo	Putah Twp	93	519
AULICK								
George	33	m	w	VA	Stanislaus	Empire Twp	92	49
AULIE								
George	36	m	w	VA	Mariposa	Maxwell Crk P O	74	140
AULINS								
Manuel	26	m	w	SCOT	San Luis Obispo	San Luis Obispo Tw	87	297
AULIS								
Ignatia	11	f	w	CA	Santa Cruz	Pajaro Twp	89	360
AULL								
Laura	12	f	w	CA	Sonoma	Russian Rvr	91	372
Thos M	64	m	w	KY	San Joaquin	Liberty Twp	86	82
AULMANN								
Lawrence	36	m	w	PRUS	Yuba	Bullards Bar P O	93	550
AULT								
Andrew J	32	m	w	OH	Inyo	Bishop Crk Twp	73	312
Anne	42	f	w	IL	Nevada	Rough & Ready Twp	75	324
Edwd	31	m	w	CANA	Yuba	Marysville	93	593
John M	38	m	w	PA	Fresno	Millerton P O	72	149
Louis	9	m	w	CA	Amador	Volcano P O	69	377
Mathias	43	m	w	NY	San Francisco	San Francisco P O	83	199
Peter	7	m	w	CA	Amador	Volcano P O	69	375
Peter	47	m	w	HDAR	Amador	Volcano P O	69	375
Sally	36	f	w	CA	Fresno	Millerton P O	72	194
AULY								
John	22	m	w	IREL	Solano	Vallejo	90	197
AUMEND								
Alfred	29	m	w	CANA	Sonoma	Bodega Twp	91	262
AUMER								
Francis	37	m	w	BAVA	Nevada	Grass Valley Twp	75	177
AUN								
Ye	30	m	c	CHIN	Amador	Fiddletown P O	69	437
AUNG								
Yong	30	m	c	CHIN	Yuba	Marysville	93	630
AUNON								
John	26	m	w	CANA	Colusa	Butte Twp	71	270
AUNSPACH								
Jacob	22	m	w	PA	San Francisco	1-Wd San Francisco	79	63
AUNSPAUGH								
Benj	44	m	w	OH	Sutter	Vernon Twp	92	135
AUR								
Ah	30	f	c	CHIN	Los Angeles	Los Angeles	73	524
Ah	20	m	c	CHIN	San Francisco	6-Wd San Francisco	81	85
AURADON								
Jule	40	m	w	FRAN	San Francisco	San Francisco P O	80	380
AURAG								
Fredrick	33	m	w	SWED	San Francisco	San Francisco P O	83	23
AURAN								
Frances	36	f	w	FRAN	San Francisco	8-Wd San Francisco	82	321
AURBERG								
Mary	71	f	w	SWED	Yuba	Marysville	93	611
AURETA								
Bruanka	46	m	w	MEXI	Tulare	Tule Rvr Twp	92	266
AURIE								
Eugene	42	m	w	FRAN	Los Angeles	Los Angeles	73	527
AURIELA								
Joseph	32	m	w	ITAL	San Francisco	San Francisco P O	80	352
AURTHA								
William S	56	m	w	MA	San Francisco	San Francisco P O	83	371
AURZAN								
Charles	27	m	w	FRAN	San Francisco	San Francisco P O	80	341
AUSER								
E W	51	m	w	NY	Sonoma	Santa Rosa	91	418
AUSLEY								
Stockdale	41	m	w	PA	El Dorado	Placerville Twp	72	103
AUSMAS								
Clara	20	f	w	PORT	Alameda	Alameda	68	10
AUSSENAC								
Catharine	44	f	w	FRAN	Yuba	Parks Bar Twp	93	649
AUST								
Frederick	40	m	w	PRUS	San Francisco	8-Wd San Francisco	82	432
John	35	m	w	SAXO	San Joaquin	Castoria Twp	86	5
AUSTERLAN								
Joseph	46	m	w	PORT	Alameda	Eden Twp	68	90
AUSTGE								
Fred	16	f	w	ENGL	San Francisco	11-Wd San Francisc	84	689
AUSTIN								
A	40	m	w	CT	Humboldt	Eureka Twp	72	269
A	33	m	w	IA	San Joaquin	Liberty Twp	86	94
A	21	f	w	MI	Amador	Drytown P O	69	422
Albert C	45	m	w	VA	San Francisco	8-Wd San Francisco	82	336
Algernon	36	m	w	ENGL	San Francisco	San Francisco P O	80	425
Alva	41	m	w	MA	San Francisco	11-Wd San Francisc	84	500
Amos	50	m	w	ME	Sonoma	Petaluma Twp	91	342
Andrew	52	m	w	VT	Contra Costa	Martinez Twp	71	349
Arnold R	52	m	w	RI	Los Angeles	Los Angeles Twp	73	484
Avendon M	32	m	w	ME	Nevada	Grass Valley Twp	75	209
B C	38	m	w	NY	Alameda	Oakland	68	218
Charles	29	m	w	NY	Kern	Havilah P O	73	337
Chas	23	m	w	NY	San Francisco	11-Wd San Francisc	84	694
Corneilus	25	m	w	NY	San Francisco	1-Wd San Francisco	79	63
D W	34	m	w	CANA	Sierra	Forest Twp	89	530
Edw	28	m	w	NY	Alameda	Oakland	68	257
Edward	48	m	w	NY	San Francisco	6-Wd San Francisco	81	94
Edwd	36	m	w	NY	San Francisco	1-Wd San Francisco	79	132
Edwin	23	m	w	VT	San Luis Obispo	Santa Rosa Twp	87	318
Frank K	23	m	w	MS	Santa Barbara	San Buenaventura P	87	448
Freeman W	41	m	w	VT	Nevada	Grass Valley Twp	75	180
George	41	m	w	MA	Monterey	Monterey	74	356
Gran S	33	m	w	TN	Sonoma	Mendocino Twp	91	295

© 2001 by Heritage Quest. All rights reserved.

Name	Age	S	R	B-PL	County	Locale	Series M593 Roll	Pg
H A	49	m	w	RI	Tuolumne	Big Oak Flat P O	93	392
H S	31	m	w	AL	Sacramento	Natomas Twp	77	166
Heman	40	m	w	VT	Nevada	Grass Valley Twp	75	188
Henry	53	m	w	ENGL	San Francisco	1-Wd San Francisco	79	109
Henry	49	m	w	MA	Sacramento	4-Wd Sacramento	77	373
Henry	43	m	w	MD	San Joaquin	2-Wd Stockton	86	209
Henry C	34	m	w	MA	Los Angeles	Los Angeles	73	542
Hiram	51	m	w	OH	Marin	San Rafael	74	55
Hiram	39	m	w	PA	Nevada	Rough & Ready Twp	75	336
Hood	30	m	w	VA	Sonoma	Analy Twp	91	232
Ira	50	m	w	CANA	Solano	Vallejo	90	213
J	25	m	w	IREL	San Francisco	1-Wd San Francisco	79	65
J A	42	m	w	US	San Joaquin	Castoria Twp	86	9
J B	49	m	w	NY	San Joaquin	Douglas Twp	86	30
J B	35	m	w	NY	San Joaquin	3-Wd Stockton	86	230
J S	55	m	w	TN	San Joaquin	Douglas Twp	86	30
James	51	m	w	VA	San Joaquin	Douglas Twp	86	35
James Thomas	33	m	w	MO	Plumas	Plumas Twp	77	26
Jno	44	m	w	MA	Butte	Kimshew Tpw	70	86
Jo	15	m	w	ME	San Joaquin	Dent Twp	86	21
Joel S	42	m	w	CANA	Tulare	Venice Twp	92	278
John	37	m	w	ME	Monterey	San Benito Twp	74	383
John	36	m	w	PRUS	San Francisco	7-Wd San Francisco	81	209
Jose	40	m	w	CA	Santa Clara	Gilroy Twp	88	93
Joseph	40	m	w	SCOT	San Francisco	5-Wd San Francisco	81	35
Levi B	52	m	w	VT	Monterey	San Juan Twp	74	400
Lewis	40	m	w	IREL	Placer	Colfax P O	76	389
M E	53	f	w	IREL	Alameda	Alameda	68	9
M F	24	f	w	MA	Alameda	Oakland	68	237
Marcius	61	m	w	NY	Alameda	Brooklyn	68	26
Margaret	34	f	w	AUSL	San Joaquin	2-Wd Stockton	86	168
Martha	38	f	w	IREL	Plumas	Quartz Twp	77	40
Minna F	30	f	w	MA	San Francisco	8-Wd San Francisco	82	353
Morris	68	m	w	NH	Calaveras	Copperopolis P O	70	262
Norman	58	m	w	NY	Santa Barbara	Santa Barbara P O	87	471
Obidiah	53	m	w	NY	Santa Clara	Santa Clara Twp	88	159
Otto	42	m	w	AUST	Placer	Bath P O	76	460
Peter K	37	m	w	ME	Marin	San Rafael	74	56
Robert	39	m	w	NY	Calaveras	San Andreas P O	70	192
Sally	51	f	w	TN	Santa Clara	Fremont Twp	88	46
Silas	39	m	w	NY	Nevada	Nevada Twp	75	283
Susan	66	f	w	MA	Alameda	Oakland	68	216
T D	40	m	w	MA	Siskiyou	Scott Rvr Twp	89	604
Thomas	34	m	w	IREL	Nevada	Meadow Lake Twp	75	265
Thomas	33	m	w	ENGL	San Francisco	San Francisco P O	83	358
W B	32	m	w	MD	San Joaquin	2-Wd Stockton	86	209
Warden	54	m	w	MS	San Luis Obispo	Salinas Twp	87	290
William	32	m	w	NJ	Santa Clara	1-Wd San Jose	88	226
William	25	m	w	ENGL	Mariposa	Mariposa P O	74	130
William	24	m	w	MI	Sacramento	2-Wd Sacramento	77	235
William H	39	m	w	CT	Santa Cruz	Watsonville	89	374
Wm	27	m	w	ENGL	San Francisco	1-Wd San Francisco	79	70
Wm H	30	m	w	MA	Butte	Kimshew Tpw	70	78
Zylpha	15	f	w	CA	Amador	Volcano P O	69	381
AUSTON								
James T	29	m	w	MO	Monterey	Castroville Twp	74	329
AUTENRIETH								
Lewis	38	m	w	FRAN	Siskiyou	Yreka	89	659
Sarah	49	f	w	IREL	Siskiyou	Yreka	89	657
AUTHEMAN								
Aug	34	m	w	FRAN	Tuolumne	Sonora P O	93	320
AUTREY								
William	64	m	w	SC	Nevada	Grass Valley Twp	75	182
AUZERAIS								
Edward	44	m	w	FRAN	Santa Clara	1-Wd San Jose	88	264
John	48	m	w	FRAN	Santa Clara	1-Wd San Jose	88	264
AUZZINI								
John	26	m	w	SWIT	Marin	San Antonio Twp	74	61
AVADGA								
Jose	37	m	w	CHIL	Amador	Sutter Crk P O	69	401
AVALA								
Angelo	23	m	w	ITAL	San Francisco	San Francisco P O	80	483
Ascension	52	f	w	CA	Santa Barbara	San Buenaventura P	87	428
Ramon	58	m	w	MEXI	Santa Barbara	Santa Barbara P O	87	454
W S	30	m	w	PORT	Amador	Jackson P O	69	343
AVALOS								
Escoba	16	m	w	MEXI	San Francisco	San Francisco P O	80	339
Guadalupe	42	m	w	MEXI	Santa Clara	2-Wd San Jose	88	308
Hosea	38	f	w	MEXI	San Francisco	San Francisco P O	80	342
Manilo	46	f	w	MEXI	San Francisco	San Francisco P O	80	476
Quesman	50	m	w	MEXI	San Francisco	San Francisco P O	80	476
AVANA								
Joseph	30	m	w	MEXI	Tuolumne	Chinese Camp P O	93	387
AVANCENO								
Nicoli	25	m	w	ITAL	El Dorado	Diamond Springs Tw	72	29
AVANNALUS								
J	18	m	w	MEXI	Alameda	Oakland	68	229
AVARA								
Antone	30	m	w	PORT	Alameda	Washington Twp	68	299
Jasa	30	m	w	PORT	Alameda	Washington Twp	68	299
AVARANA								
Jose	35	m	w	CA	Contra Costa	San Pablo Twp	71	359
AVARDO								
Domingo	22	m	i	CA	Inyo	Lone Pine Twp	73	334
AVAREZ								
Antonio	32	m	w	MEXI	Marin	San Rafael Twp	74	42

Name	Age	S	R	B-PL	County	Locale	Series M593 Roll	Pg
AVARIL								
Santiago	55	m	w	CA	San Diego	San Luis Rey	78	514
AVARISTO								
Jose	30	m	w	MEXI	San Joaquin	Douglas Twp	86	39
AVARUS								
Marcelius	45	m	w	CHIL	Santa Barbara	Santa Barbara P O	87	457
Seriaca	45	f	i	CA	Santa Barbara	Santa Barbara P O	87	457
AVEGIO								
Nicholas	39	m	w	ITAL	Calaveras	San Andreas P O	70	203
AVEL								
Francisco	49	m	w	MEXI	Monterey	Alisal Twp	74	295
AVELAR								
James	25	m	w	AZOR	San Francisco	1-Wd San Francisco	79	130
AVELINE								
L D	48	m	w	FRAN	San Francisco	3-Wd San Francisco	79	303
AVELLANO								
Juan	60	m	w	CHIL	Contra Costa	Martinez P O	71	452
AVEMENDO								
Angelo	29	m	w	ITAL	Calaveras	San Andreas P O	70	176
AVERDALE								
Michael	22	m	w	PRUS	San Francisco	San Francisco P O	85	773
AVERETA								
Leonard	20	m	w	PORT	Alameda	Washington Twp	68	273
AVERHORME								
Peter	36	m	w	WURT	Fresno	Millerton P O	72	152
AVERILL								
Alfred	25	m	w	OR	Los Angeles	Los Nietos Twp	73	580
Anson	45	m	w	ME	San Francisco	8-Wd San Francisco	82	423
C R	20	f	w	NY	San Francisco	San Francisco P O	85	779
Charles	37	m	w	NH	Calaveras	Copperopolis P O	70	250
H S	40	m	w	NJ	Amador	Ione City P O	69	351
I M	47	m	w	MA	Santa Clara	Gilroy Twp	88	71
J H M	43	m	w	TN	Monterey	Alisal Twp	74	296
Jackson L	45	m	w	NY	San Francisco	San Francisco P O	83	28
Volney	23	m	w	VT	Santa Clara	Redwood Twp	88	132
Wales	33	m	w	VT	Santa Clara	1-Wd San Jose	88	261
William E	44	m	w	ME	Amador	Jackson P O	69	342
AVERILLE								
Henry	24	m	w	FRAN	San Francisco	8-Wd San Francisco	82	352
AVERILLO								
Dolores	38	f	w	MEXI	Calaveras	San Andreas P O	70	207
AVERNA								
Francisco	32	m	w	CHIL	Calaveras	San Andreas P O	70	210
AVERNOISE								
Francis	45	m	w	CHIL	Calaveras	San Andreas P O	70	186
AVERON								
Joseph	42	m	w	FRAN	Santa Cruz	Soquel Twp	89	438
AVERRETT								
Albert E	24	m	w	GA	Santa Cruz	Watsonville	89	368
AVERSIA								
Anidito	43	m	w	CHIL	Calaveras	San Andreas P O	70	210
AVERY								
Able	55	m	w	NY	Placer	Colfax P O	76	391
Alfred	24	m	w	IL	Los Angeles	Los Nietos Twp	73	577
Ambrose G	26	m	w	NY	Yolo	Washington Twp	93	537
Benjamin	29	m	w	MI	Placer	Cisco P O	76	495
Benjamin P	41	m	w	NY	San Francisco	San Francisco P O	83	195
Chas S	35	m	w	NY	Butte	Chico Twp	70	38
Clark	42	m	w	NH	San Francisco	San Francisco P O	85	756
Dean R	36	m	w	CT	San Francisco	San Francisco P O	83	169
E W	60	m	w	NJ	Nevada	Nevada Twp	75	276
Edwd C	45	m	w	MA	San Francisco	1-Wd San Francisco	79	93
Elihu	43	m	w	CT	Monterey	Monterey Twp	74	346
Elizabeth	61	f	w	OH	San Mateo	Pescadero P O	87	410
Francis	34	m	w	OH	San Francisco	8-Wd San Francisco	82	406
Frank	28	m	w	IA	Sacramento	4-Wd Sacramento	77	345
Geo	35	m	w	ME	San Joaquin	Dent Twp	86	21
George H	40	m	w	ME	Stanislaus	Empire Twp	92	38
George R	40	m	w	IA	San Mateo	Pescadero P O	87	410
H	3	f	w	CA	San Francisco	San Francisco P O	85	828
Henery	29	m	w	ME	San Francisco	7-Wd San Francisco	81	189
Henry	7	m	w	CA	San Francisco	San Francisco P O	85	826
Henry R	42	m	w	NY	Contra Costa	Martinez P O	71	379
Ira	32	m	w	ME	Placer	Blue Canyon P O	76	418
J H	70	m	w	NH	Del Norte	Smith Rvr Twp	71	479
J M	36	m	w	MI	Sacramento	3-Wd Sacramento	77	308
James	53	m	w	CT	San Francisco	11-Wd San Francisc	84	686
James	32	m	w	IREL	Los Angeles	Los Nietos Twp	73	584
James M	35	m	w	IN	Santa Cruz	Santa Cruz Twp	89	400
Jesse	23	m	w	ME	San Joaquin	Dent Twp	86	21
John W	61	m	w	ME	Sacramento	2-Wd Sacramento	77	237
Mathew F	26	m	w	IA	San Mateo	Half Moon Bay P O	87	403
Minnie	8	f	w	CA	San Francisco	San Francisco P O	85	826
Oliver	84	f	w	VT	Yolo	Buckeye Twp	93	408
Peter	64	m	w	ME	Calaveras	Copperopolis P O	70	257
Robt	35	m	w	ME	San Francisco	8-Wd San Francisco	82	353
Ross	37	m	w	NY	San Francisco	11-Wd San Francisc	84	577
Samuel D	41	m	w	VT	Nevada	Grass Valley Twp	75	143
Sarah J	35	f	w	ME	Sacramento	2-Wd Sacramento	77	239
William	68	m	w	ENGL	Sacramento	2-Wd Sacramento	77	206
William	21	m	w	NY	Contra Costa	Martinez P O	71	374
AVES								
Clouze	35	m	w	SHOL	San Mateo	Half Moon Bay P O	87	403
AVESENTIA								
Avela	38	m	w	MEXI	Santa Clara	2-Wd San Jose	88	315
AVEY								
Jno C	30	m	w	ENGL	Butte	Hamilton Twp	70	71

© 2001 by Heritage Quest. All rights reserved.

Name	Age	S	R	B-PL	County	Locale	Roll	Pg
AVIAS								
Barnardino	26	m	w	CA	Santa Clara	Gilroy Twp	88	107
Casons	40	m	w	MEXI	Marin	San Rafael Twp	74	42
AVICHE								
Francisco	32	f	w	CA	Los Angeles	Los Angeles	73	514
AVILA								
Francisco	43	m	w	CA	Santa Clara	Santa Clara Twp	88	158
Gabriel	55	m	w	FRAN	Monterey	Pajaro Twp	74	369
Mary	13	f	w	CA	Santa Clara	Santa Clara Twp	88	157
Ramon	49	m	w	MEXI	Monterey	Alisal Twp	74	289
Salena	16	f	w	MEXI	Santa Clara	1-Wd San Jose	88	264
AVILLA								
Jose	16	m	i	CA	San Luis Obispo	San Luis Obispo Tw	87	302
Jose A	36	m	w	CA	San Luis Obispo	San Luis Obispo Tw	87	302
Miguel	62	m	w	CA	San Luis Obispo	San Luis Obispo Tw	87	297
San Fana	30	m	w	CA	San Luis Obispo	San Luis Obispo Tw	87	297
AVILLO								
Louisa	3	f	w	CA	San Francisco	San Francisco P O	80	418
AVINDRIAL								
Jesus	41	m	w	MEXI	Mariposa	Mariposa P O	74	110
AVIONER								
John	26	m	w	SWIT	San Francisco	San Francisco P O	80	538
AVIS								
Jacob	38	m	w	DENM	Alameda	Washington Twp	68	301
James	41	m	w	NJ	Amador	Jackson P O	69	335
John	48	m	w	CT	Los Angeles	Los Nietos Twp	73	581
John	38	m	w	BADE	Amador	Ione City P O	69	370
AVISAU								
Charles	42	m	w	FRAN	San Francisco	San Francisco P O	80	347
Charles	42	m	w	FRAN	San Francisco	San Francisco P O	80	348
AVISE								
Jesus	51	m	w	NJ	Los Angeles	Soledad Twp	73	630
AVISSEAU								
Charles	47	m	w	FRAN	San Francisco	8-Wd San Francisco	82	384
AVON								
John	27	m	w	ENGL	San Francisco	San Francisco P O	83	129
AVTIN								
Aug	56	m	w	FRAN	Butte	Ophir Twp	70	100
AVY								
Charles	40	m	w	FRAN	Monterey	San Juan Twp	74	385
AW								
Chow	26	m	c	CHIN	Colusa	Colusa	71	298
Chung	40	m	c	CHIN	Inyo	Cerro Gordo Twp	73	321
Hee	32	m	c	CHIN	Inyo	Lone Pine Twp	73	332
Kee	27	m	c	CHIN	Inyo	Lone Pine Twp	73	332
Mow	31	m	c	CHIN	Inyo	Cerro Gordo Twp	73	321
Sam	34	m	c	CHIN	Inyo	Independence Twp	73	328
AWARA								
Clement	27	m	w	CHIL	Fresno	Millerton P O	72	165
Jesus	21	m	w	MEXI	Santa Clara	Redwood Twp	88	127
AWATA								
Felecine	18	f	w	ITAL	San Francisco	2-Wd San Francisco	79	151
AWATI								
Francisco	27	m	w	ITAL	San Francisco	6-Wd San Francisco	81	124
AWE								
Cong	26	m	c	CHIN	Inyo	Independence Twp	73	326
John	25	m	w	MI	Santa Clara	Santa Clara Twp	88	163
Yon	28	m	c	CHIN	Inyo	Independence Twp	73	326
AWH								
Ah	32	m	c	CHIN	Nevada	Nevada Twp	75	298
AWROW								
Thos	25	m	w	ENGL	Sacramento	Center Twp	77	82
AWSLING								
Peter	43	m	w	FRAN	Butte	Wyandotte Twp	70	144
AX								
Cromwell	59	m	w	VA	Tulare	Tule Rvr Twp	92	262
AXE								
Frederick	29	m	w	PA	Humboldt	Eureka Twp	72	266
AXELL								
William	42	m	w	ENGL	Marin	Sausalito Twp	74	67
AXMAN								
Fred	25	m	w	BADE	San Francisco	1-Wd San Francisco	79	60
AXTELL								
Alexander	67	m	w	VT	Mendocino	Calpella Twp	74	189
David	53	m	w	OH	Yolo	Putah Twp	93	518
E	35	m	w	PA	Mendocino	Calpella Twp	74	189
Frank	35	m	w	MD	Sacramento	2-Wd Sacramento	77	248
Frank	30	m	w	IL	Sacramento	2-Wd Sacramento	77	220
J H	54	m	w	NJ	San Joaquin	2-Wd Stockton	86	176
Jane	57	f	w	PA	San Joaquin	2-Wd Stockton	86	165
John	25	m	w	IREL	San Francisco	7-Wd San Francisco	81	194
William	36	m	w	AR	Stanislaus	Empire Twp	92	64
Wm	20	m	w	IL	San Francisco	8-Wd San Francisco	82	359
AXTON								
Henry	41	m	w	KY	Humboldt	Eel Rvr Twp	72	246
John	21	m	w	IN	Humboldt	Eel Rvr Twp	72	246
AY								
Ah	27	m	c	CHIN	Sacramento	Granite Twp	77	138
Ah	19	m	c	CHIN	San Francisco	San Francisco P O	83	190
Ah Lee	23	m	c	CHIN	Calaveras	San Andreas P O	70	177
Lin	25	m	c	CHIN	Amador	Ione City P O	69	366
Nu	34	m	c	CHIN	El Dorado	Salmon Falls Twp	72	129
Yee	48	m	c	CHIN	Calaveras	San Andreas P O	70	199
AYALA								
Abran	28	m	w	CA	Santa Barbara	Santa Barbara P O	87	486
Apoliaro	51	m	w	CA	Santa Barbara	San Buenaventura P	87	441
Francisco	40	m	w	CA	Santa Barbara	San Buenaventura P	87	433
Francisco	30	m	w	MEXI	Santa Barbara	Las Cruces P O	87	515
Joaquina	59	f	w	CA	Santa Barbara	Santa Barbara P O	87	486
Jose M	63	m	w	CA	Santa Barbara	Santa Barbara P O	87	465
Jose M J	36	m	w	CA	Santa Barbara	Santa Barbara P O	87	481
Jose R	25	m	w	CA	Santa Barbara	San Buenaventura P	87	442
Juan P	55	m	w	CA	Santa Barbara	Santa Barbara P O	87	490
Maria A	68	f	w	CA	Santa Barbara	Santa Barbara P O	87	462
Marian	32	f	w	MEXI	Santa Clara	Almaden Twp	88	15
Mescala	23	m	w	CA	Santa Barbara	San Buenaventura P	87	442
Rafel	67	m	w	CA	Santa Barbara	Santa Barbara P O	87	485
Rafel	4	f	w	CA	Santa Barbara	Santa Barbara P O	87	485
Ramon	45	m	w	CA	Santa Barbara	San Buenaventura P	87	442
Ramon	30	m	w	CA	Santa Barbara	Santa Barbara P O	87	501
Ramon	23	m	w	CA	Santa Barbara	Santa Barbara P O	87	465
Ventura	37	m	w	CA	Santa Barbara	San Buenaventura P	87	442
Ventura	32	m	w	CA	Santa Barbara	San Buenaventura P	87	436
AYALER								
Gervasio	73	m	w	CA	Santa Barbara	Santa Barbara P O	87	456
AYARES								
James	66	m	w	IREL	San Francisco	11-Wd San Francisc	84	612
AYAZA								
Jose	21	m	w	CA	San Francisco	2-Wd San Francisco	79	183
AYDT								
Edelbert	26	m	w	PRUS	San Francisco	1-Wd San Francisco	79	63
AYE								
Ah	25	m	c	CHIN	Trinity	Lewiston Pct	92	212
Sung	18	m	c	CHIN	Sonoma	Petaluma Twp	91	342
AYECH								
Ennis	49	m	w	NORW	Plumas	Mineral Twp	77	20
AYELLA								
Raphael	50	m	w	CHIL	El Dorado	Diamond Springs Tw	72	34
AYER								
Abbie A	27	f	w	ME	San Mateo	San Mateo P O	87	357
Amos	50	m	w	MS	San Francisco	5-Wd San Francisco	81	9
Annenus S	35	m	w	OH	Yolo	Cottonwood Twp	93	467
Catherine	14	f	w	CA	San Joaquin	3-Wd Stockton	86	222
Charles	31	m	w	MA	Napa	Napa	75	15
Charles S	27	m	w	CANA	Monterey	San Juan Twp	74	398
Clarance	17	m	w	CA	Solano	Vallejo	90	191
Cyrus H	56	m	w	NH	Mendocino	Point Arena Twp	74	210
David W	24	m	w	VA	San Francisco	8-Wd San Francisco	82	335
Edward W	28	m	w	ME	Nevada	Little York Twp	75	245
Isaac	36	m	w	ME	San Francisco	2-Wd San Francisco	79	281
Jas	31	m	w	IREL	San Francisco	7-Wd San Francisco	81	266
Mary	50	f	w	KY	San Bernardino	San Bernardino Twp	78	436
Orvill F	37	m	w	OH	Yolo	Cottonwood Twp	93	467
Oscar F	48	m	w	PA	San Francisco	5-Wd San Francisco	81	17
Samuel F	30	m	w	CANA	Santa Clara	Milpitas Twp	88	110
Tigman	32	m	w	CANA	Sacramento	Georgianna Twp	77	131
Washington	47	m	w	MA	San Francisco	5-Wd San Francisco	81	1
AYERES								
John	45	m	w	IN	Fresno	Kings Rvr P O	72	211
AYERS								
A T	39	m	w	OH	San Joaquin	Elkhorn Twp	86	65
Bonauchi	47	m	w	CT	Sacramento	2-Wd Sacramento	77	247
Charles	34	m	w	VA	San Diego	Warners Rancho Dis	78	529
Charles	18	m	w	MA	Marin	San Rafael Twp	74	43
Charles L	50	m	w	ENGL	Butte	Ophir Twp	70	95
D	45	m	w	MA	San Joaquin	Elliott Twp	86	72
Daniel	32	m	w	MA	San Francisco	San Francisco P O	83	260
David	41	m	w	IREL	Sonoma	Petaluma Twp	91	359
David M	35	m	w	OH	Contra Costa	Martinez P O	71	375
Elijah S	61	m	w	NJ	Santa Cruz	Watsonville	89	368
Geo	22	m	w	CHIL	Yuba	Marysville	93	604
George	22	m	w	WI	San Francisco	8-Wd San Francisco	82	309
Humphrey	40	m	w	ME	San Francisco	San Francisco P O	85	856
Irving	37	m	w	NY	Siskiyou	Surprise Valley Tw	89	638
J A M	44	m	w	CT	Tuolumne	Big Oak Flat P O	93	393
James	52	m	w	NH	San Joaquin	Elliott Twp	86	73
Joseph	18	m	w	MO	Butte	Chico Twp	70	55
Joshua	34	m	w	IL	San Francisco	11-Wd San Francisc	84	441
Levi	65	m	w	NY	Nevada	Bloomfield Twp	75	98
Lorenzo	38	m	w	MA	Sonoma	Salt Point	91	386
Margaret	13	f	w	MO	Sonoma	Mendocino Twp	91	302
Mary	51	f	w	MD	San Francisco	San Francisco P O	83	84
Mary O	33	f	w	CHIL	Sacramento	2-Wd Sacramento	77	247
Robert	44	m	w	IREL	Santa Barbara	San Buenaventura P	87	444
W W	42	m	w	TN	Sutter	Nicolaus Twp	92	114
William	68	m	w	IREL	Santa Barbara	San Buenaventura P	87	434
William	45	m	w	IREL	Sonoma	Petaluma Twp	91	359
William	34	m	w	IREL	San Francisco	11-Wd San Francisc	84	706
William	29	m	w	ENGL	Solano	Silveyville Twp	90	89
William O	52	m	w	CT	San Francisco	San Francisco P O	83	261
William W	32	m	w	IA	Santa Cruz	Watsonville	89	368
AYHENS								
Auguste	45	m	w	FRAN	San Francisco	San Francisco P O	83	63
AYLER								
Charles F	40	m	w	NY	El Dorado	Coloma Twp	72	4
Edward	30	m	w	IN	San Francisco	7-Wd San Francisco	81	188
AYLES								
Stephen	46	m	w	ENGL	Klamath	South Fork Twp	73	383
AYLESWORTH								
John W	43	m	w	PA	Santa Cruz	Santa Cruz	89	404
AYLETT								
Alice	12	f	w	CA	San Francisco	8-Wd San Francisco	82	335
AYLLON								
Facundo	40	m	w	MEXI	Los Angeles	San Juan Twp	73	625

Series M593

© 2001 by Heritage Quest. All rights reserved.

California 1870 Census

Name	Age	S	R	B-PL	County	Locale	Series M593 Roll	Pg
Trinidad	25	m	w	MEXI	Los Angeles	Santa Ana Twp	73	616
AYLSWORTH								
Eibert	45	m	w	NY	San Diego	San Diego	78	503
AYLWARD								
John	29	m	w	IREL	Alameda	Washington Twp	68	290
AYLWIN								
F S	22	m	w	VA	Solano	Vallejo	90	202
AYN								
Lee	16	f	c	CHIN	Sacramento	1-Wd Sacramento	77	191
AYNLAR								
Dolores	25	f	w	CA	Los Angeles	Los Angeles	73	511
AYOLA								
Julia	19	f	w	CAME	San Francisco	San Francisco P O	80	539
AYRBALLA								
Santos	80	m	w	MEXI	Los Angeles	Santa Ana Twp	73	615
AYRE								
Henry	29	m	w	ME	Santa Clara	2-Wd San Jose	88	324
John	35	m	w	ENGL	Kern	Havilah P O	73	340
AYREN								
William	44	m	w	SWED	El Dorado	Placerville Twp	72	104
AYRES								
Alexander	38	m	w	IL	Sonoma	Petaluma Twp	91	323
Andrew	24	m	w	IL	Santa Barbara	San Buenaventura P	87	436
David W	37	m	w	IL	Mendocino	Round Valley Twp	74	216
Emma	37	f	w	NY	San Francisco	8-Wd San Francisco	82	305
Franklin	44	m	w	MA	Stanislaus	Empire Twp	92	61
J W	45	m	w	MD	San Francisco	8-Wd San Francisco	82	365
James M	33	m	w	TN	El Dorado	Mud Springs Twp	72	84
Janes	56	f	w	NY	Sacramento	4-Wd Sacramento	77	361
Jasper N	29	m	w	IA	Santa Cruz	Watsonville	89	377
Maria	26	f	w	ENGL	San Mateo	Redwood Twp	87	365
Maria A	24	f	w	NH	Sacramento	Franklin Twp	77	105
Mary	40	f	w	NY	San Francisco	8-Wd San Francisco	82	427
Matthias W	42	m	w	CT	Santa Clara	Alviso Twp	88	22
Meriner	27	m	w	CANA	San Mateo	Woodside P O	87	386
Thomas	33	m	w	IREL	Stanislaus	Branch Twp	92	5
W H	40	m	w	VT	Solano	Vallejo	90	182
William	31	m	w	TN	Kern	Havilah P O	73	339
AYRIS								
Charles	41	m	w	ENGL	San Mateo	Redwood Twp	87	366
AYRS								
N B	57	m	w	NY	Merced	Snelling P O	74	250
AYTMAN								
George	37	m	w	BADE	Amador	Sutter Crk P O	69	398
AYUS								
Obed	42	m	w	ME	Contra Costa	Martinez P O	71	451
AYWAITE								
Joe P	31	m	w	PORT	Marin	Sausalito Twp	74	68
AZANCIVIA								
Ancelnes	52	m	w	CHIL	Plumas	Rich Bar Twp	77	8
AZBELL								
Jasper	22	m	w	MO	Santa Barbara	San Buenaventura P	87	429
John	37	m	w	MO	Santa Barbara	San Buenaventura P	87	429
Wm T	39	m	w	IL	Santa Barbara	San Buenaventura P	87	429
AZBERGER								
Charles	41	m	w	BAVA	San Francisco	San Francisco P O	80	470
AZELAR								
Ignacio	56	m	w	MEXI	Plumas	Mineral Twp	77	20
AZESTASES								
Manuel	52	m	w	MEXI	San Diego	Fort Yuma Dist	78	463
AZEVEDO								
John J	27	m	w	SCOT	Siskiyou	Scott Valley Twp	89	611
AZINI								
Jaco	25	m	w	SWIT	Marin	Nicasio Twp	74	15
AZLE								
John	36	m	w	PRUS	El Dorado	Greenwood Twp	72	51
AZONE								
Lo	25	m	w	MEXI	Alameda	Alameda	68	10
AZPELL								
Thomas F	42	m	w	PA	Klamath	Camp Gaston	73	372
AZUINGA								
Jacinto	60	f	w	CA	Santa Cruz	Pajaro Twp	89	357
AZULIM								
Jesus	30	m	w	MEXI	San Diego	Coronado	78	466
AZWAITE								
Frank	20	m	w	AZOR	Marin	Sausalito Twp	74	71
BA								
Cee	30	m	c	CHIN	Yuba	Marysville	93	629
Kow Ney	34	m	c	CHIN	Siskiyou	Hamburg Twp	89	597
Po	65	m	c	CHIN	El Dorado	Mud Springs Twp	72	90
BAA								
---	30	m	c	CHIN	Siskiyou	Cottonwood Twp	89	592
---	27	m	c	CHIN	Siskiyou	Hamburg Twp	89	596
BAAB								
Conrab	38	m	w	BAVA	Amador	Ione City P O	69	357
BAACK								
Fred	38	m	w	PRUS	Solano	Vacaville Twp	90	131
BAALAM								
Alfred	30	m	w	KY	Tulare	Farmersville Twp	92	250
Edwin	27	m	w	AR	Tulare	Farmersville Twp	92	241
Francis	23	m	w	KY	Tulare	Farmersville Twp	92	241
George	64	m	w	ENGL	Tulare	Farmersville Twp	92	250
BAALMOOS								
M	35	m	w	CA	San Bernardino	San Bernardino Twp	78	439
BAAS								
Charles	38	m	w	PRUS	San Francisco	San Francisco P O	80	472
Chester	42	m	b	NY	San Francisco	San Francisco P O	80	398
BABACOCK								
Robert	24	m	w	MO	Santa Barbara	Arroyo Burro P O	87	509
BABB								
George	45	m	w	ME	Plumas	Goodwin Twp	77	5
L H	51	m	w	NH	Yuba	Marysville	93	634
Lyman	22	m	w	ME	Alameda	Washington Twp	68	281
Nathaniel	34	m	w	ME	Alameda	Washington Twp	68	281
Richard	43	m	w	KY	San Diego	Poway Dist	78	482
Soloman	38	m	w	OH	Plumas	Quartz Twp	77	36
BABBE								
Frederick	46	m	w	DENM	Contra Costa	Martinez P O	71	404
BABBET								
Ruth	26	f	w	PRUS	Yolo	Cache Crk Twp	93	434
William	52	m	w	IL	San Mateo	Half Moon Bay P O	87	400
BABBETT								
Columbus	33	m	w	IL	Solano	Silveyville Twp	90	76
Henry	43	m	w	MA	Sacramento	2-Wd Sacramento	77	244
BABBI								
John	40	m	w	PORT	San Francisco	2-Wd San Francisco	79	286
BABBITT								
C A	37	m	w	NY	Lake	Upper Lake	73	413
D	25	m	w	MO	Calaveras	Copperopolis P O	70	235
Jane	16	f	w	CANA	San Francisco	8-Wd San Francisco	82	481
BABBLE								
Kate	22	f	w	PRUS	San Francisco	11-Wd San Francisc	84	665
BABCOCK								
Aaron	61	m	w	VT	Santa Clara	San Jose Twp	88	179
Albert	19	m	w	ME	San Francisco	8-Wd San Francisco	82	298
Amanda	64	f	w	NY	Alameda	Brooklyn	68	31
Annie	30	f	w	IREL	San Francisco	6-Wd San Francisco	81	40
B E	46	m	w	RI	San Francisco	San Francisco P O	85	855
Charles M	44	m	w	PA	Plumas	Plumas Twp	77	28
Chas	36	m	w	NY	San Joaquin	Elkhorn Twp	86	61
Chester	43	m	w	PA	Yuba	North East Twp	93	645
E R	39	m	w	ME	Yuba	Marysville	93	612
Ethan	41	m	w	NY	Stanislaus	Empire Twp	92	53
F A	51	m	w	NJ	Nevada	Nevada Twp	75	303
Geo	33	m	w	MA	Alameda	Oakland	68	234
George	38	m	w	NY	Alameda	Brooklyn	68	29
George	30	m	w	OH	San Francisco	11-Wd San Francisc	84	564
George	15	m	w	NY	Solano	Maine Prairie Twp	90	50
H C	40	m	w	NY	Humboldt	Table Bluff Twp	72	306
H C	30	m	w	OH	Alameda	Oakland	68	234
H E	50	m	w	PA	Sacramento	4-Wd Sacramento	77	376
H T	22	f	w	MI	Amador	Jackson P O	69	319
Henry	45	m	w	LA	San Francisco	7-Wd San Francisco	81	283
Henry	33	m	w	NY	San Francisco	San Francisco P O	83	259
Hora	11	f	w	CA	Sonoma	Santa Rosa	91	396
Isaac N	41	m	w	RI	Sacramento	American Twp	77	67
J F	25	m	w	CANA	San Joaquin	1-Wd Stockton	86	134
J T	50	m	w	NY	San Francisco	San Francisco P O	83	288
Jacob	52	m	w	OH	Butte	Ophir Twp	70	111
James	45	m	w	OH	Butte	Ophir Twp	70	111
James H	29	m	w	IN	Mendocino	Ukiah Twp	74	238
John	47	m	w	NY	San Francisco	6-Wd San Francisco	81	96
Joseph	56	m	w	OH	Amador	Ione City P O	69	357
Leonard	44	m	w	NY	Yolo	Grafton Twp	93	482
M D	52	m	w	NY	Monterey	San Juan Twp	74	400
M J	56	f	w	CT	Alameda	Oakland	68	195
Mart	51	m	w	PA	Sacramento	San Joaquin Twp	77	405
Melisa	43	f	w	NY	Solano	Maine Prairie Twp	90	54
Milan	54	m	w	OH	Butte	Ophir Twp	70	111
Milton S	26	m	w	OH	Shasta	Shasta P O	89	463
Nancy	74	f	w	VA	Butte	Ophir Twp	70	111
Nathan J	41	m	w	NY	San Luis Obispo	Santa Rosa Twp	87	320
Pardon	55	m	w	VT	Santa Barbara	Arroyo Burro P O	87	509
Richard	33	m	w	IN	Mendocino	Sanel Twp	74	227
Riley	45	m	w	MA	San Francisco	6-Wd San Francisco	81	89
Robert	25	m	w	MO	Santa Barbara	Arroyo Grande P O	87	508
S	40	f	w	NY	Solano	Vallejo	90	193
Sherman	35	m	w	PA	Calaveras	San Andreas P O	70	191
Washington	38	m	w	NY	Santa Clara	Fremont Twp	88	47
Wm	38	m	w	NY	Yuba	Marysville	93	595
Wm F	40	m	w	MA	San Francisco	7-Wd San Francisco	81	283
BABEL								
Bridget A	38	f	w	IREL	Nevada	Meadow Lake Twp	75	246
Fredrick	52	m	w	BADE	Yolo	Merritt Twp	93	507
BABER								
A G	43	m	w	MO	Mendocino	Ukiah Twp	74	237
A J	40	m	w	IL	Alameda	Oakland	68	147
Ann	20	f	w	MO	Sonoma	Santa Rosa	91	429
Luella	17	f	w	MO	Sonoma	Santa Rosa	91	412
O	42	m	w	IN	Alameda	Oakland	68	164
BABET								
Levor	21	m	w	FRAN	San Francisco	11-Wd San Francisc	84	480
BABNER								
Elizabeth	42	f	w	HANO	San Francisco	7-Wd San Francisco	81	164
BABOKA								
Benina	37	f	w	MEXI	Mariposa	Mariposa P O	74	123
BABOVIC								
Christopher	29	m	w	AUST	Amador	Amador City P O	69	394
BABSON								
Martha	29	f	w	MA	Alameda	Oakland	68	198
Seth	41	m	w	ME	Sacramento	3-Wd Sacramento	77	282
BABTIST								
Jean	38	m	w	FRAN	San Joaquin	2-Wd Stockton	86	166

© 2001 by Heritage Quest. All rights reserved.

Name	Age	S	R	B-PL	County	Locale	Series M593 Roll	Pg
BABTISTA								
Juan	55	m	w	PERU	Butte	Kimshew Tpw	70	83
BABTISTE								
Juan	35	m	w	CA	San Diego	Warners Rancho Dis	78	530
BABTISTO								
Tenetto	38	f	w	CAME	Placer	Auburn P O	76	370
BABY								
David	35	m	w	MI	Contra Costa	San Pablo Twp	71	358
BAC								
Jow	33	m	c	CHIN	Trinity	Junction City Pct	92	208
BACA								
Custus	20	m	w	CA	Solano	Tremont Twp	90	28
Manuel	25	m	w	CA	San Bernardino	San Bernardino Twp	78	415
Pablo	24	m	w	NM	San Francisco	6-Wd San Francisco	81	78
BACALA								
Baptiste	30	m	w	SWIT	Plumas	Seneca Twp	77	51
BACALU								
L C	24	m	w	ITAL	Tuolumne	Big Oak Flat P O	93	395
BACCAGALUPA								
John	40	m	w	ITAL	Calaveras	San Andreas P O	70	178
BACCALAR								
Guttall	32	m	w	SWIT	Napa	Napa Twp	75	72
BACCALIO								
Antone	47	m	w	ITAL	Marin	Novato Twp	74	12
BACCHUS								
Kate	9	f	w	CA	Nevada	Grass Valley Twp	75	229
Lucretia	10	f	w	CA	Nevada	Grass Valley Twp	75	229
BACCIGALIE								
Antonio	30	m	w	ITAL	San Francisco	2-Wd San Francisco	79	232
BACCIGALUPI								
Antone	22	m	w	ITAL	Calaveras	San Andreas P O	70	160
Antonio	31	m	w	ITAL	San Francisco	2-Wd San Francisco	79	237
Joseph	35	m	w	ITAL	San Francisco	2-Wd San Francisco	79	256
BACCIGALUPO								
Giusep	47	m	w	ITAL	Calaveras	San Andreas P O	70	174
BACEGALUPI								
Andre	29	m	w	ITAL	San Francisco	3-Wd San Francisco	79	289
BACEGLUPI								
J	28	m	w	ITAL	Tuolumne	Big Oak Flat P O	93	395
BACH								
Adolph	18	m	w	BAVA	San Francisco	8-Wd San Francisco	82	438
Charles H	28	m	w	PRUS	Amador	Jackson P O	69	319
Dora	54	f	w	PRUS	San Francisco	San Francisco P O	80	358
Ferdinand	38	m	w	PRUS	Calaveras	San Andreas P O	70	199
Fredrick	39	m	w	PRUS	Sonoma	Petaluma Twp	91	311
Gee	43	m	c	CHIN	Plumas	Mineral Twp	77	23
Herman	17	m	w	PRUS	Los Angeles	Los Nietos Twp	73	587
John	45	m	w	HDAR	San Francisco	8-Wd San Francisco	82	392
John	35	m	w	HDAR	Nevada	Bridgeport Twp	75	102
John E	44	m	w	BAVA	Mariposa	Mariposa P O	74	129
Theresa	30	f	w	PRUS	San Francisco	7-Wd San Francisco	81	249
William	36	m	w	PRUS	Stanislaus	Buena Vista Twp	92	14
BACHA								
John	45	m	w	AUST	Tuolumne	Sonora P O	93	306
BACHAGALLOPO								
J	51	m	w	ITAL	Amador	Jackson P O	69	335
BACHART								
August	30	m	w	PRUS	San Francisco	2-Wd San Francisco	79	170
BACHAS								
---	35	m	w	PRUS	Monterey	Alisal Twp	74	299
BACHBELUTE								
Carlotta	18	f	w	CA	Santa Clara	Santa Clara Twp	88	146
King	35	m	w	AZ	Santa Clara	Santa Clara Twp	88	146
BACHCHEGOLDPAH								
Frank	32	m	w	ITAL	San Francisco	11-Wd San Francisc	84	701
BACHE								
Louis	65	m	w	PA	Sacramento	Sutter Twp	77	381
BACHECO								
Juan	75	m	w	CA	Santa Clara	San Jose Twp	88	195
BACHEGALUPE								
J	48	m	w	ITAL	Yuba	Marysville	93	616
BACHELDER								
Cleaveland	41	m	w	NY	Santa Clara	2-Wd San Jose	88	291
F J	34	m	w	ME	San Francisco	3-Wd San Francisco	79	308
Jas E	45	m	w	ME	Sonoma	Mendocino Twp	91	302
John	40	m	w	ME	Calaveras	San Andreas P O	70	212
John H	38	m	w	NH	Santa Cruz	Santa Cruz Twp	89	379
Jonathan B	44	m	w	VT	Plumas	Indian Twp	77	14
Levi L	51	m	w	ME	San Francisco	6-Wd San Francisco	81	130
Martha	65	f	w	ME	Sierra	Table Rock Twp	89	573
P	52	m	w	ME	Alameda	Oakland	68	189
P N	51	m	w	MA	Alameda	Oakland	68	226
T	46	m	w	ME	Alameda	Oakland	68	164
William	46	m	w	NH	Trinity	Weaverville Pct	92	227
BACHELDOR								
Joseph G	52	m	w	NH	San Mateo	San Mateo P O	87	352
BACHELOR								
David	50	m	w	MA	San Francisco	San Francisco P O	83	32
John	37	m	w	IL	El Dorado	Coloma Twp	72	10
Sam	29	m	w	MO	San Joaquin	2-Wd Stockton	86	206
Sarah	10	f	w	CA	San Francisco	San Francisco P O	83	32
BACHELVER								
Low	39	m	w	NY	Klamath	Trinidad Twp	73	392
BACHER								
Antoine	38	m	w	BADE	Plumas	Indian Twp	77	19
John H	22	m	w	PRUS	San Francisco	8-Wd San Francisco	82	408

Name	Age	S	R	B-PL	County	Locale	Series M593 Roll	Pg
BACHERE								
Takue	41	m	w	FRAN	San Francisco	San Francisco P O	80	535
BACHIES								
Charles	17	m	w	OR	San Francisco	2-Wd San Francisco	79	196
BACHMAN								
A	36	m	w	HANO	Klamath	Trinidad Twp	73	392
Alver	55	m	w	AUST	Trinity	Hayfork Valley	92	238
Henry	32	m	w	PA	Inyo	Lone Pine Twp	73	331
Henry	32	m	w	SWIT	Plumas	Mineral Twp	77	22
John H	55	m	w	NY	Calaveras	San Andreas P O	70	177
L	31	f	w	HANO	San Francisco	San Francisco P O	85	789
Leopold	19	m	w	BAVA	Alameda	Washington Twp	68	291
Nathan	60	m	w	TN	Fresno	Millerton P O	72	152
Wm	23	m	w	AR	Tehama	Tehama Twp	92	192
BACHNICH								
August	57	m	w	PRUS	Sacramento	Granite Twp	77	142
BACHNON								
John	45	m	w	SWIT	Alameda	Oakland	68	215
BACHO								
Wm	39	m	w	HANO	San Francisco	San Francisco P O	85	779
BACHTELL								
William L	25	m	w	MD	Nevada	Grass Valley Twp	75	147
BACHUCRAZ								
Claro	36	m	w	FRAN	Stanislaus	Branch Twp	92	9
BACHUS								
John	50	m	w	OH	Sacramento	Natomas Twp	77	168
Peter	51	m	w	PRUS	Mendocino	Point Arena Twp	74	206
BACIGALUPE								
Charles	23	m	w	ITAL	Mariposa	Mariposa P O	74	114
F	56	m	w	ITAL	Calaveras	Copperopolis P O	70	230
Francis	33	m	w	ITAL	Calaveras	San Andreas P O	70	176
BACIGALUPI								
Frances	48	m	w	ITAL	Calaveras	Copperopolis P O	70	245
John	31	m	w	ITAL	Calaveras	Copperopolis P O	70	244
Joseph	45	m	w	ITAL	Calaveras	San Andreas P O	70	206
Louis	16	m	w	NY	San Francisco	11-Wd San Francisc	84	586
BACILET								
William	53	m	w	FRAN	San Francisco	San Francisco P O	80	342
BACILUPI								
John	33	m	w	ITAL	Tuolumne	Columbia P O	93	345
BACK								
Ah	40	m	c	CHIN	Marin	Tomales Twp	74	85
Ah	32	f	c	CHIN	San Francisco	San Francisco P O	80	494
Ah	25	m	c	CHIN	San Francisco	1-Wd San Francisco	79	80
Ah	22	m	c	CHIN	Sacramento	1-Wd Sacramento	77	193
Ah	13	m	c	CHIN	Yuba	Marysville	93	610
C	38	m	w	WURT	Sierra	Downieville Twp	89	518
John Adam	61	m	w	FRAN	Amador	Fiddletown P O	69	433
Lyman L	45	m	w	VT	Sonoma	Petaluma Twp	91	311
BACKAR								
Christ	31	m	w	DENM	El Dorado	Salmon Falls Twp	72	130
BACKER								
C E	17	m	w	CA	Sutter	Sutter Twp	92	119
Henry	46	m	w	HANO	Sierra	Eureka Twp	89	524
John	21	m	w	PRUS	Kern	Havilah P O	73	350
Michl	40	m	w	PRUS	San Francisco	5-Wd San Francisco	81	3
William	45	m	w	HANO	San Francisco	6-Wd San Francisco	81	139
BACKERS								
Samuel	26	m	w	NY	San Francisco	San Francisco P O	80	358
BACKESTO								
John P	38	m	w	IN	Santa Clara	2-Wd San Jose	88	296
BACKHAUS								
Frank W	33	m	w	HANO	San Francisco	6-Wd San Francisco	81	78
BACKMAN								
Benj F	41	m	w	PA	Mariposa	Mariposa P O	74	123
C	40	m	w	PRUS	San Joaquin	2-Wd Stockton	86	205
Ellen	13	f	w	CA	Siskiyou	Surprise Valley Tw	89	642
BACKMOTT								
Richard	24	m	w	OH	Sacramento	San Joaquin Twp	77	407
BACKNELL								
H A	53	m	w	PA	Tuolumne	Big Oak Flat P O	93	391
BACKSTER								
Thos	33	m	w	IREL	San Francisco	1-Wd San Francisco	79	100
BACKUS								
Gurdon	49	m	w	VT	Napa	Napa	75	2
Herman	45	m	w	MA	Stanislaus	Empire Twp	92	35
J	45	m	w	NY	Alameda	Oakland	68	190
James	38	m	w	CT	Santa Barbara	Santa Barbara P O	87	472
John	35	m	w	LA	San Francisco	8-Wd San Francisco	82	343
Lucy	74	f	w	NH	San Francisco	San Francisco P O	85	728
O J	40	m	w	NY	Alameda	Oakland	68	215
Peter M	57	m	w	NY	San Francisco	6-Wd San Francisco	81	80
Richard	27	m	w	LA	San Francisco	8-Wd San Francisco	82	413
Thomas	64	m	w	PRUS	Tuolumne	Chinese Camp P O	93	382
BACKUST								
Peter	48	m	w	PRUS	Alameda	Oakland	68	140
BACLA								
Victor	21	m	w	SWIT	Plumas	Seneca Twp	77	48
BACLIAN								
Jacob	33	m	w	FRAN	San Francisco	1-Wd San Francisco	79	61
BACMASTER								
Fred	22	m	w	PA	Mono	Bridgeport P O	74	284
BACO								
Patrico	31	m	w	NM	Solano	Silveyville Twp	90	73
BACOGALUPI								
Dominic	38	m	w	ITAL	San Francisco	2-Wd San Francisco	79	180

© 2001 by Heritage Quest. All rights reserved.

Name	Age	S	R	B-PL	County	Locale	Roll	Pg
						Series M593		
BACON								
Alexander	31	m	w	NY	Santa Clara	Redwood Twp	88	129
Andrew J	20	m	w	MO	Stanislaus	Branch Twp	92	2
Asa	39	m	w	OH	Tuolumne	Columbia P O	93	338
B T	31	m	w	MO	Amador	Fiddletown P O	69	430
Charles	26	m	w	NJ	Santa Clara	Santa Clara Twp	88	163
Chas W	39	m	w	PA	Santa Barbara	San Buenaventura P	87	421
Clara	22	f	w	OH	Sutter	Yuba Twp	92	141
Deane	54	m	w	MA	San Francisco	11-Wd San Francisc	84	496
Edwin	42	m	w	MA	Stanislaus	Empire Twp	92	35
Ellen	29	f	w	DC	San Francisco	6-Wd San Francisco	81	122
Fielding	58	m	w	MO	Tulare	Venice Twp	92	274
Frank	33	m	w	PA	Santa Clara	2-Wd San Jose	88	296
Frank	23	m	w	NY	San Francisco	8-Wd San Francisco	82	347
George C	35	m	w	MA	San Francisco	6-Wd San Francisco	81	82
H D	51	m	w	MD	Alameda	Oakland	68	150
Henry	22	m	w	NZEA	San Francisco	San Francisco P O	85	848
Hiram	52	m	w	ME	El Dorado	Mud Springs Twp	72	77
J B	29	m	w	OH	Tuolumne	Sonora P O	93	310
J E	29	m	w	IA	Sutter	Butte Twp	92	91
J H	30	m	w	NY	Lake	Lower Lake	73	416
J H L	43	m	w	MA	Klamath	Orleans Twp	73	379
J S	45	m	w	NH	San Francisco	8-Wd San Francisco	82	310
Jacob	36	m	w	ME	Alameda	Oakland	68	203
James	50	m	w	MA	San Francisco	San Francisco P O	80	471
James	30	m	w	MO	Tulare	Venice Twp	92	278
John	39	m	w	PA	Tulare	Venice Twp	92	279
John	34	m	w	HANO	San Francisco	San Francisco P O	85	756
John	29	m	w	NY	Alameda	Oakland	68	176
John C	30	m	w	PA	Sacramento	2-Wd Sacramento	77	246
John D	57	m	w	TN	Tehama	Battle Crk Twp	92	158
John L	40	m	w	OH	Placer	Rocklin Twp	76	468
John W	38	m	w	CANA	Santa Clara	1-Wd San Jose	88	249
Joseph	29	m	w	MA	Alameda	Oakland	68	168
Louis S	56	m	w	FRAN	San Francisco	8-Wd San Francisco	82	366
Martin	32	m	w	ENGL	Tuolumne	Chinese Camp P O	93	386
Mary	27	f	w	ME	San Joaquin	3-Wd Stockton	86	228
Mary	20	f	w	CA	Santa Cruz	Santa Cruz Twp	89	386
Mary	10	f	w	CA	Fresno	Kings Rvr P O	72	203
Myron	49	m	w	IL	Monterey	San Benito Twp	74	382
Nellie	26	f	w	NY	San Francisco	San Francisco P O	85	714
O H	25	m	w	MA	San Francisco	San Francisco P O	85	867
Oscar	34	m	w	CT	Inyo	Independence Twp	73	327
P B	34	m	w	OH	Tuolumne	Columbia P O	93	351
Perces	29	f	w	AR	Tulare	Visalia Twp	92	281
Perris	20	f	w	AR	Fresno	Millerton P O	72	194
Samuel	37	m	w	MA	Contra Costa	Martinez P O	71	437
Sarah	44	f	w	IREL	San Francisco	7-Wd San Francisco	81	173
T F	35	m	w	NY	Alameda	Oakland	68	164
Thomas L	29	m	w	MO	Tulare	Venice Twp	92	273
Thos	34	m	w	AR	Fresno	Kings Rvr P O	72	214
Thos E	31	m	w	MO	Fresno	Millerton P O	72	188
Toydall	40	m	w	KY	Sutter	Sutter Twp	92	124
W F	26	m	w	IL	Alameda	Oakland	68	145
Walter	46	m	w	ENGL	San Joaquin	Castoria Twp	86	1
Warren M	40	m	w	NY	Sacramento	American Twp	77	67
William	63	m	w	KY	Tulare	Venice Twp	92	277
William	41	m	w	CANA	Placer	Lincoln P O	76	492
William	30	m	w	IREL	San Francisco	San Francisco P O	83	271
William J	41	m	w	IN	San Francisco	3-Wd San Francisco	79	327
BAD								
Ah	35	m	c	CHIN	Fresno	Millerton P O	72	201
BADAGUE								
Sebastion	43	m	w	SPAI	Yuba	Parks Bar Twp	93	649
BADANOL								
Julen	22	m	w	FRAN	San Francisco	San Francisco P O	83	350
BADARACA								
G B	42	m	w	ITAL	Amador	Sutter Crk P O	69	402
BADARACCO								
Jacoman	35	m	w	ITAL	Amador	Jackson P O	69	334
BADARACEO								
D	20	m	w	ITAL	Amador	Jackson P O	69	327
BADAROUS								
Helen F	15	f	w	CA	San Francisco	San Francisco P O	83	178
BADASET								
August	50	m	w	FRAN	Calaveras	San Andreas P O	70	216
BADDEN								
James	65	m	w	PA	Yuba	Slate Range Bar Tw	93	675
James	37	m	w	ENGL	Santa Clara	Redwood Twp	88	129
William	38	m	w	ENGL	Calaveras	San Andreas P O	70	217
BADDER								
Jonathan	34	m	w	ENGL	El Dorado	Salmon Falls Twp	72	132
Jules	48	m	w	MO	Nevada	Rough & Ready Twp	75	332
William	40	m	w	MO	Nevada	Rough & Ready Twp	75	333
BADDERLY								
Wm	31	m	w	ENGL	Napa	Napa	75	45
BADDLEY								
Henry J	31	m	w	ENGL	Napa	Napa	75	52
BADE								
Henry	30	m	w	HANO	San Francisco	San Francisco P O	83	81
Louis	44	m	w	HANO	San Francisco	11-Wd San Francisc	84	492
BADEAU								
Augustus	36	m	w	FRAN	Yuba	Parks Bar Twp	93	649
BADEL								
John L	29	m	w	OH	Inyo	Bishop Crk Twp	73	311
BADEMAN								
Charles	54	m	w	HANO	Mariposa	Mariposa P O	74	105
Herman	19	m	w	SHOL	Santa Cruz	Soquel Twp	89	446
BADEN								
Elisha A	32	m	w	TN	Plumas	Plumas Twp	77	33
Frederick	40	m	w	WURT	Nevada	Washington Twp	75	341
G F	40	m	w	WURT	Alameda	Oakland	68	214
Jacob	37	m	w	NORW	Contra Costa	San Pablo Twp	71	363
Luisa	30	f	w	PRUS	Monterey	Salinas Twp	74	309
Peter	34	m	w	PRUS	Butte	Hamilton Twp	70	61
Saml	35	m	w	MO	Santa Clara	Gilroy Twp	88	100
William J	30	m	w	LA	Yuba	Slate Range Bar Tw	93	678
BADENA								
James	29	m	w	ENGL	Amador	Amador City P O	69	392
BADER								
Albert	45	m	w	SWIT	Calaveras	San Andreas P O	70	185
Chas	48	m	w	PRUS	Butte	Kimshew Tpw	70	76
John	40	m	w	BAVA	Tuolumne	Chinese Camp P O	93	365
John	31	m	w	WURT	Colusa	Grand Island Twp	71	303
Josephine	23	f	w	BAVA	San Francisco	8-Wd San Francisco	82	467
Manuel	55	m	w	CHIL	El Dorado	Mountain Twp	72	67
Martha	14	f	w	CA	Calaveras	San Andreas P O	70	205
Mary	61	f	w	SWIT	Sacramento	San Joaquin Twp	77	404
Mathis	39	m	w	PRUS	Butte	Kimshew Tpw	70	76
Wm	28	m	w	PRUS	San Francisco	1-Wd San Francisco	79	70
BADGE								
Henry	25	m	w	NY	Contra Costa	Martinez P O	71	435
BADGELEY								
Charles	44	m	w	IREL	Santa Clara	2-Wd San Jose	88	335
James	42	m	w	IREL	Amador	Ione City P O	69	352
BADGELY								
Eugene	29	m	w	NY	San Francisco	San Francisco P O	83	298
BADGER								
Benjamin	24	m	w	IREL	San Francisco	11-Wd San Francisc	84	541
David	45	m	w	VT	Alameda	Eden Twp	68	71
Ella F	18	f	w	MA	San Francisco	8-Wd San Francisco	82	423
G W	43	m	w	MA	Sacramento	1-Wd Sacramento	77	175
H F	10	f	w	CA	Alameda	Oakland	68	258
Leroy	26	m	w	IN	Marin	Tomales Twp	74	83
M H	45	m	w	US	Sacramento	1-Wd Sacramento	77	185
Mary A	40	f	w	MA	San Mateo	Pescadero P O	87	411
Oliver	30	m	w	MA	San Francisco	San Francisco P O	83	145
Patk	30	m	w	IREL	Solano	Vallejo	90	173
Thomas	40	m	w	VA	Alameda	Brooklyn	68	23
William	45	m	w	MA	Alameda	Brooklyn Twp	68	54
William	39	m	w	ENGL	San Francisco	11-Wd San Francisc	84	541
Wm	22	m	w	IN	Sonoma	Santa Rosa	91	422
BADGET								
Ellen	36	f	w	NY	San Francisco	11-Wd San Francisc	84	679
BADGLEY								
Charles	29	m	w	NY	Santa Clara	2-Wd San Jose	88	317
O E	34	m	w	NY	Sierra	Forest	89	536
William H	40	m	w	NY	San Francisco	8-Wd San Francisco	82	380
Wm	60	m	w	NY	San Francisco	8-Wd San Francisco	82	357
BADIEN								
Sarah	50	f	w	IREL	San Francisco	San Francisco P O	83	414
BADILLA								
Tomasa	37	f	w	CA	Los Angeles	Los Angeles	73	521
BADILLO								
Felipe	36	m	w	CA	Santa Barbara	Santa Barbara P O	87	452
Indian	30	m	i	MEXI	Santa Barbara	San Buenaventura P	87	429
Jose F	27	m	w	CA	Santa Barbara	Santa Barbara P O	87	467
BADIT								
Sanprica	35	m	i	MEXI	Inyo	Lone Pine Twp	73	334
BADLAM								
Alex	61	m	w	MA	Napa	Napa	75	17
Alex	33	m	w	OH	San Francisco	6-Wd San Francisco	81	155
BADLEY								
Josephin	9	f	i	CA	Humboldt	South Fork Twp	72	301
Zeb	30	m	w	PA	Placer	Lincoln P O	76	492
Zephaniah	32	m	w	PA	Nevada	Rough & Ready Twp	75	324
BADLONG								
Jerome B	48	m	w	NY	Santa Cruz	Santa Cruz	89	404
BADNER								
Frances	17	f	w	AUST	San Francisco	San Francisco P O	85	817
BADO								
Chas	26	m	w	PRUS	San Francisco	8-Wd San Francisco	82	375
BADON								
William	45	m	w	IREL	Los Angeles	Los Angeles	73	522
BADRONT								
John	42	m	w	WURT	Calaveras	San Andreas P O	70	179
BADT								
Aaron	31	m	w	PRUS	Tehama	Tehama Twp	92	194
Alex	32	m	w	PRUS	San Francisco	8-Wd San Francisco	82	299
Morris	39	m	w	PRUS	San Francisco	8-Wd San Francisco	82	468
BADWHOPE								
Henry	42	m	w	HANO	San Francisco	11-Wd San Francisc	84	669
BADYN								
James	40	m	w	IREL	San Francisco	11-Wd San Francisc	84	466
BAECHTEL								
M	38	m	w	MD	Mendocino	Little Lake Twp	74	198
S S	42	m	w	MD	Mendocino	Little Lake Twp	74	200
BAEHR								
Walter	26	m	w	PRUS	San Francisco	San Francisco P O	80	344
BAEL								
Laurence	49	m	w	FRAN	Del Norte	Happy Camp Twp	71	468
BAENGON								
Louie	40	m	w	FRAN	Nevada	Nevada Twp	75	309

© 2001 by Heritage Quest. All rights reserved.

Name	Age	S	R	B-PL	County	Locale	Series M593 Roll	Pg
BAER								
Barnard	39	m	w	BAVA	Tulare	Visalia	92	296
Christ	23	m	w	DENM	Alameda	Eden Twp	68	59
Hannah	18	f	w	PRUS	San Francisco	8-Wd San Francisco	82	418
Henry	30	m	w	PRUS	Plumas	Washington Twp	77	56
Jacob	52	m	w	PRUS	Napa	Napa Twp	75	30
John	23	m	w	PRUS	Placer	Colfax P O	76	389
Manger	40	m	w	GERM	Tuolumne	Sonora P O	93	309
BAESE								
Patrick	5	m	w	CA	San Francisco	San Francisco P O	85	818
BAETTASS								
Peter	40	m	w	SHOL	Sonoma	Sonoma Twp	91	444
BAETY								
Adison	42	m	w	KY	Alameda	Eden Twp	68	66
BAETZ								
John	51	m	w	HDAR	San Francisco	San Francisco P O	83	163
BAFERMARCK								
C	40	m	w	PRUS	San Francisco	San Francisco P O	83	293
BAFFERT								
Peter	30	m	w	FRAN	Los Angeles	Los Angeles	73	552
BAFFO								
Giobatto	32	m	w	ITAL	Mariposa	Mariposa P O	74	94
BAG								
Ah	24	m	c	CHIN	Trinity	North Fork Twp	92	220
William	37	m	w	ENGL	Mariposa	Maxwell Crk P O	74	145
BAGALUPI								
Joseph	32	m	w	ITAL	Mariposa	Mariposa P O	74	121
BAGANENI								
Bat	33	m	w	ITAL	El Dorado	Diamond Springs Tw	72	29
BAGARIA								
Jerome	37	m	w	ITAL	Mariposa	Mariposa P O	74	91
BAGBY								
Edmund	52	m	w	IL	Monterey	Pajaro Twp	74	371
Richard A	50	m	w	VA	El Dorado	Mud Springs Twp	72	76
BAGEL								
Theodore	7	m	w	CA	San Francisco	San Francisco P O	80	416
BAGELEY								
William	22	m	w	MS	Sonoma	Petaluma Twp	91	336
BAGER								
Appolonio	31	f	w	MEXI	Contra Costa	Martinez P O	71	439
Samuel	48	m	w	NY	Santa Clara	Redwood Twp	88	119
BAGG								
William	36	m	w	IN	San Francisco	San Francisco P O	80	472
BAGGA								
Carl F	51	m	w	DENM	Alameda	Eden Twp	68	70
BAGGARO								
F	22	m	w	ITAL	San Francisco	3-Wd San Francisco	79	317
BAGGE								
E	42	m	w	DENM	Alameda	Oakland	68	193
Fredk C	28	m	w	EIND	San Francisco	San Francisco P O	85	724
Theo	49	m	w	DENM	Alameda	Oakland	68	220
BAGGS								
H C	50	m	w	MO	Lake	Kelsey Crk	73	402
Isaac	45	m	w	MD	San Francisco	San Francisco P O	83	404
Joseph	22	m	w	IL	Santa Clara	Gilroy Twp	88	83
Peter	25	m	w	SCOT	San Joaquin	Elkhorn Twp	86	66
Robt	20	m	w	OH	Yuba	Rose Bar Twp	93	662
Samuel	34	m	w	IA	Stanislaus	Branch Twp	92	2
Thomas	37	m	w	IREL	San Francisco	8-Wd San Francisco	82	396
Thomas	22	m	w	CANA	Marin	Point Reyes Twp	74	23
W M	47	m	w	MD	San Joaquin	1-Wd Stockton	86	120
BAGIN								
P	37	m	w	IREL	Lassen	Susanville Twp	73	440
BAGLEY								
Augustus L	40	m	w	ME	Nevada	Rough & Ready Twp	75	324
Bridget	23	f	w	IREL	San Francisco	San Francisco P O	83	239
Daniel	33	m	w	IREL	Colusa	Colusa Twp	71	276
David	48	m	w	LA	San Francisco	11-Wd San Francisc	84	500
Domenic	44	m	w	IREL	Contra Costa	Martinez P O	71	419
E M	29	m	w	ME	Monterey	Castroville Twp	74	336
Edward	64	m	w	RI	San Joaquin	Oneal Twp	86	103
Edward T	49	m	w	MO	Mendocino	Point Arena Twp	74	215
Eli	66	m	w	OH	Humboldt	Mattole Twp	72	284
Eli	20	m	w	IA	Humboldt	Mattole Twp	72	284
Hiram	46	m	w	KY	Mendocino	Round Valley Twp	74	216
Hudson W	33	m	w	ME	Alpine	Monitor P O	69	313
Jno W	42	m	w	NY	Sonoma	Mendocino Twp	91	302
Johanna	35	f	w	PA	San Francisco	San Francisco P O	83	203
John	79	m	w	IREL	San Francisco	11-Wd San Francisc	84	660
John	42	m	w	AR	Siskiyou	Butte Twp	89	584
John Sr	78	m	w	IREL	San Francisco	San Francisco P O	83	346
John W	35	m	w	NY	San Francisco	1-Wd San Francisco	79	54
Julia	19	f	w	IREL	San Francisco	6-Wd San Francisco	81	86
Luther	60	m	w	RI	Butte	Ophir Twp	70	106
Maggie	27	f	w	ENGL	San Francisco	5-Wd San Francisco	81	27
Newton	50	m	w	NY	Santa Barbara	San Buenaventura P	87	424
Paul	32	m	w	IREL	Colusa	Colusa Twp	71	277
Phebe	65	f	w	PA	Sonoma	Analy Twp	91	220
Richard	47	m	w	SWED	Plumas	Quartz Twp	77	43
Townsend	66	m	w	NY	San Francisco	San Francisco P O	83	168
W H	59	m	w	NH	Sacramento	3-Wd Sacramento	77	309
William	45	m	w	ME	Nevada	Eureka Twp	75	132
Wm	8	m	w	WA	San Francisco	San Francisco P O	85	800
Wm A	65	m	w	KY	Santa Clara	Gilroy Twp	88	82
Wm P	34	m	w	NY	San Francisco	11-Wd San Francisc	84	660
BAGLIN								
Tannie	10	f	w	CA	Colusa	Spring Valley Twp	71	337
BAGMAN								
Jacob	40	m	w	PRUS	San Francisco	San Francisco P O	85	765
John	46	m	w	PA	San Francisco	3-Wd San Francisco	79	308
BAGNAL								
James	27	m	w	ENGL	Sacramento	4-Wd Sacramento	77	367
BAGNALL								
Grace	38	f	w	IREL	San Francisco	1-Wd San Francisco	79	20
John D	46	m	w	MA	Santa Cruz	Santa Cruz	89	420
Richd	34	m	w	NY	San Francisco	1-Wd San Francisco	79	111
Timothy	45	m	w	IREL	San Francisco	1-Wd San Francisco	79	90
BAGNELL								
Cornelius	66	m	w	ENGL	Sacramento	4-Wd Sacramento	77	366
Cornelius	28	m	w	ENGL	Sacramento	4-Wd Sacramento	77	366
Eliza	42	f	w	NJ	San Francisco	San Francisco P O	83	220
Geo	50	m	w	IREL	Butte	Concow Twp	70	9
James	8	m	w	AL	San Francisco	11-Wd San Francisc	84	587
James	36	m	w	MO	Sutter	Sutter Twp	92	121
Joseph	41	m	w	UNKN	San Joaquin	2-Wd Stockton	86	173
BAGO								
Jose	33	m	w	MEXI	Stanislaus	Empire Twp	92	27
Otto	45	m	w	FRAN	Los Angeles	Los Angeles	73	560
BAGOR								
Henry C	49	m	w	NY	Inyo	Cerro Gordo Twp	73	323
BAGORT								
Elisha	27	m	w	MI	Inyo	Lone Pine Twp	73	331
BAGS								
Fannie	30	f	w	VA	San Francisco	7-Wd San Francisco	81	204
James	38	m	w	IREL	San Francisco	San Francisco P O	85	862
BAGSINE								
Rafell	28	m	w	ITAL	San Joaquin	Oneal Twp	86	119
BAGWELL								
Geo	38	m	w	NY	Sacramento	Lee Twp	77	159
J W	35	m	w	MO	Sutter	Sutter Twp	92	128
BAH								
Ah	30	m	c	CHIN	Marin	Tomales Twp	74	84
Ah	25	m	c	CHIN	Yolo	Grafton Twp	93	495
Ah	18	m	c	CHIN	Sonoma	Healdsburg & Mendo	91	278
Ah	18	m	c	CHIN	Yolo	Cache Crk Twp	93	445
On	26	m	c	CHIN	Marin	Novato Twp	74	11
Quoon	14	m	c	CHIN	San Francisco	11-Wd San Francisc	84	503
Tow	12	m	c	CHIN	San Francisco	San Francisco P O	85	877
Wan	18	m	c	CHIN	San Francisco	San Francisco P O	83	238
BAHAMS								
Daniel	30	m	w	NY	San Francisco	1-Wd San Francisco	79	71
BAHAN								
Bridget	35	f	w	IREL	San Francisco	San Francisco P O	85	822
Dennis	23	m	w	IREL	Fresno	Millerton P O	72	150
Martin V	26	m	w	VT	San Luis Obispo	Arroyo Grande Twp	87	274
BAHLAR								
Chas	48	m	w	PRUS	San Francisco	11-Wd San Francisc	84	663
BAHLER								
August	30	m	w	FRAN	San Francisco	San Francisco P O	80	478
BAHLS								
F W	29	m	w	PRUS	San Francisco	San Francisco P O	83	300
BAHM								
Erich	40	m	w	DENM	Nevada	Nevada Twp	75	274
BAHN								
David	26	m	w	IREL	Sierra	Gibson Twp	89	540
Frederick	45	m	w	HANO	Contra Costa	Martinez P O	71	391
Ludwick	26	m	w	BADE	Los Angeles	Los Angeles Twp	73	487
BAHNEY								
Wm H	45	m	w	OH	Tehama	Red Bluff	92	179
BAHO								
Andrew	46	m	w	FRAN	Klamath	Salmon Twp	73	387
BAHR								
Ferdinand	24	m	w	PRUS	San Francisco	2-Wd San Francisco	79	233
John	59	m	w	HANO	Santa Clara	1-Wd San Jose	88	276
Matilda	70	f	w	ENGL	San Francisco	11-Wd San Francisc	84	600
Michael	34	m	w	BAVA	Napa	Yountville Twp	75	89
BAHRENBURG								
J	51	m	w	HANO	Yuba	Linda Twp	93	554
BAHRS								
Andrew	37	m	w	HOLL	San Francisco	1-Wd San Francisco	79	124
BAHWELL								
Adam	38	m	w	HDAR	Tulare	Visalia Twp	92	281
BAICIGALLAPO								
John B	51	m	w	ITAL	Amador	Volcano P O	69	382
BAIER								
G C	38	m	w	BADE	Tuolumne	Sonora P O	93	303
BAIL								
John	40	m	w	ME	Inyo	Bishop Crk Twp	73	310
BAILARD								
Andrew	40	m	w	BADE	Santa Barbara	Santa Barbara P O	87	484
Mette	38	f	b	MO	Santa Barbara	Santa Barbara P O	87	484
BAILBEORDZ								
Jules	45	m	w	FRAN	Calaveras	San Andreas P O	70	216
BAILER								
John	51	m	w	PRUS	Santa Clara	1-Wd San Jose	88	257
BAILEY								
---	36	m	w	MO	Alameda	Oakland	68	245
A J	42	m	w	VT	El Dorado	Greenwood Twp	72	51
A J	40	m	w	VT	San Joaquin	Douglas Twp	86	30
A P	40	m	w	NY	Sacramento	3-Wd Sacramento	77	286
Ada A	28	f	w	VT	Santa Cruz	Santa Cruz	89	411
Alexander	73	m	w	KY	Santa Barbara	Santa Barbara P O	87	484
Alexr	35	m	w	NH	San Francisco	San Francisco P O	83	88
Amos J	37	m	w	NY	San Francisco	8-Wd San Francisco	82	334

© 2001 by Heritage Quest. All rights reserved.

Name	Age	S	R	B-PL	County	Locale	Roll	Pg
						Series M593		
Andrew	49	m	w	TN	Santa Clara	Santa Clara Twp	88	159
Ann	35	f	w	IREL	San Francisco	San Francisco P O	83	65
Anna	38	f	w	MA	San Francisco	8-Wd San Francisco	82	383
Augustus	40	m	w	NY	San Francisco	5-Wd San Francisco	81	10
Augustus	28	m	w	ME	Marin	Point Reyes Twp	74	22
B M	27	m	w	NY	San Francisco	7-Wd San Francisco	81	220
B R	43	m	w	TN	Santa Clara	Almaden Twp	88	18
Benjamin	70	m	w	MA	San Francisco	1-Wd San Francisco	79	129
Benjamin	35	m	w	ME	Mendocino	Big Rvr Twp	74	162
Bridget	25	f	w	IREL	San Francisco	11-Wd San Francisc	84	580
C H	41	m	w	MA	Santa Barbara	San Buenaventura P	87	435
C M	37	m	w	ME	Siskiyou	Klamath Twp	89	600
C P	28	m	w	WI	Monterey	Alisal Twp	74	290
Caleb	43	m	w	MO	Mendocino	Calpella Twp	74	181
Charles	32	m	w	MO	Tulare	Packwood Twp	92	257
Charles	32	m	w	NJ	Stanislaus	Empire Twp	92	44
Charles	29	m	w	NY	Stanislaus	Empire Twp	92	48
Charles	27	m	w	RI	San Francisco	San Francisco P O	83	253
Charles	24	m	w	SCOT	San Francisco	11-Wd San Francisc	84	518
Charles	24	m	w	NY	Alameda	Washington Twp	68	272
Charles G	44	m	w	NH	San Francisco	3-Wd San Francisco	79	323
Charles W	36	m	w	NY	Sutter	Nicolaus Twp	92	110
Chas	36	m	w	VA	Siskiyou	Scott Valley Twp	89	620
Chas	22	m	w	WI	Sacramento	4-Wd Sacramento	77	349
Chas O	32	m	w	VT	San Francisco	1-Wd San Francisco	79	103
D	14	m	w	CA	Solano	Benicia	90	20
D W	46	m	w	VT	Mendocino	Little Lake Twp	74	199
Daniel C	39	m	w	ME	Santa Clara	2-Wd San Jose	88	298
Darsy	24	f	w	AL	San Francisco	11-Wd San Francisc	84	611
David	61	m	w	NY	Santa Clara	1-Wd San Jose	88	242
David	24	m	w	VT	San Francisco	11-Wd San Francisc	84	646
Dennis	19	m	w	CANA	Santa Clara	Santa Clara Twp	88	159
Doctor B	39	m	w	TN	Santa Clara	Fremont Twp	88	47
E	17	m	w	MA	Solano	Vallejo	90	172
E F	20	m	w	ME	Merced	Snelling P O	74	252
Edw	23	m	w	IL	Tehama	Tehama Twp	92	191
Elbridge A	36	m	w	ME	Napa	Napa	75	38
Eliza	35	f	w	ENGL	San Francisco	11-Wd San Francisc	84	692
Elizabeth	16	f	w	NY	San Francisco	San Francisco P O	83	221
Ellen	16	f	w	CA	Alameda	Oakland	68	237
Elsie	73	f	w	AL	Marin	Tomales Twp	74	80
F C	32	m	w	IREL	Sacramento	1-Wd Sacramento	77	184
Frances	45	m	w	ITAL	San Francisco	1-Wd San Francisco	79	120
Francisco	25	m	w	GA	San Diego	Julian Dist	78	469
Frank	32	m	w	MA	San Francisco	8-Wd San Francisco	82	460
Fred	14	m	w	MA	Santa Cruz	Watsonville	89	374
Frederik E	52	m	w	VT	Santa Cruz	Santa Cruz	89	411
G W	35	m	w	KY	Sutter	Sutter Twp	92	120
Geo	55	m	w	PA	Solano	Vallejo	90	183
Geo	22	m	w	IN	Monterey	Monterey Twp	74	348
Geo E	14	m	w	CA	Alameda	Oakland	68	245
George	37	m	w	MO	Contra Costa	Martinez Twp	71	346
George	35	m	w	ENGL	San Francisco	3-Wd San Francisco	79	314
George	34	m	w	NY	Placer	Rocklin Twp	76	465
George	34	m	w	ENGL	Santa Clara	Fremont Twp	88	60
George	30	m	w	AUST	San Francisco	3-Wd San Francisco	79	298
George	28	m	w	NJ	Nevada	Meadow Lake Twp	75	249
George	24	m	w	ENGL	Nevada	Grass Valley Twp	75	217
George A	42	m	m	MA	Shasta	Shasta P O	89	462
George B	33	m	w	OH	El Dorado	Placerville	72	126
George K	29	m	w	ENGL	San Bernardino	San Bernardino Twp	78	415
H	49	m	b	VA	Amador	Sutter Crk P O	69	401
H	40	m	w	NY	Alameda	Murray Twp	68	119
H	35	m	w	OH	Solano	Vallejo	90	210
Hannibal	26	m	w	ENGL	Nevada	Grass Valley Twp	75	191
Hannibal	18	m	w	ENGL	Nevada	Grass Valley Twp	75	202
Henry	54	m	w	MO	Tulare	Visalia Twp	92	285
Henry	45	m	w	PRUS	San Francisco	San Francisco P O	85	744
Henry	28	m	w	NY	Solano	Vacaville Twp	90	126
Henry	27	m	w	ENGL	San Francisco	2-Wd San Francisco	79	213
Henry	26	m	w	MO	Fresno	Millerton P O	72	186
Henry	21	m	w	OH	Sacramento	Lee Twp	77	158
Henry	15	m	w	CA	San Francisco	11-Wd San Francisc	84	586
Hernan	23	m	w	NY	Alameda	Eden Twp	68	68
I F	40	m	w	VT	Alameda	Murray Twp	68	113
Ida Grey	24	f	w	PA	Santa Clara	1-Wd San Jose	88	245
Isaac L	40	m	w	ME	San Francisco	San Francisco P O	83	30
J E	33	m	w	NY	Alameda	Oakland	68	245
J L	45	m	w	ENGL	Tuolumne	Big Oak Flat P O	93	396
J R	50	m	w	KY	Lake	Big Valley	73	396
J R	40	m	w	NY	Lassen	Janesville Twp	73	434
Jacob	38	m	w	PA	San Francisco	7-Wd San Francisco	81	192
James	50	m	w	ENGL	Alameda	Brooklyn	68	24
James	44	m	w	IREL	El Dorado	Placerville	72	109
James	31	m	w	ENGL	San Francisco	1-Wd San Francisco	79	57
James	30	m	w	MA	San Francisco	8-Wd San Francisco	82	425
James	22	m	w	CANA	Alameda	Eden Twp	68	72
James	14	m	w	CA	San Francisco	11-Wd San Francisc	84	586
James B	24	m	w	MI	San Francisco	8-Wd San Francisco	82	405
James G	42	m	w	OH	El Dorado	Mud Springs Twp	72	84
Jefferson	42	m	w	OH	Santa Clara	Fremont Twp	88	42
Jerry	37	m	w	CT	San Joaquin	2-Wd Stockton	86	191
Jesse	17	f	w	ENGL	San Francisco	11-Wd San Francisc	84	494
Joel	40	m	w	ME	San Francisco	San Francisco P O	83	192
Johana	23	f	w	MA	Solano	Benicia	90	12
John	49	m	w	ENGL	Sonoma	Petaluma Twp	91	364
John	47	m	w	ENGL	Fresno	Millerton P O	72	167

Name	Age	S	R	B-PL	County	Locale	Roll	Pg
						Series M593		
John	45	m	w	NY	Contra Costa	Martinez P O	71	412
John	45	m	w	PA	San Francisco	8-Wd San Francisco	82	458
John	42	m	w	ENGL	Fresno	Millerton P O	72	166
John	41	m	w	ENGL	San Francisco	3-Wd San Francisco	79	323
John	22	m	w	IREL	Placer	Rocklin Twp	76	465
John A	44	m	w	MO	Tulare	Visalia Twp	92	286
John D	37	m	w	NY	Del Norte	Smith Rvr Twp	71	478
John E	25	m	w	MA	Marin	Nicasio Twp	74	18
John T	60	m	w	KY	Sacramento	Brighton Twp	77	79
Jonathan	33	m	w	MO	Sonoma	Analy Twp	91	245
Jos H	38	m	w	NY	Shasta	Shasta P O	89	452
Joseph	46	m	w	ME	Sacramento	4-Wd Sacramento	77	345
Juster	33	m	w	NY	Alameda	Washington Twp	68	283
L D	31	m	w	IL	Mendocino	Calpella Twp	74	186
Laurence H	61	m	w	VT	San Francisco	6-Wd San Francisco	81	37
Lewis	12	m	w	MA	Placer	Dutch Flat P O	76	404
Lewis N	31	m	w	KY	San Diego	San Diego	78	505
Lucinda A	16	f	w	CA	Shasta	Millville P O	89	492
Lucy	30	f	b	MA	Nevada	Nevada Twp	75	274
M O	56	m	w	ENGL	Tuolumne	Chinese Camp P O	93	375
Mark	45	m	w	MA	Sonoma	Petaluma Twp	91	336
Mark	36	m	w	NY	Tehama	Paskenta Twp	92	165
Mark B	30	m	w	GA	Stanislaus	Empire Twp	92	32
Martha	10	f	w	CA	Sutter	Vernon Twp	92	134
Martha D	30	f	w	IL	Santa Clara	2-Wd San Jose	88	327
Mary	30	f	w	KY	Stanislaus	Empire Twp	92	51
Mellissa	31	f	w	OH	Plumas	Seneca Twp	77	50
Michael	35	m	w	IREL	San Francisco	1-Wd San Francisco	79	93
Mind	26	m	w	VT	San Francisco	11-Wd San Francisc	84	684
Nathaniel	50	m	w	NJ	Nevada	Nevada Twp	75	275
Orian W	61	m	w	NC	Amador	Fiddletown P O	69	429
Patrick	65	m	w	IREL	Santa Clara	San Jose Twp	88	217
Patrick	34	m	w	IREL	San Francisco	San Francisco P O	83	15
Patrick	25	m	w	IREL	Merced	Snelling P O	74	255
Peter	50	m	w	VA	Solano	Silveyville Twp	90	76
Peter	44	m	w	IREL	San Francisco	San Francisco P O	83	350
Peter D	49	m	w	IREL	Napa	Napa Twp	75	33
Reuben	17	m	w	CA	Stanislaus	Empire Twp	92	63
Robert	48	m	w	IREL	Sonoma	Bodega Twp	91	264
Robert	42	m	w	KY	Marin	Tomales Twp	74	80
Robert	39	m	w	NC	San Diego	San Diego	78	494
Robert	38	m	w	CANA	Marin	Bolinas Twp	74	7
Robert S	50	m	w	VT	Marin	San Rafael	74	57
Robt	18	m	w	CA	Sacramento	4-Wd Sacramento	77	330
Rosa	75	f	w	ENGL	San Francisco	San Francisco P O	80	362
S A	17	f	w	CA	Alameda	Oakland	68	218
S J	38	m	w	OH	San Francisco	3-Wd San Francisco	79	316
S M	43	m	w	VA	Monterey	Alisal Twp	74	290
Saml	24	m	w	ENGL	Santa Clara	Gilroy Twp	88	93
Sanford H	29	m	w	ME	Santa Cruz	Santa Cruz	89	418
Sarah	37	f	w	ENGL	San Francisco	San Francisco P O	83	205
Sarah	30	f	w	SCOT	San Francisco	11-Wd San Francisc	84	603
Sheppard	33	m	w	ME	Marin	Point Reyes Twp	74	21
Stephen	29	m	w	NY	Stanislaus	Empire Twp	92	44
Thomas	53	m	w	MA	San Francisco	1-Wd San Francisco	79	129
Thomas	35	m	w	IREL	San Francisco	1-Wd San Francisco	79	41
Thomas	28	m	w	ENGL	Nevada	Grass Valley Twp	75	211
Thornton	45	m	w	PA	Plumas	Seneca Twp	77	48
Thos	34	m	w	IREL	San Francisco	San Francisco P O	83	126
W B	41	m	w	TN	Del Norte	Happy Camp Twp	71	472
W M	29	m	w	MI	Nevada	Nevada Twp	75	273
Walker	46	m	w	VA	San Luis Obispo	Santa Rosa Twp	87	320
Washington	41	m	w	MO	Shasta	Portugese Flat P O	89	471
William	52	m	w	OH	San Francisco	San Francisco P O	83	56
William	40	m	w	ENGL	Monterey	San Benito Twp	74	378
William	40	m	b	VA	San Francisco	11-Wd San Francisc	84	552
William	39	m	w	ENGL	Sutter	Yuba Twp	92	144
William	33	m	w	ENGL	San Francisco	8-Wd San Francisco	82	448
William	32	m	w	OH	San Francisco	7-Wd San Francisco	81	188
William	30	m	w	IREL	Santa Clara	San Jose Twp	88	194
William B	33	m	w	GA	Los Angeles	Santa Ana Twp	73	608
William E	18	m	w	MO	Tulare	Visalia Twp	92	286
William H	38	m	w	KY	Nevada	Grass Valley Twp	75	167
William H	33	m	w	VA	Colusa	Colusa	71	294
William P	46	m	w	TN	Inyo	Cerro Gordo Twp	73	323
Wm	44	m	w	GA	Tuolumne	Sonora P O	93	306
Wm	18	m	w	BADE	San Francisco	San Francisco P O	85	787
Wm C	33	m	w	IL	Del Norte	Smith Rvr Twp	71	478
Wm E	35	m	w	ME	Siskiyou	Scott Rvr Twp	89	602
Wm L	28	m	b	KY	Napa	Napa	75	49
Wright B	52	m	w	MO	Fresno	Millerton P O	72	187
BAILHACHE								
Henry	32	m	w	IL	Contra Costa	Martinez Twp	71	347
Jno	42	m	w	OH	Sonoma	Russian Rvr	91	375
BAILIFF								
John	45	m	w	ENGL	Sonoma	Santa Rosa	91	428
BAILING								
Frank	21	m	w	BAVA	San Francisco	San Francisco P O	83	165
BAILISS								
Samuel	49	m	w	OH	Yolo	Putah Twp	93	509
BAILLE								
John A	78	m	w	SCOT	Fresno	Millerton P O	72	163
Marcelene	25	m	w	FRAN	San Francisco	2-Wd San Francisco	79	159
Maylaine	43	m	w	FRAN	Yuba	Parks Bar Twp	93	649
BAILLEY								
Achilles	24	m	w	FRAN	San Francisco	2-Wd San Francisco	79	186
Arthur	26	m	w	FRAN	San Francisco	2-Wd San Francisco	79	186

© 2001 by Heritage Quest. All rights reserved.

Name	Age	S	R	B-PL	County	Locale	Roll	Pg
						Series M593		
David	35	m	w	MO	Colusa	Monroe Twp	71	320
Fredk N	37	m	w	SCOT	San Francisco	1-Wd San Francisco	79	79
Joseph	55	m	w	ME	San Francisco	2-Wd San Francisco	79	254
BAILLIE								
Hannah	40	f	w	NY	Santa Clara	1-Wd San Jose	88	233
Margaret	54	f	w	ENGL	San Francisco	7-Wd San Francisco	81	240
BAILLON								
Cecelia	30	m	w	MEXI	Kern	Bakersfield P O	73	362
BAILOW								
Abraham	43	m	w	PRUS	Tuolumne	Sonora P O	93	311
BAILS								
Jessee	30	m	w	MEXI	Amador	Jackson P O	69	324
BAILY								
A C	31	m	w	IL	Sutter	Yuba Twp	92	140
Ada M	20	f	w	MD	San Francisco	San Francisco P O	85	759
Anna	49	f	w	PA	San Francisco	2-Wd San Francisco	79	177
C K	40	m	w	MA	San Joaquin	Douglas Twp	86	45
C M	39	m	w	VA	Humboldt	South Fork Twp	72	300
Charles	40	m	w	NH	Calaveras	San Andreas P O	70	209
D A	13	f	w	CA	Alameda	Oakland	68	258
Frederick	60	m	w	ME	Butte	Wyandotte Twp	70	145
George	43	m	w	MA	Sacramento	Franklin Twp	77	116
George	29	m	w	MA	Alameda	Oakland	68	203
George B	61	m	w	VA	Yuba	Slate Range Bar Tw	93	671
George L	22	m	w	NY	San Mateo	Redwood Twp	87	365
Gibbert B	42	m	w	NH	Placer	Gold Run Twp	76	398
Horace	19	m	w	VT	Sutter	Butte Twp	92	92
J C	40	m	w	VA	San Joaquin	Liberty Twp	86	82
J F	40	m	w	ME	Yuba	Marysville	93	591
James	54	m	w	IREL	San Mateo	Menlo Park P O	87	379
James S	24	m	w	ENGL	San Mateo	Redwood Twp	87	367
Joel D	32	m	w	WI	Amador	Fiddletown P O	69	440
John C	25	m	w	TN	San Mateo	Woodside P O	87	384
Joseph C	35	m	w	PA	San Francisco	San Francisco P O	85	757
Joshua	39	m	w	OH	Sacramento	Lee Twp	77	160
Marion	23	m	w	IA	San Joaquin	Elkhorn Twp	86	55
Moses	42	m	w	MO	Sacramento	Franklin Twp	77	113
Orin	55	m	w	PA	San Joaquin	Elkhorn Twp	86	54
Orrin	54	m	w	PA	San Joaquin	Elkhorn Twp	86	61
Patrick	30	m	w	IREL	Butte	Chico Twp	70	47
R	35	m	w	ENGL	Alameda	Oakland	68	209
Robert	33	m	w	OH	El Dorado	Cosumnes Twp	72	15
Robt	29	m	w	IL	San Joaquin	Dent Twp	86	29
Sallie	55	f	w	MD	San Francisco	San Francisco P O	80	411
Sarah J	10	f	w	IA	San Joaquin	Elkhorn Twp	86	64
W H	51	m	w	ME	Sacramento	3-Wd Sacramento	77	309
Wash	22	m	w	MO	San Joaquin	Elliott Twp	86	74
William	39	m	w	NY	Placer	Pino Twp	76	470
William	28	m	w	ENGL	Placer	Newcastle Twp	76	474
BAIN								
Alexander	35	m	w	SCOT	San Francisco	2-Wd San Francisco	79	183
Blanche	27	f	w	FRAN	San Francisco	San Francisco P O	80	475
George	35	m	w	MA	San Francisco	8-Wd San Francisco	82	334
James	25	m	w	ENGL	Marin	San Rafael	74	57
James	19	m	w	CA	El Dorado	Cosumnes Twp	72	16
Maria	40	f	b	MD	San Francisco	San Francisco P O	80	417
Robert	41	m	w	IREL	Shasta	Stillwater P O	89	479
William	44	m	w	PA	Alameda	Brooklyn Twp	68	43
William	33	m	w	IN	San Francisco	San Francisco P O	83	149
Wm	42	m	w	SCOT	Butte	Concow Twp	70	9
Zach	74	m	w	MD	San Joaquin	Elkhorn Twp	86	53
BAINARD								
Isaac	38	m	w	PA	San Francisco	2-Wd San Francisco	79	139
BAINBRIDGE								
C W	27	m	w	ENGL	Alameda	Oakland	68	216
Fredk	48	m	w	KY	Stanislaus	Empire Twp	92	52
J	46	m	w	ENGL	Lake	Lower Lake	73	422
J G	46	m	w	ENGL	Lake	Lower Lake	73	420
John E	30	m	w	CT	Sacramento	Franklin Twp	77	109
John P	47	m	w	KY	Colusa	Colusa Twp	71	286
Levi	56	m	w	VA	Yuba	New York Twp	93	637
BAINE								
George	32	m	w	SCOT	Nevada	Grass Valley Twp	75	216
James A	18	m	w	WI	Amador	Ione City P O	69	350
Melinda	58	f	w	VA	San Francisco	San Francisco P O	83	292
Thomas	50	m	w	ENGL	Alameda	Oakland	68	171
BAINES								
James	27	m	w	SCOT	San Francisco	7-Wd San Francisco	81	243
Mary	18	f	w	IREL	San Francisco	San Francisco P O	83	322
R T	67	m	w	ME	Klamath	Trinidad Twp	73	389
BAINGER								
Martha	35	f	w	IREL	San Francisco	San Francisco P O	83	86
BAINS								
John K	45	m	w	SCOT	San Luis Obispo	Morro Twp	87	284
BAINWEBER								
Charles	43	m	w	CANA	San Francisco	11-Wd San Francisc	84	534
BAIR								
Abraham	56	m	w	BAVA	Los Angeles	Los Angeles	73	533
William H	41	m	w	ENGL	San Francisco	2-Wd San Francisco	79	281
BAIRD								
Alfred	40	m	w	OH	Santa Clara	Santa Clara Twp	88	151
Alvin	74	m	w	NY	San Joaquin	Oneal Twp	86	108
America	40	f	w	KY	Sierra	Gibson Twp	89	542
B P	42	m	w	NY	San Joaquin	Oneal Twp	86	108
Charles	57	m	w	IREL	Siskiyou	Callahan P O	89	629
Charles	50	m	w	OH	Yuba	Long Bar Twp	93	565
Curtis	44	m	w	NY	San Mateo	Redwood Twp	87	370
Edward	25	m	w	MI	Yolo	Washington Twp	93	535
Ellen	24	f	w	OH	Yolo	Fremont Twp	93	476
G W	26	m	w	DC	Solano	Vallejo	90	200
Geo W	38	m	w	NY	San Francisco	5-Wd San Francisco	81	22
Henry	34	m	w	OH	Solano	Vacaville Twp	90	122
Henry C	35	m	w	VT	Mendocino	Little Rvr Twp	74	171
Isabella	49	f	w	ENGL	Santa Clara	2-Wd San Jose	88	308
James	56	m	w	SCOT	Yuba	New York Twp	93	636
Jeffrson	43	m	w	PA	El Dorado	Mountain Twp	72	69
John	34	m	w	IREL	Solano	Vallejo	90	203
M L	37	m	w	PA	San Joaquin	Union Twp	86	265
Milliken	37	m	w	IN	El Dorado	Mud Springs Twp	72	76
Robert	32	m	w	PA	San Francisco	San Francisco P O	83	55
S L	38	m	w	NY	San Joaquin	Oneal Twp	86	108
Samuel	43	m	w	KY	San Francisco	San Francisco P O	80	418
Samuel	27	m	w	CANA	Alameda	Brooklyn	68	35
Thomas	48	m	w	ENGL	Yolo	Cache Crk Twp	93	446
Thomas	35	m	w	CANA	Humboldt	Eureka Twp	72	271
Thomas	35	m	w	CANA	Humboldt	Eureka Twp	72	281
Thos	43	m	w	SCOT	Sierra	Eureka Twp	89	524
Vincent L	45	m	w	TN	Sonoma	Cloverdale Twp	91	268
William	26	m	w	VT	Santa Cruz	Santa Cruz Twp	89	394
BAISE								
Chas	35	m	w	FRAN	Alameda	Oakland	68	154
BAISERN								
J	38	f	w	SPAI	San Francisco	San Francisco P O	85	792
BAISON								
Antone	40	m	w	SCOT	Alameda	Brooklyn Twp	68	56
BAISTER								
Louis A	35	m	w	IL	Butte	Chico Twp	70	13
BAITH								
Geo	47	m	w	BAVA	Humboldt	Eureka Twp	72	272
Geo	47	m	w	BAVA	Humboldt	Arcata Twp	72	235
BAIZLEY								
S E	41	m	w	CANA	Solano	Vallejo	90	180
BAJIEL								
Julien	35	m	w	NM	San Luis Obispo	San Luis Obispo Tw	87	313
BAJORKIS								
Ramon	27	m	w	CA	Santa Clara	2-Wd San Jose	88	321
Sebastian	36	m	w	CA	Santa Clara	Fremont Twp	88	62
BAK								
Ah	30	m	c	CHIN	Butte	Concow Twp	70	8
Ah	19	m	c	CHIN	San Francisco	3-Wd San Francisco	79	329
Hop	22	m	c	CHIN	Solano	Suisun Twp	90	105
Koa	14	m	c	CHIN	San Francisco	6-Wd San Francisco	81	47
BAKAIN								
Byron L	34	m	w	OH	Santa Cruz	Santa Cruz	89	432
BAKE								
Ah	17	m	c	CHIN	San Francisco	3-Wd San Francisco	79	329
BAKEMAN								
Henry	40	m	w	OH	Nevada	Nevada Twp	75	302
Jas	31	m	w	VA	Sacramento	3-Wd Sacramento	77	278
Lewis	35	m	w	SAXO	Nevada	Eureka Twp	75	128
Luther	22	m	w	ME	Sacramento	2-Wd Sacramento	77	229
P	28	m	w	HANO	Sierra	Table Rock Twp	89	575
BAKER								
---	40	m	w	CT	Humboldt	Eureka Twp	72	273
---	20	m	w	ENGL	Sacramento	4-Wd Sacramento	77	373
A	24	m	w	NY	Alameda	Oakland	68	182
A D	48	m	w	KY	Merced	Snelling P O	74	259
A J	38	m	w	NY	San Francisco	8-Wd San Francisco	82	299
A M	34	m	w	CANA	Sonoma	Mendocino Twp	91	299
A P	50	m	w	ME	Alameda	Oakland	68	228
A R	32	m	w	AR	San Joaquin	Liberty Twp	86	88
Abraham	25	m	w	NY	San Diego	Milquaty Dist	78	478
Abram	31	m	w	NY	Butte	Ophir Twp	70	108
Adam	46	m	w	BAVA	El Dorado	Placerville	72	116
Adam J	24	m	w	CANA	Humboldt	Bucksport Twp	72	244
Albert	19	m	w	IL	Colusa	Grand Island Twp	71	310
Albt	25	m	w	NJ	Butte	Chico Twp	70	26
Alferd	43	m	w	KY	Colusa	Colusa Twp	71	274
Alfred	40	m	w	IL	San Francisco	San Francisco P O	80	532
Alfred D	50	m	w	ME	San Francisco	1-Wd San Francisco	79	30
Alfred S	27	m	w	ENGL	San Francisco	San Francisco P O	83	163
Alfred W	30	m	w	IL	San Francisco	San Francisco P O	83	203
Alice C	4	f	w	CA	San Francisco	San Francisco P O	83	23
Almareane W	26	m	w	KY	Shasta	Horsetown P O	89	506
Amelia	39	f	w	KY	Butte	Oregon Twp	70	130
Andrew	36	m	w	MA	Shasta	Millville P O	89	485
Andrew	12	m	w	CA	Calaveras	Copperopolis P O	70	249
Andrew J	39	m	w	TN	Santa Barbara	San Buenaventura P	87	421
Angelo	30	m	w	PA	Sacramento	2-Wd Sacramento	77	232
Anne	30	f	w	ENGL	San Francisco	11-Wd San Francisc	84	447
Arrah	19	f	w	NY	Sacramento	1-Wd Sacramento	77	177
Asa G	45	m	w	NY	San Diego	Julian Dist	78	468
Auther	9	m	w	CA	Colusa	Stony Crk Twp	71	334
Avic	37	f	w	OH	Yuba	Marysville	93	585
Barbara	37	f	w	BAVA	San Francisco	8-Wd San Francisco	82	421
Barney	42	m	w	NY	Sacramento	Franklin Twp	77	114
Ben B	45	m	w	MA	Butte	Chico Twp	70	22
Benjamin	40	m	w	POLA	Yolo	Cache Crk Twp	93	419
Benjamin F	46	m	w	NY	Plumas	Goodwin Twp	77	7
Burton	16	m	w	ME	Humboldt	Eureka Twp	72	257
C E	16	m	w	CA	Sutter	Nicolaus Twp	92	110
Caroline	8	f	w	IL	San Francisco	San Francisco P O	85	798
Caroline	70	f	w	ME	San Francisco	San Francisco P O	83	253
Caspar	39	m	w	PRUS	San Francisco	San Francisco P O	83	366

© 2001 by Heritage Quest. All rights reserved.

California 1870 Census

Name	Age	S	R	B-PL	County	Locale	Series M593 Roll	Pg
Casper	33	m	w	PRUS	San Francisco	11-Wd San Francisc	84	707
Catherine	36	f	w	ME	San Francisco	San Francisco P O	83	242
Charles	53	m	w	ME	Placer	Lincoln P O	76	489
Charles	35	m	w	CANA	Sacramento	2-Wd Sacramento	77	240
Charles	32	m	w	DENM	San Francisco	San Francisco P O	83	363
Charles	32	m	w	ENGL	San Francisco	2-Wd San Francisco	79	166
Charles	30	m	w	NY	San Mateo	Schoolhouse Statio	87	342
Charles	29	m	w	ENGL	Contra Costa	Martinez P O	71	443
Charles	22	m	w	MA	San Diego	Julian Dist	78	468
Chas	9	m	w	CA	Santa Clara	Gilroy Twp	88	73
Chas	35	m	w	ENGL	Shasta	Millville P O	89	488
Chas	33	m	w	ENGL	Sonoma	Mendocino Twp	91	303
Chas	30	m	w	ENGL	San Francisco	11-Wd San Francisc	84	427
Chas	30	m	w	MA	San Francisco	7-Wd San Francisco	81	239
Chas L	38	m	w	OH	Butte	Ophir Twp	70	93
Chris	28	m	w	PRUS	Sutter	Nicolaus Twp	92	112
Christian	34	m	w	PRUS	San Francisco	San Francisco P O	83	391
Christian	29	m	w	DENM	Sonoma	Petaluma Twp	91	349
Christian	24	m	w	DENM	Sacramento	Brighton Twp	77	75
Christopher	35	m	w	MO	Stanislaus	Empire Twp	92	38
Clem	30	m	m	NC	Sacramento	3-Wd Sacramento	77	280
Clifford	45	m	w	CANA	Yolo	Buckeye Twp	93	414
Conrad	40	m	w	PA	San Francisco	San Francisco P O	83	364
Constantine	45	m	w	BADE	Sonoma	Salt Point	91	384
D S	36	m	w	IL	Tehama	Tehama Twp	92	186
Dan S	44	m	w	ME	Nevada	Nevada Twp	75	288
Daniel S	52	m	w	NY	Plumas	Seneca Twp	77	51
David	42	m	w	NY	San Francisco	San Francisco P O	83	124
David T	23	m	w	VA	San Luis Obispo	Santa Rosa Twp	87	326
Dryden	50	m	w	MA	Plumas	Indian Twp	77	18
E T	30	f	w	IREL	Alameda	Oakland	68	217
Ed	35	m	w	IN	Alameda	Oakland	68	264
Ede	33	m	w	NY	Santa Clara	2-Wd San Jose	88	293
Edward	45	m	w	PRUS	San Joaquin	2-Wd Stockton	86	159
Edward	32	m	w	CANA	Humboldt	Eureka Twp	72	282
Edward	19	m	w	NY	Nevada	Rough & Ready Twp	75	323
Edwin	19	m	w	ENGL	Los Angeles	Santa Ana Twp	73	603
Edwin P	34	m	w	NY	Inyo	Bishop Crk Twp	73	314
Eli	29	m	w	CANA	Sacramento	3-Wd Sacramento	77	283
Elijah D	49	m	w	PA	Shasta	Horsetown P O	89	504
Eliza	49	f	w	IN	Sonoma	Analy Twp	91	230
Eliza	23	f	w	IL	Mendocino	Little Lake Twp	74	193
Elizabeth	30	f	w	IREL	San Francisco	San Francisco P O	85	759
Elton	43	m	w	VA	San Joaquin	3-Wd Stockton	86	232
Erastus	40	m	w	MA	Humboldt	Pacific Twp	72	289
Eugene	27	m	w	IREL	San Francisco	San Francisco P O	83	244
Fines E	32	m	w	IL	Nevada	Nevada Twp	75	322
Francis	40	f	w	ME	San Francisco	11-Wd San Francisc	84	539
Frank	41	m	w	MA	Los Angeles	Los Angeles	73	567
Frank	34	m	w	BADE	Sierra	Table Rock Twp	89	576
Frank	28	m	w	MA	San Francisco	7-Wd San Francisco	81	218
Frank	20	m	i	CANA	Yolo	Grafton Twp	93	494
Frank	18	m	w	MEXI	San Joaquin	3-Wd Stockton	86	237
Franklin	30	m	w	OH	Yolo	Grafton Twp	93	497
Fred	52	m	w	PRUS	Merced	Snelling P O	74	247
Fred	28	m	w	PRUS	Sacramento	3-Wd Sacramento	77	278
Frederick	48	m	w	VA	San Mateo	Woodside P O	87	384
Frederick	43	m	w	PRUS	San Francisco	3-Wd San Francisco	79	292
Frederick	38	m	w	PRUS	San Francisco	1-Wd San Francisco	79	89
Frederick	11	m	w	CA	San Francisco	San Francisco P O	85	828
Fredrick	55	m	w	OH	Yolo	Grafton Twp	93	489
Friend	52	m	w	ENGL	Butte	Kimshew Tpw	70	83
G	42	m	w	KY	San Joaquin	2-Wd Stockton	86	191
G W	20	m	w	IN	Sutter	Sutter Twp	92	117
Gee	30	m	w	MI	Sacramento	Brighton Twp	77	73
Geo	46	m	w	OH	Yuba	Marysville Twp	93	567
Geo	28	m	w	PRUS	San Francisco	2-Wd San Francisco	79	168
Geo	26	m	w	ENGL	San Mateo	San Mateo P O	87	359
Geo	19	m	w	HAMB	San Francisco	1-Wd San Francisco	79	127
Geo W	49	m	w	KY	Sacramento	4-Wd Sacramento	77	343
George	45	m	w	OH	Shasta	Horsetown P O	89	506
George	40	m	w	ENGL	San Francisco	San Francisco P O	83	200
George	40	m	w	ENGL	Nevada	Bloomfield Twp	75	97
George	39	m	w	MA	San Francisco	11-Wd San Francisc	84	467
George	25	m	w	NY	Marin	San Rafael Twp	74	43
George	24	m	w	SAXO	Marin	Sausalito Twp	74	72
George	24	m	w	SAXO	Marin	Sausalito Twp	74	73
George H	32	m	w	ME	Colusa	Stony Crk Twp	71	327
George J	45	m	w	BAVA	San Francisco	8-Wd San Francisco	82	389
George M	42	m	w	MA	San Francisco	6-Wd San Francisco	81	119
H	39	m	w	PRUS	San Joaquin	2-Wd Stockton	86	199
H N	39	m	w	MD	Butte	Oroville Twp	70	137
H W	39	m	w	NH	Lake	Lower Lake	73	418
Hannah	9	f	w	CA	Alameda	Washington Twp	68	273
Harry	22	m	w	NY	San Francisco	7-Wd San Francisco	81	158
Henry	65	m	w	MD	Santa Cruz	Santa Cruz	89	426
Henry	43	m	w	HCAS	San Francisco	San Francisco P O	83	27
Henry	42	m	w	MA	San Francisco	San Francisco P O	83	348
Henry	40	m	w	BADE	Solano	Tremont Twp	90	30
Henry	39	m	w	PA	San Francisco	2-Wd San Francisco	79	174
Henry	34	m	w	GERM	San Francisco	7-Wd San Francisco	81	248
Henry G	45	m	w	ENGL	Santa Barbara	Santa Barbara P O	87	477
Henry H	52	m	w	NY	Shasta	Fort Crook P O	89	476
Henry H	31	m	w	PRUS	Mendocino	Little Rvr Twp	74	165
Henry J	50	m	w	HESS	El Dorado	Diamond Springs Tw	72	25
Henry S	13	m	w	TX	Los Angeles	Los Nietos Twp	73	579
Henry W	51	m	w	MO	Mendocino	Calpella Twp	74	188

Name	Age	S	R	B-PL	County	Locale	Series M593 Roll	Pg
Hilton	40	m	w	TN	Del Norte	Crescent Twp	71	455
Hiram	37	m	w	ME	Siskiyou	Surprise Valley Tw	89	639
Hiram	35	m	w	IA	Monterey	San Benito Twp	74	383
Ira	32	m	w	OH	Marin	San Rafael Twp	74	37
Isaac	45	m	w	NH	San Francisco	11-Wd San Francisc	84	601
Isaac L	25	m	w	IA	Siskiyou	Yreka	89	652
Isaac M	49	m	w	MO	San Mateo	Pescadero P O	87	410
Isabella	36	f	w	ME	San Francisco	8-Wd San Francisco	82	391
Isaiah	52	m	w	MA	San Francisco	San Francisco P O	80	357
J	40	m	w	ME	Alameda	Oakland	68	173
J	31	m	w	BAVA	San Joaquin	Liberty Twp	86	83
J	30	m	w	MO	San Joaquin	Liberty Twp	86	90
J B	39	m	w	NY	San Francisco	San Francisco P O	85	788
J C	54	m	w	KY	Lake	Lower Lake	73	421
J C	34	m	w	IL	San Joaquin	Tulare Twp	86	260
J H	25	m	w	CANA	Monterey	Salinas Twp	74	309
J H G	40	m	w	ME	Alameda	Oakland	68	217
J W	51	m	w	MO	San Joaquin	1-Wd Stockton	86	150
Jacob C	56	m	w	OH	Placer	Auburn P O	76	366
Jake	36	m	w	OH	Butte	Ophir Twp	70	113
James	69	m	w	ENGL	Placer	Roseville P O	76	349
James	67	m	w	VA	Tulare	Visalia	92	299
James	40	m	w	NY	Merced	Snelling P O	74	257
James	39	m	w	IREL	San Francisco	3-Wd San Francisco	79	310
James	30	m	w	IREL	Los Angeles	Los Angeles Twp	73	487
James	28	m	w	IA	Tulare	Visalia	92	296
James	22	m	w	IL	San Joaquin	Dent Twp	86	18
James C	53	m	w	TN	Sonoma	Salt Point	91	388
James C	37	m	w	MO	San Diego	Milquaty Dist	78	476
Jane	38	f	w	IREL	San Francisco	San Francisco P O	80	401
Jas S	25	m	w	MA	Klamath	Trinidad Twp	73	391
Jas W	37	m	w	MO	Sacramento	Alabama Twp	77	62
Jesse	61	m	w	MO	San Joaquin	Liberty Twp	86	95
Jesse R	26	m	w	MO	Sacramento	Alabama Twp	77	62
Jim	50	m	w	NY	San Francisco	5-Wd San Francisco	81	14
Jno	55	m	w	GERM	Santa Clara	Burnett Twp	88	30
Jno	40	m	w	BADE	Butte	Ophir Twp	70	118
Jno	39	m	w	IA	San Joaquin	2-Wd Stockton	86	180
Jno	22	m	w	PA	Butte	Kimshew Tpw	70	83
Jno H C	39	m	w	ME	Butte	Chico Twp	70	20
John	8	m	w	MO	Santa Cruz	Santa Cruz Twp	89	396
John	52	m	w	NY	Calaveras	San Andreas P O	70	188
John	51	m	w	HDAR	Calaveras	Copperopolis P O	70	241
John	51	m	w	DENM	Mendocino	Round Valley Twp	74	218
John	51	m	w	PA	Contra Costa	Martinez P O	71	379
John	45	m	w	ENGL	Amador	Ione City P O	69	350
John	45	m	w	BELG	Calaveras	Copperopolis P O	70	244
John	43	m	w	BADE	Fresno	Millerton P O	72	156
John	43	m	w	NC	Monterey	Alisal Twp	74	291
John	42	m	m	VA	Fresno	Kings Rvr P O	72	206
John	40	m	w	MO	Nevada	Grass Valley Twp	75	218
John	40	m	w	PRUS	El Dorado	Cosumnes Twp	72	19
John	39	m	w	IREL	Siskiyou	Yreka Twp	89	666
John	39	m	w	IREL	San Francisco	7-Wd San Francisco	81	260
John	35	m	w	IREL	Nevada	Washington Twp	75	343
John	35	m	w	GERM	San Francisco	7-Wd San Francisco	81	255
John	35	m	w	IL	San Joaquin	Oneal Twp	86	118
John	32	m	w	FRAN	Los Angeles	Los Angeles	73	541
John	32	m	w	NY	San Francisco	11-Wd San Francisc	84	707
John	28	m	b	AR	Fresno	Kings Rvr P O	72	211
John	27	m	w	NY	San Francisco	11-Wd San Francisc	84	707
John	25	m	w	ME	San Francisco	San Francisco P O	83	88
John	23	m	w	MO	Tulare	Venice Twp	92	273
John	13	m	w	DENM	Marin	San Antonio Twp	74	65
John B	71	m	w	KY	Colusa	Colusa	71	297
John C	48	m	w	VA	San Luis Obispo	Santa Rosa Twp	87	321
John E	35	m	w	NY	San Francisco	6-Wd San Francisco	81	90
John E	27	m	w	NY	Sacramento	Georgianna Twp	77	132
John F	53	m	w	BAVA	El Dorado	Placerville	72	117
John H	31	m	w	NY	San Bernardino	San Bernardino Twp	78	452
John M	49	m	w	NY	Calaveras	Copperopolis P O	70	227
Joseph	41	m	w	KY	Sonoma	Vallejo Twp	91	455
Joseph	34	m	w	MA	San Francisco	2-Wd San Francisco	79	154
Joseph	26	m	w	FRNK	San Francisco	San Francisco P O	80	332
Joseph	25	m	w	NY	San Francisco	5-Wd San Francisco	81	18
Joseph	19	m	w	NY	San Francisco	San Francisco P O	80	400
Joshuay	23	m	w	MO	Sutter	Vernon Twp	92	139
Julia	52	f	w	NY	Santa Clara	Santa Clara Twp	88	150
L	40	m	w	IN	San Joaquin	Liberty Twp	86	88
L A	47	f	w	OH	San Francisco	San Francisco P O	85	815
Len P	23	m	w	IL	Yolo	Grafton Twp	93	483
Leonard	52	m	w	CHIL	El Dorado	Placerville Twp	72	92
Livingston	43	m	w	ME	San Francisco	8-Wd San Francisco	82	475
Loretta	13	f	w	CA	El Dorado	Placerville	72	127
Louis F	47	m	w	MA	San Francisco	6-Wd San Francisco	81	142
Louis S	21	m	w	IL	San Francisco	San Francisco P O	85	758
Louisa	32	f	i	CA	Tehama	Tehama Twp	92	186
Lucy A	46	f	w	MA	Placer	Bath P O	76	432
Lucy E	25	f	w	ME	San Francisco	San Francisco P O	83	23
M	35	m	w	KY	Nevada	Washington Twp	75	346
Maria C	45	f	w	PA	Santa Clara	Santa Clara Twp	88	135
Maria J	51	f	w	MD	San Francisco	San Francisco P O	85	772
Martin	45	m	w	PA	Tulare	Visalia	92	293
Martin	35	m	w	SWIT	San Joaquin	3-Wd Stockton	86	231
Mary	37	f	w	PA	San Francisco	7-Wd San Francisco	81	267
Mary	36	f	w	RI	San Francisco	San Francisco P O	83	208
Mary	33	f	w	MA	San Francisco	San Francisco P O	83	50

© 2001 by Heritage Quest. All rights reserved.

Name	Age	S	R	B-PL	County	Locale	Series M593 Roll	Pg
Mary	17	f	w	PRUS	San Francisco	1-Wd San Francisco	79	87
Mary	15	f	w	CA	Siskiyou	Surprise Valley Tw	89	637
Mary	14	f	w	US	Nevada	Grass Valley Twp	75	229
Mary A	59	f	w	MA	San Francisco	6-Wd San Francisco	81	99
Mary B	10	f	w	CA	Mendocino	Point Arena Twp	74	210
Mary E	29	f	w	MO	Sacramento	4-Wd Sacramento	77	366
Mary J	40	f	w	CT	Santa Clara	2-Wd San Jose	88	327
Mat	35	m	w	GA	El Dorado	Georgetown Twp	72	40
Mathew	47	m	w	NY	Placer	Dutch Flat P O	76	403
Melville	38	m	w	ME	Santa Clara	2-Wd San Jose	88	336
Merchant	65	m	w	MA	Humboldt	Pacific Twp	72	291
Merritt	55	m	w	NY	Mariposa	Mariposa P O	74	133
Michl	35	m	w	IREL	Fresno	Millerton P O	72	150
Milton	48	m	w	NY	Santa Clara	2-Wd San Jose	88	294
Milton	35	m	w	IL	Humboldt	South Fork Twp	72	301
Minnie	12	f	w	CA	Trinity	Weaverville Pct	92	225
Morgan	27	m	w	IREL	San Joaquin	1-Wd Stockton	86	135
Mortimer	37	m	w	OH	Yuba	Rose Bar Twp	93	660
N	50	m	w	PRUS	San Francisco	San Francisco P O	85	839
Nathan	53	m	w	OH	Tulare	Tule Rvr Twp	92	270
Nicholas	35	m	w	PRUS	Solano	Tremont Twp	90	35
Noah	37	m	w	ENGL	San Mateo	Woodside P O	87	386
Norman	52	m	w	VT	Colusa	Spring Valley Twp	71	338
Norman J	29	m	w	NY	Placer	Gold Run Twp	76	398
O B	40	m	w	RI	Alameda	Oakland	68	215
Osborne F	30	m	w	ME	San Francisco	1-Wd San Francisco	79	106
Oscar	37	m	w	VA	Santa Clara	Redwood Twp	88	127
Otis	41	m	w	MI	Nevada	Nevada Twp	75	310
Peter	54	m	w	PA	San Joaquin	Douglas Twp	86	33
Peter	34	m	w	NY	Alameda	Oakland	68	175
Peter	30	m	w	SWIT	San Joaquin	2-Wd Stockton	86	176
Peter	21	m	w	OH	San Francisco	3-Wd San Francisco	79	323
Phillip	65	m	w	PA	Merced	Snelling P O	74	255
Prince P	35	m	w	ME	Shasta	Shasta P O	89	455
R P	58	m	w	NY	Sacramento	Cosumnes Twp	77	95
R R	26	m	w	CANA	Tuolumne	Sonora P O	93	308
Raphael	46	m	w	PRUS	San Francisco	San Francisco P O	83	197
Richard	41	m	w	IREL	Yuba	Bullards Bar P O	93	547
Richard	40	m	w	ENGL	Trinity	Weaverville Pct	92	230
Richard	35	m	w	VA	Monterey	San Juan Twp	74	393
Riley	52	m	w	NY	Los Angeles	Los Angeles Twp	73	494
Robert	44	m	w	RI	Kern	Tehachapi P O	73	356
Robert	36	m	w	MO	Yolo	Cottonwood Twp	93	461
Robert	20	m	w	KY	Kern	Havilah P O	73	351
Robert	15	m	w	CA	Los Angeles	Soledad Twp	73	631
Robert	11	m	w	CA	Santa Barbara	Santa Barbara P O	87	492
Robert M	19	m	w	IL	Los Angeles	Soledad Twp	73	631
Robt	30	m	w	KY	Butte	Hamilton Twp	70	63
Robt C	49	m	w	OH	Shasta	French Gulch P O	89	465
S C	26	m	w	CANA	Solano	Vallejo	90	189
S N	60	m	w	NY	Sacramento	Brighton Twp	77	77
S S	45	m	w	ME	Sierra	Lincoln Twp	89	550
Salvador	25	m	w	CA	Santa Barbara	Santa Barbara P O	87	488
Saml	23	m	w	PA	Solano	Vallejo	90	140
Saml D	45	m	w	NH	San Francisco	San Francisco P O	83	274
Samuel	43	m	w	NY	San Francisco	San Francisco P O	83	334
Samuel	42	m	w	FRAN	Los Angeles	Los Nietos Twp	73	590
Samuel	38	m	w	ENGL	Nevada	Grass Valley Twp	75	194
Samuel	36	m	w	ENGL	Nevada	Grass Valley Twp	75	190
Samuel	35	m	w	KY	Colusa	Colusa	71	293
Samuel	33	m	w	NY	Placer	Dutch Flat P O	76	402
Samuel	32	m	b	MO	Marin	San Rafael Twp	74	41
Samuel	26	m	w	MA	San Francisco	San Francisco P O	83	202
Samuel	25	m	w	NY	San Francisco	7-Wd San Francisco	81	204
Samuel C	28	m	w	MA	San Mateo	Pescadero P O	87	414
Samuel J	49	m	w	RI	Mendocino	Point Arena Twp	74	210
Samuel R	34	m	w	MO	Solano	Vacaville Twp	90	137
Sarah	11	f	w	VT	San Francisco	11-Wd San Francisc	84	580
Sarah A E	27	f	w	VA	Inyo	Independence Twp	73	327
Sarar	10	f	w	CA	Sutter	Sutter Twp	92	128
Schnyder	38	m	w	OH	Placer	Dutch Flat P O	76	414
Silas	49	m	w	CANA	Alameda	Washington Twp	68	283
Simeon	32	m	w	MI	Monterey	San Juan Twp	74	389
Stephen N	45	m	w	NY	San Francisco	San Francisco P O	83	56
Sylvester	52	m	w	MA	San Francisco	8-Wd San Francisco	82	300
T O	35	m	w	RI	Alameda	Oakland	68	204
Temer	72	f	w	NC	Monterey	Alisal Twp	74	291
Thomas	59	m	w	OH	Kern	Bakersfield P O	73	360
Thomas	42	m	w	ENGL	Alameda	Eden Twp	68	62
Thomas	41	m	w	ENGL	Sacramento	2-Wd Sacramento	77	252
Thomas	40	m	w	ENGL	Santa Clara	Redwood Twp	88	127
Thomas	38	m	b	WIND	San Francisco	San Francisco P O	80	458
Thomas	38	m	w	IREL	San Francisco	11-Wd San Francisc	84	461
Thomas	37	m	w	VA	Trinity	Lewiston Pct	92	211
Thomas	34	m	w	IL	Solano	Silveyville Twp	90	76
Thomas	22	m	w	MO	Stanislaus	Empire Twp	92	63
Thomas J	39	m	w	ENGL	Los Angeles	Los Angeles	73	540
Thomas K	40	m	w	CANA	Yuba	Long Bar Twp	93	565
Thomas W	37	m	w	MA	San Francisco	6-Wd San Francisco	81	99
Thos	31	m	w	IREL	San Francisco	1-Wd San Francisco	79	98
Thos	24	m	b	AR	Fresno	Kings Rvr P O	72	211
Thos C	39	m	w	KY	San Francisco	San Francisco P O	83	199
Virgil P	45	m	w	NY	Tehama	Red Bluff	92	180
W J	46	m	w	NY	Lake	Big Valley	73	398
W J	42	m	w	TN	Tehama	Tehama Twp	92	192
W W	42	m	w	NY	San Joaquin	2-Wd Stockton	86	206
Walker	47	m	w	NY	Alameda	Washington Twp	68	270
Weighstell	48	m	w	CANA	Santa Clara	Santa Clara Twp	88	155
William	55	m	w	MO	Amador	Lancha Plana P O	69	368
William	49	m	w	PRUS	Sonoma	Santa Rosa	91	407
William	44	m	w	SPAI	Alameda	Brooklyn	68	29
William	37	m	w	OH	San Francisco	5-Wd San Francisco	81	21
William	37	m	w	OH	Kern	Bakersfield P O	73	360
William	37	m	w	MA	San Francisco	3-Wd San Francisco	79	292
William	36	m	w	MO	Solano	Vacaville Twp	90	137
William	35	m	w	KY	Santa Cruz	Santa Cruz Twp	89	396
William	34	m	w	ENGL	San Francisco	San Francisco P O	83	381
William	34	m	w	AR	Stanislaus	Branch Twp	92	1
William	33	m	w	PRUS	San Francisco	2-Wd San Francisco	79	239
William	32	m	w	KY	Alameda	Washington Twp	68	272
William	31	m	w	ENGL	Tehama	Merrill	92	197
William	30	m	w	IREL	San Francisco	San Francisco P O	83	396
William	16	m	w	CA	San Francisco	3-Wd San Francisco	79	314
William A	40	m	w	VA	Inyo	Bishop Crk Twp	73	316
William H	37	m	w	NC	Alameda	Washington Twp	68	296
Wm	64	m	w	IL	San Joaquin	Liberty Twp	86	94
Wm	43	m	w	ENGL	Sacramento	4-Wd Sacramento	77	364
Wm	41	m	w	ME	El Dorado	Lake Valley Twp	72	63
Wm	34	m	w	ENGL	San Francisco	San Francisco P O	83	133
Wm	32	m	w	HAMB	Sacramento	Sutter Twp	77	385
Wm	24	m	w	OR	Lassen	Susanville Twp	73	445
Wm A	22	m	w	VA	Tuolumne	Sonora P O	93	321
Wm B	40	m	w	NY	Santa Barbara	San Buenaventura P	87	448
Wm G	27	m	w	WI	Butte	Chico Twp	70	31
Wm H	42	m	w	PA	Siskiyou	Scott Valley Twp	89	621
Wm H	40	m	w	OH	Shasta	Millville P O	89	492
Wm M	32	m	w	CANA	Sacramento	Brighton Twp	77	77
Zenetta	48	f	w	NY	Mendocino	Point Arena Twp	74	210
BAKEY								
John	30	m	w	NY	San Francisco	2-Wd San Francisco	79	152
BAKKER								
Regan	36	m	w	HOLL	San Francisco	2-Wd San Francisco	79	154
BAKMAN								
Andros	25	m	w	FINL	San Francisco	3-Wd San Francisco	79	293
Martin	24	m	w	SWED	San Francisco	3-Wd San Francisco	79	292
BAKSIN								
---	15	m	c	CHIN	Shasta	Horsetown P O	89	507
BAL								
Thos	32	m	w	MO	Sacramento	Franklin Twp	77	120
BALAAM								
George	47	m	w	ENGL	San Luis Obispo	Santa Rosa Twp	87	322
BALADA								
Pasqual	31	m	w	FRAN	Monterey	San Antonio Twp	74	322
BALAFERE								
Antoine	26	m	w	AUST	Plumas	Quartz Twp	77	35
BALAN								
James	35	m	w	IREL	San Francisco	1-Wd San Francisco	79	129
Mercado	40	f	w	CHIL	San Francisco	San Francisco P O	80	461
Thomas	36	m	w	PA	Inyo	Cerro Gordo Twp	73	318
BALANAY								
Amus	39	m	w	CT	San Francisco	11-Wd San Francisc	84	679
BALANDER								
Henry	40	m	w	GERM	San Francisco	11-Wd San Francisc	84	445
BALANDO								
Peter	42	m	w	ITAL	San Francisco	San Francisco P O	80	482
BALANSWARDO								
Jesus	22	m	w	CA	Mariposa	Mariposa P O	74	129
BALANTI								
Andrew	31	m	w	ITAL	Tuolumne	Chinese Camp P O	93	368
BALANTINE								
H	43	m	w	CANA	Solano	Vallejo	90	155
H C	56	m	w	IREL	Mariposa	Maxwell Crk P O	74	144
BALARD								
S	25	m	w	ME	Alameda	Oakland	68	160
BALARDA								
Luis	33	m	w	CA	San Luis Obispo	Salinas Twp	87	289
BALAS								
Jesus	23	m	i	MEXI	Inyo	Cerro Gordo Twp	73	322
BALASKES								
Frank	40	f	w	SAME	San Joaquin	1-Wd Stockton	86	133
BALATTES								
Victor	30	m	w	SWIT	Monterey	Alisal Twp	74	297
BALAUGULA								
F	37	m	w	MEXI	San Joaquin	2-Wd Stockton	86	172
BALBACH								
John	48	m	w	WURT	Santa Clara	1-Wd San Jose	88	259
BALBONADO								
Petra	45	m	w	CA	Los Angeles	Wilmington Twp	73	637
BALCE								
John	40	m	w	PRUS	Sacramento	2-Wd Sacramento	77	220
William	38	m	w	NY	Alameda	Eden Twp	68	81
BALCH								
Caroline	50	f	w	MA	Stanislaus	Emory Twp	92	19
Casper	32	m	w	GERM	Marin	San Rafael Twp	74	25
Henry F	46	m	w	MA	Stanislaus	Emory Twp	92	19
Horace	39	m	w	MA	San Francisco	8-Wd San Francisco	82	300
Jno Riley	36	m	w	TN	Nevada	Rough & Ready Twp	75	333
John A	36	m	w	ME	San Francisco	San Francisco P O	83	351
Lizzie	47	f	w	HAMB	San Francisco	2-Wd San Francisco	79	242
Newton	45	m	b	MO	Tehama	Tehama Twp	92	195
William	25	m	w	MA	Tehama	Merrill	92	198
BALCOM								
C F	28	m	w	MA	San Francisco	San Francisco P O	85	783
L	40	f	w	MA	San Francisco	San Francisco P O	85	798

© 2001 by Heritage Quest. All rights reserved.

Series M593

Name	Age	S	R	B-PL	County	Locale	Roll	Pg
Miles	7	m	w	CA	Alameda	San Leandro	68	96
R George	24	m	w	CANA	San Diego	San Diego	78	495
BALCOME								
John	23	m	w	MA	San Francisco	7-Wd San Francisco	81	190
BALCON								
W A	40	m	w	CANA	Alameda	Oakland	68	236
BALDACCI								
S	35	m	w	ITAL	Santa Clara	Gilroy Twp	88	68
BALDEFEROUS								
Jo	38	m	w	SWIT	San Francisco	5-Wd San Francisco	81	16
BALDENADO								
Dolores	12	m	w	CA	Los Angeles	San Juan Twp	73	627
BALDENAG								
Edward	60	m	w	MEXI	Calaveras	San Andreas P O	70	208
BALDENAGRO								
Pablo	27	m	w	MEXI	Napa	Napa	75	54
BALDENAVO								
Santioss	24	m	w	CA	San Diego	San Jacinto Dist	78	517
BALDENGRO								
Maria	30	f	w	CA	Los Angeles	San Juan Twp	73	627
BALDER								
Francisca	18	m	w	CA	Monterey	Monterey Twp	74	352
BALDERMAN								
A	42	m	w	HAMB	San Francisco	San Francisco P O	85	839
BALDES								
Jesus Antonio	40	m	w	MEXI	Monterey	San Antonio Twp	74	317
Juan	60	m	w	CA	Monterey	San Antonio Twp	74	322
Pedro	36	m	w	CA	Santa Clara	Gilroy Twp	88	90
BALDEZ								
Josephine	33	f	w	MEXI	San Francisco	San Francisco P O	80	486
Juan	30	m	w	MEXI	Santa Cruz	Soquel Twp	89	448
BALDHAGLE								
Paul	24	m	w	PRUS	San Francisco	11-Wd San Francisc	84	662
BALDI								
Jean	38	m	w	NY	Los Angeles	Los Angeles	73	537
BALDICK								
John	38	m	w	PRUS	Sacramento	Granite Twp	77	141
BALDIE								
Marco	25	m	w	ITAL	San Francisco	1-Wd San Francisco	79	110
BALDIN								
Clide	8	m	w	IA	Sacramento	Lee Twp	77	157
Thomas C	37	m	w	MA	Los Angeles	Wilmington Twp	73	642
BALDINA								
Jose	65	m	w	MEXI	San Diego	San Diego	78	505
Manuel	40	m	w	MEXI	San Diego	San Diego	78	505
BALDING								
Chas	38	m	w	PRUS	Yuba	Marysville	93	581
BALDIS								
Masiah	35	m	i	MEXI	Inyo	Cerro Gordo Twp	73	323
BALDMAN								
Sequin	40	m	w	ARGE	Calaveras	San Andreas P O	70	170
BALDO								
Ara	40	m	w	MEXI	San Joaquin	3-Wd Stockton	86	227
BALDOZ								
Juan	60	m	w	CA	Monterey	Monterey Twp	74	352
BALDREAS								
Jose	40	m	w	MEXI	Calaveras	San Andreas P O	70	203
Pedro	39	m	w	MEXI	Calaveras	San Andreas P O	70	201
BALDRIDGE								
E C	37	m	w	OH	Nevada	Nevada Twp	75	283
Wm	49	m	w	TN	Napa	Yountville Twp	75	77
BALDWIN								
A H	32	m	w	NY	San Francisco	San Francisco P O	83	334
A J	22	m	w	OH	Sonoma	Petaluma Twp	91	349
A W	40	m	w	CT	San Francisco	San Francisco P O	83	297
Abel	23	m	w	NY	San Francisco	1-Wd San Francisco	79	50
Abigail	61	f	w	CT	Merced	Snelling P O	74	254
Abigal H	23	f	w	MA	San Francisco	3-Wd San Francisco	79	328
Albert	26	m	w	CANA	Solano	Vacaville Twp	90	135
Albert S	46	m	w	OH	San Francisco	5-Wd San Francisco	81	2
Alex	36	m	w	CANA	Alameda	Eden Twp	68	87
Alex R	49	m	w	NJ	San Francisco	San Francisco P O	83	201
Alfred	54	m	w	NY	Santa Cruz	Santa Cruz	89	407
Allen	31	m	w	ENGL	San Bernardino	San Bernardino Twp	78	434
Alonzo C	23	m	w	NJ	Mendocino	Navarro & Big Rvr	74	174
Amos	47	m	w	NY	Napa	Napa	75	15
Andrew	30	m	w	OH	Santa Clara	Fremont Twp	88	58
Andrew	27	m	w	OH	Marin	Tomales Twp	74	86
Annie	3	f	w	CA	Contra Costa	Martinez P O	71	416
Antonio	28	m	w	MEXI	San Diego	San Diego	78	504
Bally	26	m	w	ENGL	Contra Costa	Martinez P O	71	435
C H	47	m	w	NY	Solano	Vallejo	90	199
Catherine	33	f	w	IN	Sacramento	Alabama Twp	77	61
Charles	43	m	w	NH	San Francisco	6-Wd San Francisco	81	81
Chas	18	m	w	OH	Marin	Tomales Twp	74	79
Chas H	50	m	w	ENGL	San Francisco	3-Wd San Francisco	79	327
Chs H	38	m	w	MALT	San Francisco	San Francisco P O	83	288
Col	45	m	w	MA	Sierra	Downieville Twp	89	521
D C	49	m	w	TN	Butte	Oroville Twp	70	139
D J	34	m	w	NY	Sierra	Downieville Twp	89	518
D M	50	m	w	VT	Alameda	Oakland	68	199
E C	34	m	w	NY	Napa	Napa	75	7
E F	55	m	w	CT	San Francisco	San Francisco P O	85	796
Ebenezer	47	m	w	PA	Contra Costa	Martinez P O	71	405
Edwin	40	m	w	SWIT	Santa Clara	Fremont Twp	88	58
Elias J	45	m	w	KY	San Francisco	8-Wd San Francisco	82	394
Elkranah	47	m	w	VT	Sacramento	Franklin Twp	77	116
F F	40	m	w	MO	San Joaquin	2-Wd Stockton	86	183
Fred D	24	m	w	MA	Monterey	Castroville Twp	74	335
G H	3	m	w	CA	Tuolumne	Chinese Camp P O	93	370
Geo	9	m	w	CA	Yuba	East Bear Rvr Twp	93	543
Geo	40	m	w	VA	Butte	Ophir Twp	70	99
Geo S	54	m	w	MEXI	San Joaquin	1-Wd Stockton	86	120
Geo W	38	m	w	NY	Nevada	Nevada Twp	75	295
George	35	m	w	US	Nevada	Grass Valley Twp	75	222
George W	37	m	w	NJ	Santa Cruz	Santa Cruz Twp	89	400
H A	48	m	w	NY	Mariposa	Maxwell Crk P O	74	145
H L	33	m	w	IN	Alameda	Brooklyn	68	27
H S	50	m	w	NY	San Francisco	8-Wd San Francisco	82	300
Hannah	73	f	w	NJ	Santa Cruz	Santa Cruz Twp	89	400
Henry W	24	m	w	OH	San Francisco	San Francisco P O	85	758
Herbert	25	m	w	MA	San Joaquin	3-Wd Stockton	86	229
Herry C	9	m	w	CA	Sacramento	San Joaquin Twp	77	399
Horace	40	m	w	NY	Nevada	Meadow Lake Twp	75	247
Isaac	47	m	w	OH	Humboldt	Pacific Twp	72	289
J A	41	m	w	MA	Klamath	Trinidad Twp	73	391
J O	33	m	w	ME	San Francisco	8-Wd San Francisco	82	363
Jabez	44	m	w	PA	Solano	Green Valley Twp	90	37
James	32	m	w	ME	Sonoma	Petaluma Twp	91	343
James C	38	m	w	IN	Los Angeles	Santa Ana Twp	73	611
James W	45	m	w	NJ	El Dorado	Georgetown Twp	72	42
Jas H	53	m	w	VT	Shasta	Millville P O	89	488
Jeremiah	32	m	w	KY	Solano	Vacaville Twp	90	123
Jno	47	m	w	MO	San Joaquin	Douglas Twp	86	38
John	60	m	w	NY	Los Angeles	Los Angeles	73	571
John	50	m	w	NY	Monterey	Pajaro Twp	74	372
John	45	m	w	ME	Contra Costa	Martinez P O	71	408
John	40	m	w	IL	Colusa	Monroe Twp	71	316
John	35	m	i	ME	Sacramento	Sutter Twp	77	384
John	35	m	w	ENGL	San Bernardino	Chino Twp	78	411
John	32	m	w	PA	Los Angeles	Los Angeles	73	534
John	32	m	w	VA	Los Angeles	Los Angeles	73	540
John E D	28	m	w	PA	Santa Cruz	Santa Cruz	89	418
John S	37	m	w	TN	Nevada	Grass Valley Twp	75	223
John W	38	m	w	CANA	San Mateo	Half Moon Bay P O	87	400
Josephene	13	f	w	NY	Sonoma	Petaluma Twp	91	310
Kate	18	f	w	IREL	San Francisco	8-Wd San Francisco	82	423
Lawrance	47	m	w	MA	Calaveras	San Andreas P O	70	187
Lewis K	50	m	w	MA	Marin	Bolinas Twp	74	2
Lizzie	16	f	w	NY	San Francisco	11-Wd San Francisc	84	620
Lucy	26	f	w	NY	Solano	Suisun Twp	90	100
M H	42	m	w	VT	Humboldt	Eureka Twp	72	260
M H	30	f	w	NJ	Sacramento	4-Wd Sacramento	77	378
Macarta	56	m	w	KY	Solano	Maine Prairie Twp	90	50
Man J	60	f	w	WALE	San Francisco	2-Wd San Francisco	79	284
Maran M	44	m	w	NJ	San Francisco	San Francisco P O	85	717
Mari	55	m	w	GERM	San Diego	San Diego	78	508
Maria	19	f	w	CA	San Diego	San Diego	78	504
Mary I	10	f	w	KS	Sacramento	Dry Crk Twp	77	98
Miner P	41	m	w	NY	El Dorado	Georgetown Twp	72	38
Nahum	45	m	w	ME	Napa	Napa	75	16
Nebraska	16	f	w	NE	Sacramento	Brighton Twp	77	71
Nellie	14	f	w	IREL	San Francisco	San Francisco P O	83	134
Oliver	36	m	w	NY	San Francisco	San Francisco P O	80	371
Orrille	26	m	w	NY	Napa	Yountville Twp	75	81
Percis	58	f	w	WURT	San Francisco	San Francisco P O	80	351
Ralf	37	m	w	OH	Nevada	Bloomfield Twp	75	96
Robert	50	m	w	ENGL	San Bernardino	San Bernardino Twp	78	444
Robert C	40	m	w	OH	Contra Costa	Martinez P O	71	393
S	50	m	w	AL	Alameda	Oakland	68	208
S D	64	m	w	MA	Yuba	Marysville	93	576
S S	30	m	w	NY	Sacramento	1-Wd Sacramento	77	203
Saml	72	m	w	NH	Sonoma	Petaluma Twp	91	341
Susan	39	f	w	NY	Nevada	Meadow Lake Twp	75	260
T J	36	m	w	FL	Tuolumne	Chinese Camp P O	93	370
Thomas	38	m	w	NY	Tulare	Tule Rvr Twp	92	262
Thomas	26	m	w	MO	Nevada	Eureka Twp	75	139
Tim	64	m	w	VT	Sutter	Butte Twp	92	101
Truman	36	m	w	NY	Placer	Auburn P O	76	379
W	30	m	w	CANA	Humboldt	Eureka Twp	72	274
William	66	m	w	CT	San Bernardino	San Bernardino Twp	78	414
William	60	m	w	NY	Mendocino	Big Rvr Twp	74	161
William	42	m	w	NY	Contra Costa	Martinez Twp	71	352
William	34	m	w	MA	San Mateo	San Mateo P O	87	349
Wm	50	m	w	NY	San Francisco	11-Wd San Francisc	84	666
Wm	45	m	w	MA	Sutter	Vernon Twp	92	137
Wm H	46	m	w	MD	San Francisco	San Francisco P O	83	79
Wm L	49	m	w	NJ	Nevada	Rough & Ready Twp	75	331
Zenas A	43	m	w	NH	Yolo	Grafton Twp	93	501
BALDWINE								
George	46	m	w	MA	San Francisco	5-Wd San Francisco	81	23
Isaac	23	m	w	CANA	Humboldt	Arcata Twp	72	225
BALE								
Edward	25	m	w	CA	Napa	Napa	75	41
Mary	55	f	w	CA	Napa	Napa	75	11
BALENGER								
Joseph	23	m	w	KY	Contra Costa	Martinez P O	71	429
Saml	37	m	w	VA	Monterey	Monterey Twp	74	350
BALENGO								
Angel	56	m	w	CHIL	El Dorado	Mud Springs Twp	72	73
BALENSMELLA								
Anton	35	m	w	CA	San Diego	Warners Rancho Dis	78	529
BALENSON								
Gertrude	80	f	w	MEXI	San Diego	Coronado	78	466

© 2001 by Heritage Quest. All rights reserved.

Name	Age	S	R	B-PL	County	Locale	Series M593 Roll	Pg
BALENSUELA								
Jose	65	m	w	MEXI	San Bernardino	San Salvador Twp	78	456
BALENSWELLA								
Frank	35	m	w	MEXI	Napa	Napa	75	55
BALENTINE								
Saml	45	m	w	OH	Humboldt	Eel Rvr Twp	72	249
BALER								
C J H	25	m	w	WURT	Sacramento	3-Wd Sacramento	77	283
Christian	44	m	w	DENM	Sonoma	Salt Point	91	389
BALERO								
John	38	m	w	FRAN	Nevada	Bloomfield Twp	75	94
BALEROSE								
Michel	45	m	w	FRAN	Calaveras	San Andreas P O	70	219
BALERSON								
Alex J	23	m	w	IL	Monterey	San Antonio Twp	74	318
BALES								
Boawter	68	m	w	NC	Solano	Maine Prairie Twp	90	53
Charles	44	m	w	IN	Alameda	Eden Twp	68	68
Charles S	23	m	w	TN	Nevada	Grass Valley Twp	75	145
J C	35	m	w	MO	Sacramento	4-Wd Sacramento	77	373
J D	22	m	w	VA	San Joaquin	Liberty Twp	86	95
Job J	43	m	w	NY	Sacramento	Alabama Twp	77	59
Stephen	34	m	w	NY	Inyo	Independence Twp	73	325
Wm	22	m	w	MO	San Joaquin	Elkhorn Twp	86	64
BALESS								
J	40	m	w	WI	San Joaquin	Elliott Twp	86	73
BALESTS								
William	22	m	w	MO	Inyo	Lone Pine Twp	73	333
BALEVAR								
Santiago	28	m	w	MEXI	Santa Clara	2-Wd San Jose	88	300
BALEW								
John	39	m	w	BELG	Nevada	Nevada Twp	75	321
BALEY								
Albert	1	m	w	CA	San Francisco	San Francisco P O	85	836
Henry	15	m	w	KY	El Dorado	Placerville Twp	72	99
John	34	m	w	ENGL	Humboldt	South Fork Twp	72	302
BALF								
Michael	28	m	w	IREL	San Francisco	5-Wd San Francisco	81	32
BALFE								
James	32	m	w	ENGL	San Francisco	8-Wd San Francisco	82	455
BALFOR								
Richard	28	m	w	SCOT	San Francisco	8-Wd San Francisco	82	341
BALFOUR								
Chas	60	m	m	JAMA	Solano	Vallejo	90	198
Robert	26	m	w	SCOT	Alameda	Brooklyn	68	24
BALFREY								
John	40	m	w	IREL	Colusa	Colusa	71	290
Wm	42	m	w	IREL	San Francisco	San Francisco P O	83	59
BALGAR								
Aberto	16	m	w	SWIT	Marin	San Antonio Twp	74	60
BALGER								
John	36	m	w	IREL	Santa Clara	2-Wd San Jose	88	306
BALGOS								
Gideon	90	m	w	MO	Calaveras	San Andreas P O	70	181
BALINGER								
Saml	40	m	w	TX	Monterey	Monterey Twp	74	347
BALINK								
Herman	27	m	w	BAVA	San Francisco	San Francisco P O	83	212
BALIS								
Geo W	45	m	w	NY	Sacramento	Lee Twp	77	160
Martin	53	m	w	TN	Sacramento	San Joaquin Twp	77	407
BALITA								
Alfonsa	21	m	w	ITAL	San Mateo	Schoolhouse Statio	87	343
BALITZ								
A P	35	m	w	FRAN	Santa Clara	Burnett Twp	88	33
Josefa	43	f	w	MEXI	Calaveras	San Andreas P O	70	185
BALK								
Frederick	26	m	w	PRUS	San Francisco	2-Wd San Francisco	79	157
Stephen S	45	m	w	ENGL	San Francisco	San Francisco P O	85	735
BALKE								
William	35	m	w	HANO	San Francisco	1-Wd San Francisco	79	77
BALKEIMER								
Charles	36	m	w	BAVA	San Francisco	8-Wd San Francisco	82	456
BALKLEY								
Matilda	35	f	w	CANA	San Francisco	San Francisco P O	85	826
BALKWELL								
John	35	m	w	ENGL	San Joaquin	Oneal Twp	86	100
BALL								
---	35	m	c	CHIN	Siskiyou	Cottonwood Twp	89	592
A	26	m	w	MO	Sacramento	1-Wd Sacramento	77	185
A Everit	24	m	w	NY	San Francisco	8-Wd San Francisco	82	333
Albion John	22	m	w	ME	Plumas	Goodwin Twp	77	8
Alfred	53	m	w	ENGL	Sacramento	Cosumnes Twp	77	91
Amasa	47	m	w	IL	Siskiyou	Butte Twp	89	586
Andrew	60	m	w	NJ	San Francisco	8-Wd San Francisco	82	316
Andrew	36	m	w	NY	San Francisco	3-Wd San Francisco	79	326
Armory F	40	m	w	MA	San Francisco	San Francisco P O	85	768
Benj	34	m	w	NY	Yuba	Marysville	93	612
C D	60	m	w	TN	Santa Clara	Gilroy Twp	88	93
Captain	23	f	i	CA	Klamath	Orleans Twp	73	380
Catharine	40	f	w	MA	San Francisco	San Francisco P O	85	810
Chas	51	m	w	NY	Butte	Chico Twp	70	14
David	48	m	w	NY	San Francisco	7-Wd San Francisco	81	176
E M	18	f	w	IL	Napa	Napa	75	8
Edgar	28	m	w	KY	Siskiyou	Table Rock Twp	89	647
Edward	38	m	w	OH	San Bernardino	San Bernardino Twp	78	451
Edward	37	m	w	VT	San Bernardino	San Bernardino Twp	78	435
Edward	30	m	w	ENGL	Santa Clara	2-Wd San Jose	88	329
Edwin	30	m	w	CT	Nevada	Washington Twp	75	340
Elbridge	38	m	w	KY	Siskiyou	Table Rock Twp	89	647
Eldridge B	26	m	w	MO	Yolo	Cache Crk Twp	93	454
Elizabeth	39	f	w	KY	Monterey	Castroville Twp	74	339
Elizabeth	30	f	w	CANA	San Francisco	San Francisco P O	83	353
Erastus	44	m	w	CANA	Nevada	Nevada Twp	75	293
Erastus	20	m	w	DENM	Yolo	Cottonwood Twp	93	463
Felander	46	m	w	VT	Monterey	Castroville Twp	74	337
Frances	13	f	w	CA	Santa Cruz	Santa Cruz	89	433
Francis	51	m	w	ITAL	Alameda	Oakland	68	203
Frank	44	m	w	VT	Monterey	Castroville Twp	74	337
George	48	m	w	OH	Shasta	Horsetown P O	89	503
George	40	m	w	IN	Santa Clara	San Jose Twp	88	183
George	35	m	w	MA	San Francisco	5-Wd San Francisco	81	3
George	30	m	w	NY	San Francisco	8-Wd San Francisco	82	337
H S	38	m	w	NY	Monterey	Alisal Twp	74	294
Harry	36	m	w	ENGL	Napa	Napa	75	43
Henry	46	m	w	KY	Los Angeles	Los Angeles	73	562
Herman	31	m	w	PRUS	Yuba	Marysville	93	579
Hugh	45	m	w	MO	San Bernardino	San Bernardino Twp	78	442
J S	49	m	w	NJ	San Francisco	San Francisco P O	85	830
James	40	m	w	IREL	Santa Cruz	Soquel Twp	89	436
James	25	m	w	CT	San Francisco	7-Wd San Francisco	81	223
James H	50	m	w	NY	Siskiyou	Table Rock Twp	89	648
Janey	22	f	w	OH	Humboldt	Mattole Twp	72	287
Jay	14	m	w	WI	Tehama	Battle Crk Twp	92	172
Jefferson D	43	m	w	NY	Mendocino	Anderson Twp	74	150
Jennett	54	f	w	NY	Amador	Drytown P O	69	423
Jno W	59	m	w	AL	Sonoma	Washington Twp	91	469
Joel	50	m	w	PA	San Francisco	2-Wd San Francisco	79	265
John	39	m	w	VA	San Francisco	2-Wd San Francisco	79	214
John	36	m	w	ENGL	Monterey	San Antonio Twp	74	315
John	31	m	w	OH	Plumas	Plumas Twp	77	27
John	24	m	w	OH	Humboldt	Mattole Twp	72	287
John	22	m	w	IL	Santa Clara	2-Wd San Jose	88	281
John	21	m	w	MO	Yolo	Grafton Twp	93	491
John A	35	m	w	IL	Nevada	Rough & Ready Twp	75	326
John C	38	m	w	VA	Yolo	Cache Crk Twp	93	423
John M	31	m	w	MO	Yolo	Grafton Twp	93	487
John O	16	m	w	IL	Siskiyou	Table Rock Twp	89	647
John P	36	m	w	IREL	Colusa	Monroe Twp	71	322
Joseph	29	m	w	OH	Humboldt	Mattole Twp	72	287
Joseph	26	m	w	CANA	Santa Cruz	Santa Cruz Twp	89	394
Joseph	25	m	w	OH	Yolo	Cache Crk Twp	93	451
Joseph L	24	m	w	OH	Yolo	Cache Crk Twp	93	423
Lucy	45	f	w	MEXI	Tuolumne	Sonora P O	93	316
Maggie	12	f	w	CA	Sacramento	2-Wd Sacramento	77	214
Martin	66	m	w	IREL	Santa Clara	Redwood Twp	88	118
Martin R	42	m	w	NY	Shasta	Millville P O	89	484
Mary	14	f	w	CA	Monterey	Pajaro Twp	74	369
Mary F	64	f	w	ENGL	San Francisco	San Francisco P O	85	763
Nancy	16	f	w	NC	Santa Clara	2-Wd San Jose	88	285
Newton	39	m	w	KY	Siskiyou	Table Rock Twp	89	645
Nich	35	m	w	PRUS	San Francisco	5-Wd San Francisco	81	13
Oliver	31	m	w	IN	Amador	Fiddletown P O	69	435
Reubin	38	m	w	IN	Amador	Drytown P O	69	423
Richard	30	m	w	NY	San Francisco	11-Wd San Francisc	84	458
Robb L	24	m	w	OH	Butte	Ophir Twp	70	105
Saml W	48	m	w	VA	San Francisco	8-Wd San Francisco	82	335
Samuel	32	m	w	NY	San Francisco	11-Wd San Francisc	84	519
Stephen	45	m	w	VA	Klamath	Orleans Twp	73	380
W	24	m	w	MO	Sacramento	1-Wd Sacramento	77	185
William	24	m	w	ENGL	Marin	Novato Twp	74	12
William H	35	m	w	ENGL	San Francisco	7-Wd San Francisco	81	178
William H	30	m	w	CT	San Francisco	7-Wd San Francisco	81	176
William L	37	m	w	US	Nevada	Little York Twp	75	242
William P	27	m	w	MO	Yolo	Cache Crk Twp	93	454
Wm Gassaway	56	m	w	SC	Plumas	Washington Twp	77	52
Wm W	43	m	w	NY	Shasta	Millville P O	89	484
Y M	36	m	w	OH	Sierra	Sierra Twp	89	569
BALLA								
Antoine	32	m	w	ITAL	San Mateo	Schoolhouse Statio	87	343
Jesus	30	m	w	MEXI	San Diego	Coronado	78	465
John	22	m	w	ITAL	San Mateo	Schoolhouse Statio	87	345
John	16	m	w	ITAL	San Mateo	Schoolhouse Statio	87	347
BALLAD								
Carie	26	f	w	ME	Sonoma	Petaluma Twp	91	312
BALLARD								
Abner H	51	m	w	OH	Colusa	Monroe Twp	71	322
Andrew J	20	m	w	US	San Mateo	Schoolhouse Statio	87	336
Arthur	4	m	w	CA	Solano	Montezuma Twp	90	65
Byron	48	m	w	MO	Tulare	Visalia Twp	92	284
C	20	f	w	IA	Santa Clara	Gilroy Twp	88	68
Charles	64	m	w	ENGL	San Francisco	3-Wd San Francisco	79	314
Charles	41	m	w	IL	Calaveras	San Andreas P O	70	153
Chas	39	m	w	MI	San Joaquin	Union Twp	86	268
Curtis	30	m	w	NY	Tehama	Antelope Twp	92	158
Dora	14	f	b	CA	Los Angeles	Los Angeles	73	530
Duane	35	m	w	NY	San Francisco	8-Wd San Francisco	82	377
Edgar	23	m	w	ENGL	Humboldt	Pacific Twp	72	290
Elizabeth	30	f	w	TX	Stanislaus	Branch Twp	92	7
Ephriam L	38	m	w	ME	Yolo	Washington Twp	93	534
Grand	34	m	w	AR	Tuolumne	Sonora P O	93	307
Harrison	55	m	w	ME	El Dorado	Georgetown Twp	72	47
Irvine C	45	m	w	VA	Calaveras	San Andreas P O	70	172
Isaac C	31	m	w	TN	Contra Costa	Martinez P O	71	382

© 2001 by Heritage Quest. All rights reserved.

California 1870 Census

Name	Age	S	R	B-PL	County	Locale	Roll	Pg
J G	30	m	w	KY	Amador	Drytown P O	69	418
J P	53	m	w	KY	Tuolumne	Chinese Camp P O	93	381
J W	58	m	w	VA	Sacramento	4-Wd Sacramento	77	342
James	53	m	w	NY	Tuolumne	Big Oak Flat P O	93	398
James A	20	m	w	OH	Contra Costa	Martinez P O	71	376
James S	51	m	w	VA	Santa Clara	San Jose Twp	88	179
Jas L	32	m	w	IL	Shasta	Stillwater P O	89	481
Jas M	53	m	w	SC	Nevada	Eureka Twp	75	135
John	55	m	w	NC	Contra Costa	Martinez P O	71	433
John	50	m	w	ENGL	Solano	Montezuma Twp	90	65
John	40	m	b	KY	Los Angeles	Los Angeles	73	503
John	40	m	w	VA	Stanislaus	San Joaquin Twp	92	81
John H	45	m	w	GA	Amador	Jackson P O	69	321
John H	26	m	w	IN	Colusa	Monroe Twp	71	322
John Q L	45	m	w	KY	El Dorado	Placerville	72	111
John W	27	m	w	IL	Solano	Green Valley Twp	90	37
Jos	40	m	w	MA	Solano	Vallejo	90	210
Joseph	45	m	w	MA	San Francisco	San Francisco P O	80	428
Lucy	15	m	w	CA	Amador	Volcano P O	69	375
M A	38	m	w	MO	Tuolumne	Chinese Camp P O	93	381
Manuel	49	m	b	MO	Sacramento	2-Wd Sacramento	77	232
Nathan	36	m	w	TX	Kern	Tehachapi P O	73	352
Newell	36	m	w	NY	Tehama	Antelope Twp	92	158
Oscar	37	m	w	CA	Stanislaus	Branch Twp	92	6
Simon	40	m	w	ME	Sonoma	Mendocino Twp	91	303
Smithfield	43	m	w	NY	Sonoma	Analy Twp	91	236
W N	38	m	w	OH	San Bernardino	San Bernardino Twp	78	429
William	44	m	w	IN	Tulare	Visalia Twp	92	280
William	38	m	w	OH	Santa Barbara	Las Cruces P O	87	515
William	35	m	w	MO	Stanislaus	Empire Twp	92	53
William	22	m	w	MO	Stanislaus	Branch Twp	92	6
Wm	15	m	w	CA	Butte	Ophir Twp	70	119
BALLDIN								
Leon	22	m	w	PA	San Francisco	8-Wd San Francisco	82	324
BALLE								
Rufus	25	m	w	MA	Mendocino	Albion & Big Rvr T	74	167
BALLEN								
Charles R	38	m	w	VT	San Mateo	Half Moon Bay P O	87	397
George	51	m	w	GREE	Placer	Bath P O	76	458
J W	21	m	w	IL	Alameda	Oakland	68	215
John	23	m	w	IREL	San Francisco	8-Wd San Francisco	82	498
Rollo	36	m	w	AUST	San Francisco	2-Wd San Francisco	79	144
William J	39	m	w	NC	Placer	Gold Run Twp	76	394
BALLENCIA								
Jesus	50	m	w	MEXI	Monterey	San Antonio Twp	74	319
BALLENGER								
John M	50	m	w	OH	Placer	Dutch Flat P O	76	415
William	46	m	w	SC	Sonoma	Mendocino Twp	91	291
BALLENSONILLA								
Pablo	35	m	w	MEXI	Napa	Napa Twp	75	68
BALLENTINE								
James	70	m	w	VA	San Francisco	11-Wd San Francisc	84	491
W	38	m	w	CANA	Alameda	Oakland	68	176
BALLENTYNE								
James	41	m	w	SCOT	San Diego	San Diego	78	487
John	44	m	w	NY	San Francisco	11-Wd San Francisc	84	497
BALLERY								
George	41	m	w	GERM	Sonoma	Petaluma Twp	91	365
BALLES								
Curim	34	m	w	MEXI	San Diego	Temecula Dist	78	527
James	21	m	w	FRAN	Calaveras	San Andreas P O	70	203
John	24	m	w	FRAN	Calaveras	San Andreas P O	70	203
BALLESTIN								
Jesus	25	m	w	MEXI	Los Angeles	El Monte Twp	73	463
BALLETH								
William	34	m	w	ITAL	San Francisco	11-Wd San Francisc	84	480
BALLETINE								
James	37	m	w	PA	Yolo	Washington Twp	93	533
BALLETT								
David	45	m	w	PA	Plumas	Seneca Twp	77	48
BALLEW								
Michael	38	m	w	IREL	Santa Clara	Alviso Twp	88	28
BALLEZ								
Louisa	50	f	w	MEXI	Napa	Napa	75	54
BALLEZA								
Ellridge	37	m	w	KY	Monterey	San Juan Twp	74	387
BALLHAUS								
Fred	55	m	w	PRUS	San Francisco	2-Wd San Francisco	79	276
BALLIER								
John	24	m	w	PA	Alameda	Oakland	68	202
BALLIGE								
G	24	m	w	ME	Nevada	Eureka Twp	75	135
BALLIGER								
Joseph	37	m	w	KY	Tehama	Tehama Twp	92	196
BALLIMOE								
Edward	46	m	w	PRUS	San Francisco	2-Wd San Francisco	79	164
BALLIN								
P	34	m	w	PRUS	San Francisco	San Francisco P O	85	809
BALLINGER								
Andrew	35	m	w	IREL	San Francisco	San Francisco P O	83	5
G H	40	m	w	PRUS	San Joaquin	3-Wd Stockton	86	219
John	39	m	w	ENGL	San Francisco	San Francisco P O	83	409
Nicholi	21	m	w	MO	San Francisco	3-Wd San Francisco	79	287
Wm	35	m	w	GA	San Francisco	2-Wd San Francisco	79	251
BALLMBHEHR								
Call	63	m	w	PRUS	Sacramento	4-Wd Sacramento	77	365
BALLME								
Jas	31	m	w	ME	Humboldt	Eureka Twp	72	277
BALLOCRADIFF								
J	28	m	w	ITAL	Alameda	Murray Twp	68	128
BALLON								
A L	44	f	w	CANA	Alameda	Murray Twp	68	122
C	65	m	w	MO	Yuba	Marysville	93	632
George	23	m	w	MA	Santa Barbara	Santa Barbara P O	87	492
John D A	43	m	w	VT	Santa Clara	San Jose Twp	88	191
Louis	42	m	w	PRUS	Siskiyou	Cottonwood Twp	89	593
Mary	38	f	w	IREL	Yuba	East Bear Rvr Twp	93	543
Mary A	55	f	w	TN	Colusa	Grand Island Twp	71	304
Vol J	41	m	w	NY	Sonoma	Santa Rosa	91	405
BALLONE								
Samuel	48	m	w	SC	Plumas	Seneca Twp	77	49
BALLOU								
George	35	m	w	OH	Tulare	Visalia	92	300
BALLOW								
Henry G	45	m	w	RI	Yolo	Washington Twp	93	534
J	47	m	w	RI	Calaveras	Copperopolis P O	70	230
BALLOWS								
Chas	47	m	w	----	San Joaquin	2-Wd Stockton	86	170
BALLS								
Fred	42	m	w	MO	Sacramento	Sutter Twp	77	383
G	39	m	w	ITAL	Sierra	Downieville Twp	89	517
R E	31	m	w	NY	San Joaquin	2-Wd Stockton	86	173
BALLSCHUETT								
S	34	m	w	HOLL	Humboldt	Eureka Twp	72	257
BALLSON								
Wm	27	m	w	ENGL	Sacramento	Franklin Twp	77	115
BALLUE								
John	24	m	w	NH	Stanislaus	Empire Twp	92	65
BALLUROES								
Antone	30	m	w	AUST	Calaveras	San Andreas P O	70	203
BALLY								
Antonio	36	m	w	ITAL	San Mateo	Schoolhouse Statio	87	345
BALMAN								
Peter	17	m	w	MEXI	San Francisco	San Francisco P O	83	130
BALMFORTH								
R	40	m	w	ENGL	Alameda	Oakland	68	153
BALMIRE								
Germano	35	m	w	ITAL	San Francisco	7-Wd San Francisco	81	245
BALMSWALER								
Jose	46	m	w	CHIL	Amador	Jackson P O	69	338
BALON								
W W	14	m	w	CA	Alameda	Oakland	68	159
BALOTTI								
Francis	23	m	w	SWIT	Sonoma	Bodega Twp	91	264
BALOW								
Mary A	10	f	w	CA	Butte	Kimshew Tpw	70	76
BALRODA								
J	40	m	w	MEXI	Tuolumne	Big Oak Flat P O	93	392
BALSAR								
Pedro	22	m	w	SAXO	Santa Clara	2-Wd San Jose	88	301
BALSARINA								
Carlo	29	m	w	SWIT	Marin	San Antonio Twp	74	64
BALSER								
Geo W	21	m	w	US	Sonoma	Analy Twp	91	232
Henry	37	m	w	OH	Sonoma	Analy Twp	91	233
John	23	m	w	HDAR	Santa Clara	2-Wd San Jose	88	328
Valentine	53	m	w	HDAR	Santa Clara	1-Wd San Jose	88	248
Valentine	50	m	w	PRUS	Santa Clara	2-Wd San Jose	88	294
BALSES								
Herman	26	m	w	SHOL	Sonoma	Salt Point	91	391
BALSLEY								
Amos	50	m	w	NY	Placer	Roseville P O	76	353
BALSTADT								
Wilhelm	58	m	w	PRUS	Sacramento	Sutter Twp	77	385
BALSTON								
Henry	42	m	w	PRUS	Kern	Havilah P O	73	350
BALTA								
Paul	35	m	i	CA	Mariposa	Mariposa P O	74	117
BALTASAR								
Frank	32	m	w	PRUS	San Francisco	San Francisco P O	80	531
BALTAZAR								
Louis	60	m	w	FRAN	El Dorado	Mud Springs Twp	72	76
BALTE								
Mares	29	m	w	ITAL	San Francisco	1-Wd San Francisco	79	114
BALTER								
R A	22	m	w	ENGL	Tuolumne	Sonora P O	93	315
BALTESMALD								
A C	45	m	w	MEXI	Amador	Jackson P O	69	345
BALTHAZARD								
Amphion	50	m	w	FRAN	Santa Clara	1-Wd San Jose	88	256
BALTIMORE								
Chas	39	m	w	IN	Butte	Kimshew Tpw	70	86
Chas	39	m	w	OH	Butte	Chico Twp	70	32
Chas	39	m	w	SAXO	Butte	Oregon Twp	70	133
BALTOGE								
Wick	35	m	w	GERM	San Joaquin	2-Wd Stockton	86	175
BALTON								
J	39	m	w	CANA	Nevada	Eureka Twp	75	139
Phillip	28	m	w	NY	San Francisco	11-Wd San Francisc	84	452
W	38	m	w	PA	Lake	Morgan Valley	73	425
Wm	42	m	w	ENGL	Sacramento	Granite Twp	77	150
BALTS								
Rincon V	46	m	w	PRUS	San Francisco	San Francisco P O	83	358

Series M593

© 2001 by Heritage Quest. All rights reserved.

Series M593

Name	Age	S	R	B-PL	County	Locale	Roll	Pg
BALTZ								
Peter	39	m	w	FRAN	Santa Clara	2-Wd San Jose	88	323
BALTZER								
Chas	40	m	w	HCAS	San Francisco	11-Wd San Francisc	84	471
BALTZLEY								
Step	36	m	w	IL	Merced	Snelling P O	74	267
BALTZLY								
S	39	m	w	OH	Merced	Snelling P O	74	279
BALUE								
Wm	38	m	w	NY	Alameda	Oakland	68	152
BALUS								
Martin	6	m	w	CA	Sacramento	San Joaquin Twp	77	407
BALWIN								
Edw	26	m	w	ENGL	Alameda	Oakland	68	163
Henry	50	m	w	NY	San Francisco	7-Wd San Francisco	81	206
John	27	m	w	NY	San Francisco	7-Wd San Francisco	81	176
BALY								
Jo	47	m	w	OH	San Joaquin	Castoria Twp	86	13
John	30	m	w	FRAN	Shasta	Horsetown P O	89	504
Moses W	43	m	w	MO	Sacramento	Georgianna Twp	77	122
BALZ								
Adolph	39	m	w	PRUS	San Francisco	San Francisco P O	85	824
BALZARI								
Celes	16	m	w	SWIT	Sonoma	Analy Twp	91	223
BALZER								
Chris	35	m	w	HAMB	Yuba	Marysville	93	616
BALZIE								
Henery	60	m	w	ENGL	San Francisco	7-Wd San Francisco	81	164
BAMAN								
David	25	m	w	BAVA	Yolo	Cache Crk Twp	93	426
BAMBAU								
Cohn	48	m	w	PRUS	Stanislaus	Branch Twp	92	1
BAMBER								
Chas	26	m	w	PRUS	San Francisco	5-Wd San Francisco	81	10
John	37	m	w	ENGL	Solano	Green Valley Twp	90	37
John	37	m	w	IL	San Francisco	1-Wd San Francisco	79	39
Joseph	25	m	w	IL	San Francisco	1-Wd San Francisco	79	39
William	40	m	w	IREL	San Francisco	6-Wd San Francisco	81	80
BAMBERGER								
Louis	25	m	w	SWIT	San Francisco	8-Wd San Francisco	82	387
BAMBRICK								
William	29	m	w	IREL	San Diego	Julian Dist	78	472
BAMBRIDGE								
Eliza	18	f	w	ENGL	Sacramento	Center Twp	77	84
Frederick	45	m	w	KY	Stanislaus	Emory Twp	92	23
Mathew	60	m	w	ENGL	Nevada	Bloomfield Twp	75	92
Sarah	47	f	w	MO	Shasta	Shasta P O	89	453
William	35	m	w	ENGL	Contra Costa	Martinez P O	71	396
BAMBURG								
Fred	29	m	w	PRUS	Colusa	Colusa	71	296
BAMBURGER								
Silas	35	m	w	BAVA	San Francisco	San Francisco P O	83	211
BAMBURY								
Mary	20	f	w	IREL	San Francisco	1-Wd San Francisco	79	65
BAMCOLI								
A	48	m	w	AUST	Amador	Jackson P O	69	329
BAMEBURY								
Jordon	30	m	w	IL	San Luis Obispo	Arroyo Grande Twp	87	278
BAMEY								
Lewis N	36	m	w	NY	Plumas	Plumas Twp	77	28
BAMFIELD								
Briean	45	m	w	TN	Colusa	Monroe Twp	71	311
John F	60	m	w	ENGL	San Francisco	San Francisco P O	83	243
Marks	32	m	w	RUSS	San Francisco	San Francisco P O	83	241
BAMFORD								
Alfred	30	m	w	ENGL	San Francisco	San Francisco P O	80	349
Edmond	21	m	w	IN	Colusa	Colusa	71	289
William	50	m	w	IREL	Alameda	Brooklyn Twp	68	54
William	49	m	w	ENGL	Santa Barbara	Santa Barbara P O	87	472
BAMGARTEL								
Chris	39	m	w	BAVA	Sacramento	Franklin Twp	77	105
BAMLES								
Joseph	55	m	w	FRAN	Calaveras	San Andreas P O	70	216
BAMM								
Anna	34	f	w	IREL	San Joaquin	2-Wd Stockton	86	164
BAMPTON								
Richard L	69	m	w	ENGL	Yolo	Washington Twp	93	532
BAMSTER								
Stokes	45	m	w	TN	Humboldt	Eel Rvr Twp	72	247
BAMUS								
Chas	25	m	w	BADE	Monterey	Alisal Twp	74	300
BAN								
Ah	47	m	c	CHIN	Butte	Kimshew Tpw	70	86
Ah	46	m	c	CHIN	Fresno	Millerton P O	72	199
Ah	39	m	c	CHIN	Butte	Ophir Twp	70	121
Ah	38	m	c	CHIN	Butte	Hamilton Twp	70	73
Ah	36	m	c	CHIN	Placer	Newcastle Twp	76	477
Ah	35	m	c	CHIN	Los Angeles	Los Angeles	73	527
Ah	34	m	c	CHIN	Butte	Hamilton Twp	70	73
Ah	30	m	c	CHIN	Calaveras	San Andreas P O	70	204
Ah	29	m	c	CHIN	Butte	Chico Twp	70	53
Ah	28	m	c	CHIN	Butte	Chico Twp	70	53
Ah	24	m	c	CHIN	Tuolumne	Chinese Camp P O	93	370
Ah	23	m	c	CHIN	Butte	Hamilton Twp	70	67
Ah	21	m	c	CHIN	Sierra	Table Rock Twp	89	571
Ah	20	m	c	CHIN	Butte	Concow Twp	70	10
Ah	14	m	c	CHIN	San Francisco	11-Wd San Francisc	84	533
Kee	37	m	c	CHIN	Yuba	Marysville	93	630
Lee	38	m	c	CHIN	Yuba	Marysville	93	626
Sing	51	m	c	CHIN	Del Norte	Crescent	71	463
BANA								
Henry	30	m	w	SPAI	San Francisco	San Francisco P O	83	355
John	36	m	w	HANO	Alameda	Oakland	68	251
BANADY								
James	75	m	w	IREL	San Francisco	San Francisco P O	83	165
Josephine	30	f	w	IREL	San Francisco	San Francisco P O	83	165
BANAGA								
Jose M	54	m	w	CHIL	Butte	Kimshew Tpw	70	82
BANAHAN								
Henry	28	m	w	IREL	San Francisco	5-Wd San Francisco	81	7
Patk	22	m	w	IREL	San Francisco	5-Wd San Francisco	81	7
BANALES								
Adalpho	19	m	w	CA	Santa Clara	Almaden Twp	88	21
N	60	m	w	MEXI	Santa Clara	Almaden Twp	88	21
BANAS								
John	60	m	w	ENGL	Alameda	Murray Twp	68	117
Lewis	22	m	w	PRUS	San Francisco	San Francisco P O	83	141
BANAYA								
R	50	m	w	CA	Santa Clara	Gilroy Twp	88	93
BANBE								
Draper	27	m	w	PA	Sacramento	Sutter Twp	77	386
BANBERRY								
Thomas	32	m	w	IREL	Placer	Summit P O	76	496
BANCA								
Joseph	21	m	i	MEXI	Inyo	Cerro Gordo Twp	73	322
BANCH								
Catherine	24	f	w	PRUS	Alameda	Alameda	68	10
BANCHARD								
Eli	45	m	w	VA	Butte	Ophir Twp	70	114
BANCHOR								
Eli	69	m	w	NH	Yolo	Buckeye Twp	93	416
BANCROFT								
Azariah A	71	m	w	MA	San Francisco	San Francisco P O	85	734
Chas E	19	m	w	CA	Butte	Ophir Twp	70	116
Chas H	47	m	w	OH	Butte	Ophir Twp	70	116
E	50	m	w	MA	San Francisco	8-Wd San Francisco	82	376
Henry	18	m	w	OH	San Francisco	2-Wd San Francisco	79	248
Hubert H	35	m	w	OH	San Francisco	San Francisco P O	85	734
Jno	40	m	w	OH	Santa Clara	Gilroy Twp	88	81
Lucy D	71	f	w	VT	San Francisco	San Francisco P O	85	734
William	53	m	w	CT	Placer	Auburn P O	76	380
Willm	37	m	w	NY	Siskiyou	Yreka	89	650
Wilton	40	m	w	ENGL	Colusa	Colusa Twp	71	280
Wm B	23	m	w	MO	San Diego	San Diego	78	495
BAND								
Abm	37	m	w	NY	San Francisco	5-Wd San Francisco	81	31
Henry	26	m	w	ENGL	Los Angeles	Wilmington Twp	73	638
Wm E	43	m	w	SCOT	Butte	Oregon Twp	70	133
BANDANCE								
Peter	45	m	w	FRAN	Santa Clara	2-Wd San Jose	88	304
BANDE								
Geo	33	m	w	ENGL	San Francisco	1-Wd San Francisco	79	78
BANDEEN								
Wm	44	m	w	SCOT	Sacramento	Dry Crk Twp	77	97
BANDEL								
Eugene	34	m	w	PRUS	Solano	Benicia	90	12
BANDERO								
Jose	109	m	i	CA	Santa Barbara	Santa Barbara P O	87	497
BANDHOLT								
Fred	37	m	w	SHOL	San Francisco	11-Wd San Francisc	84	449
BANDINE								
Dolores	9	f	w	CA	Los Angeles	Los Angeles Twp	73	497
BANDINI								
Alfred	23	m	w	CA	San Diego	San Luis Rey	78	512
Dolores	9	f	w	CA	Los Angeles	Los Angeles	73	568
Juan	35	m	w	CA	San Diego	San Luis Rey	78	512
Juan	30	m	w	CA	San Diego	San Diego	78	503
Refugia	56	f	w	CA	Los Angeles	Los Angeles	73	568
BANDIRT								
Victor	45	m	w	FRAN	Santa Clara	2-Wd San Jose	88	315
BANDMAN								
Frederick	34	m	w	PRUS	Nevada	Eureka Twp	75	130
BANDOIN								
Charles	55	m	w	FRAN	Nevada	Bridgeport Twp	75	117
BANDS								
Ed	12	m	w	CA	San Joaquin	Liberty Twp	86	82
BANDT								
Frederick	44	m	w	PRUS	Santa Clara	Milpitas Twp	88	116
BANDY								
Cornelia C	20	f	w	TN	Sacramento	San Joaquin Twp	77	407
J B	36	m	w	TN	Monterey	Castroville Twp	74	326
James	26	m	w	ENGL	San Francisco	2-Wd San Francisco	79	193
James W	33	m	w	TN	Yolo	Grafton Twp	93	498
Jesse	39	m	w	TN	Sacramento	San Joaquin Twp	77	394
Jesse A	40	m	w	FL	Monterey	Castroville Twp	74	326
Mary A	29	f	w	TN	Monterey	Castroville Twp	74	330
Reuben	50	m	w	TN	Sacramento	San Joaquin Twp	77	394
BANE								
Alexander	38	m	w	CANA	Stanislaus	San Joaquin Twp	92	78
C S	43	m	w	VA	Sierra	Forest Twp	89	531
David	36	m	w	VA	Alameda	Washington Twp	68	274
Edward F	33	m	w	MO	Yolo	Putah Twp	92	510
George B	38	m	w	PA	Stanislaus	Emory Twp	92	26
J W	22	m	w	MO	Monterey	San Juan Twp	74	400

© 2001 by Heritage Quest. All rights reserved.

Series M593

Name	Age	S	R	B-PL	County	Locale	Roll	Pg
James	30	m	w	IREL	San Francisco	San Francisco P O	83	251
Mary	14	f	w	IL	Butte	Oroville Twp	70	138
Peter	40	m	w	MO	Sacramento	American Twp	77	64
Wm R	52	m	w	KY	Santa Clara	Gilroy Twp	88	89
BANER								
August	34	m	w	WURT	Sacramento	4-Wd Sacramento	77	359
Chas	39	m	w	SHOL	San Francisco	11-Wd San Francisc	84	582
Daniel	30	m	w	PRUS	San Francisco	San Francisco P O	80	467
Emile	29	m	w	HDAR	San Francisco	2-Wd San Francisco	79	154
Gustavus A	29	m	w	PA	Santa Cruz	Santa Cruz Twp	89	396
Heinrich	45	m	w	WURT	Los Angeles	Santa Ana Twp	73	615
John	35	m	w	BADE	San Francisco	11-Wd San Francisc	84	584
Michl	39	m	w	BAVA	Sierra	Table Rock Twp	89	577
Peter	40	m	w	FRNK	San Francisco	San Francisco P O	80	349
BANES								
Jones C	30	m	w	MO	Los Angeles	El Monte Twp	73	460
BANET								
G D	24	m	w	NC	Tuolumne	Big Oak Flat P O	93	396
John	30	m	w	KY	San Francisco	5-Wd San Francisco	81	15
BANETT								
A	44	m	w	PRUS	Alameda	Oakland	68	196
Mary	15	f	w	ENGL	Alameda	Oakland	68	195
Thomas	25	m	w	US	Amador	Drytown P O	69	422
BANEY								
John	76	m	w	PA	Placer	Auburn P O	76	382
BANFIELD								
John	26	m	w	ENGL	Nevada	Grass Valley Twp	75	168
Thomas	25	m	w	ENGL	Nevada	Grass Valley Twp	75	190
W K	26	m	w	RI	Sacramento	1-Wd Sacramento	77	185
BANFORD								
Charles	38	m	w	ENGL	San Francisco	7-Wd San Francisco	81	220
BANFRETON								
Alexis	39	m	w	FRAN	Solano	Green Valley Twp	90	39
BANG								
---	25	m	c	CHIN	Siskiyou	Hamburg Twp	89	596
A	40	m	w	MEXI	Sierra	Butte Twp	89	509
Ah	41	m	c	CHIN	Tuolumne	Chinese Camp P O	93	390
Ah	40	m	c	CHIN	Trinity	Canyon City Pct	92	202
Ah	39	m	c	CHIN	Amador	Jackson P O	69	347
Ah	35	m	c	CHIN	Siskiyou	Yreka	89	650
Ah	27	m	c	CHIN	Plumas	Washington Twp	77	58
Ah	25	m	c	CHIN	Trinity	Junction City Pct	92	207
Ah	25	m	c	CHIN	San Francisco	6-Wd San Francisco	81	56
Ah	20	m	c	CHIN	San Francisco	6-Wd San Francisco	81	57
Ah	19	m	c	CHIN	Contra Costa	San Pablo Twp	71	364
Ah	17	m	c	CHIN	Plumas	Goodwin Twp	77	4
Gee	37	m	c	CHIN	Yuba	Marysville	93	625
Gee	27	m	c	CHIN	Plumas	Mineral Twp	77	23
James	45	m	w	IREL	Tuolumne	Chinese Camp P O	93	365
Lang	35	m	c	CHIN	Yuba	Marysville	93	622
Wah	22	m	c	CHIN	Marin	Novato Twp	74	9
BANGARD								
L F	44	m	w	NC	San Francisco	3-Wd San Francisco	79	320
BANGES								
Gillan	27	m	w	MEXI	Fresno	Millerton P O	72	159
BANGHAM								
E G	38	m	w	NY	Lassen	Janesville Twp	73	435
Geo	29	m	w	MI	Lassen	Janesville Twp	73	435
BANGHART								
Woolston	42	m	w	NJ	Shasta	Shasta P O	89	456
BANGILUPPO								
Louis	23	m	w	ITAL	El Dorado	Diamond Springs Tw	72	28
BANGLE								
Amos	30	m	w	ENGL	Alameda	Brooklyn	68	27
Branson	35	m	w	ENGL	Alameda	Brooklyn	68	27
Edward	41	m	w	ENGL	Alameda	Brooklyn	68	26
BANGS								
Daniel	40	m	w	MI	Plumas	Quartz Twp	77	34
Joe	40	m	w	ME	Alameda	Murray Twp	68	116
Patrick	38	m	w	IREL	San Francisco	7-Wd San Francisco	81	209
Roland	32	m	w	MEXI	Stanislaus	Empire Twp	92	37
Vital E	34	m	w	MEXI	Stanislaus	Empire Twp	92	36
William	55	m	w	NH	Alameda	Eden Twp	68	67
BANIFORD								
William	21	m	w	ENGL	San Bernardino	San Bernardino Twp	78	433
BANIN								
Henry	33	m	w	NY	Sacramento	4-Wd Sacramento	77	321
BANISTER								
John	30	m	w	GA	San Bernardino	San Bernardino Twp	78	430
John	30	m	w	ENGL	San Francisco	8-Wd San Francisco	82	323
Osmand	17	m	w	NY	Yuba	Marysville	93	581
Theo	39	m	w	VT	Sacramento	1-Wd Sacramento	77	185
BANK								
Ah	22	m	c	CHIN	Plumas	Quartz Twp	77	40
Anis	38	m	w	ME	Alameda	Murray Twp	68	119
Jesse F	16	f	i	CA	Colusa	Colusa	71	298
Oliver P	52	m	w	TN	Colusa	Spring Valley Twp	71	339
Thomas J	38	m	b	MO	Colusa	Colusa	71	298
Valentine	10	m	w	AZ	Los Angeles	Los Angeles	73	522
Wm	57	m	w	WI	Butte	Chico Twp	70	34
BANKAN								
Herman	21	m	w	PRUS	San Francisco	San Francisco P O	83	325
BANKE								
Andrew	37	m	w	OH	Stanislaus	Empire Twp	92	29
Anne	17	f	w	PRUS	San Francisco	6-Wd San Francisco	81	103
Matias	63	m	w	ENGL	Los Angeles	El Monte Twp	73	454
BANKER								
John	61	m	w	ENGL	Inyo	Cerro Gordo Twp	73	319
BANKERO								
Charles	29	m	w	ITAL	San Mateo	Schoolhouse Statio	87	332
Louis	25	m	w	ITAL	San Mateo	Schoolhouse Statio	87	332
BANKHART								
Henry	35	m	w	SWIT	Sacramento	Center Twp	77	85
BANKHEAD								
M	49	m	w	SCOT	Alameda	Oakland	68	139
Thomas	25	m	w	IREL	Colusa	Monroe Twp	71	324
William	28	m	w	VA	Humboldt	Mattole Twp	72	283
BANKIN								
Francis	20	m	w	ITAL	San Mateo	Schoolhouse Statio	87	334
John	32	m	w	ITAL	San Mateo	Schoolhouse Statio	87	346
BANKINS								
John	30	m	w	MA	Santa Clara	Redwood Twp	88	118
BANKO								
Chas	19	m	w	AZOR	San Francisco	1-Wd San Francisco	79	102
BANKOFER								
John	39	m	w	BAVA	Butte	Wyandotte Twp	70	144
BANKS								
Albert	33	m	w	PA	Contra Costa	Martinez P O	71	371
Caroline	47	f	w	CANA	San Francisco	8-Wd San Francisco	82	447
Frances A	9	f	w	KY	Los Angeles	Wilmington Twp	73	644
Frederick	42	m	w	HANO	Nevada	Bridgeport Twp	75	105
George S	42	m	w	ME	San Francisco	8-Wd San Francisco	82	379
Isabella	68	f	w	SCOT	San Francisco	San Francisco P O	80	374
J	55	m	w	PA	Alameda	Oakland	68	229
James	58	m	w	NC	Plumas	Plumas Twp	77	29
James	35	m	w	NY	San Francisco	1-Wd San Francisco	79	132
James	35	m	w	NY	San Bernardino	San Bernardino Twp	78	447
James	30	m	w	ENGL	San Bernardino	San Bernardino Twp	78	448
James	25	m	w	MO	Colusa	Spring Valley Twp	71	340
James	17	m	w	CA	San Francisco	11-Wd San Francisc	84	444
John	35	m	w	NY	San Francisco	8-Wd San Francisco	82	366
John W	30	m	b	MA	El Dorado	Mud Springs Twp	72	79
Joseph	52	m	w	ENGL	Placer	Bath P O	76	435
Joseph	37	m	w	OH	Calaveras	Copperopolis P O	70	237
Katie	10	f	w	CA	Sonoma	Russian Rvr	91	371
Lewis	41	m	w	BAVA	Butte	Oregon Twp	70	122
Martin	37	m	w	KY	Sonoma	Healdsburg & Mendo	91	280
Mary	50	f	w	PA	San Francisco	11-Wd San Francisc	84	599
Miller	34	m	w	KY	Inyo	Lone Pine Twp	73	330
R M	53	m	w	IL	San Francisco	3-Wd San Francisco	79	319
Robert	46	m	w	MI	San Francisco	7-Wd San Francisco	81	213
Robt	20	m	w	CA	Monterey	Alisal Twp	74	299
Sarah	70	f	w	IN	Placer	Rocklin Twp	76	468
Scott	26	m	w	MO	Tehama	Cottonwood Twp	92	161
Thomas C	49	m	w	CT	San Francisco	6-Wd San Francisco	81	96
W S	20	m	w	MO	Tehama	Cottonwood Twp	92	162
William	47	m	w	ENGL	San Bernardino	San Bernardino Twp	78	430
William	45	m	w	SCOT	San Francisco	6-Wd San Francisco	81	145
Wm F	38	m	w	NY	San Francisco	1-Wd San Francisco	79	88
BANLEN								
Isaac	38	m	w	POLA	San Francisco	7-Wd San Francisco	81	208
BANN								
Fredrick	35	m	w	PRUS	San Francisco	San Francisco P O	80	352
BANNACK								
Joseph	44	m	w	IREL	San Francisco	11-Wd San Francisc	84	575
BANNAHAN								
Bridget	14	f	w	CA	Santa Clara	Santa Clara Twp	88	175
Eliza	20	f	w	IREL	San Francisco	6-Wd San Francisco	81	95
BANNAN								
H	40	m	w	BAVA	Humboldt	Eureka Twp	72	279
Jacob	39	m	w	NJ	San Francisco	San Francisco P O	83	210
John	44	m	w	IREL	San Francisco	2-Wd San Francisco	79	162
Lawrence	43	m	w	IREL	Placer	Newcastle Twp	76	478
Mary	35	f	w	IREL	San Francisco	8-Wd San Francisco	82	465
BANNBERGER								
Louis	36	m	w	BAVA	San Francisco	San Francisco P O	83	201
BANNEN								
Frank	35	m	w	IREL	Sacramento	4-Wd Sacramento	77	346
Mathew	24	m	w	CANA	Plumas	Washington Twp	77	54
BANNER								
P	29	m	w	PRUS	Nevada	Nevada Twp	75	275
Simon	33	m	w	PRUS	San Francisco	8-Wd San Francisco	82	462
BANNEROT								
Eugene	29	m	w	PRUS	San Francisco	San Francisco P O	83	164
BANNET								
Etienne	41	m	w	FRAN	Alameda	Washington Twp	68	292
BANNING								
George	41	m	w	VT	Tulare	Kings Rvr Twp	92	253
Hugh	55	m	w	IREL	San Francisco	6-Wd San Francisco	81	114
John	35	m	w	MI	San Francisco	8-Wd San Francisco	82	384
John	30	m	w	IREL	San Francisco	2-Wd San Francisco	79	211
William L	28	m	w	DE	Los Angeles	Wilmington Twp	73	639
BANNINGER								
Conrad	48	m	w	SWIT	El Dorado	Salmon Falls Twp	72	132
John	40	m	w	SWIT	San Bernardino	San Bernardino Twp	78	417
BANNISTER								
Alfred	30	m	w	ENGL	San Francisco	San Francisco P O	83	147
Cramner	47	m	w	VT	Santa Cruz	Santa Cruz Twp	89	387
Ed	56	m	w	NY	Alameda	Alameda	68	7
Edw	26	m	w	NY	San Diego	San Diego	78	497
James	38	m	w	ENGL	Yolo	Cache Crk Twp	93	421
Jos	42	m	w	MD	San Francisco	San Francisco P O	83	116
L R	36	m	w	MO	Santa Clara	Gilroy Twp	88	88

© 2001 by Heritage Quest. All rights reserved.

Name	Age	S	R	B-PL	County	Locale	Roll	Pg
BANNON								
Carl	35	m	w	PA	Humboldt	Eel Rvr Twp	72	253
Cathe	34	f	w	IREL	San Francisco	San Francisco P O	83	114
Chas	30	m	w	CANA	San Francisco	San Francisco P O	85	875
Christopher	54	m	w	IREL	Marin	Novato Twp	74	10
Jane	30	f	w	IREL	Marin	San Rafael	74	52
John	56	m	w	IREL	Sonoma	Vallejo Twp	91	457
John	43	m	w	IREL	San Francisco	San Francisco P O	85	715
Pat	31	m	w	IREL	San Francisco	11-Wd San Francisc	84	666
Patrick	39	m	w	IREL	Placer	Gold Run Twp	76	394
Patrick	34	m	w	IREL	Plumas	Washington Twp	77	56
Phillips	35	m	w	IREL	San Francisco	11-Wd San Francisc	84	439
Thomas	40	m	w	IREL	Marin	Tomales Twp	74	77
BANNONI								
John	43	m	w	ITAL	San Francisco	3-Wd San Francisco	79	317
BANNSTER								
John H	21	m	w	MD	San Francisco	San Francisco P O	83	65
BANOCHI								
Hinrico	27	m	w	ITAL	San Mateo	Schoolhouse Statio	87	346
BANOCHO								
Bassalio	25	m	w	ITAL	San Mateo	Schoolhouse Statio	87	334
BANON								
Antonio	24	m	w	ITAL	Amador	Sutter Crk P O	69	399
James	36	m	w	IN	Sutter	Butte Twp	92	104
Mary	24	f	w	IREL	Amador	Sutter Crk P O	69	398
Samuel	40	m	w	NY	San Francisco	San Francisco P O	83	372
BANORA								
Jesus	24	m	w	MEXI	Fresno	Millerton P O	72	151
Ramon	26	m	w	MEXI	Fresno	Millerton P O	72	159
BANOS								
Henry	35	m	w	FRAN	Calaveras	Copperopolis P O	70	241
BANOWFT								
Martin	41	m	w	OH	Placer	Gold Run Twp	76	395
BANQUARS								
B	25	m	w	MEXI	Amador	Jackson P O	69	328
BANQUE								
Jean	52	m	w	FRAN	Calaveras	San Andreas P O	70	167
BANQUIER								
Joseph	56	m	w	FRAN	Sacramento	4-Wd Sacramento	77	362
BANS								
Ah	52	m	c	CHIN	Fresno	Millerton P O	72	200
BANSCOMB								
Jas	19	m	w	MI	Butte	Chico Twp	70	55
BANSEY								
Geo	45	m	w	NY	El Dorado	Coloma Twp	72	11
BANSON								
Leonora	8M	f	w	CA	Los Angeles	El Monte Twp	73	452
BANSTALLER								
David	34	m	w	HOLL	El Dorado	Cosumnes Twp	72	15
BANT								
Nathan	20	m	w	HOLL	San Joaquin	1-Wd Stockton	86	134
BANTA								
Abram	39	m	w	NY	Plumas	Indian Twp	77	12
H A	18	f	w	CA	Tuolumne	Big Oak Flat P O	93	402
Henry	62	m	w	KY	Nevada	Rough & Ready Twp	75	337
John D	33	m	w	GA	Yuba	New York Twp	93	642
Stephen C	33	m	w	NY	Plumas	Indian Twp	77	13
BANTADINA								
August	22	m	w	SWIT	Calaveras	San Andreas P O	70	216
BANTEN								
Jos N	33	m	w	HANO	San Francisco	San Francisco P O	83	127
BANTER								
H C	34	m	w	MO	San Joaquin	Tulare Twp	86	251
Thomas	30	m	w	KY	Mendocino	Anderson Twp	74	152
BANTING								
William	60	m	w	ENGL	Sutter	Sutter Twp	92	120
BANTLY								
A	34	m	w	WURT	Lassen	Susanville Twp	73	441
BANTON								
John	40	m	w	KY	Mariposa	Mariposa P O	74	112
BANTONN								
Julius	40	m	w	HAMB	San Francisco	2-Wd San Francisco	79	217
BANTY								
Don	37	m	w	OH	Sutter	Vernon Twp	92	130
Henry	56	m	w	TN	Sutter	Nicolaus Twp	92	112
R	42	m	w	IN	Los Angeles	Los Nietos Twp	73	586
Thomas A	41	m	w	IN	Siskiyou	Yreka	89	653
BANUN								
Josiah	30	m	w	CANA	Santa Cruz	Pajaro Twp	89	350
BANY								
John	35	m	w	VA	Sutter	Nicolaus Twp	92	113
BANZ								
John	55	m	w	SWIT	San Francisco	San Francisco P O	85	797
BANZIGER								
John	44	m	w	SWIT	Del Norte	Crescent	71	463
BAOW								
Ling	41	m	c	CHIN	Yuba	Marysville	93	628
BAP								
Ah	45	m	c	CHIN	Alameda	Eden Twp	68	61
BAPLER								
Alex	33	m	w	PRUS	San Francisco	San Francisco P O	85	809
BAPPLER								
John	25	m	w	PRUS	San Francisco	2-Wd San Francisco	79	181
BAPTASTE								
Giovanni	28	m	w	ITAL	San Francisco	1-Wd San Francisco	79	114
BAPTESE								
Juan	38	m	w	FRAN	Contra Costa	Martinez P O	71	450
BAPTIS								
John	28	m	w	OH	San Francisco	7-Wd San Francisco	81	194
BAPTIST								
Alvis	31	m	w	AZOR	San Francisco	1-Wd San Francisco	79	102
Jean	64	m	w	FRAN	San Francisco	San Francisco P O	80	472
Jean	46	m	w	FRAN	San Francisco	San Francisco P O	80	480
Jean	29	m	w	FRAN	San Francisco	San Francisco P O	80	468
John	23	m	w	BELG	San Francisco	San Francisco P O	80	343
M	42	m	w	MA	San Joaquin	2-Wd Stockton	86	178
Manuel	21	m	w	AZOR	San Francisco	1-Wd San Francisco	79	102
Manwell	33	m	w	PORT	San Mateo	Half Moon Bay P O	87	390
Robert	19	m	b	VA	San Francisco	11-Wd San Francisc	84	660
Robert	17	m	b	VA	San Francisco	6-Wd San Francisco	81	110
Thomas	50	m	w	PORT	Marin	San Rafael Twp	74	32
BAPTISTA								
Barrilla	30	m	w	SWIT	Santa Cruz	Santa Cruz	89	426
Jacinto	29	m	i	CA	Monterey	Monterey Twp	74	345
John	40	m	w	ITAL	San Mateo	Schoolhouse Statio	87	345
Jose M	22	m	w	CA	Contra Costa	Martinez P O	71	379
Papa	31	m	w	SWIT	Nevada	Grass Valley Twp	75	229
Tavertiti	47	m	w	SWIT	El Dorado	Placerville Twp	72	104
BAPTISTE								
Antone	25	m	w	PORT	Marin	San Rafael Twp	74	59
Antonio	45	m	w	BRAZ	Fresno	Millerton P O	72	156
Frank	37	m	w	PORT	San Francisco	1-Wd San Francisco	79	113
Jean	36	m	w	FRAN	San Francisco	San Francisco P O	80	468
John	47	m	w	FRAN	Yuba	Parks Bar Twp	93	649
John	25	m	w	ITAL	San Francisco	2-Wd San Francisco	79	164
John	22	m	w	ITAL	Calaveras	San Andreas P O	70	176
John	20	m	w	FRAN	San Francisco	San Francisco P O	80	423
Lewis	30	m	w	ITAL	San Mateo	Schoolhouse Statio	87	343
Robert	18	m	b	VA	San Francisco	6-Wd San Francisco	81	84
BAPTISTI								
John	28	m	w	ITAL	San Mateo	Schoolhouse Statio	87	345
Jovane	30	m	w	ITAL	San Mateo	San Mateo P O	87	349
BAPTISTO								
Alfonso	35	m	w	ITAL	San Mateo	Schoolhouse Statio	87	343
Henrico	17	m	w	ITAL	San Mateo	Schoolhouse Statio	87	346
Jeon	45	m	w	FRAN	Yuba	Bullards Bar P O	93	551
John	40	m	w	ITAL	San Mateo	Schoolhouse Statio	87	344
John	36	m	w	ITAL	San Mateo	Schoolhouse Statio	87	334
John	27	m	w	ITAL	San Mateo	Menlo Park P O	87	378
John	24	m	w	ITAL	San Mateo	Schoolhouse Statio	87	333
John	21	m	w	ITAL	San Mateo	Schoolhouse Statio	87	345
John	20	m	w	ITAL	San Mateo	Schoolhouse Statio	87	345
John	18	m	w	ITAL	San Mateo	Schoolhouse Statio	87	340
John	17	m	w	ITAL	San Mateo	Schoolhouse Statio	87	347
Jumbo	30	m	w	ITAL	San Mateo	Schoolhouse Statio	87	332
Louis	20	m	w	ITAL	San Mateo	Schoolhouse Statio	87	347
BAR								
Ah	35	m	c	CHIN	Butte	Ophir Twp	70	103
Patrick	45	m	w	IREL	San Francisco	8-Wd San Francisco	82	300
BARA								
Ah	22	m	c	CHIN	Sierra	Downieville Twp	89	520
BARABOO								
Antrozine	39	m	w	IL	Tulare	Tule Rvr Twp	92	263
BARACELO								
Francisco	23	m	w	ME	Los Angeles	San Gabriel Twp	73	594
Gabriel	26	m	w	MEXI	Los Angeles	San Gabriel Twp	73	594
Propan	45	m	w	MEXI	Los Angeles	San Gabriel Twp	73	594
BARADA								
L	44	m	w	FRAN	San Joaquin	1-Wd Stockton	86	135
M	27	m	w	CHIL	Amador	Fiddletown P O	69	440
BARADER								
Jose	28	m	w	MEXI	Napa	Napa Twp	75	33
BARADON								
Basilia	27	m	w	SWIT	Sonoma	Santa Rosa	91	396
BARAGAN								
Philip	40	m	w	IREL	Solano	Vallejo	90	149
BARAGANA								
Celia	43	f	w	MEXI	Contra Costa	Martinez P O	71	409
BARAKE								
Hanah	25	f	w	PRUS	San Francisco	7-Wd San Francisco	81	161
BARAL								
Alfred	27	m	w	FRAN	San Francisco	San Francisco P O	85	831
Dominguez	30	m	w	ITAL	Santa Barbara	San Buenaventura P	87	433
BARALES								
Colenia	45	f	w	CA	Los Angeles	Los Angeles	73	514
BARALOS								
McGregor	34	m	w	CANA	Contra Costa	San Pablo Twp	71	365
BARAMAN								
Sarah J	25	f	w	NY	Santa Clara	Santa Clara Twp	88	138
BARAMENS								
Jose	25	m	w	CA	Santa Barbara	Santa Barbara P O	87	479
BARAMORA								
Jonas	23	m	w	MEXI	San Bernardino	San Bernardino Twp	78	444
BARAMORE								
John	27	m	w	IREL	Marin	San Rafael Twp	74	25
BARANKAMP								
A	10	m	w	CA	Sacramento	3-Wd Sacramento	77	315
BARANTINE								
Sarane	74	m	w	MEXI	Shasta	American Ranch P O	89	496
BARAR								
Pedro	38	m	w	MEXI	Tuolumne	Sonora P O	93	313
BARARA								
Peter	40	m	w	ITAL	San Francisco	2-Wd San Francisco	79	235

© 2001 by Heritage Quest. All rights reserved.

California 1870 Census

Series M593

Name	Age	S	R	B-PL	County	Locale	Roll	Pg
BARAROGUIM								
A	14	m	w	CANA	Alameda	Oakland	68	146
BARASALOPS								
F	46	m	w	ITAL	Amador	Jackson P O	69	341
BARASS								
John	28	m	w	IREL	Mendocino	Point Arena Twp	74	209
BARATA								
Buchelo	18	m	w	MEXI	San Mateo	Half Moon Bay P O	87	400
BARATARA								
Charles	32	m	w	ITAL	Amador	Amador City P O	69	393
BARATINA								
Lorenzo	35	m	w	ITAL	Calaveras	San Andreas P O	70	206
BARATT								
D C	39	m	w	TN	Amador	Sutter Crk P O	69	407
Wm	24	m	w	IN	Sacramento	Sutter Twp	77	388
BARATTA								
John	34	m	w	ITAL	Mariposa	Mariposa P O	74	108
BARBA								
Barnardino	25	m	w	MEXI	San Luis Obispo	Salinas Twp	87	291
E	40	m	w	FRAN	Calaveras	Copperopolis P O	70	226
Jose	34	m	w	MEXI	San Luis Obispo	San Luis Obispo Tw	87	306
Ramon	22	m	w	MEXI	San Luis Obispo	Salinas Twp	87	291
Thomas	22	m	w	MEXI	San Luis Obispo	San Luis Obispo Tw	87	299
BARBAIRES								
Felix	54	m	w	FRAN	Solano	Benicia	90	11
BARBANE								
John	17	m	m	WIND	San Francisco	8-Wd San Francisco	82	366
BARBAR								
George W	44	m	w	VA	Inyo	Independence Twp	73	325
BARBARA								
Gabriel	22	m	w	MEXI	Santa Clara	2-Wd San Jose	88	315
Ricarda	40	m	w	SPAI	Santa Clara	2-Wd San Jose	88	326
BARBARIE								
Leopold	33	m	w	SWIT	Mariposa	Mariposa P O	74	130
BARBARY								
Ed	42	f	w	BAVA	Alameda	Oakland	68	163
Franz	40	m	w	BADE	Contra Costa	Martinez P O	71	380
BARBAT								
John	60	m	w	FRAN	San Francisco	San Francisco P O	80	416
BARBATINA								
Peter	18	m	w	SWIT	Marin	Tomales Twp	74	77
BARBE								
Ange	47	m	w	FRAN	San Francisco	8-Wd San Francisco	82	359
Hubert	38	m	w	FRAN	San Francisco	San Francisco P O	83	52
J	30	m	w	FRAN	Alameda	Oakland	68	181
Jean	37	m	w	FRAN	San Francisco	San Francisco P O	85	770
Joseph	27	m	w	FRAN	Marin	San Rafael Twp	74	43
BARBEE								
Elizabeth	50	f	w	ME	San Francisco	San Francisco P O	85	853
J D	42	m	w	KY	Sutter	Nicolaus Twp	92	106
V	46	m	w	FRAN	El Dorado	Greenwood Twp	72	50
BARBENA								
James	41	m	w	ITAL	Amador	Amador City P O	69	393
BARBER								
A J	40	m	w	NY	Mendocino	Round Valley Twp	74	220
Amos	24	m	w	CT	Napa	Napa Twp	75	67
Arthur	50	m	w	ENGL	Alameda	Alameda	68	2
B W	64	m	w	NH	Tehama	Hunters Twp	92	187
Benjamin	37	m	w	NY	Siskiyou	Table Rock Twp	89	646
C J	42	m	w	RI	Humboldt	Pacific Twp	72	294
Charles	50	m	w	OH	Sacramento	Lee Twp	77	159
Christ	30	m	w	BADE	Butte	Ophir Twp	70	118
Christopha	38	m	w	NY	Monterey	San Juan Twp	74	413
Clara	1	f	w	CA	Butte	Chico Twp	70	57
E T	32	m	w	RI	Humboldt	Eureka Twp	72	277
Edward	60	m	b	VA	San Francisco	6-Wd San Francisco	81	104
Edward W	33	m	w	ENGL	Sonoma	Petaluma Twp	91	316
Elizabeth	35	f	w	OH	Calaveras	Copperopolis P O	70	227
F	43	m	w	SWIT	Yuba	Marysville Twp	93	567
G C	37	m	w	RI	Humboldt	Pacific Twp	72	289
George	13	m	w	NY	San Francisco	7-Wd San Francisco	81	156
George W	46	m	w	NY	San Diego	Milquaty Dist	78	478
H A	59	m	w	VT	Placer	Newcastle Twp	76	473
Hernan	34	m	w	CANA	Siskiyou	Surprise Valley Tw	89	643
Isaac	49	m	w	CANA	Humboldt	Bucksport Twp	72	244
Isaac	45	m	w	CANA	Humboldt	Eureka Twp	72	261
Isaac	34	m	w	OH	Sacramento	3-Wd Sacramento	77	262
James	50	m	w	MO	Nevada	Grass Valley Twp	75	218
James	32	m	w	VA	Butte	Chico Twp	70	57
James	24	m	w	ENGL	San Francisco	7-Wd San Francisco	81	158
James M	64	m	w	KY	Placer	Clipper Gap P O	76	376
Jesse	71	m	w	NC	Siskiyou	Yreka	89	655
Jno	25	m	w	ENGL	Sierra	Gibson Twp	89	541
Jo	45	m	w	OH	Butte	Chico Twp	70	39
John	70	m	w	CT	Napa	Napa Twp	75	67
John	41	m	w	FRAN	Yolo	Grafton Twp	93	492
John	39	m	w	OH	Nevada	Bridgeport Twp	75	100
John	38	m	m	MA	San Francisco	San Francisco P O	80	401
John	32	m	w	KY	San Francisco	San Francisco P O	85	814
John	27	m	m	AL	San Francisco	San Francisco P O	80	342
John N	31	m	w	CT	Alpine	Silver Mtn P O	69	308
Katy	26	f	w	IREL	Santa Clara	2-Wd San Jose	88	305
L	29	m	w	PRUS	Alameda	Murray Twp	68	113
Laura	71	f	w	VT	Sacramento	3-Wd Sacramento	77	256
M	43	m	w	OH	Sacramento	3-Wd Sacramento	77	277
Marie	26	f	w	FRAN	San Joaquin	2-Wd Stockton	86	163
Mary	38	f	w	MA	San Francisco	8-Wd San Francisco	82	465
Mathew	54	m	w	OH	Contra Costa	Martinez Twp	71	352
Mathew O	44	m	w	IREL	Mariposa	Mariposa P O	74	101
Nathan	38	m	w	VT	Placer	Bath P O	76	448
Otis	71	m	w	VT	Sacramento	3-Wd Sacramento	77	256
Peter J	39	m	w	OH	Santa Barbara	Santa Barbara P O	87	474
Pleasant	67	m	w	VA	Butte	Chico Twp	70	43
R C	35	m	w	PA	Yuba	Marysville	93	616
Remone	36	m	i	MEXI	Inyo	Independence Twp	73	325
Richard	40	m	b	VA	San Francisco	3-Wd San Francisco	79	322
Robt	41	m	w	OH	San Francisco	5-Wd San Francisco	81	16
S	40	m	w	MO	Alameda	Oakland	68	264
S P	55	m	w	TURK	Calaveras	Copperopolis P O	70	233
Sarah	4M	f	w	CA	Placer	Gold Run Twp	76	395
Simeons	38	m	w	MO	Napa	Napa Twp	75	65
Thomas	23	m	m	MO	Alpine	Woodfords P O	69	315
Trueman	35	m	w	CANA	Siskiyou	Surprise Valley Tw	89	643
W C	49	m	w	NY	Tehama	Merrill	92	197
William	50	m	w	ENGL	San Francisco	8-Wd San Francisco	82	468
William	48	m	w	IREL	Marin	Point Reyes Twp	74	23
William	42	m	w	ENGL	Marin	San Rafael Twp	74	30
William	40	m	w	NY	Siskiyou	Surprise Valley Tw	89	642
William	40	m	w	ENGL	Placer	Gold Run Twp	76	395
William	27	m	w	MO	Los Angeles	Wilmington Twp	73	639
Wm	58	m	w	NY	Sacramento	Cosumnes Twp	77	93
Wm	57	m	w	NY	San Francisco	11-Wd San Francisc	84	625
Wm	30	m	w	IREL	San Francisco	San Francisco P O	83	130
Wyman	8	m	w	PA	Amador	Jackson P O	69	318
BARBERA								
Catharina	50	f	w	ITAL	San Francisco	11-Wd San Francisc	84	591
BARBERE								
Jacques	39	m	w	FRAN	Santa Barbara	Santa Barbara P O	87	474
Terresa	16	f	w	BADE	Monterey	Castroville Twp	74	339
BARBETTO								
Frederick	40	m	w	ITAL	San Francisco	3-Wd San Francisco	79	290
BARBIER								
Armand	37	m	w	NY	San Francisco	San Francisco P O	83	340
J B	40	m	w	FRAN	Sacramento	3-Wd Sacramento	77	290
Leonie	42	f	w	FRAN	San Francisco	6-Wd San Francisco	81	79
Paul	56	m	w	FRAN	San Francisco	11-Wd San Francisc	84	440
BARBIERA								
Manuel	36	m	w	AZOR	San Francisco	1-Wd San Francisco	79	130
Manuel	29	m	w	AZOR	San Francisco	1-Wd San Francisco	79	130
BARBIERI								
G	34	m	w	AUST	Amador	Jackson P O	69	330
Rose	14	f	w	ITAL	San Francisco	1-Wd San Francisco	79	41
BARBO								
William	40	m	w	ITAL	Amador	Volcano P O	69	386
BARBOLLA								
Juliana	46	f	w	MEXI	Alameda	Brooklyn	68	30
Luis	60	m	w	SPAI	Alameda	Hayward	68	76
BARBOR								
A	42	m	w	NY	Amador	Ione City P O	69	370
Amos	47	m	w	PA	Amador	Lancha Plana P O	69	368
Antonio	38	m	i	MEXI	Inyo	Cerro Gordo Twp	73	323
BARBORA								
Nick	23	m	w	AUST	San Joaquin	2-Wd Stockton	86	158
BARBOST								
Austin	41	m	w	FRAN	San Francisco	6-Wd San Francisco	81	89
BARBOT								
Michael	49	m	w	FRAN	Santa Clara	2-Wd San Jose	88	303
BARBOUR								
J H K	43	m	w	PA	Solano	Vallejo	90	178
John B	53	m	w	PA	Solano	Suisun Twp	90	109
Nathan	58	m	w	NY	Solano	Suisun Twp	90	99
William	46	m	w	VA	Siskiyou	Surprise Valley Tw	89	640
BARBRA								
Luciano	47	m	w	MEXI	Los Angeles	Los Nietos Twp	73	583
Maguil	40	m	w	MEXI	Mariposa	Mariposa P O	74	107
BARBREE								
Joseph	33	m	w	KY	Alameda	Washington Twp	68	282
BARBRIDGE								
Wm	43	m	w	IREL	Tuolumne	Columbia P O	93	353
BARBUSA								
Josephine	22	f	w	PA	Sacramento	4-Wd Sacramento	77	375
BARBY								
Frank	38	m	w	SWIT	Sierra	Gibson Twp	89	538
BARCARAMANTEZ								
Juan	25	m	w	MEXI	Los Angeles	Los Angeles	73	515
BARCELEAUX								
Charles	45	m	w	FRAN	Siskiyou	Yreka	89	662
BARCELLO								
Peter A	32	m	w	MEXI	Santa Clara	Santa Clara Twp	88	175
Solano	53	m	w	MEXI	Sonoma	Mendocino Twp	91	294
BARCELONE								
Juan	32	m	w	MEXI	Monterey	San Juan Twp	74	385
BARCELOUX								
Peter	32	m	w	CANA	Yolo	Cache Crk Twp	93	448
BARCH								
John	54	m	w	NY	San Joaquin	2-Wd Stockton	86	190
Wm	29	m	w	MI	San Joaquin	2-Wd Stockton	86	170
BARCIGALLUPI								
Luigi	24	m	w	ITAL	Amador	Volcano P O	69	385
BARCINA								
M	35	m	w	MEXI	Alameda	Murray Twp	68	104
BARCKLEY								
John	28	m	w	SCOT	San Francisco	7-Wd San Francisco	81	224

© 2001 by Heritage Quest. All rights reserved.

Name	Age	S	R	B-PL	County	Locale	Series M593 Roll	Pg
BARCKLY								
Stephn	47	m	w	MO	Tuolumne	Sonora P O	93	323
BARCLAY								
Andrew	56	m	w	KY	Santa Barbara	Santa Barbara P O	87	475
Charles	17	m	w	CA	San Francisco	6-Wd San Francisco	81	140
Isaac	32	m	w	ENGL	Nevada	Grass Valley Twp	75	224
James	45	m	w	KY	Calaveras	San Andreas P O	70	164
Laura	14	f	w	CA	San Francisco	San Francisco P O	83	56
Mary	44	f	w	NY	San Francisco	11-Wd San Francisc	84	430
Thomas	48	m	w	ENGL	Trinity	North Fork Twp	92	218
Thos	43	m	w	NY	San Francisco	11-Wd San Francisc	84	430
Wm	35	m	w	PA	Sacramento	Sutter Twp	77	383
BARCLE								
Isaac	26	m	w	WI	Trinity	Weaverville Pct	92	229
James	28	m	w	WI	Trinity	Weaverville Pct	92	229
BARCLY								
John	45	m	w	NY	Sacramento	Sutter Twp	77	392
Robert	26	m	w	VA	San Francisco	6-Wd San Francisco	81	114
BARCO								
Antone	40	m	w	ITAL	San Francisco	8-Wd San Francisco	82	336
Jacob	32	m	w	PRUS	Sutter	Nicolaus Twp	92	107
Lewis M	55	m	w	ITAL	Santa Clara	Santa Clara Twp	88	175
BARCOELHET								
Jessie	24	f	w	ME	San Francisco	11-Wd San Francisc	84	689
BARCOM								
J	46	m	w	PRUS	Calaveras	Copperopolis P O	70	234
BARCOT								
Jake	30	m	w	HOLL	San Joaquin	2-Wd Stockton	86	211
BARCQUER								
Francis	40	m	w	FRAN	San Francisco	San Francisco P O	83	335
BARCROFT								
Ralph	40	m	w	OH	Mariposa	Mariposa P O	74	92
BARD								
C B	20	m	w	VT	Sierra	Forest Twp	89	529
E J	32	m	w	VT	Sierra	Forest Twp	89	529
Emma M	25	f	w	OH	Los Angeles	Santa Ana Twp	73	606
Ephraham	39	m	w	IREL	Solano	Silveyville Twp	90	74
Geo	35	m	w	IN	San Joaquin	3-Wd Stockton	86	229
James	46	m	w	NJ	Shasta	Dog Crk P O	89	471
Joel	24	m	w	MO	Solano	Green Valley Twp	90	42
Joseph	26	m	w	CANA	Mendocino	Navarro & Big Rvr	74	177
Mathew	37	m	w	SCOT	San Francisco	3-Wd San Francisco	79	291
Thos	34	m	w	OH	Lassen	Susanville Twp	73	447
Thos R	28	m	w	PA	Santa Barbara	San Buenaventura P	87	443
BARDAT								
Constance	36	f	w	FRAN	San Francisco	San Francisco P O	80	466
BARDEA								
Jose	42	m	w	MEXI	Santa Cruz	Pajaro Twp	89	361
BARDEAUX								
Louis	51	m	w	FRAN	Calaveras	San Andreas P O	70	190
BARDELINE								
A	37	m	w	ITAL	Alameda	Murray Twp	68	127
BARDELLINI								
Angelo	34	m	w	ITAL	San Francisco	1-Wd San Francisco	79	121
BARDEN								
Michl	30	m	w	PRUS	San Francisco	5-Wd San Francisco	81	15
BARDENWERFER								
Otto	37	m	w	BRUN	Sacramento	4-Wd Sacramento	77	352
BARDENWERPEN								
Albert	35	m	w	PRUS	Sacramento	2-Wd Sacramento	77	241
BARDES								
Manuel	52	m	w	MEXI	Monterey	Monterey Twp	74	345
BARDETT								
Daniel	46	m	w	ENGL	Contra Costa	Martinez P O	71	418
Washington	46	m	w	GA	San Francisco	8-Wd San Francisco	82	438
BARDIN								
Henry H	53	m	w	NC	Santa Cruz	Pajaro Twp	89	353
James	60	m	w	NC	Monterey	Alisal Twp	74	304
Wm	26	m	w	MS	Monterey	Monterey	74	367
BARDNE								
Benjamin	46	m	w	PA	Santa Cruz	Pajaro Twp	89	339
BARDO								
A	18	m	w	NY	San Joaquin	2-Wd Stockton	86	161
BARDON								
Snelling	45	m	w	IREL	San Francisco	11-Wd San Francisc	84	427
BARDSLY								
John	42	m	w	ENGL	Calaveras	San Andreas P O	70	210
BARDSTEIN								
George	17	m	w	CA	San Francisco	6-Wd San Francisco	81	112
BARDUE								
Sarah	18	f	w	IA	Santa Cruz	Watsonville	89	376
BARDWELL								
David	40	m	w	PA	Mariposa	Mariposa P O	74	131
John L	39	m	w	NY	San Francisco	6-Wd San Francisco	81	123
John M	41	m	w	IN	Placer	Bath P O	76	458
Sarah	25	f	w	ENGL	Santa Clara	1-Wd San Jose	88	229
BARDY								
Pauline	57	f	w	FRAN	San Francisco	San Francisco P O	80	340
BARE								
David E	40	m	w	NY	San Mateo	Belmont P O	87	374
Jno	26	m	w	MO	Butte	Hamilton Twp	70	63
Jno G	35	m	w	PA	Butte	Kimshew Tpw	70	81
BAREAS								
Juan	50	m	w	MEXI	Santa Clara	San Jose Twp	88	209
BAREAU								
Joseph	40	m	w	FRAN	Calaveras	San Andreas P O	70	186
BAREDEN								
M J	5	f	w	IL	Solano	Vallejo	90	156
BAREFIELD								
John	32	m	w	ENGL	Contra Costa	Martinez P O	71	404
Margarett	73	f	w	KY	Merced	Snelling P O	74	277
BAREILLES								
Thomas	24	m	w	FRAN	San Francisco	San Francisco P O	85	753
BAREISA								
J	36	m	w	CHIL	Alameda	Oakland	68	250
BARELARI								
Peter	27	m	w	ITAL	San Joaquin	1-Wd Stockton	86	141
BARENA								
Charles	35	m	w	POLA	Colusa	Spring Valley Twp	71	343
BARENGO								
Antonio	45	m	w	FRAN	Fresno	Millerton P O	72	164
BARENKAMP								
Elizabeth	34	f	w	MI	Sacramento	2-Wd Sacramento	77	221
BARENTI								
Pedro	19	m	w	SWIT	Marin	San Antonio Twp	74	62
BARERAS								
Jesus	30	m	w	CA	Los Angeles	Los Angeles Twp	73	485
BARES								
Nicholas	27	m	w	MEXI	Fresno	Millerton P O	72	166
BARETA								
Antone	45	m	w	SWIT	Marin	Tomales Twp	74	77
BAREY								
Mary	23	f	w	IREL	Santa Clara	1-Wd San Jose	88	227
BARFIELD								
Sholi	22	m	i	CA	Merced	Snelling P O	74	252
BARFLED								
Bertha	18	f	w	PRUS	San Francisco	8-Wd San Francisco	82	403
BARG								
John	16	m	w	NY	San Francisco	1-Wd San Francisco	79	77
BARGAMAN								
H	40	m	w	GERM	San Joaquin	2-Wd Stockton	86	175
BARGAN								
Emillery	62	f	w	NORW	San Francisco	San Francisco P O	80	348
BARGAS								
Cecelia	29	m	w	MEXI	Santa Clara	Santa Clara Twp	88	157
Jose Antonio	63	m	w	CHIL	Los Angeles	Los Angeles Twp	73	466
BARGE								
George	39	m	w	HANO	Amador	Fiddletown P O	69	427
Lambert	43	m	w	HANO	Stanislaus	Empire Twp	92	55
BARGEMAN								
Anna	15	f	w	CA	Santa Clara	2-Wd San Jose	88	290
Christine	45	f	w	PRUS	Tulare	Visalia	92	294
BARGEN								
Henry	45	m	w	BAVA	Solano	Benicia	90	19
BARGER								
Henry	42	m	w	MA	San Francisco	8-Wd San Francisco	82	498
James	7	m	w	MO	Yolo	Cottonwood Twp	93	460
Joseph	46	m	w	CHIL	San Francisco	San Francisco P O	80	340
Parqurel	25	m	i	MEXI	Inyo	Lone Pine Twp	73	335
W F	36	m	w	IL	Nevada	Bridgeport Twp	75	120
BARGESS								
Patrick	42	m	w	IREL	Stanislaus	Emory Twp	92	22
BARGHORN								
August	34	m	w	PRUS	San Francisco	San Francisco P O	80	467
BARGIN								
Eusebe	19	m	w	FRAN	Santa Clara	Gilroy Twp	88	78
Peter	40	m	w	VT	San Joaquin	1-Wd Stockton	86	120
BARGION								
Manuel	39	m	w	CANA	San Joaquin	1-Wd Stockton	86	124
BARGLET								
John	45	m	w	ENGL	San Francisco	8-Wd San Francisco	82	292
BARGLEY								
John	17	m	w	CA	Calaveras	San Andreas P O	70	200
BARGMAN								
John	40	m	w	SAXO	Calaveras	San Andreas P O	70	204
BARGMANN								
H J	40	m	w	HANO	San Joaquin	2-Wd Stockton	86	203
BARGON								
Martin	35	m	w	PRUS	San Francisco	8-Wd San Francisco	82	435
BARGOS								
Christoval	37	m	w	MEXI	Fresno	Millerton P O	72	165
BARHAM								
A	35	m	w	CANA	San Joaquin	Dent Twp	86	28
Abraham H	37	m	w	NETH	Yuba	Bullards Bar P O	93	547
Aubrey	8	m	w	CA	Sonoma	Vallejo Twp	91	459
B H	41	m	w	ME	San Joaquin	Douglas Twp	86	32
C	32	m	w	KY	Lassen	Janesville Twp	73	432
D	38	m	w	MA	San Joaquin	Douglas Twp	86	49
Emeline	15	m	w	WI	San Joaquin	Douglas Twp	86	32
H	67	m	w	VA	San Joaquin	Douglas Twp	86	32
James F	42	m	w	KY	Los Angeles	Santa Ana Twp	73	608
Jno J	38	m	w	KY	Butte	Chico Twp	70	16
John	37	m	w	AR	Butte	Chico Twp	70	21
John A	26	m	w	MO	Santa Cruz	Watsonville	89	369
Konda	33	m	w	NY	Sonoma	Vallejo Twp	91	459
Richard M	31	m	w	IL	Santa Cruz	Watsonville	89	372
T M	29	m	w	MO	Lassen	Janesville Twp	73	432
BARHGAR								
Charles	24	m	w	NY	Colusa	Monroe Twp	71	312
BARIC								
Eugene	33	m	w	CA	Santa Clara	Burnett Twp	88	34
BARICHIEVICH								
John	35	m	w	AUST	San Francisco	8-Wd San Francisco	82	484

© 2001 by Heritage Quest. All rights reserved.

California 1870 Census

Name	Age	S	R	B-PL	County	Locale	Series M593 Roll	Pg
BARICKMAN								
Jasper N	35	m	w	KY	San Luis Obispo	Santa Rosa Twp	87	321
BARICKS								
Uriah	30	m	w	PA	San Francisco	11-Wd San Francisc	84	629
BARICLAW								
James C	42	m	w	IN	Sacramento	American Twp	77	67
BARIE								
Louis	35	m	w	FRAN	Sacramento	2-Wd Sacramento	77	248
BARIENTOS								
Florence	36	m	w	MEXI	Marin	San Rafael Twp	74	43
BARIGHT								
Mary G	8	f	w	CA	Santa Clara	2-Wd San Jose	88	298
BARILA								
Henry	34	m	w	MEXI	San Francisco	San Francisco P O	80	465
BARILE								
E	27	m	w	NJ	Nevada	Eureka Twp	75	139
BARILLAS								
Leone	60	m	w	MEXI	San Francisco	2-Wd San Francisco	79	223
BARIS								
Juan J	28	m	w	MEXI	Fresno	Millerton P O	72	166
BARISH								
Lue	45	m	b	MD	Monterey	Castroville Twp	74	330
BARITA								
Encarnacion	23	m	w	MEXI	Los Angeles	Los Nietos Twp	73	586
BARK								
Ah	19	m	c	CHIN	Solano	Vallejo	90	174
Andrew W	30	m	w	SWED	San Francisco	6-Wd San Francisco	81	40
Ar	21	m	c	CHIN	Sonoma	Petaluma Twp	91	363
Edward	28	m	w	IREL	Solano	Silveyville Twp	90	85
John	36	m	w	IREL	San Joaquin	2-Wd Stockton	86	174
Micheal	33	m	w	IREL	San Francisco	7-Wd San Francisco	81	173
William M	30	m	w	IREL	San Mateo	Half Moon Bay P O	87	398
BARKALL								
Clark	24	m	w	NY	Solano	Silveyville Twp	90	74
BARKDOLL								
J L	46	m	w	OH	Humboldt	Mattole Twp	72	287
BARKE								
Jane	25	f	w	NY	Contra Costa	Martinez Twp	71	346
BARKELOO								
John	47	m	w	NY	San Francisco	San Francisco P O	83	147
BARKEMAN								
John	30	m	w	IREL	San Francisco	San Francisco P O	83	81
BARKER								
A	39	m	w	AUST	Alameda	Oakland	68	174
A F	13	m	w	CA	Alameda	Oakland	68	242
Aaron	39	m	w	ENGL	Calaveras	Copperopolis P O	70	227
Abial	73	m	w	KY	Yolo	Grafton Twp	93	495
Alfred	21	m	w	TN	San Francisco	11-Wd San Francisc	84	643
Andrew J	42	m	w	OH	Amador	Volcano P O	69	387
Anne	22	f	w	HANO	Alameda	Oakland	68	194
Anne	15	f	w	NY	San Francisco	8-Wd San Francisco	82	498
Annie	25	f	w	ENGL	San Francisco	2-Wd San Francisco	79	141
Benj	42	m	w	ENGL	Fresno	Millerton P O	72	163
C S	62	f	w	MA	San Francisco	San Francisco P O	85	774
Charles	59	m	w	NH	El Dorado	Georgetown Twp	72	46
Charles	44	m	w	NH	Nevada	Grass Valley Twp	75	154
Charles W	44	m	w	TN	Santa Cruz	Soquel Twp	89	442
Chas	34	m	w	ENGL	Humboldt	Table Bluff Twp	72	307
David M	45	m	w	NH	Nevada	Grass Valley Twp	75	222
Dewight	8	m	i	CA	Trinity	Hayfork Valley	92	238
Don H	35	m	w	NY	Alpine	Woodfords P O	69	315
Edward	40	m	w	MA	Tuolumne	Sonora P O	93	323
Edward	36	m	w	MA	San Francisco	11-Wd San Francisc	84	585
Edward	33	m	w	NY	San Francisco	San Francisco P O	80	531
Edward	26	m	w	TX	Los Angeles	Los Nietos Twp	73	591
Elizth	55	f	w	NY	San Francisco	San Francisco P O	83	112
Emmett	35	m	w	IL	Placer	Lincoln P O	76	482
Francis	13	m	w	OH	Sutter	Sutter Twp	92	121
Francis	13	m	w	PA	Sutter	Sutter Twp	92	121
Frank	46	m	w	MA	San Francisco	11-Wd San Francisc	84	704
Frank	30	m	w	ENGL	Alameda	Oakland	68	147
Frank	21	m	w	NCOD	Contra Costa	Martinez P O	71	441
Fredrick	30	m	w	MA	San Francisco	San Francisco P O	80	384
George	45	m	w	NY	San Francisco	8-Wd San Francisco	82	440
George	37	m	w	ENGL	Inyo	Cerro Gordo Twp	73	320
George	37	m	w	VA	Shasta	Millville P O	89	493
George	33	m	w	ENGL	Inyo	Lone Pine Twp	73	331
George	28	m	w	RI	San Mateo	San Mateo P O	87	352
George	22	m	w	MI	Plumas	Indian Twp	77	10
George	21	m	w	IREL	San Francisco	San Francisco P O	80	471
George F	40	m	w	NH	Solano	Vacaville Twp	90	134
Grace	63	f	w	ENGL	San Francisco	11-Wd San Francisc	84	502
Harry	54	m	w	CT	Alameda	Alameda	68	2
Henry	46	m	b	HI	Siskiyou	Cottonwood Twp	89	590
Henry	40	m	w	MA	Solano	Montezuma Twp	90	67
Henry	36	m	w	MA	Marin	San Rafael Twp	74	25
Henry	33	m	w	PA	San Francisco	11-Wd San Francisc	84	653
Henry	32	m	w	IL	San Francisco	11-Wd San Francisc	84	674
Henry	32	m	w	SHOL	Nevada	Washington Twp	75	346
Henry T	38	m	w	NH	Napa	Napa	75	35
Hosea	56	m	w	TN	San Francisco	11-Wd San Francisc	84	485
Howard	25	m	w	MA	San Francisco	7-Wd San Francisco	81	223
Hugh	45	m	w	PA	El Dorado	Placerville	72	124
Ida	13	f	w	CA	Solano	Benicia	90	16
J	39	m	w	CANA	Alameda	Oakland	68	212
J	35	m	w	CT	Alameda	Oakland	68	157
J D	33	m	w	IL	Lassen	Susanville Twp	73	446
J L	22	m	w	NC	Santa Clara	Gilroy Twp	88	98
J M	43	m	w	MA	Nevada	Bloomfield Twp	75	99
J M	38	m	w	CANA	San Joaquin	Castoria Twp	86	2
Jacob	40	m	w	PRUS	San Francisco	5-Wd San Francisco	81	35
James	40	m	w	MO	Sutter	Vernon Twp	92	139
James	35	m	w	VA	Stanislaus	San Joaquin Twp	92	83
James	25	m	w	TN	San Francisco	11-Wd San Francisc	84	485
James S	40	m	w	KY	Santa Clara	Santa Clara Twp	88	162
Jane	25	f	w	IREL	Alameda	Oakland	68	160
Jas A	44	m	w	MO	Santa Barbara	San Buenaventura P	87	431
Jas L	30	m	w	MA	San Francisco	8-Wd San Francisco	82	325
Jas L	23	m	w	MA	Santa Barbara	Santa Barbara P O	87	502
Jesse G	35	m	w	IN	Santa Cruz	Pajaro Twp	89	354
John	44	m	w	ENGL	Calaveras	San Andreas P O	70	173
John	42	m	w	PA	Sonoma	Cloverdale Twp	91	268
John	40	m	w	NY	Plumas	Plumas Twp	77	30
John	34	m	w	MO	Sonoma	Cloverdale Twp	91	266
John	23	m	w	ENGL	Monterey	Castroville Twp	74	335
John	17	m	w	MO	Sonoma	Sonoma Twp	91	445
John S	44	m	w	NY	Santa Cruz	Santa Cruz Twp	89	385
Joseph	54	m	w	OH	Plumas	Rich Bar Twp	77	46
Joshua	39	m	w	KY	Santa Cruz	Pajaro Twp	89	354
Josie E	20	f	w	LA	Nevada	Grass Valley Twp	75	150
Julius	46	m	w	NY	Nevada	Nevada Twp	75	282
Lucy	11	f	w	CA	Santa Clara	Santa Clara Twp	88	158
M C	37	m	w	GA	El Dorado	Georgetown Twp	72	41
Maria	30	f	w	IREL	Alameda	Oakland	68	210
Martha H	53	f	w	ME	Contra Costa	Martinez P O	71	379
Mary	49	f	w	MO	Los Angeles	Los Nietos Twp	73	591
Mary	30	f	w	IREL	San Francisco	11-Wd San Francisc	84	569
N	40	m	w	PA	Alameda	Oakland	68	154
Oscar Charles	39	m	w	PA	Plumas	Mineral Twp	77	20
Paul	33	m	w	NM	San Francisco	San Francisco P O	83	360
R	40	m	w	MA	San Joaquin	3-Wd Stockton	86	223
R J	52	f	w	OH	Santa Clara	Almaden Twp	88	16
Rebecca	30	f	w	ME	San Francisco	11-Wd San Francisc	84	563
Richard	46	m	w	ENGL	Contra Costa	Martinez P O	71	421
Samuel A	36	m	w	ME	Santa Clara	San Jose Twp	88	216
Samuel O	35	m	w	OH	Yolo	Putah Twp	93	526
Sidney D	32	m	w	ME	Santa Clara	Milpitas Twp	88	115
Stephen	36	m	w	ME	Nevada	Little York Twp	75	240
Taylor	21	m	w	KY	Solano	Tremont Twp	90	28
Theodore	36	m	w	SWIT	Calaveras	Copperopolis P O	70	246
Thomas	25	m	w	OH	Solano	Denverton Twp	90	25
Thoms	38	m	w	IREL	San Francisco	2-Wd San Francisco	79	214
Thos	60	m	w	MA	Sonoma	Bodega Twp	91	258
Thos	36	m	w	ENGL	San Joaquin	3-Wd Stockton	86	222
Timothy L	40	m	w	CT	San Francisco	8-Wd San Francisco	82	429
Vine	40	m	w	IL	Kern	Bakersfield P O	73	365
W S	39	m	w	MA	Humboldt	Pacific Twp	72	295
William	41	m	w	ME	El Dorado	Placerville Twp	72	105
William	36	m	w	NJ	San Francisco	3-Wd San Francisco	79	310
William	33	m	w	ME	San Mateo	Half Moon Bay P O	87	402
William	30	m	w	MO	Santa Cruz	Pajaro Twp	89	351
William	28	m	w	IREL	Yolo	Cache Crk Twp	93	421
William	25	m	w	IN	Los Angeles	Los Angeles	73	519
William	24	m	w	NY	San Francisco	3-Wd San Francisco	79	311
William O	42	m	w	ME	Santa Clara	1-Wd San Jose	88	265
Williamson	35	m	w	IL	Nevada	Rough & Ready Twp	75	336
Willie	5	m	w	CA	Santa Clara	1-Wd San Jose	88	236
Wm	54	m	w	KY	Santa Clara	Burnett Twp	88	39
Wm C	48	m	w	NY	Nevada	Little York Twp	75	237
BARKERVILLE								
Richd	48	m	w	MA	San Francisco	San Francisco P O	83	29
BARKET								
Harry	40	m	w	PRUS	Calaveras	Copperopolis P O	70	258
BARKETT								
William	40	m	w	MO	Amador	Volcano P O	69	385
BARKHAUS								
Wm F	33	m	w	PRUS	San Francisco	8-Wd San Francisco	82	313
BARKHOUSE								
Dietrich	46	m	w	HAMB	San Francisco	8-Wd San Francisco	82	482
Henry	50	m	w	HANO	Placer	Auburn P O	76	364
BARKLA								
Isaac	25	m	w	ENGL	Nevada	Grass Valley Twp	75	148
John	38	m	w	ENGL	Nevada	Grass Valley Twp	75	147
John S	30	m	w	ENGL	El Dorado	Diamond Springs Tw	72	26
BARKLAGE								
G H	42	m	w	HANO	El Dorado	Georgetown Twp	72	40
BARKLEY								
Danl	33	m	w	SCOT	San Francisco	1-Wd San Francisco	79	94
Henry	25	m	w	OH	San Francisco	7-Wd San Francisco	81	176
John	28	m	w	CANA	Sutter	Sutter Twp	92	122
Thomas	57	m	w	KY	Placer	Roseville P O	76	355
William	68	m	w	IREL	San Francisco	2-Wd San Francisco	79	283
BARKLY								
Chas	40	m	w	VA	San Joaquin	2-Wd Stockton	86	196
BARKMAN								
A	35	m	w	BAVA	Sutter	Butte Twp	92	97
P	49	m	w	GERM	San Joaquin	2-Wd Stockton	86	162
BARKWAY								
Robert	37	m	w	ENGL	Solano	Maine Prairie Twp	90	48
Thomas	34	m	w	ENGL	Santa Clara	San Jose Twp	88	201
BARLAGE								
Henry	54	m	w	PRUS	San Francisco	6-Wd San Francisco	81	121
BARLAND								
A	31	m	w	SCOT	San Joaquin	Elkhorn Twp	86	54

© 2001 by Heritage Quest. All rights reserved.

Name	Age	S	R	B-PL	County	Locale	Roll	Pg
						Series M593		
Frances	32	m	w	FINL	San Francisco	3-Wd San Francisco	79	291
BARLAW								
Charles	25	m	w	FRAN	San Francisco	2-Wd San Francisco	79	147
BARLAY								
John	32	m	w	PRUS	San Francisco	San Francisco P O	80	350
BARLEBEL								
Robert	25	m	w	PRUS	Sacramento	2-Wd Sacramento	77	242
BARLEN								
Pat	30	m	w	IREL	San Francisco	11-Wd San Francisc	84	707
BARLEY								
A H	42	m	w	PA	San Francisco	San Francisco P O	85	822
Benj	35	m	w	MD	Sacramento	Cosumnes Twp	77	90
David	70	m	w	PA	San Francisco	San Francisco P O	85	822
Evans	32	m	w	VA	Tehama	Merrill	92	197
George	32	m	w	NY	Alameda	Oakland	68	154
James	20	m	w	NY	San Francisco	5-Wd San Francisco	81	36
James B	60	m	w	VA	Colusa	Monroe Twp	71	311
Seth	41	m	w	MO	El Dorado	Cosumnes Twp	72	14
Seth	41	m	w	MO	El Dorado	Cosumnes Twp	72	13
BARLEYCORN								
John	54	m	w	HAMB	Trinity	Canyon City Pct	92	202
BARLIER								
Thomas	40	m	w	ENGL	San Francisco	San Francisco P O	80	386
BARLING								
Frank	29	m	w	NY	Stanislaus	Empire Twp	92	58
Geo	56	m	w	NY	Butte	Kimshew Tpw	70	83
Henry	38	m	w	ENGL	Stanislaus	Empire Twp	92	58
John	6	m	w	MA	Marin	San Rafael Twp	74	29
Nellie	29	f	w	MA	Marin	Novato Twp	74	12
BARLO								
Thos	70	m	w	MEXI	San Francisco	8-Wd San Francisco	82	361
BARLOCK								
Giuseppi	29	m	w	SWIT	Marin	San Rafael Twp	74	26
BARLOOPO								
F	48	m	w	ITAL	Amador	Jackson P O	69	338
BARLOS								
Manuel	29	m	w	MEXI	Stanislaus	Empire Twp	92	60
BARLOW								
Aarisey	26	m	w	NY	Calaveras	San Andreas P O	70	220
Agnes	42	f	w	MO	Nevada	Meadow Lake Twp	75	261
Alexander	41	m	w	MO	Amador	Fiddletown P O	69	437
Ben	22	m	w	ENGL	San Francisco	San Francisco P O	83	36
Billy	20	m	i	CA	Del Norte	Smith Rvr Twp	71	481
Carrie	22	f	w	NY	San Francisco	6-Wd San Francisco	81	104
Charles	44	m	w	NY	Alameda	Oakland	68	192
Charles B	39	m	w	MA	Placer	Bath P O	76	433
Charles O	18	m	w	MA	Santa Clara	2-Wd San Jose	88	329
Davie	22	m	w	RI	Sonoma	Petaluma Twp	91	350
Deborah	10	f	w	CA	Nevada	Grass Valley Twp	75	230
Eliza	64	f	w	VT	San Francisco	11-Wd San Francisc	84	681
Geo W	35	m	w	PA	El Dorado	Placerville Twp	72	97
George	64	m	w	ENGL	San Mateo	Half Moon Bay P O	87	406
Henry	50	m	w	OH	Alameda	Alameda	68	4
James	23	m	w	NY	Santa Clara	2-Wd San Jose	88	329
James	23	m	w	NY	Santa Clara	1-Wd San Jose	88	255
John	60	m	w	KY	Colusa	Colusa	71	291
John	30	m	w	IREL	San Francisco	San Francisco P O	83	262
Luke	43	m	w	ENGL	Sonoma	Healdsburg & Mendo	91	280
Michl	35	m	w	CA	San Francisco	1-Wd San Francisco	79	97
Richd	12	m	w	AR	Butte	Kimshew Tpw	70	78
Sarah	37	f	w	IREL	Alameda	Oakland	68	147
Saxon	43	m	w	KY	Sutter	Butte Twp	92	90
Soloman	33	m	w	NY	Sonoma	Petaluma Twp	91	355
Sophia	27	f	w	ME	Santa Cruz	Santa Cruz Twp	89	394
Thomas	45	m	w	ENGL	Tuolumne	Chinese Camp P O	93	364
Thomas	42	m	w	NY	Butte	Ophir Twp	70	113
W L	39	m	w	NY	Monterey	Monterey Twp	74	351
Wm	32	m	w	MI	Sacramento	4-Wd Sacramento	77	378
Wm	26	m	w	NY	San Joaquin	2-Wd Stockton	86	167
Wm L	39	m	w	NY	Monterey	Monterey Twp	74	350
BARLTES								
Teodoro	25	m	w	MEXI	Monterey	San Antonio Twp	74	321
BARLY								
David G	30	m	w	AR	Sacramento	Sutter Twp	77	391
G W	32	m	w	PA	Alameda	Oakland	68	157
BARM								
Francis	22	m	w	PRUS	Santa Clara	2-Wd San Jose	88	335
BARMAN								
David	25	m	w	BAVA	Yolo	Cache Crk Twp	93	422
Jas	29	m	w	CT	Butte	Kimshew Tpw	70	86
Jonas	42	m	w	BAVA	San Francisco	11-Wd San Francisc	84	513
Malachi	23	m	w	IREL	San Francisco	11-Wd San Francisc	84	566
Mayo	25	m	w	GERM	Humboldt	Eureka Twp	72	273
BARMER								
Mark	25	m	w	PRUS	San Francisco	San Francisco P O	83	46
BARMES								
George W	50	m	w	PA	San Luis Obispo	San Luis Obispo Tw	87	299
BARMEYER								
Hanry	44	m	w	GERM	Tuolumne	Columbia P O	93	351
BARMON								
Susan	66	f	w	NY	Placer	Auburn P O	76	363
BARMORE								
James	42	m	w	NY	Santa Cruz	Santa Cruz Twp	89	390
James S	63	m	w	NY	Contra Costa	Martinez P O	71	393
BARMOSER								
Simon	53	m	w	PRUS	San Francisco	11-Wd San Francisc	84	614

Name	Age	S	R	B-PL	County	Locale	Roll	Pg
						Series M593		
BARMS								
Thomas	26	m	w	MA	Tuolumne	Columbia P O	93	350
BARN								
Charlott	2	f	w	CA	San Francisco	11-Wd San Francisc	84	711
Laura	4	f	w	CA	San Francisco	11-Wd San Francisc	84	711
Thomas	21	m	w	IREL	Plumas	Quartz Twp	77	34
BARNABY								
Kate	29	f	w	NH	Santa Clara	1-Wd San Jose	88	232
BARNAK								
Helena	29	f	w	PRUS	San Diego	San Diego	78	485
BARNAMAYON								
Marian	17	f	w	FRAN	San Francisco	11-Wd San Francisc	84	517
BARNARD								
Abby	30	f	w	ME	Alameda	Eden Twp	68	60
Abner	19	m	w	MI	Placer	Alta P O	76	411
Austin D	40	m	w	ME	Santa Barbara	San Buenaventura P	87	438
Frank	30	m	w	MA	San Francisco	8-Wd San Francisco	82	469
Frederick	43	m	w	FRAN	Tulare	Visalia	92	296
H	30	m	w	SAXO	Sacramento	3-Wd Sacramento	77	293
Isaac	22	m	w	POLA	Mendocino	Albion & Big Rvr T	74	167
J E	26	m	w	ME	Humboldt	Arcata Twp	72	226
J K P	30	m	w	IL	Del Norte	Happy Camp Twp	71	471
James	60	m	w	PRUS	San Francisco	San Francisco P O	83	212
James	57	m	w	FRAN	San Francisco	San Francisco P O	83	217
Jane	30	f	b	WIND	San Francisco	San Francisco P O	80	333
John	32	m	w	POLA	San Francisco	7-Wd San Francisco	81	194
John	25	m	w	MA	San Francisco	7-Wd San Francisco	81	282
John	14	m	w	IL	Monterey	Pajaro Twp	74	368
Lewis	25	m	w	WI	Alameda	Brooklyn Twp	68	42
Louis	31	m	w	SC	Marin	San Rafael	74	55
Mathew	27	m	w	MA	San Francisco	San Francisco P O	83	333
Max	12	m	w	CA	San Francisco	11-Wd San Francisc	84	466
Samuel	58	m	w	MA	Contra Costa	Martinez Twp	71	350
Ulric	36	m	w	CANA	San Francisco	7-Wd San Francisco	81	206
W M	28	m	w	IL	Del Norte	Happy Camp Twp	71	468
W M	28	m	w	IL	Del Norte	Happy Camp Twp	71	468
William	47	m	w	MA	Marin	San Rafael	74	54
Willm	22	m	w	MI	Siskiyou	Table Rock Twp	89	645
Wm E	37	m	w	MA	Santa Barbara	San Buenaventura P	87	420
BARNARDS								
Ira	41	m	w	ME	Mendocino	Big Rvr Twp	74	160
BARNASTER								
Alexander	39	m	w	NY	Contra Costa	Martinez P O	71	401
BARNATH								
Simeon	36	m	w	MEXI	Santa Clara	Alviso Twp	88	26
BARNE								
Dennis	40	m	w	IREL	San Francisco	San Francisco P O	83	146
George	36	m	w	SCOT	Alameda	Oakland	68	263
BARNEAS								
Geo	35	m	w	FRAN	Alameda	Oakland	68	181
BARNELL								
H B	40	m	w	NY	Tuolumne	Sonora P O	93	333
R	40	m	w	NY	San Joaquin	Tulare Twp	86	258
BARNEM								
Daniel	50	m	w	NY	San Joaquin	Oneal Twp	86	104
BARNEO								
Charles	16	m	w	PRUS	San Diego	Julian Dist	78	469
BARNES								
A E	10	f	m	CA	Solano	Benicia	90	2
A O	38	m	w	NY	San Joaquin	2-Wd Stockton	86	167
A P	46	m	w	OH	Yuba	Marysville	93	606
Abraham	54	m	w	MO	Yolo	Cache Crk Twp	93	443
Abraham	30	m	w	MO	Stanislaus	Emory Twp	92	23
Abram	54	m	w	MO	Yolo	Putah Twp	93	521
Aletha	23	f	w	CANA	Santa Clara	1-Wd San Jose	88	244
Alfred	39	m	w	ENGL	Calaveras	Copperopolis P O	70	244
Alfred	33	m	w	ENGL	Santa Clara	Gilroy Twp	88	96
Alfred H	52	m	w	PA	Sonoma	Petaluma Twp	91	309
Amos	44	m	w	NY	Plumas	Seneca Twp	77	51
Andrew	51	m	w	MO	Los Angeles	El Monte Twp	73	460
Andrew J	40	m	w	MO	Sacramento	2-Wd Sacramento	77	220
Anna	45	f	w	CANA	San Francisco	San Francisco P O	85	747
B G	44	m	w	NY	Alameda	Oakland	68	174
Belton	40	m	w	IL	Merced	Snelling P O	74	279
Benj M	42	m	w	KY	Sacramento	Natomas Twp	77	169
Benjamin W	50	m	w	NY	Plumas	Goodwin Twp	77	6
Betsey T	74	f	w	CT	San Francisco	San Francisco P O	83	52
Betsy	71	f	w	CT	San Joaquin	2-Wd Stockton	86	165
Charles	45	m	w	PA	San Francisco	11-Wd San Francisc	84	622
Charles	37	m	w	MA	Alameda	Hayward	68	74
Charles	23	m	w	CT	Santa Clara	San Jose Twp	88	213
Chas	48	m	w	PRUS	Sacramento	3-Wd Sacramento	77	295
Chas	36	m	w	OH	Sacramento	1-Wd Sacramento	77	189
D P	47	m	w	IN	Siskiyou	Big Valley Twp	89	582
Daniel	65	m	w	NY	San Francisco	3-Wd San Francisco	79	308
Daniel	33	m	w	OH	Santa Cruz	Pajaro Twp	89	351
Daniel	25	m	w	IL	Los Angeles	Santa Ana Twp	73	600
David	34	m	w	OH	Contra Costa	San Pablo Twp	71	355
Douglas	43	m	w	NY	Solano	Vallejo	90	197
E H	42	m	w	KY	Sonoma	Russian Rvr	91	373
E T	22	m	w	TN	Lassen	Susanville Twp	73	443
Ea P	23	m	w	MO	Sonoma	Santa Rosa	91	427
Edward	46	m	w	ENGL	Napa	Napa Twp	75	59
Elisha	35	m	w	MO	Yolo	Cache Crk Twp	93	443
Eliza B	28	f	w	RI	San Francisco	San Francisco P O	83	340
Ellen	16	f	w	CA	Santa Barbara	Santa Barbara P O	87	494
Emma	23	f	w	MI	San Francisco	8-Wd San Francisco	82	472

© 2001 by Heritage Quest. All rights reserved.

Name	Age	S	R	B-PL	County	Locale	Series M593 Roll	Pg
Ephr M	31	m	w	MO	Butte	Chico Twp	70	20
Ephraim W	30	m	w	MO	Sacramento	Franklin Twp	77	111
F B	45	m	w	ENGL	Tuolumne	Big Oak Flat P O	93	392
F S	42	m	w	NY	Sacramento	1-Wd Sacramento	77	186
Florence	23	f	w	NY	Alameda	Hayward	68	76
Frances	6	f	w	CA	Nevada	Eureka Twp	75	131
Frank	51	m	w	VA	Sonoma	Santa Rosa	91	422
Frank J	34	m	w	MO	Yolo	Putah Twp	93	521
Geo	40	m	w	NY	Tehama	Cottonwood Twp	92	161
Geo R	47	m	w	NY	Alameda	Oakland	68	135
Geo W	45	m	w	OH	Butte	Chico Twp	70	23
Geo W	44	m	w	VA	Nevada	Grass Valley Twp	75	152
Geo W	40	m	w	VA	Monterey	Monterey	74	354
George	52	m	w	MO	Fresno	Millerton P O	72	160
George	28	m	w	ME	Tuolumne	Sonora P O	93	321
George H	30	m	w	OH	Yolo	Putah Twp	93	522
Grace	74	f	w	KY	Yolo	Cache Crk Twp	93	444
Grace	15	f	w	MO	Yolo	Putah Twp	93	526
Hannah	76	f	w	NY	Yuba	Marysville	93	606
Hariett	30	f	w	IREL	San Francisco	5-Wd San Francisco	81	25
Henry	31	m	w	NY	Alameda	Oakland	68	174
Henry L	43	m	w	RI	Santa Clara	San Jose Twp	88	195
Henry L	35	m	w	OH	Santa Cruz	Watsonville	89	368
Henry L	32	m	w	OH	Santa Cruz	Pajaro Twp	89	344
Henry S	73	m	w	CT	El Dorado	Placerville	72	125
Henry S	29	m	w	PA	Sonoma	Salt Point	91	381
Isaac	28	m	w	IL	Humboldt	Arcata Twp	72	229
J T	32	m	w	NY	Sacramento	4-Wd Sacramento	77	335
J W	28	m	w	NY	Alameda	Oakland	68	259
Jacob	65	m	w	NY	Klamath	Trinidad Twp	73	390
James	37	m	w	IREL	San Francisco	San Francisco P O	83	146
James	35	m	w	ENGL	Yolo	Grafton Twp	93	481
James	27	m	w	PA	Alameda	Washington Twp	68	296
James	21	m	w	CANA	Mendocino	Navarro & Big Rvr	74	174
James E	42	m	w	KY	Yolo	Cache Crk Twp	93	439
James L	32	m	w	MD	Stanislaus	Washington Twp	92	87
Jas H	22	m	w	MA	Santa Barbara	Santa Barbara P O	87	503
Jehu	41	m	w	TN	Sonoma	Vallejo Twp	91	459
Jno	32	m	w	IREL	Sacramento	1-Wd Sacramento	77	179
Jno	27	m	w	WALE	Butte	Kimshew Tpw	70	80
Jo	22	m	w	MO	San Joaquin	Castoria Twp	86	13
John	58	m	w	PA	Placer	Lincoln P O	76	490
John	52	m	w	OH	Napa	Napa Twp	75	31
John	45	m	w	ENGL	San Joaquin	Castoria Twp	86	13
John	31	m	w	MO	Solano	Montezuma Twp	90	65
John	28	m	w	CANA	Sonoma	Petaluma Twp	91	321
John	28	m	w	IL	Butte	Mountain Spring Tw	70	87
John	28	m	w	IREL	Solano	Maine Prairie Twp	90	51
John	24	m	b	PA	Solano	Vallejo	90	203
John	22	m	w	IREL	Stanislaus	Emory Twp	92	25
John	21	m	w	OH	Solano	Vallejo	90	200
John	10	m	w	NJ	San Francisco	5-Wd San Francisco	81	25
John Frank	22	m	w	TX	Tulare	Venice Twp	92	274
John J	29	m	w	CANA	Sonoma	Petaluma Twp	91	337
John W	43	m	w	GA	San Diego	San Pasqual	78	523
Jos	50	m	w	IREL	Sacramento	1-Wd Sacramento	77	190
Joseph	42	m	w	HANO	San Francisco	San Francisco P O	85	782
Joseph	40	m	w	SCOT	San Joaquin	Elliott Twp	86	71
Joseph	23	m	w	TX	Stanislaus	San Joaquin Twp	92	78
Julia	30	f	w	NY	Sacramento	2-Wd Sacramento	77	243
Julia	25	f	w	IREL	Nevada	Grass Valley Twp	75	193
L	72	f	w	NY	Alameda	Oakland	68	174
Larkin	66	m	w	KY	Los Angeles	El Monte Twp	73	461
Lewis	66	m	b	MD	Sonoma	Petaluma Twp	91	323
Lorenzo A	45	m	w	NY	Calaveras	Copperopolis P O	70	249
Luck	30	m	w	MO	Butte	Chico Twp	70	17
Lucy	43	f	w	NY	Kern	Bakersfield P O	73	360
M	37	m	w	IN	Mendocino	Calpella Twp	74	189
M	35	f	w	IREL	San Joaquin	2-Wd Stockton	86	165
Maggie	54	f	w	NC	Butte	Chico Twp	70	55
Margaret	80	f	b	VA	Sonoma	Petaluma Twp	91	323
Margaret	35	f	w	CANA	San Francisco	San Francisco P O	85	749
Martha	17	f	w	OH	Sonoma	Salt Point	91	385
Marthe	78	f	w	VA	Tehama	Paynes Crk Twp	92	167
Martin	30	m	w	NY	Santa Clara	1-Wd San Jose	88	233
Mary	27	f	w	MO	Colusa	Butte Twp	71	267
Mary	23	f	w	IA	Tehama	Paskenta Twp	92	165
Michael	35	m	w	IREL	San Francisco	San Francisco P O	85	758
Nathan	39	m	w	OH	Solano	Denverton Twp	90	24
Noah	31	m	w	IN	Mendocino	Little Lake Twp	74	192
O F	33	m	w	IREL	Yuba	Marysville	93	585
Peter	31	m	w	NY	Solano	Vacaville Twp	90	123
Peter	25	m	w	UNKN	San Joaquin	2-Wd Stockton	86	166
R A	45	m	w	ENGL	Tuolumne	Big Oak Flat P O	93	399
Richard	50	m	w	MO	Yolo	Cache Crk Twp	93	426
Robert	40	m	w	GERM	Yolo	Cottonwood Twp	93	465
Sally	63	f	w	VA	Sonoma	Vallejo Twp	91	462
Samuel	46	m	w	KY	Yolo	Cottonwood Twp	93	472
Sarah	15	f	w	OH	Santa Cruz	Watsonville	89	377
Silas	32	m	w	NH	Tuolumne	Sonora P O	93	326
Silas P	67	m	w	NH	Yolo	Grafton Twp	93	493
Stella	6	f	w	CA	Solano	Silveyville Twp	90	92
Stephen	35	m	w	IREL	Solano	Silveyville Twp	90	81
Susan	63	f	w	VA	Sutter	Nicolaus Twp	92	107
T	55	m	w	NY	Monterey	San Juan Twp	74	416
Thatcher F	42	m	w	NY	Santa Clara	Alviso Twp	88	28
Thomas	47	m	w	KY	Yolo	Cache Crk Twp	93	424
Thomas	45	m	w	IREL	Alameda	Oakland	68	184
Thomas	43	m	w	NC	Kern	Bakersfield P O	73	365
Thomas	40	m	w	NJ	San Francisco	San Francisco P O	80	336
Thomas	39	m	w	KY	Solano	Silveyville Twp	90	92
Thomas	27	m	w	IREL	Alameda	Oakland	68	207
Thomas	26	m	w	CANA	Sonoma	Petaluma Twp	91	321
Thos	51	m	w	RI	San Joaquin	2-Wd Stockton	86	159
Thos	50	m	w	RI	San Joaquin	2-Wd Stockton	86	194
Thos	40	m	w	OH	Butte	Hamilton Twp	70	70
Thos	26	m	w	IREL	Solano	Vallejo	90	199
Thos J	61	m	w	MA	Sacramento	4-Wd Sacramento	77	341
Thos J	38	m	w	KY	Sonoma	Salt Point	91	390
Thos L	58	m	w	NC	Mendocino	Ukiah Twp	74	233
Timothy	54	m	w	NY	Solano	Suisun Twp	90	95
Vincent	50	m	w	KY	Yolo	Cache Crk Twp	93	457
W A L	35	m	w	NY	San Francisco	San Francisco P O	85	857
Walter	44	m	w	MA	Calaveras	San Andreas P O	70	208
Walter	33	m	w	NJ	San Francisco	5-Wd San Francisco	81	25
Wardner	35	m	w	VT	Placer	Bath P O	76	422
Washington	18	m	w	MO	Nevada	Eureka Twp	75	134
Wed	40	m	w	OH	Butte	Chico Twp	70	22
William	63	m	w	ENGL	Klamath	Klamath Twp	73	370
William	49	m	w	ME	Calaveras	Copperopolis P O	70	251
William	48	m	w	IREL	San Francisco	San Francisco P O	83	312
William	40	m	w	NC	Napa	Napa Twp	75	30
William	39	m	w	MO	Yolo	Putah Twp	93	521
William	33	m	w	GA	Tehama	Paynes Crk Twp	92	167
William	31	m	w	ENGL	Santa Clara	1-Wd San Jose	88	254
William	30	m	w	NY	San Francisco	1-Wd San Francisco	79	54
William	3	m	w	CA	Marin	San Rafael Twp	74	29
William	26	m	w	ME	Yuba	North East Twp	93	644
William	16	m	w	CA	Monterey	San Juan Twp	74	411
William A	48	m	w	IREL	Mendocino	Point Arena Twp	74	224
William A	38	m	w	NY	Nevada	Grass Valley Twp	75	219
William T	38	m	w	MO	Yolo	Cache Crk Twp	93	443
Wm	50	m	w	NY	Sonoma	Santa Rosa	91	401
Wm	40	m	w	KY	Sutter	Butte Twp	92	95
Wm B	35	m	w	IN	Butte	Oregon Twp	70	129
Wm D	34	m	w	RI	San Francisco	San Francisco P O	85	758
Wm L	29	m	w	KY	Santa Barbara	San Buenaventura P	87	429
Wm R	47	m	w	NY	Sacramento	4-Wd Sacramento	77	365
Wm W	33	m	w	OH	Mariposa	Mariposa P O	74	116
BARNET								
Alfred	44	m	w	DE	Mendocino	Round Valley Twp	74	217
Anestacia	35	f	w	IREL	Los Angeles	Los Angeles	73	566
Chas	36	m	w	ENGL	Yuba	Marysville	93	605
Danl M	40	m	w	KY	Mono	Bridgeport P O	74	286
H	36	m	w	ENGL	Yuba	Marysville	93	605
Harry	47	m	w	ENGL	Yuba	Marysville	93	591
J J	45	m	w	KY	El Dorado	Coloma Twp	72	1
John	39	m	w	OH	Alameda	Oakland	68	185
Joseph	42	m	w	RUSS	San Francisco	San Francisco P O	83	380
Louis	40	m	w	FRAN	San Francisco	6-Wd San Francisco	81	86
Morris	43	m	w	PRUS	San Francisco	San Francisco P O	80	484
Samuel	39	m	w	POLA	Santa Cruz	Santa Cruz	89	413
Silas	58	m	w	OH	Los Angeles	El Monte Twp	73	451
BARNETT								
Augustine	53	m	w	NY	Santa Clara	San Jose Twp	88	187
B B	61	m	w	TN	San Joaquin	2-Wd Stockton	86	190
Caroline	19	f	w	PRUS	Marin	San Rafael	74	54
Charles	40	m	w	BADE	Amador	Ione City P O	69	367
Chas E	32	m	w	CT	Sacramento	4-Wd Sacramento	77	368
Christopher	68	m	w	NJ	Alameda	Eden Twp	68	85
Edward	32	m	w	IREL	Mendocino	Anderson Twp	74	155
Ellen	12	f	w	CA	Sacramento	2-Wd Sacramento	77	238
H	32	m	w	NY	San Francisco	San Francisco P O	85	787
Henry	25	m	w	NY	Yolo	Cottonwood Twp	93	474
Henry H	35	m	w	ENGL	Colusa	Colusa	71	296
Isaac	43	m	w	PRUS	San Francisco	San Francisco P O	83	268
Jacob	29	m	w	ENGL	San Francisco	San Francisco P O	80	335
James	35	m	w	ENGL	Mariposa	Mariposa P O	74	118
James	35	m	w	ENGL	Alameda	Murray Twp	68	101
Jesse	43	m	w	AR	Siskiyou	Butte Twp	89	587
Jesser	44	m	w	KY	Napa	Napa	75	25
Joe	35	m	w	PA	San Joaquin	Douglas Twp	86	34
John	48	m	w	IREL	Solano	Vallejo	90	170
John	46	m	w	ENGL	Mariposa	Mariposa P O	74	119
John	37	m	w	TN	Sutter	Sutter Twp	92	117
John	26	m	w	IL	Santa Barbara	San Buenaventura P	87	425
John	16	m	w	CA	San Francisco	8-Wd San Francisco	82	302
Joseph	23	m	w	AR	Mariposa	Mariposa P O	74	118
Juliana	57	f	w	MEXI	San Bernardino	San Salvador Twp	78	456
L	34	m	w	POLA	Mendocino	Little Lake Twp	74	200
Mary	20	f	w	CA	Santa Clara	1-Wd San Jose	88	251
Micheal	35	m	w	IREL	San Francisco	11-Wd San Francisc	84	442
Richard	48	m	w	IN	Sutter	Yuba Twp	92	150
Richard	17	m	w	ENGL	Inyo	Cerro Gordo Twp	73	323
Robert	45	m	w	KY	Santa Clara	2-Wd San Jose	88	309
Robert	23	m	w	LA	Colusa	Colusa	71	294
Saml	35	m	w	PA	Santa Barbara	San Buenaventura P	87	432
Samuel	66	m	w	VT	Santa Barbara	San Buenaventura P	87	435
Thomas	39	m	w	IREL	Amador	Ione City P O	69	362
Thos A	29	m	w	MO	Sonoma	Analy Twp	91	226
W	40	m	w	ENGL	Sierra	Butte Twp	89	511
W B	57	m	w	PA	Mendocino	Ukiah Twp	74	234
William	40	m	w	PA	Yolo	Grafton Twp	93	483
William	35	m	w	CANA	Humboldt	Eel Rvr Twp	72	251

© 2001 by Heritage Quest. All rights reserved.

Series M593

Name	Age	S	R	B-PL	County	Locale	Roll	Pg
William	30	m	w	ENGL	Santa Cruz	Santa Cruz Twp	89	395
Wm	38	m	w	NY	Santa Barbara	San Buenaventura P	87	436
Wm R	14	m	w	CA	Sacramento	4-Wd Sacramento	77	371
Wolf	59	m	w	POLA	San Francisco	2-Wd San Francisco	79	232
BARNETTE								
William	39	m	w	NY	Los Angeles	Soledad Twp	73	632
BARNEY								
Aaron	54	m	w	PA	Sonoma	Analy Twp	91	228
Ah	25	m	c	CHIN	El Dorado	Mud Springs Twp	72	81
Amelia	60	f	w	PA	San Francisco	San Francisco P O	83	205
Ar	66	m	w	NY	Marin	San Rafael	74	48
Aurelius	54	m	w	OH	Sacramento	Franklin Twp	77	110
Benj A	46	m	w	NY	San Francisco	San Francisco P O	85	800
Carey	51	m	w	PA	Yolo	Grafton Twp	93	484
Charles S	28	m	w	MD	Marin	San Rafael	74	48
Chas	46	m	w	NY	San Joaquin	Oneal Twp	86	106
De Witt	19	m	w	IN	Del Norte	Happy Camp Twp	71	472
E	22	m	w	OR	Lassen	Susanville Twp	73	444
Frances	18	f	w	MI	Santa Clara	Santa Clara Twp	88	148
Frank	42	m	w	SPAI	Calaveras	San Andreas P O	70	200
George	40	m	w	IREL	Sonoma	Sonoma Twp	91	443
George H	40	m	w	ENGL	Placer	Auburn P O	76	359
Isabell	13	f	w	CA	San Joaquin	Oneal Twp	86	106
J H	47	m	w	MD	San Joaquin	2-Wd Stockton	86	183
J H	29	m	w	MO	San Joaquin	3-Wd Stockton	86	219
Jacob	38	m	w	NY	Amador	Drytown P O	69	423
Jacob M	18	m	w	CA	Santa Clara	Fremont Twp	88	44
James	32	m	w	NY	Placer	Rocklin Twp	76	464
James G	30	m	w	IA	Santa Clara	Santa Clara Twp	88	137
Jerome	36	m	w	MD	Marin	San Rafael	74	48
Jesse	37	m	w	NY	Placer	Lincoln P O	76	482
John	48	m	w	IREL	San Francisco	7-Wd San Francisco	81	233
John	40	m	w	IREL	Sacramento	Dry Crk Twp	77	101
John	27	m	m	IL	Sacramento	2-Wd Sacramento	77	226
Joseph	43	m	w	NY	El Dorado	Cosumnes Twp	72	17
M C	50	m	w	NY	Sierra	Table Rock Twp	89	572
Manly	46	m	w	OH	Sonoma	Russian Rvr	91	369
Michl	38	m	w	NY	Santa Clara	Gilroy Twp	88	82
Milton	75	m	w	MA	Alameda	Brooklyn	68	24
Milton	74	m	w	CT	Sacramento	4-Wd Sacramento	77	376
P T	38	m	w	NY	Sacramento	4-Wd Sacramento	77	373
Patrick	30	m	w	IREL	Contra Costa	Martinez P O	71	428
Richard	30	m	w	IREL	Alameda	Murray Twp	68	117
Richard	20	m	w	LA	Amador	Amador City P O	69	391
Richard A	42	m	w	VT	Nevada	Little York Twp	75	242
Thomas	40	m	w	SWIT	Santa Clara	Gilroy Twp	88	90
Thomas	30	m	w	IREL	Alameda	Oakland	68	183
Thomas V	41	m	w	MA	Santa Clara	Fremont Twp	88	53
William	36	m	w	PA	El Dorado	Cosumnes Twp	72	16
William	35	m	w	TN	Contra Costa	Martinez P O	71	410
Wm	60	m	w	ENGL	Sacramento	Mississippi Twp	77	163
BARNFIND								
George	20	m	w	WI	Inyo	Lone Pine Twp	73	330
BARNHAM								
Catherine	35	f	w	NY	San Francisco	6-Wd San Francisco	81	99
E	60	m	w	NY	San Joaquin	Tulare Twp	86	263
BARNHARD								
Julius	30	m	w	PRUS	San Diego	San Diego	78	485
BARNHARDT								
Edwin	30	m	w	OH	San Diego	San Diego	78	497
Jacob	44	m	w	BAVA	Calaveras	San Andreas P O	70	204
BARNHART								
Ali	23	m	w	NY	Placer	Alta P O	76	413
Ann	41	f	w	NY	Yolo	Cache Crk Twp	93	436
Benjamin	46	m	w	HCAS	Placer	Auburn P O	76	374
Charles	42	m	w	NY	Placer	Gold Run Twp	76	397
David	55	m	w	PA	Monterey	Castroville Twp	74	334
George W	42	m	w	NC	Stanislaus	Empire Twp	92	66
Heny	40	m	w	PA	San Joaquin	Liberty Twp	86	92
Jas	37	m	w	CANA	Butte	Chico Twp	70	21
John	39	m	w	PA	Nevada	Rough & Ready Twp	75	323
Joseph	40	m	w	TN	Colusa	Monroe Twp	71	312
Lewis	50	m	w	IREL	San Joaquin	2-Wd Stockton	86	166
Nicholas	37	m	w	PA	Nevada	Rough & Ready Twp	75	336
P A	44	m	w	PA	Amador	Sutter Crk P O	69	396
Samuel	20	m	b	VA	Sacramento	2-Wd Sacramento	77	243
Van	39	m	w	TN	Colusa	Monroe Twp	71	312
William	27	m	w	PRUS	Solano	Silveyville Twp	90	91
BARNHAZLE								
Henry	38	m	w	OH	Solano	Rio Vista Twp	90	59
BARNHILL								
Marcus	40	m	w	KY	Stanislaus	Emory Twp	92	18
BARNHISEL								
Expinebar	29	m	w	OH	San Francisco	11-Wd San Francisc	84	507
Jacob	57	m	w	OH	Alameda	Brooklyn	68	36
Lewis	33	m	w	OH	Santa Clara	San Jose Twp	88	189
BARNHOPE								
Isaac	50	m	w	ENGL	Solano	Denverton Twp	90	22
BARNHU								
A F	43	m	w	IL	Monterey	Monterey Twp	74	348
BARNICH								
Henry	28	m	w	PRUS	Sonoma	Healdsburg & Mendo	91	279
BARNING								
Phineas	40	m	w	DE	Los Angeles	Wilmington Twp	73	643
BARNOID								
Nicholas	27	m	w	HOLL	Sacramento	Natomas Twp	77	168

Series M593

Name	Age	S	R	B-PL	County	Locale	Roll	Pg
BARNS								
Abbie	20	f	w	ENGL	San Joaquin	Elliott Twp	86	71
Bernard A	29	m	w	PRUS	El Dorado	Mud Springs Twp	72	84
George	54	m	w	ENGL	Mariposa	Maxwell Crk P O	74	142
George	41	m	w	MA	Siskiyou	Callahan P O	89	628
Isaac B	29	m	w	IL	Klamath	Trinidad Twp	73	390
J B	48	m	w	IREL	Yuba	Marysville	93	608
John	46	m	w	OH	Sonoma	Santa Rosa	91	396
John	32	m	w	IREL	Inyo	Lone Pine Twp	73	333
John F	61	m	w	NC	Sonoma	Petaluma Twp	91	355
L	48	m	w	KY	Lake	Coyote Valley	73	401
Lewis	29	m	w	HANO	Sierra	Gibson Twp	89	540
Mark	24	m	w	MA	San Joaquin	2-Wd Stockton	86	170
Mike	27	m	w	IREL	San Joaquin	3-Wd Stockton	86	217
Peter	39	m	w	IREL	San Francisco	1-Wd San Francisco	79	76
S L	35	m	w	OH	Sutter	Nicolaus Twp	92	112
Tertias	25	m	w	CANA	Plumas	Indian Twp	77	14
Wm H	31	m	w	MO	Sonoma	Healdsburg & Mendo	91	286
BARNSTEAD								
Thos S	58	m	w	CANA	Napa	Napa Twp	75	72
BARNSTEIN								
Peter	21	m	w	POLA	San Francisco	8-Wd San Francisco	82	320
BARNSTIEN								
Nathan	22	m	w	PRUS	Napa	Napa	75	44
BARNUM								
A	54	m	w	OH	Lassen	Susanville Twp	73	446
August	50	m	w	GA	San Francisco	San Francisco P O	83	175
Charles	32	m	w	MI	Nevada	Grass Valley Twp	75	146
E W	76	m	w	VT	Nevada	Nevada Twp	75	295
Ed	42	m	w	OH	Humboldt	Eureka Twp	72	258
Edward	29	m	w	CT	Yolo	Cache Crk Twp	93	425
Edwd	39	m	w	US	San Joaquin	2-Wd Stockton	86	166
Eli	53	m	w	NY	Siskiyou	Table Rock Twp	89	645
Grace	35	f	w	MD	Nevada	Bridgeport Twp	75	112
Graham	29	m	w	NY	Humboldt	Eureka Twp	72	256
Henry M	32	m	w	NY	Sonoma	Bodega Twp	91	251
Joseph	50	m	w	PRUS	San Francisco	San Francisco P O	83	270
Marvin J	33	m	w	NY	Shasta	Fort Crook P O	89	477
Samuel	44	m	w	OH	San Bernardino	San Bernardino Twp	78	414
William S	38	m	w	OH	Yuba	Parks Bar Twp	93	648
BARNY								
Edward	35	m	w	IREL	San Joaquin	3-Wd Stockton	86	222
Elizabeth	71	f	w	IA	Sutter	Vernon Twp	92	132
Henry	27	m	w	IA	Sutter	Vernon Twp	92	132
James S	41	m	w	NY	El Dorado	Cosumnes Twp	72	13
Jas D	35	m	w	IREL	San Joaquin	2-Wd Stockton	86	173
John	70	m	w	IA	Sutter	Vernon Twp	92	132
BAROCO								
Andrew	30	m	w	ITAL	Santa Clara	1-Wd San Jose	88	236
BARODELL								
Mary	33	f	w	SCOT	Colusa	Spring Valley Twp	71	335
BAROGALUPPI								
Paul	30	m	w	ITAL	San Francisco	2-Wd San Francisco	79	176
BAROGUS								
Catharine	28	f	w	ENGL	Monterey	San Juan Twp	74	408
BAROLA								
Antonio	35	m	w	MEXI	Los Angeles	Soledad Twp	73	631
BARON								
Abram	45	m	w	PRUS	San Francisco	1-Wd San Francisco	79	128
Adolph	49	m	w	PRUS	San Francisco	11-Wd San Francisc	84	531
August	44	m	w	PORT	Contra Costa	San Pablo Twp	71	361
E G	41	m	w	OH	Tuolumne	Columbia P O	93	343
Henry	67	m	w	MA	Tuolumne	Sonora P O	93	324
Henry	22	m	w	PRUS	Solano	Silveyville Twp	90	79
James B	28	m	w	ME	Sacramento	Georgianna Twp	77	133
Jerrid	42	m	w	NY	San Francisco	11-Wd San Francisc	84	644
John	42	m	w	FRAN	San Diego	Milquaty Dist	78	476
Pedro	40	m	w	FRAN	Santa Barbara	Las Cruces P O	87	505
BARONE								
Luegi	36	m	w	ITAL	San Francisco	11-Wd San Francisc	84	594
BARONI								
Julia	40	f	w	AZOR	San Francisco	1-Wd San Francisco	79	102
BARONS								
Joseph A	29	m	w	SCOT	San Francisco	11-Wd San Francisc	84	699
BAROSA								
George	45	m	w	IREL	Santa Clara	Fremont Twp	88	51
BAROTEAU								
August	36	m	w	FRAN	San Francisco	San Francisco P O	80	338
John	42	m	w	FRAN	San Francisco	San Francisco P O	80	341
BAROVITCH								
A	25	m	w	AUST	Amador	Sutter Crk P O	69	404
BAROWN								
Y	37	m	w	IREL	Sierra	Butte Twp	89	509
BARQUALO								
John	23	m	w	ITAL	San Mateo	Schoolhouse Statio	87	346
BARQUARDT								
Henry	38	m	w	PRUS	Kern	Bakersfield P O	73	359
BARQUES								
Felis	35	m	w	CHIL	Placer	Bath P O	76	427
Jose V	54	m	w	CA	San Luis Obispo	Morro Twp	87	283
BARQUEZ								
Tomas	36	m	w	MEXI	San Francisco	San Francisco P O	80	470
BARQUWASKI								
Simon	32	m	w	PRUS	Mendocino	Point Arena Twp	74	206
BARR								
Allen	28	m	w	IN	San Diego	San Jacinto Dist	78	517
Charles	40	m	w	ENGL	Santa Clara	1-Wd San Jose	88	233

© 2001 by Heritage Quest. All rights reserved.

California 1870 Census

Name	Age	S	R	B-PL	County	Locale	Series M593 Roll	Pg
Chas	48	m	w	IREL	Solano	Vallejo	90	178
Christie A	14	f	w	KS	Yolo	Merritt Twp	93	503
Corbly	22	m	w	MO	Yolo	Cache Crk Twp	93	421
Daniel W	45	m	w	SC	Solano	Suisun Twp	90	115
G W	50	m	w	MA	Amador	Jackson P O	69	337
Hannah	34	f	w	IREL	San Francisco	San Francisco P O	85	829
Harrison	16	m	w	MO	Sacramento	Franklin Twp	77	113
Henry	34	m	w	KY	Solano	Montezuma Twp	90	68
Hiram	31	m	w	PA	Solano	Vacaville Twp	90	124
J D	22	m	w	NY	Solano	Vallejo	90	202
James	60	m	w	OH	Tulare	Visalia	92	293
Joe	24	m	w	PRUS	San Joaquin	1-Wd Stockton	86	134
John	40	m	w	IREL	San Francisco	San Francisco P O	85	745
John	30	m	w	PA	San Francisco	San Francisco P O	83	18
John D	41	m	w	NY	San Francisco	San Francisco P O	83	320
John R	30	m	w	PA	El Dorado	Mud Springs Twp	72	87
Maggie	21	f	w	OH	Sacramento	Granite Twp	77	144
Margaret	30	f	w	MD	San Francisco	San Francisco P O	85	746
Martha	34	f	w	PA	Santa Clara	Santa Clara Twp	88	148
Michael T	35	m	w	NY	Sacramento	4-Wd Sacramento	77	371
Neal	40	m	w	IREL	San Francisco	7-Wd San Francisco	81	188
Neil	45	m	w	IREL	San Francisco	11-Wd San Francisc	84	669
Nicholas	26	m	w	BAVA	Santa Clara	1-Wd San Jose	88	245
Oren	22	m	w	IL	Tulare	Visalia	92	293
R B	35	m	w	ME	Solano	Vallejo	90	211
Robert	51	m	w	SCOT	Siskiyou	Klamath Twp	89	600
Sam M	23	m	w	IA	San Francisco	7-Wd San Francisco	81	250
Samuel	28	m	w	IREL	Nevada	Washington Twp	75	339
Susan	78	f	w	MA	Stanislaus	Empire Twp	92	33
Thomas	35	m	w	MO	Humboldt	Arcata Twp	72	234
Thos	38	m	w	PA	Nevada	Nevada Twp	75	302
BARRA								
Alex	35	m	w	FRAN	San Francisco	3-Wd San Francisco	79	326
Andr	13	m	w	HANO	Alameda	Oakland	68	251
Jesus	25	f	w	MEXI	San Francisco	San Francisco P O	83	101
Martin	60	m	w	CHIL	San Mateo	Half Moon Bay P O	87	390
Tomaso	58	m	w	CA	Marin	San Antonio Twp	74	65
BARRACHMAN								
Jno	24	m	w	IN	San Joaquin	Douglas Twp	86	34
BARRAGAN								
John	24	m	w	IREL	San Francisco	7-Wd San Francisco	81	169
BARRAN								
Wm R	45	m	w	IREL	San Francisco	San Francisco P O	85	766
BARRARAS								
Teresa	12	f	w	CA	Santa Clara	Fremont Twp	88	47
BARRARO								
Francisco	40	m	w	SPAI	Siskiyou	Yreka Twp	89	668
BARRAS								
H B	38	m	w	PA	San Francisco	8-Wd San Francisco	82	290
Miguel	53	m	w	CHIL	Placer	Auburn P O	76	359
Peter	31	m	w	ENGL	San Luis Obispo	Arroyo Grande Twp	87	278
BARRAT								
James	50	m	w	ENGL	Inyo	Cerro Gordo Twp	73	323
John	30	m	w	IREL	Inyo	Cerro Gordo Twp	73	321
BARRATEY								
Frank	45	m	w	FRAN	San Francisco	San Francisco P O	83	187
BARRATH								
John	28	m	w	ENGL	Tuolumne	Sonora P O	93	325
BARRATT								
Thomas	35	m	w	ENGL	Napa	Napa	75	24
BARRE								
Ednund	38	m	w	IREL	San Francisco	11-Wd San Francisc	84	584
Parine	2	f	w	CA	Nevada	Grass Valley Twp	75	151
BARREAS								
M	70	f	w	MEXI	Napa	Napa	75	55
BARREAU								
Joseph	38	m	w	FRAN	San Francisco	1-Wd San Francisco	79	54
Pat	40	m	w	IREL	San Joaquin	Dent Twp	86	18
BARRELSON								
John	17	m	w	PRUS	San Francisco	San Francisco P O	85	752
BARREN								
Caroline	26	f	w	IREL	San Francisco	6-Wd San Francisco	81	83
William	31	m	w	IREL	San Francisco	6-Wd San Francisco	81	83
BARRER								
Leonard	31	m	w	WURT	San Francisco	2-Wd San Francisco	79	198
Stella	41	f	w	MI	Alameda	Eden Twp	68	90
BARRERAS								
Scholastico	30	m	w	MEXI	San Luis Obispo	Arroyo Grande Twp	87	271
BARRERES								
Deonisio	27	m	w	MEXI	Monterey	San Benito Twp	74	380
BARREROS								
Pedro	60	m	i	MEXI	Santa Barbara	Las Cruces P O	87	505
BARRES								
Sarah	32	f	w	PA	San Francisco	8-Wd San Francisco	82	395
BARRET								
Anna	2	f	w	CA	San Francisco	5-Wd San Francisco	81	30
Catherine	66	f	w	IREL	Sonoma	Bodega Twp	91	263
Chas	24	m	w	ENGL	San Francisco	7-Wd San Francisco	81	287
David	19	m	w	IREL	Sonoma	Bodega Twp	91	263
E	42	m	w	MA	Yuba	Marysville	93	604
George	60	m	w	NY	Contra Costa	San Pablo Twp	71	359
George	51	m	w	ENGL	Placer	Colfax P O	76	389
Henry	40	m	w	IREL	Merced	Snelling P O	74	249
Henry S	21	m	w	MA	Tuolumne	Sonora P O	93	318
James	55	m	w	IREL	Trinity	Canyon City Pct	92	202
John	40	m	w	AL	Yuba	Marysville	93	591
John	16	m	w	CA	Colusa	Monroe Twp	71	311
Louis	30	m	w	AUSL	San Mateo	Half Moon Bay P O	87	406
Louis	28	m	w	TN	San Francisco	5-Wd San Francisco	81	30
Richard	40	m	w	IREL	Sonoma	Salt Point	91	390
Thos	45	m	w	IREL	San Francisco	7-Wd San Francisco	81	275
BARRETT								
A	60	m	w	VA	Lake	Upper Lake	73	411
A	36	m	w	RUSS	Yuba	East Bear Rvr Twp	93	542
Adams	42	m	w	OH	Placer	Bath P O	76	447
Affred H	41	m	w	ENGL	Nevada	Grass Valley Twp	75	178
Alexander	32	m	w	IREL	San Francisco	7-Wd San Francisco	81	181
Alf	41	m	w	ENGL	San Francisco	11-Wd San Francisc	84	424
Ann	48	f	w	IREL	Placer	Gold Run Twp	76	395
Annie	47	f	w	IREL	Solano	Vacaville Twp	90	136
Benjamin H	28	m	w	IL	Stanislaus	Empire Twp	92	27
Brid	40	f	w	IREL	Alameda	Oakland	68	218
C N	40	m	w	PA	Alameda	Oakland	68	151
Caroline	43	f	w	SWIT	Solano	Vallejo	90	186
Caroline	42	f	w	SWIT	Solano	Vallejo	90	199
Catherine	25	f	w	IREL	San Francisco	San Francisco P O	83	228
Charles R	45	m	w	ME	Santa Clara	1-Wd San Jose	88	265
Cooper	31	m	w	NJ	Solano	Vacaville Twp	90	127
Danl	24	m	w	IREL	Sierra	Table Rock Twp	89	574
E	54	m	w	PA	Lake	Lakeport	73	407
Edw	16	m	w	PA	San Francisco	7-Wd San Francisco	81	248
Edward	55	m	w	IREL	San Francisco	7-Wd San Francisco	81	200
Edward	38	m	w	IREL	Nevada	Grass Valley Twp	75	224
Edward	35	m	w	IREL	Placer	Bath P O	76	444
Eliza	46	f	b	WIND	San Joaquin	2-Wd Stockton	86	196
F	30	m	w	IREL	Sierra	Eureka Twp	89	523
Francis A	43	m	w	ME	San Francisco	11-Wd San Francisc	84	699
Geo	27	m	w	IREL	San Francisco	San Francisco P O	83	41
Geo	23	m	w	ENGL	San Francisco	2-Wd San Francisco	79	225
George	40	m	w	OH	Contra Costa	San Pablo Twp	71	358
George	33	m	w	NJ	Solano	Vacaville Twp	90	117
George	33	m	w	OH	Yuba	Linda Twp	93	557
George	30	m	w	OH	Kern	Linns Valley P O	73	348
Guillaume	48	m	w	CANA	El Dorado	Mud Springs Twp	72	82
H	42	m	w	VA	Yuba	Marysville	93	582
Hanna	39	f	w	IREL	San Francisco	San Francisco P O	83	289
Horace F	21	m	w	MA	San Francisco	8-Wd San Francisco	82	338
J	50	m	w	OH	Sacramento	3-Wd Sacramento	77	312
J	45	m	w	IREL	Mariposa	Maxwell Crk P O	74	147
J	26	m	w	ENGL	Sierra	Table Rock Twp	89	576
J J	37	m	w	IREL	San Francisco	San Francisco P O	85	805
J S	40	m	w	IREL	Sacramento	4-Wd Sacramento	77	374
Jack S	32	m	w	IREL	San Diego	San Diego	78	498
Jacob	40	m	w	OH	Sutter	Yuba Twp	92	140
James	57	m	w	PA	Sacramento	Georgianna Twp	77	126
James	40	m	w	IREL	San Francisco	San Francisco P O	83	371
James	34	m	w	IREL	San Francisco	11-Wd San Francisc	84	459
James	30	m	w	IREL	San Francisco	San Francisco P O	83	329
James	30	m	w	IREL	Santa Cruz	Santa Cruz	89	432
James	30	m	w	IREL	Santa Cruz	Santa Cruz	89	416
James	26	m	w	IREL	San Francisco	7-Wd San Francisco	81	170
James	25	m	w	IREL	Amador	Jackson P O	69	329
James B	38	m	w	ME	Nevada	Little York Twp	75	234
Jas	40	m	w	IREL	Sierra	Sears Twp	89	561
Jas	22	m	w	VT	Butte	Kimshew Tpw	70	82
Jas S Jr	33	m	w	ME	Sierra	Table Rock Twp	89	573
Jerome	38	m	w	CANA	El Dorado	White Oak Twp	72	135
John	40	m	w	IREL	San Francisco	San Francisco P O	83	243
John	40	m	w	GA	San Francisco	San Francisco P O	83	77
John	35	m	w	ME	Alameda	Oakland	68	264
John	34	m	w	NJ	Solano	Vacaville Twp	90	122
John R	43	m	w	IN	Yolo	Cottonwood Twp	93	461
Jos J	45	m	w	PA	San Francisco	1-Wd San Francisco	79	54
Joseph	34	m	w	IREL	Solano	Suisun Twp	90	113
Josephine	11	f	w	CA	San Francisco	7-Wd San Francisco	81	169
Josiah	40	m	w	CANA	El Dorado	White Oak Twp	72	143
Julia	22	f	w	FRAN	San Francisco	8-Wd San Francisco	82	362
Kate	8	f	w	CA	Placer	Gold Run Twp	76	394
Kate	27	f	w	IREL	San Francisco	San Francisco P O	80	532
Louis	26	m	w	FRAN	San Francisco	6-Wd San Francisco	81	73
M C	6	f	w	CA	San Francisco	San Francisco P O	85	784
M T	44	f	w	IL	Solano	Vallejo	90	143
Maddison H	36	m	w	MO	Sonoma	Petaluma Twp	91	324
Maggie	19	f	w	IREL	San Francisco	San Francisco P O	83	133
Margaret	40	f	w	IREL	San Francisco	San Francisco P O	80	370
Margaret	21	f	w	NY	San Francisco	San Francisco P O	83	414
Margaret	20	f	w	IREL	Solano	Vallejo	90	161
Maria	42	f	w	IREL	San Francisco	San Francisco P O	80	458
Mary	40	f	w	IREL	Santa Clara	2-Wd San Jose	88	318
Mary	35	f	w	NY	San Francisco	8-Wd San Francisco	82	410
Mary	28	f	w	IREL	San Francisco	San Francisco P O	83	222
Mary J	43	f	w	TN	Placer	Roseville P O	76	351
Mathew	32	m	w	CA	San Joaquin	3-Wd Stockton	86	218
Michael	60	m	w	IREL	Placer	Gold Run Twp	76	394
Michael	36	m	w	IREL	San Francisco	6-Wd San Francisco	81	132
Michael	34	m	w	IREL	Sierra	Gibson Twp	89	538
Michael	30	m	w	IREL	Solano	Vallejo	90	161
Michael	25	m	w	IREL	Placer	Roseville P O	76	352
Minnie	14	f	w	CA	San Francisco	San Francisco P O	80	420
Moses	40	m	w	RUSS	San Francisco	San Francisco P O	80	465
Naomi	70	f	w	KY	Yolo	Cottonwood Twp	93	461
P	42	m	w	IREL	Napa	Napa Twp	75	75
P A	36	m	w	CANA	Tuolumne	Columbia P O	93	341
Pat	35	m	w	IREL	Alameda	Oakland	68	176

© 2001 by Heritage Quest. All rights reserved.

Series M593

Name	Age	S	R	B-PL	County	Locale	Roll	Pg
Patrick	28	m	w	IREL	Santa Clara	1-Wd San Jose	88	233
Patsey	28	m	w	NJ	Solano	Vacaville Twp	90	120
Paul	60	m	w	MI	Amador	Drytown P O	69	422
Paul	30	m	w	IREL	Alameda	Oakland	68	231
Peter	53	m	w	IREL	Solano	Vallejo	90	170
Richard	37	m	w	ENGL	Nevada	Grass Valley Twp	75	142
Richd	24	m	w	IREL	San Francisco	1-Wd San Francisco	79	45
Samuel	28	m	w	ENGL	Nevada	Grass Valley Twp	75	193
T H	27	m	w	OH	Amador	Ione City P O	69	349
Thomas	39	m	w	OH	Solano	Silveyville Twp	90	72
Thomas	30	m	w	NJ	Solano	Vacaville Twp	90	122
Thos	51	m	w	IREL	Sierra	Eureka Twp	89	523
W C	39	m	w	ME	Sacramento	3-Wd Sacramento	77	307
William	46	m	w	VT	San Francisco	6-Wd San Francisco	81	138
William	35	m	w	IREL	Santa Cruz	Santa Cruz Twp	89	400
William	28	m	w	IREL	Sonoma	Vallejo Twp	91	459
William	22	m	w	IREL	Nevada	Grass Valley Twp	75	198
William	15	m	w	MA	San Francisco	7-Wd San Francisco	81	186
Willie E	8	m	w	CA	El Dorado	Mud Springs Twp	72	73
Wm	50	m	w	ENGL	Santa Clara	Almaden Twp	88	9
Wm	46	m	w	ENGL	Sierra	Alleghany & Forest	89	534
Wm	42	m	w	ENGL	San Joaquin	2-Wd Stockton	86	193
Wm	40	m	w	IREL	Solano	Benicia	90	18
Wm	31	m	w	IREL	San Francisco	1-Wd San Francisco	79	91
Wm	25	m	w	IREL	Merced	Snelling P O	74	259
Wm C	40	m	w	NY	Sacramento	San Joaquin Twp	77	400
BARRETTO								
Peter	35	m	w	ITAL	San Francisco	3-Wd San Francisco	79	288
BARREY								
James W	28	m	w	IREL	Inyo	Lone Pine Twp	73	331
William	39	m	w	DC	Santa Clara	San Jose Twp	88	205
Wm	40	m	w	IREL	San Francisco	7-Wd San Francisco	81	250
BARRIAS								
Luis	50	m	w	MEXI	Santa Barbara	Santa Barbara P O	87	479
BARRIBAULT								
Margaret	33	f	w	FRAN	San Francisco	5-Wd San Francisco	81	5
BARRIC								
Louis E	30	m	w	CA	Santa Clara	1-Wd San Jose	88	265
BARRICH								
H V B	40	m	w	NY	San Joaquin	1-Wd Stockton	86	128
BARRICK								
John	45	m	w	PRUS	San Francisco	11-Wd San Francisc	84	423
BARRIDAL								
Archibald	36	m	w	SCOT	Placer	Colfax P O	76	392
BARRIE								
David	22	m	w	SCOT	San Francisco	3-Wd San Francisco	79	323
BARRIER								
Charles	48	m	w	FRAN	San Francisco	San Francisco P O	83	234
BARRIES								
Caesar	22	m	w	MEXI	San Joaquin	Douglas Twp	86	38
BARRIET								
John	23	m	w	SC	Santa Clara	Fremont Twp	88	48
BARRIGAN								
May	18	f	w	NY	Amador	Sutter Crk P O	69	396
W T	5	m	w	CA	Amador	Jackson P O	69	342
BARRIL								
Chas	24	m	w	CANA	Humboldt	Arcata Twp	72	226
BARRILLE								
Carmillo	22	m	w	ITAL	San Francisco	2-Wd San Francisco	79	231
BARRILLO								
Mariano	35	m	w	MEXI	Kern	Bakersfield P O	73	358
BARRINAS								
Ignacio	27	m	w	CA	San Joaquin	Tulare Twp	86	251
BARRING								
John	62	m	w	PRUS	San Francisco	11-Wd San Francisc	84	614
Rudolph	37	m	w	PRUS	Solano	Benicia	90	5
BARRINGER								
Frank	30	m	w	PA	San Francisco	1-Wd San Francisco	79	96
Saml	36	m	w	NY	Calaveras	Copperopolis P O	70	235
BARRINGIN								
J	40	m	w	FRAN	Alameda	Oakland	68	248
BARRINGTON								
Alex	40	m	w	OH	San Francisco	6-Wd San Francisco	81	111
George	34	m	w	HOLL	San Francisco	San Francisco P O	85	724
J	42	m	w	CANA	Yuba	Marysville Twp	93	569
J C	41	m	w	TN	San Joaquin	Oneal Twp	86	110
James	50	m	w	IREL	Kern	Linns Valley P O	73	349
Stephn W	40	m	w	ME	Yuba	Slate Range Bar Tw	93	677
William	28	m	w	IREL	San Mateo	Half Moon Bay P O	87	389
Wm B	42	m	w	IREL	San Francisco	1-Wd San Francisco	79	35
BARRINS								
Danial	47	m	w	RI	San Francisco	7-Wd San Francisco	81	206
BARRIOS								
Manuel	49	m	w	CHIL	Marin	San Rafael Twp	74	46
Provincio	38	m	w	MEXI	Kern	Bakersfield P O	73	362
BARRIS								
Alexander	55	m	w	NY	Santa Clara	Santa Clara Twp	88	135
George	19	m	w	MA	Marin	Sausalito Twp	74	69
Lawson	31	m	w	IREL	San Mateo	Half Moon Bay P O	87	405
T M	42	m	w	PA	Lake	Coyote Valley	73	400
BARRISTER								
E	22	m	w	WI	San Francisco	8-Wd San Francisco	82	362
BARRITINI								
David	30	m	w	ITAL	Calaveras	Copperopolis P O	70	252
BARRO								
Pedro	57	m	w	MEXI	Mariposa	Mariposa P O	74	117
BARROLL								
Samuel	45	m	w	ME	San Francisco	San Francisco P O	83	196
BARRON								
C I	34	m	w	IREL	San Francisco	San Francisco P O	83	285
Chas	30	m	w	FRAN	Sacramento	4-Wd Sacramento	77	375
David	54	m	w	NY	Amador	Volcano P O	69	381
David	42	m	w	PA	Santa Cruz	Pajaro Twp	89	339
Edward	40	m	w	IREL	San Francisco	8-Wd San Francisco	82	481
Edwin	27	m	w	IL	San Joaquin	Elkhorn Twp	86	58
F	61	m	w	MO	San Joaquin	Elkhorn Twp	86	58
F	11	m	w	CA	Solano	Benicia	90	20
Frank	36	m	w	CANA	Nevada	Nevada Twp	75	296
Gracio	32	m	w	FRAN	Los Angeles	Los Angeles Twp	73	476
Gustavus	33	m	w	MO	Marin	San Rafael Twp	74	39
J M	39	m	w	KY	Del Norte	Crescent Twp	71	457
J T	35	m	w	NY	Sacramento	3-Wd Sacramento	77	269
James	42	m	w	IREL	Alameda	Alvarado	68	305
James	32	m	w	MO	Placer	Auburn P O	76	365
James T	37	m	w	CA	Sacramento	2-Wd Sacramento	77	253
John E	40	m	w	ENGL	Alpine	Silver Mtn P O	69	307
Joseph	30	m	w	SCOT	Alameda	Washington Twp	68	285
M	40	m	w	CANA	San Francisco	San Francisco P O	85	792
M D	42	m	w	IREL	San Francisco	San Francisco P O	85	832
Mary	34	f	w	IREL	San Mateo	Redwood Twp	87	364
Mary	16	f	w	CA	San Francisco	San Francisco P O	80	404
Mathew J	21	m	w	IL	Sacramento	4-Wd Sacramento	77	326
Oscar	23	m	w	BAVA	San Francisco	7-Wd San Francisco	81	218
Richard	43	m	w	IREL	Alameda	Eden Twp	68	58
Saml	17	m	w	NY	San Francisco	11-Wd San Francisc	84	587
T A	27	m	w	ENGL	Amador	Amador City P O	69	392
Victorine	46	f	w	FRAN	San Francisco	San Francisco P O	80	475
William	36	m	w	AL	Placer	Lincoln P O	76	487
William	31	m	w	NY	Colusa	Colusa	71	298
William E	45	m	w	SPAI	San Francisco	6-Wd San Francisco	81	90
Wm	22	m	w	ENGL	Tuolumne	Sonora P O	93	325
BARRONI								
Jerome	33	m	w	ITAL	Amador	Volcano P O	69	372
Peter	35	m	w	ITAL	Amador	Volcano P O	69	372
Steven	33	m	w	ITAL	Amador	Volcano P O	69	376
BARRONIO								
Joseph	35	m	w	ITAL	Amador	Volcano P O	69	373
Thomas	25	m	w	ITAL	Amador	Volcano P O	69	372
BARRONS								
Robert	34	m	w	NY	Colusa	Colusa	71	290
BARROS								
Nicholas	35	m	w	MEXI	San Joaquin	Douglas Twp	86	38
BARROTRAS								
John	31	m	w	FRAN	Marin	Sausalito Twp	74	69
BARROTT								
John	48	m	w	IREL	San Francisco	San Francisco P O	85	764
John	43	m	w	ENGL	San Joaquin	Elkhorn Twp	86	59
BARROUNS								
Chas	40	m	w	ME	Nevada	Meadow Lake Twp	75	266
BARROUR								
Eugene	56	m	w	FRAN	Mariposa	Mariposa P O	74	128
BARROW								
Ellen	50	f	w	MA	San Francisco	San Francisco P O	83	386
Get	35	m	w	OH	San Joaquin	Elliott Twp	86	78
Harriet	65	f	w	NY	Nevada	Meadow Lake Twp	75	258
Henry	33	m	w	WI	San Francisco	San Francisco P O	85	874
James	25	m	w	ENGL	Tuolumne	Sonora P O	93	325
Joseph	32	m	w	ENGL	Tuolumne	Sonora P O	93	317
Marius	19	m	w	FRAN	Los Angeles	Los Angeles Twp	73	478
William	35	m	w	MS	Solano	Vacaville Twp	90	138
BARROWS								
Andrew	24	m	w	ME	Mendocino	Gualala Twp	74	226
C	15	m	w	CA	Solano	Benicia	90	21
Camelia	35	f	w	CT	Los Angeles	Los Angeles	73	507
G M	34	m	w	VT	Alameda	Oakland	68	165
Harvey	34	m	w	NY	Nevada	Grass Valley Twp	75	227
Henry	45	m	w	CT	Los Angeles	Los Angeles	73	529
John	44	m	w	ENGL	Tuolumne	Sonora P O	93	313
Laura	27	f	w	NY	San Francisco	8-Wd San Francisco	82	493
Rufus	17	m	w	IL	Santa Clara	Redwood Twp	88	132
Sam M	40	m	w	NY	San Francisco	3-Wd San Francisco	79	315
Samuel W	37	m	w	NY	Nevada	Grass Valley Twp	75	146
Thomas	56	m	w	ENGL	Placer	Bath P O	76	438
Thos A	43	m	w	VT	Klamath	Liberty Twp	73	376
BARRUS								
A	70	m	w	CHIL	Alameda	Oakland	68	232
BARRY								
Albert	20	m	w	ME	Mariposa	Mariposa P O	74	98
Amos	44	m	w	ME	Humboldt	Eureka Twp	72	266
Andrew	40	m	w	SWED	Nevada	Nevada Twp	75	321
Anthony	50	m	w	ENGL	Solano	Benicia	90	9
Barry	34	m	b	CANA	Marin	San Rafael Twp	74	43
Bridget	30	f	w	IREL	San Francisco	8-Wd San Francisco	82	329
Bridget R	39	f	w	IREL	San Francisco	San Francisco P O	85	764
Catharine	30	f	w	IREL	San Francisco	San Francisco P O	83	331
Catherine	50	f	w	IREL	San Francisco	8-Wd San Francisco	82	396
Catherine	28	f	w	IREL	San Francisco	8-Wd San Francisco	82	452
Catherine	13	f	w	MO	Santa Barbara	San Buenaventura P	87	438
Charles	29	m	w	ENGL	San Francisco	San Francisco P O	85	801
Charles	28	m	w	LA	San Francisco	San Francisco P O	80	393
Charles	22	m	w	CANA	San Francisco	6-Wd San Francisco	81	41
Chas A	48	m	w	SWED	Napa	Napa	75	7
Daniel	63	m	w	IREL	San Francisco	San Francisco P O	83	53

© 2001 by Heritage Quest. All rights reserved.

California 1870 Census

Name	Age	S	R	B-PL	County	Locale	Series M593 Roll	Pg
Daniel	35	m	w	IREL	Kern	Havilah P O	73	350
Danl	43	m	w	IREL	Alameda	Oakland	68	194
David	57	m	w	IREL	San Francisco	San Francisco P O	83	267
David	35	m	w	IREL	San Francisco	2-Wd San Francisco	79	189
David	29	m	w	IREL	San Francisco	7-Wd San Francisco	81	265
David	28	m	w	IREL	San Francisco	1-Wd San Francisco	79	84
Edmund	32	m	w	IREL	Marin	San Rafael Twp	74	31
Edward	40	m	w	NY	San Francisco	7-Wd San Francisco	81	194
Edward	36	m	w	IREL	San Francisco	2-Wd San Francisco	79	207
Edward	35	m	w	IREL	San Francisco	11-Wd San Francisc	84	646
Edward	33	m	w	IREL	San Francisco	11-Wd San Francisc	84	542
Edward	21	m	w	AUST	Sierra	Sears Twp	89	555
Edwd	35	m	w	NORW	San Francisco	1-Wd San Francisco	79	126
Edwd	33	m	w	IREL	San Francisco	1-Wd San Francisco	79	99
Edwin	17	m	w	MO	Calaveras	San Andreas P O	70	196
Eliza	45	f	w	IREL	San Francisco	2-Wd San Francisco	79	253
Ella	16	f	w	CA	Santa Clara	2-Wd San Jose	88	336
Ellen	75	f	w	IREL	Sutter	Sutter Twp	92	118
Ellen	70	f	w	IREL	San Francisco	San Francisco P O	83	235
Ellen	25	f	w	IREL	San Francisco	5-Wd San Francisco	81	35
Emile	26	m	w	SWED	Marin	San Rafael	74	56
Emma	57	f	w	LA	San Francisco	San Francisco P O	80	413
Emmet	27	m	w	IREL	Santa Barbara	San Buenaventura P	87	437
Eugene	36	m	w	IREL	Marin	Tomales Twp	74	81
Evan	16	m	w	CA	San Joaquin	Douglas Twp	86	32
Francis	13	m	w	MA	San Francisco	San Francisco P O	85	868
George	25	m	w	OH	Alameda	Alameda	68	13
Hannah	44	f	w	IREL	San Joaquin	Castoria Twp	86	12
Henrietta	10	f	w	CA	Nevada	Grass Valley Twp	75	229
Henry	29	m	w	NY	San Francisco	5-Wd San Francisco	81	23
Henry	23	m	w	AUST	Santa Clara	1-Wd San Jose	88	229
J B	30	m	w	IREL	Solano	Benicia	90	13
J H	33	m	w	IREL	San Francisco	San Francisco P O	85	848
James	6	m	w	CA	San Francisco	11-Wd San Francisc	84	586
James	56	m	w	IREL	San Joaquin	Douglas Twp	86	32
James	48	m	w	IREL	San Francisco	8-Wd San Francisco	82	467
James	37	m	w	NY	Nevada	Rough & Ready Twp	75	335
James	33	m	w	KY	Yuba	Marysville	93	582
James	32	m	w	ME	San Francisco	1-Wd San Francisco	79	99
James	30	m	w	IREL	Sacramento	American Twp	77	65
James	28	m	w	ENGL	Kern	Bakersfield P O	73	357
James	27	m	w	IREL	San Francisco	11-Wd San Francisc	84	487
James	26	m	w	IREL	San Francisco	San Francisco P O	85	764
James	26	m	w	IREL	Alameda	San Leandro	68	96
James	21	m	w	IREL	Santa Cruz	Santa Cruz	89	429
James	15	m	w	NY	San Francisco	San Francisco P O	80	386
James J	37	m	w	IREL	San Francisco	San Francisco P O	83	268
James R	38	m	w	LA	Yolo	Grafton Twp	93	482
James W	51	m	w	KY	Napa	Napa	75	5
Jane	18	f	w	CA	Santa Cruz	Pajaro Twp	89	339
Jas	48	m	w	IREL	Solano	Benicia	90	8
Jno	27	m	w	IREL	Sacramento	1-Wd Sacramento	77	190
Jno	23	m	w	IREL	Sacramento	1-Wd Sacramento	77	188
Jno	22	m	w	KY	Sacramento	1-Wd Sacramento	77	174
John	50	m	w	IREL	Solano	Benicia	90	10
John	45	m	w	IREL	San Francisco	San Francisco P O	83	231
John	45	m	w	IREL	Solano	Vallejo	90	175
John	41	m	w	IREL	Tehama	Antelope Twp	92	154
John	40	m	w	SWED	Tuolumne	Columbia P O	93	343
John	40	m	w	IREL	San Francisco	San Francisco P O	83	8
John	38	m	w	CANA	Yuba	W Bear Rvr Twp	93	684
John	36	m	w	IREL	San Francisco	San Francisco P O	80	332
John	35	m	w	IREL	San Francisco	11-Wd San Francisc	84	441
John	35	m	w	IREL	Solano	Denverton Twp	90	26
John	35	m	w	IREL	Santa Clara	1-Wd San Jose	88	244
John	34	m	w	IREL	Tuolumne	Sonora P O	93	310
John	34	m	w	IREL	San Francisco	San Francisco P O	83	289
John	34	m	w	MA	San Joaquin	1-Wd Stockton	86	152
John	33	m	w	WIND	San Francisco	San Francisco P O	83	377
John	31	m	w	IREL	San Francisco	San Francisco P O	83	162
John	26	m	w	IREL	Solano	Vallejo	90	193
John A	25	m	w	WI	Santa Barbara	San Buenaventura P	87	440
John H V	37	m	w	IREL	Siskiyou	Hamburg Twp	89	597
John J	51	m	w	IREL	Solano	Benicia	90	7
John T	29	m	w	IREL	San Francisco	San Francisco P O	85	877
John W	48	m	w	MO	Shasta	Millville P O	89	493
Jos	21	m	w	NY	Sacramento	1-Wd Sacramento	77	182
Joseph	51	m	w	IREL	San Francisco	San Francisco P O	83	311
Joseph	34	m	w	PA	San Diego	Coronado	78	467
Joseph	28	m	w	IREL	Alameda	Oakland	68	152
Joseph	23	m	w	IREL	Marin	San Rafael Twp	74	45
Julia	31	f	w	IREL	San Francisco	San Francisco P O	83	413
Katharine	25	f	w	VA	San Francisco	San Francisco P O	83	172
Laurence	20	m	w	IREL	San Francisco	1-Wd San Francisco	79	64
Lawrence	46	m	w	IREL	Solano	Benicia	90	18
Lawrence	21	m	w	IREL	San Francisco	1-Wd San Francisco	79	63
Louis	60	m	w	IREL	San Francisco	5-Wd San Francisco	81	6
Margaret	26	f	w	IREL	San Francisco	11-Wd San Francisc	84	555
Margrett	40	f	w	IREL	San Francisco	1-Wd San Francisco	79	99
Martin	40	m	w	IREL	Tuolumne	Sonora P O	93	328
Martin	40	m	w	CANA	San Francisco	San Francisco P O	85	844
Martin V	33	m	w	MA	Sacramento	Lee Twp	77	158
Mary	60	f	w	IREL	San Francisco	6-Wd San Francisco	81	97
Mary	43	f	w	IREL	San Francisco	2-Wd San Francisco	79	281
Mary	35	f	w	IREL	Sonoma	Petaluma Twp	91	336
Mary	30	f	w	IREL	San Francisco	6-Wd San Francisco	81	129
Mary	30	f	w	IREL	San Joaquin	2-Wd Stockton	86	174

Name	Age	S	R	B-PL	County	Locale	Series M593 Roll	Pg
Mary	27	f	w	IREL	San Francisco	7-Wd San Francisco	81	179
Mary	25	f	w	IREL	San Francisco	11-Wd San Francisc	84	436
Mary J	15	f	w	CA	Yolo	Buckeye Twp	93	408
Mary P	8	f	w	CA	Santa Clara	2-Wd San Jose	88	338
Mathew	36	m	w	IREL	San Francisco	11-Wd San Francisc	84	647
Mathew	35	m	w	IREL	Placer	Colfax P O	76	390
Michael	55	m	w	IREL	Solano	Tremont Twp	90	34
Michael	33	m	w	IREL	San Francisco	San Francisco P O	85	852
Michael	32	m	w	IREL	San Francisco	San Francisco P O	83	355
Michael	23	m	w	IREL	Solano	Benicia	90	19
Michael	13	m	w	MA	San Francisco	11-Wd San Francisc	84	586
Michael J	58	m	w	IREL	San Francisco	3-Wd San Francisco	79	310
Mike	30	m	w	IREL	Contra Costa	Martinez P O	71	420
Patrick	48	m	w	IREL	Tuolumne	Sonora P O	93	332
Patrick	47	m	w	IREL	Tuolumne	Sonora P O	93	327
Patrick	45	m	w	IREL	Klamath	Sawyers Bar	73	378
Patrick	40	m	w	IREL	San Francisco	11-Wd San Francisc	84	428
Patrick	35	m	w	IREL	San Francisco	11-Wd San Francisc	84	493
Patrick	32	m	w	IREL	San Francisco	1-Wd San Francisco	79	134
Patrick	28	m	w	IREL	San Francisco	1-Wd San Francisco	79	84
Patrick	28	m	w	IREL	Los Angeles	Wilmington Twp	73	645
Patrick	27	m	w	IREL	Colusa	Colusa	71	296
Patrick	25	m	w	CANA	Klamath	Trinidad Twp	73	392
Peter	47	m	w	NORW	San Francisco	1-Wd San Francisco	79	74
Quen	50	m	w	IREL	Calaveras	San Andreas P O	70	194
Richard	39	m	w	IREL	San Francisco	San Francisco P O	83	393
Richard	38	m	w	IREL	Nevada	Grass Valley Twp	75	210
Richd	30	m	w	NY	Yuba	Rose Bar Twp	93	659
Robert	45	m	w	WALE	Contra Costa	Martinez P O	71	427
Robert	42	m	w	NY	San Francisco	11-Wd San Francisc	84	557
Saml	27	m	w	SWED	San Francisco	7-Wd San Francisco	81	259
Terresa	44	f	w	CHIL	Sacramento	Franklin Twp	77	119
Theodore A	44	m	w	MA	San Francisco	8-Wd San Francisco	82	411
Thomas	45	m	w	IREL	San Francisco	San Francisco P O	83	209
Thomas	40	m	w	IREL	San Francisco	2-Wd San Francisco	79	205
Thomas	38	m	w	IREL	Nevada	Grass Valley Twp	75	200
Thomas	35	m	w	IREL	San Francisco	San Francisco P O	83	320
Thomas	29	m	w	ENGL	San Francisco	San Francisco P O	80	414
Thomas	20	m	w	IREL	San Francisco	8-Wd San Francisco	82	447
Thos	41	m	w	IREL	San Francisco	1-Wd San Francisco	79	93
Thos	37	m	w	NY	San Francisco	7-Wd San Francisco	81	238
Thos	29	m	w	IREL	Solano	Vallejo	90	141
W H	42	m	w	TN	Tuolumne	Big Oak Flat P O	93	400
William	57	m	w	PA	Alameda	Alameda	68	19
William	55	m	w	TN	San Francisco	7-Wd San Francisco	81	205
William	52	m	w	IREL	Sacramento	4-Wd Sacramento	77	333
William	45	m	w	IREL	San Francisco	8-Wd San Francisco	82	387
William	42	m	w	IREL	San Francisco	San Francisco P O	80	377
William	40	m	w	IREL	Alameda	Washington Twp	68	280
William	39	m	w	IREL	San Francisco	11-Wd San Francisc	84	530
William	35	m	w	IREL	San Francisco	8-Wd San Francisco	82	413
William	31	m	w	NY	Stanislaus	Empire Twp	92	49
William	31	m	w	IREL	Solano	Rio Vista Twp	90	70
William	30	m	w	IREL	Mariposa	Mariposa P O	74	130
William	26	m	w	IREL	Santa Cruz	Santa Cruz	89	411
William	25	m	w	IREL	Nevada	Meadow Lake Twp	75	251
William	25	m	w	IREL	Santa Clara	Santa Clara Twp	88	169
William	19	m	w	BADE	Placer	Dutch Flat P O	76	415
William A	38	m	w	MO	Sonoma	Sonoma Twp	91	448
Wm	46	m	w	IREL	Santa Barbara	Santa Barbara P O	87	492
Wm	37	m	w	IREL	San Francisco	11-Wd San Francisc	84	495
Wm	36	m	w	IREL	San Francisco	1-Wd San Francisco	79	73
Wm	33	m	w	IREL	San Francisco	1-Wd San Francisco	79	79
Wm	28	m	w	IREL	San Francisco	1-Wd San Francisco	79	62
Wm R	35	m	w	IREL	San Francisco	San Francisco P O	85	739
Zeikel	45	m	w	IREL	San Francisco	7-Wd San Francisco	81	179
BARRYNANO								
Clement	54	m	w	ITAL	Sonoma	Sonoma Twp	91	444
BARS								
D C	33	m	w	LA	Marin	San Rafael Twp	74	41
BARSHAT								
Nicholas	54	m	w	FRAN	Yuba	Bullards Bar P O	93	552
BARSON								
Fred	30	m	w	ENGL	Santa Cruz	Santa Cruz	89	408
John	21	m	w	FRAN	San Francisco	San Francisco P O	80	340
BARSS								
Frederick F	40	m	w	ENGL	El Dorado	Placerville	72	111
Julia	15	f	w	CA	San Francisco	8-Wd San Francisco	82	369
BARSTOW								
Anson	38	m	w	NH	San Francisco	2-Wd San Francisco	79	229
D P	42	m	w	NY	Alameda	Oakland	68	246
George	54	m	w	NH	San Francisco	8-Wd San Francisco	82	332
Josh	44	m	w	ENGL	San Joaquin	2-Wd Stockton	86	198
Kit	28	m	w	NY	San Luis Obispo	Salinas Twp	87	293
Mary	47	f	w	MD	Napa	Yountville Twp	75	89
R C	48	m	w	MO	San Joaquin	Liberty Twp	86	86
Simeon	32	m	w	CT	San Francisco	6-Wd San Francisco	81	116
William	28	m	w	WI	San Francisco	1-Wd San Francisco	79	17
Wm	47	m	w	NH	San Francisco	1-Wd San Francisco	79	131
BART								
Bernard	43	m	w	NY	San Francisco	5-Wd San Francisco	81	23
Hannah	26	f	w	OH	Nevada	Bridgeport Twp	75	100
John	7	m	w	CA	San Francisco	5-Wd San Francisco	81	23
BARTA								
C O	54	m	w	DENM	Tuolumne	Chinese Camp P O	93	367
BARTALO								
L S	28	m	w	ITAL	Tuolumne	Sonora P O	93	303

© 2001 by Heritage Quest. All rights reserved.

Name	Age	S	R	B-PL	County	Locale	Series M593 Roll	Pg
William	44	m	w	ITAL	Tuolumne	Sonora P O	93	303
BARTALOTT								
M	50	m	w	PA	Trinity	Weaverville Pct	92	227
BARTAN								
James	50	m	w	MO	Sacramento	Dry Crk Twp	77	99
BARTCH								
Geo	28	m	w	BADE	Santa Barbara	San Buenaventura P	87	444
BARTE								
Agnes	30	f	w	IREL	San Francisco	2-Wd San Francisco	79	234
BARTEL								
Isaac	22	m	w	ENGL	Nevada	Grass Valley Twp	75	159
J J	27	m	w	NY	Yuba	Rose Bar Twp	93	662
Jules	22	m	w	FRAN	San Francisco	San Francisco P O	80	350
BARTELL								
Charles	24	m	w	ENGL	Alameda	Alameda	68	5
J A	58	m	w	MA	Humboldt	Arcata Twp	72	235
J J	43	m	w	MA	Sacramento	3-Wd Sacramento	77	264
Wm G	28	m	w	CANA	San Joaquin	3-Wd Stockton	86	234
BARTELLA								
Peter	33	m	w	ITAL	San Francisco	2-Wd San Francisco	79	232
BARTELLS								
Conrad	43	m	w	HANO	San Francisco	2-Wd San Francisco	79	139
Wm	51	m	w	HANO	Amador	Volcano P O	69	374
BARTELONI								
Ritzani	36	m	w	ITAL	Sacramento	4-Wd Sacramento	77	351
BARTELOTE								
C	32	m	w	ITAL	Mariposa	Maxwell Crk P O	74	140
BARTELS								
Joseph	25	m	w	HANO	San Francisco	1-Wd San Francisco	79	87
Marx	22	m	w	PRUS	San Francisco	8-Wd San Francisco	82	432
William	25	m	w	BREM	Sacramento	2-Wd Sacramento	77	219
BARTELSMAN								
Carl	46	m	w	HCAS	Santa Clara	1-Wd San Jose	88	232
BARTELSON								
Andrew	40	m	w	NORW	San Joaquin	1-Wd Stockton	86	131
BARTER								
George W	29	m	w	NY	Los Angeles	Los Angeles	73	542
T W	64	m	w	NY	San Joaquin	Douglas Twp	86	46
William	42	m	w	IN	Placer	Newcastle Twp	76	475
BARTH								
Adam	51	m	w	PRUS	Sonoma	Russian Rvr	91	378
Christian	45	m	w	GERM	El Dorado	White Oak Twp	72	137
Frederick	44	m	w	BAVA	Butte	Mountain Spring Tw	70	88
Gotlerl	48	m	w	SAXO	Napa	Napa	75	46
Kate	17	f	w	AUST	San Francisco	8-Wd San Francisco	82	424
BARTHA								
Alice	21	f	w	IN	Santa Clara	Gilroy Twp	88	71
Philomena	36	f	w	MEXI	Sacramento	2-Wd Sacramento	77	226
BARTHALMEW								
Nelson	18	m	w	IL	Tehama	Tehama Twp	92	186
BARTHAMEW								
O C	38	m	w	IL	Tehama	Tehama Twp	92	186
BARTHE								
Eugene	32	m	w	FRAN	Yuba	Marysville	93	614
BARTHEL								
Chas	26	m	w	PRUS	San Francisco	5-Wd San Francisco	81	20
Edward	54	m	w	PRUS	Santa Clara	1-Wd San Jose	88	255
BARTHELEMY								
Maline	18	f	w	CA	San Francisco	San Francisco P O	83	373
BARTHELOME								
Adelia Mrs	30	f	w	MA	Monterey	Monterey	74	357
BARTHELOW								
Adelia	35	f	w	MA	Contra Costa	Martinez P O	71	386
BARTHEN								
Frank	40	m	w	PRUS	San Francisco	San Francisco P O	85	776
BARTHEO								
Johanna	24	f	w	MEXI	San Bernardino	San Salvador Twp	78	458
BARTHER								
Henry	28	m	w	PA	Inyo	Independence Twp	73	328
BARTHET								
Anson	33	m	w	FRAN	Calaveras	San Andreas P O	70	186
BARTHO								
August	21	m	w	BREM	San Joaquin	1-Wd Stockton	86	152
BARTHOL								
Michael	45	m	w	FRAN	Contra Costa	Martinez P O	71	434
BARTHOLEMEW								
Jefferson	42	m	w	VT	Nevada	Grass Valley Twp	75	170
M	30	m	w	NH	Solano	Vallejo	90	207
Paul	58	m	w	ITAL	San Francisco	San Francisco P O	80	426
BARTHOLEMY								
Barbaro	40	m	w	ITAL	Tuolumne	Sonora P O	93	332
BARTHOLEW								
N	38	m	w	FRAN	Amador	Lancha Plana P O	69	368
BARTHOLMEW								
Lewis	63	m	w	IA	Fresno	Millerton P O	72	158
BARTHOLOMEW								
Alan	33	m	w	BADE	San Joaquin	Douglas Twp	86	34
Alfred	47	m	w	OH	El Dorado	Placerville Twp	72	94
Asa	40	m	w	VT	Stanislaus	Branch Twp	92	2
Austin	53	m	w	FRAN	Calaveras	San Andreas P O	70	154
B	60	f	w	NY	Sacramento	3-Wd Sacramento	77	283
Campbell	30	m	w	TX	Sacramento	San Joaquin Twp	77	402
Frank	47	m	w	NY	Contra Costa	San Pablo Twp	71	357
George	36	m	w	NY	Shasta	Shasta P O	89	454
Henry G	40	m	w	SAXO	San Francisco	San Francisco P O	85	771
Jac	31	m	w	KY	San Joaquin	Elkhorn Twp	86	69
John	28	m	w	IREL	Contra Costa	Martinez P O	71	446
BARTHOVLO								
Elizabeth	42	f	w	WURT	El Dorado	Placerville	72	119
BARTHROP								
Edward	42	m	w	ENGL	San Francisco	8-Wd San Francisco	82	393
Jane	66	f	w	ENGL	San Francisco	San Francisco P O	83	95
BARTIDAS								
Pedro	38	m	w	CA	Santa Clara	Burnett Twp	88	32
BARTILAMI								
Louis	60	m	w	FRAN	Plumas	Mineral Twp	77	20
BARTILL								
A	47	m	w	FRAN	Sierra	Butte Twp	89	513
BARTIN								
Herman	14	m	w	HANO	Alameda	Brooklyn Twp	68	44
BARTINA								
John	28	m	w	FRAN	San Francisco	San Francisco P O	80	538
BARTINE								
Antonio	40	m	w	ITAL	Amador	Volcano P O	69	372
George	16	m	w	CA	Contra Costa	Martinez P O	71	410
BARTINELLO								
Chs	27	m	w	ITAL	San Francisco	2-Wd San Francisco	79	215
BARTINETT								
David	37	m	w	IREL	Contra Costa	Martinez P O	71	433
Garrett	28	m	w	IREL	Contra Costa	Martinez P O	71	438
BARTINI								
Charles	40	m	w	ITAL	Santa Clara	2-Wd San Jose	88	317
BARTINS								
Lorenzo	33	m	w	SWIT	Placer	Bath P O	76	425
BARTISON								
James	30	m	w	ENGL	Amador	Amador City P O	69	392
BARTISTO								
James	35	m	w	ITAL	Tulare	Visalia	92	294
BARTLE								
Anson	52	m	w	PA	Yuba	Linda Twp	93	557
Peter	38	m	w	PA	Yuba	Linda Twp	93	557
William	28	m	w	ENGL	Nevada	Grass Valley Twp	75	215
BARTLES								
Richard	22	m	w	WURT	San Francisco	7-Wd San Francisco	81	224
BARTLESON								
Albert	23	m	w	DENM	Placer	Lincoln P O	76	493
Edward A	24	m	w	MI	Nevada	Grass Valley Twp	75	179
Martin	48	m	w	MO	Nevada	Eureka Twp	75	139
BARTLET								
Ada	40	f	w	NY	San Francisco	7-Wd San Francisco	81	240
Austin B	39	m	w	MD	Colusa	Monroe Twp	71	319
Beniah	45	m	w	TN	San Francisco	5-Wd San Francisco	81	18
Chas	45	m	w	OH	Yuba	Linda Twp	93	557
Eliza	16	f	w	CA	San Francisco	1-Wd San Francisco	79	25
Frank	22	m	w	IREL	Colusa	Monroe Twp	71	319
G E	40	m	w	VT	Sacramento	3-Wd Sacramento	77	257
J C	41	m	w	ME	Amador	Sutter Crk P O	69	407
J H	32	m	w	NY	San Joaquin	Oneal Twp	86	112
BARTLETT								
---	25	m	w	IL	Tehama	Tehama Twp	92	196
---	13	m	w	CA	Solano	Benicia	90	21
Albert	30	m	w	HANO	Santa Clara	1-Wd San Jose	88	245
Albert	16	m	w	MO	Stanislaus	Branch Twp	92	2
Alfred	29	m	w	ENGL	San Francisco	San Francisco P O	83	334
Allan M	40	m	w	NH	Santa Clara	2-Wd San Jose	88	302
Allen F	39	m	w	ME	Stanislaus	Emory Twp	92	20
Amanda	16	f	w	CA	El Dorado	Placerville	72	109
Caleb	49	m	w	ME	Sonoma	Analy Twp	91	229
Charles	45	m	w	NH	Trinity	Junction City Pct	92	209
Chas A	36	m	w	ME	Placer	Gold Run Twp	76	400
Chas E	27	m	w	MA	Sacramento	4-Wd Sacramento	77	326
Chas H	28	m	w	PA	San Francisco	San Francisco P O	83	200
Columbus	34	m	w	FL	San Francisco	8-Wd San Francisco	82	449
D F	40	m	w	NY	Tuolumne	Chinese Camp P O	93	376
E E	38	m	w	MA	Alameda	Oakland	68	264
E E	31	m	w	MA	Alameda	Oakland	68	147
E W	53	m	w	ME	Lassen	Janesville Twp	73	432
Edward	45	m	w	ME	Placer	Gold Run Twp	76	400
Edward	21	m	w	IREL	San Francisco	7-Wd San Francisco	81	218
Edward G	40	m	w	ENGL	Nevada	Rough & Ready Twp	75	330
Eugene H	21	m	w	MA	Contra Costa	Martinez P O	71	375
Frank	14	m	w	NY	San Francisco	11-Wd San Francisc	84	586
Fred	31	m	w	HANO	Shasta	American Ranch P O	89	498
Fredk	14	m	w	ME	San Francisco	San Francisco P O	83	72
Fredk E	53	m	w	VT	Santa Barbara	Santa Barbara P O	87	460
G	37	m	w	KY	Lake	Lower Lake	73	423
George	30	m	w	ME	Marin	San Rafael Twp	74	47
Gideon T	30	m	w	ME	Placer	Gold Run Twp	76	394
Gideon T	29	m	w	MO	Placer	Gold Run Twp	76	398
H A	40	m	w	MA	Alameda	Oakland	68	182
Henry	52	m	w	KY	Solano	Suisun Twp	90	95
Henry	40	m	w	MA	Alameda	Oakland	68	211
Henry	40	m	w	ME	Nevada	Meadow Lake Twp	75	269
Henry E	32	m	w	CT	Santa Cruz	Santa Cruz Twp	89	395
Horace D	42	m	w	MA	Santa Clara	Redwood Twp	88	132
J L	51	m	w	OH	San Joaquin	1-Wd Stockton	86	122
James	64	m	w	OH	San Francisco	11-Wd San Francisc	84	566
James	51	m	w	ENGL	El Dorado	Mountain Twp	72	67
James	43	m	w	VA	Tulare	Farmersville Twp	92	247
James	41	m	w	TN	Mendocino	Ukiah Twp	74	238
James	33	m	w	US	San Joaquin	Castoria Twp	86	9
James H	35	m	w	ENGL	San Francisco	San Francisco P O	83	370
Jane	50	f	w	MO	Stanislaus	Branch Twp	92	2
Jarret S	30	m	w	OH	Colusa	Butte Twp	71	270

© 2001 by Heritage Quest. All rights reserved.

California 1870 Census

Series M593

Name	Age	S	R	B-PL	County	Locale	Roll	Pg
Jas E	30	m	w	GA	Santa Barbara	San Buenaventura P	87	446
Jas F	44	m	w	NH	Humboldt	Table Bluff Twp	72	304
Job C	40	m	w	ME	San Francisco	8-Wd San Francisco	82	464
John	42	m	w	MA	San Francisco	7-Wd San Francisco	81	199
Jonathan	50	m	w	NH	San Francisco	11-Wd San Francisc	84	529
Joseph	48	m	w	CT	Santa Barbara	San Buenaventura P	87	439
Joseph W	34	m	w	NY	San Mateo	Redwood Twp	87	365
Josiah	13	m	w	CA	San Joaquin	Castoria Twp	86	1
Josiah W	36	m	w	OH	Placer	Alta P O	76	412
Kate	27	f	w	IREL	San Francisco	San Francisco P O	83	361
L	51	m	w	VA	Sierra	Downieville Twp	89	516
M P	25	f	w	MA	Alameda	Oakland	68	182
Maria	70	f	w	NY	San Francisco	San Francisco P O	80	342
Mary A	36	f	w	ME	San Francisco	San Francisco P O	83	26
Mikel	65	m	w	IREL	Sonoma	Petaluma Twp	91	312
Peter	21	m	w	PRUS	Stanislaus	Buena Vista Twp	92	12
R P	50	m	w	SWIT	Sacramento	3-Wd Sacramento	77	309
Robert	37	m	w	MA	San Francisco	San Francisco P O	85	822
Robt	30	m	w	ENGL	San Francisco	San Francisco P O	83	130
S H	48	m	w	MA	Amador	Jackson P O	69	336
Saml A	58	m	w	NY	Santa Cruz	Santa Cruz	89	404
Thomas D	31	m	w	PA	Santa Cruz	Santa Cruz	89	409
W	32	m	w	MA	Tehama	Tehama Twp	92	191
W W	21	m	w	ME	Merced	Snelling P O	74	264
William	29	m	w	IL	Solano	Suisun Twp	90	94
William	26	m	w	IN	San Francisco	8-Wd San Francisco	82	466
William	25	m	w	MA	El Dorado	White Oak Twp	72	139
William C	50	m	w	CT	San Francisco	6-Wd San Francisco	81	140
BARTLEY								
David	54	m	w	SCOT	San Francisco	San Francisco P O	83	259
James	32	m	w	IREL	Los Angeles	Los Angeles	73	545
James	21	m	w	CANA	Santa Cruz	Soquel Twp	89	445
Joseph	23	m	w	ENGL	Nevada	Grass Valley Twp	75	215
Robert	38	m	w	IREL	Nevada	Grass Valley Twp	75	200
BARTLINO								
Wm	51	m	w	PA	Alameda	Oakland	68	138
BARTLY								
Bartholomew	50	m	w	IREL	Sacramento	Granite Twp	77	154
Henry H	37	m	w	IN	Sonoma	Petaluma Twp	91	337
Horace	41	m	w	NY	San Joaquin	Elkhorn Twp	86	61
Jerrod	36	m	w	CANA	Solano	Rio Vista Twp	90	56
Richard	20	m	w	CANA	San Mateo	Woodside P O	87	387
BARTMAN								
Mary	22	f	w	HANO	San Francisco	San Francisco P O	83	200
Matthias	68	m	w	BADE	San Francisco	2-Wd San Francisco	79	181
BARTMANN								
Chs	37	m	w	BADE	San Francisco	2-Wd San Francisco	79	236
BARTO								
Daniel	43	m	w	HDAR	San Francisco	8-Wd San Francisco	82	442
BARTOL								
John	65	m	w	NY	Siskiyou	Butte Twp	89	584
BARTOLA								
Jose	37	m	w	CA	Santa Clara	2-Wd San Jose	88	334
Joseph	40	m	w	FRAN	Calaveras	San Andreas P O	70	188
Juan	41	m	w	MEXI	Santa Clara	2-Wd San Jose	88	319
Ramon	24	m	w	CA	Santa Clara	2-Wd San Jose	88	335
BARTOLEMY								
Isaac	21	m	w	ENGL	Contra Costa	Martinez P O	71	375
BARTOLI								
Antone	43	m	w	ITAL	Nevada	Grass Valley Twp	75	168
BARTOLO								
Antone	40	m	w	ITAL	Contra Costa	Martinez P O	71	432
Battise	45	m	w	ITAL	Amador	Jackson P O	69	342
John	11	m	w	CA	Contra Costa	Martinez P O	71	434
Juan	26	m	w	CA	Marin	San Rafael Twp	74	37
BARTOLOMEO								
Carda	25	m	w	SWIT	Marin	Novato Twp	74	11
Jose	31	m	w	AZOR	San Francisco	1-Wd San Francisco	79	118
Rollo	21	m	w	ITAL	Santa Clara	2-Wd San Jose	88	317
BARTOLUAS								
Joseph	27	m	w	BADE	Calaveras	San Andreas P O	70	182
BARTON								
Abe	39	m	w	OH	Butte	Concow Twp	70	9
Alfred	28	m	w	ENGL	San Francisco	8-Wd San Francisco	82	376
Alfred	23	m	w	ENGL	Sacramento	Franklin Twp	77	115
Alfred S	35	m	w	ME	Nevada	Grass Valley Twp	75	189
Andrew	31	m	w	OH	Amador	Jackson P O	69	330
Arthur	34	m	w	OH	Nevada	Nevada Twp	75	282
B B	42	m	w	NY	Sierra	Sierra Twp	89	566
Birmingham	5	m	w	CA	Butte	Wyandotte Twp	70	148
Carrie	10	f	w	IA	Yolo	Putah Twp	93	509
Charles	52	m	w	VT	Santa Clara	Santa Clara Twp	88	142
Charles	45	m	w	NY	San Francisco	San Francisco P O	83	239
Chester R	14	m	w	CA	Butte	Chico Twp	70	13
David	54	m	w	NY	Sacramento	4-Wd Sacramento	77	342
Dexter	46	m	w	NY	Amador	Volcano P O	69	386
Ed	33	m	w	DC	San Joaquin	3-Wd Stockton	86	224
Enos D	20	m	w	IL	Tulare	Venice Twp	92	276
Frank	12	m	w	CA	Napa	Yountville Twp	75	79
Frank A	34	m	w	MA	Butte	Chico Twp	70	17
Gale	54	m	w	VT	San Diego	San Diego	78	511
Geo	45	m	w	ENGL	Sierra	Downieville Twp	89	519
George	64	m	w	ENGL	San Francisco	San Francisco P O	83	77
George	42	m	w	SHOL	Mariposa	Mariposa P O	74	117
Guy Wm	34	m	w	VT	San Diego	San Diego	78	505
H	13	m	w	CA	San Joaquin	3-Wd Stockton	86	230
Harry	22	m	w	MI	Santa Clara	Santa Clara Twp	88	150
Hattie M	20	f	w	MI	Santa Clara	Santa Clara Twp	88	143
Heman D	34	m	w	NY	Alpine	Woodfords P O	69	309
Henry	57	m	w	VT	Amador	Jackson P O	69	319
Henry	32	m	w	CT	Butte	Chico Twp	70	55
Henry	22	m	w	CANA	San Diego	San Diego	78	511
Henry	21	m	w	OH	Amador	Volcano P O	69	386
Henry C	25	m	w	NY	Sacramento	4-Wd Sacramento	77	320
Henry C	15	m	w	CA	Shasta	Millville P O	89	486
Hiram	64	m	w	MA	Yolo	Putah Twp	93	509
Hiram E	36	m	w	NY	Alpine	Woodfords P O	69	309
Hudson D	26	m	w	NJ	Tulare	Venice Twp	92	276
J	32	m	w	OH	Sierra	Sierra Twp	89	566
J	27	m	w	PA	San Francisco	San Francisco P O	83	286
J L	41	m	w	VA	Sutter	Vernon Twp	92	131
J S	28	m	w	PA	Sierra	Lincoln Twp	89	545
James	62	m	w	PA	Sutter	Vernon Twp	92	131
James	50	m	w	NJ	Tulare	Venice Twp	92	275
James	38	m	w	MO	Sacramento	4-Wd Sacramento	77	360
James	36	m	w	IREL	San Francisco	1-Wd San Francisco	79	66
James	19	m	w	CA	Los Angeles	Los Angeles	73	570
James	17	m	w	CA	Los Angeles	El Monte Twp	73	459
James W	38	m	w	MO	Yuba	Long Bar Twp	93	562
Jesse	19	f	w	US	San Joaquin	Liberty Twp	86	82
John	50	m	w	ENGL	Humboldt	Eureka Twp	72	263
John	50	m	w	MA	San Francisco	7-Wd San Francisco	81	284
John	43	m	w	ENGL	Siskiyou	Hamburg Twp	89	597
John	27	m	w	GERM	San Luis Obispo	Santa Rosa Twp	87	321
John	26	m	w	OH	Amador	Volcano P O	69	387
Johnethan	40	m	w	MO	Sacramento	Alabama Twp	77	61
Joseph	49	m	w	TN	Santa Clara	Fremont Twp	88	63
Josh	19	m	w	MO	San Joaquin	Elliott Twp	86	80
Joshua	54	m	w	MD	San Francisco	San Francisco P O	83	142
Joshua	50	m	w	MO	Sacramento	Alabama Twp	77	61
L	36	m	w	WI	Nevada	Bridgeport Twp	75	107
Lewis	53	m	b	MS	Santa Cruz	Pajaro Twp	89	345
Margaret	82	f	w	NC	San Joaquin	Liberty Twp	86	94
Margaret	81	f	w	NC	Sacramento	Alabama Twp	77	61
Mary	21	f	w	IL	Alameda	Washington Twp	68	286
Mary H	73	f	w	VT	Amador	Jackson P O	69	319
Oliver	27	m	w	OH	San Diego	Fort Yuma Dist	78	463
Peter	40	m	w	PRUS	Alameda	Murray Twp	68	117
R	32	m	w	VT	Lake	Lower Lake	73	419
R	20	m	w	MO	San Joaquin	Liberty Twp	86	82
Robert	31	m	w	LA	San Francisco	1-Wd San Francisco	79	81
Robt	20	m	w	MO	San Joaquin	Liberty Twp	86	83
Rowland	52	m	w	NY	Humboldt	Arcata Twp	72	227
Royal M	24	m	w	VT	San Diego	San Diego	78	505
Ruel D	28	m	w	ME	Mendocino	Albion & Big Rvr T	74	166
Sarah	21	f	w	VT	Sonoma	Bodega Twp	91	250
Sophy	43	f	w	ENGL	San Francisco	San Francisco P O	80	349
T	23	m	w	MO	San Joaquin	Liberty Twp	86	82
Thomas	46	m	w	KY	Mendocino	Calpella Twp	74	182
Thos	42	m	w	TN	Butte	Chico Twp	70	56
Thos	28	m	w	IREL	Solano	Vallejo	90	161
Thos A	45	m	w	MO	San Luis Obispo	San Luis Obispo Tw	87	304
Thos C	42	m	w	PA	Sonoma	Healdsburg & Mendo	91	282
Willard	32	m	w	OH	Santa Clara	2-Wd San Jose	88	335
William	9	m	w	CA	Sacramento	2-Wd Sacramento	77	244
William	48	m	w	ME	San Francisco	6-Wd San Francisco	81	133
William	41	m	w	IREL	San Francisco	2-Wd San Francisco	79	264
Wm	43	m	w	ENGL	San Francisco	2-Wd San Francisco	79	208
Wm	39	m	w	OH	Nevada	Nevada Twp	75	282
Wm	32	m	w	MD	Mono	Bridgeport P O	74	283
Wm A	66	m	w	DE	San Bernardino	San Bernardino Twp	78	422
Wm S	21	m	w	NY	San Francisco	7-Wd San Francisco	81	287
BARTONELLI								
Francis	32	m	w	ITAL	Santa Clara	Santa Clara Twp	88	175
BARTOS								
Colotto	37	m	w	ITAL	Los Angeles	Los Angeles	73	531
BARTRAM								
Isaac	52	m	w	CT	Merced	Snelling P O	74	272
Salina	47	f	w	OH	Placer	Roseville P O	76	354
Wheeler	61	m	w	CT	El Dorado	Diamond Springs Tw	72	27
BARTSCH								
Christian	44	m	w	SWIT	Yuba	Slate Range Bar Tw	93	673
BARTTLETT								
Wm B	3M	m	w	CA	Yuba	Long Bar Twp	93	563
BARTWELL								
A D	62	f	w	CANA	Alameda	Oakland	68	215
Josephine	5	f	w	CA	Santa Clara	1-Wd San Jose	88	252
BARTY								
Roger	35	m	w	IREL	San Francisco	8-Wd San Francisco	82	389
BARUH								
A	47	m	w	BAVA	Nevada	Nevada Twp	75	274
Kerman	50	m	w	BAVA	Sonoma	Petaluma Twp	91	319
BARUTH								
Ernest	27	m	w	GERM	San Francisco	8-Wd San Francisco	82	290
BARVA								
Beronica P	72	f	w	MEXI	Napa	Napa	75	54
De Loresa	65	m	w	MEXI	Napa	Napa	75	54
BARVADOLE								
B	30	m	w	SWIT	San Joaquin	Oneal Twp	86	110
BARVANOUSKI								
Henry	38	m	w	POLA	Los Angeles	Wilmington Twp	73	642
BARVIN								
Jas	40	m	w	CANA	San Joaquin	Oneal Twp	86	104

© 2001 by Heritage Quest. All rights reserved.

Name	Age	S	R	B-PL	County	Locale	Roll	Pg
						Series M593		
BARWELL								
Jordon B	38	m	w	TN	Butte	Ophir Twp	70	114
BARWICK								
Maggie	24	f	w	IREL	Santa Clara	2-Wd San Jose	88	292
BARWIS								
Armand	50	m	w	FRAN	San Francisco	San Francisco P O	83	165
BARY								
Richd	24	m	w	IREL	Sonoma	Mendocino Twp	91	303
BARYMAN								
Peter	48	m	w	HAMB	Santa Clara	Almaden Twp	88	12
Thos H	26	m	w	ENGL	Nevada	Nevada Twp	75	300
BARYN								
Michael	34	m	w	IREL	Plumas	Goodwin Twp	77	5
BARZ								
August	32	m	w	SHOL	San Francisco	3-Wd San Francisco	79	297
BARZENO								
Beyo	34	m	w	MEXI	Tulare	Visalia	92	294
BARZIL								
Joseph	20	m	w	SWIT	San Francisco	2-Wd San Francisco	79	159
BASAC								
Pedro	35	m	w	FRAN	Los Angeles	Los Angeles	73	557
BASAGNO								
Joachino	30	m	w	ITAL	San Francisco	11-Wd San Francisc	84	587
BASANIE								
Antone	46	m	w	ITAL	Amador	Jackson P O	69	337
BASAS								
Guadalupe	21	m	w	MEXI	Los Angeles	El Monte Twp	73	462
BASAYE								
Rafael	36	m	w	MEXI	Los Angeles	El Monte Twp	73	453
BASBERG								
Charles	42	m	w	SWED	Yuba	North East Twp	93	644
BASCH								
Mary	72	f	w	BAVA	San Francisco	11-Wd San Francisc	84	551
BASCHETOUPE								
Angelo	30	m	w	ITAL	Santa Clara	Santa Clara Twp	88	157
Antonio	27	m	w	ITAL	Santa Clara	Santa Clara Twp	88	157
BASCOM								
Alpheus L	32	m	w	KY	Santa Clara	San Jose Twp	88	200
George	24	m	w	OH	Siskiyou	Callahan P O	89	631
Lewis H	58	m	w	NY	Santa Clara	Santa Clara Twp	88	159
BASCON								
L	45	m	w	ENGL	San Joaquin	Liberty Twp	86	89
BASCOS								
Florencia	31	m	i	CA	Los Angeles	Los Angeles	73	501
Jose	33	m	w	MEXI	Fresno	Millerton P O	72	159
BASCULEG								
Pedro	42	m	w	FRAN	Los Angeles	Los Angeles Twp	73	474
BASCULUPIC								
John	20	m	w	ITAL	Stanislaus	Empire Twp	92	45
BASCUM								
Phillip	29	m	w	FRAN	Butte	Ophir Twp	70	118
BASCUS								
Jose	60	m	w	MEXI	Mariposa	Mariposa P O	74	95
Joseph	36	m	w	CHIL	Santa Clara	2-Wd San Jose	88	302
Ventura	17	m	w	CA	San Luis Obispo	San Luis Obispo Tw	87	303
BASDEN								
James	45	m	w	IN	Colusa	Grand Island Twp	71	308
BASELINE								
Alex	46	m	w	SPAI	San Francisco	2-Wd San Francisco	79	216
BASEMAN								
Antone	40	m	w	PRUS	Contra Costa	Martinez P O	71	414
BASER								
Elizabeth	49	f	w	PA	Mariposa	Mariposa P O	74	117
Leonide	30	f	w	MEXI	San Francisco	6-Wd San Francisco	81	81
BASETENA								
Jacob	32	m	w	GERM	Santa Clara	1-Wd San Jose	88	236
BASEY								
Joseph	29	m	w	AR	Sonoma	Mendocino Twp	91	287
BASFORD								
E N	36	m	w	MA	San Francisco	San Francisco P O	85	753
F	25	m	w	NH	Solano	Vallejo	90	177
Jas	50	m	w	IREL	Solano	Vallejo	90	170
Jas K	46	m	w	ME	San Francisco	8-Wd San Francisco	82	292
Mary	16	f	w	CA	San Francisco	6-Wd San Francisco	81	139
BASGALUPA								
Louis	39	m	w	ITAL	San Mateo	Schoolhouse Statio	87	332
BASH								
A C	34	m	w	HANO	Sierra	Butte Twp	89	512
Frederick	56	m	w	PRUS	San Mateo	San Mateo P O	87	359
H F	24	m	w	HANO	Sierra	Butte Twp	89	510
Henry	30	m	w	PRUS	San Francisco	San Francisco P O	83	367
M	20	m	w	PRUS	San Joaquin	1-Wd Stockton	86	131
Sherman	50	m	w	BAVA	Stanislaus	Emory Twp	92	24
BASHART								
L P	30	m	w	PA	San Joaquin	Liberty Twp	86	93
BASHAW								
Ellen	8	f	w	CA	San Francisco	San Francisco P O	85	827
Emma	8	f	w	CA	San Francisco	San Francisco P O	85	827
John	46	m	w	KY	Napa	Napa Twp	75	70
Mary	10	f	w	CA	San Francisco	San Francisco P O	85	827
BASHEIM								
Frederick	49	m	w	ENGL	San Francisco	8-Wd San Francisco	82	476
BASHERA								
Joseph	31	m	w	ITAL	Sonoma	Petaluma Twp	91	327
BASHERE								
John	34	m	w	VA	Colusa	Spring Valley Twp	71	339
BASHFORD								
Oscar	32	m	w	MI	San Diego	Julian Dist	78	473
BASHIELDS								
Sarah	12	f	w	CA	Mendocino	Ukiah Twp	74	234
BASHIER								
M	30	m	w	CA	Alameda	Murray Twp	68	127
BASHIR								
Cegar	42	m	w	ITAL	Santa Clara	Santa Clara Twp	88	175
BASHLOT								
J C	32	m	w	GA	Humboldt	Mattole Twp	72	287
BASHORE								
Terman	32	m	w	VA	Colusa	Spring Valley Twp	71	340
William	32	m	w	IA	Colusa	Spring Valley Twp	71	340
BASHTON								
James	30	m	w	ENGL	Nevada	Grass Valley Twp	75	199
BASIE								
Jas	32	m	w	KY	Solano	Benicia	90	18
BASIL								
Henry	34	m	w	FRAN	San Francisco	San Francisco P O	80	468
BASILISCO								
Luige	37	m	w	ITAL	San Francisco	11-Wd San Francisc	84	594
BASKEEN								
W H	24	m	w	ENGL	Yuba	Rose Bar Twp	93	656
BASKERS								
Delores	57	f	w	MEXI	Colusa	Colusa Twp	71	281
BASKERVILLE								
George G	23	m	w	OH	Santa Clara	2-Wd San Jose	88	330
George G	21	m	w	MA	Santa Clara	1-Wd San Jose	88	254
BASLE								
Antone	46	m	w	PRUS	Calaveras	San Andreas P O	70	212
BASLER								
Joseph	39	m	w	BADE	Santa Clara	2-Wd San Jose	88	319
BASLEY								
Aaron	34	m	w	PA	Yolo	Putah Twp	93	509
Frank	35	m	w	WALE	Lake	Little Borax	73	419
Martin J	44	m	w	SWIT	Sacramento	American Twp	77	64
BASLIE								
Anna	28	f	w	ENGL	San Francisco	8-Wd San Francisco	82	338
BASNEY								
Nicholas	64	m	w	CANA	Yuba	Linda Twp	93	554
Oscar	38	m	w	CT	Yuba	Marysville	93	612
BASON								
W B	47	m	w	IL	Alameda	Oakland	68	179
BASONJIR								
Joseph	35	m	w	FRAN	Calaveras	San Andreas P O	70	186
BASQUALA								
Dominico	18	m	w	ITAL	San Mateo	Schoolhouse Statio	87	345
Francis	30	m	w	ITAL	San Mateo	Schoolhouse Statio	87	345
John	22	m	w	ITAL	San Mateo	Schoolhouse Statio	87	344
Martin	25	m	w	ITAL	San Mateo	Schoolhouse Statio	87	345
BASQUALABA								
Joseph	26	m	w	ITAL	San Mateo	Menlo Park P O	87	378
BASQUALLA								
Lino	24	m	w	ITAL	San Mateo	Schoolhouse Statio	87	344
Peter	21	m	w	ITAL	San Mateo	Schoolhouse Statio	87	344
BASQUALO								
Florez	18	m	w	ITAL	San Mateo	Schoolhouse Statio	87	343
John	25	m	w	ITAL	San Mateo	Schoolhouse Statio	87	347
BASQUE								
Jarman	40	m	w	MEXI	San Diego	Temecula Dist	78	527
BASQUES								
B	62	m	w	SPAI	Monterey	Monterey	74	364
Jose	42	m	w	MEXI	San Francisco	San Francisco P O	80	472
Lino	23	m	w	CA	Santa Barbara	Las Cruces P O	87	506
Pedro	42	m	w	MEXI	San Francisco	San Francisco P O	80	540
Vincent	20	m	w	CAME	San Francisco	1-Wd San Francisco	79	117
BASQUEZ								
Anton	44	m	w	CA	Monterey	Monterey Twp	74	344
Francisco	40	m	w	CA	Los Angeles	Soledad Twp	73	631
Geryono	50	m	w	CA	Monterey	Monterey Twp	74	352
Jose	54	m	w	MEXI	San Francisco	San Francisco P O	80	471
Jose Jesus	30	m	w	CA	Monterey	Monterey Twp	74	352
Lucy	33	f	w	MEXI	San Francisco	San Francisco P O	80	486
Margarita	10	f	w	CA	Los Angeles	Santa Ana Twp	73	616
Pauble	27	m	w	CA	Monterey	Monterey Twp	74	352
Refugio	24	m	w	CA	Los Angeles	San Juan Twp	73	627
BASS								
Burtiz	32	m	w	FRAN	San Francisco	San Francisco P O	80	335
Edmund	21	m	w	CANA	Santa Clara	San Jose Twp	88	196
Edward	32	m	w	PRUS	Santa Clara	2-Wd San Jose	88	313
F H	40	m	w	NY	San Joaquin	Castoria Twp	86	4
Frances	32	f	m	OH	Sacramento	2-Wd Sacramento	77	239
Henry	45	m	w	BRUN	El Dorado	Diamond Springs Tw	72	23
Henry	43	m	w	PA	Marin	San Rafael	74	50
Jno S P	47	m	w	MO	Shasta	Stillwater P O	89	478
Joel	45	m	w	MA	Fresno	Millerton P O	72	149
John	23	m	w	CANA	Sonoma	Cloverdale Twp	91	269
John B	43	m	w	OH	Amador	Volcano P O	69	380
John E	51	m	w	VA	Placer	Lincoln P O	76	485
Joseph	35	m	w	ITAL	Los Angeles	Wilmington Twp	73	640
Joseph	35	m	w	ENGL	Solano	Vallejo	90	190
R	49	m	w	KY	Lassen	Janesville Twp	73	433
Robert	55	m	w	NY	Amador	Ione City P O	69	351
Thomas J	35	m	w	NY	San Francisco	San Francisco P O	85	740
Wm	30	m	w	MA	Solano	Vallejo	90	141
BASSADORE								
Laura	19	f	w	PRUS	San Bernardino	San Bernardino Twp	78	425

© 2001 by Heritage Quest. All rights reserved.

California 1870 Census

Series M593

Name	Age	S	R	B-PL	County	Locale	Roll	Pg
BASSAGLOUPI								
L	32	m	w	ITAL	Mariposa	Maxwell Crk P O	74	140
BASSCHE								
Francisco	24	m	w	SWIT	San Francisco	San Francisco P O	80	477
BASSE								
Peter	62	m	w	FRAN	Amador	Volcano P O	69	386
BASSECH								
Uschi	29	m	w	FRAN	San Francisco	San Francisco P O	80	477
BASSELL								
Geo	35	m	w	WALE	Butte	Kimshew Tpw	70	80
BASSERTO								
Virgillo	35	m	w	ITAL	San Francisco	San Francisco P O	80	400
BASSET								
Augustus	30	m	w	ITAL	Sacramento	4-Wd Sacramento	77	345
D	40	m	w	NY	San Joaquin	Dent Twp	86	28
Danl	40	m	w	IREL	San Francisco	7-Wd San Francisco	81	247
John	27	m	w	MA	San Joaquin	1-Wd Stockton	86	152
John S	47	m	w	NY	Butte	Oregon Twp	70	125
Robert	36	m	w	ENGL	San Francisco	2-Wd San Francisco	79	258
BASSETT								
A C	33	m	w	OH	Alameda	Oakland	68	260
Alonzo	37	m	w	ME	Alameda	Oakland	68	197
Ambrose	39	m	w	WI	Santa Clara	San Jose Twp	88	201
Austin	17	m	w	IL	Butte	Chico Twp	70	35
Bernard	62	m	w	NY	Solano	Vacaville Twp	90	127
C D	28	m	w	ME	San Francisco	1-Wd San Francisco	79	71
Charles	40	m	w	VT	San Francisco	11-Wd San Francisc	84	507
Daniel	49	m	w	NH	Santa Clara	2-Wd San Jose	88	294
David	24	m	w	WALE	Marin	Tomales Twp	74	81
Douglas	14	m	w	IL	Solano	Vacaville Twp	90	123
Edwin	27	m	w	ME	Plumas	Goodwin Twp	77	8
Elizabeth J	38	f	w	NY	Santa Clara	1-Wd San Jose	88	241
Geo	20	m	w	NY	Tehama	Red Bluff	92	182
George	45	m	w	ENGL	Santa Clara	Redwood Twp	88	128
H	31	m	w	NY	Santa Cruz	Santa Cruz Twp	89	387
Hariett	49	f	w	VT	Butte	Chico Twp	70	36
Henry	25	m	w	NY	San Francisco	San Francisco P O	83	230
Isaac	34	m	w	IN	Solano	Maine Prairie Twp	90	49
J D	49	m	w	ENGL	San Joaquin	Dent Twp	86	16
J M	39	m	w	KY	San Joaquin	2-Wd Stockton	86	183
James	35	m	w	IREL	Los Angeles	Soledad Twp	73	630
James A	23	m	w	PA	Monterey	San Antonio Twp	74	322
James H	35	m	w	OH	Santa Cruz	Pajaro Twp	89	342
John	35	m	w	ENGL	San Francisco	San Francisco P O	83	66
John	24	m	w	MD	Siskiyou	Surprise Valley Tw	89	640
Joseph	40	m	w	NY	Alameda	Brooklyn Twp	68	40
Joseph	33	m	w	MA	Merced	Snelling P O	74	265
Joseph	30	m	w	PA	Los Angeles	Soledad Twp	73	633
Manton E	21	m	w	IA	Santa Clara	2-Wd San Jose	88	327
Mitchell	30	m	w	CANA	Santa Clara	San Jose Twp	88	197
Nath	80	m	w	NY	San Francisco	8-Wd San Francisco	82	361
Nymphas B	36	m	w	IN	Solano	Maine Prairie Twp	90	49
Robert T	37	m	w	PA	Santa Cruz	Santa Cruz	89	418
S	54	m	w	NY	Lake	Lower Lake	73	415
Simon E	36	m	w	NY	San Francisco	1-Wd San Francisco	79	103
Thomas	22	m	w	WALE	Marin	Tomales Twp	74	81
U	36	m	w	CANA	Alameda	Oakland	68	165
William	32	m	w	NY	Sacramento	2-Wd Sacramento	77	220
William	24	m	w	CT	Kern	Bakersfield P O	73	361
Wilton	28	m	w	PA	Butte	Chico Twp	70	34
BASSETTE								
Emily	4	f	w	CA	Santa Cruz	Santa Cruz	89	417
BASSFORD								
Clara	12	f	w	CA	Santa Cruz	Santa Cruz Twp	89	390
Hohn W	43	m	w	MD	Santa Cruz	Santa Cruz Twp	89	392
Joseph	47	m	w	NY	Solano	Vacaville Twp	90	134
Sarah J	24	f	w	MO	Sonoma	Mendocino Twp	91	289
BASSHAM								
Green	33	m	w	AL	Trinity	Weaverville Pct	92	226
Greene B	34	m	w	AL	Shasta	Stillwater P O	89	480
William	48	m	w	KY	Santa Clara	Santa Clara Twp	88	162
BASSI								
Carolina	39	f	w	SWIT	San Francisco	11-Wd San Francisc	84	594
Joseph	36	m	w	SWIT	Marin	Bolinas Twp	74	3
BASSIDY								
James	32	m	w	IREL	San Francisco	8-Wd San Francisco	82	474
BASSILIO								
Jno	40	m	w	ITAL	San Joaquin	1-Wd Stockton	86	133
BASSING								
Adam	37	m	w	BAVA	San Diego	Milquaty Dist	78	476
H	45	m	w	PRUS	Sierra	Downieville Twp	89	522
BASSINI								
Bernando	24	m	w	FRAN	San Francisco	San Francisco P O	80	375
Ed	25	m	w	VA	San Francisco	8-Wd San Francisco	82	375
BASSLER								
Charles	40	m	w	SWIT	San Francisco	San Francisco P O	83	420
Fred	50	m	w	BADE	San Francisco	3-Wd San Francisco	79	326
BASSO								
Andrew	28	m	w	ITAL	Mariposa	Mariposa P O	74	108
Angelo	25	m	w	ITAL	Merced	Snelling P O	74	250
John	21	m	w	ITAL	Tuolumne	Big Oak Flat P O	93	398
Juan	35	m	w	ITAL	San Francisco	3-Wd San Francisco	79	289
Paubla	35	m	w	CA	Monterey	Monterey Twp	74	351
Phillip	16	m	w	CA	San Francisco	San Francisco P O	80	486
BASSOCK								
Ella	15	f	w	MO	Yolo	Cache Crk Twp	93	435

Series M593

Name	Age	S	R	B-PL	County	Locale	Roll	Pg
BASSONET								
Ann B	53	f	w	FRAN	San Francisco	6-Wd San Francisco	81	122
BASSORE								
Saml	25	m	w	OH	Yuba	W Bear Rvr Twp	93	682
BASSOTT								
J H	40	m	w	NJ	Sierra	Downieville Twp	89	514
BASSOU								
Eugene	45	m	w	FRAN	Calaveras	San Andreas P O	70	216
Jean De	41	m	w	FRAN	Sacramento	4-Wd Sacramento	77	376
Victor	40	m	w	FRAN	Calaveras	San Andreas P O	70	216
BASSOUT								
F	38	m	w	CANA	Sierra	Lincoln Twp	89	551
J	41	m	w	CANA	Sierra	Lincoln Twp	89	551
BASSY								
Frank	50	m	w	HOLL	Tuolumne	Big Oak Flat P O	93	393
BASTARD								
James	35	m	w	ENGL	Nevada	Grass Valley Twp	75	179
BASTEIN								
J	27	m	w	GERM	Lake	Morgan Valley	73	425
BASTEL								
John	87	m	w	FRAN	San Francisco	2-Wd San Francisco	79	241
Mary	71	f	w	FRAN	San Francisco	2-Wd San Francisco	79	241
BASTELETT								
A	12	m	w	CA	Alameda	Oakland	68	159
A L	17	m	w	CA	Alameda	Oakland	68	159
BASTERA								
Louisa	50	f	w	MEXI	San Mateo	Half Moon Bay P O	87	396
BASTERS								
Fernanda	33	m	w	CHIL	Placer	Bath P O	76	442
BASTIAN								
G L	32	m	w	ME	Sierra	Sierra Twp	89	562
Henry	62	m	w	ENGL	Fresno	Millerton P O	72	166
Jame J	26	m	w	ENGL	Amador	Amador City P O	69	392
James	33	m	w	ENGL	Amador	Amador City P O	69	392
James	33	m	w	ENGL	Nevada	Grass Valley Twp	75	198
James	32	m	w	ENGL	Amador	Amador City P O	69	392
James	12	m	w	ENGL	Amador	Amador City P O	69	394
John	33	m	w	ENGL	El Dorado	Mud Springs Twp	72	81
John	29	m	w	ENGL	Amador	Sutter Crk P O	69	402
Mary	80	f	w	CANA	Nevada	Grass Valley Twp	75	176
Richard	30	m	w	ENGL	Nevada	Grass Valley Twp	75	197
S M	40	f	w	ENGL	Amador	Sutter Crk P O	69	409
BASTIANI								
Egeneri	27	m	w	ITAL	San Francisco	1-Wd San Francisco	79	105
BASTIDEX								
Pedro	40	m	w	CA	Santa Clara	Burnett Twp	88	33
BASTILLE								
Philip	35	m	w	HAMB	San Francisco	2-Wd San Francisco	79	227
BASTINE								
Alexander	41	m	w	NY	Sacramento	American Twp	77	67
W	59	m	w	BADE	Sierra	Eureka Twp	89	525
BASTION								
William	40	m	b	WIND	Calaveras	Copperopolis P O	70	257
BASTON								
A F	36	m	w	MA	San Francisco	San Francisco P O	85	847
Emma	56	f	w	MA	Sonoma	Petaluma Twp	91	330
BASTONIA								
Ceffiro	35	m	w	ITAL	Santa Clara	2-Wd San Jose	88	301
BASTOW								
A	38	m	w	TN	Lake	Lower Lake	73	414
BASTROP								
Chris	33	m	w	DENM	Sutter	Nicolaus Twp	92	112
BASTSTO								
John	40	m	w	ITAL	Amador	Sutter Crk P O	69	406
BASYE								
Lisband	38	m	w	IN	San Francisco	1-Wd San Francisco	79	95
BAT								
To	44	m	c	CHIN	Calaveras	San Andreas P O	70	159
BATANA								
Jos	32	m	b	MO	San Joaquin	3-Wd Stockton	86	218
BATANCO								
Frank	24	m	w	PORT	Alameda	Washington Twp	68	269
BATANIS								
Lorenzo	32	m	w	MEXI	Merced	Snelling P O	74	251
BATASSOGE								
Joseph	42	m	w	ITAL	San Joaquin	1-Wd Stockton	86	126
BATAUL								
F	57	m	w	LA	Amador	Jackson P O	69	345
BATAVI								
Ingr	27	m	w	TX	San Joaquin	Castoria Twp	86	8
BATCHELDER								
Adowinn J	50	m	w	MA	Yuba	Bullards Bar P O	93	553
Albert	17	m	w	NH	San Mateo	San Mateo P O	87	355
C S	28	m	w	ME	Amador	Sutter Crk P O	69	396
James	40	m	w	NH	Alameda	Brooklyn	68	37
John	50	m	w	ME	San Francisco	2-Wd San Francisco	79	170
John	40	m	w	NH	Amador	Jackson P O	69	343
John	28	m	w	NY	San Francisco	6-Wd San Francisco	81	90
John R	40	m	w	MA	Santa Cruz	Santa Cruz	89	421
Mary	13	f	w	NY	San Francisco	2-Wd San Francisco	79	191
Sally	75	f	w	VT	Sonoma	Petaluma Twp	91	345
Wm H	45	m	w	MA	San Francisco	San Francisco P O	85	726
BATCHELER								
August	64	m	w	MA	Solano	Suisun Twp	90	116
Orlando C	37	m	w	ME	Calaveras	Copperopolis P O	70	247
BATCHELLER								
C S	23	m	w	ME	Amador	Sutter Crk P O	69	398

© 2001 by Heritage Quest. All rights reserved.

Name	Age	S	R	B-PL	County	Locale	Series M593 Roll	Pg
J W	40	m	w	ME	Solano	Vallejo	90	188
Jos B	35	m	w	NY	Shasta	Horsetown P O	89	502
Joseph	44	m	w	VT	Marin	San Antonio Twp	74	62
BATCHELOR								
M	51	m	w	NY	San Francisco	San Francisco P O	83	263
BATCHELTER								
H A	30	m	w	ME	Tuolumne	Chinese Camp P O	93	367
BATCHELTOR								
H V	35	m	w	NY	Napa	Napa	75	43
BATCHER								
C	45	m	w	PRUS	Sacramento	3-Wd Sacramento	77	310
John	38	m	w	BREM	Sacramento	2-Wd Sacramento	77	235
BATCHIE								
Anton	40	m	w	AUST	San Francisco	7-Wd San Francisco	81	260
BATCHLER								
Nathaniel	30	m	w	NH	Napa	Napa	75	14
BATE								
Harry	21	m	w	ENGL	San Francisco	7-Wd San Francisco	81	246
Wm H	37	m	w	ENGL	San Francisco	San Francisco P O	83	188
Wm H	11	m	w	MA	San Francisco	San Francisco P O	83	200
BATEAUX								
Louis	40	m	w	FRAN	San Francisco	6-Wd San Francisco	81	41
BATELLE								
Narsiso	60	m	w	MEXI	Los Angeles	Los Angeles	73	548
BATELMENO								
John	35	m	w	PORT	San Mateo	Half Moon Bay P O	87	394
BATEMAN								
Amos C	39	m	w	IREL	San Francisco	San Francisco P O	85	715
Ashly S	47	m	w	OH	Monterey	Monterey	74	357
Charles	20	m	w	IN	Colusa	Spring Valley Twp	71	344
Edwin	21	m	w	CANA	Santa Cruz	Santa Cruz	89	429
Edwin W M	21	m	w	CANA	Santa Cruz	Santa Cruz	89	410
Frank	35	m	w	IREL	Stanislaus	San Joaquin Twp	92	80
George	37	m	w	PA	Colusa	Monroe Twp	71	315
Henry K	22	m	w	TX	Butte	Chico Twp	70	20
Hilda	17	f	w	ENGL	San Joaquin	3-Wd Stockton	86	219
J	48	m	w	NY	Napa	Yountville Twp	75	78
J W	56	m	w	VA	Tehama	Tehama Twp	92	192
James	49	m	w	CANA	San Francisco	3-Wd San Francisco	79	302
John	46	m	w	NY	San Joaquin	2-Wd Stockton	86	163
L N	38	m	w	OH	Del Norte	Happy Camp Twp	71	470
Miles	21	m	w	ENGL	San Francisco	7-Wd San Francisco	81	246
Richard	22	m	w	ENGL	Stanislaus	Buena Vista Twp	92	13
T	28	m	w	IREL	Solano	Vallejo	90	170
William	8	m	w	CA	Alameda	Oakland	68	257
William	28	m	w	GA	San Francisco	8-Wd San Francisco	82	483
Wm	29	m	w	HANO	San Francisco	1-Wd San Francisco	79	14
Wm A	39	m	w	RI	San Francisco	8-Wd San Francisco	82	332
BATERACO								
Johanan	32	m	w	ITAL	Calaveras	San Andreas P O	70	175
BATES								
Alanson	35	m	w	VT	Sacramento	Georgianna Twp	77	128
Alfred	29	m	w	ENGL	Marin	San Rafael	74	55
Andrew J	41	m	w	OH	Yuba	Slate Range Bar Tw	93	671
Andrew T	47	m	w	VA	Los Angeles	Santa Ana Twp	73	602
Asa B	56	m	w	MA	Santa Barbara	Santa Barbara P O	87	477
Asher B	60	m	w	NY	San Francisco	8-Wd San Francisco	82	334
Ashley B	45	m	w	SC	El Dorado	White Oak Twp	72	140
Benj F	40	m	w	SC	Sacramento	Granite Twp	77	146
Benjamin	50	m	w	ENGL	Sacramento	Franklin Twp	77	114
C D	38	m	w	NY	Alameda	Oakland	68	146
Calvin	63	m	w	VT	Sacramento	Dry Crk Twp	77	97
Catherine	45	f	w	IREL	San Francisco	San Francisco P O	83	244
Charles E	31	m	w	ME	Santa Cruz	Santa Cruz Twp	89	389
Christopher	40	m	w	IREL	Sacramento	2-Wd Sacramento	77	225
Daniel S	42	m	w	NY	Calaveras	San Andreas P O	70	194
Edward H	40	m	w	OH	Monterey	San Antonio Twp	74	319
Edwin	37	m	w	ME	Plumas	Plumas Twp	77	33
Eliza	73	f	w	MD	Mariposa	Mariposa P O	74	118
Ella	18	f	w	CA	Amador	Fiddletown P O	69	433
Ella	11	f	w	CA	San Luis Obispo	Santa Rosa Twp	87	318
F	50	m	w	MA	Sacramento	1-Wd Sacramento	77	178
Fordice	47	m	w	NY	Trinity	Minersville Pct	92	203
Franklin	73	m	w	MA	Nevada	Nevada Twp	75	287
Fred A	43	m	w	MA	Placer	Clipper Gap P O	76	376
Frederick	55	m	w	ME	Sacramento	2-Wd Sacramento	77	252
Geo	22	m	w	ENGL	San Joaquin	Tulare Twp	86	255
Geo O	41	m	w	NY	Sacramento	San Joaquin Twp	77	405
Geo O	34	m	w	CT	San Francisco	8-Wd San Francisco	82	377
George	49	m	w	FRAN	Los Angeles	San Juan Twp	73	629
George	30	m	w	ENGL	San Francisco	6-Wd San Francisco	81	119
Harry N	21	m	w	IL	Merced	Snelling P O	74	247
Henry	54	m	w	VA	Yolo	Cache Crk Twp	93	423
Henry	40	m	w	ME	Kern	Havilah P O	73	340
Isaac	37	m	w	MI	San Francisco	8-Wd San Francisco	82	362
J C	31	m	w	MI	San Francisco	8-Wd San Francisco	82	365
J P	30	m	w	IL	Sacramento	1-Wd Sacramento	77	190
Jacob	66	m	w	WURT	San Francisco	6-Wd San Francisco	81	115
James E	42	m	w	MO	Amador	Fiddletown P O	69	431
John	53	m	w	VA	Tehama	Red Bluff	92	178
John	45	m	w	ENGL	Nevada	Grass Valley Twp	75	176
John	42	m	w	ENGL	San Mateo	Menlo Park P O	87	379
John	29	m	w	ENGL	San Francisco	3-Wd San Francisco	79	287
John	25	m	w	MO	Yolo	Cache Crk Twp	93	423
John	21	m	w	NY	Marin	Bolinas Twp	74	8
John B	40	m	w	VA	San Luis Obispo	Santa Rosa Twp	87	317
John C	25	m	w	MO	Yolo	Cache Crk Twp	93	422
John L	20	m	w	MA	Sonoma	Healdsburg & Mendo	91	281
John S	59	m	w	MA	Mariposa	Mariposa P O	74	92
Joseph	51	m	w	NY	Napa	Napa	75	25
Joseph C	32	m	w	ME	San Francisco	6-Wd San Francisco	81	115
Josiah	61	m	w	ENGL	Los Angeles	Santa Ana Twp	73	609
Lafayette	44	m	w	OH	Shasta	Dog Crk P O	89	471
Lafayette	38	m	w	AR	Calaveras	Copperopolis P O	70	230
Lizzie	16	f	w	CA	San Francisco	1-Wd San Francisco	79	75
Moses	38	m	w	IL	Nevada	Washington Twp	75	346
Nelson	55	m	w	NY	Trinity	Douglas	92	235
Peter	56	m	w	FRAN	Amador	Jackson P O	69	346
Philip	38	m	w	PA	Solano	Vallejo	90	160
Phillip	37	m	w	IL	Sonoma	Cloverdale Twp	91	269
R A	57	m	w	VA	Yuba	Marysville	93	617
R S	44	m	w	CT	San Joaquin	2-Wd Stockton	86	203
S C	40	m	w	PA	San Joaquin	Tulare Twp	86	260
S H	32	m	w	IL	Sacramento	1-Wd Sacramento	77	190
Samuel	40	m	w	NH	San Francisco	8-Wd San Francisco	82	379
Samuel C	29	m	w	MA	Mariposa	Mariposa P O	74	92
Samuel L	40	m	w	MO	El Dorado	Cosumnes Twp	72	19
Stephen	40	m	w	ME	San Luis Obispo	Morro Twp	87	286
V J	33	m	w	ENGL	Del Norte	Crescent	71	465
W F	47	m	w	ENGL	Sierra	Lincoln Twp	89	546
Walter C	36	m	w	WI	El Dorado	Cosumnes Twp	72	19
William	46	m	w	ENGL	San Francisco	11-Wd San Francisc	84	463
William	39	m	w	WURT	Calaveras	Copperopolis P O	70	222
William	25	m	w	NY	Kern	Linns Valley P O	73	348
William	14	m	w	CA	Stanislaus	North Twp	92	69
Wm Henry	32	m	w	OH	Plumas	Quartz Twp	77	43
Zealous	39	m	w	IA	Sonoma	Petaluma Twp	91	365
BATEY								
George	41	m	w	KY	Humboldt	South Fork Twp	72	301
Marlow	67	m	b	KY	Shasta	Shasta P O	89	454
William	40	m	w	SCOT	Contra Costa	Martinez P O	71	422
Wm	33	m	w	MA	Sonoma	Mendocino Twp	91	301
BATFORD								
Geo	22	m	w	CANA	Solano	Vallejo	90	164
BATGER								
J	32	m	w	FRAN	Tuolumne	Big Oak Flat P O	93	391
BATH								
Albert L	40	m	w	CANA	Santa Cruz	Soquel Twp	89	442
George	46	m	w	BAVA	Del Norte	Crescent	71	462
John	33	m	w	ITAL	Calaveras	San Andreas P O	70	214
Joseph	43	m	w	ENGL	Santa Barbara	San Buenaventura P	87	420
Peter	35	m	w	FRAN	San Joaquin	Castoria Twp	86	4
BATHEL								
Zac	21	m	w	GERM	Sacramento	1-Wd Sacramento	77	184
BATHERO								
Bartola	47	m	w	CHIL	Calaveras	San Andreas P O	70	217
BATHERS								
Edward T	47	m	w	MD	San Francisco	8-Wd San Francisco	82	410
BATHEUNES								
John	34	m	w	HCAS	San Francisco	11-Wd San Francisc	84	475
BATHOILA								
Louis	42	m	w	ITAL	Mariposa	Mariposa P O	74	113
BATHRE								
Totolaro	56	f	w	MEXI	Sacramento	1-Wd Sacramento	77	203
BATHSKY								
W N	27	m	w	CANA	San Francisco	3-Wd San Francisco	79	323
BATHURST								
William	35	m	w	IREL	Sacramento	2-Wd Sacramento	77	217
BATIAN								
Henry	40	m	w	ENGL	Fresno	Millerton P O	72	167
BATIO								
Leoncia	17	m	w	CA	Los Angeles	Los Angeles	73	532
BATISE								
Ada	33	f	w	BAVA	Solano	Suisun Twp	90	113
BATISTA								
Bale	36	m	w	ITAL	San Francisco	San Francisco P O	85	849
John	32	m	w	ITAL	Calaveras	Copperopolis P O	70	249
John	30	m	w	ITAL	Calaveras	Copperopolis P O	70	247
Juan	40	m	i	CA	Monterey	Monterey Twp	74	345
Juan	30	m	w	ITAL	San Francisco	3-Wd San Francisco	79	289
BATISTE								
Joseph	35	m	w	AZOR	San Francisco	San Francisco P O	83	203
BATLEY								
James	30	m	w	IREL	Inyo	Cerro Gordo Twp	73	318
BATLY								
Charles H	35	m	w	PRUS	San Francisco	7-Wd San Francisco	81	282
BATMAN								
Christian	21	m	w	SHOL	San Francisco	6-Wd San Francisco	81	70
George	27	m	w	IREL	Humboldt	South Fork Twp	72	302
John W	38	m	w	MO	Sonoma	Vallejo Twp	91	456
BATOLIA								
F	40	m	w	ITAL	Amador	Jackson P O	69	337
BATON								
Hugh	27	m	w	SCOT	Butte	Wyandotte Twp	70	146
BATOSTA								
Gitanna	39	m	w	ITAL	San Francisco	3-Wd San Francisco	79	288
BATRINO								
John	25	m	w	ITAL	San Mateo	Schoolhouse Statio	87	343
BATS								
Henry F	55	m	w	BAVA	Sonoma	Sonoma Twp	91	448
John	30	m	w	IL	Sonoma	Petaluma Twp	91	353
BATSCHE								
Charles	31	m	w	BADE	Contra Costa	Martinez P O	71	380

© 2001 by Heritage Quest. All rights reserved.

Name	Age	S	R	B-PL	County	Locale	Series M593 Roll	Pg
BATSON								
Jas	63	m	w	ENGL	San Francisco	7-Wd San Francisco	81	247
BATT								
Ah	35	m	c	CHIN	Calaveras	San Andreas P O	70	155
Major	29	m	w	VA	San Joaquin	3-Wd Stockton	86	218
Raffet	25	m	w	ITAL	El Dorado	Diamond Springs Tw	72	28
BATTA								
John	50	m	w	FRAN	Mariposa	Mariposa P O	74	129
BATTAMS								
Thos	43	m	w	ENGL	Shasta	Buckeye P O	89	482
Wm	36	m	w	OH	San Francisco	8-Wd San Francisco	82	332
BATTAZAN								
Jose	17	m	w	CA	Fresno	Millerton P O	72	167
BATTE								
James	37	m	w	LA	Merced	Snelling P O	74	251
Joseph	54	m	w	FRAN	Calaveras	San Andreas P O	70	216
Joseph	27	m	w	ITAL	Amador	Amador City P O	69	390
BATTEAUX								
Frank	36	m	w	FRAN	San Joaquin	Castoria Twp	86	4
Louis	43	m	w	FRAN	San Francisco	San Francisco P O	80	488
BATTEE								
John M	41	m	w	MD	Santa Clara	San Jose Twp	88	187
BATTEL								
Philip	55	m	w	HCAS	San Francisco	2-Wd San Francisco	79	239
BATTELLA								
John	16	m	w	ITAL	San Mateo	Schoolhouse Statio	87	345
BATTELLCIO								
Alegracia	29	f	w	CA	Los Angeles	Los Angeles	73	503
BATTELLE								
Y F	34	m	w	PA	Sierra	Sierra Twp	89	569
Y S	58	m	w	OH	Sierra	Sierra Twp	89	569
BATTEN								
Henery	26	m	w	ME	San Francisco	7-Wd San Francisco	81	176
John	49	m	w	ENGL	Calaveras	Copperopolis P O	70	247
Joseph	40	m	w	ENGL	Nevada	Grass Valley Twp	75	221
Joseph	29	m	w	ENGL	Nevada	Grass Valley Twp	75	189
Saml	42	m	w	OH	Sonoma	Santa Rosa	91	405
Sampson	42	m	w	ENGL	San Francisco	San Francisco P O	85	771
William	34	m	w	PA	Plumas	Goodwin Twp	77	8
Wm	48	m	w	ENGL	San Francisco	2-Wd San Francisco	79	269
BATTENFELL								
George	60	m	w	PA	Stanislaus	San Joaquin Twp	92	74
BATTENFIELD								
George	21	m	w	OH	Stanislaus	San Joaquin Twp	92	75
John	28	m	w	OH	Stanislaus	San Joaquin Twp	92	75
BATTER								
John	22	m	w	ME	Mendocino	Point Arena Twp	74	206
BATTERFIELD								
John A	42	m	w	NH	Amador	Volcano P O	69	387
BATTERMAN								
John	22	m	w	IREL	Solano	Suisun Twp	90	112
BATTERS								
John	38	m	w	VA	San Joaquin	Tulare Twp	86	253
William	24	m	w	POLA	San Francisco	8-Wd San Francisco	82	358
BATTERSBEE								
John	34	m	w	IREL	Santa Cruz	Santa Cruz	89	427
BATTERSBY								
Jas	50	m	w	CANA	Solano	Vallejo	90	167
BATTERSON								
Wm	38	m	w	MA	Humboldt	Table Bluff Twp	72	304
BATTERTON								
William	35	m	w	IREL	San Mateo	Schoolhouse Statio	87	344
BATTEST								
Joseph	30	m	w	SCOT	Napa	Napa	75	25
BATTEY								
Henry	21	m	w	PA	Santa Clara	Milpitas Twp	88	110
Thomas	46	m	w	IREL	Plumas	Rich Bar Twp	77	45
BATTHERS								
Rosa	1	f	w	NV	San Joaquin	Tulare Twp	86	254
BATTI								
Joseph	33	m	w	ITAL	Tuolumne	Sonora P O	93	327
BATTIE								
Andrew C	50	m	w	SCOT	San Luis Obispo	Salinas Twp	87	292
Geo	41	m	w	SCOT	El Dorado	Georgetown Twp	72	40
William	25	m	w	NY	San Francisco	San Francisco P O	80	427
Wm	37	m	w	NY	San Francisco	San Francisco P O	83	132
BATTIETE								
Francis	45	m	w	FRAN	Nevada	Bridgeport Twp	75	117
BATTIS								
Fayette	42	m	w	PORT	Nevada	Eureka Twp	75	133
Frank	20	m	w	VT	Nevada	Nevada Twp	75	282
Langder	33	m	w	FRAN	Placer	Auburn P O	76	364
Manuel	32	m	w	SCOT	Siskiyou	Table Rock Twp	89	648
BATTISTE								
Jean	50	m	w	FRAN	Marin	San Rafael Twp	74	34
John	80	m	w	IL	Nevada	Nevada Twp	75	296
John	54	m	w	FRAN	Marin	San Rafael	74	54
John	41	m	w	ITAL	Marin	San Rafael Twp	74	30
Manuel	21	m	w	PORT	Marin	Sausalito Twp	74	71
Pezzoni	24	m	w	SWIT	Marin	Novato Twp	74	9
Thomas	59	m	w	PORT	Marin	San Rafael Twp	74	34
Thomas	54	m	w	AZOR	Marin	San Rafael Twp	74	32
BATTISTI								
Tight	31	m	w	ITAL	San Francisco	11-Wd San Francisc	84	614
BATTISTO								
John	17	m	w	ITAL	Mariposa	Maxwell Crk P O	74	143

Name	Age	S	R	B-PL	County	Locale	Series M593 Roll	Pg
BATTLE								
John	65	m	w	IREL	San Francisco	8-Wd San Francisco	82	398
John S	39	m	w	NY	Sacramento	Sutter Twp	77	381
Jos	48	m	w	FRAN	Solano	Vallejo	90	161
Thomas	44	m	w	VA	San Diego	San Diego	78	486
BATTLES								
Alice	20	f	w	IL	San Luis Obispo	Arroyo Grande Twp	87	273
Geo W	55	m	w	NY	Santa Barbara	Santa Maria P O	87	511
Henry	64	m	w	HANO	Sacramento	4-Wd Sacramento	77	376
Jane	37	f	w	IREL	San Francisco	1-Wd San Francisco	79	88
John	35	m	w	IREL	San Francisco	1-Wd San Francisco	79	88
Luke	26	m	w	IREL	San Francisco	San Francisco P O	83	350
Rollin E	21	m	w	PA	Santa Barbara	Santa Maria P O	87	511
Wm H	1	m	w	CA	San Francisco	1-Wd San Francisco	79	88
BATTMAN								
J H	26	m	w	NY	Mariposa	Maxwell Crk P O	74	140
BATTO								
Michael	25	m	w	ITAL	Amador	Volcano P O	69	383
BATTON								
Hiram	25	m	w	IA	Alameda	Eden Twp	68	66
James	36	m	w	IREL	San Francisco	7-Wd San Francisco	81	166
John	30	m	w	MO	Sonoma	Russian Rvr	91	377
Joseph	58	m	w	OH	Alameda	Eden Twp	68	66
BATTRELL								
Geo H	1	m	w	ENGL	Sonoma	Analy Twp	91	227
BATTS								
George	39	m	w	ENGL	Yuba	New York Twp	93	639
Mary	40	f	w	IREL	Yuba	Marysville	93	584
BATTY								
J	40	m	w	IREL	Sierra	Butte Twp	89	510
James	34	m	w	ENGL	Santa Barbara	San Buenaventura P	87	427
John	30	m	w	ENGL	San Francisco	San Francisco P O	85	871
John L	38	m	w	MD	Placer	Bath P O	76	433
Philip	32	m	w	FRAN	Nevada	Nevada Twp	75	293
R C	47	m	w	NC	San Joaquin	Dent Twp	86	28
BATURA								
Petra	22	f	w	CA	Los Angeles	Los Angeles	73	523
BATUS								
John	50	m	w	AZOR	Amador	Jackson P O	69	347
BATY								
Agnes	18	f	w	IREL	San Francisco	8-Wd San Francisco	82	413
David	25	m	w	IL	Siskiyou	Surprise Valley Tw	89	638
James	23	m	w	CANA	Sonoma	Sonoma Twp	91	448
John	27	m	w	IL	Siskiyou	Surprise Valley Tw	89	638
Robert	28	m	w	IREL	Solano	Montezuma Twp	90	65
Thomas	40	m	w	TN	Sutter	Nicolaus Twp	92	114
BAU								
Charles	65	m	w	CT	San Francisco	11-Wd San Francisc	84	628
BAUB								
John	20	m	w	FRAN	San Francisco	San Francisco P O	83	136
BAUC								
E J	54	m	w	IREL	Lake	Knoxville Mines	73	405
BAUCH								
Frederick	45	m	w	PRUS	Stanislaus	North Twp	92	69
BAUCHE								
Serfano	37	m	w	SWIT	San Francisco	San Francisco P O	80	477
BAUCHER								
David	41	m	w	PA	Butte	Chico Twp	70	35
Jas	20	m	w	MA	San Joaquin	2-Wd Stockton	86	192
Josiah	50	m	w	PA	Butte	Chico Twp	70	35
BAUCOM								
Joseph	38	m	w	TN	Santa Cruz	Soquel Twp	89	436
BAUDEN								
William H	32	m	w	ENGL	Nevada	Grass Valley Twp	75	232
BAUDINE								
Alfredo	21	m	w	CA	Los Angeles	Los Angeles	73	570
Arturo	18	m	w	CA	Los Angeles	Los Angeles	73	570
BAUDON								
Nancy	61	f	w	TN	Tulare	Visalia	92	300
BAUDOUIN								
Henry	36	m	w	FRAN	Nevada	Grass Valley Twp	75	168
BAUDOUN								
Alfred	38	m	w	FRAN	Monterey	Monterey Twp	74	352
BAUEN								
Margt	40	f	w	AUST	Fresno	Millerton P O	72	148
BAUENBAUM								
S	29	m	w	PRUS	Solano	Vallejo	90	147
BAUER								
Charles	32	m	w	PA	San Francisco	San Francisco P O	83	151
Chas	38	m	w	WURT	Santa Clara	Gilroy Twp	88	80
J J	33	m	w	FRAN	Sacramento	1-Wd Sacramento	77	189
John	38	m	w	BAVA	San Francisco	8-Wd San Francisco	82	352
Joseph	61	m	w	WURT	San Francisco	San Francisco P O	83	347
Joseph	40	m	w	PRUS	San Francisco	San Francisco P O	80	540
Louis	25	m	w	BAVA	San Francisco	San Francisco P O	83	179
Rosa	25	f	w	BAVA	San Francisco	8-Wd San Francisco	82	406
Ulyses	51	m	w	BADE	San Joaquin	1-Wd Stockton	86	122
William	17	m	w	PA	San Francisco	San Francisco P O	83	182
BAUERS								
Fredk	45	m	w	WURT	Shasta	Shasta P O	89	452
BAUERSCHMIDT								
Joseph	26	m	w	PRUS	Los Angeles	Santa Ana Twp	73	614
BAUFFMAN								
William	30	m	w	PA	Yolo	Grafton Twp	93	484
BAUFMAN								
John	42	m	w	PRUS	San Joaquin	Castoria Twp	86	12

© 2001 by Heritage Quest. All rights reserved.

Series M593

Name	Age	S	R	B-PL	County	Locale	Roll	Pg
BAUG								
Ah	40	m	c	CHIN	Placer	Auburn P O	76	371
BAUGH								
Benjamin	42	m	w	VA	Plumas	Indian Twp	77	18
James M G	31	m	w	GA	Yolo	Cache Crk Twp	93	448
John	59	m	w	VA	Placer	Roseville P O	76	350
John	38	m	w	PA	Shasta	French Gulch P O	89	469
Jos F	57	m	w	MO	Sonoma	Mendocino Twp	91	295
Josephine	25	f	w	PA	San Francisco	San Francisco P O	83	98
T E	38	m	w	PA	San Francisco	San Francisco P O	85	782
William	31	m	w	PA	San Francisco	3-Wd San Francisco	79	308
BAUGHMAN								
A	40	m	w	PA	Amador	Fiddletown P O	69	435
Adam	39	m	w	PA	Amador	Fiddletown P O	69	440
William	20	m	w	IL	Placer	Auburn P O	76	364
BAULAINE								
Joseph	31	m	w	FRAN	Nevada	Eureka Twp	75	138
BAULANT								
Celeste	30	m	w	FRAN	Santa Cruz	Watsonville	89	365
BAULCOPI								
Francisco	21	m	w	ITAL	Santa Clara	Fremont Twp	88	48
Theodore	28	m	w	ITAL	Santa Clara	Fremont Twp	88	48
BAULEY								
Allen H	41	m	w	PA	Los Angeles	Los Angeles	73	569
BAULICUER								
Jo	29	m	w	ME	San Joaquin	2-Wd Stockton	86	161
BAULMORE								
Marion	36	m	w	OH	Butte	Hamilton Twp	70	71
BAULSIR								
Nimrod	40	m	w	NY	San Francisco	San Francisco P O	80	389
BAUM								
Adam P	30	m	w	IN	Santa Cruz	Pajaro Twp	89	356
Charles	50	m	w	RUSS	Alameda	Alameda	68	10
Christopher	30	m	w	GERM	Contra Costa	Martinez P O	71	407
Gustave	35	m	w	PRUS	San Francisco	San Francisco P O	80	536
Henry	28	m	w	SWIT	San Joaquin	2-Wd Stockton	86	200
John W	39	m	w	KY	Colusa	Colusa Twp	71	286
Julius	40	m	w	BAVA	San Francisco	San Francisco P O	83	352
Peter	38	m	w	OH	Solano	Denverton Twp	90	23
Valentine	18	f	w	PRUS	Kern	Havilah P O	73	336
Veronia	16	f	w	OR	Sonoma	Santa Rosa	91	397
Wm	24	m	w	PRUS	San Francisco	8-Wd San Francisco	82	362
BAUMAN								
Chas	33	m	w	BADE	San Francisco	1-Wd San Francisco	79	26
E	32	m	w	SWIT	San Francisco	3-Wd San Francisco	79	319
Jacob H	46	m	w	BAVA	Solano	Suisun Twp	90	100
John	44	m	w	BAVA	San Francisco	8-Wd San Francisco	82	383
Joseph	25	m	w	BAVA	San Francisco	San Francisco P O	80	333
Louis	59	m	w	BADE	San Francisco	San Francisco P O	80	534
Moritz	38	m	w	SWIT	San Francisco	San Francisco P O	80	480
BAUMBERGER								
Casper	36	m	w	SWIT	Alameda	Eden Twp	68	83
Felix	33	m	w	SWIT	Alameda	Hayward	68	78
BAUME								
Milton C	21	m	w	IL	San Francisco	1-Wd San Francisco	79	64
BAUMEISTER								
Christ	40	m	w	PRUS	El Dorado	Salmon Falls Twp	72	129
John	30	m	w	BAVA	San Francisco	San Francisco P O	83	315
Wm	28	m	w	PRUS	Siskiyou	Surprise Valley Tw	89	638
BAUMER								
Peter	40	m	w	FRAN	Calaveras	San Andreas P O	70	174
BAUMGARD								
Philip	23	m	w	BAVA	San Francisco	11-Wd San Francisc	84	512
BAUMGARDNER								
Frank	31	m	w	BADE	Alameda	Washington Twp	68	290
BAUMGARTEN								
Anton	29	m	w	HUNG	San Francisco	3-Wd San Francisco	79	326
Chas	35	m	w	PRUS	Sacramento	4-Wd Sacramento	77	341
Henriett	30	f	w	HOLL	Tehama	Tehama Twp	92	194
Joseph	22	m	w	IA	Colusa	Monroe Twp	71	314
BAUMGARTNER								
Valentine	35	m	w	BAVA	San Francisco	8-Wd San Francisco	82	418
BAUMGERDNER								
L	40	m	w	MA	San Francisco	8-Wd San Francisco	82	347
BAUMHOGGER								
John	48	m	w	PRUS	Calaveras	Copperopolis P O	70	240
BAUMONT								
Jessey	23	f	w	WI	Amador	Sutter Crk P O	69	398
W H	27	m	w	MS	San Joaquin	Oneal Twp	86	98
BAUMRI								
George	34	m	w	PRUS	San Francisco	San Francisco P O	80	459
Henry	31	m	w	PRUS	San Francisco	San Francisco P O	80	459
BAUN								
---	20	m	c	CHIN	Siskiyou	Cottonwood Twp	89	592
J F	34	m	w	WURT	Yuba	East Bear Rvr Twp	93	541
BAUND								
Wm	52	m	w	KY	San Luis Obispo	Salinas Twp	87	289
BAUPTISTE								
Gustav	38	m	w	FRAN	San Francisco	6-Wd San Francisco	81	70
BAUR								
Herman	27	m	w	PA	San Joaquin	2-Wd Stockton	86	175
John	44	m	w	BREM	Placer	Roseville P O	76	351
John	30	m	w	SWIT	Sonoma	Petaluma Twp	91	310
BAURCH								
August	40	m	w	PRUS	San Francisco	San Francisco P O	83	194
BAURDIO								
Baptist	28	m	w	ITAL	San Francisco	San Francisco P O	80	482
BAURHYTE								
Rot H	43	m	w	NY	San Francisco	8-Wd San Francisco	82	289
BAURLE								
John	15	m	w	WI	San Francisco	11-Wd San Francisc	84	587
BAUSAN								
Louis	41	m	w	FRAN	Fresno	Millerton P O	72	164
BAUSCH								
Henry	42	m	w	HDAR	Santa Cruz	Santa Cruz	89	432
BAUSE								
William G	24	m	w	CANA	Inyo	Bishop Crk Twp	73	313
BAUSMAN								
William	50	m	w	PA	San Francisco	San Francisco P O	83	321
BAUSTADT								
J C	36	m	w	HAMB	Alameda	Oakland	68	222
BAUTAUT								
Richard	27	m	w	FRAN	San Francisco	San Francisco P O	80	350
BAUTIER								
Charles	34	m	w	NY	Siskiyou	Surprise Valley Tw	89	637
BAUTISTA								
Juan	25	m	w	ECUA	San Francisco	11-Wd San Francisc	84	478
BAUTISTE								
Louis	35	m	w	ITAL	San Francisco	San Francisco P O	85	741
BAUVARD								
Ewen M	49	m	w	NY	Placer	Alta P O	76	411
BAUX								
J B	49	m	w	FRAN	Alameda	Oakland	68	177
BAUXES								
Jenny	28	f	w	FRAN	Sierra	Table Rock Twp	89	579
Jno Fr	3	m	w	FRAN	Sierra	Table Rock Twp	89	579
John	31	m	w	FRAN	Sierra	Table Rock Twp	89	579
BAVARAI								
John	28	m	w	MEXI	Tuolumne	Sonora P O	93	316
BAVARIA								
Aylla	38	m	w	SWIT	El Dorado	Lake Valley Twp	72	64
BAVERA								
John	23	m	w	NM	Solano	Tremont Twp	90	28
BAVERDA								
Incarnacion	60	m	w	MEXI	San Luis Obispo	San Luis Obispo Tw	87	302
BAVERLE								
John	47	m	w	WURT	San Francisco	San Francisco P O	80	478
BAVESTA								
Andrew	50	m	w	ITAL	Calaveras	San Andreas P O	70	177
BAVIA								
John	47	m	w	ITAL	Inyo	Cerro Gordo Twp	73	320
Manuel	36	m	w	MEXI	Santa Barbara	Las Cruces P O	87	515
BAVILLA								
A	44	m	w	IREL	Nevada	Eureka Twp	75	139
BAVOUZET								
George	44	m	w	FRAN	Yuba	Slate Range Bar Tw	93	670
BAW								
Ah	22	m	c	CHIN	Nevada	Little York Twp	75	234
Gee	42	m	c	CHIN	Plumas	Mineral Twp	77	24
Jo	63	m	c	CHIN	Mariposa	Mariposa P O	74	132
BAWAZER								
G W	15	m	w	CA	Alameda	Oakland	68	159
BAWBAUR								
D	42	m	w	PRUS	San Joaquin	2-Wd Stockton	86	207
BAWDEN								
Francis	19	m	w	ENGL	Nevada	Grass Valley Twp	75	143
James	26	m	w	ENGL	Nevada	Grass Valley Twp	75	217
Joseph	32	m	w	ENGL	Nevada	Grass Valley Twp	75	199
Nellie	18	f	w	ENGL	San Francisco	San Francisco P O	80	412
Nicholas	37	m	w	ENGL	Nevada	Grass Valley Twp	75	198
Samuel	22	m	w	ENGL	Nevada	Grass Valley Twp	75	220
William	32	m	w	ENGL	Nevada	Grass Valley Twp	75	147
William	25	m	w	ENGL	Nevada	Grass Valley Twp	75	181
Wm T	35	m	w	ENGL	Nevada	Grass Valley Twp	75	185
BAWEDON								
W	38	m	w	ENGL	Sierra	Sierra Twp	89	562
BAWER								
Bachla	38	m	w	BOHE	Sacramento	Georgianna Twp	77	132
BAWERS								
Daniel	39	m	w	PA	Trinity	Weaverville Pct	92	224
John C	37	m	w	GERM	San Francisco	San Francisco P O	83	143
BAWKES								
Mary	19	f	w	IREL	Alameda	Oakland	68	186
BAWL								
Homer	18	m	w	IA	Inyo	Bishop Crk Twp	73	312
BAWLS								
Joseph	62	m	w	MA	Trinity	Junction City Pct	92	206
BAWMAN								
Henry	50	m	w	BAVA	Alameda	Eden Twp	68	67
BAWN								
Ah	15	f	c	CHIN	San Francisco	6-Wd San Francisco	81	76
David	30	m	w	NY	San Francisco	1-Wd San Francisco	79	71
BAWSER								
Ferdinand	42	m	w	PRUS	San Francisco	San Francisco P O	85	756
BAXLER								
Rosanna	14	f	w	CA	San Francisco	11-Wd San Francisc	84	711
BAXMAN								
Lewis	24	m	w	SHOL	Sonoma	Salt Point	91	391
BAXSTER								
Joseph P	34	m	w	MA	San Francisco	3-Wd San Francisco	79	311
BAXTER								
A	65	f	w	SCOT	Calaveras	Copperopolis P O	70	229
Bell M	20	f	w	NJ	Sacramento	4-Wd Sacramento	77	372
Benjamin	27	m	w	CANA	Inyo	Cerro Gordo Twp	73	321

© 2001 by Heritage Quest. All rights reserved.

California 1870 Census

Series M593

Name	Age	S	R	B-PL	County	Locale	Roll	Pg
Carl	9	m	w	CA	Marin	San Rafael Twp	74	29
Chas C	28	m	w	MA	San Luis Obispo	Arroyo Grande Twp	87	272
Chas M	25	m	w	NY	Sonoma	Petaluma Twp	91	322
D J	46	m	w	NY	Tuolumne	Sonora P O	93	316
Daniel	45	m	w	MO	Placer	Roseville P O	76	351
David H	44	m	w	MA	Santa Cruz	Santa Cruz	89	409
E J	34	m	w	WALE	Siskiyou	Scott Rvr Twp	89	603
Francis M	33	m	w	IN	Santa Cruz	Santa Cruz Twp	89	400
Frank	25	m	w	MA	Alameda	Alameda	68	14
Geo W	43	m	w	MD	Shasta	Stillwater P O	89	481
George	40	m	w	ENGL	Tuolumne	Sonora P O	93	325
George C	39	m	w	NY	Alameda	Eden Twp	68	71
Henry V	26	m	w	NY	Santa Cruz	Santa Cruz	89	408
Hugh	29	m	w	IREL	Alameda	Eden Twp	68	69
Hugh	29	m	w	IREL	Alameda	Eden Twp	68	70
I W	37	m	w	PA	Nevada	Washington Twp	75	346
J A	42	m	w	MA	Santa Clara	Gilroy Twp	88	73
J B	41	m	w	MA	Alameda	Oakland	68	248
J W	24	m	w	NY	San Joaquin	2-Wd Stockton	86	158
James	50	m	w	SCOT	Yolo	Cache Crk Twp	93	426
James	39	m	w	NY	San Joaquin	1-Wd Stockton	86	128
James	31	m	w	PRUS	Alameda	Oakland	68	264
James	28	m	w	CANA	Stanislaus	Empire Twp	92	58
James	27	m	w	MA	San Francisco	1-Wd San Francisco	79	130
James D	21	m	w	MO	Yolo	Cache Crk Twp	93	423
Jas	22	m	w	IL	San Joaquin	2-Wd Stockton	86	164
John	75	m	w	MA	San Joaquin	2-Wd Stockton	86	207
John	50	m	w	SWED	San Francisco	11-Wd San Francisc	84	511
John	48	m	w	SCOT	Yuba	Bullards Bar P O	93	550
John	42	m	w	MO	Stanislaus	Empire Twp	92	38
John	30	m	w	SCOT	Alameda	Oakland	68	186
John	29	m	w	TN	Santa Cruz	Soquel Twp	89	441
John	21	m	w	NY	San Francisco	11-Wd San Francisc	84	523
John A	30	m	w	CANA	Inyo	Cerro Gordo Twp	73	321
Joseph T	55	m	w	MA	Monterey	Alisal Twp	74	292
Lester	65	m	w	CANA	Alameda	Hayward	68	76
Lloyd	34	m	w	OH	Nevada	Little York Twp	75	245
Louisa	58	f	w	MA	San Francisco	11-Wd San Francisc	84	434
Mansel	32	m	w	PA	Tulare	Venice Twp	92	278
Marshal L	31	m	w	MO	Yolo	Grafton Twp	93	494
Mary	78	f	w	IREL	San Francisco	11-Wd San Francisc	84	467
Mary	73	f	w	MA	San Joaquin	2-Wd Stockton	86	207
Mary	13	f	w	VA	Alameda	Washington Twp	68	273
Mary J	24	f	w	MO	Placer	Roseville P O	76	352
Morris A	36	m	w	VT	Sacramento	2-Wd Sacramento	77	250
Noah W	40	m	w	NC	Placer	Bath P O	76	424
Patrick	38	m	w	IREL	Shasta	Shasta P O	89	459
Robert	49	m	w	IREL	Solano	Denverton Twp	90	27
Robert	40	m	w	MA	San Francisco	6-Wd San Francisco	81	117
Samuel	21	m	w	IREL	San Francisco	7-Wd San Francisco	81	170
Saul	23	m	w	IREL	San Francisco	7-Wd San Francisco	81	257
Silas	44	m	w	MO	Stanislaus	Empire Twp	92	44
Sutliffe	28	m	w	ENGL	San Francisco	7-Wd San Francisco	81	248
T G	49	m	w	KY	Napa	Napa	75	37
Thersa M	21	f	w	ME	San Mateo	Half Moon Bay P O	87	407
Thomas	34	m	w	PA	San Luis Obispo	Morro Twp	87	283
Warren	7	m	w	CA	Napa	Napa	75	37
William	45	m	w	NY	Napa	Napa Twp	75	67
William	43	m	w	MO	Stanislaus	Branch Twp	92	1
Wm	60	m	w	NY	San Joaquin	Elkhorn Twp	86	66
Wm	40	m	w	ENGL	San Joaquin	Elliott Twp	86	70
Wm	21	m	w	IN	El Dorado	Greenwood Twp	72	52
Wm	12	m	w	CA	San Francisco	San Francisco P O	85	828
Y J	34	m	c	KY	Del Norte	Happy Camp Twp	71	470
BAXTON								
Frank	23	m	w	MA	Alameda	Oakland	68	168
H Clay	26	m	w	MO	Humboldt	Eel Rvr Twp	72	246
Hannah	70	f	w	VA	Humboldt	Eel Rvr Twp	72	246
Henry	30	m	w	NH	Calaveras	San Andreas P O	70	157
James	69	m	w	KY	Humboldt	Eel Rvr Twp	72	246
BAY								
Ah	40	m	c	CHIN	Sierra	Gibson Twp	89	540
Ah	28	m	c	CHIN	Alameda	Eden Twp	68	85
Harmon	48	m	w	NY	Butte	Chico Twp	70	30
Mary	65	f	w	IREL	San Francisco	San Francisco P O	83	194
BAYARD								
Herman	37	m	w	PRUS	San Francisco	San Francisco P O	85	737
John	62	m	w	FRAN	Amador	Volcano P O	69	376
BAYASTRO								
Jose	9	m	w	CA	Los Angeles	Los Angeles	73	561
BAYER								
E	19	m	w	PRUS	Sacramento	3-Wd Sacramento	77	316
John	24	m	w	SWIT	San Francisco	1-Wd San Francisco	79	69
Joseph	30	m	w	HANO	Tuolumne	Chinese Camp P O	93	380
Theobald	35	m	w	BAVA	San Luis Obispo	Arroyo Grande Twp	87	276
Ulrich	50	m	w	PRUS	Sacramento	2-Wd Sacramento	77	254
BAYERQUE								
E M	27	f	w	SC	San Francisco	San Francisco P O	83	277
BAYERSDORFER								
Wm	36	m	w	BAVA	San Francisco	1-Wd San Francisco	79	63
BAYERSSDORFFER								
---	25	m	w	BAVA	Yuba	Marysville	93	604
BAYES								
Margaret	30	f	w	IREL	San Francisco	San Francisco P O	83	168
Sarah	32	f	w	KY	San Francisco	San Francisco P O	83	80
Thomas	40	m	w	MI	Inyo	Independence Twp	73	327
BAYFIELD								
Chas	39	m	w	CANA	San Francisco	11-Wd San Francisc	84	614
BAYLA								
Wm	49	m	w	IREL	Merced	Snelling P O	74	255
BAYLE								
Andrew	51	m	w	IREL	Los Angeles	Los Angeles	73	514
August	36	m	w	FRAN	Kern	Bakersfield P O	73	358
Bautiste	27	m	w	FRAN	Santa Clara	1-Wd San Jose	88	267
Caroline	44	f	w	FRAN	Santa Clara	2-Wd San Jose	88	313
John	40	m	w	IREL	Los Angeles	Los Angeles	73	559
John A	37	m	w	MD	San Diego	Milquaty Dist	78	477
Louis	32	m	w	FRAN	Santa Clara	2-Wd San Jose	88	313
Mary	34	f	w	IREL	Tuolumne	Big Oak Flat P O	93	406
Washington	40	m	w	MO	Butte	Chico Twp	70	56
BAYLER								
Gottlieb	46	m	w	SAXO	El Dorado	Placerville Twp	72	101
John	35	m	w	WURT	Sonoma	Mendocino Twp	91	298
BAYLES								
A W	41	m	w	ENGL	Lake	Lower Lake	73	418
Isaac	44	m	w	ENGL	Sierra	Gibson Twp	89	540
John	64	m	w	IL	Solano	Maine Prairie Twp	90	46
John	24	m	w	ENGL	Sierra	Table Rock Twp	89	577
John M	40	m	w	OH	Placer	Bath P O	76	422
Smith	38	m	w	OH	Placer	Bath P O	76	422
Watson	36	m	w	ENGL	Sierra	Table Rock Twp	89	575
Wm	35	m	w	ENGL	Alameda	Oakland	68	174
BAYLESS								
A D	57	m	w	NY	Trinity	Hayfork Valley	92	238
Chas E	36	m	w	OH	San Francisco	3-Wd San Francisco	79	323
Edward	52	m	w	ENGL	Sacramento	Georgianna Twp	77	129
Fredrick	28	m	w	PRUS	San Francisco	7-Wd San Francisco	81	222
Henry	32	m	w	AL	Calaveras	San Andreas P O	70	176
BAYLEY								
Byron	40	m	w	ME	San Francisco	San Francisco P O	83	231
Charles	27	m	w	BELG	San Francisco	San Francisco P O	83	229
Chas Alfred	39	m	w	ENGL	San Francisco	San Francisco P O	83	73
Daniel	31	m	w	AR	Siskiyou	Butte Twp	89	587
Evaline	50	f	w	MS	Solano	Silveyville Twp	90	84
G W	45	m	w	NH	Sierra	Sears Twp	89	553
George	34	m	w	AR	Siskiyou	Butte Twp	89	584
James	36	m	w	AR	Siskiyou	Butte Twp	89	584
John	9M	m	w	CA	San Francisco	San Francisco P O	83	74
Joshua	38	m	w	GA	Solano	Silveyville Twp	90	84
Sam	30	m	w	NJ	Alameda	Oakland	68	163
Saml	33	m	w	NY	Yuba	Rose Bar Twp	93	664
Thomas S	35	m	w	MS	Solano	Silveyville Twp	90	84
Thos	28	m	w	CANA	Alameda	Oakland	68	186
W J	43	m	w	ENGL	Alameda	Oakland	68	173
Wilbur	28	m	w	MA	San Francisco	San Francisco P O	80	393
BAYLEYARD								
John	25	m	w	FRAN	Napa	Napa Twp	75	74
BAYLIE								
Paulina	29	f	w	MO	Stanislaus	Emory Twp	92	16
BAYLIES								
D W	58	m	w	MA	Nevada	Meadow Lake Twp	75	246
David W	58	m	w	MA	Placer	Colfax P O	76	388
F G	32	m	w	MA	Nevada	Meadow Lake Twp	75	246
BAYLIS								
Anna B	8	f	w	MO	San Luis Obispo	Santa Rosa Twp	87	329
Charles	38	m	w	OH	El Dorado	Georgetown Twp	72	42
David	26	m	w	NY	Yolo	Putah Twp	93	523
H Mrs	40	f	w	IREL	Sonoma	Petaluma Twp	91	329
Isaac	30	m	w	NY	Yolo	Putah Twp	93	509
BAYLISS								
Abrm M	40	m	w	OH	Shasta	Dog Crk P O	89	471
Samuel	51	m	w	OH	Yolo	Putah Twp	93	513
William	10	m	w	CA	Marin	San Rafael Twp	74	29
Wm Hy	50	m	w	OH	San Francisco	San Francisco P O	83	14
BAYLORD								
Frank	29	m	w	HOLL	Solano	Suisun Twp	90	109
BAYMAN								
John C	39	m	w	IL	Tulare	Venice Twp	92	273
BAYME								
C	45	m	w	IREL	Alameda	Oakland	68	235
Jno	40	m	w	IREL	Alameda	Oakland	68	235
BAYMO								
Jos	51	m	w	ITAL	San Francisco	San Francisco P O	83	311
BAYNAR								
Julius	42	m	w	FRAN	Monterey	San Benito Twp	74	378
BAYNE								
Ah	22	m	c	CHIN	Butte	Bidwell Twp	70	1
George	63	m	w	VA	Santa Cruz	Soquel Twp	89	438
BAYO								
Rossuth	25	m	w	MEXI	El Dorado	Mud Springs Twp	72	76
BAYOHAT								
---	58	m	c	CHIN	Sierra	Eureka Twp	89	526
BAYOME								
Joseph	45	m	w	FRAN	Nevada	Grass Valley Twp	75	208
BAYOR								
H	23	m	w	GERM	San Joaquin	2-Wd Stockton	86	170
BAYRAITHER								
Ann	36	f	w	GERM	San Francisco	8-Wd San Francisco	82	360
BAYREUTHER								
G	42	m	w	PRUS	San Francisco	3-Wd San Francisco	79	310
BAYS								
Henry	35	m	w	VA	San Francisco	San Francisco P O	83	80
John	35	m	w	ENGL	San Francisco	San Francisco P O	85	777

© 2001 by Heritage Quest. All rights reserved.

Name	Age	S	R	B-PL	County	Locale	Series M593 Roll	Pg
Washington	60	m	w	TN	Nevada	Grass Valley Twp	75	208
BAYSTER								
Jno	41	m	w	IA	Butte	Chico Twp	70	45
BAYTER								
Hugh	60	m	w	IREL	Santa Clara	1-Wd San Jose	88	225
BAZ								
Hyppolite	37	m	w	FRAN	Alameda	Washington Twp	68	293
BAZAND								
V	27	m	w	ITAL	Solano	Vallejo	90	200
BAZANIO								
Louis	48	m	w	ITAL	San Francisco	San Francisco P O	80	419
BAZARETTA								
John	28	m	w	FRAN	Marin	San Rafael Twp	74	39
BAZAZER								
Ed	40	m	w	VA	Mendocino	Round Valley Twp	74	221
BAZELL								
J	50	m	w	FRAN	Alameda	Oakland	68	150
Logan	30	m	w	IREL	Kern	Bakersfield P O	73	357
BAZELY								
Thomas	28	m	w	ENGL	Nevada	Grass Valley Twp	75	215
BAZILE								
John	28	m	w	ENGL	San Francisco	7-Wd San Francisco	81	280
BAZIN								
Victor	61	m	w	FRAN	San Francisco	8-Wd San Francisco	82	358
BAZZANO								
Pasquale	36	m	w	ITAL	San Francisco	11-Wd San Francisc	84	591
BAZZLE								
William	40	m	w	VA	Placer	Lincoln P O	76	492
BE								
Gin	35	m	c	CHIN	Yuba	Marysville	93	626
Kim	20	f	c	CHIN	Yuba	Marysville	93	627
BEA								
Geo	41	m	w	ITAL	San Francisco	1-Wd San Francisco	79	106
BEABLE								
Edwin	29	m	w	ENGL	San Francisco	11-Wd San Francisc	84	518
BEACH								
Alfred	30	m	w	CANA	Sonoma	Salt Point	91	392
Andrw	36	m	w	CT	San Francisco	San Francisco P O	83	355
Bridget	35	f	w	IREL	San Francisco	San Francisco P O	83	192
C D	42	m	w	NY	San Joaquin	Dent Twp	86	16
C E	40	m	w	NY	Klamath	Trinidad Twp	73	390
Charles	36	m	w	IN	Nevada	Bridgeport Twp	75	102
Charles L	42	m	w	NY	Yolo	Cache Crk Twp	93	429
Chilean	42	m	w	NJ	San Francisco	San Francisco P O	83	195
Colombus	36	m	w	VA	Contra Costa	Martinez P O	71	396
Elisha	52	m	w	MD	Fresno	Millerton P O	72	168
Eliza	54	f	w	NY	San Francisco	San Francisco P O	80	539
Elizabeth	74	f	w	CT	Placer	Roseville P O	76	350
Geo H	52	m	w	CT	San Francisco	San Francisco P O	83	326
George W	30	m	w	MO	Placer	Roseville P O	76	349
H	45	m	w	CT	San Francisco	San Francisco P O	83	294
H M	41	m	w	NY	San Francisco	San Francisco P O	85	774
Harriett	45	f	w	MA	San Francisco	11-Wd San Francisc	84	693
Harry	40	m	w	NY	San Francisco	5-Wd San Francisco	81	20
Henri	30	m	w	FRAN	San Francisco	5-Wd San Francisco	81	17
Henry B	30	m	w	NY	Santa Cruz	Santa Cruz Twp	89	390
Henry J	40	m	w	NY	Santa Clara	San Jose Twp	88	181
Henry S	35	m	w	MI	Sonoma	Analy Twp	91	239
Horace	44	m	w	NY	San Francisco	San Francisco P O	83	203
Horace	43	m	w	NY	San Francisco	8-Wd San Francisco	82	336
J W	27	m	w	MO	Sutter	Vernon Twp	92	135
James	28	m	w	NY	Stanislaus	Empire Twp	92	53
James G	40	m	w	NY	Monterey	San Juan Twp	74	399
John	32	m	w	CANA	Santa Clara	San Jose Twp	88	216
John C	32	m	w	PA	San Francisco	3-Wd San Francisco	79	312
John F	34	m	w	CT	Yolo	Cache Crk Twp	93	454
John W	31	m	w	NY	Placer	Dutch Flat P O	76	401
John W	18	m	w	MO	Sonoma	Bodega Twp	91	249
Joseph	57	m	w	NY	Colusa	Stony Crk Twp	71	332
Joseph	40	m	w	NJ	San Francisco	11-Wd San Francisc	84	602
Joseph	28	m	w	NY	Mendocino	Point Arena Twp	74	204
Julius	70	m	w	CT	Placer	Roseville P O	76	350
Julius C	45	m	w	OH	Sacramento	Franklin Twp	77	107
Lewis	8	m	w	MEXI	El Dorado	Placerville Twp	72	95
M L	42	m	w	VT	Yuba	Marysville	93	607
Mary E	39	f	w	NY	Santa Clara	2-Wd San Jose	88	328
Miller	40	m	w	TN	Plumas	Quartz Twp	77	42
Moses	24	m	w	NY	Fresno	Millerton P O	72	192
Sidney	62	m	w	NY	Fresno	Kings Rvr P O	72	211
Silas	51	m	w	VA	Santa Clara	Santa Clara Twp	88	154
Theodore S	35	m	w	CT	San Francisco	6-Wd San Francisco	81	96
Thos	32	m	w	NC	Butte	Chico Twp	70	58
Tyler	37	m	w	NY	Santa Clara	2-Wd San Jose	88	282
W M	22	m	w	CT	Solano	Vallejo	90	200
BEACHAM								
Charles	22	m	w	MD	Marin	Sausalito Twp	74	74
Richd H	32	m	w	IL	Santa Cruz	Santa Cruz	89	404
Van R	40	m	w	IL	Santa Cruz	Santa Cruz	89	414
BEACHAN								
Micheal	35	m	w	IREL	San Francisco	7-Wd San Francisco	81	178
BEACHER								
Albert	30	m	w	NY	Santa Clara	2-Wd San Jose	88	324
William	51	m	w	BAVA	San Francisco	7-Wd San Francisco	81	214
BEACHNER								
Charles	33	m	w	PA	Monterey	San Antonio Twp	74	319
BEACOM								
Thomas	50	m	w	IREL	Sonoma	Bodega Twp	91	261

Name	Age	S	R	B-PL	County	Locale	Series M593 Roll	Pg
BEAD								
William S	30	m	w	CANA	San Francisco	San Francisco P O	83	262
BEADE								
Thos	82	m	w	CT	San Joaquin	Douglas Twp	86	30
Thos	53	m	w	CT	San Joaquin	Douglas Twp	86	30
BEADEY								
James	36	m	w	IREL	Mendocino	Point Arena Twp	74	207
BEADIE								
Jas	29	m	w	ENGL	Sacramento	3-Wd Sacramento	77	273
BEADLE								
C F	50	m	w	NY	San Joaquin	Oneal Twp	86	98
Harry	47	m	w	MO	El Dorado	Mud Springs Twp	72	85
John S	56	m	w	VA	Yolo	Cottonwood Twp	93	460
Latitia	77	f	w	DC	Yolo	Cottonwood Twp	93	461
BEADLEY								
John	28	m	w	IREL	San Francisco	San Francisco P O	83	141
BEADY								
Joseph	32	m	w	TX	San Bernardino	San Bernardino Twp	78	453
Owen	44	m	w	IREL	San Francisco	San Francisco P O	85	825
BEAGERS								
C	25	f	w	MEXI	Alameda	Oakland	68	229
BEAGLE								
Daniel	28	m	w	OH	Siskiyou	Scott Valley Twp	89	614
BEAGLEHOLE								
Wm H	32	m	w	ENGL	Nevada	Grass Valley Twp	75	194
BEAGLES								
Wm H	38	m	w	TN	Napa	Napa Twp	75	66
BEAGRANT								
Francisco	30	m	w	MEXI	San Diego	San Diego	78	506
BEAGS								
Sarah	30	f	w	MA	Sacramento	3-Wd Sacramento	77	294
BEAHASS								
Jose	56	m	w	MEXI	San Bernardino	San Bernardino Twp	78	449
BEAKLY								
Absolm	38	m	w	OH	San Francisco	11-Wd San Francisc	84	491
BEAL								
Adda	11	f	w	US	Yuba	Marysville	93	609
Alice	16	f	w	US	Yuba	Marysville	93	609
Benjamin	28	m	w	ME	Shasta	Fort Crook P O	89	473
C C	45	m	w	ME	Santa Clara	Gilroy Twp	88	73
Charles A	36	m	w	NH	Placer	Colfax P O	76	389
Era	39	m	w	NH	Calaveras	San Andreas P O	70	212
Gorham	40	m	w	NY	Santa Clara	San Jose Twp	88	183
H	24	m	w	NH	San Joaquin	Liberty Twp	86	94
Israel	25	m	w	VA	San Bernardino	San Bernardino Twp	78	450
Johanea	35	m	w	MA	Alameda	Washington Twp	68	288
John	51	m	w	OH	Butte	Ophir Twp	70	106
Johnson	35	m	w	ENGL	Sacramento	3-Wd Sacramento	77	293
Martin T	48	m	w	TN	Sacramento	San Joaquin Twp	77	395
Mary	17	f	w	MO	Butte	Hamilton Twp	70	61
Oliver	30	m	w	IN	Lassen	Janesville Twp	73	431
Richard	50	m	w	NY	San Francisco	San Francisco P O	83	283
Samuel	37	m	w	MA	San Francisco	San Francisco P O	83	112
Susan	38	f	w	IN	Sonoma	Analy Twp	91	234
Tennessee	12	f	w	CA	Santa Cruz	Santa Cruz	89	417
Thomas	45	m	w	ENGL	San Francisco	San Francisco P O	83	270
Vestal	40	m	w	OH	Santa Clara	Gilroy Twp	88	105
William	42	m	w	VA	Colusa	Spring Valley Twp	71	344
William	37	m	w	OH	Stanislaus	Empire Twp	92	61
William C	42	m	w	TN	El Dorado	Mud Springs Twp	72	71
Wm	26	m	w	NY	Solano	Vallejo	90	145
Wm L	26	m	w	TN	Monterey	Castroville Twp	74	327
BEALBELER								
Lemuel	35	m	w	PRUS	San Francisco	5-Wd San Francisco	81	16
BEALE								
Jeremiah M	58	f	w	VA	Yolo	Grafton Twp	93	493
John P	49	m	w	NY	Calaveras	San Andreas P O	70	213
Louis E	7	m	w	OR	Shasta	Millville P O	89	489
Lucinda D	29	f	w	IL	Santa Cruz	Soquel Twp	89	442
Maria L	25	f	w	MO	Shasta	Millville P O	89	487
Simon P	35	m	w	ME	Santa Cruz	Santa Cruz	89	429
Thos J	42	m	w	VA	Shasta	Millville P O	89	494
BEALER								
Nathnil	45	m	b	MS	Yuba	Long Bar Twp	93	566
BEALES								
Channing	55	m	w	NY	San Francisco	San Francisco P O	80	396
BEALINGBERG								
Paul	52	m	w	DENM	El Dorado	Kelsey Twp	72	59
BEALL								
Andrew	24	m	w	MO	Mendocino	Ten Mile Rvr Twp	74	172
Harvey L	37	m	w	TN	Mendocino	Ten Mile Rvr Twp	74	172
Lloyd	26	m	w	TN	Mendocino	Ten Mile Rvr Twp	74	172
Loyd	66	m	w	TN	San Francisco	San Francisco P O	83	133
Reaim	35	m	w	OH	Plumas	Quartz Twp	77	41
Samuel J	40	m	w	TN	Mendocino	Ten Mile Rvr Twp	74	172
BEALLE								
Joseph	32	m	w	PRUS	Mendocino	Navarro & Big Rvr	74	177
BEALLIE								
Spencer P	25	m	w	NY	Mendocino	Little Lake Twp	74	195
BEALORE								
Stephen	26	m	w	NY	Monterey	San Antonio Twp	74	316
BEALS								
Edward	64	m	w	ME	San Mateo	Redwood Twp	87	364
John P	41	m	w	MA	San Mateo	San Mateo P O	87	358
Nathaniel	50	m	w	MA	Calaveras	San Andreas P O	70	189
S H	45	m	w	MA	Tuolumne	Big Oak Flat P O	93	394
William	28	m	w	IL	Solano	Silveyville Twp	90	79

© 2001 by Heritage Quest. All rights reserved.

California 1870 Census

Name	Age	S	R	B-PL	County	Locale	Roll	Pg
						Series M593		
BEAM								
B L	27	m	w	IL	Amador	Jackson P O	69	340
Catherine	49	f	w	IL	Del Norte	Smith Rvr Twp	71	478
Christian	46	m	w	PA	Butte	Oregon Twp	70	129
Daniel	49	m	w	OH	Amador	Jackson P O	69	340
Edwd	35	m	w	CANA	Butte	Oregon Twp	70	136
Jerymiah	56	m	w	NY	Sonoma	Petaluma Twp	91	310
John	34	m	w	PA	Yuba	Linda Twp	93	556
John	24	m	w	WI	Colusa	Colusa Twp	71	286
Louis	35	m	w	OH	Solano	Suisun Twp	90	104
Mary C	7	f	w	PA	Butte	Oregon Twp	70	130
BEAMAN								
G W	33	m	w	VT	Napa	Napa	75	51
George W	33	m	w	MA	Nevada	Grass Valley Twp	75	185
R	18	m	w	VT	Solano	Vallejo	90	202
Tho	38	m	w	CA	El Dorado	Kelsey Twp	72	60
BEAMES								
S J	35	m	b	MD	Tehama	Tehama Twp	92	194
BEAMISH								
George	38	m	w	IREL	Marin	San Rafael Twp	74	35
BEAMON								
John H	48	m	w	VT	Yuba	Slate Range Bar Tw	93	676
BEAN								
---	30	m	c	CHIN	San Francisco	San Francisco P O	85	721
A	64	m	w	ME	Sierra	Table Rock Twp	89	578
Abner	32	m	w	TN	Amador	Volcano P O	69	385
Ah	29	m	c	CHIN	San Francisco	San Francisco P O	85	801
Ah	16	m	c	CHIN	San Francisco	7-Wd San Francisco	81	278
Albert	50	m	w	ENGL	Napa	Napa Twp	75	31
Alex	27	m	w	OH	Mendocino	Round Valley Twp	74	221
Alexander	44	m	w	ME	Marin	Tomales Twp	74	82
Andrew	45	m	w	ME	Stanislaus	Empire Twp	92	59
Belaew	41	m	w	CHIL	Calaveras	San Andreas P O	70	191
Charles	36	m	w	VA	Los Angeles	Los Angeles	73	524
Chas M	62	m	w	ME	Santa Cruz	Santa Cruz Twp	89	385
Chas T	20	m	w	ASEA	San Francisco	San Francisco P O	85	754
Cornelius	30	m	w	IL	Alameda	Brooklyn Twp	68	44
David	27	m	w	MO	Mendocino	Little Lake Twp	74	201
David M	49	m	w	TN	Siskiyou	Yreka Twp	89	670
E C	41	m	w	KY	San Francisco	8-Wd San Francisco	82	368
E F	35	m	w	ME	Nevada	Nevada Twp	75	278
Edwin F	35	m	w	ME	San Francisco	San Francisco P O	83	202
Ezekiel	36	m	w	ME	Nevada	Nevada Twp	75	310
Frances	14	f	w	CA	Tuolumne	Columbia P O	93	335
G W	30	m	w	IA	Alameda	Murray Twp	68	107
Geo H	29	m	w	VA	Sonoma	Analy Twp	91	223
George	32	m	w	NY	San Francisco	11-Wd San Francisc	84	502
George H	30	m	w	ME	Yuba	North East Twp	93	643
Harry	49	m	w	ME	Placer	Bath P O	76	459
Ira	49	m	w	ME	Nevada	Bloomfield Twp	75	94
Jackson	37	m	w	MO	Butte	Ophir Twp	70	91
Jackson	35	m	w	MO	Yuba	Marysville	93	581
James	77	m	w	VA	Sonoma	Mendocino Twp	91	303
James	35	m	w	IA	Alameda	Washington Twp	68	276
James	27	m	w	IREL	San Francisco	San Francisco P O	80	477
James R	45	m	w	NH	Solano	Silveyville Twp	90	85
Jas	29	m	w	IA	Santa Clara	Gilroy Twp	88	105
Joel	30	m	w	ME	Sierra	Sears Twp	89	553
John	42	m	w	HANO	Monterey	San Juan Twp	74	401
John	34	m	w	ME	Sonoma	Analy Twp	91	221
John	28	m	w	IREL	San Francisco	San Francisco P O	83	5
John P	35	m	w	VA	Butte	Wyandotte Twp	70	141
John W	17	m	w	IA	Sonoma	Petaluma Twp	91	313
Joseph W	39	m	w	ME	San Francisco	San Francisco P O	83	148
L	25	m	w	MA	Alameda	Murray Twp	68	100
Lana	26	f	w	GERM	Los Angeles	Los Angeles	73	511
Louis B	36	m	w	TN	Solano	Suisun Twp	90	103
Lucy	30	f	w	IREL	San Francisco	8-Wd San Francisco	82	405
Lydia	30	f	w	ENGL	San Francisco	San Francisco P O	83	67
Martin	23	m	w	IREL	San Francisco	San Francisco P O	83	236
Michael	26	m	w	IREL	San Francisco	2-Wd San Francisco	79	215
Micheal	35	m	w	IREL	Sonoma	Petaluma Twp	91	339
Moses	52	m	w	NH	San Francisco	2-Wd San Francisco	79	230
Oren	45	m	w	IREL	Solano	Vallejo	90	180
Otter	28	m	w	SHOL	San Mateo	Half Moon Bay P O	87	391
Palmer	46	m	w	VA	Butte	Wyandotte Twp	70	143
Peten	40	m	w	VA	Humboldt	Table Bluff Twp	72	308
Philip	45	m	w	HAMB	Santa Clara	2-Wd San Jose	88	281
Redman	43	m	w	NH	San Francisco	7-Wd San Francisco	81	227
Russell T	45	m	w	TN	El Dorado	Diamond Springs Tw	72	30
Samuel	32	m	w	NH	Tulare	Farmersville Twp	92	249
Sarah	13	f	w	ME	Stanislaus	Empire Twp	92	51
Thomas	26	m	w	IREL	Napa	Napa Twp	75	31
Thomas	21	m	w	PORT	Alameda	Murray Twp	68	112
Warren	50	m	w	KY	Calaveras	San Andreas P O	70	204
William	42	m	w	CANA	San Francisco	San Francisco P O	83	341
William	25	m	w	ME	Merced	Snelling P O	74	260
William E	42	m	w	GA	Calaveras	San Andreas P O	70	218
Wm	40	m	w	NJ	San Francisco	5-Wd San Francisco	81	25
BEANE								
Archd B	49	m	w	MA	San Francisco	San Francisco P O	83	49
L W	50	m	w	VT	Solano	Vallejo	90	187
BEANER								
Jacob	30	m	w	HDAR	San Francisco	1-Wd San Francisco	79	60
BEANNER								
Peter	28	m	w	BOHE	Santa Cruz	Santa Cruz	89	412

Name	Age	S	R	B-PL	County	Locale	Roll	Pg
						Series M593		
BEANS								
Ben	43	m	w	PRUS	Solano	Vallejo	90	172
Sam S	41	m	w	PA	Merced	Snelling P O	74	265
Thomas E	41	m	w	OH	Santa Clara	2-Wd San Jose	88	295
BEANY								
James	28	m	w	NJ	Colusa	Monroe Twp	71	325
BEAR								
Abram	23	m	w	PA	Humboldt	Eureka Twp	72	279
Anne	35	f	w	PRUS	Santa Clara	1-Wd San Jose	88	267
Catharine	54	f	w	VA	Sonoma	Healdsburg & Mendo	91	281
Christopher	14	m	w	CA	Stanislaus	North Twp	92	67
Dennis	54	m	w	FRAN	El Dorado	White Oak Twp	72	143
Geo H	30	m	w	ENGL	Santa Barbara	San Buenaventura P	87	443
Job	24	m	w	PRUS	San Francisco	8-Wd San Francisco	82	368
Jonas	40	m	w	MD	Colusa	Colusa Twp	71	283
Josiah	5	m	w	OH	Siskiyou	Callahan P O	89	629
Martin	54	m	w	PRUS	Stanislaus	North Twp	92	67
Solomon	35	m	w	BOHE	Marin	San Rafael	74	54
Uriah	38	m	w	PA	Sonoma	Mendocino Twp	91	287
BEARCE								
James C	45	m	w	OH	Butte	Mountain Spring Tw	70	87
BEARD								
Ada	42	f	w	MA	Alameda	Brooklyn	68	22
Andy	40	m	w	TN	Placer	Newcastle Twp	76	473
Charles	42	m	w	IL	Sacramento	Granite Twp	77	141
Charles	34	m	w	IN	Plumas	Quartz Twp	77	43
Charles R	43	m	w	ENGL	Monterey	Salinas Twp	74	310
David I	30	m	w	IN	Santa Clara	Santa Clara Twp	88	136
E D	26	m	w	AL	Napa	Napa	75	49
Elias L	54	m	w	NY	Alameda	Washington Twp	68	291
Elihu B	44	m	w	IN	Stanislaus	Branch Twp	92	1
Frank	35	m	w	KY	Contra Costa	Martinez P O	71	396
Gardner G	68	m	w	VT	Nevada	Little York Twp	75	234
George	30	m	w	OH	Yuba	Linda Twp	93	554
Jas R	46	m	w	GA	San Francisco	San Francisco P O	83	175
Jno C	55	m	w	VA	Butte	Kimshew Tpw	70	86
John	44	m	w	OH	Alameda	Murray Twp	68	126
John	32	m	w	IN	Tulare	Visalia	92	290
John F	30	m	w	IN	Tulare	Visalia	92	297
John L	25	m	w	IN	Alameda	Washington Twp	68	269
John S	34	m	w	PA	Siskiyou	Callahan P O	89	631
Joseph	46	m	w	IREL	San Francisco	1-Wd San Francisco	79	86
Michael	56	m	w	OH	San Joaquin	Douglas Twp	86	46
Norman	22	m	w	CANA	Sacramento	4-Wd Sacramento	77	359
P S	44	m	w	NY	Mendocino	Round Valley Twp	74	218
Percival	30	m	w	CANA	Santa Clara	Redwood Twp	88	124
Rufus	36	m	w	ME	Alameda	Oakland	68	189
Samuel	23	m	w	CA	Alameda	Oakland	68	176
Thomas	25	m	w	ENGL	Placer	Summit P O	76	496
William	32	m	w	PA	Colusa	Stony Crk Twp	71	328
Wilson	60	m	w	IL	Monterey	Alisal Twp	74	288
BEARDEN								
Andrew J	38	m	w	SC	Santa Clara	2-Wd San Jose	88	313
Jas	41	m	w	TN	Sonoma	Santa Rosa	91	429
Lucretia	31	f	w	IN	Marin	Nicasio Twp	74	17
BEARDSALL								
Zadoc	45	m	w	NY	San Francisco	6-Wd San Francisco	81	104
BEARDSELY								
Sophia	39	f	w	IREL	San Francisco	8-Wd San Francisco	82	447
BEARDSLEE								
Edgar	38	m	w	NY	Solano	Maine Prairie Twp	90	53
BEARDSLEY								
A J	40	m	w	PA	Calaveras	Copperopolis P O	70	225
Barclay	26	m	w	CANA	San Francisco	6-Wd San Francisco	81	113
C	38	m	w	NY	Lake	Big Valley	73	399
Cyrus	35	m	w	CT	San Francisco	2-Wd San Francisco	79	179
G S	30	m	w	NY	Solano	Vallejo	90	202
Geo	9	m	w	CA	Sacramento	4-Wd Sacramento	77	378
Henry	28	m	w	MI	Alameda	Washington Twp	68	283
Henry	26	m	w	MI	Tehama	Tehama Twp	92	193
Heru H	25	m	w	MO	Los Angeles	El Monte Twp	73	461
Isaac	50	m	w	ENGL	Santa Clara	San Jose Twp	88	203
James	71	m	w	NY	San Francisco	San Francisco P O	80	473
James	37	m	w	NY	Plumas	Indian Twp	77	16
James	32	m	w	IREL	San Francisco	San Francisco P O	83	317
James	27	m	w	MO	Los Angeles	El Monte Twp	73	461
Johanna	24	f	w	NY	Santa Clara	Santa Clara Twp	88	141
John	40	m	w	ENGL	Tuolumne	Sonora P O	93	319
M W	33	m	w	NY	Santa Barbara	Santa Barbara P O	87	455
Nehemiah	61	m	w	NY	Los Angeles	El Monte Twp	73	461
Seth	36	m	w	NY	Santa Cruz	Santa Cruz Twp	89	390
Sophia E	20	f	w	VT	Nevada	Grass Valley Twp	75	146
W	47	m	w	CANA	San Joaquin	3-Wd Stockton	86	219
William	33	m	w	CT	Los Angeles	Soledad Twp	73	631
BEARDSLIE								
Martha	32	f	w	PA	Stanislaus	Buena Vista Twp	92	12
BEARDSLY								
A G	58	f	w	NY	Napa	Yountville Twp	75	77
John W	35	m	w	NY	Yolo	Cache Crk Twp	93	435
Lewis A	37	m	w	NY	Tulare	Tule Rvr Twp	92	261
William R	20	m	w	MO	Los Angeles	El Monte Twp	73	461
BEARDWELL								
John	35	m	w	NY	Siskiyou	Surprise Valley Tw	89	643
BEARER								
Thomas	40	m	w	PA	Amador	Fiddletown P O	69	440
BEARESLEY								
G S	32	m	w	NY	Solano	Vallejo	90	188

© 2001 by Heritage Quest. All rights reserved.

Series M593

Name	Age	S	R	B-PL	County	Locale	Roll	Pg
BEARFOOT								
L	24	f	w	ITAL	Calaveras	Copperopolis P O	70	236
BEARIN								
Dolores	24	f	w	CHIL	Los Angeles	Los Angeles	73	509
BEARING								
William	21	m	w	CANA	Yolo	Merritt Twp	93	506
BEARLING								
Martin	40	m	w	FRAN	Alpine	Markleeville P O	69	312
BEARLY								
Philip	49	m	w	TN	Sacramento	Georgianna Twp	77	128
BEARN								
Andrew	38	m	w	TN	San Diego	San Jacinto Dist	78	517
Nicholas	50	m	w	BREM	San Francisco	8-Wd San Francisco	82	397
BEARNHARD								
L	47	m	w	PRUS	Sierra	Butte Twp	89	513
BEARNS								
Samuel	30	m	w	MO	San Luis Obispo	Arroyo Grande Twp	87	273
BEARNWALD								
Celia	10	f	w	CA	San Francisco	San Francisco P O	83	370
Louis	64	m	w	POLA	San Francisco	San Francisco P O	83	368
BEARSE								
Alfred J	30	m	w	ENGL	San Francisco	6-Wd San Francisco	81	92
Annie	35	f	w	IREL	San Francisco	San Francisco P O	80	477
Edward J	27	m	w	ENGL	San Francisco	6-Wd San Francisco	81	92
James	15	m	w	NY	San Francisco	San Francisco P O	80	477
BEARSLEY								
John	30	m	w	OH	San Francisco	6-Wd San Francisco	81	119
BEARTLEY								
George	12	m	w	CA	San Francisco	San Francisco P O	83	112
BEARWALD								
George	29	m	w	POLA	San Francisco	11-Wd San Francisc	84	460
BEASE								
Simon	40	m	w	ME	San Francisco	San Francisco P O	83	67
BEASELL								
Morris	20	m	w	PA	Stanislaus	Emory Twp	92	26
BEASELY								
James	22	m	w	IREL	Marin	San Rafael	74	55
Johanna	38	f	w	IREL	Yuba	Rose Bar Twp	93	660
BEASLEY								
A	35	m	w	MO	Monterey	Monterey Twp	74	349
B F	42	m	w	TN	Nevada	Nevada Twp	75	316
C	23	m	w	CA	Napa	Napa Twp	75	73
Chas	37	m	w	MD	Sacramento	3-Wd Sacramento	77	260
Chas	37	m	w	MO	San Joaquin	3-Wd Stockton	86	222
E M	29	f	w	TX	Santa Clara	Gilroy Twp	88	107
Edward C	40	m	w	ENGL	Santa Cruz	Santa Cruz	89	421
Henry	70	m	w	NY	San Francisco	7-Wd San Francisco	81	263
Jonas	76	f	w	MD	Yolo	Cache Crk Twp	93	426
Lewis	18	m	w	CA	Napa	Napa Twp	75	61
Mary	47	f	w	IREL	San Joaquin	2-Wd Stockton	86	166
Robt	55	m	w	TN	Sacramento	Georgianna Twp	77	127
Thomas J	53	m	w	VA	Tulare	Tule Rvr Twp	92	265
Thos N	44	m	w	ENGL	Monterey	San Antonio Twp	74	316
Wm	14	m	w	CA	San Luis Obispo	Arroyo Grande Twp	87	278
BEASLY								
Jesse L	54	m	w	KY	Sonoma	Mendocino Twp	91	287
William	24	m	w	PRUS	Solano	Rio Vista Twp	90	70
William	14	m	w	CA	San Luis Obispo	Santa Rosa Twp	87	318
BEASON								
Isaac	35	m	w	KY	Mendocino	Anderson Twp	74	152
Zella	13	f	w	CA	Mendocino	Calpella Twp	74	184
BEASTON								
Robert	24	m	w	ENGL	Inyo	Cerro Gordo Twp	73	323
BEASUNE								
John	82	m	w	MA	Mendocino	Anderson Twp	74	153
BEATEN								
Mathew	23	m	w	CANA	Placer	Colfax P O	76	389
BEATES								
John	35	m	w	VA	Solano	Vacaville Twp	90	120
BEATH								
Lizzie	21	f	w	MA	Nevada	Meadow Lake Twp	75	253
BEATHAZER								
Reiner	31	m	w	SWIT	San Francisco	San Francisco P O	80	479
BEATHCY								
Geo H	25	m	w	LA	Tehama	Cottonwood Twp	92	161
BEATHOLL								
Adam	37	m	w	FRAN	San Francisco	2-Wd San Francisco	79	148
BEATHUM								
John	29	m	w	CANA	Mendocino	Point Arena Twp	74	214
BEATIE								
Robert C	39	m	w	VA	Santa Clara	2-Wd San Jose	88	292
Wm J	31	m	w	MD	Sacramento	1-Wd Sacramento	77	172
BEATING								
H	52	m	w	IREL	Sacramento	1-Wd Sacramento	77	190
Thos	32	m	w	NY	Sacramento	3-Wd Sacramento	77	257
BEATON								
John	22	m	w	CANA	Placer	Bath P O	76	453
Peter	25	m	w	CANA	San Francisco	San Francisco P O	83	107
BEATS								
Philip Wm	30	m	w	AUSL	San Francisco	San Francisco P O	83	59
BEATSE								
William	46	m	w	NY	Santa Clara	San Jose Twp	88	222
BEATTEY								
James	40	m	w	CANA	San Francisco	San Francisco P O	83	317
John	36	m	w	KY	Kern	Havilah P O	73	338
BEATTIE								
C B	50	m	w	IREL	Mendocino	Little Lake Twp	74	196
David	35	m	w	IREL	San Francisco	San Francisco P O	83	50
John	59	m	w	PA	Yolo	Cottonwood Twp	93	474
T F	39	m	w	VA	Mendocino	Ukiah Twp	74	244
Thomas	36	m	w	SCOT	San Francisco	1-Wd San Francisco	79	120
BEATTS								
David	35	m	w	IREL	Colusa	Monroe Twp	71	314
BEATTY								
Adam	52	m	w	AR	San Diego	Julian Dist	78	473
Andrew	28	m	w	IREL	Solano	Vallejo	90	141
Annie	20	f	w	IREL	Sacramento	4-Wd Sacramento	77	372
Augusta	48	f	w	VT	Sutter	Butte Twp	92	92
Ellen	19	f	w	CT	Santa Clara	2-Wd San Jose	88	330
Frank	29	m	w	PA	Nevada	Grass Valley Twp	75	146
George	30	m	w	NY	Yolo	Grafton Twp	93	480
Henry O	57	m	w	KY	Sacramento	4-Wd Sacramento	77	336
James	30	m	w	IREL	San Francisco	11-Wd San Francisc	84	434
James	29	m	w	IREL	San Francisco	11-Wd San Francisc	84	477
James	25	m	w	CANA	Sonoma	Bodega Twp	91	252
James B	12	m	w	CA	Contra Costa	Martinez P O	71	377
John	30	m	w	IREL	San Francisco	1-Wd San Francisco	79	59
John	28	m	w	IREL	Santa Clara	2-Wd San Jose	88	330
John	27	m	w	NY	San Francisco	San Francisco P O	83	297
John	25	m	w	CANA	Monterey	San Juan Twp	74	394
Launcelot	60	m	w	IREL	Nevada	Grass Valley Twp	75	154
Lizzie	20	f	w	NY	San Francisco	San Francisco P O	80	486
Mary	18	f	w	NY	Alameda	Oakland	68	188
Moses F	27	m	w	PA	Nevada	Grass Valley Twp	75	200
Patrick	42	m	w	IREL	San Francisco	8-Wd San Francisco	82	450
Robert	25	m	w	IREL	Solano	Denverton Twp	90	26
Samuel	46	m	w	IREL	Yuba	Long Bar Twp	93	562
Samuel G	42	m	w	PA	San Francisco	8-Wd San Francisco	82	463
Thos	40	m	w	IREL	Sonoma	Analy Twp	91	225
Timothy	40	m	w	PA	Monterey	San Juan Twp	74	390
W	35	m	w	MO	Mendocino	Round Valley Twp	74	218
William H	39	m	w	MO	Placer	Lincoln P O	76	491
Wm	35	m	w	SCOT	Sacramento	3-Wd Sacramento	77	298
Wm F	52	m	w	OH	Sonoma	Analy Twp	91	234
Wm H	22	m	w	AUST	San Francisco	3-Wd San Francisco	79	326
BEATY								
Abraham S	50	m	w	NJ	Santa Clara	2-Wd San Jose	88	293
Archie	42	m	w	IREL	Sutter	Yuba Twp	92	150
Elisabeth	28	f	w	IREL	Alameda	Oakland	68	189
James	50	m	w	IREL	Sierra	Eureka Twp	89	523
Jno C	26	m	w	IREL	Sonoma	Cloverdale Twp	91	271
John	31	m	w	IREL	San Joaquin	2-Wd Stockton	86	165
Mary	50	f	w	IREL	Sonoma	Cloverdale Twp	91	271
Michael	46	m	w	IREL	Sierra	Eureka Twp	89	523
Richard	46	m	w	IREL	Yuba	Rose Bar Twp	93	661
Samuel	50	m	w	MO	Santa Clara	2-Wd San Jose	88	324
Samuel	46	m	w	IREL	Sutter	Yuba Twp	92	150
Samul	68	m	w	PA	Sutter	Nicolaus Twp	92	109
William	29	m	w	IREL	Sonoma	Cloverdale Twp	91	271
BEAU								
Edward	38	m	w	CANA	Los Angeles	Los Angeles	73	571
F	44	m	w	FRAN	Sacramento	4-Wd Sacramento	77	326
BEAUCHAMP								
Ashley	36	m	w	MO	Colusa	Colusa Twp	71	276
Charles	31	m	w	MO	Stanislaus	Empire Twp	92	29
Eugene	22	m	w	FRAN	San Francisco	San Francisco P O	80	341
F	15	f	w	CA	Solano	Vallejo	90	188
Felix G	60	m	w	KY	San Luis Obispo	Santa Rosa Twp	87	319
Joseph	42	m	w	CANA	Sacramento	2-Wd Sacramento	77	237
L	40	m	w	CANA	Sierra	Lincoln Twp	89	545
Stevn	55	m	w	CANA	San Francisco	3-Wd San Francisco	79	308
BEAUCHINE								
Marcus	33	m	w	ITAL	San Francisco	6-Wd San Francisco	81	112
BEAUCOURT								
Francine	59	f	w	FRAN	San Francisco	San Francisco P O	83	135
Jane	60	f	w	FRAN	San Francisco	San Francisco P O	80	341
BEAUDET								
Thomas	28	m	w	CANA	Nevada	Grass Valley Twp	75	180
BEAUDON								
Tousaint	43	m	w	FRAN	Marin	San Rafael Twp	74	25
BEAUDRY								
Pruanet	50	m	w	CANA	Los Angeles	Los Angeles	73	540
Victor	40	m	w	CANA	Inyo	Cerro Gordo Twp	73	319
BEAUFILUS								
B	30	m	w	FRAN	Siskiyou	Callahan P O	89	628
BEAUGHAN								
John	42	m	w	NY	Siskiyou	Butte Twp	89	584
BEAUHARIS								
Alvin	35	m	w	FRAN	San Joaquin	1-Wd Stockton	86	155
Ed	29	m	w	FRAN	San Joaquin	1-Wd Stockton	86	155
BEAUHARNIS								
Maria	33	f	w	FRAN	San Francisco	San Francisco P O	80	341
BEAULIEU								
Peter	51	m	w	FRAN	Marin	Sausalito Twp	74	73
BEAUMAN								
Chas	32	m	w	PRUS	Butte	Chico Twp	70	56
BEAUMOND								
D	35	m	w	NY	Sacramento	3-Wd Sacramento	77	318
E	35	m	w	MS	San Joaquin	Dent Twp	86	16
BEAUMONT								
E	55	m	w	NY	Mendocino	Little Lake Twp	74	197
Geo	66	m	w	PA	Butte	Kimshew Tpw	70	83
Jno H	34	m	w	PRUS	Butte	Chico Twp	70	43
William	29	m	w	ENGL	Nevada	Little York Twp	75	237

© 2001 by Heritage Quest. All rights reserved.

California 1870 Census

Name	Age	S	R	B-PL	County	Locale	Roll (Series M593)	Pg
BEAUMOUNT								
Sarah	64	f	w	MA	San Joaquin	2-Wd Stockton	86	210
BEAUPAERIE								
S	54	m	w	FRAN	Contra Costa	San Pablo Twp	71	361
BEAUPRE								
Narcisso	56	m	w	FRAN	Calaveras	San Andreas P O	70	203
Narcisso	46	m	w	CANA	Calaveras	San Andreas P O	70	216
BEAUR								
John	23	m	w	WURT	Sonoma	Petaluma Twp	91	347
Paul	35	m	w	ME	San Francisco	5-Wd San Francisco	81	33
William	12	m	w	CA	Calaveras	San Andreas P O	70	198
BEAUREGARD								
Bapt	55	m	w	FRAN	Tuolumne	Sonora P O	93	330
Pauline	26	f	w	NY	San Francisco	6-Wd San Francisco	81	45
Peter	60	m	w	FRAN	Plumas	Goodwin Twp	77	7
Sarah	31	f	w	VA	San Francisco	6-Wd San Francisco	81	72
BEAUSANG								
John F	41	m	w	SWED	Stanislaus	Branch Twp	92	6
BEAUSTON								
Peter	27	m	w	SCOT	San Francisco	San Francisco P O	85	845
BEAUSUKER								
Charles	22	m	w	SWIT	Mariposa	Mariposa P O	74	131
BEAUTIGER								
Mary	42	f	w	SWIT	San Francisco	11-Wd San Francisc	84	597
Mary	13	f	w	CA	San Francisco	11-Wd San Francisc	84	597
BEAUVEAU								
Leopold	41	m	w	FRAN	San Francisco	1-Wd San Francisco	79	50
BEAUVILLE								
Augustus	43	m	w	FRAN	San Francisco	1-Wd San Francisco	79	95
Mary	25	f	w	IREL	San Francisco	1-Wd San Francisco	79	95
William	2	m	w	CA	San Francisco	1-Wd San Francisco	79	95
BEAUX								
Francis	38	m	w	FRAN	San Francisco	San Francisco P O	85	835
BEAVER								
Benjamin	24	m	w	MO	Mendocino	Big Rvr Twp	74	159
David	52	m	w	PA	Yuba	New York Twp	93	639
David L	18	m	w	CA	Yuba	New York Twp	93	639
Gideon	34	m	w	OH	Yolo	Buckeye Twp	93	414
Hamilton	25	m	w	MO	Mendocino	Navarro & Big Rvr	74	176
Henry	57	m	w	OH	Monterey	Alisal Twp	74	300
Henry	45	m	w	VA	Sonoma	Analy Twp	91	238
J W	29	m	w	MO	Monterey	Alisal Twp	74	300
John	73	m	w	NY	El Dorado	White Oak Twp	72	142
L T	33	m	w	IL	El Dorado	Lake Valley Twp	72	63
Napoleon B	29	m	w	MO	Mendocino	Big Rvr Twp	74	161
Netta	12	f	w	IA	El Dorado	Kelsey Twp	72	61
Samuel	30	m	w	NY	San Francisco	8-Wd San Francisco	82	382
Samuel	22	m	w	MO	Mendocino	Albion & Big Rvr T	74	166
Thomas	32	m	w	PA	San Francisco	San Francisco P O	83	343
Thomas	20	m	w	MO	Mendocino	Big Rvr Twp	74	159
Thos	45	m	w	RI	San Francisco	5-Wd San Francisco	81	11
Tunis S	39	m	w	OH	Sacramento	2-Wd Sacramento	77	222
William R	20	m	w	MO	Mendocino	Big Rvr Twp	74	159
BEAVERS								
Almond	39	m	w	AR	Butte	Bidwell Twp	70	3
Eliza D	20	f	w	IN	San Luis Obispo	Arroyo Grande Twp	87	274
John	39	m	w	MO	San Diego	San Diego	78	502
T B	41	m	w	PA	Amador	Drytown P O	69	418
BEAVIS								
Wm	25	m	w	KY	Sacramento	Franklin Twp	77	110
BEAYS								
Joseph	28	m	w	ENGL	Inyo	Bishop Crk Twp	73	310
BEAZ								
Damon	45	m	w	CHIL	Calaveras	San Andreas P O	70	219
BEAZELL								
Thomas B	36	m	w	PA	Alameda	Washington Twp	68	283
BEAZOTA								
Dominica	51	m	w	ITAL	Amador	Volcano P O	69	372
BEBA								
Joseph	35	m	w	CANA	Trinity	Hayfork Valley	92	239
BEBB								
E	40	f	w	WALE	Lassen	Long Valley Twp	73	437
BEBBIANA								
Devela	39	m	w	MEXI	Mariposa	Mariposa P O	74	105
BEBBINS								
Amelia	5	f	w	CA	San Francisco	San Francisco P O	85	799
L	9	m	w	AUSL	San Francisco	San Francisco P O	85	800
BEBBY								
John	54	m	w	ENGL	Sacramento	Franklin Twp	77	120
BEBEE								
Chris C	35	m	w	IA	Santa Barbara	Santa Barbara P O	87	498
Nelson	37	m	w	NY	Siskiyou	Surprise Valley Tw	89	640
Wm L	40	m	w	NY	San Luis Obispo	San Luis Obispo Tw	87	308
BEBENSTEIN								
Ann	50	f	w	PRUS	San Joaquin	2-Wd Stockton	86	200
BEBER								
Adam	50	m	w	PRUS	Butte	Chico Twp	70	42
BECENTE								
A	47	m	w	CHIL	El Dorado	Greenwood Twp	72	50
Maria L	16	f	w	CA	Monterey	Monterey	74	354
BECH								
Constantine C	47	m	w	BAVA	Calaveras	San Andreas P O	70	198
Geo W	28	m	w	IL	Santa Barbara	Santa Barbara P O	87	486
BECHA								
Joseph	56	m	w	FRAN	Tuolumne	Sonora P O	93	314
BECHAFER								
Andrew	30	m	w	BAVA	Santa Clara	Fremont Twp	88	44
BECHEEL								
N	45	m	w	MA	Alameda	Oakland	68	260
BECHEN								
J W	20	m	w	GERM	San Francisco	8-Wd San Francisco	82	375
BECHERAS								
Beatris	21	f	w	MEXI	Sacramento	2-Wd Sacramento	77	239
BECHERER								
Chas	21	m	w	PRUS	San Francisco	8-Wd San Francisco	82	375
BECHIN								
Rose	30	f	w	FRAN	San Francisco	San Francisco P O	85	790
BECHLER								
Joseph	24	m	w	PRUS	San Francisco	3-Wd San Francisco	79	302
BECHNER								
Frank	24	m	w	PRUS	San Francisco	San Francisco P O	80	478
BECHOL								
A	20	m	w	OH	Lassen	Janesville Twp	73	432
BECHT								
Joseph	40	m	w	BAVA	Alameda	Brooklyn	68	33
BECHTAL								
Jacob	43	m	w	OH	Nevada	Nevada Twp	75	319
BECHTER								
Conrad	36	m	w	BAVA	San Francisco	8-Wd San Francisco	82	457
BECHTIGER								
Hans	28	m	w	SWIT	Sacramento	4-Wd Sacramento	77	341
BECK								
A G	53	m	w	MD	San Francisco	3-Wd San Francisco	79	311
Aaron	38	m	w	IA	Nevada	Eureka Twp	75	133
Adam	63	m	w	FRAN	Amador	Jackson P O	69	325
Ah	41	m	c	CHIN	Amador	Ione City P O	69	364
Ah	40	m	c	CHIN	Sacramento	Franklin Twp	77	113
Amanda	24	f	w	IN	Solano	Tremont Twp	90	31
Andrew	26	m	w	NORW	Monterey	Pajaro Twp	74	370
Anthon H	36	m	w	BAVA	San Francisco	2-Wd San Francisco	79	138
Antonio	60	m	w	BELG	Amador	Jackson P O	69	343
August	50	m	w	FRAN	San Francisco	2-Wd San Francisco	79	202
August	41	m	w	PA	Mendocino	Point Arena Twp	74	206
Barbara	57	f	w	SWIT	San Francisco	11-Wd San Francisc	84	457
Bartholomw	60	m	w	FRAN	San Francisco	2-Wd San Francisco	79	137
C E	43	m	w	NY	San Francisco	3-Wd San Francisco	79	323
Charles	25	m	w	PRUS	San Francisco	San Francisco P O	85	744
Charles	21	m	w	GERM	Yolo	Cottonwood Twp	93	459
Christiana	59	f	w	WURT	Yolo	Putah Twp	93	526
Christopher	47	m	w	PRUS	Plumas	Plumas Twp	77	33
David H	50	m	w	PA	Alameda	Washington Twp	68	277
David L	54	m	w	NY	San Francisco	San Francisco P O	83	112
Eddie	8	m	w	CA	San Bernardino	San Bernardino Twp	78	430
Eugene	46	m	w	FRAN	Sierra	Sears Twp	89	554
Fred	22	m	w	PA	Santa Cruz	Pajaro Twp	89	342
Frederick	27	m	w	HUNG	Marin	San Rafael Twp	74	45
Frederick	27	m	w	PRUS	Kern	Kernville P O	73	368
Fredk	31	m	w	DENM	San Francisco	1-Wd San Francisco	79	71
Fritz	25	m	w	HDAR	San Francisco	11-Wd San Francisc	84	478
George	43	m	w	ENGL	San Francisco	7-Wd San Francisco	81	156
H	17	m	w	NY	San Francisco	San Francisco P O	85	821
H P	14	m	w	CA	Alameda	Oakland	68	242
Henry	50	m	w	ENGL	San Joaquin	Liberty Twp	86	88
Henry	38	m	w	BADE	San Francisco	8-Wd San Francisco	82	429
Henry	26	m	w	PRUS	San Francisco	11-Wd San Francisc	84	646
Hiram J	42	m	w	KY	Marin	Tomales Twp	74	78
Isaac	24	m	w	IN	Kern	Bakersfield P O	73	360
J C	60	m	w	ME	Alameda	Oakland	68	194
Jacob	38	m	w	HDAR	San Francisco	11-Wd San Francisc	84	566
James G	41	m	w	MA	San Francisco	San Francisco P O	83	280
Jane	30	f	w	ENGL	San Francisco	San Francisco P O	85	860
John	45	m	w	PA	San Francisco	5-Wd San Francisco	81	33
John	42	m	w	PA	Nevada	Bridgeport Twp	75	109
John	38	m	w	FRAN	Nevada	Bridgeport Twp	75	116
John	33	m	w	ENGL	Stanislaus	Washington Twp	92	86
John	31	m	w	PRUS	San Francisco	San Francisco P O	83	232
John	29	m	w	PRUS	San Francisco	San Francisco P O	80	539
John	28	m	w	OH	El Dorado	Coloma Twp	72	3
John	27	m	w	NY	Sacramento	Center Twp	77	85
John K	54	m	w	MO	Santa Clara	San Jose Twp	88	198
Joseph	4	m	w	CA	San Francisco	San Francisco P O	85	799
Joseph	30	m	w	ENGL	Sonoma	Salt Point	91	389
Joseph	29	m	w	FRAN	San Francisco	2-Wd San Francisco	79	215
Julia	35	f	w	PA	San Francisco	5-Wd San Francisco	81	33
Lena	28	f	w	HAMB	Yolo	Putah Twp	93	526
Lin	36	m	c	CHIN	Kern	Bakersfield P O	73	365
Louis	35	m	w	PRUS	Tuolumne	Sonora P O	93	318
Maria	60	f	w	LA	San Francisco	San Francisco P O	80	416
Mary	42	f	w	DENM	Nevada	Bridgeport Twp	75	105
Mary	38	f	m	LA	San Francisco	7-Wd San Francisco	81	217
Milton W	40	m	w	PA	Santa Clara	Santa Clara Twp	88	151
N	6	m	w	CA	San Francisco	San Francisco P O	85	799
Nat	50	m	w	MA	San Francisco	11-Wd San Francisc	84	662
Nicholas	35	m	w	DENM	San Francisco	7-Wd San Francisco	81	261
Peter	37	m	w	HANO	San Francisco	11-Wd San Francisc	84	499
Peter J	29	m	w	DENM	Marin	Sausalito Twp	74	67
Philip	33	m	w	GERM	Yolo	Cache Crk Twp	93	439
Phillip	71	m	w	GERM	Placer	Bath P O	76	436
Robt	53	m	w	PA	Sacramento	4-Wd Sacramento	77	350
Rose	20	f	w	PRUS	Yuba	Marysville	93	593
Samuel	8	m	w	CA	San Francisco	San Francisco P O	85	799
Samuel T E	38	m	w	SCOT	San Francisco	8-Wd San Francisco	82	426
Thomas	38	m	w	IREL	Santa Cruz	Pajaro Twp	89	344
Thomas	32	m	w	ENGL	Alameda	Oakland	68	203

© 2001 by Heritage Quest. All rights reserved.

Name	Age	S	R	B-PL	County	Locale	Series M593 Roll	Pg
Thomas	27	m	w	NCOD	Santa Clara	Redwood Twp	88	128
W	10	m	w	CA	San Francisco	San Francisco P O	85	799
Walter	22	m	w	VA	San Francisco	2-Wd San Francisco	79	213
William	45	m	w	ENGL	San Francisco	7-Wd San Francisco	81	187
William G	58	m	w	ENGL	San Mateo	Redwood Twp	87	364
Willm	38	m	w	IN	Alameda	Murray Twp	68	119
Wm	58	m	w	PA	Alameda	Murray Twp	68	126
Wm D	50	m	w	TN	Shasta	Millville P O	89	491
BECKENBO								
Sarah	37	f	w	OH	San Francisco	San Francisco P O	83	207
BECKER								
Albert	28	m	w	HANO	San Francisco	11-Wd San Francisc	84	687
Barbara	5	f	w	CA	San Francisco	8-Wd San Francisco	82	310
Charles	45	m	w	PRUS	San Francisco	San Francisco P O	80	469
Charles	26	m	w	HANO	San Francisco	7-Wd San Francisco	81	223
Charles	19	m	w	PRUS	San Francisco	7-Wd San Francisco	81	170
Chas	42	m	w	CANA	Sierra	Gibson Twp	89	542
Chas	38	m	w	PRUS	Humboldt	Eel Rvr Twp	72	248
Chas	32	m	w	PRUS	San Francisco	1-Wd San Francisco	79	69
Danial	31	m	w	BADE	San Francisco	7-Wd San Francisco	81	220
Diedrich	24	m	w	HANO	San Francisco	1-Wd San Francisco	79	129
Ellen	18	f	w	OH	Colusa	Grand Island Twp	71	304
F C	35	m	w	PRUS	Sierra	Downieville Twp	89	517
Francis	38	m	w	HANO	San Francisco	3-Wd San Francisco	79	324
Fredrika	19	f	w	PRUS	San Francisco	San Francisco P O	85	719
George	39	m	w	AUST	San Francisco	San Francisco P O	83	369
Hannah	37	f	w	IREL	San Francisco	San Francisco P O	85	830
Henry	43	m	w	DENM	San Francisco	2-Wd San Francisco	79	207
Henry	32	m	w	PRUS	San Francisco	San Francisco P O	83	242
John	40	m	w	MA	San Francisco	7-Wd San Francisco	81	216
John	26	m	w	NY	San Francisco	San Francisco P O	80	533
John H	30	m	w	PRUS	San Diego	San Diego	78	496
Joseph	55	m	w	PRUS	San Francisco	8-Wd San Francisco	82	310
Louis	37	m	w	DENM	San Francisco	2-Wd San Francisco	79	275
Martin	26	m	w	HANO	San Francisco	San Francisco P O	83	193
Michael	28	m	w	HDAR	Sonoma	Petaluma Twp	91	322
Otto	45	m	w	PRUS	San Francisco	San Francisco P O	80	532
Peter	46	m	w	BADE	San Francisco	2-Wd San Francisco	79	142
Peter	33	m	w	SWIT	San Francisco	8-Wd San Francisco	82	352
Philip	25	m	w	HDAR	San Francisco	1-Wd San Francisco	79	53
Robert	22	m	w	SAXO	Tulare	Tule Rvr Twp	92	259
Thomas	46	m	w	PRUS	Tuolumne	Chinese Camp P O	93	368
William	30	m	w	PRUS	Napa	Napa	75	56
William	26	m	w	BAVA	San Francisco	8-Wd San Francisco	82	433
BECKERLY								
William	40	m	w	ENGL	Colusa	Grand Island Twp	71	306
William	32	m	w	ENGL	Klamath	Liberty Twp	73	376
BECKERSDORFF								
John	40	m	w	PRUS	San Francisco	San Francisco P O	83	350
BECKERT								
Chas	36	m	w	SAXO	San Francisco	1-Wd San Francisco	79	86
BECKERTICH								
Samuel	34	m	w	AUST	Sacramento	2-Wd Sacramento	77	245
BECKET								
Conrad	37	m	w	PRUS	San Francisco	San Francisco P O	80	429
John F	52	m	w	ME	Calaveras	San Andreas P O	70	163
Lama L	32	m	w	LA	Los Angeles	Los Nietos Twp	73	582
Laura	17	f	w	CA	San Francisco	8-Wd San Francisco	82	384
Peter	35	m	w	IN	Placer	Bath P O	76	433
Thos J	25	m	w	MO	San Luis Obispo	San Luis Obispo Tw	87	308
William H	27	m	w	ENGL	Los Angeles	Wilmington Twp	73	642
BECKETT								
Elisha	27	m	w	PA	Sonoma	Healdsburg & Mendo	91	286
Eugene	17	m	w	CA	Nevada	Grass Valley Twp	75	176
Francis	37	m	w	WIND	San Joaquin	2-Wd Stockton	86	169
Henry	39	m	w	MO	Shasta	Millville P O	89	484
Henry	27	m	w	ENGL	San Francisco	3-Wd San Francisco	79	293
James	32	m	w	ENGL	Sacramento	2-Wd Sacramento	77	206
James F	35	m	w	VA	Nevada	Grass Valley Twp	75	152
Jas M	37	m	w	ME	Marin	San Rafael Twp	74	42
John F	23	m	w	IA	San Luis Obispo	San Luis Obispo Tw	87	316
Lemuel	52	m	w	NJ	San Luis Obispo	Arroyo Grande Twp	87	277
Solon	50	m	b	NY	San Francisco	6-Wd San Francisco	81	104
Thomas J	24	m	w	CANA	San Francisco	San Francisco P O	83	160
BECKFORD								
A	39	m	w	NH	Amador	Drytown P O	69	423
Chas	35	m	w	MA	Solano	Benicia	90	15
Daniel R	40	m	w	MA	Santa Clara	1-Wd San Jose	88	239
BECKHAM								
Henry	36	m	w	OH	Yuba	North East Twp	93	644
Lucy	4	f	w	CA	Yuba	North East Twp	93	643
Lucy A	25	f	w	ME	Sierra	Sears Twp	89	553
BECKHARD								
Michael	44	m	w	IREL	San Francisco	2-Wd San Francisco	79	214
BECKHOLD								
Chs	35	m	w	HDAR	San Francisco	2-Wd San Francisco	79	139
BECKHOLT								
A P	64	m	w	DENM	Del Norte	Happy Camp Twp	71	468
N P	26	m	w	DENM	Del Norte	Happy Camp Twp	71	468
BECKLE								
Adam	47	m	w	PRUS	Nevada	Grass Valley Twp	75	232
BECKLEY								
Ed	43	m	w	PA	Lake	Lower Lake	73	422
Edward	21	m	w	OH	Sacramento	Franklin Twp	77	113
Gabriel	33	m	w	OH	Sacramento	Brighton Twp	77	79
BECKLY								
Charles	23	m	w	WI	Los Angeles	Los Nietos Twp	73	578

Name	Age	S	R	B-PL	County	Locale	Series M593 Roll	Pg
Pyram	34	m	w	OH	Sacramento	Franklin Twp	77	110
BECKMAN								
Aldwell M	26	m	w	SWED	Placer	Bath P O	76	437
C	47	m	w	NORW	Nevada	Nevada Twp	75	272
C	40	m	w	PRUS	San Joaquin	Elkhorn Twp	86	56
Chas W	51	m	w	SWED	San Francisco	3-Wd San Francisco	79	295
Conrad	38	m	w	MECK	Placer	Bath P O	76	428
Erwin	24	m	w	IN	San Francisco	11-Wd San Francisc	84	498
Fred	28	m	w	FINL	San Francisco	3-Wd San Francisco	79	291
H	43	m	w	PRUS	Tuolumne	Big Oak Flat P O	93	402
H F	24	m	w	LA	Yuba	Marysville	93	616
Henry	37	m	w	PRUS	San Joaquin	Elkhorn Twp	86	56
John	66	m	w	NORW	San Francisco	2-Wd San Francisco	79	145
Joseph	22	m	w	HANO	San Francisco	11-Wd San Francisc	84	449
Julius	5	m	w	CA	San Francisco	7-Wd San Francisco	81	253
Louis	46	m	w	HANO	El Dorado	Mud Springs Twp	72	77
M	9	f	w	CA	Yuba	Marysville	93	616
M	17	f	w	CA	Sacramento	3-Wd Sacramento	77	317
O P	44	m	w	TN	Monterey	San Juan Twp	74	388
P	39	m	w	IL	Monterey	San Juan Twp	74	388
Peter	63	m	w	SWED	Mendocino	Casper & Big Rvr	74	164
R	32	m	w	SWIT	Sacramento	3-Wd Sacramento	77	302
S H	50	m	w	HANO	Tuolumne	Chinese Camp P O	93	367
Wm	58	m	w	TN	Nevada	Nevada Twp	75	308
Wm	39	m	w	NY	Sacramento	San Joaquin Twp	77	394
BECKMANN								
J	65	m	w	PRUS	San Francisco	San Francisco P O	83	134
BECKMEN								
Henry	19	m	w	PRUS	San Joaquin	Oneal Twp	86	119
BECKNELL								
John C	52	m	w	MO	Mariposa	Mariposa P O	74	118
BECKNER								
Jonathan	50	m	w	IL	Santa Barbara	Santa Barbara P O	87	471
William S	38	m	w	KY	Yolo	Cottonwood Twp	93	467
BECKRAM								
Joseph	33	m	w	OH	Siskiyou	Cottonwood Twp	89	590
BECKSTEAD								
Nancy	11	f	w	UT	San Bernardino	San Bernardino Twp	78	423
BECKSTED								
J L	35	m	w	CA	Del Norte	Smith Rvr Twp	71	477
BECKSTRO								
R	54	m	w	PA	San Joaquin	Castoria Twp	86	11
BECKTELL								
Max	25	m	w	PRUS	San Francisco	San Francisco P O	80	537
BECKTOL								
John	36	m	w	PA	Calaveras	San Andreas P O	70	215
BECKWELL								
James	56	m	w	TN	Los Angeles	Los Angeles	73	543
BECKWITH								
B D	30	m	w	OH	San Joaquin	Elkhorn Twp	86	64
Eliza	40	f	w	KY	Monterey	Alisal Twp	74	291
Geo	45	m	w	MA	Alameda	Oakland	68	179
Henry	36	m	w	NY	Mariposa	Mariposa P O	74	100
Huron	60	m	w	CT	Santa Barbara	Santa Barbara P O	87	499
J W	22	m	w	WI	Lake	Lower Lake	73	419
James	25	m	w	CANA	San Francisco	San Francisco P O	83	283
John	40	m	w	MA	Solano	Vallejo	90	146
John W	45	m	w	NY	San Francisco	San Francisco P O	83	366
L C	41	m	w	CT	Humboldt	Eel Rvr Twp	72	249
Mary	17	f	w	MEXI	Santa Clara	Santa Clara Twp	88	154
Nancy	12	f	w	CANA	San Francisco	San Francisco P O	83	90
S L	49	m	w	CT	San Francisco	San Francisco P O	85	796
Samuel	65	m	w	NY	Sacramento	Alabama Twp	77	61
W J	42	m	w	CANA	Tuolumne	Chinese Camp P O	93	378
Ward A	30	m	w	NY	Santa Cruz	Santa Cruz	89	407
William	14	m	w	CANA	Solano	Suisun Twp	90	108
BECKWORTH								
A W	46	m	w	NY	Sutter	Sutter Twp	92	122
Henry	34	m	w	SCOT	Los Angeles	Los Angeles Twp	73	476
John	37	m	c	CHIN	Sutter	Sutter Twp	92	122
BECQUERZ								
Antonio	40	m	w	FRAN	San Francisco	2-Wd San Francisco	79	207
BECRAFT								
John	40	m	w	MO	Los Angeles	Los Angeles Twp	73	487
BECTHEL								
John	27	m	w	PA	Alameda	Alvarado	68	303
BEDABBI								
M	29	m	w	FRAN	Santa Clara	Almaden Twp	88	20
BEDALBE								
Giles	21	m	w	MEXI	San Diego	Fort Yuma Dist	78	463
BEDASH								
Piero	24	m	w	FRAN	Monterey	Monterey Twp	74	346
BEDAT								
Paul	50	m	w	FRAN	San Francisco	San Francisco P O	80	464
BEDDIS								
Rebecca	12	f	b	CA	Mariposa	Mariposa P O	74	120
BEDDOW								
Leonard	67	m	w	VA	Butte	Wyandotte Twp	70	142
BEDELL								
Albert	32	m	w	NH	Santa Clara	Redwood Twp	88	119
Alex	34	m	w	NH	Santa Clara	Gilroy Twp	88	96
Ed A	26	m	w	NY	Santa Barbara	Santa Barbara P O	87	455
Moody B	43	m	w	NH	Alpine	Markleeville P O	69	311
Virginia	41	f	w	PA	Sierra	Sears Twp	89	527
Wm	40	m	w	NY	San Francisco	11-Wd San Francisc	84	570
BEDEN								
John	45	m	w	WALE	Nevada	Eureka Twp	75	137

© 2001 by Heritage Quest. All rights reserved.

Series M593

Name	Age	S	R	B-PL	County	Locale	Roll	Pg
BEDFORD								
Geo M	49	m	w	KY	Tuolumne	Sonora P O	93	321
Henry	58	m	w	ENGL	Calaveras	Copperopolis P O	70	239
Jas A	38	m	w	SC	Shasta	Millville P O	89	491
Jas M	54	m	w	NC	Shasta	American Ranch P O	89	497
Jno A	36	m	w	SC	Shasta	American Ranch P O	89	499
John	30	m	w	IREL	San Francisco	1-Wd San Francisco	79	71
John F	46	m	w	VT	Mariposa	Mariposa P O	74	109
Thomas	53	m	w	KY	Colusa	Stony Crk Twp	71	332
Thomas	44	m	w	KY	San Bernardino	San Salvador Twp	78	457
BEDINE								
Sarah	48	f	w	DC	San Francisco	11-Wd San Francisc	84	685
BEDINGTON								
Eliza	42	f	w	PRUS	San Joaquin	2-Wd Stockton	86	192
Jno	52	m	w	PRUS	San Joaquin	2-Wd Stockton	86	192
BEDLE								
Albert	16	m	w	IL	Sonoma	Santa Rosa	91	395
BEDNER								
John	34	m	w	PRUS	San Francisco	San Francisco P O	83	43
BEDO								
Lewis	51	m	w	FRAN	Placer	Lincoln P O	76	482
William	7	m	w	CA	Placer	Lincoln P O	76	482
BEDOES								
Antonio	35	m	w	PORT	Alameda	Washington Twp	68	272
BEDOL								
Andreas	36	m	w	CHIL	Santa Clara	Alviso Twp	88	23
BEDOLFE								
Vicenzi	34	m	w	ITAL	San Francisco	1-Wd San Francisco	79	110
BEDONA								
John	30	m	w	PA	Nevada	Rough & Ready Twp	75	332
BEDWEL								
Frank	60	m	w	TN	Sonoma	Russian Rvr	91	378
BEDWELL								
Barbara	81	f	w	VA	Sonoma	Washington Twp	91	466
Ira	40	m	w	MO	Sonoma	Mendocino Twp	91	288
Jno B	45	m	w	MO	Sonoma	Washington Twp	91	466
John	45	m	w	KY	Sacramento	Sutter Twp	77	389
Robert D	50	m	w	TN	Los Angeles	Los Nietos Twp	73	576
William	48	m	w	MO	Mendocino	Little Lake Twp	74	200
BEE								
Ah	60	f	c	CHIN	San Francisco	San Francisco P O	80	506
Ah	44	m	c	CHIN	Tuolumne	Chinese Camp P O	93	380
Ah	42	m	c	CHIN	Yolo	Cache Crk Twp	93	455
Ah	40	m	c	CHIN	Sierra	Sears Twp	89	554
Ah	36	m	c	CHIN	Stanislaus	Empire Twp	92	64
Ah	32	m	c	CHIN	San Francisco	San Francisco P O	80	502
Ah	30	m	c	CHIN	San Francisco	6-Wd San Francisco	81	54
Ah	28	m	c	CHIN	San Francisco	San Francisco P O	80	515
Ah	26	f	c	CHIN	Nevada	Bridgeport Twp	75	111
Ah	25	f	c	CHIN	San Francisco	San Francisco P O	80	497
Ah	24	m	c	CHIN	Trinity	Junction City Pct	92	206
Ah	17	m	c	CHIN	Santa Clara	Fremont Twp	88	52
Antonio	16	m	w	CA	Santa Clara	1-Wd San Jose	88	266
Barlow B	59	m	w	NY	Santa Clara	San Jose Twp	88	186
Chong	14	m	c	CHIN	San Francisco	6-Wd San Francisco	81	44
Delfina	23	f	w	MEXI	Santa Clara	2-Wd San Jose	88	315
Fredrick	43	m	w	NY	Sonoma	Vallejo Twp	91	457
Henry	62	m	w	ENGL	Santa Clara	1-Wd San Jose	88	266
Lee	36	m	c	CHIN	Yuba	Marysville	93	626
Lorenza	22	f	w	MEXI	Santa Clara	2-Wd San Jose	88	315
Macly	29	f	w	IREL	Santa Clara	Gilroy Twp	88	89
Short	42	m	c	CHIN	Lake	Little Borax	73	419
William	32	m	w	ENGL	Nevada	Grass Valley Twp	75	143
Woo	30	m	c	CHIN	San Francisco	11-Wd San Francisc	84	448
BEEBE								
A C	42	m	w	NY	El Dorado	Georgetown Twp	72	38
Alonzo	41	m	w	ME	Santa Cruz	Santa Cruz Twp	89	395
Benjamin	39	m	w	NY	Contra Costa	Martinez P O	71	439
C H	54	m	w	CT	Solano	Vallejo	90	155
C P	40	m	w	CT	San Francisco	San Francisco P O	85	877
Charles A	39	m	w	CT	Los Angeles	Los Angeles	73	525
Elijah	56	m	w	IN	Mendocino	Point Arena Twp	74	213
Ervin	---	m	w	NJ	Nevada	Nevada Twp	75	322
Esther	42	f	w	OH	El Dorado	Coloma Twp	72	10
George	26	m	w	MA	Alameda	Murray Twp	68	109
I G	12	f	w	MN	San Francisco	San Francisco P O	85	822
James	39	m	w	NY	Alameda	Oakland	68	241
Joseph	40	m	w	NY	Placer	Roseville P O	76	356
Joseph	34	m	w	NY	Sacramento	4-Wd Sacramento	77	324
Mich	38	m	w	NY	Merced	Snelling P O	74	271
Seth G	36	m	w	NY	Alameda	Eden Twp	68	57
T C	45	m	w	KY	Sacramento	3-Wd Sacramento	77	302
Watson	56	m	w	MO	Mendocino	Big Rvr Twp	74	170
William S	33	m	w	ME	Mendocino	Bourns Landing Twp	74	223
BEEBEE								
Alexander M	38	m	w	OH	Stanislaus	San Joaquin Twp	92	78
Day	35	m	w	PA	Yolo	Buckeye Twp	93	417
John	50	m	w	MO	Yolo	Cache Crk Twp	93	443
Wm S	42	m	w	MA	San Francisco	San Francisco P O	85	733
BEEBLES								
Cary	62	m	w	KY	Santa Clara	Santa Clara Twp	88	145
BEECH								
Margaret	20	f	w	NY	San Francisco	San Francisco P O	83	408
BEECHER								
G W	21	m	w	OH	Tehama	Tehama Twp	92	187
Henry	34	m	w	WURT	San Francisco	San Francisco P O	85	836
Lizzie	27	f	w	OH	Yuba	Marysville	93	596
Y A	41	m	w	MI	Sierra	Lincoln Twp	89	549
BEECHERLY								
John	45	m	w	GERM	Yolo	Cottonwood Twp	93	464
BEECHING								
Robert	50	m	w	ENGL	San Francisco	6-Wd San Francisco	81	121
BEECRAFT								
James Thomas	42	m	w	KY	Plumas	Indian Twp	77	18
BEECROFT								
John T	44	m	w	CANA	San Francisco	San Francisco P O	83	70
BEEDE								
Henry	23	m	w	IL	Contra Costa	Martinez P O	71	396
John E	35	m	w	NH	El Dorado	Mud Springs Twp	72	76
BEEDING								
Franklin	35	m	w	IA	San Mateo	Pescadero P O	87	411
BEEDLE								
Chas W	32	m	w	ME	Nevada	Nevada Twp	75	300
Louis	39	m	w	VA	Sonoma	Bodega Twp	91	253
W H	25	m	w	ME	Nevada	Meadow Lake Twp	75	247
William	24	m	w	IN	Nevada	Grass Valley Twp	75	227
BEEDY								
Jermia	21	m	w	IREL	San Francisco	7-Wd San Francisco	81	275
BEEGAN								
John	55	m	w	IREL	San Francisco	San Francisco P O	83	46
Louisa	22	f	w	NY	San Francisco	5-Wd San Francisco	81	33
Mary	24	f	w	NY	San Francisco	5-Wd San Francisco	81	33
BEEGLES								
Hiram	40	m	w	PA	San Joaquin	2-Wd Stockton	86	191
BEEH								
Christian	43	m	w	BADE	Amador	Volcano P O	69	382
BEEK								
Frederick	39	m	w	BADE	Yuba	New York Twp	93	640
BEEKMAN								
Dora	25	f	w	PRUS	San Francisco	8-Wd San Francisco	82	291
Henry	29	m	w	PRUS	San Francisco	San Francisco P O	83	220
BEEL								
Louis	28	m	w	OH	Sacramento	4-Wd Sacramento	77	354
BEELER								
George	37	m	w	BADE	Sacramento	2-Wd Sacramento	77	217
Jacob	29	m	w	OH	San Francisco	San Francisco P O	80	418
Nicholas	28	m	w	FRAN	Yuba	Slate Range Bar Tw	93	669
Oscar	42	m	w	TN	Calaveras	San Andreas P O	70	206
Peter	38	m	w	CANA	Calaveras	San Andreas P O	70	160
BEELS								
William	29	m	w	MO	Solano	Silveyville Twp	90	75
BEEM								
Ah	16	f	c	CHIN	San Francisco	6-Wd San Francisco	81	74
Tap	28	m	c	CHIN	San Francisco	6-Wd San Francisco	81	65
BEEMAN								
Henry	19	m	w	BREM	Tulare	Visalia	92	297
Lowella	12	f	w	CA	San Francisco	San Francisco P O	80	404
Mary	60	f	w	MA	Alameda	Brooklyn	68	26
Truman	45	m	w	NY	Monterey	Monterey	74	356
BEEMEAN								
John	22	m	w	IREL	Monterey	San Antonio Twp	74	315
BEEN								
A M	65	m	w	CT	San Francisco	San Francisco P O	83	277
Ah	40	m	c	CHIN	San Francisco	6-Wd San Francisco	81	57
Ah	35	m	c	CHIN	Butte	Kimshew Tpw	70	84
Ah	30	m	c	CHIN	Yuba	Marysville	93	621
Ah	24	m	c	CHIN	Butte	Bidwell Twp	70	1
Ah	20	m	c	CHIN	San Francisco	6-Wd San Francisco	81	67
Ah	15	m	c	CHIN	San Francisco	6-Wd San Francisco	81	68
John D	42	m	w	ME	San Francisco	3-Wd San Francisco	79	322
Le Roy S	28	m	w	ME	Tehama	Bell Mills Twp	92	159
Micheal	34	m	w	IREL	Sonoma	Petaluma Twp	91	320
Thomas	41	m	w	FRAN	San Francisco	1-Wd San Francisco	79	50
William J	35	m	w	CANA	San Francisco	7-Wd San Francisco	81	178
BEENE								
Joseph	29	m	w	NY	Sonoma	Analy Twp	91	231
BEENEY								
G W	53	m	w	NY	Yuba	Linda Twp	93	556
BEENS								
John	60	m	w	IREL	Merced	Snelling P O	74	260
BEER								
Ah	29	m	c	CHIN	Solano	Rio Vista Twp	90	59
Catharine	44	f	w	KY	Monterey	Pajaro Twp	74	376
Geo M	38	m	w	NY	Alameda	Oakland	68	234
John	38	m	w	ENGL	San Francisco	San Francisco P O	85	739
John	30	m	w	SCOT	San Luis Obispo	San Luis Obispo Tw	87	300
BEERANCE								
Henry	25	m	w	HANO	Alameda	Brooklyn	68	37
BEERMAN								
Henry	28	m	w	HANO	San Francisco	7-Wd San Francisco	81	223
Henry C	40	m	w	GERM	Santa Cruz	Soquel Twp	89	450
BEEROTH								
Samuel	13	m	w	CA	Amador	Ione City P O	69	359
BEERS								
Geo A	45	m	w	CT	San Francisco	2-Wd San Francisco	79	215
Hiram	60	m	w	CT	Solano	Vacaville Twp	90	121
J B	57	m	w	NY	San Francisco	San Francisco P O	85	783
John	94	m	w	MO	San Luis Obispo	San Luis Obispo Tw	87	312
John	38	m	w	OH	Placer	Bath P O	76	428
William	32	m	w	MA	San Francisco	San Francisco P O	80	531
BEES								
B L	45	m	w	KY	Sierra	Butte Twp	89	511
BEESE								
George	40	m	w	ENGL	San Francisco	7-Wd San Francisco	81	188

© 2001 by Heritage Quest. All rights reserved.

Name	Age	S	R	B-PL	County	Locale	Series M593 Roll	Pg
BEESLEY								
Wm	43	m	w	KY	Sonoma	Analy Twp	91	247
BEESON								
E B	49	m	w	NC	Amador	Ione City P O	69	361
Edward M	43	m	w	NC	San Mateo	Menlo Park P O	87	378
Emma	8	f	w	CA	Sonoma	Analy Twp	91	228
George	29	m	w	OH	Plumas	Indian Twp	77	19
Isaac	74	m	w	NC	Sonoma	Washington Twp	91	464
Jno B	50	m	w	NC	Sonoma	Healdsburg & Mendo	91	283
Orville W	24	m	w	IL	Sonoma	Washington Twp	91	464
Robert	53	m	w	ENGL	Sonoma	Vallejo Twp	91	458
Wm S	46	m	w	NC	Sonoma	Washington Twp	91	464
BEETE								
A G	35	m	w	GA	Merced	Snelling P O	74	262
BEETMAN								
J J	35	m	w	BAVA	Alameda	Oakland	68	147
BEEY								
Ah	50	m	c	CHIN	Trinity	Weaverville Pct	92	231
BEEZ								
Frederick	33	m	w	PRUS	San Francisco	6-Wd San Francisco	81	115
BEEZER								
Edward	30	m	w	PA	Colusa	Stony Crk Twp	71	332
BEEZLEY								
Silas	59	m	w	OH	Nevada	Rough & Ready Twp	75	330
BEFELL								
John	25	m	w	IREL	Alameda	Oakland	68	240
BEFFA								
Gustavius	25	m	w	ITAL	Alpine	Woodfords P O	69	309
BEFFEY								
Jno	22	m	w	ME	Butte	Kimshew Tpw	70	80
BEG								
Ah	27	m	c	CHIN	San Francisco	San Francisco P O	83	131
Ah	19	m	c	CHIN	Santa Clara	Fremont Twp	88	55
BEGAL								
Ernst	24	m	w	OLDE	Alameda	Eden Twp	68	93
BEGAN								
John	27	m	w	IREL	Marin	San Rafael Twp	74	38
Josephine	17	f	w	MI	San Luis Obispo	Santa Rosa Twp	87	317
BEGARDA								
Ramon	40	m	w	CHIL	Mariposa	Mariposa P O	74	129
BEGER								
Henry	35	m	w	SAXO	Monterey	San Juan Twp	74	407
BEGERDBEWER								
John	38	m	w	VA	Sutter	Vernon Twp	92	133
BEGERMAN								
August	49	m	w	PRUS	Marin	Sausalito Twp	74	66
BEGEROLE								
Louis	12	m	w	CA	Marin	San Rafael Twp	74	27
BEGERT								
Emil	32	m	w	FRAN	San Francisco	San Francisco P O	80	350
BEGG								
J	40	m	w	SCOT	Santa Clara	Gilroy Twp	88	74
BEGGIN								
Jas E G	47	m	w	OH	San Joaquin	3-Wd Stockton	86	241
BEGGS								
Bird	25	f	w	CT	Sacramento	3-Wd Sacramento	77	294
James	36	m	w	NJ	San Francisco	8-Wd San Francisco	82	445
John	31	m	w	IREL	San Francisco	1-Wd San Francisco	79	83
Pat	50	m	w	IREL	Santa Clara	Burnett Twp	88	31
Robert	21	m	w	NY	Nevada	Grass Valley Twp	75	172
Thomas	38	m	w	IREL	Marin	Tomales Twp	74	79
William	38	m	w	IL	Marin	Tomales Twp	74	87
BEGHANT								
E C	40	m	w	FRAN	Tuolumne	Columbia P O	93	353
BEGIN								
James	29	m	w	OH	Sutter	Sutter Twp	92	117
BEGLAR								
Michael	39	m	w	IREL	Siskiyou	Scott Valley Twp	89	614
BEGLES								
---	38	m	w	BADE	Napa	Napa	75	36
BEGLEY								
Benj	17	m	w	SWIT	Sacramento	American Twp	77	64
Michael	35	m	w	IREL	San Francisco	11-Wd San Francisc	84	583
Peter	35	m	w	IREL	San Francisco	7-Wd San Francisco	81	275
BEGNAM								
L	40	m	w	ITAL	Alameda	Oakland	68	186
BEGNE								
Peter	35	m	w	FRAN	Los Angeles	Los Angeles	73	552
BEGO								
Antonio	38	m	w	AUST	Santa Clara	2-Wd San Jose	88	317
BEGOING								
Henry	25	m	w	CANA	Yolo	Cache Crk Twp	93	448
BEGONE								
Joseph	50	m	w	BELG	Mariposa	Mariposa P O	74	130
BEGUELTE								
Deville	54	m	w	MO	San Francisco	San Francisco P O	83	137
BEGUHL								
Henry	42	m	w	PRUS	Solano	Rio Vista Twp	90	61
BEGUIR								
Gabriel	31	m	w	FRAN	San Francisco	1-Wd San Francisco	79	109
BEGUR								
Juan	53	m	w	MEXI	San Diego	San Pasqual Valley	78	524
BEGURRA								
Lorenzo	40	m	b	PHIL	Mariposa	Mariposa P O	74	104
BEHAKEY								
Jesus	50	m	w	MEXI	San Bernardino	San Salvador Twp	78	458
BEHAN								
Berrie	20	m	w	IREL	Sacramento	3-Wd Sacramento	77	316
Clinton	65	m	w	IREL	San Francisco	11-Wd San Francisc	84	489
Dennis	41	m	w	IREL	San Francisco	San Francisco P O	83	339
Thos	28	m	w	NY	San Joaquin	2-Wd Stockton	86	170
BEHANE								
Frederick	34	m	w	HAMB	Marin	Sausalito Twp	74	73
BEHARNAM								
Julius	26	m	w	PRUS	San Francisco	San Francisco P O	83	241
BEHART								
Jean	48	m	w	FRAN	San Francisco	11-Wd San Francisc	84	612
BEHASQUE								
Lavier	47	m	w	FRAN	Los Angeles	Los Angeles	73	518
BEHENKE								
Henry	46	m	w	NCOD	Siskiyou	Callahan P O	89	630
BEHENS								
Geo	40	m	w	HANO	El Dorado	Kelsey Twp	72	60
BEHENSEN								
Adolph	52	m	w	FRAN	Mariposa	Mariposa P O	74	91
BEHERER								
Jacob	47	m	w	BADE	El Dorado	Mountain Twp	72	67
BEHERNS								
Richard	22	m	w	PRUS	San Diego	Fort Yuma Dist	78	464
BEHLER								
Henry	38	m	w	BADE	Solano	Suisun Twp	90	112
Nancy J	31	f	w	IN	El Dorado	Placerville	72	118
BEHLOW								
Chs J	27	m	w	PRUS	San Francisco	2-Wd San Francisco	79	279
Wm	29	m	w	PRUS	San Francisco	San Francisco P O	83	88
BEHMER								
Herman	40	m	w	PRUS	Nevada	Meadow Lake Twp	75	249
BEHN								
Hanora	23	f	w	PRUS	San Francisco	San Francisco P O	83	210
BEHNKE								
H P C	34	m	w	HAMB	Siskiyou	Scott Valley Twp	89	619
BEHORCAS								
John	21	m	w	CA	Santa Clara	Fremont Twp	88	60
BEHR								
Henry	50	m	w	PRUS	San Francisco	5-Wd San Francisco	81	4
Hermann	51	m	w	SAXO	San Francisco	San Francisco P O	83	30
John	56	m	w	SWIT	San Francisco	San Francisco P O	80	455
John	28	m	w	HANO	San Francisco	1-Wd San Francisco	79	96
Julius	40	m	w	PRUS	San Francisco	San Francisco P O	85	728
Otto	36	m	w	SHOL	San Francisco	San Francisco P O	83	165
BEHRANS								
Charles	44	m	w	RUSS	Nevada	Bridgeport Twp	75	115
W	46	f	w	SHOL	Nevada	Bridgeport Twp	75	115
BEHRE								
Frederick	43	m	w	PRUS	San Francisco	8-Wd San Francisco	82	494
BEHREND								
Edward	34	m	w	GERM	Santa Clara	2-Wd San Jose	88	330
BEHRENDAT								
Edward	28	m	w	PRUS	Santa Clara	2-Wd San Jose	88	317
BEHRENDT								
Herman	31	m	w	PRUS	San Francisco	San Francisco P O	85	719
BEHRENIS								
George H	30	m	w	PRUS	San Francisco	San Francisco P O	83	408
BEHRENS								
Christopher	42	m	w	SAXO	Santa Barbara	Santa Barbara P O	87	456
Henry C F	60	m	w	HANO	San Francisco	San Francisco P O	83	344
James	45	m	w	GERM	San Francisco	1-Wd San Francisco	79	4
John	25	m	w	HANO	San Francisco	3-Wd San Francisco	79	287
Ludwig	44	m	w	MECK	Shasta	Shasta P O	89	456
BEHRENT								
August	45	m	w	PRUS	Contra Costa	Martinez P O	71	380
BEHRISCH								
Charles	55	m	w	SAXO	Nevada	Grass Valley Twp	75	178
BEHRLE								
Louis	19	m	w	NY	Shasta	Shasta P O	89	457
BEHRMAN								
Christian	38	m	w	PRUS	San Francisco	8-Wd San Francisco	82	440
John	26	m	w	PRUS	San Francisco	San Francisco P O	80	469
Otto	16	m	w	PRUS	San Francisco	8-Wd San Francisco	82	439
BEHRNS								
Fred	22	m	w	BAVA	Tehama	Deer Crk Twp	92	170
BEHUNIN								
Philo M	35	m	w	NY	Placer	Rocklin Twp	76	466
BEI								
Ah	43	m	c	CHIN	San Francisco	San Francisco P O	80	492
Ah	32	m	c	CHIN	San Francisco	San Francisco P O	80	500
BEIBLEY								
Mary	58	f	w	NY	San Francisco	11-Wd San Francisc	84	687
BEIDERMAN								
Charles	33	m	w	BAVA	San Francisco	8-Wd San Francisco	82	494
BEIDLEMAN								
Augdine	36	f	w	NY	San Francisco	2-Wd San Francisco	79	201
BEIGHLEY								
M M	40	m	w	PA	Sutter	Butte Twp	92	91
BEIGHTAL								
U Lewis	33	m	w	MD	Nevada	Nevada Twp	75	295
BEILER								
James	23	m	w	BADE	Butte	Oregon Twp	70	131
BEILEY								
M A	23	f	w	RI	San Francisco	San Francisco P O	85	842
BEILLY								
James	32	m	w	TX	San Francisco	7-Wd San Francisco	81	275

© 2001 by Heritage Quest. All rights reserved.

Name	Age	S	R	B-PL	County	Locale (Series M593)	Roll	Pg
BEIMER								
Augusta	17	f	w	OH	San Francisco	5-Wd San Francisco	81	16
BEIN								
Ah	32	m	c	CHIN	Sierra	Sears Twp	89	553
Ah	30	m	c	CHIN	Sierra	Eureka Twp	89	527
Henry	32	m	w	IREL	San Francisco	8-Wd San Francisco	82	294
Henry	28	m	w	HANO	San Francisco	7-Wd San Francisco	81	250
Soloman	33	m	w	PRUS	San Francisco	San Francisco P O	83	137
William	56	m	w	PRUS	San Francisco	San Francisco P O	83	138
William	29	m	w	NJ	Contra Costa	Martinez P O	71	442
BEINE								
George	50	m	w	IREL	Yolo	Grafton Twp	93	495
BEING								
Ah	32	m	c	CHIN	Calaveras	San Andreas P O	70	202
BEINIMAN								
Caroline	70	f	w	PRUS	Santa Clara	1-Wd San Jose	88	255
BEIRAT								
Oschield	37	m	w	FRAN	San Francisco	2-Wd San Francisco	79	174
BEIRNE								
Margret	25	f	w	IREL	San Francisco	1-Wd San Francisco	79	44
Patk	34	m	w	IREL	San Francisco	1-Wd San Francisco	79	44
BEIROTH								
Prudent	10	f	w	CA	Amador	Ione City P O	69	357
BEIRS								
Harriet	50	f	w	NY	San Diego	Julian Dist	78	471
BEIRSO								
G	40	m	w	ITAL	San Joaquin	Castoria Twp	86	1
BEISEL								
Fredrick	41	m	w	PRUS	San Francisco	San Francisco P O	80	474
BEISET								
Peter	30	m	w	ITAL	San Francisco	11-Wd San Francisc	84	712
BEISLER								
John	43	m	w	BAVA	Placer	Gold Run Twp	76	395
BEISSER								
Richard	28	m	w	BAVA	San Francisco	San Francisco P O	83	241
BEISTERO								
Dionicio	25	m	w	MEXI	San Diego	Coronado	78	465
BEITH								
A	27	m	w	CANA	San Joaquin	Douglas Twp	86	47
James	77	m	w	SCOT	Humboldt	Arcata Twp	72	226
James	39	m	w	SCOT	Klamath	Sawyers Bar	73	377
BEITZEL								
Jacob	32	m	w	PRUS	Alameda	Brooklyn	68	35
BEJA								
Guadloupe	10	f	w	MEXI	San Francisco	San Francisco P O	80	428
BEJER								
Louis	47	m	w	HDAR	San Francisco	San Francisco P O	80	346
BEJOT								
M	31	m	w	SPAI	San Francisco	8-Wd San Francisco	82	373
BEK								
Yeck	30	m	c	CHIN	San Francisco	11-Wd San Francisc	84	546
BEKAN								
Edward	33	m	w	IREL	San Francisco	11-Wd San Francisc	84	650
Rebecca	54	f	w	IREL	Mariposa	Mariposa P O	74	116
BEKINA								
Isabell	22	f	w	IREL	San Joaquin	2-Wd Stockton	86	171
BEKNAN								
Frank	50	m	w	FRAN	Santa Clara	Redwood Twp	88	119
BEKSTONE								
John	25	m	b	MD	San Joaquin	3-Wd Stockton	86	218
BELA								
Ah	20	m	c	CHIN	Placer	Dutch Flat P O	76	411
Philer	51	m	w	FRAN	San Francisco	8-Wd San Francisco	82	295
BELAGERA								
Jesus	49	m	w	MEXI	Calaveras	San Andreas P O	70	181
Terresa	13	f	w	CA	Calaveras	San Andreas P O	70	181
BELALONGA								
August	50	m	w	SPAI	San Francisco	1-Wd San Francisco	79	122
BELAM								
Jerome	20	m	w	SWIT	Napa	Napa Twp	75	72
BELANBERG								
M Y	56	m	w	SHOL	Merced	Snelling P O	74	255
BELAND								
Nicholas	38	m	w	FRAN	Inyo	Independence Twp	73	328
BELANDA								
Ascension	29	m	w	MEXI	Santa Barbara	Santa Barbara P O	87	487
John	32	m	w	SWED	San Francisco	San Francisco P O	80	429
BELANS								
David	47	m	w	PRUS	San Joaquin	Tulare Twp	86	259
BELANTO								
Legaro	44	m	w	MEXI	Fresno	Millerton P O	72	167
BELARDA								
Lynares	42	m	w	NM	San Bernardino	San Salvador Twp	78	460
BELARDE								
Bernardo	15	m	w	CA	Monterey	San Juan Twp	74	401
Jose	42	m	w	MEXI	Monterey	San Juan Twp	74	401
Juan	18	m	w	CA	Monterey	San Juan Twp	74	401
BELARDEZ								
Teresa	17	f	w	CA	Los Angeles	Los Angeles	73	542
BELARDO								
Kernillo	36	m	w	MEXI	San Bernardino	San Salvador Twp	78	457
BELASCO								
Abra	40	m	w	ENGL	San Francisco	San Francisco P O	83	36
R	34	m	w	SPAI	Yuba	Marysville	93	589
BELAU								
Michael	48	m	w	PRUS	San Francisco	2-Wd San Francisco	79	156
BELAVAN								
Amelia	17	f	w	CA	San Bernardino	Belleville Twp	78	408
BELAY								
Antonin	50	m	w	BOHE	San Francisco	11-Wd San Francisc	84	544
BELCAR								
Byron	37	m	w	PA	Shasta	Horsetown P O	89	505
BELCH								
Joseph	13	m	w	CA	San Diego	San Luis Rey	78	516
BELCHE								
John	37	m	w	NY	San Joaquin	1-Wd Stockton	86	124
BELCHER								
E A	22	m	w	VT	Yuba	Marysville	93	599
Elizabeth	45	f	w	PA	San Francisco	San Francisco P O	83	72
F R	54	m	w	NY	San Joaquin	Tulare Twp	86	253
Francis	21	m	w	NY	Stanislaus	Empire Twp	92	43
Fred P	44	m	w	NY	San Francisco	2-Wd San Francisco	79	257
Hugh	30	m	w	NY	San Joaquin	1-Wd Stockton	86	141
I S	45	m	w	VT	Yuba	Marysville	93	597
John	26	m	w	IREL	Sacramento	2-Wd Sacramento	77	239
John C	50	m	w	MA	Sacramento	Lee Twp	77	158
Lucy	25	f	w	IL	Sacramento	3-Wd Sacramento	77	261
Mariah	67	m	w	ENGL	Sacramento	Georgianna Twp	77	131
Philips	60	m	w	ENGL	San Francisco	11-Wd San Francisc	84	687
Richard	20	m	w	MO	Yolo	Buckeye Twp	93	414
Robert	38	m	w	NY	San Francisco	2-Wd San Francisco	79	259
S	22	m	w	PRUS	Sierra	Sierra Twp	89	568
W C	48	m	w	VT	Yuba	Marysville	93	597
BELCOUR								
J	38	m	w	FRAN	San Francisco	San Francisco P O	85	820
BELDEN								
David	38	m	w	CT	Santa Clara	2-Wd San Jose	88	324
Edwin	26	m	w	CT	Yuba	Marysville	93	582
Enma J	28	f	w	NH	San Francisco	8-Wd San Francisco	82	382
Fanny	22	f	w	OH	Siskiyou	Butte Twp	89	585
Fredk	29	m	w	OH	Yuba	East Bear Rvr Twp	93	542
Harvy	38	m	w	ME	San Joaquin	1-Wd Stockton	86	128
Henry	21	m	w	NY	San Francisco	8-Wd San Francisco	82	390
Ida	27	f	w	NY	El Dorado	Placerville	72	113
John	46	m	w	NY	Placer	Pino Twp	76	472
John	35	m	w	CT	Nevada	Nevada Twp	75	285
John H	24	m	w	NY	Nevada	Meadow Lake Twp	75	266
Josiah	50	m	w	CT	Santa Clara	2-Wd San Jose	88	295
Lizzy	31	f	w	CT	San Francisco	San Francisco P O	83	288
M E	16	f	w	CA	Alameda	Oakland	68	237
Margt	45	f	w	SCOT	San Francisco	8-Wd San Francisco	82	310
Philander H	31	m	w	ME	Nevada	Nevada Twp	75	318
Richard	18	m	w	ME	Nevada	Meadow Lake Twp	75	264
Samuel	37	m	w	NY	Tulare	Tule Rvr Twp	92	261
Sarah	18	f	w	CA	San Francisco	8-Wd San Francisco	82	382
BELDER								
J W	24	m	w	MA	San Francisco	San Francisco P O	85	789
BELDIN								
E	38	m	w	OH	Sierra	Sierra Twp	89	562
BELDING								
C C	39	m	w	NY	Amador	Sutter Crk P O	69	396
Chas	39	m	w	MA	San Joaquin	1-Wd Stockton	86	140
Orrin	55	m	w	NY	San Francisco	San Francisco P O	83	109
W J	39	m	w	NY	San Joaquin	1-Wd Stockton	86	139
BELDONA								
G	40	m	w	ITAL	Alameda	Oakland	68	241
BELDUTE								
Joseph	26	m	w	CANA	San Francisco	San Francisco P O	83	360
BELE								
Jose	35	m	w	AZOR	Monterey	Castroville Twp	74	334
BELEAU								
Thos	40	m	w	IREL	San Francisco	11-Wd San Francisc	84	671
BELECH								
Mary	18	f	w	LA	San Francisco	8-Wd San Francisco	82	290
BELEHASSER								
---	40	m	w	PRUS	Contra Costa	Martinez Twp	71	352
BELEND								
Edward	28	m	w	CANA	Yuba	W Bear Rvr Twp	93	684
BELENDER								
Chas	38	m	w	SAXO	San Francisco	San Francisco P O	85	811
BELENEUST								
Mathew	28	m	w	PORT	Sonoma	Petaluma Twp	91	358
BELER								
Jacob	35	m	w	WURT	San Francisco	San Francisco P O	85	756
Philip	21	m	w	OH	San Francisco	San Francisco P O	85	876
BELERD								
Abraham	39	m	w	BADE	Solano	Suisun Twp	90	116
BELERMANN								
Emile	30	m	w	SAXO	San Francisco	2-Wd San Francisco	79	144
BELETTA								
Grabila	29	m	w	ITAL	San Francisco	11-Wd San Francisc	84	614
BELEVEAU								
Onnesime	29	m	w	CANA	Nevada	Grass Valley Twp	75	225
BELEW								
John	50	m	w	VA	San Joaquin	3-Wd Stockton	86	222
BELF								
Geo	23	m	w	NY	San Francisco	11-Wd San Francisc	84	610
BELFILS								
Louis	38	m	w	FRAN	Alameda	Oakland	68	181
Peter	28	m	w	FRAN	San Francisco	1-Wd San Francisco	79	81
BELFOR								
Thomas	25	m	w	CANA	Solano	Silveyville Twp	90	83

© 2001 by Heritage Quest. All rights reserved.

Name	Age	S	R	B-PL	County	Locale	Series M593 Roll	Pg
BELFORE								
Elizabeth	30	f	w	SCOT	San Francisco	7-Wd San Francisco	81	223
BELFRAGE								
John	40	m	w	SWED	San Francisco	7-Wd San Francisco	81	218
BELGE								
Stephen	38	m	w	AUST	Amador	Jackson P O	69	329
BELGOMIE								
Gabriel	36	m	w	ITAL	Alpine	Woodfords P O	69	310
BELGRANT								
Augusta	11	f	w	MO	Yolo	Cache Crk Twp	93	453
BELGUD								
Anton	35	m	w	SWIT	San Francisco	11-Wd San Francisc	84	499
BELHAM								
Ludie	21	f	w	AR	Butte	Ophir Twp	70	92
BELHON								
Eugine	42	m	w	FRAN	Inyo	Lone Pine Twp	73	332
BELHUGUE								
Charles	39	m	w	FRAN	Santa Clara	2-Wd San Jose	88	302
BELICK								
John	37	m	w	NY	El Dorado	Cosumnes Twp	72	17
BELICONVICH								
Baldo	23	m	w	AUST	Santa Clara	San Jose Twp	88	193
BELIEN								
John G	33	m	w	MO	San Luis Obispo	Santa Rosa Twp	87	328
BELIN								
Anna	29	f	w	FRAN	San Francisco	San Francisco P O	83	136
Anna	27	f	w	FRAN	San Francisco	San Francisco P O	80	345
BELK								
Charles	7	m	w	AR	Lassen	Janesville Twp	73	433
BELKNAP								
A W	30	f	w	NY	San Francisco	San Francisco P O	85	782
C	42	m	w	CANA	Yuba	East Bear Rvr Twp	93	542
Cangton	39	m	w	OH	Alameda	San Leandro	68	97
Henry	46	m	w	PA	Placer	Cisco P O	76	494
Maggie	35	f	w	NH	Calaveras	Copperopolis P O	70	222
Silas	60	m	w	KY	Tulare	Tule Rvr Twp	92	260
BELKOSTZ								
Peter	35	m	w	POLA	San Francisco	San Francisco P O	83	103
BELL								
---	40	m	w	MO	El Dorado	White Oak Twp	72	139
Aaron	37	m	w	PA	Nevada	Meadow Lake Twp	75	246
Aaron M	58	m	w	NY	Sonoma	Salt Point	91	386
Ada	20	f	w	PRUS	San Francisco	6-Wd San Francisco	81	71
Agnes	15	f	w	IL	El Dorado	Mud Springs Twp	72	90
Albert K	29	m	w	MO	Sonoma	Mendocino Twp	91	293
Alexander	69	m	w	PA	Los Angeles	Los Angeles	73	525
Alexander	45	m	w	PA	Los Angeles	Los Angeles	73	540
Alexander	37	m	w	TN	Placer	Auburn P O	76	378
Alexander D	42	m	w	ENGL	San Francisco	6-Wd San Francisco	81	123
Alfred H	24	m	w	MI	Santa Cruz	Santa Cruz Twp	89	379
Alice	25	f	w	SC	San Francisco	San Francisco P O	83	172
Andrew	46	m	w	NC	Inyo	Independence Twp	73	327
Andy	40	m	w	MI	San Joaquin	2-Wd Stockton	86	206
Anna	25	f	w	NY	San Francisco	5-Wd San Francisco	81	33
Augustus	38	m	w	GA	Santa Clara	Fremont Twp	88	41
Benj F	42	m	w	OH	Sacramento	3-Wd Sacramento	77	312
Benjamin	40	m	w	VA	Sonoma	Salt Point	91	380
Catharine	40	f	w	IREL	San Francisco	San Francisco P O	83	74
Charles	30	m	w	WALE	San Francisco	1-Wd San Francisco	79	126
Charles	28	m	w	ENGL	San Francisco	7-Wd San Francisco	81	204
Charles	27	m	w	DENM	San Francisco	2-Wd San Francisco	79	214
Charles	22	m	w	VA	Humboldt	Bucksport Twp	72	243
Charles C	22	m	w	ENGL	Inyo	Lone Pine Twp	73	333
Charles H	43	m	w	GA	Stanislaus	San Joaquin Twp	92	78
Charles M	20	m	w	CA	Yolo	Buckeye Twp	93	412
Chas	45	m	w	PA	San Francisco	5-Wd San Francisco	81	18
Chas	30	m	w	NY	San Francisco	1-Wd San Francisco	79	65
Chas	16	m	w	NY	Sacramento	1-Wd Sacramento	77	181
Chas E	43	m	w	CT	Solano	Vallejo	90	211
Christiana	57	f	w	PA	El Dorado	Georgetown Twp	72	43
D P	48	m	w	CA	San Francisco	San Francisco P O	85	797
Daniel E	28	m	w	NY	Nevada	Grass Valley Twp	75	230
David	35	m	w	SCOT	San Francisco	2-Wd San Francisco	79	222
David	24	m	w	WI	Yuba	W Bear Rvr Twp	93	683
E G Mrs	48	f	w	IREL	Sonoma	Petaluma Twp	91	328
Edwd	41	m	w	FRAN	Alameda	Oakland	68	180
Elizabeth	17	f	w	NY	Amador	Volcano P O	69	380
Ellen	45	f	m	DC	San Francisco	San Francisco P O	80	419
Emma	12	f	w	CA	San Mateo	Pescadero P O	87	410
Emma S	18	f	w	IL	Sacramento	San Joaquin Twp	77	402
Fanny	24	f	w	LA	San Francisco	8-Wd San Francisco	82	312
Fellmon	27	m	w	TN	Yuba	North East Twp	93	644
Fidellow	32	m	w	NC	Inyo	Independence Twp	73	326
Frank	46	m	w	SCOT	Trinity	Junction City Pct	92	210
Frank	35	m	w	IL	Yuba	Marysville	93	614
Frank	24	m	w	MS	Klamath	Trinidad Twp	73	392
Frank	23	m	w	US	Yuba	Marysville	93	576
Frank L	41	m	w	TN	Stanislaus	Empire Twp	92	43
G	26	f	w	MA	Alameda	Alameda	68	5
G W	38	m	w	NC	Merced	Snelling P O	74	272
Gabriel	40	m	w	IREL	San Mateo	Schoolhouse Statio	87	333
Geo	32	m	w	MD	El Dorado	Georgetown Twp	72	37
Geo	26	m	w	SCOT	Butte	Ophir Twp	70	110
Geo	24	m	w	MA	Butte	Concow Twp	70	9
George	67	m	w	ENGL	Calaveras	San Andreas P O	70	207
George	34	m	w	IREL	Tuolumne	Columbia P O	93	339
George	27	m	w	NY	Marin	Sausalito Twp	74	73

Name	Age	S	R	B-PL	County	Locale	Series M593 Roll	Pg
George	27	m	w	ENGL	Sonoma	Sonoma Twp	91	440
George	13	m	w	WI	Shasta	Horsetown P O	89	503
George H	55	m	w	NY	San Francisco	San Francisco P O	85	775
George H	45	m	w	IN	Solano	Rio Vista Twp	90	57
George R	46	m	w	IN	Mendocino	Calpella Twp	74	188
George T	15	m	w	CA	Calaveras	San Andreas P O	70	217
George W	55	m	w	PA	Yolo	Washington Twp	93	534
Gustavus	43	m	w	RUSS	Sacramento	Brighton Twp	77	74
H B	27	m	w	NH	Solano	Vallejo	90	141
H C	44	m	w	KY	San Joaquin	Liberty Twp	86	85
Hanson	58	m	b	MD	Shasta	Shasta P O	89	458
Harry J	29	m	w	NY	Placer	Rocklin Twp	76	468
Henry	45	m	w	NY	Sonoma	Russian Rvr	91	370
Henry	24	m	w	PA	Sutter	Sutter Twp	92	125
Henry C	39	m	w	MD	Klamath	Sawyers Bar	73	377
Henry H	30	m	w	PA	San Francisco	San Francisco P O	83	245
Henry L	45	m	w	SCOT	San Francisco	San Francisco P O	85	781
Horace C	39	m	w	IN	Los Angeles	Los Angeles	73	502
Hugh	70	m	w	NY	Amador	Fiddletown P O	69	438
Hugh H	35	m	w	MO	Amador	Fiddletown P O	69	438
Hugh R	62	m	w	ENGL	Amador	Volcano P O	69	387
I M	43	m	w	TN	Sacramento	Brighton Twp	77	78
Ida	35	f	w	NY	San Francisco	San Francisco P O	83	83
J C	23	f	w	CANA	San Francisco	San Francisco P O	85	863
J D	44	m	w	SCOT	San Francisco	San Francisco P O	83	304
J E	27	m	w	IREL	San Joaquin	3-Wd Stockton	86	218
J M	27	m	w	SCOT	Lake	Morgan Valley	73	425
James	55	m	w	SCOT	El Dorado	Mud Springs Twp	72	84
James	50	m	w	ENGL	Mendocino	Navarro & Big Rvr	74	175
James	44	m	w	PA	San Bernardino	San Bernardino Twp	78	452
James	44	m	w	AL	San Diego	Julian Dist	78	470
James	42	m	w	ENGL	Tuolumne	Big Oak Flat P O	93	403
James	38	m	w	PA	Siskiyou	Yreka Twp	89	665
James	38	m	w	IREL	Yolo	Buckeye Twp	93	414
James	31	m	w	AR	Sonoma	Analy Twp	91	246
James	28	m	w	NY	San Francisco	5-Wd San Francisco	81	6
James	25	m	w	IREL	Yuba	Rose Bar Twp	93	661
James B	40	m	w	PA	Tulare	Visalia	92	295
James G	40	m	w	TN	Mariposa	Mariposa P O	74	119
James H	54	m	b	DC	San Francisco	8-Wd San Francisco	82	341
James J	23	m	w	WALE	Los Angeles	Los Angeles	73	542
James W	42	m	w	IREL	San Mateo	Pescadero P O	87	409
Jannett	17	f	b	MO	Butte	Hamilton Twp	70	69
Jas S	36	m	w	MO	Sonoma	Mendocino Twp	91	298
Jno	50	m	w	IREL	Butte	Kimshew Tpw	70	80
Jno W	26	m	w	MO	Sonoma	Mendocino Twp	91	293
John	59	m	w	PRUS	Sacramento	4-Wd Sacramento	77	346
John	50	m	w	NY	San Francisco	5-Wd San Francisco	81	31
John	45	m	b	VA	Sacramento	2-Wd Sacramento	77	246
John	45	m	w	SCOT	Nevada	Meadow Lake Twp	75	263
John	45	m	w	PRUS	Nevada	Grass Valley Twp	75	227
John	44	m	w	IREL	San Francisco	San Francisco P O	80	349
John	44	m	w	ENGL	El Dorado	Greenwood Twp	72	53
John	44	m	w	VA	San Joaquin	Elkhorn Twp	86	54
John	41	m	w	SCOT	Solano	Vallejo	90	154
John	40	m	w	SCOT	Stanislaus	San Joaquin Twp	92	72
John	40	m	w	HANO	Nevada	Grass Valley Twp	75	218
John	39	m	w	MA	Inyo	Bishop Crk Twp	73	317
John	39	m	w	MO	El Dorado	Georgetown Twp	72	48
John	38	m	w	CANA	San Francisco	San Francisco P O	80	486
John	38	m	w	SCOT	Sierra	Table Rock Twp	89	574
John	35	m	w	IL	El Dorado	Coloma Twp	72	4
John	34	m	w	IL	Butte	Chico Twp	70	26
John	30	m	w	FRAN	San Francisco	2-Wd San Francisco	79	145
John	30	m	w	MA	San Francisco	7-Wd San Francisco	81	220
John	26	m	w	CANA	San Francisco	11-Wd San Francisc	84	578
John	25	m	w	SCOT	Yolo	Washington Twp	93	532
John	25	m	w	LA	Calaveras	San Andreas P O	70	191
John	24	m	w	OH	Solano	Denverton Twp	90	25
John	24	m	w	CHIL	San Francisco	San Francisco P O	80	336
John	22	m	w	ENGL	San Francisco	7-Wd San Francisco	81	204
John	21	m	w	ENGL	Sacramento	Granite Twp	77	144
John	16	m	w	CA	San Francisco	11-Wd San Francisc	84	564
John B	41	m	w	SCOT	Yolo	Washington Twp	93	530
John C	45	m	w	MA	San Francisco	2-Wd San Francisco	79	283
John J	41	m	w	KY	Humboldt	Bald Hills	72	239
John P	31	m	w	NY	San Francisco	8-Wd San Francisco	82	330
John S	26	m	w	POLY	Santa Barbara	Santa Maria P O	87	514
John W	45	m	w	NY	San Francisco	San Francisco P O	83	65
Jos J	45	m	w	PA	Shasta	American Ranch P O	89	499
Joseph	28	m	w	IREL	San Joaquin	Elliott Twp	86	78
Josiah	32	m	w	CT	Sonoma	Bodega Twp	91	261
Julia	19	f	w	AR	San Diego	San Diego	78	487
Kimsey	34	m	w	MO	Sonoma	Mendocino Twp	91	298
L F	44	m	w	NY	Santa Clara	Gilroy Twp	88	87
Lewis	63	m	w	ENGL	Nevada	Nevada Twp	75	296
Lewis	41	m	w	WI	Butte	Bidwell Twp	70	1
Lillie	28	f	w	VA	Santa Clara	2-Wd San Jose	88	327
Louisa	17	f	m	CA	Shasta	Shasta P O	89	455
Louisa	13	f	w	CA	Nevada	Grass Valley Twp	75	215
Lucius	25	m	m	LA	Stanislaus	Empire Twp	92	49
Lucy	16	f	b	TN	Tuolumne	Sonora P O	93	329
Lucy	13	f	w	NY	San Francisco	San Francisco P O	80	482
Lyman	41	m	w	NY	El Dorado	Cosumnes Twp	72	14
M E	20	f	w	CA	San Francisco	San Francisco P O	85	781
Margaret	37	f	w	IREL	San Francisco	San Francisco P O	83	227
Maria	50	f	w	NY	San Francisco	San Francisco P O	83	277

© 2001 by Heritage Quest. All rights reserved.

Series M593

Name	Age	S	R	B-PL	County	Locale	Roll	Pg
Martin	40	m	w	NY	San Francisco	5-Wd San Francisco	81	33
Martin	35	m	w	SCOT	Contra Costa	Martinez P O	71	383
Mary	5	f	w	CT	San Joaquin	Douglas Twp	86	47
Mary	37	f	b	MD	San Francisco	San Francisco P O	80	418
Mary	36	f	w	IREL	San Francisco	2-Wd San Francisco	79	227
Mary	34	f	w	CANA	Sonoma	Petaluma Twp	91	346
Mary	30	f	w	IREL	San Francisco	7-Wd San Francisco	81	177
Mary	30	f	w	IREL	Solano	Vallejo	90	205
Mary	18	f	w	US	Santa Cruz	Watsonville	89	368
Mary	11	f	w	IL	El Dorado	Mud Springs Twp	72	84
Mary Ann	13	f	w	CA	Nevada	Nevada Twp	75	278
Mary S	31	f	w	WI	Solano	Benicia	90	16
Mattie	35	f	w	PA	Butte	Ophir Twp	70	105
Mattie	3	f	w	CA	Sonoma	Cloverdale Twp	91	268
Maurice	27	m	w	FRAN	Marin	San Rafael Twp	74	32
Michael	33	m	w	CANA	Marin	San Rafael Twp	74	32
Nancy	66	f	w	KY	Colusa	Colusa Twp	71	276
Otto	22	m	w	VA	Marin	Sausalito Twp	74	73
Peter	35	m	w	SCOT	Contra Costa	Martinez P O	71	415
Philip A	62	m	m	NY	San Francisco	1-Wd San Francisco	79	83
R Clarance	19	m	w	VA	Yuba	Marysville	93	579
Richard	44	m	w	SCOT	Yuba	Rose Bar Twp	93	657
Richd	24	m	w	NY	San Francisco	1-Wd San Francisco	79	42
Richd	20	m	w	ENGL	San Francisco	1-Wd San Francisco	79	134
Robert	35	m	w	OH	Humboldt	Arcata Twp	72	229
Robert	27	m	w	OH	Yuba	Parks Bar Twp	93	648
Robt	58	m	w	DENM	Sacramento	Mississippi Twp	77	163
Ronald	34	m	w	MA	San Francisco	2-Wd San Francisco	79	261
S D	40	m	w	OH	Sacramento	3-Wd Sacramento	77	280
S D	26	m	w	MS	Klamath	Trinidad Twp	73	392
Saml C	42	m	w	VA	Butte	Hamilton Twp	70	63
Samuel	34	m	w	OH	Klamath	Sawyers Bar	73	378
Samuel	31	m	w	KY	San Francisco	7-Wd San Francisco	81	177
Solomon	45	m	w	IREL	Nevada	Bridgeport Twp	75	125
Stephen	52	m	m	MO	El Dorado	Coloma Twp	72	9
Thomas	48	m	w	SCOT	San Francisco	6-Wd San Francisco	81	90
Thomas	43	m	w	PA	San Francisco	San Francisco P O	83	364
Thomas	27	m	w	MA	Monterey	San Juan Twp	74	415
Thomas	26	m	w	CANA	Alameda	Oakland	68	158
Thomas J	47	m	w	NC	Inyo	Bishop Crk Twp	73	316
Thos B	48	m	w	ENGL	San Francisco	San Francisco P O	83	10
V G	48	m	w	VA	Nevada	Bridgeport Twp	75	117
W J	41	m	w	PA	El Dorado	Lake Valley Twp	72	63
William	55	m	w	IREL	San Francisco	San Francisco P O	83	335
William	49	m	w	IL	San Francisco	San Francisco P O	85	743
William	44	m	w	AL	San Francisco	11-Wd San Francisc	84	552
William	42	m	w	MO	Nevada	Eureka Twp	75	132
William	41	m	w	MO	Nevada	Eureka Twp	75	136
William	37	m	w	PA	Los Angeles	El Monte Twp	73	457
William	36	m	w	IREL	Contra Costa	Martinez P O	71	416
William	35	m	w	IREL	San Francisco	San Francisco P O	83	150
William	24	m	w	CANA	Klamath	Trinidad Twp	73	392
William C	37	m	w	PA	Los Angeles	El Monte Twp	73	448
William H	28	m	w	ENGL	San Francisco	6-Wd San Francisco	81	135
William S	41	m	w	NY	Yolo	Cache Crk Twp	93	448
Wm	55	m	w	KY	Santa Clara	Gilroy Twp	88	100
Wm	50	m	w	SCOT	San Francisco	11-Wd San Francisc	84	689
Wm	34	m	w	IREL	San Francisco	7-Wd San Francisco	81	265
Wm H	38	m	w	OH	Mono	Bridgeport P O	74	282
Zadock F	35	m	w	NY	San Francisco	San Francisco P O	83	107
BELLA								
Antonio	53	m	w	CHIL	Santa Clara	Alviso Twp	88	28
BELLACH								
Fermond	55	m	w	CHIL	San Mateo	Schoolhouse Statio	87	339
BELLADIN								
Albert	48	m	w	NORW	San Francisco	7-Wd San Francisco	81	281
BELLAH								
Cyrus	46	m	w	AR	Sonoma	Cloverdale Twp	91	270
Saml	47	m	w	AR	Santa Barbara	San Buenaventura P	87	420
BELLAIR								
Eugene	44	m	w	FRAN	San Francisco	6-Wd San Francisco	81	105
BELLAM								
E J	40	m	w	ENGL	Santa Clara	Almaden Twp	88	19
BELLAMY								
George	31	m	w	MO	San Bernardino	San Bernardino Twp	78	438
Jesusa	62	f	w	CA	Santa Clara	1-Wd San Jose	88	264
BELLANCOURT								
Noel	43	m	w	FRAN	San Francisco	San Francisco P O	83	136
BELLAND								
Edward	36	m	w	NY	San Francisco	5-Wd San Francisco	81	11
BELLANENT								
T C	36	m	w	AZOR	Monterey	Monterey	74	360
BELLANG								
Anna	35	f	w	ENGL	Alameda	Murray Twp	68	121
BELLANI								
Gottard	30	m	w	SWIT	Napa	Napa Twp	75	59
BELLAR								
Asa	44	m	w	ME	Humboldt	Mattole Twp	72	285
BELLE								
Alfred	36	m	w	IL	Colusa	Butte Twp	71	268
Soloman	48	m	w	PRUS	Alameda	Oakland	68	151
BELLEAU								
Ann	47	f	w	LA	San Francisco	San Francisco P O	80	363
BELLECOMB								
Andrew	11	m	w	CA	San Luis Obispo	Salinas Twp	87	289
BELLEHMY								
Geo L	40	m	w	CANA	Monterey	Salinas Twp	74	311
BELLEMERE								
Louis	70	m	w	FRAN	San Francisco	11-Wd San Francisc	84	444
BELLEN								
B T	28	m	w	IL	Lake	Lower Lake	73	415
James	46	m	w	NC	Tuolumne	Big Oak Flat P O	93	402
BELLENDA								
Rafael	36	m	w	MEXI	San Luis Obispo	San Luis Obispo Tw	87	312
BELLEW								
James	23	m	w	IREL	San Francisco	1-Wd San Francisco	79	41
John	56	m	w	IREL	San Francisco	1-Wd San Francisco	79	41
Joseph M	40	m	w	LA	Santa Clara	1-Wd San Jose	88	243
Wm	8	m	w	CA	Butte	Kimshew Tpw	70	85
BELLEY								
Charles	35	m	w	ENGL	Santa Clara	2-Wd San Jose	88	303
BELLI								
Francis	40	m	w	FRAN	San Francisco	2-Wd San Francisco	79	212
Victor	35	m	w	FRAN	Amador	Volcano P O	69	373
BELLIER								
Eugene	35	m	w	FRAN	San Francisco	San Francisco P O	83	136
BELLINA								
Antone	38	m	w	PORT	Alameda	Eden Twp	68	69
BELLINGALL								
Peter	26	m	w	IL	San Francisco	8-Wd San Francisco	82	448
BELLINGER								
David	44	m	w	NY	Sierra	Table Rock Twp	89	572
John	32	m	w	NY	Nevada	Meadow Lake Twp	75	259
BELLINGHAM								
Abraham	37	m	w	IREL	Sonoma	Bodega Twp	91	255
Rob	55	m	w	ENGL	San Francisco	2-Wd San Francisco	79	259
BELLINGHUFF								
Cyrus	35	m	w	OH	Solano	Silveyville Twp	90	79
BELLINGS								
Wm H	31	m	w	ME	Sacramento	Georgianna Twp	77	131
BELLIPS								
Edwd	87	m	w	VA	Butte	Chico Twp	70	42
BELLISLE								
Frank	36	m	w	CANA	San Francisco	11-Wd San Francisc	84	560
BELLISTENOS								
Ramon	19	m	w	CA	Marin	San Rafael Twp	74	37
BELLITS								
W	29	m	w	ENGL	Sierra	Butte Twp	89	510
BELLIX								
Wm	21	m	w	VA	Sonoma	Bodega Twp	91	261
BELLKNAP								
Margret	38	f	w	CANA	San Joaquin	3-Wd Stockton	86	219
BELLMAN								
Antone	22	m	w	BADE	San Bernardino	Chino Twp	78	410
Charles	30	m	w	PA	San Francisco	San Francisco P O	83	216
Fredk	30	m	w	HDAR	San Francisco	San Francisco P O	83	295
Herman	33	m	w	BREM	San Francisco	San Francisco P O	83	326
John	35	m	w	FRAN	Alameda	Murray Twp	68	123
BELLMANAP								
Ida	9	f	w	CA	San Francisco	San Francisco P O	85	798
BELLMER								
Jno	37	m	w	HANO	Sacramento	3-Wd Sacramento	77	295
Mary	20	f	w	NY	San Francisco	11-Wd San Francisc	84	609
BELLOLI								
Joseph	28	m	w	ITAL	Santa Clara	Santa Clara Twp	88	145
BELLON								
Lewis	30	m	w	CANA	Sonoma	Sonoma Twp	91	431
BELLOTS								
Julius	38	m	w	SWIT	San Francisco	1-Wd San Francisco	79	128
BELLOUS								
Charles D	40	m	w	NY	Colusa	Colusa	71	288
BELLOW								
John	39	m	w	HI	Yolo	Merritt Twp	93	507
Peter	31	m	w	AUST	San Francisco	1-Wd San Francisco	79	128
BELLOWS								
Albert	32	m	w	VT	Sonoma	Vallejo Twp	91	459
Ed St John	30	m	w	NY	San Francisco	San Francisco P O	83	112
Geo	38	m	w	KY	El Dorado	Coloma Twp	72	3
George	39	m	w	GREE	Plumas	Indian Twp	77	16
Horace	36	m	w	NY	Inyo	Cerro Gordo Twp	73	323
James	40	m	w	ENGL	San Joaquin	2-Wd Stockton	86	168
Lewis	28	m	w	NY	San Francisco	8-Wd San Francisco	82	298
Wm	32	m	w	TN	San Joaquin	2-Wd Stockton	86	193
BELLRUDE								
John	42	m	w	NORW	Marin	Sausalito Twp	74	69
BELLS								
Enoch A	22	m	w	IL	Siskiyou	Callahan P O	89	629
Jennie	21	f	w	SCOT	Solano	Vallejo	90	177
Sherman	46	m	w	OH	Sonoma	Petaluma Twp	91	365
BELLSCH								
J	30	m	w	NY	Alameda	Oakland	68	147
BELLSTEDT								
John	48	m	w	HANO	San Francisco	11-Wd San Francisc	84	476
BELLTIER								
Joseph	37	m	w	FRAN	San Francisco	1-Wd San Francisco	79	136
BELLTRAN								
Francisca	56	f	w	MEXI	Santa Clara	2-Wd San Jose	88	310
BELLUE								
Cornelle	24	m	w	FRAN	Yuba	Slate Range Bar Tw	93	670
BELLUGAUD								
Charles	30	m	w	FRAN	San Francisco	San Francisco P O	80	538
BELLUOMINI								
G	34	m	w	ITAL	Amador	Jackson P O	69	333
John	38	m	w	ITAL	Amador	Jackson P O	69	333

© 2001 by Heritage Quest. All rights reserved.

Series M593

Name	Age	S	R	B-PL	County	Locale	Roll	Pg
BELLVILLE								
Charles	27	m	w	CANA	San Francisco	San Francisco P O	83	217
John	32	m	w	OH	Colusa	Butte Twp	71	266
Jules	45	m	w	FRAN	Siskiyou	Callahan P O	89	628
Michael	32	m	w	CANA	Marin	San Rafael Twp	74	32
W W	54	m	w	DE	San Joaquin	Elkhorn Twp	86	61
BELLY								
Ah	19	m	c	CHIN	Placer	Dutch Flat P O	76	409
BELMARE								
Alexandrine	28	f	w	NY	San Francisco	8-Wd San Francisco	82	444
BELMONT								
Gaspar	32	m	w	FRAN	Santa Barbara	Santa Barbara P O	87	454
BELMORE								
Harris	29	m	w	ME	Placer	Emigrant Gap P O	76	417
John	34	m	w	ME	Placer	Emigrant Gap P O	76	417
Jos	30	m	w	NY	Solano	Vallejo	90	160
BELNAP								
Francis	18	f	w	CA	San Joaquin	Douglas Twp	86	45
BELOF								
Margaret	34	f	w	HCAS	San Francisco	2-Wd San Francisco	79	220
BELON								
Sarah	29	f	w	IREL	Alameda	Oakland	68	219
BELOSA								
Marqueta	28	f	w	CHIL	Santa Clara	2-Wd San Jose	88	315
BELSHAW								
Benjn L	36	m	w	NY	San Francisco	5-Wd San Francisco	81	6
John F	36	m	w	NY	Inyo	Cerro Gordo Twp	73	319
Mortimer	40	m	w	NY	Inyo	Bishop Crk Twp	73	310
BELSHE								
Robert F	19	m	w	CA	Yolo	Cottonwood Twp	93	462
BELSON								
Wm	40	m	w	ENGL	Sacramento	Granite Twp	77	149
BELT								
George	35	m	w	ASEA	San Francisco	7-Wd San Francisco	81	158
R K	44	m	w	KY	San Joaquin	Dent Twp	86	25
Rufus K	53	m	w	MD	Stanislaus	Empire Twp	92	33
Thomas	35	m	w	NY	San Francisco	5-Wd San Francisco	81	29
Thos	45	m	w	ENGL	Nevada	Nevada Twp	75	296
Venania	38	f	w	CHIL	Merced	Snelling P O	74	270
BELTAN								
Gerolamo	39	m	w	ITAL	San Francisco	11-Wd San Francisc	84	591
BELTMAN								
Galino	21	m	w	MEXI	Santa Clara	Almaden Twp	88	5
BELTON								
Henrietta	66	f	w	PRUS	San Francisco	6-Wd San Francisco	81	103
Nathaniel	37	m	w	ENGL	San Francisco	1-Wd San Francisco	79	98
William H	29	m	w	NC	Colusa	Colusa	71	295
BELTONIS								
Mateo	38	m	w	MEXI	Kern	Kernville P O	73	367
BELTRAM								
Garina	24	m	w	MEXI	Santa Clara	Burnett Twp	88	34
Rosa	30	f	w	MEXI	San Francisco	6-Wd San Francisco	81	71
BELTRAN								
Bantuss	47	m	i	MEXI	Inyo	Lone Pine Twp	73	333
Giuseppe	28	m	w	SPAI	San Francisco	11-Wd San Francisc	84	591
BELTRON								
Peter	23	m	w	MEXI	Butte	Oregon Twp	70	123
BELTS								
Beldner S	5	m	w	CA	Stanislaus	North Twp	92	67
James	35	m	w	PA	Stanislaus	Empire Twp	92	54
BELUIN								
Heny	26	m	w	ENGL	San Joaquin	Douglas Twp	86	30
BELUS								
Juan	43	m	w	MEXI	Calaveras	San Andreas P O	70	180
BELVAL								
Jose	43	m	w	CHIL	Los Angeles	Los Angeles Twp	73	485
BELVINNE								
Francis	54	m	w	FRAN	San Francisco	2-Wd San Francisco	79	189
BELYAN								
H	35	m	w	ME	Alameda	Oakland	68	263
BELZEN								
Harriet	35	f	w	NY	San Francisco	8-Wd San Francisco	82	417
BELZER								
Gustavus A	38	m	w	WURT	Santa Cruz	Pajaro Twp	89	348
BELZITCH								
N	31	m	w	AUST	San Joaquin	1-Wd Stockton	86	130
BELZONE								
L	35	m	w	ITAL	Alameda	Oakland	68	221
BEM								
Ah	35	m	c	CHIN	Butte	Hamilton Twp	70	72
Valentine	30	m	w	SWED	Monterey	San Juan Twp	74	390
BEMAN								
Alfred	63	m	w	MA	San Francisco	6-Wd San Francisco	81	112
John	65	m	w	NY	San Francisco	8-Wd San Francisco	82	363
Wm Floyd	21	m	b	MS	San Joaquin	Douglas Twp	86	38
BEMENS								
Sam	38	m	w	OH	Trinity	Weaverville Pct	92	231
BEMENT								
Geo	42	m	w	NY	Napa	Napa Twp	75	72
BEMER								
Fred	32	m	w	SWIT	San Francisco	2-Wd San Francisco	79	200
Kate	20	f	w	NY	San Francisco	8-Wd San Francisco	82	455
Rudolphe	17	m	w	CA	San Francisco	11-Wd San Francisc	84	587
BEMIS								
Ames	41	m	w	NY	San Bernardino	San Bernardino Twp	78	419
Eugene	34	m	w	OH	El Dorado	Diamond Springs Tw	72	34
George A	40	m	w	CT	San Bernardino	San Bernardino Twp	78	451
John	43	m	w	MO	Yolo	Putah Twp	93	511
Levi	9	m	w	CA	San Bernardino	San Bernardino Twp	78	420
O S	55	m	w	CT	Tuolumne	Sonora P O	93	309
Robert	39	m	w	ME	Calaveras	San Andreas P O	70	198
Samuel	60	m	w	MA	Placer	Rocklin Twp	76	468
BEMISS								
Frank	35	m	w	CANA	Solano	Vallejo	90	166
BEMIUS								
Iago	40	m	w	MEXI	Calaveras	San Andreas P O	70	182
BEMMERLY								
John	46	m	w	GERM	Yolo	Grafton Twp	93	489
Michael	44	m	w	GERM	Yolo	Cache Crk Twp	93	452
BEMUS								
Harman	50	m	w	PRUS	Placer	Summit P O	76	496
James S	23	m	w	IA	Yolo	Fremont Twp	93	477
BEMVAIS								
A B	41	m	w	MA	Tuolumne	Columbia P O	93	337
BEN								
Ah	61	m	c	CHIN	Tuolumne	Big Oak Flat P O	93	402
Ah	58	m	c	CHIN	Trinity	Lewiston Pct	92	214
Ah	56	m	c	CHIN	Placer	Lincoln P O	76	484
Ah	55	m	c	CHIN	Stanislaus	Emory Twp	92	17
Ah	49	m	c	CHIN	Tuolumne	Big Oak Flat P O	93	400
Ah	46	m	c	CHIN	Amador	Fiddletown P O	69	426
Ah	46	m	c	CHIN	Sierra	Eureka Twp	89	526
Ah	41	m	c	CHIN	Mariposa	Mariposa P O	74	134
Ah	40	m	c	CHIN	Placer	Newcastle Twp	76	477
Ah	33	m	c	CHIN	Butte	Ophir Twp	70	117
Ah	32	m	c	CHIN	Placer	Auburn P O	76	373
Ah	32	m	c	CHIN	Placer	Dutch Flat P O	76	408
Ah	30	m	c	CHIN	Tuolumne	Chinese Camp P O	93	390
Ah	30	m	c	CHIN	Sierra	Sears Twp	89	554
Ah	30	m	c	CHIN	Shasta	American Ranch P O	89	497
Ah	28	m	c	CHIN	Tuolumne	Columbia P O	93	350
Ah	28	m	c	CHIN	Placer	Gold Run Twp	76	398
Ah	28	m	c	CHIN	Nevada	Meadow Lake Twp	75	257
Ah	27	m	c	CHIN	Butte	Hamilton Twp	70	68
Ah	24	m	c	CHIN	Sacramento	Georgianna Twp	77	124
Ah	24	m	c	CHIN	Nevada	Meadow Lake Twp	75	256
Ah	24	m	c	CHIN	Amador	Sutter Crk P O	69	409
Ah	20	m	c	CHIN	Nevada	Meadow Lake Twp	75	249
Ah	19	m	c	CHIN	Sacramento	3-Wd Sacramento	77	309
Ah	16	m	c	CHIN	Placer	Bath P O	76	460
Ah	13	m	c	CHIN	San Francisco	7-Wd San Francisco	81	284
Ardilla	47	f	w	FRAN	Los Angeles	Los Angeles	73	517
Charles	26	m	w	PRUS	Contra Costa	Martinez P O	71	393
Chu	42	m	c	CHIN	Santa Clara	Santa Clara Twp	88	165
Lee	45	m	c	CHIN	Siskiyou	Yreka	89	661
Me	26	m	c	CHIN	Yuba	Marysville	93	626
Thomas	25	m	w	IREL	San Francisco	11-Wd San Francisc	84	431
U	18	m	c	CHIN	San Francisco	San Francisco P O	83	131
Yet	28	m	c	CHIN	Yuba	Slate Range Bar Tw	93	678
BENADON								
John	45	m	w	OH	Stanislaus	Branch Twp	92	1
BENAGAR								
William	40	m	w	NORW	San Francisco	7-Wd San Francisco	81	217
BENAIR								
Frank A	24	m	w	BRAN	Fresno	Kingston P O	72	219
BENAN								
Jno	27	m	w	IREL	San Joaquin	Dent Twp	86	29
Martha	7	f	w	CA	Colusa	Monroe Twp	71	321
BENANDER								
Julia	27	f	w	IREL	San Francisco	San Francisco P O	80	347
BENARD								
Alexander	45	m	w	FRAN	Amador	Jackson P O	69	338
John	33	m	w	FRAN	Marin	San Rafael Twp	74	39
Joseph H	54	m	w	PA	Santa Cruz	Soquel Twp	89	445
Louis	46	m	w	AUST	Amador	Sutter Crk P O	69	400
Manuel	34	m	w	PORT	Alameda	Eden Twp	68	72
BENARDE								
Frank	38	m	w	FRAN	Los Angeles	Los Angeles	73	552
BENARDITCH								
J	40	m	w	AUST	Amador	Sutter Crk P O	69	406
BENARDO								
A	36	m	w	FRAN	Santa Clara	Almaden Twp	88	5
BENARTS								
Peter	27	m	w	FRAN	San Francisco	8-Wd San Francisco	82	373
BENAVOUR								
Frank	37	m	w	FRAN	Calaveras	Copperopolis P O	70	241
BENBEN								
David	30	m	w	WALE	Sacramento	4-Wd Sacramento	77	364
BENBOW								
Thomas	47	m	w	ENGL	Alameda	Washington Twp	68	283
BENBRIDGE								
Arness	37	m	w	ENGL	San Francisco	2-Wd San Francisco	79	160
BENBROOK								
Charles M	46	m	w	KY	Los Angeles	Los Angeles	73	567
BENC								
Chals	46	m	w	FRAN	San Francisco	2-Wd San Francisco	79	145
BENCE								
Dennis P	49	m	w	IN	Placer	Bath P O	76	460
BENCER								
Alexander	56	m	w	FRAN	Santa Cruz	Soquel Twp	89	449
BENCH								
Mark	27	m	w	MA	Santa Clara	Gilroy Twp	88	100
BENCHLEY								
Lem B	47	m	w	NY	San Francisco	6-Wd San Francisco	81	116

© 2001 by Heritage Quest. All rights reserved.

California 1870 Census

Series M593

Name	Age	S	R	B-PL	County	Locale	Roll	Pg
BENCKE								
D	27	m	w	PRUS	San Francisco	San Francisco P O	83	289
BENCLEIE								
Dalilia	49	f	w	FRAN	San Francisco	2-Wd San Francisco	79	175
BENCON								
Guadalupa	15	m	w	CA	Monterey	Monterey Twp	74	349
Roman	40	m	w	MEXI	Kern	Havilah P O	73	341
BENDEL								
Chas	35	m	w	IA	Butte	Ophir Twp	70	119
BENDELBEN								
Lather	30	m	w	BAVA	Santa Clara	San Jose Twp	88	218
BENDELL								
Joseph	30	m	w	NY	Yuba	Long Bar Twp	93	564
BENDEN								
B S	38	m	w	PA	San Joaquin	3-Wd Stockton	86	231
BENDER								
Adam	47	m	w	PA	Amador	Volcano P O	69	383
Chas	45	m	w	PRUS	San Francisco	5-Wd San Francisco	81	5
D A	26	m	w	OH	Sacramento	3-Wd Sacramento	77	315
Edward	32	m	w	BAVA	Yolo	Cache Crk Twp	93	429
Edward	29	m	w	MD	Santa Cruz	Santa Cruz	89	407
Elias	48	m	w	PA	Napa	Napa	75	39
Flora	22	f	w	OH	Sacramento	2-Wd Sacramento	77	214
Fred	28	m	w	FRAN	Tehama	Cottonwood Twp	92	161
Fred	23	m	w	BADE	Alameda	Eden Twp	68	58
Geo	15	m	w	PA	Solano	Vallejo	90	213
J	47	m	w	PA	Yuba	Marysville	93	590
Jacob	48	m	w	DC	San Francisco	San Francisco P O	80	384
James	36	m	w	HANO	San Francisco	1-Wd San Francisco	79	51
John	36	m	w	BAVA	Tuolumne	Big Oak Flat P O	93	393
Josiah	41	m	w	DC	San Francisco	San Francisco P O	83	90
Madelin	43	f	w	SWIT	San Francisco	5-Wd San Francisco	81	5
Mary J	37	f	w	CANA	Nevada	Grass Valley Twp	75	150
Nicholas	38	m	w	HDAR	Sonoma	Vallejo Twp	91	453
Nicola	19	m	w	PRUS	San Francisco	San Francisco P O	80	469
Thos	40	m	w	PRUS	Tehama	Tehama Twp	92	191
BENDERMAN								
Abm	46	m	w	HOLL	San Francisco	San Francisco P O	85	745
BENDET								
Morris	45	m	w	PRUS	San Francisco	11-Wd San Francisc	84	493
BENDICT								
Charles	50	m	w	FRAN	San Francisco	2-Wd San Francisco	79	241
BENDIG								
F C	52	m	w	PRUS	Napa	Napa	75	4
BENDING								
A	18	m	w	WI	Solano	Vallejo	90	193
BENDIT								
Isaac	52	m	w	PRUS	San Francisco	San Francisco P O	83	365
Samuel	36	m	w	PRUS	San Francisco	San Francisco P O	80	475
BENDITI								
Lewis	34	m	w	ITAL	Tuolumne	Big Oak Flat P O	93	393
BENDITO								
Felix	28	m	w	PORT	San Francisco	3-Wd San Francisco	79	330
BENDIXON								
Jacob	24	m	w	DENM	Contra Costa	Martinez P O	71	443
BENDIXSON								
James L	60	m	w	FRAN	San Francisco	8-Wd San Francisco	82	489
BENDLE								
John S	36	m	w	NY	Butte	Bidwell Twp	70	1
BENDOR								
W	44	m	w	PRUS	Sierra	Butte Twp	89	513
BENDSON								
A	32	m	w	PRUS	San Joaquin	Tulare Twp	86	264
BENDUS								
Jesus	40	m	w	CHIL	Calaveras	San Andreas P O	70	180
BENDY								
L N	40	m	w	CANA	Alameda	Oakland	68	201
BENE								
Selim	38	m	w	CANA	Amador	Volcano P O	69	380
BENEDET								
Louisa	25	m	w	ITAL	Santa Clara	Fremont Twp	88	48
BENEDICK								
C W	24	m	w	VA	Solano	Vallejo	90	148
E	25	f	w	IA	Sonoma	Santa Rosa	91	414
Martha	10	f	w	CA	Placer	Bath P O	76	423
BENEDICT								
Adolph	40	m	w	FRAN	San Francisco	San Francisco P O	83	241
B	40	m	w	IL	Alameda	Alameda	68	3
Chas B	19	m	w	VA	San Francisco	5-Wd San Francisco	81	19
Christian	29	m	w	MECK	Sacramento	Franklin Twp	77	120
Cortland	31	m	w	NY	San Francisco	11-Wd San Francisc	84	517
David	47	m	w	NY	Contra Costa	Martinez P O	71	408
Henry	19	m	w	NY	San Francisco	San Francisco P O	83	350
Jacob	40	m	w	CANA	San Francisco	11-Wd San Francisc	84	585
Jos	35	m	w	KY	Butte	Ophir Twp	70	110
M P	38	f	w	NY	Alameda	Oakland	68	204
Marrie	61	f	w	NY	Los Angeles	Los Angeles	73	535
Mary	76	f	w	VT	Alameda	Oakland	68	137
Newell	40	m	w	NY	Santa Cruz	Santa Cruz Twp	89	387
Newton	44	m	w	RI	San Francisco	11-Wd San Francisc	84	511
O	64	m	w	PRUS	Sierra	Lincoln Twp	89	552
Sophia	42	f	w	VT	San Francisco	San Francisco P O	83	149
Wm A	50	m	w	VA	San Francisco	5-Wd San Francisco	81	19
BENEDICTO								
John	46	m	w	ITAL	Santa Clara	Santa Clara Twp	88	157
BENEDIX								
John C H	47	m	w	SAXO	Placer	Bath P O	76	461
BENEFIELD								
Francis	25	m	w	MA	Santa Barbara	Santa Barbara P O	87	500
R W	48	m	w	IN	Santa Barbara	Santa Barbara P O	87	498
BENEKE								
John	21	m	w	HANO	San Francisco	2-Wd San Francisco	79	185
BENEKI								
A L	45	m	w	CHIL	Tuolumne	Chinese Camp P O	93	373
BENELLE								
Wm	30	m	w	CANA	San Francisco	11-Wd San Francisc	84	643
BENER								
Adolphus	41	m	w	BAVA	Calaveras	San Andreas P O	70	179
F M	40	m	w	PA	Alameda	Oakland	68	201
BENERITE								
J	7	f	i	CA	Alameda	Murray Twp	68	103
BENEUGH								
John	40	m	w	PRUS	San Francisco	San Francisco P O	83	415
BENEVIDES								
Madeline	1	f	w	CA	Sacramento	4-Wd Sacramento	77	378
BENEVIDUS								
Wm	4	m	w	CA	Sacramento	4-Wd Sacramento	77	378
BENFELD								
Conrad	32	m	w	SHOL	San Francisco	3-Wd San Francisco	79	287
BENFELDT								
Henry F H	42	m	w	MECK	Placer	Bath P O	76	437
BENFIELD								
Frederick	40	m	w	GERM	El Dorado	Placerville Twp	72	102
BENFORD								
Wm	24	m	w	AUST	Solano	Vallejo	90	200
BENFORT								
George	22	m	w	IN	Yolo	Cottonwood Twp	93	473
BENG								
---	42	m	c	CHIN	Siskiyou	Cottonwood Twp	89	592
Ah	45	m	c	CHIN	Contra Costa	Martinez P O	71	430
Ah	30	m	c	CHIN	San Francisco	6-Wd San Francisco	81	65
Henry	35	m	w	NY	Nevada	Meadow Lake Twp	75	269
Joseph	30	m	w	OH	Los Angeles	El Monte Twp	73	455
BENGEE								
G	20	m	w	CANA	Alameda	Oakland	68	175
BENGER								
Frank	45	m	w	SWIT	Siskiyou	Callahan P O	89	628
J W	20	m	w	IL	Sierra	Forest Twp	89	530
Louis	45	m	w	IL	Stanislaus	Branch Twp	92	9
BENGHAM								
William	37	m	w	ENGL	Monterey	San Juan Twp	74	406
BENGLER								
Jno	47	m	w	PA	San Francisco	5-Wd San Francisco	81	21
BENGLES								
Gr	50	m	w	ENGL	Sierra	Lincoln Twp	89	551
BENGOUGH								
Elizabeth	39	f	w	ENGL	Los Angeles	Los Angeles	73	537
BENHAM								
A A	40	m	w	PRUS	Tuolumne	Chinese Camp P O	93	390
Calhoun	46	m	w	OH	San Francisco	6-Wd San Francisco	81	73
Case	35	m	w	IL	Santa Cruz	Pajaro Twp	89	351
David	28	m	w	IL	Napa	Napa Twp	75	63
Elvira	70	f	w	NY	Santa Cruz	Watsonville	89	375
Henry V	50	m	w	OH	Plumas	Seneca Twp	77	49
Ira	51	m	w	VA	Napa	Napa Twp	75	63
John A	51	m	w	NY	San Francisco	1-Wd San Francisco	79	103
Mary L	57	f	w	VA	Sonoma	Salt Point	91	392
Peter	43	m	w	TN	Siskiyou	Big Valley Twp	89	580
Robert	36	m	w	KY	Yolo	Putah Twp	93	521
W	42	m	w	KY	Lassen	Susanville Twp	73	444
William	45	m	w	TN	Siskiyou	Big Valley Twp	89	581
BENHAN								
Joseph	35	m	w	NY	San Francisco	San Francisco P O	83	347
S W	27	m	w	NY	Solano	Vallejo	90	202
BENHARD								
Samuel	48	m	w	PA	San Francisco	San Francisco P O	83	365
BENHKE								
Fredrick	30	m	w	BREM	Napa	Napa	75	11
BENHOFF								
Frederika	31	f	w	HANO	San Francisco	2-Wd San Francisco	79	171
BENHPER								
S	25	m	w	ITAL	Sierra	Butte Twp	89	508
BENIGHT								
William	35	m	w	MO	Colusa	Colusa Twp	71	274
BENIGO								
Sevarac	46	m	w	MEXI	Los Angeles	Los Angeles	73	560
BENINA								
Manuel	34	m	i	CA	Inyo	Cerro Gordo Twp	73	320
Thomas	36	m	w	MEXI	San Francisco	San Francisco P O	80	465
BENING								
Andrew J	42	m	w	HESS	Sacramento	2-Wd Sacramento	77	210
BENIO								
Juana	45	f	w	CA	Santa Clara	Almaden Twp	88	19
BENIRES								
Joses	43	m	w	AZOR	San Francisco	1-Wd San Francisco	79	130
BENIS								
Henry	45	m	w	PRUS	Santa Barbara	Santa Barbara P O	87	485
BENISON								
George	53	m	w	ENGL	Sacramento	American Twp	77	66
BENITA								
Manuel	23	m	w	CA	Santa Barbara	Arroyo Burro P O	87	509
Martin	28	m	w	MEXI	Santa Clara	Almaden Twp	88	13
BENITO								
Antone	28	m	w	ITAL	Nevada	Nevada Twp	75	321

© 2001 by Heritage Quest. All rights reserved.

Series M593

Name	Age	S	R	B-PL	County	Locale	Roll	Pg
Carle	29	m	w	SPAI	San Francisco	11-Wd San Francisc	84	661
Jose	38	m	w	CA	Tulare	Visalia	92	299
Manuel	45	m	w	CHIL	Santa Barbara	Santa Maria P O	87	511
BENITOS								
Andrea	40	f	w	MEXI	San Mateo	Half Moon Bay P O	87	393
Ramon	33	m	w	CA	Los Angeles	Los Angeles	73	551
William	48	m	w	MEXI	San Mateo	Half Moon Bay P O	87	393
BENITZ								
Wm	56	m	w	BADE	Alameda	Oakland	68	149
BENIVER								
Joseph	15	m	w	ITAL	San Francisco	2-Wd San Francisco	79	179
BENJ								
Harry A	35	m	w	NY	San Francisco	5-Wd San Francisco	81	19
BENJAMIN								
Alexander	12	m	w	CA	Sacramento	2-Wd Sacramento	77	231
Alice	8	f	w	CA	Santa Cruz	Pajaro Twp	89	356
Augsts	40	m	w	MA	Sonoma	Petaluma Twp	91	343
B	19	m	w	MO	San Francisco	San Francisco P O	83	137
Bazellae	38	m	w	CT	San Francisco	11-Wd San Francisc	84	613
Ben	30	m	w	ENGL	San Francisco	7-Wd San Francisco	81	260
C D	39	m	w	OH	San Joaquin	Douglas Twp	86	51
Carrie	25	f	w	PA	San Francisco	San Francisco P O	80	428
Charles	47	m	b	NY	San Francisco	San Francisco P O	80	422
Charles E	29	m	w	NY	San Mateo	Redwood Twp	87	366
E	43	m	w	NY	Solano	Vallejo	90	213
E C	24	m	w	MA	San Francisco	8-Wd San Francisco	82	340
Edwin	39	m	w	NY	Klamath	Orleans Twp	73	379
F J	44	m	w	NY	Sonoma	Santa Rosa	91	423
Fred	37	m	w	NY	San Francisco	San Francisco P O	83	48
Geo W	41	m	w	VT	Sonoma	Washington Twp	91	469
Hector	53	m	w	NY	Butte	Bidwell Twp	70	2
J C	37	m	w	NY	Amador	Sutter Crk P O	69	405
Jacob	42	m	w	STHO	San Francisco	11-Wd San Francisc	84	443
James	35	m	w	NC	Del Norte	Happy Camp Twp	71	468
Jerome	30	m	w	MA	San Luis Obispo	Morro Twp	87	284
John	50	m	w	WALE	Amador	Sutter Crk P O	69	404
John	46	m	b	NY	Butte	Ophir Twp	70	92
John	43	m	w	OH	Placer	Bath P O	76	425
Joseph	38	m	w	NJ	San Joaquin	2-Wd Stockton	86	167
Joseph	33	m	w	CANA	Amador	Jackson P O	69	323
Julia	20	f	w	NY	San Francisco	San Francisco P O	83	115
Lizzie	7	f	w	NY	San Francisco	San Francisco P O	85	799
Louis	30	m	w	FRAN	Butte	Oregon Twp	70	133
Louisa	30	f	w	ENGL	San Francisco	7-Wd San Francisco	81	207
Lucien	59	m	b	FRAN	San Francisco	San Francisco P O	80	423
Nelson	35	m	w	NY	San Francisco	7-Wd San Francisco	81	220
Peter	30	m	w	CANA	Sacramento	American Twp	77	66
Peter	27	m	w	CANA	Calaveras	San Andreas P O	70	160
Philip	8	m	w	NY	San Francisco	San Francisco P O	85	800
Richard	51	m	w	IN	Santa Cruz	Pajaro Twp	89	356
Saml	56	m	w	VT	Alameda	Brooklyn	68	32
Sarah	30	f	w	SC	San Francisco	San Francisco P O	80	403
Sophia	15	f	w	CA	Butte	Ophir Twp	70	97
W H	26	m	w	CANA	Santa Clara	Gilroy Twp	88	92
William	48	m	w	ENGL	Placer	Colfax P O	76	388
Wm	35	m	w	GERM	San Francisco	8-Wd San Francisco	82	291
Wm C	44	m	w	CT	Butte	Hamilton Twp	70	64
BENJIMAN								
Isaac	38	m	w	PRUS	Los Angeles	Los Angeles	73	548
Reese P	53	m	w	ENGL	Butte	Oregon Twp	70	126
Sinon	37	m	w	POLA	Los Angeles	Los Angeles	73	548
BENKIRE								
John	32	m	w	PRUS	San Francisco	San Francisco P O	83	91
BENLIT								
John	24	m	w	PRUS	Inyo	Cerro Gordo Twp	73	323
BENMAN								
Frank	42	m	w	OH	Colusa	Monroe Twp	71	325
BENMIO								
Peter	34	m	w	FRAN	Alameda	Brooklyn Twp	68	39
BENMORE								
Dick	14	m	i	CA	Colusa	Stony Crk Twp	71	327
BENN								
George	36	m	w	OH	San Francisco	San Francisco P O	80	384
George	26	m	w	ENGL	Santa Barbara	Santa Barbara P O	87	484
Jno	42	m	w	IREL	Sonoma	Mendocino Twp	91	294
John	30	m	w	IREL	San Francisco	San Francisco P O	83	145
John	28	m	w	GERM	Santa Clara	San Jose Twp	88	205
John E	40	m	w	IREL	Tulare	Visalia	92	293
John S	30	m	w	IREL	San Francisco	7-Wd San Francisco	81	229
Jonathan	24	m	w	ENGL	Santa Barbara	Santa Barbara P O	87	483
Joseph	40	m	w	MA	San Francisco	San Francisco P O	83	269
Peyton W	40	m	w	MO	El Dorado	Diamond Springs Tw	72	26
Walter C	34	m	w	IREL	San Francisco	San Francisco P O	83	341
William	58	m	w	ENGL	Santa Barbara	Santa Barbara P O	87	488
BENNALLACK								
Eliza	35	f	w	ENGL	Nevada	Grass Valley Twp	75	165
BENNALLECK								
Clarrissa	10	f	w	CHIL	Nevada	Grass Valley Twp	75	188
James	34	m	w	ENGL	Nevada	Grass Valley Twp	75	198
Joseph	31	m	w	ENGL	Nevada	Grass Valley Twp	75	193
BENNAM								
Lewis	28	m	w	OH	Butte	Kimshew Tpw	70	78
BENNARD								
Cyrus	43	m	w	ME	Sacramento	Sutter Twp	77	381
John	36	m	w	IREL	San Francisco	11-Wd San Francisc	84	707
BENNARO								
Pablo	12	m	w	CA	San Francisco	San Francisco P O	80	332
BENNAUGH								
Jas	33	m	w	FRAN	Sierra	Sears Twp	89	560
BENNDORF								
Charles	27	m	w	SAXO	Nevada	Grass Valley Twp	75	178
BENNEDETTI								
Pasqualo	27	m	w	ITAL	San Francisco	6-Wd San Francisco	81	124
BENNEET								
John	40	m	w	SCOT	San Luis Obispo	San Luis Obispo Tw	87	297
BENNEFIELD								
Francis	50	m	w	HUNG	Tulare	Visalia	92	297
Willis	64	m	w	TN	Shasta	Fort Crook P O	89	476
BENNEHMAN								
Heny	29	m	w	PRUS	San Francisco	8-Wd San Francisco	82	337
BENNER								
Alden	36	m	w	ME	Stanislaus	Empire Twp	92	51
Clair	24	m	w	ME	Santa Clara	Redwood Twp	88	133
Danl J	23	m	w	PA	Yolo	Cache Crk Twp	93	425
David	45	m	w	OH	Butte	Chico Twp	70	20
David	39	m	w	PA	Butte	Oregon Twp	70	133
Henry	27	m	w	MA	Mariposa	Mariposa P O	74	135
Henry E	28	m	w	WI	Butte	Oregon Twp	70	133
Isaac	28	m	w	ME	Mendocino	Navarro & Big Rvr	74	174
Jacob	68	m	w	PA	Plumas	Seneca Twp	77	50
Jacob	65	m	w	PA	Butte	Oregon Twp	70	133
James B	35	m	w	MO	Tulare	Farmersville Twp	92	244
John	39	m	w	PA	Butte	Chico Twp	70	54
John	30	m	w	GERM	Los Angeles	Los Angeles	73	544
Paulina	8	f	w	PA	Santa Cruz	Santa Cruz	89	415
Thadius	26	m	w	PA	Butte	Oregon Twp	70	133
Wm Sr	33	m	w	PA	Butte	Oregon Twp	70	133
BENNERDA								
Maria	14	f	w	CA	San Diego	San Luis Rey	78	514
BENNERSCHIED								
Bruno	28	m	w	PRUS	San Francisco	8-Wd San Francisco	82	434
BENNERTS								
Charles	30	m	w	ENGL	Plumas	Indian Twp	77	17
BENNES								
Henry	30	m	w	GREE	Sacramento	4-Wd Sacramento	77	342
BENNET								
A J	6	f	w	CA	Klamath	Orleans Twp	73	380
Antone	26	m	w	SWIT	San Mateo	San Mateo P O	87	350
Charles	22	m	w	IA	San Mateo	Woodside P O	87	380
Charles	21	m	w	PA	Colusa	Colusa	71	295
Chas	38	m	w	TN	Humboldt	Arcata Twp	72	235
E P	39	m	w	NH	Trinity	North Fork Twp	92	221
E P	36	m	w	CANA	Fresno	Millerton P O	72	183
Edward	54	m	w	ME	San Mateo	Redwood Twp	87	364
Ellen	20	f	w	IREL	San Mateo	San Mateo P O	87	350
Erast	42	m	w	MS	Sonoma	Santa Rosa	91	419
Frank	50	m	w	NY	San Francisco	5-Wd San Francisco	81	26
Fred	29	m	w	PRUS	San Joaquin	2-Wd Stockton	86	202
G	63	m	w	PA	Calaveras	Copperopolis P O	70	236
George	27	m	w	MI	Sutter	Sutter Twp	92	122
H	18	m	w	NY	Alameda	Oakland	68	187
Henry	35	m	w	NY	San Francisco	San Francisco P O	80	532
Henry	27	m	w	NY	San Mateo	Schoolhouse Statio	87	333
Horan	28	m	w	MA	San Francisco	5-Wd San Francisco	81	14
J	62	m	w	VA	Calaveras	Copperopolis P O	70	229
J	31	m	w	IL	Calaveras	Copperopolis P O	70	236
James	44	m	w	KY	San Luis Obispo	Salinas Twp	87	288
James	31	m	w	IREL	Sonoma	Bodega Twp	91	260
James C	56	m	w	PA	San Mateo	Half Moon Bay P O	87	404
James P	35	m	w	NY	San Mateo	Redwood Twp	87	368
Jas	32	m	w	IREL	San Francisco	7-Wd San Francisco	81	235
Jerrey	42	m	w	MA	Trinity	Douglas	92	233
Jesse	29	m	w	IL	Yolo	Buckeye Twp	93	413
Jessee	47	m	w	TN	Colusa	Monroe Twp	71	315
John	53	m	w	ENGL	Sacramento	Natomas Twp	77	170
John	40	m	w	PORT	San Mateo	Pescadero P O	87	414
John	32	m	w	PORT	San Mateo	Pescadero P O	87	414
John	26	m	w	BADE	San Joaquin	1-Wd Stockton	86	127
John	21	m	w	IA	Humboldt	Pacific Twp	72	296
John	20	m	w	IL	Yuba	W Bear Rvr Twp	93	681
John D	29	m	w	WI	Sacramento	Brighton Twp	77	78
Joseph	35	m	w	IL	Yolo	Buckeye Twp	93	416
Louisa	21	f	w	CHIL	Sacramento	Franklin Twp	77	119
Marcos	28	m	w	ME	Trinity	Weaverville Pct	92	230
Michl	31	m	w	MA	San Francisco	5-Wd San Francisco	81	29
Paris	35	m	w	MO	Monterey	San Benito Twp	74	378
Paul W	34	m	w	MA	Inyo	Independence Twp	73	324
Peter	48	m	w	AUST	San Francisco	San Francisco P O	80	354
Rodney M	27	m	w	IL	Yolo	Buckeye Twp	93	413
Sam	36	m	w	IL	Sacramento	American Twp	77	65
T S	38	m	w	OH	Lassen	Susanville Twp	73	442
Thomas B	14	m	w	CA	Amador	Ione City P O	69	354
William	25	m	w	NY	San Mateo	Belmont P O	87	373
BENNETT								
A	54	m	w	PRUS	San Joaquin	2-Wd Stockton	86	192
A A	45	m	w	NY	Sacramento	3-Wd Sacramento	77	292
A B	43	m	w	NY	San Joaquin	2-Wd Stockton	86	159
A B	35	m	w	UNKN	San Joaquin	2-Wd Stockton	86	166
Abram E	28	m	w	MA	Nevada	Grass Valley Twp	75	201
Albert	42	m	w	CT	Solano	Maine Prairie Twp	90	46
Alfred	22	m	w	SCOT	San Francisco	1-Wd San Francisco	79	112
Alfred E	29	m	w	ENGL	San Francisco	6-Wd San Francisco	81	154
Allen	25	m	w	TX	Los Angeles	Los Angeles	73	516
Andrew	27	m	w	IREL	Yolo	Washington Twp	93	530

© 2001 by Heritage Quest. All rights reserved.

Name	Age	S	R	B-PL	County	Locale	Roll	Pg
						Series M593		
Ann D	45	f	w	GA	Fresno	Millerton P O	72	147
Anna	29	f	w	IL	San Bernardino	San Bernardino Twp	78	449
Ball	21	m	w	NY	Santa Cruz	Santa Cruz	89	425
C C	36	m	w	OH	Amador	Sutter Crk P O	69	406
C J	41	m	b	MD	San Joaquin	2-Wd Stockton	86	173
Caspar M	40	m	w	IN	Fresno	Millerton P O	72	184
Catherin	39	f	w	HANO	Sacramento	2-Wd Sacramento	77	244
Celestia	42	f	w	NY	Sacramento	Lee Twp	77	159
Charles	38	m	w	NY	San Francisco	7-Wd San Francisco	81	158
Chas	60	m	w	NH	Butte	Kimshew Tpw	70	82
Chas	39	m	w	ENGL	Butte	Ophir Twp	70	98
Chas	33	m	w	MA	Monterey	Pajaro Twp	74	368
Chas	26	m	w	ENGL	San Joaquin	Liberty Twp	86	88
Claude	19	m	w	MA	San Joaquin	Elkhorn Twp	86	58
Cornelius	41	m	w	IREL	Placer	Clipper Gap P O	76	392
Cristo	27	m	w	GREE	Placer	Bath P O	76	436
D C	36	m	w	GERM	San Joaquin	2-Wd Stockton	86	213
Daniel	24	m	w	CANA	Mendocino	Little Rvr Twp	74	171
David	49	m	w	IN	El Dorado	White Oak Twp	72	140
David	38	m	w	VA	Stanislaus	Empire Twp	92	66
Edwin S	41	m	w	MA	San Francisco	8-Wd San Francisco	82	321
Elihu	52	m	w	NY	Santa Cruz	Santa Cruz Twp	89	396
Eliza Ann	18	f	w	WI	Santa Cruz	Santa Cruz	89	416
Elphonzo	54	m	w	NY	Solano	Vacaville Twp	90	124
Emanuel	45	m	w	FRAN	Los Angeles	Los Angeles	73	553
Erasmus	27	m	w	IL	El Dorado	White Oak Twp	72	140
Erastus	23	m	w	ME	Santa Clara	Santa Clara Twp	88	167
Eugene	15	m	w	CA	Alameda	Oakland	68	258
F	23	m	w	ITAL	San Joaquin	Castoria Twp	86	1
F B	33	m	w	KY	Monterey	San Juan Twp	74	407
F M	35	m	w	IL	Humboldt	Table Bluff Twp	72	308
Fannie	22	f	w	AUSL	San Francisco	3-Wd San Francisco	79	320
Francis	45	m	w	NY	Sacramento	Cosumnes Twp	77	90
Francis	26	m	w	ENGL	Amador	Amador City P O	69	390
Frank	44	m	w	NY	Sacramento	Lee Twp	77	158
Frank	32	m	w	VT	Stanislaus	Empire Twp	92	49
G E	37	m	w	CT	Santa Clara	Gilroy Twp	88	102
G L	21	m	w	WI	San Francisco	8-Wd San Francisco	82	376
G W	37	m	w	ME	Lassen	Janesville Twp	73	430
G W	30	m	w	IREL	San Francisco	San Francisco P O	85	831
G W	28	m	w	NY	Merced	Snelling P O	74	268
Genoa	27	m	w	NY	Santa Clara	Redwood Twp	88	124
Geo	25	m	w	IA	San Joaquin	3-Wd Stockton	86	231
Geo H	14	m	w	CA	Colusa	Spring Valley Twp	71	335
Geo W	71	m	w	ENGL	Sonoma	Analy Twp	91	236
George	45	m	w	PA	San Francisco	2-Wd San Francisco	79	240
George	36	m	w	SCOT	Siskiyou	Callahan P O	89	633
George	28	m	w	PA	San Francisco	7-Wd San Francisco	81	181
George	21	m	w	MS	Los Angeles	Soledad Twp	73	632
George	21	m	w	VT	San Francisco	8-Wd San Francisco	82	330
George W	28	m	w	NY	Santa Clara	Santa Clara Twp	88	155
H	46	m	w	PA	Amador	Fiddletown P O	69	440
H	28	m	w	MI	Sacramento	3-Wd Sacramento	77	294
Hans	43	m	w	PRUS	San Francisco	8-Wd San Francisco	82	345
Henry	52	m	w	ENGL	San Francisco	San Francisco P O	83	163
Henry	40	m	w	FINL	Placer	Lincoln P O	76	486
Henry	39	m	w	ENGL	Calaveras	San Andreas P O	70	209
Henry	26	m	w	NJ	Shasta	Millville P O	89	484
Henry	19	m	w	CANA	Santa Clara	Fremont Twp	88	53
Henry C	56	m	w	ENGL	San Francisco	6-Wd San Francisco	81	127
Hy	45	m	w	ENGL	San Francisco	11-Wd San Francisc	84	613
Hy	45	m	w	ENGL	San Francisco	11-Wd San Francisc	84	613
Iri R	38	m	w	NY	Butte	Chico Twp	70	59
Isaac	49	m	w	ENGL	San Diego	San Diego	78	507
J	65	m	w	OH	Alameda	Oakland	68	239
J	60	m	w	NY	Alameda	Murray Twp	68	104
J	45	m	w	ENGL	Yuba	Marysville	93	604
J M	12	m	w	CA	Alameda	Oakland	68	242
J P	37	m	w	NY	San Francisco	3-Wd San Francisco	79	315
J W	41	m	w	SC	Amador	Sutter Crk P O	69	396
J W	32	m	w	ME	San Joaquin	3-Wd Stockton	86	240
James	42	m	w	NY	San Francisco	11-Wd San Francisc	84	686
James	28	m	w	NY	Stanislaus	Emory Twp	92	21
James F Jr	52	m	w	NY	Santa Cruz	Santa Cruz	89	428
James M	54	m	w	OH	Napa	Napa	75	14
James S	40	m	w	MD	San Francisco	3-Wd San Francisco	79	312
James W	46	m	w	MD	Calaveras	San Andreas P O	70	210
Jas	35	m	w	CANA	Solano	Vallejo	90	161
Jas	27	m	w	ENGL	Klamath	Liberty Twp	73	374
Jessie	23	m	w	CA	Yolo	Putah Twp	93	526
Jno W	24	m	w	MI	Butte	Chico Twp	70	44
John	64	m	w	NH	San Francisco	San Francisco P O	83	330
John	46	m	w	ENGL	Nevada	Grass Valley Twp	75	145
John	45	m	w	IREL	Sacramento	4-Wd Sacramento	77	321
John	40	m	w	MA	San Joaquin	Elkhorn Twp	86	53
John	4	m	w	CA	Klamath	South Fork Twp	73	384
John	36	m	w	MI	San Joaquin	2-Wd Stockton	86	162
John	33	m	w	ENGL	San Joaquin	2-Wd Stockton	86	191
John	33	m	w	IREL	Merced	Snelling P O	74	255
John	30	m	w	ENGL	Contra Costa	Martinez P O	71	414
John	24	m	w	IREL	San Francisco	San Francisco P O	83	312
John	18	m	w	SCOT	San Francisco	San Francisco P O	83	282
John	14	m	w	AR	Tulare	Venice Twp	92	274
John F	24	m	w	WI	Nevada	Grass Valley Twp	75	145
John J	48	m	w	NY	Placer	Auburn P O	76	366
John M	43	m	w	TN	Sierra	Sears Twp	89	556
John N	42	m	w	MA	Placer	Dutch Flat P O	76	409
John W	34	m	w	VA	Stanislaus	Washington Twp	92	86
Joseph	65	m	w	VA	Nevada	Rough & Ready Twp	75	335
Joseph	36	m	w	CANA	Marin	San Rafael	74	52
Joseph	35	m	w	ENGL	Alameda	Hayward	68	74
Joseph	32	m	w	SCOT	Alameda	Eden Twp	68	70
Joseph	31	m	w	NY	Marin	Sausalito Twp	74	70
Joseph	30	m	w	FRAN	San Francisco	2-Wd San Francisco	79	146
Joseph	25	m	w	IL	Los Angeles	Los Angeles Twp	73	468
Joseph L	60	m	w	VA	Los Angeles	Santa Ana Twp	73	600
Joseph W	38	m	w	MO	El Dorado	Mud Springs Twp	72	87
Kate	35	f	w	IREL	Santa Clara	2-Wd San Jose	88	335
L W	64	m	w	NY	Santa Clara	Almaden Twp	88	17
Lawrence	44	m	w	IREL	Sacramento	4-Wd Sacramento	77	324
Leah	75	f	w	PRUS	Yolo	Cottonwood Twp	93	463
Lizzie	12	f	w	CA	Santa Clara	Santa Clara Twp	88	167
Louis	33	m	w	ITAL	San Francisco	2-Wd San Francisco	79	164
M J	62	f	w	NH	Sacramento	1-Wd Sacramento	77	176
M S	35	f	w	NY	Sacramento	1-Wd Sacramento	77	183
Mahala	63	f	w	NY	Yuba	Long Bar Twp	93	563
Mansel V	35	m	w	AR	Santa Cruz	Santa Cruz	89	414
Maria	33	f	w	NY	San Francisco	11-Wd San Francisc	84	565
Mark	30	m	w	NY	Butte	Chico Twp	70	47
Marrion F	14	m	w	WI	San Joaquin	Elliott Twp	86	75
Martha	19	f	w	NY	San Francisco	6-Wd San Francisco	81	114
Martin	56	m	w	KY	Merced	Snelling P O	74	270
Martin	47	m	w	OH	Shasta	Fort Crook P O	89	476
Martin	16	m	w	POLA	San Francisco	8-Wd San Francisco	82	374
Mary	47	f	w	SCOT	San Francisco	11-Wd San Francisc	84	626
Mary	4	f	w	CA	Amador	Fiddletown P O	69	438
Mary	33	f	w	IREL	Sonoma	Petaluma Twp	91	322
Mary	20	f	b	NY	San Francisco	San Francisco P O	80	428
Mary A	42	f	w	IREL	San Francisco	San Francisco P O	83	71
Mathew	28	m	w	MA	San Francisco	11-Wd San Francisc	84	548
Michael	40	m	w	POLA	San Francisco	San Francisco P O	83	60
Morris	35	m	w	IREL	San Francisco	San Francisco P O	85	732
Nathl J	45	m	w	MA	Santa Cruz	Santa Cruz	89	433
Nicholas F	58	m	w	SWED	Butte	Ophir Twp	70	96
Norridan S	28	m	w	NY	Sacramento	2-Wd Sacramento	77	227
O R	24	m	w	IL	Mendocino	Little Lake Twp	74	195
Oley W	36	m	w	NORW	Inyo	Bishop Crk Twp	73	312
Orvil	31	m	w	NY	San Francisco	7-Wd San Francisco	81	162
Pat	47	m	w	IREL	Merced	Snelling P O	74	255
Patrick	45	m	w	IREL	Napa	Napa	75	47
Pedra	50	f	w	FRAN	Los Angeles	Los Angeles Twp	73	476
Peter	46	m	w	IREL	Los Angeles	Los Angeles	73	543
R H	42	m	w	MD	Alameda	Oakland	68	188
R J	31	m	w	MO	Santa Clara	Gilroy Twp	88	99
R M	26	m	w	IL	Santa Clara	Burnett Twp	88	30
R W	41	m	w	NY	Sacramento	1-Wd Sacramento	77	186
Reed	32	m	w	NY	Santa Clara	Redwood Twp	88	124
Richard	42	m	w	VT	El Dorado	Placerville Twp	72	102
Richard	30	m	w	ENGL	Amador	Amador City P O	69	393
Richard	23	m	w	ENGL	Sacramento	3-Wd Sacramento	77	273
Robert W	35	m	w	IL	Placer	Colfax P O	76	391
Robt	30	m	w	MO	San Joaquin	Oneal Twp	86	114
Rufus B	30	m	w	AR	Tulare	Venice Twp	92	274
S S	68	m	w	CANA	Mendocino	Little Lake Twp	74	195
Sam	25	m	w	NY	San Joaquin	Tulare Twp	86	264
Saml W	40	m	w	CT	Nevada	Rough & Ready Twp	75	327
Samuel	49	m	w	MA	San Francisco	San Francisco P O	80	381
Samuel	48	m	w	PRUS	San Francisco	11-Wd San Francisc	84	551
Sanford	53	m	w	NY	Sonoma	Mendocino Twp	91	295
Sophia	62	f	w	VT	San Francisco	8-Wd San Francisco	82	343
Stephen D	47	m	w	AL	Fresno	Millerton P O	72	147
T J	28	m	w	IL	Santa Clara	Burnett Twp	88	30
T Y	46	m	w	GA	Lake	Scotts Crk	73	427
Thomas	50	m	w	ENGL	San Francisco	6-Wd San Francisco	81	115
Thomas	31	m	w	ENGL	Nevada	Grass Valley Twp	75	166
Thomas	30	m	w	IREL	Los Angeles	Soledad Twp	73	630
Thos	52	m	w	AUST	San Francisco	1-Wd San Francisco	79	110
Thos M	34	m	w	ENGL	Nevada	Grass Valley Twp	75	181
W H	34	m	w	OH	Solano	Vallejo	90	196
W P	37	m	w	IL	Klamath	South Fork Twp	73	384
Walter	35	m	w	NY	San Diego	San Diego	78	493
Weston	48	m	w	GA	Santa Clara	Redwood Twp	88	134
William	62	m	w	ENGL	Nevada	Grass Valley Twp	75	154
William	36	m	w	IN	Santa Clara	1-Wd San Jose	88	254
William	32	m	w	ENGL	Inyo	Cerro Gordo Twp	73	318
William	32	m	w	ENGL	Calaveras	San Andreas P O	70	217
William	31	m	w	ENGL	Nevada	Grass Valley Twp	75	224
William	30	m	w	BAVA	Inyo	Cerro Gordo Twp	73	319
William	30	m	w	NY	Colusa	Grand Island Twp	71	306
William	29	m	w	MO	Monterey	San Benito Twp	74	378
William	22	m	w	ENGL	Amador	Amador City P O	69	394
William F	24	m	w	IL	Yolo	Cache Crk Twp	93	448
William T	37	m	w	IN	San Francisco	6-Wd San Francisco	81	106
Willm	54	m	w	ENGL	San Francisco	San Francisco P O	83	10
Wm	47	m	w	ENGL	Solano	Benicia	90	7
Wm	45	m	w	ENGL	Nevada	Nevada Twp	75	277
Wm	35	m	w	ENGL	Santa Clara	Almaden Twp	88	9
Wm	35	m	w	ENGL	San Bernardino	San Bernardino Twp	78	415
Wm	35	m	w	VT	Sacramento	1-Wd Sacramento	77	179
Wm	30	m	w	NY	Sacramento	3-Wd Sacramento	77	308
Wm	28	m	w	PRUS	San Francisco	1-Wd San Francisco	79	104
Wm C	43	m	w	CT	Santa Clara	Gilroy Twp	88	95
Wm E	39	m	w	CANA	Shasta	Horsetown P O	89	506
Wm L	25	m	w	IL	Mariposa	Maxwell Crk P O	74	144

© 2001 by Heritage Quest. All rights reserved.

Name	Age	S	R	B-PL	County	Locale	Roll	Pg
						Series M593		
Wrifield	30	m	w	MO	Monterey	San Benito Twp	74	378
BENNETTE								
Henry	15	m	w	WI	Stanislaus	Empire Twp	92	40
BENNETTI								
Agost	44	m	w	FRAN	Monterey	San Benito Twp	74	378
BENNETTO								
James	24	m	w	ENGL	Amador	Amador City P O	69	394
W A	24	m	w	ENGL	Amador	Amador City P O	69	392
BENNETTS								
George	34	m	w	ENGL	Nevada	Grass Valley Twp	75	148
James	23	m	w	ENGL	Amador	Amador City P O	69	392
John	43	m	w	ENGL	Nevada	Grass Valley Twp	75	190
John	25	m	w	ENGL	Amador	Amador City P O	69	390
Marya	38	f	w	ENGL	Nevada	Grass Valley Twp	75	223
Richard	35	m	w	ENGL	Placer	Colfax P O	76	392
Thomas	37	m	w	ENGL	Nevada	Grass Valley Twp	75	232
BENNIA								
Ale	42	m	w	FRAN	Amador	Volcano P O	69	378
BENNIGHT								
Lot	56	m	w	OH	Colusa	Monroe Twp	71	317
BENNIN								
Susan	23	f	w	IREL	Solano	Vallejo	90	146
BENNINGER								
Samuel	39	m	w	PA	El Dorado	Placerville	72	107
BENNINGTON								
E M	29	m	w	CANA	Alameda	Oakland	68	222
BENNIS								
A J	16	m	w	MO	Amador	Sutter Crk P O	69	396
Salomon	28	m	w	PRUS	Tuolumne	Sonora P O	93	311
Wm	40	m	w	OH	Sacramento	Center Twp	77	87
BENNISON								
Edward	51	m	w	CANA	Humboldt	Eureka Twp	72	268
BENNIX								
Thomas	50	m	w	NY	Kern	Tehachapi P O	73	355
BENNOVA								
Joseph	35	m	w	PORT	Marin	Sausalito Twp	74	68
BENNSON								
Minnie	2	f	w	CA	Humboldt	Table Bluff Twp	72	306
BENOIG								
Amidee	15	m	w	FRAN	San Francisco	3-Wd San Francisco	79	327
BENOIST								
Edward	26	m	w	LA	Amador	Jackson P O	69	337
William	19	m	w	CA	Mendocino	Big Rvr Twp	74	170
BENOIT								
Edward	22	m	w	CANA	Nevada	Grass Valley Twp	75	214
Gilbert	32	m	i	CANA	Inyo	Cerro Gordo Twp	73	320
Henry	40	m	w	HCAS	Placer	Auburn P O	76	380
Hubert	40	m	w	FRAN	San Francisco	2-Wd San Francisco	79	150
K	57	m	w	FRAN	Amador	Jackson P O	69	347
Philip	45	m	w	FRAN	San Francisco	1-Wd San Francisco	79	49
Seraphino	30	m	w	CANA	Nevada	Grass Valley Twp	75	213
BENONA								
R A	50	m	w	MEXI	Tuolumne	Sonora P O	93	307
BENORAS								
Bitala	28	m	i	MEXI	Inyo	Lone Pine Twp	73	334
BENORDEE								
Alfred	55	m	w	FRAN	San Mateo	Schoolhouse Statio	87	343
BENOT								
Juare	50	m	w	ITAL	San Luis Obispo	Arroyo Grande Twp	87	279
BENOUF								
Alphonse	29	m	w	FRAN	Marin	San Rafael Twp	74	37
BENRIMO								
Joseph	32	m	w	NY	San Francisco	6-Wd San Francisco	81	87
M A	35	m	w	ENGL	San Luis Obispo	San Luis Obispo Tw	87	297
BENRIST								
Torin S	52	m	w	MO	Mendocino	Big Rvr Twp	74	175
BENROSA								
Emanuel	51	m	w	MEXI	Fresno	Millerton P O	72	154
BENSACA								
Giovanni	25	m	w	SWIT	Santa Cruz	Pajaro Twp	89	358
BENSACCA								
Giuseppi	35	m	w	SWIT	Santa Cruz	Pajaro Twp	89	342
BENSE								
Charles	27	m	w	GERM	Contra Costa	Martinez P O	71	438
BENSEL								
Chas W	35	m	w	NY	San Francisco	San Francisco P O	83	62
BENSELL								
Geo A	64	m	w	PA	Sonoma	Cloverdale Twp	91	268
Herman M	26	m	w	PA	San Diego	San Diego	78	503
BENSEN								
Chas A	36	m	w	FRAN	San Francisco	7-Wd San Francisco	81	245
Mary	47	f	w	IREL	Sacramento	4-Wd Sacramento	77	327
BENSING								
John	19	m	w	WURT	San Francisco	7-Wd San Francisco	81	222
BENSINGER								
Danl	36	m	w	BADE	San Francisco	11-Wd San Francisc	84	607
BENSIT								
Alexr J	37	m	w	FRAN	San Francisco	1-Wd San Francisco	79	50
BENSLEY								
J L	36	m	w	NY	Napa	Napa	75	15
S	21	f	w	CA	Napa	Napa Twp	75	74
BENSO								
Eliza J	40	f	w	IREL	Sonoma	Vallejo Twp	91	453
BENSON								
A	46	m	w	MA	Lake	Big Valley	73	395
A	45	m	w	MA	Lake	Big Valley	73	394
Ada	37	f	w	KY	San Joaquin	Elkhorn Twp	86	67
Adeline	23	f	w	OH	Butte	Hamilton Twp	70	62
Alanson	35	m	w	NY	Contra Costa	San Pablo Twp	71	353
Alfred	53	m	w	NY	San Bernardino	San Bernardino Twp	78	427
Andw	34	m	w	IREL	San Francisco	1-Wd San Francisco	79	2
Anne	42	f	w	KY	San Francisco	11-Wd San Francisc	84	629
Augustine L	38	m	w	NY	San Mateo	San Mateo P O	87	371
Benj	34	m	w	SWIT	Solano	Vallejo	90	154
Benjamin	29	m	w	NORW	San Francisco	San Francisco P O	80	365
Capt	31	m	w	CT	San Joaquin	Tulare Twp	86	258
Catherine	78	f	w	IREL	San Francisco	8-Wd San Francisco	82	451
Charles	28	m	w	MA	San Francisco	7-Wd San Francisco	81	223
David	60	m	w	ENGL	Tuolumne	Columbia P O	93	351
Dora	18	f	w	PRUS	San Francisco	8-Wd San Francisco	82	498
Dora	13	f	w	CA	Sonoma	Analy Twp	91	241
Edwd	40	m	w	DENM	Fresno	Kings Rvr P O	72	203
Francis	40	m	w	IREL	Santa Clara	2-Wd San Jose	88	329
Francis	37	m	w	IREL	Sonoma	Analy Twp	91	229
Geo	21	m	w	MA	Alameda	Oakland	68	191
George S	23	m	w	NORW	Los Angeles	Los Angeles	73	542
Gerome	21	m	w	UT	San Bernardino	San Bernardino Twp	78	448
Henery	51	m	w	ENGL	San Francisco	7-Wd San Francisco	81	157
Henery	27	m	w	NORW	San Francisco	7-Wd San Francisco	81	218
Henry	53	m	w	NY	Contra Costa	San Pablo Twp	71	365
Henry	39	m	w	KY	Mendocino	Anderson Twp	74	154
Henry	21	m	w	HANO	San Francisco	San Francisco P O	83	23
Henry C	51	m	w	OH	Santa Clara	Santa Clara Twp	88	153
Isaac	35	m	w	NY	Tehama	Tehama Twp	92	191
J	48	m	w	SCOT	Alameda	Murray Twp	68	122
James	55	m	w	IREL	Calaveras	San Andreas P O	70	173
James	50	m	w	ENGL	San Francisco	San Francisco P O	83	16
James	30	m	w	ME	San Francisco	8-Wd San Francisco	82	493
James	20	m	w	NY	San Francisco	San Francisco P O	83	282
Jane	32	f	w	OH	San Joaquin	Union Twp	86	266
Jennie	24	f	w	IREL	San Francisco	San Francisco P O	80	349
Jenny	37	f	w	NY	San Francisco	5-Wd San Francisco	81	4
Jerome	58	m	w	NY	San Diego	San Jacinto Dist	78	517
John	54	m	w	SWED	Tehama	Cottonwood Twp	92	161
John	45	m	w	NY	San Francisco	6-Wd San Francisco	81	95
John	44	m	w	NY	Contra Costa	Martinez P O	71	367
John	37	m	w	IN	San Joaquin	Elkhorn Twp	86	66
John	32	m	w	IREL	Santa Clara	Fremont Twp	88	51
John	30	m	w	AR	San Joaquin	Union Twp	86	266
John	21	m	w	IREL	San Francisco	2-Wd San Francisco	79	213
John W	43	m	w	MA	Sonoma	Petaluma Twp	91	365
L S	51	m	w	VT	Napa	Yountville Twp	75	86
Lyman D	53	m	w	VT	Calaveras	San Andreas P O	70	164
M F	45	f	w	IREL	San Francisco	San Francisco P O	83	132
Maggie	22	f	w	IREL	Sacramento	4-Wd Sacramento	77	344
Margaret	52	f	w	DE	Solano	Vacaville Twp	90	121
Martin	26	m	w	PRUS	Solano	Maine Prairie Twp	90	53
Mary	20	f	w	IREL	San Francisco	5-Wd San Francisco	81	2
Nemasio	39	m	w	TX	Santa Cruz	Soquel Twp	89	449
Peer	31	m	w	SWED	Napa	Napa Twp	75	33
R N	52	m	w	RI	San Joaquin	1-Wd Stockton	86	135
Rachel	32	f	w	WI	Sonoma	Analy Twp	91	233
Richard	31	m	w	SCOT	Siskiyou	Scott Valley Twp	89	619
Robert	27	m	w	IREL	Mendocino	Albion & Big Rvr T	74	166
Sandford	27	m	w	IREL	Contra Costa	Martinez P O	71	445
Sarah	21	f	w	IREL	San Francisco	11-Wd San Francisc	84	494
Theodore	21	m	w	MS	Santa Barbara	San Buenaventura P	87	424
Thomas	24	m	w	MO	Solano	Vacaville Twp	90	133
Thomas A	52	m	w	NORW	San Francisco	3-Wd San Francisco	79	287
W	23	m	w	IA	Lassen	Susanville Twp	73	446
William H	43	m	w	PA	Nevada	Grass Valley Twp	75	150
BENSSON								
Ada	46	f	w	FRAN	Los Angeles	Los Angeles	73	541
BENSTEN								
Jennettie	59	f	w	SCOT	San Francisco	San Francisco P O	85	846
BENSWEGER								
Leo	22	m	w	PA	San Francisco	5-Wd San Francisco	81	13
BENSWINGER								
Louis	60	m	w	BAVA	San Francisco	2-Wd San Francisco	79	236
BENT								
Ah	28	m	c	CHIN	Sacramento	1-Wd Sacramento	77	198
E F	31	m	w	MA	San Francisco	San Francisco P O	85	777
Edward	53	m	w	OH	Contra Costa	Martinez Twp	71	349
Eliza	51	f	w	ENGL	San Joaquin	3-Wd Stockton	86	215
Henry K	38	m	w	MA	Los Angeles	Los Angeles	73	540
Jesse	46	m	m	CT	Sonoma	Analy Twp	91	225
John W	30	m	w	NY	Los Angeles	El Monte Twp	73	460
Joseph	26	m	w	NY	Los Angeles	Santa Ana Twp	73	599
Louis	38	m	w	KY	San Francisco	5-Wd San Francisco	81	30
Margaret	30	f	w	IREL	San Francisco	San Francisco P O	83	109
Mary E	26	f	w	IREL	Placer	Colfax P O	76	384
Mathew	35	m	w	FRAN	Los Angeles	Los Angeles Twp	73	473
N C	59	m	w	NY	San Joaquin	3-Wd Stockton	86	231
Nathan	22	m	w	MA	San Joaquin	1-Wd Stockton	86	141
Prince S	34	m	b	CT	Sacramento	Granite Twp	77	145
Sacaria	41	f	w	MEXI	Mariposa	Mariposa P O	74	94
Silas	43	m	w	CANA	Contra Costa	Martinez P O	71	433
Silas S	51	m	w	MA	San Francisco	2-Wd San Francisco	79	199
Tupper	23	m	w	MO	Contra Costa	Martinez Twp	71	349
Wm	29	m	w	ENGL	San Francisco	7-Wd San Francisco	81	254
BENTEEN								
T C	33	m	w	VA	Sacramento	4-Wd Sacramento	77	330
BENTEN								
Josh	20	m	w	US	San Joaquin	Castoria Twp	86	9

© 2001 by Heritage Quest. All rights reserved.

						Series M593		
Name	Age	S	R	B-PL	County	Locale	Roll	Pg
BENTER								
David	66	m	w	KY	San Joaquin	Oneal Twp	86	118
Ellen	20	f	w	AUSL	San Francisco	San Francisco P O	83	254
BENTHAM								
Henry	24	m	w	ENGL	San Francisco	7-Wd San Francisco	81	231
BENTHY								
James	52	m	w	IREL	San Francisco	8-Wd San Francisco	82	319
BENTIL								
May	40	f	w	IREL	San Joaquin	2-Wd Stockton	86	172
BENTIN								
Matt	40	m	w	CHIL	Calaveras	San Andreas P O	70	157
Meracildo	40	m	w	CHIL	Calaveras	San Andreas P O	70	157
BENTINE								
Pine	30	m	w	FRAN	Siskiyou	Callahan P O	89	629
BENTLER								
Antone	30	m	w	PRUS	El Dorado	Placerville Twp	72	98
BENTLEY								
Edgar	25	m	w	MI	Stanislaus	Empire Twp	92	35
Edwin	38	m	w	CT	San Francisco	San Francisco P O	85	746
Elisha M	47	m	w	NY	Tulare	Visalia Twp	92	284
George W	45	m	w	KY	Yolo	Cache Crk Twp	93	428
H H	45	m	w	IN	Sacramento	3-Wd Sacramento	77	302
Horatio N B	58	m	w	NY	Solano	Maine Prairie Twp	90	52
James	38	m	w	NY	Butte	Ophir Twp	70	114
Jefferson	42	m	w	KY	Stanislaus	Empire Twp	92	39
John M	29	m	w	MO	Stanislaus	Branch Twp	92	1
Margaret	24	f	w	IREL	San Francisco	2-Wd San Francisco	79	196
Richard	34	m	w	IL	Stanislaus	San Joaquin Twp	92	79
Robt	32	m	w	ENGL	San Francisco	San Francisco P O	83	330
Samuel	79	m	w	VA	Placer	Bath P O	76	447
Symond	44	m	w	NY	El Dorado	Georgetown Twp	72	38
Thomas	40	m	w	KY	Placer	Bath P O	76	450
Thomas S	34	m	w	NY	Stanislaus	Empire Twp	92	35
William	75	m	w	NY	Tulare	Visalia Twp	92	284
William	45	m	w	KY	Placer	Bath P O	76	452
BENTLY								
Edward	21	m	w	ENGL	San Francisco	11-Wd San Francisc	84	518
George	27	m	b	VA	Napa	Napa	75	37
George W	29	m	b	VA	Sonoma	Sonoma Twp	91	438
Horace	22	m	b	MD	San Francisco	San Francisco P O	80	409
James	45	m	w	NY	Butte	Bidwell Twp	70	1
John	50	m	w	ENGL	San Francisco	1-Wd San Francisco	79	88
John	40	m	w	IREL	Alameda	Oakland	68	230
Robert	54	m	w	ENGL	Contra Costa	Martinez P O	71	442
Simon	42	m	w	NY	Santa Cruz	Pajaro Twp	89	349
William	35	m	w	IREL	Alameda	Alameda	68	13
BENTON								
A P	54	m	w	PA	Nevada	Meadow Lake Twp	75	253
A P	54	m	w	PA	Nevada	Meadow Lake Twp	75	266
Abijah	60	m	w	MA	Alameda	Washington Twp	68	296
Adelbert D	17	m	w	CA	Sonoma	Petaluma Twp	91	360
Albert	23	m	w	BREM	San Francisco	11-Wd San Francisc	84	480
Anna	37	f	w	ENGL	Sonoma	Petaluma Twp	91	338
Anson S	53	m	w	MA	Placer	Gold Run Twp	76	400
Charles B	21	m	w	RI	San Mateo	San Mateo P O	87	357
Chas	42	m	w	ENGL	San Francisco	1-Wd San Francisco	79	116
Cordelia	33	f	w	ENGL	San Joaquin	Tulare Twp	86	250
Edwd	23	m	w	IN	San Francisco	1-Wd San Francisco	79	132
George	19	m	w	NY	Sonoma	Russian Rvr	91	371
George	14	m	w	CA	Sonoma	Petaluma Twp	91	345
George H	26	m	w	DE	Los Angeles	Wilmington Twp	73	641
H P	54	m	w	VT	Mendocino	Ukiah Twp	74	241
Helen	56	f	w	OH	San Francisco	11-Wd San Francisc	84	622
Henry A	62	m	w	CT	San Francisco	8-Wd San Francisco	82	383
J A	49	m	w	CT	Alameda	Oakland	68	151
J B	48	m	w	KY	Mendocino	Little Lake Twp	74	192
James	39	m	w	SCOT	Trinity	Weaverville Pct	92	224
Jno H	37	m	w	MO	Shasta	Millville P O	89	487
Joel A	52	m	w	CT	Placer	Bath P O	76	458
Joell	46	m	w	VT	Humboldt	Mattole Twp	72	284
John	33	m	w	MO	San Francisco	1-Wd San Francisco	79	44
John H	52	m	w	CT	Sonoma	Bodega Twp	91	250
John R	34	m	w	MO	Placer	Gold Run Twp	76	395
Joseph	23	m	w	PA	Marin	Sausalito Twp	74	72
Joseph A	50	m	w	CT	San Francisco	6-Wd San Francisco	81	140
Katie	16	f	w	CA	San Francisco	San Francisco P O	83	296
L	20	m	w	IREL	Lake	Knoxville Mines	73	404
Leonard T	37	m	w	IN	Shasta	Millville P O	89	483
Lewis	7	m	w	CA	Sonoma	Petaluma Twp	91	360
Marcus A	22	m	w	IL	San Luis Obispo	Santa Rosa Twp	87	318
Mary	12	f	w	CA	Sonoma	Analy Twp	91	224
Parry	10	m	w	CA	Marin	Tomales Twp	74	81
Richard	35	m	w	IREL	San Francisco	2-Wd San Francisco	79	175
Romena	34	f	w	MO	Santa Clara	2-Wd San Jose	88	295
Saml	6	m	w	AR	Butte	Oregon Twp	70	122
T H	25	m	w	OH	Mendocino	Ukiah Twp	74	233
Thomas	34	m	w	MO	Mendocino	Calpella Twp	74	181
Thomas	10	m	w	CA	Marin	San Rafael Twp	74	28
Thos	30	m	b	MO	Siskiyou	Scott Valley Twp	89	617
Wallace W	36	m	w	KY	Butte	Ophir Twp	70	96
Wm	41	m	w	ME	Butte	Ophir Twp	70	106
BENTRA								
Austalia	80	m	w	CA	Monterey	Alisal Twp	74	304
BENTRAS								
Frank	27	m	w	OH	Los Angeles	Los Angeles Twp	73	490
BENTREN								
Chris	29	m	w	DENM	San Francisco	6-Wd San Francisco	81	155
BENTS								
Francis A	46	m	w	PRUS	Tuolumne	Sonora P O	93	320
BENTURA								
Antoinette	30	f	w	MEXI	Sacramento	2-Wd Sacramento	77	238
BENTY								
Wm	45	m	w	IREL	Sonoma	Salt Point	91	391
BENTZ								
Guadlupe	35	m	w	PRUS	Solano	Tremont Twp	90	35
BENTZE								
John H	23	m	w	BADE	Siskiyou	Scott Valley Twp	89	609
BENUS								
Edmond	21	m	w	MA	Alameda	San Leandro	68	93
BENUTH								
Antonio	30	m	w	ITAL	San Francisco	3-Wd San Francisco	79	289
BENVIDOR								
Bella	6	f	w	CA	Sacramento	4-Wd Sacramento	77	378
BENWER								
William	36	m	w	MO	Tulare	Farmersville Twp	92	250
BENZ								
F M	37	m	w	MO	Siskiyou	Scott Valley Twp	89	620
Jacob	30	m	w	SWIT	Monterey	Monterey	74	355
Joseph	47	m	w	SWIT	Siskiyou	Hamburg Twp	89	599
Vitomi	22	m	w	SWIT	Marin	San Antonio Twp	74	61
W H	24	m	w	IA	Siskiyou	Callahan P O	89	624
BENZEN								
Conrad	21	m	w	PRUS	San Francisco	San Francisco P O	83	384
BEO								
Patrick	37	m	w	IREL	Yuba	Rose Bar Twp	93	665
BEOBAR								
Antonio	43	m	w	MEXI	San Luis Obispo	San Luis Obispo Tw	87	299
BEOHMKER								
Hans	36	m	w	GERM	Yolo	Putah Twp	93	517
BEOLOBES								
Cerselda	29	f	w	CA	Mariposa	Mariposa P O	74	123
BEOMETO								
Thomas	52	m	w	AUST	San Francisco	3-Wd San Francisco	79	299
BEON								
Augustus	34	m	w	ME	Yuba	North East Twp	93	643
BEORD								
J E	44	m	w	OH	Sierra	Butte Twp	89	512
S	35	m	w	ENGL	Sierra	Butte Twp	89	509
BEP								
Ah	20	m	c	CHIN	San Francisco	8-Wd San Francisco	82	420
BEPENTIS								
Beraro	40	m	i	MEXI	Inyo	Cerro Gordo Twp	73	323
BEPLER								
Justus	42	m	w	PRUS	Marin	Novato Twp	74	10
BEQUETTE								
Benjamin	34	m	w	MO	Tulare	Farmersville Twp	92	241
Charles	36	m	w	MO	Tulare	Farmersville Twp	92	242
Cyrian	45	m	w	MO	Tulare	Farmersville Twp	92	241
Henry D	36	m	w	WI	San Francisco	San Francisco P O	83	203
BER								
Louis	35	m	w	SWIT	Sacramento	4-Wd Sacramento	77	347
BERA								
Alphonz	43	m	w	FRAN	Calaveras	Copperopolis P O	70	251
Jebosis	46	m	w	CHIL	Fresno	Millerton P O	72	146
BERAL								
Miguel	35	m	w	MEXI	Santa Clara	Almaden Twp	88	4
BERAMAN								
Lewis	45	m	w	HCAS	Tuolumne	Sonora P O	93	327
BERAND								
John	49	m	w	FRAN	San Francisco	San Francisco P O	83	199
BERANGER								
George	21	m	w	SPAI	San Francisco	11-Wd San Francisc	84	661
BERARD								
Felecier	35	m	w	FRAN	San Francisco	2-Wd San Francisco	79	231
BERARU								
Peter	30	m	w	FRAN	Mendocino	Anderson Twp	74	155
BERAUD								
Loran	29	m	w	FRAN	Sacramento	2-Wd Sacramento	77	248
BERBAN								
Henry	34	m	w	IREL	Solano	Vallejo	90	215
BERBE								
William	34	m	w	NH	Trinity	North Fork Twp	92	221
BERBERICK								
Augustus	30	m	w	PRUS	San Francisco	5-Wd San Francisco	81	10
BERCH								
William	55	m	w	ENGL	Del Norte	Mountain Twp	71	474
BERCHEM								
John	27	m	w	MI	San Joaquin	2-Wd Stockton	86	206
BERCHERMANN								
Chs	34	m	w	NY	San Francisco	2-Wd San Francisco	79	238
BERCHERWITZ								
Meyer	43	m	w	POLA	San Francisco	2-Wd San Francisco	79	189
BERCHOLD								
Louis	39	m	w	PRUS	San Francisco	1-Wd San Francisco	79	74
BERCKHAUSEN								
Julius	49	m	w	HANO	San Francisco	San Francisco P O	85	802
BERCLAY								
Richard	28	m	w	MO	Trinity	Junction City Pct	92	210
BERCOURTEN								
Herman	34	m	w	FRAN	San Francisco	2-Wd San Francisco	79	147
BERD								
Patrick	48	m	w	IREL	San Francisco	8-Wd San Francisco	82	393
BERDAN								
Abraham	49	m	w	NY	Santa Clara	Santa Clara Twp	88	139

© 2001 by Heritage Quest. All rights reserved.

Name	Age	S	R	B-PL	County	Locale	Roll	Pg
						Series M593		
BERDELL								
Frank	20	m	w	OH	Sacramento	Franklin Twp	77	105
BERDEMAN								
Jacob	25	m	w	SWIT	Mariposa	Mariposa P O	74	91
BERDEN								
James	45	m	w	KY	San Joaquin	2-Wd Stockton	86	174
BERDETTE								
Julius	45	m	w	FRAN	San Francisco	San Francisco P O	85	753
BERDICK								
Alden	34	m	w	OH	Inyo	Bishop Crk Twp	73	315
Elias	68	m	w	NY	Inyo	Bishop Crk Twp	73	315
BERDIGEL								
Delifina	22	f	w	MEXI	San Francisco	2-Wd San Francisco	79	170
BERDING								
A	42	m	w	GERM	Humboldt	Pacific Twp	72	298
BERDOLT								
E	42	m	w	PRUS	Sacramento	4-Wd Sacramento	77	370
BERDUE								
Pablo	50	m	w	MEXI	San Diego	Coronado	78	465
Paratra	27	m	w	MEXI	San Diego	Warners Rancho Dis	78	528
BERDUGO								
Domingo	46	m	w	MEXI	Monterey	Alisal Twp	74	290
Nicolas	35	m	w	CA	Monterey	San Juan Twp	74	417
BEREANA								
John	48	m	w	CHIL	Sacramento	Sutter Twp	77	384
BERELUS								
C	34	f	w	MEXI	Alameda	Murray Twp	68	110
BERENBAUM								
Charles	32	m	w	IL	Siskiyou	Callahan P O	89	628
E J	12	m	w	IL	Siskiyou	Callahan P O	89	628
J G	59	m	w	PRUS	Siskiyou	Callahan P O	89	628
BEREND								
August	18	m	w	HAMB	San Francisco	1-Wd San Francisco	79	127
BERENSTEIN								
Daniel	35	m	w	POLA	San Francisco	San Francisco P O	83	232
Louis	40	m	w	PRUS	San Francisco	San Francisco P O	83	228
BERESFORD								
Joseph	32	m	w	ENGL	Sacramento	4-Wd Sacramento	77	377
BERESSO								
Maria	35	f	w	CA	Santa Clara	Almaden Twp	88	11
BERETA								
Carmelita	41	f	w	MEXI	San Francisco	2-Wd San Francisco	79	244
BERETTA								
Manuel	37	m	w	ITAL	Mariposa	Mariposa P O	74	91
William	40	m	w	ITAL	San Francisco	2-Wd San Francisco	79	250
BERFARTA								
Larcon	60	m	w	MEXI	Mariposa	Mariposa P O	74	124
BERFORD								
Hemming B	40	m	w	ENGL	San Diego	San Diego	78	508
John	50	m	w	FRAN	Stanislaus	Emory Twp	92	24
BERFTOL								
Anton	62	m	w	BADE	Sacramento	3-Wd Sacramento	77	288
BERG								
A	34	m	w	DENM	Santa Clara	Gilroy Twp	88	74
Alfred	26	m	w	SWED	Nevada	Grass Valley Twp	75	157
Andrew	42	m	w	SWED	Nevada	Little York Twp	75	235
Antonio	36	m	w	NORW	Yolo	Grafton Twp	93	481
August	40	m	w	PRUS	Monterey	Castroville Twp	74	335
August	37	m	w	SWED	Sacramento	3-Wd Sacramento	77	289
Augustin	28	m	w	SWED	Mendocino	Big Rvr Twp	74	161
Augustus	30	m	w	SWED	Plumas	Washington Twp	77	54
Charles	27	m	w	SWED	Mendocino	Casper & Big Rvr	74	163
Charles	25	m	w	SWED	Plumas	Washington Twp	77	54
Emanuel	43	m	w	BAVA	Yolo	Cache Crk Twp	93	423
Fredrick	29	m	w	HANO	San Francisco	11-Wd San Francisc	84	477
John	40	m	w	NORW	Mendocino	Big Rvr Twp	74	159
Julius	36	m	w	PRUS	San Francisco	1-Wd San Francisco	79	52
Oscar	50	m	w	FINL	Nevada	Little York Twp	75	238
Oscar	45	m	w	RUSS	Placer	Dutch Flat P O	76	401
Peter	43	m	w	NORW	San Francisco	7-Wd San Francisco	81	228
Robt	33	m	w	SWED	Shasta	American Ranch P O	89	496
Simeon	35	m	w	BADE	Los Angeles	Los Angeles	73	554
BERGAMIN								
James	25	m	w	CANA	Colusa	Butte Twp	71	270
BERGAN								
Rafel	34	m	i	MEXI	Inyo	Cerro Gordo Twp	73	323
BERGANEAU								
Sherrie	36	m	w	FRAN	Plumas	Mineral Twp	77	20
BERGANIETTI								
Chas	38	m	w	DENM	San Francisco	San Francisco P O	83	7
BERGANT								
E	56	m	w	FRAN	Calaveras	Copperopolis P O	70	250
BERGARD								
Martin	49	m	w	FRAN	Plumas	Indian Twp	77	15
BERGDEN								
Johanna	36	f	w	PRUS	San Francisco	3-Wd San Francisco	79	300
BERGE								
Andrew	57	m	w	OH	Stanislaus	Empire Twp	92	54
Augustus	43	m	w	PRUS	Plumas	Washington Twp	77	25
Cristina	19	f	w	PRUS	Sutter	Yuba Twp	92	149
Errick O	42	m	w	NORW	San Francisco	1-Wd San Francisco	79	19
Frederick	20	m	w	PRUS	Sutter	Yuba Twp	92	149
Harmon	15	m	w	IA	Sutter	Yuba Twp	92	149
Hector	26	m	w	NORW	San Francisco	7-Wd San Francisco	81	218
Henry	45	m	w	NY	Fresno	Millerton P O	72	168
Henry	26	m	w	PRUS	Sutter	Yuba Twp	92	149
J B	27	m	w	AL	San Joaquin	2-Wd Stockton	86	204
John	28	m	w	PRUS	Sutter	Yuba Twp	92	149
John	23	m	w	IA	Stanislaus	Empire Twp	92	54
Joseph	31	m	w	PRUS	Sutter	Yuba Twp	92	149
Minor	60	m	w	PA	San Joaquin	Elkhorn Twp	86	58
Saml	27	m	w	RUSS	San Luis Obispo	San Luis Obispo Tw	87	309
BERGEE								
Antons	22	m	w	SWIT	Placer	Emigrant Gap P O	76	416
Frank	28	m	w	ITAL	San Francisco	7-Wd San Francisco	81	260
BERGEIN								
Felix	50	m	w	CANA	Santa Cruz	Santa Cruz Twp	89	393
BERGEL								
Sigmond	30	m	w	PRUS	San Bernardino	San Bernardino Twp	78	421
Wm	49	m	w	PRUS	Tuolumne	Columbia P O	93	337
BERGEN								
Adolph	34	m	w	ITAL	San Francisco	San Francisco P O	80	421
Adrien	35	m	w	PRUS	San Francisco	1-Wd San Francisco	79	56
Alfd	38	m	w	OH	Sierra	Sears Twp	89	553
Bridget	26	f	w	IREL	San Francisco	San Francisco P O	80	357
Charles	35	m	w	OH	Solano	Vacaville Twp	90	125
Christopher	36	m	w	IREL	San Francisco	1-Wd San Francisco	79	63
Edward J	40	m	w	PA	San Francisco	6-Wd San Francisco	81	119
Elizth	36	f	w	PA	San Francisco	San Francisco P O	83	31
Fanny	20	f	w	PRUS	San Francisco	6-Wd San Francisco	81	113
Florenti	26	m	w	ITAL	San Francisco	2-Wd San Francisco	79	163
Harrison	22	m	w	CA	Fresno	Millerton P O	72	160
Henry	18	m	w	PRUS	San Francisco	8-Wd San Francisco	82	442
John	41	m	w	OH	Butte	Wyandotte Twp	70	144
John	35	m	w	IREL	Solano	Vallejo	90	143
John	31	m	w	MD	Santa Clara	Fremont Twp	88	66
William	20	m	w	SWED	San Francisco	San Francisco P O	80	413
Wm	26	m	w	AUST	Fresno	Kings Rvr P O	72	213
BERGENDAHL								
Daniel	30	m	w	SWED	San Francisco	3-Wd San Francisco	79	287
BERGENER								
Herman	30	m	w	PRUS	Marin	Bolinas Twp	74	5
BERGENS								
Charles	30	m	w	RUSS	San Francisco	San Francisco P O	83	337
BERGEOL								
Alexander	35	m	w	FRAN	Santa Barbara	Santa Barbara P O	87	452
BERGEON								
Michael	30	m	w	DENM	Marin	Sausalito Twp	74	72
BERGER								
Addam	40	m	w	FRAN	Trinity	Canyon City Pct	92	202
Ann	21	f	w	SAXO	San Francisco	6-Wd San Francisco	81	71
C T	29	m	w	BADE	Sacramento	3-Wd Sacramento	77	309
George W	43	m	w	MO	Mendocino	Anderson Twp	74	150
J W	54	m	w	VA	Tuolumne	Sonora P O	93	314
Joel F E	45	m	w	VA	San Mateo	Woodside P O	87	380
John	26	m	w	FRAN	Trinity	Canyon City Pct	92	202
John G	41	m	w	PRUS	Plumas	Washington Twp	77	56
Julius	42	m	w	PRUS	San Francisco	3-Wd San Francisco	79	322
Lewis	26	m	w	HANO	San Francisco	San Francisco P O	83	65
Moses	41	m	w	POLA	Sonoma	Petaluma Twp	91	320
Nathaniel	26	m	w	MO	Inyo	Bishop Crk Twp	73	310
Philip	30	m	w	HDAR	Marin	Sausalito Twp	74	72
Rosana	46	f	w	IREL	Santa Clara	Gilroy Twp	88	85
William	40	m	w	NY	Trinity	Weaverville Pct	92	231
William	35	m	w	PRUS	San Francisco	San Francisco P O	83	397
William	23	m	w	POLA	Marin	San Rafael Twp	74	42
Wm	50	m	w	PRUS	San Joaquin	1-Wd Stockton	86	153
Wm	43	m	w	DENM	Santa Clara	Gilroy Twp	88	68
Wm	22	m	w	AUST	San Francisco	San Francisco P O	83	134
BERGERET								
John	38	m	w	FRAN	San Francisco	2-Wd San Francisco	79	139
BERGES								
Joe	36	m	w	KY	San Joaquin	Elkhorn Twp	86	69
BERGESEN								
Charles	34	m	w	SWED	Marin	Bolinas Twp	74	8
BERGEVENE								
N	26	m	w	FRAN	Sacramento	3-Wd Sacramento	77	318
BERGGREN								
August	41	m	w	SWED	San Francisco	San Francisco P O	80	428
BERGH								
Henry	46	m	w	SWED	Shasta	Stillwater P O	89	478
BERGHEN								
M	45	m	w	PRUS	Alameda	Murray Twp	68	110
BERGHISER								
C A	43	m	w	PRUS	Tuolumne	Columbia P O	93	360
BERGHOLD								
William	40	m	w	BADE	San Francisco	San Francisco P O	83	271
BERGIEN								
William	44	m	w	IREL	San Francisco	11-Wd San Francisc	84	523
BERGIN								
Daniel	35	m	w	IREL	Santa Clara	Santa Clara Twp	88	145
Ellen	30	f	w	IREL	San Francisco	2-Wd San Francisco	79	141
Emma	22	f	w	SWED	San Francisco	San Francisco P O	83	364
J J	27	m	w	CT	Solano	Vallejo	90	185
James J	39	m	w	IREL	San Francisco	2-Wd San Francisco	79	140
Mary	30	f	w	IREL	Santa Cruz	Santa Cruz	89	415
Michael P	70	m	w	IREL	Nevada	Grass Valley Twp	75	158
Thomas	50	m	w	IREL	Santa Cruz	Santa Cruz Twp	89	382
W S	21	m	w	MO	Amador	Ione City P O	69	351
BERGINER								
Henry	29	m	w	HANO	Alameda	Eden Twp	68	82
BERGIVEN								
Peter	27	m	w	CANA	San Francisco	1-Wd San Francisco	79	133

© 2001 by Heritage Quest. All rights reserved.

Name	Age	S	R	B-PL	County	Locale (Series M593)	Roll	Pg
BERGLAND								
Andrew	46	m	w	SWED	Santa Clara	2-Wd San Jose	88	308
H	42	m	w	SWED	San Francisco	3-Wd San Francisco	79	293
BERGLUR								
Louis	50	m	w	GERM	Santa Clara	Burnett Twp	88	38
BERGMAN								
A W	51	m	w	BAVA	Santa Clara	Gilroy Twp	88	85
Adam	46	m	w	BAVA	Sacramento	4-Wd Sacramento	77	339
August	49	m	w	HDAR	Sacramento	American Twp	77	65
Frank	25	m	w	PRUS	Sacramento	2-Wd Sacramento	77	245
Frederick	47	m	w	HANO	Santa Clara	2-Wd San Jose	88	330
Fredericka	19	f	w	BAVA	San Francisco	8-Wd San Francisco	82	425
Jacob	38	m	w	HDAR	San Diego	Temecula Dist	78	526
Julius	25	m	w	BAVA	San Francisco	6-Wd San Francisco	81	120
M	27	m	w	SWED	Sacramento	3-Wd Sacramento	77	267
BERGNER								
Alford	40	m	w	NY	San Francisco	7-Wd San Francisco	81	211
Julius	30	m	w	PRUS	San Francisco	6-Wd San Francisco	81	92
BERGOLD								
Chas	33	m	w	HDAR	San Francisco	8-Wd San Francisco	82	332
Edward	23	m	w	FRAN	San Francisco	8-Wd San Francisco	82	332
BERGORA								
Conaceon	70	f	w	MEXI	San Mateo	Redwood Twp	87	368
BERGOT								
August	45	m	w	FRAN	Calaveras	San Andreas P O	70	157
BERGREEN								
Ben	30	m	w	SWED	Solano	Vallejo	90	163
BERGSON								
Ole	40	m	w	NORW	San Francisco	San Francisco P O	85	815
BERGSTEIN								
Louis	55	m	w	BAVA	San Francisco	San Francisco P O	83	413
Louis	55	m	w	PRUS	San Francisco	San Francisco P O	83	399
BERGSTROM								
Gustave	24	m	w	SWED	San Francisco	San Francisco P O	80	332
John	40	m	w	SWED	San Francisco	11-Wd San Francisc	84	659
William	30	m	w	SWED	San Francisco	3-Wd San Francisco	79	292
BERGUIN								
John	56	m	b	SC	Nevada	Nevada Twp	75	296
BERGWALL								
Gustaff	59	m	w	SWED	Solano	Vallejo	90	163
BERHAM								
Thomas	29	m	w	CANA	San Francisco	San Francisco P O	83	20
BERHAUS								
J	25	m	w	FRAN	Alameda	Murray Twp	68	118
BERHENS								
Chas	29	m	w	MECK	San Joaquin	1-Wd Stockton	86	138
F W	40	m	w	PRUS	Napa	Napa Twp	75	59
BERHNS								
Charles	26	m	w	PRUS	Solano	Rio Vista Twp	90	70
BERHOFER								
Conrad	40	m	w	PRUS	San Francisco	7-Wd San Francisco	81	245
BERIAN								
Machel	49	m	w	FRAN	Tuolumne	Columbia P O	93	335
BERIER								
Joseph	55	m	w	FRAN	Sacramento	4-Wd Sacramento	77	351
BERIGAN								
James	35	m	w	IREL	Amador	Jackson P O	69	334
John	36	m	w	IREL	Trinity	Junction City Pct	92	205
BERIL								
Alfred	20	m	w	CANA	Placer	Bath P O	76	454
Jerry	24	m	w	CANA	Placer	Bath P O	76	454
BERILLSON								
Gians	38	m	w	MEXI	Santa Clara	Almaden Twp	88	7
BERILOCHWAY								
Peter	35	m	w	ITAL	Sonoma	Cloverdale Twp	91	272
BERING								
John P	42	m	w	PA	San Francisco	2-Wd San Francisco	79	222
William T	38	m	w	CANA	Stanislaus	Branch Twp	92	1
BERINGER								
Frederick	38	m	w	FRNK	El Dorado	Placerville	72	111
BERINGHAM								
John	18	m	w	NY	Amador	Jackson P O	69	321
BERINS								
Isaac H	34	m	w	NC	Fresno	Kings Rvr P O	72	206
BERIT								
J	42	m	w	FRAN	Alameda	Oakland	68	132
BERK								
Chas	27	m	w	FRAN	Napa	Napa	75	14
Thos	13	m	w	NY	San Francisco	11-Wd San Francisc	84	670
BERKA								
John	24	m	w	AUSL	San Francisco	San Francisco P O	83	81
BERKELY								
Ferdinand	23	m	w	GERM	Los Angeles	Santa Ana Twp	73	599
BERKENKAMP								
Henry	32	m	w	PRUS	Yolo	Merritt Twp	93	505
BERKER								
Jacob	26	m	w	IL	San Francisco	San Francisco P O	83	74
Josiah	19	m	w	MA	Contra Costa	Martinez P O	71	414
BERKES								
Henry	40	m	w	GERM	Klamath	Trinidad Twp	73	392
BERKHARDT								
James	43	m	w	HAMB	San Francisco	San Francisco P O	85	808
BERKHOFF								
B	40	m	w	PRUS	Nevada	Meadow Lake Twp	75	249
BERKHOUSE								
Cath	50	f	w	HAMB	San Francisco	2-Wd San Francisco	79	161
BERKLE								
Andrew	34	m	w	WURT	Colusa	Spring Valley Twp	71	342
BERKLEY								
L W	30	m	w	ENGL	Tehama	Red Bluff	92	181
Mary	26	f	w	NY	San Francisco	8-Wd San Francisco	82	451
S M	30	m	w	MO	Tehama	Red Bluff	92	174
BERKMAN								
George	22	m	w	PRUS	San Francisco	8-Wd San Francisco	82	395
Sophia	40	f	w	SWED	Sacramento	Brighton Twp	77	74
BERKNES								
Andrew	34	m	w	PRUS	Solano	Tremont Twp	90	31
BERKS								
Augustin	40	m	w	GERM	Los Angeles	Los Angeles	73	563
BERKSLEY								
John C	28	m	w	ENGL	Stanislaus	Empire Twp	92	62
BERLACK								
M	23	m	w	ENGL	San Francisco	8-Wd San Francisco	82	371
BERLAND								
Aaron	32	m	w	SWED	San Francisco	8-Wd San Francisco	82	435
Walter	38	m	w	IN	Siskiyou	Scott Rvr Twp	89	602
BERLE								
Ernst	30	m	w	GERM	San Joaquin	2-Wd Stockton	86	213
Henry	21	m	w	PA	Marin	San Rafael	74	54
BERLEMANN								
Bernardina	56	f	w	PRUS	San Francisco	San Francisco P O	83	2
BERLENA								
P	24	m	w	MD	Yuba	Marysville	93	591
BERLENGON								
Mathew	36	m	w	PRUS	Contra Costa	Martinez P O	71	407
BERLET								
Anton	45	m	w	SARD	San Diego	Julian Dist	78	469
BERLEY								
John	24	m	w	OH	Solano	Vacaville Twp	90	138
Owen	26	m	w	IREL	Contra Costa	Martinez P O	71	427
BERLHOUSE								
Jane	65	f	w	HANO	San Francisco	2-Wd San Francisco	79	273
BERLIE								
Victor	35	m	w	FRAN	San Bernardino	Chino Twp	78	412
BERLIMER								
Isadore	34	m	w	PRUS	San Francisco	San Francisco P O	83	255
BERLIN								
Charles	47	m	w	IREL	Sacramento	Georgianna Twp	77	125
Charles	24	m	w	SWED	Sacramento	Georgianna Twp	77	123
John G	53	m	w	PA	Stanislaus	San Joaquin Twp	92	74
Lars	20	m	w	SWED	Sacramento	Georgianna Twp	77	125
BERLINER								
Abraham	50	m	w	RUSS	San Francisco	8-Wd San Francisco	82	432
Emily	37	f	w	PRUS	San Francisco	San Francisco P O	83	386
H A	42	m	w	PRUS	San Francisco	San Francisco P O	83	272
BERLIUS								
John	30	m	w	GERM	Los Angeles	Los Angeles	73	565
BERLOZE								
Berbier	25	f	w	FRAN	San Francisco	6-Wd San Francisco	81	106
BERMAN								
Edward	35	m	w	FRAN	San Francisco	6-Wd San Francisco	81	73
Ethelinda F	32	f	w	ENGL	Sierra	Sears Twp	89	560
Henry	33	m	w	ENGL	Sierra	Eureka Twp	89	523
Wm	48	m	w	WI	San Joaquin	Dent Twp	86	25
BERMAYON								
Isedore	27	m	w	FRAN	Monterey	San Juan Twp	74	408
BERMEYSLIN								
Morgan	45	m	w	PRUS	San Francisco	5-Wd San Francisco	81	13
BERMING								
Jane M	65	f	w	IREL	San Francisco	San Francisco P O	85	784
BERMINGHAM								
Eliza	40	f	w	ENGL	San Joaquin	2-Wd Stockton	86	169
J	18	m	w	NY	Amador	Jackson P O	69	334
John	44	m	w	IREL	Monterey	San Juan Twp	74	404
John	26	m	w	NY	Santa Clara	2-Wd San Jose	88	320
Thos	24	m	w	ENGL	San Joaquin	Elkhorn Twp	86	56
BERMINS								
Joel	21	m	w	CANA	San Francisco	2-Wd San Francisco	79	231
BERMONT								
John	39	m	w	AUST	Stanislaus	San Joaquin Twp	92	80
Sophia	19	f	w	HANO	Alameda	Eden Twp	68	89
BERMUDA								
Francisco	34	m	w	MEXI	Santa Clara	1-Wd San Jose	88	226
Juan	31	m	w	CA	Mendocino	Round Valley Twp	74	218
BERMUDAS								
Alphonso	39	m	w	LA	Kern	Havilah P O	73	336
Casimir	33	m	w	CA	Santa Barbara	Santa Barbara P O	87	477
Wan	31	m	w	MEXI	Tehama	Red Bluff	92	183
BERMUDES								
Dolnes	16	m	w	CA	Los Angeles	El Monte Twp	73	454
Gertrudes	20	f	w	CA	Los Angeles	Santa Ana Twp	73	604
Maria A	60	f	w	CA	Los Angeles	El Monte Twp	73	453
Petra	28	f	w	CA	Los Angeles	El Monte Twp	73	453
Pilar	31	f	w	CA	Los Angeles	Wilmington Twp	73	637
Rita	45	f	w	CA	Los Angeles	El Monte Twp	73	453
Tomas	33	m	w	CA	San Luis Obispo	San Luis Obispo Tw	87	299
Ventina	42	f	w	CA	Los Angeles	El Monte Twp	73	453
Viante	27	m	w	CA	Los Angeles	El Monte Twp	73	453
BERMUDEZ								
Juan	35	m	w	CA	Marin	San Rafael Twp	74	38
BERMYHAN								
Patrick	30	m	w	IREL	Los Angeles	Los Angeles	73	566

© 2001 by Heritage Quest. All rights reserved.

Name	Age	S	R	B-PL	County	Locale	Series M593 Roll	Pg
BERN								
Frank	29	m	w	IREL	San Joaquin	1-Wd Stockton	86	141
BERNADACIO								
Charles	23	m	w	SWIT	Marin	Point Reyes Twp	74	21
Patrias	23	m	w	SWIT	Marin	San Antonio Twp	74	62
BERNADES								
Gonsales	41	m	w	CHIL	Amador	Jackson P O	69	336
BERNADIA								
Joan	25	m	w	SWIT	Marin	San Antonio Twp	74	61
BERNAL								
Antonia	14	f	w	CA	Santa Clara	2-Wd San Jose	88	337
Antonio	14	m	w	CA	Santa Clara	Santa Clara Twp	88	176
Berhena	27	f	w	MEXI	Santa Clara	2-Wd San Jose	88	304
Bernard	34	m	w	GERM	Santa Clara	2-Wd San Jose	88	330
Blande Carla	33	f	w	CA	Monterey	Castroville Twp	74	332
Burno	24	m	w	CA	Los Angeles	Wilmington Twp	73	636
Cipean	19	m	w	CA	Santa Clara	San Jose Twp	88	213
Clementina	22	f	w	MEXI	San Francisco	6-Wd San Francisco	81	96
Francisco	45	m	w	CA	Santa Clara	San Jose Twp	88	220
Francisco	44	m	w	CA	Santa Clara	San Jose Twp	88	207
Francisco	40	m	w	MEXI	Santa Cruz	Pajaro Twp	89	362
Guadalupe	32	m	w	CA	Santa Cruz	Soquel Twp	89	437
Gudalupe	37	m	w	CA	Santa Clara	San Jose Twp	88	211
Gutalupe	36	m	w	CA	Monterey	Alisal Twp	74	295
Ignacio	63	m	w	MEXI	Santa Clara	2-Wd San Jose	88	312
Ignacio	29	m	w	CA	Santa Clara	San Jose Twp	88	211
Jesus	31	m	w	MEXI	Monterey	San Juan Twp	74	408
Jesus	24	m	w	CA	Contra Costa	Martinez P O	71	439
John	10	m	w	CA	Santa Clara	Fremont Twp	88	56
Jose J	32	m	w	CA	Santa Clara	San Jose Twp	88	218
Josefa	65	f	w	CA	Santa Clara	2-Wd San Jose	88	328
Joseph	12	m	w	CA	San Francisco	11-Wd San Francisc	84	592
Josepha	52	f	w	CA	Santa Clara	1-Wd San Jose	88	230
Josi	40	m	w	CA	Santa Clara	San Jose Twp	88	211
Luis	31	m	w	CA	Santa Clara	San Jose Twp	88	211
Manuel	16	m	w	CA	Santa Clara	Santa Clara Twp	88	176
Maria L	18	f	w	CA	Santa Barbara	Santa Barbara P O	87	489
Pablo	60	m	w	CA	Santa Clara	1-Wd San Jose	88	265
Pedro	42	m	w	CA	Santa Clara	San Jose Twp	88	211
R	17	f	w	CA	Alameda	Oakland	68	242
Rosaria	50	f	w	CA	Santa Clara	2-Wd San Jose	88	302
Serepina	49	f	w	CA	Los Angeles	Los Angeles	73	522
Uadalupe	35	m	w	CA	Alameda	Brooklyn Twp	68	40
BERNALD								
Alejo	33	m	w	CA	Los Angeles	San Gabriel Twp	73	595
BERNAMAN								
Katy	60	f	w	HAMB	Santa Clara	1-Wd San Jose	88	230
BERNANAYON								
Marcel	66	m	w	FRAN	Alameda	Brooklyn Twp	68	39
BERNARD								
Alex	25	m	w	FRAN	San Francisco	8-Wd San Francisco	82	364
Almond D	57	m	w	FRAN	Placer	Bath P O	76	452
Amelia	8	f	w	CA	San Francisco	San Francisco P O	80	409
Anna	15	f	w	IREL	San Francisco	8-Wd San Francisco	82	299
Aracia	40	m	w	LA	Solano	Vacaville Twp	90	120
B	26	m	w	IREL	Nevada	Meadow Lake Twp	75	265
B	25	m	w	SWIT	San Francisco	San Francisco P O	85	861
Bernard	33	m	w	HDAR	San Francisco	6-Wd San Francisco	81	114
Bernard	26	m	w	IREL	San Francisco	11-Wd San Francisc	84	688
Bernard G	40	m	w	ENGL	Sonoma	Petaluma Twp	91	321
Carrie	37	f	w	PRUS	San Francisco	7-Wd San Francisco	81	284
Celesti	30	m	w	FRAN	San Diego	San Diego	78	503
Chas	39	m	w	FRAN	San Francisco	San Francisco P O	85	829
Chas A	45	m	w	MA	San Francisco	6-Wd San Francisco	81	94
Clarance	25	m	w	IREL	San Francisco	San Francisco P O	83	400
Felice	31	f	w	SWIT	El Dorado	Diamond Springs Tw	72	28
Francis	41	m	w	NY	San Francisco	6-Wd San Francisco	81	152
Frederick	22	m	w	SWED	Plumas	Plumas Twp	77	32
Henry	30	m	w	PRUS	San Francisco	8-Wd San Francisco	82	382
Henry	22	m	w	HAMB	San Francisco	1-Wd San Francisco	79	128
Hypolite	56	m	w	FRAN	Sierra	Sears Twp	89	556
Isaac	50	m	w	POLA	San Francisco	11-Wd San Francisc	84	524
J M	24	m	w	MO	Sutter	Yuba Twp	92	140
James	26	m	w	FRAN	San Francisco	San Francisco P O	80	535
Jocemo	25	m	w	SWIT	Marin	San Antonio Twp	74	61
Johana	50	f	w	IREL	San Francisco	8-Wd San Francisco	82	311
John	50	m	w	GERM	Trinity	North Fork Twp	92	218
John	40	m	w	HAMB	San Francisco	6-Wd San Francisco	81	81
Joseph	74	m	w	FRAN	El Dorado	Placerville	72	125
Joseph	40	m	w	CA	Marin	Bolinas Twp	74	4
Joseph	39	m	w	PRUS	San Francisco	San Francisco P O	83	366
Joseph	34	m	w	MA	Contra Costa	Martinez P O	71	418
Joseph	22	m	w	PORT	Marin	San Rafael Twp	74	25
Joseph	15	m	w	CA	Marin	Nicasio Twp	74	20
Kate	27	f	w	NY	San Francisco	8-Wd San Francisco	82	345
Louis	30	m	w	GERM	San Mateo	Half Moon Bay P O	87	403
Louisa	24	f	w	NY	San Francisco	2-Wd San Francisco	79	234
M A	56	f	w	VA	Tuolumne	Columbia P O	93	356
Michl S	47	m	w	CANA	San Francisco	1-Wd San Francisco	79	22
Penan	58	m	w	FRAN	San Francisco	San Francisco P O	80	534
Stephen	41	m	w	NY	Santa Barbara	Santa Barbara P O	87	472
Thomas	46	m	w	IREL	San Francisco	8-Wd San Francisco	82	496
Thos	62	m	w	MA	San Francisco	San Francisco P O	83	113
William	40	m	w	CT	Calaveras	San Andreas P O	70	181
William	30	m	w	IREL	Santa Clara	San Jose Twp	88	217
BERNARDE								
Aqueline	40	m	w	SWIT	Calaveras	San Andreas P O	70	189
Jacob	32	m	w	SWIT	Calaveras	San Andreas P O	70	189
BERNARDEN								
Pedro	29	m	w	CA	San Bernardino	San Bernardino Twp	78	451
BERNARDI								
Carlotto	26	m	w	SWIT	San Francisco	San Francisco P O	80	479
Frank	33	m	w	FRAN	Calaveras	San Andreas P O	70	167
BERNARDINO								
Jose	21	m	i	CA	Santa Barbara	Santa Barbara P O	87	472
BERNARDO								
Francis	45	m	w	MEXI	Santa Clara	2-Wd San Jose	88	309
Juan	45	m	w	SWIT	Los Angeles	Los Angeles	73	562
Juan	29	m	w	ITAL	San Francisco	San Francisco P O	85	741
Juan	20	m	w	SWIT	Marin	San Antonio Twp	74	64
Peter	28	m	w	SWIT	Marin	San Antonio Twp	74	61
Y	33	m	w	ITAL	Mariposa	Maxwell Crk P O	74	144
BERNARDS								
David	18	m	w	POLA	Sonoma	Healdsburg & Mendo	91	278
BERNARDY								
Antone	29	m	w	SWIT	Placer	Bath P O	76	425
BERNASCONI								
Frank	38	m	w	SWIT	Calaveras	Copperopolis P O	70	242
BERNAT								
C	36	m	w	SWIT	Napa	Napa	75	20
BERNATO								
John B	39	m	w	MEXI	Amador	Ione City P O	69	357
BERNBROCK								
Theodore	38	m	w	PA	Placer	Bath P O	76	437
BERNE								
Bridget	23	f	w	IREL	Santa Clara	San Jose Twp	88	186
Dominick	31	m	w	IREL	Santa Clara	1-Wd San Jose	88	242
BERNEIR								
Covill	52	m	w	ENGL	Butte	Oregon Twp	70	122
BERNEL								
Jesus	30	m	w	MEXI	Fresno	Millerton P O	72	163
Jesus M	31	m	w	MEXI	Fresno	Millerton P O	72	154
BERNELL								
Wm	32	m	w	NY	San Francisco	San Francisco P O	83	66
BERNELLA								
B	45	m	w	ITAL	Amador	Sutter Crk P O	69	404
BERNEM								
William	31	m	w	PRUS	Santa Cruz	Pajaro Twp	89	350
BERNER								
Ella	11	f	w	CA	Sacramento	Lee Twp	77	157
Emanuel	32	m	w	HUNG	San Francisco	San Francisco P O	83	191
Fredrick	45	m	w	PRUS	Calaveras	San Andreas P O	70	200
Henry	40	m	w	HANO	Sacramento	Granite Twp	77	143
Richard L	54	m	w	VA	Yolo	Cache Crk Twp	93	431
BERNERT								
David	39	m	w	BADE	San Francisco	11-Wd San Francisc	84	524
John	41	m	w	BADE	San Francisco	San Francisco P O	80	428
BERNES								
Thomas H	44	m	w	VT	Tuolumne	Chinese Camp P O	93	363
BERNET								
Joseph	33	m	w	AUST	San Francisco	11-Wd San Francisc	84	703
BERNETT								
Edward	70	m	w	CANA	Monterey	Castroville Twp	74	336
Edwd	30	m	w	WI	San Francisco	San Francisco P O	83	77
George	28	m	w	OH	Contra Costa	Martinez P O	71	435
H A	38	m	w	MA	Sacramento	4-Wd Sacramento	77	334
John B	39	m	w	IREL	Sacramento	2-Wd Sacramento	77	218
Martha	70	f	w	CANA	Monterey	Castroville Twp	74	336
Wm	40	m	w	TN	San Joaquin	Castoria Twp	86	14
BERNETTI								
Vincent	58	m	w	SWIT	San Francisco	2-Wd San Francisco	79	198
BERNEY								
James	55	m	w	NC	Stanislaus	Empire Twp	92	41
John	35	m	w	IREL	Contra Costa	Martinez P O	71	368
BERNHARD								
C	21	m	w	HDAR	Sacramento	4-Wd Sacramento	77	341
F	41	m	w	FRAN	Sierra	Alleghany & Forest	89	534
George	42	m	w	HDAR	Mariposa	Mariposa P O	74	118
Isaac	49	m	w	BAVA	Sonoma	Petaluma Twp	91	321
J	50	m	w	FRAN	Amador	Ione City P O	69	371
William	35	m	w	OH	Solano	Silveyville Twp	90	87
BERNHARDT								
Antone	40	m	w	FRAN	Calaveras	San Andreas P O	70	195
Bertha	17	f	w	SHOL	San Francisco	San Francisco P O	83	69
BERNHART								
Maurice	35	m	w	FRAN	San Francisco	7-Wd San Francisco	81	276
BERNHEIM								
A	25	m	w	PRUS	Monterey	Castroville Twp	74	325
Celia	18	f	w	PRUS	San Francisco	8-Wd San Francisco	82	458
Emanuel	38	m	w	PRUS	Santa Cruz	Santa Cruz	89	412
Jacob	36	m	w	PRUS	Santa Cruz	Santa Cruz	89	413
Reuben	41	m	w	PRUS	Santa Cruz	Santa Cruz	89	413
Rose	20	f	w	LA	San Francisco	San Francisco P O	83	71
BERNICE								
Herman	37	m	w	HAMB	San Francisco	6-Wd San Francisco	81	94
BERNIE								
John	41	m	w	FRAN	San Francisco	6-Wd San Francisco	81	111
BERNIN								
Hannah	16	f	w	CA	San Francisco	San Francisco P O	83	352
Pincus	42	m	w	PRUS	San Francisco	8-Wd San Francisco	82	293
BERNINGS								
Lepole	37	m	w	GERM	San Joaquin	2-Wd Stockton	86	213
BERNIS								
Chas C	39	m	w	MA	San Francisco	San Francisco P O	83	100

© 2001 by Heritage Quest. All rights reserved.

California 1870 Census

Series M593

Name	Age	S	R	B-PL	County	Locale	Roll	Pg
Tho S	40	m	w	MD	Nevada	Nevada Twp	75	310
BERNOL								
Jesus	31	m	w	MEXI	Los Angeles	Santa Ana Twp	73	600
BERNS								
James	24	m	w	IREL	Inyo	Independence Twp	73	328
BERNSAUGHAN								
Eliza	30	f	w	NY	San Francisco	11-Wd San Francisc	84	688
BERNSEN								
Roland	24	m	w	MA	San Francisco	7-Wd San Francisco	81	238
BERNSER								
Frank	24	m	w	PRUS	San Francisco	8-Wd San Francisco	82	401
BERNSIDE								
Geo	35	m	m	CISL	San Francisco	2-Wd San Francisco	79	213
BERNSTADEN								
Christian	41	m	w	HANO	Santa Clara	Fremont Twp	88	63
BERNSTEIN								
George	37	m	w	PRUS	San Francisco	San Francisco P O	83	166
Goodfred F	45	m	w	SAXO	Alpine	Markleeville P O	69	311
Henry	49	m	w	RUSS	San Francisco	San Francisco P O	83	262
Julius	30	m	w	PRUS	San Francisco	San Francisco P O	83	37
Julius	25	m	w	PRUS	San Francisco	San Francisco P O	83	276
Louis	24	m	w	PRUS	San Francisco	San Francisco P O	80	537
Morris	35	m	w	PRUS	San Francisco	San Francisco P O	80	482
Samuel	53	m	w	HAMB	San Francisco	San Francisco P O	80	408
BERNSTINE								
Jos	51	m	w	POLA	San Francisco	8-Wd San Francisco	82	293
BERNY								
Ellen	14	m	w	CA	Amador	Amador City P O	69	393
BEROLDO								
F	50	m	w	FRAN	San Francisco	8-Wd San Francisco	82	371
BEROLINE								
Joseph	29	m	w	SWIT	Marin	San Rafael Twp	74	33
BERON								
Louis	30	m	w	FRAN	Napa	Napa	75	41
BERONA								
Peter	40	m	w	ITAL	San Francisco	2-Wd San Francisco	79	205
BERONAS								
Romana	30	f	w	CA	Santa Clara	Milpitas Twp	88	109
BERONDA								
---	23	m	w	CA	Monterey	Alisal Twp	74	290
Esiguel	25	m	w	CA	Monterey	Alisal Twp	74	290
BERONIO								
Augusto	26	m	w	ITAL	San Francisco	1-Wd San Francisco	79	105
Gaetano	45	m	w	ITAL	San Francisco	1-Wd San Francisco	79	105
Mary	36	f	w	ITAL	San Francisco	1-Wd San Francisco	79	105
Pietro	40	m	w	ITAL	San Francisco	1-Wd San Francisco	79	105
BEROTH								
Charles	38	m	w	BAVA	Tulare	Kings Rvr Twp	92	252
Ellen	15	m	w	CA	Amador	Ione City P O	69	358
BERQUISD								
Antonio	26	m	w	ITAL	San Francisco	2-Wd San Francisco	79	164
BERR								
John	75	m	w	FRAN	Los Angeles	Los Angeles	73	543
BERRA								
Joaquine	25	m	i	CA	Inyo	Lone Pine Twp	73	334
BERRAN								
Edd	23	m	w	MO	San Francisco	5-Wd San Francisco	81	22
BERRET								
Jacob	50	m	w	PRUS	San Francisco	San Francisco P O	80	534
BERRGESS								
Lewis	13	m	w	CA	Sonoma	Sonoma Twp	91	436
BERRI								
Charles	23	m	w	SWIT	Marin	Nicasio Twp	74	17
BERRICK								
Julian	37	m	i	MEXI	Inyo	Lone Pine Twp	73	332
BERRIER								
John	70	m	w	FRAN	Tuolumne	Sonora P O	93	320
John	48	m	w	CA	Tuolumne	Sonora P O	93	324
BERRIESSO								
Francesco	55	m	w	CA	Yolo	Cottonwood Twp	93	475
BERRIMAN								
George	21	m	w	ENGL	Nevada	Grass Valley Twp	75	201
Nicholas	35	m	w	ENGL	Nevada	Grass Valley Twp	75	173
Robert	35	m	w	ENGL	Nevada	Grass Valley Twp	75	220
BERRIN								
Emanuel	48	m	w	AUST	San Francisco	2-Wd San Francisco	79	169
BERRING								
Chas	35	m	w	PRUS	San Francisco	San Francisco P O	83	114
Mattie	22	f	w	VT	San Francisco	7-Wd San Francisco	81	247
BERRINGER								
Henrietta	42	f	w	FRAN	San Francisco	8-Wd San Francisco	82	459
William	32	m	w	OH	Santa Clara	2-Wd San Jose	88	289
BERRIT								
Aleck	52	m	w	FRAN	Calaveras	Copperopolis P O	70	246
Francois	40	m	w	FRAN	San Francisco	1-Wd San Francisco	79	55
BERROULA								
Lorenzo	50	m	w	SPAI	Calaveras	San Andreas P O	70	156
Martin	65	m	w	SPAI	Calaveras	San Andreas P O	70	156
BERRY								
A	40	f	w	FRAN	San Joaquin	1-Wd Stockton	86	133
A A Mrs	33	f	w	OH	Santa Cruz	Santa Cruz	89	403
Agnes	22	f	w	NC	Los Angeles	Los Angeles	73	524
Ah	26	m	c	CHIN	Monterey	Castroville Twp	74	325
Albert	62	m	w	ME	Sonoma	Santa Rosa	91	428
Albert A	26	m	w	OH	Yolo	Putah Twp	93	523
Albion P	23	m	w	CANA	Mendocino	Little Rvr Twp	74	171
Alexander	31	m	w	NY	Mendocino	Anderson Twp	74	150
Alexander	30	m	w	SWED	Nevada	Rough & Ready Twp	75	328
Alice	40	f	w	NY	Sonoma	Santa Rosa	91	410
Amie	30	f	w	IREL	San Francisco	San Francisco P O	83	96
Andrew B	45	m	w	ENGL	Yolo	Putah Twp	93	511
Andrew W	27	m	w	MA	Santa Cruz	Santa Cruz Twp	89	401
Anna	35	f	w	IREL	San Mateo	Belmont P O	87	374
Augustus	44	m	w	SWED	San Francisco	3-Wd San Francisco	79	293
Baxter B	62	m	w	TN	Sonoma	Analy Twp	91	234
Benjamin	60	m	b	VA	Sutter	Nicolaus Twp	92	109
Benjamin	33	m	w	PA	Sierra	Sears Twp	89	527
Benjamin	33	m	w	MO	Colusa	Grand Island Twp	71	307
Bridget	30	f	w	IREL	El Dorado	Placerville Twp	72	92
C C	24	m	w	ME	Solano	Vallejo	90	160
C C	23	m	w	ME	Solano	Vallejo	90	168
Catharine	12	f	w	AUST	Sacramento	2-Wd Sacramento	77	248
Charles	6	m	w	CA	Alameda	Eden Twp	68	83
Charles	30	m	w	IREL	San Francisco	2-Wd San Francisco	79	137
Charles	30	m	w	IREL	Yuba	New York Twp	93	639
Charles E	40	m	w	NH	Santa Clara	San Jose Twp	88	187
Charlott	73	f	w	CT	Solano	Suisun Twp	90	109
Chas	37	m	w	PRUS	San Francisco	8-Wd San Francisco	82	375
Chas	22	m	w	ME	Butte	Chico Twp	70	33
Daniel	46	m	w	KY	Contra Costa	Martinez P O	71	408
Daniel	37	m	w	NY	Yuba	East Bear Rvr Twp	93	539
Danl	30	m	w	IREL	San Francisco	7-Wd San Francisco	81	272
David	35	m	w	IREL	Alameda	Oakland	68	225
David	30	m	w	IREL	Alameda	Oakland	68	129
David E	43	m	w	KY	Yuba	North East Twp	93	643
Davis	45	m	w	IREL	Yolo	Washington Twp	93	528
E D	58	m	w	ME	Nevada	Nevada Twp	75	284
Edward	20	m	w	CA	Santa Cruz	Santa Cruz	89	411
Edward M	56	m	w	KY	Stanislaus	Empire Twp	92	66
Elizabeth	7	f	w	CA	San Francisco	11-Wd San Francisc	84	711
Ellen	65	f	w	SCOT	Yuba	Parks Bar Twp	93	648
Esther	36	f	w	IREL	Plumas	Goodwin Twp	77	6
Francis	35	m	w	DENM	Sutter	Yuba Twp	92	143
Frank	40	m	w	PORT	Santa Clara	Redwood Twp	88	121
Fredk	32	m	w	FRAN	Humboldt	Arcata Twp	72	231
Fulton G	36	m	w	ME	San Francisco	6-Wd San Francisco	81	87
Geo C	37	m	w	GA	El Dorado	Georgetown Twp	72	36
Geo R	25	m	w	NY	San Francisco	5-Wd San Francisco	81	19
Geo W	27	m	w	NH	San Joaquin	Oneal Twp	86	114
George	34	m	w	ME	San Francisco	11-Wd San Francisc	84	540
George	30	m	w	ME	San Francisco	5-Wd San Francisco	81	11
George	23	m	w	IL	Solano	Suisun Twp	90	99
George S	22	m	w	MO	Stanislaus	Empire Twp	92	57
George W	56	m	w	OH	Santa Clara	Santa Clara Twp	88	135
George W	40	m	w	NC	Napa	Napa	75	8
Gideon	30	m	w	ENGL	San Francisco	San Francisco P O	83	100
Gideon	29	m	w	WIND	San Francisco	San Francisco P O	80	411
Gilbert	45	m	w	FRAN	El Dorado	Diamond Springs Tw	72	34
Graane	26	m	w	SWIT	Monterey	Alisal Twp	74	290
Hamilton	50	m	b	MA	San Francisco	1-Wd San Francisco	79	97
Hamilton	44	m	b	MA	San Francisco	San Francisco P O	80	358
Harrison	41	m	w	IN	Alpine	Woodfords P O	69	309
Henderson	54	m	w	TN	Yuba	East Bear Rvr Twp	93	541
Henry	30	m	w	IREL	Calaveras	San Andreas P O	70	180
J H	37	m	w	IL	Lake	Coyote Valley	73	401
J H	30	m	w	AL	El Dorado	Kelsey Twp	72	61
Jacob	42	m	w	MO	Stanislaus	Empire Twp	92	38
James	57	m	w	VT	Placer	Dutch Flat P O	76	415
James	52	m	w	NC	San Luis Obispo	Salinas Twp	87	296
James	50	m	w	NY	Mendocino	Round Valley Twp	74	216
James	35	m	w	PA	Yuba	East Bear Rvr Twp	93	544
James	34	m	w	ENGL	San Francisco	San Francisco P O	83	121
James	24	m	w	CANA	Sacramento	Sutter Twp	77	385
James	24	m	w	IREL	San Francisco	8-Wd San Francisco	82	374
James	20	m	w	NJ	San Bernardino	San Bernardino Twp	78	418
James C	54	m	w	MO	Amador	Fiddletown P O	69	437
James E	31	m	w	ME	Sierra	Gibson Twp	89	540
James H	28	m	w	AL	El Dorado	Diamond Springs Tw	72	26
Jas	28	m	w	ENGL	Sierra	Table Rock Twp	89	576
Jehu	43	m	w	OH	Siskiyou	Yreka	89	652
Jno	31	m	w	IREL	Alameda	Oakland	68	222
John	50	m	w	SCOT	Solano	Denverton Twp	90	27
John	50	m	w	IREL	Fresno	Millerton P O	72	150
John	45	m	w	NJ	San Francisco	8-Wd San Francisco	82	317
John	40	m	w	IREL	San Francisco	7-Wd San Francisco	81	250
John	39	m	w	MO	Amador	Fiddletown P O	69	437
John	38	m	w	IREL	San Francisco	San Francisco P O	83	174
John	38	m	w	CANA	Solano	Vallejo	90	216
John	37	m	w	ENGL	San Bernardino	San Bernardino Twp	78	419
John	37	m	w	SWED	Santa Cruz	Santa Cruz Twp	89	401
John	25	m	w	PRUS	Alameda	Murray Twp	68	110
John	24	m	w	CANA	Humboldt	Eureka Twp	72	263
John	24	m	w	SWED	Yuba	Marysville Twp	93	568
John	21	m	w	OH	Mariposa	Mariposa P O	74	117
John A	31	m	w	SWED	Mendocino	Big Rvr Twp	74	158
John F	23	m	w	NY	Marin	San Rafael Twp	74	38
John J	43	m	w	VA	Yolo	Grafton Twp	93	485
John M	47	m	w	MO	Stanislaus	Empire Twp	92	57
John S	37	m	w	IL	Monterey	Castroville Twp	74	342
John W	27	m	w	IL	Shasta	Millville P O	89	483
Joseph	38	m	w	MA	Sacramento	4-Wd Sacramento	77	371
Joseph	24	m	w	ENGL	Yolo	Cache Crk Twp	93	445
Joseph	23	m	w	ENGL	Yolo	Cache Crk Twp	93	448
Josephine	19	f	w	MO	El Dorado	Cosumnes Twp	72	17

© 2001 by Heritage Quest. All rights reserved.

Name	Age	S	R	B-PL	County	Locale	Roll	Pg
						Series M593		
Julia M	9M	f	w	CA	Alameda	Oakland	68	221
Louis H	32	m	w	VA	San Francisco	San Francisco P O	85	760
Margaret	56	f	w	WALE	Mariposa	Mariposa P O	74	116
Mary	72	f	w	TN	Monterey	San Juan Twp	74	402
Mary	32	f	w	IREL	San Francisco	San Francisco P O	80	459
Michael	28	m	w	IREL	Colusa	Monroe Twp	71	313
Narcissa	50	f	w	VA	San Francisco	11-Wd San Francisc	84	565
Nicholas	49	m	w	SWED	Mendocino	Gualala Twp	74	226
Oreta	20	f	w	OR	Sacramento	1-Wd Sacramento	77	180
Orlando R	48	m	w	NORW	Inyo	Bishop Crk Twp	73	317
Parker S	26	m	w	PA	Placer	Rocklin Twp	76	465
Patrick	36	m	w	IREL	San Francisco	San Francisco P O	85	813
Peter	47	m	w	SPAI	San Francisco	8-Wd San Francisco	82	293
Peter	46	m	w	CHIL	Fresno	Millerton P O	72	163
R C	33	m	w	AL	Sutter	Nicolaus Twp	92	108
Rebecca	17	f	w	WY	San Bernardino	San Bernardino Twp	78	436
Reuben K	56	m	w	NY	El Dorado	Salmon Falls Twp	72	130
Rich N	59	m	w	MA	San Francisco	5-Wd San Francisco	81	22
Richard	60	m	w	IREL	Sonoma	Petaluma Twp	91	347
Richard	56	m	w	KY	Tulare	Farmersville Twp	92	247
Richard	51	m	w	ME	Marin	San Rafael	74	51
Richard	34	m	w	ENGL	San Francisco	7-Wd San Francisco	81	228
S	47	m	w	ME	Sierra	Sierra Twp	89	565
Samuel	28	m	w	IL	Lake	Coyote Valley	73	400
Sarah	48	f	w	IREL	El Dorado	Mountain Twp	72	68
Silas	46	m	w	NJ	Stanislaus	Empire Twp	92	40
Soloman A	62	m	w	ME	El Dorado	Georgetown Twp	72	46
Susan	33	f	b	PA	San Francisco	6-Wd San Francisco	81	100
Susan	32	f	m	SC	San Francisco	San Francisco P O	85	760
T E W	23	m	w	AL	Sutter	Nicolaus Twp	92	108
Theodore	16	m	w	IN	Alpine	Woodfords P O	69	316
Thomas	45	m	w	IREL	San Francisco	8-Wd San Francisco	82	352
Thomas	37	m	w	IL	Solano	Denverton Twp	90	23
Thomas	35	m	w	PA	Nevada	Eureka Twp	75	133
Thomas	30	m	w	IL	Solano	Denverton Twp	90	25
Thomas	27	m	w	IL	Solano	Montezuma Twp	90	65
Thomas	27	m	w	PA	San Francisco	San Francisco P O	83	254
Thomas	26	m	w	SWED	San Mateo	Woodside P O	87	385
Thomas	24	m	w	CA	Yolo	Cache Crk Twp	93	453
Thomas	16	m	w	CA	Nevada	Grass Valley Twp	75	151
Thomas A	24	m	w	PA	Placer	Roseville P O	76	350
Thos	38	m	w	CANA	San Francisco	San Francisco P O	83	42
Tom	50	m	b	TN	San Joaquin	Castoria Twp	86	3
Uriah	53	m	w	ENGL	Merced	Snelling P O	74	256
W J	20	m	w	ME	San Joaquin	Dent Twp	86	16
W O M	32	m	w	ME	San Francisco	San Francisco P O	85	863
William	38	m	w	OH	Nevada	Grass Valley Twp	75	216
William	35	m	w	US	Humboldt	Eureka Twp	72	278
William	34	m	w	OH	El Dorado	White Oak Twp	72	142
William	32	m	b	NY	San Francisco	San Francisco P O	80	481
William	31	m	w	KY	Monterey	San Juan Twp	74	402
William	29	m	w	ENGL	Sonoma	Petaluma Twp	91	340
Winne	5	f	w	WA	San Francisco	5-Wd San Francisco	81	6
Wm	35	m	w	IREL	Alameda	Oakland	68	246
Wm	35	m	w	IL	Alameda	Oakland	68	217
Wm	30	m	w	ME	Monterey	Alisal Twp	74	292
Wm	29	m	w	ENGL	Sonoma	Petaluma Twp	91	345
Wm C	28	m	w	AL	Plumas	Quartz Twp	77	42
Wm J	29	m	w	MO	Mendocino	Little Lake Twp	74	201
Wm P	33	m	w	IL	Sonoma	Analy Twp	91	234
BERRYANN								
Geo	40	m	w	IREL	San Joaquin	1-Wd Stockton	86	124
BERRYESA								
Francis	59	m	w	MEXI	Colusa	Spring Valley Twp	71	341
Guadalupe	17	f	w	CA	Contra Costa	Martinez Twp	71	348
BERRYESSA								
Antonio	43	m	w	CA	Santa Clara	San Jose Twp	88	184
Augustine	34	m	w	CA	Santa Clara	San Jose Twp	88	184
Berhemia	14	f	w	CA	Santa Clara	1-Wd San Jose	88	225
Carlos	60	m	w	CA	Santa Clara	San Jose Twp	88	184
Carlos	19	m	w	CA	Santa Clara	San Jose Twp	88	184
Cista	54	m	w	CA	Napa	Yountville Twp	75	90
Fernando	40	m	w	CA	Santa Cruz	Pajaro Twp	89	351
Francisco	46	m	w	CA	Santa Clara	San Jose Twp	88	184
Guadalupe	23	m	w	CA	Santa Clara	Alviso Twp	88	22
Ignacia	17	f	w	CA	Santa Clara	1-Wd San Jose	88	231
Jesus	28	m	w	CA	Santa Clara	San Jose Twp	88	184
Jose	46	m	w	CA	Santa Clara	San Jose Twp	88	184
M	20	m	w	CA	Napa	Yountville Twp	75	89
Magil	40	m	w	CA	Colusa	Stony Crk Twp	71	330
Mariano	35	m	w	CA	Santa Clara	San Jose Twp	88	184
Nicholas	86	m	w	CA	Santa Clara	San Jose Twp	88	184
Nicholas	54	m	w	CA	Santa Clara	San Jose Twp	88	184
Pablina	45	f	w	CA	Santa Clara	2-Wd San Jose	88	310
BERRYEZA								
Carolina	33	f	w	CA	Contra Costa	Martinez Twp	71	350
BERRYHILL								
John R	51	m	w	GA	El Dorado	Placerville Twp	72	99
BERRYMAN								
A	37	m	w	ENGL	Amador	Jackson P O	69	333
Albert	37	m	w	DC	Napa	Napa Twp	75	33
Arthur	36	m	w	ENGL	Fresno	Millerton P O	72	164
Benj	35	m	w	ENGL	San Francisco	1-Wd San Francisco	79	112
Frank	37	m	w	PRUS	Sacramento	4-Wd Sacramento	77	376
H	30	m	w	IL	Lassen	Long Valley Twp	73	437
L	32	m	w	VA	Napa	Napa Twp	75	30
BERRYSON								
John	30	m	w	CANA	San Francisco	6-Wd San Francisco	81	104
Martin	31	m	w	SWED	Los Angeles	Santa Ana Twp	73	601
BERS								
John	24	m	w	PRUS	San Francisco	1-Wd San Francisco	79	57
BERSE								
Joseph	35	m	w	FRAN	Santa Clara	2-Wd San Jose	88	324
BERSELIA								
Panse	42	m	m	CHIL	Placer	Bath P O	76	420
BERSEM								
W Lewis	28	m	w	CANA	Sierra	Table Rock Twp	89	576
BERSEMTA								
Martine	65	m	w	SPAI	Calaveras	San Andreas P O	70	210
BERSFORD								
Jno	36	m	w	ENGL	Santa Clara	Gilroy Twp	88	104
BERSON								
James	31	m	w	PRUS	San Francisco	1-Wd San Francisco	79	73
John	70	m	w	FRAN	San Francisco	San Francisco P O	80	346
Pierce	37	m	w	FRAN	San Francisco	8-Wd San Francisco	82	370
BERT								
Amelia	20	f	w	PA	San Francisco	11-Wd San Francisc	84	618
Antonia	50	f	w	FRAN	San Francisco	8-Wd San Francisco	82	330
Fred	26	m	w	PA	San Francisco	11-Wd San Francisc	84	609
George F	30	m	w	ME	Santa Clara	Santa Clara Twp	88	150
John	47	m	w	BADE	Plumas	Washington Twp	77	53
Marie	22	f	w	HAMB	San Francisco	6-Wd San Francisco	81	73
BERTANA								
Antone	35	m	w	ITAL	Mariposa	Mariposa P O	74	134
BERTE								
Joseph	36	m	w	ITAL	Tuolumne	Sonora P O	93	304
BERTEAU								
Stephen	38	m	w	FRAN	San Diego	Milquaty Dist	78	476
BERTENSHAW								
Mary	24	f	w	CANA	Sonoma	Mendocino Twp	91	298
BERTH								
Christian	32	m	w	GERM	Yolo	Cache Crk Twp	93	420
John	40	m	w	FRAN	San Francisco	San Francisco P O	80	469
R	55	m	w	FRAN	Sierra	Butte Twp	89	511
Wendall	48	m	w	HAMB	Sacramento	Franklin Twp	77	119
BERTHA								
Masernette	40	m	w	SWIT	Calaveras	San Andreas P O	70	216
BERTHEN								
G	17	f	w	PRUS	Santa Clara	Gilroy Twp	88	74
BERTHER								
Edward	18	m	w	PRUS	San Francisco	San Francisco P O	83	269
BERTHET								
Andrew	45	m	w	FRAN	Sacramento	2-Wd Sacramento	77	247
Arne	36	m	w	FRAN	Calaveras	San Andreas P O	70	176
BERTHIA								
Julias	15	m	w	NY	San Francisco	San Francisco P O	83	358
BERTHIER								
Albert	18	m	w	MO	San Francisco	8-Wd San Francisco	82	405
John B	65	m	w	FRAN	Santa Clara	2-Wd San Jose	88	323
BERTHOLA								
Dominico	30	m	w	ITAL	San Mateo	Schoolhouse Statio	87	340
BERTHOLANI								
Peter	25	m	w	ITAL	San Francisco	1-Wd San Francisco	79	121
BERTHOLDE								
Cothern	51	f	w	SWIT	Los Angeles	Los Angeles	73	510
BERTHOLDSON								
Otto	27	m	w	SHOL	San Francisco	2-Wd San Francisco	79	273
BERTHOLO								
Frank	43	m	w	FRAN	Calaveras	San Andreas P O	70	168
BERTHOME								
Louis	52	m	w	FRAN	El Dorado	Mountain Twp	72	69
BERTHRAND								
John	50	m	w	OH	Sacramento	Natomas Twp	77	171
BERTHRIGHT								
Lucy	78	f	w	VA	Yolo	Putah Twp	93	526
BERTIC								
Eugene	41	m	w	FRAN	Yuba	Bullards Bar P O	93	547
BERTKEN								
George	41	m	w	HANO	Mariposa	Mariposa P O	74	124
BERTLING								
Christ	28	m	w	PRUS	Santa Clara	2-Wd San Jose	88	287
BERTO								
Jeannette	58	f	w	FRAN	San Francisco	11-Wd San Francisc	84	534
Mary	38	f	w	IREL	Santa Clara	1-Wd San Jose	88	227
BERTODY								
Charles	47	m	w	FRAN	San Francisco	San Francisco P O	80	485
BERTOLA								
Passo	39	m	w	ITAL	San Francisco	3-Wd San Francisco	79	288
BERTOLLACCI								
Lebas	40	m	w	ITAL	San Francisco	2-Wd San Francisco	79	163
BERTOLOME								
Giuseppe	40	m	w	ITAL	San Francisco	1-Wd San Francisco	79	114
BERTOMA								
Lacouneti	28	m	w	ITAL	Amador	Jackson P O	69	339
BERTON								
Francis	40	m	w	SWIT	San Francisco	San Francisco P O	83	341
John H	46	m	w	ENGL	Fresno	Millerton P O	72	166
Persia	50	f	w	FRAN	San Francisco	2-Wd San Francisco	79	216
Sam	40	m	w	KY	San Joaquin	Oneal Twp	86	118
BERTOREL								
Christopher	50	m	w	ITAL	San Mateo	Belmont P O	87	372
BERTOSCK								
Laura	12	f	w	CA	Mariposa	Mariposa P O	74	123

© 2001 by Heritage Quest. All rights reserved.

Name	Age	S	R	B-PL	County	Locale	Roll	Pg
						Series M593		
BERTRAM								
Charles	27	m	w	HANO	Merced	Snelling P O	74	252
Edd	35	m	w	SCOT	San Francisco	5-Wd San Francisco	81	35
Fred	29	m	w	HANO	Merced	Snelling P O	74	252
George	14	m	w	CA	Merced	Snelling P O	74	272
John	30	m	w	FRAN	San Francisco	San Francisco P O	80	342
R	40	m	w	IREL	San Joaquin	2-Wd Stockton	86	163
Theodore	31	m	w	LA	San Francisco	San Francisco P O	85	737
BERTRAN								
A	28	m	w	FRAN	Solano	Vallejo	90	200
Alfred	45	m	w	FRAN	San Francisco	6-Wd San Francisco	81	51
Francisco	30	f	i	CA	Los Angeles	Los Angeles	73	500
BERTRAND								
Alfred	42	m	w	FRAN	Nevada	Grass Valley Twp	75	191
Andrew	62	m	w	BELG	San Francisco	San Francisco P O	80	345
Charles	28	m	w	FRAN	San Francisco	8-Wd San Francisco	82	395
Dorous	46	m	w	FRAN	Yuba	Bullards Bar P O	93	553
Joseph	51	m	w	FRAN	Marin	Novato Twp	74	12
Joseph	42	m	w	CANA	Nevada	Grass Valley Twp	75	156
Joseph	22	m	w	FRAN	San Francisco	5-Wd San Francisco	81	3
Louis	50	m	w	FRAN	Santa Clara	1-Wd San Jose	88	258
Louis	42	m	w	FRAN	San Joaquin	3-Wd Stockton	86	244
Marie	26	f	w	FRAN	San Francisco	11-Wd San Francisc	84	595
Parama	40	m	w	FRAN	Los Angeles	Los Angeles Twp	73	473
Wm	36	m	w	CANA	San Francisco	San Francisco P O	83	81
BERTSCHY								
Lena	16	f	w	IL	San Francisco	2-Wd San Francisco	79	257
BERTTA								
Comino	44	m	w	ITAL	Mariposa	Mariposa P O	74	109
BERTZ								
Geo W	55	m	w	PA	Sonoma	Mendocino Twp	91	297
Jacob	27	m	w	TX	San Francisco	6-Wd San Francisco	81	80
BERTZHOLD								
Karl	29	m	w	GERM	Santa Clara	2-Wd San Jose	88	336
BERWICK								
Azariah	31	m	w	AUST	Placer	Bath P O	76	460
Joseph	29	m	w	IREL	Santa Clara	2-Wd San Jose	88	313
Maggie	25	f	w	IREL	Santa Clara	2-Wd San Jose	88	313
Thos	34	m	w	CANA	San Francisco	2-Wd San Francisco	79	229
BERWIN								
Hattie	14	f	w	CA	San Francisco	San Francisco P O	85	788
Isaac	41	m	w	PRUS	Los Angeles	Los Angeles	73	546
Simon	30	m	w	PRUS	Yolo	Cache Crk Twp	93	427
BERY								
C P	35	m	w	AL	Sutter	Nicolaus Twp	92	108
Charles	27	m	w	IREL	Sacramento	2-Wd Sacramento	77	251
Harmon	48	m	w	NY	Alameda	Oakland	68	200
BERYANT								
E	47	m	w	KY	San Joaquin	Elliott Twp	86	75
BESA								
Bernardi	49	m	w	ITAL	Calaveras	Copperopolis P O	70	246
BESAGNO								
Maria	3	f	w	CA	San Francisco	11-Wd San Francisc	84	587
BESALIA								
Joseph	29	m	w	AUSL	San Francisco	1-Wd San Francisco	79	19
BESANTE								
Felipe	28	m	w	MEXI	Plumas	Mineral Twp	77	20
BESBY								
Henry	31	m	w	IREL	San Francisco	8-Wd San Francisco	82	291
BESCAN								
John	43	m	w	PRUS	Nevada	Bloomfield Twp	75	92
BESCHAUMAN								
Chs	33	m	w	NY	San Francisco	2-Wd San Francisco	79	276
BESCHEINEN								
Henry	26	m	w	GERM	Sacramento	1-Wd Sacramento	77	177
BESCHINO								
Minna	34	f	w	PRUS	San Francisco	San Francisco P O	80	364
William	38	m	w	PRUS	San Francisco	San Francisco P O	80	364
BESELY								
Martha	24	f	w	MA	San Francisco	11-Wd San Francisc	84	684
BESENT								
Isaac	50	m	w	ENGL	San Bernardino	San Bernardino Twp	78	429
Stephen	25	m	w	ENGL	San Bernardino	San Bernardino Twp	78	429
BESENTA								
Casseo	55	m	w	MEXI	Mariposa	Mariposa P O	74	98
BESENTO								
Carrese	80	m	w	CHIL	Calaveras	San Andreas P O	70	159
BESER								
John	45	m	w	FRAN	San Francisco	San Francisco P O	80	536
BESHERIE								
John	38	m	w	FRAN	San Francisco	8-Wd San Francisco	82	296
BESHORMAN								
Augustus	59	m	w	PRUS	San Francisco	San Francisco P O	83	192
BESIN								
John	37	m	w	FRAN	San Francisco	San Francisco P O	80	348
John	37	m	w	FRAN	San Francisco	San Francisco P O	80	347
BESING								
Antonio	32	m	w	AUST	Monterey	San Antonio Twp	74	315
BESIT								
Adam	43	m	w	PRUS	San Francisco	San Francisco P O	80	342
BESKER								
G W	28	m	w	MO	Monterey	Alisal Twp	74	299
BESLER								
B	47	m	w	PRUS	Alameda	Alameda	68	15
BESLEY								
William	42	m	w	ENGL	San Francisco	2-Wd San Francisco	79	256
BESLIN								
James	35	m	w	IREL	Placer	Blue Canyon P O	76	418
BESMARDO								
Juan	47	m	w	CHIL	Calaveras	San Andreas P O	70	181
BESON								
Frederick	38	m	w	ENGL	San Francisco	8-Wd San Francisco	82	408
BESORE								
John	41	m	w	OH	Fresno	Millerton P O	72	168
BESOVIAN								
John	44	m	m	CHIL	Placer	Bath P O	76	428
BESOVILLE								
Desirie	18	m	w	FRAN	Los Angeles	Wilmington Twp	73	644
BESS								
Thomas	37	m	w	OH	San Francisco	7-Wd San Francisco	81	159
BESSA								
Charles	51	m	w	ITAL	Contra Costa	Martinez P O	71	443
BESSAC								
Lewis	35	m	w	IA	Colusa	Monroe Twp	71	320
BESSAN								
Felip	29	m	w	FRAN	San Francisco	San Francisco P O	80	348
Felip	29	m	w	FRAN	San Francisco	San Francisco P O	80	347
BESSE								
John	62	m	w	FRAN	El Dorado	White Oak Twp	72	135
John D	39	m	w	ME	Santa Cruz	Santa Cruz	89	407
Jos O	48	m	w	CANA	San Francisco	San Francisco P O	83	286
BESSELL								
Gustavus	39	m	w	MA	El Dorado	White Oak Twp	72	136
BESSER								
Matthias	38	m	w	NJ	Placer	Pino Twp	76	472
BESSEY								
Racheal	47	f	w	DC	San Francisco	7-Wd San Francisco	81	207
Samuel	34	m	w	PA	Mendocino	Little Lake Twp	74	192
W R	43	m	w	ENGL	Monterey	Salinas Twp	74	309
BESSINGER								
Conrad	27	m	w	AUST	San Francisco	1-Wd San Francisco	79	51
Geo	20	m	w	MI	Santa Clara	Almaden Twp	88	17
John	32	m	w	BAVA	San Francisco	San Francisco P O	80	533
Rugma	26	f	w	MI	Sacramento	4-Wd Sacramento	77	319
BESSLER								
Fredene C	40	m	w	BAVA	San Luis Obispo	Santa Rosa Twp	87	320
BESSLIN								
Jacob	39	m	w	WURT	El Dorado	Greenwood Twp	72	55
BESSMER								
H L	35	m	w	POLA	San Francisco	San Francisco P O	83	298
BESSON								
Adolph	48	m	w	FRAN	San Francisco	San Francisco P O	80	538
Emile	5	m	w	CA	San Francisco	3-Wd San Francisco	79	319
Felix	38	m	w	FRAN	San Francisco	3-Wd San Francisco	79	318
BESSONET								
Peter	60	m	w	FRAN	Siskiyou	Yreka Twp	89	673
BESSY								
Samuel H	48	m	w	ME	San Mateo	Pescadero P O	87	416
BEST								
Addie	19	f	w	ME	Alameda	Brooklyn	68	38
Bridget	29	f	w	IREL	San Francisco	6-Wd San Francisco	81	70
Edward	27	m	w	NY	Santa Clara	Redwood Twp	88	119
Henry	37	m	w	OH	Sutter	Sutter Twp	92	128
James	40	m	w	IREL	San Francisco	7-Wd San Francisco	81	178
James	35	m	w	ENGL	San Bernardino	Belleville Twp	78	408
James D	35	m	w	KY	El Dorado	Mud Springs Twp	72	71
James T	24	m	w	MA	San Francisco	6-Wd San Francisco	81	79
John	44	m	w	OH	Stanislaus	Empire Twp	92	28
John	36	m	w	IREL	San Francisco	San Francisco P O	80	365
John R	40	m	w	KY	San Joaquin	3-Wd Stockton	86	231
Josiah	43	m	w	TN	Solano	Suisun Twp	90	101
Maria	44	f	w	NY	San Francisco	San Francisco P O	83	236
Martha	40	f	w	ENGL	San Francisco	8-Wd San Francisco	82	333
Martin	25	m	w	HDAR	Sierra	Eureka Twp	89	524
N W	31	m	w	CANA	Monterey	San Benito Twp	74	379
Nancy	46	f	w	IN	Stanislaus	Empire Twp	92	61
Richard	44	m	w	OH	Sutter	Sutter Twp	92	128
Samuel	42	m	w	OH	Sutter	Sutter Twp	92	128
Samuel M	35	m	w	MO	Solano	Suisun Twp	90	101
William	37	m	w	CANA	Siskiyou	Hamburg Twp	89	596
William	31	m	w	NY	San Francisco	8-Wd San Francisco	82	415
Zach	30	m	w	MO	Sutter	Sutter Twp	92	128
BESTER								
John	32	m	w	SHOL	San Francisco	2-Wd San Francisco	79	186
BESTERS								
Elizabeth	69	f	w	PRUS	San Francisco	8-Wd San Francisco	82	295
BESTHORN								
Herman	29	m	w	SHOL	San Francisco	11-Wd San Francisc	84	474
BESTON								
Margaret	26	f	w	IREL	San Francisco	San Francisco P O	80	459
Mary	14	f	w	CA	San Francisco	San Francisco P O	85	739
Thomas	50	m	w	ME	El Dorado	Diamond Springs Tw	72	21
BESTOR								
Henry	32	m	w	CT	San Francisco	11-Wd San Francisc	84	600
BESUILLIARD								
Frank	24	m	w	CANA	Marin	San Rafael Twp	74	34
BESWICH								
William	35	m	w	MI	Placer	Dutch Flat P O	76	401
BESWICK								
Frank	37	m	w	ENGL	San Joaquin	3-Wd Stockton	86	222
Henry	15	m	w	CA	San Joaquin	1-Wd Stockton	86	140
James	64	m	w	ENGL	El Dorado	Diamond Springs Tw	72	29
Jno W	37	m	w	IN	Santa Clara	Gilroy Twp	88	84

© 2001 by Heritage Quest. All rights reserved.

Name	Age	S	R	B-PL	County	Locale	Roll	Pg
						Series M593		
John	14	m	w	CA	San Joaquin	1-Wd Stockton	86	140
Nathan	32	m	w	ME	Siskiyou	Table Rock Twp	89	647
Richard	32	m	w	ME	Siskiyou	Yreka Twp	89	668
BESWINGER								
Louis	27	m	w	WURT	Los Angeles	Los Angeles	73	543
BESY								
Marie	27	f	w	FRAN	San Francisco	San Francisco P O	85	835
BET								
Ah	40	m	c	CHIN	San Francisco	San Francisco P O	80	503
Ah	36	m	c	CHIN	San Francisco	San Francisco P O	80	491
Ah	32	m	c	CHIN	San Francisco	San Francisco P O	80	492
Ah	30	m	c	CHIN	Sierra	Table Rock Twp	89	544
Ah	30	m	c	CHIN	San Francisco	San Francisco P O	80	501
Ah	20	f	c	CHIN	San Francisco	San Francisco P O	80	495
Ah	20	m	c	CHIN	Sutter	Butte Twp	92	92
Ah	18	f	c	CHIN	San Francisco	San Francisco P O	80	492
Shong	48	m	c	CHIN	El Dorado	Diamond Springs Tw	72	32
BETA								
Pablo	17	m	w	CA	Santa Barbara	San Buenaventura P	87	442
BETANCIA								
Joseph	57	m	w	PORT	Alameda	Oakland	68	144
BETANCOARA								
Frank	40	m	w	PORT	Santa Cruz	Santa Cruz	89	429
BETCHENER								
Robert V	35	m	w	MD	San Francisco	San Francisco P O	83	160
BETER								
Williard	38	m	w	WURT	San Francisco	2-Wd San Francisco	79	216
BETGE								
William	24	m	w	HANO	San Francisco	7-Wd San Francisco	81	218
BETGER								
Edward	40	m	w	SAXO	San Francisco	2-Wd San Francisco	79	139
BETGOLD								
Jacob	23	m	w	BADE	San Francisco	11-Wd San Francisc	84	467
BETH								
James	40	m	w	NY	San Francisco	7-Wd San Francisco	81	239
P	28	m	w	BAVA	Sierra	Butte Twp	89	508
BETHE								
Antone	40	m	w	SWIT	El Dorado	Lake Valley Twp	72	66
BETHEL								
Frank	36	m	w	IN	Santa Clara	1-Wd San Jose	88	231
James H	37	m	w	MO	Fresno	Millerton P O	72	168
Joseph	43	m	w	IREL	Yuba	Marysville	93	611
BETHELL								
Samuel	46	m	w	ENGL	Placer	Auburn P O	76	367
Warren R	46	m	w	IN	Santa Clara	1-Wd San Jose	88	231
BETHENSTER								
Manuel	22	m	w	PORT	Santa Clara	Redwood Twp	88	123
BETHNAL								
Moriah	35	f	w	NGRA	Sacramento	2-Wd Sacramento	77	238
BETHOLAMEW								
Caneson P	27	m	w	NY	Yolo	Putah Twp	93	517
BETLETZ								
August	40	m	w	FRAN	San Francisco	San Francisco P O	80	334
BETMAN								
Moses	39	m	w	BAVA	San Francisco	6-Wd San Francisco	81	130
BETONCOURT								
Antonio J	44	m	w	AZOR	Santa Clara	San Jose Twp	88	189
BETSELL								
Jacob	36	m	w	OH	Mendocino	Round Valley India	74	180
BETSHER								
Ormando M	23	m	w	ME	Santa Cruz	Soquel Twp	89	445
BETSOLD								
Andrew	26	m	w	BADE	Santa Clara	Fremont Twp	88	62
BETSONI								
Louis	27	m	w	ITAL	San Francisco	6-Wd San Francisco	81	155
BETSTERLING								
William	46	m	w	VA	Yolo	Grafton Twp	93	483
BETSY								
Brown	14	m	w	CA	Butte	Concow Twp	70	7
BETT								
Adolf	21	m	w	HANO	San Francisco	3-Wd San Francisco	79	325
BETTA								
Amico	38	m	w	FRAN	Calaveras	San Andreas P O	70	186
BETTE								
Augustus	48	m	w	HANO	Placer	Bath P O	76	451
BETTEE								
John	29	m	w	MA	San Francisco	11-Wd San Francisc	84	639
BETTELY								
Edwd	19	m	w	ENGL	San Francisco	1-Wd San Francisco	79	91
BETTEN								
David	40	m	w	PA	Los Angeles	Los Angeles	73	552
George H	25	m	w	SALT	Placer	Gold Run Twp	76	394
Louisa	23	f	w	BAVA	San Francisco	San Francisco P O	80	488
William	31	m	w	SALT	Placer	Gold Run Twp	76	394
BETTENCIENT								
J	35	m	w	AZOR	Monterey	Monterey	74	364
BETTENGER								
Frank	45	m	w	PRUS	Sierra	Table Rock Twp	89	579
Herman	30	m	w	PRUS	San Francisco	6-Wd San Francisco	81	91
BETTER								
Jennie	38	f	w	NY	Sacramento	Cosumnes Twp	77	92
BETTERTON								
James L	33	m	w	TN	Plumas	Quartz Twp	77	43
BETTGAR								
Mary	40	f	w	IREL	San Francisco	San Francisco P O	80	458
BETTI								
Paulina	37	f	w	CA	Los Angeles	Los Angeles	73	562
BETTICK								
Joseph	42	m	w	AL	Merced	Snelling P O	74	251
BETTIGER								
John	45	m	w	BAVA	San Francisco	2-Wd San Francisco	79	218
BETTINI								
Paulo	39	m	w	ITAL	San Francisco	11-Wd San Francisc	84	660
BETTIS								
Elijah	42	m	w	MS	Los Angeles	Los Angeles	73	531
John	30	m	w	MA	Alameda	Alameda	68	12
John W	60	m	w	NY	Los Angeles	Los Angeles	73	527
Lizzie	18	f	w	CA	San Diego	San Luis Rey	78	512
O J	44	m	w	NY	San Francisco	San Francisco P O	83	18
R S	40	m	w	MO	Tehama	Red Bluff	92	179
Truckee	41	m	w	CANA	Sierra	Sears Twp	89	557
William	64	m	w	NY	Nevada	Grass Valley Twp	75	186
BETTON								
Henry	45	m	w	OLDE	Marin	Bolinas Twp	74	7
Maria	20	f	w	NY	Sonoma	Santa Rosa	91	408
Samuel	48	m	w	SWIT	Placer	Auburn P O	76	370
BETTS								
Ebenezer M	31	m	w	NY	Santa Barbara	Santa Barbara P O	87	501
Frances	55	f	w	PA	Stanislaus	North Twp	92	69
James	23	m	w	IA	Humboldt	Eel Rvr Twp	72	246
John	42	m	w	PA	Tuolumne	Chinese Camp P O	93	368
John J	25	m	w	OH	Humboldt	Mattole Twp	72	288
Maxamillion	29	f	w	PRUS	Contra Costa	Martinez P O	71	436
William M	42	m	w	ENGL	San Francisco	San Francisco P O	83	348
Wm	28	m	w	NY	San Joaquin	3-Wd Stockton	86	217
BETTUM								
G	32	m	w	ITAL	Amador	Jackson P O	69	337
BETTZ								
John	93	m	w	HANO	Placer	Bath P O	76	447
Mary	48	f	w	IREL	Alameda	Oakland	68	179
BETZ								
Charles	41	m	w	PRUS	San Francisco	San Francisco P O	83	232
Isiah	41	m	w	OH	Yolo	Grafton Twp	93	497
Jacob	26	m	w	BAVA	San Francisco	2-Wd San Francisco	79	218
James	40	m	w	PRUS	San Francisco	8-Wd San Francisco	82	376
Joseph	34	m	w	WURT	San Francisco	8-Wd San Francisco	82	439
Joseph	23	m	w	BADE	San Francisco	8-Wd San Francisco	82	354
Louize	37	f	w	VA	Yuba	Marysville	93	613
Mary	42	f	w	GERM	San Joaquin	2-Wd Stockton	86	170
Paul	34	m	w	WURT	Santa Clara	2-Wd San Jose	88	302
BETZEL								
Charles	40	m	w	PRUS	Santa Cruz	Soquel Twp	89	446
Louis	40	m	w	PRUS	San Francisco	8-Wd San Francisco	82	414
BEU								
Ah	32	m	c	CHIN	Tuolumne	Big Oak Flat P O	93	392
BEUC								
John	44	m	w	PRUS	San Francisco	San Francisco P O	83	381
BEUCHEL								
John	64	m	w	SAXO	San Francisco	2-Wd San Francisco	79	256
BEUCHLEY								
Ruth	65	f	w	NY	Sacramento	3-Wd Sacramento	77	291
BEUCLER								
Philip	35	m	w	PRUS	Nevada	Nevada Twp	75	279
BEUDER								
Joseph	40	m	w	FRAN	Siskiyou	Hamburg Twp	89	598
BEUHM								
Mary	16	f	i	CA	Trinity	Weaverville Pct	92	222
BEUHREN								
William	60	m	w	PRUS	Napa	Napa	75	42
BEUL								
Neal G	13	m	w	PA	Yolo	Cache Crk Twp	93	453
BEULE								
Oscar	35	m	w	IL	San Bernardino	San Bernardino Twp	78	445
BEULES								
H S	46	m	w	CT	Sacramento	3-Wd Sacramento	77	266
BEULING								
Frank	25	m	w	BAVA	San Francisco	San Francisco P O	83	195
BEUMONT								
Jennie	25	f	w	CANA	Nevada	Meadow Lake Twp	75	249
BEURHYTE								
Isaac	36	m	w	NY	San Francisco	San Francisco P O	83	63
BEUTEL								
Henry	31	m	w	PRUS	Colusa	Spring Valley Twp	71	339
BEUTLER								
John B	46	m	w	BADE	San Francisco	San Francisco P O	83	200
BEUZ								
Nicholas	65	m	w	DALM	San Francisco	1-Wd San Francisco	79	96
BEVAN								
Edwn	35	m	w	WALE	Sierra	Table Rock Twp	89	579
James	38	m	w	ENGL	San Francisco	11-Wd San Francisc	84	550
John	21	m	w	CHIL	San Francisco	7-Wd San Francisco	81	270
Louis	25	m	w	WALE	Siskiyou	Scott Valley Twp	89	611
BEVANS								
Charles	35	m	w	ENGL	San Francisco	San Francisco P O	80	462
Dorothy	42	f	w	NY	San Francisco	San Francisco P O	85	829
Thomas	50	m	w	ENGL	San Francisco	San Francisco P O	80	369
Thos	59	m	w	NY	San Francisco	San Francisco P O	83	125
BEVEL								
William T	25	m	w	VA	Colusa	Colusa	71	293
BEVELL								
Richd	38	m	w	ENGL	San Francisco	San Francisco P O	83	25
BEVEN								
James	32	m	w	ENGL	San Francisco	2-Wd San Francisco	79	187

© 2001 by Heritage Quest. All rights reserved.

California 1870 Census

Name	Age	S	R	B-PL	County	Locale	Roll	Pg
BEVENER								
Frederick	24	m	w	HANO	Sacramento	2-Wd Sacramento	77	230
BEVER								
Mountford	18	m	w	IL	Yuba	New York Twp	93	639
BEVERAGE								
John	30	m	w	NY	Inyo	Cerro Gordo Twp	73	321
BEVERE								
Charles	39	m	w	PRUS	Nevada	Grass Valley Twp	75	158
BEVERIDGE								
David	52	m	w	SCOT	Sacramento	3-Wd Sacramento	77	286
David	43	m	w	MD	Sacramento	4-Wd Sacramento	77	328
Horatio	29	m	w	SCOT	San Francisco	7-Wd San Francisco	81	286
Ida F	15	f	w	ME	Contra Costa	Martinez P O	71	394
James	40	m	w	MO	Siskiyou	Yreka	89	651
BEVERLEY								
Walter	25	m	w	ENGL	Sacramento	3-Wd Sacramento	77	318
BEVERLY								
Frank	15	m	w	CA	Santa Clara	Santa Clara Twp	88	176
Frank	15	m	w	CA	Santa Clara	Fremont Twp	88	64
Jno	22	m	w	MA	Alameda	Oakland	68	211
Thos	20	m	w	ENGL	San Luis Obispo	Salinas Twp	87	291
BEVERS								
Charles	13	m	w	NY	Colusa	Stony Crk Twp	71	328
BEVERTON								
Samuel	42	m	w	ENGL	Nevada	Grass Valley Twp	75	157
BEVINS								
Alex	34	m	w	NY	Fresno	Millerton P O	72	183
Hamilton	3	m	w	CA	San Francisco	San Francisco P O	85	799
Horace	34	m	w	NY	Solano	Silveyville Twp	90	82
Peter C	45	m	w	IREL	San Francisco	1-Wd San Francisco	79	113
William	45	m	w	NY	Sacramento	2-Wd Sacramento	77	246
Wm M	53	m	w	NY	San Francisco	San Francisco P O	85	855
BEVIS								
G W	50	m	w	MO	Merced	Snelling P O	74	273
BEVISO								
John	64	m	w	FRAN	Fresno	Millerton P O	72	158
BEW								
Ah	48	m	c	CHIN	El Dorado	Placerville	72	115
BEWA								
Tebosio	37	m	w	CHIL	Fresno	Millerton P O	72	153
BEWERS								
Edward B	42	m	w	MA	Amador	Volcano P O	69	380
Elias	50	m	w	OH	Sacramento	4-Wd Sacramento	77	376
George	83	m	w	ENGL	Amador	Volcano P O	69	380
George W	30	m	w	MA	Amador	Volcano P O	69	380
BEWLEY								
Allen	40	m	w	PA	San Francisco	San Francisco P O	80	404
BEXTINE								
Margaret	9	f	w	CA	San Bernardino	Chino Twp	78	410
BEY								
Ah	28	m	c	CHIN	El Dorado	Diamond Springs Tw	72	25
Ah	21	m	c	CHIN	San Francisco	San Francisco P O	80	498
Clouse	60	m	w	HANO	El Dorado	Mud Springs Twp	72	86
Henry	62	m	w	HANO	El Dorado	Mud Springs Twp	72	86
Him	50	m	c	CHIN	Trinity	North Fork Twp	92	216
BEYA								
Miguel	28	m	w	CHIL	Fresno	Millerton P O	72	165
BEYAR								
James	35	m	w	SCOT	San Francisco	11-Wd San Francisc	84	548
BEYENDOFFER								
L	34	m	w	GERM	Solano	Vallejo	90	202
BEYER								
Anthony	32	m	w	DENM	Tulare	Tule Rvr Twp	92	270
George	19	m	w	PRUS	San Francisco	San Francisco P O	80	459
BEYERLE								
Christian	35	m	w	BAVA	San Francisco	11-Wd San Francisc	84	536
BEYLIN								
Barney	29	m	w	IREL	Sacramento	3-Wd Sacramento	77	273
James	45	m	w	IREL	Sonoma	Analy Twp	91	221
BEYREISS								
Gottleib	38	m	w	PRUS	San Francisco	San Francisco P O	80	531
BEYRNE								
Mary	18	f	w	SCOT	San Francisco	11-Wd San Francisc	84	431
BEZAR								
Mortin	25	m	w	DE	Placer	Emigrant Gap P O	76	416
BEZEL								
Mary	8	f	w	CA	San Francisco	San Francisco P O	80	405
BEZIL								
Adam	37	m	w	HDAR	Colusa	Colusa Twp	71	283
BEZONT								
James	22	m	w	ENGL	San Bernardino	Belleville Twp	78	408
BHEMANN								
John	54	m	w	HAMB	Yuba	Linda Twp	93	554
BHEN								
Michael	48	m	w	FRAN	Santa Clara	2-Wd San Jose	88	281
BHERLE								
Fredk	40	m	w	BADE	Marin	Sausalito Twp	74	70
BHERNS								
Harvey	49	m	w	UNKN	San Joaquin	2-Wd Stockton	86	166
BHETLER								
Wm	39	m	w	SWIT	El Dorado	Georgetown Twp	72	36
BHIRUD								
Alexander	52	m	w	IREL	Contra Costa	Martinez P O	71	405
BI								
Ah	27	m	c	CHIN	Sacramento	1-Wd Sacramento	77	205
Ah	19	f	c	CHIN	Santa Barbara	Santa Barbara P O	87	459
Ah	17	m	c	CHIN	San Francisco	San Francisco P O	83	188
Chung	20	m	c	CHIN	Trinity	North Fork Twp	92	219
Tee	41	m	c	CHIN	Alameda	Oakland	68	223
BIACH								
Geo	77	m	w	ME	San Joaquin	Douglas Twp	86	48
BIAIS								
Chiri	35	m	w	FRAN	Inyo	Cerro Gordo Twp	73	319
BIAL								
Johana	25	f	w	IREL	San Francisco	8-Wd San Francisco	82	297
BIANCHETTI								
Luize	43	m	w	ITAL	San Francisco	11-Wd San Francisc	84	594
Phillip	25	m	w	ASEA	Amador	Volcano P O	69	382
BIANCHI								
Giovanni	40	m	w	ITAL	San Francisco	11-Wd San Francisc	84	603
BIANCHINI								
Marta	52	f	w	SWIT	San Francisco	11-Wd San Francisc	84	594
BIANCI								
Peter	23	m	w	SWIT	Santa Clara	Fremont Twp	88	66
BIANCKI								
Edward	15	m	w	ITAL	San Francisco	3-Wd San Francisco	79	288
BIANCO								
A	40	m	w	ITAL	Amador	Sutter Crk P O	69	411
BIANKIE								
Angelo	28	m	w	ITAL	Placer	Newcastle Twp	76	476
BIANO								
Ambrose	62	m	w	AUST	San Francisco	3-Wd San Francisco	79	295
BIAR								
Thomas	32	m	w	DENM	Alameda	Eden Twp	68	59
BIAS								
Elario	32	m	w	CHIL	Fresno	Millerton P O	72	153
Ramon	40	m	w	MEXI	Santa Clara	Almaden Twp	88	10
Robert H	35	m	w	PA	Solano	Maine Prairie Twp	90	50
William	36	m	b	DC	San Francisco	3-Wd San Francisco	79	308
BIASCIO								
Carlo	28	m	w	ITAL	San Francisco	1-Wd San Francisco	79	35
BIASES								
Joseph	45	m	w	NJ	San Bernardino	San Bernardino Twp	78	430
BIAZOTA								
Dominca	27	m	w	ITAL	Amador	Volcano P O	69	372
BIBB								
Daniel	16	m	w	CA	San Francisco	11-Wd San Francisc	84	648
Enma	31	f	w	NY	San Francisco	11-Wd San Francisc	84	619
Harriet	11	f	w	CA	San Francisco	8-Wd San Francisco	82	466
Samuel	21	m	w	MO	Yolo	Cottonwood Twp	93	469
William	22	m	w	MO	Sutter	Sutter Twp	92	120
William	21	m	w	VA	Sutter	Sutter Twp	92	124
BIBBER								
Chas	28	m	w	ME	Alameda	Oakland	68	211
BIBBINS								
B F	30	m	w	VT	Sacramento	1-Wd Sacramento	77	178
Tracy L	40	m	w	IL	San Francisco	6-Wd San Francisco	81	144
BIBBY								
Rosa	15	f	w	CA	Monterey	San Antonio Twp	74	323
BIBE								
Jarome	36	m	w	PA	Siskiyou	Scott Rvr Twp	89	604
BIBEMELTT								
Monal	37	m	w	CANA	Santa Cruz	Santa Cruz Twp	89	392
BIBENS								
Thos W	35	m	b	VA	San Francisco	San Francisco P O	85	874
BIBER								
Adam	30	m	w	DENM	Butte	Oregon Twp	70	135
Adolph	32	m	w	PRUS	San Francisco	San Francisco P O	83	401
BIBLE								
Bettison	49	f	w	TN	Tehama	Deer Crk Twp	92	171
R R	22	m	w	MS	Tehama	Tehama Twp	92	192
BIBRICH								
Margaret	59	m	w	GERM	Yolo	Cache Crk Twp	93	431
BICE								
Cornelius	51	m	w	KY	Sonoma	Mendocino Twp	91	297
Edward	40	m	w	CA	Monterey	San Antonio Twp	74	321
Mary	36	f	w	ENGL	Nevada	Grass Valley Twp	75	153
Nicholas	49	m	w	ENGL	Nevada	Grass Valley Twp	75	143
BICHVED								
A C	38	m	w	NY	Sacramento	4-Wd Sacramento	77	333
BICK								
Ah	50	m	c	CHIN	Amador	Fiddletown P O	69	428
Ah	40	m	c	CHIN	Santa Clara	1-Wd San Jose	88	256
Berry	14	m	w	CA	Butte	Ophir Twp	70	94
Edwd	38	m	w	BELG	San Francisco	1-Wd San Francisco	79	98
William	28	m	w	IA	Alameda	Washington Twp	68	295
BICKEN								
John	15	m	w	KY	Alameda	Oakland	68	214
BICKENDORF								
Peter	34	m	w	PRUS	Sacramento	Brighton Twp	77	80
BICKERS								
Henry C	53	m	w	VA	San Diego	Julian Dist	78	471
BICKERSTAFF								
Jona	37	m	w	MO	Marin	Sausalito Twp	74	66
BICKERT								
C	21	f	w	PRUS	Sierra	Table Rock Twp	89	573
BICKET								
Frances	27	f	w	NY	Humboldt	Eureka Twp	72	270
Marian	7	f	w	CA	Napa	Napa	75	3
BICKFORD								
A	15	f	w	CA	Sacramento	3-Wd Sacramento	77	317
Chauncey	48	m	w	ME	San Francisco	1-Wd San Francisco	79	90
Danl	46	m	w	MA	Siskiyou	Callahan P O	89	628
Edwan	21	m	w	ME	Santa Cruz	Santa Cruz Twp	89	393

Series M593

© 2001 by Heritage Quest. All rights reserved.

Series M593

Name	Age	S	R	B-PL	County	Locale	Roll	Pg
George	38	m	w	OH	Tulare	Kings Rvr Twp	92	253
Ira	41	m	w	NY	San Francisco	8-Wd San Francisco	82	369
John	59	m	w	ME	Butte	Oroville Twp	70	137
Leonard	45	m	w	ME	Nevada	Bridgeport Twp	75	103
Leonard H	24	m	w	ME	Nevada	Nevada Twp	75	307
Lorenz D	40	m	w	ME	Shasta	Stillwater P O	89	478
Melvina	22	f	w	ME	Nevada	Nevada Twp	75	307
R A	26	m	w	ME	Tuolumne	Sonora P O	93	321
Sophronia	43	f	w	OH	Nevada	Grass Valley Twp	75	219
Wm H	42	m	w	MA	Shasta	Millville P O	89	486
BICKING								
Chas	24	m	w	GERM	San Francisco	8-Wd San Francisco	82	375
Sarah	42	f	w	FRAN	Shasta	Shasta P O	89	461
BICKINGS								
G	24	m	w	RI	San Francisco	8-Wd San Francisco	82	374
BICKLE								
Wm	42	m	w	LA	Calaveras	Copperopolis P O	70	232
BICKLEY								
Joseph	43	m	w	SWED	Sutter	Sutter Twp	92	118
BICKLY								
John F	35	m	w	VA	Sutter	Yuba Twp	92	140
BICKMAN								
Fred	50	m	w	HANO	Sacramento	Georgianna Twp	77	128
J S	51	m	w	NORW	Tuolumne	Big Oak Flat P O	93	392
BICKMORE								
Geo	30	m	w	MA	San Francisco	7-Wd San Francisco	81	243
Thomas	28	m	w	IL	Santa Cruz	Pajaro Twp	89	355
William	71	m	w	ME	Santa Cruz	Pajaro Twp	89	355
BICKNAL								
David	28	m	w	CANA	Santa Clara	San Jose Twp	88	216
BICKNALL								
Alijah	38	m	w	NY	San Diego	Julian Dist	78	471
BICKNELL								
Daniel	37	m	w	ME	Sonoma	Petaluma Twp	91	348
Elizabeth	30	f	w	CANA	Sonoma	Petaluma Twp	91	340
Isaac	54	m	w	CANA	Santa Clara	San Jose Twp	88	215
J	25	m	w	ME	Humboldt	Bucksport Twp	72	243
J F	40	m	w	VT	Nevada	Meadow Lake Twp	75	250
James	39	m	w	IREL	San Francisco	San Francisco P O	80	405
John	41	m	w	CANA	San Luis Obispo	San Luis Obispo Tw	87	309
BICKNER								
Edward	40	m	w	MA	Los Angeles	Los Angeles	73	559
BICKWEDEL								
John	35	m	w	HANO	San Francisco	San Francisco P O	85	870
BICKWELL								
J R	23	m	w	CANA	San Joaquin	Tulare Twp	86	260
BICKWORTH								
Thos	73	m	w	ME	San Francisco	11-Wd San Francisc	84	612
BIDACHE								
Victor	42	m	w	FRAN	Monterey	Monterey	74	363
BIDAL								
Rufus	50	m	w	MEXI	Tehama	Red Bluff	92	182
BIDALL								
Marie	50	f	w	FRAN	San Francisco	San Francisco P O	80	479
BIDDELL								
Frederick	27	m	w	PA	San Francisco	8-Wd San Francisco	82	442
Mary	27	f	w	OH	San Francisco	San Francisco P O	83	266
BIDDEN								
Jas S	36	m	w	WV	Klamath	Liberty Twp	73	374
BIDDLE								
Amos	46	m	w	PA	Tuolumne	Columbia P O	93	336
E M	28	m	w	PA	Tuolumne	Columbia P O	93	336
Edwin	20	m	w	IL	San Francisco	San Francisco P O	83	262
Francis	45	m	w	OH	Butte	Wyandotte Twp	70	147
Jacob	29	m	w	PA	Tuolumne	Columbia P O	93	349
Jacob	28	m	w	PA	Tuolumne	Columbia P O	93	345
John	52	m	w	PA	Yuba	Marysville	93	618
Philip	64	m	w	GERM	San Luis Obispo	Salinas Twp	87	290
BIDDLECUM								
Casimira	35	f	w	CA	San Luis Obispo	San Luis Obispo Tw	87	300
BIDDNY								
John A	41	m	w	PA	Humboldt	Arcata Twp	72	229
BIDDY								
Anthony	40	m	w	PRUS	Monterey	San Benito Twp	74	380
BIDER								
Edward	24	m	w	ENGL	Yolo	Grafton Twp	93	488
BIDERMAN								
Jno	41	m	w	PA	Sacramento	1-Wd Sacramento	77	174
BIDFORD								
Henry	75	m	b	MO	El Dorado	Cosumnes Twp	72	14
John C	35	m	w	KY	Los Angeles	Los Nietos Twp	73	578
BIDLAN								
Mary Ann	42	f	w	FL	Sacramento	Alabama Twp	77	62
BIDLEMAN								
Carrie	7	f	w	CA	Solano	Benicia	90	16
Enoch	37	m	w	NJ	San Francisco	San Francisco P O	80	532
Joseph	50	m	w	NJ	San Francisco	San Francisco P O	80	532
Kate	14	f	w	CA	Solano	Benicia	90	16
Wm	29	m	w	NJ	San Francisco	11-Wd San Francisc	84	481
BIDSTROUPE								
Fernantero	26	m	w	DENM	El Dorado	Mud Springs Twp	72	81
Hans W	35	m	w	DENM	El Dorado	Mud Springs Twp	72	80
BIDSWORTH								
J	29	m	w	MO	Yuba	Marysville	93	633
BIDULE								
Madaline	38	f	w	FRAN	San Francisco	6-Wd San Francisco	81	37

Series M593

Name	Age	S	R	B-PL	County	Locale	Roll	Pg
BIDWELL								
Abrm B	37	m	w	NY	Butte	Chico Twp	70	26
Andrew	48	m	w	ME	Stanislaus	San Joaquin Twp	92	81
F	19	m	w	IL	Sacramento	1-Wd Sacramento	77	189
H E	24	m	w	IL	Alameda	Oakland	68	212
Henry	40	m	w	VT	Plumas	Seneca Twp	77	51
James	52	m	w	CT	San Francisco	San Francisco P O	83	374
Jno H	48	m	w	NY	Shasta	Millville P O	89	490
John	50	m	w	NY	Butte	Chico Twp	70	45
Theresa	39	f	w	CANA	San Francisco	11-Wd San Francisc	84	565
BIE								
Ah	14	m	c	CHIN	Napa	Napa	75	56
War	25	f	c	CHIN	Sacramento	1-Wd Sacramento	77	195
BIEARD								
Geo	39	m	w	ENGL	San Francisco	1-Wd San Francisco	79	4
BIEBE								
Elijah T	38	m	w	AR	Mendocino	Point Arena Twp	74	212
Francis M	37	m	w	IL	Mendocino	Point Arena Twp	74	212
George W	34	m	w	MO	Mendocino	Point Arena Twp	74	212
BIEBEE								
Chas	14	m	w	AR	San Francisco	11-Wd San Francisc	84	648
BIEBER								
Julius	16	m	w	PRUS	San Francisco	San Francisco P O	83	23
BIEBRACH								
Frederick	39	m	w	PRUS	Santa Clara	1-Wd San Jose	88	262
BIEGERTON								
Robt	24	m	w	VA	Sacramento	Mississippi Twp	77	164
BIEGLER								
Fr	27	m	w	SWIT	San Francisco	San Francisco P O	83	134
BIEHL								
Julius	32	m	w	DENM	San Francisco	3-Wd San Francisco	79	311
BIEL								
Frank	32	m	w	FRAN	Los Angeles	Los Angeles	73	568
BIELA								
Juan	40	m	i	CA	San Luis Obispo	Santa Rosa Twp	87	330
BIELAR								
Henry	59	m	w	SWIT	Butte	Bidwell Twp	70	3
BIELER								
Adolf	30	m	w	BADE	San Francisco	3-Wd San Francisco	79	311
BIELO								
Bautisto	23	m	w	CA	Los Angeles	Los Angeles	73	513
BIEMER								
Minna	20	f	w	PRUS	San Francisco	8-Wd San Francisco	82	339
BIEN								
Amelia	20	f	w	BADE	San Francisco	8-Wd San Francisco	82	419
Emanuel	70	m	w	HESS	Sacramento	4-Wd Sacramento	77	323
Henry	37	m	w	HOLL	Nevada	Meadow Lake Twp	75	268
Joseph	41	m	w	PRUS	San Francisco	8-Wd San Francisco	82	456
Lyman	30	m	w	NY	Mendocino	Little Lake Twp	74	203
Philip	45	m	w	HAMB	Santa Clara	2-Wd San Jose	88	310
William	24	m	w	ME	San Francisco	8-Wd San Francisco	82	460
BIENCHE								
Conrad	34	m	w	SWIT	San Francisco	San Francisco P O	80	479
BIENCKE								
Castro	25	m	w	ITAL	San Francisco	San Francisco P O	80	427
BIENFIELD								
Elias	32	m	w	AUST	San Francisco	San Francisco P O	80	425
BIER								
Gotlief	54	m	w	HDAR	San Francisco	8-Wd San Francisco	82	293
BIERABENT								
Jose M	36	m	w	FRAN	Santa Barbara	Santa Barbara P O	87	498
BIERBRANKER								
John	38	m	w	HANO	San Francisco	2-Wd San Francisco	79	244
BIERBROW								
Chs	32	m	w	PRUS	San Francisco	2-Wd San Francisco	79	172
BIERCE								
R H	37	m	w	NY	Tehama	Red Bluff	92	178
BIERD								
Joseph	28	m	w	AR	Yuba	W Bear Rvr Twp	93	682
Platt	50	m	w	NY	Yuba	Marysville	93	618
S C	30	m	w	AR	Yuba	W Bear Rvr Twp	93	682
BIERDENHOLTZ								
Henry	45	m	w	SWIT	Tulare	Packwood Twp	92	256
BIERMAN								
Henry	34	m	w	PRUS	San Francisco	2-Wd San Francisco	79	229
BIERNAN								
Julius	33	m	w	WURT	Sacramento	2-Wd Sacramento	77	209
BIERNBAUM								
Wm	30	m	w	IL	Siskiyou	Scott Valley Twp	89	621
BIEROTTO								
Chas	39	m	w	BAVA	Fresno	Kingston P O	72	222
BIERUCH								
Fred	26	m	w	GERM	Sacramento	1-Wd Sacramento	77	173
BIESMAN								
Louis	45	m	w	PRUS	San Francisco	San Francisco P O	85	851
BIESTERFIELD								
Lorenz	41	m	w	PRUS	San Francisco	San Francisco P O	80	478
BIETENBACH								
August	38	m	w	BADE	San Francisco	San Francisco P O	83	150
BIG								
Lee	28	m	c	CHIN	San Francisco	6-Wd San Francisco	81	98
BIGAN								
William	48	m	w	TN	Napa	Napa	75	14
BIGARMS								
Joseph	45	m	w	OH	Plumas	Rich Bar Twp	77	46
BIGELOW								
A	58	m	w	US	San Joaquin	Liberty Twp	86	88

© 2001 by Heritage Quest. All rights reserved.

Series M593

Name	Age	S	R	B-PL	County	Locale	Roll	Pg
A W	49	m	w	MI	San Joaquin	Dent Twp	86	26
Alexander	47	m	w	NY	Tulare	Farmersville Twp	92	241
Allen	68	m	w	NY	Sutter	Butte Twp	92	95
Ashely S	43	m	w	VT	Calaveras	San Andreas P O	70	168
Benj	46	m	w	CANA	Yuba	Marysville	93	593
C E	42	m	w	PA	Humboldt	Eureka Twp	72	259
Chas	34	m	w	NY	San Francisco	11-Wd San Francisc	84	599
Daniel	35	m	w	IREL	San Francisco	11-Wd San Francisc	84	470
Du Boise	40	m	w	IL	Monterey	San Antonio Twp	74	319
Eli	29	m	w	NY	Mendocino	Calpella Twp	74	187
Elija	58	m	w	MA	Alameda	Oakland	68	199
Ezra	41	m	w	NY	Plumas	Seneca Twp	77	50
Francis H	26	m	w	NY	San Francisco	San Francisco P O	83	73
Geo W	40	m	w	PA	Klamath	Sawyers Bar	73	377
George	56	m	w	MA	Amador	Drytown P O	69	422
H D	21	m	w	RI	Solano	Vallejo	90	200
Jacob	60	m	w	MA	Solano	Vallejo	90	164
Jno E	31	m	w	MA	San Francisco	8-Wd San Francisco	82	301
John	59	m	w	MA	Marin	San Rafael	74	53
L G	26	m	w	MA	Sutter	Butte Twp	92	95
Marcus J	29	m	w	NY	Yuba	New York Twp	93	639
Phoebe	84	f	w	RI	San Francisco	San Francisco P O	83	143
Ralph R	39	m	w	NY	Siskiyou	Butte Twp	89	587
S W	35	m	w	NY	Nevada	Nevada Twp	75	286
T B	71	m	w	MA	Alameda	Oakland	68	199
BIGELY								
John Q	39	m	w	HI	Sutter	Vernon Twp	92	133
Joseph	60	m	w	HI	Sutter	Vernon Twp	92	133
BIGENOUGH								
Charls	36	m	w	SCOT	San Joaquin	2-Wd Stockton	86	167
BIGETY								
R C	50	m	w	CANA	Tuolumne	Columbia P O	93	353
BIGGER								
Alexander	45	m	w	IREL	San Francisco	11-Wd San Francisc	84	582
BIGGEY								
Terrance	50	m	w	IREL	San Francisco	San Francisco P O	85	868
BIGGI								
Angelo	29	m	w	ITAL	San Francisco	San Francisco P O	80	466
BIGGINS								
Frank	22	m	w	IL	Sacramento	Natomas Twp	77	165
James	42	m	w	IREL	Sonoma	Sonoma Twp	91	431
Patk	36	m	w	IREL	Marin	San Rafael Twp	74	31
Thomas	41	m	w	IREL	Marin	San Rafael Twp	74	31
Wm	30	m	w	IREL	Solano	Vallejo	90	197
Wm	26	m	w	IA	Sutter	Vernon Twp	92	135
BIGGIO								
Angello	51	m	w	ITAL	Amador	Sutter Crk P O	69	408
Watkin	26	m	w	WALE	Amador	Sutter Crk P O	69	408
BIGGIS								
Angelo	30	m	w	ITAL	San Francisco	1-Wd San Francisco	79	109
BIGGLE								
Loyan	22	m	w	IL	Kern	Bakersfield P O	73	361
BIGGS								
Abel R	53	m	w	NY	San Francisco	2-Wd San Francisco	79	267
Adam	40	m	w	PA	San Francisco	5-Wd San Francisco	81	33
Alexander D	42	m	w	TN	Santa Clara	San Jose Twp	88	207
Benjamin	30	m	w	ENGL	Santa Clara	2-Wd San Jose	88	302
Bennett	36	m	w	AR	Los Angeles	Los Nietos Twp	73	579
Berry F	62	m	w	KY	Tehama	Merrill	92	198
Christopher	24	m	w	TX	Kern	Bakersfield P O	73	360
Clinton	40	m	w	AR	Kern	Linns Valley P O	73	345
E	44	m	w	PA	Napa	Napa	75	56
Henry	19	m	w	TX	San Bernardino	San Bernardino Twp	78	444
J J	38	m	w	IL	Humboldt	Bald Hills	72	237
James	27	m	w	MO	Stanislaus	Empire Twp	92	33
James	18	m	w	TN	San Bernardino	Belleville Twp	78	408
Jessie E	30	m	w	NY	San Francisco	San Francisco P O	83	282
John	49	m	w	ENGL	San Francisco	11-Wd San Francisc	84	677
John	29	m	w	AR	San Luis Obispo	Morro Twp	87	287
John A	49	m	w	ENGL	San Francisco	11-Wd San Francisc	84	707
Marion	46	m	w	MO	Butte	Hamilton Twp	70	70
Matthew	42	m	w	PA	San Francisco	2-Wd San Francisco	79	196
Matthew H	43	m	w	PERU	Santa Barbara	Santa Barbara P O	87	450
Milton	39	m	w	IL	Mendocino	Ukiah Twp	74	243
Nancy F	52	f	w	CT	San Francisco	8-Wd San Francisco	82	298
Napoleon B	42	m	w	AL	Calaveras	Copperopolis P O	70	246
Thomas	47	m	w	IREL	Santa Barbara	Santa Barbara P O	87	453
Thos	37	m	w	VA	Sacramento	Granite Twp	77	155
William	55	m	w	ENGL	Nevada	Grass Valley Twp	75	158
BIGHAM								
David H	29	m	w	MO	Tulare	Farmersville Twp	92	245
J C	34	m	w	MO	Merced	Snelling P O	74	256
James	53	m	w	OH	Sacramento	Center Twp	77	84
James W	60	m	w	TN	Tulare	Farmersville Twp	92	245
John	53	m	w	KY	Santa Cruz	Soquel Twp	89	441
William	23	m	w	MO	Siskiyou	Surprise Valley Tw	89	641
BIGHER								
John	28	m	w	PRUS	San Francisco	8-Wd San Francisco	82	321
BIGKEL								
Conrad	57	m	w	BAVA	San Francisco	San Francisco P O	85	824
BIGLE								
Adommica	49	m	w	VT	Sacramento	Georgianna Twp	77	128
BIGLER								
Gotlieb	30	m	w	PRUS	Sacramento	4-Wd Sacramento	77	367
John	65	m	w	PA	Sacramento	3-Wd Sacramento	77	315
John	60	m	w	IREL	Sacramento	4-Wd Sacramento	77	376
John	40	m	w	BAVA	Stanislaus	Emory Twp	92	19
John	32	m	w	MA	San Francisco	8-Wd San Francisco	82	355
Maggie	16	f	w	MO	Mariposa	Mariposa P O	74	109
Margaret	30	f	w	PRUS	San Joaquin	2-Wd Stockton	86	168
Sue	35	f	i	CA	Sacramento	1-Wd Sacramento	77	201
Winn	40	m	w	OH	Los Angeles	Los Angeles	73	503
BIGLEY								
Catherine	48	f	w	ENGL	San Francisco	8-Wd San Francisco	82	494
John	42	m	w	RI	Monterey	San Juan Twp	74	410
John	30	m	w	NY	San Francisco	San Francisco P O	85	778
Thomas	43	m	w	ENGL	San Francisco	San Francisco P O	83	277
BIGLOW								
Geo H	37	m	w	MA	San Francisco	San Francisco P O	83	84
George	48	m	w	MA	Placer	Lincoln P O	76	481
Harry	40	m	w	MA	San Francisco	11-Wd San Francisc	84	514
J	35	m	w	PA	Alameda	Oakland	68	164
Lewis	32	m	w	VT	San Francisco	11-Wd San Francisc	84	512
O	52	m	w	VT	Sierra	Butte Twp	89	509
Phebe	84	f	w	RI	San Francisco	7-Wd San Francisco	81	207
BIGNALL								
James	27	m	w	IREL	San Francisco	2-Wd San Francisco	79	192
BIGNER								
William	40	m	w	BADE	San Francisco	7-Wd San Francisco	81	204
BIGNOLI								
Thos	53	m	w	IREL	Butte	Chico Twp	70	47
BIGNOTTE								
James	30	m	w	ITAL	San Francisco	2-Wd San Francisco	79	165
BIGOLD								
Charles	32	m	w	MI	Inyo	Lone Pine Twp	73	331
BIGOT								
Agostin	40	m	w	LA	Los Angeles	Santa Ana Twp	73	602
Louis	41	m	w	FRAN	Butte	Ophir Twp	70	91
W G	32	m	w	ENGL	Nevada	Nevada Twp	75	271
BIGOTT								
Adolphus	31	m	w	FRAN	Nevada	Eureka Twp	75	139
BIGSBY								
Charles B	55	m	w	NY	Sonoma	Petaluma Twp	91	316
Harriet	28	f	w	NY	Sonoma	Washington Twp	91	468
BIGTON								
Mary	17	f	w	WI	San Joaquin	Elkhorn Twp	86	65
BIHAN								
Emilie	16	f	w	OR	Santa Clara	2-Wd San Jose	88	337
BIHER								
Louis	29	m	w	CANA	San Joaquin	3-Wd Stockton	86	227
BIHIN								
Amelia	15	f	w	OR	Santa Clara	1-Wd San Jose	88	264
BIHLER								
William	42	m	w	BADE	Sonoma	Vallejo Twp	91	455
BIK								
Ah	16	m	c	CHIN	San Francisco	6-Wd San Francisco	81	67
BIL								
Ah	30	m	c	CHIN	Yuba	Marysville	93	608
BILANCO								
John	35	m	w	PORT	Alameda	Eden Twp	68	64
BILBAO								
Francisco	43	m	w	CHIL	Santa Clara	Santa Clara Twp	88	157
BILBARD								
Nidalucio	64	m	w	MEXI	Fresno	Millerton P O	72	154
BILBERRY								
Ephraim	40	m	w	GA	Tuolumne	Sonora P O	93	317
BILBY								
Mary	46	f	w	IREL	San Francisco	11-Wd San Francisc	84	504
BILDASALA								
Manuel	46	m	w	MEXI	San Diego	San Pasqual	78	519
BILDERAIN								
Refugio	19	m	w	CA	Los Angeles	Los Angeles	73	548
BILDERBACK								
Danl	41	m	w	OH	Nevada	Grass Valley Twp	75	228
BILDERBECK								
Charles	5	m	w	CA	Los Angeles	Los Angeles Twp	73	481
BILDERBEE								
Dora	29	f	w	MD	Los Angeles	Los Angeles	73	565
BILDERIAN								
Guadelupa	14	f	w	CA	Los Angeles	Los Angeles	73	540
BILE								
Ah	41	m	c	CHIN	Amador	Fiddletown P O	69	428
BILEMAN								
Henry	25	m	w	BADE	Colusa	Monroe Twp	71	325
BILER								
Peter	39	m	w	SWIT	Colusa	Colusa Twp	71	284
Sevier	29	m	w	SWIT	Colusa	Colusa Twp	71	284
Timothy B	22	m	w	CANA	Colusa	Stony Crk Twp	71	326
BILES								
C	40	m	w	PA	Alameda	Alameda	68	6
Jacob	30	m	w	PRUS	San Francisco	1-Wd San Francisco	79	33
W	49	m	w	PA	Lake	Big Valley	73	394
BILFINGER								
Mary	47	f	w	WURT	San Francisco	San Francisco P O	80	459
BILICKE								
Gustavus	40	m	w	PRUS	Santa Clara	Santa Clara Twp	88	160
BILIGAO								
Georgi	30	m	w	ITAL	San Francisco	11-Wd San Francisc	84	617
BILINGSLEY								
Thom	25	m	w	MS	Monterey	Alisal Twp	74	304
BILKEY								
Edward	14	m	w	CA	Placer	Bath P O	76	426
BILL								
Ah	38	m	c	CHIN	San Francisco	San Francisco P O	80	498

© 2001 by Heritage Quest. All rights reserved.

Name	Age	S	R	B-PL	County	Locale	Series M593 Roll	Pg
Ah	38	m	c	CHIN	Amador	Jackson P O	69	322
Ah	34	m	c	CHIN	Amador	Sutter Crk P O	69	407
Charles H	33	m	w	NY	Santa Clara	2-Wd San Jose	88	325
Emily	18	f	w	US	Nevada	Grass Valley Twp	75	229
John	50	m	w	IREL	San Joaquin	1-Wd Stockton	86	152
Lir	39	m	c	CHIN	Sierra	Downieville Twp	89	521
Margaret	42	f	w	PRUS	San Francisco	San Francisco P O	80	422
Margaret	22	f	w	PRUS	San Francisco	San Francisco P O	80	470
Phillip	66	m	w	HDAR	San Francisco	San Francisco P O	83	238
Thomas	41	m	w	ENGL	Mendocino	Big Rvr Twp	74	171
BILLA								
Francisco	63	f	w	CA	Santa Cruz	Santa Cruz Twp	89	381
Jose Anto	20	m	w	CA	Los Angeles	Santa Ana Twp	73	606
Miguel	51	m	w	CA	Santa Cruz	Santa Cruz Twp	89	381
Suserno	40	m	w	MEXI	Mariposa	Mariposa P O	74	95
Trinidad	27	m	w	MEXI	San Diego	Coronado	78	467
BILLAK								
Charles	35	m	w	FRAN	Santa Clara	2-Wd San Jose	88	302
BILLALON								
David	35	m	w	CHIL	Amador	Fiddletown P O	69	432
BILLARES								
Bernardo	17	m	w	MEXI	Fresno	Millerton P O	72	164
BILLAREZ								
Peter	29	m	w	FRAN	Los Angeles	Los Angeles	73	508
BILLBERG								
Phillip	35	m	w	PRUS	San Francisco	6-Wd San Francisco	81	81
BILLEPS								
Richard	56	m	w	VA	Tulare	Visalia	92	291
BILLERS								
Henry	33	m	w	ENGL	San Francisco	San Francisco P O	83	255
BILLERUS								
Benjom	12	m	i	CA	Los Angeles	Los Angeles	73	500
BILLET								
James	38	m	w	ENGL	Sonoma	Bodega Twp	91	265
BILLETT								
Maria	49	f	w	ENGL	San Francisco	San Francisco P O	83	310
BILLEW								
Frand	4	m	w	OR	Sonoma	Cloverdale Twp	91	271
BILLEY								
Ah	32	m	c	CHIN	Tuolumne	Sonora P O	93	330
William L	52	m	w	NY	Monterey	San Benito Twp	74	379
BILLHACH								
Peter	36	m	w	IREL	San Francisco	1-Wd San Francisco	79	53
BILLHARTZ								
August	49	m	w	BADE	Yuba	Marysville	93	588
BILLIARD								
John	53	m	w	FRAN	Amador	Jackson P O	69	347
BILLING								
E	64	m	w	ENGL	Calaveras	Copperopolis P O	70	237
Edwin	50	m	w	ENGL	Sutter	Yuba Twp	92	146
Flora	19	f	w	PORT	Sacramento	Sutter Twp	77	386
Francis H	26	m	w	ENGL	Plumas	Mineral Twp	77	21
William	76	m	w	NH	Sacramento	2-Wd Sacramento	77	247
BILLINGALL								
Cath	54	f	w	IREL	Alameda	Oakland	68	150
BILLINGAR								
E	48	m	w	ENGL	Calaveras	Copperopolis P O	70	230
BILLINGER								
William	41	m	w	MO	Colusa	Colusa	71	300
BILLINGHAM								
Raymond	65	m	w	NY	San Francisco	8-Wd San Francisco	82	415
BILLINGS								
Alfred W	41	m	w	ME	Santa Cruz	Watsonville	89	375
Annie	28	f	w	IREL	Santa Cruz	Watsonville	89	376
B F	39	m	w	ME	Tuolumne	Columbia P O	93	354
Benjamin	43	m	w	VT	Placer	Rocklin Twp	76	464
Chas	40	m	w	NY	Mono	Bridgeport P O	74	284
David	35	m	w	MA	San Francisco	7-Wd San Francisco	81	247
E D	41	m	w	CT	Sacramento	1-Wd Sacramento	77	202
E P	36	m	w	MA	Sacramento	4-Wd Sacramento	77	322
Ellen	12	f	w	IL	San Diego	San Jacinto Dist	78	517
James A	25	m	w	PA	Los Angeles	Los Nietos Twp	73	589
James M	46	m	w	ME	Santa Clara	Santa Clara Twp	88	151
Jane	8	f	w	NY	San Francisco	5-Wd San Francisco	81	25
Jennet	18	m	w	NY	San Francisco	5-Wd San Francisco	81	25
John	30	m	w	LA	Marin	San Rafael Twp	74	37
John	27	m	w	IREL	San Francisco	San Francisco P O	80	345
John F	42	m	w	NY	San Francisco	San Francisco P O	85	722
John R	33	m	w	ME	Santa Clara	Santa Clara Twp	88	166
Joseph	40	m	w	PRUS	Santa Clara	Santa Clara Twp	88	175
Julia	10	f	w	NY	San Francisco	5-Wd San Francisco	81	25
Jus	41	m	w	NY	San Francisco	1-Wd San Francisco	79	70
Lydia	70	f	w	ME	Santa Clara	Santa Clara Twp	88	149
Matilda	34	f	w	PA	San Francisco	San Francisco P O	83	175
O C	55	m	w	ME	Lake	Upper Lake	73	412
Rhoda	65	f	w	ENGL	Los Angeles	Los Angeles	73	558
Susan	37	f	w	MD	Butte	Ophir Twp	70	110
Thomas	50	m	w	OH	Yolo	Cottonwood Twp	93	459
William	31	m	w	IA	Mendocino	Noyo & Big Rvr Twp	74	173
Wm	45	m	w	ENGL	Sutter	Butte Twp	92	102
BILLINGSLEY								
Richard C	29	m	w	CANA	Sacramento	2-Wd Sacramento	77	229
Susan	14	f	w	AR	Tulare	Packwood Twp	92	256
W C	28	m	w	MO	Sacramento	3-Wd Sacramento	77	285
BILLINGSLY								
B F	38	m	w	KY	Butte	Bidwell Twp	70	3
John	46	m	w	MS	Tulare	Packwood Twp	92	256
BILLINGTON								
A	23	m	w	NY	Sonoma	Russian Rvr	91	373
Arther	5	m	w	CA	Amador	Ione City P O	69	356
Elya	32	m	w	ENGL	Placer	Bath P O	76	451
George W	28	m	w	ENGL	Plumas	Plumas Twp	77	26
Jo	25	m	w	ENGL	Placer	Colfax P O	76	392
M J	24	f	w	MO	Amador	Ione City P O	69	353
BILLINS								
William	21	m	w	MI	Placer	Dutch Flat P O	76	406
BILLION								
Joseph	29	m	w	MO	Colusa	Monroe Twp	71	315
BILLIPS								
Geo	34	m	w	OH	Shasta	Millville P O	89	487
BILLIS								
Phillipe	30	m	w	MEXI	Kern	Tehachapi P O	73	356
BILLMAN								
George	42	m	w	BADE	Sutter	Butte Twp	92	103
Goodlep	50	m	w	GA	Mariposa	Mariposa P O	74	99
BILLOCK								
George	54	m	w	PA	Colusa	Monroe Twp	71	312
John	16	m	w	IL	Colusa	Monroe Twp	71	312
Sallie	15	f	w	MI	Sacramento	4-Wd Sacramento	77	357
BILLON								
John	39	m	w	MO	Colusa	Monroe Twp	71	325
BILLOT								
Peter	47	m	w	FRAN	San Francisco	11-Wd San Francisc	84	611
BILLOW								
Mary	30	f	w	ENGL	Butte	Oregon Twp	70	136
BILLS								
Anna R	22	f	w	MI	San Francisco	8-Wd San Francisco	82	466
David L	28	m	w	WI	Humboldt	Bald Hills	72	238
Jane	25	f	w	AUSL	San Bernardino	San Bernardino Twp	78	441
John L	49	m	w	NY	Napa	Napa Twp	75	34
L	50	m	w	NY	Siskiyou	Callahan P O	89	629
Pantaleon	21	m	w	MEXI	Los Angeles	Los Angeles Twp	73	473
Robert	29	m	w	IL	Los Angeles	Los Angeles	73	543
Robt Mccoy	54	m	w	TN	Butte	Wyandotte Twp	70	149
Wm	31	m	w	OH	Butte	Oregon Twp	70	131
BILLSBORO								
Richard	35	m	w	MO	Nevada	Grass Valley Twp	75	142
BILLUPS								
I H	26	m	w	MO	Lake	Lower Lake	73	428
BILLY								
---	36	m	c	CHIN	Lassen	Janesville Twp	73	431
Ah Foa	22	m	c	CHIN	Siskiyou	Butte Twp	89	588
BILONE								
Pasqual	35	m	w	SPAI	Santa Clara	Burnett Twp	88	34
BILPO								
Chas	21	m	w	ME	San Joaquin	Tulare Twp	86	253
BILSER								
Robert	41	m	w	PRUS	San Francisco	San Francisco P O	80	467
BILTZ								
George	44	m	w	PRUS	San Francisco	5-Wd San Francisco	81	8
Theodore	45	m	w	HOLL	San Francisco	San Francisco P O	80	481
BILUPS								
Lewis	18	m	w	IA	Plumas	Seneca Twp	77	51
BIM								
Emanuel	55	m	w	PORT	Alameda	Washington Twp	68	275
BIMA								
Barney	45	m	w	IREL	San Francisco	7-Wd San Francisco	81	185
BIN								
Ah	62	m	c	CHIN	El Dorado	Mud Springs Twp	72	88
Ah	48	m	c	CHIN	San Francisco	San Francisco P O	80	514
Ah	44	m	c	CHIN	San Francisco	San Francisco P O	80	514
Ah	42	m	c	CHIN	Shasta	French Gulch P O	89	465
Ah	38	m	c	CHIN	San Francisco	San Francisco P O	80	501
Ah	37	m	c	CHIN	Nevada	Eureka Twp	75	140
Ah	34	m	c	CHIN	San Francisco	San Francisco P O	80	512
Ah	33	m	c	CHIN	Shasta	French Gulch P O	89	467
Ah	29	m	c	CHIN	Solano	Suisun Twp	90	107
Ah	29	m	c	CHIN	Butte	Hamilton Twp	70	67
Ah	28	m	c	CHIN	El Dorado	Diamond Springs Tw	72	32
Ah	28	m	c	CHIN	Nevada	Eureka Twp	75	127
Ah	27	m	c	CHIN	Butte	Hamilton Twp	70	68
Ah	24	m	c	CHIN	San Francisco	San Francisco P O	80	512
Ah	23	m	c	CHIN	Butte	Hamilton Twp	70	72
Ah	23	m	c	CHIN	Butte	Concow Twp	70	11
Ah	22	m	c	CHIN	Santa Clara	Gilroy Twp	88	75
Ah	21	m	c	CHIN	San Francisco	San Francisco P O	80	443
Ah	18	m	c	CHIN	Shasta	Horsetown P O	89	506
Ah	18	m	c	CHIN	Tuolumne	Chinese Camp P O	93	380
Ah	18	m	c	CHIN	San Francisco	San Francisco P O	80	372
Ah	17	m	c	CHIN	Tuolumne	Chinese Camp P O	93	389
Fa	36	m	c	CHIN	El Dorado	Mud Springs Twp	72	79
BINADA								
A C	34	m	w	ITAL	Tuolumne	Chinese Camp P O	93	382
BINANS								
Sarah A	16	f	w	OH	Nevada	Bridgeport Twp	75	104
BINARD								
Geo	27	m	w	ENGL	Sierra	Butte Twp	89	511
BINCATZ								
Francis	47	m	w	ITAL	Humboldt	Arcata Twp	72	228
BINCH								
Everett C	41	m	w	NY	Santa Cruz	Santa Cruz Twp	89	400
BINCK								
Geo	30	m	w	IREL	San Francisco	11-Wd San Francisc	84	692

© 2001 by Heritage Quest. All rights reserved.

California 1870 Census

Name	Age	S	R	B-PL	County	Locale	Roll	Pg
						Series M593		
BINCKLEY								
William	19	m	w	NY	San Bernardino	San Bernardino Twp	78	418
BINCONA								
A	26	m	w	SWIT	Alameda	Oakland	68	241
BIND								
R	26	m	w	IREL	Alameda	Oakland	68	209
BINDER								
George I	24	m	w	NY	San Francisco	San Francisco P O	83	364
BINDIS								
Benedito	24	m	w	ITAL	San Francisco	1-Wd San Francisco	79	105
BINDLE								
Charles T	35	m	w	NY	Yuba	North East Twp	93	643
BINDOM								
David D	56	m	w	CANA	Butte	Chico Twp	70	26
BINE								
Leet	40	m	c	CHIN	Shasta	American Ranch P O	89	499
Solomon	30	m	w	FRAN	San Francisco	San Francisco P O	83	233
BINELLI								
George	29	m	w	ITAL	Solano	Montezuma Twp	90	67
BINEY								
Ah	25	m	c	CHIN	El Dorado	Placerville Twp	72	92
Walter	21	m	w	NY	San Joaquin	1-Wd Stockton	86	128
BING								
---	40	m	c	CHIN	San Francisco	6-Wd San Francisco	81	64
---	35	m	c	CHIN	Siskiyou	Hamburg Twp	89	597
Ac	27	m	c	CHIN	Sacramento	Georgianna Twp	77	124
Ah	50	m	c	CHIN	El Dorado	Diamond Springs Tw	72	25
Ah	50	m	c	CHIN	San Francisco	San Francisco P O	80	508
Ah	50	m	c	CHIN	El Dorado	Mud Springs Twp	72	73
Ah	49	m	c	CHIN	San Francisco	San Francisco P O	80	501
Ah	47	m	c	CHIN	Sierra	Butte Twp	89	512
Ah	47	m	c	CHIN	San Francisco	San Francisco P O	80	508
Ah	46	m	c	CHIN	El Dorado	Salmon Falls Twp	72	131
Ah	42	m	c	CHIN	Placer	Auburn P O	76	374
Ah	42	m	c	CHIN	San Francisco	San Francisco P O	80	522
Ah	41	m	c	CHIN	San Francisco	6-Wd San Francisco	81	56
Ah	40	m	c	CHIN	Sierra	Forest Twp	89	528
Ah	40	m	c	CHIN	El Dorado	Mud Springs Twp	72	74
Ah	38	m	c	CHIN	Trinity	Lewiston Pct	92	212
Ah	37	m	c	CHIN	Santa Clara	Alviso Twp	88	27
Ah	36	m	c	CHIN	San Francisco	San Francisco P O	80	457
Ah	35	m	c	CHIN	El Dorado	Mud Springs Twp	72	77
Ah	35	m	c	CHIN	Santa Clara	1-Wd San Jose	88	275
Ah	35	m	c	CHIN	El Dorado	Placerville Twp	72	101
Ah	34	m	c	CHIN	Nevada	Bridgeport Twp	75	110
Ah	34	m	c	CHIN	San Francisco	San Francisco P O	80	437
Ah	34	m	c	CHIN	Butte	Hamilton Twp	70	68
Ah	34	m	c	CHIN	Butte	Wyandotte Twp	70	142
Ah	34	m	c	CHIN	Santa Clara	1-Wd San Jose	88	270
Ah	32	m	c	CHIN	El Dorado	Mud Springs Twp	72	89
Ah	32	m	c	CHIN	El Dorado	Cosumnes Twp	72	20
Ah	32	m	c	CHIN	Butte	Concow Twp	70	12
Ah	32	m	c	CHIN	El Dorado	Mud Springs Twp	72	87
Ah	31	m	c	CHIN	San Francisco	San Francisco P O	80	511
Ah	30	m	c	CHIN	El Dorado	Placerville Twp	72	97
Ah	30	m	c	CHIN	Butte	Hamilton Twp	70	66
Ah	30	f	c	CHIN	San Francisco	San Francisco P O	80	505
Ah	30	m	c	CHIN	San Francisco	San Francisco P O	80	502
Ah	30	m	c	CHIN	El Dorado	Mud Springs Twp	72	74
Ah	29	m	c	CHIN	Placer	Clipper Gap P O	76	393
Ah	29	m	c	CHIN	Yuba	Marysville	93	619
Ah	28	m	c	CHIN	El Dorado	Placerville Twp	72	103
Ah	28	m	c	CHIN	San Francisco	6-Wd San Francisco	81	75
Ah	28	m	c	CHIN	El Dorado	Placerville	72	125
Ah	28	m	c	CHIN	Butte	Chico Twp	70	53
Ah	28	m	c	CHIN	El Dorado	Mountain Twp	72	70
Ah	28	m	c	CHIN	Butte	Ophir Twp	70	103
Ah	27	m	c	CHIN	El Dorado	Cosumnes Twp	72	18
Ah	26	m	c	CHIN	San Francisco	San Francisco P O	83	127
Ah	26	m	c	CHIN	Placer	Lincoln P O	76	484
Ah	25	m	c	CHIN	El Dorado	Mud Springs Twp	72	78
Ah	25	m	c	CHIN	El Dorado	Placerville Twp	72	96
Ah	25	m	c	CHIN	El Dorado	Placerville	72	115
Ah	25	m	c	CHIN	El Dorado	Mud Springs Twp	72	88
Ah	25	m	c	CHIN	El Dorado	Mountain Twp	72	69
Ah	25	m	c	CHIN	Butte	Ophir Twp	70	103
Ah	24	m	c	CHIN	Alameda	Oakland	68	134
Ah	23	m	c	CHIN	Butte	Chico Twp	70	51
Ah	22	m	c	CHIN	San Francisco	6-Wd San Francisco	81	58
Ah	22	m	c	CHIN	Trinity	North Fork Twp	92	217
Ah	21	m	c	CHIN	San Francisco	8-Wd San Francisco	82	310
Ah	21	m	c	CHIN	Butte	Bidwell Twp	70	4
Ah	20	m	c	CHIN	San Francisco	6-Wd San Francisco	81	53
Ah	20	m	c	CHIN	Alameda	Alvarado	68	303
Ah	2	m	c	CHIN	Butte	Hamilton Twp	70	75
Ah	19	m	c	CHIN	Santa Clara	Fremont Twp	88	52
Ah	18	f	c	CHIN	San Francisco	San Francisco P O	80	529
Ah	17	m	c	CHIN	Santa Clara	San Jose Twp	88	195
Ah	16	f	c	CHIN	Santa Clara	1-Wd San Jose	88	272
Ah	15	m	c	CHIN	San Francisco	7-Wd San Francisco	81	269
Ar	30	m	c	CHIN	Sonoma	Petaluma Twp	91	363
Charley	28	m	c	CHIN	Colusa	Colusa Twp	71	284
Coak	19	f	c	CHIN	Placer	Bath P O	76	429
Cow	31	m	c	CHIN	El Dorado	Coloma Twp	72	6
H A	40	m	w	US	San Joaquin	2-Wd Stockton	86	167
Hong	45	m	c	CHIN	Yuba	Marysville	93	621
Hop	20	m	c	CHIN	San Francisco	6-Wd San Francisco	81	53
Hung	35	m	c	CHIN	Yuba	Marysville	93	625
Lee	29	m	c	CHIN	San Francisco	6-Wd San Francisco	81	52
Leet	45	f	c	CHIN	San Francisco	6-Wd San Francisco	81	55
M	47	m	w	FRAN	San Joaquin	1-Wd Stockton	86	130
Pee	25	m	c	CHIN	San Francisco	6-Wd San Francisco	81	58
Pee	20	m	c	CHIN	San Francisco	6-Wd San Francisco	81	85
Tee	30	m	c	CHIN	Napa	Napa	75	7
Wing	34	m	c	CHIN	San Francisco	8-Wd San Francisco	82	357
Yoo	30	m	c	CHIN	San Francisco	3-Wd San Francisco	79	308
BINGAY								
J N	40	m	w	CANA	Sacramento	4-Wd Sacramento	77	345
BINGER								
William	40	m	w	HESS	Alameda	Alvarado	68	302
BINGERMAN								
John	50	m	w	PA	Trinity	Lewiston Pct	92	214
BINGHAM								
A W	49	m	w	NY	Sonoma	Vallejo Twp	91	458
C	30	m	w	CANA	Yuba	Marysville	93	586
C B	32	m	w	NY	San Francisco	3-Wd San Francisco	79	311
Dora	29	f	w	KY	San Francisco	San Francisco P O	83	64
H N	32	m	w	ME	Sierra	Lincoln Twp	89	549
Henry	38	m	w	NH	Solano	Maine Prairie Twp	90	48
Henry C	36	m	w	ENGL	Los Angeles	Santa Ana Twp	73	613
Homer T	26	m	w	PA	San Diego	San Diego	78	493
John	56	m	w	NH	Solano	Maine Prairie Twp	90	50
John	50	m	w	IREL	San Francisco	1-Wd San Francisco	79	128
John	38	m	w	ME	Yolo	Grafton Twp	93	491
John	35	m	w	CANA	San Francisco	San Francisco P O	83	9
John	32	m	w	TN	Mendocino	Ukiah Twp	74	241
John	30	m	w	AR	Los Angeles	Los Nietos Twp	73	581
John	28	m	w	ENGL	Nevada	Grass Valley Twp	75	147
Joseph	40	m	w	NH	Solano	Maine Prairie Twp	90	48
Loren	46	m	w	NY	Placer	Colfax P O	76	391
Mary M	10	f	w	CA	Humboldt	Arcata Twp	72	229
U C	33	m	w	NY	Yuba	Marysville	93	595
Wm	44	m	w	PA	San Francisco	5-Wd San Francisco	81	31
BINGOFF								
Austin	25	m	w	PRUS	San Francisco	5-Wd San Francisco	81	14
BINGON								
Peter	38	m	w	HANO	San Francisco	2-Wd San Francisco	79	219
BINGYMAN								
Heny	38	m	w	GERM	Los Angeles	San Juan Twp	73	628
BINING								
J	33	m	w	PRUS	Sierra	Forest Twp	89	529
BINK								
Jason	27	m	w	NY	Placer	Gold Run Twp	76	396
Phillip P	45	m	w	NY	Merced	Snelling P O	74	252
BINKE								
George W	23	m	w	AL	Los Angeles	Los Nietos Twp	73	586
BINKLEMAN								
Adam	42	m	w	HDAR	San Francisco	11-Wd San Francisc	84	678
David	42	m	w	WURT	Nevada	Grass Valley Twp	75	188
BINKLEY								
Frank	46	m	w	MO	San Bernardino	San Salvador Twp	78	458
BINLEY								
Harriet	21	f	w	UT	San Bernardino	San Bernardino Twp	78	425
BINN								
Arabella	10	f	w	AUST	San Francisco	11-Wd San Francisc	84	648
Joseph	22	m	w	PRUS	San Francisco	11-Wd San Francisc	84	533
Wm	46	m	w	NY	San Joaquin	2-Wd Stockton	86	181
BINNCHI								
Antonio	30	m	w	ITAL	Amador	Sutter Crk P O	69	403
BINNEY								
Isaac B	49	m	w	MA	Santa Cruz	Santa Cruz	89	431
BINNIE								
C C	23	m	w	PA	San Francisco	3-Wd San Francisco	79	319
BINNING								
H	42	m	w	HANO	Sierra	Alleghany & Forest	89	533
BINNINGER								
Alice	18	f	w	CA	Yuba	Marysville Twp	93	567
Augustus C	28	m	w	IL	Sacramento	2-Wd Sacramento	77	226
Emanual M	36	m	w	IL	Yuba	Long Bar Twp	93	564
G J	53	m	w	PRUS	Sierra	Forest Twp	89	529
Wm T	41	m	w	OH	Yuba	Long Bar Twp	93	564
BINNINGHAM								
T J	37	m	w	IREL	Mariposa	Mariposa P O	74	117
BINNY								
Chas	50	m	w	PA	Yuba	Marysville	93	587
BINSTON								
Daniel	27	m	w	PRUS	San Francisco	San Francisco P O	83	253
BINTON								
John	19	m	w	IL	San Bernardino	San Bernardino Twp	78	451
BINUM								
Samuel	50	m	m	MO	Calaveras	San Andreas P O	70	178
BIPEN								
James	33	m	w	VT	Alameda	Oakland	68	187
BIPETT								
John	50	m	w	ME	Solano	Vallejo	90	180
BIRA								
Jeremiah	34	m	w	PA	Colusa	Monroe Twp	71	313
BIRCE								
Frank	30	m	w	ME	San Francisco	7-Wd San Francisco	81	273
Thos	50	m	w	WI	San Joaquin	Castoria Twp	86	14
BIRCH								
Ada	17	f	w	CA	Yuba	Marysville	93	598
Ann	50	f	w	ENGL	San Francisco	San Francisco P O	83	394
Anna	38	f	w	SWIT	El Dorado	Greenwood Twp	72	53

© 2001 by Heritage Quest. All rights reserved.

Name	Age	S	R	B-PL	County	Locale	Roll	Pg
						Series M593		
Charles	40	m	w	SAXO	Mendocino	Round Valley Twp	74	217
Ellen	36	f	w	NY	San Francisco	San Francisco P O	83	137
French	31	m	w	NY	Fresno	Millerton P O	72	158
George	33	m	w	ENGL	San Bernardino	San Bernardino Twp	78	441
Harris	10	m	w	CA	San Francisco	11-Wd San Francisc	84	592
Henry	40	m	w	PRUS	San Francisco	1-Wd San Francisco	79	117
James	32	m	w	ENGL	Tulare	Visalia Twp	92	285
Joseph	22	m	w	CT	San Francisco	5-Wd San Francisco	81	36
Joshua	35	m	w	PA	El Dorado	Kelsey Twp	72	62
May J	30	f	w	MD	San Francisco	San Francisco P O	83	256
Samuel	36	m	w	ENGL	San Francisco	11-Wd San Francisc	84	567
Thos J	50	m	w	PA	Butte	Kimshew Tpw	70	77
William	34	m	w	OH	Yuba	Marysville	93	588
William T	37	m	w	IL	San Mateo	Menlo Park P O	87	378
BIRCHAM								
William	34	m	w	NY	Placer	Rocklin Twp	76	465
BIRCHER								
Rob	19	m	w	ENGL	Alameda	Oakland	68	251
BIRCHES								
J	40	m	w	DENM	Alameda	Murray Twp	68	123
BIRCHETT								
E M	38	m	w	AR	Sutter	Vernon Twp	92	138
James	27	m	w	AR	Los Angeles	Los Nietos Twp	73	576
Mary	70	f	w	AR	Sutter	Vernon Twp	92	138
BIRCHIM								
James G	41	m	w	OH	Inyo	Bishop Crk Twp	73	314
BIRD								
A Cortier	34	m	w	MA	Santa Clara	Santa Clara Twp	88	159
Albert B	46	m	w	KY	Sacramento	4-Wd Sacramento	77	320
Alfred D	12	m	w	MO	Santa Barbara	San Buenaventura P	87	439
Alice	4	f	w	CA	Sacramento	3-Wd Sacramento	77	294
Ann S	42	f	w	VA	San Francisco	8-Wd San Francisco	82	295
Anne	33	f	w	CANA	San Francisco	San Francisco P O	83	262
Austin	25	m	w	MO	Colusa	Colusa	71	293
Benjamin	22	m	w	ENGL	Santa Barbara	Santa Barbara P O	87	478
Charles	34	m	w	IN	San Francisco	2-Wd San Francisco	79	277
Charles	30	m	w	MA	San Francisco	San Francisco P O	80	336
Chas E	38	m	w	NY	San Francisco	1-Wd San Francisco	79	53
Christopher	30	m	w	NY	Santa Cruz	Santa Cruz	89	429
Cooper B	48	m	w	GA	Placer	Bath P O	76	449
Daniel	16	m	w	CA	San Francisco	11-Wd San Francisc	84	586
David E	50	m	w	VA	Colusa	Colusa	71	289
Dennis	24	m	w	IREL	Marin	Point Reyes Twp	74	21
F P	30	m	w	KY	Sacramento	Dry Crk Twp	77	100
Franklin W	40	m	w	ENGL	Placer	Bath P O	76	435
Geo B	39	m	w	ENGL	San Francisco	1-Wd San Francisco	79	1
George	35	m	w	ENGL	Alameda	Alameda	68	13
George W	46	m	w	NY	Monterey	Monterey	74	356
Henry	42	m	w	PA	Butte	Ophir Twp	70	108
Hiram	32	m	w	NH	San Francisco	San Francisco P O	83	87
Hugh	27	m	w	IREL	Solano	Tremont Twp	90	29
Isabella	36	f	w	IREL	San Francisco	6-Wd San Francisco	81	79
J M	47	m	w	SCOT	Marin	San Rafael Twp	74	39
J W	35	m	w	ENGL	San Joaquin	Tulare Twp	86	250
Jacob	45	m	w	KY	Colusa	Colusa Twp	71	287
John	46	m	w	OR	San Diego	San Diego	78	507
John	45	m	w	TN	Tehama	Paynes Crk Twp	92	167
John	33	m	w	NY	Solano	Montezuma Twp	90	66
John	19	m	w	MO	San Joaquin	2-Wd Stockton	86	173
John P	35	m	w	TN	Tehama	Paynes Crk Twp	92	160
John W	26	m	w	ENGL	Siskiyou	Yreka	89	652
Joseph	7	m	w	PA	Stanislaus	San Joaquin Twp	92	75
Lee	32	m	i	CA	Siskiyou	Table Rock Twp	89	647
Lucy	54	f	w	VT	Contra Costa	Martinez P O	71	450
M A	26	m	w	CANA	San Francisco	7-Wd San Francisco	81	218
M J	36	m	w	CANA	Alameda	Oakland	68	197
M L	45	m	w	VT	San Joaquin	2-Wd Stockton	86	160
Mary	64	f	w	IREL	San Francisco	San Francisco P O	85	819
Matilda	45	f	w	NY	Sacramento	3-Wd Sacramento	77	294
Morgan	37	m	w	MO	Calaveras	San Andreas P O	70	188
Ralph	72	m	w	PA	Butte	Ophir Twp	70	94
Robert A	48	m	w	NY	Sacramento	2-Wd Sacramento	77	224
Samuel	55	m	w	PA	Santa Cruz	Santa Cruz	89	409
Samuel	30	m	w	KY	El Dorado	Georgetown Twp	72	45
Simon C	22	m	w	ME	Placer	Alta P O	76	413
Thomas	58	m	w	ENGL	San Francisco	1-Wd San Francisco	79	31
Thomas	35	m	w	GA	Yuba	Slate Range Bar Tw	93	673
Thomas	32	m	w	IREL	Santa Clara	San Jose Twp	88	195
Thos	30	m	w	ENGL	San Francisco	San Francisco P O	83	133
William	50	m	w	IREL	San Francisco	6-Wd San Francisco	81	129
William	40	m	w	MO	Santa Cruz	Watsonville	89	368
William	31	m	w	ENGL	Santa Clara	1-Wd San Jose	88	232
William	30	m	w	ENGL	San Francisco	7-Wd San Francisco	81	168
William	25	m	w	ENGL	Yolo	Putah Twp	93	509
William	19	m	w	NY	Santa Clara	Santa Clara Twp	88	147
Wm	30	m	w	WI	Butte	Oregon Twp	70	132
BIRDALL								
---	40	m	w	PRUS	Sacramento	4-Wd Sacramento	77	356
Catherine	35	f	w	IREL	Sacramento	4-Wd Sacramento	77	370
BIRDE								
Edward	26	m	w	ENGL	Sacramento	4-Wd Sacramento	77	341
BIRDEE								
James	31	m	w	NY	San Francisco	7-Wd San Francisco	81	164
BIRDS								
Isaac	55	m	w	ENGL	Santa Clara	1-Wd San Jose	88	277
N	43	m	w	HUNG	Sierra	Eureka Twp	89	523

Name	Age	S	R	B-PL	County	Locale	Roll	Pg
						Series M593		
BIRDSALL								
Edwd	27	m	w	NY	Solano	Vallejo	90	217
Fredk	42	m	w	NY	Sacramento	4-Wd Sacramento	77	334
George	54	m	w	NY	San Francisco	San Francisco P O	83	78
John	36	m	w	NY	San Francisco	San Francisco P O	85	784
Silas H	45	m	w	NY	Klamath	Sawyers Bar	73	377
BIRDSAN								
J	42	m	w	FRAN	Nevada	Eureka Twp	75	139
BIRDSELL								
Elizabeth	19	f	w	NY	San Francisco	San Francisco P O	83	248
Susan	25	f	w	NY	San Francisco	8-Wd San Francisco	82	467
BIRDSLEY								
C	20	f	w	VT	Sacramento	3-Wd Sacramento	77	275
BIREN								
Isaac	44	m	w	WALE	San Francisco	2-Wd San Francisco	79	249
BIRGE								
George S	28	m	w	IA	Siskiyou	Scott Valley Twp	89	618
Joel	49	m	w	OH	San Joaquin	Elkhorn Twp	86	67
Richard	40	m	w	PRUS	San Francisco	San Francisco P O	80	460
S S	36	m	w	VA	San Joaquin	Liberty Twp	86	94
BIRGER								
James	33	m	w	OH	Solano	Tremont Twp	90	28
BIRK								
Wm	33	m	w	CANA	El Dorado	Kelsey Twp	72	58
BIRKLAND								
Neils	27	m	w	FINL	Marin	San Rafael	74	55
BIRKS								
John	37	m	w	ENGL	Sutter	Butte Twp	92	96
BIRLY								
O L	48	m	w	NY	Sutter	Sutter Twp	92	125
R A	38	m	w	NY	Sutter	Sutter Twp	92	126
BIRMINGHAM								
Annie	32	f	w	IREL	Marin	San Rafael Twp	74	27
Bridget	33	f	w	IREL	San Francisco	8-Wd San Francisco	82	441
Ed	30	m	w	IREL	San Francisco	1-Wd San Francisco	79	50
Edgar	29	m	w	LA	San Francisco	5-Wd San Francisco	81	19
Edward J	60	m	w	IREL	Yuba	Slate Range Bar Tw	93	672
James T	37	m	w	PA	Yuba	North East Twp	93	643
John	41	m	w	IREL	Yuba	New York Twp	93	639
John	30	m	w	IREL	San Francisco	San Francisco P O	80	400
John	26	m	w	NY	Santa Clara	2-Wd San Jose	88	310
M	40	f	w	IREL	San Francisco	San Francisco P O	83	313
Peter	31	m	w	IREL	Marin	San Rafael Twp	74	27
S	30	f	w	IREL	San Francisco	San Francisco P O	85	857
Thos	70	m	w	IREL	San Francisco	5-Wd San Francisco	81	19
Wm	42	m	w	IREL	San Francisco	2-Wd San Francisco	79	214
BIRMMINGHAM								
John	35	m	w	IREL	San Joaquin	3-Wd Stockton	86	232
BIRNBRES								
Johannah	20	f	w	PRUS	Sacramento	2-Wd Sacramento	77	226
BIRNES								
H	35	m	w	MO	Humboldt	South Fork Twp	72	302
BIRNEY								
Carson P	46	m	w	AL	Plumas	Quartz Twp	77	37
Thomas C	36	m	w	OH	Tuolumne	Columbia P O	93	360
BIRNINGER								
Louis	51	m	w	BADE	Sacramento	2-Wd Sacramento	77	223
BIROL								
T	23	m	w	MEXI	Alameda	Alameda	68	11
BIROLA								
Gumiciendo	33	m	w	MEXI	Santa Barbara	Santa Barbara P O	87	462
BIRON								
Hyam	90	m	w	LA	San Francisco	6-Wd San Francisco	81	82
J	29	m	w	IREL	Sacramento	1-Wd Sacramento	77	179
BIRT								
John	21	m	w	PA	Mono	Bridgeport P O	74	286
BIRTHRIGHT								
James	50	m	w	VA	Yolo	Cache Crk Twp	93	443
Lucy	80	f	w	VA	Yolo	Buckeye Twp	93	413
Lucy	69	f	w	VA	Yolo	Cache Crk Twp	93	443
BIRWICK								
Edward	27	m	w	ENGL	Monterey	Monterey Twp	74	346
BISBEE								
Allen K	48	m	w	NY	Nevada	Grass Valley Twp	75	201
Arga	62	m	w	MA	Placer	Bath P O	76	448
John G	33	m	w	ME	Placer	Bath P O	76	449
William	45	m	w	MA	Siskiyou	Yreka	89	656
Wilson	38	m	w	NH	Calaveras	Copperopolis P O	70	263
BISBY								
Francis	25	m	w	NY	Santa Barbara	Santa Barbara P O	87	453
John	39	m	w	ME	Los Angeles	Wilmington Twp	73	634
L	44	m	w	ME	Monterey	San Juan Twp	74	415
L R	52	m	w	MA	Alameda	Oakland	68	179
Seymour	26	m	w	NY	Santa Barbara	Santa Barbara P O	87	472
BISCANO								
Josefa	27	f	w	ITAL	San Francisco	San Francisco P O	80	459
BISCHEL								
Henry	39	m	w	PRUS	Santa Cruz	Soquel Twp	89	443
BISCHKE								
Mary	17	f	w	CA	Sacramento	3-Wd Sacramento	77	275
BISCHOF								
Anton	25	m	w	BREM	San Francisco	1-Wd San Francisco	79	90
John	32	m	w	GERM	San Joaquin	2-Wd Stockton	86	169
BISCHOFF								
Anton	23	m	w	BADE	San Francisco	San Francisco P O	83	235
Aug	34	m	w	PRUS	San Francisco	San Francisco P O	83	135
Hans	42	m	w	PRUS	San Francisco	5-Wd San Francisco	81	16

© 2001 by Heritage Quest. All rights reserved.

Series M593

Name	Age	S	R	B-PL	County	Locale	Roll	Pg
Kate	25	f	w	PRUS	San Francisco	8-Wd San Francisco	82	399
Richd	26	m	w	BREM	San Francisco	San Francisco P O	83	273
BISCHOIR								
Louis	32	m	w	FRAN	San Francisco	1-Wd San Francisco	79	56
BISCOE								
F	24	m	w	IREL	Nevada	Meadow Lake Twp	75	249
F	19	m	w	CA	Nevada	Meadow Lake Twp	75	249
Fernand	19	m	w	CA	Sacramento	Mississippi Twp	77	162
Fernandes	18	m	w	CA	Placer	Rocklin Twp	76	465
BISCOMBES								
F	43	m	w	OH	Sierra	Table Rock Twp	89	579
BISEN								
Camillo	28	m	w	AUST	San Francisco	1-Wd San Francisco	79	121
BISENTIO								
Charles	40	m	w	CHIL	Calaveras	San Andreas P O	70	157
BISER								
Louis	44	m	w	FRAN	San Joaquin	1-Wd Stockton	86	152
BISH								
Thos	16	m	w	MO	Sonoma	Santa Rosa	91	418
BISHAP								
Samuel	39	m	w	AL	Colusa	Colusa	71	293
BISHER								
George W	17	m	w	IN	Mendocino	Little Lake Twp	74	198
BISHO								
J L	43	m	w	AZOR	Monterey	Monterey Twp	74	343
BISHOFF								
Brown	50	m	w	PRUS	Solano	Tremont Twp	90	35
Valentine	35	m	w	FRAN	Sonoma	Sonoma Twp	91	438
BISHOFFBERGER								
Jacob	38	m	w	SWIT	Amador	Volcano P O	69	378
BISHOP								
A K	53	m	w	VA	Sierra	Alleghany & Forest	89	533
A W	37	m	w	VT	San Francisco	San Francisco P O	85	774
Adelbert	26	m	w	CANA	Santa Clara	San Jose Twp	88	207
Andrew J	41	m	w	NY	Placer	Bath P O	76	458
Benjamin	49	m	w	PA	San Francisco	11-Wd San Francisc	84	524
Charles	40	m	w	NY	Sacramento	Sutter Twp	77	383
Charles	39	m	w	NY	San Francisco	San Francisco P O	83	59
Charles S	46	m	w	CANA	Sonoma	Petaluma Twp	91	347
D L	15	m	w	CA	Lake	Lower Lake	73	421
Daniel A	38	m	w	NY	Mariposa	Mariposa P O	74	114
Edger	30	m	w	NY	San Francisco	8-Wd San Francisco	82	302
Fletcher M	36	m	w	NY	Contra Costa	Martinez P O	71	372
Frances	12	f	w	CA	Santa Barbara	Santa Barbara P O	87	501
Francis A	40	m	w	CT	El Dorado	Mud Springs Twp	72	85
Frank	16	m	w	ME	Sacramento	3-Wd Sacramento	77	256
Fruma	27	m	w	CANA	San Mateo	Schoolhouse Statio	87	333
G	47	m	w	OH	Lake	Lower Lake	73	423
Gordon	54	m	w	CT	El Dorado	Mud Springs Twp	72	74
Gurdon	54	m	w	CT	San Francisco	San Francisco P O	80	364
Harvey N	52	m	w	KY	San Mateo	Redwood Twp	87	369
Henry	42	m	w	PA	San Mateo	Half Moon Bay P O	87	391
Henry	41	m	w	NY	Amador	Sutter Crk P O	69	410
Henry	40	m	w	HANO	San Francisco	2-Wd San Francisco	79	210
Henry	37	m	w	KY	San Bernardino	San Salvador Twp	78	459
Henry C	37	m	w	KY	Los Angeles	Los Nietos Twp	73	576
I H	36	m	w	NY	Tuolumne	Chinese Camp P O	93	374
J	46	m	w	NY	Sierra	Sierra Twp	89	565
James	61	m	w	ENGL	Napa	Napa	75	39
Jeremiah	19	m	w	CANA	Marin	San Rafael	74	58
John	62	m	w	SCOT	Nevada	Eureka Twp	75	131
John	50	m	w	MD	El Dorado	Coloma Twp	72	3
John	50	m	w	SCOT	San Francisco	8-Wd San Francisco	82	296
John	45	m	w	CANA	Nevada	Grass Valley Twp	75	225
John	34	m	w	NY	Contra Costa	Martinez P O	71	450
John	30	m	w	NY	San Francisco	San Francisco P O	80	538
John	27	m	w	HANO	Tulare	Farmersville Twp	92	246
John	25	m	w	ENGL	Santa Clara	1-Wd San Jose	88	237
John	23	m	w	CANA	Mendocino	Point Arena Twp	74	205
John	16	m	w	CANA	Sonoma	Petaluma Twp	91	354
John A	37	m	w	AR	Nevada	Bridgeport Twp	75	114
Jon	30	m	w	ENGL	Nevada	Grass Valley Twp	75	232
Joseph	21	m	w	PRUS	San Francisco	8-Wd San Francisco	82	320
Jules	41	m	w	FRAN	Santa Clara	2-Wd San Jose	88	315
Lester	47	m	w	NY	San Francisco	11-Wd San Francisc	84	669
Lizzy	26	f	w	NJ	San Francisco	6-Wd San Francisco	81	72
M F	28	m	w	IL	San Joaquin	Oneal Twp	86	109
M W	14	m	w	ME	Alameda	Oakland	68	173
Mary	26	f	w	IREL	San Francisco	8-Wd San Francisco	82	292
Mary	19	f	w	IA	Mendocino	Round Valley Twp	74	219
Nelson	44	m	w	NY	Tuolumne	Chinese Camp P O	93	374
Nimrod	31	m	w	KY	Santa Clara	1-Wd San Jose	88	224
Nimrod G	33	m	w	KY	San Francisco	San Francisco P O	83	5
Noey D	32	m	w	OH	Butte	Chico Twp	70	24
Oliver	28	m	w	CT	San Francisco	11-Wd San Francisc	84	534
Ransom	49	m	w	ME	San Francisco	11-Wd San Francisc	84	560
Rebecca	65	f	w	VA	Mendocino	Round Valley Twp	74	220
Richd	32	m	w	IREL	San Francisco	1-Wd San Francisco	79	32
S C W	25	m	w	ENGL	Solano	Vallejo	90	181
Samuel A	42	m	w	MO	Santa Clara	San Jose Twp	88	186
Samuel D	25	m	w	MO	Santa Clara	2-Wd San Jose	88	291
Silas	39	m	w	OH	Stanislaus	Branch Twp	92	3
Stephen	56	m	w	ENGL	Stanislaus	Emory Twp	92	23
Tennessee	40	m	w	TN	Sonoma	Mendocino Twp	91	298
Thomas	31	m	w	ENGL	Nevada	Grass Valley Twp	75	180
Thos B	29	m	w	MA	San Francisco	San Francisco P O	83	94
W B	27	m	w	VT	Napa	Napa	75	13
W D	33	m	w	MI	San Joaquin	Oneal Twp	86	109
Walter	24	m	w	ENGL	Solano	Suisun Twp	90	109
Watson	22	m	w	CANA	Santa Clara	Gilroy Twp	88	100
William	56	m	w	BAVA	Mariposa	Mariposa P O	74	120
William M	37	m	w	NY	Santa Cruz	Santa Cruz	89	433
William S	33	m	w	NY	Yolo	Putah Twp	93	513
Wm	25	m	w	OH	Sacramento	Brighton Twp	77	73
Wm	22	m	w	CANA	Sonoma	Salt Point	91	386
Wm A	35	m	w	MA	San Francisco	San Francisco P O	83	35
Z D	49	m	w	VT	Sierra	Lincoln Twp	89	550
BISHOPS								
Chas	55	m	w	CT	Sutter	Vernon Twp	92	130
G A	21	f	w	IL	Sutter	Butte Twp	92	90
BISKOWITZ								
M	13	m	w	CA	Alameda	Oakland	68	159
BISKY								
Charles	12	m	w	CA	Sacramento	Sutter Twp	77	392
BISLEY								
D F	45	m	w	SCOT	Yuba	Marysville	93	586
BISLOPE								
Frederick	40	m	w	PRUS	Sacramento	Granite Twp	77	142
BISMO								
Antonio	33	m	w	ITAL	San Francisco	11-Wd San Francisc	84	712
BISPO								
Domingo	31	m	w	SPAI	San Francisco	8-Wd San Francisco	82	371
BISS								
W C	29	m	w	ENGL	Alameda	Alameda	68	5
BISSAIN								
Antonio	49	m	w	FRAN	Los Angeles	Los Angeles	73	568
BISSEL								
Celestina	18	f	m	WIND	San Francisco	6-Wd San Francisco	81	72
Charles T	25	m	w	MI	San Francisco	San Francisco P O	85	757
Henry	46	m	w	MA	Tuolumne	Chinese Camp P O	93	386
BISSELL								
A M	14	f	w	CA	Alameda	Oakland	68	258
Allen	38	m	m	VA	San Francisco	6-Wd San Francisco	81	71
D O	46	m	w	CT	Siskiyou	Surprise Valley Tw	89	636
M L	12	m	w	CA	Napa	Napa Twp	75	75
Mary L	12	f	w	CA	Napa	Napa	75	27
BISSELLE								
Louisa	15	f	w	CA	Santa Clara	2-Wd San Jose	88	337
BISSEN								
Joseph	51	m	w	TN	Trinity	Trinity Center Pct	92	204
BISSET								
H M	56	m	w	CANA	Alameda	Alameda	68	7
BISSETT								
William	63	m	w	SCOT	Placer	Auburn P O	76	370
BISSILL								
Mary Mrs	40	f	w	MO	Lake	Lower Lake	73	422
BISTAS								
John	50	m	i	MEXI	Inyo	Cerro Gordo Twp	73	322
BISTEMON								
J M	36	m	w	HANO	Sierra	Butte Twp	89	510
BISTHREP								
William	33	m	w	NORW	San Francisco	8-Wd San Francisco	82	482
BISTRAN								
Anthony	40	m	w	NY	Mariposa	Maxwell Crk P O	74	141
BISWELL								
James	50	m	w	ENGL	San Mateo	Pescadero P O	87	409
Jane	47	f	w	ENGL	Alameda	Oakland	68	211
Joseph	50	m	w	ENGL	San Mateo	Pescadero P O	87	409
Norval B	38	m	w	MO	Colusa	Stony Crk Twp	71	333
BIT								
Ah	28	m	c	CHIN	San Joaquin	1-Wd Stockton	86	145
Ah	27	m	c	CHIN	Placer	Bath P O	76	429
Ah	22	m	c	CHIN	San Francisco	San Francisco P O	80	514
BITE								
Ah	40	m	c	CHIN	Yuba	Marysville Twp	93	569
BITHA								
Tyler	45	m	w	ME	Stanislaus	San Joaquin Twp	92	76
BITHEL								
Thomas	28	m	w	IREL	San Francisco	San Francisco P O	83	156
BITHELL								
Jas	43	m	w	NY	Sacramento	3-Wd Sacramento	77	318
BITHER								
M S	39	m	w	ME	San Joaquin	Castoria Twp	86	2
Peter	31	m	w	ME	San Diego	San Diego	78	505
BITLEY								
Walter B	49	m	w	NY	Placer	Bath P O	76	422
BITNER								
Jacob	30	m	w	PA	Siskiyou	Surprise Valley Tw	89	642
BITSCHRIAN								
Joseph	36	m	w	FRAN	San Bernardino	San Bernardino Twp	78	417
BITT								
Ah	23	m	c	CHIN	San Francisco	6-Wd San Francisco	81	62
Philip M	38	m	w	NY	Sacramento	Sutter Twp	77	392
BITTELLE								
Edward	28	m	w	FRAN	Placer	Rocklin Twp	76	465
BITTEN								
Harvey	30	m	w	CANA	Solano	Vallejo	90	172
BITTENCOURT								
John	67	m	w	WIND	Sacramento	2-Wd Sacramento	77	220
BITTER								
George	60	m	w	HDAR	San Francisco	San Francisco P O	80	533
William	43	m	w	HDAR	San Francisco	San Francisco P O	80	532
BITTERMANN								
Chas	30	m	w	AUSL	San Francisco	11-Wd San Francisc	84	663

© 2001 by Heritage Quest. All rights reserved.

Name	Age	S	R	B-PL	County	Locale	Series M593 Roll	Pg
BITTERS								
Jonas	41	m	w	PA	El Dorado	Georgetown Twp	72	48
BITTI								
Joseph	34	m	w	ITAL	Tuolumne	Big Oak Flat P O	93	393
BITTLE								
Samuel	28	m	w	PRUS	San Francisco	8-Wd San Francisco	82	357
BITTONI								
John	34	m	w	ITAL	San Francisco	San Francisco P O	80	426
BITTS								
Phillip	48	m	w	HDAR	Contra Costa	San Pablo Twp	71	357
BITZ								
Adam	35	m	w	PRUS	San Francisco	5-Wd San Francisco	81	34
BITZE								
Auguste	75	f	w	PRUS	Alameda	Alameda	68	18
BITZER								
John	43	m	w	WURT	San Francisco	8-Wd San Francisco	82	311
Uriah	50	m	w	PA	Amador	Fiddletown P O	69	437
BIVEN								
Ansparo	30	f	w	MEXI	San Francisco	2-Wd San Francisco	79	197
BIVENS								
George K	38	m	w	MO	Tulare	Kings Rvr Twp	92	253
John	45	m	w	MD	Mendocino	Calpella Twp	74	190
John	27	m	m	OH	San Francisco	San Francisco P O	80	417
Mary	72	f	b	PA	San Francisco	San Francisco P O	80	417
Mary	54	f	w	MD	Mendocino	Ukiah Twp	74	241
BIVIAN								
George	26	m	w	ENGL	Nevada	Grass Valley Twp	75	191
BIXBEE								
Chas	19	m	w	NY	San Francisco	1-Wd San Francisco	79	67
BIXBY								
A M	31	m	w	VT	Sierra	Forest Twp	89	531
A S	38	m	w	ME	Monterey	San Juan Twp	74	407
Charles	32	m	w	NY	Sonoma	Salt Point	91	388
Emmie	20	f	w	IA	Sonoma	Petaluma Twp	91	317
James	38	m	w	MO	Los Angeles	Santa Ana Twp	73	611
Marcellus	46	m	w	ME	Los Angeles	Wilmington Twp	73	634
Nelson A	41	m	w	NY	Santa Cruz	Soquel Twp	89	440
Thomas F	30	m	w	ME	Los Angeles	Wilmington Twp	73	634
BIXEL								
Joseph	51	m	w	GERM	Tuolumne	Columbia P O	93	337
BIXFORD								
Luther P	56	m	w	NH	Sonoma	Sonoma Twp	91	431
BIXLEE								
Robert	38	m	w	CT	San Francisco	8-Wd San Francisco	82	471
BIXLEER								
John	40	m	w	MA	San Francisco	7-Wd San Francisco	81	279
BIXLER								
Marion T	41	m	w	IN	Nevada	Grass Valley Twp	75	188
BIXLEY								
John	45	m	w	ME	Tuolumne	Sonora P O	93	318
Wm	56	m	w	NY	El Dorado	Georgetown Twp	72	42
BIZARIO								
Joseph	36	m	w	CANA	Yolo	Grafton Twp	93	482
BIZZANO								
Francisco	37	m	w	ITAL	Marin	San Rafael Twp	74	36
BJERKE								
Harry T	54	m	w	NORW	San Francisco	San Francisco P O	83	410
BJORKMAN								
Ellen	34	f	w	IREL	San Francisco	San Francisco P O	83	39
BLA								
Ah	40	m	c	CHIN	Tuolumne	Big Oak Flat P O	93	397
BLAANI								
John	35	m	w	ITAL	San Francisco	1-Wd San Francisco	79	122
BLABIN								
Walter	40	m	w	ME	Santa Clara	Redwood Twp	88	122
BLABON								
Francis O	40	m	w	ME	Santa Clara	2-Wd San Jose	88	303
BLABORN								
George	25	m	w	ME	Santa Clara	Santa Clara Twp	88	166
M W	36	m	w	ME	Klamath	Trinidad Twp	73	392
BLACH								
Charles	41	m	w	BADE	San Francisco	8-Wd San Francisco	82	401
BLACHLEY								
William	40	m	w	OH	Merced	Snelling P O	74	269
BLACK								
A	40	m	w	US	Del Norte	Crescent Twp	71	457
A	39	m	w	ME	Sierra	Sierra Twp	89	570
A	36	m	w	PA	Sierra	Butte Twp	89	508
Adan	54	m	w	IREL	San Francisco	11-Wd San Francisc	84	444
Albert	32	m	w	PA	Sutter	Sutter Twp	92	122
Alex	47	m	w	PA	Sonoma	Mendocino Twp	91	304
Alex G	47	m	w	IREL	Mariposa	Mariposa P O	74	135
Alex G	44	m	w	ME	Mariposa	Mariposa P O	74	99
Alexander	30	m	w	SCOT	San Francisco	7-Wd San Francisco	81	255
Alexander	27	m	w	SCOT	San Francisco	8-Wd San Francisco	82	460
Alice	12	f	w	IL	San Bernardino	San Bernardino Twp	78	433
Alsberry A	28	m	w	GA	Fresno	Kings Rvr P O	72	211
Andrew	58	m	w	VA	Solano	Suisun Twp	90	99
Andrew	40	m	w	IREL	Sacramento	2-Wd Sacramento	77	240
Andrew	27	m	w	PA	Tehama	Tehama Twp	92	195
Andy	28	m	w	PA	Tehama	Tehama Twp	92	186
Ann	36	f	w	IREL	San Joaquin	2-Wd Stockton	86	173
Anne	60	f	w	IREL	San Francisco	6-Wd San Francisco	81	97
Annie	4	f	w	CA	San Francisco	San Francisco P O	83	11
Arthur	45	m	w	DENM	Tehama	Antelope Twp	92	155
Barry	39	m	w	VA	San Diego	Warners Rancho Dis	78	528
Boyd	27	m	w	NY	San Francisco	5-Wd San Francisco	81	11

Name	Age	S	R	B-PL	County	Locale	Series M593 Roll	Pg
Caroline	29	f	w	WI	Nevada	Nevada Twp	75	271
Charles	26	m	w	PA	San Francisco	11-Wd San Francisc	84	622
Charles S	37	m	w	ME	San Bernardino	San Bernardino Twp	78	443
Charles S	34	m	w	OH	Amador	Ione City P O	69	353
Chs	20	m	w	MA	Yuba	Marysville	93	591
D A	30	m	w	PA	Humboldt	Pacific Twp	72	296
Danl	25	m	w	IREL	Alameda	Brooklyn Twp	68	50
David	47	m	w	OH	San Diego	San Diego	78	492
David	22	m	w	CANA	San Francisco	San Francisco P O	85	758
Dolly	17	f	b	VA	San Joaquin	2-Wd Stockton	86	160
Edmund	34	m	w	IREL	San Francisco	San Francisco P O	83	81
Edward	44	m	w	ME	Nevada	Eureka Twp	75	135
Edwin	33	m	w	KY	Fresno	Millerton P O	72	158
Edwin	23	m	w	ME	San Francisco	11-Wd San Francisc	84	554
Elizabeth	22	f	w	MA	San Francisco	2-Wd San Francisco	79	194
Ellen	14	f	w	CA	Contra Costa	Martinez P O	71	432
Ellenor	71	f	w	PA	Sonoma	Mendocino Twp	91	306
Frederick	40	m	w	GERM	Tulare	Visalia	92	297
Frederick	39	m	w	SHOL	Plumas	Plumas Twp	77	27
G	20	m	w	CANA	Sierra	Butte Twp	89	508
Geo	45	m	w	MO	San Joaquin	Castoria Twp	86	14
Geo	35	m	w	SCOT	Alameda	Oakland	68	221
George	47	m	w	IREL	San Francisco	San Francisco P O	85	872
George	35	m	w	NY	San Francisco	San Francisco P O	80	465
George	29	m	w	SCOT	San Francisco	11-Wd San Francisc	84	518
Henry	43	m	m	PA	Calaveras	San Andreas P O	70	193
Henry	41	m	w	OH	Sonoma	Mendocino Twp	91	306
Henry	40	m	w	PRUS	Butte	Hamilton Twp	70	65
Henry M	36	m	w	ME	San Francisco	San Francisco P O	83	348
Isaac S	42	m	w	ME	Tulare	Tule Rvr Twp	92	270
J F	35	m	w	NY	Alameda	Murray Twp	68	111
J F	35	m	w	IL	Monterey	San Juan Twp	74	414
J G	49	m	w	GA	San Joaquin	Dent Twp	86	23
Jack	45	m	i	CA	Fresno	Kings Rvr P O	72	207
Jacob	28	m	w	IA	Napa	Napa	75	26
Jacob	25	m	w	NY	San Francisco	1-Wd San Francisco	79	135
Jacob S	33	m	w	PA	Colusa	Butte Twp	71	269
James	61	m	w	IREL	Marin	Novato Twp	74	9
James	43	m	w	SWED	El Dorado	Salmon Falls Twp	72	129
James	35	m	w	IREL	Santa Clara	1-Wd San Jose	88	253
James	35	m	w	IREL	Santa Clara	Fremont Twp	88	54
James	27	m	w	CANA	Monterey	Alisal Twp	74	299
James	21	m	w	MO	Yolo	Putah Twp	93	522
James	19	m	i	----	Marin	Tomales Twp	74	89
James J	32	m	w	IL	Yolo	Grafton Twp	93	490
James S	50	m	w	MO	Monterey	San Juan Twp	74	405
Jane	45	f	w	IREL	San Francisco	San Francisco P O	83	293
Jas	19	m	w	ENGL	Sierra	Table Rock Twp	89	578
Jeremiah	31	m	w	PA	San Francisco	11-Wd San Francisc	84	517
Jno H	45	m	b	PA	Sierra	Table Rock Twp	89	573
John	49	m	w	MA	San Francisco	7-Wd San Francisco	81	260
John	48	m	w	MA	San Francisco	7-Wd San Francisco	81	245
John	45	m	w	AUST	San Francisco	San Francisco P O	80	341
John	42	m	w	NY	San Joaquin	Tulare Twp	86	254
John	40	m	w	SCOT	Contra Costa	Martinez P O	71	417
John	40	m	w	IREL	Tuolumne	Chinese Camp P O	93	371
John	39	m	w	ENGL	San Francisco	7-Wd San Francisco	81	267
John	39	m	w	OH	Lake	Upper Lake	73	412
John	37	m	w	ME	Nevada	Rough & Ready Twp	75	323
John	36	m	w	BADE	Placer	Auburn P O	76	363
John	35	m	w	IREL	Inyo	Independence Twp	73	328
John	32	m	w	SCOT	San Francisco	11-Wd San Francisc	84	563
John	30	m	w	ME	Contra Costa	Martinez P O	71	429
John	29	m	w	IREL	San Francisco	7-Wd San Francisco	81	166
John	27	m	w	ME	Humboldt	Table Bluff Twp	72	305
John A	43	m	w	PA	Calaveras	Copperopolis P O	70	225
John A	34	m	w	IL	Yolo	Grafton Twp	93	479
John C	36	m	w	PA	Santa Clara	1-Wd San Jose	88	226
John H	37	m	w	HANO	San Joaquin	2-Wd Stockton	86	168
John W	29	m	w	NY	San Francisco	7-Wd San Francisco	81	239
John W	26	m	w	IL	Yolo	Grafton Twp	93	490
Joseph	42	m	w	AUST	Monterey	Salinas Twp	74	313
Joseph	31	m	w	OH	Butte	Hamilton Twp	70	71
Joseph H	40	m	w	PA	Santa Cruz	Watsonville	89	373
Lawrence L	41	m	w	SWED	Tuolumne	Sonora P O	93	324
Lewis	20	m	w	NY	Yuba	Marysville Twp	93	571
Mary	3	f	w	CA	Alameda	Oakland	68	238
Mary	19	f	w	NY	San Francisco	5-Wd San Francisco	81	21
Matheas	38	m	w	OH	Contra Costa	Martinez P O	71	439
Mathew	40	m	w	IREL	Solano	Vallejo	90	214
Michael	45	m	w	IREL	Calaveras	Copperopolis P O	70	248
Michl	30	m	w	IREL	San Francisco	San Francisco P O	83	81
Morton	41	m	w	IA	Napa	Napa	75	26
P J	38	m	w	IREL	San Francisco	San Francisco P O	85	861
P N	40	m	w	IL	Humboldt	Pacific Twp	72	290
Patrick W	36	m	w	IREL	San Francisco	8-Wd San Francisco	82	494
Peter	48	m	w	NY	San Francisco	San Francisco P O	83	140
Peter P	41	m	w	MO	Trinity	Minersville Pct	92	215
Preston	32	m	w	IN	Contra Costa	Martinez P O	71	396
R C	50	m	w	ENGL	Nevada	Bloomfield Twp	75	94
Richd	51	m	w	SWED	San Francisco	San Francisco P O	83	36
Robert	35	m	w	PA	Napa	Napa	75	22
Robt	59	m	w	KY	Tehama	Red Bluff	92	173
Robt	37	m	w	CT	Sacramento	4-Wd Sacramento	77	357
Robt B	17	m	w	CA	Colusa	Butte Twp	71	265
Rolph	21	m	w	IL	Butte	Chico Twp	70	29
Sally	20	f	i	CA	Fresno	Millerton P O	72	192

© 2001 by Heritage Quest. All rights reserved.

Name	Age	S	R	B-PL	County	Locale	Roll	Pg
Saml	64	m	w	ME	El Dorado	Georgetown Twp	72	36
Saml	30	m	w	OH	Plumas	Plumas Twp	77	26
Samuel	49	m	w	IN	Santa Clara	Redwood Twp	88	129
Samuel	38	m	w	VA	Tulare	Farmersville Twp	92	242
Samuel	24	m	w	PA	San Diego	Julian Dist	78	470
Samuel F	45	m	w	IA	Napa	Napa	75	26
Samuel M	30	m	w	NY	Monterey	Castroville Twp	74	339
Sylvia	19	f	b	MO	San Joaquin	Elliott Twp	86	74
Thos	36	m	w	LA	San Francisco	8-Wd San Francisco	82	359
Victor I	15	m	w	IN	Santa Clara	Redwood Twp	88	129
Virginia J	15	f	w	IL	Yolo	Grafton Twp	93	483
W D	37	m	w	ENGL	Nevada	Bloomfield Twp	75	95
W M	24	m	w	NC	Yuba	Marysville	93	602
William	51	m	w	PA	San Francisco	San Francisco P O	83	220
William	38	m	w	SCOT	Nevada	Nevada Twp	75	318
William	37	m	w	IA	Napa	Napa	75	26
William	37	m	w	ENGL	Plumas	Washington Twp	77	53
William	34	m	w	PA	Marin	San Rafael Twp	74	43
William	33	m	w	IREL	San Francisco	San Francisco P O	83	330
William	15	m	b	CA	Contra Costa	Martinez P O	71	449
William S	34	m	w	AL	Los Angeles	El Monte Twp	73	462
Wm	48	m	w	ME	San Joaquin	3-Wd Stockton	86	239
Wm	39	m	w	MA	San Diego	San Diego	78	503
Wm	30	m	w	GERM	San Joaquin	2-Wd Stockton	86	167
Wm	30	m	w	ENGL	San Joaquin	2-Wd Stockton	86	164
Wm W	35	m	w	KY	San Francisco	1-Wd San Francisco	79	43
BLACKBERN								
Charles	20	m	w	IL	Inyo	Bishop Crk Twp	73	315
Hiram	14	m	w	UT	Mono	Bridgeport P O	74	286
John C	51	m	w	OH	Merced	Snelling P O	74	249
BLACKBURN								
A	47	m	w	OH	San Bernardino	San Bernardino Twp	78	428
Bruce	17	m	w	MO	Santa Cruz	Santa Cruz	89	427
Burt	35	m	w	TN	Stanislaus	Empire Twp	92	63
C E	23	m	w	IL	Sacramento	4-Wd Sacramento	77	322
Chas	48	m	w	ENGL	Sonoma	Petaluma Twp	91	318
Cornelius	23	m	w	OH	Placer	Lincoln P O	76	492
Daniel D	50	m	w	VA	San Luis Obispo	Salinas Twp	87	295
E	70	f	w	PA	San Bernardino	San Bernardino Twp	78	424
Felix	30	m	w	CANA	Humboldt	Bucksport Twp	72	244
Frank	21	m	w	IA	Butte	Chico Twp	70	49
Harriet M	38	f	w	MA	Santa Cruz	Santa Cruz	89	432
Isaac	66	m	w	PA	San Francisco	San Francisco P O	83	329
J	50	m	w	IREL	Calaveras	Copperopolis P O	70	230
J	35	m	w	VA	San Joaquin	Dent Twp	86	16
J M	31	m	w	OH	Sierra	Gibson Twp	89	544
J W	43	m	w	PA	Siskiyou	Callahan P O	89	625
Jacob	26	m	w	OH	Merced	Snelling P O	74	249
Jacob A	47	m	w	OH	Santa Cruz	Pajaro Twp	89	344
James	37	m	w	ENGL	Placer	Bath P O	76	438
James	20	m	w	CA	Sacramento	Brighton Twp	77	79
James H	43	m	w	VA	San Luis Obispo	Salinas Twp	87	295
Jas	60	m	b	AL	Butte	Chico Twp	70	30
Jas	21	m	w	VA	Butte	Chico Twp	70	31
Joseph	42	m	w	KY	Placer	Bath P O	76	437
Kate	46	f	w	IREL	San Francisco	11-Wd San Francisc	84	440
Leroy	16	m	w	CA	San Bernardino	San Bernardino Twp	78	424
Mary	15	f	w	LA	Monterey	Pajaro Twp	74	370
Nancy	56	f	w	OH	Santa Cruz	Santa Cruz Twp	89	379
R T	53	m	w	NY	Solano	Vallejo	90	217
BLACKBURNE								
Danl	48	m	w	ENGL	San Francisco	5-Wd San Francisco	81	11
BLACKBURNS								
James	32	m	w	OH	Stanislaus	Empire Twp	92	48
BLACKELEY								
Francis	45	m	w	IREL	San Francisco	8-Wd San Francisco	82	444
BLACKET								
Wm	26	m	w	NY	San Francisco	5-Wd San Francisco	81	36
BLACKFORD								
Eliza E	19	f	w	MO	Santa Clara	San Jose Twp	88	212
George M	35	m	w	OH	Santa Clara	Santa Clara Twp	88	175
John	60	m	w	PA	Nevada	Grass Valley Twp	75	142
John	40	m	w	MA	Calaveras	San Andreas P O	70	217
P	14	m	w	CA	Yuba	Rose Bar Twp	93	666
Simeon	38	m	w	IN	El Dorado	Mud Springs Twp	72	77
BLACKHALL								
H	35	m	w	SCOT	Sierra	Gibson Twp	89	543
BLACKIE								
Frances	29	m	w	SCOT	Monterey	Castroville Twp	74	340
BLACKINGTON								
E J	26	m	w	MA	Solano	Vallejo	90	212
Robert	46	m	w	OH	Sonoma	Healdsburg & Mendo	91	283
BLACKISTER								
M A	21	f	w	ENGL	San Francisco	San Francisco P O	83	132
BLACKISTON								
Willm	35	m	w	MD	Siskiyou	Table Rock Twp	89	645
BLACKLEACH								
D W	1	f	w	CA	Sacramento	3-Wd Sacramento	77	281
BLACKLOCK								
James	31	m	w	SCOT	Solano	Denverton Twp	90	24
William	37	m	w	SCOT	El Dorado	Placerville Twp	72	94
BLACKLY								
Charles	32	m	w	ENGL	Los Angeles	El Monte Twp	73	452
BLACKMAN								
Abram	44	m	w	PRUS	San Francisco	8-Wd San Francisco	82	437
Clark	22	m	w	MA	Placer	Cisco P O	76	494
John	54	m	w	VT	San Diego	San Diego	78	485
John	33	m	w	WI	Sutter	Vernon Twp	92	137
John	28	m	w	ENGL	San Joaquin	2-Wd Stockton	86	171
John	25	m	w	PRUS	San Francisco	San Francisco P O	80	411
John	19	m	w	PA	San Mateo	Half Moon Bay P O	87	408
Julius	30	m	w	CT	San Bernardino	San Bernardino Twp	78	428
Mark	34	m	w	ME	San Joaquin	2-Wd Stockton	86	161
Saml	38	m	w	PRUS	San Francisco	8-Wd San Francisco	82	370
BLACKMAR								
Ransin	23	m	w	MI	Marin	Point Reyes Twp	74	23
BLACKMER								
E S	44	m	w	NY	San Joaquin	1-Wd Stockton	86	141
Wm T	53	m	w	MA	Mariposa	Maxwell Crk P O	74	139
BLACKMORE								
Aaron	38	m	w	MI	Mendocino	Big Rvr Twp	74	170
James	41	m	c	CHIN	Trinity	Lewiston Pct	92	211
Wm	34	m	w	ENGL	Mariposa	Mariposa P O	74	99
BLACKS								
H W	35	m	w	OH	Sonoma	Russian Rvr	91	368
J L	47	m	w	ME	San Joaquin	Douglas Twp	86	51
BLACKSHIRE								
G	45	m	w	MO	Amador	Ione City P O	69	349
BLACKSTONE								
Corbin	55	m	b	VA	Santa Barbara	Santa Barbara P O	87	488
BLACKSWELL								
H F	32	m	w	TN	Merced	Snelling P O	74	275
BLACKWAY								
Charles	44	m	w	PA	Sacramento	2-Wd Sacramento	77	237
BLACKWEDEL								
John H	37	m	w	HANO	Mariposa	Mariposa P O	74	90
BLACKWELL								
A J	38	m	w	IN	Sonoma	Vallejo Twp	91	461
Alexr	44	m	w	VA	Santa Clara	Fremont Twp	88	49
D M	39	m	w	TN	Amador	Sutter Crk P O	69	399
John	47	m	w	IREL	Trinity	Weaverville Pct	92	224
John	12	m	w	OR	San Mateo	Belmont P O	87	388
John R	11	m	w	CA	Stanislaus	Empire Twp	92	54
L C	39	m	w	TN	Nevada	Eureka Twp	75	131
Nathaniel	25	m	w	ENGL	Contra Costa	Martinez P O	71	423
S	29	m	w	ME	Sacramento	3-Wd Sacramento	77	273
S L	38	m	w	NC	Nevada	Eureka Twp	75	132
Thomas	43	m	w	LA	San Mateo	Belmont P O	87	388
Thos H	25	m	w	ENGL	Nevada	Grass Valley Twp	75	183
W	44	m	w	IREL	San Francisco	3-Wd San Francisco	79	317
W D	76	m	w	NC	Tuolumne	Chinese Camp P O	93	385
BLACKWOOD								
Horatio	22	m	w	NJ	Sacramento	1-Wd Sacramento	77	186
R H	40	m	w	NY	Nevada	Nevada Twp	75	309
S W	31	m	w	MI	Sacramento	4-Wd Sacramento	77	366
W	12	m	w	CA	Alameda	Oakland	68	242
William	57	m	w	NY	Alameda	Eden Twp	68	65
Wm	42	m	w	IREL	San Francisco	San Francisco P O	83	26
BLACOW								
John	50	m	w	ENGL	Alameda	Washington Twp	68	281
Robert	55	m	w	ENGL	Alameda	Washington Twp	68	280
BLADE								
Samuel	37	m	w	MD	Kern	Linns Valley P O	73	343
BLADT								
Ludwig	59	m	w	BADE	San Francisco	San Francisco P O	83	183
BLAESE								
Joseph	52	m	w	FRAN	Yuba	Slate Range Bar Tw	93	670
BLAESO								
Louis	42	m	w	FRAN	Santa Clara	2-Wd San Jose	88	302
BLAGG								
Elijah	25	m	w	AR	Mariposa	Mariposa P O	74	130
BLAIKEE								
Andrew	50	m	w	SCOT	San Francisco	7-Wd San Francisco	81	282
BLAIKIE								
James	40	m	w	NY	San Francisco	6-Wd San Francisco	81	108
BLAIKLEY								
---	26	m	w	US	Humboldt	Eureka Twp	72	273
BLAIN								
George	31	m	w	VT	Solano	Maine Prairie Twp	90	48
Henry	49	m	w	NY	Sacramento	Lee Twp	77	159
James	42	m	w	VT	Solano	Maine Prairie Twp	90	48
John	30	m	w	IA	San Joaquin	Douglas Twp	86	46
Lewis	40	m	w	DENM	Nevada	Eureka Twp	75	130
Redman P	43	m	w	NY	San Francisco	6-Wd San Francisco	81	144
Robert P	30	m	w	NY	Solano	Maine Prairie Twp	90	53
BLAIND								
George	44	m	w	TN	Placer	Gold Run Twp	76	400
BLAINE								
Francis	31	m	w	CANA	Nevada	Bloomfield Twp	75	93
BLAINEY								
Patk	40	m	w	IREL	San Francisco	San Francisco P O	83	119
BLAIR								
Agnes	70	f	w	SCOT	El Dorado	Placerville	72	120
Alexr	65	m	w	VA	Sonoma	Mendocino Twp	91	305
Alvy	35	m	w	NY	Yolo	Putah Twp	93	520
Andrew	33	m	w	SCOT	San Francisco	1-Wd San Francisco	79	71
Andrew	28	m	w	SCOT	San Francisco	11-Wd San Francisc	84	520
B H	43	m	w	PA	Solano	Vallejo	90	152
Calvin H	40	m	w	AR	Tulare	Farmersville Twp	92	248
Charles	36	m	w	MA	San Francisco	San Francisco P O	83	254
Charles	32	m	w	SWIT	Napa	Napa	75	2
D B	33	m	w	SCOT	Alameda	Oakland	68	188
D C	48	m	w	NY	Mendocino	Little Lake Twp	74	197
Daniel	48	m	w	PA	Colusa	Colusa Twp	71	275

© 2001 by Heritage Quest. All rights reserved.

Name	Age	S	R	B-PL	County	Locale	Series M593 Roll	Pg
Edward	34	m	w	NY	Yolo	Cottonwood Twp	93	470
Elisha W	35	m	w	ME	Mendocino	Big Rvr Twp	74	159
Elizabeth	35	f	w	SCOT	San Francisco	7-Wd San Francisco	81	236
Ernestine	60	f	w	SCOT	San Francisco	San Francisco P O	83	70
Ezra	38	m	w	IN	San Joaquin	Dent Twp	86	19
G M	38	m	w	MA	Alameda	Oakland	68	188
Geo W	68	m	w	PA	Sonoma	Mendocino Twp	91	287
Henry	10	m	w	CA	San Francisco	San Francisco P O	85	828
Hugh	43	m	w	CANA	Napa	Napa Twp	75	63
Hugh	36	m	w	CANA	Napa	Napa	75	27
J F	30	m	w	VT	San Joaquin	1-Wd Stockton	86	126
James	63	m	w	VA	Stanislaus	Emory Twp	92	18
James	40	m	w	SCOT	El Dorado	Placerville Twp	72	105
James	28	m	w	KY	San Joaquin	Union Twp	86	265
James	18	m	w	OH	El Dorado	Placerville Twp	72	105
James D	40	m	w	ME	Tulare	Visalia	92	297
Jas H	49	m	w	IN	Humboldt	Pacific Twp	72	299
John	49	m	w	OH	Sonoma	Bodega Twp	91	261
John	42	m	w	SCOT	El Dorado	Placerville	72	119
John	36	m	w	VA	Inyo	Bishop Crk Twp	73	313
John	30	m	w	IREL	Sacramento	Dry Crk Twp	77	101
John	30	m	w	AUST	Sacramento	Brighton Twp	77	75
John	25	m	w	CANA	Mendocino	Calpella Twp	74	183
John H	29	m	w	SCOT	El Dorado	Placerville	72	111
Jonathan	65	m	w	TN	Tulare	Venice Twp	92	273
L	37	m	w	TN	San Joaquin	2-Wd Stockton	86	171
Lena	13	f	w	MI	Sacramento	3-Wd Sacramento	77	300
Louisa	17	f	w	CA	Los Angeles	Los Angeles	73	566
Mathew	49	m	w	VT	San Francisco	San Francisco P O	85	824
Matthew	21	m	w	SCOT	El Dorado	Placerville Twp	72	105
Phineas S	48	m	w	MA	San Francisco	San Francisco P O	83	169
Robert	42	m	w	IREL	El Dorado	Georgetown Twp	72	38
Robt	38	m	w	SCOT	Shasta	Horsetown P O	89	505
Robt L	26	m	w	OH	Sonoma	Healdsburg & Mendo	91	279
S M	47	m	w	CANA	Sacramento	4-Wd Sacramento	77	367
Saml	40	m	w	IREL	San Francisco	7-Wd San Francisco	81	236
Samuel	60	m	w	MO	Plumas	Washington Twp	77	58
Susan	40	f	w	PA	San Francisco	3-Wd San Francisco	79	324
Thomas	43	m	w	SCOT	Calaveras	Copperopolis P O	70	238
Thomas	34	m	w	OH	Mendocino	Little Lake Twp	74	197
Thomas	34	m	w	MO	Contra Costa	Martinez P O	71	407
Thomas	27	m	w	NY	Alameda	Washington Twp	68	301
Thomas	23	m	w	SCOT	San Francisco	San Francisco P O	83	168
Thomas	22	m	w	SCOT	San Francisco	San Francisco P O	80	345
Thompson	41	m	w	VA	San Francisco	San Francisco P O	83	323
Thos	23	m	w	SCOT	Sacramento	3-Wd Sacramento	77	275
Thos M	36	m	w	NY	San Francisco	8-Wd San Francisco	82	354
Thos N	34	m	w	AR	Sonoma	Santa Rosa	91	419
Walter	39	m	w	VT	Alameda	Oakland	68	203
William	22	m	w	CANA	Mendocino	Calpella Twp	74	183
William J	27	m	w	VT	San Francisco	11-Wd San Francisc	84	708
Wm	62	m	w	PA	Nevada	Nevada Twp	75	271
BLAIRE								
Spencer	48	m	w	NY	Tuolumne	Sonora P O	93	323
BLAIS								
Edward	25	m	w	CANA	Sacramento	Brighton Twp	77	76
T	12	m	w	CA	Solano	Benicia	90	21
BLAISDELL								
Alonzo G	29	m	w	ME	Placer	Gold Run Twp	76	396
E H F	49	f	w	NH	San Francisco	San Francisco P O	83	104
Elijah S	50	m	w	ME	Santa Barbara	Santa Barbara P O	87	491
Enoch W	39	m	w	IN	Santa Clara	1-Wd San Jose	88	241
Frank	18	m	w	ME	Stanislaus	Empire Twp	92	47
I	30	m	w	NY	San Joaquin	Oneal Twp	86	112
J L	32	m	w	MA	Santa Clara	Gilroy Twp	88	98
Jay	32	m	w	VT	San Francisco	8-Wd San Francisco	82	383
John	19	m	w	CA	Marin	Bolinas Twp	74	6
M C	25	f	w	PA	Santa Clara	Gilroy Twp	88	98
Olario	10	m	w	CA	Marin	Bolinas Twp	74	6
Sabine	24	f	w	ME	Stanislaus	Empire Twp	92	44
Saml	40	m	w	NY	San Francisco	7-Wd San Francisco	81	232
BLAKALL								
Manda	24	f	w	IN	Colusa	Monroe Twp	71	319
BLAKE								
A	37	m	w	NY	San Joaquin	Douglas Twp	86	48
A N	53	m	w	ENGL	San Joaquin	2-Wd Stockton	86	186
Alex	31	m	w	NJ	Mendocino	Round Valley Twp	74	218
Anna	25	f	w	DENM	Sacramento	4-Wd Sacramento	77	325
Anna	19	f	w	CANA	Alameda	San Leandro	68	94
Benja	26	m	w	OH	San Francisco	8-Wd San Francisco	82	298
Betsy R	67	f	w	ME	Placer	Newcastle Twp	76	473
C	50	m	w	MA	San Francisco	San Francisco P O	83	112
Calvin T	48	m	w	MA	San Francisco	1-Wd San Francisco	79	18
Charles	24	m	w	ME	Stanislaus	San Joaquin Twp	92	79
Chas	21	m	w	ME	San Francisco	San Francisco P O	83	31
Chas	21	m	w	CANA	Solano	Vallejo	90	200
Cornelius	54	m	w	NY	Marin	Tomales Twp	74	83
David	30	m	w	VT	Kern	Linns Valley P O	73	349
Eleck	43	m	w	VA	Solano	Montezuma Twp	90	68
Electa	82	f	w	VT	Nevada	Meadow Lake Twp	75	258
Elizabeth	40	f	w	IREL	San Francisco	8-Wd San Francisco	82	291
Frances	14	f	w	CA	San Francisco	San Francisco P O	83	327
Francis	50	m	w	ME	Alameda	Oakland	68	234
Francis	40	m	w	IREL	Nevada	Grass Valley Twp	75	209
Frank	35	m	w	IREL	Calaveras	San Andreas P O	70	192
Fred	42	m	w	HANO	Sierra	Eureka Twp	89	524
Fred W	35	m	w	ENGL	Tulare	Visalia	92	290

Name	Age	S	R	B-PL	County	Locale	Series M593 Roll	Pg
G A	39	m	w	MA	San Francisco	San Francisco P O	85	805
Geo	11	m	w	CA	San Francisco	11-Wd San Francisc	84	587
Geo M	48	m	w	NY	Alameda	Oakland	68	259
Geo M	40	m	w	NY	San Francisco	San Francisco P O	83	272
George	35	m	w	NY	San Francisco	5-Wd San Francisco	81	36
George H	55	m	w	LA	San Mateo	San Mateo P O	87	349
Harvey B	39	m	w	NY	Santa Barbara	Santa Barbara P O	87	466
Henry	42	m	w	ENGL	Alameda	Alameda	68	17
Henry	39	m	w	OH	Butte	Kimshew Tpw	70	86
Henry H	32	m	w	MA	San Francisco	8-Wd San Francisco	82	465
Hiram	40	m	w	MO	Solano	Rio Vista Twp	90	71
J	30	m	w	MO	Lassen	Susanville Twp	73	443
J C	38	m	w	VA	Lassen	Susanville Twp	73	440
J R	34	m	w	PA	Amador	Sutter Crk P O	69	413
J R	28	m	w	MA	Amador	Sutter Crk P O	69	407
James	47	m	w	IREL	San Francisco	San Francisco P O	83	401
James	40	m	w	VA	Solano	Green Valley Twp	90	38
James	33	m	w	IREL	Yuba	Rose Bar Twp	93	663
James	26	m	w	VA	San Mateo	Pescadero P O	87	413
James S	33	m	w	MD	Santa Clara	2-Wd San Jose	88	303
James W	26	m	w	ENGL	Tulare	Visalia	92	293
Jeremiah	38	m	w	ME	Nevada	Nevada Twp	75	320
Jerry	50	m	w	ME	Nevada	Nevada Twp	75	308
Jerry	36	m	w	NH	Marin	Tomales Twp	74	77
Jno	21	m	w	ENGL	Sierra	Table Rock Twp	89	576
John	43	m	w	ENGL	San Francisco	8-Wd San Francisco	82	378
John	40	m	w	IREL	Sacramento	4-Wd Sacramento	77	355
John	40	m	b	MD	San Francisco	San Francisco P O	80	419
John	40	m	w	NJ	Monterey	Castroville Twp	74	340
John	40	m	w	IREL	San Francisco	San Francisco P O	83	420
John	32	m	w	IREL	San Francisco	San Francisco P O	83	38
John	25	m	w	CANA	Humboldt	Arcata Twp	72	234
John	23	m	w	OH	San Francisco	8-Wd San Francisco	82	387
John	23	m	w	CT	San Francisco	6-Wd San Francisco	81	90
John	19	m	w	NY	San Francisco	San Francisco P O	83	163
John M	37	m	w	MA	Shasta	Shasta P O	89	453
John O	24	m	w	CT	Napa	Napa	75	11
Katie	20	f	w	NY	Santa Clara	1-Wd San Jose	88	252
Lewis	24	m	w	NJ	Colusa	Grand Island Twp	71	309
Lizzie	28	f	w	IREL	San Francisco	San Francisco P O	80	337
Maggie	33	f	w	IL	San Francisco	San Francisco P O	80	424
Mary	55	f	w	IREL	San Francisco	6-Wd San Francisco	81	143
Mary	30	f	w	IREL	Napa	Napa	75	51
Mary A	29	f	w	MA	San Francisco	San Francisco P O	83	261
Maurice B	25	m	w	ME	San Francisco	6-Wd San Francisco	81	78
May A	35	f	w	ME	San Francisco	8-Wd San Francisco	82	352
Michael	45	m	w	IREL	Siskiyou	Yreka Twp	89	667
Morris	50	m	w	ME	San Francisco	11-Wd San Francisc	84	574
Nicholas	40	m	w	IREL	San Francisco	San Francisco P O	83	294
Oliver	23	m	w	IREL	San Francisco	1-Wd San Francisco	79	104
Orlando	33	m	w	ME	Merced	Snelling P O	74	252
P H	37	m	w	MA	San Francisco	San Francisco P O	85	873
Patrick	42	m	w	IREL	Nevada	Grass Valley Twp	75	175
Peter	37	m	w	IREL	Butte	Kimshew Tpw	70	80
Peter	35	m	w	BADE	San Francisco	7-Wd San Francisco	81	160
Reuben E	38	m	w	VA	Los Angeles	El Monte Twp	73	460
Richard	7	m	w	CA	San Francisco	San Francisco P O	85	800
Robert	39	m	w	ENGL	San Luis Obispo	Santa Rosa Twp	87	324
Robert A	50	m	w	SCOT	Mendocino	Point Arena Twp	74	212
Saml A	40	m	w	PA	Butte	Hamilton Twp	70	70
Silas	32	m	w	ME	Napa	Napa	75	1
Sumner	33	m	w	ME	San Francisco	San Francisco P O	80	389
Thomas	37	m	w	ENGL	San Francisco	San Francisco P O	83	230
Thomas M	44	m	w	FL	Tulare	Farmersville Twp	92	250
Thos	37	m	w	IREL	San Joaquin	3-Wd Stockton	86	233
Thos	27	m	w	IREL	San Francisco	8-Wd San Francisco	82	375
Willard L	27	m	w	ME	Placer	Dutch Flat P O	76	409
William	60	m	w	NY	Solano	Silveyville Twp	90	91
William	58	m	w	NY	Los Angeles	San Jose Twp	73	620
William	55	m	w	VA	Tulare	Packwood Twp	92	255
William	35	m	m	MD	San Francisco	San Francisco P O	80	402
William	30	m	w	IREL	Sutter	Sutter Twp	92	123
William	28	m	w	IREL	San Joaquin	2-Wd Stockton	86	173
William	27	m	w	MI	San Francisco	8-Wd San Francisco	82	379
William H	25	m	w	VT	San Francisco	6-Wd San Francisco	81	81
Wm	52	m	w	IREL	Butte	Oregon Twp	70	135
Wm	48	m	w	IREL	Solano	Benicia	90	3
Wm	24	m	w	ENGL	San Francisco	8-Wd San Francisco	82	375
BLAKELEY								
Wm H	38	m	w	IREL	San Francisco	San Francisco P O	83	104
BLAKELY								
Alburn J	42	m	w	PA	El Dorado	Placerville Twp	72	104
Calvin	36	m	w	CANA	San Francisco	11-Wd San Francisc	84	654
F N	31	f	w	US	San Joaquin	2-Wd Stockton	86	164
James	36	m	w	CANA	San Joaquin	Elkhorn Twp	86	59
Jno A	47	m	w	TN	Sonoma	Santa Rosa	91	409
John	53	m	w	OH	Merced	Snelling P O	74	262
John	35	m	w	IREL	San Francisco	San Francisco P O	83	148
John M	39	m	w	NY	San Francisco	8-Wd San Francisco	82	385
Saml	68	m	w	KY	Santa Barbara	San Buenaventura P	87	421
Samuel	29	m	w	IREL	San Francisco	11-Wd San Francisc	84	480
Samuel W	36	m	w	CANA	Santa Cruz	Santa Cruz	89	434
Susan	19	f	w	IREL	San Francisco	San Francisco P O	83	102
William	53	m	w	IREL	Amador	Volcano P O	69	379
Wm	26	m	w	NY	Sonoma	Salt Point	91	387
BLAKEMORE								
E	30	f	w	AR	Merced	Snelling P O	74	255

© 2001 by Heritage Quest. All rights reserved.

Series M593

Name	Age	S	R	B-PL	County	Locale	Roll	Pg
George	36	m	w	TN	Tulare	Packwood Twp	92	256
William B	34	m	w	TN	Tulare	Packwood Twp	92	256
BLAKENY								
Fras	48	m	w	IREL	Santa Barbara	San Buenaventura P	87	444
J T	30	m	w	NY	Sacramento	3-Wd Sacramento	77	301
BLAKERLY								
Chauncy	32	m	w	IN	Solano	Silveyville Twp	90	86
BLAKESLEE								
George H	42	m	w	PA	Santa Clara	San Jose Twp	88	213
S	37	m	w	OH	Alameda	Oakland	68	164
Stephen B	51	m	w	CT	Los Angeles	El Monte Twp	73	454
BLAKESLEY								
Abram H	38	m	w	IN	Santa Cruz	Santa Cruz	89	429
M A	29	f	w	IL	Yuba	East Bear Rvr Twp	93	543
Warren A	39	m	w	OH	Plumas	Plumas Twp	77	32
BLAKESLY								
A H	68	m	w	NY	Butte	Wyandotte Twp	70	148
George A	48	m	w	OH	San Luis Obispo	Salinas Twp	87	293
H A	27	m	w	MI	Butte	Wyandotte Twp	70	148
BLAKEY								
Sarah	60	f	w	PA	San Francisco	San Francisco P O	85	853
BLAKLEY								
Ambrose	31	m	w	IREL	Amador	Volcano P O	69	380
BLALOCK								
J P	59	m	w	NC	Del Norte	Smith Rvr Twp	71	479
BLAMHOLTZ								
Thos	30	m	w	IREL	San Francisco	2-Wd San Francisco	79	253
BLAMYER								
James	40	m	w	ENGL	Contra Costa	San Pablo Twp	71	354
BLANC								
Charles	38	m	w	FRAN	Nevada	Grass Valley Twp	75	213
Lawrence	46	m	w	FRAN	Plumas	Rich Bar Twp	77	45
Stewart	40	m	w	IREL	San Francisco	San Francisco P O	83	364
BLANCE								
F	51	m	w	FRAN	Sacramento	1-Wd Sacramento	77	175
Francisco	25	m	w	CA	Monterey	Alisal Twp	74	289
Henry	35	m	w	HDAR	San Francisco	8-Wd San Francisco	82	416
Juaquin	9	m	w	CA	San Luis Obispo	San Luis Obispo Tw	87	300
Louis	29	m	w	ITAL	San Francisco	2-Wd San Francisco	79	163
Mathew	40	m	w	PRUS	Contra Costa	Martinez P O	71	407
BLANCER								
Prosper	40	m	w	FRAN	Calaveras	San Andreas P O	70	179
BLANCH								
Chas	39	m	w	ENGL	San Luis Obispo	Morro Twp	87	281
Eliza	24	f	w	BADE	San Francisco	2-Wd San Francisco	79	140
Trinidad	32	f	w	MEXI	Fresno	Millerton P O	72	163
William	42	m	w	ENGL	Nevada	Eureka Twp	75	131
BLANCHAR								
J D	45	m	w	NY	Napa	Yountville Twp	75	76
BLANCHARD								
A	21	m	w	FRAN	Alameda	Oakland	68	169
Adrian	21	m	w	FRAN	San Francisco	San Francisco P O	80	429
Aime	42	m	w	FRAN	Butte	Bidwell Twp	70	3
Albert	21	m	w	ME	Yolo	Cache Crk Twp	93	425
Albert S	21	m	w	ME	Yolo	Cache Crk Twp	93	444
Andrew	41	m	w	FRAN	San Francisco	2-Wd San Francisco	79	153
Arza	23	m	w	IL	Marin	Tomales Twp	74	81
August	18	m	w	FRAN	Marin	San Rafael Twp	74	34
Candace	41	f	w	MA	San Francisco	8-Wd San Francisco	82	471
Charles	38	m	w	FRAN	Santa Clara	2-Wd San Jose	88	331
Charles	37	m	w	NH	Stanislaus	Empire Twp	92	29
D	40	m	w	ME	San Francisco	San Francisco P O	85	822
David	34	m	w	IREL	San Francisco	8-Wd San Francisco	82	396
David L	42	m	w	NY	Santa Clara	2-Wd San Jose	88	293
E B	39	m	w	ME	San Joaquin	3-Wd Stockton	86	246
Ed	23	m	w	ENGL	San Francisco	2-Wd San Francisco	79	283
Epolito	56	m	w	FRAN	Marin	Sausalito Twp	74	68
Frances	54	f	w	BADE	Sonoma	Salt Point	91	391
Fred	24	m	w	CANA	San Francisco	7-Wd San Francisco	81	282
G	50	m	w	FRAN	San Francisco	San Francisco P O	83	319
George G	46	m	w	NY	El Dorado	Placerville	72	127
H P	44	m	w	MA	San Francisco	3-Wd San Francisco	79	327
Henry	39	m	w	FRAN	San Francisco	San Francisco P O	80	334
Henry	30	m	w	IL	Siskiyou	Yreka Twp	89	673
Hiram	35	m	w	CANA	Solano	Vallejo	90	192
Jas W	45	m	w	KY	Placer	Newcastle Twp	76	475
Jesse M	36	m	w	ME	Sonoma	Salt Point	91	391
John B	17	m	m	CA	Placer	Bath P O	76	422
Joseph	41	m	w	RI	Nevada	Little York Twp	75	239
Lewis	37	m	w	NY	Butte	Chico Twp	70	44
Lott	73	m	w	MA	San Francisco	8-Wd San Francisco	82	467
Louis	46	m	w	FRAN	Tuolumne	Sonora P O	93	329
Louis	35	m	w	NY	San Mateo	Woodside P O	87	381
Lucy	42	f	w	RI	San Francisco	8-Wd San Francisco	82	318
Melvill W	34	m	w	NY	Yolo	Putah Twp	93	525
N B	35	m	w	MA	San Francisco	7-Wd San Francisco	81	259
Nozello	34	m	w	NY	Contra Costa	Martinez P O	71	397
Peter	29	m	w	FRAN	Santa Clara	Redwood Twp	88	119
Phillip	40	m	w	FRAN	San Mateo	Belmont P O	87	388
Sarah J	17	f	w	NY	Placer	Bath P O	76	447
Seth	48	m	w	MA	Santa Cruz	Santa Cruz	89	424
Victor	32	m	w	FRAN	San Francisco	San Francisco P O	80	538
William	51	m	w	PRUS	San Francisco	San Francisco P O	80	423
Wm	35	m	w	VT	San Joaquin	Douglas Twp	86	39
Wm	28	m	w	IL	Humboldt	Eureka Twp	72	279
Wm K	48	m	w	MA	Santa Barbara	Santa Barbara P O	87	450
BLANCHART								
C	40	m	w	FRAN	Butte	Mountain Spring Tw	70	87
BLANCHAY								
John	34	m	w	FRAN	Santa Clara	2-Wd San Jose	88	311
BLANCHE								
Euphema	70	f	w	NJ	San Francisco	San Francisco P O	83	174
BLANCHETTE								
V	33	m	w	CANA	San Francisco	San Francisco P O	83	328
BLANCHEUSE								
Pedro	35	m	w	FRAN	Santa Cruz	Soquel Twp	89	440
BLANCHFIELD								
C	40	m	w	IREL	San Francisco	San Francisco P O	85	822
J B	63	m	w	IREL	Tuolumne	Columbia P O	93	349
BLANCHO								
Teresa	32	f	w	CHIL	San Francisco	San Francisco P O	80	348
BLANCHY								
John	30	m	w	NY	Contra Costa	Martinez P O	71	367
BLANCK								
Henry	55	m	w	SWIT	Los Angeles	Los Angeles	73	517
BLANCO								
Antonio	36	m	w	MEXI	Fresno	Kings Rvr P O	72	214
John	31	m	w	CHIL	Nevada	Little York Twp	75	238
Jose	34	m	w	CA	San Luis Obispo	San Luis Obispo Tw	87	305
Juana	36	f	w	CA	Los Angeles	Los Angeles	73	555
Louis	35	m	w	SWIT	Santa Clara	Gilroy Twp	88	97
Maria	15	f	w	MEXI	Santa Clara	2-Wd San Jose	88	318
Pablo	26	m	w	CA	San Diego	Julian Dist	78	473
Pedro	38	m	w	CA	Los Angeles	Santa Ana Twp	73	610
BLANCTOE								
Joseph	53	m	w	FRAN	Butte	Ophir Twp	70	96
BLAND								
Adam	47	m	w	VA	Santa Clara	Santa Clara Twp	88	160
Amelia	37	f	w	ME	San Diego	San Luis Rey	78	513
E	7	f	w	CA	Los Angeles	Los Angeles	73	569
Edward	14	m	w	CA	San Luis Obispo	Salinas Twp	87	290
Ezekial	35	m	w	IA	San Mateo	San Mateo P O	87	349
H J	47	m	w	VA	Sutter	Butte Twp	92	93
Isaac	21	m	w	TX	Los Angeles	Los Angeles	73	517
Jefferson D	8	m	w	CA	San Luis Obispo	Salinas Twp	87	290
John C	42	m	w	NC	Santa Clara	Santa Clara Twp	88	175
M	40	f	w	UNKN	San Joaquin	2-Wd Stockton	86	166
Samuel	40	m	w	ME	Los Angeles	Los Nietos Twp	73	589
Samuel	34	m	w	ME	San Diego	San Pasqual	78	522
Samuel	27	m	w	PRUS	San Francisco	San Francisco P O	83	399
William	41	m	w	KY	Sutter	Nicolaus Twp	92	108
William A	33	m	w	TX	Los Angeles	Los Nietos Twp	73	574
Wm	56	m	w	VA	Yuba	Marysville	93	615
BLANDI								
Francesco	35	m	w	ITAL	San Francisco	1-Wd San Francisco	79	122
BLANDING								
Edward	35	m	w	RI	San Francisco	11-Wd San Francisc	84	625
Maria	15	f	w	NY	San Francisco	San Francisco P O	85	722
Wm	45	m	w	SC	Alameda	Oakland	68	161
BLANE								
Alexander	50	m	w	IREL	San Francisco	11-Wd San Francisc	84	460
George	40	m	w	NY	Santa Clara	San Jose Twp	88	196
Mary	50	f	w	IREL	Santa Clara	2-Wd San Jose	88	296
Mary	25	f	w	FRAN	San Francisco	6-Wd San Francisco	81	81
Stewart	41	m	w	IREL	San Francisco	1-Wd San Francisco	79	113
BLANER								
John	25	m	w	SWIT	Santa Clara	1-Wd San Jose	88	230
BLANEY								
Andrew	36	m	w	MA	Marin	Tomales Twp	74	83
Dennis	34	m	w	IREL	Mariposa	Mariposa P O	74	124
Henry	39	m	w	IREL	Nevada	Meadow Lake Twp	75	260
J H	35	m	w	IREL	San Francisco	San Francisco P O	85	792
James	42	m	w	IREL	Nevada	Meadow Lake Twp	75	251
James	28	m	w	IREL	San Francisco	San Francisco P O	83	184
John	49	m	w	NC	San Francisco	8-Wd San Francisco	82	471
Margaret	34	f	w	HDAR	Inyo	Independence Twp	73	324
W	31	m	w	CANA	Alameda	Oakland	68	263
BLANEZ								
George	36	m	w	VA	Mariposa	Mariposa P O	74	93
BLANFIELD								
Louis	68	m	w	FRAN	San Joaquin	3-Wd Stockton	86	225
BLANGER								
Eugene	42	m	w	FRAN	San Francisco	6-Wd San Francisco	81	41
BLANK								
Dan	45	m	b	VA	San Joaquin	2-Wd Stockton	86	169
G A	23	m	w	SWIT	Sacramento	1-Wd Sacramento	77	176
Martin	30	m	w	PRUS	Colusa	Colusa	71	288
BLANKEN								
John	42	m	w	HANO	Nevada	Washington Twp	75	345
Nicholas	39	m	w	PRUS	San Francisco	San Francisco P O	80	473
BLANKENBURG								
John	30	m	w	PRUS	San Francisco	San Francisco P O	80	408
BLANKENHEIM								
Fritz	26	m	w	WURT	San Francisco	San Francisco P O	80	359
BLANKENSHIP								
Jas	41	m	w	GA	Monterey	Pajaro Twp	74	374
Noble P	23	m	w	VA	Tulare	Visalia Twp	92	284
William	39	m	w	VA	Tulare	Visalia	92	292
William	34	m	w	MO	Stanislaus	Empire Twp	92	46
William M	60	m	w	VA	Tulare	Visalia	92	294
BLANKENSTEIN								
Myer	35	m	w	PRUS	San Francisco	8-Wd San Francisco	82	458

© 2001 by Heritage Quest. All rights reserved.

Name	Age	S	R	B-PL	County	Locale	Series M593 Roll	Pg
BLANKING								
Jacob	39	m	w	PRUS	San Francisco	San Francisco P O	85	747
BLANKMAN								
H G	57	m	w	NETH	Monterey	Monterey	74	358
Joseph	19	m	w	NY	San Francisco	San Francisco P O	80	484
BLANKS								
Bell	23	f	w	CT	Sacramento	3-Wd Sacramento	77	291
BLANKSTEIN								
Louisa	49	f	w	ENGL	San Francisco	8-Wd San Francisco	82	428
BLANNCHUSETT								
Richard	26	m	w	IREL	San Francisco	7-Wd San Francisco	81	157
BLANNER								
Ernest	25	m	w	WURT	Sacramento	4-Wd Sacramento	77	323
BLANNON								
Jno	40	m	w	IREL	Sacramento	3-Wd Sacramento	77	303
BLANSFIELD								
Ellen	35	f	w	IREL	San Francisco	7-Wd San Francisco	81	252
James	35	m	w	IREL	San Francisco	7-Wd San Francisco	81	252
BLANTLEY								
Kate	27	f	w	IREL	San Francisco	7-Wd San Francisco	81	281
BLANTYRE								
M	13	f	w	SCOT	Mendocino	Sanel Twp	74	227
BLANTZ								
Joseph	36	m	w	SWIT	Yolo	Putah Twp	93	511
BLANVELT								
Richard	40	m	w	NY	San Francisco	8-Wd San Francisco	82	449
BLARD								
M	58	m	w	CHIL	Amador	Jackson P O	69	345
BLARE								
M J	46	m	w	MA	Sutter	Sutter Twp	92	116
S A	28	m	w	CANA	Santa Clara	Almaden Twp	88	19
BLAS								
June	27	m	w	MEXI	San Joaquin	3-Wd Stockton	86	223
BLASAUF								
John	54	m	w	SWIT	Nevada	Nevada Twp	75	281
BLASCO								
Miquel	30	m	w	MEXI	Napa	Napa	75	53
BLASDELL								
F	28	m	w	ME	Solano	Vallejo	90	160
Geo W	35	m	w	IREL	San Francisco	San Francisco P O	83	200
George	42	m	w	NY	San Francisco	San Francisco P O	83	253
BLASE								
Chas	27	m	w	RUSS	San Francisco	8-Wd San Francisco	82	375
H	47	m	w	ME	San Joaquin	Tulare Twp	86	263
BLASEDALE								
Lawrance	25	m	w	CANA	San Francisco	7-Wd San Francisco	81	156
William	21	m	w	OH	San Francisco	7-Wd San Francisco	81	158
BLASINGAME								
John	30	m	w	GA	Nevada	Bridgeport Twp	75	103
BLASKA								
Frank	55	m	w	PRUS	Calaveras	Copperopolis P O	70	262
Henry	34	m	w	RUSS	Calaveras	San Andreas P O	70	204
BLASKE								
Albert	43	m	w	PRUS	Siskiyou	Cottonwood Twp	89	592
BLASS								
Charles	31	m	w	VT	Siskiyou	Table Rock Twp	89	647
Frank	46	m	w	PRUS	Stanislaus	Washington Twp	92	84
Franklin	42	m	w	VA	Trinity	Trinity Center Pct	92	204
Gill	30	m	w	CA	Santa Clara	Gilroy Twp	88	93
John	26	m	w	HAMB	San Francisco	1-Wd San Francisco	79	124
Mason	50	m	w	PRUS	San Francisco	San Francisco P O	83	396
Tebo	40	m	w	AUST	Butte	Mountain Spring Tw	70	88
BLASSOM								
Thomas J	18	m	w	ME	Tuolumne	Sonora P O	93	330
BLASWICK								
Charles	44	m	w	PRUS	Colusa	Monroe Twp	71	321
BLATE								
John W	47	m	w	CT	Colusa	Butte Twp	71	271
BLATNER								
John	35	m	w	SWIT	San Diego	San Diego	78	501
BLATTER								
M	32	m	w	GERM	San Joaquin	2-Wd Stockton	86	213
BLATTNER								
John J	49	m	w	SWIT	San Francisco	San Francisco P O	83	105
BLAUN								
G	58	m	w	KY	Lake	Lower Lake	73	423
BLAVEL								
Thomas	37	m	w	ENGL	Marin	San Antonio Twp	74	62
BLAWELT								
Charles J	45	m	w	FRAN	Los Angeles	Wilmington Twp	73	639
BLAXLY								
Joseph	38	m	w	NY	Sutter	Yuba Twp	92	149
BLAY								
John	45	m	w	CANA	San Mateo	Belmont P O	87	373
S G	22	m	w	AR	Tuolumne	Big Oak Flat P O	93	396
Thomas	28	m	w	CANA	Colusa	Colusa Twp	71	283
BLAYLOCK								
David	59	m	w	AL	Calaveras	Copperopolis P O	70	262
BLAYNEY								
John M	38	m	w	PA	Klamath	Camp Gaston	73	372
BLAZE								
Chas	60	m	w	FRAN	Alameda	Oakland	68	154
John	34	m	w	NY	Nevada	Eureka Twp	75	139
BLAZEBACK								
Jno	28	m	w	PA	San Francisco	8-Wd San Francisco	82	376
BLAZENHOOK								
James W	60	m	w	IN	Yuba	North East Twp	93	644
BLAZER								
Catharine	26	f	w	HAMB	San Francisco	San Francisco P O	85	724
George W	21	m	w	MO	Tulare	Visalia	92	297
John	48	m	w	OH	Sonoma	Mendocino Twp	91	306
Margaret	72	f	w	MO	Sonoma	Mendocino Twp	91	306
BLAZKOWER								
P	45	m	w	PRUS	San Francisco	San Francisco P O	83	309
BLAZO								
Anthony	44	m	w	HUNG	San Francisco	8-Wd San Francisco	82	366
Joseph	40	m	w	PRUS	San Francisco	8-Wd San Francisco	82	358
BLAZZY								
Ernest	40	m	w	FRAN	San Francisco	San Francisco P O	80	348
BLEADENHUZEN								
Wm	56	m	w	MD	San Francisco	11-Wd San Francisc	84	611
BLEAKLEY								
R P	36	m	w	IREL	Solano	Vallejo	90	193
BLEAKO								
Sam	44	m	w	VA	San Joaquin	2-Wd Stockton	86	163
BLEAKS								
John	39	m	w	VA	Placer	Bath P O	76	438
BLEARWE								
William	41	m	w	ENGL	Los Angeles	Los Nietos Twp	73	573
BLEAUVELT								
W H	35	m	w	NJ	San Francisco	6-Wd San Francisco	81	117
BLECH								
Henry	36	m	w	HAMB	San Francisco	2-Wd San Francisco	79	150
BLECHER								
Christian	39	m	w	HDAR	San Francisco	San Francisco P O	80	423
BLECHSCHMIDT								
Leopold	41	m	w	BRUN	San Francisco	1-Wd San Francisco	79	64
BLEDSOE								
A	50	m	w	TN	Mendocino	Round Valley Twp	74	218
Antho C	57	m	w	TN	Sonoma	Mendocino Twp	91	303
Edward	30	m	w	MO	Los Angeles	San Jose Twp	73	623
Ella	14	f	w	TX	Santa Cruz	Soquel Twp	89	442
Henry	8	m	w	CA	Sonoma	Mendocino Twp	91	291
Howard	39	m	w	KY	San Bernardino	San Bernardino Twp	78	435
Isaac A	40	m	w	MO	Tulare	Farmersville Twp	92	242
John C	34	m	w	KY	Shasta	Millville P O	89	492
William	46	m	w	MO	Amador	Ione City P O	69	357
William	31	m	w	LA	Los Angeles	Los Nietos Twp	73	589
Wm H	40	m	w	MO	Amador	Volcano P O	69	388
BLEECHER								
Jacob	40	m	w	TN	Napa	Napa Twp	75	70
BLEN								
Lewis	27	m	w	ME	San Francisco	11-Wd San Francisc	84	609
Unice	82	f	w	MA	San Francisco	7-Wd San Francisco	81	233
BLENCHARD								
N V	38	m	w	ME	Placer	Dutch Flat P O	76	405
BLENCOE								
Lydia G	6	f	w	CA	Sonoma	Salt Point	91	390
BLENDON								
Jno	40	m	w	IL	Butte	Chico Twp	70	37
BLENG								
Ah	25	m	c	CHIN	Calaveras	Copperopolis P O	70	238
BLENHAUGHT								
Joseph	24	m	w	IREL	San Francisco	7-Wd San Francisco	81	184
BLERRING								
Louis	31	m	w	FRAN	Placer	Cisco P O	76	494
BLESCH								
Thomas	47	m	w	BELG	Calaveras	Copperopolis P O	70	226
BLESH								
Preston	9	m	w	CA	Alameda	Oakland	68	257
BLESLAN								
William	30	m	w	IREL	San Francisco	7-Wd San Francisco	81	210
BLESSE								
Ernest	43	m	w	PRUS	San Francisco	2-Wd San Francisco	79	184
BLESSEN								
Louis	25	m	w	PRUS	Yolo	Washington Twp	93	538
BLESSING								
E J	40	m	w	KY	Sacramento	4-Wd Sacramento	77	372
Fred	30	m	w	NY	San Francisco	8-Wd San Francisco	82	360
Jake	39	m	w	PRUS	San Joaquin	2-Wd Stockton	86	190
James A	41	m	w	VA	Placer	Alta P O	76	412
BLESSINGTON								
Andre	36	m	w	ENGL	San Francisco	3-Wd San Francisco	79	325
BLESSNER								
Jo	22	m	w	PRUS	San Francisco	5-Wd San Francisco	81	9
BLESY								
Caspar	27	m	w	HDAR	San Francisco	11-Wd San Francisc	84	677
BLETCHER								
George	34	m	w	BAVA	San Francisco	San Francisco P O	85	756
Moses	39	m	w	ENGL	Tuolumne	Chinese Camp P O	93	368
BLETHEN								
Andrew W	31	m	w	ME	Nevada	Nevada Twp	75	318
Clement	38	m	w	ME	San Francisco	San Francisco P O	80	355
James	42	m	w	ME	Alameda	Brooklyn Twp	68	55
James H	50	m	w	ME	San Francisco	8-Wd San Francisco	82	466
Robert	30	m	w	IREL	San Francisco	3-Wd San Francisco	79	311
BLETIER								
Peter	24	m	w	CANA	San Francisco	8-Wd San Francisco	82	312
BLEVENS								
Alexander	70	m	w	KY	Santa Barbara	San Buenaventura P	87	438
BLEVIN								
David	22	m	w	TN	Fresno	Millerton P O	72	185
James J	36	m	w	CT	San Francisco	San Francisco P O	83	410
W I	46	m	w	VA	Sutter	Butte Twp	92	101

© 2001 by Heritage Quest. All rights reserved.

Name	Age	S	R	B-PL	County	Locale	Roll	Pg
						Series M593		
BLEVINS								
Alex	61	m	w	KY	Santa Barbara	San Buenaventura P	87	434
Francis M	38	m	w	IN	Siskiyou	Callahan P O	89	629
BLEW								
Thaddeus	50	m	w	ME	Santa Clara	Fremont Twp	88	43
BLEWBAUGH								
David	45	m	w	OH	Sacramento	Brighton Twp	77	74
BLEY								
Abraham	34	m	w	PRUS	San Francisco	San Francisco P O	83	277
BLGUHL								
Adolph	40	m	w	MECK	San Francisco	11-Wd San Francisc	84	654
BLICHER								
Cony G	27	f	w	BAVA	San Francisco	San Francisco P O	85	756
BLICK								
Peter	43	m	w	FRAN	San Francisco	11-Wd San Francisc	84	669
BLIDON								
Thomas	28	m	w	MO	Mendocino	Albion & Big Rvr T	74	167
BLIDSALKER								
Ulrich	28	m	w	SWIT	San Francisco	11-Wd San Francisc	84	647
BLIGE								
John J	45	m	w	NY	San Francisco	5-Wd San Francisco	81	1
BLIGH								
Anna	29	f	w	IREL	San Francisco	San Francisco P O	83	64
BLIGHT								
Andrew	28	m	w	ENGL	Nevada	Grass Valley Twp	75	186
James	25	m	w	NY	Nevada	Nevada Twp	75	309
William	30	m	w	ENGL	Nevada	Rough & Ready Twp	75	327
BLIGON								
Pietro	29	m	w	FRAN	San Francisco	1-Wd San Francisco	79	50
BLINCOE								
Thomas	36	m	w	KY	Sonoma	Salt Point	91	384
BLINE								
R T	23	m	w	VA	San Joaquin	Tulare Twp	86	252
BLING								
H R	25	m	w	VA	Sutter	Butte Twp	92	94
Ti He	22	f	c	CHIN	Nevada	Meadow Lake Twp	75	255
BLINN								
Charles H	23	m	w	VT	San Francisco	6-Wd San Francisco	81	104
Geo W	28	m	w	NY	Sonoma	Bodega Twp	91	263
H	54	m	w	NY	Sacramento	Natomas Twp	77	171
Jacob	44	m	w	BAVA	Shasta	Shasta P O	89	452
M	58	m	w	NY	Sonoma	Bodega Twp	91	250
Morris	36	m	w	RUSS	Sonoma	Santa Rosa	91	420
Samuel	46	m	w	ME	San Francisco	San Francisco P O	83	94
BLINNMAN								
John	51	m	w	ENGL	Sierra	Sears Twp	89	555
BLISS								
Albert	50	m	w	FRAN	Calaveras	San Andreas P O	70	210
Benjamin	31	m	w	MA	San Francisco	8-Wd San Francisco	82	488
C W	48	m	w	NY	Sierra	Lincoln Twp	89	549
Chester A	36	m	w	NY	Yuba	Slate Range Bar Tw	93	676
Daniel M	60	m	w	NY	Nevada	Rough & Ready Twp	75	324
Edgar	39	m	w	NY	Yuba	Marysville Twp	93	570
F	42	m	w	MA	Sierra	Downieville Twp	89	516
George	33	m	w	WI	San Francisco	8-Wd San Francisco	82	369
George G	43	m	w	NY	San Francisco	San Francisco P O	85	716
George H	50	m	w	MA	San Francisco	San Francisco P O	83	169
Gott	36	m	w	CT	San Joaquin	2-Wd Stockton	86	202
H H	43	m	w	NY	Sierra	Lincoln Twp	89	549
Henry	37	m	w	SAXO	San Francisco	San Francisco P O	83	26
J	34	m	w	PA	Amador	Drytown P O	69	421
Jas W	37	m	w	MA	San Francisco	5-Wd San Francisco	81	23
John	35	m	w	NY	San Francisco	1-Wd San Francisco	79	5
John S	35	m	w	PA	San Francisco	1-Wd San Francisco	79	61
Louis C	50	m	w	NH	San Francisco	5-Wd San Francisco	81	12
Mathew	36	m	w	ENGL	Mariposa	Mariposa P O	74	98
Oliver H	49	m	w	KY	Fresno	Kingston P O	72	217
Peter	47	m	w	FRAN	Calaveras	San Andreas P O	70	210
S M	46	m	w	MA	Yuba	Marysville	93	591
Sadie S	17	f	w	NV	San Francisco	San Francisco P O	83	175
Theodore	35	m	w	RI	San Francisco	1-Wd San Francisco	79	10
William D	43	m	w	MA	Sonoma	Petaluma Twp	91	362
Wm Y	50	m	w	NY	Butte	Ophir Twp	70	108
BLISSEY								
S	40	m	w	SWIT	San Francisco	San Francisco P O	85	812
BLITS								
Olvius	40	m	w	BADE	San Joaquin	Douglas Twp	86	39
BLITZ								
Carrie	36	f	w	PA	San Francisco	San Francisco P O	80	418
BLIVEN								
Minnie	11	f	w	CA	Butte	Chico Twp	70	14
S M	36	m	w	OH	Nevada	Nevada Twp	75	280
BLIVENS								
H	50	m	w	RI	Solano	Vallejo	90	161
BLIZE								
Jonathan	39	m	w	MO	Calaveras	San Andreas P O	70	194
BLIZZARD								
Benm A	40	m	w	OH	Santa Cruz	Pajaro Twp	89	356
BLOCH								
Abraham	52	m	w	FRAN	San Francisco	San Francisco P O	80	460
Abraham	35	m	w	MO	San Francisco	8-Wd San Francisco	82	484
Charles	40	m	w	FRAN	San Francisco	San Francisco P O	80	485
J F	40	m	w	FRAN	San Francisco	San Francisco P O	85	788
John	45	m	w	FRAN	San Francisco	2-Wd San Francisco	79	141
John	40	m	w	PRUS	San Francisco	8-Wd San Francisco	82	426
BLOCHMAN								
A	35	m	w	FRAN	San Francisco	San Francisco P O	85	788
Emanul	43	m	w	FRAN	San Francisco	8-Wd San Francisco	82	417
Emanul	43	m	w	FRAN	San Francisco	8-Wd San Francisco	82	481
BLOCK								
A	30	m	w	FRAN	San Joaquin	Tulare Twp	86	251
Alfred	38	m	w	SWED	San Mateo	Half Moon Bay P O	87	407
Antone	26	m	w	SHOL	Alameda	Eden Twp	68	65
E D	35	m	w	BAVA	Alameda	Oakland	68	191
Eben D	30	m	w	BAVA	San Francisco	8-Wd San Francisco	82	324
Em	37	m	w	GERM	San Joaquin	3-Wd Stockton	86	232
J	40	m	w	IREL	Sierra	Lincoln Twp	89	550
John	40	m	w	BREM	San Francisco	1-Wd San Francisco	79	15
Manuel	21	m	w	AUST	San Francisco	8-Wd San Francisco	82	321
Nathan	45	m	w	FRAN	San Francisco	San Francisco P O	80	534
Robert M	46	m	w	BREM	San Francisco	6-Wd San Francisco	81	129
Sarah	67	f	w	VT	San Joaquin	2-Wd Stockton	86	186
William	36	m	w	FRAN	San Francisco	San Francisco P O	80	475
Y	36	m	w	IREL	Sierra	Lincoln Twp	89	550
BLOCKAR								
Thomas	7	m	w	WURT	Santa Cruz	Pajaro Twp	89	342
BLOCKBERGER								
Henry	39	m	w	BAVA	Sierra	Gibson Twp	89	541
BLOCKHEY								
J F	33	m	w	PRUS	Alameda	Oakland	68	180
BLOCKLINGER								
G	22	m	w	IA	Solano	Vallejo	90	200
BLOCKWAY								
William	28	m	w	MO	Colusa	Monroe Twp	71	312
BLODGET								
Asma	54	f	w	NY	Stanislaus	Empire Twp	92	33
Charles	17	m	w	OH	Stanislaus	Empire Twp	92	44
Hiram D	43	m	w	NH	Sacramento	Brighton Twp	77	71
James	39	m	w	OH	Stanislaus	Empire Twp	92	41
Jas	20	m	w	MO	Butte	Ophir Twp	70	100
John	45	m	w	CT	Sacramento	Natomas Twp	77	166
S H	40	m	w	VT	Sutter	Yuba Twp	92	143
Wm	37	m	w	IREL	Butte	Ophir Twp	70	118
BLODGETT								
Charles	42	m	w	NY	San Francisco	11-Wd San Francisc	84	524
Charles	39	m	w	MA	Sacramento	2-Wd Sacramento	77	223
Edwin	21	m	w	OH	Yolo	Grafton Twp	93	498
Eli	27	m	w	OH	Plumas	Seneca Twp	77	47
Fred K	42	m	w	NH	Marin	San Rafael Twp	74	41
G C	22	m	w	NH	Alameda	Oakland	68	182
Geo	23	m	w	NH	San Francisco	San Francisco P O	83	48
George	25	m	w	IREL	Marin	Point Reyes Twp	74	22
George	25	m	w	MA	Marin	San Rafael	74	58
Jos H	31	m	w	IN	Shasta	Millville P O	89	484
Lutheria	77	f	w	VT	Santa Clara	1-Wd San Jose	88	250
Oscar	43	m	w	CANA	Yolo	Grafton Twp	93	493
Oscar J	40	m	w	OH	Stanislaus	Washington Twp	92	85
Philip	41	m	w	IL	Shasta	Dog Crk P O	89	471
Silas	42	m	w	NH	Nevada	Grass Valley Twp	75	226
Soloman	45	m	w	CANA	Yolo	Grafton Twp	93	498
William	28	m	w	NY	Marin	Bolinas Twp	74	6
BLOED								
Charles	44	m	w	BADE	Mariposa	Mariposa P O	74	133
BLOGG								
Harry	24	m	w	CANA	Solano	Vallejo	90	149
BLOHM								
Annie	23	f	w	HANO	San Francisco	San Francisco P O	85	779
Henry	37	m	w	PRUS	San Francisco	San Francisco P O	83	386
J A	34	m	w	PRUS	Sierra	Downieville Twp	89	518
Peter	47	m	w	HANO	San Francisco	7-Wd San Francisco	81	211
BLOHME								
John	24	m	w	PRUS	San Francisco	San Francisco P O	83	191
BLOHN								
C C	41	m	w	SHOL	Sacramento	4-Wd Sacramento	77	344
J F	54	m	w	OLDE	Monterey	Castroville Twp	74	338
BLOIR								
J	30	m	w	TX	Sierra	Sierra Twp	89	565
BLOIS								
James	22	m	w	CANA	San Joaquin	Oneal Twp	86	114
BLOMM								
Andy	37	m	w	NY	San Joaquin	2-Wd Stockton	86	194
BLONDA								
John	52	m	w	FRAN	Stanislaus	Empire Twp	92	52
BLONDE								
Joe	35	m	w	FRAN	Alameda	Murray Twp	68	123
BLONDEL								
Agnes	12	f	w	CANA	San Francisco	2-Wd San Francisco	79	251
BLONDELF								
J R	23	m	w	ENGL	Alameda	Murray Twp	68	100
BLONDELL								
Edwin	21	m	w	PA	San Bernardino	San Bernardino Twp	78	449
BLONDIN								
Lamie	36	m	w	FRAN	Marin	Sausalito Twp	74	67
Louisa	22	f	w	FRAN	San Francisco	6-Wd San Francisco	81	71
BLONDINETTE								
Christin	25	f	w	PRUS	San Francisco	8-Wd San Francisco	82	350
BLONDQUIST								
Oliver	30	m	w	SWED	San Francisco	6-Wd San Francisco	81	96
BLONIGAN								
Joseph	30	m	w	PRUS	San Francisco	San Francisco P O	80	460
BLONK								
John	50	m	w	PRUS	Calaveras	Copperopolis P O	70	247
BLONNER								
John	32	m	w	GERM	San Joaquin	2-Wd Stockton	86	213

© 2001 by Heritage Quest. All rights reserved.

Name	Age	S	R	B-PL	County	Locale	Series M593 Roll	Pg
BLONONDEN								
Francis	35	m	w	FRAN	San Francisco	San Francisco P O	83	241
BLONQUIST								
Ada	23	f	w	SWED	San Mateo	Pescadero P O	87	410
Chas	35	m	w	FINL	San Francisco	3-Wd San Francisco	79	291
BLONTISM								
---	25	m	w	CANA	Alameda	Oakland	68	248
BLOOD								
Amos	37	m	w	NY	Butte	Chico Twp	70	23
August	27	m	w	PRUS	San Francisco	11-Wd San Francisc	84	683
Ethalinda H	43	f	w	PA	San Francisco	San Francisco P O	85	725
Frank J	19	m	w	NH	Alpine	Silver Mtn P O	69	306
Harvey S	30	m	w	NH	Alpine	Silver Mtn P O	69	306
Jacob	60	m	w	NY	San Francisco	8-Wd San Francisco	82	338
James	35	m	w	IREL	San Francisco	2-Wd San Francisco	79	206
Jas A	52	m	w	MA	Santa Barbara	Santa Barbara P O	87	486
John	53	m	w	ITAL	Butte	Wyandotte Twp	70	143
John	20	m	w	IREL	Marin	Point Reyes Twp	74	22
John Nelson	40	m	w	NY	Plumas	Indian Twp	77	19
Laura	17	f	w	NY	Alameda	Oakland	68	259
Mary	32	f	w	FRAN	San Francisco	8-Wd San Francisco	82	370
Mary	19	f	w	IREL	Alameda	Oakland	68	213
Noah	37	m	w	RUSS	El Dorado	Lake Valley Twp	72	64
Stillman	36	m	w	MA	Contra Costa	Martinez P O	71	376
Susan E	36	f	w	ME	Santa Clara	Fremont Twp	88	49
Wm	30	m	w	NY	Plumas	Indian Twp	77	14
BLOODGOOD								
Emery	35	m	w	NY	Santa Clara	San Jose Twp	88	194
BLOODSANE								
Willis	28	m	w	TN	Stanislaus	Branch Twp	92	5
BLOODSHAW								
W	33	m	w	KY	Amador	Ione City P O	69	355
BLOODSTONE								
G	40	m	w	AUST	Amador	Jackson P O	69	329
BLOODWORTH								
Georgia	12	f	w	CA	Santa Clara	2-Wd San Jose	88	338
BLOOK								
John	22	m	w	MO	Sonoma	Petaluma Twp	91	365
BLOOM								
Aaron	26	m	w	NH	Sonoma	Salt Point	91	393
Chs	40	m	w	SWED	San Francisco	8-Wd San Francisco	82	306
Dora	24	f	w	HANO	San Francisco	San Francisco P O	83	176
Emily	17	f	w	AUST	San Francisco	San Francisco P O	85	877
George	41	m	w	HANO	San Francisco	San Francisco P O	83	78
Henry	47	m	w	PRUS	San Francisco	San Francisco P O	83	205
Henry	33	m	w	PRUS	Contra Costa	San Pablo Twp	71	361
Henry	22	m	w	HANO	San Francisco	7-Wd San Francisco	81	223
Henry	22	m	w	PRUS	San Luis Obispo	Salinas Twp	87	293
Jacob	46	m	w	PRUS	San Francisco	San Francisco P O	80	379
James	52	m	w	NY	San Francisco	5-Wd San Francisco	81	12
James	28	m	w	SWIT	Marin	San Antonio Twp	74	63
John	31	m	w	GERM	Solano	Benicia	90	13
John	22	m	w	PA	Colusa	Spring Valley Twp	71	335
John B	38	m	w	PA	Solano	Silveyville Twp	90	73
Joseph	32	m	w	PRUS	Sonoma	Healdsburg & Mendo	91	278
Joseph	21	m	w	SWIT	Marin	Bolinas Twp	74	2
Josephine	14	f	w	AUST	San Francisco	8-Wd San Francisco	82	332
Meyer	25	m	w	POLA	Santa Clara	2-Wd San Jose	88	314
Samuel	33	m	w	POLA	San Francisco	11-Wd San Francisc	84	511
William	43	m	w	HESS	Colusa	Spring Valley Twp	71	335
William	30	m	w	PRUS	San Francisco	1-Wd San Francisco	79	29
Wm H	52	m	w	OH	Sacramento	Franklin Twp	77	113
BLOOMENTHAL								
Julius	24	m	w	PRUS	Alameda	Brooklyn Twp	68	43
BLOOMENTHALL								
Abe	23	m	w	NJ	San Joaquin	1-Wd Stockton	86	135
BLOOMER								
H R	23	m	w	NY	San Francisco	5-Wd San Francisco	81	36
Hiram J	50	m	w	NY	San Francisco	6-Wd San Francisco	81	121
BLOOMFIELD								
Arthur	28	m	w	NJ	Santa Clara	Alviso Twp	88	26
D	18	m	w	CA	Alameda	Oakland	68	159
Hamer	28	m	w	NJ	San Francisco	5-Wd San Francisco	81	31
Isaac	28	m	w	VT	Butte	Chico Twp	70	46
James	19	m	w	ASEA	San Francisco	San Francisco P O	80	538
Stephen	57	m	w	NJ	Santa Clara	Alviso Twp	88	22
Thos	47	m	w	AUSL	San Francisco	1-Wd San Francisco	79	25
William	41	m	w	KY	Yolo	Grafton Twp	93	482
BLOOMINGCAMP								
John F	36	m	w	PRUS	Siskiyou	Yreka	89	651
BLOOMINGDALE								
Emanuel	45	m	w	PRUS	San Francisco	2-Wd San Francisco	79	170
BLOOMINGTON								
Adolphus	18	m	w	CA	San Francisco	11-Wd San Francisc	84	615
BLOS								
Joseph	37	m	w	BADE	San Francisco	San Francisco P O	83	318
BLOSEDALE								
J H	42	m	w	VT	Sacramento	Brighton Twp	77	76
BLOSS								
Alsy A	41	m	w	PA	Nevada	Bridgeport Twp	75	100
Antonio	28	m	w	AUST	Calaveras	San Andreas P O	70	203
David	32	m	w	MO	Nevada	Grass Valley Twp	75	219
David W	37	m	w	MO	Nevada	Rough & Ready Twp	75	336
Henry	48	m	w	IL	San Francisco	11-Wd San Francisc	84	609
BLOSSER								
Jacob	60	m	w	PA	Mendocino	Little Lake Twp	74	199
Lorenzo W	26	m	w	VA	Santa Barbara	Arroyo Grande P O	87	508
N J	36	m	w	PA	Mendocino	Little Lake Twp	74	199
S M	31	m	w	VA	Mendocino	Little Lake Twp	74	203
William	42	m	w	NY	Monterey	San Benito Twp	74	379
BLOSSOM								
Charles	46	m	w	OH	Stanislaus	San Joaquin Twp	92	71
Susan	50	f	w	NY	San Francisco	San Francisco P O	83	202
Wm H	54	m	w	NY	San Francisco	San Francisco P O	83	201
BLOSSON								
Ira	37	m	w	NY	Tulare	Farmersville Twp	92	248
Robt H	41	m	w	OH	Tehama	Red Bluff	92	180
BLOTE								
J H	47	m	w	HANO	Alameda	Oakland	68	162
BLOUGH								
William	45	m	w	PA	Plumas	Indian Twp	77	10
BLOUNDELL								
Thos	45	m	w	FRAN	San Francisco	San Francisco P O	85	836
BLOUNT								
David T	33	m	w	NY	San Francisco	8-Wd San Francisco	82	465
BLOUS								
William	32	m	w	PRUS	Sonoma	Mendocino Twp	91	302
BLOW								
J	50	m	w	ENGL	Alameda	Oakland	68	164
Mary A	27	f	w	MS	Alameda	Oakland	68	139
BLOWER								
George W	42	m	w	OH	San Francisco	6-Wd San Francisco	81	107
John	32	m	w	ENGL	Amador	Fiddletown P O	69	431
Richard	20	m	w	WALE	Contra Costa	Martinez P O	71	430
BLOWERS								
Cassius M	25	m	w	IN	Yolo	Cache Crk Twp	93	421
Elijah	45	m	w	NY	Marin	San Rafael	74	49
Russell B	40	m	w	OH	Yolo	Cache Crk Twp	93	421
BLOXHAM								
Thomas	31	m	w	ENGL	Yolo	Cottonwood Twp	93	467
BLOY								
Ah	19	m	c	CHIN	San Francisco	1-Wd San Francisco	79	101
BLOYD								
Emberson	51	m	w	IN	Sutter	Butte Twp	92	104
Frank	25	m	w	IL	Sutter	Butte Twp	92	104
L J	25	m	w	IL	Sutter	Butte Twp	92	104
Wm	59	m	w	KY	Merced	Snelling P O	74	275
Wm W	35	m	w	IL	Merced	Snelling P O	74	275
BLUANDES								
Freeman	19	m	w	CA	San Diego	Temecula Dist	78	526
BLUBAW								
David	47	m	w	CHIN	Sacramento	Granite Twp	77	137
BLUCHER								
Matilda	24	f	w	PRUS	San Francisco	San Francisco P O	85	734
BLUCK								
Samuel T	25	m	w	ENGL	Yuba	Slate Range Bar Tw	93	676
BLUCKHORN								
Fielding	60	m	b	KY	Yuba	Long Bar Twp	93	560
BLUDWORTH								
Fannie	27	f	w	MO	Merced	Snelling P O	74	247
BLUE								
Cupid	65	m	b	VA	Yuba	Marysville	93	600
Daniel	73	m	b	KY	Sacramento	4-Wd Sacramento	77	361
Frank	43	m	w	FRAN	Yuba	Marysville	93	608
Frank	22	m	w	US	Yuba	Marysville	93	576
George	33	m	w	NY	Sacramento	4-Wd Sacramento	77	337
J A	32	m	w	KY	Sutter	Nicolaus Twp	92	107
J F	20	m	w	KY	Yuba	Marysville Twp	93	569
Louis	45	m	w	FRAN	Mariposa	Mariposa P O	74	101
Robert	32	m	w	SCOT	San Francisco	San Francisco P O	80	364
S S	40	m	w	NY	El Dorado	Greenwood Twp	72	50
Thomas P	38	m	w	TN	Nevada	Little York Twp	75	237
BLUEGAITS								
Andrew	24	m	w	SWED	Monterey	Alisal Twp	74	303
BLUETOE								
Godfrey	58	m	w	CANA	Yuba	Rose Bar Twp	93	657
BLUETT								
Ed	27	m	w	ENGL	Fresno	Millerton P O	72	159
Henry	25	m	w	ENGL	Nevada	Grass Valley Twp	75	144
Isaac	40	m	w	CANA	Solano	Vallejo	90	154
John	43	m	w	ENGL	Nevada	Nevada Twp	75	295
Saml	30	m	w	ENGL	Santa Clara	Almaden Twp	88	9
BLUFORD								
Dan	25	m	w	AL	San Joaquin	Castoria Twp	86	8
BLUGRARE								
B	32	m	w	WI	Trinity	Lewiston Pct	92	211
William	38	m	w	MO	Trinity	Lewiston Pct	92	211
BLUIT								
Gabriel	33	m	w	ENGL	Tuolumne	Sonora P O	93	326
Jeremiah	44	m	m	KY	Sacramento	2-Wd Sacramento	77	207
John F	29	m	w	ENGL	Tuolumne	Sonora P O	93	320
BLUITT								
Edward	28	m	w	IREL	Mendocino	Point Arena Twp	74	214
BLUM								
Charles	40	m	w	PRUS	Siskiyou	Scott Valley Twp	89	611
Chas	34	m	w	FINL	San Francisco	1-Wd San Francisco	79	128
Christopher	50	m	w	PRUS	Calaveras	Copperopolis P O	70	259
Ed	36	m	w	ENGL	Alameda	Alameda	68	18
Emily	21	f	w	HDAR	San Francisco	San Francisco P O	83	109
Ernest	30	m	w	PRUS	San Francisco	San Francisco P O	80	336
Eugene	40	m	w	FRAN	Sacramento	4-Wd Sacramento	77	324
George	14	m	w	HANO	Nevada	Meadow Lake Twp	75	252
Henry	38	m	w	BAVA	San Francisco	San Francisco P O	83	352
Henry	38	m	w	PRUS	San Joaquin	Douglas Twp	86	42

© 2001 by Heritage Quest. All rights reserved.

California 1870 Census

Name	Age	S	R	B-PL	County	Locale	Series M593 Roll	Pg
Henry	37	m	w	HCAS	San Francisco	2-Wd San Francisco	79	233
Herman	45	m	w	PRUS	San Francisco	6-Wd San Francisco	81	87
Hortense	18	f	w	FRAN	San Francisco	San Francisco P O	83	418
Isaac	37	m	w	FRAN	Santa Cruz	Santa Cruz	89	408
Isaac	24	m	w	PRUS	Contra Costa	Martinez Twp	71	347
Isidor	38	m	w	PRUS	San Francisco	3-Wd San Francisco	79	327
Jacob	55	m	w	POLA	San Francisco	8-Wd San Francisco	82	422
Jacob	47	m	w	FRAN	Solano	Silveyville Twp	90	90
Jacob	45	m	w	FRAN	San Francisco	8-Wd San Francisco	82	453
Jacob	41	m	w	FRAN	San Francisco	8-Wd San Francisco	82	470
James	19	m	w	FRAN	San Francisco	8-Wd San Francisco	82	352
John	45	m	w	HANO	Calaveras	Copperopolis P O	70	229
Joseph	18	m	w	MS	Nevada	Nevada Twp	75	276
L R	45	m	w	PRUS	San Francisco	San Francisco P O	83	135
Louis	37	m	w	PRUS	San Francisco	8-Wd San Francisco	82	416
Louis	35	m	w	PRUS	San Francisco	1-Wd San Francisco	79	86
Marietta	52	f	w	GERM	Nevada	Nevada Twp	75	284
Moses	42	m	w	FRAN	Solano	Vacaville Twp	90	120
Peter	35	m	w	CANA	Colusa	Colusa	71	298
Robert	13	m	w	CA	Humboldt	Pacific Twp	72	298
Simon	36	m	w	FRAN	Contra Costa	Martinez Twp	71	349
Simon	35	m	w	SAXO	San Francisco	7-Wd San Francisco	81	274
BLUMA								
W	18	m	w	IL	Sierra	Sierra Twp	89	569
BLUMAN								
Frederick L	35	m	w	DENM	Alpine	Monitor P O	69	313
BLUMAR								
Carl	26	m	w	ROMA	San Francisco	11-Wd San Francisc	84	644
BLUMAT								
Julius	50	m	w	PRUS	San Francisco	11-Wd San Francisc	84	672
Laborechs	55	m	w	PRUS	San Francisco	11-Wd San Francisc	84	672
BLUMB								
Henry	35	m	w	HDAR	Shasta	Shasta P O	89	461
BLUMBERG								
John	33	m	w	SWED	Siskiyou	Callahan P O	89	624
Peter	35	m	w	SWED	Mendocino	Point Arena Twp	74	208
BLUME								
Conrad	34	m	w	PRUS	San Francisco	1-Wd San Francisco	79	63
F G	54	m	w	PRUS	Sonoma	Bodega Twp	91	252
George	40	m	w	TX	Kern	Tehachapi P O	73	355
Henry	55	m	w	GERM	Yolo	Cache Crk Twp	93	457
Julius	26	m	w	PRUS	Sonoma	Petaluma Twp	91	320
BLUMENBERG								
Julius	47	m	w	PRUS	San Francisco	11-Wd San Francisc	84	541
BLUMENDALE								
Henry	25	m	w	HANO	San Francisco	11-Wd San Francisc	84	459
BLUMENSCHEAR								
Philip	45	m	w	HDAR	San Francisco	11-Wd San Francisc	84	569
BLUMENTHAL								
A	24	m	w	PRUS	Nevada	Nevada Twp	75	274
Harry	43	m	w	RUSS	San Francisco	San Francisco P O	83	418
Isaac	45	m	w	POLA	San Francisco	San Francisco P O	83	367
Mark	34	m	w	PRUS	Santa Clara	1-Wd San Jose	88	245
BLUMER								
Charles	21	m	w	PRUS	San Francisco	11-Wd San Francisc	84	533
Hiram B	21	m	w	NY	Siskiyou	Yreka	89	656
Jacob	41	m	w	SWIT	Solano	Vallejo	90	167
R	38	m	w	NY	Alameda	Murray Twp	68	127
BLUN								
Marcus	22	m	w	GERM	Nevada	Nevada Twp	75	279
BLUNBERG								
Peter	38	m	w	SWED	San Francisco	1-Wd San Francisco	79	126
BLUNDELL								
Elizabeth	58	f	w	IL	Sonoma	Healdsburg & Mendo	91	281
James	35	m	w	ENGL	San Francisco	San Francisco P O	80	425
John	37	m	w	NJ	Mariposa	Maxwell Crk P O	74	145
Levi I	40	m	w	IL	Nevada	Grass Valley Twp	75	192
BLUNETT								
Phil	40	m	w	ENGL	Santa Clara	Almaden Twp	88	5
BLUNIER								
John	30	m	w	WURT	San Francisco	San Francisco P O	83	236
BLUNK								
Henry	19	m	w	SHOL	Colusa	Spring Valley Twp	71	344
BLUNKALL								
Robt H	32	m	w	MO	Colusa	Monroe Twp	71	319
BLUNT								
David	53	m	w	ME	Plumas	Seneca Twp	77	51
J T	23	m	w	IN	Merced	Snelling P O	74	260
Joseph	68	m	w	PA	Merced	Snelling P O	74	248
Levi	47	m	w	KY	San Luis Obispo	Santa Rosa Twp	87	319
Margretha	30	f	w	MEXI	San Francisco	6-Wd San Francisco	81	98
Phineas A	60	m	w	MA	San Francisco	8-Wd San Francisco	82	338
Thos	38	m	w	IN	Merced	Snelling P O	74	248
BLUR								
Saml	40	m	w	OH	Sacramento	4-Wd Sacramento	77	322
BLUSARCHE								
Lena	19	f	w	FRAN	San Francisco	6-Wd San Francisco	81	87
BLUTE								
Mike	28	m	w	IREL	San Francisco	11-Wd San Francisc	84	694
BLUXOM								
Gertrude	28	f	w	MO	Sonoma	Cloverdale Twp	91	267
BLUXOME								
Isaac	43	m	w	NY	San Francisco	San Francisco P O	83	337
Joseph	39	m	w	NY	San Francisco	San Francisco P O	83	341
BLY								
Andrew	40	m	w	IREL	Butte	Oregon Twp	70	126
Andrew	31	m	w	IREL	Butte	Oregon Twp	70	124
James	50	m	w	IREL	Butte	Ophir Twp	70	114
John	45	m	w	IREL	Butte	Oregon Twp	70	127
Leander	32	m	w	MA	San Francisco	6-Wd San Francisco	81	116
Mary	45	f	w	MO	Butte	Ophir Twp	70	105
BLYDEE								
John	41	m	w	WURT	Fresno	Millerton P O	72	152
BLYE								
George	35	m	w	NY	Santa Barbara	Santa Barbara P O	87	503
Joseph	50	m	w	SCOT	Solano	Denverton Twp	90	24
William	42	m	w	OH	Solano	Denverton Twp	90	25
BLYMAN								
Edward	50	m	w	HDAR	San Francisco	San Francisco P O	80	346
BLYN								
H	24	m	w	FRAN	Alameda	Oakland	68	129
BLYTHE								
Frank S	28	m	w	MA	San Francisco	3-Wd San Francisco	79	312
Haynes	43	m	w	ME	Stanislaus	Branch Twp	92	2
Henry	47	m	w	ENGL	San Francisco	7-Wd San Francisco	81	278
James	45	m	w	RI	Solano	Montezuma Twp	90	65
Relief	54	f	w	MO	Santa Clara	San Jose Twp	88	189
Saml	40	m	w	ME	Solano	Benicia	90	3
Samuel	26	m	w	OH	San Francisco	San Francisco P O	83	276
Samuel A	44	m	w	TN	Santa Clara	Redwood Twp	88	127
BLYTHER								
John	43	m	w	ME	Amador	Lancha Plana P O	69	368
BO								
Ah	48	m	c	CHIN	El Dorado	Diamond Springs Tw	72	35
Ah	42	m	c	CHIN	Sierra	Downieville Twp	89	520
Ah	35	m	c	CHIN	Placer	Roseville P O	76	348
Ah	35	m	c	CHIN	Trinity	North Fork Twp	92	221
Ah	34	m	c	CHIN	El Dorado	Placerville	72	116
Ah	31	m	c	CHIN	El Dorado	Mountain Twp	72	70
Ah	30	f	c	CHIN	Nevada	Grass Valley Twp	75	205
Ah	26	m	c	CHIN	El Dorado	Placerville	72	114
Ah	26	m	c	CHIN	Nevada	Grass Valley Twp	75	202
Ah	25	m	c	CHIN	Sacramento	Georgianna Twp	77	124
Ah	24	m	c	CHIN	Nevada	Little York Twp	75	245
Ah	22	m	c	CHIN	Sacramento	1-Wd Sacramento	77	201
Ah	22	f	c	CHIN	El Dorado	Placerville	72	114
Ah	20	m	c	CHIN	Nevada	Grass Valley Twp	75	204
Ah	20	m	c	CHIN	Santa Clara	Fremont Twp	88	64
Dacy	30	m	c	CHIN	Trinity	Junction City Pct	92	206
I	29	m	c	CHIN	Yuba	Marysville	93	632
Koelo	24	m	c	CHIN	Sierra	Lincoln Twp	89	546
Lee	35	m	c	CHIN	Nevada	Nevada Twp	75	312
Ling	30	m	c	CHIN	Sierra	Forest Twp	89	528
See	17	m	c	CHIN	San Francisco	6-Wd San Francisco	81	69
Sung	54	m	c	CHIN	Nevada	Rough & Ready Twp	75	328
Wee Ah	20	m	c	CHIN	San Francisco	6-Wd San Francisco	81	57
BOADT								
George G	41	m	w	NY	San Diego	San Diego	78	491
BOAG								
Isaac	24	m	w	PRUS	Sacramento	2-Wd Sacramento	77	231
Thomas A	24	m	w	SCOT	Placer	Auburn P O	76	370
BOAGSDALE								
C A	2	f	w	CA	Sutter	Nicolaus Twp	92	115
BOAKE								
Ah	23	m	c	CHIN	Sierra	Sears Twp	89	561
BOALES								
Samuel	53	m	w	OH	Calaveras	San Andreas P O	70	203
BOALT								
C M	29	m	w	AR	San Joaquin	Elkhorn Twp	86	69
BOAN								
Wm	23	m	w	WI	Solano	Vallejo	90	182
BOANE								
Andrew	39	m	w	SPAI	El Dorado	Greenwood Twp	72	51
BOAQUET								
Fred	40	m	w	BAVA	Contra Costa	San Pablo Twp	71	355
BOARD								
David	51	m	w	MO	Stanislaus	North Twp	92	67
Phillip	27	m	w	MO	Stanislaus	North Twp	92	67
William	44	m	w	MO	Sonoma	Mendocino Twp	91	306
Wm	32	m	w	IREL	Marin	San Rafael Twp	74	30
BOARDMAN								
C F	25	m	w	CT	Nevada	Bridgeport Twp	75	114
Chas	40	m	w	NH	San Diego	San Diego	78	509
Frank	35	m	w	SWIT	Santa Barbara	San Buenaventura P	87	430
G T	24	m	w	ENGL	San Francisco	8-Wd San Francisco	82	365
George	49	m	w	ENGL	Santa Cruz	Santa Cruz Twp	89	379
Henry	35	m	w	VT	Colusa	Monroe Twp	71	315
J H	41	m	w	ENGL	Nevada	Nevada Twp	75	275
J M	35	m	w	IREL	Sacramento	3-Wd Sacramento	77	293
John	35	m	w	AUST	Amador	Jackson P O	69	329
John	26	m	w	IN	Calaveras	San Andreas P O	70	208
Joseph	36	m	w	NY	Santa Clara	San Jose Twp	88	222
Ozias S	32	m	w	NY	Alpine	Woodfords P O	69	310
S B	56	m	w	IN	Amador	Volcano P O	69	379
Samuel	35	m	w	OH	Sacramento	Alabama Twp	77	60
T H	38	m	w	CT	San Joaquin	Douglas Twp	86	40
W F	45	m	w	CT	Alameda	Oakland	68	163
William A	38	m	w	NY	Contra Costa	Martinez P O	71	373
Wm	42	m	w	NY	Mono	Bridgeport P O	74	286
BOARDWELL								
John R	34	m	w	NY	Yuba	Long Bar Twp	93	563
BOARMAN								
C H	39	m	w	VA	Amador	Jackson P O	69	325
Mary	45	f	w	IREL	Tehama	Red Bluff	92	180

© 2001 by Heritage Quest. All rights reserved.

Name	Age	S	R	B-PL	County	Locale	Series M593 Roll	Pg
BOAS								
Paula	18	f	w	PRUS	San Francisco	8-Wd San Francisco	82	439
BOASAL								
Auguste	32	m	w	PRUS	San Francisco	San Francisco P O	83	140
BOASE								
Wm H	34	m	w	ENGL	Napa	Napa	75	19
BOASUIT								
Alfonse	40	m	w	FRAN	San Francisco	8-Wd San Francisco	82	485
BOATCHLY								
W L	32	m	w	NY	Sierra	Sierra Twp	89	563
BOATHILLIER								
Alphonse	23	m	w	CANA	San Francisco	11-Wd San Francisc	84	570
BOATMAN								
Wm	46	m	w	OH	Tehama	Red Bluff	92	181
BOATWRIGHTS								
Wm	46	m	w	TN	Shasta	American Ranch P O	89	500
BOB								
Ah	33	m	c	CHIN	Nevada	Bridgeport Twp	75	110
Ah	33	m	c	CHIN	Stanislaus	Washington Twp	92	84
Ah	18	f	c	CHIN	San Francisco	San Francisco P O	80	523
BOBB								
Daniel	24	m	w	ME	Santa Clara	2-Wd San Jose	88	318
BOBBINS								
John	36	m	w	ITAL	Amador	Sutter Crk P O	69	403
BOBBY								
P	25	m	w	IREL	Alameda	Oakland	68	265
BOBENREITH								
John	37	m	w	FRAN	San Francisco	8-Wd San Francisco	82	416
BOBIER								
John	35	m	w	IREL	San Francisco	11-Wd San Francisc	84	552
BOBILLION								
Peter	41	m	w	FRAN	San Francisco	6-Wd San Francisco	81	89
BOBIO								
John	55	m	w	ITAL	Mariposa	Mariposa P O	74	129
Peter	36	m	w	ITAL	Mariposa	Maxwell Crk P O	74	138
BOBLES								
Abram	40	m	w	MO	Mendocino	Little Lake Twp	74	193
BOBO								
Benjamin F	40	m	w	VA	Plumas	Quartz Twp	77	40
C D	50	m	w	SC	Yuba	Marysville	93	590
BOBYER								
Wm L	43	m	w	CANA	San Francisco	8-Wd San Francisco	82	300
BOCALETTI								
Peter	32	m	w	ITAL	Amador	Sutter Crk P O	69	398
BOCARICH								
John	20	m	w	AUST	Solano	Vallejo	90	161
BOCART								
Chas	21	m	w	ME	Sacramento	3-Wd Sacramento	77	300
BOCARTE								
Joseph	31	m	w	ITAL	Santa Clara	San Jose Twp	88	203
BOCAST								
August	39	m	w	FRAN	Stanislaus	Branch Twp	92	8
BOCAURRET								
Peter	32	m	w	AUST	Santa Clara	Milpitas Twp	88	109
BOCHANT								
Louis	44	m	w	CANA	Sacramento	Alabama Twp	77	59
BOCHEM								
Charles	7	m	w	CA	San Francisco	San Francisco P O	83	68
BOCHENOOGEN								
Geo J	23	m	w	PA	Monterey	Alisal Twp	74	290
BOCHFELSKY								
Saml	23	f	w	PRUS	San Francisco	5-Wd San Francisco	81	15
BOCHINE								
Ferdinand	24	m	w	BREM	San Francisco	8-Wd San Francisco	82	380
BOCHMAN								
H	28	m	w	PRUS	Alameda	Murray Twp	68	100
W	25	m	w	HANO	Alameda	Murray Twp	68	100
BOCHOW								
Frank	26	m	w	PRUS	San Francisco	2-Wd San Francisco	79	261
BOCK								
Adolph	51	m	w	HAMB	Alameda	Alameda	68	14
Ah	40	m	c	CHIN	Sierra	Downieville Twp	89	521
Ah	30	m	c	CHIN	Sacramento	1-Wd Sacramento	77	201
Chou	31	m	c	CHIN	Yuba	Marysville	93	631
Coo	36	m	c	CHIN	Yuba	Marysville	93	629
David	48	m	w	PA	Sonoma	Petaluma Twp	91	360
Emma	6	f	w	CA	San Francisco	San Francisco P O	85	738
Eng	39	m	c	CHIN	Yuba	Marysville	93	629
Ferdinand	48	m	w	PRUS	Shasta	Shasta P O	89	458
Harman	35	m	w	PRUS	Placer	Dutch Flat P O	76	405
Henry	27	m	w	PRUS	San Francisco	6-Wd San Francisco	81	100
Hoan	19	m	c	CHIN	Klamath	Liberty Twp	73	375
Hong	25	m	c	CHIN	Klamath	Liberty Twp	73	375
Joseph	33	m	w	PRUS	San Francisco	San Francisco P O	85	803
M	43	m	w	WI	Yuba	Marysville Twp	93	569
One	42	m	c	CHIN	Yuba	Marysville	93	624
Set	30	m	c	CHIN	Yuba	Marysville	93	632
BOCKER								
A	42	m	w	HOLL	Sierra	Downieville Twp	89	514
BOCKINS								
C G	48	m	w	PA	Yuba	Marysville	93	599
Godfrey M	52	m	w	PA	Santa Cruz	Watsonville	89	376
BOCKMAN								
Henry	29	m	w	HANO	San Francisco	1-Wd San Francisco	79	77
John C	40	m	w	HANO	San Francisco	San Francisco P O	83	75
Stephen	42	m	w	PRUS	Sutter	Butte Twp	92	102
BOCKRATH								
Henry	37	m	w	MO	Sacramento	3-Wd Sacramento	77	299
BOCKSCH								
Charles	38	m	w	PRUS	Santa Clara	Redwood Twp	88	126
BOCKSTIN								
Anna	30	f	w	IREL	San Francisco	8-Wd San Francisco	82	316
BOCLE								
Louis	43	m	w	FRAN	El Dorado	White Oak Twp	72	143
BOCQUERO								
Andrew	44	m	w	ITAL	San Francisco	2-Wd San Francisco	79	232
BODA								
Edward	38	m	w	CANA	Placer	Auburn P O	76	381
William	28	m	w	HAMB	San Francisco	3-Wd San Francisco	79	297
BODAN								
Danl	34	m	w	ITAL	Santa Clara	Burnett Twp	88	33
BODATT								
Charles	45	m	w	FRAN	Butte	Bidwell Twp	70	4
BODDIN								
Joseph	35	m	w	IREL	San Francisco	San Francisco P O	83	238
BODDY								
James	48	m	w	IREL	Sacramento	Sutter Twp	77	393
Wm	12	m	w	CA	San Francisco	11-Wd San Francisc	84	592
BODE								
Carrod	24	m	w	GERM	San Joaquin	2-Wd Stockton	86	213
Dedrick	34	m	w	HANO	Alameda	Eden Twp	68	59
H W	27	m	w	HANO	San Francisco	San Francisco P O	83	84
BODECKER								
Charles	36	m	w	NORW	San Francisco	2-Wd San Francisco	79	155
BODEGA								
Calisto	60	m	w	MEXI	El Dorado	Mud Springs Twp	72	76
BODELL								
Saml	44	m	w	OH	Sacramento	1-Wd Sacramento	77	183
BODEMAN								
Gabriel	48	m	w	FRAN	San Francisco	San Francisco P O	80	348
Gabriel	48	m	w	FRAN	San Francisco	San Francisco P O	80	347
BODEN								
Penelope	60	f	w	ENGL	San Francisco	2-Wd San Francisco	79	243
William	66	m	w	IREL	San Francisco	2-Wd San Francisco	79	268
BODENSKIN								
---	52	m	w	PRUS	Santa Cruz	Soquel Twp	89	436
BODER								
Geo	45	m	w	PRUS	San Francisco	San Francisco P O	83	277
BODERHAMER								
Emily	38	f	w	MO	Placer	Auburn P O	76	377
BODESSON								
G	23	m	w	WURT	San Joaquin	Tulare Twp	86	264
BODEVITCH								
Antonio	28	m	w	AUST	Amador	Sutter Crk P O	69	406
BODFISH								
S A	47	f	w	LA	Santa Clara	Gilroy Twp	88	92
William	34	m	w	MA	San Francisco	San Francisco P O	83	346
BODGER								
E P	46	m	w	ENGL	Siskiyou	Surprise Valley Tw	89	636
Joseph	30	m	w	CANA	San Mateo	Woodside P O	87	386
Samuel	36	m	w	OH	El Dorado	Placerville Twp	72	97
BODI								
Joseph	40	m	w	SWIT	San Joaquin	Oneal Twp	86	110
BODIE								
Edmond	43	m	w	ENGL	Santa Barbara	Santa Barbara P O	87	472
Herman	44	m	w	PRUS	Calaveras	San Andreas P O	70	163
BODIER								
Frank	45	m	w	PRUS	Solano	Silveyville Twp	90	81
BODINE								
Charles	31	m	w	NY	Mariposa	Mariposa P O	74	135
BODKIN								
Sarah	32	f	w	IREL	San Francisco	8-Wd San Francisco	82	395
Thomas	34	m	w	IREL	San Francisco	San Francisco P O	83	402
BODKINS								
David H	36	m	w	VA	Yuba	Bullards Bar P O	93	548
BODLEHLER								
Fred	50	m	w	PRUS	Sonoma	Santa Rosa	91	407
BODLEY								
Joseph	24	m	w	OH	Alameda	Oakland	68	158
Thomas	49	m	w	KY	Santa Clara	1-Wd San Jose	88	233
BODO								
Mary	20	f	w	FRAN	Santa Cruz	Santa Cruz	89	409
BODON								
John F	36	m	w	HAMB	San Francisco	2-Wd San Francisco	79	233
BODONIA								
Virgilio	24	m	w	SWIT	San Francisco	San Francisco P O	83	257
BODOSSI								
Chs	32	m	w	SWIT	Monterey	Alisal Twp	74	292
BODRA								
Frank	25	m	w	FRAN	Alameda	San Leandro	68	96
BODRI								
Lumbee	35	m	w	FRAN	San Joaquin	2-Wd Stockton	86	167
BODSFORD								
Gibson	35	m	w	IN	San Bernardino	San Bernardino Twp	78	452
BODSNOST								
J F	30	m	w	VT	Sierra	Sierra Twp	89	569
BODWELL								
Chas A	47	m	w	CT	Sonoma	Vallejo Twp	91	453
Harry	41	m	w	NY	San Francisco	11-Wd San Francisc	84	631
Joseph	43	m	w	MA	San Francisco	2-Wd San Francisco	79	148
BODY								
Charles	60	m	w	FRAN	Marin	Novato Twp	74	9
Eliza	60	f	w	IREL	San Francisco	San Francisco P O	83	318

© 2001 by Heritage Quest. All rights reserved.

Name	Age	S	R	B-PL	County	Locale	Roll	Pg
						Series M593		
Mark	24	m	w	ENGL	Contra Costa	Martinez P O	71	430
William	28	m	w	ENGL	Kern	Havilah P O	73	350
BODYLY								
O E	30	m	w	CANA	Sierra	Forest Twp	89	530
BOE								
Ah	40	m	c	CHIN	Alameda	Oakland	68	247
Ah	30	m	c	CHIN	Trinity	Weaverville Pct	92	230
Ah	20	f	c	CHIN	Santa Clara	Gilroy Twp	88	75
Le	19	m	c	CHIN	Los Angeles	Los Angeles	73	520
BOECHER								
Elizabeth	22	f	w	PRUS	San Francisco	San Francisco P O	80	343
BOECK								
Christian	27	m	w	PRUS	San Francisco	San Francisco P O	80	536
BOEDEFIELD								
Joseph	26	m	w	PRUS	Colusa	Colusa	71	290
BOEGE								
Timothy	32	m	w	SHOL	Los Angeles	Santa Ana Twp	73	611
BOEHLE								
Jos	42	m	w	BADE	Sacramento	1-Wd Sacramento	77	186
BOEHME								
Geo	40	m	w	FRAN	Sacramento	3-Wd Sacramento	77	265
BOEHN								
Phillip	34	m	w	PRUS	San Bernardino	San Bernardino Twp	78	425
BOEHNE								
Fred	39	m	w	PRUS	San Francisco	2-Wd San Francisco	79	254
BOEJENI								
Antonio	37	m	w	SWIT	Sonoma	Petaluma Twp	91	348
BOELIUS								
Jas	59	m	w	MI	Butte	Ophir Twp	70	119
BOELL								
Chas	54	m	w	BAVA	Shasta	Shasta P O	89	460
BOEN								
Thos	39	m	w	ENGL	Yuba	W Bear Rvr Twp	93	682
BOENER								
Charles	33	m	w	PA	San Francisco	6-Wd San Francisco	81	102
BOERAM								
C F	41	m	w	SCOT	Merced	Snelling P O	74	265
BOERDER								
L	44	m	w	PRUS	Lake	Morgan Valley	73	425
BOERNER								
Chas	26	m	w	PRUS	Alameda	Brooklyn Twp	68	52
BOESCH								
Sophia	29	f	w	PRUS	San Francisco	8-Wd San Francisco	82	429
BOESH								
A	44	m	w	FRAN	San Joaquin	1-Wd Stockton	86	133
BOESICKE								
Wm	21	m	w	SAXO	San Francisco	8-Wd San Francisco	82	348
BOETEL								
Louis	40	m	w	FRAN	Shasta	Shasta P O	89	456
BOETTCHEN								
John	36	m	w	MECK	San Mateo	Woodside P O	87	381
BOFERGNES								
Louis	30	m	w	MEXI	Marin	San Rafael Twp	74	42
BOFFMON								
David	39	m	w	KY	Santa Cruz	Santa Cruz Twp	89	379
BOFFORD								
N H	44	m	w	ME	San Joaquin	Dent Twp	86	22
BOFINGER								
Jacob	51	m	w	WURT	San Francisco	3-Wd San Francisco	79	325
W F	40	m	w	PRUS	Tehama	Red Bluff	92	175
BOG								
Ah	18	m	c	CHIN	San Francisco	San Francisco P O	83	131
BOGA								
Joseph	30	m	w	ENGL	Stanislaus	Emory Twp	92	22
BOGAN								
Charles	41	m	w	IREL	San Francisco	San Francisco P O	83	16
Charles	41	m	w	IREL	Mariposa	Mariposa P O	74	118
Charles	35	m	w	IREL	San Francisco	San Francisco P O	80	376
Thomas	33	m	w	IREL	Mariposa	Mariposa P O	74	120
BOGARD								
Charles	30	m	w	FRAN	Santa Clara	San Jose Twp	88	199
Frank	31	m	w	CANA	Alameda	Brooklyn	68	38
J W	12	m	w	CA	Yuba	Marysville	93	590
Moses	23	m	w	SCOT	Yolo	Merritt Twp	93	508
Sarah	16	f	w	MO	Tehama	Merrill	92	197
BOGARDAS								
Gregorio	38	m	w	MEXI	Calaveras	San Andreas P O	70	210
Michel	33	m	w	MEXI	Calaveras	Copperopolis P O	70	259
BOGARDO								
Louis	30	m	w	ITAL	San Francisco	1-Wd San Francisco	79	105
BOGARDUS								
Harvy	38	m	w	NY	Santa Clara	Santa Clara Twp	88	175
John P	44	m	w	NY	San Francisco	2-Wd San Francisco	79	266
Theodore	65	m	w	FRAN	San Francisco	San Francisco P O	80	419
Wm	21	m	w	NY	San Francisco	7-Wd San Francisco	81	256
BOGART								
Benjn	24	m	w	MI	San Francisco	5-Wd San Francisco	81	10
Edwin	26	m	w	NY	Marin	Tomales Twp	74	77
Eliza	48	f	w	NY	Sacramento	3-Wd Sacramento	77	298
F	30	m	w	NY	Solano	Vallejo	90	210
Horace	26	m	w	PA	Yolo	Washington Twp	93	529
John	35	m	w	NY	Alameda	Oakland	68	194
John	20	m	w	MO	Tehama	Paynes Crk Twp	92	160
Joseph M	23	m	w	CANA	Nevada	Grass Valley Twp	75	160
Orlando	40	m	w	NY	San Francisco	11-Wd San Francisc	84	537
Simon	40	m	w	NY	Placer	Bath P O	76	427
Wm	32	m	w	ME	Butte	Chico Twp	70	35
BOGASH								
Charles	28	m	w	PRUS	San Francisco	San Francisco P O	80	334
BOGASS								
Joseph	48	m	w	FRAN	Amador	Jackson P O	69	338
BOGE								
Henry	35	m	w	SHOL	Los Angeles	Santa Ana Twp	73	609
Henry	26	m	w	SHOL	Los Angeles	Santa Ana Twp	73	611
Isadore	51	m	w	FRAN	Amador	Fiddletown P O	69	429
BOGEL								
Theodorre	31	m	w	PRUS	San Francisco	San Francisco P O	80	407
BOGES								
George	30	m	w	PRUS	San Francisco	San Francisco P O	83	282
BOGG								
Wm W	38	m	w	OH	Nevada	Washington Twp	75	345
BOGGAN								
Henry H	47	m	w	MS	Tulare	Farmersville Twp	92	250
Owen	45	m	w	IREL	San Francisco	San Francisco P O	85	739
BOGGE								
John	30	m	w	SHOL	Santa Clara	Milpitas Twp	88	109
BOGGS								
Abiel L	40	m	w	MO	Yolo	Cache Crk Twp	93	420
Alabama	21	f	w	AL	Sonoma	Santa Rosa	91	408
Albert G	38	m	w	MO	Napa	Napa	75	51
Alonzo	33	m	w	MA	San Joaquin	2-Wd Stockton	86	172
Angus S	50	m	w	MO	Santa Clara	1-Wd San Jose	88	230
Anthony B	74	m	w	VA	Sonoma	Cloverdale Twp	91	273
Ermon	36	m	w	ME	Sacramento	Georgianna Twp	77	130
Ezekiel	37	m	w	OH	Santa Clara	Fremont Twp	88	58
Fanthen	69	f	w	KY	Napa	Yountville Twp	75	76
G V	24	m	w	CA	Napa	Napa Twp	75	28
George W	30	m	w	MO	Stanislaus	San Joaquin Twp	92	79
J O	62	m	w	KY	Napa	Napa	75	52
Jackson	26	m	w	IA	Placer	Lincoln P O	76	481
James	34	m	w	CANA	Sonoma	Vallejo Twp	91	455
Jno	41	m	w	IREL	Santa Clara	Almaden Twp	88	2
John	40	m	w	MO	Colusa	Monroe Twp	71	311
John C	44	m	w	PA	Placer	Auburn P O	76	373
Mary	72	f	w	PA	Sonoma	Cloverdale Twp	91	273
Nellie	14	f	i	CA	Napa	Napa	75	51
Paul	32	m	w	ME	San Francisco	11-Wd San Francisc	84	638
William	59	m	w	OH	Yolo	Cache Crk Twp	93	450
William A	39	m	w	ME	Santa Cruz	Watsonville	89	372
William M	43	m	w	MO	Napa	Napa	75	40
BOGIE								
John	38	m	w	PRUS	San Francisco	8-Wd San Francisco	82	295
Wm	52	m	w	SCOT	San Francisco	San Francisco P O	85	870
BOGIMAN								
Fred	12	m	w	CA	San Francisco	2-Wd San Francisco	79	238
BOGLE								
C M	35	m	w	IREL	San Francisco	7-Wd San Francisco	81	220
E A	35	f	w	GA	Solano	Benicia	90	5
Henry A	38	m	w	AL	Tulare	Visalia	92	296
J H	36	m	w	CANA	Sierra	Sierra Twp	89	567
J S	35	m	w	NY	Solano	Vallejo	90	186
Joseph	34	m	w	NY	Contra Costa	Martinez P O	71	403
Rosalie	18	f	w	GA	Solano	Benicia	90	5
BOGLEW								
Turner	30	m	w	IREL	Sonoma	Petaluma Twp	91	328
BOGLIOLA								
John	47	m	w	ITAL	Mariposa	Maxwell Crk P O	74	139
BOGLIOLO								
Rudolph M	43	m	w	MO	Plumas	Rich Bar Twp	77	8
BOGN								
A	57	m	w	PRUS	Alameda	Oakland	68	244
BOGON								
J	45	m	w	IREL	Sierra	Alleghany & Forest	89	534
BOGS								
John	18	m	w	OH	Sacramento	Sutter Twp	77	381
BOGUE								
Bernard	28	m	w	IREL	San Francisco	San Francisco P O	83	29
James	27	m	w	PA	San Joaquin	Castoria Twp	86	13
Mary	30	f	w	IREL	Marin	San Rafael	74	50
BOH								
Ah	22	m	c	CHIN	Shasta	American Ranch P O	89	497
Hi	16	m	c	CHIN	San Francisco	8-Wd San Francisco	82	401
BOHALL								
Edwin	19	m	w	WI	Humboldt	Arcata Twp	72	234
Mary	30	f	w	IL	Santa Clara	San Jose Twp	88	180
Milo	40	m	w	IL	Humboldt	Arcata Twp	72	228
Wathe	36	m	w	NY	Humboldt	Eureka Twp	72	274
Wathe	35	m	w	OH	Humboldt	Eureka Twp	72	269
Wm	64	m	w	NY	Humboldt	Arcata Twp	72	232
Wm M	41	m	w	NY	Klamath	Trinidad Twp	73	390
BOHAN								
James	40	m	w	IREL	San Francisco	San Francisco P O	83	26
John	35	m	w	IREL	San Francisco	8-Wd San Francisco	82	395
John	30	m	w	IREL	San Francisco	8-Wd San Francisco	82	433
Michael	30	m	w	IREL	Nevada	Eureka Twp	75	130
Michael	29	m	w	IREL	Nevada	Eureka Twp	75	128
Patrick	32	m	w	IREL	San Francisco	1-Wd San Francisco	79	44
BOHANAN								
John	21	m	w	AR	San Diego	Julian Dist	78	474
BOHANEN								
Eliza	18	f	w	CA	San Joaquin	3-Wd Stockton	86	217
BOHANNAN								
Elliot	65	m	w	KY	Shasta	Horsetown P O	89	503
George W	45	m	w	AL	Los Angeles	El Monte Twp	73	455

© 2001 by Heritage Quest. All rights reserved.

Series M593

Name	Age	S	R	B-PL	County	Locale	Roll	Pg
James	13	m	w	CA	San Francisco	11-Wd San Francisc	84	592
John	16	m	w	CA	San Francisco	11-Wd San Francisc	84	592
John P	40	m	w	IL	Los Angeles	El Monte Twp	73	455
Michael	38	m	w	IREL	Nevada	Eureka Twp	75	134
W E	30	m	w	IL	Humboldt	Eel Rvr Twp	72	249
BOHANNEN								
Jerry	42	m	w	TN	San Joaquin	Castoria Twp	86	5
BOHANS								
Elisabeth	30	f	w	BAVA	San Francisco	11-Wd San Francisc	84	548
BOHE								
John	43	m	w	HCAS	Trinity	Canyon City Pct	92	201
BOHEM								
Simon	28	m	w	BADE	San Francisco	8-Wd San Francisco	82	450
BOHEN								
Andrew	35	m	w	TN	San Francisco	San Francisco P O	85	864
Bartholmew	24	m	w	IREL	Solano	Vallejo	90	193
Bridget	25	f	w	IREL	San Francisco	2-Wd San Francisco	79	142
Christina	27	f	w	NY	San Francisco	3-Wd San Francisco	79	287
Edward	34	m	w	PA	San Francisco	San Francisco P O	80	338
Geo T	47	m	w	MD	San Francisco	8-Wd San Francisco	82	362
Heny	32	m	w	HANO	San Francisco	2-Wd San Francisco	79	274
Johanna	52	f	w	IREL	San Francisco	San Francisco P O	83	214
Patrick	30	m	w	IREL	San Francisco	San Francisco P O	85	857
BOHL								
John	38	m	w	BAVA	San Francisco	8-Wd San Francisco	82	439
Peter	38	m	w	OH	Sacramento	4-Wd Sacramento	77	346
BOHLE								
Margaret	11	f	w	SHOL	San Francisco	11-Wd San Francisc	84	641
BOHLEN								
John	36	m	w	BAVA	El Dorado	Greenwood Twp	72	50
BOHLIN								
Francisco	73	m	w	SWED	Santa Clara	Santa Clara Twp	88	149
BOHLING								
H E	23	m	w	HANO	San Francisco	San Francisco P O	83	87
Louis	20	m	w	HANO	San Francisco	San Francisco P O	85	782
BOHLMAN								
Cecelia	24	f	w	PRUS	San Francisco	8-Wd San Francisco	82	423
Henry	40	m	w	OLDE	Alameda	Eden Twp	68	61
BOHLS								
Henry	17	m	w	HANO	San Francisco	11-Wd San Francisc	84	422
BOHM								
George	60	m	w	ENGL	Marin	Nicasio Twp	74	18
John A	37	m	w	BAVA	Sacramento	4-Wd Sacramento	77	330
Wm	37	m	w	SWED	San Francisco	San Francisco P O	85	811
BOHMAN								
Edwd	35	m	w	SWED	San Francisco	1-Wd San Francisco	79	108
BOHMEN								
Chas	25	m	w	KY	Butte	Chico Twp	70	25
BOHN								
August	23	m	w	PRUS	San Bernardino	San Bernardino Twp	78	448
Deethrick	33	m	w	PRUS	Mendocino	Albion & Big Rvr T	74	166
Elisa	27	f	w	GERM	San Francisco	11-Wd San Francisc	84	504
Hober	28	m	w	PRUS	San Francisco	San Francisco P O	80	460
Jacob	37	m	w	BAVA	Nevada	Little York Twp	75	244
John	41	m	w	SAXO	San Francisco	11-Wd San Francisc	84	423
John	38	m	w	ENGL	San Francisco	San Francisco P O	80	462
John	36	m	w	DENM	San Francisco	8-Wd San Francisco	82	391
John	34	m	w	WURT	Santa Clara	2-Wd San Jose	88	320
John H	30	m	w	NC	Stanislaus	Empire Twp	92	32
L L	30	m	w	IREL	Tuolumne	Chinese Camp P O	93	377
Mary	57	f	w	CANA	San Francisco	2-Wd San Francisco	79	217
Patrick	34	m	w	SWIT	Marin	San Rafael Twp	74	46
Peter	42	m	w	HDAR	Sierra	Table Rock Twp	89	579
Peter	21	m	w	BADE	San Francisco	San Francisco P O	80	478
Rudolph	23	m	w	PRUS	Mendocino	Point Arena Twp	74	215
Thomas	35	m	w	IREL	Marin	San Rafael	74	56
Zac	26	m	w	GERM	Solano	Vallejo	90	200
BOHNA								
Christian	66	m	w	PRUS	Kern	Linns Valley P O	73	345
Henry	27	m	w	AR	Kern	Linns Valley P O	73	345
BOHNARD								
Francois	35	m	w	FRAN	San Francisco	1-Wd San Francisco	79	50
BOHNEAU								
Thos	22	m	w	MA	Sonoma	Bodega Twp	91	264
BOHNERT								
Charles	30	m	w	BADE	Siskiyou	Yreka	89	657
BOHNMESTER								
John	32	m	w	PRUS	San Francisco	8-Wd San Francisco	82	320
BOHNSON								
Jacob	26	m	w	BADE	San Francisco	8-Wd San Francisco	82	355
BOHODARA								
Fritz	32	m	w	WURT	San Francisco	11-Wd San Francisc	84	681
BOHOKIN								
Jno	31	m	w	BADE	Butte	Chico Twp	70	17
BOHOLTES								
Raphael	50	m	w	MEXI	Fresno	Millerton P O	72	161
BOHOMAN								
C	32	m	w	HAMB	Alameda	Oakland	68	185
BOHORKS								
Cheardo	60	m	w	CA	Los Angeles	Los Angeles Twp	73	487
BOHORQUEZ								
B	17	m	w	CA	Sonoma	Santa Rosa	91	403
BOHS								
Geo	37	m	w	FRAN	San Francisco	11-Wd San Francisc	84	605
BOHU								
William	29	m	w	HDAR	Solano	Rio Vista Twp	90	70
BOHY								
Ah	15	m	c	CHIN	San Francisco	San Francisco P O	80	335
BOI								
Ah	28	m	c	CHIN	San Francisco	6-Wd San Francisco	81	56
BOIBE								
Henry	24	m	w	HESS	San Francisco	11-Wd San Francisc	84	678
BOICE								
Charles	45	m	w	MA	San Francisco	San Francisco P O	83	258
Henry B	42	m	w	NY	San Luis Obispo	Arroyo Grande Twp	87	279
John	26	m	w	CANA	Santa Clara	Alviso Twp	88	29
Paul	35	m	w	VT	Santa Clara	1-Wd San Jose	88	239
Silas	65	m	w	NH	Santa Clara	San Jose Twp	88	196
BOICO								
Nath	44	m	w	NJ	Sacramento	3-Wd Sacramento	77	261
BOID								
Geo T	24	m	w	NY	Sacramento	American Twp	77	66
James	20	m	w	IREL	Colusa	Monroe Twp	71	319
John	30	m	w	ENGL	Sacramento	Brighton Twp	77	77
S P	40	m	w	IREL	Sacramento	Granite Twp	77	146
BOIDE								
Dominic	45	m	w	ITAL	San Francisco	2-Wd San Francisco	79	143
BOIE								
Ah	20	m	c	CHIN	Sacramento	1-Wd Sacramento	77	198
John	30	m	w	GERM	San Mateo	Schoolhouse Statio	87	335
BOIGLE								
Chas	25	m	w	WURT	San Francisco	11-Wd San Francisc	84	683
BOIL								
Toll	35	m	w	ME	Mendocino	Anderson Twp	74	156
BOIN								
Nancy	65	f	b	MO	Sacramento	Granite Twp	77	145
BOINTON								
Raphal	58	m	w	FRAN	Fresno	Millerton P O	72	146
BOIS								
Ann	50	f	w	IREL	San Joaquin	1-Wd Stockton	86	139
John D	38	m	w	IREL	Santa Clara	Redwood Twp	88	129
BOISAT								
Hans	28	m	w	DENM	San Francisco	2-Wd San Francisco	79	158
BOISE								
Edward	23	m	w	FRAN	Butte	Ophir Twp	70	115
Franscoway	47	m	w	FRAN	Mariposa	Maxwell Crk P O	74	140
BOISIER								
Annette	68	f	w	FRAN	San Francisco	San Francisco P O	83	259
BOISO								
Louis	51	m	w	FRAN	San Francisco	San Francisco P O	80	356
BOISON								
Francis	18	m	w	FRAN	San Francisco	2-Wd San Francisco	79	143
John	23	m	w	SHOL	Santa Cruz	Pajaro Twp	89	341
BOISSE								
Eugene	40	m	w	FRAN	San Francisco	2-Wd San Francisco	79	167
Jean R	38	m	w	FRAN	Marin	Novato Twp	74	10
BOISSEAU								
John	32	m	w	FRAN	San Francisco	8-Wd San Francisco	82	355
BOISSEAW								
Alexander	44	m	w	FRAN	Plumas	Goodwin Twp	77	8
BOITAN								
Gisome	25	m	w	ITAL	Amador	Volcano P O	69	383
BOITANO								
Angelo	31	m	w	ITAL	Amador	Sutter Crk P O	69	411
BOITEUX								
Margaret	71	f	w	FRAN	San Francisco	8-Wd San Francisco	82	295
BOJAN								
Edward	45	m	w	FRAN	San Francisco	San Francisco P O	80	344
BOJANDA								
Dionesios	40	m	w	CA	San Luis Obispo	Arroyo Grande Twp	87	270
BOJORAGO								
Francisco	26	m	w	MEXI	Santa Barbara	San Buenaventura P	87	427
BOJORKAS								
Gabriel	28	m	w	CA	Santa Clara	1-Wd San Jose	88	259
Juan Jr	50	m	w	CA	Santa Clara	1-Wd San Jose	88	262
BOJORKES								
Bastoba	2	f	w	CA	Yuba	Linda Twp	93	558
Rafael	55	m	b	MEXI	Yuba	Marysville	93	578
S	51	m	w	MEXI	Yuba	Marysville	93	588
BOJORQUES								
Clara	40	f	w	CA	Marin	San Antonio Twp	74	63
Lorenzo	21	m	w	CA	Marin	San Antonio Twp	74	63
Pedro	31	m	w	CA	Marin	San Antonio Twp	74	65
Rafael	33	m	w	CA	Marin	San Antonio Twp	74	63
BOJORTES								
Ramon	44	m	w	MEXI	Santa Cruz	Soquel Twp	89	440
BOK								
Ah	25	m	c	CHIN	San Francisco	6-Wd San Francisco	81	75
Ah	22	m	c	CHIN	San Francisco	6-Wd San Francisco	81	53
Ah	20	m	c	CHIN	San Francisco	6-Wd San Francisco	81	85
Ah	20	m	c	CHIN	San Francisco	6-Wd San Francisco	81	68
Ah	18	m	c	CHIN	San Francisco	6-Wd San Francisco	81	68
Lam	18	m	c	CHIN	San Francisco	6-Wd San Francisco	81	66
Luen	27	m	c	CHIN	San Francisco	6-Wd San Francisco	81	53
Quoi	43	m	c	CHIN	San Francisco	6-Wd San Francisco	81	43
BOKE								
Ah	40	m	c	CHIN	Sierra	Downieville Twp	89	520
John H	42	m	w	SCOG	Placer	Dutch Flat P O	76	404
Nick	32	m	w	GERM	Placer	Dutch Flat P O	76	405
BOKEMAN								
Frank	44	m	w	PRUS	San Francisco	1-Wd San Francisco	79	39
BOKER								
David	31	m	w	NY	San Francisco	6-Wd San Francisco	81	154

© 2001 by Heritage Quest. All rights reserved.

California 1870 Census

Series M593

Name	Age	S	R	B-PL	County	Locale	Roll	Pg
Henry	42	m	w	PRUS	San Joaquin	3-Wd Stockton	86	235
Jas	40	m	w	US	Solano	Vallejo	90	141
Richard	40	m	w	ENGL	San Joaquin	2-Wd Stockton	86	165
BOKHOMMER								
John	44	m	w	DENM	San Francisco	2-Wd San Francisco	79	188
BOLA								
Eliza	38	f	w	FRAN	San Joaquin	2-Wd Stockton	86	171
Jaconda	29	m	w	SWIT	Marin	Nicasio Twp	74	14
Juana	12	f	w	CA	Los Angeles	Los Angeles	73	523
BOLADO								
Soaquire	46	m	w	SPAI	San Francisco	8-Wd San Francisco	82	353
BOLAI								
Nicholas	34	m	w	AUST	Tuolumne	Columbia P O	93	344
BOLAN								
Bridget	24	f	w	IREL	San Francisco	San Francisco P O	83	226
George	42	m	w	IN	Colusa	Colusa Twp	71	277
James	35	m	w	PRUS	Alameda	Oakland	68	246
Jas	40	m	w	US	Solano	Vallejo	90	139
Johanna	60	f	w	ITAL	Calaveras	San Andreas P O	70	174
Michael	40	m	w	GA	San Francisco	2-Wd San Francisco	79	216
BOLANC								
Maurice	45	m	w	FRAN	San Francisco	San Francisco P O	83	213
BOLAND								
A Jr	38	m	w	IN	Siskiyou	Scott Rvr Twp	89	604
Andrew J	33	m	w	MO	Santa Clara	Santa Clara Twp	88	170
Bridget	32	f	w	IREL	San Francisco	San Francisco P O	83	390
Danl	42	m	w	IREL	Sierra	Table Rock Twp	89	579
Danl	28	m	w	IREL	Sierra	Gibson Twp	89	542
Edward	35	m	w	CANA	Monterey	Alisal Twp	74	300
James	35	m	w	OH	San Francisco	11-Wd San Francisc	84	622
Jno	29	m	w	IREL	Sierra	Table Rock Twp	89	579
John	45	m	w	IREL	San Francisco	8-Wd San Francisco	82	446
Maggie	17	f	w	CA	San Francisco	3-Wd San Francisco	79	328
Martin	44	m	w	IREL	San Francisco	San Francisco P O	80	332
Mary	19	f	w	IREL	San Francisco	8-Wd San Francisco	82	290
Patrick	35	m	w	IREL	San Francisco	11-Wd San Francisc	84	629
Richard	24	m	w	ENGL	San Mateo	San Mateo P O	87	351
William	31	m	w	IN	Colusa	Colusa Twp	71	280
Wm	36	m	w	IN	Siskiyou	Scott Rvr Twp	89	604
Wm E	41	m	w	DC	San Luis Obispo	San Luis Obispo Tw	87	297
BOLANDER								
John	38	m	w	OH	El Dorado	Mud Springs Twp	72	91
BOLANGA								
Francis	31	m	w	FRAN	Nevada	Nevada Twp	75	315
BOLANGER								
Ida	4	f	w	CA	Nevada	Nevada Twp	75	290
BOLARDIA								
Andre	30	f	w	MEXI	Santa Clara	1-Wd San Jose	88	263
BOLARES								
Juan H	40	m	w	MEXI	Los Angeles	Los Angeles Twp	73	467
BOLAVA								
John	34	m	b	HI	Sutter	Butte Twp	92	97
Wha	40	m	b	HI	Sutter	Butte Twp	92	97
BOLCOFF								
Andrew	44	m	c	CA	San Mateo	San Mateo P O	87	348
Dolores H	28	m	w	CA	San Mateo	San Mateo P O	87	348
Francisco	43	m	w	CA	Santa Cruz	Pajaro Twp	89	359
BOLCOM								
Manuel	25	m	w	PORT	Alameda	Eden Twp	68	61
BOLDEN								
Joe	38	m	w	US	San Joaquin	Castoria Twp	86	9
John	30	m	w	SHOL	San Francisco	1-Wd San Francisco	79	35
Mary	35	f	w	CANA	Sonoma	Petaluma Twp	91	336
Nelson	30	m	w	DENM	Nevada	Grass Valley Twp	75	217
Samuel	41	m	w	PA	Sonoma	Salt Point	91	393
Thomas	55	m	b	VA	El Dorado	White Oak Twp	72	140
W S	42	m	w	CT	San Joaquin	Castoria Twp	86	12
BOLDER								
Jos	36	m	w	GERM	Mono	Bridgeport P O	74	285
BOLDES								
Francisco	52	m	w	MEXI	Tulare	Tule Rvr Twp	92	270
BOLDGET								
S	52	m	w	NY	Yuba	Marysville	93	579
BOLDING								
Eben	71	m	w	VT	Solano	Benicia	90	7
BOLDRINI								
F	40	m	w	ITAL	Sacramento	1-Wd Sacramento	77	189
BOLDS								
William	38	m	w	MO	Sonoma	Santa Rosa	91	424
BOLDT								
Criss	42	m	w	PRUS	Sonoma	Mendocino Twp	91	297
Henry E	45	m	w	MECK	Los Angeles	Santa Ana Twp	73	613
BOLDTHAN								
Andrew	29	m	w	SHOL	El Dorado	Diamond Springs Tw	72	34
BOLDUE								
Francois	58	m	w	CANA	Monterey	San Benito Twp	74	383
BOLDWAY								
Delia	25	f	w	PA	San Francisco	11-Wd San Francisc	84	688
BOLE								
Francis	20	m	w	CANA	Tulare	Tule Rvr Twp	92	264
Henry	34	m	w	PA	Yolo	Buckeye Twp	93	408
Isebella	25	f	w	IREL	San Francisco	San Francisco P O	83	174
James	30	m	w	IREL	San Francisco	San Francisco P O	83	60
Joseph	23	m	w	IN	San Luis Obispo	Morro Twp	87	280
BOLELA								
John	40	m	w	ITAL	San Mateo	Schoolhouse Statio	87	344
BOLELLO								
Tadaee	20	m	w	CA	Los Angeles	Los Angeles Twp	73	478
BOLEMAN								
Richard	33	m	w	ME	Nevada	Eureka Twp	75	132
Robt	25	m	w	IREL	Solano	Vallejo	90	204
BOLEN								
Nancy	10	f	w	CA	Colusa	Colusa Twp	71	282
William	32	m	w	IN	Colusa	Monroe Twp	71	315
BOLENA								
Manuel	45	m	w	PORT	Alameda	Eden Twp	68	89
BOLENGER								
John	25	m	w	FRAN	Siskiyou	Scott Valley Twp	89	614
BOLER								
Rosina	78	f	w	BAVA	Sonoma	Sonoma Twp	91	440
BOLES								
Alvy	58	m	w	OH	Siskiyou	Big Valley Twp	89	582
Daniel	38	m	w	IREL	Sacramento	4-Wd Sacramento	77	344
Jas L	40	m	w	OH	Butte	Chico Twp	70	54
John	40	m	w	IREL	San Francisco	San Francisco P O	85	871
John	35	m	w	ENGL	Humboldt	Table Bluff Twp	72	306
Margaret	40	f	w	IREL	San Francisco	San Francisco P O	85	873
Ralph	54	m	w	PA	Placer	Auburn P O	76	365
Robt	32	m	w	OH	Humboldt	Eureka Twp	72	275
BOLETTE								
D	41	m	w	ITAL	Amador	Jackson P O	69	342
BOLEVANA								
Leonora	32	f	w	MEXI	Merced	Snelling P O	74	251
BOLEY								
Louisa	15	f	w	KY	Sacramento	3-Wd Sacramento	77	301
Matty	24	f	w	OH	Sacramento	1-Wd Sacramento	77	185
Susan	61	f	w	VT	San Francisco	San Francisco P O	83	200
BOLF								
Nelson	51	m	w	VA	Merced	Snelling P O	74	253
BOLGAR								
Thomas	63	m	w	IREL	Santa Clara	Fremont Twp	88	59
BOLGER								
Anne	37	f	w	IREL	San Francisco	7-Wd San Francisco	81	233
Bridget	24	f	w	IREL	Monterey	San Juan Twp	74	418
George	27	m	w	NY	Sacramento	2-Wd Sacramento	77	219
John	28	m	w	IREL	San Francisco	San Francisco P O	83	379
Miles	8	m	w	CA	San Francisco	7-Wd San Francisco	81	233
Peter	26	m	w	NY	San Mateo	Redwood City P O	87	376
Peter	23	m	w	IREL	Alameda	Brooklyn	68	33
Thomas	57	m	w	IREL	San Bernardino	San Bernardino Twp	78	417
BOLHALTER								
Joseph	45	m	w	PRUS	Placer	Roseville P O	76	355
BOLHINN								
Minnie	22	f	w	PRUS	San Francisco	11-Wd San Francisc	84	606
BOLIAS								
Henry	35	m	w	MEXI	Fresno	Millerton P O	72	151
BOLICK								
Robert	60	m	b	MA	San Francisco	3-Wd San Francisco	79	324
BOLIEW								
Oliver	60	m	w	CANA	Santa Clara	San Jose Twp	88	197
BOLIN								
Ann	30	f	w	IREL	San Joaquin	2-Wd Stockton	86	162
Hercules	30	m	w	KY	Yolo	Grafton Twp	93	501
Jacob	45	m	w	SWED	Stanislaus	Branch Twp	92	1
Joseph	21	m	w	BADE	San Francisco	8-Wd San Francisco	82	375
Michael	28	m	w	IREL	Marin	Sausalito Twp	74	72
Thomas	24	m	w	TX	Yolo	Cottonwood Twp	93	461
Wm	53	m	w	KY	Plumas	Washington Twp	77	52
BOLING								
Danl	37	m	w	MO	Santa Clara	Gilroy Twp	88	78
Henry	46	m	w	HANO	El Dorado	Placerville Twp	72	101
J F	14	m	w	CA	Calaveras	Copperopolis P O	70	224
Nathan H	26	m	w	IA	Placer	Dutch Flat P O	76	414
P	50	m	w	IREL	Lake	Knoxville Mines	73	404
R J	31	m	w	VA	Sutter	Butte Twp	92	94
BOLINGER								
Frank	4	m	w	CA	Tulare	Venice Twp	92	277
S	39	m	w	SC	Lake	Upper Lake	73	412
Sarah	15	f	w	MO	Solano	Vacaville Twp	90	136
William G	40	m	w	OH	San Francisco	San Francisco P O	83	360
BOLITHO								
S	53	f	w	KY	Calaveras	Copperopolis P O	70	237
Sampson	32	m	w	ENGL	Nevada	Grass Valley Twp	75	200
BOLIVER								
Saml	24	m	w	MO	Butte	Chico Twp	70	17
BOLKEN								
Tim	50	m	w	IREL	San Joaquin	2-Wd Stockton	86	173
BOLL								
Henry	43	m	w	SHOL	Mariposa	Maxwell Crk P O	74	144
Michael	40	m	w	BADE	San Luis Obispo	San Luis Obispo Tw	87	309
Samuel	30	m	w	IREL	Alameda	Murray Twp	68	106
Wm P	41	m	w	VA	Monterey	San Juan Twp	74	402
BOLLA								
Peter	25	m	w	SWIT	Santa Clara	2-Wd San Jose	88	301
BOLLARD								
D B	63	f	w	MA	San Francisco	San Francisco P O	85	778
William	35	m	w	NY	San Francisco	7-Wd San Francisco	81	188
BOLLAY								
Jacob	26	m	w	KY	San Joaquin	2-Wd Stockton	86	213
BOLLD								
Amos	54	m	w	MA	Kern	Havilah P O	73	336
BOLLE								
Henry	22	m	w	ITAL	San Mateo	Schoolhouse Statio	87	344

© 2001 by Heritage Quest. All rights reserved.

Name	Age	S	R	B-PL	County	Locale	Series M593 Roll	Pg
BOLLEN								
Sarah	65	f	w	PA	Sonoma	Salt Point	91	380
BOLLENHAGEN								
Henry	21	m	w	HANO	San Francisco	San Francisco P O	83	181
BOLLER								
Joseph	27	m	w	BADE	San Francisco	San Francisco P O	80	349
BOLLES								
Fredk	30	m	w	MA	San Francisco	San Francisco P O	83	27
James H	22	m	w	AL	Santa Barbara	San Buenaventura P	87	425
BOLLIGAN								
S	45	m	w	PRUS	San Joaquin	Douglas Twp	86	51
BOLLIGER								
Jacob	34	m	w	SWIT	Klamath	Camp Gaston	73	372
BOLLIN								
John H	43	m	w	NY	San Francisco	6-Wd San Francisco	81	78
Simon	21	m	m	VA	San Francisco	1-Wd San Francisco	79	132
BOLLING								
George	43	m	w	VA	San Francisco	San Francisco P O	83	355
Gr	45	m	w	PRUS	Sierra	Lincoln Twp	89	551
Henry	32	m	w	MA	San Francisco	11-Wd San Francisc	84	630
Sarah J	31	f	w	MO	Sonoma	Russian Rvr	91	376
BOLLINGER								
Adam J	59	m	w	MO	Contra Costa	Martinez P O	71	391
Christopher	54	m	w	MO	San Mateo	Belmont P O	87	373
Christopher C	33	m	w	MO	Contra Costa	Martinez P O	71	391
Francis	30	m	w	MO	Santa Barbara	Santa Barbara P O	87	452
Francis M	36	m	w	MO	Contra Costa	Martinez P O	71	391
Geo	27	m	w	MO	San Francisco	11-Wd San Francisc	84	687
Jacob	37	m	w	BAVA	El Dorado	Placerville	72	121
John	44	m	w	MO	Santa Clara	Santa Clara Twp	88	173
John	33	m	w	SWIT	San Francisco	San Francisco P O	80	378
John	19	m	w	MO	Contra Costa	Martinez P O	71	391
Joseph	26	m	w	MO	Contra Costa	Martinez P O	71	391
Joshua	60	m	w	MO	Contra Costa	Martinez P O	71	394
BOLLIS								
Elisha F	60	m	w	NY	Sacramento	Mississippi Twp	77	163
BOLLMAIN								
---	43	m	w	PRUS	Sonoma	Petaluma Twp	91	362
BOLLMAN								
Elizabeth	43	f	w	PRUS	San Francisco	2-Wd San Francisco	79	192
F	23	m	w	BADE	Sacramento	3-Wd Sacramento	77	317
John	28	m	w	PRUS	San Francisco	San Francisco P O	80	334
BOLLNAN								
Persio	22	m	w	FRAN	Monterey	San Juan Twp	74	402
BOLLO								
Thomas	47	m	w	ITAL	San Francisco	6-Wd San Francisco	81	98
BOLONQUE								
John	33	m	w	FRAN	San Francisco	1-Wd San Francisco	79	35
BOLPY								
Charles	23	m	w	CANA	Monterey	San Juan Twp	74	390
BOLSTER								
Patrick	43	m	w	IREL	San Francisco	San Francisco P O	83	263
BOLT								
Benjamin	40	m	w	IL	Mendocino	Gualala Twp	74	226
Benjamin	30	m	w	IREL	San Francisco	1-Wd San Francisco	79	49
C M	27	m	w	NY	San Joaquin	Elkhorn Twp	86	65
Geo S	31	m	w	OH	San Joaquin	Elkhorn Twp	86	65
Saml	26	m	w	ENGL	San Francisco	1-Wd San Francisco	79	131
BOLTE								
Henry	42	m	w	PRUS	San Francisco	San Francisco P O	80	473
Henry	38	m	w	SHOL	San Francisco	1-Wd San Francisco	79	129
Jacob	32	m	w	PRUS	San Francisco	San Francisco P O	80	408
Mary	10	f	w	CA	San Francisco	1-Wd San Francisco	79	127
BOLTER								
Fletcher	27	m	w	ENGL	Stanislaus	Empire Twp	92	53
William	42	m	w	ENGL	Stanislaus	Empire Twp	92	53
William	22	m	w	NY	Stanislaus	Empire Twp	92	53
Wm J	50	m	w	ENGL	Tuolumne	Columbia P O	93	352
BOLTMAN								
Geo	20	m	w	NY	San Francisco	1-Wd San Francisco	79	73
BOLTMANN								
Henry	12	m	w	HANO	San Francisco	11-Wd San Francisc	84	623
BOLTON								
Abraham B	38	m	w	NY	Mariposa	Mariposa P O	74	131
Adolph	30	m	w	HAMB	San Francisco	8-Wd San Francisco	82	452
Alfred	72	m	w	MA	Nevada	Grass Valley Twp	75	170
Bryan J	62	m	w	IREL	Santa Cruz	Santa Cruz Twp	89	399
Curtis	32	m	w	NY	Sacramento	Alabama Twp	77	59
Edward	50	m	w	ENGL	Shasta	Shasta P O	89	453
Edwd	28	m	w	IL	Santa Clara	Gilroy Twp	88	67
Ellen	45	f	w	IREL	San Francisco	11-Wd San Francisc	84	522
Frank	43	m	w	CANA	Butte	Chico Twp	70	38
Free	42	m	w	CANA	Butte	Chico Twp	70	35
George	51	m	w	ENGL	Placer	Pino Twp	76	471
Henry	28	m	w	ENGL	San Francisco	1-Wd San Francisco	79	73
James	27	m	w	ENGL	San Joaquin	1-Wd Stockton	86	135
James R	53	m	w	NY	San Francisco	2-Wd San Francisco	79	282
James W	21	m	w	ENGL	Santa Clara	Santa Clara Twp	88	144
John	39	m	w	IREL	Sonoma	Petaluma Twp	91	354
John C	24	m	w	AR	Mendocino	Calpella Twp	74	182
Lizzie	30	f	w	ENGL	San Francisco	San Francisco P O	80	540
Michael	40	m	w	IREL	Placer	Newcastle Twp	76	480
Nelson	38	m	w	OH	Mariposa	Mariposa P O	74	120
Pat	40	m	w	IREL	Solano	Benicia	90	11
Patrick	40	m	w	IREL	Sonoma	Petaluma Twp	91	353
Redman	37	m	w	CANA	Sonoma	Petaluma Twp	91	359
Robert	55	m	w	ENGL	San Francisco	3-Wd San Francisco	79	313
Sarah	70	f	w	VT	Nevada	Grass Valley Twp	75	170
Sarah A	33	f	w	NY	Sonoma	Healdsburg & Mendo	91	283
Thoma G	46	m	w	ENGL	Tulare	Tule Rvr Twp	92	262
W	52	m	w	ENGL	Alameda	Oakland	68	211
William	43	m	w	ENGL	Santa Clara	1-Wd San Jose	88	252
BOLTS								
John	33	m	w	HANO	Alpine	Silver Mtn P O	69	308
BOLTZZ								
Albert	35	m	w	PRUS	San Francisco	2-Wd San Francisco	79	156
BOLVERAM								
Peter	31	m	w	CHIL	Shasta	American Ranch P O	89	496
BOLYER								
Abram	47	m	w	PA	Plumas	Rich Bar Twp	77	8
Soloman	35	m	w	IREL	San Francisco	11-Wd San Francisc	84	455
BOLZA								
Anna	19	f	w	NY	Solano	Benicia	90	12
BOM								
Ah	16	m	c	CHIN	San Francisco	San Francisco P O	80	351
BOMALETT								
Peter	14	m	w	CA	Klamath	Klamath Twp	73	371
BOMAN								
David	41	m	w	ENGL	Contra Costa	Martinez P O	71	422
Edward	43	m	w	PA	Alameda	Alvarado	68	302
Fred	38	m	w	HANO	Fresno	Millerton P O	72	150
John	31	m	w	PRUS	Sutter	Nicolaus Twp	92	108
Mary	20	f	w	HANO	San Francisco	8-Wd San Francisco	82	294
Stephen	25	m	w	SWIT	Sacramento	American Twp	77	66
BOMARE								
Peter	33	m	w	FRAN	Santa Clara	San Jose Twp	88	200
BOMBAY								
John	50	m	w	EIND	Santa Clara	2-Wd San Jose	88	289
BOMBEE								
---	25	m	c	CHIN	San Francisco	7-Wd San Francisco	81	227
BOMBY								
Jacob W	49	m	w	PA	Placer	Bath P O	76	458
BOMEFORD								
G	40	m	w	FRAN	San Francisco	San Francisco P O	83	269
BOMER								
Barbara	58	f	w	BAVA	San Francisco	8-Wd San Francisco	82	339
Sarah	48	f	w	IREL	San Francisco	San Francisco P O	83	317
BOMEZ								
Jesus	23	m	w	MEXI	Santa Clara	Gilroy Twp	88	93
BOMGARTEN								
David	32	m	w	PRUS	Yolo	Putah Twp	93	523
BOMHAM								
William	25	m	w	ME	San Mateo	Woodside P O	87	386
BOMHEIM								
Henry	52	m	w	GERM	Tuolumne	Columbia P O	93	338
BOMHOFF								
Wm	15	m	w	CA	Del Norte	Smith Rvr Twp	71	479
BOMMAN								
James	50	m	w	PA	San Francisco	San Francisco P O	80	352
BOMMONSITT								
Louis	44	m	w	FRAN	Amador	Volcano P O	69	379
BOMPARD								
Bautiste	38	m	w	FRAN	Santa Clara	2-Wd San Jose	88	311
M L	30	f	w	FRAN	Alameda	Oakland	68	259
BOMSON								
Benjamin	22	m	w	SWED	San Mateo	Half Moon Bay P O	87	407
BOMSTELL								
C K	15	m	w	CA	Alameda	Oakland	68	242
BOMYEA								
Kate	23	f	w	IL	Yuba	Marysville	93	599
BON								
---	26	m	c	CHIN	San Francisco	11-Wd San Francisc	84	503
Ah	48	m	c	CHIN	Kern	Bakersfield P O	73	359
Ah	46	m	c	CHIN	Placer	Pino Twp	76	471
Ah	41	m	c	CHIN	San Francisco	San Francisco P O	80	502
Ah	40	m	c	CHIN	Kern	Havilah P O	73	338
Ah	40	m	c	CHIN	Placer	Newcastle Twp	76	477
Ah	40	m	c	CHIN	San Francisco	6-Wd San Francisco	81	60
Ah	37	m	c	CHIN	Tuolumne	Sonora P O	93	331
Ah	37	m	c	CHIN	Butte	Mountain Spring Tw	70	90
Ah	31	m	c	CHIN	Nevada	Nevada Twp	75	276
Ah	26	m	c	CHIN	Solano	Silveyville Twp	90	85
Ah	21	m	c	CHIN	San Mateo	Pescadero P O	87	416
Ah	20	m	c	CHIN	Placer	Lincoln P O	76	484
Ah	16	m	c	CHIN	Sacramento	3-Wd Sacramento	77	315
Augustus	31	m	w	POLA	Alameda	Murray Twp	68	108
E Dr	38	m	w	FRAN	Sierra	Sierra Twp	89	568
Prudencia	50	m	w	MEXI	Santa Barbara	Santa Barbara P O	87	458
Rosaleno	25	m	w	MEXI	Yuba	Marysville	93	614
BONA								
F	45	m	w	ITAL	Sierra	Gibson Twp	89	542
Ferdinando	45	m	w	ITAL	San Francisco	11-Wd San Francisc	84	594
G B	47	m	w	FRAN	Alameda	Oakland	68	154
Peter	50	m	w	ITAL	San Francisco	San Francisco P O	80	463
BONAFACHE								
Gilare	18	m	w	ITAL	San Francisco	San Francisco P O	85	860
BONAHEUR								
Mary	37	f	w	OH	San Francisco	San Francisco P O	80	425
BONAPARTE								
---	25	m	w	MO	Yolo	Grafton Twp	93	495
Louis	16	m	b	MO	Colusa	Spring Valley Twp	71	339
Napoleon	39	m	w	FRAN	San Francisco	11-Wd San Francisc	84	616
BONARD								
Felis	40	m	w	FRAN	Plumas	Plumas Twp	77	32

© 2001 by Heritage Quest. All rights reserved.

Name	Age	S	R	B-PL	County	Locale	Series M593 Roll	Pg
BONARIA								
Juan	50	f	w	MEXI	San Joaquin	3-Wd Stockton	86	222
BONAS								
George	28	m	w	TN	Kern	Bakersfield P O	73	357
Rachel	59	f	w	KY	Stanislaus	Branch Twp	92	8
BONAVENTURA								
Albina	35	f	w	CA	Monterey	San Juan Twp	74	403
BONBERGIER								
John	29	m	w	CANA	Placer	Bath P O	76	454
BONBERI								
Luigi	40	m	w	ITAL	Amador	Sutter Crk P O	69	413
BONCH								
C	20	f	w	PRUS	Alameda	Alameda	68	11
BONCHER								
Charles	52	m	w	ENGL	San Francisco	7-Wd San Francisco	81	209
E C	43	m	w	AL	Santa Cruz	Pajaro Twp	89	347
Emma	21	f	w	PRUS	San Francisco	6-Wd San Francisco	81	71
Jefferson	25	m	w	CANA	San Francisco	8-Wd San Francisco	82	381
BONCHIP								
Ernst	46	m	w	FRAN	Siskiyou	Callahan P O	89	627
BONCIVANA								
Nuncio	50	m	w	ITAL	Santa Clara	1-Wd San Jose	88	251
BOND								
Augustus	40	m	w	NY	Sacramento	San Joaquin Twp	77	400
C J	30	m	w	CANA	Alameda	Murray Twp	68	127
Charles R	50	m	w	MA	San Francisco	6-Wd San Francisco	81	124
Chas	20	m	w	MA	San Francisco	San Francisco P O	83	103
Eda	5	f	w	CA	Yolo	Grafton Twp	93	488
Erastus	41	m	w	NY	Nevada	Nevada Twp	75	293
Fred	26	m	w	NY	Sonoma	Mendocino Twp	91	301
Fredrick	23	m	w	GERM	Sonoma	Vallejo Twp	91	463
George K	31	m	w	VT	Marin	San Rafael	74	57
George W	55	m	w	ENGL	Alameda	Washington Twp	68	276
Hannah	18	f	w	MA	San Francisco	8-Wd San Francisco	82	462
Harry	38	m	w	ENGL	Lake	Morgan Valley	73	424
Henrietta	31	f	m	MO	Yuba	Marysville	93	599
James	30	m	w	CANA	Colusa	Colusa	71	290
James	21	m	w	IA	Stanislaus	San Joaquin Twp	92	75
John	37	m	w	ENGL	Nevada	Nevada Twp	75	296
John	28	m	w	MO	Solano	Silveyville Twp	90	74
John F	42	m	w	AL	Tulare	Tule Rvr Twp	92	265
Joshua	53	m	w	TN	Sonoma	Petaluma Twp	91	319
Joshua W	30	m	w	OH	Sonoma	Vallejo Twp	91	458
Julia	24	f	w	NY	San Francisco	San Francisco P O	83	196
Levi	42	m	w	MA	Tulare	Tule Rvr Twp	92	261
Lizzie	36	f	w	KY	Stanislaus	Empire Twp	92	35
M H	49	m	w	NY	San Joaquin	2-Wd Stockton	86	193
Merritt D	52	m	w	OH	Colusa	Colusa	71	291
Mosses	32	m	w	IL	Sonoma	Mendocino Twp	91	297
Rezobia	61	f	w	VT	Sonoma	Healdsburg & Mendo	91	283
Richard	70	m	w	VA	San Francisco	San Francisco P O	80	394
Sabarian	56	m	w	FRAN	Monterey	Monterey Twp	74	352
Sallie	41	f	w	NY	San Francisco	San Francisco P O	80	457
Sam Lee	36	m	c	CHIN	Monterey	Monterey Twp	74	352
Samuel	30	m	w	POLA	San Francisco	6-Wd San Francisco	81	94
Seth H	24	m	w	IA	Stanislaus	San Joaquin Twp	92	75
Silas	41	m	w	IN	Santa Barbara	Santa Barbara P O	87	488
Stephen	38	m	w	NY	Kern	Bakersfield P O	73	358
Thomas	13	m	w	CA	San Francisco	San Francisco P O	85	813
William	8	m	w	CA	Sonoma	Petaluma Twp	91	362
William	53	m	w	ENGL	El Dorado	Placerville Twp	72	102
William H	35	m	w	KY	Stanislaus	Empire Twp	92	31
William R	40	m	w	VA	Yuba	Parks Bar Twp	93	648
Wm H	37	m	w	PA	Sonoma	Santa Rosa	91	410
BONDEN								
Simon	35	m	w	ENGL	Mariposa	Mariposa P O	74	131
BONDIELLI								
John	32	m	w	ITAL	Santa Clara	Santa Clara Twp	88	176
BONDIL								
Pierre	40	m	w	FRAN	San Francisco	San Francisco P O	83	135
BONDINE								
Eliza	58	f	w	ENGL	San Joaquin	2-Wd Stockton	86	174
BONDREAU								
Emile	39	m	w	LA	Santa Clara	San Jose Twp	88	193
BONDS								
James	23	m	w	ENGL	Nevada	Grass Valley Twp	75	191
James G	40	m	w	TN	Inyo	Bishop Crk Twp	73	311
BONDURANT								
Jesse H	59	m	w	VA	Fresno	Millerton P O	72	156
BONE								
Ah	35	m	c	CHIN	Placer	Dutch Flat P O	76	414
Ah	20	m	c	CHIN	San Francisco	11-Wd San Francisc	84	528
Baptiste	34	m	w	ITAL	Tuolumne	Sonora P O	93	303
Benj	19	m	w	ENGL	Yuba	Rose Bar Twp	93	655
Chas	32	m	w	ENGL	San Francisco	5-Wd San Francisco	81	13
Edward	50	m	w	ENGL	Tuolumne	Columbia P O	93	351
Henry	50	m	w	ENGL	Placer	Bath P O	76	448
J P	29	m	w	IREL	San Francisco	San Francisco P O	85	796
John	29	m	w	IA	Sonoma	Analy Twp	91	246
Katy	18	m	w	NJ	San Francisco	5-Wd San Francisco	81	13
Shadrach	46	m	w	ENGL	Tuolumne	Columbia P O	93	351
W G	48	m	w	ENGL	Tuolumne	Columbia P O	93	351
BONEAR								
Francisco	12	m	w	CA	San Diego	San Pasqual Valley	78	524
BONEE								
Hiram	58	m	w	VA	Sonoma	Washington Twp	91	464
Sencion	24	m	w	CAME	Sacramento	2-Wd Sacramento	77	242
Wm	31	m	w	MO	Sonoma	Washington Twp	91	464
BONEFACIO								
Jose	10	m	w	CA	Monterey	Alisal Twp	74	293
BONEFAN								
A	55	m	w	FRAN	Alameda	Murray Twp	68	118
BONER								
James	39	m	w	MS	Kern	Havilah P O	73	341
John	30	m	w	IREL	San Joaquin	2-Wd Stockton	86	168
John	28	m	w	LA	Kern	Havilah P O	73	341
Lewis	41	m	w	PRUS	Sonoma	Petaluma Twp	91	313
Margaret	44	f	w	IREL	Alameda	Eden Twp	68	57
BONES								
Charles	22	m	w	MO	Colusa	Spring Valley Twp	71	341
F M	39	m	w	MO	Mendocino	Sanel Twp	74	228
J W	52	m	w	PA	Alameda	Alameda	68	8
Robert	50	m	w	MD	Plumas	Plumas Twp	77	26
BONESTAL								
Charles	40	m	w	MA	San Francisco	6-Wd San Francisco	81	117
Charles	30	m	w	NY	San Francisco	6-Wd San Francisco	81	115
John T	34	m	w	NY	San Francisco	6-Wd San Francisco	81	115
BONESTALL								
August	44	m	w	NY	Alameda	Washington Twp	68	299
BONESTELL								
Louis H	45	m	w	NY	San Francisco	8-Wd San Francisco	82	344
BONETA								
John	37	m	w	SWIT	Sacramento	Sutter Twp	77	389
BONETTE								
Grucon	27	m	w	SWIT	Santa Clara	2-Wd San Jose	88	323
Leticia	17	f	w	CA	Los Angeles	Los Angeles	73	554
Lucas	24	m	w	SWED	San Mateo	Pescadero P O	87	414
BONEY								
Barney	30	m	w	IREL	San Francisco	San Francisco P O	83	169
Patrick	50	m	w	IREL	Nevada	Bloomfield Twp	75	94
BONFANTON								
Maurice	35	m	w	SWIT	Santa Cruz	Santa Cruz Twp	89	386
BONFEYLIO								
Joseph	17	m	w	MEXI	Alameda	Oakland	68	159
BONFORY								
Henry	27	m	w	PRUS	Tulare	Visalia	92	298
BONG								
---	44	m	c	CHIN	Siskiyou	Yreka Twp	89	673
Ah	55	m	c	CHIN	El Dorado	Coloma Twp	72	3
Ah	44	m	c	CHIN	Trinity	Douglas	92	233
Ah	42	m	c	CHIN	Yuba	Marysville	93	622
Ah	40	m	c	CHIN	Sierra	Downieville Twp	89	521
Ah	38	m	c	CHIN	San Francisco	San Francisco P O	80	489
Ah	34	m	c	CHIN	San Francisco	6-Wd San Francisco	81	75
Ah	30	m	c	CHIN	San Francisco	6-Wd San Francisco	81	45
Ah	29	m	c	CHIN	Klamath	Orleans Twp	73	380
Ah	28	m	c	CHIN	Santa Clara	1-Wd San Jose	88	232
Ah	27	m	c	CHIN	San Francisco	6-Wd San Francisco	81	48
Ah	26	m	c	CHIN	Nevada	Nevada Twp	75	311
Ah	25	m	c	CHIN	Calaveras	San Andreas P O	70	161
Ah	25	m	c	CHIN	Sierra	Downieville Twp	89	521
Ah	25	m	c	CHIN	San Francisco	3-Wd San Francisco	79	301
Ah	24	m	c	CHIN	Napa	Napa	75	9
Ah	24	m	c	CHIN	San Francisco	6-Wd San Francisco	81	60
Ah	22	m	c	CHIN	Nevada	Nevada Twp	75	312
Ah	20	m	c	CHIN	San Francisco	6-Wd San Francisco	81	48
Ah	20	m	c	CHIN	San Francisco	6-Wd San Francisco	81	43
Ah	20	m	c	CHIN	Placer	Auburn P O	76	377
Ah	18	m	c	CHIN	San Francisco	6-Wd San Francisco	81	53
Ah	18	m	c	CHIN	San Francisco	6-Wd San Francisco	81	85
Ah	18	m	c	CHIN	San Francisco	6-Wd San Francisco	81	67
Ah	17	m	c	CHIN	San Francisco	6-Wd San Francisco	81	55
Ah	13	m	c	CHIN	San Francisco	6-Wd San Francisco	81	46
Am	47	m	c	CHIN	Placer	Bath P O	76	446
Chik	18	m	c	CHIN	Napa	Napa	75	9
Foi	40	m	c	CHIN	San Francisco	6-Wd San Francisco	81	67
Gee	24	m	c	CHIN	Plumas	Mineral Twp	77	24
He	27	m	c	CHIN	Calaveras	San Andreas P O	70	211
Len	25	m	c	CHIN	Sacramento	1-Wd Sacramento	77	187
Sue	26	m	c	CHIN	Yuba	Marysville	93	625
Tee	31	m	c	CHIN	San Francisco	6-Wd San Francisco	81	56
Wing	30	m	c	CHIN	Nevada	Grass Valley Twp	75	184
BONGE								
Charles	62	m	w	ENGL	San Francisco	7-Wd San Francisco	81	210
BONGLEHM								
Fred	40	m	w	HANO	San Francisco	1-Wd San Francisco	79	7
BONGLET								
Cellestine	40	f	w	FRAN	San Francisco	San Francisco P O	85	831
BONHAM								
A J	32	m	w	OH	Nevada	Nevada Twp	75	316
Albert	45	m	w	ENGL	Napa	Napa Twp	75	34
Alla M	26	m	w	IA	Santa Barbara	Santa Barbara P O	87	470
B	50	m	w	TN	San Joaquin	Castoria Twp	86	5
Benjamin B	43	m	w	TN	Yolo	Putah Twp	93	515
Chas	41	m	w	NJ	Humboldt	Eureka Twp	72	271
Elisha	55	m	w	OH	Solano	Green Valley Twp	90	40
James	25	m	w	MA	Napa	Napa	75	26
William	35	m	w	PA	Placer	Bath P O	76	459
BONHEART								
Sarah	28	f	w	CANA	San Mateo	Pescadero P O	87	413
BONHOMNE								
Victoria	14	f	w	MEXI	San Francisco	San Francisco P O	80	399
BONHORST								
B	22	m	w	PRUS	San Francisco	San Francisco P O	85	797

© 2001 by Heritage Quest. All rights reserved.

Name	Age	S	R	B-PL	County	Locale	Series M593 Roll	Pg
BONI								
Jacob	26	m	w	SWIT	Marin	San Antonio Twp	74	60
BONIFACIO								
Juan	42	m	w	CA	Monterey	Monterey	74	367
BONIFIELD								
James	24	m	w	OH	San Francisco	7-Wd San Francisco	81	268
Maggie	17	f	w	NE	Solano	Benicia	90	16
Nannie	14	f	w	CA	Solano	Benicia	90	16
BONIG								
Henry	24	m	w	SHOL	Napa	Napa Twp	75	71
BONILLA								
Mariano	62	m	w	MEXI	San Luis Obispo	San Luis Obispo Tw	87	310
BONILLAS								
Maria	29	f	w	CA	Los Angeles	Santa Ana Twp	73	606
BONILLO								
Francisco	19	m	w	CA	Marin	San Rafael Twp	74	37
Patricio	66	m	m	MEXI	Santa Barbara	Santa Barbara P O	87	488
Ramon	31	m	w	CA	Santa Clara	Fremont Twp	88	49
Teodocio	26	m	w	MEXI	Santa Barbara	Santa Barbara P O	87	488
BONINA								
Jose	36	m	w	MEXI	Santa Clara	Almaden Twp	88	5
BONING								
Ida	15	f	w	CA	Alameda	Oakland	68	242
BONIO								
Joseph	30	m	w	ITAL	Amador	Volcano P O	69	384
BONIS								
Marcellin	42	m	w	FRAN	San Francisco	8-Wd San Francisco	82	386
Pierre	52	m	w	FRAN	San Francisco	San Francisco P O	83	169
BONITA								
Jose V	28	m	w	CHIL	Fresno	Millerton P O	72	165
Patrick	47	m	w	SWIT	Sacramento	Sutter Twp	77	389
BONITO								
Arratto	35	m	w	ITAL	Calaveras	Copperopolis P O	70	261
O	27	m	w	FRAN	San Joaquin	2-Wd Stockton	86	173
BONITOS								
Refufio	30	m	w	MEXI	Kern	Bakersfield P O	73	358
BONIVERT								
Peter J	30	m	w	BELG	Nevada	Grass Valley Twp	75	153
BONJARE								
Madalin	46	f	w	FRAN	Nevada	Nevada Twp	75	289
BONKOFSKY								
Augustus	28	m	w	PRUS	Tulare	Visalia	92	296
Henry	25	m	w	PRUS	Tulare	Visalia	92	296
BONLEY								
Robert T	49	m	w	ME	Placer	Bath P O	76	455
BONLUN								
W T	46	m	w	KY	Alameda	Oakland	68	188
BONMAN								
Frank	22	m	w	ME	San Francisco	San Francisco P O	83	80
BONN								
Henry	25	m	w	GERM	Sonoma	Washington Twp	91	471
Joseph	43	m	w	HANO	Calaveras	Copperopolis P O	70	264
BONNA								
Henri	36	m	w	FRAN	Calaveras	San Andreas P O	70	218
BONNARD								
Francis	53	m	w	SCOT	San Francisco	San Francisco P O	80	374
BONNASSIS								
Peter	38	m	w	FRAN	Calaveras	San Andreas P O	70	216
BONNEAU								
Abraham	50	m	w	CANA	Sonoma	Bodega Twp	91	252
Nargle	38	m	w	FRAN	Calaveras	San Andreas P O	70	151
BONNELL								
Allison	69	m	w	NJ	San Francisco	11-Wd San Francisc	84	565
Ben F	35	m	w	MO	Santa Barbara	San Buenaventura P	87	434
Edwin	32	m	w	OH	San Francisco	8-Wd San Francisco	82	325
John T	45	m	w	MA	San Francisco	8-Wd San Francisco	82	445
BONNER								
Alfred	28	m	w	NY	Mendocino	Gualala Twp	74	225
Chas E	36	m	w	IREL	San Francisco	1-Wd San Francisco	79	95
David	35	m	w	WALE	San Francisco	2-Wd San Francisco	79	175
Eph	56	m	w	NY	San Joaquin	2-Wd Stockton	86	173
Hattie E	20	f	w	SCOT	San Francisco	San Francisco P O	83	23
J D	50	m	w	KY	Mendocino	Calpella Twp	74	183
Jeshue	55	m	w	PA	Humboldt	Eureka Twp	72	269
John	63	m	w	SCOT	Santa Clara	2-Wd San Jose	88	332
John	30	m	w	NY	San Francisco	7-Wd San Francisco	81	214
John H	31	m	w	OH	Siskiyou	Surprise Valley Tw	89	642
John W	29	m	w	MO	San Francisco	7-Wd San Francisco	81	183
Joseph	65	m	w	PRUS	San Francisco	8-Wd San Francisco	82	353
L B	24	m	w	MO	San Francisco	7-Wd San Francisco	81	182
Mary	35	f	w	ENGL	Contra Costa	Martinez P O	71	443
Nancy	22	f	w	NV	San Francisco	San Francisco P O	83	278
Polle	20	m	w	FRAN	San Mateo	Schoolhouse Statio	87	332
Robert	45	m	w	SCOT	Alameda	Washington Twp	68	289
S L W	48	m	w	IL	Sacramento	4-Wd Sacramento	77	359
Saml	35	m	w	IL	Fresno	Millerton P O	72	158
Samuel	33	m	w	IL	Monterey	San Benito Twp	74	382
Stephen	29	m	w	NY	San Francisco	2-Wd San Francisco	79	174
T	35	m	w	GERM	Lake	Knoxville Mines	73	405
William	49	m	w	IL	Alameda	Eden Twp	68	70
William	43	m	w	ENGL	San Francisco	San Francisco P O	80	335
William	42	m	w	OH	Santa Clara	Milpitas Twp	88	112
William	33	m	w	ENGL	San Bernardino	San Bernardino Twp	78	448
William	23	m	w	HANO	Alameda	Brooklyn	68	33
Willis	48	m	w	KY	Mendocino	Calpella Twp	74	184
BONNERFIELD								
Cyrus	27	m	w	NY	Solano	Suisun Twp	90	111
BONNESS								
Antone	44	m	w	FRAN	Butte	Oregon Twp	70	133
Wm	62	m	w	ENGL	Butte	Kimshew Tpw	70	82
Wm	39	m	w	IL	Butte	Chico Twp	70	32
BONNET								
Fred	22	m	w	GERM	Solano	Vallejo	90	203
BONNETT								
Benjamin	60	m	w	VA	Mendocino	Anderson Twp	74	153
Laurence	20	m	w	FRAN	San Francisco	1-Wd San Francisco	79	81
Morris	44	m	w	SWIT	Marin	San Antonio Twp	74	61
Seely	36	m	w	OH	Contra Costa	Martinez Twp	71	349
BONNETTA								
Antonie	17	m	w	SWIT	Sonoma	Petaluma Twp	91	352
BONNETTI								
Albert	16	m	w	SWIT	Marin	Tomales Twp	74	77
Antone	24	m	w	SWIT	Marin	Nicasio Twp	74	17
Battiste	15	m	w	SWIT	Marin	San Antonio Twp	74	62
Luke	18	m	w	SWIT	Sonoma	Bodega Twp	91	260
Michl	45	m	w	SWIT	Marin	Nicasio Twp	74	14
Peter	18	m	w	SWIT	Marin	Nicasio Twp	74	14
BONNEY								
August	49	m	w	AUST	Calaveras	San Andreas P O	70	209
Bridget	39	f	w	IREL	San Francisco	1-Wd San Francisco	79	98
J A	28	m	w	ME	San Joaquin	Tulare Twp	86	255
James	40	m	w	ENGL	San Francisco	1-Wd San Francisco	79	59
John	44	m	w	ENGL	Nevada	Bloomfield Twp	75	98
Jos	40	m	w	CANA	Tehama	Paskenta Twp	92	166
Joseph	28	m	w	IREL	San Francisco	San Francisco P O	83	381
Surtin	47	m	w	FRAN	San Francisco	San Francisco P O	80	394
BONNEZ								
Conrad	30	m	w	HANO	San Francisco	San Francisco P O	83	30
BONNIFIELD								
Allen	25	m	w	VA	Santa Clara	San Jose Twp	88	183
Arnold	57	m	w	VA	Fresno	Millerton P O	72	193
Jesse	52	m	w	IN	Humboldt	Eel Rvr Twp	72	253
John	52	m	w	IREL	Humboldt	Pacific Twp	72	292
BONNY								
Alpha	36	m	w	ME	San Francisco	11-Wd San Francisc	84	582
George	40	m	w	MA	San Francisco	5-Wd San Francisco	81	27
James L	40	m	w	MO	Calaveras	Copperopolis P O	70	245
John	41	m	w	WALE	San Francisco	6-Wd San Francisco	81	97
BONO								
Wah	33	m	c	CHIN	Marin	San Rafael Twp	74	59
BONOIER								
J	47	m	w	FRAN	Sierra	Downieville Twp	89	518
BONOSOTO								
John	25	m	w	ITAL	Amador	Sutter Crk P O	69	413
BONOVIO								
Nicolas	27	m	w	ITAL	San Francisco	7-Wd San Francisco	81	245
BONQUICELL								
Edmond	50	m	w	FRAN	Marin	San Rafael Twp	74	32
BONSAL								
James	48	m	w	PA	Tulare	Tule Rvr Twp	92	260
BONSALL								
Elizabeth	24	f	w	NY	San Francisco	11-Wd San Francisc	84	704
BONSELL								
George	24	m	w	OH	Alameda	Washington Twp	68	295
BONSFIELD								
William	43	m	w	MA	Placer	Colfax P O	76	389
BONSON								
Jake	27	m	w	CT	San Joaquin	Tulare Twp	86	258
Joseph	53	m	w	CANA	Contra Costa	Martinez P O	71	398
BONSTRADE								
John	25	m	w	ENGL	Marin	Sausalito Twp	74	73
BONSWORT								
Nancy	43	f	w	KY	Colusa	Monroe Twp	71	313
BONTAGUE								
Edward	55	m	w	NY	Trinity	North Fork Twp	92	218
BONTAN								
Henry	41	m	w	FRAN	Nevada	Grass Valley Twp	75	219
BONTE								
Louis	40	m	w	HANO	Marin	Novato Twp	74	10
BONTELL								
Louisa	30	f	w	FRAN	San Francisco	8-Wd San Francisco	82	348
BONTELLO								
T	40	m	w	ITAL	Mariposa	Maxwell Crk P O	74	142
BONTEMOND								
H W	36	m	w	PRUS	Sutter	Nicolaus Twp	92	108
BONTEMPI								
Joseph	37	m	w	SWIT	Marin	San Rafael Twp	74	32
BONTEN								
Leonard	36	m	w	FRAN	Alameda	Brooklyn Twp	68	49
BONTERA								
Juan	60	m	w	MEXI	Los Angeles	Los Angeles	73	552
BONTERES								
Miguel	45	m	w	MEXI	Los Angeles	Los Angeles	73	514
BONTERRIOUS								
A	25	m	w	PERU	Sacramento	4-Wd Sacramento	77	321
BONTES								
P	60	m	w	FRAN	Calaveras	Copperopolis P O	70	236
BONTICE								
J	48	m	w	NY	Alameda	Murray Twp	68	122
BONTILLA								
A	40	m	w	FRAN	San Francisco	8-Wd San Francisco	82	373
BONTKLE								
Wm	54	m	w	NH	San Francisco	San Francisco P O	83	55

© 2001 by Heritage Quest. All rights reserved.

Name	Age	S	R	B-PL	County	Locale	Series M593 Roll	Pg
BONTZ								
Leon	24	m	w	FRAN	San Francisco	San Francisco P O	80	351
BONUM								
J H	39	m	w	IL	Amador	Ione City P O	69	370
BONVIER								
Eustache	46	m	w	PA	Plumas	Quartz Twp	77	40
BONYARD								
Walter	35	m	w	ENGL	Santa Clara	2-Wd San Jose	88	329
BOO								
Ah	40	m	c	CHIN	San Francisco	San Francisco P O	83	285
Ah	35	m	c	CHIN	Alameda	Oakland	68	157
Ah	31	m	c	CHIN	San Francisco	11-Wd San Francisc	84	546
Ah	30	m	c	CHIN	Nevada	Bridgeport Twp	75	110
Ah	29	m	c	CHIN	Sierra	Alleghany & Forest	89	535
Ah	28	m	c	CHIN	San Francisco	6-Wd San Francisco	81	103
Ah	27	m	c	CHIN	San Francisco	San Francisco P O	80	500
Ah	27	m	c	CHIN	San Francisco	6-Wd San Francisco	81	61
Ah	27	m	c	CHIN	Sierra	Lincoln Twp	89	549
Ah	26	m	c	CHIN	Sierra	Forest Twp	89	532
Ah	26	m	c	CHIN	Solano	Suisun Twp	90	105
Ah	19	m	c	CHIN	Alameda	Washington Twp	68	268
Bam	28	m	c	CHIN	Placer	Lincoln P O	76	493
Jam	26	m	c	CHIN	San Mateo	Schoolhouse Statio	87	335
BOOBAR								
Edward	52	m	w	ME	San Francisco	11-Wd San Francisc	84	428
James	21	m	w	ME	San Francisco	7-Wd San Francisco	81	245
BOOBE								
John	40	m	w	PA	Tulare	Visalia	92	297
BOOCHRA								
Fidella	35	m	w	FRAN	Butte	Bidwell Twp	70	3
BOODER								
Frank	25	m	w	CANA	Inyo	Bishop Crk Twp	73	311
BOODY								
Daniel	40	m	w	VT	Nevada	Eureka Twp	75	132
P	36	m	w	NY	Lassen	Janesville Twp	73	433
R	53	f	w	NY	Lassen	Janesville Twp	73	431
BOOG								
John	35	m	w	SCOT	Yolo	Cache Crk Twp	93	422
BOOGAR								
E A	26	m	w	CANA	Sacramento	3-Wd Sacramento	77	298
BOOGER								
Phillip	40	m	w	PRUS	Alameda	Oakland	68	184
BOOHAN								
Patrick	40	m	w	IREL	San Francisco	San Francisco P O	85	835
Wm	34	m	w	IREL	Solano	Vallejo	90	215
BOOHER								
David	36	m	w	VA	Colusa	Colusa Twp	71	277
Isaac	29	m	w	OH	Colusa	Grand Island Twp	71	302
BOOK								
Ah	34	m	c	CHIN	El Dorado	Placerville	72	124
Ah	25	m	c	CHIN	San Mateo	Schoolhouse Statio	87	334
George	45	m	w	MO	Stanislaus	Empire Twp	92	64
Jane	33	f	w	VA	San Joaquin	1-Wd Stockton	86	127
BOOKE								
John F	59	m	w	GA	Alameda	Eden Twp	68	72
BOOKEN								
Christ	35	m	w	WURT	Alameda	Eden Twp	68	66
John	40	m	w	WURT	Alameda	Hayward	68	74
BOOKENKASHEN								
A	25	m	w	PRUS	San Francisco	6-Wd San Francisco	81	101
BOOKER								
Dick	31	m	i	CA	Fresno	Kings Rvr P O	72	214
Geo	18	m	w	ME	San Francisco	7-Wd San Francisco	81	235
Helen	45	f	w	ME	San Francisco	7-Wd San Francisco	81	235
Helen E	47	f	w	ME	San Francisco	San Francisco P O	83	137
James	38	m	w	NC	Napa	Napa	75	10
John H	30	m	w	OH	San Bernardino	San Bernardino Twp	78	453
Thos H	53	m	w	IN	Fresno	Kings Rvr P O	72	214
W N	45	m	w	VA	Tuolumne	Sonora P O	93	313
William W	35	m	w	AL	Santa Clara	Redwood Twp	88	118
Wm L	45	m	w	ENGL	San Francisco	3-Wd San Francisco	79	327
BOOKINE								
John	32	m	w	PA	Napa	Yountville Twp	75	85
BOOKMAN								
Jesse	44	m	w	PA	Sacramento	American Twp	77	64
Wm	49	m	w	NY	San Joaquin	Tulare Twp	86	257
BOOKMEYER								
Otto W	33	m	w	SHOL	San Francisco	3-Wd San Francisco	79	287
BOOKSIN								
Henry	43	m	w	HESS	Colusa	Colusa Twp	71	275
BOOKSTAVER								
Samuel	51	m	w	NY	San Francisco	San Francisco P O	80	395
BOOL								
Frank	35	m	w	ENGL	Yuba	Rose Bar Twp	93	656
BOOLE								
George	27	m	w	CANA	San Francisco	San Francisco P O	83	296
Wm	28	m	w	CANA	San Francisco	7-Wd San Francisco	81	277
BOOLLEY								
Pat	35	m	w	MA	Alameda	Oakland	68	203
BOOLYONG								
Louis	38	m	w	FRAN	Sacramento	1-Wd Sacramento	77	180
BOOM								
James	37	m	b	NC	San Francisco	San Francisco P O	80	426
BOOMAN								
Joseph	29	m	w	SWIT	San Francisco	San Francisco P O	85	753
BOOMANN								
George	51	m	w	FRAN	San Francisco	San Francisco P O	83	135

Name	Age	S	R	B-PL	County	Locale	Series M593 Roll	Pg
BOOMER								
Aaron	25	m	w	CANA	Santa Cruz	Soquel Twp	89	445
George	34	m	w	CANA	Santa Cruz	Santa Cruz	89	406
George	26	m	w	CANA	Santa Cruz	Soquel Twp	89	445
George	26	m	w	CANA	Santa Cruz	Santa Cruz	89	432
Harvey	22	m	w	CANA	Santa Cruz	Soquel Twp	89	445
Henry	24	m	w	CANA	San Francisco	11-Wd San Francisc	84	646
W	34	m	w	KY	Lake	Lower Lake	73	419
BOOMERSHINE								
A B	35	m	w	IREL	Tuolumne	Chinese Camp P O	93	387
BOOMHOW								
Alias	32	m	w	GA	San Mateo	Woodside P O	87	384
BOON								
Ah	39	m	c	CHIN	Tuolumne	Chinese Camp P O	93	388
Ah	39	m	c	CHIN	Placer	Pino Twp	76	471
Ah	35	m	c	CHIN	Mariposa	Mariposa P O	74	114
Ah	31	m	c	CHIN	Placer	Newcastle Twp	76	479
Ah	30	m	c	CHIN	Sacramento	American Twp	77	68
Ah	28	m	c	CHIN	San Francisco	6-Wd San Francisco	81	55
Ah	26	m	c	CHIN	Amador	Ione City P O	69	371
Ah	20	m	c	CHIN	Plumas	Plumas Twp	77	31
Charles	64	m	w	ME	San Mateo	Schoolhouse Statio	87	343
D H	16	m	w	CA	Amador	Sutter Crk P O	69	397
Hong	54	m	c	CHIN	Plumas	Seneca Twp	77	48
J	28	m	w	LA	San Joaquin	2-Wd Stockton	86	162
Jacob	64	m	w	OH	Santa Clara	Fremont Twp	88	45
John	32	m	w	US	San Joaquin	2-Wd Stockton	86	171
John W	47	m	w	OH	Amador	Sutter Crk P O	69	405
Josiah	62	m	w	NJ	Calaveras	San Andreas P O	70	168
Pollie	21	f	w	ENGL	San Francisco	8-Wd San Francisco	82	361
Richard	38	m	w	KY	Mariposa	Mariposa P O	74	129
Samuel	23	m	b	NC	Mendocino	Anderson Twp	74	153
Sing	42	m	c	CHIN	San Francisco	6-Wd San Francisco	81	48
William D	47	m	w	OH	Santa Clara	Santa Clara Twp	88	168
William W	42	m	w	NC	Mendocino	Anderson Twp	74	151
BOOND								
Marion	32	m	w	NH	Colusa	Monroe Twp	71	314
BOONE								
Edward	37	m	w	MO	Colusa	Colusa Twp	71	287
J T	47	m	w	PA	Lake	Lower Lake	73	415
James	47	m	w	MA	San Joaquin	Dent Twp	86	25
James O	42	m	w	MO	Contra Costa	Martinez P O	71	382
Joel H	31	m	w	MO	Contra Costa	Martinez P O	71	382
John	28	m	w	IA	San Francisco	11-Wd San Francisc	84	581
M E	20	m	w	CA	Amador	Drytown P O	69	415
Perry	54	m	m	MD	San Francisco	2-Wd San Francisco	79	257
T B	40	m	w	MD	Tuolumne	Chinese Camp P O	93	385
Wellington T	39	m	w	MO	Contra Costa	Martinez P O	71	382
William	43	m	w	KY	Sacramento	2-Wd Sacramento	77	231
William	39	m	w	FRAN	San Francisco	2-Wd San Francisco	79	213
BOONEY								
F	38	m	w	ENGL	Sierra	Lincoln Twp	89	546
Thomas	26	m	w	IREL	San Francisco	San Francisco P O	85	744
BOONGENDER								
Jacob	29	m	w	SWED	San Mateo	Schoolhouse Statio	87	333
BOONHOMER								
Elias	30	m	w	NY	Monterey	San Juan Twp	74	398
BOONING								
John	24	m	w	HANO	San Francisco	7-Wd San Francisco	81	255
BOONSEN								
Hans	62	m	w	DENM	Sacramento	3-Wd Sacramento	77	308
BOOP								
John D	38	m	w	PA	San Francisco	San Francisco P O	83	200
Maggie	5	f	w	CA	San Francisco	San Francisco P O	83	200
BOOR								
Frank	44	m	w	HESS	Calaveras	San Andreas P O	70	159
BOORDEAUX								
Nelson	22	m	w	CANA	Yolo	Cache Crk Twp	93	456
BOOREM								
Thomas	42	m	w	NY	San Francisco	San Francisco P O	83	53
BOORMAN								
Louisa	14	f	w	CA	Yuba	Marysville	93	609
Maggie	11	f	w	CA	Yuba	Marysville	93	609
BOORMEISTER								
Amelia	25	f	w	HANO	Santa Cruz	Santa Cruz	89	410
BOOS								
Frank	45	m	w	BADE	San Mateo	Woodside P O	87	387
BOOSANASKI								
Zanah	30	m	w	ITAL	Amador	Sutter Crk P O	69	412
BOOSE								
Sohil	32	m	w	CANA	Solano	Vallejo	90	143
BOOSH								
T J	39	m	w	GA	San Joaquin	Douglas Twp	86	47
BOOSS								
Wilhelm	25	m	w	SWED	Sacramento	3-Wd Sacramento	77	287
BOOSTAMAT								
Julia	36	m	w	MEXI	Napa	Napa	75	55
BOOT								
Chong	34	m	c	CHIN	San Francisco	6-Wd San Francisco	81	40
Christene	18	f	w	BADE	Alameda	Alameda	68	5
BOOTGA								
James	42	m	w	SWIT	Klamath	Orleans Twp	73	379
BOOTH								
Ada T	23	f	w	ME	San Francisco	6-Wd San Francisco	81	45
Adam	56	m	w	ENGL	San Francisco	11-Wd San Francisc	84	555
Alice	18	f	w	SCOT	San Francisco	2-Wd San Francisco	79	278
Alma	30	m	w	CT	Solano	Benicia	90	5

© 2001 by Heritage Quest. All rights reserved.

Name	Age	S	R	B-PL	County	Locale	Series M593 Roll	Pg
Ann	29	f	w	IREL	Colusa	Colusa	71	294
Arthur	50	m	w	NC	Placer	Bath P O	76	424
Arthur A	22	m	w	MO	San Francisco	1-Wd San Francisco	79	69
Bertha	33	f	w	IREL	San Francisco	8-Wd San Francisco	82	452
Bessey	20	f	w	ENGL	Santa Clara	Redwood Twp	88	129
Chas	36	m	w	ME	Humboldt	Arcata Twp	72	232
Collins	55	m	b	VA	El Dorado	Mud Springs Twp	72	90
Ed	22	m	b	WIND	San Joaquin	2-Wd Stockton	86	163
Edward	46	m	w	MO	Nevada	Eureka Twp	75	135
Edward	36	m	w	ENGL	Placer	Roseville P O	76	349
Elija	55	m	w	OH	Humboldt	Mattole Twp	72	286
Elijah	40	m	b	MD	Nevada	Nevada Twp	75	281
Elijah	33	m	w	KY	Tulare	Tule Rvr Twp	92	264
Elisha	28	m	w	MI	San Francisco	San Francisco P O	85	720
Eliza	21	f	b	MD	Nevada	Nevada Twp	75	287
Frances	22	f	w	MA	San Francisco	San Francisco P O	80	459
Garrett	42	m	w	KY	Placer	Bath P O	76	455
Geo	42	m	b	MD	Sacramento	4-Wd Sacramento	77	329
George	39	m	w	IREL	Humboldt	Eureka Twp	72	278
George	32	m	w	MD	San Francisco	3-Wd San Francisco	79	312
George	28	m	w	MA	San Francisco	San Francisco P O	83	230
Henry	24	m	w	IREL	Solano	Silveyville Twp	90	89
Henry	23	m	w	OH	Solano	Silveyville Twp	90	72
Hiram	23	m	w	IREL	Solano	Tremont Twp	90	28
Hosea	73	m	w	NH	San Francisco	11-Wd San Francisc	84	678
Hy J	40	m	w	ENGL	San Francisco	San Francisco P O	83	111
J	49	m	w	IREL	Sierra	Alleghany & Forest	89	535
J H B	27	m	w	MO	Sierra	Downieville Twp	89	516
James	22	m	w	ENGL	San Francisco	San Francisco P O	85	747
James	22	m	w	IREL	Stanislaus	Emory Twp	92	25
James R	48	m	w	VA	Solano	Suisun Twp	90	115
Jesse	58	m	w	NY	Sonoma	Santa Rosa	91	415
John	31	m	w	MO	Solano	Silveyville Twp	90	83
John W	35	m	w	US	Nevada	Grass Valley Twp	75	228
Jonathan	59	m	w	ENGL	Santa Clara	Redwood Twp	88	129
Joseph	40	m	w	DE	San Francisco	San Francisco P O	83	258
L A	55	m	w	NY	Alameda	Oakland	68	235
Laura	15	f	w	MA	San Francisco	5-Wd San Francisco	81	26
Louis M	61	m	w	NY	Stanislaus	Buena Vista Twp	92	12
M G	42	m	w	NH	Yuba	East Bear Rvr Twp	93	542
Mary	62	f	m	MD	San Francisco	6-Wd San Francisco	81	128
Mary	60	f	m	MD	San Francisco	2-Wd San Francisco	79	154
Mary A	44	f	b	MD	Nevada	Nevada Twp	75	287
Michael	32	m	w	ME	San Francisco	8-Wd San Francisco	82	357
Minor	35	f	w	VA	Napa	Napa Twp	75	30
Minor	23	m	w	IL	Stanislaus	North Twp	92	69
Nate	30	m	w	ENGL	San Joaquin	3-Wd Stockton	86	237
Nathan B	60	m	w	CT	Los Angeles	El Monte Twp	73	463
Newton	39	m	w	IN	San Francisco	San Francisco P O	80	486
Reuben H	42	m	w	CT	Shasta	Shasta P O	89	461
Robert	40	m	w	AUSL	San Francisco	7-Wd San Francisco	81	185
Robert	37	m	w	IREL	San Francisco	11-Wd San Francisc	84	521
Robert	30	m	w	NY	San Mateo	Woodside P O	87	380
Samuel	38	m	w	ENGL	San Francisco	11-Wd San Francisc	84	605
Samuel	37	m	w	ENGL	Yolo	Grafton Twp	93	497
Sarah	37	f	w	NY	San Joaquin	3-Wd Stockton	86	242
Sarah E	32	f	w	MO	Placer	Bath P O	76	455
Scott J	35	m	w	IA	San Francisco	7-Wd San Francisco	81	226
Thomas	35	m	w	ENGL	Yuba	Rose Bar Twp	93	654
Thomas	24	m	w	OH	Solano	Montezuma Twp	90	69
Thomas	24	m	w	IREL	Alameda	Murray Twp	68	100
Thos	39	m	w	VA	Solano	Vallejo	90	146
W	38	m	w	IL	Yuba	Marysville	93	608
W H	33	m	w	IREL	Sierra	Forest Twp	89	529
Wells O	19	m	w	NY	Sonoma	Analy Twp	91	218
William	40	m	w	IREL	Siskiyou	Yreka Twp	89	666
William	36	m	w	OH	Solano	Denverton Twp	90	25
William	25	m	w	GERM	San Luis Obispo	Salinas Twp	87	293
William	21	m	w	OH	Solano	Tremont Twp	90	31
Wm	49	m	w	ENGL	San Francisco	7-Wd San Francisco	81	232
Wm	33	m	w	IREL	San Francisco	1-Wd San Francisco	79	82
Y	25	m	w	CT	Alameda	Oakland	68	222
BOOTHBY								
Adolf F	33	m	w	HANO	San Francisco	3-Wd San Francisco	79	293
August	36	m	w	HAMB	Mendocino	Gualala Twp	74	226
Moses	43	m	w	ME	Contra Costa	Martinez P O	71	412
William L	37	m	w	ME	San Francisco	8-Wd San Francisco	82	479
BOOTHE								
Poppelston	41	m	w	NC	Yuba	Rose Bar Twp	93	653
BOOTHMAN								
Geo	24	m	w	NY	Solano	Vallejo	90	162
BOOTHOLD								
Amelia	20	f	w	PRUS	San Mateo	Searsville P O	87	383
BOOTHROD								
Thos	42	m	w	ENGL	Sacramento	Sutter Twp	77	390
BOOTS								
Albert W	28	m	w	OH	Santa Clara	Santa Clara Twp	88	167
Jesse	52	m	w	VA	Nevada	Washington Twp	75	341
William	45	m	w	OH	Santa Clara	Alviso Twp	88	28
BOOTZ								
Adam	40	m	w	PRUS	San Francisco	11-Wd San Francisc	84	636
BOOVORX								
Alex	36	m	w	MA	Alameda	Oakland	68	265
BOOW								
Loon	40	m	c	CHIN	San Mateo	San Mateo P O	87	351
BOOY								
Chas	23	m	w	ITAL	Solano	Vallejo	90	213
Daniel	38	m	w	MO	Mendocino	Anderson Twp	74	155
BOOYER								
Maria	65	f	w	CANA	Sacramento	4-Wd Sacramento	77	352
BOPE								
Ada	17	f	w	CA	Santa Clara	2-Wd San Jose	88	337
BOPES								
Eliza	13	f	w	IA	Sacramento	4-Wd Sacramento	77	364
BOPP								
Charles F	35	m	w	WURT	Colusa	Colusa Twp	71	275
John	42	m	w	HOLL	San Francisco	7-Wd San Francisco	81	265
BOQUET								
Fredk	45	m	w	FRAN	Shasta	Horsetown P O	89	505
John	34	m	w	FRAN	San Francisco	San Francisco P O	80	345
BOQUIER								
Peter	27	m	w	IL	Sacramento	San Joaquin Twp	77	397
BOQUIST								
Charles V	35	m	w	SWED	Sonoma	Petaluma Twp	91	314
BORAH								
Jacob	48	m	w	KY	Stanislaus	Empire Twp	92	55
Nathaniel	44	m	w	IL	Placer	Alta P O	76	419
BORAS								
Jesus	27	m	i	MEXI	Inyo	Cerro Gordo Twp	73	322
John	27	m	w	IREL	Solano	Rio Vista Twp	90	59
BORBON								
Giuseppe	40	m	w	ITAL	Santa Barbara	Santa Barbara P O	87	456
BORBORN								
Alphonso	43	m	w	FRAN	San Francisco	1-Wd San Francisco	79	50
BORCAS								
Ramon	29	m	w	MEXI	Santa Clara	Fremont Twp	88	51
BORCE								
Peter	38	m	w	FRAN	Santa Clara	1-Wd San Jose	88	267
BORCHA								
Nicholas	40	m	w	HANO	San Francisco	2-Wd San Francisco	79	143
BORCHARD								
Charles	38	m	w	PRUS	San Francisco	6-Wd San Francisco	81	127
Chas	40	m	w	PRUS	San Francisco	1-Wd San Francisco	79	115
John E	22	m	w	IA	Santa Barbara	San Buenaventura P	87	423
Mary	28	f	w	MI	San Francisco	1-Wd San Francisco	79	115
BORCHARDT								
Herman	37	m	w	PRUS	San Francisco	San Francisco P O	83	379
BORCHEGROIN								
Gaston	46	m	w	FRAN	Amador	Ione City P O	69	359
BORCHELD								
John	47	m	w	BADE	San Francisco	2-Wd San Francisco	79	259
BORCHERS								
Fabian	30	m	w	HANO	San Francisco	1-Wd San Francisco	79	78
Henry	18	m	w	PRUS	San Francisco	San Francisco P O	80	469
Margaret	20	f	w	BAVA	San Francisco	8-Wd San Francisco	82	474
Wm	56	m	w	MECK	Sacramento	3-Wd Sacramento	77	260
Wm	39	m	w	PRUS	San Francisco	7-Wd San Francisco	81	264
BORCKEUS								
Jno H	33	m	w	HAMB	San Francisco	San Francisco P O	83	121
BORCO								
Dominick	38	m	w	ITAL	El Dorado	Placerville	72	109
BORCOVICH								
John	33	m	w	AUST	San Francisco	1-Wd San Francisco	79	105
BORD								
Harry	25	m	w	IREL	Solano	Silveyville Twp	90	79
BORDA								
Catherin	21	f	w	FRAN	San Francisco	11-Wd San Francisc	84	449
Mary	17	f	w	PRUS	San Joaquin	2-Wd Stockton	86	185
BORDAN								
James	46	m	w	NY	San Francisco	1-Wd San Francisco	79	125
Patrick	30	m	w	IREL	San Francisco	11-Wd San Francisc	84	697
BORDAT								
Silas	28	m	w	FRAN	San Francisco	6-Wd San Francisco	81	90
BORDDONA								
Alfredo	40	m	w	FRAN	Monterey	Monterey	74	366
BORDE								
Antonette	47	f	w	FRAN	San Francisco	2-Wd San Francisco	79	180
Frederick	38	m	w	PRUS	San Francisco	2-Wd San Francisco	79	169
Julian	40	f	w	FRAN	San Francisco	San Francisco P O	80	347
BORDEAUX								
Victor	39	m	w	FRAN	San Francisco	6-Wd San Francisco	81	41
BORDEAX								
Jean	47	m	w	FRAN	San Francisco	1-Wd San Francisco	79	46
BORDELE								
Charles	30	m	w	MO	Alameda	Oakland	68	264
BORDEN								
Anne E	25	f	w	CANA	El Dorado	Placerville Twp	72	95
B A	32	m	w	OH	Amador	Ione City P O	69	365
Burney	35	m	w	NY	Sacramento	Dry Crk Twp	77	99
Ellen	15	f	w	CA	Solano	Benicia	90	16
F G	15	m	w	CA	Solano	Benicia	90	20
George R	54	m	w	NY	San Mateo	Half Moon Bay P O	87	402
H M	7	f	w	CA	Solano	Vallejo	90	172
Henry	26	m	w	CANA	Plumas	Plumas Twp	77	28
Henry W	21	m	w	IN	Los Angeles	Santa Ana Twp	73	608
Joseph	64	m	w	NC	Fresno	Millerton P O	72	152
Joseph	26	m	w	ENGL	Amador	Sutter Crk P O	69	412
Joseph Jr	40	m	w	NC	Fresno	Millerton P O	72	151
Michael	40	m	w	ENGL	San Francisco	San Francisco P O	83	419
Oscar H	49	m	w	KY	Los Angeles	Santa Ana Twp	73	608
W	36	m	w	NY	Solano	Vallejo	90	172
William	41	m	w	MD	Napa	Napa	75	23
BORDENAC								
Pierre	42	m	w	FRAN	San Francisco	San Francisco P O	80	476

© 2001 by Heritage Quest. All rights reserved.

Series M593

Name	Age	S	R	B-PL	County	Locale	Roll	Pg
BORDER								
J A	30	m	w	NY	Solano	Vallejo	90	209
Jacob	40	m	w	PRUS	San Francisco	5-Wd San Francisco	81	18
John	40	m	w	FRAN	Trinity	North Fork Twp	92	220
BORDERE								
Esta	45	f	w	SAME	San Joaquin	2-Wd Stockton	86	174
John	68	m	w	FRAN	Yuba	Rose Bar Twp	93	655
BORDGES								
Edward	65	m	w	KY	Sacramento	Georgianna Twp	77	128
BORDLEY								
Perry	86	m	b	MD	Nevada	Nevada Twp	75	282
BORDMAN								
I H	35	m	w	CT	San Joaquin	Douglas Twp	86	45
Maria	28	f	w	MI	Yolo	Cottonwood Twp	93	467
BORDO								
Henry	21	m	w	CANA	El Dorado	Mud Springs Twp	72	75
BORDON								
Henry	38	m	w	HDAR	Calaveras	San Andreas P O	70	178
Jacob	48	m	w	HDAR	Calaveras	San Andreas P O	70	178
BORDUE								
Chas	30	m	w	ENGL	Sacramento	4-Wd Sacramento	77	326
BORDWELL								
Chester	58	m	w	NY	Plumas	Goodwin Twp	77	5
George	48	m	w	NY	San Francisco	San Francisco P O	83	57
H F W	40	m	w	NY	San Francisco	San Francisco P O	83	60
BORE								
Chas	14	m	w	HANO	Solano	Vallejo	90	181
Tolman	36	m	w	NORW	San Francisco	7-Wd San Francisco	81	274
BOREAUGARD								
Nap	30	m	w	CANA	San Francisco	11-Wd San Francisc	84	690
BOREE								
W R	33	m	w	VT	San Francisco	3-Wd San Francisco	79	317
BOREL								
Alfred	42	m	w	SWIT	San Francisco	6-Wd San Francisco	81	96
Florentin	37	m	w	FRAN	Butte	Bidwell Twp	70	3
BORELAND								
F W	32	m	w	IREL	San Joaquin	2-Wd Stockton	86	163
BORELLI								
Santi	33	m	w	ITAL	Solano	Benicia	90	12
BOREMAN								
Albert	40	m	w	HDAR	San Diego	Fort Yuma Dist	78	463
BOREMASTER								
Fred	45	m	w	MECK	San Francisco	6-Wd San Francisco	81	113
BOREN								
Absolem	38	m	w	IN	Yolo	Cache Crk Twp	93	419
Ally D	52	m	w	IL	San Bernardino	San Bernardino Twp	78	421
B	33	m	w	MO	San Joaquin	Douglas Twp	86	41
Beverly	46	m	w	IL	San Bernardino	San Bernardino Twp	78	429
Hiram	30	m	w	MO	San Bernardino	San Bernardino Twp	78	435
Hiram L	29	m	w	IL	San Bernardino	San Bernardino Twp	78	448
BORER								
Jno	49	m	w	AR	Sonoma	Santa Rosa	91	417
John	20	m	w	MO	Contra Costa	Martinez P O	71	369
BORES								
George W	40	m	w	VA	Colusa	Spring Valley Twp	71	337
Thomas	47	m	w	VA	Colusa	Spring Valley Twp	71	337
BORG								
Peter	39	m	w	PRUS	San Francisco	2-Wd San Francisco	79	214
BORGA								
Louis	20	m	w	ITAL	Amador	Volcano P O	69	378
BORGAN								
Peter	24	m	w	PORT	Santa Clara	San Jose Twp	88	193
BORGAS								
Antonio	19	m	w	PORT	Santa Clara	Milpitas Twp	88	110
BORGEA								
Antonio	42	m	w	ITAL	San Mateo	Menlo Park P O	87	377
BORGEN								
Neil	27	m	w	SWED	San Francisco	6-Wd San Francisco	81	114
BORGENS								
Joseph	45	m	w	ENGL	San Francisco	1-Wd San Francisco	79	49
BORGER								
Alfred N	28	m	w	CANA	San Mateo	Woodside P O	87	384
Christopher	30	m	w	PRUS	San Francisco	San Francisco P O	83	116
BORGES								
J S	30	m	w	PORT	Sierra	Sears Twp	89	560
Manuel	44	m	w	PORT	Alameda	Hayward	68	76
Mary	21	f	w	NY	San Joaquin	2-Wd Stockton	86	161
BORGEVA								
Lewis	28	m	i	MEXI	Inyo	Cerro Gordo Twp	73	319
BORGEWOOD								
Ebenizer B	30	m	w	OH	Calaveras	San Andreas P O	70	213
BORGIA								
Charles	19	m	w	ITAL	San Francisco	2-Wd San Francisco	79	185
BORGIAS								
Louis	53	m	w	ITAL	San Francisco	San Francisco P O	80	426
BORGIER								
Chas D	59	m	w	MO	San Francisco	6-Wd San Francisco	81	93
BORGLER								
Louisa	61	f	w	BAVA	San Francisco	8-Wd San Francisco	82	416
BORGMAN								
John	40	m	w	SWED	Calaveras	San Andreas P O	70	219
BORGNER								
Harry	36	m	w	HANO	Marin	Sausalito Twp	74	67
BORGSTROM								
Charles	20	m	w	SWED	San Francisco	San Francisco P O	80	428
BORGUS								
William	21	m	w	PRUS	San Francisco	8-Wd San Francisco	82	384
BORHA								
Nelly	24	f	w	IREL	San Joaquin	1-Wd Stockton	86	134
BORHAM								
Barney	23	m	w	IREL	Solano	Vallejo	90	216
BORHWELL								
John	29	m	w	IREL	Santa Cruz	Pajaro Twp	89	346
BORIES								
Benjm	25	m	w	NJ	San Francisco	8-Wd San Francisco	82	360
BORILA								
Chas	30	m	w	DENM	Alameda	Oakland	68	219
BORILE								
Joseph	27	m	w	RUSS	Mendocino	Casper & Big Rvr	74	163
BORIN								
James	66	m	w	IREL	Mendocino	Big Rvr Twp	74	161
BORINE								
Giuseppe	21	m	w	ITAL	San Francisco	11-Wd San Francisc	84	594
BORING								
Isaac C	38	m	w	KY	Plumas	Plumas Twp	77	26
Samuel W	45	m	w	TN	Santa Clara	2-Wd San Jose	88	322
BORINI								
Giuseppe	45	m	w	ITAL	San Francisco	11-Wd San Francisc	84	594
Giuseppe	27	m	w	ITAL	San Francisco	11-Wd San Francisc	84	594
BORIS								
Hippolite	49	m	w	FRAN	Plumas	Goodwin Twp	77	6
Jacob	30	m	m	DE	San Francisco	2-Wd San Francisco	79	212
BORK								
Charles	26	m	w	GERM	Yolo	Cache Crk Twp	93	453
Peter	23	m	w	IREL	Colusa	Monroe Twp	71	314
BORKE								
L	56	m	w	IREL	Sierra	Lincoln Twp	89	546
BORKHALDER								
Lucitta	38	f	w	BAVA	San Francisco	2-Wd San Francisco	79	159
BORKHEIM								
Henry	44	m	w	PRUS	San Francisco	8-Wd San Francisco	82	382
BORKUS								
Orsota	104	f	w	MEXI	Napa	Napa	75	55
BORL								
Jacob	35	m	w	MEXI	San Joaquin	2-Wd Stockton	86	173
John	69	m	w	FRAN	San Francisco	2-Wd San Francisco	79	145
BORLAN								
M A	48	f	w	IREL	San Joaquin	2-Wd Stockton	86	172
P M	48	m	w	IREL	Sacramento	1-Wd Sacramento	77	203
BORLAND								
Alx	51	m	w	SCOT	El Dorado	Coloma Twp	72	8
James	44	m	w	SCOT	Placer	Bath P O	76	428
John	39	m	w	CANA	Tehama	Merrill	92	197
Lee	32	m	w	PA	Sonoma	Petaluma Twp	91	322
Lewis	45	m	w	ENGL	San Francisco	3-Wd San Francisco	79	297
Saml H	25	m	w	TX	San Francisco	San Francisco P O	83	30
BORLE								
Gustavus	27	m	w	NY	San Francisco	San Francisco P O	83	326
Louis	34	m	w	NY	San Francisco	San Francisco P O	83	326
BORLEY								
Wm	45	m	w	ENGL	Plumas	Washington Twp	77	52
BORLIS								
Delfina	18	f	w	CA	Los Angeles	Los Angeles	73	558
BORLY								
William	4	m	w	NY	Alameda	Oakland	68	186
BORMANN								
Lewis	25	m	w	HANO	San Francisco	San Francisco P O	83	156
BORMER								
Wm	20	m	w	NY	San Joaquin	Elliott Twp	86	72
BORMESTER								
Henry	30	m	w	SHOL	Napa	Napa Twp	75	29
BORN								
Andrew	42	m	b	MD	San Francisco	11-Wd San Francisc	84	509
John	43	m	w	SWIT	Sonoma	Healdsburg & Mendo	91	277
Sarah	15	f	w	CA	Sonoma	Petaluma Twp	91	312
BORNA								
James	21	m	w	ITAL	Amador	Sutter Crk P O	69	399
BORNAS								
Phillippa	50	m	w	MEXI	El Dorado	Mud Springs Twp	72	76
BORNE								
Henry	30	m	w	NY	Solano	Vacaville Twp	90	124
BORNEMAN								
L	44	m	w	BRUN	El Dorado	Kelsey Twp	72	58
BORNEMANN								
Francis	48	m	w	HANO	San Francisco	11-Wd San Francisc	84	539
BORNEOVER								
Antone	21	m	w	ITAL	San Mateo	San Mateo P O	87	358
Joseph	22	m	w	ITAL	San Mateo	San Mateo P O	87	358
BORNHAM								
H J	40	m	w	MO	San Joaquin	Oneal Twp	86	113
BORNHEIMER								
F	46	m	w	PRUS	San Francisco	San Francisco P O	85	850
BORNHILL								
Agnes	25	f	w	ENGL	San Francisco	San Francisco P O	83	206
BORNHORD								
F	41	m	w	FRAN	Sierra	Alleghany & Forest	89	535
BORNOMON								
Salvador	9	m	w	MEXI	Santa Clara	2-Wd San Jose	88	309
BORNON								
Charles	34	m	w	BAVA	San Francisco	8-Wd San Francisco	82	390
BORNS								
Wm	11	m	w	CA	Solano	Benicia	90	21
BORNSEH								
?dier	28	m	w	BRUN	Sonoma	Petaluma Twp	91	365

© 2001 by Heritage Quest. All rights reserved.

Series M593

Name	Age	S	R	B-PL	County	Locale	Roll	Pg
BORNSTEIN								
Charles	21	m	w	MA	Contra Costa	Martinez P O	71	383
Herman	44	m	w	PRUS	San Mateo	Redwood Twp	87	368
Julius	53	m	w	PRUS	San Francisco	8-Wd San Francisco	82	405
BORNSTIEN								
Isaac N	29	m	w	PRUS	San Francisco	6-Wd San Francisco	81	84
S	53	m	w	PRUS	Sierra	Lincoln Twp	89	552
BORNT								
Ligimione	64	m	w	NY	San Francisco	11-Wd San Francisc	84	683
BORO								
John	55	m	w	NCOD	Sacramento	Cosumnes Twp	77	89
BOROLI								
Herman	44	m	w	MEXI	Tuolumne	Columbia P O	93	354
BOROLLIA								
Antonio	30	m	w	CA	Santa Barbara	Santa Maria P O	87	514
BOROMON								
Louis	27	m	w	SWED	San Diego	Warners Rancho Dis	78	528
BORONDA								
Agness	12	f	w	CA	Monterey	Castroville Twp	74	328
Canuto	66	m	w	CA	Monterey	San Juan Twp	74	403
Dolores	10	f	w	CA	Monterey	San Antonio Twp	74	317
Estevan	60	m	w	CA	Monterey	Alisal Twp	74	300
Francisco	37	m	w	CA	Monterey	San Antonio Twp	74	323
Francisco	32	m	w	CA	Monterey	Alisal Twp	74	300
Juan M	49	m	w	CA	Monterey	Monterey	74	358
Manuel	35	m	w	CA	Monterey	San Antonio Twp	74	323
Manuel	35	m	w	CA	Monterey	San Antonio Twp	74	323
BOROUSKY								
Michael	51	m	w	POLA	Nevada	Meadow Lake Twp	75	252
BOROZONA								
Louis	30	m	w	ITAL	San Francisco	3-Wd San Francisco	79	289
BORPHY								
Edward	37	m	w	GERM	Santa Clara	2-Wd San Jose	88	336
BORQUANTY								
Peter	63	m	w	FRAN	San Francisco	2-Wd San Francisco	79	211
BORQUE								
Dominique	40	m	w	FRAN	San Francisco	2-Wd San Francisco	79	241
BORQUES								
Antonio	55	m	w	MEXI	Contra Costa	Martinez Twp	71	351
BORQUGUS								
Juan	63	m	w	CA	Santa Clara	Santa Clara Twp	88	158
BORRELY								
Francisco	61	m	w	FRAN	Marin	Sausalito Twp	74	69
BORRES								
Felix	34	m	w	ITAL	Napa	Napa	75	43
BORRETT								
Elizabeth	67	f	w	ENGL	Sacramento	4-Wd Sacramento	77	357
BORRETTE								
A S	48	m	w	PA	Lassen	Susanville Twp	73	442
V J	40	m	w	PA	Lassen	Susanville Twp	73	442
BORRIMAN								
J S	19	f	w	NY	Alameda	Oakland	68	237
BORROSEY								
George	43	m	w	GREE	Santa Clara	Fremont Twp	88	54
BORROW								
James	29	m	w	ITAL	Amador	Sutter Crk P O	69	411
BORRUS								
R S	37	m	w	NY	Sierra	Alleghany & Forest	89	534
BORRY								
J	28	m	w	NY	Sierra	Sierra Twp	89	563
BORS								
Michael	37	m	w	IREL	San Francisco	San Francisco P O	83	412
Pleasent	60	m	b	VA	Los Angeles	El Monte Twp	73	455
BORSCH								
Harriett	17	f	w	BADE	Sacramento	3-Wd Sacramento	77	302
BORSE								
A	31	m	w	ITAL	Alameda	Oakland	68	241
Doratha	22	f	w	MO	Los Angeles	Los Angeles	73	516
Hans	31	m	w	PRUS	San Mateo	Half Moon Bay P O	87	406
BORSLAND								
Jas	21	m	w	IREL	San Francisco	7-Wd San Francisco	81	237
BORSTEL								
Henry	31	m	w	HANO	San Francisco	San Francisco P O	83	135
BORSTROM								
Constantine	40	m	w	SWED	San Francisco	3-Wd San Francisco	79	312
BORTAN								
John	37	m	w	NY	Los Angeles	Wilmington Twp	73	642
BORTESCHEY								
A	44	m	w	GERM	Solano	Vallejo	90	194
BORTFELD								
F C	37	m	w	PRUS	San Francisco	3-Wd San Francisco	79	320
BORTLEY								
Joseph	38	m	w	IREL	Kern	Tehachapi P O	73	353
BORTMAN								
John	34	m	w	BAVA	San Francisco	2-Wd San Francisco	79	187
BORTON								
George	30	m	w	OH	Sonoma	Petaluma Twp	91	351
Jos	36	m	w	HANO	Solano	Vallejo	90	157
Ruben	40	m	w	OH	Sonoma	Petaluma Twp	91	351
W C	47	m	w	OH	Sierra	Sierra Twp	89	562
BORTONA								
Inigei	40	m	w	ITAL	Sonoma	Vallejo Twp	91	463
BORTOW								
Alfred	17	m	w	CA	Monterey	Castroville Twp	74	338
BORUCK								
Marcus D	36	m	w	NY	San Francisco	8-Wd San Francisco	82	479
Michael	32	m	w	IREL	San Francisco	San Francisco P O	85	767
BORUNDA								
Dolores	22	f	w	CA	San Luis Obispo	Arroyo Grande Twp	87	276
Ygnacio	32	m	w	CA	Monterey	Monterey	74	356
BORWEA								
Antonio	47	m	w	CHIL	Contra Costa	San Pablo Twp	71	359
BORWELL								
Wm	45	m	w	CANA	Solano	Vallejo	90	167
BORWIN								
Martin	33	m	w	CANA	Solano	Vallejo	90	194
BORYWARITT								
M A	15	f	w	CA	Alameda	Oakland	68	258
BORZAINE								
John	50	m	w	ENGL	San Francisco	7-Wd San Francisco	81	241
BOS								
Benardo	44	m	w	CA	Los Angeles	San Juan Twp	73	626
Santiago	68	m	w	CA	Los Angeles	San Juan Twp	73	626
BOSANKO								
Henry	40	m	w	ENGL	Tehama	Red Bluff	92	183
BOSCA								
Charles	60	m	w	PRUS	San Francisco	San Francisco P O	80	338
BOSCACI								
D	24	m	w	SWIT	Alameda	Oakland	68	241
S	22	m	w	SWIT	Alameda	Oakland	68	241
BOSCAS								
Ardrea	40	m	w	MEXI	Yuba	Marysville	93	614
BOSCHA								
Nicolas	38	m	w	MA	San Francisco	San Francisco P O	83	171
BOSCHAN								
Nicholas	35	m	w	HANO	San Francisco	San Francisco P O	83	273
BOSCOE								
Harding	32	m	w	IL	Sutter	Sutter Twp	92	117
BOSCOWVITZ								
Blast	28	m	w	POLA	Amador	Amador City P O	69	392
BOSE								
Charles	33	m	w	OLDE	San Francisco	San Francisco P O	83	184
John	31	m	w	PRUS	Alameda	Oakland	68	227
BOSEKE								
Albert	42	m	w	PRUS	Santa Barbara	Santa Barbara P O	87	454
BOSENBURG								
Louis	16	m	w	CA	Sacramento	4-Wd Sacramento	77	338
BOSETEVITCH								
Antonio	25	m	w	AUST	Santa Clara	2-Wd San Jose	88	301
BOSFOOT								
John	30	m	w	PRUS	Alameda	Murray Twp	68	112
BOSFORD								
Gibbon	33	m	w	OH	Tulare	Visalia	92	289
BOSH								
Edward	30	m	w	OH	Placer	Alta P O	76	412
Wm	25	m	w	GERM	San Joaquin	2-Wd Stockton	86	171
BOSHA								
Peter	31	m	w	WI	San Francisco	San Francisco P O	83	142
BOSHEN								
Henry	40	m	w	HANO	San Joaquin	1-Wd Stockton	86	126
BOSHER								
Emil	26	m	w	WURT	San Francisco	1-Wd San Francisco	79	134
John	40	m	w	PRUS	San Joaquin	1-Wd Stockton	86	130
BOSHFACIO								
Carmen P	59	f	w	CA	Monterey	Monterey	74	355
BOSHFORD								
William	40	m	w	IREL	Los Angeles	Los Angeles Twp	73	471
BOSINA								
Rodryc	40	m	w	CA	Tehama	Red Bluff	92	183
BOSK								
Thos	30	m	w	IREL	Alameda	Oakland	68	230
BOSKA								
Catania	36	m	w	MEXI	Santa Clara	2-Wd San Jose	88	310
Oscar	35	m	w	FRAN	San Mateo	San Mateo P O	87	348
BOSKMAN								
Charles	24	m	w	PRUS	Sacramento	2-Wd Sacramento	77	244
BOSKOWITS								
Frank	21	m	w	NY	Sonoma	Petaluma Twp	91	316
BOSLAMONTA								
D	60	m	w	MEXI	San Bernardino	San Salvador Twp	78	455
BOSLAND								
William	21	m	w	HDAR	Solano	Vacaville Twp	90	120
BOSLER								
Harry	42	m	w	PA	Sacramento	2-Wd Sacramento	77	246
BOSLEY								
Mary A	21	f	w	LA	San Francisco	8-Wd San Francisco	82	393
Wm	32	m	w	NY	Merced	Snelling P O	74	279
BOSLO								
F	39	m	w	PRUS	Sierra	Downieville Twp	89	520
BOSMAN								
Saml P	36	m	w	NY	San Francisco	1-Wd San Francisco	79	106
BOSNER								
John	22	m	w	PRUS	San Francisco	San Francisco P O	80	338
BOSQ								
Romain	30	m	w	FRAN	San Francisco	8-Wd San Francisco	82	296
BOSQUALO								
Henrico	17	m	w	ITAL	San Mateo	Schoolhouse Statio	87	344
BOSQUE								
Catonna	37	m	w	MEXI	Santa Clara	San Jose Twp	88	185
Eliza	38	f	w	CHIL	San Francisco	1-Wd San Francisco	79	47
BOSQUES								
John	62	m	w	FRAN	Santa Clara	2-Wd San Jose	88	314
BOSQUETTE								
Melanie	42	f	w	FRAN	San Francisco	San Francisco P O	83	75

© 2001 by Heritage Quest. All rights reserved.

Series M593

Name	Age	S	R	B-PL	County	Locale	Roll	Pg
BOSQUEZ								
Lorenzo	46	m	w	MEXI	Monterey	San Benito Twp	74	378
BOSQUI								
Andrew	37	m	w	PRUS	San Francisco	San Francisco P O	80	378
Edward	38	m	w	CANA	San Francisco	2-Wd San Francisco	79	275
Hanna	57	f	w	CANA	Sonoma	Sonoma Twp	91	445
Kenneth J	29	m	w	CANA	Sonoma	Sonoma Twp	91	442
BOSQUIT								
Rose	40	f	w	PA	Placer	Auburn P O	76	363
BOSQUY								
Morris	28	m	w	CT	Humboldt	Arcata Twp	72	226
BOSS								
Alexander	47	m	w	NC	Contra Costa	Martinez P O	71	448
Annetta	7	f	w	CA	Contra Costa	Martinez P O	71	372
David	70	m	w	NC	Contra Costa	Martinez P O	71	372
Edmond	20	m	w	MA	Merced	Snelling P O	74	249
Henry	22	m	w	PRUS	San Francisco	San Francisco P O	85	785
Mary	64	f	w	VA	San Francisco	San Francisco P O	80	352
Wm	31	m	w	MA	Solano	Vallejo	90	139
BOSSART								
John	38	m	w	BELG	Nevada	Nevada Twp	75	286
BOSSE								
Charles	50	m	w	MA	Solano	Denverton Twp	90	23
Henry	42	m	w	PRUS	Placer	Auburn P O	76	357
Henry	25	m	w	GERM	San Luis Obispo	Arroyo Grande Twp	87	274
BOSSEL								
James	40	m	w	PA	Alameda	Murray Twp	68	126
Peter	28	m	w	GERM	San Francisco	2-Wd San Francisco	79	146
BOSSELLS								
Lewis	8	m	w	CA	Butte	Ophir Twp	70	113
BOSSEMAN								
S	53	m	w	OH	Amador	Ione City P O	69	359
BOSSER								
Christian	46	m	w	DENM	Plumas	Mineral Twp	77	22
Henry	25	m	w	CANA	San Diego	San Diego	78	508
BOSSETT								
Carl	21	m	w	HDAR	San Francisco	6-Wd San Francisco	81	139
BOSSETTI								
James	39	m	w	SWIT	San Francisco	2-Wd San Francisco	79	198
BOSSIDO								
Darden	30	m	w	SWIT	San Francisco	San Francisco P O	80	478
BOSSING								
Henry	25	m	w	NY	Humboldt	Eureka Twp	72	258
BOSSINGER								
Jno	48	m	w	WURT	Sacramento	3-Wd Sacramento	77	317
BOSSMER								
August	29	m	w	BADE	Los Angeles	Los Angeles	73	528
BOSSON								
Philip	40	m	w	PORT	Monterey	Pajaro Twp	74	373
BOSSUIT								
F J	34	m	w	NY	Sierra	Eureka Twp	89	526
BOSSYNS								
John	45	m	w	BELG	Shasta	Horsetown P O	89	502
BOST								
Jacob	37	m	w	NC	Yuba	Marysville	93	598
John	38	m	w	BAVA	Nevada	Nevada Twp	75	282
Jos W	36	m	w	NC	San Francisco	8-Wd San Francisco	82	336
BOSTER								
Wm	50	m	w	ENGL	Monterey	Castroville Twp	74	337
BOSTHEIM								
Joseph	29	m	w	HOLL	San Francisco	8-Wd San Francisco	82	455
BOSTHLY								
David	25	m	w	IREL	San Francisco	5-Wd San Francisco	81	27
BOSTICK								
Merritt	16	m	w	CA	Santa Clara	San Jose Twp	88	200
BOSTON								
Alice	65	f	w	ENGL	Santa Cruz	Santa Cruz	89	420
Antionette	14	f	w	CA	Nevada	Grass Valley Twp	75	186
Emily	9	f	w	NY	Nevada	Grass Valley Twp	75	168
Geo E	47	m	w	VA	Mariposa	Maxwell Crk P O	74	141
George	47	m	w	OH	Plumas	Seneca Twp	77	48
Joseph	46	m	w	PA	Santa Cruz	Santa Cruz	89	403
Lizzie	12	f	w	CA	San Francisco	San Francisco P O	80	537
Louis	50	m	w	CUBA	San Francisco	1-Wd San Francisco	79	80
Rebecca	7	f	w	CA	Nevada	Grass Valley Twp	75	208
Samuel	16	m	w	CA	Nevada	Grass Valley Twp	75	153
William A	20	m	w	NY	Nevada	Grass Valley Twp	75	149
Wm	38	m	w	OH	Butte	Kimshew Tpw	70	83
BOSTONIA								
Antoine	34	m	w	ITAL	San Francisco	8-Wd San Francisco	82	295
BOSTROM								
John	31	m	w	SWED	Monterey	Monterey	74	361
BOSTRUCK								
Noble	52	m	w	PA	Sutter	Vernon Twp	92	135
W H	24	m	w	MO	Sutter	Vernon Twp	92	135
BOSTWICH								
Edward R	44	m	w	VT	Sacramento	2-Wd Sacramento	77	228
John	47	m	w	GA	San Francisco	2-Wd San Francisco	79	276
BOSTWICK								
H J	60	m	w	VA	Amador	Jackson P O	69	328
Henry A	42	m	w	CANA	Tulare	Visalia	92	291
Mary	21	f	w	NY	San Francisco	6-Wd San Francisco	81	129
N W	36	m	w	NY	Sonoma	Santa Rosa	91	402
Oscar	45	m	w	NY	Sonoma	Healdsburg	91	275
S C	61	m	w	KY	Monterey	San Antonio Twp	74	319
Saml	27	m	w	IL	San Francisco	5-Wd San Francisco	81	3
Sarah	66	f	w	NY	San Francisco	5-Wd San Francisco	81	3
Wm M	55	m	w	NY	Sacramento	Natomas Twp	77	168
BOSWA								
D	40	m	w	FRAN	Alameda	Oakland	68	235
BOSWELL								
Andrew	46	m	w	TN	Colusa	Colusa	71	296
C D	30	m	w	IN	Santa Clara	Gilroy Twp	88	98
Eliza	50	f	w	ENGL	San Joaquin	Elliott Twp	86	77
F	24	m	w	NY	San Joaquin	Elkhorn Twp	86	60
George B	30	m	w	IN	El Dorado	Placerville	72	111
Herman	29	m	w	PRUS	Butte	Chico Twp	70	55
Jos Q	37	m	w	AL	Shasta	French Gulch P O	89	467
Josiah	40	m	w	ENGL	Yolo	Cache Crk Twp	93	442
Levi	24	m	w	MO	Monterey	San Juan Twp	74	400
Richd	56	m	w	NC	Santa Clara	Gilroy Twp	88	98
Robert P	50	m	w	TX	Los Angeles	Santa Ana Twp	73	603
Thomas	35	m	w	IREL	Marin	San Rafael Twp	74	41
William	54	m	w	TN	Colusa	Colusa Twp	71	280
William	25	m	w	ENGL	Yolo	Cache Crk Twp	93	442
Wm	51	m	b	VA	Sacramento	Granite Twp	77	145
BOSWICK								
Henry	34	m	w	PA	San Francisco	San Francisco P O	80	427
J S	39	m	w	CANA	San Joaquin	2-Wd Stockton	86	179
BOSWORTH								
Almann E	24	m	w	ME	Santa Cruz	Pajaro Twp	89	341
Cal M	42	m	w	ME	Sonoma	Cloverdale Twp	91	266
Charles	40	m	w	ENGL	El Dorado	Placerville Twp	72	94
Charles W	38	m	w	NY	Sacramento	2-Wd Sacramento	77	219
E A	33	m	w	VT	Napa	Napa Twp	75	59
H M	31	m	w	OH	San Francisco	San Francisco P O	85	776
Jas D	33	m	w	ME	Sonoma	Cloverdale Twp	91	271
M	37	m	w	ME	Sutter	Sutter Twp	92	127
Marcus	32	m	w	AL	San Francisco	San Francisco P O	80	406
Martin	30	m	w	NY	Marin	Point Reyes Twp	74	21
R C	54	m	w	NY	San Joaquin	2-Wd Stockton	86	183
R D	47	m	w	ME	Sierra	Sears Twp	89	527
Solomon	45	m	w	MA	Nevada	Grass Valley Twp	75	155
William	51	m	w	NY	San Francisco	8-Wd San Francisco	82	462
BOSYNY								
Abram	25	m	w	MEXI	Los Angeles	Los Angeles	73	556
BOT								
Ah	41	m	c	CHIN	Tuolumne	Big Oak Flat P O	93	394
Ah	37	m	c	CHIN	Tuolumne	Big Oak Flat P O	93	403
Ah	35	m	c	CHIN	Sacramento	1-Wd Sacramento	77	200
Ah	25	m	c	CHIN	Sacramento	1-Wd Sacramento	77	199
Ah	22	m	c	CHIN	Sacramento	Georgianna Twp	77	123
Joaquin	35	m	w	SPAI	Santa Barbara	Santa Barbara P O	87	467
BOTAES								
Edward	70	m	w	MEXI	Amador	Jackson P O	69	338
BOTALLY								
James	24	m	w	ITAL	Santa Clara	Santa Clara Twp	88	176
BOTANCO								
Joseph	40	m	w	PORT	Alameda	Alvarado	68	303
BOTARD								
Hypolite	40	m	i	FRAN	Monterey	San Juan Twp	74	412
BOTARES								
Joseph	36	m	w	CHIL	Amador	Jackson P O	69	326
BOTELER								
Jesus	22	m	w	CA	Los Angeles	Santa Ana Twp	73	609
BOTELLER								
Narciso	45	m	w	ENGL	Los Angeles	El Monte Twp	73	461
BOTELLO								
Francisca	60	f	w	MEXI	Los Angeles	Los Angeles	73	522
Francisco	50	m	w	CA	Los Angeles	Los Angeles	73	509
BOTERO								
Antonio	5	m	w	CA	Fresno	Millerton P O	72	156
Maria	37	f	w	MEXI	Fresno	Millerton P O	72	156
BOTGER								
Jno	39	m	w	HANO	Butte	Ophir Twp	70	102
BOTGERS								
Alfred	28	m	w	PRUS	San Francisco	7-Wd San Francisco	81	246
BOTH								
Richd	30	m	w	SAXO	San Francisco	1-Wd San Francisco	79	119
W	37	m	w	GA	San Joaquin	Douglas Twp	86	38
BOTHE								
David	26	m	w	BREM	San Francisco	2-Wd San Francisco	79	227
Sophea	62	f	w	HANO	San Francisco	San Francisco P O	83	151
BOTHECK								
John	35	m	w	OH	Yuba	Marysville	93	604
BOTHMANN								
Fredk	33	m	w	SAXO	San Francisco	San Francisco P O	83	11
BOTHMER								
A C	29	m	w	BAVA	Alameda	Alameda	68	11
BOTHSON								
Christian	44	m	w	DENM	Alameda	Eden Twp	68	59
BOTHULDER								
Jo	40	m	w	PRUS	Alameda	Alameda	68	19
BOTHWELL								
Bruce	36	m	w	PA	Santa Clara	2-Wd San Jose	88	288
Chas	33	m	w	SCOT	Sacramento	Franklin Twp	77	112
James	35	m	w	IREL	Alameda	Brooklyn	68	36
Richard	48	m	w	IREL	Alameda	Brooklyn Twp	68	51
BOTHWICK								
Chas	22	m	w	SCOT	San Francisco	7-Wd San Francisco	81	236
Robert	36	m	w	SCOT	Tuolumne	Columbia P O	93	337
Robt	35	m	w	ENGL	San Francisco	San Francisco P O	83	267
BOTIER								
Mary	14	f	w	CA	Santa Cruz	Pajaro Twp	89	360

© 2001 by Heritage Quest. All rights reserved.

Name	Age	S	R	B-PL	County	Locale	Series M593 Roll	Pg
BOTILLE								
Joaquin	38	m	w	CA	Monterey	San Antonio Twp	74	323
BOTILLER								
Pascual	50	m	w	CA	Santa Barbara	Santa Barbara P O	87	462
BOTILLO								
Concepciona	38	f	w	CA	Los Angeles	Los Angeles	73	548
Encarnaciona	30	f	w	MEXI	Los Angeles	Los Angeles	73	560
Refugio	46	m	w	MEXI	Los Angeles	Los Angeles	73	553
Rosaria	49	f	w	MEXI	Los Angeles	Los Angeles	73	554
BOTIN								
F F	37	m	w	AL	San Joaquin	Castoria Twp	86	13
BOTION								
Ferdinand	46	m	w	SWIT	San Francisco	2-Wd San Francisco	79	239
BOTLER								
L M	34	m	w	BAVA	Sutter	Yuba Twp	92	144
BOTO								
John B	26	m	w	ITAL	Calaveras	Copperopolis P O	70	244
BOTOY								
Ah	30	m	c	CHIN	San Francisco	3-Wd San Francisco	79	301
BOTSCH								
Frederick	39	m	w	WURT	San Mateo	Redwood Twp	87	364
BOTSFORD								
James M	44	m	w	NY	Santa Clara	1-Wd San Jose	88	246
John R	38	m	w	CT	Placer	Roseville P O	76	351
Simeon	41	m	w	NY	Yuba	New York Twp	93	637
BOTT								
Henry W	13	m	w	CA	Contra Costa	Martinez P O	71	388
Mary	13	f	w	CA	Tulare	Tule Rvr Twp	92	266
BOTTA								
Mes	21	m	w	SWIT	Marin	Nicasio Twp	74	16
BOTTCHER								
Andrew	34	m	w	PRUS	San Francisco	5-Wd San Francisco	81	15
BOTTE								
Joseph	25	m	w	ITAL	San Francisco	3-Wd San Francisco	79	289
BOTTEAR								
Alfonsina	39	f	w	FRAN	Santa Clara	1-Wd San Jose	88	267
BOTTELER								
Susana	10	f	w	CA	Los Angeles	Los Angeles Twp	73	478
BOTTELLIA								
Francisco	18	m	w	CA	Santa Barbara	Santa Maria P O	87	512
BOTTELLO								
Louis	32	m	w	FRAN	Santa Clara	2-Wd San Jose	88	316
BOTTENHOUSE								
Wm	16	m	w	MO	Sonoma	Mendocino Twp	91	290
BOTTER								
Benjiman J	33	m	w	OH	Los Angeles	Los Angeles	73	524
Thos	35	m	w	NY	Tehama	Tehama Twp	92	193
BOTTGER								
John	42	m	w	SHOL	San Francisco	11-Wd San Francisc	84	551
BOTTING								
Griffith	33	m	w	WALE	Contra Costa	Martinez P O	71	428
BOTTIS								
D	50	m	w	CHIL	Amador	Jackson P O	69	327
John	44	m	w	AUST	Amador	Jackson P O	69	333
BOTTIWICH								
Louis	33	m	w	AUST	Santa Clara	2-Wd San Jose	88	319
BOTTLEMAN								
Joseph	25	m	w	ITAL	Tuolumne	Sonora P O	93	322
BOTTLER								
John	15	m	w	MO	Sutter	Yuba Twp	92	144
BOTTO								
Angelo	23	m	w	ITAL	Amador	Sutter Crk P O	69	414
J	41	m	w	ITAL	Amador	Sutter Crk P O	69	414
John	42	m	w	AUST	Amador	Jackson P O	69	345
John	38	m	w	ITAL	Amador	Sutter Crk P O	69	404
BOTTOM								
John	27	m	w	KY	Sutter	Yuba Twp	92	140
BOTTOMLEY								
Chas	30	m	w	ENGL	San Francisco	San Francisco P O	83	335
BOTTOMLY								
James	53	m	w	ENGL	Nevada	Little York Twp	75	239
James	49	m	w	ENGL	Calaveras	San Andreas P O	70	208
James M	55	m	w	ENGL	Placer	Lincoln P O	76	489
BOTTOMS								
A W	36	m	w	KY	Siskiyou	Scott Valley Twp	89	619
John F	28	m	w	TN	San Diego	Milquaty Dist	78	475
Mattie	16	f	w	NY	San Francisco	1-Wd San Francisco	79	34
BOTTON								
James	55	m	w	IREL	Placer	Rocklin P O	76	462
John	50	m	w	ENGL	Nevada	Bridgeport Twp	75	117
John J	26	m	w	SCOT	San Francisco	6-Wd San Francisco	81	98
BOTTONIES								
Joseph	64	m	w	ITAL	Amador	Jackson P O	69	338
BOTTORFF								
Peter S	44	m	w	KY	Napa	Yountville Twp	75	88
BOTTREL								
Julia	40	f	w	ENGL	Alameda	Alameda	68	2
BOTTS								
Augustus	28	m	w	ITAL	Amador	Ione City P O	69	353
Chas	60	m	w	VT	San Francisco	8-Wd San Francisco	82	335
Christian	40	m	w	ITAL	Amador	Sutter Crk P O	69	400
Geo	38	m	w	IN	Humboldt	Arcata Twp	72	231
John	42	m	w	NY	San Francisco	7-Wd San Francisco	81	164
Levi M	45	m	w	NY	Yolo	Cache Crk Twp	93	430
Newton	32	m	w	OH	San Joaquin	Castoria Twp	86	4
BOTTZE								
Charles	20	m	w	GA	Mendocino	Little Lake Twp	74	196

Name	Age	S	R	B-PL	County	Locale	Series M593 Roll	Pg
BOTZER								
Herman	36	m	w	PRUS	Calaveras	San Andreas P O	70	192
BOUBES								
Lourrus	26	m	w	ITAL	Santa Barbara	San Buenaventura P	87	439
BOUCE								
Robert	45	m	w	SCOT	San Francisco	San Francisco P O	85	766
BOUCH								
Christ	62	m	w	BELG	San Joaquin	Douglas Twp	86	40
BOUCHARD								
Andy	40	m	w	CANA	Yolo	Putah Twp	93	518
Frank	53	m	w	ENGL	Los Angeles	Los Nietos Twp	73	587
Louis	50	m	w	FRAN	Solano	Silveyville Twp	90	84
Pauline	27	f	w	FRAN	San Francisco	6-Wd San Francisco	81	71
BOUCHE								
George	26	m	w	FRAN	Monterey	San Juan Twp	74	408
Nelson	31	m	w	CANA	Santa Clara	1-Wd San Jose	88	231
Reine	60	f	w	FRAN	San Francisco	2-Wd San Francisco	79	246
BOUCHER								
Henry	43	m	w	PRUS	Plumas	Indian Twp	77	15
James	45	m	w	IREL	San Francisco	San Francisco P O	83	333
James	28	m	w	ENGL	San Francisco	San Francisco P O	83	273
John	45	m	w	PA	Nevada	Grass Valley Twp	75	150
John	42	m	w	MA	San Francisco	7-Wd San Francisco	81	242
Leon	52	m	w	FRAN	San Francisco	6-Wd San Francisco	81	87
Peter	51	m	w	FRAN	Marin	Bolinas Twp	74	3
T E	43	m	w	TN	Mendocino	Calpella Twp	74	181
Wesley L	42	m	w	OH	Calaveras	San Andreas P O	70	194
BOUCHET								
Barcillea	62	f	w	CA	Los Angeles	Los Angeles	73	566
Falis	41	m	w	FRAN	Los Angeles	Los Angeles	73	565
BOUCOAT								
Charles	21	m	w	FRAN	Colusa	Grand Island Twp	71	306
BOUDIN								
A A	54	m	w	FRAN	Tuolumne	Big Oak Flat P O	93	394
Louis	38	m	w	SWIT	San Francisco	11-Wd San Francisc	84	628
BOUDINOT								
Jean	47	m	w	FRAN	San Francisco	San Francisco P O	80	536
BOUDRE								
Felix	64	m	w	FRAN	Marin	Novato Twp	74	10
BOUDROS								
Fred	37	m	w	FRAN	San Joaquin	Castoria Twp	86	15
BOUFERINCA								
John	32	m	w	ITAL	Amador	Sutter Crk P O	69	412
BOUGEOIS								
Louis	40	m	w	FRAN	Calaveras	San Andreas P O	70	193
BOUGERT								
John	51	m	w	FRAN	San Francisco	San Francisco P O	80	348
BOUGERTI								
John	26	m	w	SWIT	Santa Clara	Fremont Twp	88	66
BOUGET								
Alexander	55	m	w	FRAN	San Francisco	San Francisco P O	80	345
BOUGHAM								
Peter	20	m	w	IREL	San Francisco	San Francisco P O	83	137
BOUGHTON								
James	40	m	w	MO	Humboldt	Eel Rvr Twp	72	246
BOUGUS								
Mathew	31	m	w	PORT	Solano	Maine Prairie Twp	90	49
BOUILLO								
Florentino	29	m	w	CA	Santa Barbara	Santa Barbara P O	87	456
BOUISSELLE								
Edward	38	m	w	FRAN	San Francisco	2-Wd San Francisco	79	152
BOUKOFSKI								
Mike	44	m	w	PRUS	Santa Barbara	San Buenaventura P	87	438
BOUKOLSKY								
Nelson	39	m	w	PRUS	San Francisco	San Francisco P O	83	343
BOUKON								
Oscar	44	m	w	SWED	Stanislaus	Emory Twp	92	24
BOULAID								
Chas	32	m	w	FRAN	San Francisco	San Francisco P O	85	831
BOULAN								
James	38	m	w	NY	San Francisco	11-Wd San Francisc	84	668
James	27	m	w	IREL	San Francisco	San Francisco P O	83	168
BOULANGE								
Charles J	37	m	w	FRAN	Los Angeles	Los Angeles	73	542
BOULANGER								
August	60	m	w	FRAN	Los Angeles	San Gabriel Twp	73	593
Marcus	48	m	w	FRAN	San Francisco	11-Wd San Francisc	84	436
BOULDER								
Peter	30	m	w	HANO	San Francisco	11-Wd San Francisc	84	687
BOULDIN								
Thomas	32	m	w	VA	San Francisco	11-Wd San Francisc	84	509
BOULE								
Henri	55	m	w	FRAN	Sacramento	4-Wd Sacramento	77	321
Mathew	28	m	w	IREL	Marin	San Rafael Twp	74	25
BOULEN								
Jas	45	m	w	IREL	Sacramento	1-Wd Sacramento	77	202
Pierce	57	m	w	FRAN	San Francisco	2-Wd San Francisco	79	180
BOULENGAIR								
Louis	58	m	w	FRAN	San Francisco	2-Wd San Francisco	79	160
BOULET								
Orilla	17	f	w	CA	Santa Clara	2-Wd San Jose	88	321
BOULEVARD								
Lampriere	65	m	w	FRAN	Santa Cruz	Pajaro Twp	89	362
BOULGER								
Jno R	23	m	w	PA	Butte	Chico Twp	70	42
BOULGIEN								
Peter	46	m	w	FRAN	San Francisco	2-Wd San Francisco	79	147

© 2001 by Heritage Quest. All rights reserved.

Series M593

Name	Age	S	R	B-PL	County	Locale	Roll	Pg
BOULIARD								
F	60	m	w	FRAN	Amador	Jackson P O	69	347
BOULIN								
Albert C	35	m	w	MO	Solano	Maine Prairie Twp	90	50
James G	29	m	w	KY	Santa Clara	1-Wd San Jose	88	249
BOULING								
A E	17	m	w	MI	Amador	Jackson P O	69	337
Thomas	53	m	w	ME	San Francisco	11-Wd San Francisc	84	431
BOULLET								
Joseph	60	m	w	FRAN	San Francisco	San Francisco P O	83	372
BOULMORE								
Harvey	21	m	w	NY	Butte	Chico Twp	70	50
Thos	40	m	w	OH	Butte	Hamilton Twp	70	71
BOULNER								
M	57	m	w	KY	Sutter	Nicolaus Twp	92	111
BOULON								
Pierce	57	m	w	FRAN	San Francisco	2-Wd San Francisco	79	175
BOULT								
C M	35	m	w	TN	San Joaquin	Elkhorn Twp	86	67
BOULTON								
E W	43	m	w	KY	Amador	Sutter Crk P O	69	412
BOULWARE								
John T	29	m	w	KY	Yolo	Cache Crk Twp	93	427
W T	37	m	w	IL	Butte	Hamilton Twp	70	62
BOUMA								
Sol	46	m	w	PA	Sutter	Butte Twp	92	90
BOUMAN								
E W	47	m	w	ME	Monterey	San Juan Twp	74	403
John	40	m	w	SAXO	San Francisco	2-Wd San Francisco	79	164
Peter	24	m	w	SWIT	San Francisco	San Francisco P O	85	763
BOUMNI								
Henry	47	m	w	HANO	El Dorado	White Oak Twp	72	143
BOUND								
Wm	49	m	w	VA	Sonoma	Bodega Twp	91	262
BOUNDA								
Bermedila	27	m	w	ITAL	Nevada	Nevada Twp	75	310
BOUNDS								
Elkanah	44	m	w	MD	Fresno	Millerton P O	72	147
Geo	31	m	w	ENGL	San Francisco	11-Wd San Francisc	84	685
Joseph	52	m	w	OH	Colusa	Butte Twp	71	269
Milton	25	m	w	OH	Yolo	Cache Crk Twp	93	426
BOUNER								
Frank	46	m	w	NY	Stanislaus	Empire Twp	92	47
BOUNG								
Ah	50	m	c	CHIN	Nevada	Nevada Twp	75	311
BOUNGARD								
David	40	m	w	IL	Fresno	Millerton P O	72	182
BOUNSEL								
Charles	28	m	w	ME	Alameda	Murray Twp	68	123
Geo	33	m	w	ME	Alameda	Murray Twp	68	123
BOUR								
Alexander	18	m	w	BADE	San Francisco	San Francisco P O	85	756
BOURBON								
Peter	56	m	w	FRAN	Plumas	Washington Twp	77	53
Robert	40	m	w	IREL	Del Norte	Crescent Twp	71	454
BOURCHA								
Adam	24	m	w	FRAN	Amador	Ione City P O	69	355
Mat	21	m	w	FRAN	Amador	Ione City P O	69	355
BOURCHARD								
Chris	54	m	w	HANO	Santa Barbara	San Buenaventura P	87	422
Edward	22	m	w	IA	Santa Barbara	San Buenaventura P	87	422
Geo	25	m	w	FRAN	San Francisco	2-Wd San Francisco	79	146
BOURCHER								
John C	54	m	w	PRUS	San Francisco	6-Wd San Francisco	81	91
BOURDAN								
Peter	33	m	w	IREL	Santa Clara	Alviso Twp	88	25
BOURDEN								
Ellen	72	f	w	IREL	Santa Clara	Alviso Twp	88	22
Terence	38	m	w	IREL	Santa Clara	Alviso Twp	88	24
BOURDET								
Peter	39	m	w	FRAN	San Francisco	11-Wd San Francisc	84	449
BOURDMAN								
Augustus	19	m	w	NY	Santa Clara	Milpitas Twp	88	111
BOURG								
Mercelin	37	m	w	LA	Yuba	Long Bar Twp	93	561
BOURGE								
Peter	53	m	w	SHOL	Nevada	Bloomfield Twp	75	98
BOURGEIOS								
Alexander	41	m	w	FRAN	San Francisco	San Francisco P O	80	343
BOURGEOIS								
Pierre	33	m	w	FRAN	San Francisco	1-Wd San Francisco	79	54
BOURGHARD								
Louis	26	m	w	HANO	Sonoma	Bodega Twp	91	264
BOURGHARDT								
Gustaf	21	m	w	HANO	Sonoma	Bodega Twp	91	262
BOURGOIN								
Adele	54	f	w	FRAN	San Francisco	San Francisco P O	85	841
BOURGOING								
Andrew	40	m	w	FRAN	San Francisco	San Francisco P O	80	539
BOURGOIS								
Lewis	48	m	w	FRAN	San Francisco	7-Wd San Francisco	81	241
BOURITE								
Julius	48	m	w	FRAN	San Francisco	2-Wd San Francisco	79	137
BOURKE								
David H	54	m	w	IREL	San Francisco	San Francisco P O	83	355
James	50	m	w	IREL	San Francisco	San Francisco P O	83	228
Margaret	49	f	w	PA	San Francisco	San Francisco P O	83	216
Mary	50	f	w	IREL	San Francisco	San Francisco P O	83	251
Wm	40	m	w	IREL	Marin	San Antonio Twp	74	61
BOURKS								
John	19	m	w	IREL	Solano	Benicia	90	17
BOURLAND								
Joseph	19	m	w	AR	Stanislaus	Emory Twp	92	18
BOURLANDA								
Lemuel	27	m	w	MO	Sonoma	Analy Twp	91	239
BOURN								
Morton	40	m	w	VA	Mendocino	Point Arena Twp	74	224
W	13	m	w	CA	Solano	Benicia	90	21
BOURNE								
Alfred	24	m	w	CANA	Santa Clara	Redwood Twp	88	119
Charles	30	m	w	NY	San Joaquin	1-Wd Stockton	86	121
Chas H	40	m	w	MA	Mendocino	Round Valley Twp	74	218
Elijah W	49	m	w	MA	San Francisco	San Francisco P O	83	105
Florence	2	f	w	CA	Sacramento	4-Wd Sacramento	77	362
Fred	51	m	w	MA	Placer	Blue Canyon P O	76	418
George	64	m	w	VA	San Francisco	11-Wd San Francisc	84	572
George M	64	m	w	VA	San Francisco	6-Wd San Francisco	81	73
John B	45	m	w	ME	San Francisco	6-Wd San Francisco	81	140
M Ellen	4	f	w	CA	Napa	Napa Twp	75	60
Richard	27	m	w	OH	San Francisco	San Francisco P O	83	162
Richard	25	m	w	ME	San Francisco	San Francisco P O	83	236
William B	56	m	w	MA	San Francisco	6-Wd San Francisco	81	136
William H	56	m	w	HOLL	San Francisco	6-Wd San Francisco	81	90
BOURNES								
Francis C	34	m	w	IREL	Sonoma	Washington Twp	91	468
M A	41	f	w	SCOT	Solano	Benicia	90	7
BOURNONVILLE								
Charlotte	58	f	w	FRAN	San Francisco	8-Wd San Francisco	82	411
BOURNS								
James	69	m	w	IREL	Sonoma	Washington Twp	91	470
BOURONDA								
Jose M	65	m	w	CA	Monterey	Castroville Twp	74	327
BOUROUGH								
Paul	41	m	w	SWIT	San Francisco	11-Wd San Francisc	84	685
BOURQUEGNON								
Aug	60	m	w	FRAN	San Francisco	1-Wd San Francisco	79	47
BOURQUEOIS								
Antonio	53	m	w	FRAN	San Francisco	2-Wd San Francisco	79	146
BOURQUIGNON								
Argent J	61	m	w	FRAN	Santa Clara	Santa Clara Twp	88	143
BOURQUIN								
Adele	20	f	w	SWIT	San Francisco	6-Wd San Francisco	81	97
Charles	30	m	w	FRAN	San Francisco	San Francisco P O	80	538
Emile	40	m	w	SWIT	San Francisco	2-Wd San Francisco	79	270
BOUS								
Ar	29	m	c	CHIN	Sonoma	Petaluma Twp	91	363
BOUSE								
John	29	m	w	ENGL	Nevada	Grass Valley Twp	75	231
BOUSER								
Saml	39	m	b	NJ	Sacramento	3-Wd Sacramento	77	256
BOUSHEY								
Loce	45	f	w	CANA	Los Angeles	Los Angeles	73	545
BOUSLY								
Henry	61	m	w	MA	Placer	Bath P O	76	458
BOUSSIEN								
Louis	36	m	w	FRAN	San Francisco	2-Wd San Francisco	79	146
BOUST								
Elsworth B	41	m	w	VA	Santa Barbara	Santa Barbara P O	87	453
BOUTCHER								
Henry	40	m	w	HANO	Calaveras	Copperopolis P O	70	223
BOUTELL								
John	46	m	w	NH	Nevada	Grass Valley Twp	75	167
BOUTENTHISTLE								
Benjamin	43	m	w	BADE	Yuba	New York Twp	93	638
BOUTIENNE								
Etienne	51	m	w	FRAN	San Francisco	2-Wd San Francisco	79	170
BOUTIN								
Andrew	44	m	w	ENGL	Nevada	Grass Valley Twp	75	228
BOUTINON								
George	36	m	w	FRAN	San Francisco	San Francisco P O	80	539
BOUTO								
Herman	32	m	w	BAVA	San Francisco	San Francisco P O	80	458
BOUTON								
A P	50	m	w	NY	San Francisco	San Francisco P O	83	324
Andrew	39	m	w	NY	Sonoma	Washington Twp	91	467
Daniel	65	m	w	NY	San Francisco	San Francisco P O	80	484
Manles	39	m	w	NY	Calaveras	San Andreas P O	70	195
BOUTRELLA								
Louis	26	m	w	FRAN	San Francisco	6-Wd San Francisco	81	73
BOUTRIE								
Achilles	53	m	w	FRAN	Siskiyou	Callahan P O	89	627
BOUTSER								
D E	30	m	w	SCOT	Alameda	Oakland	68	264
BOUTWELL								
Stephen	34	m	w	AR	Fresno	Millerton P O	72	181
Stephen A	44	m	w	IL	Placer	Roseville P O	76	355
BOUVIER								
Chas T	39	m	w	FRAN	Nevada	Nevada Twp	75	302
Louis	52	m	w	FRAN	Santa Clara	2-Wd San Jose	88	314
BOUVILLE								
Louis	33	m	w	FRAN	San Francisco	1-Wd San Francisco	79	95
BOUX								
John	29	m	w	FRAN	San Francisco	San Francisco P O	80	535

© 2001 by Heritage Quest. All rights reserved.

Name	Age	S	R	B-PL	County	Locale	Series M593 Roll	Pg
BOUY								
Ah Ton	30	m	c	CHIN	Humboldt	Arcata Twp	72	233
BOVART								
Jane	30	f	w	KY	San Joaquin	Elliott Twp	86	74
M	35	m	w	CANA	San Joaquin	Elliott Twp	86	74
BOVEE								
J	39	m	w	NY	Sierra	Forest Twp	89	531
James S	43	m	w	NY	San Francisco	San Francisco P O	85	732
William H	48	m	w	NY	San Francisco	2-Wd San Francisco	79	246
BOVER								
Margaret	29	f	w	WI	San Joaquin	Castoria Twp	86	4
BOVEY								
Charles	32	m	w	ENGL	Tuolumne	Sonora P O	93	317
Rueben	30	m	w	IREL	San Francisco	8-Wd San Francisco	82	435
William	38	m	w	ENGL	Nevada	Grass Valley Twp	75	184
William T	32	m	w	ME	Santa Clara	San Jose Twp	88	193
BOVIE								
Mary	15	f	w	NY	San Francisco	8-Wd San Francisco	82	450
BOVYER								
David	50	m	w	ENGL	San Francisco	5-Wd San Francisco	81	18
BOW								
---	26	m	c	CHIN	Siskiyou	Cottonwood Twp	89	594
Ah	52	m	c	CHIN	Butte	Kimshew Tpw	70	84
Ah	48	m	c	CHIN	El Dorado	Mud Springs Twp	72	88
Ah	40	m	c	CHIN	San Francisco	6-Wd San Francisco	81	77
Ah	38	m	c	CHIN	Trinity	Douglas	92	233
Ah	34	m	c	CHIN	San Francisco	San Francisco P O	80	498
Ah	34	m	c	CHIN	Placer	Bath P O	76	442
Ah	33	m	c	CHIN	El Dorado	Coloma Twp	72	12
Ah	29	m	c	CHIN	San Francisco	6-Wd San Francisco	81	47
Ah	27	m	c	CHIN	Placer	Auburn P O	76	362
Ah	25	f	c	CHIN	San Francisco	6-Wd San Francisco	81	75
Ah	24	m	c	CHIN	San Francisco	6-Wd San Francisco	81	59
Ah	24	m	c	CHIN	Placer	Alta P O	76	412
Ah	24	m	c	CHIN	Placer	Dutch Flat P O	76	408
Ah	23	m	c	CHIN	San Francisco	6-Wd San Francisco	81	56
Ah	22	m	c	CHIN	Santa Clara	San Jose Twp	88	195
Ah	21	m	c	CHIN	San Francisco	6-Wd San Francisco	81	59
Ah	20	f	c	CHIN	San Francisco	6-Wd San Francisco	81	76
Ah	20	m	c	CHIN	San Francisco	6-Wd San Francisco	81	57
Ah	20	f	c	CHIN	San Francisco	6-Wd San Francisco	81	74
Ah	20	m	c	CHIN	San Francisco	11-Wd San Francisc	84	561
Ah	20	m	c	CHIN	Trinity	North Fork Twp	92	216
Ah	19	m	c	CHIN	Butte	Bidwell Twp	70	1
Ah	19	m	c	CHIN	San Francisco	11-Wd San Francisc	84	535
Ah	15	m	c	CHIN	San Francisco	6-Wd San Francisco	81	60
Ah	10	m	c	CA	San Francisco	6-Wd San Francisco	81	44
Am	28	m	c	CHIN	Colusa	Colusa	71	299
Ann E	4	f	w	CA	Sacramento	Brighton Twp	77	75
Christina	45	f	w	SCOT	San Francisco	3-Wd San Francisco	79	313
Chung	15	m	c	CHIN	Yuba	Marysville	93	621
Edmond	35	m	w	IREL	Sacramento	Brighton Twp	77	75
Joseph	30	m	w	NY	San Francisco	San Francisco P O	83	211
Kee	44	m	c	CHIN	El Dorado	Coloma Twp	72	12
Kip	47	m	c	CHIN	El Dorado	Coloma Twp	72	12
Lee	40	m	c	CHIN	San Francisco	6-Wd San Francisco	81	77
Legs	41	m	c	CHIN	Klamath	Dillon Twp	73	369
Peter	35	m	w	IREL	San Francisco	San Francisco P O	85	834
Sum	30	m	c	CHIN	Yuba	Marysville	93	631
Yap	17	m	c	CHIN	San Francisco	1-Wd San Francisco	79	87
BOWAIN								
Peter R	31	m	w	IL	Alameda	San Leandro	68	93
BOWAN								
Augustus	30	m	w	ENGL	Napa	Napa Twp	75	70
John	41	m	w	IREL	San Francisco	San Francisco P O	80	406
BOWCY								
William	48	m	w	NC	Colusa	Grand Island Twp	71	309
BOWD								
Jerry	28	m	w	OH	Lassen	Janesville Twp	73	433
BOWDAR								
Jacques	41	m	w	FRAN	San Francisco	San Francisco P O	83	63
BOWDEL								
Jacob L	42	m	w	VA	Shasta	Stillwater P O	89	481
BOWDELL								
Henry	52	m	w	OH	Amador	Jackson P O	69	338
Jacob L	42	m	w	PA	Shasta	Stillwater P O	89	481
BOWDEN								
Alex	46	m	w	FRAN	San Francisco	2-Wd San Francisco	79	224
Briget	38	f	w	IREL	San Francisco	7-Wd San Francisco	81	199
Fred	37	m	w	ENGL	Butte	Oregon Twp	70	128
Fredk	36	m	w	ENGL	Butte	Ophir Twp	70	113
J C	40	m	w	NY	San Joaquin	Douglas Twp	86	49
Jno	51	m	w	IREL	Sierra	Table Rock Twp	89	579
John	46	m	w	IREL	San Francisco	2-Wd San Francisco	79	218
John	45	m	w	MA	San Francisco	1-Wd San Francisco	79	116
John	40	m	w	IREL	San Francisco	San Francisco P O	83	80
John	34	m	w	PA	Yuba	Marysville	93	587
John	14	m	w	ME	Monterey	Pajaro Twp	74	372
Joseph	36	m	w	AUSL	San Francisco	2-Wd San Francisco	79	268
Joseph	31	m	w	ENGL	Nevada	Nevada Twp	75	305
Lafayette	45	m	w	FRAN	Calaveras	San Andreas P O	70	205
Richard	56	m	w	IREL	Sacramento	2-Wd Sacramento	77	234
Richd	28	m	w	ENGL	Fresno	Millerton P O	72	167
S H N	45	m	w	ENGL	San Francisco	San Francisco P O	83	55
Samuel	9	m	w	ENGL	San Francisco	San Francisco P O	85	800
Sophia	7	f	w	ENGL	San Francisco	San Francisco P O	85	799
Thomas	33	m	w	ENGL	Nevada	Grass Valley Twp	75	165

Name	Age	S	R	B-PL	County	Locale	Series M593 Roll	Pg
William H	33	m	w	ENGL	Santa Cruz	Pajaro Twp	89	339
BOWDER								
John	39	m	w	ENGL	El Dorado	Greenwood Twp	72	55
BOWDES								
Richd	40	m	w	IREL	San Francisco	1-Wd San Francisco	79	44
BOWDEY								
Martin	50	m	w	FRAN	Butte	Ophir Twp	70	101
BOWDITCH								
M S	33	m	w	NY	Solano	Benicia	90	9
BOWDOIN								
Joseph	40	m	w	MA	Butte	Chico Twp	70	25
BOWDREN								
Michael	30	m	w	IREL	Napa	Napa	75	25
BOWE								
Ah	46	m	c	CHIN	El Dorado	Coloma Twp	72	1
Eugene	28	m	w	FRAN	Santa Clara	2-Wd San Jose	88	317
Henry	50	m	w	OH	Calaveras	San Andreas P O	70	206
James	23	m	w	IREL	San Francisco	San Francisco P O	85	745
William	30	m	w	IREL	San Francisco	11-Wd San Francisc	84	543
BOWELL								
Edward	34	m	w	PRUS	Tulare	Farmersville Twp	92	246
F M	33	m	w	PA	Amador	Sutter Crk P O	69	412
BOWELLE								
Henry	31	m	w	OH	Amador	Volcano P O	69	380
BOWELS								
Francis	28	m	w	SCOT	San Francisco	San Francisco P O	83	412
BOWEN								
Ahab	33	m	w	AR	Tulare	Tule Rvr Twp	92	268
And	35	m	w	AUST	El Dorado	Kelsey Twp	72	58
Anna	21	f	w	IREL	Solano	Vallejo	90	179
Annie	22	f	w	IREL	San Francisco	San Francisco P O	83	334
Archie J	40	m	w	ENGL	San Francisco	1-Wd San Francisco	79	11
Asa M	52	m	w	OH	San Francisco	2-Wd San Francisco	79	223
Augustus	25	m	w	RUSS	Alameda	Murray Twp	68	107
Carroll	41	m	w	TN	Stanislaus	Empire Twp	92	62
Charles	23	m	w	RI	Marin	Point Reyes Twp	74	21
Chas F	31	m	w	MA	Sacramento	4-Wd Sacramento	77	326
Chas P	40	m	w	BRUN	Santa Barbara	Santa Barbara P O	87	453
Clara	10	f	w	CA	Tulare	Tule Rvr Twp	92	264
D L	38	m	w	OH	El Dorado	Georgetown Twp	72	48
Dar D	47	m	w	WALE	Mono	Bridgeport P O	74	285
David	55	m	w	MA	San Francisco	1-Wd San Francisco	79	124
David	42	m	w	WALE	Nevada	Bridgeport Twp	75	105
David	40	m	w	WALE	Nevada	Bridgeport Twp	75	104
Dennis	45	m	w	IREL	San Francisco	6-Wd San Francisco	81	82
E J	58	m	w	IREL	Solano	Benicia	90	19
E S	35	m	w	NY	San Francisco	8-Wd San Francisco	82	299
Edward	32	m	w	IREL	San Francisco	3-Wd San Francisco	79	316
Eliza	28	f	w	MO	Los Angeles	Los Angeles	73	545
Elizabeth	46	f	w	KY	Sonoma	Petaluma Twp	91	326
Ezeikel	45	m	w	PA	San Francisco	San Francisco P O	80	368
F W	44	f	w	NY	Sacramento	1-Wd Sacramento	77	172
Frederick	30	m	w	NY	San Francisco	6-Wd San Francisco	81	101
G H	37	m	w	MA	San Francisco	San Francisco P O	85	865
Geo W	21	m	w	IL	Siskiyou	Yreka	89	651
H	33	m	w	MA	Nevada	Washington Twp	75	346
H C	25	m	w	PA	Solano	Vallejo	90	160
Helen	23	f	w	IREL	San Francisco	8-Wd San Francisco	82	476
Henry	35	m	w	OH	Los Angeles	Los Angeles	73	559
Henry	30	m	w	ME	San Francisco	6-Wd San Francisco	81	99
Henry	28	m	w	OH	Solano	Vacaville Twp	90	134
Henry	20	m	w	RI	Marin	Point Reyes Twp	74	22
Henry	18	m	w	PA	Sonoma	Salt Point	91	389
Horace	60	m	w	NH	Nevada	Nevada Twp	75	273
J	40	m	w	CANA	Solano	Vallejo	90	208
J	30	m	w	IREL	Lake	Knoxville Mines	73	404
J C	30	m	w	VA	Alameda	Oakland	68	188
J L Robert	43	m	w	CA	San Diego	San Diego	78	508
James	55	m	w	ENGL	San Diego	Julian Dist	78	470
James	35	m	w	IREL	Nevada	Bloomfield Twp	75	92
James H	28	m	w	NY	San Francisco	1-Wd San Francisco	79	63
Jane	19	f	w	NY	Sonoma	Mendocino Twp	91	293
Jas A	40	m	w	TN	Alameda	Murray Twp	68	99
Jennie	20	f	b	PA	Santa Clara	1-Wd San Jose	88	237
Jesse	38	m	w	MD	Napa	Napa	75	50
John	42	m	w	IREL	Nevada	Grass Valley Twp	75	231
John	35	m	w	PA	Sonoma	Vallejo Twp	91	451
John	25	m	w	IREL	San Francisco	8-Wd San Francisco	82	356
John	22	m	w	IREL	San Francisco	San Francisco P O	83	162
John	20	m	w	AZOR	Monterey	Castroville Twp	74	334
John	14	m	w	CA	Placer	Auburn P O	76	382
John J	41	m	w	IN	Santa Clara	1-Wd San Jose	88	254
Joseph	38	m	w	CT	Mariposa	Maxwell Crk P O	74	145
Joseph P	30	m	w	NY	Marin	Sausalito Twp	74	74
Kate	25	f	w	IREL	San Francisco	5-Wd San Francisco	81	33
M E	40	f	b	VA	Amador	Sutter Crk P O	69	401
Marcus	32	m	w	MO	Solano	Silveyville Twp	90	74
Margaret	27	f	w	IREL	San Francisco	5-Wd San Francisco	81	33
Mary	72	f	w	IREL	San Francisco	8-Wd San Francisco	82	471
Mary	70	f	w	KY	Sonoma	Analy Twp	91	236
Mary	13	f	w	CA	Los Angeles	Los Angeles	73	568
Michael	45	m	w	IREL	San Francisco	7-Wd San Francisco	81	270
Nathan	46	m	w	OH	Contra Costa	Martinez Twp	71	347
P M	43	m	w	MA	San Francisco	San Francisco P O	85	775
Peter	42	m	w	FRAN	Los Angeles	Los Angeles	73	558
Peter L	44	m	w	MA	Marin	Bolinas Twp	74	8
Robert J	36	m	w	MO	Calaveras	San Andreas P O	70	217

© 2001 by Heritage Quest. All rights reserved.

Series M593

Name	Age	S	R	B-PL	County	Locale	Roll	Pg
Sam	40	m	w	MA	San Joaquin	2-Wd Stockton	86	183
T	35	m	w	PA	Yuba	Marysville	93	604
T D	44	m	w	OH	Sacramento	3-Wd Sacramento	77	260
Thomas	31	m	w	NY	San Francisco	8-Wd San Francisco	82	299
Thomas	19	m	w	SCOT	Alameda	Brooklyn Twp	68	56
Thomas D	25	m	w	WALE	Placer	Bath P O	76	438
Timothy	40	m	w	IREL	San Francisco	8-Wd San Francisco	82	312
W	30	m	w	IN	Amador	Ione City P O	69	358
W J	53	m	w	MA	Alameda	Oakland	68	251
William W	39	m	w	KY	Tulare	Visalia	92	291
Wm	68	m	w	KY	Sonoma	Analy Twp	91	236
Wm	43	m	w	WALE	Siskiyou	Scott Valley Twp	89	612
BOWENE								
Geo	36	m	w	MO	Yuba	Marysville	93	596
William	34	m	w	IN	Placer	Blue Canyon P O	76	418
BOWER								
Andrew	45	m	w	PRUS	Yolo	Merritt Twp	93	506
Carrie	23	f	w	NY	San Francisco	San Francisco P O	83	64
Charles	20	m	w	WURT	San Francisco	San Francisco P O	83	299
Chas	21	m	w	BADE	San Francisco	San Francisco P O	85	873
Christian	19	m	w	BADE	San Francisco	San Francisco P O	85	752
Christopher	38	m	w	PRUS	Alameda	Oakland	68	144
David	16	m	w	PA	Sonoma	Petaluma Twp	91	346
Eliza	20	f	w	CA	San Francisco	2-Wd San Francisco	79	152
Englebert	63	m	w	PRUS	Santa Clara	1-Wd San Jose	88	254
George	37	m	w	PA	Nevada	Grass Valley Twp	75	209
George	31	m	w	OH	Yolo	Cottonwood Twp	93	467
Gustave	36	m	w	SAXO	San Francisco	2-Wd San Francisco	79	218
Henry	30	m	w	BADE	Monterey	San Juan Twp	74	399
J	33	m	w	GERM	Lake	Morgan Valley	73	425
John	24	m	w	IN	Los Angeles	Los Angeles Twp	73	477
Josephine	13	f	w	PA	San Francisco	7-Wd San Francisco	81	277
Kate	14	f	w	CA	Sonoma	Petaluma Twp	91	342
Leopold	28	m	w	BADE	San Francisco	San Francisco P O	85	754
Marshal	30	m	w	BADE	Tehama	Tehama Twp	92	193
Mary	50	f	w	NC	San Francisco	2-Wd San Francisco	79	236
Nehemiah	32	m	w	OH	Alpine	Silver Mtn P O	69	306
BOWERMAN								
John	44	m	w	NY	Trinity	Minersville Pct	92	203
BOWERS								
A	40	m	w	PA	Siskiyou	Scott Valley Twp	89	618
Adam	35	m	w	PA	Marin	Bolinas Twp	74	8
Aketa	52	m	w	BADE	Mariposa	Mariposa P O	74	92
Alfonzo	39	m	w	ME	San Francisco	7-Wd San Francisco	81	229
Anna	10	f	w	CA	Mendocino	Round Valley Twp	74	220
B D	49	m	w	NH	San Francisco	San Francisco P O	83	294
Barbara A	70	f	w	VA	Los Angeles	El Monte Twp	73	451
Benjamin	59	m	w	VT	Placer	Dutch Flat P O	76	415
Benjamin B	37	m	w	NY	Plumas	Plumas Twp	77	28
C	34	m	w	PRUS	Alameda	Oakland	68	144
Charles	29	m	w	BADE	Contra Costa	Martinez P O	71	380
Conrad	26	m	w	CANA	Placer	Roseville P O	76	352
Cornelius	38	m	w	OH	Nevada	Grass Valley Twp	75	224
Danl	30	m	w	IREL	San Francisco	5-Wd San Francisco	81	27
David L	38	m	w	OH	Placer	Bath P O	76	429
Eliza	30	f	w	SCOT	San Bernardino	San Bernardino Twp	78	448
Frank	28	m	w	OH	San Joaquin	Oneal Twp	86	107
Fred	22	m	w	ENGL	Trinity	Trinity Center Pct	92	204
George	35	m	w	WURT	Los Angeles	Santa Ana Twp	73	612
Henry	38	m	w	PA	Placer	Gold Run Twp	76	395
Jacob	48	m	w	GERM	Lake	Lower Lake	73	418
Jas	63	m	w	NY	San Joaquin	2-Wd Stockton	86	187
Jefferson	75	m	w	VA	Los Angeles	El Monte Twp	73	451
Joe	30	m	w	BAVA	Santa Clara	San Jose Twp	88	215
John	44	m	w	NH	San Francisco	11-Wd San Francisc	84	487
John	36	m	w	PA	Alameda	Eden Twp	68	62
John	35	m	w	PRUS	San Francisco	2-Wd San Francisco	79	191
John	33	m	w	KY	San Joaquin	Tulare Twp	86	254
John	30	m	w	PRUS	Sacramento	4-Wd Sacramento	77	357
John G	45	m	w	PA	Yolo	Grafton Twp	93	487
Jordan	39	m	b	MO	San Francisco	San Francisco P O	80	416
Jos W	36	m	w	NY	San Diego	San Diego	78	494
Joseph	40	m	w	NY	Nevada	Meadow Lake Twp	75	261
Joseph	30	m	w	IL	Calaveras	Copperopolis P O	70	263
M L	46	m	w	VA	Sutter	Butte Twp	92	96
Mary	50	f	w	HAMB	San Francisco	6-Wd San Francisco	81	71
Mary	45	f	w	IL	Alameda	Oakland	68	171
Michael	31	m	w	OH	San Joaquin	Oneal Twp	86	107
Minerva	20	f	w	MO	San Joaquin	Oneal Twp	86	113
Nancy	20	f	w	CA	Santa Cruz	Pajaro Twp	89	354
Nehemiah	30	m	w	IL	Sacramento	Dry Crk Twp	77	102
Oliver	65	m	w	ME	San Diego	Julian Dist	78	470
Oscar	31	m	w	PRUS	San Francisco	7-Wd San Francisco	81	211
Patterson	45	m	w	VA	Los Angeles	Los Nietos Twp	73	575
Phoebe	74	f	w	NH	San Francisco	San Francisco P O	80	410
Sam	30	m	w	IA	San Joaquin	Douglas Twp	86	50
Saml	35	m	w	MA	Butte	Kimshew Tpw	70	79
Samuel T	44	m	w	MD	Yuba	New York Twp	93	640
Seth	28	m	w	CA	Sacramento	3-Wd Sacramento	77	257
Susan	22	f	w	IL	Colusa	Spring Valley Twp	71	338
T A	24	f	w	OH	Alameda	Alameda	68	6
T J	41	m	w	TN	San Francisco	San Francisco P O	85	792
Thomas	35	m	w	MA	San Francisco	San Francisco P O	80	531
Wesley	33	m	w	OH	Plumas	Seneca Twp	77	48
William	46	m	w	NJ	Sonoma	Mendocino Twp	91	302
William	39	m	w	KY	Kern	Havilah P O	73	337
William H	36	m	w	TN	Stanislaus	Emory Twp	92	21
William J	25	m	w	IL	Yolo	Grafton Twp	93	487
BOWERY								
John	53	m	w	ENGL	Monterey	Castroville Twp	74	336
John	43	m	w	ENGL	Contra Costa	Martinez Twp	71	348
BOWES								
Edward	40	m	w	IREL	Santa Clara	Milpitas Twp	88	115
Geo C	22	m	w	ME	Santa Clara	Gilroy Twp	88	97
John M	31	m	w	IL	San Francisco	7-Wd San Francisco	81	248
Nathan	25	m	w	ME	Santa Cruz	Santa Cruz Twp	89	394
BOWEY								
Aug G	24	m	w	MD	San Francisco	San Francisco P O	83	102
James	25	m	w	PA	Trinity	Douglas	92	235
BOWIE								
Adam	48	m	w	SCOT	Santa Cruz	Watsonville	89	366
Agness	24	f	w	NY	Sacramento	2-Wd Sacramento	77	243
Alexander	74	m	w	SCOT	Monterey	San Juan Twp	74	404
Augustus J	55	m	w	MD	San Francisco	8-Wd San Francisco	82	345
Geo	4	m	w	CA	Solano	Benicia	90	18
George W	47	m	w	MD	San Francisco	San Francisco P O	83	147
James	30	m	w	SCOT	Napa	Napa	75	1
Thomas	25	m	w	LA	Yolo	Grafton Twp	93	494
William	24	m	w	MD	San Francisco	11-Wd San Francisc	84	539
BOWIN								
Auguste	25	m	w	FRAN	Sacramento	2-Wd Sacramento	77	248
BOWKER								
Gideon F	42	m	w	VT	El Dorado	Diamond Springs Tw	72	31
H L	21	m	w	VT	Humboldt	South Fork Twp	72	302
J J	28	m	w	WI	Sacramento	1-Wd Sacramento	77	173
BOWL								
John	25	m	w	IREL	San Francisco	1-Wd San Francisco	79	77
BOWLAN								
Jerry	48	m	w	OH	San Joaquin	2-Wd Stockton	86	166
BOWLAND								
Feilding	38	m	w	MO	San Bernardino	San Bernardino Twp	78	417
J L	36	m	w	AL	Tuolumne	Sonora P O	93	307
James	48	m	w	ENGL	San Francisco	1-Wd San Francisco	79	46
William	39	m	w	NY	San Francisco	7-Wd San Francisco	81	163
William	16	m	w	IA	Colusa	Colusa Twp	71	275
BOWLER								
Albert	48	m	w	ME	Trinity	Weaverville Pct	92	223
Frank F	45	m	w	VA	San Diego	San Diego	78	502
BOWLES								
Amos	38	m	w	CT	Sonoma	Vallejo Twp	91	462
Anthany	42	m	w	OH	Humboldt	South Fork Twp	72	300
Charles	38	m	w	MO	San Luis Obispo	Santa Rosa Twp	87	321
E B	45	m	w	OH	Lake	Big Valley	73	397
Estelle	16	f	w	CA	Santa Clara	2-Wd San Jose	88	337
George	45	m	w	OH	San Francisco	8-Wd San Francisco	82	363
George	43	m	w	OH	San Francisco	8-Wd San Francisco	82	306
Harry	15	m	w	CA	Santa Clara	Fremont Twp	88	60
Henry	15	m	w	CA	Santa Clara	Santa Clara Twp	88	176
Horace	21	m	w	PA	Santa Barbara	San Buenaventura P	87	426
J	39	m	w	IL	Alameda	Murray Twp	68	114
Jessie	18	f	w	IL	San Francisco	San Francisco P O	83	68
Jno D	55	m	w	NH	Sacramento	3-Wd Sacramento	77	300
John	36	m	w	MO	Butte	Chico Twp	70	44
John D	43	m	w	ME	Sacramento	4-Wd Sacramento	77	374
Mary	15	f	w	CA	Santa Clara	2-Wd San Jose	88	337
Moses	39	m	w	ME	Santa Cruz	Santa Cruz Twp	89	394
Obadiah W	40	m	w	KY	El Dorado	Diamond Springs Tw	72	32
Ruth	75	f	w	KY	Los Angeles	Los Angeles Twp	73	489
William	35	m	w	NY	Nevada	Little York Twp	75	244
Wm	45	m	m	AL	Mariposa	Maxwell Crk P O	74	143
BOWLET								
Louisa	50	f	w	FRAN	Alameda	Oakland	68	140
BOWLEY								
George	35	m	w	ENGL	Nevada	Nevada Twp	75	310
James D	49	m	w	MA	San Francisco	6-Wd San Francisco	81	106
John Q A	45	m	w	ME	Placer	Bath P O	76	448
Louis	27	m	w	MO	Napa	Napa Twp	75	73
Saml C	40	m	w	NY	San Francisco	San Francisco P O	83	101
William	38	m	w	ME	Santa Clara	Fremont Twp	88	54
BOWLI								
John	50	m	w	ITAL	Tuolumne	Columbia P O	93	350
BOWLIN								
John	45	m	w	KY	Fresno	Millerton P O	72	150
John	39	m	w	KY	Solano	Suisun Twp	90	102
BOWLING								
James	38	m	w	VA	Marin	San Rafael Twp	74	43
BOWLIS								
Martha	44	f	w	OH	Sacramento	Brighton Twp	77	72
BOWLLARD								
Charles	56	m	w	FRAN	Calaveras	San Andreas P O	70	216
BOWLS								
Joseph M	52	m	w	KY	Sonoma	Petaluma Twp	91	356
Stephen	46	m	w	KY	Merced	Snelling P O	74	260
William	64	m	b	JAMA	Sonoma	Petaluma Twp	91	338
BOWLWARE								
John W	40	m	w	KY	Santa Clara	Fremont Twp	88	56
Phillip	60	m	w	MO	Butte	Hamilton Twp	70	62
BOWM								
Charles W	38	m	w	MA	Alameda	Alameda	68	2
BOWMAN								
A W	38	m	w	MA	Alameda	Oakland	68	240
Adam	44	m	w	HANO	Calaveras	San Andreas P O	70	154
Alexander	22	m	w	PRUS	San Francisco	San Francisco P O	80	335
Alfred	55	m	w	KY	Mendocino	Point Arena Twp	74	209

© 2001 by Heritage Quest. All rights reserved.

Name	Age	S	R	B-PL	County	Locale	Roll (Series M593)	Pg
Amos	38	m	w	NY	San Francisco	5-Wd San Francisco	81	36
Amos	35	m	w	CANA	Yuba	Rose Bar Twp	93	663
Andrew	29	m	w	NY	Los Angeles	Los Angeles	73	532
Arthur	35	m	w	MA	San Francisco	7-Wd San Francisco	81	286
Besharus	43	m	w	PA	Sonoma	Petaluma Twp	91	310
Betsey	51	f	b	MO	San Francisco	San Francisco P O	80	475
Bur	57	m	w	HOLL	San Francisco	11-Wd San Francisc	84	672
C C	55	m	w	NH	San Francisco	1-Wd San Francisco	79	109
C E	29	m	w	SWED	San Francisco	San Francisco P O	85	877
Charles	35	m	w	OH	Tulare	Visalia	92	298
Charles	28	m	w	IA	San Mateo	Woodside P O	87	384
Chas	65	m	w	BADE	San Francisco	San Francisco P O	85	874
Chas	28	m	w	KY	Butte	Chico Twp	70	25
Chas H	43	m	w	PA	Nevada	Washington Twp	75	346
Christ	37	m	w	OH	Butte	Chico Twp	70	34
D	49	m	w	TN	Mariposa	Maxwell Crk P O	74	148
Daniel	42	m	w	NY	El Dorado	Cosumnes Twp	72	17
Daniel	31	m	w	KY	Humboldt	Bald Hills	72	238
Danl	35	m	w	IA	Butte	Ophir Twp	70	121
David	45	m	w	OH	Sonoma	Analy Twp	91	244
E	39	f	w	MO	Mendocino	Little Lake Twp	74	195
Elisha J	49	m	w	NY	El Dorado	Placerville	72	124
Frank	27	m	w	OH	Los Angeles	Los Angeles	73	526
Frank	17	m	w	CA	Santa Clara	Almaden Twp	88	13
Fred	38	m	w	BREM	San Francisco	1-Wd San Francisco	79	49
Geo	32	m	w	PRUS	San Francisco	San Francisco P O	83	313
Geo	28	m	w	ME	Alameda	Oakland	68	171
George	41	m	w	NY	San Francisco	5-Wd San Francisco	81	25
George	26	m	w	IA	Napa	Napa	75	18
George B	58	m	w	NC	Santa Clara	2-Wd San Jose	88	285
George Mrs	30	f	w	NY	San Francisco	5-Wd San Francisco	81	25
Gustavus	38	m	w	OH	Santa Cruz	Santa Cruz	89	419
H	45	m	w	NY	Alameda	Alameda	68	3
Henry	46	m	w	CANA	Sacramento	4-Wd Sacramento	77	331
Henry	35	m	w	PA	San Francisco	5-Wd San Francisco	81	31
Henry	22	m	w	MO	Solano	Montezuma Twp	90	65
Henry G	17	m	w	NY	Nevada	Rough & Ready Twp	75	330
Ira	44	m	w	KY	Siskiyou	Scott Valley Twp	89	620
Ivory	20	m	w	ME	Nevada	Nevada Twp	75	271
J	40	m	w	ME	Alameda	Oakland	68	255
J	37	m	w	SWIT	Alameda	Oakland	68	181
J E	24	m	w	MA	San Francisco	San Francisco P O	85	849
J H	43	m	w	OH	Yuba	Marysville	93	617
James	30	m	w	TN	Kern	Havilah P O	73	341
James	29	m	w	PA	Santa Clara	1-Wd San Jose	88	244
James	29	m	w	OH	Yolo	Putah Twp	93	520
James	24	m	w	IA	Sonoma	Petaluma Twp	91	313
James E	48	m	w	NY	Yuba	Marysville	93	582
James F	44	m	w	NY	San Francisco	6-Wd San Francisco	81	131
Jane	44	f	w	IREL	Yuba	Rose Bar Twp	93	666
Jno	45	m	w	BREM	Santa Clara	Almaden Twp	88	1
Joel	56	m	w	PA	San Francisco	San Francisco P O	83	231
John	65	m	w	PA	Sonoma	Petaluma Twp	91	339
John	61	m	w	NY	Monterey	Alisal Twp	74	296
John	45	m	w	IREL	Solano	Tremont Twp	90	34
John	45	m	w	NY	Placer	Auburn P O	76	357
John	39	m	w	OH	Santa Cruz	Santa Cruz Twp	89	384
John	37	m	w	PRUS	San Francisco	San Francisco P O	85	763
John C	34	m	w	PA	Sonoma	Petaluma Twp	91	314
John H	50	m	w	NJ	San Francisco	3-Wd San Francisco	79	322
Jos	45	m	w	WURT	Sierra	Gibson Twp	89	538
Joseph	39	m	w	AUST	Calaveras	San Andreas P O	70	219
Julia	50	f	w	PA	Marin	San Rafael Twp	74	27
Kate	30	f	w	IREL	San Francisco	San Francisco P O	83	271
Lena	11	f	w	NY	San Francisco	San Francisco P O	80	467
Louisa	12	f	w	MO	Los Angeles	Wilmington Twp	73	643
M	20	m	w	ENGL	Butte	Chico Twp	70	48
Michael	37	m	w	IREL	Inyo	Cerro Gordo Twp	73	320
Michael	20	m	w	ENGL	San Francisco	San Francisco P O	83	302
Michl	34	m	w	IREL	Marin	Sausalito Twp	74	74
N M	36	m	w	TN	Amador	Jackson P O	69	337
Nelly	20	f	w	NY	San Francisco	6-Wd San Francisco	81	62
Oliver G	59	m	w	PA	Tuolumne	Sonora P O	93	331
Peter	60	m	w	PA	San Francisco	1-Wd San Francisco	79	29
Richard	36	m	w	GERM	Nevada	Washington Twp	75	346
Robt	28	m	w	NY	Colusa	Butte Twp	71	270
Sam E	17	m	w	IN	Nevada	Nevada Twp	75	307
Saml	34	m	w	IREL	San Francisco	San Francisco P O	85	830
Saml	23	m	w	OH	El Dorado	Georgetown Twp	72	48
Sarah	39	f	w	PRUS	San Francisco	San Francisco P O	80	469
Silas	32	m	w	KY	Merced	Snelling P O	74	261
Simon	35	m	w	SCOT	Butte	Chico Twp	70	37
W C	35	m	w	ME	Alameda	Oakland	68	202
W J	26	m	w	MO	Napa	Napa	75	50
Wat	30	m	w	ME	Mono	Bridgeport P O	74	284
Watson	28	m	w	ME	Inyo	Bishop Crk Twp	73	314
William	49	m	w	PA	Santa Clara	Fremont Twp	88	57
William	30	m	w	PA	Marin	San Rafael Twp	74	27
William J	57	m	w	ME	Solano	Rio Vista Twp	90	55
Wm	34	m	w	PA	San Francisco	1-Wd San Francisco	79	53
Wm	30	m	w	MA	San Francisco	San Francisco P O	85	807
Wm C	33	m	w	MO	Butte	Oregon Twp	70	129
BOWMASTER								
M	29	f	w	SHOL	Humboldt	Eureka Twp	72	270
BOWMER								
J C	51	m	w	KY	Siskiyou	Surprise Valley Tw	89	641
BOWN								
August	45	m	w	PA	Sonoma	Sonoma Twp	91	434
Elias	56	m	w	NY	El Dorado	Coloma Twp	72	12
Elizabeth	25	f	w	IREL	San Francisco	San Francisco P O	83	85
George W	50	m	w	NY	Napa	Napa	75	43
Herman	37	m	w	NY	San Joaquin	Elliott Twp	86	79
BOWNAN								
Isreal	28	m	w	OH	El Dorado	Georgetown Twp	72	48
BOWNE								
Adelaide	24	f	w	TN	San Francisco	1-Wd San Francisco	79	52
Alex	40	m	w	NY	Yuba	East Bear Rvr Twp	93	541
Peter	31	m	w	PRUS	Solano	Tremont Twp	90	34
William F	53	m	w	NY	San Francisco	8-Wd San Francisco	82	444
BOWNING								
Sam	38	m	w	ENGL	Butte	Concow Twp	70	7
BOWNS								
John H	40	m	w	ENGL	San Francisco	11-Wd San Francisc	84	709
BOWREN								
Edwd	51	m	w	ENGL	Butte	Ophir Twp	70	93
BOWRNE								
Robert C	63	m	w	VA	Nevada	Rough & Ready Twp	75	330
BOWS								
Martin	31	m	w	ME	San Francisco	1-Wd San Francisco	79	70
BOWSE								
Thos F	16	m	w	CA	San Luis Obispo	Morro Twp	87	280
BOWSEN								
Jas	50	m	w	ENGL	Butte	Ophir Twp	70	104
BOWSER								
George	29	m	b	VA	Santa Clara	2-Wd San Jose	88	283
BOWSON								
Geo H	48	m	w	MD	El Dorado	Placerville Twp	72	94
BOWTELL								
Alice	27	f	w	VT	San Francisco	8-Wd San Francisco	82	413
BOWVITCH								
Peter	30	m	w	AUST	Amador	Sutter Crk P O	69	406
BOX								
Ah	30	m	c	CHIN	San Francisco	6-Wd San Francisco	81	130
J A	20	m	w	OR	Mendocino	Round Valley Twp	74	220
James	35	m	w	ENGL	San Francisco	11-Wd San Francisc	84	638
Lucy	53	f	w	AL	Sonoma	Sonoma Twp	91	433
Norah	13	f	i	CA	San Francisco	San Francisco P O	83	325
Sing	20	m	c	CHIN	San Francisco	2-Wd San Francisco	79	172
Stephen	40	m	w	KY	Stanislaus	North Twp	92	68
Thomas	30	m	w	ENGL	San Francisco	6-Wd San Francisco	81	130
Thomas A	53	m	w	ENGL	Calaveras	San Andreas P O	70	179
BOXALL								
James	47	m	w	ENGL	Yuba	Linda Twp	93	556
William	34	m	w	ENGL	Amador	Jackson P O	69	326
BOXEL								
Louis	38	m	w	FRAN	Plumas	Rich Bar Twp	77	45
BOXLEY								
Josiah	40	m	w	OH	Colusa	Monroe Twp	71	325
BOXON								
Stephen	43	m	w	VT	Tulare	Farmersville Twp	92	247
BOXTON								
Thos H	43	m	w	ENGL	Butte	Chico Twp	70	36
BOY								
Ah	45	m	c	CHIN	El Dorado	Coloma Twp	72	12
Ah	40	m	c	CHIN	Amador	Drytown P O	69	422
Ah	39	m	c	CHIN	San Francisco	San Francisco P O	80	493
Ah	35	m	c	CHIN	Yolo	Grafton Twp	93	479
Ah	32	m	c	CHIN	San Francisco	San Francisco P O	80	497
Ah	28	m	c	CHIN	San Francisco	6-Wd San Francisco	81	62
Ah	22	m	c	CHIN	Santa Clara	Santa Clara Twp	88	166
Ah	18	m	c	CHIN	Sierra	Sierra Twp	89	566
Ah	17	f	c	CHIN	San Francisco	6-Wd San Francisco	81	76
Ar	20	m	c	CHIN	Sonoma	Petaluma Twp	91	363
Koo	36	m	c	CHIN	Yuba	Marysville	93	625
Tong	22	f	c	CHIN	Placer	Dutch Flat P O	76	409
Yen	27	m	c	CHIN	Butte	Chico Twp	70	27
BOYARD								
Annetta	14	f	w	PA	San Francisco	11-Wd San Francisc	84	688
Jackson	28	m	w	IL	Tehama	Tehama Twp	92	196
John	22	m	w	IL	Tehama	Tehama Twp	92	196
BOYARE								
John B	40	m	w	ITAL	San Francisco	6-Wd San Francisco	81	57
BOYARRI								
Jaco	44	m	w	SWIT	Marin	San Antonio Twp	74	63
BOYCE								
Aleric	44	m	w	NY	Merced	Snelling P O	74	276
Augustus	25	m	w	TN	San Francisco	5-Wd San Francisco	81	19
Clara L	13	f	w	CA	Shasta	Stillwater P O	89	481
Daniel	35	m	w	NY	Yolo	Merritt Twp	93	502
David	28	m	w	CANA	Santa Clara	Milpitas Twp	88	108
E W	49	m	w	NH	Sierra	Sears Twp	89	553
Edwin	29	m	w	IL	Napa	Napa	75	19
Isaac E	45	m	w	MO	Los Angeles	Los Nietos Twp	73	588
J C	36	m	w	VA	Tehama	Red Bluff	92	181
Jane	4	f	w	CA	Santa Clara	2-Wd San Jose	88	321
Jno F	44	m	w	NY	Sonoma	Santa Rosa	91	406
John	60	m	w	IREL	Solano	Vallejo	90	161
John	47	m	w	IREL	Shasta	Shasta P O	89	461
John	35	m	w	OH	Solano	Montezuma Twp	90	69
John	30	m	w	ENGL	San Francisco	2-Wd San Francisco	79	219
John	29	m	w	NY	San Francisco	11-Wd San Francisc	84	469
John B	31	m	w	PA	Tehama	Red Bank Twp	92	169
Jonathan	62	m	w	ENGL	San Joaquin	Liberty Twp	86	92

© 2001 by Heritage Quest. All rights reserved.

Name	Age	S	R	B-PL	County	Locale	Roll	Pg
						Series M593		
Josephine	27	f	w	IREL	San Francisco	8-Wd San Francisco	82	432
Mary	40	f	w	IREL	San Francisco	6-Wd San Francisco	81	122
Mary J	35	f	w	OH	Yolo	Merritt Twp	93	507
Otto	28	m	w	HAMB	San Francisco	11-Wd San Francisc	84	596
Patrick	38	m	w	IREL	San Mateo	San Mateo P O	87	354
Paul	37	m	w	VT	Stanislaus	San Joaquin Twp	92	78
S M	48	m	w	NH	Sierra	Sears Twp	89	553
Samuel	61	m	w	NY	Siskiyou	Table Rock Twp	89	645
Samuel	50	m	w	NY	San Diego	Julian Dist	78	470
Samuel	22	m	w	MO	Alameda	San Leandro	68	95
Silas	65	m	w	NH	Yuba	Long Bar Twp	93	561
Thomas	42	m	w	IREL	San Francisco	San Francisco P O	83	61
Thos H	30	m	b	MD	Butte	Ophir Twp	70	100
William	35	m	w	MO	Sonoma	Mendocino Twp	91	298
Wm R	38	m	w	TN	Mendocino	Calpella Twp	74	189
Wm T	40	m	w	OH	Sierra	Gibson Twp	89	543
Worden	40	m	w	PA	Alameda	Brooklyn	68	32
BOYD								
---	23	m	w	TN	Sonoma	Santa Rosa	91	419
--- [Dr]	36	m	w	IL	Yuba	Marysville	93	587
A B	28	m	w	IL	Los Angeles	Los Angeles	73	541
Agnes	53	f	w	IREL	San Francisco	8-Wd San Francisco	82	386
Alex	49	m	w	PA	San Francisco	8-Wd San Francisco	82	377
Alice	40	f	w	CANA	Alameda	Eden Twp	68	91
Alice	12	f	w	CA	Solano	Vacaville Twp	90	119
Amand	35	f	w	IN	Siskiyou	Surprise Valley Tw	89	638
Andrew	45	m	w	AR	Tulare	Farmersville Twp	92	243
Andrew	26	m	w	OH	Solano	Suisun Twp	90	102
Andrew J	43	m	w	AR	Tulare	Venice Twp	92	277
Andrew J	32	m	w	NY	Mendocino	Bourns Landing Twp	74	223
Anna	30	f	w	PA	San Francisco	7-Wd San Francisco	81	159
B B	25	m	w	PA	Tuolumne	Sonora P O	93	313
Bridget	25	f	w	IREL	San Mateo	Menlo Park P O	87	378
C E	45	m	w	NY	Amador	Jackson P O	69	319
Charles	35	m	w	CANA	Napa	Napa Twp	75	59
Charles	14	m	w	HI	Santa Clara	Santa Clara Twp	88	137
Chas P	28	m	w	MO	Siskiyou	Surprise Valley Tw	89	641
Colin M	40	m	w	SCOT	San Francisco	8-Wd San Francisco	82	324
Cornelius	49	m	w	IREL	Contra Costa	Martinez P O	71	417
D C	40	m	w	NY	San Francisco	8-Wd San Francisco	82	325
Daniel	37	m	w	IREL	San Mateo	Menlo Park P O	87	377
Daniel	34	m	w	ENGL	San Diego	San Diego	78	505
David	22	m	w	NY	Mendocino	Albion & Big Rvr T	74	167
Edward H	34	m	w	AL	Los Angeles	Los Nietos Twp	73	582
Edward T	34	m	w	ENGL	San Francisco	6-Wd San Francisco	81	41
Eliza	23	f	w	IREL	Sonoma	Bodega Twp	91	261
Francis	51	m	w	DENM	Tuolumne	Chinese Camp P O	93	390
Frank	40	m	w	IREL	Solano	Denverton Twp	90	22
Frank	38	m	w	BADE	San Francisco	2-Wd San Francisco	79	218
George	45	m	w	ME	San Francisco	11-Wd San Francisc	84	572
George	25	m	w	VA	Inyo	Independence Twp	73	325
George	24	m	w	ME	San Francisco	San Francisco P O	83	205
George	21	m	w	AR	Napa	Napa Twp	75	62
H C	34	m	w	DE	San Francisco	3-Wd San Francisco	79	317
Henry	44	m	w	VA	Marin	San Rafael	74	50
Henry	36	m	w	NY	San Francisco	5-Wd San Francisco	81	31
Henry	18	m	w	NY	San Francisco	San Francisco P O	83	390
Henry	10	m	w	CA	San Francisco	8-Wd San Francisco	82	363
Hepsebah	35	f	w	ENGL	San Mateo	Menlo Park P O	87	377
Isaac	25	m	w	SC	San Francisco	5-Wd San Francisco	81	18
J H	32	m	w	VA	Yuba	Marysville	93	577
James	50	m	w	SCOT	San Francisco	2-Wd San Francisco	79	213
James	45	m	w	ENGL	San Francisco	San Francisco P O	83	58
James	45	m	w	NY	San Francisco	11-Wd San Francisc	84	561
James	45	m	w	VA	Solano	Green Valley Twp	90	42
James	41	m	w	AR	Tulare	Venice Twp	92	276
James	37	m	w	VA	Sutter	Butte Twp	92	100
James	36	m	w	ENGL	Contra Costa	San Pablo Twp	71	364
James	35	m	w	IREL	San Francisco	San Francisco P O	80	373
James	30	m	w	CANA	San Francisco	2-Wd San Francisco	79	196
James	24	m	w	AR	Tulare	Venice Twp	92	277
James	24	m	w	MA	Solano	Vacaville Twp	90	135
James	19	m	w	NY	Contra Costa	San Pablo Twp	71	355
Jane	50	f	w	IREL	San Francisco	2-Wd San Francisco	79	202
Jas	28	m	w	NY	Solano	Vallejo	90	161
Jas	25	m	w	LA	Solano	Vallejo	90	163
Jas H	25	m	w	NY	Solano	Vallejo	90	141
John	45	m	w	MO	Tuolumne	Chinese Camp P O	93	375
John	40	m	w	NY	Los Angeles	San Gabriel Twp	73	594
John	34	m	w	IREL	Solano	Montezuma Twp	90	65
John	32	m	w	MI	Nevada	Meadow Lake Twp	75	265
John	30	m	w	IREL	San Francisco	San Francisco P O	85	780
John	26	m	w	IL	Solano	Vacaville Twp	90	133
John	24	m	w	IREL	Solano	Vacaville Twp	90	120
John	18	m	w	CT	Sonoma	Bodega Twp	91	254
John B	24	m	w	PA	San Diego	San Diego	78	492
John M	34	m	w	IREL	San Diego	San Diego	78	511
John W	59	m	w	ENGL	San Francisco	San Francisco P O	83	234
Joseph	50	m	w	IREL	San Francisco	1-Wd San Francisco	79	11
Joseph	48	m	w	IREL	Contra Costa	San Pablo Twp	71	362
Joseph	47	m	w	PA	San Francisco	San Francisco P O	83	401
Julia	19	f	w	NY	San Francisco	San Francisco P O	85	826
L A	38	m	w	TN	San Joaquin	2-Wd Stockton	86	172
Leon	49	m	w	US	San Joaquin	2-Wd Stockton	86	166
M N	44	f	w	MO	San Joaquin	2-Wd Stockton	86	206
Mary	29	f	w	IREL	Alameda	Alameda	68	13
Michael	33	m	w	SCOT	San Francisco	3-Wd San Francisco	79	294

Name	Age	S	R	B-PL	County	Locale	Roll	Pg
						Series M593		
Miller	22	m	w	MD	Marin	Nicasio Twp	74	17
Nancy	49	f	w	SCOT	San Mateo	Redwood Twp	87	368
Oliver	36	m	w	NY	San Francisco	2-Wd San Francisco	79	243
R M	50	m	w	PA	Tuolumne	Sonora P O	93	313
Ralph	40	m	w	MA	San Francisco	5-Wd San Francisco	81	11
Redman	22	m	w	CANA	San Francisco	7-Wd San Francisco	81	167
Robert	67	m	w	LA	Stanislaus	Branch Twp	92	1
Robert	62	m	w	GA	Monterey	Pajaro Twp	74	371
Robert B	37	m	w	ME	San Mateo	Pescadero P O	87	411
Robert C	56	m	w	SC	Calaveras	Copperopolis P O	70	246
Rufina	11	f	w	CA	Monterey	Monterey	74	367
S L	22	m	w	IL	Yuba	Marysville	93	587
Saml	46	m	w	MI	Butte	Ophir Twp	70	108
Samuel	40	m	w	KY	Amador	Fiddletown P O	69	438
Samuel	40	m	w	SCOT	Sutter	Nicolaus Twp	92	110
Stewart	21	m	w	CANA	Santa Clara	Santa Clara Twp	88	165
T C	41	m	w	PA	San Joaquin	1-Wd Stockton	86	138
Thomas	39	m	w	AR	Tulare	Venice Twp	92	277
Thomas	38	m	w	IN	Yolo	Fremont Twp	93	476
Thomas	31	m	w	SCOT	San Mateo	Woodside P O	87	385
Thos	26	m	w	KY	Tehama	Red Bluff	92	173
Thos L	39	m	w	VA	Sutter	Yuba Twp	92	140
W H	29	m	w	MO	Amador	Jackson P O	69	337
Walter M	52	m	w	ME	San Francisco	6-Wd San Francisco	81	116
William	48	m	w	IREL	Shasta	Horsetown P O	89	502
William	40	m	w	IREL	Yolo	Washington Twp	93	534
William	36	m	w	NY	San Francisco	7-Wd San Francisco	81	168
William	35	m	w	CANA	Contra Costa	Martinez P O	71	370
William	34	m	w	IREL	Marin	San Rafael	74	50
William	31	m	w	MO	Solano	Denverton Twp	90	25
William	27	m	w	IREL	Sonoma	Bodega Twp	91	262
William	25	m	w	PA	San Mateo	Pescadero P O	87	409
William	23	m	w	TN	San Bernardino	San Salvador Twp	78	458
William G	37	m	w	TN	Amador	Volcano P O	69	382
William R	39	m	w	TN	Klamath	Salmon Twp	73	388
Wm	28	m	w	CANA	Sonoma	Salt Point	91	384
Wm	28	m	w	IREL	San Francisco	2-Wd San Francisco	79	205
Wm B	21	m	w	VT	Sonoma	Analy Twp	91	233
Wm H	37	m	w	ME	Sonoma	Salt Point Twp	91	383
Wm S	42	m	w	MA	Amador	Volcano P O	69	377
BOYDE								
Anna	18	f	w	IL	Napa	Napa	75	2
Dan W	17	m	w	OR	Amador	Ione City P O	69	349
John	65	m	w	ENGL	Alameda	Alameda	68	11
BOYDEN								
Allen	46	m	w	MA	Placer	Lincoln P O	76	484
Wm S	63	m	w	MA	Nevada	Little York Twp	75	242
BOYDON								
George W	36	m	w	NY	Plumas	Indian Twp	77	13
BOYDSON								
Robt W	31	m	w	AR	Butte	Chico Twp	70	38
BOYDSTON								
David S	40	m	w	OH	Amador	Volcano P O	69	377
Jno	27	m	w	AR	Butte	Chico Twp	70	37
Joseph	30	m	w	TN	Butte	Chico Twp	70	37
BOYDSTONE								
Jas W	58	m	w	IN	Butte	Chico Twp	70	38
BOYE								
Charles F	38	m	w	PRUS	Siskiyou	Callahan P O	89	628
Claus	30	m	w	DENM	Sacramento	Brighton Twp	77	74
Wilhelmina	22	f	w	PRUS	San Francisco	7-Wd San Francisco	81	241
BOYED								
S B	68	m	w	IREL	Sacramento	1-Wd Sacramento	77	188
BOYEN								
Alice	55	f	w	ENGL	Placer	Lincoln P O	76	489
George C	28	m	w	CANA	Yolo	Cache Crk Twp	93	426
BOYENVUE								
Louis	30	m	w	FRAN	San Francisco	San Francisco P O	80	462
BOYER								
Christian	54	m	w	DENM	Solano	Vallejo	90	213
E A	44	m	w	PA	Mariposa	Maxwell Crk P O	74	146
George	28	m	w	CANA	Yuba	Marysville	93	586
Hiram	63	m	w	NY	Sutter	Nicolaus Twp	92	106
Jacob	37	m	w	KY	Yuba	W Bear Rvr Twp	93	682
John	43	m	w	NY	Shasta	Portugese Flat P O	89	472
John	38	m	w	IREL	Solano	Silveyville Twp	90	73
John	37	m	w	OH	Yuba	Rose Bar Twp	93	652
Joseph	28	m	w	IL	Solano	Silveyville Twp	90	83
Julieus	24	m	w	FRAN	Napa	Napa	75	56
P	21	m	w	FRAN	Butte	Bidwell Twp	70	3
S G	38	m	w	PA	Sierra	Sierra Twp	89	564
Thos	28	m	w	OH	Yuba	Marysville	93	589
William	28	m	w	PA	San Francisco	8-Wd San Francisco	82	442
BOYERS								
Betty	78	f	b	VA	Contra Costa	Martinez P O	71	389
J W	38	m	w	MO	Sutter	Butte Twp	92	90
BOYES								
Ella	19	f	w	MO	San Francisco	San Francisco P O	83	284
Fletcher	33	m	w	MO	Sonoma	Analy Twp	91	231
John R	63	m	w	NC	Sonoma	Analy Twp	91	228
William	33	m	w	OH	Alameda	Oakland	68	140
Wm	61	m	w	NC	Shasta	Millville P O	89	492
BOYHAM								
John	34	m	w	IREL	San Francisco	San Francisco P O	83	290
BOYHAN								
Luke	32	m	w	IREL	San Francisco	1-Wd San Francisco	79	132

© 2001 by Heritage Quest. All rights reserved.

Name	Age	S	R	B-PL	County	Locale	Roll	Pg
BOYINGTON								
F H	9	m	w	UT	Sutter	Butte Twp	92	89
BOYL								
Edward	13	m	w	CA	Solano	Tremont Twp	90	35
Frank	38	m	w	IREL	Monterey	Castroville Twp	74	341
Joseph	31	m	w	SCOT	Alameda	Oakland	68	255
Martin	50	m	w	IREL	Yolo	Putah Twp	93	515
Thomas	34	m	w	IREL	Mendocino	Navarro & Big Rvr	74	167
BOYLAN								
Barnard	38	m	w	IREL	San Francisco	San Francisco P O	80	402
Jas	30	m	w	IREL	Sacramento	1-Wd Sacramento	77	183
BOYLAND								
Margt	26	f	w	IREL	San Francisco	8-Wd San Francisco	82	330
W M	25	m	w	NY	Solano	Vallejo	90	200
BOYLE								
A T	36	m	w	MO	Tuolumne	Sonora P O	93	307
Alice	14	f	w	ENGL	San Francisco	San Francisco P O	83	185
Andrew	31	m	w	MA	Los Angeles	Santa Ana Twp	73	600
Anna	37	f	w	IREL	San Francisco	8-Wd San Francisco	82	309
B	34	m	w	IREL	Sacramento	3-Wd Sacramento	77	267
Barney	37	m	w	IREL	Marin	San Rafael Twp	74	40
Bernard	35	m	w	IREL	San Francisco	San Francisco P O	85	727
Bridget	18	f	w	IREL	San Francisco	San Francisco P O	83	236
C	27	f	w	NY	Solano	Vallejo	90	194
Carmilita	45	f	w	CA	San Francisco	2-Wd San Francisco	79	141
Catherine	17	f	w	IREL	San Francisco	7-Wd San Francisco	81	172
Charles	40	m	w	IREL	Nevada	Rough & Ready Twp	75	326
Charles	36	m	w	IREL	Calaveras	Copperopolis P O	70	221
Charles	30	m	w	IL	San Francisco	San Francisco P O	80	406
Charles	28	m	w	IREL	San Diego	Julian Dist	78	469
Chas	44	m	w	NY	Marin	San Rafael Twp	74	41
Christopher C	39	m	w	PA	Plumas	Plumas Twp	77	28
Danial	24	m	w	IREL	San Francisco	7-Wd San Francisco	81	182
Daniel	47	m	w	IREL	Nevada	Grass Valley Twp	75	228
Daniel	38	m	w	IREL	San Francisco	11-Wd San Francisc	84	432
Delia	30	f	w	NY	Sacramento	4-Wd Sacramento	77	342
Dennis	22	m	w	PA	Contra Costa	Martinez P O	71	419
E P	45	m	w	ENGL	San Francisco	San Francisco P O	85	857
Edward	38	m	w	IREL	San Francisco	San Francisco P O	83	368
Edward F	34	m	w	PA	Yolo	Cache Crk Twp	93	426
Edwd	50	m	w	IREL	Solano	Vallejo	90	188
Ellen	38	f	w	IREL	San Francisco	San Francisco P O	83	296
Ellen	23	f	w	MA	Solano	Benicia	90	16
G P	26	m	w	MO	Tuolumne	Sonora P O	93	307
George	50	m	w	ENGL	San Mateo	Schoolhouse Statio	87	340
George	39	m	w	CANA	Mendocino	Navarro & Big Rvr	74	167
George	33	m	w	IREL	Santa Clara	San Jose Twp	88	196
H	39	m	w	FRAN	San Joaquin	Elkhorn Twp	86	56
Hannah	60	f	w	NJ	San Francisco	2-Wd San Francisco	79	194
Henry	40	m	w	IREL	Sacramento	4-Wd Sacramento	77	355
Henry	32	m	w	ENGL	Mariposa	Mariposa P O	74	112
Henry	26	m	w	IREL	Marin	San Rafael Twp	74	25
Henry	26	m	w	NY	Alameda	Alameda	68	4
Henry	25	m	w	MA	Sonoma	Mendocino Twp	91	297
J	32	m	w	MO	Alameda	Oakland	68	262
J P	50	m	w	PA	Alameda	Oakland	68	176
James	70	m	w	IREL	San Francisco	1-Wd San Francisco	79	38
James	45	m	w	IREL	San Joaquin	Oneal Twp	86	119
James	38	m	w	IREL	Stanislaus	North Twp	92	67
James	35	m	w	IREL	San Francisco	San Francisco P O	83	40
James	31	m	w	IREL	San Francisco	San Francisco P O	83	43
James	30	m	w	IREL	San Francisco	8-Wd San Francisco	82	373
James	27	m	w	NY	San Francisco	8-Wd San Francisco	82	376
James	20	m	w	IREL	San Francisco	8-Wd San Francisco	82	373
Jane	32	f	w	IREL	San Francisco	7-Wd San Francisco	81	164
Jas	40	m	w	IREL	San Francisco	11-Wd San Francisc	84	625
Jas	32	m	w	RI	Solano	Vallejo	90	210
Jno	45	m	w	MD	Santa Clara	Burnett Twp	88	30
Jno	41	m	w	IREL	Sacramento	1-Wd Sacramento	77	178
John	60	m	w	IREL	San Francisco	2-Wd San Francisco	79	184
John	40	m	w	IREL	San Francisco	7-Wd San Francisco	81	185
John	39	m	w	CANA	San Francisco	San Francisco P O	85	859
John	37	m	w	MD	San Francisco	11-Wd San Francisc	84	422
John	26	m	w	ME	Los Angeles	Los Nietos Twp	73	578
John	25	m	w	IREL	Solano	Vallejo	90	200
John	25	m	w	MA	San Francisco	3-Wd San Francisco	79	296
John	24	m	w	IREL	Yolo	Cache Crk Twp	93	449
John G	36	m	w	MA	Santa Cruz	Pajaro Twp	89	343
John S	25	m	w	IREL	San Francisco	1-Wd San Francisco	79	30
Julia	16	f	w	NY	San Francisco	San Francisco P O	83	193
Laurence	32	m	w	IREL	San Francisco	San Francisco P O	83	41
Lawrence	30	m	w	IREL	Humboldt	Bucksport Twp	72	242
Lucy A	20	f	w	MO	Sonoma	Mendocino Twp	91	289
Manius	45	m	w	IREL	San Francisco	8-Wd San Francisco	82	434
Margaret	76	f	w	IREL	San Francisco	San Francisco P O	83	90
Margaret	30	f	w	IREL	Santa Cruz	Watsonville	89	367
Margaret	30	f	w	IREL	San Francisco	San Francisco P O	80	424
Maria	75	f	w	MD	San Francisco	2-Wd San Francisco	79	260
Mary	22	f	w	IREL	Sacramento	2-Wd Sacramento	77	229
Mary A	21	f	w	CT	Los Angeles	Santa Ana Twp	73	600
Mary A	19	f	w	IREL	San Francisco	San Francisco P O	83	227
Mary Ann	23	f	w	IREL	San Francisco	San Francisco P O	83	58
Matthew O	64	m	w	IREL	Los Angeles	Santa Ana Twp	73	600
Michael	41	m	w	IREL	Alameda	Washington Twp	68	295
Michael	32	m	w	IREL	Nevada	Grass Valley Twp	75	215
Michael	28	m	w	IREL	San Francisco	San Francisco P O	85	758
Michael	28	m	w	IREL	San Francisco	2-Wd San Francisco	79	162
Micheal	28	m	w	IREL	San Francisco	7-Wd San Francisco	81	185
Michl	28	m	w	IREL	San Francisco	1-Wd San Francisco	79	94
Minna	32	f	w	IREL	San Francisco	8-Wd San Francisco	82	318
Oscar	19	m	w	WI	San Joaquin	Dent Twp	86	22
Owen	40	m	w	IREL	Napa	Napa Twp	75	30
Owen	26	m	w	IREL	San Francisco	7-Wd San Francisco	81	217
Pat	45	m	w	IREL	Alameda	Oakland	68	250
Patrick	44	m	w	IREL	Shasta	Shasta P O	89	453
Patrick	30	m	w	IREL	Nevada	Little York Twp	75	243
Patrick	24	m	w	IREL	San Francisco	7-Wd San Francisco	81	169
Peter	60	m	w	IREL	Santa Barbara	San Buenaventura P	87	431
Peter	59	m	w	PRUS	Butte	Ophir Twp	70	118
Peter	36	m	w	IREL	San Francisco	7-Wd San Francisco	81	225
Peter	36	m	w	IREL	Sacramento	3-Wd Sacramento	77	303
Peter	26	m	w	IREL	Marin	Sausalito Twp	74	73
Robert	79	m	w	IREL	Tuolumne	Sonora P O	93	327
Robert	41	m	w	IREL	San Francisco	11-Wd San Francisc	84	615
Robt	48	m	w	IREL	Solano	Vallejo	90	170
Rosa	24	f	w	IREL	San Francisco	San Francisco P O	83	287
Rose Anna	23	f	w	IREL	San Francisco	San Francisco P O	85	877
Sarah	27	f	w	IREL	San Francisco	8-Wd San Francisco	82	304
Sarah	17	f	w	IREL	San Francisco	San Francisco P O	83	226
Stephen	38	m	w	NY	San Francisco	San Francisco P O	83	139
Thomas	49	m	w	CANA	San Francisco	San Francisco P O	85	739
Thomas	47	m	w	IREL	Stanislaus	North Twp	92	67
Thomas	45	m	w	IREL	Calaveras	Copperopolis P O	70	262
Thomas	40	m	w	TX	Kern	Linns Valley P O	73	344
Thomas	20	m	w	IREL	Santa Cruz	Watsonville	89	367
Thos	41	m	w	ME	Nevada	Nevada Twp	75	304
Thos	37	m	w	IREL	Siskiyou	Scott Valley Twp	89	614
Thos	31	m	w	IREL	Butte	Chico Twp	70	55
Thos	29	m	w	MA	San Francisco	1-Wd San Francisco	79	95
W W	34	m	w	MO	Tuolumne	Sonora P O	93	307
William	45	m	w	IREL	San Francisco	San Francisco P O	83	348
William	40	m	w	GA	Amador	Sutter Crk P O	69	412
William	33	m	w	ENGL	El Dorado	Placerville Twp	72	96
William	32	m	w	IREL	San Francisco	San Francisco P O	83	354
William	25	m	w	IREL	San Francisco	3-Wd San Francisco	79	313
William	19	m	w	IREL	Solano	Silveyville Twp	90	72
Wm	50	m	w	MA	San Francisco	1-Wd San Francisco	79	96
Wm	23	m	w	IREL	San Francisco	7-Wd San Francisco	81	278
Wm H	4	m	w	CA	Sacramento	3-Wd Sacramento	77	303
BOYLEN								
Charles	38	m	w	NY	San Francisco	2-Wd San Francisco	79	171
Jane	30	f	w	IREL	San Francisco	San Francisco P O	83	381
Mary	35	f	w	IREL	San Francisco	2-Wd San Francisco	79	255
Peter	27	m	w	IL	Solano	Vallejo	90	185
BOYLES								
James W W	22	m	w	IL	Contra Costa	Martinez P O	71	387
Jas H	45	m	w	OH	Butte	Oregon Twp	70	136
W	30	m	w	ME	Alameda	Oakland	68	201
BOYLESS								
William	34	m	w	AL	Calaveras	San Andreas P O	70	189
BOYLIN								
Mark	23	m	w	IL	Solano	Vallejo	90	139
BOYLON								
Alonzo	36	m	w	NY	Monterey	Monterey Twp	74	350
Isabelle	35	f	w	IREL	San Francisco	2-Wd San Francisco	79	276
BOYLS								
A C	22	m	w	IREL	Alameda	Oakland	68	173
BOYN								
Annie M	3	f	w	CA	San Francisco	San Francisco P O	83	121
Lup	40	m	c	CHIN	Sierra	Table Rock Twp	89	544
BOYNAN								
Patrick	32	m	w	IREL	San Francisco	San Francisco P O	83	142
BOYNE								
David	32	m	w	SCOT	San Francisco	San Francisco P O	83	376
Elizabeth	36	f	w	IREL	San Francisco	1-Wd San Francisco	79	74
George	35	m	w	ENGL	Sacramento	2-Wd Sacramento	77	217
Thomas	45	m	w	IREL	San Francisco	1-Wd San Francisco	79	74
BOYNS								
Melinda	17	f	w	IA	Sacramento	San Joaquin Twp	77	395
BOYNTON								
A W	37	m	w	ME	Trinity	Trinity Center Pct	92	204
Amos	38	m	w	NY	Sonoma	Analy Twp	91	230
Chas E	35	m	w	ME	San Francisco	San Francisco P O	83	70
Eben V	42	m	w	CANA	Santa Cruz	Santa Cruz	89	407
Edwin W	42	m	w	NY	Napa	Napa	75	43
Enne	15	f	w	CANA	Humboldt	Eureka Twp	72	263
F Z	42	m	w	VT	Humboldt	Pacific Twp	72	293
George	40	m	w	VT	Placer	Dutch Flat P O	76	410
Hugh	53	m	w	NY	San Francisco	San Francisco P O	83	174
Jennie C	78	f	w	NH	Sonoma	Analy Twp	91	230
Jno C	43	m	w	ME	Nevada	Rough & Ready Twp	75	323
John	47	m	w	ME	Merced	Snelling P O	74	261
Joseph	42	m	w	NH	Tuolumne	Columbia P O	93	336
Joseph	24	m	w	ME	Placer	Cisco P O	76	494
Joseph S	52	m	w	ME	Plumas	Indian Twp	77	10
Lamour A	22	m	w	CT	San Francisco	1-Wd San Francisco	79	131
Nancy F	47	f	w	MA	Yuba	New York Twp	93	639
S S	32	m	w	MA	Alameda	Oakland	68	201
W H	40	m	w	CT	Alameda	Oakland	68	185
BOYO								
George	21	m	w	CANA	San Mateo	Belmont P O	87	374
BOYOCHES								
Juan J	50	m	w	MEXI	San Diego	San Pasqual	78	523

© 2001 by Heritage Quest. All rights reserved.

Name	Age	S	R	B-PL	County	Locale	Series M593 Roll	Pg
BOYRA								
John	60	m	w	FRAN	Calaveras	San Andreas P O	70	154
BOYRIE								
Arthur	40	m	w	FRAN	Tuolumne	Sonora P O	93	325
J	49	m	w	FRAN	Amador	Jackson P O	69	338
BOYROAN								
Chas	68	m	w	FRAN	San Francisco	8-Wd San Francisco	82	354
BOYSE								
David	21	m	w	AR	Santa Cruz	Pajaro Twp	89	353
Millie	15	f	w	AR	Los Angeles	Los Nietos Twp	73	573
BOYSEN								
Henry	29	m	w	HAMB	San Francisco	1-Wd San Francisco	79	49
Jas	45	m	w	AUST	San Francisco	8-Wd San Francisco	82	356
Julius	40	m	w	HAMB	San Francisco	6-Wd San Francisco	81	86
Lawrence	23	m	w	PRUS	San Francisco	San Francisco P O	85	863
Lorz	22	m	w	PRUS	San Francisco	San Francisco P O	83	134
BOYSER								
Chas	45	m	w	PRUS	San Francisco	5-Wd San Francisco	81	1
BOYSON								
K M	24	m	w	DENM	Sonoma	Sonoma Twp	91	446
Lawrence	24	m	w	HOLL	Tulare	Farmersville Twp	92	247
P N	55	m	w	PRUS	Alameda	Alameda	68	9
BOYSTON								
Peter	66	m	w	IREL	Santa Clara	Redwood Twp	88	124
Theresa	16	f	w	MA	San Francisco	San Francisco P O	83	61
BOYT								
---	38	m	w	IL	Humboldt	Arcata Twp	72	226
BOYTANO								
G	26	m	w	ITAL	Amador	Jackson P O	69	347
BOYUERO								
Estoques	14	m	w	MEXI	San Francisco	2-Wd San Francisco	79	183
BOZ								
Ah	40	m	c	CHIN	San Mateo	San Mateo P O	87	351
BOZAR								
David	30	m	w	MA	Colusa	Monroe Twp	71	324
BOZEMAN								
John	35	m	w	MS	Fresno	Kingston P O	72	224
Preston	30	m	w	MS	Fresno	Kingston P O	72	222
Thos	54	m	w	MS	Fresno	Kingston P O	72	222
Wm F	22	m	w	LA	Fresno	Kingston P O	72	222
BOZENO								
Jesus	35	m	w	MEXI	Tulare	Visalia	92	298
BOZER								
August	36	m	w	ME	San Joaquin	2-Wd Stockton	86	170
BOZILSKIE								
Alphonso	43	m	w	FRAN	Nevada	Bridgeport Twp	75	117
BOZZIE								
Emanuel	47	m	w	ITAL	San Francisco	San Francisco P O	80	353
BOZZIO								
John	52	m	w	ITAL	Santa Clara	Santa Clara Twp	88	176
BRABANT								
Felip	34	m	w	MEXI	San Francisco	San Francisco P O	80	342
BRABANTI								
Hector	20	m	w	ITAL	San Francisco	San Francisco P O	80	426
BRABBAN								
Dixon	41	m	w	ENGL	Plumas	Goodwin Twp	77	2
Richard	24	m	w	ENGL	Plumas	Washington Twp	77	55
BRABRANDT								
Chas	26	m	w	HANO	Nevada	Nevada Twp	75	279
BRACCO								
Charlotte	42	f	w	FRAN	San Francisco	8-Wd San Francisco	82	381
BRACE								
Barney	50	m	w	ME	San Francisco	San Francisco P O	83	130
E M	37	m	w	KY	Amador	Fiddletown P O	69	431
Francis	35	m	w	CANA	Sonoma	Petaluma Twp	91	351
M S	35	m	w	KY	Amador	Fiddletown P O	69	431
Mat	35	m	w	KY	El Dorado	Mud Springs Twp	72	78
William	23	m	w	HANO	Los Angeles	Los Nietos Twp	73	590
Wm	58	m	w	NY	Solano	Vallejo	90	197
Wm	37	m	w	SCOT	San Joaquin	2-Wd Stockton	86	206
BRACELAND								
Cornelius	42	m	w	PA	Nevada	Nevada Twp	75	294
BRACELYN								
Dennis	42	m	w	IREL	Nevada	Grass Valley Twp	75	173
BRACHER								
Herman	38	m	w	WURT	Santa Clara	San Jose Twp	88	203
BRACK								
Alex	23	m	w	JAMA	Sonoma	Santa Rosa	91	420
Uswald	47	m	w	PRUS	San Francisco	San Francisco P O	85	730
BRACKEN								
George	26	m	w	NY	San Francisco	San Francisco P O	83	354
John	46	m	w	IREL	Placer	Colfax P O	76	389
Judith	27	f	w	WIND	Los Angeles	Los Angeles	73	520
Laurence	34	m	w	IREL	San Francisco	11-Wd San Francisc	84	470
BRACKENRIDGE								
Davis	20	m	b	MO	Santa Clara	San Jose Twp	88	188
Frank	14	m	b	MO	Santa Clara	1-Wd San Jose	88	234
BRACKER								
C A	26	m	w	GERM	Solano	Vallejo	90	203
BRACKET								
Charles	37	m	w	MO	San Mateo	Woodside P O	87	386
Charles	30	m	w	ME	San Mateo	Half Moon Bay P O	87	407
John	40	m	w	ME	Calaveras	San Andreas P O	70	188
BRACKETT								
Chas A B	21	m	w	MA	San Francisco	San Francisco P O	83	53
Ellen	23	f	w	IREL	Santa Clara	1-Wd San Jose	88	254
Jacob H	31	m	w	ME	Nevada	Grass Valley Twp	75	150
Jerry	28	m	w	IREL	Solano	Vallejo	90	212
Jno B	27	m	w	VT	Santa Barbara	Santa Barbara P O	87	501
Jos W	34	m	w	OH	Shasta	Shasta P O	89	456
Joseph	34	m	w	MA	San Francisco	San Francisco P O	80	376
Louis P	19	m	w	MA	San Francisco	2-Wd San Francisco	79	202
Nathaniel	51	m	w	NH	Santa Clara	Alviso Twp	88	27
Rufus	45	m	w	MA	Contra Costa	Martinez P O	71	433
Thomas	35	m	w	NH	Humboldt	Mattole Twp	72	284
Walter	26	m	w	MA	San Francisco	2-Wd San Francisco	79	236
Warren	40	m	w	MA	Sonoma	Petaluma Twp	91	315
William L	40	m	w	MA	San Francisco	8-Wd San Francisco	82	422
BRACKIMENTE								
M	25	m	w	MEXI	Butte	Oroville Twp	70	137
BRACKIN								
John	40	m	w	IREL	San Francisco	11-Wd San Francisc	84	708
BRACKLE								
Ambrose	35	m	w	BADE	Solano	Suisun Twp	90	97
BRACKMAN								
Charles	30	m	w	ENGL	Stanislaus	Branch Twp	92	2
Sol H	25	m	w	RUSS	Tehama	Tehama Twp	92	191
BRACKON								
Jas	48	m	w	IREL	San Francisco	11-Wd San Francisc	84	708
BRADBELT								
Edward	40	m	w	ENGL	Yolo	Washington Twp	93	529
BRADBERRY								
David	34	m	w	PA	Nevada	Bridgeport Twp	75	105
Wm	27	m	w	IL	Napa	Napa	75	10
BRADBERY								
Anna	28	f	w	ME	Amador	Jackson P O	69	321
David	25	m	w	IREL	San Francisco	2-Wd San Francisco	79	214
Frank	42	m	w	ME	Calaveras	Copperopolis P O	70	231
BRADBURN								
A C	40	m	w	AR	San Joaquin	Douglas Twp	86	44
A C	40	m	w	IA	San Joaquin	2-Wd Stockton	86	163
BRADBURRY								
John	45	m	w	MA	Humboldt	Eureka Twp	72	279
BRADBURY								
Benj R	40	m	w	ME	Shasta	Dog Crk P O	89	471
C E	31	f	w	MA	Solano	Benicia	90	5
Chas	27	m	w	KY	Nevada	Washington Twp	75	344
Elisha	37	m	w	ME	Santa Clara	Santa Clara Twp	88	146
Emaline	45	f	w	ME	Sonoma	Petaluma Twp	91	318
Emery	50	m	w	NY	Butte	Wyandotte Twp	70	144
Erastus J	42	m	w	ME	El Dorado	Diamond Springs Tw	72	23
Henry	28	m	w	VT	Solano	Maine Prairie Twp	90	51
Hiram	23	m	w	ME	Santa Clara	Gilroy Twp	88	85
J T	43	m	w	ENGL	Sierra	Alleghany & Forest	89	533
John	30	m	w	ME	Santa Clara	Fremont Twp	88	50
Matthew	35	m	w	OH	El Dorado	Mud Springs Twp	72	76
Nathl F	30	m	w	ME	San Francisco	San Francisco P O	85	729
Quincy	28	m	w	ME	Sonoma	Petaluma Twp	91	335
Wallace	22	m	w	ME	Santa Clara	Gilroy Twp	88	83
Wm	36	m	w	NC	San Francisco	11-Wd San Francisc	84	618
Wm B	34	m	w	ME	San Francisco	San Francisco P O	85	725
BRADDEN								
James	32	m	w	MO	Santa Clara	Santa Clara Twp	88	166
BRADE								
John	30	m	w	CANA	Placer	Dutch Flat P O	76	415
BRADELL								
Edward	46	m	w	PRUS	Trinity	Weaverville Pct	92	230
BRADEN								
Francis P	38	m	w	TN	Shasta	American Ranch P O	89	499
Henrietta	16	f	w	CA	Santa Clara	Santa Clara Twp	88	152
James	27	m	w	OH	Solano	Silveyville Twp	90	75
James W	46	m	w	PA	Yuba	Marysville	93	599
Joseph	27	m	w	PA	Plumas	Plumas Twp	77	27
Samuel R	31	m	w	IL	Sonoma	Bodega Twp	91	260
Thomas	40	m	w	IREL	San Francisco	San Francisco P O	85	861
Wm	28	m	w	IL	Sonoma	Bodega Twp	91	258
BRADER								
Anna	66	f	w	SWIT	San Francisco	San Francisco P O	80	351
Christian	34	m	w	SWIT	San Francisco	San Francisco P O	80	352
Henry	41	m	w	SWIT	San Francisco	San Francisco P O	80	352
Jennie	24	f	w	FRAN	San Francisco	San Francisco P O	80	467
Peter	39	m	w	SWIT	San Francisco	2-Wd San Francisco	79	275
Thos	30	m	w	ME	Butte	Ophir Twp	70	118
Wm	25	m	w	PRUS	Sacramento	4-Wd Sacramento	77	367
BRADES								
Pat	29	m	w	IREL	San Joaquin	Tulare Twp	86	262
BRADESHOFF								
Henry	33	m	w	HANO	Contra Costa	San Pablo Twp	71	363
BRADEY								
Peter	27	m	w	IREL	San Francisco	San Francisco P O	83	318
BRADFIELD								
Benj F	37	m	w	VA	Nevada	Grass Valley Twp	75	207
M H	62	m	w	OH	Sacramento	3-Wd Sacramento	77	280
BRADFORD								
A	39	m	w	ENGL	El Dorado	Greenwood Twp	72	54
A	20	m	w	IN	Merced	Snelling P O	74	265
Abigal	58	f	w	KY	San Joaquin	Oneal Twp	86	119
Alain	52	m	w	MA	Humboldt	Eel Rvr Twp	72	253
Anna M	46	f	w	ENGL	Santa Clara	2-Wd San Jose	88	328
C	24	f	w	IA	Yuba	Marysville	93	582
Caleb	48	m	w	VT	San Mateo	Belmont P O	87	373
Charles	17	m	w	DE	San Francisco	San Francisco P O	83	170
Charlie	23	m	i	CA	Del Norte	Smith Rvr Twp	71	481
Chas	32	m	w	MO	Nevada	Bridgeport Twp	75	115

© 2001 by Heritage Quest. All rights reserved.

Name	Age	S	R	B-PL	County	Locale	Roll	Pg
Chas	31	m	w	RUSS	Nevada	Bridgeport Twp	75	115
E	32	m	w	IREL	Lassen	Long Valley Twp	73	436
E W	46	m	w	MA	Lake	Lower Lake	73	416
Edward W	39	m	w	ENGL	Placer	Bath P O	76	435
Elizabeth	18	f	w	MO	Stanislaus	Empire Twp	92	46
Etta	2	f	w	CA	San Francisco	San Francisco P O	85	828
Eugeni	12	m	w	CA	Santa Cruz	Pajaro Twp	89	352
F	50	f	w	KY	Sacramento	3-Wd Sacramento	77	312
F	14	f	w	MA	Solano	Vallejo	90	141
G W	35	m	w	KY	Santa Clara	Gilroy Twp	88	94
Geo P	55	m	w	MA	San Francisco	7-Wd San Francisco	81	235
George	30	m	w	ENGL	Sacramento	4-Wd Sacramento	77	342
J W	33	m	w	OH	San Joaquin	Elkhorn Twp	86	56
James	52	m	w	KY	San Diego	Julian Dist	78	473
James	27	m	w	NY	Yolo	Grafton Twp	93	481
Jas	45	m	w	MO	Alameda	Oakland	68	260
Jas	42	m	w	MO	Butte	Chico Twp	70	54
John	51	m	w	NY	Solano	Maine Prairie Twp	90	47
John	51	m	w	GA	Colusa	Colusa Twp	71	279
Joseph	39	m	w	ENGL	El Dorado	Coloma Twp	72	3
K	21	f	w	IA	Sierra	Lincoln Twp	89	549
Kate	42	f	w	NY	San Francisco	San Francisco P O	83	112
Lucy	14	f	w	AUSL	San Francisco	11-Wd San Francisc	84	688
M	31	m	w	MO	Sierra	Forest Twp	89	530
M J	52	m	w	VA	Tuolumne	Chinese Camp P O	93	382
Mary	23	f	w	LA	San Francisco	San Francisco P O	85	751
Mary	20	f	w	LA	San Francisco	6-Wd San Francisco	81	142
Noble	49	m	w	MA	Yuba	Rose Bar Twp	93	652
Otis	30	m	w	VA	San Francisco	6-Wd San Francisco	81	108
Philip	30	m	w	IN	Sacramento	Franklin Twp	77	120
Rebecca	53	f	w	VT	Contra Costa	Martinez P O	71	418
Rebecca	51	f	b	MD	San Francisco	6-Wd San Francisco	81	110
S S	45	m	w	ME	Tuolumne	Sonora P O	93	309
W	9	m	w	CA	Solano	Benicia	90	21
William	45	m	w	DE	Tulare	Kings Rvr Twp	92	253
William	40	m	w	ENGL	San Francisco	6-Wd San Francisco	81	109
William	24	m	w	MO	Solano	Silveyville Twp	90	75
Wm	60	m	w	ME	Solano	Vallejo	90	180
Wm	54	m	w	MO	Merced	Snelling P O	74	257
Wm	47	m	w	IL	Humboldt	Arcata Twp	72	225
Wm	39	m	w	MA	San Francisco	11-Wd San Francisc	84	579
Wm	25	m	w	MA	Napa	Napa Twp	75	34
Wm H	29	m	w	NJ	San Francisco	1-Wd San Francisco	79	53
Woodbury	48	m	w	VT	San Francisco	2-Wd San Francisco	79	238
BRADHAW								
Thos	57	m	w	TN	Contra Costa	Martinez P O	71	435
BRADHOFF								
Henry	39	m	w	PRUS	San Francisco	2-Wd San Francisco	79	143
BRADIER								
Mary	25	f	w	PA	San Joaquin	2-Wd Stockton	86	162
BRADIGAN								
Amelia	14	f	w	MA	San Francisco	3-Wd San Francisco	79	289
Henry	23	m	w	IL	Amador	Fiddletown P O	69	433
BRADING								
Samuel	44	m	w	MO	Stanislaus	Empire Twp	92	64
BRADIRD								
Victoria	21	f	w	FRAN	San Francisco	6-Wd San Francisco	81	101
BRADJADO								
Frances	20	f	w	DC	San Francisco	11-Wd San Francisc	84	688
BRADLE								
W H	52	m	w	VA	Humboldt	South Fork Twp	72	301
BRADLEE								
Ezra S	47	m	w	MA	Santa Clara	2-Wd San Jose	88	336
S H	49	m	w	MA	San Francisco	San Francisco P O	85	845
Stephen	22	m	w	MA	San Francisco	11-Wd San Francisc	84	445
BRADLEY								
A G	28	m	w	VT	Humboldt	Mattole Twp	72	288
A S	38	m	w	VT	Tehama	Mill Crk Twp	92	168
Ann	3	f	w	CA	San Francisco	11-Wd San Francisc	84	691
Ann	25	f	w	IREL	San Francisco	San Francisco P O	83	259
Anne	25	f	w	IREL	San Francisco	11-Wd San Francisc	84	661
Anthony	44	m	w	IREL	Fresno	Millerton P O	72	148
Aron	38	m	w	KY	Marin	San Antonio Twp	74	60
Arthur	30	m	w	NORW	San Francisco	1-Wd San Francisco	79	122
Ben F	26	m	w	MO	Butte	Hamilton Twp	70	71
Bennett	45	m	w	IREL	Solano	Suisun Twp	90	116
Bennett T	55	m	w	TN	San Francisco	San Francisco P O	85	736
Bernard	5	m	w	CA	Solano	Suisun Twp	90	99
C	35	m	w	IA	Alameda	Oakland	68	198
Catherine	24	f	w	IREL	San Francisco	11-Wd San Francisc	84	661
Charles	37	m	w	IREL	San Francisco	San Francisco P O	83	38
Charles	30	m	w	ENGL	Santa Barbara	Santa Maria P O	87	511
Charles C	45	m	w	IREL	Sacramento	Natomas Twp	77	169
Charley	35	m	w	PA	Santa Cruz	Santa Cruz Twp	89	398
Daniel	56	m	w	KY	Stanislaus	Empire Twp	92	59
Edmond	37	m	w	NY	Inyo	Independence Twp	73	325
Edward	35	m	w	MO	San Francisco	6-Wd San Francisco	81	82
Edward	29	m	w	NY	Inyo	Independence Twp	73	328
Elias	27	m	w	MO	Santa Cruz	Pajaro Twp	89	358
Elisha L	45	m	w	NY	Placer	Dutch Flat P O	76	406
Eliza	45	f	w	PA	San Francisco	San Francisco P O	80	539
Ellen	30	f	w	IREL	San Francisco	San Francisco P O	83	111
Felix	28	m	w	IREL	San Francisco	1-Wd San Francisco	79	127
Francis	40	m	w	IREL	San Mateo	Redwood Twp	87	363
Frank	34	m	w	NY	Yolo	Cache Crk Twp	93	426
Frederick W	39	m	w	VT	Plumas	Plumas Twp	77	30
Geo L	40	m	w	MA	San Francisco	8-Wd San Francisco	82	318

Name	Age	S	R	B-PL	County	Locale	Roll	Pg
George	40	m	w	ENGL	San Francisco	11-Wd San Francisc	84	496
George	29	m	w	IREL	San Diego	Warners Rancho Dis	78	530
George Y	30	m	w	MA	Los Angeles	El Monte Twp	73	458
H	40	m	w	SC	Alameda	Alameda	68	18
Henry	31	m	w	IL	Napa	Napa Twp	75	70
Henry	26	m	w	NY	Fresno	Millerton P O	72	167
Henry	22	m	w	NY	Alameda	Hayward	68	79
Henry	17	m	w	PA	San Francisco	11-Wd San Francisc	84	586
Hugh	65	m	w	IN	Santa Clara	2-Wd San Jose	88	284
I W	51	m	w	TN	Merced	Snelling P O	74	275
J	33	m	w	MO	Sacramento	4-Wd Sacramento	77	373
J C	68	m	w	TN	Tehama	Antelope Twp	92	158
J C	40	m	w	SCOT	Yuba	Marysville	93	587
J D	38	m	w	TN	Merced	Snelling P O	74	275
J M	41	m	w	KY	Lake	Lakeport	73	403
J T	36	m	w	KY	Calaveras	Copperopolis P O	70	230
James	46	m	w	TX	Merced	Snelling P O	74	276
James	40	m	w	NY	Siskiyou	Yreka Twp	89	664
James	37	m	w	NH	Colusa	Colusa Twp	71	276
James	35	m	w	IREL	Calaveras	Copperopolis P O	70	248
James	30	m	w	IL	Tulare	Visalia	92	292
James	3	m	w	CA	Marin	San Rafael Twp	74	29
James	27	m	w	IREL	San Francisco	11-Wd San Francisc	84	575
James A	13	m	w	CA	San Mateo	Half Moon Bay P O	87	395
James H	39	m	w	KY	El Dorado	Placerville	72	124
Jane	27	f	w	IREL	Alameda	Oakland	68	199
Jane	22	f	w	MO	Sacramento	2-Wd Sacramento	77	220
Jim	35	m	w	MO	San Joaquin	Tulare Twp	86	251
John	49	m	w	ENGL	San Francisco	2-Wd San Francisco	79	179
John	33	m	w	ENGL	San Joaquin	Tulare Twp	86	252
John	29	m	w	ME	Santa Cruz	Santa Cruz Twp	89	399
John	27	m	w	IREL	San Francisco	7-Wd San Francisco	81	204
John H	42	m	w	OH	Santa Barbara	Santa Barbara P O	87	502
John S	42	m	w	MO	Amador	Jackson P O	69	319
John T	34	m	w	KY	Nevada	Grass Valley Twp	75	156
Jos	40	m	w	IREL	Sacramento	3-Wd Sacramento	77	271
Joseph	4	m	w	CA	Marin	San Rafael Twp	74	29
Kate	6	f	w	CA	San Francisco	8-Wd San Francisco	82	465
Lewis R	65	m	w	VA	Santa Clara	1-Wd San Jose	88	259
M	34	m	w	IREL	San Joaquin	1-Wd Stockton	86	153
Maggie	22	f	w	IREL	Tulare	Visalia	92	297
Marcus	40	m	w	ENGL	Santa Clara	2-Wd San Jose	88	335
Marcus	22	m	w	MO	Siskiyou	Callahan P O	89	624
Margaret	27	f	w	IREL	San Francisco	7-Wd San Francisco	81	285
Margart	60	f	w	KY	Tehama	Paynes Crk Twp	92	160
Margery	39	f	w	IREL	San Francisco	11-Wd San Francisc	84	606
Margret	50	f	w	IREL	Trinity	Lewiston Pct	92	212
Maria	42	f	w	IREL	Santa Clara	San Jose Twp	88	185
Mark	40	m	w	IREL	Santa Clara	2-Wd San Jose	88	301
Mary	67	f	w	MO	Colusa	Monroe Twp	71	325
Mary	60	f	w	IREL	Amador	Sutter Crk P O	69	397
Mary	60	f	w	IREL	Amador	Amador City P O	69	392
Mary	45	f	w	IREL	San Francisco	8-Wd San Francisco	82	447
Mary	44	f	w	MEXI	San Joaquin	3-Wd Stockton	86	217
Mary	29	f	w	IREL	Santa Clara	1-Wd San Jose	88	236
Mary	26	f	w	IREL	San Francisco	11-Wd San Francisc	84	423
Mary F	30	f	w	PA	San Francisco	8-Wd San Francisco	82	322
Michael	55	m	w	IREL	San Mateo	San Mateo P O	87	371
Michael	22	m	w	IREL	Alameda	Eden Twp	68	87
Michael	22	m	w	IREL	Alameda	Eden Twp	68	61
Minus	36	m	w	IREL	Contra Costa	Martinez P O	71	427
Mitchell	22	m	w	IREL	Stanislaus	Empire Twp	92	65
Myron W	41	m	w	VT	Santa Clara	2-Wd San Jose	88	319
Pat	30	m	w	IREL	Butte	Chico Twp	70	29
Patrick	44	m	w	IREL	Los Angeles	San Gabriel Twp	73	594
Patrick	24	m	w	IREL	San Francisco	San Francisco P O	83	251
Paul	47	m	w	ENGL	Santa Barbara	Santa Maria P O	87	511
Peter	36	m	w	PA	Santa Clara	Milpitas Twp	88	112
Peter	30	m	w	IREL	San Francisco	8-Wd San Francisco	82	487
Peter	18	m	w	NJ	San Francisco	7-Wd San Francisco	81	259
R E	33	m	w	NY	Alameda	Alameda	68	13
Ransford	39	m	w	CANA	Santa Cruz	Watsonville	89	369
Renj	23	m	w	PA	San Francisco	2-Wd San Francisco	79	214
Richmond	47	m	w	MO	Santa Cruz	Pajaro Twp	89	358
Robert	36	m	w	IREL	San Francisco	San Francisco P O	85	723
Rose	29	f	w	ME	San Francisco	7-Wd San Francisco	81	235
Saml	33	m	w	NY	Yuba	Marysville	93	607
Samuel	34	m	w	ENGL	San Francisco	San Francisco P O	83	131
Samuel R	67	m	w	MA	Placer	Rocklin P O	76	462
Samuel R	38	m	w	ME	Placer	Bath P O	76	424
T C	66	m	w	VA	Sacramento	Cosumnes Twp	77	91
Theo	30	m	w	CT	San Francisco	7-Wd San Francisco	81	232
Thomas	69	m	w	TN	Sonoma	Analy Twp	91	232
Thomas	41	m	w	MO	Contra Costa	Martinez P O	71	441
Thomas S	46	m	w	ENGL	Santa Clara	2-Wd San Jose	88	299
Thos W	40	m	w	KY	Sonoma	Analy Twp	91	232
W	60	m	w	NC	Yuba	Linda Twp	93	558
W	34	m	w	CT	Sutter	Nicolaus Twp	92	111
W	30	m	w	NY	Yuba	Linda Twp	93	558
W O	28	m	w	MA	Solano	Vallejo	90	140
W T	34	m	w	MO	Napa	Yountville Twp	75	80
Warren	22	m	w	CA	Contra Costa	Martinez P O	71	376
Whettcar	32	m	w	ENGL	Contra Costa	Martinez P O	71	414
William	48	m	w	MS	Nevada	Nevada Twp	75	319
William	46	m	w	SCOT	San Francisco	San Francisco P O	80	339
William	36	m	w	CANA	San Francisco	11-Wd San Francisc	84	531
William	32	m	w	OH	Alameda	Alvarado	68	302

© 2001 by Heritage Quest. All rights reserved.

Series M593

Name	Age	S	R	B-PL	County	Locale	Roll	Pg
William	24	m	w	IREL	Santa Clara	Fremont Twp	88	46
William S	30	m	w	IN	Santa Clara	1-Wd San Jose	88	277
Wilson	43	m	w	IN	Stanislaus	Empire Twp	92	59
Wm	40	m	w	ENGL	Sonoma	Santa Rosa	91	421
Wm	26	m	w	IL	San Francisco	8-Wd San Francisco	82	370
Wm L	43	m	w	TN	Butte	Chico Twp	70	23
BRADLY								
Elias	42	m	w	OH	Santa Cruz	Soquel Twp	89	443
Fanny	41	f	w	ENGL	San Joaquin	2-Wd Stockton	86	170
James	36	m	w	KY	Sacramento	Sutter Twp	77	388
John	90	m	w	IREL	Lassen	Janesville Twp	73	431
John	35	m	w	MS	Inyo	Bishop Crk Twp	73	316
Joseph	26	m	w	IREL	San Francisco	8-Wd San Francisco	82	352
M	75	f	w	IREL	Lassen	Janesville Twp	73	431
Otho	25	m	w	NY	San Francisco	San Francisco P O	83	394
Peter	35	m	w	IREL	San Joaquin	Elkhorn Twp	86	66
Richard	49	m	b	RI	San Francisco	San Francisco P O	80	422
S S	40	m	b	SC	Tuolumne	Chinese Camp P O	93	387
BRADOL								
Andrew	58	m	w	NORW	Sonoma	Analy Twp	91	231
BRADONSHELL								
Leon	45	m	w	FRAN	El Dorado	Diamond Springs Tw	72	30
BRADORD								
James	40	m	w	IN	Sacramento	Franklin Twp	77	120
BRADSHAW								
A R	30	f	w	MA	Alameda	Oakland	68	162
Benj	25	m	w	ENGL	Napa	Napa	75	39
Benjam	28	m	w	AUSL	Santa Cruz	Santa Cruz	89	415
Charles	48	m	w	IL	Santa Barbara	San Buenaventura P	87	447
Ed	40	m	w	KY	San Diego	San Diego	78	483
Ellen	19	f	w	TN	San Francisco	6-Wd San Francisco	81	121
Helen	19	f	w	TN	San Francisco	San Francisco P O	80	401
Henry	48	m	w	NC	Fresno	Millerton P O	72	183
I G	50	m	w	TN	Napa	Napa Twp	75	63
James	3	m	w	CA	San Francisco	11-Wd San Francisc	84	711
James B	45	m	w	ENGL	Los Angeles	Wilmington Twp	73	634
John	38	m	w	PA	Amador	Volcano P O	69	380
John	37	m	w	ENGL	El Dorado	Placerville Twp	72	102
John	30	m	w	TN	Santa Cruz	Pajaro Twp	89	358
John	28	m	w	PA	Sutter	Nicolaus Twp	92	111
John	23	m	w	IL	Sutter	Nicolaus Twp	92	108
Joseph	33	m	w	CANA	Santa Clara	Redwood Twp	88	118
Malinda	49	f	w	LA	San Francisco	San Francisco P O	80	383
Richd	38	m	w	MO	San Francisco	San Francisco P O	83	73
Robert	44	m	w	IREL	Monterey	Castroville Twp	74	336
Robert M	30	m	w	VA	Yolo	Cache Crk Twp	93	419
Saml C	56	m	w	MA	San Francisco	8-Wd San Francisco	82	293
Samuel	56	m	w	MA	San Francisco	8-Wd San Francisco	82	469
Samuel	27	m	w	ENGL	Yolo	Grafton Twp	93	492
T	46	f	w	KY	Sonoma	Santa Rosa	91	409
Thomas A	35	m	w	NY	Yolo	Grafton Twp	93	482
Tyrrell	37	m	w	MA	San Francisco	8-Wd San Francisco	82	493
W W	41	m	w	SCOT	Alameda	Oakland	68	173
Wm	8M	m	w	CA	Yuba	East Bear Rvr Twp	93	540
Wm	29	m	w	CANA	Butte	Oregon Twp	70	131
Wm	11	m	w	NY	San Francisco	San Francisco P O	85	818
BRADSTER								
George J	26	m	w	BAVA	San Mateo	Redwood Twp	87	364
BRADT								
Aaron	40	m	w	NY	Napa	Napa	75	55
Charles	27	m	w	NY	San Francisco	11-Wd San Francisc	84	527
George G	38	m	w	NY	San Francisco	6-Wd San Francisco	81	110
Henry	29	m	w	BELG	Santa Clara	1-Wd San Jose	88	232
John A	43	m	w	NY	San Francisco	11-Wd San Francisc	84	699
John M	34	m	w	NY	San Francisco	San Francisco P O	83	310
BRADWAY								
Able S	39	m	w	MA	Mendocino	Cuffeys Cove Twp	74	168
J R	52	m	w	NY	Tehama	Red Bluff	92	179
Nathaniel	56	m	w	KY	Mendocino	Navarro & Big Rvr	74	177
Thomas	16	m	w	IL	Placer	Auburn P O	76	363
BRADWELL								
Isaac	31	m	w	PA	El Dorado	Mud Springs Twp	72	90
BRADY								
A	45	f	w	IREL	Yuba	Marysville	93	590
Alexander B	43	m	w	CT	Nevada	Grass Valley Twp	75	178
Alfred	42	m	b	VA	Santa Barbara	San Buenaventura P	87	443
Ann	34	f	w	IREL	Yuba	Long Bar Twp	93	561
Anna M	37	f	w	IREL	Trinity	Weaverville Pct	92	223
Anne	32	f	w	IREL	San Francisco	1-Wd San Francisco	79	31
Annie	28	f	w	IREL	San Francisco	San Francisco P O	83	254
Barney	43	m	w	IREL	Marin	San Rafael Twp	74	36
Belinda	25	f	w	IREL	San Francisco	11-Wd San Francisc	84	644
Benjamin	42	m	w	MD	San Francisco	2-Wd San Francisco	79	144
Bernard	70	m	w	IREL	San Francisco	San Francisco P O	83	402
Bernard	38	m	w	IREL	Sacramento	Lee Twp	77	157
Bridget	36	f	w	IREL	San Francisco	8-Wd San Francisco	82	389
Bridget	30	f	w	IREL	San Francisco	2-Wd San Francisco	79	189
Briget	31	f	w	PA	San Francisco	7-Wd San Francisco	81	202
Caroline	58	f	w	NJ	San Francisco	San Francisco P O	85	716
Cathine	31	f	w	IREL	San Francisco	San Francisco P O	85	863
Chally	70	m	w	IREL	San Francisco	San Francisco P O	83	402
Charles	35	m	w	IREL	San Francisco	7-Wd San Francisco	81	160
Chas	41	m	w	IREL	Tehama	Red Bluff	92	178
Chas	35	m	w	MI	Humboldt	Arcata Twp	72	232
Chas	32	m	w	IREL	Sacramento	4-Wd Sacramento	77	334
D D	44	m	w	KY	Sonoma	Petaluma Twp	91	356
Daniel	39	m	w	IREL	San Francisco	San Francisco P O	83	363
David	35	m	w	OH	Solano	Suisun Twp	90	112
E F	47	m	w	IREL	Santa Clara	Gilroy Twp	88	78
Edward	41	m	w	ME	San Francisco	5-Wd San Francisco	81	33
Edward	40	m	w	IREL	San Francisco	8-Wd San Francisco	82	466
Edward	34	m	w	IREL	San Francisco	11-Wd San Francisc	84	433
Edward	33	m	w	IREL	Marin	Tomales Twp	74	88
Elizabeth	11	f	w	CA	Stanislaus	Empire Twp	92	27
Ellen	30	f	w	IREL	San Francisco	7-Wd San Francisco	81	169
Erwin	32	m	w	OH	Marin	San Antonio Twp	74	61
Eugene	12	m	w	CA	San Francisco	8-Wd San Francisco	82	497
F	50	m	w	IREL	San Joaquin	Castoria Twp	86	1
F R	43	m	w	NY	El Dorado	Greenwood Twp	72	53
Francis	29	m	w	IREL	San Francisco	San Francisco P O	85	877
Frank	42	m	w	IREL	Yuba	Rose Bar Twp	93	663
Frank	34	m	w	MA	Solano	Vallejo	90	140
Frank	28	f	w	AUSL	Sacramento	4-Wd Sacramento	77	333
George W	43	m	w	KY	Inyo	Independence Twp	73	325
H J	30	m	w	IREL	Sutter	Sutter Twp	92	128
H J	26	m	w	IREL	San Francisco	San Francisco P O	85	833
Hannah	40	f	w	IREL	San Francisco	San Francisco P O	85	739
Henry J	26	m	w	NY	San Francisco	San Francisco P O	83	203
Hugh	44	m	w	IREL	San Francisco	1-Wd San Francisco	79	82
J H	26	m	w	IREL	Solano	Vallejo	90	154
James	77	m	w	CANA	Inyo	Bishop Crk Twp	73	310
James	45	m	w	IREL	San Francisco	11-Wd San Francisc	84	541
James	40	m	w	IREL	Amador	Sutter Crk P O	69	407
James	40	m	w	IREL	Placer	Dutch Flat P O	76	403
James	38	m	w	IREL	Alpine	Monitor P O	69	314
James	37	m	w	IREL	Marin	Nicasio Twp	74	15
James	35	m	w	IREL	Nevada	Little York Twp	75	239
James	35	m	w	IREL	San Francisco	11-Wd San Francisc	84	454
James	31	m	w	IREL	Santa Clara	2-Wd San Jose	88	294
James	30	m	w	IREL	San Francisco	San Francisco P O	85	864
James	28	m	w	IREL	Sutter	Sutter Twp	92	129
James	26	m	w	IREL	San Francisco	San Francisco P O	80	335
James	24	m	w	IREL	San Francisco	7-Wd San Francisco	81	170
James	24	m	w	SCOT	San Francisco	7-Wd San Francisco	81	223
James T	52	m	w	NY	Sacramento	4-Wd Sacramento	77	357
Jane	23	f	w	ENGL	San Francisco	2-Wd San Francisco	79	243
John	52	m	w	IREL	Siskiyou	Butte Twp	89	584
John	49	m	w	IREL	Marin	San Rafael	74	54
John	42	m	w	NORW	San Mateo	Half Moon Bay P O	87	404
John	40	m	w	IREL	San Francisco	San Francisco P O	83	368
John	40	m	w	IREL	San Francisco	8-Wd San Francisco	82	340
John	39	m	w	IREL	Siskiyou	Cottonwood Twp	89	591
John	38	m	w	IREL	San Francisco	San Francisco P O	83	359
John	38	m	w	IREL	San Mateo	Schoolhouse Statio	87	342
John	36	m	w	IREL	San Francisco	11-Wd San Francisc	84	485
John	35	m	w	IREL	Tehama	Red Bluff	92	178
John	35	m	w	IREL	Yuba	Rose Bar Twp	93	665
John	33	m	w	IREL	Tehama	Red Bluff	92	184
John	33	m	w	IREL	San Francisco	1-Wd San Francisco	79	47
John	31	m	w	IREL	San Francisco	San Francisco P O	80	341
John	30	m	w	IREL	Kern	Bakersfield P O	73	357
John	27	m	w	IREL	Solano	Vallejo	90	211
John	26	m	w	IREL	Santa Clara	Santa Clara Twp	88	166
John	26	m	w	IREL	San Mateo	Schoolhouse Statio	87	342
John J	46	m	w	IREL	San Francisco	1-Wd San Francisco	79	74
John J	35	m	w	IREL	Marin	San Rafael Twp	74	36
John T	30	m	w	IREL	San Francisco	6-Wd San Francisco	81	96
John W	53	m	w	KY	Placer	Bath P O	76	440
John W	32	m	w	NY	San Francisco	San Francisco P O	83	222
Joseph	40	m	w	PRUS	Butte	Hamilton Twp	70	64
Jus J	32	m	w	MD	Sierra	Eureka Twp	89	524
Kate	35	f	w	IREL	San Francisco	11-Wd San Francisc	84	643
Kate	20	f	w	IREL	San Francisco	2-Wd San Francisco	79	267
Levi	51	m	w	TN	Siskiyou	Yreka	89	661
M	27	m	w	IREL	San Francisco	San Francisco P O	83	62
M	27	m	w	IREL	San Joaquin	Liberty Twp	86	94
Mar	53	f	w	IREL	Sacramento	3-Wd Sacramento	77	297
Maria	29	f	w	IREL	San Francisco	6-Wd San Francisco	81	72
Martha	38	f	w	IREL	San Francisco	San Francisco P O	85	814
Martin	32	m	w	IREL	Plumas	Quartz Twp	77	34
Mary	65	f	w	IREL	Sonoma	Petaluma Twp	91	361
Mary	60	f	w	IREL	San Mateo	Half Moon Bay P O	87	405
Mary	46	f	w	IREL	San Francisco	San Francisco P O	83	143
Mary	35	f	w	IREL	Sonoma	Petaluma Twp	91	361
Mary	34	f	w	IREL	Sonoma	Petaluma Twp	91	314
Mary E	4	f	w	CA	Mono	Bridgeport P O	74	282
Mathew	43	m	w	IREL	Tuolumne	Columbia P O	93	338
Michael	44	m	w	IREL	San Francisco	2-Wd San Francisco	79	190
Michael	35	m	w	IREL	Nevada	Little York Twp	75	235
Michael	32	m	w	IREL	San Francisco	2-Wd San Francisco	79	242
Michael	27	m	w	IREL	San Mateo	Schoolhouse Statio	87	332
Michael	20	m	w	IREL	Sacramento	2-Wd Sacramento	77	250
Mike	35	m	w	IREL	Solano	Vallejo	90	174
Mike	24	m	w	IREL	Solano	Vallejo	90	200
Nelly	9	f	w	CA	Yuba	Rose Bar Twp	93	653
Nelly	19	f	w	CA	Yuba	Marysville	93	604
Nelly	18	f	w	CA	Yuba	Marysville	93	591
Nicholas	40	m	w	CANA	San Francisco	11-Wd San Francisc	84	448
Nicholas	35	m	w	IREL	San Francisco	San Francisco P O	83	310
Nichols	25	m	w	IREL	San Francisco	7-Wd San Francisco	81	160
P	33	m	w	IL	San Francisco	San Francisco P O	83	130
Patrick	50	m	w	IREL	San Francisco	11-Wd San Francisc	84	637
Patrick	50	m	w	NY	Solano	Tremont Twp	90	30
Patrick	40	m	w	IREL	Sutter	Yuba Twp	92	149

© 2001 by Heritage Quest. All rights reserved.

Name	Age	S	R	B-PL	County	Locale	Series M593 Roll	Pg
Patrick	37	m	w	IREL	Placer	Bath P O	76	434
Patrick	36	m	w	IREL	Tuolumne	Columbia P O	93	347
Patrick	35	m	w	IREL	San Francisco	6-Wd San Francisco	81	143
Patrick	35	m	w	IREL	San Francisco	8-Wd San Francisco	82	340
Patrick	32	m	w	TN	Sonoma	Mendocino Twp	91	287
Patrick	28	m	w	ENGL	San Francisco	7-Wd San Francisco	81	192
Patrick	26	m	w	IREL	San Francisco	1-Wd San Francisco	79	135
Patrick	23	m	w	IREL	Santa Clara	1-Wd San Jose	88	242
Peter	40	m	w	IREL	San Francisco	7-Wd San Francisco	81	264
Peter	27	m	w	IREL	Kern	Havilah P O	73	337
Philip	39	m	w	IREL	San Francisco	11-Wd San Francisc	84	598
Philip	37	m	w	IREL	San Francisco	San Francisco P O	83	12
Philip	27	m	w	IREL	Inyo	Independence Twp	73	328
Philip	26	m	w	IREL	San Francisco	San Francisco P O	83	373
Phillip	55	m	b	VA	Santa Barbara	Santa Barbara P O	87	458
Phillip	30	m	w	IREL	San Francisco	7-Wd San Francisco	81	275
Phillip	27	m	w	IREL	Los Angeles	Los Angeles	73	550
Richard	40	m	w	IREL	Amador	Sutter Crk P O	69	402
Robert	33	m	w	IREL	San Francisco	11-Wd San Francisc	84	516
Robt	29	m	w	CANA	Sierra	Eureka Twp	89	523
Sarah	27	f	w	IREL	Sonoma	Petaluma Twp	91	325
Susan	65	f	w	IREL	Sacramento	2-Wd Sacramento	77	240
T	31	m	w	IREL	Alameda	Oakland	68	178
Terno	52	m	w	IREL	San Francisco	San Francisco P O	83	4
Terrence	30	m	w	IREL	San Francisco	San Francisco P O	83	263
Thomas	57	m	w	NY	Solano	Tremont Twp	90	30
Thomas	50	m	w	IREL	San Francisco	San Francisco P O	83	291
Thomas	45	m	w	IREL	San Francisco	1-Wd San Francisco	79	74
Thomas	42	m	w	IL	San Diego	Julian Dist	78	468
Thomas	36	m	w	IREL	San Francisco	2-Wd San Francisco	79	264
Thomas	36	m	w	IREL	Amador	Jackson P O	69	323
Thomas	34	m	w	IREL	San Francisco	San Francisco P O	83	377
Thomas	25	m	w	NJ	Trinity	Lewiston Pct	92	211
Thomas	24	m	w	IREL	Solano	Silveyville Twp	90	87
Thomas	24	m	w	IREL	San Francisco	San Francisco P O	85	730
Thomas	19	m	w	IREL	Sacramento	2-Wd Sacramento	77	246
Thos	37	m	w	VA	San Francisco	2-Wd San Francisco	79	215
Thos	35	m	w	IREL	Solano	Vallejo	90	161
Thos	28	m	w	IREL	Solano	Vallejo	90	170
Thos	22	m	w	IREL	San Francisco	1-Wd San Francisco	79	62
Thos F	22	m	w	MA	San Francisco	San Francisco P O	83	43
Thos T	26	m	w	NY	San Francisco	San Francisco P O	85	735
William	30	m	w	IREL	San Francisco	11-Wd San Francisc	84	532
William	30	m	w	IREL	Los Angeles	Los Angeles	73	521
Winefred	27	f	w	IREL	San Francisco	1-Wd San Francisco	79	99
Wm	42	m	w	IREL	Yuba	Marysville	93	595
Wm	23	m	w	PA	San Francisco	San Francisco P O	85	757
Wm H	29	m	w	NC	Sonoma	Petaluma Twp	91	313
BRAFFNES								
Chas	16	m	w	MO	Sonoma	Sonoma Twp	91	446
BRAG								
Augustine	25	f	w	LA	San Francisco	11-Wd San Francisc	84	563
Edward G	33	m	w	TN	Yolo	Buckeye Twp	93	415
BRAGAR								
Jose	36	m	w	CHIL	Santa Clara	Alviso Twp	88	26
BRAGARD								
Joseph	25	m	w	HI	Yolo	Merritt Twp	93	505
BRAGAW								
Abram I	26	m	w	NY	Contra Costa	Martinez P O	71	383
BRAGDON								
C	27	m	w	NH	Alameda	Murray Twp	68	118
Charles	40	m	w	ME	El Dorado	Diamond Springs Tw	72	31
Clifford	28	m	w	MA	Alameda	Washington Twp	68	298
Edward	22	m	w	NH	San Francisco	11-Wd San Francisc	84	572
Stanwood	27	m	w	ME	San Mateo	Half Moon Bay P O	87	408
BRAGENBERGER								
Andrew	36	m	w	FINL	Placer	Bath P O	76	457
BRAGET								
Teresa	52	f	w	FRAN	San Francisco	2-Wd San Francisco	79	166
BRAGG								
A G	40	m	w	CANA	Sacramento	3-Wd Sacramento	77	257
A M	37	m	w	ME	Monterey	Castroville Twp	74	328
Alonzo	34	m	w	MA	San Francisco	11-Wd San Francisc	84	530
B F	40	m	w	AZ	San Bernardino	San Bernardino Twp	78	418
Chas	45	m	w	VT	Napa	Napa	75	14
Edward	31	m	w	MI	Napa	Napa Twp	75	63
Frank	3	m	w	VT	San Joaquin	Oneal Twp	86	112
Geo F	53	m	w	NY	San Francisco	5-Wd San Francisco	81	25
Geo F	50	m	w	NY	San Francisco	5-Wd San Francisco	81	33
H S	60	m	w	ME	San Joaquin	1-Wd Stockton	86	132
James	22	m	w	ME	Trinity	North Fork Twp	92	219
James N	28	m	w	MI	Mono	Bridgeport P O	74	284
John	50	m	w	ME	San Joaquin	Oneal Twp	86	110
Robert	43	m	w	MA	San Francisco	7-Wd San Francisco	81	269
William	40	m	w	IREL	Solano	Silveyville Twp	90	79
William	28	m	w	ENGL	Yolo	Putah Twp	93	523
BRAGGE								
E M	44	m	w	VA	Sutter	Butte Twp	92	95
BRAGGER								
A L	58	m	w	PORT	Butte	Wyandotte Twp	70	141
Jacob	43	m	w	SWIT	Calaveras	Copperopolis P O	70	231
BRAGKI								
Rinaldo	51	m	w	ITAL	San Francisco	San Francisco P O	83	1
BRAGLY								
Nova	48	f	w	BADE	Colusa	Spring Valley Twp	71	337
BRAGMART								
Henr	31	m	w	ME	Sonoma	Petaluma Twp	91	321
BRAGRANO								
Diago	60	m	w	MEXI	Santa Clara	Burnett Twp	88	35
BRAHAM								
Edward	38	m	w	SCOT	San Francisco	San Francisco P O	83	209
BRAHANS								
Henry	47	m	w	SHOL	San Francisco	11-Wd San Francisc	84	595
BRAHEN								
Bernard	35	m	w	MECK	San Francisco	11-Wd San Francisc	84	596
BRAIDS								
Charles	47	m	w	ENGL	Calaveras	Copperopolis P O	70	227
BRAIDY								
Chas	40	m	w	MA	San Francisco	7-Wd San Francisco	81	228
BRAILEY								
Thos	50	m	w	ENGL	Monterey	Monterey Twp	74	346
BRAIN								
C	34	m	w	CT	Yuba	Marysville	93	587
Edward	40	m	w	MA	San Francisco	6-Wd San Francisco	81	94
Joseph	38	m	w	FRAN	San Francisco	San Francisco P O	80	393
Samuel	52	m	w	ENGL	Sonoma	Analy Twp	91	241
BRAINARD								
G S	35	m	w	NY	Sutter	Nicolaus Twp	92	111
Gilbert	41	m	w	OH	Sacramento	Franklin Twp	77	109
William N	23	m	w	NY	El Dorado	Placerville	72	111
BRAINARDS								
W H	53	m	w	NY	Sacramento	4-Wd Sacramento	77	363
BRAINE								
H C	38	m	w	DENM	San Francisco	3-Wd San Francisco	79	300
BRAINERD								
Frank	21	m	w	WI	Santa Clara	Fremont Twp	88	43
Henry C	36	m	w	NY	San Francisco	8-Wd San Francisco	82	439
Richard	35	m	w	IL	San Francisco	8-Wd San Francisco	82	414
BRAINGIN								
Saml	37	m	w	ME	San Francisco	San Francisco P O	85	831
BRAISLAND								
Jas	23	m	w	IREL	Solano	Vallejo	90	202
BRAKE								
George W	48	m	w	VA	Solano	Suisun Twp	90	99
BRAKELSBERG								
F	34	m	w	PRUS	San Francisco	San Francisco P O	83	134
BRAKEMAN								
Mary	14	f	w	CA	Tulare	Tule Rvr Twp	92	260
BRAKER								
James	31	m	w	MO	Contra Costa	Martinez P O	71	434
BRAKEWELL								
James	22	m	w	ENGL	San Francisco	San Francisco P O	85	837
BRAKLEY								
H	28	m	w	ENGL	Sierra	Butte Twp	89	511
BRALEY								
Albert G	55	m	w	MA	Yolo	Grafton Twp	93	484
Daniel	48	m	w	MA	Stanislaus	Empire Twp	92	49
James M	45	m	w	MO	Santa Clara	1-Wd San Jose	88	230
John E	65	m	w	NC	Santa Clara	Santa Clara Twp	88	167
BRALISH								
Lucus	31	m	w	AUST	Los Angeles	Los Angeles	73	538
BRALLIERE								
Helene	27	f	w	FRAN	San Francisco	6-Wd San Francisco	81	73
BRALY								
Charles	40	m	w	IL	Calaveras	Copperopolis P O	70	263
Finis E	28	m	w	MO	Santa Clara	Fremont Twp	88	42
Geo A	60	m	w	MA	San Francisco	1-Wd San Francisco	79	103
John H	35	m	w	MO	Santa Clara	Santa Clara Twp	88	167
BRALZARD								
Emil	39	m	w	FRAN	San Francisco	San Francisco P O	80	534
BRAM								
Geo W	32	m	w	IL	Solano	Rio Vista Twp	90	62
BRAMA								
Meta	28	f	w	HANO	San Francisco	San Francisco P O	85	789
BRAMALL								
Geo	63	m	w	ENGL	San Francisco	7-Wd San Francisco	81	232
BRAMAN								
David	35	m	w	PA	San Diego	San Luis Rey	78	515
Hyatt	24	m	w	IN	San Diego	San Luis Rey	78	515
J J	45	m	w	NY	San Francisco	San Francisco P O	85	813
John	40	m	w	IREL	San Francisco	5-Wd San Francisco	81	6
Lavinia	26	f	w	NY	Santa Clara	Alviso Twp	88	27
Sarah	37	f	w	IREL	San Francisco	11-Wd San Francisc	84	642
BRAMAR								
A W	50	m	w	OH	Humboldt	Eureka Twp	72	276
BRAMBERGER								
Benjamin	31	m	w	PRUS	Santa Clara	2-Wd San Jose	88	317
BRAMBLE								
George	68	m	w	ENGL	Shasta	Shasta P O	89	453
BRAMDT								
Andrew	30	m	w	PRUS	San Francisco	6-Wd San Francisco	81	118
BRAME								
John S	50	m	w	NC	Napa	Napa	75	17
BRAMELL								
William T	40	m	w	MO	Alpine	Woodfords P O	69	309
BRAMER								
Andrew	37	m	w	PA	San Diego	Julian Dist	78	471
Cornelia	8	f	w	MO	Santa Clara	2-Wd San Jose	88	308
John	35	m	w	PRUS	Santa Clara	Santa Clara Twp	88	164
Martin	36	m	w	HOLL	Napa	Napa Twp	75	59
BRAMES								
F W	44	m	w	OLDE	Monterey	Castroville Twp	74	338
BRAMFIELD								
Wm	45	m	w	IN	San Francisco	11-Wd San Francisc	84	606

© 2001 by Heritage Quest. All rights reserved.

Name	Age	S	R	B-PL	County	Locale (Series M593)	Roll	Pg
BRAMLET								
Caleb B	34	m	w	IN	Napa	Yountville Twp	75	91
Jackson	14	m	w	CA	Los Angeles	Los Angeles Twp	73	494
BRAMLETT								
C A	34	m	w	IN	Merced	Snelling P O	74	261
William H	32	m	w	IL	Yolo	Putah Twp	93	524
Wm S	22	m	w	VA	San Francisco	1-Wd San Francisco	79	107
BRAMLETTE								
Bluford	38	m	w	IL	Santa Cruz	Pajaro Twp	89	350
BRAMMER								
Cobb	25	m	w	IN	Butte	Kimshew Tpw	70	78
BRAMS								
Joseph	35	m	w	HANO	Butte	Hamilton Twp	70	69
BRAMSTEDT								
John	25	m	w	HANO	San Francisco	7-Wd San Francisco	81	262
BRAMWELL								
Aaron	42	m	w	SCOT	San Francisco	1-Wd San Francisco	79	12
BRAN								
Clara	30	f	w	OH	Stanislaus	Branch Twp	92	1
Pat	38	m	w	IREL	San Joaquin	1-Wd Stockton	86	123
Susan	35	f	w	IREL	Sacramento	4-Wd Sacramento	77	335
BRANARD								
John	16	m	w	NY	Los Angeles	Los Angeles	73	568
BRANASSIN								
F P	13	m	w	CA	Alameda	Oakland	68	243
BRANCH								
A W	52	m	w	SWED	Monterey	Salinas Twp	74	309
Alexander	50	m	w	ENGL	Nevada	Grass Valley Twp	75	165
Edwin	37	m	w	ENGL	Nevada	Grass Valley Twp	75	224
Frank	26	m	w	CA	San Luis Obispo	Arroyo Grande Twp	87	272
Frank Z	67	m	w	NY	San Luis Obispo	Arroyo Grande Twp	87	272
Frederick	14	m	w	CA	Santa Barbara	Santa Barbara P O	87	493
George W	42	m	w	TN	Stanislaus	Emory Twp	92	23
J P	42	m	w	NY	Lake	Lower Lake	73	416
Matilda	14	f	w	CA	Monterey	Alisal Twp	74	294
Ramon	33	m	w	CA	San Luis Obispo	Arroyo Grande Twp	87	274
Roman	32	m	w	CA	San Luis Obispo	Arroyo Grande Twp	87	273
T F	40	m	w	ENGL	San Joaquin	Douglas Twp	86	47
William	42	m	w	ENGL	San Francisco	San Francisco P O	80	379
BRANCHER								
A	40	m	w	OH	Nevada	Bloomfield Twp	75	98
Steven	41	m	w	PA	Contra Costa	Martinez P O	71	413
BRAND								
A	46	m	w	FRAN	Alameda	Alameda	68	19
Agust	49	m	w	PRUS	San Francisco	7-Wd San Francisco	81	190
Albert	23	m	w	ITAL	San Francisco	1-Wd San Francisco	79	110
Chris	48	m	w	SWIT	Marin	San Antonio Twp	74	64
Felix	48	m	w	FRAN	Calaveras	San Andreas P O	70	203
Harriet	44	f	w	ME	Shasta	Millville P O	89	485
Henry	47	m	w	GERM	Tuolumne	Columbia P O	93	358
Hermann	34	m	w	PRUS	San Francisco	San Francisco P O	83	22
Isadore	30	m	w	POLA	San Francisco	San Francisco P O	83	255
John	48	m	w	WURT	San Francisco	1-Wd San Francisco	79	52
Joseph	48	m	w	HESS	Calaveras	Copperopolis P O	70	264
Joseph	40	m	w	PORT	Tuolumne	Columbia P O	93	358
Loren	40	m	w	ME	San Francisco	11-Wd San Francisc	84	687
Louis	58	m	w	AUST	San Francisco	1-Wd San Francisco	79	56
Michael	37	m	w	BAVA	Contra Costa	Martinez P O	71	375
Richard	50	m	w	ENGL	Klamath	South Fork Twp	73	385
Susan	40	f	w	MO	San Joaquin	2-Wd Stockton	86	171
Wm	47	m	w	GERM	San Joaquin	2-Wd Stockton	86	168
BRANDAGE								
Mark D	41	m	w	TN	Los Angeles	Los Angeles	73	540
BRANDAN								
H	25	m	w	PRUS	Napa	Napa	75	19
Richard	28	m	w	MO	Solano	Silveyville Twp	90	89
BRANDANA								
Herick	42	m	w	ITAL	El Dorado	Diamond Springs Tw	72	29
BRANDEL								
John	40	m	w	HDAR	Sacramento	3-Wd Sacramento	77	293
BRANDELLE								
Reuben	25	m	w	IL	Fresno	Millerton P O	72	150
BRANDEN								
James	25	m	w	IREL	San Francisco	5-Wd San Francisco	81	28
William	28	m	w	PRUS	San Francisco	San Francisco P O	80	388
BRANDENBURG								
Charles	39	m	w	OH	Santa Clara	Santa Clara Twp	88	166
O C W	62	m	w	MA	San Francisco	3-Wd San Francisco	79	315
BRANDENBURGH								
Jas	35	m	w	OH	Sierra	Gibson Twp	89	540
BRANDER								
Morris	33	m	w	SWED	San Francisco	1-Wd San Francisco	79	8
Thos	36	m	w	SWED	San Francisco	1-Wd San Francisco	79	8
BRANDESTEIN								
Joseph	41	m	w	PRUS	San Francisco	8-Wd San Francisco	82	481
BRANDIDGE								
Benjamin	74	m	w	NY	El Dorado	Mud Springs Twp	72	78
BRANDIFF								
Isaac	49	m	w	NJ	San Luis Obispo	Santa Rosa Twp	87	321
BRANDING								
William	35	m	w	MO	Tulare	Tule Rvr Twp	92	262
BRANDITH								
Albert	29	m	w	PRUS	Solano	Silveyville Twp	90	88
BRANDLE								
John	45	m	w	BAVA	Shasta	Horsetown P O	89	504
BRANDLY								
John	26	m	w	WURT	San Francisco	3-Wd San Francisco	79	296
BRANDMAN								
James	40	m	w	IREL	San Francisco	2-Wd San Francisco	79	204
BRANDO								
Frank	50	m	w	PRUS	San Francisco	San Francisco P O	83	282
Margarett	75	f	w	NY	Solano	Rio Vista Twp	90	57
BRANDON								
Alex	49	m	w	AR	San Joaquin	Dent Twp	86	25
Alex	49	m	w	MD	Colusa	Monroe Twp	71	314
Andrew	35	m	w	IL	Santa Cruz	Pajaro Twp	89	352
Benjamin	42	m	w	NY	Los Angeles	Los Nietos Twp	73	586
Charles	37	m	w	ENGL	Nevada	Rough & Ready Twp	75	336
E	39	m	w	PA	Napa	Napa	75	53
Emma	13	f	w	CA	San Francisco	2-Wd San Francisco	79	152
Geo W	17	m	w	CA	El Dorado	Lake Valley Twp	72	63
George W	54	m	w	TN	Stanislaus	Empire Twp	92	66
J	44	m	w	DENM	El Dorado	Greenwood Twp	72	55
J W	36	m	w	VA	Nevada	Washington Twp	75	346
James	38	m	w	VA	Colusa	Grand Island Twp	71	306
James	15	m	w	CA	Monterey	Pajaro Twp	74	376
James	15	m	w	CA	Santa Cruz	Watsonville	89	367
James	11	m	w	CA	Sacramento	San Joaquin Twp	77	394
Joseph	42	m	w	BARB	San Francisco	11-Wd San Francisc	84	660
Margaret	25	f	w	IREL	San Francisco	6-Wd San Francisco	81	151
Margaret	25	f	w	IREL	San Francisco	San Francisco P O	83	60
Patrick	38	m	w	IREL	San Francisco	San Francisco P O	83	60
William	37	m	w	TN	Tulare	White Rvr Twp	92	301
William	34	m	w	IREL	Sonoma	Vallejo Twp	91	453
Zar P	49	m	w	OH	El Dorado	Mud Springs Twp	72	73
BRANDRETH								
E S	35	m	w	DENM	Nevada	Eureka Twp	75	129
BRANDROP								
James	28	m	w	DENM	Nevada	Eureka Twp	75	128
Jes	18	m	w	SHOL	Nevada	Nevada Twp	75	322
BRANDS								
James	10	m	w	CA	Marin	San Rafael Twp	74	27
Mary	14	f	w	CA	San Joaquin	Castoria Twp	86	12
May	17	f	w	IREL	San Joaquin	Tulare Twp	86	262
BRANDT								
Andrew	40	m	w	SWED	San Francisco	San Francisco P O	83	144
August	21	m	w	IA	Nevada	Nevada Twp	75	287
B R	43	m	w	HANO	San Francisco	San Francisco P O	85	804
Chas	32	m	w	MA	San Francisco	7-Wd San Francisco	81	279
Edwd	26	m	w	PRUS	San Francisco	1-Wd San Francisco	79	11
Fred	20	m	w	HANO	San Francisco	San Francisco P O	83	107
Geo E	39	m	w	DENM	San Francisco	2-Wd San Francisco	79	181
George	30	m	w	DENM	Mendocino	Point Arena Twp	74	224
H	35	m	w	CANA	San Joaquin	Castoria Twp	86	10
Henry	27	m	w	HANO	Alameda	Eden Twp	68	63
Henry	23	m	w	BAVA	San Francisco	8-Wd San Francisco	82	439
James	23	m	w	SCOT	San Francisco	7-Wd San Francisco	81	286
James	23	m	w	PRUS	Placer	Dutch Flat P O	76	402
Jno C	52	m	w	PRUS	Nevada	Rough & Ready Twp	75	335
Johana	48	f	w	PRUS	San Francisco	2-Wd San Francisco	79	261
John G	58	m	w	HAMB	San Francisco	San Francisco P O	83	23
L	39	m	w	DENM	Alameda	Oakland	68	181
Leonhardt	33	m	w	WURT	San Francisco	1-Wd San Francisco	79	35
Louis	34	m	w	HANO	Amador	Jackson P O	69	322
Louis	28	m	w	PRUS	San Francisco	San Francisco P O	83	227
M	40	m	w	SWED	San Francisco	8-Wd San Francisco	82	375
Minna	19	f	w	PRUS	San Francisco	San Francisco P O	83	280
Otto	31	m	w	PRUS	San Francisco	8-Wd San Francisco	82	485
Peter	50	m	w	GERM	Sonoma	Salt Point	91	390
Wm	47	m	w	PRUS	San Joaquin	Castoria Twp	86	12
BRANDY								
Jacob	29	m	w	SWIT	Sutter	Sutter Twp	92	116
Joel	37	m	w	NY	Placer	Dutch Flat P O	76	401
BRANEGAN								
J	32	m	w	IREL	Sierra	Butte Twp	89	508
Patrick	48	m	w	IREL	San Mateo	San Mateo P O	87	355
Y	30	m	w	IREL	Sierra	Butte Twp	89	508
BRANER								
Sabastian	44	m	w	BAVA	El Dorado	Georgetown Twp	72	46
BRANERLY								
M	45	m	w	IREL	Solano	Vallejo	90	195
BRANES								
Lewis	15	m	w	SWIT	Sonoma	Sonoma Twp	91	445
BRANET								
Louis	46	m	w	FRAN	Yuba	Parks Bar Twp	93	649
BRANEY								
Geo	35	m	w	GERM	San Francisco	7-Wd San Francisco	81	254
BRANFORT								
A C	42	m	w	FRAN	Tuolumne	Sonora P O	93	310
BRANGER								
John	43	m	w	FRAN	San Francisco	6-Wd San Francisco	81	104
BRANGES								
Diedrich	51	m	w	HANO	San Francisco	11-Wd San Francisc	84	617
BRANGON								
Rich N	38	m	w	ENGL	San Francisco	6-Wd San Francisco	81	155
BRANHAM								
Isaac	66	m	w	KY	Santa Clara	San Jose Twp	88	198
John	62	m	w	NY	San Francisco	11-Wd San Francisc	84	613
BRANIA								
Martha	55	f	w	ITAL	San Francisco	1-Wd San Francisco	79	27
BRANIFF								
Anna	21	f	w	PA	Sonoma	Petaluma Twp	91	325
BRANIGAN								
Arthur	43	m	w	IREL	Monterey	San Benito Twp	74	382

© 2001 by Heritage Quest. All rights reserved.

Series M593

Name	Age	S	R	B-PL	County	Locale	Roll	Pg
B	59	m	w	IREL	Sutter	Butte Twp	92	95
Bridget	23	f	w	IREL	San Francisco	San Francisco P O	83	261
James	27	m	w	IREL	Alameda	Eden Twp	68	87
Patk	35	m	w	SCOT	Sacramento	4-Wd Sacramento	77	348
William	50	m	w	IREL	San Francisco	7-Wd San Francisco	81	194
BRANING								
William	30	m	w	HANO	San Francisco	3-Wd San Francisco	79	296
BRANKEA								
Maria	22	f	w	MEXI	San Francisco	8-Wd San Francisco	82	309
BRANKEN								
Michael	37	m	w	IREL	San Francisco	2-Wd San Francisco	79	220
BRANLEY								
Thos	35	m	w	IREL	Solano	Benicia	90	18
BRANMAN								
Mary	35	f	w	IREL	San Francisco	11-Wd San Francisc	84	682
BRANN								
J A	30	f	w	OH	Solano	Vallejo	90	185
Philip	25	m	w	BAVA	San Francisco	1-Wd San Francisco	79	63
Robert	45	m	w	ME	San Francisco	7-Wd San Francisco	81	245
BRANNA								
B	23	f	w	IREL	Sacramento	1-Wd Sacramento	77	200
Santa	19	f	b	CA	Alameda	Brooklyn Twp	68	53
Thomas	34	m	w	IREL	San Francisco	11-Wd San Francisc	84	505
BRANNAGAN								
M J	26	f	w	US	Yuba	Marysville	93	609
Mary	61	f	w	IREL	Sacramento	4-Wd Sacramento	77	348
BRANNAM								
Frances L	8	f	w	CA	Santa Cruz	Watsonville	89	366
BRANNAN								
A	25	m	w	WI	San Joaquin	Liberty Twp	86	90
Bridget	35	f	w	IREL	San Joaquin	Douglas Twp	86	33
Daniel	45	m	w	IREL	Mariposa	Mariposa P O	74	131
Daniel	40	m	w	IREL	Santa Cruz	Pajaro Twp	89	343
Daniel	16	m	w	NY	Los Angeles	Los Angeles	73	570
Donald	14	m	w	NY	Los Angeles	Los Angeles	73	542
Edwin	32	m	w	SWIT	Yolo	Cache Crk Twp	93	425
Ella	17	f	w	IREL	San Francisco	7-Wd San Francisco	81	249
Ellen	46	m	w	IREL	San Francisco	8-Wd San Francisco	82	356
Ellen	24	f	w	IREL	San Francisco	San Francisco P O	85	798
Ellen	24	f	w	IREL	San Francisco	San Francisco P O	83	256
Ellen	17	f	w	IREL	San Francisco	7-Wd San Francisco	81	181
Frank	32	m	w	IREL	Santa Cruz	Pajaro Twp	89	344
Gim	35	m	w	IREL	San Francisco	7-Wd San Francisco	81	285
Harbert	28	m	w	OH	Del Norte	Crescent	71	463
Horace	19	m	w	MA	Alameda	Brooklyn	68	22
J B	46	m	w	TN	Monterey	San Juan Twp	74	389
James	45	m	w	IREL	San Francisco	San Francisco P O	83	251
James	43	m	w	IREL	Trinity	Douglas	92	233
James	40	m	w	IREL	San Francisco	San Francisco P O	80	379
James	35	m	w	IREL	San Francisco	San Francisco P O	85	771
James	32	m	w	IREL	San Francisco	2-Wd San Francisco	79	193
James	32	m	w	IREL	San Joaquin	1-Wd Stockton	86	139
James	22	m	w	IREL	San Francisco	7-Wd San Francisco	81	190
James	15	m	w	CA	Stanislaus	Buena Vista Twp	92	15
Jane	57	f	w	IREL	San Francisco	San Francisco P O	80	461
Jane	30	f	w	IREL	San Francisco	San Francisco P O	83	131
Jno H	43	m	w	IREL	Alameda	Brooklyn Twp	68	50
Joe	27	m	w	IREL	San Francisco	1-Wd San Francisco	79	59
John	50	m	w	IREL	Stanislaus	San Joaquin Twp	92	71
John	40	m	w	IREL	Solano	Vallejo	90	149
John	37	m	w	NY	Monterey	Alisal Twp	74	292
John	37	m	w	BAVA	Tuolumne	Sonora P O	93	307
John	35	m	w	IREL	Alameda	Eden Twp	68	61
John	30	m	w	IREL	Mendocino	Point Arena Twp	74	206
John	30	m	w	IREL	San Francisco	San Francisco P O	83	126
John	30	m	w	IREL	Sonoma	Salt Point	91	390
John	28	m	w	US	El Dorado	Diamond Springs Tw	72	28
John	24	m	w	PA	San Francisco	7-Wd San Francisco	81	165
John	16	m	w	CT	Stanislaus	Emory Twp	92	20
John C	33	m	w	IREL	San Francisco	8-Wd San Francisco	82	351
Jos	43	m	w	PA	Sacramento	3-Wd Sacramento	77	277
Joseph	50	m	w	IL	Sacramento	4-Wd Sacramento	77	354
Julia	16	f	w	IREL	San Francisco	2-Wd San Francisco	79	192
Kate	19	f	w	IREL	Yolo	Cache Crk Twp	93	429
L	22	m	w	US	Solano	Vallejo	90	141
Maggie	19	f	w	MA	Solano	Vallejo	90	196
Margaret	25	f	w	IREL	San Francisco	San Francisco P O	80	405
Martin	45	m	w	IREL	San Francisco	San Francisco P O	83	23
Martin	36	m	w	IREL	San Francisco	11-Wd San Francisc	84	540
Michael	40	m	w	IREL	Yuba	Long Bar Twp	93	560
Micheal	29	m	w	IREL	San Francisco	7-Wd San Francisco	81	180
Michel	39	m	w	IREL	Napa	Napa Twp	75	71
Michell	41	m	w	IREL	Los Angeles	Los Angeles	73	570
Mike	22	m	w	IREL	Solano	Vallejo	90	200
P	24	m	w	IREL	Yuba	Marysville	93	594
Pat	66	m	w	IREL	Sacramento	1-Wd Sacramento	77	188
Peter	50	m	w	IREL	Solano	Maine Prairie Twp	90	47
Peter	40	m	w	MA	San Francisco	11-Wd San Francisc	84	684
S	45	f	w	NY	San Francisco	7-Wd San Francisco	81	280
Saml	29	m	w	NY	San Francisco	San Francisco P O	83	130
Samuel	52	m	w	ME	San Francisco	6-Wd San Francisco	81	105
Thomas	50	m	w	IREL	Yolo	Cache Crk Twp	93	453
Thomas	45	m	w	IREL	Yolo	Grafton Twp	93	495
Thomas	30	m	w	IREL	San Francisco	7-Wd San Francisco	81	173
Thomas	28	m	w	IREL	San Francisco	7-Wd San Francisco	81	220
Thomas	24	m	w	IREL	San Francisco	San Francisco P O	83	344
Thos	45	m	w	IREL	San Joaquin	2-Wd Stockton	86	166
Thos	39	m	w	IA	Alameda	Murray Twp	68	118
Timothy	40	m	w	IREL	San Francisco	7-Wd San Francisco	81	229
William	25	m	w	VT	Alameda	Alvarado	68	302
Wm	45	m	w	IREL	Solano	Vallejo	90	142
Wm	39	m	w	IREL	Santa Clara	Gilroy Twp	88	74
Wm	30	m	w	IREL	San Francisco	7-Wd San Francisco	81	276
BRANNAR								
J	35	m	w	IREL	Mariposa	Maxwell Crk P O	74	140
BRANNEGAN								
J W	20	m	w	WI	Sacramento	3-Wd Sacramento	77	257
BRANNEN								
F	40	m	w	IREL	San Joaquin	2-Wd Stockton	86	162
James	29	m	w	IREL	Marin	San Rafael Twp	74	43
John	40	m	w	IREL	Alameda	Brooklyn Twp	68	50
Martha	39	f	w	IREL	Contra Costa	Martinez P O	71	420
BRANNER								
B F	37	m	w	IN	Alameda	Murray Twp	68	118
Geo F	36	m	w	PRUS	Sacramento	4-Wd Sacramento	77	354
BRANNIGAN								
Arthur	38	m	w	IREL	San Francisco	1-Wd San Francisco	79	62
John	68	m	w	IREL	Nevada	Nevada Twp	75	278
Margaret	25	f	w	IREL	San Francisco	11-Wd San Francisc	84	572
Peter	31	m	w	IREL	Yolo	Putah Twp	93	524
Thos	27	m	w	LA	Nevada	Nevada Twp	75	280
BRANNIN								
John	30	m	w	IREL	Merced	Snelling P O	74	255
Thomas	40	m	w	IREL	San Francisco	San Francisco P O	85	755
BRANNOCK								
L H	52	m	w	NY	San Joaquin	Oneal Twp	86	102
L M	26	f	w	OH	San Joaquin	Oneal Twp	86	102
BRANNON								
I	28	m	w	TN	Calaveras	Copperopolis P O	70	236
Kate	35	f	w	IREL	San Francisco	8-Wd San Francisco	82	377
Kate	27	f	w	IREL	San Francisco	San Francisco P O	85	788
Mike	34	m	w	IREL	Butte	Hamilton Twp	70	63
Samuel	37	m	w	AL	Amador	Jackson P O	69	346
Thomas	27	m	w	IREL	Inyo	Bishop Crk Twp	73	316
Thos	20	m	w	IREL	San Joaquin	2-Wd Stockton	86	175
William	55	m	w	IREL	Stanislaus	San Joaquin Twp	92	77
BRANO								
Ignacio	34	m	w	MEXI	San Francisco	San Francisco P O	80	472
BRANS								
Benj F	30	m	w	PA	Sacramento	San Joaquin Twp	77	401
Chas C	24	m	w	CANA	Butte	Chico Twp	70	18
James	28	m	w	ME	San Francisco	San Francisco P O	83	222
BRANSCOMB								
John	40	m	w	ME	Butte	Bidwell Twp	70	4
BRANSCOMBIE								
Robert	27	m	w	CANA	Solano	Green Valley Twp	90	40
BRANSFORD								
Milford B	37	m	w	KY	Plumas	Indian Twp	77	18
Robt	41	m	w	VA	Fresno	Millerton P O	72	181
Thos	25	m	w	MO	Mendocino	Round Valley Twp	74	216
Walter L	68	m	w	VA	Sonoma	Petaluma Twp	91	327
Zerel W	36	m	w	KY	Sonoma	Petaluma Twp	91	327
BRANSON								
Benj	40	m	w	MO	Sonoma	Mendocino Twp	91	304
Isaac	36	m	w	MO	Mariposa	Mariposa P O	74	95
John	47	m	w	TN	Mariposa	Mariposa P O	74	95
Lewis	25	m	w	WI	Sonoma	Petaluma Twp	91	316
Mary	11	f	w	KY	Santa Clara	2-Wd San Jose	88	338
Ruben	26	m	w	MO	Mono	Bridgeport P O	74	284
Sarah	14	f	w	CA	Santa Clara	Redwood Twp	88	118
BRANSTADSTEDER								
H M	49	m	w	IL	Monterey	Salinas Twp	74	311
BRANSTETTER								
Martin	43	m	w	MO	Humboldt	Pacific Twp	72	290
Wm J	34	m	w	WI	Placer	Roseville P O	76	350
BRANT								
Castel	36	m	w	PRUS	Napa	Napa Twp	75	67
Chas P	27	m	w	CANA	Humboldt	Bucksport Twp	72	242
Edward	22	m	w	MO	Kern	Havilah P O	73	340
Frederick	32	m	w	DENM	Los Angeles	Los Angeles	73	533
Jones	27	m	w	HCAS	Calaveras	San Andreas P O	70	209
Louis	31	m	w	CHIL	Tuolumne	Chinese Camp P O	93	383
Louisa	18	f	w	PRUS	Sonoma	Petaluma Twp	91	364
William	40	m	w	PA	San Francisco	San Francisco P O	80	363
William	31	m	w	PRUS	Los Angeles	Los Angeles	73	520
BRANTER								
John	40	m	w	PA	San Francisco	11-Wd San Francisc	84	540
BRANTHAVEN								
Daniel	39	m	w	PA	Sonoma	Analy Twp	91	237
BRANTLACT								
Joseph	52	m	w	PRUS	Siskiyou	Yreka	89	660
BRANTORE								
James	40	m	w	MO	Santa Clara	San Jose Twp	88	212
BRANTOVER								
Adam	41	m	w	PA	El Dorado	Mountain Twp	72	69
David	36	m	w	PA	El Dorado	Kelsey Twp	72	61
BRANTZ								
Berry	48	m	w	DENM	Butte	Oregon Twp	70	123
BRANUM								
George	22	m	w	MS	Santa Cruz	Soquel Twp	89	447
BRANYAN								
George	29	m	w	MI	Colusa	Monroe Twp	71	320
BRAPHY								
John	58	m	w	IREL	Merced	Snelling P O	74	266

© 2001 by Heritage Quest. All rights reserved.

California 1870 Census

Series M593

Name	Age	S	R	B-PL	County	Locale	Roll	Pg
BRAQUET								
Archilla	54	m	w	FRAN	Mariposa	Mariposa P O	74	118
BRAREN								
Christina	22	f	w	PRUS	Trinity	Weaverville Pct	92	224
BRARENS								
Fred	28	m	w	PRUS	San Francisco	San Francisco P O	83	84
BRARMAN								
M I	31	m	w	CANA	San Francisco	7-Wd San Francisco	81	249
BRAS								
Elias	35	m	w	TN	Colusa	Butte Twp	71	267
BRASCH								
Claus	40	m	w	PRUS	San Francisco	San Francisco P O	80	469
BRASCHE								
Geo H	48	m	w	HANO	San Francisco	San Francisco P O	83	108
BRASFIELD								
Wiley	32	m	w	MO	Colusa	Colusa	71	296
BRASH								
Elizabeth	27	f	w	NY	San Francisco	San Francisco P O	80	537
John	31	m	w	SCOT	Plumas	Washington Twp	77	52
William	19	m	w	PRUS	San Francisco	San Francisco P O	83	366
BRASHEARS								
Colman	40	m	w	MO	San Mateo	Pescadero P O	87	411
Wm	24	m	w	MD	Marin	San Rafael Twp	74	37
BRASK								
Chas	30	m	w	SWED	San Francisco	1-Wd San Francisco	79	116
Nicholas	37	m	w	DENM	Del Norte	Smith Rvr Twp	71	479
BRASLAN								
James	24	m	w	MA	Santa Clara	1-Wd San Jose	88	237
BRASS								
Bartholomew	40	m	w	SWED	San Mateo	Redwood Twp	87	361
Benjamin	59	m	w	MA	Shasta	French Gulch P O	89	467
Bridget	75	f	w	IREL	Los Angeles	San Gabriel Twp	73	597
Frank	28	m	w	HOLL	Fresno	Kingston P O	72	219
J	37	m	w	ITAL	Yuba	Marysville	93	586
Joseph	40	m	w	FRAN	Yuba	Marysville	93	615
S	39	m	w	NY	Los Angeles	Los Angeles	73	533
BRASSE								
Henry	69	m	w	FRAN	Santa Clara	2-Wd San Jose	88	326
BRASSEL								
Frank	32	m	w	IREL	San Francisco	San Francisco P O	83	36
BRASSETT								
Mark A	21	m	w	FRAN	San Francisco	6-Wd San Francisco	81	109
BRASSFIELD								
J E	49	m	w	MO	Calaveras	Copperopolis P O	70	228
BRASSIL								
John	26	m	w	IREL	Alameda	Oakland	68	171
BRASSY								
Frederick	33	m	w	FRAN	Santa Clara	1-Wd San Jose	88	267
BRASTED								
Ann	22	f	w	IREL	Alameda	Oakland	68	153
BRATLY								
F S	35	m	w	PA	Monterey	San Juan Twp	74	390
BRATON								
William	53	m	w	SCOT	San Mateo	Schoolhouse Statio	87	331
BRATOR								
Victor	20	m	w	MEXI	Los Angeles	Los Angeles	73	555
BRATOS								
Urich	29	m	w	AUST	Calaveras	San Andreas P O	70	203
BRATSCHNIEDER								
Fred	31	m	w	SAXO	San Francisco	2-Wd San Francisco	79	145
BRATT								
Adam	56	m	w	NY	Santa Clara	1-Wd San Jose	88	244
Carlos	42	m	w	IN	Mendocino	Round Valley Twp	74	216
Delos	38	m	w	IN	Mendocino	Calpella Twp	74	185
BRATTAN								
Martin A	61	m	w	VT	Colusa	Spring Valley Twp	71	337
BRATTON								
A C	37	m	w	KY	Calaveras	Copperopolis P O	70	256
Solomon	34	m	w	ENGL	Santa Barbara	Santa Barbara P O	87	496
BRATZ								
Edward	32	m	w	PRUS	Yolo	Cottonwood Twp	93	470
BRAUDA								
Henry W	46	m	w	NY	San Francisco	San Francisco P O	83	183
BRAUM								
H	43	m	w	PRUS	Alameda	Alameda	68	11
Walter	33	m	w	IREL	San Francisco	San Francisco P O	83	54
BRAUMAN								
Bridget	36	f	w	IREL	San Joaquin	1-Wd Stockton	86	127
BRAUN								
Charles	30	m	w	BAVA	San Francisco	8-Wd San Francisco	82	476
Mitchell	41	m	w	AUST	Butte	Mountain Spring Tw	70	89
BRAUNSHWEIGER								
H	32	m	w	BRUN	Solano	Vallejo	90	173
BRAUS								
Jacob	28	m	w	HDAR	San Francisco	8-Wd San Francisco	82	350
BRAVER								
Charles	44	m	w	GERM	Monterey	Castroville Twp	74	338
Richd	41	m	w	MD	San Francisco	5-Wd San Francisco	81	24
BRAVERMAN								
Louis	44	m	w	PRUS	San Francisco	8-Wd San Francisco	82	426
BRAVO								
Juan	63	m	w	CHIL	Santa Barbara	San Buenaventura P	87	432
Louis	43	m	w	PA	Napa	Napa	75	55
BRAWBIN								
Henry	27	m	w	NY	San Francisco	1-Wd San Francisco	79	94
BRAWLEY								
Andw J	32	m	w	TN	Fresno	Millerton P O	72	185
Ira M	1M	m	w	CA	Fresno	Millerton P O	72	150
J G	47	m	w	TN	Monterey	Castroville Twp	74	340
BRAWNER								
J B	34	m	w	KY	Mendocino	Little Lake Twp	74	193
BRAWSON								
W	48	m	w	NY	Alameda	Oakland	68	215
BRAXTON								
H	46	m	w	VA	Solano	Vallejo	90	200
BRAY								
Ann	48	f	w	IREL	Sacramento	Cosumnes Twp	77	91
Degory	28	m	w	ENGL	Contra Costa	Martinez P O	71	428
Edmund	69	m	w	IREL	Sacramento	4-Wd Sacramento	77	376
Elisha	40	m	w	OH	Solano	Vacaville Twp	90	131
Elisha	18	m	w	MO	Sonoma	Santa Rosa	91	395
Elisha	18	m	w	MO	Sonoma	Analy Twp	91	230
Francis	30	m	w	MO	Santa Clara	Santa Clara Twp	88	146
Harrell	29	m	w	OH	Sonoma	Mendocino Twp	91	288
Harrold	67	m	w	NC	Sonoma	Santa Rosa	91	404
Henry	36	m	w	ENGL	Nevada	Nevada Twp	75	309
Henry	29	m	w	IREL	San Francisco	San Francisco P O	80	360
Iredell	34	m	w	TN	Yuba	Slate Range Bar Tw	93	672
James	36	m	w	ENGL	Nevada	Grass Valley Twp	75	164
Jane	52	f	w	ENGL	Siskiyou	Yreka	89	660
Jno	31	m	w	ENGL	Sierra	Table Rock Twp	89	572
John	43	m	w	ME	Tuolumne	Chinese Camp P O	93	367
John	38	m	w	ENGL	Nevada	Grass Valley Twp	75	215
John	27	m	w	MO	San Francisco	8-Wd San Francisco	82	442
John	24	m	w	OH	Solano	Silveyville Twp	90	80
John G	57	m	w	NJ	Santa Clara	Santa Clara Twp	88	146
Joseph	38	m	w	ME	Tuolumne	Sonora P O	93	307
Joyle T B	33	m	w	NY	Monterey	Salinas Twp	74	314
Margaret	26	f	w	IREL	San Francisco	11-Wd San Francisc	84	459
Mary	35	f	w	IREL	Sacramento	Granite Twp	77	148
Melinda	19	f	w	ENGL	Santa Clara	Almaden Twp	88	10
Moses	33	m	w	VT	Santa Clara	Almaden Twp	88	18
Nathan	28	m	w	MO	Yolo	Buckeye Twp	93	412
Owen	28	m	w	NY	San Francisco	7-Wd San Francisco	81	206
Pal	28	m	w	IREL	San Joaquin	Oneal Twp	86	107
Peter	24	m	w	ENGL	Contra Costa	Martinez P O	71	428
Preston M	38	m	w	IL	Sacramento	3-Wd Sacramento	77	286
Samuel	22	m	w	ENGL	Nevada	Grass Valley Twp	75	203
Samuel	20	m	w	ENGL	Nevada	Grass Valley Twp	75	168
Thomas	35	m	w	NY	Solano	Suisun Twp	90	102
Watson	35	m	w	NJ	Alameda	Brooklyn Twp	68	39
William	43	m	w	KY	Colusa	Monroe Twp	71	315
William	37	m	w	KY	Yolo	Cache Crk Twp	93	442
Wm	60	m	w	ENGL	San Joaquin	2-Wd Stockton	86	189
Zacharias	39	m	w	ENGL	Nevada	Grass Valley Twp	75	144
BRAYDEN								
R	25	m	w	NH	Alameda	Murray Twp	68	118
BRAYED								
Louis	29	m	w	CANA	Napa	Napa Twp	75	73
BRAYENZER								
Louis	32	m	w	PRUS	Santa Cruz	Santa Cruz Twp	89	394
BRAYLES								
Benj F	17	m	w	RI	Yuba	Bullards Bar P O	93	552
BRAYLY								
Joseph	20	m	w	IN	Colusa	Colusa	71	295
BRAYMON								
A K	50	f	w	IREL	Sierra	Downieville Twp	89	519
BRAYNARD								
C P	50	m	w	MA	Tehama	Red Bluff	92	178
H A	25	m	w	NY	Tehama	Red Bluff	92	178
BRAYNOD								
O V	16	m	w	OH	Alameda	Oakland	68	226
BRAYS								
Jas H	54	m	w	NY	San Diego	San Diego	78	496
BRAYSON								
Henry	28	m	w	IA	Mendocino	Big Rvr Twp	74	171
BRAYTON								
Albert	42	m	w	NY	Alameda	Oakland	68	160
Amelia	18	f	w	CA	Contra Costa	San Pablo Twp	71	358
Edwin	42	m	w	NY	Mendocino	Navarro & Big Rvr	74	167
Horatio	22	m	w	OH	Mendocino	Cuffeys Cove Twp	74	168
John G	43	m	w	MA	Napa	Napa	75	46
Mary	35	f	w	NJ	Alameda	Oakland	68	161
BRAZ								
Joaquin	51	m	w	PORT	Contra Costa	San Pablo Twp	71	362
BRAZEL								
George	36	m	w	CANA	San Francisco	San Francisco P O	83	36
BRAZELL								
George	29	m	w	NY	Nevada	Nevada Twp	75	317
William	33	m	w	TN	Tehama	Bell Mills Twp	92	159
BRAZELTON								
James A	38	m	w	IL	San Bernardino	San Bernardino Twp	78	418
BRAZER								
John	44	m	w	MA	Santa Cruz	Santa Cruz	89	407
Solomon	40	m	w	NC	Sacramento	Dry Crk Twp	77	103
BRAZIA								
Antoine	28	m	w	AZOR	Santa Cruz	Santa Cruz	89	429
BRAZIL								
Antone	19	m	w	PORT	Marin	Point Reyes Twp	74	21
Antonio	42	m	w	PORT	San Francisco	1-Wd San Francisco	79	19
Frank	18	m	w	PORT	Marin	Point Reyes Twp	74	22
Joseph	36	m	w	AZOR	Yuba	Parks Bar Twp	93	649
Joseph	35	m	w	PORT	Marin	Bolinas Twp	74	4
Joseph	35	m	w	PORT	Santa Clara	Santa Clara Twp	88	137

© 2001 by Heritage Quest. All rights reserved.

Name	Age	S	R	B-PL	County	Locale	Series M593 Roll	Pg
Manuel	24	m	w	PORT	Marin	Point Reyes Twp	74	22
Thos	27	m	w	IREL	Solano	Vallejo	90	194
BRAZILL								
Joanna	25	f	w	IREL	Solano	Vallejo	90	140
John	31	m	w	PORT	Solano	Maine Prairie Twp	90	49
BRAZIN								
Emanuel	32	m	w	SCOT	Siskiyou	Scott Valley Twp	89	619
BRAZLETON								
Cissaro A	30	f	w	GA	Butte	Oregon Twp	70	133
Jas	40	m	w	GA	Butte	Oregon Twp	70	133
BRAZZLE								
Timothy	24	m	w	IREL	Los Angeles	Los Nietos Twp	73	576
BREAD								
John	35	m	w	IREL	San Francisco	7-Wd San Francisco	81	181
BREADLOVE								
John A	32	m	w	OH	Santa Clara	Redwood Twp	88	123
BREADY								
Charles	45	m	w	IREL	San Francisco	7-Wd San Francisco	81	177
BREAND								
John	34	m	w	TX	Los Angeles	Los Angeles	73	534
BREANTON								
William	49	m	w	ENGL	El Dorado	Mud Springs Twp	72	81
BREAS								
Adolph	22	m	w	LA	San Francisco	San Francisco P O	80	350
BREASE								
Frank	49	m	w	NY	Contra Costa	Martinez Twp	71	347
BREASER								
Henry D	34	m	w	TX	Fresno	Kingston P O	72	220
BREAT								
Antone	35	m	w	FRAN	San Francisco	8-Wd San Francisco	82	361
BREAUX								
Etienne	32	m	w	FRAN	San Francisco	San Francisco P O	85	817
BREBACA								
Joaquin	31	m	w	CA	Santa Clara	Gilroy Twp	88	87
BREBART								
M L	30	f	w	HOLL	Alameda	Oakland	68	199
BRECHMAN								
John B	34	m	w	HOLL	Stanislaus	Empire Twp	92	51
BRECHT								
August	25	m	w	BADE	San Francisco	San Francisco P O	85	804
John	35	m	w	BAVA	San Francisco	8-Wd San Francisco	82	336
William	37	m	w	GERM	San Francisco	8-Wd San Francisco	82	366
BRECK								
Charles	60	m	w	FRAN	San Francisco	2-Wd San Francisco	79	286
Earnest	43	m	w	HDAR	Yuba	Marysville	93	592
Francis	49	m	w	NH	Solano	Suisun Twp	90	95
J Lloyd	51	m	w	KY	Solano	Benicia	90	14
Matilda	12	f	w	CA	Santa Barbara	Santa Barbara P O	87	502
Samuel	45	m	w	NH	Solano	Suisun Twp	90	95
Samuel	36	m	w	MA	San Francisco	8-Wd San Francisco	82	474
William	67	m	w	MA	Santa Barbara	Santa Barbara P O	87	476
BRECKENFELD								
John D	56	m	w	DENM	Santa Clara	2-Wd San Jose	88	290
BRECKENFELDT								
J	37	m	w	PRUS	San Joaquin	1-Wd Stockton	86	154
BRECKENRIDGE								
John	20	m	b	MO	Santa Clara	Santa Clara Twp	88	172
R G	36	m	w	KY	Sacramento	4-Wd Sacramento	77	322
Robert G	38	m	w	KY	Yolo	Cache Crk Twp	93	440
Sellie	16	f	b	MO	Santa Clara	Santa Clara Twp	88	172
BRECKTEL								
Wm F	38	m	w	BADE	Santa Barbara	Santa Barbara P O	87	488
BRECKWEDEL								
R	30	f	w	HANO	San Francisco	San Francisco P O	85	819
BREDEMAN								
Henry	35	m	w	HANO	Siskiyou	Callahan P O	89	632
BREDEMIRER								
D	30	m	w	PRUS	Napa	Napa Twp	75	31
BREDEN								
Emma	21	f	b	LA	Yuba	Marysville	93	606
J N	56	m	m	KY	Yuba	Marysville Twp	93	568
Peggy	47	f	b	TN	Yuba	Marysville Twp	93	568
S	28	m	m	MS	Yuba	Marysville Twp	93	568
BREDFORD								
John	37	m	w	ENGL	Calaveras	San Andreas P O	70	211
BREDHAL								
Jane	35	f	w	NY	San Francisco	5-Wd San Francisco	81	33
BREDHOFF								
C	40	m	w	HANO	Alameda	Oakland	68	140
BREDRE								
Alexandre	33	m	w	IREL	Monterey	San Antonio Twp	74	321
BREDSO								
Stephen	37	m	w	CHIL	Calaveras	San Andreas P O	70	210
BREE								
Frank	50	m	w	FRAN	Los Angeles	Los Angeles	73	517
John	53	m	w	IREL	San Francisco	7-Wd San Francisco	81	183
John	26	m	w	ENGL	Nevada	Grass Valley Twp	75	227
BREECE								
Abraham	46	m	w	VA	Placer	Bath P O	76	446
Henry	60	m	w	NY	Santa Barbara	Las Cruces P O	87	506
BREED								
Danl C	35	m	w	MA	San Francisco	San Francisco P O	85	731
Francis	41	m	w	FRAN	San Francisco	San Francisco P O	85	771
Henry	39	m	w	MA	San Francisco	San Francisco P O	80	539
J H	39	m	w	NY	Lassen	Janesville Twp	73	431
L N	37	m	w	NY	Lassen	Janesville Twp	73	431
Ramsey	54	m	w	MO	Stanislaus	San Joaquin Twp	92	83
BREEDEN								
Nelly	16	f	w	TX	Stanislaus	Empire Twp	92	62
Robert	30	m	w	IL	Stanislaus	Empire Twp	92	62
BREEDING								
Wm	44	m	w	VA	Sacramento	Cosumnes Twp	77	95
BREEDLOVE								
Columbus	40	m	w	TN	Yolo	Cottonwood Twp	93	463
James M	10	f	w	CA	Yolo	Cottonwood Twp	93	463
James W	43	m	w	TN	El Dorado	Georgetown Twp	72	48
Jane	37	m	w	VA	El Dorado	Georgetown Twp	72	48
W N	38	m	w	VA	Amador	Amador City P O	69	395
BREEN								
A A	35	m	w	MO	Siskiyou	Scott Valley Twp	89	613
Daniel M	53	m	w	IREL	Mariposa	Mariposa P O	74	116
J C	34	m	w	IREL	Merced	Snelling P O	74	246
J S	29	m	i	MO	Monterey	San Juan Twp	74	412
John	38	m	w	CANA	Monterey	San Juan Twp	74	415
John	37	m	w	IREL	Monterey	Castroville Twp	74	333
John	33	m	w	CANA	San Francisco	8-Wd San Francisco	82	288
John	28	m	w	IREL	Sacramento	Georgianna Twp	77	130
John	21	m	w	IREL	Solano	Vallejo	90	202
Joseph	52	m	w	IREL	Sacramento	2-Wd Sacramento	77	209
Joseph H	30	m	w	IREL	Sacramento	2-Wd Sacramento	77	253
Margaret	70	f	w	IREL	Monterey	San Juan Twp	74	412
Mary	38	f	w	IREL	San Francisco	San Francisco P O	83	374
Nicholas	37	m	w	IREL	Merced	Snelling P O	74	246
O C	25	m	w	NY	Santa Clara	Gilroy Twp	88	93
Patrick	32	m	w	IA	Monterey	San Juan Twp	74	416
Peter	22	m	w	IREL	San Francisco	7-Wd San Francisco	81	162
Richd	51	m	w	IREL	Sacramento	3-Wd Sacramento	77	289
Richd	28	m	w	IREL	Sacramento	3-Wd Sacramento	77	300
Simon P	31	m	w	IA	Monterey	San Juan Twp	74	411
Thomas	45	m	w	IREL	San Francisco	San Francisco P O	85	825
Thomas	38	m	w	MO	Santa Barbara	San Buenaventura P	87	446
Thomas	24	m	w	IREL	San Francisco	8-Wd San Francisco	82	375
Tymothy	40	m	w	IREL	San Francisco	San Francisco P O	85	764
William	20	m	w	CA	Santa Clara	Santa Clara Twp	88	176
Wm	48	m	w	IREL	Santa Barbara	Santa Barbara P O	87	494
Wm	26	m	w	NY	San Joaquin	1-Wd Stockton	86	128
Wm	26	m	w	IREL	San Joaquin	1-Wd Stockton	86	135
BREENE								
Hannah	39	f	w	IREL	San Francisco	2-Wd San Francisco	79	204
BREENEN								
John	25	m	w	OH	San Joaquin	Oneal Twp	86	112
BREER								
Peter	30	m	w	IREL	San Francisco	5-Wd San Francisco	81	33
BREESE								
Isa	28	m	w	NY	Humboldt	Bald Hills	72	239
BREEZE								
Hamilton	65	m	w	VA	San Diego	Warners Rancho Dis	78	528
Helen F	32	f	w	NY	San Francisco	8-Wd San Francisco	82	446
James	28	m	w	VA	San Francisco	San Francisco P O	83	231
John	31	m	w	IL	Alameda	Brooklyn	68	37
Joseph	25	m	w	NY	San Francisco	San Francisco P O	80	414
Louis	40	m	w	FRAN	San Francisco	8-Wd San Francisco	82	464
Louis A	27	m	w	IREL	San Francisco	San Francisco P O	83	26
BREEZEE								
Ira	27	m	w	NY	Humboldt	Eel Rvr Twp	72	251
BREGARD								
Leander	28	m	w	CANA	Contra Costa	Martinez P O	71	379
BREGGEMAN								
Henry	48	m	w	PRUS	San Francisco	2-Wd San Francisco	79	161
BREGGEMANN								
A	29	f	w	PRUS	Alameda	Alameda	68	1
BREGGS								
Mary A	26	f	w	IN	Los Angeles	Los Angeles	73	516
Thos L	31	m	w	ENGL	Sacramento	Dry Crk Twp	77	100
BREIDENSTEIN								
Leonard	35	m	w	GERM	San Francisco	2-Wd San Francisco	79	152
BREIGHTON								
Edward	45	m	w	IL	Santa Clara	2-Wd San Jose	88	327
BREILING								
John	31	m	w	BAVA	San Francisco	San Francisco P O	83	299
BREINAN								
Cathrain	35	f	w	IREL	San Francisco	San Francisco P O	80	408
BREINDS								
John	40	m	w	NY	San Joaquin	1-Wd Stockton	86	141
BREIS								
S	42	m	w	NY	Amador	Sutter Crk P O	69	401
BREISATHER								
L	40	m	w	BADE	San Francisco	San Francisco P O	83	327
BREISLAND								
Jas	23	m	w	IREL	Solano	Vallejo	90	198
BREITENBACH								
Leopold	44	m	w	PRUS	San Francisco	San Francisco P O	80	420
BREITHAUP								
Felix	38	m	w	BADE	San Francisco	San Francisco P O	80	461
BREITHAUPT								
Geo	39	m	w	BADE	San Francisco	11-Wd San Francisc	84	656
BREITKOPH								
Jos	57	m	w	NCOD	Mariposa	Mariposa P O	74	117
BREITLAUGH								
Wm	44	m	w	PRUS	Sonoma	Santa Rosa	91	420
BREITLING								
Philipine	55	f	w	PRUS	San Francisco	San Francisco P O	85	820
BREITWIESCA								
Charles	30	m	w	GERM	Alameda	Washington Twp	68	287

© 2001 by Heritage Quest. All rights reserved.

Name	Age	S	R	B-PL	County	Locale	Roll	Pg
BREJOT								
Eugene	32	m	w	FRAN	Santa Clara	1-Wd San Jose	88	267
BREKEN								
James	32	m	w	IREL	Santa Barbara	San Buenaventura P	87	438
BREKERFELDT								
Josephine	22	f	w	IREL	San Joaquin	2-Wd Stockton	86	172
BREKLE								
Gotleib	48	m	w	WURT	San Francisco	San Francisco P O	80	359
BREKWITH								
J L	37	m	w	NY	Sierra	Downieville Twp	89	518
BREL								
Rufus	66	m	w	MA	El Dorado	Mud Springs Twp	72	88
BRELLEY								
Abram	29	m	w	SWIT	Trinity	North Fork Twp	92	221
BREM								
Charles	21	m	w	DENM	Sutter	Yuba Twp	92	150
BREMAN								
D J	40	m	w	IREL	Solano	Vallejo	90	207
Jack	34	m	w	VA	Sacramento	Sutter Twp	77	380
John	22	m	w	IREL	San Joaquin	2-Wd Stockton	86	169
Jos	40	m	w	PRUS	San Francisco	8-Wd San Francisco	82	336
Joseph	24	m	w	IREL	San Luis Obispo	Arroyo Grande Twp	87	274
Mary	58	f	w	IREL	San Francisco	7-Wd San Francisco	81	157
Thomas	35	m	w	IREL	Marin	San Rafael Twp	74	25
BREMBURG								
John	38	m	w	SWED	Napa	Napa	75	10
BREME								
Charlie	35	m	w	OH	Sacramento	4-Wd Sacramento	77	325
BREMEIER								
John	31	m	w	IREL	San Joaquin	1-Wd Stockton	86	136
BREMEN								
Geo	35	m	w	PRUS	Alameda	Murray Twp	68	102
Herman	24	m	w	PRUS	San Francisco	11-Wd San Francisc	84	681
J	24	m	w	CA	Alameda	Murray Twp	68	101
Thomas	26	m	w	ENGL	San Francisco	San Francisco P O	85	873
Thos	25	m	w	IREL	San Joaquin	2-Wd Stockton	86	173
Wm	30	m	w	SHOL	San Francisco	1-Wd San Francisco	79	116
BREMER								
George K	31	m	w	WURT	Los Angeles	Wilmington Twp	73	641
Henry	34	m	w	PRUS	San Francisco	San Francisco P O	80	478
John H	35	m	w	PRUS	Santa Clara	1-Wd San Jose	88	253
Jos	31	m	w	PRUS	Sacramento	1-Wd Sacramento	77	172
Nichol	45	m	w	PRUS	Sonoma	Russian Rvr	91	378
William	36	m	w	PRUS	San Francisco	San Francisco P O	83	141
Wm	40	m	w	PRUS	Sacramento	Granite Twp	77	148
BREMETT								
Francis	38	m	w	ENGL	Solano	Vallejo	90	163
BREMHER								
Conrad	68	m	w	OH	Humboldt	Bald Hills	72	238
BREMMAN								
Henry	42	m	w	BREM	Solano	Vallejo	90	197
James	27	m	w	OH	Calaveras	San Andreas P O	70	162
BREMMER								
Hannah	55	f	w	PA	Humboldt	Eureka Twp	72	276
Helena	21	f	w	AUST	San Francisco	11-Wd San Francisc	84	626
BREMMON								
John	17	m	w	PRUS	Alameda	Murray Twp	68	100
BREMON								
H N	35	m	w	MO	Sacramento	Franklin Twp	77	120
BREMOND								
M	56	m	w	FRAN	Nevada	Bloomfield Twp	75	95
BRENAGER								
John	28	m	w	WURT	San Francisco	San Francisco P O	80	480
BRENAN								
Ellen	22	f	w	IREL	San Francisco	1-Wd San Francisco	79	42
Jacob	33	m	w	NY	San Joaquin	1-Wd Stockton	86	130
John	28	m	w	ENGL	San Francisco	3-Wd San Francisco	79	291
Joseph	48	m	w	IREL	San Francisco	1-Wd San Francisco	79	91
Julia	30	f	w	IREL	Nevada	Grass Valley Twp	75	152
Margret	48	f	w	IREL	San Francisco	1-Wd San Francisco	79	76
Martin	48	m	w	IREL	San Francisco	1-Wd San Francisco	79	76
Martin	33	m	w	IREL	San Francisco	1-Wd San Francisco	79	95
Owen	25	m	w	NY	San Francisco	1-Wd San Francisco	79	104
Patrick	28	m	w	IREL	San Francisco	1-Wd San Francisco	79	132
BRENCHELL								
Edward	32	m	w	PRUS	Stanislaus	Buena Vista Twp	92	12
BRENDRES								
H	42	m	w	HOLL	Nevada	Eureka Twp	75	135
BRENEAU								
Mary	36	f	w	HDAR	San Francisco	2-Wd San Francisco	79	245
BRENEN								
Ed	39	m	w	IREL	San Joaquin	2-Wd Stockton	86	171
BRENER								
D	29	m	w	SWIT	San Joaquin	Oneal Twp	86	110
Thomas	60	m	w	ENGL	Sutter	Nicolaus Twp	92	109
BRENET								
James	35	m	w	OH	Los Angeles	Los Angeles Twp	73	483
BRENGLE								
Oscar	23	m	w	IL	San Francisco	7-Wd San Francisco	81	262
BRENHAM								
Chas	44	m	w	KY	San Francisco	11-Wd San Francisc	84	561
E W	31	m	w	PRUS	Sutter	Sutter Twp	92	127
BRENING								
E	19	f	w	HDAR	Sacramento	4-Wd Sacramento	77	326
John	25	m	w	PRUS	San Francisco	San Francisco P O	83	414
BRENISER								
Joseph	34	m	w	IL	Los Angeles	El Monte Twp	73	461
BRENKAMP								
Aug	37	m	w	PRUS	San Francisco	11-Wd San Francisc	84	490
BRENMAN								
H	25	f	w	PRUS	San Francisco	San Francisco P O	83	323
BRENMER								
Sarah	30	f	w	IREL	San Francisco	11-Wd San Francisc	84	708
BRENNA								
Jno	50	m	w	PRUS	San Francisco	5-Wd San Francisco	81	35
Nicholas	40	m	w	IREL	San Francisco	8-Wd San Francisco	82	303
BRENNAN								
Anne	28	f	w	RI	San Francisco	11-Wd San Francisc	84	445
Auguste	29	m	w	BAVA	San Francisco	11-Wd San Francisc	84	577
Bridget	19	f	w	IREL	San Francisco	8-Wd San Francisco	82	470
Carberry	41	m	w	IREL	Tehama	Antelope Twp	92	154
Cecelia	15	f	w	IREL	San Francisco	8-Wd San Francisco	82	472
Charles	23	m	w	GA	Marin	San Rafael	74	57
Danl	35	m	w	IREL	San Francisco	11-Wd San Francisc	84	431
Edward	27	m	w	IREL	Marin	Point Reyes Twp	74	21
Francis	46	m	w	ENGL	Nevada	Grass Valley Twp	75	231
James	42	m	w	IREL	Santa Cruz	Watsonville	89	371
James	37	m	w	IREL	San Francisco	San Francisco P O	83	306
James	32	m	w	IREL	Nevada	Grass Valley Twp	75	194
James	32	m	w	IREL	Nevada	Grass Valley Twp	75	180
James	30	m	w	CANA	San Francisco	11-Wd San Francisc	84	449
John	44	m	w	IREL	San Francisco	7-Wd San Francisco	81	215
John	39	m	w	IREL	San Francisco	8-Wd San Francisco	82	419
John	35	m	w	IREL	San Francisco	6-Wd San Francisco	81	86
John	35	m	w	IREL	Nevada	Grass Valley Twp	75	193
John	34	m	w	IREL	Tuolumne	Sonora P O	93	329
John	27	m	w	IREL	Nevada	Grass Valley Twp	75	227
John A	65	m	w	IREL	San Francisco	San Francisco P O	83	168
Joseph	34	m	w	PRUS	San Francisco	3-Wd San Francisco	79	317
Kate	40	f	w	IREL	San Francisco	8-Wd San Francisco	82	437
Kate	26	f	w	IREL	San Francisco	6-Wd San Francisco	81	148
Kate	24	f	w	IREL	San Francisco	San Francisco P O	83	195
Margaret	34	f	w	IREL	San Francisco	11-Wd San Francisc	84	509
Martin	29	m	w	IREL	Marin	Sausalito Twp	74	73
Mary	60	f	w	IREL	San Francisco	8-Wd San Francisco	82	426
Michael	36	m	w	IREL	San Francisco	San Francisco P O	83	394
Pat	68	m	w	IREL	San Joaquin	3-Wd Stockton	86	222
Pat	40	m	w	IREL	Santa Clara	Almaden Twp	88	14
Patrick	35	m	w	IREL	San Francisco	11-Wd San Francisc	84	557
Peter	24	m	w	IREL	San Francisco	San Francisco P O	83	333
Richard	51	m	w	IREL	San Francisco	11-Wd San Francisc	84	537
Richard P	27	m	w	IREL	San Francisco	6-Wd San Francisco	81	80
Thomas	43	m	w	PA	San Joaquin	Oneal Twp	86	101
Thomas	30	m	w	IREL	San Joaquin	Oneal Twp	86	107
Thomas	25	m	w	PA	Nevada	Grass Valley Twp	75	178
Thos	28	m	w	IREL	San Francisco	1-Wd San Francisco	79	55
Thos W	44	m	w	NY	San Francisco	San Francisco P O	83	178
William	22	m	w	NY	Santa Clara	Fremont Twp	88	61
BRENNARD								
James	17	m	w	IL	Marin	Tomales Twp	74	82
Jesse	40	m	w	PA	San Francisco	San Francisco P O	83	139
BRENNEL								
John	28	m	w	IREL	Santa Clara	2-Wd San Jose	88	304
BRENNEN								
Geo L	39	m	w	ME	San Francisco	7-Wd San Francisco	81	273
James	27	m	w	IREL	Humboldt	Eureka Twp	72	279
John	35	m	w	PA	Sierra	Eureka Twp	89	525
Thos	30	m	w	IREL	Solano	Vallejo	90	199
BRENNENS								
J	33	m	w	NY	Monterey	Salinas Twp	74	311
BRENNER								
Fred	34	m	w	BAVA	Calaveras	Copperopolis P O	70	235
Gus	35	m	w	BAVA	Calaveras	Copperopolis P O	70	235
Katt	32	f	w	IREL	Napa	Napa	75	43
Selintha	18	f	w	NY	San Francisco	San Francisco P O	83	166
BRENNING								
John	39	m	w	MECK	San Francisco	1-Wd San Francisco	79	96
BRENNON								
James	42	m	w	ENGL	San Luis Obispo	Arroyo Grande Twp	87	270
John	62	m	w	NY	San Francisco	11-Wd San Francisc	84	614
Terry	36	m	w	IREL	Klamath	Orleans Twp	73	380
BRENOCK								
Richd	22	m	w	IREL	San Francisco	1-Wd San Francisco	79	69
BRENON								
James	30	m	w	CANA	Contra Costa	San Pablo Twp	71	365
John	40	m	w	PRUS	Alameda	Murray Twp	68	108
Luke	40	m	w	IREL	Calaveras	San Andreas P O	70	203
BRENSON								
Lucy	47	f	w	ME	San Francisco	8-Wd San Francisco	82	303
BRENT								
James	17	m	w	IA	Yolo	Putah Twp	93	524
Martin J	42	m	w	DENM	Marin	Novato Twp	74	12
Thomas	28	m	w	LA	Marin	San Rafael	74	56
William	20	m	w	WI	Stanislaus	Empire Twp	92	54
BRENTNER								
George W	39	m	w	VA	Sacramento	2-Wd Sacramento	77	218
BRENTON								
Chas	29	m	w	IN	San Joaquin	3-Wd Stockton	86	216
Samuel	22	m	w	MA	Contra Costa	Martinez P O	71	369
BRENTZ								
William	49	m	w	KY	Colusa	Colusa Twp	71	286
BRENTZEL								
John	19	m	w	NY	Contra Costa	Martinez P O	71	369

© 2001 by Heritage Quest. All rights reserved.

Name	Age	S	R	B-PL	County	Locale	Roll	Pg
						Series M593		
BRERETON								
James	50	m	w	IREL	San Francisco	San Francisco P O	83	93
BRESABACHER								
Jacob	37	m	w	BADE	San Francisco	11-Wd San Francisc	84	677
BRESCA								
Rosaria	26	f	w	MEXI	Santa Clara	2-Wd San Jose	88	304
BRESCIA								
G B	38	m	w	ITAL	Amador	Jackson P O	69	347
BRESEE								
David	42	m	w	CANA	El Dorado	Mud Springs Twp	72	76
S B	37	m	w	CANA	Sonoma	Santa Rosa	91	415
BRESETT								
John	56	m	w	NY	Tuolumne	Sonora P O	93	331
BRESHLEDT								
John	22	m	w	ENGL	San Francisco	11-Wd San Francisc	84	694
BRESHNER								
Ellen	24	f	w	IREL	San Francisco	2-Wd San Francisco	79	281
BRESINHAM								
David	30	m	w	IREL	San Francisco	11-Wd San Francisc	84	662
BRESLAN								
Mat	22	m	w	PRUS	Solano	Vallejo	90	172
BRESLAUER								
Alf	20	m	w	NY	Butte	Hamilton Twp	70	66
Ben	38	m	w	PRUS	Butte	Chico Twp	70	13
Bette	33	f	w	PRUS	Butte	Chico Twp	70	13
Danl	25	m	w	PRUS	Butte	Oregon Twp	70	123
Henry	39	m	w	PRUS	San Francisco	8-Wd San Francisco	82	454
Manuel	24	m	w	PRUS	Butte	Chico Twp	70	13
Theo	30	m	w	PRUS	San Francisco	8-Wd San Francisco	82	370
BRESLAW								
Patrick	27	m	w	IREL	Contra Costa	Martinez P O	71	423
BRESLIN								
Cathrine	30	f	w	IREL	San Francisco	1-Wd San Francisco	79	50
Jane	28	f	w	IREL	San Francisco	1-Wd San Francisco	79	107
John	27	m	w	IREL	San Francisco	7-Wd San Francisco	81	257
Patk	28	m	w	IREL	San Francisco	San Francisco P O	83	133
BRESLOW								
Michael	40	m	w	IREL	Butte	Ophir Twp	70	114
BRESLUER								
Marus	18	m	w	PRUS	Butte	Chico Twp	70	13
BRESNEHAN								
Corns	33	m	w	IREL	San Francisco	1-Wd San Francisco	79	40
BRESNEY								
Jerry	30	m	w	IREL	Santa Clara	Santa Clara Twp	88	135
Margaret	60	f	w	IREL	Santa Clara	Santa Clara Twp	88	135
BRESNIHAM								
Corneilus	36	m	w	NY	San Francisco	1-Wd San Francisco	79	67
BRESON								
Joseph	34	m	w	CANA	Los Angeles	Los Angeles	73	546
BRESSELL								
John	25	m	w	NY	Sacramento	2-Wd Sacramento	77	234
BRESSERT								
Louis	18	m	w	SWIT	San Francisco	6-Wd San Francisco	81	90
BRESSIA								
Andrea	39	m	w	ITAL	Amador	Jackson P O	69	347
BRESSLER								
Geo	45	m	w	PA	San Joaquin	Elkhorn Twp	86	57
Henry	34	m	w	CANA	Tehama	Antelope Twp	92	154
BRESSLIN								
Ann	63	f	w	IREL	Yuba	Bullards Bar P O	93	549
Eunice	20	f	w	PRUS	San Francisco	San Francisco P O	83	201
BRESSON								
Honore	41	m	w	FRAN	San Francisco	San Francisco P O	83	136
Joseph	59	m	w	FRAN	San Francisco	2-Wd San Francisco	79	203
Joseph	26	m	w	FRAN	Marin	San Rafael Twp	74	33
BREST								
Alfred	31	m	w	BRUN	San Francisco	1-Wd San Francisco	79	51
BRESTART								
August	40	m	w	CA	San Francisco	San Francisco P O	83	406
BRESTLAND								
John	45	m	w	IREL	San Francisco	6-Wd San Francisco	81	126
BRESTLIN								
Danl	39	m	w	IREL	San Francisco	7-Wd San Francisco	81	229
BRESTON								
John	26	m	w	IREL	Butte	Chico Twp	70	56
BRESWATTER								
Agatha	63	f	w	FRAN	Los Angeles	Los Angeles	73	508
BRET								
Henry	30	m	w	SHOL	San Mateo	Half Moon Bay P O	87	403
BRETON								
Charles	57	m	w	SWIT	Siskiyou	Yreka	89	657
Joseph	32	m	w	FRAN	San Francisco	1-Wd San Francisco	79	50
BRETRERAS								
Isabel	25	m	w	TX	Los Angeles	Los Angeles	73	511
BRETSNEIDER								
J A	43	m	w	PRUS	Sierra	Table Rock Twp	89	575
BRETT								
George	26	m	w	IREL	San Francisco	San Francisco P O	80	408
H	22	m	w	ENGL	Humboldt	Eureka Twp	72	279
Henry	56	m	b	NC	El Dorado	Mud Springs Twp	72	78
James	28	m	w	NC	Mendocino	Noyo & Big Rvr Twp	74	173
John	47	m	w	IREL	Santa Clara	1-Wd San Jose	88	235
John B	51	m	w	ME	San Francisco	8-Wd San Francisco	82	419
Merrel	39	m	w	OH	Stanislaus	Buena Vista Twp	92	13
Michael F	36	m	w	IREL	Yolo	Cache Crk Twp	93	424
W R	51	m	w	ENGL	Humboldt	Eureka Twp	72	279
BRETTNACHER								
Nickelos	29	m	w	PRUS	Sonoma	Salt Point Twp	91	384
BRETTON								
Chs	30	m	w	JAMA	San Francisco	2-Wd San Francisco	79	216
BRETZ								
Henry	42	m	w	FRAN	San Francisco	San Francisco P O	80	536
BREUSIS								
Henry	39	m	w	HANO	Nevada	Washington Twp	75	344
BREUSTER								
Edward	32	m	w	NY	Stanislaus	Empire Twp	92	38
Jos	22	m	w	PA	San Francisco	8-Wd San Francisco	82	344
William	47	m	w	MA	San Francisco	2-Wd San Francisco	79	248
BREVARIA								
Jesus	50	m	w	MEXI	Mariposa	Mariposa P O	74	104
BREVART								
M D	35	m	w	PA	San Joaquin	Liberty Twp	86	96
BREVER								
Mary J	14	f	w	CA	San Luis Obispo	Salinas Twp	87	292
BREW								
Frank	31	m	w	IREL	Solano	Vallejo	90	173
Michael	32	m	w	IREL	San Francisco	7-Wd San Francisco	81	263
Timothy	37	m	w	IREL	Yuba	Rose Bar Twp	93	663
BREWE								
C	39	m	w	NY	Santa Clara	Gilroy Twp	88	67
BREWEN								
Eli	45	m	w	MO	Contra Costa	Martinez P O	71	390
BREWER								
Alfred L	39	m	w	CA	San Mateo	San Mateo P O	87	352
Antoine	35	m	w	PRUS	Sacramento	2-Wd Sacramento	77	223
D J	45	m	w	NY	Santa Clara	Burnett Twp	88	32
Edward	50	m	w	OH	Nevada	Grass Valley Twp	75	154
Geo	39	m	w	HI	San Francisco	11-Wd San Francisc	84	581
George	31	m	w	SPAI	Placer	Summit P O	76	497
H H	52	m	w	NY	El Dorado	Coloma Twp	72	4
Harvey	42	m	w	PRUS	San Joaquin	2-Wd Stockton	86	186
Henry	34	m	w	ME	Contra Costa	Martinez P O	71	397
Henry S	26	m	w	NY	Los Angeles	Wilmington Twp	73	644
J H	45	m	w	MA	Alameda	Oakland	68	199
Jacob	45	m	w	PRUS	San Francisco	8-Wd San Francisco	82	387
James	34	m	w	NY	Alameda	Washington Twp	68	281
James	30	m	w	ENGL	Mariposa	Mariposa P O	74	112
Jargen	36	m	w	DENM	Plumas	Seneca Twp	77	47
John	39	m	w	MO	San Joaquin	Oneal Twp	86	113
John	28	m	w	ENGL	San Francisco	1-Wd San Francisco	79	62
John F	33	m	w	GA	Fresno	Kings Rvr P O	72	211
John M	35	m	w	SC	Fresno	Millerton P O	72	188
Michael	47	m	w	PRUS	Shasta	Horsetown P O	89	505
Nelly	23	f	w	CANA	San Francisco	6-Wd San Francisco	81	135
Peter	33	m	w	BELG	Sacramento	Georgianna Twp	77	128
R F	23	m	w	OH	Solano	Vallejo	90	200
Rachael	63	f	w	IL	Mariposa	Mariposa P O	74	128
Samuel	54	m	w	MO	Mendocino	Point Arena Twp	74	214
Samuel G	37	m	w	NY	Los Angeles	Santa Ana Twp	73	605
Thos	23	m	w	ENGL	Sacramento	3-Wd Sacramento	77	315
William	35	m	w	OH	El Dorado	Diamond Springs Tw	72	27
William	28	m	w	ENGL	San Francisco	7-Wd San Francisco	81	158
William E	12	m	w	CA	El Dorado	Diamond Springs Tw	72	27
Wm	26	m	w	ENGL	San Francisco	1-Wd San Francisco	79	106
BREWERS								
Herman	43	m	w	PRUS	San Francisco	San Francisco P O	83	315
BREWESTER								
J W	51	m	w	VA	Lake	Big Valley	73	398
BREWINGTON								
Gevl	34	m	w	MD	Monterey	Pajaro Twp	74	374
BREWSTER								
Albert	43	m	w	NY	Los Angeles	San Gabriel Twp	73	598
Augustus	45	m	w	CT	Monterey	San Juan Twp	74	405
Benjiman	36	m	w	MO	Los Angeles	El Monte Twp	73	463
Caroline	79	f	w	NY	El Dorado	Placerville	72	123
Charles W	41	m	w	NY	El Dorado	Placerville	72	111
Edwd	37	m	w	ME	Solano	Vallejo	90	151
G A	42	f	w	CT	Sacramento	3-Wd Sacramento	77	258
James	35	m	w	NY	Colusa	Spring Valley Twp	71	343
James	30	m	w	PRUS	San Francisco	5-Wd San Francisco	81	13
John	53	m	w	ENGL	San Francisco	San Francisco P O	85	843
John	39	m	w	NY	Sacramento	Dry Crk Twp	77	102
John C	22	m	w	MI	El Dorado	Diamond Springs Tw	72	24
Joseph	22	m	w	ENGL	Marin	Novato Twp	74	10
Leonard O	38	m	w	VT	Stanislaus	Empire Twp	92	31
N J	47	f	w	OH	Solano	Vallejo	90	206
Richard E	44	m	w	NY	San Francisco	6-Wd San Francisco	81	112
Samuel T	42	m	w	NY	Plumas	Goodwin Twp	77	6
Stephen	37	m	w	NY	Sonoma	Salt Point	91	388
Stephen G	51	m	w	NY	El Dorado	Placerville Twp	72	102
Stephen M	50	m	w	NY	Plumas	Seneca Twp	77	48
BREWSTON								
C W	28	m	w	IN	San Joaquin	3-Wd Stockton	86	229
BREYEN								
Duncan	19	m	w	CANA	Mendocino	Ten Mile Rvr Twp	74	172
BREYFOGLE								
William C	33	m	w	OH	Santa Clara	1-Wd San Jose	88	243
BREYFONTAINE								
Chas	27	m	w	MA	San Francisco	6-Wd San Francisco	81	102
BREZENGA								
Peter	25	m	w	SWIT	Monterey	Monterey Twp	74	344
BRGAN								
Powhattan	60	m	w	VA	Nevada	Grass Valley Twp	75	200

© 2001 by Heritage Quest. All rights reserved.

Name	Age	S	R	B-PL	County	Locale	Roll	Pg
BRIAESSOLI								
Phillup	48	m	w	SWIT	Colusa	Colusa Twp	71	281
BRIALS								
Peter	32	m	w	HOLL	San Joaquin	Tulare Twp	86	255
BRIAN								
D O	45	m	w	IREL	San Mateo	San Mateo P O	87	359
Henry	50	m	w	BADE	El Dorado	Placerville	72	110
John	60	m	w	ENGL	Amador	Drytown P O	69	425
John	31	m	w	IREL	Placer	Alta P O	76	412
Lise	4	f	w	CA	El Dorado	Placerville	72	110
BRIAND								
Andrew	35	m	w	DENM	Marin	Nicasio Twp	74	18
BRIANS								
Benj W K	34	m	w	MO	Sonoma	Bodega Twp	91	253
George W	25	m	w	MO	San Luis Obispo	Arroyo Grande Twp	87	278
John C	55	m	w	KY	San Luis Obispo	Arroyo Grande Twp	87	272
Wm	58	m	w	KY	Sonoma	Analy Twp	91	225
BRIANT								
J W	27	m	w	WI	San Joaquin	Elkhorn Twp	86	64
BRIARCLIFF								
Stephen	39	m	w	ENGL	Tehama	Red Bluff	92	176
BRIARD								
Geo H	31	m	w	MA	Sonoma	Bodega Twp	91	250
BRIARTON								
James	35	m	w	IREL	Marin	San Rafael Twp	74	30
Mathew	23	m	w	IREL	Marin	San Rafael Twp	74	32
BRIASLIAN								
Patrick	37	m	w	IREL	San Francisco	San Francisco P O	85	874
BRICAUD								
Catherin	19	f	w	SPAI	San Francisco	5-Wd San Francisco	81	33
BRICE								
Agness	75	f	w	MO	Sutter	Butte Twp	92	98
Agness	69	f	w	IREL	Sutter	Butte Twp	92	89
Alfred	31	m	w	ENGL	San Francisco	11-Wd San Francisc	84	639
Bernard	45	m	w	ME	San Francisco	San Francisco P O	83	130
Daubanton	66	m	w	FRAN	Mariposa	Mariposa P O	74	120
Ellen	28	f	w	IREL	San Francisco	8-Wd San Francisco	82	452
G W	61	m	w	KY	Amador	Fiddletown P O	69	430
G W	61	m	w	KY	Amador	Fiddletown P O	69	435
Geo	27	m	w	MO	San Joaquin	Douglas Twp	86	34
Geo	22	m	w	MI	San Joaquin	Castoria Twp	86	8
J P	31	m	w	KY	Sutter	Butte Twp	92	89
James	63	m	w	IREL	San Francisco	11-Wd San Francisc	84	422
James	32	m	w	MO	Calaveras	Copperopolis P O	70	254
William	37	m	w	ENGL	San Francisco	8-Wd San Francisco	82	288
Wm	24	m	w	CA	San Joaquin	2-Wd Stockton	86	193
BRICELAND								
John	47	m	w	WV	San Francisco	San Francisco P O	83	408
John	38	m	w	VA	Humboldt	South Fork Twp	72	300
BRICH								
Benjamin	35	m	w	MO	Mendocino	Round Valley Twp	74	217
James	24	m	w	CT	San Joaquin	Castoria Twp	86	14
Pauline	22	f	w	WURT	San Francisco	8-Wd San Francisco	82	381
BRICHETT								
Paul	40	m	w	OH	San Joaquin	Elliott Twp	86	81
BRICHTI								
John	51	m	w	ITAL	San Francisco	8-Wd San Francisco	82	459
BRICKEL								
John	41	m	w	PA	Yuba	Rose Bar Twp	93	663
BRICKELL								
Josiah	38	m	w	MI	Alameda	Eden Twp	68	71
BRICKETT								
Edward J	49	m	w	IN	Nevada	Meadow Lake Twp	75	251
BRICKEY								
F J	33	m	w	MO	Amador	Jackson P O	69	326
BRICKFORD								
Anson	35	m	w	ME	San Francisco	11-Wd San Francisc	84	531
BRICKHOUSE								
Nathan	63	m	w	NC	Siskiyou	Cottonwood Twp	89	594
BRICKING								
John	31	m	w	OLDE	San Francisco	San Francisco P O	83	65
BRICKLAY								
Helen	64	f	w	IREL	San Francisco	11-Wd San Francisc	84	487
BRICKLEY								
David	33	m	w	CANA	San Francisco	San Francisco P O	83	187
John	27	m	w	IREL	San Francisco	San Francisco P O	83	408
Richard	29	m	w	ENGL	San Francisco	11-Wd San Francisc	84	519
Richd	26	m	w	ENGL	San Francisco	1-Wd San Francisco	79	126
William	32	m	w	IREL	San Francisco	3-Wd San Francisco	79	315
BRICKLY								
John	33	m	w	IREL	Yolo	Grafton Twp	93	500
BRICKNEL								
Jno	34	m	w	PA	San Francisco	5-Wd San Francisco	81	24
BRICKNER								
Henry	31	m	w	NORW	San Francisco	7-Wd San Francisco	81	281
John	36	m	w	SAXO	San Francisco	8-Wd San Francisco	82	384
BRICKOTTLE								
Chris	28	m	w	PRUS	San Francisco	5-Wd San Francisco	81	9
BRICKWEDEL								
Chas H	44	m	w	HANO	San Francisco	San Francisco P O	83	127
H	46	m	w	HANO	San Francisco	San Francisco P O	85	804
BRIDE								
Ellen	28	f	w	IREL	San Francisco	11-Wd San Francisc	84	504
Hannah	27	f	w	IREL	San Francisco	8-Wd San Francisco	82	478
John	21	m	w	BAVA	San Joaquin	Castoria Twp	86	7
Morris	25	m	w	IREL	San Mateo	Pescadero P O	87	413
Richard	64	m	w	IREL	Stanislaus	San Joaquin Twp	92	72

Name	Age	S	R	B-PL	County	Locale	Roll	Pg
BRIDEN								
David	56	m	w	OH	Yuba	Linda Twp	93	556
BRIDENBACK								
C	37	m	w	WURT	San Joaquin	Oneal Twp	86	110
BRIDER								
Chas J	38	m	w	DENM	San Francisco	San Francisco P O	83	85
Cyrus	47	m	w	VA	Sacramento	Franklin Twp	77	110
BRIDERCHE								
Bendotte	30	m	w	MEXI	Fresno	Millerton P O	72	164
BRIDESON								
Richard	29	m	w	ENGL	Nevada	Grass Valley Twp	75	172
BRIDEWAY								
Wm	45	m	w	PRUS	Sacramento	Natomas Twp	77	168
BRIDEWELL								
John	36	m	w	KY	Sacramento	Brighton Twp	77	76
BRIDGE								
Charles T	40	m	w	NY	Los Angeles	Los Angeles	73	529
Martin	36	m	w	NY	San Francisco	5-Wd San Francisco	81	31
Matthew	39	m	w	MA	San Francisco	San Francisco P O	85	716
Thos	50	m	w	ENGL	Yuba	Rose Bar Twp	93	656
Walter	22	m	w	NY	San Francisco	5-Wd San Francisco	81	31
BRIDGEMAN								
John	30	m	w	NY	San Francisco	8-Wd San Francisco	82	408
Lauretta	28	f	w	NY	Santa Cruz	Watsonville	89	369
BRIDGENS								
Annie	12	f	w	CA	San Francisco	San Francisco P O	85	714
BRIDGER								
Barney	60	m	w	IREL	Santa Clara	Almaden Twp	88	15
Henry	39	m	w	IL	Siskiyou	Callahan P O	89	631
James	34	m	w	TN	Kern	Havilah P O	73	350
Thomas	38	m	w	TN	Kern	Havilah P O	73	350
BRIDGES								
Calvin	56	m	w	MA	Tuolumne	Columbia P O	93	349
D	33	m	w	TN	Sonoma	Santa Rosa	91	418
Geo	28	m	w	MA	San Francisco	San Francisco P O	85	855
Joseph	40	m	w	TN	San Bernardino	Chino Twp	78	412
Mary	44	f	w	ENGL	San Francisco	11-Wd San Francisc	84	506
O L	36	m	w	MO	Butte	Oroville Twp	70	140
P	76	f	w	ENGL	San Joaquin	2-Wd Stockton	86	210
William	47	m	w	MO	Klamath	Camp Gaston	73	372
Wm	30	m	w	IL	Humboldt	Eureka Twp	72	275
BRIDGET								
Chas	21	m	w	PRUS	San Joaquin	2-Wd Stockton	86	179
BRIDGEWOODS								
Saml	39	m	w	IREL	San Francisco	1-Wd San Francisco	79	6
BRIDGLAND								
Sml	23	m	w	CANA	San Diego	San Diego	78	502
BRIDGMAN								
Cass	38	m	w	AR	Amador	Fiddletown P O	69	440
BRIDGWOOD								
E	53	f	w	ENGL	Napa	Napa	75	5
BRIDISON								
William	35	m	w	ENGL	San Francisco	11-Wd San Francisc	84	540
BRIECK								
Henry	30	m	w	PRUS	Marin	San Rafael Twp	74	46
Herman	47	m	w	RUSS	San Francisco	San Francisco P O	83	376
BRIEDENBACK								
R	36	m	w	PRUS	San Joaquin	2-Wd Stockton	86	202
BRIEDY								
Patrick	48	m	w	IREL	San Francisco	6-Wd San Francisco	81	113
BRIEFNER								
Pinkus	28	m	w	AUST	San Luis Obispo	San Luis Obispo Tw	87	309
BRIEGER								
Minna	12	f	w	CA	San Francisco	8-Wd San Francisco	82	345
BRIELEY								
Gillum	56	m	w	IL	Fresno	Millerton P O	72	145
BRIEMER								
Frank	25	m	w	NORW	San Francisco	1-Wd San Francisco	79	126
BRIEN								
Ellen	20	f	w	IREL	San Francisco	San Francisco P O	83	97
John	36	m	w	IREL	San Francisco	11-Wd San Francisc	84	614
John	34	m	w	FRAN	San Francisco	2-Wd San Francisco	79	226
John	29	m	w	IREL	Solano	Denverton Twp	90	27
John	28	m	w	CANA	Solano	Green Valley Twp	90	38
Joseph	18	m	w	BAVA	Contra Costa	San Pablo Twp	71	355
Margaret	65	f	w	IREL	Monterey	San Juan Twp	74	418
O C F	36	m	w	MI	Santa Clara	Almaden Twp	88	9
O Ed	28	m	w	NY	Sacramento	3-Wd Sacramento	77	308
Rosa	25	f	w	IREL	San Francisco	San Francisco P O	83	183
Wm	24	m	w	AUST	San Francisco	1-Wd San Francisco	79	128
Wm	18	m	w	IREL	Solano	Benicia	90	19
BRIENE								
August	20	m	w	PRUS	San Francisco	San Francisco P O	83	191
BRIENEY								
Pauline	10	f	w	PRUS	San Francisco	San Francisco P O	85	836
BRIER								
C C	30	m	w	IN	Alameda	Oakland	68	162
Geo	48	m	w	OH	Sacramento	4-Wd Sacramento	77	358
James	55	m	w	OH	Solano	Silveyville Twp	90	85
William H	48	m	w	OH	Alameda	Washington Twp	68	270
BRIERE								
Eugene	30	m	w	FRAN	Sacramento	2-Wd Sacramento	77	248
BRIERLY								
Isaac M	33	m	w	IA	Amador	Sutter Crk P O	69	403
John R	31	m	w	NH	Santa Clara	2-Wd San Jose	88	336
BRIERRE								
Eugene	35	m	w	FRAN	Sacramento	4-Wd Sacramento	77	344

© 2001 by Heritage Quest. All rights reserved.

Name	Age	S	R	B-PL	County	Locale	Series M593 Roll	Pg
BRIERS								
Annie	60	f	w	IREL	San Francisco	San Francisco P O	80	486
BRIERTON								
Patrick	41	m	w	IREL	San Francisco	1-Wd San Francisco	79	112
BRIERY								
John	40	m	w	ENGL	San Francisco	7-Wd San Francisco	81	171
BRIES								
Antonio B	36	m	w	CANA	San Francisco	1-Wd San Francisco	79	127
Richd	50	m	w	WALE	Butte	Chico Twp	70	49
BRIESLY								
Washington	22	m	w	IA	Amador	Volcano P O	69	380
BRIETENBACH								
Francis	44	m	w	HANO	Sonoma	Sonoma Twp	91	444
BRIFIN								
Chas	28	m	w	SWIT	San Francisco	San Francisco P O	85	875
BRIGANT								
Ansel	45	m	w	OH	San Joaquin	Dent Twp	86	24
BRIGANTEE								
William	43	m	w	PRUS	Shasta	Horsetown P O	89	507
BRIGARD								
Henry	18	m	w	CA	San Joaquin	3-Wd Stockton	86	221
BRIGARDS								
J H	26	m	w	BELG	San Francisco	San Francisco P O	85	860
BRIGG								
John A	56	m	w	VA	Mariposa	Mariposa P O	74	97
BRIGGARD								
Alex	31	m	w	FRAN	Humboldt	Arcata Twp	72	230
BRIGGARTS								
Girard	31	m	w	BELG	San Francisco	San Francisco P O	85	860
BRIGGI								
Philip	23	m	w	ITAL	Santa Clara	2-Wd San Jose	88	315
BRIGGS								
---	36	m	w	IA	Monterey	San Antonio Twp	74	324
A R	46	m	w	RI	Nevada	Nevada Twp	75	273
Albert	23	m	w	IL	San Francisco	2-Wd San Francisco	79	197
Alfred	49	m	w	NY	Sacramento	Sutter Twp	77	388
Alvah K	27	m	w	MI	Inyo	Cerro Gordo Twp	73	320
Ann M	53	f	w	CANA	Sacramento	3-Wd Sacramento	77	285
Anson	45	m	w	NY	Nevada	Nevada Twp	75	278
Bruce	2	m	w	CA	Calaveras	San Andreas P O	70	207
C G	40	m	w	NY	San Joaquin	2-Wd Stockton	86	176
Caleb A	34	m	w	MA	Yuba	Parks Bar Twp	93	650
Charles F	32	m	w	MA	Yolo	Cache Crk Twp	93	422
Cks O	47	m	w	MA	San Francisco	San Francisco P O	83	312
Clarmont C	31	m	w	WI	Sonoma	Healdsburg	91	275
Cyrus	52	m	w	MA	Sacramento	Natomas Twp	77	165
D E	35	m	w	MO	San Joaquin	Liberty Twp	86	91
D M	64	f	w	RI	San Joaquin	3-Wd Stockton	86	234
Daniel	74	m	w	NY	San Francisco	11-Wd San Francisc	84	538
Daniel	49	m	w	NY	Amador	Lancha Plana P O	69	368
Daniel	38	m	w	CT	Amador	Ione City P O	69	351
Daniel	38	m	w	IN	Amador	Ione City P O	69	357
E A	40	m	w	MA	Tuolumne	Columbia P O	93	336
E A	16	m	w	LA	Alameda	Oakland	68	258
E F	23	f	w	CO	Solano	Benicia	90	20
Ebenezer M	43	m	w	MO	Amador	Volcano P O	69	372
Edward	49	m	w	NY	Santa Clara	1-Wd San Jose	88	230
Edward	43	m	w	NY	San Francisco	11-Wd San Francisc	84	538
Elijah	32	m	w	MA	Contra Costa	Martinez P O	71	445
Elijah	24	m	w	MI	San Joaquin	Union Twp	86	267
Eliza	42	f	w	ME	San Joaquin	Oneal Twp	86	103
Eliza	16	f	w	CA	San Francisco	8-Wd San Francisco	82	420
Fanny	66	f	w	MA	San Francisco	San Francisco P O	83	103
Frances	66	f	w	VT	Sonoma	Santa Rosa	91	427
Fred C	19	m	w	IA	Santa Clara	Gilroy Twp	88	80
Fredrick	24	m	w	DENM	San Francisco	11-Wd San Francisc	84	519
G	48	m	w	MO	San Joaquin	Elkhorn Twp	86	62
G G	45	m	w	NY	Alameda	Oakland	68	219
Geo	45	m	w	PRUS	San Francisco	San Francisco P O	83	311
George	44	m	w	MA	Santa Clara	Fremont Twp	88	64
George G	45	m	w	OH	Solano	Tremont Twp	90	28
H	19	m	w	CA	Napa	Napa Twp	75	28
H N	15	f	w	CA	Sacramento	3-Wd Sacramento	77	317
H T	42	m	w	NY	Sierra	Downieville Twp	89	517
H W	50	m	w	NY	Santa Clara	Gilroy Twp	88	83
Harry	48	m	w	VA	Tuolumne	Sonora P O	93	318
Henry M	24	m	w	TN	Tulare	Visalia	92	296
Henry S	28	m	w	CANA	Yolo	Putah Twp	93	514
Hiram	29	m	w	IA	Sonoma	Mendocino Twp	91	288
Hiram H	23	m	w	IL	Contra Costa	Martinez P O	71	387
Hiram H	23	m	w	NY	Contra Costa	Martinez P O	71	374
Ira	41	m	w	NY	Contra Costa	Martinez P O	71	388
Isabel	10	f	w	CA	Contra Costa	Martinez P O	71	385
J H	36	m	w	MO	Mendocino	Ukiah Twp	74	241
J L	57	m	w	NH	Sacramento	4-Wd Sacramento	77	323
J O	40	m	w	NY	Sierra	Alleghany & Forest	89	534
J T	48	m	w	RI	Sutter	Nicolaus Twp	92	111
J T	43	m	w	RI	Sutter	Nicolaus Twp	92	111
J W	38	m	w	NY	Yuba	Marysville	93	592
James	40	m	w	ENGL	Nevada	Bridgeport Twp	75	103
James	36	m	w	PA	San Francisco	San Francisco P O	83	314
James C	26	m	w	ENGL	San Francisco	2-Wd San Francisco	79	214
James H	36	m	w	MO	Sonoma	Petaluma Twp	91	332
James R	43	m	w	PA	Stanislaus	Empire Twp	92	38
Jerome B	39	m	w	NY	Santa Clara	San Jose Twp	88	182
John	39	m	w	NY	Sutter	Yuba Twp	92	144
John	26	m	w	MO	Yolo	Buckeye Twp	93	410
John S	27	m	w	ME	Mendocino	Anderson Twp	74	154
Joseph	40	m	w	PORT	Butte	Kimshew Tpw	70	77
Joseph D	27	m	w	NY	San Francisco	3-Wd San Francisco	79	317
Joseph D	25	m	w	MA	Yolo	Cache Crk Twp	93	421
L C	31	m	w	MO	Monterey	San Juan Twp	74	405
Lawrence M	45	m	w	NY	Tuolumne	Sonora P O	93	318
Lewis M	40	m	w	NC	El Dorado	Placerville Twp	72	98
Mannola	48	f	w	CHIL	El Dorado	Greenwood Twp	72	54
Margaret	54	f	w	ENGL	San Francisco	8-Wd San Francisco	82	412
Martin S	46	m	w	NY	Santa Clara	Santa Clara Twp	88	160
Mary	70	f	w	PA	Stanislaus	Empire Twp	92	38
Mary J	32	f	w	MA	Solano	Silveyville Twp	90	77
O W	50	m	w	MA	Alameda	Alameda	68	11
Oliver	19	m	w	ME	Sutter	Vernon Twp	92	136
Otis	40	m	w	MA	Solano	Vallejo	90	146
Peter C	34	m	w	NY	Sonoma	Healdsburg	91	275
R M	54	m	w	KY	Amador	Jackson P O	69	323
Robert	23	m	w	MO	Mendocino	Calpella Twp	74	186
Robert C	55	m	w	KY	Yolo	Buckeye Twp	93	415
Russell	40	m	w	OH	Mariposa	Mariposa P O	74	101
S R	42	m	w	NY	San Francisco	San Francisco P O	85	821
Saml G	71	m	w	KY	Amador	Volcano P O	69	372
Samuel	37	m	w	NY	Yolo	Cottonwood Twp	93	464
Sebra	52	m	w	ME	Napa	Napa Twp	75	66
Simon B	37	m	w	OH	Nevada	Grass Valley Twp	75	186
Theodora	35	f	w	CANA	San Francisco	San Francisco P O	80	385
W	24	m	w	NY	Alameda	Oakland	68	222
W B	32	m	w	NY	Sacramento	4-Wd Sacramento	77	373
W F	21	m	w	IA	Santa Clara	Gilroy Twp	88	79
W H	30	m	w	MA	Solano	Vallejo	90	210
W O	35	m	w	IL	Sutter	Yuba Twp	92	147
Wallace	41	m	w	MO	Calaveras	San Andreas P O	70	207
Walter	26	m	w	ENGL	San Francisco	3-Wd San Francisco	79	312
William	42	m	w	MA	Tuolumne	Big Oak Flat P O	93	403
William	29	m	w	MO	Calaveras	San Andreas P O	70	208
William	12	m	w	CA	Stanislaus	Empire Twp	92	53
Wm W	26	m	w	NY	Butte	Hamilton Twp	70	63
BRIGHAM								
Alexander	26	m	w	MO	Yolo	Grafton Twp	93	492
Benj	50	m	w	IN	Nevada	Nevada Twp	75	303
C O	46	m	w	VT	San Francisco	San Francisco P O	83	297
Chas A	46	m	w	NH	Placer	Rocklin Twp	76	468
Davis	45	m	w	MA	Sacramento	4-Wd Sacramento	77	342
Elijah P	51	m	w	MA	Placer	Blue Canyon P O	76	418
Fannie	24	f	w	MA	Sonoma	Analy Twp	91	230
G R	50	m	w	PA	Sacramento	1-Wd Sacramento	77	184
Henry	22	m	w	UT	Tulare	Visalia	92	292
Henry A	32	m	w	MA	Nevada	Bridgeport Twp	75	106
L B	26	m	w	MA	San Joaquin	Elkhorn Twp	86	52
Wiley	55	m	w	TN	Nevada	Bloomfield Twp	75	98
BRIGHENSTIUS								
J	50	m	w	SWED	El Dorado	Georgetown Twp	72	48
BRIGHT								
Chas	28	m	w	GERM	San Francisco	8-Wd San Francisco	82	375
D	47	m	w	ENGL	San Joaquin	Elliott Twp	86	80
E C	53	m	w	VA	Alameda	Murray Twp	68	113
Fred	25	m	w	ENGL	Alameda	Oakland	68	164
Hannah	62	f	w	ENGL	Calaveras	San Andreas P O	70	173
Henry	40	m	w	VA	Amador	Drytown P O	69	422
Henry A	24	m	w	OH	Sacramento	Cosumnes Twp	77	92
J L	40	m	w	MD	Solano	Benicia	90	12
James	43	m	w	OH	Stanislaus	Empire Twp	92	54
James B	29	m	w	LA	Contra Costa	Martinez P O	71	393
John	49	m	w	ENGL	El Dorado	Greenwood Twp	72	55
John	47	m	m	BRAZ	Yuba	Marysville	93	613
John	42	m	w	ENGL	San Francisco	1-Wd San Francisco	79	80
John	40	m	w	ENGL	San Francisco	1-Wd San Francisco	79	62
John	18	m	w	NY	San Francisco	11-Wd San Francisc	84	694
Julias	29	m	w	PRUS	San Joaquin	2-Wd Stockton	86	197
Robert	53	m	w	IREL	San Francisco	8-Wd San Francisco	82	483
Samuel	39	m	w	MA	Amador	Jackson P O	69	321
Thomas	39	m	w	OH	Yolo	Washington Twp	93	534
William	46	m	w	MO	Sonoma	Sonoma Twp	91	442
William	34	m	w	UNKN	San Joaquin	2-Wd Stockton	86	172
William M	33	m	w	NJ	Nevada	Rough & Ready Twp	75	333
Wm J	41	m	w	IREL	Butte	Ophir Twp	70	97
BRIGHTENSTEIN								
Wm	23	m	w	PA	Santa Clara	Milpitas Twp	88	114
BRIGHTENSTINE								
Thos	18	m	w	MO	Sonoma	Mendocino Twp	91	298
BRIGHTMAN								
F H	31	m	w	MA	Trinity	Douglas	92	236
Henry	40	m	w	MA	El Dorado	Placerville Twp	72	105
BRIGHTMEISTER								
Charles	31	m	w	AUST	San Francisco	6-Wd San Francisco	81	81
BRIGHTON								
Fred	40	m	w	OH	Butte	Ophir Twp	70	108
Geo	29	m	w	NY	San Francisco	7-Wd San Francisco	81	236
John	36	m	w	ENGL	San Francisco	San Francisco P O	80	488
William	28	m	w	SCOT	Mendocino	Albion & Big Rvr T	74	167
BRIGLEY								
R L	38	m	w	VA	Alameda	Murray Twp	68	113
BRIGMAN								
Caswell	40	m	w	KY	Amador	Volcano P O	69	386
Jos	36	m	w	PRUS	Alameda	Murray Twp	68	112
BRIGNARDELLI								
G J	37	m	w	ITAL	San Francisco	6-Wd San Francisco	81	97

© 2001 by Heritage Quest. All rights reserved.

Series M593

Name	Age	S	R	B-PL	County	Locale	Roll	Pg
BRIGNARDELLO								
Josh	33	m	w	ITAL	San Francisco	1-Wd San Francisco	79	45
BRIGNOLE								
Anton	37	m	w	ITAL	San Joaquin	1-Wd Stockton	86	155
Tuicut	28	m	w	ITAL	San Joaquin	Castoria Twp	86	2
BRIGNOLI								
B	42	m	w	ITAL	Amador	Sutter Crk P O	69	399
Joseph	40	m	w	ITAL	Amador	Sutter Crk P O	69	405
BRIGNOLIO								
Angelo	38	m	w	ITAL	Mariposa	Maxwell Crk P O	74	140
BRIGOLARD								
Louis	31	m	w	ITAL	San Francisco	6-Wd San Francisco	81	124
BRIGOLE								
Sylvester	38	m	w	ITAL	Solano	Montezuma Twp	90	67
BRIGS								
Mary	31	f	w	MA	Napa	Yountville Twp	75	90
BRIHABA								
Antonio	50	m	w	MEXI	Fresno	Millerton P O	72	159
BRIJALVA								
Pedro	40	m	w	CA	San Luis Obispo	San Luis Obispo Tw	87	304
BRILL								
Abram	48	m	w	KY	Sacramento	1-Wd Sacramento	77	172
John	26	m	w	AUST	San Francisco	1-Wd San Francisco	79	85
BRILLA								
Gonzalez	38	m	w	MEXI	Kern	Bakersfield P O	73	364
BRILLON								
Charles	41	m	w	FRAN	San Francisco	6-Wd San Francisco	81	88
BRIM								
John	35	m	w	TN	Colusa	Spring Valley Twp	71	335
John	27	m	w	NY	Solano	Suisun Twp	90	102
BRIMACOMB								
Wm	40	m	w	ENGL	Yuba	Slate Range Bar Tw	93	672
BRIMAN								
John	26	m	w	CANA	Solano	Vallejo	90	150
BRIMBLECOM								
Francis A	42	m	w	ME	Santa Cruz	Santa Cruz Twp	89	395
Saml A	46	m	w	MA	Santa Cruz	Santa Cruz Twp	89	396
BRIMBLECUM								
Harriet	72	f	w	MA	Santa Cruz	Santa Cruz Twp	89	396
BRIMER								
Alfred	45	m	w	MS	Tulare	White Rvr Twp	92	301
John	38	m	w	PRUS	Sutter	Sutter Twp	92	123
John	26	m	w	ME	Mendocino	Point Arena Twp	74	211
BRIMHALL								
Andrew	41	m	w	IN	Santa Clara	Redwood Twp	88	122
BRIMMER								
Chris	43	m	w	PRUS	Sutter	Yuba Twp	92	147
BRIMSKILL								
E	39	m	w	IREL	Nevada	Washington Twp	75	339
BRIMWELL								
Wm	52	m	w	ENGL	Monterey	Salinas Twp	74	308
BRIN								
Charles	24	m	w	PRUS	Sutter	Yuba Twp	92	149
Kate	40	f	w	IREL	Sacramento	3-Wd Sacramento	77	278
BRINCARD								
James	16	m	w	CA	Shasta	Shasta P O	89	462
BRINCHMAN								
Fredrick	22	m	w	HANO	San Francisco	7-Wd San Francisco	81	216
BRIND								
Caleb	32	m	w	ENGL	San Francisco	San Francisco P O	83	285
BRINDAGO								
Stephen	57	m	w	CANA	Santa Clara	Santa Clara Twp	88	151
BRINDEAU								
Adrian	49	m	w	FRAN	San Francisco	San Francisco P O	80	485
BRINDELL								
Ernest	37	m	w	PRUS	Santa Clara	2-Wd San Jose	88	287
G W	39	m	w	PA	Amador	Sutter Crk P O	69	403
BRINDIRILLE								
Morris	33	m	w	IREL	San Francisco	San Francisco P O	83	150
BRINDLE								
Henry J	31	m	w	PA	Sierra	Table Rock Twp	89	573
Peter	40	m	w	NORW	San Francisco	11-Wd San Francisc	84	615
BRINDLEY								
Joseph	42	m	w	ENGL	El Dorado	Placerville	72	108
BRINDLY								
E	40	m	w	MI	Yuba	Marysville	93	604
BRINDUPKY								
Frederick	36	m	w	PRUS	El Dorado	Mud Springs Twp	72	82
BRINE								
David	37	m	w	KY	Mendocino	Albion & Big Rvr T	74	167
Emily	19	f	b	GA	Los Angeles	Los Angeles	73	530
Jane	80	f	w	PA	San Francisco	San Francisco P O	80	390
Michael	22	m	w	IREL	Mendocino	Albion & Big Rvr T	74	167
S	30	m	w	IREL	Alameda	Oakland	68	261
BRINER								
Frinklin	40	m	w	PRUS	Placer	Bath P O	76	421
BRINES								
James W	41	m	w	IL	Santa Cruz	Pajaro Twp	89	345
BRINGER								
Levi	31	m	w	CT	San Francisco	1-Wd San Francisco	79	108
BRINGHAM								
Wm C	44	m	w	IN	Plumas	Quartz Twp	77	42
BRINK								
Abram	35	m	w	NJ	Solano	Vallejo	90	158
Alfred	45	m	w	VT	Contra Costa	Martinez P O	71	428
Frank	30	m	w	HANO	Colusa	Spring Valley Twp	71	344
Isaac	72	m	w	VA	Tuolumne	Sonora P O	93	329
John S	46	m	w	DENM	Sacramento	Franklin Twp	77	119
Marcus	24	m	w	SWED	San Francisco	6-Wd San Francisco	81	115
O F	63	m	w	NY	Napa	Napa Twp	75	46
William B	60	m	w	PA	Los Angeles	Los Angeles	73	541
BRINKE								
Mary	25	f	w	IREL	San Francisco	San Francisco P O	83	199
BRINKENHOOF								
A E	35	m	w	OH	Butte	Chico Twp	70	22
BRINKER								
David	31	m	w	PRUS	Alameda	Oakland	68	153
BRINKERHOFF								
Edward	38	m	w	IL	Solano	Maine Prairie Twp	90	48
Isaac	40	m	w	NY	Solano	Silveyville Twp	90	84
John	42	m	w	NY	Solano	Silveyville Twp	90	88
Saml B	50	m	w	NY	Santa Barbara	Santa Barbara P O	87	466
Stephen	27	m	w	IL	Solano	Silveyville Twp	90	81
BRINKERS								
John	39	m	w	BAVA	Butte	Mountain Spring Tw	70	87
John	32	m	w	HANO	Plumas	Mineral Twp	77	22
BRINKHEART								
John	35	m	w	ME	San Francisco	11-Wd San Francisc	84	680
BRINKLEY								
George	25	m	w	VA	Napa	Napa	75	47
BRINKMAN								
Fred	25	m	w	PRUS	San Francisco	San Francisco P O	83	307
H	25	m	w	HANO	Sierra	Sierra Twp	89	562
J	50	m	w	ENGL	Sacramento	3-Wd Sacramento	77	265
John	39	m	w	PA	Sonoma	Sonoma Twp	91	448
John	27	m	w	HANO	Santa Clara	Fremont Twp	88	63
Joseph	34	m	w	PRUS	Placer	Dutch Flat P O	76	404
BRINKMEYER								
Henry	38	m	w	PRUS	San Francisco	San Francisco P O	80	479
BRINKS								
Benjamin	35	m	w	ENGL	Santa Clara	1-Wd San Jose	88	233
BRINLEY								
Eben	43	m	w	NY	San Diego	San Diego	78	485
BRINNEN								
James	27	m	w	IREL	Contra Costa	Martinez P O	71	368
BRINNESS								
Joseph	37	m	w	CANA	Placer	Bath P O	76	423
BRINNI								
Joseph	25	m	w	ITAL	Santa Clara	2-Wd San Jose	88	316
BRINNLEY								
Ivan	45	m	w	ITAL	Amador	Sutter Crk P O	69	414
BRINOLA								
Domingo	34	m	w	ITAL	Amador	Jackson P O	69	339
BRINOLIA								
Jacob	28	m	w	SWIT	Amador	Jackson P O	69	321
BRINSON								
Danl	36	m	w	IN	Santa Clara	Almaden Twp	88	11
BRIODY								
Edward	34	m	w	IREL	Santa Cruz	Santa Cruz	89	407
Margret	37	f	w	IREL	San Francisco	1-Wd San Francisco	79	51
Mike	34	m	w	IREL	Solano	Vallejo	90	170
BRIOLA								
Doningo	29	m	w	ITAL	San Mateo	Belmont P O	87	374
BRIONE								
Isabel	40	f	w	CHIL	Contra Costa	San Pablo Twp	71	355
BRIONES								
Casimer	46	m	w	CA	Contra Costa	Martinez Twp	71	351
Gabriel	24	m	w	CA	Contra Costa	Martinez P O	71	375
Joseph	33	m	w	CA	Marin	Bolinas Twp	74	6
Juanna	68	f	w	CA	Santa Clara	Fremont Twp	88	60
Mary	20	f	w	CA	Marin	San Rafael	74	53
Mary L	73	f	w	CA	San Mateo	Half Moon Bay P O	87	397
Pablo	55	m	w	CA	Marin	Bolinas Twp	74	4
Ramona	60	f	w	CA	Marin	Bolinas Twp	74	7
Susan	20	f	w	CA	Marin	Bolinas Twp	74	5
Walupe	75	m	w	CA	San Mateo	Half Moon Bay P O	87	397
BRIORDY								
Maggie	40	f	w	IREL	San Francisco	8-Wd San Francisco	82	347
BRISAC								
Felix	56	m	w	FRAN	San Francisco	8-Wd San Francisco	82	326
BRISBINE								
Samuel W	45	m	w	OH	Alpine	Woodfords P O	69	315
BRISCAS								
Tim	42	m	w	IREL	San Francisco	11-Wd San Francisc	84	673
BRISCH								
William	41	m	w	NC	Contra Costa	Martinez P O	71	427
BRISCO								
Barnard	38	m	w	IREL	Alameda	Washington Twp	68	293
Bill	25	m	i	CA	Colusa	Stony Crk Twp	71	326
Hannah	40	f	w	IREL	Alameda	San Leandro	68	98
John	27	m	w	NY	Monterey	Salinas Twp	74	314
Lewis	56	m	b	MD	Nevada	Nevada Twp	75	308
Samuel	48	m	w	IREL	Alameda	Eden Twp	68	83
Samuel	14	m	w	PA	Alameda	Eden Twp	68	83
BRISCOE								
Bill	38	m	i	CA	Colusa	Stony Crk Twp	71	333
Elias H	34	m	w	KY	Napa	Napa	75	50
H P	38	m	w	OH	Butte	Chico Twp	70	17
Jasper	11	m	i	CA	Colusa	Stony Crk Twp	71	333
John	42	m	w	IREL	Inyo	Cerro Gordo Twp	73	319
Walter J	38	m	w	KY	Colusa	Stony Crk Twp	71	333
BRISCOL								
James	21	m	w	PA	Yolo	Washington Twp	93	535
Michael	17	m	w	NY	San Francisco	11-Wd San Francisc	84	491

© 2001 by Heritage Quest. All rights reserved.

Name	Age	S	R	B-PL	County	Locale	Series M593 Roll	Pg
BRISENA								
Noble	18	m	w	CA	San Diego	San Diego	78	492
BRISENO								
Estephen	37	m	w	ITAL	Calaveras	San Andreas P O	70	214
Ildefonso	36	m	w	SPAI	Santa Barbara	Santa Barbara P O	87	500
BRISH								
Mary	20	f	w	CA	Santa Clara	2-Wd San Jose	88	304
Ransom	59	m	w	NY	Sonoma	Vallejo Twp	91	454
W	27	m	w	HANO	Sierra	Butte Twp	89	508
BRISK								
Julius	43	m	w	PRUS	San Francisco	San Francisco P O	83	63
Michl	45	m	w	ENGL	San Francisco	1-Wd San Francisco	79	58
BRISLAN								
John	37	m	w	IREL	El Dorado	Placerville Twp	72	100
BRISLIN								
Neal	30	m	w	IREL	Yuba	Rose Bar Twp	93	663
BRISLOW								
John W	42	m	w	MA	Yuba	Parks Bar Twp	93	650
BRISNAHAN								
Jerry	26	m	w	IREL	San Francisco	1-Wd San Francisco	79	99
S	35	m	w	IREL	San Francisco	San Francisco P O	83	316
BRISNAN								
Patrick	30	m	w	IREL	Santa Clara	2-Wd San Jose	88	316
BRISOLARI								
Bertolomes	40	m	w	ITAL	Calaveras	Copperopolis P O	70	241
BRISON								
Geo	46	m	w	SCOT	El Dorado	Georgetown Twp	72	42
James	17	m	w	CA	Colusa	Monroe Twp	71	322
L	32	m	w	LA	San Joaquin	Oneal Twp	86	109
BRISSEL								
S R	28	m	w	CANA	Sacramento	1-Wd Sacramento	77	172
W F	29	m	w	NY	Sacramento	1-Wd Sacramento	77	181
BRISSEN								
A	33	m	w	CANA	Nevada	Eureka Twp	75	139
C	26	m	w	CANA	Nevada	Eureka Twp	75	139
H	47	m	w	CANA	Nevada	Eureka Twp	75	139
Napoleon	29	m	w	CANA	Nevada	Eureka Twp	75	139
BRISSIC								
Edward	34	m	w	HOLL	San Francisco	7-Wd San Francisco	81	218
BRISSOLAIE								
Bartolo	42	m	w	ITAL	San Luis Obispo	San Luis Obispo Tw	87	310
BRISSOLARA								
C	24	m	w	ITAL	Amador	Jackson P O	69	330
Joseph	30	m	w	ITAL	Amador	Volcano P O	69	383
BRISTATA								
Esparito	38	m	w	MEXI	Fresno	Millerton P O	72	164
BRISTLER								
William	23	m	w	IREL	Santa Barbara	Santa Barbara P O	87	503
BRISTO								
Martha	18	f	w	PA	Alameda	Eden Twp	68	86
Peter	35	m	w	CANA	Sacramento	Brighton Twp	77	72
BRISTOL								
Andrew	47	m	m	NJ	San Francisco	San Francisco P O	80	386
Frank	32	m	w	CT	Marin	San Rafael Twp	74	36
John	29	m	w	IL	Colusa	Spring Valley Twp	71	337
Justice	50	m	w	NY	Santa Clara	San Jose Twp	88	191
Sherlock	55	m	w	CT	Santa Barbara	San Buenaventura P	87	447
W H H	56	m	w	NY	Monterey	Salinas Twp	74	306
Wm A	30	m	w	OH	Butte	Chico Twp	70	46
BRISTOLL								
Hanry	29	m	w	NY	San Francisco	San Francisco P O	83	78
BRISTOR								
W E	42	m	w	ME	Solano	Vallejo	90	181
BRISTOW								
Geo	37	m	w	ENGL	Yuba	Rose Bar Twp	93	661
John	68	m	w	KY	Placer	Roseville P O	76	351
Joseph	69	m	w	ENGL	San Francisco	San Francisco P O	83	262
Levi E	28	m	w	VT	San Francisco	8-Wd San Francisco	82	316
Margaret	30	f	w	IREL	San Francisco	8-Wd San Francisco	82	455
William	39	m	w	ENGL	Amador	Jackson P O	69	339
William	29	m	w	ME	Nevada	Bridgeport Twp	75	103
BRIT								
J W	25	m	w	IREL	Alameda	Oakland	68	184
BRITAIN								
Robert	48	m	w	NY	San Francisco	5-Wd San Francisco	81	22
BRITANO								
Angelo	31	m	w	ITAL	San Francisco	11-Wd San Francisc	84	594
BRITCHARD								
Henry	35	m	w	ENGL	San Francisco	5-Wd San Francisco	81	28
BRITE								
John	47	m	w	MO	Kern	Tehachapi P O	73	354
BRITEN								
Charles W	40	m	w	PA	Inyo	Lone Pine Twp	73	335
BRITHERFORD								
John	44	m	w	PA	San Francisco	5-Wd San Francisco	81	21
BRITHING								
John	25	m	w	PRUS	Santa Barbara	Santa Barbara P O	87	503
BRITIZENS								
Denis	21	m	w	RUSS	San Francisco	1-Wd San Francisco	79	49
BRITO								
Jose	38	m	w	CHIL	Fresno	Millerton P O	72	153
Marcus	35	m	w	CHIL	Fresno	Millerton P O	72	153
BRITT								
J E	31	m	w	IREL	Alameda	Oakland	68	262
John	47	m	w	IREL	Santa Clara	2-Wd San Jose	88	303
John	40	m	w	MA	San Francisco	San Francisco P O	83	88
John	37	m	w	MI	Alameda	Oakland	68	262
John	23	m	w	IREL	San Francisco	1-Wd San Francisco	79	89
Pat	42	m	w	IREL	Alameda	Alameda	68	11
Patrick	35	m	w	IREL	San Mateo	San Mateo P O	87	357
Patrick	28	m	w	IREL	San Francisco	3-Wd San Francisco	79	296
Rachel	48	f	w	ENGL	San Francisco	6-Wd San Francisco	81	144
Thomas	37	m	w	IREL	Klamath	Klamath Twp	73	371
Wm	35	m	w	IREL	San Francisco	San Francisco P O	83	124
BRITTAIN								
August	13	m	w	CA	San Francisco	2-Wd San Francisco	79	243
G E	49	m	w	VA	Sutter	Butte Twp	92	98
Wm	26	m	w	CANA	San Francisco	11-Wd San Francisc	84	636
BRITTAN								
Arthur	17	m	w	OH	San Mateo	Half Moon Bay P O	87	404
Cam	29	m	w	WI	San Diego	Julian Dist	78	469
Elkana	34	m	w	TN	San Mateo	Redwood Twp	87	363
George	34	m	w	PA	San Francisco	San Francisco P O	80	390
Hannah	47	f	w	IREL	San Francisco	8-Wd San Francisco	82	291
J S	29	m	w	ENGL	Monterey	Salinas Twp	74	306
Laura	32	f	w	KY	Colusa	Colusa Twp	71	276
Patrick	40	m	w	IREL	San Francisco	3-Wd San Francisco	79	289
R H	45	m	w	KY	Sonoma	Santa Rosa	91	397
Sharrik	38	m	w	NY	San Mateo	Belmont P O	87	373
BRITTEN								
John	45	m	w	ENGL	San Francisco	6-Wd San Francisco	81	116
BRITTENCOURT								
Thomas	37	m	w	PORT	Placer	Bath P O	76	460
BRITTIAN								
J T	33	m	w	PA	Klamath	Trinidad Twp	73	390
BRITTINGHAM								
Kendall	21	m	w	MD	Santa Cruz	Santa Cruz Twp	89	383
William	39	m	w	MD	Santa Clara	1-Wd San Jose	88	275
BRITTO								
Jose S	38	m	w	CHIL	Placer	Bath P O	76	431
BRITTON								
Ellen	35	f	w	KY	Lake	Morgan Valley	73	424
Ephraim	23	m	w	IREL	Santa Clara	Alviso Twp	88	26
George	46	m	w	ENGL	Marin	Bolinas Twp	74	7
James	36	m	w	TN	Yuba	East Bear Rvr Twp	93	541
James	25	m	w	IREL	Marin	San Rafael Twp	74	26
John	57	m	w	IREL	El Dorado	Placerville	72	108
John	47	m	w	IREL	San Francisco	11-Wd San Francisc	84	487
John	40	m	w	NY	Sacramento	Franklin Twp	77	112
John	29	m	w	IREL	Santa Clara	1-Wd San Jose	88	276
Joseph	45	m	w	ENGL	San Francisco	2-Wd San Francisco	79	275
Louisa	19	f	w	CA	Sonoma	Petaluma Twp	91	336
Martin	50	m	w	NY	Santa Clara	San Jose Twp	88	190
Robert	32	m	w	IREL	Alameda	Washington Twp	68	287
W G	36	m	w	TN	Sierra	Forest Twp	89	529
William	25	m	w	IREL	Santa Clara	Alviso Twp	88	26
Wm	40	m	w	ME	Yuba	Rose Bar Twp	93	656
Wm	30	m	w	ME	Yuba	Rose Bar Twp	93	655
Wm	25	m	w	IREL	San Diego	San Diego	78	503
Wm	15	m	w	CA	San Francisco	11-Wd San Francisc	84	586
BRITZHOFF								
A C	52	m	w	NY	San Joaquin	3-Wd Stockton	86	216
BRIU								
Hugh	66	m	w	IREL	Sonoma	Mendocino Twp	91	308
BRIXTON								
Minnie	22	f	w	ME	Plumas	Mineral Twp	77	21
BRIYAN								
Wm E	48	m	w	KY	Sacramento	Brighton Twp	77	76
BRIZANDINE								
---	24	f	w	MO	Mendocino	Little Lake Twp	74	200
BRIZEE								
John	37	m	w	NY	Alameda	Eden Twp	68	57
BRIZELL								
Ellen	14	f	-	CA	Siskiyou	Yreka	89	663
BRIZOLARA								
Louis	39	m	w	ITAL	Sacramento	Dry Crk Twp	77	99
BRIZZALARA								
Frank	53	m	w	ITAL	Inyo	Lone Pine Twp	73	332
BRIZZARD								
Paul	65	m	w	FRAN	Humboldt	Arcata Twp	72	229
BRIZZELANG								
Vinco	34	m	w	ITAL	Stanislaus	Branch Twp	92	8
BROAD								
Charles	46	m	w	ENGL	El Dorado	Placerville Twp	72	92
Charles E	24	m	w	AUSL	San Francisco	San Francisco P O	83	185
Chas	50	m	w	ENGL	San Francisco	8-Wd San Francisco	82	314
James	56	m	w	ENGL	San Francisco	2-Wd San Francisco	79	223
John	29	m	w	ENGL	San Francisco	8-Wd San Francisco	82	298
Mary	70	f	w	ENGL	San Francisco	2-Wd San Francisco	79	223
William	37	m	w	HOLL	San Francisco	3-Wd San Francisco	79	327
William H	29	m	w	ME	Stanislaus	San Joaquin Twp	92	77
BROADBENT								
John O	22	m	w	ENGL	Santa Barbara	Santa Barbara P O	87	462
Mary A	48	f	w	ENGL	Santa Clara	San Jose Twp	88	214
Stephen F	62	m	w	ENGL	El Dorado	Mud Springs Twp	72	74
BROADDUS								
Jer	79	m	w	VA	Mendocino	Little Lake Twp	74	200
BROADERSON								
Hugh	23	m	w	IREL	San Francisco	2-Wd San Francisco	79	181
BROADHURST								
C	39	m	w	MO	Merced	Snelling P O	74	277
Joseph	52	m	w	OH	Napa	Napa Twp	75	58
BROADUS								
James	37	m	m	KY	Santa Cruz	Watsonville	89	373

© 2001 by Heritage Quest. All rights reserved.

California 1870 Census

Name	Age	S	R	B-PL	County	Locale	Roll	Pg
						Series M593		
BROADWELL								
C	44	f	w	NY	Lassen	Janesville Twp	73	434
S	45	m	w	OH	Lake	Lower Lake	73	415
BROADY								
James	45	m	w	IREL	Santa Clara	Fremont Twp	88	51
BROAS								
Margerett	34	f	w	IREL	Los Angeles	Los Angeles	73	524
BROBMEL								
Henry	25	m	w	SHOL	San Francisco	1-Wd San Francisco	79	108
BROCAS								
John W	40	m	w	OH	San Francisco	1-Wd San Francisco	79	107
BROCCO								
John	34	m	w	ITAL	San Francisco	2-Wd San Francisco	79	256
BROCH								
Christian	39	m	w	DENM	San Francisco	2-Wd San Francisco	79	226
John	39	m	w	PRUS	Sacramento	4-Wd Sacramento	77	347
BROCHELLE								
James	32	m	m	NY	San Francisco	San Francisco P O	80	383
BROCHFELT								
Charles	45	m	w	HAMB	San Francisco	2-Wd San Francisco	79	245
BROCHMAN								
Moses	33	m	w	GA	Inyo	Bishop Crk Twp	73	312
BROCHURST								
H	37	m	w	ENGL	Alameda	Oakland	68	231
BROCK								
Charles	40	m	w	MA	San Francisco	2-Wd San Francisco	79	201
Daniel	60	m	w	TN	Humboldt	South Fork Twp	72	302
Dorret	37	f	w	NY	San Joaquin	2-Wd Stockton	86	175
E Mrs	55	f	w	MS	Santa Clara	Gilroy Twp	88	101
George	43	m	w	FRAN	San Francisco	2-Wd San Francisco	79	244
Hiram	36	m	w	NY	Los Angeles	Soledad Twp	73	633
J	70	m	w	NC	Amador	Fiddletown P O	69	438
J M	34	m	w	NY	Sutter	Nicolaus Twp	92	111
Jack	44	m	w	OH	San Joaquin	Elkhorn Twp	86	69
Jacob	31	m	w	FRAN	San Francisco	2-Wd San Francisco	79	242
James	39	m	w	IA	Shasta	Stillwater P O	89	478
James J	23	m	w	IL	El Dorado	Coloma Twp	72	8
Jas A	38	m	w	IN	Shasta	Stillwater P O	89	481
John	46	m	w	IL	San Joaquin	1-Wd Stockton	86	136
John	39	m	w	IL	Humboldt	South Fork Twp	72	301
Joseph M	40	m	w	NH	Butte	Ophir Twp	70	92
Josephina	27	f	w	WI	El Dorado	Placerville	72	122
Lewellan	11	m	w	CA	Solano	Vacaville Twp	90	126
Lowelian	58	m	w	MO	Solano	Vacaville Twp	90	126
M	36	m	w	HUNG	Solano	Vallejo	90	203
Michael	54	m	w	IREL	Sacramento	2-Wd Sacramento	77	216
Michael	3M	m	w	CA	Nevada	Grass Valley Twp	75	163
Patrick	32	m	w	IREL	Nevada	Grass Valley Twp	75	163
Peter	60	m	w	ENGL	Butte	Oregon Twp	70	123
Peter	30	m	w	MO	Butte	Oregon Twp	70	135
Reuben	22	m	w	OH	San Joaquin	Elkhorn Twp	86	69
Robert	41	m	w	MA	Contra Costa	Martinez Twp	71	349
Samuel	44	m	w	MO	Stanislaus	Empire Twp	92	65
Thomas	67	m	w	NC	Amador	Fiddletown P O	69	440
Thomas	42	m	w	MA	Napa	Napa	75	38
Thomas	35	m	w	ENGL	Nevada	Nevada Twp	75	303
Tilden H	36	m	w	IN	Yolo	Buckeye Twp	93	414
W S	45	m	w	VT	Humboldt	Eureka Twp	72	260
William	32	m	w	SCOT	San Francisco	San Francisco P O	83	201
William	27	m	w	MO	Solano	Montezuma Twp	90	65
Wm M	35	m	w	IL	Sacramento	Dry Crk Twp	77	98
BROCKDORFF								
Nichs	46	m	w	SHOL	San Francisco	1-Wd San Francisco	79	86
BROCKELL								
Jno	30	m	w	VT	Sacramento	1-Wd Sacramento	77	185
BROCKELMAN								
Ernest	37	m	w	HANO	Contra Costa	Martinez P O	71	370
BROCKEN								
Michl	40	m	w	IREL	San Francisco	San Francisco P O	83	14
BROCKENBROW								
Thos	33	m	w	ENGL	Santa Barbara	Santa Barbara P O	87	482
BROCKENS								
J C	32	m	w	ENGL	Yuba	Marysville	93	583
BROCKER								
Henry	45	m	w	MECK	Marin	Novato Twp	74	12
Henry	36	m	w	PRUS	San Francisco	San Francisco P O	80	470
BROCKET								
Enos	47	m	w	BADE	Klamath	Klamath Twp	73	371
BROCKETT								
Joshua S	49	m	w	MA	Sonoma	Petaluma Twp	91	345
BROCKHOFF								
Charlotte	26	f	w	HANO	San Francisco	11-Wd San Francisc	84	623
Chas	28	m	w	HANO	San Francisco	11-Wd San Francisc	84	674
BROCKHURST								
S	64	m	w	ENGL	Alameda	Oakland	68	200
BROCKIN								
David	27	m	w	WIND	San Francisco	1-Wd San Francisco	79	69
BROCKINGTON								
William	39	m	w	ENGL	Nevada	Grass Valley Twp	75	183
BROCKLEBANK								
M T	46	m	w	NY	San Francisco	3-Wd San Francisco	79	328
BROCKLESS								
Fredk	36	m	w	BRUN	San Francisco	1-Wd San Francisco	79	65
BROCKMAN								
Charles	7	m	w	CA	Marin	San Rafael Twp	74	28
Charles	49	m	w	PRUS	San Francisco	San Francisco P O	83	197
Chas	26	m	w	NY	San Francisco	1-Wd San Francisco	79	134
Eustace	12	m	w	CA	Marin	San Rafael Twp	74	27
H F	34	m	w	WI	Napa	Napa Twp	75	70
Henry	48	m	w	GERM	Contra Costa	San Pablo Twp	71	366
Henry	30	m	w	MO	Placer	Lincoln P O	76	481
Israel	45	m	w	KY	San Diego	San Diego	78	504
Jesse	24	m	w	SWIT	Sacramento	American Twp	77	64
Jos	65	m	w	KY	San Diego	San Diego	78	504
Joseph	35	m	w	MO	Sacramento	San Joaquin Twp	77	407
M	44	m	w	MO	Sonoma	Santa Rosa	91	426
Nicholas	35	m	w	HAMB	San Francisco	8-Wd San Francisco	82	414
Peter	21	m	w	SWIT	Sacramento	American Twp	77	64
Stephen	10	m	w	CA	Marin	San Rafael Twp	74	27
William	33	m	w	PRUS	Lassen	Susanville Twp	73	439
Wm H	43	m	w	GA	Nevada	Little York Twp	75	244
BROCKMEYER								
Fred	40	m	w	DENM	San Francisco	1-Wd San Francisco	79	85
BROCKMYER								
Benj	31	m	w	HDAR	Nevada	Eureka Twp	75	139
BROCKS								
Wm R	30	m	w	MO	Sonoma	Petaluma Twp	91	325
BROCKUS								
William	35	m	w	TN	Yolo	Grafton Twp	93	494
BROCKWAY								
C P	64	m	w	NY	Sacramento	4-Wd Sacramento	77	373
Charles	58	m	w	CT	Sacramento	Sutter Twp	77	382
H S	63	f	w	NY	Merced	Snelling P O	74	254
Jesse	40	m	w	NY	Sacramento	San Joaquin Twp	77	406
John	37	m	w	NY	Nevada	Meadow Lake Twp	75	247
Louis	50	m	w	FRAN	Tuolumne	Sonora P O	93	330
S H	47	m	w	VT	El Dorado	Coloma Twp	72	7
BROCKWELL								
Frank	26	m	w	ME	Marin	Point Reyes Twp	74	22
BROCQ								
Julia	48	f	w	FRAN	San Francisco	3-Wd San Francisco	79	319
BROCY								
Alfred	42	m	w	FRAN	San Francisco	11-Wd San Francisc	84	700
BROD								
Charles	54	m	w	FRAN	San Francisco	8-Wd San Francisco	82	435
John Henry	43	m	w	HCAS	Placer	Auburn P O	76	369
BRODAY								
Bernhard	36	m	w	NY	San Francisco	San Francisco P O	83	415
BRODE								
Charles	33	m	w	GERM	Los Angeles	Los Angeles	73	538
BRODECK								
Henry	23	m	w	ENGL	Santa Clara	2-Wd San Jose	88	324
BRODEK								
Samuel	38	m	w	PRUS	San Francisco	8-Wd San Francisco	82	409
BRODER								
Jacob	37	m	w	SWIT	Sacramento	Natomas Twp	77	169
James S	36	m	w	NY	Inyo	Bishop Crk Twp	73	310
John	45	m	w	CANA	Inyo	Independence Twp	73	327
John	10	m	w	CA	Santa Clara	Santa Clara Twp	88	176
Luis	13	m	w	CA	Santa Clara	Santa Clara Twp	88	176
Oswell	40	m	w	SWIT	Sacramento	Natomas Twp	77	169
Robert	37	m	w	CANA	San Luis Obispo	Salinas Twp	87	293
BRODERED								
John W	25	m	w	TX	Los Angeles	El Monte Twp	73	457
BRODERICH								
Joseph	35	m	w	CANA	Humboldt	Eel Rvr Twp	72	250
BRODERICK								
Andrew T	35	m	w	CANA	San Francisco	San Francisco P O	83	358
Bartholemeo	38	m	w	IREL	Nevada	Grass Valley Twp	75	161
C C	34	m	w	CANA	Humboldt	Eureka Twp	72	260
D	35	f	w	IREL	Alameda	Oakland	68	219
David	48	m	w	PRUS	San Francisco	San Francisco P O	83	304
David	27	m	w	IREL	San Francisco	7-Wd San Francisco	81	239
David	24	m	w	ENGL	San Mateo	Redwood Twp	87	365
Edmund	58	m	w	IREL	San Francisco	11-Wd San Francisc	84	611
F	55	m	w	IREL	Sacramento	3-Wd Sacramento	77	275
Hugh	37	m	w	IREL	Stanislaus	Emory Twp	92	16
J C	38	m	w	IREL	Nevada	Bridgeport Twp	75	121
Jas	26	m	w	IREL	San Francisco	11-Wd San Francisc	84	657
Jno	40	m	w	ENGL	San Joaquin	2-Wd Stockton	86	163
Johanna	80	f	w	IREL	San Francisco	San Francisco P O	83	33
John	55	m	w	IREL	San Francisco	11-Wd San Francisc	84	535
John	40	m	w	IREL	Marin	Sausalito Twp	74	70
John	24	m	w	IREL	San Francisco	San Francisco P O	83	117
John	16	m	w	CA	San Francisco	11-Wd San Francisc	84	592
Jul	27	f	w	IREL	Sacramento	4-Wd Sacramento	77	329
Kate	24	f	w	IREL	Alameda	Oakland	68	157
Margaret	35	f	w	IREL	San Francisco	San Francisco P O	83	55
Mary	35	f	w	IREL	San Francisco	San Francisco P O	83	76
Nellie	11	f	w	CA	San Francisco	11-Wd San Francisc	84	486
Patrick	30	m	w	IREL	San Francisco	San Francisco P O	83	287
Patrick	29	m	w	IREL	San Francisco	11-Wd San Francisc	84	558
Regina	34	f	w	PRUS	Solano	Suisun Twp	90	98
Thomas	30	m	w	IREL	Solano	Green Valley Twp	90	42
Thos	31	m	w	IREL	San Francisco	5-Wd San Francisco	81	17
Walter	38	m	w	IREL	San Francisco	1-Wd San Francisco	79	62
William	33	m	w	IREL	San Mateo	San Mateo P O	87	353
William J	24	m	w	ENGL	Los Angeles	Los Angeles	73	546
BRODERSON								
Benedict	44	m	w	PRUS	San Francisco	3-Wd San Francisco	79	324
John	28	m	w	PRUS	San Francisco	1-Wd San Francisco	79	120
BRODEX								
Pat	46	m	w	IREL	San Francisco	7-Wd San Francisco	81	275

© 2001 by Heritage Quest. All rights reserved.

Name	Age	S	R	B-PL	County	Locale	Series M593 Roll	Pg
BRODGETT								
Joseph	60	m	w	NH	Los Angeles	Los Angeles	73	507
BRODICK								
Mary	27	f	w	IREL	San Francisco	San Francisco P O	83	320
BRODIE								
Annie	15	f	w	MEXI	Solano	Benicia	90	16
Charles	19	m	w	MEXI	Santa Clara	1-Wd San Jose	88	264
David	23	m	w	MEXI	San Bernardino	San Bernardino Twp	78	416
Edwd	22	m	w	ENGL	Butte	Chico Twp	70	34
Gustave	33	m	w	PRUS	San Francisco	San Francisco P O	83	173
James	51	m	w	SCOT	San Francisco	San Francisco P O	85	766
James F	50	m	w	OH	Solano	Rio Vista Twp	90	60
Samuel	42	m	w	KY	San Francisco	San Francisco P O	80	538
William	42	m	w	SCOT	San Francisco	San Francisco P O	83	191
Wm	23	m	w	NY	Solano	Vallejo	90	146
BRODIGAN								
Hugh	28	m	w	MA	San Francisco	2-Wd San Francisco	79	137
Nick	34	m	w	IREL	Sonoma	Bodega Twp	91	251
Teddy	18	m	w	CA	Stanislaus	Buena Vista Twp	92	12
Terrence	50	m	w	IREL	Tuolumne	Sonora P O	93	310
BRODISH								
Chrisn	58	m	w	PRUS	Calaveras	Copperopolis P O	70	256
BRODKYST								
John	21	m	w	CT	Sonoma	Petaluma Twp	91	322
BRODOOLF								
Michael	40	m	w	BAVA	San Francisco	8-Wd San Francisco	82	381
BRODRICK								
Isaac	37	m	w	OH	San Francisco	11-Wd San Francisc	84	460
John	25	m	w	IREL	San Francisco	11-Wd San Francisc	84	482
M A	23	m	w	MA	San Francisco	San Francisco P O	85	784
BRODT								
A W	35	m	w	NY	Alameda	Oakland	68	217
Ephraim	38	m	w	PA	Nevada	Nevada Twp	75	295
BRODUATE								
Guy	44	m	w	VA	Butte	Chico Twp	70	22
BRODWOLF								
George	39	m	w	BAVA	San Francisco	6-Wd San Francisco	81	113
BRODY								
A J	23	m	w	IA	Tehama	Tehama Twp	92	192
Francis M	33	m	w	AR	Fresno	Millerton P O	72	182
John	50	m	w	IREL	San Francisco	San Francisco P O	83	143
Michael	41	m	w	IREL	Nevada	Eureka Twp	75	135
BROEN								
William	25	m	w	IL	San Bernardino	San Bernardino Twp	78	448
BROFF								
Jacob	32	m	w	PRUS	San Francisco	8-Wd San Francisco	82	385
BROFFEY								
John	38	m	w	IREL	Sacramento	Sutter Twp	77	380
BROFY								
Martin	32	m	w	IREL	Solano	Maine Prairie Twp	90	52
BROGAN								
Bridget	43	f	w	IREL	San Francisco	11-Wd San Francisc	84	611
Chas E	39	m	w	NJ	Placer	Gold Run Twp	76	394
J A	31	m	w	ME	Alameda	Oakland	68	264
James	40	m	w	IREL	Yuba	Marysville	93	584
James H	32	m	w	IREL	Yolo	Cache Crk Twp	93	419
Joseph	22	m	w	MO	Placer	Bath P O	76	432
Kate	26	f	w	IREL	San Joaquin	2-Wd Stockton	86	158
Kate	26	f	w	IREL	San Francisco	San Francisco P O	83	165
Margaret	30	f	w	IREL	San Francisco	11-Wd San Francisc	84	437
Martin	46	m	w	IREL	Tuolumne	Chinese Camp P O	93	364
Mary	59	f	w	IREL	Placer	Bath P O	76	426
Mary A	18	f	w	NY	Placer	Lincoln P O	76	489
Michael	80	m	w	SCOT	San Francisco	San Francisco P O	80	370
Michael	45	m	w	SCOT	San Francisco	San Francisco P O	80	370
Patk J	37	m	w	IREL	Nevada	Grass Valley Twp	75	169
Patrick	30	m	w	IREL	San Mateo	Schoolhouse Statio	87	342
Stephen	69	m	w	IREL	San Francisco	San Francisco P O	83	92
Thomas	24	m	w	MD	Placer	Bath P O	76	426
BROGARD								
Bonaparte	29	m	w	CANA	Santa Clara	Alviso Twp	88	29
BROGER								
Katie	38	f	w	FRAN	San Francisco	San Francisco P O	80	342
Otto	28	m	w	SHOL	Santa Cruz	Santa Cruz	89	413
BROGHAM								
---	34	m	w	IREL	San Francisco	11-Wd San Francisc	84	592
Mary	62	f	w	IREL	Sacramento	3-Wd Sacramento	77	279
BROGMAN								
Minna	24	f	w	PRUS	San Francisco	8-Wd San Francisco	82	315
BROHAN								
Thos D	37	m	w	IREL	San Francisco	1-Wd San Francisco	79	136
William	62	m	w	IREL	Yuba	Slate Range Bar Tw	93	669
BROHASKY								
Gustave	42	m	w	PRUS	Santa Clara	1-Wd San Jose	88	230
BROIDICKER								
Geo	30	m	w	PRUS	San Francisco	1-Wd San Francisco	79	135
BROILLE								
Anthony	34	m	w	PRUS	San Francisco	5-Wd San Francisco	81	9
BROILS								
Thomas	31	m	w	MO	Contra Costa	Martinez P O	71	400
BROISART								
John	29	m	w	FRAN	San Francisco	2-Wd San Francisco	79	145
BROKAN								
Andrew	27	m	w	NY	Yolo	Grafton Twp	93	481
Daniel G	22	m	w	NJ	San Francisco	2-Wd San Francisco	79	210
Henry V	40	m	w	NJ	San Francisco	San Francisco P O	83	199
BROKAW								
Chas W	20	m	w	OH	Shasta	Millville P O	89	488
BROKEN								
Andrew	27	m	w	NY	Yolo	Cache Crk Twp	93	432
BROKER								
Thomas	52	m	w	BADE	Placer	Auburn P O	76	363
BROKINS								
David B	50	m	w	ME	Klamath	South Fork Twp	73	385
BROKS								
Samuel	40	m	w	RUSS	Tuolumne	Chinese Camp P O	93	384
BROKSHONE								
Thomas	26	m	w	IA	Santa Barbara	Arroyo Burro P O	87	509
BROLL								
Henry	24	m	w	PRUS	San Francisco	8-Wd San Francisco	82	435
BROLLIER								
Sarah A	33	f	w	OH	Santa Clara	2-Wd San Jose	88	281
BROM								
Jessie	11	f	w	CA	Humboldt	Eureka Twp	72	279
Mary	23	f	w	IN	San Luis Obispo	Santa Rosa Twp	87	321
BROMAN								
Bennett B	39	m	w	KY	San Diego	San Diego	78	505
BROMBERT								
Abram	34	m	w	PRUS	Butte	Chico Twp	70	14
BROME								
Henri	23	m	w	FRAN	San Francisco	11-Wd San Francisc	84	643
William	46	m	w	NJ	Placer	Bath P O	76	421
BROMENHAU								
Steph	30	m	w	ME	San Francisco	1-Wd San Francisco	79	68
BROMER								
Henry	25	m	w	HANO	San Francisco	San Francisco P O	83	23
BROMES								
Alexander	52	m	w	IREL	Contra Costa	Martinez P O	71	406
Catharine	58	f	w	IREL	Sacramento	1-Wd Sacramento	77	202
Jno	25	m	w	IREL	Sacramento	1-Wd Sacramento	77	202
Mike	28	m	w	IREL	Sacramento	1-Wd Sacramento	77	202
BROMIGAN								
Peter	26	m	w	SWIT	San Joaquin	2-Wd Stockton	86	161
BROMITT								
Wm	22	m	w	MS	Sacramento	1-Wd Sacramento	77	182
BROMLEY								
Anne	35	f	w	CANA	San Francisco	San Francisco P O	83	302
Chester	45	m	w	NY	San Francisco	6-Wd San Francisco	81	147
David	50	m	w	CT	Mendocino	Big Rvr Twp	74	160
Geo T	53	m	w	CT	San Francisco	San Francisco P O	83	95
James	31	m	w	MD	Butte	Hamilton Twp	70	71
John	49	m	w	MD	Contra Costa	Martinez P O	71	442
John	49	m	w	ENGL	Placer	Auburn P O	76	360
Micheal	58	m	w	IREL	San Francisco	11-Wd San Francisc	84	455
Seth	31	m	w	MA	Sacramento	2-Wd Sacramento	77	254
T B	38	m	w	ENGL	Solano	Vallejo	90	170
Wash L	45	m	w	MD	San Francisco	6-Wd San Francisco	81	125
William	45	m	w	CT	San Francisco	6-Wd San Francisco	81	135
BROMMEL								
Berthold	21	m	w	PRUS	San Francisco	8-Wd San Francisco	82	380
BROMMER								
Diederick	35	m	w	HANO	San Francisco	San Francisco P O	83	23
Hinry	34	m	w	HANO	San Francisco	San Francisco P O	85	812
John	27	m	w	HANO	San Francisco	San Francisco P O	85	753
BROMON								
John	31	m	w	IREL	Alameda	Alameda	68	2
BROMONBECK								
Fred	27	m	w	SHOL	San Mateo	Redwood City P O	87	375
BROMS								
John	38	m	w	IREL	San Francisco	11-Wd San Francisc	84	665
BROMWELL								
M	47	m	w	AUST	San Joaquin	Elliott Twp	86	72
BRON								
Chas	23	m	w	NY	San Joaquin	1-Wd Stockton	86	134
Thomas	44	m	w	ME	San Francisco	5-Wd San Francisco	81	25
BRONAUGH								
Aug H	45	m	w	KY	San Diego	San Diego	78	499
BRONCHER								
Ed	38	m	w	PA	Sierra	Table Rock Twp	89	579
BRONERI								
Domenico	28	m	w	ITAL	San Francisco	1-Wd San Francisco	79	110
BRONEZ								
Thomas	66	m	w	ITAL	Mariposa	Mariposa P O	74	93
BRONK								
L P	51	m	w	NY	Yuba	Marysville	93	575
BRONKER								
Fred	28	m	w	ENGL	Solano	Vallejo	90	197
BRONKHORST								
Wm	25	m	w	PRUS	Contra Costa	Martinez P O	71	371
BRONKLIN								
Charles	29	m	w	SHOL	Colusa	Spring Valley Twp	71	344
BRONN								
John F	13	m	w	MA	Marin	San Rafael Twp	74	29
BRONNAN								
Owen	23	m	w	IREL	Marin	San Rafael	74	57
BRONNELL								
Irwin W	43	m	w	MA	Colusa	Monroe Twp	71	318
Jererd D	26	m	w	MO	San Luis Obispo	Morro Twp	87	281
Louisa A	22	f	w	MO	San Francisco	San Francisco P O	83	79
BRONSDON								
Phineas	48	m	w	MA	San Francisco	San Francisco P O	83	346
BRONSON								
A H	24	m	w	PA	Lassen	Milford Twp	73	438

© 2001 by Heritage Quest. All rights reserved.

California 1870 Census

Series M593

Name	Age	S	R	B-PL	County	Locale	Roll	Pg
Amos C	52	m	w	NY	Sacramento	4-Wd Sacramento	77	361
Charles	33	m	w	SWED	Stanislaus	San Joaquin Twp	92	73
Chas	38	m	w	NORW	Sacramento	4-Wd Sacramento	77	342
Cora	16	f	w	NY	Alameda	Oakland	68	259
Geo P	52	m	w	OH	Mono	Bridgeport P O	74	285
George	27	m	w	NJ	Stanislaus	Branch Twp	92	9
H W	34	m	w	CANA	Tuolumne	Columbia P O	93	343
Harriett	44	f	w	NY	Santa Clara	San Jose Twp	88	185
Henry	35	m	w	MI	Solano	Suisun Twp	90	107
Henry	21	m	w	SC	San Francisco	8-Wd San Francisco	82	386
Howard	31	m	w	MI	Solano	Suisun Twp	90	108
J C	43	m	w	CANA	Tuolumne	Columbia P O	93	343
James C	40	m	w	IN	El Dorado	Placerville	72	121
Lewis	50	m	w	NY	Santa Cruz	Soquel Twp	89	441
M	59	m	w	CT	Lassen	Long Valley Twp	73	436
Mabel	14	f	w	CA	Alameda	Oakland	68	259
Matthew	33	m	w	HANO	El Dorado	Salmon Falls Twp	72	131
Pierson	36	m	w	RI	Solano	Tremont Twp	90	30
Russell	44	m	w	IN	El Dorado	Placerville	72	122
Sam B	39	m	w	NY	Merced	Snelling P O	74	274
BRONSTRUP								
William	42	m	w	PRUS	Santa Clara	Santa Clara Twp	88	147
BRONTE								
Chas	28	m	w	FRAN	San Francisco	11-Wd San Francisc	84	643
BRONTON								
Dovia	32	m	w	ITAL	San Joaquin	1-Wd Stockton	86	155
BRONZENA								
John	22	m	w	ITAL	Solano	Montezuma Twp	90	67
BROODERSON								
Christiana	22	f	w	SAXO	San Francisco	2-Wd San Francisco	79	220
BROOK								
Allen	46	m	w	ENGL	San Francisco	San Francisco P O	80	482
Charles	34	m	w	NY	Los Angeles	Wilmington Twp	73	638
Charles E	4	m	w	CA	San Bernardino	San Bernardino Twp	78	446
David	57	m	w	PA	Kern	Linns Valley P O	73	343
Edwin	13	m	w	NY	Santa Clara	Almaden Twp	88	19
Henry	35	m	w	ENGL	San Francisco	11-Wd San Francisc	84	664
Jacob	40	m	w	BADE	San Joaquin	Elkhorn Twp	86	67
Jno	45	m	w	ENGL	Santa Clara	Almaden Twp	88	19
John	42	m	w	IL	San Francisco	5-Wd San Francisco	81	23
Sylvester	38	m	w	IN	Mariposa	Maxwell Crk P O	74	142
BROOKBANK								
Abraham	66	m	w	KY	Los Angeles	Santa Ana Twp	73	614
Thomas	35	m	w	PA	Santa Clara	1-Wd San Jose	88	264
BROOKE								
E	14	m	w	OR	Solano	Benicia	90	21
BROOKENS								
Edward	56	m	w	VT	Colusa	Colusa Twp	71	273
BROOKERS								
G	35	m	w	MO	Santa Clara	Gilroy Twp	88	104
BROOKES								
James	55	m	w	KY	Santa Barbara	Santa Barbara P O	87	481
BROOKFIELD								
James	30	m	w	DE	Klamath	Camp Gaston	73	372
T	43	m	w	CANA	San Joaquin	Elliott Twp	86	73
BROOKING								
James	44	m	w	ENGL	Yuba	New York Twp	93	641
James	39	m	w	NH	Del Norte	Smith Rvr Twp	71	477
BROOKINS								
Henry	33	m	w	AR	Colusa	Stony Crk Twp	71	329
James	24	m	w	ME	Marin	San Antonio Twp	74	62
BROOKLAND								
M	66	m	b	VA	Amador	Amador City P O	69	395
BROOKMAN								
Bettie	24	f	w	PRUS	San Francisco	San Francisco P O	83	364
BROOKS								
---	33	m	w	ENGL	Humboldt	Eureka Twp	72	279
A W	35	m	w	WALE	San Joaquin	2-Wd Stockton	86	183
Adam	38	m	w	OH	El Dorado	Placerville	72	122
Allen H	40	m	w	TN	Stanislaus	Empire Twp	92	53
Alonzo H	58	m	w	NY	Mariposa	Mariposa P O	74	107
Andrew T	30	m	w	MO	Santa Clara	Fremont Twp	88	48
Anna	20	f	w	CA	San Francisco	7-Wd San Francisco	81	205
Benj	74	m	b	MD	Yuba	Marysville	93	613
Benj H	27	m	w	NY	San Francisco	2-Wd San Francisco	79	277
Benj S	45	m	w	NY	San Francisco	San Francisco P O	83	109
Birdsie	46	m	w	NY	San Francisco	San Francisco P O	85	752
Cathine	30	f	w	IREL	San Francisco	San Francisco P O	85	835
Cecelia	26	f	w	IREL	San Francisco	8-Wd San Francisco	82	476
Charles	37	m	w	NY	El Dorado	White Oak Twp	72	136
Charles	37	m	w	POLA	San Francisco	2-Wd San Francisco	79	212
Charles	28	m	w	BADE	San Francisco	11-Wd San Francisc	84	704
Chas	50	m	w	ENGL	Santa Barbara	San Buenaventura P	87	426
Chas	45	m	w	NY	Solano	Vallejo	90	154
Chas	41	m	w	NY	San Francisco	1-Wd San Francisco	79	108
Chas	36	m	w	DENM	Sierra	Butte Twp	89	510
Clark	45	m	w	OH	Sutter	Butte Twp	92	98
Cora M	24	f	w	TX	San Francisco	San Francisco P O	83	47
Cornelius D	40	m	w	VA	El Dorado	Diamond Springs Tw	72	23
Daniel W	30	m	w	CUBA	San Bernardino	San Bernardino Twp	78	417
David L	28	m	w	NY	Sacramento	Natomas Twp	77	166
Davis	30	m	w	TN	Placer	Alta P O	76	411
Della	21	f	w	NY	San Francisco	San Francisco P O	83	64
E L	40	m	w	NY	Sonoma	Bodega Twp	91	255
Edmund	47	m	w	MD	San Francisco	6-Wd San Francisco	81	131
Edwd A	3	m	w	CA	Butte	Ophir Twp	70	93
Edwin	30	m	w	IA	Trinity	Weaverville Pct	92	230
Edwin S	30	m	w	GA	Sonoma	Analy Twp	91	240
Elija	29	m	w	MI	Yuba	New York Twp	93	641
Elijah	27	m	w	MI	Butte	Wyandotte Twp	70	141
Eliphalet C	38	m	w	ME	Santa Barbara	San Buenaventura P	87	438
Elizabeth	16	f	w	NY	San Francisco	San Francisco P O	83	412
Ella	20	f	w	NH	Colusa	Colusa	71	293
Elmont	21	m	w	MI	Yuba	North East Twp	93	643
Francis	33	m	w	ME	San Diego	San Luis Rey	78	513
Francis	16	f	w	MO	Tehama	Red Bluff	92	179
Frank	78	m	w	MI	Alameda	Murray Twp	68	114
Frank	37	m	w	OH	Butte	Mountain Spring Tw	70	90
G W	57	m	w	OH	Butte	Wyandotte Twp	70	148
G W	24	m	w	MO	Sonoma	Petaluma Twp	91	316
Geo	49	m	w	CANA	San Francisco	1-Wd San Francisco	79	1
Geo	28	m	w	ME	San Francisco	1-Wd San Francisco	79	130
Geo G	29	m	w	PRUS	Butte	Ophir Twp	70	94
George	47	m	w	ENGL	Santa Clara	San Jose Twp	88	188
George	45	m	w	SWED	Los Angeles	Wilmington Twp	73	640
George	45	m	w	ENGL	El Dorado	Placerville	72	117
George	40	m	b	MA	San Francisco	San Francisco P O	80	358
George	30	m	w	NY	San Francisco	6-Wd San Francisco	81	71
George	22	m	w	ENGL	San Francisco	6-Wd San Francisco	81	87
George	20	m	w	ENGL	San Francisco	3-Wd San Francisco	79	312
H	30	m	w	MI	Alameda	Murray Twp	68	128
Hellen	37	f	w	VT	San Francisco	8-Wd San Francisco	82	365
Henery	35	m	w	NY	San Francisco	7-Wd San Francisco	81	183
Henry	53	m	w	NY	San Francisco	San Francisco P O	83	211
Henry	52	m	w	NJ	San Francisco	5-Wd San Francisco	81	13
Henry	38	m	w	ENGL	San Francisco	11-Wd San Francisc	84	564
Henry	36	m	w	NH	San Francisco	San Francisco P O	80	412
Henry	30	m	w	NY	San Francisco	5-Wd San Francisco	81	6
Henry C	36	m	w	PA	San Bernardino	San Bernardino Twp	78	418
Henry W	30	m	w	ENGL	San Francisco	San Francisco P O	83	190
Hiram	56	m	w	NY	Solano	Suisun Twp	90	112
Hiram	50	m	w	NY	Sacramento	Sutter Twp	77	383
Homer	45	m	w	PRUS	San Joaquin	2-Wd Stockton	86	169
Horace	35	m	w	ME	San Diego	San Luis Rey	78	513
J	23	m	w	GA	San Joaquin	Dent Twp	86	19
J C	42	m	w	OH	Sutter	Vernon Twp	92	137
James	51	m	w	KY	San Francisco	7-Wd San Francisco	81	205
James	43	m	w	ENGL	San Bernardino	San Bernardino Twp	78	447
James	32	m	w	NY	San Francisco	11-Wd San Francisc	84	619
James	30	m	w	IL	Alameda	Oakland	68	261
James	28	m	w	NY	San Francisco	3-Wd San Francisco	79	323
James	22	m	w	GA	Stanislaus	Empire Twp	92	32
James W	51	m	w	KY	Los Angeles	Los Angeles	73	527
Jas	55	m	w	IL	San Joaquin	Oneal Twp	86	106
Jas	47	m	w	MA	Sierra	Gibson Twp	89	539
Jas M	48	m	w	TN	Santa Clara	Gilroy Twp	88	106
Jay	16	m	w	CA	Butte	Mountain Spring Tw	70	89
Jerry	45	m	w	NY	Butte	Kimshew Tpw	70	80
Jo	35	m	w	PORT	Alameda	Alameda	68	10
John	50	m	w	IREL	Nevada	Eureka Twp	75	130
John	47	m	w	OH	Sutter	Vernon Twp	92	139
John	46	m	w	MD	San Francisco	San Francisco P O	80	484
John	45	m	w	IREL	San Mateo	Schoolhouse Statio	87	337
John	36	m	w	MA	San Francisco	San Francisco P O	80	339
John	34	m	w	MA	Sonoma	Salt Point	91	385
John	31	m	w	NY	Plumas	Plumas Twp	77	33
John	31	m	w	ENGL	Alameda	Hayward	68	80
John	30	m	w	ENGL	Los Angeles	Los Angeles	73	508
John	26	m	w	ENGL	Los Angeles	Los Angeles	73	568
John	24	m	w	ME	San Francisco	San Francisco P O	83	303
John	22	m	w	PORT	Sacramento	4-Wd Sacramento	77	321
John G	41	m	w	MA	Plumas	Plumas Twp	77	27
John W	22	m	w	MO	Yolo	Cache Crk Twp	93	426
Jonathan	56	m	w	ENGL	Contra Costa	Martinez P O	71	401
Joseph	42	m	w	ENGL	San Francisco	San Francisco P O	83	316
L	44	m	w	OH	Yuba	Marysville	93	595
Lafayette	40	m	w	NY	Yuba	Slate Range Bar Tw	93	677
Lewis Elbert	46	m	w	VA	Sonoma	Petaluma Twp	91	333
Margaret	50	f	w	IREL	Santa Clara	2-Wd San Jose	88	288
Margaret	45	f	b	LA	San Francisco	San Francisco P O	80	485
Margaret	26	f	w	IREL	San Francisco	San Francisco P O	80	475
Mark	28	m	w	NY	San Francisco	1-Wd San Francisco	79	115
Martin	48	m	w	MA	Alameda	Murray Twp	68	125
Mary	62	f	w	WV	Sonoma	Russian Rvr	91	378
Mary	16	f	w	CA	San Francisco	San Francisco P O	80	388
Mary B	30	f	w	MD	San Francisco	8-Wd San Francisco	82	358
Mary I	43	f	w	ENGL	San Francisco	5-Wd San Francisco	81	8
Max	35	m	w	PRUS	Butte	Ophir Twp	70	93
Micajah	43	m	w	GA	Tulare	Farmersville Twp	92	246
Mox	38	m	w	BADE	Monterey	San Juan Twp	74	409
Myres	46	m	w	ME	San Francisco	11-Wd San Francisc	84	695
N W	61	m	w	ME	Sacramento	4-Wd Sacramento	77	330
Noah	39	m	w	ME	San Francisco	San Francisco P O	80	412
Patrick	51	m	w	IREL	San Mateo	Schoolhouse Statio	87	338
Princette	17	f	w	UT	San Bernardino	San Bernardino Twp	78	423
Q A	40	m	w	PA	Sacramento	3-Wd Sacramento	77	269
Reuben	20	m	w	NJ	Sacramento	Natomas Twp	77	167
Robert A	36	m	w	PA	San Bernardino	San Bernardino Twp	78	452
Robt	49	m	w	CANA	San Francisco	11-Wd San Francisc	84	587
Robt	38	m	w	TX	Santa Clara	Gilroy Twp	88	82
Robt	30	m	w	CANA	Santa Clara	Gilroy Twp	88	77
Robt	13	m	w	NY	San Francisco	11-Wd San Francisc	84	587
Ruben	20	m	w	NY	El Dorado	Lake Valley Twp	72	65
Saml	45	m	w	ENGL	San Francisco	1-Wd San Francisco	79	58

© 2001 by Heritage Quest. All rights reserved.

Name	Age	S	R	B-PL	County	Locale	Series M593 Roll	Pg
Saml	30	m	w	ENGL	Butte	Kimshew Tpw	70	81
Samuel	73	m	w	PA	San Bernardino	San Bernardino Twp	78	436
Samuel	54	m	w	ENGL	San Francisco	11-Wd San Francisc	84	659
Samuel	43	m	w	PA	San Bernardino	San Bernardino Twp	78	423
Samuel	43	m	w	TN	Tuolumne	Columbia P O	93	354
Samuel	28	m	w	ENGL	San Francisco	3-Wd San Francisco	79	323
Sarah	38	f	w	KY	San Francisco	7-Wd San Francisco	81	205
Shadrick	56	m	w	MD	San Francisco	San Francisco P O	80	354
Silas	35	m	w	ME	Sonoma	Mendocino Twp	91	287
Smith	43	m	w	MI	Trinity	North Fork Twp	92	219
Stephens S	48	m	w	OH	San Francisco	8-Wd San Francisco	82	329
Sylvester	48	m	w	CT	Sonoma	Petaluma Twp	91	330
T	63	m	w	MA	Santa Clara	Gilroy Twp	88	69
Theo	31	m	w	DENM	Butte	Chico Twp	70	50
Theodore W	37	m	w	NY	Yuba	North East Twp	93	643
Thomas	44	m	w	ENGL	Los Angeles	Los Angeles Twp	73	480
Thomas	27	m	w	CA	Los Angeles	Los Angeles Twp	73	481
Thos H	30	m	w	OH	San Francisco	San Francisco P O	83	275
Thos W	32	m	w	NY	San Francisco	San Francisco P O	85	730
Victor T	41	m	w	NY	San Francisco	6-Wd San Francisco	81	90
Volney	47	m	w	IL	Monterey	San Juan Twp	74	389
W S	46	m	w	NY	Solano	Vallejo	90	159
Weaver M	57	m	w	PA	Tuolumne	Sonora P O	93	320
William	55	m	b	VA	Napa	Napa Twp	75	69
William	50	m	w	MA	San Francisco	3-Wd San Francisco	79	289
William	34	m	w	CT	San Francisco	8-Wd San Francisco	82	379
William	30	m	w	IL	San Bernardino	San Bernardino Twp	78	452
William	21	m	w	PA	Humboldt	Bald Hills	72	239
William	12	m	w	MO	Merced	Snelling P O	74	266
William J	29	m	w	ME	Los Angeles	Los Nietos Twp	73	585
William N	66	m	w	MA	Yolo	Washington Twp	93	533
Willis	11	m	w	CA	Yolo	Putah Twp	93	524
Wm	57	m	w	NJ	Alameda	Murray Twp	68	114
Wm	50	m	w	MA	San Francisco	2-Wd San Francisco	79	217
Wm	48	m	w	ENGL	Yuba	Linda Twp	93	556
Wm	42	m	w	ENGL	San Francisco	San Francisco P O	83	73
Wm	40	m	w	NY	Sacramento	Lee Twp	77	158
Wm	38	m	w	OH	San Joaquin	Elkhorn Twp	86	66
Wm	35	m	w	MO	Sonoma	Russian Rvr	91	378
Wm	33	m	w	TN	San Joaquin	Elliott Twp	86	73
Wm H J	34	m	w	CT	San Francisco	2-Wd San Francisco	79	210
Wm K	42	m	w	TN	Sonoma	Mendocino Twp	91	288
Wm R	29	m	w	MO	Sonoma	Analy Twp	91	224
BROOKSHIRE								
Elij	49	m	w	NC	Sonoma	Mendocino Twp	91	287
BROOKSHOR								
James	20	m	w	TX	Los Angeles	Los Nietos Twp	73	576
BROOM								
Garbelle	48	m	w	FINL	San Francisco	3-Wd San Francisco	79	291
Jefferson G	22	m	w	OH	Yuba	New York Twp	93	638
BROOMSBERG								
Jos	36	m	w	FRAN	Sutter	Sutter Twp	92	116
BROONER								
Eliza	35	f	w	PA	Butte	Ophir Twp	70	104
BROPHEY								
James	42	m	w	IREL	Nevada	Bridgeport Twp	75	121
James	35	m	w	TN	Contra Costa	Martinez P O	71	443
James	29	m	w	IREL	El Dorado	Coloma Twp	72	6
BROPHY								
Bridget	75	f	w	IREL	San Francisco	San Francisco P O	85	868
E J	23	m	w	IL	Tehama	Deer Crk Twp	92	171
John	65	m	w	IREL	Alameda	Eden Twp	68	66
John	55	m	w	IREL	Santa Clara	1-Wd San Jose	88	225
John	43	m	w	IREL	Solano	Benicia	90	1
John	38	m	w	IREL	San Francisco	11-Wd San Francisc	84	580
John	26	m	w	CANA	Placer	Bath P O	76	460
John	24	m	w	IA	Alameda	Murray Twp	68	110
John T	32	m	w	NY	Los Angeles	Wilmington Twp	73	637
Martin	45	m	w	IREL	Alameda	Washington Twp	68	278
Martin	22	m	w	IREL	San Francisco	6-Wd San Francisco	81	92
Mary	28	f	w	IREL	San Francisco	San Francisco P O	85	868
Mary R	16	f	w	UT	Colusa	Spring Valley Twp	71	339
Michael	35	m	w	IREL	San Francisco	San Francisco P O	85	729
Michell	43	m	w	IREL	Los Angeles	Los Angeles Twp	73	473
Thos	34	m	w	CANA	Sutter	Sutter Twp	92	118
W B	63	m	w	IREL	Solano	Vallejo	90	171
BROQUARD								
Louis	49	m	w	FRAN	San Francisco	1-Wd San Francisco	79	49
BROQUART								
Denis	36	m	w	FRAN	San Francisco	1-Wd San Francisco	79	49
BRORDBOCK								
J	45	m	w	PRUS	Sierra	Forest Twp	89	531
BRORUS								
Henry	33	m	w	PRUS	San Francisco	San Francisco P O	85	831
BROSE								
Charles	54	m	w	PRUS	El Dorado	Salmon Falls Twp	72	131
BROSEN								
Charles	20	m	w	SWIT	Santa Clara	San Jose Twp	88	202
BROSLAR								
Hugh	22	m	w	IREL	Humboldt	Eureka Twp	72	277
BROSMAN								
Trim	27	m	w	IREL	Humboldt	Eureka Twp	72	277
BROSNAN								
Hurlbert	23	m	w	NY	Marin	San Rafael Twp	74	43
Michael	45	m	w	IREL	San Francisco	San Francisco P O	83	86
T C	35	m	w	NY	Amador	Volcano P O	69	377
BROSO								
Louis	40	m	w	CANA	El Dorado	Mud Springs Twp	72	82
BROSS								
George	39	m	w	BAVA	San Francisco	6-Wd San Francisco	81	113
Peter [Dr]	42	m	w	VA	Placer	Colfax P O	76	386
BROSSE								
Saml	42	m	w	PA	San Francisco	San Francisco P O	83	275
BROSSEAU								
Joseph	33	m	w	CANA	Nevada	Grass Valley Twp	75	156
BROSSLEY								
Thomas	30	m	w	IREL	Santa Clara	Santa Clara Twp	88	171
BROSTROM								
John	32	m	w	FINL	San Francisco	3-Wd San Francisco	79	291
BROTADO								
Ascinto	35	m	w	MEXI	Del Norte	Mountain Twp	71	474
BROTH								
James	53	m	w	ENGL	Contra Costa	Martinez P O	71	418
BROTHER								
Aldrick	34	m	w	IREL	San Francisco	11-Wd San Francisc	84	592
Alphemas	36	m	w	IREL	San Francisco	11-Wd San Francisc	84	592
Alusth	35	m	w	NY	San Francisco	11-Wd San Francisc	84	592
Augustin	33	m	w	FRAN	San Francisco	11-Wd San Francisc	84	592
Cianan	37	m	w	IREL	San Francisco	11-Wd San Francisc	84	592
Emelian	27	m	w	HDAR	San Francisco	11-Wd San Francisc	84	592
Eustace	41	m	w	IREL	San Francisco	11-Wd San Francisc	84	592
Farley	36	m	w	ENGL	Siskiyou	Yreka	89	662
Genebern	28	m	w	SWIT	San Francisco	11-Wd San Francisc	84	592
Joseph	39	m	w	IREL	San Francisco	11-Wd San Francisc	84	592
Justin	37	m	w	IREL	San Francisco	11-Wd San Francisc	84	592
Peter	41	m	w	IREL	San Francisco	11-Wd San Francisc	84	592
Sabinian	37	m	w	IREL	San Francisco	11-Wd San Francisc	84	592
BROTHERICK								
M	33	m	w	PORT	Alameda	Alameda	68	14
BROTHERLIN								
Jerrod	37	m	w	NY	Monterey	Castroville Twp	74	338
BROTHERS								
F M	28	m	w	IA	Mendocino	Round Valley Twp	74	216
Henry	41	m	w	KY	Santa Clara	Santa Clara Twp	88	140
Nathaniel	38	m	w	OH	Yolo	Cottonwood Twp	93	469
Thomas	46	m	w	MO	Santa Clara	Santa Clara Twp	88	144
Thomas	33	m	w	IREL	San Diego	San Diego	78	486
William	40	m	w	IREL	Nevada	Eureka Twp	75	130
William	40	m	w	MO	Santa Clara	2-Wd San Jose	88	322
William	26	m	w	PRUS	San Francisco	7-Wd San Francisco	81	223
Wm	44	m	w	PRUS	Calaveras	Copperopolis P O	70	238
Wm	37	m	w	IREL	Nevada	Nevada Twp	75	308
BROTHERSON								
Knud	23	m	w	DENM	Alameda	Eden Twp	68	59
William	39	m	w	PRUS	San Francisco	San Francisco P O	83	393
BROTHERTON								
Elisha	37	m	w	MI	Colusa	Colusa	71	291
Jas R	43	m	w	PA	Butte	Kimshew Tpw	70	83
R H	35	m	w	MD	Monterey	San Juan Twp	74	410
Robert	38	m	w	IREL	San Francisco	San Francisco P O	85	737
Thomas	41	m	w	MD	San Francisco	11-Wd San Francisc	84	548
BROTOBETH								
F	22	m	w	ITAL	San Joaquin	2-Wd Stockton	86	172
BROTON								
John L	44	m	w	ENGL	Humboldt	Eureka Twp	72	270
BROTT								
Francis	31	m	w	IN	Sonoma	Mendocino Twp	91	297
BROUCHER								
Jos	35	m	w	GERM	Solano	Vallejo	90	200
BROUCK								
Alexander	34	m	w	PRUS	San Francisco	San Francisco P O	80	351
BROUDER								
Green D	36	m	w	KY	Stanislaus	Branch Twp	92	5
Minerva	56	f	w	KY	Stanislaus	Branch Twp	92	5
BROUGH								
Albert	29	m	w	PRUS	Sacramento	2-Wd Sacramento	77	246
James	49	m	w	ENGL	San Francisco	1-Wd San Francisco	79	112
James	45	m	w	ENGL	Nevada	Grass Valley Twp	75	176
BROUGHAM								
John	36	m	w	IREL	San Francisco	1-Wd San Francisco	79	25
John	30	m	w	FINL	San Francisco	3-Wd San Francisco	79	295
BROUGHERTY								
Patrick	44	m	w	IREL	Nevada	Grass Valley Twp	75	214
BROUGHTON								
Chas	40	m	w	PA	San Joaquin	Dent Twp	86	23
Fredk	20	m	w	ENGL	San Francisco	1-Wd San Francisco	79	91
Job	42	m	w	KY	Santa Clara	Milpitas Twp	88	116
John	34	m	w	OH	Santa Cruz	Pajaro Twp	89	352
N S	43	m	w	AL	San Francisco	8-Wd San Francisco	82	323
Robt J	24	m	w	IREL	Santa Barbara	Las Cruces P O	87	516
Samuel	46	m	w	KY	Santa Clara	San Jose Twp	88	192
Wm W	33	m	w	NY	Santa Cruz	Santa Cruz	89	409
BROULS								
J	20	m	w	ITAL	Sierra	Butte Twp	89	511
BROUM								
Sam	44	m	w	ME	San Joaquin	1-Wd Stockton	86	120
BROUSEL								
John	51	m	w	PRUS	Shasta	Horsetown P O	89	507
BROUST								
Louis	36	m	w	FRAN	San Francisco	San Francisco P O	80	461
BROUTH								
Silas	29	m	w	IL	San Joaquin	1-Wd Stockton	86	155

© 2001 by Heritage Quest. All rights reserved.

Series M593

Name	Age	S	R	B-PL	County	Locale	Roll	Pg
BROVER								
George W	32	m	w	MO	Colusa	Colusa Twp	71	285
L	43	m	w	PRUS	Sierra	Downieville Twp	89	517
BROVO								
Donasasio	21	m	w	CA	Monterey	San Juan Twp	74	402
F R	54	m	w	MEXI	Monterey	San Juan Twp	74	401
Francisco	50	m	w	MEXI	Monterey	San Juan Twp	74	402
BROW								
Catherine	27	f	w	BAVA	Solano	Silveyville Twp	90	88
Ezra	38	m	w	CANA	Yuba	Marysville	93	584
Phillip	20	m	w	MA	Stanislaus	North Twp	92	67
BROWDER								
Albert	41	m	m	TX	Trinity	Weaverville Pct	92	226
William	44	m	w	KY	Stanislaus	Empire Twp	92	45
William	27	m	m	TX	Trinity	Weaverville Pct	92	230
BROWELL								
Charlotte	57	f	w	NY	San Francisco	7-Wd San Francisco	81	247
Jeremiah	42	m	w	ENGL	San Francisco	2-Wd San Francisco	79	200
BROWER								
A W	30	m	w	PRUS	San Francisco	San Francisco P O	83	276
Andrew J	35	m	w	NY	San Francisco	2-Wd San Francisco	79	165
Annie	40	f	w	HANO	San Francisco	San Francisco P O	85	819
Cellus	30	m	w	MA	San Francisco	San Francisco P O	83	274
Daniel	42	m	w	NY	San Francisco	2-Wd San Francisco	79	145
Elmer	13	m	w	CA	Napa	Napa Twp	75	72
H H	56	m	w	NJ	Napa	Napa Twp	75	72
Harry	39	m	w	HANO	Calaveras	Copperopolis P O	70	230
J D	49	m	w	NJ	Alameda	Alameda	68	18
J D	30	m	w	NY	Solano	Vallejo	90	156
James	25	m	w	ENGL	San Francisco	2-Wd San Francisco	79	183
John	45	m	w	BAVA	Contra Costa	Martinez P O	71	410
John D	52	m	w	NY	Solano	Suisun Twp	90	96
Margaret	33	f	w	IREL	Santa Clara	2-Wd San Jose	88	285
BROWHART								
Benj	29	m	w	PRUS	San Bernardino	San Bernardino Twp	78	415
BROWING								
Robert	24	m	w	ENGL	Alpine	Silver Mtn P O	69	307
Saml	22	m	w	TN	San Francisco	5-Wd San Francisco	81	10
BROWKEN								
M	65	m	m	MO	Amador	Sutter Crk P O	69	413
BROWLER								
Francis	39	m	w	GERM	San Joaquin	2-Wd Stockton	86	162
BROWLS								
James	51	m	w	TN	Placer	Alta P O	76	413
BROWMEN								
John A	25	m	w	SWED	El Dorado	Placerville Twp	72	100
BROWMER								
J T	42	m	w	MD	Sacramento	Sutter Twp	77	388
BROWN								
---	28	m	w	ME	Yuba	Marysville	93	617
---	26	m	w	ME	Yuba	Marysville	93	617
--- Miss	35	f	w	IREL	Alameda	Oakland	68	179
A	50	m	w	SWIT	Del Norte	Happy Camp Twp	71	471
A	47	f	b	MA	Alameda	Oakland	68	177
A	38	m	w	MA	Alameda	Oakland	68	264
A	35	m	w	MA	Alameda	Oakland	68	212
A	22	m	w	IREL	Alameda	Murray Twp	68	100
A	19	f	w	CA	Alameda	Oakland	68	237
A B	47	m	w	NY	Alameda	Oakland	68	140
A B	45	m	w	NY	Yuba	Marysville	93	585
A C	61	m	w	MA	Alameda	Oakland	68	237
A C	54	m	w	MO	Amador	Jackson P O	69	324
A C	28	f	w	WI	Sacramento	3-Wd Sacramento	77	259
A G	68	m	w	ME	San Joaquin	1-Wd Stockton	86	138
A G	68	m	w	ME	San Joaquin	1-Wd Stockton	86	129
A H	31	m	w	IREL	Alameda	Oakland	68	202
A S	62	m	w	NY	Sutter	Butte Twp	92	103
A S	37	m	w	AR	Sutter	Sutter Twp	92	118
Aaron	56	m	w	OH	Alpine	Markleeville P O	69	311
Aaron	30	m	w	POLA	San Francisco	8-Wd San Francisco	82	310
Aaron	30	m	w	HDAR	San Francisco	8-Wd San Francisco	82	304
Ab	24	m	w	MO	Alameda	Alameda	68	12
Abba	27	m	w	CANA	Plumas	Quartz Twp	77	42
Abbot R	38	m	w	MO	Yuba	Slate Range Bar Tw	93	673
Abbott	14	m	w	ME	Butte	Oroville Twp	70	139
Abner	41	m	w	RI	Sierra	Gibson Twp	89	542
Abraham	53	m	w	PA	El Dorado	Mud Springs Twp	72	77
Abraham	45	m	m	PA	San Francisco	San Francisco P O	80	357
Abraham A	37	m	w	RI	El Dorado	Placerville	72	111
Abraham I J	53	m	w	VA	El Dorado	Placerville Twp	72	106
Absalom	45	m	w	MO	El Dorado	Mud Springs Twp	72	75
Ada	35	f	w	CHIL	San Francisco	8-Wd San Francisco	82	369
Adam	58	m	w	ENGL	Monterey	Castroville Twp	74	336
Adam	35	m	b	DC	Tuolumne	Chinese Camp P O	93	387
Adin S	45	m	w	MI	Shasta	French Gulch P O	89	466
Adolph	54	m	w	FRAN	Siskiyou	Klamath Twp	89	600
Adolph	23	m	w	WURT	Nevada	Rough & Ready Twp	75	336
Adolphus	75	m	w	NY	Santa Cruz	Santa Cruz	89	434
Agnes	55	f	w	IREL	Alameda	Oakland	68	179
Agnes	49	f	w	SCOT	San Francisco	San Francisco P O	83	188
Aham	61	m	w	ENGL	Contra Costa	Martinez P O	71	400
Albert	35	m	w	PA	Santa Cruz	Santa Cruz	89	425
Albert	34	m	w	PRUS	San Francisco	2-Wd San Francisco	79	185
Albert	24	m	w	NY	San Francisco	6-Wd San Francisco	81	84
Albert	15	m	w	CA	Amador	Ione City P O	69	358
Alex	63	m	w	PA	San Francisco	2-Wd San Francisco	79	219
Alex	37	m	w	MA	Solano	Benicia	90	15
Alex B	35	m	w	RI	San Francisco	San Francisco P O	83	62
Alex F	33	m	w	KY	Marin	Tomales Twp	74	85
Alexander	42	m	w	OH	Calaveras	San Andreas P O	70	173
Alexander	38	m	w	TN	Contra Costa	Martinez P O	71	409
Alexander C	33	m	w	NY	Amador	Volcano P O	69	384
Alexander G	55	m	w	VA	Santa Barbara	Santa Barbara P O	87	458
Alfred A	33	m	w	PRUS	Tulare	Visalia	92	294
Alice	70	f	w	ME	San Francisco	11-Wd San Francisc	84	689
Allen	50	m	w	KY	Placer	Bath P O	76	454
Alois	34	m	w	PRUS	San Francisco	2-Wd San Francisco	79	283
Alonzo	51	m	w	VT	Sacramento	Brighton Twp	77	72
Alonzo	21	m	m	MA	San Francisco	8-Wd San Francisco	82	439
Alonzo F	49	m	w	NH	San Francisco	San Francisco P O	83	22
Amalia	24	f	b	WIND	San Francisco	6-Wd San Francisco	81	99
Amy	60	f	w	MO	Solano	Vacaville Twp	90	126
Andrew	55	m	w	NC	Yuba	Slate Range Bar Tw	93	673
Andrew	40	m	w	MI	Marin	Sausalito Twp	74	69
Andrew	38	m	w	IREL	San Francisco	San Francisco P O	85	852
Andrew	32	m	w	MO	Stanislaus	Empire Twp	92	33
Andrew	26	m	w	MA	San Francisco	San Francisco P O	80	474
Andrew	26	m	w	ENGL	Colusa	Colusa	71	288
Andrew	22	m	w	NORW	San Francisco	San Francisco P O	80	348
Andrew A	39	m	w	ENGL	San Francisco	3-Wd San Francisco	79	294
Andrew D	54	m	w	NY	Santa Barbara	Santa Barbara P O	87	491
Andrew D	35	m	w	MA	San Francisco	1-Wd San Francisco	79	116
Andrew J	43	m	w	KY	Nevada	Bridgeport Twp	75	112
Andrew J	38	m	w	ME	Colusa	Colusa	71	298
Andrew J	35	m	w	ME	Nevada	Eureka Twp	75	132
Andrew T	31	m	w	MO	Nevada	Rough & Ready Twp	75	334
Ann	51	f	w	IREL	Sacramento	Lee Twp	77	159
Ann	48	f	w	OH	Mendocino	Calpella Twp	74	190
Ann	24	f	w	SAXO	San Francisco	2-Wd San Francisco	79	275
Anna	33	f	w	SWIT	Monterey	San Antonio Twp	74	315
Anna	16	f	b	NY	San Francisco	San Francisco P O	80	417
Anna M	18	f	w	ME	Santa Clara	Santa Clara Twp	88	145
Annie	31	f	w	IREL	San Francisco	San Francisco P O	80	361
Annie	27	f	w	IREL	San Francisco	San Francisco P O	83	249
Annie	19	f	i	CA	Contra Costa	Martinez Twp	71	349
Anson	54	m	w	CANA	San Joaquin	Castoria Twp	86	6
Anson A	17	m	w	CA	El Dorado	Cosumnes Twp	72	17
Anthony	27	m	w	NY	Nevada	Eureka Twp	75	138
Antoine	30	m	w	CHIN	San Mateo	Half Moon Bay P O	87	395
Archibald	45	m	w	SCOT	San Francisco	San Francisco P O	83	207
Arietta	11	f	m	CA	San Francisco	San Francisco P O	83	37
Arthur	48	m	w	CT	Santa Barbara	San Buenaventura P	87	447
Arthur F	11	m	w	CA	Napa	Napa	75	5
Asher M	39	m	w	RI	Sonoma	Washington Twp	91	466
Ashur	33	m	w	CT	Yuba	Rose Bar Twp	93	657
Aug	40	m	w	PRUS	Butte	Ophir Twp	70	98
August	32	m	w	SWED	San Francisco	3-Wd San Francisco	79	292
August	30	m	w	SWED	San Francisco	San Francisco P O	80	334
August	26	m	w	FINL	San Francisco	1-Wd San Francisco	79	126
Augustus	38	m	w	ME	Mendocino	Big Rvr Twp	74	159
Augustus	34	m	w	IL	Stanislaus	Washington Twp	92	85
Augustus	23	m	w	MO	Monterey	San Antonio Twp	74	321
Augustus	21	m	w	ENGL	Santa Clara	Milpitas Twp	88	115
Augustus F	39	m	w	PRUS	San Francisco	8-Wd San Francisco	82	416
B	25	m	w	TN	Humboldt	Pacific Twp	72	291
B	17	f	w	CA	Sacramento	4-Wd Sacramento	77	327
B B	68	m	w	VT	Alameda	Oakland	68	185
B B	48	m	w	MA	Solano	Vallejo	90	217
B E	41	m	w	NY	San Joaquin	Douglas Twp	86	45
B F	55	m	w	ME	Sierra	Sierra Twp	89	563
B H	40	m	w	ME	San Joaquin	1-Wd Stockton	86	138
B W	50	m	w	NY	San Joaquin	1-Wd Stockton	86	120
Ben	24	m	w	PRUS	Solano	Vallejo	90	203
Benj	66	m	w	NY	Humboldt	Arcata Twp	72	233
Benj	42	m	w	MA	Solano	Vallejo	90	213
Benjamin	83	m	w	VA	Solano	Suisun Twp	90	104
Benjamin	54	m	w	SC	Kern	Bakersfield P O	73	361
Benjamin	45	m	w	NY	Inyo	Independence Twp	73	327
Benjamin	42	m	w	IN	Amador	Jackson P O	69	340
Benjamin	38	m	w	MO	Amador	Jackson P O	69	333
Benjamin C	35	m	w	RI	Santa Barbara	Santa Barbara P O	87	466
Betsey	34	f	i	CA	Del Norte	Crescent	71	463
Blackstein	27	m	w	TN	Humboldt	Pacific Twp	72	294
Brainard	26	m	w	VT	San Diego	San Diego	78	496
Brainard	26	m	w	VT	San Francisco	3-Wd San Francisco	79	330
Bridget	30	f	w	IREL	Yuba	Marysville	93	582
Byron	40	m	w	NY	Sacramento	Alabama Twp	77	60
Byron	31	m	w	NC	Solano	Montezuma Twp	90	67
Byron	25	m	w	NC	San Francisco	3-Wd San Francisco	79	297
C	44	m	w	TX	Yuba	Marysville	93	612
C	31	m	w	MA	Sacramento	1-Wd Sacramento	77	189
C A	24	m	w	OH	Santa Clara	Gilroy Twp	88	82
C H	40	m	w	SWIT	Alameda	Oakland	68	220
C H	30	m	w	IL	Sacramento	3-Wd Sacramento	77	318
C J	63	m	w	GERM	Tuolumne	Columbia P O	93	345
C L	35	m	w	OH	Yuba	Marysville	93	586
C M	28	m	w	IL	San Joaquin	Elliott Twp	86	72
C N	44	m	w	SWIT	El Dorado	Greenwood Twp	72	53
C W	31	m	w	SWED	San Francisco	San Francisco P O	83	36
Caleb	43	m	w	NJ	Butte	Bidwell Twp	70	1
Calvin	54	m	w	MA	Solano	Vallejo	90	198
Calvin	23	m	w	IL	Humboldt	Pacific Twp	72	296
Carl	19	m	w	OH	Sonoma	Sonoma Twp	91	439
Carlos	21	m	w	IL	Sonoma	Sonoma Twp	91	444

© 2001 by Heritage Quest. All rights reserved.

Name	Age	S	R	B-PL	County	Locale	Roll	Pg
Caroline	7	f	w	CA	Mendocino	Calpella Twp	74	185
Caroline	53	f	w	KY	Tulare	Visalia	92	296
Caroline B	52	f	w	ME	Yuba	New York Twp	93	637
Catharine	32	f	w	NY	San Francisco	San Francisco P O	83	304
Catherin	50	f	w	MA	San Francisco	8-Wd San Francisco	82	306
Catherine	35	f	w	RI	Santa Clara	Santa Clara Twp	88	166
Catherine	32	f	w	IREL	Santa Barbara	San Buenaventura P	87	430
Catherine K	60	f	w	NH	San Francisco	8-Wd San Francisco	82	421
Charles	8	m	w	CA	San Francisco	11-Wd San Francisc	84	706
Charles	8	m	w	ME	Yolo	Washington Twp	93	532
Charles	63	m	w	SCOT	Contra Costa	Martinez P O	71	443
Charles	63	m	w	FINL	Sacramento	Georgianna Twp	77	124
Charles	62	m	w	PRUS	Placer	Auburn P O	76	365
Charles	60	m	w	SWED	Nevada	Bridgeport Twp	75	120
Charles	57	m	w	ENGL	El Dorado	Salmon Falls Twp	72	132
Charles	55	m	w	DENM	San Francisco	San Francisco P O	83	345
Charles	51	m	w	NY	Santa Cruz	Santa Cruz	89	434
Charles	48	m	w	SWED	El Dorado	Mud Springs Twp	72	73
Charles	48	m	w	SWED	San Francisco	2-Wd San Francisco	79	170
Charles	45	m	w	DENM	San Francisco	7-Wd San Francisco	81	224
Charles	44	m	w	IREL	Sacramento	4-Wd Sacramento	77	321
Charles	43	m	w	PRUS	Placer	Bath P O	76	434
Charles	42	m	w	NY	Tulare	Visalia Twp	92	284
Charles	42	m	w	NORW	San Francisco	3-Wd San Francisco	79	293
Charles	40	m	w	MA	San Mateo	San Mateo P O	87	355
Charles	40	m	w	GERM	Yolo	Merritt Twp	93	507
Charles	40	m	w	US	San Mateo	Schoolhouse Statio	87	338
Charles	40	m	w	RUSS	Del Norte	Crescent	71	463
Charles	40	m	w	SWED	Sacramento	Georgianna Twp	77	126
Charles	40	m	w	SHOL	Yuba	Slate Range Bar Tw	93	671
Charles	39	m	w	NY	Santa Clara	1-Wd San Jose	88	268
Charles	37	m	w	BAVA	San Francisco	8-Wd San Francisco	82	449
Charles	37	m	w	OH	Humboldt	Bald Hills	72	238
Charles	36	m	w	DENM	Sonoma	Mendocino Twp	91	302
Charles	35	m	w	MS	Yolo	Cache Crk Twp	93	436
Charles	35	m	w	NY	Calaveras	San Andreas P O	70	209
Charles	35	m	w	PORT	Sacramento	Georgianna Twp	77	124
Charles	35	m	w	DENM	San Francisco	3-Wd San Francisco	79	292
Charles	34	m	w	NORW	Yolo	Cache Crk Twp	93	445
Charles	34	m	w	OH	Solano	Rio Vista Twp	90	71
Charles	34	m	w	MA	San Francisco	San Francisco P O	80	458
Charles	34	m	w	GERM	Marin	San Rafael Twp	74	46
Charles	33	m	w	SWED	San Francisco	3-Wd San Francisco	79	293
Charles	33	m	w	MA	San Francisco	2-Wd San Francisco	79	243
Charles	33	m	w	MA	San Francisco	7-Wd San Francisco	81	220
Charles	32	m	w	SWED	Mendocino	Albion & Big Rvr T	74	167
Charles	32	m	w	NORW	San Francisco	3-Wd San Francisco	79	287
Charles	32	m	w	MO	Amador	Ione City P O	69	359
Charles	31	m	w	GERM	Los Angeles	Los Angeles	73	546
Charles	31	m	w	CANA	Alameda	Washington Twp	68	283
Charles	30	m	w	ME	Amador	Ione City P O	69	358
Charles	30	m	w	PRUS	San Bernardino	San Bernardino Twp	78	453
Charles	29	m	w	SWED	San Francisco	3-Wd San Francisco	79	294
Charles	29	m	w	AUSL	San Francisco	San Francisco P O	83	399
Charles	28	m	w	AZOR	Marin	Sausalito Twp	74	68
Charles	28	m	w	SWED	Contra Costa	Martinez Twp	71	351
Charles	26	m	w	NY	San Francisco	3-Wd San Francisco	79	312
Charles	25	m	c	CHIN	Sutter	Butte Twp	92	99
Charles	25	m	w	PA	San Francisco	7-Wd San Francisco	81	188
Charles	24	m	w	FINL	Mendocino	Casper & Big Rvr	74	164
Charles	23	m	w	DENM	Mendocino	Navarro & Big Rvr	74	174
Charles	23	m	w	PRUS	San Francisco	San Francisco P O	80	336
Charles	21	m	w	PORT	Yuba	New York Twp	93	640
Charles	19	m	w	HAMB	San Francisco	San Francisco P O	83	75
Charles	19	m	w	CA	Stanislaus	Empire Twp	92	66
Charles	17	m	w	CA	Santa Clara	Fremont Twp	88	65
Charles	14	m	w	CA	Monterey	San Antonio Twp	74	323
Charles A	31	m	w	KY	Yolo	Cache Crk Twp	93	433
Charles E	23	m	w	AR	Stanislaus	Buena Vista Twp	92	15
Charles F	49	m	w	ME	Yuba	Long Bar Twp	93	562
Charles F	35	m	w	MA	San Diego	San Jacinto Dist	78	517
Charles L F	44	m	w	VT	Calaveras	San Andreas P O	70	188
Charlie	8	m	w	CA	San Francisco	San Francisco P O	83	358
Charlotte	22	f	w	SWED	San Francisco	San Francisco P O	85	866
Chas	55	m	w	NY	San Francisco	11-Wd San Francisc	84	568
Chas	53	m	w	IREL	San Mateo	San Mateo P O	87	360
Chas	43	m	w	ENGL	Humboldt	Table Bluff Twp	72	306
Chas	41	m	w	NY	San Francisco	1-Wd San Francisco	79	7
Chas	40	m	w	IL	Tehama	Tehama Twp	92	186
Chas	38	m	w	MEXI	San Francisco	1-Wd San Francisco	79	54
Chas	37	m	w	OH	Sutter	Butte Twp	92	88
Chas	37	m	w	BADE	San Francisco	1-Wd San Francisco	79	52
Chas	35	m	w	SWED	San Francisco	1-Wd San Francisco	79	70
Chas	29	m	w	MI	Butte	Ophir Twp	70	116
Chas	28	m	w	NY	Monterey	San Antonio Twp	74	323
Chas	25	m	w	WURT	Tehama	Antelope Twp	92	160
Chas	24	m	w	ENGL	San Francisco	1-Wd San Francisco	79	127
Chas	22	m	w	NY	San Francisco	San Francisco P O	83	319
Chas	22	m	w	AZOR	San Francisco	1-Wd San Francisco	79	102
Chas	12	m	i	CA	San Luis Obispo	Santa Rosa Twp	87	319
Chas C	36	m	w	ME	San Francisco	7-Wd San Francisco	81	258
Chas E	25	m	w	ME	Sierra	Sears Twp	89	559
Chas F	45	m	w	MA	San Francisco	7-Wd San Francisco	81	240
Chas G	20	m	w	ME	Humboldt	Bucksport Twp	72	243
Chas H	31	m	w	ENGL	San Francisco	5-Wd San Francisco	81	29
Chas M	42	m	w	PA	Napa	Napa	75	47
Chester	60	m	w	ME	San Francisco	San Francisco P O	83	175
Christian	37	m	w	DENM	San Francisco	San Francisco P O	83	50
Christian	29	m	w	NORW	Sonoma	Salt Point	91	393
Christian	28	m	w	SWED	Sonoma	Bodega Twp	91	264
Christiana	33	f	w	IA	Monterey	Pajaro Twp	74	376
Christina	25	f	w	PA	San Joaquin	2-Wd Stockton	86	183
Christopher	47	m	m	PA	Los Angeles	Los Angeles Twp	73	481
Christopher W	39	m	w	SAXO	Santa Clara	Fremont Twp	88	53
Chs	46	m	w	IREL	San Francisco	2-Wd San Francisco	79	215
Chs A	27	m	w	IREL	San Francisco	2-Wd San Francisco	79	205
Clara S	45	f	w	OH	Yolo	Cache Crk Twp	93	424
Clark	52	m	w	NY	Contra Costa	Martinez P O	71	452
Clement	34	m	w	NORW	San Francisco	7-Wd San Francisco	81	274
Clinton T	20	m	w	NY	Tulare	Tule Rvr Twp	92	271
Coolidge B	43	m	w	VT	El Dorado	Placerville	72	113
Cornelius	29	m	w	ENGL	Santa Clara	1-Wd San Jose	88	261
Cris	40	m	w	GERM	Solano	Vallejo	90	166
Cyrenus A	21	m	w	MI	Nevada	Little York Twp	75	237
Cyrus	43	m	w	ME	Yuba	Rose Bar Twp	93	655
Cyrus	19	m	w	ME	San Francisco	11-Wd San Francisc	84	518
D	58	m	b	VA	Sierra	Downieville Twp	89	518
Daniel	53	m	w	NY	San Francisco	11-Wd San Francisc	84	540
Daniel	48	m	w	NJ	Sacramento	4-Wd Sacramento	77	342
Daniel	39	m	w	IREL	Sonoma	Petaluma Twp	91	315
Daniel	35	m	w	NY	San Francisco	11-Wd San Francisc	84	535
Daniel	24	m	w	NY	San Francisco	8-Wd San Francisco	82	369
Daniel	23	m	w	IREL	San Francisco	San Francisco P O	83	142
Daniel H	31	m	w	IL	Amador	Volcano P O	69	381
Danl	60	m	w	OH	Solano	Vallejo	90	210
Danl H	25	m	w	MA	Butte	Chico Twp	70	20
David	70	m	w	IREL	Monterey	Pajaro Twp	74	370
David	55	m	w	NY	Nevada	Rough & Ready Twp	75	331
David	53	m	b	MD	Amador	Ione City P O	69	353
David	42	m	w	OH	Colusa	Monroe Twp	71	318
David	36	m	w	ENGL	San Francisco	San Francisco P O	80	362
David	34	m	w	CANA	Marin	San Rafael Twp	74	33
David	27	m	w	IREL	San Francisco	San Francisco P O	80	540
David	27	m	w	NY	Sacramento	4-Wd Sacramento	77	328
David	25	m	w	NY	Placer	Newcastle Twp	76	478
David B	45	m	w	IREL	San Francisco	2-Wd San Francisco	79	202
Davis	32	m	w	IREL	Sacramento	2-Wd Sacramento	77	239
Deitrick	45	m	w	OLDE	Alameda	Alvarado	68	302
Dianna	57	f	b	TN	Sacramento	2-Wd Sacramento	77	238
Dick	19	m	w	CA	Sacramento	4-Wd Sacramento	77	363
Dilla	30	f	w	NY	Santa Clara	San Jose Twp	88	214
Dominick	30	m	w	IREL	San Francisco	San Francisco P O	80	360
Dora	7	f	w	CA	San Francisco	San Francisco P O	85	827
Dorius	25	m	w	CANA	Sacramento	Brighton Twp	77	73
Duncan	33	m	w	NY	San Francisco	5-Wd San Francisco	81	30
Duncan	29	m	w	CANA	Marin	San Rafael	74	58
Dustin B	48	m	w	NY	Solano	Maine Prairie Twp	90	50
Dyer	66	m	w	CANA	Stanislaus	Washington Twp	92	85
E	55	m	w	ENGL	El Dorado	Greenwood Twp	72	55
E	54	m	w	MA	Alameda	Oakland	68	206
E	29	m	w	NY	Yuba	Marysville	93	591
E	19	m	w	HANO	Calaveras	Copperopolis P O	70	231
E C	17	m	w	CA	Alameda	Oakland	68	243
E E	23	m	w	NY	Solano	Vallejo	90	200
E J	43	f	w	MD	Sacramento	1-Wd Sacramento	77	186
E J	40	m	w	PA	Siskiyou	Scott Rvr Twp	89	604
E Mrs	23	f	w	IL	Napa	Napa Twp	75	46
E P	35	m	w	ME	San Joaquin	2-Wd Stockton	86	175
E W	31	m	w	ME	Nevada	Eureka Twp	75	130
Eben	39	m	w	OH	Butte	Ophir Twp	70	98
Ed	34	m	w	IREL	Sierra	Gibson Twp	89	542
Edgar	42	m	w	CT	Sacramento	2-Wd Sacramento	77	247
Edgar	23	m	w	MA	Nevada	Nevada Twp	75	321
Edgar	23	m	w	MA	Nevada	Little York Twp	75	245
Edmond	52	m	w	ENGL	Sacramento	Franklin Twp	77	115
Edw V	50	m	w	VA	Siskiyou	Yreka	89	654
Edward	51	m	w	WALE	Sierra	Sears Twp	89	557
Edward	48	m	w	VA	Inyo	Lone Pine Twp	73	330
Edward	44	m	w	NJ	San Francisco	8-Wd San Francisco	82	354
Edward	43	m	w	IREL	Napa	Napa	75	19
Edward	42	m	w	MI	Yolo	Cache Crk Twp	93	425
Edward	37	m	w	TX	Siskiyou	Scott Valley Twp	89	614
Edward	36	m	w	IREL	San Francisco	San Francisco P O	83	384
Edward	30	m	w	ENGL	San Francisco	San Francisco P O	85	730
Edward	28	m	w	MO	Colusa	Spring Valley Twp	71	339
Edward	25	m	w	NY	Los Angeles	Wilmington Twp	73	638
Edward	25	m	w	US	Humboldt	Eureka Twp	72	277
Edward	24	m	w	VA	San Francisco	11-Wd San Francisc	84	512
Edward	24	m	w	PRUS	San Francisco	8-Wd San Francisco	82	349
Edward	23	m	w	ENGL	Napa	Napa Twp	75	32
Edward	21	m	w	ME	Alameda	Oakland	68	142
Edward	19	m	w	OH	Marin	Tomales Twp	74	87
Edward	16	m	w	NY	San Francisco	7-Wd San Francisco	81	159
Edward L	66	m	w	VA	Yolo	Putah Twp	93	516
Edward L Jr	37	m	w	VA	Yolo	Putah Twp	93	516
Edwd	51	m	w	ENGL	Marin	San Rafael Twp	74	43
Edwd	31	m	w	IREL	Butte	Chico Twp	70	25
Edwin	26	m	w	ENGL	Nevada	Nevada Twp	75	301
Edwin C	28	m	w	BELG	San Francisco	1-Wd San Francisco	79	129
Egnacio	19	m	w	CA	Placer	Bath P O	76	427
Elam	73	m	w	NY	Contra Costa	Martinez P O	71	373
Eleanor	57	f	w	MA	San Francisco	11-Wd San Francisc	84	498
Elias	40	m	w	PA	Sacramento	4-Wd Sacramento	77	330
Elias	30	m	w	POLA	Sonoma	Santa Rosa	91	402

© 2001 by Heritage Quest. All rights reserved.

Name	Age	S	R	B-PL	County	Locale	Roll	Pg
Elijah W	43	m	w	CT	Nevada	Rough & Ready Twp	75	335
Elijah W	37	m	w	MO	Yolo	Putah Twp	93	510
Elisa A	55	f	w	MD	Santa Cruz	Watsonville	89	371
Elisha	34	m	w	ME	San Bernardino	San Bernardino Twp	78	447
Eliza	48	f	w	NH	San Francisco	San Francisco P O	83	172
Eliza	14	f	w	MO	Santa Cruz	Santa Cruz	89	417
Eliza J	40	f	w	MD	Nevada	Rough & Ready Twp	75	326
Elizabeth	44	f	w	ENGL	Tuolumne	Sonora P O	93	324
Elizabeth	32	f	w	TN	Sonoma	Healdsburg & Mendo	91	284
Elizabeth	30	f	w	IREL	San Francisco	1-Wd San Francisco	79	98
Elizabeth	21	f	w	ME	Butte	Ophir Twp	70	96
Elizabeth	18	f	w	MA	San Francisco	San Francisco P O	80	414
Elizabeth	16	f	w	NY	San Francisco	8-Wd San Francisco	82	445
Elizabeth B	39	f	b	MS	San Francisco	San Francisco P O	85	752
Ella	11	f	w	PA	San Francisco	San Francisco P O	83	184
Ellen	45	f	w	IREL	San Francisco	8-Wd San Francisco	82	319
Ellen	42	f	w	IN	Santa Clara	Almaden Twp	88	2
Ellen	32	f	w	ENGL	San Francisco	7-Wd San Francisco	81	227
Ellen	31	f	m	MS	Sacramento	2-Wd Sacramento	77	241
Ellen	27	f	w	PA	Los Angeles	Wilmington Twp	73	634
Ellen	22	f	w	CA	San Diego	San Diego	78	502
Ellenor	32	f	m	MD	San Francisco	San Francisco P O	80	486
Emanuel	40	m	w	GREE	Plumas	Quartz Twp	77	35
Emanuel	26	m	w	HUNG	San Francisco	2-Wd San Francisco	79	169
Emanuel	25	m	w	PORT	Sierra	Gibson Twp	89	538
Emanuel	21	m	w	PORT	Alameda	Washington Twp	68	268
Emanul	28	m	w	IL	Napa	Napa Twp	75	31
Emely	24	f	w	ME	Yuba	Marysville	93	597
Emily	31	f	w	IN	Nevada	Rough & Ready Twp	75	334
Emily	21	f	w	LA	Santa Clara	1-Wd San Jose	88	236
Eml	30	m	w	PORT	Sierra	Sears Twp	89	561
Ephraim	65	m	w	NY	Shasta	French Gulch P O	89	467
Erasmus	40	m	w	NY	Alameda	Hayward	68	76
Erastus	21	m	w	CANA	Alameda	Eden Twp	68	71
Eugene	35	m	w	ME	Mendocino	Big Rvr Twp	74	159
Evalina	15	f	w	TX	Sonoma	Salt Point Twp	91	382
Evander	45	m	w	NH	Calaveras	Copperopolis P O	70	251
Eveline	16	f	w	TX	Sonoma	Healdsburg & Mendo	91	279
Ezra	90	m	w	NY	Nevada	Bridgeport Twp	75	123
Ezra	90	m	w	NY	Sutter	Butte Twp	92	99
F	38	m	w	PRUS	Alameda	Alameda	68	5
F	37	m	w	CANA	Sierra	Sierra Twp	89	568
F	22	m	w	PARA	Sierra	Butte Twp	89	511
F M	75	f	w	ENGL	Solano	Benicia	90	1
Fanny	35	f	w	NY	San Francisco	6-Wd San Francisco	81	79
Fanny	25	f	w	IL	San Francisco	6-Wd San Francisco	81	78
Fanny E	14	f	w	CANA	Sierra	Eureka Twp	89	526
Ferdenand	29	m	w	BADE	Colusa	Colusa	71	296
Ferdinand	53	m	w	ME	Butte	Mountain Spring Tw	70	88
Florence	18	f	w	IN	San Francisco	San Francisco P O	83	99
Florence	16	f	w	IL	Humboldt	Eureka Twp	72	257
Frances	14	f	w	CA	Santa Clara	Gilroy Twp	88	84
Francis	38	m	w	NY	Shasta	Fort Crook P O	89	473
Francis	33	m	w	ENGL	Plumas	Indian Twp	77	15
Francis	25	f	w	KY	Sonoma	Petaluma Twp	91	339
Francis	12	m	w	CA	San Francisco	San Francisco P O	85	827
Francis M	31	m	w	IL	Humboldt	Bucksport Twp	72	242
Francis M	30	m	w	IN	Yolo	Cache Crk Twp	93	431
Francisco	28	m	w	AZOR	Contra Costa	Martinez P O	71	386
Frank	40	m	w	ME	Santa Barbara	Santa Barbara P O	87	496
Frank	28	m	w	PRUS	Humboldt	Eureka Twp	72	280
Frank	27	m	w	PRUS	Colusa	Monroe Twp	71	314
Frank	23	m	w	OH	Santa Clara	2-Wd San Jose	88	305
Frank	22	m	w	PORT	San Mateo	Pescadero P O	87	415
Frank	21	m	w	NY	San Diego	Coronado	78	466
Frank	21	m	w	NY	Humboldt	Arcata Twp	72	232
Frank L	18	m	w	IL	Alpine	Woodfords P O	69	309
Frank Q	55	m	w	NY	San Francisco	San Francisco P O	83	62
Frank V	35	m	w	AZOR	Monterey	Castroville Twp	74	334
Fred	50	m	w	FRNK	Amador	Drytown P O	69	422
Fred	35	m	w	OH	Contra Costa	Martinez P O	71	447
Fred	28	m	w	GERM	Solano	Vallejo	90	212
Fred	26	m	w	ME	Humboldt	Eureka Twp	72	279
Fred G	38	m	w	VT	San Francisco	6-Wd San Francisco	81	98
Frederick	40	m	w	RI	Humboldt	Eureka Twp	72	260
Frederick	40	m	w	RI	Humboldt	Eureka Twp	72	279
Frederick	40	m	w	ME	Mendocino	Big Rvr Twp	74	159
Frederick	39	m	w	NY	Santa Clara	1-Wd San Jose	88	268
Frederick	3	m	w	CA	San Francisco	2-Wd San Francisco	79	154
Frederick	11	m	w	IA	Monterey	Castroville Twp	74	329
Fredrick	35	m	w	HDAR	San Francisco	San Francisco P O	80	332
Fredrick	30	m	w	PRUS	Napa	Napa Twp	75	32
Freelon	21	m	w	ME	Marin	Tomales Twp	74	79
G	28	m	w	IL	San Joaquin	Castoria Twp	86	13
G C	43	m	w	PA	Humboldt	Arcata Twp	72	235
G F	31	m	w	NY	Sutter	Yuba Twp	92	148
G M	41	m	w	TN	Klamath	Orleans Twp	73	380
G N	26	m	w	ME	Sierra	Sierra Twp	89	563
G W	58	m	w	VA	Sutter	Nicolaus Twp	92	108
G W	52	m	w	PA	Sacramento	3-Wd Sacramento	77	293
G W	49	m	w	MO	Sutter	Butte Twp	92	100
G W	34	m	w	ME	Amador	Ione City P O	69	357
Gallant	32	m	w	GA	Tulare	Tule Rvr Twp	92	258
Geo	57	m	w	ME	San Joaquin	1-Wd Stockton	86	150
Geo	52	m	w	PA	Butte	Chico Twp	70	56
Geo	47	m	w	ENGL	El Dorado	Georgetown Twp	72	49
Geo	45	m	w	VT	Butte	Chico Twp	70	29
Geo	45	m	w	MO	San Francisco	11-Wd San Francisc	84	613
Geo	39	m	w	MO	San Joaquin	1-Wd Stockton	86	121
Geo	32	m	w	IN	Tehama	Deer Crk Twp	92	170
Geo	32	m	w	NY	San Francisco	1-Wd San Francisco	79	130
Geo H	25	m	w	NY	San Francisco	1-Wd San Francisco	79	63
Geo T	30	m	w	NY	Merced	Snelling P O	74	277
Geo W	43	m	w	AL	Shasta	Stillwater P O	89	481
Geo W	40	m	w	IN	Mendocino	Calpella Twp	74	186
Geo W	35	m	w	OH	Yuba	New York Twp	93	642
Geo W	27	m	w	VT	San Francisco	8-Wd San Francisco	82	316
Geo W	21	m	w	PA	Nevada	Meadow Lake Twp	75	255
George	51	m	b	MA	Napa	Napa	75	34
George	50	m	w	IREL	San Francisco	San Francisco P O	83	348
George	45	m	w	ME	Alameda	Hayward	68	79
George	43	m	w	ENGL	Monterey	San Benito Twp	74	379
George	41	m	w	PRUS	Calaveras	San Andreas P O	70	186
George	40	m	w	ENGL	Santa Cruz	Santa Cruz Twp	89	393
George	40	m	w	IREL	San Francisco	11-Wd San Francisc	84	649
George	40	m	w	IREL	Kern	Kernville P O	73	367
George	40	m	w	ENGL	Mariposa	Mariposa P O	74	107
George	38	m	w	PA	El Dorado	Mud Springs Twp	72	77
George	37	m	w	NY	Placer	Bath P O	76	440
George	37	m	w	KY	Colusa	Spring Valley Twp	71	340
George	35	m	w	PRUS	Napa	Napa	75	18
George	35	m	w	PRUS	San Francisco	8-Wd San Francisco	82	323
George	31	m	w	IREL	San Mateo	Menlo Park P O	87	378
George	30	m	w	ENGL	Santa Cruz	Santa Cruz Twp	89	395
George	30	m	w	IREL	San Francisco	San Francisco P O	83	241
George	30	m	w	IL	Placer	Lincoln P O	76	491
George	30	m	w	PRUS	Napa	Napa	75	9
George	30	m	w	PRUS	Santa Barbara	Santa Barbara P O	87	481
George	27	m	w	MA	Sacramento	2-Wd Sacramento	77	253
George	27	m	w	MALT	Marin	San Rafael Twp	74	37
George	27	m	w	IN	Sonoma	Salt Point	91	381
George	24	m	w	CANA	San Luis Obispo	Arroyo Grande Twp	87	274
George	23	m	w	MI	Marin	Point Reyes Twp	74	23
George	21	m	w	NY	San Mateo	Belmont P O	87	388
George	21	m	w	HAMB	San Diego	Julian Dist	78	470
George	20	m	w	PORT	Alameda	Eden Twp	68	82
George	18	m	w	MA	San Francisco	7-Wd San Francisco	81	185
George C	40	m	w	CT	Klamath	South Fork Twp	73	384
George C	37	m	w	MI	San Mateo	Half Moon Bay P O	87	398
George E	42	m	w	ENGL	Plumas	Mineral Twp	77	22
George F	44	m	w	MA	Contra Costa	Martinez P O	71	389
George Henry	50	m	w	MA	San Francisco	San Francisco P O	83	175
George L	27	m	w	MA	Santa Clara	2-Wd San Jose	88	329
George M	52	m	w	NY	Nevada	Rough & Ready Twp	75	325
George M	28	m	w	ENGL	Santa Clara	Santa Clara Twp	88	147
George N	53	m	w	IREL	Nevada	Grass Valley Twp	75	201
George N	1	m	w	CA	San Francisco	San Francisco P O	83	191
George S	34	m	w	OH	Alameda	Oakland	68	156
George W	53	m	w	NY	Yolo	Cache Crk Twp	93	448
George W	40	m	m	MD	Placer	Clipper Gap P O	76	376
George Wm	33	m	w	OH	Plumas	Mineral Twp	77	21
Giles S	46	m	w	PA	Nevada	Little York Twp	75	241
Gilman G	39	m	w	NH	Butte	Chico Twp	70	13
Godner	25	m	w	MA	Monterey	San Juan Twp	74	397
Grafton T	29	m	m	PA	San Francisco	6-Wd San Francisco	81	41
Gustave	44	m	w	PRUS	Butte	Ophir Twp	70	110
Gustave	33	m	w	BAVA	Santa Cruz	Santa Cruz Twp	89	396
Gustavus	37	m	w	KY	San Francisco	San Francisco P O	83	340
H	64	m	w	NC	Lake	Coyote Valley	73	401
H	52	m	w	PRUS	Sierra	Butte Twp	89	511
H	40	m	w	NY	Sacramento	3-Wd Sacramento	77	288
H	40	m	w	SCOT	Alameda	Murray Twp	68	119
H C	33	m	w	MO	Monterey	San Juan Twp	74	387
H E	28	m	w	IL	Solano	Vallejo	90	178
H F M	52	m	w	IL	Alameda	Oakland	68	155
H H	38	m	w	IL	San Joaquin	Elliott Twp	86	73
H J	41	m	w	MO	Lassen	Susanville Twp	73	445
H K	41	m	w	PA	Nevada	Meadow Lake Twp	75	247
H P	17	f	w	CA	Alameda	Oakland	68	257
H R	38	m	w	MA	Sierra	Table Rock Twp	89	577
H R	37	m	w	MA	Humboldt	Eureka Twp	72	258
H S	47	m	w	NY	Alameda	Oakland	68	180
H W	39	m	w	MA	Sacramento	3-Wd Sacramento	77	300
Hamilton	46	m	w	MO	Plumas	Mineral Twp	77	25
Hamilton	46	m	w	MO	Plumas	Plumas Twp	77	33
Hannah	23	f	w	IREL	San Joaquin	1-Wd Stockton	86	136
Hark	40	m	w	BADE	Butte	Chico Twp	70	47
Harriett	60	f	b	VA	Yolo	Washington Twp	93	533
Harry	45	m	w	BREM	Placer	Dutch Flat P O	76	414
Haw E	30	m	w	MO	Sonoma	Santa Rosa	91	403
Helen	38	f	w	IREL	Solano	Vallejo	90	199
Henderson	45	m	w	KY	Yolo	Cache Crk Twp	93	444
Henery	40	m	w	MA	San Francisco	7-Wd San Francisco	81	178
Henery	40	m	w	SWED	San Francisco	7-Wd San Francisco	81	217
Henery	30	m	w	BAVA	San Francisco	7-Wd San Francisco	81	165
Henery	25	m	w	HANO	San Francisco	7-Wd San Francisco	81	218
Henery	25	m	w	HOLL	San Francisco	7-Wd San Francisco	81	220
Henry	63	m	w	NY	Contra Costa	Martinez P O	71	411
Henry	59	m	w	ENGL	Humboldt	Mattole Twp	72	283
Henry	52	m	w	CANA	Yuba	North East Twp	93	644
Henry	50	m	w	ENGL	Napa	Napa	75	35
Henry	45	m	w	SCOT	Santa Cruz	Santa Cruz Twp	89	398
Henry	43	m	w	NY	Tuolumne	Sonora P O	93	331
Henry	42	m	w	PRUS	San Francisco	8-Wd San Francisco	82	364

© 2001 by Heritage Quest. All rights reserved.

Name	Age	S	R	B-PL	County	Locale	Series M593 Roll	Pg
Henry	40	m	w	CANA	Merced	Snelling P O	74	261
Henry	40	m	w	OH	Sutter	Butte Twp	92	104
Henry	40	m	w	SHOL	San Francisco	3-Wd San Francisco	79	287
Henry	38	m	w	PRUS	Solano	Green Valley Twp	90	41
Henry	38	m	w	NORW	San Francisco	1-Wd San Francisco	79	126
Henry	37	m	m	NY	San Francisco	6-Wd San Francisco	81	110
Henry	34	m	w	PRUS	San Francisco	3-Wd San Francisco	79	311
Henry	34	m	w	NY	Contra Costa	Martinez P O	71	441
Henry	32	m	w	NY	Contra Costa	Martinez P O	71	415
Henry	31	m	b	MD	Los Angeles	Los Angeles	73	541
Henry	30	m	w	MA	San Francisco	11-Wd San Francisc	84	656
Henry	28	m	w	IREL	San Francisco	11-Wd San Francisc	84	621
Henry	28	m	w	TN	Sacramento	Lee Twp	77	160
Henry	24	m	w	HDAR	Plumas	Quartz Twp	77	42
Henry	24	m	w	BREM	San Francisco	San Francisco P O	80	338
Henry	22	m	w	ENGL	Marin	San Rafael Twp	74	46
Henry	20	m	w	HANO	Butte	Ophir Twp	70	116
Henry	19	m	w	CANA	Alameda	Eden Twp	68	71
Henry A	28	m	w	ME	Napa	Napa Twp	75	46
Henry C	27	m	w	IL	Sacramento	Franklin Twp	77	105
Henry D	40	m	w	VA	Nevada	Grass Valley Twp	75	154
Henry H	42	m	w	NH	Sacramento	2-Wd Sacramento	77	220
Henry H	41	m	w	NY	Placer	Gold Run Twp	76	399
Henry H	41	m	w	WA	San Diego	San Diego	78	496
Henry J	28	m	w	AUSL	San Francisco	San Francisco P O	83	183
Henry L	41	m	w	KY	Santa Clara	Fremont Twp	88	46
Henry L	22	m	w	NY	San Francisco	1-Wd San Francisco	79	63
Henry N	49	m	w	OH	Sacramento	Georgianna Twp	77	128
Henry W	47	m	w	OH	Colusa	Stony Crk Twp	71	330
Heny	28	m	w	MA	Butte	Chico Twp	70	32
Heny J	38	m	w	IREL	Butte	Chico Twp	70	18
Herman	32	m	w	BADE	San Francisco	2-Wd San Francisco	79	213
Herrman	34	m	w	RUSS	San Francisco	San Francisco P O	83	405
Hiram	37	m	w	OH	Sonoma	Bodega Twp	91	259
Hiram	36	m	w	ME	Calaveras	Copperopolis P O	70	262
Hiram	30	m	w	IREL	Solano	Denverton Twp	90	23
Hiram W	35	m	w	MO	Yolo	Grafton Twp	93	485
Horace	34	m	w	ME	Butte	Wyandotte Twp	70	141
Horace H	33	m	w	ME	Butte	Ophir Twp	70	96
Hugh	50	m	w	NC	San Diego	Julian Dist	78	473
Hugh	40	m	w	MO	Santa Clara	Fremont Twp	88	43
Hull	41	m	w	NY	San Francisco	San Francisco P O	80	411
I	59	m	w	MO	Nevada	Eureka Twp	75	132
Irason	42	m	w	ME	San Francisco	11-Wd San Francisc	84	571
Irene	23	f	w	NY	Sacramento	3-Wd Sacramento	77	263
Isaac	45	m	w	OH	San Joaquin	1-Wd Stockton	86	150
Isaac	44	m	w	NY	Humboldt	Mattole Twp	72	286
Isaac	40	m	b	VA	Yuba	East Bear Rvr Twp	93	540
Isaac	28	m	w	AR	Contra Costa	Martinez P O	71	368
Isaac E	49	m	w	ME	Yuba	New York Twp	93	638
Isaac S	30	m	w	NY	Sacramento	2-Wd Sacramento	77	244
Isaac Wm	34	m	w	OH	San Francisco	San Francisco P O	83	27
Isabella	14	f	w	US	Nevada	Grass Valley Twp	75	229
J	42	m	w	NC	Lake	Morgan Valley	73	425
J	40	m	w	NY	Alameda	Oakland	68	262
J	40	m	w	CANA	Solano	Vallejo	90	208
J	39	m	w	US	San Joaquin	Castoria Twp	86	9
J	34	m	w	ENGL	San Joaquin	Liberty Twp	86	95
J	31	m	w	NY	Alameda	Oakland	68	237
J	21	m	w	NY	Calaveras	Copperopolis P O	70	225
J A	34	m	w	KY	San Joaquin	Liberty Twp	86	86
J B	33	m	w	OH	Humboldt	Eureka Twp	72	274
J C	53	m	w	PA	Monterey	Alisal Twp	74	294
J C	40	m	w	TN	Sutter	Butte Twp	92	92
J Charles	22	m	w	KY	San Francisco	5-Wd San Francisco	81	6
J Earl	24	m	w	RI	Nevada	Nevada Twp	75	276
J H	33	m	w	NY	Monterey	Alisal Twp	74	303
J H	32	m	b	MD	Alameda	Oakland	68	142
J K	36	m	w	IREL	Alameda	Oakland	68	262
J L	45	m	w	NY	Alameda	Oakland	68	157
J P	57	m	w	MA	Alameda	Oakland	68	193
J P	34	m	w	CANA	Lake	Lower Lake	73	415
J S	56	m	w	NY	Sacramento	3-Wd Sacramento	77	318
J S	41	m	w	MA	Yuba	Marysville	93	608
J S	37	m	w	NY	Monterey	San Juan Twp	74	388
J S	25	m	w	CANA	Klamath	Trinidad Twp	73	390
J W	53	m	w	NY	Amador	Jackson P O	69	328
J W	32	m	w	NY	Santa Clara	Gilroy Twp	88	79
J W	28	m	w	ME	Yuba	Marysville	93	617
Jack	41	m	w	NY	Yolo	Putah Twp	93	519
Jack	26	m	w	IL	Sacramento	Franklin Twp	77	112
Jackson	40	m	w	SCOT	Alameda	Brooklyn Twp	68	44
Jackson F	35	m	w	VT	Solano	Maine Prairie Twp	90	51
Jacob	30	m	w	FRAN	San Francisco	1-Wd San Francisco	79	88
Jacob	28	m	w	TN	Stanislaus	Branch Twp	92	3
Jacob	22	m	w	BAVA	Nevada	Meadow Lake Twp	75	247
Jacob	19	m	b	MO	Colusa	Butte Twp	71	269
Jacob Berry	43	m	w	CANA	Plumas	Indian Twp	77	10
Jacob L	21	m	w	CANA	Santa Clara	San Jose Twp	88	215
Jacob Newton	33	m	w	OH	Santa Clara	2-Wd San Jose	88	281
James	9	m	w	CA	San Francisco	5-Wd San Francisco	81	26
James	63	m	w	MS	Los Angeles	Los Nietos Twp	73	579
James	60	m	m	MD	San Francisco	2-Wd San Francisco	79	230
James	56	m	w	SC	Los Angeles	Los Angeles	73	503
James	50	m	b	DC	San Francisco	San Francisco P O	80	364
James	50	m	w	OH	Alameda	Oakland	68	140
James	49	m	w	ENGL	Tuolumne	Big Oak Flat P O	93	398
James	48	m	w	NY	Trinity	Lewiston Pct	92	212
James	48	m	w	ENGL	Napa	Napa	75	39
James	45	m	w	ENGL	Nevada	Grass Valley Twp	75	148
James	44	m	w	NY	San Francisco	5-Wd San Francisco	81	8
James	43	m	w	AUST	San Diego	San Pasqual	78	522
James	42	m	w	FRAN	Butte	Chico Twp	70	54
James	41	m	w	IREL	San Francisco	2-Wd San Francisco	79	214
James	40	m	w	OH	San Francisco	San Francisco P O	80	486
James	40	m	w	IREL	San Francisco	San Francisco P O	80	464
James	40	m	w	CANA	Monterey	Pajaro Twp	74	368
James	40	m	w	SWED	Tuolumne	Columbia P O	93	335
James	40	m	w	IREL	San Bernardino	San Bernardino Twp	78	451
James	40	m	w	PRUS	Colusa	Monroe Twp	71	321
James	38	m	w	NJ	Alpine	Silver Mtn P O	69	307
James	38	m	w	ENGL	San Francisco	San Francisco P O	83	80
James	38	m	w	NY	San Francisco	3-Wd San Francisco	79	298
James	37	m	w	IREL	Mendocino	Round Valley Twp	74	217
James	36	m	w	NY	San Francisco	San Francisco P O	80	472
James	36	m	w	GREE	Placer	Bath P O	76	442
James	36	m	w	FRAN	Sacramento	Granite Twp	77	139
James	36	m	w	IREL	San Joaquin	1-Wd Stockton	86	131
James	35	m	w	IREL	Alameda	Oakland	68	178
James	35	m	w	WALE	San Francisco	2-Wd San Francisco	79	247
James	34	m	w	IL	El Dorado	Lake Valley Twp	72	63
James	34	m	w	NY	San Francisco	6-Wd San Francisco	81	70
James	32	m	w	KY	Marin	San Rafael Twp	74	46
James	31	m	w	MA	San Joaquin	1-Wd Stockton	86	125
James	30	m	w	CANA	Santa Clara	2-Wd San Jose	88	325
James	30	m	w	SCOT	San Francisco	7-Wd San Francisco	81	178
James	30	m	w	NY	San Francisco	San Francisco P O	80	471
James	30	m	w	ME	Alameda	Washington Twp	68	293
James	30	m	w	MA	San Francisco	San Francisco P O	80	414
James	27	m	w	IREL	San Francisco	11-Wd San Francisc	84	433
James	26	m	w	PRUS	San Francisco	San Francisco P O	83	183
James	26	m	w	IREL	Yolo	Cache Crk Twp	93	449
James	26	m	w	MA	San Francisco	San Francisco P O	80	459
James	25	m	w	ENGL	Nevada	Grass Valley Twp	75	232
James	25	m	w	TX	San Diego	San Luis Rey	78	513
James	25	m	w	IREL	San Francisco	San Francisco P O	80	336
James	24	m	w	HI	San Francisco	5-Wd San Francisco	81	1
James	24	m	m	MD	San Francisco	San Francisco P O	80	477
James	22	m	w	SCOT	Sonoma	Santa Rosa	91	408
James	21	m	w	IL	Sacramento	Franklin Twp	77	107
James	14	m	w	CA	San Francisco	11-Wd San Francisc	84	587
James	13	m	w	CA	San Francisco	11-Wd San Francisc	84	587
James A	41	m	w	RI	San Francisco	6-Wd San Francisco	81	135
James A	20	m	w	MA	San Francisco	8-Wd San Francisco	82	455
James B	39	m	w	PA	Placer	Auburn P O	76	358
James C	27	m	w	IN	Stanislaus	Empire Twp	92	63
James D H	40	m	w	IL	Humboldt	Bucksport Twp	72	242
James E	40	m	w	VT	San Francisco	5-Wd San Francisco	81	26
James E	29	m	w	SCOT	San Francisco	1-Wd San Francisco	79	131
James F	44	m	w	ENGL	San Francisco	1-Wd San Francisco	79	115
James F	43	m	w	ME	Placer	Bath P O	76	449
James F	38	m	w	OH	Placer	Gold Run Twp	76	400
James G	45	m	w	AL	Placer	Lincoln P O	76	492
James H	37	m	w	RI	Inyo	Bishop Crk Twp	73	311
James H	27	m	w	PA	Plumas	Quartz Twp	77	41
James H	27	m	w	NY	Sonoma	Bodega Twp	91	254
James H	25	m	w	MA	Sonoma	Bodega Twp	91	260
James M	51	m	w	IL	Alpine	Silver Mtn P O	69	307
James M	34	m	w	OH	Placer	Bath P O	76	425
James M	30	m	w	PA	San Diego	Julian Dist	78	471
James N	27	m	w	NY	Santa Clara	2-Wd San Jose	88	317
James P	20	m	w	PA	Colusa	Colusa Twp	71	286
James R	48	m	w	NY	Los Angeles	Wilmington Twp	73	637
James S	44	m	w	CT	San Francisco	6-Wd San Francisco	81	155
James S	43	m	w	CT	San Francisco	San Francisco P O	85	719
James W	49	m	w	NY	Santa Cruz	Santa Cruz	89	407
James W	45	m	w	VA	Yolo	Cache Crk Twp	93	456
James W	43	m	w	MA	San Francisco	San Francisco P O	83	200
James W	37	m	w	NJ	Sonoma	Analy Twp	91	231
James W	34	m	w	TN	Sonoma	Analy Twp	91	231
James W	32	m	w	IN	Colusa	Spring Valley Twp	71	340
Jana	42	m	w	WURT	San Francisco	11-Wd San Francisc	84	677
Jane	48	f	w	OH	San Joaquin	2-Wd Stockton	86	162
Jane	25	f	b	KY	Santa Clara	Santa Clara Twp	88	136
Jas	49	m	w	MI	Butte	Chico Twp	70	25
Jas	33	m	w	NY	Solano	Vallejo	90	211
Jas	23	m	w	PORT	Butte	Chico Twp	70	41
Jas A	32	m	w	PA	San Francisco	8-Wd San Francisco	82	308
Jas B	53	m	w	KY	Sonoma	Santa Rosa	91	428
Jas C	40	m	w	NY	Butte	Ophir Twp	70	107
Jas F	40	m	w	TN	Monterey	San Antonio Twp	74	316
Jas G	32	m	w	MA	Nevada	Rough & Ready Twp	75	329
Jas George	33	m	w	IREL	San Francisco	San Francisco P O	83	198
Jas M	50	m	w	NY	San Joaquin	3-Wd Stockton	86	242
Jas M	30	m	w	PA	San Diego	San Diego	78	497
Jas R	25	m	w	KY	Sonoma	Mendocino Twp	91	290
Jas S	30	m	w	NY	San Francisco	8-Wd San Francisco	82	362
Jas T	52	m	w	ENGL	Santa Clara	Almaden Twp	88	15
Jas W	59	m	w	NY	San Joaquin	2-Wd Stockton	86	161
Jasper	8	m	w	OH	Butte	Ophir Twp	70	108
Jennie	20	f	b	NY	San Francisco	8-Wd San Francisco	82	429
Jennie	19	f	w	IREL	San Francisco	San Francisco P O	83	276
Jere	44	m	w	NY	San Francisco	6-Wd San Francisco	81	88
Jere S	49	m	w	RI	Nevada	Nevada Twp	75	279

© 2001 by Heritage Quest. All rights reserved.

California 1870 Census

Name	Age	S	R	B-PL	County	Locale	Series M593 Roll	Pg
Jeremiah	57	m	w	WI	Kern	Linns Valley P O	73	345
Jeremiah T	40	m	w	VA	Santa Clara	2-Wd San Jose	88	317
Jerry	34	m	w	TN	Tulare	White Rvr Twp	92	301
Jerry	32	m	w	IREL	Napa	Napa	75	43
Jesse	39	m	w	NY	Santa Clara	Milpitas Twp	88	108
Jesse	34	m	w	ME	Nevada	Nevada Twp	75	289
Jessie	45	f	w	SCOT	San Francisco	11-Wd San Francisc	84	566
Jim	30	m	w	IL	Lassen	Susanville Twp	73	446
Jim	30	m	b	TX	Yuba	East Bear Rvr Twp	93	544
Jno	53	m	w	NJ	Butte	Kimshew Tpw	70	80
Jno	50	m	b	AL	Santa Clara	Almaden Twp	88	2
Jno	45	m	w	IL	Butte	Kimshew Tpw	70	80
Jno	44	m	w	VA	Sonoma	Santa Rosa	91	405
Jno	40	m	w	RI	Sacramento	1-Wd Sacramento	77	185
Jno	35	m	w	GERM	Sacramento	1-Wd Sacramento	77	189
Jno	30	m	w	NY	Sierra	Gibson Twp	89	541
Jno	29	m	w	NORW	Butte	Oregon Twp	70	135
Jno	27	m	w	PRUS	Butte	Ophir Twp	70	108
Jno J	42	m	w	NY	Santa Clara	Gilroy Twp	88	99
Jno M	32	m	w	NY	San Francisco	5-Wd San Francisco	81	21
Jno Q	41	m	w	KY	Sacramento	3-Wd Sacramento	77	306
Jno W	36	m	w	WURT	Sacramento	3-Wd Sacramento	77	288
Jo	50	m	w	ENGL	Alameda	Alameda	68	17
Joe	32	m	w	IREL	Alameda	Murray Twp	68	117
Johana	25	f	w	MEXI	Calaveras	San Andreas P O	70	210
John	9	m	w	CA	San Francisco	San Francisco P O	85	827
John	68	m	w	BADE	San Francisco	2-Wd San Francisco	79	175
John	65	m	w	PRUS	Calaveras	San Andreas P O	70	170
John	65	m	w	ME	Tuolumne	Chinese Camp P O	93	390
John	65	m	w	AUST	San Francisco	7-Wd San Francisco	81	260
John	64	m	w	CT	San Francisco	San Francisco P O	80	419
John	62	m	w	CANA	Tuolumne	Chinese Camp P O	93	335
John	62	m	w	TX	San Diego	San Luis Rey	78	513
John	60	m	w	PRUS	Mariposa	Mariposa P O	74	129
John	60	m	w	PRUS	Stanislaus	Empire Twp	92	40
John	56	m	w	PRUS	Marin	Tomales Twp	74	77
John	53	m	w	MA	San Bernardino	San Bernardino Twp	78	422
John	53	m	w	BADE	Plumas	Rich Bar Twp	77	46
John	50	m	w	MO	Mendocino	Ukiah Twp	74	244
John	50	m	w	IREL	Merced	Snelling P O	74	279
John	50	m	w	AUST	Sacramento	2-Wd Sacramento	77	240
John	50	m	w	ENGL	San Francisco	1-Wd San Francisco	79	88
John	50	m	w	IREL	Trinity	Weaverville Pct	92	222
John	49	m	w	PA	Alameda	Brooklyn Twp	68	53
John	48	m	w	DENM	Marin	San Rafael Twp	74	30
John	47	m	w	VT	Calaveras	San Andreas P O	70	196
John	47	m	w	ENGL	Shasta	Horsetown P O	89	505
John	45	m	w	NORW	San Francisco	3-Wd San Francisco	79	287
John	45	m	w	SCOT	Siskiyou	Scott Valley Twp	89	612
John	45	m	w	DENM	El Dorado	Kelsey Twp	72	59
John	45	m	w	SHOL	San Francisco	1-Wd San Francisco	79	128
John	45	m	w	SWED	Marin	Bolinas Twp	74	2
John	45	m	w	IREL	San Francisco	7-Wd San Francisco	81	251
John	45	m	w	OH	San Francisco	7-Wd San Francisco	81	272
John	44	m	w	SWED	Butte	Bidwell Twp	70	4
John	44	m	w	PRUS	Santa Clara	Alviso Twp	88	25
John	43	m	w	NY	El Dorado	Greenwood Twp	72	53
John	42	m	w	IREL	San Francisco	San Francisco P O	80	335
John	42	m	w	IREL	Santa Clara	2-Wd San Jose	88	320
John	41	m	w	KY	Sutter	Butte Twp	92	89
John	40	m	w	VA	Merced	Snelling P O	74	250
John	40	m	c	CHIN	Solano	Vallejo	90	173
John	40	m	w	IREL	San Francisco	8-Wd San Francisco	82	298
John	40	m	w	SWED	San Francisco	8-Wd San Francisco	82	305
John	40	m	w	CANA	Sutter	Yuba Twp	92	149
John	40	m	w	IREL	Santa Clara	Santa Clara Twp	88	145
John	39	m	w	IREL	Butte	Ophir Twp	70	115
John	39	m	w	SWIT	Contra Costa	Martinez P O	71	439
John	39	m	w	ME	San Francisco	7-Wd San Francisco	81	243
John	38	m	w	MA	Contra Costa	Martinez P O	71	396
John	38	m	w	IREL	San Francisco	7-Wd San Francisco	81	179
John	38	m	w	IREL	San Francisco	San Francisco P O	83	354
John	37	m	w	NJ	San Francisco	5-Wd San Francisco	81	25
John	36	m	w	IREL	Kern	Havilah P O	73	339
John	36	m	w	ME	San Francisco	San Francisco P O	80	461
John	36	m	w	MA	San Francisco	San Francisco P O	80	474
John	35	m	w	CANA	Sacramento	Natomas Twp	77	166
John	35	m	w	PRUS	San Francisco	2-Wd San Francisco	79	167
John	35	m	w	NY	San Francisco	2-Wd San Francisco	79	197
John	35	m	w	PRUS	Alameda	Brooklyn	68	31
John	35	m	w	ITAL	Sacramento	Georgianna Twp	77	129
John	35	m	w	HOLL	Marin	Bolinas Twp	74	6
John	35	m	w	SCOT	San Francisco	11-Wd San Francisc	84	640
John	34	m	w	PORT	Yuba	Bullards Bar P O	93	550
John	34	m	w	NY	Sonoma	Analy Twp	91	243
John	33	m	w	IREL	Butte	Oregon Twp	70	127
John	33	m	w	IREL	Contra Costa	Martinez P O	71	427
John	33	m	w	MA	Calaveras	Copperopolis P O	70	229
John	33	m	w	IREL	Sacramento	4-Wd Sacramento	77	356
John	32	m	w	SCOT	San Francisco	San Francisco P O	83	20
John	31	m	w	KY	Marin	San Rafael Twp	74	36
John	31	m	w	NY	San Francisco	1-Wd San Francisco	79	106
John	30	m	w	AL	Los Angeles	San Gabriel Twp	73	594
John	30	m	w	IREL	Marin	Tomales Twp	74	88
John	30	m	w	ENGL	San Francisco	3-Wd San Francisco	79	314
John	30	m	w	IREL	Solano	Green Valley Twp	90	42
John	30	m	w	MA	San Francisco	6-Wd San Francisco	81	82
John	30	m	w	NY	Nevada	Eureka Twp	75	138
John	30	m	w	IREL	San Francisco	5-Wd San Francisco	81	28
John	30	m	w	IREL	San Francisco	11-Wd San Francisc	84	608
John	30	m	w	TN	Solano	Maine Prairie Twp	90	46
John	30	m	w	TN	Yuba	Parks Bar Twp	93	650
John	29	m	w	OH	Solano	Silveyville Twp	90	77
John	28	m	w	SWIT	Mendocino	Albion & Big Rvr T	74	166
John	28	m	w	GERM	Sonoma	Vallejo Twp	91	452
John	28	m	w	NY	Yolo	Grafton Twp	93	494
John	28	m	w	RI	Yolo	Cottonwood Twp	93	465
John	28	m	w	IREL	San Joaquin	2-Wd Stockton	86	170
John	28	m	w	MA	Alameda	Oakland	68	265
John	28	m	w	DENM	Alameda	Eden Twp	68	86
John	28	m	w	PORT	San Francisco	1-Wd San Francisco	79	130
John	28	m	w	SWED	San Francisco	7-Wd San Francisco	81	218
John	28	m	w	ENGL	San Francisco	5-Wd San Francisco	81	32
John	27	m	w	ITAL	Calaveras	Copperopolis P O	70	251
John	27	m	w	WALE	Nevada	Bridgeport Twp	75	108
John	27	m	w	WURT	Marin	Novato Twp	74	9
John	27	m	w	NORW	San Francisco	7-Wd San Francisco	81	216
John	27	m	w	ENGL	Solano	Vallejo	90	203
John	26	m	w	CANA	San Francisco	San Francisco P O	83	274
John	25	m	w	NY	Yolo	Grafton Twp	93	482
John	24	m	w	ENGL	San Francisco	2-Wd San Francisco	79	255
John	24	m	w	NY	San Francisco	San Francisco P O	80	473
John	23	m	w	CA	Marin	Nicasio Twp	74	20
John	22	m	m	MA	San Francisco	San Francisco P O	80	458
John	21	m	c	CHIN	Placer	Dutch Flat P O	76	411
John	16	m	w	IA	San Joaquin	Douglas Twp	86	47
John	16	m	w	NY	San Francisco	8-Wd San Francisco	82	320
John	15	m	w	CA	San Francisco	5-Wd San Francisco	81	27
John	12	m	w	CA	Humboldt	Arcata Twp	72	227
John A	52	m	w	OH	Santa Cruz	Soquel Twp	89	443
John A	45	m	w	IN	Tehama	Battle Crk Twp	92	157
John A	40	m	w	MD	Los Angeles	Los Angeles	73	519
John A	28	m	w	ENGL	San Francisco	6-Wd San Francisco	81	94
John A	25	m	w	MA	San Francisco	1-Wd San Francisco	79	100
John A	22	m	w	ITAL	Mariposa	Maxwell Crk P O	74	140
John B	26	m	w	VA	Sacramento	San Joaquin Twp	77	395
John C	37	m	w	ME	Mariposa	Maxwell Crk P O	74	143
John C	36	m	w	PA	Stanislaus	Empire Twp	92	40
John C	30	m	w	SCOT	Los Angeles	Los Angeles	73	549
John C	27	m	w	PA	Sonoma	Petaluma Twp	91	345
John D	25	m	w	MA	San Francisco	1-Wd San Francisco	79	115
John F	56	m	w	MA	Alameda	Brooklyn	68	37
John F	28	m	w	AL	San Diego	Milquaty Dist	78	475
John F	13	m	w	RI	Santa Clara	Fremont Twp	88	42
John H	55	m	w	ENGL	Santa Cruz	Santa Cruz Twp	89	380
John H	51	m	w	DENM	Placer	Bath P O	76	430
John H	40	m	w	MA	San Francisco	7-Wd San Francisco	81	207
John H	34	m	m	DC	San Francisco	8-Wd San Francisco	82	439
John H	31	m	w	NORW	San Francisco	1-Wd San Francisco	79	74
John H	31	m	w	PA	Nevada	Bridgeport Twp	75	108
John H	30	m	w	VA	Sacramento	2-Wd Sacramento	77	232
John K	45	m	w	NY	Sonoma	Petaluma Twp	91	335
John L	46	m	w	NY	Calaveras	Copperopolis P O	70	224
John L	43	m	w	TN	El Dorado	Mud Springs Twp	72	82
John L	32	m	w	ME	Mendocino	Big Rvr Twp	74	170
John M	35	m	w	IL	Tehama	Red Bluff	92	173
John N	69	m	w	KY	Placer	Roseville P O	76	354
John O	43	m	w	ENGL	San Francisco	2-Wd San Francisco	79	165
John O	40	m	w	IREL	Sacramento	Granite Twp	77	145
John R	37	m	w	NY	Sacramento	4-Wd Sacramento	77	335
John R	35	m	w	GA	Placer	Auburn P O	76	375
John R	34	m	w	CANA	Solano	Benicia	90	5
John T	48	m	w	IN	Mendocino	Anderson Twp	74	151
John T	36	m	c	OH	Placer	Dutch Flat P O	76	407
John V	38	m	w	OH	Siskiyou	Cottonwood Twp	89	592
John W	43	m	w	NY	Sonoma	Mendocino Twp	91	308
John W	40	m	w	KY	San Francisco	8-Wd San Francisco	82	346
John W	36	m	w	CANA	Nevada	Washington Twp	75	345
John W	34	m	w	NY	Sonoma	Analy Twp	91	237
John W	30	m	w	NY	San Francisco	6-Wd San Francisco	81	96
Jonas	19	m	w	MO	Marin	San Rafael Twp	74	45
Jonathan	75	m	w	NH	Placer	Colfax P O	76	390
Jonathan	46	m	w	MA	Solano	Silveyville Twp	90	76
Jonathan	36	m	w	NH	Inyo	Lone Pine Twp	73	335
Jonathan B	47	m	w	NH	Placer	Bath P O	76	453
Jos	40	m	w	IREL	Sacramento	1-Wd Sacramento	77	179
Jos	19	m	w	CANA	San Joaquin	2-Wd Stockton	86	194
Jos E	42	m	w	VA	Shasta	Millville P O	89	494
Jos G	47	m	w	MA	Shasta	French Gulch P O	89	466
Joseph	7	m	w	CA	San Francisco	8-Wd San Francisco	82	440
Joseph	62	m	w	TN	El Dorado	Cosumnes Twp	72	19
Joseph	51	m	w	PRUS	Fresno	Millerton P O	72	147
Joseph	50	m	w	BADE	Siskiyou	Yreka	89	659
Joseph	43	m	w	WALE	Alameda	Brooklyn	68	33
Joseph	40	m	w	PORT	Sacramento	Georgianna Twp	77	122
Joseph	40	m	w	ME	Butte	Oroville Twp	70	137
Joseph	40	m	w	IREL	San Francisco	8-Wd San Francisco	82	375
Joseph	39	m	w	ME	Nevada	Eureka Twp	75	138
Joseph	38	m	w	KY	Tulare	Farmersville Twp	92	244
Joseph	37	m	w	RI	Santa Cruz	Pajaro Twp	89	352
Joseph	36	m	w	SCOT	Alameda	Brooklyn Twp	68	44
Joseph	35	m	w	BAVA	Sacramento	4-Wd Sacramento	77	326
Joseph	35	m	w	SCOT	San Francisco	1-Wd San Francisco	79	91
Joseph	35	m	w	AUST	San Francisco	San Francisco P O	83	152

© 2001 by Heritage Quest. All rights reserved.

Name	Age	S	R	B-PL	County	Locale	Series M593 Roll	Pg
Joseph	35	m	w	IREL	San Francisco	San Francisco P O	85	744
Joseph	35	m	w	ITAL	Alameda	Hayward	68	78
Joseph	34	m	w	RI	San Joaquin	2-Wd Stockton	86	169
Joseph	34	m	w	AUST	San Francisco	6-Wd San Francisco	81	45
Joseph	32	m	w	PORT	Alameda	Washington Twp	68	268
Joseph	31	m	w	NY	San Francisco	5-Wd San Francisco	81	17
Joseph	30	m	w	MI	San Francisco	San Francisco P O	83	20
Joseph	28	m	w	MD	Tuolumne	Sonora P O	93	303
Joseph	25	m	w	SWED	Sacramento	4-Wd Sacramento	77	337
Joseph A	34	m	w	NORW	Yolo	Cache Crk Twp	93	454
Joseph E	45	m	w	NY	Santa Clara	1-Wd San Jose	88	278
Joshua	43	m	w	IL	Kern	Linns Valley P O	73	346
Joshua	40	m	w	PRUS	El Dorado	Lake Valley Twp	72	63
Josiah	49	m	w	PA	Sonoma	Healdsburg & Mendo	91	285
Josiah P	43	m	w	MA	Yuba	Slate Range Bar Tw	93	676
Judson	27	m	w	PA	Monterey	Alisal Twp	74	295
Julia	7	f	w	CA	San Francisco	San Francisco P O	85	827
Julia	45	f	w	PA	San Francisco	11-Wd San Francisc	84	642
Julia	37	f	w	NY	San Francisco	8-Wd San Francisco	82	387
Julia	28	f	w	LA	San Francisco	8-Wd San Francisco	82	359
Julia B	20	f	w	IA	San Francisco	San Francisco P O	83	275
Julia B	20	f	w	IA	Yolo	Cache Crk Twp	93	428
Justo	42	m	w	FRAN	Colusa	Colusa	71	290
Justus	32	m	w	NY	San Francisco	1-Wd San Francisco	79	133
Kate	27	f	b	MO	San Francisco	8-Wd San Francisco	82	386
Kate	24	f	w	ENGL	San Francisco	8-Wd San Francisco	82	384
Kate	20	f	w	IREL	San Francisco	San Francisco P O	80	473
Kaziah	51	f	w	IN	San Joaquin	Castoria Twp	86	13
L C	25	m	w	MI	Humboldt	Table Bluff Twp	72	306
L D	38	m	w	NY	Placer	Auburn P O	76	383
L M	59	m	w	KY	Mariposa	Maxwell Crk P O	74	147
L W	26	m	w	WI	Amador	Amador City P O	69	391
Laura	65	f	w	PA	Santa Clara	1-Wd San Jose	88	246
Laurence	37	m	w	IL	Contra Costa	Martinez Twp	71	346
Lawrence	30	m	w	IREL	Solano	Benicia	90	19
Lemuel	44	m	w	MO	Placer	Bath P O	76	428
Lemuel	38	m	w	AR	Trinity	North Fork Twp	92	218
Leonard	44	m	w	ENGL	Santa Clara	Fremont Twp	88	52
Leroy	35	m	w	PA	Yolo	Cache Crk Twp	93	419
Levi	63	m	w	LA	El Dorado	Mud Springs Twp	72	74
Levi	24	m	w	POLA	San Francisco	San Francisco P O	85	777
Lewis	37	m	w	SAXO	Butte	Chico Twp	70	18
Lewis	34	m	w	NORW	San Francisco	3-Wd San Francisco	79	292
Lewis G	44	m	w	NH	Placer	Roseville P O	76	352
Lizzie	50	f	b	VA	San Joaquin	Elkhorn Twp	86	60
Lizzie	30	f	w	IREL	San Francisco	7-Wd San Francisco	81	270
Lizzie	30	f	w	MO	San Francisco	San Francisco P O	83	276
Lizzie C	30	f	w	IL	Plumas	Indian Twp	77	12
Lorenzo	39	m	w	AR	Butte	Chico Twp	70	48
Louis	28	m	w	IL	Stanislaus	San Joaquin Twp	92	82
Louis J	35	m	w	RI	San Francisco	San Francisco P O	85	777
Louisa	35	f	w	ENGL	Solano	Vallejo	90	172
Louisa	23	f	w	IL	Sacramento	3-Wd Sacramento	77	284
Louisa	21	f	w	NY	Colusa	Colusa	71	296
Louisa	14	f	w	IL	Humboldt	Eureka Twp	72	274
Lucetta	17	f	w	IL	Santa Clara	2-Wd San Jose	88	297
Lucius	29	m	w	ME	Stanislaus	Emory Twp	92	26
Lucy A	56	f	w	OH	Santa Barbara	Santa Barbara P O	87	500
Lucy A	24	f	w	VT	Tuolumne	Sonora P O	93	325
Luella	13	f	w	CA	Yolo	Grafton Twp	93	484
Luther	38	m	w	OH	Yuba	Marysville	93	583
M	45	m	w	IREL	Calaveras	Copperopolis P O	70	233
M	36	m	w	NY	Sierra	Sierra Twp	89	564
M	35	m	w	NH	Alameda	Oakland	68	187
M	27	m	w	PA	Sierra	Sierra Twp	89	569
M B	33	m	w	NC	Tehama	Tehama Twp	92	186
M D	54	m	w	PA	El Dorado	Greenwood Twp	72	50
M G	38	f	w	IREL	San Francisco	San Francisco P O	83	132
M H	26	m	w	PA	Yuba	Marysville	93	595
M M	35	m	w	NY	Trinity	Weaverville Pct	92	224
Maggie	16	f	w	NY	Napa	Napa	75	18
Mahalia	54	f	w	IL	Stanislaus	Empire Twp	92	66
Mansfield	10	m	w	IA	Butte	Oregon Twp	70	128
Manson W	35	m	w	VA	Santa Cruz	Pajaro Twp	89	352
Manual P	35	m	w	AZOR	Yuba	New York Twp	93	636
Manuel	45	m	w	AZOR	Marin	Sausalito Twp	74	71
Manuel	40	m	w	PORT	Alameda	Eden Twp	68	82
Manuel	32	m	w	PORT	Nevada	Rough & Ready Twp	75	336
Manuel	31	m	w	AZOR	Monterey	Castroville Twp	74	334
Manuell	36	m	w	PORT	San Mateo	Half Moon Bay P O	87	402
March T	43	f	w	IREL	San Francisco	San Francisco P O	83	82
Margaret	76	f	w	NY	Santa Clara	2-Wd San Jose	88	286
Margaret	74	f	w	VA	Contra Costa	Martinez P O	71	373
Margaret	48	f	w	IREL	Santa Clara	Gilroy Twp	88	78
Margaret	46	f	w	IREL	San Francisco	11-Wd San Francisc	84	508
Margaret	40	f	w	MEXI	San Francisco	San Francisco P O	80	341
Margaret	40	f	b	GA	San Francisco	San Francisco P O	80	396
Margaret	32	f	w	IREL	Sacramento	Brighton Twp	77	73
Margarett	32	f	w	IREL	Humboldt	Arcata Twp	72	229
Maria	50	f	b	VA	San Francisco	San Francisco P O	80	381
Maria T	9	f	w	CA	San Francisco	San Francisco P O	85	719
Marian	55	f	w	ENGL	San Francisco	11-Wd San Francisc	84	544
Mark	48	m	w	IREL	Sierra	Table Rock Twp	89	572
Mark	29	m	w	NY	Solano	Vallejo	90	160
Mark	28	m	w	IREL	San Francisco	1-Wd San Francisco	79	132
Mark B	43	m	w	VT	Stanislaus	Emory Twp	92	23
Martha	35	f	w	LA	San Francisco	6-Wd San Francisco	81	98

Name	Age	S	R	B-PL	County	Locale	Series M593 Roll	Pg
Martha	28	f	w	MO	Yolo	Cottonwood Twp	93	469
Martha	27	f	w	MO	Monterey	San Juan Twp	74	387
Martin	27	m	w	KY	Solano	Vacaville Twp	90	128
Mary	8	f	w	CA	Nevada	Grass Valley Twp	75	230
Mary	7	f	w	CA	Sonoma	Russian Rvr	91	370
Mary	50	f	w	NY	Sonoma	Bodega Twp	91	262
Mary	50	f	w	IREL	Sacramento	Franklin Twp	77	115
Mary	49	f	w	IREL	El Dorado	Placerville	72	118
Mary	47	f	w	ENGL	Contra Costa	Martinez P O	71	443
Mary	40	f	w	IREL	Solano	Vallejo	90	148
Mary	40	f	w	MA	San Francisco	7-Wd San Francisco	81	279
Mary	40	f	w	FRAN	San Francisco	8-Wd San Francisco	82	355
Mary	36	f	w	IREL	San Francisco	8-Wd San Francisco	82	312
Mary	35	f	w	IREL	Alameda	San Leandro	68	98
Mary	30	f	m	DE	San Francisco	1-Wd San Francisco	79	133
Mary	30	f	w	IREL	San Francisco	8-Wd San Francisco	82	476
Mary	26	f	w	MA	San Francisco	San Francisco P O	80	425
Mary	24	f	w	IREL	San Joaquin	2-Wd Stockton	86	163
Mary	23	f	w	MO	Mendocino	Little Lake Twp	74	201
Mary	20	f	w	IL	Stanislaus	Empire Twp	92	41
Mary	19	f	w	IL	San Joaquin	Dent Twp	86	19
Mary	16	f	w	IREL	San Francisco	8-Wd San Francisco	82	395
Mary A	33	f	w	OR	Siskiyou	Butte Twp	89	586
Mary A	3	f	w	CA	San Francisco	6-Wd San Francisco	81	102
Mary A	2M	f	w	CA	San Francisco	11-Wd San Francisc	84	711
Mary R	50	f	w	NY	Sacramento	3-Wd Sacramento	77	278
Mary S	35	f	w	MO	Colusa	Monroe Twp	71	315
Mason	65	m	w	ME	Yuba	Bullards Bar P O	93	551
Mathew	32	m	w	PA	Solano	Vallejo	90	200
Maurice	43	m	w	IREL	Calaveras	Copperopolis P O	70	234
Maurice	40	m	w	KY	Shasta	Fort Crook P O	89	475
May	25	f	w	ENGL	Tulare	Visalia	92	294
Mers C D	61	f	w	IREL	Santa Clara	Almaden Twp	88	13
Michael	71	m	w	IREL	San Francisco	11-Wd San Francisc	84	432
Michael	50	m	w	IREL	San Francisco	2-Wd San Francisco	79	178
Michael	48	m	w	IREL	Nevada	Nevada Twp	75	284
Michael	40	m	w	OH	San Francisco	San Francisco P O	83	50
Michael	35	m	w	IREL	San Francisco	San Francisco P O	83	55
Michael	35	m	w	IREL	Santa Clara	Santa Clara Twp	88	143
Michael	25	m	w	BAVA	Stanislaus	Empire Twp	92	34
Michael	22	m	w	IREL	Sacramento	Brighton Twp	77	77
Miles H	30	m	w	IL	Stanislaus	Empire Twp	92	49
Milton	49	m	w	KY	Mendocino	Sanel Twp	74	230
Minnie	18	f	w	NY	San Francisco	6-Wd San Francisco	81	40
Mitchel	42	m	w	MO	Siskiyou	Yreka Twp	89	666
Mordecai	38	m	w	GA	Plumas	Quartz Twp	77	42
Morris	38	m	w	POLA	San Francisco	San Francisco P O	85	777
Morris	32	m	w	PRUS	Amador	Sutter Crk P O	69	398
Moses	38	m	b	MO	San Francisco	San Francisco P O	80	347
Moses	35	m	w	ME	Yuba	Rose Bar Twp	93	654
Moses R	38	m	w	NY	Santa Clara	Milpitas Twp	88	115
Munley M	32	m	w	NY	Trinity	Lewiston Pct	92	213
N A	45	m	w	OH	Los Angeles	Los Angeles Twp	73	487
N N	23	m	w	ME	Solano	Vallejo	90	143
N P	35	m	w	MA	Nevada	Nevada Twp	75	281
Nancy C	37	f	w	EIND	San Mateo	Redwood Twp	87	364
Nathan	44	m	w	OH	Stanislaus	Branch Twp	92	1
Nathan	36	m	w	POLA	San Francisco	11-Wd San Francisc	84	468
Nathan A	42	m	w	NY	Los Angeles	Los Angeles	73	526
Nathan M	43	m	w	OH	San Mateo	Pescadero P O	87	411
Nathaniel	36	m	b	KY	Mendocino	Big Rvr Twp	74	170
Nellie	8	f	w	US	Nevada	Grass Valley Twp	75	229
Nelson	33	m	w	ME	Alameda	Hayward	68	79
Nelson	32	m	w	KY	San Joaquin	3-Wd Stockton	86	218
Neppoleon	38	m	w	NY	Mariposa	Mariposa P O	74	106
Neslon	30	m	w	CANA	Butte	Chico Twp	70	25
Nettie	19	f	w	IL	Sacramento	1-Wd Sacramento	77	201
Nevada B	17	f	w	CA	San Bernardino	San Bernardino Twp	78	441
Nich	43	m	w	SCOT	Merced	Snelling P O	74	252
Nichols	34	m	w	IREL	San Francisco	7-Wd San Francisco	81	186
Obediah	34	m	w	CT	Tehama	Deer Crk Twp	92	170
Olando A	19	m	w	IL	Yolo	Cache Crk Twp	93	454
Ops	42	m	w	ME	Sutter	Butte Twp	92	90
Orrin	32	m	w	NY	San Mateo	Pescadero P O	87	416
Oscar	35	m	w	MA	Yuba	W Bear Rvr Twp	93	681
Oscar	25	m	m	LA	San Francisco	San Francisco P O	80	473
Otis	39	m	w	NY	Placer	Rocklin P O	76	462
P	45	m	w	IREL	Humboldt	Eureka Twp	72	260
P	36	m	w	POLA	Yuba	Marysville	93	591
P	35	m	w	POLA	Yuba	Marysville	93	593
P D	43	m	w	NJ	El Dorado	Greenwood Twp	72	52
Page	15	m	w	MO	San Francisco	11-Wd San Francisc	84	648
Pardon	25	m	w	RI	Siskiyou	Surprise Valley Tw	89	637
Pat	44	m	w	IREL	San Joaquin	2-Wd Stockton	86	162
Patrick	45	m	w	IREL	Stanislaus	Buena Vista Twp	92	14
Patrick	32	m	w	IREL	San Francisco	San Francisco P O	83	23
Patrick J	48	m	w	IREL	Placer	Bath P O	76	422
Paulina	46	f	w	BAVA	Shasta	French Gulch P O	89	469
Perly	36	m	w	MA	Nevada	Grass Valley Twp	75	189
Peter	58	m	w	DENM	Marin	San Antonio Twp	74	60
Peter	55	m	w	SCOT	San Francisco	2-Wd San Francisco	79	228
Peter	54	m	w	SCOT	Yuba	New York Twp	93	641
Peter	52	m	w	SCOT	Butte	Wyandotte Twp	70	149
Peter	50	m	w	HANO	Stanislaus	Buena Vista Twp	92	13
Peter	40	m	w	NJ	Kern	Havilah P O	73	340
Peter	39	m	w	SCOT	Contra Costa	Martinez P O	71	421
Peter	39	m	w	NY	Mendocino	Navarro & Big Rvr	74	177

© 2001 by Heritage Quest. All rights reserved.

California 1870 Census

Name	Age	S	R	B-PL	County	Locale (Series M593)	Roll	Pg
Peter	37	m	w	MA	Butte	Hamilton Twp	70	61
Peter	35	m	w	PRUS	San Francisco	8-Wd San Francisco	82	381
Peter	35	m	w	PRUS	Calaveras	San Andreas P O	70	173
Peter	33	m	w	SWED	San Francisco	6-Wd San Francisco	81	102
Peter	31	m	w	BADE	Butte	Hamilton Twp	70	70
Peter	27	m	w	PA	San Francisco	8-Wd San Francisco	82	365
Peter	26	m	w	SCOT	San Francisco	8-Wd San Francisco	82	369
Peter	23	m	w	IA	Butte	Oregon Twp	70	128
Phebe	40	f	w	NJ	San Francisco	8-Wd San Francisco	82	435
Phil	30	m	w	IREL	Butte	Oregon Twp	70	129
Philip	32	m	w	IREL	San Joaquin	1-Wd Stockton	86	124
Phillbrook	56	m	w	ME	Humboldt	Eureka Twp	72	259
Phillip	27	m	w	MO	Butte	Hamilton Twp	70	62
Phillip S	35	m	w	KY	Trinity	Weaverville Pct	92	227
Placido	22	m	w	CA	Monterey	Alisal Twp	74	290
R	53	f	w	NJ	Alameda	Oakland	68	206
R	25	m	w	IN	San Joaquin	Elkhorn Twp	86	61
R C	35	m	w	CANA	San Joaquin	1-Wd Stockton	86	131
R D	35	m	w	OH	Sutter	Butte Twp	92	99
R G	23	m	w	VT	Sutter	Butte Twp	92	102
R H	45	m	w	NY	Solano	Vallejo	90	197
R J	30	m	w	CANA	Sacramento	San Joaquin Twp	77	394
R M	31	m	w	RUSS	Monterey	Salinas Twp	74	308
R T	46	m	w	NH	Sacramento	3-Wd Sacramento	77	270
Ralph	38	m	w	NY	Sonoma	Petaluma Twp	91	312
Ralph	26	m	w	ENGL	Mariposa	Mariposa P O	74	111
Rebecca	58	f	w	TN	Tulare	Visalia	92	295
Rebecca N	29	f	w	ME	San Francisco	San Francisco P O	83	113
Reed	62	m	w	VT	Solano	Maine Prairie Twp	90	51
Reuben	28	m	w	NY	San Francisco	San Francisco P O	83	25
Richard	55	m	w	ENGL	Marin	Sausalito Twp	74	66
Richard	55	m	w	IREL	San Francisco	San Francisco P O	85	756
Richard	50	m	w	MA	San Francisco	2-Wd San Francisco	79	250
Richard	40	m	w	SWED	San Francisco	11-Wd San Francisc	84	475
Richard	39	m	w	IREL	San Francisco	San Francisco P O	83	382
Richard	36	m	w	CANA	San Francisco	San Francisco P O	83	196
Richard	36	m	w	GA	Plumas	Quartz Twp	77	43
Richard	34	m	w	ENGL	San Francisco	7-Wd San Francisco	81	194
Richard	34	m	w	IA	Stanislaus	Empire Twp	92	64
Richard	33	m	w	PRUS	Inyo	Lone Pine Twp	73	333
Richard	31	m	w	IREL	Trinity	Weaverville Pct	92	229
Richard	30	m	w	NJ	Alameda	Eden Twp	68	68
Richard	28	m	w	NJ	Alameda	Eden Twp	68	71
Richd	32	m	w	NY	San Francisco	1-Wd San Francisco	79	116
Robert	55	m	w	MO	Sutter	Nicolaus Twp	92	108
Robert	41	m	w	PA	San Francisco	7-Wd San Francisco	81	220
Robert	38	m	w	NY	Los Angeles	Los Angeles Twp	73	491
Robert	38	m	m	VA	San Francisco	6-Wd San Francisco	81	110
Robert	36	m	w	IREL	San Francisco	San Francisco P O	80	458
Robert	36	m	w	IREL	San Francisco	11-Wd San Francisc	84	670
Robert	34	m	w	PRUS	Sacramento	2-Wd Sacramento	77	233
Robert	34	m	w	ME	Mendocino	Albion & Big Rvr T	74	167
Robert	30	m	w	CANA	Plumas	Indian Twp	77	18
Robert	30	m	w	OH	Solano	Silveyville Twp	90	85
Robert	30	m	w	IREL	San Francisco	San Francisco P O	83	182
Robert	27	m	w	IREL	San Francisco	San Francisco P O	83	373
Robt	58	m	w	PORT	San Francisco	2-Wd San Francisco	79	166
Robt	45	m	w	MO	San Joaquin	Tulare Twp	86	260
Robt	43	m	w	MO	San Joaquin	Liberty Twp	86	83
Robt	39	m	w	IREL	Butte	Chico Twp	70	55
Robt	37	m	w	PRUS	San Francisco	2-Wd San Francisco	79	165
Robt	35	m	w	IREL	Sacramento	Brighton Twp	77	77
Robt	25	m	w	NY	San Francisco	5-Wd San Francisco	81	14
Robt A	38	m	w	NY	Sonoma	Mendocino Twp	91	293
Robt S	28	m	w	NY	San Luis Obispo	Morro Twp	87	284
Roger C	49	m	w	VT	Santa Clara	2-Wd San Jose	88	286
Roland G	35	m	w	MA	San Francisco	8-Wd San Francisco	82	399
Rufus	49	m	w	ME	San Francisco	11-Wd San Francisc	84	493
Rufus D	28	m	w	NH	Butte	Chico Twp	70	47
Rufus G	20	m	w	AR	Stanislaus	Buena Vista Twp	92	12
Ruth J	33	f	w	KY	Yolo	Putah Twp	93	509
S A	49	m	w	NY	San Joaquin	Tulare Twp	86	250
S B	37	m	w	MA	Alameda	Oakland	68	265
S C	30	m	w	CANA	San Joaquin	Douglas Twp	86	33
S D	31	m	w	VT	Sutter	Sutter Twp	92	129
S F	52	m	w	AL	Monterey	Monterey Twp	74	344
S F	46	m	w	KY	Napa	Napa	75	3
S J	46	m	w	PA	Tuolumne	Columbia P O	93	349
S M	42	m	w	TN	Merced	Snelling P O	74	254
Sabin	60	m	w	RI	El Dorado	Kelsey Twp	72	58
Sabribus	35	f	w	MEXI	Los Angeles	Los Angeles	73	557
Sam	77	m	w	PA	San Joaquin	3-Wd Stockton	86	240
Sam Lung	30	m	c	CHIN	Sutter	Butte Twp	92	104
Samel	18	m	w	CA	Los Angeles	El Monte Twp	73	463
Saml	52	m	w	NY	San Francisco	San Francisco P O	83	116
Saml	45	m	w	CANA	San Francisco	8-Wd San Francisco	82	313
Saml	37	m	w	MO	Sonoma	Santa Rosa	91	409
Saml	34	m	w	ME	Tuolumne	Big Oak Flat P O	93	404
Saml	28	m	w	TN	Marin	San Rafael Twp	74	38
Saml H	27	m	w	ENGL	San Francisco	San Francisco P O	83	187
Saml O	39	m	w	NJ	Placer	Gold Run Twp	76	395
Samuel	52	m	w	CANA	Alameda	Washington Twp	68	283
Samuel	50	m	w	IL	Nevada	Grass Valley Twp	75	154
Samuel	48	m	w	US	Nevada	Little York Twp	75	243
Samuel	38	m	w	SWED	San Francisco	11-Wd San Francisc	84	472
Samuel	37	m	w	VA	Colusa	Butte Twp	71	271
Samuel	27	m	w	ME	Sonoma	Analy Twp	91	218

Name	Age	S	R	B-PL	County	Locale (Series M593)	Roll	Pg
Samuel	25	m	w	VT	San Francisco	San Francisco P O	85	768
Samuel	23	m	w	PA	Contra Costa	Martinez P O	71	423
Samuel A	47	m	w	PA	El Dorado	Placerville	72	121
Samuel C	42	m	w	NY	Tulare	Visalia	92	291
Samuel C	30	m	w	SC	Solano	Rio Vista Twp	90	58
Samuel F	37	m	w	PA	Alameda	Washington Twp	68	272
Samuel H	39	m	w	NY	San Francisco	San Francisco P O	83	195
Samuel M	49	m	w	TN	Sacramento	Cosumnes Twp	77	96
Sarah	59	f	w	MA	San Francisco	8-Wd San Francisco	82	329
Sarah	24	f	w	IL	Stanislaus	Empire Twp	92	66
Sarah	23	f	w	NH	San Francisco	San Francisco P O	83	199
Sarah	20	f	w	IREL	San Francisco	8-Wd San Francisco	82	427
Sarah L	20	f	w	MA	San Francisco	8-Wd San Francisco	82	428
Sarah L	18	f	b	MS	San Francisco	8-Wd San Francisco	82	313
Sarchel C	54	m	w	MO	Plumas	Mineral Twp	77	22
Selmira	73	f	w	NY	Nevada	Bridgeport Twp	75	123
Seth	50	m	w	NY	San Francisco	San Francisco P O	85	858
Sherman	41	m	w	MA	Solano	Maine Prairie Twp	90	51
Sidney	29	m	w	NY	Placer	Rocklin P O	76	462
Sidney	28	m	w	OH	Placer	Rocklin Twp	76	468
Silas	60	m	w	CT	Yolo	Washington Twp	93	536
Silas	54	m	w	ME	El Dorado	Greenwood Twp	72	51
Silas	34	m	w	NY	Alpine	Silver Mtn P O	69	306
Simon	45	m	m	MD	San Francisco	2-Wd San Francisco	79	212
Simon	40	m	m	TN	Yuba	Marysville Twp	93	568
Simon	24	m	w	AUST	San Francisco	San Francisco P O	83	155
Simon	23	m	w	WI	San Francisco	8-Wd San Francisco	82	365
Simon C	32	m	w	NY	San Francisco	San Francisco P O	83	50
Smith	52	m	w	RI	Napa	Napa	75	49
Sobrina	73	f	w	NY	Sutter	Butte Twp	92	99
Solomon	27	m	w	IL	Tehama	Tehama Twp	92	193
Stephen	30	m	w	IL	Stanislaus	San Joaquin Twp	92	82
Stephen V	21	m	w	IN	Inyo	Bishop Crk Twp	73	312
Stewart	23	m	w	IREL	Alameda	Murray Twp	68	100
Susanna	29	f	w	MA	Sonoma	Petaluma Twp	91	314
Syborn	42	m	w	PORT	Trinity	Indian Crk	92	199
Sylvester	40	m	w	MO	Sonoma	Petaluma Twp	91	366
Sylvester B	37	m	w	RI	San Francisco	6-Wd San Francisco	81	136
Sylvester F	39	m	w	NY	Siskiyou	Yreka	89	659
Sylvesti	46	m	w	MA	Sacramento	Brighton Twp	77	79
Symon	45	m	w	PRUS	San Francisco	5-Wd San Francisco	81	13
T C	39	m	w	IN	Napa	Napa	75	20
T C	31	m	w	TN	Sutter	Butte Twp	92	92
T D	33	m	w	TN	Lake	Lower Lake	73	416
T H	40	m	w	PRUS	San Francisco	5-Wd San Francisco	81	8
Telamanse	45	m	w	TN	Stanislaus	San Joaquin Twp	92	71
Theodore	30	m	w	PRUS	San Bernardino	San Bernardino Twp	78	445
Theodore	29	m	w	MA	San Francisco	6-Wd San Francisco	81	107
Theodore	28	m	w	ME	San Francisco	1-Wd San Francisco	79	106
Theodore	28	m	w	IN	Humboldt	Pacific Twp	72	298
Theodore	19	m	w	OH	Marin	Tomales Twp	74	77
Thomas	65	m	w	ENGL	Sutter	Butte Twp	92	97
Thomas	54	m	w	IREL	Klamath	South Fork Twp	73	383
Thomas	52	m	w	ENGL	Placer	Lincoln P O	76	487
Thomas	50	m	w	SWED	San Francisco	San Francisco P O	80	471
Thomas	50	m	w	ENGL	Monterey	Pajaro Twp	74	374
Thomas	47	m	w	IL	Contra Costa	Martinez Twp	71	346
Thomas	44	m	w	TN	Humboldt	Pacific Twp	72	290
Thomas	44	m	w	NY	Yolo	Washington Twp	93	529
Thomas	44	m	w	IREL	Yolo	Washington Twp	93	529
Thomas	43	m	w	PA	Solano	Silveyville Twp	90	79
Thomas	41	m	w	NY	San Francisco	San Francisco P O	83	143
Thomas	40	m	w	IREL	San Francisco	San Francisco P O	83	244
Thomas	40	m	w	IREL	San Francisco	11-Wd San Francisc	84	569
Thomas	40	m	w	PRUS	Napa	Yountville Twp	75	79
Thomas	40	m	w	PA	Placer	Gold Run Twp	76	400
Thomas	40	m	w	CANA	Humboldt	Eureka Twp	72	256
Thomas	40	m	w	ENGL	Calaveras	San Andreas P O	70	153
Thomas	40	m	w	SWIT	Calaveras	San Andreas P O	70	192
Thomas	40	m	w	ENGL	San Francisco	8-Wd San Francisco	82	342
Thomas	38	m	w	IREL	San Francisco	San Francisco P O	80	456
Thomas	38	m	w	ENGL	San Francisco	San Francisco P O	80	424
Thomas	33	m	w	IREL	San Francisco	11-Wd San Francisc	84	442
Thomas	32	m	w	SCOT	San Francisco	11-Wd San Francisc	84	451
Thomas	31	m	w	MA	San Francisco	San Francisco P O	80	477
Thomas	31	m	w	VA	San Francisco	San Francisco P O	80	335
Thomas	30	m	w	IREL	San Francisco	6-Wd San Francisco	81	92
Thomas	30	m	w	IREL	San Francisco	San Francisco P O	85	768
Thomas	29	m	w	CANA	Fresno	Millerton P O	72	194
Thomas	28	m	w	CANA	Contra Costa	Martinez P O	71	397
Thomas	28	m	w	IREL	Alameda	Brooklyn Twp	68	49
Thomas	27	m	w	MO	Tulare	Farmersville Twp	92	241
Thomas	24	m	w	OH	San Francisco	1-Wd San Francisco	79	135
Thomas	23	m	w	ENGL	Mendocino	Big Rvr Twp	74	162
Thomas C	37	m	w	VT	San Francisco	6-Wd San Francisco	81	94
Thomas D	24	m	w	KY	Santa Clara	Milpitas Twp	88	115
Thomas G	57	m	w	IREL	San Francisco	6-Wd San Francisco	81	104
Thomas H B	31	m	w	MO	Santa Cruz	Pajaro Twp	89	352
Thomas J	28	m	w	NH	Alpine	Monitor P O	69	314
Thos	6	m	w	CA	Sonoma	Russian Rvr	91	369
Thos	56	m	w	MA	San Francisco	1-Wd San Francisco	79	128
Thos	44	m	w	IREL	San Joaquin	2-Wd Stockton	86	166
Thos	40	m	w	IREL	Solano	Vallejo	90	171
Thos	29	m	w	ENGL	Solano	Vallejo	90	202
Thos	25	m	w	MA	Solano	Vallejo	90	140
Thos	25	m	w	IN	Tehama	Tehama Twp	92	186
Thos H	25	m	w	IN	Butte	Chico Twp	70	50

© 2001 by Heritage Quest. All rights reserved.

Name	Age	S	R	B-PL	County	Locale	Roll	Pg
Thos J	45	m	w	MO	Sacramento	Cosumnes Twp	77	89
V R	45	m	w	NY	Sacramento	Franklin Twp	77	109
Vaness	36	m	w	MI	Sacramento	Cosumnes Twp	77	95
Victor	44	m	w	FRAN	San Francisco	San Francisco P O	80	349
W	52	m	w	ENGL	Calaveras	Copperopolis P O	70	232
W	47	m	w	PRUS	Calaveras	Copperopolis P O	70	232
W A	35	m	w	NY	San Joaquin	Tulare Twp	86	252
W A G	27	m	m	MA	Nevada	Meadow Lake Twp	75	249
W B C	39	m	w	KY	Sacramento	3-Wd Sacramento	77	306
W C	37	m	w	NY	Yuba	Marysville	93	578
W D	43	m	w	OH	San Joaquin	Douglas Twp	86	37
W H	49	m	w	VA	Monterey	Castroville Twp	74	327
W H	41	m	w	VA	Amador	Fiddletown P O	69	429
W H	38	m	w	NJ	El Dorado	Greenwood Twp	72	53
W K	54	m	w	NY	Butte	Hamilton Twp	70	61
W K	41	m	w	CA	Sacramento	3-Wd Sacramento	77	259
W R	29	m	b	PA	San Joaquin	1-Wd Stockton	86	128
W S	33	m	w	CT	San Francisco	San Francisco P O	83	310
W T	51	m	w	VA	San Joaquin	2-Wd Stockton	86	161
W W	45	m	w	PA	San Francisco	San Francisco P O	83	307
Walter	30	m	w	ENGL	San Francisco	6-Wd San Francisco	81	79
Walter	26	m	w	ENGL	San Francisco	San Francisco P O	85	753
Walter	25	m	w	PA	Calaveras	San Andreas P O	70	203
Walter	22	m	w	IA	Stanislaus	Empire Twp	92	64
Walter S	35	m	w	CANA	San Francisco	6-Wd San Francisco	81	140
Warren	44	m	w	IL	Contra Costa	Martinez Twp	71	346
Warren A	38	m	w	NY	Yolo	Cottonwood Twp	93	471
Warren A	38	m	w	NY	Yolo	Cottonwood Twp	93	473
Washington	47	m	w	MD	El Dorado	Greenwood Twp	72	57
West H	15	m	w	MS	Sonoma	Santa Rosa	91	423
West Mrs	37	f	w	IREL	Placer	Colfax P O	76	384
Will	7	m	w	CA	Sonoma	Russian Rvr	91	369
Willard	42	m	w	CT	Nevada	Little York Twp	75	244
Willen	33	m	w	DENM	San Francisco	1-Wd San Francisco	79	71
William	7	m	w	OR	Del Norte	Smith Rvr Twp	71	479
William	69	m	w	SCOT	San Francisco	7-Wd San Francisco	81	182
William	66	m	w	IREL	Santa Cruz	Santa Cruz	89	414
William	62	m	w	MA	Shasta	French Gulch P O	89	467
William	60	m	m	WA	Los Angeles	Los Angeles	73	505
William	60	m	w	ENGL	San Francisco	8-Wd San Francisco	82	492
William	54	m	w	VT	Mariposa	Mariposa P O	74	105
William	53	m	w	ME	San Mateo	Woodside P O	87	380
William	52	m	w	ENGL	Nevada	Grass Valley Twp	75	175
William	52	m	w	VA	Los Angeles	Los Angeles	73	543
William	50	m	w	SCOT	Tuolumne	Sonora P O	93	330
William	50	m	w	SWIT	San Francisco	San Francisco P O	83	339
William	50	m	w	VT	Siskiyou	Surprise Valley Tw	89	641
William	49	m	w	VA	Kern	Havilah P O	73	339
William	48	m	w	OH	Mendocino	Anderson Twp	74	157
William	47	m	w	IREL	San Francisco	San Francisco P O	80	383
William	47	m	w	IREL	San Francisco	San Francisco P O	83	246
William	46	m	w	ENGL	Plumas	Washington Twp	77	52
William	45	m	w	IREL	San Francisco	5-Wd San Francisco	81	19
William	43	m	w	ENGL	Santa Cruz	Pajaro Twp	89	362
William	43	m	w	MO	Colusa	Colusa Twp	71	286
William	41	m	w	ENGL	Alpine	Silver Mtn P O	69	308
William	40	m	w	MA	Solano	Silveyville Twp	90	76
William	39	m	w	ENGL	San Francisco	2-Wd San Francisco	79	202
William	38	m	w	SWED	San Francisco	3-Wd San Francisco	79	292
William	37	m	w	OH	El Dorado	Placerville Twp	72	100
William	37	m	w	RI	San Francisco	San Francisco P O	83	222
William	35	m	w	GERM	Contra Costa	Martinez P O	71	396
William	34	m	w	SCOT	Contra Costa	Martinez P O	71	423
William	33	m	w	CANA	Mendocino	Cuffeys Cove Twp	74	168
William	33	m	w	NY	San Francisco	San Francisco P O	83	252
William	32	m	w	ME	Stanislaus	Empire Twp	92	35
William	32	m	w	IN	Stanislaus	Empire Twp	92	37
William	31	m	w	ENGL	San Francisco	2-Wd San Francisco	79	253
William	31	m	b	TN	Placer	Auburn P O	76	381
William	31	m	w	IL	Yolo	Grafton Twp	93	488
William	30	m	w	PRUS	Marin	Bolinas Twp	74	6
William	30	m	w	NY	San Francisco	San Francisco P O	83	413
William	30	m	w	NY	San Diego	Coronado	78	466
William	30	m	w	CANA	Sonoma	Petaluma Twp	91	320
William	30	m	w	ME	San Francisco	7-Wd San Francisco	81	204
William	29	m	w	ENGL	San Francisco	7-Wd San Francisco	81	223
William	28	m	w	KY	Yolo	Buckeye Twp	93	412
William	27	m	w	IREL	Alameda	Eden Twp	68	72
William	27	m	w	NJ	San Francisco	11-Wd San Francisc	84	530
William	26	m	b	DE	San Francisco	San Francisco P O	80	342
William	26	m	w	ENGL	Placer	Lincoln P O	76	486
William	25	m	w	NY	Alameda	Oakland	68	184
William	24	m	w	ENGL	Solano	Silveyville Twp	90	89
William	24	m	w	GERM	Contra Costa	Martinez P O	71	433
William	20	m	w	OH	Monterey	San Juan Twp	74	407
William	19	m	w	MO	Amador	Drytown P O	69	424
William	18	m	w	NY	Tulare	Tule Rvr Twp	92	258
William	10M	m	w	CA	Amador	Ione City P O	69	356
William A	40	m	w	PA	Sierra	Table Rock Twp	89	572
William A	21	m	w	IL	Yolo	Cache Crk Twp	93	454
William A	21	m	w	IL	Yolo	Cache Crk Twp	93	456
William B	44	m	w	MO	Solano	Montezuma Twp	90	68
William B	40	m	w	DENM	Yolo	Washington Twp	93	528
William D	30	m	w	AUST	Santa Clara	1-Wd San Jose	88	260
William E	42	m	w	MA	Sacramento	2-Wd Sacramento	77	213
William F	25	m	w	ME	San Luis Obispo	Salinas Twp	87	291
William G	55	m	w	MO	Placer	Gold Run Twp	76	396
William G	23	m	w	NY	San Francisco	6-Wd San Francisco	81	153
William H	59	m	w	VT	San Francisco	6-Wd San Francisco	81	41
William H	55	m	w	KY	Santa Cruz	Soquel Twp	89	436
William H	38	m	w	PA	El Dorado	Mud Springs Twp	72	89
William H	36	m	w	OH	El Dorado	Mud Springs Twp	72	84
William H	34	m	w	NY	Santa Clara	2-Wd San Jose	88	285
William H	23	m	w	PRUS	San Mateo	San Mateo P O	87	355
William L	31	m	w	WI	Mendocino	Big Rvr Twp	74	158
William S	35	m	w	NY	Santa Clara	Redwood Twp	88	132
William S	26	m	w	OH	Los Angeles	Los Angeles	73	546
William S	24	m	w	NH	Placer	Newcastle Twp	76	476
William T	55	m	w	SC	Santa Clara	2-Wd San Jose	88	282
William W	38	m	w	NH	Santa Clara	Fremont Twp	88	48
Willie	12	m	w	CA	San Joaquin	Douglas Twp	86	30
Wilson	39	m	w	IL	Contra Costa	Martinez P O	71	448
Winefred	26	f	w	ENGL	Inyo	Lone Pine Twp	73	334
Wm	62	m	w	DENM	San Francisco	7-Wd San Francisco	81	268
Wm	54	m	w	SWED	San Francisco	11-Wd San Francisc	84	695
Wm	52	m	w	ENGL	San Francisco	1-Wd San Francisco	79	136
Wm	48	m	w	SWED	Solano	Vallejo	90	156
Wm	43	m	w	PRUS	Sacramento	4-Wd Sacramento	77	324
Wm	43	m	w	OH	Marin	San Antonio Twp	74	62
Wm	42	m	w	DE	Nevada	Nevada Twp	75	313
Wm	40	m	w	MA	Butte	Ophir Twp	70	98
Wm	40	m	w	IREL	Nevada	Nevada Twp	75	293
Wm	40	m	w	PRUS	San Francisco	San Francisco P O	85	877
Wm	37	m	w	IN	San Joaquin	1-Wd Stockton	86	153
Wm	35	m	w	CANA	Solano	Vallejo	90	161
Wm	35	m	w	IREL	Solano	Vallejo	90	161
Wm	35	m	w	HANO	Sonoma	Analy Twp	91	246
Wm	35	m	w	BAVA	Monterey	Alisal Twp	74	299
Wm	34	m	w	NORW	Butte	Oregon Twp	70	135
Wm	33	m	w	NY	Butte	Ophir Twp	70	117
Wm	33	m	w	MO	Sacramento	4-Wd Sacramento	77	372
Wm	32	m	w	NY	Fresno	Millerton P O	72	164
Wm	30	m	w	SCOT	San Francisco	11-Wd San Francisc	84	683
Wm	30	m	w	MD	Marin	San Rafael Twp	74	41
Wm	3	m	w	CA	San Francisco	San Francisco P O	85	799
Wm	29	m	w	ENGL	Sacramento	American Twp	77	66
Wm	27	m	w	PRUS	San Francisco	1-Wd San Francisco	79	110
Wm	24	m	w	IA	Sonoma	Santa Rosa	91	415
Wm	24	m	w	CT	Sacramento	3-Wd Sacramento	77	273
Wm	22	m	b	DE	San Francisco	San Francisco P O	85	759
Wm	20	m	w	MO	El Dorado	Lake Valley Twp	72	65
Wm	19	m	w	MA	San Francisco	1-Wd San Francisco	79	65
Wm A	36	m	w	DENM	Tuolumne	Sonora P O	93	316
Wm A	22	m	w	TN	Sacramento	Cosumnes Twp	77	93
Wm A	21	m	w	MA	San Francisco	8-Wd San Francisco	82	376
Wm B	56	m	w	ENGL	San Francisco	8-Wd San Francisco	82	345
Wm B	42	m	w	KY	Sonoma	Santa Rosa	91	405
Wm C	37	m	w	IN	San Luis Obispo	Salinas Twp	87	291
Wm F	20	m	b	NY	San Francisco	1-Wd San Francisco	79	52
Wm H	39	m	w	MD	San Francisco	8-Wd San Francisco	82	312
Wm H	35	m	w	NY	San Francisco	1-Wd San Francisco	79	105
Wm Henry	24	m	w	KY	Napa	Yountville Twp	75	87
Wm J	34	m	w	OH	Sutter	Vernon Twp	92	132
Wm Kelley	28	m	w	RI	San Francisco	San Francisco P O	83	37
Wm M	68	m	w	ENGL	San Francisco	San Francisco P O	83	24
Wm M	42	m	w	ENGL	San Francisco	3-Wd San Francisco	79	325
Wm N	46	m	w	SCOT	Solano	Vallejo	90	148
Wm R	40	m	w	ME	Napa	Napa Twp	75	46
Wm R	40	m	w	MA	Butte	Oregon Twp	70	124
Wm T	34	m	w	TN	Monterey	San Juan Twp	74	399
Wm V	27	m	w	IA	Fresno	Millerton P O	72	149
Z B	38	m	w	CANA	Humboldt	Eel Rvr Twp	72	252
Zadok M	52	m	w	OH	Santa Clara	San Jose Twp	88	196
Zenas J	58	m	w	NY	Yolo	Grafton Twp	93	494
Zenas L	32	m	w	NY	Shasta	Millville P O	89	483
BROWNAGE								
Mary	17	f	w	NY	Alameda	Washington Twp	68	283
BROWNE								
C P	51	m	w	MO	San Joaquin	Liberty Twp	86	83
Chas E	45	m	w	ENGL	San Francisco	1-Wd San Francisco	79	112
David S	42	m	w	ENGL	San Francisco	6-Wd San Francisco	81	121
E H	38	m	w	IN	San Joaquin	Elkhorn Twp	86	62
Edward	26	m	w	NJ	Yolo	Cache Crk Twp	93	432
Henry	35	m	w	PRUS	San Francisco	1-Wd San Francisco	79	99
J M	48	m	w	NH	Solano	Vallejo	90	168
J M	46	m	w	ENGL	Santa Clara	Gilroy Twp	88	78
Jacob	57	m	w	TN	Mono	Bridgeport P O	74	284
James	34	m	w	IREL	San Francisco	1-Wd San Francisco	79	76
John	50	m	w	IREL	San Francisco	1-Wd San Francisco	79	20
John	32	m	w	IREL	San Francisco	1-Wd San Francisco	79	40
John E	29	m	w	NY	San Francisco	1-Wd San Francisco	79	111
Joseph	32	m	w	FRAN	San Mateo	San Mateo P O	87	349
Justin	32	m	w	IREL	San Francisco	1-Wd San Francisco	79	28
Kate	50	f	w	IREL	San Francisco	1-Wd San Francisco	79	72
Lucy	48	f	w	IREL	San Francisco	1-Wd San Francisco	79	30
Marks	44	m	w	IREL	San Francisco	1-Wd San Francisco	79	113
Peter	50	m	w	TN	San Diego	Warners Rancho Dis	78	530
Philip	30	m	w	ENGL	San Francisco	1-Wd San Francisco	79	8
Robert	36	m	w	IREL	San Francisco	1-Wd San Francisco	79	7
T H	46	m	w	PA	Alameda	Oakland	68	198
Thomas	30	m	w	ME	Humboldt	Eureka Twp	72	277
Thos	30	m	w	IREL	San Francisco	1-Wd San Francisco	79	81
Wm	36	m	w	NY	San Francisco	1-Wd San Francisco	79	89
Wm	28	m	w	SWED	San Francisco	1-Wd San Francisco	79	67

Series M593

© 2001 by Heritage Quest. All rights reserved.

California 1870 Census

Name	Age	S	R	B-PL	County	Locale	Series M593 Roll	Pg
Wm	28	m	w	NORW	San Francisco	1-Wd San Francisco	79	74
Wm	28	m	w	SWED	San Francisco	1-Wd San Francisco	79	121
Wm	18	m	w	HANO	San Francisco	1-Wd San Francisco	79	65
BROWNEE								
George	37	m	c	CHIN	San Joaquin	Castoria Twp	86	13
BROWNELL								
Danl R	20	m	w	UT	Sacramento	3-Wd Sacramento	77	285
James	58	m	w	MA	El Dorado	Lake Valley Twp	72	63
James A	49	m	w	NY	Yolo	Cache Crk Twp	93	424
Joseph	36	m	w	NY	Monterey	Castroville Twp	74	342
N J	60	m	w	RI	San Joaquin	3-Wd Stockton	86	234
R P	52	m	w	OH	San Joaquin	Liberty Twp	86	90
William W	36	m	w	MA	Yolo	Grafton Twp	93	483
BROWNELLE								
David	39	m	w	MA	Solano	Tremont Twp	90	34
BROWNEN								
James	29	m	w	IREL	Contra Costa	San Pablo Twp	71	363
BROWNER								
Guesippi	32	m	w	SWIT	San Francisco	3-Wd San Francisco	79	319
BROWNFIELD								
Albert	35	m	w	PA	Plumas	Indian Twp	77	9
John	40	m	w	PRUS	San Francisco	8-Wd San Francisco	82	324
Senica G	42	m	w	IL	Mariposa	Mariposa P O	74	92
BROWNHART								
Saml	32	m	w	PRUS	Santa Barbara	Santa Barbara P O	87	450
BROWNING								
August	35	m	w	PRUS	San Francisco	San Francisco P O	80	386
David	34	m	w	IA	Santa Clara	Fremont Twp	88	58
Elizabeth	68	f	w	KY	Yolo	Cache Crk Twp	93	442
George	45	m	w	MA	Amador	Volcano P O	69	383
Henry	35	m	w	NC	Tulare	Tule Rvr Twp	92	262
J	42	m	w	CANA	Alameda	Oakland	68	262
J	36	m	w	NY	San Francisco	San Francisco P O	85	784
J T	42	m	w	MD	Sacramento	4-Wd Sacramento	77	373
Jacob	45	m	w	NY	San Francisco	San Francisco P O	85	784
John	70	m	w	TN	Santa Clara	San Jose Twp	88	190
John	43	m	w	IL	Amador	Ione City P O	69	351
John	31	m	w	HANO	San Francisco	11-Wd San Francisc	84	619
Jos	35	m	w	IREL	San Francisco	8-Wd San Francisco	82	361
Joseph	94	m	w	SC	Sonoma	Petaluma Twp	91	338
L G	30	m	w	CANA	Klamath	Camp Gaston	73	373
Mary	60	f	w	MI	Yolo	Cache Crk Twp	93	440
Mary	27	f	w	NY	San Francisco	San Francisco P O	80	405
Richd	53	m	w	ENGL	Colusa	Grand Island Twp	71	307
Robert	36	m	w	KY	Yolo	Cache Crk Twp	93	442
Sam	41	m	w	IL	Placer	Dutch Flat P O	76	414
Tandy	47	m	w	KY	Sonoma	Petaluma Twp	91	338
William	42	m	w	PRUS	San Francisco	San Francisco P O	83	233
William	39	m	w	IL	Santa Clara	1-Wd San Jose	88	261
William	17	m	w	CA	Merced	Snelling P O	74	280
William Y	41	m	w	TN	Yolo	Cache Crk Twp	93	442
Wm	31	m	w	ENGL	San Joaquin	2-Wd Stockton	86	183
BROWNLEE								
Calvin	20	m	w	CANA	Sonoma	Salt Point	91	384
James	40	m	w	NY	Santa Clara	2-Wd San Jose	88	286
John	30	m	w	SCOT	San Francisco	3-Wd San Francisco	79	305
John	19	m	w	IREL	San Francisco	3-Wd San Francisco	79	323
Robert	57	m	w	SCOT	Napa	Napa Twp	75	32
BROWNLEY								
C C	48	m	w	VA	Mariposa	Maxwell Crk P O	74	141
James	39	m	w	IREL	Sonoma	Salt Point Twp	91	383
Jennie	25	f	w	OH	Humboldt	Arcata Twp	72	232
BROWNLIE								
James	57	m	w	SCOT	San Francisco	11-Wd San Francisc	84	575
Jas	34	m	w	SCOT	Solano	Vallejo	90	143
Thos	50	m	w	SCOT	Solano	Vallejo	90	192
BROWNLY								
Charles	26	m	w	PA	San Francisco	San Francisco P O	80	335
Richard	31	m	w	MD	Sutter	Yuba Twp	92	150
BROWNRIGG								
Richard	54	m	w	VT	Placer	Bath P O	76	452
BROWNS								
Jas T	42	m	w	MO	Butte	Ophir Twp	70	105
BROWNSHEE								
Peter	40	m	w	DENM	Santa Barbara	Santa Barbara P O	87	478
BROWNSLEY								
W J	22	m	w	CANA	Alameda	Oakland	68	214
BROWNSON								
Augustus	35	m	w	SWED	Stanislaus	San Joaquin Twp	92	73
Chas	50	m	w	DENM	Alameda	Oakland	68	250
John	29	m	w	SCOT	San Francisco	6-Wd San Francisco	81	129
M D	50	m	w	NY	Solano	Vallejo	90	161
M K	71	m	w	PA	Napa	Napa	75	14
BROWNSTEIN								
Jacob	38	m	w	PRUS	Tehama	Red Bluff	92	176
BROWNSTELLER								
Joseph	25	m	w	BADE	Sacramento	4-Wd Sacramento	77	351
BROWNSTINE								
David	31	m	w	PRUS	Santa Cruz	Watsonville	89	368
H	25	m	w	PRUS	San Joaquin	2-Wd Stockton	86	170
T	66	f	w	PRUS	San Joaquin	2-Wd Stockton	86	160
BROWNSTONE								
Elizth	22	f	w	GERM	Santa Clara	1-Wd San Jose	88	225
Isaac	33	m	w	FRAN	San Francisco	8-Wd San Francisco	82	293
Jacob	37	m	w	PRUS	Santa Cruz	Santa Cruz	89	404
Moses	56	m	w	FRAN	San Francisco	8-Wd San Francisco	82	293

Name	Age	S	R	B-PL	County	Locale	Series M593 Roll	Pg
BROWNT								
Brice	35	m	w	SCOT	Napa	Yountville Twp	75	78
BROWNWAY								
Samuel	35	m	w	ENGL	Stanislaus	Empire Twp	92	42
BROWNWELL								
Chas	11	m	w	MI	Alameda	Oakland	68	149
BROWSE								
Henry W	45	m	w	OH	Stanislaus	Empire Twp	92	48
BROXELL								
Henry	45	m	w	PA	Sierra	Table Rock Twp	89	579
BROYDE								
Daniel	33	m	w	CANA	San Francisco	11-Wd San Francisc	84	578
BROYER								
George	42	m	w	PRUS	San Francisco	San Francisco P O	80	474
BROYLES								
John	83	m	w	TN	Stanislaus	Empire Twp	92	35
Nicholas	44	m	w	IN	Yuba	Parks Bar Twp	93	650
Samuel W	27	m	w	TN	Stanislaus	Empire Twp	92	35
BROYT								
Jo	48	m	w	IREL	Alameda	Alameda	68	5
BROZAN								
N	30	m	w	IREL	Alameda	Alameda	68	2
BROZELLE								
Jose	27	m	w	AZOR	San Francisco	1-Wd San Francisco	79	118
BRU								
James	23	m	w	NY	Los Angeles	Los Angeles	73	529
BRUBAKER								
E P	39	m	w	PA	Lake	Lower Lake	73	414
G W	37	m	w	PA	Sacramento	Dry Crk Twp	77	101
Sarah	39	f	w	ME	San Francisco	11-Wd San Francisc	84	464
BRUCE								
A	45	m	w	SCOT	Lake	Knoxville Mines	73	404
A	20	m	w	CANA	Yuba	Marysville	93	605
Adel	23	m	w	ENGL	San Joaquin	2-Wd Stockton	86	187
Alexander	28	m	w	SCOT	Sonoma	Analy Twp	91	226
Alexander	24	m	w	SCOT	San Francisco	San Francisco P O	80	419
Alonzo	45	m	w	VA	Sonoma	Analy Twp	91	241
Charles	57	m	w	NJ	Mariposa	Mariposa P O	74	119
Charles	40	m	w	MA	San Francisco	3-Wd San Francisco	79	315
Daniel	18	m	w	MO	Calaveras	San Andreas P O	70	158
Donald	26	m	w	ENGL	San Francisco	8-Wd San Francisco	82	407
E	50	f	b	NY	Alameda	Oakland	68	157
Edward	27	m	w	SCOT	Calaveras	San Andreas P O	70	185
Eugene B	29	m	w	KY	Yuba	Long Bar Twp	93	561
G C	48	m	w	NY	Sacramento	3-Wd Sacramento	77	310
Gardiner W	31	m	w	GA	San Francisco	San Francisco P O	85	745
Geo	37	m	w	SWIT	Alameda	Oakland	68	241
George	55	m	w	SCOT	El Dorado	Placerville	72	120
Henry	46	m	w	NY	Solano	Vallejo	90	193
Henry	34	m	w	SCOT	San Francisco	San Francisco P O	83	114
Henry	25	m	w	HDAR	San Francisco	7-Wd San Francisco	81	218
Herbert	22	m	w	MA	San Francisco	11-Wd San Francisc	84	640
Horace	25	m	w	NY	Sutter	Yuba Twp	92	146
Hosea	33	m	w	NY	Monterey	Alisal Twp	74	303
J J	39	m	w	MO	Sutter	Sutter Twp	92	119
James	36	m	w	IREL	San Francisco	San Francisco P O	80	416
Janius	42	m	w	ME	San Francisco	San Francisco P O	80	387
Jno	40	m	w	PRUS	Butte	Chico Twp	70	34
John	30	m	w	NY	San Francisco	7-Wd San Francisco	81	188
John E	30	m	w	VA	Yolo	Grafton Twp	93	485
Joseph H	56	m	w	KY	Yuba	Long Bar Twp	93	561
Louis	36	m	w	MA	San Francisco	San Francisco P O	80	422
Marion	40	m	w	IA	Butte	Oregon Twp	70	128
Mary	32	f	w	MA	San Francisco	6-Wd San Francisco	81	116
Mary	12	f	m	CA	San Francisco	San Francisco P O	83	331
Maxwell M	28	m	w	SCOT	Sacramento	American Twp	77	64
May	35	f	w	IREL	Alameda	Oakland	68	146
Ralph	24	m	w	IREL	San Francisco	3-Wd San Francisco	79	312
Reuben	29	m	w	ENGL	Marin	Sausalito Twp	74	72
Rich K	41	m	w	VA	Tehama	Antelope Twp	92	153
Robert	57	m	w	SCOT	Sutter	Butte Twp	92	90
Robert	30	m	w	SCOT	San Francisco	San Francisco P O	83	337
Robt	35	m	w	IN	Sacramento	Brighton Twp	77	81
Thomas	27	m	w	IREL	Marin	Tomales Twp	74	84
Thomas	23	m	w	IREL	Marin	Point Reyes Twp	74	22
Thos	40	m	w	NY	Butte	Chico Twp	70	26
Washington	45	m	w	MA	San Francisco	San Francisco P O	83	58
William	60	m	w	NH	San Francisco	11-Wd San Francisc	84	639
William	56	m	w	VT	San Francisco	San Francisco P O	80	471
Wm	60	m	w	IL	San Joaquin	Elliott Twp	86	78
Wm	21	m	w	ENGL	San Francisco	1-Wd San Francisco	79	130
Wm	16	m	w	OH	Butte	Chico Twp	70	54
Wm A	22	m	w	MI	San Joaquin	3-Wd Stockton	86	229
BRUCH								
Charles	46	m	w	PRUS	Santa Clara	1-Wd San Jose	88	249
George	61	m	w	BAVA	San Francisco	3-Wd San Francisco	79	328
BRUCHANI								
Peter	21	m	w	ITAL	Santa Clara	San Jose Twp	88	204
BRUCHER								
Peter	36	m	w	CANA	San Bernardino	San Bernardino Twp	78	419
BRUCHI								
John	34	m	w	ITAL	Tuolumne	Columbia P O	93	345
BRUCK								
David	57	m	w	PRUS	Solano	Silveyville Twp	90	82
Esther	25	f	w	PRUS	San Francisco	San Francisco P O	83	379
John	37	m	w	SCOT	San Francisco	San Francisco P O	83	40
Louis	41	m	w	PRUS	Napa	Napa	75	37

© 2001 by Heritage Quest. All rights reserved.

Name	Age	S	R	B-PL	County	Locale (Series M593)	Roll	Pg
BRUCKEMAN								
Fred	35	m	w	PRUS	Sierra	Table Rock Twp	89	578
BRUCKERMAN								
Henry	29	m	w	PRUS	Sierra	Table Rock Twp	89	578
BRUCKHALTER								
F	35	m	w	OH	Nevada	Meadow Lake Twp	75	247
BRUCKMAN								
Alex	32	m	w	AUSL	Contra Costa	Martinez P O	71	419
Mary	15	f	w	CA	San Joaquin	1-Wd Stockton	86	139
BRUCKNEW								
Fred	28	m	w	NY	Klamath	Camp Gaston	73	372
BRUDER								
Andrew	48	m	w	CANA	Tulare	Visalia Twp	92	285
John	40	m	w	BADE	San Francisco	San Francisco P O	80	469
BRUDETT								
Henry	46	m	w	NJ	Kern	Bakersfield P O	73	358
BRUDHMAN								
Moses	38	m	w	RUSS	San Francisco	1-Wd San Francisco	79	35
BRUEN								
J H	52	m	w	NJ	Santa Clara	Gilroy Twp	88	86
James B	28	m	w	OH	Santa Cruz	Santa Cruz	89	417
BRUENING								
Rosa	30	f	w	WURT	San Francisco	San Francisco P O	85	756
BRUENS								
H	25	m	w	HANO	Yuba	Marysville	93	605
BRUERTON								
James	36	m	w	ENGL	San Francisco	1-Wd San Francisco	79	59
John	45	m	w	ENGL	San Francisco	1-Wd San Francisco	79	59
BRUESE								
Hiram	43	m	w	NY	San Joaquin	Oneal Twp	86	106
BRUFF								
G W	30	m	w	MD	Sacramento	3-Wd Sacramento	77	257
Wm	32	m	w	NY	Merced	Snelling P O	74	265
BRUFFORD								
James	47	m	w	OH	Monterey	Salinas Twp	74	310
BRUGG								
Jno B	37	m	w	MO	Butte	Chico Twp	70	48
Patrick	46	m	w	IREL	San Francisco	11-Wd San Francisc	84	454
Perry	41	m	w	MO	San Joaquin	Douglas Twp	86	36
BRUGGEMAN								
Henry	41	m	w	HANO	San Francisco	11-Wd San Francisc	84	466
BRUGGY								
Patrick	45	m	w	IREL	San Francisco	11-Wd San Francisc	84	479
BRUGHN								
H H	34	m	w	NY	Humboldt	Pacific Twp	72	291
BRUGIERE								
Lewis	53	m	w	FRAN	Alameda	Oakland	68	239
BRUGYN								
Wm	36	m	w	IREL	Butte	Oregon Twp	70	125
BRUHINS								
Henry	37	m	w	PRUS	San Francisco	2-Wd San Francisco	79	190
BRUHN								
Deidrich	25	m	w	SHOL	San Mateo	Half Moon Bay P O	87	407
BRUHNS								
Henry	43	m	w	CA	San Francisco	1-Wd San Francisco	79	9
BRUINBROECK								
Amasa S	9	m	w	MA	Santa Cruz	Santa Cruz	89	432
BRUITT								
E Jane	11	f	w	CA	Humboldt	Eel Rvr Twp	72	246
Wm	10	m	w	MEXI	San Francisco	San Francisco P O	85	828
BRUJIER								
Adolph	56	m	w	LA	Santa Clara	2-Wd San Jose	88	287
BRULLA								
Juan	57	m	w	CA	Santa Clara	Santa Clara Twp	88	157
BRUM								
David	45	m	w	IREL	Nevada	Bridgeport Twp	75	112
John	43	m	w	FRAN	San Francisco	San Francisco P O	80	535
S A	50	m	w	MO	San Joaquin	Dent Twp	86	27
BRUMAGIM								
J H	40	m	w	NY	Mariposa	Mariposa P O	74	109
John	46	m	w	NY	San Francisco	San Francisco P O	80	404
BRUMAN								
A	35	m	w	PRUS	San Francisco	San Francisco P O	85	823
BRUMBERGER								
Mark	27	m	w	PRUS	San Francisco	8-Wd San Francisco	82	345
BRUMBLE								
Joseph	25	m	w	SCOT	Alameda	San Leandro	68	96
BRUME								
Peter	32	m	w	DENM	Sacramento	2-Wd Sacramento	77	232
BRUMEGEN								
E J	10	f	w	NY	Alameda	Oakland	68	236
BRUMENTHAL								
Emma	41	f	w	UNKN	San Joaquin	2-Wd Stockton	86	166
BRUMFIELD								
Byrd	32	m	w	VA	Sonoma	Russian Rvr	91	374
Geo P	55	m	w	VA	Sonoma	Russian Rvr	91	374
Percilla	5	f	w	CA	Sonoma	Mendocino Twp	91	292
S	27	m	w	VA	Sonoma	Russian Rvr	91	374
Saml	39	m	w	KY	Shasta	Shasta P O	89	452
BRUMHALL								
F	22	m	w	ENGL	Sacramento	1-Wd Sacramento	77	181
BRUMLEY								
Wm	60	m	w	NY	Sacramento	3-Wd Sacramento	77	265
BRUMLINN								
John	25	m	w	NY	San Francisco	1-Wd San Francisco	79	133
BRUMMER								
Anne	15	f	w	CA	Alameda	Oakland	68	185
BRUMMET								
James	69	m	w	KY	Santa Clara	San Jose Twp	88	199
BRUMMETT								
Caleb	35	m	w	TN	Monterey	San Juan Twp	74	414
BRUMMIT								
Jane	58	f	w	NY	Monterey	San Juan Twp	74	416
BRUMNER								
Cloys	37	m	w	HANO	San Francisco	11-Wd San Francisc	84	561
David	39	m	w	PRUS	Butte	Concow Twp	70	8
BRUMS								
Christopher	29	m	w	PRUS	San Francisco	5-Wd San Francisco	81	16
BRUN								
Adolphus	40	m	w	PRUS	Placer	Auburn P O	76	361
Ah	38	m	c	CHIN	Yuba	Marysville	93	620
Mary	26	f	w	IREL	San Joaquin	1-Wd Stockton	86	120
BRUNA								
Philip	45	m	w	PRUS	San Francisco	5-Wd San Francisco	81	30
BRUNAN								
Mary	45	f	w	IREL	Alameda	Oakland	68	143
BRUNDAGE								
Benn	36	m	w	OH	Kern	Havilah P O	73	337
Thos J	30	m	w	OH	Tulare	Farmersville Twp	92	242
Wm J	39	m	w	NY	Butte	Wyandotte Twp	70	147
BRUNDEL								
George	24	m	w	BAVA	Alameda	Oakland	68	202
BRUNDELL								
Geo	46	m	w	PRUS	Sierra	Downieville Twp	89	521
BRUNDIGE								
Chas	43	m	w	NY	Sierra	Sears Twp	89	559
BRUNDISH								
Wm	15	m	w	MO	Fresno	Millerton P O	72	182
BRUNDRIDGE								
J	11	m	w	MO	Lassen	Janesville Twp	73	431
W	20	m	w	MO	Lassen	Long Valley Twp	73	436
BRUNDROGA								
C	35	m	w	DENM	Alameda	Oakland	68	265
BRUNE								
August	36	m	w	HANO	San Francisco	1-Wd San Francisco	79	61
John	27	m	w	NY	San Diego	San Diego	78	487
BRUNEL								
Alexander	40	m	w	FINL	San Francisco	3-Wd San Francisco	79	291
BRUNEN								
Sim	31	m	w	IREL	San Francisco	7-Wd San Francisco	81	286
BRUNENGO								
Aloysus	34	m	w	ITAL	Santa Clara	Santa Clara Twp	88	175
BRUNER								
Alfred	27	m	w	ENGL	Solano	Vallejo	90	162
Alfred	25	m	w	ENGL	San Francisco	San Francisco P O	80	338
Daniel	34	m	w	OH	Sonoma	Analy Twp	91	222
Frank	50	m	w	GERM	Yolo	Cache Crk Twp	93	450
Fredrick	38	m	w	PRUS	Sonoma	Petaluma Twp	91	310
Jacob	40	m	w	SWIT	San Francisco	2-Wd San Francisco	79	273
Jacob	25	m	w	SWIT	San Francisco	6-Wd San Francisco	81	71
James [Dr]	45	m	w	PA	San Francisco	5-Wd San Francisco	81	5
John	26	m	w	ENGL	Alameda	Oakland	68	142
Joseph	48	m	w	PRUS	Solano	Rio Vista Twp	90	60
Joseph A	49	m	w	VA	Santa Clara	Santa Clara Twp	88	146
Lassens	38	m	w	CANA	Placer	Bath P O	76	449
Lizzie	25	f	w	IREL	San Francisco	San Francisco P O	80	338
Louis	45	m	w	FRAN	San Francisco	1-Wd San Francisco	79	61
Peter	38	m	w	OH	Sonoma	Analy Twp	91	225
Philip	35	m	w	IN	Sonoma	Russian Rvr	91	374
William H	43	m	w	PA	San Francisco	San Francisco P O	83	228
BRUNERS								
Jacob	28	m	w	HANO	Alameda	Eden Twp	68	65
BRUNET								
Eugene	35	m	w	FRAN	San Francisco	San Francisco P O	80	350
BRUNETT								
Louis	51	m	w	FRAN	Tuolumne	Columbia P O	93	335
Y H	34	m	w	ENGL	Sierra	Downieville Twp	89	517
BRUNG								
David	30	m	w	BAVA	Alameda	Oakland	68	158
BRUNGIS								
John	43	m	w	HANO	San Francisco	2-Wd San Francisco	79	226
BRUNHAM								
Amelia	25	f	w	ENGL	San Francisco	San Francisco P O	83	113
BRUNI								
Carlo	23	m	w	ITAL	Santa Cruz	Pajaro Twp	89	358
BRUNICH								
Dora	31	f	w	HANO	San Francisco	2-Wd San Francisco	79	171
BRUNIE								
Balus	36	m	w	SWIT	El Dorado	Georgetown Twp	72	37
BRUNIER								
Eugene	42	m	w	FRAN	San Francisco	San Francisco P O	80	463
Eugene	33	m	w	FRAN	San Francisco	2-Wd San Francisco	79	151
BRUNING								
Bernard	37	m	w	PRUS	San Francisco	San Francisco P O	85	756
Henry	40	m	w	HANO	Shasta	Shasta P O	89	462
Henry	27	m	w	HANO	Plumas	Washington Twp	77	54
Henry N	49	m	w	HANO	Los Angeles	Wilmington Twp	73	641
BRUNK								
Caroline	23	f	w	MO	Kern	Linns Valley P O	73	345
Henry	30	m	w	IL	Sonoma	Santa Rosa	91	395
William	52	m	w	GERM	Los Angeles	Los Angeles	73	535
BRUNN								
Isaac	32	m	w	PRUS	San Bernardino	San Bernardino Twp	78	418

© 2001 by Heritage Quest. All rights reserved.

Name	Age	S	R	B-PL	County	Locale	Series M593 Roll	Pg
BRUNNEMAN								
John A	39	m	w	HANO	Nevada	Grass Valley Twp	75	147
BRUNNER								
John	42	m	w	BADE	Sacramento	4-Wd Sacramento	77	326
BRUNNIA								
Maria	40	f	w	MEXI	San Bernardino	San Bernardino Twp	78	430
BRUNNING								
John	31	m	w	ENGL	Tehama	Red Bluff	92	175
BRUNNINGS								
Martin	28	m	w	HANO	San Francisco	San Francisco P O	83	172
BRUNNIS								
Conrod	35	m	w	HANO	San Francisco	11-Wd San Francisc	84	434
BRUNO								
David	40	m	w	CHIL	Contra Costa	San Pablo Twp	71	360
Giuseppe	28	m	w	ITAL	San Francisco	11-Wd San Francisc	84	591
Peter	39	m	w	ITAL	Amador	Sutter Crk P O	69	400
BRUNON								
Joseph	23	m	w	SWIT	Sonoma	Sonoma Twp	91	440
BRUNOTTA								
Louis	40	m	w	PRUS	San Francisco	2-Wd San Francisco	79	240
BRUNS								
Christian	60	m	w	PRUS	San Francisco	8-Wd San Francisco	82	382
Geo	35	m	w	PRUS	San Francisco	7-Wd San Francisco	81	283
Geo	33	m	w	ASEA	Sacramento	3-Wd Sacramento	77	264
Geo O	37	m	w	ME	San Francisco	2-Wd San Francisco	79	173
Henry	40	m	w	HANO	San Francisco	11-Wd San Francisc	84	640
Henry	35	m	w	PRUS	San Francisco	San Francisco P O	80	343
Henry	30	m	w	BAVA	San Francisco	San Francisco P O	80	367
Henry	28	m	w	PRUS	Sacramento	2-Wd Sacramento	77	235
Henry	23	m	w	PRUS	San Francisco	San Francisco P O	83	243
John	34	m	w	HANO	San Francisco	11-Wd San Francisc	84	560
Margaret	62	f	w	IREL	San Francisco	San Francisco P O	83	20
Nicholas	43	m	w	HANO	San Francisco	11-Wd San Francisc	84	565
Nichols	36	m	w	ITAL	San Francisco	1-Wd San Francisco	79	45
Peter	39	m	w	NORW	San Francisco	San Francisco P O	80	467
Peter	38	m	w	HANO	San Francisco	San Francisco P O	83	87
Richard	27	m	w	HANO	San Francisco	7-Wd San Francisco	81	211
BRUNSBACK								
Sophia	25	f	w	HANO	San Francisco	San Francisco P O	83	44
BRUNSHAUS								
C	40	m	w	PRUS	Mariposa	Maxwell Crk P O	74	144
BRUNSING								
Mortin	51	m	w	BAVA	Mendocino	Big Rvr Twp	74	162
BRUNSON								
Albert C	34	m	w	IL	Los Angeles	El Monte Twp	73	451
Anson	36	m	w	OH	Los Angeles	Los Angeles	73	568
Edgar	30	m	w	MI	Mendocino	Cuffeys Cove Twp	74	168
Henry	29	m	w	SHOL	San Francisco	San Francisco P O	83	23
James	36	m	w	IREL	San Francisco	San Francisco P O	80	531
Richard	28	m	w	ENGL	Tulare	Tule Rvr Twp	92	271
W S	42	m	w	MA	Tuolumne	Big Oak Flat P O	93	394
BRUNST								
Frank	28	m	w	PRUS	Santa Clara	1-Wd San Jose	88	258
BRUNSTETTER								
Peter	38	m	w	PA	Nevada	Grass Valley Twp	75	142
BRUNT								
Samuel	40	m	w	ENGL	San Francisco	11-Wd San Francisc	84	631
William	51	m	w	ENGL	San Francisco	San Francisco P O	83	326
William	35	m	w	ENGL	San Francisco	11-Wd San Francisc	84	459
BRUNTCH								
Carl	27	m	w	PA	San Francisco	2-Wd San Francisco	79	220
BRUNTON								
Elleanor	55	f	w	PA	Tuolumne	Sonora P O	93	326
George	48	m	w	ENGL	Nevada	Grass Valley Twp	75	187
BRUNTY								
John T	35	m	w	MO	Siskiyou	Butte Twp	89	585
BRUSAN								
Frederick	23	m	w	VT	Nevada	Little York Twp	75	234
BRUSCHE								
Huschle	33	m	w	CANA	Nevada	Grass Valley Twp	75	156
BRUSCHER								
Fred	20	m	w	FRAN	San Francisco	2-Wd San Francisco	79	240
BRUSEN								
George	45	m	w	FRAN	Alameda	Brooklyn	68	38
BRUSH								
Albert	53	m	w	NY	San Francisco	San Francisco P O	85	857
Albert	42	m	w	CANA	Solano	Vallejo	90	165
David C	54	m	w	KY	Sonoma	Cloverdale Twp	91	269
Ellsworth	23	m	w	NY	Marin	Tomales Twp	74	79
Francisco	42	m	w	ITAL	Mariposa	Maxwell Crk P O	74	139
Harry	19	m	w	NY	Los Angeles	Los Angeles	73	525
John	56	m	w	PA	San Bernardino	San Bernardino Twp	78	438
Nelson	34	m	w	NY	Mendocino	Round Valley Twp	74	216
P	59	m	w	NY	Lake	Knoxville Mines	73	404
Philetus P	58	m	w	NY	Yolo	Cottonwood Twp	93	473
R W	65	m	w	MA	San Joaquin	2-Wd Stockton	86	203
Reuben G	35	m	w	IL	San Francisco	San Francisco P O	85	724
Thos	23	m	w	ENGL	San Francisco	7-Wd San Francisco	81	238
W T	28	m	w	PA	Mendocino	Sanel Twp	74	227
BRUSHELL								
Lucinda	41	f	m	NY	San Francisco	San Francisco P O	80	386
BRUSHER								
Adam	36	m	w	HCAS	Humboldt	Bucksport Twp	72	244
Joseph	30	m	w	NY	San Francisco	San Francisco P O	80	340
BRUSIE								
C J	49	m	w	FRAN	Tuolumne	Sonora P O	93	309
Luther	48	m	w	CT	Amador	Ione City P O	69	350
Robt	52	m	w	CT	Sacramento	Alabama Twp	77	60
BRUSIELL								
E S	48	m	w	PA	San Joaquin	Tulare Twp	86	255
BRUSKIN								
Wm	39	m	w	AUST	Tuolumne	Chinese Camp P O	93	378
BRUSLON								
Michael	44	m	w	IREL	Butte	Oregon Twp	70	127
BRUSO								
L	40	m	w	CANA	Sierra	Lincoln Twp	89	549
BRUSS								
Fred	23	m	w	PRUS	Sonoma	Russian Rvr	91	373
BRUSSEL								
Wash	46	m	w	NY	Butte	Chico Twp	70	17
BRUSTER								
Calvin	83	m	w	CT	Sonoma	Petaluma Twp	91	314
Charles	20	m	w	RI	San Francisco	7-Wd San Francisco	81	180
George	50	m	w	NORW	San Francisco	11-Wd San Francisc	84	707
Henery	26	m	w	RI	San Francisco	7-Wd San Francisco	81	180
J A	40	m	w	PA	Alameda	Oakland	68	214
BRUSTGREEN								
Henrietta	23	f	w	HANO	Alameda	Eden Twp	68	84
BRUSTGRUN								
Frederick	41	m	w	SHOL	Alameda	Eden Twp	68	60
BRUTEN								
J J	36	m	w	KY	Lake	Kelsey Crk	73	403
BRUTHBANK								
Julius	42	m	w	PRUS	Monterey	San Juan Twp	74	407
BRUTON								
James	36	m	w	IREL	Marin	San Rafael Twp	74	32
John	33	m	w	AL	San Francisco	6-Wd San Francisco	81	97
BRUTSCHER								
Adam	23	m	w	PRUS	San Francisco	8-Wd San Francisco	82	310
BRUTTIG								
Peter	20	m	w	PRUS	San Francisco	San Francisco P O	85	875
BRUTY								
Edward	31	m	w	ENGL	San Mateo	Schoolhouse Statio	87	336
BRUVETTA								
Agoosta	44	m	w	FRAN	Fresno	Millerton P O	72	146
BRUZE								
Thomas F	40	m	w	VA	El Dorado	Kelsey Twp	72	59
BRUZILL								
Antone	26	m	w	PORT	Butte	Ophir Twp	70	100
BRUZSE								
Norman	42	m	w	OH	El Dorado	Coloma Twp	72	10
BRUZZENO								
A	24	m	w	ITAL	Amador	Jackson P O	69	329
BRUZZO								
Juan	43	m	w	ITAL	Marin	San Rafael Twp	74	36
BRY								
Chow	35	m	c	CHIN	Butte	Concow Twp	70	11
Henry	11	m	w	CA	Siskiyou	Yreka Twp	89	666
William	14	m	w	CA	Siskiyou	Yreka Twp	89	665
BRYAL								
A D	38	m	w	IREL	Alameda	Oakland	68	244
BRYALDO								
Alberto	30	m	w	MEXI	Los Angeles	El Monte Twp	73	461
BRYAN								
Abner	68	m	w	MO	Monterey	San Juan Twp	74	417
Andrew	32	m	w	MA	Sacramento	2-Wd Sacramento	77	235
Annie	8	f	w	CA	San Francisco	11-Wd San Francisc	84	710
Archie	35	m	w	IL	San Francisco	11-Wd San Francisc	84	466
Benj B	37	m	w	KY	Sacramento	4-Wd Sacramento	77	333
Charles	35	m	w	ENGL	San Francisco	11-Wd San Francisc	84	566
Chas	4	m	w	CA	San Francisco	San Francisco P O	85	828
Columbus M	36	m	w	KY	Placer	Bath P O	76	422
Daniel C	63	m	w	NY	San Francisco	6-Wd San Francisco	81	90
Ed	23	m	w	IREL	Sierra	Table Rock Twp	89	575
Edward	24	m	w	IREL	Placer	Rocklin Twp	76	468
Hamlin S	38	m	w	KY	Placer	Bath P O	76	421
Isaac	33	m	w	PA	Sacramento	Franklin Twp	77	108
Jacob	57	m	w	PA	Monterey	San Juan Twp	74	391
Jacob	38	m	w	OH	San Mateo	Schoolhouse Statio	87	331
James	45	m	w	IREL	San Francisco	1-Wd San Francisco	79	62
James	34	m	w	IREL	Humboldt	Eureka Twp	72	278
James	31	m	w	IREL	San Francisco	8-Wd San Francisco	82	379
Jno E	40	m	w	SWED	Sacramento	3-Wd Sacramento	77	304
John	49	m	w	NY	El Dorado	Mud Springs Twp	72	89
John	41	m	w	IREL	Alameda	Oakland	68	181
John	33	m	w	IREL	San Francisco	San Francisco P O	83	243
John	24	m	w	PA	San Bernardino	San Bernardino Twp	78	430
John A	50	m	w	PA	Nevada	Grass Valley Twp	75	190
John V	42	m	w	IREL	Placer	Colfax P O	76	389
Joseph	44	m	w	KY	Calaveras	San Andreas P O	70	165
Louis	23	m	b	VA	Los Angeles	Los Angeles	73	547
M J	50	m	w	VA	Tehama	Merrill	92	198
Mark H	52	m	w	VT	San Francisco	8-Wd San Francisco	82	493
Mary	40	f	w	IREL	San Francisco	11-Wd San Francisc	84	539
Mary	25	f	w	IREL	San Francisco	11-Wd San Francisc	84	643
Michael	46	m	w	IREL	San Francisco	11-Wd San Francisc	84	526
P O	37	m	w	IREL	San Francisco	San Francisco P O	83	332
Patk	38	m	w	IREL	San Francisco	1-Wd San Francisco	79	72
Saml	33	m	w	MA	San Francisco	11-Wd San Francisc	84	595
Samuel	65	m	m	JAMA	San Francisco	San Francisco P O	85	743
Thomas	58	m	w	ENGL	Santa Clara	1-Wd San Jose	88	234
Thomas	45	m	w	IREL	Sonoma	Vallejo Twp	91	451
Thomas	34	m	w	IREL	San Francisco	8-Wd San Francisco	82	474
Thos	36	m	w	IREL	San Francisco	8-Wd San Francisco	82	331

© 2001 by Heritage Quest. All rights reserved.

Name	Age	S	R	B-PL	County	Locale	Roll	Pg
						Series M593		
William	50	m	w	ENGL	San Francisco	San Francisco P O	80	411
William	42	m	w	IREL	San Francisco	7-Wd San Francisco	81	173
William	36	m	w	IREL	San Francisco	8-Wd San Francisco	82	471
William	30	m	w	MO	San Francisco	11-Wd San Francisc	84	437
Wm	8	m	w	CA	San Francisco	San Francisco P O	85	828
Wm H	58	m	w	NY	San Francisco	8-Wd San Francisco	82	364
BRYAND								
C S	46	m	w	VT	Sutter	Vernon Twp	92	136
BRYANS								
Adam T	40	m	w	MO	San Luis Obispo	Arroyo Grande Twp	87	275
Prudence	85	m	w	KY	San Luis Obispo	Arroyo Grande Twp	87	275
BRYANT								
---	40	m	w	IREL	Sacramento	4-Wd Sacramento	77	346
Alexander	43	m	w	NY	San Francisco	11-Wd San Francisc	84	562
Alfred	46	m	w	NY	San Francisco	3-Wd San Francisco	79	315
Alonzo	27	m	w	NY	San Francisco	11-Wd San Francisc	84	456
And J	38	m	w	NH	San Francisco	8-Wd San Francisco	82	334
Andrew J	41	m	w	KY	Santa Barbara	San Buenaventura P	87	443
Anson B	37	m	w	OH	El Dorado	Lake Valley Twp	72	65
Anthony F	46	m	w	MA	Mono	Bridgeport P O	74	282
Barney S	40	m	w	GA	Los Angeles	Los Angeles	73	544
Bascom	38	m	w	IN	Tehama	Red Bank Twp	92	169
Berkly	41	m	w	OH	El Dorado	Lake Valley Twp	72	65
Burke	47	m	w	OH	San Joaquin	Dent Twp	86	24
C P	49	m	w	KY	Sonoma	Santa Rosa	91	425
Caleb R	65	m	w	MA	Calaveras	San Andreas P O	70	198
Calvin	51	m	w	VT	Humboldt	Eel Rvr Twp	72	255
Catherine	21	f	w	LA	Solano	Vallejo	90	210
Charles	45	m	w	SWED	Butte	Mountain Spring Tw	70	88
Charles	39	m	b	ENGL	Santa Clara	2-Wd San Jose	88	333
Charles D	37	m	w	ENGL	Santa Cruz	Watsonville	89	364
Charles G	32	m	w	ENGL	Sonoma	Petaluma Twp	91	326
Chas	34	m	w	PA	Yuba	Marysville	93	583
Chas L	28	m	w	IL	Sonoma	Cloverdale Twp	91	266
D	16	m	w	CA	Alameda	Oakland	68	243
D S	46	m	w	MA	Alameda	Oakland	68	231
Daniel M	23	m	w	VT	Mendocino	Bourns Landing Twp	74	223
E	17	m	w	CA	Alameda	Oakland	68	243
E C	23	m	w	KY	Solano	Vallejo	90	171
E J	33	m	w	IL	Santa Clara	Gilroy Twp	88	73
Edward S	49	m	w	NY	El Dorado	Mud Springs Twp	72	83
Edwd	38	m	w	IREL	San Francisco	San Francisco P O	83	42
Elbridge	44	m	w	ME	Sacramento	American Twp	77	67
Ester	24	f	w	KY	Placer	Dutch Flat P O	76	415
Frances	72	f	w	MA	San Francisco	11-Wd San Francisc	84	562
G W	50	m	w	AR	Monterey	Castroville Twp	74	325
Gardiner	38	m	w	SC	Contra Costa	Martinez P O	71	436
Geo	44	m	w	NY	Alameda	Oakland	68	240
Geo	30	m	w	ENGL	San Francisco	1-Wd San Francisco	79	46
George	49	m	w	MA	Calaveras	San Andreas P O	70	152
George	45	m	w	OH	Placer	Gold Run Twp	76	398
George	36	m	w	NH	Nevada	Nevada Twp	75	322
George H	40	m	w	MA	San Francisco	6-Wd San Francisco	81	150
George W	60	m	w	NY	Placer	Colfax P O	76	389
H	24	f	w	PRUS	Santa Clara	Gilroy Twp	88	76
H D	36	m	w	PA	Napa	Napa	75	16
Herman	32	m	w	NY	San Francisco	11-Wd San Francisc	84	562
J	46	m	w	KY	San Joaquin	Elliott Twp	86	75
J Henry	43	m	w	ME	Nevada	Nevada Twp	75	308
J N	33	m	w	ME	Napa	Yountville Twp	75	89
J S	40	m	w	ME	Tuolumne	Columbia P O	93	362
Jackson	40	m	w	ME	Humboldt	Eureka Twp	72	270
James	60	m	w	ENGL	San Francisco	1-Wd San Francisco	79	106
James	46	m	w	ENGL	Contra Costa	Martinez P O	71	425
James	40	m	m	MD	Sacramento	2-Wd Sacramento	77	229
James	38	m	w	ENGL	San Francisco	San Francisco P O	85	817
James	30	m	w	AUSL	San Bernardino	San Bernardino Twp	78	441
James	29	m	w	IREL	Siskiyou	Scott Valley Twp	89	619
James	27	m	w	NY	San Francisco	5-Wd San Francisco	81	35
James B	50	m	w	TN	Stanislaus	Emory Twp	92	26
James M	52	m	w	KY	El Dorado	White Oak Twp	72	141
James S	35	m	w	MA	San Francisco	2-Wd San Francisco	79	284
Jas	37	m	w	OH	Tehama	Antelope Twp	92	155
Jerry	35	m	w	OH	Plumas	Seneca Twp	77	48
Johanna	30	f	w	BREM	San Francisco	8-Wd San Francisco	82	427
John	40	m	w	ENGL	Plumas	Plumas Twp	77	26
John	38	m	w	ME	Butte	Chico Twp	70	39
John	35	m	w	ENGL	Yuba	Marysville	93	604
John	35	m	w	FL	San Luis Obispo	Salinas Twp	87	288
John	33	m	b	PA	San Francisco	6-Wd San Francisco	81	70
John	33	m	w	MO	Santa Clara	Fremont Twp	88	63
John	27	m	w	NY	Solano	Vallejo	90	139
John	26	m	w	ENGL	San Francisco	11-Wd San Francisc	84	633
John	23	m	w	ME	San Francisco	San Francisco P O	85	785
John G	27	m	w	WI	Yolo	Putah Twp	93	513
Joseph	47	m	w	NY	El Dorado	Diamond Springs Tw	72	33
Joshua	28	m	w	VT	Yolo	Cottonwood Twp	93	467
Julia	25	f	w	IREL	Humboldt	Eureka Twp	72	272
L H	58	m	w	NY	Sacramento	Dry Crk Twp	77	101
Lewis	38	m	w	MA	El Dorado	Georgetown Twp	72	45
Lillian	26	f	b	NY	San Francisco	6-Wd San Francisco	81	70
Mary	45	f	w	ME	San Francisco	San Francisco P O	83	215
Michael	22	m	w	NY	San Francisco	5-Wd San Francisco	81	35
Morgan	64	m	w	KY	San Luis Obispo	Santa Rosa Twp	87	327
Morrison	55	m	w	VA	Colusa	Monroe Twp	71	311
Nathaniel	42	m	w	KY	Placer	Dutch Flat P O	76	414
Nelson	44	m	w	NY	San Francisco	6-Wd San Francisco	81	70
Nora	45	f	w	IREL	Solano	Vallejo	90	160
O H	45	m	w	MA	Solano	Vallejo	90	164
Octovies	34	f	b	MO	Yuba	Slate Range Bar Tw	93	673
Orout	20	m	w	OH	Sutter	Vernon Twp	92	136
Orrin B	20	m	w	NY	Placer	Colfax P O	76	389
P M	16	m	w	CA	Alameda	Oakland	68	243
Patrick	40	m	w	MA	San Francisco	6-Wd San Francisco	81	86
Patrick	36	m	w	IREL	Sacramento	2-Wd Sacramento	77	223
Perry M	48	m	w	MO	Santa Clara	San Jose Twp	88	205
R M	46	m	w	ME	Alameda	Oakland	68	236
Richd	35	m	w	ENGL	San Francisco	1-Wd San Francisco	79	46
Richd	35	m	w	ENGL	San Francisco	1-Wd San Francisco	79	46
Robert	34	m	w	NY	San Francisco	San Francisco P O	83	353
Rolla	42	m	w	VT	Humboldt	Eel Rvr Twp	72	251
Rosa	50	f	b	LA	Nevada	Little York Twp	75	235
Rufus	26	m	w	OH	Sacramento	2-Wd Sacramento	77	243
Ruth	51	f	w	MA	Sonoma	Analy Twp	91	231
Samuel	37	m	w	MO	Monterey	Castroville Twp	74	328
Samuel	26	m	w	PA	Monterey	San Antonio Twp	74	319
Samul M	27	m	w	TX	Los Angeles	Los Angeles	73	540
T B	36	m	w	KY	San Joaquin	Elliott Twp	86	76
Thomas	50	m	w	IREL	Yolo	Cache Crk Twp	93	426
Thomas	46	m	w	MA	Marin	Bolinas Twp	74	7
Thomas	43	m	w	IL	Sonoma	Vallejo Twp	91	457
Thomas	27	m	w	ME	San Francisco	7-Wd San Francisco	81	218
Thomas	22	m	w	MO	Colusa	Monroe Twp	71	313
Thomas	10	m	m	CA	San Francisco	San Francisco P O	80	365
W S	42	m	w	IL	Napa	Napa	75	16
Warren	41	m	w	NY	San Francisco	11-Wd San Francisc	84	562
Wilford	39	m	w	GUYA	San Francisco	San Francisco P O	85	718
William	46	m	b	VA	San Francisco	San Francisco P O	80	423
William	41	m	w	PA	San Bernardino	San Bernardino Twp	78	454
William	39	m	w	ME	Nevada	Grass Valley Twp	75	175
William	36	m	w	IREL	Colusa	Spring Valley Twp	71	344
Wm	50	m	w	KY	San Joaquin	Oneal Twp	86	115
Wm	45	m	w	KY	San Joaquin	Oneal Twp	86	114
Wm	33	m	w	KY	Butte	Chico Twp	70	32
Wm	30	m	w	ENGL	Sacramento	Natomas Twp	77	170
Wm	30	m	w	ENGL	San Joaquin	2-Wd Stockton	86	168
Wm C	69	m	w	IL	Sonoma	Vallejo Twp	91	456
Wm D	26	m	w	MA	San Francisco	7-Wd San Francisco	81	248
Wm H	35	m	w	CANA	Nevada	Rough & Ready Twp	75	327
Wm H	28	m	w	CANA	Monterey	Alisal Twp	74	289
BRYANTI								
Emmanuel	37	m	w	ITAL	San Francisco	11-Wd San Francisc	84	594
BRYCE								
Robert C	43	m	w	SCOT	Santa Clara	2-Wd San Jose	88	283
Thos	32	m	w	SCOT	San Francisco	11-Wd San Francisc	84	610
BRYCH								
Mary	36	f	w	NY	Calaveras	San Andreas P O	70	213
BRYDEN								
J W	27	m	w	PA	Santa Barbara	Santa Barbara P O	87	455
James C	41	m	w	OH	Yuba	Marysville Twp	93	567
BRYDGES								
Marshal	43	m	w	ENGL	San Francisco	San Francisco P O	83	255
BRYDING								
Mary	32	f	w	FRAN	Sacramento	1-Wd Sacramento	77	190
P	40	m	w	HOLL	Sacramento	1-Wd Sacramento	77	190
BRYDON								
Joseph	28	m	w	ENGL	Contra Costa	Martinez P O	71	376
Robert	40	m	w	SCOT	Nevada	Grass Valley Twp	75	174
BRYENE								
Anna	45	f	w	IREL	San Francisco	2-Wd San Francisco	79	151
BRYER								
Charles	32	m	w	PA	Santa Clara	2-Wd San Jose	88	329
Frank	35	m	w	IL	Solano	Suisun Twp	90	102
John	39	m	w	HANO	Yuba	Linda Twp	93	555
BRYERLY								
Thomas	27	m	w	IREL	San Mateo	San Mateo P O	87	355
BRYMER								
Jasper	28	m	w	TN	Los Angeles	Los Nietos Twp	73	574
BRYNARD								
G Wm	30	m	w	CANA	San Diego	San Diego	78	491
BRYNE								
Frank	27	m	w	NY	Solano	Vallejo	90	139
James	25	m	w	ENGL	Sonoma	Salt Point	91	385
Jno	35	m	w	IREL	Alameda	Oakland	68	220
John	34	m	w	WURT	San Francisco	3-Wd San Francisco	79	289
John A	25	m	w	IREL	San Francisco	3-Wd San Francisco	79	297
Martha	35	f	w	IREL	El Dorado	Coloma Twp	72	1
William	28	m	w	ENGL	Monterey	San Juan Twp	74	404
BRYSON								
John	38	m	w	MO	Nevada	Rough & Ready Twp	75	333
Mary	21	f	w	MA	San Francisco	7-Wd San Francisco	81	269
Peter	38	m	w	IREL	San Francisco	7-Wd San Francisco	81	190
Peter	24	m	w	FRAN	Nevada	Eureka Twp	75	138
Susan	45	f	w	KY	Butte	Chico Twp	70	45
Thomas	45	m	w	VA	Kern	Bakersfield P O	73	365
Thos	14	m	w	CA	San Francisco	11-Wd San Francisc	84	586
William	18	m	w	NY	San Francisco	7-Wd San Francisco	81	161
William J	23	m	w	NY	Sacramento	2-Wd Sacramento	77	240
Wm	35	m	w	ENGL	San Diego	San Diego	78	491
Wm W	40	m	w	MI	Sacramento	Brighton Twp	77	75
BRYTE								
Mike	42	m	w	OH	Sacramento	3-Wd Sacramento	77	271
BTEYJOGGLE								
Hannah	53	f	w	NY	Alameda	San Leandro	68	94

© 2001 by Heritage Quest. All rights reserved.

California 1870 Census

Series M593

Name	Age	S	R	B-PL	County	Locale	Roll	Pg
BU								
Ah	38	m	c	CHIN	Nevada	Nevada Twp	75	312
Ah	35	m	c	CHIN	El Dorado	Cosumnes Twp	72	13
BUALAND								
John	40	m	w	NY	Monterey	Castroville Twp	74	329
BUAR								
Levi	65	m	w	CT	San Francisco	2-Wd San Francisco	79	205
BUARINIO								
Bartole	40	m	w	CHIL	Los Angeles	Los Angeles Twp	73	481
BUBAKER								
Mary	23	f	w	OH	San Francisco	7-Wd San Francisco	81	174
BUBB								
Benjamin T	32	m	w	MO	Santa Clara	Fremont Twp	88	48
John	42	m	w	MO	Santa Clara	Redwood Twp	88	122
William H	34	m	w	MO	Santa Clara	Fremont Twp	88	48
BUBBEN								
Anna	25	f	w	PRUS	San Francisco	1-Wd San Francisco	79	23
BUBBETT								
J W	23	m	w	IL	San Joaquin	Dent Twp	86	16
BUBBY								
Felix	50	m	w	GERM	Mono	Bridgeport P O	74	286
BUBEE								
David	65	m	w	NY	Santa Barbara	Santa Barbara P O	87	494
Francis M	16	m	w	CA	Santa Barbara	Santa Barbara P O	87	495
Napoleon B	29	m	w	AR	Santa Barbara	Santa Barbara P O	87	495
BUBEN								
Charles	54	m	w	PRUS	San Francisco	11-Wd San Francisc	84	504
BUBESKIMER								
P	42	m	w	PRUS	Sierra	Downieville Twp	89	520
BUBS								
Anna	33	f	w	MO	Inyo	Lone Pine Twp	73	330
BUC								
Ah	28	m	c	CHIN	El Dorado	Diamond Springs Tw	72	27
BUCACES								
Manuel	55	m	w	CA	San Diego	San Luis Rey	78	514
BUCEY								
John C	34	m	w	OH	Nevada	Eureka Twp	75	128
BUCH								
Henry	54	m	w	PRUS	San Francisco	San Francisco P O	83	375
John	25	m	w	KY	Marin	San Rafael Twp	74	37
L F	43	m	w	NORW	Nevada	Eureka Twp	75	131
BUCHAN								
Wm	47	m	w	SCOT	El Dorado	Greenwood Twp	72	50
BUCHANAN								
Andrew	22	m	w	CANA	Mendocino	Navarro & Big Rvr	74	175
Catherine	35	f	w	IREL	San Francisco	3-Wd San Francisco	79	291
Chas	25	m	w	MA	San Francisco	7-Wd San Francisco	81	275
Geo	40	m	w	ME	Humboldt	Bucksport Twp	72	243
George	35	m	w	IN	Colusa	Stony Crk Twp	71	333
George	34	m	m	OH	Colusa	Colusa	71	296
Henry	38	m	w	IREL	San Francisco	8-Wd San Francisco	82	435
Isaiah	38	m	m	PA	Sacramento	2-Wd Sacramento	77	229
J	57	m	w	TN	San Joaquin	Castoria Twp	86	2
J F	51	m	w	NY	Sutter	Butte Twp	92	98
James	33	m	w	VT	Colusa	Monroe Twp	71	314
Jas	40	m	w	OH	San Joaquin	Castoria Twp	86	15
John	50	m	w	IREL	San Francisco	7-Wd San Francisco	81	229
John	38	m	w	CANA	Mendocino	Point Arena Twp	74	224
John	35	m	w	IREL	San Francisco	3-Wd San Francisco	79	317
John	30	m	w	CANA	San Francisco	San Francisco P O	80	384
L S	22	m	w	BAVA	San Francisco	8-Wd San Francisco	82	362
M	24	m	w	CANA	Mendocino	Calpella Twp	74	183
M L	23	f	w	VT	San Francisco	8-Wd San Francisco	82	363
Phil J	48	m	w	NY	Butte	Ophir Twp	70	95
Sarah	47	f	w	KY	San Francisco	11-Wd San Francisc	84	622
Walter	32	m	w	VT	El Dorado	Mud Springs Twp	72	74
William	54	m	w	SCOT	Santa Cruz	Santa Cruz Twp	89	387
William	43	m	w	SAXO	Alameda	Alvarado	68	304
William	27	m	w	CANA	San Francisco	San Francisco P O	83	318
BUCHANNAN								
Chas L	25	m	w	MO	Placer	Colfax P O	76	390
Edwd	28	m	w	PA	Marin	San Rafael	74	54
James	26	m	w	CANA	Nevada	Grass Valley Twp	75	208
John	42	m	w	IREL	Marin	Tomales Twp	74	79
M C	14	f	w	CA	Yuba	Marysville	93	598
Will	37	m	w	NY	Placer	Colfax P O	76	391
BUCHANNON								
Puly	11	f	w	GERM	Los Angeles	Los Angeles	73	513
BUCHANON								
John W C	38	m	w	OH	Los Angeles	Los Angeles	73	541
BUCHARD								
Emil	33	m	w	FRAN	Monterey	San Juan Twp	74	412
James	46	m	w	LA	San Francisco	San Francisco P O	83	311
John	43	m	w	CANA	Siskiyou	Table Rock Twp	89	646
L A	40	f	w	VA	Santa Clara	Gilroy Twp	88	70
Sarah	18	f	w	CA	Sacramento	2-Wd Sacramento	77	221
BUCHARDT								
Frederick	24	m	w	PRUS	San Francisco	8-Wd San Francisco	82	460
BUCHART								
Anton	21	m	w	PRUS	San Francisco	San Francisco P O	80	478
Matthew	30	m	w	DENM	San Francisco	2-Wd San Francisco	79	226
BUCHELE								
Philip	37	m	w	WURT	Santa Clara	1-Wd San Jose	88	231
BUCHELL								
Henetta	44	f	w	FRAN	Nevada	Bridgeport Twp	75	102
Louis	36	m	w	NY	Nevada	Bridgeport Twp	75	103

Series M593

Name	Age	S	R	B-PL	County	Locale	Roll	Pg
BUCHENAN								
Geo M	43	m	w	HDAR	Mariposa	Mariposa P O	74	96
BUCHER								
Andrew	32	m	w	SWIT	Marin	Novato Twp	74	13
Herman S	36	m	w	NY	Placer	Bath P O	76	433
Jas	22	m	w	IREL	Sacramento	3-Wd Sacramento	77	269
John	32	m	w	OH	Siskiyou	Surprise Valley Tw	89	641
M	35	m	w	GERM	Sacramento	1-Wd Sacramento	77	185
Thomas	16	m	w	CA	Marin	San Rafael Twp	74	31
Wm	34	m	w	MO	Santa Clara	Gilroy Twp	88	99
BUCHHOLTZ								
Gottleib	41	m	w	PRUS	San Francisco	San Francisco P O	80	467
John	39	m	w	PRUS	San Francisco	San Francisco P O	80	467
BUCHLENKIERCHEN								
A	22	m	w	HANO	San Francisco	1-Wd San Francisco	79	108
BUCHLER								
John C	29	m	w	SWIT	San Francisco	San Francisco P O	85	754
BUCHLY								
--- Mr	62	m	w	ENGL	Sacramento	Sutter Twp	77	386
BUCHMAN								
C	40	m	w	PRUS	San Joaquin	1-Wd Stockton	86	131
Walker	56	m	w	VT	Solano	Tremont Twp	90	35
Wm	46	m	w	NY	Sierra	Sears Twp	89	556
BUCHNAN								
N J	48	m	w	NH	El Dorado	Georgetown Twp	72	36
BUCHNER								
Geo	40	m	w	BAVA	Siskiyou	Scott Valley Twp	89	611
BUCHO								
Samuel	38	m	w	GREE	Tuolumne	Columbia P O	93	345
BUCHOLTZ								
Catherine	21	f	w	PRUS	San Francisco	8-Wd San Francisco	82	485
BUCHTA								
F	42	m	w	PRUS	Sierra	Lincoln Twp	89	552
BUCHWALD								
Fred	31	m	w	DENM	Butte	Chico Twp	70	26
BUCIGALUPI								
John	23	m	w	ITAL	San Francisco	6-Wd San Francisco	81	92
BUCK								
A	58	m	w	SCOT	Lassen	Long Valley Twp	73	436
Ah	42	m	c	CHIN	Placer	Auburn P O	76	375
Ah	34	m	c	CHIN	Placer	Auburn P O	76	371
Ah	28	m	c	CHIN	Nevada	Washington Twp	75	339
Ah	17	m	c	CHIN	San Francisco	3-Wd San Francisco	79	320
Allen	63	m	w	NY	Amador	Jackson P O	69	341
Andrew	40	m	w	IL	San Francisco	11-Wd San Francisc	84	514
Charles	22	m	w	FRAN	Sonoma	Analy Twp	91	225
Chaw	17	m	c	CHIN	Nevada	Bridgeport Twp	75	111
Danl	45	m	w	PA	San Francisco	5-Wd San Francisco	81	31
Edward	36	m	w	NY	San Joaquin	1-Wd Stockton	86	124
Edwin	60	m	w	ME	Tuolumne	Chinese Camp P O	93	383
Elijah	49	m	w	NY	Yuba	Marysville	93	603
Fred	34	m	w	HANO	San Francisco	2-Wd San Francisco	79	275
George	38	m	w	CANA	Stanislaus	Empire Twp	92	34
George	36	m	w	IREL	San Francisco	San Francisco P O	83	240
H	57	m	w	NY	Lake	Lower Lake	73	415
Henry	26	m	w	PRUS	San Francisco	1-Wd San Francisco	79	104
Hermann	20	m	w	HANO	San Francisco	2-Wd San Francisco	79	221
Hiram M	33	m	w	NY	Santa Cruz	Pajaro Twp	89	350
Howard	56	m	w	MA	Lake	Little Borax	73	419
Hup	29	m	c	CHIN	Yuba	Marysville	93	630
J	30	m	w	OH	Sacramento	1-Wd Sacramento	77	178
James	30	m	w	ENGL	Los Angeles	Santa Ana Twp	73	600
James A	40	m	w	OH	Santa Clara	San Jose Twp	88	209
Jas S	35	m	w	CANA	San Diego	San Diego	78	490
Joel H	13	m	w	VT	San Mateo	Redwood Twp	87	363
John	51	m	w	MA	San Francisco	3-Wd San Francisco	79	303
John	37	m	w	HANO	San Francisco	San Francisco P O	85	769
John	33	m	w	IREL	San Francisco	San Francisco P O	85	810
John	30	m	w	IREL	Contra Costa	Martinez P O	71	444
Justis	66	m	w	NY	Calaveras	San Andreas P O	70	158
Lymon	65	m	w	VT	Yuba	Slate Range Bar Tw	93	673
M	30	m	w	PA	Nevada	Bloomfield Twp	75	94
Mary	18	f	w	IL	San Francisco	11-Wd San Francisc	84	595
Moses P	54	m	w	NY	Mendocino	Little Lake Twp	74	200
Ohim	49	m	w	IREL	San Joaquin	1-Wd Stockton	86	123
Patrick	35	m	w	IREL	Tuolumne	Sonora P O	93	326
Poo	21	m	c	CHIN	Yuba	Marysville	93	630
Que	30	m	c	CHIN	Yuba	Marysville	93	630
Robert	49	m	w	PA	Siskiyou	Surprise Valley Tw	89	642
S M	38	m	w	ME	Humboldt	Eureka Twp	72	269
Samuel	35	m	w	CANA	Marin	Tomales Twp	74	88
Thomas	49	m	w	HANO	Marin	Sausalito Twp	74	67
Thos	47	m	w	ME	San Joaquin	3-Wd Stockton	86	228
William	53	m	w	OH	Santa Clara	1-Wd San Jose	88	277
William H	22	m	w	CANA	Klamath	Camp Gaston	73	372
Wm	35	m	w	HANO	San Francisco	San Francisco P O	83	81
Wm	24	m	w	OLDE	San Francisco	San Francisco P O	83	73
Wm R	44	m	w	IN	Mendocino	Ukiah Twp	74	240
BUCKALEW								
Ansel S	36	m	w	NY	Colusa	Colusa	71	288
BUCKANNAN								
Elizabeth	40	f	w	PRUS	San Francisco	San Francisco P O	83	379
BUCKART								
Albert	34	m	w	BADE	Santa Clara	1-Wd San Jose	88	232
BUCKBEE								
Charles A	46	m	w	NY	San Francisco	8-Wd San Francisco	82	474
John	44	m	w	NY	San Francisco	11-Wd San Francisc	84	582

© 2001 by Heritage Quest. All rights reserved.

Series M593

Name	Age	S	R	B-PL	County	Locale	Roll	Pg
BUCKE								
Michael	30	m	w	CANA	Contra Costa	Martinez P O	71	446
BUCKEK								
J W	26	m	w	ME	Santa Clara	Gilroy Twp	88	97
BUCKELEW								
Franklin	25	m	w	OH	Marin	San Rafael	74	49
Martha	54	f	w	PA	Marin	San Rafael Twp	74	59
BUCKER								
Gustavus	22	m	w	HAMB	San Francisco	3-Wd San Francisco	79	324
Heny F	20	m	w	ME	San Francisco	8-Wd San Francisco	82	458
Jacob	40	m	w	PRUS	Butte	Hamilton Twp	70	64
William W	54	m	w	CT	El Dorado	White Oak Twp	72	137
BUCKERT								
Dehlia	10	f	w	CA	San Francisco	5-Wd San Francisco	81	1
BUCKERY								
Lovesta	13	f	w	ME	San Francisco	San Francisco P O	83	387
BUCKETT								
James	40	m	w	ENGL	Nevada	Grass Valley Twp	75	215
Thomas	37	m	w	ENGL	Nevada	Grass Valley Twp	75	231
Thomas	30	m	w	ENGL	Nevada	Grass Valley Twp	75	189
Wm Henry	37	m	w	ENGL	Nevada	Grass Valley Twp	75	189
BUCKHADER								
Lorendo	37	m	i	MEXI	Inyo	Cerro Gordo Twp	73	321
BUCKHALTER								
John	53	m	w	IN	Tulare	Visalia	92	297
BUCKHAM								
Andrew M	36	m	w	KY	Nevada	Grass Valley Twp	75	219
BUCKHANNAN								
J S	49	m	w	MO	Sonoma	Mendocino Twp	91	297
Jas	47	m	w	IN	Sonoma	Mendocino Twp	91	304
BUCKHARD								
Geo	35	m	w	DENM	San Francisco	2-Wd San Francisco	79	223
BUCKHART								
A H	47	m	w	NY	Alameda	Oakland	68	180
BUCKHOLTZ								
Henery	31	m	w	HANO	San Francisco	7-Wd San Francisco	81	218
BUCKING								
Diedrich	26	m	w	OLDE	San Francisco	1-Wd San Francisco	79	129
Domingo	22	m	w	SWIT	Monterey	Alisal Twp	74	291
Gezena	20	f	w	HANO	San Francisco	San Francisco P O	85	764
BUCKINGHAM								
C E	43	m	w	NY	San Francisco	8-Wd San Francisco	82	371
Digery	48	m	w	ENGL	Mariposa	Mariposa P O	74	134
Elen P	32	f	w	MA	San Francisco	8-Wd San Francisco	82	334
J	39	m	w	CT	Alameda	Oakland	68	189
John	20	m	w	NY	Kern	Havilah P O	73	350
Nathan	29	m	w	IL	Sonoma	Salt Point	91	389
Robert H	36	m	w	CT	Yolo	Washington Twp	93	530
Robt	40	m	w	ENGL	Santa Barbara	San Buenaventura P	87	425
S S	28	m	w	IL	Solano	Vallejo	90	160
Wm P	18	m	w	WI	San Francisco	San Francisco P O	85	824
BUCKINS								
V C	70	m	w	DC	Alameda	Oakland	68	200
BUCKLAND								
H M	39	m	w	PA	Calaveras	Copperopolis P O	70	224
James	33	m	w	CANA	Nevada	Rough & Ready Twp	75	327
John	33	m	w	FINL	San Francisco	3-Wd San Francisco	79	291
Low	40	m	w	ME	San Mateo	San Mateo P O	87	350
BUCKLAR								
John	48	m	w	FRAN	El Dorado	Georgetown Twp	72	41
BUCKLE								
Margaret	25	f	w	ENGL	San Francisco	San Francisco P O	85	788
BUCKLER								
Fanny	15	f	w	CHIN	San Francisco	San Francisco P O	83	93
BUCKLES								
Henry H	43	m	w	OH	Santa Cruz	Santa Cruz Twp	89	388
Newton	34	m	w	IREL	Solano	Silveyville Twp	90	86
Thomas	45	m	w	IN	Solano	Silveyville Twp	90	82
BUCKLEY								
Andrew	44	m	w	IREL	San Francisco	San Francisco P O	83	403
Ann Mrs	50	f	w	IREL	Amador	Ione City P O	69	362
Anna	38	f	w	IREL	Alameda	Alameda	68	2
Anne	30	f	w	IREL	San Francisco	6-Wd San Francisco	81	130
Briget	80	f	w	IREL	San Francisco	7-Wd San Francisco	81	179
Catherin	40	f	w	NY	Napa	Napa Twp	75	30
Catherine	35	f	w	IREL	San Francisco	8-Wd San Francisco	82	427
Christopher	26	m	w	OH	Los Angeles	Los Angeles	73	571
Christopher	24	m	w	NY	San Francisco	San Francisco P O	80	396
Corneilus	35	m	w	IREL	San Francisco	1-Wd San Francisco	79	92
Corneleus	35	m	w	IREL	Nevada	Grass Valley Twp	75	215
Cornelius	17	m	w	IREL	Santa Clara	1-Wd San Jose	88	246
Dan M	14	m	w	CA	Santa Cruz	Pajaro Twp	89	341
Danial	40	m	w	IREL	San Francisco	7-Wd San Francisco	81	175
David	26	m	w	NY	Sacramento	1-Wd Sacramento	77	173
Dennis	37	m	w	IREL	Alameda	Eden Twp	68	82
Dennis	30	m	w	IREL	San Francisco	7-Wd San Francisco	81	241
E J	27	m	w	AUSL	San Francisco	8-Wd San Francisco	82	358
Edmond	15	m	w	CA	Santa Clara	Santa Clara Twp	88	176
Edward	36	m	w	CANA	San Francisco	6-Wd San Francisco	81	114
Edward	34	m	w	IREL	San Francisco	2-Wd San Francisco	79	217
Edwd	26	m	w	ENGL	San Francisco	1-Wd San Francisco	79	8
Edwd J	30	m	w	IREL	San Francisco	1-Wd San Francisco	79	94
Eliza	35	f	w	IREL	San Francisco	11-Wd San Francisc	84	523
Ellen	67	f	w	IREL	Santa Cruz	Santa Cruz Twp	89	399
Francis	52	m	w	IREL	San Francisco	San Francisco P O	85	872
Francis Jr	21	m	w	CHIL	San Francisco	San Francisco P O	85	872
Frank	48	m	w	IREL	San Francisco	11-Wd San Francisc	84	460
Frank	28	m	w	IREL	San Francisco	San Francisco P O	83	380
Frank	21	m	w	IREL	Colusa	Colusa	71	292
G W	28	m	w	IA	Merced	Snelling P O	74	247
Geo	56	m	w	IREL	San Francisco	7-Wd San Francisco	81	265
Geo	49	m	w	ME	Butte	Ophir Twp	70	116
George	29	m	w	ENGL	San Francisco	8-Wd San Francisco	82	487
Hedge	35	m	w	IREL	Yuba	Rose Bar Twp	93	661
Henry	42	m	w	IREL	Plumas	Goodwin Twp	77	58
Henry	34	m	w	NY	Merced	Snelling P O	74	247
Henry	27	m	w	NY	San Francisco	5-Wd San Francisco	81	24
Homer	32	m	w	OH	Merced	Snelling P O	74	259
Horace	27	m	w	IL	Merced	Snelling P O	74	254
J	52	m	w	IREL	Sierra	Downieville Twp	89	519
J J	38	m	w	MA	San Francisco	San Francisco P O	85	848
James P	48	m	w	IREL	Mendocino	Anderson Twp	74	151
Jane	30	f	w	IREL	San Francisco	2-Wd San Francisco	79	221
Jeremia	25	m	w	IREL	San Francisco	San Francisco P O	83	272
Jeremiah	38	m	w	NY	San Francisco	San Francisco P O	85	772
Jeremiah	37	m	w	IREL	San Francisco	San Francisco P O	83	333
Jeremiah	35	m	w	IREL	San Francisco	San Francisco P O	85	864
Jno	31	m	w	NY	Sacramento	1-Wd Sacramento	77	172
Joanna	60	m	w	ITAL	Tuolumne	Sonora P O	93	330
Joanna	24	f	w	CANA	San Francisco	San Francisco P O	83	115
John	69	m	w	IREL	San Francisco	San Francisco P O	80	394
John	50	m	w	IREL	San Francisco	8-Wd San Francisco	82	423
John	48	m	w	ENGL	Santa Clara	1-Wd San Jose	88	248
John	45	m	w	IREL	Alameda	Eden Twp	68	86
John	43	m	w	IREL	Nevada	Grass Valley Twp	75	143
John	40	m	w	IREL	Nevada	Bridgeport Twp	75	115
John	30	m	w	IREL	Butte	Oregon Twp	70	124
John	27	m	w	IREL	Sonoma	Bodega Twp	91	249
John	23	m	w	IREL	San Francisco	1-Wd San Francisco	79	41
Joseph	24	m	w	NY	San Diego	San Diego	78	486
Julia	34	f	w	IREL	San Francisco	7-Wd San Francisco	81	282
M	29	m	w	IREL	Nevada	Meadow Lake Twp	75	252
M W	28	m	w	LA	Nevada	Meadow Lake Twp	75	247
Margret	30	f	w	IREL	San Francisco	1-Wd San Francisco	79	94
Mark	66	m	w	NJ	Placer	Auburn P O	76	373
Mary	45	f	w	IREL	San Francisco	8-Wd San Francisco	82	309
Mary	43	f	w	IREL	San Francisco	San Francisco P O	83	332
Mary	32	f	w	IREL	Nevada	Grass Valley Twp	75	211
Mary	21	f	w	IREL	Santa Clara	1-Wd San Jose	88	231
Mary A	20	f	w	IREL	Santa Clara	1-Wd San Jose	88	248
Michael	38	m	w	OH	Solano	Denverton Twp	90	26
Michael	34	m	w	IREL	Nevada	Grass Valley Twp	75	228
Michael	30	m	w	IREL	San Francisco	San Francisco P O	83	156
Michael	25	m	w	IREL	San Francisco	7-Wd San Francisco	81	249
Michael	25	m	w	IREL	Solano	Rio Vista Twp	90	64
Miffin	40	m	w	PA	Alameda	Washington Twp	68	296
Mike	60	m	w	IREL	San Joaquin	2-Wd Stockton	86	165
Mike	30	m	w	IREL	San Francisco	11-Wd San Francisc	84	667
Milton	27	m	w	CT	San Francisco	11-Wd San Francisc	84	550
P J	45	m	w	IREL	Sacramento	4-Wd Sacramento	77	340
Patrick	50	m	w	IREL	San Francisco	San Francisco P O	80	398
Patrick	35	m	w	IREL	San Francisco	San Francisco P O	85	870
Patrick	30	m	w	IREL	Klamath	Camp Gaston	73	372
Richard	24	m	w	IREL	San Francisco	7-Wd San Francisco	81	162
Robert	40	m	w	NY	Solano	Tremont Twp	90	30
Robert T	31	m	w	OH	Yolo	Cache Crk Twp	93	423
Rufus	27	m	w	OH	Plumas	Indian Twp	77	13
S	54	m	w	NY	Merced	Snelling P O	74	259
S P	20	m	w	IA	Merced	Snelling P O	74	247
Thomas	46	m	w	IREL	Yolo	Putah Twp	93	515
Thomas	43	m	w	MA	Calaveras	San Andreas P O	70	198
Thomas	38	m	w	IL	San Francisco	8-Wd San Francisco	82	381
Tim	28	m	w	IREL	Merced	Snelling P O	74	252
Timothy	40	m	w	IN	Sacramento	4-Wd Sacramento	77	349
Timothy	40	m	w	OH	Solano	Denverton Twp	90	26
Timothy	21	m	w	IREL	Nevada	Bloomfield Twp	75	97
William	45	m	w	MA	San Francisco	San Francisco P O	85	735
William	44	m	w	NY	Contra Costa	Martinez Twp	71	349
William	42	m	w	NY	Santa Clara	1-Wd San Jose	88	228
William	39	m	w	IREL	Calaveras	San Andreas P O	70	171
William H	48	m	w	NY	Contra Costa	Martinez P O	71	374
William H	28	m	w	IREL	San Francisco	San Francisco P O	83	339
BUCKLIN								
A G	50	m	w	RI	Amador	Sutter Crk P O	69	410
E P	41	m	w	RI	San Francisco	3-Wd San Francisco	79	313
S G	52	m	w	NY	San Francisco	8-Wd San Francisco	82	306
William R	40	m	w	IREL	Yuba	New York Twp	93	637
BUCKLOLZ								
Minnie	21	f	w	PRUS	San Francisco	San Francisco P O	83	327
BUCKLY								
J B	24	m	w	MA	San Joaquin	Elkhorn Twp	86	66
John	45	m	w	IREL	Napa	Napa Twp	75	61
John	45	m	w	KY	San Francisco	5-Wd San Francisco	81	17
John	40	m	w	IREL	Sacramento	Georgianna Twp	77	126
K	14	f	w	CA	Alameda	Oakland	68	242
Nellie	8	f	w	CA	Alameda	Oakland	68	242
Susan	28	f	w	IREL	San Mateo	Menlo Park P O	87	379
Timothy	22	m	w	IREL	San Mateo	San Mateo P O	87	350
W	12	f	w	CA	Alameda	Oakland	68	242
BUCKMAN								
---	25	m	w	US	Santa Cruz	Santa Cruz Twp	89	391
Amos	50	m	w	VT	San Diego	San Diego	78	492
Chas	33	m	w	HESS	Sacramento	4-Wd Sacramento	77	327
Clement	49	m	w	KY	Tulare	Farmersville Twp	92	244

© 2001 by Heritage Quest. All rights reserved.

Name	Age	S	R	B-PL	County	Locale	Roll	Pg
Ezra	53	m	w	ME	San Francisco	7-Wd San Francisco	81	276
F J	42	f	w	MA	Napa	Yountville Twp	75	83
G B	42	m	w	NY	Tuolumne	Sonora P O	93	321
George	58	m	w	MA	Santa Clara	Fremont Twp	88	64
Henry	41	m	w	PRUS	San Francisco	2-Wd San Francisco	79	242
Henry	35	m	w	WEST	San Francisco	6-Wd San Francisco	81	40
Jno G	27	m	w	MO	Nevada	Little York Twp	75	237
Jos	42	m	w	IREL	San Joaquin	2-Wd Stockton	86	185
Leonice	74	f	w	ME	Yolo	Washington Twp	93	528
Michael	34	m	w	HAMB	San Francisco	San Francisco P O	83	352
W	30	m	w	ENGL	San Francisco	8-Wd San Francisco	82	370
BUCKMASTER								
Charles	25	m	w	MA	Yolo	Cottonwood Twp	93	462
John	37	m	w	OH	Siskiyou	Yreka	89	657
John	32	m	w	CANA	San Francisco	San Francisco P O	83	188
L A	35	f	w	VT	San Mateo	San Mateo P O	87	357
Mary	19	f	w	CA	Sacramento	3-Wd Sacramento	77	266
BUCKMINSTER								
L	28	f	w	VT	Sacramento	3-Wd Sacramento	77	284
BUCKMIRE								
Charles	45	m	w	PRUS	Sacramento	Natomas Twp	77	169
BUCKMORE								
Geo	38	m	w	NY	San Francisco	1-Wd San Francisco	79	103
BUCKNA								
George	32	m	w	NY	Napa	Yountville Twp	75	78
BUCKNAN								
Hattie	16	f	w	US	Yuba	Marysville	93	609
BUCKNEL								
Jon G	33	m	w	NY	San Francisco	8-Wd San Francisco	82	330
BUCKNELL								
G	56	m	w	ENGL	Lake	Upper Lake	73	409
R	24	m	w	MO	Lake	Upper Lake	73	411
BUCKNER								
Charles	56	m	w	PRUS	San Mateo	Schoolhouse Statio	87	331
Charles	28	m	w	PRUS	San Francisco	San Francisco P O	83	369
George	63	m	b	KY	San Luis Obispo	Arroyo Grande Twp	87	278
J W	36	m	w	MO	El Dorado	Cosumnes Twp	72	19
James	18	m	w	MO	Monterey	San Juan Twp	74	391
John	40	m	b	VA	El Dorado	Mud Springs Twp	72	87
John C H	40	m	w	VA	Yuba	North East Twp	93	644
Mary	60	f	b	TN	Alameda	Oakland	68	193
R	39	m	w	KY	Mendocino	Sanel Twp	74	230
R B	47	m	w	KY	Santa Clara	Gilroy Twp	88	69
Tho	50	m	w	KY	El Dorado	Georgetown Twp	72	37
William	41	m	w	TN	Stanislaus	Empire Twp	92	39
William W	22	m	w	IL	Yolo	Cache Crk Twp	93	453
Wm	31	m	w	KY	Solano	Vallejo	90	213
BUCKNOR								
Jno	50	m	w	CANA	Butte	Chico Twp	70	31
BUCKSON								
Louis	36	m	w	PRUS	San Francisco	San Francisco P O	80	538
BUCKSTON								
A C	14	f	w	IA	Tuolumne	Big Oak Flat P O	93	395
BUCKUN								
Jos	37	m	w	TN	San Joaquin	Elkhorn Twp	86	56
BUCKUS								
John	37	m	w	OH	Butte	Ophir Twp	70	95
Wm L	44	m	w	OH	Butte	Ophir Twp	70	109
BUCKWALL								
Fred	28	m	w	POLA	San Francisco	3-Wd San Francisco	79	292
BUCKWELL								
Alfred	57	m	w	ENGL	Monterey	Salinas Twp	74	308
BUCKWITH								
Henry	43	m	w	CT	San Joaquin	1-Wd Stockton	86	121
BUCKWORTH								
Robert	30	m	w	PA	Colusa	Colusa	71	288
BUCKYUS								
Charles	6	m	w	MEXI	Los Angeles	Los Angeles	73	519
BUD								
Harvey	20	m	w	IL	Sacramento	Franklin Twp	77	116
Herbert	27	m	w	NJ	San Francisco	5-Wd San Francisco	81	27
Michael	28	m	w	NY	San Mateo	Half Moon Bay P O	87	400
BUDD								
Charles G	35	m	w	NY	San Diego	San Diego	78	489
E R	51	m	w	OH	Mendocino	Ukiah Twp	74	233
Edwin R	20	m	w	IN	Mendocino	Round Valley Twp	74	217
H J	39	m	w	ENGL	Sacramento	1-Wd Sacramento	77	189
J H	48	m	w	NY	San Joaquin	2-Wd Stockton	86	186
J H	19	m	w	WI	San Francisco	San Francisco P O	83	282
John	17	m	w	WI	San Francisco	11-Wd San Francisc	84	648
Wayman	29	m	w	MO	San Francisco	7-Wd San Francisco	81	284
BUDDELL								
Lyman	35	m	w	OH	Siskiyou	Callahan P O	89	628
BUDDEN								
B H	43	m	w	HANO	Yuba	Marysville	93	574
Henry	30	m	w	GERM	Los Angeles	Los Angeles	73	571
BUDDICK								
Thomas	33	m	w	ENGL	El Dorado	Kelsey Twp	72	60
BUDDIE								
Henry	29	m	w	HAMB	Sacramento	Brighton Twp	77	70
BUDDINGTON								
Edwd	25	m	w	ME	San Francisco	1-Wd San Francisco	79	71
John	45	m	w	NY	Stanislaus	Emory Twp	92	20
Nathan	51	m	w	NY	Stanislaus	Emory Twp	92	20
Walter	43	m	w	CT	San Francisco	6-Wd San Francisco	81	84
BUDDLE								
Stephen	25	m	w	ENGL	Nevada	Grass Valley Twp	75	194
BUDE								
N	42	m	w	ME	Calaveras	Copperopolis P O	70	237
S S	30	m	w	NH	Sacramento	4-Wd Sacramento	77	364
BUDELMANS								
Wm	23	m	w	HANO	San Francisco	1-Wd San Francisco	79	85
BUDEMAR								
Robert	3	m	w	CA	Los Angeles	Los Angeles Twp	73	464
BUDENBEDER								
Chas	39	m	w	PRUS	Siskiyou	Hamburg Twp	89	598
BUDERACH								
Louis	20	m	w	CA	San Joaquin	Oneal Twp	86	99
BUDICH								
Michael	22	m	w	AUST	San Francisco	3-Wd San Francisco	79	325
BUDINA								
Petra	60	f	w	MEXI	Nevada	Grass Valley Twp	75	142
BUDKE								
Henry	30	m	w	PRUS	San Francisco	5-Wd San Francisco	81	15
BUDLIN								
Thomas	39	m	w	IREL	Marin	San Rafael Twp	74	38
BUDNEY								
Chris	38	m	w	PRUS	Sacramento	4-Wd Sacramento	77	363
BUDRY								
Charles	38	m	w	CANA	Placer	Dutch Flat P O	76	402
BUDSON								
George	24	m	w	NY	Solano	Tremont Twp	90	31
BUDUA								
Pedro	50	m	w	FRAN	Calaveras	Copperopolis P O	70	221
BUDWORTH								
Wm	33	m	w	PA	Alameda	Murray Twp	68	126
BUDZILENA								
Baseli	39	m	w	ITAL	Alameda	Brooklyn	68	33
BUE								
Ah	17	m	c	CHIN	San Francisco	San Francisco P O	83	131
BUECH								
L C	35	m	w	SWIT	San Francisco	7-Wd San Francisco	81	183
BUEDIN								
Eugene	20	m	w	SWIT	San Francisco	6-Wd San Francisco	81	97
BUEFF								
Conrad	38	m	w	IL	El Dorado	Salmon Falls Twp	72	132
BUEL								
Elisha	58	m	w	MD	Sutter	Vernon Twp	92	135
Fredrick	54	m	w	MA	Alameda	Brooklyn	68	23
Harlan P	27	m	w	VT	Santa Barbara	Las Cruces P O	87	515
Horton	38	m	w	CT	Yuba	East Bear Rvr Twp	93	543
John	42	m	w	SWED	Sacramento	2-Wd Sacramento	77	241
Leon M	22	m	w	OH	Alpine	Markleeville P O	69	311
Linas	67	m	w	VT	Monterey	Salinas Twp	74	313
R T	42	m	w	VT	Monterey	Salinas Twp	74	313
BUELANA								
Carmel	56	f	w	MEXI	Santa Barbara	Santa Barbara P O	87	492
BUELDE								
Louis	28	m	w	FRAN	San Francisco	San Francisco P O	80	463
BUELER								
Joseph	28	m	w	SWIT	Siskiyou	Cottonwood Twp	89	595
BUELL								
Adam	28	m	w	PRUS	San Francisco	San Francisco P O	80	331
Alonzo	34	m	w	VT	Santa Barbara	Santa Barbara P O	87	500
E C	37	m	w	NY	Mendocino	Little Lake Twp	74	200
Elizabeth	50	f	w	CT	Placer	Bath P O	76	441
Leonard	55	m	w	VT	San Bernardino	San Bernardino Twp	78	427
Lydia	39	f	w	NY	Marin	Point Reyes Twp	74	22
Samuel	59	m	w	NY	Los Angeles	Los Nietos Twp	73	591
BUELLNIA								
Jose	49	m	i	MEXI	San Luis Obispo	Salinas Twp	87	295
BUELNA								
Albino	27	m	w	CA	Santa Clara	Santa Clara Twp	88	157
Anita	35	f	w	CA	Los Angeles	Los Angeles	73	568
Antonio	32	m	w	CA	San Mateo	Half Moon Bay P O	87	393
Antonio	26	m	w	MEXI	Los Angeles	Santa Ana Twp	73	600
Antonio	18	m	w	CA	Los Angeles	San Jose Twp	73	618
Florida	19	f	w	CA	Los Angeles	Los Angeles	73	514
Jeronimo	34	m	w	CA	San Luis Obispo	Morro Twp	87	281
Johana	42	f	i	CA	San Joaquin	2-Wd Stockton	86	171
Jose	40	m	w	MEXI	Santa Barbara	Santa Barbara P O	87	483
Juan	25	m	w	CA	Marin	Bolinas Twp	74	5
Lugarda	30	f	w	MEXI	Los Angeles	Los Angeles	73	560
Maria	8	f	w	CA	Santa Cruz	Pajaro Twp	89	362
Sarah	13	f	w	CA	San Mateo	Half Moon Bay P O	87	393
BUELOW								
F	38	m	w	PRUS	Sacramento	3-Wd Sacramento	77	289
BUELTA								
Peter	42	m	w	ITAL	San Francisco	San Francisco P O	83	139
BUELY								
Balon	40	m	w	AR	San Joaquin	3-Wd Stockton	86	236
BUEMIA								
John	46	m	w	SCOT	Alameda	Washington Twp	68	270
BUEN								
Ah	54	m	c	CHIN	San Francisco	6-Wd San Francisco	81	77
James	25	m	w	IREL	Contra Costa	Martinez P O	71	428
John	25	m	w	PRUS	Tehama	Tehama Twp	92	193
Joseph H	26	m	w	IREL	Sacramento	3-Wd Sacramento	77	289
Sing	20	m	c	CHIN	Sacramento	3-Wd Sacramento	77	296
BUERNA								
Francisco	36	m	w	CA	San Francisco	San Francisco P O	80	362
BUERST								
Leopold	25	m	w	GERM	Los Angeles	Los Angeles	73	513

Series M593

© 2001 by Heritage Quest. All rights reserved.

Name	Age	S	R	B-PL	County	Locale	Series M593 Roll	Pg
BUESS								
John A	37	m	w	AUST	Los Angeles	Los Angeles	73	543
BUEST								
Wm	26	m	w	SCOT	Santa Clara	Gilroy Twp	88	79
BUEY								
Ah	70	m	c	CHIN	Humboldt	Eureka Twp	72	266
Ah	20	f	c	CHIN	San Francisco	6-Wd San Francisco	81	77
BUFF								
John E	24	m	w	MO	San Francisco	1-Wd San Francisco	79	65
BUFFALOW								
James	22	m	i	OR	San Luis Obispo	Morro Twp	87	287
BUFFAM								
Jas	56	m	w	IN	Shasta	Dog Crk P O	89	471
BUFFAN								
Augustus	31	m	w	FRAN	Marin	San Rafael Twp	74	39
BUFFENDEAU								
Emil	33	m	w	FRAN	San Francisco	6-Wd San Francisco	81	95
BUFFER								
Catherine	42	f	w	FRAN	Napa	Napa	75	41
BUFFERT								
Henry	33	m	w	NH	San Francisco	11-Wd San Francisc	84	629
BUFFIN								
Albert	38	m	w	MA	San Francisco	San Francisco P O	83	234
BUFFINDER								
Met	35	m	w	FRAN	San Francisco	5-Wd San Francisco	81	22
BUFFINGTON								
Andrew C	50	m	w	OH	San Luis Obispo	Santa Rosa Twp	87	327
D	39	m	w	MA	Amador	Sutter Crk P O	69	408
J R	33	m	w	IL	Amador	Drytown P O	69	422
James R	45	m	w	PA	El Dorado	Diamond Springs Tw	72	31
Jefferson	40	m	w	VA	Plumas	Seneca Twp	77	47
Joseph	40	m	w	VA	Plumas	Seneca Twp	77	47
William	40	m	w	MA	Nevada	Grass Valley Twp	75	144
BUFFINTON								
Jno Mason	52	m	w	MA	San Francisco	San Francisco P O	83	57
BUFFON								
E R	40	m	w	ME	Sierra	Sierra Twp	89	562
BUFFORD								
Jos L	55	m	w	NH	San Francisco	8-Wd San Francisco	82	302
BUFFUM								
E W	36	m	w	NH	Merced	Snelling P O	74	264
Edward W	38	m	w	NH	Mariposa	Mariposa P O	74	107
James M	45	m	w	NY	San Luis Obispo	Santa Rosa Twp	87	326
BUFFY								
Gustav	38	m	w	FRAN	San Francisco	6-Wd San Francisco	81	41
BUFORD								
Charles	46	m	w	LA	Marin	San Rafael Twp	74	37
Edward L	30	m	w	MS	Santa Clara	1-Wd San Jose	88	259
S H	40	m	w	KY	Napa	Yountville Twp	75	87
Sally	25	f	w	MS	Santa Clara	1-Wd San Jose	88	241
BUFOREA								
Lorenzo	36	m	i	MEXI	Inyo	Cerro Gordo Twp	73	322
BUFOSKIE								
J	27	m	w	POLA	Lake	Morgan Valley	73	425
BUGAN								
Anthony	52	m	w	PA	San Mateo	Schoolhouse Statio	87	333
Thos	37	m	w	ENGL	Sacramento	3-Wd Sacramento	77	296
BUGBEE								
George	33	m	w	ME	San Francisco	11-Wd San Francisc	84	441
Saml C	50	m	w	ME	San Francisco	San Francisco P O	83	108
BUGBY								
Benj N	43	m	w	CT	Sacramento	Granite Twp	77	148
W D	50	m	w	NY	San Joaquin	2-Wd Stockton	86	177
BUGER								
T B	30	m	w	MO	Lake	Lakeport	73	406
BUGG								
Ulretta	24	f	w	MA	Sonoma	Analy Twp	91	228
BUGH								
C	24	m	w	WURT	Sierra	Butte Twp	89	510
BUGHAN								
Julia	28	f	w	MA	Alameda	Oakland	68	173
BUGHNER								
Sophia	14	f	w	CA	Yuba	Long Bar Twp	93	566
BUGIL								
Henry	40	m	w	PRUS	Sacramento	Lee Twp	77	161
BUGINE								
John	40	m	w	SWIT	Santa Clara	Santa Clara Twp	88	137
BUGLLEAU								
Eugene	37	m	w	LA	San Francisco	11-Wd San Francisc	84	682
BUGS								
Stephen	23	m	w	OH	San Joaquin	Union Twp	86	266
BUGSBEE								
Chas H	30	m	w	ME	Humboldt	Bucksport Twp	72	243
R J	45	m	w	NY	Humboldt	Pacific Twp	72	291
BUGUHL								
David	39	m	w	PRUS	Solano	Rio Vista Twp	90	60
BUHANAN								
T	39	m	w	SCOT	Sacramento	3-Wd Sacramento	77	299
BUHL								
Charles	32	m	w	IN	San Francisco	2-Wd San Francisco	79	211
George	42	m	w	WURT	Marin	Sausalito Twp	74	72
BUHLART								
Albert	39	m	w	PRUS	San Francisco	6-Wd San Francisco	81	104
Julius	29	m	w	PRUS	San Francisco	6-Wd San Francisco	81	104
BUHLE								
William	30	m	w	SHOL	San Francisco	3-Wd San Francisco	79	287

Name	Age	S	R	B-PL	County	Locale	Series M593 Roll	Pg
BUHLER								
J M	32	m	w	MD	San Francisco	San Francisco P O	83	300
BUHMANN								
Fritz	35	m	w	PRUS	Solano	Tremont Twp	90	32
BUHMEISTER								
Henry	38	m	w	PRUS	Solano	Green Valley Twp	90	44
BUHNE								
H H	48	m	w	DENM	Humboldt	Eureka Twp	72	270
BUHNELL								
Frank	35	m	w	SWED	Marin	San Rafael	74	58
BUHNS								
John	53	m	w	BADE	Calaveras	Copperopolis P O	70	242
BUHRING								
Adolph	28	m	w	GERM	Santa Clara	2-Wd San Jose	88	326
Louis	41	m	w	NORW	Nevada	Bridgeport Twp	75	101
BUHSEN								
D	49	m	w	HANO	Alameda	Oakland	68	212
BUHT								
Fred	24	m	w	SWED	San Francisco	San Francisco P O	83	127
BUICK								
David S K	45	m	w	SCOT	Santa Clara	Milpitas Twp	88	114
BUILDER								
Joseph	42	m	w	ENGL	Sacramento	2-Wd Sacramento	77	235
BUIS								
Nicholas	45	m	w	DALM	San Francisco	1-Wd San Francisco	79	96
BUISLAY								
Gruett	36	m	w	FRAN	San Francisco	San Francisco P O	80	339
BUISSOM								
Jeane	26	f	w	FRAN	Los Angeles	Los Angeles	73	565
BUISSON								
Charles	36	m	w	FRAN	San Francisco	San Francisco P O	80	475
BUITES								
Peter	52	m	w	NETH	Santa Cruz	Soquel Twp	89	440
BUITTNER								
Herman	38	m	w	PRUS	San Francisco	San Francisco P O	80	363
BUK								
Ah	25	m	c	CHIN	San Francisco	6-Wd San Francisco	81	69
BUKER								
Herman	57	m	w	PRUS	El Dorado	Mud Springs Twp	72	85
John	38	m	w	ME	Marin	Nicasio Twp	74	19
Levi	35	m	w	ME	San Francisco	San Francisco P O	80	377
BUKMASTER								
Richard	23	m	w	OH	Sacramento	Sutter Twp	77	391
BULACKER								
Fred	50	m	w	SWIT	Nevada	Nevada Twp	75	274
Lecticia	45	f	w	HAMB	Nevada	Nevada Twp	75	289
BULAN								
Carl	26	m	w	PRUS	Los Angeles	Los Angeles Twp	73	484
BULCH								
James R	37	m	w	ME	Trinity	Weaverville Pct	92	224
BULDER								
G F	17	m	w	CA	Alameda	Oakland	68	242
BULDRIDGE								
James	34	m	w	NY	San Bernardino	San Salvador Twp	78	459
BULENEMELLO								
Alson	21	m	w	MEXI	San Diego	Coronado	78	466
BULENS								
John L	48	m	w	FRAN	Placer	Roseville P O	76	350
BULEY								
D	30	m	w	IL	San Joaquin	Elliott Twp	86	74
BULFORM								
Robt	40	m	w	MA	San Francisco	5-Wd San Francisco	81	22
BULGER								
Anna	22	f	w	IREL	San Francisco	8-Wd San Francisco	82	304
Anna	22	f	w	IREL	San Francisco	8-Wd San Francisco	82	304
Henry	26	m	w	GERM	Contra Costa	Martinez P O	71	396
John	45	m	w	IREL	San Francisco	San Francisco P O	83	215
John	30	m	w	IREL	Colusa	Grand Island Twp	71	306
John	28	m	w	IREL	Sonoma	Bodega Twp	91	249
John	25	m	w	NY	San Francisco	1-Wd San Francisco	79	123
Martin	36	m	w	NY	San Francisco	San Francisco P O	83	349
Mary	19	f	w	SWIT	San Francisco	San Francisco P O	83	266
Mathew	31	m	w	IREL	San Francisco	11-Wd San Francisc	84	471
Raphael	27	m	w	DC	San Francisco	San Francisco P O	83	386
BULHAM								
Jacob	38	m	w	NY	San Francisco	11-Wd San Francisc	84	694
BULHEA								
Guadalupe	40	m	w	CA	Santa Cruz	Santa Cruz	89	425
BULHER								
John	40	m	w	PRUS	San Francisco	San Francisco P O	80	461
Rafaela	52	f	w	CA	Santa Cruz	Santa Cruz	89	425
BULKELEY								
L E	39	m	w	ME	San Francisco	6-Wd San Francisco	81	98
BULKLEY								
Anne	26	f	w	IREL	San Francisco	11-Wd San Francisc	84	661
E	59	m	w	PA	Humboldt	Eureka Twp	72	271
E C	30	m	w	PA	Humboldt	Bucksport Twp	72	244
Ichabod	33	m	w	CT	San Francisco	San Francisco P O	83	47
BULL								
A	65	m	w	OH	Sierra	Alleghany & Forest	89	535
Alpheus	54	m	w	NY	San Francisco	2-Wd San Francisco	79	262
Anson O	61	m	w	MA	Nevada	Little York Twp	75	244
Charles	38	m	w	NY	San Francisco	11-Wd San Francisc	84	528
E W	22	m	w	MA	Humboldt	Arcata Twp	72	235
Emma	17	f	w	SHOL	San Francisco	San Francisco P O	83	323
Frank	30	m	w	OR	Yuba	Marysville	93	591
Fredk	8	m	w	AUST	San Francisco	San Francisco P O	85	800

© 2001 by Heritage Quest. All rights reserved.

California 1870 Census

Series M593

Name	Age	S	R	B-PL	County	Locale	Roll	Pg
George	16	m	w	CA	Santa Clara	Santa Clara Twp	88	176
Isaac D	50	m	w	NY	Santa Clara	Fremont Twp	88	53
J C Jr	31	m	w	MA	Humboldt	Arcata Twp	72	235
James	36	m	w	ENGL	San Francisco	8-Wd San Francisco	82	393
Jno	26	m	w	MO	San Joaquin	2-Wd Stockton	86	212
John	52	m	w	OH	Sacramento	Georgianna Twp	77	126
John	31	m	w	ENGL	San Francisco	3-Wd San Francisco	79	310
John	30	m	w	ENGL	Solano	Vallejo	90	212
Mary	5	f	w	CA	San Francisco	San Francisco P O	85	799
Moses	40	m	w	MI	Plumas	Indian Twp	77	17
Thomas	38	m	w	OH	San Francisco	3-Wd San Francisco	79	315
W	9	m	w	AUST	San Francisco	San Francisco P O	85	800
BULLAMADO								
Dolars	30	m	w	MEXI	San Diego	Fort Yuma Dist	78	463
BULLAN								
Jonathan	55	m	w	ENGL	San Francisco	6-Wd San Francisco	81	83
BULLARD								
Austin D	38	m	w	MA	Placer	Bath P O	76	440
B	55	m	b	KY	Sacramento	3-Wd Sacramento	77	266
Benj	65	m	w	VT	Sacramento	4-Wd Sacramento	77	353
Benjamin	22	m	w	MI	Sacramento	2-Wd Sacramento	77	235
Chas	40	m	w	MA	San Joaquin	Elkhorn Twp	86	58
Eliza	43	f	w	SCOT	El Dorado	Mud Springs Twp	72	80
Ellen	28	f	w	ENGL	San Francisco	8-Wd San Francisco	82	333
Ellen	25	f	w	ENGL	San Francisco	6-Wd San Francisco	81	133
Francis	48	m	w	MA	Yolo	Putah Twp	93	521
Geo	41	m	w	MA	Tehama	Tehama Twp	92	196
Guilford	58	m	w	US	Nevada	Rough & Ready Twp	75	330
Hattie	22	f	w	IL	Yolo	Putah Twp	93	521
James	52	m	w	ENGL	Santa Clara	1-Wd San Jose	88	268
James	36	m	w	AL	Yolo	Cottonwood Twp	93	466
James H	60	m	w	KY	San Francisco	2-Wd San Francisco	79	271
John W	46	m	w	OH	El Dorado	Mountain Twp	72	69
Peter	40	m	w	ITAL	San Francisco	2-Wd San Francisco	79	151
Preston	44	m	w	MO	Monterey	San Benito Twp	74	383
S A	43	f	m	KY	Sacramento	3-Wd Sacramento	77	266
Wm	27	m	w	ENGL	San Francisco	San Francisco P O	83	3
Wm S	32	m	w	VA	Mono	Bridgeport P O	74	285
BULLEN								
Helen	30	f	w	ME	San Francisco	7-Wd San Francisco	81	233
James	58	m	w	ENGL	Placer	Bath P O	76	436
Jas	50	m	w	OH	Siskiyou	Callahan P O	89	625
Tupper	32	m	w	CANA	San Francisco	11-Wd San Francisc	84	515
BULLEND								
Benoit	31	m	w	FRAN	San Francisco	6-Wd San Francisco	81	73
BULLER								
Robert	56	m	m	MD	Placer	Colfax P O	76	385
BULLERDICK								
A G	47	m	w	PRUS	Tuolumne	Columbia P O	93	356
BULLETI								
Costa	43	m	w	SWIT	San Francisco	2-Wd San Francisco	79	199
BULLIER								
Leon	39	m	w	FRAN	Monterey	San Juan Twp	74	410
BULLINGER								
George I	35	m	w	SWIT	Placer	Auburn P O	76	359
BULLIS								
Horace	28	m	w	NY	San Francisco	San Francisco P O	83	323
Orrin	33	m	w	NY	Marin	San Rafael	74	58
Richard	39	m	w	NY	Marin	San Rafael	74	58
BULLMAN								
Henry	30	m	w	DENM	San Francisco	7-Wd San Francisco	81	223
BULLO								
Patra	32	m	w	ITAL	San Francisco	3-Wd San Francisco	79	289
BULLOCK								
Arthur	32	m	w	ENGL	Los Angeles	Los Angeles Twp	73	486
Bjm	11	m	w	CA	San Francisco	11-Wd San Francisc	84	592
Edward	30	m	w	KY	Santa Clara	2-Wd San Jose	88	328
Elizabeth	14	f	w	CA	San Mateo	Redwood Twp	87	366
Ezekiel	44	m	w	IREL	San Francisco	8-Wd San Francisco	82	416
Hannah	82	f	w	ME	Siskiyou	Butte Twp	89	585
James D	59	m	w	MA	Yuba	New York Twp	93	641
James P	41	m	w	KY	Yolo	Cache Crk Twp	93	431
Jane	56	f	w	NY	Amador	Sutter Crk P O	69	398
John W	36	m	w	IL	Placer	Emigrant Gap P O	76	417
Lathrop S	40	m	w	MA	San Francisco	2-Wd San Francisco	79	211
Lois	35	f	w	ME	Alameda	Washington Twp	68	278
Marion	29	m	w	MO	Alameda	Eden Twp	68	80
Mary	12	f	w	CA	Solano	Suisun Twp	90	116
Matthew	35	m	w	NY	San Francisco	1-Wd San Francisco	79	125
Nathaniel	34	m	w	NY	Humboldt	Eureka Twp	72	271
Osgood	40	m	w	CANA	Humboldt	Bald Hills	72	238
R R	65	m	w	OH	Amador	Drytown P O	69	418
Robert	37	m	w	MO	Santa Cruz	Pajaro Twp	89	358
S S	60	m	w	NH	Klamath	South Fork Twp	73	383
William H	38	m	w	MA	Placer	Auburn P O	76	368
William Henry	36	m	w	NY	Mendocino	Albion & Big Rvr T	74	166
Wm	41	m	w	ENGL	San Francisco	11-Wd San Francisc	84	680
Z F	33	m	w	IN	Shasta	Shasta P O	89	454
BULLOTTI								
Henri	26	m	w	SWIT	San Francisco	San Francisco P O	80	342
BULLOW								
Henry H	22	m	w	PRUS	Santa Clara	2-Wd San Jose	88	329
BULLRIDGE								
John	30	m	w	IREL	Colusa	Spring Valley Twp	71	340
BULLWELL								
Jno N	35	m	w	ENGL	San Francisco	5-Wd San Francisco	81	19
BULLWINGEL								
G	28	m	w	HANO	Klamath	Trinidad Twp	73	389
BULLWINKEL								
C	30	m	w	HANO	Klamath	Trinidad Twp	73	389
J	20	m	w	HANO	Klamath	Trinidad Twp	73	389
John F	32	m	w	PRUS	San Francisco	San Francisco P O	83	233
BULMAN								
Jas Sheare	45	m	w	NJ	San Francisco	San Francisco P O	83	29
BULMER								
Charles	28	m	w	MA	Sonoma	Salt Point	91	390
H H	53	m	w	ENGL	Alameda	Eden Twp	68	81
Isaac	42	m	w	FL	Nevada	Grass Valley Twp	75	156
BULMORE								
Robt	29	m	w	ENGL	San Francisco	2-Wd San Francisco	79	209
BULOW								
Henry A	21	m	w	PRUS	San Francisco	3-Wd San Francisco	79	315
BULS								
Jacob	29	m	w	HDAR	Siskiyou	Callahan P O	89	624
Richard W	32	m	w	ASEA	Siskiyou	Scott Valley Twp	89	621
BULSOM								
John	44	m	w	NY	San Francisco	San Francisco P O	83	416
BULTER								
Isabella	20	f	w	CA	San Francisco	8-Wd San Francisco	82	380
Israel	37	m	w	AR	Fresno	Kings Rvr P O	72	216
BULTON								
John Q	38	m	w	MA	Placer	Alta P O	76	412
Nicholas	31	m	w	SWED	San Francisco	1-Wd San Francisco	79	71
BULTRAND								
Lorenzo	38	m	w	MEXI	Mariposa	Mariposa P O	74	120
BULWER								
Andrew	33	m	w	FRAN	Marin	Nicasio Twp	74	19
John	35	m	w	KY	Yolo	Grafton Twp	93	498
Levi	26	m	w	MO	Inyo	Independence Twp	73	326
BUM								
J	28	m	w	CT	Alameda	Oakland	68	266
R M	40	m	w	CT	Nevada	Eureka Twp	75	135
BUMBER								
Charles	27	m	w	PA	San Francisco	7-Wd San Francisco	81	164
BUMGARD								
Peter	63	m	w	SWIT	Sacramento	2-Wd Sacramento	77	249
BUMGARDER								
George	37	m	w	PA	El Dorado	Mud Springs Twp	72	75
BUMGARDNER								
Daniel	43	m	w	IN	Nevada	Little York Twp	75	242
G	29	m	w	BADE	Trinity	Junction City Pct	92	209
Percilla	27	f	w	IL	El Dorado	Mud Springs Twp	72	75
BUMGARTNER								
B	34	m	w	BADE	Trinity	Canyon City Pct	92	201
BUMGNEY								
Emile	47	m	w	FRAN	Yuba	Bullards Bar P O	93	547
BUMGOERDT								
Jose	21	f	w	BAVA	San Francisco	3-Wd San Francisco	79	324
BUMM								
Jas	37	m	w	PA	San Joaquin	Castoria Twp	86	12
John	40	m	w	WURT	San Francisco	11-Wd San Francisc	84	475
BUMMEN								
H	32	m	w	PRUS	Alameda	Murray Twp	68	101
BUMNER								
Joseph	47	m	w	SCOT	Napa	Yountville Twp	75	88
BUMP								
A J	44	m	w	NY	Sacramento	Franklin Twp	77	108
Elihu	68	m	w	NY	Tehama	Red Bluff	92	173
Nelson	47	m	w	NY	Yolo	Merritt Twp	93	504
BUMPASS								
K V	56	m	w	TN	Tehama	Paynes Crk Twp	92	167
BUMPUS								
Cyrus	48	m	w	ME	Sonoma	Santa Rosa	91	409
Dolores	28	f	w	MEXI	San Francisco	2-Wd San Francisco	79	244
Silas	60	m	w	NY	Sacramento	Sutter Twp	77	381
Wm	47	m	w	MO	San Joaquin	Elkhorn Twp	86	65
BUMSIDE								
Thomas	21	m	w	IREL	Placer	Summit P O	76	495
BUN								
---	35	m	c	CHIN	Siskiyou	Cottonwood Twp	89	592
Ah	29	m	c	CHIN	Butte	Ophir Twp	70	121
Ah	18	m	c	CHIN	Sonoma	Bodega Twp	91	251
Ah	14	m	c	CHIN	Sacramento	3-Wd Sacramento	77	300
Gee	26	m	c	CHIN	Yuba	Marysville	93	624
John	40	m	w	PA	San Francisco	6-Wd San Francisco	81	93
BUNBRIDE								
C W	28	m	w	ENGL	Alameda	Oakland	68	260
BUNCE								
Daniel	54	m	w	ENGL	El Dorado	Greenwood Twp	72	51
Edward A	29	m	w	CT	Contra Costa	Martinez P O	71	386
Isaac H	37	m	w	NY	San Luis Obispo	San Luis Obispo Tw	87	298
William	50	m	w	NY	San Francisco	6-Wd San Francisco	81	138
William	39	m	w	ENGL	Calaveras	San Andreas P O	70	197
BUNCH								
Jefferson P	63	m	w	KY	Los Angeles	El Monte Twp	73	461
John	42	m	w	IN	San Joaquin	Oneal Twp	86	107
Martin	37	m	w	MI	Sonoma	Healdsburg & Mendo	91	281
Samuel	59	m	w	NY	Alameda	Eden Twp	68	86
BUND								
C	35	m	w	GERM	San Joaquin	2-Wd Stockton	86	163
Wm A Jr	39	m	w	PA	San Francisco	5-Wd San Francisco	81	22
BUNDER								
Geo	26	m	w	NY	Solano	Vallejo	90	165

© 2001 by Heritage Quest. All rights reserved.

Name	Age	S	R	B-PL	County	Locale	Series M593 Roll	Pg
BUNDESEN								
Marcus	31	m	w	DENM	Santa Cruz	Pajaro Twp	89	342
BUNDHRUA								
Rag	37	m	w	BADE	El Dorado	Georgetown Twp	72	45
BUNDS								
Alex	42	m	w	MO	San Joaquin	Castoria Twp	86	12
John C	52	m	w	KY	Stanislaus	Empire Twp	92	62
Lucella	20	f	w	AR	Stanislaus	Branch Twp	92	1
BUNDSCHUE								
Chs	27	m	w	BADE	San Francisco	2-Wd San Francisco	79	145
BUNDY								
Charles	30	m	b	PA	San Francisco	San Francisco P O	80	483
Elizabeth	65	f	b	VA	Solano	Benicia	90	5
Francis	23	m	w	IN	San Diego	San Diego	78	499
James	26	m	w	ENGL	San Francisco	3-Wd San Francisco	79	311
Joseph H	31	m	w	VT	Colusa	Colusa	71	296
Lewis	37	m	w	NY	Merced	Snelling P O	74	268
William	19	m	m	LA	San Francisco	San Francisco P O	80	402
BUNEL								
William	45	m	w	VT	Humboldt	Mattole Twp	72	286
BUNEMAN								
Chas	34	m	w	HAMB	San Francisco	San Francisco P O	85	776
Frederick	24	m	w	HAMB	Santa Clara	2-Wd San Jose	88	323
BUNG								
Ah	69	m	c	CHIN	Trinity	Canyon City Pct	92	201
Ah	42	m	c	CHIN	El Dorado	Diamond Springs Tw	72	30
Ah	40	m	c	CHIN	El Dorado	Mud Springs Twp	72	90
Ah	39	m	c	CHIN	Mariposa	Mariposa P O	74	127
Ah	38	m	c	CHIN	Solano	Benicia	90	5
Ah	37	m	c	CHIN	El Dorado	Mud Springs Twp	72	86
Ah	35	m	c	CHIN	Mariposa	Mariposa P O	74	133
Ah	34	m	c	CHIN	El Dorado	Mountain Twp	72	68
Ah	32	m	c	CHIN	Shasta	American Ranch P O	89	496
Ah	32	m	c	CHIN	El Dorado	Diamond Springs Tw	72	28
Ah	32	m	c	CHIN	El Dorado	Mud Springs Twp	72	75
Ah	32	m	c	CHIN	El Dorado	Diamond Springs Tw	72	25
Ah	31	m	c	CHIN	El Dorado	Mud Springs Twp	72	77
Ah	30	m	c	CHIN	El Dorado	Diamond Springs Tw	72	25
Ah	27	m	c	CHIN	San Francisco	6-Wd San Francisco	81	56
Ah	25	m	c	CHIN	El Dorado	Cosumnes Twp	72	13
Ah	25	m	c	CHIN	El Dorado	Mud Springs Twp	72	89
Ah	22	m	c	CHIN	El Dorado	Diamond Springs Tw	72	24
Ah	18	m	c	CHIN	Yuba	Marysville	93	591
Ah	17	m	c	CHIN	Sacramento	3-Wd Sacramento	77	304
Choon	7M	m	c	CA	Plumas	Goodwin Twp	77	5
Chung	34	m	c	CHIN	Yuba	Marysville	93	621
BUNGAR								
Thomas	34	m	w	PRUS	San Francisco	11-Wd San Francisc	84	518
BUNGASTA								
John	18	m	w	ITAL	Santa Clara	Santa Clara Twp	88	178
Joseph	26	m	w	ITAL	Santa Clara	Santa Clara Twp	88	178
BUNK								
Ah	32	m	c	CHIN	Tuolumne	Big Oak Flat P O	93	399
Thomas	38	m	w	IREL	San Mateo	Schoolhouse Statio	87	342
BUNKER								
Alfred	30	m	w	NY	San Francisco	San Francisco P O	83	274
Barrond B	30	m	w	MA	El Dorado	Placerville Twp	72	95
Cromwell	63	m	w	MA	San Francisco	San Francisco P O	80	382
Danl G	50	m	w	NH	Shasta	Horsetown P O	89	504
Elisha C	41	m	w	IN	Colusa	Butte Twp	71	266
F R	69	m	w	MA	San Francisco	San Francisco P O	83	286
Geo F	55	m	w	MA	San Francisco	San Francisco P O	83	129
Geo H	43	m	w	MA	San Francisco	San Francisco P O	83	92
Henry	50	m	w	MA	San Francisco	11-Wd San Francisc	84	507
Henry	34	m	w	MA	Alameda	Washington Twp	68	292
Jas	26	m	w	NY	Butte	Chico Twp	70	31
Louisa	13	f	w	ME	San Francisco	6-Wd San Francisco	81	149
Obadiah	34	m	w	CANA	Placer	Bath P O	76	435
P	29	m	w	ME	Mendocino	Little Lake Twp	74	199
Palmer	37	m	w	NY	Amador	Ione City P O	69	365
Paul	38	m	w	MA	San Francisco	San Francisco P O	83	55
Robert	34	m	w	MA	San Francisco	San Francisco P O	80	386
Roland	48	m	w	MA	Contra Costa	Martinez P O	71	433
Wm	63	m	w	MA	San Joaquin	1-Wd Stockton	86	140
Wm	23	m	w	NY	San Francisco	San Francisco P O	83	50
Wm B	62	m	w	MA	San Luis Obispo	Arroyo Grande Twp	87	272
BUNKERO								
Antonio	26	m	w	ITAL	San Mateo	Schoolhouse Statio	87	332
BUNKIS								
Benj B	29	m	w	NY	Sacramento	Dry Crk Twp	77	100
BUNN								
Ah	14	m	c	CHIN	San Francisco	6-Wd San Francisco	81	49
George	50	m	w	NJ	Marin	Tomales Twp	74	86
Lim	28	m	c	CHIN	Placer	Bath P O	76	429
Wesley J	42	m	w	OH	San Mateo	Redwood Twp	87	370
BUNNEL								
Fred	42	m	w	BADE	Sacramento	Sutter Twp	77	392
BUNNELL								
Abner W	47	m	w	OH	Butte	Oregon Twp	70	132
Alfred F	30	m	w	NJ	San Diego	San Diego	78	499
George	30	m	w	MA	Alameda	Brooklyn Twp	68	40
Virgil	40	m	w	CT	Butte	Bidwell Twp	70	2
Wellington	39	m	w	NH	Plumas	Seneca Twp	77	51
Wesley	29	m	w	CT	Yolo	Cache Crk Twp	93	454
BUNNER								
George W	27	m	w	PA	San Francisco	8-Wd San Francisco	82	417
J C	60	m	w	NY	San Francisco	San Francisco P O	85	783
BUNNETT								
W T	22	m	w	ENGL	Sierra	Butte Twp	89	511
Wesley	52	m	w	IN	San Luis Obispo	Arroyo Grande Twp	87	277
BUNNEY								
Alexander	38	m	w	ENGL	Nevada	Grass Valley Twp	75	178
Geo	28	m	w	NY	Butte	Oregon Twp	70	128
Wm	37	m	w	ENGL	Santa Clara	Almaden Twp	88	11
BUNNIMAN								
Henry	35	m	w	HAMB	San Francisco	2-Wd San Francisco	79	278
BUNNINGHAM								
Sabrina	30	f	w	IREL	San Francisco	San Francisco P O	83	112
BUNOL								
Philitus	37	m	w	NY	Sutter	Yuba Twp	92	146
BUNS								
Albert	25	m	w	NY	Alameda	Eden Twp	68	66
BUNSEL								
J	70	m	w	ME	Alameda	Murray Twp	68	123
BUNT								
John	35	m	w	NY	Siskiyou	Scott Valley Twp	89	615
John L	40	m	w	NY	Sacramento	Granite Twp	77	145
BUNTE								
Diedrich	37	m	w	HANO	Santa Cruz	Soquel Twp	89	439
BUNTENBACH								
August	32	m	w	PRUS	Contra Costa	Martinez P O	71	378
BUNTIELICH								
Antoine	50	m	w	FRAN	San Francisco	San Francisco P O	85	865
BUNTING								
H	53	m	w	PA	Yuba	Marysville Twp	93	570
Joseph	55	m	w	MA	San Francisco	San Francisco P O	83	77
BUNTON								
Charles	19	m	w	NY	Marin	Sausalito Twp	74	74
Edward	36	m	w	NY	Los Angeles	Santa Ana Twp	73	617
Ella	70	f	w	CA	San Diego	San Diego	78	490
William	48	m	w	MO	San Diego	San Diego	78	489
William H	42	m	w	ME	San Mateo	Pescadero P O	87	414
Wm A	49	m	w	TN	Monterey	Alisal Twp	74	294
BUNTS								
John	35	m	w	CANA	Inyo	Bishop Crk Twp	73	317
BUNUN								
Margaret	48	f	w	PA	San Francisco	8-Wd San Francisco	82	476
BUNY								
Viola C	15	f	w	OR	Santa Cruz	Santa Cruz	89	407
BUNYARD								
Lewis S	59	m	w	NC	Los Angeles	El Monte Twp	73	458
BUNZELL								
Francis	42	m	w	NY	Klamath	Salmon Twp	73	388
BUOB								
Christian	54	m	w	GERM	Yolo	Cache Crk Twp	93	452
BUOCHOLS								
---	37	m	w	SHOL	Humboldt	Eureka Twp	72	256
BUOMAN								
Chas	47	m	w	PRUS	San Francisco	11-Wd San Francisc	84	623
BUONA								
J C	60	m	w	CHIL	Amador	Jackson P O	69	342
BUONS								
Cath	20	f	w	IREL	San Francisco	San Francisco P O	85	788
BUORIS								
Ed	30	m	w	ENGL	San Francisco	San Francisco P O	85	785
BUOYINGTON								
J L	54	m	w	NY	Sutter	Vernon Twp	92	134
BUPPRICHT								
John	38	m	w	BAVA	Placer	Dutch Flat P O	76	404
BUR								
Aaron	41	m	w	BAVA	Siskiyou	Scott Valley Twp	89	609
Mamie	17	f	w	ENGL	Alameda	Oakland	68	246
BURA								
Jacob	20	m	w	SWIT	San Francisco	San Francisco P O	85	873
BURBACK								
Chas	50	m	w	WI	Butte	Concow Twp	70	7
BURBACREDUFF								
I	28	m	w	ITAL	Alameda	Murray Twp	68	124
BURBAGO								
Fred	47	m	w	GA	San Diego	San Diego	78	496
BURBANK								
Abraham P	44	m	w	NH	Santa Cruz	Watsonville	89	371
Charles H	44	m	w	NY	Yolo	Grafton Twp	93	478
Chas	30	m	w	MA	Solano	Vallejo	90	180
David	48	m	w	NH	Los Angeles	Los Angeles Twp	73	479
David	31	m	w	MA	Marin	Tomales Twp	74	81
George	40	m	w	MA	Marin	Tomales Twp	74	81
L	36	m	w	NY	San Francisco	San Francisco P O	85	811
Moss	28	m	w	ME	Humboldt	Arcata Twp	72	225
P D	65	m	w	NH	Sacramento	4-Wd Sacramento	77	349
S C	51	m	w	NH	Placer	Newcastle Twp	76	476
W T	25	m	w	ME	Mariposa	Maxwell Crk P O	74	143
Warren	35	m	w	ME	Santa Barbara	San Buenaventura P	87	434
BURBANKS								
Henry	43	m	w	MA	Amador	Amador City P O	69	393
BURBECK								
John	53	m	w	PRUS	San Francisco	San Francisco P O	80	332
Wm	31	m	w	MA	Monterey	Salinas Twp	74	313
BURBER								
William	32	m	w	NY	Trinity	North Fork Twp	92	216
BURBERG								
William	50	m	w	ENGL	San Francisco	2-Wd San Francisco	79	250
BURBLESLACK								
Anton	50	m	w	PRUS	San Francisco	8-Wd San Francisco	82	352

© 2001 by Heritage Quest. All rights reserved.

California 1870 Census

Name	Age	S	R	B-PL	County	Locale	Series M593 Roll	Pg
BURBOWER								
Uriah	38	m	w	OH	Humboldt	Pacific Twp	72	297
BURBRIDGE								
Harriet	37	f	b	DC	Nevada	Nevada Twp	75	279
Henry	20	m	w	CANA	Placer	Colfax P O	76	391
J L	39	m	b	KY	Nevada	Nevada Twp	75	279
Samuel	62	m	w	CANA	Sonoma	Sonoma Twp	91	436
BURBY								
Thomas	36	m	w	IREL	Kern	Havilah P O	73	339
BURCALO								
Darius	68	f	w	KY	Sacramento	San Joaquin Twp	77	407
BURCE								
John	77	m	w	SCOT	Mariposa	Mariposa P O	74	118
BURCELL								
Joel	57	m	w	IN	Yolo	Grafton Twp	93	484
BURCELLI								
Orazio	33	m	w	ITAL	San Francisco	11-Wd San Francisc	84	594
BURCH								
Andrew	46	m	w	NJ	Mendocino	Navarro & Big Rvr	74	174
Chas	40	m	w	PRUS	San Francisco	1-Wd San Francisco	79	117
Frank	14	m	w	IA	San Joaquin	Oneal Twp	86	103
Fred P	49	m	w	CT	Solano	Benicia	90	5
George	5	m	w	CA	Los Angeles	Santa Ana Twp	73	600
George	48	m	w	OH	Sutter	Sutter Twp	92	118
Hiram	35	m	w	IN	Shasta	Portugese Flat P O	89	472
Jno C	45	m	w	MA	Sacramento	3-Wd Sacramento	77	288
John	24	m	w	HANO	San Francisco	San Francisco P O	83	176
John C	30	m	w	KY	Marin	Nicasio Twp	74	20
Lew	34	m	w	KY	Siskiyou	Surprise Valley Tw	89	642
Richard M	38	m	w	MO	Nevada	Little York Twp	75	237
William	44	m	w	ENGL	San Francisco	6-Wd San Francisco	81	111
William	40	m	w	OH	Sutter	Sutter Twp	92	118
William A	33	m	w	MI	Placer	Emigrant Gap P O	76	416
Wm	35	m	w	OH	Sacramento	San Joaquin Twp	77	407
Wm	32	m	w	KY	Marin	San Rafael Twp	74	47
Wm	11	m	w	CA	San Francisco	11-Wd San Francisc	84	592
BURCHAM								
John	40	m	w	ENGL	San Francisco	8-Wd San Francisco	82	493
BURCHARD								
J K	37	m	w	NY	San Joaquin	Liberty Twp	86	87
James P	31	m	w	NY	Placer	Rocklin Twp	76	463
Jno	40	m	w	NY	Santa Clara	Gilroy Twp	88	106
Lucy	19	f	w	MO	Santa Clara	San Jose Twp	88	212
Thomas S	19	m	w	MO	Stanislaus	Branch Twp	92	1
William	20	m	w	NY	San Francisco	San Francisco P O	80	473
BURCHARDE								
Ernest	42	m	w	PRUS	Santa Clara	San Jose Twp	88	217
BURCHART								
Charles	27	m	w	PRUS	Marin	Bolinas Twp	74	6
BURCHEL								
Henry	41	m	w	HANO	Amador	Drytown P O	69	417
BURCHELL								
Jno	35	m	w	IREL	Santa Clara	Gilroy Twp	88	101
BURCHERS								
Bernard W	38	m	w	HAMB	Santa Clara	San Jose Twp	88	200
BURCHES								
Theodore	21	m	w	HANO	Los Angeles	Los Nietos Twp	73	591
BURCHFIELD								
Fred	35	m	w	OH	Stanislaus	Empire Twp	92	38
BURCHILL								
Alex	50	m	w	VA	San Joaquin	Elkhorn Twp	86	57
B M	54	m	w	IREL	Monterey	Alisal Twp	74	295
BURCHWALE								
Chas	42	m	w	HANO	San Francisco	San Francisco P O	83	193
BURCKERS								
Samuel S	33	m	w	MA	San Francisco	8-Wd San Francisco	82	441
BURCKHARDT								
Ann	38	f	w	AUST	San Francisco	San Francisco P O	80	342
BURCKMAN								
Hermann	36	m	w	AUST	San Francisco	2-Wd San Francisco	79	228
BURD								
Hannah	12	f	w	CA	Amador	Volcano P O	69	374
Hiram	34	m	w	OH	Solano	Montezuma Twp	90	65
Lawrence	35	m	w	IREL	San Francisco	San Francisco P O	83	386
Vinna	33	f	w	SWIT	Calaveras	San Andreas P O	70	185
BURDACIO								
James	20	m	w	SWIT	Marin	Nicasio Twp	74	16
BURDECK								
Thomas	72	m	w	NY	Los Angeles	Los Angeles	73	532
BURDED								
Dice	9	f	w	CA	San Joaquin	Castoria Twp	86	1
BURDELL								
Adam	24	m	w	BADE	San Francisco	2-Wd San Francisco	79	154
Lizzie	12	f	w	PA	San Francisco	San Francisco P O	85	798
Mary	10	f	w	CA	San Francisco	San Francisco P O	85	798
Simon	50	m	w	NH	San Francisco	8-Wd San Francisco	82	465
Wm	45	m	w	LA	San Francisco	8-Wd San Francisco	82	359
BURDEN								
Andrew	39	m	w	KY	San Luis Obispo	Santa Rosa Twp	87	330
Henry	35	m	w	PRUS	Mariposa	Mariposa P O	74	113
William	29	m	w	ENGL	Tuolumne	Sonora P O	93	325
BURDERWICK								
P	22	m	w	PRUS	Sierra	Lincoln Twp	89	550
BURDET								
Canda	35	m	w	FRAN	Calaveras	San Andreas P O	70	167
Peter	39	m	w	SWIT	Napa	Napa	75	8
BURDETT								
A	30	m	w	OH	Solano	Vallejo	90	160
A	27	m	w	CANA	Solano	Vallejo	90	161
H	27	m	w	NY	Klamath	Trinidad Twp	73	392
John	83	m	w	WIND	Calaveras	Copperopolis P O	70	257
Reuben	47	m	w	MA	Santa Clara	1-Wd San Jose	88	241
BURDETTE								
Lewis	32	m	w	HOLL	Mendocino	Casper & Big Rvr	74	163
BURDGE								
Stephen D	59	m	w	NY	Placer	Lincoln P O	76	486
BURDICK								
Amos	55	m	w	MA	Placer	Rocklin Twp	76	467
C B	44	m	w	OH	Yuba	W Bear Rvr Twp	93	683
Cyrus	35	m	w	OH	Los Angeles	Santa Ana Twp	73	599
Edward F	40	m	w	VT	San Francisco	8-Wd San Francisco	82	420
Edwin R	32	m	w	NY	Placer	Rocklin Twp	76	466
H	40	m	w	NY	Mendocino	Round Valley Twp	74	218
Henry	24	m	w	IREL	Solano	Tremont Twp	90	28
Horace	39	m	w	NY	Los Angeles	Los Angeles	73	544
John	36	m	w	RI	San Francisco	11-Wd San Francisc	84	598
Marcius	36	m	w	NY	Marin	Nicasio Twp	74	15
O L	36	m	w	NY	Mendocino	Sanel Twp	74	228
Samul	29	m	w	PA	Butte	Chico Twp	70	39
Stephen	42	m	w	RI	Marin	San Rafael Twp	74	35
Susan	28	f	w	IREL	San Francisco	San Francisco P O	83	4
Thomas H	32	m	w	OH	Los Angeles	Los Angeles	73	537
Wm L	51	m	w	VT	San Francisco	San Francisco P O	83	116
BURDIETT								
Daniel	30	m	w	ME	Contra Costa	Martinez Twp	71	350
BURDIN								
C H	22	m	w	ENGL	Tuolumne	Sonora P O	93	315
Charles	45	m	w	ENGL	Tuolumne	Sonora P O	93	315
BURDIS								
John	40	m	w	ENGL	El Dorado	Mud Springs Twp	72	85
John	20	m	w	ENGL	San Francisco	1-Wd San Francisco	79	74
BURDO								
Frank E	26	m	w	NY	Santa Clara	2-Wd San Jose	88	298
BURDON								
Lawrence	40	m	w	CANA	Mariposa	Mariposa P O	74	114
Thomas	32	m	w	ENGL	San Francisco	San Francisco P O	85	718
BURDOW								
Mary	45	f	w	IREL	Santa Clara	San Jose Twp	88	186
BURDROW								
Charles	24	m	w	CT	Santa Barbara	Santa Barbara P O	87	452
BURDT								
John	30	m	w	PRUS	San Francisco	7-Wd San Francisco	81	223
William	22	m	w	PRUS	San Francisco	San Francisco P O	80	400
BURDY								
G	19	m	w	OH	San Joaquin	Elkhorn Twp	86	62
James A	49	m	w	NH	San Francisco	3-Wd San Francisco	79	300
BUREA								
John	35	m	w	FRAN	San Francisco	8-Wd San Francisco	82	302
BUREGARD								
Jacob	50	m	w	PRUS	Sutter	Butte Twp	92	102
William	44	m	w	PRUS	Sutter	Butte Twp	92	102
BUREL								
Giusseppi	49	m	w	ITAL	Calaveras	San Andreas P O	70	174
Martin	42	m	w	PRUS	Solano	Rio Vista Twp	90	64
BUREN								
Antone	25	m	w	SWIT	Shasta	American Ranch P O	89	499
BURES								
Henry	52	m	w	NY	Santa Clara	Gilroy Twp	88	102
BURET								
Thomas C	45	m	w	FRAN	Calaveras	San Andreas P O	70	201
BURFEIND								
Hermann	40	m	w	HANO	San Francisco	11-Wd San Francisc	84	614
BURFIELD								
John	33	m	w	HANO	San Francisco	2-Wd San Francisco	79	221
BURFIEND								
Martin	38	m	w	HANO	San Francisco	2-Wd San Francisco	79	219
BURFORD								
Roland S	46	m	w	AL	Fresno	Millerton P O	72	147
BURG								
Charles	33	m	w	FRAN	San Francisco	San Francisco P O	80	462
John	51	m	w	SHOL	Placer	Auburn P O	76	363
BURGAN								
John	63	m	w	KY	Tulare	Visalia Twp	92	282
Samuel	30	m	w	MO	Tulare	Visalia Twp	92	282
Wm	13	m	w	CA	Yuba	Marysville Twp	93	567
BURGAR								
George	50	m	w	OH	San Luis Obispo	Santa Rosa Twp	87	324
BURGAS								
Henry	32	m	w	PA	San Mateo	Half Moon Bay P O	87	389
Kossuth	43	m	w	MEXI	El Dorado	Mud Springs Twp	72	76
BURGDORF								
J	36	m	w	GERM	Solano	Vallejo	90	200
BURGE								
Elizabeth	10	f	w	CA	Contra Costa	Martinez P O	71	387
Frank J	40	m	w	NY	Tehama	Red Bluff	92	177
George	40	m	w	ENGL	Marin	Bolinas Twp	74	5
James Peterson	50	m	w	NC	Plumas	Indian Twp	77	9
R K	43	m	w	PA	San Francisco	San Francisco P O	85	832
Thomas	38	m	w	NC	Plumas	Indian Twp	77	15
William	39	m	w	PRUS	San Francisco	7-Wd San Francisco	81	223
BURGEN								
Charles	32	m	w	OH	Amador	Ione City P O	69	359
Lewis	35	m	w	BADE	Alameda	Oakland	68	220

© 2001 by Heritage Quest. All rights reserved.

Series M593

Name	Age	S	R	B-PL	County	Locale	Roll	Pg
BURGER								
Anna	20	f	w	PRUS	Sacramento	2-Wd Sacramento	77	242
C H	32	m	w	MO	Napa	Napa	75	17
Edmond G	44	m	w	PA	Yolo	Grafton Twp	93	492
Gragor	54	m	w	BADE	El Dorado	Mud Springs Twp	72	72
J F	44	m	w	TN	Lake	Scotts Crk	73	428
Jacob	28	m	w	PRUS	San Francisco	San Francisco P O	80	531
James	34	m	w	IN	Sonoma	Russian Rvr	91	372
Jas S	42	m	w	PA	Sonoma	Cloverdale Twp	91	269
Joseph	35	m	w	OH	Yuba	North East Twp	93	643
Joseph	34	m	w	FRAN	Plumas	Quartz Twp	77	37
Louis	40	m	w	NY	Merced	Snelling P O	74	247
Louis	18	m	w	NY	San Francisco	8-Wd San Francisco	82	466
Lynford	42	m	w	PA	Yolo	Grafton Twp	93	491
Sarah	70	f	w	NC	Yolo	Cottonwood Twp	93	470
Thos	31	m	w	CANA	Sacramento	4-Wd Sacramento	77	361
BURGERS								
T K	52	m	w	NY	Sacramento	San Joaquin Twp	77	398
W H	56	m	w	MA	Sierra	Lincoln Twp	89	546
BURGERT								
Louis	35	m	w	PRUS	Sacramento	4-Wd Sacramento	77	370
BURGES								
Cesar	22	m	w	IL	Sacramento	Dry Crk Twp	77	100
Henry	25	m	w	ENGL	Fresno	Millerton P O	72	167
Hiram A	45	m	w	ME	Stanislaus	Washington Twp	92	84
John	40	m	w	TX	Monterey	Alisal Twp	74	292
Nelson	35	m	w	CT	San Joaquin	2-Wd Stockton	86	166
W C	41	m	w	ME	Sutter	Yuba Twp	92	148
BURGESS								
A	47	m	w	OH	Nevada	Meadow Lake Twp	75	260
Alfred	34	m	w	MI	Sonoma	Analy Twp	91	224
Amos	62	m	w	PA	Mendocino	Anderson Twp	74	150
Andrew	30	m	w	SCOT	Colusa	Monroe Twp	71	312
Ann	21	f	w	NY	San Francisco	11-Wd San Francisc	84	688
Anne F	12	m	w	CA	San Francisco	1-Wd San Francisco	79	73
Annin A	28	m	w	ME	Santa Cruz	Santa Cruz Twp	89	379
Charles	31	m	w	NY	Sacramento	Granite Twp	77	142
Charles F	26	m	w	MA	Santa Clara	Milpitas Twp	88	115
Chas	50	m	w	MA	San Joaquin	Elkhorn Twp	86	54
Chas	46	m	w	MA	Sacramento	4-Wd Sacramento	77	376
Chas E	21	m	w	ME	San Francisco	8-Wd San Francisco	82	374
Edmond	42	m	w	NY	Calaveras	San Andreas P O	70	162
Edward T	36	m	w	MI	Sonoma	Petaluma Twp	91	358
Elias	39	m	w	OH	Mendocino	Calpella Twp	74	182
Ellen	25	f	w	IREL	San Francisco	6-Wd San Francisco	81	118
Gorham E	37	m	w	ME	Contra Costa	Martinez P O	71	378
H	45	m	w	ENGL	Alameda	Oakland	68	197
Henry	36	m	w	ENGL	Santa Clara	San Jose Twp	88	181
Isabella	13	f	w	ME	Yolo	Merritt Twp	93	503
James	74	m	w	ME	Amador	Drytown P O	69	417
James	46	m	w	SCOT	San Francisco	1-Wd San Francisco	79	92
John	24	m	w	NY	Solano	Vacaville Twp	90	134
John C	40	m	w	VA	Siskiyou	Yreka	89	656
John F	37	m	w	TN	El Dorado	White Oak Twp	72	142
John W	50	m	w	CT	Tehama	Red Bluff	92	175
Levi	40	m	w	ENGL	Santa Clara	Gilroy Twp	88	91
Louis	40	m	w	IL	Solano	Vacaville Twp	90	130
Otis	40	m	w	OH	San Francisco	7-Wd San Francisco	81	283
Peter	21	m	w	MA	San Francisco	7-Wd San Francisco	81	185
Pierrinne	26	m	w	FRAN	San Francisco	San Francisco P O	85	772
R W	33	m	w	ME	Nevada	Eureka Twp	75	135
Richd	34	m	w	ENGL	Fresno	Millerton P O	72	167
Robert	39	m	w	ME	Tuolumne	Columbia P O	93	336
Robert	36	m	w	SCOT	Tuolumne	Columbia P O	93	336
Rufus	37	m	b	TN	El Dorado	Coloma Twp	72	8
Sebre G	64	m	w	VT	Sonoma	Healdsburg & Mendo	91	276
Smith	24	m	w	ME	Sutter	Butte Twp	92	95
T J	31	m	w	IA	Solano	Vallejo	90	152
Thomas	35	m	w	MD	El Dorado	Mud Springs Twp	72	90
Walter	30	m	w	SCOT	San Francisco	6-Wd San Francisco	81	155
William	46	m	w	FRAN	San Francisco	San Francisco P O	80	458
William	44	m	w	RI	Calaveras	San Andreas P O	70	184
William	33	m	w	ME	Nevada	Eureka Twp	75	137
Wm	28	m	w	ENGL	San Francisco	1-Wd San Francisco	79	60
Wm	24	m	w	ME	San Francisco	1-Wd San Francisco	79	136
BURGET								
Eley	45	m	w	OH	Sacramento	Sutter Twp	77	392
Henry	39	m	w	OH	Sutter	Butte Twp	92	91
Henry	30	m	w	PA	Sutter	Sutter Twp	92	122
M B	37	m	w	OH	Sutter	Butte Twp	92	93
BURGETT								
Henry	24	m	w	IN	Yolo	Washington Twp	93	532
Ira	32	m	w	OH	Humboldt	Pacific Twp	72	294
Jacob	34	m	w	HAMB	Marin	Sausalito Twp	74	66
Wm H	30	m	w	NY	Shasta	Fort Crook P O	89	473
BURGGETT								
Phil	40	m	w	TN	Del Norte	Crescent	71	464
BURGHAM								
Thos	40	m	w	MA	Sonoma	Salt Point	91	393
BURGI								
Jacob	44	m	w	SWIT	Sonoma	Sonoma Twp	91	446
BURGIN								
James	45	m	w	IREL	Calaveras	San Andreas P O	70	205
BURGINA								
Vincenta	33	m	w	SWIT	Marin	San Antonio Twp	74	61
BURGINGHAM								
Paul	29	m	w	CANA	Stanislaus	Empire Twp	92	44
BURGIS								
Geo H	38	m	w	ENGL	San Francisco	5-Wd San Francisco	81	36
Henry	31	m	w	HOLL	San Francisco	11-Wd San Francisc	84	644
Tristen	23	m	w	RI	San Francisco	San Francisco P O	85	779
BURGISS								
Richd	35	m	w	ENGL	Fresno	Millerton P O	72	166
BURGMAN								
Charles	46	m	w	SWED	Santa Clara	1-Wd San Jose	88	267
Henry	40	m	w	HAMB	Marin	Sausalito Twp	74	68
BURGOON								
Jacob	43	m	w	PA	El Dorado	Mud Springs Twp	72	74
John C	48	m	w	PA	El Dorado	Mud Springs Twp	72	74
BURGOS								
Miguela	5	f	w	CA	San Luis Obispo	San Luis Obispo Tw	87	310
BURGOW								
Wm	32	m	w	IREL	San Francisco	1-Wd San Francisco	79	39
BURGOYNE								
A W	32	m	w	OH	Alameda	Alameda	68	13
BURGRUS								
Richard	38	m	w	IREL	Alameda	Washington Twp	68	294
BURGTROF								
Charles	36	m	w	PRUS	Sonoma	Petaluma Twp	91	309
BURHAM								
John	25	m	w	NY	Kern	Tehachapi P O	73	354
Morris	23	m	w	MO	Butte	Chico Twp	70	25
BURHANS								
Wm	43	m	w	MA	San Francisco	8-Wd San Francisco	82	367
BURHOUSE								
Wm	37	m	w	MO	San Joaquin	Tulare Twp	86	258
BURICK								
Nathan	19	m	w	AR	Kern	Linns Valley P O	73	344
BURIELL								
George W	36	m	w	MD	Mendocino	Noyo & Big Rvr Twp	74	173
BURILLO								
Santos	30	m	w	MEXI	Santa Barbara	Santa Maria P O	87	513
BURIMAL								
Gilbert	42	m	w	IL	San Bernardino	San Salvador Twp	78	460
BURIMOND								
Maggie	25	f	w	NY	San Francisco	San Francisco P O	83	299
BURIOM								
Jno	29	m	w	SWED	Butte	Chico Twp	70	44
BURIS								
W W	28	m	w	IL	Sierra	Butte Twp	89	512
BURJ								
Peter	40	m	w	DENM	San Francisco	1-Wd San Francisco	79	122
BURK								
A	30	m	w	NY	Lake	Lower Lake	73	422
Aaron	25	m	w	SWED	Nevada	Meadow Lake Twp	75	259
Addison	26	m	w	KY	El Dorado	Georgetown Twp	72	45
Angeline	22	f	w	IN	Nevada	Meadow Lake Twp	75	248
B F	35	m	w	IREL	Alameda	Oakland	68	227
Barney	35	m	w	IREL	San Francisco	7-Wd San Francisco	81	189
Barthelmar	36	m	w	IREL	Monterey	Salinas Twp	74	306
Catherine	34	f	w	IREL	San Mateo	Belmont P O	87	388
Charles	25	m	w	NY	Nevada	Meadow Lake Twp	75	264
Chas L	26	m	w	KY	Nevada	Meadow Lake Twp	75	265
David	28	m	w	NY	San Mateo	Redwood Twp	87	367
Dominick	37	m	w	IREL	Amador	Amador City P O	69	390
Ed	19	m	w	VA	Butte	Chico Twp	70	31
Edward	1	m	w	CANA	San Francisco	11-Wd San Francisc	84	533
Edwd	19	m	w	OH	Butte	Chico Twp	70	38
Eliza	23	f	w	IREL	Yuba	Marysville	93	600
Eliza A	49	f	w	MD	San Francisco	2-Wd San Francisco	79	259
Elizabeth	50	f	w	IREL	San Mateo	San Mateo P O	87	358
Elizabeth	25	f	w	IREL	Nevada	Bridgeport Twp	75	117
Ellen	30	f	w	NY	San Francisco	6-Wd San Francisco	81	115
Ellen	20	f	w	MI	Tehama	Red Bluff	92	175
Ellen M	20	m	w	CANA	Tulare	Visalia	92	295
Emma	32	f	w	MA	San Francisco	2-Wd San Francisco	79	262
Frank	50	m	w	BELG	Sutter	Vernon Twp	92	130
Frank	40	m	w	IREL	Yuba	Marysville	93	583
Frank	30	m	w	POLA	Sonoma	Petaluma Twp	91	311
Geo	42	m	w	PA	Solano	Vallejo	90	161
George	25	m	w	FL	Los Angeles	Los Angeles Twp	73	495
George G	29	m	w	MO	Yolo	Grafton Twp	93	486
Harry	32	m	w	HANO	Sutter	Sutter Twp	92	117
Isaac	42	m	w	VA	Butte	Chico Twp	70	14
Jabic T	30	m	w	IL	Placer	Bath P O	76	422
James	60	m	w	PA	Humboldt	Table Bluff Twp	72	308
James	47	m	w	OH	El Dorado	Georgetown Twp	72	39
James	45	m	w	SCOT	Amador	Ione City P O	69	361
James	30	m	w	IREL	Alameda	Oakland	68	233
James	26	m	w	IREL	San Mateo	Half Moon Bay P O	87	390
James	24	m	w	NY	San Francisco	11-Wd San Francisc	84	707
James	22	m	w	NY	San Francisco	8-Wd San Francisco	82	343
John	40	m	w	IREL	Shasta	Horsetown P O	89	504
John	38	m	w	NY	Amador	Jackson P O	69	325
John	33	m	w	IREL	San Francisco	1-Wd San Francisco	79	67
John	31	m	w	IREL	San Francisco	11-Wd San Francisc	84	465
John	30	m	w	IREL	San Mateo	Woodside P O	87	380
John	28	m	w	BELG	San Francisco	2-Wd San Francisco	79	230
John	24	m	w	NY	Colusa	Grand Island Twp	71	302
John	24	m	w	PRUS	San Francisco	2-Wd San Francisco	79	259
John H	21	m	w	NJ	Humboldt	Table Bluff Twp	72	306
Le Roy	31	m	w	MO	Colusa	Colusa Twp	71	286
Luke	30	m	w	IREL	Nevada	Meadow Lake Twp	75	264
M K	38	m	w	OH	Nevada	Meadow Lake Twp	75	264

© 2001 by Heritage Quest. All rights reserved.

Name	Age	S	R	B-PL	County	Locale	Roll	Pg
Mary	25	f	w	IREL	San Francisco	11-Wd San Francisc	84	502
Mary A	20	f	w	IREL	Placer	Bath P O	76	426
Michael	33	m	w	IREL	San Bernardino	San Bernardino Twp	78	452
Miner	39	m	w	IREL	Mendocino	Round Valley Twp	74	217
Pat	64	m	w	IREL	Yuba	Rose Bar Twp	93	658
Pat	27	m	w	IREL	San Francisco	11-Wd San Francisc	84	672
Pat	20	m	w	IREL	Merced	Snelling P O	74	270
Patrick	80	m	w	IREL	San Mateo	Half Moon Bay P O	87	390
Patrick	53	m	w	IREL	Shasta	French Gulch P O	89	467
Patrick	42	m	w	IREL	San Mateo	Half Moon Bay P O	87	389
Patrick	39	m	w	IREL	Yuba	Marysville	93	632
Patrick	32	m	w	IREL	San Francisco	San Francisco P O	83	6
Peter	55	m	w	GERM	Nevada	Nevada Twp	75	296
Peter	28	m	w	IREL	San Mateo	Half Moon Bay P O	87	390
Peter J	2	m	w	CA	San Mateo	Half Moon Bay P O	87	390
Richard	32	m	w	IREL	Sutter	Yuba Twp	92	150
Richard	27	m	w	MA	San Francisco	2-Wd San Francisco	79	262
Sam	40	m	w	OH	Butte	Kimshew Tpw	70	78
Saml	48	m	w	PA	Solano	Benicia	90	6
Sophia	30	f	w	IREL	Alameda	Washington Twp	68	284
Terrance R	31	m	w	IREL	El Dorado	Mud Springs Twp	72	81
Thomas	30	m	w	MA	San Diego	Coronado	78	466
Thomas	28	m	w	IREL	San Francisco	7-Wd San Francisco	81	194
Thomas	16	m	w	IREL	Alameda	Brooklyn Twp	68	55
Thomas J	54	m	w	OH	Amador	Amador City P O	69	391
Thos	40	m	w	IREL	Sierra	Table Rock Twp	89	577
William	23	m	w	NY	Sonoma	Petaluma Twp	91	357
William H	31	m	w	IREL	San Mateo	Half Moon Bay P O	87	389
Wm	50	m	w	IREL	Yuba	Rose Bar Twp	93	667
Wm	40	m	w	WY	Butte	Oregon Twp	70	135
BURKE								
A J	28	m	w	NY	San Francisco	1-Wd San Francisco	79	108
Alex	62	m	w	TN	Mendocino	Ukiah Twp	74	243
Alexr	30	m	w	NY	San Francisco	5-Wd San Francisco	81	20
Andrew	40	m	w	IREL	Solano	Vacaville Twp	90	118
Andrew	30	m	w	IREL	Contra Costa	Martinez P O	71	429
Anne	30	f	w	IREL	San Francisco	11-Wd San Francisc	84	535
Anne	30	f	w	IREL	San Francisco	8-Wd San Francisco	82	469
Augustus	19	m	w	IREL	San Francisco	11-Wd San Francisc	84	576
B	40	m	w	TN	Lake	Upper Lake	73	413
Barbara	48	f	w	SCOT	San Francisco	2-Wd San Francisco	79	272
Bridget	44	f	w	IREL	Sacramento	4-Wd Sacramento	77	339
Bridget	40	f	w	IREL	San Francisco	8-Wd San Francisco	82	411
Bridget	38	f	w	IREL	Marin	San Rafael	74	53
Caroline	26	f	w	AUSL	San Francisco	8-Wd San Francisco	82	475
Charles D	35	m	w	VT	Sacramento	2-Wd Sacramento	77	244
Claud V	30	m	w	OH	Yolo	Cache Crk Twp	93	453
Daniel	40	m	w	IREL	Kern	Linns Valley P O	73	343
David	28	m	w	IREL	San Francisco	1-Wd San Francisco	79	99
David B	24	m	w	PRUS	Sacramento	2-Wd Sacramento	77	230
Denis	48	m	w	IREL	San Francisco	1-Wd San Francisco	79	94
E	53	m	w	VA	San Francisco	San Francisco P O	85	802
Edmund	43	m	w	MD	Kern	Linns Valley P O	73	343
Edward	65	m	w	MD	San Francisco	6-Wd San Francisco	81	122
Edward	30	m	w	IREL	Santa Clara	Fremont Twp	88	45
Edward	25	m	w	IREL	Sacramento	2-Wd Sacramento	77	238
Edwin	37	m	w	NY	Kern	Havilah P O	73	339
Eliza	42	f	w	IREL	San Francisco	San Francisco P O	83	125
Ellen	30	f	w	IREL	San Francisco	7-Wd San Francisco	81	274
Emily	45	f	w	MI	San Francisco	8-Wd San Francisco	82	472
Emma	24	f	w	IREL	San Francisco	8-Wd San Francisco	82	403
Erastus	54	m	w	CANA	Placer	Pino Twp	76	471
Eva	14	f	w	WI	Alameda	Oakland	68	259
F M	30	m	w	MO	Mendocino	Ukiah Twp	74	235
F T	42	m	w	NY	Sacramento	1-Wd Sacramento	77	177
F T	40	m	w	IREL	Sacramento	1-Wd Sacramento	77	172
Fred W	34	m	w	MO	Sacramento	2-Wd Sacramento	77	228
Geo	25	m	w	IREL	San Francisco	1-Wd San Francisco	79	69
Hannah	37	f	w	IREL	San Francisco	San Francisco P O	83	140
Henry	48	m	w	IREL	Placer	Bath P O	76	459
Henry	34	m	w	PA	Sacramento	2-Wd Sacramento	77	226
Henry	34	m	w	IREL	Marin	San Rafael Twp	74	45
Honora	45	f	w	IREL	Santa Clara	Santa Clara Twp	88	141
Honora M	23	f	w	NY	San Francisco	6-Wd San Francisco	81	135
J	22	m	w	CANA	Sacramento	3-Wd Sacramento	77	313
J C	23	m	w	VA	San Francisco	San Francisco P O	85	802
James	8	m	w	CA	San Francisco	San Francisco P O	83	385
James	43	m	w	IREL	San Francisco	11-Wd San Francisc	84	486
James	42	m	w	IREL	Santa Cruz	Pajaro Twp	89	346
James	41	m	w	IREL	Sacramento	Granite Twp	77	139
James	40	m	w	IREL	San Francisco	1-Wd San Francisco	79	23
James	38	m	w	BADE	San Diego	Fort Yuma Dist	78	463
James	35	m	w	IREL	San Francisco	11-Wd San Francisc	84	614
James	32	m	w	IREL	Nevada	Grass Valley Twp	75	171
James	30	m	w	IREL	San Francisco	8-Wd San Francisco	82	370
James	30	m	w	IREL	Sutter	Sutter Twp	92	123
James	28	m	w	IREL	San Francisco	3-Wd San Francisco	79	327
James	27	m	w	MO	San Luis Obispo	San Luis Obispo Tw	87	302
James	27	m	w	IREL	Sonoma	Petaluma Twp	91	319
James	22	m	w	IREL	Santa Clara	San Jose Twp	88	184
James	22	m	w	IREL	San Francisco	2-Wd San Francisco	79	213
James	15	m	w	NY	Marin	San Rafael Twp	74	27
James H	38	m	w	TN	Los Angeles	Los Nietos Twp	73	580
James W	71	m	w	IREL	Santa Barbara	Santa Barbara P O	87	459
Jane	32	f	w	IREL	San Francisco	San Francisco P O	83	99
Jane	13	f	w	ME	San Francisco	San Francisco P O	85	817
Jas H	34	m	w	MO	Mendocino	Ukiah Twp	74	242
Jeremiah	25	m	w	IL	Tehama	Cottonwood Twp	92	161
Joannah	32	f	w	IREL	San Francisco	6-Wd San Francisco	81	128
John	63	m	w	IREL	San Francisco	San Francisco P O	83	7
John	50	m	w	IREL	San Francisco	7-Wd San Francisco	81	227
John	50	m	w	IREL	Santa Clara	Fremont Twp	88	60
John	46	m	w	IREL	Sacramento	Sutter Twp	77	384
John	42	m	w	IREL	Alameda	Oakland	68	186
John	40	m	w	NY	San Francisco	San Francisco P O	80	483
John	40	m	w	IREL	Sacramento	Granite Twp	77	139
John	40	m	w	IREL	Yuba	Linda Twp	93	555
John	38	m	w	IREL	San Francisco	11-Wd San Francisc	84	582
John	38	m	w	IREL	San Francisco	1-Wd San Francisco	79	75
John	37	m	w	IREL	Alpine	Bullion P O	69	314
John	35	m	w	MA	San Francisco	11-Wd San Francisc	84	461
John	35	m	w	IREL	Humboldt	Pacific Twp	72	291
John	32	m	w	IA	Solano	Tremont Twp	90	35
John	30	m	w	IREL	San Francisco	7-Wd San Francisco	81	194
John	28	m	w	IREL	San Francisco	1-Wd San Francisco	79	134
John	26	m	w	IREL	San Francisco	8-Wd San Francisco	82	446
John	26	m	w	IREL	Santa Cruz	Santa Cruz	89	427
John	22	m	w	NY	San Francisco	7-Wd San Francisco	81	227
John	22	m	w	LA	San Francisco	San Francisco P O	80	336
John	20	m	w	IREL	Napa	Napa	75	18
John H	27	m	w	IREL	San Francisco	San Francisco P O	83	38
John H	23	m	w	NY	San Francisco	2-Wd San Francisco	79	195
John I	67	m	w	MD	San Francisco	6-Wd San Francisco	81	122
John W	32	m	w	MO	Mendocino	Ukiah Twp	74	242
Jos	26	m	w	IREL	Sacramento	1-Wd Sacramento	77	187
Joseph	43	m	w	IREL	San Francisco	San Francisco P O	83	401
Joseph	26	m	w	WI	Alpine	Markleeville P O	69	312
Julia	31	f	w	IREL	San Francisco	San Francisco P O	85	735
Julia K	10	f	w	NY	San Francisco	San Francisco P O	83	4
Julius	32	m	w	PRUS	San Francisco	8-Wd San Francisco	82	353
Kate	28	f	w	IREL	San Francisco	8-Wd San Francisco	82	480
Kate	25	f	w	IREL	Sacramento	3-Wd Sacramento	77	280
Laura	9	f	w	CA	Nevada	Grass Valley Twp	75	230
Lewis	34	m	w	PRUS	Sacramento	2-Wd Sacramento	77	227
Lewis	27	m	w	ENGL	San Francisco	7-Wd San Francisco	81	228
Louisa M	70	f	w	MD	San Francisco	6-Wd San Francisco	81	122
Luke	35	m	w	IREL	Nevada	Little York Twp	75	241
M	41	m	w	IREL	Lake	Morgan Valley	73	425
M	25	m	w	IREL	Lake	Knoxville Mines	73	405
Madden	42	m	w	IREL	San Francisco	2-Wd San Francisco	79	152
Margaret	27	f	w	IREL	San Francisco	3-Wd San Francisco	79	315
Margaret	23	f	w	IREL	San Francisco	7-Wd San Francisco	81	267
Margaret	20	f	w	IREL	Marin	San Rafael Twp	74	30
Margrett	37	f	w	IREL	Napa	Napa	75	37
Mariah	38	f	w	IREL	Sacramento	2-Wd Sacramento	77	254
Martin	60	m	w	IREL	Placer	Bath P O	76	435
Martin J	49	m	w	IREL	San Francisco	8-Wd San Francisco	82	298
Mary	73	f	w	IREL	San Francisco	San Francisco P O	83	115
Mary	73	f	w	NY	San Francisco	6-Wd San Francisco	81	125
Mary	50	f	w	IREL	San Francisco	7-Wd San Francisco	81	165
Mary	45	f	w	NY	San Francisco	7-Wd San Francisco	81	204
Mary	40	f	w	IREL	San Francisco	7-Wd San Francisco	81	282
Mary	40	f	w	IREL	San Francisco	6-Wd San Francisco	81	155
Mary	40	f	w	IREL	San Francisco	6-Wd San Francisco	81	89
Mary	35	f	w	IREL	Sonoma	Santa Rosa	91	401
Mary	35	f	w	IREL	Sacramento	1-Wd Sacramento	77	177
Mary	35	f	w	IREL	Santa Cruz	Santa Cruz	89	403
Mary	30	f	w	SALT	San Francisco	San Francisco P O	83	198
Mary	26	f	w	AUSL	San Francisco	7-Wd San Francisco	81	181
Mary	22	f	w	IREL	Sacramento	2-Wd Sacramento	77	252
Mary	19	f	w	MI	Tehama	Red Bluff	92	176
Mary	14	f	w	CA	Santa Clara	2-Wd San Jose	88	308
Mary E	11	f	w	CA	Nevada	Grass Valley Twp	75	230
Mathew	45	m	w	IREL	San Francisco	3-Wd San Francisco	79	296
Michael	69	m	w	IREL	San Francisco	2-Wd San Francisco	79	160
Michael	40	m	w	IREL	San Francisco	11-Wd San Francisc	84	605
Michael	38	m	w	IREL	Marin	San Rafael	74	54
Michael	35	m	w	IREL	San Mateo	San Mateo P O	87	359
Michael	30	m	w	IREL	San Francisco	San Francisco P O	85	780
Michael	25	m	w	IREL	Sacramento	2-Wd Sacramento	77	234
Michael	23	m	w	IREL	San Francisco	San Francisco P O	80	336
Michael	22	m	w	IREL	Klamath	Camp Gaston	73	372
Michael	20	m	w	IREL	San Francisco	San Francisco P O	83	385
Michael	13	m	w	CA	Placer	Bath P O	76	422
Michael D	27	m	w	IREL	Santa Clara	Fremont Twp	88	42
Michal P	29	m	w	IREL	San Francisco	San Francisco P O	83	363
Michl	37	m	w	IREL	San Francisco	San Francisco P O	83	11
Michl	27	m	w	NY	San Francisco	1-Wd San Francisco	79	115
Mike	45	m	w	IREL	Sacramento	3-Wd Sacramento	77	273
Milo A	43	m	w	VT	Sacramento	4-Wd Sacramento	77	361
Oscar P	35	m	w	MS	San Joaquin	3-Wd Stockton	86	233
Patrick	37	m	w	IREL	San Francisco	11-Wd San Francisc	84	656
Patrick	36	m	w	IREL	San Francisco	11-Wd San Francisc	84	645
Patrick	36	m	w	IREL	Tuolumne	Big Oak Flat P O	93	405
Patrick	32	m	w	IREL	Nevada	Grass Valley Twp	75	199
Peter	38	m	w	IREL	San Francisco	1-Wd San Francisco	79	61
Peter	24	m	w	NY	Marin	San Rafael Twp	74	47
Phillip	27	m	w	IREL	Los Angeles	Los Angeles	73	566
Robert	36	m	w	RUSS	San Francisco	1-Wd San Francisco	79	26
Robert	22	m	w	ENGL	Los Angeles	Wilmington Twp	73	636
Rose	40	f	w	IREL	San Francisco	11-Wd San Francisc	84	649
S W	65	m	w	OH	Sacramento	3-Wd Sacramento	77	281
Samuel	50	m	w	NY	San Francisco	7-Wd San Francisco	81	204
Stephen	36	m	w	IREL	Solano	Suisun Twp	90	100

Series M593

© 2001 by Heritage Quest. All rights reserved.

Name	Age	S	R	B-PL	County	Locale	Series M593 Roll	Pg
Susan	7	f	w	CA	Nevada	Grass Valley Twp	75	230
T	34	m	w	IREL	Lake	Knoxville Mines	73	405
T	26	m	w	IREL	Lake	Knoxville Mines	73	405
T H	28	m	w	OH	Sacramento	3-Wd Sacramento	77	280
Thomas	55	m	w	IREL	San Francisco	San Francisco P O	80	331
Thomas	47	m	w	IREL	San Francisco	San Francisco P O	80	333
Thomas	44	m	w	IREL	San Francisco	San Francisco P O	83	142
Thomas	40	m	w	IREL	San Francisco	San Francisco P O	85	858
Thomas	31	m	w	NY	San Francisco	6-Wd San Francisco	81	107
Thomas	30	m	w	IREL	Placer	Bath P O	76	453
Thomas	25	m	w	IREL	Solano	Montezuma Twp	90	65
Thorn P	42	m	w	NY	San Francisco	2-Wd San Francisco	79	214
Thos	40	m	w	IREL	Sacramento	3-Wd Sacramento	77	273
Thos	27	m	w	IREL	Solano	Vallejo	90	170
Thos	26	m	w	NY	San Francisco	San Francisco P O	83	123
Thos	24	m	w	ENGL	San Francisco	1-Wd San Francisco	79	95
W	54	m	w	IREL	San Francisco	San Francisco P O	85	779
W T	20	m	w	MO	Lake	Upper Lake	73	413
Walter	32	m	w	OH	Stanislaus	Empire Twp	92	37
William	36	m	w	IREL	San Francisco	San Francisco P O	83	385
William	27	m	w	VA	Siskiyou	Hamburg Twp	89	596
William	16	m	w	MD	San Francisco	1-Wd San Francisco	79	89
William A	49	m	w	CANA	San Francisco	6-Wd San Francisco	81	144
William F	38	m	w	IREL	San Francisco	6-Wd San Francisco	81	136
Winifred	36	f	w	IREL	Santa Clara	1-Wd San Jose	88	245
Wm	9	m	w	CA	San Francisco	11-Wd San Francisc	84	577
Wm	55	m	w	IREL	San Francisco	7-Wd San Francisco	81	265
Wm	33	m	w	NY	San Francisco	1-Wd San Francisco	79	123
Wm	25	m	w	IREL	San Francisco	1-Wd San Francisco	79	44
Wm A	50	m	w	CANA	San Francisco	8-Wd San Francisco	82	367
Wm N	54	m	w	OH	Sacramento	4-Wd Sacramento	77	354
Wm W	24	m	w	VT	San Francisco	1-Wd San Francisco	79	69
BURKES								
Charles	53	m	w	AL	El Dorado	Mud Springs Twp	72	82
BURKET								
Michl	40	m	w	ENGL	San Francisco	5-Wd San Francisco	81	33
Saml	20	m	w	PA	Butte	Chico Twp	70	43
BURKETT								
A	42	m	w	OH	San Joaquin	Oneal Twp	86	99
Calvin	26	m	w	ME	Santa Cruz	Santa Cruz Twp	89	394
John T	45	m	w	ME	Santa Clara	2-Wd San Jose	88	303
Lizzie	12	f	b	CA	Santa Barbara	Santa Barbara P O	87	454
Martha	23	f	w	VA	Santa Cruz	Santa Cruz	89	419
BURKETTE								
Jas	30	m	w	ME	Sierra	Gibson Twp	89	544
BURKEY								
Peter E	14	m	w	CA	Colusa	Colusa	71	292
BURKHALTER								
Erasmus	27	m	w	GA	Monterey	San Juan Twp	74	391
BURKHARD								
Fred	42	m	w	WURT	San Francisco	11-Wd San Francisc	84	450
BURKHARDT								
Adolph	36	m	w	WURT	San Francisco	8-Wd San Francisco	82	384
Anton	34	m	w	GERM	San Diego	San Diego	78	496
Charles	31	m	w	WURT	San Francisco	San Francisco P O	80	387
Christian	42	m	w	WURT	San Francisco	San Francisco P O	80	385
Frank	46	m	w	BADE	San Francisco	San Francisco P O	80	362
George	36	m	w	PRUS	San Francisco	San Francisco P O	83	23
Henry	56	m	w	PA	Solano	Tremont Twp	90	35
John	31	m	w	IA	San Diego	San Diego	78	484
Louisa	27	f	w	BAVA	San Francisco	8-Wd San Francisco	82	446
Max	50	m	w	PRUS	San Francisco	5-Wd San Francisco	81	35
Max	38	m	w	WURT	San Francisco	1-Wd San Francisco	79	136
Max	35	m	w	HAMB	San Francisco	3-Wd San Francisco	79	324
Max A	28	m	w	GERM	San Diego	San Diego	78	496
BURKHART								
Albert	31	m	b	MA	Sacramento	4-Wd Sacramento	77	365
Chas	35	m	w	WURT	Solano	Benicia	90	2
George	45	m	w	WURT	Los Angeles	Los Angeles	73	543
Mary	19	f	w	NE	Los Angeles	Los Angeles	73	534
T A	37	m	w	PRUS	Mendocino	Round Valley Twp	74	217
BURKHEAD								
Mary A	56	f	w	VA	Fresno	Millerton P O	72	194
BURKHEART								
David	22	m	w	PA	Colusa	Colusa Twp	71	285
BURKHOLDER								
Wm	35	m	w	PA	Butte	Ophir Twp	70	110
BURKINSHAW								
Susie	5	f	w	CANA	Sonoma	Petaluma Twp	91	361
BURKLEY								
Chas	28	m	w	KY	Sutter	Vernon Twp	92	130
David	34	m	w	CT	San Francisco	7-Wd San Francisco	81	256
Renequiaz	26	m	w	SWAB	Los Angeles	Santa Ana Twp	73	609
BURKMAN								
Mary	16	f	w	GERM	San Joaquin	3-Wd Stockton	86	243
BURKMIE								
Herman	40	m	w	HAMB	Los Angeles	Los Angeles Twp	73	475
BURKOFSKY								
Emil	40	m	w	PRUS	San Francisco	San Francisco P O	83	340
BURKS								
Edward	22	m	w	KY	Stanislaus	Empire Twp	92	44
John	35	m	w	IREL	San Francisco	7-Wd San Francisco	81	188
BURLAND								
Robt	40	m	w	NY	Monterey	Pajaro Twp	74	368
BURLEIGH								
John	50	m	w	FRAN	San Francisco	San Francisco P O	80	533
BURLESON								
Charles	43	m	w	OH	Santa Clara	Santa Clara Twp	88	139
BURLETT								
F	40	m	w	FRAN	Alameda	Oakland	68	182
BURLEY								
---	38	m	w	IREL	Yuba	Marysville	93	611
Bolivar	44	m	w	CT	Humboldt	Bald Hills	72	239
Jane	16	f	w	AUSL	San Francisco	8-Wd San Francisco	82	394
John	27	m	w	ENGL	Nevada	Grass Valley Twp	75	224
Robinson	32	m	w	CANA	San Francisco	San Francisco P O	83	36
Saml	40	m	w	ENGL	Sacramento	3-Wd Sacramento	77	318
Samuel	26	m	w	CANA	Santa Clara	Fremont Twp	88	64
Thomas J	22	m	w	CANA	Yolo	Cache Crk Twp	93	457
Wm J	24	m	w	CANA	Yolo	Cache Crk Twp	93	432
BURLIN								
E L	60	m	w	SWED	Sacramento	3-Wd Sacramento	77	297
BURLING								
James	31	m	w	PA	San Francisco	11-Wd San Francisc	84	483
Julian	16	m	w	CA	Santa Clara	Santa Clara Twp	88	176
Lucian	17	m	w	CA	Santa Clara	Santa Clara Twp	88	176
Margaret	33	f	w	IREL	San Francisco	5-Wd San Francisco	81	6
William	47	m	w	PA	San Francisco	11-Wd San Francisc	84	529
BURLINGAME								
B C	47	m	w	ME	Butte	Bidwell Twp	70	3
Dewitt C	43	m	w	OH	Butte	Ophir Twp	70	91
Ed	40	m	w	NY	San Francisco	5-Wd San Francisco	81	21
H B	21	m	w	MI	Sacramento	1-Wd Sacramento	77	184
Henry	44	m	w	ME	Los Angeles	Wilmington Twp	73	644
Matilda	27	f	w	ME	Sonoma	Mendocino Twp	91	292
BURLINGHAM								
J M	52	f	w	NY	Amador	Drytown P O	69	416
Nathan D	38	m	w	PA	El Dorado	Mud Springs Twp	72	81
BURLL								
Manuel	34	m	w	PORT	Stanislaus	Emory Twp	92	25
BURLUGH								
J A	36	m	w	NH	Sierra	Butte Twp	89	512
BURLY								
Hanover	70	m	w	ENGL	San Mateo	Schoolhouse Statio	87	336
BURLYHEAD								
Elwd	37	m	w	TN	San Diego	San Diego	78	485
BURMAM								
Joseph	44	m	w	MO	Placer	Bath P O	76	440
BURMAN								
Anton	25	m	w	SWIT	Tehama	Antelope Twp	92	154
John	34	m	w	ENGL	Sierra	Eureka Twp	89	523
John H	30	m	w	GERM	San Joaquin	2-Wd Stockton	86	167
BURMEISTER								
Alrich	26	m	w	HANO	San Francisco	6-Wd San Francisco	81	151
Ch H	36	m	w	HANO	San Francisco	1-Wd San Francisco	79	103
Francis	34	m	w	SHOL	San Francisco	11-Wd San Francisc	84	554
H	31	m	w	HAMB	San Francisco	1-Wd San Francisco	79	27
Henry	30	m	w	FRAN	Solano	Green Valley Twp	90	44
BURMER								
Joseph	21	m	w	IREL	Alameda	Brooklyn	68	23
BURMESTER								
Hy	47	m	w	HAMB	San Francisco	11-Wd San Francisc	84	569
BURMINGHAM								
John	30	m	w	IREL	San Joaquin	2-Wd Stockton	86	175
M	40	m	w	IREL	Trinity	Canyon City Pct	92	201
Patrick	38	m	w	IREL	Placer	Gold Run Twp	76	394
BURMUDES								
Jesus	40	m	w	MEXI	Los Angeles	Wilmington Twp	73	634
BURN								
A	31	m	w	RUSS	Alameda	Murray Twp	68	107
Am	30	m	c	CHIN	Monterey	San Juan Twp	74	399
Clemente	20	m	w	ITAL	Sonoma	Analy Twp	91	236
E J	32	m	w	IREL	Solano	Vallejo	90	203
Hannah	75	f	w	PRUS	San Francisco	8-Wd San Francisco	82	383
Henry	26	m	w	ENGL	Placer	Bath P O	76	437
J W	28	m	w	IREL	Alameda	Oakland	68	247
J W	28	m	w	IREL	Alameda	Oakland	68	247
James	43	m	w	IREL	Placer	Bath P O	76	431
John	71	m	w	SWIT	Sacramento	Sutter Twp	77	393
John	25	m	w	IREL	San Francisco	San Francisco P O	83	87
Moses	87	m	w	PRUS	San Francisco	8-Wd San Francisco	82	383
Peter	60	m	w	IREL	San Francisco	San Francisco P O	83	420
William	27	m	w	MA	Sonoma	Petaluma Twp	91	365
BURNAD								
Thos	21	m	w	IL	Sacramento	San Joaquin Twp	77	402
BURNAN								
John	53	m	w	NY	Klamath	Trinidad Twp	73	390
BURNAR								
Sarah	40	f	w	OH	Colusa	Colusa	71	295
BURNCH								
Thos J	45	m	w	MO	San Luis Obispo	San Luis Obispo Tw	87	303
BURNE								
Anna	30	f	w	IREL	Alameda	Oakland	68	152
Anna	20	f	w	MA	Santa Clara	Santa Clara Twp	88	168
James	30	m	w	NY	San Francisco	San Francisco P O	85	819
John	34	m	w	NY	Sutter	Vernon Twp	92	133
Manuel	32	m	w	PORT	Marin	San Rafael Twp	74	59
Thomas	38	m	w	IREL	San Francisco	San Francisco P O	85	811
BURNEL								
Desiderio	50	m	w	MEXI	Los Angeles	Santa Ana Twp	73	605
BURNELL								
A	35	m	w	CA	Alameda	Murray Twp	68	103
A	24	m	w	CA	Alameda	Murray Twp	68	111

© 2001 by Heritage Quest. All rights reserved.

California 1870 Census

Name	Age	S	R	B-PL	County	Locale	Roll	Pg
Antwine	55	m	w	CA	Alameda	Murray Twp	68	111
Augustin	34	m	w	MEXI	Fresno	Millerton P O	72	167
Eldrick	25	m	w	ME	Sonoma	Salt Point	91	380
Frank	32	m	w	CANA	Solano	Vallejo	90	139
James	37	m	w	NJ	Alameda	Murray Twp	68	107
Joe	38	m	w	CA	Alameda	Murray Twp	68	108
Joel	51	m	w	NY	Humboldt	Eel Rvr Twp	72	246
John	49	m	w	IREL	Nevada	Nevada Twp	75	302
Mathew	20	m	w	OH	Santa Clara	Santa Clara Twp	88	140
P	40	m	w	CA	Alameda	Murray Twp	68	104
R	44	m	w	NY	Napa	Napa	75	51
BURNER								
Charles	40	m	w	SWIT	Sacramento	American Twp	77	64
George F	25	m	w	OH	Colusa	Colusa Twp	71	275
Henry	22	m	w	OH	San Francisco	11-Wd San Francisc	84	507
Jacob	20	m	w	OH	Colusa	Colusa Twp	71	276
John	29	m	w	OH	San Francisco	11-Wd San Francisc	84	507
Louis	30	m	w	WURT	San Francisco	2-Wd San Francisco	79	233
Mary	45	f	w	OH	Tehama	Deer Crk Twp	92	171
Peter	20	m	w	IREL	Contra Costa	Martinez P O	71	423
Samuel	46	m	w	VA	Nevada	Little York Twp	75	238
Scott	16	m	w	CA	Colusa	Colusa Twp	71	275
William	39	m	w	OH	Placer	Bath P O	76	460
BURNES								
A	61	m	w	POLA	Sacramento	1-Wd Sacramento	77	176
Catie G	43	f	w	CA	Sutter	Vernon Twp	92	133
Charles	38	m	w	WURT	San Francisco	San Francisco P O	83	341
Charles A	39	m	w	MO	Monterey	Salinas Twp	74	312
Ellen	16	f	w	MO	Mendocino	Ukiah Twp	74	233
Frank	42	m	w	NY	Sonoma	Petaluma Twp	91	365
Frank	30	m	w	MO	Tulare	Tule Rvr Twp	92	266
Frank S	43	m	w	NY	Stanislaus	Emory Twp	92	20
Harmon	26	m	w	IL	Butte	Chico Twp	70	59
Henry	39	m	w	ME	San Francisco	11-Wd San Francisc	84	574
Ira	41	m	w	AUST	Amador	Sutter Crk P O	69	406
J A	27	m	b	NC	Amador	Ione City P O	69	361
J H	35	m	w	NY	Solano	Vallejo	90	216
James L	39	m	w	AL	San Luis Obispo	Morro Twp	87	280
Jas	25	m	w	IREL	Solano	Vallejo	90	162
John	30	m	w	CANA	Solano	Benicia	90	18
Lewis	31	m	w	NY	Santa Clara	1-Wd San Jose	88	250
Luke	26	m	w	IL	Amador	Amador City P O	69	392
Michael	26	m	w	IREL	Contra Costa	Martinez P O	71	413
Nellie J	13	f	w	CA	Monterey	Monterey	74	355
Nelly	21	f	w	MO	Yuba	Marysville	93	602
Samuel	23	m	w	CANA	Sonoma	Bodega Twp	91	261
Samuel K	52	m	w	AL	Monterey	Salinas Twp	74	312
Thurmer	38	m	w	NY	Butte	Chico Twp	70	56
W	20	m	w	WALE	Sacramento	1-Wd Sacramento	77	189
Watson	26	m	w	MA	Yolo	Grafton Twp	93	494
Wm	40	m	w	OH	Sacramento	1-Wd Sacramento	77	173
BURNESS								
Lorat	45	m	w	FRAN	Del Norte	Mountain Twp	71	474
BURNET								
Fred	29	m	w	MA	San Francisco	7-Wd San Francisco	81	227
James	29	m	w	PRUS	San Francisco	San Francisco P O	80	462
Jane	35	f	w	ENGL	San Francisco	San Francisco P O	80	465
John	46	m	w	TN	Sutter	Sutter Twp	92	118
John	24	m	w	PERU	Contra Costa	San Pablo Twp	71	363
Minerva	24	f	w	MO	Sacramento	Franklin Twp	77	119
William	51	m	w	ENGL	Calaveras	Copperopolis P O	70	241
BURNETT								
A	31	m	w	ENGL	San Joaquin	Douglas Twp	86	37
Albert	42	m	w	NY	Stanislaus	Emory Twp	92	16
Alexander	28	m	w	SCOT	Los Angeles	Los Angeles Twp	73	496
Alfred	44	m	w	OH	San Francisco	6-Wd San Francisco	81	90
Amer	65	m	w	VA	Plumas	Washington Twp	77	54
Augustus	20	m	w	MO	Nevada	Meadow Lake Twp	75	253
Bjn	39	m	w	FRAN	San Francisco	11-Wd San Francisc	84	643
Charles	44	m	w	NY	Tuolumne	Sonora P O	93	331
Charles	35	m	w	NY	Nevada	Little York Twp	75	242
Dwight	44	m	w	TN	Santa Clara	Santa Clara Twp	88	155
E D	37	m	w	ENGL	Mariposa	Maxwell Crk P O	74	145
Edward F	29	m	w	NY	Mendocino	Navarro & Big Rvr	74	175
Edwin F	30	m	w	CANA	Fresno	Kings Rvr P O	72	203
Elias	48	m	w	OH	Napa	Napa	75	26
Elie	16	m	w	FRAN	San Francisco	11-Wd San Francisc	84	643
Frank	36	m	w	MO	Nevada	Eureka Twp	75	135
Frank	31	m	w	NY	Alameda	Murray Twp	68	105
G	37	m	w	IREL	Nevada	Meadow Lake Twp	75	248
George	28	m	w	MA	San Francisco	6-Wd San Francisco	81	149
George O	60	m	w	TN	Solano	Vacaville Twp	90	137
Hanah	36	f	w	IREL	San Francisco	7-Wd San Francisco	81	217
Haran	24	m	w	OH	San Joaquin	Liberty Twp	86	97
Harriett	60	f	w	SCOT	San Joaquin	Douglas Twp	86	36
Harvey	16	m	w	TX	Santa Cruz	Santa Cruz Twp	89	386
Henry	24	m	w	NY	Yolo	Cottonwood Twp	93	474
Horace G	37	m	w	MO	Yolo	Cache Crk Twp	93	428
Isaac T	52	m	w	VT	Santa Cruz	Santa Cruz	89	421
Isham	40	m	w	KY	Colusa	Monroe Twp	71	321
J	13	m	w	CA	Solano	Benicia	90	21
J B	44	m	w	PA	El Dorado	Greenwood Twp	72	55
J H	30	m	w	NJ	Sacramento	American Twp	77	68
J J	24	m	w	MO	Monterey	San Juan Twp	74	398
James	28	m	w	CANA	San Francisco	San Francisco P O	83	90
James M	39	m	w	IA	Sonoma	Analy Twp	91	227
Jas	38	m	w	SCOT	San Joaquin	Douglas Twp	86	36

Name	Age	S	R	B-PL	County	Locale	Roll	Pg
John	50	m	w	PA	Nevada	Grass Valley Twp	75	162
John	34	m	w	NY	Sacramento	2-Wd Sacramento	77	234
John B	49	m	w	MO	Santa Clara	1-Wd San Jose	88	249
John M	32	m	w	MO	San Francisco	San Francisco P O	85	724
Lester	65	m	w	CT	Yuba	Long Bar Twp	93	560
Mary	37	f	w	MO	San Francisco	2-Wd San Francisco	79	268
Melvin	38	m	w	KY	Solano	Tremont Twp	90	29
Nathaniel	50	m	w	NY	San Francisco	San Francisco P O	83	339
Peter	36	m	w	OH	Butte	Chico Twp	70	35
Peter H	63	m	w	TN	San Francisco	San Francisco P O	85	724
R	36	f	w	ENGL	San Francisco	San Francisco P O	83	265
R B	31	m	w	NY	Alameda	Oakland	68	213
R P	40	m	w	MA	Alameda	Oakland	68	264
R R	13	m	w	CA	Alameda	Oakland	68	159
Robert	36	m	w	SCOT	Los Angeles	Los Angeles Twp	73	496
Robert	30	m	w	SCOT	Los Angeles	Los Angeles Twp	73	496
Robt	50	m	w	IREL	Sacramento	4-Wd Sacramento	77	333
Sindrilla	53	f	w	KY	Sonoma	Petaluma Twp	91	334
T O	11	m	w	CA	Alameda	Oakland	68	159
Thos	47	m	w	MO	Mendocino	Ukiah Twp	74	241
W C	41	m	w	CT	San Francisco	San Francisco P O	85	767
W F	39	m	w	IN	Monterey	San Juan Twp	74	414
William	42	m	w	NY	San Francisco	3-Wd San Francisco	79	311
William	40	m	w	IREL	Nevada	Little York Twp	75	237
William	39	m	w	PA	Nevada	Bridgeport Twp	75	114
William	25	m	w	NY	San Francisco	7-Wd San Francisco	81	218
Wm J	21	m	w	MO	Santa Clara	Milpitas Twp	88	111
BURNETTE								
James	17	m	w	WI	Alameda	Murray Twp	68	106
Marcella	68	m	w	FRAN	San Francisco	1-Wd San Francisco	79	49
BURNETTS								
Philetus N	63	m	w	MA	Sacramento	4-Wd Sacramento	77	334
BURNEY								
A	21	m	w	TN	San Joaquin	2-Wd Stockton	86	193
Aneseta	60	m	w	MEXI	Alameda	Brooklyn	68	36
Barnett	69	m	w	VA	Butte	Chico Twp	70	23
C S	40	m	w	NY	Mendocino	Ukiah Twp	74	237
William	36	m	w	TX	Stanislaus	Empire Twp	92	40
BURNHAM								
A	60	m	w	ME	Sonoma	Santa Rosa	91	399
Alfred	18	m	w	UT	Alpine	Silver Mtn P O	69	306
G M	50	m	w	MA	Alameda	Oakland	68	246
Geo C	42	m	w	NY	Santa Cruz	Santa Cruz Twp	89	394
George	43	m	w	CT	El Dorado	Placerville	72	108
Henry	37	m	w	MA	Sacramento	2-Wd Sacramento	77	224
J	28	m	w	ME	Sonoma	Santa Rosa	91	399
James	33	m	w	MA	San Francisco	11-Wd San Francisc	84	637
James E	44	m	w	TN	Calaveras	San Andreas P O	70	178
James H	24	m	w	TX	Sacramento	Granite Twp	77	142
John	54	m	w	HOLL	El Dorado	Placerville Twp	72	93
John	30	m	w	MA	San Francisco	8-Wd San Francisco	82	310
Jos	23	m	w	WI	Sonoma	Santa Rosa	91	399
L	1	m	w	CA	Alameda	Oakland	68	236
Lewis P	60	m	w	ME	Placer	Bath P O	76	454
Louis	52	m	w	ME	Butte	Ophir Twp	70	106
Sophia	40	f	w	ME	San Francisco	San Francisco P O	83	269
Stephen	36	m	w	ENGL	Butte	Ophir Twp	70	106
W C	43	m	w	CT	Sacramento	1-Wd Sacramento	77	178
W H	36	m	w	MA	San Francisco	San Francisco P O	83	295
BURNHAN								
O H	43	m	w	NY	Alameda	Oakland	68	154
BURNHART								
Geo	36	m	w	BADE	San Joaquin	Oneal Twp	86	102
BURNICK								
Geo	38	m	w	AUST	Santa Clara	Burnett Twp	88	38
BURNIE								
Alexander	49	m	w	OH	Nevada	Grass Valley Twp	75	158
W S	20	m	w	NY	Alameda	Oakland	68	225
BURNING								
Dora	13	f	w	HANO	San Francisco	San Francisco P O	83	341
BURNIS								
J	40	m	w	IREL	Sierra	Lincoln Twp	89	548
BURNMHLEN								
Henry	52	m	w	HANO	Placer	Bath P O	76	452
BURNS								
A	17	f	w	CA	Los Angeles	Los Angeles	73	570
A J	42	m	w	OH	Amador	Jackson P O	69	330
A V	46	m	w	NY	Santa Clara	Gilroy Twp	88	68
Aaron	44	m	w	PA	San Francisco	8-Wd San Francisco	82	378
Abner	34	m	w	NH	Sacramento	Sutter Twp	77	388
Alexander	43	m	w	PA	Siskiyou	Yreka	89	651
Amelia	7	f	w	CA	San Francisco	11-Wd San Francisc	84	711
Andrew	36	m	w	IREL	San Francisco	San Francisco P O	83	304
Ann	80	f	w	IREL	San Francisco	8-Wd San Francisco	82	397
Ann	45	f	w	IREL	San Francisco	San Francisco P O	83	185
Archer	45	m	w	NY	Solano	Tremont Twp	90	33
B	30	m	w	IN	Nevada	Meadow Lake Twp	75	261
B	20	f	w	IREL	Sierra	Lincoln Twp	89	551
Barney	35	m	w	IREL	San Francisco	San Francisco P O	83	35
Barney	30	m	w	IREL	San Francisco	8-Wd San Francisco	82	361
Benj	60	m	w	KY	Mendocino	Little Lake Twp	74	192
Bernard	25	m	w	IREL	San Francisco	5-Wd San Francisco	81	32
Bridget	40	f	w	IREL	San Francisco	San Francisco P O	80	427
Bridget	36	f	w	IREL	San Francisco	11-Wd San Francisc	84	490
Bridget	26	f	w	IREL	San Francisco	8-Wd San Francisco	82	289
Bridget	26	f	w	IREL	Sacramento	2-Wd Sacramento	77	236
Bryan	40	m	w	IREL	San Francisco	San Francisco P O	83	154

Series M593

© 2001 by Heritage Quest. All rights reserved.

Name	Age	S	R	B-PL	County	Series M593 Locale	Roll	Pg
C	38	m	w	IREL	Yuba	Marysville	93	586
Catherine	50	f	w	IREL	San Francisco	8-Wd San Francisco	82	328
Catherine	14	f	w	CA	Shasta	Shasta P O	89	455
Charles	27	m	w	IREL	Marin	San Rafael	74	55
Charles	25	m	w	IREL	Sonoma	Salt Point	91	390
Charles C	59	m	w	VA	Sacramento	Brighton Twp	77	80
Chas	55	m	w	NY	Sacramento	4-Wd Sacramento	77	325
Chas	45	m	w	IREL	Sacramento	3-Wd Sacramento	77	296
Chas	45	m	w	NY	San Francisco	5-Wd San Francisco	81	6
Chas	36	m	w	IREL	Sierra	Lincoln Twp	89	552
Christopher	35	m	w	IREL	Alameda	Washington Twp	68	276
Cornelius	31	m	w	IREL	San Francisco	San Francisco P O	85	874
D	47	m	w	VT	San Francisco	11-Wd San Francisc	84	650
D J	27	m	w	CANA	Santa Clara	Gilroy Twp	88	97
Daniel	40	m	w	IREL	San Francisco	San Francisco P O	83	351
Daniel	21	m	w	ENGL	San Francisco	San Francisco P O	83	188
Daniel M	24	m	w	TN	Yolo	Cache Crk Twp	93	426
David	40	m	w	IREL	Klamath	Liberty Twp	73	374
David	30	m	w	IREL	Alameda	Oakland	68	171
David N	43	m	w	KY	Santa Cruz	Santa Cruz Twp	89	389
Dennis	43	m	w	ENGL	Calaveras	San Andreas P O	70	215
Eddward	33	m	w	IREL	San Francisco	11-Wd San Francisc	84	607
Edmond	45	m	w	IREL	San Francisco	San Francisco P O	85	851
Edward	42	m	w	IREL	Los Angeles	El Monte Twp	73	456
Edward	38	m	w	IREL	San Francisco	San Francisco P O	83	231
Ellen	33	f	w	IREL	San Francisco	11-Wd San Francisc	84	456
Ellen	32	f	w	IREL	Santa Cruz	Santa Cruz	89	432
Ellen	3	f	w	CA	Placer	Colfax P O	76	391
Ellen	21	f	w	IREL	San Francisco	San Francisco P O	83	294
Frances	13	f	w	CA	San Francisco	6-Wd San Francisco	81	108
Francis	36	m	w	IREL	San Francisco	11-Wd San Francisc	84	479
Frank	30	m	w	VT	Yuba	East Bear Rvr Twp	93	541
Frank	18	m	w	MA	Butte	Ophir Twp	70	121
Franklin	20	m	w	MA	Butte	Ophir Twp	70	94
Fred	45	m	w	ENGL	Alameda	Oakland	68	142
Fredrick	27	m	w	IREL	San Francisco	San Francisco P O	83	228
George	46	m	w	WURT	Los Angeles	Los Angeles Twp	73	487
George	43	m	w	SCOT	Los Angeles	Los Angeles	73	570
Gustav	19	m	w	PRUS	San Francisco	7-Wd San Francisco	81	186
H E	41	m	w	IREL	Sutter	Vernon Twp	92	130
H F	30	m	w	IREL	Nevada	Meadow Lake Twp	75	265
H G	33	m	w	MO	Mendocino	Little Lake Twp	74	195
H R	28	m	w	VA	Sacramento	4-Wd Sacramento	77	325
Hannah	64	f	m	VA	Yuba	Marysville	93	588
Hannah	35	f	w	IREL	Nevada	Bridgeport Twp	75	106
Hary	26	m	w	MA	Sacramento	Brighton Twp	77	72
Helena	20	f	w	OLDE	San Francisco	8-Wd San Francisco	82	300
Henery	21	m	w	MA	San Francisco	7-Wd San Francisco	81	194
Henry	70	m	w	IREL	Monterey	Pajaro Twp	74	377
Henry	39	m	w	ME	San Bernardino	San Bernardino Twp	78	447
Henry	34	m	w	IREL	San Diego	San Luis Rey	78	515
Henry	29	m	w	BELG	San Francisco	2-Wd San Francisco	79	230
Henry	21	m	w	IL	San Mateo	Pescadero P O	87	409
Hugh	50	m	w	IREL	Sutter	Vernon Twp	92	133
Hugh	36	m	w	IREL	Placer	Auburn P O	76	367
Hugh	35	m	w	IREL	San Francisco	San Francisco P O	85	777
Humphrey	34	m	w	GA	Placer	Auburn P O	76	366
J	36	m	w	IREL	Lake	Knoxville Mines	73	404
J A	48	m	w	PA	Sacramento	4-Wd Sacramento	77	326
J G	38	m	w	MO	Mendocino	Little Lake Twp	74	196
J M	33	m	w	CANA	Solano	Vallejo	90	194
J M	33	m	w	CANA	Solano	Vallejo	90	158
Jack	24	m	b	NC	Amador	Lancha Plana P O	69	368
James	70	m	w	IREL	San Francisco	11-Wd San Francisc	84	458
James	55	m	w	IREL	Sonoma	Analy Twp	91	229
James	51	m	w	IREL	Yolo	Washington Twp	93	533
James	50	m	w	IREL	Nevada	Little York Twp	75	238
James	50	m	w	IREL	Napa	Napa	75	47
James	50	m	w	IREL	Yolo	Washington Twp	93	537
James	50	m	w	SWED	Nevada	Nevada Twp	75	273
James	45	m	w	IREL	San Francisco	1-Wd San Francisco	79	14
James	44	m	w	IREL	Placer	Colfax P O	76	391
James	41	m	w	IREL	San Francisco	San Francisco P O	80	537
James	40	m	w	IREL	San Francisco	San Francisco P O	83	164
James	40	m	w	MI	Tuolumne	Big Oak Flat P O	93	398
James	40	m	w	IREL	Placer	Bath P O	76	441
James	40	m	w	IREL	San Francisco	1-Wd San Francisco	79	113
James	38	m	w	IREL	San Francisco	7-Wd San Francisco	81	225
James	37	m	w	IREL	Placer	Blue Canyon P O	76	418
James	37	m	w	IREL	Santa Clara	Fremont Twp	88	47
James	35	m	w	IREL	San Francisco	1-Wd San Francisco	79	44
James	35	m	w	IREL	San Francisco	1-Wd San Francisco	79	95
James	33	m	w	MI	Tuolumne	Sonora P O	93	321
James	32	m	w	MD	El Dorado	Placerville	72	109
James	31	m	w	IREL	San Francisco	San Francisco P O	83	320
James	30	m	w	IREL	Marin	Nicasio Twp	74	19
James	30	m	w	IREL	Sacramento	Brighton Twp	77	70
James	25	m	w	IREL	Yuba	Rose Bar Twp	93	662
James	24	m	w	IREL	Sacramento	Franklin Twp	77	111
James	21	m	w	SCOT	Santa Cruz	Santa Cruz Twp	89	397
James	15	m	w	OR	San Francisco	11-Wd San Francisc	84	592
James F	38	m	w	NY	Los Angeles	Los Angeles	73	533
James G	36	m	w	KY	Klamath	Orleans Twp	73	379
James V	24	m	w	MA	San Francisco	1-Wd San Francisco	79	110
Jennie	19	f	w	PRUS	San Joaquin	2-Wd Stockton	86	213
Jno	25	m	w	PRUS	Butte	Chico Twp	70	36
Joe	40	m	w	IREL	San Joaquin	2-Wd Stockton	86	206
Johana	35	f	w	IREL	San Francisco	8-Wd San Francisco	82	362
John	59	m	w	SCOT	Santa Cruz	Santa Cruz Twp	89	397
John	54	m	w	MA	Santa Clara	2-Wd San Jose	88	285
John	52	m	w	IREL	Marin	San Rafael	74	56
John	49	m	w	KY	Mendocino	Calpella Twp	74	181
John	46	m	w	IREL	Sacramento	2-Wd Sacramento	77	215
John	45	m	w	PRUS	San Francisco	2-Wd San Francisco	79	202
John	43	m	w	NY	San Francisco	San Francisco P O	83	87
John	42	m	w	IREL	San Francisco	San Francisco P O	85	826
John	40	m	w	SCOT	Marin	San Rafael	74	56
John	40	m	w	PRUS	El Dorado	Diamond Springs Tw	72	27
John	40	m	w	IREL	Yuba	Marysville	93	598
John	40	m	w	ME	Alpine	Woodfords P O	69	309
John	40	m	w	IREL	Sacramento	Dry Crk Twp	77	104
John	38	m	w	IREL	San Joaquin	1-Wd Stockton	86	127
John	38	m	w	IREL	Yolo	Cache Crk Twp	93	449
John	38	m	w	IREL	Yuba	Rose Bar Twp	93	658
John	36	m	w	IREL	San Francisco	San Francisco P O	85	837
John	36	m	w	IREL	Los Angeles	Los Angeles	73	546
John	35	m	w	IREL	San Francisco	San Francisco P O	83	139
John	34	m	w	IREL	San Joaquin	2-Wd Stockton	86	170
John	33	m	w	IREL	Solano	Vallejo	90	200
John	32	m	w	IREL	Klamath	Camp Gaston	73	373
John	31	m	w	IREL	Alameda	Oakland	68	265
John	30	m	w	IREL	San Joaquin	2-Wd Stockton	86	164
John	30	m	w	IREL	San Joaquin	Tulare Twp	86	261
John	30	m	w	IREL	Los Angeles	Soledad Twp	73	630
John	30	m	w	IREL	Sacramento	American Twp	77	68
John	30	m	w	IREL	San Francisco	6-Wd San Francisco	81	142
John	28	m	w	IREL	San Francisco	7-Wd San Francisco	81	218
John	27	m	w	CANA	Inyo	Cerro Gordo Twp	73	321
John	26	m	w	IREL	Solano	Suisun Twp	90	100
John	26	m	w	IREL	Placer	Summit P O	76	495
John	25	m	w	NY	San Joaquin	Liberty Twp	86	83
John	25	m	w	IREL	Santa Clara	Fremont Twp	88	52
John	25	m	w	IREL	Siskiyou	Big Valley Twp	89	583
John	23	m	w	IREL	San Joaquin	Castoria Twp	86	14
John	23	m	w	ENGL	Solano	Denverton Twp	90	27
John	23	m	w	SCOT	Santa Cruz	Santa Cruz Twp	89	397
John	23	m	w	IREL	San Francisco	7-Wd San Francisco	81	170
John A	48	m	w	MO	Mariposa	Maxwell Crk P O	74	146
John B	45	m	w	IREL	Sacramento	2-Wd Sacramento	77	246
John J	40	m	w	PA	Santa Cruz	Santa Cruz Twp	89	394
Johnithan	48	m	w	MA	Sacramento	Natomas Twp	77	165
Jos	42	m	w	PA	Solano	Vallejo	90	197
Joseph	38	m	w	IREL	Siskiyou	Surprise Valley Tw	89	638
Joseph	38	m	w	NC	Fresno	Kings Rvr P O	72	204
Joseph	35	m	w	IREL	Sacramento	4-Wd Sacramento	77	365
Joseph	14	m	w	OR	San Francisco	11-Wd San Francisc	84	592
Kate	26	f	w	IREL	San Francisco	8-Wd San Francisco	82	336
Kate	19	f	w	IREL	San Francisco	8-Wd San Francisco	82	365
Katharine	45	f	w	IREL	San Francisco	San Francisco P O	83	203
L J	36	m	w	ME	Yuba	Rose Bar Twp	93	653
Lionel G	40	m	w	MO	Mariposa	Maxwell Crk P O	74	146
Lizzie	15	f	w	MA	Santa Clara	San Jose Twp	88	196
M	50	m	w	IREL	San Francisco	San Francisco P O	85	786
M	15	f	w	CA	Los Angeles	Los Angeles	73	570
Maggie	19	f	w	NY	San Francisco	8-Wd San Francisco	82	378
Maggie	15	f	w	IREL	Sacramento	3-Wd Sacramento	77	305
Marcella	39	f	w	IREL	San Francisco	11-Wd San Francisc	84	629
Maria	40	f	w	IREL	Yuba	Linda Twp	93	555
Martin	37	m	w	IREL	San Francisco	2-Wd San Francisco	79	249
Martin	37	m	w	IREL	San Francisco	1-Wd San Francisco	79	98
Martin	28	m	w	IREL	San Francisco	San Francisco P O	85	864
Martin	24	m	w	IREL	Inyo	Cerro Gordo Twp	73	323
Martin J	39	m	w	CANA	San Francisco	San Francisco P O	85	723
Mary	65	f	w	IREL	San Francisco	San Francisco P O	83	82
Mary	55	f	w	IREL	Placer	Bath P O	76	448
Mary	54	f	w	IREL	San Francisco	11-Wd San Francisc	84	504
Mary	49	f	w	IREL	San Francisco	San Francisco P O	83	156
Mary	45	f	w	IREL	Santa Clara	Santa Clara Twp	88	163
Mary	35	f	w	IREL	Sacramento	3-Wd Sacramento	77	308
Mary	35	f	w	IREL	San Francisco	1-Wd San Francisco	79	113
Mary	35	f	w	IREL	Plumas	Goodwin Twp	77	58
Mary	34	f	w	IREL	Sierra	Gibson Twp	89	541
Mary	30	f	w	IREL	Sacramento	4-Wd Sacramento	77	363
Mary	28	f	w	IREL	San Francisco	8-Wd San Francisco	82	401
Mary	28	f	w	IREL	San Francisco	San Francisco P O	83	114
Mary	25	f	w	NY	San Francisco	11-Wd San Francisc	84	668
Mary	22	f	w	IREL	San Francisco	San Francisco P O	83	228
Mary	22	f	w	CANA	Santa Clara	San Jose Twp	88	207
Mary	17	f	w	CANA	San Francisco	San Francisco P O	80	465
Mary	17	f	w	CANA	San Francisco	2-Wd San Francisco	79	216
Matthew J	50	m	w	KY	Santa Cruz	Santa Cruz Twp	89	389
Michael	50	m	w	IREL	Santa Clara	Redwood Twp	88	123
Michael	50	m	w	IREL	San Joaquin	2-Wd Stockton	86	166
Michael	42	m	w	IREL	Santa Clara	Gilroy Twp	88	90
Michael	41	m	w	IREL	San Francisco	San Francisco P O	83	202
Michael	40	m	w	IREL	San Francisco	11-Wd San Francisc	84	498
Michael	39	m	w	IREL	Amador	Ione City P O	69	358
Michael	37	m	w	IREL	Placer	Newcastle Twp	76	476
Michael	34	m	w	IREL	Sonoma	Analy Twp	91	225
Michael	26	m	w	IREL	Monterey	San Juan Twp	74	396
Micheal	24	m	w	IREL	San Francisco	7-Wd San Francisco	81	170
Micheal	24	m	w	MA	San Francisco	7-Wd San Francisco	81	185
Michl	11	m	w	MA	San Francisco	11-Wd San Francisc	84	587
Mike	37	m	w	IREL	Mendocino	Little Lake Twp	74	196

© 2001 by Heritage Quest. All rights reserved.

California 1870 Census

Name	Age	S	R	B-PL	County	Locale	Series M593 Roll	Pg
Mike	26	m	w	IREL	San Francisco	11-Wd San Francisc	84	649
Miles	26	m	w	TN	Humboldt	Bald Hills	72	237
Minna	21	f	w	NY	San Francisco	8-Wd San Francisco	82	349
Nicholas	29	m	w	ENGL	San Francisco	1-Wd San Francisco	79	101
Nicholas	25	m	w	IREL	Los Angeles	Wilmington Twp	73	642
Otis E	34	m	w	MA	Napa	Yountville Twp	75	83
Owen	44	m	w	IREL	Sonoma	Analy Twp	91	225
Owen	28	m	w	IREL	San Francisco	8-Wd San Francisco	82	347
P	42	m	w	IREL	Lake	Knoxville Mines	73	404
P	36	m	w	IREL	Sacramento	3-Wd Sacramento	77	297
Patk	30	m	w	IREL	San Francisco	5-Wd San Francisco	81	7
Patrick	62	m	w	IREL	San Francisco	San Francisco P O	85	772
Patrick	61	m	w	IREL	San Francisco	San Francisco P O	85	873
Patrick	58	m	w	IREL	San Francisco	San Francisco P O	85	868
Patrick	53	m	w	IREL	Nevada	Bridgeport Twp	75	121
Patrick	50	m	w	IREL	San Francisco	2-Wd San Francisco	79	214
Patrick	47	m	w	IREL	San Francisco	11-Wd San Francisc	84	462
Patrick	42	m	w	IREL	San Francisco	San Francisco P O	85	865
Patrick	40	m	w	IREL	San Francisco	11-Wd San Francisc	84	654
Patrick	40	m	w	IREL	San Francisco	11-Wd San Francisc	84	482
Patrick	40	m	w	IREL	San Francisco	11-Wd San Francisc	84	709
Patrick	39	m	w	IREL	Santa Barbara	San Buenaventura P	87	430
Patrick	37	m	w	IREL	San Francisco	11-Wd San Francisc	84	526
Patrick	37	m	w	IREL	San Francisco	San Francisco P O	83	169
Patrick	37	m	w	IREL	San Francisco	San Francisco P O	85	826
Patrick	35	m	w	IREL	Colusa	Colusa	71	298
Patrick	30	m	w	IREL	San Francisco	San Francisco P O	85	773
Patrick	30	m	w	IREL	San Francisco	San Francisco P O	83	370
Patrick	30	m	w	IREL	San Francisco	San Francisco P O	85	869
Patrick	25	m	w	IREL	Colusa	Grand Island Twp	71	310
Peter	55	m	w	IREL	Sonoma	Vallejo Twp	91	461
Peter	42	m	w	IREL	Sacramento	Sutter Twp	77	391
Peter	38	m	w	ENGL	San Francisco	11-Wd San Francisc	84	668
Peter	37	m	w	IREL	San Francisco	San Francisco P O	80	470
Peter	36	m	w	IREL	San Francisco	San Francisco P O	85	837
Peter	33	m	w	IREL	Marin	Tomales Twp	74	87
Peter	33	m	w	IREL	Marin	Tomales Twp	74	87
Peter	33	m	w	IREL	Colusa	Butte Twp	71	266
R	19	f	w	CA	Los Angeles	Los Angeles	73	570
Reer	16	f	w	PA	Sacramento	3-Wd Sacramento	77	304
Richard	46	m	w	IREL	San Joaquin	2-Wd Stockton	86	159
Richard	44	m	w	IREL	Klamath	Sawyers Bar	73	377
Richard	23	m	w	MA	San Francisco	7-Wd San Francisco	81	194
Robert	59	m	w	IREL	San Francisco	8-Wd San Francisco	82	367
Robert	38	m	w	PA	Yolo	Putah Twp	93	514
Robert	38	m	w	PA	Solano	Tremont Twp	90	29
Robert	25	m	w	CANA	Sonoma	Bodega Twp	91	261
Robt	45	m	w	NY	San Francisco	5-Wd San Francisco	81	27
Robt	35	m	w	SCOT	Humboldt	Arcata Twp	72	234
Rufus C	36	m	w	IN	Colusa	Stony Crk Twp	71	332
S	42	m	b	CUBA	Sierra	Downieville Twp	89	518
S B	65	f	w	ME	Tuolumne	Big Oak Flat P O	93	402
Samuel	20	m	w	IREL	San Francisco	7-Wd San Francisco	81	170
Sarah	26	f	w	IREL	San Joaquin	1-Wd Stockton	86	126
Sarah	20	f	w	PRUS	San Francisco	11-Wd San Francisc	84	515
Spencer	73	m	b	VA	Yuba	Marysville	93	588
Stephen	36	m	w	IREL	San Francisco	11-Wd San Francisc	84	652
T	21	m	w	LA	Sierra	Butte Twp	89	511
T J	40	m	w	KY	Tehama	Deer Crk Twp	92	170
T R	27	m	w	IREL	Alameda	Oakland	68	141
Terence	34	m	w	IREL	Sacramento	Granite Twp	77	150
Thomas	46	m	w	SCOT	El Dorado	Mud Springs Twp	72	89
Thomas	40	m	w	IREL	San Francisco	San Francisco P O	85	813
Thomas	35	m	w	IREL	Sonoma	Bodega Twp	91	257
Thomas	33	m	w	IREL	Yolo	Washington Twp	93	529
Thomas	31	m	w	IREL	Nevada	Grass Valley Twp	75	227
Thomas	30	m	w	IREL	San Francisco	San Francisco P O	83	224
Thomas	28	m	w	IREL	San Francisco	San Francisco P O	83	194
Thomas	26	m	w	SCOT	Santa Cruz	Santa Cruz Twp	89	397
Thomas	24	m	w	NY	Yuba	Marysville	93	602
Thomas	12	m	w	CA	Mendocino	Ukiah Twp	74	234
Thomas	11	m	w	CA	Solano	Suisun Twp	90	116
Thomas H	44	m	w	IREL	Nevada	Grass Valley Twp	75	199
Thomas Z	45	m	w	PA	El Dorado	Diamond Springs Tw	72	28
Thos	37	m	w	ME	San Joaquin	Douglas Twp	86	50
Thos	26	m	w	PA	Solano	Vallejo	90	200
Thos	25	m	w	IREL	San Francisco	1-Wd San Francisco	79	87
Timothy	39	m	w	IREL	San Francisco	1-Wd San Francisco	79	88
Turner	31	m	w	ME	Plumas	Washington Twp	77	25
Uriah	79	m	w	SC	Monterey	Salinas Twp	74	307
W B	25	m	w	MO	Mendocino	Little Lake Twp	74	196
W S	28	m	w	MA	Alameda	Oakland	68	201
William	52	m	w	SCOT	Tuolumne	Columbia P O	93	342
William	5	m	w	CA	San Francisco	11-Wd San Francisc	84	711
William	45	m	w	IREL	Sacramento	2-Wd Sacramento	77	231
William	43	m	w	IREL	San Francisco	1-Wd San Francisco	79	36
William	38	m	m	VA	Yuba	Marysville	93	588
William	37	m	w	IREL	San Diego	Poway Dist	78	481
William	35	m	w	IREL	Santa Barbara	Santa Barbara P O	87	465
William	34	m	w	IREL	San Luis Obispo	Santa Rosa Twp	87	325
William	32	m	w	IREL	Sacramento	2-Wd Sacramento	77	216
William	29	m	w	IREL	Klamath	Liberty Twp	73	374
William	20	m	w	NY	San Francisco	San Francisco P O	83	206
William S	53	m	w	IREL	El Dorado	Placerville	72	119
Wm	38	m	m	SCOT	Sacramento	1-Wd Sacramento	77	190
Wm	37	m	w	IREL	Plumas	Quartz Twp	77	34
Wm	28	m	w	ENGL	Nevada	Nevada Twp	75	277

Name	Age	S	R	B-PL	County	Locale	Series M593 Roll	Pg
Wm	27	m	w	MA	San Francisco	San Francisco P O	85	852
Wm	25	m	w	IREL	San Francisco	San Francisco P O	85	865
Wm B	49	m	w	NH	San Diego	San Diego	78	489
BURNSBY								
--- Miss	52	f	w	ENGL	Sacramento	Sutter Twp	77	386
BURNSELMEIR								
Mary	48	f	w	PRUS	Butte	Chico Twp	70	44
BURNSIDE								
George	29	m	w	CANA	Plumas	Indian Twp	77	14
BURNSIDES								
Wm A	37	m	w	OH	Monterey	Castroville Twp	74	335
BURNSIDS								
Chas	40	m	b	WIND	San Francisco	8-Wd San Francisco	82	292
Mary A	23	f	m	WIND	San Francisco	8-Wd San Francisco	82	292
BURNSON								
John J	62	m	w	PRUS	Yolo	Putah Twp	93	517
BURNSTEAD								
Abram	30	m	w	POLA	San Francisco	8-Wd San Francisco	82	320
BURNSTEIN								
Carl	28	m	w	PRUS	San Francisco	5-Wd San Francisco	81	36
Samuel	18	m	w	PRUS	Solano	Rio Vista Twp	90	60
BURNSTIEN								
Herman	40	m	w	PRUS	San Francisco	San Francisco P O	83	9
BURNTT								
Squire	58	m	w	NY	Butte	Wyandotte Twp	70	146
BURON								
Henry	23	m	w	MO	Fresno	Millerton P O	72	163
Victor	30	m	w	FRAN	San Francisco	San Francisco P O	83	67
BURPEE								
D	43	m	w	MA	El Dorado	Greenwood Twp	72	51
BURPU								
S A	46	m	w	NY	Alameda	Oakland	68	129
BURR								
A F	53	m	w	CT	Amador	Sutter Crk P O	69	403
Addison T	17	m	w	CA	Yolo	Grafton Twp	93	494
Amos	24	m	w	CT	Santa Clara	2-Wd San Jose	88	330
Anson	43	m	w	NY	Del Norte	Crescent	71	466
Benjamin	36	m	w	PA	San Francisco	2-Wd San Francisco	79	239
Benjamin F	43	m	w	OH	Tulare	Tule Rvr Twp	92	262
Charles	32	m	w	MI	San Francisco	7-Wd San Francisco	81	226
Clarence C	32	m	w	RI	San Francisco	San Francisco P O	85	749
David	27	m	w	CANA	San Mateo	Half Moon Bay P O	87	407
E Willard	61	m	w	RI	San Francisco	San Francisco P O	85	749
Edward	51	m	w	VA	San Diego	San Diego	78	484
Edwin A	48	m	w	CT	Sacramento	4-Wd Sacramento	77	352
Eli B	24	m	w	IN	Nevada	Grass Valley Twp	75	149
Erastus C	45	m	w	IA	Mendocino	Navarro & Big Rvr	74	176
Geo	32	m	w	CT	San Francisco	1-Wd San Francisco	79	102
Geo	28	m	w	CT	San Francisco	1-Wd San Francisco	79	43
George W	42	m	w	ME	San Francisco	San Francisco P O	83	406
H S	45	m	w	ME	San Francisco	3-Wd San Francisco	79	313
Horace H	77	m	w	NY	Yolo	Grafton Twp	93	493
Jacob	32	m	w	GERM	Marin	San Rafael Twp	74	36
James	45	m	w	NY	San Francisco	San Francisco P O	80	347
James	45	m	w	NY	San Francisco	San Francisco P O	80	348
Jos D	49	m	w	CT	San Francisco	8-Wd San Francisco	82	359
Lawrence W	65	m	w	WURT	Santa Clara	Fremont Twp	88	44
Lester L	49	m	w	OH	Yolo	Grafton Twp	93	490
Robert	36	m	w	IREL	Nevada	Eureka Twp	75	137
Robt R	53	m	w	CANA	Fresno	Millerton P O	72	158
Samuel B	47	m	w	OH	Siskiyou	Table Rock Twp	89	647
BURRAGE								
Geo S	47	m	w	MA	Napa	Napa	75	50
BURRAN								
Kolman	48	m	w	PRUS	San Francisco	7-Wd San Francisco	81	239
William	21	m	w	ENGL	Butte	Oregon Twp	70	127
BURRE								
Mary	27	f	w	FRAN	San Francisco	6-Wd San Francisco	81	89
BURREL								
Edward	40	m	w	NY	Santa Clara	Santa Clara Twp	88	164
Tomas	28	m	w	MEXI	Los Angeles	San Juan Twp	73	625
BURRELL								
A W	49	m	w	VT	Alameda	Oakland	68	137
Charles	48	m	w	NY	San Francisco	San Francisco P O	83	278
Cuthbert	45	m	w	NY	Santa Clara	1-Wd San Jose	88	241
Dave	35	m	w	DE	Sacramento	1-Wd Sacramento	77	203
Frank	21	m	w	WI	Napa	Napa Twp	75	33
Hiram	53	m	w	ME	Tuolumne	Columbia P O	93	348
J C	27	m	w	CANA	San Joaquin	3-Wd Stockton	86	243
J S	33	m	w	MO	San Joaquin	Douglas Twp	86	34
Lyman	70	m	w	MA	Santa Clara	Redwood Twp	88	133
Martin	33	m	w	NY	San Joaquin	Douglas Twp	86	39
Mary	74	f	w	ENGL	Santa Clara	1-Wd San Jose	88	241
Thomas	50	m	w	NY	Solano	Green Valley Twp	90	38
William	52	m	w	ME	Colusa	Monroe Twp	71	316
William H	34	m	w	ME	Yolo	Washington Twp	93	534
BURRES								
Balinda	49	m	w	TN	Contra Costa	Martinez P O	71	435
Chas	34	m	w	IREL	Sacramento	4-Wd Sacramento	77	352
Floyd	21	m	w	MO	Contra Costa	Martinez P O	71	436
James B	28	m	w	IN	Colusa	Butte Twp	71	272
John	30	m	w	TN	Contra Costa	Martinez P O	71	414
Oliver	39	m	w	TN	Contra Costa	Martinez P O	71	437
Wilbur	30	m	w	TN	Contra Costa	Martinez P O	71	450
Willes	53	m	w	TN	Contra Costa	Martinez P O	71	437
BURRESS								
Benj F	55	m	w	SC	Sonoma	Salt Point	91	390

© 2001 by Heritage Quest. All rights reserved.

Name	Age	S	R	B-PL	County	Locale	Roll	Pg
						Series M593		
BURRICHTER								
Henry	39	m	w	GERM	Tehama	Red Bluff	92	177
BURRIDGE								
John B	43	m	w	MA	Mendocino	Point Arena Twp	74	206
BURRIGAN								
L	23	m	w	IN	Yuba	Marysville Twp	93	568
BURRIGHT								
W	60	m	w	NY	Mendocino	Calpella Twp	74	189
BURRILL								
Andrew	46	m	w	AUSL	San Francisco	2-Wd San Francisco	79	168
E A	30	m	w	WI	Sacramento	1-Wd Sacramento	77	185
Henry	23	m	w	MO	Fresno	Millerton P O	72	193
Judson	25	m	w	CANA	Colusa	Grand Island Twp	71	310
Mary	20	f	w	MA	San Francisco	San Francisco P O	83	265
Saml	38	m	w	ME	Humboldt	Eureka Twp	72	281
BURRIS								
David	45	m	w	MO	Sonoma	Sonoma Twp	91	443
Geo W	50	m	w	VA	Sonoma	Healdsburg	91	275
Hannah	46	f	w	ENGL	Yuba	Long Bar Twp	93	566
James	55	m	w	US	El Dorado	Mud Springs Twp	72	71
James	16	m	w	MO	Mendocino	Calpella Twp	74	186
Jemima	6	f	w	CA	Sonoma	Healdsburg	91	275
Joel	37	m	w	KY	Sonoma	Salt Point	91	380
Thomas	13	m	i	CA	Sacramento	Sutter Twp	77	384
William	50	m	w	MO	Sonoma	Sonoma Twp	91	448
William	46	m	w	VA	Colusa	Colusa Twp	71	280
Wm	63	m	w	DE	San Francisco	San Francisco P O	83	76
BURRISS								
Anna	39	f	w	IL	Amador	Volcano P O	69	380
BURRITT								
Joan	66	m	w	FRAN	San Francisco	San Francisco P O	80	342
Robert	12	m	w	CA	Merced	Snelling P O	74	252
BURROUCHS								
Charles	43	m	w	VT	Inyo	Lone Pine Twp	73	332
Fredrick C	51	m	w	VT	Inyo	Lone Pine Twp	73	332
BURROUGH								
Jas	43	m	w	ENGL	Sonoma	Cloverdale Twp	91	270
Wiley	60	m	w	AR	Fresno	Kings Rvr P O	72	203
Wm	37	m	w	OH	Butte	Kimshew Tpw	70	79
BURROUGHS								
A	31	m	w	NY	Yuba	Marysville Twp	93	569
Chas	44	m	w	CT	San Francisco	5-Wd San Francisco	81	6
Chas	34	m	w	NY	Butte	Mountain Spring Tw	70	88
Chas	25	m	w	NY	Alameda	Brooklyn Twp	68	42
David	34	m	w	NY	San Diego	Temecula Dist	78	527
Edw	47	m	w	NJ	Nevada	Nevada Twp	75	277
Eliza	74	f	w	CT	Butte	Mountain Spring Tw	70	88
F	44	m	w	NY	Lassen	Susanville Twp	73	439
H D	32	m	w	ENGL	Humboldt	Eureka Twp	72	263
Henry	38	m	w	NY	Colusa	Butte Twp	71	270
J L	61	m	w	MO	Solano	Vallejo	90	190
J N	29	m	w	SC	Mendocino	Little Lake Twp	74	202
John	31	m	w	MA	Santa Clara	2-Wd San Jose	88	284
L C	50	m	w	SC	Lake	Scotts Crk	73	426
Rufus W	43	m	w	NY	Nevada	Eureka Twp	75	134
Stephen	57	m	w	BADE	San Joaquin	1-Wd Stockton	86	121
Wm	19	m	w	IN	Solano	Vallejo	90	204
BURROUS								
C A	27	m	w	MO	Nevada	Eureka Twp	75	135
Edward	42	m	w	MA	Calaveras	San Andreas P O	70	163
BURROW								
B O	40	m	w	MD	San Joaquin	Oneal Twp	86	100
George	59	m	w	NJ	San Francisco	11-Wd San Francisc	84	648
Joseph	45	m	w	BOHE	Sacramento	4-Wd Sacramento	77	325
Robt K	36	m	w	OH	Monterey	Alisal Twp	74	293
BURROWS								
Albert	32	m	w	WI	Siskiyou	Yreka	89	659
Charles	45	m	w	CT	San Francisco	2-Wd San Francisco	79	200
E	20	m	w	IL	Alameda	Oakland	68	145
Elijah	29	m	w	SWED	El Dorado	Placerville Twp	72	101
Francis	26	f	w	MS	San Bernardino	San Bernardino Twp	78	423
G W	50	m	w	NY	Calaveras	Copperopolis P O	70	223
George	29	m	w	NJ	El Dorado	Cosumnes Twp	72	14
Henry T	22	m	w	CT	San Francisco	1-Wd San Francisco	79	69
J	10	m	w	NY	Lassen	Susanville Twp	73	439
James	38	m	w	OH	Sacramento	Natomas Twp	77	165
James	26	m	w	MO	San Diego	Julian Dist	78	474
John	50	m	w	ENGL	San Francisco	11-Wd San Francisc	84	584
Jos	41	m	w	ENGL	Santa Clara	Almaden Twp	88	10
Joshua	22	m	w	TX	San Diego	Milquaty Dist	78	477
Margaret	27	f	w	CANA	El Dorado	Placerville Twp	72	101
Mat	37	m	w	OH	Mendocino	Ukiah Twp	74	237
N	50	m	w	MD	San Joaquin	Oneal Twp	86	101
Nancy	81	f	w	KY	Mendocino	Calpella Twp	74	181
Philip	45	m	w	IREL	San Joaquin	1-Wd Stockton	86	122
R R	30	m	w	OH	Sutter	Butte Twp	92	99
Robert	50	m	w	PA	San Francisco	San Francisco P O	80	344
Thomas	60	m	w	MO	San Diego	Milquaty Dist	78	477
Thos	25	m	w	ENGL	San Francisco	1-Wd San Francisco	79	65
W H	32	m	w	CANA	Santa Clara	Gilroy Twp	88	67
W O	17	m	w	CA	Amador	Ione City P O	69	358
Wm	15	m	w	NY	Yuba	Marysville	93	604
Wm M	37	m	w	PA	Siskiyou	Callahan P O	89	630
BURRS								
James	40	m	b	KY	San Francisco	8-Wd San Francisco	82	341
BURRUP								
Washn	30	m	w	IREL	San Francisco	5-Wd San Francisco	81	15
BURRUR								
James R	35	m	w	VA	Amador	Fiddletown P O	69	438
BURRY								
C H	23	m	w	CANA	San Joaquin	1-Wd Stockton	86	134
Locky	43	m	w	IREL	San Mateo	San Mateo P O	87	360
Paul	52	m	w	FRAN	Santa Clara	2-Wd San Jose	88	290
BURS								
Henry	50	m	w	MA	San Francisco	11-Wd San Francisc	84	423
J H	36	m	w	CANA	Alameda	Oakland	68	263
Stoner G	39	m	w	CT	Placer	Gold Run Twp	76	395
BURSCHELL								
Frank	44	m	w	HDAR	Del Norte	Crescent	71	465
BURSCOUGH								
Hy	50	m	w	ENGL	San Francisco	San Francisco P O	83	100
BURSE								
Ebenezer P	53	m	w	MA	Calaveras	San Andreas P O	70	199
Geo	42	m	w	MA	Sacramento	Granite Twp	77	155
BURSEE								
Mengrell	35	m	w	NY	Sacramento	Dry Crk Twp	77	104
BURSEL								
Jesse	39	m	w	PA	Tulare	Tule Rvr Twp	92	259
BURSELL								
Mary	21	f	w	WI	San Joaquin	Dent Twp	86	24
BURSKEY								
Mario	29	m	w	ITAL	San Diego	San Diego	78	488
BURSLEY								
Isaac	63	m	w	MA	Solano	Suisun Twp	90	111
Jerome	34	m	w	NY	Stanislaus	Empire Twp	92	43
BURSON								
Jas N	38	m	w	MI	San Francisco	San Francisco P O	83	24
John	35	m	w	PA	Yolo	Cache Crk Twp	93	429
L M	48	m	w	PA	San Francisco	3-Wd San Francisco	79	315
BURST								
Nicholas	52	m	w	PRUS	Colusa	Colusa Twp	71	274
BURSTON								
William	44	m	w	ENGL	El Dorado	Mud Springs Twp	72	86
BURT								
A J	41	m	w	OH	San Joaquin	Elliott Twp	86	75
Aaron	38	m	w	OH	Butte	Oregon Twp	70	127
B	49	m	w	MA	Amador	Drytown P O	69	417
Belden D	46	m	w	NY	Placer	Bath P O	76	446
Caroline W	65	f	w	MA	San Francisco	6-Wd San Francisco	81	113
Charles	35	m	w	PRUS	Alameda	Murray Twp	68	128
Chas	45	m	w	ENGL	San Francisco	7-Wd San Francisco	81	259
Clara	28	f	w	GA	Stanislaus	Emory Twp	92	18
Fletcher M	35	m	w	NY	Humboldt	Arcata Twp	72	230
Geo	21	m	w	ENGL	San Francisco	1-Wd San Francisco	79	58
Henry	26	m	w	ENGL	Nevada	Grass Valley Twp	75	203
Hiram	41	m	w	VT	Nevada	Little York Twp	75	235
Isabella	16	f	w	AR	Mariposa	Mariposa P O	74	123
J M	42	m	w	NY	San Joaquin	Elkhorn Twp	86	58
J P	51	m	w	MA	Tuolumne	Columbia P O	93	337
James	47	m	w	VT	Amador	Fiddletown P O	69	430
James	46	m	w	MA	Santa Clara	Fremont Twp	88	63
James M	53	m	w	NY	Butte	Ophir Twp	70	107
Jo	22	m	w	MO	San Joaquin	Liberty Twp	86	86
John	43	m	w	PA	Mariposa	Mariposa P O	74	125
John	30	m	w	IREL	Alameda	Murray Twp	68	106
Joseph	46	m	w	PA	San Francisco	5-Wd San Francisco	81	22
Joseph H	34	m	w	GA	San Francisco	San Francisco P O	85	833
Maria	21	f	w	NY	Santa Clara	Santa Clara Twp	88	142
Mary	30	f	w	IREL	Sonoma	Santa Rosa	91	412
Philip	65	m	w	SC	San Francisco	11-Wd San Francisc	84	620
Richard	28	m	w	VT	San Francisco	6-Wd San Francisco	81	81
Samuel B	41	m	w	NY	Placer	Bath P O	76	446
Thomas	22	m	w	MA	San Francisco	San Francisco P O	85	758
Warner	2	m	w	CA	Humboldt	Arcata Twp	72	234
William	34	m	w	NY	San Francisco	11-Wd San Francisc	84	496
Wm	34	m	w	WI	San Diego	San Diego	78	501
Wm H	42	m	w	RI	Marin	San Rafael Twp	74	35
Wm L	60	m	w	CT	Humboldt	Arcata Twp	72	227
BURTAS								
Samuel	40	m	w	NY	Mendocino	Navarro & Big Rvr	74	177
BURTCHALL								
Dora	35	f	w	IREL	Marin	Novato Twp	74	9
BURTE								
Mathus	34	m	w	BADE	Sierra	Gibson Twp	89	540
BURTELL								
Galen	41	m	w	NY	Marin	Novato Twp	74	13
Jno	40	m	w	RI	Santa Clara	Burnett Twp	88	36
BURTER								
Henry	40	m	w	IREL	San Francisco	11-Wd San Francisc	84	432
BURTHAM								
L	46	m	w	NY	Amador	Drytown P O	69	418
BURTIS								
Edwin	62	m	w	NY	Colusa	Grand Island Twp	71	306
James	28	m	w	IREL	San Francisco	1-Wd San Francisco	79	106
BURTISS								
Stephen	54	m	w	NY	Colusa	Grand Island Twp	71	306
BURTLEY								
J W	10	m	w	MO	Alameda	Oakland	68	257
Jas R	38	m	w	IN	Fresno	Millerton P O	72	181
BURTNETT								
P	48	m	w	OH	Lake	Big Valley	73	397
Wm C	27	m	w	IL	San Luis Obispo	San Luis Obispo Tw	87	303
BURTON								
---	40	m	w	LA	Yuba	Marysville	93	611

© 2001 by Heritage Quest. All rights reserved.

Name	Age	S	R	B-PL	County	Locale	Series M593 Roll	Pg
A	45	m	w	NY	San Joaquin	Tulare Twp	86	258
Albert	62	m	w	CT	Sacramento	Natomas Twp	77	165
Alfred H	50	m	w	TN	San Luis Obispo	Santa Rosa Twp	87	321
Allen	20	m	w	MO	Sonoma	Washington Twp	91	466
Angelo	35	m	w	ITAL	San Francisco	11-Wd San Francisc	84	603
Ann	19	f	w	ENGL	Santa Clara	Gilroy Twp	88	80
C O	38	m	w	NY	San Joaquin	1-Wd Stockton	86	128
Caroline	35	f	b	PA	Los Angeles	Los Angeles	73	546
Caroline	30	f	b	PA	Los Angeles	Los Angeles	73	543
Charles	40	m	w	VA	San Francisco	San Francisco P O	80	410
Charles	38	m	w	PA	Santa Clara	1-Wd San Jose	88	255
Claybourn	53	m	m	VA	Sacramento	2-Wd Sacramento	77	233
Daniel	41	m	w	ME	Tuolumne	Sonora P O	93	319
David	31	m	w	AR	San Diego	Milquaty Dist	78	477
David	29	m	w	VT	Sutter	Sutter Twp	92	125
Dixon	18	m	w	CA	Siskiyou	Cottonwood Twp	89	592
Edward	41	m	w	VA	Santa Clara	1-Wd San Jose	88	255
Erastus	35	m	w	NY	Sacramento	2-Wd Sacramento	77	244
Flem	19	m	w	MO	San Joaquin	Dent Twp	86	25
George	31	m	w	IREL	Los Angeles	Los Angeles	73	537
George	12	m	w	ME	Alameda	Eden Twp	68	81
Giovanni	24	m	w	ITAL	San Francisco	11-Wd San Francisc	84	603
Henry	26	m	w	CA	Contra Costa	Martinez P O	71	385
Henry	24	m	w	VT	Sonoma	Russian Rvr	91	367
Henry	20	m	w	SCOT	San Francisco	San Francisco P O	83	162
Herman	39	m	w	NY	Sacramento	Natomas Twp	77	166
Hiram	37	m	w	NY	Sacramento	Natomas Twp	77	166
Homer	40	m	w	NY	Sacramento	4-Wd Sacramento	77	373
Isaac	43	m	w	IN	Yolo	Merritt Twp	93	502
J	32	m	w	CANA	San Joaquin	Elliott Twp	86	73
J R	32	m	w	MS	Lassen	Susanville Twp	73	445
John	50	m	w	KY	San Joaquin	Elkhorn Twp	86	63
John	32	m	w	IREL	Fresno	Millerton P O	72	162
John	29	m	w	NY	Yolo	Grafton Twp	93	482
John G	25	m	w	LA	Colusa	Monroe Twp	71	324
Joseph	31	m	w	CANA	Monterey	San Benito Twp	74	379
Juan	35	m	w	CA	Napa	Napa	75	57
Lewis T	61	m	w	TN	Santa Barbara	Santa Barbara P O	87	450
Louisa	21	f	w	UT	Siskiyou	Cottonwood Twp	89	591
Mary	36	f	w	MEXI	Napa	Napa	75	23
Mary	26	f	w	ENGL	San Francisco	San Francisco P O	83	374
N J	40	m	w	NY	Placer	Newcastle Twp	76	473
Nathan	32	m	w	NY	Placer	Summit P O	76	495
Noah	48	m	w	ENGL	Tulare	Visalia	92	294
Richard	18	m	w	MO	Yolo	Merritt Twp	93	502
Robert	46	m	w	ME	San Francisco	7-Wd San Francisco	81	271
Robert	39	m	w	ENGL	San Joaquin	2-Wd Stockton	86	168
Robert	22	m	w	IREL	Santa Clara	Santa Clara Twp	88	162
S A	23	m	w	NY	Siskiyou	Callahan P O	89	633
Sam	35	m	w	MO	San Joaquin	2-Wd Stockton	86	187
Thomas E	40	m	w	OH	Amador	Fiddletown P O	69	434
Thomas H	13	m	w	CA	Yolo	Cache Crk Twp	93	430
Thomas M	35	m	w	MO	Yolo	Grafton Twp	93	486
Thos	37	m	w	PA	Marin	San Rafael Twp	74	37
W H	43	m	w	ME	Humboldt	Eureka Twp	72	262
W H	35	m	w	ME	Humboldt	Eureka Twp	72	261
William	25	m	w	ENGL	Solano	Vacaville Twp	90	118
William	23	m	w	ENGL	San Francisco	11-Wd San Francisc	84	645
Wm	36	m	w	TN	San Joaquin	Elliott Twp	86	79
Wm T	46	m	w	KY	Mariposa	Mariposa P O	74	125
BURTRICK								
John	35	m	w	FRAN	Nevada	Bridgeport Twp	75	116
BURTSELL								
John M	31	m	w	NY	San Francisco	8-Wd San Francisco	82	290
Maggy	15	f	w	NY	San Mateo	Belmont P O	87	388
BURTT								
George W	32	m	w	NY	Tehama	Red Bluff	92	177
H H	42	m	w	NY	Tehama	Red Bluff	92	175
Monty	48	m	w	NY	Tehama	Paskenta Twp	92	163
Nathan	39	m	w	PA	Tehama	Toomes & Grant	92	169
S F	45	m	w	ENGL	Sierra	Butte Twp	89	513
T W	24	m	w	MO	Tehama	Red Bluff	92	174
BURUCK								
Kate	22	f	w	HAMB	San Francisco	8-Wd San Francisco	82	420
BURUES								
Chas	36	m	w	NY	Sacramento	1-Wd Sacramento	77	173
BURUZI								
Antonio	21	m	w	SWIT	San Francisco	1-Wd San Francisco	79	105
BURVEE								
M T	36	m	w	CANA	Sacramento	1-Wd Sacramento	77	183
BURWASH								
Stephen	52	m	w	CANA	Mendocino	Casper & Big Rvr	74	163
BURWELL								
Elijah	37	m	w	CANA	Nevada	Washington Twp	75	345
Frederick	17	m	w	ENGL	San Francisco	San Francisco P O	83	263
H H	54	m	w	VA	Amador	Fiddletown P O	69	429
James	34	m	w	IREL	San Francisco	San Francisco P O	83	139
Jesus	42	m	w	MEXI	San Bernardino	San Salvador Twp	78	458
L S	38	m	w	CT	Amador	Sutter Crk P O	69	396
Lela	20	f	w	VA	San Francisco	San Francisco P O	80	428
Samuel	26	m	w	OH	Napa	Napa	75	17
Walter	16	m	w	CA	San Francisco	7-Wd San Francisco	81	262
BURWICK								
Chas	39	m	w	ENGL	San Francisco	8-Wd San Francisco	82	350
Peter	30	m	w	PRUS	San Francisco	San Francisco P O	83	127
BURY								
D W	30	m	w	CANA	San Joaquin	2-Wd Stockton	86	161
G A	24	m	w	MA	Sierra	Butte Twp	89	513
H V	26	m	w	IA	Sierra	Downieville Twp	89	517
John	23	m	w	MA	San Francisco	San Francisco P O	85	747
BURZE								
Baptiste	32	m	w	FRAN	Monterey	San Antonio Twp	74	322
BUSA								
Edw	27	m	w	IREL	Alameda	Oakland	68	257
BUSAN								
Andrew M	36	m	w	MO	Amador	Fiddletown P O	69	431
BUSANE								
Yanacia	35	m	w	MEXI	Mariposa	Mariposa P O	74	95
BUSANVICH								
Domingo	32	m	w	ITAL	Solano	Montezuma Twp	90	67
BUSBEE								
A	38	m	w	IREL	Calaveras	Copperopolis P O	70	257
BUSBY								
Geo W	18	m	w	IL	Siskiyou	Yreka Twp	89	665
BUSCELL								
James	32	m	w	OH	San Francisco	San Francisco P O	80	413
BUSCH								
Charles	32	m	w	BAVA	Santa Clara	2-Wd San Jose	88	323
George	43	m	w	BAVA	Amador	Fiddletown P O	69	433
Martin L	39	m	w	SWED	Napa	Napa	75	20
BUSE								
J	27	m	w	PRUS	Sierra	Butte Twp	89	508
BUSECK								
F	24	f	w	PRUS	Sacramento	3-Wd Sacramento	77	281
BUSELAN								
Blanco	30	m	w	FRAN	Los Angeles	Los Angeles Twp	73	477
BUSELMIRE								
Ansolem	30	m	w	BADE	Sonoma	Healdsburg & Mendo	91	276
BUSER								
Dora	37	f	w	SWIT	El Dorado	Diamond Springs Tw	72	30
Lena	20	f	w	WI	El Dorado	Diamond Springs Tw	72	30
BUSGAND								
D W C	30	m	w	SCOT	Alameda	Oakland	68	265
BUSGHI								
Raphael	40	m	w	AUST	San Francisco	1-Wd San Francisco	79	110
BUSH								
Albert L	60	m	w	NY	Los Angeles	Santa Ana Twp	73	604
Alex	38	m	w	CT	Humboldt	Arcata Twp	72	226
Alex	36	m	w	CANA	Humboldt	Arcata Twp	72	225
Augusta	27	f	w	PRUS	Santa Clara	Santa Clara Twp	88	160
Charles H	35	m	w	PA	Los Angeles	Los Angeles	73	540
Chas	45	m	w	PRUS	Butte	Oregon Twp	70	136
Chas P	28	m	w	NZEA	San Francisco	8-Wd San Francisco	82	376
Chauncey C	39	m	w	MA	Shasta	Shasta P O	89	462
Clarence W	21	m	w	MS	Yolo	Cache Crk Twp	93	435
Conrad	50	m	w	HCAS	Santa Cruz	Soquel Twp	89	437
Cordelia	38	f	w	NY	Sonoma	Petaluma Twp	91	324
Danl B Jr	41	m	w	MA	Shasta	Shasta P O	89	462
Danl E	37	m	w	LA	Nevada	Little York Twp	75	237
David	64	m	w	OH	Trinity	North Fork Twp	92	220
David	34	m	w	OH	Sacramento	3-Wd Sacramento	77	306
E	40	m	w	NY	Nevada	Bloomfield Twp	75	96
E	17	m	w	HANO	Sierra	Butte Twp	89	509
Edward	31	m	w	IA	San Diego	Julian Dist	78	472
Edwin R	23	m	w	MS	Yolo	Cache Crk Twp	93	435
Eliza	53	f	b	MD	San Francisco	San Francisco P O	80	396
Elizabeth	8	f	w	OH	Nevada	Eureka Twp	75	134
Ernest	30	m	w	PRUS	San Francisco	8-Wd San Francisco	82	435
Eva	15	f	w	NY	San Francisco	8-Wd San Francisco	82	399
Everett	37	m	w	NY	San Francisco	11-Wd San Francisc	84	626
F	53	m	w	HANO	Sierra	Butte Twp	89	511
F O	32	m	w	LA	Amador	Jackson P O	69	340
Frederick	20	m	w	GERM	Los Angeles	Los Angeles	73	568
G C	56	m	w	NY	Tuolumne	Sonora P O	93	303
George	60	m	b	ME	El Dorado	Mud Springs Twp	72	76
George	30	m	w	HDAR	San Francisco	San Francisco P O	83	232
George	10	m	w	MA	Sonoma	Santa Rosa	91	409
George B	36	m	w	PRUS	San Francisco	11-Wd San Francisc	84	703
George D	44	m	w	PA	Stanislaus	Empire Twp	92	39
George W	33	m	w	IL	San Diego	Julian Dist	78	472
Georgiana	25	f	w	NY	San Francisco	7-Wd San Francisco	81	159
Gustav	28	m	w	PRUS	San Francisco	6-Wd San Francisco	81	45
Henry	64	m	w	VT	Contra Costa	Martinez Twp	71	350
Henry	42	m	w	PRUS	San Francisco	1-Wd San Francisco	79	13
Henry	38	m	w	PRUS	San Francisco	San Francisco P O	83	390
Henry	37	m	w	NY	Santa Barbara	San Buenaventura P	87	418
Henry	27	m	w	PRUS	San Francisco	San Francisco P O	80	474
Henry	25	m	w	MA	San Francisco	7-Wd San Francisco	81	279
Henry	20	m	w	PRUS	Contra Costa	Martinez P O	71	415
Henry	16	m	w	MA	Solano	Vallejo	90	200
Hyman	22	m	w	NY	San Francisco	San Francisco P O	83	282
Ida S	14	f	w	CA	Humboldt	Arcata Twp	72	232
Isaac	40	m	w	PRUS	San Francisco	San Francisco P O	83	397
Isaac K	57	m	w	VA	San Diego	Julian Dist	78	472
J G	45	m	w	WURT	Del Norte	Crescent Twp	71	455
J G	43	m	w	HAMB	Mendocino	Calpella Twp	74	188
James	35	m	w	DENM	San Francisco	11-Wd San Francisc	84	701
James S	45	m	w	NY	San Francisco	6-Wd San Francisco	81	155
Jane	60	f	w	ENGL	Nevada	Grass Valley Twp	75	142
Jaren	29	m	w	IA	San Diego	Julian Dist	78	472
Jas J	37	m	w	PRUS	San Francisco	8-Wd San Francisco	82	376
Jno Do	27	m	w	PA	Butte	Kimshew Tpw	70	79
John	66	m	w	MA	El Dorado	Placerville	72	112
John	44	m	w	ENGL	San Francisco	2-Wd San Francisco	79	154

© 2001 by Heritage Quest. All rights reserved.

Name	Age	S	R	B-PL	County	Locale	Series M593 Roll	Pg
John	41	m	w	KY	Los Angeles	Santa Ana Twp	73	608
John	35	m	w	PRUS	San Francisco	5-Wd San Francisco	81	35
John	29	m	w	ENGL	San Francisco	3-Wd San Francisco	79	319
John	26	m	w	IL	Los Angeles	El Monte Twp	73	457
John	22	m	w	HANO	Alameda	Eden Twp	68	65
John	20	m	w	IN	San Joaquin	Douglas Twp	86	30
John M	39	m	w	OH	Nevada	Bloomfield Twp	75	94
Jonas	40	m	w	CANA	Stanislaus	Buena Vista Twp	92	12
Julious	32	m	w	SWIT	Trinity	North Fork Twp	92	221
Kate	35	f	w	BADE	San Francisco	8-Wd San Francisco	82	479
Klaus	37	m	w	HANO	Klamath	Liberty Twp	73	375
Lewis	40	m	w	GERM	San Francisco	7-Wd San Francisco	81	243
Lewis	37	m	w	CANA	Yuba	Rose Bar Twp	93	658
M	28	m	w	CANA	Solano	Vallejo	90	165
M L	48	m	w	NY	San Francisco	3-Wd San Francisco	79	312
Martha	31	f	b	KY	Colusa	Spring Valley Twp	71	340
Mary	39	m	w	ENGL	Contra Costa	Martinez Twp	71	347
Mary A	45	f	w	TN	Mendocino	Ukiah Twp	74	237
Mary A	35	f	w	IREL	Sonoma	Healdsburg & Mendo	91	285
Moses	55	m	w	NY	Fresno	Kingston P O	72	221
Patrick	30	m	w	IREL	San Francisco	11-Wd San Francisc	84	427
Peter	58	m	w	CANA	Colusa	Colusa	71	293
Peter	52	m	w	DENM	Napa	Napa	75	35
Peter	40	m	w	SHOL	Sacramento	Granite Twp	77	156
Sarah P	14	f	w	IREL	Lake	Big Valley	73	394
Solomon	50	m	w	NY	Santa Clara	1-Wd San Jose	88	261
Theo	29	m	w	PRUS	Butte	Concow Twp	70	7
Thomas	39	m	w	PA	San Diego	San Diego	78	483
Thos	38	m	w	NY	Yuba	Rose Bar Twp	93	662
William	64	m	w	ENGL	Nevada	Grass Valley Twp	75	165
William	35	m	w	ME	San Francisco	8-Wd San Francisco	82	369
William	34	m	w	NY	Solano	Rio Vista Twp	90	71
William	23	m	w	CT	Colusa	Monroe Twp	71	325
Wm	28	m	w	OH	Sutter	Sutter Twp	92	116
Wm	23	m	w	IREL	Sierra	Gibson Twp	89	541
BUSHA								
William	34	m	w	MI	Alameda	Oakland	68	203
William	31	m	w	CANA	Alameda	Oakland	68	264
BUSHAN								
Henery	35	m	w	ME	San Francisco	7-Wd San Francisco	81	182
William	25	m	w	ME	San Francisco	7-Wd San Francisco	81	182
BUSHBY								
Frank	40	m	w	ME	San Francisco	3-Wd San Francisco	79	293
George	39	m	w	ENGL	Yuba	Linda Twp	93	554
BUSHE								
Charles	26	m	w	ME	Solano	Tremont Twp	90	35
John	33	m	w	IREL	Santa Clara	Santa Clara Twp	88	176
BUSHELL								
John	34	m	w	PRUS	Yuba	Parks Bar Twp	93	648
BUSHEY								
Mary	28	f	w	ME	San Francisco	7-Wd San Francisco	81	213
BUSHLER								
Fredrick	25	m	w	HANO	Inyo	Independence Twp	73	328
BUSHMAN								
Chas	28	m	w	BADE	San Francisco	11-Wd San Francisc	84	649
H	42	m	w	HOLL	Nevada	Washington Twp	75	343
Henry	38	m	w	PRUS	Butte	Kimshew Tpw	70	79
Johanna	24	f	w	MA	San Francisco	5-Wd San Francisco	81	1
John	31	m	w	HANO	San Francisco	7-Wd San Francisco	81	217
Pauldo	45	m	b	GA	Los Angeles	Los Angeles Twp	73	481
Wm	37	m	w	PRUS	San Francisco	San Francisco P O	85	757
BUSHMORE								
Albert	47	m	w	NY	San Francisco	11-Wd San Francisc	84	619
BUSHNELL								
Albert	40	m	w	MA	Solano	Suisun Twp	90	96
Amaza	48	m	w	NY	Sonoma	Analy Twp	91	236
C H	44	m	w	CT	Yuba	Rose Bar Twp	93	658
David	38	m	w	OH	Plumas	Plumas Twp	77	27
H M	35	m	w	NY	Solano	Vallejo	90	151
John E	50	m	w	VT	Plumas	Plumas Twp	77	26
Olive	69	f	w	MA	Yuba	Marysville	93	576
S H	44	m	w	OH	San Francisco	San Francisco P O	85	847
BUSHNER								
T	40	m	w	PRUS	Alameda	Murray Twp	68	123
BUSHNOFF								
Frank	27	m	w	MA	San Francisco	11-Wd San Francisc	84	503
BUSHTON								
James	24	m	w	ENGL	Monterey	Monterey	74	363
BUSICK								
John M	36	m	w	IN	El Dorado	Mud Springs Twp	72	90
BUSING								
Capt J	45	m	w	NY	Alameda	Oakland	68	202
BUSKET								
Frank	49	m	w	CANA	Alameda	Oakland	68	248
BUSKEY								
Frank	40	m	w	IREL	San Francisco	7-Wd San Francisco	81	199
BUSKIRK								
Geo	24	m	w	OH	Yuba	Marysville	93	604
Van Richd	45	m	w	CANA	Butte	Chico Twp	70	25
BUSMORE								
William	66	m	w	NY	El Dorado	Placerville Twp	72	94
BUSNELL								
James M	35	m	w	MA	Yuba	New York Twp	93	637
BUSON								
Andrew M C	37	m	w	IL	Amador	Volcano P O	69	385
BUSONE								
Domingo	40	m	b	CHIL	Mariposa	Maxwell Crk P O	74	139
BUSPEN								
Juan	50	m	w	MEXI	Kern	Tehachapi P O	73	354
BUSS								
Alfred C	39	m	w	NY	Yuba	Bullards Bar P O	93	547
Frank	64	m	w	MA	Yuba	Bullards Bar P O	93	547
Geo C	33	m	w	NY	Tuolumne	Sonora P O	93	317
Jacob H	40	m	w	PRUS	San Francisco	San Francisco P O	83	225
BUSSARD								
Wilson	34	m	w	PA	Mendocino	Round Valley Twp	74	217
BUSSENI								
Joseph	42	m	w	FRAN	Santa Barbara	Santa Barbara P O	87	452
BUSSENIUS								
H R	49	m	w	GERM	Nevada	Nevada Twp	75	274
BUSSETT								
John	36	m	w	OH	San Joaquin	Union Twp	86	267
Martin	41	m	w	CANA	San Francisco	11-Wd San Francisc	84	600
BUSSEY								
Wm C	31	m	w	NY	San Francisco	1-Wd San Francisco	79	107
BUSSIE								
Jean	50	m	w	FRAN	Tuolumne	Sonora P O	93	322
BUSSINGER								
Rosa	60	f	w	FRAN	San Francisco	8-Wd San Francisco	82	464
BUSSO								
Charles	45	m	w	ITAL	Tuolumne	Chinese Camp P O	93	371
BUSSON								
George	32	m	w	PRUS	Alameda	Oakland	68	264
BUST								
Frederik	22	m	w	NY	Contra Costa	Martinez P O	71	453
George	22	m	w	NY	Contra Costa	Martinez P O	71	453
BUSTAMANTE								
Francisco	32	m	w	MEXI	Los Angeles	Los Nietos Twp	73	573
Jose	7	m	w	AZ	Los Angeles	San Juan Twp	73	626
Josefa	34	f	w	MEXI	Los Angeles	Los Angeles	73	560
Prapis	28	m	w	MEXI	Los Angeles	El Monte Twp	73	462
BUSTAMENTA								
Manuel	48	m	w	CHIL	Contra Costa	Martinez Twp	71	352
BUSTAMENTE								
Antonio	40	m	w	MEXI	Monterey	San Juan Twp	74	385
Jafa	65	m	w	CA	Los Angeles	San Gabriel Twp	73	593
Jesus	26	m	w	MEXI	Los Angeles	Santa Ana Twp	73	605
Jose	30	m	w	MEXI	Los Angeles	Soledad Twp	73	631
Pedro	50	m	w	MEXI	Los Angeles	Los Angeles	73	557
Pedro	45	m	w	MEXI	Los Angeles	San Gabriel Twp	73	598
Ralph	13	m	w	PHIL	San Francisco	11-Wd San Francisc	84	586
Ramon	27	m	w	MEXI	Los Angeles	Los Angeles	73	505
Teodoro	35	m	w	MEXI	Los Angeles	Soledad Twp	73	631
BUSTAMENTO								
Joaquin	23	m	w	FRAN	Los Angeles	Los Angeles Twp	73	492
Rosa	36	f	w	MEXI	San Francisco	San Francisco P O	80	339
BUSTAMONTE								
Ignace	26	m	w	MEXI	San Luis Obispo	San Luis Obispo Tw	87	313
BUSTELLOS								
Raio	59	m	w	MEXI	Monterey	San Benito Twp	74	380
BUSTEMENTE								
Manuel	42	m	w	MEXI	Los Angeles	Los Angeles Twp	73	468
Marie	33	f	w	MEXI	San Francisco	6-Wd San Francisco	81	111
BUSTEMINTE								
Felipe	36	m	w	MEXI	Los Angeles	Los Angeles	73	555
BUSTER								
C F	14	m	w	CA	Alameda	Oakland	68	159
Callie	15	f	w	CA	Mendocino	Ukiah Twp	74	242
Charles	10	m	w	CA	Santa Clara	San Jose Twp	88	182
Franciall	45	m	w	TN	Santa Barbara	Santa Barbara P O	87	484
John W	42	m	w	TN	Mendocino	Cuffeys Cove Twp	74	168
William	50	m	w	TN	Mendocino	Point Arena Twp	74	213
BUSTERO								
Jose	14	m	w	CA	Kern	Bakersfield P O	73	361
BUSTILLAS								
Jesus	20	f	w	MEXI	San Francisco	San Francisco P O	80	418
BUSTILLOS								
Dolores	44	m	w	MEXI	Santa Barbara	Santa Barbara P O	87	458
Jesus	33	m	w	MEXI	Plumas	Goodwin Twp	77	5
BUSTIN								
John	36	m	w	GA	Marin	San Rafael	74	53
BUSTOL								
Charles	39	m	w	CT	Klamath	Klamath Twp	73	370
BUSTON								
Timothy G	40	m	w	NY	El Dorado	White Oak Twp	72	143
BUSWELL								
Alexander	37	m	w	HANO	San Francisco	2-Wd San Francisco	79	256
Hy	40	m	w	NY	San Francisco	11-Wd San Francisc	84	643
BUT								
Ah	33	m	c	CHIN	San Joaquin	1-Wd Stockton	86	134
Ah	31	m	c	CHIN	Sacramento	1-Wd Sacramento	77	205
Ah	31	m	c	CHIN	Contra Costa	Martinez P O	71	441
Wing	25	m	c	CHIN	San Francisco	1-Wd San Francisco	79	120
BUTANCO								
Antonio	48	m	w	PORT	Alameda	Washington Twp	68	270
BUTCHART								
George	60	m	w	SCOT	San Luis Obispo	Salinas Twp	87	292
John	37	m	w	SCOT	San Mateo	Half Moon Bay P O	87	408
BUTCHEN								
C	24	m	w	SHOL	Alameda	Oakland	68	239
BUTCHER								
H	32	m	w	IL	Solano	Vallejo	90	166
Henry	30	m	w	NJ	San Francisco	6-Wd San Francisco	81	98
James	33	m	w	OH	San Francisco	11-Wd San Francisc	84	682

© 2001 by Heritage Quest. All rights reserved.

California 1870 Census

Name	Age	S	R	B-PL	County	Locale	Roll	Pg
						Series M593		
Mary	57	f	w	WURT	Sonoma	Healdsburg & Mendo	91	276
Thos	29	m	w	CANA	Butte	Chico Twp	70	31
William	48	m	w	OH	Solano	Vacaville Twp	90	125
BUTCHERS								
John	42	m	w	HAMB	San Francisco	2-Wd San Francisco	79	157
BUTE								
Barney F	38	m	w	NY	Santa Clara	Milpitas Twp	88	113
BUTEN								
Maria Josefa	43	f	w	CA	Monterey	Castroville Twp	74	332
BUTENOP								
Henry	56	m	w	PRUS	San Francisco	San Francisco P O	80	477
Peter	48	m	w	PRUS	San Francisco	San Francisco P O	80	479
BUTERWORK								
Frederick	29	m	w	PRUS	Alameda	Brooklyn Twp	68	53
BUTES								
Chas B	28	m	w	ENGL	Santa Barbara	Santa Barbara P O	87	450
BUTH								
James	30	m	w	ENGL	Trinity	Douglas	92	237
BUTHEMUTH								
Antonio	30	m	w	PRUS	San Bernardino	San Bernardino Twp	78	452
Theodore	33	m	w	MO	San Bernardino	San Bernardino Twp	78	452
BUTHEN								
John	28	m	w	VA	Alameda	Oakland	68	261
BUTIEREZ								
Florencio	9	m	w	CA	Santa Cruz	Pajaro Twp	89	357
BUTLAR								
Emma	18	f	w	US	Yuba	Marysville	93	609
BUTLER								
A G	42	m	w	ME	Sacramento	Dry Crk Twp	77	98
Albert B	27	m	w	IA	Butte	Chico Twp	70	15
Alex	29	m	w	CANA	Solano	Benicia	90	18
Alexr J	38	m	w	NY	San Francisco	5-Wd San Francisco	81	1
Alfred V	42	m	w	ME	San Francisco	San Francisco P O	83	298
Amma H	31	f	w	IREL	San Francisco	7-Wd San Francisco	81	177
Ammy	19	f	w	ENGL	San Francisco	7-Wd San Francisco	81	204
Amos	60	m	w	CANA	Sacramento	Sutter Twp	77	383
Annie	29	f	w	IREL	San Francisco	11-Wd San Francisc	84	506
B	46	m	w	WURT	Amador	Drytown P O	69	418
Bell	20	f	w	RI	Marin	San Rafael Twp	74	47
Benjamin	31	m	w	OH	Humboldt	South Fork Twp	72	300
C C	50	f	w	MA	Alameda	Oakland	68	204
C C	41	m	w	NY	San Francisco	San Francisco P O	85	857
C S	40	f	w	KY	Sacramento	3-Wd Sacramento	77	312
C S	27	m	w	CANA	San Joaquin	Elkhorn Twp	86	60
Catharine J	30	f	i	CA	Mariposa	Mariposa P O	74	124
Catherin	28	f	w	IREL	San Francisco	11-Wd San Francisc	84	635
Cathrine	34	f	w	IREL	San Francisco	San Francisco P O	83	382
Charles	42	m	b	DE	San Francisco	San Francisco P O	80	458
Charles	19	m	w	SCOT	Inyo	Independence Twp	73	328
Charles C	39	m	w	KY	Colusa	Colusa	71	298
Charles O	40	m	w	NY	Yolo	Cottonwood Twp	93	470
Charles [Adopted]	7	m	w	MO	Humboldt	South Fork Twp	72	300
Charlotte W	45	f	w	ME	San Francisco	San Francisco P O	83	151
Chas H	40	m	w	NY	Sonoma	Santa Rosa	91	424
Daniel	32	m	w	PA	San Francisco	San Francisco P O	80	461
David	42	m	w	NH	San Francisco	San Francisco P O	83	175
Delia	30	f	w	IREL	San Francisco	San Francisco P O	83	273
E A	52	m	w	KY	Sonoma	Russian Rvr	91	377
E A	23	m	w	AR	Sonoma	Russian Rvr	91	377
E D	39	f	w	IN	Napa	Napa	75	15
Edward	26	m	w	IREL	Mendocino	Anderson Twp	74	154
Edward	18	m	w	CA	San Francisco	11-Wd San Francisc	84	587
Edward P	36	m	w	PA	Santa Cruz	Santa Cruz	89	419
Elizabeth	19	f	w	SCOT	San Francisco	6-Wd San Francisco	81	98
Ellen	40	f	w	IREL	San Francisco	7-Wd San Francisco	81	216
Emily Frances	32	f	w	NY	El Dorado	Mud Springs Twp	72	71
Emma	2	f	w	CA	Monterey	Monterey	74	366
Erastus	23	m	w	AR	Sonoma	Analy Twp	91	243
Eveline	49	f	w	NY	Sonoma	Petaluma Twp	91	340
Fenton	40	m	w	UNKN	San Joaquin	2-Wd Stockton	86	167
Frances P	36	m	w	IREL	San Francisco	San Francisco P O	83	340
Francis	44	m	w	FRAN	Stanislaus	Emory Twp	92	25
Frank	29	m	m	DE	San Francisco	San Francisco P O	80	423
Frank	27	m	w	IREL	Sonoma	Petaluma Twp	91	343
G W	63	m	w	IREL	Monterey	Alisal Twp	74	290
Geo	36	m	w	NY	San Francisco	1-Wd San Francisco	79	26
George	42	m	w	PRUS	Kern	Linns Valley P O	73	344
George	24	m	w	CANA	Solano	Rio Vista Twp	90	64
George	23	m	w	ENGL	Siskiyou	Yreka	89	658
George	23	m	w	NY	San Francisco	San Francisco P O	83	305
George R	34	m	w	NY	Los Angeles	Los Angeles	73	549
Grace	65	f	w	ENGL	Butte	Ophir Twp	70	107
H R	45	m	w	NY	Lake	Big Valley	73	394
Harriet	45	f	w	NY	San Francisco	11-Wd San Francisc	84	486
Henry	35	m	w	PRUS	Contra Costa	Martinez P O	71	431
Henry M	40	m	w	ME	San Francisco	San Francisco P O	83	414
Henry W	30	m	w	VA	San Francisco	1-Wd San Francisco	79	40
Henthir	39	m	w	NY	Sacramento	Sutter Twp	77	385
Horace	45	m	w	NY	Tuolumne	Columbia P O	93	336
J	31	f	w	IREL	San Francisco	San Francisco P O	83	133
James	46	m	w	IREL	Mariposa	Mariposa P O	74	124
James	45	m	w	IREL	San Francisco	11-Wd San Francisc	84	526
James	45	m	w	IREL	San Francisco	11-Wd San Francisc	84	510
James	40	m	w	IREL	Del Norte	Happy Camp Twp	71	468
James	39	m	w	IREL	San Francisco	San Francisco P O	80	332
James	35	m	w	NY	Sacramento	Granite Twp	77	148
James	30	m	w	IREL	Solano	Green Valley Twp	90	38
James	28	m	w	IREL	San Francisco	3-Wd San Francisco	79	294
James	27	m	w	IREL	Sonoma	Santa Rosa	91	400
James	23	m	w	IREL	Nevada	Grass Valley Twp	75	214
Jas F	27	m	w	CANA	San Francisco	1-Wd San Francisco	79	69
Jed Ton	44	m	w	VT	Klamath	Salmon Twp	73	387
Jesse	12	m	w	TX	Los Angeles	San Gabriel Twp	73	595
Jno R	42	m	b	MD	Butte	Ophir Twp	70	105
John	59	m	w	ENGL	San Diego	San Diego	78	503
John	50	m	w	MD	San Francisco	San Francisco P O	83	206
John	49	m	w	KY	Contra Costa	Martinez P O	71	416
John	47	m	w	IREL	Alameda	Oakland	68	234
John	46	m	w	ME	Kern	Kernville P O	73	367
John	38	m	w	IL	Alameda	Oakland	68	245
John	36	m	w	CANA	Placer	Bath P O	76	455
John	34	m	w	NY	San Francisco	6-Wd San Francisco	81	101
John	30	m	w	ENGL	San Francisco	San Francisco P O	83	151
John	28	m	w	PRUS	San Francisco	11-Wd San Francisc	84	519
John	26	m	w	IREL	San Francisco	San Francisco P O	83	304
John	25	m	w	CANA	Alameda	San Leandro	68	96
John	24	m	w	OH	San Francisco	7-Wd San Francisco	81	281
Johnathan	47	m	w	OH	Nevada	Grass Valley Twp	75	207
Joseph	48	m	w	IREL	San Francisco	1-Wd San Francisco	79	62
Joseph	37	m	w	VA	Sonoma	Sonoma Twp	91	441
Joseph	35	m	w	IREL	San Francisco	San Francisco P O	83	4
Joseph	22	m	w	ENGL	San Bernardino	San Bernardino Twp	78	417
Joseph	22	m	w	TX	San Bernardino	San Bernardino Twp	78	453
Joseph A	33	m	w	KY	Nevada	Rough & Ready Twp	75	323
Joseph D	43	m	w	IREL	San Francisco	San Francisco P O	85	851
Joseph D	43	m	w	IREL	San Francisco	1-Wd San Francisco	79	106
Joseph E	41	m	w	ME	San Mateo	San Mateo P O	87	357
Kate	26	f	w	MA	San Joaquin	2-Wd Stockton	86	196
L	39	m	w	PA	Lake	Coyote Valley	73	400
Lillie	28	f	w	IREL	San Francisco	11-Wd San Francisc	84	628
Lily	5	f	w	CA	Solano	Vallejo	90	152
Loreza	24	m	w	MA	San Francisco	1-Wd San Francisco	79	55
M	25	m	w	CANA	Lake	Lower Lake	73	429
M F	13	m	w	CA	Alameda	Oakland	68	257
Margaret	40	f	w	IREL	San Francisco	San Francisco P O	80	534
Margaret	35	f	w	IREL	San Francisco	11-Wd San Francisc	84	432
Margaret	29	f	w	IREL	San Francisco	8-Wd San Francisco	82	426
Margaret	28	f	w	IREL	San Francisco	8-Wd San Francisco	82	384
Margaret	24	f	w	PA	Sacramento	2-Wd Sacramento	77	248
Margaret B	15	f	w	IA	Yolo	Grafton Twp	93	478
Martin	35	m	w	IREL	San Francisco	11-Wd San Francisc	84	478
Mary	73	f	w	IREL	San Francisco	San Francisco P O	80	332
Mary	36	f	w	IREL	Santa Cruz	Santa Cruz	89	414
Mary	35	f	w	IREL	San Francisco	San Francisco P O	83	55
Mary	34	f	w	MS	San Francisco	San Francisco P O	80	488
Mary	19	f	w	IREL	San Francisco	8-Wd San Francisco	82	439
Mary	18	f	w	IREL	San Francisco	8-Wd San Francisco	82	394
Matthew	39	m	w	IREL	San Francisco	San Francisco P O	85	732
Michael	35	m	w	IREL	Solano	Silveyville Twp	90	83
Michael	28	m	w	IREL	San Francisco	3-Wd San Francisco	79	327
Michael J	30	m	w	IREL	Santa Cruz	Santa Cruz	89	415
Michl	45	m	w	IREL	San Francisco	1-Wd San Francisco	79	8
Miner	44	m	w	GA	San Francisco	11-Wd San Francisc	84	565
Minnie	6	f	j	CA	San Francisco	San Francisco P O	80	488
Morris	46	m	m	MD	Nevada	Meadow Lake Twp	75	248
Mortimer D	42	m	w	VT	Colusa	Colusa Twp	71	273
Newton C	41	m	w	TN	Solano	Rio Vista Twp	90	55
Orin	32	m	w	MA	Solano	Vallejo	90	205
Oscar	14	m	w	CA	Tulare	White Rvr Twp	92	301
P H	43	m	w	TN	Nevada	Bridgeport Twp	75	100
Patk	67	m	w	IREL	Solano	Vallejo	90	184
Patrick	50	m	w	IREL	Santa Clara	1-Wd San Jose	88	225
Patrick	29	m	w	IREL	San Francisco	11-Wd San Francisc	84	457
Patrick	21	m	w	IREL	Yuba	Rose Bar Twp	93	657
Patrick	21	m	w	OH	Yuba	Rose Bar Twp	93	661
Peter	23	m	w	NY	Placer	Lincoln P O	76	492
Peter	18	m	w	NY	Alameda	Oakland	68	253
R D	22	m	w	CA	Napa	Napa Twp	75	71
Robert	32	m	w	IREL	San Francisco	7-Wd San Francisco	81	179
Roland	8	m	w	IA	Monterey	Alisal Twp	74	295
Rose	1	f	w	CA	Santa Cruz	Santa Cruz	89	417
Samuel	63	m	w	NY	El Dorado	Placerville Twp	72	100
Samuel	41	m	w	MA	Sonoma	Vallejo Twp	91	456
Sarah	35	f	b	MD	San Francisco	6-Wd San Francisco	81	89
Sarah	20	f	w	ENGL	Los Angeles	Los Angeles	73	520
Sarah E	50	f	w	ENGL	San Francisco	6-Wd San Francisco	81	115
Steph W	38	m	w	NY	Sacramento	4-Wd Sacramento	77	331
T R	27	m	w	NY	Alameda	Oakland	68	134
Thomas	60	m	w	IREL	San Mateo	Schoolhouse Statio	87	343
Thomas	52	m	w	MA	Sonoma	Petaluma Twp	91	350
Thomas	35	m	w	IREL	San Francisco	11-Wd San Francisc	84	655
Thomas	33	m	w	VT	Yuba	Long Bar Twp	93	561
Thomas	31	m	w	IREL	San Francisco	2-Wd San Francisco	79	260
Thomas	25	m	w	IREL	San Francisco	1-Wd San Francisco	79	55
Thomas J	33	m	w	NY	Sonoma	Petaluma Twp	91	366
Thomas M	53	m	w	IREL	Santa Cruz	Santa Cruz	89	409
Thos J	44	m	w	ME	Nevada	Nevada Twp	75	296
Torin G	54	m	w	VT	Sacramento	Sutter Twp	77	392
W A	35	m	w	ME	San Francisco	San Francisco P O	85	832
W H	33	m	w	IREL	Sierra	Downieville Twp	89	516
W P	27	m	w	IN	San Joaquin	Liberty Twp	86	88
W T	21	m	w	IN	Sacramento	Sutter Twp	77	388
Walter	38	m	w	CANA	Solano	Benicia	90	18
Warren C	43	m	w	NY	San Francisco	6-Wd San Francisco	81	124

© 2001 by Heritage Quest. All rights reserved.

Series M593

Name	Age	S	R	B-PL	County	Locale	Roll	Pg
William	52	m	w	ENGL	Mendocino	Point Arena Twp	74	207
William	50	m	w	MO	Siskiyou	Yreka Twp	89	673
William	45	m	w	MA	San Francisco	San Francisco P O	83	279
William	45	m	w	CANA	San Mateo	Pescadero P O	87	413
William	40	m	w	IREL	San Francisco	7-Wd San Francisco	81	172
Wm	8	m	w	CA	San Francisco	San Francisco P O	83	76
Wm	40	m	w	CANA	Solano	Vallejo	90	145
Wm	39	m	w	IREL	San Francisco	11-Wd San Francisc	84	431
Wm	38	m	w	IREL	San Francisco	San Francisco P O	83	132
Wm	37	m	w	TN	Yuba	Linda Twp	93	557
Wm G	20	m	w	NC	Shasta	Millville P O	89	483
Wm L	28	m	w	NY	Santa Barbara	Santa Barbara P O	87	501
Wm M	39	m	w	MA	Santa Barbara	Santa Barbara P O	87	493
BUTLETT								
E D	52	m	w	NY	Alameda	Oakland	68	153
BUTLEY								
Lewis	1	m	w	CA	San Mateo	Schoolhouse Statio	87	336
BUTMAN								
Fred	49	m	w	ME	San Francisco	11-Wd San Francisc	84	579
BUTNER								
Alonzo	22	m	w	PRUS	San Francisco	5-Wd San Francisco	81	8
James W	35	m	w	NY	San Francisco	1-Wd San Francisco	79	78
John	50	m	w	HDAR	San Francisco	7-Wd San Francisco	81	235
Wm	17	m	w	PA	Marin	Tomales Twp	74	87
BUTON								
Charles	58	m	w	KY	Sacramento	Franklin Twp	77	119
Charles	40	m	w	NY	Santa Clara	1-Wd San Jose	88	236
Mary	18	f	w	CA	Fresno	Millerton P O	72	163
BUTRON								
Demas	46	m	i	CA	Monterey	Castroville Twp	74	336
Jose	25	m	w	CA	Santa Cruz	Watsonville	89	367
Manuel	48	m	w	CA	Monterey	Monterey	74	363
BUTSCHER								
Clement	21	m	w	PRUS	San Francisco	San Francisco P O	85	753
BUTSENHIZER								
Henry	60	m	w	PA	Placer	Bath P O	76	447
BUTT								
L D	26	m	w	PA	Nevada	Meadow Lake Twp	75	259
Peter	31	m	w	PRUS	San Francisco	San Francisco P O	80	368
Peter	30	m	w	HANO	San Francisco	1-Wd San Francisco	79	52
Peter	19	m	w	PRUS	Alameda	Washington Twp	68	278
William	19	m	w	HANO	Alameda	Washington Twp	68	282
BUTTAR								
J C	28	m	w	IA	Humboldt	Mattole Twp	72	288
BUTTEN								
George W	44	m	w	ME	San Mateo	Schoolhouse Statio	87	333
Robt	23	m	w	WALE	Contra Costa	Martinez P O	71	426
BUTTER								
E	39	m	w	ME	Nevada	Bridgeport Twp	75	109
G R	22	m	w	OH	San Joaquin	Elkhorn Twp	86	65
Geo	40	m	w	AUSL	San Joaquin	2-Wd Stockton	86	165
John E	37	m	w	ENGL	Sacramento	Natomas Twp	77	167
John G	36	m	w	WURT	Santa Cruz	Pajaro Twp	89	342
Margaret	55	f	w	IREL	Solano	Vallejo	90	175
Norris	63	m	m	CA	Amador	Sutter Crk P O	69	413
P	29	m	m	LA	Amador	Ione City P O	69	357
W J	27	m	w	KY	Lake	Big Valley	73	399
Wm J	33	m	w	AR	Fresno	Kingston P O	72	224
BUTTERBREAD								
Frederick	40	m	w	PRUS	Kern	Havilah P O	73	351
BUTTERFELD								
R	50	m	w	OH	Sacramento	1-Wd Sacramento	77	178
BUTTERFIELD								
Alonzo	9	m	w	MT	San Francisco	11-Wd San Francisc	84	614
Alonzo	26	m	w	ME	Mendocino	Casper & Big Rvr	74	164
Andrew	31	m	w	ME	Sonoma	Salt Point	91	385
B F	52	m	w	NH	Tuolumne	Chinese Camp P O	93	372
Benjamin F	23	m	w	VT	Yuba	New York Twp	93	639
Benjamin F	23	m	w	VT	Yuba	North East Twp	93	644
Charles	50	m	w	ME	Colusa	Monroe Twp	71	315
F	15	m	w	CA	Alameda	Oakland	68	159
Geo	37	m	w	ME	Yuba	W Bear Rvr Twp	93	683
George	43	m	w	ME	Plumas	Seneca Twp	77	49
George F	37	m	w	ME	Calaveras	San Andreas P O	70	215
Gideon H	52	m	w	ME	Colusa	Monroe Twp	71	315
Harvey	47	m	w	VT	Marin	San Rafael Twp	74	33
Henry M	34	m	w	ME	Calaveras	San Andreas P O	70	215
Henry W	37	m	w	ME	Nevada	Nevada Twp	75	317
John H	47	m	w	NY	Santa Barbara	San Buenaventura P	87	419
Josiah	80	m	w	ENGL	Monterey	San Juan Twp	74	409
Josiah	75	m	w	NH	Santa Cruz	Watsonville	89	374
Josiah	35	m	w	ME	Santa Clara	2-Wd San Jose	88	287
L L	13	m	w	CA	Alameda	Oakland	68	258
Mary	25	f	w	IREL	Nevada	Grass Valley Twp	75	147
Reuben	44	m	w	PA	Placer	Roseville P O	76	356
W	37	m	w	ME	Alameda	Oakland	68	206
William	20	m	w	MI	Sacramento	2-Wd Sacramento	77	240
BUTTERFORD								
Richd	33	m	w	NY	Butte	Ophir Twp	70	116
BUTTERLY								
John	54	m	w	IREL	San Joaquin	1-Wd Stockton	86	152
BUTTERS								
Henry	52	m	w	MA	San Francisco	8-Wd San Francisco	82	424
John L	52	m	w	SCOT	San Francisco	6-Wd San Francisco	81	138
Lizzie	26	f	w	IREL	San Francisco	5-Wd San Francisco	81	29
BUTTERWORTH								
Ed	48	m	w	ENGL	San Francisco	11-Wd San Francisc	84	598

Series M593

Name	Age	S	R	B-PL	County	Locale	Roll	Pg
Edwd	32	m	w	ENGL	Marin	San Rafael	74	48
Gouthir	79	m	w	ENGL	Sacramento	4-Wd Sacramento	77	376
James	44	m	w	ENGL	San Francisco	7-Wd San Francisco	81	267
Richard	45	m	w	ENGL	San Francisco	San Francisco P O	85	749
Sam F	58	m	w	NY	San Francisco	8-Wd San Francisco	82	317
BUTTIN								
B F	54	m	w	TN	Monterey	Salinas Twp	74	309
BUTTIS								
Hannah	74	f	w	NY	Los Angeles	Wilmington Twp	73	643
James D	44	m	w	NY	Los Angeles	Wilmington Twp	73	643
Joseph J	70	m	w	NY	Los Angeles	Wilmington Twp	73	643
Phillip	30	m	w	NY	Los Angeles	Wilmington Twp	73	643
BUTTLE								
James	70	m	w	ENGL	Nevada	Grass Valley Twp	75	204
James T	34	m	w	ENGL	Nevada	Grass Valley Twp	75	204
John	32	m	w	ENGL	San Francisco	11-Wd San Francisc	84	621
Thos B	28	m	w	IL	Napa	Napa Twp	75	68
William W	42	m	w	ME	San Francisco	8-Wd San Francisco	82	404
BUTTLEMAN								
Fred	29	m	w	HANO	Yuba	Marysville	93	598
BUTTLER								
Felix	43	m	w	KY	Alameda	Oakland	68	177
Frances	33	f	w	ENGL	Yuba	Marysville	93	591
Fred	39	m	w	BAVA	Yuba	Marysville	93	588
James	27	m	w	IREL	Alameda	Oakland	68	182
Jos L	30	m	w	LA	San Francisco	8-Wd San Francisco	82	335
Mark	26	m	w	NY	Tulare	White Rvr Twp	92	301
William	30	m	w	NY	Sonoma	Vallejo Twp	91	452
Wm I	32	m	w	IREL	San Francisco	8-Wd San Francisco	82	321
BUTTMAN								
Constantine	35	m	w	GREE	Placer	Bath P O	76	437
BUTTMER								
James	46	m	w	PRUS	Trinity	North Fork Twp	92	219
BUTTNER								
Bertha	20	f	w	PA	Santa Cruz	Santa Cruz	89	420
Clara	8	f	w	CA	Sonoma	Bodega Twp	91	252
Ferdinand	34	m	w	PRUS	Mendocino	Anderson Twp	74	151
Go	42	m	w	BAVA	Alameda	Murray Twp	68	104
BUTTOMER								
J C	25	m	w	IREL	Nevada	Bridgeport Twp	75	120
BUTTON								
Adelbert T	38	m	w	PA	Monterey	San Benito Twp	74	378
Catherine	59	f	w	VT	Sonoma	Petaluma Twp	91	310
H E	52	m	w	MA	Sacramento	3-Wd Sacramento	77	282
Henry	39	m	w	NY	Santa Cruz	Soquel Twp	89	444
Isaac V	33	m	w	VT	Sonoma	Petaluma Twp	91	335
Isabell	30	f	w	NY	San Joaquin	2-Wd Stockton	86	170
Jos	36	m	w	VT	Sonoma	Santa Rosa	91	397
Lee	34	m	w	NY	Lassen	Susanville Twp	73	446
Mont	57	m	w	NY	San Bernardino	San Bernardino Twp	78	442
Nathaniel	6M	m	w	CA	Sonoma	Santa Rosa	91	396
O	43	m	w	NY	Alameda	Oakland	68	167
Orlando	47	m	w	NY	Amador	Ione City P O	69	356
William	45	m	w	MO	Tehama	Tehama Twp	92	186
BUTTRICK								
Charles	39	m	w	MA	Santa Cruz	Pajaro Twp	89	349
W H	37	m	w	MA	San Joaquin	Tulare Twp	86	253
BUTTS								
Albert	50	m	w	NY	Sonoma	Healdsburg & Mendo	91	276
Alexander	43	m	w	MO	Kern	Havilah P O	73	339
Andrew	35	m	w	OH	Contra Costa	Martinez P O	71	452
C C	27	m	w	PRUS	San Francisco	8-Wd San Francisco	82	339
Charles	58	m	w	PA	Marin	San Rafael Twp	74	35
David	43	m	w	TN	Sonoma	Mendocino Twp	91	308
George	32	m	w	KY	Placer	Auburn P O	76	369
George	30	m	w	MO	Nevada	Grass Valley Twp	75	218
Henry	42	m	w	NY	San Francisco	7-Wd San Francisco	81	222
Isabella	15	f	w	CA	Sonoma	Mendocino Twp	91	301
James	35	m	b	DC	El Dorado	Placerville	72	119
James	30	m	w	MS	Nevada	Grass Valley Twp	75	227
Jas	21	m	w	MI	San Joaquin	Elkhorn Twp	86	62
John	38	m	w	HANO	San Mateo	Half Moon Bay P O	87	404
John	11	m	w	CA	Butte	Ophir Twp	70	102
Johnson	34	m	w	VA	Trinity	Douglas	92	237
Norman	42	m	w	NY	Santa Barbara	Santa Barbara P O	87	495
Parmelia	63	f	w	TN	Calaveras	Copperopolis P O	70	238
Rufus	35	m	w	TN	Monterey	San Juan Twp	74	391
Sarah A	43	f	w	ENGL	Nevada	Grass Valley Twp	75	191
BUTZ								
Frederick	27	m	m	RUSS	Colusa	Colusa	71	295
Peter	42	m	w	BAVA	Yuba	Slate Range Bar Tw	93	675
BUTZNA								
Philip	31	m	w	WURT	San Francisco	11-Wd San Francisc	84	642
BUXDORF								
Chrisr	45	m	w	SWIT	San Francisco	3-Wd San Francisco	79	324
BUXTON								
Edmond	56	m	w	ME	Placer	Bath P O	76	425
Frank	24	m	w	MA	Alameda	Oakland	68	172
George	54	m	w	NH	San Francisco	8-Wd San Francisco	82	445
Thomas	22	m	w	IREL	San Francisco	7-Wd San Francisco	81	173
BUY								
Ah	50	m	c	CHIN	Trinity	Canyon City Pct	92	201
Dennis	33	m	w	US	Humboldt	Eureka Twp	72	279
John	33	m	w	BADE	San Francisco	San Francisco P O	83	138
Louis	30	m	w	SWIT	Tehama	Merrill	92	197
BUYAK								
John F	52	m	w	BELG	Amador	Volcano P O	69	379

© 2001 by Heritage Quest. All rights reserved.

California 1870 Census

Name	Age	S	R	B-PL	County	Locale	Series M593 Roll	Pg
BUYCK								
Flora	11	f	w	CA	Calaveras	San Andreas P O	70	212
BUYER								
William	21	m	w	HANO	San Francisco	7-Wd San Francisco	81	211
BUYOC								
Alfonse	40	m	w	FRAN	Monterey	San Juan Twp	74	414
BUZAN								
John	49	m	w	MO	Shasta	Millville P O	89	492
BUZMAN								
M	36	m	w	PRUS	Alameda	Alameda	68	13
BUZZA								
John	31	m	w	ENGL	Nevada	Grass Valley Twp	75	144
Joseph	28	m	w	ENGL	Nevada	Grass Valley Twp	75	175
BUZZARD								
Levi B	44	m	w	PA	Placer	Bath P O	76	428
BUZZEL								
Anson	34	m	w	ME	Sierra	Table Rock Twp	89	571
BUZZELL								
Albert	52	m	w	NY	San Mateo	Half Moon Bay P O	87	402
Edmund C	41	m	w	ME	Placer	Newcastle Twp	76	478
Herbert	8	m	w	CA	San Mateo	Half Moon Bay P O	87	404
John F	43	m	w	ME	Monterey	Castroville Twp	74	330
Waldo P	29	m	w	ME	Placer	Newcastle Twp	76	478
Willard	19	m	w	CA	San Joaquin	Oneal Twp	86	110
BUZZINI								
Martin	29	m	w	SWIT	San Francisco	11-Wd San Francisc	84	709
BUZZLE								
Mary	15	f	w	CA	Santa Clara	Gilroy Twp	88	70
BWINHAM								
Job	27	m	w	NY	Butte	Ophir Twp	70	100
BY								
Ah	36	m	c	CHIN	Sacramento	Georgianna Twp	77	131
Mow	41	m	c	CHIN	Butte	Ophir Twp	70	106
BYAM								
H F	41	m	w	NY	Mendocino	Sanel Twp	74	228
Henry Mrs	30	f	w	NY	San Francisco	5-Wd San Francisco	81	18
J A	30	m	w	NY	Tuolumne	Columbia P O	93	337
William	45	m	w	MO	Stanislaus	San Joaquin Twp	92	82
BYAN								
John	30	m	w	ENGL	San Francisco	San Francisco P O	85	863
T P	31	m	w	OH	Alameda	Oakland	68	190
BYANS								
Henry	44	m	w	ME	San Francisco	5-Wd San Francisco	81	11
BYANT								
Wm	53	m	w	ENGL	El Dorado	Salmon Falls Twp	72	133
BYARD								
Geo A	35	m	w	ME	Humboldt	Eel Rvr Twp	72	254
BYARLY								
Jos	48	m	w	PA	Solano	Vallejo	90	188
BYAS								
Harriet	42	f	w	ME	San Joaquin	2-Wd Stockton	86	163
Jose	62	m	w	CHIL	Contra Costa	San Pablo Twp	71	355
BYASTAN								
Romaldo	62	m	w	CA	Los Angeles	Los Angeles Twp	73	493
BYCE								
Jemima	64	f	w	NC	Merced	Snelling P O	74	254
BYCROFT								
Andrew	29	m	w	IREL	Solano	Silveyville Twp	90	78
Thos	48	m	w	ENGL	Solano	Vallejo	90	157
BYDING								
Adam	32	m	w	PRUS	Sonoma	Santa Rosa	91	394
BYE								
Ah	50	m	c	CHIN	Amador	Ione City P O	69	365
John	42	m	w	ENGL	Mariposa	Mariposa P O	74	131
Richard	50	m	w	PRUS	Placer	Bath P O	76	452
BYENARD								
Joseph	24	m	w	FRAN	Monterey	San Juan Twp	74	408
BYENE								
Edward	50	m	w	IREL	San Francisco	2-Wd San Francisco	79	163
Samuel	32	m	w	ENGL	Yuba	Long Bar Twp	93	560
BYER								
Herman	49	m	w	PRUS	San Mateo	Belmont P O	87	373
BYERLEY								
Charles	17	m	w	PRUS	San Francisco	11-Wd San Francisc	84	587
BYERLY								
Melville	28	m	w	OH	Monterey	San Juan Twp	74	399
BYERON								
James	38	m	w	ME	Amador	Volcano P O	69	380
BYERS								
A	29	m	w	ME	San Joaquin	2-Wd Stockton	86	193
Alexander	49	m	w	OH	Contra Costa	Martinez P O	71	380
Christopher	41	m	w	BADE	Plumas	Washington Twp	77	53
Ellen	21	f	w	IREL	San Francisco	2-Wd San Francisco	79	196
George	46	m	w	BADE	Nevada	Rough & Ready Twp	75	335
George	30	m	w	GERM	Marin	San Rafael Twp	74	43
Hunter J	45	m	w	PA	Colusa	Grand Island Twp	71	303
J D	45	m	w	PA	Lassen	Janesville Twp	73	432
J M	47	m	w	NH	San Joaquin	3-Wd Stockton	86	219
James	30	m	w	IREL	Santa Clara	San Jose Twp	88	188
John	45	m	w	OH	Nevada	Grass Valley Twp	75	224
John	40	m	w	IREL	San Francisco	1-Wd San Francisco	79	20
John	37	m	w	NY	Mendocino	Anderson Twp	74	155
John A	35	m	w	VA	Colusa	Spring Valley Twp	71	339
Joseph	38	m	w	PA	San Francisco	San Francisco P O	80	394
Thomas	21	m	w	ENGL	San Francisco	2-Wd San Francisco	79	213
William	68	m	w	OH	Stanislaus	Empire Twp	92	54
Wm Thomas	39	m	w	MO	Plumas	Plumas Twp	77	26
BYESTARO								
Jesus	30	m	w	CA	Los Angeles	Los Angeles	73	522
BYGATT								
Geo	36	m	w	NY	Solano	Vallejo	90	203
BYHOT								
Dominick	43	m	w	FRAN	Los Angeles	Los Angeles	73	518
BYING								
Hing	19	m	c	CHIN	San Francisco	San Francisco P O	83	105
BYINGTON								
Walter	14	m	w	CA	San Francisco	11-Wd San Francisc	84	592
BYINTON								
L	49	m	w	CT	Sierra	Downieville Twp	89	515
BYL								
James	43	m	w	ENGL	San Bernardino	San Bernardino Twp	78	430
BYLE								
Jacob	35	m	w	HDAR	San Francisco	11-Wd San Francisc	84	684
Mary	49	f	w	IREL	San Francisco	San Francisco P O	83	39
BYLES								
George	37	m	w	ENGL	San Francisco	San Francisco P O	83	407
John	35	m	w	OH	Butte	Hamilton Twp	70	65
Wm A	26	m	w	MO	Napa	Napa Twp	75	72
BYME								
Patrick	26	m	w	IREL	Placer	Gold Run Twp	76	395
BYMES								
Pat Joseph	35	m	w	IREL	El Dorado	Georgetown Twp	72	47
BYMON								
Alfred A	41	m	w	CANA	San Francisco	San Francisco P O	83	160
BYMUM								
Alexander	40	m	w	IN	Yolo	Cottonwood Twp	93	474
BYNAM								
B	15	m	w	CA	Solano	Benicia	90	21
R K	34	m	w	IL	Mendocino	Calpella Twp	74	183
BYNON								
Joseph	42	m	w	WALE	Nevada	Bridgeport Twp	75	124
BYNUM								
B	43	m	w	MO	Lake	Scotts Crk	73	428
B Mrs	52	f	w	KY	Lake	Lower Lake	73	420
Edward E	46	m	w	MO	Yolo	Cache Crk Twp	93	426
Joseph	55	m	w	KY	Yolo	Cottonwood Twp	93	475
S	55	m	w	MO	Lake	Big Valley	73	397
BYONE								
Francis Joseph	27	m	w	IREL	San Francisco	1-Wd San Francisco	79	133
Harvey	21	m	w	NY	San Francisco	1-Wd San Francisco	79	91
Michl	39	m	w	IREL	San Francisco	1-Wd San Francisco	79	116
BYORS								
John	33	m	w	NY	San Francisco	1-Wd San Francisco	79	108
BYRAM								
Peter	20	m	w	IREL	San Francisco	5-Wd San Francisco	81	28
BYRD								
Cathraine	18	f	w	IREL	San Francisco	San Francisco P O	80	541
David	30	m	w	MO	Tulare	Visalia	92	292
F J	53	m	w	VA	Tuolumne	Columbia P O	93	340
Frank	29	m	w	CANA	Yolo	Grafton Twp	93	478
Isaiah	41	m	w	AL	Tulare	Tule Rvr Twp	92	268
J D	37	m	w	MO	Santa Clara	Gilroy Twp	88	84
Jasper	27	m	w	AL	Mendocino	Point Arena Twp	74	215
Jesse A	51	m	w	AL	Tulare	Tule Rvr Twp	92	268
John H	30	m	w	GA	Fresno	Kings Rvr P O	72	214
John W	40	m	w	VA	Placer	Bath P O	76	441
John W	16	m	w	TX	Tulare	White Rvr Twp	92	301
Mary	50	f	w	TN	Tulare	Visalia	92	292
Oliver P	21	m	w	TX	San Bernardino	San Bernardino Twp	78	452
Pleasant	40	m	w	MO	Tulare	Visalia	92	295
William	50	m	w	MO	Siskiyou	Yreka Twp	89	672
BYRDY								
George	33	m	w	OH	Alameda	Eden Twp	68	87
BYRENE								
T M	30	m	w	LA	San Joaquin	3-Wd Stockton	86	218
BYRES								
Heny	35	m	w	ME	Humboldt	Arcata Twp	72	226
Randolf	40	m	w	IL	San Luis Obispo	Santa Rosa Twp	87	329
BYRING								
H M	50	m	w	NORW	San Francisco	1-Wd San Francisco	79	82
BYRINGTON								
Charles	14	m	w	IL	Stanislaus	Empire Twp	92	33
Henry W	35	m	w	NY	San Francisco	5-Wd San Francisco	81	19
BYRN								
Caroline	52	f	w	MD	Sacramento	4-Wd Sacramento	77	361
BYRNA								
Robt	45	m	w	OR	Alameda	Oakland	68	145
BYRNE								
Addie	26	f	w	NY	San Francisco	6-Wd San Francisco	81	78
Alonzo A	18	m	w	WI	San Francisco	San Francisco P O	83	142
Annie	7	f	w	CA	Nevada	Grass Valley Twp	75	155
Annie	43	f	w	IREL	Sacramento	4-Wd Sacramento	77	339
Bernard	60	m	w	IREL	San Francisco	San Francisco P O	83	242
Bridgett	43	f	w	IREL	San Francisco	San Francisco P O	83	41
C F	23	m	w	PA	Nevada	Meadow Lake Twp	75	248
Dennis	38	m	w	IREL	San Francisco	6-Wd San Francisco	81	105
Edward	42	m	w	IREL	Shasta	Shasta P O	89	456
Elizabeth	20	f	w	IREL	San Francisco	San Francisco P O	85	834
Ellen	22	f	w	MS	Santa Clara	2-Wd San Jose	88	324
Felix	48	m	w	IREL	San Francisco	San Francisco P O	83	24
Frank	35	m	w	ENGL	Nevada	Eureka Twp	75	129
Garrat J	42	m	w	IREL	San Francisco	8-Wd San Francisco	82	316
Hannah	25	f	w	IREL	San Francisco	8-Wd San Francisco	82	328
Hannah	21	f	w	IREL	Sacramento	4-Wd Sacramento	77	320

© 2001 by Heritage Quest. All rights reserved.

Name	Age	S	R	B-PL	County	Locale	Series M593 Roll	Pg
Henry	28	m	w	HANO	San Francisco	San Francisco P O	85	854
Henry H	46	m	w	NY	San Francisco	11-Wd San Francisc	84	660
Herbert	40	m	w	NY	San Francisco	8-Wd San Francisco	82	311
Hugh	35	m	w	IREL	San Francisco	11-Wd San Francisc	84	592
James	34	m	w	CANA	Sonoma	Salt Point	91	384
James	33	m	w	IREL	Amador	Sutter Crk P O	69	399
James	27	m	w	NJ	Santa Clara	2-Wd San Jose	88	291
James	22	m	w	IREL	Alameda	Washington Twp	68	296
James	17	m	w	CA	Santa Clara	Santa Clara Twp	88	176
James K	33	m	w	IL	Nevada	Grass Valley Twp	75	146
James M	50	m	w	FRAN	San Francisco	6-Wd San Francisco	81	78
Jane	8	f	w	CA	Nevada	Grass Valley Twp	75	230
Jo	43	m	w	IREL	Alameda	Alameda	68	18
John	40	m	w	IREL	Butte	Ophir Twp	70	92
John	12	m	w	CA	Santa Clara	Santa Clara Twp	88	176
John W	48	m	w	FRAN	San Francisco	8-Wd San Francisco	82	302
Joseph	35	m	w	IREL	Placer	Bath P O	76	448
Kate	40	f	w	IREL	Santa Clara	2-Wd San Jose	88	301
Kate	28	f	w	IREL	Alameda	Oakland	68	218
Kate	14	f	w	CA	Nevada	Grass Valley Twp	75	229
Lizzie	16	f	w	IREL	Santa Barbara	Santa Barbara P O	87	487
M	15	f	w	CA	Alameda	Oakland	68	241
Malachi	38	m	w	IREL	Tuolumne	Chinese Camp P O	93	386
Margaret	34	f	w	IREL	San Francisco	San Francisco P O	83	169
Maria	17	f	w	IREL	San Francisco	2-Wd San Francisco	79	167
Mary	70	f	w	IREL	San Francisco	San Francisco P O	80	390
Mary	32	f	w	IREL	San Joaquin	2-Wd Stockton	86	169
Mary	19	f	w	CA	San Joaquin	Tulare Twp	86	256
Mary	15	f	w	IN	Sacramento	3-Wd Sacramento	77	291
Mathew	30	m	w	IREL	San Bernardino	San Bernardino Twp	78	431
Michael	34	m	w	IREL	San Francisco	6-Wd San Francisco	81	134
Michael	22	m	w	IREL	Contra Costa	Martinez P O	71	388
Michael I	31	m	w	IL	Nevada	Grass Valley Twp	75	153
Michael Sr	71	m	w	IREL	Nevada	Grass Valley Twp	75	158
N B	52	m	w	MO	Alameda	Oakland	68	253
P A	22	m	w	MA	Solano	Vallejo	90	176
Patrick	46	m	w	IREL	Merced	Snelling P O	74	253
Patrick	42	m	w	IREL	Solano	Maine Prairie Twp	90	53
Patrick	38	m	w	IREL	San Francisco	8-Wd San Francisco	82	303
Patrick	35	m	w	IREL	San Francisco	San Francisco P O	80	398
Patrick	26	m	w	IREL	San Francisco	San Francisco P O	83	245
Peter	15	m	w	CA	Santa Clara	Santa Clara Twp	88	176
Philip C	21	m	w	IL	Nevada	Grass Valley Twp	75	153
Robert	69	m	w	IREL	Amador	Drytown P O	69	418
Robt	50	m	w	IREL	Butte	Chico Twp	70	21
Rodger	60	m	w	IREL	Tuolumne	Columbia P O	93	337
Theresa	23	f	w	IREL	San Francisco	8-Wd San Francisco	82	432
Thomas	52	m	w	IREL	San Francisco	San Francisco P O	83	239
Thomas	39	m	w	IREL	San Francisco	San Francisco P O	85	746
Thomas	22	m	w	NY	San Francisco	San Francisco P O	80	531
Thomas B	48	m	w	IREL	Santa Cruz	Santa Cruz	89	407
Thos	47	m	w	NY	San Francisco	11-Wd San Francisc	84	565
Thos	40	m	w	IREL	Butte	Oregon Twp	70	133
Thos	37	m	w	IREL	Sacramento	4-Wd Sacramento	77	335
Thos M	26	m	w	NY	Tuolumne	Columbia P O	93	338
Thos P	48	m	w	CA	Nevada	Nevada Twp	75	302
William	24	m	w	NY	San Francisco	San Francisco P O	80	479
Wm H	28	m	w	NY	Tuolumne	Columbia P O	93	337
BYRNES								
Edwd	62	m	w	IREL	San Francisco	San Francisco P O	83	49
Eliza	19	f	w	SCOT	San Francisco	11-Wd San Francisc	84	688
Henry	28	m	w	IREL	San Francisco	6-Wd San Francisco	81	99
James	40	m	w	IREL	Alameda	Oakland	68	187
James	23	m	w	CANA	Santa Barbara	San Buenaventura P	87	436
John	40	m	w	NY	San Francisco	1-Wd San Francisco	79	27
John	40	m	w	IREL	San Francisco	7-Wd San Francisco	81	241
John	20	m	w	CANA	San Mateo	Woodside P O	87	380
Joseph	35	m	w	ENGL	San Francisco	7-Wd San Francisco	81	241
Kate	20	f	w	NY	San Francisco	7-Wd San Francisco	81	240
M	33	m	w	IREL	San Francisco	7-Wd San Francisco	81	243
M K	50	m	w	IREL	Napa	Napa Twp	75	75
Mary	20	f	w	IREL	San Francisco	5-Wd San Francisco	81	35
Mary A	68	f	w	CT	San Mateo	San Mateo P O	87	371
Michael	36	m	w	IREL	San Mateo	Belmont P O	87	372
Nathan	36	m	w	IREL	San Mateo	Schoolhouse Statio	87	342
Susan	42	f	w	IREL	San Mateo	Redwood Twp	87	369
Thomas	63	m	w	IREL	San Francisco	San Francisco P O	80	401
Thomas	35	m	w	IREL	San Francisco	San Francisco P O	80	381
Thos	23	m	w	IREL	Sacramento	1-Wd Sacramento	77	188
William	40	m	w	MA	San Francisco	San Francisco P O	83	242
BYRNIS								
John	25	m	w	PA	San Francisco	San Francisco P O	85	758
BYRNS								
James	45	m	w	IREL	Nevada	Grass Valley Twp	75	210
James	38	m	w	IREL	Alameda	Brooklyn	68	30
James	36	m	w	IREL	Humboldt	Eureka Twp	72	274
John	45	m	w	MO	Yolo	Grafton Twp	93	494
Katie	15	f	w	LA	Sacramento	Alabama Twp	77	62
Margt	46	f	w	IREL	San Francisco	8-Wd San Francisco	82	318
Mary	82	f	w	IREL	San Francisco	11-Wd San Francisc	84	440
Michael	7	m	w	IREL	Alameda	Eden Twp	68	71
BYROM								
George	46	m	w	SCOT	Santa Clara	Santa Clara Twp	88	166
BYRON								
Ada	32	f	w	NY	San Francisco	8-Wd San Francisco	82	353
Ann	25	f	w	NY	San Francisco	11-Wd San Francisc	84	688
Anna	34	f	w	NY	San Francisco	5-Wd San Francisco	81	8
Anne	83	f	w	IREL	San Francisco	11-Wd San Francisc	84	477
Bartol	53	m	w	IREL	San Francisco	San Francisco P O	83	188
Catherine	67	f	w	IREL	Alameda	Brooklyn Twp	68	51
Cornelius	31	m	w	IREL	Inyo	Independence Twp	73	325
Franklin	24	m	w	IREL	San Mateo	Schoolhouse Statio	87	342
Jennie	18	f	w	CA	San Francisco	1-Wd San Francisco	79	131
John	45	m	w	ENGL	San Francisco	San Francisco P O	83	380
John	41	m	b	PERU	Del Norte	Crescent Twp	71	454
John P	29	m	w	CANA	Mendocino	Navarro & Big Rvr	74	175
Kate	22	f	w	NY	Sacramento	3-Wd Sacramento	77	284
Lawrence	24	m	w	NY	San Francisco	1-Wd San Francisco	79	63
Maria	35	f	w	IREL	San Francisco	8-Wd San Francisco	82	475
Martin J	49	m	w	IREL	Inyo	Cerro Gordo Twp	73	320
Mary	80	f	w	IREL	Solano	Silveyville Twp	90	92
Michael	38	m	w	NY	San Francisco	8-Wd San Francisco	82	368
Petton	40	m	w	NH	Sacramento	Lee Twp	77	159
Philip	64	m	w	IREL	Sacramento	Lee Twp	77	157
Roger	41	m	w	IREL	Sacramento	San Joaquin Twp	77	399
Thomas	43	m	w	ENGL	Contra Costa	Martinez P O	71	414
Thomas	42	m	w	WALE	Tuolumne	Chinese Camp P O	93	376
Thomas	35	m	w	IREL	Monterey	San Antonio Twp	74	324
W P	40	m	w	KY	Trinity	Indian Crk	92	200
William	35	m	w	IREL	Inyo	Independence Twp	73	328
William	34	m	w	WALE	Contra Costa	Martinez P O	71	427
Wm	21	m	w	CANA	San Joaquin	Oneal Twp	86	118
BYRUGHT								
Philip	27	m	w	PERU	Santa Clara	Santa Clara Twp	88	158
BYRUM								
Martin	35	m	w	MO	Stanislaus	Empire Twp	92	31
BYSTLE								
Danl P	49	m	w	PA	Shasta	Shasta P O	89	457
BYTHA								
James	17	m	w	CA	Stanislaus	Empire Twp	92	66
BYTHER								
Arthur	17	m	w	ME	Stanislaus	Branch Twp	92	5
Hilo	42	m	w	ME	Stanislaus	Branch Twp	92	2
BYWATER								
Joseph	42	m	w	ENGL	Klamath	Trinidad Twp	73	389
CA								
Ah	30	m	c	CHIN	Tuolumne	Big Oak Flat P O	93	395
Sin	41	m	c	CHIN	Nevada	Rough & Ready Twp	75	327
Sion	6	m	c	CHIN	San Francisco	11-Wd San Francisc	84	575
CABALLA								
Gonzella	32	m	w	PORT	San Francisco	1-Wd San Francisco	79	118
CABANAS								
Lee	24	m	c	CHIN	San Francisco	3-Wd San Francisco	79	304
CABANES								
Lewis C	38	m	w	MEXI	Los Angeles	San Gabriel Twp	73	597
CABARET								
Edward	53	m	w	FRAN	Amador	Volcano P O	69	377
CABARRETE								
Pat	60	m	w	IREL	San Francisco	2-Wd San Francisco	79	230
CABASENT								
Simion	39	m	w	MEXI	Tuolumne	Sonora P O	93	315
CABB								
Robt	31	m	w	CANA	Santa Clara	Gilroy Twp	88	80
CABBIN								
John	22	m	w	IOFM	San Diego	San Diego	78	505
CABEL								
Hezekiah	50	m	w	NY	San Bernardino	San Bernardino Twp	78	449
CABESENT								
J M	40	m	w	MEXI	Tuolumne	Sonora P O	93	310
CABIEDES								
Manuela	30	f	w	MEXI	San Francisco	San Francisco P O	83	275
CABINA								
Antonio	29	m	w	SWIT	San Francisco	San Francisco P O	80	477
CABINESS								
Emma	13	f	w	CA	Siskiyou	Scott Valley Twp	89	614
Jeremiah	53	m	w	TN	Kern	Havilah P O	73	341
T T	43	m	w	VA	Siskiyou	Scott Valley Twp	89	613
CABLE								
J	63	m	w	CT	Lake	Lower Lake	73	418
John	32	m	w	NY	Los Angeles	Los Angeles	73	526
Saml	62	m	w	PA	Butte	Chico Twp	70	23
Sarah E	39	f	w	IL	El Dorado	Cosumnes Twp	72	13
CABLENTZ								
Gustave	33	m	w	FRAN	San Francisco	San Francisco P O	83	196
CABLES								
Martin	39	m	w	IL	San Francisco	1-Wd San Francisco	79	53
CABMAN								
Augustus	42	m	w	TN	San Diego	Warners Rancho Dis	78	530
CABNER								
Mary	40	f	w	IREL	Sacramento	1-Wd Sacramento	77	187
CABOSE								
Mercele	75	m	w	CHIL	Fresno	Millerton P O	72	156
CABOYA								
Jesus	39	m	w	CA	Santa Clara	San Jose Twp	88	204
CABRAL								
John	18	m	w	PORT	Marin	Sausalito Twp	74	68
CABRARA								
David	17	m	w	MEXI	Santa Clara	2-Wd San Jose	88	310
CABRERA								
Candeline	18	f	w	CA	San Mateo	Schoolhouse Statio	87	338
CABRIANO								
Frank	15	m	w	CA	Santa Clara	San Jose Twp	88	214
CABRIE								
Frank	29	m	w	BAVA	Inyo	Bishop Crk Twp	73	310

© 2001 by Heritage Quest. All rights reserved.

California 1870 Census

Name	Age	S	R	B-PL	County	Locale	Series M593 Roll	Pg
CABRIL								
Casimer	23	m	w	PORT	San Francisco	1-Wd San Francisco	79	134
CABROLL								
Pat	40	m	w	IREL	Humboldt	Eureka Twp	72	277
CACAVITCH								
Peter	10	m	w	AUST	San Joaquin	1-Wd Stockton	86	130
CACCIART								
Frederic	28	m	w	FRAN	San Francisco	San Francisco P O	83	135
CACELLAIS								
Hipolito	42	m	w	MEXI	Monterey	Castroville Twp	74	332
CACEY								
Mary	34	f	w	IREL	Alameda	Washington Twp	68	289
CACHE								
Frank	5	m	w	CA	Sonoma	Bodega Twp	91	252
CACHMAN								
Dennis	45	m	w	IREL	San Francisco	San Francisco P O	83	103
CACHOT								
Maximilian	36	m	w	LA	San Francisco	San Francisco P O	83	170
CACHRAN								
William	40	m	w	IREL	Los Angeles	Los Angeles	73	557
CACIATTOLO								
Giuseppe	45	m	w	ITAL	San Francisco	11-Wd San Francisc	84	594
CACIOPO								
Mariano	48	m	w	ITAL	San Francisco	3-Wd San Francisco	79	318
CACKET								
Luke	34	m	w	IREL	San Francisco	11-Wd San Francisc	84	673
CACODE								
I	22	m	w	SWIT	Alameda	Oakland	68	184
CACONORA								
Hosea	42	m	w	MEXI	Fresno	Millerton P O	72	151
CACORN								
G	40	m	w	ITAL	Alameda	Oakland	68	148
CACY								
Lee	27	m	c	CHIN	San Joaquin	1-Wd Stockton	86	146
Margret	45	f	w	IREL	Trinity	Indian Crk	92	199
CADAEIN								
Patrick	40	m	w	IREL	San Francisco	San Francisco P O	83	351
CADAGE								
Hippolite	39	m	w	FRAN	Santa Clara	2-Wd San Jose	88	312
CADALINS								
Marco	39	m	w	ITAL	San Francisco	1-Wd San Francisco	79	120
CADAM								
Patrick	40	m	w	IREL	San Francisco	San Francisco P O	83	420
CADAMANTON								
Luis	60	m	w	ITAL	Tuolumne	Sonora P O	93	317
CADAMARTEN								
F	27	m	w	ITAL	Amador	Jackson P O	69	334
CADD								
Joseph	33	m	w	ENGL	San Bernardino	San Bernardino Twp	78	426
Thomas	39	m	w	ENGL	San Bernardino	San Bernardino Twp	78	423
CADDEN								
James	28	m	w	IREL	Nevada	Grass Valley Twp	75	200
John	24	m	w	IREL	Nevada	Grass Valley Twp	75	220
Peter	33	m	w	IREL	Nevada	Grass Valley Twp	75	176
CADDIGAN								
Wm	22	m	w	IREL	San Francisco	7-Wd San Francisco	81	252
CADDINGTON								
Geo	52	m	w	NY	Sacramento	1-Wd Sacramento	77	172
CADDOW								
J	31	m	w	IREL	Sierra	Lincoln Twp	89	545
John	30	m	w	IREL	San Francisco	San Francisco P O	83	192
CADDY								
Elizabeth	15	f	w	IREL	San Francisco	San Francisco P O	85	759
Hiram	32	m	w	VA	Nevada	Bloomfield Twp	75	98
Richard	22	m	w	ENGL	Nevada	Grass Valley Twp	75	224
CADEAU								
Frank	54	m	w	FRAN	Los Angeles	Wilmington Twp	73	643
CADEL								
Andrew	30	m	w	PORT	Sacramento	Georgianna Twp	77	129
Peter	57	m	w	BADE	San Francisco	2-Wd San Francisco	79	171
CADELL								
Gustave	42	m	w	PRUS	Calaveras	San Andreas P O	70	211
CADEMORTER								
Frank	24	m	w	ITAL	Trinity	Minersville Pct	92	203
CADEN								
John	31	m	w	IN	San Joaquin	3-Wd Stockton	86	216
M A	59	f	w	SCOT	San Joaquin	3-Wd Stockton	86	216
CADENASO								
C	36	m	w	ITAL	San Francisco	3-Wd San Francisco	79	318
Josph	37	m	w	ITAL	San Francisco	1-Wd San Francisco	79	18
CADENASSO								
Giuseppe	21	m	w	ITAL	San Francisco	11-Wd San Francisc	84	594
CADENESSO								
Joseph A	20	m	w	ITAL	San Francisco	6-Wd San Francisco	81	37
CADENNARTORL								
Steffano	36	m	w	ITAL	Mariposa	Mariposa P O	74	101
CADENZA								
Domingo	40	m	w	PORT	Sacramento	Georgianna Twp	77	124
CADETT								
Masondo	49	m	w	US	San Joaquin	2-Wd Stockton	86	169
CADEY								
Jerry	33	m	w	IREL	Sonoma	Vallejo Twp	91	454
Wm	18	m	w	NY	El Dorado	Lake Valley Twp	72	65
CADEZ								
Joseph	56	m	w	FRAN	San Francisco	San Francisco P O	80	411
Mary	13	f	w	CA	San Francisco	San Francisco P O	80	411
CADGEN								
Thos	44	m	w	IREL	Alameda	Oakland	68	139
CADICE								
Jean	45	m	w	FRAN	Butte	Ophir Twp	70	101
CADIE								
Frank	40	m	w	FRAN	San Francisco	San Francisco P O	80	420
CADIER								
Jean M	34	m	w	FRAN	Calaveras	San Andreas P O	70	174
CADIGAN								
Timothy	40	m	w	IREL	San Francisco	11-Wd San Francisc	84	470
CADIN								
Heny	34	m	w	WALE	San Joaquin	1-Wd Stockton	86	154
John	43	m	w	FRAN	San Joaquin	1-Wd Stockton	86	155
CADISH								
Manuel	48	m	w	PRUS	Calaveras	San Andreas P O	70	210
CADIZ								
James	60	m	w	PA	San Francisco	San Francisco P O	80	362
CADLE								
James	46	m	w	TN	Sonoma	Vallejo Twp	91	452
CADMAN								
Ann	45	f	w	WALE	Sierra	Table Rock Twp	89	572
George	27	m	w	ENGL	Solano	Vacaville Twp	90	122
N	23	m	w	ENGL	Sierra	Alleghany & Forest	89	534
CADMON								
T	50	m	w	ENGL	Sierra	Alleghany & Forest	89	534
CADOC								
Felix	35	m	w	FRAN	Butte	Kimshew Tpw	70	76
CADOGA								
J	42	m	w	IREL	Alameda	Oakland	68	207
CADOGAN								
J J	38	m	w	IREL	Sacramento	3-Wd Sacramento	77	284
Patrick	13	m	w	CA	Santa Barbara	Santa Barbara P O	87	492
William	34	m	w	IREL	Amador	Volcano P O	69	387
CADRINS								
Anna M	40	f	w	ME	San Francisco	8-Wd San Francisco	82	354
CADUC								
Phillip	40	m	w	MD	San Francisco	8-Wd San Francisco	82	322
CADUS								
James	67	m	w	NJ	Tuolumne	Sonora P O	93	319
CADWALADER								
Geo	40	m	w	OH	Sacramento	4-Wd Sacramento	77	336
Ira	27	m	w	OH	Nevada	Eureka Twp	75	138
CADWALDER								
N	40	m	w	OH	Nevada	Bridgeport Twp	75	125
CADWALLADER								
Geo	42	m	w	PA	San Francisco	5-Wd San Francisco	81	24
CADWALLEDER								
H	35	m	w	OH	Sacramento	3-Wd Sacramento	77	300
CADWELL								
Alexander	42	m	w	NY	Sonoma	Analy Twp	91	230
Ambrose	31	m	w	MI	Contra Costa	Martinez P O	71	436
Caleb	55	m	w	VT	Santa Clara	2-Wd San Jose	88	279
Caleb	29	m	w	IL	Alameda	Eden Twp	68	85
Geo W	33	m	w	IL	Butte	Hamilton Twp	70	62
Henry	45	m	w	ENGL	Nevada	Grass Valley Twp	75	203
Jacob A	35	m	w	IL	Yuba	New York Twp	93	639
Mary G	43	f	w	WALE	Shasta	Shasta P O	89	460
Orrin M	61	m	w	VT	Santa Clara	2-Wd San Jose	88	279
Oven N	40	m	w	NY	Santa Barbara	Santa Barbara P O	87	485
Philemon	57	m	w	VT	Santa Clara	2-Wd San Jose	88	279
William	25	m	w	ENGL	Nevada	Grass Valley Twp	75	147
CADY								
A	42	m	w	MA	San Joaquin	Oneal Twp	86	114
A	28	m	w	AR	San Joaquin	Elliott Twp	86	73
Alexander	36	m	w	CT	Nevada	Bloomfield Twp	75	99
Barney	21	m	w	NY	Tehama	Paskenta Twp	92	163
Chas	28	m	w	NY	San Francisco	8-Wd San Francisco	82	376
Cyrus	57	m	w	RI	Sacramento	4-Wd Sacramento	77	343
Cyrus C	47	m	w	IL	Sacramento	2-Wd Sacramento	77	240
Delia	26	f	w	IREL	Stanislaus	Emory Twp	92	24
E M	39	m	w	OH	Sierra	Forest	89	537
Edward	29	m	w	LA	San Francisco	7-Wd San Francisco	81	220
Elizabeth	25	f	w	VT	San Francisco	8-Wd San Francisco	82	467
F	26	m	w	OH	San Joaquin	Elliott Twp	86	77
George B	43	m	w	VT	San Francisco	San Francisco P O	83	211
Horatio	48	m	m	LA	Sacramento	2-Wd Sacramento	77	212
J B	23	m	w	IREL	San Francisco	San Francisco P O	83	273
J S	44	m	w	MA	Tuolumne	Sonora P O	93	307
John	63	m	w	SCOT	San Francisco	San Francisco P O	83	418
John	40	m	w	TN	Sonoma	Santa Rosa	91	421
John	30	m	w	IREL	San Joaquin	Oneal Twp	86	114
John	30	m	w	ENGL	Nevada	Eureka Twp	75	138
Josephine	40	f	w	CANA	San Francisco	5-Wd San Francisco	81	4
Lorenzo	45	m	w	VA	San Francisco	11-Wd San Francisc	84	442
Martin	23	m	w	CT	Napa	Yountville Twp	75	89
Mary	18	f	w	IREL	San Francisco	2-Wd San Francisco	79	234
Mary	14	f	w	CA	San Francisco	San Francisco P O	85	822
Mary S	40	f	w	IREL	Solano	Benicia	90	16
P H	39	m	w	MO	San Joaquin	Douglas Twp	86	36
Patrick	39	m	w	IREL	Fresno	Millerton P O	72	154
Robert	23	m	w	IREL	San Francisco	San Francisco P O	80	531
Stowel	46	m	w	NY	San Joaquin	Castoria Twp	86	3
Thos	35	m	w	IREL	Solano	Vallejo	90	154
William	22	m	w	MA	San Francisco	7-Wd San Francisco	81	184
Wm	20	m	w	IL	San Joaquin	Castoria Twp	86	7
Wm J	40	m	w	RI	San Francisco	San Francisco P O	83	23

© 2001 by Heritage Quest. All rights reserved.

Name	Age	S	R	B-PL	County	Locale	Series M593 Roll	Pg
CAE								
Land	56	m	c	CHIN	Nevada	Nevada Twp	75	312
CAEL								
Abby	35	f	w	VT	Sacramento	2-Wd Sacramento	77	235
CAELLOT								
August	49	m	w	FRAN	Plumas	Goodwin Twp	77	1
CAEN								
Ferdinand	38	m	w	FRAN	Calaveras	San Andreas P O	70	190
CAERAN								
Daniels	35	m	w	IREL	Sonoma	Vallejo Twp	91	459
CAERTOO								
Francis	39	m	w	FRAN	San Joaquin	3-Wd Stockton	86	225
CAES								
Edwd	19	m	w	NY	San Francisco	1-Wd San Francisco	79	59
CAESON								
Wm	40	m	w	CANA	Humboldt	Eureka Twp	72	267
CAFERATER								
Antonio	35	m	w	ITAL	San Francisco	2-Wd San Francisco	79	223
CAFERPRANN								
Francis	66	f	w	ITAL	San Francisco	2-Wd San Francisco	79	164
CAFFARETTO								
Peter	43	m	w	ITAL	Butte	Wyandotte Twp	70	149
CAFFARY								
M E	35	f	w	IREL	San Francisco	San Francisco P O	85	789
CAFFEE								
John A	38	m	w	KY	Napa	Napa Twp	75	64
CAFFEL								
George	40	m	w	ENGL	San Francisco	1-Wd San Francisco	79	22
CAFFERT								
Jane	30	f	w	IREL	San Francisco	5-Wd San Francisco	81	29
Mary	27	f	w	IREL	San Francisco	5-Wd San Francisco	81	29
CAFFERTY								
Edward	46	m	w	IREL	Placer	Rocklin P O	76	462
Frank	26	m	w	IREL	Marin	Tomales Twp	74	84
Neil	35	m	w	IREL	San Francisco	2-Wd San Francisco	79	213
Patrick	28	m	w	IREL	Nevada	Grass Valley Twp	75	226
Patrick W	40	m	w	IREL	Sacramento	2-Wd Sacramento	77	237
Paul	50	m	w	IREL	Placer	Rocklin P O	76	462
CAFFERY								
Patrick	63	m	w	IREL	Calaveras	San Andreas P O	70	182
Rose	25	f	w	IREL	Napa	Napa Twp	75	75
Rose	25	f	w	IREL	Napa	Napa	75	27
CAFFEY								
Esthur	43	f	w	IREL	San Francisco	2-Wd San Francisco	79	199
Phillip	16	m	w	CT	San Francisco	7-Wd San Francisco	81	194
CAFFIN								
Hasekiel	27	m	w	MA	Sonoma	Petaluma Twp	91	313
Stephen	37	m	w	IREL	Nevada	Washington Twp	75	343
CAFFMAN								
Benj S	36	m	w	NY	San Francisco	8-Wd San Francisco	82	380
CAFFRAY								
Edd	30	m	w	IREL	San Francisco	5-Wd San Francisco	81	32
George	46	m	w	CANA	Sacramento	2-Wd Sacramento	77	222
Michl	28	m	w	IREL	San Francisco	5-Wd San Francisco	81	28
CAFFREDS								
Frank	30	m	w	IREL	San Francisco	5-Wd San Francisco	81	17
CAFFREY								
Alfred	33	m	w	IREL	Nevada	Meadow Lake Twp	75	251
Edward	29	m	w	IREL	San Francisco	11-Wd San Francisc	84	575
James	33	m	w	IREL	San Francisco	2-Wd San Francisco	79	242
Thomas	25	m	w	IREL	Klamath	Camp Gaston	73	372
CAFRAY								
John	30	m	w	IREL	San Francisco	1-Wd San Francisco	79	81
CAGALA								
John	20	m	w	ITAL	Calaveras	Copperopolis P O	70	226
CAGAN								
Mary E	9	f	w	CA	San Francisco	1-Wd San Francisco	79	135
CAGE								
Edward	44	m	w	MO	Los Angeles	El Monte Twp	73	454
Julian	25	m	i	CA	Napa	Napa Twp	75	65
CAGGA								
Louis	24	m	w	ITAL	Amador	Jackson P O	69	335
CAGHLIN								
J	24	m	w	IREL	Lake	Morgan Valley	73	425
CAGIN								
Thomas	44	m	w	CANA	Solano	Montezuma Twp	90	66
CAGLE								
Henry	52	m	w	KY	Klamath	Klamath Twp	73	370
Isen	38	m	w	GA	Stanislaus	Branch Twp	92	4
Wm	64	m	w	VA	Santa Barbara	San Buenaventura P	87	421
CAGNEY								
Martin	50	m	w	IREL	San Francisco	8-Wd San Francisco	82	418
CAGON								
James	42	m	w	IREL	Nevada	Nevada Twp	75	313
CAGUNCHAN								
Erassus	37	m	w	DENM	Nevada	Eureka Twp	75	131
CAGWIN								
Chas N	40	m	w	NY	Sonoma	Washington Twp	91	468
Hamden A	59	m	w	NY	Alpine	Markleeville P O	69	311
Hamden E	19	m	w	IL	Alpine	Markleeville P O	69	311
CAH								
Ah	24	m	c	CHIN	Contra Costa	Martinez P O	71	441
CAHALAN								
John	52	m	w	IREL	San Francisco	11-Wd San Francisc	84	634
John	32	m	w	IREL	San Francisco	11-Wd San Francisc	84	497
Michael	80	m	w	IREL	Santa Clara	San Jose Twp	88	208
CAHALIN								
John	36	m	w	IREL	San Francisco	San Francisco P O	83	181
CAHALL								
James	38	m	w	IREL	San Francisco	San Francisco P O	85	849
CAHALLA								
Joseph	41	m	w	CHIL	Amador	Fiddletown P O	69	434
M	40	m	w	MEXI	Amador	Fiddletown P O	69	433
CAHARDA								
N	45	f	w	CA	Calaveras	Copperopolis P O	70	255
CAHAVI								
Mary	68	f	w	MEXI	Tuolumne	Columbia P O	93	356
CAHELL								
William	42	m	w	IREL	Alameda	Eden Twp	68	88
CAHEN								
Catharine	50	f	w	IREL	San Francisco	San Francisco P O	85	858
David	23	m	w	FRAN	Contra Costa	Martinez P O	71	390
Kate	29	f	w	IREL	San Francisco	San Francisco P O	83	320
CAHER								
G F	36	m	w	AL	San Joaquin	Douglas Twp	86	39
CAHEY								
Roland	21	m	w	CANA	Marin	Tomales Twp	74	79
CAHHILL								
John	29	m	w	MO	San Luis Obispo	Salinas Twp	87	290
CAHIL								
Patrick	43	m	w	IREL	San Francisco	6-Wd San Francisco	81	141
CAHILL								
A	41	m	w	IREL	San Francisco	San Francisco P O	83	36
Alice	45	f	w	IREL	San Francisco	7-Wd San Francisco	81	286
Anthony	40	m	w	IREL	San Mateo	Half Moon Bay P O	87	389
Bernard	35	m	w	IREL	Nevada	Little York Twp	75	241
Catharine	48	f	w	IREL	San Francisco	11-Wd San Francisc	84	475
Chas	35	m	w	NJ	San Francisco	11-Wd San Francisc	84	642
Dennis	34	m	w	IREL	Tuolumne	Columbia P O	93	350
E	50	m	w	OH	San Joaquin	Elliott Twp	86	77
E Mrs	30	f	w	IREL	Napa	Napa	75	21
Edwd	38	m	w	IREL	San Francisco	1-Wd San Francisco	79	91
Edwd	25	m	w	IREL	San Francisco	5-Wd San Francisco	81	35
Elisabeth	70	f	w	IREL	Alameda	Eden Twp	68	70
Honora	45	f	w	IREL	San Francisco	San Francisco P O	83	306
James	50	m	w	IREL	San Francisco	San Francisco P O	85	803
James	42	m	w	IREL	San Francisco	1-Wd San Francisco	79	24
James	35	m	w	IREL	San Francisco	San Francisco P O	83	250
James	31	m	w	CANA	Santa Clara	2-Wd San Jose	88	316
James H	25	m	w	MA	San Francisco	San Francisco P O	85	815
James T	42	m	w	IREL	San Francisco	8-Wd San Francisco	82	477
Jas	40	m	w	IREL	Butte	Chico Twp	70	15
John	45	m	w	IREL	San Francisco	2-Wd San Francisco	79	265
John	40	m	w	IREL	Contra Costa	San Pablo Twp	71	362
John	35	m	w	IREL	Alameda	Eden Twp	68	70
John	34	m	w	IREL	Placer	Rocklin Twp	76	467
John	34	m	w	IREL	San Francisco	1-Wd San Francisco	79	125
John	30	m	w	IREL	San Mateo	Menlo Park P O	87	377
Johnson	35	m	w	NJ	San Francisco	11-Wd San Francisc	84	585
Lewis	29	m	w	IREL	San Francisco	San Francisco P O	83	312
Lissie	3	f	w	CA	San Francisco	11-Wd San Francisc	84	516
M J	23	m	w	MA	Nevada	Nevada Twp	75	278
Martin	47	m	w	IREL	San Joaquin	3-Wd Stockton	86	234
Martin	30	m	w	IREL	Napa	Napa Twp	75	31
Mary	40	f	w	MO	Santa Clara	San Jose Twp	88	183
Mary	35	f	w	IREL	San Joaquin	2-Wd Stockton	86	168
Michael	24	m	w	IREL	San Francisco	San Francisco P O	83	350
Pat	35	m	w	IREL	San Francisco	5-Wd San Francisco	81	28
Pat	16	m	w	CA	San Francisco	11-Wd San Francisc	84	592
Patrick	55	m	w	IREL	Santa Clara	2-Wd San Jose	88	305
Patrick	46	m	w	IREL	Santa Clara	2-Wd San Jose	88	334
Patrick	45	m	w	IREL	San Francisco	11-Wd San Francisc	84	474
Patrick	45	m	w	IREL	Placer	Auburn P O	76	381
Patrick	38	m	w	IREL	San Francisco	San Francisco P O	83	220
Patrick	38	m	w	IREL	Placer	Bath P O	76	432
Patrick	35	m	w	IREL	Monterey	Castroville Twp	74	339
Patrick H	30	m	w	IREL	Sacramento	2-Wd Sacramento	77	239
Sarah	14	f	w	CA	Solano	Benicia	90	16
Thomas	28	m	w	IREL	Santa Clara	San Jose Twp	88	222
Wm	39	m	w	CANA	San Francisco	7-Wd San Francisco	81	243
CAHL								
Robert	35	m	w	LA	San Francisco	3-Wd San Francisco	79	319
CAHLIA								
Pat	29	m	w	IREL	Alameda	Murray Twp	68	126
CAHN								
A	49	m	w	FRAN	San Francisco	San Francisco P O	85	789
Armund	32	m	w	FRAN	San Francisco	11-Wd San Francisc	84	424
David	26	m	w	FRAN	San Francisco	San Francisco P O	85	791
David	26	m	w	FRAN	San Francisco	6-Wd San Francisco	81	139
Herman	37	m	w	BADE	San Francisco	8-Wd San Francisco	82	417
Hyman	33	m	w	FRAN	San Francisco	11-Wd San Francisc	84	456
J	42	m	w	FRAN	San Francisco	San Francisco P O	85	789
Jerome	66	m	w	FRAN	San Francisco	11-Wd San Francisc	84	424
L	40	m	w	FRAN	San Francisco	San Francisco P O	85	791
Lina	21	f	w	FRNK	San Francisco	2-Wd San Francisco	79	224
Morris	30	m	w	SAXO	San Francisco	6-Wd San Francisco	81	112
Nathan	31	m	w	FRAN	Los Angeles	Los Angeles	73	565
Saylvan	34	m	w	FRAN	San Francisco	2-Wd San Francisco	79	246
CAHOON								
Benjamin	70	m	w	NY	Santa Cruz	Soquel Twp	89	446
Edwin B	40	m	w	NY	Santa Cruz	Soquel Twp	89	446
Frederick	24	m	w	NY	San Francisco	8-Wd San Francisco	82	385
Fredk	38	m	w	ENGL	San Francisco	5-Wd San Francisco	81	11

© 2001 by Heritage Quest. All rights reserved.

Name	Age	S	R	B-PL	County	Locale	Roll	Pg
						Series M593		
George	33	m	w	IN	Kern	Linns Valley P O	73	343
Henry D	50	m	w	OH	Los Angeles	Wilmington Twp	73	645
Wilbur	24	m	w	OH	Santa Cruz	Santa Cruz Twp	89	399
Wm	20	m	w	NY	Tehama	Cottonwood Twp	92	161
CAHOUN								
H C	39	m	w	NY	Tuolumne	Columbia P O	93	346
CAHOW								
Abijah	24	m	w	IA	Shasta	Stillwater P O	89	479
Marietta	13	f	w	CA	Shasta	Buckeye P O	89	482
CAHU								
Rachel	24	f	w	GERM	Los Angeles	Los Angeles	73	539
CAIGIE								
John C	28	m	w	CANA	Inyo	Bishop Crk Twp	73	314
CAILLAND								
Eugene	46	m	w	FRAN	Kern	Linns Valley P O	73	343
CAILLOCE								
Jean V	41	m	w	FRAN	Santa Cruz	Santa Cruz Twp	89	392
CAILLOUX								
J F	48	m	w	FRAN	Sierra	Downieville Twp	89	518
CAIN								
Ah	40	m	c	CHIN	Sonoma	Sonoma Twp	91	435
Ah	24	m	c	CHIN	Stanislaus	Emory Twp	92	26
Andrew	36	m	w	PA	Siskiyou	Butte Twp	89	588
Anna	25	f	w	IREL	San Francisco	5-Wd San Francisco	81	35
Aquilla	31	m	w	WI	San Joaquin	Elkhorn Twp	86	58
Bernard	53	m	w	IREL	Alameda	Washington Twp	68	295
Catherine	31	f	w	IREL	Sonoma	Bodega Twp	91	260
David F	33	m	w	MA	Mendocino	Point Arena Twp	74	208
Dennis	30	m	w	IREL	Colusa	Spring Valley Twp	71	342
Dennis	17	m	w	NY	Calaveras	San Andreas P O	70	170
Edward	28	m	w	MA	San Francisco	7-Wd San Francisco	81	220
Elisha	35	m	w	MO	Mendocino	Calpella Twp	74	183
F A	48	f	w	NY	Calaveras	Copperopolis P O	70	238
Francis M	50	m	w	GA	Tuolumne	Sonora P O	93	319
Isaac W	46	m	w	MO	Colusa	Colusa	71	298
J M	44	m	w	ENGL	Sierra	Gibson Twp	89	544
James	44	m	w	NY	San Francisco	2-Wd San Francisco	79	176
James	25	m	w	OH	Lassen	Susanville Twp	73	442
James A	47	m	w	KY	Tulare	Visalia	92	299
James A	30	m	w	NY	Sonoma	Bodega Twp	91	260
James F	22	m	w	IREL	Sonoma	Petaluma Twp	91	329
Johana	35	f	w	IREL	San Joaquin	2-Wd Stockton	86	165
John	35	m	w	IREL	Kern	Tehachapi P O	73	355
John	34	m	w	IREL	San Francisco	1-Wd San Francisco	79	62
John	30	m	w	IA	San Joaquin	Douglas Twp	86	45
John	22	m	w	MA	San Francisco	7-Wd San Francisco	81	186
Jos	35	m	w	IREL	Sacramento	1-Wd Sacramento	77	181
Kate	27	f	w	MO	San Joaquin	Elkhorn Twp	86	64
Martha	59	f	w	KY	San Joaquin	Elkhorn Twp	86	54
Martin	45	m	w	IREL	San Joaquin	1-Wd Stockton	86	131
Mary E	31	f	w	FRAN	San Francisco	3-Wd San Francisco	79	295
Michael	36	m	w	IREL	Kern	Havilah P O	73	341
Michael	34	m	w	IREL	San Francisco	2-Wd San Francisco	79	232
Miles B	35	m	w	NY	Alameda	Brooklyn Twp	68	49
N G	21	m	w	AR	Mendocino	Sanel Twp	74	230
Nancy	30	f	w	IREL	San Francisco	5-Wd San Francisco	81	20
P J	38	m	w	IREL	San Joaquin	1-Wd Stockton	86	136
Patrick	36	m	w	IREL	San Francisco	San Francisco P O	85	871
Patrick	32	m	w	IREL	San Francisco	1-Wd San Francisco	79	63
R K	57	m	w	MD	San Francisco	San Francisco P O	85	825
Robert	27	m	w	SWED	San Francisco	7-Wd San Francisco	81	220
Thomas	24	m	w	IREL	Placer	Auburn P O	76	366
W M	34	m	w	MO	Lassen	Janesville Twp	73	432
William	27	m	w	IREL	Colusa	Colusa	71	298
CAINA								
John	41	m	w	IOFM	San Joaquin	Liberty Twp	86	92
CAINAN								
Adolf	16	m	w	FRAN	San Francisco	11-Wd San Francisc	84	592
Henry	19	m	w	IREL	Marin	San Rafael Twp	74	25
Wm	25	m	w	IREL	San Francisco	2-Wd San Francisco	79	139
CAINE								
Caladonia	9	f	b	CA	Santa Clara	1-Wd San Jose	88	242
Charles	25	m	w	IREL	Santa Clara	San Jose Twp	88	194
Jerry	74	m	b	TN	San Joaquin	1-Wd Stockton	86	140
Lizzie	23	f	w	IREL	Alameda	Oakland	68	209
Mary	15	f	w	CA	Alameda	Oakland	68	161
Peter	50	m	w	NY	San Joaquin	Oneal Twp	86	109
Richard	21	m	w	CANA	Shasta	Millville P O	89	486
CAINES								
John	41	m	w	KY	Santa Clara	Gilroy Twp	88	67
Thomas	35	m	w	IREL	Amador	Drytown P O	69	422
CAING								
Ah	20	m	c	CHIN	Nevada	Bridgeport Twp	75	115
CAINNAS								
James	35	m	w	MS	Stanislaus	Empire Twp	92	29
CAINOUX								
Peter	36	m	w	FRAN	Santa Cruz	Santa Cruz Twp	89	393
CAINS								
David	33	m	w	NY	Monterey	Alisal Twp	74	301
CAIO								
Jane	9	f	b	HI	Tuolumne	Big Oak Flat P O	93	399
Joseph	40	m	b	HI	Tuolumne	Big Oak Flat P O	93	400
CAIRE								
Jules	44	m	w	FRAN	San Francisco	6-Wd San Francisco	81	91
Justinian	42	m	w	FRAN	San Francisco	1-Wd San Francisco	79	24
CAIRNCROSS								
Jas	47	m	w	SCOT	San Francisco	3-Wd San Francisco	79	314

Name	Age	S	R	B-PL	County	Locale	Roll	Pg
						Series M593		
CAIRNES								
John	66	m	w	SCOT	San Francisco	6-Wd San Francisco	81	140
CAIRNS								
Francis	30	m	w	SCOT	Sacramento	2-Wd Sacramento	77	211
John	35	m	w	SCOT	San Francisco	1-Wd San Francisco	79	63
CAIRO								
Maurice	33	m	w	POLA	San Francisco	1-Wd San Francisco	79	114
CAISH								
Jos	44	m	w	FRAN	Sierra	Sears Twp	89	556
CAITANO								
Moreno	54	m	w	MEXI	Santa Barbara	San Buenaventura P	87	429
CAITY								
Paul	38	m	w	IREL	San Francisco	2-Wd San Francisco	79	200
CAJNEDO								
Monedo	41	m	w	CA	Sacramento	2-Wd Sacramento	77	215
CAKER								
Charles	45	m	w	PRUS	Sacramento	Center Twp	77	83
Gould C	26	m	w	ME	Placer	Bath P O	76	453
CAKINS								
Josiah A	39	m	w	NY	Humboldt	Pacific Twp	72	295
CALABAN								
James	40	m	w	IREL	San Francisco	San Francisco P O	85	739
CALAGHAN								
Patrick	40	m	w	IREL	San Francisco	7-Wd San Francisco	81	197
CALAGORI								
Peter	26	m	w	ITAL	Amador	Jackson P O	69	329
CALAHAN								
Bridget	25	f	w	ENGL	Klamath	Trinidad Twp	73	391
Con	41	m	w	IREL	Klamath	Trinidad Twp	73	391
Daniel	46	m	w	MO	Stanislaus	Buena Vista Twp	92	12
David	41	m	w	IREL	Sutter	Vernon Twp	92	133
Edward	58	m	w	MO	Stanislaus	Buena Vista Twp	92	12
Ellen	48	f	w	IREL	Santa Clara	Santa Clara Twp	88	164
F	45	m	w	IREL	Lake	Morgan Valley	73	425
Geo	29	m	w	NY	Alameda	Murray Twp	68	108
Hughey	40	m	w	IREL	Alameda	Washington Twp	68	269
John	32	m	w	IREL	Colusa	Monroe Twp	71	320
John	27	m	w	IREL	San Bernardino	San Bernardino Twp	78	417
Julia	24	f	w	IREL	San Joaquin	2-Wd Stockton	86	164
Kate	25	f	i	CA	Colusa	Monroe Twp	71	317
Mary	42	f	w	IREL	Alameda	Oakland	68	136
Mike	32	m	w	IL	Trinity	Junction City Pct	92	205
Stephen	52	m	w	KY	Stanislaus	Empire Twp	92	56
Thomas	30	m	w	IREL	Colusa	Monroe Twp	71	313
Thomas	29	m	w	MA	Alameda	Oakland	68	203
Thomas M	40	m	w	MO	Colusa	Monroe Twp	71	317
Timothy	25	m	w	IREL	Marin	San Rafael Twp	74	30
W	27	m	w	IL	Lake	Lower Lake	73	419
CALAHAYGA								
Jose	38	m	w	CHIL	San Francisco	San Francisco P O	80	476
CALAMANDA								
Josp	36	m	w	ITAL	Calaveras	Copperopolis P O	70	249
CALAMARA								
A	28	m	w	ITAL	Calaveras	Copperopolis P O	70	226
J	18	m	w	ITAL	Calaveras	Copperopolis P O	70	226
P	19	m	w	ITAL	Calaveras	Copperopolis P O	70	226
CALAMERA								
Augustine	26	m	w	ITAL	Calaveras	Copperopolis P O	70	241
CALAN								
Jon	33	m	w	IREL	Solano	Vallejo	90	195
CALANAN								
H	61	m	w	IREL	Nevada	Bridgeport Twp	75	118
CALANCIE								
P	45	m	w	AUST	Alameda	Murray Twp	68	127
CALANI								
Martin	51	m	w	ITAL	Tuolumne	Chinese Camp P O	93	384
CALANNES								
Eugene	40	m	w	FRAN	Sonoma	Vallejo Twp	91	458
CALARON								
Petro	52	f	w	MEXI	Fresno	Millerton P O	72	154
CALAS								
Antone	38	m	w	AUST	Sierra	Gibson Twp	89	540
CALATUNO								
Miguel	40	m	w	SPAI	Santa Barbara	Santa Barbara P O	87	500
CALAVAN								
William	26	m	w	ENGL	Stanislaus	Empire Twp	92	46
CALAVOTA								
Sylvesta	67	f	w	AUST	San Francisco	7-Wd San Francisco	81	260
CALAWAY								
George	56	m	w	GA	Yolo	Merritt Twp	93	506
Wm	36	m	w	MO	San Luis Obispo	Morro Twp	87	287
CALAYOS								
Emanuel	40	m	w	CHIL	Fresno	Millerton P O	72	159
CALBERNOT								
R S	14	m	w	CA	Solano	Benicia	90	21
CALBERT								
John	38	m	w	ENGL	San Francisco	6-Wd San Francisco	81	95
Joseph	27	m	w	ENGL	Santa Clara	Fremont Twp	88	47
Moargret	14	f	w	CA	Trinity	Weaverville Pct	92	223
CALBICK								
John A	32	m	w	CANA	Nevada	Nevada Twp	75	295
CALBORN								
Mary	31	f	w	MI	Siskiyou	Yreka	89	663
CALBY								
A A	30	m	w	ME	Tuolumne	Columbia P O	93	358
E M	35	f	w	VT	Sierra	Sierra Twp	89	567

© 2001 by Heritage Quest. All rights reserved.

Series M593

Name	Age	S	R	B-PL	County	Locale	Roll	Pg
CALCIDA								
Juan	33	m	w	MEXI	Kern	Bakersfield P O	73	361
CALCLASER								
Benjamin	35	m	w	IN	Santa Clara	Redwood Twp	88	118
CALCOAT								
Allen K	40	m	w	MS	Tulare	Visalia Twp	92	283
CALCONCO								
D	28	m	w	WI	Yuba	Marysville	93	616
CALD								
James	27	m	w	ME	San Joaquin	Liberty Twp	86	83
CALDARO								
John	24	m	w	ITAL	Santa Cruz	Santa Cruz	89	429
CALDARON								
Valentine	40	m	w	CA	Santa Barbara	Santa Barbara P O	87	468
CALDEN								
George W	23	m	w	ME	Colusa	Colusa	71	293
James	32	m	w	ME	Colusa	Monroe Twp	71	324
Jas	26	m	w	IREL	Solano	Benicia	90	18
Michael	40	m	w	IREL	San Francisco	11-Wd San Francisc	84	584
CALDER								
Alexander	67	m	w	SCOT	Sonoma	Analy Twp	91	235
Alexander	32	m	w	SCOT	San Francisco	San Francisco P O	83	342
Charles	35	m	w	MA	San Francisco	6-Wd San Francisco	81	80
George	30	m	w	OH	Santa Barbara	Santa Barbara P O	87	484
Hugh	25	m	w	CANA	Sonoma	Salt Point	91	386
Jas	40	m	w	SCOT	Tehama	Paskenta Twp	92	165
Peter	30	m	w	SCOT	Yolo	Buckeye Twp	93	407
CALDERON								
Abraham	32	m	w	MEXI	Los Angeles	Santa Ana Twp	73	611
Manuel	30	m	w	MEXI	Kern	Tehachapi P O	73	354
Thos	60	m	w	CHIL	Shasta	Horsetown P O	89	502
CALDERWOOD								
D	54	m	w	SCOT	San Francisco	3-Wd San Francisco	79	310
Geo	35	m	w	ME	El Dorado	Greenwood Twp	72	51
J F	33	m	w	ME	Sacramento	4-Wd Sacramento	77	345
J F	19	m	w	OH	Nevada	Meadow Lake Twp	75	249
M	45	m	w	VT	Alameda	Oakland	68	187
M	40	m	w	IREL	Napa	Napa	75	4
Martin H	35	m	w	ME	Placer	Auburn P O	76	381
S	20	m	w	MA	Sacramento	1-Wd Sacramento	77	200
W J	36	m	w	ME	Placer	Dutch Flat P O	76	405
CALDESON								
Santas	60	m	m	CHIL	Placer	Bath P O	76	432
Verginius	35	m	m	CHIL	Placer	Bath P O	76	432
CALDINA								
Francis	51	m	w	PORT	Alameda	Washington Twp	68	272
CALDON								
Albern	48	m	w	NH	Colusa	Monroe Twp	71	311
Daniel	27	m	w	IREL	Colusa	Colusa Twp	71	275
Danl	75	m	w	IREL	San Francisco	7-Wd San Francisco	81	239
CALDRON								
Ch	22	m	w	MEXI	Merced	Snelling P O	74	262
CALDWEL								
F M	39	m	w	TN	Sonoma	Santa Rosa	91	411
Mort A	27	m	w	MS	Sonoma	Santa Rosa	91	409
CALDWELL								
Adam	54	m	w	IREL	El Dorado	Diamond Springs Tw	72	26
Albert	42	m	w	NY	Alameda	Brooklyn	68	31
Albert	16	m	w	CA	San Francisco	11-Wd San Francisc	84	587
Andrew	54	m	w	PA	Colusa	Monroe Twp	71	316
Andrew	45	m	w	SC	Stanislaus	Empire Twp	92	28
Andrew	45	m	w	IREL	Placer	Pino Twp	76	471
Andrew	38	m	w	PA	Siskiyou	Butte Twp	89	588
Anna	62	f	w	IREL	Santa Cruz	Pajaro Twp	89	356
Arthur	47	m	w	VA	Santa Clara	Redwood Twp	88	117
Augustus B	50	m	w	KY	Santa Clara	Santa Clara Twp	88	142
C M	29	m	w	PA	San Francisco	San Francisco P O	83	12
Charles	37	m	w	PA	San Francisco	San Francisco P O	83	232
Charles T	34	m	w	OH	Santa Clara	2-Wd San Jose	88	285
Crawford	52	m	w	OH	El Dorado	Diamond Springs Tw	72	29
David	52	m	w	VA	Santa Cruz	Santa Cruz Twp	89	398
David	29	m	w	CANA	San Francisco	11-Wd San Francisc	84	659
David A	36	m	w	OH	Contra Costa	Martinez P O	71	392
E J	34	m	w	IREL	Solano	Benicia	90	9
Edward	22	m	w	IN	Santa Cruz	Santa Cruz Twp	89	401
Edwin	45	m	w	NY	Alameda	Brooklyn	68	31
Eugene	24	m	w	MA	San Francisco	11-Wd San Francisc	84	548
Eugene	23	m	w	MA	San Francisco	11-Wd San Francisc	84	548
F	18	f	w	CA	Sacramento	3-Wd Sacramento	77	315
Frank	20	m	i	CA	Colusa	Monroe Twp	71	316
Henry	24	m	w	ENGL	San Francisco	11-Wd San Francisc	84	548
Hugh	59	m	w	OH	Sonoma	Cloverdale Twp	91	273
J V	39	m	w	AL	Napa	Yountville Twp	75	85
James	43	m	w	SCOT	Mariposa	Mariposa P O	74	104
James	42	m	w	IREL	San Francisco	San Francisco P O	80	366
James	15	m	w	PA	San Francisco	11-Wd San Francisc	84	587
James P	24	m	w	OH	San Bernardino	San Bernardino Twp	78	415
Jno	31	m	w	CT	Sierra	Table Rock Twp	89	572
John	44	m	w	CANA	Nevada	Nevada Twp	75	272
John	40	m	w	CANA	San Francisco	San Francisco P O	83	167
John	40	m	w	OH	Napa	Napa	75	14
John	40	m	w	KY	Tuolumne	Sonora P O	93	325
John	29	m	w	IREL	San Francisco	7-Wd San Francisco	81	262
John E	59	m	w	NJ	Alameda	Washington Twp	68	280
John I	40	m	w	OH	Nevada	Nevada Twp	75	272
Jones P	29	m	w	TN	Los Angeles	El Monte Twp	73	452
Joseph	64	m	w	KY	Kern	Kernville P O	73	368
Joseph	25	m	w	ME	San Francisco	11-Wd San Francisc	84	574
Lucy	50	f	w	LA	Stanislaus	Empire Twp	92	41
M A	28	m	w	MS	Sonoma	Santa Rosa	91	401
Marcus L	25	m	w	MO	Santa Cruz	Soquel Twp	89	441
Marie	56	f	m	KY	San Francisco	San Francisco P O	80	406
Martha	18	f	w	IN	Santa Cruz	Santa Cruz	89	412
Mathew	28	m	w	NY	San Francisco	11-Wd San Francisc	84	548
Maxwell	18	m	w	NY	San Francisco	7-Wd San Francisco	81	276
Robert	34	m	w	PA	San Francisco	11-Wd San Francisc	84	502
Samuel	48	m	w	NH	Placer	Lincoln P O	76	492
Samuel	32	m	w	OH	Nevada	Eureka Twp	75	126
Samuel	26	m	w	MO	Sonoma	Cloverdale Twp	91	273
Silas	30	m	w	MO	San Bernardino	Chino Twp	78	410
Susan	15	m	w	CA	Siskiyou	Callahan P O	89	628
T C	38	f	w	NY	Santa Clara	Gilroy Twp	88	81
Tarlton	56	m	w	VA	Santa Barbara	San Buenaventura P	87	445
Theon K	27	m	w	NJ	Placer	Newcastle Twp	76	476
Thomas	27	m	w	CANA	Santa Clara	2-Wd San Jose	88	283
Tilman	33	m	w	MO	Los Angeles	San Gabriel Twp	73	597
William	38	m	w	IREL	Sonoma	Cloverdale Twp	91	269
William	35	m	w	MO	Colusa	Grand Island Twp	71	303
William	27	m	w	MO	Santa Clara	Redwood Twp	88	119
William	16	m	w	CA	Los Angeles	Los Angeles	73	570
William A	29	m	w	ENGL	Nevada	Grass Valley Twp	75	180
William T	28	m	w	MO	Santa Clara	Redwood Twp	88	122
Wm	36	m	w	IREL	Sacramento	American Twp	77	66
Wm C	39	m	w	TN	Fresno	Kings Rvr P O	72	211
Wm H	29	m	w	MO	Santa Barbara	San Buenaventura P	87	445
CALE								
Geo A	46	m	w	NY	San Joaquin	Douglas Twp	86	45
J A	26	m	w	IL	Sonoma	Bodega Twp	91	259
CALEAU								
Joseph	56	m	w	FRAN	Calaveras	San Andreas P O	70	181
CALEB								
Antoinella	29	f	w	ME	San Francisco	1-Wd San Francisco	79	124
Fred	6	m	w	CA	San Francisco	1-Wd San Francisco	79	124
Harry F	7	m	w	CA	San Francisco	1-Wd San Francisco	79	124
CALEDORI								
Andrew	30	m	w	ITAL	San Francisco	1-Wd San Francisco	79	35
CALEF								
Henrietta	56	f	w	WIND	San Francisco	8-Wd San Francisco	82	467
John H	28	m	w	MA	San Francisco	San Francisco P O	85	757
CALEFF								
Henry	48	m	w	CANA	Inyo	Lone Pine Twp	73	331
CALEL								
Van Buren	36	m	w	KY	Fresno	Millerton P O	72	194
CALEM								
John	34	m	w	IREL	Sacramento	2-Wd Sacramento	77	222
CALEMUS								
M D L F	52	m	w	KY	Sutter	Nicolaus Twp	92	107
CALENCODAY								
Rafal	52	m	w	MEXI	Santa Clara	Almaden Twp	88	7
CALENDEN								
Charles R	39	m	w	MA	Stanislaus	Washington Twp	92	86
Stephen	50	m	w	NY	Stanislaus	Washington Twp	92	86
CALENDER								
Peter	32	m	w	SCOT	Colusa	Colusa Twp	71	284
CALEON								
Francisco	51	m	w	ITAL	Calaveras	San Andreas P O	70	201
CALER								
Isabella	43	f	w	NY	San Francisco	11-Wd San Francisc	84	545
Jno A	48	m	w	KY	Butte	Oregon Twp	70	132
John	35	m	w	IREL	San Francisco	San Francisco P O	85	845
CALESTER								
John	39	m	w	RI	Inyo	Independence Twp	73	325
CALEY								
Henry F	30	m	w	MO	San Luis Obispo	Salinas Twp	87	293
Hervey	37	m	w	BELG	San Joaquin	Elkhorn Twp	86	66
Viola	25	f	w	OH	Alameda	Oakland	68	197
William	39	m	w	ENGL	San Bernardino	San Bernardino Twp	78	451
CALF								
W	38	m	w	IL	Alameda	Oakland	68	244
CALFE								
Chs P	43	m	w	FRAN	San Francisco	2-Wd San Francisco	79	222
CALHAM								
J W	51	m	w	VA	Sonoma	Russian Rvr	91	371
CALHOFF								
Herman	24	m	w	SAXO	San Francisco	6-Wd San Francisco	81	124
CALHOME								
John	42	m	w	IREL	San Joaquin	2-Wd Stockton	86	206
CALHONE								
Ellen	27	f	w	NY	San Francisco	San Francisco P O	83	207
CALHOON								
John	26	m	w	KY	Mono	Bridgeport P O	74	283
Lucy	68	f	w	NY	San Francisco	8-Wd San Francisco	82	374
CALHOUN								
D R	47	m	w	OH	Siskiyou	Scott Valley Twp	89	619
Frank	40	m	w	SCOT	Alameda	Brooklyn Twp	68	48
J H	43	m	w	OH	Yuba	Marysville Twp	93	569
John	24	m	w	NY	San Francisco	11-Wd San Francisc	84	586
Martha	24	f	w	NY	San Francisco	San Francisco P O	83	366
Silas	30	m	w	IA	Santa Clara	2-Wd San Jose	88	329
William	42	m	w	SC	Santa Clara	1-Wd San Jose	88	278
William	42	m	w	SC	Santa Clara	San Jose Twp	88	180
William	30	m	w	IREL	San Francisco	11-Wd San Francisc	84	536
CALHOURD								
Ezekiel	44	m	w	KY	Kern	Bakersfield P O	73	359

© 2001 by Heritage Quest. All rights reserved.

Name	Age	S	R	B-PL	County	Locale	Roll	Pg
CALIER								
M	46	f	w	VA	Sierra	Downieville Twp	89	521
CALIFF								
Hiram	35	m	w	OH	Sutter	Yuba Twp	92	145
CALIGAN								
James	24	m	w	SWIT	Marin	Tomales Twp	74	77
CALIGARI								
Peter	23	m	w	SWIT	Sonoma	Bodega Twp	91	254
CALIGHAN								
Samuel	49	m	w	ME	Yuba	Bullards Bar P O	93	550
CALIHAN								
William	35	m	w	MO	Inyo	Bishop Crk Twp	73	317
CALILLAS								
Finnin	29	m	w	MEXI	San Luis Obispo	Arroyo Grande Twp	87	271
CALIMAN								
James	34	m	w	IREL	San Francisco	11-Wd San Francisc	84	513
CALIN								
Sinclair	50	m	w	SCOT	San Francisco	2-Wd San Francisco	79	254
CALINANS								
Ellen	6	f	w	CA	Santa Cruz	Santa Cruz	89	417
CALINCINTA								
Pedro	45	m	w	MEXI	Santa Clara	Almaden Twp	88	6
Ponciana	21	m	w	MEXI	Santa Clara	Almaden Twp	88	6
CALIO								
J B	62	m	w	MO	Sacramento	Franklin Twp	77	116
John	33	m	w	IL	Sacramento	Franklin Twp	77	116
CALIS								
Augustus	30	m	w	NY	Los Angeles	Los Angeles	73	519
CALISH								
Rafeal	45	m	w	PRUS	San Francisco	6-Wd San Francisco	81	154
CALISHER								
Julia	32	f	w	PRUS	San Francisco	San Francisco P O	83	343
Martin	44	m	w	PRUS	Los Angeles	Santa Ana Twp	73	611
Woolf	44	m	w	PRUS	Los Angeles	Los Angeles	73	527
CALISSON								
John S	38	m	w	MD	San Francisco	8-Wd San Francisco	82	308
CALISTINE								
Galliano	34	m	w	ITAL	Santa Clara	Santa Clara Twp	88	175
CALISTON								
Ezekial	39	m	w	OH	Tulare	Tule Rvr Twp	92	265
Lewis A	13	m	w	CA	Tulare	Tule Rvr Twp	92	265
CALISTRO								
Jose	32	m	i	----	Marin	Nicasio Twp	74	89
CALIVAN								
James M	24	m	w	KY	Stanislaus	San Joaquin Twp	92	74
William	39	m	w	KY	Stanislaus	San Joaquin Twp	92	73
CALIWAY								
Silas	38	m	w	AL	Sacramento	Franklin Twp	77	114
CALKEN								
George	45	m	w	IREL	Mariposa	Mariposa P O	74	113
Wm	22	m	w	NY	Mono	Bridgeport P O	74	283
CALKIN								
E F	27	m	w	MI	Alameda	Oakland	68	211
Milo	60	m	w	NY	Marin	San Rafael	74	54
Milo	55	m	w	IN	San Francisco	8-Wd San Francisco	82	311
William	38	m	w	TN	Solano	Vacaville Twp	90	121
CALKINS								
Dan	35	m	w	IREL	San Joaquin	1-Wd Stockton	86	123
Delos L	38	m	w	NY	Nevada	Nevada Twp	75	306
Edd	61	m	w	CT	Sonoma	Healdsburg	91	274
J A	38	m	w	NY	Tuolumne	Chinese Camp P O	93	376
CALL								
Christopher C	29	m	w	IN	Santa Clara	2-Wd San Jose	88	298
Coverto	5	m	w	CA	San Luis Obispo	San Luis Obispo Tw	87	300
Dallas	43	m	w	NY	Santa Clara	Burnett Twp	88	30
Denis	30	m	w	IREL	San Francisco	1-Wd San Francisco	79	76
Edward	74	m	w	NY	Sonoma	Petaluma Twp	91	334
Frank	36	m	w	IREL	San Francisco	1-Wd San Francisco	79	113
Hamilton	37	m	w	PA	Stanislaus	Emory Twp	92	26
Henry	38	m	w	NH	Santa Cruz	Santa Cruz Twp	89	380
Henry C	39	m	w	PA	Stanislaus	Emory Twp	92	26
Hidensel	34	m	w	OH	Yolo	Cache Crk Twp	93	446
Jesse	21	m	w	MO	Nevada	Washington Twp	75	343
John	47	m	w	SCOT	Sonoma	Healdsburg & Mendo	91	282
John	45	m	w	IN	Solano	Vallejo	90	151
Killian	48	m	w	SPAI	Los Angeles	Los Angeles	73	566
Mary	30	f	w	MA	Contra Costa	Martinez P O	71	397
Mc Jno	24	m	w	CA	Santa Clara	Gilroy Twp	88	95
Mitchel	29	m	w	PRUS	Butte	Concow Twp	70	6
Nancy	74	f	w	MA	Sonoma	Petaluma Twp	91	334
Patrick	35	m	w	IREL	San Francisco	1-Wd San Francisco	79	76
Samuel L	12	m	w	IA	Colusa	Stony Crk Twp	71	333
Sarah	32	f	w	IN	Butte	Chico Twp	70	25
Silas B	31	m	w	NH	San Luis Obispo	San Luis Obispo Tw	87	310
William	48	m	w	NH	San Francisco	11-Wd San Francisc	84	645
William	29	m	w	IREL	Solano	Rio Vista Twp	90	64
Wm	15	m	w	IA	Sonoma	Analy Twp	91	238
CALLA								
James	31	m	w	PA	Mendocino	Round Valley Twp	74	217
John	28	m	w	IREL	Mendocino	Round Valley Twp	74	217
John B	24	m	w	ITAL	Mariposa	Maxwell Crk P O	74	140
CALLADO								
Francisco	21	f	w	CA	Los Angeles	Los Angeles	73	568
CALLAGAN								
Danl	39	m	w	IREL	Tuolumne	Columbia P O	93	348
CALLAGHAN								
Catherine	13	f	w	RI	Santa Cruz	Santa Cruz	89	417
Daniel	45	m	w	ENGL	San Francisco	11-Wd San Francisc	84	510
Delia	23	f	w	NY	San Francisco	1-Wd San Francisco	79	86
Dennis	28	m	w	IREL	San Francisco	San Francisco P O	85	817
Ellen	28	f	w	IREL	San Francisco	San Francisco P O	83	280
James	48	m	w	IREL	San Francisco	3-Wd San Francisco	79	324
Jane	58	f	w	IREL	San Francisco	7-Wd San Francisco	81	198
Jas	38	m	w	IREL	Sierra	Table Rock Twp	89	576
Jeremh	25	m	w	NY	San Francisco	1-Wd San Francisco	79	86
John	38	m	w	IREL	San Francisco	San Francisco P O	80	396
John	32	m	w	IREL	Tuolumne	Sonora P O	93	328
John A	24	m	w	IREL	San Francisco	1-Wd San Francisco	79	69
John O	36	m	w	IREL	Nevada	Grass Valley Twp	75	162
Joseph	32	m	w	IREL	San Francisco	San Francisco P O	83	213
Joseph	1	m	w	CA	San Francisco	1-Wd San Francisco	79	86
Julia	25	f	w	IREL	San Francisco	San Francisco P O	85	776
Laurs	36	m	w	IREL	Sierra	Table Rock Twp	89	576
Mary	15	f	w	CA	Solano	Benicia	90	16
Mary C	25	f	w	IREL	San Francisco	San Francisco P O	83	199
Mary Jr	2	f	w	CA	San Francisco	San Francisco P O	83	163
Michael	40	m	w	IREL	San Francisco	San Francisco P O	83	65
Michael	35	m	w	IREL	San Francisco	11-Wd San Francisc	84	577
Micheal	40	m	w	IREL	San Francisco	7-Wd San Francisco	81	187
Micheal	29	m	w	IREL	San Francisco	11-Wd San Francisc	84	432
Michl	27	m	w	IREL	Sierra	Gibson Twp	89	538
Pat	33	m	w	IREL	Sierra	Table Rock Twp	89	577
Patrick	43	m	w	IREL	Nevada	Nevada Twp	75	321
Patrick	39	m	w	IREL	San Francisco	1-Wd San Francisco	79	123
Patrick	36	m	w	IREL	San Francisco	San Francisco P O	83	163
Peter	39	m	w	IREL	San Francisco	1-Wd San Francisco	79	113
CALLAGHER								
David	36	m	w	IREL	San Francisco	San Francisco P O	83	157
CALLAHAM								
Bartholomew	27	m	w	IREL	Humboldt	Eureka Twp	72	258
Broxton	38	m	w	MO	Tulare	Tule Rvr Twp	92	264
William	34	m	w	MO	Tulare	Tule Rvr Twp	92	265
CALLAHAN								
---	35	m	w	IREL	Sonoma	Santa Rosa	91	420
Ann	36	f	w	IREL	Solano	Vallejo	90	151
Bedelia	35	f	w	IREL	Solano	Silveyville Twp	90	82
Bernard	43	m	w	DE	San Francisco	San Francisco P O	83	348
C	35	m	w	IREL	San Francisco	San Francisco P O	85	846
Catherine	39	f	w	NY	San Francisco	San Francisco P O	83	23
Charles	45	m	w	IREL	San Francisco	8-Wd San Francisco	82	457
Christopher	14	m	w	NY	San Francisco	11-Wd San Francisc	84	587
Cornelius	32	m	w	IREL	San Francisco	8-Wd San Francisco	82	414
Corns	23	m	w	IREL	San Francisco	San Francisco P O	83	119
D E	50	m	w	PA	Sacramento	3-Wd Sacramento	77	318
Dan O	36	m	w	IREL	Sonoma	Mendocino Twp	91	295
Daniel	27	m	w	IREL	Contra Costa	Martinez P O	71	379
Daniel	12	m	w	MA	San Francisco	San Francisco P O	85	817
Delia	24	f	w	IREL	San Francisco	6-Wd San Francisco	81	140
Dennis	38	m	w	IREL	Alameda	Eden Twp	68	72
Dennis	37	m	w	IREL	San Francisco	7-Wd San Francisco	81	249
Dennis	30	m	w	IREL	San Mateo	Redwood Twp	87	363
Edw	20	m	w	MA	Tehama	Red Bluff	92	178
Edwd	40	m	w	IREL	Solano	Vallejo	90	155
Eliza	45	f	w	IREL	San Francisco	6-Wd San Francisco	81	103
Ellen	28	f	w	IREL	San Francisco	6-Wd San Francisco	81	133
F T	29	m	w	NY	Mendocino	Round Valley Twp	74	217
Francis	26	m	w	IREL	Marin	San Rafael Twp	74	37
Frank	22	m	w	IREL	San Francisco	San Francisco P O	80	336
Henry	28	m	w	IREL	Nevada	Little York Twp	75	241
J	45	f	w	IREL	San Francisco	San Francisco P O	85	794
J	30	m	w	IREL	Sacramento	1-Wd Sacramento	77	190
J	25	m	w	IREL	Sierra	Sears Twp	89	559
J D	49	m	w	IREL	Monterey	Monterey	74	356
James	37	m	w	MA	Santa Clara	1-Wd San Jose	88	260
James	26	m	w	VT	San Francisco	7-Wd San Francisco	81	215
James	25	m	w	IREL	Santa Clara	Milpitas Twp	88	115
James	24	m	w	IREL	San Francisco	San Francisco P O	80	473
James	16	m	w	ENGL	San Francisco	San Francisco P O	83	350
Jas	40	m	w	IREL	Solano	Benicia	90	13
Jas	36	m	w	IREL	San Francisco	1-Wd San Francisco	79	9
Jas	22	m	w	IREL	San Francisco	8-Wd San Francisco	82	346
Jerry	40	m	w	IREL	San Joaquin	Douglas Twp	86	49
Johanna	37	f	w	IREL	San Francisco	7-Wd San Francisco	81	282
John	46	m	w	IREL	San Francisco	San Francisco P O	85	864
John	44	m	w	IREL	San Francisco	11-Wd San Francisc	84	613
John	40	m	w	IREL	San Francisco	San Francisco P O	85	777
John	40	m	w	IREL	Solano	Suisun Twp	90	98
John	35	m	w	IREL	Sonoma	Bodega Twp	91	258
John	35	m	w	IREL	San Francisco	San Francisco P O	85	739
John	35	m	w	IREL	Yuba	East Bear Rvr Twp	93	544
John	32	m	w	IREL	Solano	Silveyville Twp	90	83
John	28	m	w	IREL	San Francisco	8-Wd San Francisco	82	488
John	27	m	w	IREL	San Francisco	7-Wd San Francisco	81	253
John	26	m	w	MA	San Francisco	8-Wd San Francisco	82	434
John	24	m	w	CA	Los Angeles	San Gabriel Twp	73	593
John	24	m	w	IREL	Solano	Vacaville Twp	90	117
John	23	m	w	CANA	San Francisco	11-Wd San Francisc	84	618
John	23	m	w	MA	Nevada	Grass Valley Twp	75	209
John	22	m	w	CA	Los Angeles	San Gabriel Twp	73	594
John	18	m	w	ENGL	San Francisco	San Francisco P O	83	350
Julia	36	f	w	IREL	Santa Cruz	Santa Cruz	89	427
Julia	22	f	w	IREL	San Francisco	8-Wd San Francisco	82	426
L	40	m	w	IREL	Amador	Sutter Crk P O	69	402
L	40	m	w	IREL	Amador	Amador City P O	69	391

© 2001 by Heritage Quest. All rights reserved.

Name	Age	S	R	B-PL	County	Locale	Series M593 Roll	Pg
Luke	27	m	w	CANA	San Joaquin	2-Wd Stockton	86	162
Margaret	50	f	w	IREL	San Francisco	San Francisco P O	80	424
Margaret	50	f	w	IREL	San Francisco	8-Wd San Francisco	82	427
Margaret	21	f	w	IREL	San Francisco	8-Wd San Francisco	82	463
Martin	33	m	w	IREL	Nevada	Grass Valley Twp	75	224
Mary	64	f	w	IREL	Sonoma	Russian Rvr	91	373
Mary	45	f	w	IREL	San Francisco	San Francisco P O	83	112
Mary	40	f	w	IREL	San Francisco	San Francisco P O	83	32
Mary	38	f	w	IREL	San Francisco	2-Wd San Francisco	79	274
Mary	28	f	w	IREL	San Francisco	San Francisco P O	85	721
Mary	27	f	w	IREL	San Francisco	San Francisco P O	85	777
Mary	26	f	w	IREL	Marin	San Rafael	74	57
Mary	17	f	w	PA	Nevada	Grass Valley Twp	75	171
Mary A	31	f	w	MA	San Francisco	8-Wd San Francisco	82	381
Mat	39	m	w	ENGL	Sacramento	4-Wd Sacramento	77	332
Maynet	27	f	w	IREL	Santa Barbara	Santa Barbara P O	87	474
Michael	43	m	w	IREL	Solano	Silveyville Twp	90	77
Michael	40	m	w	IREL	Solano	Montezuma Twp	90	66
Michael	26	m	w	IREL	Solano	Maine Prairie Twp	90	52
Mike	50	m	w	IREL	El Dorado	Georgetown Twp	72	47
Mike	25	m	w	IREL	Alameda	Oakland	68	181
Minna	21	f	w	IREL	San Francisco	San Francisco P O	83	97
Owen	33	m	w	IREL	San Francisco	11-Wd San Francisc	84	649
Pat	30	m	w	IREL	San Francisco	11-Wd San Francisc	84	598
Pat	30	m	w	IREL	San Joaquin	2-Wd Stockton	86	171
Patck	30	m	w	IREL	San Francisco	San Francisco P O	85	830
Patk	43	m	w	CANA	Tuolumne	Columbia P O	93	360
Patrick	50	m	w	IREL	Nevada	Grass Valley Twp	75	143
Patrick	48	m	w	IREL	San Francisco	San Francisco P O	83	36
Patrick	40	m	w	IREL	Nevada	Grass Valley Twp	75	157
Patrick	35	m	w	IREL	San Francisco	7-Wd San Francisco	81	185
Phil	48	m	w	IREL	Sacramento	4-Wd Sacramento	77	371
Philip	30	m	w	IREL	San Francisco	San Francisco P O	83	35
Rosa	31	f	w	IREL	San Mateo	Redwood City P O	87	376
Thomas	32	m	w	PA	Yolo	Cache Crk Twp	93	421
Thomas	32	m	w	IREL	Calaveras	San Andreas P O	70	181
Thos	33	m	w	IREL	Solano	Benicia	90	21
Thos H	44	m	w	IREL	Calaveras	Copperopolis P O	70	221
Wm E	39	m	w	PA	Sacramento	Sutter Twp	77	382
CALLAL								
Matildie	16	f	w	FRAN	Napa	Napa	75	45
CALLAN								
Christopher	41	m	w	IREL	San Francisco	6-Wd San Francisco	81	143
David	32	m	w	IREL	San Francisco	San Francisco P O	83	361
Ellen	6	f	w	CA	San Francisco	San Francisco P O	85	850
Eugene	5	m	w	CA	San Mateo	Half Moon Bay P O	87	404
James	34	m	w	IREL	Yuba	Marysville	93	612
John	43	m	w	IREL	Alameda	Oakland	68	183
John	28	m	w	IREL	San Francisco	San Francisco P O	83	22
Joseph	40	m	w	ME	Placer	Lincoln P O	76	487
Mary	27	f	w	IREL	San Mateo	Menlo Park P O	87	379
Michl	25	m	w	IREL	San Francisco	1-Wd San Francisco	79	113
Thomas	78	m	w	IREL	Contra Costa	Martinez P O	71	445
Wm	32	m	w	IREL	San Francisco	1-Wd San Francisco	79	121
CALLANDEN								
Christian	45	m	w	DENM	San Francisco	8-Wd San Francisco	82	492
CALLANDER								
Saml	46	m	w	PA	Solano	Vallejo	90	167
CALLAR								
Jules	39	m	w	TX	Sacramento	4-Wd Sacramento	77	329
CALLAS								
David	33	m	w	AR	Fresno	Millerton P O	72	146
CALLASER								
Romaldo	30	m	w	MEXI	Kern	Bakersfield P O	73	364
CALLAWAN								
Patrick	50	m	w	IREL	Santa Cruz	Santa Cruz	89	430
CALLAWAY								
A E	43	m	w	VA	Amador	Ione City P O	69	370
Lellie	19	f	w	IN	Nevada	Grass Valley Twp	75	145
Milton	28	m	m	KY	Nevada	Rough & Ready Twp	75	329
Patrick H	41	m	w	MO	El Dorado	White Oak Twp	72	140
William T	46	m	w	NY	El Dorado	Placerville	72	110
CALLEHAN								
Bridget	34	f	w	IREL	Siskiyou	Yreka Twp	89	667
Catherine	25	f	w	IREL	San Francisco	2-Wd San Francisco	79	174
CALLEN								
Ellen	22	f	w	IREL	Sonoma	Analy Twp	91	222
Hiaceo	30	m	w	CHIL	Sacramento	2-Wd Sacramento	77	216
Margaret	46	f	w	IREL	San Francisco	San Francisco P O	85	834
Patrick	28	m	w	CANA	Humboldt	Arcata Twp	72	231
Thomas	12	m	w	CA	Solano	Suisun Twp	90	109
CALLENDER								
Cordelia	1	f	b	CA	San Francisco	1-Wd San Francisco	79	96
Henry	29	m	w	CT	San Francisco	San Francisco P O	83	138
John T	33	m	b	WIND	San Francisco	1-Wd San Francisco	79	96
Mary	33	f	b	PA	San Francisco	1-Wd San Francisco	79	96
CALLENIUR								
Theodore	19	m	w	PRUS	Solano	Silveyville Twp	90	78
CALLENY								
Franklin	32	m	w	IREL	San Mateo	Schoolhouse Statio	87	342
CALLER								
C M	60	m	w	IREL	Tuolumne	Big Oak Flat P O	93	395
CALLERITON								
Joseph	20	m	w	PA	Sacramento	Georgianna Twp	77	125
CALLERS								
Francis	33	m	w	VA	Tuolumne	Sonora P O	93	325
CALLESON								
Y	36	m	w	DENM	Sierra	Butte Twp	89	510
CALLESTRO								
Revis	20	m	w	MEXI	Stanislaus	Buena Vista Twp	92	15
CALLICOTT								
James	18	m	w	PA	San Francisco	11-Wd San Francisc	84	592
Wm G	22	m	w	NC	Sacramento	1-Wd Sacramento	77	182
CALLIER								
John W	41	m	w	ME	Calaveras	San Andreas P O	70	208
CALLIGAN								
Anne	40	f	w	IREL	San Francisco	11-Wd San Francisc	84	532
M	14	f	w	CA	Alameda	Oakland	68	242
Pat	33	m	w	ME	San Francisco	7-Wd San Francisco	81	268
CALLIHA								
Amelia	29	f	w	SCOT	Sacramento	2-Wd Sacramento	77	243
CALLIHAN								
Annie	24	f	w	ENGL	San Francisco	2-Wd San Francisco	79	195
Catherin	35	f	w	ENGL	San Francisco	8-Wd San Francisco	82	317
Cornelius	42	m	w	IREL	San Francisco	2-Wd San Francisco	79	249
James	40	m	w	IREL	Los Angeles	Los Angeles	73	571
K	32	f	w	IREL	Santa Clara	Gilroy Twp	88	81
Katy	18	f	w	MA	Santa Clara	Gilroy Twp	88	77
Maggi	22	f	w	IREL	San Francisco	8-Wd San Francisco	82	321
Pat	28	m	w	IREL	San Francisco	2-Wd San Francisco	79	216
Pat	24	m	w	IREL	San Francisco	2-Wd San Francisco	79	214
Thos	12	m	w	IREL	San Francisco	2-Wd San Francisco	79	167
Timothy	50	m	w	IREL	San Francisco	2-Wd San Francisco	79	249
William	48	m	w	IREL	San Francisco	2-Wd San Francisco	79	172
CALLIN								
George	7	m	w	CA	Marin	San Rafael Twp	74	28
CALLINAN								
John	27	m	w	NC	Solano	Vallejo	90	160
CALLINBERGER								
Jacob	42	m	w	BAVA	Calaveras	San Andreas P O	70	209
CALLININI								
Eugene	24	m	w	IREL	El Dorado	Placerville	72	109
CALLIS								
A	40	m	b	VA	Sierra	Downieville Twp	89	516
Antone	23	m	w	PORT	Alameda	Washington Twp	68	291
Lucinda J	60	f	w	KY	Santa Barbara	Santa Barbara P O	87	486
Robert A	27	m	w	KY	Santa Barbara	Santa Barbara P O	87	486
Thos C	26	m	w	KY	Santa Barbara	Santa Barbara P O	87	483
William S	48	m	w	VA	Santa Barbara	Santa Barbara P O	87	486
CALLISH								
Lewis	57	m	w	HAMB	Sacramento	3-Wd Sacramento	77	263
CALLISON								
Rebecca J	33	f	w	IL	Shasta	Fort Crook P O	89	474
CALLISTER								
A	18	m	w	IREL	Santa Clara	Gilroy Twp	88	93
Mc M	19	m	w	IREL	Santa Clara	Gilroy Twp	88	93
CALLMAN								
James	29	m	w	IREL	Monterey	Castroville Twp	74	333
CALLMAND								
Henry	51	m	w	FRAN	San Francisco	San Francisco P O	80	536
CALLOGHAN								
Callaghan	35	m	w	IREL	San Francisco	San Francisco P O	85	768
CALLON								
Belinde	19	f	w	IREL	Marin	Tomales Twp	74	87
Claude	36	m	w	FRAN	Marin	San Rafael Twp	74	32
Ellen	35	f	w	CA	San Francisco	San Francisco P O	83	150
John	42	m	w	NJ	San Francisco	5-Wd San Francisco	81	25
Thomas	64	m	w	VT	Calaveras	San Andreas P O	70	200
Thomas	46	m	w	IOFM	Butte	Ophir Twp	70	91
Thomas	30	m	w	IREL	Marin	Tomales Twp	74	77
Thomas	30	m	w	IREL	Marin	Tomales Twp	74	85
Thomas	10	m	w	CA	Marin	San Rafael Twp	74	27
CALLONAY								
O Peter	44	m	w	MS	San Diego	San Diego	78	511
CALLOPI								
James	34	m	w	IREL	San Francisco	San Francisco P O	83	390
CALLOR								
M	40	m	w	OH	San Joaquin	1-Wd Stockton	86	140
CALLORI								
Luigi	34	m	w	ITAL	Amador	Volcano P O	69	385
CALLOUGH								
George M	46	m	w	PA	Fresno	Millerton P O	72	149
CALLOUN								
Thomas	46	m	w	IOFM	Butte	Ophir Twp	70	91
CALLOWAY								
David	47	m	w	AL	Sonoma	Sonoma Twp	91	442
Howard A	31	m	w	MO	Los Angeles	Los Angeles	73	504
CALLS								
David	28	m	w	SCOT	San Francisco	7-Wd San Francisco	81	255
CALLSA								
Henry	32	m	w	ME	San Francisco	San Francisco P O	83	369
CALLSEN								
Peter	49	m	w	HAMB	San Francisco	San Francisco P O	80	372
CALLUM								
C A	18	f	w	NY	San Francisco	San Francisco P O	85	812
Patrick	28	m	w	IREL	Mendocino	Little Rvr Twp	74	165
CALLWELL								
Mary	45	f	w	IL	San Francisco	San Francisco P O	83	265
CALLY								
Alonzo	38	m	w	ME	Calaveras	San Andreas P O	70	211
L O	52	m	w	NH	Alameda	Oakland	68	171
CALM								
Frank	33	m	w	HI	Yolo	Merritt Twp	93	505

© 2001 by Heritage Quest. All rights reserved.

Name	Age	S	R	B-PL	County	Locale	Roll	Pg
John	35	m	w	SCOT	Butte	Ophir Twp	70	102
CALMAN								
J C	45	m	w	IN	Sacramento	3-Wd Sacramento	77	261
CALME								
Charles	52	m	w	KY	Placer	Bath P O	76	437
CALMES								
Fielding	63	m	w	KY	Colusa	Colusa Twp	71	286
Joseph	22	m	b	KY	Colusa	Colusa Twp	71	286
Waller	39	m	w	KY	Colusa	Colusa Twp	71	274
William H	39	m	w	KY	Colusa	Colusa Twp	71	287
Ziskie	32	m	w	MO	Colusa	Colusa	71	292
CALMESE								
Timothy	21	m	w	MO	Colusa	Colusa	71	292
CALMEYER								
Christian R	57	m	w	BREM	Colusa	Spring Valley Twp	71	342
CALNAN								
Ellen	28	f	w	IREL	San Francisco	San Francisco P O	83	36
John	24	m	w	CANA	Inyo	Lone Pine Twp	73	332
Julia	48	f	w	IREL	San Francisco	1-Wd San Francisco	79	26
CALNON								
August	20	m	w	GERM	San Francisco	7-Wd San Francisco	81	239
Johanna	27	f	w	IREL	San Francisco	7-Wd San Francisco	81	239
CALODA								
George	55	m	w	GREE	Nevada	Bridgeport Twp	75	100
CALOVE								
Philip	31	m	w	GERM	Santa Clara	Fremont Twp	88	53
CALOVER								
Peter	40	m	w	BADE	San Francisco	1-Wd San Francisco	79	33
CALOWAY								
Elizabeth	70	f	w	MA	Mendocino	Ukiah Twp	74	235
G L	40	m	w	OH	Sacramento	Dry Crk Twp	77	100
John	78	m	w	KY	Mendocino	Ukiah Twp	74	235
Sarah	19	f	w	NC	Santa Clara	2-Wd San Jose	88	285
CALRADO								
Jose	24	m	w	NCOD	Contra Costa	San Pablo Twp	71	366
CALREES								
Loveland	30	m	w	ITAL	Sacramento	Sutter Twp	77	383
CALRON								
James	51	m	w	VA	Mariposa	Mariposa P O	74	128
CALSADO								
Francisco	20	m	w	CA	Santa Barbara	Las Cruces P O	87	507
CALSON								
C A	32	m	w	FINL	San Francisco	3-Wd San Francisco	79	291
John	30	m	w	SWED	Stanislaus	Empire Twp	92	54
Martin	27	m	w	NORW	Mendocino	Point Arena Twp	74	204
Sophia	25	f	w	SWED	San Francisco	6-Wd San Francisco	81	86
CALT								
Charles	35	m	w	NY	San Francisco	7-Wd San Francisco	81	207
J M	40	m	w	MA	San Francisco	San Francisco P O	85	788
CALTON								
E Ford	36	m	w	VT	Calaveras	Copperopolis P O	70	256
John	58	m	w	SCOT	San Francisco	San Francisco P O	80	391
CALTRINE								
John	49	m	w	NY	Yolo	Cottonwood Twp	93	470
CALTY								
Hugh	26	m	w	IREL	Alameda	Washington Twp	68	300
CALUGAN								
Kate	25	f	w	IREL	Alameda	Oakland	68	211
CALVAN								
J	30	m	w	AUSL	Alameda	Murray Twp	68	124
CALVEN								
Daniel	45	m	w	IREL	San Francisco	San Francisco P O	83	194
CALVENERY								
Robert	40	m	w	ENGL	San Francisco	San Francisco P O	83	209
CALVER								
H	16	f	w	CA	Sacramento	3-Wd Sacramento	77	317
J B	22	m	w	WI	Sacramento	3-Wd Sacramento	77	281
Richard P	63	m	w	NY	El Dorado	Placerville Twp	72	105
CALVERLEI								
Robert	7	m	w	ENGL	San Francisco	11-Wd San Francisc	84	697
CALVERT								
Celsus	37	m	w	KY	Alameda	Brooklyn	68	25
Jackson	42	m	w	ENGL	Nevada	Nevada Twp	75	302
James	42	m	w	KY	Nevada	Grass Valley Twp	75	143
John	48	m	w	IREL	San Francisco	8-Wd San Francisco	82	321
John T	25	m	w	NY	San Francisco	6-Wd San Francisco	81	143
Mattie	21	f	w	KY	Nevada	Grass Valley Twp	75	143
Wm	46	m	w	AL	Napa	Napa Twp	75	64
Wm	46	m	w	DE	Alameda	Brooklyn	68	24
CALVI								
Ah	35	m	c	CHIN	Amador	Ione City P O	69	364
CALVIN								
A J	46	m	w	PA	Sierra	Butte Twp	89	513
David	41	m	w	MO	Yuba	Slate Range Bar Tw	93	676
Dunlap	22	m	w	TX	Kern	Linns Valley P O	73	347
Eugene	33	m	w	NY	Placer	Auburn P O	76	374
F F	48	m	w	VT	San Joaquin	Douglas Twp	86	32
Gustavus	40	m	w	SWIT	Sonoma	Vallejo Twp	91	461
J W	47	m	w	OH	Santa Clara	Gilroy Twp	88	95
James	40	m	w	AR	Tulare	Farmersville Twp	92	242
James A	44	m	w	SCOT	San Francisco	2-Wd San Francisco	79	270
John	32	m	w	IREL	Santa Clara	2-Wd San Jose	88	316
R G	41	m	w	NY	Amador	Jackson P O	69	319
Robert W	30	m	w	SCOT	San Francisco	1-Wd San Francisco	79	121
Spencer J	25	m	w	NY	Placer	Summit P O	76	496
Timothy	28	m	w	IREL	San Francisco	7-Wd San Francisco	81	187
Victor	42	m	w	FRAN	Marin	Novato Twp	74	10
Vincent	40	m	w	FRAN	Marin	San Rafael Twp	74	32
CALVINA								
Rika	22	f	w	PRUS	San Joaquin	1-Wd Stockton	86	141
CALVRET								
B	40	m	w	ITAL	San Francisco	San Francisco P O	85	859
CALWELL								
B M	43	m	w	GA	Monterey	Castroville Twp	74	333
Dennis	33	m	w	OH	Sonoma	Sonoma Twp	91	437
Edwd	34	m	w	CANA	Butte	Chico Twp	70	55
Frank	19	m	w	IL	Alameda	Washington Twp	68	279
Peter	66	m	w	SCOT	Butte	Chico Twp	70	55
William	21	m	w	IREL	San Francisco	7-Wd San Francisco	81	206
CALY								
Fredric	36	m	w	SWIT	Trinity	Weaverville Pct	92	225
CALYER								
Peter	41	m	w	NY	El Dorado	White Oak Twp	72	135
CALZIA								
Bartholemew	26	m	w	ITAL	Santa Clara	Santa Clara Twp	88	175
CAM								
Ah	59	m	c	CHIN	Amador	Ione City P O	69	354
Ah	46	m	c	CHIN	Tuolumne	Chinese Camp P O	93	380
Ah	45	m	c	CHIN	Placer	Auburn P O	76	375
Ah	42	m	c	CHIN	Amador	Fiddletown P O	69	429
Ah	40	m	c	CHIN	Kern	Linns Valley P O	73	343
Ah	39	m	c	CHIN	Amador	Drytown P O	69	423
Ah	33	m	c	CHIN	Stanislaus	Emory Twp	92	17
Ah	32	f	c	CHIN	Placer	Auburn P O	76	371
Ah	26	m	c	CHIN	Placer	Auburn P O	76	377
Ah	21	m	c	CHIN	Santa Clara	1-Wd San Jose	88	277
Ah	18	f	c	CHIN	Amador	Ione City P O	69	364
Ah	17	m	c	CHIN	San Francisco	1-Wd San Francisco	79	61
Ah	16	f	c	CHIN	Fresno	Millerton P O	72	200
Envician	47	f	w	MEXI	Humboldt	Arcata Twp	72	233
Gew	31	m	c	CHIN	El Dorado	Coloma Twp	72	1
Joo	23	m	c	CHIN	Solano	Vacaville Twp	90	131
W	28	m	w	PRUS	Sierra	Sierra Twp	89	568
Wo	24	m	c	CHIN	Santa Clara	1-Wd San Jose	88	232
CAMACH								
C N	50	m	w	MEXI	Tuolumne	Sonora P O	93	306
CAMACHA								
Pablo	23	m	m	MEXI	Santa Barbara	Santa Barbara P O	87	480
CAMACHO								
Edward	32	m	w	MEXI	Alameda	Hayward	68	78
Tomas	50	m	w	MEXI	Los Angeles	Los Nietos Twp	73	589
Wm	35	m	w	MEXI	Alameda	Hayward	68	78
CAMALA								
Creepena	4	f	w	CA	Tulare	Tule Rvr Twp	92	267
CAMALETE								
Ucen	47	f	w	MEXI	Tehama	Red Bluff	92	181
CAMALITA								
T	36	f	w	CHIL	Yuba	Marysville	93	603
CAMANCHE								
Paula	12	f	w	MEXI	Santa Clara	1-Wd San Jose	88	255
CAMARA								
Luis	58	m	w	MEXI	Tuolumne	Sonora P O	93	314
CAMAREA								
Juan	59	m	w	MEXI	Santa Barbara	San Buenaventura P	87	436
CAMARGA								
Antonio	58	m	w	MEXI	Santa Barbara	Santa Barbara P O	87	479
CAMARI								
Joe	25	m	w	SWIT	Sonoma	Bodega Twp	91	260
CAMARINDA								
Adrien	15	m	w	CA	Kern	Bakersfield P O	73	363
CAMARINO								
Antonio	50	m	w	MEXI	Santa Barbara	Las Cruces P O	87	505
CAMAY								
Charles	26	m	w	MD	Sacramento	2-Wd Sacramento	77	225
CAMAYO								
Manuella	30	f	w	MEXI	San Francisco	6-Wd San Francisco	81	96
CAMBELL								
A B	31	m	w	IL	San Joaquin	3-Wd Stockton	86	233
Alex	54	m	w	ME	San Francisco	8-Wd San Francisco	82	370
Archibald	40	m	w	CANA	Mendocino	Bourns Landing Twp	74	223
Bernard	30	m	w	IREL	Sonoma	Vallejo Twp	91	460
Berry	8	m	w	CA	Butte	Chico Twp	70	44
Daniel	27	m	w	CANA	Mendocino	Point Arena Twp	74	205
Donald	51	m	w	SCOT	San Francisco	11-Wd San Francisc	84	677
Ellen	45	f	w	IREL	Butte	Oregon Twp	70	124
G B	37	m	w	KY	Monterey	San Antonio Twp	74	320
John	54	m	w	ME	Mendocino	Albion & Big Rvr T	74	166
Jos	32	m	w	IREL	San Francisco	8-Wd San Francisco	82	346
Jos	22	m	w	IREL	San Francisco	8-Wd San Francisco	82	363
M Ann	28	f	w	WI	San Francisco	8-Wd San Francisco	82	363
Mary	27	f	w	LA	San Francisco	11-Wd San Francisc	84	688
Nicholas	40	m	w	IREL	San Francisco	8-Wd San Francisco	82	331
Wm D	44	m	w	TN	Shasta	Shasta P O	89	453
CAMBERM								
Thomas	32	m	w	IL	San Diego	Poway Dist	78	481
CAMBERMOND								
Peter	42	m	w	FRAN	San Francisco	2-Wd San Francisco	79	214
CAMBERS								
Joseph	36	m	w	OH	San Francisco	5-Wd San Francisco	81	26
CAMBLE								
Patrick	32	m	w	IREL	San Francisco	1-Wd San Francisco	79	134
CAMBRICK								
John	40	m	w	IREL	Mariposa	Mariposa P O	74	129

Series M593

© 2001 by Heritage Quest. All rights reserved.

Name	Age	S	R	B-PL	County	Locale (Series M593)	Roll	Pg
CAMBRIDGE								
John	31	m	w	KY	Merced	Snelling P O	74	252
Oliver	48	m	w	IN	Sacramento	2-Wd Sacramento	77	208
CAMBRIE								
Stephen	43	m	w	AUST	Yolo	Grafton Twp	93	490
CAMBROD								
Fred	20	m	w	NY	Solano	Suisun Twp	90	96
CAMDEN								
Ada	17	f	w	CA	Alameda	Oakland	68	259
Chas	53	m	w	ENGL	Shasta	French Gulch P O	89	464
Christa	40	f	w	NY	San Francisco	7-Wd San Francisco	81	182
Etta	18	f	w	MA	Alameda	Oakland	68	259
Grace	15	f	w	CA	Alameda	Oakland	68	259
J	40	m	w	NY	Alameda	Oakland	68	259
Kate	20	f	i	CA	Shasta	Shasta P O	89	459
Mary	8	f	w	CA	Alameda	Oakland	68	259
William	36	m	w	SCOT	San Francisco	7-Wd San Francisco	81	210
CAME								
Ah	42	m	c	CHIN	Santa Clara	1-Wd San Jose	88	271
CAMEL								
James M	44	m	w	AL	Nevada	Bridgeport Twp	75	100
CAMELE								
Nicholas B	31	m	w	MO	Mendocino	Point Arena Twp	74	215
CAMELL								
Daniel	40	m	w	TN	Mendocino	Anderson Twp	74	154
CAMEN								
Ah	15	f	c	CHIN	Monterey	Monterey	74	367
CAMENETTE								
Roch	46	m	w	SICI	San Francisco	San Francisco P O	85	754
CAMER								
Martin	26	m	w	TX	San Diego	Warners Rancho Dis	78	530
P	25	m	w	PA	Alameda	Oakland	68	262
CAMERA								
Angelos	50	m	w	ITAL	Sacramento	American Twp	77	68
Gotlip	23	m	w	SWIT	Sacramento	American Twp	77	64
CAMERDEN								
Michael	59	m	w	NY	San Francisco	San Francisco P O	85	865
CAMERELLA								
Frances	13	f	w	CA	Santa Barbara	Santa Barbara P O	87	501
Magdalina	11	f	w	CA	Santa Barbara	Santa Barbara P O	87	501
CAMERIN								
John	30	m	w	IREL	Sutter	Sutter Twp	92	116
CAMERON								
A D	29	m	w	CANA	Santa Clara	Gilroy Twp	88	73
A O	29	m	w	IA	Mendocino	Little Lake Twp	74	199
Alex	54	m	w	SCOT	Mariposa	Mariposa P O	74	127
Alex	54	m	w	SCOT	Mariposa	Mariposa P O	74	126
Alex J	18	m	w	CANA	Marin	Point Reyes Twp	74	23
Alexander	7	m	w	CA	Santa Clara	San Jose Twp	88	218
Alexander	47	m	w	TN	Los Angeles	Los Angeles Twp	73	472
Alexander	39	m	w	CANA	Mendocino	Little Rvr Twp	74	171
Archd	41	m	w	SCOT	San Francisco	San Francisco P O	85	746
Ashley	51	m	w	CANA	Alameda	Washington Twp	68	278
August	40	m	w	CANA	San Francisco	6-Wd San Francisco	81	114
B O	16	m	w	NY	Alameda	Oakland	68	260
C P	45	m	w	ENGL	Sacramento	3-Wd Sacramento	77	261
Cesthe	28	m	w	SCOT	San Diego	Fort Yuma Dist	78	463
D	49	m	w	US	Siskiyou	Scott Valley Twp	89	611
Danl	50	m	w	CANA	San Francisco	7-Wd San Francisco	81	272
David J	14	m	w	CA	Sonoma	Petaluma Twp	91	341
David P	23	m	w	CANA	Santa Clara	Santa Clara Twp	88	147
Duncan	55	m	w	CANA	Humboldt	South Fork Twp	72	300
Duncan	50	m	w	CANA	Alameda	Brooklyn	68	33
Ed	22	m	w	PA	San Joaquin	Douglas Twp	86	42
Edwin W	36	m	w	NY	Colusa	Stony Crk Twp	71	334
Elizabeth	50	f	w	PA	San Francisco	7-Wd San Francisco	81	271
Elizabeth	22	f	w	CANA	San Francisco	6-Wd San Francisco	81	120
Emily	23	f	w	ENGL	Sacramento	3-Wd Sacramento	77	295
Emma S	25	f	w	VT	San Francisco	8-Wd San Francisco	82	429
Flora	20	f	w	MA	San Francisco	7-Wd San Francisco	81	259
George	43	m	w	TN	Kern	Tehachapi P O	73	353
Gordon	24	m	w	CANA	Solano	Silveyville Twp	90	79
Hannah	25	f	w	CANA	San Francisco	San Francisco P O	83	44
Hugh	25	m	w	CANA	Sierra	Gibson Twp	89	540
J S	27	m	w	SC	Tehama	Red Bluff	92	173
Jacob	43	m	w	IL	Placer	Auburn P O	76	383
James	49	m	w	CANA	San Francisco	San Francisco P O	83	44
James	45	m	w	IREL	San Francisco	11-Wd San Francisc	84	518
James	35	m	w	IREL	San Francisco	7-Wd San Francisco	81	273
James	26	m	w	KY	Humboldt	Mattole Twp	72	283
James	20	m	w	IREL	Sonoma	Vallejo Twp	91	450
James W	30	m	w	CANA	Mendocino	Cuffeys Cove Twp	74	168
Jno	40	m	w	IREL	San Joaquin	2-Wd Stockton	86	176
Jno	38	m	w	CANA	Sierra	Table Rock Twp	89	578
John	30	m	w	IREL	San Francisco	San Francisco P O	83	32
John H	56	m	w	CANA	Santa Clara	Santa Clara Twp	88	155
John M	79	m	w	GA	Sonoma	Analy Twp	91	227
John W	40	m	w	TN	Solano	Rio Vista Twp	90	62
Julia	35	f	w	ME	San Francisco	8-Wd San Francisco	82	421
Lillie	23	f	w	MO	San Francisco	8-Wd San Francisco	82	435
M	25	f	w	IL	Sacramento	3-Wd Sacramento	77	305
Margaret	15	f	w	CA	Marin	Sausalito Twp	74	67
Margt	40	f	w	IREL	Sonoma	Petaluma Twp	91	361
Mary	76	f	w	GA	Sonoma	Analy Twp	91	227
Mary	30	f	w	NY	San Francisco	San Francisco P O	83	159
Mary	28	f	w	SCOT	San Francisco	1-Wd San Francisco	79	40
Mary	16	f	w	IA	Tehama	Red Bluff	92	175
Nathan	45	m	w	MA	San Francisco	San Francisco P O	83	163
O P	38	m	w	NY	Sacramento	3-Wd Sacramento	77	300
Peter	54	m	w	NC	Calaveras	Copperopolis P O	70	239
Phebe	58	f	w	AL	Napa	Napa	75	26
Reuben	48	m	w	IN	Humboldt	Eel Rvr Twp	72	255
Robert	55	m	w	IREL	Plumas	Indian Twp	77	18
Robert	42	m	w	IREL	Stanislaus	San Joaquin Twp	92	83
Saml	78	m	w	NY	Alameda	Brooklyn	68	33
Saml	19	m	w	IA	Tehama	Battle Crk Twp	92	157
Samuel	25	m	w	CANA	Plumas	Plumas Twp	77	33
Smith	33	m	w	PA	Placer	Lincoln P O	76	487
Thomas	50	m	w	MO	Colusa	Monroe Twp	71	321
Thomas	42	m	w	SCOT	San Diego	Milquaty Dist	78	478
Thomas	42	m	w	MA	Stanislaus	Emory Twp	92	26
William	26	m	w	IA	Contra Costa	Martinez Twp	71	346
CAMESTIA								
James	44	m	w	AZOR	San Francisco	1-Wd San Francisco	79	102
CAMET								
C W	45	m	w	US	Solano	Vallejo	90	154
CAMEY								
Henry	30	m	w	IREL	San Francisco	11-Wd San Francisc	84	672
James	35	m	w	NH	Placer	Gold Run Twp	76	395
CAMFIELD								
Charles	23	m	w	CHIL	Placer	Bath P O	76	420
CAMFORD								
Geo W	40	m	w	PA	Sacramento	Granite Twp	77	141
CAMFORT								
David	29	m	w	SCOT	San Francisco	11-Wd San Francisc	84	648
CAMICIA								
Joseph	42	m	w	ITAL	Mariposa	Mariposa P O	74	91
Lewis	29	m	w	ITAL	Siskiyou	Surprise Valley Tw	89	637
CAMIES								
Peter	25	m	w	FRAN	San Francisco	8-Wd San Francisco	82	364
CAMILE								
Peter	60	m	w	FRAN	Tuolumne	Columbia P O	93	342
CAMILLA								
Eda	27	f	w	CA	San Diego	Julian Dist	78	469
Jose	25	m	w	CA	San Diego	Fort Yuma Dist	78	463
CAMILLE								
Frank	36	m	w	ITAL	Tuolumne	Columbia P O	93	344
CAMILLO								
Antonio	32	m	w	MEXI	San Bernardino	Belleville Twp	78	408
Carlo	54	m	w	SPAI	San Francisco	11-Wd San Francisc	84	660
CAMILLON								
F	50	m	w	ITAL	Amador	Jackson P O	69	337
CAMILLONI								
George	49	m	w	ITAL	Solano	Montezuma Twp	90	67
CAMILO								
Garcia	35	m	w	MEXI	Santa Clara	Almaden Twp	88	14
CAMILUS								
Antonio	60	m	w	ITAL	Santa Clara	Burnett Twp	88	37
CAMINETTI								
C Mrs	28	f	w	MA	Amador	Jackson P O	69	322
CAMINO								
Maria	56	f	w	MEXI	Amador	Jackson P O	69	322
CAMINSKY								
Wm	38	m	w	SWED	Fresno	Kings Rvr P O	72	213
CAMIO								
Joseph	70	m	b	HI	Tuolumne	Big Oak Flat P O	93	399
CAMIRE								
Jules	31	m	w	FRAN	San Francisco	1-Wd San Francisco	79	109
CAMM								
William	41	m	w	ENGL	Marin	San Rafael	74	49
CAMMAN								
August	56	m	w	PRUS	San Francisco	San Francisco P O	83	396
Joseph	26	m	w	PA	San Francisco	San Francisco P O	80	337
CAMMANN								
Lewis	42	m	w	HANO	Alameda	Alvarado	68	303
CAMMANS								
Louis	35	m	w	PA	San Francisco	San Francisco P O	80	347
CAMMEL								
F H	36	m	w	PA	Sierra	Forest	89	537
CAMMER								
James	40	m	w	IREL	Sacramento	Dry Crk Twp	77	104
CAMMERON								
F	39	m	w	NJ	Napa	Napa	75	47
CAMMET								
C	38	m	w	ME	Solano	Vallejo	90	141
John	43	m	w	NH	San Francisco	11-Wd San Francisc	84	540
CAMMINI								
Lugi	27	m	w	ITAL	Santa Clara	2-Wd San Jose	88	316
CAMMON								
Fredk	33	m	w	HANO	Placer	Bath P O	76	430
Mary	22	f	w	PA	San Francisco	8-Wd San Francisco	82	322
CAMMONS								
Cecilia	53	f	w	IREL	Santa Clara	1-Wd San Jose	88	266
CAMMONY								
John	30	m	w	IREL	Solano	Montezuma Twp	90	66
CAMON								
Catherine	14	f	w	MEXI	Santa Clara	2-Wd San Jose	88	337
Dolores	16	f	w	MEXI	Santa Clara	2-Wd San Jose	88	337
Isabel	13	f	w	MEXI	Santa Clara	2-Wd San Jose	88	337
John	17	m	w	MEXI	San Francisco	11-Wd San Francisc	84	592
Joseph	16	m	w	MEXI	San Francisco	11-Wd San Francisc	84	592
Lupee	11	f	w	MEXI	Santa Clara	2-Wd San Jose	88	338
CAMORAN								
Margaret	74	f	w	CANA	San Francisco	8-Wd San Francisco	82	294

© 2001 by Heritage Quest. All rights reserved.

California 1870 Census

Series M593

Name	Age	S	R	B-PL	County	Locale	Roll	Pg
CAMORO								
Theodore	40	m	w	SWIT	Mariposa	Mariposa P O	74	101
CAMOSSE								
John	23	m	w	SWIT	Marin	Tomales Twp	74	79
CAMOT								
Bartello	40	m	w	FRAN	Tuolumne	Columbia P O	93	342
CAMP								
Alice	45	f	w	ENGL	Yuba	Marysville	93	602
Asa S	40	m	w	PA	El Dorado	Kelsey Twp	72	61
C	45	m	w	PRUS	Sierra	Lincoln Twp	89	549
C E	45	m	w	OH	Sacramento	4-Wd Sacramento	77	373
Carconcia	23	m	w	MEXI	San Diego	Coronado	78	466
Carrol D	27	m	w	IL	Colusa	Butte Twp	71	271
E	13	m	w	CA	Alameda	Oakland	68	243
E C	15	m	w	CA	Alameda	Oakland	68	159
E S	13	m	w	CA	Alameda	Oakland	68	185
Frederick A	23	m	w	NY	Los Angeles	Los Angeles Twp	73	477
George	29	m	w	NY	Stanislaus	Empire Twp	92	53
H	54	m	w	CANA	Del Norte	Happy Camp Twp	71	470
Henry	39	m	w	HANO	San Francisco	San Francisco P O	83	30
Isador	21	m	w	PRUS	San Francisco	San Francisco P O	83	291
J W	37	m	w	MI	San Joaquin	3-Wd Stockton	86	239
James	41	m	w	CANA	Del Norte	Happy Camp Twp	71	470
John	33	m	w	IL	Contra Costa	Martinez P O	71	392
Joseph	42	m	w	ENGL	Klamath	South Fork Twp	73	385
Louis	24	m	w	LA	San Francisco	San Francisco P O	80	335
Nickolas	26	m	w	SAXO	Sonoma	Petaluma Twp	91	366
Peter R	35	m	w	VA	San Mateo	Redwood City P O	87	376
R	38	m	w	BADE	San Francisco	8-Wd San Francisco	82	365
R J	37	m	w	IREL	Tuolumne	Big Oak Flat P O	93	394
Sarah	41	f	w	ENGL	San Francisco	2-Wd San Francisco	79	187
T K	60	m	w	NY	San Joaquin	Castoria Twp	86	6
Wasick	35	f	i	CA	Del Norte	Happy Camp Twp	71	470
CAMPA								
F	50	f	w	MEXI	Alameda	Murray Twp	68	110
Francisco	24	m	w	MEXI	Amador	Jackson P O	69	326
M	30	m	w	MEXI	Alameda	Murray Twp	68	111
Manuel	40	m	w	CHIL	San Francisco	San Francisco P O	80	340
CAMPADOICO								
Gyton	27	m	w	ITAL	San Francisco	11-Wd San Francisc	84	701
CAMPAI								
John	34	m	w	ITAL	Amador	Volcano P O	69	376
CAMPANI								
Ansell	30	m	w	SWIT	El Dorado	Diamond Springs Tw	72	33
CAMPAS								
Andrea	40	m	w	MEXI	Tulare	Tule Rvr Twp	92	258
Antone	50	m	w	MEXI	Alameda	Washington Twp	68	287
Emanuel	60	m	w	MEXI	Tulare	Tule Rvr Twp	92	258
Gregorio	35	m	w	MEXI	Los Angeles	Soledad Twp	73	631
Miguel	39	m	w	MEXI	Santa Clara	Almaden Twp	88	14
Miguel	38	m	w	MEXI	Santa Clara	Almaden Twp	88	15
CAMPBEL								
Archy	40	m	w	MA	Calaveras	San Andreas P O	70	188
Casper	35	m	w	PRUS	San Francisco	7-Wd San Francisco	81	274
Henry	28	m	w	WI	Yolo	Grafton Twp	93	493
James	34	m	w	KY	Sonoma	Russian Rvr	91	372
Jane	42	f	w	TN	Sonoma	Russian Rvr	91	368
Jas A	65	m	w	KY	Sonoma	Russian Rvr	91	368
John W	35	m	w	TN	Sonoma	Santa Rosa	91	408
William	30	m	w	MA	Sonoma	Petaluma Twp	91	333
CAMPBELL								
A	33	m	w	SCOT	Solano	Vallejo	90	204
A	31	m	w	VT	Amador	Sutter Crk P O	69	408
A	24	m	w	SCOT	San Francisco	3-Wd San Francisco	79	314
A	11	f	w	US	Yuba	Marysville	93	609
A B	39	m	w	CANA	Amador	Ione City P O	69	350
A L	38	m	w	IREL	Solano	Vallejo	90	215
Adlan	61	m	w	NC	El Dorado	Coloma Twp	72	5
Alex	60	m	w	CANA	Alameda	Oakland	68	219
Alex	38	m	w	IREL	Solano	Vallejo	90	202
Alex	37	m	w	VA	Nevada	Nevada Twp	75	299
Alex	30	m	w	ENGL	San Francisco	3-Wd San Francisco	79	291
Alex	25	m	w	SCOT	Solano	Vallejo	90	213
Alex	12	m	w	CA	Solano	Vallejo	90	215
Alex W	41	m	w	IN	Butte	Hamilton Twp	70	66
Alexander	45	m	w	NY	Santa Clara	Milpitas Twp	88	115
Alexander	42	m	w	SCOT	Santa Clara	Santa Clara Twp	88	136
Alexander	39	m	w	VA	Nevada	Nevada Twp	75	317
Alexander	38	m	w	OH	Nevada	Rough & Ready Twp	75	324
Alexander	35	m	w	IREL	San Francisco	8-Wd San Francisco	82	487
Alexander	28	m	w	SCOT	Yolo	Washington Twp	93	530
Alexander	24	m	w	CANA	San Francisco	8-Wd San Francisco	82	435
Alexander	16	m	w	CA	Santa Clara	Santa Clara Twp	88	176
Alfred	32	m	w	ENGL	San Francisco	1-Wd San Francisco	79	96
Alice	58	f	w	ENGL	San Francisco	11-Wd San Francisc	84	544
Andrew	40	m	w	IREL	Monterey	Castroville Twp	74	335
Andrew	38	m	w	NY	San Francisco	11-Wd San Francisc	84	652
Andrew	35	m	w	IREL	San Francisco	1-Wd San Francisco	79	66
Andrew	30	m	w	IREL	Alameda	Eden Twp	68	85
Andrew	30	m	w	IREL	Alameda	Eden Twp	68	61
Andrew	21	m	w	PA	Marin	Sausalito Twp	74	74
Andrew	20	m	w	PA	San Francisco	1-Wd San Francisco	79	134
Andrw	54	m	w	SCOT	San Francisco	San Francisco P O	80	540
Angus	46	m	w	SCOT	Solano	Vallejo	90	174
Ann	36	f	w	IREL	Colusa	Colusa Twp	71	274
Anna	40	f	w	IREL	San Francisco	2-Wd San Francisco	79	145
Annie	58	f	w	IREL	San Francisco	11-Wd San Francisc	84	575
Anthony	38	m	w	SCOT	Placer	Bath P O	76	453
Archy	27	m	w	CANA	Inyo	Bishop Crk Twp	73	317
Austin	25	m	w	IREL	San Francisco	7-Wd San Francisco	81	202
Basil	49	m	b	MO	Yolo	Cottonwood Twp	93	469
Ben F	33	m	w	CANA	San Francisco	San Francisco P O	83	94
Benjamin	43	m	w	KY	Santa Clara	Santa Clara Twp	88	173
Benoni	40	m	w	MD	San Diego	San Diego	78	503
Bernt F	48	m	w	IREL	Plumas	Goodwin Twp	77	6
Bridget	40	f	w	IREL	Alameda	Alameda	68	5
Bryan	28	m	w	IREL	Solano	Vallejo	90	200
C	20	f	w	IREL	Sacramento	3-Wd Sacramento	77	279
C A	34	m	w	NY	San Joaquin	Dent Twp	86	26
C A	31	m	w	WI	San Joaquin	Tulare Twp	86	254
C A	16	m	w	CA	Alameda	Oakland	68	159
C D	33	m	w	MO	Monterey	Alisal Twp	74	290
C J	30	m	w	OH	Sacramento	1-Wd Sacramento	77	181
C T	28	m	w	WI	San Joaquin	Castoria Twp	86	3
Cath	32	f	w	IREL	Marin	Sausalito Twp	74	67
Catharine	58	f	w	OH	Placer	Auburn P O	76	378
Catherin	37	f	w	TN	Sacramento	Mississippi Twp	77	162
Charles	35	m	w	PA	San Mateo	Half Moon Bay P O	87	399
Charles	35	m	w	CANA	Solano	Suisun Twp	90	109
Charles	24	m	w	MA	San Francisco	San Francisco P O	83	165
Charles E	47	m	w	ME	Santa Clara	2-Wd San Jose	88	293
Chas	43	m	w	NJ	San Francisco	San Francisco P O	83	91
Chas	38	m	w	MI	Butte	Oregon Twp	70	122
Chas E	44	m	w	PA	Butte	Ophir Twp	70	101
Chas T	23	m	w	OH	San Francisco	San Francisco P O	85	757
Christopher	42	m	w	SWED	Plumas	Washington Twp	77	54
Cyrus C	54	m	w	PA	El Dorado	Diamond Springs Tw	72	33
D T	14	m	w	CA	Alameda	Oakland	68	243
D W	38	m	w	MA	Yuba	Marysville	93	617
Daniel	47	m	w	IREL	Santa Cruz	Santa Cruz Twp	89	394
Daniel	39	m	w	SCOT	San Diego	Julian Dist	78	469
Daniel	28	m	w	KY	San Francisco	San Francisco P O	83	138
David	45	m	w	KY	Tulare	Tule Rvr Twp	92	260
David	40	m	w	IREL	Sierra	Eureka Twp	89	526
David	37	m	w	IREL	Placer	Auburn P O	76	381
David	32	m	w	NY	Santa Clara	Milpitas Twp	88	115
Delos	41	m	w	NY	Los Angeles	Los Angeles	73	517
Donald	51	m	w	SCOT	San Francisco	11-Wd San Francisc	84	707
Duncan	55	m	w	SCOT	Inyo	Bishop Crk Twp	73	311
Duncan	41	m	w	SCOT	San Francisco	1-Wd San Francisco	79	13
Duncan	40	m	w	CANA	Napa	Yountville Twp	75	78
Duncan	31	m	w	CANA	Inyo	Bishop Crk Twp	73	311
Duncan	26	m	w	CANA	Sonoma	Analy Twp	91	224
E	57	m	w	VA	San Joaquin	Tulare Twp	86	258
E	25	m	w	NY	Alameda	Murray Twp	68	104
E B	42	m	w	NY	Solano	Vallejo	90	152
E W	38	m	w	PA	Calaveras	Copperopolis P O	70	226
Ed	45	m	w	IREL	San Francisco	7-Wd San Francisco	81	250
Edward	32	m	w	IREL	Santa Clara	Fremont Twp	88	66
Edwd	45	m	w	IREL	Butte	Concow Twp	70	8
Eliza	45	f	w	IREL	San Francisco	San Francisco P O	83	334
Elizabeth	75	f	w	VA	Butte	Oregon Twp	70	136
Elizabeth	30	f	w	WI	Nevada	Grass Valley Twp	75	159
Elizabth	36	f	w	IREL	Yuba	Rose Bar Twp	93	659
Ellen	30	f	w	IREL	San Francisco	11-Wd San Francisc	84	423
Ellen	29	f	w	IREL	Sacramento	3-Wd Sacramento	77	308
Ellen	28	f	w	IREL	Santa Clara	Gilroy Twp	88	68
Ellen	27	m	w	IREL	San Francisco	San Francisco P O	80	486
Emily	33	f	w	IN	San Francisco	1-Wd San Francisco	79	132
Emma	20	f	w	NY	Alameda	Oakland	68	259
Emma	18	f	w	CA	Sacramento	3-Wd Sacramento	77	286
Emma	15	f	w	MA	Solano	Vallejo	90	157
Everatt	18	m	w	IL	Colusa	Colusa Twp	71	286
F B	41	m	w	CT	Klamath	Klamath Twp	73	370
F H	32	m	w	NY	Sierra	Sierra Twp	89	564
F M	33	m	w	NY	Alameda	Oakland	68	162
Fanny	11	f	w	CA	San Francisco	6-Wd San Francisco	81	106
Felix	30	m	w	IREL	San Francisco	San Francisco P O	85	861
Frank	44	m	w	IREL	San Francisco	11-Wd San Francisc	84	582
Frank	4	m	w	CA	Mendocino	Sanel Twp	74	229
Frank	3	m	w	CANA	Napa	Yountville Twp	75	78
Frank	27	m	w	IREL	Tehama	Tehama P O	92	193
Fred	27	m	w	ENGL	San Francisco	San Francisco P O	83	398
Geo	61	m	w	KY	Lake	Lower Lake	73	418
Geo	41	m	w	NY	San Joaquin	2-Wd Stockton	86	187
Geo W	42	m	w	ME	San Francisco	San Francisco P O	85	734
George	52	m	w	NJ	Sonoma	Vallejo Twp	91	452
George	34	m	w	OH	Stanislaus	Emory Twp	92	21
George	23	m	w	IA	Sonoma	Sonoma Twp	91	437
George	18	m	w	CA	San Joaquin	Tulare Twp	86	251
George	18	m	w	ME	Stanislaus	Branch Twp	92	1
H	65	m	b	AR	San Joaquin	2-Wd Stockton	86	172
H C	39	m	w	SCOT	Sonoma	Petaluma Twp	91	320
H J	18	m	w	IA	San Joaquin	2-Wd Stockton	86	162
Hannah	34	f	w	IREL	Sacramento	4-Wd Sacramento	77	343
Henry	35	m	w	MO	Nevada	Nevada Twp	75	283
Henry	35	m	w	IREL	Contra Costa	Martinez P O	71	417
Henry	32	m	w	IREL	Contra Costa	Martinez P O	71	419
Henry	32	m	w	IREL	Amador	Volcano P O	69	388
Henry	30	m	w	IREL	San Francisco	San Francisco P O	85	723
Henry	27	m	w	WI	Yolo	Washington Twp	93	535
Houston	35	m	w	AL	Tulare	Venice Twp	92	276
Hugh	35	m	w	SCOT	San Bernardino	San Bernardino Twp	78	449
Hugh	27	m	w	IREL	San Francisco	San Francisco P O	85	753

© 2001 by Heritage Quest. All rights reserved.

Name	Age	S	R	B-PL	County	Locale	Roll	Pg
Isac	52	m	w	SCOT	Alameda	Alameda	68	12
J	54	m	w	SCOT	Sacramento	1-Wd Sacramento	77	180
J	42	m	w	NY	Yuba	Marysville	93	591
J	39	m	w	MO	Sierra	Lincoln Twp	89	545
J	38	m	w	CANA	Lassen	Janesville Twp	73	434
J	30	m	w	IREL	Sierra	Downieville Twp	89	518
J C	47	m	w	NY	Siskiyou	Callahan P O	89	630
J D	40	m	w	NY	Alameda	Oakland	68	161
J M	40	m	w	IREL	Tuolumne	Columbia P O	93	348
J M	18	m	w	MO	Mendocino	Little Lake Twp	74	200
J N	24	m	w	OH	Lake	Lower Lake	73	422
J S	35	m	w	OH	Tehama	Antelope Twp	92	160
J S	32	m	w	MO	Amador	Jackson P O	69	326
Jacob E	21	m	w	IA	Placer	Auburn P O	76	370
James	51	m	w	CANA	Nevada	Bridgeport Twp	75	124
James	50	m	w	IREL	San Joaquin	2-Wd Stockton	86	166
James	50	m	w	NY	San Mateo	Half Moon Bay P O	87	394
James	48	m	w	ENGL	San Francisco	8-Wd San Francisco	82	460
James	44	m	w	SCOT	Contra Costa	Martinez P O	71	402
James	43	m	w	IREL	San Francisco	1-Wd San Francisco	79	12
James	39	m	w	SCOT	San Francisco	3-Wd San Francisco	79	319
James	38	m	w	IA	Amador	Fiddletown P O	69	438
James	36	m	w	ME	San Joaquin	Oneal Twp	86	110
James	36	m	w	IREL	San Francisco	11-Wd San Francisc	84	499
James	35	m	w	IREL	San Francisco	1-Wd San Francisco	79	67
James	35	m	w	NY	San Francisco	7-Wd San Francisco	81	220
James	30	m	w	IREL	Amador	Volcano P O	69	388
James	29	m	w	OH	Lake	Lower Lake	73	423
James	29	m	w	IREL	Santa Clara	Fremont Twp	88	43
James	28	m	w	SCOT	San Francisco	1-Wd San Francisco	79	63
James	27	m	w	SCOT	San Francisco	San Francisco P O	83	224
James	27	m	w	MA	Marin	San Rafael Twp	74	37
James	25	m	w	MA	Solano	Suisun Twp	90	114
James	19	m	w	CA	Santa Clara	Santa Clara Twp	88	176
James B	37	m	w	TN	Mariposa	Mariposa P O	74	116
James C	40	m	w	PRUS	San Francisco	1-Wd San Francisco	79	132
James F	22	m	w	NJ	San Francisco	San Francisco P O	83	339
James M	50	m	w	ME	Nevada	Grass Valley Twp	75	154
James S	45	m	w	VA	Trinity	Junction City Pct	92	208
James S	44	m	w	NY	Sacramento	Granite Twp	77	145
James T	32	m	w	TN	Stanislaus	Empire Twp	92	35
Jane	73	f	w	PA	San Francisco	11-Wd San Francisc	84	623
Jane	67	f	w	IREL	Santa Clara	Fremont Twp	88	56
Jane	30	f	w	CANA	Contra Costa	Martinez P O	71	418
Jared	46	m	w	PA	Sacramento	Brighton Twp	77	79
Jas	37	m	w	IREL	Sierra	Table Rock Twp	89	544
Jas A	39	m	w	PA	San Francisco	3-Wd San Francisco	79	328
Jas D	32	m	w	GA	Mariposa	Mariposa P O	74	101
Jas W H	42	m	w	CANA	San Francisco	1-Wd San Francisco	79	132
Jefferson	41	m	w	KY	Tulare	Farmersville Twp	92	242
Jein	41	m	w	CANA	San Joaquin	Castoria Twp	86	8
Jerome	34	m	w	OH	Marin	San Rafael	74	49
Jno	21	m	w	CANA	Alameda	Oakland	68	235
Jno A	31	m	w	OH	San Joaquin	Douglas Twp	86	46
Jo	42	m	w	NY	San Francisco	5-Wd San Francisco	81	22
John	65	m	w	SCOT	Los Angeles	Soledad Twp	73	632
John	56	m	w	CANA	San Francisco	San Francisco P O	83	95
John	49	m	b	EIND	San Joaquin	Douglas Twp	86	43
John	47	m	w	IREL	Butte	Ophir Twp	70	109
John	45	m	w	SCOT	Tulare	Tule Rvr Twp	92	262
John	45	m	w	IREL	Alameda	Oakland	68	155
John	45	m	w	IREL	Sacramento	2-Wd Sacramento	77	223
John	41	m	w	OH	Placer	Emigrant Gap P O	76	417
John	41	m	w	OH	Placer	Summit P O	76	496
John	40	m	w	IREL	Sierra	Table Rock Twp	89	544
John	40	m	b	DC	San Francisco	San Francisco P O	80	359
John	38	m	w	IREL	San Francisco	1-Wd San Francisco	79	107
John	37	m	w	AL	Solano	Suisun Twp	90	104
John	37	m	w	SCOT	San Francisco	1-Wd San Francisco	79	82
John	35	m	w	ENGL	San Francisco	2-Wd San Francisco	79	254
John	33	m	w	OH	Monterey	Alisal Twp	74	297
John	33	m	w	IL	San Joaquin	1-Wd Stockton	86	155
John	32	m	w	IREL	San Francisco	San Francisco P O	80	340
John	31	m	w	IREL	Nevada	Nevada Twp	75	301
John	30	m	w	IREL	Santa Clara	Fremont Twp	88	55
John	30	m	w	MO	Santa Clara	Santa Clara Twp	88	174
John	30	m	w	NCOD	Colusa	Monroe Twp	71	325
John	28	m	w	NY	San Francisco	7-Wd San Francisco	81	221
John	28	m	w	IL	San Diego	Julian Dist	78	468
John	28	m	w	IL	Alameda	Murray Twp	68	124
John	28	m	w	IREL	San Francisco	San Francisco P O	85	747
John	27	m	w	PA	Santa Clara	2-Wd San Jose	88	313
John	27	m	w	PA	Los Angeles	Los Nietos Twp	73	573
John	24	m	w	NY	San Francisco	San Francisco P O	80	472
John	22	m	w	BADE	Sacramento	Franklin Twp	77	105
John	21	m	w	CANA	Mono	Bridgeport P O	74	282
John	19	m	w	ENGL	Plumas	Seneca Twp	77	51
John	19	m	w	CANA	Merced	Snelling P O	74	259
John A	51	m	w	NC	Santa Clara	San Jose Twp	88	189
John A	32	m	w	SCOT	San Francisco	6-Wd San Francisco	81	86
John B	38	m	w	PA	Placer	Bath P O	76	459
John C	35	m	w	IL	Yolo	Putah Twp	93	523
John D	32	m	w	OH	San Luis Obispo	Santa Rosa Twp	87	319
John F	50	m	w	VA	Fresno	Kings Rvr P O	72	211
John H	44	m	w	LA	Placer	Newcastle Twp	76	479
John H	40	m	w	ENGL	Nevada	Grass Valley Twp	75	213
John O	63	m	w	PA	San Francisco	San Francisco P O	83	405
Jos	40	m	w	IREL	Mono	Bridgeport P O	74	284
Jos	40	m	w	BADE	Sacramento	3-Wd Sacramento	77	257
Joseph	43	m	w	NC	Nevada	Bridgeport Twp	75	120
Joseph	33	m	w	IREL	San Francisco	7-Wd San Francisco	81	181
Joseph	28	m	w	IREL	San Francisco	7-Wd San Francisco	81	247
Joseph	14	m	w	CA	San Francisco	11-Wd San Francisc	84	592
Jrony	35	m	w	NY	Mono	Bridgeport P O	74	285
June	30	f	w	IREL	Santa Cruz	Santa Cruz Twp	89	395
Kate	32	f	w	IREL	San Joaquin	2-Wd Stockton	86	165
Laura	2	f	w	CA	Calaveras	Copperopolis P O	70	249
Lewis	32	m	w	VT	Nevada	Nevada Twp	75	309
Louis	21	m	b	MO	Santa Clara	2-Wd San Jose	88	281
Louis	14	m	w	CA	Santa Clara	Santa Clara Twp	88	176
Louisa	46	f	w	TN	Kern	Linns Valley P O	73	347
Louisa	45	f	w	VT	San Francisco	San Francisco P O	83	266
Louisa V	18	f	w	CA	San Francisco	San Francisco P O	83	96
Lucy	20	m	w	MO	Yolo	Grafton Twp	93	500
M	60	m	w	IREL	Alameda	Oakland	68	178
M	41	m	w	CHIL	Sierra	Forest Twp	89	532
M	39	m	w	IREL	Solano	Vallejo	90	217
M B	11	m	w	MI	Alameda	Oakland	68	178
M L	34	m	w	OH	Sacramento	3-Wd Sacramento	77	291
M S	48	m	w	NY	Alameda	Oakland	68	139
Maddison	34	m	w	MI	San Francisco	11-Wd San Francisc	84	705
Mal	27	m	w	CANA	Butte	Chico Twp	70	55
Malcolm	22	m	w	CANA	Stanislaus	Emory Twp	92	20
Marcellina	33	f	w	CA	Santa Clara	1-Wd San Jose	88	275
Margaret	9	f	w	CA	Tulare	Farmersville Twp	92	245
Margaret	35	f	w	PA	San Francisco	San Francisco P O	85	751
Mark	26	m	w	IREL	San Francisco	1-Wd San Francisco	79	41
Martha	30	f	w	MO	San Joaquin	Elliott Twp	86	74
Mary	46	f	w	NY	Siskiyou	Scott Valley Twp	89	619
Mary	40	f	w	IREL	San Joaquin	3-Wd Stockton	86	232
Mary	39	f	b	KY	Sacramento	4-Wd Sacramento	77	329
Mary	36	f	w	PA	Sonoma	Bodega Twp	91	256
Mary	24	f	w	CANA	San Francisco	2-Wd San Francisco	79	234
Mary	21	f	i	CA	Trinity	North Fork Twp	92	218
Mary	16	f	w	NY	Humboldt	Eureka Twp	72	264
Mary	16	f	w	MA	San Joaquin	Douglas Twp	86	37
Mary	10	f	w	MO	Contra Costa	Martinez P O	71	396
Mary F	14	f	w	MO	Yolo	Buckeye Twp	93	416
Matt	35	m	w	ENGL	San Francisco	3-Wd San Francisco	79	295
Matthew	59	m	w	IREL	Placer	Auburn P O	76	375
Michael	36	m	w	IREL	San Francisco	San Francisco P O	80	461
Micheal	30	m	w	MA	San Francisco	7-Wd San Francisco	81	179
Milton	8M	m	w	CA	San Francisco	San Francisco P O	83	280
Milton	35	m	w	ME	Santa Clara	1-Wd San Jose	88	240
Murdock	38	m	w	IREL	Santa Clara	1-Wd San Jose	88	278
N	31	m	w	CANA	Klamath	Trinidad Twp	73	390
N C	56	m	w	SCOT	Tuolumne	Chinese Camp P O	93	383
Norman	29	m	w	CANA	Contra Costa	Martinez P O	71	447
O F	33	m	w	NY	Sacramento	4-Wd Sacramento	77	353
Oscar	29	m	w	ME	Nevada	Nevada Twp	75	309
P	43	m	w	IREL	San Francisco	San Francisco P O	83	319
P	35	m	w	IREL	Yuba	Marysville	93	583
P	30	m	w	CANA	Alameda	Oakland	68	263
P	27	m	w	CANA	Alameda	Oakland	68	214
P J	33	m	w	IREL	Alameda	Murray Twp	68	121
Pat	50	m	w	IREL	San Francisco	11-Wd San Francisc	84	576
Pat	48	m	w	CANA	San Francisco	2-Wd San Francisco	79	215
Pat	42	m	w	IREL	San Francisco	11-Wd San Francisc	84	619
Patrick	46	m	w	IREL	Nevada	Bridgeport Twp	75	114
Patrick	30	m	w	IREL	Nevada	Eureka Twp	75	139
Peter	54	m	w	ENGL	San Francisco	San Francisco P O	80	388
Peter	45	m	w	PA	San Francisco	7-Wd San Francisco	81	177
Peter	38	m	w	IREL	Alameda	Washington Twp	68	284
Peter	35	m	w	SCOT	Marin	Bolinas Twp	74	1
Peter J	64	m	w	NY	Alameda	Washington Twp	68	268
Porter	35	m	w	IREL	San Francisco	San Francisco P O	85	795
R E	60	m	w	ENGL	Tuolumne	Columbia P O	93	351
R H	31	m	w	IA	Tehama	Red Bluff	92	179
R R	45	m	w	SCOT	Solano	Vallejo	90	189
R W	30	m	w	MI	Alameda	Oakland	68	265
Reina	60	f	b	TN	San Joaquin	3-Wd Stockton	86	224
Richd	44	m	b	TN	Santa Cruz	Watsonville	89	371
Robert	54	m	w	KY	Solano	Vacaville Twp	90	128
Robert	40	m	w	NY	San Mateo	Half Moon Bay P O	87	399
Robert	36	m	w	IREL	San Francisco	7-Wd San Francisco	81	286
Robert	35	m	w	AR	Tulare	Farmersville Twp	92	246
Robert	32	m	w	SCOT	Santa Cruz	Soquel Twp	89	450
Robert	30	m	w	SCOT	San Francisco	San Francisco P O	83	187
Robert	27	m	w	PA	Plumas	Indian Twp	77	9
Robert	26	m	w	ENGL	San Francisco	11-Wd San Francisc	84	519
Robert	24	m	w	CANA	Mendocino	Navarro & Big Rvr	74	177
Robt	39	m	w	SCOT	Alameda	Oakland	68	234
Robt	35	m	w	IREL	San Francisco	2-Wd San Francisco	79	148
Robt	30	m	w	IREL	Solano	Vallejo	90	154
Robt	20	m	w	NY	Merced	Snelling P O	74	272
Robt A	27	m	w	ME	Sacramento	4-Wd Sacramento	77	348
Rosanna	57	f	w	KY	Santa Clara	2-Wd San Jose	88	297
S	50	f	b	KY	Sierra	Downieville Twp	89	519
S	29	m	w	IN	Nevada	Meadow Lake Twp	75	252
S	19	f	w	IN	Yuba	Marysville	93	605
S	16	m	w	CA	San Joaquin	Douglas Twp	86	34
S K	65	m	w	KY	San Joaquin	Castoria Twp	86	3
S S	44	m	w	KY	Tuolumne	Columbia P O	93	347
Sam	36	m	w	NY	San Joaquin	Elkhorn Twp	86	54

Series M593

© 2001 by Heritage Quest. All rights reserved.

Series M593

Name	Age	S	R	B-PL	County	Locale	Roll	Pg
Samuel D	43	m	w	NC	Solano	Suisun Twp	90	93
Samuel H	24	m	w	TX	Los Angeles	Soledad Twp	73	632
Samuel Y	65	m	w	KY	Stanislaus	San Joaquin Twp	92	78
Sarah	40	f	w	IREL	San Francisco	2-Wd San Francisco	79	148
Sarah	40	f	w	IREL	El Dorado	Placerville	72	126
Sarah	25	f	w	IREL	San Francisco	San Francisco P O	83	339
Sarah	16	f	w	CA	Nevada	Grass Valley Twp	75	230
Smith	49	m	w	NY	San Diego	San Diego	78	505
Sophia	51	f	w	MO	San Francisco	San Francisco P O	83	280
Susan	36	f	w	CANA	San Joaquin	Oneal Twp	86	102
Sydney	25	f	w	SCOT	Sacramento	4-Wd Sacramento	77	326
T G	44	m	w	KY	Trinity	North Fork Twp	92	218
Theo	25	m	w	CANA	Santa Clara	Gilroy Twp	88	94
Thobia	34	m	w	NY	Placer	Emigrant Gap P O	76	416
Thomas	63	m	w	IREL	Placer	Bath P O	76	449
Thomas	60	m	w	NH	Placer	Bath P O	76	433
Thomas	52	m	w	KY	Santa Clara	2-Wd San Jose	88	284
Thomas	36	m	b	WIND	Sacramento	2-Wd Sacramento	77	238
Thomas	36	m	w	SCOT	Marin	San Rafael Twp	74	45
Thomas	34	m	w	CANA	Contra Costa	Martinez P O	71	370
Thomas	34	m	w	CANA	San Francisco	San Francisco P O	83	221
Thomas	32	m	w	IREL	San Francisco	11-Wd San Francisc	84	502
Thomas	22	m	w	IL	Santa Clara	1-Wd San Jose	88	225
Thomas G	45	m	w	KY	Humboldt	Eureka Twp	72	275
Thomas P	30	m	w	MO	Los Angeles	Los Angeles	73	552
Thos	56	m	w	SCOT	Marin	Nicasio Twp	74	18
Thos	47	m	w	IREL	San Francisco	San Francisco P O	83	128
Thos	44	m	w	IREL	Siskiyou	Yreka	89	661
Thos	30	m	w	IREL	Solano	Vallejo	90	186
Thos	30	m	w	SCOT	San Francisco	San Francisco P O	83	91
Thos	19	m	b	MO	San Joaquin	Liberty Twp	86	84
Thos C	50	m	w	SCOT	Sonoma	Salt Point	91	392
W	44	m	w	CANA	San Joaquin	Tulare Twp	86	254
W	41	m	w	IREL	Sierra	Downieville Twp	89	517
W B	40	m	w	KY	Nevada	Meadow Lake Twp	75	264
W C	21	m	w	IA	Tehama	Red Bluff	92	179
W H	42	m	w	PA	San Francisco	San Francisco P O	85	792
W L	47	m	w	VA	San Joaquin	Elliott Twp	86	74
W R	32	m	w	NY	Alameda	San Leandro	68	96
Washington	33	m	w	WV	Calaveras	Copperopolis P O	70	250
William	78	m	w	KY	Santa Clara	Santa Clara Twp	88	174
William	54	m	w	PA	Yolo	Cache Crk Twp	93	453
William	47	m	w	PA	Amador	Fiddletown P O	69	437
William	42	m	w	SCOT	Nevada	Grass Valley Twp	75	180
William	40	m	w	NY	Placer	Summit P O	76	496
William	40	m	w	IREL	Nevada	Grass Valley Twp	75	170
William	38	m	w	SCOT	Santa Cruz	Santa Cruz	89	431
William	38	m	w	PA	San Francisco	San Francisco P O	83	238
William	35	m	w	IREL	Alameda	Eden Twp	68	84
William	34	m	w	MO	San Bernardino	San Bernardino Twp	78	438
William	32	m	w	IREL	Yolo	Grafton Twp	93	480
William	29	m	w	MO	Santa Clara	Redwood Twp	88	122
William	27	m	w	ME	San Francisco	7-Wd San Francisco	81	220
William	25	m	w	SCOT	Contra Costa	Martinez P O	71	427
William	25	m	w	IREL	San Francisco	San Francisco P O	83	350
William D	25	m	w	MO	Yolo	Buckeye Twp	93	415
William G	34	m	w	KY	Santa Clara	Santa Clara Twp	88	174
William J	40	m	w	CANA	San Francisco	11-Wd San Francisc	84	706
Wilson	41	m	w	ENGL	Yolo	Putah Twp	93	526
Wilson	35	m	w	MA	Yolo	Buckeye Twp	93	414
Wm	45	m	w	IREL	Alameda	Murray Twp	68	101
Wm	39	m	w	IREL	Butte	Ophir Twp	70	120
Wm	38	m	w	VA	San Francisco	2-Wd San Francisco	79	203
Wm	32	m	w	IREL	Solano	Vallejo	90	205
Wm	30	m	w	SCOT	San Francisco	7-Wd San Francisco	81	259
Wm	28	m	w	CANA	Solano	Benicia	90	6
Wm	15	m	w	NY	Tehama	Red Bluff	92	182
Wm A	41	m	w	FRAN	Tuolumne	Sonora P O	93	323
Wm B	58	m	w	CA	Nevada	Nevada Twp	75	297
Wm H	37	m	w	IREL	San Mateo	Half Moon Bay P O	87	400
CAMPDONICA								
Louis	29	m	w	FRAN	San Francisco	San Francisco P O	80	458
CAMPE								
G	32	m	w	SPAI	San Francisco	3-Wd San Francisco	79	318
George	16	m	w	BRAZ	San Francisco	8-Wd San Francisco	82	361
Henry	35	m	w	PRUS	San Francisco	San Francisco P O	83	223
Henry	28	m	w	LA	Marin	San Rafael	74	57
Justis	41	m	w	PRUS	San Francisco	San Francisco P O	80	406
Magnus	29	m	w	HANO	San Francisco	San Francisco P O	83	93
William	49	m	w	PRUS	San Francisco	San Francisco P O	80	490
CAMPEDONI								
Guy	30	m	w	ITAL	San Francisco	11-Wd San Francisc	84	614
CAMPEL								
Fannie	39	f	w	IREL	Monterey	Castroville Twp	74	328
CAMPELL								
Agness	14	f	w	CA	Humboldt	Eureka Twp	72	265
CAMPELLA								
Francis	20	m	w	SWIT	Marin	Tomales Twp	74	77
CAMPENS								
Loretto	34	f	w	MEXI	San Francisco	San Francisco P O	80	474
CAMPER								
Henry W	39	m	w	VA	Yuba	Bullards Bar P O	93	551
Lewis S	37	m	w	VA	Yuba	Bullards Bar P O	93	551
Lucas	50	m	w	ITAL	Calaveras	Copperopolis P O	70	244
N	24	m	w	ITAL	Calaveras	Copperopolis P O	70	233
S	34	m	w	ITAL	Calaveras	Copperopolis P O	70	233
CAMPERDONCO								
Paulo	30	m	w	ITAL	Tuolumne	Sonora P O	93	330
CAMPFIELD								
---	60	m	w	PA	El Dorado	White Oak Twp	72	142
CAMPH								
Joseph	48	m	w	SWIT	Sacramento	Franklin Twp	77	112
CAMPHENE								
Augusta	40	m	w	CA	Santa Clara	Redwood Twp	88	117
Peter	50	m	w	SWIT	El Dorado	Placerville	72	123
CAMPIEN								
Ed	27	m	w	IREL	Solano	Vallejo	90	162
CAMPILI								
Petra	23	m	w	SWIT	Marin	Bolinas Twp	74	2
CAMPILL								
Wm	50	m	w	ME	Tuolumne	Sonora P O	93	318
CAMPILLI								
Charles	20	m	w	SWIT	Marin	Nicasio Twp	74	20
CAMPIN								
Thomas	28	m	w	IREL	San Francisco	San Francisco P O	83	382
CAMPINE								
Vincent	38	m	w	SWIT	El Dorado	Placerville	72	125
CAMPION								
A	36	m	w	NY	Alameda	Oakland	68	255
A	32	m	w	ME	Alameda	Oakland	68	265
Edward	33	m	w	IREL	San Francisco	San Francisco P O	83	357
H T S	31	m	w	ENGL	Sacramento	1-Wd Sacramento	77	175
Henry	21	m	w	NY	San Francisco	San Francisco P O	83	350
J	25	m	w	IREL	Solano	Vallejo	90	196
John S	44	m	w	MA	Los Angeles	Los Angeles	73	540
Kate	22	f	w	IREL	San Francisco	2-Wd San Francisco	79	143
Michael	42	m	w	IREL	San Francisco	11-Wd San Francisc	84	469
Michal	16	m	w	IREL	San Francisco	11-Wd San Francisc	84	462
Patrick	31	m	w	IREL	Nevada	Grass Valley Twp	75	198
Thos	36	m	w	IREL	San Francisco	San Francisco P O	83	332
William	39	m	w	IREL	Butte	Oregon Twp	70	126
William S	30	m	w	ME	Los Angeles	San Juan Twp	73	624
CAMPO								
Antonio	35	m	w	ITAL	Los Angeles	Los Angeles	73	568
Francisco	25	m	w	MEXI	Monterey	San Antonio Twp	74	316
Jessee	24	f	w	MEXI	Amador	Jackson P O	69	322
Pedro	44	m	w	MEXI	Santa Clara	Burnett Twp	88	35
CAMPODONICA								
John	27	m	w	ITAL	San Francisco	San Francisco P O	80	331
Pasquale	26	m	w	ITAL	San Francisco	6-Wd San Francisco	81	124
CAMPODONICO								
Antonio	44	m	w	ITAL	Mariposa	Mariposa P O	74	94
Giuseppe	32	m	w	ITAL	San Francisco	11-Wd San Francisc	84	594
John	25	m	w	ITAL	Tulare	Visalia	92	294
CAMPOI								
Josafa	44	f	w	MEXI	Napa	Napa	75	55
P	20	m	w	MEXI	Napa	Napa	75	55
CAMPON								
David	22	m	w	MO	San Joaquin	Douglas Twp	86	33
Louis	47	m	w	FRAN	Santa Clara	Alviso Twp	88	26
CAMPONIE								
Anton	37	m	w	AUST	San Francisco	San Francisco P O	83	369
CAMPOS								
Antonio	18	m	w	CA	Santa Clara	Almaden Twp	88	15
Ignatio	45	m	w	MEXI	Shasta	Shasta P O	89	456
Louis	35	m	w	MEXI	San Francisco	1-Wd San Francisco	79	131
CAMPOWSKI								
Gustave	26	m	w	PRUS	Marin	San Rafael Twp	74	46
CAMPP								
Albert	25	m	w	NY	Solano	Maine Prairie Twp	90	54
CAMPRO								
John	45	m	w	CHIL	El Dorado	Greenwood Twp	72	54
CAMPRON								
Mary	30	f	w	IREL	Santa Clara	2-Wd San Jose	88	294
Mary	25	f	w	IREL	San Francisco	11-Wd San Francisc	84	440
CAMPS								
Jose A	37	m	w	CA	Santa Barbara	Santa Barbara P O	87	455
CAMPSIE								
William	47	m	w	IREL	Trinity	Junction City Pct	92	209
CAMPTON								
A P	53	m	w	OH	Humboldt	Eel Rvr Twp	72	254
Alfred	32	m	w	ENGL	San Francisco	1-Wd San Francisco	79	17
Caroline	44	f	w	MI	Humboldt	Eel Rvr Twp	72	250
E	19	f	w	KY	Yuba	Marysville	93	605
Emma	19	f	w	ENGL	Humboldt	Bucksport Twp	72	244
Ezre G	37	m	w	MO	Placer	Alta P O	76	412
Geo	30	m	w	MA	Solano	Vallejo	90	155
George	7M	m	w	CA	Sacramento	2-Wd Sacramento	77	238
John	29	m	w	IREL	San Francisco	1-Wd San Francisco	79	122
Susan	39	f	w	MO	Monterey	Salinas Twp	74	312
T J	27	m	w	MS	Humboldt	Eel Rvr Twp	72	248
William	39	m	w	TN	Kern	Tehachapi P O	73	356
Wm	35	m	w	MD	San Joaquin	2-Wd Stockton	86	177
Wm	27	m	w	MA	San Francisco	1-Wd San Francisco	79	130
CAMREN								
Angelica	20	f	w	IREL	San Francisco	5-Wd San Francisco	81	15
CAMRON								
John	39	m	w	PA	San Francisco	San Francisco P O	83	393
Olive	16	f	w	CA	Sonoma	Petaluma Twp	91	310
Philip	23	m	w	CANA	Placer	Bath P O	76	460
Robert	28	m	w	CANA	Placer	Bath P O	76	460
William	32	m	w	SCOT	Placer	Bath P O	76	454

© 2001 by Heritage Quest. All rights reserved.

Name	Age	S	R	B-PL	County	Locale	Series M593 Roll	Pg
CAMSO								
Henry	44	m	w	ITAL	Solano	Montezuma Twp	90	67
CAMTRON								
James E	29	m	w	IL	Plumas	Quartz Twp	77	39
CAMUEL								
Mary	23	f	w	IREL	San Francisco	8-Wd San Francisco	82	463
CAMY								
Chester	44	m	w	PA	Amador	Drytown P O	69	422
CAN								
---	15	m	c	CHIN	San Francisco	San Francisco P O	85	720
Ah	56	m	c	CHIN	Amador	Drytown P O	69	419
Ah	54	m	c	CHIN	Tuolumne	Chinese Camp P O	93	390
Ah	50	m	c	CHIN	Tuolumne	Chinese Camp P O	93	379
Ah	46	m	c	CHIN	Sacramento	Granite Twp	77	151
Ah	42	m	c	CHIN	Calaveras	San Andreas P O	70	179
Ah	40	m	c	CHIN	Siskiyou	Hamburg Twp	89	598
Ah	39	m	c	CHIN	Fresno	Millerton P O	72	199
Ah	38	m	c	CHIN	Santa Cruz	Pajaro Twp	89	344
Ah	37	m	c	CHIN	Butte	Hamilton Twp	70	68
Ah	36	m	c	CHIN	Tuolumne	Chinese Camp P O	93	364
Ah	35	m	c	CHIN	Sacramento	Cosumnes Twp	77	89
Ah	33	m	c	CHIN	Calaveras	San Andreas P O	70	183
Ah	32	m	c	CHIN	Fresno	Millerton P O	72	199
Ah	30	m	c	CHIN	Santa Cruz	Soquel Twp	89	442
Ah	30	m	c	CHIN	Tuolumne	Chinese Camp P O	93	370
Ah	29	m	c	CHIN	Amador	Ione City P O	69	364
Ah	28	m	c	CHIN	Tuolumne	Chinese Camp P O	93	388
Ah	25	m	c	CHIN	Amador	Fiddletown P O	69	428
Ah	25	m	c	CHIN	San Francisco	San Francisco P O	80	456
Ah	24	m	c	CHIN	Fresno	Millerton P O	72	163
Ah	20	m	c	CHIN	San Francisco	San Francisco P O	83	132
Ah	20	m	c	CHIN	Solano	Suisun Twp	90	105
Ah	19	m	c	CHIN	Santa Cruz	Santa Cruz	89	408
Ah	18	m	c	CHIN	Tuolumne	Big Oak Flat P O	93	403
Ah	18	f	c	CHIN	San Francisco	San Francisco P O	80	444
Ah	17	m	c	CHIN	Sacramento	Franklin Twp	77	107
Ah	17	m	c	CHIN	Nevada	Nevada Twp	75	279
Charles	34	m	w	IREL	Placer	Gold Run Twp	76	399
Dow	39	m	c	CHIN	Yuba	Marysville	93	631
Foy	55	m	c	CHIN	Calaveras	San Andreas P O	70	187
Heen	30	m	c	CHIN	Siskiyou	Cottonwood Twp	89	594
Hen	44	m	c	CHIN	Plumas	Rich Bar Twp	77	45
How	24	m	c	CHIN	Tehama	Tehama Twp	92	189
James	35	m	w	SCOT	Klamath	South Fork Twp	73	385
John	39	m	w	IL	Amador	Ione City P O	69	360
Low	40	m	c	CHIN	Calaveras	San Andreas P O	70	171
Pat	25	m	c	CHIN	Sacramento	Franklin Twp	77	116
Richard M	20	m	w	LA	Sacramento	Franklin Twp	77	116
Sing	60	m	c	CHIN	Del Norte	Happy Camp Twp	71	468
Stephen	29	m	w	TN	San Joaquin	Tulare Twp	86	262
Sui	2	f	c	CHIN	Monterey	Monterey Twp	74	351
Tan	45	m	c	CHIN	Calaveras	Copperopolis P O	70	234
Tin	39	m	c	CHIN	Yuba	Marysville	93	625
Tin	23	m	c	CHIN	Solano	Rio Vista Twp	90	70
To	40	m	c	CHIN	Calaveras	San Andreas P O	70	162
Toe He	32	f	c	CHIN	Calaveras	San Andreas P O	70	211
Tong	37	m	c	CHIN	Nevada	Nevada Twp	75	313
Wee	16	m	c	CHIN	Tehama	Tehama Twp	92	188
CANA								
Pedro	23	m	w	MEXI	Santa Clara	Almaden Twp	88	6
CANADA								
Charles	32	m	w	CANA	Sonoma	Sonoma Twp	91	431
Cora	15	f	w	OH	Colusa	Colusa Twp	71	278
Edward	25	m	w	CANA	Sacramento	Sutter Twp	77	389
Francis	15	f	w	SC	Colusa	Colusa	71	289
Humphry	35	m	w	IREL	San Francisco	San Francisco P O	85	803
James	21	m	w	CANA	Sacramento	Franklin Twp	77	117
John	38	m	w	IREL	Sacramento	Georgianna Twp	77	125
John	21	m	w	CANA	Sacramento	Franklin Twp	77	113
John	20	m	w	MD	Yolo	Cache Crk Twp	93	449
Juan	34	m	w	AZOR	San Francisco	1-Wd San Francisco	79	118
Mike	27	m	w	CANA	Sacramento	Sutter Twp	77	389
CANADO								
Dolores	36	m	w	CA	Los Angeles	Los Angeles	73	555
CANADY								
Silas	38	m	w	IL	Yuba	Long Bar Twp	93	563
CANAGERANTO								
F	33	m	w	CHIL	Santa Clara	Almaden Twp	88	10
CANALA								
Serillo	45	m	w	MEXI	Tulare	Tule Rvr Twp	92	266
CANALES								
Jose	65	m	w	CHIL	Calaveras	San Andreas P O	70	196
CANALL								
Richard	31	m	w	NY	San Diego	Julian Dist	78	471
CANAN								
J J	15	m	w	CA	Alameda	Oakland	68	243
Jerome	13	m	w	OR	Sonoma	Bodega Twp	91	255
Wm S	48	m	w	PA	Sonoma	Healdsburg & Mendo	91	284
CANAPER								
August	38	m	w	ITAL	San Francisco	2-Wd San Francisco	79	149
CANARASSIM								
John	36	m	w	ITAL	San Francisco	1-Wd San Francisco	79	105
CANARD								
James H	33	m	w	PA	Nevada	Eureka Twp	75	135
CANARES								
Peter	52	m	w	PRUS	Santa Cruz	Soquel Twp	89	436

Name	Age	S	R	B-PL	County	Locale	Series M593 Roll	Pg
CANARLY								
Patrick	38	m	w	IREL	San Francisco	8-Wd San Francisco	82	295
CANARY								
Abbia	23	f	w	CT	San Francisco	8-Wd San Francisco	82	446
John B	24	m	w	PRUS	Santa Cruz	Soquel Twp	89	444
CANAS								
Vicente	30	m	w	MEXI	Los Angeles	Los Angeles Twp	73	467
CANAT								
Adeline	11	f	w	CA	San Luis Obispo	Morro Twp	87	287
CANAVA								
Geo	27	m	w	ITAL	Tuolumne	Big Oak Flat P O	93	402
CANAVAN								
Elen	24	f	w	IREL	San Francisco	8-Wd San Francisco	82	379
Ellen	22	f	w	IREL	San Francisco	San Francisco P O	80	425
Geo	45	m	w	ITAL	Tuolumne	Big Oak Flat P O	93	403
James	71	m	w	TN	Stanislaus	San Joaquin Twp	92	73
James	48	m	w	IREL	Nevada	Meadow Lake Twp	75	260
James	45	m	w	IREL	San Francisco	11-Wd San Francisc	84	495
James	40	m	w	IREL	San Francisco	San Francisco P O	83	248
James	30	m	w	IREL	San Francisco	7-Wd San Francisco	81	190
John	29	m	w	MA	San Francisco	1-Wd San Francisco	79	123
Mark	37	m	w	IREL	Contra Costa	Martinez P O	71	409
Mary	25	f	w	IREL	San Francisco	8-Wd San Francisco	82	420
Mat	37	m	w	IREL	San Francisco	San Francisco P O	83	351
Michl	42	m	w	IREL	San Francisco	1-Wd San Francisco	79	86
Nancy	70	f	w	KY	Stanislaus	San Joaquin Twp	92	73
Patrick	41	m	w	CANA	San Francisco	1-Wd San Francisco	79	62
Peter	35	m	w	ENGL	Alameda	Washington Twp	68	282
Sabina	22	f	w	IREL	San Francisco	11-Wd San Francisc	84	574
Thomas	30	m	w	MA	San Francisco	San Francisco P O	83	218
CANAVER								
Antonio	32	m	w	ITAL	Mariposa	Mariposa P O	74	106
CANAY								
David	47	m	w	IREL	San Francisco	7-Wd San Francisco	81	166
Morris	30	m	w	IREL	San Francisco	11-Wd San Francisc	84	524
CANAZALEZ								
Leana Mina	59	f	w	CA	Santa Cruz	Pajaro Twp	89	357
CANBOY								
P	31	m	w	IREL	Lake	Knoxville Mines	73	404
CANBRE								
Celia	39	f	w	PRUS	Solano	Silveyville Twp	90	73
CANBY								
Jane	30	f	w	IREL	Alameda	Oakland	68	198
CANCORICH								
George	40	m	w	FRAN	San Francisco	3-Wd San Francisco	79	316
CANDAGE								
Wiley	25	m	w	MA	San Francisco	7-Wd San Francisco	81	156
CANDAN								
Eugene	42	m	w	FRAN	Calaveras	San Andreas P O	70	186
CANDEAU								
Joseph	23	m	w	PORT	San Mateo	Half Moon Bay P O	87	400
CANDELARIA								
Manuel	60	m	w	MEXI	Monterey	San Antonio Twp	74	319
CANDIA								
Manuel	36	m	w	PORT	Alameda	Hayward	68	77
CANDIDO								
Joseph	35	m	w	PORT	Alameda	San Leandro	68	96
Luigi	28	m	w	ITAL	El Dorado	Diamond Springs Tw	72	29
CANDILL								
Nancy	64	f	w	KY	Santa Cruz	Pajaro Twp	89	354
Theophilus	39	m	w	IL	Santa Cruz	Pajaro Twp	89	354
CANDISE								
Peter	28	m	w	FRAN	San Francisco	San Francisco P O	83	4
CANDLE								
Amelius J	23	m	w	MS	Los Angeles	Los Nietos Twp	73	573
James	37	m	w	KY	Plumas	Quartz Twp	77	36
CANDY								
Jas	38	m	w	ENGL	San Joaquin	2-Wd Stockton	86	200
CANE								
Ah	40	m	c	CHIN	Calaveras	San Andreas P O	70	197
Annie	30	f	w	IREL	Solano	Vacaville Twp	90	134
Bridget	44	f	w	IREL	Yuba	Rose Bar Twp	93	665
Chey	32	f	c	CHIN	Butte	Ophir Twp	70	104
Daniel	39	m	w	IREL	Yuba	Rose Bar Twp	93	665
Edward	3	m	w	CA	Marin	San Rafael Twp	74	29
Elizabeth	54	f	w	IREL	San Francisco	1-Wd San Francisco	79	20
John D	49	m	w	NY	Alameda	Brooklyn	68	34
Julia	21	f	w	CANA	Alameda	Oakland	68	229
Katy	14	f	w	CA	Sonoma	Sonoma Twp	91	431
Mary	40	f	w	IREL	Sacramento	2-Wd Sacramento	77	217
Michael	4	m	w	CA	Marin	San Rafael Twp	74	29
Michael	38	m	w	IREL	San Francisco	San Francisco P O	85	792
Stephen	40	m	w	NY	Alameda	Murray Twp	68	117
CANEAW								
Guillermo	37	m	w	FRAN	Marin	San Rafael Twp	74	32
CANEDA								
Maria	35	f	w	CA	Santa Barbara	Santa Barbara P O	87	475
CANEDAS								
Juan	38	m	w	CA	Los Angeles	Wilmington Twp	73	634
CANEDO								
Francisco	43	m	w	CA	Los Angeles	San Juan Twp	73	624
Irineca	30	m	w	MEXI	Los Angeles	Santa Ana Twp	73	615
Jesus	45	m	w	MEXI	Amador	Jackson P O	69	345
Jesus	18	m	w	CA	San Diego	San Luis Rey	78	515
Juan	27	m	w	CA	Los Angeles	Santa Ana Twp	73	609
Julian	45	m	w	MEXI	Calaveras	San Andreas P O	70	180

© 2001 by Heritage Quest. All rights reserved.

California 1870 Census

Name	Age	S	R	B-PL	County	Locale	Series M593 Roll	Pg
CANEDY								
Charles	52	m	w	SHOL	Inyo	Lone Pine Twp	73	331
CANELIN								
James	37	m	w	PA	Stanislaus	Buena Vista Twp	92	15
CANELO								
Francisco	28	m	w	MEXI	Los Angeles	El Monte Twp	73	462
Juan	15	m	w	CA	Santa Clara	Santa Clara Twp	88	176
CANEO								
F	35	m	w	ITAL	Amador	Jackson P O	69	337
CANEPA								
Giobetta	35	m	w	ITAL	Mariposa	Mariposa P O	74	91
CANERA								
Victor	38	m	w	SWIT	Marin	Nicasio Twp	74	15
CANESELLES								
Le Grand	40	m	w	CANA	San Diego	Julian Dist	78	469
CANET								
Frecia	12	f	w	CA	San Luis Obispo	San Luis Obispo Tw	87	310
CANETRO								
Grace	20	f	w	CA	Santa Clara	Fremont Twp	88	41
CANEUS								
Aurelia	15	f	w	CA	San Francisco	5-Wd San Francisco	81	13
CANEY								
Daniel	38	m	w	IREL	San Francisco	San Francisco P O	83	391
CANFIELD								
Albert	24	m	w	IA	Sonoma	Salt Point Twp	91	384
C A	42	m	w	OH	Monterey	Monterey	74	357
Chas	33	m	w	NJ	San Francisco	1-Wd San Francisco	79	55
Chauncy	26	m	w	CT	Solano	Suisun Twp	90	94
Chauncy L	58	m	w	CT	Solano	Suisun Twp	90	94
Cyrus C	45	m	w	OH	Placer	Auburn P O	76	374
E D	37	m	w	MI	Sacramento	Sutter Twp	77	384
Ellen	40	f	w	IREL	San Francisco	11-Wd San Francisc	84	619
Eugene	16	m	w	OH	Stanislaus	Empire Twp	92	47
George	40	m	w	NY	San Francisco	San Francisco P O	80	484
Henry	31	m	w	IREL	San Francisco	San Francisco P O	83	355
John	33	m	w	GA	Stanislaus	Empire Twp	92	37
M A	7	f	w	CA	Santa Clara	Gilroy Twp	88	94
Martha	45	f	w	PA	El Dorado	Placerville	72	114
Martha	38	f	w	CHIL	Placer	Auburn P O	76	378
Martin D	29	m	w	CANA	Yolo	Buckeye Twp	93	415
Michl	20	m	w	IREL	San Francisco	1-Wd San Francisco	79	83
Moses	56	m	w	NJ	Sutter	Sutter Twp	92	125
Oscar	30	m	w	PA	Sonoma	Salt Point Twp	91	383
Patrick	40	m	w	IREL	San Francisco	11-Wd San Francisc	84	440
R	14	m	w	CA	Solano	Benicia	90	21
Rufus	41	m	w	ME	San Francisco	San Francisco P O	80	355
Sayres	72	m	w	NY	Siskiyou	Callahan P O	89	632
Seth	33	m	w	OH	Fresno	Millerton P O	72	158
T C	41	m	w	NY	Nevada	Nevada Twp	75	274
William	52	m	w	NY	San Francisco	2-Wd San Francisco	79	142
Withington	43	m	w	NY	Kern	Bakersfield P O	73	366
Wm	59	m	w	VT	Sonoma	Analy Twp	91	225
CANFONTE								
John	54	m	w	ITAL	Monterey	San Benito Twp	74	384
CANG								
Ah	57	m	c	CHIN	Tuolumne	Big Oak Flat P O	93	394
Ah	49	m	c	CHIN	San Joaquin	1-Wd Stockton	86	145
Ah	45	m	c	CHIN	San Francisco	San Francisco P O	80	487
Ah	31	m	c	CHIN	San Joaquin	Castoria Twp	86	2
CANGER								
James	37	m	w	NY	San Francisco	San Francisco P O	83	262
CANGES								
Bitra	21	f	w	MEXI	Los Angeles	Los Angeles	73	519
CANGINA								
Jas	25	m	w	FRAN	San Francisco	8-Wd San Francisco	82	373
CANHAM								
Charles	34	m	w	ENGL	San Francisco	San Francisco P O	80	463
Robert	40	m	w	ENGL	Santa Cruz	Santa Cruz Twp	89	397
Wm F	55	m	w	ENGL	San Francisco	San Francisco P O	85	732
CANIAS								
M J	44	m	w	MEXI	Tuolumne	Columbia P O	93	344
CANIDO								
Rosaria	45	f	w	CA	Los Angeles	San Juan Twp	73	627
CANIDY								
John	35	m	w	IREL	San Francisco	5-Wd San Francisco	81	28
CANIE								
Ah	16	m	c	CHIN	Los Angeles	Los Angeles Twp	73	493
CANIEF								
Eliza	50	f	w	NY	San Francisco	San Francisco P O	83	357
CANIER								
John	38	m	w	SCOT	San Mateo	Half Moon Bay P O	87	408
CANIFF								
William H	52	m	w	NY	Mariposa	Mariposa P O	74	122
CANIGAN								
James	37	m	w	PA	Siskiyou	Scott Valley Twp	89	615
CANILI								
Pierre	38	m	w	FRAN	San Francisco	San Francisco P O	80	466
CANILLO								
Rosa	15	f	w	CA	Los Angeles	San Juan Twp	73	626
CANING								
Charles	44	m	w	IREL	Sierra	Sears Twp	89	555
CANION								
Peter	40	m	w	PRUS	Sacramento	Lee Twp	77	158
CANIPAS								
Toderico	52	m	w	ARGE	Los Angeles	Los Angeles	73	562
CANIPELKIN								
Charles	51	m	w	HANO	Amador	Jackson P O	69	346
S	22	m	w	HANO	Amador	Jackson P O	69	346
CANIPES								
John	25	m	w	ITAL	Calaveras	Copperopolis P O	70	247
Louis	20	m	w	ITAL	Calaveras	Copperopolis P O	70	247
CANIVAN								
Michael	60	m	w	IREL	San Francisco	2-Wd San Francisco	79	203
CANKLIN								
Charles	32	m	w	MA	Sacramento	Natomas Twp	77	169
Eliza	30	f	w	IREL	San Joaquin	2-Wd Stockton	86	211
CANLEN								
John	40	m	w	VA	Santa Cruz	Santa Cruz Twp	89	393
CANLEY								
Jose	50	m	w	CHIL	Monterey	Monterey Twp	74	346
William	26	m	w	IREL	Napa	Napa	75	14
CANLON								
Hanna	28	f	w	UNKN	San Joaquin	2-Wd Stockton	86	173
CANN								
Ah	32	m	c	CHIN	San Joaquin	Elkhorn Twp	86	53
Ah	30	m	c	CHIN	Nevada	Grass Valley Twp	75	197
Ah	18	m	c	CHIN	Mendocino	Point Arena Twp	74	205
Capt	54	m	w	MA	Solano	Vallejo	90	170
David	33	m	w	IA	San Francisco	San Francisco P O	83	150
Jas	19	m	w	ENGL	Calaveras	Copperopolis P O	70	238
Mc B	24	m	w	IREL	Santa Clara	Gilroy Twp	88	94
Sing	20	m	c	CHIN	San Francisco	5-Wd San Francisco	81	10
Thomas	49	m	w	NY	Santa Clara	1-Wd San Jose	88	268
CANNA								
Solomon	36	m	w	OH	Butte	Chico Twp	70	47
CANNADA								
A	10	f	m	CA	Yuba	Marysville	93	595
Anne	25	f	w	MA	Alameda	Oakland	68	170
Antoni	52	m	w	AUST	Placer	Bath P O	76	461
CANNADY								
J M	48	m	w	NY	Tuolumne	Columbia P O	93	344
James	28	m	w	IREL	San Francisco	San Francisco P O	83	265
CANNALL								
Jas	34	m	w	ENGL	Sierra	Table Rock Twp	89	579
CANNAUP								
Mary	14	f	w	MO	Sacramento	San Joaquin Twp	77	395
CANNAVAN								
Augustus	14	m	w	MA	San Francisco	San Francisco P O	83	157
Bartholomew	35	m	w	IREL	San Francisco	11-Wd San Francisc	84	536
M	22	m	w	IREL	San Francisco	San Francisco P O	85	868
Margt	28	f	w	IREL	San Francisco	8-Wd San Francisco	82	316
Martin	33	m	w	NY	San Francisco	San Francisco P O	80	377
Patrick	27	m	w	IREL	San Francisco	11-Wd San Francisc	84	539
CANNEA								
Julius	31	m	w	FRAN	Marin	San Rafael Twp	74	32
CANNEDY								
John	40	m	w	MO	Plumas	Mineral Twp	77	20
William J	41	m	w	MA	Yolo	Buckeye Twp	93	409
CANNELL								
Estelle	28	f	w	VT	San Francisco	San Francisco P O	83	138
CANNELS								
Conrado	40	m	w	MEXI	Calaveras	Copperopolis P O	70	263
CANNES								
Jose	29	m	w	CA	San Luis Obispo	Morro Twp	87	286
CANNEY								
Mary	45	f	w	NY	San Francisco	7-Wd San Francisco	81	183
CANNIN								
Michael	25	m	w	IREL	San Mateo	Schoolhouse Statio	87	334
CANNING								
Francis	48	m	w	ITAL	Placer	Newcastle Twp	76	476
James	49	m	w	IREL	Alameda	Oakland	68	199
Wm	40	m	w	IREL	San Francisco	San Francisco P O	85	780
Wm	30	m	w	IREL	San Francisco	San Francisco P O	83	4
CANNON								
A M Q	54	m	w	OH	Butte	Wyandotte Twp	70	148
B O	17	m	w	CA	Alameda	Oakland	68	216
Barry	29	m	w	IREL	San Francisco	7-Wd San Francisco	81	169
C C	28	m	w	MO	Siskiyou	Surprise Valley Tw	89	636
Charles A	20	m	w	NY	Placer	Lincoln P O	76	486
Edward	35	m	w	IREL	San Francisco	11-Wd San Francisc	84	505
Edward	30	m	w	ENGL	Humboldt	Bucksport Twp	72	243
Emma	30	f	w	NY	Napa	Napa	75	27
Franklin E	46	m	w	OH	Placer	Bath P O	76	456
George	52	m	w	PA	Alameda	Murray Twp	68	109
George	36	m	w	ENGL	Contra Costa	Martinez P O	71	427
Holman B	59	m	w	IN	Mariposa	Mariposa P O	74	120
James	46	m	w	ENGL	San Francisco	7-Wd San Francisco	81	211
James	36	m	w	IREL	San Francisco	San Francisco P O	83	107
James	33	m	w	IREL	Nevada	Grass Valley Twp	75	199
James	30	m	w	IREL	Yuba	Rose Bar Twp	93	662
James	22	m	w	IREL	San Francisco	7-Wd San Francisco	81	192
James	20	m	w	IREL	San Francisco	2-Wd San Francisco	79	216
James G	44	m	w	DE	Yuba	Long Bar Twp	93	560
Jane	54	f	w	OH	San Joaquin	2-Wd Stockton	86	204
Jas	32	m	w	AR	Sonoma	Santa Rosa	91	419
Jas	30	m	w	IREL	Solano	Benicia	90	8
Jas L	52	m	w	MO	Shasta	Fort Crook P O	89	475
Jno C	50	m	w	MO	Shasta	Fort Crook P O	89	473
John	36	m	w	IREL	Yuba	Linda Twp	93	556
John	35	m	w	IREL	Nevada	Eureka Twp	75	134
John	32	m	w	SWED	Amador	Volcano P O	69	385
John	30	m	w	PRUS	San Mateo	Half Moon Bay P O	87	404
John	25	m	w	ENGL	San Francisco	7-Wd San Francisco	81	172
John	22	m	w	MO	Siskiyou	Surprise Valley Tw	89	641

© 2001 by Heritage Quest. All rights reserved.

Series M593

Name	Age	S	R	B-PL	County	Locale	Roll	Pg
John L	35	m	w	KY	Placer	Gold Run Twp	76	396
John T	37	m	w	VA	Placer	Lincoln P O	76	485
Jones	50	m	w	IREL	Tuolumne	Columbia P O	93	359
L J	37	f	w	CANA	Nevada	Nevada Twp	75	285
L J	27	f	w	MO	Nevada	Nevada Twp	75	277
Martin	40	m	w	IREL	Santa Clara	Santa Clara Twp	88	172
Mary	38	f	w	NC	Sonoma	Analy Twp	91	221
Mary	35	f	w	IREL	San Francisco	1-Wd San Francisco	79	83
Mary	12	f	w	CA	Sonoma	Santa Rosa	91	406
Patk	35	m	w	IREL	San Francisco	San Francisco P O	83	47
Patrick	40	m	w	IREL	San Francisco	San Francisco P O	83	336
Paul	34	m	b	MO	Napa	Napa Twp	75	69
Richard	44	m	w	OH	Plumas	Goodwin Twp	77	1
Robert	40	m	w	OH	Solano	Suisun Twp	90	95
Saml	34	m	w	WI	Butte	Oregon Twp	70	131
Saml	34	m	w	MO	Butte	Chico Twp	70	54
Sophia	40	f	w	NY	San Francisco	11-Wd San Francisc	84	621
Thomas	21	m	w	IREL	San Francisco	11-Wd San Francisc	84	519
William	24	m	w	IREL	Solano	Silveyville Twp	90	78
Wm	21	m	w	MO	Butte	Hamilton Twp	70	62
Wm R	30	m	w	AR	Sonoma	Russian Rvr	91	373
CANNONE								
Joseph	18	m	w	ITAL	San Mateo	Schoolhouse Statio	87	346
CANNORAN								
Thorn	24	m	w	NY	San Diego	San Diego	78	495
CANNS								
James	30	m	w	IREL	Santa Clara	Redwood Twp	88	127
CANNY								
Annie	23	f	w	IREL	San Francisco	San Francisco P O	85	856
Caun	30	m	w	IREL	Sierra	Sears Twp	89	558
Dennis	36	m	w	IREL	Sierra	Sears Twp	89	558
Luke	13	m	w	NY	San Francisco	2-Wd San Francisco	79	221
CANO								
Antonio	35	m	w	MEXI	Fresno	Millerton P O	72	163
Roffelle	30	m	w	CA	San Luis Obispo	Morro Twp	87	285
CANON								
Adam	52	m	w	OH	Alameda	Brooklyn Twp	68	39
Frank	21	m	w	MA	Placer	Colfax P O	76	389
George W	35	m	w	MI	Colusa	Spring Valley Twp	71	339
Ida	12	f	w	CA	Sacramento	4-Wd Sacramento	77	378
James	30	m	w	IREL	San Francisco	7-Wd San Francisco	81	169
Julia	11	f	w	CA	Sacramento	4-Wd Sacramento	77	378
Thomas	20	m	w	OR	Sonoma	Salt Point	91	389
W J	38	m	w	IL	Lake	Lower Lake	73	416
CANOPER								
John	34	m	w	SWIT	Marin	Nicasio Twp	74	15
CANOR								
Francisco	67	m	w	CHIL	Los Angeles	El Monte Twp	73	462
CANOSSA								
Passamer	36	m	w	MEXI	Fresno	Millerton P O	72	157
CANOTO								
---	30	m	w	CA	San Luis Obispo	San Luis Obispo Tw	87	305
CANOVAN								
C	35	m	w	NY	Solano	Vallejo	90	160
Chas	35	m	w	CANA	Solano	Vallejo	90	181
James	40	m	w	IREL	Santa Clara	2-Wd San Jose	88	334
Jos H	45	m	w	CANA	Nevada	Meadow Lake Twp	75	265
Maggie	26	f	w	IREL	Los Angeles	Los Angeles	73	546
Margt	26	f	w	IREL	San Francisco	8-Wd San Francisco	82	302
Thomas	32	m	w	MA	San Francisco	7-Wd San Francisco	81	221
CANOVARO								
Angelo	40	m	w	ITAL	Calaveras	San Andreas P O	70	180
CANOVENE								
Joseph	18	m	w	ITAL	San Mateo	Schoolhouse Statio	87	334
CANOVER								
George H	43	m	w	OH	Yuba	New York Twp	93	641
CANPAR								
Jno	42	m	w	IN	San Joaquin	1-Wd Stockton	86	152
CANSECO								
Miguel	20	m	w	ME	San Francisco	1-Wd San Francisco	79	46
CANSO								
Pedro	36	m	w	ITAL	Tuolumne	Chinese Camp P O	93	386
CANT								
Charles	28	m	w	HAMB	San Francisco	3-Wd San Francisco	79	292
Wm	40	m	w	PA	San Diego	San Diego	78	504
CANTA								
Vincenco	40	m	w	ITAL	San Francisco	3-Wd San Francisco	79	289
CANTARO								
Frank	33	m	i	CA	San Luis Obispo	Salinas Twp	87	294
CANTEBERRY								
Augustus M	23	m	w	MO	Yolo	Cottonwood Twp	93	464
CANTELOPE								
Peter	30	m	w	FRAN	Napa	Yountville Twp	75	77
CANTELOW								
William	44	m	w	NY	Solano	Vacaville Twp	90	130
CANTENELLI								
Josh	45	m	w	FRAN	San Francisco	1-Wd San Francisco	79	47
CANTENI								
Simon	39	m	w	SWIT	Siskiyou	Callahan P O	89	627
CANTER								
Michl	38	m	w	IREL	San Francisco	1-Wd San Francisco	79	97
CANTERBURY								
Jas C	23	m	w	KY	Shasta	Millville P O	89	489
Lawrence	51	m	w	KY	Yolo	Cottonwood Twp	93	463
Milton	49	m	w	KY	Yolo	Grafton Twp	93	480
CANTERO								
Marie	11	f	w	CA	San Bernardino	San Bernardino Twp	78	416
CANTERRY								
Felix	55	m	w	VA	Yuba	Long Bar Twp	93	564
CANTHLAW								
Thomas	38	m	w	IREL	San Francisco	11-Wd San Francisc	84	472
CANTILLON								
James	53	m	w	IREL	Santa Clara	Fremont Twp	88	55
CANTILON								
William	25	m	w	PRUS	San Francisco	7-Wd San Francisco	81	220
CANTIS								
Antonio	40	m	w	MEXI	Santa Clara	Almaden Twp	88	4
John	46	m	w	PRUS	San Joaquin	3-Wd Stockton	86	216
CANTLEY								
Dennis	31	m	w	CANA	Yuba	East Bear Rvr Twp	93	539
CANTLIN								
Mary E	25	f	w	CT	Sacramento	2-Wd Sacramento	77	222
Michael	30	m	w	IREL	Sacramento	Granite Twp	77	139
CANTO								
Cave	16	m	w	CA	Los Angeles	Los Angeles	73	570
Nicholas	30	m	w	FRAN	Tulare	Visalia Twp	92	285
William	17	m	w	CA	Los Angeles	Los Angeles	73	570
CANTOLOUP								
Adolph	38	m	w	FRAN	Merced	Snelling P O	74	281
CANTON								
Chas	36	m	w	IN	Santa Clara	Gilroy Twp	88	78
J P	39	m	w	CANA	San Francisco	San Francisco P O	85	791
Lizzie	25	f	w	IREL	San Francisco	8-Wd San Francisco	82	348
Matilda	13	f	w	CA	Santa Clara	2-Wd San Jose	88	338
CANTOURA								
Joseph	15	m	i	----	Marin	No Twp Listed	74	89
CANTOWN								
Corefa	34	f	w	CA	Placer	Auburn P O	76	358
CANTRAL								
Joe	39	m	w	IL	Butte	Chico Twp	70	60
CANTRAN								
Catarinel	60	m	w	MEXI	Santa Clara	Almaden Twp	88	6
CANTRARA								
Ramon	28	m	w	MEXI	San Luis Obispo	San Luis Obispo Tw	87	313
CANTREL								
Henry	23	m	w	TN	Sonoma	Russian Rvr	91	378
CANTRELL								
Alfred	50	m	w	TN	Mendocino	Little Lake Twp	74	196
Amos	53	m	w	AL	San Joaquin	Tulare Twp	86	261
Ari	42	m	w	MO	Humboldt	South Fork Twp	72	302
Charles	14	m	w	NY	Marin	San Rafael Twp	74	30
Daniel	52	m	w	TN	Sacramento	Dry Crk Twp	77	104
Edwin	13	m	w	CA	Sonoma	Vallejo Twp	91	456
George	58	m	w	ENGL	San Francisco	San Francisco P O	83	353
Henry	21	m	w	TN	Sonoma	Mendocino Twp	91	288
J B	28	m	w	NY	San Francisco	San Francisco P O	85	842
James M	36	m	w	TN	Tulare	Tule Rvr Twp	92	262
James S	36	m	w	IL	Sonoma	Petaluma Twp	91	335
Joab	40	m	w	TN	Yolo	Washington Twp	93	529
John	44	m	w	NY	El Dorado	Cosumnes Twp	72	16
Martha	60	f	w	ENGL	San Francisco	San Francisco P O	83	366
P H	22	m	w	MO	Sonoma	Russian Rvr	91	370
R J	24	m	w	TN	Sonoma	Santa Rosa	91	403
Richd	36	m	w	IREL	San Francisco	1-Wd San Francisco	79	76
Stephen	35	m	w	IL	Siskiyou	Surprise Valley Tw	89	640
Thos	33	m	w	NY	San Francisco	8-Wd San Francisco	82	315
William	37	m	w	IL	Contra Costa	Martinez P O	71	424
William	24	m	w	IL	Siskiyou	Surprise Valley Tw	89	640
Willis	62	m	w	KY	Siskiyou	Surprise Valley Tw	89	640
Wm B	39	m	w	NY	Siskiyou	Yreka	89	657
CANTRO								
Cherpocklino	35	m	w	CHIL	Fresno	Millerton P O	72	162
CANTRON								
Wm	39	m	b	PA	Tuolumne	Sonora P O	93	333
CANTROWITZ								
M	35	m	w	POLA	San Francisco	3-Wd San Francisco	79	324
CANTRY								
James	57	m	w	IREL	San Diego	Fort Yuma Dist	78	464
CANTUA								
Guadalupe	84	m	w	CA	San Luis Obispo	Santa Rosa Twp	87	324
Ignacio	40	m	w	CA	Santa Clara	Alviso Twp	88	27
Jose	42	m	w	CA	San Luis Obispo	Santa Rosa Twp	87	327
Juan M	34	m	w	CA	Monterey	Alisal Twp	74	290
Prudencia	40	m	w	CA	Santa Clara	Alviso Twp	88	24
CANTURA								
Ireana	59	m	w	MEXI	Plumas	Rich Bar Twp	77	8
CANTUS								
George	31	m	w	PRUS	San Francisco	8-Wd San Francisco	82	442
CANTWELL								
Chas	24	m	w	KY	San Francisco	1-Wd San Francisco	79	64
Chas L	40	m	w	PA	San Francisco	San Francisco P O	85	757
Ellen	28	f	w	CANA	San Francisco	6-Wd San Francisco	81	97
H	16	m	w	CA	Solano	Benicia	90	21
J H	28	m	w	NY	Nevada	Nevada Twp	75	321
John F	30	m	w	OH	San Bernardino	San Bernardino Twp	78	452
Mathew	58	m	w	IN	Tulare	Tule Rvr Twp	92	260
Michael	38	m	w	IREL	Santa Cruz	Santa Cruz Twp	89	391
Michael	35	m	w	NY	Placer	Bath P O	76	432
Morris	36	m	w	IREL	San Francisco	San Francisco P O	83	288
W R	48	m	w	OH	Sacramento	1-Wd Sacramento	77	176
CANTY								
Daniel J	20	m	w	MA	Inyo	Lone Pine Twp	73	331
Hannah	28	f	w	IREL	San Francisco	San Francisco P O	83	124
J	18	m	w	MA	Nevada	Meadow Lake Twp	75	269

© 2001 by Heritage Quest. All rights reserved.

Name	Age	S	R	B-PL	County	Locale	Roll	Pg
Jno	25	m	w	IREL	Sacramento	1-Wd Sacramento	77	179
John	35	m	w	IREL	Solano	Vallejo	90	197
Mary	26	f	w	IREL	Yolo	Grafton Twp	93	481
Mary	26	f	w	IREL	San Francisco	8-Wd San Francisco	82	419
Michael	50	m	w	IREL	San Francisco	San Francisco P O	83	250
Michael	40	m	w	IREL	Mariposa	Mariposa P O	74	111
Patrick	28	m	w	IREL	San Francisco	San Francisco P O	83	237
Thomas	56	m	w	IREL	Mariposa	Mariposa P O	74	128
Thomas	45	m	w	IREL	San Francisco	San Francisco P O	83	241
Thomas	33	m	w	IREL	Mariposa	Mariposa P O	74	130
CANUTA								
Louisa	20	f	w	MEXI	San Francisco	2-Wd San Francisco	79	168
CANVAN								
Mathew	45	m	w	ENGL	Amador	Volcano P O	69	386
CANWELL								
Mary	28	f	w	IREL	San Francisco	1-Wd San Francisco	79	12
CANWRIGHT								
Frank	41	m	w	NY	Solano	Rio Vista Twp	90	63
CANYONAS								
Alejo	23	m	w	MEXI	San Luis Obispo	Salinas Twp	87	288
CANYRODONICO								
Stephen	29	m	w	ITAL	San Francisco	11-Wd San Francisc	84	443
CAP								
Ah	60	m	c	CHIN	Placer	Roseville P O	76	349
Ah	49	m	c	CHIN	San Mateo	Belmont P O	87	373
Ah	38	m	c	CHIN	Fresno	Millerton P O	72	199
Ah	29	m	c	CHIN	Sierra	Lincoln Twp	89	548
Ah	27	m	c	CHIN	San Francisco	1-Wd San Francisco	79	98
Ah	23	m	c	CHIN	San Francisco	8-Wd San Francisco	82	357
Ah	23	m	c	CHIN	Kern	Bakersfield P O	73	357
Joe	46	m	i	CA	Fresno	Kings Rvr P O	72	215
Lottie	19	f	w	AR	Sonoma	Mendocino Twp	91	291
Sem???	22	m	c	CHIN	Yuba	Long Bar Twp	93	560
CAPA								
Andrew	43	m	w	ITAL	Amador	Jackson P O	69	336
CAPACHA								
Juan	40	m	w	CA	Santa Barbara	Las Cruces P O	87	516
CAPAN								
Geo C	60	m	w	ME	San Francisco	5-Wd San Francisco	81	26
CAPARRO								
Antonio	57	m	w	ITAL	Los Angeles	Los Angeles	73	506
CAPDASPE								
Jean	35	m	w	FRAN	Santa Barbara	Santa Barbara P O	87	501
CAPE								
William	28	m	w	IREL	San Francisco	8-Wd San Francisco	82	375
CAPEL								
Chas	18	m	i	OR	San Luis Obispo	San Luis Obispo Tw	87	316
Julius	31	m	w	PRUS	San Mateo	Belmont P O	87	374
CAPELL								
Benson	37	m	w	KY	Sonoma	Mendocino Twp	91	300
Britton	46	m	w	TN	Napa	Napa Twp	75	72
Chas W	39	m	w	KY	Sonoma	Mendocino Twp	91	294
D C	20	m	w	CA	Alameda	Oakland	68	159
Elizabeth	66	f	w	TN	Sonoma	Mendocino Twp	91	296
Harriet	16	f	i	CA	Solano	Green Valley Twp	90	41
James	45	m	w	VA	Alameda	Brooklyn	68	27
James	43	m	w	TN	Solano	Green Valley Twp	90	41
CAPELLA								
Augustine	36	m	w	ITAL	Calaveras	Copperopolis P O	70	249
Joab	32	m	w	ITAL	Calaveras	Copperopolis P O	70	249
Josepha	40	m	w	ITAL	Calaveras	Copperopolis P O	70	251
CAPELLI								
Bartoleme	20	m	w	SWIT	Marin	San Rafael Twp	74	32
CAPELLO								
Antonio	30	m	w	ITAL	Santa Cruz	Santa Cruz	89	433
CAPENTER								
Elijah B	41	m	w	NY	Yolo	Washington Twp	93	530
CAPER								
Peter	22	m	w	SWIT	Plumas	Washington Twp	77	56
CAPERO								
Jos	40	m	w	ITAL	San Joaquin	3-Wd Stockton	86	221
CAPERS								
John	25	m	w	ENGL	San Francisco	1-Wd San Francisco	79	116
CAPERTON								
Wm	38	m	w	MA	San Francisco	1-Wd San Francisco	79	100
CAPEY								
P	1	m	w	CA	Alameda	Oakland	68	132
CAPHART								
Aron	34	m	w	VA	Sonoma	Healdsburg	91	274
CAPHORD								
A	36	m	w	PRUS	San Joaquin	2-Wd Stockton	86	165
CAPIALO								
Dominic	23	m	w	ITAL	San Francisco	2-Wd San Francisco	79	180
CAPIDY								
Jackson	31	m	w	IL	Monterey	Pajaro Twp	74	377
CAPILIAN								
Allenson	34	m	w	MI	Los Angeles	Los Angeles Twp	73	495
CAPIN								
James	26	m	w	GERM	Los Angeles	Santa Ana Twp	73	600
Martin	38	m	w	IREL	Solano	Benicia	90	9
CAPISTRANO								
Juan	25	m	w	CA	Santa Barbara	Santa Barbara P O	87	453
CAPITANI								
Feliche	26	m	w	ITAL	Sonoma	Analy Twp	91	236
CAPITHORNE								
Richard	32	m	w	IREL	San Francisco	11-Wd San Francisc	84	531
CAPITOLA								
Morris	18	m	w	FRAN	Marin	San Rafael Twp	74	34
CAPLE								
James	50	m	w	OH	Sacramento	Natomas Twp	77	165
CAPLER								
Carl	59	m	w	HANO	Santa Clara	2-Wd San Jose	88	331
Hans	50	m	w	HANO	Yolo	Merritt Twp	93	506
Rosa	18	f	w	CA	Sacramento	3-Wd Sacramento	77	317
CAPLES								
James	46	m	w	OH	Alpine	Woodfords P O	69	309
CAPLESS								
Patk	25	m	w	IREL	San Francisco	1-Wd San Francisco	79	69
CAPLICE								
John	36	m	w	IREL	San Francisco	11-Wd San Francisc	84	450
CAPLIN								
William	29	m	w	MI	Santa Clara	Santa Clara Twp	88	135
CAPLINGER								
Isaac	54	m	w	VA	Sonoma	Analy Twp	91	234
CAPONIA								
Amelia	19	f	w	SWIT	Marin	Nicasio Twp	74	14
CAPORA								
Augustus	36	m	w	ITAL	San Francisco	San Francisco P O	80	334
CAPP								
C S	39	m	w	PA	San Francisco	San Francisco P O	85	839
George	21	m	w	NY	Santa Clara	2-Wd San Jose	88	300
Gustave	55	m	w	SWIT	Santa Clara	2-Wd San Jose	88	308
Martin	50	m	w	BAVA	Los Angeles	Los Angeles	73	544
CAPPARRO								
Thos	33	m	w	ITAL	Mariposa	Maxwell Crk P O	74	139
CAPPE								
John	40	m	w	MEXI	San Luis Obispo	San Luis Obispo Tw	87	310
CAPPEL								
Annie	11	f	w	CA	Sonoma	Russian Rvr	91	374
Frank	27	m	w	ENGL	San Francisco	11-Wd San Francisc	84	613
Frederick	35	m	w	BAVA	Sacramento	2-Wd Sacramento	77	241
CAPPELL								
Francis	62	m	w	FRAN	Santa Clara	Fremont Twp	88	41
William	26	m	w	ENGL	Yolo	Grafton Twp	93	497
CAPPELLA								
Thomas	22	m	w	SWIT	Sonoma	Bodega Twp	91	264
CAPPELMAN								
H	24	m	w	NY	Alameda	Murray Twp	68	100
CAPPIE								
Joseph	40	m	w	IREL	Sacramento	2-Wd Sacramento	77	240
CAPPINGER								
Thomas	45	m	w	IREL	El Dorado	Georgetown Twp	72	42
CAPPINI								
Joseph	44	m	w	MD	San Francisco	2-Wd San Francisco	79	195
CAPPLEMAN								
Cornelius	39	m	w	HANO	Santa Cruz	Santa Cruz	89	413
CAPPRIA								
Charles	17	m	w	SWIT	Placer	Bath P O	76	443
CAPPS								
J S	44	m	w	TN	Lake	Morgan Valley	73	424
Thomas J	53	m	w	TN	San Mateo	Half Moon Bay P O	87	399
CAPRARO								
Michael	50	m	w	ITAL	El Dorado	Diamond Springs Tw	72	29
CAPRENE								
Antonio	24	m	w	ITAL	San Francisco	San Francisco P O	85	751
CAPRON								
J George	42	m	w	OH	San Diego	San Diego	78	492
CAPRONI								
Paul	32	m	w	ITAL	San Francisco	1-Wd San Francisco	79	129
CAPRORI								
Fileno D	25	m	w	SWIT	El Dorado	Placerville Twp	72	94
CAPT								
Mike	45	m	i	CA	Del Norte	Smith Rvr Twp	71	479
CAPTAIN								
Jack	40	m	i	CA	Colusa	Grand Island Twp	71	310
CAPTESTI								
John	26	m	w	ITAL	San Francisco	San Francisco P O	85	851
CAPTIAN								
El	80	m	i	CA	Yolo	Buckeye Twp	93	412
CAPTIN								
John	40	m	w	ME	Sacramento	Natomas Twp	77	166
CAPTO								
William	36	m	w	PA	San Francisco	San Francisco P O	83	239
CAPULCO								
Jose M	25	m	w	CA	Santa Cruz	Pajaro Twp	89	356
CAPURO								
Antonio	50	m	w	ITAL	San Francisco	11-Wd San Francisc	84	587
John	26	m	w	ITAL	El Dorado	Diamond Springs Tw	72	29
Juan	28	m	w	ITAL	San Francisco	11-Wd San Francisc	84	587
CAPUT								
Benerd	70	m	w	FRAN	Yuba	Parks Bar Twp	93	649
CAPWELL								
Wm D	33	m	w	RI	Marin	Point Reyes Twp	74	21
CAR								
Louisa	35	f	w	NY	San Francisco	5-Wd San Francisco	81	8
Sarah J	39	f	w	IN	Humboldt	South Fork Twp	72	302
CARA								
Francisco	30	m	w	SCOT	Alameda	Brooklyn Twp	68	45
CARABAGAY								
Antoine	35	m	w	CHIL	Sacramento	2-Wd Sacramento	77	215
CARABANA								
Antonia	35	f	w	MEXI	Los Angeles	Los Angeles	73	553

© 2001 by Heritage Quest. All rights reserved.

Name	Age	S	R	B-PL	County	Locale	Series M593 Roll	Pg
CARACOA								
Loni	19	m	w	SWIT	Marin	Novato Twp	74	9
CARADA								
John	48	m	w	ITAL	Tuolumne	Chinese Camp P O	93	382
CARADINE								
Sarah	50	f	w	ENGL	San Francisco	7-Wd San Francisco	81	257
CARADOO								
Allix	42	m	w	ITAL	Trinity	North Fork Twp	92	216
CARAFELL								
R	37	m	w	IREL	Alameda	Oakland	68	155
CARAFFA								
John B	48	m	w	ITAL	San Francisco	2-Wd San Francisco	79	146
CARAGA								
Jose	30	m	w	CHIL	San Francisco	2-Wd San Francisco	79	151
CARAGAN								
Mary	75	f	w	IREL	San Francisco	11-Wd San Francisc	84	611
CARAGHER								
Patrick	40	m	w	IREL	Sacramento	2-Wd Sacramento	77	231
CARAGNAW								
John	60	m	w	ITAL	Tuolumne	Sonora P O	93	312
CARAGOUN								
Felix	19	m	w	ITAL	San Francisco	2-Wd San Francisco	79	151
CARAHAN								
John	28	m	w	IREL	San Francisco	7-Wd San Francisco	81	172
CARAHER								
Julia	24	f	w	IREL	San Francisco	San Francisco P O	83	184
CARALLA								
Frank	52	m	w	SWIT	Amador	Jackson P O	69	335
CARALLI								
Antone	40	m	w	SWIT	San Joaquin	2-Wd Stockton	86	188
CARALLO								
Nicholas	31	m	w	ITAL	San Francisco	2-Wd San Francisco	79	176
CARALY								
Anne	43	f	w	IREL	San Francisco	1-Wd San Francisco	79	29
CARAMELLA								
Louis	44	m	w	ITAL	El Dorado	Diamond Springs Tw	72	29
CARANCIA								
Benita	18	f	w	CA	Santa Cruz	Watsonville	89	369
P	13	f	w	CA	Santa Clara	Gilroy Twp	88	94
CARANO								
Joaquin	30	m	w	MEXI	Fresno	Millerton P O	72	163
Juan	40	m	w	MEXI	Kern	Bakersfield P O	73	365
Pablo	65	m	w	MEXI	Fresno	Millerton P O	72	163
CARANOVA								
Joseph	42	m	w	ITAL	Amador	Sutter Crk P O	69	405
CARANT								
Jonah	45	m	w	MA	San Joaquin	Castoria Twp	86	6
CARANZA								
Alvino	36	m	w	CA	Santa Clara	Gilroy Twp	88	96
Poncho	48	m	w	CA	Santa Clara	Gilroy Twp	88	96
Theo	25	m	w	CA	Santa Clara	Gilroy Twp	88	96
CARARAS								
Trocundo	10	m	w	CA	Santa Clara	Milpitas Twp	88	109
CARAS								
Cristo	25	m	w	ITAL	San Francisco	11-Wd San Francisc	84	591
CARASCO								
Angel	48	m	w	MEXI	Los Angeles	Los Angeles Twp	73	480
Barnalel	36	m	w	CHIL	San Francisco	11-Wd San Francisc	84	612
Cousre	40	m	i	MEXI	Inyo	Lone Pine Twp	73	334
Isidore	40	f	w	MEXI	Fresno	Millerton P O	72	157
P	60	m	w	MEXI	Calaveras	Copperopolis P O	70	231
Sacramento	26	m	w	MEXI	Monterey	San Benito Twp	74	380
CARASHAL								
Hoza M	53	m	w	CHIL	San Mateo	Half Moon Bay P O	87	389
CARATA								
Jose	50	m	w	CHIL	Santa Clara	Alviso Twp	88	27
CARAVAHAL								
Jose	38	m	w	MEXI	Napa	Napa	75	55
CARAVAJAL								
Chapile	66	m	w	MEXI	Los Angeles	Los Angeles	73	553
CARAVANTES								
Francisco	33	m	w	MEXI	Marin	San Rafael Twp	74	41
CARAVAZAR								
Jesus	38	m	w	MEXI	Monterey	San Antonio Twp	74	316
CARAVCHAL								
Jose M	42	m	w	CHIL	San Mateo	Half Moon Bay P O	87	397
CARAVER								
John	37	m	w	IL	San Francisco	7-Wd San Francisco	81	182
CARAVIA								
Gabail	42	m	w	SWIT	Calaveras	San Andreas P O	70	199
CARAVISCO								
Jesus	34	m	w	MEXI	Los Angeles	Los Angeles Twp	73	492
CARAVOKER								
Madeline	21	f	w	MEXI	Santa Clara	2-Wd San Jose	88	318
CARAWAY								
Virgil	52	m	w	VA	Trinity	North Fork Twp	92	218
CARAY								
Peter	45	m	w	IREL	San Francisco	11-Wd San Francisc	84	600
CARBARRINO								
Antonio	47	m	w	ITAL	Mariposa	Mariposa P O	74	109
CARBARY								
Jno J	43	m	w	MI	Sacramento	1-Wd Sacramento	77	204
CARBELL								
James	29	m	w	MA	San Francisco	7-Wd San Francisco	81	169
Rob	23	m	w	IA	Merced	Snelling P O	74	265
CARBERRY								
Arron	45	m	w	MI	Yolo	Fremont Twp	93	476
Briget	37	f	w	IREL	San Francisco	7-Wd San Francisco	81	181
Cormick	30	m	w	IREL	San Francisco	San Francisco P O	83	269
Edwd	25	m	w	CANA	San Francisco	San Francisco P O	83	84
Harry	32	m	w	IREL	San Francisco	6-Wd San Francisco	81	123
James A	28	m	w	IREL	Santa Clara	Santa Clara Twp	88	147
James H	21	m	w	PA	Tulare	Tule Rvr Twp	92	260
Jenny	29	f	w	IREL	San Francisco	5-Wd San Francisco	81	35
Jo	37	m	w	IREL	San Francisco	5-Wd San Francisco	81	35
Patrick	50	m	w	IREL	Marin	Tomales Twp	74	84
Patrick	27	m	w	IREL	Santa Clara	Fremont Twp	88	56
Peter	38	m	w	IREL	Sierra	Eureka Twp	89	524
Robert	20	m	w	IREL	Santa Clara	Fremont Twp	88	56
Sarah	35	f	w	IREL	San Francisco	8-Wd San Francisco	82	390
William	54	m	w	IN	Tehama	Red Bluff	92	177
CARBERY								
Alice	24	f	w	MI	Sacramento	4-Wd Sacramento	77	373
CARBETT								
Edward	39	m	w	IOFM	Colusa	Colusa Twp	71	283
CARBHARDT								
A	18	m	w	SWIT	Solano	Benicia	90	4
CARBINE								
James	44	m	w	IREL	Sacramento	Granite Twp	77	139
CARBNHER								
M	35	m	w	PRUS	Amador	Sutter Crk P O	69	396
CARBOJAL								
F	35	m	w	CHIL	El Dorado	Greenwood Twp	72	54
CARBON								
John	19	m	w	ITAL	Contra Costa	Martinez P O	71	437
Kate	25	f	w	WIND	San Francisco	11-Wd San Francisc	84	689
Nicholas	29	m	w	ITAL	Contra Costa	Martinez P O	71	437
CARBONE								
Antonio	20	m	w	ITAL	San Francisco	11-Wd San Francisc	84	594
Antonio	19	m	w	ITAL	Napa	Napa Twp	75	75
Antonio	18	m	w	ITAL	Contra Costa	Martinez P O	71	437
CARBONI								
Frank	38	m	w	ITAL	Santa Clara	2-Wd San Jose	88	312
CARBONIER								
John	46	m	w	NY	Marin	Novato Twp	74	13
CARBONO								
Luigi	50	m	w	ITAL	Napa	Napa Twp	75	74
CARBRY								
Catherine	24	f	w	IREL	San Francisco	San Francisco P O	83	23
CARBUHN								
M	28	m	w	PRUS	Amador	Sutter Crk P O	69	402
CARBURT								
Chlarles	40	m	w	SHOL	San Mateo	Half Moon Bay P O	87	403
CARBY								
Stevens	35	m	w	IREL	San Francisco	7-Wd San Francisco	81	287
CARCEN								
Vancello	23	m	w	MEXI	San Joaquin	Tulare Twp	86	258
CARCHER								
Adolph	45	m	w	PRUS	Yuba	Rose Bar Twp	93	663
CARCILLO								
Silvester	14	m	w	CA	Los Angeles	Soledad Twp	73	632
CARCLIO								
Babtiste	27	m	w	ITAL	San Luis Obispo	Arroyo Grande Twp	87	276
CARCOVA								
Thomas	43	m	w	IREL	San Joaquin	Oneal Twp	86	111
CARD								
Alexander	36	m	w	NY	El Dorado	Diamond Springs Tw	72	33
C B	26	m	w	CANA	Alameda	Oakland	68	148
D W	46	m	w	CT	San Joaquin	Oneal Twp	86	108
Emma	29	f	w	ENGL	San Francisco	San Francisco P O	83	150
Emma	16	f	w	IA	San Joaquin	Oneal Twp	86	108
George	70	m	w	RI	San Joaquin	3-Wd Stockton	86	234
George B	36	m	w	ME	Santa Cruz	Watsonville	89	364
Henry	62	m	w	MA	Sierra	Table Rock Twp	89	571
Joel	43	m	w	NY	San Joaquin	Liberty Twp	86	93
Joseph E	39	m	w	NY	Yolo	Cache Crk Twp	93	433
M	49	m	w	ME	Sacramento	3-Wd Sacramento	77	263
M	38	m	w	IREL	Alameda	Oakland	68	181
Russel	41	m	w	RI	San Francisco	8-Wd San Francisco	82	311
Siles	35	m	w	IN	San Joaquin	Oneal Twp	86	105
W D	35	m	w	OH	Santa Clara	Almaden Twp	88	20
W M	72	m	w	MA	Alameda	Oakland	68	236
William	28	m	w	NY	San Francisco	8-Wd San Francisco	82	465
William F	38	m	w	IN	Santa Clara	San Jose Twp	88	180
William S	50	m	w	NY	Santa Cruz	Santa Cruz Twp	89	401
Wm H	55	m	w	RI	Mendocino	Round Valley Twp	74	218
CARDAGE								
John	50	m	w	GREE	Placer	Bath P O	76	440
CARDAM								
Nichlo	34	m	w	ITAL	San Francisco	11-Wd San Francisc	84	710
CARDANEO								
M	6	m	w	CA	San Bernardino	San Salvador Twp	78	455
CARDANES								
Joaquina	12	f	w	CA	Los Angeles	Santa Ana Twp	73	604
CARDASO								
Manuel	31	m	w	MEXI	Stanislaus	San Joaquin Twp	92	70
CARDEDO								
Joseph	33	m	w	ITAL	San Francisco	1-Wd San Francisco	79	121
CARDELLA								
Charles	28	m	w	ITAL	Calaveras	San Andreas P O	70	173
Joseph	27	m	w	ITAL	Calaveras	San Andreas P O	70	173
Joseph	25	m	w	ITAL	Calaveras	San Andreas P O	70	173
Stephen	19	m	w	ITAL	Calaveras	San Andreas P O	70	173

© 2001 by Heritage Quest. All rights reserved.

Series M593

Name	Age	S	R	B-PL	County	Locale	Roll	Pg
CARDEN								
Francis	28	m	w	ENGL	Sacramento	Sutter Twp	77	390
John	34	m	w	SCOT	San Francisco	1-Wd San Francisco	79	125
John C	39	m	w	NY	San Francisco	1-Wd San Francisco	79	125
Lavina	22	f	w	NY	San Francisco	11-Wd San Francisc	84	520
R C	46	m	w	TN	Sacramento	Center Twp	77	87
Thomas	65	m	w	GA	Tulare	Visalia Twp	92	283
CARDENA								
Louis	51	m	w	CHIL	Amador	Fiddletown P O	69	432
CARDENAS								
Fernando	24	m	w	PERU	Santa Barbara	Las Cruces P O	87	515
CARDENEL								
Luis	36	m	w	ITAL	Tuolumne	Sonora P O	93	318
CARDENO								
Jose	30	m	w	CHIL	Amador	Jackson P O	69	346
Thomas	45	m	w	CHIL	Amador	Jackson P O	69	346
CARDER								
D D	47	m	w	NY	Sonoma	Petaluma Twp	91	339
George	35	m	w	OH	Mendocino	Ukiah Twp	74	237
James	33	m	w	PA	San Francisco	3-Wd San Francisco	79	324
James	30	m	w	IREL	Marin	Tomales Twp	74	76
James B	40	m	w	RI	Placer	Bath P O	76	447
John	31	m	w	NY	Yuba	Marysville Twp	93	571
John B	20	m	w	NY	Placer	Dutch Flat P O	76	415
Thos	40	m	w	CANA	Santa Clara	Almaden Twp	88	2
William	43	m	w	MS	Calaveras	Copperopolis P O	70	246
Wm	13	m	w	CA	Tuolumne	Columbia P O	93	340
CARDIFF								
Margaret	25	f	w	NY	San Francisco	7-Wd San Francisco	81	227
Miles	70	m	w	IREL	San Francisco	San Francisco P O	83	10
CARDILINO								
Remo	35	m	w	ITAL	San Francisco	11-Wd San Francisc	84	712
CARDIN								
Ernist	40	m	w	MO	Mendocino	Point Arena Twp	74	212
CARDINAS								
Ant	35	m	w	MEXI	Santa Clara	Burnett Twp	88	34
Nichlo	32	m	w	ITAL	San Francisco	11-Wd San Francisc	84	710
CARDINELL								
Delia	69	f	w	MA	San Francisco	11-Wd San Francisc	84	515
John	37	m	w	CANA	San Mateo	Redwood Twp	87	369
Prestion	22	m	w	CANA	Yolo	Cache Crk Twp	93	425
Wm	34	m	w	CANA	Marin	Sausalito Twp	74	70
CARDINELLE								
Eliza	20	f	w	CANA	Solano	Benicia	90	5
CARDINET								
A	39	m	w	FRAN	Napa	Napa	75	13
Emile	39	m	w	FRAN	San Francisco	2-Wd San Francisco	79	226
CARDINI								
Frank	45	m	w	MEXI	Tuolumne	Columbia P O	93	353
Geo	30	m	w	ITAL	Tuolumne	Big Oak Flat P O	93	403
CARDINO								
James	28	m	w	CHIL	San Joaquin	2-Wd Stockton	86	163
CARDMAN								
John	48	m	w	SWIT	Napa	Napa Twp	75	70
CARDNELL								
John	29	m	w	NC	San Joaquin	Tulare Twp	86	262
CARDNES								
Mary	40	f	m	CHIL	Placer	Bath P O	76	422
CARDOFF								
Mark	58	m	w	IREL	San Francisco	San Francisco P O	83	42
CARDON								
Eligo	33	m	w	MEXI	Santa Barbara	Santa Barbara P O	87	472
Elijo	40	m	w	MEXI	Santa Barbara	Santa Barbara P O	87	494
Guillermo	60	m	w	CA	Santa Barbara	Santa Barbara P O	87	501
John	28	m	w	ME	Humboldt	Eureka Twp	72	279
Jose	40	m	w	CA	Santa Barbara	Las Cruces P O	87	516
Louis	38	m	w	FRAN	Butte	Ophir Twp	70	117
CARDONA								
Casamora	9	f	w	CA	San Luis Obispo	Arroyo Grande Twp	87	276
Manuel	52	m	w	MEXI	Santa Barbara	Santa Barbara P O	87	478
Tibucio	57	m	w	MEXI	Los Angeles	San Juan Twp	73	626
CARDONNA								
Giuseppe	25	m	w	ITAL	San Francisco	11-Wd San Francisc	84	594
CARDONOLA								
Antonio	44	m	w	WALE	Mariposa	Mariposa P O	74	130
CARDOSE								
Louis	28	m	w	PORT	San Mateo	Half Moon Bay P O	87	391
Manuel	29	m	w	PORT	Alameda	Washington Twp	68	299
Vincent	30	m	w	SCOT	Alameda	Brooklyn Twp	68	48
CARDOVA								
Hosea	47	m	w	MEXI	Mariposa	Mariposa P O	74	107
Hosepha	75	f	w	MEXI	Mariposa	Mariposa P O	74	107
CARDOZA								
Frank	21	m	w	PORT	Yuba	Bullards Bar P O	93	550
Jesus	34	f	w	MEXI	San Francisco	San Francisco P O	80	464
Joseph	40	m	w	PORT	Alameda	Eden Twp	68	72
Louisa	26	f	w	MEXI	San Francisco	San Francisco P O	80	459
Manuel	38	m	w	PORT	Nevada	Rough & Ready Twp	75	336
Ramon	26	m	w	CA	Fresno	Millerton P O	72	146
CARDOZI								
Martin J	19	m	w	PORT	Mariposa	Mariposa P O	74	90
CARDOZO								
John	45	m	w	AZOR	San Francisco	1-Wd San Francisco	79	102
Manuel	45	m	w	PORT	Alameda	Eden Twp	68	88
Manuel J	75	m	w	PORT	Alameda	Eden Twp	68	88
Reta L	72	f	w	PORT	Alameda	Eden Twp	68	88
CARDRIUS								
Jane	17	f	w	MEXI	San Francisco	8-Wd San Francisco	82	464
CARDUFF								
John	34	m	w	CANA	San Joaquin	Elliott Twp	86	81
W	34	m	w	IREL	San Joaquin	3-Wd Stockton	86	223
CARDUGAL								
Hado	33	m	w	CHIL	Fresno	Millerton P O	72	165
CARDUGIN								
Fernando	55	m	w	FRAN	Los Angeles	Los Angeles	73	553
CARDUS								
Jose	47	m	w	CHIL	Fresno	Millerton P O	72	146
CARDWELL								
Caleb W	42	m	w	TN	Contra Costa	Martinez P O	71	377
George	64	m	w	KY	Mariposa	Mariposa P O	74	119
George W	39	m	w	KY	Colusa	Colusa Twp	71	286
J T	27	m	w	IREL	Sacramento	Mississippi Twp	77	162
John H	23	m	w	NY	San Francisco	San Francisco P O	83	54
William	14	m	w	CA	Los Angeles	Los Angeles	73	510
CARDWELLE								
L	29	m	w	ITAL	Mariposa	Maxwell Crk P O	74	138
CARDWINS								
R	38	m	w	SCOT	San Joaquin	Dent Twp	86	27
CARDWOOD								
Alx	40	m	w	VT	San Joaquin	2-Wd Stockton	86	194
CARDY								
Ed	4	m	w	US	San Joaquin	2-Wd Stockton	86	180
Jose	16	m	m	MA	San Joaquin	2-Wd Stockton	86	178
Patrick	25	m	w	IREL	Inyo	Cerro Gordo Twp	73	318
CARE								
Aaron	40	m	w	OH	Sacramento	Franklin Twp	77	120
D S	40	m	w	MA	Solano	Vallejo	90	187
David	22	m	w	NY	San Francisco	8-Wd San Francisco	82	494
Martin T	43	m	w	ENGL	San Francisco	San Francisco P O	83	294
Minor	24	m	w	CANA	Santa Clara	Gilroy Twp	88	98
Rose	64	f	w	PRUS	San Francisco	3-Wd San Francisco	79	326
Thomas C	51	m	w	ENGL	San Mateo	Half Moon Bay P O	87	406
Wm	45	m	w	IREL	San Francisco	5-Wd San Francisco	81	28
CAREDDA								
Joseph	50	m	w	SARD	Santa Clara	Santa Clara Twp	88	175
CAREGEN								
Thomas	33	m	w	IREL	Sonoma	Petaluma Twp	91	313
CAREL								
Isaiah W	34	m	w	ME	Placer	Bath P O	76	440
May	18	f	w	IREL	San Joaquin	Douglas Twp	86	50
CARELO								
Diedo	24	m	w	SWIT	San Francisco	San Francisco P O	80	478
CARENCIA								
J	37	m	w	MEXI	Santa Clara	Almaden Twp	88	4
CARENNARO								
Francis	28	m	w	ITAL	San Francisco	2-Wd San Francisco	79	142
CARENO								
Guadaloup	20	m	w	MEXI	Fresno	Millerton P O	72	166
CARENS								
Augustine	40	f	i	CA	Santa Clara	Almaden Twp	88	13
Cara	45	m	w	CHIL	Santa Clara	Almaden Twp	88	13
James	35	m	w	IREL	San Joaquin	1-Wd Stockton	86	133
CAREO								
Filicita	42	f	w	CA	Los Angeles	Los Angeles	73	558
CARERAS								
Ignacio	52	m	w	MEXI	Los Angeles	Los Angeles	73	565
CARERGAN								
Margt	30	f	w	IREL	San Joaquin	2-Wd Stockton	86	162
CARERTY								
William	31	m	w	IREL	San Francisco	7-Wd San Francisco	81	171
CAREW								
Antonio	36	m	w	ITAL	Calaveras	San Andreas P O	70	217
James	43	m	w	IREL	San Francisco	San Francisco P O	85	850
Malake	40	m	w	IREL	Yuba	Marysville	93	590
CAREY								
Alice	16	f	w	MA	San Francisco	San Francisco P O	83	343
Andrew	32	m	b	VA	San Francisco	San Francisco P O	80	488
Anna	30	f	w	IREL	San Francisco	8-Wd San Francisco	82	333
Arthur J	35	m	w	IREL	Solano	Vallejo	90	171
Bridget	29	f	w	IREL	San Joaquin	2-Wd Stockton	86	208
Calvin	44	m	w	NY	Santa Clara	Milpitas Twp	88	115
Charles	35	m	w	MA	San Francisco	5-Wd San Francisco	81	32
Chas H	21	m	w	WI	San Francisco	8-Wd San Francisco	82	319
Cyrus	40	m	w	NY	Contra Costa	Martinez P O	71	406
David A	31	m	w	IREL	San Francisco	1-Wd San Francisco	79	63
Dennis	25	m	w	IREL	Santa Cruz	Pajaro Twp	89	341
Doremus	62	m	w	NY	San Francisco	5-Wd San Francisco	81	30
Elizabeth	45	f	w	NJ	Solano	Denverton Twp	90	24
Ellen	20	f	w	IREL	San Francisco	6-Wd San Francisco	81	130
James	50	m	w	NY	San Francisco	5-Wd San Francisco	81	11
James	35	m	w	IREL	Contra Costa	Martinez P O	71	402
James	34	m	w	IREL	San Francisco	7-Wd San Francisco	81	271
John	44	m	w	IREL	Fresno	Kings Rvr P O	72	203
John	40	m	w	IREL	Contra Costa	Martinez P O	71	412
John	35	m	w	IN	Napa	Napa Twp	75	70
John	34	m	w	ENGL	Alameda	Washington Twp	68	296
John	31	m	w	IREL	Solano	Tremont Twp	90	28
John	30	m	w	IREL	Merced	Snelling P O	74	262
John	28	m	w	PRUS	San Francisco	8-Wd San Francisco	82	374
John	26	m	w	NY	San Francisco	1-Wd San Francisco	79	65
John	25	m	w	IREL	Sonoma	Vallejo Twp	91	453
John	22	m	w	IREL	Solano	Vallejo	90	215
John	15	m	w	ENGL	San Francisco	1-Wd San Francisco	79	6

© 2001 by Heritage Quest. All rights reserved.

Series M593

Name	Age	S	R	B-PL	County	Locale	Roll	Pg
John D	33	m	w	IN	Tehama	Red Bluff	92	182
John E	18	m	w	IA	Placer	Cisco P O	76	494
John H	32	m	w	ENGL	San Francisco	8-Wd San Francisco	82	354
Joseph	46	m	w	NY	Santa Clara	Milpitas Twp	88	115
Joseph	42	m	w	PA	San Francisco	San Francisco P O	80	416
Joseph	37	m	w	NY	Contra Costa	Martinez P O	71	407
Kate	30	f	w	IREL	San Francisco	7-Wd San Francisco	81	273
Kate	25	f	w	IREL	San Francisco	San Francisco P O	83	287
Kate	24	f	w	IREL	Alameda	Murray Twp	68	109
Lafayette	35	m	w	IL	San Luis Obispo	Arroyo Grande Twp	87	279
Laurence	39	m	w	IREL	San Francisco	San Francisco P O	83	383
Lawrence	40	m	w	IREL	Plumas	Quartz Twp	77	37
Luther H	48	m	w	NY	Santa Clara	2-Wd San Jose	88	305
Margaret	48	f	w	IREL	Sacramento	4-Wd Sacramento	77	376
Mary	40	f	w	IREL	San Francisco	San Francisco P O	80	410
Mary	40	f	w	MA	San Francisco	8-Wd San Francisco	82	339
Mary C	46	f	w	NY	Santa Clara	1-Wd San Jose	88	228
Maurice	35	m	w	IREL	San Francisco	1-Wd San Francisco	79	28
Michael	44	m	w	PA	Santa Cruz	Pajaro Twp	89	356
Michael	34	m	w	IREL	Alameda	Hayward	68	73
Michael	30	m	w	IREL	San Francisco	San Francisco P O	83	132
Michael	26	m	w	IREL	Mariposa	Mariposa P O	74	112
Michal A	22	m	w	ME	San Francisco	San Francisco P O	83	10
Mike	36	m	w	IREL	San Francisco	11-Wd San Francisc	84	676
Morris	32	m	w	IREL	Solano	Vallejo	90	216
N P	42	m	w	IREL	Solano	Benicia	90	20
Nelson	29	m	w	ENGL	Solano	Vacaville Twp	90	118
Patrick	27	m	w	IREL	Alameda	Eden Twp	68	83
Patrick	25	m	w	IREL	Santa Clara	1-Wd San Jose	88	250
R S	42	m	w	MO	Sacramento	3-Wd Sacramento	77	262
Robt	37	m	w	IREL	Solano	Vallejo	90	197
Samuel F	38	m	w	NY	Marin	Sausalito Twp	74	72
Sarah	25	f	w	NY	San Francisco	San Francisco P O	83	406
Thomas	40	m	w	IREL	San Francisco	8-Wd San Francisco	82	463
Thomas	35	m	w	IREL	Los Angeles	Los Angeles Twp	73	489
Thomas	30	m	w	IREL	San Francisco	1-Wd San Francisco	79	133
Thomas	24	m	w	IREL	San Francisco	1-Wd San Francisco	79	105
Thos	36	m	w	IREL	San Joaquin	3-Wd Stockton	86	247
Thos	26	m	w	MA	San Francisco	11-Wd San Francisc	84	478
Thos	12	m	w	NY	San Francisco	San Francisco P O	83	83
Thos G	46	m	w	NY	Sacramento	Dry Crk Twp	77	98
W D	40	m	w	RI	Sierra	Downieville Twp	89	518
W R	42	m	w	NY	Nevada	Eureka Twp	75	132
William	32	m	w	IREL	San Mateo	Redwood City P O	87	376
William	32	m	w	IREL	Placer	Auburn P O	76	383
Wm R	33	m	w	NY	Nevada	Eureka Twp	75	135
CARFIELD								
R W	50	m	w	LA	Monterey	San Juan Twp	74	411
CARGE								
Wm B	49	m	w	VT	Santa Barbara	Santa Barbara P O	87	501
CARGELA								
Francesca	20	f	w	CHIL	Santa Clara	2-Wd San Jose	88	317
CARGHINE								
Antone	27	m	w	ITAL	Sonoma	Vallejo Twp	91	463
CARGILE								
John B	37	m	w	MO	Sonoma	Analy Twp	91	240
CARGILL								
Mathew	49	m	w	VA	Yuba	Slate Range Bar Tw	93	675
CARGLE								
Geo M	28	m	w	PA	San Francisco	1-Wd San Francisco	79	107
CARGON								
Lawrence	34	m	w	AUST	Amador	Sutter Crk P O	69	402
Ricardo	65	m	i	CA	Santa Cruz	Santa Cruz Twp	89	399
CARGYLE								
C S B	32	m	w	KY	Merced	Snelling P O	74	263
CARHATE								
William	28	m	w	HANO	Sonoma	Vallejo Twp	91	453
CARI								
Louis	28	m	w	FRAN	San Francisco	1-Wd San Francisco	79	55
CARIAG								
Francisco	18	f	w	CA	Santa Clara	Gilroy Twp	88	96
CARIAGA								
Pedro	18	m	w	CA	Monterey	San Juan Twp	74	407
Rita F	51	f	w	MEXI	Monterey	San Juan Twp	74	407
CARIAGO								
Loreta	27	m	w	MEXI	Los Angeles	Los Angeles	73	514
CARICO								
Elzy	25	m	w	KY	Nevada	Grass Valley Twp	75	199
Preelus	48	m	w	KY	Siskiyou	Callahan P O	89	624
CARIDO								
Manuel	42	m	w	MEXI	Santa Clara	Almaden Twp	88	1
CARIEN								
Angelo	49	m	w	ITAL	Calaveras	San Andreas P O	70	205
CARIER								
Francis	41	m	w	MEXI	San Francisco	San Francisco P O	80	344
T L	16	m	w	CA	Alameda	Oakland	68	243
CARIESA								
Ramon	35	m	w	CA	Fresno	Millerton P O	72	162
CARIG								
David N	29	m	w	OH	Sonoma	Vallejo Twp	91	459
CARIGAN								
Ann	35	f	w	NY	Alameda	Brooklyn	68	24
Arthur	16	m	w	CANA	San Francisco	11-Wd San Francisc	84	587
Mary	50	f	w	IREL	San Francisco	11-Wd San Francisc	84	687
Nancy	15	f	w	TN	Sacramento	Franklin Twp	77	110
CARIGER								
David	22	m	w	CA	Sonoma	Sonoma Twp	91	444
Nicholas	53	m	w	TN	Sonoma	Sonoma Twp	91	444
CARIL								
Mary	15	f	w	CA	San Francisco	2-Wd San Francisco	79	254
CARILLO								
Antone	37	m	w	MEXI	Marin	Sausalito Twp	74	68
Francis	44	m	w	MEXI	Santa Clara	Almaden Twp	88	5
Francisco	57	m	w	CA	Santa Barbara	Santa Barbara P O	87	480
Jean	24	m	w	ITAL	Calaveras	San Andreas P O	70	180
Jose C	35	m	w	CA	San Bernardino	Chino Twp	78	412
Jose M	52	m	w	CA	Santa Barbara	Santa Barbara P O	87	463
Juan	26	m	w	CA	Santa Barbara	Santa Barbara P O	87	454
Rita	35	f	w	CA	Santa Barbara	Santa Barbara P O	87	463
Romulo	17	m	w	CA	Santa Barbara	Santa Barbara P O	87	461
CARIN								
Pedro	38	m	w	MEXI	Santa Barbara	Las Cruces P O	87	507
CARINA								
Joseph	29	m	w	CANA	San Francisco	San Francisco P O	80	460
CARINES								
John	23	m	w	NY	Solano	Vallejo	90	166
CARINGER								
James W	27	m	w	MO	Sonoma	Sonoma Twp	91	431
CARINO								
Intronacio	43	m	w	MEXI	Marin	San Rafael Twp	74	36
CARIO								
Jose	30	m	w	CHIL	San Francisco	6-Wd San Francisco	81	82
CARION								
Adolph	35	m	w	FRAN	Nevada	Bridgeport Twp	75	102
Guadaloupe	15	f	w	CA	San Francisco	1-Wd San Francisco	79	27
Martina	39	f	w	CHIL	San Francisco	1-Wd San Francisco	79	28
CARIOT								
Joseph	48	m	w	FRAN	Santa Clara	Fremont Twp	88	52
CARIPIO								
Domingues	69	m	w	MEXI	San Luis Obispo	Salinas Twp	87	295
CARISMA								
John	24	m	w	PORT	San Mateo	Half Moon Bay P O	87	390
CARISOSO								
Manuel	35	m	w	MEXI	Los Angeles	Los Angeles Twp	73	492
CARITHERS								
D N	33	m	w	IL	Sonoma	Santa Rosa	91	410
George	60	m	w	IREL	Calaveras	San Andreas P O	70	189
CARKEEK								
Andrw	51	m	w	ENGL	Tuolumne	Sonora P O	93	310
CARKEEP								
Stephen	14	m	w	CA	San Francisco	11-Wd San Francisc	84	587
CARKILL								
John G	26	m	w	GERM	San Francisco	San Francisco P O	83	156
CARKINS								
John	31	m	w	ENGL	Nevada	Grass Valley Twp	75	224
CARL								
A W	26	m	w	ME	Sacramento	3-Wd Sacramento	77	274
Albert	24	m	w	MO	Yolo	Cache Crk Twp	93	448
Charles	34	m	w	NY	Alameda	Oakland	68	206
David E	35	m	w	ME	Contra Costa	Martinez P O	71	378
Edward	42	m	w	CANA	Contra Costa	Martinez Twp	71	350
Emma M	14	f	w	CA	Sonoma	Healdsburg	91	274
Jeremiah	45	m	w	IREL	San Francisco	2-Wd San Francisco	79	247
John	36	m	w	IREL	Mariposa	Mariposa P O	74	112
Michael	40	m	w	IREL	El Dorado	White Oak Twp	72	135
Michael	35	m	w	IREL	San Francisco	2-Wd San Francisco	79	177
P F	40	m	w	IREL	Alameda	Oakland	68	210
Patrick	46	m	w	NY	San Joaquin	Castoria Twp	86	1
Patrick	40	m	w	IREL	Sacramento	Brighton Twp	77	77
Patrick	32	m	w	IREL	Mariposa	Mariposa P O	74	113
Patrick	30	m	w	IREL	San Mateo	San Mateo P O	87	360
S R	42	m	w	CANA	Solano	Vallejo	90	209
Silas	34	m	w	NY	Sacramento	4-Wd Sacramento	77	355
W L	40	m	w	MI	Monterey	San Antonio Twp	74	317
CARLA								
John	60	m	w	ITAL	Tuolumne	Chinese Camp P O	93	383
CARLAGIE								
Andrew	35	m	w	IREL	San Francisco	7-Wd San Francisco	81	233
CARLAN								
Ann	27	f	w	IREL	San Francisco	8-Wd San Francisco	82	457
David	39	m	w	IREL	San Francisco	San Francisco P O	83	386
James	39	m	w	IREL	Contra Costa	Martinez P O	71	418
Pat	25	m	w	IREL	Alameda	Oakland	68	172
CARLAND								
Daniel	58	m	w	IREL	Nevada	Grass Valley Twp	75	171
CARLDERON								
Santa	17	f	w	CHIL	Sacramento	2-Wd Sacramento	77	222
CARLE								
Alonzo E	28	m	w	CA	Sacramento	3-Wd Sacramento	77	294
Anni	46	f	w	IREL	Yuba	Slate Range Bar Tw	93	671
L	57	m	w	IREL	Alameda	Oakland	68	150
Pierre	42	m	w	FRAN	Butte	Ophir Twp	70	115
CARLEN								
E	19	f	w	IREL	Alameda	Oakland	68	236
Levi	48	m	w	NY	San Joaquin	3-Wd Stockton	86	234
CARLER								
George	50	m	w	IREL	Tuolumne	Chinese Camp P O	93	387
Thomas	27	m	w	ME	Contra Costa	Martinez P O	71	431
CARLES								
James H	22	m	w	OH	Sonoma	Bodega Twp	91	264
Josephine	25	f	w	LA	San Francisco	5-Wd San Francisco	81	9
Leondas	41	m	w	AL	Merced	Snelling P O	74	279
Peter	44	m	w	AUST	Monterey	San Juan Twp	74	415
Thos	34	m	w	NY	Solano	Vallejo	90	200

© 2001 by Heritage Quest. All rights reserved.

Series M593

Name	Age	S	R	B-PL	County	Locale	Roll	Pg
CARLESS								
Beard	35	m	w	IN	Humboldt	South Fork Twp	72	303
Geo W	25	m	w	IN	Nevada	Meadow Lake Twp	75	247
CARLETON								
Charles	35	m	w	NH	El Dorado	Placerville Twp	72	103
Charles	35	m	w	TN	Solano	Vacaville Twp	90	129
Charles	34	m	w	NY	San Francisco	San Francisco P O	83	260
Charles	33	m	w	VT	Kern	Havilah P O	73	340
Frank	32	m	w	CANA	Solano	Vallejo	90	168
Hilman	8	m	w	CA	Butte	Ophir Twp	70	98
John	26	m	w	IREL	Placer	Rocklin Twp	76	465
John	25	m	w	OH	Placer	Rocklin Twp	76	467
Peter	45	m	w	BELG	Butte	Chico Twp	70	25
R L	39	m	w	IREL	Solano	Vallejo	90	197
William R	52	m	w	NY	San Diego	San Diego	78	498
CARLEY								
A B	43	m	w	NY	Nevada	Nevada Twp	75	272
Alfred	28	m	w	ENGL	Nevada	Grass Valley Twp	75	231
George	40	m	w	NY	Alameda	Oakland	68	175
George	30	m	w	NY	Calaveras	Copperopolis P O	70	241
Henry	40	m	w	IREL	Tuolumne	Chinese Camp P O	93	373
Jabez	43	m	w	ENGL	Sacramento	4-Wd Sacramento	77	324
James	35	m	w	OH	Sacramento	Dry Crk Twp	77	99
John	42	m	w	IREL	San Francisco	San Francisco P O	85	848
John	28	m	w	IREL	San Francisco	San Francisco P O	83	410
Joseph	50	m	w	ENGL	Calaveras	Copperopolis P O	70	250
M	20	m	w	IREL	Yuba	Marysville	93	588
Mark	40	m	w	NY	Calaveras	Copperopolis P O	70	241
Mary	31	f	w	IREL	Santa Cruz	Watsonville	89	364
Patrick	33	m	w	IREL	Nevada	Washington Twp	75	346
Sam	24	m	w	NY	Alameda	Murray Twp	68	125
CARLICAN								
Frances	45	f	w	MEXI	San Francisco	San Francisco P O	80	339
CARLIE								
George	23	m	w	ENGL	Los Angeles	Los Angeles	73	527
CARLILE								
---	38	m	w	ENGL	Amador	Ione City P O	69	357
J H	25	m	w	OH	Amador	Ione City P O	69	351
Louisa	75	f	w	WIND	San Francisco	San Francisco P O	83	264
W W	32	m	w	OH	Amador	Ione City P O	69	351
CARLILLE								
Jesus M	35	m	w	MEXI	Los Angeles	Los Angeles	73	545
CARLIN								
Annie	31	f	w	IREL	Marin	San Rafael	74	55
Annie	28	f	w	IREL	San Francisco	2-Wd San Francisco	79	277
Bernhard	41	m	w	PA	San Francisco	San Francisco P O	85	864
Chas H	32	m	w	PA	Placer	Dutch Flat P O	76	414
Danl	44	m	w	IREL	San Francisco	7-Wd San Francisco	81	257
Edward	30	m	w	PRUS	San Francisco	San Francisco P O	85	728
Edward	23	m	w	IREL	Placer	Cisco P O	76	495
Hugh	19	m	w	CT	Sacramento	Granite Twp	77	146
John	30	m	w	IREL	San Francisco	8-Wd San Francisco	82	343
John	25	m	w	MA	San Francisco	8-Wd San Francisco	82	351
Mary	35	f	i	CA	Trinity	North Fork Twp	92	220
Michael	24	m	w	IREL	Placer	Cisco P O	76	494
Patrick	30	m	w	IREL	San Francisco	7-Wd San Francisco	81	194
Peter	30	m	w	IREL	San Francisco	1-Wd San Francisco	79	65
Richard	27	m	w	ENGL	Nevada	Grass Valley Twp	75	224
Samul	48	m	w	OH	Trinity	North Fork Twp	92	220
William	61	m	w	IREL	Humboldt	South Fork Twp	72	300
Wm	40	m	w	IREL	San Francisco	San Francisco P O	85	782
CARLINE								
Eliza	29	f	w	IREL	Nevada	Nevada Twp	75	287
John	45	m	w	IREL	San Francisco	7-Wd San Francisco	81	240
CARLING								
Matilda	48	f	w	NJ	San Francisco	San Francisco P O	85	725
P Hubbard	33	m	w	NJ	San Diego	San Diego	78	492
CARLISLE								
Alex	21	m	w	IREL	Humboldt	Eureka Twp	72	267
B	12	f	w	CA	Los Angeles	Los Angeles	73	569
Ben F	47	m	w	MO	Butte	Ophir Twp	70	98
D C	39	m	w	NY	Sierra	Downieville Twp	89	518
Dan	44	m	w	CANA	Alameda	Oakland	68	148
Geo O	44	m	w	VT	San Francisco	San Francisco P O	85	718
George	22	m	w	PA	San Francisco	San Francisco P O	80	336
James	17	m	w	CA	Colusa	Monroe Twp	71	321
James C	32	m	w	KY	Butte	Chico Twp	70	13
Kate	6	f	w	CA	Butte	Ophir Twp	70	108
L	10	f	w	CA	Los Angeles	Los Angeles	73	569
Mary	12	f	w	CA	Los Angeles	Los Angeles	73	511
Sam	35	m	w	KY	Butte	Ophir Twp	70	102
Sam	31	m	w	MO	Butte	Ophir Twp	70	97
Samuel	52	m	w	PA	Sacramento	4-Wd Sacramento	77	346
Shubel H	45	m	w	VT	San Francisco	8-Wd San Francisco	82	391
Thomas	30	m	w	MO	Yolo	Buckeye Twp	93	407
Thomas	28	m	w	IREL	Humboldt	Table Bluff Twp	72	305
Thomas	25	m	w	MO	Yolo	Buckeye Twp	93	417
Thomas	23	m	w	OH	Nevada	Nevada Twp	75	317
Thomas	23	m	w	NY	San Francisco	11-Wd San Francisc	84	544
Turner	35	m	w	VA	Santa Clara	1-Wd San Jose	88	264
William	28	m	w	IREL	San Francisco	11-Wd San Francisc	84	519
William	28	m	w	MI	Alameda	Washington Twp	68	293
Wm	41	m	w	IREL	Sonoma	Bodega Twp	91	261
CARLITA								
Jose	27	m	w	MEXI	San Francisco	San Francisco P O	80	464
CARLITINA								
John	33	m	w	AUST	San Francisco	2-Wd San Francisco	79	201

Series M593

Name	Age	S	R	B-PL	County	Locale	Roll	Pg
CARLO								
Braga	26	m	w	ITAL	Sonoma	Analy Twp	91	236
Frank	35	m	w	SCOT	Alameda	Brooklyn Twp	68	48
Mardo	36	m	w	MEXI	Stanislaus	Emory Twp	92	26
Phillipa	38	f	w	SAME	El Dorado	Salmon Falls Twp	72	130
Thomas	45	m	w	IREL	Sacramento	3-Wd Sacramento	77	297
CARLOCK								
A B	37	m	w	OH	Siskiyou	Scott Valley Twp	89	610
F M	26	m	w	IL	Siskiyou	Scott Valley Twp	89	610
George	22	m	w	MO	Kern	Bakersfield P O	73	361
Jacob	28	m	w	OH	Kern	Bakersfield P O	73	361
W E	27	m	w	IL	El Dorado	Greenwood Twp	72	51
CARLON								
D C	15	m	w	CA	Tuolumne	Big Oak Flat P O	93	391
Francisco	23	m	w	CA	San Luis Obispo	Morro Twp	87	283
John	43	m	w	IREL	Tuolumne	Big Oak Flat P O	93	391
Juan	31	m	w	CA	San Luis Obispo	Santa Rosa Twp	87	326
CARLOS								
Ah	10	m	c	CHIN	Santa Cruz	Pajaro Twp	89	357
James	41	m	w	IREL	Nevada	Bloomfield Twp	75	94
Jesus	30	m	w	MEXI	Stanislaus	Emory Twp	92	25
John	33	m	w	KY	Sacramento	2-Wd Sacramento	77	221
Merce	22	m	w	CA	Stanislaus	Emory Twp	92	26
Ninette	24	f	w	MEXI	San Francisco	San Francisco P O	80	463
Thomas F	24	m	w	IREL	San Francisco	3-Wd San Francisco	79	300
CARLOSON								
Wm	40	m	w	IREL	San Luis Obispo	San Luis Obispo Tw	87	305
CARLOVE								
Varney	30	m	w	ITAL	Santa Clara	San Jose Twp	88	221
CARLOW								
M A	52	f	w	NY	Calaveras	Copperopolis P O	70	235
CARLSEN								
Chas	43	m	w	NORW	Tuolumne	Big Oak Flat P O	93	398
H M	28	m	w	NORW	San Francisco	3-Wd San Francisco	79	297
James	40	m	w	NORW	Trinity	Indian Crk	92	200
John	25	m	w	GERM	Klamath	Camp Gaston	73	372
Junius	35	m	w	NORW	San Francisco	1-Wd San Francisco	79	74
Oloff C	28	m	w	DENM	San Francisco	1-Wd San Francisco	79	79
W	48	m	w	SWED	Placer	Gold Run Twp	76	398
CARLSON								
C B	40	m	w	DENM	Sacramento	American Twp	77	68
Charles	22	m	w	SWED	San Francisco	7-Wd San Francisco	81	160
Charles	22	m	w	SWED	San Francisco	7-Wd San Francisco	81	217
Gastafe	26	m	w	FINL	Placer	Lincoln P O	76	486
H H T	34	m	w	DENM	Del Norte	Smith Rvr Twp	71	479
J	35	m	w	DENM	Sierra	Lincoln Twp	89	548
John	24	m	w	SWED	El Dorado	Mud Springs Twp	72	71
John	18	m	w	SWED	Santa Clara	1-Wd San Jose	88	267
John E	43	m	w	SWED	Mendocino	Big Rvr Twp	74	159
Mars	44	m	w	SWED	San Francisco	San Francisco P O	83	35
Peter	26	m	w	SWED	San Francisco	7-Wd San Francisco	81	211
Thomas	37	m	w	NORW	Alpine	Silver Mtn P O	69	308
Wilrick	35	m	w	FINL	San Francisco	3-Wd San Francisco	79	291
CARLSTON								
John	44	m	w	SWED	Placer	Bath P O	76	420
CARLT								
Emma	19	f	w	PRUS	Sacramento	3-Wd Sacramento	77	277
CARLTON								
Austin	52	m	w	NC	Sonoma	Analy Twp	91	244
Benjamin	45	m	w	MA	Calaveras	San Andreas P O	70	206
Columbus	42	m	w	NC	Sonoma	Bodega Twp	91	255
Elizabeth	71	f	w	ME	Santa Cruz	Pajaro Twp	89	342
Elizabeth	40	f	w	ME	San Francisco	7-Wd San Francisco	81	240
Francis	28	m	w	ME	San Francisco	2-Wd San Francisco	79	284
Frank	55	m	w	MA	Stanislaus	Empire Twp	92	45
G A	27	m	w	ME	Alameda	Oakland	68	176
Geo	23	m	w	MA	San Francisco	8-Wd San Francisco	82	364
Geo W	27	m	w	NY	Santa Cruz	Pajaro Twp	89	342
George	42	m	w	WI	San Diego	San Diego	78	487
George	35	m	w	KY	Siskiyou	Yreka Twp	89	665
H	36	m	w	NY	Alameda	Oakland	68	255
H E	62	m	w	ME	Alameda	Oakland	68	249
Harriet C	48	f	w	VT	San Francisco	San Francisco P O	83	115
Henry	33	m	w	MA	San Francisco	San Francisco P O	83	258
Henry P	35	m	w	MA	San Francisco	8-Wd San Francisco	82	308
J	42	m	w	MA	Alameda	Oakland	68	261
James	29	m	w	IN	Santa Clara	Fremont Twp	88	51
John	41	m	w	IREL	Nevada	Meadow Lake Twp	75	249
John	35	m	w	CANA	San Francisco	7-Wd San Francisco	81	276
John	28	m	w	SWED	Contra Costa	Martinez P O	71	415
John J	48	m	w	VT	Los Angeles	Los Angeles	73	538
Mariah	30	f	w	MA	San Francisco	San Francisco P O	83	381
Oliver B	41	m	w	ME	San Francisco	San Francisco P O	83	26
Robert	22	m	w	NC	Sonoma	Salt Point	91	387
Robert	18	m	w	PA	San Francisco	1-Wd San Francisco	79	74
Sophia	38	f	w	NY	Santa Clara	Santa Clara Twp	88	139
William	46	m	w	NJ	Mendocino	Point Arena Twp	74	210
William	29	m	w	IN	Placer	Colfax P O	76	388
CARLY								
Catherine	28	f	w	IREL	San Francisco	8-Wd San Francisco	82	440
Danl	47	m	w	ENGL	Sacramento	3-Wd Sacramento	77	304
David	49	m	w	ENGL	Napa	Napa Twp	75	46
George	25	m	w	MI	Humboldt	Mattole Twp	72	283
Stephen	32	m	w	NY	Lake	Lakeport	73	407
CARLYLE								
Irvin	45	m	w	SCOT	San Francisco	San Francisco P O	83	208
Robert	34	m	w	SCOT	Contra Costa	Martinez P O	71	418

© 2001 by Heritage Quest. All rights reserved.

Name	Age	S	R	B-PL	County	Locale	Series M593 Roll	Pg
Thomas	27	m	w	IREL	Nevada	Washington Twp	75	340
William E	35	m	w	MD	San Francisco	6-Wd San Francisco	81	79
CARLYON								
E	31	m	w	ENGL	Santa Clara	Almaden Twp	88	9
Edward	19	m	w	ENGL	Nevada	Grass Valley Twp	75	202
Jas	28	m	w	ENGL	Santa Clara	Almaden Twp	88	9
Richard	40	m	w	ENGL	Nevada	Grass Valley Twp	75	183
Thomas	28	m	w	ENGL	Nevada	Grass Valley Twp	75	148
William	32	m	w	ENGL	Nevada	Grass Valley Twp	75	187
CARM								
John	30	m	w	PRUS	Sacramento	American Twp	77	66
CARMACK								
H	42	m	w	PA	Nevada	Bridgeport Twp	75	103
Samuel	39	m	w	TN	Nevada	Rough & Ready Twp	75	331
CARMADY								
John	60	m	w	IREL	Marin	Tomales Twp	74	81
Patrick	22	m	w	IREL	Los Angeles	Los Angeles	73	541
CARMAN								
A S	20	m	w	CANA	Napa	Napa	75	3
Albt	20	m	w	CANA	Butte	Chico Twp	70	48
Alonzo	40	m	w	CANA	Plumas	Quartz Twp	77	43
Geo L	32	m	w	NY	Shasta	Fort Crook P O	89	476
John	42	m	w	ENGL	Stanislaus	Empire Twp	92	62
John	20	m	w	CA	San Mateo	Pescadero P O	87	415
Louis	49	m	w	SWED	Fresno	Millerton P O	72	194
Moses V	40	m	w	IREL	San Francisco	San Francisco P O	85	758
P J	35	m	w	NJ	Amador	Drytown P O	69	422
William	51	m	w	NY	San Francisco	San Francisco P O	83	221
Wm	49	m	w	NY	Butte	Chico Twp	70	29
CARMAND								
Sophie	6	f	w	CA	San Francisco	San Francisco P O	83	32
CARMANN								
Arvalia	56	m	w	CHIL	Sacramento	2-Wd Sacramento	77	215
CARMANY								
Cyrus	58	m	w	PA	San Francisco	San Francisco P O	80	408
CARMATI								
B J	68	m	w	ITAL	Tuolumne	Chinese Camp P O	93	371
CARMATZ								
Adolf	38	m	w	PRUS	San Francisco	3-Wd San Francisco	79	318
CARME								
Antonio	42	m	w	SWIT	Calaveras	San Andreas P O	70	209
Maria	55	f	w	CA	Santa Cruz	Pajaro Twp	89	357
CARMEGO								
Francisco	18	m	w	MEXI	Fresno	Millerton P O	72	154
CARMEL								
Jose	40	m	w	CHIL	Amador	Fiddletown P O	69	435
CARMELI								
A	33	m	w	SWIT	Alameda	Oakland	68	150
CARMELO								
Ramon	29	m	w	MEXI	Amador	Jackson P O	69	322
CARMEN								
John	36	m	w	NY	Siskiyou	Callahan P O	89	631
William	44	m	w	ENGL	Calaveras	Copperopolis P O	70	264
CARMENDO								
Rolie	40	m	w	MEXI	San Joaquin	1-Wd Stockton	86	133
CARMER								
Charles	32	m	w	NJ	Sonoma	Petaluma Twp	91	335
David E	20	m	w	CANA	Mendocino	Point Arena Twp	74	204
H L	41	f	w	NY	Solano	Vallejo	90	193
Rueben O	35	m	w	NY	Tehama	Red Bluff	92	179
CARMES								
Emil	26	m	w	FRAN	San Francisco	11-Wd San Francisc	84	643
CARMETTA								
James	32	m	w	ITAL	Calaveras	San Andreas P O	70	179
Joab	31	m	w	ITAL	Calaveras	San Andreas P O	70	179
CARMI								
Deblee	28	m	w	NY	Santa Barbara	Santa Barbara P O	87	496
CARMICHAEL								
A	50	m	w	SCOT	Sierra	Sears Twp	89	559
Annie	45	f	w	IREL	San Francisco	7-Wd San Francisco	81	229
Archi	31	m	w	NY	Butte	Oregon Twp	70	130
Archy	39	m	w	NC	Sonoma	Washington Twp	91	467
Daniel	45	m	w	SCOT	San Francisco	11-Wd San Francisc	84	519
Danl	39	m	w	IREL	San Francisco	San Francisco P O	83	319
David	40	m	w	SCOT	Solano	Tremont Twp	90	33
Jacob	35	m	w	OH	Santa Clara	1-Wd San Jose	88	266
John	47	m	w	SCOT	Monterey	San Benito Twp	74	381
John	46	m	w	SCOT	Nevada	Bridgeport Twp	75	115
John	42	m	w	IREL	Sacramento	Sutter Twp	77	389
John	34	m	w	SCOT	San Francisco	7-Wd San Francisco	81	242
John H	80	m	w	IREL	Sonoma	Washington Twp	91	467
Mary	45	f	w	IREL	Contra Costa	Martinez P O	71	394
Moses	39	m	w	PA	Solano	Silveyville Twp	90	83
Nancy	70	f	w	NC	Sonoma	Washington Twp	91	467
Robt	20	m	w	SCOT	Placer	Cisco P O	76	495
Wm	33	m	w	SCOT	San Francisco	San Francisco P O	83	316
Wm	29	m	w	MO	Sonoma	Mendocino Twp	91	301
CARMICHAL								
Jno	38	m	w	NY	San Joaquin	Elkhorn Twp	86	69
CARMICHEAL								
Wm	23	m	w	ENGL	San Joaquin	2-Wd Stockton	86	185
CARMICHLE								
John	40	m	w	PA	San Joaquin	Elkhorn Twp	86	67
CARMICHO								
Dominica	30	m	w	ITAL	Amador	Volcano P O	69	384
CARMICLE								
Ann E	39	f	w	VA	El Dorado	Placerville Twp	72	103
CARMIES								
R E	32	m	w	ME	Nevada	Bloomfield Twp	75	94
CARMIKEL								
Chas	39	m	w	NY	Shasta	Stillwater P O	89	481
CARMINE								
Mary	40	f	w	FRAN	San Francisco	6-Wd San Francisco	81	76
CARMODY								
E	33	m	w	GERM	Solano	Vallejo	90	209
John	38	m	w	IREL	San Francisco	San Francisco P O	83	313
Joseph	26	m	w	IREL	Yuba	Marysville	93	586
Martin	29	m	w	CANA	Nevada	Nevada Twp	75	322
Pat	25	m	w	IREL	San Francisco	7-Wd San Francisco	81	255
CARMON								
George	36	m	w	CANA	Contra Costa	Martinez P O	71	371
CARMONE								
John	15	m	w	ITAL	San Mateo	Schoolhouse Statio	87	334
CARMONY								
Mary	45	f	w	MEXI	Sacramento	2-Wd Sacramento	77	221
CARMOODY								
J	22	m	w	IREL	Yuba	Marysville Twp	93	567
CARMOSTI								
John	35	m	w	ITAL	Calaveras	San Andreas P O	70	177
CARN								
Catharine	35	f	w	IREL	San Francisco	San Francisco P O	85	822
David	30	m	w	NJ	Santa Clara	2-Wd San Jose	88	322
James	25	m	w	IREL	San Francisco	San Francisco P O	85	792
Mary	17	f	w	IREL	San Joaquin	2-Wd Stockton	86	197
Mary	14	f	w	IREL	Alameda	Oakland	68	187
Michl	38	m	w	IREL	San Francisco	1-Wd San Francisco	79	66
CARNA								
Manuel	20	m	w	MEXI	San Luis Obispo	Salinas Twp	87	291
CARNAG								
Charles	39	m	w	ITAL	San Francisco	2-Wd San Francisco	79	185
CARNAHAN								
J A	45	m	w	PA	Solano	Vallejo	90	151
Robt	28	m	w	PA	Santa Barbara	Santa Barbara P O	87	496
CARNAUD								
Octave	12	m	w	CA	Marin	San Rafael Twp	74	29
CARNDS								
Henry	60	m	w	EIND	San Mateo	Half Moon Bay P O	87	390
CARNDUFF								
J L	47	m	w	NY	San Joaquin	1-Wd Stockton	86	141
Samuel	52	m	w	IREL	San Mateo	Menlo Park P O	87	379
CARNE								
Ah	14	m	c	CHIN	San Mateo	Half Moon Bay P O	87	395
Ar	24	f	c	CHIN	Sonoma	Petaluma Twp	91	342
Catharine	63	f	w	ENGL	El Dorado	Placerville	72	124
Edward	45	m	w	ENGL	Tuolumne	Sonora P O	93	324
Edwin	36	m	w	ENGL	Tuolumne	Sonora P O	93	319
John	40	m	w	IREL	Alameda	Oakland	68	151
John	30	m	w	ENGL	Tuolumne	Sonora P O	93	317
John B	39	m	w	IL	Yolo	Cache Crk Twp	93	445
Timothy	30	m	w	IREL	Alameda	Murray Twp	68	106
CARNEA								
Candelario	35	m	w	CA	Santa Cruz	Pajaro Twp	89	349
CARNEDA								
Narciso	37	m	w	CA	Santa Barbara	Santa Barbara P O	87	460
CARNEDO								
Rafael	65	m	w	MEXI	Los Angeles	Los Nietos Twp	73	589
CARNEE								
Jason	34	m	w	OH	Mendocino	Calpella Twp	74	188
CARNEL								
Francis	20	f	w	PORT	Alameda	Eden Twp	68	88
CARNELL								
Margaret	40	f	w	IREL	San Francisco	San Francisco P O	83	142
CARNER								
Ambrose	63	m	w	MA	Mendocino	Calpella Twp	74	187
Hiram	40	m	w	OH	Mendocino	Calpella Twp	74	188
James	29	m	w	IREL	Sacramento	Franklin Twp	77	108
Jas M	38	m	w	OH	Mendocino	Calpella Twp	74	190
John S	52	m	w	NY	Plumas	Mineral Twp	77	22
Joseph	51	m	w	OH	Butte	Concow Twp	70	7
Peter	42	m	w	NY	San Francisco	3-Wd San Francisco	79	290
R	32	m	w	IL	Mendocino	Calpella Twp	74	189
CARNERY								
Laurenc	48	m	w	IREL	Butte	Kimshew Tpw	70	83
CARNES								
Fred G	42	m	w	NY	San Francisco	San Francisco P O	83	176
Geo A	44	m	w	NY	San Francisco	8-Wd San Francisco	82	291
Grace B	3	f	w	CA	Contra Costa	Martinez P O	71	387
Henry S	48	m	w	MA	Santa Barbara	Santa Barbara P O	87	453
James	40	m	w	IA	San Joaquin	2-Wd Stockton	86	158
James	29	m	w	NY	San Joaquin	Elkhorn Twp	86	62
Peter	27	m	w	PRUS	Solano	Tremont Twp	90	32
Robert	38	m	w	PA	Los Angeles	Wilmington Twp	73	635
CARNESA								
Louie	38	m	w	ITAL	San Francisco	San Francisco P O	85	865
CARNET								
Arom	30	m	w	SWED	Sutter	Vernon Twp	92	130
CARNETO								
Leopold	25	m	w	ITAL	Santa Clara	Fremont Twp	88	58
CARNEY								
Chas	54	m	w	OH	Siskiyou	Surprise Valley Tw	89	640
Edward	40	m	w	NY	Nevada	Little York Twp	75	235
Edward	27	m	w	IREL	San Francisco	San Francisco P O	83	298
Elizabeth	20	f	w	IREL	Napa	Napa Twp	75	30
Francis	50	m	w	ENGL	Placer	Auburn P O	76	361

© 2001 by Heritage Quest. All rights reserved.

Name	Age	S	R	B-PL	County	Locale	Roll	Pg
						Series M593		
George H	39	m	w	NY	Placer	Dutch Flat P O	76	405
Isaac T	48	m	w	TN	Mendocino	Anderson Twp	74	153
James	45	m	w	ME	Nevada	Meadow Lake Twp	75	252
James	42	m	w	ENGL	Sacramento	2-Wd Sacramento	77	234
James	15	m	w	CT	Nevada	Eureka Twp	75	128
Jno	45	m	w	IREL	Sacramento	1-Wd Sacramento	77	184
John	42	m	w	NY	El Dorado	Mud Springs Twp	72	84
John	37	m	w	IREL	Sacramento	Center Twp	77	85
John	30	m	w	IREL	San Francisco	7-Wd San Francisco	81	159
John	25	m	b	NY	San Mateo	Half Moon Bay P O	87	406
Joseph	40	m	w	NY	Mono	Bridgeport P O	74	286
Lawrence	39	m	w	IREL	San Francisco	San Francisco P O	83	315
Lizzie	14	f	w	CA	San Joaquin	Castoria Twp	86	4
Margaret	43	f	w	IREL	San Francisco	San Francisco P O	83	372
Martin	35	m	w	IREL	Sacramento	1-Wd Sacramento	77	188
Mary	44	f	w	IREL	El Dorado	Placerville	72	127
Mary	24	f	w	IREL	San Francisco	8-Wd San Francisco	82	453
Michael	50	m	w	IREL	Tuolumne	Columbia P O	93	359
Mike	45	m	w	IREL	Solano	Vallejo	90	215
Morris	42	m	w	IREL	San Francisco	11-Wd San Francisc	84	545
Oscar	22	m	w	ME	Plumas	Washington Twp	77	53
P J	30	m	w	IREL	Alameda	Oakland	68	262
Patk	40	m	w	NY	Solano	Vallejo	90	155
Peter	28	m	w	IREL	Napa	Napa	75	19
Sam	40	m	w	ME	Nevada	Eureka Twp	75	135
Smith	40	m	w	OH	Nevada	Washington Twp	75	343
Susie	69	f	w	IREL	San Francisco	San Francisco P O	85	790
William	21	m	w	CANA	Sonoma	Vallejo Twp	91	451
CARNIEZ								
Josefa	40	f	w	MEXI	San Francisco	San Francisco P O	80	475
CARNIFF								
R C	30	m	w	NY	Sutter	Sutter Twp	92	127
CARNIGHA								
John	25	m	w	ITAL	San Francisco	1-Wd San Francisco	79	114
CARNILLA								
Langlois	23	m	w	CANA	Humboldt	Table Bluff Twp	72	305
CARNIN								
J C	45	m	w	IREL	Tuolumne	Columbia P O	93	355
CARNIPER								
Angel	28	m	w	SWIT	Marin	San Antonio Twp	74	61
Antoine	21	m	w	SWIT	Marin	San Antonio Twp	74	61
Joseph	42	m	w	SWIT	Marin	San Antonio Twp	74	61
Louis	31	m	w	SWIT	Marin	San Antonio Twp	74	61
CARNISH								
Edgar	56	m	w	ENGL	Placer	Colfax P O	76	386
CARNISS								
Jacob	45	m	w	ITAL	San Francisco	1-Wd San Francisco	79	39
CARNO								
Rafael	13	m	w	CA	Monterey	Alisal Twp	74	296
Rosamon	4	f	w	CA	Santa Cruz	Soquel Twp	89	450
CARNOBY								
James	17	m	w	AUST	San Francisco	11-Wd San Francisc	84	429
CARNON								
Thos R	45	m	w	MO	Fresno	Millerton P O	72	147
CARNORI								
A	26	m	w	SWIT	Alameda	Oakland	68	241
L	23	m	w	SWIT	Alameda	Oakland	68	241
CARNPOY								
Joan	23	m	w	MEXI	Fresno	Millerton P O	72	166
CARO								
Hosea	37	m	w	MEXI	Fresno	Millerton P O	72	163
James	36	m	w	CA	San Joaquin	2-Wd Stockton	86	165
Louis	36	m	w	PRUS	San Bernardino	San Bernardino Twp	78	416
Samuel	40	m	w	PRUS	San Francisco	San Francisco P O	83	344
Simon	28	m	w	PRUS	San Bernardino	San Bernardino Twp	78	415
Wolff	40	m	w	PRUS	San Francisco	San Francisco P O	83	177
CAROL								
James	26	m	w	VT	San Mateo	Schoolhouse Statio	87	333
Jane	32	f	w	IREL	Colusa	Monroe Twp	71	324
John	40	m	w	IREL	Sutter	Butte Twp	92	99
John	34	m	w	IREL	Colusa	Butte Twp	71	266
Luke	30	m	w	IREL	Alameda	Oakland	68	171
Pat	38	m	w	IREL	Merced	Snelling P O	74	264
CAROLAN								
Abigail	24	f	w	MD	San Francisco	San Francisco P O	83	175
C A	38	m	w	ENGL	San Francisco	San Francisco P O	85	874
William	42	m	w	IREL	San Francisco	San Francisco P O	80	353
CAROLIN								
Jas	27	m	w	IREL	San Francisco	San Francisco P O	83	89
CAROLINE								
M	45	f	w	PA	Santa Cruz	Santa Cruz Twp	89	383
CAROLINSKI								
Antonio	40	m	w	MEXI	Fresno	Millerton P O	72	151
CAROLL								
Catharine	45	f	w	IREL	San Francisco	7-Wd San Francisco	81	230
James	60	m	w	SCOT	San Francisco	2-Wd San Francisco	79	180
James	34	m	w	IREL	Mendocino	Navarro & Big Rvr	74	175
Thos	45	m	w	IREL	San Francisco	7-Wd San Francisco	81	276
Thos	33	m	w	NY	San Luis Obispo	Salinas Twp	87	288
William	26	m	w	IREL	Colusa	Monroe Twp	71	324
CAROLLY								
Jas	27	m	w	IREL	San Joaquin	Tulare Twp	86	257
John	37	m	w	IREL	San Joaquin	3-Wd Stockton	86	231
CAROLTON								
John	40	m	w	IL	Plumas	Indian Twp	77	17
CARONA								
Lassida	28	f	w	MEXI	Fresno	Millerton P O	72	163

Name	Age	S	R	B-PL	County	Locale	Roll	Pg
						Series M593		
CARONET								
A	39	m	w	NICA	San Bernardino	San Salvador Twp	78	456
CARONORAS								
Corinl	21	m	i	MEXI	Inyo	Lone Pine Twp	73	334
CAROPAS								
Edecio	35	m	w	MEXI	Los Angeles	Soledad Twp	73	631
Juan Jose	26	m	w	MEXI	Los Angeles	Soledad Twp	73	631
CAROSA								
G	21	m	w	ITAL	San Joaquin	2-Wd Stockton	86	206
CAROSE								
Manwell	42	m	w	PORT	San Mateo	Half Moon Bay P O	87	390
CAROSO								
Joseph	21	m	w	PORT	Alameda	Eden Twp	68	71
CAROTHER								
Wm E	32	m	w	MI	Sacramento	San Joaquin Twp	77	399
CAROTHERS								
Andrew	67	m	w	PA	Sacramento	4-Wd Sacramento	77	356
Annie	11	f	w	MO	Santa Barbara	San Buenaventura P	87	444
Helen	21	f	w	MI	Sacramento	4-Wd Sacramento	77	361
James	46	m	w	PA	Contra Costa	Martinez P O	71	436
James H	51	m	w	OH	Sonoma	Petaluma Twp	91	314
John	33	m	w	DC	Sacramento	Sutter Twp	77	381
Maggie	21	f	w	MI	Sacramento	4-Wd Sacramento	77	376
Thos L	27	m	w	IL	Mendocino	Ukiah Twp	74	234
Walter	50	m	w	OH	Santa Clara	2-Wd San Jose	88	289
Wm	34	m	w	DC	Sacramento	Sutter Twp	77	381
CAROTHIN								
Wm	32	m	w	IREL	San Francisco	San Francisco P O	85	865
CAROW								
Thomas	60	m	w	IREL	San Francisco	San Francisco P O	85	821
CAROWAN								
James	35	m	w	IREL	Santa Clara	Redwood Twp	88	120
CARPA								
Florence	20	f	w	MEXI	San Francisco	San Francisco P O	83	100
CARPANI								
S J	28	f	w	MEXI	Tuolumne	Sonora P O	93	315
CARPE								
Jose M	40	m	w	MEXI	Santa Cruz	Soquel Twp	89	448
CARPELLI								
Chs	37	m	w	ITAL	San Francisco	2-Wd San Francisco	79	232
CARPELLO								
Joseph	34	m	w	ITAL	San Francisco	2-Wd San Francisco	79	232
CARPENA								
Josefa	38	f	w	MEXI	Santa Clara	2-Wd San Jose	88	328
CARPENETTE								
Louis	40	m	w	FRAN	Butte	Ophir Twp	70	96
CARPENTER								
---	38	m	w	IN	Sutter	Sutter Twp	92	128
---	19	f	w	CA	Los Angeles	Los Angeles	73	569
A G	38	m	w	MA	Nevada	Nevada Twp	75	321
A O	33	m	w	VT	Mendocino	Ukiah Twp	74	233
Abigal	74	f	w	MA	Napa	Napa	75	48
Alex	28	m	w	MI	Contra Costa	Martinez P O	71	431
Alexander	35	m	w	MA	San Francisco	11-Wd San Francisc	84	570
Alford	28	m	w	NY	San Francisco	7-Wd San Francisco	81	164
Alice	18	f	w	OH	Sacramento	3-Wd Sacramento	77	289
Anton	53	m	w	MEXI	Santa Clara	Almaden Twp	88	1
Augustin	45	m	w	CT	San Francisco	San Francisco P O	80	404
Benj	78	m	w	CT	San Bernardino	San Bernardino Twp	78	436
Benj	38	m	w	NY	Shasta	Shasta P O	89	455
Caleb G	53	m	w	NY	El Dorado	Diamond Springs Tw	72	23
Calvin	35	m	w	OH	Sonoma	Analy Twp	91	225
Calvin E	48	m	w	NY	Placer	Auburn P O	76	382
Catherine	50	f	w	IREL	San Francisco	6-Wd San Francisco	81	112
Chas	40	m	w	VT	San Joaquin	Douglas Twp	86	45
Chas	35	m	w	ME	Sonoma	Cloverdale Twp	91	273
Chas F	31	m	w	MS	Butte	Chico Twp	70	13
Con	50	m	w	OH	San Joaquin	Oneal Twp	86	119
Daniel	46	m	w	MA	San Francisco	San Francisco P O	80	390
Daniel	43	m	w	MA	San Francisco	6-Wd San Francisco	81	143
Daniel	40	m	w	NY	Contra Costa	Martinez P O	71	442
Darias	32	m	w	SHOL	Plumas	Washington Twp	77	54
David	41	m	w	ME	San Francisco	5-Wd San Francisco	81	25
David	40	m	w	VT	San Francisco	8-Wd San Francisco	82	465
E	40	m	w	IN	Siskiyou	Scott Valley Twp	89	617
E G	50	m	w	NY	Sacramento	Brighton Twp	77	73
Edward	45	m	w	NY	San Mateo	San Mateo P O	87	349
Edward	39	m	w	MA	San Francisco	San Francisco P O	80	351
Edwd C	38	m	w	NY	San Francisco	1-Wd San Francisco	79	88
Eli	22	m	w	MO	Sutter	Sutter Twp	92	126
Emeline	29	f	w	KY	San Francisco	11-Wd San Francisc	84	605
Eugene	49	m	w	FRAN	Butte	Ophir Twp	70	101
Ezra	46	m	w	IL	Monterey	San Antonio Twp	74	320
Frank	50	m	w	KY	Los Angeles	Los Angeles	73	541
Fred	35	m	w	OH	Butte	Chico Twp	70	49
Geo	28	m	w	IL	Sacramento	1-Wd Sacramento	77	178
George	34	m	w	IREL	Placer	Lincoln P O	76	485
George	32	m	w	WI	San Francisco	6-Wd San Francisco	81	107
George	32	m	w	CT	Sutter	Yuba Twp	92	140
George	14	m	w	CA	Santa Clara	Fremont Twp	88	64
Gideon J	48	m	w	PA	El Dorado	Placerville	72	112
H	38	m	w	CT	Solano	Vallejo	90	214
Henry	38	m	w	MI	Solano	Suisun Twp	90	102
Hill O	18	m	w	VA	Sonoma	Mendocino Twp	91	295
J	32	m	w	NY	Lake	Big Valley	73	395
Jacob	37	m	w	MO	Nevada	Nevada Twp	75	274
James	54	m	w	MO	Siskiyou	Butte Twp	89	584

© 2001 by Heritage Quest. All rights reserved.

Name	Age	S	R	B-PL	County	Locale	Series M593 Roll	Pg
James	29	m	w	VA	Stanislaus	Empire Twp	92	61
James H	45	m	w	MO	Los Angeles	San Gabriel Twp	73	594
Jas	48	m	w	ME	Sacramento	1-Wd Sacramento	77	190
Jno	40	m	w	NH	Butte	Ophir Twp	70	119
Jno	24	m	w	IN	San Joaquin	Liberty Twp	86	88
John	45	m	w	SWED	San Joaquin	Elkhorn Twp	86	58
John	43	m	w	ENGL	Stanislaus	Empire Twp	92	60
John	40	m	w	NH	Butte	Mountain Spring Tw	70	88
John	38	m	w	IN	El Dorado	Placerville Twp	72	97
John	37	m	w	NY	El Dorado	Georgetown Twp	72	38
John	34	m	w	IREL	Tuolumne	Columbia P O	93	346
John	30	m	w	MO	Los Angeles	Los Angeles Twp	73	476
John G	54	m	w	FL	Los Angeles	Los Angeles Twp	73	488
L B	40	m	w	IL	Sonoma	Petaluma Twp	91	327
L B	39	m	w	MI	Sutter	Vernon Twp	92	133
L F	42	m	w	NY	Sonoma	Petaluma Twp	91	325
L F	37	m	w	NY	Mendocino	Ukiah Twp	74	236
Lewis	35	m	w	US	El Dorado	Mud Springs Twp	72	89
Louis	38	m	w	MO	San Francisco	San Francisco P O	83	280
Louis	35	m	w	KY	San Francisco	San Francisco P O	80	400
Lucius C	36	m	w	NY	Yolo	Washington Twp	93	533
Lyman	35	m	w	OH	Sacramento	2-Wd Sacramento	77	253
M	30	f	w	MA	Sierra	Sierra Twp	89	569
M H	51	m	w	NC	Calaveras	Copperopolis P O	70	230
Mary	55	f	w	CA	Los Angeles	Los Nietos Twp	73	585
Mary	36	f	w	NY	San Joaquin	2-Wd Stockton	86	176
Mary	34	f	w	OH	San Francisco	6-Wd San Francisco	81	105
Mary	26	f	w	AL	Los Angeles	Los Angeles Twp	73	474
Mattie	22	f	w	IREL	Butte	Chico Twp	70	16
Milton	33	m	w	MO	Solano	Silveyville Twp	90	90
N B	33	m	w	RI	Merced	Snelling P O	74	267
Nichola	64	m	w	OH	El Dorado	Kelsey Twp	72	61
Nicholas	34	m	w	IA	Marin	San Rafael Twp	74	46
Noah	54	m	w	NY	Sacramento	2-Wd Sacramento	77	239
Orren F	39	m	w	OH	El Dorado	Mountain Twp	72	67
Patrick	36	m	w	IREL	San Francisco	7-Wd San Francisco	81	208
Philip	45	m	w	NY	Santa Cruz	Pajaro Twp	89	352
S	29	m	w	OH	Lake	Big Valley	73	394
S	23	m	w	VT	Yuba	East Bear Rvr Twp	93	543
Sampson	31	m	w	IA	Marin	San Rafael Twp	74	46
Samuel	38	m	w	MO	Yolo	Buckeye Twp	93	411
Secundino	24	m	w	CA	Los Angeles	Los Nietos Twp	73	588
Sitney	63	f	w	NC	Shasta	Horsetown P O	89	501
Sophie	70	f	w	ENGL	Sonoma	Bodega Twp	91	261
Stephen	38	m	w	NY	San Diego	San Diego	78	487
Susan A	44	f	w	VA	Sonoma	Mendocino Twp	91	301
T H	42	m	w	ENGL	Tuolumne	Sonora P O	93	314
Thos	45	m	w	OH	Amador	Volcano P O	69	376
Thos	39	m	w	IREL	San Francisco	11-Wd San Francisc	84	600
W A	29	m	w	NY	Sierra	Sierra Twp	89	562
W H	45	m	w	VA	San Francisco	San Francisco P O	85	782
Warren W	42	m	w	NY	Sonoma	Petaluma Twp	91	319
William	38	m	w	MA	Nevada	Nevada Twp	75	310
William	37	m	w	NY	San Francisco	San Francisco P O	80	384
William	18	m	w	MI	El Dorado	Mud Springs Twp	72	74
William H	47	m	w	VA	Colusa	Monroe Twp	71	319
William M	40	m	m	NY	El Dorado	Salmon Falls Twp	72	129
Wm	70	m	w	NY	Tehama	Battle Crk Twp	92	157
Wm	47	m	w	MA	Yuba	Rose Bar Twp	93	663
Wm	38	m	w	IN	Nevada	Meadow Lake Twp	75	248
Wm	37	m	w	WV	Sonoma	Petaluma Twp	91	324
Wm	30	m	w	NY	Monterey	Alisal Twp	74	288
Wm H	28	m	w	MA	San Francisco	San Francisco P O	83	70
Wm H	23	m	w	ENGL	Fresno	Millerton P O	72	148
Wm M	36	m	w	IN	Sacramento	Natomas Twp	77	168
Wm P	37	m	w	VT	El Dorado	Placerville Twp	72	102
CARPENTIA								
Asa L	25	m	w	VA	San Diego	San Diego	78	507
CARPENTIER								
H W	47	m	w	NY	Alameda	Oakland	68	137
CARPER								
T J	47	m	w	VA	Lake	Big Valley	73	399
CARPERELO								
Pasqued	48	m	w	SWIT	El Dorado	Georgetown Twp	72	36
CARPERO								
John	35	m	w	ITAL	San Francisco	2-Wd San Francisco	79	160
CARPERRA								
Dolores	42	f	w	MEXI	Santa Barbara	Santa Barbara P O	87	466
CARPINTER								
Chas	31	m	w	PA	Alameda	Oakland	68	137
CARPRENE								
Lorenzo	21	m	w	ITAL	San Francisco	San Francisco P O	85	751
CARPY								
Chas	20	m	w	CA	San Francisco	11-Wd San Francisc	84	592
CARQUELIN								
J	55	m	w	FRAN	Butte	Bidwell Twp	70	3
CARQUILLAT								
Jules	36	m	w	FRAN	San Francisco	San Francisco P O	80	350
CARR								
Alex	40	m	w	SCOT	Butte	Oregon Twp	70	132
Alfred	9	m	w	CA	Santa Cruz	Pajaro Twp	89	343
Andrew	48	m	w	IN	Butte	Ophir Twp	70	113
Andrew	43	m	w	IREL	Tuolumne	Columbia P O	93	356
Anna	13	f	w	ENGL	Santa Clara	Santa Clara Twp	88	144
Anthoney	23	m	w	NY	San Francisco	11-Wd San Francisc	84	647
Bridget	30	f	w	IREL	San Francisco	8-Wd San Francisco	82	447
Bridget	19	f	w	NY	San Francisco	San Francisco P O	83	89

Name	Age	S	R	B-PL	County	Locale	Series M593 Roll	Pg
Catharine	36	f	w	IREL	San Francisco	7-Wd San Francisco	81	178
Charles	34	m	w	MD	Los Angeles	Los Angeles	73	525
Charles	26	m	w	VT	San Francisco	San Francisco P O	85	863
Charles	23	m	w	NY	Yuba	Marysville	93	604
Clarence	31	m	w	RI	San Diego	San Diego	78	483
Curtis	55	m	w	ENGL	Solano	Vallejo	90	161
Daglan	33	m	w	IREL	Yuba	Marysville	93	579
Daniel	43	m	w	IREL	Marin	San Rafael Twp	74	45
Daniel	30	m	w	IREL	Sacramento	1-Wd Sacramento	77	179
Daniel D	40	m	w	ME	Amador	Fiddletown P O	69	431
David	32	m	w	POLA	San Francisco	7-Wd San Francisco	81	191
David P	37	m	w	VT	Santa Barbara	Santa Barbara P O	87	501
E M	35	m	w	NY	Alameda	Murray Twp	68	107
Edward	32	m	w	IREL	San Francisco	1-Wd San Francisco	79	82
Edward	30	m	w	CANA	Alameda	Brooklyn	68	21
Edward	30	m	w	IREL	San Francisco	7-Wd San Francisco	81	197
Francis P	36	m	w	FRAN	Calaveras	Copperopolis P O	70	255
Geo	23	m	w	CANA	San Francisco	1-Wd San Francisco	79	65
Geo C	35	m	w	PA	San Joaquin	2-Wd Stockton	86	180
Geo T	35	m	w	IL	Sacramento	Cosumnes Twp	77	96
George	55	m	w	MD	Yuba	Long Bar Twp	93	564
George	51	m	w	ENGL	Plumas	Mineral Twp	77	22
George	40	m	w	SCOT	Solano	Rio Vista Twp	90	64
H W	27	m	w	ME	Yuba	East Bear Rvr Twp	93	542
Henry	21	m	w	PRUS	San Joaquin	Oneal Twp	86	101
Hugh	43	m	w	IREL	Yuba	Marysville	93	608
J D	56	m	w	TN	Monterey	Alisal Twp	74	291
J F	32	m	w	OH	Nevada	Nevada Twp	75	271
J I	27	m	w	PA	Napa	Napa	75	52
James	52	m	w	IREL	Butte	Ophir Twp	70	102
James	50	m	w	IREL	Sonoma	Analy Twp	91	225
James	33	m	w	IREL	Contra Costa	Martinez P O	71	393
James	30	m	w	IREL	San Francisco	San Francisco P O	83	244
James C	50	m	w	TN	Trinity	Trinity Center Pct	92	204
James C	27	m	w	RI	San Francisco	1-Wd San Francisco	79	123
Jeremiah	45	m	w	PA	Marin	San Rafael Twp	74	32
John	55	m	w	OH	Santa Cruz	Pajaro Twp	89	348
John	53	m	w	IREL	Santa Cruz	Santa Cruz	89	430
John	53	m	w	IREL	Humboldt	Table Bluff Twp	72	306
John	42	m	w	IREL	Calaveras	San Andreas P O	70	188
John	41	m	w	IREL	Humboldt	Eureka Twp	72	258
John	40	m	w	PA	San Joaquin	Elliott Twp	86	73
John	38	m	w	IREL	Sacramento	2-Wd Sacramento	77	246
John	36	m	w	SCOT	San Francisco	7-Wd San Francisco	81	192
John	35	m	w	SCOT	San Francisco	7-Wd San Francisco	81	180
John	34	m	w	IREL	San Francisco	San Francisco P O	83	335
John	30	m	w	IREL	Sonoma	Vallejo Twp	91	455
John	30	m	w	IREL	Alameda	Hayward	68	78
John	27	m	w	IREL	Mendocino	Point Arena Twp	74	207
John	27	m	w	MA	Stanislaus	Emory Twp	92	20
John	25	m	w	MA	San Joaquin	Castoria Twp	86	6
John	22	m	w	IL	Nevada	Rough & Ready Twp	75	328
John	18	m	w	MA	Marin	Tomales Twp	74	79
John F	47	m	w	NY	San Francisco	San Francisco P O	83	185
John H	37	m	w	MA	San Francisco	8-Wd San Francisco	82	369
Joseph G	36	m	w	ME	El Dorado	Cosumnes Twp	72	16
L T	50	m	w	NY	San Joaquin	2-Wd Stockton	86	186
Leon M	43	m	w	NY	Nevada	Grass Valley Twp	75	187
Louie	35	m	w	PRUS	San Francisco	San Francisco P O	85	863
Lyman	29	m	w	NY	Stanislaus	Empire Twp	92	52
M E	30	f	w	IREL	Alameda	Oakland	68	134
Mark	45	m	w	ENGL	Sonoma	Vallejo Twp	91	456
Mary	34	f	w	IREL	Sonoma	Petaluma Twp	91	361
Mary	20	f	w	VA	Contra Costa	Martinez P O	71	396
Mary	16	f	w	IREL	Santa Cruz	Santa Cruz	89	426
Mary A	22	f	w	IREL	San Francisco	San Francisco P O	83	133
Mat	29	m	w	CANA	Santa Clara	Gilroy Twp	88	95
Mathew	29	m	w	IREL	Plumas	Plumas Twp	77	26
Mathew D	49	m	w	OH	San Francisco	6-Wd San Francisco	81	140
Michael	36	m	w	IREL	Solano	Benicia	90	5
Michael	29	m	w	GERM	San Mateo	Schoolhouse Statio	87	342
Michael	28	m	w	IREL	San Francisco	1-Wd San Francisco	79	5
Michael M	42	m	w	IREL	Sacramento	1-Wd Sacramento	77	180
Nelson	48	m	w	NY	Sonoma	Santa Rosa	91	402
Nelson F	32	m	w	KY	Yolo	Putah Twp	93	516
Nicholas E	57	m	w	ENGL	San Francisco	8-Wd San Francisco	82	461
O F	45	m	w	CT	Nevada	Bridgeport Twp	75	107
Owen	49	m	w	IREL	San Francisco	San Francisco P O	83	121
Pat	27	m	w	IREL	Placer	Cisco P O	76	494
Patrick	45	m	w	IREL	Calaveras	San Andreas P O	70	188
Patrick	44	m	w	IREL	San Francisco	11-Wd San Francisc	84	462
Patrick	30	m	w	IREL	Solano	Vallejo	90	170
Patrick	27	m	w	IREL	San Francisco	San Francisco P O	83	395
Peter	33	m	w	IREL	Alameda	Murray Twp	68	110
Peter	28	m	w	FRAN	Sutter	Yuba Twp	92	145
Peter	25	m	w	IREL	San Francisco	11-Wd San Francisc	84	596
R D	49	m	w	NY	Sierra	Table Rock Twp	89	579
Rebecca	27	f	w	CT	Monterey	Castroville Twp	74	329
Richd	53	m	w	ENGL	Solano	Benicia	90	3
Robt	37	m	w	ENGL	Alameda	Murray Twp	68	117
Samuel	50	m	w	MA	Plumas	Rich Bar Twp	77	8
Samuel	45	m	w	PRUS	San Francisco	San Francisco P O	85	831
Samuel	40	m	w	WALE	Alameda	Murray Twp	68	119
Samuel	26	m	w	OH	Yuba	Marysville	93	617
Samuel M	35	m	w	NY	Sacramento	Sutter Twp	77	383
Samuel W	45	m	w	KY	Mariposa	Mariposa P O	74	100
Sarah	5	f	w	CA	Santa Clara	Gilroy Twp	88	94

© 2001 by Heritage Quest. All rights reserved.

Name	Age	S	R	B-PL	County	Locale	Series M593 Roll	Pg
Sarah	30	f	w	IREL	San Francisco	San Francisco P O	85	775
Sarah	30	f	w	IREL	San Francisco	8-Wd San Francisco	82	444
Sarah	15	f	w	CA	Santa Cruz	Santa Cruz	89	408
Sarah	14	f	w	CA	Santa Cruz	Santa Cruz	89	426
Sarah A	59	f	w	IREL	Nevada	Nevada Twp	75	319
Seymour	29	m	w	NY	Sacramento	Lee Twp	77	159
Simon	32	m	w	BADE	Butte	Hamilton Twp	70	71
Susan (Mrs)	70	f	w	IREL	Monterey	Castroville Twp	74	339
Thomas	56	m	w	VA	Kern	Kernville P O	73	367
Thomas	45	m	w	IREL	Santa Clara	Fremont Twp	88	63
Thomas	43	m	w	IREL	Humboldt	Eureka Twp	72	259
Thomas	27	m	w	ENGL	Tuolumne	Big Oak Flat P O	93	402
Thomas	26	m	w	IREL	San Francisco	2-Wd San Francisco	79	140
Thomas	18	m	w	DC	San Francisco	6-Wd San Francisco	81	84
Thomas W	46	m	w	ENGL	San Francisco	3-Wd San Francisco	79	297
Timothy	45	m	w	IREL	Santa Cruz	Soquel Twp	89	448
William	40	m	w	ENGL	San Francisco	8-Wd San Francisco	82	334
William	39	m	w	IN	San Francisco	11-Wd San Francisc	84	635
William	35	m	w	IREL	San Francisco	11-Wd San Francisc	84	504
William	27	m	w	IREL	Santa Cruz	Pajaro Twp	89	350
Wm	43	m	w	IREL	Yuba	Marysville	93	577
Wm	34	m	w	IL	Santa Clara	Burnett Twp	88	33
Wm	22	m	w	IREL	Santa Clara	Almaden Twp	88	16
Wm	13	m	w	CA	San Francisco	11-Wd San Francisc	84	587
Wm B	50	m	w	NY	Marin	San Rafael Twp	74	39
Wm H	29	m	w	MO	San Francisco	1-Wd San Francisco	79	103
CARRABINE								
John	49	m	w	IREL	San Francisco	San Francisco P O	83	31
CARRAGAN								
John	39	m	w	IREL	San Francisco	11-Wd San Francisc	84	615
CARRAGHAN								
Eugene	50	m	w	IREL	San Francisco	San Francisco P O	83	171
CARRAHAN								
Sarah	28	f	w	IREL	San Francisco	San Francisco P O	83	272
CARRAL								
August	25	m	w	PORT	San Francisco	1-Wd San Francisco	79	117
CARRAN								
Anna	40	f	w	IREL	Humboldt	Eureka Twp	72	263
Laurence	40	f	w	FRAN	San Francisco	1-Wd San Francisco	79	108
Leon	13	m	w	CA	Monterey	San Juan Twp	74	408
Mary	30	f	w	IREL	Alameda	Oakland	68	198
CARRANZA								
Amelia	28	f	w	PA	San Francisco	8-Wd San Francisco	82	353
Ricardo	44	m	w	CA	Santa Cruz	Watsonville	89	373
CARRARO								
Francisco	41	m	w	MEXI	Plumas	Mineral Twp	77	22
CARRASCO								
M C	22	m	w	CHIL	Alameda	Oakland	68	170
Miguel	21	m	w	MEXI	Fresno	Millerton P O	72	157
CARRATTO								
Julia	25	f	w	ITAL	Amador	Jackson P O	69	325
CARRAVAJAL								
Transito	45	m	w	CHIL	Santa Clara	Alviso Twp	88	24
CARRAZIE								
Andrew	19	m	w	ITAL	Napa	Napa Twp	75	75
CARRE								
Clara	37	f	w	FRAN	San Francisco	11-Wd San Francisc	84	628
George	36	m	w	FRAN	San Francisco	San Francisco P O	80	477
John	25	m	w	ITAL	Stanislaus	San Joaquin Twp	92	80
Laurent	40	m	w	FRAN	Alameda	Hayward	68	76
CARREA								
Alberta	67	f	i	CA	Santa Barbara	San Buenaventura P	87	439
CARREAN								
Mathew	30	m	w	PRUS	San Francisco	5-Wd San Francisco	81	3
CARREGUE								
Joseph	28	m	w	BELG	San Francisco	1-Wd San Francisco	79	120
CARRELL								
William	52	m	w	IREL	Santa Clara	1-Wd San Jose	88	225
CARRELLY								
Jos	24	m	w	IREL	San Francisco	11-Wd San Francisc	84	694
CARREN								
Antonio	50	m	w	FRAN	Calaveras	San Andreas P O	70	158
CARRENS								
Julia	50	f	w	IREL	Contra Costa	Martinez P O	71	396
CARRERE								
Arrony	67	m	w	FRAN	San Francisco	San Francisco P O	80	408
Pascal	45	m	w	FRAN	Nevada	Grass Valley Twp	75	223
CARRERI								
Emanuel	48	m	w	MEXI	Fresno	Millerton P O	72	157
CARRERO								
Blaz	36	m	w	MEXI	San Luis Obispo	San Luis Obispo Tw	87	307
CARREY								
H M	38	m	w	CANA	Alameda	Murray Twp	68	109
James	54	m	w	IL	Alameda	Murray Twp	68	109
Jno	40	m	w	IREL	Monterey	San Juan Twp	74	406
CARRGAN								
Joseph	28	m	w	IREL	Napa	Napa	75	56
CARRGRRO								
Jose	52	m	w	CA	Fresno	Millerton P O	72	160
CARRI								
George	28	m	w	FRAN	San Francisco	San Francisco P O	83	299
CARRICK								
Bridget	80	f	w	IREL	San Francisco	11-Wd San Francisc	84	469
Daniel	32	m	w	IREL	San Francisco	11-Wd San Francisc	84	469
David	40	m	w	IN	Siskiyou	Butte Twp	89	586
David	37	m	w	ME	Alameda	Brooklyn	68	35
Elijah	38	m	w	IN	Siskiyou	Yreka	89	651
John	58	m	w	IREL	San Francisco	San Francisco P O	83	371
Kate	39	f	w	IREL	San Francisco	11-Wd San Francisc	84	510
Mary	26	f	w	IREL	Alameda	Brooklyn Twp	68	55
Mary	22	f	w	IREL	Solano	Vallejo	90	162
Patrick	32	m	w	IREL	Sonoma	Mendocino Twp	91	302
Thos	32	m	w	ENGL	San Francisco	1-Wd San Francisco	79	81
Wm	40	m	w	IREL	Solano	Vallejo	90	164
CARRICO								
Willm	36	m	w	MO	Siskiyou	Table Rock Twp	89	647
CARRIE								
Jos A	42	m	w	SC	Sonoma	Cloverdale Twp	91	270
CARRIER								
George H	45	m	w	FRAN	San Francisco	6-Wd San Francisco	81	102
Jno	34	m	w	ENGL	Sacramento	1-Wd Sacramento	77	179
Jno Q A	38	m	w	NC	Shasta	Horsetown P O	89	505
Walter	48	m	w	NY	Klamath	Trinidad Twp	73	391
CARRIG								
Thomas	17	m	w	CA	San Francisco	11-Wd San Francisc	84	640
CARRIGAN								
Andrew	41	m	w	IREL	San Francisco	11-Wd San Francisc	84	527
Andrew	33	m	w	IREL	San Francisco	8-Wd San Francisco	82	328
Anne	40	f	w	IREL	Yuba	Marysville	93	585
Corn	30	m	w	IREL	Klamath	Trinidad Twp	73	391
Edward	27	m	w	IREL	Nevada	Eureka Twp	75	130
James	45	m	w	MO	Santa Clara	Gilroy Twp	88	98
James B	26	m	w	NY	Sacramento	Cosumnes Twp	77	96
John	54	m	w	NY	Butte	Wyandotte Twp	70	142
John	38	m	w	IREL	Nevada	Rough & Ready Twp	75	328
John L	17	m	w	NY	Marin	San Rafael	74	52
Joseph	22	m	w	CANA	San Francisco	5-Wd San Francisco	81	10
Lizzie	8	f	w	CA	San Francisco	2-Wd San Francisco	79	216
Mary	27	f	w	IREL	Santa Clara	1-Wd San Jose	88	245
Mary	25	f	w	IREL	San Francisco	8-Wd San Francisco	82	328
Mich	24	m	w	MI	Alameda	Alameda	68	13
Michael	50	m	w	IREL	Sacramento	Granite Twp	77	154
Owen	22	m	w	NY	San Francisco	1-Wd San Francisco	79	65
Patrick	32	m	w	IREL	San Francisco	7-Wd San Francisco	81	180
Peter	42	m	w	IREL	San Francisco	11-Wd San Francisc	84	655
Peter	35	m	w	IREL	San Francisco	1-Wd San Francisco	79	72
Rose	27	f	w	IREL	San Francisco	San Francisco P O	83	158
Thos	26	m	w	IREL	Solano	Vallejo	90	148
CARRIGAR								
Wm	28	m	w	IREL	Sutter	Sutter Twp	92	118
CARRIGER								
A B	21	m	w	CA	Sonoma	Santa Rosa	91	419
Caleb C	37	m	w	TN	Sonoma	Sonoma Twp	91	431
CARRIGHAN								
William	30	m	w	IL	Solano	Silveyville Twp	90	90
CARRIGO								
Dolores	66	f	w	MEXI	San Francisco	San Francisco P O	80	345
CARRIGY								
Winnie	25	f	w	IREL	San Francisco	San Francisco P O	85	723
CARRIK								
Sophia	21	f	w	MI	San Francisco	6-Wd San Francisco	81	126
CARRIL								
Alexander	40	m	w	FRAN	Calaveras	San Andreas P O	70	190
CARRILLE								
Josephine	16	f	w	CA	Sonoma	Petaluma Twp	91	339
Lizzie	14	f	w	CA	Sonoma	Petaluma Twp	91	339
CARRILLO								
Anastasio	29	m	w	CA	Santa Barbara	Santa Barbara P O	87	459
Dorotea	45	m	w	MEXI	San Diego	San Pasqual	78	522
Francisco	24	m	w	CA	Santa Barbara	Santa Barbara P O	87	459
Gerno	61	m	w	FRAN	Los Angeles	Los Angeles	73	568
Ignacio	38	m	w	MEXI	Santa Clara	Almaden Twp	88	6
Joaquin	51	m	w	CA	Sonoma	Analy Twp	91	232
Joaquin	41	m	w	CA	Sonoma	Santa Rosa	91	420
John J	28	m	w	CA	Los Angeles	Los Angeles	73	535
Jose	60	m	w	CA	Santa Barbara	Santa Barbara P O	87	477
Jose	33	m	w	MEXI	San Bernardino	San Salvador Twp	78	459
Jose	26	m	w	CA	Marin	Point Reyes Twp	74	21
Julian	30	m	w	MEXI	Monterey	San Benito Twp	74	378
Julio	44	m	w	CA	Sonoma	Santa Rosa	91	403
Pedro	60	m	w	MEXI	Los Angeles	Los Angeles	73	555
Pedro C	52	m	w	CA	Los Angeles	Los Angeles	73	534
Plutarco	29	m	w	CA	Santa Barbara	Santa Barbara P O	87	460
Refugia	37	f	w	CA	Santa Barbara	Santa Barbara P O	87	466
Santiago	54	m	w	MEXI	Los Angeles	Los Angeles	73	514
Tomas	43	m	w	MEXI	Los Angeles	El Monte Twp	73	462
Vicente	18	m	w	CA	Santa Barbara	Las Cruces P O	87	515
William	47	m	w	CA	Santa Barbara	Santa Barbara P O	87	460
CARRINGTON								
C	62	m	w	CT	Solano	Vallejo	90	214
H	26	m	w	CT	Napa	Napa	75	24
Jas	32	m	b	KY	Sacramento	1-Wd Sacramento	77	172
John	66	m	w	SCOT	San Francisco	8-Wd San Francisco	82	318
John	41	m	w	IN	Solano	Denverton Twp	90	22
Joseph	31	m	w	NJ	Sacramento	San Joaquin Twp	77	394
Mariah	52	f	w	ENGL	Sacramento	San Joaquin Twp	77	395
Mary	26	f	w	VA	San Francisco	8-Wd San Francisco	82	354
T E	53	m	w	KY	Tuolumne	Columbia P O	93	354
William	19	m	w	NJ	Yolo	Putah Twp	93	510
Wm	65	m	w	ENGL	San Joaquin	3-Wd Stockton	86	233
CARRIO								
Paul	45	m	w	ME	San Francisco	2-Wd San Francisco	79	227
Ramornes	27	m	w	CA	Mendocino	Ten Mile Rvr Twp	74	172
Salvator	53	m	w	SARD	Santa Clara	Santa Clara Twp	88	175

© 2001 by Heritage Quest. All rights reserved.

Name	Age	S	R	B-PL	County	Locale	Series M593 Roll	Pg
CARRION								
Albert	35	m	w	CANA	San Francisco	5-Wd San Francisco	81	5
Fabias	40	m	w	CANA	Nevada	Eureka Twp	75	132
Satonio	25	m	w	CA	Los Angeles	San Jose Twp	73	623
CARRISON								
Ben	50	m	w	ME	Solano	Vallejo	90	180
Henry	42	m	w	SC	Alameda	Oakland	68	249
CARRO								
Ranswell	37	m	i	MEXI	Inyo	Cerro Gordo Twp	73	320
CARROL								
Andrew	26	m	w	IREL	San Mateo	San Mateo P O	87	358
Anna	28	f	w	IREL	Sacramento	2-Wd Sacramento	77	237
Anna	23	f	w	IREL	Los Angeles	Los Angeles	73	505
Bridget	37	f	w	IREL	Sacramento	4-Wd Sacramento	77	347
Bridget	35	f	w	IREL	San Francisco	8-Wd San Francisco	82	317
Chas E	35	m	w	MA	Sacramento	4-Wd Sacramento	77	331
Delia	21	f	w	IREL	Sacramento	4-Wd Sacramento	77	335
Edward	26	m	w	IREL	San Francisco	7-Wd San Francisco	81	157
Edwd	27	m	w	IREL	Solano	Benicia	90	15
Elizabeth E	5	f	w	CA	Sacramento	2-Wd Sacramento	77	228
Ellen	50	f	w	IREL	San Mateo	Redwood Twp	87	365
Isabelle	28	f	w	NY	San Francisco	8-Wd San Francisco	82	347
J C	36	m	w	MA	Sacramento	4-Wd Sacramento	77	322
J P	27	m	w	IREL	San Francisco	7-Wd San Francisco	81	226
James	43	m	w	IREL	Yuba	Marysville	93	633
James	28	m	w	IREL	San Mateo	Schoolhouse Statio	87	341
Johana	30	f	w	IL	San Francisco	7-Wd San Francisco	81	156
John	45	m	w	IREL	San Francisco	8-Wd San Francisco	82	373
John	40	m	w	IREL	San Mateo	Schoolhouse Statio	87	335
John	35	m	w	IREL	San Mateo	Schoolhouse Statio	87	340
John	29	m	w	CANA	Sacramento	4-Wd Sacramento	77	346
John	25	m	w	IREL	Alameda	Eden Twp	68	67
John	25	m	w	IREL	Merced	Snelling P O	74	260
John	24	m	w	IREL	San Francisco	7-Wd San Francisco	81	208
M	37	m	w	IREL	Alameda	Oakland	68	219
Margarett	25	f	w	IREL	Sonoma	Petaluma Twp	91	331
Martin	44	m	w	IREL	San Mateo	Schoolhouse Statio	87	340
Mehele	16	f	w	PRUS	Sutter	Nicolaus Twp	92	106
Michael	44	m	w	IREL	Solano	Vallejo	90	217
Michael	40	m	w	IREL	San Mateo	Redwood Twp	87	361
Michael	34	m	w	PA	San Francisco	2-Wd San Francisco	79	243
Micheal	32	m	w	PA	San Francisco	7-Wd San Francisco	81	223
P	36	m	w	IN	Alameda	Oakland	68	262
Pat	53	m	w	IREL	Placer	Gold Run Twp	76	400
Patk	40	m	w	IREL	Sacramento	4-Wd Sacramento	77	355
Patrick	49	m	w	IREL	Sacramento	2-Wd Sacramento	77	227
Patrick	40	m	w	IREL	Tuolumne	Sonora P O	93	322
Peter	30	m	w	IREL	Sutter	Yuba Twp	92	148
Sarah	19	f	w	IREL	Sacramento	2-Wd Sacramento	77	231
Stephen	45	m	w	IREL	Placer	Auburn P O	76	377
Susan	16	f	w	NY	Solano	Vallejo	90	181
Thomas	34	m	w	IREL	San Francisco	7-Wd San Francisco	81	217
Thos	14	m	w	CA	Solano	Benicia	90	21
CARROLAN								
Jane	26	f	w	IREL	San Francisco	San Francisco P O	83	111
CARROLD								
Michael	32	m	w	IREL	San Francisco	2-Wd San Francisco	79	221
Richard	34	m	w	NY	San Francisco	2-Wd San Francisco	79	251
Thomas	30	m	w	IREL	Inyo	Cerro Gordo Twp	73	318
CARROLE								
Mary E	28	f	w	IREL	Butte	Ophir Twp	70	95
Wm	36	m	w	NY	San Francisco	1-Wd San Francisco	79	8
CARROLL								
A	39	f	w	IREL	San Francisco	San Francisco P O	83	132
Alice	24	f	w	MA	San Francisco	7-Wd San Francisco	81	163
Andrew	32	m	w	IREL	San Francisco	11-Wd San Francisc	84	691
Ann	64	f	w	IREL	San Francisco	San Francisco P O	85	714
Anna	40	f	w	IREL	San Francisco	7-Wd San Francisco	81	191
Anna	26	f	w	IREL	San Francisco	7-Wd San Francisco	81	172
Anna	20	f	w	NY	San Francisco	8-Wd San Francisco	82	444
Annie	18	f	w	IREL	San Francisco	San Francisco P O	83	109
Annie M	14	f	w	CA	San Francisco	San Francisco P O	83	7
Benjamin	36	m	w	VA	Yuba	New York Twp	93	637
Bridget	25	f	w	IREL	San Francisco	San Francisco P O	83	237
Catharine	40	f	w	IREL	San Francisco	San Francisco P O	85	716
Catherine	70	f	w	IREL	San Joaquin	Oneal Twp	86	100
Catherine	20	f	w	IREL	San Francisco	San Francisco P O	83	217
Charles	39	m	w	MD	Nevada	Rough & Ready Twp	75	330
Chas	22	m	w	IL	San Francisco	1-Wd San Francisco	79	93
Chas E	60	m	w	IREL	San Francisco	1-Wd San Francisco	79	83
Danial	24	m	w	MI	San Francisco	7-Wd San Francisco	81	172
Daniel	39	m	w	OH	Stanislaus	San Joaquin Twp	92	70
Daniel	27	m	w	IREL	Marin	San Rafael Twp	74	31
Daniel	16	m	w	CA	San Francisco	San Francisco P O	85	854
David	34	m	w	IREL	San Francisco	San Francisco P O	83	11
Delia	18	f	w	IREL	San Francisco	8-Wd San Francisco	82	470
Dennis	60	m	w	IREL	San Francisco	San Francisco P O	85	870
Dennis	58	m	w	IREL	Nevada	Grass Valley Twp	75	174
Dennis	42	m	w	IREL	Sacramento	American Twp	77	67
Dora	30	f	w	IREL	San Francisco	San Francisco P O	83	162
Edward	31	m	w	IREL	San Francisco	11-Wd San Francisc	84	452
Eliza	33	f	w	IREL	San Francisco	San Francisco P O	83	266
Eliza	28	f	w	IREL	San Francisco	San Francisco P O	85	856
Eliza	23	f	w	IREL	San Francisco	San Francisco P O	85	775
Elizabeth	23	f	w	ME	Siskiyou	Scott Valley Twp	89	613
F Martin	47	m	w	IREL	San Diego	San Diego	78	498
Frank	15	m	w	CANA	San Francisco	3-Wd San Francisco	79	295
Geo M	34	m	w	MA	San Francisco	2-Wd San Francisco	79	213
George	36	m	w	IREL	Nevada	Bridgeport Twp	75	116
Hariett	22	f	w	IREL	San Francisco	5-Wd San Francisco	81	5
Henry	49	m	w	IREL	San Francisco	11-Wd San Francisc	84	478
Henry	38	m	w	ENGL	Stanislaus	Empire Twp	92	42
Henry	35	m	b	MD	San Francisco	8-Wd San Francisco	82	439
Herbert	55	m	w	MA	Santa Cruz	Santa Cruz	89	424
Honora	50	f	w	IREL	Nevada	Bridgeport Twp	75	125
Hugh	37	m	w	IREL	Contra Costa	Martinez P O	71	388
Hugh A	42	m	w	IREL	Fresno	Millerton P O	72	189
Isidore	17	m	w	NY	San Francisco	11-Wd San Francisc	84	494
J	30	m	w	IN	Sacramento	San Joaquin Twp	77	397
J C	46	m	w	IREL	San Francisco	7-Wd San Francisco	81	226
J C	32	m	w	MD	Siskiyou	Scott Valley Twp	89	611
J T	24	m	w	IREL	Solano	Vallejo	90	145
Jackson	22	m	w	MO	Tulare	Tule Rvr Twp	92	271
James	48	m	w	IREL	Amador	Jackson P O	69	321
James	45	m	w	IREL	San Francisco	11-Wd San Francisc	84	668
James	43	m	w	IREL	San Francisco	San Francisco P O	83	83
James	37	m	w	IREL	San Francisco	San Francisco P O	85	863
James	32	m	w	VT	Sacramento	3-Wd Sacramento	77	295
James	30	m	w	IREL	Santa Clara	Almaden Twp	88	9
James	30	m	w	IREL	Alameda	Eden Twp	68	87
James	30	m	w	IREL	Placer	Roseville P O	76	351
James	25	m	w	IREL	San Francisco	1-Wd San Francisco	79	104
James	25	m	w	IREL	San Francisco	San Francisco P O	85	785
James J	18	m	w	NY	Nevada	Nevada Twp	75	278
Jas	30	m	w	IREL	Solano	Vallejo	90	141
Jeremiah	47	m	w	IREL	Contra Costa	Martinez P O	71	444
Jeremiah	42	m	w	IREL	San Francisco	San Francisco P O	85	834
Jeremiah	40	m	w	IREL	San Francisco	San Francisco P O	83	220
Jeremiah	36	m	w	IREL	Sacramento	4-Wd Sacramento	77	356
Jno	30	m	w	IREL	Alameda	Oakland	68	226
Jno H	45	m	w	MA	Sacramento	3-Wd Sacramento	77	304
Johanna	25	f	w	IREL	Nevada	Grass Valley Twp	75	227
John	50	m	w	IREL	San Francisco	8-Wd San Francisco	82	475
John	42	m	w	MA	San Francisco	7-Wd San Francisco	81	159
John	40	m	w	IREL	Alameda	Eden Twp	68	87
John	40	m	w	IREL	San Francisco	San Francisco P O	83	5
John	40	m	w	MA	San Francisco	San Francisco P O	80	425
John	37	m	w	FL	San Bernardino	San Bernardino Twp	78	447
John	35	m	w	IREL	San Francisco	San Francisco P O	83	184
John	35	m	w	IREL	San Francisco	11-Wd San Francisc	84	694
John	35	m	w	IREL	San Francisco	San Francisco P O	85	874
John	35	m	w	MA	Solano	Suisun Twp	90	114
John	35	m	w	IL	San Francisco	1-Wd San Francisco	79	93
John	32	m	w	IREL	Tehama	Paskenta Twp	92	165
John	31	m	w	IREL	San Francisco	11-Wd San Francisc	84	535
John	30	m	w	IREL	Contra Costa	San Pablo Twp	71	364
John	30	m	w	IREL	San Francisco	1-Wd San Francisco	79	43
John	25	m	w	IREL	San Francisco	7-Wd San Francisco	81	218
John	24	m	w	NY	San Francisco	San Francisco P O	83	36
John	24	m	w	NY	San Francisco	San Francisco P O	83	48
John	22	m	w	IREL	San Francisco	1-Wd San Francisco	79	63
John	21	m	w	IREL	San Francisco	7-Wd San Francisco	81	172
John	20	m	w	ENGL	Contra Costa	Martinez Twp	71	352
John B	43	m	w	IREL	San Francisco	San Francisco P O	83	155
John C	41	m	w	IREL	San Francisco	7-Wd San Francisco	81	186
John M	12	m	w	CA	San Francisco	San Francisco P O	85	873
Joseph P	32	m	w	IREL	Mendocino	Noyo & Big Rvr Twp	74	173
Julius	33	m	w	ITAL	San Joaquin	1-Wd Stockton	86	139
Kate	33	f	w	IREL	San Francisco	San Francisco P O	83	4
Levi P	40	m	w	IL	Tulare	Venice Twp	92	273
Liza	25	f	w	CANA	San Francisco	San Francisco P O	83	64
M	43	m	w	IREL	San Joaquin	Dent Twp	86	20
M J	60	f	w	MS	Siskiyou	Scott Valley Twp	89	608
M T	30	m	w	KY	Alameda	Oakland	68	177
Maggie	16	f	w	CA	Santa Clara	2-Wd San Jose	88	336
Margaret	60	f	m	MD	San Francisco	6-Wd San Francisco	81	62
Margaret	32	f	w	IREL	Sacramento	4-Wd Sacramento	77	366
Margaret	30	f	w	IREL	San Francisco	8-Wd San Francisco	82	427
Margerett	40	f	w	IREL	Los Angeles	Los Angeles	73	570
Margret	70	f	w	IREL	San Joaquin	Oneal Twp	86	111
Martha	48	f	w	FRAN	San Francisco	San Francisco P O	83	399
Martin	45	m	w	CANA	San Francisco	11-Wd San Francisc	84	599
Mary	7	f	w	CA	Nevada	Grass Valley Twp	75	188
Mary	65	f	w	IREL	San Francisco	San Francisco P O	83	241
Mary	56	f	w	IREL	Solano	Vallejo	90	145
Mary	55	f	w	IREL	San Francisco	San Francisco P O	83	382
Mary	50	f	w	IREL	San Francisco	San Francisco P O	83	150
Mary	39	f	w	IREL	Sacramento	3-Wd Sacramento	77	306
Mary	32	f	w	IREL	San Francisco	7-Wd San Francisco	81	235
Mary	23	f	w	IREL	Alameda	Oakland	68	178
Mary A	21	f	w	IREL	Sacramento	4-Wd Sacramento	77	363
Mich	2	m	w	MA	San Francisco	1-Wd San Francisco	79	11
Michael	46	m	w	IREL	Sacramento	2-Wd Sacramento	77	250
Michael	40	m	w	IREL	Nevada	Grass Valley Twp	75	211
Michael	39	m	w	IREL	Calaveras	San Andreas P O	70	178
Michael	38	m	w	IREL	Calaveras	San Andreas P O	70	205
Michael	36	m	w	NY	San Francisco	San Francisco P O	83	263
Michael	36	m	w	IREL	Amador	Jackson P O	69	321
Michael	34	m	w	IREL	San Francisco	San Francisco P O	83	403
Michael	31	m	w	IREL	Tulare	Farmersville Twp	92	246
Michael	30	m	w	IREL	Mendocino	Little Rvr Twp	74	165
Michael	29	m	w	IREL	San Francisco	San Francisco P O	80	402
Michael	28	m	w	IREL	San Francisco	San Francisco P O	85	834
Michael	28	m	w	IREL	San Francisco	6-Wd San Francisco	81	71

© 2001 by Heritage Quest. All rights reserved.

California 1870 Census

Name	Age	S	R	B-PL	County	Locale	Series M593 Roll	Pg
Michael	27	m	w	MO	San Francisco	San Francisco P O	85	735
Michael	24	m	w	MD	Sacramento	Lee Twp	77	158
Michel	28	m	w	IREL	Napa	Napa	75	41
Mike	37	m	w	IREL	San Joaquin	1-Wd Stockton	86	139
Morris	29	m	w	NY	Yuba	W Bear Rvr Twp	93	682
O C	39	m	w	MA	San Francisco	San Francisco P O	85	849
Owen	35	m	w	IREL	San Francisco	11-Wd San Francisc	84	460
Owen	25	m	w	NY	Sonoma	Bodega Twp	91	257
Pat	27	m	w	IREL	San Francisco	11-Wd San Francisc	84	592
Pat	27	m	w	IREL	Santa Clara	Gilroy Twp	88	97
Patrick	47	m	w	IREL	San Francisco	San Francisco P O	83	367
Patrick	45	m	w	IREL	San Francisco	San Francisco P O	85	834
Patrick	40	m	w	IREL	Sutter	Nicolaus Twp	92	106
Patrick	40	m	w	IREL	San Francisco	6-Wd San Francisco	81	92
Patrick	40	m	w	IREL	Nevada	Nevada Twp	75	277
Patrick	35	m	w	IREL	San Francisco	1-Wd San Francisco	79	83
Patrick	33	m	w	IREL	Sonoma	Analy Twp	91	223
Patrick	33	m	w	IREL	San Francisco	San Francisco P O	85	871
Patrick	32	m	w	IREL	Santa Clara	2-Wd San Jose	88	316
Patrick	32	m	w	IREL	San Francisco	11-Wd San Francisc	84	548
Patrick	30	m	w	IREL	San Francisco	San Francisco P O	83	372
Patrick	28	m	w	IREL	San Francisco	San Francisco P O	85	765
Patrick	22	m	w	IREL	San Francisco	1-Wd San Francisco	79	63
Peter	30	m	w	IREL	San Francisco	San Francisco P O	85	745
Peter	28	m	w	IREL	San Francisco	3-Wd San Francisco	79	310
Ralph	44	m	w	TN	Tulare	Tule Rvr Twp	92	272
Richard	28	m	w	IREL	Mendocino	Casper & Big Rvr	74	164
Richd	32	m	w	IREL	San Francisco	1-Wd San Francisco	79	62
Robert	28	m	w	IREL	Mendocino	Point Arena Twp	74	224
Robt	32	m	w	IREL	Sutter	Sutter Twp	92	117
Sarah	16	f	w	CA	Nevada	Grass Valley Twp	75	147
Sarah E	14	f	w	CA	Tulare	Tule Rvr Twp	92	270
Thomas	70	m	w	IREL	San Francisco	8-Wd San Francisco	82	431
Thomas	46	m	w	IREL	Sutter	Vernon Twp	92	131
Thomas	39	m	w	IREL	San Francisco	San Francisco P O	83	145
Thomas	33	m	w	IREL	San Francisco	San Francisco P O	83	190
Thomas	32	m	w	NY	San Francisco	7-Wd San Francisco	81	220
Thomas	26	m	w	IREL	Santa Clara	2-Wd San Jose	88	307
Thos	38	m	w	IREL	Solano	Vallejo	90	175
Thos	21	m	w	CT	Sacramento	3-Wd Sacramento	77	264
Thos P	45	m	w	ENGL	San Francisco	2-Wd San Francisco	79	218
Timothy	30	m	w	IREL	Los Angeles	Santa Ana Twp	73	602
Topy	39	m	w	ME	Yuba	Rose Bar Twp	93	661
W	25	m	w	MI	Alameda	Oakland	68	262
W F	35	m	w	IREL	Alameda	Oakland	68	170
Warren	34	m	w	CANA	Santa Clara	Gilroy Twp	88	93
Wesley	43	m	w	PA	Alameda	Brooklyn Twp	68	54
William	35	m	w	ENGL	San Francisco	San Francisco P O	83	253
William	34	m	w	IREL	Santa Clara	2-Wd San Jose	88	316
William	30	m	w	MO	Humboldt	South Fork Twp	72	300
William	26	m	w	NY	San Francisco	San Francisco P O	83	355
William	26	m	w	NY	San Francisco	11-Wd San Francisc	84	561
William	22	m	w	ENGL	Solano	Vacaville Twp	90	136
Wm	46	m	w	IREL	Sacramento	Lee Twp	77	161
Wm	43	m	w	IREL	San Francisco	1-Wd San Francisco	79	40
Wm	40	m	w	IREL	San Francisco	1-Wd San Francisco	79	6
Wm	28	m	w	IREL	Solano	Vallejo	90	197
Wm	24	m	w	ME	Marin	Tomales Twp	74	78
Wm	10	m	w	CA	San Francisco	11-Wd San Francisc	84	587
Wm J	40	m	w	NY	Plumas	Quartz Twp	77	36
CARROLLS								
Patrick	30	m	w	IREL	San Joaquin	Douglas Twp	86	35
CARROTTO								
Giovani	30	m	w	ITAL	Amador	Volcano P O	69	385
CARRUS								
Manuel	40	m	w	PORT	Calaveras	San Andreas P O	70	175
CARRUTH								
Leavy	23	m	w	TN	Kern	Tehachapi P O	73	352
CARRUTHER								
M	59	m	w	SCOT	San Diego	San Diego	78	490
CARRUTHERS								
George	45	m	w	SCOT	San Francisco	6-Wd San Francisco	81	122
John	22	m	w	ENGL	San Francisco	6-Wd San Francisco	81	122
CARRY								
Alexander	45	m	w	OH	Solano	Rio Vista Twp	90	62
Bridget	54	f	w	IREL	San Francisco	11-Wd San Francisc	84	481
Ellen	35	f	w	IREL	San Francisco	8-Wd San Francisco	82	320
Geo	53	m	w	CT	Butte	Ophir Twp	70	117
James	28	m	w	IREL	San Francisco	7-Wd San Francisco	81	190
Mary	65	f	w	IREL	San Francisco	2-Wd San Francisco	79	175
Sam C	30	m	w	OH	Butte	Chico Twp	70	46
Wilbur F	28	m	w	AR	Napa	Napa	75	17
Wm	46	m	w	ME	Sacramento	1-Wd Sacramento	77	172
Wm C	57	m	w	PA	Napa	Napa	75	5
CARRYAN								
Daniel	50	m	w	IREL	Contra Costa	Martinez Twp	71	348
CARSAN								
James	26	m	w	IREL	Sacramento	Dry Crk Twp	77	104
CARSARLIN								
Franc	31	m	w	ITAL	Sacramento	Georgianna Twp	77	129
CARSASSA								
Charles	46	m	w	ITAL	San Francisco	2-Wd San Francisco	79	164
CARSELLE								
Ashield	57	m	w	FRAN	San Francisco	2-Wd San Francisco	79	153
CARSERAS								
Hitild	9	f	w	CA	Sonoma	Petaluma Twp	91	309

Name	Age	S	R	B-PL	County	Locale	Series M593 Roll	Pg
CARSI								
Louis	40	m	w	ITAL	Tuolumne	Chinese Camp P O	93	383
CARSO								
Manuel	62	m	w	MEXI	Calaveras	San Andreas P O	70	175
CARSON								
A J	35	m	w	IL	Lake	Upper Lake	73	410
Bernard	50	m	w	IREL	San Francisco	San Francisco P O	83	264
Bernard	26	m	w	PRUS	San Francisco	San Francisco P O	83	165
C	37	m	w	NORW	Alameda	Murray Twp	68	112
Charles	30	m	w	NY	San Francisco	San Francisco P O	83	69
Charles	30	m	w	SWED	Marin	Sausalito Twp	74	68
Chris	32	m	w	CANA	Solano	Vallejo	90	163
Chs	29	m	w	PRUS	San Francisco	2-Wd San Francisco	79	224
Conrad	31	m	w	HDAR	Butte	Oregon Twp	70	131
Daniel	41	m	w	ENGL	El Dorado	Diamond Springs Tw	72	30
Daniel	23	m	w	OH	Inyo	Cerro Gordo Twp	73	318
David	45	m	w	NC	Sonoma	Analy Twp	91	234
Fredk	33	m	w	SHOL	San Francisco	1-Wd San Francisco	79	12
George	56	m	w	VA	Nevada	Grass Valley Twp	75	153
George	38	m	w	NY	Los Angeles	Wilmington Twp	73	638
George	34	m	w	CANA	Humboldt	Eureka Twp	72	282
Henry	53	m	w	BREM	San Francisco	11-Wd San Francisc	84	464
Henry W	25	m	w	NY	San Francisco	San Francisco P O	83	183
James	45	m	w	IREL	Trinity	Weaverville Pct	92	227
James	27	m	w	CANA	Sonoma	Petaluma Twp	91	316
James M	28	m	w	PA	Santa Clara	2-Wd San Jose	88	328
Jas G	26	m	w	IREL	San Francisco	San Francisco P O	83	62
John	8	m	w	CA	San Francisco	San Francisco P O	85	828
John	35	m	w	IREL	San Francisco	11-Wd San Francisc	84	617
John	30	m	w	NY	San Francisco	7-Wd San Francisco	81	161
John	26	m	w	CANA	Sonoma	Salt Point Twp	91	383
L	51	m	w	MO	Lake	Kelsey Crk	73	402
Lodis	74	f	w	CT	Sacramento	Lee Twp	77	158
Magerate	20	f	w	IN	El Dorado	Lake Valley Twp	72	64
Margaret	74	f	w	VA	Shasta	American Ranch P O	89	498
Martha	36	f	w	ME	San Francisco	6-Wd San Francisco	81	98
Mary T	45	f	w	NY	San Francisco	8-Wd San Francisco	82	473
Mathias	52	m	w	PA	San Francisco	San Francisco P O	85	738
Menk A	53	m	w	TN	Siskiyou	Cottonwood Twp	89	590
Os Car	26	m	w	PRUS	Yuba	Marysville	93	586
Peter	27	m	w	MD	Solano	Green Valley Twp	90	39
Robert	36	m	w	PRUS	Contra Costa	San Pablo Twp	71	355
Robert	11	m	w	CA	Kern	Bakersfield P O	73	361
Samuel	25	m	w	NY	Kern	Bakersfield P O	73	360
Theodore	43	m	w	PRUS	San Francisco	11-Wd San Francisc	84	518
Thomas	42	m	w	CANA	Marin	Sausalito Twp	74	66
W Mc K	41	m	w	MD	San Joaquin	Oneal Twp	86	119
W W	30	m	w	WI	Lassen	Milford Twp	73	438
William	70	m	w	PA	Monterey	Pajaro Twp	74	369
William	48	m	w	PA	Calaveras	Copperopolis P O	70	261
William	25	m	w	IREL	Humboldt	Pacific Twp	72	292
William	22	m	w	CANA	Marin	San Antonio Twp	74	62
William H	45	m	w	OH	Santa Clara	Santa Clara Twp	88	136
Wm	39	m	w	OH	Shasta	American Ranch P O	89	498
CARSORIS								
Antonie	48	f	w	MEXI	Calaveras	San Andreas P O	70	171
CARSS								
Robert	40	m	w	ENGL	San Francisco	San Francisco P O	83	234
Robert	40	m	w	ENGL	San Francisco	San Francisco P O	83	252
CARSTEIN								
Chas	29	m	w	SHOL	San Francisco	1-Wd San Francisco	79	111
Edwd	35	m	w	SHOL	San Francisco	1-Wd San Francisco	79	97
CARSTEN								
Fred	32	m	w	PRUS	San Francisco	8-Wd San Francisco	82	364
CARSTENSEN								
Louis	19	m	w	SHOL	San Francisco	7-Wd San Francisco	81	262
CARSTENSON								
Carsten	35	m	w	DENM	San Francisco	8-Wd San Francisco	82	447
CARSTON								
Brandon	35	m	w	IREL	Sacramento	Georgianna Twp	77	129
Joseph	25	m	w	AZOR	San Francisco	1-Wd San Francisco	79	130
CARSTONBROCK								
J D	37	m	w	HANO	Yuba	Marysville	93	616
CARSTONSON								
Wm	22	m	w	PRUS	San Francisco	8-Wd San Francisco	82	337
CARSWELL								
G W	41	m	w	CT	San Francisco	San Francisco P O	85	822
John	49	m	w	NH	Alameda	Brooklyn	68	24
CART								
Ah	34	m	c	CHIN	Calaveras	Copperopolis P O	70	222
Henry	42	m	w	PRUS	Sutter	Sutter Twp	92	119
CARTAIN								
Antonio	51	m	w	MEXI	Los Angeles	Los Angeles	73	554
CARTELO								
Thomas	55	m	w	IREL	Trinity	Weaverville Pct	92	230
CARTENI								
E J	50	m	w	FRAN	Tuolumne	Chinese Camp P O	93	382
CARTER								
A	43	m	w	ITAL	Sierra	Downieville Twp	89	519
A B	24	m	w	NY	Solano	Vallejo	90	202
A C	33	m	w	TN	Tehama	Hunters Twp	92	187
A G	40	m	w	OH	Tehama	Deer Crk Twp	92	171
Ada	19	f	w	OH	Butte	Ophir Twp	70	118
Albert A	34	m	w	MO	Los Angeles	El Monte Twp	73	456
Alfd	44	m	w	ENGL	San Francisco	San Francisco P O	83	100
Alfred	32	m	w	IL	San Diego	San Diego	78	487
Annie	15	f	w	MA	Solano	Benicia	90	16

© 2001 by Heritage Quest. All rights reserved.

Name	Age	S	R	B-PL	County	Locale	Series M593 Roll	Pg
Artimus	32	m	w	MA	Colusa	Monroe Twp	71	324
Asa	44	m	b	AR	Yolo	Cottonwood Twp	93	465
Asa M	29	m	w	IA	Trinity	Trinity Center Pct	92	240
Atha	35	m	w	IN	Inyo	Lone Pine Twp	73	334
B H	44	m	w	NY	Santa Clara	Gilroy Twp	88	70
Barney	38	m	w	IN	San Bernardino	San Bernardino Twp	78	429
Barney	35	m	w	OH	Yuba	Long Bar Twp	93	561
Benjamin	31	m	w	VA	San Mateo	Schoolhouse Statio	87	343
C A	24	f	w	VA	Yuba	Marysville	93	599
C H	32	m	w	MA	San Francisco	San Francisco P O	85	790
Charles	42	m	w	IN	San Bernardino	San Bernardino Twp	78	450
Charles E	36	m	w	NH	Santa Cruz	Pajaro Twp	89	340
Chas H	41	m	w	NY	Tuolumne	Sonora P O	93	323
Daniel	44	m	w	SHOL	San Francisco	3-Wd San Francisco	79	320
Daniel P	42	m	w	NY	Butte	Ophir Twp	70	92
David	45	m	w	OH	Sonoma	Bodega Twp	91	264
David	43	m	w	OH	Sonoma	Santa Rosa	91	410
David	33	m	w	IL	San Bernardino	San Bernardino Twp	78	450
Dennis	33	m	w	IREL	San Francisco	San Francisco P O	85	848
Dora	35	f	w	IREL	San Francisco	7-Wd San Francisco	81	244
Durolt	58	m	w	KY	Yuba	Rose Bar Twp	93	657
Ed	35	m	w	DENM	Sonoma	Bodega Twp	91	258
Edward	47	m	w	OH	Sonoma	Mendocino Twp	91	301
Edward	22	m	w	NY	San Francisco	8-Wd San Francisco	82	438
Edwd	18	m	b	VA	San Francisco	1-Wd San Francisco	79	132
Edwin	23	m	w	NH	Mendocino	Round Valley Twp	74	217
Eliza	63	f	w	PA	Placer	Lincoln P O	76	493
Eliza	40	f	w	ENGL	San Francisco	San Francisco P O	80	420
Eliza	36	f	w	AUSL	Alameda	Washington Twp	68	282
Eliza	26	f	w	MO	Sonoma	Healdsburg & Mendo	91	279
Emilie	17	f	w	AUSL	San Francisco	7-Wd San Francisco	81	246
Emily	24	f	w	ENGL	San Francisco	San Francisco P O	83	95
Emma	52	f	b	PA	San Francisco	8-Wd San Francisco	82	319
Emma	10	f	i	CA	Trinity	Hayfork Valley	92	238
Francis	45	m	w	ENGL	Nevada	Grass Valley Twp	75	166
Francis	36	m	w	ENGL	Nevada	Grass Valley Twp	75	184
Frank	45	m	w	ENGL	Humboldt	Eel Rvr Twp	72	250
G W	35	m	w	TN	Tehama	Deer Crk Twp	92	171
Geo	27	m	b	ME	Butte	Chico Twp	70	18
Geo	23	m	w	TX	Monterey	Alisal Twp	74	304
Geo	14	m	w	CA	San Francisco	11-Wd San Francisc	84	592
Geo B	28	m	w	HOND	Sacramento	3-Wd Sacramento	77	282
Geo W	22	m	w	MA	Merced	Snelling P O	74	246
George	45	m	w	MA	San Francisco	5-Wd San Francisco	81	3
George	36	m	w	ENGL	Santa Cruz	Santa Cruz	89	403
George	29	m	w	ENGL	Nevada	Grass Valley Twp	75	228
George	27	m	w	ME	Marin	San Rafael Twp	74	35
George	25	m	w	IREL	San Francisco	San Francisco P O	83	162
George	21	m	w	OH	Los Angeles	Santa Ana Twp	73	601
George W T	35	m	w	NY	San Mateo	Half Moon Bay P O	87	408
Gideon	38	m	w	VT	San Bernardino	San Bernardino Twp	78	414
H A	62	m	w	NY	Amador	Ione City P O	69	358
H K	42	m	w	NY	San Francisco	San Francisco P O	85	804
Hazen	30	m	w	CANA	Santa Clara	Alviso Twp	88	23
Helen	28	f	w	PA	San Francisco	San Francisco P O	80	403
Henery	37	m	w	IREL	San Francisco	7-Wd San Francisco	81	158
Hennege	46	m	w	ENGL	San Francisco	11-Wd San Francisc	84	596
Henry	47	m	w	IL	Tehama	Antelope Twp	92	155
Henry	43	m	w	NY	San Francisco	San Francisco P O	85	857
Henry	42	m	w	IL	Tehama	Paynes Crk Twp	92	160
Henry	40	m	w	NY	Butte	Chico Twp	70	50
Henry	37	m	w	MA	San Francisco	7-Wd San Francisco	81	220
Henry	36	m	w	ENGL	Stanislaus	Emory Twp	92	24
Henry	18	m	w	CA	San Bernardino	San Bernardino Twp	78	435
Heny S	31	m	w	ME	Butte	Kimshew Tpw	70	81
Hugh	12	m	w	TN	Santa Cruz	Watsonville	89	376
J	40	f	w	IREL	San Francisco	San Francisco P O	83	287
J A	36	m	w	KY	Alameda	Oakland	68	186
J J	23	m	w	MA	Sacramento	3-Wd Sacramento	77	312
J W	30	m	w	TN	Sonoma	Russian Rvr	91	379
Jackson	48	m	w	SC	Placer	Lincoln P O	76	486
Jacob	26	m	w	IL	Merced	Snelling P O	74	270
James	50	m	w	SCOT	Sacramento	Granite Twp	77	150
James	50	m	w	DENM	Yolo	Cottonwood Twp	93	464
James	45	m	b	KY	Amador	Ione City P O	69	357
James	41	m	w	ENGL	Santa Clara	2-Wd San Jose	88	288
James	41	m	w	IL	Amador	Drytown P O	69	422
James	40	m	w	PA	Nevada	Bloomfield Twp	75	99
James	36	m	w	KY	Santa Clara	Gilroy Twp	88	79
James	35	m	w	NJ	Nevada	Eureka Twp	75	128
James	35	m	w	IREL	Nevada	Bloomfield Twp	75	98
James	30	m	w	VA	Sacramento	Cosumnes Twp	77	92
James	30	m	b	TX	Amador	Lancha Plana P O	69	368
James	30	m	w	TN	Stanislaus	Empire Twp	92	40
James	25	m	w	MS	San Bernardino	San Bernardino Twp	78	440
James	18	m	w	CA	Fresno	Kings Rvr P O	72	212
James E	32	m	w	TN	Fresno	Millerton P O	72	191
Jas	36	m	w	IL	Alameda	Oakland	68	259
Jas	28	m	w	CANA	Solano	Vallejo	90	212
Jenney	30	f	i	CA	Trinity	Hayfork Valley	92	238
Jno W	35	m	w	ME	Siskiyou	Callahan P O	89	627
Johana	34	f	w	IREL	San Francisco	San Francisco P O	80	541
John	62	m	w	ENGL	San Francisco	8-Wd San Francisco	82	449
John	45	m	w	IREL	San Francisco	San Francisco P O	80	356
John	41	m	w	IN	Tehama	Deer Crk Twp	92	171
John	40	m	w	NY	Yuba	Rose Bar Twp	93	656
John	38	m	w	TN	Tuolumne	Big Oak Flat P O	93	397
John	33	m	w	IREL	Stanislaus	Emory Twp	92	24
John	30	m	w	IREL	San Francisco	7-Wd San Francisco	81	171
John	25	m	w	IREL	San Francisco	7-Wd San Francisco	81	186
John A	38	m	w	ENGL	Sonoma	Petaluma Twp	91	340
John B	45	m	w	CT	Tuolumne	Sonora P O	93	321
John C	64	m	w	ENGL	San Bernardino	San Bernardino Twp	78	442
John E	55	m	w	PA	Monterey	San Juan Twp	74	403
John Jr	23	m	w	MO	Santa Cruz	Soquel Twp	89	445
John L	47	m	w	NY	Placer	Lincoln P O	76	492
John S	42	m	w	NH	Santa Clara	2-Wd San Jose	88	298
John W	44	m	w	TN	Trinity	Hayfork Valley	92	239
John W	30	m	w	NY	San Francisco	8-Wd San Francisco	82	413
Joseph	42	m	w	TN	Trinity	Hayfork Valley	92	238
Joseph	28	m	w	RI	San Francisco	1-Wd San Francisco	79	123
Joseph	26	m	w	MD	San Luis Obispo	Salinas Twp	87	292
Joseph	18	m	w	IL	El Dorado	Lake Valley Twp	72	65
Joseph M	22	m	w	VA	Amador	Amador City P O	69	391
Joshua	39	m	w	IREL	Napa	Napa	75	44
Josiah M	51	m	w	NC	Sonoma	Analy Twp	91	224
Josiah Starr	39	m	w	VA	Plumas	Indian Twp	77	18
Julia	42	f	w	NY	Butte	Ophir Twp	70	92
Julius E	39	m	w	NY	Yuba	Long Bar Twp	93	561
Kate M	14	f	w	IN	San Francisco	8-Wd San Francisco	82	437
Landon	50	m	w	VA	Sonoma	Santa Rosa	91	412
Lewis	46	m	w	KY	Tulare	Farmersville Twp	92	249
Lewis	26	m	w	CANA	Nevada	Grass Valley Twp	75	146
Lizzie	21	f	w	VT	Santa Cruz	Santa Cruz	89	413
Loraine	53	f	w	NH	Humboldt	Pacific Twp	72	296
Lorenzo	23	m	w	UT	San Bernardino	San Bernardino Twp	78	429
Louisa	35	f	w	ME	Los Angeles	Los Angeles Twp	73	474
Lowell	20	m	w	WI	Placer	Auburn P O	76	360
Lucio	55	m	w	MEXI	San Diego	Pala Valley Reserv	78	480
Lutien	14	f	w	MO	San Diego	San Jacinto Dist	78	517
Mabella	8	f	w	PA	San Francisco	11-Wd San Francisc	84	577
Margaret	64	f	w	KY	San Bernardino	San Bernardino Twp	78	419
Martha	33	f	w	MO	Fresno	Millerton P O	72	148
Martha	20	f	w	MO	San Joaquin	Liberty Twp	86	94
Martha E	7	f	w	CA	San Bernardino	San Bernardino Twp	78	421
Martin	37	m	w	IREL	Sutter	Sutter Twp	92	128
Mary	70	f	w	IREL	Alameda	Oakland	68	143
Mary	44	f	w	ENGL	Santa Clara	2-Wd San Jose	88	284
Mary	38	f	w	IREL	Sutter	Yuba Twp	92	141
Mary	23	f	b	DC	San Francisco	San Francisco P O	80	334
Mary A	21	f	w	MO	Contra Costa	Martinez P O	71	382
Peter	60	m	w	SCOT	San Francisco	2-Wd San Francisco	79	152
Peter	54	m	w	MO	Trinity	North Fork Twp	92	218
Peter F	35	m	w	NY	Sonoma	Salt Point	91	388
Phebe	17	f	b	MS	San Francisco	8-Wd San Francisco	82	464
R D	34	m	w	IREL	Nevada	Eureka Twp	75	139
R W	46	m	w	PA	San Francisco	8-Wd San Francisco	82	293
Rebecca	27	f	w	MA	San Francisco	San Francisco P O	83	77
Richard	45	m	w	IREL	Yuba	Slate Range Bar Tw	93	673
Richard	38	m	w	NY	Solano	Suisun Twp	90	108
Richard	27	m	w	IREL	San Francisco	San Francisco P O	83	315
Riley	35	m	w	IA	Yolo	Cottonwood Twp	93	468
Rinaldo	43	m	w	MD	Santa Clara	1-Wd San Jose	88	229
Robert	38	m	w	MO	Yolo	Cache Crk Twp	93	454
Robert C	36	m	w	ENGL	Solano	Rio Vista Twp	90	60
Robert E	49	m	w	ENGL	Nevada	Grass Valley Twp	75	230
Robt	36	m	w	DE	Solano	Vallejo	90	203
Robt F	37	m	w	OH	Butte	Chico Twp	70	15
S P	50	m	w	VA	Monterey	San Antonio Twp	74	324
S V	43	m	w	IL	Amador	Jackson P O	69	345
Samuel	41	m	w	AL	Los Angeles	Los Nietos Twp	73	577
Samuel	38	m	w	MO	Stanislaus	Empire Twp	92	66
Samuel A	37	m	w	VA	Santa Cruz	Santa Cruz Twp	89	385
Sarah	51	f	w	NY	San Francisco	11-Wd San Francisc	84	531
Solomon	49	m	w	TN	Kern	Havilah P O	73	350
Thomas J	42	m	b	KY	El Dorado	Mud Springs Twp	72	90
Thos	35	m	w	PA	San Francisco	11-Wd San Francisc	84	604
Thos	27	m	w	IA	Fresno	Millerton P O	72	186
Valeria	45	f	w	TN	Santa Cruz	Watsonville	89	367
W C	54	m	w	PA	Nevada	Bloomfield Twp	75	93
Wade	22	m	w	NC	San Diego	Julian Dist	78	471
Walter	27	m	w	ME	San Francisco	San Francisco P O	83	260
William	61	m	w	KY	Humboldt	Bald Hills	72	239
William	43	m	w	VA	Napa	Napa Twp	75	64
William	34	m	w	TN	Placer	Auburn P O	76	383
William	26	m	b	VA	Marin	San Rafael Twp	74	40
William	24	m	b	VA	San Francisco	San Francisco P O	80	383
William F	36	m	w	VA	Nevada	Grass Valley Twp	75	168
William F	30	m	w	MO	Los Angeles	Wilmington Twp	73	641
Wm	6	m	m	CA	Sacramento	4-Wd Sacramento	77	329
Wm	45	m	w	KY	San Joaquin	Liberty Twp	86	85
Wm	38	m	w	KY	Klamath	Trinidad Twp	73	391
Wm	36	m	w	PA	San Francisco	11-Wd San Francisc	84	664
Wm	32	m	w	CANA	Solano	Vallejo	90	212
Wm	22	m	w	VA	Sacramento	Brighton Twp	77	77
Wm F	30	m	w	SCOT	San Francisco	1-Wd San Francisco	79	131
Wm Henry	28	m	w	VA	San Francisco	1-Wd San Francisco	79	68
Wm L	29	m	w	IL	Shasta	Shasta P O	89	463
CARTERA								
Vincent	28	m	w	CHIL	Santa Clara	Fremont Twp	88	51
CARTERG								
Enrique	30	m	w	FRAN	Santa Barbara	Las Cruces P O	87	515
CARTET								
John	39	m	w	PRUS	San Joaquin	2-Wd Stockton	86	206

© 2001 by Heritage Quest. All rights reserved.

Name	Age	S	R	B-PL	County	Locale	Series M593 Roll	Pg
CARTEZ								
Juan	25	m	w	CHIL	Fresno	Millerton P O	72	167
CARTHE								
Patrick	40	m	w	IREL	San Joaquin	Douglas Twp	86	43
CARTHECHE								
John	47	m	w	GREE	El Dorado	Placerville	72	124
CARTHER								
John	21	m	w	CANA	San Francisco	7-Wd San Francisco	81	172
CARTHEW								
William	35	m	w	WI	Yuba	North East Twp	93	646
CARTHY								
Chas	30	m	w	IREL	Tehama	Red Bluff	92	177
Hellen	76	f	w	IREL	Solano	Vallejo	90	143
John	35	m	w	NY	Solano	Vallejo	90	143
Mary	26	f	w	IREL	San Francisco	2-Wd San Francisco	79	218
Patk	29	m	w	IREL	Solano	Vallejo	90	200
CARTICENE								
Manuel	50	m	w	CHIL	Butte	Wyandotte Twp	70	143
CARTIE								
R	28	m	w	CANA	San Joaquin	Douglas Twp	86	50
CARTIER								
Geo	29	m	w	PRUS	San Joaquin	Douglas Twp	86	51
Victor	37	m	w	FRAN	San Francisco	San Francisco P O	80	339
CARTING								
John	30	m	w	IREL	San Francisco	11-Wd San Francisc	84	616
CARTINOY								
Paul	36	m	w	ITAL	San Francisco	San Francisco P O	80	426
CARTIS								
Geo	50	m	w	MI	San Joaquin	Castoria Twp	86	14
Georgiana	22	f	w	NY	San Francisco	5-Wd San Francisco	81	1
Samuel	37	m	w	KY	San Joaquin	2-Wd Stockton	86	167
CARTLAND								
Wm	37	m	w	KY	Butte	Oroville Twp	70	139
CARTMAN								
Joseph	21	m	w	NY	San Francisco	7-Wd San Francisco	81	156
CARTNELL								
C W	26	m	w	KY	Sutter	Sutter Twp	92	117
William G	47	m	w	OH	Tulare	Packwood Twp	92	255
CARTNEY								
Honora	65	f	w	IREL	Solano	Vallejo	90	188
CARTON								
James	30	m	w	IREL	Santa Clara	Fremont Twp	88	41
Peter S	44	m	w	IREL	San Francisco	San Francisco P O	83	245
CARTOS								
Henry	19	m	w	PRUS	San Francisco	1-Wd San Francisco	79	74
CARTRES								
Emanuel	30	m	w	PORT	Alameda	Washington Twp	68	281
CARTRETT								
Richd	62	m	w	MA	Sierra	Gibson Twp	89	539
CARTRIDGE								
Peter	23	m	w	AUST	Plumas	Quartz Twp	77	35
CARTRIGHT								
John	31	m	w	NY	Santa Clara	Milpitas Twp	88	108
P	58	m	w	VT	Sacramento	San Joaquin Twp	77	396
CARTRO								
Beceata	32	m	w	MEXI	Monterey	San Antonio Twp	74	321
Florentina	72	f	w	CA	Santa Clara	Santa Clara Twp	88	157
Guadalupe	89	f	w	CA	Santa Clara	Santa Clara Twp	88	157
Joaquin	61	m	w	CA	Contra Costa	San Pablo Twp	71	358
John	35	m	w	ARGE	Contra Costa	Martinez Twp	71	348
CARTS								
Benjamin	48	m	w	FRAN	San Francisco	San Francisco P O	85	823
Jose M	52	m	w	MEXI	Monterey	Alisal Twp	74	288
CARTWRIGHT								
A	40	m	w	NY	Alameda	Oakland	68	195
Bruce	16	m	w	HI	Solano	Benicia	90	21
Carl	41	m	w	AR	Fresno	Kings Rvr P O	72	203
D C	36	m	w	NY	Yuba	East Bear Rvr Twp	93	544
David	30	m	w	IREL	San Francisco	7-Wd San Francisco	81	214
H C	39	m	w	KY	Klamath	Trinidad Twp	73	392
Heny B	43	m	w	PA	Yuba	Parks Bar Twp	93	648
Hiram	38	m	w	NY	Placer	Auburn P O	76	360
Jackson	38	m	w	IL	Butte	Chico Twp	70	37
James	30	m	w	MS	Marin	Sausalito Twp	74	74
James	27	m	w	NY	San Francisco	1-Wd San Francisco	79	127
Oscar	18	m	w	MI	Sonoma	Healdsburg & Mendo	91	281
R	31	m	w	NC	San Joaquin	Dent Twp	86	22
Redick	33	m	w	IL	Butte	Chico Twp	70	37
Thomas	45	m	w	NY	San Francisco	San Francisco P O	80	483
CARTY								
Bernard M	55	m	w	ENGL	Fresno	Millerton P O	72	150
Charles	30	m	w	VT	Santa Barbara	Las Cruces P O	87	515
Daniel	27	m	w	VT	Santa Barbara	Las Cruces P O	87	515
Ellen	11	f	w	PA	San Francisco	2-Wd San Francisco	79	278
Margaret	8	f	w	CA	Solano	Benicia	90	16
McCagon	47	m	w	MO	Stanislaus	Branch Twp	92	3
Miles	46	m	w	IREL	Solano	Benicia	90	16
Patrick	35	m	w	IREL	San Francisco	San Francisco P O	83	388
Richd	47	m	w	PA	Butte	Kimshew Tpw	70	82
Thos	47	m	w	IREL	San Joaquin	Tulare Twp	86	262
Thos	41	m	w	IREL	San Francisco	1-Wd San Francisco	79	76
CARTZ								
Jaser	60	m	w	ITAL	San Joaquin	Oneal Twp	86	119
Jno	57	m	w	MO	Butte	Kimshew Tpw	70	83
CARUANNA								
Caroline	21	f	w	AUST	Nevada	Grass Valley Twp	75	144
Francis I	32	m	w	NY	Nevada	Grass Valley Twp	75	142
CARUBENO								
Lorenzo	62	m	w	ITAL	El Dorado	Diamond Springs Tw	72	27
CARUCECH								
Lorencio	40	m	w	MEXI	Los Angeles	Los Angeles Twp	73	467
CARULLO								
Vicenta	45	f	w	CA	Los Angeles	Santa Ana Twp	73	616
CARUNOS								
Victor	40	m	w	FRAN	Contra Costa	San Pablo Twp	71	355
CARUPEN								
Michael	35	m	w	IREL	Contra Costa	Martinez P O	71	409
CARUS								
Deloss	35	m	w	NY	Yuba	Marysville	93	577
CARUSE								
Philoma	38	f	w	MEXI	Tehama	Red Bluff	92	181
CARUTH								
John	69	m	w	GA	San Diego	Milquaty Dist	78	476
CARUTHERS								
Frank	14	m	w	CA	Stanislaus	Emory Twp	92	21
George	18	m	w	VT	Stanislaus	Branch Twp	92	10
Irene	51	f	w	NY	Stanislaus	Emory Twp	92	21
James	54	m	w	PA	Tulare	Tule Rvr Twp	92	258
Samuel	49	m	w	PA	Tulare	Tule Rvr Twp	92	258
Thomes	49	m	w	OH	Humboldt	Eel Rvr Twp	72	250
Thos	38	m	w	ENGL	Marin	Tomales Twp	74	76
CARVAHAL								
Jose M	26	m	w	CA	Santa Cruz	Soquel Twp	89	437
CARVAJAL								
Manuel	38	m	w	CHIL	Plumas	Goodwin Twp	77	1
CARVAL								
Luke	30	m	w	IREL	San Joaquin	2-Wd Stockton	86	175
CARVALLO								
Chas	60	m	w	IN	Butte	Chico Twp	70	43
CARVELL								
John	47	m	w	CANA	Sonoma	Analy Twp	91	235
CARVEN								
Roell	28	m	w	MEXI	Stanislaus	Empire Twp	92	63
CARVER								
Albert G	39	m	w	ME	Stanislaus	Empire Twp	92	32
Amanda	34	f	w	MA	San Francisco	7-Wd San Francisco	81	182
Benjamin	32	m	w	ME	San Francisco	7-Wd San Francisco	81	194
E P	26	m	w	PA	Solano	Vallejo	90	195
G A	47	m	w	PA	Alameda	Oakland	68	162
Henry P	45	m	w	MD	Nevada	Grass Valley Twp	75	144
Mary	25	f	i	CA	Tehama	Battle Crk Twp	92	157
Thomas	38	m	w	IL	Kern	Linns Valley P O	73	344
W S	46	m	w	OH	Tehama	Battle Crk Twp	92	157
CARVERY								
James	30	m	w	IREL	San Francisco	7-Wd San Francisco	81	169
CARVEY								
James	35	m	w	IREL	Sonoma	Analy Twp	91	221
CARVILL								
B	38	m	w	IREL	Sacramento	3-Wd Sacramento	77	301
CARVILLE								
O S	47	m	w	ME	San Francisco	San Francisco P O	83	280
CARVOLLI								
A	44	m	w	SWIT	San Francisco	San Francisco P O	85	797
CARVY								
Henry	37	m	w	FINL	San Francisco	3-Wd San Francisco	79	291
CARWELL								
W P	40	m	w	NY	Solano	Vallejo	90	204
William	25	m	w	IL	Santa Clara	1-Wd San Jose	88	238
CARWIEVRTO								
Pedro	17	m	w	MEXI	San Francisco	11-Wd San Francisc	84	592
CARWILE								
H A	52	f	w	OH	Sacramento	1-Wd Sacramento	77	184
CARY								
Charles	30	m	w	CANA	San Francisco	8-Wd San Francisco	82	443
Daniel	67	m	w	NY	Calaveras	San Andreas P O	70	158
Edward	24	m	w	KY	San Francisco	San Francisco P O	85	863
Eugene W	34	m	w	IREL	San Francisco	San Francisco P O	83	268
Frank	33	m	w	SWIT	Humboldt	Eel Rvr Twp	72	250
Frank	25	m	w	IL	Humboldt	Eureka Twp	72	272
Frank L	46	m	w	ME	Butte	Oregon Twp	70	134
George W	20	m	w	MO	Yolo	Putah Twp	93	517
Jabez	52	m	w	MA	San Francisco	5-Wd San Francisco	81	21
James	33	m	w	IREL	Yuba	Long Bar Twp	93	563
Jeremiah	30	m	w	IREL	Marin	San Antonio Twp	74	62
Jno E	23	m	w	IN	Butte	Oregon Twp	70	136
John	82	m	w	IREL	San Francisco	11-Wd San Francisc	84	429
John	58	m	w	IREL	Siskiyou	Callahan P O	89	626
John	45	m	w	NY	Contra Costa	Martinez P O	71	408
John	45	m	w	IREL	Nevada	Bridgeport Twp	75	118
John	43	m	w	IREL	Alameda	Brooklyn	68	30
John	40	m	w	IREL	Sacramento	4-Wd Sacramento	77	360
John	38	m	w	IREL	San Francisco	San Francisco P O	85	805
John	30	m	w	IN	Sonoma	Vallejo Twp	91	463
John E	38	m	w	ME	Tuolumne	Sonora P O	93	325
John Tert	30	m	w	IN	Klamath	Orleans Twp	73	379
Joseph	42	m	w	IREL	Placer	Bath P O	76	444
Joseph	34	m	w	OH	Solano	Maine Prairie Twp	90	48
Lewis	49	m	w	NJ	Colusa	Colusa	71	296
Lizzie	9	f	w	NY	San Francisco	11-Wd San Francisc	84	656
Mary	27	f	w	IREL	San Francisco	San Francisco P O	85	798
Michael	40	m	w	IREL	Solano	Maine Prairie Twp	90	52
Mike	33	m	w	CANA	Solano	Vallejo	90	215
Morris	30	m	w	IREL	El Dorado	Mud Springs Twp	72	81
Patrick	50	m	w	IREL	San Joaquin	Douglas Twp	86	35

© 2001 by Heritage Quest. All rights reserved.

Series M593

Name	Age	S	R	B-PL	County	Locale	Roll	Pg
Peter	28	m	w	IREL	San Francisco	5-Wd San Francisco	81	9
Rosa	10	f	w	NY	Solano	Benicia	90	4
Rubin	45	m	w	CT	Alameda	Oakland	68	131
S D	40	m	w	NY	San Francisco	San Francisco P O	85	869
Sam C	30	m	w	MI	Butte	Oregon Twp	70	129
T B	48	m	w	NY	Sonoma	Vallejo Twp	91	463
Thomas	42	m	w	IREL	San Francisco	San Francisco P O	85	751
Thomas	24	m	w	IREL	San Mateo	Schoolhouse Statio	87	332
Thomas N	39	m	w	ENGL	Nevada	Meadow Lake Twp	75	249
Thos	30	m	w	IREL	Butte	Chico Twp	70	47
Timothy	83	m	w	IREL	Marin	San Antonio Twp	74	62
Tolman	30	m	w	ME	Calaveras	San Andreas P O	70	210
William	36	m	w	MO	San Luis Obispo	Arroyo Grande Twp	87	273
Wm	77	m	w	VT	Humboldt	Arcata Twp	72	230
CARYL								
B L	40	m	w	NY	Alameda	Oakland	68	156
Henry	30	m	w	PRUS	San Francisco	11-Wd San Francisc	84	633
CASA								
Antonio	35	m	w	ITAL	Santa Clara	2-Wd San Jose	88	315
CASAD								
Ellen	24	f	w	IL	Los Angeles	Los Angeles Twp	73	488
Martin	40	m	w	OH	Yuba	Marysville	93	581
Thomas	54	m	w	IL	Los Angeles	Santa Ana Twp	73	601
CASADA								
Mary	61	f	w	IREL	Sonoma	Petaluma Twp	91	310
CASADY								
Maggie	23	f	w	CANA	San Francisco	San Francisco P O	83	151
CASAFERSING								
M	21	m	w	MEXI	San Francisco	7-Wd San Francisco	81	206
CASALA								
Philip	23	m	w	MEXI	San Francisco	2-Wd San Francisco	79	142
CASALADO								
Juan	21	m	w	CA	Fresno	Millerton P O	72	159
CASALAM								
Andrew	45	m	w	ITAL	San Francisco	San Francisco P O	80	419
CASALEGIO								
Judita	20	f	w	ITAL	San Francisco	11-Wd San Francisc	84	586
Paulo	24	m	w	ITAL	San Francisco	11-Wd San Francisc	84	586
CASALINO								
Manwell	30	m	w	ITAL	San Mateo	Schoolhouse Statio	87	332
CASANUEVA								
Teresa C	39	f	w	MEXI	Santa Clara	1-Wd San Jose	88	260
CASAONOREYON								
Martha	18	f	w	FRAN	San Francisco	2-Wd San Francisco	79	176
CASAR								
Wm	34	m	w	HANO	San Francisco	11-Wd San Francisc	84	552
CASARD								
Wm	28	m	w	MO	Butte	Hamilton Twp	70	65
CASAS								
Dolores	40	f	w	CA	Santa Barbara	San Buenaventura P	87	434
John	45	m	w	MEXI	San Francisco	San Francisco P O	80	350
CASASO								
Soloman	17	m	w	MEXI	San Francisco	San Francisco P O	80	459
CASASSA								
Domienico	20	m	w	ITAL	San Francisco	San Francisco P O	85	865
Orlando	21	m	w	ITAL	San Francisco	San Francisco P O	85	865
CASBAN								
--- Mr	38	m	w	MA	Alameda	Oakland	68	205
CASCADINE								
Wilhelm	27	m	w	SHOL	San Francisco	San Francisco P O	83	85
CASCAR								
Sacremento	40	m	w	MEXI	Calaveras	San Andreas P O	70	208
CASCETTI								
Dominic	26	m	w	SWIT	Santa Clara	Santa Clara Twp	88	176
CASCHA								
S	38	m	w	ITAL	Calaveras	Copperopolis P O	70	231
CASCHIN								
J W	41	m	w	OH	Lake	Lower Lake	73	423
CASE								
A	30	m	w	HANO	Alameda	Oakland	68	152
Abner	28	m	w	OH	Solano	Green Valley Twp	90	44
Ann	50	f	w	NY	Santa Cruz	Watsonville	89	375
Austin B	47	m	w	NY	Sonoma	Petaluma Twp	91	314
B B	36	m	w	NY	Mendocino	Little Lake Twp	74	193
C E	17	m	w	CA	San Joaquin	Douglas Twp	86	32
Charles E	22	m	w	US	El Dorado	Mud Springs Twp	72	83
E G	14	m	w	CA	Alameda	Oakland	68	243
Elijah	61	m	w	NY	San Francisco	11-Wd San Francisc	84	704
Florence E	14	f	w	CA	Napa	Napa Twp	75	29
G E	24	m	w	NY	Sutter	Sutter Twp	92	122
Gardner W	49	m	w	MA	Sacramento	2-Wd Sacramento	77	215
Geo	23	m	w	CT	San Francisco	7-Wd San Francisco	81	279
George A	44	m	w	MA	San Francisco	6-Wd San Francisco	81	146
George B	43	m	w	NY	Sonoma	Petaluma Twp	91	309
Grachum	63	m	w	OH	San Bernardino	San Bernardino Twp	78	425
H S	37	m	w	PA	Humboldt	Eel Rvr Twp	72	251
Harry	19	m	w	MO	Sonoma	Santa Rosa	91	405
Isaac	41	m	w	ME	Solano	Suisun Twp	90	101
Isham	37	m	w	NY	Alameda	Brooklyn	68	33
James	49	m	w	KY	Mendocino	Little Lake Twp	74	202
James	30	m	w	IL	San Bernardino	San Bernardino Twp	78	425
James M	44	m	w	TN	Santa Clara	1-Wd San Jose	88	252
Jas M	56	m	w	KY	Sutter	Butte Twp	92	90
John	37	m	w	IREL	San Francisco	11-Wd San Francisc	84	689
John	30	m	w	IREL	Marin	Tomales Twp	74	84
John	25	m	w	ENGL	Nevada	Grass Valley Twp	75	217
John	22	m	w	MI	Sutter	Sutter Twp	92	117

Series M593

Name	Age	S	R	B-PL	County	Locale	Roll	Pg
John A	36	m	w	NY	Amador	Volcano P O	69	372
John B	49	m	w	KY	San Bernardino	San Bernardino Twp	78	451
John W	14	m	w	CA	Santa Clara	1-Wd San Jose	88	252
Joseph	33	m	w	NY	San Francisco	11-Wd San Francisc	84	597
Lafayette	38	m	w	NY	El Dorado	Placerville Twp	72	105
Laura	15	f	w	MO	San Bernardino	San Bernardino Twp	78	418
Lizzie	22	f	w	OH	Sacramento	2-Wd Sacramento	77	243
Nathan P	50	m	w	PA	Trinity	Lewiston Pct	92	213
Oscar L	32	m	w	NY	Yolo	Washington Twp	93	530
Robert C	43	m	w	MA	Santa Clara	2-Wd San Jose	88	300
Russell	28	m	w	OH	Alameda	Murray Twp	68	119
Samuel F	31	m	w	NY	Marin	Sausalito Twp	74	74
Samuel N	36	m	w	NY	Placer	Roseville P O	76	356
Simon	23	m	w	FRAN	Fresno	Millerton P O	72	193
W B	38	m	w	OH	San Joaquin	Oneal Twp	86	108
Walter	49	m	w	CT	Sonoma	Healdsburg & Mendo	91	278
Webb	40	m	w	CT	Marin	Bolinas Twp	74	7
William	33	m	w	MO	Tulare	Farmersville Twp	92	246
William	26	m	w	IL	San Bernardino	San Bernardino Twp	78	426
William H	47	m	w	NY	Calaveras	Copperopolis P O	70	228
CASEA								
Frank	39	m	w	MA	Alameda	Brooklyn Twp	68	50
CASEAUX								
Jane	28	f	w	FRAN	San Francisco	San Francisco P O	80	536
CASEBAUM								
Charles	47	m	w	PRUS	San Francisco	San Francisco P O	80	333
CASEBOLDT								
James	34	m	w	KY	Yolo	Putah Twp	93	523
CASEBOLT								
Geo	30	m	w	MO	San Francisco	7-Wd San Francisco	81	282
Henry	54	m	w	VA	San Francisco	San Francisco P O	85	764
J D	30	m	w	VA	San Francisco	San Francisco P O	83	291
CASEGENNA								
August	43	m	w	FRAN	San Francisco	San Francisco P O	83	1
CASELAR								
John	25	m	w	AUST	San Francisco	3-Wd San Francisco	79	289
CASELE								
Myra	30	f	w	MI	Santa Cruz	Santa Cruz	89	434
CASELLI								
Vacinyo	33	m	w	ITAL	Sacramento	Sutter Twp	77	387
CASELLMAN								
Esther	67	f	w	PA	Santa Clara	1-Wd San Jose	88	250
CASELMAN								
James	18	m	w	CANA	Placer	Colfax P O	76	391
CASEMENT								
William	40	m	w	IREL	San Francisco	San Francisco P O	83	210
CASENOVA								
Andrew	32	m	w	ITAL	San Francisco	2-Wd San Francisco	79	256
CASER								
Henry	33	m	w	PA	Santa Cruz	Pajaro Twp	89	353
John	38	m	w	PA	Santa Cruz	Pajaro Twp	89	353
CASERES								
Antonio	29	m	w	CA	Sonoma	Salt Point Twp	91	383
Cyrus F	24	m	w	CA	Sonoma	Bodega Twp	91	249
Francisco	43	m	w	CA	Sonoma	Bodega Twp	91	249
CASERETTA								
Joseph	43	m	w	ITAL	Mariposa	Mariposa P O	74	97
CASERLY								
Y	45	m	w	IREL	Sierra	Lincoln Twp	89	551
CASEUS								
Almeda	24	m	w	MEXI	Stanislaus	Emory Twp	92	26
Frank	17	m	w	CA	Sonoma	Santa Rosa	91	412
CASEY								
Amelia	17	f	w	MA	San Francisco	San Francisco P O	80	409
Andrew	9	m	w	PA	San Francisco	San Francisco P O	85	799
Andrew	13	m	w	CA	Yuba	Parks Bar Twp	93	649
Annie	27	f	w	IREL	San Francisco	7-Wd San Francisco	81	233
Annie	19	f	w	NY	San Francisco	San Francisco P O	85	863
Annie E	6	f	w	CA	Sonoma	Bodega Twp	91	264
Benj	60	m	w	OH	Santa Clara	Almaden Twp	88	16
Bridget	23	f	w	IREL	San Francisco	1-Wd San Francisco	79	98
Burven	30	f	w	IREL	San Francisco	San Francisco P O	83	129
Casper	28	m	w	WURT	Los Angeles	Wilmington Twp	73	642
Catharine	68	f	w	IREL	Solano	Green Valley Twp	90	37
Catherine	73	f	w	IREL	Nevada	Grass Valley Twp	75	161
Catherine	24	f	w	IREL	San Francisco	8-Wd San Francisco	82	347
Charles	11	m	w	CA	Siskiyou	Surprise Valley Tw	89	638
Cornelius	48	m	w	IREL	Marin	Tomales Twp	74	82
Daniel	8	m	w	PA	San Francisco	San Francisco P O	85	799
Daniel	48	m	w	NY	San Joaquin	Castoria Twp	86	9
Daniel	39	m	w	NY	San Joaquin	Castoria Twp	86	1
Daniel	36	m	w	IREL	San Francisco	San Francisco P O	80	397
Daniel	35	m	w	IREL	San Francisco	11-Wd San Francisc	84	492
Daniel	17	m	w	IREL	San Francisco	San Francisco P O	80	409
Daniel D	30	m	w	IREL	San Francisco	San Francisco P O	85	792
Daniel H	30	m	w	ENGL	San Francisco	San Francisco P O	83	244
Danl	38	m	w	IREL	San Francisco	1-Wd San Francisco	79	33
Dennis	27	m	w	IREL	Napa	Napa	75	18
E W	42	m	w	IL	San Francisco	San Francisco P O	85	788
Edward	21	m	w	NY	San Francisco	1-Wd San Francisco	79	98
Edward	19	m	w	WI	Sonoma	Salt Point	91	380
Ellen	30	f	w	IREL	Humboldt	Eureka Twp	72	269
Eugene	34	m	w	IREL	San Francisco	San Francisco P O	83	290
Frank	35	m	w	IREL	Sacramento	3-Wd Sacramento	77	313
Frank	25	m	w	CANA	San Francisco	San Francisco P O	85	805
Hannah	40	f	w	IREL	San Francisco	11-Wd San Francisc	84	557
Henry	39	m	w	IREL	San Francisco	8-Wd San Francisco	82	475

© 2001 by Heritage Quest. All rights reserved.

Name	Age	S	R	B-PL	County	Locale	Series M593 Roll	Pg
Henry	26	m	w	NY	San Francisco	7-Wd San Francisco	81	274
Hiram	21	m	w	WI	Sonoma	Analy Twp	91	237
Honora	67	f	w	IREL	San Francisco	8-Wd San Francisco	82	454
Hugh	50	m	w	IREL	San Francisco	San Francisco P O	83	213
Hugh	23	m	w	IREL	Sacramento	3-Wd Sacramento	77	256
Isaac W	26	m	w	MD	Nevada	Grass Valley Twp	75	147
J	35	m	w	IREL	Santa Clara	Almaden Twp	88	3
James	46	m	w	IREL	Solano	Suisun Twp	90	110
James	40	m	w	IREL	San Francisco	San Francisco P O	85	859
James	38	m	w	IREL	San Mateo	Schoolhouse Statio	87	338
James	38	m	w	IREL	San Francisco	11-Wd San Francisc	84	544
James	35	m	w	IREL	San Francisco	8-Wd San Francisco	82	393
James	32	m	w	IREL	San Francisco	11-Wd San Francisc	84	709
James	31	m	w	IREL	San Francisco	1-Wd San Francisco	79	98
James	21	m	w	IREL	San Francisco	San Francisco P O	85	764
James H	42	m	w	IREL	Calaveras	San Andreas P O	70	153
Jerry	32	m	w	IREL	Santa Clara	Almaden Twp	88	11
Johanna	28	f	w	IREL	San Francisco	11-Wd San Francisc	84	671
Johanna T	25	f	w	IREL	Shasta	Horsetown P O	89	506
John	7	m	w	CA	Marin	San Rafael Twp	74	29
John	60	m	w	TN	Los Angeles	El Monte Twp	73	460
John	55	m	w	IREL	San Mateo	San Mateo P O	87	358
John	50	m	w	IREL	San Mateo	San Mateo P O	87	353
John	48	m	w	IREL	Sacramento	American Twp	77	68
John	45	m	w	IREL	San Mateo	San Mateo P O	87	355
John	40	m	w	IREL	San Francisco	7-Wd San Francisco	81	229
John	36	m	w	IREL	Solano	Vacaville Twp	90	130
John	35	m	w	IREL	San Francisco	San Francisco P O	85	730
John	35	m	w	IREL	San Francisco	11-Wd San Francisc	84	613
John	31	m	w	IREL	Colusa	Butte Twp	71	267
John	29	m	w	IREL	Contra Costa	Martinez P O	71	379
John	29	m	w	IREL	San Francisco	7-Wd San Francisco	81	252
John	29	m	w	IREL	San Francisco	San Francisco P O	80	540
John	27	m	w	IREL	Santa Clara	Almaden Twp	88	11
John	26	m	w	IREL	San Francisco	San Francisco P O	85	751
John	25	m	w	IREL	San Diego	San Diego	78	510
John	14	m	w	NY	San Francisco	11-Wd San Francisc	84	587
John E	26	m	w	NY	San Francisco	1-Wd San Francisco	79	98
Joseph	75	m	w	IREL	San Francisco	San Francisco P O	83	218
Joseph	18	m	w	LA	Napa	Yountville Twp	75	81
Kate	25	f	w	NJ	San Francisco	San Francisco P O	85	724
Levi J	51	m	w	CANA	Sonoma	Cloverdale Twp	91	272
Lewis	52	m	w	OH	Santa Clara	Almaden Twp	88	16
Louis A	50	m	w	NJ	Los Angeles	Los Angeles Twp	73	496
Mackey	25	m	w	IREL	Colusa	Colusa Twp	71	276
Maggie	22	f	w	IREL	San Francisco	5-Wd San Francisco	81	33
Margaret	60	f	w	IREL	San Francisco	San Francisco P O	80	397
Margaret	17	f	w	NY	San Francisco	San Francisco P O	83	249
Margrett	56	f	w	IREL	San Francisco	1-Wd San Francisco	79	98
Maria	25	f	w	IREL	San Francisco	8-Wd San Francisco	82	300
Mary	57	f	w	IREL	Napa	Napa	75	42
Mary	50	f	w	IREL	San Francisco	San Francisco P O	83	27
Mary	36	f	w	IREL	San Francisco	San Francisco P O	80	419
Mary	30	f	w	IREL	San Francisco	San Francisco P O	83	107
Mary	27	f	w	IREL	Alameda	Oakland	68	154
Michael	50	m	w	IREL	Solano	Suisun Twp	90	110
Michael	45	m	w	IREL	San Mateo	Belmont P O	87	388
Michael	42	m	w	IREL	Nevada	Grass Valley Twp	75	179
Michael	40	m	w	IREL	San Francisco	8-Wd San Francisco	82	314
Michael	37	m	w	IREL	Nevada	Grass Valley Twp	75	227
Michael	35	m	w	IREL	San Francisco	San Francisco P O	80	478
Michael	32	m	w	IREL	San Mateo	Schoolhouse Statio	87	342
Michael	26	m	w	IREL	Nevada	Little York Twp	75	245
Michael	24	m	w	IREL	San Francisco	San Francisco P O	85	801
Michael	24	m	w	IREL	San Francisco	7-Wd San Francisco	81	275
Michael	20	m	w	IREL	Colusa	Colusa Twp	71	276
Michael	20	m	w	IREL	Santa Clara	Fremont Twp	88	57
Michl	35	m	w	IREL	San Francisco	1-Wd San Francisco	79	59
Nellie	19	f	w	CANA	Napa	Napa	75	18
Owen	54	m	w	IREL	San Francisco	11-Wd San Francisc	84	463
Owen	44	m	w	IREL	Sacramento	2-Wd Sacramento	77	252
Owen	28	m	w	IREL	San Francisco	11-Wd San Francisc	84	467
Pat	30	m	w	IREL	San Joaquin	1-Wd Stockton	86	157
Patrick	65	m	w	IREL	San Mateo	San Mateo P O	87	358
Patrick	52	m	w	IREL	Del Norte	Happy Camp Twp	71	470
Patrick	5	m	w	CA	Marin	San Rafael Twp	74	29
Patrick	45	m	w	IREL	Nevada	Grass Valley Twp	75	212
Patrick	40	m	w	IREL	San Francisco	San Francisco P O	83	143
Patrick	37	m	w	IREL	Yolo	Cache Crk Twp	93	438
Patrick	30	m	w	IREL	Colusa	Colusa Twp	71	276
Patrick	30	m	w	IREL	Marin	San Rafael Twp	74	46
Patrick	28	m	w	IREL	San Francisco	San Francisco P O	83	270
Patrick	23	m	w	NY	Mendocino	Point Arena Twp	74	224
Patrick	20	m	w	IREL	Santa Cruz	Santa Cruz	89	411
Patrick	18	m	w	MA	Sonoma	Sonoma Twp	91	431
Patrick B	45	m	w	IREL	San Mateo	San Mateo P O	87	359
Peter	40	m	w	IREL	Nevada	Grass Valley Twp	75	198
Peter	37	m	w	IREL	San Mateo	San Mateo P O	87	358
Richard	40	m	w	IREL	San Francisco	San Francisco P O	83	291
Robert	27	m	w	IREL	San Francisco	San Francisco P O	83	184
S W	60	m	w	CANA	Sacramento	3-Wd Sacramento	77	310
Sarah	24	f	w	IREL	San Francisco	San Francisco P O	85	812
Sarah	21	f	w	CA	San Francisco	San Francisco P O	85	789
Sophia	40	m	w	OLDE	Yuba	Marysville Twp	93	570
T C	24	m	w	CANA	Yuba	Marysville Twp	93	571
Tenna	11	f	w	AUSL	Solano	Benicia	90	16
Theresa	18	f	w	CA	Solano	Suisun Twp	90	114
Thomas	45	m	w	IREL	San Francisco	San Francisco P O	83	157
Thomas	42	m	w	IREL	Placer	Rocklin Twp	76	463
Thomas	40	m	w	IREL	Yuba	Marysville Twp	93	571
Thomas	34	m	w	LA	San Diego	Temecula Dist	78	526
Thomas	28	m	w	IREL	San Francisco	San Francisco P O	85	753
Thomas	28	m	w	IREL	Marin	Tomales Twp	74	88
Thomas	27	m	w	IREL	San Francisco	1-Wd San Francisco	79	113
Thomas	21	m	w	NY	Marin	San Rafael Twp	74	45
Thomas F	30	m	w	ME	San Francisco	6-Wd San Francisco	81	99
Thomas J	35	m	w	IREL	San Francisco	San Francisco P O	83	232
William	50	m	w	IREL	Solano	Silveyville Twp	90	72
William	40	m	w	IREL	San Mateo	Schoolhouse Statio	87	342
William	35	m	w	IREL	Nevada	Grass Valley Twp	75	230
William	33	m	w	IREL	Plumas	Quartz Twp	77	34
William	31	m	w	NY	San Diego	Julian Dist	78	472
William	31	m	w	MA	Calaveras	San Andreas P O	70	188
William	30	m	w	IREL	Nevada	Rough & Ready Twp	75	335
William	22	m	w	ENGL	Yolo	Buckeye Twp	93	407
William	12	m	w	CA	Nevada	Bridgeport Twp	75	104
Wm	36	m	w	IREL	Sacramento	Granite Twp	77	140
Wm	33	m	w	IREL	Sacramento	Granite Twp	77	139
Wm T	30	m	w	MA	Tuolumne	Columbia P O	93	343
CASGROVE								
Joseph	19	m	w	NY	San Francisco	San Francisco P O	83	240
P H	44	m	w	IREL	Tuolumne	Columbia P O	93	347
Patrick	35	m	w	IREL	San Francisco	San Francisco P O	85	842
CASH								
G A	26	m	w	NY	San Francisco	San Francisco P O	85	853
Georom	37	m	w	NY	Monterey	Castroville Twp	74	340
Jacob	38	m	w	PRUS	Nevada	Washington Twp	75	341
Martin	47	m	w	PRUS	Sacramento	Mississippi Twp	77	162
Nelson	38	m	w	KY	Siskiyou	Table Rock Twp	89	648
Oliver P	42	m	w	NY	Sonoma	Petaluma Twp	91	363
Peter	27	m	w	CANA	Nevada	Meadow Lake Twp	75	259
Rosanna	24	f	w	CA	Sonoma	Analy Twp	91	232
Samuel	40	m	w	ME	Los Angeles	Los Angeles	73	505
CASHAN								
Benj	40	m	w	IREL	San Francisco	1-Wd San Francisco	79	32
CASHBURN								
Fred	25	m	w	ME	San Mateo	Pescadero P O	87	416
CASHEEN								
Edward	22	m	w	IREL	Sutter	Sutter Twp	92	121
CASHEL								
Frank	35	m	w	IREL	San Francisco	1-Wd San Francisco	79	35
CASHELS								
Machee	29	m	w	IREL	Placer	Summit P O	76	496
CASHENDER								
James	20	m	w	ME	San Francisco	1-Wd San Francisco	79	61
Wm	50	m	w	ME	San Francisco	1-Wd San Francisco	79	61
CASHER								
John	30	m	w	IL	Solano	Suisun Twp	90	103
Peter	20	m	w	CA	Sonoma	Analy Twp	91	226
CASHIEN								
John	30	m	w	ME	Stanislaus	Emory Twp	92	24
Peter	45	m	w	NY	Amador	Drytown P O	69	418
CASHIER								
John R	21	m	w	TX	San Diego	Julian Dist	78	473
CASHILLO								
Juan	37	m	w	MEXI	San Luis Obispo	San Luis Obispo Tw	87	298
CASHIN								
Dennis	62	m	w	IREL	Nevada	Grass Valley Twp	75	147
John	42	m	w	IREL	Nevada	Nevada Twp	75	299
Michael	24	m	w	IREL	Nevada	Grass Valley Twp	75	147
Richd	30	m	w	IREL	San Francisco	1-Wd San Francisco	79	77
Thomas	38	m	w	IREL	Monterey	San Antonio Twp	74	320
CASHING								
Catherine A	39	f	w	NY	Santa Cruz	Pajaro Twp	89	339
CASHINS								
Jas D	30	m	w	IREL	Solano	Vallejo	90	176
CASHLAN								
Justin	51	m	w	FRAN	Amador	Volcano P O	69	378
CASHMAN								
Charles D	53	m	w	MA	San Francisco	8-Wd San Francisco	82	415
Henry	22	m	w	IREL	San Francisco	San Francisco P O	83	206
James	35	m	w	RI	Plumas	Plumas Twp	77	32
John	55	m	w	IREL	San Francisco	San Francisco P O	85	869
John	28	m	w	IREL	Klamath	Liberty Twp	73	376
M	27	m	w	IREL	Yuba	Marysville Twp	93	567
Martin	38	m	w	IREL	Stanislaus	Emory Twp	92	24
Mary	64	f	w	IREL	Santa Clara	2-Wd San Jose	88	287
Mary	22	f	w	IREL	San Francisco	7-Wd San Francisco	81	179
Richd	28	m	w	IREL	Marin	Tomales Twp	74	87
Wm	29	m	w	IREL	San Francisco	San Francisco P O	83	123
CASHNER								
Joseph	28	m	w	GERM	San Francisco	8-Wd San Francisco	82	337
CASHO								
Cesario	20	m	w	CA	San Luis Obispo	Arroyo Grande Twp	87	270
Jose P	50	m	w	CA	San Luis Obispo	Arroyo Grande Twp	87	275
Juan	38	m	w	CA	San Luis Obispo	Santa Rosa Twp	87	324
Ramon	32	m	w	MEXI	San Luis Obispo	Arroyo Grande Twp	87	275
CASHUE								
Joseph	62	m	w	ITAL	Plumas	Washington Twp	77	56
CASIA								
Kasas	30	m	w	CA	Santa Clara	Burnett Twp	88	39
CASICK								
John	33	m	w	IREL	Nevada	Nevada Twp	75	300

© 2001 by Heritage Quest. All rights reserved.

Name	Age	S	R	B-PL	County	Locale	Roll	Pg
CASICO								
Mike	40	m	w	VA	San Joaquin	2-Wd Stockton	86	190
CASILAS								
Librado	36	m	w	MEXI	San Francisco	San Francisco P O	80	466
CASILLAS								
Francisco	67	m	w	MEXI	Mariposa	Mariposa P O	74	110
CASILLO								
Ramona	58	f	w	CA	San Luis Obispo	San Luis Obispo Tw	87	298
CASINAGA								
Louis	36	m	w	ITAL	San Francisco	San Francisco P O	83	311
CASINOMA								
Friveda	50	f	w	CAME	Los Angeles	Los Angeles Twp	73	490
CASINTA								
Jose	50	m	w	CHIL	Amador	Jackson P O	69	345
CASIO								
Tomasa	27	f	w	CA	Los Angeles	Los Angeles	73	561
CASIUS								
Euphunin	36	m	w	ME	Humboldt	Eureka Twp	72	264
CASKAR								
Jas	38	m	w	IREL	Sierra	Table Rock Twp	89	574
CASKELL								
Tho	21	m	w	ENGL	San Joaquin	Liberty Twp	86	91
CASKER								
Valentine	25	f	w	PORT	Contra Costa	Martinez P O	71	367
CASKEY								
James	51	m	w	IREL	Humboldt	Eureka Twp	72	282
Mary	13	f	w	CA	San Francisco	San Francisco P O	85	864
Wm R	62	m	w	TN	Tuolumne	Sonora P O	93	320
CASKILL								
Calvin	40	m	w	NC	Colusa	Spring Valley Twp	71	340
CASKIN								
Clinton	15	m	w	SC	Monterey	San Juan Twp	74	385
John	19	m	w	CA	Monterey	San Benito Twp	74	384
V	18	m	w	PRUS	Alameda	Oakland	68	208
CASLAGNETTI								
Gio	24	m	w	ITAL	San Francisco	3-Wd San Francisco	79	289
CASLAGNETTO								
Peter	32	m	w	ITAL	Mariposa	Maxwell Crk P O	74	148
CASLER								
Martin M	43	m	w	OH	Yolo	Cache Crk Twp	93	444
CASLETO								
V	30	m	w	ITAL	Amador	Jackson P O	69	337
CASLEY								
---	35	m	w	IREL	Alameda	Alameda	68	13
Thomas	30	m	w	ENGL	Nevada	Grass Valley Twp	75	181
Thomas	30	m	w	IREL	Nevada	Grass Valley Twp	75	222
William	26	m	w	ENGL	Plumas	Indian Twp	77	15
CASLIN								
Anny	26	f	w	NY	San Francisco	5-Wd San Francisco	81	33
CASMAN								
Charles	55	m	w	FRAN	Calaveras	Copperopolis P O	70	262
Thedore	40	m	w	FRAN	Calaveras	Copperopolis P O	70	262
CASMER								
Freeman	28	m	w	LA	San Diego	Julian Dist	78	468
Jacob	45	m	w	FRAN	Calaveras	San Andreas P O	70	194
CASMETER								
M	53	m	w	BADE	San Joaquin	Oneal Twp	86	112
CASMO								
Daniel	48	m	w	CHIL	Calaveras	Copperopolis P O	70	245
CASNELL								
Albert	22	m	w	MS	Sonoma	Petaluma Twp	91	311
John H	34	m	w	NY	San Luis Obispo	Santa Rosa Twp	87	325
CASNER								
Isabella	27	f	w	MEXI	Calaveras	San Andreas P O	70	217
James	40	m	w	PRUS	San Francisco	San Francisco P O	83	48
Joseph	28	m	w	FRAN	Calaveras	San Andreas P O	70	195
CASNET								
John	45	m	w	ITAL	San Francisco	11-Wd San Francisc	84	710
CASNEY								
Chas	58	m	w	ME	San Francisco	11-Wd San Francisc	84	689
CASON								
J H	29	m	m	MO	Solano	Benicia	90	1
James	70	m	w	VA	El Dorado	Salmon Falls Twp	72	129
CASONOVA								
Angelo	37	m	w	ITAL	Monterey	Monterey	74	366
CASOWICK								
Christopher	35	m	w	AUST	San Francisco	San Francisco P O	83	87
CASPAR								
Adam	28	m	w	MA	San Francisco	6-Wd San Francisco	81	104
Henry	35	m	w	SWIT	San Francisco	11-Wd San Francisc	84	693
Martin	26	m	w	PRUS	San Francisco	11-Wd San Francisc	84	524
Michael	52	m	w	FRAN	El Dorado	Mud Springs Twp	72	91
CASPARE								
Joseph	29	m	w	ITAL	Marin	Sausalito Twp	74	72
CASPER								
Andrew J	15	m	w	OR	Inyo	Lone Pine Twp	73	335
Carlo	25	m	w	ITAL	Amador	Jackson P O	69	336
Chas	40	m	w	PRUS	San Francisco	7-Wd San Francisco	81	274
Frederick	40	m	w	BADE	Plumas	Indian Twp	77	19
George	40	m	w	ITAL	San Francisco	11-Wd San Francisc	84	712
Henry	45	m	w	CANA	San Francisco	San Francisco P O	83	254
Jackson A	34	m	w	KY	Fresno	Millerton P O	72	148
Mat	26	m	w	WI	Contra Costa	Martinez P O	71	411
Miser	53	m	w	BAVA	Amador	Jackson P O	69	346
Peter	38	m	w	SWED	Yuba	Marysville	93	611
Samuel L	42	m	w	PA	San Diego	San Diego	78	495
CASPERENCE								
Albert	50	m	w	FRAN	San Francisco	8-Wd San Francisco	82	350
CASPIN								
H A	54	m	w	FRAN	Tuolumne	Sonora P O	93	309
CASPINO								
John	41	m	w	ITAL	San Francisco	San Francisco P O	80	471
CASQUETTE								
Francois	17	m	w	FRAN	San Francisco	6-Wd San Francisco	81	99
CASS								
Charles	34	m	w	ME	Trinity	Weaverville Pct	92	229
Geo W	43	m	w	NY	Siskiyou	Surprise Valley Tw	89	639
James	44	m	w	ENGL	San Luis Obispo	Arroyo Grande Twp	87	277
Jno	26	m	w	IREL	Sacramento	1-Wd Sacramento	77	177
John	48	m	w	IREL	Alameda	Eden Twp	68	66
John	45	m	w	IREL	Yuba	Marysville	93	606
John	22	m	w	DENM	Colusa	Grand Island Twp	71	309
Julia	34	f	w	IREL	San Francisco	11-Wd San Francisc	84	598
Maggie	25	f	w	IREL	San Francisco	San Francisco P O	85	776
Peter	40	m	w	IREL	El Dorado	Coloma Twp	72	4
Richard	36	m	w	IREL	San Francisco	11-Wd San Francisc	84	533
Simeon	38	m	w	CANA	Sacramento	3-Wd Sacramento	77	266
Thomas	26	m	w	ENGL	Nevada	Grass Valley Twp	75	154
Wm	35	m	w	ENGL	San Francisco	7-Wd San Francisco	81	279
CASSA								
Margaret	37	f	w	SCOT	San Joaquin	2-Wd Stockton	86	167
CASSACHO								
Dominick	38	m	w	ITAL	Calaveras	San Andreas P O	70	204
CASSAD								
Horace	27	m	w	LA	Los Angeles	Wilmington Twp	73	643
CASSADA								
James	28	m	w	RI	Placer	Clipper Gap P O	76	392
CASSADAY								
Catharine	30	f	w	IREL	Sierra	Sears Twp	89	558
CASSADY								
Alex	39	m	w	PA	Nevada	Meadow Lake Twp	75	264
Catherine	37	f	w	IREL	San Mateo	San Mateo P O	87	357
Charles	30	m	w	IREL	San Francisco	San Francisco P O	83	374
Charles C	41	m	w	KY	Placer	Dutch Flat P O	76	407
F	40	m	w	IREL	Sierra	Sears Twp	89	557
James	27	m	w	IREL	Placer	Rocklin Twp	76	465
John W	47	m	w	NJ	Sonoma	Petaluma Twp	91	343
Mary	25	f	w	IREL	Santa Cruz	Soquel Twp	89	440
CASSAHI								
Pedro	45	m	w	MEXI	Tuolumne	Sonora P O	93	314
CASSAIS								
Rosa	38	f	w	MEXI	Tuolumne	Sonora P O	93	316
CASSALE								
Salvador	43	m	w	ITAL	Marin	Novato Twp	74	10
CASSALI								
John	23	m	w	ITAL	Tuolumne	Columbia P O	93	344
CASSANDRA								
Daniel	21	m	w	IL	Santa Clara	Milpitas Twp	88	111
CASSANELLI								
B G	36	m	w	SARD	Tuolumne	Chinese Camp P O	93	371
Louis	35	m	w	ITAL	Tuolumne	Columbia P O	93	348
CASSANK								
Politz	29	m	b	WIND	San Francisco	8-Wd San Francisco	82	353
CASSAR								
Frank	30	m	w	FRAN	Butte	Ophir Twp	70	119
CASSARAGO								
Aloysius	36	m	w	ITAL	Santa Clara	Santa Clara Twp	88	176
CASSARD								
Maria A	50	f	w	CA	Santa Barbara	Santa Barbara P O	87	452
CASSARETO								
B B	38	m	w	ITAL	Tuolumne	Sonora P O	93	314
CASSAS								
Charles	25	m	w	ITAL	San Francisco	2-Wd San Francisco	79	237
Elizabeth	42	f	w	IREL	Santa Clara	2-Wd San Jose	88	325
CASSASSA								
Andre	50	m	w	ITAL	Mariposa	Maxwell Crk P O	74	143
Carlo	27	m	w	ITAL	San Mateo	Schoolhouse Statio	87	340
Rosa	40	f	w	ITAL	San Francisco	2-Wd San Francisco	79	162
CASSATTA								
Manuel	21	m	w	ITAL	San Francisco	11-Wd San Francisc	84	586
Piedra	17	m	w	ITAL	San Francisco	11-Wd San Francisc	84	586
CASSAVETO								
Anton	32	m	w	ITAL	Tuolumne	Big Oak Flat P O	93	393
CASSCAS								
Juan	40	m	w	MEXI	Amador	Jackson P O	69	328
CASSDY								
John	24	m	w	IL	Monterey	Pajaro Twp	74	372
CASSEAS								
Isabel	40	f	w	MEXI	Mariposa	Mariposa P O	74	105
CASSEBONNE								
William	42	m	w	BREM	San Francisco	6-Wd San Francisco	81	123
CASSEDAY								
John	30	m	w	IREL	San Francisco	San Francisco P O	83	370
CASSEDEMATRI								
Guillame	34	m	w	FRAN	Calaveras	San Andreas P O	70	205
CASSEDO								
Ramon	48	m	w	MEXI	Kern	Bakersfield P O	73	360
CASSEDY								
John	23	m	w	TN	Los Angeles	San Gabriel Twp	73	594
William	54	m	w	IREL	Amador	Ione City P O	69	349
CASSEL								
Corsel	42	m	w	PRUS	San Francisco	2-Wd San Francisco	79	243
Dora	19	f	w	PRUS	San Francisco	2-Wd San Francisco	79	147

© 2001 by Heritage Quest. All rights reserved.

Name	Age	S	R	B-PL	County	Locale	Series M593 Roll	Pg
Henny	44	m	w	NY	Placer	Auburn P O	76	370
John	21	m	w	FRAN	San Francisco	San Francisco P O	85	753
Jos F	54	m	w	MD	San Francisco	7-Wd San Francisco	81	243
CASSELA								
James	52	m	w	NY	Sacramento	Lee Twp	77	157
CASSELLA								
Antonio	33	m	w	ITAL	San Joaquin	1-Wd Stockton	86	139
CASSELLI								
Alexander	66	m	w	FRAN	San Francisco	6-Wd San Francisco	81	88
Andrew	36	m	w	ITAL	Napa	Napa Twp	75	74
Peter	42	m	w	ITAL	San Francisco	San Francisco P O	80	479
CASSELMANE								
Fred	42	m	w	PRUS	Humboldt	Eureka Twp	72	260
CASSELO								
Michal	43	m	w	ITAL	Sacramento	3-Wd Sacramento	77	288
CASSEN								
Michael	60	m	w	IREL	Mariposa	Mariposa P O	74	104
CASSENELLI								
David	24	m	w	ITAL	Calaveras	San Andreas P O	70	168
CASSENER								
John C	41	m	w	BAVA	Sierra	Table Rock Twp	89	577
CASSENIS								
Alphonso	75	m	w	CHIL	Calaveras	San Andreas P O	70	180
Bernard	34	m	w	MEXI	Calaveras	San Andreas P O	70	180
CASSENS								
Gustave	42	m	w	SHOL	San Francisco	2-Wd San Francisco	79	237
CASSERES								
Augustine	45	m	w	CHIL	Kern	Bakersfield P O	73	360
CASSERI								
Giovanni	36	m	w	ITAL	San Francisco	1-Wd San Francisco	79	123
CASSERLEY								
John	24	m	w	IREL	Los Angeles	Los Angeles	73	569
CASSERLY								
Eugene	46	m	w	IREL	San Francisco	11-Wd San Francisc	84	661
Francis	50	m	w	IREL	San Francisco	San Francisco P O	83	8
Francis	30	m	w	HOLL	San Francisco	1-Wd San Francisco	79	117
Frank	37	m	w	PRUS	San Francisco	11-Wd San Francisc	84	674
Henry	57	m	w	IREL	Yuba	Rose Bar Twp	93	657
John	50	m	w	IREL	San Mateo	Schoolhouse Statio	87	340
John	40	m	w	NY	San Francisco	2-Wd San Francisco	79	242
Margaret	35	f	w	IREL	San Francisco	8-Wd San Francisco	82	391
Michael	30	m	w	IREL	San Francisco	2-Wd San Francisco	79	213
Michael	26	m	w	IREL	Santa Clara	2-Wd San Jose	88	296
Michl	30	m	w	IREL	San Francisco	1-Wd San Francisco	79	59
Patrick	63	m	w	CA	Humboldt	Eel Rvr Twp	72	246
Patrick	40	m	w	IREL	San Francisco	1-Wd San Francisco	79	59
CASSERMAN								
Jacob	43	m	w	FRAN	Calaveras	San Andreas P O	70	204
CASSERNY								
Philip	48	m	w	FRAN	El Dorado	Placerville Twp	72	101
CASSERTY								
John	35	m	w	IREL	San Francisco	11-Wd San Francisc	84	651
CASSERY								
Michael	37	m	w	IREL	San Francisco	11-Wd San Francisc	84	702
CASSES								
Augustus	32	m	w	ITAL	San Francisco	2-Wd San Francisco	79	164
John	41	m	w	ITAL	San Francisco	2-Wd San Francisco	79	150
Leon	40	m	w	NY	San Francisco	6-Wd San Francisco	81	98
CASSESSA								
Louis	25	m	w	ITAL	San Francisco	1-Wd San Francisco	79	36
CASSETT								
James	22	m	w	PRUS	San Francisco	7-Wd San Francisco	81	204
CASSEY								
Alice	35	f	w	IREL	Alameda	Oakland	68	196
David	45	m	w	IREL	Klamath	Liberty Twp	73	374
Frank	39	m	w	IREL	San Francisco	11-Wd San Francisc	84	543
James	27	m	w	IREL	San Francisco	7-Wd San Francisco	81	190
James	24	m	w	MA	San Francisco	7-Wd San Francisco	81	167
John	26	m	w	NY	San Francisco	7-Wd San Francisco	81	177
Joseph	27	m	w	CANA	San Francisco	San Francisco P O	83	351
Lizie	9	f	w	CA	Klamath	Sawyers Bar	73	377
Mich	46	m	w	IREL	Alameda	Oakland	68	230
Peter W	38	m	b	PA	Santa Clara	1-Wd San Jose	88	241
William	30	m	w	IREL	San Francisco	San Francisco P O	83	373
CASSHON								
James	55	m	w	IREL	Contra Costa	Martinez P O	71	426
CASSIA								
Manuel	80	m	w	MEXI	Los Angeles	Los Angeles Twp	73	483
CASSIANO								
Peter	50	m	i	MEXI	San Luis Obispo	San Luis Obispo Tw	87	298
CASSIAS								
James	35	m	w	VT	San Francisco	San Francisco P O	83	36
CASSIDA								
Dennis	21	m	w	RI	Placer	Auburn P O	76	375
CASSIDAY								
B	36	m	w	IREL	Mendocino	Sanel Twp	74	231
H	32	m	w	IREL	Solano	Vallejo	90	200
John	38	m	w	IREL	San Francisco	San Francisco P O	83	167
Mary	25	f	w	IREL	Napa	Napa	75	38
Richd	40	m	w	NY	Solano	Vallejo	90	188
Saml	41	m	w	OH	Santa Clara	Gilroy Twp	88	70
CASSIDY								
Andrew	40	m	w	IREL	San Diego	San Diego	78	483
Barney	50	m	w	IREL	Colusa	Spring Valley Twp	71	341
Bridget	45	f	w	IREL	Los Angeles	Los Angeles	73	536
Danl B	42	m	w	OH	Siskiyou	Table Rock Twp	89	647
Edward	40	m	w	IREL	Yolo	Putah Twp	93	509
Edwin	29	m	w	NY	San Francisco	8-Wd San Francisco	82	339
Ellen	14	f	w	ENGL	Los Angeles	Los Angeles	73	538
Felix	36	m	w	IREL	Sonoma	Santa Rosa	91	424
Felix F	30	m	w	MI	Nevada	Grass Valley Twp	75	170
Francis	48	m	w	IREL	San Francisco	11-Wd San Francisc	84	651
George	29	m	w	IL	Monterey	Pajaro Twp	74	369
Henery	33	m	w	IREL	San Francisco	7-Wd San Francisco	81	187
Henry	26	m	w	IL	Monterey	Pajaro Twp	74	376
Hugh	41	m	w	IREL	Nevada	Grass Valley Twp	75	228
Hugh	41	m	w	IREL	Yuba	Rose Bar Twp	93	665
Hugh	40	m	w	IREL	San Francisco	11-Wd San Francisc	84	526
James	48	m	w	IREL	Yuba	Slate Range Bar Tw	93	668
James	35	m	w	IREL	Alameda	Oakland	68	145
James	29	m	w	CANA	San Diego	San Pasqual Valley	78	525
James	27	m	w	IREL	Solano	Denverton Twp	90	27
James	26	m	w	IREL	Sonoma	Salt Point	91	387
James	25	m	w	VT	San Francisco	7-Wd San Francisco	81	234
James	25	m	w	IREL	San Francisco	6-Wd San Francisco	81	114
Jno C	36	m	w	IREL	San Francisco	San Francisco P O	83	328
John	56	m	w	NY	San Francisco	11-Wd San Francisc	84	613
John	41	m	w	IREL	San Francisco	San Francisco P O	83	250
John	32	m	w	NY	Alameda	Washington Twp	68	283
John W	47	m	w	NJ	Sonoma	Petaluma Twp	91	345
Kate	27	f	w	IREL	San Francisco	8-Wd San Francisco	82	457
Maria	19	f	w	OH	San Francisco	San Francisco P O	83	26
Mary	48	f	w	IREL	San Francisco	San Francisco P O	80	386
Michael	50	m	w	IREL	Tuolumne	Sonora P O	93	328
Michl	22	m	w	IREL	San Francisco	San Francisco P O	83	57
Mike	37	m	w	IREL	Placer	Lincoln P O	76	486
Nellie	14	f	w	NY	San Francisco	8-Wd San Francisco	82	401
P	34	m	w	IREL	Solano	Vallejo	90	141
Patrick	36	m	w	IREL	Santa Cruz	Soquel Twp	89	440
Patrick	26	m	w	IREL	San Francisco	11-Wd San Francisc	84	464
Patrick	25	m	w	IREL	Yolo	Cache Crk Twp	93	432
Philip	40	m	w	IREL	San Francisco	San Francisco P O	83	12
Reuben	55	m	w	KY	Monterey	Pajaro Twp	74	369
Susan	21	f	w	IREL	Santa Cruz	Watsonville	89	376
Terrence	84	m	w	IREL	San Francisco	7-Wd San Francisco	81	166
William	36	m	w	IREL	San Francisco	7-Wd San Francisco	81	166
CASSIE								
Wm	47	m	w	CANA	San Francisco	San Francisco P O	85	865
CASSILAGAS								
Paul	24	m	w	ITAL	San Francisco	2-Wd San Francisco	79	164
CASSILANI								
Joseph	40	m	w	ITAL	Humboldt	Eureka Twp	72	277
CASSILLA								
Hosea	40	m	w	MEXI	Tehama	Red Bluff	92	182
Margerite	45	f	i	CA	Tehama	Red Bluff	92	182
CASSILY								
Patrick	35	m	w	IREL	Yolo	Cache Crk Twp	93	449
CASSIN								
Anne	23	f	w	MA	San Francisco	San Francisco P O	83	110
Bridget	35	f	w	IREL	San Francisco	San Francisco P O	83	111
John	30	m	w	IREL	San Joaquin	Tulare Twp	86	251
John C	39	m	w	NY	San Francisco	1-Wd San Francisco	79	125
John W	60	m	w	IREL	Tehama	Red Bluff	92	179
Joseph	60	m	w	IREL	San Francisco	San Francisco P O	83	189
La Bella	24	f	w	SCOT	Butte	Chico Twp	70	20
Martin	58	m	w	IREL	San Francisco	San Francisco P O	83	214
Martin	36	m	w	IREL	Mendocino	Point Arena Twp	74	215
Mary J	50	f	w	IREL	San Francisco	San Francisco P O	83	283
P J	37	m	w	IREL	San Francisco	San Francisco P O	83	290
Peter	43	m	w	IREL	San Francisco	11-Wd San Francisc	84	516
Thomas	30	m	m	IREL	Nevada	Grass Valley Twp	75	148
CASSINILLI								
Gillamo	37	m	w	ITAL	Amador	Volcano P O	69	385
CASSINLLI								
Leuca	31	m	w	ITAL	Amador	Volcano P O	69	377
CASSINO								
Chas	35	m	w	SAXO	Santa Clara	Gilroy Twp	88	94
CASSINS								
F F	43	m	w	GERM	Humboldt	Pacific Twp	72	298
CASSION								
Dennis	26	m	w	IREL	San Francisco	San Francisco P O	83	130
Owen	57	m	w	IREL	Monterey	Pajaro Twp	74	372
CASSIYAS								
Augustine	27	m	w	MEXI	Plumas	Mineral Twp	77	20
CASSLEBERG								
William	52	m	w	IL	Stanislaus	Empire Twp	92	32
CASSMANN								
John	42	m	w	FRAN	San Francisco	2-Wd San Francisco	79	176
CASSON								
Ellen	28	f	w	IREL	San Francisco	11-Wd San Francisc	84	537
Jno	40	m	w	SCOT	San Joaquin	Douglas Twp	86	44
William	13	m	w	CA	San Francisco	6-Wd San Francisco	81	150
CASSTEL								
Edwd	33	m	w	ENGL	Solano	Vallejo	90	170
CASSUBEN								
Crecencia	28	m	w	SHOL	Santa Barbara	Santa Barbara P O	87	481
CASSWELL								
Allen	37	m	w	CT	San Francisco	7-Wd San Francisco	81	250
CASSY								
Mary	28	f	w	NY	Alameda	Oakland	68	161
CASTA								
Anton	46	m	w	MEXI	Tuolumne	Sonora P O	93	304
Carlos	44	m	w	ITAL	Calaveras	San Andreas P O	70	196
Carmin	19	f	w	CA	San Diego	Fort Yuma Dist	78	463

© 2001 by Heritage Quest. All rights reserved.

Name	Age	S	R	B-PL	County	Locale	Roll	Pg
						Series M593		
De Manuel	22	m	w	PORT	San Mateo	Schoolhouse Statio	87	337
Domingo	27	m	w	AZOR	Nevada	Washington Twp	75	346
F	31	m	w	ITAL	Calaveras	Copperopolis P O	70	232
J	36	m	w	ITAL	Tuolumne	Big Oak Flat P O	93	391
John	28	m	w	ITAL	Calaveras	Copperopolis P O	70	232
Jose	50	m	w	SPAI	San Francisco	San Francisco P O	80	349
Louis	38	m	w	ITAL	Tuolumne	Big Oak Flat P O	93	393
Manuel	58	m	w	PORT	Alameda	Eden Twp	68	82
Michael	41	m	w	SARD	Tuolumne	Sonora P O	93	332
R A	65	m	w	MEXI	Tuolumne	Sonora P O	93	316
Rafupa	31	m	i	MEXI	Inyo	Cerro Gordo Twp	73	320
CASTAGNETO								
Emanul	31	m	w	ITAL	San Francisco	3-Wd San Francisco	79	287
CASTAGNETS								
B	45	m	w	SWIT	Sierra	Downieville Twp	89	517
G B	36	m	w	ITAL	Sierra	Butte Twp	89	512
CASTAGNETT								
Maurice	32	m	w	ITAL	San Francisco	11-Wd San Francisc	84	517
CASTAGNETTE								
F	45	m	w	ITAL	Mariposa	Maxwell Crk P O	74	141
CASTAGNETTO								
Batholomew	33	m	w	ITAL	Mariposa	Mariposa P O	74	109
Domenico	55	m	w	ITAL	Mariposa	Mariposa P O	74	109
John	30	m	w	ITAL	Mariposa	Mariposa P O	74	108
John	20	m	w	ITAL	Mariposa	Mariposa P O	74	113
CASTAGNIOR								
Emanuel	35	m	w	ITAL	San Francisco	2-Wd San Francisco	79	271
CASTAGNNIO								
Lazaro	35	m	w	ITAL	San Francisco	2-Wd San Francisco	79	182
CASTALE								
Margret	32	f	w	IREL	San Francisco	11-Wd San Francisc	84	698
CASTALEW								
Angelo	48	m	w	ITAL	Calaveras	Copperopolis P O	70	250
CASTANA								
Joseppa	22	m	w	ITAL	Calaveras	San Andreas P O	70	183
Manuel	37	m	w	ITAL	Nevada	Bloomfield Twp	75	95
CASTANERO								
Luigi	28	m	w	ITAL	San Francisco	1-Wd San Francisco	79	110
CASTANGAY								
Phillipe	3	m	w	MEXI	San Francisco	San Francisco P O	80	337
CASTANIAS								
Jose M	51	m	w	MEXI	San Luis Obispo	Arroyo Grande Twp	87	277
CASTANOS								
Felipe	31	m	w	MEXI	Santa Clara	Gilroy Twp	88	77
CASTATER								
Eva	15	f	w	WI	Amador	Fiddletown P O	69	432
CASTAVEN								
Jesus	44	f	w	MEXI	San Francisco	2-Wd San Francisco	79	168
CASTE								
John	61	m	w	FRAN	Mariposa	Mariposa P O	74	91
CASTEEL								
Francis L	47	m	w	IL	Tulare	Visalia Twp	92	285
Jas A	32	m	w	IN	Siskiyou	Big Valley Twp	89	580
Pierce	46	m	w	OH	El Dorado	Georgetown Twp	72	40
William	42	m	w	IN	Siskiyou	Big Valley Twp	89	580
CASTEGNETO								
Peter	36	m	w	ITAL	San Francisco	San Francisco P O	80	463
CASTEIL								
Mary	60	f	w	IREL	Los Angeles	Los Angeles	73	545
CASTELHUN								
Frederick	28	m	w	HDAR	San Francisco	8-Wd San Francisco	82	451
CASTELING								
Jacob	47	m	w	BAVA	Colusa	Monroe Twp	71	316
CASTELL								
B S	9	m	w	LA	San Francisco	San Francisco P O	85	800
CASTELLANICH								
Sam	35	m	w	AUST	Butte	Ophir Twp	70	93
CASTELLE								
N G	54	m	w	MEXI	Monterey	Alisal Twp	74	296
CASTELLO								
Antonio	41	m	w	SPAI	San Francisco	San Francisco P O	83	69
Berhena	36	f	w	MEXI	Santa Clara	2-Wd San Jose	88	311
Bridget M	52	f	w	IREL	Sonoma	Petaluma Twp	91	335
Daniel	27	m	w	IREL	Solano	Silveyville Twp	90	75
Danl	6	m	w	CA	Sacramento	3-Wd Sacramento	77	278
Ed	42	m	w	IREL	San Joaquin	2-Wd Stockton	86	203
Edward	24	m	w	IREL	Santa Clara	Santa Clara Twp	88	161
Emanuel	48	m	w	MEXI	Plumas	Quartz Twp	77	44
Frances	36	m	w	IREL	Nevada	Washington Twp	75	345
Francisco	40	m	w	MEXI	Monterey	Castroville Twp	74	334
Francisco	38	m	w	MEXI	Fresno	Millerton P O	72	155
Francisco	12	m	w	CA	Los Angeles	Los Angeles Twp	73	465
Franquelino	37	m	w	MEXI	Los Angeles	Los Nietos Twp	73	585
Henry	44	m	w	ENGL	San Francisco	San Francisco P O	80	485
Isaac	29	m	w	AR	Siskiyou	Scott Valley Twp	89	618
James	37	m	w	IREL	Butte	Ophir Twp	70	98
James	33	m	w	PA	Sacramento	San Joaquin Twp	77	396
John	32	m	w	ECUA	Inyo	Cerro Gordo Twp	73	318
Jose	54	m	w	MEXI	Contra Costa	Martinez P O	71	440
Juan	40	m	w	CA	Monterey	San Antonio Twp	74	315
Juanna	45	f	w	MEXI	Santa Clara	1-Wd San Jose	88	255
Oliver	50	m	w	IREL	Sacramento	4-Wd Sacramento	77	323
Patrick	25	m	w	IREL	San Francisco	1-Wd San Francisco	79	105
Peter	24	m	w	IREL	Sacramento	3-Wd Sacramento	77	287
Ramon	33	m	w	MEXI	Los Angeles	Los Angeles Twp	73	465
Theodora	36	f	w	MEXI	Santa Clara	2-Wd San Jose	88	311
Thomas	36	m	w	TN	Stanislaus	Empire Twp	92	58
W R	23	m	w	CANA	San Francisco	3-Wd San Francisco	79	316
CASTELO								
James	40	m	w	IREL	San Francisco	San Francisco P O	85	763
John	23	m	w	IREL	Monterey	Salinas Twp	74	311
CASTELOVITCH								
John	30	m	w	AUST	Amador	Sutter Crk P O	69	405
CASTENEDA								
Jesus	36	m	w	MEXI	San Francisco	San Francisco P O	80	412
CASTENI								
J	35	m	w	AZOR	El Dorado	Greenwood Twp	72	51
CASTENS								
Henry	38	m	w	HANO	Sonoma	Analy Twp	91	237
CASTENSON								
Aury	26	m	w	DENM	Sutter	Nicolaus Twp	92	115
CASTER								
Charles	44	m	w	NY	San Francisco	San Francisco P O	80	390
D D	56	m	b	MO	Nevada	Nevada Twp	75	274
Elizabeth	14	f	w	CA	Alameda	Oakland	68	143
John	36	m	w	PRUS	San Francisco	2-Wd San Francisco	79	284
John	36	m	w	PRUS	San Francisco	2-Wd San Francisco	79	147
CASTERA								
Charles	31	m	w	FRAN	San Francisco	6-Wd San Francisco	81	37
CASTERHOLT								
Jonas	52	m	w	NY	Colusa	Monroe Twp	71	319
CASTERSON								
Thos	30	m	w	DENM	San Joaquin	2-Wd Stockton	86	172
CASTIA								
Antonio	48	m	w	CA	San Luis Obispo	San Luis Obispo Tw	87	307
Daniel	30	m	w	IREL	San Francisco	San Francisco P O	83	385
Joseph	34	m	w	BAVA	San Francisco	San Francisco P O	83	232
Sanon	19	m	w	MEXI	Santa Clara	Burnett Twp	88	34
CASTIDO								
Delphino	25	m	w	MEXI	Santa Clara	Burnett Twp	88	35
CASTILE								
Bicenta	4	m	w	MEXI	San Francisco	San Francisco P O	80	459
James	28	m	w	MO	Lassen	Susanville Twp	73	444
Jessee	38	m	w	OH	San Luis Obispo	Arroyo Grande Twp	87	270
Jessie	40	m	w	US	Nevada	Little York Twp	75	239
John	40	m	w	MO	Lassen	Susanville Twp	73	444
CASTILLA								
Andreas	77	m	w	MEXI	Mariposa	Mariposa P O	74	123
Lorenza	28	f	w	MEXI	Mariposa	Mariposa P O	74	96
CASTILLE								
Rafael	30	m	w	MEXI	Santa Barbara	San Buenaventura P	87	435
CASTILLIA								
Josi	30	m	w	MEXI	San Francisco	7-Wd San Francisco	81	260
CASTILLIO								
Trinidad	18	f	w	MEXI	Santa Barbara	San Buenaventura P	87	433
CASTILLO								
Adolfo	9	m	w	CA	Santa Cruz	Pajaro Twp	89	361
Amarantho	45	m	w	MEXI	Los Angeles	Wilmington Twp	73	636
Ambrose	50	m	w	CA	San Bernardino	San Bernardino Twp	78	442
Eustemio	46	m	w	MEXI	Monterey	San Benito Twp	74	380
Gervasio	50	m	w	MEXI	Los Angeles	Los Nietos Twp	73	582
Henry	25	m	w	OH	Kern	Bakersfield P O	73	365
Jacques	17	m	w	FRAN	San Francisco	11-Wd San Francisc	84	556
Jeronimo	41	m	w	MEXI	Los Angeles	Los Angeles	73	554
Jesus	30	m	w	MEXI	Los Angeles	Santa Ana Twp	73	600
Joaquin	25	m	w	MEXI	Los Angeles	Soledad Twp	73	631
Joaquin	19	m	w	MEXI	Los Angeles	Soledad Twp	73	631
John	21	m	w	PORT	Marin	Nicasio Twp	74	19
Jordon	20	m	w	MEXI	Los Angeles	Santa Ana Twp	73	614
Joseph	49	m	w	IL	San Bernardino	San Bernardino Twp	78	439
Juan	36	m	w	SPAI	Plumas	Quartz Twp	77	41
Juan	26	m	w	CA	San Diego	San Luis Rey	78	514
Loretto	46	m	w	MEXI	Placer	Auburn P O	76	358
M F	40	m	w	CA	Alameda	San Leandro	68	98
Manuel	48	m	w	MEXI	San Bernardino	San Salvador Twp	78	460
Manwell	30	m	w	ITAL	San Mateo	Half Moon Bay P O	87	391
Marcedona	33	m	w	MEXI	Plumas	Goodwin Twp	77	5
Matias	57	m	w	MEXI	San Bernardino	San Salvador Twp	78	456
Ramon	47	m	w	MEXI	Santa Barbara	San Buenaventura P	87	427
Thomas	28	m	w	ENGL	Alameda	Washington Twp	68	296
CASTILLONA								
Andrea	33	m	w	ITAL	Amador	Volcano P O	69	377
CASTIN								
Henry	26	m	w	HAMB	San Francisco	1-Wd San Francisco	79	96
Henry	22	m	w	ITAL	San Mateo	Schoolhouse Statio	87	346
Jares	25	m	w	FRAN	San Francisco	2-Wd San Francisco	79	174
John	15	m	w	ITAL	San Mateo	Schoolhouse Statio	87	346
CASTINA								
Dolores	32	f	w	MEXI	San Francisco	San Francisco P O	80	475
CASTINE								
Custer	26	m	w	ITAL	San Francisco	11-Wd San Francisc	84	712
Henry	45	m	w	GERM	Nevada	Rough & Ready Twp	75	330
Louis	55	m	w	BREM	Yuba	Bullards Bar P O	93	550
CASTINER								
Thos	28	m	w	NY	San Francisco	1-Wd San Francisco	79	14
CASTINETTE								
A	37	m	w	ITAL	Sacramento	3-Wd Sacramento	77	303
CASTINO								
Devotion	30	m	w	ITAL	San Mateo	Schoolhouse Statio	87	343
Henry	21	m	w	ITAL	San Mateo	Schoolhouse Statio	87	345
John	22	m	w	ITAL	San Mateo	Schoolhouse Statio	87	343
CASTION								
William	28	m	w	FRAN	Santa Clara	Fremont Twp	88	44

© 2001 by Heritage Quest. All rights reserved.

Name	Age	S	R	B-PL	County	Locale	Series M593 Roll	Pg
CASTLAS								
Pat	65	m	w	IREL	San Francisco	11-Wd San Francisc	84	616
CASTLE								
A S	30	m	w	IL	Nevada	Meadow Lake Twp	75	258
Albert	9	m	w	CA	Alameda	Brooklyn Twp	68	40
Albert	8	m	w	CA	Alameda	Oakland	68	159
Albert J	65	m	w	NY	Amador	Fiddletown P O	69	435
Charles	34	m	w	ENGL	San Francisco	San Francisco P O	83	76
Charlotte	68	f	w	ENGL	San Francisco	San Francisco P O	83	93
Charlotte T	12	f	w	CA	Santa Clara	1-Wd San Jose	88	245
Christ	40	m	w	NY	San Joaquin	Union Twp	86	268
Geo	47	m	w	NY	San Joaquin	Dent Twp	86	20
Geo F	40	m	w	MD	Siskiyou	Yreka	89	661
Hanah	43	f	w	NH	San Francisco	7-Wd San Francisco	81	174
Isaac	71	m	w	NY	Santa Clara	Milpitas Twp	88	110
J	22	m	w	BADE	Sacramento	3-Wd Sacramento	77	313
James	54	m	w	ENGL	Mariposa	Mariposa P O	74	111
James	38	m	w	NY	San Joaquin	Oneal Twp	86	105
Joseph	29	m	w	ENGL	San Francisco	1-Wd San Francisco	79	124
Michael	42	m	w	ENGL	San Francisco	8-Wd San Francisco	82	452
Michael	28	m	w	IREL	Placer	Newcastle Twp	76	473
Orrin	23	m	w	IL	Amador	Fiddletown P O	69	430
Sam	29	m	w	OH	San Joaquin	Elkhorn Twp	86	62
Wellman	45	m	w	NY	Santa Clara	Milpitas Twp	88	110
William	36	m	w	IL	Sonoma	Russian Rvr	91	376
William N	43	m	w	SWED	Santa Clara	2-Wd San Jose	88	284
CASTLEHAN								
John F	27	m	w	HDAR	San Francisco	6-Wd San Francisco	81	73
CASTLEMAN								
F	43	f	w	IREL	San Francisco	San Francisco P O	83	319
CASTLERING								
Edmund	23	m	w	MI	Colusa	Monroe Twp	71	315
CASTLES								
Henry M	43	m	w	CANA	Yolo	Grafton Twp	93	494
Margaret	61	f	w	VA	Santa Clara	1-Wd San Jose	88	239
CASTLEY								
William	36	m	w	CANA	Sonoma	Mendocino Twp	91	291
CASTLO								
S W	45	m	w	VT	Solano	Vallejo	90	172
CASTNER								
Daniel J	48	m	w	NY	Placer	Roseville P O	76	349
Emma D	26	f	w	IL	Placer	Bath P O	76	431
Louis	34	m	w	PRUS	Sacramento	4-Wd Sacramento	77	372
Wm H	38	m	w	ME	Solano	Vallejo	90	159
CASTO								
John	26	m	w	FINL	Sutter	Nicolaus Twp	92	109
Jonathan S	51	m	w	OH	Shasta	Horsetown P O	89	501
Tim E	42	m	w	IN	Sonoma	Santa Rosa	91	428
CASTOE								
Jas	32	m	w	PRUS	Sacramento	1-Wd Sacramento	77	203
CASTOER								
Julius	30	m	w	PRUS	San Francisco	2-Wd San Francisco	79	153
CASTON								
Fredk	28	m	w	NY	San Francisco	5-Wd San Francisco	81	30
J	35	m	w	MA	Alameda	Oakland	68	247
CASTONET								
John	35	m	w	FRAN	San Mateo	Schoolhouse Statio	87	341
CASTONS								
Jno H	25	m	w	HANO	San Francisco	San Francisco P O	83	14
CASTOR								
Alex	38	m	w	ITAL	Yuba	Marysville	93	586
Fred	25	m	w	ITAL	Yuba	Marysville	93	586
Henry	36	m	w	GERM	Los Angeles	Los Angeles	73	529
Jacob	37	m	w	OH	Calaveras	Copperopolis P O	70	234
Joe	28	m	w	ITAL	Yuba	Marysville	93	586
Wilhilma	48	f	w	PRUS	Mariposa	Mariposa P O	74	119
CASTORA								
Charles	31	m	w	FRAN	San Francisco	San Francisco P O	80	480
CASTORNA								
Jesus	24	m	w	MEXI	San Francisco	San Francisco P O	80	424
CASTRA								
Sarah	15	f	w	CA	San Francisco	San Francisco P O	83	408
CASTRE								
Jose	48	m	w	MEXI	San Joaquin	Dent Twp	86	24
Louisa	29	f	w	MEXI	Mariposa	Mariposa P O	74	95
CASTREA								
John	41	m	w	FRAN	San Francisco	San Francisco P O	80	467
CASTRO								
A	59	m	w	CA	Santa Clara	Gilroy Twp	88	89
Addie	8	f	w	MEXI	Contra Costa	Martinez P O	71	439
Agaton	26	m	w	MEXI	Santa Clara	San Jose Twp	88	184
Amendo	20	m	w	MEXI	San Diego	Coronado	78	467
Andreas	38	m	w	MEXI	Fresno	Kingston P O	72	217
Andrew	25	m	w	CA	Contra Costa	San Pablo Twp	71	356
Andrew	17	m	w	CA	Santa Clara	Almaden Twp	88	14
Angel	38	m	w	MEXI	San Mateo	Half Moon Bay P O	87	393
Antoine	36	m	w	MEXI	Stanislaus	San Joaquin Twp	92	74
Antomio	27	m	w	MEXI	Kern	Bakersfield P O	73	357
Antonia	50	f	w	MEXI	Santa Clara	Almaden Twp	88	12
Antonio	70	m	w	CA	Los Angeles	San Gabriel Twp	73	594
Antonio	45	m	w	CA	Santa Cruz	Soquel Twp	89	438
Antonio	26	m	w	MEXI	Kern	Tehachapi P O	73	356
Atelana	11	f	w	CA	Santa Clara	2-Wd San Jose	88	308
Augustin	32	m	w	CA	Los Angeles	Los Angeles Twp	73	472
Augustin	28	m	w	MEXI	San Francisco	San Francisco P O	80	472
Beatrice	40	f	w	MEXI	Santa Clara	1-Wd San Jose	88	231
Beatrice	15	f	w	CA	San Francisco	2-Wd San Francisco	79	269
Blas	50	m	w	CA	San Luis Obispo	San Luis Obispo Tw	87	306
Carlos	24	m	w	MEXI	Stanislaus	Empire Twp	92	63
Columbo	9	m	w	MEXI	Marin	Sausalito Twp	74	68
Crisanto	42	m	w	CA	Santa Clara	Fremont Twp	88	62
Crisnetimo	43	m	w	CA	Monterey	Monterey Twp	74	343
Daniel	18	m	w	CA	San Luis Obispo	Morro Twp	87	286
Dolores	37	m	w	MEXI	Santa Clara	Redwood Twp	88	119
Doroles	30	m	w	AZOR	San Luis Obispo	San Luis Obispo Tw	87	308
Emma	15	f	w	CA	San Francisco	2-Wd San Francisco	79	190
Emmo	60	m	w	MEXI	El Dorado	Placerville Twp	72	96
Essus	19	f	w	MEXI	Sacramento	2-Wd Sacramento	77	216
Esteven	10	m	w	CA	Monterey	Castroville Twp	74	326
Felipe	63	m	w	CA	Santa Cruz	Santa Cruz Twp	89	383
Felipe	37	m	w	MEXI	Kern	Bakersfield P O	73	365
Francis	24	m	w	GUAT	San Francisco	7-Wd San Francisco	81	287
Francisco	58	m	w	MEXI	Santa Clara	Burnett Twp	88	34
Francisco	50	f	w	MEXI	Santa Clara	1-Wd San Jose	88	264
Francisco	45	m	w	CA	Santa Cruz	Pajaro Twp	89	362
Francisco	40	m	w	CA	San Luis Obispo	San Luis Obispo Tw	87	298
Francisco	38	m	w	CA	Monterey	Castroville Twp	74	325
Francisco	28	m	w	CA	Monterey	San Juan Twp	74	387
Francisco	14	m	w	CA	Monterey	Monterey	74	360
Frank	35	m	w	CA	Alameda	Oakland	68	153
Frank	28	m	w	PARA	Alameda	Oakland	68	165
Genevieve	16	f	w	CA	Monterey	San Juan Twp	74	408
Geo	45	m	w	CHIL	Sierra	Table Rock Twp	89	579
Geo	35	m	w	PA	El Dorado	Greenwood Twp	72	55
George	34	m	w	CA	Monterey	San Juan Twp	74	403
Guadalupe	56	m	w	CA	Santa Cruz	Pajaro Twp	89	360
Hayo	40	m	w	MEXI	Stanislaus	Empire Twp	92	63
Ignacio	40	m	i	MEXI	Los Angeles	Los Angeles Twp	73	498
Igncio	34	m	w	MEXI	Merced	Snelling P O	74	248
J M	50	m	w	CA	Alameda	Oakland	68	133
James	26	m	w	IL	Stanislaus	Empire Twp	92	42
Jesus	85	m	w	MEXI	San Bernardino	Chino Twp	78	412
Jesus	29	m	w	MEXI	San Francisco	San Francisco P O	80	468
Jesus	28	m	w	CA	Monterey	San Juan Twp	74	387
Joaquin	50	m	w	CA	Santa Cruz	Pajaro Twp	89	362
Joaquin	40	m	w	CA	Fresno	Millerton P O	72	146
Joaquin	23	m	w	CA	Santa Cruz	Soquel Twp	89	437
Jos	21	m	w	PORT	Solano	Vallejo	90	199
Jos M	42	m	w	CA	Monterey	San Juan Twp	74	407
Jose	58	m	w	CA	Monterey	Monterey Twp	74	344
Jose	50	m	w	MEXI	Santa Clara	Almaden Twp	88	11
Jose	42	m	w	CA	Monterey	San Juan Twp	74	403
Jose	35	m	w	PA	Santa Clara	Almaden Twp	88	1
Jose	32	m	w	CA	Contra Costa	San Pablo Twp	71	358
Jose	28	m	w	CA	Marin	San Rafael	74	56
Jose	25	m	w	CA	Santa Clara	Gilroy Twp	88	91
Jose	22	m	w	CA	Los Angeles	Los Angeles	73	564
Jose	21	m	w	CA	Los Angeles	Los Angeles	73	568
Jose A	40	m	w	CA	Marin	San Rafael Twp	74	40
Jose Ig	23	m	w	CA	Santa Clara	Gilroy Twp	88	87
Jose Maria	48	m	w	CA	Monterey	Castroville Twp	74	327
Joseph	37	m	w	CHIL	Sacramento	2-Wd Sacramento	77	254
Joseph	36	m	w	MEXI	Solano	Vacaville Twp	90	125
Juan	40	m	w	MEXI	Fresno	Kingston P O	72	217
Juan	28	m	w	MEXI	San Joaquin	Dent Twp	86	29
Juan	23	m	w	CA	Marin	San Rafael Twp	74	43
Juan	20	m	w	CA	San Francisco	San Francisco P O	80	471
Juan	18	m	w	MEXI	San Francisco	1-Wd San Francisco	79	111
Juan B	35	m	w	CA	Monterey	Castroville Twp	74	325
Juan Jose	68	m	w	CA	Santa Cruz	Pajaro Twp	89	362
Juana	16	f	w	CA	Santa Clara	Gilroy Twp	88	90
Juliana	41	f	w	MEXI	Los Angeles	Los Angeles	73	562
Leandro	36	m	w	CA	Monterey	Castroville Twp	74	325
Leone	41	f	w	MEXI	San Francisco	6-Wd San Francisco	81	111
Lorencio	41	m	w	MEXI	Los Angeles	Los Angeles	73	552
Louis	27	m	w	CA	Alameda	San Leandro	68	97
Luciano	27	m	w	MEXI	Monterey	Castroville Twp	74	332
Manuel	50	m	w	CA	San Francisco	San Francisco P O	83	284
Manuel	45	m	w	CA	Santa Cruz	Pajaro Twp	89	361
Manuel	40	m	w	CHIL	El Dorado	Coloma Twp	72	5
Manuel	36	m	w	MEXI	Sacramento	2-Wd Sacramento	77	237
Manuel	14	m	w	MEXI	Monterey	Monterey Twp	74	346
Manuel A	42	m	w	CA	Monterey	Castroville Twp	74	332
Marcand	18	f	w	CA	Alameda	Oakland	68	252
Margareta	25	f	w	MEXI	Los Angeles	Los Angeles	73	555
Maria	7	f	w	CA	Los Angeles	El Monte Twp	73	453
Maria A	68	f	w	CA	Monterey	Monterey	74	362
Mariana	27	m	w	CA	San Francisco	1-Wd San Francisco	79	57
Marie A	50	f	w	CA	Santa Cruz	Santa Cruz Twp	89	382
Marino	60	m	w	MEXI	Kern	Tehachapi P O	73	355
Martin	33	m	w	CA	Santa Cruz	Soquel Twp	89	450
Martina	23	f	w	CA	Contra Costa	San Pablo Twp	71	359
Mary	37	f	w	CA	San Francisco	2-Wd San Francisco	79	189
Matthew	36	m	w	SCOT	Siskiyou	Yreka Twp	89	668
Merce O	70	f	w	CA	Monterey	Monterey	74	366
Miguel	53	m	w	CA	Monterey	San Juan Twp	74	387
Miguel Jr	25	m	w	CA	Monterey	San Juan Twp	74	387
Modesta	52	f	w	CA	San Luis Obispo	Arroyo Grande Twp	87	276
Nicholas	40	m	w	GREE	San Francisco	11-Wd San Francisc	84	523
Pablino	46	m	w	MEXI	Kern	Bakersfield P O	73	362
Pafillio	15	m	w	CA	Santa Cruz	Watsonville	89	365
Patrick	27	m	w	CA	Contra Costa	Martinez Twp	71	352
Pedro	17	m	w	MEXI	San Francisco	1-Wd San Francisco	79	14
Petra	63	f	w	CA	Contra Costa	San Pablo Twp	71	359

© 2001 by Heritage Quest. All rights reserved.

Name	Age	S	R	B-PL	County	Locale	Series M593 Roll	Pg
Philemon	21	m	w	CA	Santa Clara	Fremont Twp	88	46
Proviso	38	f	w	CA	Contra Costa	San Pablo Twp	71	365
Quando	49	m	w	MEXI	San Francisco	San Francisco P O	80	341
Rafael	67	m	w	CA	Santa Cruz	Soquel Twp	89	438
Rafiel	33	m	w	CA	Monterey	Castroville Twp	74	332
Ramon	55	m	w	CA	Santa Barbara	Santa Barbara P O	87	495
Ramon	47	m	w	CA	Contra Costa	San Pablo Twp	71	365
Ramon	33	m	w	CA	Santa Cruz	Pajaro Twp	89	357
Ramon	30	m	w	MEXI	Los Angeles	Los Angeles Twp	73	467
Ramon	22	m	w	MEXI	Santa Clara	Almaden Twp	88	6
Refufio	25	m	w	MEXI	Kern	Bakersfield P O	73	359
Remano	3	f	w	CA	Fresno	Millerton P O	72	146
Ricardo	33	m	w	CA	Santa Cruz	Pajaro Twp	89	360
Romano	32	m	w	MEXI	San Luis Obispo	San Luis Obispo Tw	87	298
Rose	5	f	w	CA	Solano	Benicia	90	16
Salvador	40	m	w	CA	Santa Clara	Gilroy Twp	88	89
Silvano	18	m	w	MEXI	Fresno	Millerton P O	72	163
Simon	30	m	w	CA	Santa Cruz	Pajaro Twp	89	360
T	20	m	w	MEXI	Yuba	Marysville	93	617
Teresa	40	f	w	MEXI	San Francisco	6-Wd San Francisco	81	71
Thomas	40	m	w	MEXI	Kern	Bakersfield P O	73	363
Timbatao	19	m	w	CA	Santa Cruz	Soquel Twp	89	440
Trevedad	28	m	w	MEXI	Los Angeles	Los Angeles	73	541
Trinidad	80	f	w	CA	Santa Clara	Santa Clara Twp	88	157
Vicente	35	m	w	CA	Santa Cruz	Soquel Twp	89	438
Victor	50	m	w	CA	Contra Costa	San Pablo Twp	71	363
Vidal	35	m	w	MEXI	Fresno	Millerton P O	72	167
William	38	m	w	MEXI	Butte	Ophir Twp	70	114
William	28	m	w	CA	Alameda	San Leandro	68	97
William	18	m	w	CA	Los Angeles	Los Angeles	73	542
Ygnacio	24	m	w	CA	Monterey	Castroville Twp	74	325
CASTRUCIO								
Peter	26	m	w	ITAL	Los Angeles	Los Angeles	73	547
CASTUE								
Ann	45	f	w	IREL	Alameda	Oakland	68	203
CASTURF								
Henry	34	m	w	PRUS	Sacramento	2-Wd Sacramento	77	230
CASTY								
John	25	m	w	IREL	San Mateo	San Mateo P O	87	360
Richard	34	m	w	IREL	San Francisco	7-Wd San Francisco	81	257
CASUAR								
Pedro	30	m	w	FRAN	Los Angeles	Los Angeles Twp	73	478
CASURE								
Martin	55	m	w	AL	San Diego	Poway Dist	78	481
CASUSO								
Jea	46	m	w	CHIL	Fresno	Millerton P O	72	153
CASWELL								
Adam	31	m	w	ME	San Diego	San Diego	78	497
Alex	29	m	w	NY	Butte	Chico Twp	70	14
Benjamin E	37	m	w	MA	Santa Clara	2-Wd San Jose	88	298
H	33	m	w	OH	Lake	Morgan Valley	73	424
Harvey	65	m	w	CT	San Francisco	8-Wd San Francisco	82	392
Henry	58	m	w	IREL	Sacramento	Sutter Twp	77	383
John	60	m	w	ME	Amador	Sutter Crk P O	69	414
John	28	m	w	NORW	San Francisco	7-Wd San Francisco	81	220
John C	47	m	w	RI	Marin	Sausalito Twp	74	67
Julia	33	f	w	ME	San Francisco	San Francisco P O	83	270
Laura	17	f	w	OH	Lake	Morgan Valley	73	424
Samuel B	42	m	w	MA	Los Angeles	Los Angeles	73	544
Thomas C	13	m	w	WI	Stanislaus	Empire Twp	92	51
Wm	44	m	w	NY	San Francisco	7-Wd San Francisco	81	241
Wm	35	m	w	NORW	San Francisco	San Francisco P O	83	115
CASY								
Edward	23	m	w	IREL	San Francisco	San Francisco P O	85	822
James F	45	m	w	OH	El Dorado	Diamond Springs Tw	72	34
John	40	m	w	NY	San Bernardino	San Bernardino Twp	78	437
Mary	30	f	w	IREL	San Mateo	San Mateo P O	87	356
CAT								
Ah	45	m	c	CHIN	Tuolumne	Chinese Camp P O	93	389
Ah	43	m	c	CHIN	Merced	Snelling P O	74	250
CATA								
Cirafica	40	m	w	MEXI	San Diego	San Pasqual	78	519
CATAGAL								
Louisa	35	f	w	MEXI	Sacramento	2-Wd Sacramento	77	225
CATAH								
J	7	f	w	CA	Amador	Drytown P O	69	415
CATALAN								
Octave	26	m	w	FRAN	San Francisco	San Francisco P O	80	535
CATANE								
Rice	64	m	w	SCOT	Sacramento	Sutter Twp	77	385
CATANEO								
Emanuel	50	m	w	CA	San Bernardino	San Salvador Twp	78	457
Frank	48	m	w	ITAL	Contra Costa	Martinez P O	71	400
Jesus	29	m	w	CA	San Bernardino	San Salvador Twp	78	455
CATANO								
Joseph	30	m	w	SCOT	Alameda	Brooklyn Twp	68	45
CATAPLDE								
Eleanor	13	f	w	CA	Calaveras	San Andreas P O	70	214
CATCHMAN								
R E	38	m	w	IL	San Joaquin	Douglas Twp	86	42
CATE								
Chas	44	m	w	ENGL	Sacramento	3-Wd Sacramento	77	270
Daniel R	46	m	w	NH	Plumas	Plumas Twp	77	30
George N	20	m	w	MA	Sacramento	2-Wd Sacramento	77	216
John K	55	m	w	NH	Butte	Wyandotte Twp	70	144
Joseph	53	m	w	MA	San Francisco	11-Wd San Francisc	84	488
Lafayette F	41	m	w	NH	Plumas	Plumas Twp	77	32

Name	Age	S	R	B-PL	County	Locale	Series M593 Roll	Pg
M E	32	f	w	ME	Sacramento	3-Wd Sacramento	77	269
Reuben	55	m	w	TN	Placer	Lincoln P O	76	490
Thomas	20	m	w	MO	Placer	Lincoln P O	76	490
CATECHI								
John	35	m	w	ITAL	San Francisco	San Francisco P O	83	222
CATEL								
Domingo	38	m	w	FRAN	Plumas	Rich Bar Twp	77	45
CATEN								
Joseph	17	m	w	PORT	Alameda	Eden Twp	68	69
CATENA								
Chas	17	m	w	OH	Butte	Chico Twp	70	17
CATER								
Charles	29	m	w	ENGL	San Francisco	6-Wd San Francisco	81	109
CATERS								
Fredrick	38	m	w	WURT	Placer	Summit P O	76	496
CATES								
Clamisse	61	f	w	ME	Monterey	Alisal Twp	74	291
James W	40	m	w	IL	Los Angeles	Los Nietos Twp	73	588
Joseph	40	m	w	ENGL	Sacramento	Sutter Twp	77	381
Lucinda	38	f	w	ME	Alameda	Washington Twp	68	285
Lucinda	36	f	w	ME	Alameda	Washington Twp	68	284
Richard	27	m	w	NY	San Mateo	Schoolhouse Statio	87	342
Thomas	68	m	w	ME	Marin	Novato Twp	74	12
CATHARINE								
M	17	f	w	NY	Klamath	Trinidad Twp	73	389
CATHARS								
Margat	65	f	w	IREL	Monterey	Pajaro Twp	74	370
CATHAY								
Andw M	25	m	w	AR	Fresno	Millerton P O	72	149
CATHCART								
Alex S	33	m	w	MA	Placer	Roseville P O	76	352
Hannah	21	f	w	NJ	Sonoma	Sonoma Twp	91	436
Isabelle	3	f	w	CA	Alameda	Eden Twp	68	61
James	46	m	w	IREL	San Francisco	1-Wd San Francisco	79	9
John	40	m	w	SCOT	San Francisco	1-Wd San Francisco	79	14
Julius	35	m	w	NY	Alameda	Eden Twp	68	89
Morris	28	m	w	IREL	San Joaquin	3-Wd Stockton	86	220
Thos	14	m	w	CA	Alameda	Eden Twp	68	83
William	40	m	w	NJ	San Francisco	San Francisco P O	83	205
Wm	42	m	w	MI	Humboldt	Eel Rvr Twp	72	251
CATHEART								
William	54	m	w	MA	San Francisco	San Francisco P O	80	413
CATHELIN								
Joseph	25	m	w	FRAN	San Francisco	8-Wd San Francisco	82	355
CATHER								
Catherine	33	m	w	WALE	Butte	Oregon Twp	70	122
Danial	55	m	w	IREL	San Francisco	7-Wd San Francisco	81	189
Mary Anne	36	f	w	IREL	San Francisco	1-Wd San Francisco	79	72
Thos	29	m	w	AL	San Joaquin	Dent Twp	86	29
CATHERWOOD								
Robt	48	m	w	IREL	Santa Clara	Almaden Twp	88	3
CATHEY								
Andrew	66	m	w	NC	Mariposa	Mariposa P O	74	90
Danl	39	m	w	NC	Fresno	Millerton P O	72	149
James	22	m	w	AR	Mariposa	Mariposa P O	74	90
John	47	m	w	MO	Humboldt	Mattole Twp	72	283
John B	34	m	w	MO	Mendocino	Anderson Twp	74	152
Nathaniel L	36	m	w	GA	Mariposa	Mariposa P O	74	90
Thomas	28	m	w	MO	Humboldt	Mattole Twp	72	283
Wm P	31	m	w	GA	Mariposa	Mariposa P O	74	125
CATHOURN								
George	35	m	w	IL	San Diego	San Diego	78	499
CATHRIN								
Susan	17	f	w	IN	Sacramento	Franklin Twp	77	120
W S	50	m	w	NY	Sacramento	4-Wd Sacramento	77	353
CATHRON								
William	49	m	w	MO	Stanislaus	San Joaquin Twp	92	82
CATIN								
Manuel	34	m	w	PORT	San Francisco	1-Wd San Francisco	79	94
CATLIN								
A P	45	m	w	NY	Sacramento	1-Wd Sacramento	77	186
Brant D F	43	m	w	NY	San Mateo	Redwood Twp	87	366
Elom	36	m	w	NY	Sonoma	Mendocino Twp	91	295
John	22	m	w	PRUS	San Francisco	San Francisco P O	85	758
John	20	m	w	NY	Santa Cruz	Pajaro Twp	89	350
Julius	31	m	w	ME	Plumas	Quartz Twp	77	36
Oliver W	38	m	w	NY	Santa Clara	Redwood Twp	88	120
Warren M	58	m	w	NY	Mariposa	Maxwell Crk P O	74	141
CATLIP								
Jacob	30	m	w	PRUS	San Francisco	San Francisco P O	83	390
CATNEY								
Edw C	39	m	w	NY	Tehama	Paskenta Twp	92	163
CATO								
Antone	28	m	w	SCOT	San Luis Obispo	San Luis Obispo Tw	87	297
John	40	m	w	MEXI	Butte	Oregon Twp	70	123
CATOIR								
Daniel	55	m	w	PRUS	San Francisco	San Francisco P O	83	373
CATON								
Emanuel	47	m	w	AZOR	San Francisco	1-Wd San Francisco	79	58
Lizzie	30	f	w	IL	Santa Clara	Milpitas Twp	88	111
Manuel	36	m	w	AZOR	San Francisco	1-Wd San Francisco	79	102
Manuel	30	m	w	AZOR	Placer	Newcastle Twp	76	474
Thomas	25	m	w	IREL	Humboldt	Eureka Twp	72	277
CATOR								
Frank	50	m	w	MD	San Francisco	1-Wd San Francisco	79	97
Frank	48	m	w	MD	San Francisco	5-Wd San Francisco	81	22
Thomas	25	m	w	IREL	San Mateo	Redwood Twp	87	367

© 2001 by Heritage Quest. All rights reserved.

Name	Age	S	R	B-PL	County	Locale	Series M593 Roll	Pg
CATOSKY								
Leander	48	m	w	NY	San Joaquin	Douglas Twp	86	34
CATRICK								
Joseph	32	m	w	NY	San Bernardino	San Bernardino Twp	78	418
CATRIN								
Joseph	52	m	w	FRAN	Trinity	Junction City Pct	92	209
CATRON								
A S	45	m	w	TN	Calaveras	Copperopolis P O	70	223
Atford G	28	m	w	ENGL	Fresno	Millerton P O	72	167
Greenbery	40	m	w	MO	Tulare	Farmersville Twp	92	243
Joseph M	35	m	w	ENGL	Nevada	Grass Valley Twp	75	187
Manuel	17	m	w	PORT	Contra Costa	Martinez P O	71	386
Martin	42	m	w	ENGL	Fresno	Millerton P O	72	159
Stephen	20	m	w	ENGL	Fresno	Millerton P O	72	159
Wm	36	m	w	ENGL	Fresno	Millerton P O	72	167
Wm C	52	m	w	TN	Sonoma	Russian Rvr	91	372
CATS								
J	38	m	w	ENGL	Sierra	Butte Twp	89	509
Louisa	65	f	w	CT	Alameda	Oakland	68	256
CATSHOFE								
Antone	30	m	w	ITAL	San Joaquin	3-Wd Stockton	86	221
CATTALDE								
Marco	44	m	w	CHIL	Calaveras	San Andreas P O	70	214
Romuldo	41	m	w	CHIL	Calaveras	San Andreas P O	70	214
CATTAM								
Joel D	19	m	w	IL	Sacramento	Lee Twp	77	158
CATTANCE								
Julius	45	m	w	ITAL	Plumas	Seneca Twp	77	48
CATTANEO								
Franco	40	m	w	ITAL	San Francisco	11-Wd San Francisc	84	591
CATTELAIN								
Gabriello	24	m	w	ITAL	San Francisco	1-Wd San Francisco	79	114
CATTELLO								
Damore	36	m	w	ITAL	San Francisco	3-Wd San Francisco	79	288
CATTER								
B B	38	m	w	NH	Sacramento	3-Wd Sacramento	77	301
CATTERALL								
Thos	27	m	w	ENGL	San Francisco	San Francisco P O	83	307
CATTEREA								
G	49	m	w	FRAN	Alameda	Oakland	68	181
CATTERSON								
John L	36	m	w	IN	Contra Costa	Martinez P O	71	383
CATTIN								
James	37	m	w	IL	Colusa	Grand Island Twp	71	307
S R	27	m	w	PA	San Francisco	7-Wd San Francisco	81	166
CATTLE								
Alvara	61	m	w	VT	Los Angeles	Los Angeles	73	536
John	51	m	w	MO	Calaveras	San Andreas P O	70	176
John	40	m	w	IREL	Placer	Rocklin P O	76	462
Marshall	36	m	w	MO	Alameda	Eden Twp	68	67
Thomas	28	m	w	SCOT	Colusa	Spring Valley Twp	71	343
CATTLETT								
Hanson J	43	m	w	KY	Yuba	New York Twp	93	637
CATTO								
William	39	m	w	SWIT	El Dorado	Diamond Springs Tw	72	31
CATTOU								
Joseph	29	m	w	ENGL	San Francisco	San Francisco P O	83	370
CATTRELL								
George R	30	m	w	NY	Los Angeles	Los Angeles	73	536
CATTROLL								
Edward	44	m	w	IREL	San Francisco	11-Wd San Francisc	84	514
CATY								
George W	16	m	w	CA	Colusa	Monroe Twp	71	316
CATZENSTINE								
G	29	m	w	FRAN	Yuba	Marysville	93	582
CAUBLE								
Cordelia J	19	f	w	MO	Fresno	Millerton P O	72	149
CAUFFMAN								
Hiram	36	m	w	PA	Santa Barbara	Santa Barbara P O	87	490
M	61	m	w	PA	Amador	Ione City P O	69	365
CAUFMAN								
Alfred	35	m	w	VA	San Francisco	8-Wd San Francisco	82	462
CAUGHEY								
Robert	34	m	w	CANA	Mendocino	Point Arena Twp	74	207
Silas W W	39	m	w	PA	Butte	Ophir Twp	70	96
CAUGHILL								
John	16	m	w	LA	Sonoma	Bodega Twp	91	260
CAUGHLAN								
James	28	m	w	IREL	San Francisco	San Francisco P O	80	473
Michael	22	m	w	IREL	Santa Cruz	Pajaro Twp	89	362
CAUGHLEY								
John	24	m	w	CANA	Mendocino	Point Arena Twp	74	207
William	28	m	w	CANA	Mendocino	Point Arena Twp	74	206
CAUGHLIN								
E	22	f	w	IREL	Alameda	Oakland	68	157
John	37	m	w	IREL	San Francisco	1-Wd San Francisco	79	18
John	34	m	w	SCOT	Alameda	Oakland	68	151
Martin	40	m	w	IREL	San Francisco	1-Wd San Francisco	79	97
Martin	35	m	w	ENGL	San Francisco	1-Wd San Francisco	79	122
Michl	24	m	w	IREL	San Francisco	1-Wd San Francisco	79	132
Stephen	33	m	w	IREL	San Francisco	1-Wd San Francisco	79	93
CAUGHRAN								
Jno	37	m	w	PA	Sacramento	3-Wd Sacramento	77	289
CAUGHTON								
Danl	50	m	w	IREL	Alameda	Oakland	68	194
CAUGHY								
John	56	m	w	IREL	Sonoma	Bodega Twp	91	261
William	28	m	w	CANA	Sonoma	Bodega Twp	91	252
CAUHISH								
Theodore	53	m	w	FRAN	San Joaquin	1-Wd Stockton	86	131
CAULDWELL								
George	30	m	w	MO	San Luis Obispo	Salinas Twp	87	296
CAULEY								
Grace	23	f	w	IREL	Alameda	Oakland	68	182
CAULFIELD								
Eleanor	71	f	w	IREL	San Francisco	San Francisco P O	83	144
Fred	31	m	w	ENGL	San Francisco	1-Wd San Francisco	79	69
Henry A	42	m	w	IREL	Sacramento	2-Wd Sacramento	77	250
Patrick	40	m	w	IREL	San Francisco	San Francisco P O	83	67
Thos E	29	m	w	OH	San Francisco	1-Wd San Francisco	79	15
CAULKINS								
Chas	40	m	w	CT	Butte	Ophir Twp	70	108
CAULKLIN								
Patrick	35	m	w	IREL	San Francisco	San Francisco P O	83	362
CAULLI								
Francis	40	m	w	SPAI	Calaveras	San Andreas P O	70	203
CAULTER								
Daniel	78	m	w	NC	Calaveras	San Andreas P O	70	217
Joseph H	38	m	w	IREL	San Francisco	1-Wd San Francisco	79	107
Wm L	37	m	w	CA	Monterey	Salinas Twp	74	313
CAULTIN								
Martin	32	m	w	IREL	San Diego	San Diego	78	497
CAULWELL								
Albert	15	m	w	IL	San Francisco	San Francisco P O	80	333
CAULY								
John	9	m	w	CA	San Francisco	11-Wd San Francisc	84	614
Thos	11	m	w	CA	San Francisco	11-Wd San Francisc	84	614
CAUN								
G	24	m	w	FRAN	Alameda	Oakland	68	242
CAUNIHIN								
John	30	m	w	IREL	San Francisco	1-Wd San Francisco	79	76
CAUNT								
Mary	38	f	w	FRAN	San Francisco	1-Wd San Francisco	79	23
CAURHAUT								
Josephine	24	f	w	BADE	San Francisco	San Francisco P O	80	473
CAURTAINE								
Harry	36	m	w	IREL	San Francisco	1-Wd San Francisco	79	106
CAURTZEN								
Andrew	31	m	w	DENM	San Francisco	1-Wd San Francisco	79	117
CAURUNGE								
Louis	24	m	w	PRUS	Solano	Silveyville Twp	90	82
CAUSBY								
Frank	20	m	i	CA	Sacramento	3-Wd Sacramento	77	274
CAUSECHRI								
Franconi	28	m	w	ITAL	San Francisco	1-Wd San Francisco	79	105
CAUSELL								
Joe	30	m	w	AUST	San Joaquin	2-Wd Stockton	86	164
CAUSEY								
Isaac	54	m	w	NC	Sacramento	Franklin Twp	77	110
CAUSIN								
Eben	38	m	w	ME	Butte	Kimshew Tpw	70	77
CAUSLAND								
Jus W	41	m	w	ME	Marin	San Rafael Twp	74	40
CAUSNEY								
Andrew	42	m	w	MI	Sacramento	1-Wd Sacramento	77	204
CAUSSE								
Gerololemo	43	m	w	ITAL	Santa Barbara	Santa Barbara P O	87	456
CAUTHRON								
Chas	43	m	w	MO	Yuba	Linda Twp	93	559
CAUTLAN								
Richard	38	m	w	IREL	San Francisco	San Francisco P O	83	179
CAVADE								
J	30	m	w	IREL	Alameda	Oakland	68	175
CAVADO								
Carlos	30	m	w	MEXI	Santa Clara	2-Wd San Jose	88	311
CAVAGANEN								
Demi	38	m	w	ITAL	Calaveras	San Andreas P O	70	160
John	32	m	w	ITAL	Calaveras	San Andreas P O	70	160
Joseph	20	m	w	ITAL	Calaveras	San Andreas P O	70	160
CAVAGARO								
Antone	37	m	w	ITAL	Calaveras	San Andreas P O	70	160
CAVAGNARO								
John	48	m	w	ITAL	Tuolumne	Big Oak Flat P O	93	392
CAVAGNARS								
Carlo	44	m	w	ITAL	Mariposa	Mariposa P O	74	101
CAVAGUARO								
Francesco	56	m	w	ITAL	San Francisco	11-Wd San Francisc	84	594
CAVAHER								
John B	45	m	w	FRAN	San Francisco	8-Wd San Francisco	82	391
CAVAI								
A C	28	m	w	ITAL	Tuolumne	Big Oak Flat P O	93	392
CAVAIGUCO								
Manuel	34	m	i	MEXI	Tuolumne	Sonora P O	93	330
CAVAJNARO								
Louis	24	m	w	ITAL	San Francisco	San Francisco P O	80	479
CAVALHO								
Eliza	27	f	w	HOLL	San Francisco	11-Wd San Francisc	84	672
CAVALI								
George	28	m	w	ITAL	Tuolumne	Big Oak Flat P O	93	395
John	25	m	w	ITAL	Tuolumne	Big Oak Flat P O	93	395
John	25	m	w	ITAL	Tuolumne	Big Oak Flat P O	93	394
CAVALIA								
Caroline	5	f	w	CA	San Francisco	San Francisco P O	83	59

© 2001 by Heritage Quest. All rights reserved.

Name	Age	S	R	B-PL	County	Locale	Series M593 Roll	Pg
CAVALITTI								
Charles	42	m	w	ITAL	San Francisco	San Francisco P O	80	348
CAVALLE								
Joseph	27	m	w	SWIT	Sonoma	Sonoma Twp	91	440
CAVALLI								
Gotardo	64	m	w	SWIT	Calaveras	San Andreas P O	70	206
Joseph	30	m	w	SWIT	Calaveras	San Andreas P O	70	206
CAVAN								
Kate	35	f	w	IREL	San Francisco	6-Wd San Francisco	81	131
William	30	m	w	CANA	Contra Costa	Martinez P O	71	447
CAVANA								
A	19	f	w	IREL	Alameda	Oakland	68	190
P	25	m	w	ITAL	San Francisco	San Francisco P O	85	755
CAVANAC								
Angelo	35	m	w	ITAL	Calaveras	Copperopolis P O	70	244
CAVANAGH								
Anne	22	f	w	IREL	Santa Clara	San Jose Twp	88	188
B	40	m	w	IREL	Sacramento	4-Wd Sacramento	77	333
Edwd	30	m	w	IREL	Alameda	Oakland	68	194
Elizabeth	34	f	w	IREL	San Francisco	San Francisco P O	80	467
Frank	2	m	w	CA	Siskiyou	Butte Twp	89	584
George	41	m	w	IREL	San Francisco	8-Wd San Francisco	82	432
J D	38	m	w	IREL	San Francisco	San Francisco P O	83	309
James	40	m	w	IREL	San Francisco	7-Wd San Francisco	81	246
James	37	m	w	IREL	San Francisco	San Francisco P O	83	349
James	30	m	w	IREL	San Francisco	8-Wd San Francisco	82	496
Joseph	42	m	w	IREL	Siskiyou	Butte Twp	89	584
M	35	m	w	IREL	Amador	Jackson P O	69	323
Nathl	45	m	w	IREL	San Francisco	San Francisco P O	85	714
Pat	55	m	w	IREL	San Francisco	7-Wd San Francisco	81	241
Patrick	33	m	w	IREL	San Francisco	San Francisco P O	83	205
Phillip	15	m	w	IREL	San Francisco	6-Wd San Francisco	81	102
Timothy	47	m	w	IREL	Contra Costa	Martinez P O	71	432
Wm	40	m	w	IREL	San Francisco	11-Wd San Francisc	84	640
CAVANARO								
James	45	m	w	ITAL	Santa Clara	Fremont Twp	88	58
CAVANAUG								
Charles	40	m	w	IREL	Mendocino	Big Rvr Twp	74	161
CAVANAUGH								
Charles	36	m	w	IREL	San Mateo	Menlo Park P O	87	379
Chas	23	m	w	IREL	San Francisco	1-Wd San Francisco	79	69
D	30	m	w	IREL	San Francisco	7-Wd San Francisco	81	165
D	26	m	w	IREL	Santa Clara	Gilroy Twp	88	95
Ed	25	m	w	IREL	Sierra	Gibson Twp	89	542
Elizth	58	f	w	IREL	San Francisco	San Francisco P O	83	121
George	28	m	w	PA	Yolo	Cottonwood Twp	93	460
Hannah	39	f	w	IREL	Sierra	Table Rock Twp	89	574
Hugh	35	m	w	IREL	Santa Cruz	Santa Cruz	89	414
J	46	m	w	IREL	San Joaquin	2-Wd Stockton	86	162
James	35	m	w	OH	Plumas	Washington Twp	77	54
Jerry	30	m	w	IREL	San Francisco	San Francisco P O	83	133
John	60	m	w	IREL	Contra Costa	Martinez P O	71	446
John	46	m	w	IREL	Sonoma	Petaluma Twp	91	328
John	40	m	w	IREL	San Francisco	11-Wd San Francisc	84	673
Joseph	35	m	w	IREL	Sonoma	Petaluma Twp	91	332
L J	20	m	w	NY	Humboldt	Eureka Twp	72	270
Lawrence	39	m	w	IREL	Nevada	Grass Valley Twp	75	197
M	55	m	w	IREL	San Francisco	7-Wd San Francisco	81	163
Mathew	23	m	w	IREL	Sonoma	Vallejo Twp	91	454
Michael	28	m	w	CANA	Contra Costa	Martinez P O	71	446
Morris	41	m	w	IREL	San Francisco	San Francisco P O	83	145
N	37	m	w	MO	San Bernardino	San Bernardino Twp	78	432
Thomas	53	m	w	IREL	Mendocino	Big Rvr Twp	74	175
Thomas	51	m	w	IREL	Plumas	Indian Twp	77	14
Thomas	32	m	w	IREL	Nevada	Grass Valley Twp	75	212
Thos	3	m	w	NY	San Francisco	7-Wd San Francisco	81	266
W	22	m	w	IREL	Solano	Benicia	90	13
Wm	50	m	w	IREL	Monterey	Alisal Twp	74	300
Wm	32	m	w	IREL	San Luis Obispo	Salinas Twp	87	293
CAVANEZ								
Juan	32	m	w	MEXI	Fresno	Millerton P O	72	167
CAVANNA								
John	40	m	w	NY	Solano	Vallejo	90	140
Mary	40	f	w	IREL	Alameda	Oakland	68	210
CAVANNAUGH								
Jas	60	m	w	IREL	San Francisco	2-Wd San Francisco	79	215
M	28	m	w	NY	Santa Clara	Gilroy Twp	88	77
Pat	23	m	w	IREL	Santa Clara	Gilroy Twp	88	78
CAVANOUGH								
J P	43	m	w	NY	Solano	Vallejo	90	184
William	34	m	w	ENGL	Nevada	Bloomfield Twp	75	92
CAVANY								
Mary	39	f	w	NY	Solano	Benicia	90	16
CAVANZO								
Luiseand	28	m	w	CA	Santa Clara	Gilroy Twp	88	88
CAVARA								
Candelora	43	f	w	CHIL	Calaveras	Copperopolis P O	70	239
CAVARCO								
Janey	14	f	w	CA	San Francisco	San Francisco P O	85	813
CAVARI								
Luke	18	m	w	ITAL	San Francisco	1-Wd San Francisco	79	93
CAVASSO								
J	45	m	w	ITAL	Alameda	Oakland	68	169
CAVE								
Ah	42	m	c	CHIN	Nevada	Nevada Twp	75	312
Colma D	66	f	w	KY	Humboldt	Arcata Twp	72	234
Hugh L	32	m	w	IA	Humboldt	Arcata Twp	72	230
Jesse H	48	m	w	KY	Yolo	Merritt Twp	93	502
Lizzy A	48	f	w	CA	San Bernardino	San Bernardino Twp	78	446
Marcus L	42	m	w	MO	Santa Clara	Fremont Twp	88	58
Richard B	36	m	w	ME	Humboldt	Arcata Twp	72	230
Ruben	25	m	w	IA	Sacramento	San Joaquin Twp	77	397
William	51	m	w	KY	Yolo	Merritt Twp	93	503
William	27	m	w	KY	San Bernardino	San Bernardino Twp	78	432
CAVEL								
Robt	27	m	w	AL	Yuba	Marysville	93	611
CAVEMAN								
William	48	m	w	IREL	San Francisco	7-Wd San Francisco	81	170
CAVEN								
George	43	m	w	IREL	San Francisco	2-Wd San Francisco	79	252
James	37	m	w	NY	Calaveras	Copperopolis P O	70	227
CAVENAGH								
John	40	m	w	IREL	Santa Clara	San Jose Twp	88	191
CAVENAUGH								
Ed	29	m	w	IREL	San Joaquin	1-Wd Stockton	86	135
Jas	36	m	w	IREL	Butte	Oregon Twp	70	130
Jerry	28	m	w	NY	Sutter	Sutter Twp	92	124
Kate	22	f	w	IREL	Alameda	Brooklyn Twp	68	40
Michal	27	m	w	IREL	San Mateo	San Mateo P O	87	359
Mikael	66	m	w	IREL	Sonoma	Salt Point	91	388
Patrick	26	m	w	IREL	Monterey	Castroville Twp	74	329
CAVENDER								
John	21	m	w	KS	Sonoma	Petaluma Twp	91	336
CAVENEE								
John	68	m	w	PA	Santa Clara	Redwood Twp	88	133
CAVENER								
John	14	m	w	ME	San Joaquin	Liberty Twp	86	83
Michael	43	m	w	IREL	San Francisco	11-Wd San Francisc	84	702
CAVENERA								
D	26	m	w	BADE	Yuba	Marysville	93	586
CAVENOR								
Thos	29	m	w	IREL	San Francisco	11-Wd San Francisc	84	669
CAVENOUGH								
---	45	m	w	IREL	Sacramento	1-Wd Sacramento	77	190
CAVERLY								
Orin	50	m	w	NH	Alameda	Brooklyn Twp	68	52
CAVERON								
Frank	45	m	w	FRAN	Tuolumne	Columbia P O	93	342
CAVERRI								
David	24	m	w	ITAL	San Francisco	San Francisco P O	85	842
CAVERS								
Adolph	45	m	w	FRAN	San Francisco	2-Wd San Francisco	79	145
CAVERT								
G W	38	m	w	IN	Sacramento	American Twp	77	66
CAVES								
Frank	48	m	w	KY	Tehama	Antelope Twp	92	154
CAVET								
Louis	53	m	w	SWIT	Santa Clara	Fremont Twp	88	50
CAVIANO								
Domingo	54	m	w	CHIL	Amador	Jackson P O	69	322
CAVIGNAS								
Joseph	52	m	w	FRAN	Kern	Havilah P O	73	350
CAVILILIER								
Henry	35	m	w	OH	Yuba	Long Bar Twp	93	564
CAVILLE								
Andrew	46	m	w	SPAI	Calaveras	San Andreas P O	70	203
CAVILLERA								
Jose	42	m	w	SPAI	Marin	Sausalito Twp	74	67
CAVILLON								
Adrian	62	m	w	FRAN	San Francisco	San Francisco P O	80	535
CAVIN								
M G	37	m	w	KY	Nevada	Bridgeport Twp	75	102
Patrick	25	m	w	IREL	Klamath	Camp Gaston	73	373
Pilock	28	m	w	IREL	Mendocino	Casper & Big Rvr	74	164
CAVINA								
John	35	m	w	IREL	Alameda	Alameda	68	7
CAVINE								
John	48	m	w	IREL	Alameda	Murray Twp	68	101
CAVIOSKI								
John	27	m	w	SWIT	San Joaquin	Castoria Twp	86	8
CAVIS								
Emma	40	f	w	NH	Tuolumne	Chinese Camp P O	93	335
CAVIZO								
P	28	m	w	MEXI	Santa Clara	Gilroy Twp	88	96
CAVO								
Joseph M	46	m	w	MEXI	Fresno	Millerton P O	72	153
CAVOLIE								
Trudell	30	m	w	SWIT	Kern	Linns Valley P O	73	344
CAW								
Ah	24	m	c	CHIN	Sacramento	Natomas Twp	77	171
Chung	39	m	c	CHIN	Alameda	Oakland	68	134
James	63	m	w	KY	Kern	Linns Valley P O	73	344
James	35	m	w	IREL	Fresno	Millerton P O	72	155
Thomas	40	m	w	IREL	San Francisco	2-Wd San Francisco	79	204
Wm W	36	m	w	VA	San Francisco	2-Wd San Francisco	79	219
CAWDEN								
Thos	40	m	w	IREL	Solano	Benicia	90	12
CAWELTI								
John	40	m	w	WURT	Santa Barbara	San Buenaventura P	87	426
CAWER								
D B	39	m	w	OH	Napa	Napa	75	3
James	30	m	w	KY	Solano	Silveyville Twp	90	74
CAWLEY								
Edward	30	m	w	MA	San Francisco	7-Wd San Francisco	81	181

© 2001 by Heritage Quest. All rights reserved.

California 1870 Census

Name	Age	S	R	B-PL	County	Locale	Series M593 Roll	Pg
John	30	m	w	IREL	San Francisco	7-Wd San Francisco	81	167
Kate	32	f	w	IREL	Alameda	Alameda	68	2
CAWNOYER								
Valentin	73	m	w	VA	Sacramento	Natomas Twp	77	169
CAWOA								
Giacomo	29	m	w	ITAL	Mariposa	Maxwell Crk P O	74	138
CAWRIDON								
Louis	26	m	w	FRAN	Yuba	Bullards Bar P O	93	550
CAWSLAS								
Stephen	40	m	w	PA	Colusa	Monroe Twp	71	315
CAXALL								
George	30	m	w	MO	Santa Clara	Santa Clara Twp	88	178
CAXTON								
James	36	m	w	TX	Stanislaus	Buena Vista Twp	92	14
CAY								
---	47	m	c	CHIN	Siskiyou	Cottonwood Twp	89	592
Ah	28	m	c	CHIN	Alameda	Washington Twp	68	299
Ah	15	m	c	CHIN	San Francisco	11-Wd San Francisc	84	571
Nelson F	43	m	w	NC	Fresno	Kingston P O	72	219
CAYA								
Michell	57	m	w	CANA	Sierra	Sears Twp	89	555
CAYAT								
A M	24	m	w	FRAN	Sierra	Table Rock Twp	89	574
CAYATANO								
Manuel	20	m	w	PORT	Monterey	Pajaro Twp	74	373
CAYHILL								
A J	42	m	w	VA	Alameda	Oakland	68	206
CAYLE								
M A	8	f	w	CA	Tuolumne	Big Oak Flat P O	93	395
CAYNOR								
John	26	m	w	VA	Mariposa	Mariposa P O	74	117
CAYOGUETTE								
David	25	m	w	CANA	Santa Cruz	Santa Cruz Twp	89	387
CAYON								
Ah	27	m	c	CHIN	Sierra	Lincoln Twp	89	551
Joseph	46	m	w	FRAN	Butte	Bidwell Twp	70	3
CAYOT								
Celeste	33	m	w	FRAN	Plumas	Goodwin Twp	77	5
Francois	35	m	w	FRAN	Plumas	Goodwin Twp	77	5
Jaques	35	m	w	FRAN	Sierra	Sears Twp	89	555
Josephine	59	f	w	FRAN	Plumas	Goodwin Twp	77	5
CAYSER								
William	23	m	w	ENGL	Alameda	Eden Twp	68	83
CAYSTILE								
Thomas	60	m	w	IOFM	El Dorado	Placerville	72	113
CAYTON								
Alvis	20	m	w	AZOR	San Francisco	1-Wd San Francisco	79	102
Joseph	18	m	w	PORT	San Mateo	Half Moon Bay P O	87	401
Nellie	25	f	w	IREL	Solano	Vallejo	90	214
Wm	56	m	w	PA	Shasta	Fort Crook P O	89	476
CAYWOOD								
Benj	70	m	w	NY	San Bernardino	Belleville Twp	78	408
CAZALA								
H	11	m	w	ITAL	Calaveras	Copperopolis P O	70	226
CAZAROVA								
Heny	35	m	w	ITAL	San Francisco	2-Wd San Francisco	79	259
CAZASSA								
Edward	12	m	w	CA	San Francisco	11-Wd San Francisc	84	587
CAZASSAS								
Antonio	33	m	w	ITAL	Mariposa	Mariposa P O	74	117
CAZELL								
John	20	m	w	ITAL	Sacramento	Sutter Twp	77	383
CAZERRA								
Antano	34	m	w	ITAL	Contra Costa	Martinez P O	71	437
CAZERWOKY								
Frank	21	m	w	NY	San Diego	San Diego	78	486
CAZNEAU								
Emma	33	f	w	AUSL	San Francisco	8-Wd San Francisco	82	344
William	25	m	w	NY	San Francisco	2-Wd San Francisco	79	186
CAZNER								
James	31	m	w	ENGL	Mendocino	Anderson Twp	74	155
CAZZERETTA								
F	38	m	w	ITAL	Calaveras	Copperopolis P O	70	231
CE								
Be	35	m	c	CHIN	Yuba	Marysville	93	628
CEAK								
Louis	38	m	w	PRUS	San Francisco	2-Wd San Francisco	79	157
CEALAI								
Martin	35	m	w	SWIT	Calaveras	San Andreas P O	70	198
CEARING								
Edman	64	m	w	NC	Alameda	Washington Twp	68	296
CEARSE								
Harriet	52	f	w	VA	Colusa	Stony Crk Twp	71	331
CEASAR								
Harriett A	54	f	b	NY	Tehama	Red Bluff	92	177
CEASER								
Julius	28	m	w	PRUS	San Francisco	8-Wd San Francisco	82	436
CEAVY								
A	45	m	w	NH	Yuba	Marysville	93	590
CEBALLAS								
Vaneule	45	m	i	MEXI	Inyo	Cerro Gordo Twp	73	320
CECEL								
James N	45	m	w	KY	Los Angeles	El Monte Twp	73	448
CECHNER								
Robert	53	m	w	PA	San Francisco	2-Wd San Francisco	79	156
CECIL								
Amanda	47	f	w	VA	Sonoma	Santa Rosa	91	430
J P	27	m	w	MO	Amador	Lancha Plana P O	69	368
John	30	m	w	INDI	San Francisco	1-Wd San Francisco	79	71
John	22	m	w	MO	Amador	Ione City P O	69	357
Jos M	35	m	w	TN	Butte	Hamilton Twp	70	63
Nathaniel	28	m	b	MO	Amador	Volcano P O	69	386
Sarah	66	f	w	AR	Tulare	Visalia	92	289
Thomas	37	m	w	WALE	Amador	Jackson P O	69	330
Thomas	30	m	w	WALE	Amador	Jackson P O	69	330
William	33	m	w	AR	Tulare	Visalia Twp	92	283
CECILE								
James	25	m	w	MO	Butte	Chico Twp	70	30
Joseph	36	m	w	TN	Butte	Chico Twp	70	54
Sebastian	51	m	w	VA	Butte	Chico Twp	70	30
CEDARBURG								
I A	42	m	w	SWED	Santa Clara	Gilroy Twp	88	104
CEDARHOME								
Adolph	6	m	w	PRUS	San Francisco	San Francisco P O	85	799
D	8	m	w	PRUS	San Francisco	San Francisco P O	85	799
CEDERSTROM								
John	78	m	w	SWED	San Francisco	2-Wd San Francisco	79	267
John	40	m	w	SWED	San Francisco	2-Wd San Francisco	79	267
CEDGARGREEN								
John C D	23	m	w	SWED	San Mateo	Redwood Twp	87	367
CEDOLE								
Pascor	35	m	w	ITAL	Alameda	Washington Twp	68	287
CEDRA								
Elena	75	f	i	CA	Santa Barbara	San Buenaventura P	87	439
CEE								
Ah	45	m	c	CHIN	Trinity	Weaverville Pct	92	227
Ah	32	m	c	CHIN	Yuba	Marysville	93	619
Ah	30	m	c	CHIN	Contra Costa	Martinez Twp	71	351
Ah	23	m	c	CHIN	San Joaquin	Castoria Twp	86	10
Ong	18	m	c	CHIN	Sierra	Eureka Twp	89	525
Yip	19	m	c	CHIN	San Francisco	8-Wd San Francisco	82	294
CEECHE								
Fredrick	49	m	w	SWIT	Sonoma	Sonoma Twp	91	435
CEEN								
Ah	30	m	c	CHIN	Butte	Hamilton Twp	70	70
CEFONS								
James	39	m	b	DC	El Dorado	Mud Springs Twp	72	79
CEFUS								
Wm	43	m	w	PRUS	San Joaquin	2-Wd Stockton	86	183
CEGER								
Valentine	23	m	w	PRUS	Monterey	Alisal Twp	74	296
CEGURA								
Edwd	36	m	i	MEXI	Santa Clara	Almaden Twp	88	21
CEICIL								
John	34	m	w	MD	Nevada	Meadow Lake Twp	75	252
CEIGEN								
Maria	35	f	w	IREL	San Francisco	8-Wd San Francisco	82	296
CEILE								
John	49	m	w	WURT	San Francisco	San Francisco P O	80	488
CEIS								
John	40	m	w	FRNK	San Francisco	2-Wd San Francisco	79	238
CELDERON								
Andrew	45	m	w	ARGE	Santa Clara	Fremont Twp	88	62
CELESTINA								
Rosa	11	f	b	CUBA	San Francisco	2-Wd San Francisco	79	194
CELESTINE								
F	34	f	w	FRAN	San Joaquin	2-Wd Stockton	86	173
CELESTINO								
Joquin	25	m	w	SWIT	San Luis Obispo	San Luis Obispo Tw	87	307
CELESTNY								
Ryan	25	m	w	FRAN	San Joaquin	2-Wd Stockton	86	173
CELEY								
Michael	35	m	w	IREL	San Mateo	Schoolhouse Statio	87	338
CELILE								
Antonio	26	m	w	SWIT	San Francisco	San Francisco P O	80	477
CELIO								
Antonio	32	m	w	SWIT	Amador	Jackson P O	69	336
Charles G	36	m	w	SWIT	El Dorado	Placerville	72	107
Francis	50	m	w	AUST	Amador	Fiddletown P O	69	436
Francis	26	m	w	NY	Amador	Fiddletown P O	69	436
John	48	m	w	SWIT	El Dorado	Placerville	72	120
CELIS								
Adolphus	19	m	w	CA	Marin	San Rafael Twp	74	46
Pastor	19	m	w	CA	Los Angeles	Los Angeles	73	570
CELL								
Ale	28	m	c	CHIN	San Joaquin	1-Wd Stockton	86	144
CELLA								
Augusta	32	f	w	ITAL	San Francisco	San Francisco P O	85	823
John W	44	m	w	ITAL	Mariposa	Maxwell Crk P O	74	140
CELLAHAR								
M	27	m	w	IREL	Yuba	Marysville	93	583
CELLANS								
James	40	m	w	SCOT	Merced	Snelling P O	74	249
CELLE								
Joseph	57	m	w	ITAL	San Francisco	2-Wd San Francisco	79	150
CELLER								
George	23	m	w	PA	San Francisco	San Francisco P O	80	418
Michael	55	m	w	PRUS	San Francisco	San Francisco P O	83	174
CELLETT								
Ezra	28	m	w	TX	Santa Barbara	Santa Barbara P O	87	496
CELLIS								
Firman A	69	m	w	FRAN	Nevada	Grass Valley Twp	75	208
CELLISER								
Victor	46	m	w	FRAN	Solano	Denverton Twp	90	27

© 2001 by Heritage Quest. All rights reserved.

Name	Age	S	R	B-PL	County	Locale	Series M593 Roll	Pg
CELLY								
Thomas	34	m	w	ME	Sutter	Sutter Twp	92	123
CELMAN								
Mathew	25	m	w	IREL	Trinity	Weaverville Pct	92	225
CELSEY								
Torty	28	m	w	SWIT	Placer	Bath P O	76	443
CEMBELLACK								
John	24	m	w	ENGL	El Dorado	Placerville Twp	72	93
CEMBER								
Martha	38	f	w	ENGL	San Francisco	7-Wd San Francisco	81	174
CEMCO								
Joseph	35	m	w	ITAL	Calaveras	San Andreas P O	70	216
CEMONE								
Alexander	45	m	w	BADE	Contra Costa	Martinez P O	71	372
CEN								
Ah	58	m	c	CHIN	Placer	Newcastle Twp	76	478
Ah	30	m	c	CHIN	Tuolumne	Columbia P O	93	352
Ah	22	m	c	CHIN	Santa Clara	Gilroy Twp	88	81
Ah	20	m	c	CHIN	Sonoma	Sonoma Twp	91	449
CENADEL								
Maria	13	f	w	CA	Los Angeles	El Monte Twp	73	453
CENALO								
Delphina	7	f	w	CA	Santa Clara	2-Wd San Jose	88	312
Fernando	44	m	w	CHIL	Santa Clara	2-Wd San Jose	88	312
CENARTEZ								
Jose	35	m	w	CA	Monterey	San Juan Twp	74	393
CENCES								
Joseph	30	m	w	GERM	Alameda	Washington Twp	68	292
CENDERLIN								
James	60	m	w	IREL	Monterey	San Juan Twp	74	393
Patrick	29	m	w	IA	Monterey	San Juan Twp	74	393
CENEY								
Carlton	36	m	w	VT	Santa Clara	Redwood Twp	88	132
CENLIN								
James	33	m	w	IREL	Colusa	Colusa Twp	71	283
CENN								
Ah	21	m	c	CHIN	Nevada	Nevada Twp	75	308
CENOBIE								
F	60	m	i	CA	Alameda	Murray Twp	68	103
CENOWETH								
Andrew F	52	m	w	KY	Sonoma	Petaluma Twp	91	318
Miles	41	m	w	KY	Sonoma	Petaluma Twp	91	318
CENQUIS								
Louis	41	m	w	FRAN	El Dorado	Mud Springs Twp	72	71
CENROW								
Wm	35	m	w	OH	Sonoma	Salt Point	91	389
CENRY								
Abraham	50	m	w	SCOT	Sonoma	Russian Rvr	91	379
CENSALAGE								
Nicholas	38	m	w	AUST	Calaveras	San Andreas P O	70	217
CENSALI								
John	41	m	w	CHIL	El Dorado	Mountain Twp	72	67
CENSAR								
Chas	42	m	w	FRAN	Shasta	Shasta P O	89	463
CENSON								
A	27	m	w	MA	San Francisco	7-Wd San Francisco	81	218
CENTA								
Hugh	21	m	w	SCOT	Napa	Napa	75	1
CENTEN								
John	26	m	w	PORT	Trinity	North Fork Twp	92	217
CENTER								
David	42	m	w	SCOT	San Francisco	11-Wd San Francisc	84	619
Edwd	19	m	w	NY	Butte	Chico Twp	70	30
Enoc	35	m	w	IL	Butte	Chico Twp	70	33
Fannie	26	f	w	MO	Colusa	Monroe Twp	71	316
George	57	m	w	SCOT	San Francisco	11-Wd San Francisc	84	518
German S	61	m	w	ME	Santa Barbara	Santa Barbara P O	87	451
Innie B	8	f	w	ME	San Francisco	San Francisco P O	83	170
James	42	m	w	SCOT	San Francisco	11-Wd San Francisc	84	510
John	55	m	w	SCOT	San Francisco	11-Wd San Francisc	84	518
John Jr	33	m	w	MA	San Francisco	San Francisco P O	83	169
Jos	29	m	w	PORT	Alameda	Eden Twp	68	63
Joseph	28	m	w	PORT	Alameda	Washington Twp	68	293
Owen	32	m	w	IREL	San Mateo	Schoolhouse Statio	87	342
Samuel S	38	m	w	ME	El Dorado	Mud Springs Twp	72	84
CENTERS								
Juan G J	43	m	w	CA	Monterey	Alisal Twp	74	288
CENTRE								
Edward	20	m	w	NY	San Francisco	5-Wd San Francisco	81	18
CENTURA								
Jose	22	m	w	CA	Santa Clara	Burnett Twp	88	37
Jose M	53	m	w	CA	Santa Clara	Burnett Twp	88	37
CENY								
Ah	27	m	c	CHIN	San Joaquin	1-Wd Stockton	86	144
CENZON								
Charles	44	m	w	BREM	Los Angeles	El Monte Twp	73	454
CEPECK								
Enna	15	f	w	NY	San Francisco	11-Wd San Francisc	84	618
CEPHUS								
Benjamin	21	m	b	VA	Tulare	Visalia Twp	92	283
CEPRICE								
George	48	m	w	CANA	San Francisco	11-Wd San Francisc	84	506
CEPWISA								
Antonio	40	m	w	MEXI	Los Angeles	El Monte Twp	73	449
CER								
Nicholas	26	m	w	AUST	Contra Costa	Martinez P O	71	383
CERALLI								
Sebastian	26	m	w	ITAL	San Francisco	1-Wd San Francisco	79	22
CERAS								
Felippi	40	m	w	FRAN	San Diego	San Pasqual	78	522
CERBY								
William	12	m	w	CA	Alameda	Washington Twp	68	295
CERCORASAD								
Thos	22	m	w	IREL	Contra Costa	San Pablo Twp	71	360
CERCOVICH								
Gio	50	m	w	AUST	San Francisco	3-Wd San Francisco	79	299
CERDON								
Henry	40	m	w	FRAN	Butte	Chico Twp	70	30
CEREGHIMI								
Carlo	24	m	w	ITAL	Sonoma	Vallejo Twp	91	463
CEREGHINO								
John	30	m	w	ITAL	San Francisco	2-Wd San Francisco	79	164
CEREN								
Frank	30	m	w	BELG	San Francisco	2-Wd San Francisco	79	148
CERESI								
Michl	40	m	w	GREE	San Francisco	1-Wd San Francisco	79	67
CERF								
Ernest	25	m	w	FRAN	San Luis Obispo	San Luis Obispo Tw	87	310
Julian	42	m	w	FRAN	San Francisco	San Francisco P O	80	351
Julius	49	m	w	FRAN	San Francisco	8-Wd San Francisco	82	289
Leon	30	m	w	FRAN	Santa Barbara	San Buenaventura P	87	433
M	38	m	w	FRAN	San Francisco	San Francisco P O	85	791
Rosa	17	f	w	IL	San Francisco	San Francisco P O	85	723
CERGE								
William	28	m	w	FRAN	San Francisco	7-Wd San Francisco	81	216
CERICHLEN								
Philip	36	m	w	BADE	Sierra	Sears Twp	89	560
CERICOLA								
Ang	43	m	w	ARGE	Amador	Fiddletown P O	69	433
CERIL								
Henry	51	m	w	MD	Tuolumne	Sonora P O	93	314
CERINE								
Frank	34	m	w	ITAL	San Francisco	San Francisco P O	83	365
CERINI								
Antone	25	m	w	SWIT	Marin	Bolinas Twp	74	3
John	16	m	w	SWIT	Sonoma	Bodega Twp	91	254
CERKEL								
Wolf	34	m	w	POLA	Solano	Suisun Twp	90	98
CERLES								
Mathew	42	m	w	PRUS	El Dorado	Placerville Twp	72	99
CERLESS								
William B	45	m	w	VT	Sonoma	Petaluma Twp	91	321
CERNEA								
Jesus	22	m	w	MEXI	Los Angeles	San Jose Twp	73	619
CERNES								
Stephen	60	m	w	ITAL	San Francisco	2-Wd San Francisco	79	232
CERNEY								
Mary	32	f	w	NY	San Francisco	2-Wd San Francisco	79	218
CERNOLE								
John	24	m	w	MI	Santa Clara	1-Wd San Jose	88	244
CERNOQOVICH								
Kessto	32	m	w	AUST	San Francisco	3-Wd San Francisco	79	288
CERQUE								
Wm R	59	m	w	NY	El Dorado	Georgetown Twp	72	46
CERRAPHIN								
J	36	m	w	ITAL	San Francisco	San Francisco P O	85	859
CERREAN								
Peogninta	50	m	w	MEXI	Placer	Auburn P O	76	360
CERRIGAN								
Edward	33	m	w	IREL	Nevada	Bloomfield Twp	75	92
CERROVANTS								
Primdeo	37	m	w	MEXI	Inyo	Lone Pine Twp	73	334
CERRUTI								
Giovani	45	m	w	ITAL	San Francisco	San Francisco P O	80	359
CERSEA								
Jesus	40	m	w	MEXI	Mariposa	Mariposa P O	74	129
CERSTA								
Lord	60	m	w	MEXI	San Joaquin	3-Wd Stockton	86	224
CERSTONE								
John	23	m	w	SWED	San Francisco	7-Wd San Francisco	81	192
CERTUZ								
Isador	20	m	w	MEXI	Los Angeles	Los Angeles	73	508
CERVANTE								
John	38	m	w	FRAN	San Francisco	San Francisco P O	80	347
John	38	m	w	FRAN	San Francisco	San Francisco P O	80	348
CERVANTES								
Cruz	83	m	w	MEXI	Fresno	Millerton P O	72	161
Leon	45	m	w	MEXI	San Luis Obispo	Arroyo Grande Twp	87	276
Refugio	52	m	w	MEXI	San Luis Obispo	Morro Twp	87	281
Santos	21	f	w	CA	Los Angeles	San Gabriel Twp	73	593
Trinidad	28	m	w	CA	Fresno	Millerton P O	72	161
CERVANTEZ								
Viriana	13	f	w	CA	San Luis Obispo	Arroyo Grande Twp	87	270
CERVELLI								
Raphael	22	m	w	ITAL	San Francisco	1-Wd San Francisco	79	110
CERWIG								
Jno	40	m	w	KY	San Francisco	5-Wd San Francisco	81	22
CERY								
Jno	27	m	w	IREL	San Joaquin	Dent Twp	86	20
Mary	22	f	w	IREL	Sacramento	3-Wd Sacramento	77	270
CESCHI								
Fedle	28	m	w	ITAL	Alameda	Washington Twp	68	287

© 2001 by Heritage Quest. All rights reserved.

Name	Age	S	R	B-PL	County	Locale	Series M593 Roll	Pg
CESEY								
George	46	m	w	ENGL	San Francisco	11-Wd San Francisc	84	707
CESINA								
Ramon	36	m	w	CA	Santa Clara	Burnett Twp	88	33
Ramon	28	m	w	MEXI	Tulare	Visalia	92	298
CESONTO								
Frank	30	m	w	PHIL	San Francisco	2-Wd San Francisco	79	151
CESSAINCEA								
Ignatio	24	m	w	MEXI	Fresno	Millerton P O	72	154
CESSOR								
Wm	37	m	w	LA	San Joaquin	3-Wd Stockton	86	234
CESTRO								
J	55	m	w	MEXI	San Joaquin	1-Wd Stockton	86	120
William	38	m	w	NY	Sutter	Nicolaus Twp	92	112
CETTERBERG								
J A	42	m	w	SWIT	El Dorado	Greenwood Twp	72	53
CEUNG								
Ah	40	m	c	CHIN	Yuba	Marysville	93	620
CEVRAS								
Juan	43	m	w	MEXI	Contra Costa	Martinez P O	71	381
CEW								
Ah	42	m	c	CHIN	El Dorado	Diamond Springs Tw	72	30
Ah	39	m	c	CHIN	El Dorado	Placerville	72	115
Ah	32	m	c	CHIN	El Dorado	Placerville	72	115
Ah	25	m	c	CHIN	El Dorado	Mud Springs Twp	72	74
CEY								
Ah	42	m	c	CHIN	Placer	Bath P O	76	445
CEYASSO								
S S	43	m	w	FRAN	Tuolumne	Columbia P O	93	345
CEYOW								
Ah	40	m	c	CHIN	Trinity	Weaverville Pct	92	227
CH								
Cho	30	m	c	CHIN	Butte	Ophir Twp	70	106
CHA								
---	24	m	c	CHIN	Siskiyou	Yreka Twp	89	667
Ah	80	m	c	CHIN	Tuolumne	Big Oak Flat P O	93	401
Ah	49	m	c	CHIN	Tuolumne	Chinese Camp P O	93	364
Ah	44	m	c	CHIN	San Luis Obispo	San Luis Obispo Tw	87	297
Ah	42	m	c	CHIN	Nevada	Nevada Twp	75	312
Ah	38	m	c	CHIN	Tuolumne	Columbia P O	93	359
Ah	34	m	c	CHIN	San Francisco	San Francisco P O	80	506
Ah	28	m	c	CHIN	Solano	Suisun Twp	90	106
Ah	27	m	c	CHIN	Butte	Chico Twp	70	51
Ah	26	m	c	CHIN	Calaveras	Copperopolis P O	70	260
Ah	25	m	c	CHIN	Santa Clara	Santa Clara Twp	88	165
Ah	20	m	c	CHIN	Tuolumne	Chinese Camp P O	93	388
Ah	20	m	c	CHIN	San Francisco	8-Wd San Francisco	82	321
Ah	17	m	c	CHIN	San Francisco	San Francisco P O	83	31
Ah	16	m	c	CHIN	Nevada	Grass Valley Twp	75	187
Ah	14	m	c	CHIN	Nevada	Grass Valley Twp	75	162
Cha	28	f	c	CHIN	Calaveras	Copperopolis P O	70	260
Foo	25	m	c	CHIN	Santa Clara	1-Wd San Jose	88	266
Pow	33	m	c	CHIN	Fresno	Millerton P O	72	184
CHAAN								
Ah	13	m	c	CHIN	San Francisco	1-Wd San Francisco	79	87
CHABBOT								
R	38	m	w	CANA	Alameda	Oakland	68	188
CHABELLA								
George	31	m	w	FRAN	Sacramento	2-Wd Sacramento	77	236
CHABES								
Rosa	9	f	i	CA	Sonoma	Salt Point Twp	91	382
CHABIS								
Juan	43	m	w	MEXI	Santa Cruz	Santa Cruz Twp	89	381
CHABOT								
Basil	38	m	w	CANA	Monterey	San Benito Twp	74	383
Hippolite	39	m	w	FRAN	Napa	Napa	75	53
CHABOY								
Padra	80	m	w	MEXI	Santa Clara	San Jose Twp	88	207
CHABOYA								
Andrew	30	m	w	CA	Santa Clara	San Jose Twp	88	218
Augustine	36	m	w	CA	Santa Clara	San Jose Twp	88	218
Francisco	27	m	w	CA	San Luis Obispo	Salinas Twp	87	292
Manwell	32	m	w	CA	Santa Clara	San Jose Twp	88	218
CHABRIETTE								
George	27	m	w	FRAN	Marin	San Rafael Twp	74	37
CHABROL								
Selven	62	m	w	FRAN	Nevada	Grass Valley Twp	75	223
CHABUT								
Milo	40	m	w	FRAN	Monterey	San Juan Twp	74	404
CHAC								
Ah	25	m	c	CHIN	El Dorado	Placerville	72	125
Ah	18	m	c	CHIN	San Francisco	8-Wd San Francisco	82	412
CHACE								
H A	45	m	w	RI	Sacramento	4-Wd Sacramento	77	320
Jane	42	f	w	NY	Contra Costa	Martinez Twp	71	352
Winfield S	21	m	w	RI	San Francisco	San Francisco P O	83	384
CHACH								
Ah	20	m	c	CHIN	San Joaquin	1-Wd Stockton	86	143
CHACK								
Ah	24	m	c	CHIN	San Francisco	2-Wd San Francisco	79	282
CHACON								
Jose	45	m	w	MEXI	Tulare	Visalia	92	298
Manul	40	m	w	CA	Los Angeles	San Jose Twp	73	618
Senforiano	73	m	w	MEXI	Los Angeles	Santa Ana Twp	73	605
CHAD								
Ah	50	f	c	CHIN	San Francisco	6-Wd San Francisco	81	77
Ah	50	f	c	CHIN	San Francisco	6-Wd San Francisco	81	76
Ah	21	m	c	CHIN	San Francisco	6-Wd San Francisco	81	85
CHADBORN								
Clara	30	f	w	CANA	Trinity	Weaverville Pct	92	225
CHADBOURN								
Joshua	36	m	w	ME	Alameda	Washington Twp	68	284
CHADBOURNE								
A J	27	m	w	ME	Alameda	Murray Twp	68	110
H	56	m	w	ME	Calaveras	Copperopolis P O	70	257
Howard	30	m	w	ME	Mendocino	Ten Mile Rvr Twp	74	172
Joseph	40	m	w	ME	Alameda	Washington Twp	68	280
CHADBURN								
Emry	38	m	w	ME	El Dorado	White Oak Twp	72	137
Levi	36	m	w	MD	Humboldt	South Fork Twp	72	301
Thomas	32	m	w	ME	San Francisco	8-Wd San Francisco	82	498
Wm	6	m	w	CA	Mendocino	Little Lake Twp	74	196
CHADBURNE								
Chas F	30	m	w	ME	San Francisco	6-Wd San Francisco	81	141
CHADD								
G W	39	m	w	IN	Humboldt	Eel Rvr Twp	72	246
Geo	69	m	w	KY	San Joaquin	2-Wd Stockton	86	200
CHADDERDON								
Jacob	39	m	w	NY	Sacramento	2-Wd Sacramento	77	230
CHADERON								
J S	34	m	w	NY	Sacramento	4-Wd Sacramento	77	321
CHADMAN								
Manuel	28	m	w	AZOR	Marin	Sausalito Twp	74	70
CHADWICK								
B	39	m	w	ME	Yuba	Rose Bar Twp	93	652
Chas P	62	m	w	MA	San Francisco	3-Wd San Francisco	79	308
Cordelia	30	f	w	ME	San Francisco	8-Wd San Francisco	82	318
George	42	m	w	PA	Sacramento	4-Wd Sacramento	77	328
Henry	41	m	w	CANA	San Bernardino	San Bernardino Twp	78	449
James	33	m	w	ENGL	Sacramento	Dry Crk Twp	77	97
Jos L	46	m	w	CT	San Francisco	San Francisco P O	83	36
Mary	72	f	w	ENGL	Calaveras	Copperopolis P O	70	246
Nathl	30	m	w	NC	San Francisco	San Francisco P O	83	154
Nathl G	33	m	w	NH	San Francisco	San Francisco P O	85	718
Sago	66	m	w	ENGL	Calaveras	Copperopolis P O	70	245
William	29	m	w	NJ	San Diego	Julian Dist	78	468
CHADWITZ								
Heny	45	m	w	PRUS	San Joaquin	Dent Twp	86	25
CHAEERY								
Prestemam	37	m	w	ITAL	San Mateo	Redwood City P O	87	375
CHAEN								
Ah	18	m	c	CHIN	Santa Clara	Alviso Twp	88	25
CHAEY								
Ah	24	m	c	CHIN	San Joaquin	3-Wd Stockton	86	230
CHAFER								
W	12	m	w	NV	San Francisco	San Francisco P O	85	800
CHAFERO								
Francisco	42	m	w	MEXI	Santa Clara	1-Wd San Jose	88	255
CHAFFAR								
Joseph	62	m	w	FRAN	Mariposa	Mariposa P O	74	91
CHAFFEE								
Rufus	64	m	w	VT	Marin	Point Reyes Twp	74	21
Walter S	42	m	w	NY	Santa Barbara	San Buenaventura P	87	437
CHAFFER								
C	11	f	w	NY	San Francisco	San Francisco P O	85	826
Elma	8	m	w	NY	San Francisco	San Francisco P O	85	826
John	24	m	w	NJ	Mendocino	Round Valley Twp	74	217
Laura	12	f	w	NY	San Francisco	San Francisco P O	85	826
Richard	33	m	w	ENGL	Nevada	Grass Valley Twp	75	167
Salina	6	f	w	NY	San Francisco	San Francisco P O	85	826
Samuel	54	m	w	CT	Nevada	Grass Valley Twp	75	204
CHAFFEY								
Lily D	6	f	w	CA	Sonoma	Analy Twp	91	245
CHAFFIN								
Aaron	46	m	w	VA	Humboldt	South Fork Twp	72	301
Bradfd	32	m	w	OH	Calaveras	Copperopolis P O	70	237
CHAFIN								
Amos	25	m	w	WI	San Francisco	7-Wd San Francisco	81	275
CHAFTON								
William	34	m	w	ENGL	San Francisco	2-Wd San Francisco	79	211
CHAG								
Ah	58	m	c	CHIN	San Francisco	11-Wd San Francisc	84	695
Si	28	m	c	CHIN	Tuolumne	Sonora P O	93	312
CHAGGE								
J M	47	m	w	CT	Tuolumne	Big Oak Flat P O	93	394
CHAGNEY								
Fred	30	m	w	ENGL	San Francisco	3-Wd San Francisco	79	302
CHAGNON								
A	34	m	w	FRAN	Sonoma	Santa Rosa	91	424
CHAH								
Ah	28	m	c	CHIN	Marin	Novato Twp	74	11
Ah	20	m	c	CHIN	Yuba	Marysville Twp	93	567
CHAI								
Ah	35	m	c	CHIN	Sacramento	Franklin Twp	77	115
Ah	29	f	c	CHIN	Calaveras	San Andreas P O	70	199
Ah	16	f	c	CHIN	Mariposa	Maxwell Crk P O	74	138
CHAIE								
Ah	25	f	c	CHIN	Mariposa	Maxwell Crk P O	74	138
CHAIGNEAU								
Victorie	45	f	w	FRAN	San Francisco	2-Wd San Francisco	79	219
CHAINE								
Gaston	12	m	w	CA	Marin	San Rafael Twp	74	29
CHAINEUX								
Joseph	27	m	w	MO	San Francisco	San Francisco P O	80	343

© 2001 by Heritage Quest. All rights reserved.

Name	Age	S	R	B-PL	County	Locale	Roll	Pg
						Series M593		
CHAING								
Lim Now	34	m	c	CHIN	Sacramento	1-Wd Sacramento	77	193
CHAISE								
Julius	35	m	w	FRAN	San Francisco	San Francisco P O	80	462
CHAIX								
Eugene	28	m	w	FRAN	Placer	Lincoln P O	76	482
CHAK								
Ah	40	m	c	CHIN	San Francisco	6-Wd San Francisco	81	64
CHAKE								
Ah	22	m	c	CHIN	Merced	Snelling P O	74	248
CHAL								
Lee	26	m	c	CHIN	Sacramento	1-Wd Sacramento	77	192
CHALEE								
Gong	19	m	c	CHIN	Del Norte	Smith Rvr Twp	71	477
CHALFANT								
Aaron	32	m	w	PA	Mendocino	Point Arena Twp	74	213
John E	45	m	w	PA	Mendocino	Anderson Twp	74	156
Pleasant	39	m	w	OH	Inyo	Independence Twp	73	325
Samel J	25	m	w	MD	Mendocino	Big Rvr Twp	74	170
CHALIFONA								
Decido	43	m	w	FRAN	Fresno	Millerton P O	72	164
CHALITTE								
Besfate	65	m	w	MEXI	Los Angeles	Los Angeles Twp	73	490
CHALL								
John	34	m	w	SWIT	El Dorado	Greenwood Twp	72	55
CHALLA								
L	24	m	w	ITAL	Calaveras	Copperopolis P O	70	233
CHALLEE								
---	26	m	c	CHIN	Shasta	Horsetown P O	89	506
CHALLENGE								
James	43	m	w	KY	Plumas	Mineral Twp	77	23
CHALLIOL								
George	50	m	w	HESS	San Francisco	2-Wd San Francisco	79	159
CHALLMAN								
A	36	m	w	SWED	San Francisco	3-Wd San Francisco	79	300
John P	45	m	w	SWED	Plumas	Goodwin Twp	77	8
CHALLONER								
Mary	40	f	m	MA	San Francisco	6-Wd San Francisco	81	112
CHALMAN								
Andrew	24	m	w	CANA	Santa Cruz	Santa Cruz Twp	89	390
John	21	m	w	SWED	San Francisco	San Francisco P O	83	390
Samuel	15	m	w	CA	Inyo	Bishop Crk Twp	73	313
CHALMER								
A C	50	m	w	ENGL	Tuolumne	Big Oak Flat P O	93	406
G G	28	m	w	PA	Tuolumne	Big Oak Flat P O	93	406
H G	50	m	w	ENGL	Tuolumne	Sonora P O	93	318
John	54	m	w	SCOT	Nevada	Nevada Twp	75	304
R J	23	m	w	PA	Tuolumne	Big Oak Flat P O	93	406
CHALMERES								
Alx	27	m	w	CANA	San Joaquin	2-Wd Stockton	86	194
CHALMERS								
Alexander	38	m	w	CA	Santa Cruz	Watsonville	89	371
Alvin	30	m	w	VA	Santa Cruz	Watsonville	89	373
George	40	m	w	SCOT	Monterey	San Juan Twp	74	416
George	32	m	w	CANA	El Dorado	Placerville	72	111
J P	54	m	w	SCOT	San Francisco	3-Wd San Francisco	79	327
Jennie	57	f	w	SCOT	San Francisco	San Francisco P O	80	356
John	41	m	w	SCOT	Alpine	Silver Mtn P O	69	308
John	39	m	w	NC	San Joaquin	3-Wd Stockton	86	236
Lewis	45	m	w	SCOT	Alpine	Silver Mtn P O	69	308
Mary	16	f	w	CA	Tuolumne	Sonora P O	93	308
Obed	39	m	w	VA	San Joaquin	Elkhorn Twp	86	68
Robt	50	m	w	SCOT	El Dorado	Coloma Twp	72	7
W L	43	m	w	SCOT	Alameda	Oakland	68	137
William P	42	m	w	NC	Santa Cruz	Pajaro Twp	89	340
Wm	37	m	w	SCOT	San Francisco	8-Wd San Francisco	82	315
CHALMES								
Luther	52	m	w	NY	San Joaquin	Douglas Twp	86	31
CHALO								
Bernard	34	m	w	FRAN	San Francisco	San Francisco P O	80	469
CHALONER								
Herbert	23	m	w	ME	Santa Clara	Redwood Twp	88	131
John	71	m	w	IREL	San Francisco	11-Wd San Francisc	84	613
T W	38	m	w	MA	San Joaquin	1-Wd Stockton	86	135
CHALSNER								
C J	31	m	w	OH	Del Norte	Mountain Twp	71	475
CHAM								
Ah	41	m	c	CHIN	Amador	Fiddletown P O	69	428
Ah	36	m	c	CHIN	Tuolumne	Chinese Camp P O	93	389
Ah	35	m	c	CHIN	Santa Clara	Alviso Twp	88	23
Ah	30	m	c	CHIN	Santa Clara	1-Wd San Jose	88	273
Ah	25	m	c	CHIN	Sierra	Gibson Twp	89	538
Ah	24	m	c	CHIN	Santa Clara	San Jose Twp	88	194
Ah	22	m	c	CHIN	Santa Clara	Alviso Twp	88	22
Ah	21	m	c	CHIN	Santa Clara	2-Wd San Jose	88	297
Ah	20	m	c	CHIN	Santa Clara	San Jose Twp	88	179
Ah	18	m	c	CHIN	Yolo	Cache Crk Twp	93	429
Ah	17	m	c	CHIN	San Francisco	1-Wd San Francisco	79	87
Ah	16	m	c	CHIN	San Francisco	1-Wd San Francisco	79	43
Ah	15	m	c	CHIN	San Francisco	6-Wd San Francisco	81	39
Ah	14	m	c	CHIN	Santa Clara	1-Wd San Jose	88	272
Sam	28	m	c	CHIN	Yolo	Merritt Twp	93	504
Sing	30	m	c	CHIN	Mariposa	Mariposa P O	74	121
CHAMBER								
C	35	m	w	ME	Alameda	Oakland	68	265
Henry C	53	m	w	LA	Colusa	Colusa	71	289
Robt	30	m	w	SCOT	Alameda	Oakland	68	183
CHAMBERLAIN								
A	47	m	w	NY	Merced	Snelling P O	74	272
A	30	m	w	ME	Alameda	Oakland	68	170
Andrew	40	m	w	NY	Humboldt	Bucksport Twp	72	242
Anne	15	f	w	ME	San Francisco	8-Wd San Francisco	82	466
Charity	45	f	w	NY	Sacramento	Granite Twp	77	137
Chas	18	f	w	LA	San Francisco	8-Wd San Francisco	82	363
E	36	f	w	IREL	San Francisco	8-Wd San Francisco	82	367
Emeline	21	f	w	NY	Plumas	Seneca Twp	77	49
F	41	m	w	MI	Sacramento	3-Wd Sacramento	77	293
Flora	22	f	w	ENGL	San Francisco	6-Wd San Francisco	81	72
Flora	22	f	w	NY	San Francisco	6-Wd San Francisco	81	45
Fred D	41	m	w	OH	Sacramento	2-Wd Sacramento	77	254
George	46	m	w	NY	Contra Costa	Martinez P O	71	427
H	20	m	w	MA	San Francisco	7-Wd San Francisco	81	180
H F	36	f	w	OH	Alameda	Oakland	68	239
Hellen	15	f	w	LA	San Francisco	8-Wd San Francisco	82	363
Henry M	35	m	w	NY	Mendocino	Point Arena Twp	74	207
Isabella	16	f	w	LA	San Francisco	8-Wd San Francisco	82	363
J	39	m	w	NY	Alameda	Washington Twp	68	291
J T	22	m	w	IA	Humboldt	Pacific Twp	72	297
Jerome	39	m	w	NY	San Mateo	Half Moon Bay P O	87	397
Joel	39	m	w	NY	Contra Costa	Martinez P O	71	410
John	24	m	w	NY	San Francisco	7-Wd San Francisco	81	232
Leyer	42	m	w	NY	Contra Costa	Martinez P O	71	427
Louis	10	m	w	WI	Santa Clara	San Jose Twp	88	206
M	20	f	w	MA	Alameda	Oakland	68	190
M	16	m	w	CA	Amador	Drytown P O	69	417
Manie	13	f	w	CA	San Mateo	San Mateo P O	87	357
Mary	60	f	w	NJ	Humboldt	Bucksport Twp	72	242
Mary	45	f	w	NY	San Francisco	8-Wd San Francisco	82	441
Mary	12	f	w	CA	Tehama	Antelope Twp	92	155
Melissa	24	f	w	RI	San Francisco	8-Wd San Francisco	82	401
P	26	m	w	MA	Napa	Napa	75	19
Paul	40	m	w	KY	Trinity	Lewiston Pct	92	213
Philander	30	m	w	OH	San Mateo	Redwood Twp	87	367
Philo B	36	m	w	OH	Colusa	Colusa	71	297
R	41	m	w	OH	Siskiyou	Scott Valley Twp	89	616
Ralson	61	m	w	VT	San Francisco	8-Wd San Francisco	82	423
S B	30	f	w	IREL	Sacramento	1-Wd Sacramento	77	173
Thos	40	m	w	IREL	San Francisco	11-Wd San Francisc	84	704
Timothy	35	m	w	IN	Solano	Suisun Twp	90	97
W	55	m	w	WI	Sacramento	3-Wd Sacramento	77	310
W	25	m	w	NY	Alameda	Oakland	68	235
W E	64	m	w	NH	Sacramento	4-Wd Sacramento	77	364
Watson	43	m	w	MA	Nevada	Little York Twp	75	244
Wm	60	m	w	NJ	Sacramento	Granite Twp	77	137
Wm	37	m	w	CANA	Yuba	Rose Bar Twp	93	657
Wm	29	m	w	NY	Nevada	Eureka Twp	75	133
CHAMBERLAINE								
E	70	f	w	MEXI	Solano	Benicia	90	8
E G	31	m	w	IL	Solano	Benicia	90	8
CHAMBERLAN								
J	41	m	w	PA	Alameda	Murray Twp	68	109
John	55	m	w	IREL	Monterey	Monterey	74	360
CHAMBERLAND								
Thos	28	m	w	CANA	Sonoma	Salt Point	91	388
CHAMBERLIN								
A	39	m	w	NH	San Francisco	San Francisco P O	85	778
A	35	m	w	MA	San Francisco	8-Wd San Francisco	82	354
Chas	50	m	w	ME	San Francisco	11-Wd San Francisc	84	663
Dav	51	m	w	NY	Sonoma	Santa Rosa	91	394
E	21	m	w	NY	Yuba	Marysville Twp	93	567
Edward	34	m	w	MA	San Francisco	San Francisco P O	83	240
Frank	15	m	w	ENGL	San Francisco	11-Wd San Francisc	84	509
Geo	31	m	w	ME	Butte	Ophir Twp	70	106
H S	46	m	w	ME	San Francisco	8-Wd San Francisco	82	352
Israel G	43	m	w	VA	El Dorado	Placerville Twp	72	99
J	38	m	w	VT	Lassen	Long Valley Twp	73	437
J P	49	m	w	VT	Tuolumne	Big Oak Flat P O	93	394
James	18	m	w	NY	San Francisco	5-Wd San Francisco	81	36
James B	36	m	w	ME	Inyo	Bishop Crk Twp	73	315
Jno	39	m	w	PA	Butte	Kimshew Tpw	70	77
Joel	30	m	w	ENGL	Nevada	Nevada Twp	75	309
Joh	34	m	w	OH	Butte	Hamilton Twp	70	61
Joseph	48	m	w	CANA	San Francisco	San Francisco P O	83	417
Joseph	38	m	w	MI	San Diego	San Pasqual	78	523
Joseph F	45	m	w	OH	Sonoma	Petaluma Twp	91	321
Lewis	65	m	w	NY	Monterey	San Juan Twp	74	389
Lewis R	51	m	w	VA	Placer	Lincoln P O	76	488
Martha	28	f	w	MA	Sonoma	Petaluma Twp	91	336
Mary	14	f	w	MI	San Francisco	8-Wd San Francisco	82	323
Paul	30	m	w	MA	San Francisco	San Francisco P O	83	53
Phillip	24	m	w	VT	San Francisco	5-Wd San Francisco	81	3
Richard	20	m	w	OR	Solano	Suisun Twp	90	108
Sarah E	14	f	w	CA	Sonoma	Washington Twp	91	466
Walter	25	m	w	NY	San Francisco	5-Wd San Francisco	81	36
Wm	25	m	w	CT	San Francisco	San Francisco P O	85	749
CHAMBERLINE								
Brigham H	39	m	w	MA	Yuba	New York Twp	93	639
O	28	m	w	ME	Solano	Vallejo	90	141
CHAMBERS								
A	45	m	w	ITAL	Tehama	Tehama Twp	92	193
Adam	34	m	w	CANA	Alpine	Markleeville P O	69	312
Alex	34	m	w	IREL	San Francisco	2-Wd San Francisco	79	193
Alexander C	34	m	w	NY	Alpine	Markleeville P O	69	316
Austin	27	m	w	OH	San Diego	Julian Dist	78	471

© 2001 by Heritage Quest. All rights reserved.

California 1870 Census

Series M593

Name	Age	S	R	B-PL	County	Locale	Roll	Pg
B	27	m	w	MO	Mendocino	Ukiah Twp	74	234
Booker	54	m	w	VA	Placer	Newcastle Twp	76	478
Bridget	60	f	w	IREL	San Francisco	8-Wd San Francisco	82	496
Charles	50	m	w	NY	Marin	Bolinas Twp	74	3
Charles	40	m	w	ENGL	Sacramento	2-Wd Sacramento	77	212
David	30	m	w	PA	Amador	Volcano P O	69	384
David C	48	m	w	KY	El Dorado	Mud Springs Twp	72	78
Eugene	37	m	w	CANA	Colusa	Colusa Twp	71	283
Frank	30	m	w	PA	San Francisco	7-Wd San Francisco	81	160
Geo	40	m	w	ENGL	San Francisco	1-Wd San Francisco	79	133
Geo	28	m	w	NY	San Francisco	1-Wd San Francisco	79	17
Geo L	22	m	w	OH	San Francisco	1-Wd San Francisco	79	115
Geo W	31	m	w	PA	Butte	Chico Twp	70	22
Henry	42	m	w	KY	Monterey	San Benito Twp	74	378
Honora	20	f	w	IREL	San Francisco	11-Wd San Francisc	84	701
J C	33	m	w	CANA	El Dorado	Coloma Twp	72	8
James	55	m	w	ENGL	Alameda	Brooklyn Twp	68	54
James	45	m	w	CANA	San Francisco	7-Wd San Francisco	81	276
James	35	m	w	IREL	San Francisco	11-Wd San Francisc	84	701
James	32	m	w	ME	Santa Clara	1-Wd San Jose	88	236
Jerome	24	m	w	IREL	Stanislaus	Emory Twp	92	25
Jerry	40	m	w	NJ	Butte	Ophir Twp	70	107
Jno	35	m	w	IREL	Butte	Oregon Twp	70	124
John	45	m	w	KY	Siskiyou	Scott Rvr Twp	89	602
John	42	m	w	GA	Mariposa	Mariposa P O	74	124
John	41	m	w	VA	San Diego	Julian Dist	78	470
John	40	m	w	DENM	San Francisco	2-Wd San Francisco	79	266
John	40	m	w	MA	Butte	Chico Twp	70	42
John	35	m	w	IREL	Humboldt	Mattole Twp	72	288
John	30	m	w	MA	San Francisco	San Francisco P O	85	873
John	28	m	w	MO	Solano	Silveyville Twp	90	75
John	27	m	w	PA	San Diego	Julian Dist	78	470
John	23	m	w	IREL	San Francisco	1-Wd San Francisco	79	46
John	22	m	w	OH	Sonoma	Petaluma Twp	91	314
John	22	m	w	MO	Sonoma	Petaluma Twp	91	344
John	21	m	w	NJ	San Francisco	11-Wd San Francisc	84	477
John	20	m	w	MO	Colusa	Grand Island Twp	71	302
John C	42	m	w	MO	Monterey	San Benito Twp	74	383
John W	20	m	w	IL	San Francisco	1-Wd San Francisco	79	100
Jonathan	29	m	w	ENGL	El Dorado	White Oak Twp	72	135
Joshua	40	m	w	CT	Plumas	Seneca Twp	77	48
Kate	34	f	w	IREL	Napa	Napa	75	57
L	28	m	w	CANA	Sierra	Gibson Twp	89	541
Mary	25	f	w	IREL	San Francisco	6-Wd San Francisco	81	108
Medora	34	f	w	IL	Sacramento	2-Wd Sacramento	77	236
Michel	37	m	w	IREL	Napa	Napa Twp	75	29
Naomi	73	f	w	NC	Monterey	Pajaro Twp	74	368
Obed	26	m	w	NY	San Joaquin	Union Twp	86	265
Robt	37	m	w	OH	Siskiyou	Cottonwood Twp	89	595
Sarah	47	f	w	IREL	Colusa	Monroe Twp	71	315
Thomas	72	m	w	PA	Colusa	Spring Valley Twp	71	340
Thos	59	m	w	VA	San Francisco	2-Wd San Francisco	79	229
Thos	36	m	w	IREL	San Francisco	San Francisco P O	83	119
Thos K	75	m	w	PA	Sonoma	Petaluma Twp	91	358
William	41	m	w	MI	Colusa	Colusa	71	294
Wm	61	m	w	CANA	Humboldt	Bucksport Twp	72	244
Wm	30	m	w	IREL	Tuolumne	Sonora P O	93	309
Wm A	37	m	w	OH	San Diego	San Diego	78	490
CHAMBERTIN								
Jas W	42	m	w	TN	Butte	Chico Twp	70	16
CHAMBILLE								
Albert	29	m	w	FRAN	San Francisco	11-Wd San Francisc	84	554
CHAMBLIN								
Marquis	41	m	w	KY	Santa Clara	1-Wd San Jose	88	225
CHAMBREY								
Alfonz	27	m	w	FRAN	San Francisco	2-Wd San Francisco	79	146
CHAMBUSH								
John	35	m	w	HAMB	San Francisco	6-Wd San Francisco	81	155
CHAMCEY								
S B	43	m	w	MO	San Joaquin	Dent Twp	86	27
CHAME								
Ah	25	m	c	CHIN	Santa Clara	Alviso Twp	88	27
CHAMICHAEL								
R	28	m	w	AL	El Dorado	Coloma Twp	72	10
CHAMLIN								
John L	38	m	w	KY	San Luis Obispo	Santa Rosa Twp	87	325
CHAMORA								
Jane	42	f	w	CHIL	San Francisco	San Francisco P O	80	461
CHAMORO								
Marano	20	m	w	MEXI	San Francisco	San Francisco P O	80	477
CHAMOT								
Estine	37	m	w	FRAN	Santa Clara	1-Wd San Jose	88	268
CHAMPBELL								
William J	49	m	w	MO	Yolo	Cottonwood Twp	93	464
CHAMPEAU								
Efran	24	m	w	CANA	Marin	San Rafael Twp	74	34
CHAMPEAUX								
Carrie	30	f	w	WALE	San Francisco	San Francisco P O	83	114
CHAMPENET								
Janet	46	f	w	FRAN	Santa Clara	2-Wd San Jose	88	300
CHAMPENEY								
Harriet	60	f	w	MA	Nevada	Meadow Lake Twp	75	264
CHAMPIN								
Margaret	45	f	w	IREL	San Francisco	San Francisco P O	85	860
CHAMPION								
A D	39	m	w	FRAN	Alameda	Oakland	68	145
Anna	46	f	w	SCOT	Amador	Sutter Crk P O	69	401
Emanuel	50	m	w	ENGL	Nevada	Grass Valley Twp	75	154
Emanul	57	m	w	ENGL	Nevada	Grass Valley Twp	75	162
Emele	43	m	w	FRAN	Yuba	New York Twp	93	641
F	21	m	w	ENGL	Nevada	Meadow Lake Twp	75	264
F W	38	m	w	MA	San Joaquin	Douglas Twp	86	46
Francis	43	m	w	ENGL	Calaveras	Copperopolis P O	70	264
Henry	30	m	w	ENGL	Nevada	Nevada Twp	75	314
Israel	50	m	w	CT	Yolo	Washington Twp	93	531
James	49	m	w	SC	Calaveras	San Andreas P O	70	152
James	31	m	w	ENGL	Nevada	Grass Valley Twp	75	182
James	23	m	w	ENGL	Fresno	Millerton P O	72	167
James D	51	m	w	NY	Los Angeles	Los Angeles	73	508
Jas	29	m	w	ENGL	Fresno	Millerton P O	72	165
John	30	m	w	ENGL	Calaveras	San Andreas P O	70	195
John	21	m	w	ENGL	Nevada	Grass Valley Twp	75	203
Joseph	24	m	w	CANA	San Francisco	1-Wd San Francisco	79	63
Joseph	23	m	w	ENGL	Nevada	Grass Valley Twp	75	152
L	34	m	w	NY	San Francisco	8-Wd San Francisco	82	374
Laroy S	26	m	w	MA	Butte	Oroville Twp	70	140
Lewis	47	m	w	ENGL	Placer	Bath P O	76	434
Robert	24	m	w	ENGL	Marin	Novato Twp	74	12
W	29	m	w	ENGL	Sierra	Butte Twp	89	513
Wm	17	m	w	TX	San Bernardino	San Bernardino Twp	78	440
CHAMPLAIN								
Erastus	52	m	w	VT	Sonoma	Cloverdale Twp	91	268
Julia	32	f	w	NY	San Francisco	San Francisco P O	83	50
CHAMPLIN								
Erastus W	42	m	w	NY	Los Angeles	Santa Ana Twp	73	612
G W	47	m	w	NY	Siskiyou	Scott Valley Twp	89	619
Geo	43	m	w	RI	Tehama	Tehama Twp	92	187
George T	63	m	w	RI	Yolo	Fremont Twp	93	477
N	42	m	w	NY	Sacramento	3-Wd Sacramento	77	291
Orrin	38	m	w	PA	Siskiyou	Yreka Twp	89	664
CHAMPLINS								
Charles	58	m	w	NY	Sonoma	Sonoma Twp	91	431
John	39	m	w	NJ	San Francisco	11-Wd San Francisc	84	498
CHAMPMAN								
Henry	28	m	w	ENGL	San Francisco	2-Wd San Francisco	79	187
CHAMPNEY								
D C	56	m	w	NY	Tuolumne	Columbia P O	93	349
CHAMPSAUR								
Lucien	18	m	w	FRAN	San Francisco	1-Wd San Francisco	79	111
CHAN								
Ah	61	m	c	CHIN	Butte	Kimshew Tpw	70	84
Ah	50	m	c	CHIN	Placer	Auburn P O	76	362
Ah	44	m	c	CHIN	Alameda	Alvarado	68	305
Ah	40	m	c	CHIN	Sacramento	Sutter Twp	77	391
Ah	40	m	c	CHIN	Placer	Auburn P O	76	361
Ah	40	m	c	CHIN	San Francisco	6-Wd San Francisco	81	67
Ah	4	f	c	CA	San Francisco	San Francisco P O	80	527
Ah	37	m	c	CHIN	Butte	Hamilton Twp	70	73
Ah	37	m	c	CHIN	San Francisco	San Francisco P O	80	465
Ah	35	m	c	CHIN	Mariposa	Maxwell Crk P O	74	147
Ah	35	m	c	CHIN	Alameda	Washington Twp	68	273
Ah	35	m	c	CHIN	Santa Clara	Fremont Twp	88	55
Ah	33	m	c	CHIN	Nevada	Nevada Twp	75	313
Ah	31	m	c	CHIN	Calaveras	San Andreas P O	70	172
Ah	31	m	c	CHIN	Placer	Dutch Flat P O	76	411
Ah	30	m	c	CHIN	Tuolumne	Columbia P O	93	352
Ah	30	m	c	CHIN	Mariposa	Maxwell Crk P O	74	147
Ah	29	m	c	CHIN	Tuolumne	Sonora P O	93	312
Ah	28	m	c	CHIN	Placer	Bath P O	76	453
Ah	28	m	c	CHIN	Placer	Dutch Flat P O	76	409
Ah	27	m	c	CHIN	Santa Clara	San Jose Twp	88	192
Ah	25	m	c	CHIN	Sacramento	Franklin Twp	77	114
Ah	25	m	c	CHIN	Amador	Ione City P O	69	367
Ah	24	m	c	CHIN	Santa Clara	2-Wd San Jose	88	288
Ah	22	m	c	CHIN	Placer	Dutch Flat P O	76	411
Ah	22	m	c	CHIN	San Francisco	6-Wd San Francisco	81	50
Ah	22	m	c	CHIN	Yuba	Marysville	93	601
Ah	21	m	c	CHIN	San Francisco	San Francisco P O	80	521
Ah	19	m	c	CHIN	Nevada	Meadow Lake Twp	75	255
Ah	18	m	c	CHIN	Siskiyou	Hamburg Twp	89	597
Ah	18	m	c	CHIN	Butte	Chico Twp	70	52
Ah	17	m	c	CHIN	San Francisco	1-Wd San Francisco	79	55
Ah	16	f	c	CA	Calaveras	San Andreas P O	70	171
Ah	14	m	c	CHIN	Placer	Dutch Flat P O	76	411
An	34	m	c	CHIN	Tuolumne	Sonora P O	93	311
Chan	17	m	c	CHIN	Contra Costa	San Pablo Twp	71	358
Choy	25	f	c	CHIN	Santa Clara	1-Wd San Jose	88	269
Eh	43	m	c	CHIN	Amador	Volcano P O	69	378
Gaw	38	m	c	CHIN	Calaveras	San Andreas P O	70	218
Hing	29	m	c	CHIN	San Mateo	Schoolhouse Statio	87	336
Isaac	37	m	w	RI	San Joaquin	1-Wd Stockton	86	134
Kee	32	m	c	CHIN	San Francisco	1-Wd San Francisco	79	118
Kin	28	f	c	CHIN	Amador	Fiddletown P O	69	428
Laing	24	m	c	CHIN	San Francisco	11-Wd San Francisc	84	529
Pan	20	m	c	CHIN	San Francisco	6-Wd San Francisco	81	53
Sat	16	m	c	CHIN	San Francisco	6-Wd San Francisco	81	52
Simeon	33	m	w	ME	Yuba	Rose Bar Twp	93	653
Sing	9	m	c	CHIN	Sacramento	3-Wd Sacramento	77	303
Tong	45	m	c	CHIN	Kern	Havilah P O	73	338
Yee	19	m	c	CHIN	San Francisco	San Francisco P O	83	404
Young	40	m	c	CHIN	Calaveras	San Andreas P O	70	161
Yuen	20	m	c	CHIN	San Francisco	6-Wd San Francisco	81	54
Yun	40	m	c	CHIN	Calaveras	San Andreas P O	70	162

© 2001 by Heritage Quest. All rights reserved.

Name	Age	S	R	B-PL	County	Locale	Roll	Pg
CHANCE								
Catharine	18	f	w	IREL	Sacramento	2-Wd Sacramento	77	238
James F	28	m	w	MO	Stanislaus	Empire Twp	92	31
Silas	35	m	w	IL	Monterey	Salinas Twp	74	307
William	28	m	w	OH	Yolo	Putah Twp	93	518
William J	30	m	w	MO	Stanislaus	Empire Twp	92	31
CHANCEL								
James	40	m	w	FRAN	San Francisco	San Francisco P O	80	463
CHANCERI								
Nicola	34	m	w	ITAL	San Francisco	San Francisco P O	80	466
CHANCEY								
Frances	43	f	w	IN	Alameda	Alvarado	68	305
CHANCY								
Edward	33	m	w	ME	Yolo	Buckeye Twp	93	407
James	35	m	w	IREL	San Francisco	11-Wd San Francisc	84	543
Mathew	29	m	w	IREL	Yolo	Putah Twp	93	519
CHANDERLAIN								
Wm	43	m	w	NY	Merced	Snelling P O	74	261
CHANDERS								
Enock W	36	m	w	IN	Colusa	Colusa	71	288
CHANDLER								
A B	49	m	w	NH	Amador	Volcano P O	69	382
A F	23	m	w	MA	Napa	Yountville Twp	75	80
A L	38	m	w	VT	Sutter	Nicolaus Twp	92	115
Albert	53	m	w	NJ	San Francisco	1-Wd San Francisco	79	39
Albert B	24	m	w	IL	Santa Clara	2-Wd San Jose	88	325
Bethia	35	f	w	ME	Santa Clara	1-Wd San Jose	88	233
Boyadial S	44	m	w	OH	Yolo	Cottonwood Twp	93	459
Bridget	48	f	w	IREL	San Francisco	1-Wd San Francisco	79	131
Chas	29	m	w	WI	Yuba	Marysville	93	633
Clark	54	m	w	MA	San Francisco	San Francisco P O	83	258
Daniel	35	m	w	SC	El Dorado	Diamond Springs Tw	72	34
David	38	m	w	OH	Humboldt	Arcata Twp	72	226
E	46	m	w	OH	Sierra	Sierra Twp	89	564
E M	56	m	w	NY	Yuba	Marysville	93	586
E M	48	m	w	NY	Yuba	Marysville	93	591
Eveline	60	f	w	PA	Santa Clara	Santa Clara Twp	88	142
Fleming	59	m	w	KY	Trinity	Minersville Pct	92	203
Fred	25	m	w	NH	Placer	Colfax P O	76	386
Frederick	38	m	w	NY	Solano	Vacaville Twp	90	118
Freeman	36	m	w	ME	Siskiyou	Yreka Twp	89	665
Gates S	46	m	w	OH	Yolo	Putah Twp	93	525
George	37	m	w	ENGL	San Francisco	11-Wd San Francisc	84	503
H L	35	m	w	MA	Solano	Vallejo	90	209
H M	54	f	w	VT	Sacramento	3-Wd Sacramento	77	265
Horatio	42	m	w	NY	San Francisco	11-Wd San Francisc	84	457
Isaac	77	m	w	NH	Santa Cruz	Santa Cruz Twp	89	395
J M	37	m	w	PA	Yuba	Marysville	93	595
James	41	m	w	NY	Sacramento	San Joaquin Twp	77	399
James D	20	m	w	TX	Santa Cruz	Santa Cruz Twp	89	400
Jeff	33	m	w	NY	Napa	Yountville Twp	75	89
Jennie	24	f	w	ENGL	San Francisco	San Francisco P O	80	457
Jessie	57	m	w	PA	Nevada	Grass Valley Twp	75	167
John A	36	m	w	PA	Yuba	Slate Range Bar Tw	93	675
Jonah	60	m	w	VT	Sonoma	Petaluma Twp	91	320
Jos	17	m	w	TN	Sonoma	Russian Rvr	91	369
Jotham L	32	m	w	ME	Santa Clara	Fremont Twp	88	50
L C	49	m	w	NY	Sacramento	1-Wd Sacramento	77	178
La Fayette	34	m	w	ME	San Mateo	Pescadero P O	87	413
Lewis	45	m	w	AR	Santa Cruz	Santa Cruz Twp	89	401
Martin	49	m	w	NY	San Francisco	5-Wd San Francisco	81	12
Mary	17	f	w	NJ	Solano	Benicia	90	16
Nathan	26	m	w	ME	Sonoma	Vallejo Twp	91	452
O S	47	m	w	MA	Tuolumne	Big Oak Flat P O	93	394
P M	5	m	w	NY	Sutter	Sutter Twp	92	127
R T	52	m	w	GA	Merced	Snelling P O	74	251
Richd D	42	m	w	ENGL	San Francisco	1-Wd San Francisco	79	98
Robert	34	m	w	ENGL	San Francisco	1-Wd San Francisco	79	133
Robt	34	m	w	ENGL	San Francisco	San Francisco P O	85	819
Russell	40	m	w	NC	El Dorado	Mud Springs Twp	72	76
Salmon	74	m	w	VT	Yolo	Putah Twp	93	525
Sam	43	m	w	ME	Placer	Gold Run Twp	76	399
Sarah M	29	f	w	NH	Sonoma	Petaluma Twp	91	342
Seth	63	m	w	OH	Plumas	Goodwin Twp	77	2
Soloman P	73	m	w	NY	Yolo	Cache Crk Twp	93	431
Stephen	47	m	w	KY	Kern	Havilah P O	73	338
T H	27	m	w	NY	Solano	Vallejo	90	188
Theo	45	m	w	ME	San Joaquin	Dent Twp	86	21
Thos	27	m	w	VA	San Francisco	1-Wd San Francisco	79	127
William	40	m	w	PA	Los Angeles	Los Angeles Twp	73	467
William	28	m	w	VA	Alameda	Washington Twp	68	289
William	25	m	w	OH	Solano	Maine Prairie Twp	90	45
Wm	40	m	w	ENGL	San Francisco	11-Wd San Francisc	84	641
Wm	40	m	w	MA	San Joaquin	Liberty Twp	86	91
Wm A	37	m	w	IL	Santa Cruz	Santa Cruz Twp	89	395
CHANDLERS								
George	37	m	w	AR	Stanislaus	Empire Twp	92	33
CHANDON								
C T	47	m	w	FRAN	Sutter	Butte Twp	92	104
F A	33	m	w	MO	Yuba	Marysville Twp	93	569
Joseph	40	m	w	MO	Yuba	Marysville Twp	93	570
M	21	f	w	BADE	Yuba	Marysville	93	616
CHANDONA								
Mathew	44	m	w	GERM	Los Angeles	Los Angeles	73	535
CHANDONER								
John	42	m	w	PRUS	Sacramento	American Twp	77	65
CHANDOUR								
E J	46	m	w	FRAN	Tuolumne	Big Oak Flat P O	93	404
CHANDRA								
Mata	20	f	w	PORT	Santa Clara	Milpitas Twp	88	110
CHANE								
Celistis	39	m	w	FRAN	Monterey	Alisal Twp	74	298
Lawrence	42	m	w	IREL	Santa Barbara	Santa Barbara P O	87	501
Mary	34	f	w	FRAN	Monterey	Castroville Twp	74	335
CHANET								
Julia	33	f	w	FRAN	Napa	Napa	75	19
CHANEY								
Anna	69	f	w	PA	Butte	Chico Twp	70	33
Henry	37	m	w	MA	Nevada	Washington Twp	75	341
John	40	m	w	IREL	San Francisco	San Francisco P O	85	845
Owen	50	m	w	IREL	San Francisco	11-Wd San Francisc	84	524
Saml	41	m	w	OH	Butte	Chico Twp	70	33
Stephen C	18	m	w	MO	Alpine	Woodfords P O	69	309
Thomas	36	m	w	MA	Nevada	Washington Twp	75	341
William W	54	m	w	TN	Los Angeles	Los Nietos Twp	73	574
CHANG								
---	32	m	c	CHIN	San Francisco	6-Wd San Francisco	81	64
---	20	m	c	CHIN	Siskiyou	Yreka Twp	89	669
A	33	m	c	CHIN	Alameda	Eden Twp	68	87
Ah	7	f	c	CHIN	San Francisco	San Francisco P O	80	448
Ah	56	m	c	CHIN	San Francisco	San Francisco P O	80	496
Ah	50	m	c	CHIN	San Francisco	San Francisco P O	80	493
Ah	46	m	c	CHIN	San Francisco	San Francisco P O	80	455
Ah	45	m	c	CHIN	Nevada	Grass Valley Twp	75	194
Ah	40	m	c	CHIN	Calaveras	Copperopolis P O	70	222
Ah	40	m	c	CHIN	Sacramento	Granite Twp	77	138
Ah	40	m	c	CHIN	Sacramento	Granite Twp	77	138
Ah	40	m	c	CHIN	Santa Clara	1-Wd San Jose	88	271
Ah	40	m	c	CHIN	San Joaquin	Castoria Twp	86	10
Ah	40	m	c	CHIN	San Francisco	San Francisco P O	80	449
Ah	39	m	c	CHIN	San Francisco	San Francisco P O	80	530
Ah	39	m	c	CHIN	San Francisco	San Francisco P O	80	525
Ah	39	m	c	CHIN	San Francisco	San Francisco P O	80	496
Ah	39	m	c	CHIN	San Francisco	San Francisco P O	80	495
Ah	38	m	c	CHIN	San Francisco	San Francisco P O	80	496
Ah	38	m	c	CHIN	Tuolumne	Big Oak Flat P O	93	394
Ah	36	m	c	CHIN	Butte	Wyandotte Twp	70	142
Ah	36	m	c	CHIN	San Francisco	San Francisco P O	80	515
Ah	36	m	c	CHIN	San Francisco	San Francisco P O	80	498
Ah	36	m	c	CHIN	San Francisco	San Francisco P O	80	497
Ah	36	m	c	CHIN	San Francisco	San Francisco P O	80	436
Ah	35	m	c	CHIN	Stanislaus	Emory Twp	92	19
Ah	35	m	c	CHIN	San Francisco	San Francisco P O	80	437
Ah	34	m	c	CHIN	San Francisco	San Francisco P O	80	522
Ah	34	m	c	CHIN	San Francisco	San Francisco P O	80	512
Ah	34	m	c	CHIN	Mariposa	Mariposa P O	74	104
Ah	34	m	c	CHIN	San Francisco	San Francisco P O	80	436
Ah	32	m	c	CHIN	San Francisco	San Francisco P O	80	497
Ah	32	m	c	CHIN	San Francisco	San Francisco P O	80	500
Ah	32	m	c	CHIN	San Francisco	San Francisco P O	80	496
Ah	32	m	c	CHIN	San Joaquin	Castoria Twp	86	12
Ah	31	m	c	CHIN	Santa Clara	1-Wd San Jose	88	277
Ah	31	m	c	CHIN	San Francisco	San Francisco P O	80	512
Ah	31	m	c	CHIN	San Joaquin	1-Wd Stockton	86	155
Ah	30	m	c	CHIN	Alameda	Washington Twp	68	273
Ah	30	m	c	CHIN	Santa Clara	1-Wd San Jose	88	274
Ah	30	m	c	CHIN	San Francisco	San Francisco P O	80	495
Ah	30	m	c	CHIN	San Francisco	San Francisco P O	80	493
Ah	30	m	c	CHIN	Santa Clara	San Jose Twp	88	192
Ah	30	m	c	CHIN	Placer	Auburn P O	76	370
Ah	30	m	c	CHIN	Placer	Auburn P O	76	371
Ah	30	m	c	CHIN	San Francisco	2-Wd San Francisco	79	282
Ah	29	m	c	CHIN	Santa Clara	2-Wd San Jose	88	325
Ah	29	f	c	CHIN	Santa Clara	1-Wd San Jose	88	274
Ah	29	m	c	CHIN	San Francisco	San Francisco P O	80	529
Ah	29	m	c	CHIN	San Francisco	San Francisco P O	80	491
Ah	29	m	c	CHIN	San Francisco	San Francisco P O	80	521
Ah	29	m	c	CHIN	San Francisco	San Francisco P O	80	514
Ah	29	m	c	CHIN	San Joaquin	Tulare Twp	86	262
Ah	28	m	c	CHIN	Trinity	Lewiston Pct	92	214
Ah	28	m	c	CHIN	Santa Clara	1-Wd San Jose	88	277
Ah	28	m	c	CHIN	San Francisco	San Francisco P O	80	453
Ah	28	m	c	CHIN	San Francisco	San Francisco P O	80	487
Ah	27	m	c	CHIN	Yuba	East Bear Rvr Twp	93	540
Ah	27	m	c	CHIN	Calaveras	Copperopolis P O	70	258
Ah	27	m	c	CHIN	Nevada	Meadow Lake Twp	75	259
Ah	27	m	c	CHIN	Nevada	Meadow Lake Twp	75	266
Ah	26	m	c	CHIN	Santa Clara	1-Wd San Jose	88	270
Ah	26	m	c	CHIN	Santa Clara	1-Wd San Jose	88	273
Ah	26	m	c	CHIN	San Francisco	San Francisco P O	80	516
Ah	26	m	c	CHIN	San Francisco	San Francisco P O	80	505
Ah	26	m	c	CHIN	San Francisco	San Francisco P O	80	514
Ah	26	m	c	CHIN	San Francisco	San Francisco P O	80	494
Ah	26	m	c	CHIN	San Francisco	11-Wd San Francisc	84	695
Ah	25	m	c	CHIN	Santa Clara	Fremont Twp	88	49
Ah	25	m	c	CHIN	Santa Clara	Fremont Twp	88	57
Ah	25	m	c	CHIN	San Francisco	7-Wd San Francisco	81	257
Ah	25	m	c	CHIN	Placer	Auburn P O	76	371
Ah	25	m	c	CHIN	San Francisco	1-Wd San Francisco	79	106
Ah	24	m	c	CHIN	San Francisco	8-Wd San Francisco	82	458
Ah	24	m	c	CHIN	San Francisco	San Francisco P O	80	509
Ah	24	m	c	CHIN	San Francisco	San Francisco P O	80	529
Ah	24	f	c	CHIN	San Francisco	San Francisco P O	80	508

© 2001 by Heritage Quest. All rights reserved.

California 1870 Census

Name	Age	S	R	B-PL	County	Locale (Series M593)	Roll	Pg
Ah	24	f	c	CHIN	San Francisco	San Francisco P O	80	503
Ah	24	f	c	CHIN	San Francisco	San Francisco P O	80	491
Ah	24	m	c	CHIN	San Francisco	11-Wd San Francisc	84	557
Ah	24	m	c	CHIN	San Francisco	2-Wd San Francisco	79	277
Ah	23	m	c	CHIN	San Joaquin	1-Wd Stockton	86	149
Ah	22	f	c	CHIN	San Francisco	San Francisco P O	80	494
Ah	22	m	c	CHIN	Tuolumne	Chinese Camp P O	93	364
Ah	21	m	c	CHIN	Santa Clara	San Jose Twp	88	196
Ah	20	m	c	CHIN	Colusa	Colusa	71	298
Ah	20	f	c	CHIN	San Francisco	San Francisco P O	80	441
Ah	19	m	c	CHIN	Nevada	Rough & Ready Twp	75	337
Ah	19	f	c	CHIN	San Francisco	San Francisco P O	80	507
Ah	19	m	c	CHIN	San Joaquin	Castoria Twp	86	15
Ah	19	m	c	CHIN	Yuba	Marysville	93	583
Ah	18	m	c	CHIN	Mariposa	Maxwell Crk P O	74	138
Ah	18	m	c	CHIN	Monterey	Monterey	74	356
Ah	18	m	c	CHIN	Sacramento	3-Wd Sacramento	77	316
Ah	17	m	c	CHIN	Santa Clara	1-Wd San Jose	88	271
Ah	17	m	c	CHIN	San Francisco	San Francisco P O	83	263
Ah	17	m	c	CHIN	San Joaquin	2-Wd Stockton	86	197
Ah	16	m	c	CHIN	Sierra	Sears Twp	89	553
Ah	15	m	c	CHIN	Placer	Auburn P O	76	377
Ah	14	m	c	CHIN	San Francisco	11-Wd San Francisc	84	557
Ar	30	m	c	CHIN	Sutter	Sutter Twp	92	121
Chang	35	m	c	CHIN	Placer	Bath P O	76	453
Choon	22	m	c	CHIN	San Francisco	11-Wd San Francisc	84	529
Con	18	m	c	CHIN	Yuba	Marysville	93	625
Dong	25	m	c	CHIN	San Francisco	11-Wd San Francisc	84	529
El	18	m	c	CHIN	San Francisco	11-Wd San Francisc	84	529
Gee	19	m	c	CHIN	Sierra	Eureka Twp	89	527
Hang	22	m	c	CHIN	San Francisco	7-Wd San Francisco	81	257
Hang	20	m	c	CHIN	San Francisco	6-Wd San Francisco	81	44
Hing	50	m	c	CHIN	Sierra	Table Rock Twp	89	578
Hing	30	m	c	CHIN	San Francisco	11-Wd San Francisc	84	528
Ho	17	m	c	CHIN	Santa Clara	San Jose Twp	88	194
Jim	22	m	c	CHIN	Sacramento	3-Wd Sacramento	77	283
Jos	30	m	c	CHIN	Monterey	San Juan Twp	74	410
Ka	59	m	c	CHIN	Tuolumne	Sonora P O	93	312
Ki	43	m	c	CHIN	Butte	Wyandotte Twp	70	143
Lee	36	m	c	CHIN	San Mateo	Schoolhouse Statio	87	335
Lee	33	m	c	CHIN	San Joaquin	1-Wd Stockton	86	146
Lee	30	m	c	CHIN	San Joaquin	1-Wd Stockton	86	147
Leong	22	m	c	CHIN	San Francisco	11-Wd San Francisc	84	556
Lo	28	m	c	CHIN	San Joaquin	1-Wd Stockton	86	147
Long	24	m	c	CHIN	San Francisco	6-Wd San Francisco	81	39
Loo	40	m	c	CHIN	Butte	Wyandotte Twp	70	148
Loo	20	m	c	CHIN	Tuolumne	Big Oak Flat P O	93	392
Lung	35	m	c	CHIN	San Francisco	11-Wd San Francisc	84	529
Lung	28	m	c	CHIN	Tulare	Kings Rvr Twp	92	252
Lung	24	f	c	CHIN	Santa Clara	1-Wd San Jose	88	274
Ming	22	m	c	CHIN	San Francisco	11-Wd San Francisc	84	529
On	40	m	c	CHIN	Yuba	Marysville	93	629
Po	24	m	c	CHIN	San Joaquin	1-Wd Stockton	86	146
Quak	24	m	c	CHIN	San Francisco	11-Wd San Francisc	84	529
Sam	31	m	c	CHIN	San Francisco	11-Wd San Francisc	84	529
San	31	m	c	CHIN	Tuolumne	Columbia P O	93	341
Sang	26	m	c	CHIN	San Francisco	11-Wd San Francisc	84	529
Seve	35	m	c	CHIN	San Francisco	11-Wd San Francisc	84	529
Si	27	m	c	CHIN	Yolo	Merritt Twp	93	504
Sing	16	m	c	CHIN	San Francisco	11-Wd San Francisc	84	529
Sum	40	m	c	CHIN	Tulare	Visalia Twp	92	286
Tchi	25	m	c	CHIN	San Francisco	11-Wd San Francisc	84	529
Tong	56	m	c	CHIN	Placer	Lincoln P O	76	483
Tow	19	m	c	CHIN	Nevada	Nevada Twp	75	316
Wang	25	m	c	CHIN	Tulare	Tule Rvr Twp	92	259
Wing	30	m	c	CHIN	San Francisco	6-Wd San Francisco	81	43
Wing	22	m	c	CHIN	Solano	Montezuma Twp	90	66
Wo	32	m	c	CHIN	Santa Clara	1-Wd San Jose	88	274
Wo	23	m	c	CHIN	San Joaquin	Douglas Twp	86	33
Wo	19	m	c	CHIN	Sonoma	Santa Rosa	91	412
Woo Gon	23	m	c	CHIN	San Francisco	11-Wd San Francisc	84	509
Yon	31	m	c	CHIN	San Francisco	11-Wd San Francisc	84	529
Yuck	36	m	c	CHIN	Yuba	Marysville	93	621
CHANGTIE								
Ah	20	m	c	CHIN	San Joaquin	1-Wd Stockton	86	155
CHANLERS								
C S	22	m	w	NY	Alameda	Oakland	68	202
CHANNELL								
John H	36	m	w	NH	El Dorado	Placerville	72	120
CHANNING								
H G	40	m	w	IREL	Tuolumne	Chinese Camp P O	93	370
CHANNON								
Caroline	32	f	w	FRAN	Sacramento	2-Wd Sacramento	77	233
John	26	m	w	ENGL	San Diego	Julian Dist	78	473
CHANO								
Gawbor	50	m	w	MEXI	San Luis Obispo	San Luis Obispo Tw	87	298
Louis	65	m	w	FRAN	Nevada	Bridgeport Twp	75	117
CHANSON								
Hilaron	32	m	w	FRAN	San Francisco	2-Wd San Francisco	79	145
CHANTIER								
George	40	m	w	FRAN	Tuolumne	Chinese Camp P O	93	383
CHANTREAU								
E	49	m	w	FRAN	Alameda	Oakland	68	175
CHANTRY								
Wm	50	m	w	NY	Solano	Vallejo	90	184
CHANVIN								
Emil	37	m	w	FRAN	Merced	Snelling P O	74	250
CHANY								
Ah	20	m	c	CHIN	Placer	Dutch Flat P O	76	411
Jonny	18	m	c	CHIN	Los Angeles	Los Angeles	73	506
CHANZ								
Jesus	38	m	w	MEXI	Los Angeles	Wilmington Twp	73	637
CHAOGA								
Macemene	20	f	w	CA	Monterey	Monterey Twp	74	349
CHAP								
Ah	50	m	c	CHIN	Amador	Jackson P O	69	331
Ah	41	m	c	CHIN	Amador	Fiddletown P O	69	428
Ah	28	m	c	CHIN	Sacramento	Granite Twp	77	138
Ah	18	m	c	CHIN	Santa Clara	San Jose Twp	88	194
CHAPA								
Antonio	14	m	w	CA	Santa Clara	Gilroy Twp	88	96
Matias	81	m	w	MEXI	Los Angeles	Los Angeles	73	550
CHAPAL								
John	22	m	w	CA	Santa Cruz	Santa Cruz	89	432
CHAPEE								
Joseph	30	m	w	FRAN	Sacramento	4-Wd Sacramento	77	330
CHAPEL								
Bartlett A	39	m	w	NY	San Diego	San Diego	78	500
Edwin	29	m	w	NY	Santa Cruz	Santa Cruz Twp	89	401
John	39	m	w	FRAN	Calaveras	San Andreas P O	70	174
Richard	58	m	w	NY	Santa Cruz	Santa Cruz Twp	89	401
CHAPELL								
Henry	35	m	w	KY	Solano	Vallejo	90	149
J	26	m	w	ENGL	Calaveras	Copperopolis P O	70	237
Thomas	28	m	w	ENGL	Amador	Sutter Crk P O	69	409
CHAPELLA								
Ann	60	f	w	MEXI	San Joaquin	1-Wd Stockton	86	132
CHAPELLE								
D La	35	m	w	CANA	Sonoma	Bodega Twp	91	253
Edw	31	m	w	IREL	Alameda	Oakland	68	228
CHAPEN								
Henry	34	m	w	CT	Stanislaus	Branch Twp	92	3
CHAPIAN								
Jose	28	m	w	CA	San Diego	Warners Rancho Dis	78	530
CHAPIN								
Addie	23	f	w	NY	San Francisco	San Francisco P O	80	484
Albert F	32	m	w	VA	San Diego	San Luis Rey	78	515
Amilia	35	f	w	VT	San Joaquin	Dent Twp	86	16
Anna	42	f	w	NY	San Francisco	San Francisco P O	83	25
Charles	42	m	w	VT	Tuolumne	Big Oak Flat P O	93	397
Charles	28	m	w	NY	San Francisco	6-Wd San Francisco	81	95
Chas	47	m	w	NY	San Francisco	5-Wd San Francisco	81	16
Dominic	38	m	w	CT	San Francisco	2-Wd San Francisco	79	274
Edwin M	41	m	w	RI	San Luis Obispo	Santa Rosa Twp	87	326
Fredk W	31	m	w	MA	Siskiyou	Yreka Twp	89	665
Geo	37	m	w	MI	San Francisco	11-Wd San Francisc	84	422
Grahm	45	m	w	NY	San Francisco	San Francisco P O	80	466
Henry	46	m	w	TN	Los Angeles	Los Nietos Twp	73	587
James	23	m	w	NY	Santa Clara	2-Wd San Jose	88	293
John E	26	m	w	NY	San Mateo	Woodside P O	87	384
Lyman	53	m	w	MA	Mariposa	Mariposa P O	74	112
Orrin	52	m	w	NY	Humboldt	Pacific Twp	72	294
Pamelia	11	f	w	CA	Monterey	Pajaro Twp	74	376
Rachel	38	f	w	OH	Santa Clara	1-Wd San Jose	88	224
Rodney	47	m	w	MA	Yuba	Rose Bar Twp	93	655
Saml L	40	m	w	NY	Nevada	Little York Twp	75	239
Saml M	52	m	w	MA	Sacramento	Franklin Twp	77	115
Samuel F	31	m	w	NY	Placer	Auburn P O	76	368
W D	51	m	w	NC	Merced	Snelling P O	74	268
William	48	m	w	CT	Marin	Bolinas Twp	74	6
CHAPINS								
Elom	41	m	w	CANA	Colusa	Colusa	71	288
Francis	3	m	w	CA	San Francisco	2-Wd San Francisco	79	278
CHAPIRA								
Edward J	25	m	w	JERU	Los Angeles	Wilmington Twp	73	645
CHAPIS								
Susannah	14	f	w	CA	Santa Cruz	Santa Cruz Twp	89	383
CHAPLAIN								
---	25	m	w	CANA	Alameda	Oakland	68	248
A D	28	m	w	CANA	Alameda	Oakland	68	211
Charles	36	m	w	FRAN	Plumas	Rich Bar Twp	77	45
G W	65	m	w	VT	Sacramento	San Joaquin Twp	77	398
Henry	52	m	w	VT	Sacramento	San Joaquin Twp	77	398
Jacques	35	m	w	FRAN	Plumas	Rich Bar Twp	77	8
Moses	49	m	w	VT	Sacramento	San Joaquin Twp	77	398
P	29	m	w	OH	Lake	Lower Lake	73	414
Yves Mary	49	m	w	FRAN	Plumas	Rich Bar Twp	77	8
CHAPLET								
H	16	m	w	FRAN	Alameda	Oakland	68	145
CHAPLIN								
Chas	40	m	w	IL	Butte	Ophir Twp	70	117
Daniel	49	m	w	NY	Butte	Wyandotte Twp	70	141
E ?	44	m	w	NY	San Joaquin	2-Wd Stockton	86	188
Hiram	37	m	w	TN	Butte	Ophir Twp	70	113
J H	41	m	w	VA	Del Norte	Crescent	71	465
James	51	m	w	ENGL	San Francisco	11-Wd San Francisc	84	554
Joseph	41	m	w	NY	San Francisco	San Francisco P O	85	861
Robt	48	m	w	IA	Butte	Ophir Twp	70	118
Samuel	18	m	w	ENGL	San Francisco	8-Wd San Francisco	82	487
CHAPLING								
C	45	m	w	NY	San Joaquin	3-Wd Stockton	86	240
CHAPMA								
Robert	35	m	w	MO	San Mateo	Half Moon Bay P O	87	403

© 2001 by Heritage Quest. All rights reserved.

Name	Age	S	R	B-PL	County	Locale	Roll	Pg
						Series M593		
CHAPMAN								
---	35	m	w	IN	Napa	Napa	75	18
A	43	m	w	NY	Nevada	Nevada Twp	75	284
A	38	f	w	MI	Amador	Jackson P O	69	339
A Mc	52	m	w	SCOT	Santa Clara	Gilroy Twp	88	86
Abraham	29	m	w	MO	Solano	Maine Prairie Twp	90	45
Alfred B	40	m	w	AL	Los Angeles	Los Angeles	73	547
Amelia	7	f	w	CA	San Francisco	San Francisco P O	83	236
And	50	m	w	SC	El Dorado	Georgetown Twp	72	36
Andrew	55	m	w	KY	Solano	Suisun Twp	90	116
Andrew	43	m	w	CT	Napa	Napa	75	35
Anson	36	m	w	NY	Calaveras	San Andreas P O	70	218
Asa	42	m	w	CT	Napa	Napa Twp	75	74
Aug H	43	m	w	NY	Butte	Chico Twp	70	14
B H	39	m	w	ENGL	Sacramento	3-Wd Sacramento	77	309
Barny	51	m	w	NC	El Dorado	Coloma Twp	72	5
C	53	f	w	NY	Sacramento	1-Wd Sacramento	77	180
C	40	m	w	WI	Sutter	Butte Twp	92	100
C	31	m	w	OH	San Joaquin	Tulare Twp	86	263
C D	52	m	w	NY	San Francisco	San Francisco P O	85	766
C W	50	m	w	VA	San Francisco	7-Wd San Francisco	81	207
Caroline	50	f	w	ENGL	San Francisco	8-Wd San Francisco	82	341
Charles	72	m	w	VT	Los Angeles	Los Angeles	73	508
Charles	32	m	w	VA	Nevada	Grass Valley Twp	75	147
Charles	28	m	w	IA	Los Angeles	Los Angeles Twp	73	495
Charles	19	m	w	CA	Sacramento	Natomas Twp	77	166
Chas	49	m	w	KY	Yuba	Rose Bar Twp	93	657
Chas C	64	m	w	NH	San Francisco	8-Wd San Francisco	82	344
Chas C	39	m	w	VA	Nevada	Little York Twp	75	240
Cyrus C	35	m	w	NH	San Francisco	San Francisco P O	83	50
Daniel	40	m	w	IREL	Marin	San Rafael Twp	74	26
Daniel	31	m	w	CANA	Colusa	Butte Twp	71	266
Danl	42	m	w	IREL	Marin	San Rafael Twp	74	34
Dennis	39	m	w	OH	Plumas	Indian Twp	77	17
Dexter	35	m	w	ME	Calaveras	San Andreas P O	70	212
E	32	f	w	MA	Sacramento	3-Wd Sacramento	77	298
E H	28	m	w	OH	San Francisco	7-Wd San Francisco	81	168
E M	13	f	w	OR	Alameda	Oakland	68	237
E W	24	m	w	OH	Merced	Snelling P O	74	262
Ed	53	m	w	ENGL	Butte	Chico Twp	70	31
Edgar M	50	m	w	NY	Santa Clara	1-Wd San Jose	88	234
Edward	29	m	w	ENGL	San Francisco	San Francisco P O	83	325
Elenor	18	f	w	CANA	Los Angeles	Los Angeles	73	531
Elias	35	m	m	KY	Sacramento	2-Wd Sacramento	77	229
Emery W	24	m	w	OH	Fresno	Millerton P O	72	151
F	52	m	i	ENGL	Del Norte	Crescent Twp	71	457
F	44	f	w	PRUS	Alameda	Oakland	68	131
F S	31	m	w	AR	Lassen	Susanville Twp	73	442
Fanny	24	f	w	IL	Stanislaus	Empire Twp	92	46
Fernessa	32	f	w	CA	Santa Barbara	Las Cruces P O	87	504
Francis M	45	m	w	DC	Los Angeles	Los Angeles	73	519
Frank	34	m	w	VT	Mendocino	Noyo & Big Rvr Twp	74	173
Freeman F	26	m	w	OH	Santa Barbara	San Buenaventura P	87	437
G	58	m	w	NY	Sacramento	1-Wd Sacramento	77	186
G F	46	m	w	NH	Sacramento	3-Wd Sacramento	77	267
Geo	20	m	w	NY	Humboldt	Eureka Twp	72	280
George	47	m	w	PA	San Francisco	5-Wd San Francisco	81	22
George	40	m	w	NY	Trinity	Junction City Pct	92	207
George	38	m	w	ME	Calaveras	San Andreas P O	70	212
George	36	m	w	VA	Nevada	Little York Twp	75	235
George	35	m	w	AL	Yolo	Buckeye Twp	93	409
George	33	m	w	CT	Stanislaus	Emory Twp	92	26
George W	30	m	w	NY	Santa Cruz	Soquel Twp	89	448
H F	35	m	w	CANA	Merced	Snelling P O	74	252
Hannah	51	f	w	IREL	Santa Clara	San Jose Twp	88	205
Harry	37	m	w	NY	Mariposa	Mariposa P O	74	92
Henry	43	m	w	CT	San Francisco	5-Wd San Francisco	81	14
Henry	30	m	w	ENGL	San Francisco	11-Wd San Francisc	84	556
Henry	29	m	w	OH	Shasta	Horsetown P O	89	507
Howard	42	m	w	CANA	San Francisco	11-Wd San Francisc	84	631
Ira	38	m	w	CT	San Francisco	8-Wd San Francisco	82	354
Isaac	32	m	w	GA	Nevada	Grass Valley Twp	75	227
Isaac N	31	m	w	OH	Sonoma	Healdsburg & Mendo	91	283
J	45	m	w	ME	Alameda	Murray Twp	68	123
J	35	m	w	MA	Solano	Vallejo	90	169
J	33	m	w	IREL	Sacramento	3-Wd Sacramento	77	292
J A	48	m	w	ME	Solano	Vallejo	90	154
J H	12	m	w	CA	Klamath	Klamath Twp	73	370
J S	28	m	w	AR	Lassen	Susanville Twp	73	445
James	56	m	w	PA	Butte	Ophir Twp	70	108
James	41	m	w	KY	Mariposa	Mariposa P O	74	136
James	24	m	w	CANA	Sonoma	Salt Point	91	393
Jas	60	m	w	VA	Butte	Ophir Twp	70	108
Jeremiah S	45	m	w	NY	Santa Cruz	Watsonville	89	364
Jesse J	34	m	w	OH	Stanislaus	Empire Twp	92	51
Jno	47	m	w	IREL	Butte	Ophir Twp	70	107
Jno	42	m	w	OH	Shasta	Horsetown P O	89	503
John	50	m	w	IN	El Dorado	Diamond Springs Tw	72	23
John	50	m	w	NJ	Stanislaus	Empire Twp	92	44
John	48	m	w	GA	El Dorado	Georgetown Twp	72	36
John	48	m	w	KY	Trinity	Hayfork Valley	92	238
John	45	m	w	PA	San Francisco	3-Wd San Francisco	79	293
John	43	m	w	OH	Plumas	Plumas Twp	77	26
John	42	m	w	ENGL	Tuolumne	Sonora P O	93	319
John	41	m	w	OH	Tuolumne	Sonora P O	93	318
John	40	m	w	ME	San Francisco	11-Wd San Francisc	84	428
John	35	m	w	OH	Los Angeles	Soledad Twp	73	632
John	28	m	w	MA	San Francisco	7-Wd San Francisco	81	207
John	23	m	w	CA	San Francisco	11-Wd San Francisc	84	518
John K	38	m	w	ENGL	Santa Clara	Santa Clara Twp	88	138
Joseph	60	m	w	VA	Tehama	Bell Mills Twp	92	159
Joseph	50	m	w	MD	Tuolumne	Columbia P O	93	340
Joseph	48	m	w	CA	Santa Barbara	San Buenaventura P	87	442
Joseph	46	m	w	IN	El Dorado	Diamond Springs Tw	72	21
Joshua	43	m	w	ME	Solano	Vallejo	90	148
Joshua	32	m	w	ENGL	Nevada	Grass Valley Twp	75	220
L J	62	f	w	MD	Lassen	Janesville Twp	73	431
Lafeytt	42	m	w	NY	Sonoma	Petaluma Twp	91	310
Lizzie	22	f	w	LA	Sacramento	2-Wd Sacramento	77	243
Lyman	49	m	w	CT	Napa	Napa Twp	75	66
M	71	f	w	PA	Napa	Napa	75	17
M V	37	m	w	ME	Nevada	Bridgeport Twp	75	101
M V	32	m	w	IN	Napa	Yountville Twp	75	86
Margrate	27	f	w	NH	San Francisco	7-Wd San Francisco	81	175
Mary	5	f	w	CA	Butte	Ophir Twp	70	118
Mary	15	f	w	IREL	Marin	San Rafael Twp	74	25
Morris	37	m	w	ME	Kern	Havilah P O	73	338
Morton	25	m	w	OH	Yolo	Cottonwood Twp	93	473
N	30	m	w	NY	San Francisco	3-Wd San Francisco	79	313
Norman	44	m	w	NY	San Francisco	5-Wd San Francisco	81	30
P A	53	m	w	CT	Sierra	Sierra Twp	89	567
R J	43	m	w	ME	San Francisco	San Francisco P O	85	858
Richard	37	m	w	ENGL	Los Angeles	Los Angeles Twp	73	469
Robert	35	m	w	ME	San Francisco	San Francisco P O	83	253
Stephen	30	m	w	CT	Napa	Napa Twp	75	60
Susan	64	f	w	MA	Santa Clara	Redwood Twp	88	120
T S	50	m	w	IA	Sonoma	Analy Twp	91	220
Thomas	52	m	w	IREL	San Francisco	5-Wd San Francisco	81	9
Thomas	36	m	w	IL	Mariposa	Mariposa P O	74	136
Thomas A	32	m	w	IREL	Contra Costa	Martinez P O	71	381
Thomas C	38	m	w	IREL	Stanislaus	San Joaquin Twp	92	77
Thos	41	m	w	BADE	San Francisco	3-Wd San Francisco	79	314
Thos	30	m	w	ME	Alameda	Oakland	68	212
Thos	26	m	w	ENGL	Butte	Oregon Twp	70	131
Thos	24	m	w	IREL	San Francisco	7-Wd San Francisco	81	260
Thos M	43	m	w	PA	Sonoma	Vallejo Twp	91	451
W A	39	m	w	ME	Siskiyou	Callahan P O	89	627
W D Mrs	45	f	w	CANA	Lake	Lakeport	73	407
Walter	30	m	w	NY	Butte	Chico Twp	70	57
Walter A	35	m	w	TN	Colusa	Monroe Twp	71	320
William	72	m	w	KY	Placer	Auburn P O	76	380
William	43	m	w	NY	San Francisco	San Francisco P O	83	418
William	42	m	w	TN	Sonoma	Petaluma Twp	91	348
William	30	m	w	ENGL	Amador	Amador City P O	69	393
William	27	m	w	NY	Amador	Amador City P O	69	391
William C	51	m	w	OH	Santa Cruz	Santa Cruz Twp	89	402
William S	37	m	w	AL	Los Angeles	San Gabriel Twp	73	597
Wm	39	m	w	OH	Nevada	Meadow Lake Twp	75	248
Wm	38	m	w	KY	Butte	Kimshew Tpw	70	78
Wm	35	m	w	IREL	Butte	Ophir Twp	70	118
Wm	34	m	w	CT	Mendocino	Round Valley Twp	74	217
Wm	34	m	w	ENGL	Yuba	Marysville	93	610
Wm H	40	m	w	CT	Napa	Napa Twp	75	71
Woodbury	42	m	w	NH	Del Norte	Crescent	71	464
CHAPMAN F								
F	35	m	w	OH	Sacramento	3-Wd Sacramento	77	312
CHAPO								
Gertrues	50	f	w	CA	San Diego	San Pasqual	78	520
CHAPONTE								
Mary	49	f	w	FRAN	Solano	Benicia	90	15
CHAPPALE								
L A	23	f	w	NY	Alameda	Oakland	68	195
CHAPPEAU								
August	41	m	w	FRAN	Calaveras	San Andreas P O	70	156
CHAPPEL								
Thomas	39	m	w	ENGL	San Francisco	11-Wd San Francisc	84	634
Thomas	35	m	w	ENGL	Amador	Jackson P O	69	322
William	36	m	w	TX	Kern	Tehachapi P O	73	353
CHAPPELE								
Fred	28	m	w	GERM	San Diego	San Diego	78	505
CHAPPELETTE								
F	42	m	w	FRAN	Alameda	Oakland	68	171
CHAPPELL								
Edwin	30	m	w	CT	Santa Barbara	Arroyo Burro P O	87	509
Jas M	45	m	w	NY	Shasta	Shasta P O	89	461
John	32	m	w	ENGL	Nevada	Grass Valley Twp	75	231
Jos	33	m	w	NY	Solano	Vallejo	90	204
Serena	4	f	w	CA	Santa Barbara	Arroyo Burro P O	87	509
Wallace H	34	m	w	NY	Butte	Ophir Twp	70	95
William	40	m	w	TN	Colusa	Spring Valley Twp	71	345
William	37	m	w	MO	Mariposa	Mariposa P O	74	118
CHAPPELLE								
Alfred	51	m	w	GA	Santa Clara	Gilroy Twp	88	101
Belle	14	f	w	CA	San Francisco	San Francisco P O	85	798
F M	22	m	w	MO	Santa Clara	Gilroy Twp	88	96
John P	54	m	w	TN	Los Angeles	El Monte Twp	73	449
CHAPPELLETT								
Henry	16	m	w	FRAN	Santa Clara	Santa Clara Twp	88	176
CHAPPIETRA								
Dominga	37	f	w	ITAL	Santa Barbara	Santa Barbara P O	87	465
CHAPPIN								
Mary	37	f	w	MA	San Joaquin	3-Wd Stockton	86	234
CHAPPLE								
Henry	44	m	w	ENGL	Plumas	Seneca Twp	77	48

© 2001 by Heritage Quest. All rights reserved.

Name	Age	S	R	B-PL	County	Locale	Series M593 Roll	Pg
John	33	m	w	ENGL	Plumas	Indian Twp	77	18
CHAPPO								
Juan	12	m	w	CA	San Diego	San Pasqual Valley	78	525
W	20	m	w	FRAN	Napa	Napa Twp	75	73
CHAPPUIS								
A	40	m	w	FRAN	Sierra	Downieville Twp	89	518
CHAPTER								
Oren	42	m	w	NY	Butte	Ophir Twp	70	117
CHAPUIS								
Charles	21	m	w	OH	Yolo	Putah Twp	93	514
Joseph	49	m	w	FRAN	San Francisco	6-Wd San Francisco	81	51
CHAPUKE								
J H	43	m	w	HAMB	El Dorado	Salmon Falls Twp	72	132
CHAQUETTE								
Ephraim	32	m	w	CANA	Inyo	Bishop Crk Twp	73	311
Octave	17	m	w	CANA	Contra Costa	Martinez P O	71	392
CHAR								
Ah	50	m	c	CHIN	San Francisco	6-Wd San Francisco	81	63
Ah	41	m	c	CHIN	San Francisco	6-Wd San Francisco	81	74
Ah	40	m	c	CHIN	San Francisco	6-Wd San Francisco	81	51
Ah	31	m	c	CHIN	San Francisco	6-Wd San Francisco	81	46
Ah	30	m	w	NJ	Calaveras	Copperopolis P O	70	233
Choy	49	m	c	CHIN	San Francisco	6-Wd San Francisco	81	51
CHARADE								
Louis	36	m	w	FRAN	San Francisco	San Francisco P O	80	339
CHARAMO								
Plutarch	35	m	w	MEXI	Fresno	Millerton P O	72	159
CHARANIS								
Joseph	34	m	w	ITAL	Amador	Jackson P O	69	339
CHARANNAT								
L	55	m	w	FRAN	Nevada	Nevada Twp	75	303
CHARBEY								
Ah	13	m	c	CHIN	San Francisco	San Francisco P O	85	823
CHARBONNET								
Fred	42	m	w	FRAN	Sierra	Sears Twp	89	557
CHARBOVA								
P	38	m	w	CANA	Alameda	Oakland	68	214
CHARBRUEX								
Antonie	40	m	w	FRAN	Nevada	Grass Valley Twp	75	191
CHARD								
Ann	40	f	w	ENGL	San Francisco	2-Wd San Francisco	79	185
George	34	m	w	PA	San Francisco	11-Wd San Francisc	84	456
W G	63	m	w	NY	Tehama	Deer Crk Twp	92	172
CHARDIN								
Augustus	50	m	w	FRAN	El Dorado	Cosumnes Twp	72	18
CHARDINE								
Aman	34	m	w	FRAN	San Francisco	San Francisco P O	80	349
CHARE								
Hiram	45	m	w	NY	Sacramento	Dry Crk Twp	77	102
CHARENTAUEX								
C	62	m	w	FRAN	Amador	Jackson P O	69	346
CHARES								
Francisco	47	m	w	CA	San Diego	Warners Rancho Dis	78	528
Gregorio	23	m	w	CA	San Diego	Warners Rancho Dis	78	528
Tiveloro	38	m	w	MEXI	San Diego	Warners Rancho Dis	78	529
CHAREST								
Theode	26	m	w	CANA	Santa Cruz	Santa Cruz	89	433
CHAREY								
Mary	19	f	w	IREL	San Francisco	San Francisco P O	83	322
CHARIG								
Concepcion	50	m	w	CA	Los Angeles	Los Nietos Twp	73	583
CHARILLON								
Levy	42	m	w	FRAN	Los Angeles	El Monte Twp	73	461
CHARIS								
Carlos	65	m	w	MEXI	Santa Clara	Almaden Twp	88	1
Jose A	52	m	w	NM	San Luis Obispo	Arroyo Grande Twp	87	276
CHARK								
Ah	40	m	c	CHIN	San Francisco	6-Wd San Francisco	81	45
CHARL								
Ah	15	m	c	CHIN	San Francisco	San Francisco P O	85	736
CHARLEMGNE								
Louis	42	m	w	FRAN	Calaveras	San Andreas P O	70	185
CHARLES								
---	40	m	w	UNKN	San Joaquin	2-Wd Stockton	86	167
Adam	56	m	b	ENGL	San Francisco	8-Wd San Francisco	82	353
Ah	44	m	c	CHIN	Placer	Auburn P O	76	379
Ah	40	m	c	CHIN	Placer	Lincoln P O	76	493
Ah	4	m	c	CHIN	Monterey	Salinas Twp	74	308
Ah	39	m	c	CHIN	Tuolumne	Sonora P O	93	324
Ah	36	m	c	CHIN	Placer	Auburn P O	76	358
Ah	33	m	c	CHIN	Placer	Auburn P O	76	357
Ah	32	m	c	CHIN	Placer	Alta P O	76	413
Ah	30	m	c	CHIN	Placer	Auburn P O	76	363
Ah	30	m	c	CHIN	Placer	Clipper Gap P O	76	393
Ah	28	m	c	CHIN	Placer	Dutch Flat P O	76	415
Ah	25	m	c	CHIN	Tuolumne	Sonora P O	93	324
Ah	23	m	c	CHIN	Placer	Auburn P O	76	360
Ah	22	m	c	CHIN	Placer	Gold Run Twp	76	398
Ah	17	m	c	CHIN	San Mateo	San Mateo P O	87	357
Ah	17	m	c	CHIN	Placer	Summit P O	76	497
Ah	16	m	c	CHIN	Placer	Alta P O	76	411
Ah	16	m	c	CHIN	Nevada	Meadow Lake Twp	75	248
Ah	15	m	c	CHIN	Placer	Clipper Gap P O	76	393
Alpheus	55	m	w	ME	Contra Costa	Martinez P O	71	374
Andrew	36	m	w	NM	San Luis Obispo	Santa Rosa Twp	87	325
Ann	50	f	w	IREL	Santa Clara	1-Wd San Jose	88	242
Base	24	m	c	CHIN	Sacramento	1-Wd Sacramento	77	193
Byron J	16	m	w	NY	San Diego	San Diego	78	496
Christopher	28	m	w	SWIT	San Francisco	San Francisco P O	80	425
D	27	m	w	OH	Lassen	Susanville Twp	73	445
David	33	m	w	WALE	Sierra	Sears Twp	89	556
Elbert R	27	m	w	IL	Sonoma	Vallejo Twp	91	462
George A	32	m	w	PA	Sonoma	Salt Point Twp	91	383
H	30	m	w	ME	San Joaquin	Tulare Twp	86	250
H	27	m	w	PRUS	San Francisco	San Francisco P O	85	830
Hanry	16	m	j	JAPA	San Francisco	San Francisco P O	80	458
Henry	50	m	w	WALE	San Francisco	2-Wd San Francisco	79	227
Henry	35	m	w	RUSS	Los Angeles	San Juan Twp	73	625
Henry A	46	m	w	NY	San Francisco	8-Wd San Francisco	82	411
James M	56	m	w	PA	Sonoma	Vallejo Twp	91	462
John	28	m	w	ENGL	San Francisco	11-Wd San Francisc	84	703
Josephine	27	f	w	NORW	El Dorado	Placerville	72	126
Kee	22	m	c	CHIN	San Mateo	Schoolhouse Statio	87	339
Levin Carroll	42	m	w	IL	Plumas	Plumas Twp	77	27
Louis	21	m	w	PRUS	San Francisco	6-Wd San Francisco	81	71
M F T	44	m	w	MO	Amador	Sutter Crk P O	69	396
Mary C	40	f	w	ENGL	San Francisco	11-Wd San Francisc	84	634
Parnalo	1	m	w	CA	Alameda	Oakland	68	178
Ross	19	m	w	WURT	Santa Cruz	Santa Cruz Twp	89	396
Sarah A	18	f	w	ENGL	San Mateo	Schoolhouse Statio	87	332
Sidney	37	m	w	NY	Shasta	Millville P O	89	489
William	36	m	w	IREL	San Francisco	San Francisco P O	80	430
William	30	m	w	NY	San Francisco	6-Wd San Francisco	81	88
CHARLESTON								
Chas	34	m	w	SWED	San Francisco	11-Wd San Francisc	84	687
George	51	m	w	SCOT	Santa Clara	Fremont Twp	88	43
CHARLETON								
Robert	41	m	w	ENGL	Kern	Bakersfield P O	73	357
CHARLEY								
Ah	49	m	c	CHIN	Santa Clara	Alviso Twp	88	24
Ah	40	m	c	CHIN	San Francisco	6-Wd San Francisco	81	46
Ah	37	m	c	CHIN	Santa Clara	1-Wd San Jose	88	277
Ah	35	m	c	CHIN	Santa Cruz	Pajaro Twp	89	346
Ah	30	m	c	CHIN	Placer	Bath P O	76	454
Ah	28	m	c	CHIN	Santa Clara	Gilroy Twp	88	75
Ah	28	m	c	CHIN	Placer	Bath P O	76	451
Ah	25	m	c	CHIN	Sierra	Lincoln Twp	89	545
Ah	23	m	c	CHIN	Yolo	Putah Twp	93	516
Ah	22	m	c	CHIN	Santa Cruz	Santa Cruz Twp	89	391
Ah	20	m	c	CHIN	Santa Cruz	Santa Cruz Twp	89	388
Ah	20	m	c	CHIN	Trinity	North Fork Twp	92	216
Ah	20	m	c	CHIN	Los Angeles	Los Angeles	73	527
August	23	m	w	GERM	Solano	Vallejo	90	200
Chine	24	m	c	CHIN	Tehama	Tehama Twp	92	189
Clone	34	m	c	CHIN	Shasta	French Gulch P O	89	465
Fallip	19	m	w	SWIT	Monterey	Alisal Twp	74	304
Hy	19	m	c	CHIN	Santa Cruz	Pajaro Twp	89	347
Luck	35	m	c	CHIN	Yuba	Marysville	93	624
Ou Kee	20	m	c	CHIN	Siskiyou	Yreka	89	659
Peter	50	m	w	FRAN	San Francisco	San Francisco P O	85	769
Ton	21	m	c	CHIN	Colusa	Monroe Twp	71	324
CHARLI								
Ah	40	m	c	CHIN	Placer	Clipper Gap P O	76	393
J	18	m	c	CHIN	Merced	Snelling P O	74	266
CHARLIE								
---	14	m	c	CHIN	Sacramento	4-Wd Sacramento	77	361
Ah	34	m	c	CHIN	Sacramento	Brighton Twp	77	79
Ah	32	m	c	CHIN	Santa Barbara	Santa Barbara P O	87	487
Ah	25	m	c	CHIN	Sonoma	Cloverdale Twp	91	269
Ah	22	m	c	CHIN	Los Angeles	Los Angeles Twp	73	493
Ah	14	m	c	CHIN	Placer	Dutch Flat P O	76	411
CHARLOT								
Jules	60	m	w	FRAN	San Francisco	6-Wd San Francisco	81	41
CHARLSTON								
Mary	24	f	w	IREL	San Francisco	San Francisco P O	83	205
CHARLTON								
Abraham	40	m	w	TN	Kern	Bakersfield P O	73	365
Chas	41	m	w	VA	Siskiyou	Surprise Valley Tw	89	639
Edward	28	m	w	CANA	San Francisco	San Francisco P O	83	193
Frank	29	m	b	WIND	San Francisco	6-Wd San Francisco	81	99
Fred	48	m	w	CT	Sacramento	3-Wd Sacramento	77	292
G	47	m	w	OH	Santa Clara	Burnett Twp	88	30
John	31	m	w	MA	Sonoma	Bodega Twp	91	248
John	20	m	w	CANA	San Mateo	Schoolhouse Statio	87	340
Nettie	19	f	w	NY	Sacramento	1-Wd Sacramento	77	205
Samuel	12	m	w	CA	Kern	Bakersfield P O	73	365
Thos	28	m	w	PA	Mendocino	Ukiah Twp	74	237
William	22	m	w	CANA	Solano	Silveyville Twp	90	75
Wm	25	m	w	IA	Alameda	Eden Twp	68	82
CHARLY								
Ah	40	m	c	CHIN	Sacramento	Franklin Twp	77	115
Ah	35	m	c	CHIN	Sacramento	Brighton Twp	77	72
Ah	27	m	c	CHIN	El Dorado	Placerville	72	113
Ah	24	m	c	CHIN	Amador	Fiddletown P O	69	427
Ah	14	m	c	CHIN	San Francisco	San Francisco P O	80	478
CHARMAK								
B	21	m	w	PRUS	Lake	Lakeport	73	406
C	20	m	w	GERM	Lake	Kelsey Crk	73	402
H	31	m	w	PRUS	Lake	Big Valley	73	396
CHARMIN								
Josefa	45	f	w	CA	Los Angeles	Los Angeles	73	506
CHARMON								
Jules	47	m	w	FRAN	Mariposa	Mariposa P O	74	91

© 2001 by Heritage Quest. All rights reserved.

Name	Age	S	R	B-PL	County	Locale	Series M593 Roll	Pg
CHARN								
Ah	33	m	c	CHIN	Trinity	Douglas	92	236
CHAROLINE								
Lewis	43	m	w	LA	San Joaquin	2-Wd Stockton	86	193
CHARP								
Chas	40	m	w	NY	Nevada	Bloomfield Twp	75	99
CHARPIE								
Laura	43	f	w	CT	Alameda	Oakland	68	161
CHARPIOT								
Joseph	56	m	w	FRAN	San Francisco	2-Wd San Francisco	79	169
CHARRE								
Jean Bte	48	m	w	FRAN	San Francisco	San Francisco P O	83	135
CHARRETT								
Henry F	33	m	w	CANA	Sonoma	Petaluma Twp	91	320
CHARREUL								
Andrew	38	m	w	CANA	Calaveras	San Andreas P O	70	159
CHARRIER								
Prosper	47	m	w	FRAN	Yuba	Slate Range Bar Tw	93	670
CHARRION								
Augustus C	43	m	w	MO	Los Angeles	Los Angeles	73	543
CHARRIS								
F	32	m	w	MEXI	Merced	Snelling P O	74	250
CHARRON								
Lawrence	35	m	w	CANA	Santa Barbara	Santa Barbara P O	87	474
Thomas	47	m	w	FRAN	Marin	San Rafael Twp	74	32
CHARRONET								
Louis	56	m	w	FRAN	San Francisco	1-Wd San Francisco	79	54
CHARST								
Philip	35	m	w	CANA	Sierra	Sears Twp	89	555
CHART								
John	16	m	w	CANA	Humboldt	Pacific Twp	72	297
Olid	63	m	w	ENGL	Sonoma	Sonoma Twp	91	446
CHARTEL								
Oscar	45	m	w	FRAN	San Francisco	San Francisco P O	80	350
CHARTER								
Ephram C	40	m	w	OH	Mariposa	Mariposa P O	74	137
Joe	38	m	w	KY	San Joaquin	Elkhorn Twp	86	62
Oliver	53	m	w	NY	Del Norte	Crescent	71	465
CHARWICH								
Lamson	23	m	w	CANA	San Francisco	11-Wd San Francisc	84	703
CHARY								
Lawrence	33	m	w	IREL	Del Norte	Happy Camp Twp	71	468
Mary	19	f	w	MA	San Francisco	San Francisco P O	83	162
CHARYIN								
Aryilo	23	m	w	ITAL	San Francisco	11-Wd San Francisc	84	710
CHARYS								
Peter	34	m	w	PRUS	Sutter	Sutter Twp	92	121
CHAS								
Ah	34	m	c	CHIN	Sierra	Eureka Twp	89	525
Ar	18	m	c	CHIN	Sonoma	Petaluma Twp	91	342
F	24	m	w	MI	Nevada	Meadow Lake Twp	75	265
Hi	29	m	c	CHIN	San Joaquin	1-Wd Stockton	86	148
Hung	22	m	c	CHIN	Tehama	Antelope Twp	92	153
Ling	20	m	c	CHIN	Tehama	Tehama Twp	92	195
CHASE								
A F	23	m	w	MA	Humboldt	Pacific Twp	72	296
A R	33	m	w	ME	Lassen	Susanville Twp	73	443
A R	25	m	w	NY	Sacramento	3-Wd Sacramento	77	303
A S	53	m	w	MA	San Joaquin	2-Wd Stockton	86	182
A W	28	m	w	OH	Del Norte	Smith Rvr Twp	71	479
Abbie	35	f	w	ME	Santa Clara	Redwood Twp	88	131
Albert C	31	m	w	MA	Tehama	Red Bluff	92	174
Alfred	29	m	w	VT	Santa Cruz	Santa Cruz Twp	89	399
Andrew H	29	m	w	ME	Santa Cruz	Santa Cruz Twp	89	389
Andrew J	58	m	w	MA	San Diego	San Diego	78	504
Benj F	45	m	w	MA	Mendocino	Casper & Big Rvr	74	163
C H	46	m	w	MA	San Joaquin	Oneal Twp	86	103
C H	39	m	w	MA	Nevada	Nevada Twp	75	293
C W	25	m	w	CT	Sacramento	1-Wd Sacramento	77	178
Capt	44	m	w	NY	San Joaquin	Castoria Twp	86	12
Charles	48	m	w	NH	Yolo	Merritt Twp	93	507
Charles	34	m	w	MA	San Francisco	San Francisco P O	80	359
Charles L	38	m	w	ME	Calaveras	San Andreas P O	70	163
Cyrus H	42	m	w	NY	Santa Barbara	Santa Barbara P O	87	485
Daniel C	29	m	w	ME	Placer	Auburn P O	76	377
Danl	40	m	w	MA	Alameda	Oakland	68	182
Dudley [Rev]	50	m	w	CT	San Francisco	San Francisco P O	83	31
E B	40	m	w	MA	Sutter	Nicolaus Twp	92	114
Edwin	22	m	w	ME	Santa Clara	Redwood Twp	88	131
Elbert G	57	m	w	NH	San Francisco	8-Wd San Francisco	82	480
Emanuel	35	m	w	PORT	Sierra	Sears Twp	89	561
Ettie	19	f	w	RI	San Francisco	6-Wd San Francisco	81	72
F C	23	m	w	MA	Napa	Napa Twp	75	28
Florence	22	f	w	MA	Los Angeles	Los Angeles	73	533
Foster W	21	m	w	ME	Santa Clara	Redwood Twp	88	130
Francis	53	m	w	NY	Mendocino	Little Lake Twp	74	199
Geo B	27	m	w	AUSL	Sacramento	Natomas Twp	77	170
Geo W	33	m	w	ME	San Francisco	7-Wd San Francisco	81	253
Geo W	27	m	w	MA	Santa Barbara	Santa Barbara P O	87	451
George	37	m	w	IL	Santa Cruz	Pajaro Twp	89	350
George	28	m	w	MA	San Francisco	2-Wd San Francisco	79	237
George	28	m	w	MA	Alameda	Brooklyn	68	22
George	18	m	w	CA	Siskiyou	Yreka Twp	89	664
George H	37	m	w	ME	Santa Clara	Redwood Twp	88	131
Henery	37	m	w	MA	San Francisco	7-Wd San Francisco	81	199
Henry	38	m	w	NY	Monterey	San Juan Twp	74	396
Henry	25	m	w	MA	San Francisco	8-Wd San Francisco	82	486
Henry	24	m	w	NJ	Mendocino	Round Valley Twp	74	217
Henry C	24	m	w	NY	Santa Cruz	Santa Cruz	89	418
Henry P	56	m	w	RI	San Francisco	3-Wd San Francisco	79	323
Hiram	38	m	w	TX	Stanislaus	Branch Twp	92	10
Hiram B	44	m	w	IL	Santa Cruz	Pajaro Twp	89	347
Hiram W	45	m	w	NY	Yuba	Long Bar Twp	93	563
Homer	64	m	w	NH	Kern	Tehachapi P O	73	355
Jacob E	50	m	w	PA	San Francisco	1-Wd San Francisco	79	29
James	53	m	w	MA	San Francisco	San Francisco P O	80	407
James	42	m	w	MA	San Francisco	San Francisco P O	80	358
James	28	m	w	NY	Solano	Denverton Twp	90	27
James	24	m	w	ME	Santa Clara	Redwood Twp	88	131
James H	34	m	w	ME	Solano	Rio Vista Twp	90	58
James W	38	m	w	MA	Klamath	Sawyers Bar	73	377
Jas	42	m	w	ME	Solano	Vallejo	90	141
Jennie	29	f	w	NH	San Francisco	8-Wd San Francisco	82	386
Jennie	25	f	w	NY	San Francisco	San Francisco P O	83	169
John	37	m	w	HUNG	Solano	Benicia	90	12
John	30	m	w	NH	Contra Costa	Martinez P O	71	396
John A	46	m	w	MA	Tehama	Merrill	92	198
John D	43	m	w	NY	Santa Cruz	Santa Cruz	89	412
John E	33	m	w	MA	San Francisco	2-Wd San Francisco	79	275
John G	26	m	w	MA	San Francisco	San Francisco P O	83	171
John S	42	m	w	ME	Calaveras	San Andreas P O	70	165
Joseph	35	m	w	MA	San Francisco	San Francisco P O	83	251
Joseph P	36	m	w	AZOR	San Francisco	1-Wd San Francisco	79	12
Josiah	34	m	w	ME	Santa Clara	Redwood Twp	88	130
Juniette	23	f	w	NY	Sacramento	3-Wd Sacramento	77	303
Lathiel T	40	m	w	MA	San Francisco	8-Wd San Francisco	82	399
Leande W	48	m	w	MA	Tehama	Battle Crk Meadows	92	168
Leary	25	m	w	IL	Sacramento	Granite Twp	77	150
Levi	46	m	w	NY	Santa Barbara	San Buenaventura P	87	447
Levi	45	m	w	ME	San Diego	San Diego	78	484
Mollie	22	f	w	MA	San Francisco	8-Wd San Francisco	82	349
Moses	63	m	w	MA	Alameda	Brooklyn	68	22
Moses	37	m	w	ME	Plumas	Plumas Twp	77	29
Newton	32	m	w	NY	Monterey	San Juan Twp	74	396
Orlando	21	m	w	VA	Colusa	Grand Island Twp	71	304
Q A	40	m	w	ME	Alameda	Oakland	68	216
R B	30	m	w	ME	Los Angeles	Soledad Twp	73	631
Rebecca	67	f	w	MA	San Francisco	6-Wd San Francisco	81	116
Robt Henry	46	m	w	MA	Nevada	Grass Valley Twp	75	165
Robt P	54	m	w	NY	San Francisco	San Francisco P O	83	266
Rowland	37	m	w	MA	Mariposa	Maxwell Crk P O	74	143
Russell	50	m	w	VT	Solano	Vallejo	90	146
Ruth	21	f	w	ENGL	Santa Clara	2-Wd San Jose	88	299
S P	50	m	w	CANA	Humboldt	Eureka Twp	72	260
Samuel	55	m	w	IL	Yolo	Grafton Twp	93	499
Sidney	34	m	w	IL	Santa Barbara	San Buenaventura P	87	424
Stephen H	36	m	w	ME	Santa Clara	Redwood Twp	88	131
Susan	61	f	w	VT	Contra Costa	Martinez P O	71	407
Susan	46	f	w	NY	Siskiyou	Yreka	89	661
Thomas	40	m	w	NH	San Francisco	San Francisco P O	83	231
Thomas	18	m	w	CA	Mendocino	Calpella Twp	74	181
Thos	34	m	w	ENGL	San Francisco	11-Wd San Francisc	84	613
Timothy	35	m	w	CANA	Santa Clara	Almaden Twp	88	16
Upton A	62	m	w	MA	Inyo	Independence Twp	73	325
Warren	35	m	w	NH	El Dorado	White Oak Twp	72	143
Warren D	28	m	w	MA	Colusa	Colusa Twp	71	282
William	53	m	w	MA	Santa Clara	Santa Clara Twp	88	136
William	40	m	w	MA	Calaveras	San Andreas P O	70	158
William	34	m	w	ME	Santa Cruz	Soquel Twp	89	448
William	27	m	w	MD	Humboldt	Mattole Twp	72	286
William T	24	m	w	MA	San Francisco	6-Wd San Francisco	81	93
Wm A	28	m	w	ME	San Francisco	5-Wd San Francisco	81	27
Wm W	39	m	w	MA	San Francisco	2-Wd San Francisco	79	230
CHASMYRE								
Wm	24	m	w	IREL	Napa	Napa	75	2
CHASSAGNE								
Antoni	20	m	w	FRAN	San Francisco	1-Wd San Francisco	79	82
CHASTERFIELD								
S	28	m	w	IN	San Joaquin	Oneal Twp	86	108
CHASTIE								
Ah	36	m	c	CHIN	Santa Cruz	Watsonville	89	377
CHASTINE								
John	45	m	w	VA	Inyo	Independence Twp	73	325
CHAT								
Ah	37	m	c	CHIN	Placer	Auburn P O	76	362
Ah	26	m	c	CHIN	Tuolumne	Chinese Camp P O	93	378
Ah	22	m	c	CHIN	Placer	Dutch Flat P O	76	409
Ah	22	m	c	CHIN	San Mateo	Schoolhouse Statio	87	336
Ah	21	m	c	CHIN	San Francisco	6-Wd San Francisco	81	53
Ah	20	m	c	CHIN	El Dorado	Mud Springs Twp	72	77
Ah	16	m	c	CHIN	Butte	Ophir Twp	70	121
Ah	15	m	c	CHIN	San Luis Obispo	Salinas Twp	87	291
Ah	14	f	c	CHIN	San Francisco	6-Wd San Francisco	81	74
Youn	32	m	c	CHIN	Yuba	Marysville	93	628
CHATA								
Maria	30	f	w	CA	San Diego	San Pasqual	78	521
CHATE								
Ah	28	m	c	CHIN	Shasta	French Gulch P O	89	465
CHATEAU								
Chris	48	m	w	FRAN	San Francisco	San Francisco P O	83	187
Eugene	30	m	w	FRAN	San Francisco	San Francisco P O	80	430
Louis	40	m	w	FRAN	San Francisco	San Francisco P O	80	456
CHATELAIN								
Honori	49	m	w	FRAN	San Francisco	1-Wd San Francisco	79	23

© 2001 by Heritage Quest. All rights reserved.

Name	Age	S	R	B-PL	County	Locale	Roll	Pg
						Series M593		
CHATELIN								
Amelia	13	f	w	CA	San Francisco	San Francisco P O	83	32
CHATELL								
Edward	33	m	w	CANA	Amador	Sutter Crk P O	69	409
CHATENUF								
Albert D	42	m	w	FRAN	Santa Barbara	San Buenaventura P	87	439
CHATFIELD								
H	50	m	w	NY	Alameda	Oakland	68	253
H	45	m	w	NY	Alameda	Oakland	68	166
James	35	m	w	NY	Alameda	Oakland	68	135
Levi	37	m	w	IL	Lassen	Milford Twp	73	438
Solon	37	m	w	OH	Yuba	Bullards Bar P O	93	547
William	40	m	w	NY	San Bernardino	San Bernardino Twp	78	453
CHATHAM								
Augt	54	m	w	DE	Shasta	Millville P O	89	494
James	62	m	w	KY	Tulare	Tule Rvr Twp	92	269
Robert F	74	m	w	NJ	Yuba	Long Bar Twp	93	563
CHATLAIN								
Samuel	35	m	w	SWIT	Monterey	San Juan Twp	74	408
CHATMAN								
Francis F	37	m	w	PA	Yuba	Long Bar Twp	93	563
Geo	28	m	w	IL	Alameda	Murray Twp	68	116
James	46	m	w	NY	San Francisco	San Francisco P O	83	208
Wm A	21	m	w	CT	Monterey	Monterey Twp	74	346
CHATORICK								
Geo	31	m	w	AUST	Sacramento	Dry Crk Twp	77	101
CHATT								
Andrew J	37	m	w	OH	Yuba	Long Bar Twp	93	563
CHATTAN								
Richard	43	m	w	CANA	Tulare	Venice Twp	92	278
CHATTAS								
Elina	11	f	w	CA	San Joaquin	3-Wd Stockton	86	229
CHATTEN								
---	30	m	w	MA	Humboldt	Eureka Twp	72	273
CHATTERDON								
P M	40	m	w	NJ	Sacramento	Sutter Twp	77	389
CHATTERTON								
E M	35	m	w	NH	Sacramento	3-Wd Sacramento	77	257
James	24	m	w	IREL	San Francisco	San Francisco P O	83	145
John	63	m	w	NY	Sacramento	Center Twp	77	82
CHATTIN								
James	46	m	w	FRAN	San Joaquin	2-Wd Stockton	86	171
CHATTOCK								
Chas	42	m	w	IREL	Butte	Chico Twp	70	45
CHATWICK								
James	36	m	w	NH	San Francisco	San Francisco P O	83	240
CHATZ								
Adolph	15	m	w	CA	San Francisco	San Francisco P O	80	348
CHAU								
Ah	30	m	c	CHIN	Los Angeles	Los Angeles	73	527
CHAUCER								
O	35	m	w	FRAN	Alameda	Oakland	68	134
CHAUFON								
Louis	47	m	w	FRAN	Plumas	Goodwin Twp	77	7
CHAUN								
Ah	34	m	c	CHIN	Plumas	Mineral Twp	77	25
CHAUNCEY								
Alfred G	57	m	w	MA	Shasta	French Gulch P O	89	465
Henry N	29	m	w	NJ	San Francisco	3-Wd San Francisco	79	327
CHAUNCY								
H M	49	m	w	NY	Trinity	Weaverville Pct	92	226
CHAUPIN								
John	25	m	w	FRAN	Fresno	Millerton P O	72	158
CHAURET								
Justin	63	m	w	FRAN	San Francisco	San Francisco P O	83	335
CHAUVAL								
Eugenie	44	f	w	FRAN	San Francisco	1-Wd San Francisco	79	55
CHAUVET								
Joshua	48	m	w	FRAN	Sonoma	Sonoma Twp	91	432
Justin	63	m	w	FRAN	San Francisco	7-Wd San Francisco	81	216
CHAUVIS								
Francisco	21	m	w	CA	San Bernardino	Belleville Twp	78	408
Francisco	12	m	w	CA	San Bernardino	Belleville Twp	78	408
Jose	21	m	w	CA	San Bernardino	Belleville Twp	78	408
Marion	50	m	w	MEXI	San Bernardino	Belleville Twp	78	408
CHAVANA								
Claro	25	m	w	MEXI	Monterey	San Juan Twp	74	416
Juan	39	m	w	CA	Monterey	San Juan Twp	74	403
Pilar	75	f	w	CA	Monterey	San Juan Twp	74	416
CHAVANCHE								
Jules	40	m	w	FRAN	San Francisco	8-Wd San Francisco	82	383
CHAVANCHIEL								
Jan	40	m	w	FRAN	San Francisco	5-Wd San Francisco	81	27
CHAVARIA								
Ramon	34	m	w	CA	Monterey	San Juan Twp	74	403
CHAVES								
Astacio	12	m	w	CA	Santa Clara	2-Wd San Jose	88	305
Dolores	30	f	w	MEXI	Santa Clara	2-Wd San Jose	88	312
Fernando	31	m	w	CA	San Diego	Warners Rancho Dis	78	529
John	30	m	w	IREL	Monterey	Monterey	74	354
Manuel	49	m	w	MEXI	Monterey	Alisal Twp	74	289
Plutarch	30	m	w	MEXI	Santa Clara	2-Wd San Jose	88	305
Santiago	70	m	w	CA	San Diego	San Pasqual	78	521
CHAVEZ								
Patricio	40	m	w	MEXI	Los Angeles	San Jose Twp	73	618
CHAVIER								
Lisandro	29	m	w	AZOR	San Francisco	11-Wd San Francisc	84	594

Name	Age	S	R	B-PL	County	Locale	Roll	Pg
						Series M593		
CHAVIEY								
L B	18	m	w	ME	Nevada	Nevada Twp	75	316
CHAVIS								
Andre	28	f	w	MEXI	Napa	Napa	75	37
Anna M	29	f	w	CA	Los Angeles	Los Angeles	73	516
Francis	16	m	w	CA	Los Angeles	Los Angeles	73	570
Gabriel	40	m	w	NM	Los Angeles	Los Angeles	73	516
Jennie	39	f	w	MEXI	Napa	Napa	75	53
John	31	m	w	FRAN	Napa	Yountville Twp	75	78
Jose Ma	50	m	w	MEXI	Los Angeles	San Jose Twp	73	620
Manuel	35	m	w	NM	Los Angeles	Los Angeles	73	516
Margareta	70	f	w	MEXI	Napa	Napa	75	37
Neanam	66	m	w	MEXI	Los Angeles	Los Angeles	73	516
Presentacen	32	m	w	CA	Los Angeles	Los Angeles	73	515
Ramon	38	m	w	MEXI	Napa	Napa Twp	75	60
Trinidad	30	m	w	MEXI	Los Angeles	Los Angeles Twp	73	476
Victorino	50	m	w	BRAZ	San Luis Obispo	San Luis Obispo Tw	87	304
William	61	m	w	MEXI	Los Angeles	Los Angeles	73	515
CHAVOREA								
Frank	24	m	w	CHIL	Santa Clara	Alviso Twp	88	27
CHAVOYA								
Elmano	16	m	w	CA	Santa Clara	San Jose Twp	88	209
CHAVRATT								
Louis	43	m	w	FRAN	Humboldt	Arcata Twp	72	229
CHAW								
Ah	49	m	c	CHIN	Mono	Bridgeport P O	74	283
Ah	43	m	c	CHIN	Placer	Bath P O	76	446
Ah	38	m	c	CHIN	Calaveras	San Andreas P O	70	178
Ah	35	m	c	CHIN	Alameda	Washington Twp	68	299
Ah	29	m	c	CHIN	Calaveras	San Andreas P O	70	204
Ah	26	m	c	CHIN	Amador	Ione City P O	69	355
Ah	26	f	c	CHIN	San Francisco	San Francisco P O	80	493
Ah	20	m	c	CHIN	Merced	Snelling P O	74	274
Ah	20	m	c	CHIN	San Francisco	8-Wd San Francisco	82	340
Ban	34	m	c	CHIN	Calaveras	San Andreas P O	70	205
CHAY								
Ah	48	m	c	CHIN	Tuolumne	Chinese Camp P O	93	364
Ah	45	m	c	CHIN	Butte	Chico Twp	70	52
Ah	41	m	c	CHIN	Placer	Dutch Flat P O	76	408
Ah	39	m	c	CHIN	Placer	Bath P O	76	429
Ah	35	m	c	CHIN	Butte	Chico Twp	70	52
Ah	34	m	c	CHIN	Calaveras	San Andreas P O	70	204
Ah	32	m	c	CHIN	San Francisco	3-Wd San Francisco	79	301
Ah	29	f	c	CHIN	Tuolumne	Columbia P O	93	342
Ah	28	m	c	CHIN	Tuolumne	Chinese Camp P O	93	379
Ah	27	m	c	CHIN	Butte	Hamilton Twp	70	68
Ah	25	m	c	CHIN	San Francisco	11-Wd San Francisc	84	695
Ah	25	m	c	CHIN	Trinity	Canyon City Pct	92	201
Ah	23	m	c	CHIN	Butte	Chico Twp	70	51
Anna	20	f	c	CHIN	Humboldt	Eureka Twp	72	266
Kow	48	m	c	CHIN	Tuolumne	Columbia P O	93	342
Lom	28	m	c	CHIN	San Francisco	6-Wd San Francisco	81	75
Toe	27	m	c	CHIN	Butte	Chico Twp	70	51
Toy	21	m	c	CHIN	Nevada	Bridgeport Twp	75	111
Yuen	23	m	c	CHIN	San Francisco	6-Wd San Francisco	81	103
CHAYNSKI								
Joseph	35	m	w	FRAN	Sacramento	2-Wd Sacramento	77	220
CHAYSE								
Frank	35	m	w	FRAN	San Francisco	San Francisco P O	80	465
CHAYTE								
Louis	34	m	w	CANA	Yolo	Cache Crk Twp	93	448
CHAZOTTE								
Stephen B	39	m	w	SC	Placer	Auburn P O	76	369
CHE								
Ah	45	m	c	CHIN	Nevada	Nevada Twp	75	311
Ah	43	m	c	CHIN	Sacramento	1-Wd Sacramento	77	196
Ah	41	m	c	CHIN	El Dorado	Placerville	72	115
Ah	40	m	c	CHIN	Yuba	Marysville	93	577
Ah	33	m	c	CHIN	Butte	Concow Twp	70	8
Ah	32	m	c	CHIN	Santa Clara	Santa Clara Twp	88	148
Ah	28	m	c	CHIN	Mariposa	Mariposa P O	74	107
Ah	26	m	c	CHIN	Sacramento	1-Wd Sacramento	77	204
Ah	26	m	c	CHIN	Butte	Chico Twp	70	53
Ah	24	m	c	CHIN	El Dorado	Placerville Twp	72	98
Ah	24	m	c	CHIN	Butte	Kimshew Tpw	70	85
Ah	23	m	c	CHIN	Butte	Concow Twp	70	11
Ah	18	m	c	CHIN	San Francisco	8-Wd San Francisco	82	387
Ah	17	m	c	CHIN	Alameda	Oakland	68	206
Ah	14	m	c	CHIN	Alameda	Oakland	68	208
Ah	12	m	c	CHIN	San Francisco	6-Wd San Francisco	81	110
Chiel	40	m	c	CHIN	Butte	Concow Twp	70	11
Chin	43	m	c	CHIN	Trinity	North Fork Twp	92	218
Cum	20	f	c	CHIN	Calaveras	San Andreas P O	70	169
Hing	23	m	c	CHIN	Yuba	Slate Range Bar Tw	93	678
Lang	57	m	c	CHIN	Butte	Chico Twp	70	49
Le	29	m	c	CHIN	Alameda	Oakland	68	152
Lem	30	m	c	CHIN	Santa Clara	1-Wd San Jose	88	277
Lo	21	f	c	CHIN	San Joaquin	1-Wd Stockton	86	153
Loh	31	m	c	CHIN	Marin	Sausalito Twp	74	68
Lung	25	m	c	CHIN	Alameda	Oakland	68	138
Mong	17	m	c	CHIN	San Luis Obispo	Arroyo Grande Twp	87	279
Ong	30	m	c	CHIN	Klamath	Sawyers Bar	73	378
Ong Ke	28	f	c	CHIN	Calaveras	San Andreas P O	70	199
Ping	45	m	c	CHIN	Amador	Volcano P O	69	383
Song	28	f	c	CHIN	Sacramento	1-Wd Sacramento	77	195
Ton	50	m	c	CHIN	Butte	Oroville Twp	70	140
Tong	42	m	c	CHIN	Butte	Hamilton Twp	70	73

© 2001 by Heritage Quest. All rights reserved.

Name	Age	S	R	B-PL	County	Locale	Roll	Pg
Wa	19	m	c	CHIN	Alameda	Washington Twp	68	301
Wah	40	m	c	CHIN	San Francisco	San Francisco P O	83	238
Wah	30	m	c	CHIN	Butte	Kimshew Tpw	70	84
Wang	31	m	c	CHIN	San Luis Obispo	Arroyo Grande Twp	87	279
War	18	m	c	CHIN	San Francisco	6-Wd San Francisco	81	64
Way	35	m	c	CHIN	Klamath	Klamath Twp	73	370
Wing	35	m	c	CHIN	San Luis Obispo	Salinas Twp	87	296
Yen	64	m	c	CHIN	Amador	Jackson P O	69	344
You	30	m	c	CHIN	Solano	Vacaville Twp	90	132
Yum	15	m	c	CHIN	Nevada	Grass Valley Twp	75	184
CHEA								
Chong	22	m	c	CHIN	San Mateo	Schoolhouse Statio	87	335
CHEADLE								
George L	36	m	w	OH	Contra Costa	Martinez P O	71	393
Raphel	41	m	w	OH	San Francisco	6-Wd San Francisco	81	153
CHEAN								
Ah	39	m	c	CHIN	Butte	Concow Twp	70	11
Bridget	30	f	w	IREL	San Francisco	San Francisco P O	85	785
CHEANG								
---	19	m	c	CHIN	Shasta	American Ranch P O	89	500
Ah	53	m	c	CHIN	Shasta	French Gulch P O	89	469
Ah	36	m	c	CHIN	Calaveras	Copperopolis P O	70	243
Ah	32	m	c	CHIN	Plumas	Plumas Twp	77	31
Ah	22	m	c	CHIN	San Francisco	6-Wd San Francisco	81	61
Ah	19	m	c	CHIN	San Francisco	6-Wd San Francisco	81	68
Eu	25	m	c	CHIN	Nevada	Washington Twp	75	342
Leung	53	m	c	CHIN	Nevada	Nevada Twp	75	298
CHEASMAN								
Ellen	33	f	w	CANA	San Francisco	6-Wd San Francisco	81	106
CHEATEL								
Austin	27	m	w	MI	Sonoma	Mendocino Twp	91	297
CHEATEM								
Dewit C	29	m	w	TN	Calaveras	Copperopolis P O	70	239
William	32	m	w	TN	Calaveras	Copperopolis P O	70	257
CHEATHAM								
Henry	23	m	w	MO	Amador	Volcano P O	69	381
J	26	m	w	MO	Merced	Snelling P O	74	250
John B	8	m	w	CA	Yolo	Buckeye Twp	93	414
CHEAW								
Ah	42	m	c	CHIN	Calaveras	Copperopolis P O	70	243
CHEBOYA								
Alexander	34	m	w	CA	Santa Clara	San Jose Twp	88	205
Augustine	36	m	w	CA	Santa Clara	1-Wd San Jose	88	249
Sixto	29	m	w	CA	Santa Clara	San Jose Twp	88	205
CHECAN								
Rodolph	17	m	i	MEXI	Inyo	Lone Pine Twp	73	334
CHECH								
Lee	23	m	c	CHIN	San Joaquin	1-Wd Stockton	86	148
CHECK								
Adam	48	m	w	AR	Fresno	Millerton P O	72	185
Ah	60	m	c	CHIN	Placer	Auburn P O	76	377
Ah	45	m	c	CHIN	Nevada	Nevada Twp	75	307
Ah	40	m	c	CHIN	Sacramento	Franklin Twp	77	118
Ah	30	m	c	CHIN	Placer	Newcastle Twp	76	477
Ah	30	m	c	CHIN	Shasta	American Ranch P O	89	497
Ah	29	m	c	CHIN	Sacramento	Granite Twp	77	137
Ah	22	f	c	CHIN	Sacramento	Granite Twp	77	151
Ah	22	m	c	CHIN	Placer	Roseville P O	76	353
Ah	20	m	c	CHIN	Plumas	Goodwin Twp	77	3
Ah	17	f	c	CHIN	Butte	Chico Twp	70	27
CHECKE								
Chief	35	m	i	CA	Colusa	Spring Valley Twp	71	338
CHECON								
Sebastiana	50	f	w	MEXI	Santa Clara	1-Wd San Jose	88	263
CHEDA								
Garatenzia	34	m	w	SWIT	Marin	Bolinas Twp	74	1
John	45	m	w	SWIT	Marin	Nicasio Twp	74	18
John	40	m	w	SWIT	Marin	Bolinas Twp	74	2
Louis	48	m	w	SWIT	Marin	San Antonio Twp	74	61
Louis	20	m	w	SWIT	Marin	Nicasio Twp	74	18
Rocco	22	m	w	SWIT	San Francisco	San Francisco P O	85	751
CHEE								
---	30	m	c	CHIN	Siskiyou	Hamburg Twp	89	598
---	22	m	c	CHIN	San Francisco	6-Wd San Francisco	81	64
Ah	62	m	c	CHIN	El Dorado	Coloma Twp	72	6
Ah	60	m	c	CHIN	Amador	Ione City P O	69	370
Ah	6	f	c	CA	San Francisco	San Francisco P O	80	530
Ah	55	m	c	CHIN	Fresno	Millerton P O	72	188
Ah	52	m	c	CHIN	Nevada	Rough & Ready Twp	75	324
Ah	50	m	c	CHIN	Nevada	Grass Valley Twp	75	217
Ah	50	m	c	CHIN	Calaveras	San Andreas P O	70	199
Ah	50	f	c	CHIN	San Francisco	San Francisco P O	80	530
Ah	50	m	c	CHIN	San Francisco	5-Wd San Francisco	81	14
Ah	48	m	c	CHIN	Amador	Jackson P O	69	331
Ah	46	m	c	CHIN	Tuolumne	Chinese Camp P O	93	366
Ah	46	m	c	CHIN	Tuolumne	Chinese Camp P O	93	384
Ah	45	m	c	CHIN	Amador	Fiddletown P O	69	438
Ah	44	m	c	CHIN	Tuolumne	Chinese Camp P O	93	379
Ah	44	m	c	CHIN	Placer	Clipper Gap P O	76	393
Ah	44	m	c	CHIN	Nevada	Grass Valley Twp	75	183
Ah	43	m	c	CHIN	Stanislaus	Emory Twp	92	25
Ah	42	m	c	CHIN	Sierra	Eureka Twp	89	526
Ah	42	m	c	CHIN	Trinity	Douglas	92	235
Ah	42	m	c	CHIN	Mariposa	Mariposa P O	74	133
Ah	42	m	c	CHIN	Trinity	North Fork Twp	92	218
Ah	42	m	c	CHIN	San Francisco	San Francisco P O	80	523
Ah	41	m	c	CHIN	San Francisco	San Francisco P O	80	502
Ah	41	f	c	CHIN	San Francisco	San Francisco P O	80	433
Ah	41	m	c	CHIN	San Francisco	San Francisco P O	80	335
Ah	41	m	c	CHIN	Plumas	Plumas Twp	77	31
Ah	41	m	w	CHIN	Plumas	Indian Twp	77	19
Ah	41	m	c	CHIN	San Francisco	San Francisco P O	80	524
Ah	40	m	c	CHIN	Tuolumne	Columbia P O	93	341
Ah	40	m	c	CHIN	San Francisco	11-Wd San Francisc	84	694
Ah	40	m	c	CHIN	San Luis Obispo	San Luis Obispo Tw	87	297
Ah	40	m	c	CHIN	Mariposa	Mariposa P O	74	102
Ah	40	m	c	CHIN	Kern	Tehachapi P O	73	356
Ah	40	m	c	CHIN	Klamath	Trinidad Twp	73	392
Ah	40	m	c	CHIN	San Francisco	San Francisco P O	80	446
Ah	40	m	c	CHIN	Placer	Bath P O	76	444
Ah	40	m	c	CHIN	Placer	Bath P O	76	458
Ah	40	m	c	CHIN	Los Angeles	Los Angeles	73	527
Ah	40	m	c	CHIN	Amador	Volcano P O	69	373
Ah	40	m	c	CHIN	Sierra	Eureka Twp	89	526
Ah	40	m	c	CHIN	San Francisco	San Francisco P O	80	505
Ah	40	m	c	CHIN	San Francisco	San Francisco P O	80	519
Ah	39	m	c	CHIN	San Francisco	San Francisco P O	80	522
Ah	38	m	c	CHIN	Tuolumne	Chinese Camp P O	93	384
Ah	38	m	c	CHIN	Tuolumne	Chinese Camp P O	93	383
Ah	38	m	c	CHIN	Mono	Bridgeport P O	74	282
Ah	38	f	c	CHIN	Mariposa	Maxwell Crk P O	74	138
Ah	38	m	c	CHIN	Nevada	Nevada Twp	75	298
Ah	38	m	c	CHIN	Alameda	Oakland	68	223
Ah	38	m	c	CHIN	Alameda	Oakland	68	229
Ah	38	m	c	CHIN	Sierra	Table Rock Twp	89	574
Ah	38	m	c	CHIN	San Francisco	San Francisco P O	80	507
Ah	37	f	c	CHIN	San Francisco	San Francisco P O	80	445
Ah	37	m	c	CHIN	Nevada	Rough & Ready Twp	75	337
Ah	37	m	c	CHIN	Butte	Bidwell Twp	70	4
Ah	37	m	c	CHIN	Amador	Drytown P O	69	420
Ah	37	m	c	CHIN	Amador	Drytown P O	69	423
Ah	36	m	c	CHIN	Marin	San Rafael Twp	74	59
Ah	36	m	c	CHIN	Marin	San Rafael Twp	74	39
Ah	36	m	c	CHIN	Calaveras	Copperopolis P O	70	244
Ah	36	m	c	CHIN	Calaveras	San Andreas P O	70	183
Ah	36	m	c	CHIN	Nevada	Rough & Ready Twp	75	338
Ah	36	m	c	CHIN	San Francisco	San Francisco P O	80	515
Ah	36	m	c	CHIN	San Francisco	San Francisco P O	80	513
Ah	36	m	c	CHIN	San Francisco	San Francisco P O	80	519
Ah	35	m	c	CHIN	Mariposa	Maxwell Crk P O	74	144
Ah	35	m	c	CHIN	Alameda	Brooklyn Twp	68	39
Ah	35	m	c	CHIN	Alameda	Oakland	68	223
Ah	35	m	c	CHIN	Sonoma	Sonoma Twp	91	442
Ah	35	m	c	CHIN	San Francisco	San Francisco P O	80	508
Ah	34	m	c	CHIN	Mariposa	Maxwell Crk P O	74	145
Ah	34	m	c	CHIN	Nevada	Nevada Twp	75	321
Ah	34	f	c	CHIN	San Francisco	San Francisco P O	80	449
Ah	34	m	c	CHIN	Placer	Lincoln P O	76	483
Ah	34	m	c	CHIN	Calaveras	Copperopolis P O	70	234
Ah	34	m	c	CHIN	San Francisco	San Francisco P O	80	516
Ah	33	m	c	CHIN	Placer	Dutch Flat P O	76	410
Ah	33	m	c	CHIN	Alameda	Eden Twp	68	61
Ah	32	m	c	CHIN	San Francisco	6-Wd San Francisco	81	62
Ah	32	m	c	CHIN	San Francisco	6-Wd San Francisco	81	69
Ah	32	m	c	CHIN	Alameda	Oakland	68	241
Ah	32	f	c	CHIN	San Francisco	San Francisco P O	80	449
Ah	32	f	c	CHIN	San Francisco	San Francisco P O	80	449
Ah	32	m	c	CHIN	Alameda	Brooklyn Twp	68	40
Ah	32	m	c	CHIN	San Francisco	11-Wd San Francisc	84	448
Ah	31	m	c	CHIN	Mariposa	Mariposa P O	74	102
Ah	31	m	c	CHIN	Nevada	Grass Valley Twp	75	218
Ah	31	m	c	CHIN	Amador	Fiddletown P O	69	428
Ah	31	m	c	CHIN	San Francisco	San Francisco P O	80	519
Ah	31	f	c	CHIN	San Francisco	San Francisco P O	80	523
Ah	30	m	c	CHIN	Sierra	Sears Twp	89	554
Ah	30	m	c	CHIN	Shasta	Shasta P O	89	454
Ah	30	m	c	CHIN	Tuolumne	Chinese Camp P O	93	388
Ah	30	m	c	CHIN	San Joaquin	1-Wd Stockton	86	134
Ah	30	m	c	CHIN	Calaveras	Copperopolis P O	70	251
Ah	30	m	c	CHIN	Placer	Pino Twp	76	470
Ah	30	m	c	CHIN	San Francisco	2-Wd San Francisco	79	241
Ah	30	m	c	CHIN	Placer	Lincoln P O	76	483
Ah	30	m	c	CHIN	Plumas	Goodwin Twp	77	3
Ah	30	m	c	CHIN	Sacramento	Granite Twp	77	148
Ah	30	m	c	CHIN	Plumas	Indian Twp	77	19
Ah	30	m	c	CHIN	Amador	Jackson P O	69	331
Ah	30	m	c	CHIN	Alameda	Oakland	68	206
Ah	30	m	c	CHIN	Santa Cruz	Watsonville	89	367
Ah	30	f	c	CHIN	San Francisco	San Francisco P O	80	525
Ah	30	f	c	CHIN	San Francisco	San Francisco P O	80	526
Ah	30	m	c	CHIN	San Francisco	San Francisco P O	80	518
Ah	30	m	c	CHIN	San Francisco	San Francisco P O	80	520
Ah	30	m	c	CHIN	San Francisco	11-Wd San Francisc	84	639
Ah	29	m	c	CHIN	Butte	Hamilton Twp	70	74
Ah	29	m	c	CHIN	Placer	Dutch Flat P O	76	402
Ah	29	m	c	CHIN	Sacramento	1-Wd Sacramento	77	196
Ah	29	m	c	CHIN	Santa Clara	1-Wd San Jose	88	272
Ah	29	m	c	CHIN	San Francisco	San Francisco P O	80	513
Ah	28	m	c	CHIN	Tuolumne	Chinese Camp P O	93	380
Ah	28	m	c	CHIN	Tuolumne	Chinese Camp P O	93	388
Ah	28	m	c	CHIN	Tuolumne	Big Oak Flat P O	93	395
Ah	28	m	c	CHIN	Trinity	Weaverville Pct	92	231
Ah	28	m	c	CHIN	San Francisco	6-Wd San Francisco	81	43
Ah	28	m	c	CHIN	Marin	San Rafael Twp	74	38

© 2001 by Heritage Quest. All rights reserved.

California 1870 Census

Name	Age	S	R	B-PL	County	Locale	Roll (Series M593)	Pg
Ah	28	m	c	CHIN	Alameda	Oakland	68	232
Ah	28	m	c	CHIN	Placer	Clipper Gap P O	76	392
Ah	28	m	c	CHIN	Napa	Napa	75	7
Ah	28	m	c	CHIN	Nevada	Little York Twp	75	245
Ah	28	f	c	CHIN	San Francisco	San Francisco P O	80	431
Ah	28	m	c	CHIN	Nevada	Grass Valley Twp	75	215
Ah	28	m	c	CHIN	Placer	Bath P O	76	423
Ah	28	m	c	CHIN	Placer	Bath P O	76	456
Ah	28	m	c	CHIN	Alameda	Oakland	68	232
Ah	28	m	c	CHIN	Sierra	Gibson Twp	89	540
Ah	27	m	c	CHIN	Butte	Hamilton Twp	70	67
Ah	27	m	c	CHIN	San Francisco	3-Wd San Francisco	79	310
Ah	27	m	c	CHIN	Marin	San Rafael Twp	74	43
Ah	27	m	c	CHIN	Placer	Auburn P O	76	360
Ah	27	m	c	CHIN	Fresno	Millerton P O	72	184
Ah	26	m	c	CHIN	Siskiyou	Cottonwood Twp	89	594
Ah	26	f	c	CHIN	San Francisco	San Francisco P O	80	503
Ah	26	m	c	CHIN	San Francisco	11-Wd San Francisc	84	478
Ah	26	m	c	CHIN	Marin	San Rafael Twp	74	37
Ah	26	f	c	CHIN	San Francisco	San Francisco P O	80	448
Ah	26	m	c	CHIN	Sierra	Table Rock Twp	89	579
Ah	26	f	c	CHIN	San Francisco	San Francisco P O	80	504
Ah	26	m	c	CHIN	San Francisco	San Francisco P O	80	524
Ah	25	m	c	CHIN	Santa Cruz	Soquel Twp	89	447
Ah	25	m	c	CHIN	Fresno	Millerton P O	72	201
Ah	25	f	c	CHIN	San Francisco	San Francisco P O	80	451
Ah	25	m	c	CHIN	Nevada	Grass Valley Twp	75	197
Ah	25	m	c	CHIN	Nevada	Grass Valley Twp	75	205
Ah	25	m	c	CHIN	Placer	Dutch Flat P O	76	406
Ah	25	m	c	CHIN	Butte	Concow Twp	70	11
Ah	25	m	c	CHIN	Siskiyou	Yreka Twp	89	669
Ah	25	m	c	CHIN	Trinity	Lewiston Pct	92	214
Ah	25	m	c	CHIN	San Francisco	6-Wd San Francisco	81	38
Ah	24	m	c	CHIN	Butte	Hamilton Twp	70	74
Ah	24	m	c	CHIN	Placer	Blue Canyon P O	76	419
Ah	24	f	c	CHIN	San Francisco	San Francisco P O	80	452
Ah	24	f	c	CHIN	San Francisco	San Francisco P O	80	438
Ah	24	m	c	CHIN	Santa Clara	1-Wd San Jose	88	272
Ah	24	m	c	CHIN	San Francisco	6-Wd San Francisco	81	128
Ah	23	f	c	CHIN	San Francisco	San Francisco P O	80	434
Ah	23	f	c	CHIN	San Francisco	San Francisco P O	80	441
Ah	22	m	c	CHIN	Calaveras	San Andreas P O	70	191
Ah	22	m	c	CHIN	Placer	Colfax P O	76	384
Ah	22	m	c	CHIN	Nevada	Rough & Ready Twp	75	329
Ah	22	f	c	CHIN	San Francisco	San Francisco P O	80	432
Ah	22	m	c	CHIN	Nevada	Grass Valley Twp	75	197
Ah	21	m	c	CHIN	San Francisco	3-Wd San Francisco	79	309
Ah	21	f	c	CHIN	San Francisco	San Francisco P O	80	431
Ah	21	m	c	CHIN	Nevada	Meadow Lake Twp	75	254
Ah	21	m	c	CHIN	Sacramento	1-Wd Sacramento	77	190
Ah	21	m	c	CHIN	Trinity	Junction City Pct	92	209
Ah	21	m	c	CHIN	San Francisco	6-Wd San Francisco	81	72
Ah	20	f	c	CHIN	Butte	Hamilton Twp	70	73
Ah	20	m	c	CHIN	Placer	Blue Canyon P O	76	419
Ah	20	f	c	CHIN	San Francisco	San Francisco P O	80	432
Ah	20	f	c	CHIN	San Francisco	San Francisco P O	80	438
Ah	20	f	c	CHIN	San Francisco	San Francisco P O	80	439
Ah	20	f	c	CHIN	San Francisco	San Francisco P O	80	440
Ah	20	m	c	CHIN	Nevada	Washington Twp	75	342
Ah	20	m	c	CHIN	Nevada	Nevada Twp	75	298
Ah	20	m	c	CHIN	Nevada	Grass Valley Twp	75	205
Ah	20	f	c	CHIN	San Francisco	San Francisco P O	80	529
Ah	20	f	c	CHIN	San Francisco	San Francisco P O	80	506
Ah	20	f	c	CHIN	San Francisco	San Francisco P O	80	506
Ah	20	f	c	CHIN	San Francisco	San Francisco P O	80	521
Ah	20	f	c	CHIN	San Francisco	San Francisco P O	80	527
Ah	20	m	c	CHIN	San Francisco	6-Wd San Francisco	81	51
Ah	19	m	c	CHIN	San Francisco	6-Wd San Francisco	81	42
Ah	19	m	c	CHIN	San Francisco	3-Wd San Francisco	79	304
Ah	19	f	c	CHIN	San Francisco	San Francisco P O	80	439
Ah	19	f	c	CHIN	San Francisco	San Francisco P O	80	431
Ah	19	m	c	CHIN	Plumas	Goodwin Twp	77	3
Ah	19	m	c	CHIN	Alameda	Oakland	68	224
Ah	19	m	c	CHIN	Alameda	Washington Twp	68	270
Ah	19	m	c	CHIN	San Francisco	11-Wd San Francisc	84	606
Ah	18	m	c	CHIN	Tuolumne	Chinese Camp P O	93	390
Ah	18	m	c	CHIN	San Francisco	San Francisco P O	83	285
Ah	18	m	c	CHIN	San Luis Obispo	San Luis Obispo Tw	87	315
Ah	18	f	c	CHIN	San Francisco	San Francisco P O	80	437
Ah	18	m	c	CHIN	San Francisco	San Francisco P O	80	429
Ah	18	m	c	CHIN	Sacramento	Granite Twp	77	144
Ah	18	m	c	CHIN	Plumas	Goodwin Twp	77	3
Ah	18	m	c	CHIN	Alameda	Oakland	68	226
Ah	18	m	c	CHIN	Santa Clara	Alviso Twp	88	27
Ah	18	m	c	CHIN	San Joaquin	Tulare Twp	86	251
Ah	17	m	c	CHIN	San Francisco	6-Wd San Francisco	81	46
Ah	17	m	c	CHIN	Nevada	Nevada Twp	75	310
Ah	16	m	c	CHIN	Tuolumne	Sonora P O	93	323
Ah	16	m	c	CHIN	San Francisco	3-Wd San Francisco	79	322
Ah	16	m	c	CHIN	San Francisco	3-Wd San Francisco	79	307
Ah	16	m	c	CHIN	Shasta	French Gulch P O	89	470
Ah	16	f	c	CHIN	San Francisco	San Francisco P O	80	526
Ah	16	m	c	CHIN	San Francisco	6-Wd San Francisco	81	49
Ah	16	m	c	CHIN	San Francisco	6-Wd San Francisco	81	42
Ah	15	m	c	CHIN	Shasta	French Gulch P O	89	469
Ah	15	m	c	CHIN	Nevada	Rough & Ready Twp	75	329
Ah	15	m	c	CHIN	Sacramento	2-Wd Sacramento	77	224
Ah	15	m	c	CHIN	Sacramento	2-Wd Sacramento	77	209
Ah	15	m	c	CHIN	San Francisco	6-Wd San Francisco	81	52
Ah	14	m	c	CHIN	San Francisco	6-Wd San Francisco	81	44
Ah	14	m	c	CHIN	San Francisco	6-Wd San Francisco	81	67
Ah	14	m	c	CHIN	Trinity	Lewiston Pct	92	211
Ah	13	f	c	CHIN	San Francisco	San Francisco P O	80	495
Ah	13	m	c	CHIN	Trinity	Junction City Pct	92	207
Ar	20	m	c	CHIN	Sonoma	Petaluma Twp	91	343
Bee	31	m	c	CHIN	Plumas	Goodwin Twp	77	3
Chow	33	m	c	CHIN	Tuolumne	Big Oak Flat P O	93	392
Chung	23	m	c	CHIN	Mariposa	Maxwell Crk P O	74	145
Comb	31	f	c	CHIN	Yuba	Marysville	93	626
Cong	50	m	c	CHIN	Shasta	Shasta P O	89	461
Cong	30	m	c	CHIN	Shasta	Shasta P O	89	453
Coon	31	f	c	CHIN	Yuba	Marysville	93	626
Cow	52	m	c	CHIN	Mariposa	Mariposa P O	74	133
Fan	21	f	c	CHIN	Butte	Oroville Twp	70	140
Fen	45	m	c	CHIN	San Mateo	San Mateo P O	87	350
Foo	21	m	c	CHIN	Solano	Rio Vista Twp	90	70
Gee	54	m	c	CHIN	Plumas	Mineral Twp	77	23
Gee	27	m	c	CHIN	Plumas	Mineral Twp	77	24
Gee	27	m	c	CHIN	Plumas	Mineral Twp	77	23
Gon	26	m	c	CHIN	Yuba	Marysville	93	622
Hay	42	m	c	CHIN	San Francisco	11-Wd San Francisc	84	695
Ho	30	m	c	CHIN	Sacramento	2-Wd Sacramento	77	250
Hock	46	m	c	CHIN	Yuba	Marysville	93	625
Hong	31	m	c	CHIN	Fresno	Millerton P O	72	184
Hung	20	m	c	CHIN	Tulare	Visalia	92	299
Jim	20	m	c	CHIN	San Francisco	6-Wd San Francisco	81	42
Kah	34	m	c	CHIN	Yuba	Marysville	93	626
Lie	26	m	c	CHIN	Fresno	Millerton P O	72	188
Loam	30	m	c	CHIN	Marin	Tomales Twp	74	77
Long	43	m	c	CHIN	Santa Clara	1-Wd San Jose	88	270
Loo	39	m	c	CHIN	San Joaquin	1-Wd Stockton	86	147
Loo	34	m	c	CHIN	Solano	Vacaville Twp	90	130
Loo	19	m	c	CHIN	San Luis Obispo	Arroyo Grande Twp	87	279
Lung	43	m	c	CHIN	Alameda	Murray Twp	68	114
Mis	23	m	c	CHIN	San Francisco	San Francisco P O	85	831
Ok	30	m	c	CHIN	Yuba	Marysville	93	601
Paw	40	m	c	CHIN	Placer	Bath P O	76	444
Quoy	42	m	c	CHIN	San Francisco	6-Wd San Francisco	81	53
Susan	21	f	c	CHIN	Tulare	Visalia	92	299
To	25	m	c	CHIN	San Francisco	6-Wd San Francisco	81	63
Toy	34	m	c	CHIN	Yuba	Marysville	93	626
Toy	27	m	c	CHIN	Nevada	Bridgeport Twp	75	111
Two	40	m	c	CHIN	Mariposa	Mariposa P O	74	114
Um	29	m	c	CHIN	Butte	Hamilton Twp	70	67
W	21	m	c	CHIN	Sutter	Yuba Twp	92	144
W Kee	42	m	c	CHIN	San Francisco	11-Wd San Francisc	84	546
Wong	20	m	c	CHIN	Los Angeles	Los Angeles	73	516
Woo	52	m	c	CHIN	Mariposa	Maxwell Crk P O	74	138
Woo	40	m	c	CHIN	Tulare	Visalia	92	299
Wung	60	m	c	CHIN	Calaveras	San Andreas P O	70	173
Yee	47	m	c	CHIN	Yuba	Marysville	93	628
Yong	27	m	c	CHIN	Kern	Havilah P O	73	338
CHEECK								
Ah	40	m	c	CHIN	Sacramento	Granite Twp	77	137
CHEEDA								
Petro	24	m	w	SWIT	Marin	San Antonio Twp	74	62
CHEEING								
Too	21	m	c	CHIN	Nevada	Nevada Twp	75	316
CHEEK								
Ah	30	m	c	CHIN	Sacramento	3-Wd Sacramento	77	304
Ah	30	m	c	CHIN	Sierra	Gibson Twp	89	538
CHEEN								
Pow	22	m	c	CHIN	Fresno	Millerton P O	72	188
CHEENEY								
Cortez D	53	m	w	NY	Santa Clara	2-Wd San Jose	88	293
Danl L	51	m	w	VT	Napa	Napa Twp	75	67
David	37	m	w	IL	Sonoma	Vallejo Twp	91	451
Delia	18	f	w	PA	San Francisco	San Francisco P O	83	265
I	42	m	w	IREL	Lake	Lower Lake	73	414
Jessie	44	m	w	VT	San Francisco	San Francisco P O	83	300
John M	31	m	w	IL	Sonoma	Sonoma Twp	91	445
Lynus	36	m	w	MA	Contra Costa	Martinez P O	71	396
Return J	33	m	w	IL	Sonoma	Vallejo Twp	91	451
Thomas	62	m	w	OH	Sonoma	Sonoma Twp	91	432
CHEENY								
Ezekell	28	m	w	OH	Inyo	Independence Twp	73	328
Kate	24	f	w	IREL	San Francisco	San Francisco P O	85	794
Wm	25	m	w	OH	Lassen	Long Valley Twp	73	437
CHEEP								
Ah	22	m	c	CHIN	San Francisco	6-Wd San Francisco	81	77
Ah	17	f	c	CHIN	San Francisco	6-Wd San Francisco	81	75
CHEER								
Ah	30	m	c	CHIN	Santa Clara	Santa Clara Twp	88	165
CHEES								
Charles	34	m	w	NH	San Joaquin	3-Wd Stockton	86	231
CHEESBRO								
Erastus	54	m	w	CT	Placer	Bath P O	76	427
CHEESE								
James F	45	m	w	MA	El Dorado	White Oak Twp	72	137
CHEESEMAN								
Marcus H	30	m	w	PA	Los Angeles	Santa Ana Twp	73	603
Thomas	30	m	w	MO	Stanislaus	Empire Twp	92	48
CHEESMAN								
Chas R	13	m	w	CA	Butte	Ophir Twp	70	116

© 2001 by Heritage Quest. All rights reserved.

Name	Age	S	R	B-PL	County	Locale	Series M593 Roll	Pg
D W	45	m	w	IN	Alameda	Oakland	68	232
Frank S	37	m	w	NY	Sonoma	Petaluma Twp	91	315
G H	36	m	w	MA	Alameda	Oakland	68	233
Jacob	55	m	w	SWIT	Calaveras	San Andreas P O	70	195
Nelson	24	m	w	IN	San Francisco	3-Wd San Francisco	79	315
Norton	40	m	w	NY	San Francisco	San Francisco P O	83	112
Robert	42	m	w	NJ	San Francisco	11-Wd San Francisc	84	630
Samuel	28	m	w	CHIL	San Mateo	Pescadero P O	87	415
William	24	m	w	CHIL	San Mateo	Pescadero P O	87	415
CHEEVER								
Christophr	45	m	w	ENGL	San Francisco	1-Wd San Francisco	79	98
Chs	40	m	w	MA	Monterey	Salinas Twp	74	310
Cyrus	35	m	w	VT	San Francisco	8-Wd San Francisco	82	454
Henry	52	m	w	MA	San Francisco	7-Wd San Francisco	81	286
Moses	29	m	w	VT	San Francisco	2-Wd San Francisco	79	239
CHEEYON								
Ah	30	m	c	CHIN	Nevada	Nevada Twp	75	298
CHEFFI								
Jennie	21	f	w	FRAN	San Francisco	11-Wd San Francisc	84	556
CHEGHAM								
Matthew	41	m	w	KY	Marin	San Rafael Twp	74	39
CHEIM								
Ah	44	m	c	CHIN	Nevada	Grass Valley Twp	75	171
CHEING								
Ah	25	m	c	CHIN	Nevada	Grass Valley Twp	75	154
Ah	21	m	c	CHIN	San Francisco	11-Wd San Francisc	84	529
CHEK								
Ah	30	m	c	CHIN	San Francisco	11-Wd San Francisc	84	522
Ah	25	m	c	CHIN	San Francisco	6-Wd San Francisco	81	39
CHEKAS								
Wm	30	m	w	ENGL	San Francisco	1-Wd San Francisco	79	58
CHELAMAN								
Juan	40	m	w	CHIL	Monterey	San Antonio Twp	74	316
CHELAND								
Margaret	22	f	w	IREL	San Francisco	2-Wd San Francisco	79	193
CHELESER								
Louis	28	m	w	ITAL	San Francisco	11-Wd San Francisc	84	512
CHELEY								
James	35	m	w	IREL	Sacramento	Dry Crk Twp	77	101
CHELIUS								
Jennie	31	f	w	IA	Santa Cruz	Santa Cruz	89	410
CHELL								
John W	48	m	w	ENGL	San Francisco	8-Wd San Francisco	82	356
CHELLEN								
Henry	40	m	w	GERM	San Joaquin	2-Wd Stockton	86	174
CHELLES								
Lewis	34	m	w	CANA	Siskiyou	Hamburg Twp	89	598
CHELLIRE								
Matilda	58	f	w	FRAN	San Francisco	6-Wd San Francisco	81	97
CHELLIS								
D M	50	m	w	ME	Sonoma	Russian Rvr	91	378
CHELMAN								
H	13	m	w	NV	Alameda	Oakland	68	160
CHELOVICH								
Elia	46	m	w	AUST	San Francisco	San Francisco P O	85	720
CHELSA								
Ramon	27	m	w	MEXI	Santa Clara	Almaden Twp	88	4
CHELTON								
John	28	m	w	IREL	Alameda	Washington Twp	68	291
CHELY								
Louis	44	m	w	HAMB	San Francisco	1-Wd San Francisco	79	66
CHEM								
Ah	42	m	c	CHIN	Sacramento	1-Wd Sacramento	77	196
Ah	17	m	c	CHIN	Nevada	Grass Valley Twp	75	190
F	24	m	c	CHIN	Solano	Green Valley Twp	90	43
Hiram	40	m	w	NY	Calaveras	San Andreas P O	70	189
CHEMEY								
Dennis	44	m	w	FRAN	Sonoma	Sonoma Twp	91	435
CHEMICKER								
Frederick	41	m	w	PRUS	San Luis Obispo	Salinas Twp	87	293
CHEMIS								
Nicholas D	35	m	w	ENGL	Nevada	Grass Valley Twp	75	230
CHEMLOCK								
Theo	40	m	w	FRAN	San Francisco	8-Wd San Francisco	82	346
CHEN								
Ah	46	m	c	CHIN	Placer	Dutch Flat P O	76	410
Ah	35	m	c	CHIN	Sierra	Downieville Twp	89	521
Ah	35	m	c	CHIN	Tuolumne	Big Oak Flat P O	93	402
Ah	35	m	c	CHIN	Calaveras	San Andreas P O	70	166
Ah	34	m	c	CHIN	Los Angeles	Los Angeles Twp	73	466
Ah	30	m	c	CHIN	Tuolumne	Chinese Camp P O	93	386
Ah	30	m	c	CHIN	Calaveras	San Andreas P O	70	169
Ah	28	m	c	CHIN	Contra Costa	Martinez P O	71	452
Ah	27	m	c	CHIN	Placer	Dutch Flat P O	76	415
Ah	27	m	c	CHIN	Butte	Concow Twp	70	11
Ah	21	m	c	CHIN	Tuolumne	Big Oak Flat P O	93	393
Ah	19	m	c	CHIN	Placer	Emigrant Gap P O	76	416
Ah	18	m	c	CHIN	Santa Clara	Alviso Twp	88	25
Ah	15	m	c	CHIN	Nevada	Little York Twp	75	234
Celia	25	f	w	IREL	Napa	Yountville Twp	75	79
Gan	43	m	c	CHIN	Butte	Ophir Twp	70	121
Geong	25	m	c	CHIN	Yuba	Slate Range Bar Tw	93	677
Goo	32	m	c	CHIN	Butte	Concow Twp	70	11
James	48	m	w	MD	Tuolumne	Big Oak Flat P O	93	399
Jim	45	m	c	CHIN	Placer	Bath P O	76	460
John	45	m	w	IREL	Yuba	Slate Range Bar Tw	93	671
Kee	41	m	c	CHIN	Butte	Hamilton Twp	70	74

Name	Age	S	R	B-PL	County	Locale	Series M593 Roll	Pg
Kee	22	m	c	CHIN	Butte	Chico Twp	70	30
Lung	25	m	c	CHIN	Butte	Hamilton Twp	70	75
Peter	30	m	w	PA	San Bernardino	San Bernardino Twp	78	450
Quan	32	m	c	CHIN	Contra Costa	Martinez P O	71	430
War	31	m	c	CHIN	Solano	Green Valley Twp	90	43
CHENACK								
Franklin	46	m	w	FRAN	Kern	Tehachapi P O	73	354
CHENCK								
Lee	35	m	c	CHIN	Nevada	Washington Twp	75	342
CHENCY								
E H	44	m	w	VT	Sonoma	Bodega Twp	91	254
CHENE								
Ah	28	m	c	CHIN	San Joaquin	Douglas Twp	86	49
CHENEE								
Albert	20	m	w	CA	San Joaquin	Oneal Twp	86	104
CHENERY								
Richard	6	m	w	CA	San Francisco	San Francisco P O	85	728
Richard	53	m	w	MA	San Francisco	San Francisco P O	83	147
Walter H	20	m	w	MA	San Francisco	1-Wd San Francisco	79	117
CHENETA								
Dona	43	f	w	MEXI	Napa	Napa	75	53
CHENEWETH								
Lem	35	m	w	MO	Sonoma	Bodega Twp	91	258
CHENEY								
Ann M	52	f	w	NY	Alameda	Washington Twp	68	280
Boyngton	36	m	w	VT	Humboldt	Bald Hills	72	237
Calvin	40	m	w	TN	Fresno	Kings Rvr P O	72	214
Charles	30	m	w	IREL	San Francisco	San Francisco P O	83	399
Charles	19	m	w	IL	Colusa	Colusa	71	288
I M	56	m	w	NY	Monterey	San Antonio Twp	74	319
James	36	m	w	SCOT	San Francisco	1-Wd San Francisco	79	77
James	34	m	w	NY	Alameda	Washington Twp	68	301
M C	38	m	w	IN	Del Norte	Happy Camp Twp	71	471
M L	34	m	w	MA	Nevada	Meadow Lake Twp	75	248
W Fitch	37	m	w	NY	Butte	Chico Twp	70	13
Winthrop	66	m	w	MA	Colusa	Stony Crk Twp	71	329
CHENG								
Ah	47	m	c	CHIN	Calaveras	San Andreas P O	70	179
Ah	42	m	c	CHIN	San Joaquin	1-Wd Stockton	86	156
Ah	30	m	c	CHIN	San Francisco	San Francisco P O	80	442
Ah	30	m	c	CHIN	Sacramento	Georgianna Twp	77	123
Ah	30	m	c	CHIN	Sacramento	Georgianna Twp	77	123
Ah	25	m	c	CHIN	Alameda	Oakland	68	175
Ah	25	m	c	CHIN	San Francisco	6-Wd San Francisco	81	65
Ah	21	m	c	CHIN	San Francisco	San Francisco P O	80	509
Ah	20	m	c	CHIN	San Francisco	6-Wd San Francisco	81	68
Ah	20	m	c	CHIN	Yolo	Putah Twp	93	511
Ah	18	m	c	CHIN	San Francisco	6-Wd San Francisco	81	44
Goon	50	m	c	CHIN	Butte	Kimshew Tpw	70	85
Luck	27	m	c	CHIN	Placer	Bath P O	76	444
Sheppe	27	m	c	CHIN	San Francisco	11-Wd San Francisc	84	546
Yeser	29	m	c	CHIN	Butte	Kimshew Tpw	70	77
CHENGTIE								
Ah	21	m	c	CHIN	San Joaquin	Castoria Twp	86	13
CHENHALL								
Nicholas	25	m	w	IL	San Bernardino	San Bernardino Twp	78	417
CHENIWORTH								
R M	36	m	w	VA	Tuolumne	Columbia P O	93	358
CHENNG								
Ah	41	m	c	CHIN	Amador	Ione City P O	69	364
Ah	19	m	c	CHIN	Siskiyou	Hamburg Twp	89	597
CHENNI								
Joseph	23	m	w	PORT	Solano	Maine Prairie Twp	90	46
CHENNY								
Ah	26	m	c	CHIN	Trinity	Lewiston Pct	92	214
CHENOT								
Eugene	44	m	w	BELG	San Francisco	San Francisco P O	83	373
CHENOW								
Robt	35	m	w	NY	Colusa	Monroe Twp	71	314
CHENOWETH								
James	32	m	w	ENGL	Mariposa	Mariposa P O	74	112
Wm	34	m	w	ENGL	Mariposa	Mariposa P O	74	112
CHENRICK								
Emma	22	f	w	PRUS	San Francisco	San Francisco P O	83	405
CHENSEY								
Harriet	21	f	w	KY	San Francisco	11-Wd San Francisc	84	637
CHENTE								
Ah	46	m	c	CHIN	San Joaquin	3-Wd Stockton	86	220
CHENWORTHY								
John	60	m	w	VA	Tuolumne	Columbia P O	93	357
CHENY								
Ah	27	m	c	CHIN	San Joaquin	1-Wd Stockton	86	154
Ah	17	m	c	CHIN	Contra Costa	Martinez P O	71	413
Lee	14	m	c	CHIN	San Joaquin	1-Wd Stockton	86	147
Myra	19	f	w	NY	San Joaquin	3-Wd Stockton	86	226
Stanford	22	m	w	AR	Kern	Havilah P O	73	339
CHEO								
Ah	52	m	c	CHIN	Amador	Drytown P O	69	419
Ah	14	m	c	CHIN	Placer	Auburn P O	76	377
CHEODER								
M S	55	m	w	IN	El Dorado	Georgetown Twp	72	37
CHEOK								
Ah	34	m	c	CHIN	San Francisco	6-Wd San Francisco	81	43
Ah	20	m	c	CHIN	San Francisco	6-Wd San Francisco	81	42
CHEON								
Ah	43	m	c	CHIN	Calaveras	San Andreas P O	70	176
Ah	40	m	c	CHIN	Butte	Kimshew Tpw	70	84

© 2001 by Heritage Quest. All rights reserved.

California 1870 Census

Series M593

Name	Age	S	R	B-PL	County	Locale	Roll	Pg
Ah	40	m	c	CHIN	Calaveras	San Andreas P O	70	161
Ah	36	m	c	CHIN	Calaveras	San Andreas P O	70	191
Ah	35	m	c	CHIN	Calaveras	Copperopolis P O	70	260
Ah	31	m	c	CHIN	Calaveras	San Andreas P O	70	199
Ah	30	m	c	CHIN	Calaveras	San Andreas P O	70	199
Ah	29	m	c	CHIN	Nevada	Nevada Twp	75	311
Ah	25	m	c	CHIN	Calaveras	San Andreas P O	70	162
Ah	22	m	c	CHIN	Sierra	Sears Twp	89	554
Ah	21	m	c	CHIN	San Francisco	6-Wd San Francisco	81	42
Ah	20	m	c	CHIN	San Francisco	6-Wd San Francisco	81	49
Owen	39	m	w	IREL	San Francisco	San Francisco P O	85	764
Un	22	m	c	CHIN	Calaveras	San Andreas P O	70	165
CHEONG								
---	30	m	c	CHIN	Siskiyou	Yreka Twp	89	673
---	15	m	c	CHIN	Santa Clara	Fremont Twp	88	47
Ah	62	m	c	CHIN	Placer	Lincoln P O	76	484
Ah	50	m	c	CHIN	Calaveras	San Andreas P O	70	210
Ah	45	m	c	CHIN	Nevada	Nevada Twp	75	317
Ah	42	m	c	CHIN	Calaveras	San Andreas P O	70	176
Ah	40	m	c	CHIN	Calaveras	San Andreas P O	70	155
Ah	37	m	c	CHIN	Amador	Fiddletown P O	69	440
Ah	37	m	c	CHIN	Nevada	Meadow Lake Twp	75	256
Ah	36	m	c	CHIN	Nevada	Meadow Lake Twp	75	259
Ah	35	m	c	CHIN	Del Norte	Happy Camp Twp	71	469
Ah	34	m	c	CHIN	San Francisco	6-Wd San Francisco	81	45
Ah	34	m	c	CHIN	Calaveras	San Andreas P O	70	187
Ah	33	m	c	CHIN	Nevada	Eureka Twp	75	127
Ah	31	m	c	CHIN	Shasta	French Gulch P O	89	470
Ah	31	m	c	CHIN	San Francisco	6-Wd San Francisco	81	38
Ah	30	m	c	CHIN	San Francisco	6-Wd San Francisco	81	45
Ah	30	m	c	CHIN	Calaveras	San Andreas P O	70	205
Ah	30	m	c	CHIN	Nevada	Eureka Twp	75	126
Ah	29	m	c	CHIN	Amador	Drytown P O	69	423
Ah	29	m	c	CHIN	Nevada	Meadow Lake Twp	75	266
Ah	29	m	c	CHIN	San Francisco	3-Wd San Francisco	79	309
Ah	25	m	c	CHIN	Shasta	French Gulch P O	89	466
Ah	25	m	c	CHIN	Nevada	Eureka Twp	75	129
Ah	24	f	c	CHIN	Calaveras	San Andreas P O	70	199
Ah	22	m	c	CHIN	San Francisco	6-Wd San Francisco	81	47
Ah	22	m	c	CHIN	San Francisco	6-Wd San Francisco	81	63
Ah	22	m	c	CHIN	Nevada	Nevada Twp	75	321
Ah	22	m	c	CHIN	San Francisco	6-Wd San Francisco	81	45
Ah	21	m	c	CHIN	Calaveras	San Andreas P O	70	155
Ah	20	m	c	CHIN	Nevada	Nevada Twp	75	318
Ah	20	m	c	CHIN	San Francisco	3-Wd San Francisco	79	304
Ah	18	m	c	CHIN	San Francisco	6-Wd San Francisco	81	67
Bun	30	m	c	CHIN	San Francisco	1-Wd San Francisco	79	101
Foon	26	m	c	CHIN	San Francisco	11-Wd San Francisc	84	546
Fu	31	m	c	CHIN	Amador	Fiddletown P O	69	428
Ki	28	m	c	CHIN	Nevada	Nevada Twp	75	312
Kooey	30	m	c	CHIN	Yuba	Marysville	93	631
Lee	35	m	c	CHIN	San Francisco	2-Wd San Francisco	79	285
Lew	36	m	c	CHIN	Yuba	Marysville	93	625
Luey	18	m	c	CHIN	San Francisco	3-Wd San Francisco	79	303
Soue	30	f	c	CHIN	Calaveras	San Andreas P O	70	210
CHEOO								
Ki Oon	26	m	c	CHIN	San Francisco	11-Wd San Francisc	84	546
CHEOW								
Ah	55	m	c	CHIN	Calaveras	San Andreas P O	70	191
Ah	24	m	c	CHIN	Nevada	Nevada Twp	75	312
Hock	40	m	c	CHIN	Nevada	Washington Twp	75	342
CHEOY								
Ah	25	m	c	CHIN	San Francisco	6-Wd San Francisco	81	48
CHEPON								
Jas	44	m	w	ENGL	Solano	Benicia	90	8
CHER								
Ah	40	m	c	CHIN	Tuolumne	Sonora P O	93	322
CHERAKENA								
Benito	30	m	w	ITAL	San Francisco	1-Wd San Francisco	79	81
CHERALE								
Antonio	20	m	w	ITAL	Solano	Vallejo	90	213
CHERARO								
Ursalia	40	m	w	MEXI	Stanislaus	Washington Twp	92	87
CHERASSUS								
Edwin	36	m	w	FRAN	San Francisco	8-Wd San Francisco	82	372
CHERBERNET								
Francis	52	m	w	FRAN	Nevada	Grass Valley Twp	75	179
CHERENY								
Pauline	51	f	w	FRAN	San Francisco	2-Wd San Francisco	79	172
CHERICE								
Morgan	30	m	w	MEXI	Tulare	Kings Rvr Twp	92	252
CHERIFF								
Chas	50	m	w	PRUS	San Francisco	1-Wd San Francisco	79	57
CHERK								
John	40	m	w	IN	Alameda	Murray Twp	68	112
CHERKINS								
Claus	28	m	w	HAMB	San Joaquin	Tulare Twp	86	254
CHERLEY								
Charles P	36	m	w	NH	San Francisco	San Francisco P O	83	185
CHERLOTA								
Huldah	29	f	w	SWIT	San Francisco	11-Wd San Francisc	84	700
CHERLSON								
John	23	m	w	SWED	San Joaquin	1-Wd Stockton	86	134
CHERNET								
Cathrine	50	f	w	IREL	San Francisco	1-Wd San Francisco	79	135
CHERRADELLI								
---	17	m	w	CA	Alameda	Oakland	68	167
CHERRARDELLE								
D	56	m	w	ITAL	Alameda	Oakland	68	168
CHERREFIELD								
Oliver	42	m	w	CANA	Nevada	Bloomfield Twp	75	94
CHERRICK								
George	33	m	w	CA	San Francisco	San Francisco P O	83	389
CHERRINGTON								
Edward	39	m	w	OH	San Mateo	Pescadero P O	87	409
CHERRISIA								
Jno	49	m	w	SWIT	Sacramento	3-Wd Sacramento	77	291
CHERRY								
Elizabeth	31	f	w	PA	San Francisco	8-Wd San Francisco	82	415
Emily	14	f	w	FRAN	San Francisco	San Francisco P O	85	720
James	10	m	w	CA	San Francisco	San Francisco P O	83	160
John	50	m	w	PA	Colusa	Colusa Twp	71	287
John	48	m	w	IREL	Alameda	Oakland	68	230
John	41	m	w	NJ	San Francisco	San Francisco P O	80	413
Mary	24	f	w	IREL	Santa Clara	Fremont Twp	88	65
Mary	15	f	w	CA	Fresno	Millerton P O	72	186
William	34	m	w	IL	Colusa	Spring Valley Twp	71	337
CHERVOILLOT								
John	56	m	w	FRAN	Nevada	Grass Valley Twp	75	178
CHERY								
Suing	25	f	c	CHIN	Humboldt	Eureka Twp	72	266
William H	52	m	w	NC	Tulare	Tule Rvr Twp	92	269
CHES								
Ah	45	m	c	CHIN	Calaveras	Copperopolis P O	70	232
Ah	34	m	c	CHIN	Calaveras	Copperopolis P O	70	235
CHESCO								
Frank	24	m	w	ITAL	San Francisco	2-Wd San Francisco	79	180
CHESDAL								
Herman	22	m	w	PRUS	San Francisco	San Francisco P O	80	479
CHESEBRO								
J J	35	m	w	CT	Napa	Napa	75	18
CHESEBROW								
P	45	m	w	NY	Yuba	Marysville	93	608
CHESHIN								
Chas	28	m	w	RUSS	San Francisco	1-Wd San Francisco	79	60
CHESHOLM								
Duncan	45	m	w	CANA	San Francisco	1-Wd San Francisco	79	30
CHESKY								
Ezra	42	m	w	PRUS	San Joaquin	2-Wd Stockton	86	200
CHESLER								
Ernest	42	m	w	PRUS	San Francisco	San Francisco P O	80	354
CHESLEY								
Geo W	51	m	w	RI	Sacramento	1-Wd Sacramento	77	174
James E	23	m	w	NH	Sacramento	1-Wd Sacramento	77	174
Lucy	45	f	w	MA	San Francisco	San Francisco P O	83	170
W	60	m	w	IREL	Sacramento	1-Wd Sacramento	77	190
Wm E	23	m	w	MA	Sacramento	1-Wd Sacramento	77	174
CHESLING								
Anna	32	f	w	SWED	San Francisco	San Francisco P O	83	202
CHESNEAU								
Francis	32	m	w	FRAN	Nevada	Grass Valley Twp	75	191
CHESNEY								
Jane S	23	f	w	KY	San Luis Obispo	Morro Twp	87	285
John W	29	m	w	KY	San Luis Obispo	Morro Twp	87	285
CHESNUT								
Andrew	29	m	w	PA	Monterey	Castroville Twp	74	335
James D	42	m	w	NY	Placer	Bath P O	76	443
John A	40	m	w	OH	Nevada	Nevada Twp	75	285
Jos M	38	m	w	IN	Shasta	Horsetown P O	89	505
Robt	32	m	w	SCOT	Solano	Vallejo	90	150
CHESNUTWOOD								
E T	60	m	w	PA	San Joaquin	Oneal Twp	86	114
CHESON								
George C	42	m	w	ME	Mendocino	Cuffeys Cove Twp	74	168
CHESROWN								
John C	29	m	w	PA	Placer	Bath P O	76	459
CHESSLEY								
William	62	m	w	NY	Sacramento	2-Wd Sacramento	77	254
CHESTER								
Alexr	28	m	w	CANA	San Francisco	San Francisco P O	83	102
Charles	40	m	w	NY	San Francisco	San Francisco P O	83	415
Chas	40	m	w	IL	Solano	Vallejo	90	145
David S	27	m	w	PA	Stanislaus	Empire Twp	92	52
Fred	21	m	w	MA	San Francisco	7-Wd San Francisco	81	274
Geo B	37	m	w	NY	San Francisco	5-Wd San Francisco	81	30
George	32	m	w	CT	Kern	Bakersfield P O	73	360
George A	28	m	m	DE	Santa Cruz	Santa Cruz	89	420
H C	39	m	w	VT	Del Norte	Happy Camp Twp	71	468
Henry	37	m	w	ENGL	San Francisco	San Francisco P O	83	199
James	24	m	w	IREL	Humboldt	Mattole Twp	72	283
Jno B	64	m	w	PA	Butte	Hamilton Twp	70	69
John	30	m	w	IREL	San Francisco	8-Wd San Francisco	82	431
John	21	m	w	CT	Tulare	Kings Rvr Twp	92	253
John Jr	23	m	w	IA	Butte	Ophir Twp	70	114
John W	37	m	w	PA	San Francisco	7-Wd San Francisco	81	222
Julius	39	m	w	CT	Kern	Bakersfield P O	73	357
Lano	40	m	w	ITAL	San Joaquin	1-Wd Stockton	86	154
Martin	24	m	w	ME	San Francisco	7-Wd San Francisco	81	223
Mary	25	f	w	IREL	Alameda	Oakland	68	154
Mary T	20	f	i	CA	Santa Cruz	Santa Cruz	89	420
Morris	34	m	w	OH	San Francisco	San Francisco P O	80	479
Reuben	19	m	w	NC	Sonoma	Analy Twp	91	224
Saml	33	m	w	IREL	San Francisco	7-Wd San Francisco	81	270

© 2001 by Heritage Quest. All rights reserved.

Name	Age	S	R	B-PL	County	Locale	Series M593 Roll	Pg
CHESTEWOOD								
John	27	m	w	NY	San Joaquin	3-Wd Stockton	86	245
CHESTNUT								
Edmund	38	m	w	MO	Colusa	Butte Twp	71	265
Jennie	22	f	w	MO	Colusa	Colusa Twp	71	277
John	42	m	w	NY	Amador	Fiddletown P O	69	430
John	38	m	w	IN	Siskiyou	Scott Valley Twp	89	616
Mary	7	f	w	CA	San Francisco	7-Wd San Francisco	81	281
Mary	18	f	w	IA	San Francisco	2-Wd San Francisco	79	187
Robert	31	m	w	CANA	Sonoma	Salt Point	91	386
CHET								
Ah	42	m	c	CHIN	Placer	Bath P O	76	456
Ah	40	m	c	CHIN	Shasta	French Gulch P O	89	467
Ah	28	m	c	CHIN	Yuba	Marysville	93	619
CHETT								
Ah	41	m	c	CHIN	Placer	Bath P O	76	442
Ah	21	m	c	CHIN	Placer	Bath P O	76	445
CHEU								
Ah	43	m	c	CHIN	Shasta	French Gulch P O	89	469
Ah	16	m	c	CHIN	Shasta	French Gulch P O	89	466
Mow	40	m	c	CHIN	Butte	Kimshew Tpw	70	84
Wing	24	m	c	CHIN	Santa Clara	Santa Clara Twp	88	164
CHEUCK								
Ah	38	m	c	CHIN	Shasta	French Gulch P O	89	464
Ah	36	m	c	CHIN	Siskiyou	Cottonwood Twp	89	594
Ah	12	m	c	CHIN	Shasta	French Gulch P O	89	469
CHEUM								
Ah	60	m	c	CHIN	Calaveras	San Andreas P O	70	180
CHEUN								
Ah	32	m	c	CHIN	Mariposa	Mariposa P O	74	135
CHEUNG								
---	44	m	c	CHIN	Siskiyou	Cottonwood Twp	89	593
---	25	m	w	CHIN	Siskiyou	Yreka Twp	89	667
---	21	m	c	CHIN	Shasta	American Ranch P O	89	500
---	13	m	c	CHIN	Shasta	Horsetown P O	89	507
Ah	51	m	c	CHIN	Calaveras	Copperopolis P O	70	258
Ah	48	m	c	CHIN	Amador	Ione City P O	69	355
Ah	48	m	c	CHIN	Nevada	Nevada Twp	75	312
Ah	47	m	c	CHIN	Shasta	Horsetown P O	89	506
Ah	40	m	c	CHIN	Calaveras	San Andreas P O	70	169
Ah	40	m	c	CHIN	Mariposa	Maxwell Crk P O	74	145
Ah	40	m	c	CHIN	Shasta	French Gulch P O	89	470
Ah	35	m	c	CHIN	Mariposa	Maxwell Crk P O	74	145
Ah	33	m	c	CHIN	Trinity	North Fork Twp	92	216
Ah	31	m	c	CHIN	Amador	Fiddletown P O	69	440
Ah	30	m	c	CHIN	Trinity	Indian Crk	92	199
Ah	30	m	c	CHIN	Nevada	Nevada Twp	75	276
Ah	29	m	c	CHIN	San Francisco	6-Wd San Francisco	81	60
Ah	28	m	c	CHIN	San Francisco	6-Wd San Francisco	81	59
Ah	28	m	c	CHIN	San Francisco	6-Wd San Francisco	81	98
Ah	28	m	c	CHIN	Nevada	Meadow Lake Twp	75	250
Ah	28	m	c	CHIN	Shasta	French Gulch P O	89	466
Ah	26	m	c	CHIN	Nevada	Nevada Twp	75	298
Ah	25	m	c	CHIN	Trinity	North Fork Twp	92	221
Ah	25	m	c	CHIN	Trinity	Douglas	92	237
Ah	24	m	c	CHIN	San Francisco	6-Wd San Francisco	81	56
Ah	24	m	c	CHIN	San Francisco	6-Wd San Francisco	81	69
Ah	22	m	c	CHIN	Shasta	French Gulch P O	89	470
Ah	22	m	c	CHIN	Trinity	Junction City Pct	92	210
Ah	22	m	c	CHIN	Trinity	Junction City Pct	92	207
Ah	22	m	c	CHIN	San Francisco	11-Wd San Francisc	84	548
Ah	22	m	c	CHIN	Shasta	French Gulch P O	89	470
Ah	21	m	c	CHIN	Amador	Lancha Plana P O	69	369
Ah	20	m	c	CHIN	Trinity	Junction City Pct	92	206
Ah	20	f	c	CHIN	San Francisco	6-Wd San Francisco	81	76
Ah	20	m	c	CHIN	Nevada	Bridgeport Twp	75	110
Ah	19	m	c	CHIN	San Francisco	6-Wd San Francisco	81	65
Ah	18	m	c	CHIN	San Francisco	6-Wd San Francisco	81	77
Ah	18	m	c	CHIN	San Francisco	6-Wd San Francisco	81	142
Ah	18	m	c	CHIN	Shasta	American Ranch P O	89	497
Ah	18	m	c	CHIN	San Francisco	6-Wd San Francisco	81	63
Ah	18	f	c	CHIN	San Francisco	6-Wd San Francisco	81	77
Ark	24	m	c	CHIN	Shasta	French Gulch P O	89	470
Hang	60	m	c	CHIN	Shasta	American Ranch P O	89	499
Hoon	54	m	c	CHIN	Siskiyou	Cottonwood Twp	89	594
Me	50	m	c	CHIN	Nevada	Nevada Twp	75	320
Toon	26	m	c	CHIN	Shasta	French Gulch P O	89	470
CHEUP								
---	20	m	c	CHIN	Siskiyou	Yreka Twp	89	666
CHEVALIER								
C J	36	m	w	PA	San Francisco	San Francisco P O	85	779
Fortuna	56	m	w	FRAN	Sacramento	2-Wd Sacramento	77	212
George	2	m	w	CA	Nevada	Nevada Twp	75	274
John	41	m	w	FRAN	San Francisco	San Francisco P O	80	461
John B	58	m	w	FRAN	San Francisco	San Francisco P O	83	224
Louis	31	m	w	FRAN	San Francisco	8-Wd San Francisco	82	485
Mary	44	f	w	SWIT	San Francisco	2-Wd San Francisco	79	161
CHEVALLEY								
Eime	22	m	w	SWIT	Nevada	Grass Valley Twp	75	219
CHEVAN								
John	39	m	w	FRAN	San Francisco	8-Wd San Francisco	82	447
CHEVARIA								
Nicholas	40	m	w	CHIL	Santa Clara	Milpitas Twp	88	109
CHEVASEO								
C B	23	m	w	ITAL	San Francisco	1-Wd San Francisco	79	28
CHEVAUNCY								
Joseph	48	m	w	FRAN	Butte	Wyandotte Twp	70	142
CHEVENOT								
Francois	39	m	w	FRAN	San Francisco	6-Wd San Francisco	81	111
CHEVERET								
Leon	48	m	w	FRAN	Humboldt	Arcata Twp	72	235
CHEVERI								
Waukena	32	f	w	MEXI	Calaveras	Copperopolis P O	70	256
CHEVERS								
Wm	41	m	w	VA	San Francisco	2-Wd San Francisco	79	197
CHEVESICH								
Emanuel	35	m	w	AUST	San Francisco	6-Wd San Francisco	81	90
CHEVINANT								
A B	24	m	w	FRAN	Alameda	Alameda	68	18
CHEVIO								
Peter	32	m	w	MEXI	San Francisco	6-Wd San Francisco	81	111
CHEVIS								
Chevin	41	m	w	FRAN	Siskiyou	Callahan P O	89	627
Raphael	45	m	w	MEXI	Tulare	Farmersville Twp	92	241
CHEVOLM								
Thos	26	m	w	IREL	San Francisco	1-Wd San Francisco	79	66
CHEVOSECH								
Charles	44	m	w	AUST	Contra Costa	San Pablo Twp	71	353
CHEVOYA								
Francisco	28	m	w	CA	Santa Clara	San Jose Twp	88	218
Joseph	35	m	w	MEXI	Santa Clara	San Jose Twp	88	218
CHEW								
Ah	63	m	c	CHIN	Nevada	Nevada Twp	75	311
Ah	60	m	c	CHIN	El Dorado	White Oak Twp	72	136
Ah	57	m	c	CHIN	El Dorado	Salmon Falls Twp	72	130
Ah	56	m	c	CHIN	Nevada	Nevada Twp	75	286
Ah	55	m	c	CHIN	Amador	Ione City P O	69	351
Ah	54	m	c	CHIN	Mariposa	Mariposa P O	74	131
Ah	54	m	c	CHIN	Mariposa	Mariposa P O	74	103
Ah	53	m	c	CHIN	El Dorado	Mountain Twp	72	67
Ah	51	m	c	CHIN	Nevada	Washington Twp	75	339
Ah	51	m	c	CHIN	Trinity	Minersville Pct	92	203
Ah	50	m	c	CHIN	Mariposa	Mariposa P O	74	125
Ah	50	m	c	CHIN	Merced	Snelling P O	74	278
Ah	50	m	c	CHIN	El Dorado	Mud Springs Twp	72	79
Ah	47	m	c	CHIN	Calaveras	San Andreas P O	70	155
Ah	45	m	c	CHIN	Shasta	Shasta P O	89	461
Ah	45	m	c	CHIN	Nevada	Rough & Ready Twp	75	337
Ah	45	m	c	CHIN	El Dorado	Mud Springs Twp	72	80
Ah	45	m	c	CHIN	Trinity	Douglas	92	234
Ah	44	m	c	CHIN	Butte	Ophir Twp	70	103
Ah	42	m	c	CHIN	Sacramento	Franklin Twp	77	114
Ah	42	m	c	CHIN	Calaveras	San Andreas P O	70	172
Ah	42	m	c	CHIN	Calaveras	Copperopolis P O	70	243
Ah	41	m	c	CHIN	Mariposa	Mariposa P O	74	126
Ah	41	m	c	CHIN	El Dorado	Diamond Springs Tw	72	27
Ah	40	m	c	CHIN	Calaveras	Copperopolis P O	70	243
Ah	40	m	c	CHIN	Nevada	Grass Valley Twp	75	210
Ah	40	m	c	CHIN	Santa Clara	Alviso Twp	88	29
Ah	39	m	c	CHIN	Sacramento	Sutter Twp	77	382
Ah	38	m	c	CHIN	Mariposa	Mariposa P O	74	104
Ah	37	m	c	CHIN	El Dorado	Cosumnes Twp	72	17
Ah	37	m	c	CHIN	Calaveras	Copperopolis P O	70	240
Ah	36	m	c	CHIN	Placer	Bath P O	76	459
Ah	35	m	c	CHIN	Calaveras	San Andreas P O	70	169
Ah	35	m	c	CHIN	Amador	Volcano P O	69	388
Ah	34	m	c	CHIN	San Francisco	San Francisco P O	85	749
Ah	34	m	c	CHIN	Placer	Bath P O	76	454
Ah	34	m	c	CHIN	El Dorado	Placerville	72	115
Ah	34	m	c	CHIN	Nevada	Nevada Twp	75	318
Ah	33	m	c	CHIN	Amador	Volcano P O	69	378
Ah	32	m	c	CHIN	Nevada	Grass Valley Twp	75	228
Ah	30	m	c	CHIN	Placer	Clipper Gap P O	76	392
Ah	30	m	c	CHIN	Mariposa	Mariposa P O	74	127
Ah	30	m	c	CHIN	Mariposa	Mariposa P O	74	126
Ah	30	m	c	CHIN	Calaveras	Copperopolis P O	70	233
Ah	30	m	c	CHIN	El Dorado	Mud Springs Twp	72	88
Ah	30	m	c	CHIN	Placer	Newcastle Twp	76	479
Ah	30	m	c	CHIN	San Francisco	6-Wd San Francisco	81	57
Ah	29	m	c	CHIN	San Joaquin	1-Wd Stockton	86	146
Ah	28	m	c	CHIN	Colusa	Colusa	71	299
Ah	28	m	c	CHIN	El Dorado	Salmon Falls Twp	72	132
Ah	28	m	c	CHIN	Nevada	Eureka Twp	75	140
Ah	26	m	c	CHIN	Trinity	Weaverville Pct	92	228
Ah	26	m	c	CHIN	Placer	Clipper Gap P O	76	392
Ah	26	m	c	CHIN	Sacramento	Franklin Twp	77	116
Ah	25	m	c	CHIN	Nevada	Rough & Ready Twp	75	329
Ah	25	m	c	CHIN	Colusa	Colusa	71	298
Ah	25	m	c	CHIN	El Dorado	White Oak Twp	72	136
Ah	25	m	c	CHIN	El Dorado	Coloma Twp	72	8
Ah	25	m	c	CHIN	Trinity	Canyon City Pct	92	202
Ah	24	m	c	CHIN	San Francisco	11-Wd San Francisc	84	710
Ah	24	m	c	CHIN	Nevada	Eureka Twp	75	126
Ah	23	m	c	CHIN	Nevada	Grass Valley Twp	75	184
Ah	22	m	c	CHIN	Nevada	Grass Valley Twp	75	171
Ah	21	m	c	CHIN	San Francisco	6-Wd San Francisco	81	60
Ah	21	m	c	CHIN	Nevada	Nevada Twp	75	279
Ah	20	m	c	CHIN	Shasta	American Ranch P O	89	500
Ah	20	m	c	CHIN	San Francisco	6-Wd San Francisco	81	59
Ah	20	m	c	CHIN	San Francisco	San Francisco P O	85	747
Ah	20	m	c	CHIN	Nevada	Nevada Twp	75	298
Ah	20	m	c	CHIN	Calaveras	San Andreas P O	70	173
Ah	20	m	c	CHIN	Calaveras	San Andreas P O	70	171
Ah	20	m	c	CHIN	Plumas	Goodwin Twp	77	2

© 2001 by Heritage Quest. All rights reserved.

Name	Age	S	R	B-PL	County	Locale	Series M593 Roll	Pg
Ah	17	m	c	CHIN	Nevada	Eureka Twp	75	141
Ah	17	m	c	CHIN	Santa Clara	Santa Clara Twp	88	163
Ah	14	m	c	CHIN	Nevada	Grass Valley Twp	75	184
Ah	12	m	c	CHIN	Santa Clara	Santa Clara Twp	88	163
Albert G	32	m	w	TN	Nevada	Little York Twp	75	236
Alfred	36	m	w	OH	Santa Clara	San Jose Twp	88	215
Allen	43	m	w	NJ	Alameda	Washington Twp	68	291
Chick	39	m	c	CHIN	El Dorado	Salmon Falls Twp	72	130
Chong	39	m	c	CHIN	El Dorado	Coloma Twp	72	1
Chung	28	m	c	CHIN	San Francisco	6-Wd San Francisco	81	86
Fong	40	m	c	CHIN	Calaveras	San Andreas P O	70	220
Foo	29	m	c	CHIN	Butte	Hamilton Twp	70	72
Fow	27	m	c	CHIN	Butte	Ophir Twp	70	106
Hang	53	m	c	CHIN	San Francisco	6-Wd San Francisco	81	54
Hong	30	m	c	CHIN	San Francisco	6-Wd San Francisco	81	39
John P H	51	m	w	GA	Colusa	Spring Valley Twp	71	345
Joseph	39	m	w	TN	Nevada	Little York Twp	75	237
Ku	34	m	c	CHIN	San Francisco	6-Wd San Francisco	81	48
Lar	40	m	c	CHIN	San Francisco	6-Wd San Francisco	81	97
Long	27	m	c	CHIN	Calaveras	San Andreas P O	70	204
Mon	50	m	c	CHIN	Nevada	Washington Twp	75	339
Pui	42	m	c	CHIN	Yuba	Slate Range Bar Tw	93	678
Yit	30	m	c	CHIN	Calaveras	San Andreas P O	70	204
CHEWETT								
Antone	32	m	w	FRAN	Contra Costa	Martinez P O	71	367
CHEWEY								
Ah	32	m	c	CHIN	Placer	Bath P O	76	442
CHEWING								
Ah	21	m	c	CHIN	San Francisco	6-Wd San Francisco	81	104
CHEWY								
Ah	18	m	c	CHIN	Yuba	Marysville	93	619
CHEY								
Ah	38	m	c	CHIN	Butte	Chico Twp	70	51
Ah	38	m	c	CHIN	San Francisco	6-Wd San Francisco	81	64
Ah	30	m	c	CHIN	San Francisco	6-Wd San Francisco	81	66
Ah	24	m	c	CHIN	Plumas	Goodwin Twp	77	4
CHEYON								
Ah	58	m	c	CHIN	Nevada	Nevada Twp	75	312
CHEYWHIDEN								
John	43	m	w	ENGL	Mariposa	Mariposa P O	74	113
CHI								
Ah	51	m	c	CHIN	San Francisco	6-Wd San Francisco	81	56
Ah	40	m	c	CHIN	Trinity	Junction City Pct	92	208
Ah	38	m	c	CHIN	Placer	Pino Twp	76	470
Ah	38	m	c	CHIN	Tuolumne	Columbia P O	93	352
Ah	36	m	c	CHIN	Butte	Ophir Twp	70	104
Ah	35	m	c	CHIN	Yolo	Washington Twp	93	528
Ah	34	m	c	CHIN	Butte	Hamilton Twp	70	67
Ah	34	m	c	CHIN	San Francisco	San Francisco P O	80	513
Ah	34	m	c	CHIN	Trinity	Weaverville Pct	92	228
Ah	32	m	c	CHIN	San Joaquin	Oneal Twp	86	117
Ah	27	m	c	CHIN	Alameda	Oakland	68	138
Ah	27	m	c	CHIN	San Joaquin	1-Wd Stockton	86	156
Ah	27	m	c	CHIN	San Joaquin	Oneal Twp	86	116
Ah	20	m	c	CHIN	Sutter	Nicolaus Twp	92	115
Ah	19	m	c	CHIN	San Francisco	3-Wd San Francisco	79	307
Ah	19	m	c	CHIN	San Francisco	6-Wd San Francisco	81	68
Ah	18	m	c	CHIN	San Francisco	3-Wd San Francisco	79	309
Amali	27	m	c	CHIN	Solano	Green Valley Twp	90	43
Chee	22	m	c	CHIN	Yuba	Marysville	93	629
Chong	54	m	c	CHIN	Santa Clara	1-Wd San Jose	88	269
Choy	28	f	c	CHIN	Calaveras	San Andreas P O	70	161
Chun	27	m	c	CHIN	Yuba	Marysville	93	624
Gi	28	m	c	CHIN	San Francisco	2-Wd San Francisco	79	285
Hing	32	m	c	CHIN	Mariposa	Mariposa P O	74	103
Hip	30	m	c	CHIN	Mariposa	Mariposa P O	74	103
Joe	15	m	c	CHIN	Yolo	Putah Twp	93	523
Kee	40	m	c	CHIN	Butte	Chico Twp	70	52
Lee	36	m	c	CHIN	Sacramento	1-Wd Sacramento	77	204
Lin	30	m	c	CHIN	Butte	Concow Twp	70	8
Lon	31	m	c	CHIN	Yuba	Marysville	93	632
Long	24	m	c	CHIN	Sierra	Alleghany & Forest	89	535
Look	34	m	c	CHIN	Yuba	Marysville	93	628
Lu	27	m	c	CHIN	Butte	Concow Twp	70	11
Lun	22	m	c	CHIN	Butte	Kimshew Tpw	70	86
Mi	24	m	c	CHIN	Amador	Jackson P O	69	331
Min	48	m	c	CHIN	Butte	Kimshew Tpw	70	86
Ning	26	f	c	CHIN	San Francisco	2-Wd San Francisco	79	216
Si	26	f	c	CHIN	Tuolumne	Big Oak Flat P O	93	399
Si	21	f	c	CHIN	Tuolumne	Big Oak Flat P O	93	400
Toe	26	m	c	CHIN	Butte	Hamilton Twp	70	72
Tong	31	m	c	CHIN	Solano	Green Valley Twp	90	42
Wi	26	m	c	CHIN	San Francisco	2-Wd San Francisco	79	285
Won	34	m	c	CHIN	Butte	Hamilton Twp	70	73
Yee	51	m	c	CHIN	San Francisco	2-Wd San Francisco	79	285
Yong	16	m	c	CHIN	San Francisco	2-Wd San Francisco	79	236
Yung	38	m	c	CHIN	San Francisco	2-Wd San Francisco	79	286
CHIA								
Jan	33	m	c	CHIN	San Mateo	Schoolhouse Statio	87	335
CHIAPARI								
Giovanni	18	m	w	ITAL	San Francisco	11-Wd San Francisc	84	642
CHIAPOCO								
Julia	45	m	w	ITAL	San Francisco	5-Wd San Francisco	81	12
CHIARMI								
Francisco	29	m	w	ITAL	San Francisco	11-Wd San Francisc	84	595
CHIBONA								
Emile	39	m	w	FRAN	Calaveras	Copperopolis P O	70	260
CHIC								
Ah	36	m	c	CHIN	Butte	Hamilton Twp	70	75
CHICA								
Ah Hun	32	m	c	CHIN	Solano	Vallejo	90	178
CHICASOLA								
Juan	40	m	w	MEXI	Calaveras	San Andreas P O	70	205
CHICH								
Ah	40	m	c	CHIN	San Francisco	1-Wd San Francisco	79	61
Ah	35	m	c	CHIN	Sacramento	San Joaquin Twp	77	395
Ah	27	m	c	CHIN	San Joaquin	1-Wd Stockton	86	146
Ah	22	m	c	CHIN	San Joaquin	1-Wd Stockton	86	147
Sing	20	m	c	CHIN	San Francisco	San Francisco P O	83	176
CHICHEL								
John	45	m	w	AUST	San Francisco	3-Wd San Francisco	79	293
CHICHESTER								
Daniel W	39	m	w	NY	El Dorado	Placerville	72	127
Deloss	14	m	w	CA	Stanislaus	Empire Twp	92	66
J R	45	m	w	MD	San Francisco	8-Wd San Francisco	82	351
Mary	42	f	w	NY	San Francisco	11-Wd San Francisc	84	452
CHICHISOLA								
Antonio	31	m	w	ITAL	Mariposa	Mariposa P O	74	104
CHICK								
Ah	60	m	c	CHIN	Plumas	Goodwin Twp	77	2
Ah	48	m	c	CHIN	Plumas	Plumas Twp	77	33
Ah	48	m	c	CHIN	Tuolumne	Chinese Camp P O	93	364
Ah	45	m	c	CHIN	Calaveras	San Andreas P O	70	169
Ah	41	m	c	CHIN	Butte	Chico Twp	70	27
Ah	41	m	c	CHIN	Butte	Ophir Twp	70	121
Ah	40	m	c	CHIN	Butte	Chico Twp	70	28
Ah	40	m	c	CHIN	El Dorado	Mud Springs Twp	72	73
Ah	39	m	c	CHIN	Butte	Hamilton Twp	70	74
Ah	38	m	c	CHIN	Tuolumne	Sonora P O	93	312
Ah	35	m	c	CHIN	El Dorado	Mud Springs Twp	72	79
Ah	34	m	c	CHIN	Butte	Chico Twp	70	53
Ah	34	m	c	CHIN	Alameda	Oakland	68	134
Ah	32	m	c	CHIN	Butte	Hamilton Twp	70	67
Ah	31	m	c	CHIN	Butte	Hamilton Twp	70	68
Ah	30	m	c	CHIN	Butte	Hamilton Twp	70	67
Ah	30	m	c	CHIN	San Francisco	6-Wd San Francisco	81	61
Ah	24	m	c	CHIN	Butte	Oregon Twp	70	133
Ah	24	m	c	CHIN	Sacramento	Georgianna Twp	77	126
Ah	24	m	c	CHIN	Placer	Pino Twp	76	470
Ah	24	m	c	CHIN	Solano	Silveyville Twp	90	85
Ah	22	m	c	CHIN	San Mateo	Pescadero P O	87	414
Ah	21	m	c	CHIN	Butte	Hamilton Twp	70	68
Ah	21	m	c	CHIN	Placer	Auburn P O	76	362
Ah	20	m	c	CHIN	Alameda	Oakland	68	135
Ah	20	f	c	CHIN	Butte	Chico Twp	70	60
Ah	19	m	c	CHIN	San Joaquin	2-Wd Stockton	86	181
Augustus	43	m	w	ME	Alameda	Oakland	68	133
E G	50	m	w	ME	Yuba	Marysville	93	591
Elwell	58	m	w	ME	San Francisco	6-Wd San Francisco	81	144
Gee	47	m	c	CHIN	Placer	Auburn P O	76	370
George	38	m	w	OH	Calaveras	San Andreas P O	70	206
Harrison	30	m	w	MA	San Francisco	6-Wd San Francisco	81	152
Mille	30	f	w	ME	Alameda	Oakland	68	226
Ora	56	f	w	ME	Alameda	Oakland	68	229
Samuel B	33	m	w	NH	Sacramento	Georgianna Twp	77	126
W	34	m	w	NY	San Francisco	8-Wd San Francisco	82	369
Wm	37	m	w	ENGL	San Francisco	11-Wd San Francisc	84	606
Yon	39	m	c	CHIN	Butte	Hamilton Twp	70	75
CHICKERING								
Andrew	47	m	w	NH	Sutter	Butte Twp	92	102
Sam G	33	m	w	NH	Butte	Ophir Twp	70	95
CHICKS								
Hall	42	m	w	PRUS	San Francisco	5-Wd San Francisco	81	15
CHICO								
Antonio	40	m	w	MEXI	Santa Clara	Fremont Twp	88	58
Louis	50	m	w	MEXI	Amador	Ione City P O	69	362
M	40	m	w	MEXI	Amador	Ione City P O	69	362
Roman	28	m	w	MEXI	Kern	Tehachapi P O	73	354
CHICONI								
M	40	f	w	ME	Yuba	Marysville	93	589
CHIDESTER								
David	47	m	w	VA	Merced	Snelling P O	74	268
John	43	m	w	OH	Fresno	Millerton P O	72	157
CHIE								
Ah	38	m	c	CHIN	Alameda	Oakland	68	238
Ah	32	m	c	CHIN	San Francisco	6-Wd San Francisco	81	66
Ah	30	m	c	CHIN	San Joaquin	Oneal Twp	86	117
Ah	26	m	c	CHIN	Sacramento	Georgianna Twp	77	132
Ah	14	m	c	CHIN	San Francisco	San Francisco P O	83	197
Wah	40	m	c	CHIN	Amador	Jackson P O	69	344
Wawn	19	f	c	CHIN	Butte	Ophir Twp	70	112
CHIEN								
---	39	m	c	CHIN	San Francisco	11-Wd San Francisc	84	696
Ah	27	m	c	CHIN	San Francisco	11-Wd San Francisc	84	695
Ah	25	m	c	CHIN	San Francisco	3-Wd San Francisco	79	290
Ah	20	m	w	CHIN	Santa Cruz	Santa Cruz	89	412
Ah	17	m	c	CHIN	San Francisco	11-Wd San Francisc	84	689
Ah	17	m	c	CHIN	San Francisco	11-Wd San Francisc	84	664
Ah	14	m	c	CHIN	San Francisco	11-Wd San Francisc	84	680
CHIERRY								
Thomas	42	m	w	FRAN	San Francisco	San Francisco P O	80	539
CHIET								
Ah	27	m	c	CHIN	San Joaquin	3-Wd Stockton	86	232

© 2001 by Heritage Quest. All rights reserved.

Name	Age	S	R	B-PL	County	Locale	Roll	Pg
CHIEX								
Peter	63	m	w	FRAN	Yuba	Slate Range Bar Tw	93	670
CHIK								
Ah	32	m	c	CHIN	San Francisco	San Francisco P O	80	487
Ah	15	m	c	CHIN	San Francisco	6-Wd San Francisco	81	66
Ch	37	m	c	CHIN	Yolo	Washington Twp	93	537
CHILCOAT								
William P	46	m	w	AL	Los Angeles	El Monte Twp	73	461
CHILCOTE								
William	50	m	w	NY	Santa Clara	Redwood Twp	88	133
CHILD								
C C	8	m	w	CA	Amador	Lancha Plana P O	69	368
E F	40	m	w	RI	San Francisco	San Francisco P O	83	301
Edward	36	m	w	MA	Sacramento	4-Wd Sacramento	77	365
Ezra	45	m	w	RI	San Francisco	2-Wd San Francisco	79	189
Mary	16	f	w	CA	El Dorado	Mud Springs Twp	72	84
Stanley F	51	m	w	NY	El Dorado	Coloma Twp	72	8
William	35	m	w	ENGL	El Dorado	Mud Springs Twp	72	73
CHILDER								
Thos	23	m	w	MO	San Joaquin	Douglas Twp	86	41
CHILDERS								
Abhm A	36	m	w	TN	Fresno	Millerton P O	72	181
Arnold	49	m	w	VA	Sonoma	Santa Rosa	91	417
Fannie	30	f	w	NY	Sacramento	2-Wd Sacramento	77	227
Henry	40	m	w	NC	Tulare	Farmersville Twp	92	248
Heny	63	m	w	VA	Butte	Ophir Twp	70	100
James H	17	m	w	MO	Trinity	Hayfork Valley	92	238
John L	34	m	w	TN	Colusa	Butte Twp	71	270
Joseph	37	m	w	VA	Sonoma	Santa Rosa	91	414
M Fr	53	m	w	VA	Amador	Ione City P O	69	357
Mary	31	f	w	AR	Tulare	Visalia Twp	92	288
Mary	21	f	w	MO	San Joaquin	2-Wd Stockton	86	158
Oliver	38	m	w	IN	Fresno	Kingston P O	72	218
Richard	34	m	w	MO	Colusa	Butte Twp	71	270
Spencer	47	m	w	VA	Monterey	Salinas Twp	74	311
CHILDES								
Isaac	41	m	w	KY	Yolo	Putah Twp	93	519
CHILDREN								
John H	35	m	w	NC	Yuba	Slate Range Bar Tw	93	676
CHILDRESS								
M W	50	f	w	MS	Alameda	Oakland	68	227
Wm I	40	m	w	TN	Nevada	Little York Twp	75	244
CHILDS								
Benjamin	45	m	w	MA	Solano	Suisun Twp	90	97
C	12	f	w	CA	Alameda	Oakland	68	237
C D	49	m	w	NY	Sacramento	Franklin Twp	77	105
Catherine	24	f	w	MA	San Francisco	San Francisco P O	83	258
Charles	35	m	w	ENGL	San Francisco	7-Wd San Francisco	81	207
Charles	25	m	w	PRUS	Marin	Sausalito Twp	74	67
David	27	m	w	OH	Solano	Vacaville Twp	90	124
E	14	f	w	CA	Alameda	Oakland	68	237
Elijah	45	m	w	PA	El Dorado	Mountain Twp	72	67
Ellen	45	f	w	IREL	San Francisco	San Francisco P O	85	775
Enma	14	f	w	CA	Napa	Napa	75	26
F H	34	m	w	ME	San Francisco	San Francisco P O	85	820
Francis	42	m	w	PRUS	Sacramento	Natomas Twp	77	170
Frank	21	m	w	WI	El Dorado	Placerville Twp	72	102
Geo E	39	m	w	MA	Santa Barbara	Santa Barbara P O	87	454
George	53	m	w	NY	Sutter	Butte Twp	92	103
George	43	m	w	MA	Tuolumne	Chinese Camp P O	93	381
George	40	m	w	MA	San Francisco	11-Wd San Francisc	84	637
George	28	m	w	MA	San Francisco	San Francisco P O	83	258
George	16	m	w	CA	Stanislaus	Branch Twp	92	6
George W	29	m	w	VA	Inyo	Lone Pine Twp	73	331
H L	23	m	w	IL	Alameda	Oakland	68	252
H W	48	m	w	NY	San Joaquin	Liberty Twp	86	85
Harry	34	m	w	ENGL	Fresno	Kings Rvr P O	72	213
J W	65	m	w	ME	Del Norte	Mountain Twp	71	474
J W	40	m	w	MA	Alameda	Oakland	68	168
James	44	m	w	ENGL	San Francisco	San Francisco P O	85	876
James M	39	m	w	MA	San Francisco	San Francisco P O	85	715
James W	42	m	w	KY	Yolo	Cache Crk Twp	93	443
John	35	m	w	VA	Santa Barbara	San Buenaventura P	87	421
John	34	m	w	MO	Sacramento	Cosumnes Twp	77	95
John E	40	m	w	MD	San Luis Obispo	San Luis Obispo Tw	87	303
John O	29	m	w	NH	Santa Cruz	Watsonville	89	371
Kate	23	f	w	MA	San Francisco	11-Wd San Francisc	84	437
Marcas W	39	m	w	VT	Los Angeles	Los Angeles	73	537
Matilda P	28	f	w	MD	Sacramento	2-Wd Sacramento	77	243
O	41	m	w	MO	San Joaquin	Elliott Twp	86	75
Oero W	43	m	w	VT	Los Angeles	Los Angeles	73	503
Tannie	17	f	w	CA	Alameda	Oakland	68	236
Thomas	35	m	w	WALE	Napa	Napa	75	24
William W	52	m	w	NY	El Dorado	Placerville Twp	72	102
Wm	65	m	w	MD	Monterey	Castroville Twp	74	330
Wm	40	m	w	ME	Klamath	Trinidad Twp	73	390
CHILES								
Joseph B	60	m	w	KY	Napa	Napa	75	26
Sarah E	16	f	w	CA	Napa	Napa	75	3
CHILEY								
Adam	28	m	w	PRUS	San Francisco	1-Wd San Francisco	79	113
CHILINO								
Joseph	2	m	w	CA	Santa Clara	Gilroy Twp	88	77
Julius	26	m	w	NY	Santa Clara	Gilroy Twp	88	77
CHILL								
Ah	31	m	c	CHIN	Tuolumne	Big Oak Flat P O	93	397
John	27	m	w	IREL	San Francisco	San Francisco P O	83	387

Name	Age	S	R	B-PL	County	Locale	Roll	Pg
Theresa	21	f	w	IREL	San Francisco	8-Wd San Francisco	82	353
CHILLENDEN								
H H	37	m	w	CT	Sierra	Table Rock Twp	89	573
CHILLES								
Charles	41	m	w	ME	Stanislaus	Empire Twp	92	47
CHILLI								
Joseph	34	m	w	ITAL	Calaveras	Copperopolis P O	70	251
CHILLIS								
M	51	m	w	VA	Amador	Ione City P O	69	354
CHILLON								
A	30	m	w	ENGL	Alameda	Oakland	68	240
CHILOVICH								
Chas	66	m	w	AUST	Butte	Ophir Twp	70	98
CHILQUET								
Jules	30	m	w	FRAN	Santa Clara	2-Wd San Jose	88	311
CHILSON								
Emer	28	m	w	IL	San Bernardino	San Salvador Twp	78	459
Mary	46	f	w	OH	San Bernardino	San Salvador Twp	78	459
Samuel	42	m	w	IN	San Bernardino	San Salvador Twp	78	458
Stephen	45	m	w	IN	San Bernardino	San Salvador Twp	78	458
Wm D	45	m	w	NY	Santa Barbara	San Buenaventura P	87	434
CHILTON								
Anselur L	48	m	w	VA	El Dorado	Mud Springs Twp	72	75
CHIM								
Ah	49	m	c	CHIN	Mono	Bridgeport P O	74	283
Ah	45	m	c	CHIN	Sierra	Table Rock Twp	89	544
Ah	44	m	c	CHIN	Alameda	Eden Twp	68	61
Ah	42	m	c	CHIN	Placer	Auburn P O	76	373
Ah	40	m	c	CHIN	Amador	Ione City P O	69	354
Ah	40	m	c	CHIN	Placer	Clipper Gap P O	76	393
Ah	33	m	c	CHIN	Nevada	Eureka Twp	75	126
Ah	30	m	c	CHIN	Calaveras	Copperopolis P O	70	238
Ah	30	m	c	CHIN	Nevada	Nevada Twp	75	307
Ah	30	m	c	CHIN	Santa Clara	San Jose Twp	88	222
Ah	28	m	c	CHIN	Placer	Auburn P O	76	373
Ah	26	m	c	CHIN	Sierra	Table Rock Twp	89	571
Ah	25	m	c	CHIN	Alameda	Eden Twp	68	61
Ah	24	m	c	CHIN	Alameda	Hayward	68	77
Ah	22	m	c	CHIN	Alameda	Eden Twp	68	62
Ah	20	m	c	CHIN	San Francisco	2-Wd San Francisco	79	277
Ah	19	f	c	CHIN	Santa Clara	1-Wd San Jose	88	254
Ah	17	m	c	CHIN	Alameda	Washington Twp	68	269
Ah	15	m	c	CHIN	San Francisco	2-Wd San Francisco	79	237
Ah	13	m	c	CHIN	San Francisco	8-Wd San Francisco	82	322
Ah	13	m	c	CHIN	Shasta	French Gulch P O	89	469
Ah	13	m	c	CHIN	San Francisco	2-Wd San Francisco	79	258
John	71	m	c	CHIN	Trinity	Weaverville Pct	92	228
Ye	35	m	c	CHIN	Alameda	Washington Twp	68	274
CHIMA								
John	15	m	c	CHIN	Sonoma	Sonoma Twp	91	448
CHIMB								
T	19	m	w	PA	Alameda	Oakland	68	229
CHIMM								
Ah	22	m	c	CHIN	San Francisco	6-Wd San Francisco	81	46
CHIN								
A	25	m	c	CHIN	Calaveras	Copperopolis P O	70	237
Ah	9	m	c	CHIN	San Francisco	San Francisco P O	80	438
Ah	7	f	c	CA	San Francisco	San Francisco P O	80	448
Ah	61	m	c	CHIN	Mariposa	Mariposa P O	74	132
Ah	60	m	c	CHIN	El Dorado	Mud Springs Twp	72	87
Ah	6	m	c	CHIN	San Francisco	6-Wd San Francisco	81	65
Ah	57	m	c	CHIN	Shasta	French Gulch P O	89	470
Ah	55	m	c	CHIN	Calaveras	Copperopolis P O	70	247
Ah	52	m	c	CHIN	Santa Clara	Alviso Twp	88	25
Ah	51	m	c	CHIN	Nevada	Bridgeport Twp	75	119
Ah	51	m	c	CHIN	Mariposa	Mariposa P O	74	103
Ah	50	m	c	CHIN	Trinity	Indian Crk	92	200
Ah	50	m	c	CHIN	Mariposa	Maxwell Crk P O	74	142
Ah	50	f	c	CHIN	San Francisco	San Francisco P O	80	434
Ah	50	m	c	CHIN	Trinity	Douglas	92	233
Ah	50	m	c	CHIN	Tuolumne	Chinese Camp P O	93	364
Ah	48	m	c	CHIN	Amador	Fiddletown P O	69	427
Ah	48	m	c	CHIN	San Francisco	6-Wd San Francisco	81	56
Ah	47	m	c	CHIN	Mono	Bridgeport P O	74	282
Ah	46	m	c	CHIN	Placer	Auburn P O	76	362
Ah	45	m	c	CHIN	Alameda	Eden Twp	68	62
Ah	45	m	c	CHIN	Mariposa	Mariposa P O	74	114
Ah	45	m	c	CHIN	Sacramento	Franklin Twp	77	114
Ah	45	m	c	CHIN	Tuolumne	Sonora P O	93	332
Ah	44	m	c	CHIN	Calaveras	San Andreas P O	70	187
Ah	44	m	c	CHIN	Mariposa	Mariposa P O	74	131
Ah	44	m	c	CHIN	Shasta	Horsetown P O	89	507
Ah	43	m	c	CHIN	Amador	Fiddletown P O	69	440
Ah	43	m	c	CHIN	Butte	Chico Twp	70	52
Ah	42	m	c	CHIN	Placer	Newcastle Twp	76	479
Ah	42	m	c	CHIN	Placer	Auburn P O	76	362
Ah	42	m	c	CHIN	Tuolumne	Sonora P O	93	312
Ah	41	m	c	CHIN	El Dorado	Salmon Falls Twp	72	130
Ah	41	m	c	CHIN	Calaveras	San Andreas P O	70	172
Ah	41	m	c	CHIN	Amador	Fiddletown P O	69	438
Ah	41	m	c	CHIN	Placer	Bath P O	76	439
Ah	40	m	c	CHIN	Butte	Ophir Twp	70	106
Ah	40	m	c	CHIN	San Francisco	San Francisco P O	80	524
Ah	40	m	c	CHIN	San Francisco	San Francisco P O	80	522
Ah	40	m	c	CHIN	San Francisco	11-Wd San Francisc	84	522
Ah	40	m	c	CHIN	Santa Clara	Alviso Twp	88	27
Ah	40	m	c	CHIN	Santa Clara	Gilroy Twp	88	93

© 2001 by Heritage Quest. All rights reserved.

California 1870 Census

Name	Age	S	R	B-PL	County	Locale	Series M593 Roll	Pg
Ah	40	m	c	CHIN	Marin	San Rafael Twp	74	59
Ah	40	m	c	CHIN	El Dorado	Placerville	72	114
Ah	40	m	c	CHIN	Calaveras	San Andreas P O	70	181
Ah	40	m	c	CHIN	Placer	Newcastle Twp	76	475
Ah	40	m	c	CHIN	San Francisco	San Francisco P O	80	446
Ah	40	f	c	CHIN	San Francisco	San Francisco P O	80	448
Ah	40	m	c	CHIN	Stanislaus	Emory Twp	92	23
Ah	39	m	c	CHIN	Nevada	Nevada Twp	75	313
Ah	38	m	c	CHIN	Trinity	Lewiston Pct	92	212
Ah	38	m	c	CHIN	San Francisco	San Francisco P O	80	447
Ah	38	m	c	CHIN	Tuolumne	Big Oak Flat P O	93	395
Ah	37	m	c	CHIN	San Francisco	San Francisco P O	80	511
Ah	37	m	c	CHIN	Butte	Hamilton Twp	70	73
Ah	37	m	c	CHIN	Butte	Chico Twp	70	28
Ah	37	m	c	CHIN	Sacramento	Franklin Twp	77	108
Ah	37	m	c	CHIN	San Francisco	San Francisco P O	80	446
Ah	37	m	c	CHIN	Tuolumne	Sonora P O	93	322
Ah	37	f	c	CHIN	San Francisco	6-Wd San Francisco	81	61
Ah	36	m	c	CHIN	Placer	Lincoln P O	76	484
Ah	36	f	c	CHIN	San Francisco	San Francisco P O	80	527
Ah	36	m	c	CHIN	San Francisco	San Francisco P O	80	511
Ah	36	m	c	CHIN	San Francisco	San Francisco P O	80	505
Ah	36	m	c	CHIN	San Francisco	San Francisco P O	80	511
Ah	36	m	c	CHIN	Mariposa	Mariposa P O	74	102
Ah	36	m	c	CHIN	Tuolumne	Big Oak Flat P O	93	403
Ah	36	m	c	CHIN	San Francisco	6-Wd San Francisco	81	61
Ah	36	m	c	CHIN	San Francisco	11-Wd San Francisc	84	477
Ah	35	m	c	CHIN	Nevada	Nevada Twp	75	307
Ah	34	m	c	CHIN	Amador	Jackson P O	69	343
Ah	34	m	c	CHIN	Nevada	Rough & Ready Twp	75	329
Ah	34	m	c	CHIN	San Francisco	San Francisco P O	80	493
Ah	34	m	c	CHIN	San Francisco	San Francisco P O	80	514
Ah	34	m	c	CHIN	San Francisco	San Francisco P O	80	515
Ah	34	m	c	CHIN	San Francisco	San Francisco P O	80	517
Ah	34	m	c	CHIN	San Francisco	San Francisco P O	80	524
Ah	34	m	c	CHIN	San Francisco	San Francisco P O	80	511
Ah	34	m	c	CHIN	San Francisco	San Francisco P O	80	512
Ah	34	m	c	CHIN	San Francisco	San Francisco P O	80	530
Ah	34	f	c	CHIN	San Francisco	San Francisco P O	80	525
Ah	34	m	c	CHIN	Trinity	North Fork Twp	92	221
Ah	34	m	c	CHIN	Placer	Auburn P O	76	377
Ah	34	m	c	CHIN	San Francisco	San Francisco P O	80	443
Ah	33	m	c	CHIN	Placer	Bath P O	76	444
Ah	33	m	c	CHIN	Placer	Dutch Flat P O	76	407
Ah	33	m	c	CHIN	San Francisco	San Francisco P O	80	514
Ah	33	m	c	CHIN	Mariposa	Mariposa P O	74	131
Ah	32	m	c	CHIN	Calaveras	Copperopolis P O	70	242
Ah	32	m	c	CHIN	Sacramento	Franklin Twp	77	108
Ah	32	m	c	CHIN	Santa Clara	Alviso Twp	88	24
Ah	32	m	c	CHIN	Mariposa	Mariposa P O	74	126
Ah	32	m	c	CHIN	San Francisco	San Francisco P O	80	435
Ah	32	f	c	CHIN	San Francisco	San Francisco P O	80	445
Ah	31	m	c	CHIN	Nevada	Grass Valley Twp	75	204
Ah	31	m	c	CHIN	San Francisco	San Francisco P O	80	490
Ah	31	m	c	CHIN	San Francisco	San Francisco P O	80	530
Ah	31	f	c	CHIN	San Francisco	San Francisco P O	80	432
Ah	31	f	c	CHIN	San Francisco	San Francisco P O	80	434
Ah	30	m	c	CHIN	Nevada	Grass Valley Twp	75	204
Ah	30	m	c	CHIN	Placer	Lincoln P O	76	484
Ah	30	m	c	CHIN	Sacramento	Franklin Twp	77	113
Ah	30	m	c	CHIN	Placer	Auburn P O	76	375
Ah	30	m	c	CHIN	San Francisco	San Francisco P O	80	530
Ah	30	m	c	CHIN	Santa Clara	Gilroy Twp	88	88
Ah	30	m	c	CHIN	Amador	Fiddletown P O	69	438
Ah	30	m	c	CHIN	Shasta	French Gulch P O	89	466
Ah	30	m	c	CHIN	Siskiyou	Hamburg Twp	89	598
Ah	30	m	c	CHIN	Tuolumne	Big Oak Flat P O	93	393
Ah	30	m	c	CHIN	San Francisco	6-Wd San Francisco	81	83
Ah	30	m	c	CHIN	San Francisco	San Francisco P O	80	489
Ah	3	m	c	CHIN	Butte	Ophir Twp	70	104
Ah	29	m	c	CHIN	Nevada	Bridgeport Twp	75	110
Ah	29	m	c	CHIN	San Francisco	San Francisco P O	80	453
Ah	29	f	c	CHIN	San Francisco	San Francisco P O	80	503
Ah	29	m	c	CHIN	San Francisco	San Francisco P O	80	527
Ah	29	m	c	CHIN	Butte	Ophir Twp	70	119
Ah	29	m	c	CHIN	San Francisco	San Francisco P O	80	435
Ah	29	m	c	CHIN	Stanislaus	Empire Twp	92	41
Ah	28	m	c	CHIN	Alameda	Eden Twp	68	59
Ah	28	m	c	CHIN	Nevada	Meadow Lake Twp	75	256
Ah	28	m	c	CHIN	San Francisco	San Francisco P O	80	513
Ah	28	m	c	CHIN	Trinity	North Fork Twp	92	216
Ah	28	m	c	CHIN	Placer	Rocklin Twp	76	468
Ah	28	m	c	CHIN	Placer	Colfax P O	76	386
Ah	28	m	c	CHIN	San Francisco	San Francisco P O	80	453
Ah	28	m	c	CHIN	Yolo	Grafton Twp	93	479
Ah	28	m	c	CHIN	San Francisco	San Francisco P O	80	494
Ah	28	m	c	CHIN	San Joaquin	Oneal Twp	86	116
Ah	27	m	c	CHIN	Santa Clara	1-Wd San Jose	88	269
Ah	27	m	c	CHIN	Contra Costa	Martinez P O	71	441
Ah	27	m	c	CHIN	Butte	Chico Twp	70	27
Ah	27	m	c	CHIN	Santa Clara	San Jose Twp	88	204
Ah	26	m	c	CHIN	El Dorado	Placerville	72	122
Ah	26	m	c	CHIN	Monterey	Monterey Twp	74	350
Ah	26	m	c	CHIN	Siskiyou	Yreka Twp	89	673
Ah	26	f	c	CHIN	San Francisco	San Francisco P O	80	438
Ah	25	m	c	CHIN	Calaveras	Copperopolis P O	70	233
Ah	25	m	c	CHIN	San Francisco	6-Wd San Francisco	81	42
Ah	25	m	c	CHIN	San Francisco	6-Wd San Francisco	81	148
Ah	25	m	c	CHIN	Santa Clara	Fremont Twp	88	41
Ah	25	m	c	CHIN	Contra Costa	Martinez P O	71	370
Ah	25	f	c	CHIN	San Francisco	San Francisco P O	80	437
Ah	25	f	c	CHIN	San Francisco	San Francisco P O	80	450
Ah	25	f	c	CHIN	San Francisco	San Francisco P O	80	451
Ah	24	m	c	CHIN	San Francisco	San Francisco P O	80	516
Ah	24	m	c	CHIN	Santa Clara	Gilroy Twp	88	75
Ah	24	m	c	CHIN	El Dorado	Mud Springs Twp	72	89
Ah	24	m	c	CHIN	Butte	Hamilton Twp	70	72
Ah	24	m	c	CHIN	Placer	Auburn P O	76	363
Ah	24	m	c	CHIN	Shasta	French Gulch P O	89	466
Ah	24	m	c	CHIN	Shasta	French Gulch P O	89	467
Ah	24	m	c	CHIN	Solano	Suisun Twp	90	106
Ah	24	m	c	CHIN	Tuolumne	Chinese Camp P O	93	381
Ah	24	m	c	CHIN	San Francisco	6-Wd San Francisco	81	68
Ah	24	m	c	CHIN	San Francisco	6-Wd San Francisco	81	42
Ah	23	m	c	CHIN	San Francisco	San Francisco P O	80	514
Ah	23	m	c	CHIN	San Francisco	San Francisco P O	80	513
Ah	23	m	c	CHIN	San Francisco	San Francisco P O	83	132
Ah	23	m	c	CHIN	Nevada	Nevada Twp	75	282
Ah	22	m	c	CHIN	Calaveras	San Andreas P O	70	199
Ah	22	m	c	CHIN	Placer	Lincoln P O	76	492
Ah	22	m	c	CHIN	San Francisco	6-Wd San Francisco	81	62
Ah	22	f	c	CHIN	San Francisco	San Francisco P O	80	434
Ah	22	m	c	CHIN	Santa Clara	San Jose Twp	88	203
Ah	22	m	c	CHIN	Tuolumne	Chinese Camp P O	93	379
Ah	21	m	c	CHIN	Colusa	Grand Island Twp	71	305
Ah	21	m	c	CHIN	San Francisco	San Francisco P O	80	466
Ah	21	m	c	CHIN	San Francisco	San Francisco P O	80	530
Ah	20	m	c	CHIN	Alameda	Eden Twp	68	64
Ah	20	m	c	CHIN	Contra Costa	Martinez P O	71	413
Ah	20	m	c	CHIN	Nevada	Grass Valley Twp	75	207
Ah	20	m	c	CHIN	San Francisco	7-Wd San Francisco	81	281
Ah	20	f	c	CHIN	San Francisco	San Francisco P O	80	526
Ah	20	m	c	CHIN	San Francisco	11-Wd San Francisc	84	521
Ah	20	m	c	CHIN	Trinity	Lewiston Pct	92	215
Ah	20	m	c	CHIN	Trinity	Minersville Pct	92	203
Ah	20	m	c	CHIN	Alameda	Alameda	68	1
Ah	20	m	c	CHIN	San Francisco	1-Wd San Francisco	79	22
Ah	20	f	c	CHIN	San Francisco	San Francisco P O	80	433
Ah	20	m	c	CHIN	Siskiyou	Hamburg Twp	89	598
Ah	20	m	c	CHIN	San Mateo	San Mateo P O	87	356
Ah	19	m	c	CHIN	Placer	Auburn P O	76	362
Ah	19	m	c	CHIN	Nevada	Grass Valley Twp	75	184
Ah	19	f	c	CHIN	San Francisco	San Francisco P O	80	505
Ah	19	m	c	CHIN	Placer	Auburn P O	76	378
Ah	19	m	c	CHIN	San Francisco	San Francisco P O	80	443
Ah	19	m	c	CHIN	Tuolumne	Chinese Camp P O	93	388
Ah	19	m	c	CHIN	San Francisco	San Francisco P O	80	503
Ah	18	m	c	CHIN	San Francisco	San Francisco P O	80	506
Ah	18	m	c	CHIN	Trinity	Junction City Pct	92	206
Ah	18	f	h	CHIN	Placer	Alta P O	76	419
Ah	18	m	c	CHIN	San Francisco	3-Wd San Francisco	79	310
Ah	18	m	c	CHIN	San Francisco	San Francisco P O	80	387
Ah	18	m	c	CHIN	San Francisco	6-Wd San Francisco	81	46
Ah	18	m	c	CHIN	San Francisco	6-Wd San Francisco	81	40
Ah	17	m	c	CHIN	Placer	Lincoln P O	76	484
Ah	17	f	c	CHIN	Calaveras	San Andreas P O	70	167
Ah	17	m	c	CHIN	Tuolumne	Chinese Camp P O	93	384
Ah	17	m	c	CHIN	San Francisco	8-Wd San Francisco	82	336
Ah	16	m	c	CHIN	Santa Clara	Gilroy Twp	88	72
Ah	16	m	c	CHIN	Marin	San Rafael	74	51
Ah	16	m	c	CHIN	San Francisco	6-Wd San Francisco	81	50
Ah	15	m	c	CHIN	Placer	Auburn P O	76	379
Ah	15	m	c	CHIN	San Francisco	3-Wd San Francisco	79	329
Ah	12	f	c	CHIN	San Francisco	San Francisco P O	80	441
Ah	11	m	c	CA	San Francisco	San Francisco P O	80	452
Ah	10	f	c	CHIN	San Francisco	San Francisco P O	80	525
Au Quon	31	m	c	CHIN	Amador	Ione City P O	69	366
Chas	22	m	c	CHIN	San Francisco	San Francisco P O	85	864
Che	12	m	c	CHIN	San Francisco	11-Wd San Francisc	84	587
Cho	32	m	c	CHIN	Solano	Green Valley Twp	90	43
Chong	22	m	c	CHIN	San Francisco	San Francisco P O	83	400
Chong	19	m	c	CHIN	Merced	Snelling P O	74	249
Chun	22	f	c	CHIN	El Dorado	Coloma Twp	72	5
Chung	41	m	c	CHIN	Calaveras	San Andreas P O	70	167
Con	31	m	c	CHIN	Trinity	Weaverville Pct	92	232
Coon	20	m	c	CHIN	Shasta	French Gulch P O	89	467
Cow	42	m	c	CHIN	El Dorado	Greenwood Twp	72	54
Cow	35	m	c	CHIN	Butte	Concow Twp	70	12
Cow	23	m	c	CHIN	Butte	Chico Twp	70	51
Cow	20	m	c	CHIN	San Francisco	6-Wd San Francisco	81	43
Cum	27	m	c	CHIN	Mariposa	Maxwell Crk P O	74	142
Fan	18	m	c	CHIN	Butte	Ophir Twp	70	121
Fin	20	m	c	CHIN	Solano	Vacaville Twp	90	132
Fon	54	m	c	CHIN	Trinity	Weaverville Pct	92	228
Foo	38	m	c	CHIN	Butte	Chico Twp	70	53
Foo	36	m	c	CHIN	Butte	Chico Twp	70	60
Foo	34	m	c	CHIN	Solano	Vacaville Twp	90	131
Foon	52	m	c	CHIN	Placer	Auburn P O	76	371
Foong Hee	20	m	c	CHIN	San Francisco	11-Wd San Francisc	84	546
Fop	31	m	c	CHIN	Yuba	North East Twp	93	646
Fu	19	m	c	CHIN	San Francisco	San Francisco P O	83	72
Gah	38	m	c	CHIN	Butte	Oroville Twp	70	140
Gah	28	m	c	CHIN	Butte	Bidwell Twp	70	5
Gee	6	m	c	CHIN	Butte	Hamilton Twp	70	72

© 2001 by Heritage Quest. All rights reserved.

Series M593

Name	Age	S	R	B-PL	County	Locale	Roll	Pg
Gee	58	m	c	CHIN	Butte	Chico Twp	70	53
Gee	26	m	c	CHIN	Yuba	Marysville	93	622
Gee	25	m	c	CHIN	Trinity	North Fork Twp	92	220
Gong	37	m	c	CHIN	Nevada	Rough & Ready Twp	75	328
Gow	37	m	c	CHIN	Trinity	North Fork Twp	92	220
Gui	24	m	c	CHIN	Calaveras	San Andreas P O	70	169
Henry	41	m	w	BADE	San Francisco	San Francisco P O	80	540
Hong	18	m	c	CHIN	San Luis Obispo	San Luis Obispo Tw	87	310
Jah	35	m	c	CHIN	Calaveras	San Andreas P O	70	155
Kan	13	m	c	CHIN	San Francisco	San Francisco P O	83	124
Kee	40	f	c	CHIN	Santa Clara	1-Wd San Jose	88	273
Kee	30	m	c	CHIN	San Francisco	5-Wd San Francisco	81	16
Kong	27	m	c	CHIN	Klamath	Sawyers Bar	73	378
Lee	27	m	c	CHIN	Calaveras	San Andreas P O	70	204
Lee	21	m	c	CHIN	Solano	Green Valley Twp	90	42
Leong	18	m	c	CHIN	San Francisco	2-Wd San Francisco	79	282
Leoon	25	m	c	CHIN	San Francisco	11-Wd San Francisc	84	556
Lew	29	m	c	CHIN	Placer	Bath P O	76	431
Li	46	m	c	CHIN	Placer	Bath P O	76	439
Lin	57	m	c	CHIN	Calaveras	San Andreas P O	70	202
Lin Gang	20	m	c	CHIN	Calaveras	San Andreas P O	70	155
Long	40	m	c	CHIN	Trinity	Weaverville Pct	92	228
Luck	36	m	c	CHIN	Yuba	Marysville	93	623
Lun	19	m	c	CHIN	San Francisco	8-Wd San Francisco	82	465
Man Cun	47	m	c	CHIN	Amador	Ione City P O	69	366
Man Two	46	m	c	CHIN	Amador	Ione City P O	69	367
Me	51	m	c	CHIN	Mariposa	Mariposa P O	74	103
Mee	46	m	c	CHIN	San Francisco	11-Wd San Francisc	84	695
Mo	27	m	c	CHIN	Butte	Chico Twp	70	31
Mon	62	m	c	CHIN	Butte	Hamilton Twp	70	68
Mow	35	m	c	CHIN	Solano	Vallejo	90	208
Mung	35	m	c	CHIN	San Francisco	2-Wd San Francisco	79	285
Ni Saw	23	m	c	CHIN	Amador	Ione City P O	69	367
Ock	43	m	c	CHIN	Shasta	Shasta P O	89	455
Pa	35	m	c	CHIN	Butte	Oroville Twp	70	139
Quen	45	m	c	CHIN	Nevada	Rough & Ready Twp	75	327
Qui	31	m	c	CHIN	Mariposa	Maxwell Crk P O	74	145
Sam	35	m	c	CHIN	El Dorado	Cosumnes Twp	72	15
Sam On	22	m	c	CHIN	Amador	Ione City P O	69	367
Saml	40	m	c	CHIN	San Francisco	1-Wd San Francisco	79	120
Seng	28	m	c	CHIN	San Francisco	11-Wd San Francisc	84	556
Share	40	m	c	CHIN	San Francisco	3-Wd San Francisco	79	328
Sin	29	f	c	CHIN	Nevada	Nevada Twp	75	299
Sing	20	m	c	CHIN	San Francisco	6-Wd San Francisco	81	41
Sing	12	m	c	CA	San Francisco	6-Wd San Francisco	81	44
Sling	50	m	c	CHIN	Shasta	Shasta P O	89	455
So	30	m	c	CHIN	Sacramento	1-Wd Sacramento	77	204
Song	37	m	c	CHIN	Klamath	Dillon Twp	73	369
Soon	30	m	c	CHIN	Shasta	French Gulch P O	89	470
Tom	28	m	c	CHIN	Solano	Suisun Twp	90	107
Ton	25	m	c	CHIN	Yuba	Marysville	93	625
Tow	29	m	c	CHIN	Yuba	Marysville	93	625
Wa Fung	52	m	c	CHIN	San Francisco	3-Wd San Francisco	79	328
Wah	43	m	c	CHIN	Placer	Pino Twp	76	471
Wak	37	m	c	CHIN	Butte	Hamilton Twp	70	67
Wan	35	m	c	CHIN	Sonoma	Salt Point	91	386
Wing	5	m	c	CA	San Francisco	6-Wd San Francisco	81	44
Wing	34	m	c	CHIN	Butte	Chico Twp	70	54
Wm	37	m	c	CHIN	San Joaquin	1-Wd Stockton	86	142
Wo	29	m	c	CHIN	Butte	Hamilton Twp	70	74
Yan	24	m	c	CHIN	Marin	Novato Twp	74	12
Yee	19	m	c	CHIN	Butte	Wyandotte Twp	70	147
Yon	16	m	c	CHIN	San Luis Obispo	Arroyo Grande Twp	87	278
You	30	m	c	CHIN	Yuba	Rose Bar Twp	93	655
You	30	f	c	CHIN	Placer	Rocklin Twp	76	464
You	27	m	c	CHIN	Yuba	East Bear Rvr Twp	93	546
Yow	30	m	c	CHIN	El Dorado	Coloma Twp	72	6
Yow	20	f	c	CHIN	San Francisco	6-Wd San Francisco	81	55
Zoca	40	f	c	CHIN	Tulare	Visalia	92	299
CHINA								
Maria	11	f	i	----	Marin	Novato Twp	74	89
CHINCE								
Ah	24	m	c	CHIN	Placer	Bath P O	76	442
Ah	17	m	c	CHIN	Nevada	Eureka Twp	75	140
CHINCOVICH								
Peter	43	m	w	AUST	San Francisco	1-Wd San Francisco	79	129
CHINE								
---	25	m	c	CHIN	Siskiyou	Hamburg Twp	89	596
Ah	40	m	c	CHIN	Sacramento	Georgianna Twp	77	129
Ah	40	m	c	CHIN	Sacramento	3-Wd Sacramento	77	316
Ah	38	f	c	CHIN	Calaveras	San Andreas P O	70	199
Ah	30	m	c	CHIN	San Mateo	San Mateo P O	87	350
Ah	30	m	c	CHIN	San Francisco	San Francisco P O	83	86
Ah	22	m	c	CHIN	Solano	Vallejo	90	208
Ah	22	m	c	CHIN	Sacramento	3-Wd Sacramento	77	288
Ah	20	m	c	CHIN	Yolo	Cache Crk Twp	93	449
Ah	19	m	c	CHIN	San Joaquin	Tulare Twp	86	262
Chas	40	m	w	GERM	San Joaquin	2-Wd Stockton	86	170
Low	19	m	c	CHIN	San Francisco	6-Wd San Francisco	81	44
Mary	6	f	w	CA	San Francisco	11-Wd San Francisc	84	710
CHINERY								
Baptiste	34	m	w	FRAN	Yuba	Parks Bar Twp	93	648
CHINEWERTH								
James	25	m	w	IL	Sonoma	Analy Twp	91	246
John	52	m	w	KY	Sonoma	Analy Twp	91	246
Presley	55	m	w	KY	Sonoma	Analy Twp	91	246

Series M593

Name	Age	S	R	B-PL	County	Locale	Roll	Pg
CHINEWORTH								
Miles	39	m	w	IL	Sonoma	Vallejo Twp	91	458
CHINEY								
Cha	29	m	c	CHIN	Solano	Suisun Twp	90	105
Charles	54	m	w	DE	Trinity	Lewiston Pct	92	211
CHING								
---	37	m	w	CHIN	Siskiyou	Yreka Twp	89	667
---	33	m	c	CHIN	San Francisco	6-Wd San Francisco	81	64
---	26	m	c	CHIN	San Francisco	11-Wd San Francisc	84	694
---	25	m	c	CHIN	Shasta	Horsetown P O	89	507
---	21	f	c	CHIN	Amador	Fiddletown P O	69	427
---	21	m	c	CHIN	Siskiyou	Yreka Twp	89	673
---	13	m	c	CHIN	Shasta	Shasta P O	89	454
Ah	61	m	c	CHIN	San Francisco	2-Wd San Francisco	79	286
Ah	61	m	c	CHIN	Trinity	Weaverville Pct	92	231
Ah	60	m	c	CHIN	Placer	Pino Twp	76	470
Ah	56	m	c	CHIN	Placer	Dutch Flat P O	76	410
Ah	56	m	c	CHIN	San Francisco	San Francisco P O	80	522
Ah	52	m	c	CHIN	Amador	Volcano P O	69	383
Ah	52	f	c	CHIN	San Francisco	San Francisco P O	80	529
Ah	50	m	c	CHIN	San Francisco	San Francisco P O	80	432
Ah	50	m	c	CHIN	Mariposa	Mariposa P O	74	107
Ah	50	m	c	CHIN	Calaveras	Copperopolis P O	70	242
Ah	50	m	c	CHIN	Nevada	Bridgeport Twp	75	107
Ah	49	m	c	CHIN	Sacramento	Franklin Twp	77	115
Ah	47	m	c	CHIN	San Francisco	6-Wd San Francisco	81	58
Ah	46	f	c	CHIN	San Francisco	San Francisco P O	80	433
Ah	46	m	c	CHIN	San Francisco	San Francisco P O	80	457
Ah	45	f	c	CHIN	San Francisco	San Francisco P O	80	447
Ah	45	f	c	CHIN	San Francisco	San Francisco P O	80	446
Ah	45	m	c	CHIN	San Francisco	San Francisco P O	80	505
Ah	44	m	c	CHIN	Calaveras	Copperopolis P O	70	226
Ah	44	m	c	CHIN	Plumas	Plumas Twp	77	32
Ah	44	m	c	CHIN	Nevada	Bloomfield Twp	75	96
Ah	43	m	c	CHIN	San Francisco	San Francisco P O	80	508
Ah	42	m	c	CHIN	Tuolumne	Big Oak Flat P O	93	394
Ah	42	m	c	CHIN	San Francisco	San Francisco P O	80	443
Ah	42	m	c	CHIN	San Francisco	San Francisco P O	80	445
Ah	42	f	c	CHIN	San Francisco	San Francisco P O	80	437
Ah	42	f	c	CHIN	San Francisco	San Francisco P O	80	432
Ah	42	m	c	CHIN	San Francisco	San Francisco P O	80	436
Ah	41	m	c	CHIN	San Joaquin	2-Wd Stockton	86	166
Ah	41	m	c	CHIN	Sierra	Gibson Twp	89	540
Ah	41	m	c	CHIN	Nevada	Meadow Lake Twp	75	259
Ah	41	m	c	CHIN	San Francisco	San Francisco P O	80	445
Ah	41	m	c	CHIN	Butte	Hamilton Twp	70	68
Ah	41	m	c	CHIN	Nevada	Bridgeport Twp	75	117
Ah	41	m	c	CHIN	San Francisco	San Francisco P O	80	528
Ah	41	m	c	CHIN	San Francisco	San Francisco P O	80	524
Ah	40	m	c	CHIN	San Joaquin	1-Wd Stockton	86	143
Ah	40	m	c	CHIN	Stanislaus	Emory Twp	92	23
Ah	40	f	c	CHIN	San Francisco	San Francisco P O	80	452
Ah	40	m	c	CHIN	San Francisco	San Francisco P O	80	451
Ah	40	m	c	CHIN	San Francisco	San Francisco P O	80	451
Ah	40	m	c	CHIN	San Francisco	San Francisco P O	80	446
Ah	40	m	c	CHIN	San Francisco	San Francisco P O	80	437
Ah	40	m	c	CHIN	Amador	Fiddletown P O	69	429
Ah	40	m	c	CHIN	San Francisco	San Francisco P O	80	524
Ah	40	m	c	CHIN	Sierra	Eureka Twp	89	526
Ah	40	m	c	CHIN	Trinity	Indian Crk	92	199
Ah	39	m	c	CHIN	San Francisco	6-Wd San Francisco	81	68
Ah	39	m	c	CHIN	Placer	Dutch Flat P O	76	407
Ah	39	m	c	CHIN	Nevada	Rough & Ready Twp	75	327
Ah	39	m	c	CHIN	San Francisco	San Francisco P O	80	518
Ah	38	m	c	CHIN	San Francisco	2-Wd San Francisco	79	286
Ah	38	m	c	CHIN	San Francisco	San Francisco P O	80	450
Ah	38	m	c	CHIN	Mariposa	Mariposa P O	74	133
Ah	38	m	c	CHIN	Mariposa	Mariposa P O	74	115
Ah	38	m	c	CHIN	Amador	Drytown P O	69	424
Ah	38	m	c	CHIN	Butte	Ophir Twp	70	116
Ah	38	m	c	CHIN	Amador	Volcano P O	69	377
Ah	38	m	c	CHIN	San Francisco	San Francisco P O	80	513
Ah	38	m	c	CHIN	San Francisco	San Francisco P O	80	519
Ah	38	m	c	CHIN	San Joaquin	Douglas Twp	86	51
Ah	37	m	w	UNKN	San Joaquin	2-Wd Stockton	86	167
Ah	37	m	c	CHIN	San Joaquin	1-Wd Stockton	86	143
Ah	37	m	c	CHIN	Tuolumne	Columbia P O	93	341
Ah	37	m	c	CHIN	San Francisco	San Francisco P O	80	442
Ah	37	m	c	CHIN	Calaveras	Copperopolis P O	70	241
Ah	37	m	c	CHIN	Nevada	Grass Valley Twp	75	203
Ah	37	m	c	CHIN	San Francisco	San Francisco P O	80	501
Ah	37	m	c	CHIN	San Francisco	San Francisco P O	80	520
Ah	36	m	c	CHIN	San Joaquin	2-Wd Stockton	86	173
Ah	36	m	c	CHIN	San Francisco	San Francisco P O	80	448
Ah	36	f	c	CHIN	San Francisco	San Francisco P O	80	452
Ah	36	f	c	CHIN	San Francisco	San Francisco P O	80	445
Ah	36	m	c	CHIN	San Francisco	San Francisco P O	80	447
Ah	36	f	c	CHIN	San Francisco	San Francisco P O	80	530
Ah	36	m	c	CHIN	San Francisco	San Francisco P O	80	509
Ah	36	m	c	CHIN	San Francisco	San Francisco P O	80	510
Ah	36	m	c	CHIN	San Francisco	San Francisco P O	80	519
Ah	36	m	c	CHIN	San Francisco	San Francisco P O	80	524
Ah	36	m	c	CHIN	San Francisco	San Francisco P O	80	518
Ah	36	m	c	CHIN	Stanislaus	Emory Twp	92	20
Ah	35	m	c	CHIN	San Joaquin	Liberty Twp	86	86
Ah	35	m	c	CHIN	Siskiyou	Cottonwood Twp	89	594
Ah	35	m	c	CHIN	Tulare	White Rvr Twp	92	301

© 2001 by Heritage Quest. All rights reserved.

California 1870 Census

Name	Age	S	R	B-PL	County	Locale	Roll	Pg
						Series M593		
Ah	35	m	c	CHIN	Sacramento	Franklin Twp	77	114
Ah	35	m	c	CHIN	San Francisco	San Francisco P O	80	336
Ah	35	m	c	CHIN	Alameda	Oakland	68	266
Ah	35	m	c	CHIN	El Dorado	Georgetown Twp	72	36
Ah	35	m	c	CHIN	San Francisco	6-Wd San Francisco	81	54
Ah	35	m	c	CHIN	Siskiyou	Yreka Twp	89	667
Ah	35	m	c	CHIN	Trinity	Canyon City Pct	92	202
Ah	34	m	c	CHIN	Sierra	Sears Twp	89	554
Ah	34	m	c	CHIN	San Francisco	San Francisco P O	80	416
Ah	34	m	c	CHIN	Mariposa	Mariposa P O	74	137
Ah	34	m	c	CHIN	Los Angeles	Santa Ana Twp	73	613
Ah	34	m	c	CHIN	Calaveras	Copperopolis P O	70	226
Ah	34	m	c	CHIN	Calaveras	San Andreas P O	70	161
Ah	34	f	c	CHIN	San Francisco	San Francisco P O	80	525
Ah	34	m	c	CHIN	San Francisco	San Francisco P O	80	526
Ah	34	m	c	CHIN	San Francisco	San Francisco P O	80	513
Ah	34	m	c	CHIN	San Francisco	San Francisco P O	80	508
Ah	34	m	c	CHIN	San Francisco	San Francisco P O	80	516
Ah	34	m	c	CHIN	San Francisco	San Francisco P O	80	516
Ah	33	m	c	CHIN	Mariposa	Mariposa P O	74	98
Ah	33	m	c	CHIN	San Francisco	San Francisco P O	80	448
Ah	32	m	c	CHIN	San Francisco	6-Wd San Francisco	81	60
Ah	32	m	c	CHIN	San Francisco	San Francisco P O	80	496
Ah	32	m	c	CHIN	Placer	Bath P O	76	453
Ah	32	m	c	CHIN	Nevada	Rough & Ready Twp	75	328
Ah	32	f	c	CHIN	San Francisco	San Francisco P O	80	438
Ah	32	f	c	CHIN	Butte	Ophir Twp	70	104
Ah	32	m	c	CHIN	Alameda	Oakland	68	172
Ah	32	m	c	CHIN	Plumas	Goodwin Twp	77	3
Ah	31	m	c	CHIN	San Francisco	San Francisco P O	80	496
Ah	31	m	c	CHIN	Plumas	Goodwin Twp	77	3
Ah	31	m	c	CHIN	San Francisco	11-Wd San Francisc	84	528
Ah	31	f	c	CHIN	San Francisco	San Francisco P O	80	527
Ah	31	f	c	CHIN	San Francisco	San Francisco P O	80	504
Ah	30	m	c	CHIN	San Francisco	6-Wd San Francisco	81	66
Ah	30	m	c	CHIN	San Francisco	San Francisco P O	85	748
Ah	30	m	c	CHIN	San Joaquin	Liberty Twp	86	82
Ah	30	m	c	CHIN	Solano	Suisun Twp	90	105
Ah	30	m	c	CHIN	Sonoma	Sonoma Twp	91	445
Ah	30	m	c	CHIN	Sonoma	Petaluma Twp	91	357
Ah	30	m	c	CHIN	Tuolumne	Chinese Camp P O	93	364
Ah	30	m	c	CHIN	Tuolumne	Sonora P O	93	311
Ah	30	m	c	CHIN	Sacramento	Franklin Twp	77	113
Ah	30	m	c	CHIN	Placer	Blue Canyon P O	76	419
Ah	30	m	c	CHIN	Placer	Lincoln P O	76	483
Ah	30	m	c	CHIN	Placer	Auburn P O	76	364
Ah	30	f	c	CHIN	San Francisco	San Francisco P O	80	448
Ah	30	f	c	CHIN	San Francisco	San Francisco P O	80	454
Ah	30	f	c	CHIN	San Francisco	San Francisco P O	80	449
Ah	30	f	c	CHIN	San Francisco	San Francisco P O	80	451
Ah	30	f	c	CHIN	San Francisco	San Francisco P O	80	452
Ah	30	f	c	CHIN	San Francisco	San Francisco P O	80	448
Ah	30	f	c	CHIN	San Francisco	San Francisco P O	80	439
Ah	30	f	c	CHIN	San Francisco	San Francisco P O	80	440
Ah	30	f	c	CHIN	San Francisco	San Francisco P O	80	449
Ah	30	f	c	CHIN	San Francisco	San Francisco P O	80	439
Ah	30	f	c	CHIN	San Francisco	San Francisco P O	80	438
Ah	30	f	c	CHIN	San Francisco	San Francisco P O	80	438
Ah	30	f	c	CHIN	San Francisco	San Francisco P O	80	437
Ah	30	m	c	CHIN	Alameda	Oakland	68	241
Ah	30	m	c	CHIN	El Dorado	Coloma Twp	72	5
Ah	30	m	c	CHIN	Placer	Bath P O	76	445
Ah	30	m	c	CHIN	Sonoma	Sonoma Twp	91	435
Ah	30	m	c	CHIN	Sonoma	Sonoma Twp	91	448
Ah	30	m	c	CHIN	Sonoma	Sonoma Twp	91	436
Ah	30	m	c	CHIN	San Joaquin	Dent Twp	86	23
Ah	29	m	c	CHIN	Placer	Auburn P O	76	370
Ah	29	m	c	CHIN	San Francisco	San Francisco P O	80	441
Ah	29	m	c	CHIN	San Francisco	San Francisco P O	80	450
Ah	29	f	c	CHIN	San Francisco	San Francisco P O	80	432
Ah	29	m	c	CHIN	Calaveras	San Andreas P O	70	199
Ah	29	m	c	CHIN	Amador	Ione City P O	69	364
Ah	29	m	c	CHIN	Nevada	Bridgeport Twp	75	110
Ah	29	m	c	CHIN	San Francisco	San Francisco P O	80	521
Ah	29	m	c	CHIN	San Francisco	San Francisco P O	80	521
Ah	28	m	c	CHIN	San Francisco	6-Wd San Francisco	81	69
Ah	28	m	c	CHIN	San Joaquin	Castoria Twp	86	13
Ah	28	m	c	CHIN	San Mateo	Schoolhouse Statio	87	335
Ah	28	m	c	CHIN	Sierra	Lincoln Twp	89	551
Ah	28	m	c	CHIN	Tuolumne	Chinese Camp P O	93	384
Ah	28	m	c	CHIN	Nevada	Meadow Lake Twp	75	256
Ah	28	m	c	CHIN	Butte	Wyandotte Twp	70	143
Ah	28	m	c	CHIN	Alameda	Alvarado	68	303
Ah	28	m	c	CHIN	Colusa	Colusa	71	300
Ah	28	m	c	CHIN	El Dorado	Placerville	72	115
Ah	28	m	c	CHIN	Sacramento	Georgianna Twp	77	126
Ah	28	m	c	CHIN	Mariposa	Maxwell Crk P O	74	147
Ah	28	m	c	CHIN	San Francisco	San Francisco P O	80	505
Ah	28	m	c	CHIN	San Francisco	San Francisco P O	80	517
Ah	28	m	c	CHIN	San Mateo	San Mateo P O	87	351
Ah	27	m	c	CHIN	San Francisco	6-Wd San Francisco	81	61
Ah	27	m	c	CHIN	San Francisco	3-Wd San Francisco	79	304
Ah	27	m	c	CHIN	San Francisco	San Francisco P O	80	445
Ah	27	m	c	CHIN	Butte	Hamilton Twp	70	67
Ah	27	m	c	CHIN	Alameda	Alameda	68	1
Ah	27	m	c	CHIN	San Francisco	San Francisco P O	80	514
Ah	27	m	c	CHIN	San Joaquin	2-Wd Stockton	86	203

Name	Age	S	R	B-PL	County	Locale	Roll	Pg
						Series M593		
Ah	26	m	c	CHIN	San Francisco	San Francisco P O	80	503
Ah	26	m	c	CHIN	Sierra	Lincoln Twp	89	548
Ah	26	m	c	CHIN	Yolo	Merritt Twp	93	503
Ah	26	f	c	CHIN	San Francisco	San Francisco P O	80	451
Ah	26	m	c	CHIN	San Francisco	San Francisco P O	80	435
Ah	26	f	c	CHIN	San Francisco	San Francisco P O	80	434
Ah	26	m	c	CHIN	San Francisco	San Francisco P O	80	503
Ah	26	m	c	CHIN	San Francisco	San Francisco P O	80	511
Ah	26	m	c	CHIN	San Francisco	San Francisco P O	80	519
Ah	26	m	c	CHIN	San Francisco	San Francisco P O	80	517
Ah	26	m	c	CHIN	San Francisco	San Francisco P O	80	465
Ah	26	m	c	CHIN	Tehama	Tehama Twp	92	189
Ah	25	m	c	CHIN	Sierra	Forest	89	537
Ah	25	m	c	CHIN	Sacramento	4-Wd Sacramento	77	355
Ah	25	m	c	CHIN	Sacramento	Brighton Twp	77	71
Ah	25	f	c	CHIN	San Francisco	San Francisco P O	80	439
Ah	25	m	c	CHIN	Los Angeles	San Gabriel Twp	73	596
Ah	25	m	c	CHIN	Butte	Bidwell Twp	70	4
Ah	25	m	c	CHIN	Colusa	Colusa	71	299
Ah	25	m	c	CHIN	Placer	Newcastle Twp	76	479
Ah	25	m	c	CHIN	San Francisco	San Francisco P O	80	511
Ah	25	m	c	CHIN	San Mateo	Menlo Park P O	87	378
Ah	24	m	c	CHIN	Sonoma	Sonoma Twp	91	449
Ah	24	m	c	CHIN	Yolo	Grafton Twp	93	484
Ah	24	m	c	CHIN	Placer	Clipper Gap P O	76	392
Ah	24	m	c	CHIN	Nevada	Meadow Lake Twp	75	259
Ah	24	m	c	CHIN	San Francisco	2-Wd San Francisco	79	283
Ah	24	f	c	CHIN	San Francisco	San Francisco P O	80	451
Ah	24	f	c	CHIN	San Francisco	San Francisco P O	80	449
Ah	24	f	c	CHIN	San Francisco	San Francisco P O	80	451
Ah	24	f	c	CHIN	San Francisco	San Francisco P O	80	434
Ah	24	m	c	CHIN	Nevada	Grass Valley Twp	75	197
Ah	24	f	c	CHIN	San Francisco	San Francisco P O	80	505
Ah	24	f	c	CHIN	San Francisco	San Francisco P O	80	454
Ah	24	m	c	CHIN	Santa Clara	1-Wd San Jose	88	273
Ah	23	m	c	CHIN	San Francisco	3-Wd San Francisco	79	328
Ah	23	m	c	CHIN	El Dorado	Coloma Twp	72	6
Ah	23	m	c	CHIN	Sierra	Forest	89	537
Ah	22	m	c	CHIN	San Francisco	6-Wd San Francisco	81	63
Ah	22	m	c	CHIN	San Francisco	San Francisco P O	80	498
Ah	22	m	c	CHIN	Yolo	Buckeye Twp	93	411
Ah	22	m	c	CHIN	Sacramento	Sutter Twp	77	391
Ah	22	m	c	CHIN	Placer	Auburn P O	76	364
Ah	22	m	c	CHIN	San Francisco	2-Wd San Francisco	79	210
Ah	22	f	c	CHIN	San Francisco	San Francisco P O	80	445
Ah	22	m	c	CHIN	Alameda	Oakland	68	255
Ah	22	m	c	CHIN	Alameda	Oakland	68	164
Ah	22	m	c	CHIN	Plumas	Goodwin Twp	77	3
Ah	22	f	c	CHIN	San Francisco	San Francisco P O	80	506
Ah	21	m	c	CHIN	San Joaquin	1-Wd Stockton	86	143
Ah	21	m	c	CHIN	San Francisco	3-Wd San Francisco	79	309
Ah	21	f	c	CHIN	San Francisco	San Francisco P O	80	448
Ah	21	f	c	CHIN	San Francisco	San Francisco P O	80	442
Ah	21	f	c	CHIN	San Francisco	San Francisco P O	80	431
Ah	21	f	c	CHIN	San Francisco	San Francisco P O	80	507
Ah	21	f	c	CHIN	San Francisco	San Francisco P O	80	527
Ah	20	m	c	CHIN	San Francisco	6-Wd San Francisco	81	63
Ah	20	m	c	CHIN	San Francisco	6-Wd San Francisco	81	62
Ah	20	m	c	CHIN	Siskiyou	Hamburg Twp	89	597
Ah	20	f	c	CHIN	San Francisco	San Francisco P O	80	444
Ah	20	m	c	CHIN	San Francisco	San Francisco P O	80	436
Ah	20	f	c	CHIN	San Francisco	San Francisco P O	80	440
Ah	20	f	c	CHIN	San Francisco	San Francisco P O	80	437
Ah	20	f	c	CHIN	San Francisco	San Francisco P O	80	435
Ah	20	m	c	CHIN	San Francisco	San Francisco P O	80	336
Ah	20	m	c	CHIN	San Francisco	6-Wd San Francisco	81	54
Ah	20	m	c	CHIN	San Francisco	6-Wd San Francisco	81	85
Ah	20	m	c	CHIN	San Francisco	San Francisco P O	80	502
Ah	20	f	c	CHIN	San Francisco	San Francisco P O	80	523
Ah	20	m	c	CHIN	San Francisco	San Francisco P O	80	523
Ah	20	f	c	CHIN	San Francisco	San Francisco P O	80	526
Ah	20	m	c	CHIN	San Francisco	San Francisco P O	80	516
Ah	2	f	c	CA	San Francisco	San Francisco P O	80	444
Ah	19	m	c	CHIN	San Francisco	San Francisco P O	85	748
Ah	19	f	c	CHIN	San Francisco	San Francisco P O	80	449
Ah	19	f	c	CHIN	San Francisco	San Francisco P O	80	449
Ah	19	m	c	CHIN	Marin	Novato Twp	74	11
Ah	19	m	c	CHIN	El Dorado	Placerville	72	122
Ah	19	m	c	CHIN	San Francisco	2-Wd San Francisco	79	241
Ah	19	f	c	CHIN	San Francisco	San Francisco P O	80	453
Ah	19	m	c	CHIN	Sonoma	Sonoma Twp	91	449
Ah	18	m	c	CHIN	San Francisco	6-Wd San Francisco	81	43
Ah	18	m	c	CHIN	San Francisco	3-Wd San Francisco	79	306
Ah	18	m	c	CHIN	San Francisco	San Francisco P O	80	453
Ah	18	m	c	CHIN	Alameda	Alameda	68	17
Ah	18	m	c	CHIN	Sacramento	3-Wd Sacramento	77	309
Ah	18	m	c	CHIN	San Francisco	San Francisco P O	83	152
Ah	18	m	c	CHIN	San Francisco	San Francisco P O	83	190
Ah	18	f	c	CHIN	San Francisco	San Francisco P O	80	528
Ah	18	m	c	CHIN	San Francisco	San Francisco P O	80	522
Ah	17	m	c	CHIN	San Francisco	2-Wd San Francisco	79	255
Ah	17	m	c	CHIN	Alameda	Eden Twp	68	62
Ah	17	m	c	CHIN	San Francisco	11-Wd San Francisc	84	512
Ah	17	f	c	CHIN	San Francisco	San Francisco P O	80	526
Ah	16	m	c	CHIN	San Francisco	11-Wd San Francisc	84	586
Ah	16	m	c	CHIN	Placer	Clipper Gap P O	76	393
Ah	16	m	c	CHIN	San Francisco	2-Wd San Francisco	79	203

© 2001 by Heritage Quest. All rights reserved.

Name	Age	S	R	B-PL	County	Locale	Series M593 Roll	Pg
Ah	16	m	c	CHIN	San Francisco	San Francisco P O	80	389
Ah	16	f	c	CHIN	San Francisco	San Francisco P O	80	528
Ah	16	m	c	CHIN	Stanislaus	Emory Twp	92	19
Ah	16	m	c	CHIN	Sonoma	Sonoma Twp	91	432
Ah	15	m	c	CHIN	Placer	Bath P O	76	456
Ah	15	m	c	CHIN	San Francisco	San Francisco P O	80	360
Ah	15	m	c	CHIN	Nevada	Bridgeport Twp	75	103
Ah	15	m	c	CHIN	Placer	Auburn P O	76	359
Ah	15	m	c	CHIN	San Francisco	San Francisco P O	83	398
Ah	14	m	c	CHIN	San Francisco	San Francisco P O	85	722
Ah	14	m	c	CHIN	Alameda	Oakland	68	215
Ah	14	m	c	CHIN	San Francisco	7-Wd San Francisco	81	277
Ah	14	m	c	CHIN	Sierra	Table Rock Twp	89	571
Ah	12	m	c	CHIN	San Francisco	San Francisco P O	80	440
Ah	1	f	c	CA	San Francisco	San Francisco P O	80	527
Ah Tie	20	m	c	CHIN	San Joaquin	Elliott Twp	86	71
An	30	m	c	CHIN	Alameda	Washington Twp	68	270
Ang	40	m	c	CHIN	Plumas	Seneca Twp	77	48
Ar	27	m	c	CHIN	Sonoma	Petaluma Twp	91	343
Ar	15	m	c	CHIN	Sonoma	Petaluma Twp	91	357
Beng	55	m	c	CHIN	Nevada	Rough & Ready Twp	75	327
Can	30	m	c	CHIN	San Francisco	San Francisco P O	83	131
Chang	33	m	c	CHIN	San Francisco	San Francisco P O	83	400
Chang	30	m	c	CHIN	San Francisco	2-Wd San Francisco	79	243
Chas	40	m	c	CHIN	Humboldt	Eureka Twp	72	270
Chew	30	m	c	CHIN	Merced	Snelling P O	74	278
Chie	21	m	c	CHIN	San Joaquin	Oneal Twp	86	115
Chon	25	m	c	CHIN	Calaveras	San Andreas P O	70	173
Chong	24	m	c	CHIN	San Francisco	2-Wd San Francisco	79	286
Chong	15	m	c	CHIN	Colusa	Colusa	71	289
Chong Wong	30	m	c	CHIN	San Francisco	11-Wd San Francisc	84	546
Chow	46	m	c	CHIN	Sierra	Butte Twp	89	510
Chow	25	m	c	CHIN	El Dorado	Greenwood Twp	72	50
Chu	26	m	c	CHIN	Tehama	Merrill	92	197
Chung	42	m	c	CHIN	Placer	Bath P O	76	429
Coo	39	m	c	CHIN	El Dorado	Salmon Falls Twp	72	133
Eig	38	m	c	CHIN	Calaveras	San Andreas P O	70	218
Eugh	49	m	c	CHIN	Calaveras	San Andreas P O	70	220
Eun Wiohap	26	m	c	CHIN	San Francisco	11-Wd San Francisc	84	546
Fo	25	m	c	CHIN	Sutter	Nicolaus Twp	92	109
Fong	36	m	c	CHIN	Shasta	French Gulch P O	89	470
Foo	42	m	c	CHIN	Yuba	Marysville	93	620
Foo	40	m	c	CHIN	El Dorado	Salmon Falls Twp	72	133
Foo	38	m	c	CHIN	Sierra	Forest Twp	89	528
Foo	38	m	c	CHIN	Placer	Bath P O	76	429
Foo	36	m	c	CHIN	San Francisco	2-Wd San Francisco	79	286
Foo	28	m	c	CHIN	Tehama	Deer Crk Twp	92	171
Foo	27	m	c	CHIN	San Luis Obispo	Arroyo Grande Twp	87	279
Foo	27	m	c	CHIN	Butte	Chico Twp	70	27
Foo	26	m	c	CHIN	Sierra	Lincoln Twp	89	552
Foo	23	m	c	CHIN	Butte	Hamilton Twp	70	68
Foo	19	m	c	CHIN	Yolo	Buckeye Twp	93	411
Foo	18	m	c	CHIN	Yolo	Grafton Twp	93	483
Foo	18	m	c	CHIN	San Luis Obispo	Arroyo Grande Twp	87	276
Foo	16	m	c	CHIN	Sacramento	2-Wd Sacramento	77	248
Foot Pow	45	m	c	CHIN	San Francisco	11-Wd San Francisc	84	547
Foot Pow	45	m	c	CHIN	San Francisco	11-Wd San Francisc	84	563
Fou	22	m	c	CHIN	Tehama	Red Bank Twp	92	169
Fou	21	m	c	CHIN	Tehama	Merrill	92	198
Foy	70	m	c	CHIN	Calaveras	San Andreas P O	70	172
Fui	20	m	c	CHIN	Tehama	Battle Crk Twp	92	157
Fum	40	m	c	CHIN	San Francisco	6-Wd San Francisco	81	64
Fung	25	m	c	CHIN	Sacramento	3-Wd Sacramento	77	304
Gar Kee	22	m	c	CHIN	San Francisco	11-Wd San Francisc	84	547
Gee	38	m	c	CHIN	Butte	Hamilton Twp	70	68
Gee	29	m	c	CHIN	Butte	Chico Twp	70	31
Gee	24	m	c	CHIN	Butte	Kimshew Tpw	70	86
Gee	12	m	c	CHIN	San Francisco	6-Wd San Francisco	81	46
Gin	50	m	c	CHIN	Nevada	Nevada Twp	75	313
Go	25	m	c	CHIN	Colusa	Colusa	71	299
Gorey	38	m	c	CHIN	Plumas	Mineral Twp	77	24
Haw	45	m	c	CHIN	Shasta	Horsetown P O	89	503
Hei	36	m	c	CHIN	San Francisco	San Francisco P O	80	489
Hi	41	m	c	CHIN	Nevada	Little York Twp	75	245
High	27	m	c	CHIN	Sierra	Lincoln Twp	89	548
Hip Foo	30	m	c	CHIN	San Francisco	11-Wd San Francisc	84	547
Ho	23	m	c	CHIN	Sonoma	Santa Rosa	91	420
Hon	35	m	c	CHIN	Colusa	Colusa	71	300
Hoo	27	m	c	CHIN	Sierra	Alleghany & Forest	89	535
Hoo Hone	30	m	c	CHIN	San Francisco	11-Wd San Francisc	84	547
Hor	27	m	c	CHIN	San Francisco	San Francisco P O	83	131
Hoy	18	m	c	CHIN	San Mateo	Half Moon Bay P O	87	395
Hu	30	m	c	CHIN	Siskiyou	Yreka Twp	89	667
Jim	25	m	c	CHIN	Sonoma	Santa Rosa	91	420
Joe	35	m	c	CHIN	Alpine	Markleeville P O	69	312
Jow	51	m	c	CHIN	Plumas	Mineral Twp	77	24
Jow	34	m	c	CHIN	Plumas	Mineral Twp	77	24
Jueng	49	m	c	CHIN	Nevada	Bridgeport Twp	75	106
Kee	36	m	c	CHIN	Yuba	Marysville	93	628
Kee	35	m	c	CHIN	Placer	Clipper Gap P O	76	393
Kee	32	m	c	CHIN	Butte	Ophir Twp	70	103
Kee	30	m	c	CHIN	El Dorado	Georgetown Twp	72	36
Kee Fee	27	m	c	CHIN	San Francisco	11-Wd San Francisc	84	547
Ken Goo	24	m	c	CHIN	San Francisco	11-Wd San Francisc	84	547
Ki	49	m	c	CHIN	San Francisco	2-Wd San Francisco	79	286
Kin Goo	24	m	c	CHIN	San Francisco	11-Wd San Francisc	84	563
King	27	m	c	CHIN	Tuolumne	Columbia P O	93	341
La	40	m	c	CHIN	San Francisco	11-Wd San Francisc	84	695
La	39	m	c	CHIN	Calaveras	San Andreas P O	70	219
Lan	22	m	c	CHIN	Calaveras	San Andreas P O	70	204
Lan	16	m	c	CHIN	Tehama	Tehama Twp	92	188
Law	40	m	c	CHIN	Klamath	Sawyers Bar	73	378
Le	36	m	c	CHIN	San Joaquin	Douglas Twp	86	46
Le	30	m	c	CHIN	Sacramento	1-Wd Sacramento	77	199
Lee	30	m	c	CHIN	San Joaquin	Elkhorn Twp	86	65
Lee	30	m	c	CHIN	Mariposa	Mariposa P O	74	121
Lee	29	m	c	CHIN	El Dorado	Coloma Twp	72	5
Lee	28	m	c	CHIN	San Francisco	San Francisco P O	83	256
Lee	17	m	c	CHIN	Santa Clara	Santa Clara Twp	88	161
Leeo Ning	28	m	c	CHIN	San Francisco	11-Wd San Francisc	84	547
Len Chee	28	m	c	CHIN	San Francisco	11-Wd San Francisc	84	546
Len Fo	22	m	c	CHIN	San Francisco	11-Wd San Francisc	84	547
Len Fo	22	m	c	CHIN	San Francisco	11-Wd San Francisc	84	563
Lik Tee	27	m	c	CHIN	San Francisco	11-Wd San Francisc	84	563
Lik Tee	27	m	c	CHIN	San Francisco	11-Wd San Francisc	84	547
Lin	31	m	c	CHIN	Butte	Hamilton Twp	70	72
Ling	31	m	c	CHIN	Solano	Silveyville Twp	90	84
Loo	40	m	c	CHIN	San Joaquin	1-Wd Stockton	86	146
Loo	37	m	c	CHIN	Sierra	Forest Twp	89	532
Loo	32	m	c	CHIN	San Joaquin	Oneal Twp	86	115
Loo	31	m	c	CHIN	Placer	Bath P O	76	456
Loo Goo	22	m	c	CHIN	San Francisco	11-Wd San Francisc	84	563
Loy	19	m	c	CHIN	Calaveras	San Andreas P O	70	204
Luck	30	m	c	CHIN	Solano	Tremont Twp	90	31
Lum	36	m	c	CHIN	Merced	Snelling P O	74	279
Lun	24	m	c	CHIN	Solano	Vacaville Twp	90	136
Lung	49	m	c	CHIN	San Francisco	2-Wd San Francisco	79	230
Lung	41	m	c	CHIN	San Francisco	2-Wd San Francisco	79	286
Lung	37	m	c	CHIN	Siskiyou	Yreka Twp	89	669
Man Soo	24	m	c	CHIN	San Francisco	11-Wd San Francisc	84	563
Man Sooy	24	m	c	CHIN	San Francisco	11-Wd San Francisc	84	547
Ming	51	m	c	CHIN	Nevada	Bridgeport Twp	75	111
Moi	40	m	c	CHIN	San Francisco	6-Wd San Francisco	81	68
Mon Loog	25	m	c	CHIN	San Francisco	11-Wd San Francisc	84	547
Moo	43	m	c	CHIN	San Francisco	11-Wd San Francisc	84	696
Moo	22	m	c	CHIN	Yolo	Merritt Twp	93	506
Mung	42	m	c	CHIN	San Francisco	2-Wd San Francisco	79	286
Mung	39	m	c	CHIN	San Francisco	2-Wd San Francisco	79	285
Mung	39	m	c	CHIN	San Francisco	2-Wd San Francisco	79	286
Nam	31	m	c	CHIN	Yolo	Grafton Twp	93	483
Nang	40	m	c	CHIN	San Joaquin	Oneal Twp	86	99
Now	27	f	c	CHIN	Butte	Chico Twp	70	27
Ock	54	m	c	CHIN	Trinity	North Fork Twp	92	216
Pat Wee	26	m	c	CHIN	San Francisco	11-Wd San Francisc	84	547
Pin	39	m	c	CHIN	Calaveras	San Andreas P O	70	205
Po	39	m	c	CHIN	San Joaquin	1-Wd Stockton	86	149
Po	34	m	c	CHIN	San Joaquin	1-Wd Stockton	86	148
Pon	26	m	c	CHIN	Tuolumne	Chinese Camp P O	93	390
Poo	48	m	c	CHIN	Sierra	Butte Twp	89	510
Poo	46	m	c	CHIN	Sierra	Lincoln Twp	89	552
Poo	44	m	c	CHIN	Sierra	Butte Twp	89	512
Poo	40	m	c	CHIN	Tuolumne	Chinese Camp P O	93	377
Poo	29	m	c	CHIN	Sierra	Forest Twp	89	528
Poo	24	m	c	CHIN	Sierra	Forest Twp	89	528
Poo	19	m	c	CHIN	Alameda	Washington Twp	68	272
Quang	21	m	c	CHIN	Sierra	Eureka Twp	89	527
Quing Toon	22	m	c	CHIN	San Francisco	11-Wd San Francisc	84	563
Quing Toon	22	m	c	CHIN	San Francisco	11-Wd San Francisc	84	547
Quong	29	m	c	CHIN	Nevada	Little York Twp	75	235
Ric	38	m	c	CHIN	Sonoma	Petaluma Twp	91	343
Sam	30	m	c	CHIN	Colusa	Grand Island Twp	71	308
Sam	25	m	c	CHIN	Yolo	Washington Twp	93	529
Sang	53	m	c	CHIN	Amador	Jackson P O	69	343
See	34	m	c	CHIN	El Dorado	Greenwood Twp	72	56
Sing	7	m	c	CA	Yuba	Marysville	93	627
Sing	39	m	c	CHIN	Tuolumne	Chinese Camp P O	93	366
Sing	38	m	c	CHIN	Sierra	Alleghany & Forest	89	535
Sing	34	m	c	CHIN	Solano	Montezuma Twp	90	66
Sing	30	m	c	CHIN	San Francisco	San Francisco P O	83	213
Sing	26	m	c	CHIN	Solano	Green Valley Twp	90	43
Sing	24	m	c	CHIN	Calaveras	San Andreas P O	70	205
Son	51	m	c	CHIN	Nevada	Bridgeport Twp	75	110
Son	33	m	c	CHIN	San Francisco	6-Wd San Francisco	81	52
Son	20	m	c	CHIN	San Joaquin	Oneal Twp	86	99
Song	19	m	c	CHIN	San Joaquin	Oneal Twp	86	115
Soo	29	m	c	CHIN	Nevada	Meadow Lake Twp	75	259
Soo Ling	24	m	c	CHIN	San Francisco	11-Wd San Francisc	84	547
Soong Kooi	32	m	c	CHIN	San Francisco	11-Wd San Francisc	84	547
Su	19	m	c	CHIN	Nevada	Eureka Twp	75	140
Sue	27	m	c	CHIN	Butte	Hamilton Twp	70	71
Sung	32	m	c	CHIN	Yuba	Marysville	93	631
Ti	28	m	c	CHIN	Nevada	Nevada Twp	75	299
Tie	42	m	c	CHIN	San Joaquin	Elkhorn Twp	86	69
Too	19	m	c	CHIN	Nevada	Nevada Twp	75	318
Too Goo	22	m	c	CHIN	San Francisco	11-Wd San Francisc	84	547
Toy	37	m	c	CHIN	Butte	Wyandotte Twp	70	143
Wah	25	m	c	CHIN	Solano	Vacaville Twp	90	134
Wah	23	m	c	CHIN	San Francisco	San Francisco P O	83	232
Wah	21	m	c	CHIN	San Francisco	11-Wd San Francisc	84	548
Wah	18	m	c	CHIN	San Francisco	San Francisco P O	83	256
Wan	21	m	c	CHIN	Tehama	Antelope Twp	92	153
Wang	32	m	c	CHIN	Tulare	Visalia	92	297
Way	40	m	c	CHIN	Siskiyou	Yreka Twp	89	667
Wing	55	m	c	CHIN	Trinity	Weaverville Pct	92	228

© 2001 by Heritage Quest. All rights reserved.

California 1870 Census

Name	Age	S	R	B-PL	County	Locale	Series M593 Roll	Pg
Wing	36	m	c	CHIN	San Francisco	2-Wd San Francisco	79	285
Wing	30	m	c	CHIN	El Dorado	Greenwood Twp	72	53
Wing Fing	22	m	c	CHIN	San Francisco	11-Wd San Franciso	84	547
Wo	32	m	c	CHIN	Nevada	Meadow Lake Twp	75	256
Won	52	m	c	CHIN	Sierra	Lincoln Twp	89	548
Wone	28	m	c	CHIN	San Mateo	Half Moon Bay P O	87	395
Woo	50	m	c	CHIN	Trinity	Weaverville Pct	92	231
Yan	34	m	c	CHIN	Calaveras	San Andreas P O	70	205
Yang	36	m	c	CHIN	Placer	Bath P O	76	455
Yass	35	m	c	CHIN	Butte	Hamilton Twp	70	72
Yee	34	m	c	CHIN	San Francisco	2-Wd San Francisco	79	286
Yee	25	m	c	CHIN	Yuba	Marysville	93	628
Yeng	61	m	c	CHIN	San Francisco	6-Wd San Francisco	81	43
Yet	29	f	c	CHIN	Butte	Chico Twp	70	28
Yik	35	m	c	CHIN	Butte	Hamilton Twp	70	75
Yik	34	m	c	CHIN	Butte	Concow Twp	70	8
Yik Choon	23	m	c	CHIN	San Francisco	11-Wd San Francisc	84	547
Yuen	37	m	c	CHIN	San Francisco	6-Wd San Francisco	81	52
Yung	32	m	c	CHIN	Mariposa	Maxwell Crk P O	74	145
Zing Low	43	m	c	CHIN	San Francisco	San Francisco P O	80	495
CHINGREN								
John	36	m	w	ITAL	Contra Costa	Martinez P O	71	447
CHINGTIE								
Ah	23	m	c	CHIN	San Joaquin	Castoria Twp	86	12
CHINK								
Ah	41	m	c	CHIN	Tuolumne	Big Oak Flat P O	93	397
Ah	25	m	c	CHIN	San Joaquin	1-Wd Stockton	86	142
Ling	28	m	c	CHIN	Solano	Vacaville Twp	90	130
CHINN								
Ah	45	m	c	CHIN	Placer	Bath P O	76	429
Ah	34	m	c	CHIN	San Francisco	6-Wd San Francisco	81	66
Ah	32	m	c	CHIN	Placer	Alta P O	76	411
Ah	30	m	c	CHIN	San Francisco	6-Wd San Francisco	81	66
Ah	27	m	c	CHIN	Nevada	Meadow Lake Twp	75	255
Ah	26	m	c	CHIN	Tuolumne	Big Oak Flat P O	93	397
Ah	25	m	c	CHIN	San Francisco	6-Wd San Francisco	81	47
Ah	20	m	c	CHIN	San Francisco	6-Wd San Francisco	81	68
Ah	18	m	c	CHIN	Napa	Napa	75	47
Ah	13	m	c	CHIN	Napa	Napa	75	51
Chas	40	m	w	IN	Sonoma	Santa Rosa	91	411
James W	47	m	w	VA	Placer	Bath P O	76	447
John B	39	m	w	KY	Placer	Emigrant Gap P O	76	416
John L	40	m	w	VA	Yuba	Long Bar Twp	93	566
Thomas	26	m	w	KY	Placer	Emigrant Gap P O	76	416
Wm	48	m	w	ENGL	Yuba	Marysville	93	594
CHINO								
Rosario	50	f	w	MEXI	Santa Clara	1-Wd San Jose	88	231
Santiago	60	m	w	MEXI	Santa Clara	1-Wd San Jose	88	262
CHINTZ								
Herman	36	m	w	SWIT	San Francisco	7-Wd San Francisco	81	191
CHINVO								
Hah	26	f	c	CHIN	Napa	Napa	75	56
CHIOGGI								
Joseph	36	m	w	ITAL	Santa Clara	San Jose Twp	88	221
CHIONG								
Ah	28	m	c	CHIN	Amador	Ione City P O	69	370
CHIOUSSE								
Joseph	49	m	w	FRAN	San Francisco	San Francisco P O	85	751
CHIP								
Ah	40	m	c	CHIN	Butte	Chico Twp	70	28
Ah	39	m	c	CHIN	Nevada	Nevada Twp	75	307
Ah	37	m	c	CHIN	Butte	Hamilton Twp	70	68
Ah	36	m	c	CHIN	El Dorado	Placerville	72	115
Ah	34	m	c	CHIN	El Dorado	Greenwood Twp	72	56
Ah	32	m	c	CHIN	Butte	Chico Twp	70	53
Ah	31	m	c	CHIN	San Francisco	San Francisco P O	80	497
Ah	30	m	c	CHIN	El Dorado	Georgetown Twp	72	48
Ah	29	m	c	CHIN	San Joaquin	1-Wd Stockton	86	147
Ah	25	m	c	CHIN	El Dorado	Coloma Twp	72	3
Ah	24	m	c	CHIN	Butte	Hamilton Twp	70	67
Ah	23	m	c	CHIN	San Francisco	8-Wd San Francisco	82	336
Ah	17	m	c	CHIN	San Francisco	6-Wd San Francisco	81	84
Cow	55	m	c	CHIN	Placer	Dutch Flat P O	76	407
Lit	32	m	c	CHIN	San Joaquin	1-Wd Stockton	86	142
Pan	46	m	c	CHIN	Tuolumne	Chinese Camp P O	93	380
See	40	m	c	CHIN	El Dorado	Kelsey Twp	72	59
Sing	15	m	c	CHIN	El Dorado	Greenwood Twp	72	56
Wong	46	m	c	CHIN	Calaveras	San Andreas P O	70	169
Yon	30	m	c	CHIN	San Joaquin	1-Wd Stockton	86	148
CHIPCHACE								
W J	28	m	w	ENGL	Solano	Vallejo	90	160
CHIPCHASE								
John M	23	m	w	CANA	Stanislaus	Buena Vista Twp	92	14
CHIPITII								
Augustine	42	m	w	SPAI	Santa Barbara	Santa Barbara P O	87	453
CHIPLEY								
Benton	36	m	w	IL	Alameda	Alvarado	68	304
CHIPMAN								
B	15	f	w	CA	Sacramento	3-Wd Sacramento	77	317
Caleb	38	m	w	MA	San Joaquin	2-Wd Stockton	86	168
Caroline	39	f	w	AL	San Francisco	8-Wd San Francisco	82	382
H C	17	m	w	CA	Sacramento	4-Wd Sacramento	77	322
Hiram	52	m	w	ME	Placer	Auburn P O	76	369
John	58	m	w	ENGL	San Francisco	San Francisco P O	83	211
John	32	m	w	MA	Alameda	San Leandro	68	96
Joshua	27	m	w	ENGL	Nevada	Grass Valley Twp	75	172
Justus	17	m	w	CA	San Bernardino	San Bernardino Twp	78	441
Layfaette	45	m	w	NY	Santa Clara	San Jose Twp	88	221
Mary	20	f	w	MO	San Bernardino	San Bernardino Twp	78	421
Norman	73	m	w	VT	Monterey	Alisal Twp	74	299
Wm	52	m	w	MA	San Francisco	1-Wd San Francisco	79	124
Wm	50	m	w	VT	San Francisco	2-Wd San Francisco	79	195
Wm	40	m	w	AL	San Joaquin	2-Wd Stockton	86	177
CHIPPS								
Sam J	40	m	w	MO	Butte	Chico Twp	70	15
CHIQUATIN								
Jose	20	m	w	CA	San Diego	San Luis Rey	78	514
CHIQUITA								
J	45	f	w	MEXI	Santa Clara	Almaden Twp	88	8
CHIRCK								
Ah	35	m	c	CHIN	Nevada	Meadow Lake Twp	75	254
CHIRE								
Charles	22	m	w	BREM	Inyo	Lone Pine Twp	73	331
CHIROKEE								
Ah	20	f	c	CHIN	Monterey	Salinas Twp	74	308
CHIROLOT								
Francis	39	m	w	FRAN	Fresno	Millerton P O	72	147
CHIRONI								
Augustine	20	m	w	SWIT	El Dorado	Diamond Springs Tw	72	28
CHISALLIAN								
L E	40	m	w	ME	Monterey	Salinas Twp	74	311
CHISCH								
Theodore	22	m	w	SWIT	Sutter	Nicolaus Twp	92	114
CHISCO								
A M	35	m	w	KY	Los Angeles	Soledad Twp	73	631
CHISE								
Ah	29	m	c	CHIN	Nevada	Meadow Lake Twp	75	256
CHISEM								
David	38	m	w	VA	Alameda	Brooklyn Twp	68	39
CHISHOLM								
Alex	27	m	w	CANA	Solano	Benicia	90	5
Alex	27	m	w	CANA	Mendocino	Ukiah Twp	74	239
Alexander	40	m	w	SCOT	Nevada	Grass Valley Twp	75	229
Alexander	40	m	w	SCOT	Nevada	Grass Valley Twp	75	203
Christopher	30	m	w	CANA	San Francisco	11-Wd San Francisc	84	698
David B	42	m	w	SCOT	San Francisco	2-Wd San Francisco	79	262
Donald	40	m	w	CANA	San Francisco	San Francisco P O	85	801
H	43	f	w	ENGL	Lassen	Janesville Twp	73	430
James	36	m	w	SCOT	Nevada	Bridgeport Twp	75	101
John	38	m	w	PRUS	San Francisco	San Francisco P O	80	347
John	30	m	w	CANA	Sacramento	2-Wd Sacramento	77	222
Susan	35	f	w	CANA	Sacramento	4-Wd Sacramento	77	359
William	39	m	w	CANA	San Francisco	2-Wd San Francisco	79	151
CHISHOLME								
Geo	42	m	w	RI	San Joaquin	Elliott Twp	86	81
CHISM								
Andrew	42	m	b	KY	Los Angeles	Los Angeles	73	528
Jas G	13	m	w	CA	Shasta	Millville P O	89	492
John	24	m	w	TX	Stanislaus	Branch Twp	92	10
Joseph T	22	m	w	KY	Yolo	Cache Crk Twp	93	444
Seth	52	m	w	ME	Humboldt	Eel Rvr Twp	72	249
Thomas	14	m	b	CA	Los Angeles	Los Angeles	73	528
William L	22	m	w	TX	Los Angeles	Los Angeles Twp	73	469
CHISOLM								
Alex	40	m	w	CANA	San Joaquin	2-Wd Stockton	86	165
CHISON								
Coline	40	m	w	CANA	San Joaquin	2-Wd Stockton	86	169
CHIST								
Charter	33	m	w	DENM	Sutter	Yuba Twp	92	149
CHISTOHER								
R T	59	m	w	MO	San Joaquin	Castoria Twp	86	9
CHISUM								
Peter G	39	m	w	AL	San Luis Obispo	Morro Twp	87	282
CHIT								
Ah	62	m	c	CHIN	Butte	Ophir Twp	70	106
Ah	46	m	c	CHIN	Tuolumne	Big Oak Flat P O	93	399
Ah	40	m	c	CHIN	Placer	Auburn P O	76	373
Ah	31	m	c	CHIN	Tuolumne	Chinese Camp P O	93	388
Ah	25	m	c	CHIN	Placer	Gold Run Twp	76	398
Ah	20	m	c	CHIN	Yolo	Cottonwood Twp	93	467
Ah	19	m	c	CHIN	Shasta	French Gulch P O	89	470
CHITTEN								
William	28	m	w	IN	Stanislaus	Branch Twp	92	3
CHITTENDEN								
C	25	m	w	NH	San Joaquin	Oneal Twp	86	114
C J	22	m	w	VT	San Joaquin	Castoria Twp	86	3
G E	31	m	w	MI	Yuba	W Bear Rvr Twp	93	680
Geo	39	m	w	ENGL	Mariposa	Mariposa P O	74	91
James H	56	m	w	CT	Santa Cruz	Santa Cruz	89	405
Jas T	30	m	w	NY	San Francisco	6-Wd San Francisco	81	96
John	40	m	w	NY	Contra Costa	Martinez P O	71	401
John E	30	m	w	IL	Stanislaus	San Joaquin Twp	92	71
Jos	42	m	w	NY	San Francisco	7-Wd San Francisco	81	287
Julia	55	f	w	MA	San Joaquin	2-Wd Stockton	86	209
L	27	f	w	MI	Alameda	Oakland	68	199
Ledin J	21	m	w	IA	Santa Cruz	Santa Cruz Twp	89	402
W A	28	m	w	MA	San Joaquin	2-Wd Stockton	86	209
Wm	32	m	w	IN	Yuba	Marysville Twp	93	571
Wm T	36	m	w	NY	Alameda	Eden Twp	68	70
CHITTENDON								
Chas R	26	m	w	CT	San Francisco	San Francisco P O	83	90
J K	38	m	w	MA	Sacramento	American Twp	77	64
CHITTICK								
Johston	30	m	w	IREL	San Francisco	San Francisco P O	83	349

© 2001 by Heritage Quest. All rights reserved.

Name	Age	S	R	B-PL	County	Locale	Series M593 Roll	Pg
CHITWOOD								
Isaac	19	m	w	MO	Amador	Ione City P O	69	367
Jas N	41	m	w	TN	Sonoma	Russian Rvr	91	379
Jos A	47	m	w	TN	Shasta	French Gulch P O	89	464
Jos T	26	m	w	MO	Sonoma	Russian Rvr	91	372
M J	15	f	w	CA	Sonoma	Russian Rvr	91	378
Russel	38	m	w	TN	Sonoma	Mendocino Twp	91	288
CHIUN								
Ah	45	m	c	CHIN	Nevada	Nevada Twp	75	316
CHIUNG								
Ah	22	m	c	CHIN	Trinity	Douglas	92	237
CHIVA								
Lee	25	m	i	CA	Del Norte	Crescent Twp	71	458
CHIVALLIE								
Victor	40	m	w	FRAN	San Francisco	8-Wd San Francisco	82	352
CHIVEL								
Joseph	35	m	w	PORT	Alameda	Washington Twp	68	299
CHIVELL								
James	22	m	w	ENGL	Nevada	Grass Valley Twp	75	193
CHIVER								
Thos	28	m	w	ENGL	Butte	Oregon Twp	70	128
CHIVERS								
Thos	50	m	w	CANA	Tehama	Red Bluff	92	175
CHIVIEL								
John	18	m	w	PORT	Alameda	Washington Twp	68	299
CHLAAY								
Hin	20	m	c	CHIN	San Francisco	1-Wd San Francisco	79	87
CHN								
Ah	37	m	c	CHIN	Sierra	Butte Twp	89	510
Ah	28	m	c	CHIN	Butte	Chico Twp	70	51
Ah	26	m	c	CHIN	El Dorado	Placerville	72	127
Ah	25	m	c	CHIN	Calaveras	Copperopolis P O	70	247
Ah	25	m	c	CHIN	Sacramento	Georgianna Twp	77	133
CHNG								
Ah	20	m	c	CHIN	San Francisco	6-Wd San Francisco	81	69
CHO								
Ah	58	m	c	CHIN	Butte	Kimshew Tpw	70	85
Ah	48	m	c	CHIN	Sierra	Forest Twp	89	532
Ah	47	m	c	CHIN	Butte	Kimshew Tpw	70	85
Ah	46	m	c	CHIN	Butte	Kimshew Tpw	70	84
Ah	39	m	c	CHIN	Butte	Chico Twp	70	51
Ah	36	m	c	CHIN	Marin	San Rafael Twp	74	37
Ah	35	m	c	CHIN	Solano	Vallejo	90	209
Ah	35	m	c	CHIN	Sacramento	Franklin Twp	77	114
Ah	34	f	c	CHIN	Santa Clara	1-Wd San Jose	88	273
Ah	32	m	c	CHIN	Los Angeles	Los Angeles	73	525
Ah	32	m	c	CHIN	Kern	Havilah P O	73	338
Ah	31	m	c	CHIN	Butte	Chico Twp	70	21
Ah	30	m	c	CHIN	Calaveras	Copperopolis P O	70	235
Ah	30	m	c	CHIN	Trinity	Indian Crk	92	199
Ah	29	m	c	CHIN	Los Angeles	Los Angeles	73	564
Ah	29	m	c	CHIN	Butte	Ophir Twp	70	121
Ah	28	m	c	CHIN	Butte	Chico Twp	70	52
Ah	26	m	c	CHIN	Butte	Kimshew Tpw	70	81
Ah	25	m	c	CHIN	Los Angeles	Los Angeles Twp	73	487
Ah	25	m	c	CHIN	Alameda	Oakland	68	134
Ah	23	m	c	CHIN	San Francisco	San Francisco P O	80	517
Ah	20	m	c	CHIN	Butte	Hamilton Twp	70	73
Ah	20	m	c	CHIN	Butte	Concow Twp	70	8
Ah	16	m	c	CHIN	Alameda	Oakland	68	208
Ay	38	m	c	CHIN	Sierra	Downieville Twp	89	520
Chong	24	m	c	CHIN	Butte	Concow Twp	70	11
Dot	43	m	c	CHIN	Butte	Concow Twp	70	10
Dot	37	m	c	CHIN	Butte	Chico Twp	70	52
Dot	30	m	c	CHIN	Butte	Chico Twp	70	51
Fat	54	m	c	CHIN	Butte	Concow Twp	70	11
Fay	29	f	c	CHIN	Yuba	Marysville	93	627
Fo	41	m	c	CHIN	Butte	Concow Twp	70	10
Foo	38	m	c	CHIN	Butte	Hamilton Twp	70	74
Fung	25	m	c	CHIN	Butte	Chico Twp	70	52
Fung	25	m	c	CHIN	Butte	Chico Twp	70	51
Gan	45	m	c	CHIN	Trinity	Douglas	92	232
Ge	37	m	c	CHIN	Butte	Concow Twp	70	8
Gee	32	m	c	CHIN	Butte	Hamilton Twp	70	72
Hon	39	m	c	CHIN	Butte	Concow Twp	70	11
Hoy	38	m	c	CHIN	Butte	Concow Twp	70	10
Ke	41	m	c	CHIN	Butte	Hamilton Twp	70	75
Kee	30	m	c	CHIN	Butte	Ophir Twp	70	103
Kin	47	m	c	CHIN	Placer	Bath P O	76	424
Ling	30	m	c	CHIN	Calaveras	San Andreas P O	70	161
Lun	32	m	c	CHIN	Butte	Concow Twp	70	11
Lung	27	m	c	CHIN	Butte	Chico Twp	70	52
Miney	26	m	c	CHIN	Butte	Hamilton Twp	70	71
Mon	30	m	c	CHIN	San Francisco	11-Wd San Francisc	84	529
On	20	m	c	CHIN	Nevada	Grass Valley Twp	75	184
Sang	32	m	c	CHIN	Siskiyou	Yreka	89	661
Say	28	f	c	CHIN	Monterey	Monterey Twp	74	351
Sook	9	f	c	CHIN	Monterey	Monterey Twp	74	352
Wing	32	m	c	CHIN	Butte	Concow Twp	70	12
CHOA								
Ah	26	m	c	CHIN	San Francisco	San Francisco P O	83	138
Gregorio	53	m	w	MEXI	Contra Costa	Martinez P O	71	416
Jesus	23	m	w	MEXI	Contra Costa	Martinez P O	71	416
CHOAT								
Edward	38	m	w	TN	Yuba	Bullards Bar P O	93	550
John	46	m	w	AL	El Dorado	Cosumnes Twp	72	19
Larkin	34	m	w	TN	Yuba	Bullards Bar P O	93	550

Name	Age	S	R	B-PL	County	Locale	Series M593 Roll	Pg
CHOATE								
Edward	38	m	w	ME	San Diego	San Diego	78	491
Edward	37	m	w	MO	Plumas	Quartz Twp	77	43
Jason	23	m	w	CANA	Santa Clara	Fremont Twp	88	47
Nehemiah	33	m	w	ME	San Francisco	San Francisco P O	83	46
Rebecca	55	f	w	MA	Sonoma	Sonoma Twp	91	437
Richd	36	m	w	CANA	Solano	Vallejo	90	200
Robt H	32	m	w	MA	San Luis Obispo	Arroyo Grande Twp	87	276
T B	44	m	w	MA	San Joaquin	1-Wd Stockton	86	134
CHOB								
Gee	37	f	c	CHIN	Yuba	Marysville	93	627
CHOBAN								
Joaquin	35	m	w	MEXI	Kern	Tehachapi P O	73	354
CHOBOLLA								
Angel A	40	m	w	CA	Monterey	San Juan Twp	74	403
CHOC								
Kim	44	m	c	CHIN	Amador	Jackson P O	69	332
CHOCK								
---	30	m	c	CHIN	Siskiyou	Yreka Twp	89	667
Ah	36	m	c	CHIN	Sierra	Downieville Twp	89	521
Ah	34	m	c	CHIN	San Mateo	San Mateo P O	87	351
Ah	32	m	c	CHIN	San Francisco	6-Wd San Francisco	81	44
Ah	25	m	c	CHIN	Sacramento	American Twp	77	68
Ah	24	m	c	CHIN	San Francisco	3-Wd San Francisco	79	309
Ah	19	m	c	CHIN	San Francisco	6-Wd San Francisco	81	66
Ah	18	m	c	CHIN	Tuolumne	Chinese Camp P O	93	384
Gee	41	m	c	CHIN	Plumas	Mineral Twp	77	24
She	30	m	c	CHIN	Nevada	Meadow Lake Twp	75	250
Ton	26	m	c	CHIN	Placer	Bath P O	76	439
We	38	m	c	CHIN	Butte	Hamilton Twp	70	73
CHODD								
Richard	26	m	w	IN	Los Angeles	Los Angeles	73	528
CHODIT								
Guttutt	78	m	w	SAXO	Humboldt	Arcata Twp	72	233
CHOE								
A G	38	m	w	FRAN	Alameda	Oakland	68	146
Ah	43	m	c	CHIN	San Francisco	6-Wd San Francisco	81	66
Ah	41	m	c	CHIN	Sutter	Butte Twp	92	88
Ah	38	m	c	CHIN	Calaveras	San Andreas P O	70	161
Ah	36	m	c	CHIN	San Francisco	6-Wd San Francisco	81	48
Ah	31	m	c	CHIN	Amador	Fiddletown P O	69	427
Ah	30	m	c	CHIN	Sacramento	Franklin Twp	77	114
Ah	26	m	c	CHIN	Santa Clara	1-Wd San Jose	88	273
Ah	25	m	c	CHIN	Calaveras	San Andreas P O	70	160
Ah	17	m	c	CHIN	Placer	Colfax P O	76	384
Juan	35	m	c	CHIN	Sonoma	Salt Point	91	386
M	47	m	w	IREL	Lake	Knoxville Mines	73	405
CHOEA								
Ah	24	m	c	CHIN	Sonoma	Sonoma Twp	91	449
CHOEN								
J	48	m	w	FRNK	San Joaquin	2-Wd Stockton	86	159
Michael	40	m	w	POLA	San Francisco	San Francisco P O	83	373
Phillip	33	m	w	RUSS	Colusa	Colusa	71	298
CHOEY								
Ah	27	m	c	CHIN	Butte	Ophir Twp	70	109
Ah	25	m	c	CHIN	San Francisco	3-Wd San Francisco	79	304
Ah	16	f	c	CHIN	Butte	Chico Twp	70	28
Ah	12	f	c	CHIN	Humboldt	Eureka Twp	72	266
CHOG								
Ah	51	m	c	CHIN	Mariposa	Mariposa P O	74	102
Ah	47	m	c	CHIN	Mariposa	Mariposa P O	74	102
Ah	43	m	c	CHIN	Mariposa	Mariposa P O	74	133
Ah	35	m	c	CHIN	Mariposa	Mariposa P O	74	114
Ah	28	m	c	CHIN	Nevada	Rough & Ready Twp	75	327
Ling	28	f	c	CHIN	Mariposa	Mariposa P O	74	125
CHOH								
Ah	24	m	c	CHIN	Yolo	Putah Twp	93	516
Ah	22	m	c	CHIN	San Francisco	6-Wd San Francisco	81	71
Wong Ah	24	m	c	CHIN	San Francisco	6-Wd San Francisco	81	88
CHOHN								
Michl Mrs	32	f	w	NY	San Francisco	5-Wd San Francisco	81	13
CHOI								
Ah	52	m	c	CHIN	Calaveras	San Andreas P O	70	167
Ah	52	m	c	CHIN	San Francisco	San Francisco P O	80	494
Ah	42	m	c	CHIN	San Francisco	San Francisco P O	80	516
Ah	41	m	c	CHIN	San Francisco	San Francisco P O	80	456
Ah	40	m	c	CHIN	Calaveras	San Andreas P O	70	155
Ah	37	m	c	CHIN	Mariposa	Maxwell Crk P O	74	145
Ah	37	m	c	CHIN	San Francisco	San Francisco P O	80	439
Ah	30	m	c	CHIN	San Francisco	San Francisco P O	80	510
Ah	28	f	c	CHIN	Calaveras	San Andreas P O	70	167
Ah	28	f	m	CHIN	Mariposa	Maxwell Crk P O	74	138
Ah	23	f	c	CHIN	Santa Clara	Gilroy Twp	88	80
Ah	22	m	c	CHIN	Calaveras	San Andreas P O	70	167
Ah	22	m	c	CHIN	Alpine	Woodfords P O	69	309
Ah	21	m	c	CHIN	San Francisco	San Francisco P O	80	496
Ah	20	m	c	CHIN	Calaveras	San Andreas P O	70	155
Ah	20	f	c	CHIN	San Francisco	San Francisco P O	80	450
Ah	12	m	c	CHIN	San Francisco	San Francisco P O	80	502
Foo	22	m	c	CHIN	Solano	Green Valley Twp	90	43
Kin	41	m	c	CHIN	Fresno	Millerton P O	72	202
Lan	30	m	c	CHIN	Fresno	Millerton P O	72	202
See	39	m	c	CHIN	Yuba	Marysville	93	630
Sing	25	m	c	CHIN	Mariposa	Maxwell Crk P O	74	138
Sun	21	m	c	CHIN	Solano	Rio Vista Twp	90	70
Ty	53	m	c	CHIN	Calaveras	San Andreas P O	70	161
Yet	55	m	c	CHIN	Calaveras	San Andreas P O	70	220

© 2001 by Heritage Quest. All rights reserved.

Series M593

Name	Age	S	R	B-PL	County	Locale	Roll	Pg
Yu	34	f	c	CHIN	Calaveras	San Andreas P O	70	181
CHOIN								
Ah	42	m	c	CHIN	San Francisco	6-Wd San Francisco	81	47
Ah	35	m	c	CHIN	San Francisco	6-Wd San Francisco	81	45
Ah	18	m	c	CHIN	San Francisco	6-Wd San Francisco	81	46
Ah	14	m	c	CHIN	San Francisco	6-Wd San Francisco	81	45
CHOISSER								
Joseph	22	m	w	IL	Mariposa	Mariposa P O	74	110
Lafayette	33	m	w	IL	Mariposa	Mariposa P O	74	110
CHOK								
---	18	m	c	CHIN	San Francisco	6-Wd San Francisco	81	64
Ah	36	m	c	CHIN	Placer	Newcastle Twp	76	479
Ah	27	m	c	CHIN	Sacramento	Franklin Twp	77	116
Ah	25	m	c	CHIN	San Francisco	6-Wd San Francisco	81	63
Ah	22	m	c	CHIN	San Francisco	6-Wd San Francisco	81	69
Ah	21	m	c	CHIN	San Francisco	6-Wd San Francisco	81	67
Lok	30	m	c	CHIN	Napa	Napa	75	8
Sun	41	m	c	CHIN	San Francisco	6-Wd San Francisco	81	67
CHOLBYE								
V	47	m	w	FRAN	Sierra	Butte Twp	89	513
CHOLEY								
Achille	33	m	w	FRAN	Tuolumne	Sonora P O	93	323
Leon	35	m	w	FRAN	Tuolumne	Sonora P O	93	323
CHOLIE								
Ah	15	m	c	CHIN	San Francisco	8-Wd San Francisco	82	407
CHOLT								
Joseph	50	m	w	FRAN	San Francisco	3-Wd San Francisco	79	319
CHOM								
Ah	39	m	c	CHIN	Santa Clara	1-Wd San Jose	88	272
Ah	32	m	c	CHIN	Alameda	Washington Twp	68	268
Ah	28	m	c	CHIN	Placer	Auburn P O	76	381
Ah	23	m	c	CHIN	Nevada	Eureka Twp	75	127
Ah	19	m	c	CHIN	Nevada	Eureka Twp	75	140
CHOMAN								
John	43	m	w	WURT	San Francisco	11-Wd San Francisc	84	678
CHOMAS								
John	58	m	w	FRAN	Calaveras	San Andreas P O	70	193
CHOMETON								
August	57	m	w	FRAN	San Francisco	2-Wd San Francisco	79	180
CHOMO								
Ah	31	m	c	CHIN	Placer	Bath P O	76	452
CHOMP								
Loo	25	m	c	CHIN	Solano	Vacaville Twp	90	132
CHON								
Ah	62	m	c	CHIN	Tuolumne	Chinese Camp P O	93	380
Ah	53	m	c	CHIN	El Dorado	Coloma Twp	72	3
Ah	45	m	c	CHIN	Napa	Napa Twp	75	58
Ah	45	m	c	CHIN	Sacramento	3-Wd Sacramento	77	300
Ah	43	m	c	CHIN	Placer	Lincoln P O	76	484
Ah	42	m	c	CHIN	Amador	Volcano P O	69	378
Ah	42	m	c	CHIN	Amador	Volcano P O	69	387
Ah	42	m	c	CHIN	Butte	Hamilton Twp	70	67
Ah	42	m	c	CHIN	Sierra	Downieville Twp	89	520
Ah	41	m	c	CHIN	Kern	Linns Valley P O	73	343
Ah	40	m	c	CHIN	Shasta	French Gulch P O	89	464
Ah	40	m	c	CHIN	San Francisco	San Francisco P O	83	82
Ah	40	m	c	CHIN	Butte	Chico Twp	70	51
Ah	39	m	c	CHIN	Calaveras	San Andreas P O	70	176
Ah	36	m	c	CHIN	Amador	Volcano P O	69	387
Ah	34	m	c	CHIN	Placer	Lincoln P O	76	484
Ah	33	m	c	CHIN	Amador	Ione City P O	69	354
Ah	32	m	c	CHIN	San Francisco	San Francisco P O	85	748
Ah	32	m	c	CHIN	Butte	Concow Twp	70	11
Ah	31	m	c	CHIN	Calaveras	San Andreas P O	70	183
Ah	30	m	c	CHIN	San Francisco	San Francisco P O	85	748
Ah	30	m	c	CHIN	Mariposa	Mariposa P O	74	121
Ah	30	m	c	CHIN	Calaveras	San Andreas P O	70	167
Ah	30	m	c	CHIN	Amador	Ione City P O	69	354
Ah	29	m	c	CHIN	Amador	Jackson P O	69	332
Ah	29	m	c	CHIN	San Francisco	6-Wd San Francisco	81	59
Ah	28	m	c	CHIN	Sierra	Eureka Twp	89	523
Ah	28	m	c	CHIN	San Francisco	6-Wd San Francisco	81	58
Ah	27	m	c	CHIN	Alameda	Eden Twp	68	62
Ah	26	m	c	CHIN	Merced	Snelling P O	74	253
Ah	25	m	c	CHIN	Butte	Concow Twp	70	11
Ah	25	m	c	CHIN	San Francisco	6-Wd San Francisco	81	139
Ah	23	m	c	CHIN	Placer	Bath P O	76	451
Ah	23	m	c	CHIN	Calaveras	San Andreas P O	70	176
Ah	22	m	c	CHIN	San Francisco	San Francisco P O	85	835
Ah	21	m	c	CHIN	San Francisco	6-Wd San Francisco	81	64
Ah	21	m	c	CHIN	Amador	Jackson P O	69	331
Ah	20	m	c	CHIN	Sierra	Table Rock Twp	89	544
Ah	20	m	c	CHIN	Sierra	Eureka Twp	89	525
Ah	18	m	c	CHIN	Alameda	Oakland	68	138
Ah	18	m	c	CHIN	Butte	Kimshew Tpw	70	86
Ah	17	m	c	CHIN	San Francisco	2-Wd San Francisco	79	196
Ah	17	f	c	CHIN	Butte	Oregon Twp	70	131
Ah	14	m	c	CA	Tuolumne	Chinese Camp P O	93	371
Ah	14	m	c	CHIN	San Francisco	3-Wd San Francisco	79	307
Ar	33	m	c	CHIN	Sonoma	Petaluma Twp	91	363
Ar	25	m	c	CHIN	Sonoma	Petaluma Twp	91	363
Chew	39	m	c	CHIN	Yuba	North East Twp	93	646
Chew	36	m	c	CHIN	Sierra	Butte Twp	89	513
Chow	35	m	c	CHIN	Nevada	Nevada Twp	75	298
Chuck	50	m	c	CHIN	Calaveras	San Andreas P O	70	161
Cow	36	m	c	CHIN	Butte	Concow Twp	70	11
Ding	55	m	c	CHIN	Calaveras	San Andreas P O	70	161

Series M593

Name	Age	S	R	B-PL	County	Locale	Roll	Pg
Flora	28	f	w	PRUS	Yolo	Cache Crk Twp	93	419
Fuc	33	m	c	CHIN	Trinity	Indian Crk	92	199
Gin	32	m	c	CHIN	Butte	Concow Twp	70	10
Gon	32	m	c	CHIN	Butte	Chico Twp	70	51
He	30	m	c	CHIN	Calaveras	San Andreas P O	70	199
Hung	26	m	c	CHIN	Calaveras	San Andreas P O	70	161
Kee	32	m	c	CHIN	Butte	Hamilton Twp	70	74
Ken	28	m	c	CHIN	Shasta	French Gulch P O	89	465
Kom	36	m	c	CHIN	San Francisco	6-Wd San Francisco	81	38
Leon	17	m	c	CHIN	Shasta	French Gulch P O	89	466
Long	48	m	c	CHIN	Shasta	French Gulch P O	89	465
Long	30	f	c	CHIN	Yuba	Marysville	93	627
Mong	50	m	c	CHIN	Mariposa	Mariposa P O	74	127
Pew	33	m	c	CHIN	San Francisco	6-Wd San Francisco	81	41
Pin	14	m	c	CHIN	San Francisco	1-Wd San Francisco	79	54
Quan	46	m	c	CHIN	Calaveras	San Andreas P O	70	211
Que	44	m	c	CHIN	Butte	Concow Twp	70	10
Sing	50	m	c	CHIN	Calaveras	Copperopolis P O	70	264
Sing	50	m	c	CHIN	Butte	Kimshew Tpw	70	84
Sing	5	m	c	CHIN	Butte	Ophir Twp	70	104
Tay	22	f	c	CHIN	Placer	Bath P O	76	439
War	26	f	c	CHIN	San Francisco	6-Wd San Francisco	81	60
Wi	31	f	c	CHIN	Tuolumne	Columbia P O	93	341
Wy	36	m	c	CHIN	Alameda	Washington Twp	68	271
Yee	40	m	c	CHIN	Yolo	Washington Twp	93	536
You	35	m	c	CHIN	Monterey	Monterey Twp	74	347
CHOND								
Ah	26	m	c	CHIN	San Francisco	3-Wd San Francisco	79	301
CHONE								
Ah	26	m	c	CHIN	Nevada	Grass Valley Twp	75	197
Ah	26	m	c	CHIN	Trinity	Junction City Pct	92	206
Ah	20	m	c	CHIN	Trinity	Canyon City Pct	92	201
Christofer	31	m	w	HANO	Inyo	Cerro Gordo Twp	73	319
CHONG								
---	37	m	c	CHIN	Shasta	Horsetown P O	89	506
---	27	m	c	CHIN	San Francisco	11-Wd San Francisc	84	702
---	19	m	c	CHIN	Siskiyou	Yreka Twp	89	668
---	19	m	c	CHIN	San Francisco	6-Wd San Francisco	81	64
Ah	56	m	c	CHIN	Amador	Volcano P O	69	383
Ah	53	m	c	CHIN	San Joaquin	1-Wd Stockton	86	148
Ah	53	m	c	CHIN	Calaveras	Copperopolis P O	70	251
Ah	52	m	c	CHIN	San Francisco	2-Wd San Francisco	79	285
Ah	51	m	c	CHIN	San Mateo	Schoolhouse Statio	87	332
Ah	50	m	c	CHIN	San Francisco	6-Wd San Francisco	81	46
Ah	50	m	c	CHIN	San Francisco	San Francisco P O	80	489
Ah	50	m	c	CHIN	San Francisco	11-Wd San Francisc	84	528
Ah	48	m	c	CHIN	Butte	Hamilton Twp	70	74
Ah	46	m	c	CHIN	San Francisco	San Francisco P O	80	515
Ah	44	m	c	CHIN	San Francisco	6-Wd San Francisco	81	43
Ah	44	m	c	CHIN	Nevada	Eureka Twp	75	127
Ah	43	m	c	CHIN	Tuolumne	Columbia P O	93	350
Ah	42	m	c	CHIN	Mariposa	Maxwell Crk P O	74	145
Ah	42	m	c	CHIN	Butte	Concow Twp	70	11
Ah	42	m	c	CHIN	Santa Clara	Fremont Twp	88	64
Ah	42	m	c	CHIN	San Francisco	San Francisco P O	80	455
Ah	42	m	c	CHIN	El Dorado	Kelsey Twp	72	59
Ah	42	m	c	CHIN	Nevada	Eureka Twp	75	136
Ah	41	m	c	CHIN	Nevada	Rough & Ready Twp	75	332
Ah	41	m	c	CHIN	Nevada	Meadow Lake Twp	75	266
Ah	40	m	c	CHIN	San Francisco	6-Wd San Francisco	81	42
Ah	40	m	c	CHIN	Tuolumne	Chinese Camp P O	93	379
Ah	40	m	c	CHIN	San Francisco	San Francisco P O	80	442
Ah	40	m	c	CHIN	Nevada	Meadow Lake Twp	75	260
Ah	40	m	c	CHIN	Butte	Chico Twp	70	40
Ah	40	m	c	CHIN	Trinity	North Fork Twp	92	216
Ah	40	m	c	CHIN	Santa Clara	1-Wd San Jose	88	254
Ah	40	m	c	CHIN	San Francisco	San Francisco P O	80	507
Ah	40	m	c	CHIN	Butte	Chico Twp	70	42
Ah	40	m	c	CHIN	Butte	Chico Twp	70	51
Ah	40	m	c	CHIN	Nevada	Grass Valley Twp	75	205
Ah	39	m	c	CHIN	Butte	Oregon Twp	70	135
Ah	39	m	c	CHIN	Butte	Hamilton Twp	70	67
Ah	38	m	c	CHIN	Santa Cruz	Pajaro Twp	89	345
Ah	38	m	c	CHIN	San Francisco	San Francisco P O	80	440
Ah	38	f	c	CHIN	Calaveras	Copperopolis P O	70	234
Ah	38	m	c	CHIN	Santa Clara	Alviso Twp	88	28
Ah	38	m	c	CHIN	Santa Clara	Alviso Twp	88	27
Ah	37	m	c	CHIN	El Dorado	White Oak Twp	72	142
Ah	37	m	c	CHIN	Santa Clara	1-Wd San Jose	88	270
Ah	37	m	c	CHIN	Santa Clara	1-Wd San Jose	88	273
Ah	37	m	c	CHIN	San Francisco	San Francisco P O	80	521
Ah	37	m	c	CHIN	Nevada	Eureka Twp	75	136
Ah	36	m	c	CHIN	Nevada	Meadow Lake Twp	75	259
Ah	36	m	c	CHIN	Merced	Snelling P O	74	279
Ah	36	m	c	CHIN	San Francisco	San Francisco P O	83	127
Ah	36	m	c	CHIN	El Dorado	Diamond Springs Tw	72	34
Ah	35	m	c	CHIN	San Francisco	6-Wd San Francisco	81	66
Ah	35	m	c	CHIN	Shasta	French Gulch P O	89	464
Ah	35	m	c	CHIN	Placer	Bath P O	76	424
Ah	35	m	c	CHIN	Amador	Fiddletown P O	69	428
Ah	35	m	c	CHIN	Calaveras	San Andreas P O	70	180
Ah	35	m	c	CHIN	Amador	Volcano P O	69	387
Ah	34	m	c	CHIN	Yuba	Marysville Twp	93	569
Ah	34	m	c	CHIN	Tuolumne	Chinese Camp P O	93	384
Ah	34	m	c	CHIN	San Francisco	2-Wd San Francisco	79	282
Ah	34	m	c	CHIN	Santa Clara	Fremont Twp	88	57
Ah	34	m	c	CHIN	San Francisco	San Francisco P O	80	510

© 2001 by Heritage Quest. All rights reserved.

Name	Age	S	R	B-PL	County	Locale	Series M593 Roll	Pg
Ah	34	m	c	CHIN	Butte	Ophir Twp	70	106
Ah	33	m	c	CHIN	San Joaquin	1-Wd Stockton	86	147
Ah	33	m	c	CHIN	San Francisco	San Francisco P O	80	436
Ah	33	m	c	CHIN	Placer	Dutch Flat P O	76	409
Ah	32	m	c	CHIN	San Francisco	6-Wd San Francisco	81	38
Ah	32	m	c	CHIN	Solano	Suisun Twp	90	105
Ah	32	m	c	CHIN	San Francisco	San Francisco P O	80	440
Ah	32	m	c	CHIN	Nevada	Rough & Ready Twp	75	324
Ah	32	m	c	CHIN	Butte	Oregon Twp	70	133
Ah	32	m	c	CHIN	Calaveras	San Andreas P O	70	172
Ah	32	m	c	CHIN	Butte	Chico Twp	70	30
Ah	32	m	c	CHIN	Butte	Hamilton Twp	70	68
Ah	32	m	c	CHIN	Santa Clara	2-Wd San Jose	88	285
Ah	31	m	c	CHIN	Nevada	Nevada Twp	75	312
Ah	31	m	c	CHIN	Placer	Auburn P O	76	371
Ah	31	m	c	CHIN	Yuba	Marysville	93	600
Ah	31	m	c	CHIN	San Mateo	Schoolhouse Statio	87	341
Ah	30	m	c	CHIN	San Joaquin	1-Wd Stockton	86	142
Ah	30	m	c	CHIN	San Joaquin	1-Wd Stockton	86	146
Ah	30	m	c	CHIN	San Francisco	6-Wd San Francisco	81	66
Ah	30	m	c	CHIN	San Francisco	6-Wd San Francisco	81	66
Ah	30	m	c	CHIN	Nevada	Rough & Ready Twp	75	324
Ah	30	m	c	CHIN	Mariposa	Mariposa P O	74	126
Ah	30	m	c	CHIN	Butte	Oregon Twp	70	131
Ah	30	m	c	CHIN	Butte	Ophir Twp	70	104
Ah	30	m	c	CHIN	Amador	Ione City P O	69	367
Ah	30	m	c	CHIN	Amador	Ione City P O	69	358
Ah	30	m	c	CHIN	Placer	Emigrant Gap P O	76	416
Ah	29	m	c	CHIN	Nevada	Meadow Lake Twp	75	266
Ah	29	m	c	CHIN	Butte	Ophir Twp	70	119
Ah	29	m	c	CHIN	Santa Clara	1-Wd San Jose	88	277
Ah	29	m	c	CHIN	San Francisco	San Francisco P O	80	525
Ah	29	m	c	CHIN	Amador	Jackson P O	69	328
Ah	29	m	c	CHIN	Nevada	Eureka Twp	75	136
Ah	28	m	c	CHIN	San Francisco	San Francisco P O	85	748
Ah	28	m	c	CHIN	San Mateo	Schoolhouse Statio	87	338
Ah	28	m	c	CHIN	Placer	Auburn P O	76	371
Ah	28	m	c	CHIN	Santa Clara	Santa Clara Twp	88	168
Ah	28	m	c	CHIN	Santa Clara	2-Wd San Jose	88	297
Ah	28	m	c	CHIN	Calaveras	San Andreas P O	70	169
Ah	28	m	c	CHIN	Nevada	Bridgeport Twp	75	114
Ah	27	m	c	CHIN	San Francisco	San Francisco P O	85	748
Ah	27	m	c	CHIN	Solano	Suisun Twp	90	106
Ah	27	m	c	CHIN	San Francisco	2-Wd San Francisco	79	286
Ah	27	m	c	CHIN	San Francisco	San Francisco P O	80	431
Ah	27	m	c	CHIN	Santa Barbara	San Buenaventura P	87	438
Ah	27	m	c	CHIN	San Francisco	San Francisco P O	80	499
Ah	26	m	c	CHIN	San Francisco	6-Wd San Francisco	81	39
Ah	26	m	c	CHIN	San Francisco	San Francisco P O	80	499
Ah	26	m	c	CHIN	Tuolumne	Chinese Camp P O	93	382
Ah	26	m	c	CHIN	Nevada	Rough & Ready Twp	75	329
Ah	26	m	c	CHIN	Colusa	Grand Island Twp	71	309
Ah	25	m	c	CHIN	Placer	Lincoln P O	76	483
Ah	25	m	c	CHIN	Placer	Clipper Gap P O	76	376
Ah	25	f	c	CHIN	Butte	Ophir Twp	70	106
Ah	25	m	c	CHIN	Trinity	North Fork Twp	92	216
Ah	25	m	c	CHIN	Santa Clara	San Jose Twp	88	179
Ah	25	m	c	CHIN	San Francisco	6-Wd San Francisco	81	38
Ah	25	m	c	CHIN	San Francisco	San Francisco P O	83	136
Ah	25	m	c	CHIN	Nevada	Eureka Twp	75	127
Ah	24	m	c	CHIN	Santa Clara	San Jose Twp	88	192
Ah	24	m	c	CHIN	Nevada	Meadow Lake Twp	75	256
Ah	24	m	c	CHIN	Butte	Ophir Twp	70	103
Ah	24	m	c	CHIN	Butte	Chico Twp	70	30
Ah	24	m	c	CHIN	Santa Clara	San Jose Twp	88	179
Ah	24	f	c	CHIN	Santa Clara	1-Wd San Jose	88	269
Ah	24	m	c	CHIN	Santa Clara	1-Wd San Jose	88	272
Ah	24	m	c	CHIN	San Francisco	San Francisco P O	83	398
Ah	24	m	c	CHIN	Placer	Bath P O	76	452
Ah	24	m	c	CHIN	Yuba	Marysville	93	619
Ah	23	m	c	CHIN	Santa Clara	San Jose Twp	88	180
Ah	23	m	c	CHIN	Butte	Concow Twp	70	11
Ah	23	m	c	CHIN	Santa Clara	1-Wd San Jose	88	277
Ah	22	m	c	CHIN	Santa Clara	Milpitas Twp	88	113
Ah	22	m	c	CHIN	Sacramento	2-Wd Sacramento	77	226
Ah	22	m	c	CHIN	Sacramento	2-Wd Sacramento	77	250
Ah	22	m	c	CHIN	Santa Clara	1-Wd San Jose	88	270
Ah	22	m	c	CHIN	San Mateo	San Mateo P O	87	351
Ah	22	m	c	CHIN	San Mateo	Schoolhouse Statio	87	344
Ah	21	m	c	CHIN	Santa Clara	San Jose Twp	88	192
Ah	21	m	c	CHIN	San Francisco	1-Wd San Francisco	79	106
Ah	21	f	c	CHIN	San Francisco	San Francisco P O	80	438
Ah	21	m	c	CHIN	Santa Clara	1-Wd San Jose	88	274
Ah	21	m	c	CHIN	Santa Clara	1-Wd San Jose	88	277
Ah	21	m	c	CHIN	San Francisco	6-Wd San Francisco	81	53
Ah	21	m	c	CHIN	Butte	Concow Twp	70	10
Ah	20	m	c	CHIN	San Francisco	San Francisco P O	83	86
Ah	20	m	c	CHIN	Shasta	French Gulch P O	89	467
Ah	20	m	c	CHIN	Yolo	Putah Twp	93	513
Ah	20	m	c	CHIN	Tuolumne	Sonora P O	93	332
Ah	20	m	c	CHIN	Trinity	Lewiston Pct	92	211
Ah	20	m	c	CHIN	Santa Clara	Fremont Twp	88	48
Ah	20	m	c	CHIN	Santa Clara	2-Wd San Jose	88	319
Ah	20	m	c	CHIN	San Francisco	6-Wd San Francisco	81	150
Ah	19	m	c	CHIN	Santa Clara	San Jose Twp	88	189
Ah	19	m	c	CHIN	San Francisco	6-Wd San Francisco	81	44
Ah	19	m	c	CHIN	Santa Cruz	Santa Cruz	89	408
Ah	19	m	c	CHIN	Santa Cruz	Soquel Twp	89	446
Ah	19	m	c	CHIN	Santa Clara	Alviso Twp	88	25
Ah	19	m	c	CHIN	San Francisco	3-Wd San Francisco	79	304
Ah	19	m	c	CHIN	San Francisco	3-Wd San Francisco	79	307
Ah	19	f	c	CHIN	San Francisco	San Francisco P O	80	450
Ah	19	m	c	CHIN	Sacramento	2-Wd Sacramento	77	234
Ah	19	f	c	CHIN	Santa Clara	1-Wd San Jose	88	269
Ah	19	m	c	CHIN	Santa Clara	Fremont Twp	88	66
Ah	18	m	c	CHIN	Santa Clara	1-Wd San Jose	88	225
Ah	18	m	c	CHIN	Trinity	Douglas	92	233
Ah	18	f	c	CHIN	San Francisco	San Francisco P O	80	431
Ah	18	m	c	CHIN	Placer	Clipper Gap P O	76	393
Ah	18	m	c	CHIN	Mendocino	Big Rvr Twp	74	170
Ah	18	m	c	CHIN	San Francisco	6-Wd San Francisco	81	119
Ah	18	f	c	CHIN	San Francisco	San Francisco P O	80	506
Ah	17	m	c	CHIN	San Joaquin	1-Wd Stockton	86	148
Ah	17	m	c	CHIN	San Francisco	6-Wd San Francisco	81	67
Ah	17	f	c	CHIN	San Francisco	6-Wd San Francisco	81	74
Ah	16	m	c	CHIN	Santa Clara	1-Wd San Jose	88	271
Ah	16	m	c	CHIN	Santa Clara	Gilroy Twp	88	81
Ah	16	m	c	CHIN	San Francisco	7-Wd San Francisco	81	239
Ah	16	m	c	CHIN	San Francisco	2-Wd San Francisco	79	172
Ah	15	m	c	CHIN	Shasta	French Gulch P O	89	465
Ah	15	m	c	CHIN	Santa Cruz	Santa Cruz	89	427
Ah	15	m	c	CHIN	San Francisco	San Francisco P O	80	417
Ah	15	m	c	CHIN	San Francisco	6-Wd San Francisco	81	142
Ah	15	m	c	CHIN	San Francisco	6-Wd San Francisco	81	69
Ah	14	m	c	CHIN	San Francisco	San Francisco P O	83	393
Ah	13	m	c	CHIN	San Francisco	2-Wd San Francisco	79	233
Ah He	45	m	c	CHIN	Calaveras	San Andreas P O	70	172
Ah Hong	26	m	c	CHIN	Monterey	Monterey	74	358
Ang	43	m	c	CHIN	Plumas	Seneca Twp	77	48
Ang	18	f	c	CHIN	Amador	Fiddletown P O	69	428
Ar	40	m	c	CHIN	Sonoma	Sonoma Twp	91	447
Ar	38	m	c	CHIN	Sonoma	Petaluma Twp	91	363
Beng	20	m	c	CHIN	Yuba	Marysville	93	632
Chon	46	m	c	CHIN	Calaveras	San Andreas P O	70	171
Co	55	m	c	CHIN	Santa Clara	Alviso Twp	88	25
Fook	20	m	c	CHIN	San Francisco	11-Wd San Francisc	84	546
Fung	33	m	c	CHIN	Alpine	Woodfords P O	69	310
Fung	20	m	c	CHIN	Nevada	Nevada Twp	75	314
Gee	41	m	c	CHIN	Butte	Wyandotte Twp	70	147
Gee	40	m	c	CHIN	Yuba	Bullards Bar P O	93	552
George	30	m	c	CHIN	Colusa	Colusa	71	299
Hi	48	m	c	CHIN	San Joaquin	1-Wd Stockton	86	148
Hi	26	m	c	CHIN	Sacramento	2-Wd Sacramento	77	233
High	41	m	c	CHIN	Yuba	Marysville	93	624
Hine	14	m	c	CHIN	Shasta	Shasta P O	89	452
Hing	40	m	c	CHIN	Tuolumne	Columbia P O	93	342
Hong	32	m	c	CHIN	Placer	Newcastle Twp	76	479
Hong	28	m	c	CHIN	Solano	Suisun Twp	90	106
Hop	30	m	c	CHIN	San Mateo	Schoolhouse Statio	87	334
Hung	30	m	c	CHIN	San Francisco	7-Wd San Francisco	81	215
Jim	31	m	c	CHIN	Santa Clara	1-Wd San Jose	88	270
Jim	30	m	c	CHIN	Colusa	Colusa	71	291
Kee	53	m	c	CHIN	San Francisco	2-Wd San Francisco	79	285
Kee	36	m	c	CHIN	Santa Clara	1-Wd San Jose	88	273
Kee	30	m	c	CHIN	Santa Clara	1-Wd San Jose	88	270
Kee	30	m	c	CHIN	San Francisco	2-Wd San Francisco	79	184
Kee	22	m	c	CHIN	Nevada	Rough & Ready Twp	75	337
Kin	29	m	c	CHIN	Nevada	Rough & Ready Twp	75	324
Kin	22	m	c	CHIN	Butte	Concow Twp	70	11
Kow	32	m	c	CHIN	San Francisco	6-Wd San Francisco	81	51
La	32	m	c	CHIN	San Francisco	11-Wd San Francisc	84	529
Lai	22	m	c	CHIN	San Francisco	6-Wd San Francisco	81	37
Le	27	m	c	CHIN	Santa Clara	1-Wd San Jose	88	277
Lee	27	m	c	CHIN	El Dorado	Cosumnes Twp	72	15
Lee	24	m	c	CHIN	San Joaquin	Liberty Twp	86	83
Lim	39	m	c	CHIN	Shasta	American Ranch P O	89	499
Lo	34	m	c	CHIN	San Joaquin	1-Wd Stockton	86	144
Lo	24	m	c	CHIN	Butte	Chico Twp	70	31
Long	30	m	c	CHIN	Sacramento	1-Wd Sacramento	77	194
Long	22	m	c	CHIN	Tehama	Tehama Twp	92	188
Long	18	m	c	CHIN	San Francisco	2-Wd San Francisco	79	158
Loy	45	m	c	CHIN	Yuba	Marysville	93	621
Lung	31	m	c	CHIN	Solano	Suisun Twp	90	107
Mong	24	m	c	CHIN	San Francisco	2-Wd San Francisco	79	229
Mung	30	m	c	CHIN	Yuba	Marysville	93	632
Noy	34	m	c	CHIN	Butte	Chico Twp	70	52
Po	31	m	c	CHIN	San Joaquin	1-Wd Stockton	86	146
Pong	24	m	c	CHIN	Solano	Suisun Twp	90	106
Quang	52	m	c	CHIN	Yuba	Marysville	93	624
San	25	m	c	CHIN	Colusa	Grand Island Twp	71	306
Sang	29	m	c	CHIN	Santa Clara	1-Wd San Jose	88	273
See	28	m	c	CHIN	Santa Clara	Alviso Twp	88	26
See	18	m	c	CHIN	Nevada	Washington Twp	75	347
Sing	39	m	c	CHIN	Yuba	Marysville	93	622
Sing	35	m	c	CHIN	Mariposa	Mariposa P O	74	113
Sloo	35	m	c	CHIN	Tulare	Visalia	92	299
Soo	31	m	c	CHIN	Yuba	Marysville	93	632
Soy	38	m	c	CHIN	Amador	Jackson P O	69	332
Tchun	14	m	c	CHIN	San Francisco	11-Wd San Francisc	84	529
Tee	40	m	c	CHIN	Colusa	Colusa	71	299
Ti	34	m	c	CHIN	Nevada	Nevada Twp	75	314
Toung	20	m	c	CHIN	San Francisco	11-Wd San Francisc	84	529
Tow	60	m	c	CHIN	Nevada	Nevada Twp	75	313
Wan	39	m	c	CHIN	Sierra	Downieville Twp	89	520

© 2001 by Heritage Quest. All rights reserved.

Name	Age	S	R	B-PL	County	Locale	Roll	Pg
Wee	41	m	c	CHIN	Santa Clara	1-Wd San Jose	88	272
Wee	32	m	c	CHIN	Santa Clara	Alviso Twp	88	25
Wi	27	m	c	CHIN	Santa Clara	San Jose Twp	88	179
Wing	27	m	c	CHIN	Solano	Suisun Twp	90	106
Wong	36	m	c	CHIN	San Francisco	6-Wd San Francisco	81	38
Yne	48	m	c	CHIN	San Joaquin	1-Wd Stockton	86	148
Yung	17	m	c	CHIN	San Francisco	11-Wd San Francisc	84	529
CHONLUR								
Antonio	35	m	w	SWIT	Amador	Jackson P O	69	333
CHOO								
---	30	m	c	CHIN	Shasta	Shasta P O	89	454
---	26	m	c	CHIN	Shasta	Shasta P O	89	454
Ah	70	m	c	CHIN	Nevada	Bridgeport Twp	75	110
Ah	50	m	c	CHIN	Tuolumne	Chinese Camp P O	93	380
Ah	50	m	c	CHIN	Tuolumne	Chinese Camp P O	93	380
Ah	50	m	c	CHIN	San Francisco	San Francisco P O	80	453
Ah	45	m	c	CHIN	Calaveras	Copperopolis P O	70	244
Ah	44	m	c	CHIN	Calaveras	Copperopolis P O	70	233
Ah	43	m	c	CHIN	Nevada	Nevada Twp	75	311
Ah	42	m	c	CHIN	San Francisco	San Francisco P O	80	524
Ah	4	f	c	CHIN	San Francisco	San Francisco P O	80	525
Ah	3M	f	c	CA	San Francisco	San Francisco P O	80	530
Ah	37	m	c	CHIN	San Francisco	San Francisco P O	80	445
Ah	37	m	c	CHIN	Calaveras	Copperopolis P O	70	234
Ah	34	m	c	CHIN	Stanislaus	Branch Twp	92	4
Ah	34	m	c	CHIN	Stanislaus	Empire Twp	92	64
Ah	34	m	c	CHIN	Tuolumne	Big Oak Flat P O	93	393
Ah	32	m	c	CHIN	Stanislaus	Empire Twp	92	64
Ah	31	m	c	CHIN	Marin	Point Reyes Twp	74	21
Ah	31	m	c	CHIN	San Francisco	San Francisco P O	80	518
Ah	30	m	c	CHIN	Calaveras	Copperopolis P O	70	225
Ah	28	m	c	CHIN	Calaveras	Copperopolis P O	70	254
Ah	28	m	c	CHIN	Calaveras	Copperopolis P O	70	257
Ah	28	m	c	CHIN	Kern	Bakersfield P O	73	361
Ah	27	m	c	CHIN	Sierra	Forest Twp	89	532
Ah	27	m	c	CHIN	Nevada	Washington Twp	75	347
Ah	26	m	c	CHIN	San Francisco	3-Wd San Francisco	79	310
Ah	26	m	c	CHIN	San Francisco	San Francisco P O	80	523
Ah	24	m	c	CHIN	Sacramento	3-Wd Sacramento	77	303
Ah	23	m	c	CHIN	San Francisco	5-Wd San Francisco	81	16
Ah	21	m	c	CHIN	Yolo	Cache Crk Twp	93	426
Ah	20	f	c	CHIN	San Francisco	San Francisco P O	80	437
Ah	20	m	c	CHIN	San Francisco	11-Wd San Francisc	84	521
Ah	20	f	c	CHIN	San Francisco	San Francisco P O	80	507
Ah	20	f	c	CHIN	San Francisco	San Francisco P O	80	506
Ah	18	f	c	CHIN	San Francisco	6-Wd San Francisco	81	77
Ah	18	f	c	CHIN	San Francisco	San Francisco P O	80	526
Chien	21	m	c	CHIN	San Francisco	11-Wd San Francisc	84	546
Coon	27	f	c	CHIN	Yuba	Marysville	93	627
Hame	61	m	c	CHIN	Shasta	American Ranch P O	89	500
He	38	m	c	CHIN	San Joaquin	1-Wd Stockton	86	149
Hoy	23	m	c	CHIN	Yolo	Cache Crk Twp	93	424
Kay	57	m	c	CHIN	Shasta	American Ranch P O	89	500
Kee	28	m	c	CHIN	Butte	Chico Twp	70	51
Lee	33	m	c	CHIN	Stanislaus	Branch Twp	92	1
Lee	24	m	c	CHIN	Marin	San Rafael Twp	74	34
Loo	38	m	c	CHIN	San Joaquin	Castoria Twp	86	13
Lum	33	m	c	CHIN	San Francisco	6-Wd San Francisco	81	50
Nimb	28	m	c	CHIN	Nevada	Nevada Twp	75	312
Ping	30	m	c	CHIN	Tulare	Visalia	92	300
Poo	26	m	c	CHIN	Tehama	Tehama Twp	92	188
Sang	15	m	c	CHIN	Shasta	American Ranch P O	89	500
Ti	28	m	c	CHIN	Santa Clara	Fremont Twp	88	66
Wan	30	m	c	CHIN	Shasta	American Ranch P O	89	500
Wing	40	m	c	CHIN	San Francisco	San Francisco P O	80	490
Wing	22	m	c	CHIN	Nevada	Nevada Twp	75	313
Yan	36	m	c	CHIN	Shasta	American Ranch P O	89	496
CHOOK								
Ah	32	m	c	CHIN	Sierra	Sears Twp	89	553
Ah	21	m	c	CHIN	Santa Clara	2-Wd San Jose	88	322
CHOOKEE								
Ah	19	m	c	CHIN	Santa Clara	Fremont Twp	88	65
CHOON								
Ah	30	m	c	CHIN	San Francisco	6-Wd San Francisco	81	75
Ah	30	m	c	CHIN	Shasta	French Gulch P O	89	465
Ah	28	m	c	CHIN	Shasta	French Gulch P O	89	467
Ah	26	m	c	CHIN	San Francisco	3-Wd San Francisco	79	307
Ah	25	m	c	CHIN	San Francisco	6-Wd San Francisco	81	75
Ah	23	m	c	CHIN	San Francisco	6-Wd San Francisco	81	56
Ah	21	m	c	CHIN	Plumas	Washington Twp	77	57
Ah	20	m	c	CHIN	Nevada	Eureka Twp	75	127
Ah	20	m	c	CHIN	Plumas	Washington Twp	77	57
Ah	19	m	c	CHIN	San Francisco	San Francisco P O	85	748
Ah	17	m	c	CHIN	San Francisco	6-Wd San Francisco	81	43
Ang	40	m	c	CHIN	Plumas	Seneca Twp	77	48
Cam	52	m	c	CHIN	Shasta	Horsetown P O	89	506
Gee	15	m	c	CHIN	Plumas	Mineral Twp	77	24
War	13	f	c	CHIN	San Francisco	6-Wd San Francisco	81	67
CHOONG								
Ah	30	m	c	CHIN	Shasta	French Gulch P O	89	466
Ah	24	m	c	CHIN	Plumas	Seneca Twp	77	48
Ong	48	m	c	CHIN	Nevada	Nevada Twp	75	315
CHOP								
Ah	67	m	c	CHIN	San Joaquin	1-Wd Stockton	86	146
Ah	47	m	c	CHIN	Nevada	Nevada Twp	75	312
Ah	45	m	c	CHIN	Sacramento	1-Wd Sacramento	77	197
Ah	37	m	c	CHIN	Siskiyou	Cottonwood Twp	89	593
Ah	36	m	c	CHIN	El Dorado	Georgetown Twp	72	41
Ah	36	m	c	CHIN	Tuolumne	Chinese Camp P O	93	377
Ah	32	m	c	CHIN	San Joaquin	1-Wd Stockton	86	148
Ah	29	m	c	CHIN	San Joaquin	Douglas Twp	86	47
Ah	29	m	c	CHIN	Tuolumne	Columbia P O	93	349
Ah	29	m	c	CHIN	San Joaquin	1-Wd Stockton	86	146
Ah	28	m	c	CHIN	Sacramento	Granite Twp	77	138
Ah	24	m	c	CHIN	Plumas	Washington Twp	77	53
Ah	24	m	c	CHIN	San Francisco	San Francisco P O	80	497
Ah	21	m	c	CHIN	San Joaquin	1-Wd Stockton	86	151
Ah	20	m	c	CHIN	San Francisco	6-Wd San Francisco	81	57
Ah	18	m	c	CHIN	San Francisco	6-Wd San Francisco	81	65
Chon	23	m	c	CHIN	Sierra	Butte Twp	89	513
Lin	26	m	c	CHIN	San Joaquin	Douglas Twp	86	49
Lo	18	m	c	CHIN	San Joaquin	1-Wd Stockton	86	146
See	37	m	c	CHIN	Sierra	Lincoln Twp	89	548
See	31	m	c	CHIN	Tuolumne	Big Oak Flat P O	93	392
Sep	22	m	c	CHIN	Solano	Vacaville Twp	90	130
Sing	28	m	c	CHIN	Sierra	Lincoln Twp	89	548
CHOPARD								
Gustave	49	m	w	FRAN	Alameda	Brooklyn Twp	68	40
Louis	31	m	w	SWIT	Santa Clara	1-Wd San Jose	88	262
CHOPAT								
Lewis	28	m	w	FRAN	San Joaquin	2-Wd Stockton	86	173
CHOPE								
Alexander	49	m	w	ENGL	Humboldt	Eureka Twp	72	268
CHOPSON								
Thos	59	m	w	VA	Napa	Yountville Twp	75	79
CHORD								
Daniel	51	m	w	OH	Napa	Napa	75	8
Mahala	32	f	w	IN	Napa	Napa	75	22
Wm	45	m	w	ENGL	San Francisco	11-Wd San Francisc	84	613
CHORE								
F W	45	m	w	MA	San Joaquin	1-Wd Stockton	86	138
CHORESS								
Francis	51	m	w	FRAN	San Francisco	11-Wd San Francisc	84	611
CHOREY								
Tallerand	43	m	w	KY	San Luis Obispo	Salinas Twp	87	289
CHORM								
Soon	70	m	c	CHIN	Amador	Fiddletown P O	69	426
CHORR								
Ah	21	m	c	CHIN	Nevada	Grass Valley Twp	75	151
CHORY								
Ah	32	m	c	CHIN	Kern	Bakersfield P O	73	357
Sin	27	f	c	CHIN	Kern	Bakersfield P O	73	359
CHOSE								
Daniel	40	m	w	ME	Calaveras	San Andreas P O	70	180
Geo C	58	m	w	NH	Sierra	Downieville Twp	89	515
Li	27	m	c	CHIN	Nevada	Bridgeport Twp	75	111
CHOSSAGNE								
Leon	27	m	w	FRAN	San Francisco	2-Wd San Francisco	79	191
CHOT								
Ah	50	m	c	CHIN	San Francisco	6-Wd San Francisco	81	48
CHOU								
Ah	40	m	c	CHIN	Yuba	Marysville	93	625
Ah	22	m	c	CHIN	Sonoma	Bodega Twp	91	261
Fow	29	f	c	CHIN	Yuba	Marysville	93	627
CHOUG								
Ah	30	m	c	CHIN	Placer	Colfax P O	76	389
CHOUN								
Chas	30	m	w	WURT	San Joaquin	Liberty Twp	86	96
CHOUR								
Eh	28	m	c	CHIN	Amador	Volcano P O	69	387
CHOUTE								
Moses	42	m	w	ME	Placer	Auburn P O	76	360
CHOVIS								
Francisco	48	m	w	MEXI	Monterey	San Juan Twp	74	415
CHOVOREN								
Joaquin	50	m	w	CA	Los Angeles	Los Angeles Twp	73	475
CHOW								
Ah	76	m	c	CHIN	Trinity	North Fork Twp	92	218
Ah	68	m	c	CHIN	Mariposa	Mariposa P O	74	114
Ah	64	m	c	CHIN	Butte	Ophir Twp	70	104
Ah	61	m	c	CHIN	El Dorado	Mud Springs Twp	72	87
Ah	60	m	c	CHIN	Santa Clara	1-Wd San Jose	88	272
Ah	58	m	c	CHIN	Mariposa	Mariposa P O	74	127
Ah	57	m	c	CHIN	Amador	Drytown P O	69	424
Ah	55	m	c	CHIN	San Mateo	San Mateo P O	87	351
Ah	54	m	c	CHIN	San Francisco	6-Wd San Francisco	81	84
Ah	54	m	c	CHIN	Mariposa	Mariposa P O	74	103
Ah	52	m	c	CHIN	Calaveras	San Andreas P O	70	171
Ah	52	m	c	CHIN	Amador	Fiddletown P O	69	427
Ah	51	m	c	CHIN	Mariposa	Maxwell Crk P O	74	139
Ah	48	m	c	CHIN	San Francisco	San Francisco P O	80	513
Ah	48	m	c	CHIN	Mariposa	Mariposa P O	74	115
Ah	46	m	c	CHIN	Butte	Ophir Twp	70	103
Ah	46	m	c	CHIN	Sierra	Lincoln Twp	89	548
Ah	46	m	c	CHIN	Stanislaus	North Twp	92	67
Ah	45	m	c	CHIN	El Dorado	Mud Springs Twp	72	73
Ah	45	m	c	CHIN	El Dorado	Diamond Springs Tw	72	25
Ah	45	m	c	CHIN	Monterey	Monterey Twp	74	352
Ah	45	m	c	CHIN	Nevada	Eureka Twp	75	127
Ah	45	m	c	CHIN	Trinity	North Fork Twp	92	219
Ah	45	m	c	CHIN	Mono	Bridgeport P O	74	283
Ah	44	m	c	CHIN	Nevada	Nevada Twp	75	298
Ah	44	m	c	CHIN	Trinity	Douglas	92	236
Ah	43	m	c	CHIN	San Mateo	Half Moon Bay P O	87	395

Series M593

© 2001 by Heritage Quest. All rights reserved.

Name	Age	S	R	B-PL	County	Locale	Series M593 Roll	Pg
Ah	42	m	c	CHIN	San Mateo	Schoolhouse Statio	87	332
Ah	41	m	c	CHIN	Amador	Lancha Plana P O	69	369
Ah	41	m	c	CHIN	Sierra	Forest Twp	89	528
Ah	41	m	c	CHIN	San Francisco	6-Wd San Francisco	81	57
Ah	41	m	c	CHIN	San Francisco	San Francisco P O	80	436
Ah	41	m	c	CHIN	Mariposa	Mariposa P O	74	105
Ah	41	m	c	CHIN	Mono	Bridgeport P O	74	283
Ah	41	m	c	CHIN	Calaveras	San Andreas P O	70	169
Ah	40	m	c	CHIN	El Dorado	Diamond Springs Tw	72	25
Ah	40	m	c	CHIN	Butte	Chico Twp	70	52
Ah	40	m	c	CHIN	Alameda	Eden Twp	68	58
Ah	40	m	c	CHIN	Mariposa	Maxwell Crk P O	74	145
Ah	40	m	c	CHIN	Plumas	Rich Bar Twp	77	45
Ah	40	m	c	CHIN	San Mateo	Schoolhouse Statio	87	344
Ah	40	m	c	CHIN	Solano	Vallejo	90	140
Ah	40	m	c	CHIN	Placer	Auburn P O	76	378
Ah	40	m	c	CHIN	Placer	Lincoln P O	76	483
Ah	40	f	c	CHIN	San Francisco	San Francisco P O	80	450
Ah	40	m	c	CHIN	San Francisco	San Francisco P O	80	446
Ah	40	m	c	CHIN	Butte	Ophir Twp	70	103
Ah	40	m	c	CHIN	Calaveras	San Andreas P O	70	211
Ah	40	m	c	CHIN	Butte	Chico Twp	70	28
Ah	40	m	c	CHIN	Shasta	French Gulch P O	89	464
Ah	39	m	c	CHIN	Trinity	Weaverville Pct	92	228
Ah	39	m	c	CHIN	Tuolumne	Big Oak Flat P O	93	392
Ah	38	m	c	CHIN	Butte	Wyandotte Twp	70	142
Ah	38	m	c	CHIN	Trinity	Weaverville Pct	92	228
Ah	38	m	c	CHIN	Mariposa	Mariposa P O	74	91
Ah	38	m	c	CHIN	Mariposa	Mariposa P O	74	103
Ah	38	m	c	CHIN	Butte	Hamilton Twp	70	73
Ah	37	m	c	CHIN	Fresno	Millerton P O	72	199
Ah	37	m	c	CHIN	Amador	Volcano P O	69	378
Ah	37	m	c	CHIN	Butte	Ophir Twp	70	117
Ah	37	m	c	CHIN	Nevada	Grass Valley Twp	75	208
Ah	37	m	c	CHIN	San Joaquin	Douglas Twp	86	51
Ah	37	m	c	CHIN	San Joaquin	3-Wd Stockton	86	215
Ah	37	m	c	CHIN	San Francisco	6-Wd San Francisco	81	57
Ah	37	m	c	CHIN	Mariposa	Mariposa P O	74	132
Ah	37	m	c	CHIN	San Joaquin	Castoria Twp	86	15
Ah	36	m	c	CHIN	Amador	Jackson P O	69	338
Ah	36	m	c	CHIN	San Francisco	San Francisco P O	80	509
Ah	36	m	c	CHIN	San Francisco	San Francisco P O	85	748
Ah	35	m	c	CHIN	El Dorado	Placerville	72	115
Ah	35	m	c	CHIN	Calaveras	Copperopolis P O	70	248
Ah	35	m	c	CHIN	San Francisco	6-Wd San Francisco	81	88
Ah	35	m	c	CHIN	Los Angeles	Wilmington Twp	73	636
Ah	35	m	c	CHIN	El Dorado	Placerville	72	124
Ah	34	m	c	CHIN	Placer	Auburn P O	76	362
Ah	34	m	c	CHIN	San Mateo	Woodside P O	87	381
Ah	34	m	c	CHIN	Nevada	Nevada Twp	75	297
Ah	34	f	w	CHIN	San Francisco	San Francisco P O	80	454
Ah	34	m	c	CHIN	Calaveras	Copperopolis P O	70	226
Ah	34	m	c	CHIN	Contra Costa	Martinez P O	71	436
Ah	34	m	c	CHIN	Sierra	Lincoln Twp	89	552
Ah	34	m	c	CHIN	Trinity	Douglas	92	236
Ah	32	m	c	CHIN	Amador	Jackson P O	69	332
Ah	32	m	c	CHIN	Placer	Auburn P O	76	372
Ah	32	m	c	CHIN	Santa Clara	1-Wd San Jose	88	272
Ah	32	m	c	CHIN	Yuba	Marysville	93	619
Ah	32	f	c	CHIN	San Francisco	San Francisco P O	80	454
Ah	32	m	c	CHIN	Mariposa	Mariposa P O	74	102
Ah	32	m	c	CHIN	Merced	Snelling P O	74	278
Ah	32	m	c	CHIN	Alameda	Oakland	68	158
Ah	32	m	c	CHIN	San Francisco	San Francisco P O	85	747
Ah	32	m	c	CHIN	Sierra	Lincoln Twp	89	549
Ah	31	m	c	CHIN	El Dorado	Kelsey Twp	72	59
Ah	31	m	c	CHIN	Amador	Ione City P O	69	371
Ah	31	m	c	CHIN	Amador	Lancha Plana P O	69	369
Ah	31	m	c	CHIN	Alameda	Alvarado	68	303
Ah	31	m	c	CHIN	Santa Clara	2-Wd San Jose	88	297
Ah	31	m	c	CHIN	San Francisco	San Francisco P O	80	506
Ah	31	m	c	CHIN	Yuba	Marysville	93	624
Ah	31	m	c	CHIN	Tuolumne	Big Oak Flat P O	93	392
Ah	31	m	c	CHIN	Yolo	Putah Twp	93	523
Ah	31	m	c	CHIN	Stanislaus	Empire Twp	92	46
Ah	30	m	c	CHIN	El Dorado	Georgetown Twp	72	36
Ah	30	m	c	CHIN	Alameda	Washington Twp	68	297
Ah	30	m	c	CHIN	Nevada	Eureka Twp	75	129
Ah	30	m	c	CHIN	Santa Clara	San Jose Twp	88	189
Ah	30	m	c	CHIN	San Francisco	6-Wd San Francisco	81	75
Ah	30	m	c	CHIN	San Francisco	6-Wd San Francisco	81	46
Ah	30	m	c	CHIN	San Francisco	6-Wd San Francisco	81	130
Ah	30	m	c	CHIN	San Francisco	San Francisco P O	80	509
Ah	30	m	c	CHIN	Stanislaus	Emory Twp	92	23
Ah	30	f	c	CHIN	San Francisco	San Francisco P O	80	454
Ah	30	f	c	CHIN	San Francisco	San Francisco P O	80	453
Ah	30	f	c	CHIN	San Francisco	San Francisco P O	80	453
Ah	30	f	c	CHIN	San Francisco	San Francisco P O	80	453
Ah	30	f	c	CHIN	San Francisco	San Francisco P O	80	438
Ah	30	f	c	CHIN	Mariposa	Mariposa P O	74	131
Ah	30	m	c	CHIN	Mariposa	Mariposa P O	74	103
Ah	30	m	c	CHIN	Mono	Bridgeport P O	74	284
Ah	30	m	c	CHIN	Butte	Chico Twp	70	29
Ah	30	m	c	CHIN	San Mateo	San Mateo P O	87	350
Ah	30	m	c	CHIN	Sierra	Forest Twp	89	528
Ah	30	m	c	CHIN	Stanislaus	Empire Twp	92	58
Ah	29	m	c	CHIN	Amador	Ione City P O	69	349
Ah	29	m	c	CHIN	Butte	Concow Twp	70	12
Ah	29	m	c	CHIN	Alameda	Eden Twp	68	61
Ah	29	m	c	CHIN	Nevada	Grass Valley Twp	75	206
Ah	29	m	c	CHIN	San Joaquin	3-Wd Stockton	86	232
Ah	29	m	c	CHIN	San Francisco	San Francisco P O	80	505
Ah	29	m	c	CHIN	San Francisco	San Francisco P O	80	457
Ah	29	m	c	CHIN	Nevada	Rough & Ready Twp	75	328
Ah	29	m	c	CHIN	San Francisco	6-Wd San Francisco	81	77
Ah	29	m	c	CHIN	Stanislaus	Empire Twp	92	45
Ah	28	m	c	CHIN	El Dorado	Coloma Twp	72	5
Ah	28	m	c	CHIN	Butte	Mountain Spring Tw	70	89
Ah	28	m	c	CHIN	El Dorado	Placerville	72	120
Ah	28	m	c	CHIN	Mendocino	Point Arena Twp	74	212
Ah	28	m	c	CHIN	Trinity	Junction City Pct	92	208
Ah	28	m	c	CHIN	Mariposa	Mariposa P O	74	111
Ah	28	m	c	CHIN	Mariposa	Mariposa P O	74	103
Ah	27	m	c	CHIN	Butte	Hamilton Twp	70	74
Ah	27	f	c	CHIN	Mendocino	Big Rvr Twp	74	170
Ah	27	m	c	CHIN	San Francisco	6-Wd San Francisco	81	48
Ah	27	m	c	CHIN	San Francisco	San Francisco P O	80	514
Ah	27	m	c	CHIN	Butte	Wyandotte Twp	70	144
Ah	27	m	c	CHIN	Butte	Bidwell Twp	70	5
Ah	27	m	c	CHIN	Butte	Chico Twp	70	60
Ah	27	m	c	CHIN	Butte	Chico Twp	70	27
Ah	27	m	c	CHIN	San Joaquin	Castoria Twp	86	10
Ah	27	m	c	CHIN	San Joaquin	2-Wd Stockton	86	178
Ah	27	m	c	CHIN	Sierra	Lincoln Twp	89	548
Ah	26	m	c	CHIN	Trinity	North Fork Twp	92	219
Ah	26	m	c	CHIN	Trinity	Weaverville Pct	92	231
Ah	26	m	c	CHIN	Mariposa	Mariposa P O	74	98
Ah	26	m	c	CHIN	El Dorado	Diamond Springs Tw	72	27
Ah	26	m	c	CHIN	Contra Costa	Martinez P O	71	452
Ah	26	m	c	CHIN	San Francisco	San Francisco P O	80	491
Ah	26	m	c	CHIN	San Joaquin	Oneal Twp	86	114
Ah	25	m	c	CHIN	El Dorado	Mountain Twp	72	68
Ah	25	m	c	CHIN	Fresno	Kings Rvr P O	72	211
Ah	25	m	c	CHIN	El Dorado	Salmon Falls Twp	72	130
Ah	25	m	c	CHIN	Amador	Jackson P O	69	331
Ah	25	m	c	CHIN	Calaveras	San Andreas P O	70	196
Ah	25	m	c	CHIN	Alameda	Alvarado	68	305
Ah	25	m	c	CHIN	Alameda	Washington Twp	68	270
Ah	25	m	c	CHIN	Alameda	Washington Twp	68	281
Ah	25	m	c	CHIN	Nevada	Grass Valley Twp	75	217
Ah	25	m	c	CHIN	Placer	Bath P O	76	444
Ah	25	m	c	CHIN	San Joaquin	Liberty Twp	86	97
Ah	25	m	c	CHIN	San Francisco	San Francisco P O	80	502
Ah	25	m	c	CHIN	San Francisco	San Francisco P O	80	513
Ah	25	f	c	CHIN	San Francisco	San Francisco P O	80	451
Ah	24	m	c	CHIN	Santa Clara	San Jose Twp	88	179
Ah	24	m	c	CHIN	San Francisco	San Francisco P O	80	518
Ah	24	m	c	CHIN	Nevada	Washington Twp	75	347
Ah	24	m	c	CHIN	San Francisco	3-Wd San Francisco	79	310
Ah	24	f	c	CHIN	San Francisco	San Francisco P O	80	454
Ah	24	f	c	CHIN	San Francisco	San Francisco P O	80	440
Ah	24	m	c	CHIN	Butte	Concow Twp	70	10
Ah	24	m	c	CHIN	El Dorado	Placerville	72	107
Ah	24	m	c	CHIN	San Francisco	8-Wd San Francisco	82	357
Ah	24	m	c	CHIN	Sierra	Butte Twp	89	510
Ah	23	m	c	CHIN	Butte	Ophir Twp	70	104
Ah	23	m	c	CHIN	San Joaquin	Liberty Twp	86	97
Ah	23	m	c	CHIN	Santa Clara	Gilroy Twp	88	75
Ah	23	m	c	CHIN	Trinity	Indian Crk	92	200
Ah	23	m	c	CHIN	San Francisco	6-Wd San Francisco	81	104
Ah	23	m	c	CHIN	San Francisco	6-Wd San Francisco	81	47
Ah	23	m	c	CHIN	San Joaquin	Castoria Twp	86	12
Ah	23	m	c	CHIN	San Francisco	San Francisco P O	85	748
Ah	22	m	c	CHIN	Alameda	San Leandro	68	98
Ah	22	m	c	CHIN	Alameda	Washington Twp	68	284
Ah	22	m	c	CHIN	Nevada	Eureka Twp	75	140
Ah	22	m	w	CHIN	Plumas	Indian Twp	77	19
Ah	22	m	c	CHIN	Solano	Vallejo	90	208
Ah	22	m	c	CHIN	San Francisco	6-Wd San Francisco	81	77
Ah	22	m	c	CHIN	Placer	Colfax P O	76	386
Ah	22	m	c	CHIN	Nevada	Meadow Lake Twp	75	262
Ah	22	m	c	CHIN	Calaveras	Copperopolis P O	70	257
Ah	22	m	c	CHIN	San Mateo	Menlo Park P O	87	377
Ah	21	m	c	CHIN	Plumas	Goodwin Twp	77	3
Ah	21	m	c	CHIN	San Francisco	2-Wd San Francisco	79	282
Ah	20	m	c	CHIN	Alameda	Eden Twp	68	62
Ah	20	m	c	CHIN	Nevada	Grass Valley Twp	75	171
Ah	20	m	c	CHIN	San Mateo	Half Moon Bay P O	87	396
Ah	20	m	c	CHIN	Trinity	Junction City Pct	92	207
Ah	20	m	c	CHIN	Sierra	Gibson Twp	89	538
Ah	20	m	c	CHIN	San Francisco	8-Wd San Francisco	82	488
Ah	20	m	c	CHIN	San Francisco	6-Wd San Francisco	81	48
Ah	20	m	c	CHIN	Nevada	Nevada Twp	75	318
Ah	20	m	c	CHIN	Sacramento	2-Wd Sacramento	77	246
Ah	20	f	c	CHIN	San Francisco	San Francisco P O	80	433
Ah	20	f	c	CHIN	San Francisco	San Francisco P O	80	432
Ah	20	m	c	CHIN	San Francisco	San Francisco P O	80	487
Ah	20	m	c	CHIN	Santa Clara	San Jose Twp	88	195
Ah	19	m	c	CHIN	Nevada	Washington Twp	75	347
Ah	19	m	c	CHIN	San Francisco	San Francisco P O	85	806
Ah	19	f	c	CHIN	Santa Clara	1-Wd San Jose	88	269
Ah	19	m	c	CHIN	Santa Clara	1-Wd San Jose	88	277
Ah	19	f	c	CHIN	San Francisco	6-Wd San Francisco	81	77
Ah	19	m	c	CHIN	San Francisco	6-Wd San Francisco	81	147

© 2001 by Heritage Quest. All rights reserved.

California 1870 Census

Name	Age	S	R	B-PL	County	Locale	Series M593 Roll	Pg
Ah	19	m	c	CHIN	San Francisco	6-Wd San Francisco	81	128
Ah	19	m	c	CHIN	San Francisco	8-Wd San Francisco	82	346
Ah	19	m	c	CHIN	San Joaquin	Castoria Twp	86	11
Ah	18	m	c	CHIN	Butte	Bidwell Twp	70	1
Ah	18	m	c	CHIN	Alameda	Washington Twp	68	288
Ah	18	m	c	CHIN	Santa Clara	Santa Clara Twp	88	161
Ah	18	f	c	CHIN	San Francisco	6-Wd San Francisco	81	76
Ah	18	m	c	CHIN	San Francisco	6-Wd San Francisco	81	85
Ah	17	m	c	CHIN	Sacramento	3-Wd Sacramento	77	292
Ah	17	m	c	CHIN	Santa Clara	Santa Clara Twp	88	165
Ah	17	m	c	CHIN	Yuba	Marysville	93	618
Ah	16	m	c	CHIN	Alameda	Brooklyn Twp	68	40
Ah	16	m	c	CHIN	Napa	Napa	75	9
Ah	16	m	c	CHIN	Sacramento	Franklin Twp	77	119
Ah	16	m	c	CHIN	Sacramento	Franklin Twp	77	117
Ah	16	m	c	CHIN	San Joaquin	Castoria Twp	86	13
Ah	16	m	c	CHIN	San Joaquin	Castoria Twp	86	13
Ah	16	m	c	CHIN	San Francisco	San Francisco P O	85	748
Ah	15	m	c	CHIN	San Francisco	6-Wd San Francisco	81	148
Ah	14	m	c	CHIN	Santa Clara	2-Wd San Jose	88	301
Ah	13	m	c	CHIN	San Francisco	6-Wd San Francisco	81	155
Ah	12	m	c	JAPA	San Francisco	San Francisco P O	83	397
Ah	10	m	c	CHIN	Yuba	Marysville	93	601
Ah Chong	31	m	c	CHIN	Nevada	Nevada Twp	75	313
Ah Slung	27	m	c	CHIN	Trinity	Junction City Pct	92	206
Aqui	28	m	c	CHIN	Solano	Vacaville Twp	90	117
Bod	40	m	c	CHIN	Sierra	Table Rock Twp	89	578
Chee	21	m	c	CHIN	Sacramento	3-Wd Sacramento	77	304
Chei	26	m	c	CHIN	Nevada	Grass Valley Twp	75	171
Chong	20	m	c	CHIN	Solano	Suisun Twp	90	107
Chow	28	m	c	CHIN	Sierra	Forest Twp	89	528
Chow	20	m	c	CHIN	San Joaquin	3-Wd Stockton	86	230
Choy	16	f	c	CHIN	San Francisco	6-Wd San Francisco	81	76
Chung	26	m	c	CHIN	Solano	Rio Vista Twp	90	70
Coon	28	m	c	CHIN	Solano	Vallejo	90	209
Eu	62	m	c	CHIN	El Dorado	Placerville	72	116
Foo	37	m	c	CHIN	Tulare	Visalia	92	299
Foo	21	m	c	CHIN	Butte	Concow Twp	70	8
Gon	50	m	c	CHIN	El Dorado	Salmon Falls Twp	72	132
Hi	28	m	c	CHIN	Butte	Bidwell Twp	70	5
Hie	41	m	c	CHIN	Mariposa	Mariposa P O	74	125
Ho	24	m	c	CHIN	San Joaquin	3-Wd Stockton	86	230
Ho	19	m	c	CHIN	San Francisco	San Francisco P O	83	404
Jim	22	m	c	CHIN	Alameda	Washington Twp	68	286
Joe	25	m	c	CHIN	Colusa	Grand Island Twp	71	308
John	27	m	c	CHIN	Santa Clara	Santa Clara Twp	88	163
Kee	39	m	c	CHIN	Santa Clara	San Jose Twp	88	190
King	30	m	c	CHIN	Solano	Vacaville Twp	90	130
King	21	m	c	CHIN	Solano	Suisun Twp	90	104
Kong	38	m	c	CHIN	Santa Clara	1-Wd San Jose	88	273
Kum	30	m	c	CHIN	Solano	Vallejo	90	209
Lap	49	m	c	CHIN	Mariposa	Mariposa P O	74	121
Le	28	m	c	CHIN	San Joaquin	3-Wd Stockton	86	230
Lee	41	m	c	CHIN	Butte	Chico Twp	70	27
Lee	40	m	c	CHIN	Yuba	Marysville	93	625
Lee	24	m	c	CHIN	San Francisco	6-Wd San Francisco	81	65
Lee	20	m	c	CHIN	San Francisco	6-Wd San Francisco	81	97
Ling	28	m	c	CHIN	San Joaquin	Oneal Twp	86	99
Lon	23	m	c	CHIN	Amador	Ione City P O	69	364
Loo	43	m	c	CHIN	Tulare	White Rvr Twp	92	301
Loo	28	m	c	CHIN	Kern	Bakersfield P O	73	359
Lung	88	m	c	CHIN	San Joaquin	Oneal Twp	86	115
Man	30	m	c	CHIN	Mariposa	Mariposa P O	74	127
Me	30	f	c	CHIN	Mariposa	Mariposa P O	74	125
Muck	34	m	c	CHIN	El Dorado	Diamond Springs Tw	72	33
Ong	43	m	c	CHIN	Trinity	Weaverville Pct	92	231
Par	36	m	c	CHIN	Nevada	Nevada Twp	75	312
Ping	51	m	c	CHIN	Mariposa	Mariposa P O	74	127
Poy	31	m	c	CHIN	Amador	Lancha Plana P O	69	369
Pung	40	m	c	CHIN	Mariposa	Mariposa P O	74	102
Sam	40	m	c	CHIN	Santa Clara	Santa Clara Twp	88	161
Sam	32	m	c	CHIN	Colusa	Grand Island Twp	71	308
Sam	30	m	c	CHIN	San Joaquin	Castoria Twp	86	10
Shoo	18	m	c	CHIN	San Joaquin	1-Wd Stockton	86	147
Sin	19	f	c	CHIN	Mariposa	Mariposa P O	74	125
Sing	30	m	c	CHIN	Nevada	Bridgeport Twp	75	107
Sing	28	f	c	CHIN	Mariposa	Mariposa P O	74	103
Sing	27	m	c	CHIN	Solano	Suisun Twp	90	105
Sing	21	m	c	CHIN	San Joaquin	Oneal Twp	86	115
Sip	24	m	c	CHIN	Colusa	Grand Island Twp	71	309
Sue	30	m	c	CHIN	San Mateo	Schoolhouse Statio	87	336
Sue	28	m	c	CHIN	Colusa	Grand Island Twp	71	302
To	37	m	c	CHIN	Nevada	Meadow Lake Twp	75	259
To	29	m	c	CHIN	Amador	Volcano P O	69	384
Too	54	m	c	CHIN	Nevada	Nevada Twp	75	321
Tow	21	m	c	CHIN	Yolo	Grafton Twp	93	483
Toy	24	m	c	CHIN	Shasta	Shasta P O	89	455
Tuchk	48	m	c	CHIN	Mendocino	Big Rvr Twp	74	170
Ty	19	m	c	CHIN	Amador	Jackson P O	69	330
We	24	m	c	CHIN	Yolo	Putah Twp	93	513
Wo	57	m	c	CHIN	Placer	Blue Canyon P O	76	417
Woi	23	m	c	CHIN	San Francisco	6-Wd San Francisco	81	39
Yon	49	m	c	CHIN	San Joaquin	1-Wd Stockton	86	156
Yon	28	f	c	CHIN	Lassen	Susanville Twp	73	441
You	31	m	c	CHIN	Solano	Suisun Twp	90	105
Yu	25	m	c	CHIN	San Francisco	6-Wd San Francisco	81	40
Yuy	32	m	c	CHIN	San Francisco	6-Wd San Francisco	81	67
CHOWE								
Ah	30	m	c	CHIN	Placer	Auburn P O	76	363
CHOWEY								
Ah	18	m	c	CHIN	Sierra	Downieville Twp	89	521
CHOWMING								
M L	55	m	w	TN	Alameda	Eden Twp	68	70
CHOWN								
He	29	m	c	CHIN	Colusa	Colusa	71	298
CHOWVEL								
John	52	m	w	FRAN	Calaveras	San Andreas P O	70	154
CHOY								
---	21	m	c	CHIN	Siskiyou	Yreka	89	660
Ah	9	f	c	CHIN	San Francisco	San Francisco P O	80	490
Ah	9	f	c	CHIN	San Francisco	San Francisco P O	80	528
Ah	9	f	c	CHIN	San Francisco	San Francisco P O	80	494
Ah	6	f	c	CA	San Francisco	San Francisco P O	80	527
Ah	6	f	c	CHIN	San Francisco	6-Wd San Francisco	81	76
Ah	59	m	c	CHIN	Amador	Volcano P O	69	378
Ah	56	f	c	CHIN	San Francisco	San Francisco P O	80	521
Ah	56	m	c	CHIN	San Francisco	San Francisco P O	80	433
Ah	50	m	c	CHIN	Yolo	Putah Twp	93	513
Ah	50	m	c	CHIN	Placer	Clipper Gap P O	76	392
Ah	50	m	c	CHIN	Placer	Clipper Gap P O	76	393
Ah	48	m	c	CHIN	Nevada	Grass Valley Twp	75	202
Ah	47	f	c	CHIN	San Francisco	San Francisco P O	80	434
Ah	47	f	c	CHIN	San Francisco	San Francisco P O	80	433
Ah	45	m	c	CHIN	San Francisco	6-Wd San Francisco	81	52
Ah	45	m	c	CHIN	Mariposa	Mariposa P O	74	114
Ah	44	m	c	CHIN	Calaveras	San Andreas P O	70	179
Ah	42	m	c	CHIN	Amador	Fiddletown P O	69	428
Ah	41	m	c	CHIN	San Francisco	San Francisco P O	80	491
Ah	41	m	c	CHIN	San Francisco	San Francisco P O	80	491
Ah	40	m	c	CHIN	San Francisco	6-Wd San Francisco	81	55
Ah	40	m	c	CHIN	Amador	Ione City P O	69	361
Ah	40	m	c	CHIN	Nevada	Nevada Twp	75	307
Ah	40	m	c	CHIN	Butte	Chico Twp	70	28
Ah	40	m	c	CHIN	San Francisco	San Francisco P O	80	449
Ah	4	m	c	CHIN	San Francisco	6-Wd San Francisco	81	77
Ah	39	m	c	CHIN	Calaveras	San Andreas P O	70	179
Ah	38	f	c	CHIN	Trinity	Indian Crk	92	199
Ah	38	m	c	CHIN	San Francisco	San Francisco P O	80	505
Ah	38	f	c	CHIN	San Francisco	San Francisco P O	80	499
Ah	38	f	c	CHIN	San Francisco	San Francisco P O	80	529
Ah	38	m	c	CHIN	Butte	Chico Twp	70	52
Ah	38	f	c	CHIN	Mariposa	Mariposa P O	74	132
Ah	37	m	c	CHIN	San Francisco	San Francisco P O	80	500
Ah	37	m	c	CHIN	San Francisco	6-Wd San Francisco	81	67
Ah	36	f	c	CHIN	San Francisco	6-Wd San Francisco	81	75
Ah	36	m	c	CHIN	San Francisco	San Francisco P O	80	522
Ah	36	m	c	CHIN	San Francisco	San Francisco P O	80	517
Ah	36	m	c	CHIN	San Francisco	San Francisco P O	80	523
Ah	36	m	c	CHIN	San Francisco	San Francisco P O	80	507
Ah	36	m	c	CHIN	Butte	Ophir Twp	70	117
Ah	36	m	c	CHIN	Amador	Drytown P O	69	423
Ah	36	m	c	CHIN	Amador	Volcano P O	69	377
Ah	36	f	c	CHIN	Nevada	Meadow Lake Twp	75	254
Ah	36	m	c	CHIN	San Francisco	San Francisco P O	80	493
Ah	36	f	c	CHIN	Fresno	Millerton P O	72	200
Ah	36	f	c	CHIN	San Francisco	San Francisco P O	80	432
Ah	35	m	c	CHIN	Santa Clara	1-Wd San Jose	88	270
Ah	35	m	c	CHIN	San Francisco	6-Wd San Francisco	81	42
Ah	35	m	c	CHIN	Mariposa	Mariposa P O	74	113
Ah	35	f	c	CHIN	San Francisco	San Francisco P O	80	449
Ah	34	m	c	CHIN	San Francisco	San Francisco P O	80	517
Ah	34	m	c	CHIN	San Francisco	San Francisco P O	80	513
Ah	34	m	c	CHIN	San Francisco	San Francisco P O	80	503
Ah	33	m	c	CHIN	Mariposa	Mariposa P O	74	137
Ah	33	m	c	CHIN	Yolo	Merritt Twp	93	503
Ah	32	m	c	CHIN	Nevada	Washington Twp	75	347
Ah	32	m	c	CHIN	Sierra	Sears Twp	89	554
Ah	32	m	c	CHIN	Mariposa	Mariposa P O	74	104
Ah	32	m	c	CHIN	Mariposa	Mariposa P O	74	132
Ah	32	f	c	CHIN	San Francisco	San Francisco P O	80	431
Ah	32	f	c	CHIN	San Francisco	San Francisco P O	80	432
Ah	31	m	c	CHIN	San Francisco	San Francisco P O	80	516
Ah	31	f	c	CHIN	San Francisco	San Francisco P O	80	521
Ah	31	m	c	CHIN	Butte	Ophir Twp	70	121
Ah	31	m	c	CHIN	Amador	Fiddletown P O	69	426
Ah	31	f	c	CHIN	San Francisco	San Francisco P O	80	494
Ah	31	f	c	CHIN	San Francisco	San Francisco P O	80	497
Ah	31	f	c	CHIN	Mariposa	Mariposa P O	74	133
Ah	30	m	c	CHIN	Santa Clara	Santa Clara Twp	88	146
Ah	30	f	c	CHIN	Santa Clara	1-Wd San Jose	88	273
Ah	30	m	c	CHIN	Santa Clara	Santa Clara Twp	88	161
Ah	30	m	c	CHIN	Butte	Ophir Twp	70	121
Ah	30	f	c	CHIN	Amador	Fiddletown P O	69	427
Ah	30	m	c	CHIN	Placer	Bath P O	76	446
Ah	30	f	c	CHIN	Nevada	Grass Valley Twp	75	204
Ah	30	m	c	CHIN	San Francisco	6-Wd San Francisco	81	39
Ah	30	m	c	CHIN	San Francisco	San Francisco P O	80	501
Ah	30	f	c	CHIN	San Francisco	11-Wd San Francisc	84	695
Ah	30	m	c	CHIN	Tuolumne	Columbia P O	93	352
Ah	30	f	c	CHIN	Tuolumne	Columbia P O	93	342
Ah	30	m	c	CHIN	Mariposa	Mariposa P O	74	127
Ah	30	f	c	CHIN	Mariposa	Mariposa P O	74	114
Ah	30	m	c	CHIN	Mariposa	Mariposa P O	74	121
Ah	30	f	c	CHIN	San Francisco	San Francisco P O	80	444

© 2001 by Heritage Quest. All rights reserved.

Name	Age	S	R	B-PL	County	Locale (Series M593)	Roll	Pg
Ah	30	f	c	CHIN	San Francisco	San Francisco P O	80	432
Ah	29	f	c	CHIN	Santa Clara	1-Wd San Jose	88	274
Ah	29	m	c	CHIN	San Francisco	6-Wd San Francisco	81	61
Ah	29	m	c	CHIN	San Francisco	San Francisco P O	80	522
Ah	29	f	c	CHIN	San Francisco	San Francisco P O	80	508
Ah	29	m	c	CHIN	San Francisco	6-Wd San Francisco	81	70
Ah	29	m	c	CHIN	Solano	Suisun Twp	90	106
Ah	29	m	c	CHIN	Mariposa	Mariposa P O	74	103
Ah	29	f	c	CHIN	Mariposa	Mariposa P O	74	126
Ah	28	f	c	CHIN	Amador	Ione City P O	69	364
Ah	28	m	c	CHIN	Nevada	Washington Twp	75	344
Ah	28	m	c	CHIN	Yuba	Marysville	93	619
Ah	28	m	c	CHIN	Trinity	Weaverville Pct	92	232
Ah	28	m	c	CHIN	Santa Clara	Redwood Twp	88	124
Ah	28	m	c	CHIN	Solano	Suisun Twp	90	106
Ah	28	m	c	CHIN	Mariposa	Mariposa P O	74	132
Ah	28	m	c	CHIN	Nevada	Nevada Twp	75	313
Ah	27	m	c	CHIN	Nevada	Nevada Twp	75	300
Ah	27	m	c	CHIN	Placer	Auburn P O	76	358
Ah	27	f	c	CHIN	San Francisco	6-Wd San Francisco	81	62
Ah	27	f	c	CHIN	Yolo	Cache Crk Twp	93	453
Ah	27	m	c	CHIN	San Francisco	3-Wd San Francisco	79	303
Ah	26	m	c	CHIN	Santa Clara	1-Wd San Jose	88	272
Ah	26	m	c	CHIN	San Francisco	San Francisco P O	80	516
Ah	26	f	c	CHIN	San Francisco	San Francisco P O	80	524
Ah	26	m	c	CHIN	Sacramento	3-Wd Sacramento	77	312
Ah	26	f	c	CHIN	San Francisco	San Francisco P O	80	444
Ah	26	f	c	CHIN	San Francisco	San Francisco P O	80	449
Ah	26	f	c	CHIN	San Francisco	San Francisco P O	80	432
Ah	25	f	c	CHIN	Santa Clara	1-Wd San Jose	88	254
Ah	25	m	c	CHIN	San Francisco	6-Wd San Francisco	81	52
Ah	25	f	c	CHIN	Monterey	San Juan Twp	74	408
Ah	25	m	c	CHIN	Solano	Suisun Twp	90	105
Ah	25	f	c	CHIN	Yolo	Washington Twp	93	528
Ah	25	f	c	CHIN	San Francisco	San Francisco P O	80	438
Ah	24	m	c	CHIN	Santa Clara	1-Wd San Jose	88	271
Ah	24	f	c	CHIN	San Francisco	6-Wd San Francisco	81	75
Ah	24	f	c	CHIN	San Francisco	6-Wd San Francisco	81	75
Ah	24	m	c	CHIN	San Francisco	6-Wd San Francisco	81	71
Ah	24	m	c	CHIN	San Francisco	6-Wd San Francisco	81	69
Ah	24	m	c	CHIN	San Francisco	San Francisco P O	80	515
Ah	24	m	c	CHIN	San Francisco	6-Wd San Francisco	81	85
Ah	24	m	c	CHIN	San Francisco	6-Wd San Francisco	81	86
Ah	24	m	c	CHIN	San Francisco	San Francisco P O	80	496
Ah	24	m	c	CHIN	Siskiyou	Hamburg Twp	89	596
Ah	24	f	c	CHIN	Amador	Fiddletown P O	69	428
Ah	24	m	c	CHIN	Placer	Auburn P O	76	362
Ah	24	m	c	CHIN	Nevada	Washington Twp	75	344
Ah	24	f	c	CHIN	San Francisco	San Francisco P O	80	433
Ah	24	f	c	CHIN	San Francisco	San Francisco P O	80	444
Ah	24	m	c	CHIN	San Francisco	3-Wd San Francisco	79	301
Ah	23	m	c	CHIN	San Francisco	6-Wd San Francisco	81	49
Ah	23	f	c	CHIN	San Francisco	San Francisco P O	80	504
Ah	22	f	c	CHIN	Santa Clara	1-Wd San Jose	88	270
Ah	22	f	c	CHIN	San Francisco	6-Wd San Francisco	81	77
Ah	22	m	c	CHIN	Amador	Jackson P O	69	331
Ah	22	f	c	CHIN	Amador	Jackson P O	69	344
Ah	22	m	c	CHIN	Napa	Napa	75	9
Ah	22	m	c	CHIN	San Francisco	6-Wd San Francisco	81	51
Ah	21	f	c	CHIN	Santa Clara	1-Wd San Jose	88	270
Ah	21	m	c	CHIN	Santa Clara	Santa Clara Twp	88	161
Ah	21	f	c	CHIN	San Francisco	6-Wd San Francisco	81	73
Ah	21	m	c	CHIN	San Francisco	San Francisco P O	80	522
Ah	21	f	c	CHIN	San Francisco	San Francisco P O	80	523
Ah	21	m	c	CHIN	San Francisco	San Francisco P O	80	511
Ah	21	m	c	CHIN	San Francisco	6-Wd San Francisco	81	68
Ah	21	f	c	CHIN	Mariposa	Mariposa P O	74	104
Ah	21	f	c	CHIN	Butte	Hamilton Twp	70	75
Ah	21	f	c	CHIN	San Francisco	San Francisco P O	80	442
Ah	21	f	c	CHIN	San Francisco	San Francisco P O	80	442
Ah	20	m	c	CHIN	San Francisco	6-Wd San Francisco	81	55
Ah	20	f	c	CHIN	El Dorado	Mud Springs Twp	72	79
Ah	20	m	c	CHIN	Yuba	Marysville	93	618
Ah	20	f	c	CHIN	San Francisco	San Francisco P O	80	435
Ah	20	f	c	CHIN	San Francisco	San Francisco P O	80	442
Ah	20	f	c	CHIN	San Francisco	San Francisco P O	80	431
Ah	2	f	c	CA	San Francisco	San Francisco P O	80	528
Ah	2	f	c	CA	San Francisco	San Francisco P O	80	452
Ah	19	f	c	CHIN	Santa Clara	1-Wd San Jose	88	274
Ah	19	f	c	CHIN	Santa Clara	1-Wd San Jose	88	269
Ah	19	f	c	CHIN	San Francisco	6-Wd San Francisco	81	76
Ah	19	f	c	CHIN	San Francisco	San Francisco P O	80	526
Ah	19	m	c	CHIN	San Francisco	6-Wd San Francisco	81	65
Ah	19	m	c	CHIN	San Francisco	6-Wd San Francisco	81	68
Ah	19	f	c	CHIN	San Francisco	San Francisco P O	80	434
Ah	18	f	c	CHIN	San Francisco	6-Wd San Francisco	81	74
Ah	18	m	c	CHIN	San Francisco	6-Wd San Francisco	81	69
Ah	18	f	c	CHIN	San Francisco	6-Wd San Francisco	81	76
Ah	18	f	c	CHIN	San Francisco	San Francisco P O	80	505
Ah	18	m	c	CHIN	San Francisco	8-Wd San Francisco	82	318
Ah	18	f	c	CHIN	El Dorado	Placerville	72	116
Ah	18	f	c	CHIN	San Francisco	6-Wd San Francisco	81	61
Ah	18	m	c	CHIN	Calaveras	Copperopolis P O	70	226
Ah	18	f	c	CHIN	San Francisco	San Francisco P O	80	434
Ah	17	f	c	CHIN	San Francisco	6-Wd San Francisco	81	77
Ah	17	f	c	CHIN	San Francisco	6-Wd San Francisco	81	75
Ah	17	m	c	CHIN	Butte	Wyandotte Twp	70	149
Ah	17	m	c	CHIN	Butte	Ophir Twp	70	114
Ah	17	f	c	CHIN	Amador	Drytown P O	69	419
Ah	17	f	c	CHIN	Amador	Drytown P O	69	421
Ah	17	m	c	CHIN	San Francisco	6-Wd San Francisco	81	85
Ah	17	m	c	CHIN	San Francisco	San Francisco P O	80	335
Ah	16	f	c	CHIN	San Francisco	6-Wd San Francisco	81	76
Ah	16	f	c	CHIN	San Francisco	6-Wd San Francisco	81	74
Ah	16	f	c	CHIN	San Francisco	6-Wd San Francisco	81	77
Ah	16	f	c	CHIN	San Francisco	San Francisco P O	80	508
Ah	16	m	c	CHIN	San Francisco	6-Wd San Francisco	81	62
Ah	15	m	c	CHIN	San Francisco	2-Wd San Francisco	79	212
Ah	15	f	c	CHIN	Trinity	Weaverville Pct	92	228
Ah	15	m	c	CHIN	San Francisco	6-Wd San Francisco	81	42
Ah	14	m	c	CHIN	San Francisco	6-Wd San Francisco	81	68
Ah	14	m	c	CHIN	San Francisco	6-Wd San Francisco	81	66
Ah	12	f	c	CHIN	San Francisco	San Francisco P O	80	431
Ah	11	f	c	CHIN	San Francisco	San Francisco P O	80	452
Ah Tin	28	f	c	CHIN	Mono	Bridgeport P O	74	282
Ay	28	m	c	CHIN	Yuba	Marysville	93	630
Cam	26	f	c	CHIN	Placer	Dutch Flat P O	76	408
Chee	30	m	c	CHIN	San Francisco	6-Wd San Francisco	81	69
Chew	36	m	c	CHIN	San Francisco	6-Wd San Francisco	81	39
Chow	30	m	c	CHIN	Napa	Napa	75	9
Chuk	20	f	c	CHIN	San Francisco	6-Wd San Francisco	81	76
Cue	35	m	c	CHIN	Trinity	Weaverville Pct	92	229
Cum	26	f	c	CHIN	Fresno	Millerton P O	72	200
Dam	34	m	c	CHIN	Amador	Lancha Plana P O	69	369
Eh	33	f	c	CHIN	El Dorado	Placerville	72	116
Eugh	28	m	c	CHIN	Calaveras	San Andreas P O	70	205
Fe	31	m	c	CHIN	Yolo	Merritt Twp	93	503
Foo	20	m	c	CHIN	San Francisco	6-Wd San Francisco	81	86
Frank	27	m	c	CHIN	Santa Clara	Redwood Twp	88	131
Gee	28	f	c	CHIN	Placer	Auburn P O	76	371
Hi	26	m	c	CHIN	Monterey	Monterey Twp	74	351
Jim	40	m	c	CHIN	Santa Clara	Santa Clara Twp	88	158
King	25	f	c	CHIN	San Francisco	6-Wd San Francisco	81	61
King	20	f	c	CHIN	Nevada	Meadow Lake Twp	75	255
Kun	29	m	c	CHIN	Yuba	Marysville	93	624
Lee	60	f	c	CHIN	Mariposa	Mariposa P O	74	103
Lim	30	f	c	CHIN	Yuba	Marysville	93	627
Lue	30	f	c	CHIN	Mariposa	Mariposa P O	74	102
Lung	29	m	c	CHIN	Butte	Ophir Twp	70	116
M	20	m	c	CHIN	Placer	Colfax P O	76	385
Mow	28	m	c	CHIN	Napa	Napa	75	7
Pee	15	f	c	CHIN	San Francisco	6-Wd San Francisco	81	78
Pung	27	f	c	CHIN	Trinity	Weaverville Pct	92	229
Sin	21	m	c	CHIN	Solano	Suisun Twp	90	107
Sin	20	f	c	CHIN	Mariposa	Mariposa P O	74	102
Su	21	f	c	CHIN	Mariposa	Mariposa P O	74	103
Sung	46	m	c	CHIN	Yuba	Marysville	93	625
Tee	40	m	c	CHIN	San Francisco	6-Wd San Francisco	81	51
Tie	20	m	c	CHIN	San Francisco	3-Wd San Francisco	79	301
Tong	35	m	c	CHIN	Nevada	Nevada Twp	75	312
Tong	21	f	c	CHIN	Mariposa	Mariposa P O	74	103
Tong	18	m	c	CHIN	Mariposa	Mariposa P O	74	103
Tung	27	m	c	CHIN	Calaveras	San Andreas P O	70	161
Tuy	35	f	c	CHIN	Merced	Snelling P O	74	279
Ty	23	f	c	CHIN	Butte	Chico Twp	70	28
Wan	25	f	c	CHIN	Yuba	Marysville	93	627
Wo	40	m	c	CHIN	Fresno	Millerton P O	72	184
Wong	23	f	c	CHIN	Nevada	Grass Valley Twp	75	205
Woo	12	f	c	CHIN	San Francisco	6-Wd San Francisco	81	76
Yik	30	m	c	CHIN	Butte	Kimshew Tpw	70	81
Yin	12	f	c	CHIN	San Francisco	6-Wd San Francisco	81	39
Yo	31	f	c	CHIN	Mariposa	Mariposa P O	74	103
Yow	18	f	c	CHIN	Mariposa	Mariposa P O	74	103
Yow	17	f	c	CHIN	San Francisco	6-Wd San Francisco	81	74
Yuen	37	m	c	CHIN	Calaveras	San Andreas P O	70	204
CHOYA								
Ah	29	m	c	CHIN	Monterey	Monterey Twp	74	351
CHOYES								
Ah	40	m	c	CHIN	Amador	Drytown P O	69	423
CHOYINSKI								
Francis	18	f	w	NY	San Francisco	5-Wd San Francisco	81	4
CHOYN								
Ah	51	m	c	CHIN	Amador	Fiddletown P O	69	427
CHOYSKA								
Isadore	35	m	w	PRUS	San Francisco	7-Wd San Francisco	81	158
CHRES								
Michl	74	m	w	PRUS	San Francisco	11-Wd San Francisc	84	614
CHRESSLY								
Ricchd	59	m	w	MA	Butte	Concow Twp	70	9
CHRETIEN								
John	16	m	w	CA	Santa Clara	Santa Clara Twp	88	176
Joseph	61	m	w	FRAN	Santa Clara	2-Wd San Jose	88	287
CHRICH								
Chas	25	m	w	NY	San Francisco	5-Wd San Francisco	81	18
CHRICHTON								
Richard	25	m	w	SCOT	Santa Clara	2-Wd San Jose	88	302
CHRIN								
Ah	26	m	c	CHIN	Placer	Bath P O	76	424
CHRIS								
A T	39	m	w	MA	Sacramento	Cosumnes Twp	77	92
CHRISHOLM								
Alex	34	m	w	CANA	San Francisco	8-Wd San Francisco	82	328
CHRISLER								
Peter	39	m	w	NY	Solano	Suisun Twp	90	94

© 2001 by Heritage Quest. All rights reserved.

California 1870 Census

Series M593

Name	Age	S	R	B-PL	County	Locale	Roll	Pg
CHRISMAN								
G	47	m	w	VA	Napa	Napa	75	9
J	37	m	w	IL	Lake	Lower Lake	73	429
Jesse	32	m	w	PA	Santa Clara	2-Wd San Jose	88	318
John P	45	m	w	VA	Contra Costa	Martinez P O	71	380
Joseph	31	m	w	VT	San Francisco	5-Wd San Francisco	81	12
Josiah	29	m	w	PA	Santa Clara	Fremont Twp	88	59
Louis C	37	m	w	TN	Placer	Blue Canyon P O	76	418
Margaret	29	f	w	MO	Siskiyou	Yreka Twp	89	665
CHRISMON								
David W	45	m	w	IN	Butte	Ophir Twp	70	116
CHRIST								
Charles	40	m	w	SWED	Mendocino	Albion & Big Rvr T	74	166
Charles	38	m	w	FRAN	Tuolumne	Columbia P O	93	345
Charles	36	m	w	PRUS	Mendocino	Point Arena Twp	74	204
E B	38	m	w	PA	Calaveras	Copperopolis P O	70	237
Henry	43	m	w	VA	El Dorado	Mud Springs Twp	72	72
James	27	m	w	DENM	Mendocino	Casper & Big Rvr	74	164
Jesus	42	m	w	ITAL	Santa Clara	Almaden Twp	88	13
John	32	m	w	SHOL	San Mateo	Redwood Twp	87	367
Nelson	35	m	w	DENM	San Mateo	Redwood Twp	87	367
Susan	24	f	w	BAVA	San Francisco	8-Wd San Francisco	82	484
CHRISTA								
J	34	m	w	IREL	San Joaquin	Elliott Twp	86	76
Thomas	50	m	w	ITAL	San Mateo	Schoolhouse Statio	87	339
CHRISTAIN								
Frank	30	m	w	BADE	Solano	Suisun Twp	90	97
CHRISTALEAR								
John	29	m	w	IA	Tehama	Bell Mills Twp	92	159
John P	70	m	w	NY	Tehama	Antelope Twp	92	160
CHRISTALEER								
---	68	m	w	IA	Tehama	Red Bluff	92	178
CHRISTAN								
Ignace	56	m	w	FRAN	Alpine	Markleeville P O	69	312
Robert	30	m	w	IREL	San Francisco	7-Wd San Francisco	81	181
CHRISTEAN								
Baptiste	36	m	w	FRAN	San Diego	Milquaty Dist	78	476
R	49	m	w	ENGL	San Francisco	San Francisco P O	85	819
CHRISTEE								
Carry	61	f	w	WIND	San Francisco	11-Wd San Francisc	84	493
Frank	21	m	w	SCOT	San Francisco	San Francisco P O	83	402
CHRISTEN								
A	61	m	w	FRAN	Yuba	Marysville	93	581
CHRISTENS								
Nicholas	25	m	w	AUST	San Francisco	San Francisco P O	80	350
CHRISTENSEN								
Chris	55	m	w	DENM	Butte	Kimshew Tpw	70	82
Henry	53	m	w	DENM	Santa Cruz	Soquel Twp	89	436
Hy	48	m	w	SHOL	San Francisco	11-Wd San Francisc	84	601
John	32	m	w	SHOL	San Francisco	3-Wd San Francisco	79	287
CHRISTENSON								
Eras	18	m	w	PRUS	Monterey	Pajaro Twp	74	374
Ferdinand	33	m	w	DENM	San Francisco	2-Wd San Francisco	79	273
J	34	m	w	DENM	San Francisco	San Francisco P O	85	780
John	19	m	w	DENM	Mendocino	Little Rvr Twp	74	171
Peter	47	m	w	DENM	San Diego	San Diego	78	492
Peter	40	m	w	DENM	Yuba	Slate Range Bar Tw	93	668
CHRISTESON								
Chas	24	m	w	DENM	San Francisco	7-Wd San Francisco	81	261
CHRISTIA								
Henry	36	m	w	CANA	Yolo	Grafton Twp	93	482
CHRISTIAN								
---	35	m	w	DENM	Santa Clara	1-Wd San Jose	88	275
Adolph	34	m	w	HDAR	Solano	Vacaville Twp	90	123
Albert	30	m	w	DENM	San Francisco	1-Wd San Francisco	79	129
B F	45	m	w	FRAN	San Francisco	1-Wd San Francisco	79	53
Bautiste	49	m	w	FRAN	Santa Clara	1-Wd San Jose	88	265
Carl	29	m	w	NORW	Sonoma	Petaluma Twp	91	314
Charles	45	m	w	SWED	Santa Cruz	Soquel Twp	89	440
Charles	34	m	b	MA	Sacramento	2-Wd Sacramento	77	217
Chas	35	m	w	GERM	San Francisco	8-Wd San Francisco	82	360
Chas	35	m	w	DENM	Humboldt	Eureka Twp	72	275
Chris	35	m	w	DENM	Santa Barbara	San Buenaventura P	87	436
Christ	24	m	w	DENM	Alameda	Eden Twp	68	61
Christ	22	m	w	DENM	Alameda	Eden Twp	68	62
Christ	22	m	w	DENM	Alameda	Washington Twp	68	297
Christian	35	m	w	SWED	San Francisco	3-Wd San Francisco	79	293
Daniel	22	m	w	IN	Solano	Silveyville Twp	90	92
Edwin	37	m	w	MA	San Francisco	11-Wd San Francisc	84	497
Emmanuel	29	m	w	SWED	Santa Clara	Alviso Twp	88	22
Evan	30	m	w	GREE	Santa Clara	Alviso Twp	88	25
Francis	67	m	w	CANA	El Dorado	Placerville	72	126
Fred	43	m	w	RUSS	Amador	Fiddletown P O	69	437
George	41	m	w	NY	Contra Costa	San Pablo Twp	71	357
H	30	m	w	OH	Alameda	Oakland	68	261
Harriett	35	f	w	FRAN	Santa Clara	2-Wd San Jose	88	306
Henry	48	m	w	NY	El Dorado	Placerville	72	107
Henry	39	m	w	BAVA	Calaveras	San Andreas P O	70	185
James	50	m	w	SWED	San Francisco	6-Wd San Francisco	81	80
Jim	40	m	w	KY	San Joaquin	Liberty Twp	86	86
John	29	m	w	IOFM	Santa Clara	1-Wd San Jose	88	229
Joseph F	22	m	w	PRUS	San Francisco	5-Wd San Francisco	81	15
Mark	58	m	w	SWIT	San Luis Obispo	Arroyo Grande Twp	87	279
Mattias	28	m	w	DENM	San Francisco	1-Wd San Francisco	79	126
Nuna J	42	m	w	FL	Yolo	Merritt Twp	93	503
Oliver	22	m	w	PRUS	Sutter	Nicolaus Twp	92	107
Peter	43	m	w	SWED	Santa Clara	Fremont Twp	88	60
Peter	19	m	w	DENM	San Joaquin	Castoria Twp	86	9
Peter	17	m	w	DENM	Alameda	Eden Twp	68	63
Peter E	42	m	w	SWED	San Francisco	1-Wd San Francisco	79	111
R	50	m	w	NCOD	Sacramento	4-Wd Sacramento	77	340
S	42	m	w	OH	Yuba	Marysville	93	614
S	34	f	w	PRUS	Alameda	Oakland	68	206
Thomas	20	m	w	CANA	San Francisco	San Francisco P O	83	262
Victor	33	m	w	FRAN	Santa Clara	1-Wd San Jose	88	256
William	26	m	w	IOFM	El Dorado	Diamond Springs Tw	72	34
Wm	51	m	w	IOFM	El Dorado	Mountain Twp	72	67
Wm	42	m	w	ENGL	San Joaquin	1-Wd Stockton	86	126
Wm	20	m	w	ENGL	San Francisco	7-Wd San Francisco	81	287
CHRISTIANCEN								
Martin	35	m	w	PRUS	Santa Clara	Redwood Twp	88	130
CHRISTIANS								
James	40	m	w	DENM	Sutter	Nicolaus Twp	92	111
Jim	25	m	c	CHIN	Sutter	Nicolaus Twp	92	111
CHRISTIANSEN								
Charles	34	m	w	SHOL	Santa Clara	2-Wd San Jose	88	313
Charles	29	m	w	NORW	San Francisco	11-Wd San Francisc	84	519
Christian	54	m	w	NORW	San Francisco	11-Wd San Francisc	84	514
Christopher	43	m	w	DENM	Marin	Sausalito Twp	74	68
James	46	m	w	NORW	San Francisco	11-Wd San Francisc	84	613
Oliver	26	m	w	NORW	San Francisco	San Francisco P O	83	106
CHRISTIANSON								
A	33	m	w	NORW	Napa	Napa	75	53
Andrew	28	m	w	DENM	San Francisco	1-Wd San Francisco	79	128
C	40	m	w	DENM	Alameda	Alameda	68	20
C M	26	m	w	NORW	Alameda	Brooklyn	68	36
Carl	33	m	w	DENM	San Francisco	11-Wd San Francisc	84	694
Christain	51	m	w	NORW	Alpine	Bullion P O	69	314
Fred	32	m	w	SHOL	Trinity	North Fork Twp	92	216
Gus	14	m	w	CA	San Francisco	8-Wd San Francisco	82	346
Hannah	18	f	w	NORW	Napa	Napa Twp	75	71
Hans	45	m	w	DENM	Calaveras	Copperopolis P O	70	246
Hans	31	m	w	PRUS	San Francisco	San Francisco P O	83	134
Henry	25	m	w	PRUS	Alameda	Brooklyn	68	38
Henry	17	m	w	PRUS	San Francisco	8-Wd San Francisco	82	297
James	23	m	w	DENM	San Francisco	7-Wd San Francisco	81	284
John	37	m	w	DENM	San Francisco	2-Wd San Francisco	79	190
Johnson	36	m	w	DENM	Alameda	Eden Twp	68	63
Louisa	14	f	w	NY	Santa Clara	Gilroy Twp	88	85
Michael	30	m	w	NORW	San Francisco	7-Wd San Francisco	81	274
Michael	30	m	w	DENM	Alameda	Brooklyn	68	31
Peter	34	m	w	SCOT	Sonoma	Petaluma Twp	91	316
Peter	32	m	w	NORW	Marin	San Rafael Twp	74	43
Robert	30	m	w	DENM	Sonoma	Salt Point	91	392
CHRISTICH								
Fred	41	m	w	WURT	Sonoma	Petaluma Twp	91	317
CHRISTIE								
Andrew	39	m	w	OH	Butte	Chico Twp	70	15
Andrew J	46	m	w	NY	El Dorado	Coloma Twp	72	6
Charles	20	m	w	IL	San Francisco	San Francisco P O	83	197
Charles J	29	m	w	CANA	Humboldt	Eureka Twp	72	261
Chas J	29	m	w	CANA	Humboldt	Eureka Twp	72	262
Fred	35	m	w	DENM	Mendocino	Casper & Big Rvr	74	163
Geo	31	m	w	SCOT	San Francisco	11-Wd San Francisc	84	608
John	40	m	w	ENGL	Tulare	Visalia	92	296
John	33	m	w	NY	Mendocino	Point Arena Twp	74	210
Margie	18	f	w	SCOT	Sonoma	Petaluma Twp	91	342
Thomas	23	m	w	CANA	Yolo	Cache Crk Twp	93	420
Wm	46	m	w	SCOT	Solano	Vallejo	90	190
Wm	39	m	w	CANA	San Joaquin	Elkhorn Twp	86	58
CHRISTIEN								
Carl	44	m	w	SWED	San Francisco	1-Wd San Francisco	79	79
CHRISTIENSEN								
Philip	28	m	w	DENM	San Francisco	1-Wd San Francisco	79	79
CHRISTIN								
Chas	43	m	w	SWIT	San Francisco	San Francisco P O	85	812
CHRISTINA								
Mary	11	f	w	CA	San Francisco	11-Wd San Francisc	84	710
CHRISTINE								
Enma	19	f	w	IA	Sonoma	Analy Twp	91	232
Joseph	26	m	w	SWIT	San Francisco	11-Wd San Francisc	84	645
CHRISTINS								
Christ	37	m	w	NORW	Mendocino	Noyo & Big Rvr Twp	74	173
Peter	29	m	w	DENM	Mendocino	Noyo & Big Rvr Twp	74	173
CHRISTISON								
Colin	24	m	w	SCOT	Shasta	Horsetown P O	89	507
H	54	f	w	NJ	Solano	Vallejo	90	183
Henry	43	m	w	DENM	San Francisco	7-Wd San Francisco	81	218
CHRISTJANSON								
Crist	47	m	w	DENM	Sonoma	Petaluma Twp	91	349
CHRISTLER								
Amaza	40	m	w	MI	Solano	Suisun Twp	90	94
CHRISTMAN								
Gabriel	36	m	w	VA	Tulare	Visalia Twp	92	282
Henry	40	m	w	VA	Tulare	Visalia Twp	92	282
J	42	m	w	NORW	Alameda	Alameda	68	3
Uler	39	m	w	NORW	Monterey	San Juan Twp	74	396
William	42	m	w	PA	Placer	Bath P O	76	458
Wm Henry	44	m	w	NY	Plumas	Seneca Twp	77	49
CHRISTMAS								
Chas	25	m	w	ENGL	Napa	Napa	75	6
Chas	25	m	w	ENGL	San Francisco	1-Wd San Francisco	79	81
Wm	44	m	w	ENGL	San Francisco	7-Wd San Francisco	81	263

© 2001 by Heritage Quest. All rights reserved.

Name	Age	S	R	B-PL	County	Locale	Series M593 Roll	Pg
CHRISTO								
James	21	m	w	ENGL	Nevada	Nevada Twp	75	304
CHRISTOE								
John	26	m	w	ENGL	Nevada	Nevada Twp	75	301
CHRISTOFF								
John	32	m	w	SHOL	San Francisco	1-Wd San Francisco	79	56
CHRISTOFFERSON								
Peter	30	m	w	DENM	San Francisco	San Francisco P O	83	93
CHRISTOLAVITCH								
J	30	m	w	AUST	Amador	Sutter Crk P O	69	402
CHRISTON								
John	36	m	w	SHOL	Sutter	Nicolaus Twp	92	107
CHRISTONSON								
O C	47	m	w	SHOL	Trinity	Douglas	92	234
CHRISTOPH								
Nicholas	48	m	w	PRUS	Sacramento	San Joaquin Twp	77	396
Razo	36	m	w	ITAL	San Francisco	San Francisco P O	85	741
CHRISTOPHER								
B F	47	m	w	TN	Mendocino	Calpella Twp	74	187
Charles	39	m	w	NORW	Plumas	Seneca Twp	77	50
Emma	30	f	w	PRUS	San Francisco	5-Wd San Francisco	81	10
F	1	m	w	CA	Klamath	Trinidad Twp	73	389
James	36	m	w	TN	Humboldt	Bucksport Twp	72	241
Louis	29	m	w	NORW	Plumas	Quartz Twp	77	34
Margaret	35	f	w	IREL	San Francisco	8-Wd San Francisco	82	406
Martin	25	m	w	SWIT	Marin	Bolinas Twp	74	2
Mary	28	f	w	DENM	Marin	San Rafael	74	51
Nath A	46	m	b	NY	Sacramento	4-Wd Sacramento	77	329
Nicholas	25	m	w	ENGL	Mariposa	Mariposa P O	74	112
Peter John	24	m	w	BAVA	Plumas	Quartz Twp	77	34
R T	39	m	w	OH	Sierra	Butte Twp	89	511
Richd	32	m	w	CANA	San Francisco	San Francisco P O	85	719
Thomas	25	m	w	ENGL	Mariposa	Mariposa P O	74	122
W M	43	m	w	TN	Mendocino	Calpella Twp	74	190
Wm	35	m	w	SWED	Plumas	Mineral Twp	77	21
Wm	33	m	w	TN	Mendocino	Calpella Twp	74	186
Wm	28	m	w	ENGL	Shasta	French Gulch P O	89	466
CHRISTOPHERSON								
Chas	40	m	w	SWED	San Francisco	1-Wd San Francisco	79	68
Christian	22	m	w	NORW	Sonoma	Salt Point	91	389
CHRISTY								
Alex	35	m	w	SCOT	San Francisco	7-Wd San Francisco	81	242
Antony	24	m	w	NORW	San Francisco	7-Wd San Francisco	81	257
Archibald	60	m	w	IREL	San Francisco	San Francisco P O	85	838
Christopher	28	m	w	SWIT	San Francisco	5-Wd San Francisco	81	9
David	26	m	w	CANA	San Mateo	Woodside P O	87	381
Edward	47	m	w	IREL	Sacramento	Granite Twp	77	148
Elijah	30	m	w	NY	Sacramento	Lee Twp	77	160
James	40	m	w	BADE	San Francisco	11-Wd San Francisc	84	687
James	32	m	w	NY	Siskiyou	Surprise Valley Tw	89	643
John	38	m	w	PA	Mendocino	Calpella Twp	74	181
Joseph	35	m	w	CANA	San Francisco	7-Wd San Francisco	81	247
L M	38	m	w	NY	Santa Clara	Gilroy Twp	88	77
Nelson	19	m	w	DENM	Placer	Bath P O	76	460
Richard	54	m	w	NC	Contra Costa	Martinez P O	71	379
Samuel	50	m	w	KY	San Francisco	San Francisco P O	80	538
Thomas	30	m	w	ENGL	San Francisco	7-Wd San Francisco	81	220
Wm	36	m	w	IN	Fresno	Millerton P O	72	188
CHRISY								
Henry	38	m	w	PRUS	Los Angeles	Los Angeles	73	527
CHRITELLON								
Clara	12	f	w	CA	San Francisco	2-Wd San Francisco	79	226
CHRONAN								
Charles	28	m	w	IREL	Nevada	Grass Valley Twp	75	206
CHRUTHERS								
Louis	65	m	b	VA	Mariposa	Mariposa P O	74	120
CHRY								
Julia	40	f	w	SAXO	Alameda	Oakland	68	148
CHRYOWETH								
William	40	m	w	ENGL	Nevada	Nevada Twp	75	309
CHRYSTY								
Henry	40	m	w	SCOT	San Francisco	San Francisco P O	83	303
CHU								
Ah	63	m	c	CHIN	El Dorado	Placerville Twp	72	96
Ah	53	m	c	CHIN	Fresno	Millerton P O	72	199
Ah	50	m	c	CHIN	El Dorado	Georgetown Twp	72	41
Ah	44	f	c	CHIN	Sierra	Downieville Twp	89	521
Ah	41	m	c	CHIN	Alameda	Oakland	68	223
Ah	40	m	c	CHIN	San Francisco	San Francisco P O	80	489
Ah	40	m	c	CHIN	Butte	Ophir Twp	70	104
Ah	40	m	c	CHIN	Alameda	Oakland	68	158
Ah	40	m	c	CHIN	Placer	Newcastle Twp	76	474
Ah	40	m	c	CHIN	Tuolumne	Columbia P O	93	352
Ah	39	m	c	CHIN	Alameda	Oakland	68	152
Ah	39	m	c	CHIN	Placer	Bath P O	76	432
Ah	38	m	c	CHIN	Amador	Volcano P O	69	377
Ah	38	m	c	CHIN	Sierra	Forest Twp	89	532
Ah	38	m	c	CHIN	Stanislaus	Buena Vista Twp	92	12
Ah	35	m	c	CHIN	San Joaquin	Elkhorn Twp	86	53
Ah	35	m	c	CHIN	Butte	Chico Twp	70	52
Ah	35	m	c	CHIN	Los Angeles	Los Angeles	73	507
Ah	35	m	c	CHIN	Siskiyou	Cottonwood Twp	89	592
Ah	34	m	c	CHIN	San Mateo	Schoolhouse Statio	87	340
Ah	34	m	c	CHIN	Alameda	Oakland	68	152
Ah	33	m	c	CHIN	Fresno	Millerton P O	72	202
Ah	32	m	c	CHIN	Amador	Fiddletown P O	69	428
Ah	29	m	c	CHIN	Butte	Hamilton Twp	70	67
Ah	29	m	c	CHIN	Yolo	Washington Twp	93	534
Ah	27	m	c	CHIN	Shasta	French Gulch P O	89	469
Ah	26	m	c	CHIN	Sierra	Alleghany & Forest	89	535
Ah	26	m	c	CHIN	Sierra	Forest	89	537
Ah	26	m	c	CHIN	Butte	Hamilton Twp	70	73
Ah	25	m	c	CHIN	San Francisco	San Francisco P O	83	355
Ah	25	m	c	CHIN	Butte	Ophir Twp	70	103
Ah	25	m	c	CHIN	El Dorado	Mud Springs Twp	72	81
Ah	25	m	c	CHIN	Placer	Clipper Gap P O	76	393
Ah	25	m	c	CHIN	Placer	Colfax P O	76	390
Ah	25	m	c	CHIN	Solano	Suisun Twp	90	98
Ah	24	m	c	CHIN	Solano	Suisun Twp	90	105
Ah	24	m	c	CHIN	Yolo	Putah Twp	93	513
Ah	22	m	c	CHIN	Alameda	Oakland	68	157
Ah	22	m	c	CHIN	Sacramento	2-Wd Sacramento	77	245
Ah	22	m	c	CHIN	Yuba	Marysville	93	593
Ah	18	m	c	CHIN	Solano	Vallejo	90	176
Ah	17	m	c	CHIN	Alameda	Oakland	68	206
Ah	16	m	c	CHIN	San Francisco	San Francisco P O	85	717
Ah	16	m	c	CHIN	San Francisco	6-Wd San Francisco	81	99
Ah	16	m	c	CHIN	Santa Clara	Fremont Twp	88	55
Ah	16	m	c	CHIN	Napa	Napa	75	57
Ah	15	m	c	CHIN	San Francisco	1-Wd San Francisco	79	80
Ah	12	m	c	CHIN	Alameda	Washington Twp	68	290
An	39	m	c	CHIN	Tuolumne	Sonora P O	93	311
Chow	29	m	c	CHIN	San Francisco	6-Wd San Francisco	81	88
Choy	48	m	c	CHIN	Siskiyou	Hamburg Twp	89	598
Gee	31	f	c	CHIN	Yuba	Marysville	93	627
Hi	49	m	c	CHIN	Calaveras	San Andreas P O	70	191
Kee	28	m	c	CHIN	Solano	Rio Vista Twp	90	70
Lee	45	m	c	CHIN	Fresno	Millerton P O	72	202
Lee	17	m	c	CHIN	Alameda	Oakland	68	158
Low	23	m	c	CHIN	Alameda	Oakland	68	152
Lum	41	m	c	CHIN	Trinity	Weaverville Pct	92	231
Quo	30	m	c	CHIN	Fresno	Millerton P O	72	201
Tong	51	m	c	CHIN	Amador	Fiddletown P O	69	428
Tuck	27	f	c	CHIN	Calaveras	Copperopolis P O	70	264
CHUAP								
Ah	35	m	c	CHIN	Placer	Bath P O	76	445
CHUB								
Oliver	30	m	w	VT	Kern	Bakersfield P O	73	366
CHUBBICK								
Barney	36	m	w	NY	Fresno	Millerton P O	72	158
CHUBBRICK								
J M	41	m	w	ME	Butte	Bidwell Twp	70	4
CHUBRICK								
A	40	m	w	LA	San Francisco	San Francisco P O	85	807
CHUC								
Ah	51	m	c	CHIN	El Dorado	Mud Springs Twp	72	73
Ah	30	f	c	CHIN	Nevada	Grass Valley Twp	75	205
CHUCH								
Ah	31	m	c	CHIN	San Joaquin	3-Wd Stockton	86	243
Ah	29	m	c	CHIN	Sacramento	Granite Twp	77	137
Ah	27	m	c	CHIN	San Joaquin	1-Wd Stockton	86	155
Ah	27	m	c	CHIN	San Joaquin	2-Wd Stockton	86	179
Ah	26	m	c	CHIN	San Joaquin	Oneal Twp	86	118
Ah	25	m	c	CHIN	San Francisco	6-Wd San Francisco	81	56
Ah	20	m	c	CHIN	San Joaquin	2-Wd Stockton	86	180
Sam	40	m	c	CHIN	San Joaquin	1-Wd Stockton	86	147
CHUCK								
Ah	60	m	c	CHIN	Butte	Ophir Twp	70	104
Ah	55	m	c	CHIN	Placer	Dutch Flat P O	76	408
Ah	46	m	c	CHIN	San Joaquin	Liberty Twp	86	88
Ah	45	m	c	CHIN	Tuolumne	Sonora P O	93	311
Ah	45	m	c	CHIN	Trinity	Douglas	92	233
Ah	40	m	c	CHIN	Placer	Auburn P O	76	364
Ah	40	m	c	CHIN	Trinity	Douglas	92	233
Ah	38	m	c	CHIN	Plumas	Goodwin Twp	77	2
Ah	36	m	c	CHIN	Alameda	Oakland	68	254
Ah	34	m	c	CHIN	El Dorado	Diamond Springs Tw	72	33
Ah	31	m	c	CHIN	Alameda	Oakland	68	138
Ah	30	m	c	CHIN	Solano	Suisun Twp	90	106
Ah	30	m	c	CHIN	Calaveras	San Andreas P O	70	161
Ah	30	m	c	CHIN	Alameda	Oakland	68	245
Ah	30	m	c	CHIN	San Francisco	San Francisco P O	83	285
Ah	30	m	c	CHIN	San Francisco	6-Wd San Francisco	81	53
Ah	29	m	c	CHIN	Solano	Suisun Twp	90	105
Ah	28	m	c	CHIN	Placer	Dutch Flat P O	76	408
Ah	28	m	c	CHIN	Alameda	Alameda	68	6
Ah	25	m	c	CHIN	Alameda	Oakland	68	172
Ah	24	m	c	CHIN	Alameda	Oakland	68	156
Ah	24	m	c	CHIN	Amador	Jackson P O	69	331
Ah	22	m	c	CHIN	San Francisco	3-Wd San Francisco	79	329
Ah	21	m	c	CHIN	Solano	Suisun Twp	90	104
Ah	21	m	c	CHIN	San Francisco	3-Wd San Francisco	79	310
Ah	21	m	c	CHIN	Placer	Auburn P O	76	379
Ah	20	m	c	CHIN	San Francisco	6-Wd San Francisco	81	65
Ah	20	m	c	CHIN	Stanislaus	Emory Twp	92	19
Ah	19	m	c	CHIN	San Francisco	6-Wd San Francisco	81	63
Ah	17	m	c	CHIN	San Francisco	6-Wd San Francisco	81	85
Ah	17	m	c	CHIN	Solano	Vallejo	90	209
Ain	25	f	c	CHIN	Sacramento	1-Wd Sacramento	77	193
Chip	35	m	c	CHIN	Placer	Newcastle Twp	76	479
Chuen	29	m	c	CHIN	San Francisco	6-Wd San Francisco	81	53
Foon	25	f	c	CHIN	Nevada	Bridgeport Twp	75	111
Goo	42	m	c	CHIN	Solano	Vallejo	90	209
Ham	20	m	c	CHIN	Tuolumne	Columbia P O	93	361

© 2001 by Heritage Quest. All rights reserved.

Name	Age	S	R	B-PL	County	Locale	Series M593 Roll	Pg
Lah	35	m	c	CHIN	Marin	Tomales Twp	74	80
Lee	29	m	c	CHIN	Tuolumne	Big Oak Flat P O	93	404
Sue	25	m	c	CHIN	Yuba	Marysville	93	630
Tuck	20	m	c	CHIN	Calaveras	San Andreas P O	70	176
Wan	52	m	c	CHIN	Solano	Suisun Twp	90	104
Wan	26	m	c	CHIN	Solano	Vacaville Twp	90	131
Won	40	m	c	CHIN	Nevada	Washington Twp	75	342
CHUDWICK								
Wm J	50	m	w	NY	El Dorado	Salmon Falls Twp	72	132
CHUE								
Ah	46	m	c	CHIN	Amador	Jackson P O	69	344
Ah	40	m	c	CHIN	Mariposa	Mariposa P O	74	136
Ah	35	m	c	CHIN	Amador	Fiddletown P O	69	427
Ah	30	m	c	CHIN	Placer	Lincoln P O	76	483
Ah	30	m	c	CHIN	San Joaquin	Castoria Twp	86	15
Ah	27	m	c	CHIN	San Joaquin	Dent Twp	86	22
Ah	24	m	c	CHIN	San Francisco	6-Wd San Francisco	81	52
Ah	22	m	c	CHIN	Placer	Lincoln P O	76	492
Ah	19	m	c	CHIN	San Francisco	6-Wd San Francisco	81	87
Loy	42	m	c	CHIN	Plumas	Mineral Twp	77	25
Newey	22	m	c	CHIN	Plumas	Mineral Twp	77	25
Sang	39	m	c	CHIN	Yuba	Marysville	93	625
Sing Yet	30	m	c	CHIN	Marin	San Rafael Twp	74	59
Toy	34	m	c	CHIN	Plumas	Mineral Twp	77	25
CHUEING								
Ah	17	m	c	CHIN	San Francisco	3-Wd San Francisco	79	309
CHUEM								
Ah	30	m	c	CHIN	Calaveras	Copperopolis P O	70	226
CHUEN								
Ah	33	m	c	CHIN	San Francisco	6-Wd San Francisco	81	66
Ah	30	m	c	CHIN	San Francisco	6-Wd San Francisco	81	44
Ah	27	m	c	CHIN	San Francisco	3-Wd San Francisco	79	309
Ah	21	m	c	CHIN	San Francisco	6-Wd San Francisco	81	55
Ah	20	m	c	CHIN	San Francisco	6-Wd San Francisco	81	84
Ah	18	m	c	CHIN	San Francisco	6-Wd San Francisco	81	59
Ah	18	m	c	CHIN	San Francisco	3-Wd San Francisco	79	309
Ah	16	m	c	CHIN	San Francisco	6-Wd San Francisco	81	69
Ah	16	m	c	CHIN	San Francisco	6-Wd San Francisco	81	85
Ah	16	m	c	CHIN	San Francisco	3-Wd San Francisco	79	320
Ah	13	m	c	CHIN	San Francisco	San Francisco P O	83	298
Choy	23	m	c	CHIN	San Francisco	6-Wd San Francisco	81	69
Lue	24	m	c	CHIN	San Francisco	6-Wd San Francisco	81	82
Lung	30	m	c	CHIN	San Francisco	6-Wd San Francisco	81	72
Sam	20	m	c	CHIN	San Francisco	6-Wd San Francisco	81	94
CHUEY								
Ah	33	m	c	CHIN	San Francisco	6-Wd San Francisco	81	130
Ah	28	m	c	CHIN	San Francisco	3-Wd San Francisco	79	301
Ah	24	m	c	CHIN	San Francisco	3-Wd San Francisco	79	318
Sing Chong	61	m	c	CHIN	San Francisco	6-Wd San Francisco	81	88
Tie	21	m	c	CHIN	San Joaquin	Liberty Twp	86	97
CHUG								
Ah	40	m	c	CHIN	Siskiyou	Cottonwood Twp	89	594
Ah	28	m	c	CHIN	San Francisco	6-Wd San Francisco	81	42
Ah	25	m	c	CHIN	San Francisco	San Francisco P O	80	492
Ah	19	m	c	CHIN	San Francisco	6-Wd San Francisco	81	43
CHUGN								
Mi	42	m	c	CHIN	Placer	Bath P O	76	442
CHUH								
---	16	m	c	CHIN	San Joaquin	1-Wd Stockton	86	142
CHUI								
Sew	33	m	c	CHIN	Yuba	North East Twp	93	646
CHUICH								
Oraville	48	m	w	NY	Butte	Chico Twp	70	21
CHUIG								
Fang	31	m	c	CHIN	Solano	Vacaville Twp	90	129
CHUING								
Ah	40	m	c	CHIN	Amador	Ione City P O	69	364
CHUK								
Ah	40	m	c	CHIN	Contra Costa	Martinez P O	71	452
Ah	40	m	c	CHIN	Nevada	Rough & Ready Twp	75	324
Ah	30	m	c	CHIN	San Francisco	6-Wd San Francisco	81	54
Ah	30	m	c	CHIN	San Francisco	6-Wd San Francisco	81	86
Ah	27	m	c	CHIN	San Francisco	6-Wd San Francisco	81	65
Ah	20	m	c	CHIN	Alameda	Oakland	68	169
Ah	20	m	c	CHIN	Sacramento	San Joaquin Twp	77	395
Ah	19	m	c	CHIN	San Francisco	6-Wd San Francisco	81	67
Ah	19	m	c	CHIN	San Francisco	6-Wd San Francisco	81	66
Ah	18	m	c	CHIN	San Francisco	3-Wd San Francisco	79	304
Ah	16	m	c	CHIN	San Francisco	8-Wd San Francisco	82	382
Luk	20	m	c	CHIN	San Francisco	6-Wd San Francisco	81	64
CHULER								
Ah	26	m	c	CHIN	Placer	Clipper Gap P O	76	392
CHUM								
Ah	52	f	c	CHIN	San Francisco	San Francisco P O	80	443
Ah	49	m	c	CHIN	Tuolumne	Chinese Camp P O	93	386
Ah	47	m	c	CHIN	Tuolumne	Big Oak Flat P O	93	400
Ah	45	m	c	CHIN	Mariposa	Mariposa P O	74	102
Ah	44	m	c	CHIN	Mariposa	Mariposa P O	74	114
Ah	44	m	c	CHIN	Tuolumne	Chinese Camp P O	93	384
Ah	42	m	c	CHIN	Butte	Ophir Twp	70	104
Ah	39	m	c	CHIN	Mariposa	Mariposa P O	74	102
Ah	38	m	c	CHIN	Tuolumne	Chinese Camp P O	93	390
Ah	37	m	c	CHIN	San Francisco	11-Wd San Francisc	84	695
Ah	35	m	c	CHIN	Mariposa	Mariposa P O	74	103
Ah	34	m	c	CHIN	Nevada	Grass Valley Twp	75	205
Ah	32	m	c	CHIN	Mariposa	Mariposa P O	74	126
Ah	30	f	c	CHIN	San Francisco	6-Wd San Francisco	81	77

Name	Age	S	R	B-PL	County	Locale	Series M593 Roll	Pg
Ah	29	m	c	CHIN	Solano	Suisun Twp	90	106
Ah	29	m	c	CHIN	Nevada	Grass Valley Twp	75	184
Ah	28	m	c	CHIN	San Francisco	11-Wd San Francisc	84	574
Ah	28	m	c	CHIN	Santa Barbara	Santa Barbara P O	87	452
Ah	28	m	c	CHIN	El Dorado	Mud Springs Twp	72	74
Ah	27	m	c	CHIN	San Francisco	3-Wd San Francisco	79	304
Ah	26	m	c	CHIN	Tuolumne	Chinese Camp P O	93	370
Ah	25	m	c	CHIN	Alameda	Murray Twp	68	124
Ah	25	f	c	CHIN	Amador	Fiddletown P O	69	428
Ah	25	m	c	CHIN	Alameda	Washington Twp	68	271
Ah	23	m	c	CHIN	Calaveras	Copperopolis P O	70	226
Ah	22	m	c	CHIN	Alameda	Oakland	68	251
Ah	22	m	c	CHIN	Nevada	Little York Twp	75	245
Ah	20	m	c	CHIN	San Francisco	6-Wd San Francisco	81	49
Ah	20	m	c	CHIN	Alameda	Eden Twp	68	59
Ah	19	m	c	CHIN	San Francisco	3-Wd San Francisco	79	304
Ah	19	m	c	CHIN	Santa Clara	1-Wd San Jose	88	274
Ah	19	m	c	CHIN	Nevada	Grass Valley Twp	75	206
Ah	18	m	c	CHIN	San Francisco	3-Wd San Francisco	79	304
Ah	18	m	c	CHIN	Santa Clara	Santa Clara Twp	88	166
Ah	13	m	c	CHIN	Tuolumne	Chinese Camp P O	93	379
Ah	1	m	c	CA	San Francisco	San Francisco P O	80	444
Choy	25	m	c	CHIN	San Francisco	6-Wd San Francisco	81	43
Chy	31	m	c	CHIN	Yuba	Marysville	93	622
Hid	37	m	c	CHIN	San Mateo	Schoolhouse Statio	87	339
Hira	27	m	c	CHIN	San Mateo	Schoolhouse Statio	87	335
Ho	20	m	c	CHIN	Sonoma	Sonoma Twp	91	431
Kee	50	m	c	CHIN	Butte	Ophir Twp	70	109
Kin	37	m	c	CHIN	Butte	Concow Twp	70	12
Lou	25	m	c	CHIN	Alameda	Oakland	68	158
Low	20	m	c	CHIN	Trinity	North Fork Twp	92	216
Lun	27	m	c	CHIN	Solano	Rio Vista Twp	90	70
Sen	45	m	c	CHIN	San Francisco	6-Wd San Francisco	81	47
Sun	24	m	c	CHIN	Solano	Rio Vista Twp	90	70
Wo	47	m	c	CHIN	Tuolumne	Big Oak Flat P O	93	394
Yap	28	m	c	CHIN	Placer	Bath P O	76	442
Yo	22	f	c	CHIN	Mariposa	Mariposa P O	74	102
Yow	54	m	c	CHIN	Trinity	Junction City Pct	92	208
Yow	38	m	c	CHIN	San Francisco	6-Wd San Francisco	81	67
CHUMWAY								
Cyrus H	42	m	w	OH	Stanislaus	Empire Twp	92	65
CHUN								
Ah	60	m	c	CHIN	Amador	Fiddletown P O	69	440
Ah	51	m	c	CHIN	Nevada	Grass Valley Twp	75	203
Ah	50	m	c	CHIN	Sacramento	Granite Twp	77	138
Ah	48	m	c	CHIN	Mariposa	Mariposa P O	74	132
Ah	48	m	c	CHIN	Placer	Auburn P O	76	372
Ah	45	m	c	CHIN	Tuolumne	Sonora P O	93	323
Ah	44	m	c	CHIN	Amador	Fiddletown P O	69	427
Ah	41	m	c	CHIN	Tuolumne	Sonora P O	93	321
Ah	41	m	c	CHIN	Amador	Fiddletown P O	69	440
Ah	41	m	c	CHIN	Placer	Auburn P O	76	374
Ah	40	m	c	CHIN	Tuolumne	Big Oak Flat P O	93	392
Ah	40	m	c	CHIN	Butte	Kimshew Tpw	70	77
Ah	40	m	c	CHIN	Stanislaus	Emory Twp	92	19
Ah	40	m	c	CHIN	Amador	Volcano P O	69	378
Ah	40	m	c	CHIN	Amador	Volcano P O	69	387
Ah	40	m	c	CHIN	Butte	Kimshew Tpw	70	86
Ah	39	m	c	CHIN	Tuolumne	Chinese Camp P O	93	366
Ah	37	m	c	CHIN	San Francisco	San Francisco P O	80	505
Ah	36	m	c	CHIN	Butte	Chico Twp	70	30
Ah	35	m	c	CHIN	San Francisco	6-Wd San Francisco	81	51
Ah	34	m	c	CHIN	Amador	Fiddletown P O	69	429
Ah	33	m	c	CHIN	Butte	Oregon Twp	70	135
Ah	33	m	c	CHIN	Placer	Colfax P O	76	384
Ah	32	f	c	CHIN	Tuolumne	Sonora P O	93	324
Ah	32	m	c	CHIN	Mariposa	Mariposa P O	74	125
Ah	32	m	c	CHIN	Merced	Snelling P O	74	279
Ah	32	m	c	CHIN	Butte	Kimshew Tpw	70	77
Ah	32	m	c	CHIN	Sacramento	Georgianna Twp	77	122
Ah	31	m	c	CHIN	Calaveras	Copperopolis P O	70	235
Ah	30	m	c	CHIN	Amador	Volcano P O	69	376
Ah	30	m	c	CHIN	Nevada	Meadow Lake Twp	75	254
Ah	29	m	c	CHIN	Calaveras	San Andreas P O	70	178
Ah	28	m	c	CHIN	Merced	Snelling P O	74	278
Ah	28	m	c	CHIN	Sacramento	Georgianna Twp	77	133
Ah	25	m	c	CHIN	Placer	Auburn P O	76	378
Ah	22	m	c	CHIN	Placer	Dutch Flat P O	76	414
Ah	22	m	c	CHIN	San Francisco	6-Wd San Francisco	81	59
Ah	21	f	c	CHIN	Santa Cruz	Watsonville	89	377
Ah	21	m	c	CHIN	Nevada	Meadow Lake Twp	75	256
Ah	21	m	c	CHIN	Yuba	Marysville	93	620
Ah	20	m	c	CHIN	Alameda	Oakland	68	198
Ah	18	m	c	CHIN	Butte	Concow Twp	70	10
Ah	16	m	c	CHIN	Tuolumne	Big Oak Flat P O	93	391
Ah	16	m	c	CHIN	Placer	Auburn P O	76	361
Ah	12	m	c	CHIN	Sacramento	1-Wd Sacramento	77	199
Ar	33	m	c	CHIN	Sonoma	Petaluma Twp	91	363
Choo	30	m	c	CHIN	Solano	Vacaville Twp	90	117
Come	20	m	c	CHIN	Yuba	Slate Range Bar Tw	93	668
Day	24	m	c	CHIN	San Francisco	6-Wd San Francisco	81	52
Dee	28	m	c	CHIN	Yuba	Marysville	93	622
Ee	30	m	c	CHIN	Sacramento	1-Wd Sacramento	77	192
Foo	36	m	c	CHIN	Butte	Chico Twp	70	53
Gee	21	m	c	CHIN	Butte	Kimshew Tpw	70	85
Haewn	28	m	c	CHIN	Calaveras	Copperopolis P O	70	253
John	28	m	c	CHIN	Solano	Vallejo	90	175

© 2001 by Heritage Quest. All rights reserved.

Name	Age	S	R	B-PL	County	Locale	Series M593 Roll	Pg
Kan	46	m	c	CHIN	Placer	Dutch Flat P O	76	407
Kee	29	m	c	CHIN	Amador	Amador City P O	69	395
King	15	m	c	CHIN	San Francisco	6-Wd San Francisco	81	39
Lee	32	m	c	CHIN	Butte	Chico Twp	70	52
Lee	28	m	c	CHIN	Butte	Chico Twp	70	51
Ling	24	m	c	CHIN	Placer	Colfax P O	76	386
Long	20	m	c	CHIN	Siskiyou	Yreka Twp	89	669
Lun	60	m	c	CHIN	Calaveras	Copperopolis P O	70	226
Lung	40	m	c	CHIN	Sacramento	1-Wd Sacramento	77	193
M	42	m	c	CHIN	Butte	Chico Twp	70	52
Mon	34	m	c	CHIN	Alameda	Washington Twp	68	299
Mon	27	m	c	CHIN	Butte	Chico Twp	70	51
Yik	38	m	c	CHIN	Butte	Ophir Twp	70	119
Yong	57	m	c	CHIN	Trinity	Weaverville Pct	92	231
Zin	40	m	c	CHIN	Trinity	Indian Crk	92	199
CHUNE								
Ah	40	m	c	CHIN	Mariposa	Mariposa P O	74	92
Ah	35	m	c	CHIN	Marin	San Rafael Twp	74	45
Ah	29	m	c	CHIN	Amador	Fiddletown P O	69	427
Ah	27	m	c	CHIN	Trinity	Indian Crk	92	199
Ah	24	m	c	CHIN	Santa Clara	1-Wd San Jose	88	253
Ah	22	m	c	CHIN	San Francisco	3-Wd San Francisco	79	309
Ah	17	m	c	CHIN	San Francisco	6-Wd San Francisco	81	111
Gee	48	m	c	CHIN	Plumas	Mineral Twp	77	23
Tie	21	m	c	CHIN	Los Angeles	Los Angeles	73	524
CHUNEY								
Hi	43	m	c	CHIN	San Joaquin	1-Wd Stockton	86	147
CHUNG								
---	55	m	c	CHIN	Amador	Fiddletown P O	69	428
---	32	m	c	CHIN	Siskiyou	Yreka	89	660
---	20	m	c	CHIN	Shasta	Shasta P O	89	454
---	12	m	c	CHIN	San Francisco	5-Wd San Francisco	81	1
Ah	78	m	c	CHIN	Nevada	Grass Valley Twp	75	205
Ah	78	m	c	CHIN	San Francisco	11-Wd San Francisc	84	574
Ah	7	f	c	CA	Calaveras	San Andreas P O	70	181
Ah	63	m	c	CHIN	Placer	Blue Canyon P O	76	419
Ah	62	m	c	CHIN	Amador	Ione City P O	69	363
Ah	60	m	c	CHIN	Nevada	Grass Valley Twp	75	206
Ah	59	m	c	CHIN	El Dorado	Placerville	72	115
Ah	56	m	c	CHIN	Placer	Newcastle Twp	76	479
Ah	56	m	c	CHIN	El Dorado	Placerville	72	114
Ah	55	m	c	CHIN	Calaveras	Copperopolis P O	70	235
Ah	54	m	c	CHIN	Tuolumne	Chinese Camp P O	93	364
Ah	53	m	c	CHIN	Nevada	Grass Valley Twp	75	206
Ah	50	m	c	CHIN	Amador	Drytown P O	69	421
Ah	50	m	c	CHIN	Calaveras	Copperopolis P O	70	233
Ah	50	m	c	CHIN	Sacramento	Granite Twp	77	138
Ah	50	m	c	CHIN	Stanislaus	Emory Twp	92	19
Ah	50	m	c	CHIN	Sierra	Downieville Twp	89	521
Ah	50	m	c	CHIN	Tuolumne	Chinese Camp P O	93	381
Ah	50	m	c	CHIN	Butte	Chico Twp	70	28
Ah	49	m	c	CHIN	Amador	Jackson P O	69	338
Ah	49	m	c	CHIN	Placer	Bath P O	76	445
Ah	48	m	c	CHIN	Amador	Ione City P O	69	351
Ah	48	m	c	CHIN	Plumas	Washington Twp	77	58
Ah	46	m	c	CHIN	Amador	Fiddletown P O	69	426
Ah	46	m	c	CHIN	Mariposa	Mariposa P O	74	102
Ah	46	m	c	CHIN	Plumas	Plumas Twp	77	31
Ah	45	m	c	CHIN	Butte	Wyandotte Twp	70	141
Ah	45	m	c	CHIN	Amador	Ione City P O	69	364
Ah	45	m	c	CHIN	Amador	Ione City P O	69	364
Ah	45	m	c	CHIN	El Dorado	Salmon Falls Twp	72	131
Ah	45	m	c	CHIN	Sacramento	Granite Twp	77	138
Ah	45	m	c	CHIN	Trinity	North Fork Twp	92	220
Ah	45	m	c	CHIN	Klamath	Orleans Twp	73	380
Ah	45	m	c	CHIN	Placer	Colfax P O	76	384
Ah	44	m	c	CHIN	Sierra	Table Rock Twp	89	544
Ah	44	m	c	CHIN	Placer	Auburn P O	76	362
Ah	43	m	c	CHIN	Klamath	Orleans Twp	73	379
Ah	43	m	c	CHIN	Kern	Tehachapi P O	73	356
Ah	42	m	c	CHIN	Placer	Auburn P O	76	367
Ah	41	m	c	CHIN	Trinity	Weaverville Pct	92	232
Ah	41	m	c	CHIN	San Francisco	11-Wd San Francisc	84	695
Ah	41	m	c	CHIN	Mariposa	Mariposa P O	74	121
Ah	41	m	c	CHIN	Placer	Lincoln P O	76	483
Ah	40	m	c	CHIN	Calaveras	San Andreas P O	70	167
Ah	40	m	c	CHIN	El Dorado	Mountain Twp	72	67
Ah	40	m	c	CHIN	Kern	Tehachapi P O	73	353
Ah	40	m	c	CHIN	Placer	Bath P O	76	445
Ah	40	m	c	CHIN	Plumas	Seneca Twp	77	48
Ah	40	m	c	CHIN	Plumas	Washington Twp	77	57
Ah	40	m	c	CHIN	Nevada	Grass Valley Twp	75	217
Ah	40	m	c	CHIN	Nevada	Grass Valley Twp	75	194
Ah	40	m	c	CHIN	San Francisco	6-Wd San Francisco	81	56
Ah	40	m	c	CHIN	Tuolumne	Chinese Camp P O	93	375
Ah	40	m	c	CHIN	Tuolumne	Sonora P O	93	327
Ah	40	m	c	CHIN	Tuolumne	Chinese Camp P O	93	363
Ah	40	m	c	CHIN	Tuolumne	Sonora P O	93	312
Ah	40	m	c	CHIN	Tulare	Visalia Twp	92	281
Ah	40	m	c	CHIN	San Joaquin	1-Wd Stockton	86	145
Ah	40	m	c	CHIN	San Francisco	6-Wd San Francisco	81	42
Ah	40	m	c	CHIN	San Francisco	6-Wd San Francisco	81	39
Ah	40	m	c	CHIN	Kern	Linns Valley P O	73	343
Ah	40	m	c	CHIN	Mariposa	Mariposa P O	74	137
Ah	40	m	c	CHIN	Mariposa	Mariposa P O	74	136
Ah	40	m	c	CHIN	Mariposa	Mariposa P O	74	103
Ah	40	m	c	CHIN	Butte	Hamilton Twp	70	66
Ah	40	m	c	CHIN	Placer	Auburn P O	76	363
Ah	40	m	c	CHIN	San Francisco	San Francisco P O	80	444
Ah	39	m	c	CHIN	El Dorado	Diamond Springs Tw	72	32
Ah	39	m	c	CHIN	Placer	Bath P O	76	445
Ah	39	m	c	CHIN	San Francisco	San Francisco P O	80	454
Ah	38	m	c	CHIN	El Dorado	Mud Springs Twp	72	74
Ah	38	m	c	CHIN	Tuolumne	Big Oak Flat P O	93	392
Ah	38	m	c	CHIN	Mariposa	Mariposa P O	74	114
Ah	38	m	c	CHIN	Mariposa	Mariposa P O	74	103
Ah	38	m	c	CHIN	Calaveras	San Andreas P O	70	183
Ah	38	m	c	CHIN	San Diego	Julian Dist	78	469
Ah	37	m	c	CHIN	Amador	Sutter Crk P O	69	403
Ah	37	m	c	CHIN	Amador	Jackson P O	69	319
Ah	37	m	c	CHIN	Kern	Kernville P O	73	367
Ah	37	m	c	CHIN	Mariposa	Mariposa P O	74	104
Ah	36	m	c	CHIN	Amador	Fiddletown P O	69	426
Ah	36	m	c	CHIN	Amador	Sutter Crk P O	69	413
Ah	36	m	c	CHIN	Alameda	Alvarado	68	303
Ah	36	m	c	CHIN	Placer	Auburn P O	76	361
Ah	36	m	c	CHIN	Mariposa	Maxwell Crk P O	74	143
Ah	35	m	c	CHIN	Alameda	Oakland	68	267
Ah	35	m	c	CHIN	El Dorado	White Oak Twp	72	142
Ah	35	m	c	CHIN	Placer	Dutch Flat P O	76	409
Ah	35	m	c	CHIN	San Francisco	6-Wd San Francisco	81	46
Ah	35	m	c	CHIN	San Francisco	11-Wd San Francisc	84	528
Ah	35	m	c	CHIN	Solano	Vallejo	90	216
Ah	35	m	c	CHIN	San Francisco	6-Wd San Francisco	81	59
Ah	35	m	c	CHIN	Kern	Havilah P O	73	337
Ah	35	m	c	CHIN	Mariposa	Mariposa P O	74	101
Ah	35	m	c	CHIN	Alameda	Oakland	68	247
Ah	35	m	c	CHIN	Calaveras	Copperopolis P O	70	222
Ah	35	m	c	CHIN	Plumas	Indian Twp	77	16
Ah	34	m	c	CHIN	San Francisco	6-Wd San Francisco	81	75
Ah	34	m	c	CHIN	Calaveras	Copperopolis P O	70	226
Ah	34	m	c	CHIN	Placer	Auburn P O	76	383
Ah	33	m	c	CHIN	Amador	Ione City P O	69	355
Ah	33	m	c	CHIN	Placer	Bath P O	76	446
Ah	33	m	c	CHIN	Placer	Auburn P O	76	362
Ah	33	m	c	CHIN	Nevada	Grass Valley Twp	75	205
Ah	33	m	c	CHIN	Nevada	Grass Valley Twp	75	202
Ah	33	m	c	CHIN	San Francisco	6-Wd San Francisco	81	56
Ah	33	m	c	CHIN	Butte	Bidwell Twp	70	5
Ah	33	m	c	CHIN	Plumas	Plumas Twp	77	32
Ah	33	m	c	CHIN	Placer	Emigrant Gap P O	76	417
Ah	33	m	c	CHIN	Placer	Lincoln P O	76	483
Ah	32	m	c	CHIN	El Dorado	Diamond Springs Tw	72	32
Ah	32	m	c	CHIN	Nevada	Nevada Twp	75	298
Ah	32	m	c	CHIN	Tuolumne	Chinese Camp P O	93	369
Ah	32	m	c	CHIN	Tuolumne	Chinese Camp P O	93	364
Ah	32	m	c	CHIN	Stanislaus	Empire Twp	92	56
Ah	32	m	c	CHIN	Stanislaus	Empire Twp	92	41
Ah	32	m	c	CHIN	San Luis Obispo	San Luis Obispo Tw	87	297
Ah	32	m	c	CHIN	San Francisco	6-Wd San Francisco	81	37
Ah	32	m	c	CHIN	Mariposa	Mariposa P O	74	132
Ah	32	m	c	CHIN	Calaveras	San Andreas P O	70	171
Ah	32	m	c	CHIN	Contra Costa	Martinez P O	71	386
Ah	32	m	c	CHIN	Plumas	Goodwin Twp	77	4
Ah	32	m	c	CHIN	Nevada	Little York Twp	75	245
Ah	31	m	c	CHIN	El Dorado	Salmon Falls Twp	72	130
Ah	31	m	c	CHIN	Kern	Bakersfield P O	73	357
Ah	31	m	c	CHIN	Plumas	Plumas Twp	77	26
Ah	31	m	c	CHIN	Placer	Gold Run Twp	76	398
Ah	30	m	c	CHIN	Los Angeles	Los Angeles	73	550
Ah	30	m	c	CHIN	Sacramento	1-Wd Sacramento	77	198
Ah	30	m	c	CHIN	Sacramento	3-Wd Sacramento	77	295
Ah	30	m	c	CHIN	Placer	Alta P O	76	413
Ah	30	m	c	CHIN	Placer	Auburn P O	76	364
Ah	30	m	c	CHIN	Nevada	Grass Valley Twp	75	227
Ah	30	m	c	CHIN	Nevada	Bridgeport Twp	75	111
Ah	30	m	c	CHIN	Nevada	Bridgeport Twp	75	119
Ah	30	m	c	CHIN	Santa Clara	1-Wd San Jose	88	275
Ah	30	m	c	CHIN	San Joaquin	Douglas Twp	86	49
Ah	30	m	c	CHIN	San Mateo	Schoolhouse Statio	87	344
Ah	30	m	c	CHIN	San Francisco	6-Wd San Francisco	81	55
Ah	30	m	c	CHIN	Sierra	Lincoln Twp	89	548
Ah	30	m	c	CHIN	Trinity	Weaverville Pct	92	230
Ah	30	m	c	CHIN	Tehama	Antelope Twp	92	156
Ah	30	m	c	CHIN	San Francisco	6-Wd San Francisco	81	47
Ah	30	m	c	CHIN	San Francisco	6-Wd San Francisco	81	62
Ah	30	m	c	CHIN	San Francisco	8-Wd San Francisco	82	378
Ah	30	m	c	CHIN	San Francisco	11-Wd San Francisc	84	429
Ah	30	m	c	CHIN	Los Angeles	Los Angeles	73	566
Ah	30	m	c	CHIN	Mariposa	Mariposa P O	74	126
Ah	30	m	c	CHIN	Mariposa	Mariposa P O	74	127
Ah	30	m	c	CHIN	Mariposa	Mariposa P O	74	122
Ah	30	f	c	CHIN	Mariposa	Mariposa P O	74	103
Ah	30	m	c	CHIN	Alameda	Oakland	68	199
Ah	30	m	c	CHIN	Calaveras	San Andreas P O	70	162
Ah	30	m	c	CHIN	Sacramento	2-Wd Sacramento	77	245
Ah	30	m	c	CHIN	Placer	Emigrant Gap P O	76	416
Ah	30	m	c	CHIN	Placer	Bath P O	76	423
Ah	30	m	c	CHIN	Placer	Bath P O	76	429
Ah	29	m	c	CHIN	Butte	Wyandotte Twp	70	147
Ah	29	m	c	CHIN	Alameda	Oakland	68	152
Ah	29	m	c	CHIN	Marin	San Rafael Twp	74	41
Ah	29	m	c	CHIN	Sierra	Eureka Twp	89	527
Ah	29	m	c	CHIN	Trinity	Douglas	92	237

© 2001 by Heritage Quest. All rights reserved.

California 1870 Census

Name	Age	S	R	B-PL	County	Locale	Roll	Pg
Ah	29	m	c	CHIN	Alameda	Oakland	68	158
Ah	29	m	c	CHIN	Butte	Oregon Twp	70	135
Ah	29	m	c	CHIN	Butte	Hamilton Twp	70	66
Ah	28	m	c	CHIN	Alameda	Alameda	68	6
Ah	28	m	c	CHIN	San Diego	San Diego	78	494
Ah	28	m	c	CHIN	Nevada	Grass Valley Twp	75	227
Ah	28	m	c	CHIN	Sonoma	Salt Point Twp	91	384
Ah	28	m	c	CHIN	Yuba	Marysville	93	619
Ah	28	m	c	CHIN	Stanislaus	Empire Twp	92	64
Ah	28	m	c	CHIN	Trinity	Douglas	92	234
Ah	28	m	c	CHIN	Trinity	Weaverville Pct	92	228
Ah	28	m	c	CHIN	San Francisco	San Francisco P O	85	748
Ah	28	m	c	CHIN	Marin	San Rafael Twp	74	45
Ah	28	m	c	CHIN	Alameda	Oakland	68	205
Ah	28	m	c	CHIN	Alameda	Alameda	68	16
Ah	28	m	c	CHIN	Alameda	Alameda	68	16
Ah	28	m	c	CHIN	Alameda	Murray Twp	68	102
Ah	28	m	c	CHIN	Butte	Wyandotte Twp	70	147
Ah	28	m	c	CHIN	El Dorado	Placerville	72	110
Ah	28	m	c	CHIN	El Dorado	Placerville Twp	72	105
Ah	28	m	c	CHIN	Placer	Auburn P O	76	362
Ah	27	m	c	CHIN	Alameda	Oakland	68	134
Ah	27	m	c	CHIN	Plumas	Plumas Twp	77	31
Ah	27	m	c	CHIN	Nevada	Grass Valley Twp	75	202
Ah	27	m	c	CHIN	Nevada	Grass Valley Twp	75	206
Ah	27	m	c	CHIN	Nevada	Grass Valley Twp	75	217
Ah	27	m	c	CHIN	Nevada	Grass Valley Twp	75	222
Ah	27	m	c	CHIN	Trinity	Lewiston Pct	92	214
Ah	27	m	c	CHIN	Santa Clara	2-Wd San Jose	88	307
Ah	27	m	c	CHIN	Sierra	Lincoln Twp	89	550
Ah	27	m	c	CHIN	Yolo	Putah Twp	93	518
Ah	27	m	c	CHIN	Stanislaus	Empire Twp	92	53
Ah	27	m	c	CHIN	Stanislaus	Washington Twp	92	85
Ah	27	m	c	CHIN	San Joaquin	Castoria Twp	86	14
Ah	27	m	c	CHIN	San Francisco	6-Wd San Francisco	81	63
Ah	27	m	c	CHIN	Placer	Gold Run Twp	76	398
Ah	27	m	c	CHIN	San Francisco	3-Wd San Francisco	79	329
Ah	27	m	c	CHIN	San Francisco	3-Wd San Francisco	79	309
Ah	26	m	c	CHIN	Alameda	Oakland	68	267
Ah	26	m	c	CHIN	El Dorado	Placerville	72	122
Ah	26	m	c	CHIN	Plumas	Plumas Twp	77	31
Ah	26	m	c	CHIN	Nevada	Grass Valley Twp	75	228
Ah	26	m	c	CHIN	Marin	San Rafael Twp	74	43
Ah	26	f	c	CHIN	San Francisco	San Francisco P O	80	454
Ah	26	m	c	CHIN	San Francisco	San Francisco P O	85	748
Ah	26	m	c	CHIN	Santa Cruz	Santa Cruz	89	434
Ah	26	m	c	CHIN	Shasta	French Gulch P O	89	470
Ah	25	m	c	CHIN	Alameda	Oakland	68	232
Ah	25	m	c	CHIN	Alameda	Murray Twp	68	122
Ah	25	m	c	CHIN	Butte	Bidwell Twp	70	4
Ah	25	m	c	CHIN	Napa	Napa Twp	75	70
Ah	25	m	c	CHIN	Napa	Napa Twp	75	30
Ah	25	m	c	CHIN	Nevada	Grass Valley Twp	75	208
Ah	25	m	c	CHIN	Solano	Vallejo	90	208
Ah	25	m	c	CHIN	Sierra	Eureka Twp	89	525
Ah	25	m	c	CHIN	San Francisco	6-Wd San Francisco	81	59
Ah	25	m	c	CHIN	Stanislaus	Buena Vista Twp	92	11
Ah	25	m	c	CHIN	Trinity	Weaverville Pct	92	230
Ah	25	m	c	CHIN	Trinity	Douglas	92	235
Ah	25	m	c	CHIN	Marin	San Rafael Twp	74	39
Ah	25	m	c	CHIN	Alameda	Oakland	68	169
Ah	25	m	c	CHIN	El Dorado	Placerville	72	122
Ah	25	m	c	CHIN	Placer	Colfax P O	76	389
Ah	25	m	c	CHIN	San Francisco	San Francisco P O	80	457
Ah	24	m	c	CHIN	El Dorado	Placerville	72	123
Ah	24	m	c	CHIN	Sacramento	1-Wd Sacramento	77	201
Ah	24	m	c	CHIN	Placer	Bath P O	76	445
Ah	24	m	c	CHIN	San Francisco	San Francisco P O	80	519
Ah	24	m	c	CHIN	Shasta	French Gulch P O	89	469
Ah	24	m	c	CHIN	Tuolumne	Chinese Camp P O	93	382
Ah	24	m	c	CHIN	San Francisco	San Francisco P O	85	748
Ah	24	m	c	CHIN	San Francisco	6-Wd San Francisco	81	43
Ah	24	m	c	CHIN	San Francisco	6-Wd San Francisco	81	60
Ah	24	m	c	CHIN	Alameda	Oakland	68	216
Ah	24	m	c	CHIN	Plumas	Quartz Twp	77	34
Ah	24	m	c	CHIN	Placer	Auburn P O	76	362
Ah	23	m	c	CHIN	Butte	Bidwell Twp	70	4
Ah	23	m	c	CHIN	Placer	Alta P O	76	413
Ah	23	m	c	CHIN	Nevada	Grass Valley Twp	75	145
Ah	23	m	c	CHIN	San Francisco	6-Wd San Francisco	81	52
Ah	23	m	c	CHIN	San Francisco	San Francisco P O	85	748
Ah	23	m	c	CHIN	San Francisco	6-Wd San Francisco	81	62
Ah	23	m	c	CHIN	San Francisco	San Francisco P O	83	172
Ah	23	m	c	CHIN	Alameda	Oakland	68	169
Ah	23	m	c	CHIN	Placer	Blue Canyon P O	76	419
Ah	22	m	c	CHIN	El Dorado	Mud Springs Twp	72	76
Ah	22	m	c	CHIN	Sacramento	1-Wd Sacramento	77	199
Ah	22	m	c	CHIN	Plumas	Rich Bar Twp	77	45
Ah	22	m	c	CHIN	Trinity	Douglas	92	232
Ah	22	m	c	CHIN	San Francisco	San Francisco P O	85	748
Ah	22	m	c	CHIN	San Francisco	6-Wd San Francisco	81	63
Ah	22	m	c	CHIN	Alameda	Alameda	68	10
Ah	22	m	c	CHIN	Sacramento	1-Wd Sacramento	77	193
Ah	21	m	c	CHIN	Alameda	Oakland	68	246
Ah	21	m	c	CHIN	Santa Clara	Fremont Twp	88	47
Ah	21	m	c	CHIN	San Mateo	Belmont P O	87	372
Ah	21	m	c	CHIN	San Francisco	6-Wd San Francisco	81	55
Ah	21	m	c	CHIN	Sierra	Sears Twp	89	561
Ah	21	m	c	CHIN	Sierra	Table Rock Twp	89	544
Ah	21	m	c	CHIN	Solano	Suisun Twp	90	105
Ah	21	m	c	CHIN	Mariposa	Mariposa P O	74	102
Ah	21	m	c	CHIN	Alameda	Oakland	68	201
Ah	20	m	c	CHIN	Alameda	Murray Twp	68	119
Ah	20	m	c	CHIN	Alameda	Oakland	68	189
Ah	20	f	c	CHIN	Butte	Kimshew Tpw	70	77
Ah	20	m	c	CHIN	El Dorado	Placerville	72	122
Ah	20	m	c	CHIN	Sacramento	3-Wd Sacramento	77	292
Ah	20	m	c	CHIN	Sacramento	3-Wd Sacramento	77	301
Ah	20	m	c	CHIN	Plumas	Goodwin Twp	77	4
Ah	20	m	c	CHIN	Nevada	Nevada Twp	75	311
Ah	20	m	c	CHIN	Santa Clara	Milpitas Twp	88	109
Ah	20	m	c	CHIN	San Francisco	6-Wd San Francisco	81	145
Ah	20	m	c	CHIN	San Francisco	San Francisco P O	80	481
Ah	20	f	c	CHIN	San Francisco	6-Wd San Francisco	81	76
Ah	20	m	c	CHIN	San Francisco	6-Wd San Francisco	81	99
Ah	20	m	c	CHIN	San Francisco	6-Wd San Francisco	81	48
Ah	20	m	c	CHIN	Trinity	Weaverville Pct	92	230
Ah	20	m	c	CHIN	Sonoma	Sonoma Twp	91	436
Ah	20	m	c	CHIN	Yolo	Grafton Twp	93	486
Ah	20	m	c	CHIN	San Mateo	Pescadero P O	87	412
Ah	20	m	c	CHIN	San Francisco	6-Wd San Francisco	81	42
Ah	20	m	c	CHIN	San Francisco	6-Wd San Francisco	81	66
Ah	20	m	c	CHIN	San Francisco	6-Wd San Francisco	81	85
Ah	20	m	c	CHIN	Calaveras	San Andreas P O	70	162
Ah	20	m	c	CHIN	Butte	Hamilton Twp	70	61
Ah	20	m	c	CHIN	Nevada	Nevada Twp	75	314
Ah	20	m	c	CHIN	Nevada	Rough & Ready Twp	75	329
Ah	20	m	c	CHIN	Placer	Auburn P O	76	382
Ah	20	m	c	CHIN	Placer	Auburn P O	76	378
Ah	20	m	c	CHIN	Placer	Clipper Gap P O	76	392
Ah	20	m	c	CHIN	Placer	Bath P O	76	429
Ah	20	m	c	CHIN	San Francisco	3-Wd San Francisco	79	309
Ah	20	m	c	CHIN	San Francisco	3-Wd San Francisco	79	304
Ah	20	m	c	CHIN	San Francisco	3-Wd San Francisco	79	310
Ah	20	m	c	CHIN	San Francisco	2-Wd San Francisco	79	264
Ah	19	m	c	CHIN	Calaveras	San Andreas P O	70	156
Ah	19	m	c	CHIN	Amador	Jackson P O	69	330
Ah	19	m	c	CHIN	Alameda	Brooklyn Twp	68	40
Ah	19	m	c	CHIN	Santa Clara	2-Wd San Jose	88	314
Ah	19	m	c	CHIN	Santa Clara	Fremont Twp	88	60
Ah	19	m	c	CHIN	San Francisco	6-Wd San Francisco	81	55
Ah	19	m	c	CHIN	Santa Cruz	Santa Cruz	89	434
Ah	18	m	c	CHIN	Alameda	Brooklyn Twp	68	43
Ah	18	m	c	CHIN	Alameda	Oakland	68	237
Ah	18	m	c	CHIN	Alameda	Oakland	68	264
Ah	18	m	c	CHIN	Alameda	Oakland	68	135
Ah	18	m	c	CHIN	Nevada	Little York Twp	75	234
Ah	18	m	c	CHIN	San Mateo	Schoolhouse Statio	87	332
Ah	18	m	c	CHIN	Santa Barbara	San Buenaventura P	87	438
Ah	18	f	c	CHIN	San Francisco	San Francisco P O	80	507
Ah	18	m	c	CHIN	San Francisco	6-Wd San Francisco	81	60
Ah	18	m	c	CHIN	San Francisco	6-Wd San Francisco	81	86
Ah	18	m	c	CHIN	San Francisco	6-Wd San Francisco	81	68
Ah	18	m	c	CHIN	Alameda	Oakland	68	199
Ah	18	m	c	CHIN	Alameda	Oakland	68	189
Ah	18	m	c	CHIN	Alameda	Alameda	68	15
Ah	18	m	c	CHIN	Contra Costa	Martinez P O	71	397
Ah	18	m	c	CHIN	Sacramento	1-Wd Sacramento	77	195
Ah	18	m	c	CHIN	Placer	Lincoln P O	76	486
Ah	17	m	c	CHIN	Plumas	Goodwin Twp	77	6
Ah	17	m	c	CHIN	San Francisco	6-Wd San Francisco	81	44
Ah	17	m	c	CHIN	Sierra	Downieville Twp	89	520
Ah	17	m	c	CHIN	San Francisco	6-Wd San Francisco	81	44
Ah	17	m	c	CHIN	Alameda	Oakland	68	187
Ah	16	m	c	CHIN	San Francisco	11-Wd San Francisc	84	427
Ah	16	m	c	CHIN	Solano	Silveyville Twp	90	91
Ah	16	m	c	CHIN	San Francisco	6-Wd San Francisco	81	57
Ah	15	m	c	CHIN	Alameda	Oakland	68	135
Ah	15	m	c	CHIN	Yuba	Linda Twp	93	555
Ah	15	m	c	CHIN	San Francisco	6-Wd San Francisco	81	39
Ah	14	m	c	CHIN	Alameda	Oakland	68	230
Ah	14	m	c	CHIN	El Dorado	Greenwood Twp	72	52
Ah	14	m	c	CHIN	Sacramento	3-Wd Sacramento	77	300
Ah	14	m	c	CHIN	Placer	Alta P O	76	413
Ah	14	m	c	CHIN	Shasta	French Gulch P O	89	470
Ah	14	m	c	CHIN	San Francisco	6-Wd San Francisco	81	66
Ah	14	m	c	CHIN	San Francisco	8-Wd San Francisco	82	334
Ah	14	m	c	CHIN	Alameda	Oakland	68	144
Ah	14	m	c	CHIN	Nevada	Nevada Twp	75	284
Ah	12	m	c	CHIN	San Francisco	6-Wd San Francisco	81	104
Ah	11	m	c	CHIN	San Francisco	8-Wd San Francisco	82	427
Ah You	30	m	c	CHIN	Solano	Suisun Twp	90	106
Ale	25	m	c	CHIN	Sacramento	3-Wd Sacramento	77	306
Ar	39	m	c	CHIN	Sonoma	Petaluma Twp	91	362
Ar	35	m	c	CHIN	Sonoma	Petaluma Twp	91	359
Ar	23	m	c	CHIN	Sonoma	Petaluma Twp	91	342
Au	35	m	c	CHIN	Alameda	Oakland	68	148
Ban	20	m	c	CHIN	Yuba	Marysville	93	628
Ca	36	m	c	CHIN	Trinity	Weaverville Pct	92	228
Can Poo	52	m	c	CHIN	Amador	Fiddletown P O	69	428
Chong	30	m	c	CHIN	Calaveras	San Andreas P O	70	190
Chow	33	m	c	CHIN	San Francisco	6-Wd San Francisco	81	47
Chow	23	m	c	CHIN	Solano	Suisun Twp	90	105
Chu	28	m	c	CHIN	El Dorado	Mud Springs Twp	72	88

Series M593

© 2001 by Heritage Quest. All rights reserved.

Name	Age	S	R	B-PL	County	Locale	Series M593 Roll	Pg
Chum	52	m	c	CHIN	Trinity	Weaverville Pct	92	229
Chum	20	m	c	CHIN	San Mateo	Schoolhouse Statio	87	336
Coey	56	m	c	CHIN	Klamath	South Fork Twp	73	382
Far	32	f	c	CHIN	Yuba	Marysville	93	627
Fi	38	m	c	CHIN	Yuba	Marysville	93	623
Fi	35	m	c	CHIN	San Francisco	11-Wd San Francisc	84	547
Fo	40	m	c	CHIN	Monterey	San Juan Twp	74	407
Fong	22	m	c	CHIN	San Mateo	Schoolhouse Statio	87	336
Foo	26	m	c	CHIN	Solano	Vallejo	90	209
Foo	20	m	c	CHIN	Sacramento	2-Wd Sacramento	77	253
Foo	13	m	c	CHIN	San Luis Obispo	Arroyo Grande Twp	87	279
Foo Ah	17	m	c	CHIN	Sacramento	1-Wd Sacramento	77	195
Fow	24	f	c	CHIN	Amador	Ione City P O	69	354
Gee	41	m	c	CHIN	Plumas	Mineral Twp	77	24
Gee	38	m	c	CHIN	Plumas	Mineral Twp	77	24
Gee	37	m	c	CHIN	Butte	Hamilton Twp	70	66
Gee	35	m	c	CHIN	Plumas	Washington Twp	77	52
Gee	30	m	c	CHIN	Plumas	Mineral Twp	77	24
Gee	27	m	c	CHIN	Plumas	Rich Bar Twp	77	46
Gee	19	m	c	CHIN	Butte	Oregon Twp	70	131
Geung	40	m	c	CHIN	Trinity	Weaverville Pct	92	229
Go	70	m	c	CHIN	Trinity	North Fork Twp	92	216
Goon	19	m	c	CHIN	San Francisco	San Francisco P O	85	866
Hang	30	m	c	CHIN	Shasta	Horsetown P O	89	503
Hay	30	m	c	CHIN	Trinity	Douglas	92	233
He	58	m	c	CHIN	Placer	Bath P O	76	428
Hen	27	m	c	CHIN	Kern	Havilah P O	73	336
Henry	21	m	c	CHIN	Sacramento	1-Wd Sacramento	77	185
Hey	44	m	c	CHIN	Mariposa	Maxwell Crk P O	74	147
Ho	30	f	c	CHIN	Nevada	Nevada Twp	75	299
Hoe	20	m	c	CHIN	Monterey	San Juan Twp	74	407
Hoi	39	f	c	CHIN	Yuba	Marysville	93	627
Hong	30	m	c	CHIN	Solano	Vallejo	90	162
Hop	45	m	c	CHIN	Placer	Auburn P O	76	382
Hop	30	m	c	CHIN	Placer	Auburn P O	76	372
Hoy	35	m	c	CHIN	Stanislaus	Emory Twp	92	20
Hue	19	m	c	CHIN	San Francisco	6-Wd San Francisco	81	53
Hy	25	m	c	CHIN	Placer	Newcastle Twp	76	473
Jim	20	m	c	CHIN	Colusa	Spring Valley Twp	71	338
Jin	35	m	c	CHIN	Stanislaus	Empire Twp	92	49
Joh	18	m	c	CHIN	Placer	Bath P O	76	429
Kim	38	m	c	CHIN	Placer	Dutch Flat P O	76	402
Kit	43	m	c	CHIN	Placer	Auburn P O	76	372
Koo	50	m	c	CHIN	Yuba	Marysville	93	623
Ku	30	m	c	CHIN	Alameda	Oakland	68	144
La	14	f	c	CHIN	Los Angeles	Los Angeles	73	565
Law	35	m	c	CHIN	Plumas	Rich Bar Twp	77	46
Le	50	m	c	CHIN	Del Norte	Crescent	71	464
Le	38	m	c	CHIN	Stanislaus	Emory Twp	92	25
Le	20	m	c	CHIN	El Dorado	Mud Springs Twp	72	87
Lee	40	m	c	CHIN	Alameda	Oakland	68	224
Lee	38	m	c	CHIN	Alameda	Oakland	68	223
Lee	38	m	c	CHIN	Alameda	Oakland	68	224
Lee	37	m	c	CHIN	Alameda	Murray Twp	68	111
Lee	36	m	c	CHIN	Alameda	Oakland	68	158
Lee	35	m	c	CHIN	Nevada	Little York Twp	75	245
Lee	34	m	c	CHIN	Alameda	Oakland	68	158
Lee	33	m	c	CHIN	Calaveras	San Andreas P O	70	184
Lee	30	m	c	CHIN	Calaveras	Copperopolis P O	70	263
Lee	30	m	c	CHIN	Butte	Wyandotte Twp	70	141
Lee	29	m	c	CHIN	Alameda	Oakland	68	158
Lee	27	m	c	CHIN	Sacramento	1-Wd Sacramento	77	200
Lee	22	m	c	CHIN	Butte	Ophir Twp	70	119
Lee	19	m	c	CHIN	San Francisco	7-Wd San Francisco	81	167
Lee	13	m	c	CHIN	San Luis Obispo	Arroyo Grande Twp	87	279
Lem	40	m	c	CHIN	Placer	Lincoln P O	76	483
Leng	49	m	c	CHIN	Calaveras	Copperopolis P O	70	226
Leng	35	m	c	CHIN	Plumas	Seneca Twp	77	51
Lin	50	m	c	CHIN	Placer	Auburn P O	76	371
Lind	25	m	c	CHIN	Sacramento	1-Wd Sacramento	77	193
Ling	36	m	c	CHIN	Placer	Colfax P O	76	384
Lo	31	m	c	CHIN	El Dorado	Placerville	72	115
Lo	27	m	c	CHIN	Placer	Clipper Gap P O	76	393
Lo	14	m	c	CHIN	Trinity	North Fork Twp	92	216
Long	38	m	c	CHIN	Calaveras	San Andreas P O	70	184
Loo	21	m	c	CHIN	San Francisco	6-Wd San Francisco	81	53
Loon	55	m	c	CHIN	Sacramento	1-Wd Sacramento	77	193
Luck	50	m	c	CHIN	Placer	Auburn P O	76	373
Lung	30	m	c	CHIN	Siskiyou	Yreka Twp	89	666
Lyn	24	f	c	CHIN	Sacramento	1-Wd Sacramento	77	193
Ming	27	m	c	CHIN	Yuba	Marysville	93	629
Moo	36	m	c	CHIN	Placer	Auburn P O	76	362
Ni	15	m	c	CHIN	Sonoma	Sonoma Twp	91	440
Oh	35	m	c	CHIN	Yuba	Marysville	93	629
Pat	25	m	c	CHIN	San Francisco	6-Wd San Francisco	81	41
Peow	37	m	c	CHIN	Nevada	Nevada Twp	75	314
Ping	45	m	c	CHIN	Calaveras	San Andreas P O	70	161
Ping Sung	25	m	c	CHIN	San Francisco	11-Wd San Francisc	84	546
Pong	50	m	c	CHIN	Placer	Auburn P O	76	371
Quack	30	m	c	CHIN	Placer	Lincoln P O	76	491
Quan	25	m	c	CHIN	Placer	Lincoln P O	76	483
Que	26	m	c	CHIN	Plumas	Washington Twp	77	57
Rebecca	32	f	w	ENGL	Sacramento	3-Wd Sacramento	77	295
Sam	31	m	c	CHIN	San Francisco	3-Wd San Francisco	79	306
Sam	18	m	c	CHIN	San Francisco	1-Wd San Francisco	79	55
Se	32	m	c	CHIN	Mono	Bridgeport P O	74	284
See	24	m	c	CHIN	Nevada	Meadow Lake Twp	75	259
Sen	14	m	c	CHIN	Yuba	Marysville	93	602
Shee	11	m	c	CHIN	Trinity	North Fork Twp	92	216
Sing	30	f	c	CHIN	Mariposa	Mariposa P O	74	132
Sing	28	m	c	CHIN	San Francisco	3-Wd San Francisco	79	317
Sir	21	m	c	CHIN	Los Angeles	Soledad Twp	73	632
Soy Ah	32	m	c	CHIN	San Francisco	3-Wd San Francisco	79	301
Sue	30	f	c	CHIN	Sacramento	1-Wd Sacramento	77	193
Sung	50	m	c	CHIN	San Francisco	2-Wd San Francisco	79	285
Ti	33	m	c	CHIN	Nevada	Nevada Twp	75	271
Tong	12	m	c	CHIN	San Francisco	11-Wd San Francisc	84	556
Too	28	m	c	CHIN	Placer	Auburn P O	76	362
Tow	53	m	c	CHIN	Nevada	Rough & Ready Twp	75	327
Toy	21	m	c	CHIN	Placer	Bath P O	76	439
Toy	17	m	c	CHIN	San Francisco	1-Wd San Francisco	79	114
Tung	29	m	c	CHIN	Marin	San Rafael Twp	74	45
Un	55	m	c	CHIN	Amador	Jackson P O	69	331
Wa	50	m	c	CHIN	Nevada	Grass Valley Twp	75	205
Wing	24	m	c	CHIN	Nevada	Nevada Twp	75	293
Wo	13	m	c	CHIN	San Francisco	8-Wd San Francisco	82	294
Wo Hip	31	m	c	CHIN	Solano	Suisun Twp	90	104
Woa	17	m	c	CHIN	San Mateo	Schoolhouse Statio	87	335
Woe	18	m	c	CHIN	San Francisco	San Francisco P O	83	404
Wog	14	m	c	CHIN	San Francisco	11-Wd San Francisc	84	529
Woo	4	f	c	CA	Mariposa	Maxwell Crk P O	74	138
Yang Wa	50	m	c	CHIN	San Francisco	6-Wd San Francisco	81	39
Ye	35	m	c	CHIN	Yuba	Rose Bar Twp	93	655
Ye	33	m	c	CHIN	Yuba	East Bear Rvr Twp	93	546
Ye	31	m	c	CHIN	Yuba	East Bear Rvr Twp	93	546
Yee	31	m	c	CHIN	Yuba	Marysville	93	629
Yek	24	m	c	CHIN	Solano	Green Valley Twp	90	43
Yet	50	m	c	CHIN	Amador	Jackson P O	69	332
Yo	30	m	c	CHIN	San Joaquin	Castoria Twp	86	6
Yon	36	m	c	CHIN	Placer	Bath P O	76	442
You	47	m	c	CHIN	Placer	Blue Canyon P O	76	417
You	26	m	c	CHIN	San Francisco	San Francisco P O	85	866
Yu	35	m	c	CHIN	Mariposa	Mariposa P O	74	137
CHUNGAN								
Jno	18	m	w	CA	San Joaquin	Douglas Twp	86	43
CHUNGE								
Quese	23	m	c	CHIN	Inyo	Independence Twp	73	327
CHUNK								
Ah	40	m	c	CHIN	San Joaquin	Oneal Twp	86	116
Ah	23	m	c	CHIN	San Joaquin	1-Wd Stockton	86	123
Ah	14	m	c	CHIN	San Francisco	8-Wd San Francisco	82	425
CHUNN								
Nathan	41	m	w	AL	Kern	Tehachapi P O	73	355
Nathan	41	m	w	AL	Kern	Havilah P O	73	341
CHUNNG								
Ah	25	m	c	CHIN	Trinity	Junction City Pct	92	210
CHUNO								
Ah	19	m	c	CHIN	Alameda	Oakland	68	134
Ah	19	m	c	CHIN	Santa Cruz	Santa Cruz	89	427
CHUNY								
Ah	24	m	c	CHIN	San Diego	San Diego	78	485
Wen	30	m	c	CHIN	Sacramento	1-Wd Sacramento	77	191
CHUNYGO								
Tony	48	m	c	CHIN	Sacramento	1-Wd Sacramento	77	191
CHUOGIN								
Joseph	20	m	w	ITAL	Santa Clara	Santa Clara Twp	88	157
CHUONG								
Ah	36	m	c	CHIN	Amador	Fiddletown P O	69	439
CHUP								
Ah	37	m	c	CHIN	San Joaquin	Oneal Twp	86	116
Ah	19	m	c	CHIN	San Joaquin	1-Wd Stockton	86	148
Me	26	m	c	CHIN	San Joaquin	1-Wd Stockton	86	147
Yow	43	m	c	CHIN	Placer	Bath P O	76	439
CHUPIN								
Stella	10	f	w	MA	San Joaquin	Dent Twp	86	17
CHUPP								
Ah	25	m	c	CHIN	San Francisco	6-Wd San Francisco	81	68
CHUR								
A B	37	m	w	BAVA	Alameda	Oakland	68	167
CHURBUMAN								
G	35	m	w	PRUS	Alameda	Oakland	68	263
CHURCH								
A	18	m	w	DENM	Alameda	Murray Twp	68	113
A D	37	m	w	VT	Sierra	Sierra Twp	89	567
Abi	54	f	w	NY	San Joaquin	Liberty Twp	86	82
Abner	24	m	w	NY	Solano	Vacaville Twp	90	124
Ah	24	m	c	CHIN	Nevada	Nevada Twp	75	312
Albert R	25	m	w	ME	San Francisco	San Francisco P O	85	732
Almira	24	f	w	FRAN	San Francisco	2-Wd San Francisco	79	255
Alonzo	43	m	w	NY	El Dorado	Cosumnes Twp	72	17
Amos	35	m	w	NY	San Francisco	5-Wd San Francisco	81	30
Antonio	27	m	w	ITAL	Amador	Jackson P O	69	330
Augh M	54	m	w	NY	Sonoma	Healdsburg & Mendo	91	278
Augustus	19	m	w	ENGL	Monterey	Castroville Twp	74	335
Ben	22	m	w	MO	San Joaquin	Liberty Twp	86	83
Catherine	35	f	w	IREL	San Francisco	7-Wd San Francisco	81	178
Charles	32	m	w	NY	San Francisco	8-Wd San Francisco	82	441
Charles	18	m	w	NY	Sonoma	Bodega Twp	91	248
Colby	28	m	w	MI	Solano	Vacaville Twp	90	125
Douglas	39	m	w	PA	Sonoma	Sonoma Twp	91	446
E B	69	m	w	VT	Sierra	Sierra Twp	89	567
E J	44	m	w	NY	Napa	Napa	75	3
Edward B	25	m	w	MA	San Mateo	San Mateo P O	87	352
Ephriam	50	m	w	NY	Solano	Vacaville Twp	90	124

© 2001 by Heritage Quest. All rights reserved.

Name	Age	S	R	B-PL	County	Locale	Series M593 Roll	Pg
Florence	18	f	w	CA	San Francisco	7-Wd San Francisco	81	285
Gardner	50	m	w	NY	Marin	San Rafael	74	57
Geo A	35	m	w	NY	Nevada	Nevada Twp	75	271
Gideon	57	m	w	ME	Alameda	Brooklyn Twp	68	54
Harry	45	m	w	ENGL	Solano	Vallejo	90	178
Henry	52	m	w	MA	Sonoma	Petaluma Twp	91	348
Henry	24	m	w	PA	Nevada	Washington Twp	75	339
I S	40	m	w	VT	Sierra	Sierra Twp	89	569
Isaac S	45	m	w	MA	San Francisco	6-Wd San Francisco	81	143
J E	46	m	w	RI	Tehama	Red Bluff	92	176
J H	30	m	w	NY	San Francisco	3-Wd San Francisco	79	317
James	18	m	w	IREL	Alameda	Brooklyn	68	33
James C	46	m	w	IN	Plumas	Plumas Twp	77	32
James H	40	m	w	NY	Yolo	Cottonwood Twp	93	461
James W	28	m	w	IL	San Francisco	3-Wd San Francisco	79	317
Jeremiah	41	m	w	CANA	Santa Clara	1-Wd San Jose	88	244
Jno E	32	m	w	NY	San Francisco	5-Wd San Francisco	81	33
John	25	m	w	IL	Stanislaus	Empire Twp	92	39
John	24	m	w	SCOT	San Francisco	7-Wd San Francisco	81	205
John A	28	m	w	ME	Nevada	Nevada Twp	75	310
John F	24	m	w	MI	Nevada	Rough & Ready Twp	75	335
John M	23	m	w	GA	Fresno	Kings Rvr P O	72	211
Joseph	40	m	w	NY	Yolo	Cache Crk Twp	93	450
L	24	m	w	IN	Lake	Lower Lake	73	416
Lemuel	33	m	w	RI	Humboldt	Pacific Twp	72	290
Luke	35	m	w	CANA	Humboldt	Pacific Twp	72	289
Luke A	38	m	w	OH	Stanislaus	Empire Twp	92	49
M B	46	m	w	CT	Amador	Drytown P O	69	415
M C	32	f	w	MA	Monterey	Castroville Twp	74	335
M M	39	m	w	VT	Calaveras	Copperopolis P O	70	225
Mary	45	f	w	IREL	San Francisco	11-Wd San Francisc	84	611
Mary A	50	f	w	IREL	San Francisco	San Francisco P O	83	201
Moses J	57	m	w	NY	Fresno	Kings Rvr P O	72	211
Nathaniel	64	m	w	CANA	Santa Barbara	Santa Barbara P O	87	495
Robert	40	m	w	OH	San Francisco	7-Wd San Francisco	81	188
Robert R	30	m	w	NJ	Santa Clara	2-Wd San Jose	88	296
S W	34	m	w	MA	Monterey	Castroville Twp	74	335
Saml H	40	m	w	NY	Marin	Tomales Twp	74	76
Samuel	36	m	w	NY	San Francisco	11-Wd San Francisc	84	523
Sichery	30	m	w	ENGL	San Joaquin	Douglas Twp	86	39
Thomas	40	m	w	NY	San Francisco	8-Wd San Francisco	82	337
Thomas	23	m	w	ITAL	San Francisco	3-Wd San Francisco	79	289
William	42	m	w	CT	Mendocino	Calpella Twp	74	190
William D	45	m	w	NY	San Mateo	Half Moon Bay P O	87	405
Wm	50	m	w	ENGL	San Luis Obispo	Arroyo Grande Twp	87	276
Wm	31	m	w	ENGL	San Francisco	2-Wd San Francisco	79	238
CHURCHER								
William	49	m	w	ENGL	Trinity	Weaverville Pct	92	232
CHURCHHILL								
Jas B	46	m	w	CANA	San Francisco	1-Wd San Francisco	79	84
CHURCHILL								
Benjam	48	m	w	NY	San Francisco	11-Wd San Francisc	84	522
Caroline	30	f	w	CANA	Santa Clara	2-Wd San Jose	88	293
Charles	40	m	w	MO	San Francisco	6-Wd San Francisco	81	78
Enos	41	m	w	NY	Monterey	San Juan Twp	74	391
F	15	f	w	IL	Santa Clara	Gilroy Twp	88	100
H	41	m	w	VT	Sutter	Butte Twp	92	88
J	50	m	w	MA	San Joaquin	3-Wd Stockton	86	229
James	44	m	w	NY	Siskiyou	Yreka	89	658
James	33	m	b	MO	Yuba	Marysville	93	610
James	28	m	w	ME	Mariposa	Mariposa P O	74	131
Jno	45	m	w	IREL	Klamath	Liberty Twp	73	376
Joe	26	m	w	NY	San Joaquin	3-Wd Stockton	86	231
John	7	m	b	CA	San Joaquin	Liberty Twp	86	84
John	38	m	w	ENGL	Nevada	Grass Valley Twp	75	145
L B	53	m	w	PA	Sacramento	3-Wd Sacramento	77	259
Lenas	51	m	w	NY	Monterey	San Juan Twp	74	391
Leonard C [Dr]	50	m	w	OH	San Francisco	San Francisco P O	83	159
P	55	m	m	KY	Yuba	Marysville	93	610
Seth	49	m	w	VT	Santa Clara	1-Wd San Jose	88	228
W B	42	m	w	NY	Nevada	Eureka Twp	75	132
W B	29	m	w	NY	Solano	Vallejo	90	202
W B	28	m	w	NY	Solano	Vallejo	90	198
William	9	m	w	CA	Placer	Bath P O	76	423
William	50	m	w	PA	Nevada	Meadow Lake Twp	75	269
Winslow	15	m	w	MI	Alameda	San Leandro	68	98
CHURCHMAN								
Ann	21	f	w	CA	Sonoma	Vallejo Twp	91	459
Caroline	58	f	w	NY	Sonoma	Petaluma Twp	91	331
George	27	m	w	IL	Sonoma	Analy Twp	91	245
Henry	34	m	w	IN	Sonoma	Analy Twp	91	245
John	66	m	w	PA	Sonoma	Analy Twp	91	245
T C	40	m	w	OH	Sacramento	3-Wd Sacramento	77	278
W	51	m	w	IN	Sonoma	Santa Rosa	91	414
CHURCHWARD								
Francis	20	m	w	ENGL	Marin	San Rafael	74	57
Jas	42	m	w	NY	San Francisco	11-Wd San Francisc	84	468
CHURCHWELL								
R B	38	m	w	TN	Siskiyou	Scott Valley Twp	89	618
CHURDIN								
Stephen	47	m	w	FRAN	El Dorado	Cosumnes Twp	72	18
CHURG								
Pat Wer	26	m	c	CHIN	San Francisco	11-Wd San Francisc	84	560
CHURK								
Ah	38	m	c	CHIN	San Joaquin	Oneal Twp	86	116
CHURLEY								
Ah	40	m	c	CHIN	Trinity	Trinity Center Pct	92	204

Name	Age	S	R	B-PL	County	Locale	Series M593 Roll	Pg
Ah	35	m	c	CHIN	El Dorado	Placerville	72	125
Ah	34	m	c	CHIN	El Dorado	Mud Springs Twp	72	90
CHURLY								
William	54	m	w	SCOT	Lake	Lakeport	73	403
CHURT								
Charles	40	m	w	SCOT	San Francisco	San Francisco P O	80	346
CHUSTER								
M C	19	f	w	IREL	Solano	Benicia	90	11
CHUSTIS								
William	29	m	w	PRUS	Solano	Maine Prairie Twp	90	52
CHUT								
---	24	m	c	CHIN	San Joaquin	1-Wd Stockton	86	142
Ah	46	m	c	CHIN	Tuolumne	Chinese Camp P O	93	374
Ah	35	f	c	CHIN	El Dorado	Placerville	72	116
Ah	27	m	c	CHIN	San Joaquin	Oneal Twp	86	117
Ah	26	m	c	CHIN	San Joaquin	1-Wd Stockton	86	142
Ah	21	m	c	CHIN	San Mateo	Half Moon Bay P O	87	396
Ah	20	m	c	CHIN	San Francisco	6-Wd San Francisco	81	59
Go	34	m	c	CHIN	San Joaquin	Douglas Twp	86	49
Lee	18	m	c	CHIN	San Joaquin	1-Wd Stockton	86	146
CHUTE								
Richard	26	m	w	NY	San Francisco	3-Wd San Francisco	79	320
CHUTON								
Vesta	50	f	b	LA	San Francisco	San Francisco P O	83	69
CHUY								
Ah	30	m	c	CHIN	Stanislaus	Emory Twp	92	17
Lu	19	m	c	CHIN	Sonoma	Sonoma Twp	91	449
Quing	23	m	c	CHIN	San Francisco	5-Wd San Francisco	81	1
CHW								
Ah	54	m	c	CHIN	Nevada	Grass Valley Twp	75	193
CHY								
Ah	41	m	c	CHIN	Butte	Chico Twp	70	53
Ah	40	m	c	CHIN	Butte	Hamilton Twp	70	74
Ah	40	m	c	CHIN	Butte	Chico Twp	70	53
Ah	34	m	c	CHIN	Stanislaus	Emory Twp	92	17
Ah	32	m	c	CHIN	Tuolumne	Big Oak Flat P O	93	393
Ah	31	m	c	CHIN	San Joaquin	1-Wd Stockton	86	132
Ah	30	m	c	CHIN	Butte	Hamilton Twp	70	67
Ah	29	m	c	CHIN	San Francisco	6-Wd San Francisco	81	61
Ah	28	m	c	CHIN	Butte	Hamilton Twp	70	67
Ah	25	f	c	CHIN	Nevada	Grass Valley Twp	75	205
Ah	21	m	c	CHIN	San Francisco	6-Wd San Francisco	81	56
Ah	21	m	c	CHIN	San Francisco	6-Wd San Francisco	81	61
Ah	12	m	c	CHIN	San Francisco	San Francisco P O	83	103
Ching	16	m	c	CHIN	San Francisco	8-Wd San Francisco	82	294
Dot	34	m	c	CHIN	Butte	Chico Twp	70	53
Fing	30	m	c	CHIN	Butte	Chico Twp	70	53
Foo	26	m	c	CHIN	Butte	Hamilton Twp	70	67
Foo	21	f	c	CHIN	Butte	Ophir Twp	70	121
Foo	14	f	c	CHIN	Butte	Chico Twp	70	27
Fung	52	m	c	CHIN	Butte	Kimshew Tpw	70	85
Gee	34	m	c	CHIN	Butte	Hamilton Twp	70	73
I	37	f	c	CHIN	Stanislaus	Emory Twp	92	17
Lim	51	m	c	CHIN	Butte	Kimshew Tpw	70	86
Lin	42	m	c	CHIN	Butte	Hamilton Twp	70	74
Lon	28	m	c	CHIN	Butte	Kimshew Tpw	70	84
Loy	37	m	c	CHIN	Butte	Ophir Twp	70	117
Lung	40	m	c	CHIN	Butte	Kimshew Tpw	70	79
Lung	25	m	c	CHIN	Butte	Chico Twp	70	53
Mo Foy	50	m	c	CHIN	San Francisco	6-Wd San Francisco	81	57
Ock	15	f	c	CHIN	Butte	Ophir Twp	70	103
Sen	49	m	c	CHIN	Butte	Ophir Twp	70	119
Sing	29	m	c	CHIN	Butte	Kimshew Tpw	70	77
Ton	46	m	c	CHIN	Butte	Hamilton Twp	70	73
Ton	20	f	c	CHIN	Butte	Hamilton Twp	70	74
Wang	40	m	c	CHIN	Butte	Chico Twp	70	53
Wee	28	m	c	CHIN	San Francisco	6-Wd San Francisco	81	46
Wing	20	f	c	CHIN	Butte	Hamilton Twp	70	73
Wun	27	m	c	CHIN	Butte	Chico Twp	70	51
Yee	50	m	c	CHIN	Yuba	Marysville	93	621
Yuen	44	m	c	CHIN	Calaveras	Copperopolis P O	70	264
CHYCY								
Joseph	30	m	w	PRUS	Siskiyou	Callahan P O	89	624
CI								
Mung	38	m	c	CHIN	Trinity	Weaverville Pct	92	231
CIALINTO								
Aloysius	27	m	w	ITAL	Santa Clara	Santa Clara Twp	88	175
CIBERS								
Albert	29	m	w	SWED	Nevada	Meadow Lake Twp	75	248
CIBY								
John	63	m	w	SPAI	San Francisco	2-Wd San Francisco	79	168
CICARIA								
Francisco	50	m	w	MEXI	San Luis Obispo	Salinas Twp	87	294
CICIL								
James M	35	m	w	OH	Placer	Blue Canyon P O	76	419
CICILEY								
Geo	27	m	w	AUST	Solano	Vallejo	90	212
CIDWELL								
Robert	24	m	w	OH	Solano	Rio Vista Twp	90	57
CIE								
Ah	29	m	c	CHIN	Sacramento	1-Wd Sacramento	77	196
CIEGO								
Drinido	25	f	w	CA	San Diego	San Luis Rey	78	515
CIENIGA								
Ventinus	23	m	w	MEXI	San Francisco	2-Wd San Francisco	79	182
CIERA								
Timotao	30	m	w	MEXI	San Luis Obispo	Arroyo Grande Twp	87	272

© 2001 by Heritage Quest. All rights reserved.

Series M593

Name	Age	S	R	B-PL	County	Locale	Roll	Pg
CIGARLA								
Paul	37	m	w	ITAL	Calaveras	Copperopolis P O	70	253
CIHALLA								
Allicia	40	m	w	MEXI	Napa	Napa	75	55
CILCALOUS								
James	25	m	i	CA	Trinity	Trinity Center Pct	92	240
CILGORE								
Wm	20	m	w	IA	Sacramento	Brighton Twp	77	73
CILKER								
John	33	m	w	PRUS	Santa Clara	Redwood Twp	88	127
CILLAGRAN								
D	30	f	w	MEXI	Santa Clara	Almaden Twp	88	8
CILLEN								
John	31	m	w	SWED	Nevada	Washington Twp	75	340
CILLEY								
Augustus	40	m	w	ME	Yuba	Slate Range Bar Tw	93	678
H K	47	f	w	NH	Tuolumne	Columbia P O	93	356
J W	42	m	w	ME	Solano	Vallejo	90	157
William	48	m	w	NH	Stanislaus	Empire Twp	92	51
CILLISTINO								
Pedro	32	m	w	CA	Marin	San Rafael Twp	74	39
CILLS								
John	29	m	w	GA	Solano	Silveyville Twp	90	81
Rufas	46	m	w	NH	Yolo	Cache Crk Twp	93	419
CILLSI								
John	38	m	w	NH	Nevada	Meadow Lake Twp	75	258
CILLY								
Mary	45	f	w	NY	San Francisco	5-Wd San Francisco	81	33
CIM								
Ah	40	m	c	CHIN	Trinity	Lewiston Pct	92	214
Ah	38	m	c	CHIN	Amador	Fiddletown P O	69	428
CIMONET								
John	36	m	w	SWIT	Siskiyou	Table Rock Twp	89	647
CIN								
Ah	22	m	c	CHIN	Placer	Dutch Flat P O	76	408
CINDRAS								
Lonicio	30	m	w	CHIL	Santa Clara	Almaden Twp	88	21
CINEZA								
Isabella	24	f	w	MEXI	San Francisco	11-Wd San Francisc	84	645
CING								
Ah	52	f	c	CHIN	San Francisco	San Francisco P O	80	523
Ah	23	m	c	CHIN	Tuolumne	Big Oak Flat P O	93	397
Lot	48	m	c	CHIN	Calaveras	San Andreas P O	70	161
CINGUEJUNGUS								
Jose M	40	m	w	MEXI	San Luis Obispo	San Luis Obispo Tw	87	306
CINK								
Joseph	31	m	w	BADE	Amador	Ione City P O	69	352
CINKIUS								
Frederico	30	m	w	GERM	Los Angeles	Los Angeles	73	541
CINN								
Ty	23	f	c	CHIN	Placer	Dutch Flat P O	76	409
CINNER								
Andres T	30	m	w	ME	Los Angeles	San Jose Twp	73	623
CINORA								
Casi	30	m	w	MEXI	Santa Clara	Almaden Twp	88	4
CINVERMAN								
John	34	m	w	HDAR	San Francisco	11-Wd San Francisc	84	681
CINVICH								
Zelia	34	m	w	AUST	Plumas	Quartz Twp	77	35
CIOSI								
Louis	30	m	w	ITAL	Santa Clara	2-Wd San Jose	88	315
CIRCELLO								
Stephen	27	m	w	ITAL	Solano	Montezuma Twp	90	67
CIRE								
Tim	60	m	c	CHIN	Nevada	Nevada Twp	75	311
CIRETANA								
Pares	38	m	w	MEXI	Plumas	Goodwin Twp	77	1
CIRIACA								
Gomica	58	f	w	MEXI	Santa Clara	San Jose Twp	88	211
CIRVAN								
Frank	29	m	w	ENGL	Placer	Gold Run Twp	76	395
CISAL								
Michail	49	m	w	OH	Tuolumne	Columbia P O	93	352
CISCO								
Elizabeth	40	f	m	PA	Sacramento	2-Wd Sacramento	77	242
Orande	38	m	w	SWIT	El Dorado	Georgetown Twp	72	48
CISE								
Peter	29	m	w	PRUS	San Francisco	5-Wd San Francisco	81	9
CISEN								
F	35	m	w	PRUS	Alameda	Oakland	68	139
CISGROVE								
Chas E	23	m	w	SWIT	Placer	Emigrant Gap P O	76	416
CISNERO								
Manuel	30	m	w	SPAI	San Diego	San Luis Rey	78	513
CISSNA								
Evins	35	m	w	OH	Sacramento	San Joaquin Twp	77	406
Samuel	39	m	w	OH	Solano	Vacaville Twp	90	129
William	37	m	w	OH	Solano	Vacaville Twp	90	129
CISTANIOS								
Francisco	13	f	w	NV	San Francisco	San Francisco P O	80	409
CISTERNOS								
Nocane	21	m	w	CHIL	Fresno	Millerton P O	72	159
CIT								
Ah	39	m	c	CHIN	Tuolumne	Big Oak Flat P O	93	397
CITERSON								
Mary	23	f	w	IREL	San Francisco	San Francisco P O	83	213
CITNOR								
Jesus	35	m	w	MEXI	Santa Clara	Almaden Twp	88	10
CITPA								
Thos	34	m	w	SWIT	Sacramento	American Twp	77	64
CITRINO								
Capriano	22	m	w	SWIT	Marin	Bolinas Twp	74	1
CITRON								
Abraham	22	m	w	POLA	San Francisco	1-Wd San Francisco	79	97
Maurice	35	m	w	POLA	San Francisco	San Francisco P O	80	414
CIVILICH								
Mathew	22	m	w	AUST	San Francisco	3-Wd San Francisco	79	288
CIZEK								
Joseph P	37	m	w	POLA	San Francisco	11-Wd San Francisc	84	703
CLAASSEN								
Cornelius	47	m	w	PRUS	Santa Clara	2-Wd San Jose	88	331
CLACEY								
James	24	m	w	IREL	Contra Costa	Martinez P O	71	416
CLACK								
Jno W	39	m	w	KY	Sonoma	Healdsburg & Mendo	91	279
CLADWELL								
John	26	m	w	SCOT	San Francisco	1-Wd San Francisco	79	31
CLAEK								
Ah	4	m	c	CA	San Francisco	11-Wd San Francisc	84	695
CLAFER								
A G	49	m	w	PRUS	Tuolumne	Chinese Camp P O	93	390
W J	46	m	w	PRUS	Tuolumne	Chinese Camp P O	93	390
CLAFFEY								
Delia	18	f	w	CA	San Francisco	San Francisco P O	83	180
Edward	22	m	w	WI	Colusa	Colusa Twp	71	276
Hubert	34	m	w	PRUS	San Francisco	San Francisco P O	80	379
James	35	m	w	IREL	San Francisco	San Francisco P O	83	100
James	14	m	w	CA	Marin	Novato Twp	74	9
John	24	m	w	IREL	Santa Cruz	Santa Cruz	89	410
John	23	m	w	IREL	San Francisco	11-Wd San Francisc	84	487
Mary	37	f	w	IREL	San Francisco	11-Wd San Francisc	84	633
CLAFFY								
Ellen	16	f	w	IREL	Alameda	Brooklyn	68	37
John	41	m	w	IREL	San Mateo	Belmont P O	87	388
CLAFREY								
M	50	m	w	IREL	Yuba	Marysville	93	586
CLAHAN								
Mary	42	f	w	IREL	San Francisco	7-Wd San Francisco	81	178
CLAHN								
Benjamin	60	m	w	SHOL	Butte	Wyandotte Twp	70	142
CLAIBORN								
Mary	38	f	w	NY	San Francisco	6-Wd San Francisco	81	101
CLAIBORNE								
Gilbert	43	m	w	VA	San Joaquin	1-Wd Stockton	86	153
CLAIBOURNE								
R K	39	m	w	TN	El Dorado	Cosumnes Twp	72	16
CLAIG								
E H	20	m	w	ENGL	Monterey	Castroville Twp	74	335
CLAIR								
Nicholas	41	m	w	FRAN	Inyo	Cerro Gordo Twp	73	318
CLAIRE								
John	45	m	w	PA	Sutter	Yuba Twp	92	151
CLAIRFIELD								
Lucas	29	m	w	BAVA	San Joaquin	2-Wd Stockton	86	199
CLAIRMONT								
Rudolph	37	m	w	FRAN	San Francisco	2-Wd San Francisco	79	219
CLAISEN								
Charles	45	m	w	SHOL	Solano	Tremont Twp	90	33
CLAK								
John	35	m	w	IREL	Colusa	Colusa Twp	71	282
CLAM								
Ah	16	m	c	CHIN	San Francisco	11-Wd San Francisc	84	626
CLAMON								
Daniel	32	m	w	KY	Sutter	Sutter Twp	92	120
Wm	31	m	w	KY	Sutter	Sutter Twp	92	120
CLAMPET								
James	34	m	w	IN	Sutter	Yuba Twp	92	141
CLAMSEY								
W	27	m	w	IREL	San Francisco	San Francisco P O	85	785
CLANARD								
Henry	42	m	w	OLDE	Placer	Bath P O	76	430
CLANCEY								
Daniel	40	m	w	IREL	Nevada	Nevada Twp	75	271
Julia	14	f	w	IREL	San Francisco	San Francisco P O	80	400
Peter	38	m	w	IREL	San Francisco	San Francisco P O	83	205
Thomas	34	m	w	IREL	San Francisco	7-Wd San Francisco	81	189
CLANCHY								
Phillip	34	m	w	IREL	San Mateo	Schoolhouse Statio	87	338
CLANCY								
C	23	m	w	CANA	Solano	Vallejo	90	216
Catherine	17	f	w	CANA	Humboldt	Bucksport Twp	72	243
Cecilia	50	f	w	IREL	San Francisco	San Francisco P O	83	103
Daniel	47	m	w	IREL	Contra Costa	San Pablo Twp	71	357
Daniel	30	m	w	IREL	Humboldt	Eureka Twp	72	277
Danl	34	m	w	IREL	Humboldt	Eureka Twp	72	261
Danl	34	m	w	IREL	Humboldt	Eureka Twp	72	262
Dennis	54	m	w	IREL	Los Angeles	Los Angeles	73	537
Elizth	48	f	w	IREL	San Francisco	San Francisco P O	83	92
Geo	35	m	w	CANA	Solano	Vallejo	90	216
George	40	m	w	IREL	Kern	Havilah P O	73	340
J G	34	m	w	VT	San Francisco	3-Wd San Francisco	79	315
John	46	m	w	IREL	Yuba	Rose Bar Twp	93	661
John	32	m	w	IREL	Nevada	Grass Valley Twp	75	214

© 2001 by Heritage Quest. All rights reserved.

Series M593

Name	Age	S	R	B-PL	County	Locale	Roll	Pg
John	30	m	w	IREL	El Dorado	White Oak Twp	72	135
John	30	m	w	IREL	Humboldt	Bucksport Twp	72	243
John	28	m	w	IREL	San Francisco	5-Wd San Francisco	81	32
Martin	31	m	w	IREL	San Francisco	San Francisco P O	83	3
Michael	34	m	w	IREL	Placer	Bath P O	76	432
Michl	21	m	w	IREL	San Francisco	1-Wd San Francisco	79	63
Owen	29	m	w	IREL	San Francisco	6-Wd San Francisco	81	120
Patrick	35	m	w	IREL	San Francisco	San Francisco P O	80	378
Phillip	30	m	w	IREL	San Francisco	11-Wd San Francisc	84	578
Thomas	52	m	w	IREL	Los Angeles	Los Angeles	73	569
Thos	50	m	w	IREL	San Francisco	San Francisco P O	83	106
Thos	40	m	w	NY	San Francisco	1-Wd San Francisco	79	134
Thos B	41	m	w	IREL	San Francisco	San Francisco P O	83	310
Wm	18	m	w	NY	San Francisco	1-Wd San Francisco	79	95
CLANNEY								
Charles	36	m	w	IREL	Marin	Novato Twp	74	12
CLANNIN								
Ann F	53	f	w	PA	San Francisco	San Francisco P O	83	373
CLANSEY								
John	22	m	w	IREL	Stanislaus	Emory Twp	92	24
Mariann	10	f	w	CA	San Francisco	11-Wd San Francisc	84	703
CLANSON								
Asmus	35	m	w	PRUS	El Dorado	White Oak Twp	72	139
Pheobe	55	f	w	MO	Sonoma	Sonoma Twp	91	443
CLANSY								
Philip	29	m	w	IREL	Solano	Vallejo	90	178
CLANTON								
Drewry M	38	m	w	MO	Yolo	Cache Crk Twp	93	442
E A	6	m	m	CA	Solano	Benicia	90	2
Emma	26	f	w	IL	Butte	Chico Twp	70	43
John M	62	m	w	MO	Yolo	Cache Crk Twp	93	441
John W	25	m	w	MO	Inyo	Lone Pine Twp	73	330
Newman H	52	m	w	TN	Santa Barbara	San Buenaventura P	87	419
S J	29	f	m	OH	Solano	Benicia	90	2
Thomas	56	m	w	TN	Colusa	Spring Valley Twp	71	336
CLAP								
Ah	19	m	c	CHIN	San Francisco	1-Wd San Francisco	79	46
CLAPEW								
G P	49	m	w	PRUS	Sonoma	Petaluma Twp	91	355
CLAPP								
Alexander	64	m	w	MA	Santa Clara	San Jose Twp	88	196
Belle	16	f	w	CA	Mono	Bridgeport P O	74	287
Benj	18	m	w	MO	Monterey	San Antonio Twp	74	318
Charles	14	m	w	CA	Monterey	Pajaro Twp	74	368
Chas	17	m	w	CA	Alameda	Oakland	68	159
Christopher C	42	m	w	NY	Tulare	Tule Rvr Twp	92	271
Cyrus F	19	m	w	ME	Humboldt	Bucksport Twp	72	244
Edward L	25	m	w	OH	Santa Barbara	Santa Maria P O	87	514
Elvira	45	f	w	NY	Santa Cruz	Watsonville	89	372
George	46	m	w	MA	Placer	Auburn P O	76	381
George	38	m	w	ME	San Francisco	San Francisco P O	83	354
George	35	m	w	MA	Stanislaus	Empire Twp	92	48
George H	36	m	w	MA	San Francisco	San Francisco P O	83	342
Henry C	47	m	w	PA	Sacramento	2-Wd Sacramento	77	235
Henry O	23	m	w	MA	Stanislaus	San Joaquin Twp	92	76
Jacob	33	m	w	HANO	Stanislaus	North Twp	92	69
James	29	m	w	NY	Nevada	Meadow Lake Twp	75	267
Jason	55	m	w	MA	San Francisco	7-Wd San Francisco	81	284
John	60	m	w	NY	Amador	Volcano P O	69	384
John	38	m	w	GERM	San Joaquin	2-Wd Stockton	86	174
John	30	m	w	NY	San Francisco	6-Wd San Francisco	81	88
John E	17	m	w	UT	Los Angeles	Los Angeles Twp	73	467
John W	28	m	w	TX	Siskiyou	Callahan P O	89	630
Joseph	19	m	w	US	San Joaquin	Castoria Twp	86	9
Joseph C	32	m	w	MO	Sonoma	Vallejo Twp	91	459
Joseph L	42	m	w	MA	Nevada	Grass Valley Twp	75	154
Louisa	40	f	w	MA	San Francisco	San Francisco P O	80	391
Mary	54	f	w	IN	Los Angeles	Los Angeles Twp	73	467
Nellie	17	f	w	MI	San Joaquin	2-Wd Stockton	86	181
Peter	40	m	w	ME	San Joaquin	Castoria Twp	86	4
Stephen	49	m	w	ME	Humboldt	Bucksport Twp	72	244
Theodore J	27	m	w	IA	San Diego	San Diego	78	497
Thomas	15	m	w	UT	Monterey	Castroville Twp	74	340
Totham	32	m	w	NH	Marin	Sausalito Twp	74	74
W	20	f	w	MO	San Joaquin	2-Wd Stockton	86	175
Wm	23	m	w	MA	Fresno	Kings Rvr P O	72	214
CLAPPER								
Henry	69	m	w	PA	Placer	Dutch Flat P O	76	415
CLAPRICH								
John	43	m	w	PRUS	Los Angeles	Los Angeles	73	533
CLAPSTEIN								
Joseph	44	m	w	OH	San Francisco	8-Wd San Francisco	82	341
CLAR								
John	57	m	w	SPAI	San Francisco	San Francisco P O	85	774
CLARA								
Berger	50	f	w	VA	San Mateo	Schoolhouse Statio	87	343
Chas	22	m	w	IREL	Yuba	Linda Twp	93	555
Henrietto	52	m	w	FRAN	Los Angeles	Los Angeles	73	527
John	40	m	w	IREL	Yuba	Linda Twp	93	555
Thomas	40	m	w	CANA	San Francisco	11-Wd San Francisc	84	532
CLARANCE								
S C	38	m	w	ME	Alameda	Oakland	68	156
CLARCK								
George	28	m	w	WI	Alameda	Alameda	68	12
J W	47	m	w	ME	Alameda	Alameda	68	11
John	35	m	w	ENGL	Alameda	Alameda	68	5
CLARE								
Charles	42	m	w	CHIL	San Francisco	7-Wd San Francisco	81	223
Henry	63	m	w	HESS	Sutter	Yuba Twp	92	142
Jan Jos	32	m	w	IREL	Nevada	Nevada Twp	75	287
John	60	m	w	IREL	San Francisco	1-Wd San Francisco	79	100
Law	35	m	c	CHIN	Sutter	Yuba Twp	92	142
Thomas	30	m	w	IREL	Alameda	Oakland	68	151
CLAREE								
Clarissa	19	f	w	CHIL	San Francisco	San Francisco P O	80	409
CLAREN								
Ed	35	m	w	PRUS	Alameda	Oakland	68	163
CLARENCE								
Geo	27	m	w	CANA	San Francisco	1-Wd San Francisco	79	65
Isaac	19	m	w	CANA	Sonoma	Bodega Twp	91	264
Martin	30	m	w	NY	San Mateo	Half Moon Bay P O	87	407
CLARENCY								
William	52	m	w	ME	Solano	Suisun Twp	90	107
CLARESSY								
Wm	44	m	w	MA	Sonoma	Petaluma Twp	91	324
CLAREY								
John	40	m	w	HANO	Siskiyou	Cottonwood Twp	89	592
Thomas	21	m	w	AUSL	Santa Clara	2-Wd San Jose	88	325
William	31	m	w	ENGL	Stanislaus	Washington Twp	92	84
CLARING								
Michl	40	m	w	IREL	Alameda	Murray Twp	68	107
CLARK								
A	49	m	w	NJ	San Joaquin	Douglas Twp	86	40
A	17	m	w	OH	Sierra	Forest	89	537
A G	50	m	w	OH	Napa	Yountville Twp	75	76
A G	36	m	w	PA	Santa Clara	Gilroy Twp	88	76
A G Mrs	34	f	w	AR	Sutter	Yuba Twp	92	151
A H	32	m	w	ME	Nevada	Meadow Lake Twp	75	265
A H	30	m	w	NY	Nevada	Meadow Lake Twp	75	259
A J	5	m	w	CANA	Yuba	Marysville	93	577
A J	41	m	w	TN	Solano	Benicia	90	20
A L	28	m	w	ENGL	Nevada	Bloomfield Twp	75	94
A P	24	m	w	NY	Nevada	Meadow Lake Twp	75	261
A T	28	m	w	IL	San Joaquin	Elkhorn Twp	86	65
A V	27	m	w	OH	Nevada	Meadow Lake Twp	75	267
Aaron	40	m	w	RI	Nevada	Grass Valley Twp	75	160
Abbott	15	m	w	MA	San Francisco	11-Wd San Francisc	84	648
Abner G	35	m	w	VT	San Diego	San Diego	78	495
Abner L	39	m	w	ME	Plumas	Plumas Twp	77	29
Abraham	65	m	w	NJ	Monterey	Pajaro Twp	74	369
Abraham	50	m	w	ENGL	Napa	Yountville Twp	75	88
Ada	29	f	w	PA	San Francisco	5-Wd San Francisco	81	8
Adam R	66	m	w	NH	Placer	Lincoln P O	76	489
Addison R	40	m	w	NY	Nevada	Grass Valley Twp	75	185
Agnes	4	f	w	CA	San Francisco	1-Wd San Francisco	79	2
Albert	46	m	w	NY	Butte	Ophir Twp	70	120
Albert C	35	m	w	NY	Butte	Chico Twp	70	46
Albert P	41	m	w	RI	Nevada	Little York Twp	75	234
Alex	23	m	w	SCOT	San Francisco	8-Wd San Francisco	82	303
Alfred	40	m	w	ENGL	San Francisco	3-Wd San Francisco	79	314
Alfred	38	m	w	IREL	San Francisco	11-Wd San Francisc	84	501
Alfred	26	m	w	ENGL	Butte	Bidwell Twp	70	3
Alfred B	48	m	w	VT	Butte	Oregon Twp	70	123
Alice	8	f	w	CA	Contra Costa	Martinez P O	71	373
Alice	55	f	w	IREL	Marin	Tomales Twp	74	83
Alice	30	f	w	IREL	San Francisco	8-Wd San Francisco	82	299
Almer	47	m	w	PA	Sonoma	Vallejo Twp	91	451
Alson	33	m	w	MI	Alameda	Washington Twp	68	289
Alvah	41	m	w	NY	Colusa	Colusa Twp	71	285
Alvord	38	m	w	HI	Contra Costa	Martinez P O	71	443
Amanda	21	f	w	MEXI	San Francisco	7-Wd San Francisco	81	220
Anderville	50	m	w	VA	Yolo	Cottonwood Twp	93	471
Andrew	40	m	w	NY	San Francisco	5-Wd San Francisco	81	33
Andrew	37	m	w	PA	Inyo	Bishop Crk Twp	73	311
Andrew	35	m	w	SWED	Sonoma	Petaluma Twp	91	317
Andrew	24	m	w	MO	Marin	Tomales Twp	74	76
Andrew C	51	m	w	IA	Butte	Hamilton Twp	70	62
Andrew Me	52	m	w	VA	Yolo	Cottonwood Twp	93	466
Angus M	39	m	w	MS	Fresno	Millerton P O	72	147
Ann	45	f	w	IREL	Alameda	Brooklyn Twp	68	49
Ann	40	f	w	IREL	Amador	Ione City P O	69	356
Anna	32	f	w	IREL	San Francisco	5-Wd San Francisco	81	27
Anna E	28	f	w	ENGL	San Francisco	San Francisco P O	85	718
Anna G	69	f	w	NH	San Francisco	2-Wd San Francisco	79	249
Annie	40	f	w	IREL	Napa	Napa Twp	75	46
Annie	17	f	w	NY	San Francisco	San Francisco P O	83	240
Annie	17	f	w	IREL	Alpine	Markleeville P O	69	311
Annie W	60	f	w	NY	El Dorado	Placerville	72	119
Anson	38	m	w	ME	Solano	Vallejo	90	167
Anthony	45	m	w	ENGL	Placer	Bath P O	76	433
Anthony	26	m	w	MO	Solano	Vallejo	90	214
Asa	42	m	w	ME	San Joaquin	2-Wd Stockton	86	197
Asa B	57	m	w	VT	Yuba	Bullards Bar P O	93	547
B F	38	m	w	ME	San Joaquin	3-Wd Stockton	86	237
B S	49	m	m	KY	San Joaquin	1-Wd Stockton	86	129
Backus	60	m	b	TN	Sutter	Yuba Twp	92	151
Barney	43	m	w	IREL	Sacramento	1-Wd Sacramento	77	172
Bartholmew	51	m	w	IREL	Tehama	Tehama Twp	92	190
Basuel	50	m	w	IA	San Mateo	Half Moon Bay P O	87	405
Bela W	59	m	w	ME	Plumas	Plumas Twp	77	30
Benjamin	28	m	w	NH	Yolo	Grafton Twp	93	493
Benjamin	15	m	w	CA	San Francisco	11-Wd San Francisc	84	587
Benjan	45	m	w	IN	Sonoma	Russian Rvr	91	374

© 2001 by Heritage Quest. All rights reserved.

Name	Age	S	R	B-PL	County	Locale	Series M593 Roll	Pg
Bentley	40	m	m	KY	San Joaquin	1-Wd Stockton	86	129
Bernard	38	m	w	IREL	San Francisco	11-Wd San Francisc	84	609
Bridget	64	f	w	IREL	Santa Cruz	Pajaro Twp	89	348
Bridget	31	f	w	IREL	Sacramento	1-Wd Sacramento	77	173
Burnett	38	m	w	MA	San Francisco	11-Wd San Francisc	84	502
C	24	m	w	CT	Yuba	Marysville	93	581
C C	60	m	w	KY	Sacramento	4-Wd Sacramento	77	349
C R	28	m	w	HI	Alameda	Oakland	68	187
C W	42	m	w	IN	Sacramento	4-Wd Sacramento	77	368
Calvin R	39	m	w	IN	Nevada	Grass Valley Twp	75	147
Cardwell	60	m	w	VA	Sonoma	Mendocino Twp	91	299
Casander	36	m	w	VA	Yolo	Cottonwood Twp	93	471
Catherine	40	f	w	IREL	San Francisco	7-Wd San Francisco	81	183
Catherine	33	f	w	IREL	Humboldt	Eureka Twp	72	257
Catherine	25	f	w	SC	San Francisco	8-Wd San Francisco	82	494
Chares H	34	m	w	NY	Placer	Bath P O	76	449
Charles	52	m	w	IN	Sonoma	Russian Rvr	91	369
Charles	50	m	w	MA	San Francisco	6-Wd San Francisco	81	120
Charles	50	m	w	OH	Santa Clara	Milpitas Twp	88	109
Charles	50	m	w	ME	Marin	Point Reyes Twp	74	23
Charles	49	m	w	ME	San Francisco	11-Wd San Francisc	84	554
Charles	48	m	w	ENGL	Humboldt	Mattole Twp	72	288
Charles	48	m	w	NY	Contra Costa	Martinez P O	71	417
Charles	43	m	w	IREL	Contra Costa	San Pablo Twp	71	355
Charles	43	m	w	MA	San Francisco	San Francisco P O	83	174
Charles	42	m	w	CANA	Napa	Napa	75	18
Charles	40	m	w	IL	Napa	Napa Twp	75	31
Charles	38	m	w	ENGL	San Francisco	5-Wd San Francisco	81	21
Charles	38	m	w	NY	San Francisco	7-Wd San Francisco	81	213
Charles	32	m	w	NH	Santa Clara	San Jose Twp	88	180
Charles	30	m	w	IREL	Alameda	Oakland	68	184
Charles	27	m	w	KY	Kern	Bakersfield P O	73	360
Charles	22	m	w	NY	Yolo	Grafton Twp	93	489
Charles	17	m	w	LA	San Francisco	San Francisco P O	80	335
Charles	12	m	w	CA	Contra Costa	Martinez P O	71	436
Charles A	56	m	w	RI	Placer	Dutch Flat P O	76	404
Charles H	33	m	w	NY	San Francisco	6-Wd San Francisco	81	73
Charles H	31	m	w	VT	Santa Barbara	Las Cruces P O	87	506
Charles J	43	m	w	KY	Yuba	Long Bar Twp	93	563
Charles P	49	m	w	VT	San Francisco	San Francisco P O	83	215
Charlie	17	m	i	CA	Napa	Napa Twp	75	71
Charlotte	52	f	w	NH	San Francisco	San Francisco P O	83	149
Chas	66	m	w	PRUS	Sacramento	3-Wd Sacramento	77	271
Chas	49	m	w	CANA	Humboldt	Arcata Twp	72	232
Chas	45	m	w	MA	Mariposa	Maxwell Crk P O	74	144
Chas	35	m	w	IL	Solano	Vallejo	90	216
Chas	23	m	w	ME	Butte	Chico Twp	70	47
Chas A	34	m	w	ME	Nevada	Nevada Twp	75	316
Chas A	34	m	w	NY	Sonoma	Mendocino Twp	91	295
Chas E	39	m	w	NY	San Francisco	1-Wd San Francisco	79	49
Chas F	27	m	w	NY	San Francisco	San Francisco P O	83	175
Chas H	25	m	w	MO	Sacramento	4-Wd Sacramento	77	337
Chas R	38	m	w	NY	San Diego	San Diego	78	499
Chas T	31	m	w	OH	Napa	Napa	75	49
Chas W	36	m	w	NY	Shasta	Fort Crook P O	89	476
Clara	14	f	w	CA	Sacramento	2-Wd Sacramento	77	224
Claus	42	m	w	SHOL	San Mateo	San Mateo P O	87	354
Columbus	36	m	w	KY	Yolo	Cottonwood Twp	93	471
Cora	32	f	w	CT	Sacramento	4-Wd Sacramento	77	352
Costmer	60	m	w	WI	Napa	Napa Twp	75	71
Crawford C	2	m	c	CA	Nevada	Grass Valley Twp	75	227
Curtis	77	m	w	VT	Santa Cruz	Santa Cruz	89	433
Cyrus P	38	m	w	MA	Mendocino	Point Arena Twp	74	205
D	30	m	w	NY	Alameda	Murray Twp	68	109
Dana B	39	m	w	ME	Santa Barbara	Santa Barbara P O	87	488
Daniel	47	m	w	NY	San Diego	San Diego	78	486
Daniel	40	m	w	IREL	San Francisco	San Francisco P O	85	849
Daniel	40	m	w	OH	El Dorado	Placerville Twp	72	92
Daniel	37	m	w	ME	Stanislaus	Buena Vista Twp	92	15
Daniel	28	m	w	MS	Calaveras	Copperopolis P O	70	243
Daniel F	30	m	w	MO	Calaveras	San Andreas P O	70	175
David	57	m	w	OH	Sonoma	Santa Rosa	91	412
David	53	m	w	NH	Mariposa	Mariposa P O	74	130
David	37	m	w	OH	Yolo	Grafton Twp	93	497
David	20	m	w	OH	Butte	Ophir Twp	70	101
Delia	23	f	w	NY	Alameda	Murray Twp	68	115
Dexter	19	m	w	IL	San Diego	San Diego	78	493
Dorcas	55	f	w	CANA	San Francisco	San Francisco P O	85	859
E	46	m	w	ENGL	Lake	Morgan Valley	73	425
E	13	f	w	CA	San Francisco	San Francisco P O	85	798
E J	56	m	w	MA	Sacramento	3-Wd Sacramento	77	282
E N	54	m	w	NY	Tehama	Antelope Twp	92	160
E N	27	m	w	CT	Amador	Volcano P O	69	381
E R	36	m	w	CT	Humboldt	Bald Hills	72	239
E W	40	m	w	ME	Solano	Vallejo	90	171
Ed	40	m	w	NH	Alameda	Oakland	68	194
Ed F	39	m	w	NY	San Diego	San Diego	78	493
Edgar B	36	m	w	CT	San Francisco	6-Wd San Francisco	81	101
Edmond	60	m	w	VA	Yolo	Cottonwood Twp	93	471
Edmund	21	m	w	MO	Yolo	Cottonwood Twp	93	471
Edward	40	m	w	MD	San Francisco	7-Wd San Francisco	81	220
Edward	37	m	w	OH	Sonoma	Petaluma Twp	91	324
Edward	35	m	w	IREL	Santa Barbara	San Buenaventura P	87	429
Edward	28	m	w	IREL	San Francisco	7-Wd San Francisco	81	165
Edward	27	m	w	ASEA	Marin	Tomales Twp	74	87
Edwd	28	m	w	IREL	Sacramento	1-Wd Sacramento	77	188
Edwin A	37	m	b	WIND	San Francisco	6-Wd San Francisco	81	144

Name	Age	S	R	B-PL	County	Locale	Series M593 Roll	Pg
Eli	24	m	w	MO	Colusa	Grand Island Twp	71	304
Eli D	16	m	w	IA	El Dorado	Placerville	72	126
Elias G	60	m	w	ME	Yuba	Parks Bar Twp	93	650
Elias W	56	m	w	AR	Sutter	Nicolaus Twp	92	113
Elija M	40	m	w	KY	Colusa	Butte Twp	71	265
Elijah	7	m	w	NE	Yuba	Marysville	93	618
Elijah	40	m	w	AR	Shasta	Portugese Flat P O	89	472
Elisha	54	m	w	CT	Sacramento	Sutter Twp	77	380
Elisha	47	m	w	NY	Santa Cruz	Santa Cruz Twp	89	386
Elisha	45	m	w	NY	Humboldt	Table Bluff Twp	72	307
Elisha D	54	m	w	VT	Butte	Oregon Twp	70	134
Eliza	66	f	w	PA	Mariposa	Maxwell Crk P O	74	147
Eliza	35	f	w	IREL	Nevada	Little York Twp	75	242
Eliza J	39	f	w	MA	San Francisco	San Francisco P O	85	722
Elizabeth	64	f	w	NY	San Francisco	8-Wd San Francisco	82	420
Elizabeth	23	f	w	CANA	Santa Clara	Fremont Twp	88	53
Ellen	50	f	w	IREL	San Francisco	San Francisco P O	80	412
Ellen	43	f	w	IREL	San Francisco	San Francisco P O	83	48
Emma	49	f	w	LA	San Francisco	San Francisco P O	85	744
Emma	40	f	w	IREL	San Francisco	11-Wd San Francisc	84	632
Erena	44	f	w	TN	Mariposa	Mariposa P O	74	97
Eulentheros A	43	m	w	OH	Santa Clara	1-Wd San Jose	88	246
F	35	m	w	NY	Sierra	Sierra Twp	89	566
Fannie	60	f	w	TN	Monterey	Castroville Twp	74	330
Foster	42	m	w	OH	Alameda	Brooklyn	68	32
Francis	60	m	b	MO	Butte	Wyandotte Twp	70	144
Francis	56	m	w	NY	San Francisco	San Francisco P O	80	345
Francis	45	m	w	IREL	San Francisco	San Francisco P O	83	125
Francis	10	m	b	CA	Sacramento	2-Wd Sacramento	77	226
Frank	35	m	w	IN	Sacramento	Franklin Twp	77	116
Frank	26	m	w	LA	Marin	San Rafael Twp	74	37
Frank	22	m	w	PA	San Francisco	8-Wd San Francisco	82	370
Frank	20	m	w	NY	Yolo	Cache Crk Twp	93	457
Frank	19	m	w	IL	Yolo	Putah Twp	93	519
Frank B	25	m	w	CT	Los Angeles	Los Angeles Twp	73	491
Frank G	28	m	w	OH	Napa	Napa Twp	75	71
Franklin	37	m	w	PA	El Dorado	Georgetown Twp	72	49
Fred	60	m	w	ENGL	Sonoma	Santa Rosa	91	424
Fred P	47	m	w	CT	San Francisco	2-Wd San Francisco	79	183
Fredrick	32	m	w	NY	San Francisco	7-Wd San Francisco	81	220
G	21	m	w	CANA	Alameda	Oakland	68	222
G A	29	m	w	NY	Alameda	Oakland	68	262
G W	36	m	w	MI	Sacramento	1-Wd Sacramento	77	178
Galen	56	m	w	NC	Mariposa	Mariposa P O	74	134
Geo	40	m	w	ME	San Francisco	7-Wd San Francisco	81	235
Geo	37	m	w	VT	Alameda	Oakland	68	255
Geo	37	m	w	IREL	San Francisco	7-Wd San Francisco	81	253
Geo	28	m	w	WALE	Sierra	Gibson Twp	89	540
Geo	20	m	w	IA	Sacramento	4-Wd Sacramento	77	373
Geo	15	m	w	IL	San Francisco	11-Wd San Francisc	84	587
Geo T	35	m	w	NY	Santa Clara	Gilroy Twp	88	81
Geo W	46	m	w	NY	Napa	Napa Twp	75	63
Geo W	45	m	w	VT	San Francisco	2-Wd San Francisco	79	236
George	59	m	w	MA	San Francisco	6-Wd San Francisco	81	98
George	55	m	w	NY	San Francisco	7-Wd San Francisco	81	175
George	43	m	w	ENGL	San Francisco	San Francisco P O	85	777
George	42	m	w	NY	San Francisco	7-Wd San Francisco	81	201
George	37	m	w	OH	San Francisco	5-Wd San Francisco	81	12
George	35	m	w	IREL	San Francisco	7-Wd San Francisco	81	188
George	33	m	w	IREL	San Francisco	7-Wd San Francisco	81	170
George	31	m	w	CANA	Stanislaus	Buena Vista Twp	92	14
George	29	m	w	MO	Sonoma	Mendocino Twp	91	299
George	26	m	w	MO	Stanislaus	Emory Twp	92	24
George	25	m	w	MO	Yolo	Cottonwood Twp	93	471
George	23	m	w	CANA	Mendocino	Point Arena Twp	74	205
George	21	m	w	IA	Napa	Yountville Twp	75	88
George	16	m	w	NJ	Alpine	Woodfords P O	69	310
George A	38	m	w	ME	Placer	Auburn P O	76	357
George C	38	m	w	MI	Amador	Jackson P O	69	341
George L	52	m	w	MA	San Diego	Fort Yuma Dist	78	463
George R	30	m	w	MA	San Francisco	San Francisco P O	83	169
George T	32	m	w	ENGL	San Diego	Julian Dist	78	472
George T	18	m	w	NH	Calaveras	Copperopolis P O	70	227
George W	45	m	w	MA	Sonoma	Sonoma Twp	91	438
George W	44	m	w	KY	Amador	Fiddletown P O	69	434
George W	36	m	w	NY	Inyo	Bishop Crk Twp	73	312
George W	23	m	w	IA	Yolo	Cottonwood Twp	93	471
Gilbert	35	m	w	CT	San Francisco	7-Wd San Francisco	81	185
Gilman W	40	m	w	MA	Sacramento	2-Wd Sacramento	77	247
H	25	m	w	CANA	Humboldt	Eureka Twp	72	269
H A	26	m	w	PA	Yuba	Marysville	93	583
H H	24	m	w	MI	Alameda	Oakland	68	176
H J	32	m	w	IN	Sacramento	3-Wd Sacramento	77	271
H S	21	m	w	TN	Santa Barbara	San Buenaventura P	87	421
Harry	44	m	w	IREL	Humboldt	Eureka Twp	72	279
Hasen K	78	m	w	NH	Merced	Snelling P O	74	255
Heman H	59	m	w	VT	Sonoma	Vallejo Twp	91	459
Henry	38	m	w	OR	Humboldt	Arcata Twp	72	233
Henry	38	m	w	OH	Alameda	Brooklyn Twp	68	42
Henry	36	m	b	MD	Nevada	Rough & Ready Twp	75	334
Henry	33	m	w	MO	Siskiyou	Yreka Twp	89	665
Henry	22	m	w	IL	Los Angeles	Soledad Twp	73	631
Henry	21	m	w	IREL	Solano	Silveyville Twp	90	76
Henry A	33	m	w	IREL	Santa Cruz	Santa Cruz Twp	89	390
Henry D	48	m	w	PA	San Francisco	8-Wd San Francisco	82	421
Hervey F	13	m	w	CA	San Francisco	San Francisco P O	85	821
Highposian	16	m	w	TN	Mendocino	Point Arena Twp	74	212

© 2001 by Heritage Quest. All rights reserved.

Series M593

Name	Age	S	R	B-PL	County	Locale	Roll	Pg
Hiram	40	m	w	OH	San Joaquin	3-Wd Stockton	86	221
Horace	51	m	w	NY	San Francisco	8-Wd San Francisco	82	451
Horace	43	m	w	ME	San Francisco	11-Wd San Francisc	84	576
Horace	38	m	w	NY	San Bernardino	San Bernardino Twp	78	422
Howard	43	m	w	MA	Sonoma	Sonoma Twp	91	437
Howel	59	m	w	NY	Sacramento	4-Wd Sacramento	77	368
Hugh	38	m	w	IREL	Amador	Ione City P O	69	349
Hugh	37	m	w	IREL	San Francisco	11-Wd San Francisc	84	458
Hugh	31	m	w	IREL	Alameda	Murray Twp	68	102
Hugh J	46	m	w	IREL	Napa	Napa	75	43
Hugh W	35	m	w	AR	Fresno	Kings Rvr P O	72	212
Hugh Wm	39	m	w	NY	San Francisco	8-Wd San Francisco	82	288
Hulett	59	m	w	VT	San Bernardino	San Bernardino Twp	78	441
Ida	9	f	w	CA	Santa Clara	Santa Clara Twp	88	154
Ida	25	f	w	MA	Alameda	Oakland	68	182
Ida	1	f	w	CA	Sacramento	1-Wd Sacramento	77	172
Isaac	41	m	w	VA	San Francisco	2-Wd San Francisco	79	214
Isaac	40	m	w	ENGL	Marin	San Rafael	74	48
Isaac	30	m	w	NJ	Solano	Vallejo	90	200
Isabel	36	f	w	ITAL	San Diego	San Diego	78	489
J	40	m	w	NY	El Dorado	Greenwood Twp	72	51
J A	39	m	w	NY	Sutter	Sutter Twp	92	125
J B	48	m	w	VT	Merced	Snelling P O	74	271
J B	41	m	w	OH	Sierra	Table Rock Twp	89	576
J B	21	m	w	IL	Solano	Vallejo	90	197
J C	36	m	w	ME	Alameda	Oakland	68	267
J C	30	m	w	NY	Monterey	Castroville Twp	74	336
J F	41	m	w	NY	Sacramento	3-Wd Sacramento	77	311
J F	40	m	w	NY	Sacramento	3-Wd Sacramento	77	277
J F	38	m	w	OH	Sutter	Butte Twp	92	88
J H	29	m	w	MO	Sutter	Yuba Twp	92	140
J J	50	m	w	IL	Alameda	Murray Twp	68	124
J Martin	50	m	w	PA	San Diego	San Diego	78	509
J R	51	m	w	MA	El Dorado	Salmon Falls Twp	72	133
J S	26	m	w	LA	Solano	Vallejo	90	200
J S	25	m	w	PA	Alameda	Alameda	68	13
J T	49	m	w	KY	Sacramento	3-Wd Sacramento	77	297
J W	47	m	w	ENGL	Monterey	San Juan Twp	74	416
J W	40	m	w	PA	San Francisco	8-Wd San Francisco	82	375
J W	37	m	w	PA	Yuba	W Bear Rvr Twp	93	680
J W	33	m	w	MI	San Francisco	3-Wd San Francisco	79	314
Jabal	50	m	w	NY	Solano	Vallejo	90	160
Jacob	35	m	w	ME	Yuba	Rose Bar Twp	93	654
Jacob	30	m	w	AR	Siskiyou	Surprise Valley Tw	89	641
Jacob B	54	m	w	TN	Sutter	Yuba Twp	92	141
Jacob C	34	m	w	MO	Santa Clara	2-Wd San Jose	88	280
Jaine	32	m	w	IREL	Amador	Jackson P O	69	329
James	65	m	w	SCOT	Tuolumne	Big Oak Flat P O	93	394
James	55	m	w	NY	Contra Costa	Martinez P O	71	414
James	53	m	w	ENGL	Alameda	Oakland	68	251
James	50	m	w	IREL	Sonoma	Vallejo Twp	91	460
James	50	m	w	CANA	Mendocino	Point Arena Twp	74	205
James	49	m	w	OH	Colusa	Monroe Twp	71	322
James	47	m	w	IREL	San Francisco	San Francisco P O	80	396
James	46	m	w	NY	San Francisco	7-Wd San Francisco	81	213
James	45	m	w	KY	Kern	Linns Valley P O	73	344
James	43	m	w	IREL	Sonoma	Petaluma Twp	91	337
James	41	m	w	IREL	Sonoma	Bodega Twp	91	252
James	41	m	w	KY	Solano	Vacaville Twp	90	123
James	40	m	w	IREL	Humboldt	Mattole Twp	72	285
James	40	m	w	IREL	Tuolumne	Columbia P O	93	348
James	40	m	w	TN	Yolo	Putah Twp	93	512
James	39	m	w	OH	Butte	Chico Twp	70	24
James	38	m	w	IREL	San Francisco	11-Wd San Francisc	84	481
James	38	m	w	NY	San Francisco	San Francisco P O	83	317
James	37	m	w	IREL	Yuba	W Bear Rvr Twp	93	682
James	37	m	w	IREL	Tuolumne	Sonora P O	93	328
James	35	m	w	NY	Amador	Jackson P O	69	318
James	35	m	w	ENGL	Nevada	Grass Valley Twp	75	224
James	35	m	w	IREL	San Francisco	11-Wd San Francisc	84	598
James	34	m	w	ENGL	Solano	Silveyville Twp	90	81
James	32	m	w	NY	San Francisco	1-Wd San Francisco	79	134
James	30	m	w	IREL	Amador	Jackson P O	69	329
James	30	m	w	IA	Sacramento	Lee Twp	77	157
James	28	m	w	ME	Nevada	Meadow Lake Twp	75	267
James	27	m	w	IREL	Santa Clara	1-Wd San Jose	88	229
James	26	m	w	IREL	San Francisco	7-Wd San Francisco	81	165
James	26	m	w	NY	San Francisco	1-Wd San Francisco	79	69
James	25	m	w	AUSL	Marin	Tomales Twp	74	87
James	25	m	w	PA	Mariposa	Mariposa P O	74	90
James	24	m	w	PA	Marin	San Rafael Twp	74	40
James	23	m	w	AUSL	San Francisco	San Francisco P O	80	337
James	16	m	w	IL	Sacramento	3-Wd Sacramento	77	297
James	16	m	w	CA	Sonoma	Washington Twp	91	468
James A	43	m	w	NY	Butte	Chico Twp	70	21
James A	22	m	w	MO	San Luis Obispo	Morro Twp	87	282
James C	34	m	w	NY	Trinity	Junction City Pct	92	208
James L	42	m	w	VT	Sacramento	Sutter Twp	77	382
James L	27	m	w	IL	Los Angeles	Los Nietos Twp	73	587
James M	33	m	w	IL	Santa Clara	Alviso Twp	88	24
James P	33	m	w	MO	Mendocino	Ukiah Twp	74	241
James R	45	m	w	SCOT	Inyo	Cerro Gordo Twp	73	319
James W	54	m	w	NY	Los Angeles	Santa Ana Twp	73	603
James W	34	m	w	NY	Santa Cruz	Watsonville	89	376
Jane	5	f	w	CA	Alameda	Murray Twp	68	115
Jane A	39	f	w	NY	San Francisco	San Francisco P O	83	174
Jane F	49	f	w	MI	Sonoma	Petaluma Twp	91	313
Jas	50	m	w	VT	Sonoma	Santa Rosa	91	428
Jas	44	m	w	ME	San Francisco	7-Wd San Francisco	81	262
Jas	38	m	w	IREL	San Francisco	7-Wd San Francisco	81	258
Jas	31	m	w	VT	Solano	Vallejo	90	212
Jas	30	m	w	NY	Butte	Chico Twp	70	26
Jas B	25	m	w	VT	Butte	Chico Twp	70	35
Jas H	44	m	w	KY	San Luis Obispo	Arroyo Grande Twp	87	277
Jas P	49	m	w	TN	Sonoma	Santa Rosa	91	400
Jas P	47	m	w	ENGL	Sonoma	Santa Rosa	91	400
Jefferson	33	m	w	TN	Stanislaus	San Joaquin Twp	92	75
Jeremiah	50	m	w	NY	San Francisco	San Francisco P O	80	364
Jerome	21	m	w	IL	Yolo	Putah Twp	93	515
Jessie	47	m	w	KY	Yolo	Cache Crk Twp	93	424
Jessie	35	m	w	ENGL	San Francisco	San Francisco P O	83	141
Jno	40	m	w	ENGL	Sierra	Table Rock Twp	89	575
Jno	28	m	w	IREL	Sacramento	1-Wd Sacramento	77	188
Jno C	50	m	w	MO	Butte	Ophir Twp	70	113
Jno R O	45	m	w	NY	Butte	Hamilton Twp	70	70
Johah	37	f	w	IREL	Alameda	Washington Twp	68	278
John	73	m	w	KY	Marin	San Rafael Twp	74	36
John	65	m	w	TN	San Diego	San Diego	78	508
John	60	m	w	IREL	San Francisco	11-Wd San Francisc	84	431
John	55	m	b	DC	San Francisco	6-Wd San Francisco	81	89
John	53	m	w	NY	San Mateo	Half Moon Bay P O	87	396
John	51	m	w	ENGL	Tehama	Red Bluff	92	173
John	50	m	w	IREL	Nevada	Grass Valley Twp	75	196
John	48	m	w	PA	Plumas	Plumas Twp	77	27
John	48	m	w	ENGL	Stanislaus	Buena Vista Twp	92	15
John	45	m	w	NC	Alameda	Eden Twp	68	66
John	45	m	w	NY	Inyo	Bishop Crk Twp	73	316
John	43	m	w	TN	Santa Clara	Redwood Twp	88	118
John	39	m	w	ENGL	Alameda	Alameda	68	13
John	38	m	w	WALE	Solano	Benicia	90	2
John	38	m	w	OH	Santa Cruz	Soquel Twp	89	436
John	37	m	w	IREL	Sonoma	Bodega Twp	91	254
John	37	m	w	SWED	San Francisco	6-Wd San Francisco	81	150
John	37	m	w	IREL	San Francisco	3-Wd San Francisco	79	320
John	37	m	w	ENGL	Monterey	Castroville Twp	74	336
John	36	m	w	NY	San Francisco	2-Wd San Francisco	79	248
John	36	m	w	CANA	Stanislaus	Empire Twp	92	46
John	35	m	w	IREL	Santa Barbara	San Buenaventura P	87	448
John	35	m	w	IREL	San Francisco	7-Wd San Francisco	81	173
John	35	m	w	FRAN	San Francisco	3-Wd San Francisco	79	295
John	33	m	w	MA	Marin	San Rafael Twp	74	43
John	33	m	w	ENGL	Yolo	Buckeye Twp	93	408
John	32	m	w	ME	Merced	Snelling P O	74	260
John	32	m	w	US	Nevada	Grass Valley Twp	75	224
John	32	m	w	ENGL	San Francisco	San Francisco P O	83	285
John	32	m	w	ME	San Joaquin	2-Wd Stockton	86	193
John	30	m	w	NY	San Francisco	7-Wd San Francisco	81	220
John	30	m	w	IREL	San Francisco	7-Wd San Francisco	81	216
John	30	m	w	IREL	Sacramento	2-Wd Sacramento	77	225
John	30	m	w	IREL	Sonoma	Vallejo Twp	91	459
John	30	m	w	NY	Shasta	Portugese Flat P O	89	472
John	29	m	w	ENGL	Marin	Tomales Twp	74	83
John	28	m	w	ENGL	San Francisco	7-Wd San Francisco	81	204
John	28	m	w	IREL	San Francisco	11-Wd San Francisc	84	600
John	27	m	w	CANA	Siskiyou	Callahan P O	89	629
John	27	m	w	IREL	Santa Clara	1-Wd San Jose	88	230
John	27	m	w	IN	San Francisco	San Francisco P O	80	456
John	24	m	w	CANA	Sacramento	Sutter Twp	77	381
John	24	m	w	NY	San Francisco	8-Wd San Francisco	82	334
John	24	m	w	PRUS	Solano	Silveyville Twp	90	79
John	23	m	w	NY	Marin	San Rafael Twp	74	40
John	23	m	w	VA	Sutter	Nicolaus Twp	92	114
John	21	m	w	LA	Colusa	Monroe Twp	71	314
John	20	m	w	ME	Solano	Vallejo	90	202
John	15	m	w	UT	San Bernardino	San Bernardino Twp	78	434
John C	46	m	w	AL	Monterey	San Antonio Twp	74	321
John E	41	m	w	VA	Sonoma	Sonoma Twp	91	433
John G	38	m	w	DC	San Francisco	8-Wd San Francisco	82	464
John H	30	m	w	IREL	Inyo	Independence Twp	73	326
John I	27	m	w	ENGL	Sacramento	Granite Twp	77	146
John L	31	m	w	OH	Tulare	Tule Rvr Twp	92	263
John M	47	m	w	ME	Nevada	Washington Twp	75	346
John Q A	43	m	w	NH	Placer	Newcastle Twp	76	477
John S	39	m	w	OH	Stanislaus	Branch Twp	92	6
John W	56	m	w	NY	Napa	Napa	75	3
Johnston	63	m	w	SCOT	Sonoma	Analy Twp	91	218
Jonathan	44	m	w	IN	Humboldt	Eureka Twp	72	257
Jonathan	42	m	w	ENGL	Nevada	Nevada Twp	75	280
Jos B	48	m	w	ME	San Francisco	San Francisco P O	83	46
Jos W	56	m	w	CT	San Francisco	San Francisco P O	83	109
Joseph	50	m	w	KY	Nevada	Grass Valley Twp	75	199
Joseph	43	m	w	NY	Colusa	Monroe Twp	71	324
Joseph	40	m	c	IL	Del Norte	Happy Camp Twp	71	470
Joseph	39	m	w	TX	San Bernardino	Chino Twp	78	412
Joseph	38	m	w	BELG	Nevada	Nevada Twp	75	288
Joseph	37	m	w	IREL	Mariposa	Mariposa P O	74	129
Joseph	34	m	w	NY	Sacramento	2-Wd Sacramento	77	218
Joseph	34	m	b	PA	Butte	Chico Twp	70	18
Joseph	25	m	w	IREL	San Francisco	7-Wd San Francisco	81	165
Joseph C	40	m	w	SCOT	San Luis Obispo	Santa Rosa Twp	87	323
Josiah	41	m	w	VA	Butte	Chico Twp	70	45
Judson	36	m	w	ME	San Francisco	San Francisco P O	83	369
Julia	42	f	m	TN	Yuba	Marysville	93	610
Kate	20	f	w	NJ	Butte	Chico Twp	70	41

© 2001 by Heritage Quest. All rights reserved.

Name	Age	S	R	B-PL	County	Locale	Series M593 Roll	Pg
Kate	16	f	w	CA	San Francisco	2-Wd San Francisco	79	203
L C	38	m	w	TN	Butte	Wyandotte Twp	70	147
L M	30	f	w	MA	Lassen	Susanville Twp	73	442
L M	21	m	w	CANA	Mendocino	Little Lake Twp	74	199
L R	40	m	w	NY	Alameda	Murray Twp	68	128
L S	30	m	w	OH	San Francisco	San Francisco P O	85	787
Lander J	39	m	w	VA	Yolo	Cottonwood Twp	93	471
Larah	25	f	w	NY	San Francisco	San Francisco P O	83	44
Lawrence	40	m	w	HOLL	Sutter	Sutter Twp	92	120
Layfaette	14	m	w	IN	Solano	Silveyville Twp	90	92
Leonard	38	m	w	ME	Santa Barbara	Santa Barbara P O	87	476
Lester G	38	m	w	MA	Santa Cruz	Pajaro Twp	89	344
Levi B	48	m	w	PA	Santa Clara	Santa Clara Twp	88	149
Lewis	35	m	w	CANA	Kern	Kernville P O	73	367
Lewis A	6	m	w	NV	Santa Barbara	San Buenaventura P	87	439
Lewis B	23	m	w	NY	Nevada	Nevada Twp	75	309
Lewis M	30	m	w	AL	Colusa	Spring Valley Twp	71	340
Lizzie	40	f	w	IREL	Alameda	Oakland	68	259
Lizzy	25	f	w	IREL	San Francisco	6-Wd San Francisco	81	153
Lorenzo B	30	m	w	ME	San Francisco	San Francisco P O	83	183
Lucien	32	m	w	NY	Mendocino	Casper & Big Rvr	74	163
Lucretia W	50	f	w	PA	Colusa	Colusa	71	298
M B	41	m	w	PA	Alameda	Oakland	68	171
M B	40	m	w	NY	Santa Clara	Gilroy Twp	88	85
M D	27	m	w	TX	Yuba	Marysville Twp	93	569
M J	24	m	w	OH	San Joaquin	2-Wd Stockton	86	162
Margaret	40	f	w	IREL	San Francisco	San Francisco P O	83	144
Margaret	33	f	w	NJ	Santa Clara	Fremont Twp	88	65
Margaret	32	f	w	IREL	San Francisco	San Francisco P O	85	721
Margaret	21	f	w	MO	San Francisco	San Francisco P O	83	260
Margt	25	f	w	IREL	San Francisco	San Francisco P O	83	98
Maria	60	f	w	NY	Contra Costa	Martinez P O	71	437
Maria	18	f	w	IREL	San Francisco	11-Wd San Francisc	84	479
Mark H	38	m	w	TN	Monterey	Alisal Twp	74	297
Martha	26	f	w	SCOT	Marin	Point Reyes Twp	74	21
Martin B	28	m	w	NY	Santa Clara	Redwood Twp	88	131
Mary	45	f	w	IREL	San Francisco	San Francisco P O	83	120
Mary	40	f	w	RI	San Francisco	San Francisco P O	83	222
Mary	25	f	w	WI	Alameda	Murray Twp	68	115
Mary	25	f	w	IL	Sonoma	Analy Twp	91	230
Mary	24	f	w	IREL	Marin	San Rafael	74	57
Mary	23	f	w	IREL	Santa Clara	2-Wd San Jose	88	317
Mary	15	f	w	US	Nevada	Grass Valley Twp	75	229
Mary A	45	f	w	IREL	Sacramento	Georgianna Twp	77	130
Mary E	35	f	w	CT	San Francisco	8-Wd San Francisco	82	329
Mathew	37	m	w	KY	Sacramento	Georgianna Twp	77	124
Matilda	18	f	b	MO	Sutter	Yuba Twp	92	151
Matilda	10	f	w	CA	Shasta	Millville P O	89	483
Matthew	46	m	w	PA	Los Angeles	San Juan Twp	73	628
Melville	30	m	w	NY	San Joaquin	2-Wd Stockton	86	182
Michael	41	m	w	IREL	Placer	Bath P O	76	436
Michael	39	m	w	IREL	Alameda	Hayward	68	78
Michael	29	m	w	IREL	San Francisco	11-Wd San Francisc	84	539
Michael	28	m	w	IREL	Nevada	Eureka Twp	75	139
Miles	32	m	w	VT	Solano	Silveyville Twp	90	73
Milton S	30	m	w	PA	Inyo	Bishop Crk Twp	73	316
Minnie L	12	f	w	CA	Placer	Newcastle Twp	76	473
Molly	23	f	w	PA	Sacramento	3-Wd Sacramento	77	290
Molly	19	f	w	NY	San Francisco	6-Wd San Francisco	81	71
N	54	m	w	MA	Lassen	Janesville Twp	73	430
N	37	m	w	MA	Sierra	Lincoln Twp	89	547
N A	39	m	w	ME	Tuolumne	Columbia P O	93	359
Nancy	49	f	w	TN	Mariposa	Mariposa P O	74	91
Nathan	40	m	w	NY	San Francisco	San Francisco P O	80	395
Nathan	30	m	w	VT	Sonoma	Petaluma Twp	91	351
Nathan	28	m	w	NY	Monterey	Salinas Twp	74	307
Nathan	27	m	w	IREL	Los Angeles	Santa Ana Twp	73	600
Nehemiah	40	m	w	DE	Sacramento	Sutter Twp	77	390
Nellie	8	f	w	CA	Colusa	Grand Island Twp	71	308
Nellie	25	f	m	MA	San Francisco	San Francisco P O	80	486
Nimrod	55	m	w	VA	Sutter	Yuba Twp	92	143
Noah G	53	m	w	ME	Sonoma	Petaluma Twp	91	340
Noble	38	m	w	IREL	Yolo	Grafton Twp	93	491
Olin	35	m	w	NY	Placer	Dutch Flat P O	76	415
Olive J	41	f	w	NH	San Francisco	San Francisco P O	83	147
Oliver L	33	m	w	VT	Butte	Chico Twp	70	30
Osmer	35	m	w	VT	San Francisco	11-Wd San Francisc	84	483
Otis	31	m	w	OH	Sutter	Butte Twp	92	102
P	26	m	w	IREL	Lake	Upper Lake	73	408
Pa Le	35	m	w	CT	Sacramento	Dry Crk Twp	77	100
Pat	38	m	w	IREL	San Joaquin	3-Wd Stockton	86	236
Patrick	60	m	w	IREL	Sonoma	Santa Rosa	91	428
Patrick	60	m	w	IREL	San Francisco	San Francisco P O	83	402
Patrick	50	m	w	IREL	San Mateo	Pescadero P O	87	415
Patrick	37	m	w	IREL	Tuolumne	Chinese Camp P O	93	366
Patrick	22	m	w	IREL	San Francisco	San Francisco P O	83	403
Patrk	36	m	w	IREL	Sacramento	4-Wd Sacramento	77	327
Peter	53	m	w	IREL	Lake	Lakeport	73	406
Peter	41	m	w	IREL	Butte	Chico Twp	70	41
Peter	37	m	w	IREL	Lake	Big Valley	73	395
Peter	28	m	w	DENM	San Francisco	7-Wd San Francisco	81	259
Peter B	36	m	w	VT	Placer	Colfax P O	76	390
Pharez A	24	m	w	IL	Alpine	Monitor P O	69	313
Philander	24	m	w	OH	Santa Clara	Milpitas Twp	88	109
Philip	32	m	w	PA	San Francisco	San Francisco P O	85	745
Philip Margt	45	f	w	IREL	Sonoma	Petaluma Twp	91	341
Phillip N	52	m	w	NY	San Mateo	San Mateo P O	87	371
Pomeroy B	51	m	w	CT	Marin	San Rafael	74	57
R	30	m	w	IL	Alameda	Murray Twp	68	110
R J	29	m	w	KY	Sonoma	Santa Rosa	91	410
R L	33	m	w	ENGL	Nevada	Eureka Twp	75	134
Rebecca	37	f	w	PA	Alameda	Oakland	68	151
Reuben	54	m	w	MA	Contra Costa	Martinez Twp	71	348
Reuben	41	m	w	MS	San Joaquin	2-Wd Stockton	86	190
Richard	36	m	m	WIND	San Francisco	San Francisco P O	80	375
Richard	28	m	w	NY	San Francisco	8-Wd San Francisco	82	334
Richard A	48	m	w	VA	Colusa	Colusa Twp	71	286
Robert	46	m	w	NY	Sonoma	Washington Twp	91	470
Robert	42	m	w	NC	Kern	Havilah P O	73	339
Robert	42	m	w	ENGL	Napa	Napa	75	35
Robert	40	m	w	ENGL	San Mateo	Redwood City P O	87	376
Robert	36	m	w	IREL	Mendocino	Navarro & Big Rvr	74	177
Robert	23	m	w	AUSL	Marin	Tomales Twp	74	87
Robert	19	m	w	IL	Contra Costa	Martinez P O	71	369
Robert M	44	m	w	MA	Solano	Suisun Twp	90	98
Robert O	50	m	w	CANA	Stanislaus	Emory Twp	92	20
Robin	54	m	b	KY	Sonoma	Petaluma Twp	91	323
Robt	33	m	w	IREL	San Francisco	San Francisco P O	83	299
Robt A	47	m	w	KY	El Dorado	Lake Valley Twp	72	63
Robt C	47	m	w	MD	Marin	Novato Twp	74	13
Robt V	20	m	w	IN	El Dorado	Coloma Twp	72	8
Rosa	28	f	w	CHIL	San Francisco	San Francisco P O	85	860
Rosa	20	f	w	BELG	San Francisco	San Francisco P O	80	394
Roxana	48	f	w	VT	El Dorado	Georgetown Twp	72	45
Rufus A	36	m	w	VA	Shasta	Millville P O	89	485
S D	46	m	w	NY	Santa Clara	Gilroy Twp	88	75
S F	30	f	w	MO	San Joaquin	2-Wd Stockton	86	179
S G	35	m	w	CANA	Napa	Napa	75	9
S P	39	m	w	PA	Mendocino	Little Lake Twp	74	200
S P	37	m	w	ENGL	Solano	Vallejo	90	163
S P	34	m	w	ME	Humboldt	Pacific Twp	72	292
S T	36	m	w	ME	Sacramento	3-Wd Sacramento	77	287
Sam	25	m	w	CANA	Solano	Vallejo	90	143
Sam J P	21	m	w	ME	San Francisco	San Francisco P O	83	94
Saml	45	m	w	CT	Yuba	Rose Bar Twp	93	659
Saml	43	m	w	IN	Sacramento	3-Wd Sacramento	77	287
Saml	30	m	w	TN	Sonoma	Santa Rosa	91	397
Saml	22	m	w	ME	Solano	Vallejo	90	139
Saml F	43	m	w	PA	San Francisco	5-Wd San Francisco	81	31
Saml J	44	m	w	CANA	San Luis Obispo	San Luis Obispo Tw	87	308
Samuel	54	m	w	NY	Napa	Napa Twp	75	72
Samuel	50	m	w	IREL	Nevada	Nevada Twp	75	278
Samuel	44	m	w	AUST	Plumas	Quartz Twp	77	35
Samuel	40	m	w	PA	Marin	Bolinas Twp	74	7
Samuel	35	m	w	ME	Sacramento	3-Wd Sacramento	77	303
Samuel	26	m	w	FRAN	San Mateo	Schoolhouse Statio	87	333
Samuel B	38	m	w	NY	San Francisco	6-Wd San Francisco	81	116
Sandy	50	m	b	VA	Yuba	Marysville	93	610
Sarah	22	f	w	LA	San Francisco	8-Wd San Francisco	82	384
Sarah	17	f	w	AUSL	San Francisco	San Francisco P O	83	412
Skillman	26	m	w	IN	Yolo	Cache Crk Twp	93	447
Soloman	54	m	w	KY	Plumas	Quartz Twp	77	36
Solomon A	47	m	w	MA	Santa Clara	1-Wd San Jose	88	246
Stephen	39	m	w	NY	San Francisco	11-Wd San Francisc	84	574
Stephen	22	m	w	CANA	Solano	Vallejo	90	139
Susan	33	f	w	IREL	San Francisco	San Francisco P O	83	6
Susan	15	f	w	CA	San Francisco	11-Wd San Francisc	84	606
T	47	m	w	ENGL	Lake	Knoxville Mines	73	404
T B	47	m	w	CT	Alameda	Oakland	68	176
T I	42	m	w	IREL	Tuolumne	Big Oak Flat P O	93	395
T J	38	m	w	MO	Amador	Drytown P O	69	418
T S	60	m	w	MA	Amador	Jackson P O	69	341
T S	38	m	w	OH	Solano	Vallejo	90	207
Terrence	51	m	w	VA	Tuolumne	Sonora P O	93	304
Terrence	35	m	w	IREL	San Francisco	8-Wd San Francisco	82	389
Thadius	40	m	w	NY	Humboldt	Arcata Twp	72	225
Thomas	73	m	w	IREL	San Francisco	11-Wd San Francisc	84	505
Thomas	70	m	w	PA	Inyo	Bishop Crk Twp	73	315
Thomas	65	m	w	IREL	Tuolumne	Columbia P O	93	348
Thomas	59	m	w	ENGL	Mendocino	Little Lake Twp	74	192
Thomas	54	m	w	ENGL	Humboldt	Mattole Twp	72	288
Thomas	48	m	w	MO	Yolo	Cache Crk Twp	93	453
Thomas	43	m	w	IREL	San Francisco	San Francisco P O	85	781
Thomas	40	m	w	ENGL	San Francisco	1-Wd San Francisco	79	88
Thomas	40	m	b	PA	San Francisco	2-Wd San Francisco	79	244
Thomas	38	m	w	IOFM	El Dorado	Mountain Twp	72	67
Thomas	38	m	w	ENGL	Nevada	Rough & Ready Twp	75	328
Thomas	35	m	w	IREL	San Francisco	San Francisco P O	83	143
Thomas	34	m	w	CANA	Santa Clara	1-Wd San Jose	88	259
Thomas	34	m	w	IREL	San Francisco	San Francisco P O	83	318
Thomas	34	m	w	PA	Inyo	Bishop Crk Twp	73	315
Thomas	33	m	w	IREL	San Francisco	11-Wd San Francisc	84	451
Thomas	33	m	w	IREL	Sacramento	3-Wd Sacramento	77	258
Thomas	28	m	w	IREL	Santa Barbara	San Buenaventura P	87	444
Thomas	22	m	w	IREL	Santa Clara	1-Wd San Jose	88	226
Thomas C	57	m	w	NJ	Tuolumne	Columbia P O	93	340
Thomas H	30	m	w	AL	Santa Cruz	Pajaro Twp	89	342
Thomas H	17	m	w	IN	Inyo	Bishop Crk Twp	73	316
Thomas L	51	m	w	DE	Yolo	Cache Crk Twp	93	455
Thos	9	m	w	CA	Sacramento	Cosumnes Twp	77	91
Thos	42	m	w	IREL	Solano	Vallejo	90	192
Thos	39	m	w	NY	Sacramento	4-Wd Sacramento	77	327
Thos F	37	m	w	ME	San Francisco	San Francisco P O	83	10
Thos W	41	m	w	NY	Sonoma	Bodega Twp	91	260

© 2001 by Heritage Quest. All rights reserved.

Series M593

Name	Age	S	R	B-PL	County	Locale	Roll	Pg
W C	23	m	w	NY	Alameda	Oakland	68	240
W E	38	m	w	ME	Sacramento	4-Wd Sacramento	77	365
W H	37	m	w	NY	Amador	Sutter Crk P O	69	398
W H	28	m	w	VT	Sutter	Vernon Twp	92	135
W I	47	m	w	MA	Tuolumne	Chinese Camp P O	93	377
W N	60	m	w	NY	Tuolumne	Sonora P O	93	313
W O	53	m	w	IN	Amador	Drytown P O	69	416
W T	33	m	w	NY	Trinity	Minersville Pct	92	203
Walter	25	m	w	CANA	San Francisco	San Francisco P O	83	29
Wan	27	m	w	NY	San Joaquin	Tulare Twp	86	261
Warren V	47	m	w	CT	Calaveras	San Andreas P O	70	218
Willard	49	m	w	ME	Siskiyou	Surprise Valley Tw	89	643
William	66	m	w	SCOT	Nevada	Little York Twp	75	237
William	60	m	w	NY	San Bernardino	San Bernardino Twp	78	427
William	53	m	w	GA	San Diego	Julian Dist	78	468
William	52	m	w	GA	Shasta	Shasta P O	89	456
William	51	m	w	KY	Napa	Napa Twp	75	63
William	49	m	w	IL	Placer	Bath P O	76	447
William	41	m	w	TN	Plumas	Quartz Twp	77	38
William	41	m	w	OH	Lake	Lakeport	73	406
William	40	m	w	ENGL	Los Angeles	El Monte Twp	73	450
William	39	m	w	ENGL	Klamath	Trinidad Twp	73	392
William	37	m	w	IL	Stanislaus	Empire Twp	92	43
William	35	m	w	NY	Yolo	Putah Twp	93	511
William	34	m	w	MO	Stanislaus	Emory Twp	92	24
William	34	m	w	LA	San Francisco	3-Wd San Francisco	79	323
William	32	m	w	IREL	Marin	Tomales Twp	74	83
William	28	m	w	IREL	San Francisco	San Francisco P O	85	747
William	28	m	w	NY	Solano	Rio Vista Twp	90	71
William	25	m	w	NY	San Francisco	7-Wd San Francisco	81	220
William	24	m	w	MA	Sacramento	2-Wd Sacramento	77	237
William	24	m	w	NY	San Francisco	1-Wd San Francisco	79	63
William	22	m	w	NY	Yolo	Merritt Twp	93	507
William	21	m	w	NY	Alameda	Eden Twp	68	81
William	21	m	w	CANA	Mendocino	Point Arena Twp	74	205
William	14	m	w	MA	Contra Costa	Martinez Twp	71	349
William A	48	m	w	CT	San Luis Obispo	Santa Rosa Twp	87	329
William A	40	m	w	IL	San Mateo	Redwood Twp	87	369
William C	53	m	w	HDAR	Nevada	Eureka Twp	75	126
William H	55	m	w	ME	San Francisco	6-Wd San Francisco	81	88
William H	40	m	w	NY	El Dorado	Mud Springs Twp	72	87
William H	36	m	w	NY	San Mateo	San Mateo P O	87	358
William H	26	m	w	ENGL	San Bernardino	San Bernardino Twp	78	452
William J	48	m	w	IREL	Yolo	Grafton Twp	93	496
William L	36	m	w	CT	Yolo	Merritt Twp	93	507
William S	60	m	w	MD	Santa Clara	2-Wd San Jose	88	330
William V	36	m	w	IL	Los Angeles	Los Angeles	73	506
Winnie	25	f	w	IREL	San Francisco	5-Wd San Francisco	81	20
Wm	70	m	w	IL	Butte	Ophir Twp	70	99
Wm	70	m	w	NH	Butte	Ophir Twp	70	97
Wm	66	m	w	CANA	Alameda	Murray Twp	68	115
Wm	49	m	w	OH	Butte	Oregon Twp	70	128
Wm	36	m	w	HAMB	San Francisco	1-Wd San Francisco	79	124
Wm	35	m	w	IREL	San Francisco	11-Wd San Francisc	84	468
Wm	32	m	w	NY	San Francisco	San Francisco P O	83	127
Wm	30	m	w	IREL	Yuba	Rose Bar Twp	93	660
Wm	28	m	w	ME	Humboldt	Eureka Twp	72	279
Wm	28	m	w	CT	Napa	Napa Twp	75	66
Wm	13	m	w	IA	Shasta	Portugese Flat P O	89	472
Wm A	34	m	w	VA	Tuolumne	Sonora P O	93	309
Wm E	49	m	w	IREL	Butte	Concow Twp	70	6
Wm E	39	m	w	NY	Sacramento	1-Wd Sacramento	77	180
Wm G	29	m	w	IN	Sacramento	San Joaquin Twp	77	399
Wm H	50	m	w	ME	San Francisco	San Francisco P O	83	203
Wm H	48	m	w	NH	San Francisco	8-Wd San Francisco	82	377
Wm H	27	m	w	CT	San Francisco	1-Wd San Francisco	79	22
Wm H G	57	m	w	ENGL	San Francisco	San Francisco P O	83	172
Wm J	34	m	w	IREL	San Francisco	San Francisco P O	83	63
Wm L	35	m	w	NY	Sacramento	Franklin Twp	77	106
Wm M	35	m	w	MI	San Francisco	San Francisco P O	85	875
Wm S	38	m	w	IN	Sonoma	Russian Rvr	91	378
Wm S	22	m	w	IREL	Plumas	Quartz Twp	77	41
Woodruff	33	m	w	NY	Colusa	Spring Valley Twp	71	337
Wright	40	m	w	IREL	Yuba	Rose Bar Twp	93	659
Zerah P	27	m	w	OH	San Francisco	San Francisco P O	83	147
Zeyltha	33	f	w	MS	Los Angeles	Los Nietos Twp	73	578
CLARKE								
Alfred	38	m	w	ENGL	San Francisco	San Francisco P O	85	816
Charles	31	m	w	ENGL	San Francisco	San Francisco P O	85	724
Chas	25	m	w	MA	Solano	Vallejo	90	200
Edw	27	m	w	PA	Alameda	Oakland	68	228
Edwards D	37	m	w	OH	Placer	Dutch Flat P O	76	401
Elizabeth	73	f	w	IREL	Solano	Vacaville Twp	90	124
Elizabeth	45	f	w	CANA	San Francisco	San Francisco P O	80	392
Emma	16	f	w	CA	Santa Clara	2-Wd San Jose	88	337
Francis	13	m	w	KS	Santa Barbara	Santa Barbara P O	87	498
George	32	m	w	ENGL	San Francisco	San Francisco P O	83	20
George	26	m	w	NY	San Francisco	San Francisco P O	80	411
George J	53	m	w	NH	Los Angeles	Los Angeles	73	545
George W	26	m	w	MI	Inyo	Cerro Gordo Twp	73	321
Henry	40	m	w	DE	Solano	Vacaville Twp	90	124
Henry L	39	m	w	VT	Solano	Tremont Twp	90	32
Hugh	33	m	w	IREL	Alameda	Oakland	68	228
Isaac N	45	m	w	IN	Santa Barbara	Santa Barbara P O	87	495
James	34	m	w	NY	Amador	Jackson P O	69	321
James E	42	m	w	VT	San Diego	San Diego	78	493
Jane	53	f	w	IREL	Solano	Vallejo	90	166
John	35	m	w	MO	Solano	Silveyville Twp	90	88
John	30	m	w	IREL	San Francisco	7-Wd San Francisco	81	237
Joseph	3	m	w	CA	San Francisco	San Francisco P O	85	818
M E	35	m	w	MA	San Francisco	San Francisco P O	83	292
Michl	31	m	w	IREL	San Francisco	1-Wd San Francisco	79	78
Robert	51	m	w	NH	Solano	Maine Prairie Twp	90	52
Sarah	73	f	w	ENGL	San Francisco	San Francisco P O	85	816
Sarah M	50	f	w	OH	Santa Cruz	Santa Cruz Twp	89	392
W H	38	m	w	US	Amador	Sutter Crk P O	69	411
W H	28	m	w	SCOT	Solano	Vallejo	90	200
Warren	39	m	w	ME	Placer	Cisco P O	76	494
William	71	m	w	CANA	Solano	Vacaville Twp	90	124
Wm	49	m	w	ENGL	San Francisco	7-Wd San Francisco	81	242
Wm	3	m	w	CA	San Francisco	7-Wd San Francisco	81	270
CLARKEN								
R	12	m	w	US	Sacramento	3-Wd Sacramento	77	318
CLARKIN								
Emily	23	f	w	SC	Sacramento	Granite Twp	77	149
CLARKLIN								
Thomas	44	m	w	MA	Calaveras	San Andreas P O	70	192
CLARKS								
Sydney	39	m	w	KY	Solano	Suisun Twp	90	110
CLARKSON								
Henry	51	m	w	KY	San Francisco	San Francisco P O	83	148
James	45	m	w	ENGL	Nevada	Grass Valley Twp	75	155
Jane	32	f	w	PRUS	San Francisco	San Francisco P O	80	430
Jas	45	m	w	ENGL	Siskiyou	Yreka	89	650
Mary	23	f	w	IREL	San Francisco	San Francisco P O	83	148
Susan	30	f	w	OH	San Francisco	San Francisco P O	83	277
CLARNE								
G W	45	m	w	OH	Del Norte	Smith Rvr Twp	71	477
G W Jr	20	m	w	IL	Del Norte	Smith Rvr Twp	71	477
CLARNO								
Wm H H	38	m	w	OH	Del Norte	Smith Rvr Twp	71	478
CLARO								
Franciso	40	m	i	CA	Sonoma	Analy Twp	91	235
T B Field	44	m	w	NGRA	Amador	Sutter Crk P O	69	404
CLARREN								
William	35	m	w	BAVA	San Francisco	2-Wd San Francisco	79	147
CLARRIDGE								
George A	40	m	w	IA	Solano	Rio Vista Twp	90	59
CLART								
William	34	m	w	NY	Colusa	Monroe Twp	71	325
CLARVILLE								
Walter	27	m	w	KY	San Francisco	3-Wd San Francisco	79	294
CLARY								
Annie	38	f	w	IREL	San Francisco	7-Wd San Francisco	81	226
Boucher James	51	m	w	IREL	Calaveras	San Andreas P O	70	164
Charles	32	m	w	ME	Santa Clara	Fremont Twp	88	61
Charles W	39	m	w	CANA	Calaveras	San Andreas P O	70	164
Edmund	45	m	w	IREL	San Francisco	11-Wd San Francisc	84	500
Frank	34	m	w	IREL	San Francisco	11-Wd San Francisc	84	622
James M	27	m	w	VA	Yolo	Grafton Twp	93	484
John	38	m	w	NY	Yolo	Grafton Twp	93	501
Michael	45	m	w	IREL	Butte	Mountain Spring Tw	70	88
Nellie	24	f	w	CANA	San Francisco	8-Wd San Francisco	82	289
Patrick	38	m	w	IREL	San Francisco	11-Wd San Francisc	84	622
Peter	35	m	w	IREL	San Francisco	7-Wd San Francisco	81	168
Richard	27	m	w	IREL	San Mateo	San Mateo P O	87	350
Thomas	50	m	w	IREL	San Bernardino	San Bernardino Twp	78	453
Thomas	40	m	w	IREL	San Francisco	11-Wd San Francisc	84	704
Thomas	16	m	w	IREL	San Francisco	8-Wd San Francisco	82	433
Thos	37	m	w	IREL	San Francisco	San Francisco P O	85	793
William	40	m	w	NY	San Francisco	8-Wd San Francisco	82	400
William	23	m	w	NY	San Francisco	San Francisco P O	83	284
CLAS								
Frank	42	m	w	ITAL	Sacramento	Georgianna Twp	77	129
CLASBEY								
John	30	m	w	IREL	Yolo	Grafton Twp	93	495
Owen	30	m	w	IREL	Contra Costa	Martinez P O	71	423
CLASBY								
Annie	30	f	w	IREL	San Francisco	San Francisco P O	80	410
John	46	m	w	IREL	San Francisco	2-Wd San Francisco	79	270
Martin	28	m	w	IREL	Sonoma	Bodega Twp	91	262
Patrick	39	m	w	IREL	Contra Costa	Martinez P O	71	421
CLASE								
Mariella	27	f	w	ENGL	Los Angeles	Los Angeles	73	540
CLASKY								
John	64	m	w	ENGL	Tuolumne	Sonora P O	93	304
CLASON								
Paul	26	m	w	ENGL	El Dorado	Coloma Twp	72	8
Peter M	67	m	w	ENGL	El Dorado	Coloma Twp	72	8
CLASPEY								
James	30	m	w	IREL	San Francisco	1-Wd San Francisco	79	136
CLASPY								
Anne	35	f	w	IREL	San Francisco	11-Wd San Francisc	84	602
CLASSEN								
Henry	41	m	w	SHOL	San Francisco	11-Wd San Francisc	84	605
Jacob	43	m	w	PRUS	Santa Clara	2-Wd San Jose	88	329
James	47	m	w	NY	San Francisco	San Francisco P O	85	728
John	50	m	w	HAMB	San Francisco	2-Wd San Francisco	79	211
Peter	44	m	w	PRUS	Santa Clara	2-Wd San Jose	88	330
CLASSLER								
John	18	m	w	IREL	Napa	Napa Twp	75	64
CLATHUR								
W B	39	m	w	CANA	Trinity	Junction City Pct	92	208

© 2001 by Heritage Quest. All rights reserved.

Name	Age	S	R	B-PL	County	Locale	Series M593 Roll	Pg
CLAUD								
George	26	m	w	OH	Yolo	Cache Crk Twp	93	450
Henry	14	m	w	CA	San Francisco	San Francisco P O	83	148
Wm	47	m	w	TN	Butte	Chico Twp	70	29
CLAUDE								
---	40	m	w	FRAN	Contra Costa	Martinez P O	71	442
Mari	33	m	w	MEXI	Stanislaus	Empire Twp	92	60
CLAUGH								
Elijah	31	m	w	NH	Butte	Chico Twp	70	29
H H	37	m	w	NY	San Joaquin	Elliott Twp	86	74
Mary	38	f	w	SCOT	San Diego	Julian Dist	78	470
CLAUGHTON								
Margaret F	40	f	w	MO	San Luis Obispo	Morro Twp	87	281
CLAUS								
Abby	70	f	w	FRAN	Solano	Benicia	90	8
Diedrich	34	m	w	PRUS	San Francisco	San Francisco P O	83	174
George	28	m	w	FRAN	Santa Clara	2-Wd San Jose	88	327
Henry	21	m	w	PRUS	Napa	Napa	75	46
John H	44	m	w	HCAS	San Francisco	San Francisco P O	85	758
CLAUSE								
George	23	m	w	BADE	San Francisco	7-Wd San Francisco	81	176
CLAUSEMAN								
L	25	m	w	FRAN	San Francisco	7-Wd San Francisco	81	188
CLAUSEN								
August	40	m	w	GERM	Solano	Vallejo	90	195
Benjamin	34	m	w	PRUS	San Francisco	7-Wd San Francisco	81	224
C P	55	m	w	SHOL	Mariposa	Maxwell Crk P O	74	146
David	42	m	w	NJ	San Francisco	5-Wd San Francisco	81	22
Ebenezer	65	m	w	NJ	Siskiyou	Scott Valley Twp	89	617
Elias	57	m	w	NY	Sonoma	Santa Rosa	91	398
Erasmus	32	m	w	DENM	San Luis Obispo	San Luis Obispo Tw	87	302
Eschel	29	m	w	SHOL	Alameda	Eden Twp	68	82
Francis	43	m	w	DENM	San Francisco	San Francisco P O	85	813
George	30	m	w	DENM	Alameda	Eden Twp	68	85
Henry	29	m	w	DENM	Stanislaus	Emory Twp	92	26
Jacob	40	m	w	PRUS	San Francisco	5-Wd San Francisco	81	13
CLAUSER								
Asel	26	m	w	PRUS	San Francisco	San Francisco P O	80	478
Herman	24	m	w	PRUS	San Francisco	5-Wd San Francisco	81	15
Peter	36	m	w	PRUS	San Francisco	San Francisco P O	80	470
Richard	33	m	w	IREL	San Francisco	7-Wd San Francisco	81	262
CLAUSHER								
Harry	36	m	w	ME	Mendocino	Noyo & Big Rvr Twp	74	173
CLAUSMAN								
L	21	m	w	FRAN	San Francisco	7-Wd San Francisco	81	213
CLAUSON								
Chas	2	m	w	CA	Monterey	Alisal Twp	74	301
J	38	m	w	SHOL	Monterey	Alisal Twp	74	301
Margart	12	f	w	CA	Tehama	Merrill	92	197
Nancy A	36	f	w	TN	Tehama	Merrill	92	197
CLAUSONSINS								
Geo	34	m	w	HOLL	San Francisco	2-Wd San Francisco	79	200
CLAUSS								
Carl	35	m	w	WURT	San Joaquin	Tulare Twp	86	261
George	44	m	w	FRAN	Santa Clara	2-Wd San Jose	88	323
CLAUSSE								
Jacob	76	m	w	PRUS	Napa	Napa	75	41
CLAUSSEN								
Benjamin	47	m	w	PRUS	San Francisco	8-Wd San Francisco	82	392
Frank	45	m	w	DENM	Solano	Vallejo	90	139
George	35	m	w	DENM	Plumas	Indian Twp	77	9
John	25	m	w	PRUS	San Francisco	San Francisco P O	83	135
Nicholas	48	m	w	DENM	San Francisco	11-Wd San Francisc	84	601
CLAUSSON								
Sophia	38	f	w	PRUS	San Francisco	8-Wd San Francisco	82	386
CLAUTON								
Jas	36	m	w	NC	Butte	Oregon Twp	70	133
CLAVEAU								
Antonio	55	m	w	FRAN	San Francisco	San Francisco P O	80	360
CLAVEL								
Teodore	38	m	w	CA	Santa Barbara	Las Cruces P O	87	516
CLAVEN								
Ellen	40	f	w	IREL	San Francisco	7-Wd San Francisco	81	197
Mary	35	f	w	IREL	San Francisco	8-Wd San Francisco	82	475
CLAVERE								
John	30	m	w	FRAN	San Francisco	San Francisco P O	80	537
CLAVERY								
Kate	40	f	w	IREL	San Francisco	San Francisco P O	83	201
CLAVETT								
Frank	27	m	w	FRAN	Santa Clara	Almaden Twp	88	9
CLAVLOT								
Chas	40	m	w	NY	Santa Barbara	San Buenaventura P	87	426
CLAVO								
Agnes	26	f	w	PRUS	San Francisco	San Francisco P O	85	850
Nicholas	34	m	w	HOLL	Solano	Vallejo	90	142
CLAW								
Step	30	m	c	CHIN	San Mateo	San Mateo P O	87	351
CLAWFORD								
John	34	m	w	NY	San Mateo	Schoolhouse Statio	87	342
CLAWITER								
Edward	52	m	w	PRUS	Alameda	Eden Twp	68	60
CLAWSON								
Cornelius C	35	m	w	VA	Nevada	Grass Valley Twp	75	145
Essex O	34	m	w	NY	San Mateo	Schoolhouse Statio	87	338
Peter	45	m	w	PRUS	San Francisco	6-Wd San Francisco	81	86
CLAXTO								
Wm C	35	m	w	ENGL	Calaveras	Copperopolis P O	70	236
CLAXTON								
George W	47	m	w	PA	Mendocino	Ten Mile Rvr Twp	74	172
Harry	35	m	w	ENGL	Calaveras	Copperopolis P O	70	258
CLAY								
Anne	22	f	w	IREL	San Francisco	8-Wd San Francisco	82	480
Charles	43	m	w	NH	Yolo	Washington Twp	93	536
Edwin R	49	m	w	VA	Santa Clara	Santa Clara Twp	88	156
Effie	9	f	w	WI	Sonoma	Santa Rosa	91	399
Fred	34	m	w	ENGL	San Francisco	11-Wd San Francisc	84	609
George W	46	m	w	KY	Nevada	Nevada Twp	75	322
Henry	57	m	w	PRUS	Shasta	Shasta P O	89	462
Henry	24	m	w	SHOL	San Francisco	3-Wd San Francisco	79	323
Jabez	50	m	w	VT	San Francisco	11-Wd San Francisc	84	555
James	31	m	w	SCOT	Yuba	Slate Range Bar Tw	93	674
John	53	m	w	OH	Yuba	Slate Range Bar Tw	93	677
Mary	35	f	w	IREL	San Mateo	San Mateo P O	87	357
R S	33	m	w	NY	Merced	Snelling P O	74	261
William	46	m	w	TN	Mendocino	Point Arena Twp	74	212
Wilmoth	35	f	w	AL	Sutter	Vernon Twp	92	132
Wm	25	m	w	MI	Sacramento	3-Wd Sacramento	77	318
Wm T	34	m	w	VA	Monterey	Castroville Twp	74	330
CLAYBORN								
Binga	18	f	w	NY	San Francisco	11-Wd San Francisc	84	688
George S	47	m	w	GA	El Dorado	Cosumnes Twp	72	16
James	60	m	w	MI	Butte	Chico Twp	70	47
Lafeyette	31	m	w	IA	Lassen	Susanville Twp	73	447
Lemul	50	m	w	VA	Sacramento	Dry Crk Twp	77	98
Perry	35	m	w	IL	Sutter	Sutter Twp	92	126
CLAYBROOK								
Mitzer F	35	m	w	WI	El Dorado	Cosumnes Twp	72	16
CLAYBURG								
Albert	35	m	w	PRUS	San Francisco	8-Wd San Francisco	82	446
Myer	25	m	w	NCOD	Colusa	Colusa	71	290
CLAYBURGH								
Moses	36	m	w	PRUS	San Francisco	San Francisco P O	83	307
CLAYES								
Charles W	25	m	w	IL	San Francisco	San Francisco P O	83	376
Joe	28	m	w	IL	San Joaquin	2-Wd Stockton	86	205
CLAYMAN								
Benj	63	m	w	PA	Shasta	Stillwater P O	89	479
CLAYPOOL								
Jus S	32	m	w	OH	Amador	Volcano P O	69	388
Mathew M	36	m	w	OH	El Dorado	Placerville Twp	72	105
Thornton	32	m	w	IA	Sonoma	Analy Twp	91	220
CLAYPOOLE								
Jesse	45	m	w	KY	Sonoma	Santa Rosa	91	408
CLAYS								
O M	33	m	w	IL	San Joaquin	2-Wd Stockton	86	181
CLAYTON								
---	43	m	w	OH	Sacramento	3-Wd Sacramento	77	282
A B F	36	m	w	VA	Merced	Snelling P O	74	263
Agness	19	f	w	LA	Alameda	Oakland	68	139
Chas	40	m	w	ENGL	San Francisco	7-Wd San Francisco	81	249
Cornelius	23	m	w	IREL	Colusa	Colusa	71	289
David	26	m	w	MO	Napa	Napa Twp	75	61
David J	58	m	w	KY	Solano	Suisun Twp	90	115
Della	12	f	w	CA	Sonoma	Sonoma Twp	91	442
Eliza	51	f	w	NY	San Francisco	San Francisco P O	80	373
Frank	24	m	w	WI	Contra Costa	Martinez P O	71	443
Furman	59	m	w	NJ	San Francisco	San Francisco P O	80	373
G	28	m	w	NY	Solano	Vallejo	90	144
Geo H	38	m	w	OH	El Dorado	Greenwood Twp	72	55
George	42	m	w	VA	Marin	San Rafael	74	49
Henry	48	m	w	ENGL	Solano	Vallejo	90	217
Isaac	24	m	w	NY	Humboldt	Mattole Twp	72	288
James	38	m	w	ENGL	Santa Clara	2-Wd San Jose	88	299
James	11	m	w	MO	Solano	Vacaville Twp	90	130
Jas D	19	m	w	MO	Sonoma	Healdsburg & Mendo	91	285
Jno	37	m	w	BADE	Butte	Kimshew Tpw	70	80
Jno M	40	m	w	KY	Shasta	Fort Crook P O	89	473
Joel	60	m	w	ENGL	Santa Barbara	Las Cruces P O	87	507
Joel	50	m	w	ENGL	Contra Costa	Martinez P O	71	443
John	28	m	w	MO	Stanislaus	Buena Vista Twp	92	12
John	28	m	w	MO	Stanislaus	Buena Vista Twp	92	12
John	22	m	w	MO	Stanislaus	Branch Twp	92	3
John J	31	m	w	IL	Los Angeles	Wilmington Twp	73	637
Jonas	20	m	w	CANA	San Joaquin	Elliott Twp	86	70
Joseph H	29	m	w	MA	Inyo	Independence Twp	73	328
Joshua	50	m	w	NC	Alameda	Brooklyn	68	29
M	55	f	w	NJ	Sacramento	3-Wd Sacramento	77	279
M A	19	f	w	IREL	Alameda	Oakland	68	212
Margaret	33	f	w	IREL	San Joaquin	2-Wd Stockton	86	168
Maria	35	f	w	IREL	San Francisco	11-Wd San Francisc	84	523
Patrick	34	m	w	NY	Tuolumne	Sonora P O	93	315
Randolph	22	m	w	MD	Santa Clara	Fremont Twp	88	64
Robert	24	m	w	ENGL	Colusa	Grand Island Twp	71	302
Saml	31	m	w	PA	Solano	Vallejo	90	159
Thomas	26	m	w	CANA	Santa Clara	San Jose Twp	88	196
Wm	24	m	w	ME	Alameda	Oakland	68	176
CLBY								
Wm	37	m	w	VT	Sierra	Downieville Twp	89	517
CLEACY								
Thomas	40	m	w	MI	Alameda	Murray Twp	68	126
CLEAIROUX								
Sophia	47	f	w	CANA	Yolo	Putah Twp	93	517
CLEAL								
Catherine	68	f	w	ENGL	Santa Clara	1-Wd San Jose	88	245

© 2001 by Heritage Quest. All rights reserved.

California 1870 Census

Series M593

Name	Age	S	R	B-PL	County	Locale	Roll	Pg
Charles A	23	m	w	CANA	Santa Clara	1-Wd San Jose	88	261
Thomas L	25	m	w	ENGL	Santa Clara	1-Wd San Jose	88	261
CLEANES								
Jeremiah	44	m	w	ME	Santa Clara	San Jose Twp	88	183
CLEANS								
James	38	m	w	ME	Humboldt	Eel Rvr Twp	72	246
CLEARCLAD								
Septimus	50	m	w	VT	Stanislaus	Empire Twp	92	34
CLEARE								
John	26	m	w	ENGL	Nevada	Nevada Twp	75	283
CLEARES								
Arastrus	38	m	w	ME	Stanislaus	Washington Twp	92	84
CLEAREY								
Alice	15	f	w	MA	San Francisco	San Francisco P O	83	162
James	23	m	w	IREL	San Francisco	San Francisco P O	83	370
CLEARY								
Daniel	28	m	m	WIND	San Francisco	San Francisco P O	80	371
Edward	30	m	w	IREL	San Francisco	San Francisco P O	83	419
F J	35	m	w	IREL	San Francisco	San Francisco P O	85	817
Hannah	48	f	w	IREL	San Francisco	San Francisco P O	83	145
James	27	m	w	IREL	San Francisco	1-Wd San Francisco	79	67
Lena	19	f	w	NY	San Francisco	San Francisco P O	83	219
Michael	25	m	w	IREL	Sacramento	Georgianna Twp	77	128
Micheal	40	m	w	IREL	San Francisco	7-Wd San Francisco	81	195
Micheal	25	m	w	IREL	San Francisco	7-Wd San Francisco	81	211
Michl	30	m	w	IREL	San Francisco	1-Wd San Francisco	79	69
Patrick	43	m	w	IREL	San Francisco	San Francisco P O	83	256
Patrick	36	m	w	IREL	San Francisco	7-Wd San Francisco	81	185
Robt	29	m	w	IL	San Francisco	5-Wd San Francisco	81	24
Thomas	41	m	w	IREL	San Francisco	San Francisco P O	80	401
Thomas	37	m	w	IREL	Klamath	Camp Gaston	73	372
William	27	m	w	IREL	San Francisco	7-Wd San Francisco	81	194
CLEAVE								
Daniel	29	m	w	NY	Contra Costa	Martinez P O	71	398
CLEAVELAND								
A	63	m	w	MA	Nevada	Nevada Twp	75	295
Aron	21	m	w	OH	Siskiyou	Surprise Valley Tw	89	640
C B	23	m	w	IL	Santa Clara	Gilroy Twp	88	70
Charles D	37	m	w	NY	Santa Cruz	Santa Cruz Twp	89	379
Charles E	52	m	w	OH	Santa Cruz	Watsonville	89	377
Isabel	70	f	w	SC	Mendocino	Ukiah Twp	74	241
Joseph	57	m	w	CANA	El Dorado	Placerville Twp	72	104
L C	31	m	w	IL	Santa Clara	Gilroy Twp	88	70
M	22	f	w	ALOR	Santa Clara	Gilroy Twp	88	82
M V	36	m	w	AL	Mendocino	Ukiah Twp	74	239
Wm	19	m	w	IL	Santa Clara	Gilroy Twp	88	70
CLEAVER								
Christis	35	m	w	SHOL	San Mateo	Half Moon Bay P O	87	404
Clark	43	m	w	IN	Mariposa	Mariposa P O	74	90
Payne E	36	m	w	ME	Sonoma	Salt Point	91	390
CLEAVES								
Caire	16	f	w	CT	San Francisco	San Francisco P O	83	9
CLEAVLAND								
Chas	44	m	w	NY	Nevada	Nevada Twp	75	320
Ham	34	m	w	NY	San Francisco	5-Wd San Francisco	81	31
M S	56	m	w	NY	Sutter	Butte Twp	92	91
Mary	75	f	w	MA	San Francisco	San Francisco P O	85	816
Reuben	63	m	w	MA	Tuolumne	Sonora P O	93	313
Sarah	30	f	w	NY	San Francisco	8-Wd San Francisco	82	302
CLEAVY								
Can	50	m	w	IREL	San Joaquin	1-Wd Stockton	86	152
CLEE								
Ah	20	m	c	CHIN	San Francisco	6-Wd San Francisco	81	63
Ah	20	m	c	CHIN	Sierra	Sears Twp	89	553
CLEEK								
Andrew S	52	m	w	VA	Colusa	Monroe Twp	71	316
Thomas J	33	m	w	TN	Colusa	Colusa Twp	71	287
CLEEN								
Ah	24	m	c	CHIN	San Francisco	6-Wd San Francisco	81	56
CLEENEY								
Joseph	60	m	w	IREL	San Francisco	11-Wd San Francisc	84	613
CLEENIUS								
Dalnith	30	m	w	PRUS	Santa Clara	Redwood Twp	88	129
CLEEPUSEE								
Mary	20	f	w	CHIN	San Francisco	11-Wd San Francisc	84	688
CLEER								
Tie	34	f	c	CHIN	Mariposa	Maxwell Crk P O	74	138
CLEERY								
Alfred	29	m	w	IREL	San Francisco	5-Wd San Francisco	81	7
CLEESE								
John P	36	m	w	HOLL	El Dorado	Placerville	72	108
CLEEVE								
Hannah	33	f	w	IREL	San Francisco	San Francisco P O	83	167
CLEFFORD								
Alfred	23	m	w	CANA	Sacramento	Brighton Twp	77	80
George	28	m	w	VT	Contra Costa	Martinez P O	71	419
CLEFT								
John	18	m	w	CA	Los Angeles	Los Angeles Twp	73	475
CLEFTON								
James J	30	m	w	KY	Santa Barbara	Santa Barbara P O	87	450
CLEGG								
Mary E	53	f	w	ENGL	San Francisco	San Francisco P O	83	100
Thomas	47	m	w	ENGL	Alameda	Alameda	68	3
CLEGGETT								
J	33	m	w	VA	San Joaquin	Tulare Twp	86	251
James	40	m	m	VA	San Joaquin	2-Wd Stockton	86	178
CLEGHORN								
Isaac	45	m	w	KY	Colusa	Colusa Twp	71	280
John	50	m	w	SCOT	Napa	Napa	75	4
P M	50	m	w	SCOT	Tehama	Paskenta Twp	92	163
Serena	37	f	w	IN	San Bernardino	San Bernardino Twp	78	454
T C	63	m	w	SCOT	Sierra	Table Rock Twp	89	579
Thos	21	m	w	NY	Sierra	Gibson Twp	89	539
CLEGUET								
Louis	33	m	w	FRAN	San Francisco	2-Wd San Francisco	79	223
CLEIOS								
Joseph	30	m	w	MO	San Bernardino	San Bernardino Twp	78	429
CLEISDALE								
Edwin	30	m	w	ENGL	Napa	Napa	75	19
CLELAND								
Alfred	28	m	w	DE	Marin	Point Reyes Twp	74	22
David	35	m	w	NY	Siskiyou	Yreka	89	656
Fanny	62	f	w	SCOT	San Francisco	11-Wd San Francisc	84	544
John	40	m	w	IREL	Alameda	Brooklyn	68	21
John S	45	m	w	NY	Siskiyou	Yreka	89	656
CLELLAN								
Francis G	40	m	w	NY	San Mateo	Pescadero P O	87	417
CLEM								
---	26	m	c	CHIN	Siskiyou	Hamburg Twp	89	597
Ah	16	m	c	CHIN	San Francisco	San Francisco P O	85	722
Charles	41	m	w	SAXO	San Francisco	San Francisco P O	80	343
John	30	m	w	TN	Yolo	Grafton Twp	93	495
CLEMAN								
John	1	m	w	CA	Monterey	Castroville Twp	74	329
CLEMENCE								
E H	50	m	w	GA	Sutter	Butte Twp	92	103
James E	36	m	w	VA	Yolo	Putah Twp	93	516
CLEMENCET								
Chas	23	m	w	FRAN	San Francisco	1-Wd San Francisco	79	50
CLEMENO								
Angelo	24	m	w	ITAL	Alpine	Woodfords P O	69	309
CLEMENS								
A C	2	f	w	CA	Amador	Sutter Crk P O	69	409
Andrew	42	m	w	ME	San Francisco	San Francisco P O	83	84
Charles	44	m	w	OH	Sacramento	Cosumnes Twp	77	88
Charles	37	m	w	IREL	San Francisco	San Francisco P O	85	745
Chas	47	m	w	BADE	Butte	Concow Twp	70	6
Ely	55	m	w	FRAN	Inyo	Cerro Gordo Twp	73	320
Hiram M	36	m	w	OH	Plumas	Plumas Twp	77	33
Isaac	44	m	w	MA	Inyo	Cerro Gordo Twp	73	318
James	39	m	w	IREL	Amador	Drytown P O	69	416
Jessy	28	m	w	ENGL	Nevada	Nevada Twp	75	309
John	42	m	w	ENGL	Amador	Sutter Crk P O	69	396
Levi	55	m	w	NY	Monterey	San Juan Twp	74	386
Reuben Z	46	m	w	CANA	San Francisco	8-Wd San Francisco	82	487
Richard	40	m	w	MA	Calaveras	San Andreas P O	70	194
Richard	36	m	w	ENGL	Alpine	Monitor P O	69	313
Robt E	23	m	w	OH	Butte	Chico Twp	70	20
Rufus H	33	m	w	NH	San Francisco	San Francisco P O	85	717
CLEMENT								
Annie	27	f	w	SCOT	San Francisco	San Francisco P O	83	166
Barckly	48	m	w	DE	Santa Cruz	Santa Cruz	89	405
Belle	16	f	w	CA	Nevada	Rough & Ready Twp	75	323
C W	60	m	w	NJ	Solano	Vallejo	90	183
Daniel	43	m	w	HDAR	San Francisco	8-Wd San Francisco	82	308
Edward	40	m	w	NC	Los Angeles	El Monte Twp	73	455
Edward	35	m	w	ME	Siskiyou	Hamburg Twp	89	597
Elizabeth	40	f	w	NY	San Francisco	11-Wd San Francisc	84	607
Emma	20	f	w	NH	Trinity	Indian Crk	92	200
Eph	55	m	w	NH	El Dorado	Lake Valley Twp	72	63
Frank	44	m	w	SWIT	Siskiyou	Yreka	89	660
G	23	m	w	SWIT	Santa Clara	Gilroy Twp	88	95
Gilbert H	39	m	w	NY	Sonoma	Bodega Twp	91	251
Henry	30	m	w	NY	Merced	Snelling P O	74	280
Henry	26	m	w	NH	Santa Cruz	Santa Cruz	89	427
J	33	m	w	NY	Alameda	Alameda	68	1
Joseph	66	m	w	NY	El Dorado	Placerville Twp	72	96
Joseph	60	m	w	NY	San Francisco	2-Wd San Francisco	79	165
L	29	m	w	VT	San Francisco	San Francisco P O	83	303
Louis	33	m	w	CANA	Sacramento	4-Wd Sacramento	77	347
Lucius	38	m	w	NY	Alameda	Brooklyn Twp	68	42
Mary	11	f	w	CA	Solano	Maine Prairie Twp	90	52
Matilda	17	f	w	PA	San Francisco	8-Wd San Francisco	82	296
Peter	42	m	w	FRAN	San Francisco	2-Wd San Francisco	79	223
Peter	32	m	w	HDAR	San Francisco	San Francisco P O	85	727
Rebecca	52	f	w	MD	Nevada	Grass Valley Twp	75	177
Robert	35	m	w	CANA	Plumas	Washington Twp	77	54
Rosewell	44	m	w	NY	San Francisco	11-Wd San Francisc	84	628
W B	45	m	w	NY	Alameda	Alameda	68	1
William	44	m	w	NH	Trinity	Weaverville Pct	92	223
Wm	45	m	w	WALE	Sierra	Table Rock Twp	89	577
Wm H	32	m	w	MO	Shasta	Millville P O	89	484
CLEMENTE								
C	12	f	w	CA	Los Angeles	Los Angeles	73	569
Michell	49	m	w	FRAN	Los Angeles	Los Angeles	73	508
CLEMENTICT								
Joseph	35	m	w	AUST	Yolo	Grafton Twp	93	490
CLEMENTS								
A	59	m	w	NY	Yuba	Linda Twp	93	554
A	21	f	w	IN	San Francisco	San Francisco P O	83	295
Bell	16	f	w	CA	Nevada	Meadow Lake Twp	75	248
Benjamin	38	m	b	OH	San Francisco	San Francisco P O	83	245
C F	35	m	w	NY	Yuba	Marysville	93	604

© 2001 by Heritage Quest. All rights reserved.

Name	Age	S	R	B-PL	County	Locale	Series M593 Roll	Pg
Charles	9M	m	w	CA	Santa Clara	San Jose Twp	88	201
Charles	42	m	w	NY	Santa Clara	1-Wd San Jose	88	247
David	44	m	w	IREL	Amador	Jackson P O	69	334
David	32	m	w	OH	Butte	Ophir Twp	70	117
E B	20	m	w	GA	Sierra	Downieville Twp	89	522
Genera	43	m	w	DC	San Francisco	11-Wd San Francisc	84	442
George B	29	m	w	OH	Mendocino	Anderson Twp	74	154
J	38	m	w	ITAL	Alameda	Oakland	68	241
J E	61	m	w	MA	San Joaquin	Oneal Twp	86	102
Jno	25	m	w	OH	Butte	Chico Twp	70	46
Jno F	45	m	w	SC	Butte	Hamilton Twp	70	61
John	71	m	w	ENGL	Los Angeles	El Monte Twp	73	448
John	40	m	w	NORW	San Francisco	2-Wd San Francisco	79	200
John J	27	m	w	PA	Los Angeles	El Monte Twp	73	448
Julia	30	f	w	NY	San Francisco	6-Wd San Francisco	81	71
Lambert B	47	m	w	PA	Santa Cruz	Soquel Twp	89	440
Mary	6	f	w	CA	Sacramento	2-Wd Sacramento	77	242
Mathew	31	m	w	IREL	San Mateo	Schoolhouse Statio	87	342
O C	28	m	w	IL	Humboldt	Bucksport Twp	72	242
Reuben	9	m	w	OR	San Francisco	11-Wd San Francisc	84	592
Thomas	31	m	w	IREL	Amador	Jackson P O	69	333
William	33	m	w	ENGL	Santa Clara	San Jose Twp	88	204
CLEMINGER								
John	28	m	w	PRUS	San Francisco	San Francisco P O	80	531
CLEMINSON								
James	37	m	w	MO	San Bernardino	San Bernardino Twp	78	430
CLEMMANS								
John	30	m	w	IREL	Yolo	Washington Twp	93	533
CLEMMENS								
Andrew	34	m	w	DENM	Santa Barbara	San Buenaventura P	87	422
Maggie	25	f	w	IREL	San Francisco	San Francisco P O	83	134
William	26	m	w	ENGL	Nevada	Nevada Twp	75	309
CLEMMENTS								
John	27	m	w	NY	Solano	Silveyville Twp	90	74
Wm	40	m	w	NY	Alameda	Oakland	68	165
CLEMMER								
Anthony	28	m	w	OH	Nevada	Rough & Ready Twp	75	327
G	30	m	w	VA	Yuba	Marysville	93	605
CLEMO								
James	33	m	w	ENGL	Yuba	Rose Bar Twp	93	663
Samuel	28	m	w	ENGL	Tuolumne	Sonora P O	93	323
CLEMONS								
N Y	13	m	w	CA	Alameda	Oakland	68	243
S J	37	f	w	NY	San Francisco	San Francisco P O	83	328
CLEMONT								
John	63	m	w	IREL	Inyo	Cerro Gordo Twp	73	321
Louis	37	m	w	FRAN	El Dorado	White Oak Twp	72	139
CLEN								
Ah	15	m	c	CHIN	Solano	Vallejo	90	175
CLENAN								
Samuel	48	m	w	IREL	Alameda	Brooklyn Twp	68	47
CLENCH								
William C	43	m	w	CANA	San Francisco	San Francisco P O	83	244
CLENCY								
Michael	32	m	w	IREL	San Francisco	San Francisco P O	83	139
CLENDENAN								
Robt	45	m	w	ENGL	Butte	Ophir Twp	70	101
CLENDENEN								
Andrew W	24	m	w	ENGL	Mariposa	Mariposa P O	74	114
Atamesis	31	f	w	NY	Shasta	Buckeye P O	89	482
Calvin	36	m	w	WI	Shasta	Fort Crook P O	89	476
Thos G	41	m	w	PA	San Luis Obispo	Santa Rosa Twp	87	326
CLENDENING								
L A	43	m	w	KY	Santa Clara	Gilroy Twp	88	99
W S	57	m	w	IL	San Joaquin	Castoria Twp	86	3
Wellington	20	m	w	MI	San Francisco	8-Wd San Francisco	82	485
CLENDENNAN								
A	35	m	w	CANA	Humboldt	Arcata Twp	72	231
A	33	m	w	CANA	Humboldt	Eureka Twp	72	264
Francis	36	m	w	CANA	Humboldt	Eureka Twp	72	278
H	31	m	w	ME	Humboldt	Eureka Twp	72	278
CLENDENNIE								
Wm H	41	m	w	NC	Napa	Napa Twp	75	60
CLENDENNIN								
Samuel	44	m	w	IL	Napa	Napa	75	20
CLENDENNING								
Charlotte	30	f	w	MO	San Francisco	San Francisco P O	80	488
Jack	41	m	w	MO	Shasta	Stillwater P O	89	478
Margaret	39	f	w	SCOT	Santa Clara	Santa Clara Twp	88	169
Wm	28	m	w	CANA	San Diego	San Diego	78	505
CLENDERING								
Wallace	28	m	w	KY	Santa Clara	San Jose Twp	88	206
CLENEY								
Peter	40	m	w	IREL	San Francisco	7-Wd San Francisco	81	176
CLENFORD								
Chas	30	m	w	MA	Monterey	Alisal Twp	74	304
John	68	m	w	GERM	Monterey	Monterey	74	354
CLENICK								
John	40	m	w	ENGL	Mariposa	Maxwell Crk P O	74	143
CLENIS								
Wm	22	m	w	ENGL	Nevada	Nevada Twp	75	302
CLENNY								
Jas	28	m	w	MA	Solano	Vallejo	90	141
CLENT								
James	33	m	w	MO	Los Angeles	Soledad Twp	73	633
CLENTICK								
Samuel	45	m	w	CANA	San Francisco	7-Wd San Francisco	81	217
CLENTON								
Henry	37	m	w	GERM	San Joaquin	2-Wd Stockton	86	167
William	35	m	w	IREL	San Francisco	11-Wd San Francisc	84	472
CLERE								
Mary	41	f	w	FRAN	San Francisco	7-Wd San Francisco	81	171
CLEREDMAN								
Oscar	28	m	w	ME	Placer	Gold Run Twp	76	398
CLERK								
James	35	m	w	IREL	San Francisco	3-Wd San Francisco	79	314
William	18	m	w	CA	Contra Costa	Martinez Twp	71	352
CLERKIN								
P	39	m	w	NY	Sierra	Forest Twp	89	529
CLERLAND								
Thos	45	m	w	OH	San Joaquin	Elkhorn Twp	86	53
CLERNAN								
Lilia	12	f	w	CA	Solano	Vallejo	90	169
CLERO								
Wm	37	m	w	PRUS	San Joaquin	Elkhorn Twp	86	63
CLERRY								
A E	28	m	w	MO	Sutter	Vernon Twp	92	135
John	40	m	w	IREL	Trinity	Junction City Pct	92	210
CLERTRE								
H N	30	f	w	WI	Alameda	Oakland	68	191
CLERY								
D C	25	m	w	AL	Kern	Bakersfield P O	73	357
John	52	m	w	IREL	Santa Clara	Fremont Twp	88	63
Kate	24	f	w	IREL	Contra Costa	Martinez P O	71	414
CLESLEND								
H	36	m	w	KY	Sierra	Sierra Twp	89	568
CLEURA								
Henry	27	m	w	PRUS	Colusa	Colusa	71	292
CLEVELAND								
A	56	m	w	AR	San Joaquin	Douglas Twp	86	49
A	51	m	w	VT	Alameda	Alameda	68	3
Abby	35	f	w	ME	Napa	Napa	75	35
Annie	24	f	w	NY	San Francisco	8-Wd San Francisco	82	384
Chas	44	m	w	MO	San Francisco	11-Wd San Francisc	84	505
David	32	m	w	NY	San Diego	San Diego	78	497
Elva	24	m	w	ME	Mendocino	Point Arena Twp	74	206
Ezra	67	m	w	NY	Sonoma	Petaluma Twp	91	348
Fannie J	23	f	w	OH	Alpine	Markleeville P O	69	311
Francis J	38	m	w	NY	Amador	Volcano P O	69	376
Frank	42	m	w	VA	Nevada	Grass Valley Twp	75	150
Geo	38	m	w	VT	Butte	Chico Twp	70	59
J C	40	m	w	NY	San Joaquin	Douglas Twp	86	43
J J	40	m	w	NY	Sonoma	Vallejo Twp	91	456
J M	35	m	w	AL	San Francisco	San Francisco P O	85	770
M L	35	f	w	MO	Lassen	Susanville Twp	73	440
Rebecca	66	f	w	NY	Sonoma	Petaluma Twp	91	309
Russell W	45	m	w	NY	Los Angeles	Los Angeles	73	542
Timothy P	33	m	w	NY	Yolo	Putah Twp	93	524
W J	49	m	w	SC	Mendocino	Calpella Twp	74	181
William	52	m	w	NY	Santa Cruz	Pajaro Twp	89	347
William	40	m	w	ME	Mendocino	Point Arena Twp	74	214
William	23	m	w	MO	Humboldt	Pacific Twp	72	293
Wm	31	m	w	OH	Shasta	American Ranch P O	89	497
Wm	20	m	w	IL	Santa Cruz	Pajaro Twp	89	347
CLEVEN								
Mary	29	f	w	IREL	San Francisco	2-Wd San Francisco	79	189
CLEVENGER								
Esther	52	f	w	IN	Santa Clara	1-Wd San Jose	88	237
John	37	m	w	MO	Santa Clara	Redwood Twp	88	117
Jonas S	40	m	w	PA	Yolo	Buckeye Twp	93	417
Stephen	27	m	w	MO	Monterey	San Juan Twp	74	399
Thomas	29	m	w	MO	Santa Clara	1-Wd San Jose	88	227
Thos B	47	m	w	NJ	Sonoma	Healdsburg & Mendo	91	278
CLEVENLAND								
Dan G	58	m	w	VT	Siskiyou	Scott Valley Twp	89	614
CLEVINGER								
James R	22	m	w	MO	Santa Clara	San Jose Twp	88	218
CLEW								
John	35	m	w	KY	El Dorado	Greenwood Twp	72	50
John P	37	m	w	FRAN	San Francisco	2-Wd San Francisco	79	217
CLEWETT								
James	21	m	w	IREL	Yuba	Marysville	93	588
CLEXTON								
C G	37	m	w	IREL	San Francisco	San Francisco P O	85	842
Thomas	35	m	w	IREL	San Francisco	7-Wd San Francisco	81	160
CLEYNE								
Robert	51	m	w	SCOT	San Francisco	7-Wd San Francisco	81	170
CLICH								
George	32	m	w	AUST	Amador	Sutter Crk P O	69	405
CLICK								
Ah	63	m	c	CHIN	El Dorado	Kelsey Twp	72	60
Daniel	39	m	w	PRUS	Placer	Lincoln P O	76	482
Mart	25	m	w	OH	Placer	Lincoln P O	76	488
Philip	32	m	w	BAVA	Placer	Lincoln P O	76	492
CLIDE								
J H	46	m	w	NY	Sierra	Alleghany & Forest	89	534
CLIDESDALE								
Richard	61	m	w	SCOT	Mendocino	Anderson Twp	74	156
CLIDET								
Louis	26	m	w	FRAN	San Francisco	San Francisco P O	80	477
CLIEN								
Joseph	45	m	w	ENGL	San Diego	San Diego	78	509
CLIFF								
John F	35	m	w	KY	Yolo	Putah Twp	93	513

© 2001 by Heritage Quest. All rights reserved.

Name	Age	S	R	B-PL	County	Locale	Roll	Pg
						Series M593		
Nathaniel	25	m	w	CT	Santa Clara	1-Wd San Jose	88	252
CLIFFE								
Rebecca	19	f	w	IN	Santa Clara	1-Wd San Jose	88	240
CLIFFERD								
Lewis	42	m	w	HANO	El Dorado	Coloma Twp	72	12
CLIFFMAN								
Chas	44	m	w	HANO	Butte	Hamilton Twp	70	65
CLIFFORD								
A	36	m	w	NY	Lake	Lower Lake	73	423
Alfred	23	m	w	CANA	Sacramento	Brighton Twp	77	76
Bridget	32	f	w	IREL	San Francisco	7-Wd San Francisco	81	249
Catherine	40	f	w	ENGL	Alameda	Brooklyn Twp	68	39
Charles	25	m	w	IREL	Contra Costa	Martinez P O	71	368
Daniel	50	m	w	IREL	San Francisco	San Francisco P O	83	83
David A	32	m	w	PA	Nevada	Grass Valley Twp	75	151
Edrian	40	m	w	NY	Humboldt	Eel Rvr Twp	72	247
Edward	28	m	w	IREL	San Mateo	Redwood Twp	87	362
Elijah	39	m	w	NH	San Francisco	11-Wd San Francisc	84	708
Ellen	18	f	i	CA	Trinity	Weaverville Pct	92	223
George	46	m	w	IN	Napa	Napa Twp	75	65
George	41	m	w	RI	San Francisco	San Francisco P O	80	412
George B	38	m	w	MA	Napa	Napa	75	44
H K	40	m	w	IN	San Joaquin	2-Wd Stockton	86	180
Hiram	48	m	w	ME	San Francisco	11-Wd San Francisc	84	585
J	30	f	w	PRUS	Alameda	Alameda	68	8
J H	48	m	w	MO	San Joaquin	2-Wd Stockton	86	209
James	55	m	w	IREL	Sacramento	4-Wd Sacramento	77	357
Janna	25	f	w	IREL	San Francisco	8-Wd San Francisco	82	430
Jeremiah	40	m	w	IREL	San Francisco	San Francisco P O	83	149
Johanna	30	f	w	IREL	San Francisco	11-Wd San Francisc	84	661
John	50	m	w	IREL	San Francisco	San Francisco P O	83	358
John	50	m	w	IREL	Sonoma	Petaluma Twp	91	309
John	40	m	w	IREL	Alameda	Alameda	68	12
John H	45	m	w	NH	Sacramento	Granite Twp	77	150
Lotty	20	f	w	NY	San Francisco	6-Wd San Francisco	81	92
Michael	42	m	w	IREL	El Dorado	White Oak Twp	72	141
Michael	30	m	w	IREL	San Mateo	Schoolhouse Statio	87	338
Nathaniel	45	m	w	ME	Santa Cruz	Santa Cruz Twp	89	394
Nelly	22	f	w	IREL	Solano	Suisun Twp	90	112
Nelly	21	f	w	IREL	San Francisco	1-Wd San Francisco	79	135
Patrick	36	m	w	IREL	San Francisco	11-Wd San Francisc	84	551
Richard	43	m	w	IREL	Trinity	Weaverville Pct	92	223
Richard	35	m	w	NY	Santa Cruz	Santa Cruz Twp	89	396
Sam	30	m	w	NY	Monterey	San Juan Twp	74	417
Saml	21	m	w	ME	Marin	Nicasio Twp	74	19
Seth	38	m	w	OH	Butte	Chico Twp	70	14
T C	28	m	w	ME	San Francisco	San Francisco P O	85	863
Thomas	33	m	w	IREL	San Francisco	11-Wd San Francisc	84	545
William	34	m	w	CANA	Sacramento	2-Wd Sacramento	77	238
Wm	34	m	w	NY	Sacramento	1-Wd Sacramento	77	188
Wm	27	m	w	CANA	San Francisco	San Francisco P O	83	74
CLIFICAL								
L A	58	m	w	PRUS	Tuolumne	Chinese Camp P O	93	384
CLIFT								
Alfred	19	m	w	ENGL	Nevada	Grass Valley Twp	75	175
Charles	26	m	w	ENGL	Nevada	Grass Valley Twp	75	182
James P	35	m	w	KY	San Bernardino	San Bernardino Twp	78	422
Ostro	46	m	w	NY	Mendocino	Anderson Twp	74	157
Rebecca	19	f	w	OH	Santa Clara	Burnett Twp	88	33
William	38	m	w	ENGL	Nevada	Grass Valley Twp	75	182
CLIFTON								
C M	33	m	w	PA	Marin	San Rafael Twp	74	41
Chas	34	m	w	IREL	San Francisco	1-Wd San Francisco	79	85
Geo	36	m	w	CHIN	San Joaquin	Elliott Twp	86	76
Henry	50	m	b	DE	San Francisco	San Francisco P O	80	486
Henry	32	m	w	AR	Merced	Snelling P O	74	268
Henry	27	m	w	TX	San Bernardino	San Bernardino Twp	78	445
Henry	23	m	w	NY	Los Angeles	Los Angeles	73	527
Ida	14	f	w	CA	Santa Clara	Redwood Twp	88	134
J W	43	m	w	IN	Santa Clara	Gilroy Twp	88	77
James	29	m	w	IA	Amador	Ione City P O	69	359
May A	46	f	w	ENGL	El Dorado	Placerville Twp	72	95
Robert B	24	m	w	NY	Sacramento	2-Wd Sacramento	77	247
Thomas	54	m	w	OH	Amador	Ione City P O	69	359
Thos	52	m	w	ENGL	San Francisco	11-Wd San Francisc	84	612
W G	28	m	w	ENGL	San Francisco	San Francisco P O	83	282
CLIMA								
Francis	40	m	w	WI	Sutter	Butte Twp	92	88
CLIMAES								
L	50	m	w	MEXI	Alameda	Murray Twp	68	121
CLINCH								
Conrad	42	m	w	ME	Sacramento	Granite Twp	77	144
Eliza	29	f	w	AUSL	Nevada	Grass Valley Twp	75	158
Henry	40	m	w	ENGL	San Francisco	11-Wd San Francisc	84	659
John	38	m	w	ENGL	Plumas	Washington Twp	77	56
Robert W	34	m	w	CANA	Placer	Colfax P O	76	385
Wm	49	m	w	ENGL	Plumas	Washington Twp	77	54
CLINCKENBARD								
A J	52	m	w	KY	Napa	Napa Twp	75	59
CLINE								
Annie	38	f	w	OH	San Francisco	San Francisco P O	83	279
C J	38	m	w	WURT	Sierra	Butte Twp	89	508
Cornelius	23	m	w	PA	Klamath	Camp Gaston	73	373
D A	37	m	w	MO	El Dorado	Lake Valley Twp	72	63
E M	45	m	w	VA	Alameda	Oakland	68	242
E W	38	m	w	IL	Tuolumne	Big Oak Flat P O	93	402
Ellen	19	f	w	NY	San Francisco	San Francisco P O	83	129
Emma	32	f	w	ME	San Francisco	7-Wd San Francisco	81	184
Emma	30	f	w	ME	San Francisco	11-Wd San Francisc	84	618
Geo	33	m	w	PA	Shasta	Stillwater P O	89	481
Henry	45	m	w	DENM	San Francisco	7-Wd San Francisco	81	210
Henry	33	m	w	PRUS	San Francisco	San Francisco P O	83	386
Henry	28	m	w	WURT	Sonoma	Mendocino Twp	91	302
Henry	23	m	w	NY	San Francisco	8-Wd San Francisco	82	372
John	44	m	w	IREL	San Francisco	San Francisco P O	80	375
John	32	m	w	GERM	Mono	Bridgeport P O	74	286
John	20	m	w	PA	San Mateo	San Mateo P O	87	350
John T	39	m	w	TN	Nevada	Eureka Twp	75	133
Joseph	43	m	w	PA	Solano	Silveyville Twp	90	81
Joseph	39	m	w	PRUS	San Joaquin	3-Wd Stockton	86	223
Joseph	35	m	w	ENGL	Nevada	Nevada Twp	75	289
Marion	28	m	w	IA	Sonoma	Washington Twp	91	467
Mary	6	f	w	CA	Colusa	Grand Island Twp	71	302
Michael	42	m	w	IREL	Nevada	Meadow Lake Twp	75	267
Mike	53	m	w	IREL	Nevada	Nevada Twp	75	283
Peter	44	m	w	IREL	San Francisco	San Francisco P O	80	376
S	28	m	w	MA	Alameda	Oakland	68	263
Simeon	29	m	w	PRUS	San Francisco	6-Wd San Francisco	81	131
Thomas	19	m	w	IREL	Nevada	Washington Twp	75	346
William	50	m	w	PA	San Francisco	6-Wd San Francisco	81	79
William	26	m	w	IREL	San Francisco	San Francisco P O	83	295
Wm	45	m	w	OH	San Joaquin	2-Wd Stockton	86	202
Wm	32	m	w	OH	Lassen	Long Valley Twp	73	437
CLINES								
John	71	m	w	PA	Stanislaus	Buena Vista Twp	92	14
Thomas	29	m	w	IREL	Alameda	Eden Twp	68	62
CLINESMITH								
Augustus F	33	m	w	HANO	El Dorado	Mud Springs Twp	72	83
CLING								
Ah	8	f	c	CHIN	Mariposa	Mariposa P O	74	125
Ah	26	m	c	CHIN	San Francisco	San Francisco P O	80	527
Ah	25	m	c	CHIN	El Dorado	Placerville Twp	72	97
Ah	20	m	c	CHIN	Santa Clara	Santa Clara Twp	88	161
Foo	27	m	c	CHIN	Sierra	Lincoln Twp	89	546
Ling	19	m	c	CHIN	San Joaquin	Oneal Twp	86	115
Lo	19	m	c	CHIN	Tehama	Tehama Twp	92	188
William	45	m	w	SWED	San Francisco	San Francisco P O	80	377
Won	18	m	c	CHIN	San Francisco	2-Wd San Francisco	79	191
CLINGAN								
David	41	m	w	MD	Marin	Sausalito Twp	74	66
CLINGENBURGH								
Chas	26	m	w	BREM	San Francisco	1-Wd San Francisco	79	120
CLINGER								
Benjamin	30	m	w	PRUS	Sonoma	Sonoma Twp	91	432
John	78	m	w	PA	Solano	Suisun Twp	90	116
CLINGHAM								
Mary	25	f	w	SCOT	San Francisco	San Francisco P O	83	270
Robert	27	m	w	IREL	Los Angeles	Los Nietos Twp	73	588
William	32	m	w	TN	Santa Cruz	Soquel Twp	89	445
William	30	m	w	MO	Santa Cruz	Soquel Twp	89	447
CLINGOR								
R	38	m	w	PA	Napa	Napa Twp	75	61
CLINGSTON								
Louis	24	m	w	PRUS	San Francisco	7-Wd San Francisco	81	223
CLINK								
Ah	44	m	c	CHIN	Sacramento	Granite Twp	77	151
Richd	43	m	w	GERM	Santa Clara	Almaden Twp	88	14
CLINKER								
H	48	m	w	HAMB	San Joaquin	Elliott Twp	86	77
Henry	48	m	w	HANO	Humboldt	Table Bluff Twp	72	307
CLINKINGBEARD								
Kinsley S	27	m	w	MO	Placer	Bath P O	76	460
CLINN								
Thos	51	m	w	IREL	San Francisco	San Francisco P O	83	37
CLINNA								
Thomas	36	m	w	WI	Sutter	Butte Twp	92	100
CLINNG								
Ah	18	m	c	CHIN	Napa	Napa Twp	75	58
CLINSLAN								
Cornelius	23	m	w	IREL	Sacramento	Georgianna Twp	77	129
CLINT								
Chas	40	m	w	MECK	San Francisco	1-Wd San Francisco	79	4
Chas N	26	m	w	SWED	San Francisco	1-Wd San Francisco	79	4
CLINTON								
Alexander	70	m	w	MD	Sacramento	San Joaquin Twp	77	399
Charles	31	m	w	IREL	San Francisco	San Francisco P O	85	745
Chas W	42	m	w	OH	Butte	Bidwell Twp	70	4
David C	27	m	w	IL	Mendocino	Point Arena Twp	74	210
De Witt	37	m	w	ME	Santa Clara	2-Wd San Jose	88	303
Fred	35	m	w	PRUS	Contra Costa	Martinez P O	71	416
Henry	27	m	w	ENGL	San Francisco	1-Wd San Francisco	79	125
I F	37	m	w	KY	Tuolumne	Columbia P O	93	339
James	60	m	w	IREL	Contra Costa	San Pablo Twp	71	362
James	50	m	w	IREL	San Francisco	San Francisco P O	83	287
James	44	m	w	NY	San Francisco	11-Wd San Francisc	84	650
James	31	m	w	IREL	Sonoma	Analy Twp	91	219
Malachi	25	m	w	IREL	Klamath	Camp Gaston	73	372
Mary	24	f	w	CANA	San Francisco	11-Wd San Francisc	84	480
Sally	33	f	w	CANA	San Francisco	6-Wd San Francisco	81	46
Sally	23	f	w	MO	San Francisco	6-Wd San Francisco	81	72
Shane	30	m	w	MI	San Francisco	San Francisco P O	83	356
Thos	18	m	w	LA	San Francisco	1-Wd San Francisco	79	65
Walter	24	m	w	PA	San Francisco	San Francisco P O	80	335

© 2001 by Heritage Quest. All rights reserved.

Name	Age	S	R	B-PL	County	Locale	Roll	Pg
						Series M593		
CLINY								
Ah	27	m	c	CHIN	Sierra	Forest Twp	89	528
CLIPPER								
John	55	m	w	GERM	San Luis Obispo	Salinas Twp	87	293
CLIPPERTON								
William H	34	m	w	ENGL	Santa Clara	Fremont Twp	88	53
CLIPPIN								
Henry	37	m	w	ENGL	Colusa	Spring Valley Twp	71	341
CLIPPINGER								
J A	27	m	w	OH	Sacramento	Brighton Twp	77	71
CLIPPLE								
Jno	25	m	w	WI	San Joaquin	Douglas Twp	86	41
CLIVER								
William	35	m	w	GERM	Los Angeles	Los Angeles	73	511
CLOATHE								
George	21	m	w	PRUS	San Francisco	7-Wd San Francisco	81	177
CLOCK								
Abraham	49	m	w	MA	Napa	Napa	75	9
Charles W	18	m	w	FRAN	Los Angeles	El Monte Twp	73	448
William	29	m	w	ME	Humboldt	Eureka Twp	72	270
Wm	37	m	w	WURT	San Francisco	11-Wd San Francisc	84	689
CLOCKENBAUM								
D	66	f	w	BREM	Yuba	Marysville	93	602
CLOCKER								
P	30	m	w	DENM	Alameda	Murray Twp	68	107
CLODI								
Louis	29	m	w	BRUN	San Francisco	6-Wd San Francisco	81	40
CLODIE								
Charles	23	m	w	BRAN	Siskiyou	Yreka	89	657
CLOE								
Eh	16	m	c	CHIN	San Francisco	11-Wd San Francisc	84	504
CLOFF								
James J	15	m	w	CA	Los Angeles	Los Angeles	73	525
CLOGIN								
Martin	25	m	w	PORT	Alameda	Washington Twp	68	270
CLOGSTON								
William M	32	m	w	OH	Alpine	Woodfords P O	69	315
CLOHESEY								
M A	28	f	w	IREL	San Francisco	San Francisco P O	85	863
CLOHOSON								
H M	33	m	w	TN	Marin	San Rafael Twp	74	38
CLOHSEY								
Ellen	27	f	w	IREL	San Joaquin	2-Wd Stockton	86	171
CLOIS								
J S	35	m	w	MA	Alameda	Oakland	68	259
CLOK								
Ah	22	m	c	CHIN	Sacramento	Georgianna Twp	77	132
CLON								
Ah	40	m	c	CHIN	Napa	Napa Twp	75	58
CLOND								
George	38	m	w	MA	Sacramento	San Joaquin Twp	77	396
CLONE								
Daniel	28	m	w	NY	Colusa	Monroe Twp	71	319
CLONEN								
John	48	m	w	IREL	Solano	Vallejo	90	142
CLONEY								
Margery	35	f	w	IREL	Nevada	Nevada Twp	75	291
CLONG								
Loy	30	f	c	CHIN	Tulare	Visalia	92	299
CLONTRER								
Jos	34	m	w	CANA	Sierra	Sears Twp	89	557
CLOOK								
Ah	22	m	c	CHIN	San Francisco	11-Wd San Francisc	84	695
CLOON								
Michael	33	m	w	IREL	Yolo	Cache Crk Twp	93	430
CLOONAN								
Edward	40	m	w	IREL	Shasta	Shasta P O	89	463
Michael	40	m	w	IREL	Nevada	Grass Valley Twp	75	177
CLOONEY								
James	79	m	w	IREL	Yolo	Cottonwood Twp	93	461
Mary	30	f	w	IREL	San Francisco	San Francisco P O	83	99
Thomas	36	m	w	IREL	Nevada	Nevada Twp	75	321
CLOONY								
Patrick	44	m	w	IREL	Nevada	Nevada Twp	75	288
CLOPENBERG								
D W	45	m	w	BREM	Solano	Vallejo	90	205
CLOPTON								
W G	39	m	w	TN	Tuolumne	Big Oak Flat P O	93	402
CLORAN								
John	40	m	w	IREL	Calaveras	Copperopolis P O	70	253
CLOREN								
Thos	25	m	w	SCOT	San Francisco	11-Wd San Francisc	84	694
CLORES								
John H	15	m	w	MO	Colusa	Colusa Twp	71	284
CLORN								
Mark	59	m	w	IREL	Solano	Rio Vista Twp	90	55
CLORY								
Mary K	1	f	w	CA	San Francisco	San Francisco P O	83	103
CLOS								
Pedro	35	m	w	FRAN	Los Angeles	Soledad Twp	73	633
CLOSE								
Andrew	39	m	w	IN	San Diego	Julian Dist	78	469
Andrew J	45	m	w	PA	Inyo	Independence Twp	73	325
C P	23	m	w	IREL	San Francisco	3-Wd San Francisco	79	315
Hugh	40	m	w	IREL	San Francisco	11-Wd San Francisc	84	687
Nellie	31	f	w	MA	San Francisco	San Francisco P O	80	475
Robt	44	m	w	NY	Shasta	Horsetown P O	89	503

Name	Age	S	R	B-PL	County	Locale	Roll	Pg
						Series M593		
Seymour	70	m	w	NY	El Dorado	Mud Springs Twp	72	81
Thompson M	46	m	w	NY	San Francisco	San Francisco P O	83	54
William	34	m	w	NY	San Francisco	8-Wd San Francisco	82	434
CLOSKEY								
Joseph	18	m	w	ENGL	San Francisco	San Francisco P O	83	219
CLOSNER								
David	38	m	w	SWIT	Mendocino	Ukiah Twp	74	238
CLOSSEN								
Louisa	24	f	w	MO	San Francisco	San Francisco P O	83	335
CLOSSY								
Ellen	25	f	w	IREL	San Francisco	11-Wd San Francisc	84	443
CLOSTER								
Paul	33	m	w	DENM	Sierra	Table Rock Twp	89	573
CLOSTLER								
Floxler	50	m	w	BADE	Colusa	Stony Crk Twp	71	332
CLOTHIER								
James	59	m	w	ENGL	Calaveras	Copperopolis P O	70	228
Samuel	60	m	w	CANA	Calaveras	Copperopolis P O	70	264
CLOTHUS								
James	29	m	w	ENGL	Amador	Sutter Crk P O	69	409
CLOTMAN								
Jeddiah	30	m	w	IL	Sutter	Butte Twp	92	103
CLOTZBACH								
Antone	45	m	w	HESS	Colusa	Spring Valley Twp	71	335
CLOU								
Robt Mrs	43	f	w	ENGL	Alameda	Oakland	68	234
CLOUCHOT								
Antonin	50	m	w	FRAN	Yuba	Slate Range Bar Tw	93	671
CLOUD								
Alfred	32	m	w	PRUS	Contra Costa	San Pablo Twp	71	355
Clara	69	f	w	SC	San Joaquin	3-Wd Stockton	86	224
Jesse	14	m	w	TN	Alameda	Oakland	68	192
John C	46	m	w	TN	San Luis Obispo	Arroyo Grande Twp	87	278
Joseph J	48	m	w	PA	San Mateo	Half Moon Bay P O	87	405
Manuel	35	m	w	PORT	Alameda	Eden Twp	68	91
Willie	12	f	w	CA	San Francisco	San Francisco P O	83	148
Wm	35	m	w	WI	Butte	Ophir Twp	70	112
Wm G	26	m	w	MO	Butte	Chico Twp	70	31
CLOUDMAN								
Chas H	51	m	w	ME	Placer	Gold Run Twp	76	395
D C	57	m	w	ME	Tuolumne	Chinese Camp P O	93	385
H	23	m	w	ME	Alameda	Oakland	68	148
Wm	56	m	w	ME	Tuolumne	Chinese Camp P O	93	365
CLOUG								
Hee	20	m	c	CHIN	Inyo	Independence Twp	73	327
CLOUGH								
Abner P	63	m	w	NY	Amador	Volcano P O	69	381
Albion	42	m	w	ME	Siskiyou	Surprise Valley Tw	89	637
Alfred W	39	m	w	NH	Mariposa	Mariposa P O	74	101
Amos	51	m	w	ME	San Francisco	San Francisco P O	83	206
Barclay	45	m	w	NY	Alameda	Washington Twp	68	279
David	46	m	w	NH	Monterey	Pajaro Twp	74	374
Elijah	39	m	w	CANA	San Francisco	San Francisco P O	83	326
Emma J	26	f	w	NH	Santa Cruz	Santa Cruz	89	414
Frank M	15	m	w	CA	Merced	Snelling P O	74	252
Frank S	31	m	w	NH	Los Angeles	Los Angeles Twp	73	471
Frederick	29	m	w	ME	San Mateo	Half Moon Bay P O	87	398
Greenleaf	34	m	w	ME	Plumas	Goodwin Twp	77	7
Henry M	40	m	w	ME	Santa Cruz	Santa Cruz	89	419
Jas	35	m	w	ME	San Francisco	8-Wd San Francisco	82	370
Jas P	44	m	w	AL	San Francisco	8-Wd San Francisco	82	331
John	45	m	w	ENGL	Tuolumne	Sonora P O	93	318
John	40	m	w	CANA	San Joaquin	Douglas Twp	86	46
John	37	m	w	ENGL	Tuolumne	Columbia P O	93	348
John	28	m	w	ME	San Francisco	11-Wd San Francisc	84	465
John W	39	m	w	ENGL	San Francisco	San Francisco P O	83	53
Johnathan C	50	m	w	CT	Nevada	Grass Valley Twp	75	194
Michael	30	m	w	IREL	San Francisco	San Francisco P O	83	137
Myron	26	m	w	IL	San Francisco	San Francisco P O	80	357
Nathan B	50	m	w	IL	Santa Barbara	Santa Barbara P O	87	455
Orrison	50	m	w	ME	Tehama	Cottonwood Twp	92	162
Orson	47	m	w	NY	Amador	Volcano P O	69	381
Sidney A	30	m	w	ME	San Francisco	San Francisco P O	85	732
CLOUGHLEY								
David	7	m	w	CA	Marin	San Rafael Twp	74	28
CLOUPENBRUCK								
A	35	m	w	BADE	San Francisco	8-Wd San Francisco	82	356
CLOUS								
D	35	m	w	IREL	Alameda	Oakland	68	234
Fredrick	44	m	w	AUST	Calaveras	Copperopolis P O	70	241
CLOUSE								
Belknap	41	m	w	DENM	Calaveras	San Andreas P O	70	164
George	23	m	w	PRUS	San Francisco	San Francisco P O	83	224
George W	34	m	w	OH	Los Angeles	Los Nietos Twp	73	587
Hans	35	m	w	SHOL	Sonoma	Petaluma Twp	91	349
Jacob	29	m	w	NY	San Joaquin	2-Wd Stockton	86	169
M R	35	m	w	SAXO	San Joaquin	2-Wd Stockton	86	189
Moses	30	m	w	SHOL	Napa	Napa Twp	75	67
N J	32	m	w	OH	San Joaquin	2-Wd Stockton	86	164
CLOUSEN								
John	25	m	w	PRUS	Sutter	Vernon Twp	92	138
CLOUSER								
F S	29	m	w	LA	Amador	Fiddletown P O	69	434
CLOUSON								
A	37	m	w	PA	Sutter	Butte Twp	92	102
Daniel	34	m	w	PA	Sutter	Butte Twp	92	102
Ferdinand	40	m	w	PRUS	San Francisco	6-Wd San Francisco	81	94

© 2001 by Heritage Quest. All rights reserved.

Name	Age	S	R	B-PL	County	Locale	Series M593 Roll	Pg
Henry	44	m	w	GERM	Yolo	Grafton Twp	93	493
John	50	m	w	DENM	Calaveras	Copperopolis P O	70	247
CLOUSS								
Heny	35	m	w	HAMB	San Joaquin	Douglas Twp	86	31
CLOUT								
A J	40	m	w	OH	Monterey	Salinas Twp	74	309
Able	23	m	w	MO	Solano	Silveyville Twp	90	75
CLOUTMAN								
Joseph	45	m	w	NH	Solano	Tremont Twp	90	30
CLOVER								
Milton	37	m	w	IN	Sonoma	Analy Twp	91	237
Theobea	67	f	w	OH	El Dorado	Cosumnes Twp	72	17
CLOW								
A F	30	m	w	NY	Sierra	Forest Twp	89	530
Ah	53	m	c	CHIN	Amador	Ione City P O	69	354
Andrew	50	m	w	SCOT	Alameda	Oakland	68	180
Francis	60	m	w	NY	El Dorado	Diamond Springs Tw	72	21
Henry	53	m	w	PRUS	Mendocino	Anderson Twp	74	155
John R	37	m	w	NY	Yuba	Slate Range Bar Tw	93	671
Richard	41	m	w	NY	Yuba	Slate Range Bar Tw	93	671
Stephen	42	m	w	VT	Placer	Newcastle Twp	76	473
CLOWDER								
Adam	44	m	w	PRUS	San Francisco	7-Wd San Francisco	81	230
CLOWE								
Mifflin E	25	m	w	VA	Yolo	Grafton Twp	93	483
CLOWES								
J C	34	m	w	MA	Sacramento	4-Wd Sacramento	77	323
CLOWN								
C	23	m	w	PRUS	Alameda	Oakland	68	184
CLOWSON								
Emma	15	f	w	CA	Inyo	Bishop Crk Twp	73	315
John	23	m	w	HANO	San Francisco	11-Wd San Francisc	84	603
John W	55	m	w	PRUS	Inyo	Bishop Crk Twp	73	313
CLOY								
Ah	46	m	c	CHIN	Santa Clara	1-Wd San Jose	88	274
Ah	29	m	c	CHIN	San Francisco	6-Wd San Francisco	81	67
Wong	25	m	c	CHIN	San Francisco	6-Wd San Francisco	81	43
CLOYD								
David	17	m	b	VA	San Francisco	San Francisco P O	80	486
Robert	48	m	w	TN	Calaveras	San Andreas P O	70	180
CLOYES								
Charles E	30	m	w	IN	San Francisco	6-Wd San Francisco	81	129
Jo	47	m	w	MA	Alameda	Alameda	68	9
CLUE								
Ah	30	m	c	CHIN	San Joaquin	2-Wd Stockton	86	162
J C	24	m	w	ENGL	Sutter	Nicolaus Twp	92	115
Perrie	45	m	w	FRAN	Tuolumne	Chinese Camp P O	93	376
CLUFF								
Charles	14	m	w	CA	Stanislaus	Branch Twp	92	10
William	35	m	w	IREL	San Francisco	San Francisco P O	83	231
CLUGH								
Pike	43	m	w	AL	Stanislaus	San Joaquin Twp	92	75
CLUM								
Kee	20	m	c	CHIN	Alameda	Brooklyn	68	34
Samuel	33	m	w	NJ	San Bernardino	San Bernardino Twp	78	450
CLUN								
Ah	20	m	c	CHIN	Yolo	Grafton Twp	93	479
CLUNAN								
John	23	m	w	IREL	Nevada	Meadow Lake Twp	75	255
CLUNE								
Ellen	19	f	w	IREL	Santa Clara	San Jose Twp	88	205
Michael	37	m	w	IREL	San Francisco	San Francisco P O	85	852
CLUNESS								
W R	35	m	w	CANA	Sacramento	1-Wd Sacramento	77	181
CLUNEY								
Dennis	37	m	w	IREL	San Francisco	San Francisco P O	83	316
Jas	30	m	w	MA	Solano	Vallejo	90	143
John P	37	m	w	CANA	San Francisco	6-Wd San Francisco	81	121
CLUNG								
Ah	30	m	c	CHIN	Placer	Clipper Gap P O	76	393
Ah	19	m	c	CHIN	Santa Cruz	Santa Cruz Twp	89	388
CLUNIE								
T J	21	m	w	CANA	Sacramento	1-Wd Sacramento	77	187
CLUNIN								
Michael	44	m	w	SCOT	Placer	Auburn P O	76	359
CLUNN								
Ah	12	m	c	CHIN	San Francisco	2-Wd San Francisco	79	169
Samuel	33	m	w	NJ	San Bernardino	San Bernardino Twp	78	430
CLUNTON								
Ethabutt J	38	m	w	IL	Yolo	Cache Crk Twp	93	441
CLUP								
Yo	23	m	c	CHIN	San Joaquin	1-Wd Stockton	86	149
CLUPP								
Byron	21	m	w	IL	El Dorado	Diamond Springs Tw	72	27
CLURGER								
Thos	57	m	w	PRUS	San Joaquin	Elliott Twp	86	70
CLURY								
Joanna	17	f	w	MA	Alameda	Oakland	68	205
CLUSH								
Charles	26	m	w	HAMB	Colusa	Monroe Twp	71	314
CLUSKY								
Charles	63	m	w	KY	San Bernardino	San Bernardino Twp	78	417
CLUSS								
Augustus	26	m	w	HANO	Colusa	Spring Valley Twp	71	344
CLUSTA								
Juan	22	m	w	MEXI	Fresno	Millerton P O	72	163
CLUTE								
Alva	7	m	w	CA	San Francisco	San Francisco P O	85	788
Edwin	21	m	w	WI	San Francisco	7-Wd San Francisco	81	157
Peter A	34	m	w	NY	Amador	Volcano P O	69	374
CLUTTER								
Samuel	32	m	w	OH	Nevada	Nevada Twp	75	282
CLYD								
A	26	m	w	WI	Nevada	Meadow Lake Twp	75	265
CLYDE								
Abel	24	m	w	MO	Solano	Denverton Twp	90	25
Almon	36	m	w	NY	San Bernardino	San Bernardino Twp	78	435
Edward	9	m	w	NY	San Francisco	San Francisco P O	85	799
Edward	38	m	w	NY	San Bernardino	San Bernardino Twp	78	434
G W	41	m	w	NY	Amador	Drytown P O	69	422
Isabella	37	f	w	CANA	Siskiyou	Yreka	89	661
John	29	m	w	IREL	Solano	Silveyville Twp	90	79
K K	27	m	w	NY	Humboldt	Table Bluff Twp	72	309
Peter	26	m	w	IREL	Solano	Maine Prairie Twp	90	51
Robert S	54	m	w	SCOT	San Francisco	3-Wd San Francisco	79	321
Soloman	48	m	w	NY	San Bernardino	San Bernardino Twp	78	434
Tryphina Y	47	f	w	NY	Humboldt	Table Bluff Twp	72	309
W	10	m	w	NY	San Francisco	San Francisco P O	85	799
William	26	m	w	IREL	Solano	Silveyville Twp	90	78
CLYESDALE								
John	40	m	w	IREL	Placer	Rocklin Twp	76	465
CLYMAN								
James	78	m	w	VA	Napa	Napa Twp	75	65
Lancaster	50	m	w	OH	Sonoma	Analy Twp	91	243
CLYMER								
Allen	25	m	w	IN	Butte	Chico Twp	70	40
James J	70	m	w	VA	Butte	Oregon Twp	70	128
CLYMO								
John	60	m	w	ENGL	Marin	Sausalito Twp	74	68
CLYMORE								
John	36	m	w	ENGL	Santa Clara	San Jose Twp	88	209
CLYNCH								
Patrick	40	m	w	IREL	Butte	Chico Twp	70	25
CLYNE								
Jas	22	m	w	IREL	Solano	Benicia	90	4
Margaret	32	f	w	IREL	San Francisco	San Francisco P O	83	202
N	37	m	w	NY	Alameda	Oakland	68	239
Patrick	29	m	w	IREL	San Francisco	11-Wd San Francisc	84	453
Samuel	29	m	w	FRAN	San Francisco	San Francisco P O	83	9
CNOTHRIC								
Saml	37	m	w	NY	San Francisco	San Francisco P O	83	96
CO								
Ah	50	m	c	CHIN	Stanislaus	Emory Twp	92	17
Ah	38	m	c	CHIN	Amador	Jackson P O	69	343
Ah	23	m	c	CHIN	Sacramento	Georgianna Twp	77	132
Chu	53	m	c	CHIN	Calaveras	San Andreas P O	70	183
Chung	40	m	c	CHIN	Calaveras	San Andreas P O	70	211
Peh	56	m	c	CHIN	Calaveras	San Andreas P O	70	161
Quey	5	m	c	CA	Yuba	Marysville	93	627
Sun	20	m	c	CHIN	Yuba	Marysville	93	628
Tip	32	m	c	CHIN	Butte	Hamilton Twp	70	73
Yong	30	m	c	CHIN	Trinity	North Fork Twp	92	217
COA								
David	55	m	w	VA	Monterey	San Juan Twp	74	386
COACH								
Benjamin	29	m	w	TN	Santa Cruz	Santa Cruz Twp	89	390
COACHELL								
Abulan	59	m	w	PA	Trinity	Weaverville Pct	92	226
COAD								
Alfred	35	m	w	ENGL	San Francisco	San Francisco P O	83	70
COADY								
Wm	31	m	w	IREL	Solano	Vallejo	90	200
COAH								
Ah	30	m	c	CHIN	Los Angeles	Los Angeles	73	527
COAKLEY								
Caleb	46	m	w	IREL	Stanislaus	Branch Twp	92	8
Danl	35	m	w	NY	Humboldt	Eureka Twp	72	276
J F	20	m	w	MA	San Francisco	3-Wd San Francisco	79	311
John	25	m	w	IREL	Marin	San Rafael Twp	74	25
Nora	14	f	w	NY	Sacramento	4-Wd Sacramento	77	360
Wm	40	m	w	IREL	Sierra	Sears Twp	89	561
Wm	39	m	w	IREL	Sacramento	4-Wd Sacramento	77	376
COALBURM								
James	45	m	w	OH	Yuba	Marysville	93	618
COALES								
Elisha A	48	m	w	MA	Mendocino	Point Arena Twp	74	214
Maria	30	f	w	MEXI	San Joaquin	2-Wd Stockton	86	165
COALING								
John H	47	m	w	ENGL	Trinity	Trinity Center Pct	92	204
COAN								
Ah	40	m	c	CHIN	Yolo	Washington Twp	93	533
Ah	32	m	w	CHIN	Siskiyou	Yreka Twp	89	667
Ah	30	m	c	CHIN	Placer	Bath P O	76	446
James	23	m	w	OH	Solano	Tremont Twp	90	29
John T	31	m	w	VT	El Dorado	White Oak Twp	72	135
COANG								
Keen	26	m	c	CHIN	San Francisco	11-Wd San Francisc	84	546
COANS								
Edward H	43	m	w	VA	El Dorado	Placerville	72	120
COAPLAND								
Alexr	52	m	w	SC	Monterey	Castroville Twp	74	338
COARES								
Emanuel	30	m	w	PORT	Alameda	Washington Twp	68	269

© 2001 by Heritage Quest. All rights reserved.

Name	Age	S	R	B-PL	County	Locale	Series M593 Roll	Pg
COATES								
Abner	69	m	w	PA	Mendocino	Little Lake Twp	74	203
Benjamin	72	m	w	PA	Mendocino	Little Lake Twp	74	203
Caleb	30	m	w	ENGL	San Francisco	8-Wd San Francisco	82	446
Claiborne M	38	m	w	TN	Placer	Auburn P O	76	363
Elizabeth	58	f	w	KY	Mendocino	Little Lake Twp	74	192
Eva	12	f	m	CA	Fresno	Millerton P O	72	188
Frank	37	m	w	ENGL	San Francisco	3-Wd San Francisco	79	318
Geo W	60	m	w	PA	Mendocino	Little Lake Twp	74	203
George W	12	m	w	MO	Placer	Newcastle Twp	76	478
Horace	18	m	w	MO	San Francisco	San Francisco P O	83	198
James B	19	m	w	WI	Mendocino	Little Lake Twp	74	197
John	29	m	w	OH	San Joaquin	Tulare Twp	86	263
John	25	m	w	IREL	Stanislaus	Empire Twp	92	65
John P	38	m	w	IN	Mendocino	Round Valley Twp	74	219
Moses	62	m	w	PA	San Francisco	11-Wd San Francisc	84	630
Newton M	46	m	w	TN	Santa Barbara	Santa Barbara P O	87	491
Rebecca	18	f	w	WI	Mendocino	Little Lake Twp	74	192
Thomas	29	m	w	CANA	San Francisco	3-Wd San Francisco	79	294
William	50	m	w	ENGL	Sacramento	2-Wd Sacramento	77	211
William H	34	m	w	PA	Placer	Bath P O	76	425
COATS								
Amos	18	m	w	MO	Sutter	Sutter Twp	92	117
Arthur	30	m	w	MO	Sutter	Sutter Twp	92	120
Arthur	18	m	w	MO	Sutter	Sutter Twp	92	120
C G	34	m	w	VT	Tuolumne	Columbia P O	93	350
Catherine	57	f	w	KY	Colusa	Spring Valley Twp	71	337
Charles	36	m	w	IREL	San Francisco	2-Wd San Francisco	79	151
Charlie	22	m	w	OH	Contra Costa	Martinez P O	71	378
Chas	19	m	w	OH	San Francisco	San Francisco P O	85	819
Felix G	42	m	w	MO	Contra Costa	Martinez P O	71	384
G C	60	m	w	VA	Tuolumne	Columbia P O	93	357
George	36	m	w	WI	El Dorado	Placerville Twp	72	99
George	34	m	w	VT	Tuolumne	Big Oak Flat P O	93	405
George	17	m	w	LA	San Francisco	11-Wd San Francisc	84	630
H	44	m	w	ENGL	Sacramento	3-Wd Sacramento	77	277
Harry	52	m	w	SHOL	Butte	Mountain Spring Tw	70	89
J J	25	m	w	MO	Sutter	Sutter Twp	92	116
James	60	m	w	KY	San Mateo	Searsville P O	87	382
James	23	m	w	IREL	San Francisco	7-Wd San Francisco	81	170
Jas M	32	m	w	MO	San Francisco	8-Wd San Francisco	82	331
Jesse	55	m	w	TN	Tuolumne	Sonora P O	93	317
John	44	m	w	ME	Contra Costa	Martinez P O	71	407
John P	57	m	w	PA	Humboldt	Eel Rvr Twp	72	251
John R	27	m	w	MO	Contra Costa	Martinez P O	71	386
Lemuel	33	m	w	MO	Contra Costa	Martinez P O	71	384
M E	24	f	w	ENGL	Tuolumne	Chinese Camp P O	93	363
Mary	14	f	w	CA	Tulare	Visalia Twp	92	284
Niles	20	m	w	OH	Nevada	Little York Twp	75	240
Robert	34	m	w	MO	Sutter	Vernon Twp	92	139
Talbott	52	m	w	VA	Nevada	Eureka Twp	75	132
William	26	m	w	ENGL	Sutter	Yuba Twp	92	145
Wilson	67	m	w	TN	Contra Costa	Martinez P O	71	384
Wm	40	m	w	VA	Sacramento	1-Wd Sacramento	77	202
Wm	38	m	w	MO	Sutter	Sutter Twp	92	116
Wm	36	m	w	NY	Lake	Lakeport	73	408
Wm J	41	m	w	IN	El Dorado	Placerville Twp	72	103
Wm L	39	m	w	MO	Merced	Snelling P O	74	254
COATTES								
Alexander	35	m	w	SCOT	San Mateo	Redwood Twp	87	361
COATZ								
John	30	m	w	IREL	Santa Clara	Redwood Twp	88	118
COBAIN								
Thomas	26	m	w	CANA	Plumas	Washington Twp	77	53
COBAL								
John	39	m	w	TN	Tulare	Farmersville Twp	92	248
COBALLERO								
Francisco	56	m	w	ITAL	Santa Barbara	Santa Barbara P O	87	476
COBB								
A V	23	m	w	NC	Sonoma	Santa Rosa	91	415
Alvin	45	m	w	KY	Colusa	Colusa Twp	71	286
C	23	f	w	IA	Sierra	Sierra Twp	89	564
Caroline	68	f	w	ENGL	San Francisco	San Francisco P O	80	395
Charles	50	m	w	CT	Sonoma	Petaluma Twp	91	330
David	29	m	w	ENGL	San Francisco	San Francisco P O	83	211
Eldridge	53	m	w	MA	San Francisco	San Francisco P O	83	375
George	40	m	w	NY	Santa Clara	Alviso Twp	88	22
George	36	m	w	PA	Yolo	Cache Crk Twp	93	456
Grey L	47	m	w	VT	Sonoma	Healdsburg	91	275
H C	21	f	w	IA	Sierra	Sierra Twp	89	569
Hattie M	24	f	w	ENGL	San Francisco	San Francisco P O	83	202
Henry	53	m	w	IOFG	San Francisco	San Francisco P O	80	359
Henry A	43	m	w	ENGL	San Francisco	5-Wd San Francisco	81	33
Heny	28	m	w	FRAN	San Francisco	2-Wd San Francisco	79	276
James	25	m	w	ME	Nevada	Little York Twp	75	245
James C	63	m	w	NY	Santa Clara	2-Wd San Jose	88	325
John	56	m	w	KY	Lake	Lower Lake	73	422
John	28	m	w	ME	San Francisco	San Francisco P O	85	807
John	13	m	w	CA	San Francisco	5-Wd San Francisco	81	33
Joseph	31	m	w	IREL	Santa Clara	Santa Clara Twp	88	154
Joseph L	30	m	w	ME	Santa Clara	Fremont Twp	88	43
L L	55	m	w	ME	Nevada	Bloomfield Twp	75	95
Lyman E	25	m	w	NY	Napa	Napa	75	39
Martha	30	f	w	NY	Alameda	Oakland	68	137
Nathan	64	m	w	RI	Tuolumne	Big Oak Flat P O	93	402
Nina	12	f	w	CA	Santa Clara	2-Wd San Jose	88	337
Samuel	52	m	w	ENGL	Santa Clara	San Jose Twp	88	212
Samuel	39	m	w	MA	Amador	Sutter Crk P O	69	400
Thop	55	m	w	VA	El Dorado	Georgetown Twp	72	47
W A B	52	m	w	ME	San Francisco	San Francisco P O	83	194
William H	40	m	w	MA	San Francisco	6-Wd San Francisco	81	130
Wm	39	m	w	ENGL	Alameda	Murray Twp	68	118
Y	52	m	w	MA	Sierra	Sierra Twp	89	569
COBBERT								
John	58	m	w	IREL	Nevada	Grass Valley Twp	75	212
COBBERTEY								
J	17	m	w	FRAN	San Joaquin	Tulare Twp	86	251
COBBLEDICK								
James	40	m	w	ENGL	Alameda	Brooklyn	68	22
COBBLES								
John F	45	m	w	IN	Mendocino	Little Lake Twp	74	195
COBBY								
A B	47	f	w	NH	Solano	Vallejo	90	164
M E	15	f	w	CA	Solano	Vallejo	90	164
COBE								
John M	52	m	w	VA	Sutter	Butte Twp	92	88
COBEL								
Wesley	36	m	w	NC	Santa Barbara	San Buenaventura P	87	419
COBELICH								
Paulo	40	m	w	AUST	El Dorado	Salmon Falls Twp	72	131
COBERT								
Geo P	48	m	w	PA	Shasta	Stillwater P O	89	479
Mariah	18	f	w	MO	Sonoma	Washington Twp	91	466
Saml H	43	m	w	VA	Shasta	Stillwater P O	89	479
COBINER								
T	32	m	w	OH	Alameda	Oakland	68	144
COBIO								
Louis	35	m	w	CANA	Calaveras	San Andreas P O	70	186
COBIONI								
Frank	10	m	w	CA	San Joaquin	3-Wd Stockton	86	242
COBLE								
Frank	38	m	w	ME	Tehama	Red Bluff	92	184
Thomas	49	m	w	GERM	Contra Costa	Martinez P O	71	439
COBLEIGH								
John	42	m	w	NH	San Francisco	San Francisco P O	85	728
COBLENTZ								
Cerf	21	m	w	FRAN	El Dorado	Mud Springs Twp	72	78
Felix	24	m	w	FRAN	Amador	Sutter Crk P O	69	398
Joseph	30	m	w	FRAN	Los Angeles	Los Angeles	73	525
Lambert	22	m	w	FRAN	Amador	Fiddletown P O	69	430
COBLER								
Charles	35	m	w	MO	Los Angeles	Soledad Twp	73	631
Margarete	17	f	w	SWED	Mendocino	Little Rvr Twp	74	165
COBLEY								
Margaret	8	f	w	CA	Sonoma	Sonoma Twp	91	449
COBLINER								
John	35	m	w	FRAN	San Francisco	8-Wd San Francisco	82	364
COBO								
Jose	42	m	w	SPAI	San Francisco	2-Wd San Francisco	79	237
COBRY								
Henry	52	m	w	IREL	Inyo	Independence Twp	73	325
COBS								
James	30	m	w	NY	San Francisco	San Francisco P O	83	356
COBURN								
F H	30	m	w	RI	San Francisco	San Francisco P O	85	766
George	14	m	w	NY	Santa Clara	San Jose Twp	88	199
George A	24	m	w	VT	San Mateo	Schoolhouse Statio	87	331
Gilbert	42	m	w	OH	Solano	Vacaville Twp	90	123
Gilbert	42	m	w	OH	Solano	Vacaville Twp	90	125
James	52	m	w	IN	San Bernardino	San Bernardino Twp	78	444
John	61	m	w	NY	Plumas	Plumas Twp	77	27
John	40	m	w	OH	Sonoma	Santa Rosa	91	395
John	33	m	w	IREL	San Mateo	Schoolhouse Statio	87	342
Loren	44	m	w	VT	San Mateo	Woodside P O	87	381
Lulu	10	f	w	CA	Santa Clara	San Jose Twp	88	190
M J	28	f	w	IREL	Alameda	Oakland	68	247
Man	31	m	w	VA	Sonoma	Santa Rosa	91	395
Naham	47	m	w	ME	Siskiyou	Scott Valley Twp	89	619
Nelson F	44	m	w	OH	Inyo	Lone Pine Twp	73	330
S A	47	m	w	VT	Alameda	Oakland	68	229
Samuel S	45	m	w	ME	Tulare	Visalia Twp	92	284
Sylvanus P	43	m	w	ME	San Mateo	Pescadero P O	87	412
William	34	m	w	LA	Colusa	Monroe Twp	71	313
COCH								
Edward	34	m	w	HANO	San Francisco	San Francisco P O	83	191
COCHLAN								
Mary P	42	f	w	IREL	El Dorado	Kelsey Twp	72	61
COCHLIN								
J L	37	m	w	IREL	San Joaquin	2-Wd Stockton	86	208
Jas	25	m	w	IREL	San Joaquin	2-Wd Stockton	86	185
Jerry	37	m	w	IREL	San Joaquin	3-Wd Stockton	86	234
Timothy	40	m	w	IREL	San Mateo	Redwood Twp	87	361
COCHRAINE								
William	45	m	w	IREL	San Francisco	San Francisco P O	80	388
COCHRAM								
Ann	40	f	w	IREL	Placer	Bath P O	76	426
Richard	8	m	m	CA	San Francisco	San Francisco P O	80	375
T A	36	m	w	CANA	Tuolumne	Sonora P O	93	325
COCHRAN								
Aaron	38	m	w	VA	Kern	Bakersfield P O	73	366
Alexander W	35	m	w	IREL	Inyo	Bishop Crk Twp	73	311
Alfred H	30	m	w	SCOT	Los Angeles	Wilmington Twp	73	641
David R	45	m	w	CANA	Santa Cruz	Santa Cruz Twp	89	394
Dennis	55	m	w	IREL	Santa Clara	Santa Clara Twp	88	135

© 2001 by Heritage Quest. All rights reserved.

California 1870 Census

Name	Age	S	R	B-PL	County	Locale (Series M593)	Roll	Pg
Evangline	22	f	w	CANA	San Joaquin	2-Wd Stockton	86	174
George	38	m	w	IREL	Placer	Bath P O	76	425
George	12	m	w	IL	Sutter	Yuba Twp	92	145
Henry	48	m	w	IN	Nevada	Eureka Twp	75	135
Hiram	35	m	w	ME	Nevada	Washington Twp	75	346
Hiram	29	m	w	NY	Alameda	Brooklyn Twp	68	52
Holton	42	m	w	OH	Shasta	Millville P O	89	486
Horace	57	m	w	VT	Tehama	Red Bluff	92	179
J	40	m	w	MO	Yuba	Marysville	93	608
J	30	m	w	IREL	Yuba	Rose Bar Twp	93	660
Jacob	38	m	w	PA	Butte	Ophir Twp	70	109
James	38	m	w	OH	Marin	Sausalito Twp	74	70
James	38	m	w	TX	Kern	Bakersfield P O	73	357
James	38	m	w	OH	Colusa	Colusa Twp	71	287
James	37	m	w	OH	Butte	Hamilton Twp	70	61
Jerry	56	m	w	KY	Tehama	Battle Crk Twp	92	157
Jerry	40	m	w	IREL	Sacramento	4-Wd Sacramento	77	370
Jno H	52	m	w	OH	Butte	Ophir Twp	70	113
John	52	m	w	OH	Butte	Hamilton Twp	70	61
John	47	m	w	IREL	Tuolumne	Big Oak Flat P O	93	393
John	41	m	w	AL	Kern	Kernville P O	73	368
John	34	m	w	ME	Tuolumne	Big Oak Flat P O	93	398
John	30	m	w	IL	Monterey	Alisal Twp	74	290
John	25	m	w	IREL	San Francisco	San Francisco P O	85	852
Josph	15	m	w	VT	Monterey	San Juan Twp	74	401
M J	4	f	w	CA	Tuolumne	Big Oak Flat P O	93	398
Maggie	17	f	w	OR	Los Angeles	Los Angeles	73	536
Mary	56	f	w	IREL	San Francisco	San Francisco P O	83	59
Mary	42	f	w	SCOT	Sacramento	4-Wd Sacramento	77	324
Mary	40	f	w	IREL	Santa Barbara	Santa Barbara P O	87	452
Mary	24	f	w	MA	Sacramento	1-Wd Sacramento	77	205
Mary	21	f	w	MO	Santa Cruz	Santa Cruz	89	418
Michael	25	m	w	IREL	Alameda	Eden Twp	68	68
P	35	m	w	IREL	Sutter	Butte Twp	92	91
Pat	45	m	w	IREL	Solano	Benicia	90	19
Rufus	39	m	w	MS	Butte	Chico Twp	70	21
Saml T	63	m	w	PA	Shasta	Millville P O	89	484
Samuel	18	m	w	FRAN	San Francisco	2-Wd San Francisco	79	141
Simon	58	m	w	IREL	San Francisco	San Francisco P O	83	399
T J	41	m	w	OH	Sacramento	Brighton Twp	77	78
W	36	f	w	IREL	Sacramento	3-Wd Sacramento	77	290
W A	38	m	w	ME	Tuolumne	Big Oak Flat P O	93	398
William	33	m	w	MO	Alameda	Washington Twp	68	285
William A	32	m	w	AL	Los Angeles	Los Nietos Twp	73	576
Wm	25	m	w	IREL	Santa Barbara	Santa Barbara P O	87	503
Wm W	39	m	w	MD	Yuba	Slate Range Bar Tw	93	672
COCHRANBAUGH								
I	40	m	w	PA	Nevada	Nevada Twp	75	275
COCHRANE								
Anne	22	f	w	IREL	San Francisco	11-Wd San Francisc	84	661
Fannie	12	f	w	CA	San Francisco	San Francisco P O	83	170
Jas	35	m	w	IREL	San Francisco	San Francisco P O	83	262
Jno	45	m	w	VT	Santa Clara	Burnett Twp	88	30
John	33	m	w	MO	San Francisco	7-Wd San Francisco	81	277
Mariah	27	f	w	NY	San Francisco	San Francisco P O	83	404
Mary	38	f	w	IREL	Placer	Lincoln P O	76	489
Mary	30	f	w	IREL	San Francisco	7-Wd San Francisco	81	282
Mary	26	f	w	ENGL	San Francisco	7-Wd San Francisco	81	245
Mary	10	f	i	CA	Placer	Lincoln P O	76	490
Richard	20	m	w	CA	Santa Clara	Santa Clara Twp	88	176
Wm	33	m	w	IREL	San Francisco	7-Wd San Francisco	81	232
COCHREN								
Asa H	41	m	w	NY	Alameda	Brooklyn	68	29
COCK								
Ah	28	m	c	CHIN	Solano	Suisun Twp	90	105
Isaac F	37	m	w	IN	Sonoma	Santa Rosa	91	398
Nicholas	38	m	w	ENGL	Nevada	Grass Valley Twp	75	203
Wm E	59	m	w	KY	Sonoma	Santa Rosa	91	409
COCKBILL								
James	41	m	w	ENGL	El Dorado	Coloma Twp	72	5
COCKBORN								
Jane	24	f	w	ENGL	San Francisco	San Francisco P O	83	356
COCKBURN								
Andrew	26	m	w	SCOT	San Francisco	1-Wd San Francisco	79	96
Thos	40	m	w	SCOT	Tehama	Paskenta Twp	92	164
COCKE								
John	26	m	w	MO	San Luis Obispo	Morro Twp	87	286
COCKEFARE								
William H	37	m	w	NJ	Alameda	Alvarado	68	304
COCKEREL								
C	49	m	w	KY	Yuba	Marysville	93	577
COCKERELL								
C M	23	m	w	MO	Monterey	Alisal Twp	74	304
James	34	m	w	KY	Plumas	Quartz Twp	77	39
Jennette	14	f	w	CA	Monterey	Alisal Twp	74	304
COCKERILL								
Chas H	38	m	w	ENGL	Shasta	Stillwater P O	89	479
COCKERTIE								
A	40	m	w	IL	Alameda	Murray Twp	68	121
COCKIN								
Henry	43	m	w	ENGL	Mariposa	Mariposa P O	74	122
Mary A	42	f	w	ENGL	Mariposa	Mariposa P O	74	121
COCKING								
George	30	m	w	ENGL	Santa Cruz	Santa Cruz Twp	89	393
Nicholas	28	m	w	ENGL	Nevada	Grass Valley Twp	75	232
Stephen	31	m	w	ENGL	El Dorado	Mud Springs Twp	72	81
William	32	m	w	ENGL	Nevada	Grass Valley Twp	75	191

Name	Age	S	R	B-PL	County	Locale (Series M593)	Roll	Pg
William	24	m	w	ENGL	Placer	Bath P O	76	452
COCKLEY								
William	37	m	w	OH	Calaveras	San Andreas P O	70	215
COCKLIN								
Ellen	60	f	w	IREL	San Francisco	11-Wd San Francisc	84	692
COCKMAN								
John	45	m	w	ENGL	San Francisco	1-Wd San Francisco	79	58
COCKNELL								
Saml R	38	m	w	NY	San Francisco	5-Wd San Francisco	81	26
COCKRAN								
Edwd	35	m	w	IL	Alameda	Murray Twp	68	114
J	24	m	w	IREL	Lake	Knoxville Mines	73	405
John	42	m	w	ENGL	San Joaquin	2-Wd Stockton	86	169
John D	43	m	w	MA	Nevada	Washington Twp	75	345
Kate	40	f	w	IREL	Santa Clara	Santa Clara Twp	88	163
Maggie	3	f	w	NY	San Francisco	2-Wd San Francisco	79	257
Mary	25	f	w	IREL	San Francisco	7-Wd San Francisco	81	207
Rugles S	35	m	w	PA	Mariposa	Mariposa P O	74	134
COCKREL								
Mary	40	f	w	IREL	San Francisco	8-Wd San Francisco	82	340
COCKRELL								
R B	25	m	w	MO	Monterey	Alisal Twp	74	304
Theodore	35	m	w	KY	San Francisco	11-Wd San Francisc	84	643
Walter	17	m	w	CA	Santa Clara	1-Wd San Jose	88	252
COCKRILL								
Cassey	61	f	w	MD	Sonoma	Analy Twp	91	243
Larkin D	50	m	w	SC	Sonoma	Analy Twp	91	219
R	91	m	w	SC	Monterey	Alisal Twp	74	300
Robert	21	m	w	MO	Mendocino	Cuffeys Cove Twp	74	169
Sterling R	43	m	w	TN	Fresno	Kings Rvr P O	72	211
COCKS								
Henry	44	m	w	ENGL	Tulare	Tule Rvr Twp	92	272
Miguela	36	f	w	CA	Monterey	Monterey	74	366
Nicholas	25	m	w	ENGL	Sonoma	Salt Point	91	392
COCKSWORTH								
Harrison	32	m	w	ENGL	Humboldt	Pacific Twp	72	297
COCKUMRY								
C	16	f	w	OH	Yuba	Marysville	93	582
COCKWOOD								
Jemma	15	f	w	AUSL	Contra Costa	Martinez P O	71	445
COCLADA								
Chas	65	m	w	FRAN	Calaveras	Copperopolis P O	70	231
COCORAN								
J	38	m	w	IREL	Alameda	Oakland	68	220
COCRINO								
Jose	35	m	w	CA	San Diego	Warners Rancho Dis	78	530
COCUS								
Nicholas	55	m	w	FRAN	San Francisco	11-Wd San Francisc	84	520
CODA								
John	40	m	w	IREL	San Francisco	San Francisco P O	83	415
CODAMORTORE								
N	19	m	w	ITAL	Calaveras	Copperopolis P O	70	232
CODDEN								
H H	38	m	w	CT	Nevada	Eureka Twp	75	130
CODDING								
Geo R	42	m	w	NY	Sonoma	Petaluma Twp	91	330
CODDINGHAM								
William	28	m	w	ME	San Francisco	8-Wd San Francisco	82	441
CODDINGTON								
Charles	14	m	w	CA	Santa Clara	Santa Clara Twp	88	177
James	15	m	w	CA	Santa Clara	Santa Clara Twp	88	177
William	42	m	w	NY	San Francisco	8-Wd San Francisco	82	492
William	27	m	w	MS	San Bernardino	San Bernardino Twp	78	440
Wm	50	m	w	NJ	Calaveras	Copperopolis P O	70	234
CODE								
Henry	44	m	w	ENGL	San Francisco	8-Wd San Francisco	82	403
J K	42	m	w	MO	Sierra	Downieville Twp	89	515
Julia M	33	f	w	MO	Nevada	Grass Valley Twp	75	146
Philip	27	m	w	NY	San Francisco	11-Wd San Francisc	84	552
CODEINATRE								
John	45	m	w	ITAL	San Francisco	San Francisco P O	85	860
CODEY								
Charles	41	m	w	NJ	Sonoma	Salt Point	91	386
Mary	40	f	w	IREL	Sacramento	4-Wd Sacramento	77	344
CODIN								
Noel	39	m	w	FRAN	Siskiyou	Scott Valley Twp	89	614
CODINA								
Francis	38	m	w	SPAI	Santa Barbara	Santa Barbara P O	87	492
CODINGHAM								
William	18	m	w	IA	Humboldt	Pacific Twp	72	298
CODRICK								
George	40	m	w	OH	San Francisco	San Francisco P O	83	339
CODRILL								
Johana	28	f	w	IREL	San Francisco	San Francisco P O	80	485
William	35	m	w	ENGL	Stanislaus	Empire Twp	92	42
CODY								
Andrew	25	m	w	IREL	Placer	Newcastle Twp	76	477
B F	40	m	w	OH	Sierra	Table Rock Twp	89	578
Canote	20	f	w	MEXI	Fresno	Millerton P O	72	154
E	60	m	w	VT	Sierra	Alleghany & Forest	89	535
Edmund	35	m	w	IREL	Sacramento	4-Wd Sacramento	77	369
Edward	40	m	w	IREL	Tuolumne	Sonora P O	93	315
Ellin	5	f	w	CA	San Francisco	11-Wd San Francisc	84	711
Felix	28	m	w	AR	San Joaquin	Oneal Twp	86	109
J M	33	m	w	IN	Lake	Lakeport	73	407
James	25	m	w	IREL	Sutter	Nicolaus Twp	92	115
John	48	m	w	IREL	Sutter	Nicolaus Twp	92	115

© 2001 by Heritage Quest. All rights reserved.

Name	Age	S	R	B-PL	County	Locale	Roll	Pg
John	40	m	w	IREL	San Mateo	Schoolhouse Statio	87	342
John	35	m	w	IREL	Santa Clara	2-Wd San Jose	88	313
John	35	m	w	IREL	San Francisco	San Francisco P O	83	15
John	22	m	w	IREL	San Mateo	Woodside P O	87	381
John	22	m	w	IREL	San Francisco	5-Wd San Francisco	81	7
Margaret	40	f	w	KY	San Francisco	5-Wd San Francisco	81	17
Mary	27	f	w	IREL	San Francisco	8-Wd San Francisco	82	333
Mary	20	f	w	IREL	San Francisco	2-Wd San Francisco	79	192
Mathew	32	m	w	IREL	Contra Costa	Martinez P O	71	415
Michael	36	m	w	IREL	Santa Clara	Milpitas Twp	88	109
Michael	29	m	w	IREL	Marin	San Rafael Twp	74	25
Michail	39	m	w	IREL	Monterey	San Benito Twp	74	378
N T	49	m	w	NY	Mariposa	Maxwell Crk P O	74	139
Patrick	36	m	w	IREL	San Francisco	11-Wd San Francisc	84	641
Thomas	45	m	w	IREL	Humboldt	Pacific Twp	72	297
Thomas	37	m	w	OH	El Dorado	Placerville	72	123
Thos	13	m	w	CA	San Francisco	11-Wd San Francisc	84	592
COE								
A A	73	m	w	IREL	Tuolumne	Chinese Camp P O	93	385
Ah	50	m	c	CHIN	Tuolumne	Chinese Camp P O	93	388
Ah	41	m	c	CHIN	Sierra	Lincoln Twp	89	548
Ah	17	m	c	CHIN	San Mateo	Half Moon Bay P O	87	398
Ah	17	m	c	CHIN	Santa Clara	San Jose Twp	88	183
Archibald	57	m	w	OH	Nevada	Nevada Twp	75	320
E G	31	m	w	NY	Alameda	Murray Twp	68	124
Edwd H	45	m	w	NY	San Francisco	1-Wd San Francisco	79	18
Frank H	46	m	w	NY	Sonoma	Santa Rosa	91	420
G	37	m	w	ITAL	Alameda	Murray Twp	68	128
G	27	m	w	ITAL	Alameda	Murray Twp	68	124
Geo	36	m	w	OH	San Francisco	1-Wd San Francisco	79	59
Henry W	50	m	w	NH	Santa Clara	San Jose Twp	88	188
J P	50	m	w	NY	Alameda	Oakland	68	208
John	35	m	w	NJ	Sutter	Sutter Twp	92	126
John	32	m	w	IL	Alpine	Woodfords P O	69	309
John	27	m	w	IL	Sacramento	Natomas Twp	77	165
Joo	32	m	c	CHIN	San Joaquin	1-Wd Stockton	86	142
Lawrence W	39	m	w	NY	San Francisco	8-Wd San Francisco	82	384
Lee	42	m	c	CHIN	San Joaquin	1-Wd Stockton	86	149
Mi	19	m	c	CHIN	Tuolumne	Columbia P O	93	341
W	36	m	w	NH	Nevada	Washington Twp	75	346
Wells S	37	m	w	NY	Nevada	Washington Twp	75	347
Wm	67	m	w	OH	El Dorado	Kelsey Twp	72	59
Wm	33	m	w	OH	Sacramento	Granite Twp	77	147
Wm R	37	m	w	NY	Nevada	Nevada Twp	75	287
Wm R	37	m	w	NY	Nevada	Nevada Twp	75	287
COEDARRESS								
Louis	32	m	w	FRAN	Los Angeles	Los Angeles	73	567
COEG								
Ah	27	m	c	CHIN	El Dorado	Mud Springs Twp	72	77
COELHO								
Antone J	23	m	w	AZOR	Contra Costa	Martinez P O	71	391
COELING								
Bridget	22	f	w	IREL	San Francisco	2-Wd San Francisco	79	197
COEMEN								
Prucia	49	m	w	MEXI	Los Angeles	Los Angeles	73	509
COEN								
Ah	20	m	c	CHIN	Yuba	Marysville	93	621
Mary A	43	f	w	OH	Shasta	Fort Crook P O	89	475
COENISH								
Minnie	8	f	w	CA	Nevada	Grass Valley Twp	75	229
COERMBS								
Alexr	27	m	w	NY	San Francisco	5-Wd San Francisco	81	24
COEY								
Ah	30	m	c	CHIN	Yolo	Washington Twp	93	537
Ah	30	m	c	CHIN	Sacramento	3-Wd Sacramento	77	316
Ah	28	m	c	CHIN	Santa Clara	Alviso Twp	88	25
Choy	21	f	c	CHIN	Yuba	Rose Bar Twp	93	656
James	29	m	w	NY	San Francisco	San Francisco P O	83	255
Mary L	28	f	w	PA	San Francisco	San Francisco P O	83	255
Nicolas	35	m	w	PRUS	Yolo	Putah Twp	93	512
COFER								
Ephriam	68	m	w	NC	Santa Clara	Redwood Twp	88	132
George W	42	m	w	MO	San Diego	San Diego	78	493
James	36	m	w	MO	Inyo	Independence Twp	73	326
R D	26	m	w	MO	Sutter	Vernon Twp	92	130
Wm W	37	m	w	MO	Sonoma	Petaluma Twp	91	323
COFF								
Joseph	22	m	w	FRAN	Sacramento	4-Wd Sacramento	77	369
Thos	38	m	w	IREL	Alameda	Oakland	68	225
COFFAY								
P	24	m	w	IREL	Sierra	Sierra Twp	89	569
COFFE								
Dennis	39	m	w	IREL	Sacramento	3-Wd Sacramento	77	274
Edward	29	m	w	NY	Sacramento	2-Wd Sacramento	77	227
Jacques	44	m	w	FRAN	Yuba	Slate Range Bar Tw	93	671
Robt	47	m	w	MA	San Joaquin	Elliott Twp	86	79
COFFEE								
A J	51	m	w	TN	Alameda	Oakland	68	246
Alfred	33	m	w	TN	Stanislaus	Empire Twp	92	40
Alvin A	44	m	m	KY	Shasta	Shasta P O	89	461
Ann	24	f	w	RI	San Joaquin	3-Wd Stockton	86	224
Charles	30	m	w	IREL	Solano	Denverton Twp	90	27
Dennis	31	m	w	IREL	San Francisco	7-Wd San Francisco	81	196
Eli	38	m	w	IN	San Luis Obispo	Santa Rosa Twp	87	318
Ellen E	31	f	w	IREL	Nevada	Grass Valley Twp	75	146
Frank	25	m	w	TN	Stanislaus	Empire Twp	92	40
Geo	48	m	w	PA	San Francisco	7-Wd San Francisco	81	239

Name	Age	S	R	B-PL	County	Locale	Roll	Pg
Geo	25	m	w	NY	El Dorado	Placerville Twp	72	104
Harris	20	m	w	PRUS	San Francisco	San Francisco P O	83	141
Henry	38	m	w	NY	Contra Costa	Martinez P O	71	400
James	48	m	w	IREL	Sonoma	Bodega Twp	91	258
James	47	m	w	IREL	San Joaquin	3-Wd Stockton	86	227
James	45	m	w	PA	Sacramento	3-Wd Sacramento	77	318
James	33	m	w	NY	Stanislaus	Empire Twp	92	55
James	30	m	w	IREL	San Francisco	San Francisco P O	85	765
James	26	m	w	IREL	Sacramento	2-Wd Sacramento	77	234
Jas S	47	m	w	IN	San Luis Obispo	Santa Rosa Twp	87	318
Jeremiah	29	m	w	IREL	Sacramento	2-Wd Sacramento	77	233
John	63	m	w	IREL	Sacramento	4-Wd Sacramento	77	319
John	41	m	w	ENGL	San Francisco	San Francisco P O	83	168
John	34	m	w	IREL	San Bernardino	San Bernardino Twp	78	452
John	22	m	w	MA	San Francisco	7-Wd San Francisco	81	173
John W	23	m	b	MO	Tehama	Tehama Twp	92	194
Lewis	46	m	w	NY	San Francisco	8-Wd San Francisco	82	344
Mahala	49	f	b	VA	Shasta	Shasta P O	89	461
Mary	38	f	w	IREL	San Francisco	San Francisco P O	83	331
Mary	30	f	w	IREL	San Francisco	8-Wd San Francisco	82	345
Mary	22	f	w	NY	Sonoma	Santa Rosa	91	405
Mary	13	f	w	CA	Fresno	Kings Rvr P O	72	205
Mary	1	f	w	CA	Alameda	Oakland	68	183
Mary E	14	f	w	CA	Butte	Ophir Twp	70	96
Michael	36	m	w	IREL	Sacramento	2-Wd Sacramento	77	233
Michael	31	m	w	IREL	San Francisco	San Francisco P O	85	755
Michael	30	m	w	IREL	Tuolumne	Columbia P O	93	342
Micheal	11	m	w	MA	San Francisco	7-Wd San Francisco	81	173
Patrick	39	m	w	IREL	Sacramento	2-Wd Sacramento	77	209
Patrick	36	m	w	IREL	Sacramento	4-Wd Sacramento	77	348
Patrick	25	m	w	IREL	San Francisco	San Francisco P O	85	848
Richard	40	m	w	TN	Stanislaus	Empire Twp	92	40
Thomas	48	m	w	IREL	Santa Clara	2-Wd San Jose	88	320
Thomas	30	m	w	TX	Sacramento	Franklin Twp	77	112
Tom	26	m	c	CHIN	Alameda	San Leandro	68	97
W H	45	m	w	PA	Yuba	Marysville	93	604
Washington	41	m	w	IN	San Luis Obispo	Santa Rosa Twp	87	322
William R	32	m	w	MO	Nevada	Rough & Ready Twp	75	323
Wm	28	m	w	NY	San Francisco	11-Wd San Francisc	84	565
Wyatt	33	m	w	TN	Plumas	Indian Twp	77	13
COFFEEN								
Wm	55	m	w	MEXI	Mariposa	Mariposa P O	74	110
COFFER								
E V	31	m	w	MO	Siskiyou	Surprise Valley Tw	89	637
John	21	m	w	CA	Alameda	Oakland	68	171
Richard	30	m	w	IREL	Sutter	Nicolaus Twp	92	113
COFFERS								
J	38	m	w	MA	Alameda	Oakland	68	264
COFFEY								
Ann	37	f	w	IREL	San Francisco	San Francisco P O	83	341
Catharine	19	f	w	CANA	San Francisco	San Francisco P O	83	78
Danl	28	m	w	IREL	San Francisco	San Francisco P O	83	17
David	22	m	w	CANA	San Francisco	1-Wd San Francisco	79	63
Francis	36	m	w	CANA	Nevada	Bridgeport Twp	75	115
James	32	m	w	NY	Merced	Snelling P O	74	275
Johanna	45	f	w	IREL	San Francisco	1-Wd San Francisco	79	85
John	31	m	w	MA	San Francisco	San Francisco P O	80	414
Joseph	49	m	w	IREL	Santa Barbara	Santa Barbara P O	87	492
Joseph	45	m	w	IREL	San Francisco	San Francisco P O	83	3
Joseph	13	m	w	CA	San Francisco	San Francisco P O	83	178
Michael	32	m	w	IREL	San Francisco	San Francisco P O	85	785
Michael	30	m	w	IREL	Santa Clara	Fremont Twp	88	49
Micheal	30	m	w	IREL	San Francisco	7-Wd San Francisco	81	189
Thos	26	m	w	IREL	Solano	Vallejo	90	200
William	25	m	w	CANA	San Francisco	1-Wd San Francisco	79	63
COFFIELD								
John	48	m	w	IREL	Colusa	Monroe Twp	71	322
John	27	m	w	IREL	Yolo	Putah Twp	93	525
Thomas	35	m	w	IREL	San Francisco	8-Wd San Francisco	82	398
COFFIN								
Albert	50	m	w	MA	San Francisco	San Francisco P O	83	186
Albert	30	m	w	ME	Alameda	Oakland	68	247
Alonzo	24	m	w	MA	San Francisco	6-Wd San Francisco	81	92
Charles	23	m	w	NY	San Francisco	11-Wd San Francisc	84	464
Christph C	36	m	w	MA	Santa Cruz	Santa Cruz	89	431
Cyrus S	45	m	w	MA	Sacramento	3-Wd Sacramento	77	301
Dan	82	m	w	MA	San Francisco	11-Wd San Francisc	84	665
David Jr	55	m	w	ME	Santa Clara	Santa Clara Twp	88	166
E F	16	m	w	CA	Alameda	Oakland	68	243
Ed A	45	m	w	MA	San Francisco	San Francisco P O	83	105
Edward	28	m	w	RI	San Francisco	7-Wd San Francisco	81	173
F	32	m	w	MA	Alameda	Oakland	68	247
Fannie	12	f	w	AUSL	Santa Clara	2-Wd San Jose	88	337
Frank	40	m	w	MA	Alameda	Oakland	68	261
Frederick	35	m	w	ME	Santa Clara	2-Wd San Jose	88	284
Frederick F	30	m	w	MA	Santa Clara	2-Wd San Jose	88	291
Fredk E	37	m	w	OH	San Francisco	San Francisco P O	85	729
Geo	40	m	w	ITAL	San Joaquin	2-Wd Stockton	86	210
George	58	m	w	MA	San Francisco	San Francisco P O	83	85
George	43	m	w	MA	Contra Costa	Martinez Twp	71	351
Gilbert	49	m	w	MA	San Francisco	6-Wd San Francisco	81	94
Henry	54	m	w	MA	San Francisco	8-Wd San Francisco	82	413
Henry	31	m	w	NH	San Francisco	1-Wd San Francisco	79	22
Isaac T	37	m	w	NH	Placer	Dutch Flat P O	76	404
J W	35	m	w	MA	Mendocino	Calpella Twp	74	184
James	24	m	w	NY	San Francisco	San Francisco P O	83	75
John	9	m	w	CA	Santa Clara	Santa Clara Twp	88	177

© 2001 by Heritage Quest. All rights reserved.

Name	Age	S	R	B-PL	County	Locale (Series M593)	Roll	Pg
John	62	m	w	NY	San Francisco	San Francisco P O	80	360
John	29	m	w	ENGL	San Francisco	2-Wd San Francisco	79	236
John F	47	m	w	MA	San Francisco	8-Wd San Francisco	82	494
Joseph	47	m	w	MA	Contra Costa	Martinez Twp	71	351
Kate	25	f	w	WI	San Francisco	8-Wd San Francisco	82	359
Lewis	36	m	w	MA	Solano	Vallejo	90	166
Lincoln A	30	m	w	ME	San Francisco	San Francisco P O	83	15
Louisa	35	f	w	RUSS	San Francisco	7-Wd San Francisco	81	245
Mary	65	f	w	MA	San Francisco	11-Wd San Francisc	84	543
Mary	49	f	w	OH	Solano	Suisun Twp	90	114
Matilda	13	f	w	AR	Tulare	Visalia Twp	92	284
Michael	45	m	w	IREL	San Francisco	San Francisco P O	83	357
N M	67	m	w	NY	El Dorado	Greenwood Twp	72	51
Obed	22	m	w	MA	San Joaquin	Tulare Twp	86	254
Oliver	57	m	w	MA	Contra Costa	Martinez Twp	71	352
Oliver	36	m	w	IN	El Dorado	Placerville Twp	72	94
Oliver	35	m	w	MA	San Joaquin	Castoria Twp	86	11
Oliver	34	m	w	IN	El Dorado	Placerville Twp	72	93
Peter	49	m	w	MA	San Francisco	San Francisco P O	80	381
Robert	52	m	w	MA	San Francisco	7-Wd San Francisco	81	171
Rodolphus	31	m	w	MA	San Francisco	11-Wd San Francisc	84	559
Samuel	30	m	w	ME	Stanislaus	Empire Twp	92	42
W	36	m	w	ME	Alameda	Oakland	68	255
William H	24	m	w	IL	El Dorado	White Oak Twp	72	140
William L	40	m	w	MA	Placer	Bath P O	76	423
Wm	48	m	w	IREL	San Francisco	11-Wd San Francisc	84	612
Wm	16	m	w	CA	Butte	Ophir Twp	70	107
Zenas	38	m	w	MA	San Francisco	San Francisco P O	83	41
COFFINS								
Albert	29	m	w	CANA	Placer	Lincoln P O	76	492
COFFLE								
Solomon	32	m	w	POLA	Monterey	Monterey	74	366
COFFLIN								
C A	39	m	w	VA	Santa Clara	Gilroy Twp	88	99
William	41	m	w	IREL	Yuba	Marysville	93	607
COFFMAN								
Charissa J	27	f	w	AL	El Dorado	White Oak Twp	72	141
Charles A	37	m	w	VA	Los Angeles	Los Angeles	73	504
Daniel	61	m	w	OH	Mendocino	Calpella Twp	74	188
Dick	20	m	i	CA	Monterey	San Benito Twp	74	382
E	38	m	w	TN	Lake	Lower Lake	73	414
E R	32	m	w	VA	Yuba	W Bear Rvr Twp	93	684
George	43	m	w	PRUS	San Bernardino	Chino Twp	78	412
I N	38	m	w	TN	Lake	Lower Lake	73	420
J	55	m	w	OH	Amador	Ione City P O	69	365
Jacob	37	m	w	PRUS	San Francisco	1-Wd San Francisco	79	57
John	33	m	w	MO	Colusa	Colusa Twp	71	278
John	21	m	w	MO	Nevada	Grass Valley Twp	75	221
John J	20	m	w	VA	Sonoma	Bodega Twp	91	264
L J Mrs	27	f	w	IL	Lake	Upper Lake	73	409
Martin	53	m	w	VA	Sonoma	Bodega Twp	91	264
W	34	m	w	IL	Lake	Upper Lake	73	408
W C	33	m	w	IL	Del Norte	Smith Rvr Twp	71	479
Wm F	37	m	w	VA	Mariposa	Mariposa P O	74	123
COFFRAN								
Adriana	23	f	w	MA	Solano	Suisun Twp	90	113
F C	43	m	w	KY	Marin	San Rafael Twp	74	41
COFFREN								
Elizabeth	54	f	w	IREL	San Francisco	San Francisco P O	83	198
COFFREY								
Marnence	42	m	w	CHIL	Sacramento	2-Wd Sacramento	77	222
COFFRIN								
James	33	m	w	ME	Santa Clara	Santa Clara Twp	88	148
COFFRON								
John	48	m	w	NY	San Francisco	8-Wd San Francisco	82	364
COFFROTH								
Edwin	28	m	w	VA	Sacramento	1-Wd Sacramento	77	172
Jas	40	m	w	PA	Sacramento	3-Wd Sacramento	77	259
COFFYN								
David	38	m	w	ENGL	Placer	Emigrant Gap P O	76	416
Steven	46	m	w	ENGL	Placer	Emigrant Gap P O	76	416
COFIELD								
F	38	m	w	HANO	Sierra	Forest Twp	89	531
J	69	m	w	HANO	Sierra	Forest Twp	89	531
COFLIN								
Daniel N	29	m	w	NY	Alpine	Monitor P O	69	313
Dennis	38	m	w	IREL	Solano	Silveyville Twp	90	79
COFMAN								
Isaac	50	m	w	VA	San Diego	San Diego	78	509
COG								
Ah	29	m	c	CHIN	Nevada	Meadow Lake Twp	75	266
Ah	24	m	c	CHIN	Nevada	Eureka Twp	75	141
COGAN								
Ann	30	f	w	IREL	San Francisco	San Francisco P O	85	746
Ellen	50	f	w	IREL	San Francisco	San Francisco P O	83	2
Hannah	29	f	w	IREL	San Joaquin	2-Wd Stockton	86	163
Joannah	32	f	w	IREL	San Francisco	6-Wd San Francisco	81	118
John	40	m	w	IREL	San Francisco	1-Wd San Francisco	79	19
John	28	m	w	IREL	San Francisco	7-Wd San Francisco	81	197
Michael	64	m	w	IREL	Tuolumne	Columbia P O	93	355
Michael	36	m	w	IREL	San Francisco	San Francisco P O	83	70
Morris	42	m	w	IREL	San Francisco	7-Wd San Francisco	81	198
Patrick	33	m	w	IREL	San Francisco	San Francisco P O	85	745
Thomas	32	m	w	IREL	San Francisco	2-Wd San Francisco	79	184
Wm	21	m	w	IREL	San Francisco	11-Wd San Francisc	84	695
COGANTES								
Ruciano	37	m	w	MEXI	San Luis Obispo	San Luis Obispo Tw	87	313

Name	Age	S	R	B-PL	County	Locale (Series M593)	Roll	Pg
COGAR								
Benjamin	35	m	m	IL	Sacramento	2-Wd Sacramento	77	241
John	32	m	w	ENGL	Nevada	Nevada Twp	75	315
William	6	m	m	CA	Sacramento	2-Wd Sacramento	77	241
COGART								
Chas	36	m	w	FRAN	San Joaquin	1-Wd Stockton	86	132
COGEN								
James	45	m	w	IREL	San Francisco	San Francisco P O	83	419
COGER								
Matilda	61	f	w	VA	Sonoma	Healdsburg & Mendo	91	278
COGET								
J	45	m	w	FRAN	Sierra	Lincoln Twp	89	550
COGGENS								
Wm	13	m	w	CA	San Joaquin	Dent Twp	86	19
COGGER								
John	30	m	w	ENGL	San Francisco	San Francisco P O	83	7
COGGESHALL								
E	42	f	w	MA	San Francisco	San Francisco P O	83	277
F	50	m	w	MA	Alameda	Oakland	68	232
Jno H	46	m	w	RI	Shasta	Stillwater P O	89	479
COGGIN								
John R	37	m	w	GA	San Diego	San Diego	78	505
COGGINS								
Edward H	47	m	w	ME	Sacramento	2-Wd Sacramento	77	241
Isaac	33	m	w	NH	San Francisco	7-Wd San Francisco	81	163
Praschal	47	m	w	PA	San Francisco	San Francisco P O	83	302
S M	27	f	w	NY	Sacramento	3-Wd Sacramento	77	266
Zacchariah	46	m	w	GA	Butte	Mountain Spring Tw	70	87
COGGSHELL								
George	44	m	w	MA	Sacramento	4-Wd Sacramento	77	362
Uriah	38	m	w	PA	San Francisco	5-Wd San Francisco	81	33
COGGSWELL								
Jno K	27	m	w	MA	San Francisco	5-Wd San Francisco	81	23
Lucius	54	m	w	CT	Calaveras	Copperopolis P O	70	241
Oliver A	39	m	w	CT	Amador	Volcano P O	69	386
COGHEN								
James	30	m	w	MA	San Francisco	6-Wd San Francisco	81	115
COGHILL								
R A	12	m	w	CA	Alameda	Oakland	68	243
W	12	m	w	CA	Solano	Benicia	90	21
William E	40	m	w	NY	San Francisco	6-Wd San Francisco	81	100
COGHLAN								
Jas	32	m	w	IREL	San Francisco	7-Wd San Francisco	81	252
COGLAN								
John M	35	m	w	KY	Solano	Suisun Twp	90	94
Mik	56	m	w	IREL	Butte	Kimshew Tpw	70	82
COGLEY								
James	51	m	w	IREL	Butte	Oregon Twp	70	132
COGLIN								
Chas	23	m	w	CANA	Sacramento	4-Wd Sacramento	77	338
Daniel	42	m	w	IREL	Nevada	Eureka Twp	75	139
Jerry	40	m	w	IREL	Butte	Concow Twp	70	7
Micheal	41	m	w	IREL	San Francisco	7-Wd San Francisco	81	172
COGSDIL								
Samuel D	45	m	w	NY	Placer	Emigrant Gap P O	76	416
COGSHALL								
A	54	m	w	KY	San Joaquin	2-Wd Stockton	86	200
COGSWELL								
E B	47	m	w	MA	San Joaquin	Douglas Twp	86	37
Edson	35	m	w	NY	Stanislaus	Branch Twp	92	1
Henry D	50	m	w	CT	San Francisco	1-Wd San Francisco	79	103
J P	53	m	w	NY	Alameda	Oakland	68	162
James	40	m	w	CT	San Francisco	11-Wd San Francisc	84	640
James K	22	m	w	WI	San Francisco	San Francisco P O	83	147
Louisa	30	f	w	VT	San Mateo	San Mateo P O	87	356
Nathl	63	m	w	PA	Santa Cruz	Santa Cruz Twp	89	383
Samuel	52	m	w	NY	Placer	Auburn P O	76	375
W	35	m	w	CT	Lake	Upper Lake	73	408
Warren	40	m	w	CANA	Solano	Vallejo	90	149
COGUARD								
Joseph	42	m	w	FRAN	Nevada	Little York Twp	75	235
COGUN								
Jno	54	m	w	IREL	Santa Clara	Burnett Twp	88	38
COGWELL								
F	32	m	w	CT	Sacramento	Natomas Twp	77	170
COH								
Hem	40	m	c	CHIN	Calaveras	San Andreas P O	70	171
COHA								
J W	27	m	w	PORT	Santa Clara	Gilroy Twp	88	95
COHAM								
Abraham P	33	m	w	PRUS	Sonoma	Petaluma Twp	91	312
Nancy	46	f	w	NY	Butte	Ophir Twp	70	94
COHAN								
E	45	m	w	MI	San Joaquin	Elkhorn Twp	86	62
L B	40	m	w	BADE	Alameda	Oakland	68	180
Patrick	38	m	w	IREL	Calaveras	San Andreas P O	70	170
COHEA								
Geroldine	35	f	w	NY	San Francisco	11-Wd San Francisc	84	523
COHEL								
John	40	m	w	OH	Alameda	Murray Twp	68	115
COHELANE								
Honora	23	f	w	IREL	San Francisco	11-Wd San Francisc	84	671
COHEN								
A	37	m	w	PRUS	San Joaquin	Elliott Twp	86	74
A	35	f	w	GERM	San Joaquin	2-Wd Stockton	86	172
A A	40	m	w	ENGL	Alameda	Alameda	68	1
Abraham	49	m	w	POLA	San Francisco	San Francisco P O	83	366

© 2001 by Heritage Quest. All rights reserved.

Name	Age	S	R	B-PL	County	Locale	Series M593 Roll	Pg
Abram	39	m	w	PRUS	San Francisco	San Francisco P O	83	9
Abram	24	m	w	PRUS	San Francisco	San Francisco P O	80	348
Adolph	31	m	w	PRUS	Los Angeles	Los Angeles	73	525
Alex	48	m	w	ENGL	Alameda	Alameda	68	14
Alfred	12	m	w	CA	San Francisco	11-Wd San Francisc	84	648
Ann	40	f	w	IREL	San Francisco	San Francisco P O	83	171
B	42	m	w	PRUS	Solano	Vallejo	90	172
B	22	m	w	PRUS	Yuba	Marysville	93	595
Benjm	40	m	w	RUSS	San Francisco	8-Wd San Francisco	82	343
Bernard	22	m	w	PRUS	San Francisco	8-Wd San Francisco	82	345
Bernhartz	32	m	w	PRUS	Los Angeles	Los Angeles	73	532
Bridget	28	f	w	IREL	San Francisco	8-Wd San Francisco	82	311
C	40	m	w	RUSS	Sacramento	1-Wd Sacramento	77	177
C A	15	f	w	CA	Tuolumne	Sonora P O	93	307
Caroline F	30	f	w	NY	San Francisco	1-Wd San Francisco	79	111
Casper	31	m	w	PRUS	Los Angeles	Los Angeles	73	567
Casper	20	m	w	PRUS	Los Angeles	Los Angeles	73	525
Charles L	30	m	w	PRUS	San Francisco	6-Wd San Francisco	81	40
Daniel	40	m	w	IREL	San Francisco	San Francisco P O	83	163
Daniel	28	m	w	POLA	Sacramento	4-Wd Sacramento	77	342
David	80	m	w	RUSS	San Francisco	11-Wd San Francisc	84	565
David	44	m	w	PRUS	San Francisco	11-Wd San Francisc	84	466
Dora	17	f	w	PRUS	San Francisco	11-Wd San Francisc	84	423
E	36	m	w	PRUS	Yuba	Marysville	93	595
Edmund	23	m	w	FRAN	San Francisco	6-Wd San Francisco	81	112
Edward	10	m	w	CA	San Francisco	11-Wd San Francisc	84	648
Ellen	22	f	w	IREL	San Francisco	8-Wd San Francisco	82	321
Frank	30	m	w	PRUS	San Joaquin	1-Wd Stockton	86	151
Frank	22	m	w	SWED	San Francisco	1-Wd San Francisco	79	121
George	26	m	w	PRUS	San Francisco	San Francisco P O	80	429
Gerson	29	m	w	PRUS	Colusa	Grand Island Twp	71	302
Godfrey	40	m	w	BADE	Monterey	San Juan Twp	74	409
Harris	49	m	w	PRUS	San Francisco	San Francisco P O	80	485
Henry	50	m	w	PRUS	Calaveras	San Andreas P O	70	191
Henry	49	m	w	ENGL	San Francisco	San Francisco P O	83	363
Henry L	32	m	w	PA	San Francisco	San Francisco P O	83	50
Herman	46	m	w	PRUS	Los Angeles	Los Angeles	73	549
Hypolite	21	m	w	AFRI	San Francisco	6-Wd San Francisco	81	112
Isaac	60	m	w	RUSS	San Francisco	1-Wd San Francisco	79	60
Isaac	22	m	w	PRUS	Los Angeles	Los Angeles	73	524
Isaac H	36	m	w	PRUS	San Francisco	8-Wd San Francisco	82	397
Isador	44	m	w	PRUS	Los Angeles	Los Angeles	73	548
Isadore	33	m	w	PRUS	Yuba	Marysville	93	584
Isaiah	55	m	w	POLA	San Francisco	8-Wd San Francisco	82	313
Iseral L	52	m	w	PRUS	Sonoma	Healdsburg & Mendo	91	280
Jacob	56	m	w	PRUS	San Francisco	San Francisco P O	83	390
Jacob	45	m	w	PRUS	San Francisco	San Francisco P O	83	377
Jacob	29	m	w	HOLL	San Francisco	11-Wd San Francisc	84	447
Jacob	25	m	w	PRUS	San Joaquin	1-Wd Stockton	86	134
James	40	m	w	ENGL	San Francisco	San Francisco P O	80	484
James	37	m	w	PRUS	San Francisco	San Francisco P O	83	379
James	32	m	w	CT	El Dorado	Cosumnes Twp	72	18
Joseph	25	m	w	PRUS	Los Angeles	Los Angeles	73	567
Julia	24	f	w	BAVA	San Francisco	8-Wd San Francisco	82	474
Julia	18	f	w	PRUS	San Francisco	San Francisco P O	80	414
Louis	42	m	w	PRUS	San Francisco	San Francisco P O	83	306
Louis	38	m	w	PRUS	San Francisco	San Francisco P O	80	475
Louis	33	m	w	PRUS	San Francisco	San Francisco P O	83	367
Louis	32	m	w	PRUS	Siskiyou	Yreka	89	652
Lydia	18	f	w	IA	San Joaquin	Douglas Twp	86	41
M	49	m	w	ENGL	San Joaquin	2-Wd Stockton	86	159
Maggie	20	f	w	IREL	San Francisco	11-Wd San Francisc	84	580
Marcus	28	m	w	POLA	San Francisco	San Francisco P O	83	218
Margaret	37	f	w	IREL	San Francisco	San Francisco P O	83	301
Martin	50	m	w	PRUS	San Francisco	8-Wd San Francisco	82	351
Mary G	28	f	w	CHIL	Sacramento	Franklin Twp	77	119
Mary J	30	f	w	NY	San Francisco	8-Wd San Francisco	82	384
Maurice	28	m	w	PRUS	San Francisco	San Francisco P O	83	197
Max	30	m	w	PRUS	San Diego	San Diego	78	487
Michael	41	m	w	PRUS	San Bernardino	San Bernardino Twp	78	414
Michel	52	m	w	FRAN	Contra Costa	Martinez P O	71	383
Morris	43	m	w	BADE	San Francisco	San Francisco P O	83	24
Morris	36	m	w	SAXO	San Francisco	2-Wd San Francisco	79	145
Morris	36	m	w	PRUS	San Francisco	San Francisco P O	83	280
Morris	26	m	w	PRUS	San Francisco	San Francisco P O	83	370
Nathan	35	m	w	POLA	San Francisco	San Francisco P O	83	199
Oscar	27	m	w	AL	Marin	San Rafael Twp	74	45
Peter	54	m	w	BAVA	San Francisco	2-Wd San Francisco	79	283
Phillip	26	m	w	OH	Siskiyou	Butte Twp	89	587
Rachel	28	f	w	PRUS	San Francisco	6-Wd San Francisco	81	113
Rudolph	32	m	w	PRUS	San Francisco	8-Wd San Francisco	82	299
Sam	30	m	w	PRUS	San Joaquin	Elliott Twp	86	74
Simon	43	m	w	HAMB	San Francisco	5-Wd San Francisco	81	3
Simon	40	m	w	POLA	Sacramento	Granite Twp	77	143
Simon	39	m	w	FRAN	Los Angeles	Los Angeles	73	542
Simon	32	m	w	PRUS	San Francisco	San Francisco P O	83	23
Simon	32	m	w	POLA	San Francisco	8-Wd San Francisco	82	294
Simon	18	m	w	POLA	San Francisco	San Francisco P O	83	352
Solomon	59	m	w	PRUS	San Francisco	San Francisco P O	83	61
Solomon	25	m	w	PRUS	San Francisco	San Francisco P O	80	476
Thomas	35	m	w	IREL	San Francisco	6-Wd San Francisco	81	95
Thomas	29	m	w	PRUS	San Francisco	San Francisco P O	80	428
William	49	m	w	ENGL	San Francisco	1-Wd San Francisco	79	53
William	22	m	w	PRUS	Marin	San Rafael Twp	74	35
Wm	56	m	w	IREL	San Joaquin	2-Wd Stockton	86	188
Wm	45	m	w	IREL	San Joaquin	3-Wd Stockton	86	242
Wm	21	m	w	OH	Lassen	Susanville Twp	73	443

Name	Age	S	R	B-PL	County	Locale	Series M593 Roll	Pg
COHENS								
John	43	m	w	NY	San Francisco	8-Wd San Francisco	82	445
COHIGILL								
Charles	19	m	w	NY	San Francisco	San Francisco P O	80	421
COHILL								
Augustus	32	m	w	CANA	Humboldt	Bucksport Twp	72	244
COHIMO								
Nicolas	35	m	w	CA	Los Angeles	Los Nietos Twp	73	585
COHIN								
Nathan	30	m	w	POLA	San Francisco	1-Wd San Francisco	79	118
S	36	m	w	PRUS	Sierra	Downieville Twp	89	517
COHL								
Frank	1	m	w	CA	San Francisco	San Francisco P O	83	141
Frederick	34	m	w	PRUS	Sacramento	2-Wd Sacramento	77	208
COHLE								
John	34	m	w	FRAN	Solano	Vallejo	90	200
COHLER								
Nicholas	40	m	w	PRUS	Solano	Rio Vista Twp	90	59
COHN								
A	39	m	w	PRUS	San Joaquin	1-Wd Stockton	86	135
A	36	m	w	PRUS	Sierra	Downieville Twp	89	514
Aaron	38	m	w	HAMB	San Francisco	1-Wd San Francisco	79	52
Abraham	22	m	w	BADE	Solano	Suisun Twp	90	103
Abram	46	m	w	PRUS	San Francisco	8-Wd San Francisco	82	377
Abram	30	m	w	PRUS	Solano	Suisun Twp	90	97
Adam	44	m	w	BAVA	Santa Barbara	Santa Barbara P O	87	451
Asher	33	m	w	PRUS	Plumas	Plumas Twp	77	33
Charles	49	m	w	HOLL	Stanislaus	Emory Twp	92	25
Chas	37	m	w	PRUS	Sacramento	3-Wd Sacramento	77	311
David	34	m	w	PRUS	Inyo	Independence Twp	73	324
David	32	m	w	PRUS	San Francisco	8-Wd San Francisco	82	380
Edward	45	m	w	PRUS	San Francisco	6-Wd San Francisco	81	118
Edward	43	m	w	PRUS	El Dorado	Placerville	72	111
Edward	42	m	w	BAVA	San Francisco	2-Wd San Francisco	79	284
Edward	13	m	w	CA	San Francisco	8-Wd San Francisco	82	443
Elias	34	m	w	PRUS	Kern	Havilah P O	73	336
Elkan	43	m	w	PRUS	San Francisco	8-Wd San Francisco	82	411
Fanny	30	f	w	IREL	San Francisco	11-Wd San Francisc	84	524
Francis	35	m	w	BADE	Solano	Montezuma Twp	90	65
Frederika	22	f	w	BAVA	San Francisco	2-Wd San Francisco	79	140
Godfrey	43	m	w	ENGL	San Francisco	8-Wd San Francisco	82	470
Gretchen	19	f	w	PRUS	San Francisco	San Francisco P O	85	820
H	44	m	w	RUSS	Lake	Lakeport	73	403
Hannah	25	f	w	NY	San Francisco	San Francisco P O	83	328
Harris	43	m	w	PRUS	San Francisco	San Francisco P O	83	290
Harris	37	m	w	RUSS	Santa Cruz	Watsonville	89	365
Henery	22	m	w	PRUS	San Francisco	7-Wd San Francisco	81	194
Henretta	19	f	w	PRUS	San Francisco	8-Wd San Francisco	82	418
Henry	45	m	w	BAVA	San Francisco	8-Wd San Francisco	82	472
Henry	40	m	w	POLA	Butte	Kimshew Tpw	70	76
Henry	35	m	w	PRUS	Santa Barbara	San Buenaventura P	87	433
Herman	26	m	w	PRUS	San Francisco	3-Wd San Francisco	79	322
I	25	m	w	GERM	Sacramento	1-Wd Sacramento	77	184
Ike	13	m	w	CA	San Francisco	San Francisco P O	83	307
Isaac	35	m	w	PRUS	San Francisco	San Francisco P O	83	282
Isaac	24	m	w	POLA	Mendocino	Ukiah Twp	74	236
Isaac	24	m	w	ENGL	Mendocino	Ukiah Twp	74	236
Isaac H	58	m	w	BAVA	Sonoma	Petaluma Twp	91	328
Isadore	38	m	w	PRUS	San Francisco	San Francisco P O	83	165
Isadore	32	m	w	POLA	San Francisco	7-Wd San Francisco	81	186
Isidore	55	m	w	POLA	San Francisco	7-Wd San Francisco	81	199
J C	45	f	w	MO	Lassen	Susanville Twp	73	444
Jabus	30	m	w	BADE	San Joaquin	Douglas Twp	86	47
Jacob	39	m	w	PRUS	San Francisco	8-Wd San Francisco	82	463
Jacob	37	m	w	PRUS	San Francisco	8-Wd San Francisco	82	477
Jacob	36	m	w	PRUS	San Francisco	1-Wd San Francisco	79	40
Jacob	20	m	w	PRUS	Kern	Bakersfield P O	73	360
Jacob M	44	m	w	POLA	San Francisco	San Francisco P O	83	22
James H	60	m	w	PRUS	Yolo	Cache Crk Twp	93	420
John	35	m	w	PRUS	San Francisco	8-Wd San Francisco	82	317
Julius	32	m	w	PRUS	San Francisco	5-Wd San Francisco	81	18
Lena	20	f	w	PRUS	Yolo	Cache Crk Twp	93	420
Lewis	19	m	w	PRUS	San Francisco	8-Wd San Francisco	82	338
Louis	40	m	w	PRUS	San Francisco	1-Wd San Francisco	79	45
Louis	39	m	w	NY	San Francisco	11-Wd San Francisc	84	443
Louis	31	m	w	PRUS	Los Angeles	Los Angeles	73	525
Louis	24	m	w	PRUS	San Francisco	8-Wd San Francisco	82	478
Louis M	42	m	w	PRUS	San Francisco	8-Wd San Francisco	82	450
Marcus	46	m	w	BAVA	San Francisco	11-Wd San Francisc	84	496
Martin	27	m	w	PRUS	San Francisco	6-Wd San Francisco	81	96
Marx	22	m	w	PRUS	San Francisco	8-Wd San Francisco	82	479
Mary	31	f	w	PRUS	San Francisco	7-Wd San Francisco	81	196
Mary	29	f	w	IREL	San Francisco	8-Wd San Francisco	82	313
Meyers	59	m	w	HAMB	San Francisco	San Francisco P O	83	328
Michael	32	m	w	PRUS	San Joaquin	3-Wd Stockton	86	236
Mina	38	f	w	BADE	San Luis Obispo	San Luis Obispo Tw	87	307
Morris B	35	m	w	PRUS	San Francisco	1-Wd San Francisco	79	115
Morris D	52	m	w	PRUS	San Francisco	3-Wd San Francisco	79	326
Myer	45	m	w	PRUS	Nevada	Grass Valley Twp	75	148
Nathan	40	m	w	GERM	San Francisco	8-Wd San Francisco	82	319
Nathan	28	m	w	PRUS	Solano	Silveyville Twp	90	88
Phil	40	m	w	GERM	Sacramento	1-Wd Sacramento	77	185
Phillip	51	m	w	PRUS	Solano	Vacaville Twp	90	117
Phillip	45	m	w	PRUS	Santa Clara	Gilroy Twp	88	81
R	39	f	w	FRAN	San Francisco	San Francisco P O	85	788
Rachel	70	f	w	PRUS	Amador	Jackson P O	69	325
Rosa	17	f	w	AUST	San Francisco	8-Wd San Francisco	82	424

© 2001 by Heritage Quest. All rights reserved.

Series M593

Name	Age	S	R	B-PL	County	Locale	Roll	Pg
S	42	m	w	NY	San Francisco	San Francisco P O	85	830
S L	25	m	w	HI	San Francisco	7-Wd San Francisco	81	250
Sam	32	m	w	PRUS	Alameda	Alameda	68	5
Samuel	32	m	w	PRUS	Los Angeles	Los Angeles	73	530
Simon	39	m	w	PRUS	San Francisco	8-Wd San Francisco	82	425
Simon	35	m	w	GERM	Los Angeles	Los Angeles	73	537
Simon	29	m	w	POLA	Butte	Kimshew Tpw	70	76
Simon	24	m	w	PRUS	San Francisco	San Francisco P O	83	141
Sinond	30	m	w	PRUS	Inyo	Bishop Crk Twp	73	312
Solomon	36	m	w	BAVA	San Francisco	11-Wd San Francisc	84	493
Solomon	26	m	w	PRUS	San Francisco	San Francisco P O	80	532
Thomas	30	m	w	IREL	Sonoma	Vallejo Twp	91	461
William	26	m	w	PRUS	San Francisco	San Francisco P O	83	177
Wm	37	m	w	PRUS	Yuba	Marysville	93	595
Wm	25	m	w	PRUS	San Francisco	8-Wd San Francisco	82	359
Wm	20	m	w	POLA	Yuba	Marysville	93	591
Wolf	26	m	w	PRUS	Colusa	Stony Crk Twp	71	331
COHNAN								
Wm P	41	m	w	KY	Sacramento	1-Wd Sacramento	77	173
COHORN								
William	59	m	w	PA	Inyo	Lone Pine Twp	73	331
COHRON								
Ed	25	m	w	NY	San Joaquin	2-Wd Stockton	86	192
Sam	40	m	w	NY	San Joaquin	2-Wd Stockton	86	192
COI								
Ah	32	m	c	CHIN	Sacramento	1-Wd Sacramento	77	200
COIL								
Charles	39	m	w	PA	Yolo	Cache Crk Twp	93	450
Dewitt	37	m	w	MO	Santa Clara	San Jose Twp	88	209
Harry	33	m	w	NY	San Francisco	5-Wd San Francisco	81	33
James	60	m	w	TN	Mendocino	Little Lake Twp	74	198
James	45	m	w	IREL	Sacramento	Sutter Twp	77	380
James	26	m	w	IREL	Humboldt	Eureka Twp	72	268
Mary	70	f	w	IREL	Trinity	Trinity Center Pct	92	205
Thomas	42	m	w	IREL	Trinity	Trinity Center Pct	92	204
COILE								
Francis	40	m	w	IREL	El Dorado	White Oak Twp	72	136
COIN								
Ann M	34	f	w	CANA	Monterey	San Juan Twp	74	416
Charles	25	m	c	CHIN	Alameda	Oakland	68	184
James	40	m	w	IREL	Solano	Tremont Twp	90	28
Santiago	45	m	w	CA	San Diego	San Luis Rey	78	514
COINE								
Winnefred	40	f	w	IREL	Yuba	Rose Bar Twp	93	659
COINER								
Alexr	28	m	w	VA	Monterey	Castroville Twp	74	333
Daniel	37	m	w	VA	Monterey	Alisal Twp	74	301
COING								
Martin	22	m	w	GERM	Santa Clara	Gilroy Twp	88	75
COJO								
Bill	20	m	i	CA	San Diego	San Luis Rey	78	512
COK								
Hung	39	m	c	CHIN	Nevada	Grass Valley Twp	75	206
COKE								
Thomas	24	m	w	ENGL	Santa Clara	1-Wd San Jose	88	254
COKELAND								
Evaline	38	f	w	MO	Sacramento	2-Wd Sacramento	77	226
COKELEY								
Mary	25	f	w	IREL	San Francisco	San Francisco P O	83	167
COKELY								
Catharine	2M	f	w	CA	San Francisco	11-Wd San Francisc	84	711
Jane	5	f	w	CA	San Francisco	11-Wd San Francisc	84	711
John	29	m	w	IREL	San Francisco	1-Wd San Francisco	79	83
Margaret	40	f	w	IREL	Sacramento	4-Wd Sacramento	77	368
COKER								
Edwd	45	m	w	ENGL	San Francisco	San Francisco P O	83	19
F B	28	m	w	GA	San Joaquin	Douglas Twp	86	43
Frances	75	f	w	VA	Tulare	Visalia Twp	92	283
Henry	70	m	w	GA	Tulare	Tule Rvr Twp	92	260
William H	30	m	w	ME	Placer	Bath P O	76	454
COKLEY								
Tim	31	m	w	IREL	Solano	Vallejo	90	194
COLA								
Peter	39	m	w	TUSC	Amador	Jackson P O	69	324
Sebastian	28	m	w	MEXI	Los Angeles	El Monte Twp	73	450
COLADA								
John	13	m	w	ITAL	San Mateo	Schoolhouse Statio	87	337
COLAHAN								
John T	31	m	w	MD	Santa Clara	1-Wd San Jose	88	240
William J	29	m	w	IREL	Santa Clara	1-Wd San Jose	88	243
COLAMER								
Geo W	34	m	w	OH	Tehama	Red Bluff	92	175
COLAN								
Marie	70	f	w	MEXI	Stanislaus	Empire Twp	92	27
COLANDER								
Mary	54	f	w	PRUS	San Francisco	San Francisco P O	83	385
COLANES								
Martini	31	m	w	AZOR	San Francisco	1-Wd San Francisco	79	130
COLARD								
W D	36	m	w	ME	Humboldt	Eureka Twp	72	282
COLARZEZ								
Ametata	6	f	w	MEXI	Los Angeles	Los Angeles Twp	73	480
COLASA								
Francisco	23	m	w	MEXI	Santa Clara	Burnett Twp	88	35
John	42	m	w	SWIT	El Dorado	Coloma Twp	72	10
COLB								
J R	40	m	w	NY	Sutter	Vernon Twp	92	135
COLBACK								
Wm	50	m	w	CANA	San Francisco	7-Wd San Francisco	81	234
COLBAKER								
Albert	28	m	w	OH	Placer	Roseville P O	76	353
Floren	59	m	w	BAVA	Sacramento	Center Twp	77	83
COLBERG								
Samuel	53	m	w	KY	Mendocino	Ukiah Twp	74	234
COLBERGER								
George	52	m	w	BADE	Nevada	Grass Valley Twp	75	204
COLBERN								
Charles	48	m	w	NY	Sonoma	Petaluma Twp	91	311
COLBERT								
Arthur	36	m	w	IREL	San Francisco	San Francisco P O	83	84
Edmund	45	m	w	IREL	San Francisco	1-Wd San Francisco	79	127
Elizth	23	f	w	IREL	San Francisco	San Francisco P O	83	94
James	30	m	w	IREL	Alameda	Murray Twp	68	101
John	26	m	w	MA	San Francisco	San Francisco P O	83	84
John	20	m	w	MA	Trinity	Junction City Pct	92	205
Mary	26	f	w	IREL	San Francisco	2-Wd San Francisco	79	204
Nicholas	40	m	w	IREL	San Francisco	8-Wd San Francisco	82	473
Patrick	35	m	w	IREL	San Francisco	7-Wd San Francisco	81	192
Peter	40	m	w	DENM	Mendocino	Big Rvr Twp	74	159
COLBERTSON								
J C	21	m	w	MS	Sacramento	Brighton Twp	77	73
COLBEY								
Jeremiah	30	m	w	MA	San Francisco	San Francisco P O	83	223
Michael	31	m	w	NY	Solano	Vacaville Twp	90	126
COLBIRTH								
Pelatiah	70	m	w	ME	Placer	Roseville P O	76	348
COLBORN								
E L	30	m	w	NY	Sutter	Yuba Twp	92	141
John C	44	m	w	ME	Sonoma	Petaluma Twp	91	347
Jos	30	m	w	CANA	Sierra	Sears Twp	89	557
Rebecca	28	f	w	MA	San Francisco	6-Wd San Francisco	81	114
COLBORTE								
Joanna	25	f	w	CA	San Francisco	11-Wd San Francisc	84	689
COLBRACH								
Thos E	38	m	w	MD	Siskiyou	Scott Valley Twp	89	615
COLBURN								
A H	56	m	w	MA	Tuolumne	Sonora P O	93	327
Brewer	27	m	w	IL	Sonoma	Analy Twp	91	218
Chas H	34	m	w	MA	San Francisco	6-Wd San Francisco	81	83
David S	32	m	w	ME	Solano	Maine Prairie Twp	90	45
E E	22	m	w	MA	Solano	Vallejo	90	200
Edwin A	44	m	w	ME	Stanislaus	Emory Twp	92	22
Geo S	40	m	w	VT	San Francisco	2-Wd San Francisco	79	203
Harvey	27	m	w	OH	Sonoma	Analy Twp	91	218
Henry S	42	m	w	ME	Napa	Napa	75	56
James B	57	m	w	MA	Placer	Roseville P O	76	355
Joseph E	45	m	w	ME	Napa	Napa	75	48
Phoebe	48	f	m	AL	Shasta	Shasta P O	89	459
Saml	51	m	w	VT	El Dorado	Kelsey Twp	72	58
Sanford A	27	m	w	MO	Yolo	Cache Crk Twp	93	445
Thomas	54	m	w	MA	San Francisco	San Francisco P O	80	403
Warren R	43	m	w	VT	Sonoma	Petaluma Twp	91	345
COLBURNE								
Richd	40	m	w	IREL	San Francisco	1-Wd San Francisco	79	17
COLBY								
A D	49	m	w	NH	Alameda	Oakland	68	225
Abram L	43	m	w	NY	Santa Cruz	Soquel Twp	89	445
Alonzo	33	m	w	ME	Santa Cruz	Santa Cruz	89	421
Anna	63	f	w	VT	Sonoma	Vallejo Twp	91	451
Arnold E	18	m	w	WI	Santa Barbara	Santa Barbara P O	87	490
C K	47	m	w	MA	Solano	Vallejo	90	142
Charles	39	m	w	NY	San Francisco	San Francisco P O	80	382
Claus	28	m	w	PRUS	San Francisco	San Francisco P O	80	467
E H	36	m	w	ME	Tuolumne	Columbia P O	93	340
Ebben E	25	m	w	MO	Humboldt	Bucksport Twp	72	244
Eben E	25	m	w	ME	Santa Cruz	Santa Cruz Twp	89	392
Edwin	12	m	w	WI	Sonoma	Analy Twp	91	222
F M	39	m	w	ME	Alameda	Oakland	68	267
G H	27	m	w	VT	Nevada	Nevada Twp	75	271
H H	30	m	w	VT	San Francisco	San Francisco P O	85	779
Helen	14	f	w	CA	San Francisco	11-Wd San Francisc	84	520
Hy Eugene	39	m	w	NY	San Francisco	San Francisco P O	83	21
James	60	m	w	IREL	San Francisco	San Francisco P O	83	258
James	47	m	w	MA	San Francisco	11-Wd San Francisc	84	542
James	27	m	w	MI	Nevada	Meadow Lake Twp	75	268
James Henry	22	m	w	ME	Plumas	Washington Twp	77	52
Jeramiah	42	m	w	NH	Placer	Rocklin Twp	76	468
Jeremiah	48	m	w	NH	Sacramento	4-Wd Sacramento	77	345
John	27	m	w	NY	San Francisco	San Francisco P O	83	418
Maddison	28	m	w	NH	Marin	San Rafael	74	51
Martha	30	f	w	VT	Marin	Bolinas Twp	74	5
Phillip	42	m	w	NJ	Kern	Havilah P O	73	337
William	42	m	w	ME	Mendocino	Albion & Big Rvr T	74	167
COLCLASUNE								
John	40	m	w	IN	Sutter	Butte Twp	92	96
COLCOTT								
Francis	14	f	w	CA	Nevada	Nevada Twp	75	287
COLDA								
Antone	26	m	w	PORT	Alameda	Eden Twp	68	84
COLDATI								
Alisandro	16	m	w	SWIT	Marin	San Antonio Twp	74	62
COLDBUCK								
Thomas	40	m	w	ENGL	Yolo	Cache Crk Twp	93	449

© 2001 by Heritage Quest. All rights reserved.

Series M593

Name	Age	S	R	B-PL	County	Locale	Roll	Pg
COLDER								
John	19	m	w	CA	Sonoma	Petaluma Twp	91	317
COLDREN								
Jasper	35	m	w	PA	Placer	Bath P O	76	457
COLDWELL								
Ellen	14	f	w	VA	San Francisco	8-Wd San Francisco	82	472
J B	32	m	w	GA	San Joaquin	Dent Twp	86	25
J C	38	m	w	MO	Monterey	Salinas Twp	74	310
James	48	m	w	MO	Stanislaus	San Joaquin Twp	92	81
John B	32	m	w	TN	Stanislaus	Empire Twp	92	64
Thomas A	34	m	w	TN	Stanislaus	Emory Twp	92	22
Thos	63	m	w	NY	Butte	Concow Twp	70	9
William	76	m	w	KY	Stanislaus	Buena Vista Twp	92	14
COLE								
A	43	m	w	MO	Lassen	Susanville Twp	73	444
A G	44	m	w	NY	Santa Clara	Gilroy Twp	88	72
Adam	28	m	w	OH	Sacramento	2-Wd Sacramento	77	225
Albert	31	m	w	NY	San Francisco	8-Wd San Francisco	82	426
Alexander	42	m	w	ME	Nevada	Little York Twp	75	242
Alexander	31	m	w	NY	Inyo	Lone Pine Twp	73	334
Alva	49	m	w	ME	Plumas	Plumas Twp	77	27
Andrew J	40	m	w	IL	Los Angeles	Los Nietos Twp	73	579
Annie	25	f	w	IREL	San Francisco	San Francisco P O	85	716
Asa	53	m	w	OR	San Joaquin	Tulare Twp	86	255
Asa	53	m	w	OH	Stanislaus	Buena Vista Twp	92	12
Austin	34	m	w	MA	San Francisco	5-Wd San Francisco	81	26
Barnard	55	m	w	IREL	San Luis Obispo	Morro Twp	87	287
Benjiman	35	m	w	IL	San Bernardino	San Salvador Twp	78	459
Benone	52	m	w	MO	Stanislaus	Empire Twp	92	63
Carrie	46	f	w	CT	San Francisco	San Francisco P O	80	344
Carrie E	27	f	w	CANA	San Francisco	3-Wd San Francisco	79	320
Casper	45	m	w	ITAL	Los Angeles	Los Angeles	73	526
Cassious	18	m	w	IL	San Joaquin	Oneal Twp	86	99
Charles	28	m	w	IL	Los Angeles	Santa Ana Twp	73	599
Charles H	23	m	w	PA	Stanislaus	Empire Twp	92	46
Charles L	47	m	w	NY	San Francisco	8-Wd San Francisco	82	372
Chas	47	m	w	NY	San Joaquin	Tulare Twp	86	264
Chas J	39	m	w	ENGL	Nevada	Rough & Ready Twp	75	330
Clementina	56	f	w	ME	San Francisco	11-Wd San Francisc	84	623
Conrad	31	m	w	PRUS	Butte	Ophir Twp	70	114
Cornelia	7	f	w	CA	San Francisco	6-Wd San Francisco	81	153
Cornelius	50	m	w	NY	Santa Cruz	Santa Cruz	89	435
Cornelius	47	m	w	NY	San Francisco	6-Wd San Francisco	81	153
D F	38	m	w	VT	Sierra	Lincoln Twp	89	545
Daniel	69	m	w	MO	Napa	Napa	75	27
Daniel	25	m	w	NY	Yuba	Marysville	93	577
David	46	m	w	NY	Napa	Napa	75	8
David J	22	m	w	NJ	Los Angeles	Santa Ana Twp	73	603
David J	20	m	w	NY	San Francisco	3-Wd San Francisco	79	314
David M	40	m	w	IREL	San Francisco	7-Wd San Francisco	81	287
Delos	44	m	w	NY	Santa Clara	San Jose Twp	88	182
Edmond C	52	m	w	MA	Napa	Napa	75	42
Edward	61	m	w	ENGL	San Francisco	San Francisco P O	85	850
Edward	26	m	w	NY	Sacramento	Franklin Twp	77	109
Edward	24	m	w	IREL	San Francisco	San Francisco P O	80	334
Edwd	28	m	w	NY	San Francisco	1-Wd San Francisco	79	71
Edwin M	43	m	w	NY	Santa Clara	Santa Clara Twp	88	142
Elija T	52	m	w	NY	San Francisco	6-Wd San Francisco	81	90
Ellen	38	f	w	IREL	San Francisco	San Francisco P O	83	348
Francis	30	m	w	ENGL	San Francisco	San Francisco P O	83	382
Frank	35	m	w	PRUS	Alameda	Murray Twp	68	124
G D	62	m	w	RI	Amador	Ione City P O	69	365
G W	38	m	w	NY	Amador	Lancha Plana P O	69	368
G W	37	m	w	NY	Sacramento	Center Twp	77	82
G W	30	m	w	MI	El Dorado	Coloma Twp	72	3
Geo C	33	m	w	OH	Alameda	Oakland	68	184
George A	36	m	w	ME	Santa Clara	Santa Clara Twp	88	145
George J	25	m	w	NY	Yolo	Cache Crk Twp	93	426
George M	44	m	w	VT	San Luis Obispo	Santa Rosa Twp	87	317
George W	43	m	w	IL	Los Angeles	Los Nietos Twp	73	579
Gustave	34	m	w	OH	San Francisco	7-Wd San Francisco	81	156
H V	20	m	w	MO	Sacramento	Franklin Twp	77	111
Harry	22	m	w	PRUS	Alameda	Oakland	68	213
Hattie	28	f	m	DE	Sacramento	4-Wd Sacramento	77	347
Henry	43	m	w	PA	Yolo	Cache Crk Twp	93	450
Henry	42	m	w	NY	Contra Costa	Martinez Twp	71	349
Henry	29	m	w	MO	San Joaquin	2-Wd Stockton	86	168
Hugh	62	m	w	NJ	San Bernardino	San Bernardino Twp	78	422
J	35	m	w	IREL	Alameda	Oakland	68	184
J F	48	m	w	NY	Sierra	Table Rock Twp	89	578
J H	48	m	w	NY	San Joaquin	Oneal Twp	86	112
Jacob	33	m	w	CANA	Humboldt	Eureka Twp	72	282
James	42	m	w	NY	Stanislaus	Empire Twp	92	49
James	39	m	w	NJ	Amador	Jackson P O	69	330
James	39	m	w	OH	San Bernardino	San Bernardino Twp	78	440
James	35	m	w	IREL	Nevada	Bloomfield Twp	75	93
James	30	m	b	MD	Sacramento	4-Wd Sacramento	77	347
James	28	m	w	NY	San Francisco	San Francisco P O	83	254
James	16	m	w	TX	Kern	Tehachapi P O	73	352
James A	29	m	w	NY	Butte	Chico Twp	70	23
James H	52	m	w	NY	Butte	Chico Twp	70	18
James H	30	m	w	AR	Los Angeles	San Juan Twp	73	628
Jas	57	m	w	IREL	Solano	Benicia	90	8
Jas J	43	m	w	OH	Siskiyou	Big Valley Twp	89	580
Jeremiah	36	m	w	NY	Humboldt	Arcata Twp	72	231
Jesse	64	m	w	ME	San Francisco	2-Wd San Francisco	79	228
Jesse	42	m	w	IN	Kern	Bakersfield P O	73	362
Jessie	21	m	w	MO	Nevada	Rough & Ready Twp	75	325
Jno	45	m	w	NY	Santa Clara	Gilroy Twp	88	100
John	72	m	i	CA	Tehama	Battle Crk Twp	92	172
John	60	m	w	IREL	Placer	Dutch Flat P O	76	404
John	54	m	w	ME	Santa Clara	Santa Clara Twp	88	142
John	42	m	w	ENGL	San Francisco	San Francisco P O	83	126
John	40	m	w	IREL	San Francisco	San Francisco P O	85	746
John	40	m	w	NY	Colusa	Stony Crk Twp	71	328
John	40	m	w	ME	San Francisco	11-Wd San Francisc	84	625
John	40	m	w	IREL	San Francisco	7-Wd San Francisco	81	218
John	39	m	w	ENGL	Humboldt	Eureka Twp	72	279
John	32	m	w	AL	Fresno	Kingston P O	72	218
John B	37	m	w	KY	Yolo	Cottonwood Twp	93	466
John H	34	m	w	ENGL	Solano	Vacaville Twp	90	118
John H	32	m	w	IA	Santa Cruz	Santa Cruz Twp	89	392
Joseph	31	m	w	NY	Santa Clara	Santa Clara Twp	88	167
Joseph	20	m	w	ENGL	Plumas	Indian Twp	77	17
Joseph	15	m	w	CA	Santa Cruz	Soquel Twp	89	439
Joseph H	38	m	w	ME	Santa Clara	Santa Clara Twp	88	142
Josiah	60	m	w	MA	San Francisco	San Francisco P O	80	404
Juan	23	m	w	NY	San Francisco	1-Wd San Francisco	79	115
Julian	23	m	w	NY	San Francisco	5-Wd San Francisco	81	13
L A	42	m	w	NY	San Francisco	San Francisco P O	83	282
Lamas	35	m	w	OH	Stanislaus	Empire Twp	92	40
Lewis	48	m	w	IREL	Mendocino	Anderson Twp	74	154
Lizzie	14	f	w	UT	San Francisco	San Francisco P O	83	47
Lomira	36	f	w	NY	San Francisco	11-Wd San Francisc	84	582
Lucius	21	m	w	OH	San Joaquin	2-Wd Stockton	86	171
Lyman	37	m	w	NY	San Francisco	1-Wd San Francisco	79	54
Lysander	57	m	w	ME	Stanislaus	Emory Twp	92	20
Maranda	30	f	w	ME	Humboldt	Eureka Twp	72	282
Marrowi	37	m	w	MO	Alameda	Washington Twp	68	296
Mary	36	f	w	IREL	San Francisco	11-Wd San Francisc	84	459
Mary	30	f	w	IREL	San Francisco	2-Wd San Francisco	79	193
Mary	20	f	w	BADE	Alameda	Eden Twp	68	58
N B	38	m	w	NY	Napa	Yountville Twp	75	79
Nathan	44	m	w	NY	Butte	Oroville Twp	70	140
Nathan P	39	m	w	NH	San Francisco	6-Wd San Francisco	81	117
Nathaniel	46	m	w	ME	San Francisco	11-Wd San Francisc	84	609
Nesbit	47	m	w	IREL	Siskiyou	Callahan P O	89	633
Obed	47	m	w	NY	San Joaquin	Tulare Twp	86	260
R B	43	m	w	VA	Alameda	Oakland	68	222
R E	50	m	w	OH	Alameda	Oakland	68	208
Reuben	43	m	w	ME	Tehama	Battle Crk Twp	92	172
Robert	42	m	w	NY	El Dorado	Placerville Twp	72	94
Robert	35	m	w	IN	Amador	Sutter Crk P O	69	411
Robert	35	m	w	OH	Amador	Sutter Crk P O	69	410
Robert	35	m	w	MI	Amador	Sutter Crk P O	69	400
Rufus	47	m	w	NY	Siskiyou	Cottonwood Twp	89	593
Saml	31	m	w	VA	Fresno	Kings Rvr P O	72	210
Sampson	69	m	w	TN	Los Angeles	Los Nietos Twp	73	579
Samuel	27	m	w	NJ	Alameda	Brooklyn	68	37
T Jefferson	26	m	w	MI	Amador	Ione City P O	69	361
Thomas	40	m	w	MA	San Francisco	San Francisco P O	85	782
Thomas	18	m	w	CA	Santa Clara	1-Wd San Jose	88	257
Thos S	47	m	w	TN	Nevada	Meadow Lake Twp	75	267
W H	47	m	w	MA	Sierra	Forest Twp	89	532
W L	22	m	w	NY	Sierra	Lincoln Twp	89	545
Warren	39	m	w	OH	Yolo	Grafton Twp	93	493
Wesley	35	m	w	OH	Plumas	Washington Twp	77	25
Willard	21	m	w	RI	Colusa	Colusa Twp	71	281
William	44	m	w	IREL	Santa Clara	2-Wd San Jose	88	326
William	41	m	w	IREL	Tehama	Red Bluff	92	183
William	38	m	w	IL	Napa	Napa	75	26
William	38	m	w	MA	San Francisco	3-Wd San Francisco	79	288
William	29	m	w	ENGL	Plumas	Rich Bar Twp	77	46
William	28	m	w	WALE	San Francisco	San Francisco P O	83	148
William J	33	m	w	ME	Santa Cruz	Watsonville	89	364
Wm	44	m	w	IOFM	El Dorado	Mountain Twp	72	67
Wm	28	m	w	IL	San Joaquin	Tulare Twp	86	249
Wm T	45	m	w	MO	Fresno	Kings Rvr P O	72	212
COLEBANK								
William	23	m	w	ENGL	San Mateo	Schoolhouse Statio	87	340
COLEDGE								
Sarah	5	f	w	CA	Amador	Volcano P O	69	379
COLEFORD								
John	29	m	w	CANA	Yuba	Marysville	93	610
COLEGAN								
Margaret	28	f	w	IREL	San Mateo	San Mateo P O	87	358
COLEGROVE								
John S	51	m	w	RI	San Mateo	San Mateo P O	87	359
COLEHAN								
Alice G	23	f	w	OH	San Mateo	San Mateo P O	87	352
COLEHOFF								
Philip	36	m	w	BAVA	Santa Clara	Fremont Twp	88	50
COLEHOWER								
L Mrs	26	f	w	MI	Amador	Jackson P O	69	326
Louisa	32	f	w	IL	Amador	Jackson P O	69	338
COLEMAN								
A N	46	m	w	NY	San Francisco	8-Wd San Francisco	82	379
Adam	54	m	w	PA	Solano	Green Valley Twp	90	40
Adna	30	m	w	OH	Humboldt	South Fork Twp	72	303
Adoram	38	m	w	NY	Shasta	Shasta P O	89	459
Alfred	49	m	w	ME	San Francisco	8-Wd San Francisco	82	344
Augustus	27	m	w	MA	Solano	Silveyville Twp	90	86
Bernard	32	m	w	POLA	Santa Clara	Fremont Twp	88	54
Catherine	41	f	w	IREL	San Francisco	7-Wd San Francisco	81	214

© 2001 by Heritage Quest. All rights reserved.

Name	Age	S	R	B-PL	County	Locale	Roll	Pg
						Series M593		
Charles	35	m	w	PRUS	San Francisco	San Francisco P O	83	234
Charles	33	m	w	PRUS	San Francisco	2-Wd San Francisco	79	238
Charles	21	m	w	POLA	Santa Clara	Fremont Twp	88	53
Christina	40	f	w	PRUS	San Francisco	San Francisco P O	80	359
Christopher	43	m	w	IN	Santa Clara	Fremont Twp	88	47
Clara B	24	f	w	LA	San Francisco	8-Wd San Francisco	82	312
Cris	24	m	w	NORW	Del Norte	Crescent Twp	71	456
Cyrus	30	m	w	PA	Alpine	Markleeville P O	69	311
D	25	m	w	IREL	Alameda	Oakland	68	150
D H	29	m	w	IREL	San Francisco	San Francisco P O	83	1
D O	22	m	w	IA	San Joaquin	Oneal Twp	86	104
Daniel	39	m	w	OH	Placer	Roseville P O	76	351
Daniel	27	m	w	IREL	San Francisco	San Francisco P O	83	153
David	72	m	w	NJ	Alameda	Eden Twp	68	89
David	44	m	w	ME	Butte	Kimshew Tpw	70	83
David	25	m	w	WI	Tehama	Toomes & Grant	92	169
David	24	m	w	NY	San Francisco	1-Wd San Francisco	79	128
David R	44	m	w	MA	San Francisco	8-Wd San Francisco	82	471
Ed	11	m	w	NV	San Francisco	11-Wd San Francisc	84	592
Edward	39	m	w	ENGL	Nevada	Grass Valley Twp	75	167
Edward J	29	m	w	OH	Calaveras	San Andreas P O	70	203
Edwin D	55	m	w	GA	Plumas	Plumas Twp	77	33
Ezekiel	67	m	w	ME	Mendocino	Little Lake Twp	74	203
Ezra	60	m	w	MA	San Francisco	San Francisco P O	83	170
Fred	26	m	w	MA	Napa	Napa	75	38
Frederick	47	m	w	HANO	Placer	Bath P O	76	437
Garry	26	m	w	IREL	San Francisco	1-Wd San Francisco	79	94
Geo G	33	m	w	GERM	Nevada	Eureka Twp	75	133
George	25	m	w	NY	Los Angeles	Los Angeles	73	545
George	23	m	w	BOHE	San Francisco	San Francisco P O	83	172
George W	30	m	w	TN	Los Angeles	Los Angeles	73	537
Green G	33	m	w	MO	Colusa	Colusa Twp	71	282
Gustus	13	m	w	CA	Santa Barbara	Santa Barbara P O	87	492
H G	38	m	w	IN	Santa Clara	Gilroy Twp	88	82
Harris	38	m	w	PRUS	Calaveras	San Andreas P O	70	193
Harry	6	m	w	CA	Santa Clara	Fremont Twp	88	54
Hartwell G	40	m	w	ME	Nevada	Grass Valley Twp	75	168
Henoria	70	f	w	DENM	San Francisco	11-Wd San Francisc	84	699
Hyman	40	m	w	POLA	San Francisco	San Francisco P O	83	177
J	28	m	w	IREL	Lake	Knoxville Mines	73	404
Jacob	49	m	w	POLA	Solano	Benicia	90	17
James	40	m	w	IREL	San Francisco	11-Wd San Francisc	84	668
James	33	m	w	OH	Siskiyou	Scott Valley Twp	89	608
James	28	m	w	NY	San Francisco	San Francisco P O	83	45
James	24	m	w	CANA	San Francisco	11-Wd San Francisc	84	706
James	24	m	w	IREL	Alameda	San Leandro	68	93
James P	41	m	w	IREL	Sonoma	Bodega Twp	91	264
Jas	47	m	w	NY	San Francisco	7-Wd San Francisco	81	277
Jas	27	m	w	NY	Sacramento	4-Wd Sacramento	77	322
Jas	23	m	w	MO	Sonoma	Santa Rosa	91	407
Jno	56	m	w	ENGL	San Francisco	11-Wd San Francisc	84	708
John	63	m	w	IREL	San Francisco	San Francisco P O	85	786
John	56	m	w	CT	Marin	Nicasio Twp	74	17
John	49	m	w	AL	Tulare	Venice Twp	92	277
John	37	m	w	IREL	San Francisco	2-Wd San Francisco	79	137
John	36	m	w	MS	Santa Clara	San Jose Twp	88	195
John	36	m	w	IREL	San Francisco	2-Wd San Francisco	79	243
John	35	m	w	SC	Sonoma	Salt Point	91	392
John	32	m	w	IREL	Contra Costa	Martinez Twp	71	346
John	31	m	w	NY	San Luis Obispo	San Luis Obispo Tw	87	303
John	29	m	w	IREL	San Francisco	San Francisco P O	80	374
John	28	m	w	IREL	Los Angeles	Los Angeles	73	504
John	27	m	w	IREL	Marin	Point Reyes Twp	74	23
John	26	m	w	ENGL	Plumas	Mineral Twp	77	23
John	26	m	w	IREL	San Francisco	San Francisco P O	83	14
John	25	m	w	IREL	Solano	Vallejo	90	159
John	25	m	w	LA	Inyo	Independence Twp	73	326
John	21	m	w	IREL	San Francisco	San Francisco P O	83	141
John	20	m	w	MO	Tehama	Red Bluff	92	174
John C	46	m	w	ENGL	Nevada	Grass Valley Twp	75	161
Joseph	66	m	w	NY	San Francisco	11-Wd San Francisc	84	494
Joseph	40	m	w	IREL	San Francisco	11-Wd San Francisc	84	476
Lucas	44	m	b	OH	San Francisco	San Francisco P O	80	423
Lysander	32	m	w	IN	Sonoma	Santa Rosa	91	406
Maggie	25	f	w	IREL	San Francisco	11-Wd San Francisc	84	537
Margaret	68	f	w	IREL	San Francisco	11-Wd San Francisc	84	460
Martha M	31	f	w	IREL	San Francisco	5-Wd San Francisco	81	5
Martin	40	m	w	PRUS	San Francisco	6-Wd San Francisco	81	105
Martin	35	m	w	IREL	San Francisco	San Francisco P O	83	158
Martin	25	m	w	IREL	Sacramento	Franklin Twp	77	119
Martin	24	m	w	IREL	San Mateo	Belmont P O	87	388
Mary A	25	f	w	IREL	San Francisco	8-Wd San Francisco	82	323
Michael	43	m	w	IREL	Santa Clara	Santa Clara Twp	88	155
Michael	40	m	w	IREL	Monterey	San Juan Twp	74	408
Michael	37	m	w	IREL	San Francisco	11-Wd San Francisc	84	584
Michael	25	m	w	IREL	Sacramento	2-Wd Sacramento	77	240
Morris	40	m	w	POLA	Contra Costa	Martinez P O	71	433
N E	28	m	w	IA	Sonoma	Washington Twp	91	471
N J	20	f	w	IREL	San Francisco	San Francisco P O	85	798
Napoleon	39	m	w	KY	Solano	Silveyville Twp	90	72
Oliver H	55	m	w	MO	Nevada	Grass Valley Twp	75	232
Oliver H	55	m	w	KY	Nevada	Grass Valley Twp	75	218
Oliver H P	55	m	w	KY	El Dorado	Diamond Springs Tw	72	33
Patrick	38	m	w	IREL	San Francisco	San Francisco P O	83	406
Patrick	30	m	w	IREL	San Francisco	San Francisco P O	83	247
Peter J	40	m	w	MD	Fresno	Millerton P O	72	150
Phineas	72	m	w	PA	Napa	Yountville Twp	75	84

Name	Age	S	R	B-PL	County	Locale	Roll	Pg
						Series M593		
Robt	41	m	w	IREL	San Francisco	11-Wd San Francisc	84	585
Sairoz	20	m	w	POLA	San Francisco	11-Wd San Francisc	84	505
Samuel	35	m	w	PA	Napa	Yountville Twp	75	84
Thomas	44	m	w	IREL	San Mateo	San Mateo P O	87	356
Thomas	35	m	w	MO	Colusa	Colusa Twp	71	282
Thomas	35	m	w	IREL	Santa Clara	2-Wd San Jose	88	316
Thomas	33	m	w	IREL	San Francisco	San Francisco P O	83	216
Thomas	32	m	w	MA	San Diego	Fort Yuma Dist	78	464
Thomas	30	m	w	IREL	Los Angeles	Los Angeles	73	557
Thomas	27	m	w	CANA	Nevada	Meadow Lake Twp	75	264
Thomas	24	m	w	MA	San Francisco	2-Wd San Francisco	79	251
Thomas E	37	m	w	IREL	Yolo	Grafton Twp	93	480
Thorn	29	m	w	IREL	San Francisco	2-Wd San Francisco	79	186
Thos	67	m	w	IREL	San Francisco	8-Wd San Francisco	82	342
Thos	42	m	w	IREL	Sierra	Table Rock Twp	89	579
Thos	30	m	w	IREL	San Francisco	1-Wd San Francisco	79	124
Thos	30	m	w	IREL	Butte	Kimshew Tpw	70	83
Thos	25	m	w	IREL	San Francisco	1-Wd San Francisco	79	59
Timothy	45	m	w	IREL	Nevada	Grass Valley Twp	75	180
Timothy	30	m	w	CANA	Placer	Rocklin Twp	76	465
William	43	m	w	VA	Placer	Alta P O	76	413
William	40	m	w	IREL	Santa Clara	1-Wd San Jose	88	233
William	37	m	w	ENGL	San Francisco	San Francisco P O	83	178
William	24	m	w	FRAN	San Francisco	San Francisco P O	80	484
Witton	43	m	w	MI	Solano	Vallejo	90	152
Wm	47	m	w	KY	Sonoma	Santa Rosa	91	406
Wm	36	m	w	PRUS	San Francisco	San Francisco P O	83	42
Wm	30	m	w	ME	San Francisco	1-Wd San Francisco	79	68
Wm	28	m	w	PRUS	San Francisco	1-Wd San Francisco	79	86
Wm	21	m	w	NORW	San Francisco	7-Wd San Francisco	81	281
Wm H	28	m	w	MO	Nevada	Grass Valley Twp	75	232
Wm Jas	35	m	w	ENGL	San Francisco	1-Wd San Francisco	79	115
COLEMBOCK								
Geo	53	m	w	BAVA	San Joaquin	2-Wd Stockton	86	199
COLEMORE								
Mary	22	f	w	IREL	Alameda	Oakland	68	203
COLENS								
Levi F	45	m	w	ME	San Francisco	San Francisco P O	83	14
COLER								
Benjamin	23	m	w	PA	Inyo	Bishop Crk Twp	73	317
Marie	33	f	w	PRUS	San Francisco	8-Wd San Francisco	82	437
COLERY								
Frank	61	m	w	CT	San Joaquin	3-Wd Stockton	86	240
COLES								
Augustus	40	m	w	MD	San Francisco	San Francisco P O	83	143
Eibert S	28	m	w	NY	San Diego	San Diego	78	500
George	46	m	w	ME	San Francisco	San Francisco P O	85	813
Thoms	47	m	w	NY	San Francisco	2-Wd San Francisco	79	247
COLESTACK								
William	31	m	w	OH	Alameda	Eden Twp	68	68
COLESTIEN								
Jobe	29	m	w	ITAL	San Joaquin	2-Wd Stockton	86	170
COLESWORTHY								
William A	41	m	w	MA	Calaveras	Copperopolis P O	70	248
COLET								
Louis	18	m	w	FRAN	San Francisco	2-Wd San Francisco	79	241
COLEY								
Elisabeth	25	f	w	OH	San Joaquin	Tulare Twp	86	253
Frederick	25	m	w	MA	Monterey	Monterey	74	361
H C	32	m	w	NY	San Joaquin	Tulare Twp	86	252
Henry M	20	m	w	OH	San Francisco	3-Wd San Francisco	79	318
Libbie	25	f	w	OH	San Joaquin	Castoria Twp	86	2
COLFER								
John	38	m	w	IREL	Alameda	Brooklyn Twp	68	53
Patrick	35	m	w	IREL	Santa Clara	2-Wd San Jose	88	309
COLFIN								
John	55	m	w	IREL	San Francisco	8-Wd San Francisco	82	318
COLGAN								
E A P	51	m	w	NY	Sonoma	Santa Rosa	91	399
Francis	32	m	w	IREL	Tulare	Visalia	92	297
COLGATE								
Henry	42	m	b	DE	Butte	Wyandotte Twp	70	143
John	14	m	m	CA	Butte	Wyandotte Twp	70	143
Luis G	50	m	w	ENGL	San Luis Obispo	Arroyo Grande Twp	87	276
Polly	28	f	i	CA	Butte	Wyandotte Twp	70	143
COLGEN								
Chs	25	m	w	IREL	San Francisco	2-Wd San Francisco	79	280
John	27	m	w	IREL	San Francisco	7-Wd San Francisco	81	168
COLGENON								
Louis	30	m	w	FRAN	San Francisco	San Francisco P O	80	347
Louis	30	m	w	FRAN	San Francisco	San Francisco P O	80	348
COLGIN								
William	28	m	w	IREL	Yolo	Grafton Twp	93	480
COLGLESSER								
Solomon D	34	m	w	OH	Sacramento	Brighton Twp	77	75
COLGROVE								
Henry H	46	m	w	NY	Santa Barbara	San Buenaventura P	87	434
J S	51	m	w	NY	Placer	Dutch Flat P O	76	401
Martin	21	m	w	IL	Placer	Blue Canyon P O	76	418
COLHORN								
R	37	m	w	PA	Sierra	Sierra Twp	89	565
COLHOWER								
Hattie	27	f	w	OH	Amador	Volcano P O	69	382
COLI								
James	42	m	w	NY	Placer	Dutch Flat P O	76	415
COLIER								
Peter	40	m	w	IREL	Alameda	Murray Twp	68	128

© 2001 by Heritage Quest. All rights reserved.

Series M593

Name	Age	S	R	B-PL	County	Locale	Roll	Pg
William	55	m	w	OH	Humboldt	South Fork Twp	72	300
COLIGEN								
John	33	m	w	IREL	Alameda	Murray Twp	68	128
COLIHAN								
William	22	m	w	IREL	Los Angeles	Los Angeles Twp	73	488
COLIMA								
Alfredo	20	m	w	CA	Los Angeles	Los Nietos Twp	73	589
COLIN								
Antonio	72	m	w	FRAN	Calaveras	San Andreas P O	70	186
John	37	m	w	US	San Joaquin	3-Wd Stockton	86	218
COLINE								
Christiana	34	f	w	NY	San Francisco	7-Wd San Francisco	81	202
Manuel	18	m	w	MEXI	Santa Clara	1-Wd San Jose	88	256
COLINS								
Charles W	40	m	w	MO	Inyo	Bishop Crk Twp	73	310
Hedley	38	m	w	OH	San Joaquin	Tulare Twp	86	263
John	42	m	w	IREL	Sacramento	Granite Twp	77	142
COLISON								
Joseph	48	m	w	ME	San Diego	San Diego	78	492
COLL								
Matilda E	25	f	w	MO	Stanislaus	Empire Twp	92	37
Nancy	75	f	w	MA	San Luis Obispo	Santa Rosa Twp	87	321
Peter	34	m	w	IREL	Nevada	Rough & Ready Twp	75	337
Thomas	37	m	w	KY	Nevada	Meadow Lake Twp	75	267
William	41	m	w	VT	San Francisco	8-Wd San Francisco	82	478
COLLAIS								
Maurice	14	m	w	DC	San Francisco	11-Wd San Francisc	84	587
COLLAMORE								
Andrew J	36	m	w	ME	Santa Cruz	Santa Cruz Twp	89	394
Peter	39	m	w	ME	Placer	Summit P O	76	496
Richard	50	m	w	ME	Santa Cruz	Santa Cruz Twp	89	391
COLLAN								
Thomas	38	m	w	IREL	San Francisco	8-Wd San Francisco	82	336
COLLANS								
Wm	38	m	w	ENGL	Calaveras	Copperopolis P O	70	238
COLLAR								
---	44	m	w	NY	Sacramento	4-Wd Sacramento	77	373
Mary	26	f	w	IREL	San Francisco	San Francisco P O	83	387
COLLARY								
John	31	m	w	IREL	San Francisco	San Francisco P O	85	780
COLLEEN								
James	20	m	w	IL	Mendocino	Ukiah Twp	74	238
Mary	27	f	w	ENGL	San Joaquin	1-Wd Stockton	86	141
COLLEER								
George	27	m	w	MO	Stanislaus	San Joaquin Twp	92	79
COLLEN								
Charles	32	m	w	ENGL	San Francisco	San Francisco P O	83	39
Louis	54	m	w	FRAN	Amador	Ione City P O	69	359
COLLENBERG								
Wilhelmina	44	f	w	PRUS	El Dorado	Cosumnes Twp	72	17
COLLER								
F	29	m	w	CANA	Alameda	Oakland	68	264
Thos	27	m	w	IREL	San Joaquin	2-Wd Stockton	86	192
COLLERTON								
M	35	m	w	NY	San Francisco	8-Wd San Francisco	82	374
COLLERY								
Edwin	12	m	w	CA	Alameda	Oakland	68	257
COLLES								
Eleshen	42	m	w	VT	San Joaquin	3-Wd Stockton	86	245
COLLET								
Alice	13	f	w	MO	Yolo	Cottonwood Twp	93	464
Samuel	41	m	b	CANA	Tuolumne	Sonora P O	93	321
William T	34	m	w	MO	Yolo	Buckeye Twp	93	408
COLLETT								
Alphonse	32	m	w	FRAN	Calaveras	San Andreas P O	70	200
Christopher	41	m	w	PRUS	San Francisco	San Francisco P O	80	425
John	37	m	w	PRUS	San Francisco	San Francisco P O	80	425
Joseph	65	m	w	ENGL	Butte	Mountain Spring Tw	70	89
William	35	m	w	NY	Stanislaus	Empire Twp	92	62
COLLETTI								
Patrice	24	m	w	ITAL	San Francisco	San Francisco P O	80	472
COLLEY								
James	42	m	w	ME	Nevada	Nevada Twp	75	275
James	32	m	w	OH	Amador	Drytown P O	69	417
Margaret	40	f	w	NY	San Francisco	San Francisco P O	83	312
Nellie	34	f	w	CHIL	Nevada	Meadow Lake Twp	75	263
Wm H	32	m	w	ME	Nevada	Nevada Twp	75	275
COLLICOTT								
T	62	m	w	ENGL	Sierra	Alleghany & Forest	89	534
Wm G	37	m	w	MA	Sacramento	Center Twp	77	85
COLLIE								
Susan	39	f	w	POLY	Alameda	Brooklyn Twp	68	39
COLLIEN								
William F	53	m	w	VA	Calaveras	Copperopolis P O	70	227
COLLIER								
Amos	26	m	w	MO	Placer	Bath P O	76	460
Benj H	48	m	w	NY	Santa Barbara	Santa Barbara P O	87	456
David	24	m	w	MO	Sonoma	Santa Rosa	91	404
David H	52	m	w	NY	Butte	Bidwell Twp	70	2
F S	13	f	w	CA	Sierra	Eureka Twp	89	525
Franklin	45	m	w	PA	Shasta	Millville P O	89	489
George	58	m	w	MA	Sacramento	2-Wd Sacramento	77	223
Ira	52	m	w	VA	Sonoma	Santa Rosa	91	394
Irba R	52	m	w	SC	Mariposa	Mariposa P O	74	107
J Warren	34	m	w	NH	Sacramento	2-Wd Sacramento	77	222
James H	46	m	w	NY	Nevada	Grass Valley Twp	75	190
Jane	59	f	w	NY	Santa Clara	1-Wd San Jose	88	260

Series M593

Name	Age	S	R	B-PL	County	Locale	Roll	Pg
John	57	m	w	ENGL	Nevada	Grass Valley Twp	75	216
John	56	m	w	NY	Nevada	Grass Valley Twp	75	190
John	40	m	w	IREL	Amador	Sutter Crk P O	69	405
Julia A	45	f	w	MA	El Dorado	Salmon Falls Twp	72	132
Kate	24	f	w	NY	Sacramento	4-Wd Sacramento	77	341
Michl	40	m	w	IREL	Alameda	Murray Twp	68	113
Orrin	33	m	w	NY	Sacramento	3-Wd Sacramento	77	312
Patrick	34	m	w	IREL	Amador	Sutter Crk P O	69	406
Robert	56	m	w	VT	Sacramento	2-Wd Sacramento	77	247
Wm G	42	m	w	KY	Merced	Snelling P O	74	267
Wm H	34	m	w	KY	Monterey	Castroville Twp	74	327
COLLIERE								
Peter	35	m	w	ITAL	San Francisco	1-Wd San Francisco	79	33
COLLIGAN								
John	36	m	w	IREL	San Francisco	San Francisco P O	85	801
Terence	30	m	w	IREL	San Francisco	San Francisco P O	80	369
Wm	25	m	w	IREL	San Francisco	San Francisco P O	83	130
COLLIN								
Aug	42	m	w	FRAN	Sierra	Sears Twp	89	555
Hattie	4	f	w	CA	Stanislaus	Empire Twp	92	40
Henry	46	m	w	ENGL	San Francisco	San Francisco P O	80	380
J H	33	m	w	PA	San Joaquin	3-Wd Stockton	86	229
John	27	m	w	IREL	San Francisco	San Francisco P O	83	269
Josephine	57	f	w	FRAN	San Francisco	11-Wd San Francisc	84	617
Margaret	24	f	w	IREL	San Francisco	8-Wd San Francisco	82	489
Robt	36	m	w	IREL	Sacramento	4-Wd Sacramento	77	323
Thomas	29	m	w	IREL	San Francisco	5-Wd San Francisco	81	35
COLLING								
A	38	m	w	IREL	San Joaquin	2-Wd Stockton	86	171
Daniel G	40	m	w	ME	San Luis Obispo	San Luis Obispo Tw	87	297
COLLINGE								
John	33	m	w	ENGL	Placer	Bath P O	76	457
COLLINGHAM								
Wm	28	m	w	ENGL	San Francisco	8-Wd San Francisco	82	331
COLLINGRIDGE								
Joseph	64	m	w	ENGL	Contra Costa	Martinez P O	71	384
COLLINGS								
John	33	m	w	ENGL	San Francisco	San Francisco P O	83	190
COLLINGSWOOD								
Charles	28	m	w	ENGL	Amador	Sutter Crk P O	69	397
COLLINGSWORTH								
John	40	m	w	ENGL	Plumas	Quartz Twp	77	41
COLLINGWOOD								
Andrew	58	m	w	NY	Mariposa	Mariposa P O	74	122
Geo	49	m	w	ENGL	San Joaquin	3-Wd Stockton	86	233
COLLINS								
---	37	m	w	IREL	San Joaquin	1-Wd Stockton	86	121
A W	39	m	w	SC	Santa Clara	Gilroy Twp	88	101
Aca	43	m	w	CANA	Alameda	Eden Twp	68	93
Albert F	29	m	w	VT	San Francisco	San Francisco P O	85	721
Anda	50	m	w	PA	El Dorado	Georgetown Twp	72	47
Andrew	45	m	w	IREL	San Francisco	8-Wd San Francisco	82	434
Andrew	35	m	w	IREL	Alameda	Eden Twp	68	92
Andrew W	33	m	w	PA	Calaveras	Copperopolis P O	70	262
Ann	65	f	w	IREL	Yolo	Grafton Twp	93	482
Ann	46	f	w	IREL	Yuba	Marysville	93	588
Anna	45	f	w	IREL	San Francisco	2-Wd San Francisco	79	283
Annie	85	f	w	OH	Stanislaus	Empire Twp	92	54
Anthony	52	m	w	MA	Butte	Chico Twp	70	16
Arnold	38	m	w	TN	Stanislaus	San Joaquin Twp	92	82
Barnard	30	m	w	SWED	San Francisco	7-Wd San Francisco	81	218
Barney	32	m	w	PRUS	San Francisco	San Francisco P O	83	395
Benjamin	28	m	w	IREL	Los Angeles	Wilmington Twp	73	638
Benjamin R	44	m	w	MA	San Francisco	San Francisco P O	83	358
Bridget	40	f	w	IREL	San Francisco	San Francisco P O	83	387
Bridget	40	f	w	IREL	Solano	Benicia	90	16
Bridget	30	f	w	IREL	San Francisco	8-Wd San Francisco	82	403
Bridget	29	f	w	IREL	Marin	Point Reyes Twp	74	22
C W	47	m	w	NY	Amador	Jackson P O	69	342
Can	50	m	w	IREL	San Joaquin	1-Wd Stockton	86	131
Charles	38	m	w	KY	Kern	Kernville P O	73	368
Charles	30	m	w	SWIT	Alameda	Murray Twp	68	123
Charles	22	m	w	PA	San Francisco	3-Wd San Francisco	79	323
Chas	55	m	w	PA	San Francisco	5-Wd San Francisco	81	21
Chas C	36	m	w	NY	Nevada	Little York Twp	75	240
Christian	33	m	w	IREL	San Francisco	San Francisco P O	80	387
Clara	29	f	w	MO	Santa Clara	Gilroy Twp	88	76
Clinton	38	m	w	OH	San Bernardino	San Bernardino Twp	78	432
Cornelious	50	m	w	IREL	San Francisco	11-Wd San Francisc	84	644
Cornelious	33	m	w	IREL	San Francisco	11-Wd San Francisc	84	458
Cornelius	40	m	w	IREL	Placer	Rocklin Twp	76	463
D J	49	m	w	NY	Tuolumne	Big Oak Flat P O	93	405
Damis	22	m	w	IREL	Napa	Napa Twp	75	75
Daniel	53	m	w	IREL	Placer	Bath P O	76	453
Daniel	41	m	m	IREL	Nevada	Grass Valley Twp	75	148
Daniel	40	m	w	IREL	Sacramento	2-Wd Sacramento	77	240
Daniel	24	m	w	IREL	San Francisco	San Francisco P O	83	318
Danl	35	m	w	NY	Sacramento	3-Wd Sacramento	77	262
David	70	m	w	MA	San Francisco	San Francisco P O	83	358
David	50	m	w	IREL	San Francisco	San Francisco P O	80	389
David	37	m	w	OH	Siskiyou	Scott Rvr Twp	89	604
David	32	m	w	NY	San Diego	Temecula Dist	78	526
Davis	38	m	w	IREL	San Joaquin	1-Wd Stockton	86	131
Dennis	49	m	w	IREL	Alameda	Oakland	68	146
Dennis	45	m	w	IREL	San Mateo	Belmont P O	87	374
Dennis	36	m	w	IREL	San Francisco	3-Wd San Francisco	79	296
Dennis	32	m	w	IREL	San Francisco	San Francisco P O	83	138

© 2001 by Heritage Quest. All rights reserved.

California 1870 Census

Name	Age	S	R	B-PL	County	Locale	Roll	Pg
Dennis	32	m	w	IREL	San Francisco	San Francisco P O	83	160
Dennis	28	m	w	IREL	San Francisco	5-Wd San Francisco	81	28
Dennis	27	m	w	IREL	San Francisco	7-Wd San Francisco	81	200
Dennis B	40	m	w	IREL	San Francisco	6-Wd San Francisco	81	117
Dennis D	50	m	w	IREL	San Francisco	San Francisco P O	83	37
E P	48	m	w	KY	Sacramento	San Joaquin Twp	77	401
Ed	30	m	w	OH	Humboldt	Pacific Twp	72	289
Edgar	32	m	w	NY	San Francisco	5-Wd San Francisco	81	12
Edward	39	m	w	ENGL	Mariposa	Mariposa P O	74	121
Edward	35	m	w	IREL	San Francisco	San Francisco P O	83	170
Edwd	50	m	w	IREL	Sonoma	Petaluma Twp	91	321
Edwd	40	m	w	PA	San Francisco	1-Wd San Francisco	79	33
Edwd	38	m	w	IREL	San Francisco	1-Wd San Francisco	79	4
Edwd	24	m	w	IREL	San Francisco	1-Wd San Francisco	79	135
Elizabeth	38	f	w	IREL	San Francisco	7-Wd San Francisco	81	186
Elizabeth	30	f	w	IREL	San Francisco	6-Wd San Francisco	81	94
Ellen	73	f	w	KY	Sacramento	3-Wd Sacramento	77	263
Ellen	20	f	w	IREL	San Francisco	2-Wd San Francisco	79	273
Ellen	15	f	w	IREL	Nevada	Grass Valley Twp	75	156
Ernstine	14	f	w	CA	San Francisco	San Francisco P O	83	182
Eugene	9	m	w	CA	Marin	San Rafael Twp	74	29
Eunice	71	f	w	NH	Santa Clara	1-Wd San Jose	88	276
Eunice	49	f	m	PA	San Francisco	6-Wd San Francisco	81	135
Felix	35	m	w	BELG	San Francisco	2-Wd San Francisco	79	146
Francis	62	m	w	VA	Yuba	Bullards Bar P O	93	549
Frank	55	m	w	PORT	Placer	Auburn P O	76	369
Frank	40	m	w	AL	Fresno	Kings Rvr P O	72	210
Franklin	26	m	w	NY	Mendocino	Point Arena Twp	74	209
Frederick	38	m	w	MA	El Dorado	Placerville	72	124
G	41	m	w	NH	Lassen	Janesville Twp	73	430
Geo	54	m	w	NY	Amador	Volcano P O	69	372
Geo	45	m	w	MD	El Dorado	Georgetown Twp	72	39
Geo	30	m	w	CANA	San Francisco	1-Wd San Francisco	79	69
Geo E	13	m	w	CA	Butte	Wyandotte Twp	70	144
Geo H	29	m	w	MA	San Francisco	8-Wd San Francisco	82	325
Geo N	45	m	w	OH	Santa Barbara	Santa Barbara P O	87	460
Geo W	16	m	w	CA	El Dorado	Cosumnes Twp	72	14
George	53	m	w	NY	Monterey	San Benito Twp	74	382
George	45	m	w	ENGL	Humboldt	Mattole Twp	72	287
George	40	m	w	MS	Tulare	Visalia	92	299
George	28	m	w	ME	Del Norte	Crescent Twp	71	457
George	28	m	w	OH	Monterey	San Juan Twp	74	397
George	26	m	w	CANA	Sonoma	Analy Twp	91	221
George U	35	m	w	ME	Santa Cruz	Santa Cruz	89	422
Germania	34	m	w	NY	San Diego	Temecula Dist	78	526
H	28	m	w	IL	Alameda	Oakland	68	212
Harry	38	m	w	NY	Tehama	Red Bluff	92	184
Henry	38	m	w	MO	Nevada	Eureka Twp	75	132
Henry	38	m	w	MO	Nevada	Bloomfield Twp	75	95
Henry	35	m	w	MO	Nevada	Eureka Twp	75	129
Henry C	21	m	b	MO	Santa Clara	San Jose Twp	88	180
Henry M	38	m	w	NY	El Dorado	Placerville	72	116
Henry T	34	m	w	ENGL	Nevada	Grass Valley Twp	75	182
Hin	29	m	w	NY	San Joaquin	3-Wd Stockton	86	228
Irene	30	f	w	MA	Alameda	Brooklyn	68	27
Isaac	62	m	w	MA	Nevada	Nevada Twp	75	273
J	28	m	w	LA	Yuba	Marysville	93	591
J B	48	m	w	IREL	Sacramento	4-Wd Sacramento	77	334
J C	43	m	w	ENGL	San Francisco	San Francisco P O	85	877
J F	22	m	w	NY	Yuba	Marysville	93	594
J J	33	m	w	MO	San Joaquin	Elkhorn Twp	86	61
J L	32	m	w	RI	Amador	Amador City P O	69	391
J M	34	m	w	IN	Lake	Coyote Valley	73	400
J W	57	m	w	CANA	Solano	Vallejo	90	196
J W	30	m	w	MS	San Joaquin	Liberty Twp	86	82
James	54	m	w	ENGL	San Francisco	San Francisco P O	83	166
James	49	m	w	KY	Placer	Auburn P O	76	369
James	46	m	w	ENGL	San Francisco	3-Wd San Francisco	79	313
James	42	m	w	OH	Solano	Vacaville Twp	90	122
James	41	m	w	SWED	Fresno	Millerton P O	72	149
James	40	m	w	IREL	Santa Clara	2-Wd San Jose	88	309
James	40	m	w	IREL	Alameda	Eden Twp	68	71
James	40	m	w	IREL	Trinity	North Fork Twp	92	218
James	36	m	w	IREL	Yolo	Cache Crk Twp	93	446
James	36	m	w	IREL	Sacramento	2-Wd Sacramento	77	240
James	35	m	w	IREL	San Francisco	7-Wd San Francisco	81	240
James	35	m	w	IREL	Alameda	Oakland	68	266
James	34	m	w	VA	Mendocino	Casper & Big Rvr	74	164
James	31	m	w	IL	Marin	San Rafael Twp	74	42
James	30	m	w	IREL	San Francisco	7-Wd San Francisco	81	287
James	27	m	w	IREL	San Francisco	San Francisco P O	83	417
James	26	m	w	IREL	Santa Clara	Burnett Twp	88	36
James	21	m	w	NY	San Mateo	Pescadero P O	87	409
James	17	m	w	MA	Alameda	Hayward	68	76
James C	50	m	w	ENGL	San Francisco	6-Wd San Francisco	81	149
James T	42	m	w	KY	Monterey	San Juan Twp	74	411
James W	35	m	w	ENGL	San Francisco	8-Wd San Francisco	82	459
Jane	50	f	w	PA	Sacramento	4-Wd Sacramento	77	335
Jane	38	f	w	IREL	San Francisco	7-Wd San Francisco	81	201
Jane	24	f	w	IREL	Alameda	Oakland	68	181
Jas	38	m	w	IREL	Solano	Vallejo	90	198
Jas	24	m	w	IREL	Solano	Vallejo	90	197
Jas D	48	m	w	IREL	Sacramento	4-Wd Sacramento	77	334
Jeremiah	39	m	w	ENGL	San Francisco	San Francisco P O	83	184
Jeremiah	34	m	w	TN	El Dorado	Georgetown Twp	72	37
Jeremiah	30	m	w	IREL	Alameda	Oakland	68	204
Jeremiah	17	m	w	MA	Santa Clara	Santa Clara Twp	88	175

Name	Age	S	R	B-PL	County	Locale	Roll	Pg
Jerome	33	m	w	IREL	Napa	Napa	75	18
Jerry	45	m	w	IREL	Los Angeles	Los Angeles	73	507
Jerry	28	m	w	IREL	San Joaquin	2-Wd Stockton	86	203
Jessie	19	f	w	NY	San Francisco	5-Wd San Francisco	81	12
Johanna	25	f	w	MA	Sacramento	3-Wd Sacramento	77	305
Johanna	11	f	w	CA	San Francisco	11-Wd San Francisc	84	611
John	83	m	w	VA	El Dorado	Cosumnes Twp	72	13
John	75	m	w	IREL	Yolo	Grafton Twp	93	485
John	66	m	w	IREL	Sonoma	Bodega Twp	91	265
John	52	m	w	PRUS	San Francisco	1-Wd San Francisco	79	115
John	50	m	w	IREL	San Francisco	7-Wd San Francisco	81	202
John	50	m	w	IREL	Butte	Wyandotte Twp	70	142
John	50	m	w	MO	Siskiyou	Cottonwood Twp	89	592
John	48	m	w	NY	San Francisco	5-Wd San Francisco	81	12
John	47	m	w	PRUS	San Francisco	San Francisco P O	83	344
John	46	m	w	PRUS	San Francisco	1-Wd San Francisco	79	127
John	46	m	w	IREL	Calaveras	San Andreas P O	70	190
John	43	m	w	OH	Kern	Linns Valley P O	73	348
John	43	m	w	IREL	San Francisco	San Francisco P O	83	106
John	42	m	w	IREL	San Francisco	11-Wd San Francisc	84	426
John	40	m	w	MA	San Francisco	11-Wd San Francisc	84	457
John	40	m	w	IREL	San Francisco	11-Wd San Francisc	84	666
John	40	m	b	DE	San Francisco	San Francisco P O	80	417
John	38	m	w	NY	San Francisco	San Francisco P O	80	406
John	36	m	w	IREL	Napa	Napa Twp	75	74
John	36	m	w	IREL	Alameda	Eden Twp	68	87
John	36	m	w	IREL	San Francisco	7-Wd San Francisco	81	157
John	36	m	w	IREL	San Francisco	2-Wd San Francisco	79	213
John	35	m	w	ENGL	Amador	Sutter Crk P O	69	409
John	35	m	w	IREL	Contra Costa	Martinez P O	71	367
John	34	m	w	NY	Santa Cruz	Santa Cruz Twp	89	395
John	34	m	w	IREL	San Francisco	San Francisco P O	83	53
John	33	m	w	ENGL	Nevada	Grass Valley Twp	75	181
John	32	m	w	IREL	San Francisco	11-Wd San Francisc	84	425
John	32	m	w	IREL	Yolo	Putah Twp	93	512
John	31	m	w	ENGL	Nevada	Grass Valley Twp	75	183
John	31	m	w	ENGL	Nevada	Grass Valley Twp	75	183
John	30	m	w	NY	Amador	Amador City P O	69	390
John	30	m	w	IREL	San Francisco	San Francisco P O	83	2
John	30	m	w	IREL	Trinity	Hayfork Valley	92	239
John	29	m	w	TN	Contra Costa	Martinez P O	71	439
John	28	m	w	IREL	San Francisco	1-Wd San Francisco	79	101
John	27	m	w	IREL	Kern	Tehachapi P O	73	354
John	27	m	w	MD	Mendocino	Navarro & Big Rvr	74	174
John	27	m	w	IREL	San Francisco	1-Wd San Francisco	79	82
John	25	m	w	NY	Marin	San Rafael Twp	74	26
John	25	m	w	IREL	San Francisco	11-Wd San Francisc	84	535
John	25	m	w	NY	San Francisco	5-Wd San Francisco	81	31
John	24	m	w	IREL	San Francisco	7-Wd San Francisco	81	169
John	23	m	w	IREL	Nevada	Nevada Twp	75	310
John	23	m	w	NY	Contra Costa	Martinez P O	71	443
John	22	m	w	AL	Los Angeles	El Monte Twp	73	457
John	21	m	w	MA	San Francisco	San Francisco P O	85	811
John	20	m	w	IN	Alameda	Washington Twp	68	268
John	19	m	w	IREL	Napa	Napa Twp	75	75
John	19	m	w	BREM	Santa Clara	Gilroy Twp	88	81
John	18	m	w	CA	Tulare	Tule Rvr Twp	92	271
John A	55	m	w	VT	San Francisco	6-Wd San Francisco	81	128
John M	32	m	w	ENGL	Nevada	Grass Valley Twp	75	183
John P	55	m	w	GA	Los Angeles	Santa Ana Twp	73	612
John R	45	m	w	IREL	Mariposa	Maxwell Crk P O	74	139
John S	23	m	w	SCOT	Santa Barbara	San Buenaventura P	87	447
John T	24	m	w	NY	San Francisco	6-Wd San Francisco	81	95
Jose	45	m	w	IREL	Los Angeles	Wilmington Twp	73	636
Joseph	56	m	w	PA	Santa Clara	San Jose Twp	88	217
Joseph	35	m	w	IREL	Alameda	Brooklyn Twp	68	50
Joseph	30	m	w	IREL	Solano	Suisun Twp	90	111
Joseph	28	m	w	MD	San Joaquin	Elkhorn Twp	86	53
Joseph	21	m	w	IREL	San Francisco	7-Wd San Francisco	81	185
Joseph C	26	m	w	OH	Santa Clara	San Jose Twp	88	217
Josephus	44	m	w	OH	Stanislaus	Branch Twp	92	2
Jules	39	m	w	FRAN	Calaveras	San Andreas P O	70	216
Julia	33	f	w	IREL	San Francisco	2-Wd San Francisco	79	262
Julia	20	f	w	IREL	Monterey	Pajaro Twp	74	375
Julia	16	f	w	ENGL	Santa Clara	2-Wd San Jose	88	321
Julius	28	m	w	SCOT	San Francisco	2-Wd San Francisco	79	145
July	28	f	w	IREL	Yuba	Marysville	93	608
Kate	26	f	w	IREL	Sacramento	4-Wd Sacramento	77	336
Kate	24	f	w	IREL	San Francisco	San Francisco P O	80	410
L P	40	m	w	MN	Alameda	Oakland	68	217
Lewis	60	m	w	KY	Stanislaus	Empire Twp	92	32
Lilie	10	f	w	NH	Solano	Vallejo	90	217
Lot	52	m	w	IREL	Santa Clara	San Jose Twp	88	191
Louisa	30	f	w	NY	San Francisco	San Francisco P O	80	474
Louisa	24	f	w	HCAS	San Francisco	6-Wd San Francisco	81	70
Lucy	43	f	w	ENGL	San Francisco	San Francisco P O	85	740
Lysander	42	m	w	PA	Santa Clara	Redwood Twp	88	131
M	9	f	w	CA	Los Angeles	Los Angeles	73	569
M H	29	m	w	IREL	Sacramento	3-Wd Sacramento	77	274
M W	42	m	w	MA	Solano	Vallejo	90	148
Margaret	35	f	w	IREL	San Mateo	Menlo Park P O	87	377
Margaret	31	f	w	IREL	Sacramento	3-Wd Sacramento	77	287
Margaret	27	f	w	IREL	San Francisco	San Francisco P O	85	770
Martin	29	m	w	NY	San Francisco	2-Wd San Francisco	79	179
Mary	67	f	w	SCOT	San Francisco	11-Wd San Francisc	84	456
Mary	60	f	w	IREL	San Francisco	8-Wd San Francisco	82	443
Mary	56	f	w	IREL	San Francisco	San Francisco P O	83	386

© 2001 by Heritage Quest. All rights reserved.

Name	Age	S	R	B-PL	County	Locale	Series M593 Roll	Pg
Mary	47	f	w	IREL	Alameda	Oakland	68	191
Mary	39	f	w	IREL	Yolo	Cache Crk Twp	93	431
Mary	2M	f	w	CA	San Francisco	11-Wd San Francisc	84	711
Mary	28	f	w	IREL	San Francisco	San Francisco P O	83	325
Mary	25	f	w	IREL	Sonoma	Sonoma Twp	91	432
Mary	25	f	w	IREL	San Francisco	1-Wd San Francisco	79	27
Mary	22	f	w	MA	San Francisco	3-Wd San Francisco	79	327
Mary	17	f	w	MA	Solano	Benicia	90	16
Mary	15	f	w	NY	San Francisco	2-Wd San Francisco	79	218
Mary	14	f	w	IREL	San Francisco	San Francisco P O	83	17
Mathew	45	m	w	IREL	Klamath	Trinidad Twp	73	391
Matthew	25	m	w	IREL	San Francisco	1-Wd San Francisco	79	68
Melvina	26	f	w	IL	San Francisco	San Francisco P O	83	263
Michael	54	m	w	IREL	San Francisco	San Francisco P O	83	215
Michael	48	m	w	IREL	San Francisco	San Francisco P O	85	860
Michael	43	m	w	IREL	San Francisco	San Francisco P O	80	363
Michael	34	m	w	RI	San Francisco	11-Wd San Francisc	84	529
Michael	32	m	w	IREL	San Francisco	San Francisco P O	85	736
Michael	27	m	w	IREL	Yolo	Washington Twp	93	530
Michael	21	m	w	IREL	Sacramento	Georgianna Twp	77	130
Micheal	36	m	w	IREL	San Francisco	7-Wd San Francisco	81	189
Michl	35	m	w	IREL	San Francisco	1-Wd San Francisco	79	67
Michl	27	m	w	IREL	San Francisco	1-Wd San Francisco	79	59
Mike	33	m	w	IREL	San Francisco	11-Wd San Francisc	84	675
Mike	27	m	w	IREL	San Joaquin	1-Wd Stockton	86	140
Nathan E	44	m	w	MA	San Francisco	6-Wd San Francisco	81	154
O H	42	m	w	NY	Tehama	Red Bluff	92	176
Octave	26	f	w	FRAN	Santa Clara	1-Wd San Jose	88	267
P M	39	m	w	IREL	San Francisco	San Francisco P O	85	843
Patk	28	m	w	IREL	San Francisco	1-Wd San Francisco	79	133
Patrick	45	m	w	IREL	Shasta	French Gulch P O	89	468
Patrick	42	m	w	IREL	San Francisco	San Francisco P O	83	309
Patrick	40	m	w	CANA	San Mateo	Half Moon Bay P O	87	405
Patrick	40	m	w	IREL	San Francisco	San Francisco P O	83	233
Patrick	38	m	w	CANA	San Mateo	Half Moon Bay P O	87	406
Patrick	33	m	w	IREL	Siskiyou	Scott Valley Twp	89	613
Patrick	32	m	w	MA	San Francisco	San Francisco P O	83	379
Patrick	31	m	w	IREL	Santa Clara	1-Wd San Jose	88	225
Patrick	28	m	w	NY	San Francisco	San Francisco P O	80	337
Patrick	24	m	w	IREL	San Mateo	Belmont P O	87	374
Peleg	70	m	w	RI	Los Angeles	Los Angeles	73	505
Perry	40	m	w	VT	Santa Clara	Fremont Twp	88	65
Peter	43	m	w	MA	San Francisco	11-Wd San Francisc	84	539
Peter	37	m	w	IREL	Nevada	Grass Valley Twp	75	193
Peter	36	m	w	IREL	San Francisco	San Francisco P O	83	404
Peter	35	m	w	IREL	Nevada	Grass Valley Twp	75	196
Philip	26	m	w	IREL	Monterey	Alisal Twp	74	290
R C	40	m	w	ENGL	Santa Clara	Gilroy Twp	88	67
Richard	44	m	w	IREL	Trinity	Douglas	92	234
Richard	39	m	w	IREL	San Francisco	11-Wd San Francisc	84	526
Richard	31	m	w	MA	San Mateo	San Mateo P O	87	348
Richard	28	m	w	MD	Sacramento	San Joaquin Twp	77	399
Richard	24	m	w	ENGL	Placer	Newcastle Twp	76	474
Richard	22	m	w	IREL	San Francisco	7-Wd San Francisco	81	181
Richard	14	m	w	CA	San Francisco	2-Wd San Francisco	79	230
Richard W	55	m	w	PA	San Francisco	8-Wd San Francisco	82	465
Robert	24	m	w	CANA	San Francisco	7-Wd San Francisco	81	177
S	47	m	w	US	San Joaquin	Castoria Twp	86	9
S	37	m	w	PA	Sacramento	Natomas Twp	77	171
S T	35	m	w	ME	San Francisco	San Francisco P O	83	87
Saml A	25	m	w	NY	San Francisco	5-Wd San Francisco	81	12
Samuel	67	m	b	OH	Mariposa	Mariposa P O	74	123
Samuel	33	m	w	ENGL	Alameda	Brooklyn	68	34
Samuel	30	m	w	ME	San Francisco	San Francisco P O	83	366
Samuel H	36	m	w	ENGL	Tulare	Visalia	92	296
Samuel J	44	m	w	ENGL	Nevada	Rough & Ready Twp	75	333
Sarah L	20	f	w	IA	Yolo	Washington Twp	93	536
Savory	45	m	w	MA	San Francisco	San Francisco P O	80	420
Savory W	35	m	w	NH	San Francisco	8-Wd San Francisco	82	332
Silas H	42	m	w	MA	San Francisco	San Francisco P O	83	361
Stephen	38	m	w	ME	Nevada	Rough & Ready Twp	75	323
Susan	18	f	w	ENGL	Santa Clara	2-Wd San Jose	88	321
T	31	m	w	IREL	Lake	Big Valley	73	395
Thomas	45	m	w	IREL	San Francisco	11-Wd San Francisc	84	595
Thomas	40	m	w	IREL	Napa	Napa	75	39
Thomas	40	m	w	CT	Mariposa	Mariposa P O	74	129
Thomas	35	m	w	IREL	Tuolumne	Sonora P O	93	329
Thomas	29	m	w	IREL	Marin	Bolinas Twp	74	4
Thomas	24	m	w	ENGL	San Francisco	8-Wd San Francisco	82	344
Thomas	16	m	w	OH	Alameda	Brooklyn	68	32
Thomas A	40	m	w	TN	Stanislaus	Empire Twp	92	28
Thomas B	45	m	w	OH	Yolo	Putah Twp	93	516
Thomes	28	m	w	IREL	San Joaquin	2-Wd Stockton	86	173
Thos	25	m	w	IREL	San Francisco	1-Wd San Francisco	79	107
Thos	22	m	w	ENGL	San Francisco	11-Wd San Francisc	84	595
Timothy	30	m	w	IREL	San Francisco	San Francisco P O	83	86
Timothy	26	m	w	IREL	San Francisco	11-Wd San Francisc	84	642
Timothy	19	m	w	IREL	Nevada	Grass Valley Twp	75	210
Victor	40	m	w	IN	Solano	Silveyville Twp	90	92
W	47	m	w	SCOT	Alameda	Oakland	68	240
W C	37	m	w	MS	San Joaquin	Liberty Twp	86	83
W H	28	m	w	IREL	San Joaquin	1-Wd Stockton	86	132
W L	45	m	w	IREL	Humboldt	Table Bluff Twp	72	308
W N	47	m	w	RI	Sacramento	3-Wd Sacramento	77	256
W R	14	m	w	MO	Los Angeles	Soledad Twp	73	630
William	59	m	w	ENGL	Contra Costa	Martinez P O	71	444
William	53	m	w	CT	Mariposa	Mariposa P O	74	129
William	48	m	w	PRUS	Trinity	North Fork Twp	92	216
William	46	m	w	ENGL	Amador	Ione City P O	69	356
William	24	m	w	NY	San Francisco	7-Wd San Francisco	81	208
William	23	m	w	NY	San Francisco	6-Wd San Francisco	81	95
William E	36	m	w	KY	Los Angeles	El Monte Twp	73	457
William H	30	m	w	NY	Santa Clara	San Jose Twp	88	186
William L	33	m	w	IN	Yolo	Cottonwood Twp	93	461
William P	26	m	w	CANA	Santa Clara	2-Wd San Jose	88	317
Winslow	20	m	w	ME	San Mateo	Woodside P O	87	386
Wm	62	m	w	IN	El Dorado	Georgetown Twp	72	37
Wm J	36	m	w	IN	Santa Clara	Gilroy Twp	88	84
Wm S	36	m	w	VT	Plumas	Washington Twp	77	25
Wm W	40	m	w	MS	Butte	Chico Twp	70	13
COLLINSON								
Thomas	37	m	w	ENGL	San Francisco	San Francisco P O	83	418
COLLINWOOD								
William	52	m	w	ENGL	Stanislaus	Branch Twp	92	1
COLLIPY								
John	38	m	w	IREL	Trinity	Lewiston Pct	92	214
COLLIS								
Aaron	28	m	w	HANO	Mariposa	Mariposa P O	74	135
Albert	35	m	w	ME	Sonoma	Petaluma Twp	91	358
Edward	41	m	w	IREL	San Francisco	2-Wd San Francisco	79	215
N H	54	m	w	OH	Monterey	Alisal Twp	74	299
Robert	38	m	w	IREL	San Francisco	San Francisco P O	80	339
William	21	m	w	MI	Marin	Bolinas Twp	74	2
Wm	43	m	w	ENGL	San Francisco	San Francisco P O	83	86
COLLISCHONN								
Chas	36	m	w	FRNK	San Francisco	San Francisco P O	83	35
COLLISON								
James	32	m	w	SCOT	San Francisco	11-Wd San Francisc	84	658
Robert	42	m	w	MD	Mariposa	Mariposa P O	74	117
COLLISTER								
William	30	m	w	ENGL	Nevada	Grass Valley Twp	75	232
COLLIVAR								
Thomas	22	m	w	ENGL	Nevada	Grass Valley Twp	75	203
William	50	m	w	ENGL	Nevada	Grass Valley Twp	75	203
COLLMAN								
John	36	m	w	MA	Marin	Bolinas Twp	74	1
Wm	26	m	w	IREL	Marin	San Rafael Twp	74	39
COLLOGAN								
John	34	m	w	WI	Nevada	Grass Valley Twp	75	186
COLLOM								
Eliza	35	f	w	IREL	San Joaquin	2-Wd Stockton	86	171
COLLON								
Mick	29	m	w	IREL	Alameda	Oakland	68	235
COLLONNA								
August	38	m	w	ITAL	Solano	Vallejo	90	200
COLLOPY								
George	26	m	w	VT	San Mateo	Schoolhouse Statio	87	331
Mary	23	f	w	IREL	San Francisco	San Francisco P O	85	857
Timothy	40	m	w	IREL	Santa Cruz	Santa Cruz	89	430
COLLOSON								
Mary	67	f	w	SCOT	San Francisco	San Francisco P O	83	417
COLLOUGH								
Mc C	33	m	w	PA	Santa Clara	Gilroy Twp	88	92
Roger	54	m	w	IREL	Nevada	Bloomfield Twp	75	94
COLLUM								
Thomas	30	m	w	NY	San Francisco	3-Wd San Francisco	79	293
COLLY								
Ferdinand J	42	m	w	ME	Nevada	Bridgeport Twp	75	112
Fred A	21	m	w	ME	San Francisco	8-Wd San Francisco	82	298
Harney	8	m	w	CA	San Francisco	San Francisco P O	83	193
S	25	m	w	ME	Humboldt	Eureka Twp	72	258
Zebulon	39	m	w	NH	San Francisco	2-Wd San Francisco	79	219
COLLYER								
C A	47	m	w	NY	Yuba	Marysville Twp	93	569
Edward	38	m	w	NY	San Francisco	San Francisco P O	80	482
Jacob	35	m	w	NJ	San Francisco	San Francisco P O	83	81
Wm W	45	m	w	ENGL	San Diego	San Diego	78	496
COLMAN								
Abraham	35	m	w	PRUS	San Francisco	8-Wd San Francisco	82	427
C	40	m	w	ENGL	Sacramento	3-Wd Sacramento	77	269
Chas	18	m	w	NY	San Francisco	1-Wd San Francisco	79	84
J S	40	m	w	MA	San Joaquin	3-Wd Stockton	86	234
J W C	38	m	w	VA	Sacramento	3-Wd Sacramento	77	263
James	24	m	w	NY	San Francisco	1-Wd San Francisco	79	67
John	37	m	w	IREL	Calaveras	Copperopolis P O	70	240
John	36	m	w	ENGL	San Francisco	San Francisco P O	80	368
John	26	m	w	NY	San Francisco	1-Wd San Francisco	79	67
Julius	37	m	w	PRUS	Amador	Volcano P O	69	377
Lewis	35	m	w	CA	Sacramento	3-Wd Sacramento	77	284
Marie	45	f	w	VT	San Joaquin	2-Wd Stockton	86	162
Mary	21	f	w	IREL	San Francisco	San Francisco P O	85	718
Michl	29	m	w	IREL	Marin	Nicasio Twp	74	18
Owen	40	m	w	IREL	Sacramento	3-Wd Sacramento	77	305
Patrick	32	m	w	IREL	Santa Cruz	Santa Cruz Twp	89	391
Peter	27	m	w	IREL	Marin	Sausalito Twp	74	74
T	72	m	w	TN	San Joaquin	Liberty Twp	86	85
William	26	m	w	IREL	Marin	Tomales Twp	74	81
COLMER								
Caleb	31	m	w	ENGL	Sierra	Gibson Twp	89	538
Robert	33	m	w	GERM	Los Angeles	Los Angeles	73	546
COLMON								
Aimwell F	32	m	w	ENGL	San Francisco	8-Wd San Francisco	82	400
COLMORE								
Peter J	38	m	w	SWED	Fresno	Millerton P O	72	147

© 2001 by Heritage Quest. All rights reserved.

Name	Age	S	R	B-PL	County	Locale	Series M593 Roll	Pg
COLNON								
Catherine	21	f	w	CANA	Inyo	Lone Pine Twp	73	335
COLOMBET								
Clement	16	m	w	CA	Santa Clara	Santa Clara Twp	88	177
Joseph	48	m	w	FRAN	Alameda	Washington Twp	68	292
Peter	52	m	w	FRAN	Contra Costa	Martinez P O	71	431
Peter	14	m	w	CA	Santa Clara	Santa Clara Twp	88	177
Thomas	17	m	w	CA	Santa Clara	Santa Clara Twp	88	177
COLOMBO								
Dominic	35	m	w	DALM	San Francisco	1-Wd San Francisco	79	95
Pierini	32	m	w	ITAL	San Francisco	11-Wd San Francisc	84	617
COLON								
Christopher	21	m	w	NY	San Francisco	11-Wd San Francisc	84	560
Christopher	20	m	w	NJ	San Francisco	San Francisco P O	83	48
John	14	m	w	MEXI	San Francisco	1-Wd San Francisco	79	14
Lizzie	14	f	w	NY	San Francisco	San Francisco P O	83	48
Mary	16	f	m	NJ	San Francisco	11-Wd San Francisc	84	599
COLONE								
Peter	28	m	w	FRAN	San Francisco	2-Wd San Francisco	79	148
COLONEL								
Joseph	68	m	w	FRAN	Santa Barbara	San Buenaventura P	87	436
COLONNE								
Joseph	18	m	w	FRAN	San Francisco	11-Wd San Francisc	84	568
COLONS								
Mary	47	f	w	FRAN	Alameda	Oakland	68	246
COLONY								
U L	50	m	w	NY	Sierra	Downieville Twp	89	517
COLORADO								
J	47	m	w	MEXI	Sierra	Lincoln Twp	89	550
COLORES								
Andrew	47	m	w	VA	Colusa	Colusa Twp	71	283
COLORI								
Pedro	17	m	w	ITAL	Sonoma	Salt Point	91	391
COLOSINA								
Callina	25	m	w	MEXI	Fresno	Millerton P O	72	164
COLQUHAN								
Elizabeth	46	f	w	SCOT	San Francisco	San Francisco P O	83	230
COLRIDGE								
Henry	33	m	w	IREL	Calaveras	San Andreas P O	70	205
COLSHIER								
Fred	52	m	w	GERM	San Francisco	8-Wd San Francisco	82	314
COLSON								
E A	51	m	w	SWED	San Francisco	San Francisco P O	83	330
James	36	m	w	VT	Stanislaus	San Joaquin Twp	92	81
John	35	m	w	ENGL	Nevada	Grass Valley Twp	75	228
John	26	m	w	SWED	Merced	Snelling P O	74	252
Nicholas	47	m	w	FRAN	Sonoma	Mendocino Twp	91	290
Wm P	53	m	w	NH	Tuolumne	Columbia P O	93	335
COLSTON								
Chas	36	m	w	SWED	Humboldt	Bucksport Twp	72	242
Edward	9	m	w	CA	San Francisco	San Francisco P O	85	828
COLT								
Ah	17	f	c	CHIN	San Francisco	San Francisco P O	80	490
Elizabeth	23	f	w	CANA	San Francisco	8-Wd San Francisco	82	444
Geo W	42	m	w	PA	Lassen	Janesville Twp	73	430
Jabes	41	m	b	LA	San Joaquin	Liberty Twp	86	86
John C	60	m	w	NY	Yolo	Putah Twp	93	511
COLTE								
Jennie	19	f	w	VT	San Francisco	8-Wd San Francisco	82	444
COLTEN								
George	31	m	w	PA	Sacramento	2-Wd Sacramento	77	234
COLTER								
Ann	37	f	w	CANA	San Francisco	8-Wd San Francisco	82	332
Charles L	10	m	w	CA	Yolo	Cache Crk Twp	93	434
David D	37	m	w	ME	San Francisco	8-Wd San Francisco	82	332
E C	39	m	w	MD	Humboldt	Eureka Twp	72	280
Frank	50	m	w	IREL	San Francisco	6-Wd San Francisco	81	137
James	20	m	w	MA	San Francisco	San Francisco P O	83	143
John	46	m	w	IREL	San Francisco	San Francisco P O	85	740
Patrick	65	m	w	IREL	San Francisco	11-Wd San Francisc	84	638
Thomas	54	m	w	IREL	Merced	Snelling P O	74	260
William	6	m	w	CA	Yolo	Putah Twp	93	513
William J	7	m	w	CA	Yolo	Putah Twp	93	511
COLTHURST								
J	45	m	w	ENGL	Lassen	Janesville Twp	73	434
COLTMAN								
Mathew	32	m	w	ENGL	Sacramento	Franklin Twp	77	117
William	36	m	w	PRUS	Nevada	Rough & Ready Twp	75	328
COLTON								
Charles E	35	m	w	MI	San Bernardino	San Bernardino Twp	78	421
Charles W	42	m	w	OH	Los Angeles	Wilmington Twp	73	644
Chester F	45	m	w	CT	Sacramento	4-Wd Sacramento	77	354
David	41	m	w	TN	Tulare	Tule Rvr Twp	92	262
Elizabeth	23	f	w	IL	Sacramento	Alabama Twp	77	60
F C	26	m	w	NY	San Joaquin	1-Wd Stockton	86	131
Franklin D	46	m	w	VT	Sonoma	Petaluma Twp	91	330
J R	37	m	w	IREL	Solano	Vallejo	90	184
James	37	m	w	ENGL	Nevada	Grass Valley Twp	75	195
John	30	m	w	IREL	Santa Clara	Santa Clara Twp	88	143
John	26	m	w	NY	Mendocino	Little Rvr Twp	74	170
Louis	50	m	w	NY	Sacramento	San Joaquin Twp	77	406
Samuel	28	m	w	ENGL	Kern	Bakersfield P O	73	357
Sidney	41	m	w	IL	Yuba	Long Bar Twp	93	560
William	35	m	w	IREL	San Francisco	11-Wd San Francisc	84	517
William F	43	m	w	VT	Calaveras	San Andreas P O	70	164
COLTRIN								
Hugh	61	m	w	NY	Alpine	Monitor P O	69	317

Name	Age	S	R	B-PL	County	Locale	Series M593 Roll	Pg
COLTS								
Lewis	35	m	b	MD	San Joaquin	Elkhorn Twp	86	61
Samuel	54	m	w	MD	San Joaquin	1-Wd Stockton	86	136
COLUMBER								
William	48	m	w	VA	Inyo	Lone Pine Twp	73	331
COLUMBET								
Clemente	52	m	w	FRAN	Santa Clara	2-Wd San Jose	88	282
COLUMBO								
John	35	m	w	AR	Marin	San Rafael Twp	74	36
COLUMBUS								
Alfred	30	m	w	FRAN	San Francisco	8-Wd San Francisco	82	302
Cathrain	38	f	w	IREL	San Francisco	San Francisco P O	80	465
M	4	f	w	CA	San Francisco	San Francisco P O	85	799
Mary	2	f	w	CA	San Francisco	11-Wd San Francisc	84	475
COLUNCO								
Peter	30	m	w	GREE	Sacramento	Georgianna Twp	77	130
COLVER								
Alexander	40	m	w	NY	Los Angeles	Wilmington Twp	73	638
COLVERMAKER								
Frank	54	m	w	SAXO	San Francisco	2-Wd San Francisco	79	235
COLVIL								
James A	48	m	w	MO	Sonoma	Russian Rvr	91	370
COLVILL								
Aug E	7	m	w	CA	Sonoma	Russian Rvr	91	370
COLVILLE								
James	35	m	w	SCOT	Tulare	Kings Rvr Twp	92	253
Wm Henry	7	m	w	NV	Plumas	Quartz Twp	77	38
COLVIN								
A	33	m	w	PRUS	San Joaquin	2-Wd Stockton	86	185
Augustus	25	m	w	NY	Siskiyou	Table Rock Twp	89	647
Benj F	44	m	w	RI	Nevada	Grass Valley Twp	75	215
Christian	34	f	w	NY	Alameda	Washington Twp	68	291
Elijah T	35	m	w	AL	Tulare	Farmersville Twp	92	249
Frank M	25	m	w	IN	Sonoma	Cloverdale Twp	91	269
Hugh	40	m	w	SCOT	San Francisco	San Francisco P O	80	355
Jacob	21	m	w	PORT	Santa Clara	Santa Clara Twp	88	169
Jno	26	m	w	MO	Butte	Kimshew Tpw	70	86
John	52	m	w	KY	Colusa	Spring Valley Twp	71	337
John J	25	m	w	SCOT	San Francisco	2-Wd San Francisco	79	236
Presley W	11	m	w	CA	Santa Clara	Santa Clara Twp	88	177
S T	31	m	w	NY	Placer	Rocklin Twp	76	466
Thos S	52	m	w	IN	Sonoma	Cloverdale Twp	91	269
Wm	38	m	w	KY	Plumas	Indian Twp	77	12
Wm	26	m	w	PA	Solano	Vallejo	90	146
COLWELL								
Alonzo	9	m	w	CA	Placer	Bath P O	76	423
Anderson	30	m	w	NY	Contra Costa	Martinez Twp	71	351
Anturtus	49	m	w	NY	Santa Clara	Santa Clara Twp	88	151
Benj	25	m	w	NY	Monterey	San Antonio Twp	74	323
Dave	35	m	w	IREL	Butte	Chico Twp	70	55
E B	33	m	w	ENGL	San Joaquin	2-Wd Stockton	86	162
George	62	m	w	VA	Tulare	Visalia Twp	92	283
James	50	m	w	OH	Santa Barbara	San Buenaventura P	87	437
James	43	m	w	IREL	Merced	Snelling P O	74	264
James M	28	m	w	OH	San Francisco	2-Wd San Francisco	79	187
Jane	49	f	w	VT	Placer	Bath P O	76	430
Jennie	11	f	w	CA	San Francisco	San Francisco P O	80	388
Jesse	37	m	w	OH	Marin	Bolinas Twp	74	5
John	32	m	w	PA	Siskiyou	Cottonwood Twp	89	593
Julius	40	m	w	AL	Placer	Lincoln P O	76	485
M J	22	m	w	CANA	Alameda	Oakland	68	148
Nicholas	54	m	w	ENGL	Solano	Montezuma Twp	90	68
O	18	m	w	IA	San Joaquin	Elkhorn Twp	86	56
S R	41	m	w	AL	Sacramento	3-Wd Sacramento	77	266
Samuel	23	m	w	CANA	Yolo	Cache Crk Twp	93	434
Terrence	36	m	w	IREL	San Francisco	San Francisco P O	85	876
William	48	m	w	IREL	Sutter	Yuba Twp	92	150
William B	37	m	w	OH	Los Angeles	Los Angeles	73	551
COLY								
James	40	m	w	ENGL	Colusa	Spring Valley Twp	71	338
COLYEAR								
Andrw J	52	m	w	KY	Monterey	Castroville Twp	74	326
George	74	m	w	TN	Monterey	Castroville Twp	74	326
COLYER								
Charles Jr	41	m	w	KY	Plumas	Plumas Twp	77	32
James	40	m	b	NY	San Francisco	San Francisco P O	80	423
Joseph	39	m	w	NY	Solano	Vacaville Twp	90	118
Maria	40	f	w	NY	San Francisco	5-Wd San Francisco	81	16
Thomas	41	m	w	NY	San Francisco	5-Wd San Francisco	81	16
W J	36	m	w	GA	Solano	Vallejo	90	155
William	25	m	w	IL	Kern	Tehachapi P O	73	354
COLYIAR								
Richard J	28	m	w	MO	Monterey	Castroville Twp	74	334
COLYN								
Jas N	42	m	w	NY	Sacramento	4-Wd Sacramento	77	363
COM								
Ah	4	f	c	CHIN	Placer	Auburn P O	76	371
Ah	35	m	c	CHIN	Mariposa	Maxwell Crk P O	74	145
Ah	34	m	c	CHIN	Fresno	Millerton P O	72	201
Ah	32	f	c	CHIN	Calaveras	Copperopolis P O	70	232
Ah	28	m	c	CHIN	El Dorado	Coloma Twp	72	3
Ah	25	m	c	CHIN	Sacramento	Granite Twp	77	141
Ah	18	m	c	CHIN	Plumas	Plumas Twp	77	31
Ah	18	f	c	CHIN	San Francisco	6-Wd San Francisco	81	61
Au	26	f	c	CHIN	Tulare	Visalia	92	299
Bee	32	m	c	CHIN	Fresno	Millerton P O	72	202
Boo	50	m	c	CHIN	Yuba	Slate Range Bar Tw	93	668

© 2001 by Heritage Quest. All rights reserved.

California 1870 Census

Name	Age	S	R	B-PL	County	Locale	Series M593 Roll	Pg
Cor	23	f	c	CHIN	Tulare	Visalia	92	299
Cow	30	m	c	CHIN	Tehama	Tehama Twp	92	189
Fank	40	m	c	CHIN	Tuolumne	Big Oak Flat P O	93	397
James	22	m	w	IREL	San Francisco	San Francisco P O	85	865
Mow	64	m	c	CHIN	Trinity	Weaverville Pct	92	228
Sam Sun	29	m	c	CHIN	Placer	Auburn P O	76	374
See	33	m	c	CHIN	Sonoma	Sonoma Twp	91	431
Yuck	37	m	c	CHIN	Mariposa	Maxwell Crk P O	74	145
COMACHO								
Blas	35	m	w	MEXI	Fresno	Millerton P O	72	153
John	50	m	w	MADE	Nevada	Nevada Twp	75	272
COMADI								
Daniel	25	m	w	PRUS	Calaveras	San Andreas P O	70	213
COMAGHTEN								
Bridget	44	f	w	IREL	San Francisco	San Francisco P O	80	398
COMAHREWS								
John	44	m	w	HANO	San Mateo	San Mateo P O	87	354
COMAN								
Joe	16	m	w	MA	Humboldt	Eureka Twp	72	278
Samuel	43	m	w	MI	Trinity	North Fork Twp	92	217
COMANCHO								
Antone	51	m	w	AZOR	Nevada	Washington Twp	75	339
Romana	30	f	w	MEXI	Santa Clara	Fremont Twp	88	41
COMANS								
Peter	40	m	w	SCOT	Colusa	Spring Valley Twp	71	344
COMAPLA								
John B	47	m	w	SPAI	Santa Barbara	San Buenaventura P	87	448
COMAR								
Julius	48	m	w	IREL	San Francisco	11-Wd San Francisc	84	695
COMARD								
Bernard	30	m	w	FRAN	San Mateo	Belmont P O	87	374
COMARFORD								
Edward	34	m	w	IREL	San Francisco	11-Wd San Francisc	84	456
COMARIO								
Louis	19	m	w	ITAL	Amador	Sutter Crk P O	69	403
COMARZHAT								
Antonio	32	m	w	AZOR	Monterey	Monterey Twp	74	343
COMAS								
Anna	14	f	w	NY	San Francisco	San Francisco P O	83	309
Emanuel	36	m	w	FRAN	San Francisco	San Francisco P O	80	350
COMB								
Ah	38	m	c	CHIN	Fresno	Millerton P O	72	199
Sarah	67	f	w	MO	San Joaquin	2-Wd Stockton	86	189
Si	26	f	c	CHIN	Amador	Drytown P O	69	421
COMBE								
Mary	75	f	w	FRAN	Santa Clara	1-Wd San Jose	88	248
Wm	43	m	w	IN	Nevada	Nevada Twp	75	275
COMBES								
Jno W	32	m	w	NY	Sonoma	Healdsburg & Mendo	91	281
Mary	35	f	w	IREL	San Francisco	2-Wd San Francisco	79	199
Stephen	56	m	w	NY	San Francisco	7-Wd San Francisco	81	266
COMBS								
C T	59	m	w	ME	Solano	Vallejo	90	155
Calvin	36	m	w	KY	Sonoma	Healdsburg & Mendo	91	285
Charles	44	m	w	NY	Placer	Colfax P O	76	391
Chas	42	m	w	NY	Tehama	Battle Crk Twp	92	172
Daniel	47	m	w	VA	Butte	Wyandotte Twp	70	141
G W	55	m	w	NY	Sacramento	4-Wd Sacramento	77	338
Jas	50	m	w	KY	Solano	Vallejo	90	165
John	76	m	b	VA	Santa Clara	Santa Clara Twp	88	149
John	39	m	w	ENGL	Trinity	Indian Crk	92	200
John W	33	m	w	NY	Santa Clara	2-Wd San Jose	88	285
John W	22	m	w	OR	Sonoma	Santa Rosa	91	409
Laura S	43	f	w	NH	Santa Clara	1-Wd San Jose	88	238
M	39	m	w	KY	Alameda	Alameda	68	6
Marca	10	f	w	CA	Los Angeles	Los Angeles Twp	73	468
Martha	48	m	m	ME	Butte	Ophir Twp	70	112
Mena	20	f	i	CA	Tehama	Battle Crk Twp	92	172
Pierce	17	m	w	CA	Siskiyou	Table Rock Twp	89	646
Polly	51	f	w	NY	Sacramento	2-Wd Sacramento	77	220
Richd	20	m	w	OR	Sonoma	Santa Rosa	91	407
Saml	26	m	w	CA	Tehama	Battle Crk Twp	92	172
Thomas	25	m	w	MO	Tulare	Tule Rvr Twp	92	271
Thomas J	24	m	w	KY	Tulare	Tule Rvr Twp	92	259
W S	42	m	w	PA	Amador	Ione City P O	69	353
William	46	m	w	NY	Stanislaus	Empire Twp	92	63
William	44	m	w	IN	Placer	Auburn P O	76	380
William J	26	m	w	IN	Siskiyou	Table Rock Twp	89	647
Wm	50	m	w	KY	Butte	Oregon Twp	70	136
Wm	50	m	w	PA	Napa	Napa	75	19
Wm C	53	m	w	NY	Santa Barbara	Santa Barbara P O	87	453
COMBSTOCK								
C B	42	m	w	NY	Sutter	Nicolaus Twp	92	106
COMBY								
Augustus	45	m	w	FRAN	Nevada	Grass Valley Twp	75	219
Ell	20	m	w	BERM	Sacramento	1-Wd Sacramento	77	182
COMCETO								
N	20	m	w	MEXI	Alameda	Oakland	68	159
COME								
Ah	37	m	c	CHIN	Placer	Dutch Flat P O	76	408
Ah	24	f	c	CHIN	Nevada	Bridgeport Twp	75	111
Ah	19	f	c	CHIN	Trinity	Weaverville Pct	92	228
D S	60	m	w	NY	San Diego	San Luis Rey	78	512
Toy	23	f	c	CHIN	Nevada	Bridgeport Twp	75	111
Yow	20	f	c	CHIN	Nevada	Nevada Twp	75	299
COMEFORD								
Richard	40	m	w	IREL	Sonoma	Petaluma Twp	91	350
COMEGANO								
Jack	35	m	w	ITAL	San Francisco	3-Wd San Francisco	79	288
COMEGYRS								
Jacob	73	m	w	KY	Santa Clara	1-Wd San Jose	88	238
COMEHIGH								
John	30	m	b	HI	San Francisco	6-Wd San Francisco	81	114
COMELICH								
Geo	49	m	w	AUST	San Francisco	San Francisco P O	83	266
COMELIO								
Antonio	60	m	w	ITAL	Santa Clara	1-Wd San Jose	88	239
COMENCE								
Asurus	19	m	w	DENM	Alameda	Eden Twp	68	65
COMENFORT								
Michl	72	m	w	IREL	San Francisco	11-Wd San Francisc	84	641
COMEO								
Doningo	31	m	w	ITAL	San Francisco	2-Wd San Francisco	79	235
Gromeo	35	m	w	ITAL	San Francisco	2-Wd San Francisco	79	235
COMER								
Frank	26	m	w	IREL	Santa Clara	2-Wd San Jose	88	320
Mary	24	f	w	IREL	Yolo	Cottonwood Twp	93	463
Samuel R	36	m	w	KY	Yolo	Cache Crk Twp	93	442
Wm	38	m	w	MI	Butte	Chico Twp	70	34
COMERFORD								
Edwd J	36	m	w	IREL	San Francisco	San Francisco P O	83	201
John	19	m	w	MD	San Francisco	11-Wd San Francisc	84	592
Joseph	19	m	w	AUSL	San Mateo	Schoolhouse Statio	87	335
Lizzie	15	f	w	CA	Santa Clara	2-Wd San Jose	88	337
Lottie	10	f	w	CA	Santa Clara	2-Wd San Jose	88	338
Moses	44	m	w	IREL	San Francisco	11-Wd San Francisc	84	481
Patk	40	m	w	IREL	San Francisco	1-Wd San Francisco	79	43
Theresa	45	f	w	IREL	San Francisco	8-Wd San Francisco	82	471
Wm	34	m	w	IREL	San Francisco	1-Wd San Francisco	79	66
COMERFORT								
Catherine	36	f	w	IREL	San Francisco	2-Wd San Francisco	79	234
COMERS								
A	10	f	w	CA	Los Angeles	Los Angeles	73	569
COMES								
Ida	12	f	w	CA	San Joaquin	Castoria Twp	86	6
COMEY								
D W	49	m	w	MA	Sacramento	3-Wd Sacramento	77	257
COMFORT								
Chas	60	m	w	PA	Sierra	Eureka Twp	89	525
Daniel	68	m	w	NY	Solano	Tremont Twp	90	31
E	46	m	w	PA	Calaveras	Copperopolis P O	70	224
Jabez	35	m	w	ENGL	Santa Clara	Fremont Twp	88	48
John R	39	m	w	ENGL	Monterey	San Juan Twp	74	402
S M	33	m	w	MO	Santa Clara	Gilroy Twp	88	78
COMGAMA								
Christ	27	m	w	CANA	Placer	Gold Run Twp	76	394
COMIDI								
Antonio	36	m	w	ITAL	San Francisco	1-Wd San Francisco	79	110
COMING								
Sarah	26	f	w	NY	El Dorado	Placerville	72	124
COMINS								
John	46	m	w	IREL	San Joaquin	Douglas Twp	86	30
Paschall	61	m	w	MA	San Francisco	San Francisco P O	80	393
COMINSKY								
P	46	m	w	IREL	Mendocino	Sanel Twp	74	230
COMISEOME								
Angela	55	f	w	ITAL	Mariposa	Mariposa P O	74	100
COMITO								
Laurent	19	m	w	FRAN	San Francisco	San Francisco P O	80	340
Martin	40	m	w	FRAN	San Francisco	San Francisco P O	80	340
COMLIN								
Edw	30	m	w	SCOT	Alameda	Oakland	68	258
COMMARY								
P	56	m	w	CANA	San Francisco	San Francisco P O	83	300
COMMEFORD								
Edd	28	m	w	IREL	San Francisco	11-Wd San Francisc	84	703
COMMELANO								
Benito	30	m	w	ITAL	San Francisco	3-Wd San Francisco	79	289
COMMENICA								
Antone	39	m	w	SCOT	Alameda	Brooklyn	68	38
COMMENPO								
Joseph	23	m	w	SWIT	Marin	Point Reyes Twp	74	23
COMMER								
Chas	30	m	w	SHOL	San Francisco	San Francisco P O	83	265
COMMERFORD								
J	28	m	w	IREL	San Francisco	3-Wd San Francisco	79	318
COMMERLEN								
John	32	m	w	NC	Tulare	Farmersville Twp	92	247
COMMERS								
Ed	46	m	w	GERM	San Diego	San Diego	78	508
Frank	45	m	w	FRAN	Calaveras	San Andreas P O	70	168
COMMERSTON								
Jane	22	f	w	FL	San Francisco	11-Wd San Francisc	84	688
COMMESUL								
Hermann	50	m	w	HOLL	San Francisco	2-Wd San Francisco	79	223
COMMETT								
David	46	m	w	SWIT	San Francisco	6-Wd San Francisco	81	93
COMMINGES								
Aime	58	m	w	FRAN	San Francisco	San Francisco P O	83	135
COMMINGHAM								
J S	52	m	w	RI	Monterey	Castroville Twp	74	325
COMMINGST								
Jo	24	m	w	SWIT	Sacramento	3-Wd Sacramento	77	317

© 2001 by Heritage Quest. All rights reserved.

Name	Age	S	R	B-PL	County	Locale	Roll	Pg
						Series M593		
COMMON								
Thomas	38	m	w	IREL	Alameda	Oakland	68	209
COMMONFERT								
Mary	40	f	w	ENGL	Los Angeles	Los Angeles	73	510
N	10	f	w	CA	Los Angeles	Los Angeles	73	569
COMMONFORT								
John	45	m	w	MO	Yolo	Cache Crk Twp	93	457
John	40	m	w	IREL	San Bernardino	San Bernardino Twp	78	447
COMMONUZE								
Alex	40	m	w	FRAN	San Francisco	1-Wd San Francisco	79	83
COMMORA								
Lorenzo	24	m	w	ITAL	Merced	Snelling P O	74	252
COMO								
Ah Chow	22	f	c	CHIN	San Francisco	San Francisco P O	83	82
Me	35	m	c	CHIN	Sonoma	Sonoma Twp	91	431
COMOSE								
C W	44	m	w	OH	Alameda	Oakland	68	212
COMOSO								
John	19	m	w	SWIT	San Francisco	2-Wd San Francisco	79	235
COMPA								
Antonio	18	m	w	ITAL	San Mateo	Schoolhouse Statio	87	340
COMPAN								
Gussip	39	m	w	SWIT	Calaveras	San Andreas P O	70	204
COMPASANA								
Jose	36	m	w	MEXI	Stanislaus	Empire Twp	92	63
COMPASS								
Manuela	34	f	w	CHIL	Yuba	Marysville	93	614
Simon A	61	m	w	MS	Nevada	Rough & Ready Twp	75	324
COMPENDE								
Desire	34	m	w	FRAN	San Francisco	San Francisco P O	80	485
COMPENE								
Eugene	22	m	w	SWIT	San Francisco	San Francisco P O	85	756
COMPHER								
Jacob B	41	m	w	PA	San Luis Obispo	Arroyo Grande Twp	87	278
John H	32	m	w	IL	Santa Cruz	Watsonville	89	377
COMPKINS								
Danl D	37	m	w	NY	Santa Cruz	Santa Cruz Twp	89	397
COMPLEDA								
E	40	f	w	MEXI	Yuba	Marysville	93	600
COMPLIN								
Thomas	31	m	w	MO	Alameda	Washington Twp	68	278
COMPOS								
Frank	38	m	w	MEXI	San Mateo	Half Moon Bay P O	87	393
COMPTE								
Auguste	30	m	w	MO	Sacramento	2-Wd Sacramento	77	245
COMPTEN								
Valentine	56	m	w	NORW	Calaveras	San Andreas P O	70	166
COMPTON								
Alozzo G	27	m	w	NY	Nevada	Grass Valley Twp	75	152
Andrew J	36	m	w	OH	Santa Cruz	Watsonville	89	377
Anne M	16	f	w	NY	San Francisco	8-Wd San Francisco	82	412
Beale	40	m	w	DC	Marin	Sausalito Twp	74	74
Chs	39	m	w	NY	Yuba	Rose Bar Twp	93	653
George D	49	m	w	VA	Los Angeles	Wilmington Twp	73	644
H	43	m	w	VT	Lake	Lakeport	73	403
H T	48	m	w	MD	San Joaquin	2-Wd Stockton	86	196
Henry	32	m	w	OH	Tehama	Battle Crk Meadows	92	168
Henry	30	m	w	KY	Yolo	Cottonwood Twp	93	462
Henry C	37	m	w	CANA	Butte	Chico Twp	70	38
Hiram D	42	m	w	KY	Alameda	Washington Twp	68	277
Isiah	42	m	w	SCOT	Placer	Rocklin Twp	76	468
James	43	m	w	KY	San Mateo	Half Moon Bay P O	87	398
Jno	48	m	w	PRUS	Butte	Ophir Twp	70	117
Jno	39	m	w	NJ	Santa Clara	Burnett Twp	88	37
Jno R	27	m	w	NY	Monterey	San Juan Twp	74	415
John	54	m	w	VA	Colusa	Colusa	71	291
John	32	m	w	NY	Solano	Rio Vista Twp	90	62
John B	42	m	w	KY	Stanislaus	Empire Twp	92	43
John D	38	m	w	NJ	Plumas	Indian Twp	77	15
John H	22	m	w	OH	Santa Barbara	Santa Barbara P O	87	499
Jos C	35	m	w	VA	Sonoma	Russian Rvr	91	372
Joseph	18	m	w	CA	Colusa	Colusa	71	295
Joshua	39	m	w	MO	Yuba	New York Twp	93	637
Kenneth	31	m	w	NJ	Plumas	Indian Twp	77	16
L F	43	m	w	KY	Alameda	Oakland	68	261
L F	41	m	w	MO	San Francisco	San Francisco P O	83	87
Lewis	34	m	w	NY	San Francisco	San Francisco P O	83	389
Mark	19	m	w	MO	Butte	Hamilton Twp	70	62
Matilda	30	f	w	MS	Fresno	Millerton P O	72	156
Nathan	36	m	w	NY	Mendocino	Anderson Twp	74	150
Nathan H	30	m	w	OH	San Mateo	Woodside P O	87	385
P H	44	m	w	GA	Santa Clara	Gilroy Twp	88	104
Peter	70	m	w	NY	Nevada	Grass Valley Twp	75	169
Stephan	42	m	w	MO	Yuba	New York Twp	93	636
T J	25	m	w	MO	Sutter	Butte Twp	92	89
William	28	m	w	VA	Solano	Vacaville Twp	90	119
Wm	40	m	w	LA	Yuba	Marysville Twp	93	570
COMSOUR								
Edgar	33	m	w	NJ	Alameda	Oakland	68	132
COMSTOCK								
A M	47	m	w	NY	San Francisco	7-Wd San Francisco	81	207
Arnold	47	m	w	NY	San Francisco	San Francisco P O	83	143
Asa	38	m	w	ME	Amador	Fiddletown P O	69	436
Byron	38	m	w	MO	Stanislaus	Branch Twp	92	2
C	28	m	w	OH	Sacramento	1-Wd Sacramento	77	189
C C	29	m	w	NY	Alameda	Oakland	68	239
Charles	30	m	w	VT	Placer	Alta P O	76	412
Charles B	24	m	w	PA	Los Angeles	Los Angeles	73	567
Chas E	36	m	w	CT	Napa	Napa	75	48
Chester	52	m	w	NY	Tuolumne	Sonora P O	93	319
Daniel	30	m	w	ME	Contra Costa	Martinez P O	71	387
David	25	m	w	VT	Kern	Bakersfield P O	73	360
Elijah	45	m	w	VA	Yolo	Washington Twp	93	535
Elmira	10	f	w	CA	San Francisco	7-Wd San Francisco	81	207
George	35	m	w	WI	Placer	Gold Run Twp	76	397
H P	38	m	w	MI	Sierra	Sierra Twp	89	568
H S	45	m	w	PA	Humboldt	Eureka Twp	72	274
Harry	32	m	w	NY	San Mateo	Pescadero P O	87	410
Harvey	42	m	w	NY	San Francisco	5-Wd San Francisco	81	21
J	60	m	w	NY	Siskiyou	Callahan P O	89	627
James	19	m	w	NY	San Francisco	San Francisco P O	80	346
Jared	23	m	w	CT	Santa Cruz	Santa Cruz Twp	89	397
Lewis H	37	m	w	NY	San Mateo	Pescadero P O	87	410
M B	26	m	w	OH	Sacramento	1-Wd Sacramento	77	189
Mary	42	f	w	ENGL	San Francisco	6-Wd San Francisco	81	115
Mary	30	f	w	ME	Tehama	Red Bluff	92	183
Nathan	62	m	w	RI	San Mateo	Half Moon Bay P O	87	406
Peter	40	m	w	ME	Tehama	Red Bluff	92	182
Ralph	59	m	w	CT	Yuba	Long Bar Twp	93	565
Saml	71	m	w	CT	Santa Cruz	Watsonville	89	367
Seth	37	m	w	NY	San Joaquin	Douglas Twp	86	37
Smith	28	m	w	MA	Santa Cruz	Soquel Twp	89	444
Sylvester	33	m	w	RI	Nevada	Eureka Twp	75	135
W D	29	m	w	NH	Sacramento	3-Wd Sacramento	77	312
William	40	m	w	CT	Sonoma	Vallejo Twp	91	457
COMTE								
A	64	m	w	FRAN	Sacramento	4-Wd Sacramento	77	350
COMTIE								
Edward	16	m	w	CA	Solano	Denverton Twp	90	24
COMUSE								
Melinda	35	f	w	ME	Fresno	Millerton P O	72	145
COMY								
Emily H	35	f	w	ENGL	Alameda	Oakland	68	197
COMYNS								
Morris	31	m	w	IREL	San Francisco	San Francisco P O	83	319
CON								
Ah	50	m	c	CHIN	Santa Barbara	Santa Barbara P O	87	459
Ah	50	m	c	CHIN	Los Angeles	Los Angeles	73	546
Ah	50	m	w	CHIN	Placer	Roseville P O	76	348
Ah	40	m	c	CHIN	Tuolumne	Chinese Camp P O	93	364
Ah	40	m	c	CHIN	San Francisco	San Francisco P O	80	525
Ah	39	m	c	CHIN	Tuolumne	Big Oak Flat P O	93	396
Ah	39	m	c	CHIN	Butte	Hamilton Twp	70	72
Ah	38	m	c	CHIN	Sierra	Table Rock Twp	89	544
Ah	38	m	c	CHIN	Placer	Pino Twp	76	471
Ah	38	m	c	CHIN	San Francisco	San Francisco P O	80	523
Ah	37	m	c	CHIN	San Francisco	San Francisco P O	80	448
Ah	37	m	c	CHIN	San Francisco	San Francisco P O	80	447
Ah	36	m	c	CHIN	Sacramento	Cosumnes Twp	77	90
Ah	35	m	c	CHIN	Tuolumne	Big Oak Flat P O	93	393
Ah	35	m	c	CHIN	Butte	Chico Twp	70	28
Ah	35	m	c	CHIN	Mariposa	Mariposa P O	74	132
Ah	35	m	c	CHIN	Kern	Kernville P O	73	367
Ah	34	m	c	CHIN	Sacramento	1-Wd Sacramento	77	204
Ah	32	m	c	CHIN	Tuolumne	Big Oak Flat P O	93	394
Ah	32	m	c	CHIN	Tuolumne	Chinese Camp P O	93	380
Ah	31	m	c	CHIN	Tuolumne	Chinese Camp P O	93	390
Ah	30	m	c	CHIN	Tuolumne	Big Oak Flat P O	93	392
Ah	30	m	c	CHIN	Kern	Havilah P O	73	336
Ah	30	m	c	CHIN	Sacramento	Natomas Twp	77	165
Ah	30	m	c	CHIN	Placer	Colfax P O	76	384
Ah	30	m	c	CHIN	Kern	Kernville P O	73	368
Ah	30	m	c	CHIN	Trinity	Weaverville Pct	92	227
Ah	30	f	c	CHIN	San Francisco	San Francisco P O	80	528
Ah	3	m	c	CA	Mariposa	Mariposa P O	74	102
Ah	29	m	c	CHIN	Tuolumne	Chinese Camp P O	93	377
Ah	29	m	c	CHIN	Butte	Oregon Twp	70	131
Ah	29	m	c	CHIN	Calaveras	San Andreas P O	70	184
Ah	28	m	c	CHIN	Tuolumne	Chinese Camp P O	93	385
Ah	28	m	c	CHIN	Butte	Concow Twp	70	10
Ah	28	m	c	CHIN	San Mateo	San Mateo P O	87	351
Ah	27	m	c	CHIN	Tuolumne	Chinese Camp P O	93	370
Ah	27	m	c	CHIN	Placer	Blue Canyon P O	76	419
Ah	27	m	c	CHIN	Butte	Chico Twp	70	54
Ah	26	m	c	CHIN	Kern	Havilah P O	73	338
Ah	25	m	c	CHIN	Tuolumne	Chinese Camp P O	93	369
Ah	25	m	c	CHIN	Butte	Kimshew Tpw	70	86
Ah	25	m	c	CHIN	Butte	Mountain Spring Tw	70	88
Ah	23	m	c	CHIN	Solano	Suisun Twp	90	107
Ah	22	m	c	CHIN	Sacramento	1-Wd Sacramento	77	200
Ah	21	m	c	CHIN	Marin	Bolinas Twp	74	1
Ah	20	m	c	CHIN	San Mateo	Half Moon Bay P O	87	396
Ah	20	m	c	CHIN	Sacramento	Georgianna Twp	77	127
Ah	20	m	c	CHIN	San Francisco	San Francisco P O	80	497
Ah	20	m	c	CHIN	San Francisco	San Francisco P O	85	806
Ah	19	m	c	CHIN	Amador	Jackson P O	69	330
Ah	18	f	c	CHIN	San Francisco	San Francisco P O	80	432
Ah	18	m	c	CHIN	Sacramento	1-Wd Sacramento	77	197
Ah	16	m	c	CHIN	San Francisco	8-Wd San Francisco	82	358
Ah	11	m	c	CHIN	Placer	Dutch Flat P O	76	408
Chon	41	m	c	CHIN	Placer	Pino Twp	76	471
Com	4	f	c	CHIN	Monterey	Monterey	74	367
Die	30	f	c	CHIN	Kern	Havilah P O	73	338
Doen	21	m	c	CHIN	Trinity	Junction City Pct	92	206

© 2001 by Heritage Quest. All rights reserved.

Name	Age	S	R	B-PL	County	Locale	Series M593 Roll	Pg
Fong	21	m	c	CHIN	Butte	Chico Twp	70	51
Frick	27	m	c	CHIN	Trinity	Junction City Pct	92	206
Hip	50	m	c	CHIN	Calaveras	San Andreas P O	70	181
Lee	26	m	c	CHIN	Placer	Bath P O	76	445
Lin	32	m	c	CHIN	Butte	Concow Twp	70	11
Lin	30	m	c	CHIN	Butte	Hamilton Twp	70	71
Lon	30	m	c	CHIN	Butte	Hamilton Twp	70	73
Loo	32	m	c	CHIN	Kern	Bakersfield P O	73	359
Loy	28	m	c	CHIN	Yuba	Marysville	93	622
Lung	28	m	c	CHIN	San Francisco	7-Wd San Francisco	81	185
Mow	24	m	c	CHIN	El Dorado	Greenwood Twp	72	54
On	32	m	c	CHIN	Tuolumne	Chinese Camp P O	93	380
Quinn	30	m	c	CHIN	Nevada	Grass Valley Twp	75	208
Sa	25	m	c	CHIN	Sonoma	Sonoma Twp	91	447
Sen	18	m	c	CHIN	Yuba	Marysville	93	621
Shu	10	m	c	CHIN	Sacramento	1-Wd Sacramento	77	197
Sing	30	m	c	CHIN	El Dorado	Greenwood Twp	72	54
Sing	21	m	c	CHIN	Solano	Vacaville Twp	90	132
Son	32	m	c	CHIN	Butte	Concow Twp	70	11
Toc	21	m	c	CHIN	Butte	Concow Twp	70	11
Tong	27	m	c	CHIN	Butte	Hamilton Twp	70	74
Tong	23	m	c	CHIN	Butte	Hamilton Twp	70	73
Ye	31	m	c	CHIN	Butte	Chico Twp	70	51
Yee	32	m	c	CHIN	Butte	Chico Twp	70	52
Yow	42	m	c	CHIN	Trinity	Weaverville Pct	92	231
CONA								
Ah	45	m	c	CHIN	Calaveras	Copperopolis P O	70	232
CONACA								
Joseph	54	m	w	PRUS	Stanislaus	North Twp	92	69
CONAFLY								
John	50	m	w	IREL	Alameda	Washington Twp	68	281
CONALLY								
James	13	m	w	CA	Sonoma	Vallejo Twp	91	460
Michael	64	m	w	IREL	Nevada	Nevada Twp	75	305
CONALY								
James	48	m	w	IREL	Tuolumne	Sonora P O	93	304
Mikel W	36	m	w	IREL	Sonoma	Petaluma Twp	91	315
CONAN								
Andrew W	29	m	w	TN	San Luis Obispo	Morro Twp	87	287
CONANT								
Abram	48	m	w	ME	Butte	Ophir Twp	70	117
Auguste	30	m	w	ME	San Francisco	San Francisco P O	83	187
Benjamin	42	m	w	MA	San Francisco	11-Wd San Francisc	84	443
Manson	23	m	w	ME	Sonoma	Petaluma Twp	91	353
Roger	33	m	w	ME	Santa Cruz	Santa Cruz	89	413
CONAPHER								
A	41	m	w	ITAL	Amador	Sutter Crk P O	69	411
CONARDDO								
Maria J	7	f	w	CA	Monterey	Alisal Twp	74	294
CONAT								
Prosper	45	m	w	FRAN	Nevada	Grass Valley Twp	75	208
CONATY								
Thomas	25	m	w	IREL	San Francisco	San Francisco P O	85	864
CONAWAY								
John	39	m	w	PA	Mariposa	Mariposa P O	74	134
Patrick	26	m	w	OH	Colusa	Colusa Twp	71	283
CONBAY								
Richd	30	m	w	IREL	Santa Clara	Gilroy Twp	88	83
CONBOIE								
Mary G	64	f	w	IREL	Sacramento	4-Wd Sacramento	77	327
CONBOIS								
J A	32	m	w	IREL	Sacramento	1-Wd Sacramento	77	176
CONBOY								
Mary	55	f	w	IREL	Alameda	Oakland	68	247
Patrick	27	m	w	IREL	Napa	Napa	75	19
CONBRE								
George	26	m	w	NY	San Francisco	San Francisco P O	83	145
CONCANA								
Luke	50	m	w	IREL	Alameda	Alameda	68	8
CONCANNON								
Eliza	27	f	w	IREL	San Francisco	San Francisco P O	83	105
Harriet	22	f	w	IREL	San Francisco	San Francisco P O	83	64
CONCANON								
Kate	24	f	w	WI	El Dorado	Diamond Springs Tw	72	21
Mary	19	f	w	IREL	Placer	Bath P O	76	436
CONCEPCION								
Mary	38	f	w	MEXI	San Francisco	1-Wd San Francisco	79	47
CONCEPTION								
Mary	29	f	w	MEXI	Tuolumne	Columbia P O	93	338
CONCH								
Jesse	50	m	w	GA	El Dorado	Mud Springs Twp	72	72
CONCHA								
Daras	40	f	w	SPAI	San Joaquin	1-Wd Stockton	86	141
J C	43	m	w	CHIL	Amador	Jackson P O	69	322
CONCKLEMAN								
Jeannette	29	f	w	CT	San Francisco	8-Wd San Francisco	82	382
CONCKLIN								
Emma	15	f	w	MI	Yolo	Cache Crk Twp	93	441
Frances	28	f	w	IREL	San Francisco	8-Wd San Francisco	82	434
Platt	38	m	w	NY	San Francisco	8-Wd San Francisco	82	489
CONCOOL								
Julia A	14	f	w	WI	San Francisco	San Francisco P O	83	344
CONCORSA								
Hosea	45	m	w	CHIL	Calaveras	Copperopolis P O	70	245
CONDA								
Aston	18	m	w	SARD	Tuolumne	Big Oak Flat P O	93	404
James	46	m	w	IREL	Yolo	Putah Twp	93	519

Name	Age	S	R	B-PL	County	Locale	Series M593 Roll	Pg
CONDAY								
Joseph	36	m	w	ENGL	El Dorado	Mountain Twp	72	68
CONDE								
Albert	31	m	w	CA	Marin	San Rafael Twp	74	38
George M	35	m	w	NY	San Francisco	San Francisco P O	85	738
CONDEE								
John	30	m	w	SCOT	Contra Costa	Martinez P O	71	427
CONDELL								
Fred	40	m	w	IREL	San Joaquin	3-Wd Stockton	86	226
CONDEN								
J	38	m	w	IREL	San Joaquin	1-Wd Stockton	86	153
T W	43	m	w	OH	Monterey	Salinas Twp	74	311
William	38	m	w	IREL	Trinity	Weaverville Pct	92	224
CONDER								
James	52	m	w	PA	Butte	Ophir Twp	70	97
CONDERO								
Manuel	30	m	w	MEXI	Stanislaus	San Joaquin Twp	92	72
CONDET								
Amos	23	m	w	OH	Monterey	Pajaro Twp	74	368
CONDICH								
John	32	m	w	IREL	San Francisco	2-Wd San Francisco	79	214
CONDILE								
May	12	f	w	CA	Alameda	Oakland	68	168
CONDILLA								
Maria	16	f	w	CA	San Diego	San Pasqual	78	519
CONDIRA								
Apostel	50	m	w	GREE	Placer	Bath P O	76	442
CONDIT								
J H	42	m	w	NY	Tuolumne	Sonora P O	93	307
Lorenzo W	49	m	w	NJ	Mariposa	Mariposa P O	74	97
CONDO								
John	37	m	w	PA	Amador	Fiddletown P O	69	437
Nicklas	40	m	i	MEXI	Inyo	Cerro Gordo Twp	73	320
CONDON								
Adelia	40	f	w	CANA	San Francisco	8-Wd San Francisco	82	340
Alexander	30	m	w	OH	Santa Cruz	Santa Cruz Twp	89	394
Anna	7	f	w	OR	Humboldt	Eureka Twp	72	279
Anna	21	f	w	ME	Sonoma	Washington Twp	91	467
Anne	45	f	w	IREL	San Francisco	8-Wd San Francisco	82	478
Asaph	36	m	w	ME	Placer	Bath P O	76	434
David	35	m	w	OH	Santa Barbara	San Buenaventura P	87	421
Eliza	25	f	w	IREL	San Francisco	San Francisco P O	83	166
Frank	39	m	w	OH	Humboldt	Eureka Twp	72	278
Henry M	30	m	w	MA	San Francisco	San Francisco P O	85	876
Isaac	48	m	w	ME	Humboldt	Pacific Twp	72	295
J B	44	m	w	NY	Yuba	Marysville	93	611
J C D	24	m	w	IREL	San Francisco	San Francisco P O	85	785
James	35	m	w	NY	Nevada	Washington Twp	75	340
James	28	m	w	IREL	Contra Costa	Martinez P O	71	372
John	29	m	w	PA	Contra Costa	Martinez P O	71	420
John	28	m	w	MA	Fresno	Millerton P O	72	160
John	23	m	w	MI	San Francisco	6-Wd San Francisco	81	92
Maggie	18	f	w	IREL	San Francisco	San Francisco P O	83	281
Mary	40	f	w	IREL	San Francisco	2-Wd San Francisco	79	239
Mary	24	f	w	IREL	San Francisco	San Francisco P O	83	113
Michael	51	m	w	IREL	San Francisco	San Francisco P O	83	153
Morris	32	m	w	IREL	San Francisco	San Francisco P O	83	367
Patrick	69	m	w	IREL	Fresno	Millerton P O	72	160
Patrick	25	m	w	IREL	San Francisco	San Francisco P O	83	272
Richard T	21	m	w	MO	San Francisco	6-Wd San Francisco	81	114
Thomas	33	m	w	IREL	San Francisco	7-Wd San Francisco	81	216
Thomas	33	m	w	MA	San Francisco	11-Wd San Francisc	84	519
Thomas	30	m	w	CANA	Inyo	Bishop Crk Twp	73	311
Wm	38	m	w	CANA	Tuolumne	Sonora P O	93	322
CONDRA								
Ed H	28	m	w	WI	Santa Barbara	Santa Barbara P O	87	500
CONDRAY								
Furney G	50	m	w	TN	Placer	Newcastle Twp	76	477
James	52	m	w	KY	Sonoma	Analy Twp	91	224
CONDREY								
James	26	m	w	MO	Sacramento	2-Wd Sacramento	77	249
CONDRICH								
Annie	5	f	w	CA	San Francisco	11-Wd San Francisc	84	711
Ellen	7	f	w	CA	San Francisco	11-Wd San Francisc	84	711
CONDRIN								
J T	30	m	w	MA	San Francisco	San Francisco P O	85	858
CONDRON								
J H	22	m	w	MA	Solano	Benicia	90	5
CONDRY								
Benj	30	m	w	VA	Mariposa	Mariposa P O	74	111
Henry	20	m	w	NJ	Santa Clara	Santa Clara Twp	88	147
James	17	m	w	NJ	Santa Clara	Santa Clara Twp	88	147
CONE								
Ah	33	m	c	CHIN	Trinity	Lewiston Pct	92	214
Ah	28	f	c	CHIN	Santa Clara	1-Wd San Jose	88	274
Ah	20	m	c	CHIN	Placer	Colfax P O	76	387
Ah	15	m	c	CHIN	San Francisco	6-Wd San Francisco	81	85
Ephraim	37	m	w	GA	Sacramento	Sutter Twp	77	380
Francis I	40	m	w	OH	San Francisco	San Francisco P O	83	160
George	55	m	w	OH	Sacramento	American Twp	77	64
Isaac	30	m	w	IA	Alameda	Hayward	68	80
J B	41	m	w	NY	Amador	Volcano P O	69	384
Jas L	47	m	w	OH	Tehama	Antelope Twp	92	156
Joseph	40	m	w	NY	San Francisco	San Francisco P O	83	207
Lewis	28	m	w	PRUS	San Francisco	San Francisco P O	83	381
Patrick	24	m	w	IREL	Los Angeles	Los Angeles	73	557
Sing	19	m	c	CHIN	San Francisco	6-Wd San Francisco	81	44

© 2001 by Heritage Quest. All rights reserved.

Series M593

Name	Age	S	R	B-PL	County	Locale	Roll	Pg
Timothy	43	m	w	OH	Tehama	Antelope Twp	92	156
William	37	m	w	MI	San Francisco	11-Wd San Francisc	84	560
Yie	7	f	c	CA	Sierra	Downieville Twp	89	521
CONEGHAN								
Michael	24	m	w	IREL	Contra Costa	Martinez P O	71	370
CONELL								
Peter T	28	m	w	IREL	Mendocino	Big Rvr Twp	74	158
Phillip	28	m	w	ENGL	San Francisco	7-Wd San Francisco	81	238
CONELLO								
Jose	41	m	w	CHIL	Amador	Jackson P O	69	343
CONELLY								
Michael	55	m	w	IREL	San Francisco	7-Wd San Francisco	81	252
Pat	30	m	w	IREL	San Francisco	7-Wd San Francisco	81	265
Pathrick	29	m	w	IREL	Monterey	Pajaro Twp	74	375
Patrick	35	m	w	IREL	Santa Clara	San Jose Twp	88	195
CONELY								
R	43	m	w	ENGL	San Joaquin	2-Wd Stockton	86	181
Robert	52	m	w	IREL	Sacramento	San Joaquin Twp	77	401
CONEN								
Mary	25	f	w	IREL	San Francisco	San Francisco P O	83	371
CONENY								
John J	44	m	w	PA	Santa Clara	2-Wd San Jose	88	332
CONEO								
Joseph	40	m	w	ITAL	Amador	Volcano P O	69	385
Rosario	42	f	w	MEXI	El Dorado	Mud Springs Twp	72	76
CONERCO								
Stephen	24	m	w	AUST	Marin	San Rafael Twp	74	46
CONERS								
Thos	25	m	w	NY	Sacramento	San Joaquin Twp	77	399
CONERTHY								
Ellen	28	f	w	IREL	Mendocino	Big Rvr Twp	74	158
CONERWAY								
Margaret	70	f	b	VA	Solano	Suisun Twp	90	113
CONES								
Anton	---	m	w	ITAL	San Francisco	San Francisco P O	83	2
CONESTA								
Achilla	17	m	w	SWIT	Marin	Nicasio Twp	74	14
CONETT								
Jason	50	m	w	ME	Amador	Fiddletown P O	69	440
Samuel	45	m	w	ME	Amador	Fiddletown P O	69	440
CONEY								
Alexander	50	m	w	HAMB	San Francisco	San Francisco P O	85	722
Bautiste	20	m	w	ITAL	Santa Clara	Fremont Twp	88	48
E	28	m	w	MA	El Dorado	Greenwood Twp	72	56
James	24	m	w	CT	Yolo	Fremont Twp	93	476
Leonard	43	m	w	ENGL	San Francisco	San Francisco P O	83	28
Michael	39	m	w	IREL	San Mateo	Belmont P O	87	388
Michael	34	m	w	IREL	Sacramento	1-Wd Sacramento	77	178
Michael J	24	m	w	IREL	Yolo	Grafton Twp	93	481
Patrick	20	m	w	MA	Marin	San Rafael Twp	74	32
Rosalie	47	f	w	FRAN	San Francisco	2-Wd San Francisco	79	224
Soloman	48	m	w	PRUS	Sacramento	2-Wd Sacramento	77	232
Thomas	25	m	w	IREL	San Francisco	1-Wd San Francisco	79	70
CONEZA								
J B	27	m	w	CHIL	Mendocino	Ukiah Twp	74	237
CONFER								
Albert	25	m	w	HOLL	San Bernardino	San Bernardino Twp	78	418
CONFEY								
Jeremiah	26	m	w	IREL	Yolo	Cache Crk Twp	93	449
CONG								
Ah	60	m	c	CHIN	Nevada	Grass Valley Twp	75	217
Ah	60	m	c	CHIN	Amador	Ione City P O	69	351
Ah	60	m	c	CHIN	Stanislaus	Emory Twp	92	20
Ah	49	m	c	CHIN	Amador	Sutter Crk P O	69	411
Ah	47	m	c	CHIN	Butte	Bidwell Twp	70	5
Ah	45	m	c	CHIN	Amador	Ione City P O	69	371
Ah	44	m	c	CHIN	Nevada	Nevada Twp	75	318
Ah	44	m	c	CHIN	Sacramento	1-Wd Sacramento	77	195
Ah	41	m	c	CHIN	San Francisco	San Francisco P O	80	451
Ah	41	m	c	CHIN	Nevada	Grass Valley Twp	75	202
Ah	40	m	c	CHIN	Nevada	Grass Valley Twp	75	207
Ah	39	m	c	CHIN	San Francisco	San Francisco P O	80	454
Ah	39	m	c	CHIN	Calaveras	San Andreas P O	70	183
Ah	38	m	c	CHIN	Amador	Jackson P O	69	332
Ah	37	m	c	CHIN	Santa Barbara	Santa Barbara P O	87	459
Ah	36	m	c	CHIN	Amador	Drytown P O	69	424
Ah	35	m	c	CHIN	Tuolumne	Chinese Camp P O	93	370
Ah	34	m	c	CHIN	Calaveras	San Andreas P O	70	205
Ah	33	m	c	CHIN	Placer	Dutch Flat P O	76	408
Ah	32	m	c	CHIN	Nevada	Bridgeport Twp	75	119
Ah	31	f	c	CHIN	San Francisco	San Francisco P O	80	433
Ah	31	m	c	CHIN	Butte	Concow Twp	70	10
Ah	30	f	c	CHIN	San Francisco	San Francisco P O	80	433
Ah	30	m	c	CHIN	Sonoma	Salt Point	91	380
Ah	30	m	c	CHIN	Yuba	Marysville	93	626
Ah	29	m	c	CHIN	Solano	Suisun Twp	90	106
Ah	29	m	c	CHIN	Sonoma	Petaluma Twp	91	342
Ah	28	m	c	CHIN	Nevada	Nevada Twp	75	314
Ah	28	m	c	CHIN	Merced	Snelling P O	74	280
Ah	28	m	c	CHIN	Placer	Bath P O	76	445
Ah	28	m	c	CHIN	San Francisco	San Francisco P O	80	510
Ah	26	m	c	CHIN	Nevada	Nevada Twp	75	318
Ah	26	m	c	CHIN	San Francisco	San Francisco P O	80	528
Ah	24	m	c	CHIN	San Francisco	San Francisco P O	80	489
Ah	21	m	c	CHIN	San Francisco	San Francisco P O	80	428
Ah	20	m	c	CHIN	San Francisco	San Francisco P O	80	492
Ah	20	m	c	CHIN	San Francisco	San Francisco P O	80	429
Ah	20	m	c	CHIN	Alameda	Oakland	68	175
Ah	19	m	c	CHIN	Santa Clara	San Jose Twp	88	179
Ah	18	m	c	CHIN	Amador	Jackson P O	69	331
Chin	26	m	c	CHIN	Klamath	South Fork Twp	73	384
Foo	20	m	c	CHIN	Nevada	Grass Valley Twp	75	223
He	19	m	c	CHIN	Sonoma	Petaluma Twp	91	344
Ho	41	m	c	CHIN	Amador	Jackson P O	69	332
Hung	38	m	c	CHIN	Yuba	Marysville	93	626
I	28	f	c	CHIN	Stanislaus	San Joaquin Twp	92	78
Leang	40	m	c	CHIN	Nevada	Bridgeport Twp	75	111
Lie	24	m	c	CHIN	Yuba	Marysville	93	625
Me	41	m	c	CHIN	San Joaquin	1-Wd Stockton	86	147
Mung	21	m	c	CHIN	Yuba	Marysville	93	622
See	45	m	c	CHIN	El Dorado	Salmon Falls Twp	72	133
Toy	28	m	c	CHIN	Yuba	Marysville	93	628
We	31	m	c	CHIN	Santa Clara	Santa Clara Twp	88	167
Yon	31	m	c	CHIN	Placer	Bath P O	76	442
CONGDON								
Amelia	38	f	w	VT	San Francisco	6-Wd San Francisco	81	135
Anna	45	f	b	MA	San Francisco	6-Wd San Francisco	81	133
Arnold	46	m	w	VT	Del Norte	Smith Rvr Twp	71	479
Benj	41	m	w	MA	San Francisco	7-Wd San Francisco	81	227
Charles	38	m	w	SHOL	Calaveras	San Andreas P O	70	207
Edward	26	m	w	IREL	San Francisco	2-Wd San Francisco	79	246
F D	40	m	w	CT	Yuba	Rose Bar Twp	93	653
Fanny	12	f	i	CA	Del Norte	Smith Rvr Twp	71	479
George C	54	m	w	NY	El Dorado	Placerville	72	119
Hannah	16	f	w	IREL	San Francisco	8-Wd San Francisco	82	433
Horace W	43	m	w	OH	Monterey	Salinas Twp	74	307
Hy B	35	m	w	CT	San Francisco	San Francisco P O	83	85
J S	25	m	w	RI	Tuolumne	Chinese Camp P O	93	386
Joel R	32	m	w	CT	Los Angeles	San Juan Twp	73	625
L	72	f	w	CT	Yuba	Rose Bar Twp	93	658
N C	55	m	w	VT	Calaveras	Copperopolis P O	70	257
Patrick	25	m	w	IREL	San Francisco	San Francisco P O	83	365
CONGDONE								
Edward	38	m	w	CT	San Francisco	11-Wd San Francisc	84	659
CONGELLY								
Wm	24	m	w	ENGL	Santa Clara	Almaden Twp	88	10
CONGELTON								
A C	56	m	w	NY	Nevada	Nevada Twp	75	317
CONGER								
E	26	m	w	OR	Lassen	Susanville Twp	73	443
James	30	m	w	CANA	Mendocino	Little Rvr Twp	74	171
Leonard	45	m	w	NY	San Bernardino	San Bernardino Twp	78	425
CONGIATO								
Nicholas	50	m	w	ITAL	Santa Clara	2-Wd San Jose	88	309
CONGLETON								
G W	12	m	w	CA	Sonoma	Washington Twp	91	466
CONGLTON								
Aden C	56	m	w	NY	Mendocino	Navarro & Big Rvr	74	176
CONGREVE								
John	45	m	w	IREL	Los Angeles	Los Angeles	73	526
CONGROVE								
Johnathan	47	m	w	KY	Sonoma	Petaluma Twp	91	331
CONGUIS								
Louis	40	m	w	FRAN	El Dorado	White Oak Twp	72	143
CONHEIM								
Max	42	m	w	PRUS	San Francisco	San Francisco P O	83	274
CONIA								
Emma	40	f	w	MEXI	Los Angeles	Los Angeles Twp	73	475
Jesus	38	m	w	MEXI	Kern	Havilah P O	73	339
John	35	m	w	PORT	Nevada	Rough & Ready Twp	75	329
CONICK								
Otto	33	m	w	PRUS	Alameda	San Leandro	68	95
CONIFF								
John	42	m	w	IREL	Sonoma	Petaluma Twp	91	325
Michael	52	m	w	IREL	San Francisco	San Francisco P O	83	117
Peter	46	m	w	IREL	San Francisco	1-Wd San Francisco	79	12
Peter	45	m	w	IREL	San Francisco	11-Wd San Francisc	84	498
CONIGAN								
Eliza	40	f	w	IREL	San Francisco	2-Wd San Francisco	79	161
CONILL								
Louis Felix	38	m	w	FRAN	Los Angeles	Los Angeles	73	562
CONIO								
Angilo	25	m	w	ITAL	Nevada	Grass Valley Twp	75	186
CONIPER								
Antonio	41	m	w	CRIC	Calaveras	San Andreas P O	70	203
CONISS								
D B	12	m	w	CA	Alameda	Oakland	68	243
CONKEY								
Adelaide	50	f	w	HAMB	San Francisco	8-Wd San Francisco	82	491
William W	40	m	w	NY	Placer	Auburn P O	76	366
CONKLE								
Isiah	42	m	w	OH	Butte	Kimshew Tpw	70	83
CONKLEY								
Timothy	7	m	w	CA	Marin	San Rafael Twp	74	29
William	10	m	w	CA	Marin	San Rafael Twp	74	29
CONKLIN								
A C	55	m	w	NY	San Francisco	San Francisco P O	83	303
Conner	40	m	w	NY	Mariposa	Mariposa P O	74	97
Daniel	45	m	w	NY	San Francisco	San Francisco P O	83	119
Ed B	46	m	w	NY	Santa Barbara	San Buenaventura P	87	439
Emma	16	f	w	NY	San Francisco	San Francisco P O	83	49
Geo	44	m	w	NY	San Francisco	11-Wd San Francisc	84	428
Hiram	62	m	w	NY	Mariposa	Mariposa P O	74	92
Jessy	39	m	w	OH	San Joaquin	2-Wd Stockton	86	175

© 2001 by Heritage Quest. All rights reserved.

Name	Age	S	R	B-PL	County	Locale	Series M593 Roll	Pg
John	37	m	w	IREL	Nevada	Meadow Lake Twp	75	270
John K	36	m	w	IREL	Nevada	Little York Twp	75	241
Kate	25	f	w	IREL	San Francisco	8-Wd San Francisco	82	290
Levi	55	m	w	MO	Colusa	Stony Crk Twp	71	332
Levi	43	m	w	NY	Santa Barbara	Santa Barbara P O	87	488
N	41	m	w	NY	Del Norte	Crescent	71	467
S W	40	m	w	NY	Monterey	Salinas Twp	74	307
Silas	38	m	w	NY	Stanislaus	Empire Twp	92	65
Thaddeus	19	m	w	NY	Shasta	Buckeye P O	89	482
Timothy	57	m	w	NY	Shasta	Shasta P O	89	458
W R	20	m	w	NY	Marin	San Rafael Twp	74	37
Wm	23	m	w	IREL	Santa Barbara	Santa Barbara P O	87	503
Wm S	52	m	w	NY	Sonoma	Healdsburg	91	275
CONKLING								
Charles	37	m	w	NY	Humboldt	Mattole Twp	72	288
Charles	33	m	w	NY	El Dorado	Salmon Falls Twp	72	130
David	30	m	w	OH	San Francisco	San Francisco P O	80	487
Frank	39	m	w	NY	San Francisco	8-Wd San Francisco	82	307
M J	46	m	w	NY	Humboldt	Mattole Twp	72	285
Pheobe J	33	f	w	NY	San Francisco	8-Wd San Francisco	82	305
CONKRIGHT								
Emanuel	30	m	w	MI	Sonoma	Analy Twp	91	224
CONLAN								
Allan H	29	m	w	MA	Siskiyou	Cottonwood Twp	89	591
Ann	25	f	w	IREL	Yolo	Putah Twp	93	519
Ann	25	f	w	IREL	San Francisco	7-Wd San Francisco	81	193
Annie	25	f	w	IREL	San Francisco	1-Wd San Francisco	79	44
Catherine	28	f	w	IREL	Nevada	Grass Valley Twp	75	176
Danl	34	m	w	IREL	Sierra	Sears Twp	89	559
James	35	m	w	IREL	Marin	San Rafael Twp	74	38
John P	38	m	w	IREL	San Francisco	11-Wd San Francisc	84	698
Michael	28	m	w	IREL	Yolo	Putah Twp	93	523
Patrick	40	m	w	IREL	Sacramento	2-Wd Sacramento	77	213
Saml	32	m	w	IREL	Sierra	Sears Twp	89	559
Sarah	35	f	w	IREL	San Francisco	8-Wd San Francisco	82	472
Thomas	32	m	w	IREL	Yolo	Putah Twp	93	519
CONLAND								
Michael	39	m	w	IREL	San Francisco	San Francisco P O	83	13
CONLEE								
L	37	m	w	NY	Sierra	Sierra Twp	89	570
CONLEN								
Mary	30	f	w	IREL	San Francisco	11-Wd San Francisc	84	513
CONLEY								
Annie	23	f	w	IREL	San Francisco	San Francisco P O	83	169
Arthur	35	m	w	IREL	San Francisco	1-Wd San Francisco	79	77
Barney	45	m	w	IREL	Tulare	Visalia	92	295
Christopher	36	m	w	MI	Siskiyou	Yreka Twp	89	672
Columbus	28	m	w	TN	Colusa	Spring Valley Twp	71	335
Cornelius	37	m	w	IREL	Solano	Vallejo	90	163
Daniel	37	m	w	IREL	San Francisco	San Francisco P O	83	117
Ellen	32	f	w	IREL	Sacramento	1-Wd Sacramento	77	186
F	36	m	w	IREL	Alameda	Oakland	68	261
Frank	51	m	w	NY	Sacramento	2-Wd Sacramento	77	235
Frank	23	m	w	IREL	San Francisco	1-Wd San Francisco	79	132
George	30	m	w	TN	Colusa	Spring Valley Twp	71	335
George	20	m	w	ENGL	San Mateo	Redwood Twp	87	365
Henry	29	m	w	IREL	Marin	Tomales Twp	74	77
J T	8	m	w	CA	Amador	Ione City P O	69	364
James	75	m	w	IREL	San Francisco	San Francisco P O	83	304
James	38	m	w	IREL	Solano	Vacaville Twp	90	133
James	30	m	w	IREL	San Francisco	1-Wd San Francisco	79	70
James L	30	m	w	IREL	Yuba	Marysville	93	589
John	50	m	w	NY	San Francisco	8-Wd San Francisco	82	398
John	40	m	w	IREL	Santa Clara	1-Wd San Jose	88	250
John	38	m	w	IREL	Santa Clara	Redwood Twp	88	128
John	35	m	w	OH	Tehama	Tehama Twp	92	192
John	26	m	w	IREL	Napa	Napa	75	48
John	20	m	w	MA	San Francisco	San Francisco P O	83	107
John W	26	m	w	MA	San Francisco	8-Wd San Francisco	82	290
Joseph	24	m	w	IREL	Monterey	Castroville Twp	74	335
Maggie	17	f	w	ME	Tulare	Visalia	92	292
Margaret	22	f	w	IREL	San Francisco	8-Wd San Francisco	82	490
Mathew	37	m	w	IREL	Mariposa	Maxwell Crk P O	74	142
Michael	29	m	w	IREL	Yuba	Rose Bar Twp	93	655
Milton	26	m	w	IN	Colusa	Colusa	71	289
Pat	25	m	w	IREL	Solano	Benicia	90	4
Patrick	46	m	w	IREL	Santa Clara	San Jose Twp	88	181
Patrick	40	m	w	IREL	San Francisco	San Francisco P O	83	239
Peter	10	m	w	CA	San Mateo	Redwood City P O	87	375
Philip	27	m	w	IREL	Marin	Tomales Twp	74	85
Richd	26	m	w	IREL	San Francisco	1-Wd San Francisco	79	84
Samuel	24	m	w	AR	Colusa	Spring Valley Twp	71	336
Susan	23	f	w	IREL	San Francisco	7-Wd San Francisco	81	267
Thomas	30	m	w	IREL	San Francisco	San Francisco P O	85	838
Thomas	25	m	w	NY	San Francisco	1-Wd San Francisco	79	136
Thomas G	33	m	w	OH	Tulare	Tule Rvr Twp	92	262
Thos	24	m	w	IREL	San Francisco	1-Wd San Francisco	79	132
William	45	m	w	IL	Santa Clara	Redwood Twp	88	128
William	28	m	w	IREL	San Francisco	2-Wd San Francisco	79	243
CONLIER								
John	26	m	w	IREL	Yolo	Grafton Twp	93	479
CONLIFFE								
James	64	m	w	ENGL	San Francisco	3-Wd San Francisco	79	322
CONLIN								
Catharine	27	f	w	IREL	Butte	Ophir Twp	70	115
Francis	35	m	w	IREL	Nevada	Grass Valley Twp	75	159
James	40	m	w	IREL	Tuolumne	Columbia P O	93	348
James	35	m	w	IREL	San Francisco	San Francisco P O	85	734
James	24	m	w	IREL	San Francisco	San Francisco P O	83	150
John	40	m	w	IREL	Tuolumne	Columbia P O	93	344
John	37	m	w	IREL	Tuolumne	Columbia P O	93	343
John	32	m	w	IREL	San Francisco	11-Wd San Francisc	84	425
John	31	m	w	IREL	San Francisco	San Francisco P O	83	401
John F	35	m	w	IREL	San Francisco	8-Wd San Francisco	82	331
L	43	m	w	MA	Solano	Vallejo	90	193
Margt	33	f	w	IREL	San Francisco	8-Wd San Francisco	82	318
Martin	59	m	w	IREL	San Francisco	San Francisco P O	83	34
Mary	20	f	w	IREL	Sonoma	Petaluma Twp	91	361
Mathew	28	m	w	IREL	San Francisco	San Francisco P O	83	363
Palsey	40	m	w	IREL	San Francisco	11-Wd San Francisc	84	512
Simon	43	m	w	IREL	Plumas	Quartz Twp	77	35
Thos	37	m	w	IREL	Yuba	Rose Bar Twp	93	661
Winfred	23	f	w	IREL	San Francisco	11-Wd San Francisc	84	510
CONLON								
Anne	60	f	w	IREL	San Francisco	San Francisco P O	83	265
Bernard	37	m	w	IREL	San Francisco	San Francisco P O	83	161
Cathrine	23	f	w	IREL	San Francisco	1-Wd San Francisco	79	103
Ellen	31	f	w	IREL	San Francisco	San Francisco P O	83	320
Emile	33	m	w	FRAN	San Francisco	8-Wd San Francisco	82	394
Francis	40	m	w	IREL	San Francisco	San Francisco P O	83	161
H	40	m	w	IREL	Sierra	Lincoln Twp	89	547
Ida	24	f	w	LA	Sacramento	1-Wd Sacramento	77	181
John	36	m	w	IREL	San Francisco	San Francisco P O	83	265
John	30	m	w	IREL	Solano	Benicia	90	13
John	26	m	w	IREL	San Francisco	1-Wd San Francisco	79	105
John	25	m	w	IREL	San Francisco	8-Wd San Francisco	82	443
John B	43	m	w	IREL	Nevada	Grass Valley Twp	75	228
M	28	m	w	CANA	Solano	Vallejo	90	145
Mary	31	f	w	NY	Sacramento	1-Wd Sacramento	77	181
Michl	29	m	w	IREL	San Francisco	1-Wd San Francisco	79	85
Owen	36	m	w	IREL	San Francisco	1-Wd San Francisco	79	72
Patk	40	m	w	IREL	Sacramento	1-Wd Sacramento	77	179
Patrick	40	m	w	IREL	San Francisco	11-Wd San Francisc	84	458
Patrick	21	m	w	IREL	San Francisco	8-Wd San Francisco	82	461
Peter	33	m	w	IREL	San Francisco	1-Wd San Francisco	79	99
Thomas	37	m	w	IREL	Amador	Jackson P O	69	321
CONLUE								
Ed	40	m	w	IREL	Alameda	Oakland	68	205
CONLY								
Alexander B	23	m	w	IL	San Luis Obispo	Santa Rosa Twp	87	327
Andres F	26	m	w	IL	Los Angeles	Wilmington Twp	73	642
Bridget	28	f	w	IREL	Monterey	San Juan Twp	74	411
Catherin	26	f	w	IREL	San Francisco	11-Wd San Francisc	84	491
Charles	30	m	w	IREL	San Francisco	8-Wd San Francisco	82	376
Cyrus B	39	m	w	OH	Stanislaus	San Joaquin Twp	92	77
Edward	40	m	w	IREL	San Mateo	San Mateo P O	87	349
Ellen	21	f	w	IREL	San Francisco	8-Wd San Francisco	82	289
Hannah	30	f	w	IREL	Alameda	Oakland	68	266
James	36	m	w	IREL	Solano	Suisun Twp	90	93
James	28	m	w	IREL	San Francisco	11-Wd San Francisc	84	599
James	23	m	w	ENGL	Santa Clara	Fremont Twp	88	41
John	50	m	w	IREL	Napa	Napa Twp	75	34
John	38	m	w	IREL	San Francisco	11-Wd San Francisc	84	496
John	19	m	w	CANA	Marin	Tomales Twp	74	77
Joseph W	38	m	w	PA	Solano	Rio Vista Twp	90	61
Mary	27	f	w	IREL	San Joaquin	1-Wd Stockton	86	121
Nicholas	32	m	w	IREL	Sonoma	Petaluma Twp	91	352
Pat	32	m	w	IREL	San Francisco	7-Wd San Francisco	81	257
Patrick	23	m	w	IREL	San Francisco	8-Wd San Francisco	82	329
Sarah Ann	27	f	w	TN	Santa Clara	Fremont Twp	88	45
Thomas	49	m	w	IREL	Sutter	Vernon Twp	92	132
William	56	m	w	CT	San Luis Obispo	Santa Rosa Twp	87	327
CONN								
Ah	38	m	c	CHIN	Tuolumne	Sonora P O	93	323
Edward J	38	m	w	NY	Mendocino	Big Rvr Twp	74	160
Francis	23	m	w	CT	San Francisco	6-Wd San Francisco	81	125
Furgeson	38	m	w	PA	Mariposa	Mariposa P O	74	124
Henry D	65	m	w	KY	Fresno	Millerton P O	72	145
Herman	25	m	w	MA	Siskiyou	Yreka Twp	89	665
James	40	m	w	IREL	Nevada	Bloomfield Twp	75	93
John	37	m	w	CANA	Santa Cruz	Watsonville	89	366
John B	37	m	w	IREL	Nevada	Eureka Twp	75	133
Kate	6	f	w	CA	San Francisco	2-Wd San Francisco	79	280
Thomas	28	m	w	IREL	Nevada	Bloomfield Twp	75	92
William	49	m	w	ENGL	Nevada	Washington Twp	75	342
William	46	m	w	WIND	San Bernardino	San Bernardino Twp	78	429
William	42	m	w	IREL	San Diego	Warners Rancho Dis	78	530
Zachariah	66	m	w	PRUS	San Diego	San Diego	78	486
CONNAHAN								
Cornelius	40	m	w	IREL	San Francisco	11-Wd San Francisc	84	616
Frank	44	m	w	IREL	San Francisco	San Francisco P O	83	291
Frank	31	m	w	IREL	Contra Costa	Martinez P O	71	415
CONNAL								
John	42	m	w	IREL	Nevada	Grass Valley Twp	75	208
CONNALAY								
Andy	77	m	w	IREL	Nevada	Nevada Twp	75	273
Ann	73	f	w	IREL	Nevada	Nevada Twp	75	273
CONNALLON								
Ellen	21	f	w	IREL	San Francisco	San Francisco P O	83	195
CONNALLY								
Bernard	22	m	w	IREL	Sonoma	Vallejo Twp	91	460
Henry	32	m	w	IREL	Calaveras	San Andreas P O	70	170
CONNALY								
J A	45	m	w	IREL	Tuolumne	Columbia P O	93	343

© 2001 by Heritage Quest. All rights reserved.

Series M593

Name	Age	S	R	B-PL	County	Locale	Roll	Pg
CONNATO								
Lorenzo	30	m	w	ITAL	Santa Cruz	Santa Cruz	89	433
CONNAUGHTON								
John	9	m	w	CA	Marin	San Rafael Twp	74	27
CONNAY								
Edwin N	28	m	w	AR	San Luis Obispo	Santa Rosa Twp	87	317
J J B	28	m	w	NY	Sierra	Butte Twp	89	508
Phillip	33	m	w	IREL	San Francisco	San Francisco P O	83	6
William	22	m	w	IREL	Kern	Linns Valley P O	73	343
CONNE								
Ellen	18	f	w	IREL	San Francisco	San Francisco P O	83	171
CONNEAL								
A	27	m	w	IL	Amador	Ione City P O	69	353
CONNEAUX								
James	30	m	w	ENGL	San Francisco	6-Wd San Francisco	81	92
CONNEFF								
Ellen	17	f	w	MA	San Francisco	San Francisco P O	83	183
Micheal	35	m	w	IREL	Sonoma	Petaluma Twp	91	333
Patrick	48	m	w	IREL	Sonoma	Petaluma Twp	91	333
CONNEFRY								
John	33	m	w	IREL	Placer	Rocklin Twp	76	464
CONNEL								
Dennis	45	m	w	IREL	Alameda	Oakland	68	210
James	27	m	w	IREL	Nevada	Meadow Lake Twp	75	265
Jennie	41	f	w	IREL	Santa Clara	San Jose Twp	88	195
John	35	m	w	IREL	Solano	Vallejo	90	197
Joseph	35	m	w	IN	Siskiyou	Scott Valley Twp	89	620
Mary	18	f	w	IREL	Alameda	Oakland	68	188
Pat	23	m	w	IREL	Solano	Vallejo	90	215
Stephen	26	m	w	IREL	Solano	Vallejo	90	215
CONNELEY								
Michael	33	m	w	IREL	Amador	Sutter Crk P O	69	396
Patrick	40	m	w	IREL	San Francisco	San Francisco P O	83	419
CONNELL								
Agnes M	30	f	w	IREL	San Francisco	1-Wd San Francisco	79	56
Bridget	42	f	w	IREL	Solano	Suisun Twp	90	113
Catherine	30	f	w	IREL	San Francisco	San Francisco P O	83	385
Chas D	37	m	w	IREL	San Francisco	1-Wd San Francisco	79	56
Chas S	5	m	w	CA	San Francisco	1-Wd San Francisco	79	56
Danl	35	m	w	IREL	Solano	Benicia	90	18
David	72	m	w	SCOT	San Francisco	2-Wd San Francisco	79	219
Dennis	45	m	w	IREL	San Francisco	San Francisco P O	85	743
Dennis	40	m	w	IREL	San Francisco	San Francisco P O	83	296
E	30	f	w	IREL	Alameda	Oakland	68	150
Giles	64	m	w	TN	Marin	Tomales Twp	74	77
Hiram	27	m	w	IL	Solano	Vacaville Twp	90	135
Honora	45	f	w	IREL	San Francisco	11-Wd San Francisc	84	453
Hugh	39	m	w	IREL	Napa	Napa Twp	75	75
Hugh	36	m	w	IREL	Marin	San Rafael Twp	74	26
James	52	m	w	ENGL	San Francisco	San Francisco P O	80	399
James	38	m	w	IREL	San Diego	San Diego	78	488
James	34	m	w	IREL	San Francisco	11-Wd San Francisc	84	450
Johanna	71	f	w	IREL	San Francisco	11-Wd San Francisc	84	625
John	46	m	w	IREL	Merced	Snelling P O	74	280
John	40	m	w	IREL	San Francisco	1-Wd San Francisco	79	15
John	38	m	w	IREL	San Joaquin	3-Wd Stockton	86	232
John	37	m	w	NY	San Francisco	11-Wd San Francisc	84	692
John	35	m	w	IREL	San Francisco	San Francisco P O	85	714
John	28	m	w	IREL	San Francisco	6-Wd San Francisco	81	62
John	28	m	w	IREL	San Francisco	1-Wd San Francisco	79	65
John	27	m	w	IREL	Sutter	Yuba Twp	92	149
John	26	m	w	VA	Mono	Bridgeport P O	74	287
Katie	25	f	w	IREL	San Francisco	1-Wd San Francisco	79	132
Laurence	80	m	w	IREL	San Francisco	San Francisco P O	83	75
Lizzie	30	f	w	IREL	San Francisco	San Francisco P O	83	98
Mary	50	f	w	IREL	San Francisco	8-Wd San Francisco	82	485
Michael	36	m	w	CANA	San Francisco	San Francisco P O	83	349
Michael	25	m	w	IREL	Sutter	Sutter Twp	92	129
Michl	40	m	w	IREL	Sutter	Sutter Twp	92	117
Michl	26	m	w	IREL	San Francisco	1-Wd San Francisco	79	133
Michl	22	m	w	IREL	San Francisco	1-Wd San Francisco	79	32
Mike	37	m	w	IREL	San Francisco	11-Wd San Francisc	84	693
Nicholas	35	m	w	IREL	Amador	Amador City P O	69	391
Patk	40	m	w	IREL	Solano	Vallejo	90	144
Patk	26	m	w	IREL	Solano	Vallejo	90	203
Patrick	40	m	w	IREL	San Francisco	San Francisco P O	83	313
Patrick	36	m	w	IREL	San Francisco	1-Wd San Francisco	79	125
Patrick	36	m	w	IREL	San Francisco	3-Wd San Francisco	79	308
Peter	35	m	w	IREL	Santa Clara	Fremont Twp	88	61
Reny	29	m	w	PA	Solano	Silveyville Twp	90	84
Richd	49	m	w	IREL	San Francisco	1-Wd San Francisco	79	91
Richd	39	m	w	IREL	San Francisco	1-Wd San Francisco	79	79
Richd	37	m	w	NY	San Francisco	San Francisco P O	83	130
Rose	21	f	w	IREL	Santa Barbara	Santa Barbara P O	87	451
Thompson	46	m	w	OH	Colusa	Monroe Twp	71	311
Thos	51	m	w	IREL	San Francisco	11-Wd San Francisc	84	624
William	30	m	w	ENGL	Sonoma	Petaluma Twp	91	353
William	21	m	w	CANA	San Francisco	San Francisco P O	80	336
Wm	40	m	w	IREL	Sacramento	3-Wd Sacramento	77	255
Wm	30	m	w	NY	Sacramento	1-Wd Sacramento	77	182
Wm	30	m	w	IREL	San Francisco	5-Wd San Francisco	81	35
CONNELLEY								
Michael	47	m	w	IREL	San Francisco	San Francisco P O	83	263
Peter	50	m	w	IREL	San Francisco	San Francisco P O	83	335
Peter	28	m	w	IREL	San Francisco	San Francisco P O	83	266
CONNELLS								
Danl	59	m	w	IREL	San Diego	San Diego	78	491

Series M593

Name	Age	S	R	B-PL	County	Locale	Roll	Pg
CONNELLY								
A H	38	m	w	MA	Napa	Napa	75	18
Ann	19	f	w	NY	San Francisco	San Francisco P O	85	722
Annie	29	f	w	NY	San Francisco	11-Wd San Francisc	84	510
Bartlett	48	m	w	IREL	Monterey	San Antonio Twp	74	321
Bridget	45	f	w	IREL	San Francisco	11-Wd San Francisc	84	564
Bridgett	17	f	w	IREL	San Francisco	1-Wd San Francisco	79	89
Christopher	47	m	w	IREL	Placer	Roseville P O	76	350
Colman	51	m	w	IREL	Placer	Auburn P O	76	373
Dan	23	m	w	IREL	San Francisco	5-Wd San Francisco	81	27
David	30	m	w	PA	Nevada	Eureka Twp	75	133
E	56	f	w	IREL	San Francisco	San Francisco P O	83	133
Edward	48	m	w	ENGL	San Francisco	2-Wd San Francisco	79	201
Edwd	32	m	w	IREL	San Francisco	San Francisco P O	83	81
Ellen	24	f	w	IREL	Nevada	Grass Valley Twp	75	167
Ellen	20	f	w	IREL	San Francisco	8-Wd San Francisco	82	412
Ellen	19	f	w	IREL	San Francisco	San Francisco P O	83	179
Felix	30	m	w	IREL	Marin	Tomales Twp	74	83
Florida	14	f	w	CA	Sonoma	Cloverdale Twp	91	267
Francis	30	m	w	IREL	San Francisco	San Francisco P O	83	219
Frank	45	m	w	CANA	Alameda	Oakland	68	225
Frank J	18	m	w	IL	Butte	Chico Twp	70	20
J W	32	m	w	NY	Sierra	Table Rock Twp	89	572
James	65	m	w	IREL	San Francisco	San Francisco P O	83	66
James	22	m	w	IREL	San Francisco	San Francisco P O	85	764
James J	43	m	w	ENGL	Placer	Bath P O	76	451
James M	36	m	w	IREL	Yolo	Cache Crk Twp	93	430
Jane	18	f	w	IREL	San Francisco	San Francisco P O	83	35
Johanna	18	f	w	IREL	San Francisco	8-Wd San Francisco	82	453
John	45	m	w	NY	San Francisco	2-Wd San Francisco	79	185
John	36	m	w	MA	San Francisco	San Francisco P O	85	763
John	36	m	w	ENGL	Alpine	Markleeville P O	69	312
John	30	m	w	MA	San Francisco	5-Wd San Francisco	81	32
John	30	m	w	IREL	Contra Costa	Martinez P O	71	389
John	26	m	w	IREL	San Francisco	San Francisco P O	85	873
John D	40	m	w	IREL	San Francisco	1-Wd San Francisco	79	62
Kate	30	f	w	IREL	San Francisco	San Francisco P O	80	407
Margaret	8	f	w	CA	San Francisco	San Francisco P O	83	53
Mark	35	m	w	IREL	San Francisco	2-Wd San Francisco	79	156
Mary	19	f	w	CA	San Francisco	11-Wd San Francisc	84	711
Mary	17	f	w	ENGL	San Francisco	San Francisco P O	83	105
Mary	12	f	w	CA	San Francisco	San Francisco P O	80	379
Michael	33	m	w	IREL	San Francisco	San Francisco P O	85	840
Michael	30	m	w	IREL	Santa Clara	Alviso Twp	88	28
Michael	26	m	w	IREL	Sutter	Sutter Twp	92	129
Michl	27	m	w	IREL	San Francisco	5-Wd San Francisco	81	32
Mike	40	m	w	IREL	San Francisco	11-Wd San Francisc	84	671
P	57	m	w	IREL	Sierra	Eureka Twp	89	526
Patrick	32	m	w	IREL	Santa Clara	Alviso Twp	88	28
Patrick	30	m	w	NY	San Francisco	San Francisco P O	83	408
Patrick	24	m	w	IREL	San Francisco	San Francisco P O	83	224
Theophlus F A	37	m	w	KY	Inyo	Bishop Crk Twp	73	317
Thomas	28	m	w	NY	San Francisco	San Francisco P O	83	216
Thomas	27	m	w	CANA	Alpine	Markleeville P O	69	312
Thos	25	m	w	IREL	San Francisco	San Francisco P O	83	123
Thos	25	m	w	IREL	San Francisco	San Francisco P O	83	130
Timothy	43	m	w	IREL	Monterey	Monterey Twp	74	349
Timothy	24	m	w	IREL	Nevada	Rough & Ready Twp	75	333
William	45	m	w	IREL	San Francisco	San Francisco P O	83	416
Wm C	36	m	w	AL	Tuolumne	Sonora P O	93	324
CONNELY								
Bridget	30	f	w	IREL	San Francisco	8-Wd San Francisco	82	303
George	29	m	w	WURT	Sonoma	Petaluma Twp	91	348
John	32	m	w	MD	San Francisco	11-Wd San Francisc	84	691
CONNEN								
John	37	m	w	CANA	Solano	Vallejo	90	144
CONNENS								
John	38	m	w	PA	Mariposa	Maxwell Crk P O	74	144
CONNER								
Alexandre	29	m	w	VA	Monterey	San Antonio Twp	74	319
Alice M	20	f	w	MA	San Francisco	San Francisco P O	83	23
Amelia	15	f	w	NY	San Mateo	Half Moon Bay P O	87	391
Ann	50	f	w	IREL	San Francisco	San Francisco P O	83	381
Anna	9	f	w	MA	Sacramento	2-Wd Sacramento	77	252
Arthur	45	m	w	OH	Sacramento	Lee Twp	77	158
Bartholemew	45	m	w	IREL	San Francisco	San Francisco P O	83	161
Caswell M	56	m	w	SC	Sacramento	Brighton Twp	77	71
Catherine	32	f	w	HDAR	Inyo	Independence Twp	73	324
D	30	m	w	IREL	Lake	Knoxville Mines	73	404
Daniel	62	m	w	ME	Trinity	Douglas	92	234
Daniel	39	m	w	IREL	Tuolumne	Sonora P O	93	326
E	23	m	w	MA	Napa	Napa Twp	75	68
Edwd W	33	m	w	CT	Butte	Chico Twp	70	26
Fanny	11	f	w	CA	Santa Clara	Burnett Twp	88	38
Francis E	56	m	w	IREL	Sacramento	Cosumnes Twp	77	88
Geo D	43	m	w	KY	Sacramento	Lee Twp	77	160
H S	30	m	w	NH	Sacramento	Franklin Twp	77	114
J	45	m	w	IREL	Lake	Lower Lake	73	418
J H	26	m	w	CANA	Alameda	Alameda	68	7
J P	30	m	w	IREL	Lake	Lower Lake	73	428
J Whitcomb	49	m	w	VT	Contra Costa	Martinez P O	71	378
Jack	35	m	w	IREL	Placer	Roseville P O	76	354
James	49	m	w	VA	San Diego	San Diego	78	486
James	48	m	w	IREL	Calaveras	San Andreas P O	70	183
James	40	m	w	IREL	Nevada	Grass Valley Twp	75	212
James	31	m	w	IREL	Alameda	Washington Twp	68	278
James	26	m	w	IREL	Alameda	Washington Twp	68	294

© 2001 by Heritage Quest. All rights reserved.

Series M593

Name	Age	S	R	B-PL	County	Locale	Roll	Pg
James	25	m	w	IREL	Sacramento	San Joaquin Twp	77	407
James H	23	m	w	MA	Santa Cruz	Pajaro Twp	89	350
Jerry	35	m	w	IREL	Sierra	Sears Twp	89	561
Jessie	16	f	w	CA	San Francisco	11-Wd San Francisc	84	608
Jno	27	m	w	IREL	Sierra	Gibson Twp	89	541
Jno W	40	m	w	NY	San Francisco	San Francisco P O	83	129
John	50	m	w	IN	El Dorado	Diamond Springs Tw	72	32
John	46	m	w	ME	Mendocino	Little Rvr Twp	74	171
John	36	m	w	IREL	Contra Costa	Martinez P O	71	415
John	35	m	w	IREL	San Francisco	San Francisco P O	83	142
John	32	m	w	IREL	Plumas	Indian Twp	77	19
John	31	m	w	SCOT	Placer	Rocklin Twp	76	467
John	25	m	w	IREL	Napa	Yountville Twp	75	76
John	21	m	w	IREL	Solano	Vallejo	90	217
John C	36	m	w	SC	Sacramento	Sutter Twp	77	391
John L	48	m	w	ENGL	Stanislaus	Emory Twp	92	20
John S	37	m	w	NH	Santa Clara	Santa Clara Twp	88	173
Joseph	26	m	w	OH	Santa Clara	2-Wd San Jose	88	323
Joseph	24	m	w	MO	Yolo	Buckeye Twp	93	413
Julia	50	f	w	IREL	San Francisco	San Francisco P O	83	84
L B	28	m	w	MI	Alameda	Alameda	68	13
M	27	m	w	IREL	Solano	Vallejo	90	213
Mary	43	f	w	IREL	San Francisco	San Francisco P O	83	258
Mary	30	f	w	CANA	Santa Clara	1-Wd San Jose	88	238
Mary A	16	f	w	NY	Santa Clara	Alviso Twp	88	22
Nora	19	f	w	IREL	San Francisco	San Francisco P O	85	813
Patk	25	m	w	IA	Marin	San Rafael Twp	74	38
Patrick	30	m	w	IREL	Marin	San Rafael Twp	74	31
Peter	40	m	w	PRUS	Alameda	Murray Twp	68	119
Philip	30	m	w	IREL	Santa Clara	1-Wd San Jose	88	241
Richard	34	m	w	IREL	Humboldt	Eureka Twp	72	271
T	39	m	w	IREL	Lake	Knoxville Mines	73	404
Thomas	39	m	w	IREL	Marin	San Rafael Twp	74	43
Thos	35	m	w	MA	San Francisco	5-Wd San Francisco	81	35
Thos	32	m	w	IREL	San Joaquin	3-Wd Stockton	86	216
Thos E	22	m	w	ENGL	San Francisco	5-Wd San Francisco	81	19
Timothy	40	m	w	IREL	Solano	Vallejo	90	189
Washington	30	m	w	CANA	Humboldt	Bucksport Twp	72	243
William	49	m	w	IREL	Santa Clara	Santa Clara Twp	88	172
William	44	m	w	OH	Colusa	Colusa Twp	71	281
William	43	m	w	IREL	Shasta	French Gulch P O	89	470
William	28	m	w	ME	Alameda	Brooklyn Twp	68	42
Wm	42	m	w	IREL	El Dorado	Coloma Twp	72	8
Wm	32	m	w	AL	Sacramento	Dry Crk Twp	77	98
CONNERLY								
David	35	m	w	IREL	San Francisco	8-Wd San Francisco	82	322
Kate	19	f	w	IREL	San Francisco	8-Wd San Francisco	82	289
CONNERO								
Ardora	21	m	i	MEXI	Inyo	Lone Pine Twp	73	333
CONNERS								
Abbie	21	f	w	IREL	San Francisco	San Francisco P O	83	260
Anna	35	f	w	NY	Alameda	Oakland	68	177
Anna Mrs	34	f	w	IREL	Amador	Amador City P O	69	395
Bridget	49	f	w	IREL	San Francisco	San Francisco P O	83	190
Frank	35	m	w	IREL	Trinity	Junction City Pct	92	205
Geo	28	m	w	CANA	Humboldt	Arcata Twp	72	234
J	42	m	w	IREL	Lake	Knoxville Mines	73	404
J	35	m	w	IREL	Alameda	Oakland	68	262
John	42	m	w	IREL	San Francisco	1-Wd San Francisco	79	76
John	41	m	w	IREL	San Joaquin	3-Wd Stockton	86	231
John	35	m	w	IREL	San Francisco	San Francisco P O	83	215
John	34	m	w	IREL	Amador	Amador City P O	69	392
John	30	m	w	NY	San Francisco	1-Wd San Francisco	79	42
John	28	m	w	IREL	Amador	Amador City P O	69	394
John	21	m	w	IREL	Sacramento	San Joaquin Twp	77	399
John J	36	m	w	IREL	Stanislaus	Empire Twp	92	64
Lamer	32	m	w	IREL	Siskiyou	Scott Valley Twp	89	611
Laurence	28	m	w	IREL	San Francisco	San Francisco P O	83	229
Mary	50	f	w	SCOT	Tuolumne	Sonora P O	93	310
Mary	35	f	w	IREL	Solano	Vallejo	90	208
Norah	24	f	w	IREL	Monterey	San Juan Twp	74	396
Richard	29	m	w	IREL	San Diego	Julian Dist	78	471
Robt	36	m	w	IREL	San Francisco	San Francisco P O	83	83
Thomas	35	m	w	IREL	Alameda	Washington Twp	68	276
Thomas	31	m	w	IREL	Colusa	Butte Twp	71	269
Thomas	30	m	w	NJ	Colusa	Colusa Twp	71	277
Thomas	28	m	w	CANA	Humboldt	Eureka Twp	72	282
CONNERTON								
Matthew	35	m	w	IREL	San Francisco	1-Wd San Francisco	79	72
CONNERTY								
Mary Ann	50	f	w	IREL	San Francisco	San Francisco P O	83	57
CONNERY								
Benj	40	m	w	WALE	Calaveras	Copperopolis P O	70	241
Matthew	50	m	w	IREL	Santa Clara	2-Wd San Jose	88	319
CONNESSE								
Jeaques	42	m	w	ITAL	San Francisco	San Francisco P O	85	851
CONNETT								
Wm L	23	m	w	NY	Siskiyou	Table Rock Twp	89	645
Wm L	22	m	w	IA	Shasta	Millville P O	89	487
CONNEY								
F E C	25	m	w	NH	Santa Clara	2-Wd San Jose	88	322
John	35	m	w	IREL	San Francisco	2-Wd San Francisco	79	213
Luke	35	m	w	IREL	Alameda	Oakland	68	150
CONNIC								
Leonard	56	m	w	CANA	Humboldt	Eureka Twp	72	264
CONNICK								
Harris	50	m	w	CANA	Humboldt	Eureka Twp	72	274

Series M593

Name	Age	S	R	B-PL	County	Locale	Roll	Pg
CONNIE								
Amos	26	m	w	CANA	Humboldt	Arcata Twp	72	225
F G	28	m	w	CANA	Humboldt	Arcata Twp	72	225
John	30	m	w	CANA	Humboldt	Arcata Twp	72	225
John	26	m	w	CANA	Santa Clara	Redwood Twp	88	131
CONNIEL								
Dominico	18	m	w	ITAL	San Mateo	Schoolhouse Statio	87	333
Dominico	16	m	w	ITAL	San Mateo	Schoolhouse Statio	87	346
John	20	m	w	ITAL	San Mateo	Schoolhouse Statio	87	346
CONNIELIES								
James	24	m	w	IREL	San Francisco	1-Wd San Francisco	79	132
CONNIFF								
James	36	m	w	IREL	San Francisco	1-Wd San Francisco	79	2
James	22	m	w	AUSL	San Francisco	1-Wd San Francisco	79	104
John	45	m	w	IREL	Alameda	Brooklyn	68	38
M	15	f	w	CA	Alameda	Oakland	68	237
O M	36	m	w	ME	Nevada	Meadow Lake Twp	75	248
CONNIHAN								
John	42	m	w	IREL	San Francisco	San Francisco P O	83	1
CONNISS								
John	38	m	w	IREL	Sonoma	Petaluma Twp	91	333
Mary	18	f	w	NY	Alameda	Oakland	68	157
CONNLY								
John	35	m	w	IREL	San Francisco	11-Wd San Francisc	84	431
CONNOGG								
Eunice	82	f	w	NJ	Contra Costa	Martinez P O	71	376
CONNOL								
Tim	35	m	w	IREL	San Francisco	5-Wd San Francisco	81	35
CONNOLEY								
John	34	m	w	IREL	San Francisco	7-Wd San Francisco	81	180
John	28	m	w	NY	San Francisco	7-Wd San Francisco	81	195
Mary	40	f	w	IREL	San Francisco	7-Wd San Francisco	81	186
CONNOLLEY								
Thos	42	m	w	IREL	San Francisco	San Francisco P O	83	286
CONNOLLY								
Ann	50	f	w	IREL	San Francisco	6-Wd San Francisco	81	147
Anne	40	f	w	IREL	San Francisco	8-Wd San Francisco	82	399
Bryan	32	m	w	IREL	Nevada	Bloomfield Twp	75	97
Catherine	28	f	w	IREL	San Francisco	8-Wd San Francisco	82	471
Cornelious	28	m	w	IREL	San Francisco	11-Wd San Francisc	84	541
D W	64	m	w	VA	San Francisco	3-Wd San Francisco	79	327
Dan	22	m	w	IREL	San Francisco	San Francisco P O	83	372
Edward	39	m	w	IREL	San Francisco	8-Wd San Francisco	82	473
Eliza	20	f	w	AUSL	San Francisco	11-Wd San Francisc	84	711
Ellen	23	f	w	IREL	Alameda	Oakland	68	175
Gilbert	50	m	w	IREL	Santa Cruz	Santa Cruz Twp	89	390
James	40	m	w	IREL	San Francisco	8-Wd San Francisco	82	436
James	36	m	w	CANA	Alameda	Oakland	68	148
Jane	15	f	w	RI	San Francisco	8-Wd San Francisco	82	467
Jas	37	m	w	IREL	San Francisco	San Francisco P O	85	786
Jetty	30	f	w	IREL	San Francisco	6-Wd San Francisco	81	94
John	40	m	w	IREL	San Francisco	San Francisco P O	85	757
John	40	m	w	IREL	Nevada	Grass Valley Twp	75	213
John	32	m	w	IREL	Santa Cruz	Pajaro Twp	89	350
John	31	m	w	IREL	San Francisco	8-Wd San Francisco	82	490
Joseph	19	m	w	CANA	San Francisco	8-Wd San Francisco	82	461
Kate	40	f	w	IREL	Alameda	Oakland	68	182
Margaret	40	f	w	NY	San Francisco	San Francisco P O	83	23
Margaret	30	f	w	IREL	Nevada	Grass Valley Twp	75	150
Martin	48	m	w	IREL	San Francisco	San Francisco P O	83	393
Mary	30	f	w	NY	Alameda	Oakland	68	193
Mary	19	f	w	MA	Nevada	Rough & Ready Twp	75	330
Mary	19	f	w	IREL	San Francisco	2-Wd San Francisco	79	208
Mathias	24	m	w	IREL	Nevada	Grass Valley Twp	75	220
Michl	63	m	w	IREL	San Francisco	San Francisco P O	85	869
Michl	33	m	w	IREL	San Francisco	1-Wd San Francisco	79	64
N	35	m	w	IREL	San Francisco	San Francisco P O	85	825
Nicholas	22	m	w	LA	San Francisco	San Francisco P O	85	851
Owen	48	m	w	IREL	San Francisco	San Francisco P O	85	825
Owen	23	m	w	IREL	Santa Clara	2-Wd San Jose	88	333
Patk	36	m	w	IREL	San Francisco	San Francisco P O	83	36
Patrick	37	m	w	IREL	San Francisco	6-Wd San Francisco	81	92
Patrick	30	m	w	IREL	San Francisco	San Francisco P O	83	279
Patrick	26	m	w	IREL	San Francisco	San Francisco P O	85	773
Patrick	26	m	w	IREL	Nevada	Grass Valley Twp	75	213
Patrick	25	m	w	IREL	San Francisco	San Francisco P O	83	384
Patrick	25	m	w	IREL	Nevada	Grass Valley Twp	75	217
Peter	36	m	w	IREL	San Francisco	8-Wd San Francisco	82	487
Peter	26	m	w	IREL	San Francisco	San Francisco P O	83	29
Philip	36	m	w	IREL	Nevada	Rough & Ready Twp	75	324
Richard	21	m	w	IREL	Nevada	Rough & Ready Twp	75	333
Rodgers	28	m	w	IREL	San Francisco	7-Wd San Francisco	81	238
Thomas	32	m	w	IREL	Nevada	Grass Valley Twp	75	231
Timothy	45	m	w	IREL	San Francisco	1-Wd San Francisco	79	83
Timothy	45	m	w	IREL	San Francisco	11-Wd San Francisc	84	579
Tom	29	m	w	NY	San Francisco	San Francisco P O	83	399
William	21	m	w	IREL	San Francisco	5-Wd San Francisco	81	28
Wm	38	m	w	IREL	San Francisco	1-Wd San Francisco	79	63
Wm J	36	m	w	IREL	San Francisco	San Francisco P O	83	105
CONNOLY								
Briget	31	f	w	IREL	San Francisco	7-Wd San Francisco	81	196
Coleman	25	m	w	IREL	San Francisco	7-Wd San Francisco	81	197
Henry	43	m	w	IREL	Solano	Vallejo	90	144
James	40	m	w	IREL	Santa Barbara	San Buenaventura P	87	437
James	26	m	w	IREL	San Francisco	7-Wd San Francisco	81	184
John	42	m	w	IREL	San Francisco	San Francisco P O	83	163
John	36	m	w	IREL	Amador	Sutter Crk P O	69	410

© 2001 by Heritage Quest. All rights reserved.

California 1870 Census

Name	Age	S	R	B-PL	County	Locale	Roll	Pg
						Series M593		
John	30	m	w	IREL	San Francisco	7-Wd San Francisco	81	203
Kate	20	f	w	IREL	San Francisco	San Francisco P O	85	776
Margaret	14	f	w	NY	San Francisco	6-Wd San Francisco	81	115
Mary	49	f	w	IREL	Alameda	Oakland	68	180
Mary A	30	f	w	PA	Nevada	Grass Valley Twp	75	173
Mathew	30	m	w	IREL	San Francisco	7-Wd San Francisco	81	180
Patrick	35	m	w	IREL	San Francisco	7-Wd San Francisco	81	201
Patrick	30	m	w	IREL	San Francisco	7-Wd San Francisco	81	196
William	37	m	w	RI	San Francisco	3-Wd San Francisco	79	320
CONNON								
Larcus	45	m	w	IREL	Contra Costa	San Pablo Twp	71	362
Mary Ann	35	f	w	MA	San Francisco	San Francisco P O	83	84
CONNONE								
Dominic	34	m	w	ITAL	San Mateo	Schoolhouse Statio	87	345
CONNOR								
--- Mrs	35	m	w	IREL	Sacramento	4-Wd Sacramento	77	373
Alma	17	f	w	CA	Sacramento	3-Wd Sacramento	77	317
Bridget	47	f	w	IREL	San Francisco	11-Wd San Francisc	84	572
Bridget	38	f	w	IREL	San Mateo	Half Moon Bay P O	87	389
C R	23	m	w	NY	San Francisco	3-Wd San Francisco	79	322
Charles M	25	m	w	MA	San Francisco	San Francisco P O	83	171
Chas	40	m	w	OH	San Francisco	11-Wd San Francisc	84	694
Christian	40	m	w	MA	San Francisco	2-Wd San Francisco	79	212
Daniel	35	m	w	IREL	San Francisco	11-Wd San Francisc	84	504
Daniel	25	m	w	MA	Nevada	Grass Valley Twp	75	193
Danl	27	m	w	IREL	Alameda	Murray Twp	68	106
David	40	m	w	IREL	San Francisco	San Francisco P O	85	778
David	32	m	w	SC	Santa Barbara	San Buenaventura P	87	420
Dennis	24	m	w	IREL	San Francisco	3-Wd San Francisco	79	313
Dennis	22	m	w	MA	San Francisco	7-Wd San Francisco	81	237
Edmund	28	m	w	NY	Alpine	Monitor P O	69	314
Edward	50	m	w	IREL	Yolo	Putah Twp	93	521
Edward W	48	m	w	NY	Siskiyou	Yreka	89	663
Eliza	23	f	w	IREL	San Francisco	8-Wd San Francisco	82	481
Ellen	23	f	w	MA	San Francisco	8-Wd San Francisco	82	463
Ellen	22	f	w	IREL	San Francisco	San Francisco P O	83	288
Fannie	8	f	w	CA	Alameda	Oakland	68	146
Francis	43	m	w	MO	San Francisco	7-Wd San Francisco	81	245
Frank	38	m	w	IREL	San Francisco	1-Wd San Francisco	79	118
Frank	26	m	w	IREL	Sacramento	1-Wd Sacramento	77	186
Frank	25	m	w	IREL	San Francisco	11-Wd San Francisc	84	550
Frank	25	m	w	OH	Sacramento	4-Wd Sacramento	77	369
Graham	26	m	w	PRUS	San Francisco	7-Wd San Francisco	81	224
Hamilton	30	m	w	NY	Yolo	Merritt Twp	93	503
Hanah	48	f	w	IREL	San Francisco	7-Wd San Francisco	81	163
Hannah	20	f	w	IREL	San Francisco	San Francisco P O	80	469
Henry	40	m	w	CANA	San Francisco	2-Wd San Francisco	79	274
Henry	28	m	w	NY	Merced	Snelling P O	74	252
Henry	27	m	w	MECK	San Francisco	11-Wd San Francisc	84	434
Hugh	39	m	w	IREL	Alameda	Oakland	68	225
J	29	m	w	NY	Alameda	Oakland	68	184
James	47	m	w	IREL	San Mateo	Redwood Twp	87	363
James	45	m	w	IREL	San Francisco	San Francisco P O	80	462
James	37	m	w	NY	Contra Costa	Martinez P O	71	412
James	33	m	w	NY	San Francisco	1-Wd San Francisco	79	102
James	31	m	w	NY	San Francisco	1-Wd San Francisco	79	71
James	26	m	w	MD	Napa	Napa	75	26
James	23	m	w	SCOT	San Francisco	11-Wd San Francisc	84	519
James	21	m	w	IREL	Contra Costa	Martinez P O	71	413
Jane	28	f	w	IREL	Alameda	Oakland	68	256
Jeremiah	19	m	w	IREL	San Francisco	San Francisco P O	83	197
Jerry	40	m	w	ME	San Joaquin	2-Wd Stockton	86	171
Jno	7	m	w	NY	Santa Clara	Burnett Twp	88	32
John	60	m	w	WALE	Yolo	Cache Crk Twp	93	457
John	55	m	w	IREL	Shasta	Portugese Flat P O	89	472
John	52	m	w	CANA	Santa Cruz	Pajaro Twp	89	344
John	50	m	w	IREL	San Francisco	San Francisco P O	85	857
John	39	m	w	IREL	San Mateo	San Mateo P O	87	359
John	36	m	b	HI	Tuolumne	Big Oak Flat P O	93	400
John	36	m	w	IREL	San Francisco	1-Wd San Francisco	79	61
John	33	m	w	SCOT	San Francisco	7-Wd San Francisco	81	190
John	31	m	w	IREL	San Francisco	6-Wd San Francisco	81	88
John	31	m	w	RI	Placer	Auburn P O	76	383
John	29	m	w	IREL	Mendocino	Navarro & Big Rvr	74	174
John	22	m	w	IREL	San Francisco	San Francisco P O	85	764
John	22	m	w	IREL	San Francisco	7-Wd San Francisco	81	171
John	21	m	w	IREL	Yolo	Washington Twp	93	534
John E	48	m	w	IL	Tulare	Tule Rvr Twp	92	270
John E	44	m	w	IREL	San Francisco	6-Wd San Francisco	81	105
John J	26	m	w	IREL	San Francisco	7-Wd San Francisco	81	239
Joseph	36	m	w	IREL	San Francisco	1-Wd San Francisco	79	91
Joseph	35	m	w	IL	Del Norte	Mountain Twp	71	475
Julia	26	f	w	IREL	Marin	Tomales Twp	74	82
Kate	30	f	w	IREL	San Francisco	6-Wd San Francisco	81	131
Kate	30	f	w	IREL	San Francisco	San Francisco P O	83	109
Katie	38	f	w	IREL	San Francisco	1-Wd San Francisco	79	120
Katie	36	f	w	IREL	San Francisco	1-Wd San Francisco	79	3
Laurence	29	m	w	IREL	San Francisco	1-Wd San Francisco	79	82
Lizzie	35	f	w	IREL	Nevada	Nevada Twp	75	291
Louis	56	m	w	IN	Contra Costa	Martinez P O	71	442
M A	38	f	w	IREL	San Francisco	San Francisco P O	83	296
Maria	22	f	w	IREL	Nevada	Bloomfield Twp	75	97
Mary	40	f	w	IREL	San Francisco	8-Wd San Francisco	82	464
Mary	30	f	w	IREL	San Francisco	San Francisco P O	85	825
Mary	29	f	w	IREL	San Francisco	2-Wd San Francisco	79	201
Mary	1M	f	w	CA	San Francisco	11-Wd San Francisc	84	496
Mary A	18	f	w	IA	Napa	Napa	75	27
Nicholas	48	m	w	IREL	San Francisco	San Francisco P O	83	74
Nicholas	33	m	w	IREL	Siskiyou	Butte Twp	89	586
Owen	30	m	w	IREL	San Francisco	1-Wd San Francisco	79	103
Pat	21	m	w	IREL	Alameda	Murray Twp	68	106
Patrick	44	m	w	IREL	San Francisco	7-Wd San Francisco	81	187
Patrick	42	m	w	IREL	San Francisco	1-Wd San Francisco	79	91
Patrick	32	m	w	IREL	Solano	Denverton Twp	90	26
Patrick	30	m	w	IREL	San Francisco	6-Wd San Francisco	81	139
Patrick	28	m	w	IREL	Yolo	Washington Twp	93	530
Patrick	19	m	w	ME	Mendocino	Navarro & Big Rvr	74	174
Pauline	21	f	b	WIND	San Francisco	San Francisco P O	80	465
Robert	32	m	w	OH	San Francisco	11-Wd San Francisc	84	694
Simon P	28	m	w	MA	San Francisco	1-Wd San Francisco	79	110
Stephen	35	m	w	IREL	Marin	Tomales Twp	74	82
Thomas	48	m	w	IREL	San Francisco	San Francisco P O	85	872
Thomas	40	m	w	IREL	Yolo	Buckeye Twp	93	410
Thomas	30	m	w	IREL	San Francisco	San Francisco P O	85	762
Thomas	27	m	w	MD	San Francisco	7-Wd San Francisco	81	176
Thos	50	m	w	SCOT	Butte	Kimshew Tpw	70	82
Timothy	44	m	w	IREL	Nevada	Grass Valley Twp	75	158
Timothy	37	m	w	IREL	San Mateo	Schoolhouse Statio	87	339
W J	45	m	w	PA	Solano	Vallejo	90	217
W J	35	m	w	PA	Santa Clara	Gilroy Twp	88	73
W T	27	m	w	IL	Alameda	Oakland	68	148
William	70	m	w	CA	Mendocino	Ukiah Twp	74	236
William	35	m	w	IREL	San Francisco	San Francisco P O	83	250
William	25	m	w	IN	Contra Costa	Martinez P O	71	444
Wm	35	m	w	PA	San Francisco	7-Wd San Francisco	81	269
Wm	23	m	w	IREL	San Francisco	1-Wd San Francisco	79	134
CONNORS								
Anna	30	f	w	IREL	Alameda	Oakland	68	239
David	41	m	w	IREL	San Mateo	San Mateo P O	87	359
David	24	m	w	IREL	San Francisco	San Francisco P O	83	121
Denis	25	m	w	IREL	San Francisco	1-Wd San Francisco	79	67
Edward	35	m	w	IREL	San Francisco	7-Wd San Francisco	81	172
Edward	22	m	w	IREL	San Francisco	6-Wd San Francisco	81	93
James	44	m	w	IREL	San Francisco	1-Wd San Francisco	79	115
James	36	m	w	IREL	San Francisco	San Francisco P O	83	320
John	50	m	w	IREL	San Francisco	2-Wd San Francisco	79	180
John	40	m	w	NY	Sacramento	4-Wd Sacramento	77	377
John	33	m	w	ENGL	San Francisco	1-Wd San Francisco	79	126
John	32	m	w	IREL	San Francisco	11-Wd San Francisc	84	481
John	32	m	w	IREL	Nevada	Grass Valley Twp	75	221
John	28	m	w	IREL	San Francisco	San Francisco P O	83	1
John	26	m	w	IREL	San Francisco	7-Wd San Francisco	81	190
Katy	25	f	w	IREL	San Francisco	San Francisco P O	80	539
Larry	37	m	w	IREL	San Francisco	11-Wd San Francisc	84	654
M	28	m	w	IREL	Yuba	Linda Twp	93	556
Margt	25	f	w	IREL	San Francisco	San Francisco P O	85	863
Mary	24	f	w	IREL	San Francisco	San Francisco P O	83	326
Michael	47	m	w	IREL	Nevada	Bridgeport Twp	75	118
Michael	27	m	w	IREL	San Mateo	Schoolhouse Statio	87	342
Michl	46	m	w	IREL	San Francisco	1-Wd San Francisco	79	92
Michl	35	m	w	IREL	San Francisco	1-Wd San Francisco	79	67
Patrick	40	m	w	IREL	Nevada	Grass Valley Twp	75	196
Patrick	36	m	w	IREL	Nevada	Grass Valley Twp	75	206
Patrick	36	m	w	IREL	San Francisco	11-Wd San Francisc	84	654
Patrick	31	m	w	IREL	San Bernardino	San Bernardino Twp	78	452
Patrick	30	m	w	IREL	San Francisco	San Francisco P O	83	12
Patrick	26	m	w	CANA	San Francisco	7-Wd San Francisco	81	214
Robert	31	m	w	MA	San Francisco	San Francisco P O	80	488
Thomas	27	m	w	IREL	Marin	Tomales Twp	74	78
Thomas	26	m	w	IREL	San Francisco	7-Wd San Francisco	81	180
Thos	28	m	w	NY	San Francisco	1-Wd San Francisco	79	85
Tomothy	31	m	w	IREL	San Francisco	San Francisco P O	83	417
William	25	m	w	IREL	San Francisco	7-Wd San Francisco	81	197
Wm	35	m	w	IREL	San Francisco	11-Wd San Francisc	84	578
CONNORTON								
Thos	46	m	w	IREL	San Francisco	2-Wd San Francisco	79	194
CONNORTY								
Patrick	43	m	w	IREL	Nevada	Grass Valley Twp	75	196
CONNOWAY								
Patrick	40	m	w	IREL	San Francisco	San Francisco P O	85	773
CONNRALL								
Theodosia	76	f	w	CT	San Francisco	San Francisco P O	83	110
CONNWAY								
Maggie	25	f	w	IREL	San Francisco	San Francisco P O	83	30
CONNY								
Margt	36	f	w	IREL	San Francisco	8-Wd San Francisco	82	342
CONNYON								
B	27	m	w	MO	San Joaquin	Douglas Twp	86	37
CONOLAN								
Roger	50	m	w	IREL	Nevada	Nevada Twp	75	304
CONOLE								
Joaquin	50	m	w	SPAI	Fresno	Millerton P O	72	166
CONOLEY								
Alice	37	f	w	IREL	San Francisco	7-Wd San Francisco	81	172
Alice	3	f	w	CA	San Francisco	7-Wd San Francisco	81	172
Frank	8M	m	w	CA	San Francisco	7-Wd San Francisco	81	172
Michael	44	m	w	IREL	Sacramento	Cosumnes Twp	77	91
CONOLLY								
Andrew	37	m	w	IREL	Los Angeles	Los Angeles Twp	73	469
Christopher	15	m	w	NY	San Francisco	11-Wd San Francisc	84	587
Edward	50	m	w	IREL	San Francisco	San Francisco P O	83	402
James	37	m	w	IREL	Santa Clara	2-Wd San Jose	88	334
Jno	34	m	w	IREL	San Joaquin	Douglas Twp	86	49
M	25	f	w	CA	Los Angeles	Los Angeles	73	569

© 2001 by Heritage Quest. All rights reserved.

Name	Age	S	R	B-PL	County	Locale	Series M593 Roll	Pg
Mariah	61	f	w	IREL	Alameda	Oakland	68	144
Patrick	28	m	w	IREL	Santa Clara	2-Wd San Jose	88	330
CONOLY								
Ann	28	f	w	IREL	Alameda	Oakland	68	209
C C	31	m	w	TX	Los Angeles	Los Angeles	73	516
John	47	m	w	IREL	San Joaquin	2-Wd Stockton	86	206
John	13	m	w	NY	Alameda	Oakland	68	253
Maggie	30	f	w	IREL	Los Angeles	Los Angeles	73	533
Patrick	45	m	w	IREL	San Francisco	7-Wd San Francisco	81	163
Patrick	36	m	w	IREL	Los Angeles	Los Angeles Twp	73	492
Thomas	26	m	w	NY	San Luis Obispo	Arroyo Grande Twp	87	274
CONONE								
John	18	m	w	ITAL	San Mateo	Schoolhouse Statio	87	346
CONOPISO								
S B	31	m	w	ITAL	Tuolumne	Big Oak Flat P O	93	395
CONOTEE								
Balensuel	50	m	w	CA	San Bernardino	San Bernardino Twp	78	442
CONOVAN								
Darius	70	m	w	IREL	San Joaquin	3-Wd Stockton	86	231
Jno	34	m	w	IREL	Santa Clara	Almaden Twp	88	13
CONOVER								
Elizabth	38	f	w	NJ	Sonoma	Santa Rosa	91	408
Geo	39	m	w	IA	Butte	Ophir Twp	70	115
Jas	11	m	w	CA	Siskiyou	Yreka Twp	89	665
John	31	m	w	IREL	Sacramento	2-Wd Sacramento	77	232
Libbie	14	f	w	CA	Santa Cruz	Watsonville	89	375
Sydney	23	m	w	NJ	Santa Cruz	Watsonville	89	364
CONOWAY								
James	38	m	w	IREL	Sacramento	2-Wd Sacramento	77	206
William	26	m	w	IREL	San Francisco	7-Wd San Francisco	81	180
CONOY								
Juan	25	m	m	CA	Santa Barbara	Santa Barbara P O	87	472
CONRAD								
Andrew	42	m	w	RUSS	San Francisco	11-Wd San Francisc	84	439
B S	34	m	w	NY	Alameda	Murray Twp	68	115
Benjamin	54	m	w	NY	Mendocino	Point Arena Twp	74	204
Charles	50	m	w	PRUS	San Francisco	2-Wd San Francisco	79	238
Charles	36	m	w	KY	Klamath	Dillon Twp	73	369
Charles	21	m	w	WI	Siskiyou	Yreka Twp	89	669
Chas	28	m	w	PRUS	San Francisco	San Francisco P O	83	271
Christopher	65	m	w	NY	San Francisco	3-Wd San Francisco	79	316
David	42	m	w	OH	San Francisco	7-Wd San Francisco	81	277
E C	50	f	w	BAVA	Tuolumne	Sonora P O	93	304
Eli P	46	m	w	PA	Butte	Ophir Twp	70	114
Elias	12	m	w	TN	Solano	Tremont Twp	90	35
Ephraim	58	m	w	NC	Stanislaus	Empire Twp	92	36
Frank	26	m	w	PRUS	Santa Clara	2-Wd San Jose	88	319
Fritz	21	m	w	BAVA	Los Angeles	Santa Ana Twp	73	609
Geo	46	m	w	BADE	San Francisco	2-Wd San Francisco	79	225
Geo W	43	m	w	PA	Butte	Ophir Twp	70	113
George	43	m	w	NY	Calaveras	Copperopolis P O	70	259
H A	36	m	w	NJ	Tuolumne	Big Oak Flat P O	93	391
Henrietta	22	f	w	SWED	San Francisco	2-Wd San Francisco	79	237
Henry	26	m	w	BAVA	San Francisco	7-Wd San Francisco	81	231
Herrman	39	m	w	PRUS	San Francisco	San Francisco P O	83	416
Hiram C	19	m	w	CANA	Stanislaus	Empire Twp	92	65
Jacob	47	m	w	PRUS	San Joaquin	1-Wd Stockton	86	134
James	34	m	w	OH	Stanislaus	Empire Twp	92	52
James	21	m	w	NY	San Francisco	San Francisco P O	83	212
James W	35	m	w	OH	Stanislaus	Empire Twp	92	64
Jas	22	m	w	PA	Sierra	Gibson Twp	89	540
Jerry	55	m	w	ENGL	Stanislaus	Empire Twp	92	53
Jno	46	m	w	POLA	Sacramento	1-Wd Sacramento	77	175
Jno	38	m	w	PA	Sierra	Table Rock Twp	89	573
John	39	m	w	PA	Yolo	Washington Twp	93	534
John	35	m	w	MD	Santa Cruz	Pajaro Twp	89	341
John	28	m	w	CANA	Mendocino	Little Rvr Twp	74	171
Joseph	50	m	w	FRAN	Butte	Ophir Twp	70	101
Joseph	29	m	w	GERM	San Joaquin	2-Wd Stockton	86	168
Mariah	30	f	w	CANA	Humboldt	Eureka Twp	72	264
Michael	36	m	w	FRAN	Los Angeles	Santa Ana Twp	73	612
Pat	36	m	w	IREL	Alameda	Oakland	68	148
Rank	40	m	w	PA	Mariposa	Maxwell Crk P O	74	143
Rued	28	m	w	SWIT	San Francisco	3-Wd San Francisco	79	324
Samuel	66	m	w	PA	Yolo	Washington Twp	93	536
Simon	51	m	w	PA	Sonoma	Petaluma Twp	91	325
Smuel	54	m	w	AUST	Tuolumne	Chinese Camp P O	93	365
T L	35	m	w	CANA	San Francisco	7-Wd San Francisco	81	287
Thomas	40	m	w	PRUS	San Francisco	San Francisco P O	83	328
Thos	32	m	w	GA	Butte	Oroville Twp	70	139
White W	42	m	w	OH	Stanislaus	Empire Twp	92	52
William	40	m	w	WI	El Dorado	Diamond Springs Tw	72	21
Wilson	24	m	w	NC	Stanislaus	Empire Twp	92	32
Wm A	33	m	w	SAXO	San Francisco	San Francisco P O	85	783
CONRADES								
William	30	m	w	HANO	Santa Clara	1-Wd San Jose	88	236
CONRADS								
D R	28	m	w	FRAN	Sutter	Sutter Twp	92	127
Gilbert	35	m	i	CA	Santa Barbara	San Buenaventura P	87	439
CONRAGO								
John	53	m	w	FRAN	Tuolumne	Sonora P O	93	331
CONRALS								
Frank	23	m	w	PRUS	Santa Clara	2-Wd San Jose	88	314
CONRALTO								
C	31	m	w	CHIL	Santa Clara	Almaden Twp	88	21
CONRAN								
Chas P	60	m	w	MI	Fresno	Millerton P O	72	194
Thos L	38	m	w	CANA	San Francisco	San Francisco P O	83	23
CONRAUTY								
Ed	34	m	w	PRUS	San Francisco	2-Wd San Francisco	79	229
CONRAY								
Frank	37	m	w	IREL	Santa Clara	Almaden Twp	88	13
James	29	m	w	IREL	San Francisco	11-Wd San Francisc	84	639
CONRERAS								
Bernardo	62	m	w	MEXI	Los Angeles	Los Angeles Twp	73	480
CONREY								
Henry	42	m	w	NY	San Francisco	5-Wd San Francisco	81	19
CONRO								
Cassius M	25	m	w	NY	San Francisco	8-Wd San Francisco	82	469
Fredrick	52	m	w	VT	San Francisco	San Francisco P O	80	419
CONROW								
Ephriam	35	m	w	IN	Plumas	Quartz Twp	77	42
CONROY								
Barnard	42	m	w	IREL	Shasta	Horsetown P O	89	502
Bernard	50	m	w	IREL	San Francisco	1-Wd San Francisco	79	54
Bernard	32	m	w	IREL	San Francisco	1-Wd San Francisco	79	95
Bridget	25	f	w	IREL	San Francisco	6-Wd San Francisco	81	136
Cora	21	f	w	MO	San Francisco	6-Wd San Francisco	81	45
Cornelius	16	m	w	MO	Humboldt	Bucksport Twp	72	244
Dennis	37	m	w	IREL	Santa Clara	Gilroy Twp	88	82
Dennis	23	m	w	IREL	Monterey	Alisal Twp	74	297
Dora	25	f	w	NY	San Francisco	6-Wd San Francisco	81	72
Ellen	20	f	w	IREL	San Francisco	6-Wd San Francisco	81	112
Eugene	14	m	w	MA	Nevada	Grass Valley Twp	75	180
Francis	58	m	w	IREL	San Francisco	San Francisco P O	85	739
George	38	m	w	ENGL	Sonoma	Vallejo Twp	91	454
Henry	28	m	w	CANA	Humboldt	Arcata Twp	72	225
James	40	m	w	IREL	San Francisco	1-Wd San Francisco	79	87
James	35	m	w	IREL	San Francisco	San Francisco P O	85	770
Johanna	32	f	w	IREL	San Francisco	5-Wd San Francisco	81	20
John	45	m	w	NY	San Francisco	8-Wd San Francisco	82	361
John	43	m	w	IREL	San Francisco	1-Wd San Francisco	79	37
John	40	m	w	IREL	Solano	Vallejo	90	170
John	36	m	w	IREL	Nevada	Grass Valley Twp	75	161
John	30	m	w	IREL	San Francisco	11-Wd San Francisc	84	616
John	27	m	w	IREL	San Francisco	6-Wd San Francisco	81	88
Jon	27	m	w	IREL	Solano	Vallejo	90	197
Joseph	45	m	w	IREL	San Francisco	1-Wd San Francisco	79	102
Julia	25	f	w	IREL	San Francisco	8-Wd San Francisco	82	342
Kate	21	f	w	IREL	San Francisco	8-Wd San Francisco	82	453
Laura J	29	f	w	PA	Siskiyou	Yreka	89	660
Margaret	35	f	w	IREL	San Francisco	San Francisco P O	83	258
Mary	4	f	w	CA	San Francisco	San Francisco P O	83	250
Mary	36	f	w	NY	San Francisco	San Francisco P O	80	355
Michael	7	m	w	CA	Santa Cruz	Santa Cruz	89	410
Michael	47	m	w	IREL	Placer	Auburn P O	76	366
Michael	45	m	w	IREL	San Francisco	San Francisco P O	83	80
Michael	40	m	w	IREL	Santa Clara	2-Wd San Jose	88	323
Michael	25	m	w	IREL	San Francisco	San Francisco P O	83	294
Michl	24	m	w	IREL	San Francisco	5-Wd San Francisco	81	27
Ora	21	f	w	MO	Sacramento	2-Wd Sacramento	77	243
Ottis	40	m	w	ME	San Francisco	7-Wd San Francisco	81	216
Patrick	44	m	w	IREL	Santa Clara	Santa Clara Twp	88	135
Patrick	27	m	w	IREL	San Francisco	1-Wd San Francisco	79	63
Peter	40	m	w	IREL	Monterey	Monterey Twp	74	346
Peter	29	m	w	IREL	San Francisco	2-Wd San Francisco	79	283
William	40	m	w	PRUS	Sutter	Butte Twp	92	101
Wm	16	m	w	MA	Yuba	East Bear Rvr Twp	93	543
CONRY								
Bridget	26	f	w	IREL	Sacramento	4-Wd Sacramento	77	344
Martin	30	m	w	ME	Alameda	Oakland	68	204
CONS								
Agnes	35	f	w	IREL	San Francisco	San Francisco P O	85	877
Patrick	37	m	w	IREL	Santa Barbara	Santa Barbara P O	87	451
CONSADINE								
Edward	28	m	w	IREL	San Francisco	San Francisco P O	80	377
J	25	m	w	IREL	Alameda	Oakland	68	160
CONSAL								
Reuben	21	m	w	CHIL	Colusa	Spring Valley Twp	71	344
CONSALIS								
Am	46	m	w	MEXI	Tuolumne	Big Oak Flat P O	93	392
CONSALUERO								
Louis	25	m	w	ITAL	Calaveras	San Andreas P O	70	159
CONSATES								
Francisca	15	f	i	CA	Monterey	Castroville Twp	74	335
CONSEJA								
Jeane	40	m	w	ITAL	Amador	Jackson P O	69	327
CONSELLA								
Ramon	26	m	w	CHIL	Santa Clara	2-Wd San Jose	88	320
CONSEN								
Laura	38	f	w	FRAN	Alameda	Brooklyn Twp	68	40
CONSIDINE								
Margt	26	f	w	IREL	San Francisco	6-Wd San Francisco	81	116
CONSIGLIER								
Simon	40	m	w	FRAN	San Mateo	San Mateo P O	87	350
CONSOLASIO								
Joseph	31	m	w	SWIT	San Francisco	1-Wd San Francisco	79	105
CONSOR								
John	42	m	w	NY	San Francisco	7-Wd San Francisco	81	193
CONSTABLE								
Amanda J	19	f	w	OR	Santa Barbara	San Buenaventura P	87	430
Charles	51	m	w	ENGL	Placer	Bath P O	76	421
Chas W	40	m	w	ENGL	Nevada	Grass Valley Twp	75	149
Elizabeth	55	f	w	ENGL	Placer	Bath P O	76	421

© 2001 by Heritage Quest. All rights reserved.

Name	Age	S	R	B-PL	County	Locale	Series M593 Roll	Pg
Henry	19	m	w	CA	Placer	Bath P O	76	420
J L	56	m	w	NY	San Francisco	San Francisco P O	83	323
CONSTANCE								
Job	42	m	w	ME	San Francisco	1-Wd San Francisco	79	122
CONSTANDT								
John	34	m	w	AUST	Marin	San Rafael	74	54
CONSTANT								
Alex	50	m	w	FRAN	San Francisco	8-Wd San Francisco	82	360
Jane	50	f	w	IREL	San Francisco	6-Wd San Francisco	81	141
Louis	45	m	w	FRAN	San Francisco	San Francisco P O	80	348
Louis	45	m	w	FRAN	San Francisco	San Francisco P O	80	347
Mangin	25	m	w	FRAN	Santa Clara	Redwood Twp	88	132
Verner	37	m	w	FRAN	San Francisco	San Francisco P O	80	535
CONSTANTIA								
Carlotta	3	f	w	CA	Santa Barbara	San Buenaventura P	87	436
Peter	47	m	w	ITAL	Santa Barbara	San Buenaventura P	87	437
CONSTANTIN								
P	33	m	w	IREL	Alameda	Oakland	68	132
CONSTANTINE								
Brick	26	m	w	ITAL	Mariposa	Mariposa P O	74	113
Charles	8	m	w	CA	Santa Cruz	Soquel Twp	89	439
Margat	18	m	w	SWIT	Kern	Bakersfield P O	73	361
Nick	40	m	w	GREE	Calaveras	San Andreas P O	70	157
Varillo	24	m	w	TURK	San Francisco	San Francisco P O	80	345
CONSTANTINO								
Phillip	44	m	w	ITAL	San Mateo	Schoolhouse Statio	87	339
CONSTANZA								
Raphael	35	m	w	AZOR	San Francisco	1-Wd San Francisco	79	130
CONSTINE								
A	44	m	w	BAVA	Sacramento	3-Wd Sacramento	77	281
CONSULA								
Louis	22	m	w	ITAL	San Francisco	11-Wd San Francisc	84	709
CONSULMAN								
Geo	28	m	w	PRUS	San Francisco	11-Wd San Francisc	84	686
CONSUS								
P	15	f	w	CA	Alameda	Murray Twp	68	106
CONT								
Ah	42	m	c	CHIN	Amador	Ione City P O	69	359
Emile	15	f	w	CA	San Francisco	San Francisco P O	83	32
CONTARD								
Felistra	35	f	w	FRAN	Nevada	Nevada Twp	75	273
CONTARDO								
Maria	30	f	w	CA	San Luis Obispo	Salinas Twp	87	295
CONTAT								
B	58	m	w	SWIT	Amador	Drytown P O	69	422
CONTATIN								
Dioze	38	m	w	FRAN	San Francisco	San Francisco P O	80	342
CONTE								
Germain	36	m	w	FRAN	San Francisco	San Francisco P O	83	136
Joseph	16	m	w	SWIT	Marin	San Antonio Twp	74	61
CONTEAS								
Victor	42	m	w	FRAN	Calaveras	Copperopolis P O	70	255
CONTEL								
Alexis	54	m	w	FRAN	San Francisco	6-Wd San Francisco	81	41
CONTELL								
Chas	26	m	w	IA	Sutter	Nicolaus Twp	92	113
J H	6	m	w	CA	Sacramento	3-Wd Sacramento	77	312
CONTENT								
Wm	21	m	w	IL	Monterey	Monterey Twp	74	348
CONTER								
Peter	38	m	w	PRUS	Napa	Napa	75	20
Wm B	54	m	w	KY	Sonoma	Russian Rvr	91	367
CONTERIAS								
Jesus	38	m	w	MEXI	Fresno	Millerton P O	72	163
CONTERO								
Petra	23	m	w	MEXI	San Luis Obispo	Santa Rosa Twp	87	330
CONTERS								
W H	45	m	w	VT	Del Norte	Crescent	71	462
CONTI								
John	50	m	w	ITAL	El Dorado	Diamond Springs Tw	72	29
CONTIE								
Jean	34	m	w	FRAN	San Francisco	8-Wd San Francisco	82	373
CONTILAINTA								
Ramon	26	m	w	CA	Marin	San Rafael Twp	74	41
CONTIN								
W	42	m	w	IREL	Lake	Knoxville Mines	73	404
CONTON								
Bridget	30	f	w	IREL	Yolo	Grafton Twp	93	481
Caterine	27	f	w	IREL	Yolo	Grafton Twp	93	481
John	44	m	w	MEXI	Tuolumne	Sonora P O	93	314
CONTOYS								
William	48	m	w	ENGL	San Francisco	6-Wd San Francisco	81	101
CONTRALO								
Emanuel	28	m	w	MEXI	Tulare	Tule Rvr Twp	92	269
CONTRAOS								
Mary	70	f	w	MEXI	Alameda	Eden Twp	68	93
CONTRARAS								
Adinaco	50	m	w	MEXI	Tuolumne	Sonora P O	93	330
Amanda	36	f	w	MEXI	Mariposa	Mariposa P O	74	123
Juan	45	m	w	MEXI	Mariposa	Mariposa P O	74	94
CONTRARES								
Carman	22	f	w	MEXI	San Francisco	San Francisco P O	80	337
Cesar	26	m	w	MEXI	San Francisco	San Francisco P O	80	337
Lantana	40	m	w	MEXI	San Luis Obispo	San Luis Obispo Tw	87	314
Martinez	63	m	w	MEXI	Kern	Bakersfield P O	73	363
CONTRAS								
Ramon	27	m	w	MEXI	Santa Barbara	Santa Barbara P O	87	486

Name	Age	S	R	B-PL	County	Locale	Series M593 Roll	Pg
CONTRENE								
D	34	m	w	MEXI	Alameda	Murray Twp	68	110
CONTRERA								
Joseph	46	m	w	CHIL	El Dorado	Diamond Springs Tw	72	34
CONTRERAS								
Antonio	25	m	w	MEXI	Los Angeles	Los Angeles Twp	73	473
Bernard	50	m	w	CHIL	Contra Costa	Martinez P O	71	440
Camilia	45	m	w	MEXI	Los Angeles	Los Angeles	73	564
E	30	m	w	MEXI	Alameda	Murray Twp	68	110
Guadalupe	35	f	w	MEXI	San Francisco	1-Wd San Francisco	79	48
Jesus	48	m	w	MEXI	Los Angeles	Los Nietos Twp	73	583
Jesus	48	f	w	MEXI	Los Angeles	Los Nietos Twp	73	585
Joseph	11	m	w	MEXI	Placer	Auburn P O	76	382
Manuel	26	m	w	MEXI	Los Angeles	Los Angeles	73	513
Mark	23	m	w	MEXI	Los Angeles	Los Nietos Twp	73	585
Matias	14	m	w	CA	Los Angeles	Los Angeles	73	556
Nasario	48	m	w	MEXI	Los Angeles	Los Angeles Twp	73	473
Refugio	23	m	w	CA	Marin	San Rafael Twp	74	41
Santana	39	m	i	MEXI	San Luis Obispo	San Luis Obispo Tw	87	312
Trenidad	40	f	w	MEXI	Los Angeles	Los Angeles	73	521
Victoriano	53	m	w	MEXI	Kern	Bakersfield P O	73	361
CONTRERE								
C	50	m	w	MEXI	Alameda	Murray Twp	68	111
CONTRERO								
Jesus	29	m	w	MEXI	San Luis Obispo	San Luis Obispo Tw	87	310
CONTRESES								
Lucas	25	m	w	MEXI	San Diego	Temecula Dist	78	527
CONTRO								
Ignacio	30	m	w	MEXI	Santa Clara	Almaden Twp	88	12
CONTROWITH								
Joseph	40	m	w	RUSS	San Francisco	San Francisco P O	83	407
CONTS								
Blunt	40	m	w	TN	San Diego	San Luis Rey	78	512
Cave J	48	m	w	TN	San Diego	San Luis Rey	78	512
CONTURE								
Alex	20	m	w	VT	Sacramento	3-Wd Sacramento	77	288
CONTURO								
Augh C	19	m	w	MEXI	San Francisco	11-Wd San Francisc	84	422
CONTUSON								
John B	34	m	w	FRAN	San Francisco	8-Wd San Francisco	82	310
CONTZ								
Malon	40	m	w	OH	Butte	Ophir Twp	70	111
Wm	37	m	w	IREL	San Francisco	San Francisco P O	83	115
CONUS								
Ralph	24	m	w	CANA	Napa	Napa Twp	75	61
CONVER								
Mary	26	f	w	IREL	Santa Clara	2-Wd San Jose	88	298
CONVERSE								
Chas C	34	m	w	NY	Fresno	Millerton P O	72	148
Myres	28	m	w	NY	Los Angeles	Soledad Twp	73	630
CONVERY								
Patrick	40	m	w	IREL	San Francisco	1-Wd San Francisco	79	123
CONVEY								
John	30	m	w	ENGL	Nevada	Grass Valley Twp	75	187
CONVILL								
Ann	35	f	w	IREL	San Francisco	San Francisco P O	83	379
Winefreed	76	f	w	IREL	San Francisco	San Francisco P O	83	379
CONVOISIEN								
Albert	52	m	w	SWIT	Amador	Volcano P O	69	384
CONVOY								
John	32	m	w	IREL	San Francisco	San Francisco P O	80	372
CONWAY								
Adelaide	24	f	w	IREL	San Francisco	San Francisco P O	83	79
Alphonse	37	m	w	NH	San Francisco	8-Wd San Francisco	82	369
Ama	23	f	w	IREL	San Francisco	7-Wd San Francisco	81	159
Amie	6	f	w	CA	Sonoma	Salt Point	91	384
Andrew	54	m	w	VA	Siskiyou	Callahan P O	89	625
Anna	35	f	w	IREL	San Francisco	7-Wd San Francisco	81	159
Barney	50	m	w	IREL	Mariposa	Mariposa P O	74	122
Bernard	33	m	w	IREL	San Francisco	San Francisco P O	83	276
Bridget	25	f	w	IREL	San Francisco	San Francisco P O	83	256
C	29	m	w	IREL	Solano	Vallejo	90	206
Carville	60	m	w	MD	Nevada	Grass Valley Twp	75	170
Catharine	35	f	w	IREL	San Francisco	11-Wd San Francisc	84	572
Charles	37	m	w	IREL	San Francisco	7-Wd San Francisco	81	212
Cornelius	40	m	w	IREL	Sacramento	4-Wd Sacramento	77	368
Cornelius	35	m	w	IREL	San Francisco	San Francisco P O	85	733
David	30	m	w	IREL	Sacramento	3-Wd Sacramento	77	255
Edward	27	m	w	CANA	Mendocino	Point Arena Twp	74	215
Edward	18	m	w	IL	Santa Clara	Santa Clara Twp	88	145
Edwd	42	m	w	NY	San Francisco	San Francisco P O	83	85
Frances	64	f	w	ENGL	Alameda	Oakland	68	197
Francis	35	m	w	IREL	San Francisco	San Francisco P O	83	191
Francis	22	m	w	IN	Colusa	Grand Island Twp	71	307
George	45	m	w	IREL	Stanislaus	Empire Twp	92	56
George	45	m	w	WALE	Yolo	Washington Twp	93	530
J P	40	m	w	TX	Lake	Big Valley	73	399
Jacob	40	m	w	PRUS	San Joaquin	2-Wd Stockton	86	160
James	59	m	w	VA	Mendocino	Ukiah Twp	74	239
James	41	m	w	IREL	Sacramento	4-Wd Sacramento	77	342
James	40	m	w	OH	Sonoma	Petaluma Twp	91	359
James	30	m	w	IREL	San Francisco	San Francisco P O	80	368
James	30	m	w	IREL	Contra Costa	Martinez P O	71	422
James	28	m	w	IREL	San Francisco	San Francisco P O	83	184
James	21	m	w	MA	Colusa	Colusa Twp	71	276
James	19	m	w	IREL	San Joaquin	Elkhorn Twp	86	66
Jas	30	m	w	VA	Butte	Chico Twp	70	58

© 2001 by Heritage Quest. All rights reserved.

Name	Age	S	R	B-PL	County	Locale	Series M593 Roll	Pg
Jas H	39	m	w	MO	San Francisco	San Francisco P O	85	737
John	60	m	w	IREL	San Francisco	1-Wd San Francisco	79	21
John	51	m	w	IREL	Amador	Jackson P O	69	319
John	50	m	w	IREL	San Francisco	San Francisco P O	80	400
John	50	m	w	IREL	San Francisco	11-Wd San Francisc	84	507
John	47	m	w	IA	Tehama	Tehama Twp	92	194
John	40	m	w	IREL	Sacramento	Dry Crk Twp	77	101
John	39	m	w	IREL	Contra Costa	Martinez P O	71	383
John	32	m	w	IREL	San Francisco	1-Wd San Francisco	79	92
John	26	m	w	NY	San Francisco	8-Wd San Francisco	82	329
John	24	m	w	AUSL	San Francisco	San Francisco P O	83	399
John	10	m	w	NY	San Francisco	1-Wd San Francisco	79	4
John M	35	m	w	IREL	Mendocino	Big Rvr Twp	74	175
John M	30	m	w	IREL	Mendocino	Navarro & Big Rvr	74	175
Kitty	50	f	w	IREL	San Francisco	6-Wd San Francisco	81	89
Maggie	31	f	w	IREL	San Francisco	11-Wd San Francisc	84	583
Margret	15	f	w	CA	Trinity	Weaverville Pct	92	224
Mary	60	f	w	IREL	San Francisco	11-Wd San Francisc	84	653
Mary	35	f	w	IREL	San Francisco	San Francisco P O	83	133
Mary	34	f	w	IREL	San Francisco	1-Wd San Francisco	79	22
Mary	30	f	w	ME	San Francisco	San Francisco P O	83	377
Mary	22	f	w	NY	San Francisco	2-Wd San Francisco	79	234
May	37	f	w	IREL	Butte	Ophir Twp	70	109
Michael	59	m	w	IREL	San Francisco	San Francisco P O	83	3
Michael	50	m	w	IREL	San Francisco	8-Wd San Francisco	82	445
Michael	42	m	w	IREL	San Mateo	San Mateo P O	87	360
Michael	40	m	w	IREL	San Francisco	San Francisco P O	80	388
Michael	37	m	w	NJ	San Francisco	2-Wd San Francisco	79	230
Michael	32	m	w	IREL	San Francisco	11-Wd San Francisc	84	515
Michael	28	m	w	IREL	San Francisco	7-Wd San Francisco	81	265
Micheal	30	m	w	IREL	San Francisco	7-Wd San Francisco	81	173
Morris	40	m	w	IREL	San Francisco	San Francisco P O	85	733
Nicholson	55	m	w	IREL	San Mateo	Schoolhouse Statio	87	342
Patrick	53	m	w	IREL	San Francisco	San Francisco P O	85	786
Patrick	28	m	w	IREL	San Francisco	11-Wd San Francisc	84	699
Peter	49	m	w	IREL	San Francisco	11-Wd San Francisc	84	613
Peter	48	m	w	IREL	Sonoma	Petaluma Twp	91	316
Phillipine	19	f	w	CA	San Luis Obispo	Santa Rosa Twp	87	325
Richd	37	m	w	IREL	San Francisco	1-Wd San Francisco	79	83
Robt	35	m	w	MA	San Francisco	11-Wd San Francisc	84	426
Sarah J	30	f	w	IREL	San Francisco	San Francisco P O	85	721
Saul	35	m	w	SCOT	Solano	Suisun Twp	90	116
Scott	22	m	w	IA	Trinity	Weaverville Pct	92	226
Silas	39	m	w	IN	Santa Clara	Fremont Twp	88	58
Thomas	42	m	w	IREL	San Francisco	11-Wd San Francisc	84	703
Thomas	35	m	w	IREL	San Francisco	6-Wd San Francisco	81	144
Thomas	34	m	w	OH	Trinity	Weaverville Pct	92	231
Thomas	33	m	w	CANA	Mendocino	Little Rvr Twp	74	171
Thomas	12	m	w	CA	Los Angeles	San Gabriel Twp	73	593
Thos	31	m	w	IREL	Alameda	Oakland	68	253
Thos	23	m	w	CANA	San Francisco	San Francisco P O	85	848
William	9	m	w	OR	Stanislaus	Empire Twp	92	36
William	34	m	w	KY	Stanislaus	Emory Twp	92	25
CONWELL								
H A	37	m	w	DE	Butte	Wyandotte Twp	70	148
J W	37	m	w	DE	Butte	Wyandotte Twp	70	148
Mary	6	f	w	CA	Calaveras	Copperopolis P O	70	245
S	57	m	w	CANA	Calaveras	Copperopolis P O	70	230
CONWEY								
George	40	m	w	NY	Napa	Napa	75	13
CONY								
Felix	36	m	w	FRAN	Los Angeles	Los Angeles	73	523
CONYADO								
Jose	44	m	w	CA	Amador	Jackson P O	69	322
CONYEN								
H	23	m	w	DENM	Alameda	Murray Twp	68	113
CONYER								
Allas	7	f	i	CA	Humboldt	South Fork Twp	72	300
CONYERS								
Benjamin L	42	m	w	TN	Tulare	Visalia	92	293
Sanford H	42	m	w	KY	Plumas	Indian Twp	77	11
CONYES								
George S	8	m	w	CA	Humboldt	South Fork Twp	72	301
CONZONSINS								
Geo	35	m	w	BADE	Humboldt	Eureka Twp	72	257
COO								
Ah	58	m	c	CHIN	Tuolumne	Chinese Camp P O	93	364
Ah	55	m	c	CHIN	Tuolumne	Chinese Camp P O	93	364
Ah	48	m	c	CHIN	Trinity	Weaverville Pct	92	227
Ah	44	m	c	CHIN	Tuolumne	Big Oak Flat P O	93	394
Ah	42	m	c	CHIN	San Mateo	Belmont P O	87	388
Ah	40	m	c	CHIN	Alameda	Oakland	68	238
Ah	37	m	c	CHIN	Kern	Havilah P O	73	338
Ah	35	f	c	CHIN	Placer	Lincoln P O	76	484
Ah	30	m	c	CHIN	Alameda	Murray Twp	68	120
Ah	30	m	c	CHIN	Sierra	Gibson Twp	89	538
Ah	30	m	c	CHIN	Sierra	Eureka Twp	89	525
Ah	28	m	c	CHIN	Tuolumne	Chinese Camp P O	93	378
Ah	26	m	c	CHIN	Alameda	Brooklyn	68	34
Ah	25	m	c	CHIN	Sierra	Lincoln Twp	89	546
Ah	24	m	c	CHIN	Sierra	Allegheny & Forest	89	535
Ah	20	m	c	CHIN	Tuolumne	Big Oak Flat P O	93	397
Chong	42	m	c	CHIN	Calaveras	San Andreas P O	70	167
Hi	25	m	c	CHIN	Alameda	Washington Twp	68	295
Hoo	30	m	c	CHIN	Yuba	Marysville	93	630
Kay	31	f	c	CHIN	Yuba	Marysville	93	627
Mary	28	f	w	ME	San Joaquin	1-Wd Stockton	86	128

Name	Age	S	R	B-PL	County	Locale	Series M593 Roll	Pg
Nan	22	m	c	CHIN	Los Angeles	Los Angeles	73	507
See	34	m	c	CHIN	Yuba	Marysville	93	622
COOANG								
Ah	20	m	c	CHIN	San Francisco	6-Wd San Francisco	81	42
COOBY								
Peter P	49	m	w	VT	Monterey	Monterey	74	359
COOCHARD								
Oscar	27	m	w	SWIT	Colusa	Stony Crk Twp	71	331
COOCK								
Isaac	44	m	w	NY	Humboldt	Mattole Twp	72	284
COOD								
James	41	m	w	ENGL	Nevada	Grass Valley Twp	75	175
John	23	m	w	NY	San Francisco	San Francisco P O	83	180
COODMAN								
William	42	m	w	IREL	Colusa	Spring Valley Twp	71	344
COOE								
Ah Chong	30	m	c	CHIN	Monterey	Monterey	74	358
COOEY								
Sook	40	m	c	CHIN	Yuba	Marysville	93	622
COOFER								
John	24	m	w	DENM	Stanislaus	Washington Twp	92	84
COOGAN								
Anna	33	f	w	IREL	San Francisco	7-Wd San Francisco	81	176
Dave	40	m	w	IREL	Butte	Chico Twp	70	55
Henry	31	m	w	IREL	Marin	San Rafael Twp	74	39
James	45	m	w	IREL	Calaveras	San Andreas P O	70	165
COOIL								
Wm	28	m	w	IOFM	San Francisco	11-Wd San Francisc	84	478
COOK								
---	18	m	c	CHIN	Napa	Napa	75	9
A	42	m	w	HDAR	San Francisco	San Francisco P O	85	839
A A	38	m	w	NY	Sacramento	4-Wd Sacramento	77	349
A G	28	m	w	NH	Sonoma	Santa Rosa	91	429
A H	30	m	w	OH	San Diego	Julian Dist	78	469
A J	37	m	w	PA	Napa	Napa	75	57
A J	35	m	w	PA	Nevada	Meadow Lake Twp	75	269
A S	40	m	w	MA	Sacramento	4-Wd Sacramento	77	372
Ah	64	m	c	CHIN	Tuolumne	Chinese Camp P O	93	366
Ah	60	m	c	CHIN	Sacramento	Granite Twp	77	153
Ah	49	m	c	CHIN	Plumas	Goodwin Twp	77	2
Ah	42	m	c	CHIN	Tuolumne	Chinese Camp P O	93	388
Ah	32	m	c	CHIN	Sonoma	Petaluma Twp	91	365
Ah	28	m	c	CHIN	Mariposa	Mariposa P O	74	108
Ah	26	m	c	CHIN	Mariposa	Mariposa P O	74	114
Ah	17	m	c	CHIN	Santa Clara	San Jose Twp	88	194
Albert	48	m	w	HANO	Amador	Jackson P O	69	320
Albert S	23	m	w	KY	Colusa	Colusa	71	297
Alex	25	m	w	NY	San Francisco	7-Wd San Francisco	81	242
Alexander	50	m	w	SCOT	San Luis Obispo	Santa Rosa Twp	87	329
Alexander	47	m	w	NY	Santa Clara	Santa Clara Twp	88	160
Alfred	40	m	w	ENGL	Sutter	Yuba Twp	92	149
Algernon	47	m	w	RI	San Francisco	11-Wd San Francisc	84	526
Alonzo	26	m	w	ME	Mendocino	Point Arena Twp	74	207
Alvin	60	m	w	MS	Yolo	Putah Twp	93	511
Amanda	59	f	w	PRUS	Sacramento	Sutter Twp	77	382
Amelia	16	f	w	CA	Santa Clara	Almaden Twp	88	12
Andr	59	m	w	PRUS	Sierra	Gibson Twp	89	542
Andrew	25	m	w	MO	Los Angeles	Los Nietos Twp	73	590
Andrew	18	m	w	IA	Stanislaus	Emory Twp	92	22
Andrew J	38	m	w	SC	Nevada	Grass Valley Twp	75	152
Andrw	40	m	w	KY	Butte	Kimshew Tpw	70	78
Anna	5	f	w	NY	San Francisco	11-Wd San Francisc	84	711
Anna	46	f	w	IREL	San Francisco	6-Wd San Francisco	81	79
Anna	41	f	w	IREL	San Francisco	San Francisco P O	83	47
Anne	34	f	w	PRUS	San Francisco	8-Wd San Francisco	82	424
Annie	40	f	w	OH	Butte	Ophir Twp	70	111
Ansel	25	m	w	MO	Contra Costa	Martinez P O	71	368
Arthur	40	m	w	ENGL	San Luis Obispo	Arroyo Grande Twp	87	278
August	36	m	w	PRUS	Sacramento	Sutter Twp	77	392
B F	36	m	w	IN	El Dorado	Kelsey Twp	72	62
Benj F	35	m	w	ME	Napa	Napa Twp	75	73
Benjamin	30	m	w	CANA	Santa Clara	Santa Clara Twp	88	148
Bradford	31	m	w	NY	Santa Clara	2-Wd San Jose	88	335
Calvin	38	m	w	VT	Sutter	Nicolaus Twp	92	114
Caroline	42	f	w	SCOG	San Francisco	6-Wd San Francisco	81	79
Catherine	67	f	w	IREL	San Francisco	11-Wd San Francisc	84	635
Catherine	30	f	w	IREL	Santa Clara	1-Wd San Jose	88	233
Cathraine	54	f	w	CANA	San Francisco	San Francisco P O	80	392
Charles	6	m	w	IREL	San Francisco	11-Wd San Francisc	84	711
Charles	55	m	w	NY	San Francisco	2-Wd San Francisco	79	267
Charles	51	m	w	SCOT	San Francisco	3-Wd San Francisco	79	300
Charles	43	m	w	PA	Humboldt	Mattole Twp	72	283
Charles	35	m	w	MA	Calaveras	Copperopolis P O	70	260
Charles	26	m	w	CANA	San Luis Obispo	Morro Twp	87	285
Charles	20	m	w	NY	Sonoma	Salt Point	91	380
Charles	19	m	w	ENGL	Santa Clara	Santa Clara Twp	88	170
Charles	13	m	w	NY	San Francisco	11-Wd San Francisc	84	649
Charles C	44	m	w	IN	Santa Clara	2-Wd San Jose	88	299
Charles O	6	m	w	CA	Colusa	Colusa	71	297
Charles W	50	m	w	MA	San Francisco	2-Wd San Francisco	79	277
Charles W	40	m	w	MA	Placer	Bath P O	76	457
Chas	30	m	w	FRAN	Sonoma	Cloverdale Twp	91	268
Chas	28	m	w	VT	San Francisco	1-Wd San Francisco	79	69
Chas	28	m	w	SWED	San Francisco	1-Wd San Francisco	79	122
Chas	19	m	w	PA	Yuba	Marysville	93	611
Chas A	23	m	w	SCOT	San Francisco	San Francisco P O	85	758
Chas F	40	m	w	IL	San Francisco	1-Wd San Francisco	79	103

© 2001 by Heritage Quest. All rights reserved.

Name	Age	S	R	B-PL	County	Locale	Series M593 Roll	Pg
Chee Tak	22	m	c	CHIN	San Francisco	11-Wd San Francisc	84	546
Christian	46	m	w	PA	Sutter	Sutter Twp	92	118
Churchill	20	m	w	AR	San Diego	Julian Dist	78	473
Clara	49	f	w	ENGL	San Francisco	6-Wd San Francisco	81	137
Clara	21	f	w	NH	Humboldt	Pacific Twp	72	294
Columbus	19	m	w	MO	Napa	Napa	75	7
Cristopher	35	m	w	PRUS	Alameda	Murray Twp	68	104
Cune	32	f	c	CHIN	El Dorado	Placerville	72	115
Cynthia A	24	f	w	MO	Mendocino	Little Lake Twp	74	192
D	32	m	w	IREL	Nevada	Meadow Lake Twp	75	265
D O	22	m	w	NY	Sacramento	1-Wd Sacramento	77	182
Danial	35	m	w	NY	San Francisco	7-Wd San Francisco	81	207
Daniel	25	m	w	IL	Colusa	Monroe Twp	71	320
David	66	m	w	KY	Sonoma	Sonoma Twp	91	439
David P	58	m	w	KY	Sonoma	Analy Twp	91	247
David S	47	m	w	VT	San Mateo	San Mateo P O	87	356
David W	52	m	w	VA	Sonoma	Healdsburg & Mendo	91	284
Delia	32	f	w	IREL	San Francisco	San Francisco P O	83	189
Dennis	50	m	w	RI	Santa Cruz	Santa Cruz Twp	89	398
Edgar	75	m	w	ENGL	Nevada	Grass Valley Twp	75	158
Edward	6	m	w	CA	San Francisco	San Francisco P O	80	410
Edward	25	m	w	MO	Colusa	Monroe Twp	71	325
Edwd	40	m	w	MA	Solano	Vallejo	90	140
Eli	49	m	w	MA	San Francisco	8-Wd San Francisco	82	394
Elisha	46	m	w	NY	San Francisco	San Francisco P O	83	290
Elizabeth	40	f	w	ENGL	Sacramento	4-Wd Sacramento	77	364
Ellridge G	50	m	w	MA	San Francisco	San Francisco P O	83	18
Emily	34	f	w	NY	Amador	Ione City P O	69	363
Ephriam	41	m	w	OH	Yolo	Putah Twp	93	527
Eziah	19	m	w	CA	Stanislaus	Emory Twp	92	18
F	49	m	w	PRUS	San Joaquin	Dent Twp	86	21
F	49	m	w	OH	Alameda	Oakland	68	174
F D	37	m	w	ME	Tuolumne	Columbia P O	93	347
F H	20	m	w	MA	Sacramento	1-Wd Sacramento	77	181
F M	38	m	w	GA	Amador	Jackson P O	69	338
Ferdinand	24	m	w	PA	San Francisco	San Francisco P O	83	304
Fill	37	m	w	OH	Alameda	Oakland	68	191
Francis D	35	m	w	ME	Tuolumne	Sonora P O	93	321
Francis F	23	m	w	NY	San Francisco	1-Wd San Francisco	79	93
Frank	8	m	w	CA	Sacramento	Franklin Twp	77	118
Frank	16	m	w	ME	Butte	Chico Twp	70	54
Frank M	42	m	w	GA	Amador	Volcano P O	69	379
Fred	13	m	w	CA	San Francisco	11-Wd San Francisc	84	587
Frederick	53	m	w	SHOL	San Francisco	1-Wd San Francisco	79	92
Frederick	38	m	w	US	Nevada	Rough & Ready Twp	75	332
Frederick	25	m	w	NY	San Francisco	San Francisco P O	83	273
Fung	40	m	c	CHIN	Yuba	Marysville	93	629
Gee	25	m	c	CHIN	Yuba	Marysville	93	628
Geo	24	m	w	PRUS	San Francisco	7-Wd San Francisco	81	236
Geo	22	m	w	ME	San Joaquin	1-Wd Stockton	86	121
Geo A	47	m	w	OH	Sonoma	Mendocino Twp	91	291
Geo E	35	m	w	NY	Sierra	Table Rock Twp	89	578
Geo H	18	m	w	NY	Solano	Vallejo	90	200
George	54	m	w	ENGL	Placer	Bath P O	76	454
George	39	m	w	NJ	Siskiyou	Butte Twp	89	586
George	38	m	w	NY	Yuba	Rose Bar Twp	93	654
George	38	m	w	NY	Yuba	Rose Bar Twp	93	654
George	35	m	w	NY	Plumas	Quartz Twp	77	34
George	30	m	w	MO	Monterey	San Antonio Twp	74	321
George	24	m	w	HANO	San Francisco	7-Wd San Francisco	81	218
George	23	m	w	ENGL	Santa Clara	Santa Clara Twp	88	170
George H	30	m	w	MA	Yolo	Grafton Twp	93	496
George M	46	m	w	OH	Sonoma	Mendocino Twp	91	294
George T	27	m	w	KY	Yolo	Cache Crk Twp	93	448
George W	43	m	w	MA	Alameda	Washington Twp	68	292
George W	24	m	w	MA	Calaveras	San Andreas P O	70	220
Gordon A	57	m	w	NY	Sonoma	Healdsburg & Mendo	91	282
Green L	35	m	w	KY	Calaveras	Copperopolis P O	70	246
H A	34	m	w	MO	Yuba	Marysville	93	616
Hannah	75	f	w	ENGL	El Dorado	Placerville	72	108
Hannah	35	f	w	MA	San Francisco	6-Wd San Francisco	81	138
Hariet	46	f	w	KY	Colusa	Colusa	71	293
Harriet	49	f	w	KY	Colusa	Colusa	71	289
Harris H	35	m	w	PA	Santa Clara	Santa Clara Twp	88	147
Harry	44	m	w	PRUS	Sacramento	Franklin Twp	77	119
Henry	62	m	w	NY	San Francisco	San Francisco P O	83	45
Henry	62	m	w	MD	Yuba	Marysville	93	634
Henry	60	m	w	NY	San Francisco	11-Wd San Francisc	84	564
Henry	49	m	w	PRUS	Inyo	Cerro Gordo Twp	73	321
Henry	48	m	w	NY	Colusa	Stony Crk Twp	71	332
Henry	44	m	w	ME	Kern	Linns Valley P O	73	348
Henry	29	m	w	HOLL	Butte	Chico Twp	70	56
Henry	26	m	w	IREL	Sacramento	2-Wd Sacramento	77	244
Henry	25	m	w	CANA	Alameda	Oakland	68	169
Henry	25	m	w	GA	Sonoma	Analy Twp	91	235
Henry	21	m	w	GERM	Los Angeles	Los Angeles	73	546
Henry	21	m	w	GA	Sonoma	Analy Twp	91	234
Henry	19	m	w	PRUS	San Francisco	San Francisco P O	80	402
Henry E	40	m	w	ENGL	Yolo	Grafton Twp	93	495
Henry F	42	m	w	KY	Mendocino	Anderson Twp	74	150
Henry H	45	m	w	KY	Santa Clara	1-Wd San Jose	88	241
Herman	30	m	w	CANA	San Francisco	San Francisco P O	83	55
Herrman	23	m	w	PRUS	San Francisco	7-Wd San Francisco	81	228
Hiram	40	m	w	NY	Sacramento	3-Wd Sacramento	77	285
Holmes	36	m	w	ENGL	San Francisco	San Francisco P O	85	768
Horace	49	m	b	HI	Tuolumne	Big Oak Flat P O	93	399
Horatio	29	m	w	ME	San Francisco	San Francisco P O	80	392
Horatio	27	m	w	ME	San Francisco	San Francisco P O	80	407
Horatio	20	m	w	MA	San Francisco	1-Wd San Francisco	79	66
Ira	35	m	w	MA	San Francisco	San Francisco P O	83	418
Isaac	44	m	w	MA	San Francisco	San Francisco P O	85	839
Isaac	36	m	w	PRUS	San Francisco	8-Wd San Francisco	82	411
Israel	35	m	w	PA	Sonoma	Vallejo Twp	91	451
J	35	m	w	IN	Alameda	Oakland	68	264
J A H	53	m	w	TN	Monterey	Alisal Twp	74	294
J B	34	m	w	ENGL	Nevada	Bridgeport Twp	75	106
J G	58	m	w	KY	Monterey	Alisal Twp	74	300
J H	36	m	w	NY	Nevada	Nevada Twp	75	291
J L	39	m	w	MO	Napa	Yountville Twp	75	77
J S	40	m	w	WI	Santa Clara	2-Wd San Jose	88	331
Jacob	34	m	w	PA	Amador	Volcano P O	69	380
Jacob	30	m	w	CANA	Napa	Napa	75	16
Jacob A	19	m	w	HCAS	Santa Barbara	Santa Barbara P O	87	456
James	52	m	w	SCOT	Santa Clara	Fremont Twp	88	41
James	45	m	w	AR	Los Angeles	San Jose Twp	73	621
James	40	m	w	TN	Placer	Auburn P O	76	377
James	40	m	w	SCOT	Alameda	Murray Twp	68	109
James	39	m	w	VT	Nevada	Grass Valley Twp	75	177
James	39	m	w	NY	San Francisco	San Francisco P O	83	240
James	38	m	w	ENGL	Placer	Colfax P O	76	392
James	35	m	w	IL	Santa Clara	Burnett Twp	88	31
James	34	m	w	PA	Alameda	Alameda	68	20
James	33	m	w	CT	Yuba	Marysville	93	600
James	33	m	w	KY	Inyo	Independence Twp	73	327
James	29	m	w	NY	San Francisco	11-Wd San Francisc	84	446
James	28	m	w	ENGL	San Francisco	3-Wd San Francisco	79	295
James	27	m	w	SCOT	Napa	Napa Twp	75	34
James	20	m	w	CANA	Santa Clara	Almaden Twp	88	18
James	14	m	w	CA	Calaveras	San Andreas P O	70	212
James B	60	m	w	PA	Napa	Napa	75	22
James F	18	m	w	CA	Mendocino	Cuffeys Cove Twp	74	169
James M	48	m	w	VA	Placer	Bath P O	76	456
James R	41	m	w	OH	Monterey	San Antonio Twp	74	322
James R	31	m	w	KY	San Diego	Milquaty Dist	78	478
James W	34	m	w	MO	Stanislaus	Empire Twp	92	39
Jane	40	f	w	IREL	San Francisco	2-Wd San Francisco	79	138
Jas C	49	m	w	KY	Sonoma	Mendocino Twp	91	307
Jas W	35	m	w	OH	Butte	Chico Twp	70	19
Jay Juz	33	m	w	NY	Mariposa	Mariposa P O	74	118
Jefferson	47	m	w	TN	San Diego	Milquaty Dist	78	475
Jesse D	26	m	w	MO	Monterey	Castroville Twp	74	341
Jessie	40	f	w	NY	San Francisco	8-Wd San Francisco	82	433
Jessie F	58	m	w	MS	Yuba	Slate Range Bar Tw	93	674
Jno B	56	m	w	KY	Sonoma	Santa Rosa	91	422
Jno L	28	m	w	MO	Sonoma	Santa Rosa	91	423
John	73	m	w	IOFW	Santa Clara	Santa Clara Twp	88	137
John	63	m	w	OH	Alameda	Oakland	68	176
John	46	m	w	IREL	Solano	Benicia	90	5
John	45	m	w	NY	Santa Barbara	Santa Barbara P O	87	472
John	44	m	b	HI	Tuolumne	Big Oak Flat P O	93	399
John	43	m	w	ME	Nevada	Nevada Twp	75	315
John	42	m	w	MD	El Dorado	Placerville	72	127
John	40	m	w	IREL	Calaveras	San Andreas P O	70	159
John	38	m	w	IREL	San Francisco	11-Wd San Francisc	84	523
John	38	m	w	MO	San Francisco	San Francisco P O	80	376
John	38	m	w	MI	Tuolumne	Columbia P O	93	345
John	36	m	w	NY	San Francisco	3-Wd San Francisco	79	297
John	36	m	w	NC	San Bernardino	San Bernardino Twp	78	425
John	35	m	w	VA	Mariposa	Maxwell Crk P O	74	147
John	35	m	w	IREL	Nevada	Nevada Twp	75	293
John	35	m	w	IN	Sonoma	Mendocino Twp	91	294
John	32	m	w	ITAL	San Francisco	San Francisco P O	80	338
John	32	m	w	GERM	San Francisco	8-Wd San Francisco	82	342
John	27	m	w	BAVA	Santa Barbara	Santa Barbara P O	87	451
John	27	m	w	PRUS	Marin	Novato Twp	74	12
John	25	m	w	CANA	San Francisco	1-Wd San Francisco	79	121
John	25	m	w	ENGL	Yuba	Rose Bar Twp	93	657
John	23	m	w	TX	Lake	Lower Lake	73	421
John	21	m	w	PRUS	San Francisco	San Francisco P O	83	352
John F	25	m	w	ENGL	Santa Clara	Santa Clara Twp	88	170
John H	64	m	w	HAMB	El Dorado	Mud Springs Twp	72	86
John J	40	m	w	MI	Yolo	Grafton Twp	93	487
John L	24	m	w	OH	Placer	Bath P O	76	427
John M	26	m	w	MO	Yolo	Cache Crk Twp	93	445
John V	35	m	w	KY	Sonoma	Sonoma Twp	91	436
John W	34	m	w	MO	Colusa	Colusa	71	289
Jos	50	m	b	MO	San Joaquin	3-Wd Stockton	86	218
Jos E	43	m	w	MO	Shasta	Shasta P O	89	458
Jos S	36	m	w	ME	Santa Barbara	San Buenaventura P	87	421
Joseph	56	m	w	KY	Yolo	Cache Crk Twp	93	445
Joseph	55	m	w	SAXO	San Francisco	2-Wd San Francisco	79	171
Joseph	45	m	b	MD	San Joaquin	1-Wd Stockton	86	128
Joseph	18	m	w	PRUS	Sacramento	Franklin Twp	77	114
Josiah	37	m	w	KY	Nevada	Meadow Lake Twp	75	268
Kate	27	f	w	MA	San Francisco	San Francisco P O	83	68
L B	32	m	w	OH	Santa Clara	Burnett Twp	88	30
L H	40	m	w	NY	Monterey	San Juan Twp	74	391
L T	26	m	w	MO	Monterey	Salinas Twp	74	306
Larkin	36	m	w	OH	Santa Barbara	Santa Maria P O	87	511
Lawrence	27	m	w	PA	Solano	Vallejo	90	140
Lena	24	f	w	HAMB	San Francisco	San Francisco P O	83	27
Leonard	43	m	w	VT	Sutter	Sutter Twp	92	120
Lewis D	49	m	w	NY	Sacramento	2-Wd Sacramento	77	246
Lim	35	m	c	CHIN	Yuba	Marysville	93	620

© 2001 by Heritage Quest. All rights reserved.

Series M593

Name	Age	S	R	B-PL	County	Locale	Roll	Pg
Louis	38	m	w	PRUS	San Francisco	2-Wd San Francisco	79	153
Louis H	21	m	w	NY	Shasta	Fort Crook P O	89	473
Luke	36	m	w	PRUS	San Francisco	2-Wd San Francisco	79	210
M	39	m	w	HDAR	San Francisco	8-Wd San Francisco	82	368
M M	32	m	w	MA	San Francisco	San Francisco P O	85	862
Magdaline	79	f	w	NY	San Francisco	2-Wd San Francisco	79	267
Mariah	28	f	w	PA	Sacramento	4-Wd Sacramento	77	349
Mark	26	m	w	HANO	Stanislaus	Empire Twp	92	59
Martin	39	m	w	HDAR	Santa Clara	Fremont Twp	88	58
Martin	20	m	w	CA	Marin	San Rafael Twp	74	40
Mary	50	f	w	IREL	San Francisco	2-Wd San Francisco	79	138
Mary	47	f	w	IREL	Santa Clara	Fremont Twp	88	56
Mary	30	f	w	MA	Butte	Chico Twp	70	21
Mary E	19	f	w	MO	Sonoma	Healdsburg & Mendo	91	276
Mary F	38	f	b	MD	San Francisco	2-Wd San Francisco	79	143
Mary M	40	f	w	CANA	San Francisco	San Francisco P O	83	160
Mather	40	m	w	IREL	Sacramento	3-Wd Sacramento	77	257
Matt	41	m	w	IREL	Sacramento	3-Wd Sacramento	77	296
Michael	62	m	w	NY	Placer	Bath P O	76	454
Michael	58	m	w	NY	Placer	Bath P O	76	446
Michal	30	m	w	MA	Sacramento	3-Wd Sacramento	77	296
Mike	50	m	w	IREL	Solano	Vallejo	90	176
Mrijah C	43	m	w	NY	Placer	Gold Run Twp	76	399
Murroe V	50	m	w	MO	Sonoma	Santa Rosa	91	422
N B	30	m	w	MS	Nevada	Bloomfield Twp	75	99
N S	50	m	w	IREL	San Francisco	San Francisco P O	85	873
Napoleon	42	m	w	PA	San Francisco	11-Wd San Francisc	84	541
Nathaniel	50	m	w	ENGL	Santa Clara	Santa Clara Twp	88	151
Nathaniel	40	m	w	NY	Yolo	Putah Twp	93	518
Nelson	47	m	b	NY	San Francisco	San Francisco P O	83	185
O F	43	m	w	NY	Solano	Benicia	90	3
Oliver	23	m	w	CANA	Santa Clara	Santa Clara Twp	88	167
P	56	m	w	NY	Amador	Sutter Crk P O	69	400
Pardon W	52	m	w	NY	Stanislaus	Empire Twp	92	57
Pat	30	m	w	IREL	Alameda	Murray Twp	68	107
Patrick	33	m	w	IREL	Stanislaus	Empire Twp	92	34
Paul	41	m	w	NY	San Francisco	5-Wd San Francisco	81	12
Peter	42	m	w	SHOL	Mariposa	Maxwell Crk P O	74	148
Peter	30	m	w	NY	San Francisco	San Francisco P O	85	718
Ph Henry	25	m	w	ENGL	San Francisco	7-Wd San Francisco	81	247
Phil	27	m	w	LA	San Joaquin	2-Wd Stockton	86	211
Philmron	57	m	w	NY	Amador	Sutter Crk P O	69	408
R W	48	m	w	NH	San Francisco	8-Wd San Francisco	82	359
Richard	45	m	w	ENGL	San Francisco	7-Wd San Francisco	81	191
Richard	30	m	w	ENGL	San Bernardino	San Bernardino Twp	78	452
Richd	40	m	w	ENGL	San Francisco	5-Wd San Francisco	81	28
Ronald	46	m	w	SCOT	San Francisco	San Francisco P O	83	93
Rudolph	38	m	w	OH	Santa Barbara	Santa Maria P O	87	510
Saml R	34	m	w	AL	Napa	Napa Twp	75	71
Samuel	49	m	w	NY	San Francisco	2-Wd San Francisco	79	229
Samuel	47	m	w	ENGL	Plumas	Plumas Twp	77	33
Samuel	46	m	w	PA	Napa	Yountville Twp	75	85
Samuel	46	m	w	ENGL	Plumas	Mineral Twp	77	22
Samuel	23	m	w	CT	Butte	Oroville Twp	70	140
Samuel M	47	m	w	NY	San Mateo	Redwood Twp	87	365
Sarah	17	f	w	PA	Placer	Auburn P O	76	366
Sarah A	61	f	w	ENGL	Placer	Dutch Flat P O	76	406
Saxton	40	m	w	NY	Sonoma	Cloverdale Twp	91	271
Simon	43	m	w	BAVA	San Francisco	3-Wd San Francisco	79	321
Sing	30	m	c	CHIN	Trinity	North Fork Twp	92	216
T	48	m	w	IREL	Lake	Knoxville Mines	73	404
Theodore	41	m	w	PRUS	San Francisco	1-Wd San Francisco	79	52
Thomas	66	m	w	ENGL	Tuolumne	Sonora P O	93	320
Thomas	40	m	w	IREL	Calaveras	San Andreas P O	70	154
Thomas	35	m	w	IN	Alameda	Alameda	68	19
Thomas	30	m	w	MD	San Bernardino	San Bernardino Twp	78	448
Thomas	30	m	w	MO	San Francisco	San Francisco P O	83	314
Thomas E	32	m	w	IN	Yuba	Long Bar Twp	93	563
Thomas J	43	m	w	IN	Santa Clara	Santa Clara Twp	88	136
Thomas R	27	m	w	NY	Yolo	Grafton Twp	93	480
Thomas W	36	m	w	NY	Placer	Dutch Flat P O	76	406
Thos	37	m	m	VA	Sacramento	3-Wd Sacramento	77	256
Timothy	35	m	w	ENGL	Monterey	Alisal Twp	74	293
Tuey	26	m	c	CHIN	Yuba	Marysville	93	628
Undine	21	m	w	PRUS	Sacramento	Franklin Twp	77	114
Valentine B	52	m	w	MO	Napa	Napa Twp	75	69
Vining	29	m	w	OH	San Diego	Julian Dist	78	470
Virginia	16	f	w	ENGL	Alameda	Brooklyn Twp	68	42
W	23	m	w	ENGL	Lake	Knoxville Mines	73	405
W J	45	m	w	VA	San Joaquin	2-Wd Stockton	86	206
W L	26	m	w	MO	Yuba	Marysville	93	583
W R	25	m	w	OH	Napa	Yountville Twp	75	76
W S	39	m	w	AL	Lake	Lakeport	73	407
Walter H	31	m	w	ME	Santa Barbara	San Buenaventura P	87	424
Warren	38	m	w	ME	Placer	Bath P O	76	457
Warren	13	m	w	CA	Colusa	Monroe Twp	71	311
William	48	m	w	OH	Yolo	Buckeye Twp	93	414
William	46	m	w	IREL	Placer	Bath P O	76	433
William	45	m	w	WALE	Contra Costa	Martinez P O	71	426
William	40	m	w	HESS	Amador	Ione City P O	69	363
William	35	m	w	MD	Nevada	Little York Twp	75	239
William	35	m	w	RI	San Francisco	8-Wd San Francisco	82	494
William	35	m	w	WALE	San Francisco	11-Wd San Francisc	84	705
William	28	m	w	CANA	Alpine	Silver Mtn P O	69	308
William	26	m	w	AR	Los Angeles	Los Nietos Twp	73	590
William	24	m	w	ENGL	Napa	Napa	75	24
William	24	m	w	CANA	Siskiyou	Callahan P O	89	629
William C	75	m	w	ENGL	El Dorado	Placerville	72	108
William S	41	m	w	GA	El Dorado	Mud Springs Twp	72	90
Wm	40	m	w	ENGL	Sacramento	Mississippi Twp	77	163
Wm A	37	m	w	VA	San Francisco	San Francisco P O	85	792
Wm N	49	m	w	MD	San Francisco	2-Wd San Francisco	79	269
COOKE								
Alexr	45	m	w	NY	San Francisco	San Francisco P O	83	72
Bernard	30	m	w	IREL	San Francisco	11-Wd San Francisc	84	634
Chas	20	m	w	PA	Butte	Chico Twp	70	26
Geo	32	m	w	NH	San Francisco	1-Wd San Francisco	79	92
Geo	19	m	w	NY	San Francisco	1-Wd San Francisco	79	82
Henry	53	m	w	IA	Solano	Denverton Twp	90	24
Henry	53	m	w	PA	Solano	Denverton Twp	90	23
Henry	21	m	w	GERM	Santa Clara	Burnett Twp	88	32
James	56	m	w	ENGL	Solano	Silveyville Twp	90	86
Jno	24	m	w	IL	Santa Clara	Burnett Twp	88	36
John	48	m	w	ENGL	Placer	Lincoln P O	76	493
Joseph B	34	m	w	ENGL	Colusa	Colusa	71	296
Mary	19	f	w	CA	Solano	Denverton Twp	90	22
Niel	53	m	w	SCOT	Solano	Rio Vista Twp	90	56
Robert	44	m	w	IREL	Sonoma	Mendocino Twp	91	288
Wm N	34	m	w	MO	El Dorado	Georgetown Twp	72	48
Wm R	37	m	w	IREL	San Francisco	1-Wd San Francisco	79	112
COOKERLY								
John C	35	m	w	MD	Nevada	Eureka Twp	75	131
COOKES								
Benj	41	m	w	IREL	San Diego	San Diego	78	492
COOKLEY								
Francis	30	m	w	IREL	San Francisco	11-Wd San Francisc	84	652
James	28	m	w	IREL	San Diego	Julian Dist	78	472
Pat	35	m	w	IREL	San Francisco	11-Wd San Francisc	84	710
COOKS								
Barzilla	45	m	w	CT	San Francisco	7-Wd San Francisco	81	232
COOKSEN								
Richard B	24	m	w	ME	San Mateo	Belmont P O	87	373
COOKSEY								
James	37	m	w	IL	Sierra	Gibson Twp	89	543
COOKSLY								
Henry	42	m	w	ENGL	Sacramento	4-Wd Sacramento	77	323
COOKSON								
Alex	36	m	w	CANA	Humboldt	Eureka Twp	72	267
Sam	33	m	w	ME	San Joaquin	Dent Twp	86	20
COOL								
Frederick	57	m	w	PA	Yuba	New York Twp	93	642
Peter Y	39	m	w	NY	Santa Barbara	Santa Barbara P O	87	466
Sylvester	36	m	w	NY	San Francisco	5-Wd San Francisco	81	31
COOLAGE								
Gray	3	m	w	CANA	Solano	Silveyville Twp	90	86
Joseph	55	m	w	ME	San Francisco	San Francisco P O	85	759
Mary	23	f	w	MA	San Francisco	7-Wd San Francisco	81	206
COOLBAUGH								
David	32	m	w	PA	San Joaquin	Oneal Twp	86	109
COOLBRITH								
Saml W	42	m	w	ME	Sonoma	Bodega Twp	91	251
COOLE								
Patrick	39	m	w	IREL	San Francisco	11-Wd San Francisc	84	592
COOLEDGE								
C H	67	m	w	ME	Amador	Fiddletown P O	69	430
Joseph	50	m	w	MA	San Francisco	8-Wd San Francisco	82	437
Sabine	38	m	w	MD	Amador	Fiddletown P O	69	430
W S	43	m	w	MA	Amador	Jackson P O	69	318
COOLEGE								
Isaac B	37	m	w	NH	Sacramento	2-Wd Sacramento	77	239
COOLER								
John	40	m	w	ENGL	San Francisco	7-Wd San Francisco	81	188
COOLEY								
Abner	34	m	w	MO	Solano	Vacaville Twp	90	123
Abram	21	m	w	OH	Solano	Tremont Twp	90	30
Alexander W	33	m	w	IN	Colusa	Butte Twp	71	268
Andrew S	40	m	w	NY	Plumas	Goodwin Twp	77	2
C P	43	m	w	OH	Sacramento	Cosumnes Twp	77	92
Caleb	45	m	w	OH	Nevada	Bridgeport Twp	75	116
Catherine	47	f	w	IREL	Nevada	Grass Valley Twp	75	216
Charles B	62	m	w	VA	Sacramento	2-Wd Sacramento	77	254
Chas B	64	m	w	NY	Sacramento	4-Wd Sacramento	77	364
Chas H	47	m	w	OH	Sonoma	Cloverdale Twp	91	272
Chauncy	30	m	w	IL	Siskiyou	Scott Valley Twp	89	608
E K	46	m	w	VT	San Francisco	San Francisco P O	85	832
Ervin	37	m	w	MO	El Dorado	White Oak Twp	72	136
F P	20	m	w	NY	Solano	Vallejo	90	200
Francis	72	m	w	MA	Santa Barbara	Santa Barbara P O	87	476
Geo	45	m	w	ENGL	El Dorado	Georgetown Twp	72	39
George	36	m	w	ENGL	San Bernardino	San Bernardino Twp	78	439
Jarome B	47	m	w	TN	El Dorado	Georgetown Twp	72	47
John	42	m	w	ENGL	Siskiyou	Yreka Twp	89	670
John	38	m	w	SWED	Calaveras	Copperopolis P O	70	236
John D	39	m	w	IREL	San Francisco	7-Wd San Francisco	81	159
John E	23	m	w	IREL	San Francisco	San Francisco P O	83	36
John W	33	m	w	MO	Tulare	Farmersville Twp	92	247
Joseph S	46	m	w	IN	Yolo	Cottonwood Twp	93	473
Lester	32	m	w	VT	San Francisco	11-Wd San Francisc	84	627
Lester P	32	m	w	VT	San Mateo	Menlo Park P O	87	379
Margaret	30	f	w	IREL	San Francisco	San Francisco P O	85	804
Mary	33	f	w	IREL	San Francisco	1-Wd San Francisco	79	72
Menzo	26	m	w	NY	Placer	Rocklin Twp	76	463
Michael	40	m	w	IREL	San Francisco	San Francisco P O	83	24
Micheal	32	m	w	IREL	San Francisco	7-Wd San Francisco	81	189

© 2001 by Heritage Quest. All rights reserved.

Name	Age	S	R	B-PL	County	Locale	Series M593 Roll	Pg
Ralph	40	m	w	NY	Alameda	Eden Twp	68	93
S B	40	m	w	CT	Sacramento	1-Wd Sacramento	77	200
Squire	52	m	w	MA	Siskiyou	Scott Valley Twp	89	608
Van	19	m	w	IL	Siskiyou	Yreka Twp	89	673
William	63	m	w	KY	Siskiyou	Yreka	89	652
William H	35	m	w	NY	Placer	Rocklin Twp	76	467
Wm R	26	m	w	MI	Santa Barbara	Santa Barbara P O	87	454
COOLGAN								
M	38	m	w	IREL	San Joaquin	Tulare Twp	86	263
COOLIDGE								
Samuel	36	m	w	PA	San Diego	Julian Dist	78	469
Wm M	33	m	w	MA	Fresno	Kingston P O	72	218
COOLIE								
Lydia	18	f	w	IA	San Joaquin	Oneal Twp	86	108
Thompson	32	m	w	SCOT	San Francisco	San Francisco P O	83	118
COOLIGE								
John P	40	m	w	MA	San Francisco	San Francisco P O	83	358
COOLLEY								
T J	38	m	w	IN	Mendocino	Calpella Twp	74	186
COOLOT								
Antony	47	m	w	AUST	Sacramento	3-Wd Sacramento	77	286
COOLS								
John	42	m	w	IL	San Francisco	11-Wd San Francisc	84	500
COOLWINE								
Bernard	44	m	w	WURT	San Francisco	8-Wd San Francisco	82	361
COOLY								
Charles	30	m	w	MA	Sacramento	San Joaquin Twp	77	400
Dwight	42	m	w	NY	Solano	Tremont Twp	90	31
Ephram	24	m	w	NY	Solano	Silveyville Twp	90	80
Geo W	27	m	w	NY	Sonoma	Salt Point	91	386
Han	38	m	w	IREL	Alameda	Oakland	68	264
Nicholas	18	m	i	CA	Yolo	Cottonwood Twp	93	465
COOM								
Ah	19	m	c	CHIN	San Francisco	6-Wd San Francisco	81	38
COOMB								
Elizabeth	74	f	w	ENGL	Nevada	Rough & Ready Twp	75	323
William	33	m	w	ENGL	Nevada	Grass Valley Twp	75	159
COOMBE								
John	30	m	w	ENGL	Santa Clara	1-Wd San Jose	88	244
W	32	m	w	ENGL	Amador	Drytown P O	69	418
COOMBS								
Charles	27	m	w	NY	Napa	Yountville Twp	75	84
Edward	59	m	w	MA	Marin	Bolinas Twp	74	7
Fannie	43	f	w	MO	Merced	Snelling P O	74	247
Fredrick	40	m	w	MA	Napa	Napa	75	22
Henry	37	m	w	ENGL	Alameda	Oakland	68	153
Jacob L	41	m	w	PA	Nevada	Grass Valley Twp	75	170
John H	40	m	w	CA	San Francisco	San Francisco P O	85	864
Jos	20	m	w	IN	Tehama	Red Bluff	92	182
Joseph	45	m	w	ENGL	El Dorado	Placerville Twp	72	95
Matthew R	61	m	w	NY	Yolo	Putah Twp	93	527
Nathan	45	m	w	MA	Napa	Napa Twp	75	65
O	30	m	w	SCOT	Sacramento	1-Wd Sacramento	77	174
Peter	42	m	w	ENGL	El Dorado	Georgetown Twp	72	49
S C	43	m	w	ME	Solano	Vallejo	90	212
Silas	52	m	w	ME	Mendocino	Little Rvr Twp	74	165
William	38	m	w	ENGL	Nevada	Rough & Ready Twp	75	338
COOMIS								
Albert N	26	m	w	MA	Sacramento	Franklin Twp	77	110
COOMLEY								
Marich	24	f	w	MA	Los Angeles	Los Angeles	73	568
COOMS								
Levi	39	m	w	ENGL	El Dorado	Placerville	72	126
William L	38	m	w	ME	Santa Clara	2-Wd San Jose	88	284
COON								
Ah	57	m	c	CHIN	Sacramento	Georgianna Twp	77	134
Ah	54	m	c	CHIN	Placer	Newcastle Twp	76	479
Ah	54	m	c	CHIN	Shasta	Horsetown P O	89	507
Ah	50	m	c	CHIN	Sacramento	Natomas Twp	77	171
Ah	50	m	c	CHIN	Placer	Auburn P O	76	375
Ah	48	m	c	CHIN	Sacramento	Cosumnes Twp	77	90
Ah	47	m	c	CHIN	Sacramento	Natomas Twp	77	171
Ah	45	m	c	CHIN	Trinity	Lewiston Pct	92	212
Ah	45	m	c	CHIN	Sacramento	Mississippi Twp	77	162
Ah	45	m	c	CHIN	Merced	Snelling P O	74	279
Ah	44	m	c	CHIN	Amador	Jackson P O	69	343
Ah	44	m	c	CHIN	El Dorado	Coloma Twp	72	10
Ah	44	m	c	CHIN	Sacramento	American Twp	77	68
Ah	43	m	c	CHIN	Sacramento	Cosumnes Twp	77	95
Ah	42	m	c	CHIN	Trinity	Weaverville Pct	92	227
Ah	42	m	c	CHIN	Yuba	Marysville	93	618
Ah	42	m	c	CHIN	Sacramento	Dry Crk Twp	77	101
Ah	41	m	c	CHIN	Sacramento	American Twp	77	67
Ah	41	m	c	CHIN	Stanislaus	Empire Twp	92	62
Ah	40	m	c	CHIN	Calaveras	Copperopolis P O	70	234
Ah	40	m	c	CHIN	Sacramento	Granite Twp	77	155
Ah	40	m	c	CHIN	Sacramento	Cosumnes Twp	77	94
Ah	40	m	c	CHIN	Sacramento	Cosumnes Twp	77	94
Ah	40	m	c	CHIN	El Dorado	Coloma Twp	72	10
Ah	40	m	c	CHIN	Sacramento	Natomas Twp	77	168
Ah	40	m	c	CHIN	Sacramento	Natomas Twp	77	168
Ah	40	m	c	CHIN	Sacramento	Granite Twp	77	155
Ah	40	m	c	CHIN	Tuolumne	Chinese Camp P O	93	388
Ah	39	m	c	CHIN	Marin	San Rafael Twp	74	36
Ah	38	m	c	CHIN	Sacramento	Center Twp	77	86
Ah	37	m	c	CHIN	Sacramento	Granite Twp	77	153
Ah	37	m	c	CHIN	Sacramento	Center Twp	77	86

Name	Age	S	R	B-PL	County	Locale	Series M593 Roll	Pg
Ah	36	m	c	CHIN	Amador	Volcano P O	69	377
Ah	36	m	c	CHIN	Plumas	Plumas Twp	77	32
Ah	35	m	c	CHIN	Amador	Ione City P O	69	363
Ah	35	m	c	CHIN	Placer	Auburn P O	76	363
Ah	34	m	c	CHIN	Placer	Rocklin Twp	76	468
Ah	34	m	c	CHIN	Trinity	Weaverville Pct	92	227
Ah	34	m	c	CHIN	Sierra	Downieville Twp	89	521
Ah	32	m	c	CHIN	Sacramento	Center Twp	77	86
Ah	32	m	c	CHIN	Plumas	Plumas Twp	77	31
Ah	31	m	c	CHIN	Tuolumne	Chinese Camp P O	93	388
Ah	30	m	c	CHIN	Alameda	Washington Twp	68	297
Ah	30	m	c	CHIN	Sacramento	1-Wd Sacramento	77	205
Ah	30	m	c	CHIN	Sacramento	Georgianna Twp	77	134
Ah	30	m	c	CHIN	Sacramento	Georgianna Twp	77	124
Ah	30	m	c	CHIN	Sacramento	Georgianna Twp	77	125
Ah	30	m	c	CHIN	Sacramento	Natomas Twp	77	171
Ah	30	m	c	CHIN	San Francisco	1-Wd San Francisco	79	87
Ah	30	m	c	CHIN	San Francisco	3-Wd San Francisco	79	307
Ah	29	m	c	CHIN	Amador	Fiddletown P O	69	429
Ah	29	m	c	CHIN	Plumas	Goodwin Twp	77	5
Ah	29	m	c	CHIN	Sacramento	American Twp	77	68
Ah	29	m	c	CHIN	Placer	Bath P O	76	429
Ah	28	m	c	CHIN	Solano	Suisun Twp	90	106
Ah	28	m	c	CHIN	Sacramento	Granite Twp	77	141
Ah	28	m	c	CHIN	Sacramento	Cosumnes Twp	77	94
Ah	28	m	c	CHIN	Sacramento	Georgianna Twp	77	128
Ah	28	m	c	CHIN	Placer	Newcastle Twp	76	475
Ah	28	m	c	CHIN	Tuolumne	Big Oak Flat P O	93	397
Ah	28	m	c	CHIN	Sierra	Lincoln Twp	89	548
Ah	27	m	c	CHIN	Sacramento	Granite Twp	77	152
Ah	26	m	c	CHIN	Shasta	Shasta P O	89	453
Ah	25	m	c	CHIN	Alameda	Eden Twp	68	64
Ah	25	m	c	CHIN	Sacramento	3-Wd Sacramento	77	269
Ah	25	m	c	CHIN	San Francisco	8-Wd San Francisco	82	361
Ah	24	m	c	CHIN	Placer	Rocklin P O	76	462
Ah	22	m	c	CHIN	Placer	Bath P O	76	446
Ah	21	m	c	CHIN	Alameda	Eden Twp	68	61
Ah	20	f	c	CHIN	Sacramento	Granite Twp	77	153
Ah	20	m	c	CHIN	Placer	Bath P O	76	429
Ah	20	m	c	CHIN	Shasta	French Gulch P O	89	470
Ah	20	m	c	CHIN	San Francisco	San Francisco P O	83	28
Ah	19	m	c	CHIN	Santa Clara	Redwood Twp	88	126
Ah	18	m	c	CHIN	Los Angeles	Los Angeles	73	565
Ah	18	m	c	CHIN	Contra Costa	Martinez P O	71	384
Ah	17	m	c	CHIN	Placer	Bath P O	76	429
Ah	17	m	c	CHIN	San Francisco	San Francisco P O	80	402
Ah	15	m	c	CHIN	San Francisco	8-Wd San Francisco	82	312
Ah	15	m	c	CHIN	San Francisco	3-Wd San Francisco	79	304
Ah	14	m	c	CHIN	San Francisco	San Francisco P O	85	728
Albert	26	m	w	IL	Butte	Oregon Twp	70	136
Alonzo	30	m	w	KY	Santa Clara	Santa Clara Twp	88	156
Andrew	33	m	w	IL	Butte	Chico Twp	70	32
Charley Ah	21	m	c	CHIN	Placer	Bath P O	76	436
Chas D	34	m	w	NY	San Francisco	8-Wd San Francisco	82	323
Chin	38	m	c	CHIN	Yuba	Marysville	93	631
Chung Long	25	m	c	CHIN	Sacramento	1-Wd Sacramento	77	194
Conly	38	m	w	IREL	Napa	Napa	75	22
David P	41	m	w	PA	Colusa	Spring Valley Twp	71	336
Dennis	40	m	w	IREL	Colusa	Butte Twp	71	266
Elisha	53	m	w	NY	Marin	Tomales Twp	74	83
Elizabeth	54	f	w	VA	Sonoma	Analy Twp	91	245
Ezra F	28	m	w	MA	Sonoma	Salt Point	91	380
Fee	27	m	c	CHIN	Yuba	Marysville	93	628
Fi	30	m	c	CHIN	Alameda	Eden Twp	68	64
Fred	31	m	w	ENGL	Alameda	Oakland	68	265
Frederick	35	m	w	PRUS	San Francisco	San Francisco P O	83	19
Geo W	53	m	w	KY	Sacramento	San Joaquin Twp	77	405
George	35	m	w	NY	San Francisco	San Francisco P O	83	30
Git	49	m	c	CHIN	El Dorado	Diamond Springs Tw	72	22
Gup	40	m	c	CHIN	Sacramento	1-Wd Sacramento	77	199
Hiram	43	m	w	NY	Tuolumne	Sonora P O	93	321
Hiram	24	m	w	WI	Tuolumne	Sonora P O	93	307
How	39	m	c	CHIN	Yuba	Marysville	93	628
John	60	m	w	OH	Yolo	Cache Crk Twp	93	447
John	38	m	w	OH	Amador	Volcano P O	69	379
John	26	m	w	SHOL	San Francisco	1-Wd San Francisco	79	129
John A	43	m	w	NY	Humboldt	Mattole Twp	72	284
Lap	30	m	c	CHIN	Sacramento	1-Wd Sacramento	77	196
Lorenzo	30	m	w	NY	San Francisco	11-Wd San Francisc	84	531
Louis	27	m	w	POLA	Sacramento	2-Wd Sacramento	77	245
Mike	34	m	w	OH	Butte	Chico Twp	70	40
Mo	28	m	c	CHIN	Tuolumne	Columbia P O	93	342
N B	40	m	w	NY	Sacramento	3-Wd Sacramento	77	271
Norman	47	m	w	NY	San Francisco	11-Wd San Francisc	84	619
Perry	19	m	w	IL	Butte	Chico Twp	70	37
R W	30	m	w	VA	Tehama	Red Bluff	92	196
Riley M	65	m	w	VA	Butte	Chico Twp	70	40
Robert	45	m	w	NY	Amador	Lancha Plana P O	69	368
Robt	10	m	w	CA	Butte	Chico Twp	70	37
Sarah	40	f	w	IN	Butte	Chico Twp	70	37
Simmon	22	m	w	BADE	San Francisco	7-Wd San Francisco	81	161
Sing	33	m	c	CHIN	Yuba	Long Bar Twp	93	561
Ty	36	m	c	CHIN	San Francisco	1-Wd San Francisco	79	101
William	38	m	w	PRUS	Alameda	Brooklyn	68	35
William	35	m	w	IREL	San Francisco	11-Wd San Francisc	84	502
Wm	50	m	w	OH	Butte	Chico Twp	70	41
Wm	35	m	w	SC	San Francisco	8-Wd San Francisco	82	368

© 2001 by Heritage Quest. All rights reserved.

Name	Age	S	R	B-PL	County	Locale	Roll	Pg
Woo	26	m	c	CHIN	Sacramento	1-Wd Sacramento	77	196
Y	28	m	c	CHIN	Yuba	Marysville	93	630
Yon	15	m	c	CHIN	San Francisco	8-Wd San Francisco	82	301
Yop	16	m	c	CHIN	San Francisco	1-Wd San Francisco	79	58
COONAN								
James F	14	m	w	CA	Santa Clara	2-Wd San Jose	88	324
Mary	14	f	w	CA	Santa Cruz	Santa Cruz	89	417
COONES								
James	36	m	w	PA	Nevada	Eureka Twp	75	136
COONEY								
Anne	28	f	w	IREL	San Francisco	San Francisco P O	83	97
Bridget	18	f	w	CA	Sacramento	Granite Twp	77	143
Daniel	40	m	w	IREL	San Francisco	11-Wd San Francisc	84	585
Ellen	40	f	w	IREL	San Francisco	San Francisco P O	83	160
Hanah	56	f	w	PA	Butte	Chico Twp	70	44
Honora	25	f	w	IREL	San Francisco	7-Wd San Francisco	81	259
J	57	m	w	IREL	Sierra	Downieville Twp	89	514
James	41	m	w	IREL	Yolo	Washington Twp	93	530
James	40	m	w	IREL	Yolo	Washington Twp	93	529
James	40	m	w	IREL	San Francisco	7-Wd San Francisco	81	283
James	32	m	w	IREL	San Francisco	7-Wd San Francisco	81	282
James	25	m	w	IREL	Napa	Napa Twp	75	61
Johanna	33	f	w	IREL	San Francisco	8-Wd San Francisco	82	399
John	38	m	w	FRAN	Inyo	Cerro Gordo Twp	73	318
John	38	m	w	IREL	San Francisco	8-Wd San Francisco	82	303
Kate	30	f	w	IREL	San Francisco	8-Wd San Francisco	82	405
Margaret	40	f	w	IREL	Sacramento	Granite Twp	77	142
Mary	72	f	w	IREL	San Francisco	11-Wd San Francisc	84	585
Mary	25	f	w	IREL	Santa Clara	Milpitas Twp	88	108
Michael	29	m	w	IREL	San Francisco	San Francisco P O	83	14
Mike	29	m	w	IREL	San Francisco	11-Wd San Francisc	84	424
Patrick	40	m	w	IREL	San Francisco	7-Wd San Francisco	81	190
Patrick	30	m	w	IREL	San Francisco	8-Wd San Francisco	82	482
Peter	33	m	w	IREL	San Francisco	5-Wd San Francisco	81	32
Peter	21	m	w	IREL	San Francisco	1-Wd San Francisco	79	100
Peter E	33	m	w	IREL	San Francisco	1-Wd San Francisco	79	33
Richard	22	m	w	NY	San Francisco	3-Wd San Francisco	79	314
Sarah	30	f	w	IREL	San Francisco	San Francisco P O	85	735
Terence	25	m	w	IREL	San Francisco	1-Wd San Francisco	79	100
Thomas	53	m	w	IREL	Placer	Alta P O	76	419
Thos	29	m	w	IREL	Sonoma	Santa Rosa	91	401
Ying	20	m	c	CHIN	Siskiyou	Butte Twp	89	586
COONIE								
Chas	29	m	w	IREL	Sacramento	1-Wd Sacramento	77	183
COONIN								
Cornelius	37	m	w	IREL	San Francisco	San Francisco P O	83	189
John	24	m	w	IREL	Yolo	Buckeye Twp	93	407
COONROD								
Edward	33	m	w	OH	Siskiyou	Table Rock Twp	89	648
Jno	35	m	w	GERM	Santa Clara	Gilroy Twp	88	107
COONS								
Andrew	40	m	w	BAVA	San Francisco	3-Wd San Francisco	79	299
Pat	30	m	w	IREL	Alameda	Oakland	68	258
William	33	m	w	KY	Kern	Havilah P O	73	337
Wm N	36	m	w	IL	Sacramento	Cosumnes Twp	77	88
COONSMAN								
Wm	34	m	w	PA	Sacramento	American Twp	77	65
COONY								
James	29	m	w	IREL	Sacramento	Brighton Twp	77	70
James	28	m	w	IREL	San Mateo	Woodside P O	87	384
Mary	39	f	w	IREL	San Francisco	6-Wd San Francisco	81	117
Peter	24	m	w	IREL	Los Angeles	Los Angeles	73	566
COOP								
Adam	35	m	w	BADE	Alameda	Oakland	68	156
Green	45	m	w	TN	Mariposa	Mariposa P O	74	120
Herman	44	m	w	PRUS	Mendocino	Navarro & Big Rvr	74	174
Horatio	37	m	w	MO	Fresno	Millerton P O	72	150
Isaac	48	m	w	PA	San Joaquin	Castoria Twp	86	3
John	31	m	w	ENGL	San Francisco	11-Wd San Francisc	84	648
Josephine	27	f	w	MO	San Joaquin	2-Wd Stockton	86	164
Michael	37	m	w	LUXE	Butte	Kimshew Tpw	70	81
COOPE								
Antony	36	m	w	ITAL	Inyo	Cerro Gordo Twp	73	318
COOPER								
A C	46	m	w	MO	Sutter	Vernon Twp	92	132
A H	28	m	w	ENGL	Santa Clara	Gilroy Twp	88	79
Aaron	25	m	w	NY	Amador	Jackson P O	69	333
Agnes	29	f	w	SCOT	Yolo	Washington Twp	93	529
Allen	19	m	w	MO	Sonoma	Cloverdale Twp	91	271
Alonzo	34	m	w	NH	Nevada	Little York Twp	75	243
Amos	30	m	w	MD	San Joaquin	1-Wd Stockton	86	154
Andrew	31	m	w	IREL	Solano	Silveyville Twp	90	72
Ann	72	f	w	PA	Sonoma	Santa Rosa	91	410
Anna	26	f	w	TN	Sacramento	2-Wd Sacramento	77	248
Annie	30	f	w	ENGL	Santa Clara	Gilroy Twp	88	78
Anthoney	50	m	w	ENGL	Amador	Ione City P O	69	355
Arthur	38	m	w	SCOT	Nevada	Grass Valley Twp	75	230
Arthur	37	m	w	ENGL	Nevada	Grass Valley Twp	75	201
Augusta	40	f	w	GERM	Los Angeles	Los Angeles	73	542
Augusta A	38	m	w	KY	Butte	Chico Twp	70	46
B F	28	m	w	NY	Alameda	Murray Twp	68	107
Benjamin	34	m	w	MO	Solano	Tremont Twp	90	28
Benjamin F	38	m	w	OH	San Mateo	Redwood Twp	87	366
Brayton	52	m	w	MO	Mendocino	Calpella Twp	74	188
Bridget	26	f	w	IREL	San Francisco	7-Wd San Francisco	81	232
Cathrain	21	f	w	NY	San Francisco	San Francisco P O	80	479
Celeste	6	f	w	IA	San Luis Obispo	Santa Rosa Twp	87	319
Charles	34	m	w	OH	Solano	Denverton Twp	90	24
Charles	15	m	w	CA	Sierra	Eureka Twp	89	524
Charles W	23	m	w	NY	Yuba	Long Bar Twp	93	563
Chas	39	m	w	PRUS	San Francisco	1-Wd San Francisco	79	39
Chas H	36	m	w	IREL	Shasta	Shasta P O	89	463
Chas R	16	m	w	CA	San Luis Obispo	Arroyo Grande Twp	87	277
Columbus	38	m	w	ME	Sierra	Eureka Twp	89	524
Cyrus	26	m	m	NY	Colusa	Monroe Twp	71	311
D	34	m	w	MO	Amador	Ione City P O	69	361
D A	45	m	w	NJ	Amador	Sutter Crk P O	69	407
D F	40	m	w	VA	Amador	Drytown P O	69	424
D L	33	m	w	ME	Alameda	Oakland	68	217
David	57	m	b	NY	Nevada	Meadow Lake Twp	75	253
David	50	m	w	SCOT	Placer	Gold Run Twp	76	398
David	26	m	w	CA	Tehama	Merrill	92	197
Delfina	8	f	w	CA	Monterey	Castroville Twp	74	328
E B	45	m	w	NY	San Francisco	San Francisco P O	85	846
E T	31	f	w	NY	San Francisco	San Francisco P O	85	792
Ed	30	m	w	VA	Sierra	Sears Twp	89	558
Edmund	36	m	w	BELG	Santa Clara	San Jose Twp	88	189
Edward	17	m	w	NY	San Francisco	7-Wd San Francisco	81	178
Edwd E	32	m	w	NY	San Francisco	1-Wd San Francisco	79	7
Edwin	29	m	w	KY	Solano	Benicia	90	19
Eliza Ann	17	f	w	IL	Tehama	Cottonwood Twp	92	162
Elwood	40	m	w	PA	Santa Barbara	Santa Barbara P O	87	475
Emma	38	f	w	NY	Santa Cruz	Santa Cruz	89	413
Emma J	16	f	w	CA	Sonoma	Healdsburg & Mendo	91	285
Ezekiel	50	m	b	MA	San Francisco	6-Wd San Francisco	81	132
Francis	6	m	w	CA	Santa Clara	Gilroy Twp	88	78
Frank	56	m	w	PA	Santa Cruz	Santa Cruz	89	427
Frank	41	m	w	HAMB	San Francisco	11-Wd San Francisc	84	446
Fred L	31	m	w	ME	Nevada	Nevada Twp	75	309
Frederick	19	m	b	TX	Santa Clara	1-Wd San Jose	88	235
Geo F	50	m	w	CANA	Nevada	Nevada Twp	75	306
George	8	m	w	MA	Sacramento	Brighton Twp	77	80
George	40	m	w	OH	Marin	San Rafael Twp	74	41
George	30	m	w	KS	Solano	Silveyville Twp	90	72
George	21	m	w	NY	San Francisco	8-Wd San Francisco	82	321
George W	31	m	w	MO	Mendocino	Gualala Twp	74	226
George W	23	m	w	TN	Colusa	Spring Valley Twp	71	337
Grace	50	f	w	SCOT	San Francisco	6-Wd San Francisco	81	92
Halsey F	42	m	w	NY	San Francisco	San Francisco P O	83	178
Halsey F	33	m	w	NY	San Francisco	San Francisco P O	83	178
Haman	42	m	w	KY	Stanislaus	Empire Twp	92	63
Harmon	42	m	w	TN	Stanislaus	Empire Twp	92	59
Harvey	32	m	w	ME	Nevada	Nevada Twp	75	309
Henry	54	m	w	NY	Yolo	Buckeye Twp	93	410
Henry	52	m	w	PA	San Francisco	San Francisco P O	80	531
Henry	21	m	w	IN	Tehama	Red Bluff	92	180
Henry H	60	m	w	NY	Sonoma	Petaluma Twp	91	313
J A	36	m	w	GA	Merced	Snelling P O	74	270
J B	44	m	w	ME	San Joaquin	Elliott Twp	86	81
J B	43	m	w	VT	San Francisco	San Francisco P O	85	782
J C	54	m	w	NY	Amador	Ione City P O	69	363
J F	28	m	w	KY	Sacramento	3-Wd Sacramento	77	290
J H	51	m	w	MO	Lake	Big Valley	73	397
J H	35	m	w	VA	Sacramento	4-Wd Sacramento	77	351
J H	19	m	w	NY	Klamath	South Fork Twp	73	385
J J	37	m	w	NY	Sutter	Sutter Twp	92	124
Jackson	33	m	w	NY	Butte	Chico Twp	70	60
Jacob	25	m	w	NY	Sutter	Yuba Twp	92	143
James	48	m	w	NY	Butte	Wyandotte Twp	70	142
James	38	m	w	NY	San Francisco	1-Wd San Francisco	79	56
James	30	m	w	IREL	Sonoma	Sonoma Twp	91	441
James	29	m	w	SCOT	San Francisco	San Francisco P O	83	69
James	27	m	w	ENGL	Nevada	Grass Valley Twp	75	145
James	24	m	w	KY	Butte	Oregon Twp	70	136
James	21	m	w	MO	Mendocino	Gualala Twp	74	226
James A	48	m	w	TN	Los Angeles	El Monte Twp	73	449
James A	48	m	w	PA	Santa Cruz	Watsonville	89	369
James B	41	m	w	NY	Yolo	Merritt Twp	93	506
James C	54	m	w	NY	Calaveras	San Andreas P O	70	157
James G	40	m	w	NY	San Francisco	San Francisco P O	83	144
James R	34	m	w	PA	San Francisco	8-Wd San Francisco	82	436
Jas	50	m	w	MA	Humboldt	Eel Rvr Twp	72	247
Jas H	48	m	w	NY	Butte	Ophir Twp	70	120
Jeff	26	m	w	MI	Sacramento	Franklin Twp	77	116
Jervay	16	m	w	PA	Butte	Concow Twp	70	9
Jno A	66	m	w	OH	Sonoma	Santa Rosa	91	411
Jno D	34	m	w	MO	Sonoma	Santa Rosa	91	408
Joe	26	m	w	MO	Sonoma	Bodega Twp	91	262
John	52	m	w	ENGL	Humboldt	Eel Rvr Twp	72	252
John	50	m	w	VT	Amador	Jackson P O	69	343
John	50	m	w	MA	Amador	Jackson P O	69	334
John	47	m	w	IA	Monterey	San Antonio Twp	74	322
John	38	m	w	OH	Solano	Maine Prairie Twp	90	46
John	37	m	w	KY	Sonoma	Cloverdale Twp	91	273
John	35	m	w	SCOT	San Francisco	11-Wd San Francisc	84	613
John	35	m	w	IREL	Nevada	Little York Twp	75	240
John	32	m	w	ENGL	San Francisco	8-Wd San Francisco	82	326
John	28	m	w	KY	Sacramento	4-Wd Sacramento	77	350
John	25	m	w	ENGL	Solano	Vacaville Twp	90	117
John	24	m	w	CA	Solano	Denverton Twp	90	22
John	20	m	w	NY	Santa Clara	Redwood Twp	88	123
John	15	m	w	BAVA	Alameda	Eden Twp	68	67
John	14	m	w	CA	Santa Barbara	Santa Barbara P O	87	478
John B R	67	m	w	ENGL	San Francisco	8-Wd San Francisco	82	333

© 2001 by Heritage Quest. All rights reserved.

Series M593

Name	Age	S	R	B-PL	County	Locale	Roll	Pg
John C	55	m	w	MA	San Bernardino	San Bernardino Twp	78	445
John G	49	m	w	ENGL	San Mateo	Schoolhouse Statio	87	332
John L	40	m	w	PA	Santa Cruz	Santa Cruz	89	413
Joseph	45	m	w	NY	San Francisco	5-Wd San Francisco	81	25
Joseph	25	m	w	POLA	San Francisco	8-Wd San Francisco	82	385
Joseph H	28	m	w	MO	Santa Barbara	Las Cruces P O	87	506
Joseph W	42	m	w	KY	Santa Barbara	Las Cruces P O	87	506
Joshua	68	m	w	PA	Sacramento	Sutter Twp	77	385
Juan B H	39	m	w	CA	Monterey	Monterey	74	362
Julia	16	f	w	IREL	San Francisco	2-Wd San Francisco	79	234
L	20	f	w	NY	Sacramento	3-Wd Sacramento	77	317
Lewis S	41	m	w	IL	Sonoma	Santa Rosa	91	398
Lucius	30	m	w	PA	Santa Barbara	Santa Barbara P O	87	452
Lucy	66	f	w	VT	San Francisco	San Francisco P O	80	357
M A	45	m	w	IREL	Alameda	Murray Twp	68	121
Maggie	14	f	w	PA	Plumas	Seneca Twp	77	50
Mary	70	f	w	TN	Solano	Maine Prairie Twp	90	52
Mary	48	f	w	MO	Los Angeles	San Gabriel Twp	73	596
Mathew	47	m	w	TN	Solano	Suisun Twp	90	109
Mathew	40	m	w	IREL	San Francisco	7-Wd San Francisco	81	233
Milton	27	m	w	KY	Solano	Silveyville Twp	90	77
Nancy	30	f	i	CA	Butte	Wyandotte Twp	70	142
Peter	45	m	w	SWED	Calaveras	San Andreas P O	70	215
R	45	m	w	MO	Calaveras	Copperopolis P O	70	225
Randolph	56	m	b	MA	Santa Clara	2-Wd San Jose	88	283
Richard	30	m	w	CANA	Mendocino	Casper & Big Rvr	74	162
Richd	28	m	w	MO	Sonoma	Cloverdale Twp	91	271
Robert	80	m	w	NC	Solano	Maine Prairie Twp	90	52
Robert	32	m	w	CANA	San Francisco	7-Wd San Francisco	81	199
Rosa	5	f	w	CA	Marin	San Rafael Twp	74	26
Rose	28	f	w	NY	San Francisco	11-Wd San Francisc	84	688
S R	31	m	w	OH	Sonoma	Santa Rosa	91	395
Samel E	35	m	w	NY	Sonoma	Petaluma Twp	91	339
Saml	35	m	w	NY	Shasta	Shasta P O	89	459
Saml Davis	43	m	w	PA	Plumas	Plumas Twp	77	32
Saml V	33	m	w	PA	Napa	Yountville Twp	75	90
Samuel	20	m	w	MO	Colusa	Monroe Twp	71	311
Sarah	72	f	w	ENGL	San Francisco	San Francisco P O	85	863
Sarah	60	f	w	VA	Santa Clara	2-Wd San Jose	88	326
Sashel	40	m	w	MO	Colusa	Colusa Twp	71	286
Sidney	36	m	w	KY	Santa Clara	Gilroy Twp	88	106
Solomone	47	m	w	ENGL	Humboldt	Eureka Twp	72	264
Stephen	73	m	w	KY	Colusa	Colusa Twp	71	286
T B	33	m	w	KY	San Francisco	San Francisco P O	85	785
Theodore	50	m	m	NY	San Francisco	San Francisco P O	80	464
Theresa	20	f	w	IREL	San Francisco	8-Wd San Francisco	82	471
Thomas	43	m	w	ENGL	Placer	Bath P O	76	458
Thomas	33	m	b	VA	San Francisco	6-Wd San Francisco	81	109
Thomas	28	m	w	NC	San Francisco	San Francisco P O	80	486
Thomas	28	m	w	ENGL	Contra Costa	Martinez P O	71	411
Thomas	22	m	w	CA	Sonoma	Sonoma Twp	91	437
Thomas S	43	m	w	PA	Santa Cruz	Watsonville	89	369
Thos	47	m	w	PA	Sonoma	Cloverdale Twp	91	266
Thos	23	m	w	INDI	Merced	Snelling P O	74	280
W B	38	m	w	MI	Santa Clara	Gilroy Twp	88	69
W B	29	m	w	NJ	San Joaquin	Elkhorn Twp	86	58
W J	25	m	w	IL	Amador	Volcano P O	69	380
W W	42	m	w	KY	Sierra	Forest Twp	89	531
Wesley H	25	m	w	OH	Sacramento	4-Wd Sacramento	77	368
Wiley	26	m	w	IL	Butte	Chico Twp	70	19
William	56	m	w	NY	San Luis Obispo	Santa Rosa Twp	87	320
William	50	m	w	PRUS	San Francisco	3-Wd San Francisco	79	288
William	43	m	w	VT	San Francisco	8-Wd San Francisco	82	430
William	37	m	w	IN	Solano	Vacaville Twp	90	127
William	30	m	w	TN	Los Angeles	Santa Ana Twp	73	599
William F	46	m	w	PA	Santa Cruz	Santa Cruz	89	413
William F	45	m	w	IN	Stanislaus	Buena Vista Twp	92	12
William F	24	m	w	MO	Los Angeles	Los Nietos Twp	73	576
William H	69	m	w	ENGL	El Dorado	Placerville	72	118
Wm	36	m	w	NY	San Francisco	1-Wd San Francisco	79	125
Wm	35	m	w	ENGL	San Francisco	1-Wd San Francisco	79	121
Wm	32	m	w	TN	San Joaquin	Union Twp	86	267
Wm	30	m	w	IL	Butte	Chico Twp	70	37
Wm	26	m	w	PRUS	San Francisco	2-Wd San Francisco	79	213
Wm M	67	m	w	PA	Sonoma	Santa Rosa	91	410
Wm M	37	m	w	IL	Sonoma	Santa Rosa	91	411
Wm R	40	m	w	NY	Napa	Napa	75	38
Wm S	42	m	w	ME	Tuolumne	Sonora P O	93	310
Yam	40	m	w	VA	Trinity	Douglas	92	234
COOPERS								
H R	48	m	w	AR	San Joaquin	Dent Twp	86	29
COOPERTHWAITE								
Wm	42	m	w	ENGL	San Francisco	11-Wd San Francisc	84	466
COOPMAN								
F	48	m	w	MECK	Yuba	Rose Bar Twp	93	664
COOPR								
Albert S	18	m	w	IL	Sacramento	Brighton Twp	77	79
C A	38	m	w	OH	Sacramento	American Twp	77	67
Stephen T	47	m	w	VA	Sacramento	American Twp	77	67
COOR								
Samuel	21	m	w	MO	Mendocino	Anderson Twp	74	155
COOREE								
Ah	42	m	c	CHIN	Mariposa	Maxwell Crk P O	74	145
COOREILLA								
Derroughter	50	m	w	MEXI	San Diego	Pala Valley Reserv	78	480
COOT								
Ah	59	m	c	CHIN	San Francisco	6-Wd San Francisco	81	129
Kean	14	m	c	CHIN	Sacramento	1-Wd Sacramento	77	191
COOTH								
Seth	33	m	w	MA	San Francisco	5-Wd San Francisco	81	12
COOTS								
Brittan R	38	m	w	OH	Butte	Ophir Twp	70	92
Richd	27	m	w	AL	Butte	Kimshew Tpw	70	78
COOVER								
Benjamin	20	m	w	PA	Colusa	Butte Twp	71	267
John H	44	m	w	MO	San Mateo	Half Moon Bay P O	87	403
COOVY								
E B	28	m	w	NY	Sierra	Butte Twp	89	508
COOW								
Lung	16	m	c	CHIN	Sacramento	1-Wd Sacramento	77	193
COOY								
How	20	f	c	CHIN	Yuba	Marysville	93	626
COP								
Ah	54	m	c	CHIN	Nevada	Eureka Twp	75	136
Ah	28	m	c	CHIN	Sacramento	1-Wd Sacramento	77	195
Ah	25	m	c	CHIN	Sacramento	1-Wd Sacramento	77	201
COPALI								
Carlo	26	m	w	ITAL	Santa Clara	2-Wd San Jose	88	315
COPE								
Benjamin	35	m	w	PA	El Dorado	Cosumnes Twp	72	13
Chas	40	m	w	PA	San Joaquin	2-Wd Stockton	86	164
Frank	41	m	w	PA	Mariposa	Mariposa P O	74	118
Frederick R	31	m	w	PA	Mariposa	Maxwell Crk P O	74	142
Jessie M	37	m	w	OH	Sutter	Butte Twp	92	99
John F	42	m	w	PA	Mariposa	Maxwell Crk P O	74	142
R	36	m	w	ENGL	San Joaquin	Elkhorn Twp	86	65
Richd	37	m	w	ENGL	San Joaquin	Elkhorn Twp	86	61
W	67	m	w	PA	Solano	Vallejo	90	202
Warner	46	m	w	KY	San Francisco	11-Wd San Francisc	84	550
COPEFIELD								
Edwd	36	m	w	IREL	San Francisco	1-Wd San Francisco	79	29
COPELAN								
John	18	m	w	CA	Monterey	Castroville Twp	74	340
COPELAND								
A J	37	m	w	VA	Yuba	W Bear Rvr Twp	93	682
Alexander	24	m	w	CANA	Santa Clara	Redwood Twp	88	123
Anthony	38	m	w	IREL	Nevada	Grass Valley Twp	75	217
Benj T	53	m	w	NY	Nevada	Little York Twp	75	240
Benjamin H	37	m	w	VA	El Dorado	Mud Springs Twp	72	85
Chas	36	m	w	SHOL	San Francisco	1-Wd San Francisco	79	129
D W	26	m	w	OH	Tehama	Paskenta Twp	92	166
Elisabeth	11	f	w	CA	San Joaquin	Douglas Twp	86	46
Eliza	38	f	w	ENGL	San Francisco	7-Wd San Francisco	81	234
Fred	37	m	w	MA	San Diego	San Diego	78	510
George	58	m	w	PA	Contra Costa	Martinez P O	71	415
George E	38	m	w	SCOT	Stanislaus	San Joaquin Twp	92	72
H	42	m	w	NY	Tehama	Red Bluff	92	183
H C	47	m	w	OH	Tehama	Antelope Twp	92	155
Henry	42	m	w	MA	San Francisco	San Francisco P O	85	816
I	25	m	w	CANA	Sierra	Gibson Twp	89	544
J S	35	m	w	NY	Tehama	Deer Crk Twp	92	170
Jane A	38	f	b	VA	Colusa	Butte Twp	71	267
John	38	m	w	IREL	San Francisco	7-Wd San Francisco	81	236
John	35	m	w	IREL	Tuolumne	Columbia P O	93	342
John	32	m	w	SCOT	Santa Barbara	Santa Maria P O	87	514
John B	33	m	w	MO	Stanislaus	Empire Twp	92	41
Johnson	39	m	w	PA	Calaveras	Copperopolis P O	70	264
Marion	26	m	w	MO	Stanislaus	Empire Twp	92	62
Maurice	22	m	w	NY	Monterey	San Juan Twp	74	405
Piety	55	f	w	NC	Stanislaus	Empire Twp	92	41
Silas N	36	m	w	IL	Plumas	Indian Twp	77	12
Stepn	55	m	w	GA	Sutter	Sutter Twp	92	117
Timothy	40	m	w	IREL	San Francisco	San Francisco P O	83	178
William	37	m	w	SCOT	Plumas	Indian Twp	77	14
William S	46	m	w	IL	Stanislaus	Emory Twp	92	21
Wm	42	m	w	SWED	San Francisco	1-Wd San Francisco	79	119
Wm	30	m	w	ENGL	San Francisco	2-Wd San Francisco	79	254
Wm	28	m	w	VA	Santa Barbara	San Buenaventura P	87	420
Wm H	36	m	w	OH	Siskiyou	Cottonwood Twp	89	592
Zechariah	48	m	m	VA	Colusa	Butte Twp	71	267
COPELEY								
John	35	m	w	IREL	Solano	Vallejo	90	182
COPELL								
David	23	m	w	MO	Solano	Denverton Twp	90	27
COPELLA								
Joseph	34	m	w	ITAL	Contra Costa	Martinez P O	71	437
COPELLE								
Nicholas	16	m	w	ITAL	Contra Costa	Martinez P O	71	437
COPELLO								
Giuseppe	50	m	w	ITAL	Santa Cruz	Santa Cruz	89	433
COPELON								
Thos	40	m	w	ME	Alameda	Murray Twp	68	117
COPEMAN								
Eva	18	f	w	IL	San Joaquin	Elkhorn Twp	86	58
J	39	m	w	PRUS	Alameda	Murray Twp	68	112
COPEN								
Geo	29	m	w	ENGL	Sonoma	Bodega Twp	91	264
John	30	m	w	FRAN	Santa Clara	Redwood Twp	88	119
Louis	25	m	w	PRUS	San Francisco	11-Wd San Francisc	84	662
COPENA								
Matthias	23	m	w	SHOL	San Mateo	Half Moon Bay P O	87	403
COPENGER								
P	45	m	w	IREL	Lake	Lakeport	73	403

© 2001 by Heritage Quest. All rights reserved.

Name	Age	S	R	B-PL	County	Locale	Series M593 Roll	Pg
COPENHAVER								
Henry	35	m	w	PA	Butte	Oroville Twp	70	139
COPER								
Henry W	24	m	w	AR	Tulare	Farmersville Twp	92	249
COPERAS								
George	22	m	w	KY	Nevada	Eureka Twp	75	135
COPEZ								
Luis	30	m	w	MEXI	San Luis Obispo	Morro Twp	87	283
COPHER								
Allen	19	m	w	IA	Sonoma	Analy Twp	91	226
James M	28	m	w	MO	Sonoma	Analy Twp	91	226
COPIO								
Antone	64	m	w	ITAL	San Joaquin	3-Wd Stockton	86	220
M	64	m	w	ITAL	San Joaquin	3-Wd Stockton	86	220
COPITO								
James	42	m	w	IREL	Butte	Chico Twp	70	36
COPLAND								
Edward	30	m	w	IREL	San Francisco	5-Wd San Francisco	81	7
George	45	m	w	FRAN	Santa Clara	2-Wd San Jose	88	315
J	43	m	w	MO	San Joaquin	Tulare Twp	86	254
Jas	51	m	w	TN	San Joaquin	Castoria Twp	86	8
William	50	m	w	TN	Sonoma	Sonoma Twp	91	445
COPLEY								
A J	40	m	w	NY	Monterey	San Antonio Twp	74	321
Michael	29	m	w	CANA	Santa Cruz	Santa Cruz Twp	89	380
Thomas	40	m	w	ENGL	Los Angeles	Los Angeles	73	532
COPLINTZ								
Clara	23	f	w	FRAN	San Francisco	San Francisco P O	80	357
COPMEYER								
Chas	50	m	w	NH	Butte	Concow Twp	70	6
COPO								
John	36	m	w	ITAL	Placer	Bath P O	76	437
COPORN								
Michael	25	m	w	SWIT	Plumas	Quartz Twp	77	34
COPP								
Benjn	48	m	w	NY	San Francisco	5-Wd San Francisco	81	9
Carl G	41	m	w	WURT	Stanislaus	San Joaquin Twp	92	72
Charles O	39	m	w	WI	Yolo	Grafton Twp	93	484
George	40	m	w	NY	Nevada	Bloomfield Twp	75	98
George	27	m	w	NC	San Francisco	San Francisco P O	80	531
John	50	m	w	NY	San Francisco	San Francisco P O	83	205
John E	70	m	w	CANA	Yolo	Grafton Twp	93	495
John G	55	m	w	ME	San Francisco	1-Wd San Francisco	79	83
Michael	31	m	w	NJ	San Francisco	5-Wd San Francisco	81	7
William H H	35	m	w	NY	Yolo	Grafton Twp	93	480
COPPAGE								
John	30	m	w	VA	San Francisco	2-Wd San Francisco	79	280
COPPE								
Victor	48	m	w	FRAN	San Francisco	San Francisco P O	85	771
COPPEN								
Daniel	60	m	w	ENGL	Tehama	Battle Crk Twp	92	158
COPPER								
Frank	29	m	w	ENGL	San Francisco	2-Wd San Francisco	79	215
John	54	m	w	NJ	Siskiyou	Scott Valley Twp	89	613
William	46	m	w	OH	Amador	Fiddletown P O	69	438
COPPERAL								
Joseph	35	m	w	SWIT	Placer	Bath P O	76	443
Paul	25	m	w	SWIT	Placer	Bath P O	76	443
COPPERSMITH								
J H	21	m	w	PA	Sacramento	3-Wd Sacramento	77	302
COPPERWAIT								
Thomas	22	m	w	IREL	San Francisco	6-Wd San Francisco	81	94
COPPERWHITE								
Saml	46	m	w	NY	San Francisco	1-Wd San Francisco	79	86
COPPIER								
Claude	49	m	w	FRAN	San Francisco	San Francisco P O	83	136
COPPIN								
Jno	33	m	w	VT	Santa Clara	Burnett Twp	88	36
John	64	m	w	ENGL	Contra Costa	Martinez P O	71	397
Robt	50	m	w	ENGL	Sacramento	Alabama Twp	77	59
Selina	28	f	w	FRAN	San Francisco	6-Wd San Francisco	81	78
COPPING								
Fred	24	m	w	BAVA	Solano	Silveyville Twp	90	88
COPPINGER								
Mary	56	f	w	IREL	San Francisco	1-Wd San Francisco	79	20
Wm	27	m	w	IREL	Marin	Sausalito Twp	74	73
COPPLE								
Mary	15	f	w	MO	Sonoma	Washington Twp	91	467
Milton Wm	36	m	w	IL	Plumas	Seneca Twp	77	49
COPPLEMAN								
John	55	m	w	SC	El Dorado	Coloma Twp	72	9
COPPLES								
B F	38	m	w	IN	Mendocino	Little Lake Twp	74	203
Louis	15	m	w	CA	Mendocino	Ukiah Twp	74	242
COPPMAN								
John L	38	m	w	IL	Monterey	San Benito Twp	74	379
COPREN								
A	35	m	w	VA	Sacramento	3-Wd Sacramento	77	269
COPSE								
George	25	m	w	NC	Sacramento	2-Wd Sacramento	77	249
COPSEY								
C C	72	m	w	MD	Lake	Lower Lake	73	422
D M	37	m	w	IN	Lake	Lower Lake	73	420
John	26	m	w	MO	Lake	Lower Lake	73	423
O J	40	m	w	IN	Lake	Lower Lake	73	421
S A	47	m	w	IN	Lake	Lower Lake	73	421
S E Mrs	28	f	w	MO	Lake	Lower Lake	73	420

Name	Age	S	R	B-PL	County	Locale	Series M593 Roll	Pg
COPSTEIN								
Nicholas	44	m	w	LUXE	Santa Clara	Redwood Twp	88	121
COQUART								
Alexander	34	m	w	FRAN	Santa Clara	1-Wd San Jose	88	249
COQUEL								
N Robert	58	m	w	FRAN	Calaveras	Copperopolis P O	70	231
COR								
Ah	35	m	c	CHIN	Yuba	Marysville	93	619
CORA								
Bassie	14	f	w	US	Yuba	Marysville	93	609
Jno C	50	m	w	OH	Butte	Chico Twp	70	35
Jno W	35	m	w	IN	Butte	Chico Twp	70	38
John	18	m	w	IA	Yuba	Rose Bar Twp	93	665
Mary	47	f	w	MD	Yuba	Rose Bar Twp	93	654
Wm	29	m	w	IN	Butte	Chico Twp	70	38
CORACO								
J S	40	m	w	EIND	San Joaquin	Tulare Twp	86	252
CORADELL								
George	11	m	w	CA	Napa	Yountville Twp	75	82
CORAH								
N	33	m	w	ENGL	Sierra	Butte Twp	89	508
CORAIL								
Jose	20	m	w	MEXI	Santa Clara	San Jose Twp	88	221
CORALAN								
Jere	43	m	w	IREL	San Francisco	6-Wd San Francisco	81	92
CORALES								
Ignacio	60	m	w	MEXI	Los Angeles	Los Angeles Twp	73	475
CORALIS								
Gee	36	m	w	HANO	Calaveras	Copperopolis P O	70	232
CORALL								
Abigail	50	f	w	OH	Yuba	Marysville	93	615
CORALLES								
Jesus	30	m	w	MEXI	San Luis Obispo	San Luis Obispo Tw	87	298
CORAN								
Ann	33	f	w	IREL	San Francisco	2-Wd San Francisco	79	234
CORANADO								
R	37	m	w	PERU	El Dorado	Greenwood Twp	72	55
CORANCE								
Jose	42	m	w	PORT	Trinity	Indian Crk	92	199
CORANE								
Charles	31	m	w	MEXI	Tuolumne	Columbia P O	93	345
CORARRUBIAS								
Seferino	54	m	w	MEXI	Los Angeles	Santa Ana Twp	73	612
CORASMA								
Juan	25	m	w	AZOR	Solano	Rio Vista Twp	90	57
CORASO								
Pedro	41	m	w	FRAN	Santa Clara	1-Wd San Jose	88	256
CORBAN								
Caroline	48	f	w	CT	Colusa	Stony Crk Twp	71	330
CORBATT								
John	40	m	w	IREL	Santa Clara	2-Wd San Jose	88	318
CORBELL								
George	37	m	w	MD	San Francisco	San Francisco P O	80	410
Lawrence	35	m	w	IREL	San Francisco	11-Wd San Francisc	84	543
CORBEN								
Ann	18	f	w	IL	Sonoma	Vallejo Twp	91	458
CORBET								
Amos	56	m	w	IL	Alameda	Washington Twp	68	287
Henry	34	m	w	OH	Solano	Vacaville Twp	90	124
John	33	m	w	IREL	Kern	Havilah P O	73	336
Joseph	42	m	w	SWIT	Humboldt	Mattole Twp	72	283
Joseph	29	m	w	CANA	Alpine	Markleeville P O	69	312
Leon	24	m	w	FRAN	San Francisco	San Francisco P O	83	200
Wm	40	m	w	NY	Sacramento	Dry Crk Twp	77	97
CORBETT								
Alex C	36	m	w	CANA	San Francisco	8-Wd San Francisco	82	299
Alexander	66	m	w	SCOT	Santa Cruz	Santa Cruz	89	429
Andrew	35	m	w	ME	Sierra	Gibson Twp	89	544
Anne	35	f	w	CANA	San Francisco	8-Wd San Francisco	82	444
Charles	42	m	w	ENGL	Stanislaus	Empire Twp	92	62
David	33	m	w	CANA	Sierra	Sears Twp	89	559
Dennis	28	m	w	IREL	Solano	Vallejo	90	202
Edward	23	m	w	TX	Los Angeles	Los Nietos Twp	73	577
Edward	21	m	w	IL	Sacramento	4-Wd Sacramento	77	325
Edward W	39	m	w	NY	San Francisco	6-Wd San Francisco	81	109
Ellen	9	f	w	CA	Nevada	Grass Valley Twp	75	158
Frances	15	f	w	MA	San Francisco	San Francisco P O	85	767
Hamilton	40	m	w	IREL	San Francisco	1-Wd San Francisco	79	91
J Ellis	62	m	w	NY	San Diego	San Diego	78	498
James	52	m	w	IREL	San Francisco	San Francisco P O	83	249
Jas	32	m	w	IREL	Solano	Vallejo	90	200
Jessie	23	m	w	IL	San Bernardino	San Bernardino Twp	78	445
John	40	m	w	IREL	Solano	Vallejo	90	185
John	40	m	w	IREL	Santa Clara	2-Wd San Jose	88	326
John	38	m	w	IREL	Nevada	Grass Valley Twp	75	213
John	37	m	w	NY	San Francisco	11-Wd San Francisc	84	523
John	34	m	w	IREL	San Francisco	San Francisco P O	83	133
John H	43	m	w	CANA	Sonoma	Petaluma Twp	91	325
John J	41	m	w	CANA	San Francisco	8-Wd San Francisco	82	446
John J	23	m	w	IREL	San Francisco	San Francisco P O	83	185
John W	47	m	w	CANA	San Francisco	8-Wd San Francisco	82	407
Julia	75	f	w	IREL	San Francisco	San Francisco P O	85	767
Lawrence	35	m	w	IREL	San Francisco	11-Wd San Francisc	84	610
Malace	32	m	w	IREL	Napa	Napa Twp	75	31
Malike	22	m	w	IREL	San Mateo	Schoolhouse Statio	87	338
Mary A	28	f	w	CANA	Santa Cruz	Santa Cruz	89	430
Michael	34	m	w	IREL	San Francisco	11-Wd San Francisc	84	496

© 2001 by Heritage Quest. All rights reserved.

Name	Age	S	R	B-PL	County	Locale (Series M593)	Roll	Pg
Miles T	33	m	w	PA	Plumas	Quartz Twp	77	39
P J	35	m	w	IREL	San Francisco	San Francisco P O	83	316
Patrick	45	m	w	IREL	San Francisco	San Francisco P O	80	391
Richard	25	m	w	IREL	San Francisco	San Francisco P O	85	745
Saml J	33	m	w	NY	San Francisco	San Francisco P O	83	266
Thomas	38	m	w	IREL	San Francisco	8-Wd San Francisco	82	326
Thomas	35	m	w	IREL	San Francisco	San Francisco P O	85	767
Thomas	30	m	w	NY	San Francisco	8-Wd San Francisco	82	330
William	33	m	w	IREL	Santa Clara	2-Wd San Jose	88	334
Wm	79	m	w	SCOT	San Francisco	San Francisco P O	85	780
Wm	50	m	w	IREL	San Joaquin	2-Wd Stockton	86	166
Wm A	24	m	w	PA	Sierra	Table Rock Twp	89	573
CORBIERE								
Casie C	9	f	w	CA	Colusa	Grand Island Twp	71	310
Charles	43	m	w	VT	Colusa	Grand Island Twp	71	310
Joseph	41	m	w	VT	Colusa	Grand Island Twp	71	306
William	77	m	w	FRAN	Colusa	Grand Island Twp	71	310
CORBIN								
David	32	m	w	PA	Colusa	Stony Crk Twp	71	334
Mary	35	f	w	FRAN	San Francisco	San Francisco P O	80	350
Robert	53	m	m	VA	Sacramento	2-Wd Sacramento	77	231
CORBISIER								
F	46	m	w	FRAN	Sacramento	3-Wd Sacramento	77	296
CORBIT								
John	38	m	w	IREL	San Luis Obispo	San Luis Obispo Tw	87	316
Martin	53	m	w	IREL	Mendocino	Round Valley Twp	74	216
Mehetibel	42	f	w	ME	San Luis Obispo	San Luis Obispo Tw	87	316
CORBLY								
William	23	m	w	VA	Solano	Vacaville Twp	90	123
CORBON								
William	50	m	w	NY	San Francisco	7-Wd San Francisco	81	188
CORBREY								
Kate	9	f	w	NY	San Francisco	San Francisco P O	83	144
CORBULZ								
J J	38	m	w	IN	Sutter	Butte Twp	92	88
CORBUS								
A T	38	m	w	OH	Trinity	Indian Crk	92	200
CORBY								
Charles	35	m	w	MI	Sonoma	Salt Point	91	381
CORBYN								
Harry	26	m	w	NY	San Francisco	San Francisco P O	80	349
James H	25	m	w	NY	Sacramento	2-Wd Sacramento	77	254
Newell	40	m	w	NY	Yolo	Cottonwood Twp	93	461
CORCAS								
Salome	12	f	i	CA	San Luis Obispo	San Luis Obispo Tw	87	304
CORCHARAN								
Cornelius	40	m	w	IREL	Nevada	Bridgeport Twp	75	121
CORCHOG								
Cornelius	37	m	w	IREL	Nevada	Bridgeport Twp	75	118
CORCKER								
James B	30	m	w	MA	Placer	Dutch Flat P O	76	401
CORCKRAN								
Harvey	24	m	w	IREL	Nevada	Meadow Lake Twp	75	268
CORCORAL								
J	55	m	w	IREL	Sierra	Downieville Twp	89	518
CORCORAN								
Alexander	13	m	w	NY	San Francisco	11-Wd San Francisc	84	572
Anna	26	f	w	IREL	Trinity	Weaverville Pct	92	226
Bridget	28	f	w	IREL	San Francisco	3-Wd San Francisco	79	314
Charles	45	m	w	IREL	Calaveras	San Andreas P O	70	178
Daniel	20	m	w	IREL	San Francisco	8-Wd San Francisco	82	430
Dennis	45	m	w	IREL	San Francisco	San Francisco P O	83	121
Eliza	21	f	w	IREL	Marin	Nicasio Twp	74	14
Elizabeth	44	f	w	IREL	Sacramento	2-Wd Sacramento	77	231
Francis	20	m	w	NY	San Francisco	11-Wd San Francisc	84	556
Frank	42	m	w	DC	San Francisco	San Francisco P O	83	196
Honora	28	f	w	IREL	Solano	Vallejo	90	166
J	35	f	w	IREL	Alameda	Oakland	68	249
James	49	m	w	IREL	Santa Cruz	Soquel Twp	89	444
James	22	m	w	IREL	Alameda	Brooklyn Twp	68	42
Jas H	9	m	w	CA	Santa Barbara	Santa Barbara P O	87	492
Jeremiah	35	m	w	IREL	Santa Clara	Santa Clara Twp	88	153
Johanna	40	f	w	IREL	Yolo	Buckeye Twp	93	410
John	50	m	w	IREL	Santa Clara	Fremont Twp	88	54
John	34	m	w	IREL	San Francisco	San Francisco P O	80	406
John	32	m	w	OH	Placer	Bath P O	76	461
John	30	m	w	IREL	San Joaquin	2-Wd Stockton	86	166
John	25	m	w	NY	San Francisco	6-Wd San Francisco	81	98
John M	36	m	w	KY	Mariposa	Mariposa P O	74	116
Lou	3	f	w	CA	San Francisco	San Francisco P O	83	196
M	28	m	w	PA	Solano	Vallejo	90	209
Magie	25	f	w	IREL	Alameda	Murray Twp	68	106
Martin	44	m	w	CANA	Santa Clara	2-Wd San Jose	88	329
Mary	45	f	w	IREL	San Francisco	8-Wd San Francisco	82	396
Mary	38	f	w	IREL	San Francisco	7-Wd San Francisco	81	181
Mary	35	f	w	IREL	San Francisco	11-Wd San Francisc	84	627
Mary	19	f	w	IREL	San Mateo	Redwood City P O	87	376
Michael	62	m	w	IREL	Sacramento	4-Wd Sacramento	77	335
Michael	26	m	w	IREL	Sacramento	2-Wd Sacramento	77	229
Michl	42	m	w	IREL	San Francisco	San Francisco P O	83	70
Mike	40	m	w	IREL	San Francisco	11-Wd San Francisc	84	670
Patrick	56	m	w	IREL	Contra Costa	Martinez P O	71	401
Patrick	32	m	w	IREL	San Francisco	2-Wd San Francisco	79	157
Patrick	21	m	w	IREL	Placer	Bath P O	76	429
Philip	28	m	w	IREL	Nevada	Eureka Twp	75	126
Philip	25	m	w	IREL	Nevada	Eureka Twp	75	129
Robert	38	m	w	IREL	San Francisco	San Francisco P O	83	216
Simon	40	m	w	IREL	Solano	Vallejo	90	212
Thomas	29	m	w	IREL	Trinity	Junction City Pct	92	209
Thos	60	m	w	IREL	Siskiyou	Scott Valley Twp	89	619
Timothy	52	m	w	IREL	San Francisco	San Francisco P O	83	416
Tymothy	24	m	w	IREL	San Francisco	San Francisco P O	85	758
William	40	m	w	IREL	San Francisco	San Francisco P O	80	381
William	40	m	w	IREL	San Francisco	11-Wd San Francisc	84	539
William	36	m	w	OH	Placer	Bath P O	76	461
William	36	m	w	OH	Placer	Bath P O	76	443
Wm	48	m	w	MD	San Francisco	San Francisco P O	85	825
CORCRAN								
Daniel	40	m	w	IREL	San Francisco	San Francisco P O	83	415
CORCROFT								
John	27	m	w	ENGL	Inyo	Bishop Crk Twp	73	310
CORCUT								
Antonio	51	m	w	PORT	San Mateo	Half Moon Bay P O	87	390
CORD								
A	40	m	w	NY	Alameda	Murray Twp	68	119
Cora May	7	f	w	CA	Santa Clara	Milpitas Twp	88	112
George W	42	m	w	KY	Yolo	Putah Twp	93	514
John	35	m	w	IREL	Alameda	Oakland	68	209
Thomas A	40	m	w	KY	Yolo	Putah Twp	93	509
Wm J	35	m	w	IREL	San Francisco	1-Wd San Francisco	79	83
CORDA								
Antonio	22	m	w	SWIT	Humboldt	Mattole Twp	72	283
CORDAN								
Antonio	26	m	w	ITAL	Tuolumne	Sonora P O	93	327
Louis	47	m	w	MEXI	Los Angeles	Los Angeles	73	555
Victoria	5	f	w	CA	Los Angeles	Los Angeles	73	560
CORDANA								
Antonio	36	m	w	ITAL	San Francisco	11-Wd San Francisc	84	710
CORDANO								
Frank	20	m	w	ITAL	Tuolumne	Big Oak Flat P O	93	393
CORDARNO								
Louis	16	m	w	ITAL	San Francisco	San Francisco P O	85	751
CORDAY								
Ellen	43	f	m	WIND	Kern	Havilah P O	73	336
CORDAZO								
Nancy	35	f	w	KY	El Dorado	Coloma Twp	72	2
CORDE								
Frank	30	m	w	PRUS	San Francisco	6-Wd San Francisco	81	123
CORDELIN								
Carlos	30	m	w	SPAI	Stanislaus	Empire Twp	92	58
CORDELL								
Geo	20	m	w	MEXI	Solano	Vallejo	90	140
Wilm	30	m	w	IA	Monterey	Pajaro Twp	74	374
CORDELLA								
Anita	12	f	w	CA	San Francisco	San Francisco P O	80	409
CORDELLERON								
Wm	68	m	w	FRAN	Contra Costa	Martinez P O	71	368
CORDENS								
B	44	m	w	SWED	El Dorado	Greenwood Twp	72	55
CORDER								
Francisco	30	m	i	MEXI	Inyo	Lone Pine Twp	73	332
Frank	50	m	w	ENGL	San Diego	San Diego	78	490
John	29	m	w	IL	Santa Clara	Burnett Twp	88	40
Sevina	60	f	w	NY	Mendocino	Ukiah Twp	74	236
Thomas	39	m	w	ENGL	Trinity	Lewiston Pct	92	211
W T	24	m	w	ENGL	Yuba	Marysville	93	600
CORDERA								
Calisto	31	m	w	MEXI	Fresno	Millerton P O	72	156
CORDERF								
Quello	34	m	w	SWIT	San Francisco	San Francisco P O	80	477
CORDERO								
Emedia	38	f	w	CA	Santa Barbara	Santa Barbara P O	87	469
Francisco	57	m	w	CA	Santa Barbara	Santa Barbara P O	87	452
Francisco	26	m	w	CA	Santa Barbara	Santa Barbara P O	87	468
Francisco	20	m	w	CA	Monterey	Castroville Twp	74	330
Gregorio	40	m	i	CA	Santa Barbara	Las Cruces P O	87	506
Guadalupe	43	m	w	CA	Santa Barbara	Santa Barbara P O	87	469
Jose	34	m	w	CA	Santa Barbara	Santa Barbara P O	87	471
Jose A	48	m	w	CA	Santa Barbara	Santa Barbara P O	87	464
Jose A	30	m	w	CA	Santa Barbara	Santa Barbara P O	87	468
Jose J	40	m	w	CA	Santa Barbara	Santa Barbara P O	87	487
Jose J	37	m	w	CA	Santa Barbara	Santa Barbara P O	87	469
Juan	70	m	w	CA	Santa Barbara	Santa Barbara P O	87	468
Mariana	31	m	w	CA	Santa Barbara	Santa Barbara P O	87	469
Matthias	70	m	i	CA	San Luis Obispo	Arroyo Grande Twp	87	270
Rita	30	f	w	CA	Santa Barbara	Las Cruces P O	87	506
Romaldo	36	m	w	CA	Monterey	Castroville Twp	74	332
Thomas	35	m	w	CA	San Luis Obispo	Arroyo Grande Twp	87	270
Vicente	45	m	w	CA	Santa Barbara	Las Cruces P O	87	504
CORDERS								
Antonio J	36	m	w	PORT	Fresno	Millerton P O	72	146
CORDES								
D	41	m	w	HANO	Sierra	Forest Twp	89	530
H	42	m	w	HANO	Alameda	Oakland	68	219
Henry	32	m	w	BREM	San Francisco	11-Wd San Francisc	84	666
John	40	m	w	PRUS	San Francisco	San Francisco P O	80	469
N	35	m	w	ITAL	Alameda	Oakland	68	241
P H	42	m	w	ME	San Joaquin	Tulare Twp	86	264
P H	29	m	w	HANO	Alameda	Oakland	68	231
Wallace	35	m	w	SWED	San Francisco	7-Wd San Francisco	81	176
William	47	m	w	MSCH	Contra Costa	Martinez P O	71	391
Wm	46	m	w	MECK	San Francisco	San Francisco P O	85	769
Wm	41	m	w	PRUS	San Francisco	11-Wd San Francisc	84	675

© 2001 by Heritage Quest. All rights reserved.

Series M593

Name	Age	S	R	B-PL	County	Locale	Roll	Pg
CORDEVANT								
Louis	53	m	w	FRAN	Butte	Chico Twp	70	57
CORDI								
Manuele	40	m	w	MEXI	Santa Clara	Almaden Twp	88	13
CORDIL								
Marion B	37	m	w	KY	Los Angeles	Los Nietos Twp	73	587
CORDILIN								
John	28	m	w	ITAL	San Francisco	11-Wd San Francisc	84	710
CORDIMARTI								
John	21	m	w	ITAL	San Francisco	11-Wd San Francisc	84	614
CORDIN								
Gustav	32	m	w	ITAL	San Francisco	11-Wd San Francisc	84	712
CORDING								
Joseph H	45	m	w	ENGL	San Francisco	11-Wd San Francisc	84	700
CORDIS								
A J F	35	m	w	HAMB	Solano	Vallejo	90	188
D	30	m	w	MEXI	Santa Clara	Almaden Twp	88	7
CORDIVANT								
Leroy	7	m	w	CA	Butte	Chico Twp	70	58
CORDIVIOLA								
Josh	42	m	w	ITAL	San Francisco	1-Wd San Francisco	79	45
CORDLEY								
Minnie	14	f	w	MI	San Francisco	San Francisco P O	85	805
CORDO								
Ignacio	54	m	i	MEXI	Inyo	Cerro Gordo Twp	73	322
Maxima	55	f	w	MEXI	Santa Clara	Almaden Twp	88	6
CORDOMA								
Antonea	21	m	w	ITAL	Sonoma	Vallejo Twp	91	463
CORDON								
Antonio	37	m	w	PORT	San Francisco	1-Wd San Francisco	79	18
Patrick	32	m	w	IREL	Nevada	Eureka Twp	75	126
S E	36	m	w	ENGL	Sacramento	Sutter Twp	77	390
Stephen	25	m	w	ITAL	Santa Clara	Fremont Twp	88	48
CORDONA								
Frank	48	m	w	ITAL	Sonoma	Vallejo Twp	91	463
Joseph	49	m	w	ITAL	San Francisco	San Francisco P O	80	331
CORDORA								
Dolorey	55	f	w	MEXI	Yuba	Linda Twp	93	558
Francisco	25	m	w	CA	San Luis Obispo	Arroyo Grande Twp	87	279
Guadalupe	38	m	w	MEXI	Fresno	Millerton P O	72	154
CORDORES								
Guadalupe	30	m	w	CA	San Luis Obispo	Salinas Twp	87	289
CORDOSA								
Mary	49	f	w	CA	Sacramento	2-Wd Sacramento	77	207
CORDOVA								
Anisetto	18	m	w	MEXI	Marin	Sausalito Twp	74	69
Antonia	50	f	w	MEXI	Mariposa	Mariposa P O	74	107
Antonio	45	m	w	MEXI	Kern	Bakersfield P O	73	359
Calisto	32	m	w	MEXI	Santa Cruz	Pajaro Twp	89	346
Carlotta	50	f	w	MEXI	Santa Clara	2-Wd San Jose	88	310
Damjan	35	m	w	MEXI	Plumas	Goodwin Twp	77	1
Dolores	40	m	w	MEXI	Los Angeles	Los Angeles Twp	73	473
Ephrio	70	m	w	MEXI	Calaveras	San Andreas P O	70	168
Guadelupe	30	m	w	MEXI	Los Angeles	Los Angeles Twp	73	468
Jesus	22	m	w	MEXI	San Luis Obispo	Salinas Twp	87	291
Jose	40	m	w	MEXI	Los Angeles	San Gabriel Twp	73	594
Jose	32	m	w	MEXI	Marin	San Rafael Twp	74	36
Juan	55	m	w	MEXI	Calaveras	San Andreas P O	70	174
Juan	33	m	w	MEXI	San Luis Obispo	San Luis Obispo Tw	87	306
Lewis	31	m	w	ITAL	Tuolumne	Big Oak Flat P O	93	398
Manuel	5	m	w	CA	San Luis Obispo	San Luis Obispo Tw	87	306
Manuel	39	m	w	MEXI	Calaveras	San Andreas P O	70	177
Nicha	50	m	w	MEXI	Kern	Bakersfield P O	73	359
Paulonio	35	m	w	MEXI	San Luis Obispo	San Luis Obispo Tw	87	306
Venabel	16	m	w	MEXI	San Luis Obispo	San Luis Obispo Tw	87	299
CORDOVER								
J	35	m	w	MEXI	Sierra	Downieville Twp	89	514
CORDOVIA								
Joseph	21	m	w	SWIT	Marin	Bolinas Twp	74	2
Juan	36	m	w	MEXI	Kern	Bakersfield P O	73	364
CORDOWER								
Mary	30	f	w	MEXI	San Luis Obispo	San Luis Obispo Tw	87	299
CORDOZA								
Leandro	71	m	w	MEXI	Fresno	Millerton P O	72	156
CORDRAY								
Charles	28	m	w	IL	Contra Costa	Martinez P O	71	415
CORDROS								
Manuel	20	m	w	AZOR	Monterey	Monterey	74	364
CORDS								
David	26	m	w	HAMB	San Francisco	2-Wd San Francisco	79	264
Henry	52	m	w	HAMB	San Francisco	2-Wd San Francisco	79	227
CORDT								
Frank	22	m	w	PRUS	San Francisco	5-Wd San Francisco	81	16
CORDTS								
Minnie	22	f	w	HANO	San Francisco	San Francisco P O	83	97
CORDWELL								
James	37	m	w	IREL	Placer	Summit P O	76	495
CORE								
Thos	46	m	w	IREL	San Francisco	7-Wd San Francisco	81	267
COREA								
Joaquin	35	m	w	PORT	San Francisco	3-Wd San Francisco	79	288
COREAD								
Francis	30	m	w	SCOT	San Luis Obispo	San Luis Obispo Tw	87	300
COREAL								
Juan	19	m	w	ENGL	San Francisco	1-Wd San Francisco	79	74
CORELL								
R	70	f	w	NY	San Joaquin	Liberty Twp	86	93
COREN								
Wm	60	m	w	MA	Sacramento	Granite Twp	77	136
CORENS								
Qurus	27	m	w	MEXI	San Joaquin	2-Wd Stockton	86	174
CORERA								
Antonio	35	m	w	IREL	San Luis Obispo	San Luis Obispo Tw	87	314
CORES								
Fred	27	m	w	GERM	Santa Clara	Gilroy Twp	88	100
CORESO								
Yavanah	25	f	w	CA	Tehama	Red Bluff	92	183
COREY								
Chas	23	m	w	CANA	Sacramento	3-Wd Sacramento	77	316
D W	62	m	w	NY	El Dorado	Georgetown Twp	72	40
E A	36	f	w	OH	Solano	Vallejo	90	153
Ellen	24	f	w	WI	San Mateo	Menlo Park P O	87	378
Franklin	54	m	w	NY	San Mateo	Woodside P O	87	384
J H	36	m	w	VT	Santa Clara	Gilroy Twp	88	80
Jane	32	f	w	MO	Sacramento	1-Wd Sacramento	77	202
Jas A	31	m	w	CANA	Santa Barbara	San Buenaventura P	87	434
Johanna	75	f	w	IREL	San Joaquin	Douglas Twp	86	36
John	35	m	w	WI	San Francisco	8-Wd San Francisco	82	303
John Calvin	55	m	w	OH	Plumas	Seneca Twp	77	49
John G	42	m	w	OH	Solano	Suisun Twp	90	93
Josiah	40	m	w	IREL	Stanislaus	Branch Twp	92	1
Luther	38	m	w	OH	Santa Cruz	Santa Cruz	89	416
Noah	43	m	w	CANA	Sonoma	Analy Twp	91	219
Reuben	69	m	w	MA	Sonoma	Analy Twp	91	224
Serril	60	m	w	RI	Alameda	Eden Twp	68	71
Thomas	45	m	w	AR	Siskiyou	Butte Twp	89	586
Thos	40	m	w	IREL	San Francisco	1-Wd San Francisco	79	84
William	37	m	w	CANA	Santa Cruz	Santa Cruz	89	416
CORF								
John	43	m	w	FRAN	Contra Costa	San Pablo Twp	71	353
CORFIELD								
Olive B	24	f	w	NY	San Francisco	San Francisco P O	83	339
CORGE								
Ah	34	m	c	CHIN	Santa Clara	2-Wd San Jose	88	314
CORGELL								
J	28	m	w	PRUS	Alameda	Oakland	68	148
CORGI								
Ah	18	m	c	CHIN	Los Angeles	Los Angeles	73	544
CORHDALLOS								
A B	6	f	w	NY	Sonoma	Petaluma Twp	91	330
CORIAN								
James	34	m	w	FRAN	Calaveras	San Andreas P O	70	190
CORICA								
Francisco	26	m	w	ITAL	Calaveras	San Andreas P O	70	215
John	27	m	w	ITAL	Calaveras	San Andreas P O	70	215
CORICK								
Adam	32	m	w	VA	Marin	Tomales Twp	74	77
CORIDALE								
William	36	m	w	IL	Nevada	Grass Valley Twp	75	217
CORIDON								
John	45	m	w	BELG	Butte	Ophir Twp	70	101
CORIE								
Eleni	40	f	w	IREL	San Joaquin	1-Wd Stockton	86	120
CORIGAN								
Patrick	25	m	w	IREL	San Francisco	San Francisco P O	85	857
CORIN								
Ah	35	m	c	CHIN	San Luis Obispo	Arroyo Grande Twp	87	276
CORINE								
Jos	23	m	w	SCOT	Alameda	Brooklyn Twp	68	47
CORINGTON								
Simeon	32	m	w	ENGL	Mendocino	Big Rvr Twp	74	159
CORINSON								
Elizabeth	75	f	w	POLA	San Francisco	San Francisco P O	85	756
Morris	50	m	w	POLA	San Francisco	San Francisco P O	85	756
CORIO								
Francisco	22	m	w	MEXI	Fresno	Millerton P O	72	160
CORK								
Barry	35	m	w	ENGL	San Francisco	7-Wd San Francisco	81	188
George	35	m	w	ENGL	Del Norte	Mountain Twp	71	474
Julia	25	f	i	CA	Del Norte	Mountain Twp	71	474
Lewis	35	m	w	BELG	Sierra	Eureka Twp	89	523
CORKAN								
Mary	23	f	w	IREL	San Francisco	8-Wd San Francisco	82	425
CORKERY								
Charles	65	m	w	IREL	San Francisco	San Francisco P O	80	541
Dennis	36	m	w	IREL	Santa Clara	2-Wd San Jose	88	319
Hannah	25	f	w	IREL	San Francisco	2-Wd San Francisco	79	168
Joanna	60	f	w	IREL	Santa Clara	Fremont Twp	88	43
Thomas	32	m	w	CANA	Stanislaus	Empire Twp	92	51
CORKHOUSE								
August	60	m	w	PRUS	Amador	Volcano P O	69	388
CORKLE								
Thomas	34	m	w	ENGL	Plumas	Indian Twp	77	16
CORKLEY								
Bridget	50	f	w	IREL	San Francisco	8-Wd San Francisco	82	473
CORKREY								
James	30	m	w	IREL	San Francisco	San Francisco P O	85	770
CORLAN								
Jack	19	m	w	MO	San Joaquin	1-Wd Stockton	86	155
CORLEAN								
---	35	m	h	MEXI	Colusa	Spring Valley Twp	71	343
CORLEN								
W L	23	m	w	MO	San Joaquin	1-Wd Stockton	86	155
William	24	m	w	IREL	San Francisco	2-Wd San Francisco	79	147

© 2001 by Heritage Quest. All rights reserved.

							Series M593	
Name	Age	S	R	B-PL	County	Locale	Roll	Pg
CORLESS								
Edward	10	m	w	CA	San Francisco	11-Wd San Francisc	84	587
Henry	35	m	w	VT	Sutter	Nicolaus Twp	92	115
CORLETT								
William	41	m	w	IOFM	San Francisco	1-Wd San Francisco	79	20
CORLEW								
Andrew J	32	m	w	MO	Alpine	Woodfords P O	69	315
CORLEY								
Henry	35	m	w	WALE	San Francisco	7-Wd San Francisco	81	281
Ida	23	f	w	IL	San Francisco	San Francisco P O	83	286
CORLIES								
James L	23	m	w	NY	San Francisco	3-Wd San Francisco	79	322
CORLIN								
Edward	32	m	w	IREL	Trinity	Hayfork Valley	92	239
Roger	34	m	w	IREL	San Francisco	San Francisco P O	83	29
CORLIS								
Aaron Jr	34	m	w	CUBA	San Francisco	2-Wd San Francisco	79	189
CORLISS								
C P	32	m	w	NY	Sacramento	4-Wd Sacramento	77	324
Ellen	39	f	w	IREL	San Francisco	7-Wd San Francisco	81	252
Jas	45	m	w	NY	Sacramento	4-Wd Sacramento	77	324
Mary	39	f	w	VT	San Francisco	11-Wd San Francisc	84	618
Wm	39	m	w	MN	Sacramento	3-Wd Sacramento	77	309
CORLIZLE								
Jno W	40	m	w	OH	Butte	Ophir Twp	70	117
CORMACHE								
Ann	21	f	w	IREL	San Francisco	8-Wd San Francisco	82	471
CORMACK								
J W	47	m	w	CANA	Alameda	Oakland	68	187
Jas	39	m	w	NY	San Francisco	7-Wd San Francisco	81	236
Mc	67	m	w	MS	Santa Clara	Gilroy Twp	88	100
Richard	30	m	w	PA	Los Angeles	Wilmington Twp	73	635
CORMAHREM								
H	46	m	w	PRUS	San Francisco	San Francisco P O	83	289
CORMANA								
Joseph	43	m	w	CHIL	Inyo	Cerro Gordo Twp	73	319
CORMICCLE								
Charles	35	m	w	IL	Colusa	Colusa	71	289
CORMICK								
Albert	26	m	w	CANA	Sonoma	Salt Point	91	380
G F	42	m	w	ME	Monterey	San Juan Twp	74	394
John	22	m	w	ENGL	Contra Costa	Martinez P O	71	427
CORMISKI								
Charles	18	m	w	SWED	Sacramento	Dry Crk Twp	77	102
CORMOELL								
E	33	m	w	NY	Solano	Vallejo	90	200
CORN								
Ah	21	m	c	CHIN	San Francisco	1-Wd San Francisco	79	84
Ah	20	f	c	CHIN	San Francisco	1-Wd San Francisco	79	52
Hiram S	40	m	w	NY	San Francisco	2-Wd San Francisco	79	280
William	55	m	w	IREL	San Francisco	San Francisco P O	83	155
CORNADO								
Christopher	53	m	w	MEXI	Plumas	Goodwin Twp	77	1
CORNADRA								
Pedro	48	m	w	MEXI	Plumas	Goodwin Twp	77	1
CORNALL								
P M	38	m	w	NY	Butte	Oroville Twp	70	139
CORNATO								
G	47	m	i	CA	Santa Clara	Almaden Twp	88	21
CORNAY								
Bryan	38	m	w	IREL	San Mateo	Half Moon Bay P O	87	406
CORNAZ								
Julius F	38	m	w	SWIT	Shasta	Fort Crook P O	89	476
CORNDE								
Fannie	40	f	w	FRAN	San Francisco	San Francisco P O	83	372
CORNE								
Ah	20	f	c	CHIN	Sierra	Downieville Twp	89	521
Isaac H	44	m	w	NY	San Francisco	6-Wd San Francisco	81	87
CORNEALISON								
W	39	m	w	TN	Lassen	Janesville Twp	73	431
CORNEILSON								
Joseph	43	m	w	PA	Marin	San Rafael Twp	74	42
CORNEILUS								
James	20	m	w	IREL	San Francisco	San Francisco P O	80	430
CORNEL								
Philip	30	m	w	PA	Placer	Lincoln P O	76	485
CORNELA								
Roman	28	m	w	CHIL	Calaveras	San Andreas P O	70	180
CORNELE								
Mahela	36	m	w	CHIL	Sacramento	2-Wd Sacramento	77	222
CORNELIA								
A	16	f	w	CA	Los Angeles	Los Angeles	73	569
George	24	m	w	MN	Alpine	Woodfords P O	69	316
CORNELIE								
Patrick	35	m	w	IREL	Solano	Green Valley Twp	90	38
CORNELIN								
A	27	m	w	IREL	San Francisco	7-Wd San Francisco	81	220
CORNELIOUS								
L	37	m	w	HCAS	San Francisco	San Francisco P O	83	264
Peter	42	m	w	DENM	Inyo	Cerro Gordo Twp	73	318
CORNELIUS								
Amos	43	m	w	NY	San Francisco	5-Wd San Francisco	81	26
Fred	42	m	w	OH	Butte	Ophir Twp	70	120
George	30	m	w	BREM	Sonoma	Sonoma Twp	91	438
George	19	m	w	PA	Yolo	Cache Crk Twp	93	456
Jacob	46	m	w	BAVA	Santa Clara	1-Wd San Jose	88	232
James	28	m	w	PA	Yolo	Grafton Twp	93	490
John	19	m	w	ENGL	El Dorado	Salmon Falls Twp	72	133
John F	42	m	w	NH	San Francisco	San Francisco P O	83	131
Joseph	30	m	w	ENGL	Plumas	Indian Twp	77	17
Joseph	25	m	w	ITAL	San Francisco	11-Wd San Francisc	84	709
Martin	41	m	w	ENGL	Nevada	Grass Valley Twp	75	169
Peter	29	m	w	CANA	Amador	Volcano P O	69	383
Thomas	24	m	w	TN	Yolo	Grafton Twp	93	487
Thomas	24	m	w	TN	Yolo	Grafton Twp	93	487
CORNELL								
Alonso	41	m	w	OH	Trinity	Weaverville Pct	92	227
Anson F	22	m	w	PA	San Mateo	Redwood Twp	87	366
Benj W	45	m	w	MA	Placer	Roseville P O	76	348
Chas	11	m	w	MA	San Francisco	11-Wd San Francisc	84	680
Chas A	23	m	w	ENGL	San Francisco	San Francisco P O	83	159
Chas H	22	m	w	MA	San Francisco	San Francisco P O	83	162
Chas W	52	m	w	NY	Nevada	Nevada Twp	75	276
Chauncey	26	m	w	NY	San Francisco	11-Wd San Francisc	84	610
Chauncy	5	m	w	CA	Butte	Wyandotte Twp	70	145
D W	28	m	w	IA	San Joaquin	Douglas Twp	86	42
Daniel	35	m	w	IREL	Sacramento	2-Wd Sacramento	77	206
E	25	m	w	RI	Sierra	Lincoln Twp	89	547
Ed	49	m	w	ENGL	San Joaquin	3-Wd Stockton	86	227
H K	46	m	w	NY	Lassen	Susanville Twp	73	445
Henry	40	m	w	OH	Calaveras	San Andreas P O	70	218
Henry	33	m	w	ENGL	Tehama	Antelope Twp	92	156
Herbert S	33	m	w	NY	Tehama	Red Bluff	92	177
J D	40	m	w	IL	San Joaquin	Douglas Twp	86	42
J G	61	m	w	NY	Yuba	Marysville Twp	93	568
Jacob	45	m	w	NY	San Francisco	2-Wd San Francisco	79	278
James	38	m	w	IREL	Sacramento	Brighton Twp	77	75
James D	38	m	w	NY	Nevada	Grass Valley Twp	75	166
Jerry W	42	m	w	MO	Butte	Ophir Twp	70	93
John	37	m	w	SWED	San Francisco	7-Wd San Francisco	81	220
John	36	m	w	TN	Solano	Maine Prairie Twp	90	45
John	36	m	w	NY	Stanislaus	San Joaquin Twp	92	79
Julia	27	f	w	IREL	San Francisco	7-Wd San Francisco	81	232
Jus	34	m	w	IREL	Sacramento	3-Wd Sacramento	77	271
Lizzie	11	f	w	CA	Mendocino	Sanel Twp	74	228
Louisa	16	f	w	LA	San Francisco	8-Wd San Francisco	82	440
M	42	f	w	NY	San Francisco	San Francisco P O	85	811
M S	50	m	w	OH	San Francisco	8-Wd San Francisco	82	310
Mary E	24	f	w	CANA	Santa Barbara	Santa Barbara P O	87	481
Michael	25	m	w	IREL	San Francisco	2-Wd San Francisco	79	167
Nora	6	f	w	CA	Butte	Wyandotte Twp	70	145
Norman	37	m	w	NY	Butte	Wyandotte Twp	70	146
Richard	25	m	w	ENGL	San Francisco	San Francisco P O	83	150
Samuel F	44	m	w	OH	Stanislaus	San Joaquin Twp	92	81
Susan	23	f	w	AR	Mariposa	Mariposa P O	74	137
Thomas	36	m	w	IREL	Contra Costa	Martinez P O	71	386
Thomas	33	m	w	ENGL	Amador	Sutter Crk P O	69	402
Timothy	40	m	w	IREL	San Francisco	7-Wd San Francisco	81	192
William	28	m	w	NY	San Francisco	8-Wd San Francisco	82	486
William	16	m	w	MA	San Francisco	San Francisco P O	80	333
William J	44	m	w	ENGL	Santa Clara	1-Wd San Jose	88	275
Wm	26	m	w	NY	Butte	Chico Twp	70	26
CORNEN								
Patrick	20	m	w	CANA	San Mateo	Redwood Twp	87	361
CORNENS								
Maria	34	f	w	IREL	Nevada	Bridgeport Twp	75	100
CORNEPS								
Annie	10	f	w	CA	San Francisco	San Francisco P O	85	827
Catherine	15	f	w	CA	San Francisco	8-Wd San Francisco	82	487
Emma	13	f	w	CA	San Francisco	San Francisco P O	85	827
Katie	14	f	w	CA	San Francisco	San Francisco P O	83	329
Mary	12	f	w	CA	San Francisco	San Francisco P O	85	827
CORNER								
Harvey	39	m	w	PRUS	San Joaquin	2-Wd Stockton	86	191
Henry	36	m	w	PA	Nevada	Little York Twp	75	240
Robert T	39	m	w	NY	San Francisco	8-Wd San Francisco	82	437
CORNESSO								
A	25	m	w	ITAL	Amador	Jackson P O	69	329
CORNET								
William	28	m	w	IREL	Napa	Napa	75	2
CORNETTE								
A	16	f	w	NY	Sierra	Butte Twp	89	512
CORNEY								
Ellen	22	f	w	IREL	San Francisco	8-Wd San Francisco	82	491
Jerry	24	m	w	IREL	Yolo	Putah Twp	93	523
John	55	m	w	IREL	San Francisco	1-Wd San Francisco	79	17
John	35	m	w	IREL	Solano	Benicia	90	12
CORNFOOT								
Henry	36	m	w	SCOT	San Francisco	San Francisco P O	83	74
CORNG								
Ah	40	m	c	CHIN	Calaveras	San Andreas P O	70	183
CORNIA								
Jos	25	m	w	PORT	Solano	Benicia	90	6
CORNIBE								
Guiacoma	39	m	w	ITAL	Calaveras	San Andreas P O	70	209
CORNICO								
Lewis	19	m	w	SWIT	San Francisco	2-Wd San Francisco	79	173
CORNIDES								
Gabriel	56	m	w	MEXI	Los Angeles	San Jose Twp	73	622
CORNIFF								
Thomas	30	m	w	IREL	San Mateo	Half Moon Bay P O	87	389
Thomas	12	m	w	MA	San Mateo	San Mateo P O	87	371
William	17	m	w	MA	San Mateo	Belmont P O	87	373

© 2001 by Heritage Quest. All rights reserved.

Name	Age	S	R	B-PL	County	Locale	Series M593 Roll	Pg
CORNIN								
Pat	39	m	w	IREL	Alameda	Oakland	68	244
CORNING								
Jefferson	38	m	w	NY	Santa Clara	1-Wd San Jose	88	268
Jno	41	m	w	NY	Sacramento	1-Wd Sacramento	77	189
CORNIPS								
Cathrain	38	f	w	PRUS	San Francisco	San Francisco P O	80	353
CORNISH								
Benjamin	52	m	w	VT	Plumas	Washington Twp	77	52
Cornelius	49	m	w	NY	Siskiyou	Yreka Twp	89	671
E	54	f	w	ENGL	Sierra	Forest	89	536
F H	40	m	w	ENGL	Sierra	Forest	89	537
George F	31	m	w	IL	Yolo	Merritt Twp	93	503
Harry	25	m	w	ENGL	Colusa	Monroe Twp	71	325
Henry	47	m	w	ENGL	Placer	Roseville P O	76	349
John	35	m	w	ENGL	Nevada	Grass Valley Twp	75	231
Mark	35	m	w	PA	Santa Clara	Redwood Twp	88	121
Thos	30	m	b	MD	Sacramento	4-Wd Sacramento	77	329
CORNNETTE								
Frederick	30	m	w	MA	Los Angeles	Los Angeles Twp	73	476
CORNSTOCK								
Eph S	62	m	w	MA	Butte	Kimshew Tpw	70	79
Henry	31	m	w	NY	San Francisco	1-Wd San Francisco	79	120
CORNT								
Ah	24	m	c	CHIN	Placer	Dutch Flat P O	76	414
CORNTHWAIT								
James	43	m	w	MD	Santa Clara	San Jose Twp	88	192
CORNUE								
Robert	31	m	w	IREL	Calaveras	Copperopolis P O	70	245
CORNWALL								
A	14	m	w	CA	Solano	Benicia	90	21
Abigail	61	f	w	NJ	Santa Clara	Redwood Twp	88	117
Daniel	23	m	w	MI	Santa Clara	Santa Clara Twp	88	142
Geo A	31	m	w	AR	Santa Barbara	San Buenaventura P	87	445
George	35	m	w	VT	Contra Costa	Martinez P O	71	416
Joseph	37	m	w	AR	Kern	Linns Valley P O	73	346
Joseph A	72	m	w	GA	Santa Barbara	San Buenaventura P	87	445
Mary	34	f	w	IREL	Contra Costa	Martinez P O	71	367
Mathew	40	m	w	CANA	Plumas	Washington Twp	77	53
P	55	m	w	VA	Amador	Sutter Crk P O	69	411
Pierre B	46	m	w	NY	San Francisco	San Francisco P O	83	110
Sam	70	m	w	NY	San Bernardino	San Bernardino Twp	78	426
Susan	74	f	w	VT	San Bernardino	San Bernardino Twp	78	426
William A	46	m	w	NY	Santa Cruz	Santa Cruz	89	432
CORNWAY								
Bernard	45	m	w	IREL	San Francisco	7-Wd San Francisco	81	264
CORNWELL								
A	30	m	w	ENGL	Alameda	Oakland	68	164
Abigail	51	f	w	NJ	Santa Clara	Redwood Twp	88	125
Andrew	42	m	w	OH	Tulare	Visalia	92	297
Betsey A	34	f	w	MI	Santa Clara	Redwood Twp	88	125
Craton	35	m	w	NC	Sonoma	Petaluma Twp	91	363
Edward	22	m	w	IN	Sonoma	Petaluma Twp	91	330
F B	20	m	w	NY	Solano	Vallejo	90	177
George	33	m	w	MA	Santa Clara	2-Wd San Jose	88	297
George W	45	m	w	NY	Napa	Napa	75	50
Herbert	14	m	w	MI	San Francisco	11-Wd San Francisc	84	587
Ida	18	f	w	IL	Yolo	Grafton Twp	93	483
James	33	m	w	MO	Tulare	Visalia	92	296
James F	40	m	w	TN	Colusa	Colusa Twp	71	278
John	44	m	w	NY	Solano	Rio Vista Twp	90	59
John	42	m	w	NY	Napa	Napa	75	45
John	35	m	w	MO	Monterey	San Benito Twp	74	384
Jonathan	41	m	w	ENGL	Stanislaus	Emory Twp	92	25
CORNY								
J B	15	m	w	CA	Alameda	Oakland	68	243
John	38	m	w	IREL	San Francisco	2-Wd San Francisco	79	216
CORNYERS								
John	39	m	w	IREL	San Francisco	11-Wd San Francisc	84	471
CORNYN								
Felix	23	m	w	IREL	San Francisco	1-Wd San Francisco	79	94
Jas	45	m	w	IREL	San Francisco	1-Wd San Francisco	79	94
John	28	m	w	IREL	San Francisco	1-Wd San Francisco	79	94
COROLIS								
Timothy	56	m	w	VT	Monterey	San Juan Twp	74	408
CORONA								
Alviah	36	f	w	MEXI	San Francisco	6-Wd San Francisco	81	91
Ancel	15	m	w	MEXI	San Mateo	Half Moon Bay P O	87	399
Athus	40	m	w	MEXI	Stanislaus	San Joaquin Twp	92	82
Dolores	22	f	w	MEXI	San Francisco	San Francisco P O	80	359
Jose Ma	28	m	w	MEXI	Los Angeles	Santa Ana Twp	73	606
Victoriana	50	f	w	CA	Los Angeles	San Gabriel Twp	73	597
CORONADO								
Loritta	35	m	w	MEXI	Napa	Napa	75	54
Raphael	49	m	w	MEXI	Napa	Napa	75	54
CORONATHA								
Marcelina	30	f	w	MEXI	Santa Clara	2-Wd San Jose	88	312
CORONDO								
Pedro	47	m	w	MEXI	Butte	Oroville Twp	70	138
CORONEL								
A F	45	m	w	CA	Sacramento	3-Wd Sacramento	77	315
Francisco	71	f	w	MEXI	Los Angeles	Los Angeles	73	510
Manuel	40	m	w	MEXI	Los Angeles	Los Angeles	73	513
Manuel	35	m	w	MEXI	Los Angeles	Los Angeles Twp	73	465
Mercedes	10	f	w	CA	Sacramento	3-Wd Sacramento	77	315
Stephen	10	m	w	MEXI	San Francisco	San Francisco P O	80	422
Sugro	80	m	w	MEXI	Los Angeles	Los Angeles	73	513

Name	Age	S	R	B-PL	County	Locale	Series M593 Roll	Pg
CORONERS								
Kate	19	f	w	IREL	San Francisco	8-Wd San Francisco	82	402
CORONIL								
Carlos	23	m	w	PRUS	San Francisco	San Francisco P O	80	411
COROORAN								
Josh P	40	m	w	PA	San Francisco	1-Wd San Francisco	79	56
COROSASO								
Ranon	31	m	w	MEXI	Kern	Tehachapi P O	73	356
COROTA								
Felipe	28	m	w	MEXI	Santa Clara	2-Wd San Jose	88	312
COROTHERS								
J	35	m	w	ENGL	Amador	Sutter Crk P O	69	411
James H	54	m	w	VA	Amador	Sutter Crk P O	69	414
COROTTO								
Giovanni	53	m	w	ITAL	San Francisco	11-Wd San Francisc	84	594
COROVA								
Wm	26	m	w	ITAL	San Joaquin	2-Wd Stockton	86	206
CORPER								
C S	38	m	w	MA	San Joaquin	1-Wd Stockton	86	121
CORPORAN								
Naerons	38	m	w	CANA	Contra Costa	Martinez P O	71	367
CORPSTEIN								
Mary	20	f	w	IA	Santa Clara	Redwood Twp	88	118
CORPY								
John	33	m	w	ITAL	Santa Cruz	Santa Cruz	89	422
CORR								
Annie	25	f	w	IREL	San Francisco	San Francisco P O	80	428
Edward	30	m	w	IREL	Alameda	Washington Twp	68	285
Frank	33	m	w	AUST	Amador	Jackson P O	69	330
Margaret	50	f	w	IREL	San Francisco	San Francisco P O	83	348
Moses	39	m	w	VA	Calaveras	San Andreas P O	70	219
Patrick	40	m	w	IREL	Yuba	Marysville	93	594
CORRACA								
Emasando	16	m	w	CA	Los Angeles	Los Angeles	73	503
CORRALES								
Francisco	26	m	w	MEXI	Santa Barbara	Las Cruces P O	87	515
Jesus	24	m	w	CA	Santa Barbara	Las Cruces P O	87	515
Jose	24	m	w	CA	Contra Costa	Martinez P O	71	369
Manuel	33	m	w	MEXI	Los Angeles	San Gabriel Twp	73	598
Santiago	9	m	w	CA	Santa Barbara	Las Cruces P O	87	515
CORRAN								
Diez	41	m	w	MEXI	San Francisco	San Francisco P O	80	465
John	28	m	w	IREL	San Mateo	Redwood Twp	87	361
CORRAS								
Anselmo	20	m	w	MEXI	Fresno	Millerton P O	72	159
CORRE								
Francis	50	m	w	FRAN	Amador	Fiddletown P O	69	429
Jose	34	m	w	CA	Santa Barbara	Arroyo Burro P O	87	509
CORREA								
Joe A	24	m	w	WI	San Francisco	1-Wd San Francisco	79	65
John	52	m	w	AZOR	Contra Costa	San Pablo Twp	71	360
Joseph K	39	m	w	AZOR	Placer	Newcastle Twp	76	474
CORREIA								
John	21	m	w	PORT	Alameda	Hayward	68	79
CORRELE								
G A	50	m	w	FRAN	Merced	Snelling P O	74	250
CORRELL								
Jacob	37	m	w	PRUS	Santa Clara	Gilroy Twp	88	85
John J	45	m	w	BAVA	San Francisco	8-Wd San Francisco	82	443
Peter L	54	m	w	NC	Santa Barbara	San Buenaventura P	87	420
CORREVEYA								
Jose	45	m	w	MEXI	San Diego	Pala Valley Reserv	78	480
CORREY								
B	40	f	w	IREL	Alameda	Oakland	68	190
Carrie	23	f	w	IL	Solano	Suisun Twp	90	98
John	40	m	w	MA	San Francisco	7-Wd San Francisco	81	244
Thomas	40	m	w	MA	San Francisco	San Francisco P O	83	36
CORRICK								
John	48	m	w	SCOT	Santa Clara	Milpitas Twp	88	114
John M	27	m	w	VA	Sonoma	Vallejo Twp	91	453
CORRIDELL								
Johana	28	f	w	IREL	San Francisco	8-Wd San Francisco	82	299
CORRIEO								
Stephen	32	m	w	ITAL	Los Angeles	Los Angeles	73	509
CORRIF								
P	29	m	w	IREL	Merced	Snelling P O	74	269
CORRIGAN								
Henry	35	m	w	PA	San Mateo	Searsville P O	87	383
Henry	33	m	w	PA	San Mateo	Searsville P O	87	382
M	29	m	w	IREL	Yuba	Rose Bar Twp	93	654
Martin	39	m	w	IREL	Tehama	Red Bluff	92	177
P	48	m	w	IREL	Yuba	Marysville	93	591
Pat	50	m	w	IREL	Yuba	Rose Bar Twp	93	666
Thos	42	m	w	IREL	Yuba	Rose Bar Twp	93	657
Wm	31	m	w	IREL	Solano	Vallejo	90	186
CORRIGON								
John	38	m	w	IREL	Placer	Newcastle Twp	76	476
CORRILLA								
Carlos	36	m	w	SPAI	San Francisco	San Francisco P O	80	468
Tomas	36	m	w	MEXI	San Francisco	San Francisco P O	80	471
CORRILLIS								
Jose	25	m	w	MEXI	Butte	Chico Twp	70	42
CORRIN								
John	35	m	w	ENGL	Nevada	Grass Valley Twp	75	175
Manuel	48	m	w	SCOT	Alameda	Brooklyn Twp	68	47
Simon	45	m	w	IREL	San Francisco	San Francisco P O	83	78

© 2001 by Heritage Quest. All rights reserved.

Name	Age	S	R	B-PL	County	Locale	Series M593 Roll	Pg
CORRINO								
Merino	42	m	w	MEXI	Fresno	Millerton P O	72	154
CORRO								
Jas W	46	m	w	NC	Monterey	San Antonio Twp	74	317
CORROLL								
Chas	26	m	w	IREL	San Francisco	San Francisco P O	83	132
Richd	42	m	w	IREL	San Francisco	San Francisco P O	83	18
CORROTIA								
Michael	42	m	w	NCOD	San Joaquin	2-Wd Stockton	86	168
CORRY								
Albert B	33	m	w	CT	Placer	Auburn P O	76	377
Jas	29	m	w	IREL	Sacramento	1-Wd Sacramento	77	187
Laurence	38	m	w	IREL	Calaveras	Copperopolis P O	70	253
Michael	25	m	w	IREL	San Francisco	2-Wd San Francisco	79	213
CORSAN								
H	45	m	w	OH	Sacramento	1-Wd Sacramento	77	184
CORSARO								
Lucien	39	m	w	ITAL	Solano	Montezuma Twp	90	67
CORSBY								
Josiah	42	m	w	MA	Klamath	South Fork Twp	73	383
CORSER								
Henry Harrison	49	m	w	NY	Plumas	Rich Bar Twp	77	46
CORSIA								
W	19	f	w	CA	Santa Clara	Gilroy Twp	88	74
CORSICA								
Basater	45	f	w	CA	San Mateo	Woodside P O	87	380
Joseph	35	m	w	ITAL	San Mateo	Schoolhouse Statio	87	332
Joseph	34	m	w	ITAL	San Mateo	Menlo Park P O	87	378
CORSON								
Chas W	34	m	w	ME	Butte	Chico Twp	70	19
Geo M	48	m	w	PA	Shasta	Horsetown P O	89	507
John	38	m	w	PA	Solano	Vallejo	90	139
Mary	25	f	w	CANA	Sonoma	Bodega Twp	91	251
Sylvester	34	m	w	ME	Santa Clara	Gilroy Twp	88	69
CORT								
George	25	m	w	FINL	Santa Clara	Fremont Twp	88	62
CORTA								
Antonio	41	m	w	ITAL	Tuolumne	Chinese Camp P O	93	384
John	30	m	w	ITAL	Tuolumne	Chinese Camp P O	93	384
Lernardo	45	m	w	CA	San Bernardino	Chino Twp	78	409
CORTALO								
V	19	m	w	MEXI	Santa Clara	Almaden Twp	88	21
CORTEEL								
John	35	m	w	IREL	Sutter	Sutter Twp	92	122
CORTELLI								
Andrew	30	m	w	ITAL	Tuolumne	Chinese Camp P O	93	376
CORTELLO								
Michael	42	m	w	IREL	El Dorado	Coloma Twp	72	7
Michael	27	m	w	IREL	San Francisco	San Francisco P O	83	148
CORTER								
Sarah	28	f	w	NY	San Francisco	11-Wd San Francisc	84	562
CORTERLE								
Patrick	45	m	w	IREL	Alameda	Washington Twp	68	291
CORTERO								
Dennis	30	m	i	CA	Fresno	Kings Rvr P O	72	216
CORTES								
Ahuno	36	m	w	CHIL	Calaveras	Copperopolis P O	70	255
Charles	45	m	w	IREL	San Francisco	6-Wd San Francisco	81	96
Cor	26	m	w	MEXI	Santa Clara	Almaden Twp	88	10
Francisco	46	m	w	MEXI	Los Angeles	Los Angeles	73	567
Francisco	45	m	w	MEXI	Los Angeles	Los Angeles	73	560
Martha	60	f	w	LA	San Francisco	8-Wd San Francisco	82	354
Ramon	51	m	w	MEXI	Tuolumne	Sonora P O	93	314
CORTEZ								
Antone	26	m	w	PRUS	San Francisco	1-Wd San Francisco	79	34
Antonio	23	m	w	ITAL	Santa Clara	2-Wd San Jose	88	310
Antwine	30	m	w	PORT	Alameda	Murray Twp	68	112
Manuel	24	m	w	PORT	Alameda	Murray Twp	68	112
Panfe A	40	m	w	MEXI	Alameda	Murray Twp	68	112
Rachael	26	f	w	ENGL	San Mateo	San Mateo P O	87	356
Ramon	28	m	w	MEXI	Fresno	Millerton P O	72	153
CORTEZE								
M	31	m	w	CHIN	Sierra	Lincoln Twp	89	549
CORTHAY								
Alex	27	m	w	SWIT	Napa	Napa	75	22
Louis	40	m	w	SWIT	San Francisco	San Francisco P O	83	335
CORTIGAN								
Jno	31	m	w	IL	Santa Clara	Gilroy Twp	88	71
CORTIN								
Piedro	20	m	w	SWIT	Sonoma	Santa Rosa	91	395
CORTIS								
H A	37	m	w	GERM	Solano	Vallejo	90	213
CORTNEY								
Ann	39	f	w	IREL	Santa Clara	1-Wd San Jose	88	236
CORTON								
Katharine	37	f	w	IREL	San Francisco	San Francisco P O	83	152
CORTRAS								
Malaads	18	f	i	MEXI	Inyo	Lone Pine Twp	73	335
CORTRIGHT								
Homer	12	m	w	CA	Sacramento	Alabama Twp	77	60
Isaac	41	m	w	OH	Tuolumne	Sonora P O	93	309
James	35	m	w	IN	Tuolumne	Sonora P O	93	322
CORTS								
Paul	31	m	w	ITAL	Santa Clara	Fremont Twp	88	46
CORTTY								
James	26	m	w	IREL	San Francisco	6-Wd San Francisco	81	97
CORTWRIGHT								
Chas	17	m	w	CA	San Joaquin	Castoria Twp	86	6
Philip	30	m	w	NY	Sacramento	Cosumnes Twp	77	89
CORUCHAN								
R	41	m	w	NY	Yuba	Marysville	93	608
CORVALL								
Morgan	43	m	w	PA	Santa Clara	Redwood Twp	88	128
CORVALLI								
Carlo	40	m	w	SWIT	Santa Clara	1-Wd San Jose	88	257
CORVELLE								
Antonio	42	m	w	MEXI	Fresno	Millerton P O	72	151
CORVEY								
Archibald	29	m	w	SCOT	Contra Costa	Martinez P O	71	424
CORVIN								
Albert	33	m	w	PA	Colusa	Grand Island Twp	71	307
Joseph	17	m	w	ITAL	Inyo	Lone Pine Twp	73	332
Robert	51	m	w	VA	Sacramento	Sutter Twp	77	392
CORVIOLE								
James P	21	m	w	NY	Butte	Chico Twp	70	13
CORWELL								
Anthony	38	m	w	IREL	San Francisco	San Francisco P O	83	122
James	33	m	w	ENGL	San Francisco	San Francisco P O	80	381
John D	45	m	w	NY	San Francisco	7-Wd San Francisco	81	261
Tobin B	27	m	w	SCOT	San Diego	San Diego	78	506
CORWIN								
E C	10	f	w	NY	Solano	Benicia	90	15
Elie W	60	m	w	NY	Colusa	Colusa	71	292
Fanny	65	f	w	NY	San Francisco	7-Wd San Francisco	81	280
James	58	m	w	SC	Los Angeles	Wilmington Twp	73	645
Joseph	43	m	w	NY	San Francisco	San Francisco P O	80	423
Lewis M	39	m	w	IN	Napa	Napa	75	44
Nellie	23	f	w	IREL	San Francisco	5-Wd San Francisco	81	14
Samuel T	40	m	w	ME	Los Angeles	Los Nietos Twp	73	592
Sarah	21	f	w	NY	Sacramento	Granite Twp	77	147
Stephen	41	m	w	MI	Nevada	Grass Valley Twp	75	150
William S	47	m	w	IN	Nevada	Rough & Ready Twp	75	334
CORWISH								
Henry	47	m	w	ENGL	Placer	Auburn P O	76	379
CORWYNN								
Micheal	40	m	w	IREL	San Francisco	7-Wd San Francisco	81	193
CORY								
Andrew J	37	m	w	OH	Santa Clara	San Jose Twp	88	185
Benjamin	47	m	w	OH	Santa Clara	1-Wd San Jose	88	229
Benjamin F	43	m	w	VT	Yuba	Slate Range Bar Tw	93	678
Charles	49	m	w	NY	Colusa	Colusa	71	296
Chas	42	m	w	NY	San Francisco	5-Wd San Francisco	81	26
David	32	m	w	IREL	Stanislaus	Washington Twp	92	85
Henry C	40	m	w	IN	Siskiyou	Scott Valley Twp	89	621
Isaac	12	m	w	CA	Nevada	Rough & Ready Twp	75	332
J B	53	m	w	RI	San Joaquin	Oneal Twp	86	112
James	72	m	w	NH	Santa Clara	Santa Clara Twp	88	136
James	52	m	w	NJ	Santa Clara	Santa Clara Twp	88	168
James C	42	m	w	CANA	San Francisco	2-Wd San Francisco	79	278
James M	40	m	w	OH	Santa Clara	Santa Clara Twp	88	168
Josephine	33	f	w	OH	Placer	Bath P O	76	457
Manuel	28	m	w	SCOT	Alameda	Brooklyn Twp	68	48
Parkus	67	m	w	PA	Calaveras	Copperopolis P O	70	251
Rubin	32	m	w	CANA	Sonoma	Petaluma Twp	91	365
Thomas	64	m	w	RI	Monterey	Monterey	74	360
Thomas	46	m	w	OH	Shasta	Portugese Flat P O	89	471
Thomas H	43	m	w	NY	Colusa	Colusa	71	289
Thoms	45	m	w	IREL	Yuba	Rose Bar Twp	93	658
W N	28	m	w	OH	Amador	Jackson P O	69	333
William	38	m	w	LA	San Francisco	San Francisco P O	83	225
William	17	m	w	CA	Nevada	Rough & Ready Twp	75	324
William	16	m	w	CA	Nevada	Rough & Ready Twp	75	332
CORYDON								
Simon	25	m	w	IREL	San Francisco	5-Wd San Francisco	81	15
CORYELL								
Amy	70	f	w	MO	San Francisco	San Francisco P O	80	363
John	42	m	w	LA	San Francisco	San Francisco P O	80	363
CORZA								
Josph	32	m	w	ITAL	San Joaquin	1-Wd Stockton	86	141
COSANE								
Chino	8	m	w	CA	San Diego	San Luis Rey	78	514
COSAREGULA								
Dominico	21	m	w	ITAL	San Francisco	San Francisco P O	85	782
COSAS								
Martinos	36	m	w	MEXI	Stanislaus	Empire Twp	92	59
COSAY								
Bartholomew	52	m	w	IREL	Sonoma	Petaluma Twp	91	327
Jas	23	m	w	IREL	Solano	Vallejo	90	215
COSBEDO								
Gerado	27	m	w	MEXI	San Francisco	San Francisco P O	80	347
Gerado	27	m	w	MEXI	San Francisco	San Francisco P O	80	348
COSBY								
Frank	28	m	w	KY	San Francisco	8-Wd San Francisco	82	437
Samuel	46	m	w	SC	Yuba	Long Bar Twp	93	564
COSE								
Martha	14	f	w	MO	San Francisco	San Francisco P O	83	342
COSEN								
Isaac	49	m	w	FINL	San Francisco	11-Wd San Francisc	84	652
COSEY								
Frank	39	m	w	IREL	San Francisco	11-Wd San Francisc	84	521
James	41	m	w	IREL	San Francisco	11-Wd San Francisc	84	500
Jeremiah	40	m	w	IREL	Monterey	San Antonio Twp	74	322

© 2001 by Heritage Quest. All rights reserved.

Series M593

Name	Age	S	R	B-PL	County	Locale	Roll	Pg
COSGRAVE								
M L	27	m	w	OH	San Joaquin	1-Wd Stockton	86	128
COSGRIFF								
Charles P	36	m	w	IREL	San Francisco	San Francisco P O	85	714
John	29	m	w	IREL	San Francisco	8-Wd San Francisco	82	454
COSGRIFTH								
Michael	28	m	w	IREL	San Francisco	San Francisco P O	85	868
COSGROV								
Henry	50	m	w	IREL	Calaveras	San Andreas P O	70	156
COSGROVE								
Andrew	35	m	w	IREL	Sacramento	1-Wd Sacramento	77	203
Ann	64	f	w	IREL	San Francisco	8-Wd San Francisco	82	353
Annie	13	f	w	CA	Solano	Benicia	90	16
Bridget	35	f	w	IREL	Sacramento	4-Wd Sacramento	77	363
Catherine	38	f	w	IREL	San Francisco	2-Wd San Francisco	79	216
Catherine	30	f	w	IREL	San Francisco	2-Wd San Francisco	79	228
Chas	17	m	w	CA	Calaveras	Copperopolis P O	70	235
Edward	26	m	w	IREL	San Francisco	San Francisco P O	83	184
Felix	17	m	w	NY	San Francisco	11-Wd San Francisc	84	433
Felix	17	m	w	IREL	San Francisco	11-Wd San Francisc	84	649
Frank	5	m	w	CA	Marin	San Rafael Twp	74	28
Hugh	60	m	w	IREL	Mariposa	Mariposa P O	74	101
James	40	m	w	IREL	San Francisco	8-Wd San Francisco	82	496
James	30	m	w	IREL	San Francisco	2-Wd San Francisco	79	271
James	26	m	w	IREL	San Francisco	11-Wd San Francisc	84	598
Jane	40	f	w	IREL	San Francisco	San Francisco P O	80	418
John	55	m	w	IREL	San Francisco	2-Wd San Francisco	79	244
John	40	m	w	IREL	San Joaquin	1-Wd Stockton	86	133
John	40	m	w	NY	San Francisco	San Francisco P O	83	357
John	39	m	w	IREL	Yuba	Rose Bar Twp	93	652
John	35	m	w	MA	San Francisco	1-Wd San Francisco	79	102
John	35	m	w	IREL	San Francisco	1-Wd San Francisco	79	21
John	35	m	w	NY	San Francisco	1-Wd San Francisco	79	133
John	34	m	w	NY	Alameda	Oakland	68	190
John	32	m	w	IN	San Francisco	San Francisco P O	83	263
John	29	m	w	AL	Solano	Vacaville Twp	90	125
John	23	m	w	AUSL	San Francisco	San Francisco P O	83	336
John J	26	m	w	IREL	San Francisco	2-Wd San Francisco	79	214
John P	22	m	w	ENGL	San Francisco	San Francisco P O	83	238
Kate	30	f	w	IREL	San Francisco	6-Wd San Francisco	81	116
Margaret	27	f	w	IREL	San Francisco	7-Wd San Francisco	81	273
Mary A	18	f	w	IREL	San Francisco	San Francisco P O	83	133
Michael	49	m	w	IREL	Calaveras	Copperopolis P O	70	242
Pat	48	m	w	IREL	San Joaquin	3-Wd Stockton	86	231
Patrick	35	m	w	IREL	San Francisco	San Francisco P O	80	381
Patrick	32	m	w	IREL	San Francisco	11-Wd San Francisc	84	654
Patrick	30	m	w	IREL	San Mateo	San Mateo P O	87	354
Peter	6	m	w	CA	Marin	San Rafael Twp	74	28
Peter	39	m	w	ME	San Francisco	San Francisco P O	83	324
Peter	31	m	w	PRUS	Solano	Silveyville Twp	90	74
Peter	29	m	w	ENGL	Sacramento	1-Wd Sacramento	77	188
Philip	40	m	w	IREL	San Francisco	San Francisco P O	83	105
Thomas	36	m	w	IREL	San Francisco	San Francisco P O	85	756
Thomas	28	m	w	IREL	Contra Costa	Martinez P O	71	416
Thos	40	m	w	IREL	San Joaquin	1-Wd Stockton	86	154
Thos	40	m	w	OH	Butte	Chico Twp	70	60
Thos	30	m	w	IREL	San Francisco	2-Wd San Francisco	79	208
Tim	21	m	w	IREL	San Joaquin	3-Wd Stockton	86	231
Tim	18	m	w	IREL	San Joaquin	Douglas Twp	86	49
COSHBOW								
Augustus A	34	m	w	OH	Inyo	Bishop Crk Twp	73	313
COSI								
Ah	40	m	c	CHIN	Fresno	Millerton P O	72	201
COSIA								
Francisco	35	m	w	CA	Monterey	San Antonio Twp	74	318
COSIANSLO								
Jose	29	m	w	CHIL	Calaveras	San Andreas P O	70	177
COSICH								
Louis	28	m	w	AUST	San Francisco	3-Wd San Francisco	79	301
COSILLIA								
Charles	28	m	w	ITAL	San Francisco	2-Wd San Francisco	79	161
COSINI								
Gabriello	41	m	w	ITAL	San Francisco	1-Wd San Francisco	79	110
COSIO								
Francois	35	m	w	MEXI	Kern	Bakersfield P O	73	358
Jesus	52	m	w	MEXI	Monterey	Monterey Twp	74	349
Nicholas	21	m	w	MEXI	Kern	Bakersfield P O	73	357
COSION								
Marshall C	50	m	w	VA	Colusa	Colusa	71	298
COSLIN								
Anna	28	f	w	MA	Alameda	Alameda	68	8
COSLING								
Quoi	30	f	c	CHIN	Calaveras	San Andreas P O	70	155
COSMINSKI								
H	34	m	w	PRUS	Yuba	Marysville	93	616
J	43	m	w	IREL	Yuba	Marysville	93	615
COSNER								
William	45	m	w	IA	Calaveras	San Andreas P O	70	206
COSOMO								
Giovanni	60	m	w	HUNG	Calaveras	Copperopolis P O	70	226
COSOVICH								
Chrisn	32	m	w	AUST	San Francisco	3-Wd San Francisco	79	292
COSS								
Urias	34	m	w	CANA	Plumas	Plumas Twp	77	31
COSSA								
Jean	59	m	w	FRAN	Santa Clara	Alviso Twp	88	26
COSSAN								
Eugene	35	m	w	FRAN	Santa Clara	Alviso Twp	88	23
COSSER								
Edward K	27	m	w	MO	San Luis Obispo	Santa Rosa Twp	87	317
COSSOFOOM								
Henry	27	m	w	CANA	San Francisco	San Francisco P O	85	871
COSSON								
James	31	m	w	FRAN	San Francisco	San Francisco P O	80	533
COSSULEI								
George B	33	m	w	ITAL	San Francisco	San Francisco P O	85	751
COSSUM								
Daniel	39	m	w	NY	Santa Clara	1-Wd San Jose	88	254
COSTA								
Antonio	43	m	w	PORT	Nevada	Rough & Ready Twp	75	328
Antonio	41	m	w	SARD	Tuolumne	Columbia P O	93	350
Charles	30	m	w	ME	San Francisco	2-Wd San Francisco	79	150
Francesco	25	m	w	ITAL	San Francisco	3-Wd San Francisco	79	289
Frank	40	m	w	PORT	San Francisco	San Francisco P O	83	83
Georgiana	21	f	w	NY	San Francisco	6-Wd San Francisco	81	45
Georgiana	20	f	w	ENGL	San Francisco	6-Wd San Francisco	81	72
Jas	37	m	w	ITAL	Santa Clara	Almaden Twp	88	1
Jas	27	m	w	PORT	Sierra	Table Rock Twp	89	579
Joe	18	m	w	PORT	Sacramento	Sutter Twp	77	386
John	37	m	w	PORT	Marin	Sausalito Twp	74	71
John	25	m	w	ITAL	Calaveras	San Andreas P O	70	197
John B	45	m	w	ITAL	Calaveras	San Andreas P O	70	197
John B	38	m	w	ITAL	San Francisco	2-Wd San Francisco	79	146
Joseph	47	m	w	AZOR	Nevada	Nevada Twp	75	317
Joseph	40	m	w	ITAL	San Francisco	1-Wd San Francisco	79	114
Joseph	35	m	w	ITAL	San Francisco	San Francisco P O	80	332
Joseph	27	m	w	PORT	San Francisco	1-Wd San Francisco	79	37
Juan	25	m	w	ITAL	San Francisco	11-Wd San Francisc	84	660
Louis	42	m	w	ITAL	Calaveras	San Andreas P O	70	177
Louis	40	m	c	CHIN	San Francisco	6-Wd San Francisco	81	50
Louis	35	m	w	ITAL	Yuba	Marysville	93	594
Louis	28	m	w	ITAL	Amador	Jackson P O	69	327
Lozerre	37	m	w	ITAL	San Francisco	1-Wd San Francisco	79	41
Miguel	33	m	w	PORT	Santa Clara	1-Wd San Jose	88	256
Nicholas	64	m	w	ITAL	Calaveras	San Andreas P O	70	196
Nicolas	22	m	w	ITAL	Calaveras	San Andreas P O	70	197
Pablo	18	m	w	CA	San Francisco	1-Wd San Francisco	79	84
Parronila	29	f	w	CHIL	Los Angeles	Los Angeles	73	554
Peter	35	m	w	ITAL	San Francisco	2-Wd San Francisco	79	243
Peters	35	m	w	ITAL	San Francisco	11-Wd San Francisc	84	659
Rosa	25	f	w	ITAL	San Francisco	1-Wd San Francisco	79	114
Theodore	45	m	w	PRUS	San Francisco	1-Wd San Francisco	79	47
Thos L	52	m	w	AZOR	Nevada	Nevada Twp	75	317
COSTALE								
Ellen	25	f	w	IREL	San Francisco	11-Wd San Francisc	84	539
COSTANCES								
J	45	m	i	CA	Alameda	Murray Twp	68	103
COSTAR								
Frederick	22	m	w	HOLL	San Francisco	8-Wd San Francisco	82	389
Thomas	44	m	w	ENGL	Plumas	Seneca Twp	77	49
COSTELL								
Daniel	25	m	w	ENGL	Sutter	Yuba Twp	92	143
COSTELLA								
Ella	19	f	w	IL	Santa Clara	Gilroy Twp	88	75
Michael	37	m	w	IREL	San Francisco	San Francisco P O	83	198
Rafonkes	38	m	w	MEXI	Tuolumne	Sonora P O	93	327
COSTELLO								
Daniel	38	m	w	VENE	San Francisco	San Francisco P O	83	200
Delia	19	f	w	IREL	San Francisco	5-Wd San Francisco	81	29
Edward	34	m	w	IREL	San Francisco	San Francisco P O	83	242
Edward	31	m	w	IREL	San Francisco	11-Wd San Francisc	84	424
Edward	27	m	w	IREL	San Francisco	2-Wd San Francisco	79	215
Ellen	26	f	w	IREL	San Francisco	8-Wd San Francisco	82	470
Ellen	25	f	w	IREL	Yuba	Rose Bar Twp	93	663
F	45	m	w	BADE	San Joaquin	1-Wd Stockton	86	122
Francisca	32	f	w	MEXI	Solano	Vallejo	90	212
Irving	50	m	w	MA	San Francisco	San Francisco P O	83	159
Isabella	32	f	w	SPAI	San Francisco	5-Wd San Francisco	81	10
James	44	m	w	IREL	San Francisco	San Francisco P O	83	60
James	39	m	w	IREL	Placer	Auburn P O	76	365
James	35	m	w	IREL	San Francisco	8-Wd San Francisco	82	488
James	32	m	w	IREL	San Francisco	San Francisco P O	83	38
James	29	m	w	ENGL	Santa Clara	2-Wd San Jose	88	296
Jas	36	m	w	IREL	Sutter	Sutter Twp	92	116
Jas	32	m	w	IREL	Solano	Vallejo	90	149
Jno	24	m	w	IREL	Santa Clara	Gilroy Twp	88	78
John	50	m	w	NY	Santa Clara	Gilroy Twp	88	102
John	36	m	w	IREL	Santa Clara	Santa Clara Twp	88	157
John	35	m	w	IREL	San Francisco	2-Wd San Francisco	79	191
John	10	m	w	CA	Marin	San Rafael Twp	74	28
Joseph	50	m	w	MEXI	Santa Clara	2-Wd San Jose	88	302
Julia	40	f	w	IREL	Solano	Vallejo	90	199
Lucy	25	f	w	IREL	Trinity	Hayfork Valley	92	238
M	36	m	w	IREL	San Joaquin	2-Wd Stockton	86	165
Martin	30	m	w	IREL	San Francisco	5-Wd San Francisco	81	32
Mary	22	f	w	IREL	San Francisco	5-Wd San Francisco	81	29
Michael	30	m	w	NY	Santa Clara	San Jose Twp	88	194
Michael	23	m	w	IREL	Marin	Sausalito Twp	74	71
Nich	50	m	w	IREL	Santa Clara	Gilroy Twp	88	70
Patrick	41	m	w	IREL	Santa Clara	Gilroy Twp	88	96
Pierce	46	m	w	IREL	Tuolumne	Columbia P O	93	359
Saml	28	m	w	IREL	San Francisco	11-Wd San Francisc	84	576
Sarah	19	f	w	IREL	San Francisco	San Francisco P O	83	50

© 2001 by Heritage Quest. All rights reserved.

Name	Age	S	R	B-PL	County	Locale	Roll	Pg
						Series M593		
Sylvester	35	m	w	IREL	Santa Clara	Gilroy Twp	88	90
Walter	36	m	w	IREL	San Francisco	San Francisco P O	83	235
William	26	m	w	IREL	San Francisco	6-Wd San Francisco	81	118
William	23	m	w	CANA	Santa Clara	2-Wd San Jose	88	329
COSTELLOE								
James A	27	m	w	IREL	San Francisco	6-Wd San Francisco	81	88
Mary	65	f	w	IREL	Del Norte	Smith Rvr Twp	71	476
COSTELOW								
Alice	27	f	w	IREL	Yolo	Cache Crk Twp	93	422
COSTENS								
Henry	34	m	w	HANO	San Mateo	Redwood Twp	87	367
COSTER								
Coster	38	m	w	PRUS	San Francisco	San Francisco P O	85	839
Isaac	22	m	w	CANA	San Francisco	San Francisco P O	85	756
John L	29	m	w	SC	San Francisco	San Francisco P O	85	783
Lawrence	26	m	w	ENGL	Placer	Pino Twp	76	471
Peter	29	m	w	PRUS	Sutter	Sutter Twp	92	116
COSTES								
Jaquine	18	m	w	MEXI	Inyo	Cerro Gordo Twp	73	319
COSTIGAN								
John	48	m	w	IREL	Trinity	Junction City Pct	92	206
John	32	m	w	IREL	San Francisco	San Francisco P O	83	282
P M	26	m	w	NY	San Francisco	San Francisco P O	85	840
Patrick	35	m	w	IREL	San Francisco	San Francisco P O	85	745
Peter	31	m	w	IREL	San Francisco	1-Wd San Francisco	79	115
William J	34	m	w	NY	Solano	Suisun Twp	90	93
COSTILLE								
Wm	40	m	w	IREL	Mono	Bridgeport P O	74	284
COSTILLO								
Danl	37	m	w	VENE	San Francisco	7-Wd San Francisco	81	258
Jno	23	m	w	NY	Butte	Chico Twp	70	38
Thomas	37	m	w	IREL	Sonoma	Petaluma Twp	91	363
COSTIN								
August	41	m	w	HESS	Shasta	Shasta P O	89	456
J	55	m	w	CHIL	Sierra	Forest Twp	89	530
Voloney G	48	m	w	NY	Sonoma	Healdsburg & Mendo	91	276
COSTLE								
James	32	m	w	IREL	San Francisco	11-Wd San Francisc	84	610
Mary J	50	f	w	IREL	Sacramento	Brighton Twp	77	81
COSTLO								
Michael	30	m	w	IREL	San Francisco	San Francisco P O	85	811
Thomas	34	m	w	IREL	San Francisco	11-Wd San Francisc	84	500
COSTLOW								
Joseph	18	m	w	CA	San Francisco	7-Wd San Francisco	81	254
P	36	m	w	IREL	Sierra	Table Rock Twp	89	575
COSTNEL								
Peter	47	m	w	ITAL	San Francisco	2-Wd San Francisco	79	232
COSTO								
C	57	f	w	IN	Sierra	Alleghany & Forest	89	533
Joseph	27	m	w	PORT	Marin	Nicasio Twp	74	20
COSTOLLO								
Henry	44	m	w	ENGL	San Francisco	11-Wd San Francisc	84	586
COSTOM								
Matilda	38	f	w	DENM	San Francisco	8-Wd San Francisco	82	471
COSTRA								
Ivart	37	m	w	MEXI	San Joaquin	3-Wd Stockton	86	221
COSTRO								
Louis	28	m	w	SWED	Santa Clara	Almaden Twp	88	3
COSTRY								
Perie	37	m	w	CHIL	Alameda	Oakland	68	170
COSWALL								
Andreas	15	m	w	CHIL	Fresno	Millerton P O	72	167
COSWELL								
T H	46	m	w	NY	Nevada	Nevada Twp	75	291
COT								
Ah	27	m	c	CHIN	Stanislaus	Empire Twp	92	63
At	29	m	c	CHIN	Yuba	Marysville	93	622
Walter	30	m	w	WI	Humboldt	Mattole Twp	72	284
COTA								
Antonio	17	m	w	CA	Los Angeles	Los Angeles	73	536
David	29	m	w	MEXI	Los Angeles	Wilmington Twp	73	634
Emilio	29	m	w	CA	Santa Cruz	Watsonville	89	377
Felipa	24	f	w	CA	Santa Barbara	Santa Barbara P O	87	473
Francisco	47	m	w	CA	Los Angeles	Los Angeles Twp	73	485
Francisco	33	m	w	CA	Los Angeles	Santa Ana Twp	73	599
Francisco	29	m	w	CA	Santa Barbara	Santa Barbara P O	87	466
Francisco	27	m	w	CA	Santa Barbara	Las Cruces P O	87	504
Frank	35	m	w	VT	San Francisco	San Francisco P O	85	753
Gabriel	30	m	w	MEXI	Santa Clara	Almaden Twp	88	10
Henry	40	m	w	AZOR	Nevada	Washington Twp	75	340
Ignatio	55	m	w	MEXI	Fresno	Millerton P O	72	151
Isidore	19	m	w	CA	San Diego	San Pasqual	78	520
Jesus	34	m	w	CA	Los Angeles	Los Angeles	73	523
Joaquin	64	m	w	CA	Santa Barbara	Las Cruces P O	87	504
Jose	35	m	w	CA	Santa Barbara	Santa Barbara P O	87	485
Jose	33	m	w	MEXI	Santa Clara	1-Wd San Jose	88	265
Jose	18	m	w	MEXI	Santa Clara	Santa Clara Twp	88	163
Jose J	39	m	w	CA	Santa Barbara	Santa Barbara P O	87	485
Jose J	38	m	w	CA	Santa Barbara	Santa Barbara P O	87	490
Jose Jesus	30	m	w	CA	Los Angeles	Los Angeles	73	522
Jose M	69	m	w	CA	Santa Barbara	Santa Barbara P O	87	482
Jose M	39	m	w	CA	Santa Barbara	Santa Barbara P O	87	482
Joseph	30	m	w	VT	Plumas	Goodwin Twp	77	8
Joseph	22	m	w	MEXI	Alameda	Hayward	68	78
Juan	26	m	w	CA	Santa Barbara	Santa Barbara P O	87	451
Juana	23	f	w	CA	Santa Barbara	Santa Barbara P O	87	482
Lamacio	40	m	w	MEXI	Los Angeles	Los Angeles	73	553

Name	Age	S	R	B-PL	County	Locale	Roll	Pg
						Series M593		
Leonardo	52	m	w	CA	Los Angeles	Los Angeles	73	552
Lorela	45	f	w	CA	Los Angeles	Los Angeles	73	554
Luis	33	m	w	CA	Santa Barbara	Las Cruces P O	87	506
Luisa	30	f	w	CA	Los Angeles	Los Angeles	73	560
Manuel	60	m	w	CA	Santa Barbara	Santa Barbara P O	87	483
Manuel	45	m	w	CA	San Diego	San Pasqual	78	522
Manuel	33	m	w	CA	Los Angeles	Los Angeles	73	506
Manuela	53	f	w	CA	Santa Barbara	Santa Barbara P O	87	467
Maria A	15	f	w	CA	Santa Barbara	Santa Barbara P O	87	476
Maria J	80	f	w	CA	Santa Barbara	Santa Barbara P O	87	466
Maria J	41	f	w	CA	Santa Barbara	Santa Barbara P O	87	479
Maria J	20	f	w	CA	Santa Barbara	Las Cruces P O	87	505
Maria L	73	f	w	CA	Santa Barbara	Santa Barbara P O	87	462
Mary P	28	f	w	CANA	Nevada	Grass Valley Twp	75	191
Mitchell	40	m	w	CANA	Nevada	Grass Valley Twp	75	224
Pacifico	46	m	w	CA	Santa Barbara	Santa Barbara P O	87	467
Pedro	31	m	w	CA	Napa	Napa	75	55
Ramon	36	m	w	CA	Santa Barbara	Santa Barbara P O	87	482
Refugia	43	f	w	CA	Los Angeles	Los Angeles	73	502
Refugio	55	m	w	MEXI	Marin	San Rafael Twp	74	41
Savilla	30	f	w	CA	Los Angeles	Los Angeles	73	506
Seraphico	40	m	w	MEXI	San Diego	San Pasqual Valley	78	524
Valentine	75	m	w	CA	Santa Barbara	Santa Barbara P O	87	462
COTANCH								
James	35	m	m	NC	Nevada	Grass Valley Twp	75	156
COTE								
Hermine	25	f	w	CANA	San Francisco	11-Wd San Francisc	84	562
COTEE								
John	21	m	w	MEXI	San Francisco	3-Wd San Francisco	79	328
COTES								
Isabella	33	f	w	WURT	Santa Clara	Gilroy Twp	88	80
John	28	m	w	MO	Colusa	Colusa Twp	71	286
M K	38	m	w	IREL	Sierra	Downieville Twp	89	519
Victor	27	m	w	CA	Santa Barbara	Santa Barbara P O	87	456
COTESWORTH								
Thomas	52	m	w	ENGL	El Dorado	White Oak Twp	72	141
COTHBAR								
Charles	41	m	b	CANA	San Francisco	San Francisco P O	80	474
COTHERS								
James	45	m	w	IREL	Sacramento	Georgianna Twp	77	128
COTHLIN								
Dennis	29	m	w	IN	Sutter	Sutter Twp	92	126
COTHRAN								
Henry W	37	m	w	VA	Santa Cruz	Pajaro Twp	89	349
COTIGA								
Peter	20	m	w	SWIT	Santa Cruz	Santa Cruz Twp	89	401
COTINGER								
J	30	m	w	PRUS	Alameda	Murray Twp	68	108
COTLE								
Emil	32	m	w	FRAN	San Francisco	San Francisco P O	80	535
COTLER								
Thos	36	m	w	IREL	Sacramento	4-Wd Sacramento	77	371
COTO								
Asuncem	45	f	w	CA	Alameda	Washington Twp	68	292
COTREL								
Charles	6	m	w	CA	San Francisco	San Francisco P O	85	799
Frank	8	m	w	CA	San Francisco	San Francisco P O	85	799
Henry	4	m	w	CA	San Francisco	San Francisco P O	85	799
W	10	m	w	CA	San Francisco	San Francisco P O	85	799
COTRELL								
Alexr	26	m	w	MI	Siskiyou	Big Valley Twp	89	581
Michael	41	m	w	IL	Sacramento	Dry Crk Twp	77	98
Otis	45	m	w	NY	Sacramento	Cosumnes Twp	77	96
COTT								
Jefferson	30	m	w	IREL	San Francisco	8-Wd San Francisco	82	430
T T	32	m	w	MO	Lake	Big Valley	73	397
COTTA								
John	25	m	w	SWIT	Marin	Bolinas Twp	74	2
Manuel	22	m	w	MEXI	San Francisco	1-Wd San Francisco	79	28
R J	41	m	w	MEXI	Tuolumne	Big Oak Flat P O	93	392
Ramon	19	m	w	CA	San Luis Obispo	Salinas Twp	87	289
COTTE								
Francois	30	m	w	FRAN	San Francisco	San Francisco P O	80	350
Pierone	57	m	w	FRAN	Calaveras	San Andreas P O	70	200
COTTELIN								
Markus	49	m	w	PRUS	Sacramento	Center Twp	77	83
COTTER								
Charles	30	m	w	ME	Nevada	Meadow Lake Twp	75	264
Cornelius	42	m	w	IREL	San Francisco	8-Wd San Francisco	82	418
Edward B	30	m	w	NY	San Francisco	6-Wd San Francisco	81	87
Hannah	34	f	w	IREL	San Francisco	11-Wd San Francisc	84	540
Henry	30	m	w	NY	Sonoma	Santa Rosa	91	409
Henry F	34	m	w	IN	Sonoma	Washington Twp	91	467
James	28	m	w	IREL	San Francisco	San Francisco P O	83	192
John	50	m	w	IREL	San Francisco	San Francisco P O	85	783
John	40	m	w	NY	San Francisco	San Francisco P O	80	429
John	36	m	w	IREL	Mendocino	Point Arena Twp	74	215
Lawrence	27	m	w	IREL	San Francisco	San Francisco P O	83	148
Margaret	32	f	w	IREL	San Francisco	11-Wd San Francisc	84	622
Morris	33	m	w	IREL	San Francisco	San Francisco P O	83	158
Nicholas	27	m	w	IREL	San Francisco	8-Wd San Francisco	82	397
Pat	28	m	w	IREL	Yuba	Marysville	93	605
Richard	38	m	w	IREL	San Francisco	11-Wd San Francisc	84	702
William	54	m	w	ENGL	Calaveras	San Andreas P O	70	151
Wm	36	m	w	IREL	Solano	Vallejo	90	145
Wm	30	m	w	SCOT	San Francisco	7-Wd San Francisco	81	242

© 2001 by Heritage Quest. All rights reserved.

Name	Age	S	R	B-PL	County	Locale	Series M593 Roll	Pg
COTTEREL								
John W	41	m	w	NY	Calaveras	San Andreas P O	70	196
Richard	44	m	w	AL	Fresno	Millerton P O	72	148
COTTERELL								
Byron	30	m	w	NY	Nevada	Meadow Lake Twp	75	255
H	33	f	w	IL	Napa	Napa	75	50
COTTING								
Eben	53	m	w	MA	San Francisco	2-Wd San Francisco	79	202
Henry B	46	m	w	MA	Solano	Suisun Twp	90	93
COTTINGHAM								
Alfred B	49	m	w	KY	Amador	Volcano P O	69	374
James	51	m	w	KY	Plumas	Indian Twp	77	16
Robt	38	m	w	KY	Marin	Bolinas Twp	74	5
Wm M	25	m	w	IL	Plumas	Indian Twp	77	12
COTTLE								
Annetta	16	f	w	OR	San Francisco	San Francisco P O	85	791
Benjamin H	35	m	w	ME	Santa Clara	2-Wd San Jose	88	332
Chas	64	m	w	MA	Tuolumne	Big Oak Flat P O	93	403
Chris A	30	m	w	ME	San Francisco	6-Wd San Francisco	81	88
Edward	32	m	w	IREL	Santa Clara	San Jose Twp	88	195
Edwd	25	m	w	IL	Santa Clara	Gilroy Twp	88	103
Frank	26	m	w	IA	Santa Clara	Redwood Twp	88	133
Franklin	52	m	w	MA	San Francisco	San Francisco P O	83	337
Henry	46	m	w	MO	Santa Clara	San Jose Twp	88	210
Ira	50	m	w	MO	Santa Clara	San Jose Twp	88	196
J A	22	m	w	CA	Santa Clara	Gilroy Twp	88	84
James	42	m	w	IREL	Placer	Lincoln P O	76	485
John	40	m	w	ENGL	San Francisco	6-Wd San Francisco	81	151
John A	58	m	w	VT	Santa Clara	San Jose Twp	88	189
Marion F	33	m	w	MO	Stanislaus	Washington Twp	92	84
Melville	30	m	w	ME	Stanislaus	Empire Twp	92	42
Oliver	56	m	w	MO	Santa Clara	San Jose Twp	88	189
Orville B	56	m	w	VT	Santa Clara	San Jose Twp	88	212
Royal	60	m	w	MO	Santa Clara	San Jose Twp	88	197
Taylor	21	m	w	MO	Santa Clara	San Jose Twp	88	222
William I	38	m	w	MO	Santa Clara	San Jose Twp	88	210
Zora	53	f	w	MO	Stanislaus	Washington Twp	92	84
COTTMAN								
Bell	12	f	w	CA	Yuba	Marysville	93	609
Celia	10	f	w	CA	Yuba	Marysville	93	609
COTTON								
A	47	m	w	NY	Sutter	Butte Twp	92	95
Albert F	20	m	w	IL	Sacramento	Franklin Twp	77	107
Alexander M	53	m	w	ENGL	San Mateo	Redwood Twp	87	362
Benjamin	40	m	w	RI	San Francisco	San Francisco P O	80	421
David E	45	m	w	NY	San Diego	San Diego	78	499
Edw	28	m	w	IREL	Alameda	Oakland	68	248
J	24	m	w	ENGL	San Joaquin	Elliott Twp	86	72
J A	34	m	w	MA	Tuolumne	Big Oak Flat P O	93	401
J C	29	m	w	NY	Alameda	Oakland	68	156
James	30	m	w	KY	Solano	Vacaville Twp	90	134
James F	47	m	w	VT	San Francisco	6-Wd San Francisco	81	88
John P	33	m	w	MA	San Francisco	1-Wd San Francisco	79	35
Josephine	19	f	w	CA	Sacramento	Franklin Twp	77	107
P	50	m	w	CANA	Solano	Vallejo	90	164
Patrick	20	m	w	IREL	San Mateo	San Mateo P O	87	359
William F	42	m	w	NY	El Dorado	Mud Springs Twp	72	91
Zelotus	50	m	w	NY	San Francisco	8-Wd San Francisco	82	465
COTTOR								
Patrick	50	m	w	IREL	San Francisco	San Francisco P O	85	875
William	50	m	w	IREL	San Francisco	San Francisco P O	80	359
COTTRALL								
Walter	32	m	w	PA	Mendocino	Point Arena Twp	74	213
COTTRELL								
Annie	13	f	w	CA	San Francisco	11-Wd San Francisc	84	544
Charles	30	m	w	RI	Santa Clara	1-Wd San Jose	88	275
Cornelius F	28	m	w	NY	El Dorado	Mud Springs Twp	72	71
E M	42	m	w	IREL	Solano	Vallejo	90	166
Gordon	54	m	w	RI	Santa Clara	1-Wd San Jose	88	275
John C	44	m	w	PA	Santa Cruz	Pajaro Twp	89	352
Mike	32	m	w	NY	San Luis Obispo	Salinas Twp	87	295
William	36	m	w	ENGL	Stanislaus	Washington Twp	92	86
COTTRILL								
Augustus	30	m	w	CANA	Humboldt	Eureka Twp	72	270
COTTS								
Felicity	9	f	w	IL	Humboldt	Arcata Twp	72	225
COTY								
Alexander	28	m	w	CANA	San Francisco	San Francisco P O	80	477
Eli	30	m	w	CANA	San Mateo	San Mateo P O	87	348
COU								
Ah	24	m	c	CHIN	Tehama	Tehama Twp	92	192
Ah	20	m	c	CHIN	Alameda	Oakland	68	245
COUCH								
Henry	24	m	w	SWED	San Mateo	Schoolhouse Statio	87	334
John	43	m	w	ENGL	San Francisco	11-Wd San Francisc	84	565
John B	41	m	w	MA	San Francisco	6-Wd San Francisco	81	142
Pablo	42	m	w	CA	San Diego	Warners Rancho Dis	78	530
Thos	35	m	w	IREL	Solano	Vallejo	90	165
COUCHMAN								
D R	25	m	w	IL	Merced	Snelling P O	74	258
COUDRY								
Margaret	35	f	w	IREL	San Joaquin	2-Wd Stockton	86	165
COUDY								
J	40	m	w	ENGL	San Joaquin	2-Wd Stockton	86	211
COUETSER								
Cihisire	40	m	w	SWIT	Sonoma	Petaluma Twp	91	348
COUFHARD								
Christopher	35	m	w	CANA	Monterey	Monterey Twp	74	352
COUGAN								
George	35	m	w	AL	Marin	San Rafael Twp	74	45
COUGH								
Wm	13	m	w	CA	Santa Clara	Almaden Twp	88	3
COUGHAN								
Alexander	40	m	w	SC	Nevada	Eureka Twp	75	131
COUGHDEN								
Daniel	33	m	w	IREL	Plumas	Indian Twp	77	15
COUGHEN								
John	30	m	w	IREL	San Francisco	San Francisco P O	83	6
COUGHER								
Pat	20	m	w	IREL	San Joaquin	Union Twp	86	265
COUGHLAN								
Danl	35	m	w	IREL	Shasta	Horsetown P O	89	502
John	35	m	w	IREL	Nevada	Bloomfield Twp	75	97
Mary	47	f	w	CA	Nevada	Nevada Twp	75	294
Michael	44	m	w	IREL	Nevada	Nevada Twp	75	293
Michl	30	m	w	IREL	Marin	San Rafael	74	49
Nora	50	f	w	IREL	San Francisco	7-Wd San Francisco	81	194
P	20	m	w	IREL	Nevada	Nevada Twp	75	280
Thos	60	m	w	IREL	San Francisco	11-Wd San Francisc	84	597
COUGHLEN								
Cornelius	29	m	w	IREL	Monterey	San Juan Twp	74	415
COUGHLIN								
Daniel	45	m	w	IREL	San Francisco	San Francisco P O	80	483
Daniel	38	m	w	IREL	Nevada	Grass Valley Twp	75	199
Danl	40	m	w	IREL	San Francisco	7-Wd San Francisco	81	236
Ellen	24	f	w	IREL	San Francisco	San Francisco P O	83	278
George	33	m	w	NY	San Francisco	5-Wd San Francisco	81	28
J I	33	m	w	NY	Alameda	Oakland	68	172
James	35	m	w	ENGL	San Francisco	5-Wd San Francisco	81	23
Jeremiah	35	m	w	IREL	Shasta	Horsetown P O	89	502
John	46	m	w	IREL	San Francisco	San Francisco P O	85	765
John	40	m	w	IREL	San Francisco	San Francisco P O	80	365
John	38	m	w	IREL	San Francisco	San Francisco P O	80	375
John	35	m	w	IREL	Sierra	Table Rock Twp	89	571
John	34	m	w	IREL	Calaveras	San Andreas P O	70	154
John	32	m	w	IREL	San Francisco	8-Wd San Francisco	82	398
John	25	m	w	IREL	San Francisco	San Francisco P O	80	337
Jos	27	m	w	MA	Klamath	Liberty Twp	73	374
N	27	m	w	IREL	Alameda	Oakland	68	260
Richd	44	m	w	IREL	San Francisco	San Francisco P O	83	136
Timothy	25	m	w	IREL	Santa Clara	2-Wd San Jose	88	320
William	38	m	w	IREL	San Francisco	7-Wd San Francisco	81	164
William	32	m	w	IREL	San Mateo	Half Moon Bay P O	87	392
COUGHRAN								
James	68	m	w	KY	Tulare	Packwood Twp	92	257
James	36	m	w	AR	Tulare	Packwood Twp	92	257
John L	29	m	w	AR	Mariposa	Mariposa P O	74	118
Lewis P	43	m	w	AR	Tulare	Packwood Twp	92	257
Thomas	41	m	w	AR	Tulare	Packwood Twp	92	256
Wiley	42	m	w	AR	Tulare	Packwood Twp	92	256
Wiley	40	m	w	MO	Kern	Havilah P O	73	350
William W	33	m	w	AR	Tulare	Packwood Twp	92	257
COUGHS								
H C	22	m	w	PRUS	Alameda	Murray Twp	68	113
COULAND								
John	35	m	w	IREL	San Francisco	11-Wd San Francisc	84	678
COULDER								
M	39	m	w	PRUS	Sierra	Downieville Twp	89	515
COULER								
Martin	62	m	w	FRAN	El Dorado	Diamond Springs Tw	72	33
COULES								
Alfred	84	m	w	CT	San Diego	San Diego	78	510
COULEY								
A B	36	m	w	ME	San Joaquin	Tulare Twp	86	256
COULL								
Joseph	28	m	w	PRUS	San Francisco	San Francisco P O	83	37
COULLER								
J L	40	m	w	TN	Humboldt	Arcata Twp	72	227
COULON								
Edward	46	m	w	FRAN	San Francisco	2-Wd San Francisco	79	148
COULSON								
Robt	40	m	w	ENGL	San Francisco	San Francisco P O	83	262
COULT								
E A	22	f	w	NY	Yuba	Marysville	93	593
Mary	30	f	w	MO	San Francisco	11-Wd San Francisc	84	552
COULTAS								
John R	36	m	w	IL	Siskiyou	Cottonwood Twp	89	591
COULTEN								
George W	38	m	w	IL	Yolo	Putah Twp	93	513
COULTER								
Adolphin H	43	m	w	NC	Calaveras	San Andreas P O	70	163
Alex S	15	m	w	CA	Mariposa	Maxwell Crk P O	74	144
Andrew	25	m	w	SCOT	San Francisco	7-Wd San Francisco	81	241
B C	33	m	w	TN	Santa Clara	Gilroy Twp	88	84
David	42	m	w	IREL	Santa Clara	Fremont Twp	88	62
Dora	9	f	w	CA	Alameda	Oakland	68	258
G H	35	m	w	ENGL	Alameda	Oakland	68	265
George	52	m	w	PA	San Francisco	San Francisco P O	83	412
George	43	m	w	NY	Plumas	Washington Twp	77	54
George	40	m	w	NJ	San Francisco	5-Wd San Francisco	81	31
George	22	m	w	MEXI	Mariposa	Maxwell Crk P O	74	140
George	17	m	w	CA	San Francisco	San Francisco P O	80	532
Henry	50	m	w	NY	Mariposa	Mariposa P O	74	101

© 2001 by Heritage Quest. All rights reserved.

Name	Age	S	R	B-PL	County	Locale	Roll	Pg
						Series M593		
James	45	m	w	CANA	San Francisco	7-Wd San Francisco	81	156
James L	33	m	w	TN	Humboldt	Eureka Twp	72	276
Joel	43	m	w	NY	Amador	Fiddletown P O	69	433
Joseph	22	m	w	BADE	San Francisco	San Francisco P O	83	217
Joseph H	37	m	w	MD	Alpine	Bullion P O	69	314
Josephine	15	f	w	CA	Sacramento	3-Wd Sacramento	77	293
L	35	m	w	OH	Siskiyou	Surprise Valley Tw	89	641
Lewis	35	m	w	NC	Santa Cruz	Pajaro Twp	89	354
Martin L	35	m	w	IL	Santa Barbara	San Buenaventura P	87	418
Rachael F	44	f	w	MO	Nevada	Rough & Ready Twp	75	327
Robt	25	m	w	OH	Sierra	Gibson Twp	89	543
S T	43	m	w	KY	Sonoma	Santa Rosa	91	416
Sarah	58	f	w	CANA	Butte	Bidwell Twp	70	1
William	49	m	w	NY	Yuba	Slate Range Bar Tw	93	671
William	40	m	w	IREL	San Francisco	7-Wd San Francisco	81	209
Wm	29	m	w	OH	Sierra	Gibson Twp	89	542
COULTERVIEL								
Fred	28	m	w	PRUS	San Francisco	2-Wd San Francisco	79	222
COULTIS								
Nancy	20	m	w	IL	Siskiyou	Cottonwood Twp	89	591
COULTON								
Saml F	45	m	w	IREL	San Francisco	1-Wd San Francisco	79	86
Wm	53	m	w	ENGL	San Francisco	2-Wd San Francisco	79	222
COULY								
Thos	44	m	w	IREL	San Joaquin	1-Wd Stockton	86	153
COUNCIL								
S S	55	f	w	SC	San Francisco	San Francisco P O	85	856
COUNCILMAN								
Chas	6	m	w	NV	Solano	Benicia	90	20
COUNS								
Charles	35	m	w	MA	San Francisco	7-Wd San Francisco	81	206
COUNTA								
Joseph	23	m	w	SWIT	Marin	Nicasio Twp	74	15
COUNTE								
Joseph	46	m	w	SWIT	Marin	Point Reyes Twp	74	22
COUNTER								
J	50	m	w	PRUS	Sierra	Butte Twp	89	513
M	40	m	w	PRUS	Sierra	Butte Twp	89	511
COUNTRYMAN								
Eli	40	m	w	OH	Yuba	Bullards Bar P O	93	547
Jacob	72	m	w	CANA	Napa	Napa	75	34
John	64	m	w	NY	Napa	Napa	75	56
COUNTS								
Courthat	27	m	w	SWED	San Mateo	Searsville P O	87	383
F	25	m	w	OH	Alameda	Alameda	68	13
George	64	m	w	TN	Mariposa	Mariposa P O	74	116
J P	38	m	w	KY	Sacramento	1-Wd Sacramento	77	176
Peter	21	m	w	OH	Placer	Lincoln P O	76	492
S B	40	m	w	CANA	Sacramento	1-Wd Sacramento	77	185
W S	28	m	w	IN	Nevada	Meadow Lake Twp	75	247
COUNTZ								
J C	42	m	w	TN	Humboldt	Pacific Twp	72	297
COUPE								
Charles	27	m	w	NY	San Francisco	San Francisco P O	83	222
Geo	22	m	w	NY	San Francisco	7-Wd San Francisco	81	237
Magnis	30	m	w	HANO	San Francisco	11-Wd San Francisc	84	428
COUPEL								
George	32	m	w	SWIT	Contra Costa	Martinez P O	71	408
COURANTS								
Michael	45	m	w	IREL	Sacramento	Lee Twp	77	159
COURCY								
John	29	m	w	IREL	Solano	Vallejo	90	175
COURELL								
Thos	30	m	w	IREL	San Francisco	11-Wd San Francisc	84	676
COURLANDT								
John	25	m	w	BELG	San Francisco	1-Wd San Francisco	79	129
COURLY								
Ann	35	f	w	IREL	San Francisco	San Francisco P O	83	98
COURSAN								
William	40	m	w	MO	Colusa	Colusa Twp	71	273
COURSE								
Jerry	20	m	w	NH	San Joaquin	Douglas Twp	86	48
COURSEN								
Gershon	40	m	w	NJ	San Francisco	8-Wd San Francisco	82	407
COURT								
Alfred	21	m	w	ENGL	San Francisco	3-Wd San Francisco	79	302
Joseph	39	m	w	CANA	Sacramento	2-Wd Sacramento	77	236
COURTAIN								
Thos	42	m	w	IREL	San Francisco	San Francisco P O	83	38
COURTAINE								
Henry	34	m	w	IREL	San Francisco	2-Wd San Francisco	79	203
COURTENAY								
Ann	18	f	w	CA	Solano	Benicia	90	14
COURTENEY								
Gregory	30	m	w	IREL	San Francisco	11-Wd San Francisc	84	575
COURTER								
Mongenty	50	m	w	NY	Alameda	Washington Twp	68	272
COURTES								
Y H	25	m	w	ENGL	Sierra	Butte Twp	89	509
COURTIER								
Edmond	34	m	w	BAVA	San Francisco	2-Wd San Francisco	79	272
Richard	21	m	w	AUSL	San Francisco	8-Wd San Francisco	82	343
COURTIN								
Heun	47	m	w	FRAN	San Francisco	San Francisco P O	83	135
Joseph	38	m	w	FRAN	San Francisco	San Francisco P O	80	533
COURTNAS								
M	23	m	w	MEXI	Sierra	Sierra Twp	89	568
COURTNAY								
Patrick	28	m	w	IREL	Marin	San Rafael Twp	74	32
COURTNER								
Amzi	40	m	w	TN	Merced	Snelling P O	74	268
COURTNEY								
C T	35	m	w	NY	San Francisco	7-Wd San Francisco	81	188
Daniel	56	m	w	IREL	Los Angeles	Wilmington Twp	73	644
Ellen	25	f	w	IREL	San Francisco	San Francisco P O	80	376
George	22	m	w	IREL	San Francisco	5-Wd San Francisco	81	32
J	50	m	w	IREL	Sacramento	3-Wd Sacramento	77	264
J E	37	m	w	NY	San Francisco	7-Wd San Francisco	81	217
James	21	m	w	IREL	Inyo	Independence Twp	73	324
Jeptha D	32	m	w	IN	Plumas	Plumas Twp	77	29
Martin	29	m	w	IREL	Nevada	Bridgeport Twp	75	101
Mary	35	f	w	IREL	San Francisco	7-Wd San Francisco	81	255
Mary	35	f	w	IREL	Santa Clara	1-Wd San Jose	88	238
Mary	16	f	w	CA	San Francisco	7-Wd San Francisco	81	180
Mary	16	f	w	CA	San Francisco	7-Wd San Francisco	81	241
Michael	27	m	w	IREL	Placer	Newcastle Twp	76	476
Michl	22	m	w	IREL	San Francisco	5-Wd San Francisco	81	28
Mike	26	m	w	IREL	San Joaquin	1-Wd Stockton	86	131
William	30	m	w	ENGL	Monterey	San Juan Twp	74	389
COURTNY								
William C	46	m	w	CT	Placer	Gold Run Twp	76	398
COURTRARIS								
Charles	40	m	w	CA	Placer	Emigrant Gap P O	76	416
COURTRIGHT								
A	44	m	w	OH	Sierra	Table Rock Twp	89	571
R	32	m	w	OH	Amador	Amador City P O	69	390
COURTS								
Francis	48	m	w	ENGL	El Dorado	Mud Springs Twp	72	71
Henry	34	m	w	PRUS	San Francisco	San Francisco P O	80	408
J A	29	m	w	WI	Nevada	Meadow Lake Twp	75	247
J P	39	m	w	AL	San Joaquin	Dent Twp	86	24
Jas R	39	m	w	KY	Siskiyou	Scott Rvr Twp	89	603
COURTWRIGHT								
A T	53	m	w	NY	Sonoma	Bodega Twp	91	258
Edwd	38	m	w	IL	Butte	Chico Twp	70	33
James	22	m	w	IL	Sonoma	Bodega Twp	91	258
John	21	m	w	OH	Sonoma	Bodega Twp	91	250
Mary	16	f	w	WI	Butte	Ophir Twp	70	112
Robt	30	m	w	PA	Butte	Ophir Twp	70	115
William H	46	m	w	NY	Santa Cruz	Watsonville	89	371
COURTZ								
William	27	m	m	PA	Sacramento	2-Wd Sacramento	77	217
COUSALAGE								
Joseph	29	m	w	ITAL	Calaveras	San Andreas P O	70	204
COUSAR								
Lewis	50	m	w	FRAN	San Joaquin	2-Wd Stockton	86	169
COUSE								
William	39	m	w	NY	Kern	Kernville P O	73	368
COUSEN								
Nicholas	42	m	w	FRAN	Alameda	Brooklyn Twp	68	40
COUSENS								
C N	40	m	w	MA	San Francisco	San Francisco P O	85	853
Ralph	25	m	w	CANA	Napa	Napa Twp	75	66
Richard	30	m	w	CANA	Napa	Napa Twp	75	66
COUSIN								
Charles	45	m	w	PORT	Santa Cruz	Santa Cruz Twp	89	394
Mary	45	f	w	FRAN	San Francisco	2-Wd San Francisco	79	169
COUSINS								
E B	32	m	w	ME	Humboldt	Eureka Twp	72	268
Geo	23	m	w	FRAN	San Francisco	11-Wd San Francisc	84	682
H B	41	m	w	US	Humboldt	Eureka Twp	72	279
Henry	40	m	w	IREL	Tulare	Visalia	92	296
Jacob	41	m	w	ME	Humboldt	Eureka Twp	72	273
James	46	m	w	SCOT	San Francisco	2-Wd San Francisco	79	209
James	42	m	m	VA	Yuba	Marysville	93	613
James	35	m	w	IN	Napa	Napa Twp	75	67
Mathew J	41	m	w	ENGL	El Dorado	Placerville Twp	72	97
Robert	65	m	w	IREL	Tuolumne	Chinese Camp P O	93	375
William	50	m	w	ENGL	San Francisco	San Francisco P O	80	391
William	37	m	w	ME	Sacramento	Franklin Twp	77	109
COUST								
Charles	19	m	w	HANO	Santa Barbara	Santa Barbara P O	87	503
COUSTEO								
Manuel	52	m	w	GREE	San Bernardino	San Bernardino Twp	78	443
COUSTING								
Michal	25	m	w	IREL	San Joaquin	1-Wd Stockton	86	125
COUTIE								
James	47	m	w	SCOT	Klamath	Klamath Twp	73	370
COUTLEE								
Henry	41	m	w	CANA	Sacramento	3-Wd Sacramento	77	286
COUTS								
Hannah	35	f	w	IREL	Napa	Napa Twp	75	74
Thomas	11	m	w	CA	Kern	Bakersfield P O	73	365
COUTU								
Ceasar	39	m	w	CANA	Siskiyou	Hamburg Twp	89	598
Leon	26	m	w	CANA	Siskiyou	Hamburg Twp	89	598
COUTZ								
Timothy	24	m	w	IREL	Kern	Havilah P O	73	337
COUY								
I	24	f	c	CHIN	Stanislaus	Emory Twp	92	17
COUZ								
Henry	41	m	w	PORT	Contra Costa	San Pablo Twp	71	360
COV								
Ah	28	m	c	CHIN	Placer	Pino Twp	76	471

© 2001 by Heritage Quest. All rights reserved.

Name	Age	S	R	B-PL	County	Locale	Series M593 Roll	Pg
COVACHICH								
Anto	47	m	w	AUST	San Francisco	San Francisco P O	85	735
COVALL								
Allen	44	m	w	NY	Alameda	Eden Twp	68	91
Lyman	48	m	w	NY	Sutter	Yuba Twp	92	143
COVARIAS								
Andro	52	m	w	MEXI	Tuolumne	Columbia P O	93	340
COVARRUBIA								
Onesimo	28	m	w	CA	Santa Barbara	Santa Barbara P O	87	463
COVARRUBIAS								
Maria	55	f	w	CA	Santa Barbara	Santa Barbara P O	87	464
COVARUBIAS								
Nicholas	31	m	w	CA	Santa Barbara	Santa Barbara P O	87	460
COVE								
Robert	39	m	w	ENGL	San Francisco	11-Wd San Francisc	84	542
COVEINGTON								
William	36	m	w	NC	Inyo	Lone Pine Twp	73	333
COVELEY								
John	52	m	w	IREL	Santa Cruz	Soquel Twp	89	438
COVELL								
C H	40	m	w	MA	San Joaquin	2-Wd Stockton	86	198
Calvin	31	m	w	PA	Santa Clara	Redwood Twp	88	133
Chas R	22	m	w	MA	San Francisco	San Francisco P O	83	107
Henry	28	m	w	PA	Santa Clara	Redwood Twp	88	133
P H	38	m	w	MA	Sacramento	3-Wd Sacramento	77	274
COVENTSKI								
Caroline	30	f	w	PRUS	Sacramento	4-Wd Sacramento	77	367
COVER								
Thomas W	36	m	w	MD	Los Angeles	Los Angeles	73	521
COVERALLAS								
Hosa	45	m	w	CHIL	Amador	Fiddletown P O	69	433
COVERDALE								
Robt	40	m	w	MO	Solano	Vallejo	90	157
COVERDILL								
Martha	15	f	w	CA	Napa	Yountville Twp	75	76
COVERT								
Andrew	38	m	w	IN	Tehama	Paynes Crk Twp	92	160
Darius	36	m	w	NY	Santa Clara	Redwood Twp	88	125
Enoch	51	m	w	PA	Santa Barbara	Santa Barbara P O	87	454
Henry	47	m	w	ME	Stanislaus	Empire Twp	92	33
Isaac	45	m	w	NY	Santa Clara	Redwood Twp	88	125
Jno W	38	m	w	IN	Sonoma	Washington Twp	91	464
John	59	m	w	ME	Stanislaus	Empire Twp	92	35
Mary	29	f	w	OH	Sacramento	3-Wd Sacramento	77	285
Schell	35	m	w	IL	Stanislaus	San Joaquin Twp	92	71
Steph H	46	m	w	MA	San Francisco	San Francisco P O	83	49
William	32	m	w	IN	Stanislaus	Empire Twp	92	30
COVEY								
H R	40	m	w	NY	San Francisco	San Francisco P O	83	280
Jno G	44	m	w	PA	San Francisco	5-Wd San Francisco	81	24
Nancy	12	f	w	CA	Sonoma	Mendocino Twp	91	303
Stephen	33	m	w	NY	Monterey	San Juan Twp	74	410
Urial	36	m	w	OH	Sonoma	Mendocino Twp	91	300
COVILLAND								
C	15	m	w	CA	Yuba	Marysville	93	579
COVILLE								
Henry	15	m	w	CA	El Dorado	Mud Springs Twp	72	86
M M	20	m	w	MEXI	Alameda	Oakland	68	159
R F	18	m	w	MEXI	Alameda	Oakland	68	159
COVILLO								
J	35	m	w	CA	Santa Clara	Almaden Twp	88	8
COVINGTON								
Ann E	36	f	w	IN	Los Angeles	Los Angeles	73	543
J S	49	m	w	VA	El Dorado	Coloma Twp	72	2
James	52	m	w	OH	Yolo	Fremont Twp	93	477
James	51	m	w	OH	Yolo	Fremont Twp	93	476
Nathaniel	66	m	w	MA	Contra Costa	Martinez P O	71	446
Saml	50	m	w	IL	Sacramento	4-Wd Sacramento	77	337
Wm	61	m	w	TN	San Luis Obispo	Santa Rosa Twp	87	328
COVIO								
Alahe	28	m	w	CA	Sacramento	Cosumnes Twp	77	92
COVITDE								
Peter	32	m	w	AUST	Calaveras	San Andreas P O	70	203
COVOLT								
Abram	55	m	w	VA	Plumas	Rich Bar Twp	77	46
COVVEY								
Abram	46	m	w	NY	Shasta	Horsetown P O	89	506
COW								
Abraham	29	m	w	POLA	San Francisco	San Francisco P O	85	790
Ah	9	f	c	CHIN	San Francisco	6-Wd San Francisco	81	75
Ah	6	m	c	CHIN	Placer	Dutch Flat P O	76	409
Ah	55	m	c	CHIN	El Dorado	Coloma Twp	72	6
Ah	50	m	c	CHIN	Trinity	Junction City Pct	92	208
Ah	50	m	c	CHIN	Alameda	Washington Twp	68	298
Ah	50	m	c	CHIN	Placer	Auburn P O	76	383
Ah	45	m	c	CHIN	Trinity	Lewiston Pct	92	212
Ah	45	m	c	CHIN	Amador	Jackson P O	69	331
Ah	44	m	c	CHIN	Sierra	Eureka Twp	89	525
Ah	41	m	c	CHIN	Calaveras	San Andreas P O	70	183
Ah	41	m	c	CHIN	Mariposa	Mariposa P O	74	93
Ah	41	f	c	CHIN	Mariposa	Mariposa P O	74	125
Ah	40	m	c	CHIN	Trinity	Trinity Center Pct	92	205
Ah	40	m	c	CHIN	San Joaquin	Oneal Twp	86	118
Ah	40	m	c	CHIN	Butte	Concow Twp	70	10
Ah	39	m	c	CHIN	Trinity	North Fork Twp	92	221
Ah	38	m	c	CHIN	Placer	Auburn P O	76	372
Ah	38	m	c	CHIN	Mariposa	Mariposa P O	74	133

Name	Age	S	R	B-PL	County	Locale	Series M593 Roll	Pg
Ah	37	m	c	CHIN	Sierra	Eureka Twp	89	525
Ah	37	m	c	CHIN	Nevada	Eureka Twp	75	141
Ah	36	m	c	CHIN	Amador	Volcano P O	69	384
Ah	35	m	c	CHIN	Santa Clara	1-Wd San Jose	88	273
Ah	35	m	c	CHIN	San Francisco	San Francisco P O	80	452
Ah	35	m	c	CHIN	El Dorado	Cosumnes Twp	72	19
Ah	34	m	c	CHIN	Mariposa	Mariposa P O	74	126
Ah	33	m	c	CHIN	Amador	Ione City P O	69	349
Ah	32	m	c	CHIN	Trinity	Junction City Pct	92	208
Ah	32	m	c	CHIN	Nevada	Eureka Twp	75	136
Ah	32	m	c	CHIN	Monterey	Monterey	74	354
Ah	32	m	c	CHIN	Mendocino	Noyo & Big Rvr Twp	74	173
Ah	31	m	c	CHIN	El Dorado	Greenwood Twp	72	56
Ah	31	m	c	CHIN	Mariposa	Mariposa P O	74	114
Ah	30	m	c	CHIN	Trinity	North Fork Twp	92	221
Ah	30	m	c	CHIN	Nevada	Rough & Ready Twp	75	329
Ah	3	f	c	CA	Amador	Jackson P O	69	344
Ah	29	m	c	CHIN	Plumas	Indian Twp	77	19
Ah	29	m	c	CHIN	Amador	Drytown P O	69	424
Ah	29	m	c	CHIN	Amador	Ione City P O	69	364
Ah	29	m	c	CHIN	El Dorado	Placerville Twp	72	103
Ah	29	m	c	CHIN	Calaveras	San Andreas P O	70	176
Ah	29	m	c	CHIN	Mariposa	Mariposa P O	74	103
Ah	28	m	c	CHIN	Santa Barbara	San Buenaventura P	87	438
Ah	28	m	c	CHIN	Fresno	Millerton P O	72	200
Ah	28	m	c	CHIN	El Dorado	White Oak Twp	72	140
Ah	28	m	c	CHIN	Butte	Hamilton Twp	70	72
Ah	27	m	c	CHIN	Alameda	Washington Twp	68	281
Ah	27	m	c	CHIN	Trinity	Douglas	92	234
Ah	27	m	c	CHIN	Butte	Oregon Twp	70	135
Ah	27	m	c	CHIN	Mariposa	Mariposa P O	74	105
Ah	26	m	c	CHIN	Santa Clara	2-Wd San Jose	88	297
Ah	26	m	c	CHIN	Tehama	Tehama Twp	92	188
Ah	26	m	c	CHIN	San Francisco	San Francisco P O	80	498
Ah	26	m	c	CHIN	Fresno	Kings Rvr P O	72	211
Ah	25	m	c	CHIN	San Francisco	6-Wd San Francisco	81	58
Ah	25	m	c	CHIN	San Francisco	1-Wd San Francisco	79	131
Ah	25	m	c	CHIN	Sacramento	Georgianna Twp	77	126
Ah	25	m	c	CHIN	Monterey	San Juan Twp	74	405
Ah	25	m	c	CHIN	El Dorado	Diamond Springs Tw	72	24
Ah	24	m	c	CHIN	Santa Clara	Burnett Twp	88	35
Ah	24	m	c	CHIN	Trinity	Junction City Pct	92	206
Ah	24	m	c	CHIN	Plumas	Plumas Twp	77	31
Ah	24	m	c	CHIN	San Mateo	Half Moon Bay P O	87	396
Ah	24	m	c	CHIN	Plumas	Goodwin Twp	77	4
Ah	23	m	c	CHIN	Santa Barbara	San Buenaventura P	87	440
Ah	23	m	c	CHIN	Yuba	Marysville	93	594
Ah	22	m	c	CHIN	Trinity	Weaverville Pct	92	230
Ah	21	m	c	CHIN	Yuba	Marysville	93	613
Ah	20	m	c	CHIN	San Francisco	San Francisco P O	85	806
Ah	20	m	c	CHIN	Mendocino	Point Arena Twp	74	205
Ah	20	m	c	CHIN	Mendocino	Point Arena Twp	74	205
Ah	20	f	c	CHIN	Mariposa	Mariposa P O	74	132
Ah	20	m	c	CHIN	Yuba	Marysville	93	593
Ah	2	f	c	CHIN	Monterey	Monterey Twp	74	351
Ah	19	m	c	CHIN	Santa Clara	1-Wd San Jose	88	271
Ah	19	m	c	CHIN	Plumas	Goodwin Twp	77	3
Ah	19	m	c	CHIN	San Francisco	8-Wd San Francisco	82	336
Ah	19	m	c	CHIN	Santa Clara	San Jose Twp	88	192
Ah	18	m	c	CHIN	San Francisco	6-Wd San Francisco	81	84
Ah	18	m	c	CHIN	San Francisco	6-Wd San Francisco	81	69
Ah	18	m	c	CHIN	Tehama	Tehama Twp	92	189
Ah	18	m	c	CHIN	Plumas	Washington Twp	77	57
Ah	18	f	c	CHIN	Monterey	Monterey Twp	74	351
Ah	18	m	c	CHIN	San Francisco	6-Wd San Francisco	81	68
Ah	18	m	c	CHIN	Butte	Chico Twp	70	15
Ah	17	m	c	CHIN	Mendocino	Point Arena Twp	74	208
Ah	17	m	c	CHIN	Nevada	Nevada Twp	75	312
Ah	16	f	c	CHIN	San Francisco	6-Wd San Francisco	81	76
Ah	16	f	c	CHIN	San Francisco	6-Wd San Francisco	81	77
Ah	16	m	c	CHIN	San Francisco	1-Wd San Francisco	79	80
Ah	14	m	c	CHIN	Yuba	Marysville	93	590
Chee	30	m	c	CHIN	Yuba	Marysville	93	632
Chow	28	m	c	CHIN	Sierra	Alleghany & Forest	89	535
Cow	27	m	c	CHIN	El Dorado	Kelsey Twp	72	58
Fan	22	m	c	CHIN	Butte	Hamilton Twp	70	72
Foney	27	f	c	CHIN	Butte	Ophir Twp	70	109
Foney	25	m	c	CHIN	Butte	Hamilton Twp	70	72
Fong	31	m	c	CHIN	Butte	Chico Twp	70	53
Foo	32	m	c	CHIN	Placer	Bath P O	76	444
Foy	28	m	c	CHIN	Butte	Chico Twp	70	52
Fuke	40	m	c	CHIN	Monterey	Monterey Twp	74	351
Gee	42	m	c	CHIN	Butte	Chico Twp	70	53
Gun	30	m	c	CHIN	Sacramento	Franklin Twp	77	119
He	43	m	c	CHIN	Butte	Chico Twp	70	53
Ho	43	m	c	CHIN	Butte	Concow Twp	70	10
Lee	30	m	c	CHIN	Colusa	Colusa	71	294
Loe	24	m	c	CHIN	Santa Clara	San Jose Twp	88	180
Low	30	f	c	CHIN	Yuba	Marysville	93	627
Man	18	m	c	CHIN	San Mateo	Pescadero P O	87	416
Oh	39	m	c	CHIN	Yuba	Marysville	93	629
Qui	42	m	c	CHIN	Butte	Ophir Twp	70	121
Sam	35	m	c	CHIN	Placer	Auburn P O	76	372
Sang	40	m	c	CHIN	El Dorado	Coloma Twp	72	6
Sing	45	m	c	CHIN	Mariposa	Mariposa P O	74	128
Sow	37	m	c	CHIN	El Dorado	Coloma Twp	72	6
Su	27	m	c	CHIN	Butte	Chico Twp	70	27

© 2001 by Heritage Quest. All rights reserved.

Series M593

Name	Age	S	R	B-PL	County	Locale	Roll	Pg
Sun	20	f	c	CHIN	Butte	Hamilton Twp	70	73
Ti	25	m	c	CHIN	Santa Clara	Fremont Twp	88	45
Toney	48	m	c	CHIN	Butte	Hamilton Twp	70	72
Toy	25	m	c	CHIN	Trinity	North Fork Twp	92	219
W B	62	m	w	IREL	Nevada	Eureka Twp	75	136
Wah	60	m	c	CHIN	El Dorado	Georgetown Twp	72	43
Y	64	m	c	CHIN	Amador	Drytown P O	69	423
COWADEL								
Maria	45	f	w	CA	Los Angeles	El Monte Twp	73	453
COWAN								
Bennett	35	m	w	POLA	Sacramento	3-Wd Sacramento	77	286
D H	26	m	w	ENGL	Solano	Benicia	90	12
D W C	40	m	w	PA	Sacramento	Alabama Twp	77	60
Dan	36	m	w	SCOT	Alameda	Oakland	68	263
David	24	m	w	SCOT	Marin	San Rafael Twp	74	30
E C	32	m	w	MN	Solano	Benicia	90	20
Francis	43	m	w	IREL	Mendocino	Point Arena Twp	74	209
George W	32	m	w	CT	San Diego	San Diego	78	500
Hugh	48	m	w	SCOT	San Francisco	San Francisco P O	83	29
James	36	m	w	SCOT	San Francisco	5-Wd San Francisco	81	10
Jas	25	m	w	SCOT	Sacramento	1-Wd Sacramento	77	183
John	37	m	w	ENGL	Mariposa	Mariposa P O	74	99
John	21	m	w	ENGL	Santa Clara	Fremont Twp	88	47
John T	35	m	w	AR	Mariposa	Mariposa P O	74	137
Joseph H	37	m	w	IN	Napa	Napa	75	24
Mary J	17	f	w	PA	El Dorado	Placerville	72	127
Oliver	43	m	w	NY	Tuolumne	Sonora P O	93	333
Peter	42	m	w	KY	Nevada	Grass Valley Twp	75	219
Robert	30	m	w	IREL	San Francisco	11-Wd San Francisc	84	659
S	31	m	w	OH	Nevada	Eureka Twp	75	139
S F	40	m	w	KY	Monterey	San Juan Twp	74	398
Samuel	52	m	w	TN	Sacramento	Georgianna Twp	77	132
William W	46	m	w	SCOT	El Dorado	Placerville Twp	72	101
William W	34	m	w	PA	Santa Clara	San Jose Twp	88	191
Wm	40	m	w	IREL	San Francisco	1-Wd San Francisco	79	136
COWANS								
John	13	m	w	IA	Santa Clara	Gilroy Twp	88	100
COWARD								
H	38	m	w	MD	Alameda	Oakland	68	145
John	66	m	w	BAVA	Mendocino	Anderson Twp	74	152
John	38	m	w	NC	Stanislaus	Empire Twp	92	66
COWART								
Jane	38	f	w	GA	Solano	Silveyville Twp	90	86
COWAY								
Stephen	37	m	w	OH	Nevada	Little York Twp	75	241
COWD								
Ah	25	m	c	CHIN	Fresno	Millerton P O	72	201
COWDARA								
Antonio	27	m	w	CA	Monterey	Monterey	74	360
COWDELL								
John	40	m	w	OH	Santa Clara	2-Wd San Jose	88	284
COWDEN								
Alfred	29	m	w	MO	Alameda	Washington Twp	68	285
Ambrose H	35	m	w	NY	Placer	Bath P O	76	428
D N	32	m	w	OH	Sierra	Downieville Twp	89	518
Jas	42	m	w	IREL	San Joaquin	Elkhorn Twp	86	53
John D	40	m	w	PA	Monterey	Castroville Twp	74	325
COWDER								
Davis	34	m	w	MI	Merced	Snelling P O	74	259
Robt	37	m	w	MI	San Francisco	5-Wd San Francisco	81	24
COWDERY								
Tabez F	35	m	w	NY	San Francisco	San Francisco P O	83	197
COWDRY								
Job	42	m	w	TN	Los Angeles	Los Nietos Twp	73	587
COWE								
Ah	35	f	c	CHIN	Nevada	Nevada Twp	75	298
COWEFAUD								
M	14	f	w	CA	Los Angeles	Los Angeles	73	569
COWELL								
Alfred H	36	m	w	OH	Yolo	Cache Crk Twp	93	419
Belle	15	f	w	CA	San Francisco	San Francisco P O	83	97
Francis	23	m	w	WI	Stanislaus	Empire Twp	92	66
H W	33	m	w	NY	San Joaquin	Castoria Twp	86	4
Henry	50	m	w	MA	Santa Cruz	Santa Cruz	89	428
Henry	33	m	w	NY	Stanislaus	Empire Twp	92	66
Henry	30	m	w	ENGL	San Francisco	6-Wd San Francisco	81	155
John	30	m	w	ENGL	Alameda	Brooklyn	68	28
Joseph	27	m	w	MS	San Diego	Warners Rancho Dis	78	528
Lydia	6	f	w	NY	San Francisco	1-Wd San Francisco	79	29
M J	8	f	w	NV	San Joaquin	Douglas Twp	86	40
Richard	38	m	w	ENGL	Nevada	Grass Valley Twp	75	227
Richard	38	m	w	IREL	Alameda	Alameda	68	10
Richard	37	m	w	ENGL	Nevada	Grass Valley Twp	75	144
Wm	28	m	w	IREL	Alameda	Oakland	68	137
COWEN								
E Le [Dr]	42	m	w	PA	Sacramento	Alabama Twp	77	60
G	35	m	w	GREE	Solano	Vallejo	90	180
George	35	m	w	ME	Alameda	Oakland	68	184
George M	39	m	w	OH	Placer	Blue Canyon P O	76	418
James	26	m	w	IREL	Inyo	Independence Twp	73	328
Philip	38	m	w	PRUS	Sonoma	Petaluma Twp	91	312
Thomas	38	m	w	PA	Merced	Snelling P O	74	269
Thos	41	m	w	AR	Fresno	Millerton P O	72	148
COWENSTEIN								
Isaac	44	m	w	PRUS	San Francisco	San Francisco P O	80	457
COWES								
Chin D	26	m	c	CHIN	San Francisco	6-Wd San Francisco	81	37
Martha	40	f	m	NY	San Francisco	San Francisco P O	80	430
Rebecca	28	f	m	NY	San Francisco	7-Wd San Francisco	81	281
COWFE								
Ah	40	m	c	CHIN	Placer	Auburn P O	76	379
COWFER								
Saml	32	m	w	OH	San Joaquin	2-Wd Stockton	86	182
Wm	41	m	w	OH	San Joaquin	2-Wd Stockton	86	182
COWFORD								
Jacob	48	m	w	DENM	Placer	Bath P O	76	457
COWGILL								
Elisha	53	m	w	KY	Placer	Bath P O	76	437
COWIE								
Geo W	38	m	w	SCOT	Butte	Ophir Twp	70	109
James	44	m	w	SCOT	El Dorado	Mud Springs Twp	72	80
John	47	m	w	SCOT	Tuolumne	Sonora P O	93	315
William	30	m	w	MA	San Francisco	6-Wd San Francisco	81	108
COWING								
Calvin	41	m	w	ME	Alameda	Eden Twp	68	66
Charley	38	m	c	CHIN	Inyo	Independence Twp	73	327
Turner	57	m	w	ME	San Francisco	11-Wd San Francisc	84	651
W B	34	m	w	NY	San Francisco	3-Wd San Francisco	79	312
COWL								
Thomas	61	m	w	RI	Calaveras	San Andreas P O	70	187
COWLES								
Allen B	21	m	w	MA	Santa Cruz	Watsonville	89	365
Amey D	30	f	w	CANA	Nevada	Meadow Lake Twp	75	251
Heny B	45	m	w	NH	Butte	Concow Twp	70	8
John	37	m	w	NC	Sonoma	Petaluma Twp	91	354
John	30	m	w	CA	San Diego	Poway Dist	78	481
Moses	40	m	w	MA	Amador	Drytown P O	69	421
Percy	57	f	w	NY	Placer	Auburn P O	76	382
Samuel	44	m	w	OH	San Francisco	11-Wd San Francisc	84	536
COWLEY								
D	56	m	w	IOFM	Sierra	Lincoln Twp	89	546
Edward J	53	m	w	ENGL	Sonoma	Petaluma Twp	91	341
James	34	m	w	IL	Stanislaus	Empire Twp	92	45
Robt	39	m	w	NY	Sacramento	4-Wd Sacramento	77	346
Wm A	25	m	w	ENGL	Napa	Napa Twp	75	69
COWLING								
Henry J	28	m	w	ENGL	Santa Cruz	Santa Cruz Twp	89	393
COWLSON								
Elson	34	m	w	NJ	Stanislaus	Branch Twp	92	1
COWLTER								
J B	40	m	w	NY	Amador	Fiddletown P O	69	427
COWN								
Ah	19	m	c	CHIN	Mendocino	Point Arena Twp	74	215
Cown	36	m	c	CHIN	Placer	Bath P O	76	453
Margaret	16	f	w	IL	San Francisco	San Francisco P O	83	151
Yon	51	m	c	CHIN	Sacramento	3-Wd Sacramento	77	316
COWNEY								
Ah	25	m	c	CHIN	Mendocino	Point Arena Twp	74	208
COWNOVER								
Geo	44	m	w	SC	Butte	Wyandotte Twp	70	141
COWO								
Ah	33	m	c	CHIN	Monterey	Castroville Twp	74	337
COWPER								
George	27	m	w	ENGL	Placer	Bath P O	76	436
COWSERT								
David	45	m	w	TN	Mendocino	Ukiah Twp	74	238
COWY								
Ah	40	m	c	CHIN	Nevada	Nevada Twp	75	311
COX								
---	47	m	w	ENGL	El Dorado	Coloma Twp	72	1
A F C	46	f	w	NY	Amador	Ione City P O	69	356
A G	40	m	w	VA	San Francisco	1-Wd San Francisco	79	74
Aaron	26	m	w	MA	San Joaquin	Douglas Twp	86	50
Abraham	47	m	w	NJ	Santa Cruz	Pajaro Twp	89	349
Ada W	35	f	w	OH	Mariposa	Mariposa P O	74	119
Albert T	23	m	w	NY	Sonoma	Petaluma Twp	91	320
Andrew	55	m	w	AL	San Bernardino	San Bernardino Twp	78	425
Andrew	40	m	w	ENGL	Santa Clara	Gilroy Twp	88	106
Annie	4	f	w	MO	San Francisco	11-Wd San Francisc	84	699
Benjamin	31	m	w	NY	Sonoma	Petaluma Twp	91	341
Benjamin F	32	m	w	NY	Sonoma	Petaluma Twp	91	315
Berry	61	m	b	MO	Placer	Auburn P O	76	381
C M	36	m	w	VA	Lake	Morgan Valley	73	424
C S	21	m	w	OH	San Joaquin	Tulare Twp	86	263
Camelia A	47	f	w	VA	San Luis Obispo	Morro Twp	87	283
Carter	42	m	w	VA	Placer	Bath P O	76	429
Cate	27	f	w	NY	Humboldt	Eureka Twp	72	276
Charles	55	m	w	NH	Amador	Ione City P O	69	362
Charles	55	m	w	IREL	Sacramento	Brighton Twp	77	75
Charles	24	m	w	MI	Sacramento	2-Wd Sacramento	77	254
Charles	22	m	w	ENGL	Sacramento	2-Wd Sacramento	77	237
Charles	19	m	w	NY	Sacramento	2-Wd Sacramento	77	254
Chas L	22	m	w	ME	Klamath	Trinidad Twp	73	389
Christopher	34	m	w	ENGL	San Francisco	1-Wd San Francisco	79	102
Connor	36	m	w	IREL	Nevada	Bridgeport Twp	75	121
D M	36	m	w	KY	Tehama	Paskenta Twp	92	165
D N	39	m	w	NY	Sacramento	3-Wd Sacramento	77	255
D W	31	m	w	IL	Siskiyou	Surprise Valley Tw	89	643
David	65	m	w	PA	Sacramento	1-Wd Sacramento	77	177
Ed	23	m	w	IL	San Joaquin	Douglas Twp	86	36
Edmund	35	m	w	AUSL	San Francisco	8-Wd San Francisco	82	496
Edward	67	m	w	IREL	San Francisco	8-Wd San Francisco	82	432
Edward	45	m	w	OH	Sutter	Butte Twp	92	98
Edward	38	m	w	OH	Mendocino	Ukiah Twp	74	240

© 2001 by Heritage Quest. All rights reserved.

Name	Age	S	R	B-PL	County	Locale	Roll	Pg
Edward	32	m	w	AR	Colusa	Stony Crk Twp	71	327
Edwin	35	m	w	VA	Santa Clara	1-Wd San Jose	88	236
Elisabeth	20	f	i	CA	Trinity	North Fork Twp	92	220
Elizabeth	59	f	w	IREL	Placer	Lincoln P O	76	491
Elizabeth	35	f	w	ENGL	San Francisco	6-Wd San Francisco	81	90
Elizabeth	28	f	w	IREL	Sacramento	4-Wd Sacramento	77	325
Ellen	25	f	w	IREL	Sacramento	2-Wd Sacramento	77	224
Ellen	14	f	w	CA	Sacramento	Franklin Twp	77	112
Elmer H	63	m	w	VA	Contra Costa	Martinez P O	71	394
Emiley	4	f	w	CA	Napa	Napa	75	57
Emma	32	f	w	HDAR	San Francisco	San Francisco P O	83	266
Frances	29	f	w	IREL	San Francisco	8-Wd San Francisco	82	443
Frances	14	f	w	CA	Sutter	Butte Twp	92	97
Francis	50	m	w	ENGL	Sacramento	San Joaquin Twp	77	406
Francis	50	m	w	NY	Marin	San Rafael Twp	74	35
Franklin	43	m	w	IN	Placer	Auburn P O	76	366
Franklin	36	m	w	MO	Butte	Mountain Spring Tw	70	87
Fred	42	m	w	ENGL	Sacramento	4-Wd Sacramento	77	368
Geo	45	m	w	ENGL	San Francisco	11-Wd San Francisco	84	601
Geo	44	m	w	TN	San Joaquin	Liberty Twp	86	93
Geo	42	m	w	CO	Sacramento	3-Wd Sacramento	77	300
Geo	31	m	c	CHIN	Placer	Bath P O	76	444
Geo W	37	m	w	IN	Sierra	Table Rock Twp	89	571
George	30	m	w	MO	Siskiyou	Surprise Valley Tw	89	639
George	28	m	w	ENGL	Nevada	Grass Valley Twp	75	196
George M S	30	m	w	ME	Los Angeles	Los Angeles	73	541
George W	38	m	w	KY	Los Angeles	Los Nietos Twp	73	581
H E	7	f	w	CA	Sutter	Butte Twp	92	95
Henry	45	m	w	OH	Mendocino	Calpella Twp	74	188
Henry	45	m	w	ENGL	San Francisco	San Francisco P O	80	409
Henry	29	m	w	TN	El Dorado	Diamond Springs Tw	72	35
Henry A	38	m	w	VA	Placer	Colfax P O	76	384
Henry J	28	m	w	IN	Tulare	Farmersville Twp	92	248
Henry P	45	m	w	PA	Placer	Dutch Flat P O	76	406
I R	41	m	w	OH	Sutter	Sutter Twp	92	118
Ida	8	f	w	CA	Sacramento	3-Wd Sacramento	77	278
Isreal	52	m	w	IN	Tulare	Farmersville Twp	92	247
Ivey H	42	m	w	VA	San Diego	Milquaty Dist	78	478
J	35	m	w	CANA	Solano	Vallejo	90	168
J C	53	m	w	KY	Siskiyou	Big Valley Twp	89	582
J Clement	35	m	w	PA	Los Angeles	Los Angeles	73	532
J D	32	m	w	CANA	San Joaquin	2-Wd Stockton	86	191
J E	25	m	w	NY	Alameda	Oakland	68	261
J L	62	m	w	VA	Lake	Kelsey Crk	73	402
J V R	52	m	w	PA	Sierra	Alleghany & Forest	89	534
James F	43	m	w	OH	Placer	Lincoln P O	76	485
James F	20	m	w	MO	Yolo	Cache Crk Twp	93	454
James H	34	m	w	IL	Stanislaus	Empire Twp	92	56
James H	33	m	w	IL	Merced	Snelling P O	74	251
James J	54	m	w	TN	Merced	Snelling P O	74	267
James M	38	m	w	CANA	Humboldt	Eel Rvr Twp	72	249
Jane	67	f	w	IREL	San Francisco	San Francisco P O	83	162
Jerome	40	m	w	VA	San Francisco	11-Wd San Francisc	84	556
Jesse C	42	m	w	OH	Sonoma	Analy Twp	91	246
Jno W	46	m	w	MO	Butte	Kimshew Tpw	70	83
John	50	m	w	ENGL	Amador	Fiddletown P O	69	430
John	46	m	w	ENGL	San Francisco	3-Wd San Francisco	79	330
John	43	m	w	ENGL	Contra Costa	Martinez P O	71	419
John	40	m	w	ENGL	San Francisco	San Francisco P O	83	327
John	40	m	w	OH	Mendocino	Ukiah Twp	74	239
John	40	m	w	TN	Solano	Suisun Twp	90	113
John	39	m	w	MI	San Joaquin	2-Wd Stockton	86	194
John	34	m	w	IREL	Solano	Vallejo	90	154
John	34	m	w	IL	Plumas	Washington Twp	77	56
John	24	m	w	MO	Santa Clara	1-Wd San Jose	88	228
John	24	m	w	IREL	San Joaquin	1-Wd Stockton	86	135
John	19	m	w	WI	Contra Costa	Martinez P O	71	423
John	19	m	w	IREL	Sonoma	Analy Twp	91	233
John B	33	m	w	CANA	San Diego	Julian Dist	78	469
John D	34	m	w	PA	San Joaquin	Tulare Twp	86	258
John F	45	m	w	VA	Santa Clara	1-Wd San Jose	88	247
John H	38	m	w	CANA	Amador	Volcano P O	69	387
John J	36	m	w	KY	Sonoma	Salt Point	91	381
John J	30	m	w	ENGL	San Francisco	8-Wd San Francisco	82	370
John S	29	m	w	ENGL	Napa	Napa	75	19
John S	24	m	w	NY	San Francisco	8-Wd San Francisco	82	434
John W	64	m	w	KY	Stanislaus	Empire Twp	92	62
Jordan	42	m	w	CANA	Sonoma	Russian Rvr	91	371
Joseph	55	m	w	ENGL	Sacramento	San Joaquin Twp	77	406
Joseph	45	m	w	MO	Colusa	Monroe Twp	71	311
Joseph	27	m	w	ENGL	Amador	Amador City P O	69	392
Joseph A	10	m	w	CA	Napa	Napa Twp	75	71
Joseph B	30	m	w	OH	Sonoma	Sonoma Twp	91	440
Joshua	60	m	w	VA	Sonoma	Santa Rosa	91	426
L D	54	m	w	NY	Amador	Ione City P O	69	353
Levi	71	m	w	VA	Placer	Bath P O	76	443
Levi	69	m	w	VA	Nevada	Grass Valley Twp	75	172
Levi	34	m	w	OH	Plumas	Plumas Twp	77	26
Lewis	45	m	w	NY	Santa Clara	1-Wd San Jose	88	261
Louis M	17	m	w	NJ	Santa Clara	2-Wd San Jose	88	330
M E	13	f	w	CA	Sacramento	3-Wd Sacramento	77	317
Maria	25	f	w	IREL	San Francisco	8-Wd San Francisco	82	428
Mary	66	f	w	SC	San Bernardino	San Bernardino Twp	78	432
Mary J	16	f	w	UT	Sutter	Butte Twp	92	89
Mary J	16	f	w	UT	Sutter	Butte Twp	92	94
Nellie Barnes	7	f	w	CA	Mendocino	Ukiah Twp	74	233
Newton	28	m	w	IN	Placer	Lincoln P O	76	486
Nicholas	36	m	w	ENGL	Nevada	Little York Twp	75	244
Palmer	30	m	w	CANA	San Francisco	San Francisco P O	83	210
Pat	46	m	w	IREL	Sacramento	3-Wd Sacramento	77	284
Patrick	37	m	w	IREL	San Francisco	7-Wd San Francisco	81	161
Patrick	24	m	w	IREL	San Francisco	San Francisco P O	83	141
Paul	46	m	w	OH	Placer	Lincoln P O	76	481
Peter	45	m	w	NY	Monterey	Pajaro Twp	74	370
Phineas	35	m	w	NY	Sacramento	Mississippi Twp	77	163
Phineas	32	m	w	KY	Sacramento	Natomas Twp	77	169
Phoebe	29	f	w	MO	Los Angeles	Los Angeles	73	502
Preston T	37	m	w	VA	Solano	Green Valley Twp	90	37
Richard	45	m	w	ENGL	San Francisco	6-Wd San Francisco	81	90
Richard	35	m	w	ENGL	Santa Barbara	San Buenaventura P	87	419
Richard	28	m	w	NY	San Francisco	San Francisco P O	83	273
Richard	23	m	w	MO	Sutter	Sutter Twp	92	125
Richd	27	m	w	IN	San Joaquin	2-Wd Stockton	86	206
Richd	24	m	w	ENGL	San Francisco	1-Wd San Francisco	79	102
Rose	45	f	w	IREL	San Joaquin	2-Wd Stockton	86	166
Russell	67	m	b	KY	Placer	Auburn P O	76	378
S S	32	m	w	KY	Sonoma	Vallejo Twp	91	450
S S	28	m	w	IN	Santa Clara	Gilroy Twp	88	94
Samuel	42	m	w	OH	Butte	Chico Twp	70	32
Simon B	38	m	w	IL	Los Angeles	Los Angeles Twp	73	491
Stephen	45	m	w	DENM	San Francisco	6-Wd San Francisco	81	120
Teresa	16	f	w	KS	Santa Clara	2-Wd San Jose	88	331
Theodore M	36	m	w	IL	Sacramento	San Joaquin Twp	77	399
Thomas	46	m	w	ENGL	Calaveras	Copperopolis P O	70	249
Thomas	42	m	w	IREL	San Francisco	7-Wd San Francisco	81	198
Thomas	39	m	w	ENGL	Trinity	North Fork Twp	92	220
Thomas	30	m	w	IREL	San Mateo	Half Moon Bay P O	87	404
Thomas	26	m	w	ENGL	Calaveras	Copperopolis P O	70	249
Thomas	17	m	w	MA	San Francisco	8-Wd San Francisco	82	308
Thomas O	23	m	w	IREL	San Francisco	3-Wd San Francisco	79	297
Thos	50	m	w	MO	Butte	Ophir Twp	70	112
Thos	31	m	w	IREL	San Joaquin	Douglas Twp	86	35
Thos	27	m	w	ENGL	Butte	Hamilton Twp	70	62
Tipton	30	m	w	MO	Yolo	Cache Crk Twp	93	448
V H	31	m	w	IREL	Merced	Snelling P O	74	257
Wash	19	m	w	BADE	San Joaquin	Liberty Twp	86	85
William	70	m	w	TN	Santa Clara	San Jose Twp	88	191
William	61	m	w	TN	Santa Clara	2-Wd San Jose	88	320
William	48	m	w	IREL	San Francisco	11-Wd San Francisc	84	525
William	43	m	w	OH	Santa Clara	Redwood Twp	88	124
William	36	m	w	IL	Alameda	Eden Twp	68	70
William	30	m	w	OH	Colusa	Grand Island Twp	71	309
William	28	m	w	ENGL	Calaveras	Copperopolis P O	70	248
William	23	m	w	MO	Colusa	Colusa Twp	71	284
William A	21	m	w	TN	Calaveras	Copperopolis P O	70	257
William B	50	m	w	KY	Los Angeles	Los Angeles Twp	73	481
William B	30	m	w	MO	Colusa	Butte Twp	71	270
William P	26	m	w	TN	Colusa	Stony Crk Twp	71	334
William W	37	m	w	IN	Contra Costa	Martinez P O	71	394
Wm	70	m	w	KY	Fresno	Kings Rvr P O	72	204
Wm	39	m	w	VA	Butte	Chico Twp	70	56
Wm	24	m	w	CANA	San Francisco	8-Wd San Francisco	82	314
Wm E	30	m	w	NY	Sonoma	Petaluma Twp	91	324
Wm H	53	m	w	PA	Butte	Chico Twp	70	26
Wm J	41	m	w	PA	Sutter	Vernon Twp	92	136
Wm J	23	m	w	MO	San Luis Obispo	Santa Rosa Twp	87	325
COXE								
Henry E	36	m	w	ME	San Francisco	1-Wd San Francisco	79	91
James	36	m	w	IREL	San Francisco	1-Wd San Francisco	79	62
Margret E	32	f	w	NY	San Francisco	1-Wd San Francisco	79	111
Wm	26	m	w	IREL	San Francisco	1-Wd San Francisco	79	65
COXHERD								
D C	46	m	w	ENGL	Alameda	Oakland	68	192
COY								
Abner	27	m	w	IREL	Solano	Denverton Twp	90	23
Ah	42	m	c	CHIN	Mariposa	Mariposa P O	74	93
Ah	40	m	c	CHIN	El Dorado	Coloma Twp	72	12
Ah	40	m	c	CHIN	Placer	Lincoln P O	76	483
Ah	39	m	c	CHIN	Amador	Ione City P O	69	362
Ah	38	m	c	CHIN	Yuba	Rose Bar Twp	93	656
Ah	37	m	c	CHIN	Nevada	Washington Twp	75	343
Ah	36	m	c	CHIN	Nevada	Washington Twp	75	347
Ah	35	m	c	CHIN	Kern	Bakersfield P O	73	357
Ah	35	m	c	CHIN	San Mateo	San Mateo P O	87	351
Ah	32	m	c	CHIN	Amador	Drytown P O	69	422
Ah	31	m	c	CHIN	Yuba	Marysville	93	628
Ah	30	m	c	CHIN	San Francisco	8-Wd San Francisco	82	359
Ah	30	m	c	CHIN	Sacramento	1-Wd Sacramento	77	200
Ah	29	m	c	CHIN	Calaveras	San Andreas P O	70	176
Ah	29	m	c	CHIN	Butte	Hamilton Twp	70	68
Ah	29	m	c	CHIN	Yuba	Marysville	93	587
Ah	29	m	c	CHIN	Butte	Wyandotte Twp	70	142
Ah	28	m	c	CHIN	Amador	Drytown P O	69	419
Ah	27	m	c	CHIN	Nevada	Bloomfield Twp	75	96
Ah	25	m	c	CHIN	Sacramento	Sutter Twp	77	388
Ah	25	m	c	CHIN	Siskiyou	Yreka	89	654
Ah	22	m	c	CHIN	San Francisco	3-Wd San Francisco	79	306
Ah	22	m	c	CHIN	Plumas	Goodwin Twp	77	3
Ah	21	m	c	CHIN	Nevada	Bloomfield Twp	75	96
Ah	20	f	c	CHIN	Butte	Hamilton Twp	70	74
Ah	19	m	c	CHIN	Butte	Bidwell Twp	70	5
Ah	19	m	c	CHIN	Yuba	Marysville	93	603
Ah	18	m	c	CHIN	San Francisco	11-Wd San Francisc	84	666
Ah	17	m	c	CHIN	Butte	Wyandotte Twp	70	147

© 2001 by Heritage Quest. All rights reserved.

Series M593

Name	Age	S	R	B-PL	County	Locale	Roll	Pg
Ah	16	m	c	CHIN	Alameda	Oakland	68	138
Ah	14	m	c	CHIN	Placer	Auburn P O	76	367
Ah	12	m	c	CHIN	Yuba	Marysville	93	597
Ashley	41	m	w	OH	Solano	Montezuma Twp	90	65
Benj B	34	m	w	MA	El Dorado	Lake Valley Twp	72	64
Benjamin	34	m	w	IL	Nevada	Meadow Lake Twp	75	265
Burns I	36	m	w	CANA	Sacramento	San Joaquin Twp	77	402
Frank	36	m	w	NY	Alameda	Alameda	68	14
Fy	55	m	c	CHIN	Santa Clara	1-Wd San Jose	88	254
Gay	31	m	c	CHIN	Solano	Vacaville Twp	90	130
Horace	35	m	w	KY	Marin	San Rafael	74	51
Horace	30	m	w	NY	San Francisco	11-Wd San Francisc	84	653
J M	27	m	w	IREL	San Francisco	3-Wd San Francisco	79	319
Long	22	m	c	CHIN	Butte	Concow Twp	70	11
Manuel	34	m	w	PORT	Marin	San Rafael	74	58
Mary A	18	f	w	WI	Amador	Drytown P O	69	416
Min	30	m	c	CHIN	Yuba	Marysville	93	631
Pee	21	m	c	CHIN	Yuba	Marysville	93	632
Peter	36	m	w	IREL	San Francisco	1-Wd San Francisco	79	132
Rosanna	35	f	w	IREL	San Francisco	1-Wd San Francisco	79	38
Sam	25	m	c	CHIN	Sacramento	3-Wd Sacramento	77	316
See	40	m	c	CHIN	Amador	Drytown P O	69	422
Tong	47	m	c	CHIN	Butte	Concow Twp	70	11
COYADO								
Jose B	34	m	w	CHIL	Calaveras	San Andreas P O	70	182
COYAN								
John	22	m	w	PA	Sutter	Yuba Twp	92	150
W D	42	m	w	OH	Napa	Napa Twp	75	65
COYD								
John	27	m	w	MI	Alameda	Oakland	68	263
COYE								
Albert	21	m	w	IREL	Solano	Vacaville Twp	90	123
David	30	m	w	MA	San Francisco	8-Wd San Francisco	82	353
Jos	37	m	w	IREL	Sacramento	1-Wd Sacramento	77	189
Robert	29	m	w	MA	San Francisco	San Francisco P O	80	335
Young	40	m	c	CHIN	Placer	Dutch Flat P O	76	408
COYEN								
Aaron	23	m	w	POLA	San Francisco	3-Wd San Francisco	79	295
COYENS								
Saml	40	m	b	VA	Calaveras	Copperopolis P O	70	241
COYER								
George	24	m	w	NY	Nevada	Meadow Lake Twp	75	268
COYINE								
Rosanna	15	f	w	CA	Yuba	Marysville	93	598
COYL								
Cornelius	48	m	w	CANA	Sonoma	Petaluma Twp	91	320
James	45	m	w	IREL	Alameda	Oakland	68	154
COYLE								
Alexander	21	m	w	CANA	Mendocino	Point Arena Twp	74	206
Andrew	35	m	w	IREL	Solano	Silveyville Twp	90	73
Andrew	27	m	w	IREL	Solano	Silveyville Twp	90	89
Arthur	23	m	w	CANA	Mendocino	Point Arena Twp	74	206
Barnard	50	m	w	IREL	Sierra	Gibson Twp	89	538
Barney	40	m	w	IREL	Contra Costa	Martinez P O	71	369
Bridget	30	f	w	IREL	San Francisco	San Francisco P O	83	274
Bridget	12	f	w	NY	Santa Barbara	Santa Barbara P O	87	452
Charles	16	m	w	ME	Marin	Bolinas Twp	74	1
Chas	30	m	w	IREL	San Francisco	8-Wd San Francisco	82	348
David	51	m	w	TN	Solano	Vacaville Twp	90	124
Edward	40	m	w	IREL	Sacramento	Center Twp	77	84
Francis M	33	m	w	IL	Yuba	New York Twp	93	640
Frank	40	m	w	IREL	Sierra	Gibson Twp	89	538
Frank	30	m	w	NY	San Francisco	7-Wd San Francisco	81	287
George	38	m	w	ME	Placer	Summit P O	76	496
Georgiana	25	f	w	NY	San Francisco	8-Wd San Francisco	82	425
Henry	31	m	w	IREL	San Francisco	San Francisco P O	83	241
Hugh	50	m	w	IREL	San Francisco	11-Wd San Francisc	84	511
Hugh	36	m	w	IREL	Tuolumne	Columbia P O	93	349
James	50	m	w	IREL	San Francisco	San Francisco P O	83	378
James	42	m	w	IREL	San Francisco	8-Wd San Francisco	82	400
James	27	m	w	IREL	San Francisco	7-Wd San Francisco	81	228
John	51	m	w	IREL	San Francisco	San Francisco P O	83	329
John	50	m	w	IREL	San Francisco	San Francisco P O	83	398
John	38	m	w	IREL	Santa Barbara	Santa Barbara P O	87	487
John	35	m	w	IREL	San Francisco	7-Wd San Francisco	81	190
John	30	m	w	IREL	San Joaquin	2-Wd Stockton	86	170
John	30	m	w	IREL	Klamath	Trinidad Twp	73	393
Kate	22	f	w	IREL	San Francisco	8-Wd San Francisco	82	471
Katy	23	f	w	SCOT	Santa Clara	Gilroy Twp	88	76
Kitty	15	f	w	NY	Santa Barbara	Santa Barbara P O	87	474
Luke	40	m	w	IREL	Calaveras	Copperopolis P O	70	250
Maggie	30	f	w	IREL	San Francisco	8-Wd San Francisco	82	379
Margrett	23	f	w	IREL	Napa	Napa	75	52
Mary	59	f	w	ME	San Francisco	7-Wd San Francisco	81	285
Mary	35	f	w	IREL	San Francisco	San Francisco P O	83	162
Mary	30	f	w	PA	San Francisco	8-Wd San Francisco	82	494
Mary	24	f	w	IREL	San Francisco	11-Wd San Francisc	84	539
Mary	18	f	w	MA	San Francisco	8-Wd San Francisco	82	476
Mary	12	f	w	CA	Santa Barbara	Santa Barbara P O	87	502
Michael	30	m	w	IREL	Butte	Ophir Twp	70	95
Michial	29	m	w	IREL	Sonoma	Petaluma Twp	91	337
Owen	60	m	w	IREL	San Francisco	7-Wd San Francisco	81	182
Patrick	45	m	w	IREL	San Francisco	San Francisco P O	83	287
Patrick	29	m	w	IREL	San Francisco	7-Wd San Francisco	81	196
Patrick	25	m	w	IREL	Santa Clara	Santa Clara Twp	88	178
Peter	40	m	w	IREL	Santa Barbara	Santa Barbara P O	87	494
Peter	20	m	w	IREL	Contra Costa	Martinez P O	71	369
R S	49	m	w	KY	Merced	Snelling P O	74	275
Reuben S	49	m	w	KY	Stanislaus	Empire Twp	92	55
Samuel	23	m	w	IREL	Sacramento	2-Wd Sacramento	77	246
Sarah	24	f	w	IREL	San Francisco	8-Wd San Francisco	82	378
William	47	m	w	KY	Merced	Snelling P O	74	277
William	27	m	w	MA	Sonoma	Analy Twp	91	233
COYLES								
John	42	m	w	TN	Solano	Vacaville Twp	90	124
COYN								
Jack	40	m	w	IREL	Mariposa	Mariposa P O	74	114
Ramon	38	m	w	FRAN	San Francisco	San Francisco P O	83	334
COYNE								
Denis	28	m	w	IREL	San Francisco	1-Wd San Francisco	79	132
John	28	m	w	IREL	San Francisco	San Francisco P O	83	296
Lewis	60	m	w	FRAN	Stanislaus	Branch Twp	92	7
Michael	43	m	w	IREL	Santa Clara	Santa Clara Twp	88	168
Pat	39	m	w	IREL	Sacramento	1-Wd Sacramento	77	180
Patrick	28	m	w	IREL	Klamath	Camp Gaston	73	373
Patrick	25	m	w	IREL	San Francisco	San Francisco P O	85	758
Peter	48	m	w	IREL	Mariposa	Mariposa P O	74	130
Thomas	29	m	w	IREL	San Francisco	San Francisco P O	83	402
COYNER								
Eliza	40	f	w	ENGL	San Francisco	6-Wd San Francisco	81	103
James B	23	m	w	VA	Amador	Volcano P O	69	372
COYNES								
Ines	18	f	w	OH	San Joaquin	Castoria Twp	86	6
COYT								
Henry	22	m	w	PA	Solano	Denverton Twp	90	25
COZ								
Sam	30	m	c	CHIN	Nevada	Nevada Twp	75	311
COZART								
William	51	m	w	TN	Alameda	Brooklyn	68	21
COZINE								
Albert	41	m	w	KY	Contra Costa	Martinez P O	71	398
Charity	73	f	w	KY	Contra Costa	Martinez P O	71	398
William	51	m	w	KY	Contra Costa	Martinez P O	71	398
COZNO								
Argo	48	m	w	PRUS	Sacramento	1-Wd Sacramento	77	195
COZONA								
Hannah	33	f	w	IREL	San Francisco	San Francisco P O	83	351
COZZENS								
Edward	11	m	w	CA	Stanislaus	Emory Twp	92	16
George	32	m	w	MO	Santa Clara	San Jose Twp	88	181
Henry B	40	m	b	LA	Siskiyou	Scott Valley Twp	89	618
William W	51	m	w	MA	Nevada	Little York Twp	75	238
COZZINS								
John H	48	m	w	NJ	Placer	Roseville P O	76	349
Thos	40	m	w	ENGL	San Joaquin	Dent Twp	86	16
CRAB								
Stephen	36	m	w	IN	Tuolumne	Columbia P O	93	347
William	34	m	w	CANA	Alameda	Oakland	68	147
CRABB								
Alexr	44	m	w	SCOT	San Francisco	San Francisco P O	83	62
Charles	40	m	w	NY	Santa Cruz	Soquel Twp	89	443
D	17	m	w	HI	Sacramento	3-Wd Sacramento	77	276
Edward	40	m	w	ENGL	Sacramento	Center Twp	77	84
H W	40	m	w	OH	Napa	Yountville Twp	75	78
James M	46	m	w	NY	Santa Barbara	Santa Maria P O	87	514
Jessica	34	f	w	SCOT	San Francisco	11-Wd San Francisc	84	467
John	46	m	w	ENGL	Marin	San Rafael Twp	74	46
Lewis	18	m	w	VT	San Mateo	Pescadero P O	87	415
Lucius	14	m	w	WI	San Mateo	Pescadero P O	87	414
Sylvanus	42	m	w	NY	Santa Cruz	Soquel Twp	89	443
Thos	50	m	w	PRUS	San Francisco	San Francisco P O	83	83
CRABER								
A S	29	m	w	MI	Sacramento	3-Wd Sacramento	77	308
CRABTREE								
Abner	35	m	w	ME	Tuolumne	Sonora P O	93	321
Allen	35	m	w	IL	Amador	Ione City P O	69	360
Benjam	59	m	w	NY	Sutter	Nicolaus Twp	92	108
Benjamin	60	m	w	IL	Sacramento	2-Wd Sacramento	77	235
C	21	m	w	MO	Lake	Lower Lake	73	429
Edward	24	m	w	CANA	San Francisco	7-Wd San Francisco	81	199
Ezra J	27	m	w	TX	San Luis Obispo	Santa Rosa Twp	87	323
Francis A	44	m	w	VA	El Dorado	Cosumnes Twp	72	16
Frank	32	m	w	ME	Humboldt	Eureka Twp	72	266
Harriet	45	f	w	CANA	San Francisco	1-Wd San Francisco	79	123
J	46	m	w	VA	Lake	Lower Lake	73	415
J	44	m	w	MO	San Joaquin	Elliott Twp	86	71
James	40	m	w	IL	Tulare	Tule Rvr Twp	92	271
James	27	m	w	MO	San Diego	Milquaty Dist	78	477
John	75	m	w	TN	Tulare	Tule Rvr Twp	92	271
John	27	m	w	MI	San Joaquin	Castoria Twp	86	9
John F	32	m	w	TX	Tulare	Tule Rvr Twp	92	261
M B	40	m	w	CANA	Tuolumne	Chinese Camp P O	93	384
May	4	f	i	CA	Humboldt	South Fork Twp	72	302
T	50	m	w	VA	Lake	Coyote Valley	73	401
William M	30	m	w	TX	Tulare	Tule Rvr Twp	92	261
CRACK								
Peter	39	m	w	DENM	San Francisco	San Francisco P O	83	130
CRACKBON								
Chas	37	m	w	NY	San Francisco	11-Wd San Francisc	84	533
Frank	36	m	w	NY	Sacramento	2-Wd Sacramento	77	245
Jos	45	m	w	MA	Sacramento	3-Wd Sacramento	77	305
CRACKEN								
Joseph	22	m	w	NY	Marin	San Rafael Twp	74	37

© 2001 by Heritage Quest. All rights reserved.

Name	Age	S	R	B-PL	County	Locale	Series M593 Roll	Pg
CRACKOW								
John	36	m	w	GERM	Mono	Bridgeport P O	74	284
CRADDOC								
Chas D	22	m	w	MD	Butte	Chico Twp	70	36
CRADDOCK								
Anna	28	f	w	IREL	San Francisco	San Francisco P O	83	193
C W	40	m	w	NY	Nevada	Meadow Lake Twp	75	248
Chas F	32	m	w	KY	San Francisco	San Francisco P O	83	27
E	39	m	w	VA	Napa	Yountville Twp	75	81
H J	3	m	w	CA	Napa	Napa Twp	75	59
J H	32	m	w	KY	Sutter	Yuba Twp	92	146
James	35	m	w	IREL	Sonoma	Analy Twp	91	233
John	37	m	w	MO	Shasta	Shasta P O	89	462
John E	5	m	w	CA	Napa	Napa	75	25
Maria	25	f	w	IREL	San Francisco	San Francisco P O	83	113
Rolla	34	m	w	TN	Santa Cruz	Pajaro Twp	89	347
S J	8	m	w	CA	Napa	Napa	75	25
Sam	25	m	c	CHIN	Sutter	Yuba Twp	92	146
Silas	44	m	w	VA	Santa Cruz	Pajaro Twp	89	347
CRADE								
Henry	41	m	w	CHIL	Tuolumne	Chinese Camp P O	93	383
CRADEN								
Pat	46	m	w	IREL	Sacramento	1-Wd Sacramento	77	180
CRADES								
Jacob	39	m	w	IL	Sacramento	Franklin Twp	77	112
CRADLEY								
Christ	35	m	w	SWIT	Sutter	Butte Twp	92	100
Martin	45	m	w	SWIT	Santa Clara	San Jose Twp	88	202
CRADOCK								
John	46	m	w	ENGL	El Dorado	Placerville Twp	72	94
Richard	25	m	w	ENGL	El Dorado	Placerville Twp	72	94
William	24	m	w	IREL	San Francisco	San Francisco P O	83	399
CRADOLOCK								
E J	50	f	w	IN	Alameda	Oakland	68	204
CRADON								
Anna	25	f	w	IREL	San Francisco	11-Wd San Francisc	84	539
Samuel	35	m	w	IREL	San Francisco	8-Wd San Francisco	82	463
CRADWICK								
John	40	m	w	ENGL	Napa	Yountville Twp	75	85
CRADY								
John	38	m	w	HDAR	San Francisco	11-Wd San Francisc	84	533
CRAEY								
James	44	m	w	OH	Napa	Napa	75	22
CRAFF								
Peter	32	m	w	PRUS	Sutter	Vernon Twp	92	137
CRAFFORD								
John	31	m	w	OH	Sonoma	Petaluma Twp	91	353
CRAFT								
August	45	m	w	PRUS	Colusa	Colusa	71	300
Benjamin	50	m	w	NY	Santa Clara	Santa Clara Twp	88	169
Frank	27	m	w	PRUS	Napa	Napa	75	7
George	66	m	w	GERM	Tulare	Visalia	92	297
George F	40	m	w	DC	Tulare	Visalia	92	291
Harry	53	m	w	PRUS	San Joaquin	2-Wd Stockton	86	200
Henry	65	m	w	PRUS	San Francisco	11-Wd San Francisc	84	509
Homer	45	m	w	WI	Alameda	Eden Twp	68	68
Justin	79	m	w	MA	Humboldt	Eel Rvr Twp	72	247
Levi F	51	m	w	PA	Yolo	Cache Crk Twp	93	432
Robert	30	m	w	PRUS	San Francisco	1-Wd San Francisco	79	60
CRAFTE								
Henry	64	m	w	FRAN	Alameda	Brooklyn Twp	68	49
CRAFTON								
George	60	m	w	IREL	Trinity	Weaverville Pct	92	222
CRAFTS								
Edward	3	m	w	CA	San Francisco	San Francisco P O	85	799
George	50	m	w	MA	San Francisco	San Francisco P O	80	539
John H	41	m	w	MA	Yuba	New York Twp	93	640
M	13	m	w	GA	Solano	Benicia	90	20
Moses	33	m	w	NY	San Francisco	5-Wd San Francisco	81	21
Myron	53	m	w	MA	San Bernardino	San Bernardino Twp	78	450
CRAGAN								
Peter	60	m	w	IREL	Yuba	Rose Bar Twp	93	663
CRAGAR								
Jac	31	m	w	NJ	Santa Clara	Burnett Twp	88	38
CRAGE								
I	42	m	w	CANA	Sierra	Lincoln Twp	89	545
J	35	m	w	OH	Sierra	Lincoln Twp	89	545
CRAGEN								
James	42	m	w	IREL	Nevada	Rough & Ready Twp	75	328
CRAGER								
Jacob	59	m	w	OH	Alpine	Monitor P O	69	317
CRAGG								
Abel	24	m	w	NY	Stanislaus	Emory Twp	92	26
CRAGIE								
D	26	m	w	MI	Lassen	Milford Twp	73	438
CRAGIN								
Elizabeth	55	f	w	IREL	San Francisco	San Francisco P O	83	190
Enma J	9	f	w	CA	El Dorado	Placerville Twp	72	105
Sylvester	43	m	w	VT	San Diego	San Diego	78	497
William S	25	m	w	MA	San Francisco	6-Wd San Francisco	81	117
CRAGO								
Jacob	50	m	w	IL	Santa Clara	Redwood Twp	88	118
CRAGS								
Jas	26	m	w	ENGL	Fresno	Millerton P O	72	165
CRAHAM								
J G	29	m	w	CANA	Humboldt	South Fork Twp	72	302
John F	30	m	w	DENM	Sonoma	Salt Point	91	392
CRAHER								
Manly	25	m	w	CA	Sacramento	Dry Crk Twp	77	99
CRAIDLEBON								
James	35	m	w	PRUS	Kern	Havilah P O	73	351
CRAIG								
Alexander	45	m	w	CANA	Santa Cruz	Watsonville	89	367
Alexr	36	m	w	SCOT	San Francisco	San Francisco P O	83	122
Andrew	34	m	w	OH	Santa Cruz	Watsonville	89	369
Ann	48	f	w	KY	Merced	Snelling P O	74	261
Archibald	45	m	w	IREL	Sonoma	Bodega Twp	91	264
Charles	53	m	w	DENM	Santa Clara	2-Wd San Jose	88	314
Charles	30	m	w	PRUS	San Francisco	San Francisco P O	83	79
Charles	15	m	w	CA	Solano	Maine Prairie Twp	90	52
Chas S	42	m	w	OH	Klamath	South Fork Twp	73	383
Daniel B	52	m	w	NY	El Dorado	Georgetown Twp	72	43
David	40	m	w	OH	Yuba	Bullards Bar P O	93	547
Dennis	47	m	w	IREL	San Francisco	San Francisco P O	83	4
Edward A	24	m	w	CANA	San Francisco	8-Wd San Francisco	82	394
Edward L	32	m	w	KY	Placer	Auburn P O	76	368
Elias	70	m	w	MA	San Joaquin	Oneal Twp	86	109
Ella	17	f	w	IL	Butte	Ophir Twp	70	105
Frederick	43	m	w	NY	Kern	Kernville P O	73	368
George	30	m	w	MI	Monterey	San Juan Twp	74	403
George	26	m	w	ENGL	El Dorado	Lake Valley Twp	72	64
Hugh	41	m	w	CANA	Alpine	Markleeville P O	69	312
Hugh	31	m	w	IREL	San Francisco	San Francisco P O	83	314
J W	25	m	w	AR	San Joaquin	Castoria Twp	86	3
Jackson	40	m	w	OH	Santa Clara	Fremont Twp	88	47
James	68	m	w	KY	San Francisco	San Francisco P O	80	349
James	43	m	w	SCOT	Tuolumne	Sonora P O	93	326
James	37	m	w	ENGL	Placer	Bath P O	76	461
James	36	m	w	SCOT	San Mateo	Schoolhouse Statio	87	342
James	36	m	w	IREL	San Francisco	San Francisco P O	83	281
James	30	m	w	CANA	Mendocino	Navarro & Big Rvr	74	177
James	29	m	w	IREL	Los Angeles	San Gabriel Twp	73	594
James	20	m	w	MI	Yolo	Cache Crk Twp	93	440
Joel	40	m	w	IREL	Sonoma	Petaluma Twp	91	344
John	46	m	w	FRAN	San Francisco	San Francisco P O	80	415
John	45	m	w	IREL	Calaveras	San Andreas P O	70	156
John	43	m	w	OH	San Joaquin	Elkhorn Twp	86	55
John	43	m	w	SCOT	San Francisco	San Francisco P O	83	285
John	40	m	w	IREL	San Francisco	11-Wd San Francisc	84	654
John	40	m	w	IREL	El Dorado	White Oak Twp	72	144
John	38	m	w	PA	Solano	Denverton Twp	90	23
John	37	m	w	IREL	San Francisco	11-Wd San Francisc	84	600
John	35	m	w	SCOT	Kern	Kernville P O	73	368
John	24	m	w	DENM	Alameda	Eden Twp	68	84
John A	39	m	w	VA	Nevada	Bridgeport Twp	75	123
John W	44	m	w	AL	Sonoma	Petaluma Twp	91	356
Joseph	32	m	w	CANA	Alameda	Hayward	68	77
Julia	30	f	w	IREL	San Francisco	2-Wd San Francisco	79	209
Julia	19	f	b	PA	San Francisco	6-Wd San Francisco	81	153
Louisa	5	f	w	CA	San Francisco	11-Wd San Francisc	84	598
Louisa	29	f	w	IREL	San Francisco	6-Wd San Francisco	81	155
M	58	m	w	OH	Lassen	Susanville Twp	73	440
Mary	60	f	w	OH	Nevada	Nevada Twp	75	294
Michael	40	m	w	IREL	San Francisco	11-Wd San Francisc	84	652
Michael	27	m	w	IREL	Yuba	Rose Bar Twp	93	662
Micheal	37	m	w	IREL	San Francisco	11-Wd San Francisc	84	467
Olliver W	61	m	w	NH	Sonoma	Sonoma Twp	91	437
P M	40	m	w	ME	Alameda	Oakland	68	205
Peter	53	m	w	SCOT	San Francisco	8-Wd San Francisco	82	441
Peter A	40	m	w	VT	Mono	Bridgeport P O	74	282
Quincy	38	m	w	AL	San Joaquin	3-Wd Stockton	86	216
R R	55	m	w	KY	Nevada	Nevada Twp	75	305
Robert	67	m	w	IREL	San Francisco	San Francisco P O	83	399
Robert	31	m	w	CANA	Santa Clara	Redwood Twp	88	131
Robert	24	m	w	NY	Sacramento	Franklin Twp	77	110
Robt	60	m	w	NY	Siskiyou	Scott Rvr Twp	89	603
Robt	50	m	w	NY	San Joaquin	Oneal Twp	86	103
Samuel	42	m	w	WV	Santa Cruz	Soquel Twp	89	447
Silas	42	m	b	KY	Siskiyou	Yreka	89	654
Thomas	30	m	w	NY	San Francisco	3-Wd San Francisco	79	293
Thomas H	32	m	w	PA	San Francisco	3-Wd San Francisco	79	329
Timothy	40	m	w	IREL	Monterey	Pajaro Twp	74	376
Tracy	11	m	w	CA	Humboldt	Arcata Twp	72	232
W C	22	m	w	MS	Alameda	Oakland	68	257
William	6	m	w	CA	Santa Clara	San Jose Twp	88	180
William	43	m	w	AL	Stanislaus	Empire Twp	92	35
William	43	m	w	SCOT	San Francisco	6-Wd San Francisco	81	118
Wm	40	m	w	IREL	Sacramento	4-Wd Sacramento	77	322
Wm	31	m	w	ME	Sacramento	1-Wd Sacramento	77	190
Wm D	41	m	w	NJ	Nevada	Nevada Twp	75	275
CRAIGE								
Homer A	23	m	w	IA	Butte	Ophir Twp	70	96
Nehelous	35	m	w	AUST	Trinity	Lewiston Pct	92	213
CRAIGER								
M	35	m	w	NJ	Solano	Vallejo	90	171
CRAIGG								
Frederick	40	m	w	NY	Yolo	Putah Twp	93	518
Robert	30	m	w	SCOT	Contra Costa	Martinez P O	71	427
CRAIGH								
Michael	46	m	w	IREL	San Francisco	San Francisco P O	83	363
CRAIGLAN								
M	35	f	w	IREL	Alameda	Oakland	68	227
CRAIGS								
John	50	m	w	IREL	San Francisco	11-Wd San Francisc	84	432

© 2001 by Heritage Quest. All rights reserved.

California 1870 Census

Name	Age	S	R	B-PL	County	Locale	Series M593 Roll	Pg
CRAILE								
G	65	m	w	KY	Amador	Ione City P O	69	363
CRAILEY								
Patrick	35	m	w	IREL	Solano	Denverton Twp	90	27
CRAILY								
Martin	31	m	w	IREL	Sonoma	Petaluma Twp	91	325
CRAIMER								
Henry	25	m	w	CA	Merced	Snelling P O	74	262
CRAIN								
Catherine	34	f	w	IREL	Alameda	Brooklyn Twp	68	55
D S	40	m	w	ME	Merced	Snelling P O	74	252
Elisha	53	m	w	NH	San Francisco	7-Wd San Francisco	81	277
Fred	37	m	w	PRUS	San Joaquin	1-Wd Stockton	86	123
George	19	m	w	ME	Colusa	Monroe Twp	71	314
James S	43	m	w	OH	Butte	Hamilton Twp	70	65
John	40	m	w	OH	Solano	Rio Vista Twp	90	71
William	52	m	w	OH	Klamath	Trinidad Twp	73	389
CRAINE								
Wm C	33	m	w	OH	Sonoma	Mendocino Twp	91	308
CRAKER								
Judson	25	m	w	WI	San Francisco	San Francisco P O	83	85
CRALL								
I S	43	m	w	PA	Nevada	Bridgeport Twp	75	107
James	25	m	w	KY	Sacramento	Brighton Twp	77	71
Samuel N	26	m	w	PA	Nevada	Bridgeport Twp	75	108
CRAM								
Ashley A	22	m	w	IN	San Francisco	1-Wd San Francisco	79	104
C C	49	m	w	KY	Sutter	Sutter Twp	92	120
Charles	56	m	w	ENGL	Mendocino	Albion & Big Rvr T	74	166
Dora B	8	f	w	CA	El Dorado	White Oak Twp	72	142
Elizabeth	71	f	w	ME	San Francisco	San Francisco P O	85	847
Frank	19	m	w	CA	Sutter	Yuba Twp	92	145
Goodsell	48	m	w	IA	San Bernardino	San Bernardino Twp	78	435
J T	40	m	w	IREL	Solano	Vallejo	90	166
John	26	m	w	SCOT	San Francisco	8-Wd San Francisco	82	448
Joseph	29	m	w	IREL	San Francisco	1-Wd San Francisco	79	128
Judith	30	f	w	MO	El Dorado	White Oak Twp	72	142
Perry	40	m	w	NY	Siskiyou	Yreka Twp	89	669
Sidny	55	m	w	NH	Yuba	Long Bar Twp	93	564
Sylvester K	39	m	w	NH	El Dorado	White Oak Twp	72	142
William	42	m	w	ME	San Francisco	7-Wd San Francisco	81	200
CRAMBO								
Arsa	26	m	w	ITAL	San Francisco	11-Wd San Francisc	84	709
CRAMEAN								
Otella	6	f	w	CA	Los Angeles	Los Angeles	73	509
CRAMER								
---	25	m	w	PA	Yuba	Marysville	93	617
A D	30	m	w	NY	Solano	Vallejo	90	209
Abraham	52	m	w	NY	Sonoma	Petaluma Twp	91	349
Adolf	35	m	w	PRUS	San Francisco	3-Wd San Francisco	79	324
Albert	45	m	w	PA	Placer	Gold Run Twp	76	396
Andrew	36	m	w	CANA	Butte	Chico Twp	70	33
Anna	19	f	w	BAVA	Santa Clara	Santa Clara Twp	88	155
Annie	15	f	w	IREL	San Francisco	11-Wd San Francisc	84	568
C A	35	m	w	PRUS	Amador	Drytown P O	69	420
Charles	28	m	w	HANO	Sonoma	Petaluma Twp	91	318
Charles	24	m	w	SAXO	Santa Barbara	San Buenaventura P	87	434
Chas L	37	m	w	CANA	San Francisco	5-Wd San Francisco	81	1
David	70	m	w	PA	Nevada	Bridgeport Twp	75	105
Edon	60	m	w	VA	Plumas	Quartz Twp	77	42
Ellen	10M	f	w	CA	San Francisco	San Francisco P O	83	13
Francis	45	m	w	PRUS	San Francisco	3-Wd San Francisco	79	300
Frank	39	m	w	HOLL	Nevada	Washington Twp	75	341
Frank	22	m	w	IA	Plumas	Quartz Twp	77	41
H P	33	m	w	SAXO	San Francisco	San Francisco P O	83	143
Henry	44	m	w	HANO	San Francisco	3-Wd San Francisco	79	301
Henry	36	m	w	GERM	Tuolumne	Sonora P O	93	305
Jacob	39	m	w	NY	Tulare	Tule Rvr Twp	92	263
Jacob	38	m	w	PA	Nevada	Nevada Twp	75	320
James	27	m	w	GERM	San Francisco	8-Wd San Francisco	82	375
John	60	m	w	FRAN	Tehama	Cottonwood Twp	92	161
John	36	m	w	BADE	San Francisco	San Francisco P O	83	39
John	26	m	w	SWIT	Stanislaus	Empire Twp	92	52
John	25	m	w	NY	Stanislaus	Empire Twp	92	45
John	24	m	w	PRUS	Santa Clara	1-Wd San Jose	88	254
John D	37	m	w	NY	San Francisco	San Francisco P O	85	731
Jos	24	m	w	BADE	Santa Clara	Gilroy Twp	88	81
Joseph	21	m	w	PRUS	Monterey	Monterey	74	366
Joseph C	22	m	w	PA	Butte	Chico Twp	70	14
L	29	m	w	GERM	Yuba	Marysville	93	605
Louis	37	m	w	OH	Yolo	Cache Crk Twp	93	454
Philopena	42	f	w	GERM	Contra Costa	Martinez P O	71	403
Samuel	60	m	w	VA	Los Angeles	El Monte Twp	73	451
Silas	40	m	w	NY	San Francisco	8-Wd San Francisco	82	321
Sylvester	48	m	w	IL	Yolo	Grafton Twp	93	500
Thomas J	53	m	w	VA	Los Angeles	El Monte Twp	73	450
Virginia	47	f	w	PRUS	San Francisco	8-Wd San Francisco	82	354
W	23	m	w	PA	San Francisco	8-Wd San Francisco	82	370
William	21	m	w	IN	Santa Clara	2-Wd San Jose	88	282
Wm	30	m	w	WURT	Sierra	Sears Twp	89	556
CRAMFORD								
Thos	36	m	w	IREL	Merced	Snelling P O	74	261
W R	45	m	w	MO	San Joaquin	Liberty Twp	86	87
CRAMI								
William	45	m	w	IOFM	San Francisco	1-Wd San Francisco	79	109
CRAMLET								
Chas	40	m	w	MD	San Joaquin	3-Wd Stockton	86	240

Name	Age	S	R	B-PL	County	Locale	Series M593 Roll	Pg
CRAMM								
J A	54	m	w	NY	San Joaquin	2-Wd Stockton	86	164
CRAMMER								
Julias	38	m	w	PRUS	Monterey	Salinas Twp	74	307
CRAMP								
Martha	38	f	w	ENGL	San Francisco	2-Wd San Francisco	79	188
William	24	m	w	ENGL	Solano	Suisun Twp	90	98
CRAMPEY								
Wm	30	m	w	IREL	Yuba	Rose Bar Twp	93	662
CRAMTON								
Nelson	22	m	w	IL	Yolo	Cache Crk Twp	93	445
CRAN								
Stephen	24	m	w	NY	San Francisco	San Francisco P O	85	873
CRANA								
Catharine	32	f	w	IREL	Sacramento	2-Wd Sacramento	77	244
CRANAGE								
William H	46	m	w	ENGL	Placer	Bath P O	76	434
CRANAM								
John	45	m	w	IREL	Stanislaus	Emory Twp	92	18
CRANBY								
Robert	33	m	w	HDAR	Colusa	Colusa Twp	71	283
CRANDAL								
H	45	m	w	NY	Alameda	Oakland	68	235
Samuel	50	m	w	NY	Siskiyou	Surprise Valley Tw	89	638
CRANDALL								
Alice	10	f	w	CA	Nevada	Grass Valley Twp	75	230
Annie	65	f	w	OH	Santa Cruz	Pajaro Twp	89	340
B P	39	m	w	NY	Butte	Mountain Spring Tw	70	89
Chas	30	m	w	OH	Tehama	Red Bluff	92	175
Chas	28	m	w	PA	San Francisco	1-Wd San Francisco	79	65
Cyrenius	45	m	w	NY	El Dorado	Diamond Springs Tw	72	33
David A	34	m	w	OH	San Diego	San Diego	78	499
George H	42	m	w	RI	Nevada	Grass Valley Twp	75	178
Gills G	31	m	w	NY	Colusa	Colusa	71	295
Jared B	58	m	w	MA	Santa Clara	Santa Clara Twp	88	144
Jas P	17	m	w	NY	San Francisco	San Francisco P O	83	47
John R	62	m	w	MA	Placer	Auburn P O	76	366
Jones	37	m	w	OH	Contra Costa	Martinez P O	71	444
Joseph	28	m	w	PORT	Alameda	Washington Twp	68	295
Lucian	38	m	w	NY	San Bernardino	San Bernardino Twp	78	430
Marcus	64	m	w	NY	San Diego	San Diego	78	499
Mathew	28	m	w	IL	San Bernardino	San Bernardino Twp	78	435
May	35	f	w	CT	San Francisco	8-Wd San Francisco	82	369
Oliver L	47	m	w	NY	Santa Clara	San Jose Twp	88	195
Peter	56	m	w	NY	Sacramento	4-Wd Sacramento	77	367
Sarah	73	f	w	NY	San Bernardino	San Bernardino Twp	78	453
Simon	74	m	w	NY	San Bernardino	San Bernardino Twp	78	453
T P	36	m	w	NY	Nevada	Eureka Twp	75	135
William G	28	m	w	GA	Santa Clara	Santa Clara Twp	88	144
CRANDELL								
Benj	27	m	w	RI	Marin	Point Reyes Twp	74	22
C	28	m	w	WALE	San Joaquin	2-Wd Stockton	86	187
Charles	40	m	w	NY	San Francisco	6-Wd San Francisco	81	89
I	24	m	w	NY	San Francisco	3-Wd San Francisco	79	323
N R	31	f	w	UNKN	San Joaquin	2-Wd Stockton	86	172
Oliver	41	m	w	NJ	San Francisco	5-Wd San Francisco	81	23
Orman	54	m	w	NY	San Francisco	7-Wd San Francisco	81	167
S	50	m	w	NY	Del Norte	Crescent	71	466
Thomas	29	m	w	RI	Marin	Point Reyes Twp	74	22
Wm	40	m	w	NY	San Joaquin	3-Wd Stockton	86	217
CRANDLE								
J B	26	m	w	MI	Los Angeles	Los Angeles	73	571
Jno	15	m	w	CA	Sonoma	Mendocino Twp	91	296
John	56	m	w	ME	Colusa	Grand Island Twp	71	307
John	13	m	w	CA	Sonoma	Mendocino Twp	91	299
Joseph	28	m	w	GERM	San Francisco	8-Wd San Francisco	82	307
William O L	41	m	w	SC	Alameda	Alvarado	68	304
CRANDRES								
F	44	m	w	PRUS	Sierra	Forest Twp	89	532
CRANE								
A N	38	m	w	OH	Nevada	Bridgeport Twp	75	104
Aaron A	22	m	w	IN	San Francisco	8-Wd San Francisco	82	331
Albert E	36	m	w	NY	San Francisco	6-Wd San Francisco	81	117
Amos	25	m	w	CANA	San Diego	San Diego	78	511
Andrew E	35	m	w	NJ	Alameda	Washington Twp	68	274
Andrew J	38	m	w	MO	Amador	Fiddletown P O	69	439
Ann	40	f	w	IREL	San Mateo	San Mateo P O	87	356
B G	27	m	w	NY	San Francisco	San Francisco P O	85	779
Bella	9	f	w	CA	San Francisco	11-Wd San Francisc	84	618
Caleb	45	m	w	NY	Amador	Ione City P O	69	352
Caleb	44	m	w	VA	Amador	Ione City P O	69	357
Carrie	28	f	w	OH	Santa Clara	Gilroy Twp	88	79
Charles	28	m	w	KY	El Dorado	Greenwood Twp	72	57
Chas	25	m	w	ENGL	Sacramento	3-Wd Sacramento	77	316
Conecpain	40	f	w	CA	Monterey	San Juan Twp	74	412
Donald	30	m	w	ENGL	Yuba	Marysville	93	615
Edward A	45	m	w	NJ	Placer	Bath P O	76	421
Emerson	48	m	w	NY	Alameda	Eden Twp	68	84
Frank	23	m	w	MO	San Joaquin	Castoria Twp	86	7
Fred	35	m	w	SWIT	Stanislaus	Empire Twp	92	44
Geo L	55	m	w	OH	Sonoma	Russian Rvr	91	369
Gertrude	50	f	w	NY	San Diego	San Diego	78	505
Henry	12	m	w	CA	Marin	Bolinas Twp	74	5
Henry A	37	m	w	NY	San Francisco	8-Wd San Francisco	82	378
Henry M	37	m	w	NY	San Francisco	8-Wd San Francisco	82	472
Hezekiah G	42	m	w	NY	Santa Barbara	Santa Barbara P O	87	477
J K	33	m	w	IREL	Santa Clara	Gilroy Twp	88	69

© 2001 by Heritage Quest. All rights reserved.

Name	Age	S	R	B-PL	County	Locale	Series M593 Roll	Pg
James	64	m	w	MA	Marin	San Rafael	74	54
James	60	m	w	US	Nevada	Grass Valley Twp	75	194
James A	28	m	w	IL	San Francisco	1-Wd San Francisco	79	53
Jas E	41	m	w	KY	Santa Barbara	San Buenaventura P	87	425
Jeff L	31	m	w	OH	Santa Barbara	San Buenaventura P	87	444
Jeremiah	50	m	w	IREL	San Francisco	7-Wd San Francisco	81	260
Joel	38	m	w	KY	Sonoma	Santa Rosa	91	394
John	39	m	w	MA	Alameda	Oakland	68	171
John	38	m	w	CHIL	Tuolumne	Chinese Camp P O	93	383
John	25	m	w	IREL	Santa Cruz	Soquel Twp	89	437
John D	17	m	w	MA	Marin	San Rafael Twp	74	43
Josiah H	49	m	w	OH	Sonoma	Petaluma Twp	91	320
L P	47	m	w	PA	Sutter	Butte Twp	92	94
Lemual T	51	m	w	ME	Yuba	New York Twp	93	640
Levi	44	m	w	NY	El Dorado	Georgetown Twp	72	36
Lewis	19	m	w	NY	San Joaquin	2-Wd Stockton	86	164
Martin	40	m	w	IREL	San Francisco	7-Wd San Francisco	81	157
Martin	30	m	w	IREL	Sonoma	Santa Rosa	91	405
Mary	52	f	w	IREL	San Joaquin	2-Wd Stockton	86	197
Mary	26	f	w	AUSL	San Francisco	5-Wd San Francisco	81	7
Mathew T	55	m	w	NY	Los Angeles	Los Angeles Twp	73	470
Nathan	53	m	w	US	San Francisco	11-Wd San Francisc	84	619
Owen	47	m	w	IREL	San Francisco	1-Wd San Francisco	79	34
Owen	33	m	w	IREL	San Francisco	San Francisco P O	83	392
Richd	40	m	w	KY	Sonoma	Santa Rosa	91	397
Robert	30	m	w	NH	San Mateo	Pescadero P O	87	414
Robert	27	m	w	PA	Yuba	Marysville	93	582
Robert C	24	m	w	MO	Calaveras	Copperopolis P O	70	256
Robt	47	m	w	KY	Sonoma	Santa Rosa	91	399
Samuel	44	m	w	NJ	San Francisco	San Francisco P O	83	353
Samuel L	64	m	w	KY	Yolo	Cottonwood Twp	93	474
Simon	35	m	w	NY	Sacramento	Brighton Twp	77	75
Theodosia	8	f	w	CA	Tulare	Visalia Twp	92	287
Thomas	30	m	w	IREL	Yolo	Putah Twp	93	511
Thos J	52	m	w	KY	Sonoma	Santa Rosa	91	394
W H	31	m	w	NY	Lassen	Susanville Twp	73	442
Walter	28	m	w	IREL	Nevada	Meadow Lake Twp	75	250
William	58	m	w	MA	Marin	Bolinas Twp	74	6
William	35	m	w	IREL	San Francisco	San Francisco P O	83	252
William	31	m	w	IL	Inyo	Cerro Gordo Twp	73	321
William	17	m	w	MA	Marin	Sausalito Twp	74	71
William M	53	m	w	ME	Yuba	New York Twp	93	640
William T	55	m	w	NY	Santa Clara	Fremont Twp	88	46
CRANER								
Adolph	45	m	w	PRUS	San Francisco	San Francisco P O	83	371
Alexander	32	m	w	PRUS	El Dorado	Diamond Springs Tw	72	31
Benjamin	53	m	w	PRUS	Calaveras	San Andreas P O	70	209
Chas	45	m	w	WURT	San Francisco	8-Wd San Francisco	82	356
Henry H	30	m	w	PRUS	Yolo	Buckeye Twp	93	415
Phillip	50	m	w	HCAS	Amador	Sutter Crk P O	69	410
Samuel	24	m	w	PRUS	Solano	Rio Vista Twp	90	60
Wm L	40	m	w	PRUS	Placer	Rocklin Twp	76	465
CRANERT								
Augt	39	m	w	PRUS	San Francisco	8-Wd San Francisco	82	354
CRANES								
James S	24	m	w	CANA	Nevada	Grass Valley Twp	75	186
CRANFIELD								
William	30	m	w	IREL	San Francisco	San Francisco P O	83	302
CRANGLE								
Alfred	45	m	w	ENGL	Santa Barbara	Santa Barbara P O	87	455
Wm	32	m	w	NY	San Francisco	San Francisco P O	83	79
CRANK								
Ruener	14	f	w	OR	Humboldt	Mattole Twp	72	284
Sarah	33	f	w	IL	Humboldt	Mattole Twp	72	288
Suzan	55	f	w	KY	Humboldt	Mattole Twp	72	286
W D	9	m	w	OR	Humboldt	Mattole Twp	72	287
William	23	m	w	MO	Humboldt	Mattole Twp	72	286
CRANLEY								
Patrick	28	m	w	IREL	Colusa	Colusa Twp	71	282
Wm	34	m	w	IREL	San Francisco	San Francisco P O	85	871
CRANLY								
Jeremiah	36	m	w	MO	Sutter	Nicolaus Twp	92	115
CRANNA								
William	29	m	w	NY	San Francisco	6-Wd San Francisco	81	120
CRANNEY								
James	54	m	w	IREL	San Francisco	San Francisco P O	85	869
CRANNIS								
Phillip	52	m	w	ENGL	Amador	Jackson P O	69	346
CRANNY								
Ada	15	f	w	IA	Stanislaus	Empire Twp	92	38
CRANOR								
C M	50	m	w	PA	San Joaquin	2-Wd Stockton	86	210
CRANS								
Charles	46	m	w	PRUS	Nevada	Grass Valley Twp	75	169
John	35	m	w	PA	Sacramento	Georgianna Twp	77	127
CRANSHAW								
Louis	31	m	w	IA	Mono	Bridgeport P O	74	284
CRANSON								
A B	35	m	w	IL	San Joaquin	1-Wd Stockton	86	123
William	30	m	w	PRUS	Stanislaus	Empire Twp	92	47
CRANSTON								
David	30	m	w	SCOT	Nevada	Grass Valley Twp	75	157
Josephine	29	f	w	MEXI	San Francisco	San Francisco P O	80	486
Wm	27	m	w	MO	Nevada	Washington Twp	75	340
CRANSTUN								
Albert	39	m	w	SCOT	Santa Barbara	Santa Barbara P O	87	474
CRANTON								
Thos	39	m	w	IREL	Sacramento	1-Wd Sacramento	77	179
CRANTS								
Charles	47	m	w	PRUS	Nevada	Grass Valley Twp	75	188
CRANTZ								
Elizabeth	22	f	w	HANO	Santa Clara	1-Wd San Jose	88	255
CRANZ								
Theodore	47	m	w	PRUS	San Francisco	8-Wd San Francisco	82	408
CRANZA								
Chas	34	m	w	MECK	San Francisco	1-Wd San Francisco	79	87
CRAPEAU								
John	44	m	w	FRAN	San Francisco	San Francisco P O	80	420
CRAPS								
Alonzo	24	m	w	IL	Sutter	Butte Twp	92	100
CRARY								
James	23	m	w	ENGL	Santa Clara	1-Wd San Jose	88	255
Leroy	20	m	w	IL	Yuba	Rose Bar Twp	93	662
Milton W	40	m	w	OH	Placer	Auburn P O	76	365
R L	51	m	w	NY	Yuba	Rose Bar Twp	93	662
Stephen H	41	m	w	MA	Siskiyou	Hamburg Twp	89	596
CRASADA								
Jesus	66	m	w	MEXI	Santa Clara	Burnett Twp	88	34
CRASBY								
Ada L	15	f	w	CA	Placer	Rocklin Twp	76	467
B F	37	m	w	MA	Tuolumne	Columbia P O	93	357
John	45	m	w	ENGL	Tuolumne	Sonora P O	93	327
CRASCROW								
Peter	38	m	w	CHIL	Mariposa	Mariposa P O	74	129
CRASE								
Eli	24	m	w	OH	Santa Clara	Redwood Twp	88	117
Henry	33	m	w	ENGL	Nevada	Grass Valley Twp	75	181
James	36	m	w	ENGL	Nevada	Meadow Lake Twp	75	258
John	45	m	w	ENGL	Nevada	Grass Valley Twp	75	211
Mary A	47	f	w	ENGL	Nevada	Grass Valley Twp	75	182
Richard	26	m	w	ENGL	Nevada	Grass Valley Twp	75	202
Richard	25	m	w	ENGL	Nevada	Grass Valley Twp	75	145
William	43	m	w	MO	El Dorado	Mud Springs Twp	72	87
William J	43	m	w	ENGL	Nevada	Grass Valley Twp	75	159
CRASEY								
P	30	m	w	IREL	San Joaquin	Tulare Twp	86	255
CRASS								
John	36	m	w	HOLL	Tuolumne	Columbia P O	93	340
CRASTON								
Thomas J	42	m	w	OH	Yolo	Cottonwood Twp	93	472
CRATES								
Sylvester	19	m	w	CA	Mendocino	Point Arena Twp	74	214
CRATTAN								
G W	15	m	w	NY	Solano	Vallejo	90	195
CRATTY								
John	30	m	w	OH	Siskiyou	Surprise Valley Tw	89	641
Mary	28	f	w	IREL	Solano	Vallejo	90	144
CRATZ								
Augustus	45	m	w	PRUS	Santa Clara	Fremont Twp	88	62
CRAUFORD								
David P	23	m	w	CANA	San Luis Obispo	Santa Rosa Twp	87	329
CRAUNTOR								
Christin	23	m	w	DENM	El Dorado	Salmon Falls Twp	72	132
CRAUS								
A	46	m	w	PRUS	San Joaquin	2-Wd Stockton	86	173
CRAUSE								
Rudalph	32	m	w	PRUS	San Joaquin	2-Wd Stockton	86	164
Wilhelm G F	46	m	w	PRUS	San Francisco	San Francisco P O	83	56
CRAUSTER								
Wm	43	m	w	OH	San Joaquin	Castoria Twp	86	15
CRAVEN								
Ann	38	f	w	IREL	San Francisco	San Francisco P O	83	376
Briget	35	f	w	IREL	San Francisco	7-Wd San Francisco	81	181
H S	24	m	w	NY	Solano	Vallejo	90	188
J	36	m	w	NY	Sacramento	3-Wd Sacramento	77	271
John	27	m	w	IREL	Santa Clara	Milpitas Twp	88	109
M	12	m	w	NY	Solano	Benicia	90	21
Michael	36	m	w	IREL	Sacramento	Sutter Twp	77	381
Phillip	50	m	w	IREL	San Francisco	7-Wd San Francisco	81	174
T G	60	m	w	DC	Solano	Vallejo	90	188
Thomas	53	m	w	PA	Plumas	Washington Twp	77	52
CRAVENS								
Jessie P	73	m	w	KY	Plumas	Plumas Twp	77	28
Joshua D	30	m	w	MO	Fresno	Kings Rvr P O	72	206
Robt O	42	m	w	VA	Sacramento	4-Wd Sacramento	77	353
CRAVER								
Catharine	22	f	w	LA	Calaveras	Copperopolis P O	70	256
Daniel	40	m	w	SC	Butte	Mountain Spring Tw	70	87
CRAVIN								
Peter	35	m	w	IREL	San Francisco	San Francisco P O	85	823
CRAW								
Adherbal	65	m	w	NY	Sacramento	Sutter Twp	77	383
Charles J	35	m	w	MO	San Bernardino	San Bernardino Twp	78	414
Eugene	25	m	w	NY	Monterey	San Juan Twp	74	396
George A	26	m	w	IA	San Bernardino	San Bernardino Twp	78	446
Hiram	33	m	w	MI	San Bernardino	San Bernardino Twp	78	445
James	32	m	w	AL	Mendocino	Navarro & Big Rvr	74	167
Jane A	60	f	w	NY	San Bernardino	San Bernardino Twp	78	419
John P	55	m	w	NY	Santa Clara	2-Wd San Jose	88	281
W H	30	m	w	KY	San Joaquin	Castoria Twp	86	2
CRAWAY								
Patrick	33	m	w	IREL	Santa Clara	Santa Clara Twp	88	167

© 2001 by Heritage Quest. All rights reserved.

Name	Age	S	R	B-PL	County	Locale	Roll	Pg
						Series M593		
CRAWBACK								
Rose	38	f	w	GERM	San Joaquin	2-Wd Stockton	86	171
CRAWE								
John	43	m	w	MD	Alameda	Oakland	68	130
CRAWELL								
H L	60	m	w	MA	Tuolumne	Columbia P O	93	357
Henry	37	m	w	ENGL	Marin	San Rafael Twp	74	39
CRAWFORD								
A K	40	m	w	CANA	Santa Clara	Gilroy Twp	88	76
Adam	38	m	w	PA	Sonoma	Analy Twp	91	234
Adam	25	m	w	IREL	Napa	Napa Twp	75	29
Andrew	37	m	w	IREL	San Francisco	7-Wd San Francisco	81	222
Andrew J	33	m	w	TN	El Dorado	Mud Springs Twp	72	72
Arthur	33	m	w	IREL	San Francisco	San Francisco P O	83	27
C	24	m	w	IREL	San Joaquin	2-Wd Stockton	86	193
Caroline	50	f	w	ENGL	Calaveras	San Andreas P O	70	218
Charles	27	m	w	ENGL	Kern	Linns Valley P O	73	343
Chas H	43	m	w	KY	Sonoma	Santa Rosa	91	412
David	41	m	w	NY	Monterey	Pajaro Twp	74	369
David	21	m	w	SCOT	Siskiyou	Yreka	89	653
E L	37	m	w	ME	El Dorado	Georgetown Twp	72	41
Edward	40	m	w	NY	San Francisco	San Francisco P O	83	213
Edward	35	m	w	MI	Stanislaus	Empire Twp	92	41
Edward	30	m	w	IREL	San Francisco	6-Wd San Francisco	81	106
Elizabeth	73	f	w	NC	Mendocino	Ukiah Twp	74	240
Elizabeth	49	f	w	KY	Santa Cruz	Santa Cruz	89	409
Ellen	28	f	w	OH	San Diego	Poway Dist	78	481
Ellen	26	f	w	MO	San Diego	San Diego	78	496
F M	32	m	w	NY	Napa	Napa	75	50
Frances	23	m	w	MO	Contra Costa	Martinez P O	71	405
Francis	22	m	w	NY	Santa Clara	Fremont Twp	88	61
Frederck	39	m	w	NY	Yolo	Putah Twp	93	515
Fredk	31	m	w	ENGL	San Francisco	San Francisco P O	83	132
G W	48	m	w	ME	Tuolumne	Sonora P O	93	317
Geo	46	m	w	ENGL	Santa Clara	Burnett Twp	88	32
Geo	33	m	w	IREL	San Francisco	11-Wd San Francisc	84	658
Geo O	47	m	w	ME	Calaveras	Copperopolis P O	70	228
Geo R	34	m	w	NY	Nevada	Nevada Twp	75	284
George B	39	m	w	CANA	Santa Cruz	Pajaro Twp	89	352
H	26	m	w	IREL	San Joaquin	2-Wd Stockton	86	193
Harriet	18	f	b	MS	Los Angeles	Los Nietos Twp	73	575
Henry	35	m	w	NY	San Francisco	8-Wd San Francisco	82	487
Henry A	20	m	w	MO	Stanislaus	Washington Twp	92	87
Hiram K	38	m	w	OH	Santa Clara	San Jose Twp	88	181
Hugh	46	m	w	TN	Stanislaus	Branch Twp	92	1
J	41	m	w	NY	Sierra	Eureka Twp	89	525
J	21	m	w	CANA	Yuba	Marysville Twp	93	569
J B	42	m	w	TN	Sacramento	4-Wd Sacramento	77	350
J H	19	m	w	MO	Lake	Upper Lake	73	413
J T	58	m	w	SCOT	Calaveras	Copperopolis P O	70	228
J W	45	m	w	CANA	Alameda	Oakland	68	248
James	50	m	w	IREL	Calaveras	Copperopolis P O	70	244
James	46	m	w	NY	Alameda	Washington Twp	68	280
James	40	m	w	VT	El Dorado	Salmon Falls Twp	72	129
James	37	m	w	MO	Placer	Auburn P O	76	365
James	34	m	w	NY	San Diego	Fort Yuma Dist	78	464
James	33	m	w	VA	Alameda	Oakland	68	173
James	32	m	w	NY	Los Angeles	Los Angeles	73	535
James	30	m	w	IREL	Alameda	Oakland	68	132
James	26	m	w	OH	Plumas	Plumas Twp	77	30
James	24	m	w	MO	Sutter	Butte Twp	92	101
James	24	m	w	OH	Solano	Vacaville Twp	90	135
James S	32	m	w	NY	Los Angeles	Los Angeles	73	567
Jane	32	f	w	IREL	San Francisco	11-Wd San Francisc	84	463
Jeane	23	f	w	CANA	Alameda	Alameda	68	5
Jno	45	m	w	VA	Sierra	Table Rock Twp	89	579
Jno	30	m	w	NY	Butte	Chico Twp	70	26
Jno H	52	m	w	IREL	Sacramento	3-Wd Sacramento	77	308
John	38	m	w	WI	San Joaquin	Elkhorn Twp	86	59
John	33	m	w	IN	Mendocino	Ukiah Twp	74	240
John	31	m	w	OH	Sonoma	Bodega Twp	91	248
John	30	m	w	KY	Los Angeles	Los Nietos Twp	73	576
John	25	m	w	IL	San Joaquin	Oneal Twp	86	118
John	20	m	w	NY	Santa Clara	Fremont Twp	88	41
John A	44	m	w	CANA	Plumas	Plumas Twp	77	30
John F	44	m	w	PA	Sacramento	4-Wd Sacramento	77	336
John M	41	m	w	MO	Solano	Vacaville Twp	90	135
John O	30	m	w	TN	Los Angeles	Los Nietos Twp	73	574
Levi	40	m	w	NY	Stanislaus	Empire Twp	92	41
Luke	28	m	w	MA	Humboldt	Eureka Twp	72	282
M A	64	f	w	IREL	Solano	Vallejo	90	176
M D	49	m	w	NC	Los Angeles	Los Nietos Twp	73	574
M J	38	m	w	NY	Yuba	Rose Bar Twp	93	652
Margaret	45	f	w	IREL	San Francisco	8-Wd San Francisco	82	388
Mary	64	f	w	IREL	Klamath	Orleans Twp	73	379
Mathi	64	m	w	SC	Yuba	Slate Range Bar Tw	93	669
Michl G	37	m	w	IREL	Santa Barbara	Santa Barbara P O	87	482
R C	42	m	w	ME	Siskiyou	Callahan P O	89	625
Rebecca	7	f	w	CA	San Joaquin	Liberty Twp	86	94
Richard	22	m	w	GA	San Francisco	San Francisco P O	83	403
Robert	40	m	w	IREL	San Francisco	3-Wd San Francisco	79	297
Robert	38	m	w	SCOT	San Francisco	San Francisco P O	83	226
Robert	23	m	w	IREL	San Francisco	7-Wd San Francisco	81	168
Robt	45	m	w	IREL	San Diego	Warners Rancho Dis	78	529
S F	44	m	w	CANA	Monterey	San Juan Twp	74	414
Samuel	28	m	w	IL	Solano	Vacaville Twp	90	136
Samuel B	46	m	w	PA	Nevada	Washington Twp	75	339
Sarah A W	35	f	w	VA	Placer	Bath P O	76	452
T P	45	m	w	TN	San Joaquin	Castoria Twp	86	5
Thomas	24	m	w	IREL	San Francisco	11-Wd San Francisc	84	474
Thos	40	m	w	CANA	Sonoma	Bodega Twp	91	258
Thos	40	m	w	SCOT	San Joaquin	1-Wd Stockton	86	125
Thos	40	m	w	PA	San Joaquin	1-Wd Stockton	86	139
Thos	34	m	w	GA	Mariposa	Mariposa P O	74	131
Thos M	45	m	w	OH	Shasta	Horsetown P O	89	502
Travers	52	m	w	SCOT	Contra Costa	Martinez P O	71	418
Tutton	41	m	w	TN	Trinity	Weaverville Pct	92	225
W B	31	m	w	VA	Nevada	Meadow Lake Twp	75	268
W D	41	m	w	OH	Tuolumne	Big Oak Flat P O	93	403
W W	37	m	w	OH	Lassen	Milford Twp	73	438
Walter	37	m	w	ENGL	Alameda	Oakland	68	130
William	70	m	w	MI	Nevada	Nevada Twp	75	279
William	40	m	w	VA	Plumas	Quartz Twp	77	40
William	21	m	w	OH	Kern	Havilah P O	73	350
Wm	42	m	w	PA	El Dorado	Coloma Twp	72	5
Wm	40	m	w	SCOT	Plumas	Mineral Twp	77	23
Wm	40	m	w	IL	San Joaquin	Liberty Twp	86	96
Wm	35	m	w	IREL	Humboldt	Pacific Twp	72	290
Wm	30	m	w	IREL	Del Norte	Crescent	71	467
Wm	29	m	w	IREL	Sonoma	Santa Rosa	91	399
Wm	27	m	w	IREL	San Francisco	1-Wd San Francisco	79	115
Wm H	34	m	w	NY	Nevada	Grass Valley Twp	75	224
Wood	39	m	w	OH	Lake	Big Valley	73	397
CRAWHALL								
John	37	m	w	ENGL	San Francisco	San Francisco P O	80	406
CRAWLEY								
Blanch	9	f	w	CA	Los Angeles	Los Angeles	73	547
D S	37	m	w	IL	San Joaquin	Liberty Twp	86	90
Dennis	28	m	w	IREL	Nevada	Washington Twp	75	342
F R	30	m	w	IREL	Sacramento	4-Wd Sacramento	77	376
Geo W	47	m	w	MA	San Francisco	San Francisco P O	83	130
George	26	m	w	IREL	Solano	Vacaville Twp	90	117
J	9	f	w	CA	Alameda	Oakland	68	138
J	56	m	w	IREL	Alameda	Oakland	68	235
James	35	m	w	IREL	Monterey	San Antonio Twp	74	315
John	30	m	w	MA	San Francisco	San Francisco P O	83	128
M J	20	m	b	MD	Sutter	Nicolaus Twp	92	115
Mary	22	f	w	IREL	San Joaquin	2-Wd Stockton	86	198
Thomas	26	m	w	IREL	Monterey	Castroville Twp	74	337
Timothy	30	m	w	IREL	San Francisco	San Francisco P O	83	81
CRAWMER								
Thos J	55	m	w	KY	Fresno	Millerton P O	72	183
CRAWSBEE								
Wm	41	m	w	ENGL	San Luis Obispo	Salinas Twp	87	295
CRAWSON								
C	22	m	w	MI	San Joaquin	1-Wd Stockton	86	138
CRAY								
Cormick	36	m	w	IREL	Alameda	Brooklyn	68	29
Ella	17	f	w	CA	Colusa	Butte Twp	71	270
Francis	40	m	w	MEXI	Calaveras	Copperopolis P O	70	261
Geo	50	m	w	OH	Santa Clara	Almaden Twp	88	18
Isaac	21	m	w	MO	San Joaquin	Tulare Twp	86	262
Thomas	28	m	w	SC	Inyo	Cerro Gordo Twp	73	319
CRAYCROFT								
George	28	m	w	CANA	Fresno	Millerton P O	72	158
CRAYTON								
Isabella	55	f	w	CANA	Alameda	Alameda	68	8
Robert	35	m	w	NH	San Francisco	6-Wd San Francisco	81	145
Wm	29	m	w	IREL	San Francisco	San Francisco P O	85	773
CRAYTOR								
Robert	32	m	w	ENGL	Amador	Amador City P O	69	392
CREADON								
Dennis	30	m	w	IREL	Santa Clara	2-Wd San Jose	88	316
Patrick	32	m	w	IREL	San Francisco	11-Wd San Francisc	84	583
CREADY								
Frank	30	m	w	FRAN	Contra Costa	San Pablo Twp	71	365
CREAGAN								
James	40	m	w	IREL	Nevada	Bloomfield Twp	75	97
CREAGER								
William	23	m	w	PRUS	San Francisco	7-Wd San Francisco	81	199
CREAL								
Michael	40	m	w	OH	Calaveras	San Andreas P O	70	203
CREAMER								
Aaron	45	m	w	PA	San Francisco	8-Wd San Francisco	82	330
Allen S	27	m	w	ME	Placer	Lincoln P O	76	493
Caspar	40	m	w	PRUS	San Francisco	San Francisco P O	83	388
James	40	m	w	IREL	San Francisco	San Francisco P O	80	373
John	43	m	w	BELG	San Francisco	11-Wd San Francisc	84	598
John	30	m	w	IREL	San Francisco	11-Wd San Francisc	84	558
Mary	27	f	w	IREL	San Francisco	11-Wd San Francisc	84	511
Thomas	38	m	w	HANO	Santa Cruz	Santa Cruz	89	430
Tim	32	m	w	IREL	Santa Barbara	Santa Barbara P O	87	501
William	44	m	w	HCAS	Placer	Auburn P O	76	360
William	32	m	w	IREL	San Francisco	3-Wd San Francisco	79	295
CREAN								
Wm	56	m	w	IREL	Butte	Chico Twp	70	25
CREANER								
C	14	m	w	CA	Solano	Benicia	90	21
CREANN								
Charles	21	m	w	SWIT	San Francisco	2-Wd San Francisco	79	175
CREARY								
A	59	m	w	NY	Amador	Ione City P O	69	364
James L	23	m	w	ENGL	Santa Clara	2-Wd San Jose	88	329
Jas Chas	37	m	w	ME	San Francisco	San Francisco P O	83	26

© 2001 by Heritage Quest. All rights reserved.

Series M593

Name	Age	S	R	B-PL	County	Locale	Roll	Pg
Martin	38	m	w	IREL	Alameda	Oakland	68	258
CREASER								
James	30	m	w	CANA	Alameda	Oakland	68	207
CREASON								
Thos A	19	m	w	MO	San Luis Obispo	Santa Rosa Twp	87	325
CREASOR								
Sterling P	28	m	w	MO	Yolo	Grafton Twp	93	498
CREAY								
Thomas	69	m	w	IREL	El Dorado	White Oak Twp	72	143
CREAYO								
Joseph	35	m	w	TX	Napa	Napa	75	56
CREBER								
Walter	42	m	w	ENGL	San Francisco	2-Wd San Francisco	79	219
CRECCARD								
Thomas	38	m	w	IREL	Trinity	Douglas	92	233
CRECH								
W H	23	m	w	NY	Merced	Snelling P O	74	253
CREDE								
Frederick	40	m	w	HCAS	Santa Clara	2-Wd San Jose	88	324
CREDEN								
Fannie	22	f	w	IREL	San Francisco	3-Wd San Francisco	79	315
CREDIFORD								
Daniel	25	m	w	ME	Santa Cruz	Santa Cruz Twp	89	395
CREDON								
Cornelius	32	m	w	IREL	San Francisco	1-Wd San Francisco	79	98
CREECH								
L L	38	m	w	MO	San Joaquin	3-Wd Stockton	86	236
CREED								
Daniel	40	m	w	IREL	Yolo	Cache Crk Twp	93	442
Daniel	13	m	w	ENGL	San Francisco	San Francisco P O	83	237
Demnis	28	m	w	IREL	Colusa	Spring Valley Twp	71	341
Dennis	40	m	w	IREL	Sacramento	2-Wd Sacramento	77	240
James	29	m	w	IREL	San Francisco	San Francisco P O	83	382
John	28	m	w	OH	San Francisco	San Francisco P O	80	408
CREEDEN								
Hannah	23	f	w	IREL	San Francisco	San Francisco P O	83	110
James	21	m	w	IREL	San Francisco	11-Wd San Francisc	84	435
Jno	40	m	w	IREL	Sacramento	3-Wd Sacramento	77	317
CREEDON								
Danl	27	m	w	IREL	San Francisco	1-Wd San Francisco	79	131
Jeremiah	27	m	w	IREL	Placer	Rocklin Twp	76	467
Jerry	28	m	w	IREL	Placer	Rocklin Twp	76	468
William	40	m	w	IREL	San Francisco	3-Wd San Francisco	79	298
CREEKMER								
Oscar	19	m	w	VA	San Diego	San Diego	78	483
CREELEY								
Isaac	42	m	w	IREL	Napa	Napa Twp	75	66
CREEN								
John	30	m	w	IREL	San Joaquin	Elkhorn Twp	86	55
CREENAN								
Thos	25	m	w	MA	San Francisco	7-Wd San Francisco	81	241
CREETER								
Margrate	27	f	w	IREL	San Francisco	7-Wd San Francisco	81	166
CREGAN								
Ellen	79	f	w	IREL	San Francisco	San Francisco P O	83	330
James	45	m	w	OH	Nevada	Bloomfield Twp	75	95
Martin	45	m	w	IREL	San Francisco	San Francisco P O	83	7
Mary J	36	f	w	MA	San Francisco	San Francisco P O	83	68
Micheal	35	m	w	IREL	San Francisco	7-Wd San Francisco	81	184
Peter	47	m	w	IREL	San Francisco	San Francisco P O	83	330
CREGAR								
W V	36	m	w	OH	Solano	Benicia	90	12
CREGIER								
William	37	m	w	PRUS	Contra Costa	San Pablo Twp	71	366
CREGO								
Henry M	49	m	w	NY	Calaveras	Copperopolis P O	70	256
CREIG								
C W	21	m	w	PA	Trinity	Junction City Pct	92	209
Jas	37	m	w	IN	Sierra	Eureka Twp	89	523
Joseph	48	m	w	ENGL	Trinity	Weaverville Pct	92	224
CREIGH								
Henry	9	m	w	CA	Solano	Vallejo	90	158
John	69	m	w	PA	San Francisco	11-Wd San Francisc	84	609
Samuel	39	m	w	PA	San Francisco	11-Wd San Francisc	84	537
CREIGHAN								
James D	33	m	w	IREL	Mariposa	Mariposa P O	74	92
CREIGHTON								
C	22	f	w	NY	San Francisco	7-Wd San Francisco	81	184
C W	36	m	w	IL	Sutter	Butte Twp	92	92
Cornelius	33	m	w	IREL	San Francisco	1-Wd San Francisco	79	94
David	55	m	w	IREL	Solano	Vacaville Twp	90	124
Fred	50	m	w	OH	San Francisco	11-Wd San Francisc	84	634
Frederick	45	m	w	ENGL	Santa Clara	1-Wd San Jose	88	227
Fredk	39	m	w	IREL	San Francisco	1-Wd San Francisco	79	125
George	20	m	w	CA	Humboldt	Bald Hills	72	238
H	47	m	w	IREL	San Joaquin	Elkhorn Twp	86	57
Henry	50	m	w	ME	San Joaquin	Elkhorn Twp	86	54
James	70	m	w	SCOT	San Francisco	8-Wd San Francisco	82	299
James	47	m	w	ME	El Dorado	Placerville Twp	72	102
James	36	m	w	OH	Calaveras	San Andreas P O	70	153
James	22	m	w	CANA	San Francisco	San Francisco P O	83	332
Jas	19	m	w	ENGL	Humboldt	Eureka Twp	72	279
John	28	m	w	IL	Humboldt	Bald Hills	72	238
John	22	m	w	IREL	San Francisco	3-Wd San Francisco	79	294
John L	21	m	w	CANA	San Francisco	8-Wd San Francisco	82	299
Kenedy	27	m	w	PA	Solano	Vallejo	90	163
Michl	45	m	w	IREL	San Francisco	1-Wd San Francisco	79	44
Pat	40	m	w	IREL	San Francisco	2-Wd San Francisco	79	255
Patk	38	m	w	IREL	San Francisco	1-Wd San Francisco	79	58
Patrick	34	m	w	IREL	San Francisco	San Francisco P O	83	362
Terrence	48	m	w	IREL	San Francisco	7-Wd San Francisco	81	243
Thomas	52	m	w	PA	Humboldt	Bucksport Twp	72	244
Thos	33	m	w	PA	Sonoma	Santa Rosa	91	403
Thos	18	m	w	CA	San Francisco	11-Wd San Francisc	84	663
W J	22	m	w	PA	Amador	Amador City P O	69	392
William	31	m	w	CANA	San Diego	Julian Dist	78	473
Wm	40	m	w	IREL	San Francisco	1-Wd San Francisco	79	44
Wm	23	m	w	IREL	San Francisco	1-Wd San Francisco	79	119
CREIST								
Antoine	30	m	w	SCOT	Siskiyou	Yreka Twp	89	666
CRELAND								
Mary E	50	f	w	IREL	San Francisco	8-Wd San Francisco	82	353
CRELLEN								
Sarah	15	f	w	CA	Yolo	Grafton Twp	93	487
CRELLER								
Eugene	22	m	w	CANA	Nevada	Grass Valley Twp	75	200
CRELLEY								
Neil	40	m	w	IREL	Butte	Ophir Twp	70	96
CRELLIN								
Jas	45	m	w	ENGL	Solano	Vallejo	90	180
Sarah A	16	f	w	CA	Yolo	Grafton Twp	93	480
CRELLY								
James	33	m	w	IREL	San Francisco	San Francisco P O	83	66
CREM								
Yon	26	f	c	CHIN	Plumas	Indian Twp	77	9
CREMAN								
Felix	60	m	w	FRAN	Marin	San Rafael Twp	74	32
CREMENS								
Catharine	20	f	w	IREL	Sacramento	2-Wd Sacramento	77	253
CREMER								
David K	26	m	w	IL	Sonoma	Petaluma Twp	91	365
Herman	58	m	w	PRUS	San Francisco	8-Wd San Francisco	82	423
Thos	38	m	w	IREL	Solano	Vallejo	90	169
CREMIN								
Timothy	35	m	w	IREL	Yuba	W Bear Rvr Twp	93	683
CREMO								
Lazaro	34	m	w	ITAL	San Francisco	2-Wd San Francisco	79	165
CREMONE								
William	35	m	w	IOFM	San Francisco	San Francisco P O	83	190
CREMONY								
John C	45	m	w	MA	San Francisco	6-Wd San Francisco	81	98
Juan	13	m	w	MEXI	San Francisco	11-Wd San Francisc	84	587
CREMOR								
Bertha	46	f	w	PRUS	San Francisco	6-Wd San Francisco	81	81
Jenny	27	f	w	MA	San Francisco	6-Wd San Francisco	81	84
CRENEN								
John	10	m	w	CA	San Francisco	11-Wd San Francisc	84	587
CRENGIZER								
Matilda	18	f	w	NY	Marin	San Rafael	74	58
CRENN								
James	31	m	w	MD	Nevada	Meadow Lake Twp	75	268
CRENNEN								
Francois	48	m	w	FRAN	San Francisco	11-Wd San Francisc	84	613
CRENNEY								
James	50	m	w	IREL	San Francisco	8-Wd San Francisco	82	303
CRENO								
Sam	25	m	i	CA	Yolo	Grafton Twp	93	479
CRENSHAW								
John A	29	m	w	VA	Santa Clara	Santa Clara Twp	88	148
Overton	40	m	w	IL	Sonoma	Mendocino Twp	91	289
Susa	21	f	w	VA	Santa Clara	Santa Clara Twp	88	154
CREOLING								
Georg W	39	m	w	PA	Placer	Gold Run Twp	76	400
CREPPS								
John	25	m	w	ENGL	Contra Costa	Martinez P O	71	444
CREPS								
Wm	40	m	w	PA	Yuba	East Bear Rvr Twp	93	540
CREQUE								
Antoine	57	m	w	FRAN	Colusa	Grand Island Twp	71	308
CRESENT								
Aquinna	29	m	m	CHIL	Placer	Bath P O	76	431
CRESIMOND								
Horace F	40	m	w	VA	Mariposa	Mariposa P O	74	131
CRESON								
James	82	m	w	VA	Sacramento	San Joaquin Twp	77	407
William	22	m	w	MO	Tulare	Venice Twp	92	278
CRESS								
Edward	42	m	w	PA	Del Norte	Smith Rvr Twp	71	478
Frank	38	m	w	VA	Butte	Wyandotte Twp	70	150
Manuel	41	m	w	----	San Joaquin	2-Wd Stockton	86	168
Morgan	38	m	w	NC	Calaveras	San Andreas P O	70	218
Thos A	18	m	w	IA	Sacramento	Alabama Twp	77	60
CRESSEY								
John	25	m	w	MA	San Francisco	San Francisco P O	85	846
Oliver S	34	m	w	MA	Nevada	Nevada Twp	75	317
Theodore	27	m	w	MI	Santa Barbara	San Buenaventura P	87	447
CRESSLER								
William	33	m	w	PA	Siskiyou	Surprise Valley Tw	89	642
CRESSLEY								
John	24	m	w	PORT	Sacramento	Georgianna Twp	77	133
CRESSWELL								
Joseph	34	m	w	ENGL	Del Norte	Crescent Twp	71	455
CRESSY								
Albert	36	m	w	NH	Merced	Snelling P O	74	252

© 2001 by Heritage Quest. All rights reserved.

Name	Age	S	R	B-PL	County	Locale	Roll	Pg
Caleb E	40	m	w	NH	Stanislaus	Empire Twp	92	51
Curtis	65	m	w	ME	Merced	Snelling P O	74	252
Theodore S	33	m	w	MA	San Francisco	1-Wd San Francisco	79	32
CREST								
Joseph	14	m	w	CA	San Francisco	11-Wd San Francisc	84	587
CRESTENA								
Stephen	37	m	w	MEXI	Sacramento	2-Wd Sacramento	77	207
CRESTHWAITE								
Francis	21	m	w	CA	San Diego	San Diego	78	485
CRESWELL								
Elizabeth	40	f	w	IN	Sacramento	Brighton Twp	77	76
CRETAR								
Alexander	34	m	w	TX	Calaveras	San Andreas P O	70	190
CRETEAU								
Joseph	32	m	w	NY	San Francisco	San Francisco P O	83	198
CREVAS								
Steward	21	m	w	CANA	Sonoma	Sonoma Twp	91	447
CREVENS								
Thos A	39	m	w	AL	Santa Barbara	Santa Barbara P O	87	482
CREVESTA								
Ravesel	23	m	w	FRAN	Santa Clara	San Jose Twp	88	195
CREVISON								
Jacob	40	m	w	IN	Los Angeles	Soledad Twp	73	631
CREW								
Ada	7	f	w	CA	San Francisco	San Francisco P O	85	798
Anne	23	f	w	IREL	San Francisco	8-Wd San Francisco	82	431
Jane E	38	f	w	ENGL	Santa Clara	2-Wd San Jose	88	318
Joe	32	m	w	MI	San Joaquin	Dent Twp	86	29
Mary	10	f	w	CA	San Francisco	San Francisco P O	85	798
Pleasent	44	m	w	TN	Sacramento	Georgianna Twp	77	124
T	5	f	w	CA	San Francisco	San Francisco P O	85	798
CREWDSON								
George	26	m	w	KY	Alpine	Woodfords P O	69	310
Samuel W	31	m	w	KY	Alpine	Woodfords P O	69	310
CREWETAR								
Miguel	30	m	i	MEXI	Los Angeles	Los Angeles Twp	73	499
CREWS								
Benjamin	36	m	w	KY	Monterey	Pajaro Twp	74	371
Caleb	36	m	w	MO	Santa Clara	Gilroy Twp	88	87
Henry	8	m	w	CA	Santa Clara	Gilroy Twp	88	88
James	38	m	w	MO	Santa Clara	Gilroy Twp	88	93
CREWZIGER								
Hugo	44	m	w	WURT	San Francisco	San Francisco P O	85	717
CREY								
Antone	40	m	w	MEXI	Alameda	Murray Twp	68	103
Rose	14	f	w	CA	Alameda	Oakland	68	168
CREYE								
Wm	37	m	w	ENGL	Nevada	Nevada Twp	75	282
CREZIA								
Jesus	45	m	w	MEXI	Sacramento	1-Wd Sacramento	77	202
CRIASSANT								
Chas	34	m	w	BAVA	Butte	Chico Twp	70	23
CRIBBEN								
William	9	m	w	CA	Marin	San Rafael Twp	74	27
CRIBBONS								
Ellen	16	f	w	NY	Sacramento	4-Wd Sacramento	77	328
May E	6	f	w	CA	San Francisco	11-Wd San Francisc	84	710
CRIBINS								
Patrick	35	m	w	IREL	San Francisco	8-Wd San Francisco	82	369
CRIBNER								
John	45	m	w	SAXO	Yuba	Marysville	93	605
CRIBONS								
Patrick	27	m	w	IREL	Amador	Amador City P O	69	394
CRICHTON								
John	50	m	w	SCOT	Tulare	Farmersville Twp	92	248
John	27	m	w	IL	Santa Clara	2-Wd San Jose	88	317
CRICKARD								
Mary	49	f	w	IREL	San Francisco	San Francisco P O	83	331
CRICKTON								
George	50	m	w	SCOT	Tulare	Farmersville Twp	92	245
William	35	m	w	CANA	Contra Costa	Martinez P O	71	432
CRIDER								
James C	45	m	w	PA	Yolo	Putah Twp	93	511
William	40	m	w	GERM	Los Angeles	Los Angeles	73	527
William	38	m	w	TN	Los Angeles	Los Angeles	73	544
CRIEGH								
Jennie	22	f	w	PA	San Francisco	11-Wd San Francisc	84	537
CRIERVITO								
Rafael	56	m	w	MEXI	Mariposa	Mariposa P O	74	110
CRIESEN								
Joseph	22	m	w	FRAN	Calaveras	San Andreas P O	70	190
CRIG								
John	45	m	w	IREL	El Dorado	White Oak Twp	72	141
CRIGER								
August	31	m	w	PRUS	Alameda	Eden Twp	68	83
CRIGHTON								
David	55	m	w	SCOT	Humboldt	Bald Hills	72	239
CRIGLER								
J C	50	m	w	KY	Lake	Lower Lake	73	429
James	22	m	w	MO	Mendocino	Sanel Twp	74	229
Michael	28	m	w	IREL	Yolo	Buckeye Twp	93	413
Wm E	45	m	w	VA	Sonoma	Cloverdale Twp	91	268
CRIGLOW								
Henry	39	m	w	MA	Amador	Drytown P O	69	416
CRIJABOA								
Jesus	30	m	w	MEXI	Los Angeles	Los Angeles	73	557

Name	Age	S	R	B-PL	County	Locale	Roll	Pg
CRILISH								
Charles	31	m	w	PRUS	San Francisco	San Francisco P O	85	867
CRILL								
L M	25	m	w	PA	Lassen	Susanville Twp	73	446
CRILLEY								
Thompson	33	m	w	SCOT	San Francisco	San Francisco P O	83	116
CRILLY								
Patrick	34	m	w	IREL	San Francisco	1-Wd San Francisco	79	90
Wm	55	m	w	ENGL	Solano	Benicia	90	9
CRIMLEY								
Wm	38	m	w	IREL	Sacramento	1-Wd Sacramento	77	188
CRIMLY								
Wm	48	m	w	IREL	Yuba	Marysville	93	608
CRIMMENS								
Wm	27	m	w	IREL	San Francisco	San Francisco P O	83	133
CRIMMINS								
Wm	48	m	w	IREL	San Francisco	San Francisco P O	83	168
CRIMMONS								
Hanah	18	f	w	MA	San Francisco	7-Wd San Francisco	81	175
CRINE								
Samuel	52	m	w	PA	San Francisco	11-Wd San Francisc	84	606
Samuel	29	m	w	CA	Calaveras	San Andreas P O	70	198
CRING								
William	38	m	w	IREL	Placer	Bath P O	76	428
CRININ								
James	27	m	w	IREL	Solano	Suisun Twp	90	115
CRINKLAW								
John	49	m	w	NY	Santa Barbara	San Buenaventura P	87	426
CRINSEN								
G W	58	m	w	OH	Amador	Ione City P O	69	371
John	34	m	w	AR	Amador	Lancha Plana P O	69	368
CRIPE								
Elias	34	m	w	IN	San Joaquin	Castoria Twp	86	12
Samuel	40	m	w	IN	Yolo	Cache Crk Twp	93	442
Wm	55	m	w	PA	Napa	Napa Twp	75	64
CRIPMAN								
Benjamin	35	m	w	HDAR	Placer	Bath P O	76	453
CRIPPEN								
Charles	47	m	w	OH	El Dorado	Placerville	72	119
John	69	m	w	DE	El Dorado	Placerville	72	114
Jonas J	43	m	w	OH	El Dorado	Placerville	72	121
Joshua D	41	m	w	DE	Mariposa	Mariposa P O	74	116
Nancy	65	f	w	VA	El Dorado	Placerville	72	119
CRIPPIN								
Stephen	38	m	w	PA	Humboldt	Mattole Twp	72	288
CRIPPLIN								
James	27	m	w	IA	Stanislaus	Empire Twp	92	41
CRIPS								
Wellington	28	m	w	CANA	Solano	Vacaville Twp	90	118
CRIPSEY								
H	28	m	w	IREL	Sacramento	1-Wd Sacramento	77	188
CRISLAND								
Chas B	60	m	w	ENGL	Butte	Chico Twp	70	56
CRISMAN								
A	46	f	w	TN	Humboldt	Pacific Twp	72	294
Benjamin	65	m	w	HDAR	Placer	Auburn P O	76	369
Christopher	38	m	w	IREL	Sacramento	2-Wd Sacramento	77	240
George	38	m	w	HDAR	Placer	Auburn P O	76	368
Gilpin	21	m	w	MO	Santa Barbara	San Buenaventura P	87	447
J	35	m	w	PA	San Joaquin	Tulare Twp	86	249
Jeremiah	60	m	w	PA	Placer	Newcastle Twp	76	478
John	23	m	w	NY	Placer	Auburn P O	76	369
CRISP								
Daniel	24	m	w	IL	Sutter	Sutter Twp	92	124
James	52	m	w	VA	Sutter	Nicolaus Twp	92	112
John	13	m	w	CA	Sonoma	Russian Rvr	91	368
Sarah	15	f	w	CA	Sonoma	Russian Rvr	91	378
CRISPEL								
Oliver	66	m	w	FRAN	San Francisco	San Francisco P O	83	135
CRISPIN								
Francisco	22	m	w	MEXI	Los Angeles	Los Angeles	73	550
Nate W	40	m	w	OH	Sonoma	Mendocino Twp	91	288
William	53	m	w	ENGL	Calaveras	Copperopolis P O	70	255
CRISPINO								
Anton	26	m	w	MEXI	San Francisco	San Francisco P O	80	342
CRISS								
Jacob	44	m	w	IL	Humboldt	Pacific Twp	72	292
John	24	m	w	IL	San Joaquin	Elkhorn Twp	86	60
John W	37	m	w	OH	Shasta	Horsetown P O	89	507
CRISSMAN								
Lewis	33	m	w	GERM	Placer	Bath P O	76	453
Louis	22	m	w	ME	Humboldt	Eel Rvr Twp	72	252
CRIST								
Antoine	41	m	w	SCOT	Siskiyou	Yreka Twp	89	668
G F	39	m	w	BAVA	Butte	Oroville Twp	70	139
Geo	36	m	w	NY	San Joaquin	Elkhorn Twp	86	65
H B	59	m	w	MD	Alameda	Alameda	68	6
John	41	m	w	PA	Shasta	Stillwater P O	89	481
R	35	m	w	SWIT	Sacramento	1-Wd Sacramento	77	190
William	30	m	w	SCOT	Alameda	Oakland	68	265
Wm	36	m	w	PA	Sonoma	Analy Twp	91	233
CRISTANA								
Satenina	27	f	w	CA	Los Angeles	Los Angeles	73	552
CRISTIE								
Rene	50	m	w	FRAN	San Francisco	11-Wd San Francisc	84	557
Robert	25	m	w	IREL	Napa	Napa Twp	75	29

© 2001 by Heritage Quest. All rights reserved.

Name	Age	S	R	B-PL	County	Locale	Series M593 Roll	Pg
CRISTO								
Giuseppi	25	m	w	ITAL	Marin	Novato Twp	74	11
CRISTOPHER								
Con	43	m	w	UNKN	San Joaquin	2-Wd Stockton	86	166
CRISTOVA								
Nicolas	30	m	w	MEXI	San Luis Obispo	Morro Twp	87	281
CRISTY								
William	31	m	w	IREL	Placer	Bath P O	76	453
CRITCHER								
Henry	43	m	w	VA	Alameda	Brooklyn	68	27
CRITCHFIELD								
Geo W	39	m	w	OH	Sonoma	Washington Twp	91	469
CRITES								
Allice	17	f	w	CA	Sacramento	3-Wd Sacramento	77	264
Angus	30	m	w	NY	Kern	Tehachapi P O	73	352
Ephriam Q	31	m	w	OH	Yolo	Grafton Twp	93	479
Wm	46	m	w	PA	Sacramento	Brighton Twp	77	74
CRITIES								
A	28	m	w	CANA	Sierra	Sierra Twp	89	568
CRITSON								
Abraham	40	m	w	PA	Yuba	W Bear Rvr Twp	93	681
CRITTEN								
Joseph M	44	m	w	OH	Placer	Bath P O	76	461
CRITTENDEN								
B L	34	m	w	MA	Merced	Snelling P O	74	277
Charles	33	m	w	OH	Kern	Tehachapi P O	73	353
Charles P	41	m	w	NY	Santa Clara	1-Wd San Jose	88	255
Chas S	43	m	w	NY	San Francisco	San Francisco P O	83	199
D	46	m	w	KY	Yuba	Marysville	93	604
D	40	m	w	FL	Yuba	Marysville	93	591
H	31	m	w	NY	Santa Clara	Gilroy Twp	88	68
John	40	m	w	ENGL	Yolo	Cache Crk Twp	93	446
Orrin	56	m	w	MI	Santa Clara	Fremont Twp	88	42
Parker	21	m	w	TX	San Francisco	6-Wd San Francisco	81	117
T	12	m	w	GA	Solano	Benicia	90	20
Wm	45	m	w	IL	Sutter	Sutter Twp	92	121
CRITTENDON								
N W	54	m	w	NY	San Francisco	8-Wd San Francisco	82	370
CRIVICHICH								
Mateo	36	m	w	AUST	El Dorado	Salmon Falls Twp	72	131
CRIZER								
Andrew F	25	m	w	VA	Santa Clara	1-Wd San Jose	88	278
CROACH								
Jno	27	m	w	SWIT	Santa Clara	Gilroy Twp	88	93
CROAGE								
William	30	m	w	MA	San Francisco	7-Wd San Francisco	81	178
CROAK								
Patrick	27	m	w	IREL	Alameda	Washington Twp	68	294
CROAKER								
A	30	m	w	MA	Alameda	Oakland	68	263
CROALL								
Janet	34	f	w	SCOT	Santa Clara	Fremont Twp	88	51
CROAN								
Luis	40	m	w	MEXI	Santa Clara	Almaden Twp	88	8
CROCE								
Churubino	22	m	w	SWIT	San Francisco	3-Wd San Francisco	79	319
Peter	52	m	w	SWIT	San Francisco	3-Wd San Francisco	79	321
Rose	25	f	w	SWIT	San Francisco	San Francisco P O	83	341
CROCH								
Nelson	49	m	w	NY	Humboldt	Mattole Twp	72	286
CROCHER								
Horace	40	m	w	CT	San Francisco	San Francisco P O	83	404
James	38	m	w	OH	El Dorado	Coloma Twp	72	1
John	46	m	w	MD	El Dorado	Coloma Twp	72	1
CROCHET								
Emma	26	f	w	ENGL	San Francisco	San Francisco P O	83	139
CROCHRAN								
Richard	40	m	w	LA	San Bernardino	San Bernardino Twp	78	452
CROCK								
David	64	m	w	PA	Yuba	Marysville	93	594
John	49	m	b	PA	Yuba	Marysville	93	606
CROCKELL								
William	29	m	w	PRUS	Marin	San Rafael	74	55
CROCKEN								
George	24	m	w	IL	Sacramento	4-Wd Sacramento	77	349
CROCKER								
A	11	m	w	IL	Sierra	Forest Twp	89	529
A S	48	m	w	MA	Tuolumne	Big Oak Flat P O	93	394
Albert W	40	m	w	MA	Mono	Bridgeport P O	74	282
Asa	34	m	w	MA	Solano	Suisun Twp	90	95
Benj R	43	m	w	CT	Sacramento	4-Wd Sacramento	77	326
Benjamin S	43	m	w	VA	El Dorado	Placerville	72	121
C E	35	m	w	IN	Sacramento	3-Wd Sacramento	77	308
C W	43	m	w	NY	Sacramento	3-Wd Sacramento	77	264
Charles	35	m	w	NY	Trinity	Trinity Center Pct	92	204
Chas	47	m	w	NY	Sacramento	3-Wd Sacramento	77	286
Chas A	47	m	w	ME	Nevada	Nevada Twp	75	310
Chas W	45	m	w	IL	San Francisco	5-Wd San Francisco	81	24
D H	29	m	w	ME	San Francisco	San Francisco P O	83	286
Daniel B	54	m	w	NY	Placer	Roseville P O	76	350
Dexter	41	m	w	PA	Yolo	Cache Crk Twp	93	435
Edward	54	m	w	ENGL	El Dorado	White Oak Twp	72	137
Edward	35	m	w	MI	San Luis Obispo	Salinas Twp	87	290
Edward B	53	m	w	NY	Sacramento	2-Wd Sacramento	77	252
Ellen	30	f	w	IREL	San Francisco	San Francisco P O	83	276
Everett	47	m	w	ME	Shasta	Shasta P O	89	455
G N	50	m	w	CT	Calaveras	Copperopolis P O	70	238
H S	38	m	w	NY	Sacramento	1-Wd Sacramento	77	181
J B	55	m	w	MD	Siskiyou	Scott Valley Twp	89	610
J C	36	m	w	NY	Santa Clara	Gilroy Twp	88	76
James	43	m	w	MA	San Francisco	11-Wd San Francisc	84	428
James	36	m	w	NY	Kern	Bakersfield P O	73	366
James M	26	m	w	TN	Sonoma	Salt Point	91	390
John	30	m	w	NY	Solano	Vallejo	90	148
John	28	m	w	ENGL	Monterey	Alisal Twp	74	302
John R	43	m	w	NY	Nevada	Grass Valley Twp	75	143
Mary A	40	f	w	CT	San Francisco	San Francisco P O	83	50
Nathan	24	m	w	PRUS	San Luis Obispo	Salinas Twp	87	293
R	55	f	w	NY	Sierra	Forest Twp	89	529
Roland R	32	m	w	MA	San Francisco	San Francisco P O	83	342
Samuel S	44	m	w	ME	Nevada	Nevada Twp	75	322
Sanford	29	m	w	TN	Kern	Havilah P O	73	339
Sarah R	40	f	w	MA	Yolo	Cache Crk Twp	93	446
Stephen	55	m	w	MA	Sacramento	American Twp	77	65
Thomas	40	m	w	ENGL	Tuolumne	Sonora P O	93	316
W	46	m	w	MA	Alameda	Oakland	68	200
W H	43	m	w	MA	Tuolumne	Big Oak Flat P O	93	394
William H	38	m	w	MO	El Dorado	Placerville	72	122
Wm	46	m	w	PRUS	San Francisco	5-Wd San Francisco	81	15
CROCKERD								
Hugh	38	m	w	IREL	San Francisco	11-Wd San Francisc	84	697
CROCKET								
Jame	24	m	w	OH	Lassen	Long Valley Twp	73	437
Samuel	40	m	w	ME	Calaveras	San Andreas P O	70	211
Thomas	15	m	w	CA	San Mateo	Half Moon Bay P O	87	401
CROCKETT								
D C	40	m	w	TN	Mendocino	Ukiah Twp	74	236
David	50	m	w	MA	San Francisco	San Francisco P O	83	88
David	45	m	w	NY	San Francisco	San Francisco P O	83	87
David	40	m	w	IL	Siskiyou	Cottonwood Twp	89	592
David	16	m	i	CA	Los Angeles	Los Angeles	73	500
Henry	30	m	w	ME	Placer	Bath P O	76	427
John	32	m	w	CANA	San Diego	San Diego	78	511
William	31	m	w	CANA	Mendocino	Cuffeys Cove Twp	74	168
CROCO								
Sneider	30	m	w	OH	Yolo	Cache Crk Twp	93	445
CRODAN								
John	50	m	w	IREL	San Francisco	San Francisco P O	85	852
CRODY								
Alexr	35	m	w	VT	San Francisco	5-Wd San Francisco	81	19
CROELL								
C J	27	m	w	NJ	San Francisco	San Francisco P O	85	779
CROEN								
Henry	35	m	w	SWED	San Francisco	2-Wd San Francisco	79	238
CROERZIN								
Alex	57	m	w	SCOT	San Joaquin	1-Wd Stockton	86	155
CROFF								
John	38	m	w	NY	Amador	Fiddletown P O	69	433
CROFFEY								
Jno	20	m	w	CANA	Butte	Chico Twp	70	29
CROFFORD								
H M	47	m	w	OH	Amador	Fiddletown P O	69	430
Theresa	9	f	w	MA	San Francisco	San Francisco P O	83	128
CROFFORTH								
Henry	48	m	w	OH	Amador	Fiddletown P O	69	439
CROFFREN								
John	41	m	w	ENGL	San Francisco	7-Wd San Francisco	81	166
CROFOLIO								
O	36	f	w	MEXI	Sierra	Downieville Twp	89	520
CROFT								
Jas	27	m	w	ENGL	San Joaquin	Liberty Twp	86	90
Thomas B	34	m	w	ENGL	San Francisco	3-Wd San Francisco	79	297
CROFTER								
John	41	m	w	IREL	San Joaquin	1-Wd Stockton	86	120
CROFTON								
James	45	m	w	IREL	San Francisco	1-Wd San Francisco	79	11
John	40	m	w	IREL	Sacramento	Georgianna Twp	77	122
Kate	22	f	w	MA	Sacramento	4-Wd Sacramento	77	333
Saml W	33	m	w	CT	Butte	Chico Twp	70	18
CROFTS								
John	37	m	w	ENGL	San Francisco	San Francisco P O	83	377
Julius C	42	m	w	IREL	San Francisco	1-Wd San Francisco	79	112
Montague	28	m	w	IREL	San Francisco	1-Wd San Francisco	79	62
S S	48	m	w	OH	Sierra	Alleghany & Forest	89	534
CROGAN								
Bernard	85	m	w	IREL	San Francisco	8-Wd San Francisco	82	486
Ellen	35	f	w	IREL	San Joaquin	2-Wd Stockton	86	174
James	32	m	w	IREL	San Francisco	San Francisco P O	83	286
Joseph	30	m	w	OH	Sacramento	4-Wd Sacramento	77	366
Mary	26	f	w	IREL	Alameda	Brooklyn	68	31
Pat	20	m	w	IREL	San Joaquin	Castoria Twp	86	15
CROGEN								
Pat	27	m	w	IREL	Sierra	Gibson Twp	89	542
CROGER								
George	25	m	w	HAMB	Alameda	Eden Twp	68	68
Henry	60	m	w	BAVA	Santa Clara	2-Wd San Jose	88	286
William G	27	m	w	PRUS	Nevada	Grass Valley Twp	75	144
CROGGS								
William	39	m	w	IREL	Solano	Silveyville Twp	90	78
CROGHAN								
John	40	m	w	NORW	San Francisco	3-Wd San Francisco	79	292
Lillie	16	f	w	NY	Alameda	Brooklyn Twp	68	39
Peter	35	m	w	IREL	San Francisco	San Francisco P O	80	361

© 2001 by Heritage Quest. All rights reserved.

Name	Age	S	R	B-PL	County	Locale	Series M593 Roll	Pg
CROGIER								
William	31	m	w	ENGL	Santa Clara	Santa Clara Twp	88	139
CROHAIN								
John	26	m	w	IREL	Santa Clara	Santa Clara Twp	88	171
CROHAN								
Mary	33	f	w	IREL	San Francisco	11-Wd San Francisc	84	552
CROHURST								
Wm	25	m	w	ENGL	Solano	Vallejo	90	212
CROIZER								
Robert	40	m	w	IREL	San Francisco	San Francisco P O	83	216
CROKE								
James	45	m	w	IREL	San Francisco	6-Wd San Francisco	81	80
Kate	17	f	w	NY	San Francisco	8-Wd San Francisco	82	340
CROKSAW								
Julius	42	m	w	KY	San Francisco	6-Wd San Francisco	81	125
CROLEY								
James	31	m	w	SCOT	Alameda	Oakland	68	220
James Jr	27	m	w	MO	Tulare	Farmersville Twp	92	247
James Sr	60	m	w	TN	Tulare	Farmersville Twp	92	247
John	26	m	w	IREL	Humboldt	Eel Rvr Twp	72	248
CROM								
C A	38	m	w	ME	Placer	Alta P O	76	413
CROMAR								
William	30	m	w	PRUS	San Francisco	6-Wd San Francisco	81	106
CROMARA								
Domingo	40	m	w	SWIT	Santa Clara	2-Wd San Jose	88	323
CROMBECK								
Christ	30	m	w	HANO	San Francisco	San Francisco P O	83	105
CROMBIE								
B	60	m	w	NH	Merced	Snelling P O	74	266
John H	36	m	w	MA	San Francisco	7-Wd San Francisco	81	254
Lewis	30	m	w	SCOT	Los Angeles	El Monte Twp	73	462
CROME								
Henry	22	m	w	SHOL	San Mateo	Half Moon Bay P O	87	403
John	54	m	w	BAVA	Amador	Drytown P O	69	418
CROMER								
Harrison	23	m	w	MI	Colusa	Colusa Twp	71	284
CROMLESS								
Daniel	24	m	w	IREL	San Francisco	1-Wd San Francisco	79	76
James	22	m	w	IREL	San Francisco	1-Wd San Francisco	79	76
CROMLEY								
Aaron	38	m	w	OH	Tulare	Visalia Twp	92	288
CROMM								
Michael	34	m	w	IREL	Alameda	Washington Twp	68	294
CROMMETT								
Thos J	39	m	w	ME	Mariposa	Mariposa P O	74	131
CROMPT								
M V	21	f	w	KY	Del Norte	Crescent	71	467
CROMPTON								
G F	34	m	w	ME	Del Norte	Happy Camp Twp	71	470
John	42	m	w	ENGL	Alameda	Brooklyn	68	28
Thos	34	m	w	ENGL	Solano	Vallejo	90	212
CROMWELL								
N J	19	m	w	CA	Sonoma	Petaluma Twp	91	355
Olaver	60	m	w	KY	Inyo	Bishop Crk Twp	73	315
Sadie	18	f	w	GA	San Francisco	San Francisco P O	85	718
Sadie	17	f	w	GA	San Francisco	San Francisco P O	83	274
William	61	m	w	MD	Sonoma	Petaluma Twp	91	309
CRON								
Adalbert	38	m	w	PRUS	San Francisco	San Francisco P O	83	139
John	50	m	w	FRAN	San Francisco	2-Wd San Francisco	79	180
Launcelet	40	m	w	SCOT	San Francisco	8-Wd San Francisco	82	454
CRONAL								
S A	28	m	w	CHIL	Tuolumne	Chinese Camp P O	93	383
CRONAMILLER								
Susan	8	f	w	CA	Placer	Lincoln P O	76	487
CRONAN								
Anne	30	f	w	IREL	San Francisco	8-Wd San Francisco	82	402
Cathrain	34	f	w	IREL	San Francisco	San Francisco P O	80	459
D	24	m	w	IREL	Alameda	Oakland	68	260
Edward	35	m	w	CANA	Alameda	Brooklyn	68	29
Hugh	35	m	w	IREL	Sutter	Sutter Twp	92	129
James	70	m	w	IREL	San Francisco	8-Wd San Francisco	82	483
John	61	m	w	IREL	San Mateo	Schoolhouse Statio	87	337
John	38	m	w	IREL	Klamath	South Fork Twp	73	385
John	38	m	w	IREL	Placer	Bath P O	76	444
John	19	m	w	CANA	Solano	Vallejo	90	163
Kate	9	f	w	CA	Sacramento	3-Wd Sacramento	77	298
Margt	27	f	w	IREL	San Francisco	8-Wd San Francisco	82	334
Mary	56	f	w	IREL	Nevada	Grass Valley Twp	75	162
Mary	35	f	w	IREL	San Francisco	8-Wd San Francisco	82	430
Mary	22	f	w	IREL	San Francisco	San Francisco P O	83	297
Michael	22	m	w	IREL	Yolo	Washington Twp	93	533
Michel	27	m	w	IREL	Trinity	Weaverville Pct	92	231
Pat	40	m	w	IREL	Sacramento	3-Wd Sacramento	77	298
Patrick	43	m	w	IREL	Butte	Chico Twp	70	42
Patrick	37	m	w	IREL	Klamath	Liberty Twp	73	376
Patrick	36	m	w	IREL	Alameda	San Leandro	68	98
Patrick	20	m	w	IREL	Alameda	Eden Twp	68	86
Patrick	20	m	w	IREL	Alameda	Eden Twp	68	87
Peter	32	m	w	IREL	San Francisco	8-Wd San Francisco	82	496
Tim	50	m	w	IREL	Solano	Vallejo	90	192
William	40	m	w	IREL	San Francisco	11-Wd San Francisc	84	653
Willie	23	m	w	IREL	San Francisco	7-Wd San Francisco	81	273
CRONDLE								
James	23	m	w	NY	Mendocino	Noyo & Big Rvr Twp	74	173
CRONE								
David H	35	m	w	PRUS	San Francisco	San Francisco P O	83	187
John	38	m	w	SCOT	Yolo	Buckeye Twp	93	410
L E	27	m	w	NY	Sierra	Alleghany & Forest	89	533
Mary	22	f	w	IREL	San Francisco	8-Wd San Francisco	82	474
Michael	42	m	w	IREL	Sacramento	4-Wd Sacramento	77	334
CRONEL								
Mary	16	f	w	CA	Santa Clara	1-Wd San Jose	88	241
CRONELL								
Cornelious	30	m	w	IREL	San Francisco	11-Wd San Francisc	84	646
CRONEN								
Cathrine	55	f	w	IREL	San Francisco	1-Wd San Francisco	79	87
Jerry	37	m	w	IREL	San Francisco	1-Wd San Francisco	79	121
John	31	m	w	IREL	San Francisco	1-Wd San Francisco	79	87
Joseph	33	m	w	IREL	San Francisco	2-Wd San Francisco	79	215
Mary	30	f	w	IREL	Santa Clara	San Jose Twp	88	210
Mary	28	f	w	IREL	San Francisco	1-Wd San Francisco	79	29
Peter	30	m	w	IREL	San Mateo	Belmont P O	87	371
CRONER								
Emma	25	f	w	KY	Nevada	Nevada Twp	75	274
CRONEY								
Kate	47	f	w	IREL	Solano	Suisun Twp	90	94
Patrick	38	m	w	IREL	Siskiyou	Scott Valley Twp	89	610
CRONG								
Wm	27	m	w	CANA	Sonoma	Salt Point	91	386
CRONIG								
Christian	23	m	w	GERM	Yolo	Merritt Twp	93	508
CRONIN								
Bridget	35	f	w	IREL	San Francisco	6-Wd San Francisco	81	99
Bridget	21	f	w	IREL	San Francisco	11-Wd San Francisc	84	510
Catherine	28	f	w	IREL	Nevada	Grass Valley Twp	75	160
Cornelus	35	m	w	IREL	San Francisco	7-Wd San Francisco	81	160
Daniel	38	m	w	IREL	San Francisco	San Francisco P O	85	854
Daniel	26	m	w	IREL	Sonoma	Analy Twp	91	241
Daniel	25	m	w	IREL	Yolo	Cache Crk Twp	93	421
Daniel	21	m	w	IREL	Contra Costa	San Pablo Twp	71	365
James	39	m	w	IREL	San Francisco	San Francisco P O	83	34
James	36	m	w	IREL	San Francisco	5-Wd San Francisco	81	29
John	33	m	w	IREL	San Francisco	1-Wd San Francisco	79	72
John	30	m	w	IREL	Marin	Nicasio Twp	74	15
John	24	m	w	NY	Solano	Suisun Twp	90	97
Kate	26	f	w	IREL	Alameda	Oakland	68	228
Kate	18	f	w	IREL	San Francisco	6-Wd San Francisco	81	87
Lizzie	10	f	w	VA	San Francisco	San Francisco P O	80	424
Maggie	16	f	w	VA	San Francisco	San Francisco P O	80	371
Margt	25	f	w	IREL	Sacramento	4-Wd Sacramento	77	328
Mary	61	f	w	IREL	San Francisco	11-Wd San Francisc	84	601
Mary	45	f	w	IREL	Alameda	Oakland	68	165
Mary	38	f	w	IREL	San Francisco	San Francisco P O	83	390
Mary	16	f	w	CA	Santa Clara	2-Wd San Jose	88	333
Michael	60	m	w	IREL	San Francisco	San Francisco P O	83	403
Michael	38	m	w	IREL	San Francisco	San Francisco P O	83	269
Michael	35	m	w	IREL	San Francisco	San Francisco P O	83	365
Michael	32	m	w	IREL	Alameda	Washington Twp	68	284
Michael	24	m	w	IREL	Siskiyou	Callahan P O	89	626
Michael	23	m	w	IREL	San Francisco	San Francisco P O	83	372
Michael	15	m	w	MA	San Francisco	11-Wd San Francisc	84	587
Michal	47	m	w	IREL	San Joaquin	1-Wd Stockton	86	131
Norah	58	f	w	IREL	San Francisco	San Francisco P O	83	21
Patric	39	m	w	IREL	Trinity	Lewiston Pct	92	211
Patrick	29	m	w	ENGL	Marin	Nicasio Twp	74	15
Robt	30	m	w	IREL	San Francisco	2-Wd San Francisco	79	216
S D	24	m	w	IREL	Alameda	Oakland	68	186
Thos	27	m	w	NY	San Francisco	5-Wd San Francisco	81	31
Timothy	55	m	w	IREL	San Francisco	San Francisco P O	83	194
William	25	m	w	NY	San Francisco	San Francisco P O	83	146
William	10	m	w	CA	Marin	San Rafael Twp	74	27
Wm P	32	m	w	IREL	Sacramento	3-Wd Sacramento	77	275
CRONING								
Cornelius	36	m	w	IREL	San Mateo	Redwood Twp	87	363
Dennis	27	m	w	IREL	Placer	Auburn P O	76	375
Michael	34	m	w	IREL	San Mateo	Redwood Twp	87	362
Patrick	25	m	w	IREL	Yolo	Putah Twp	93	515
William	46	m	w	RUSS	Amador	Fiddletown P O	69	437
CRONISE								
Christina	22	f	w	KY	San Francisco	1-Wd San Francisco	79	88
Wm H	45	m	w	MD	San Francisco	2-Wd San Francisco	79	165
CRONK								
Herbert	20	m	w	NY	Santa Cruz	Santa Cruz Twp	89	386
J	38	m	w	HANO	Sierra	Forest Twp	89	530
John	66	m	w	NY	Calaveras	San Andreas P O	70	152
CRONKITE								
Hosea	46	m	w	NY	Sacramento	Brighton Twp	77	79
John	41	m	w	NY	Alpine	Markleeville P O	69	311
CRONKRETE								
John W	51	m	w	CANA	Sonoma	Petaluma Twp	91	317
CRONLAND								
Victor	42	m	w	SWED	Tuolumne	Sonora P O	93	328
CRONNER								
Chs	35	m	w	OH	Lassen	Susanville Twp	73	445
CRONOGUE								
James	32	m	w	IREL	Marin	San Rafael Twp	74	35
CRONON								
Denis	33	m	w	IREL	San Francisco	1-Wd San Francisco	79	132
P	39	m	w	IREL	Sierra	Butte Twp	89	511
William	10	m	w	NY	Alameda	Washington Twp	68	294

© 2001 by Heritage Quest. All rights reserved.

Name	Age	S	R	B-PL	County	Locale	Roll	Pg
CRONY								
Wm	5	m	w	IL	Sutter	Sutter Twp	92	116
CRONYNN								
Elisa	54	f	w	CANA	San Francisco	11-Wd San Francisc	84	544
CROOK								
A J	42	m	w	OH	Calaveras	Copperopolis P O	70	235
Alvias	32	m	w	VT	Stanislaus	San Joaquin Twp	92	74
Charles	28	m	w	ME	San Francisco	8-Wd San Francisco	82	480
Christ	38	m	w	DENM	Placer	Lincoln P O	76	488
Edwin R	32	m	w	NH	San Bernardino	San Bernardino Twp	78	453
James	71	m	w	MD	San Francisco	6-Wd San Francisco	81	148
James	43	m	w	IREL	San Francisco	11-Wd San Francisc	84	484
Jane	45	f	w	ENGL	San Joaquin	2-Wd Stockton	86	175
Jno	35	m	w	MI	Butte	Chico Twp	70	36
John	34	m	w	PRUS	Placer	Auburn P O	76	360
John	23	m	w	SWED	San Francisco	San Francisco P O	80	348
John R	63	m	w	VT	Stanislaus	San Joaquin Twp	92	74
John T	37	m	w	NY	San Francisco	6-Wd San Francisco	81	124
Josiah	29	m	w	IN	Yolo	Buckeye Twp	93	417
Mary	34	f	w	IREL	Contra Costa	Martinez P O	71	392
Mary	30	f	w	IREL	San Francisco	2-Wd San Francisco	79	138
W H	30	m	w	NH	Yuba	Marysville	93	602
William	40	m	w	MO	Stanislaus	Empire Twp	92	48
William C	42	m	w	ENGL	San Mateo	Half Moon Bay P O	87	401
CROOKE								
George	44	m	w	SCOT	El Dorado	Salmon Falls Twp	72	130
CROOKER								
D C	32	m	w	NY	San Francisco	8-Wd San Francisco	82	310
Ellen	18	f	w	ME	San Francisco	8-Wd San Francisco	82	484
George F	26	m	w	NY	Yolo	Cache Crk Twp	93	435
John S	55	m	w	ME	Marin	Tomales Twp	74	78
Mary	20	f	w	ME	Marin	Novato Twp	74	11
Susan	24	f	w	ME	Marin	Tomales Twp	74	78
Zacheus	24	m	w	ME	Marin	Novato Twp	74	11
CROOKS								
Andrew	35	m	w	MO	Solano	Silveyville Twp	90	74
Bridget	71	f	w	IREL	El Dorado	Placerville	72	125
David	37	m	w	NJ	El Dorado	Mountain Twp	72	67
Donzy	24	m	w	ENGL	Marin	Sausalito Twp	74	72
George	40	m	w	IN	Shasta	Portugese Flat P O	89	471
Henry	21	m	w	IL	Solano	Silveyville Twp	90	75
J B	46	m	w	OH	Sierra	Eureka Twp	89	525
J B	17	m	w	IA	Humboldt	Pacific Twp	72	291
James	40	m	w	IREL	San Francisco	San Francisco P O	85	840
James	17	m	w	CA	Placer	Bath P O	76	436
Mathew	57	m	w	IREL	San Francisco	San Francisco P O	83	79
Michael	71	m	w	IREL	El Dorado	Placerville	72	125
Newel	46	m	w	NY	Monterey	San Juan Twp	74	410
Oliver	28	m	w	MEXI	San Joaquin	3-Wd Stockton	86	237
Richard	41	m	w	IREL	San Francisco	San Francisco P O	85	797
Samuel J	26	m	w	IREL	San Francisco	San Francisco P O	85	877
Thomas	50	m	w	SCOT	Santa Cruz	Santa Cruz Twp	89	383
W I	22	m	w	NY	San Francisco	San Francisco P O	83	333
Wiley	55	m	w	IN	Tulare	Tule Rvr Twp	92	262
Wm H	35	m	w	NY	Fresno	Millerton P O	72	148
CROOKSON								
Thomas	60	m	w	ME	Stanislaus	Empire Twp	92	45
CROOL								
Charles D	12	m	w	CA	Santa Clara	Redwood Twp	88	123
CROOLEY								
Patrick	22	m	w	IREL	Nevada	Meadow Lake Twp	75	268
CROON								
Francis	46	m	w	HOLL	San Francisco	1-Wd San Francisco	79	38
Jim	40	m	c	CHIN	Sacramento	3-Wd Sacramento	77	278
CROOS								
J J	32	m	w	PA	San Joaquin	Douglas Twp	86	47
Robert	35	m	w	NH	Contra Costa	Martinez P O	71	422
CROP								
J H	50	m	w	NY	Sutter	Sutter Twp	92	128
CROPLEY								
Abram	36	m	w	ME	Mendocino	Little Lake Twp	74	200
William	26	m	w	MA	Santa Cruz	Pajaro Twp	89	355
CROPMAN								
Wm	18	m	w	ENGL	Fresno	Millerton P O	72	165
CROPPER								
Eliza	41	f	b	PA	San Francisco	San Francisco P O	80	417
Oliver	22	m	w	TX	San Diego	San Luis Rey	78	513
William	24	m	w	ME	Sacramento	2-Wd Sacramento	77	221
CROPSY								
George	30	m	w	NY	Alameda	Eden Twp	68	82
CROS								
Geo	10	m	w	CA	San Francisco	San Francisco P O	83	275
CROSBEY								
Pat	40	m	w	IREL	Mono	Bridgeport P O	74	283
CROSBIE								
John	35	m	w	NY	Amador	Jackson P O	69	321
John	27	m	w	OH	Amador	Jackson P O	69	318
CROSBRIDGE								
Jerry	33	m	w	IREL	Calaveras	San Andreas P O	70	189
CROSBY								
Benj S	36	m	w	NY	Shasta	French Gulch P O	89	468
Berthold	27	m	w	IREL	Placer	Auburn P O	76	381
Bridget	22	f	w	IREL	Marin	San Rafael	74	51
C	28	m	w	MA	Alameda	Oakland	68	264
Charles C	30	m	w	WI	Placer	Auburn P O	76	367
Daniel E	40	m	w	MA	Solano	Suisun Twp	90	94
Edward	42	m	w	IREL	Alameda	Washington Twp	68	278
Eli	55	m	w	PRUS	Marin	Novato Twp	74	12
Eliah	72	m	w	OH	San Diego	San Diego	78	506
Elizabeth	23	f	w	NC	San Francisco	8-Wd San Francisco	82	471
Ellen	4	f	w	CA	San Francisco	11-Wd San Francisc	84	676
Frank	28	m	w	IREL	Stanislaus	Emory Twp	92	25
Fred	39	m	w	IREL	San Francisco	11-Wd San Francisc	84	597
Fredrick	42	m	w	PA	San Francisco	San Francisco P O	80	411
George O	51	m	w	VT	San Francisco	8-Wd San Francisco	82	455
Heny R	40	m	w	PA	San Francisco	8-Wd San Francisco	82	419
Isaac B	40	m	w	NY	Santa Barbara	San Buenaventura P	87	436
James	36	m	w	TN	Stanislaus	Washington Twp	92	85
James	29	m	w	CANA	Sacramento	2-Wd Sacramento	77	254
James	24	m	w	ENGL	San Francisco	5-Wd San Francisco	81	32
Jane E	11	f	w	CA	San Francisco	San Francisco P O	83	143
John	42	m	w	MA	Sonoma	Bodega Twp	91	256
John	33	m	w	IREL	Solano	Vallejo	90	213
John	30	m	w	IREL	Solano	Vallejo	90	215
John	28	m	w	IREL	San Francisco	11-Wd San Francisc	84	610
Joseph	32	m	w	ENGL	San Francisco	8-Wd San Francisco	82	361
Josiah	37	m	w	ME	Placer	Lincoln P O	76	489
Lawrance	25	m	w	IREL	Humboldt	Pacific Twp	72	297
Maria	67	f	w	NY	San Francisco	6-Wd San Francisco	81	132
Mary	33	f	w	IREL	Marin	San Rafael	74	52
Patrick	27	m	w	IREL	Marin	Tomales Twp	74	85
Patrick	25	m	w	IREL	Marin	Tomales Twp	74	78
Porter	65	m	w	NY	Alameda	Oakland	68	233
Robert	25	m	w	IREL	Solano	Green Valley Twp	90	38
Saml A	39	m	w	CT	Napa	Napa	75	6
Samuel	64	m	w	NY	Placer	Bath P O	76	425
Simon	50	m	w	IREL	Solano	Benicia	90	15
Thomas	40	m	w	IREL	Placer	Bath P O	76	435
William	54	m	w	SWED	Marin	Sausalito Twp	74	69
William	49	m	w	IREL	Marin	Sausalito Twp	74	69
William	37	m	w	MA	Marin	Bolinas Twp	74	7
William	28	m	w	MA	San Francisco	6-Wd San Francisco	81	87
CROSDALE								
John	35	m	w	IL	Yolo	Cache Crk Twp	93	442
CROSE								
John	29	m	w	IN	Sonoma	Analy Twp	91	219
Samuel	58	m	w	IREL	Sacramento	3-Wd Sacramento	77	301
Samuel	38	m	w	KY	Stanislaus	San Joaquin Twp	92	77
CROSEGO								
Antoine	17	m	w	ITAL	San Francisco	San Francisco P O	85	849
CROSER								
Elizabeth	45	f	w	CANA	Sonoma	Vallejo Twp	91	455
CROSETT								
James L	52	m	w	MA	San Francisco	San Francisco P O	83	28
CROSGROVE								
Edward	22	m	w	MD	Sacramento	San Joaquin Twp	77	407
CROSKEY								
Robert	43	m	w	IREL	San Francisco	San Francisco P O	85	803
CROSLEY								
Charles	19	m	w	ME	Santa Clara	Redwood Twp	88	133
J S	35	m	w	OH	Alameda	Oakland	68	152
William	60	m	w	KY	El Dorado	Placerville Twp	72	103
CROSLY								
Edgar	30	m	w	MA	Calaveras	San Andreas P O	70	209
James	44	m	w	OH	Calaveras	San Andreas P O	70	192
Jno	18	m	w	IREL	San Joaquin	Oneal Twp	86	106
CROSMAN								
John	52	m	w	ENGL	Fresno	Millerton P O	72	167
M A	41	f	w	PA	Alameda	Oakland	68	228
CROSMORE								
George	36	m	w	MD	Tulare	Packwood Twp	92	255
Henry	34	m	w	MD	Tulare	Packwood Twp	92	255
CROSO								
Vadman	29	m	w	NY	Solano	Silveyville Twp	90	86
CROSON								
William	15	m	w	CA	Stanislaus	Branch Twp	92	4
CROSORDIO								
Penoso	40	m	w	MEXI	El Dorado	Mud Springs Twp	72	77
CROSQUER								
Adan	25	m	w	FRAN	San Francisco	San Francisco P O	80	484
CROSS								
Alfd	35	m	w	CANA	Butte	Hamilton Twp	70	70
Alfred	49	m	w	NY	Sacramento	1-Wd Sacramento	77	188
Alfred	39	m	w	TN	Yuba	Linda Twp	93	555
Ann E	23	f	w	WI	Napa	Napa	75	10
Annie	15	f	w	MA	San Francisco	San Francisco P O	85	775
Anson	45	m	w	NY	Kern	Havilah P O	73	341
Anthony	45	m	w	IREL	San Francisco	2-Wd San Francisco	79	145
Apolet	50	m	w	FRAN	Nevada	Grass Valley Twp	75	165
Betsy	49	f	w	ME	San Francisco	1-Wd San Francisco	79	109
Brown L	50	m	w	KY	Placer	Bath P O	76	438
C B	5	f	w	NV	Sierra	Sierra Twp	89	569
Carrie	37	f	w	OH	Yolo	Cache Crk Twp	93	434
Charles	35	m	w	PORT	Alameda	Eden Twp	68	64
Daniel	40	m	w	CANA	San Francisco	8-Wd San Francisco	82	416
David	39	m	w	OH	Sacramento	3-Wd Sacramento	77	265
David	38	m	w	MD	El Dorado	Kelsey Twp	72	59
De Los	36	m	w	NY	Placer	Colfax P O	76	389
Dennis	26	m	w	NH	Butte	Kimshew Tpw	70	80
E W	45	m	w	NY	Nevada	Nevada Twp	75	302
Elizabeth	39	f	w	ME	San Francisco	11-Wd San Francisc	84	638
Frank	48	m	w	MEXI	Alameda	Murray Twp	68	108
G J	43	m	w	US	Sacramento	1-Wd Sacramento	77	185
Geo W	40	m	w	MA	Mono	Bridgeport P O	74	282

© 2001 by Heritage Quest. All rights reserved.

Name	Age	S	R	B-PL	County	Locale	Roll	Pg
George	47	m	w	MO	San Francisco	11-Wd San Francisc	84	705
George	44	m	w	SCOT	Santa Clara	San Jose Twp	88	207
George	35	m	w	MI	Santa Clara	Milpitas Twp	88	113
Hellen	14	f	w	ME	San Francisco	8-Wd San Francisco	82	347
Henry	40	m	w	ENGL	Los Angeles	Los Angeles	73	517
Henry	32	m	w	GERM	San Mateo	Schoolhouse Statio	87	342
Henry F	47	m	w	CANA	Los Angeles	Los Angeles	73	568
Howard	23	m	w	NY	Kern	Bakersfield P O	73	366
Isaac	63	m	w	PA	Sacramento	3-Wd Sacramento	77	310
J F	48	m	w	ME	Sacramento	Center Twp	77	84
J R	38	m	w	PA	Nevada	Meadow Lake Twp	75	262
James	32	m	w	MI	Stanislaus	Empire Twp	92	58
Jas	33	m	w	MI	San Joaquin	2-Wd Stockton	86	188
Jenny	28	f	w	NY	San Francisco	6-Wd San Francisco	81	106
Joel	38	m	w	IL	Kern	Linns Valley P O	73	344
John	62	m	w	IREL	Santa Barbara	Santa Barbara P O	87	484
John	21	m	w	PORT	Alameda	Hayward	68	79
John A	44	m	w	NC	Plumas	Quartz Twp	77	40
John C	38	m	w	NY	Amador	Fiddletown P O	69	433
Joshua A	71	m	w	MD	Nevada	Nevada Twp	75	283
Lavilla	10	f	w	OH	Sacramento	Sutter Twp	77	380
M L	25	m	w	VA	Nevada	Meadow Lake Twp	75	247
Mary	29	f	w	PA	San Francisco	11-Wd San Francisc	84	661
Nellie	17	f	w	MA	San Francisco	8-Wd San Francisco	82	291
Nicholas M	26	m	w	MA	Sacramento	Georgianna Twp	77	126
Richd	44	m	w	ENGL	San Francisco	1-Wd San Francisco	79	41
Sarah	50	f	w	PA	Nevada	Bridgeport Twp	75	105
Thomas	29	m	w	ENGL	Nevada	Grass Valley Twp	75	201
Thos	41	m	w	SCOT	Sacramento	Granite Twp	77	154
V A	41	m	w	NY	Tuolumne	Big Oak Flat P O	93	406
W B	45	m	w	MA	Sacramento	1-Wd Sacramento	77	181
CROSSAN								
Wm	19	m	w	IREL	San Joaquin	Tulare Twp	86	261
CROSSE								
William T	46	m	w	CANA	San Francisco	8-Wd San Francisco	82	498
CROSSEN								
John	34	m	w	ENGL	Tehama	Tehama Twp	92	193
Samuel	34	m	w	MS	Santa Barbara	San Buenaventura P	87	425
CROSSER								
W	44	m	w	ENGL	Alameda	Oakland	68	137
CROSSETT								
Frank M	32	m	w	MA	Santa Clara	1-Wd San Jose	88	247
James	40	m	w	NY	Yuba	Rose Bar Twp	93	655
Sam	46	m	w	IREL	Calaveras	Copperopolis P O	70	230
Thomas	38	m	w	IREL	Calaveras	Copperopolis P O	70	243
Truman	52	m	w	VT	San Francisco	11-Wd San Francisc	84	562
CROSSETTE								
G H	42	m	w	NY	Butte	Ophir Twp	70	107
Mary C	7	f	w	CA	Sacramento	4-Wd Sacramento	77	336
CROSSHEE								
John	25	m	w	AUST	Amador	Jackson P O	69	318
CROSSLAND								
J	25	m	w	IA	Yuba	Marysville	93	604
John	33	m	w	IREL	Sacramento	4-Wd Sacramento	77	339
CROSSLEY								
Charles	23	m	w	CANA	Alameda	Washington Twp	68	286
Limon	22	m	w	ENGL	Alameda	Oakland	68	133
Powell	56	m	w	OH	Santa Clara	1-Wd San Jose	88	237
CROSSLIN								
James M	34	m	w	MS	Los Angeles	San Jose Twp	73	621
Richard	36	m	w	GA	Kern	Linns Valley P O	73	347
CROSSMAN								
Charles	41	m	w	BAVA	Calaveras	Copperopolis P O	70	226
Harry	26	m	w	PA	Santa Clara	San Jose Twp	88	222
James H	50	m	w	MA	San Bernardino	San Bernardino Twp	78	452
John	30	m	w	ENGL	Fresno	Millerton P O	72	165
R	26	m	w	NY	Sierra	Downieville Twp	89	519
Williak H	27	m	w	PA	San Mateo	Half Moon Bay P O	87	405
CROSSMORE								
Geo	47	m	w	MD	San Joaquin	Dent Twp	86	16
CROSSON								
Saml	37	m	w	NY	Tehama	Bell Mills Twp	92	159
CROSSWHITE								
A D	31	m	w	MO	Sonoma	Cloverdale Twp	91	271
CROST								
John	36	m	w	HAMB	San Francisco	2-Wd San Francisco	79	194
CROSTA								
John	40	m	w	ITAL	San Mateo	Schoolhouse Statio	87	332
CROSWELL								
Elisabeth	35	f	w	ME	Alameda	Eden Twp	68	84
CROTHERS								
James	39	m	w	IREL	Sutter	Sutter Twp	92	117
John	23	m	w	PA	Colusa	Monroe Twp	71	324
Wm	45	m	w	PA	Napa	Napa	75	16
CROTOLEY								
Nora	40	f	w	IREL	Yuba	Marysville	93	579
CROTON								
Fannie	15	f	w	CA	Contra Costa	Martinez P O	71	415
Francis	21	m	w	CANA	El Dorado	Placerville Twp	72	97
Ransom	24	m	w	NY	Yolo	Fremont Twp	93	477
CROTTI								
Anthony	55	m	w	ITAL	Santa Clara	Santa Clara Twp	88	176
CROTTY								
Jane	50	f	w	CT	San Francisco	6-Wd San Francisco	81	96
John	35	m	w	IREL	San Francisco	11-Wd San Francisc	84	557
Maggie	3	f	w	NY	San Francisco	11-Wd San Francisc	84	557
Maria	56	f	w	MA	Santa Clara	Alviso Twp	88	23

Name	Age	S	R	B-PL	County	Locale	Roll	Pg
CROTY								
John	19	m	w	IREL	Yuba	Rose Bar Twp	93	657
Pat	32	m	w	IREL	Yuba	Rose Bar Twp	93	657
CROTZEN								
John L	22	m	w	KY	San Joaquin	Douglas Twp	86	38
CROUCH								
Elisha	39	m	w	WI	Butte	Chico Twp	70	34
Harrison	53	m	w	VA	Plumas	Mineral Twp	77	20
Henry W	36	m	w	VA	Nevada	Rough & Ready Twp	75	331
Herbert	30	m	w	ENGL	San Diego	San Luis Rey	78	513
James	41	m	w	ENGL	San Francisco	2-Wd San Francisco	79	183
Jno	40	m	w	IL	Butte	Chico Twp	70	34
Julia	25	f	w	CANA	Yolo	Cache Crk Twp	93	446
Robert	46	m	w	OH	Napa	Napa	75	43
Robert	40	m	w	OH	Colusa	Colusa	71	292
Rosina	30	f	i	CA	Shasta	Dog Crk P O	89	471
Simon	40	m	w	IL	Butte	Chico Twp	70	32
Thomas S	50	m	w	VA	Los Angeles	Wilmington Twp	73	643
W T	38	m	w	MD	Sacramento	3-Wd Sacramento	77	272
Wm	45	m	w	CT	Shasta	Dog Crk P O	89	471
CROUDACE								
Fredrick	35	m	w	ENGL	San Francisco	7-Wd San Francisco	81	204
CROUDER								
Frank	39	m	w	IL	Butte	Ophir Twp	70	120
CROUGH								
Edward	46	m	w	IREL	Tuolumne	Sonora P O	93	305
CROUNKLE								
Charles	40	m	w	NY	San Francisco	7-Wd San Francisco	81	217
CROUSE								
Bernard	38	m	w	PRUS	Calaveras	San Andreas P O	70	209
Charles	40	m	w	PRUS	San Francisco	2-Wd San Francisco	79	160
Charles	25	m	w	BADE	Inyo	Independence Twp	73	328
John	30	m	w	NY	San Francisco	5-Wd San Francisco	81	6
John	21	m	w	BAVA	San Francisco	11-Wd San Francisc	84	694
Wellington	46	m	w	CANA	Yolo	Washington Twp	93	529
CROUSIT								
Chas	28	m	w	HAMB	Solano	Vallejo	90	216
CROUSON								
John	45	m	w	AR	Stanislaus	Empire Twp	92	44
CROUSTAN								
John	19	m	w	CANA	Sonoma	Salt Point	91	392
CROUT								
Walter	36	m	w	SCOT	Alameda	Oakland	68	262
CROVAT								
Caperton	12	m	w	CA	San Francisco	8-Wd San Francisco	82	426
CROVELL								
Manuel	43	m	w	SCOT	Siskiyou	Table Rock Twp	89	646
CROVEY								
Joseph	55	m	w	NY	Placer	Bath P O	76	420
CROW								
A M	44	m	w	MO	San Joaquin	2-Wd Stockton	86	203
Ah	28	m	c	CHIN	Yolo	Grafton Twp	93	488
Alexander Hill	35	m	w	ENGL	Plumas	Goodwin Twp	77	8
Allen	30	m	w	NY	San Francisco	11-Wd San Francisc	84	484
Andrew	45	m	w	IL	Colusa	Monroe Twp	71	322
Benjamin H	46	m	w	KY	Stanislaus	San Joaquin Twp	92	81
C B	39	m	w	MO	San Joaquin	2-Wd Stockton	86	210
C T	31	m	w	CANA	Sutter	Nicolaus Twp	92	115
Charles	48	m	w	PRUS	Plumas	Seneca Twp	77	47
Chas	34	m	w	IREL	San Francisco	1-Wd San Francisco	79	107
Christian	29	m	w	PA	Solano	Green Valley Twp	90	37
Edward	20	m	w	NY	Tuolumne	Sonora P O	93	318
Edward E	35	m	w	TN	Yolo	Grafton Twp	93	498
F M	29	m	w	IA	Alameda	Murray Twp	68	115
Frederick	23	m	w	SHOL	San Mateo	Half Moon Bay P O	87	403
George M	48	m	w	VA	Santa Cruz	Watsonville	89	378
Henry	40	m	w	PA	Los Angeles	Los Angeles	73	507
Isaac	51	m	w	NC	Shasta	Horsetown P O	89	506
Isaac	50	m	w	KY	Stanislaus	San Joaquin Twp	92	81
Isaac	40	m	w	PA	Solano	Green Valley Twp	90	37
J A	49	m	w	MO	San Joaquin	2-Wd Stockton	86	204
J W	19	m	w	CA	Alameda	Oakland	68	159
James	33	m	w	NY	San Francisco	2-Wd San Francisco	79	213
James	30	m	w	IREL	San Mateo	Redwood Twp	87	369
James	28	m	w	TN	San Francisco	6-Wd San Francisco	81	82
James R	70	m	w	TN	Plumas	Quartz Twp	77	44
Jas G	50	m	w	NC	Shasta	Horsetown P O	89	505
Jasper	37	m	w	MO	Alameda	Eden Twp	68	68
Joe	30	m	w	IL	San Francisco	7-Wd San Francisco	81	274
John	24	m	w	DENM	San Francisco	7-Wd San Francisco	81	242
John	22	m	w	MA	Inyo	Bishop Crk Twp	73	316
John	10	m	w	CA	Contra Costa	Martinez P O	71	442
John B	44	m	w	MO	Stanislaus	San Joaquin Twp	92	81
John J	34	m	w	IA	Alameda	Eden Twp	68	68
John Logan	40	m	w	AR	Plumas	Quartz Twp	77	42
John M	35	m	w	ENGL	Trinity	Lewiston Pct	92	211
Joseph	23	m	w	LA	San Mateo	San Mateo P O	87	349
Louis	41	m	w	MO	Stanislaus	Emory Twp	92	16
Luther C	12	m	w	CANA	Alameda	Washington Twp	68	276
M J	38	f	w	VA	San Joaquin	Elkhorn Twp	86	52
Margaret	27	f	w	IREL	San Francisco	11-Wd San Francisc	84	654
Matthew	39	m	w	IREL	San Francisco	San Francisco P O	83	206
Otto	30	m	w	SHOL	San Mateo	Half Moon Bay P O	87	403
R	40	m	w	IREL	Nevada	Meadow Lake Twp	75	249
Rankin	35	m	w	MO	Sonoma	Mendocino Twp	91	302
Robert	76	m	w	TN	Placer	Auburn P O	76	379
Thomas	25	m	w	NJ	San Francisco	San Francisco P O	85	719

© 2001 by Heritage Quest. All rights reserved.

Name	Age	S	R	B-PL	County	Locale	Series M593 Roll	Pg
W G	37	m	w	MO	Alameda	Murray Twp	68	115
William	44	m	w	IL	Stanislaus	Branch Twp	92	3
William	28	m	w	OH	Siskiyou	Table Rock Twp	89	647
William J	27	m	w	MO	Santa Clara	Santa Clara Twp	88	174
Wm N	44	m	w	TN	San Luis Obispo	Santa Rosa Twp	87	318
Zenas	42	m	w	BADE	San Joaquin	2-Wd Stockton	86	212
CROWAIN								
James	44	m	w	CA	Santa Clara	Santa Clara Twp	88	149
CROWAN								
Catharine	40	f	w	IREL	Alameda	Brooklyn	68	27
John	40	m	w	IREL	Alameda	Eden Twp	68	64
CROWCHER								
Wm	51	m	w	RI	Fresno	Millerton P O	72	148
CROWDEN								
Geo	40	m	w	ENGL	Humboldt	Eureka Twp	72	268
John	50	m	w	IREL	San Francisco	San Francisco P O	85	852
CROWDER								
D A	60	m	w	BADE	Tuolumne	Big Oak Flat P O	93	391
George W	24	m	w	IL	Yolo	Grafton Twp	93	480
Godfry C	59	m	w	NC	Butte	Chico Twp	70	58
Phillip	89	m	w	TN	Yolo	Grafton Twp	93	480
Phillip	45	m	w	IL	Yolo	Grafton Twp	93	487
CROWE								
Hannah	28	f	w	IREL	San Francisco	San Francisco P O	83	285
William D	26	m	w	ENGL	Yolo	Washington Twp	93	530
CROWELL								
A J	24	m	w	OH	Yuba	Marysville	93	587
Abner B	21	m	w	OH	Yuba	Bullards Bar P O	93	548
Abraham	34	m	w	NH	Solano	Rio Vista Twp	90	62
Charles	35	m	w	IL	Santa Clara	1-Wd San Jose	88	235
Charles H	38	m	w	NH	Santa Clara	1-Wd San Jose	88	247
Charles H	29	m	w	MA	San Francisco	8-Wd San Francisco	82	497
Cyrus	36	m	w	NY	Sacramento	Brighton Twp	77	71
D	35	m	w	IREL	Yuba	Marysville	93	611
David	28	m	w	MA	Stanislaus	Emory Twp	92	23
Edward	14	m	w	CA	Mendocino	Ukiah Twp	74	235
Eugine E	50	m	w	OH	San Francisco	8-Wd San Francisco	82	304
F H	18	m	w	CA	El Dorado	Lake Valley Twp	72	64
Geo	17	m	w	LA	Sonoma	Bodega Twp	91	262
Geo C	33	m	w	MA	San Francisco	2-Wd San Francisco	79	198
George	34	m	w	MA	San Francisco	7-Wd San Francisco	81	159
Herman	41	m	w	CANA	Alameda	Washington Twp	68	283
J L	38	m	w	NY	Tehama	Paynes Crk Twp	92	160
James	47	m	w	IREL	Santa Clara	2-Wd San Jose	88	313
John	38	m	w	NY	San Francisco	1-Wd San Francisco	79	39
Lizza A	14	f	w	CA	Yuba	Slate Range Bar Tw	93	673
M T	64	m	w	NH	Sacramento	4-Wd Sacramento	77	361
Martin L	26	m	w	ME	Santa Clara	2-Wd San Jose	88	298
Mary	30	f	w	IREL	Santa Clara	Gilroy Twp	88	86
Mary M	20	f	w	OH	Yuba	Slate Range Bar Tw	93	678
Mike	33	m	w	IREL	San Joaquin	3-Wd Stockton	86	219
Patrick	37	m	w	IREL	Nevada	Washington Twp	75	344
Patrick	29	m	w	IREL	San Francisco	11-Wd San Francisc	84	548
Thos	39	m	w	ME	Butte	Ophir Twp	70	98
W H E	26	m	w	IL	Sacramento	4-Wd Sacramento	77	323
William	45	m	w	NH	Plumas	Mineral Twp	77	22
William	29	m	w	IREL	San Francisco	San Francisco P O	80	474
Wm	50	m	w	MA	Siskiyou	Scott Rvr Twp	89	604
Zena	50	m	w	MA	San Joaquin	3-Wd Stockton	86	243
Zenas	40	m	w	MA	San Francisco	8-Wd San Francisco	82	402
CROWEY								
G W	55	m	w	NC	Napa	Yountville Twp	75	83
CROWFORD								
C	34	m	w	ME	Sierra	Forest Twp	89	530
C	34	m	w	ME	Sierra	Lincoln Twp	89	549
Eugene	15	m	w	NY	Calaveras	Copperopolis P O	70	243
James	29	m	w	CISL	San Francisco	2-Wd San Francisco	79	213
Jno	30	m	w	MA	Butte	Chico Twp	70	54
Jno D	43	m	w	IL	Butte	Oregon Twp	70	122
John	42	m	w	PA	Santa Cruz	Pajaro Twp	89	353
W	43	m	w	FRAN	Alameda	Murray Twp	68	126
CROWIN								
Dennis	28	m	w	IREL	Colusa	Butte Twp	71	266
James	28	m	w	IREL	San Joaquin	Oneal Twp	86	118
John	45	m	w	IREL	San Francisco	1-Wd San Francisco	79	8
Martin	36	m	w	IREL	San Francisco	1-Wd San Francisco	79	103
CROWL								
Catharine	35	f	w	IREL	San Francisco	San Francisco P O	85	760
Milton	26	m	w	PA	San Diego	Julian Dist	78	468
CROWLEY								
Bart	36	m	w	IREL	San Francisco	11-Wd San Francisc	84	663
Bartholemeo	53	m	w	IREL	Nevada	Grass Valley Twp	75	216
Bath	36	m	w	IREL	San Francisco	San Francisco P O	83	54
Bridget	25	f	w	IREL	San Francisco	8-Wd San Francisco	82	399
Catharine	32	f	w	IREL	San Francisco	11-Wd San Francisc	84	575
Catherine	60	f	w	IREL	Nevada	Grass Valley Twp	75	181
Catherine	42	f	w	IREL	San Francisco	7-Wd San Francisco	81	180
Catherine	36	f	w	IREL	San Francisco	6-Wd San Francisco	81	144
Catherine	29	f	w	IREL	San Francisco	2-Wd San Francisco	79	234
Cathraine	35	f	w	IREL	San Francisco	San Francisco P O	80	389
Chas	30	m	w	IREL	San Francisco	San Francisco P O	85	837
Ches	24	m	w	IREL	Sacramento	1-Wd Sacramento	77	188
Con	30	m	w	IREL	Santa Clara	Fremont Twp	88	41
Cornelius	7	m	w	NCOD	San Francisco	5-Wd San Francisco	81	4
Cornelius	48	m	w	IREL	San Francisco	San Francisco P O	83	241
Cornelius	25	m	w	IREL	San Francisco	San Francisco P O	83	195
Cornelus	17	m	w	IREL	San Francisco	7-Wd San Francisco	81	180

Name	Age	S	R	B-PL	County	Locale	Series M593 Roll	Pg
Dan	33	m	w	IREL	Solano	Benicia	90	13
Daniel	46	m	w	IREL	San Francisco	11-Wd San Francisc	84	550
Daniel	41	m	w	IREL	San Francisco	San Francisco P O	83	269
Daniel	40	m	w	IREL	Alameda	Washington Twp	68	271
Daniel	30	m	w	IREL	San Francisco	6-Wd San Francisco	81	143
Daniel	27	m	w	IREL	Plumas	Plumas Twp	77	31
Daniel	27	m	w	IREL	San Francisco	1-Wd San Francisco	79	65
Daniel	24	m	w	NY	San Francisco	San Francisco P O	83	223
Daniel	17	m	w	MA	Santa Clara	Santa Clara Twp	88	175
Daniel	14	m	w	CA	San Francisco	San Francisco P O	83	166
Danl	40	m	w	IREL	San Francisco	7-Wd San Francisco	81	272
David	45	m	w	IREL	Santa Clara	Santa Clara Twp	88	135
Edward	51	m	w	PA	Tuolumne	Chinese Camp P O	93	367
Eliza	30	f	w	IREL	Solano	Benicia	90	13
Ellen	50	f	w	IREL	Sierra	Table Rock Twp	89	574
Florance	28	m	w	IREL	San Joaquin	1-Wd Stockton	86	130
Florence	37	m	w	IREL	Shasta	American Ranch P O	89	497
Greenbury	37	m	w	MO	Inyo	Lone Pine Twp	73	330
Hannah	40	f	w	IREL	San Francisco	8-Wd San Francisco	82	438
Hannah	30	f	w	IREL	San Francisco	8-Wd San Francisco	82	428
Hannah	17	f	w	IREL	Nevada	Grass Valley Twp	75	146
Henry	30	m	w	IREL	San Francisco	San Francisco P O	85	773
Isaac	25	m	w	CANA	Mendocino	Point Arena Twp	74	215
J	45	f	w	IREL	San Francisco	San Francisco P O	83	134
J J	28	m	w	MA	San Francisco	7-Wd San Francisco	81	189
Jake	30	m	w	IREL	Solano	Vallejo	90	215
James	48	m	w	IREL	San Francisco	7-Wd San Francisco	81	199
James	29	m	w	IREL	Shasta	Stillwater P O	89	479
James	25	m	w	IREL	San Francisco	1-Wd San Francisco	79	63
Jas	50	m	w	IREL	Solano	Vallejo	90	149
Jas	23	m	w	IREL	San Francisco	San Francisco P O	83	310
Jeremiah	25	m	w	IREL	San Francisco	11-Wd San Francisc	84	523
Jeremiah	25	m	w	IREL	San Mateo	Searsville P O	87	383
Jerry	27	m	w	IREL	Solano	Vallejo	90	197
Jno	40	m	w	IREL	Butte	Chico Twp	70	44
Jno	30	m	w	IREL	Sierra	Table Rock Twp	89	575
Johanna	35	f	w	IREL	San Francisco	8-Wd San Francisco	82	402
Johanna	24	f	w	IREL	San Francisco	8-Wd San Francisco	82	415
John	55	m	w	IREL	Siskiyou	Yreka	89	659
John	54	m	w	IREL	San Francisco	San Francisco P O	83	166
John	40	m	w	IREL	San Francisco	San Francisco P O	83	322
John	40	m	w	IREL	Alameda	Oakland	68	258
John	38	m	w	IREL	San Francisco	San Francisco P O	83	403
John	37	m	w	IL	Sutter	Butte Twp	92	96
John	35	m	w	CANA	San Francisco	7-Wd San Francisco	81	281
John	34	m	w	IREL	San Mateo	Redwood Twp	87	367
John	34	m	w	IREL	San Francisco	11-Wd San Francisc	84	558
John	32	m	w	IREL	San Francisco	11-Wd San Francisc	84	640
John	30	m	w	IREL	San Francisco	5-Wd San Francisco	81	17
John	29	m	w	IREL	San Francisco	San Francisco P O	85	862
John	28	m	w	IREL	San Francisco	8-Wd San Francisco	82	433
John	25	m	w	IREL	San Francisco	1-Wd San Francisco	79	136
John	22	m	w	MI	San Francisco	3-Wd San Francisco	79	323
John	22	m	w	IREL	Alameda	Oakland	68	172
John	22	m	w	IREL	Santa Clara	2-Wd San Jose	88	315
John	19	m	w	IREL	San Francisco	7-Wd San Francisco	81	215
John	11	m	w	CA	San Francisco	11-Wd San Francisc	84	587
John D	49	m	w	IREL	Sacramento	2-Wd Sacramento	77	209
Joseph	18	m	w	NY	San Francisco	8-Wd San Francisco	82	372
Julia	40	f	w	IREL	San Francisco	11-Wd San Francisc	84	455
Julia	29	f	w	IREL	San Francisco	2-Wd San Francisco	79	276
Kate	27	f	w	IREL	San Francisco	11-Wd San Francisc	84	538
Kate	20	f	w	IREL	Sonoma	Russian Rvr	91	370
Lawrance	26	m	w	IREL	San Francisco	7-Wd San Francisco	81	183
Lawrence	36	m	w	IREL	San Francisco	San Francisco P O	83	256
Lawrence	30	m	w	IREL	San Francisco	5-Wd San Francisco	81	27
Lula	14	f	i	CA	Santa Clara	Burnett Twp	88	30
M	45	m	w	IREL	Solano	Vallejo	90	165
M	43	m	w	IREL	San Francisco	San Francisco P O	85	794
Margaret	65	f	w	IREL	Nevada	Grass Valley Twp	75	174
Margaret	50	f	w	IREL	San Francisco	San Francisco P O	83	44
Margaret	29	f	w	IREL	San Francisco	San Francisco P O	85	845
Margaret	20	f	w	IREL	San Francisco	San Francisco P O	85	875
Maria	30	f	w	IREL	San Francisco	7-Wd San Francisco	81	199
Mary	40	f	w	IREL	San Francisco	1-Wd San Francisco	79	98
Mary	23	f	w	IREL	San Francisco	8-Wd San Francisco	82	305
Mary	20	f	w	LA	Nevada	Grass Valley Twp	75	150
Mary	19	f	w	MA	Alameda	Alameda	68	17
Michael	40	m	w	IREL	Nevada	Grass Valley Twp	75	195
Michael	40	m	w	IREL	San Francisco	San Francisco P O	83	310
Michael	32	m	w	IREL	San Francisco	7-Wd San Francisco	81	163
Michl	22	m	w	IREL	Alameda	Oakland	68	175
Pat	40	m	w	IREL	San Joaquin	Oneal Twp	86	111
Pat	37	m	w	IREL	San Joaquin	1-Wd Stockton	86	123
Patk	38	m	w	NY	San Francisco	1-Wd San Francisco	79	25
Patk	30	m	w	IREL	Solano	Vallejo	90	197
Patrick	26	m	w	IREL	San Francisco	San Francisco P O	83	58
Peter	50	m	w	ENGL	Santa Clara	Santa Clara Twp	88	137
Richard	40	m	w	IREL	Los Angeles	Los Nietos Twp	73	574
Richd	40	m	w	IREL	San Francisco	1-Wd San Francisco	79	61
T	35	m	w	IREL	Yuba	Marysville	93	605
T J	53	m	w	TN	Santa Clara	Burnett Twp	88	30
Thos	30	m	w	DC	Solano	Vallejo	90	180
Tim	24	m	w	IREL	Alameda	Murray Twp	68	116
Timothy	69	m	w	IREL	Shasta	Shasta P O	89	462
Timothy	45	m	w	IREL	San Francisco	San Francisco P O	83	119
Timothy	40	m	w	IREL	San Francisco	San Francisco P O	80	397

© 2001 by Heritage Quest. All rights reserved.

Name	Age	S	R	B-PL	County	Locale (Series M593)	Roll	Pg
Timothy	35	m	w	IREL	San Francisco	5-Wd San Francisco	81	16
Timothy	31	m	w	IREL	Santa Clara	Fremont Twp	88	41
Timothy	30	m	w	IREL	Sacramento	Cosumnes Twp	77	89
Timothy	26	m	w	ASEA	San Francisco	San Francisco P O	83	1
Timothy	25	m	w	MA	San Francisco	7-Wd San Francisco	81	174
Timothy	22	m	w	IREL	Santa Clara	Fremont Twp	88	58
Timothy	21	m	w	IREL	Alameda	Washington Twp	68	294
Vincent	22	m	w	MI	Sonoma	Salt Point	91	392
W C	23	m	w	IREL	San Francisco	San Francisco P O	85	785
William	30	m	w	IREL	San Francisco	11-Wd San Francisc	84	487
William	29	m	w	CT	Kern	Bakersfield P O	73	363
William	24	m	w	IREL	Contra Costa	Martinez P O	71	419
Wm	50	m	w	IREL	San Joaquin	3-Wd Stockton	86	245
CROWLING								
Mary	29	f	w	IREL	Alameda	Oakland	68	161
CROWLLEY								
John	60	m	w	IREL	Contra Costa	San Pablo Twp	71	361
CROWLS								
Mary	18	f	w	MA	San Francisco	2-Wd San Francisco	79	241
CROWLY								
F	22	m	w	IREL	Alameda	Oakland	68	143
James	43	m	w	ENGL	Los Angeles	Wilmington Twp	73	638
Jeremiah	32	m	w	IREL	San Francisco	San Francisco P O	83	406
John	36	m	w	IREL	Los Angeles	Wilmington Twp	73	638
John	28	m	w	PRUS	San Francisco	5-Wd San Francisco	81	32
Joseph	24	m	w	IREL	Solano	Suisun Twp	90	111
Mary	27	f	w	IREL	San Mateo	San Mateo P O	87	359
Michael	44	m	w	IREL	San Francisco	San Francisco P O	83	392
Thos	30	m	w	IREL	Sacramento	4-Wd Sacramento	77	339
Timothy	30	m	w	IREL	Los Angeles	Wilmington Twp	73	638
CROWN								
Augustus	28	m	w	VT	Santa Cruz	Santa Cruz	89	409
Bridget	15	f	w	NY	Santa Cruz	Santa Cruz	89	417
Harris	38	m	w	POLA	San Francisco	11-Wd San Francisc	84	511
Helen	26	f	w	IREL	Butte	Chico Twp	70	45
Henry	27	m	w	DENM	San Francisco	San Francisco P O	80	536
Sol	37	m	w	OH	Sacramento	3-Wd Sacramento	77	318
CROWNER								
Charles	46	m	w	NY	Santa Clara	Milpitas Twp	88	108
Ezra A	45	m	w	NY	Santa Cruz	Watsonville	89	374
John	30	m	w	IREL	Solano	Vallejo	90	197
CROWNEY								
Ellen	25	f	w	CANA	San Francisco	San Francisco P O	83	380
Jno	55	m	w	IREL	Butte	Chico Twp	70	29
CROWNINBERG								
Johan	74	m	w	PRUS	San Francisco	San Francisco P O	83	25
CROWNING								
Jacob Sheile	27	m	w	MA	Fresno	Millerton P O	72	164
CROWNINSHIELD								
C R	44	m	w	MA	Trinity	Weaverville Pct	92	223
J	38	m	w	NY	San Francisco	6-Wd San Francisco	81	103
CROWTHER								
Geo D	54	m	w	ENGL	San Francisco	San Francisco P O	83	335
Mary	30	f	w	SHOL	San Francisco	San Francisco P O	83	27
CROXFORD								
Asa	40	m	w	ME	San Luis Obispo	Morro Twp	87	285
CROXON								
Warren	10	m	w	CA	Santa Clara	Fremont Twp	88	53
CROYLE								
Prentice	46	m	w	MA	San Francisco	11-Wd San Francisc	84	686
CROZADA								
Alphonse	62	m	w	FRAN	Marin	San Rafael Twp	74	33
CROZEON								
Charles	35	m	w	HANO	Contra Costa	Martinez P O	71	450
CROZER								
James	32	m	w	IREL	San Francisco	San Francisco P O	85	764
CROZIER								
A B	28	m	w	KY	Los Angeles	Los Nietos Twp	73	582
Arthur	36	m	w	IREL	Sacramento	4-Wd Sacramento	77	327
James	44	m	w	OH	Colusa	Monroe Twp	71	324
James	39	m	w	FRAN	San Francisco	San Francisco P O	80	347
James	39	m	w	FRAN	San Francisco	San Francisco P O	80	348
James	28	m	w	CANA	Santa Clara	2-Wd San Jose	88	314
Jas	25	m	w	MA	Sacramento	4-Wd Sacramento	77	349
Munroe	50	m	w	OH	Marin	San Rafael Twp	74	41
William	50	m	w	IREL	Calaveras	Copperopolis P O	70	246
William	27	m	w	AFRI	San Francisco	San Francisco P O	80	372
CRUBEY								
J	23	m	w	IREL	Lake	Knoxville Mines	73	404
CRUCKSHANK								
John	39	m	w	NY	Contra Costa	Martinez P O	71	417
William	48	m	w	NY	Contra Costa	Martinez P O	71	417
CRUDDEN								
Henry	44	m	w	IREL	El Dorado	White Oak Twp	72	144
William	39	m	w	IREL	San Francisco	11-Wd San Francisc	84	472
CRUDE								
D	40	m	w	IL	Alameda	Oakland	68	262
Jerry	60	m	w	IREL	San Joaquin	Tulare Twp	86	255
CRUESS								
Lambert	40	m	w	IREL	San Luis Obispo	Salinas Twp	87	295
CRUEY								
Elias	34	m	w	OH	Sacramento	3-Wd Sacramento	77	270
CRUG								
Wm	40	m	w	MO	San Joaquin	Liberty Twp	86	96
CRUGAL								
Vincent	23	m	w	GERM	Contra Costa	Martinez P O	71	433
CRUGAR								
Henry	30	m	w	HANO	San Francisco	2-Wd San Francisco	79	226
CRUGHWELL								
Ernest	30	m	w	POLA	San Francisco	1-Wd San Francisco	79	85
CRUIKSHANKS								
Danl	28	m	w	SCOT	San Francisco	1-Wd San Francisco	79	94
CRUIS								
Charles	42	m	w	CHIL	Del Norte	Crescent	71	467
CRUISE								
H	32	m	w	IL	Santa Clara	Gilroy Twp	88	76
Wm	35	m	w	IREL	San Francisco	11-Wd San Francisc	84	670
CRULAN								
Jas	32	m	w	IREL	Sutter	Butte Twp	92	90
CRULY								
James	37	m	w	IREL	San Joaquin	3-Wd Stockton	86	234
CRUM								
Alvin O	39	m	w	MA	Los Angeles	Santa Ana Twp	73	603
Andrew	39	m	w	IL	Butte	Oregon Twp	70	129
Jno H	26	m	w	IL	Butte	Oregon Twp	70	128
John Edwin	30	m	w	OH	Plumas	Seneca Twp	77	47
John H	25	m	w	MO	Sacramento	Franklin Twp	77	112
Michael	37	m	w	IL	Butte	Chico Twp	70	47
Wm H	30	m	w	IL	Butte	Oregon Twp	70	129
CRUMB								
J M	45	m	w	OH	Sutter	Butte Twp	92	101
Lana	11	f	w	CA	Humboldt	South Fork Twp	72	303
CRUMBAUGH								
Peter	42	m	w	OH	Tehama	Mill Crk Twp	92	167
CRUMBELL								
John	40	m	w	IREL	Alameda	Eden Twp	68	69
CRUME								
Jesse	43	m	w	KY	Shasta	Stillwater P O	89	478
CRUMEL								
Saline	45	f	w	FRAN	San Francisco	2-Wd San Francisco	79	231
CRUMER								
C E	33	m	w	ENGL	Alameda	Oakland	68	264
CRUMEY								
Owen	43	m	w	IREL	San Francisco	11-Wd San Francisc	84	682
CRUMIS								
Thomas	31	m	w	IREL	Humboldt	Eureka Twp	72	263
CRUMLEY								
D W	31	m	w	AR	Tehama	Mill Crk Twp	92	168
James	42	m	w	KY	Merced	Snelling P O	74	277
CRUMLY								
Kendrick	43	m	w	TN	Inyo	Independence Twp	73	324
CRUMM								
Helen	23	f	w	IL	Butte	Oregon Twp	70	129
CRUMMELL								
George	32	m	w	OH	Napa	Napa	75	18
CRUMMER								
Abbie	33	f	w	MA	San Francisco	7-Wd San Francisco	81	206
Crist	36	m	w	NY	Colusa	Colusa	71	295
Hugh	39	m	w	IREL	San Francisco	7-Wd San Francisco	81	206
CRUMMEY								
John W	53	m	w	IREL	San Francisco	San Francisco P O	85	744
CRUMMINGS								
Dennis	34	m	w	IREL	San Francisco	7-Wd San Francisco	81	261
CRUMP								
David	47	m	w	CANA	Yolo	Merritt Twp	93	504
Emma J	15	f	w	CA	Sacramento	2-Wd Sacramento	77	227
F F	23	m	w	VA	Sacramento	1-Wd Sacramento	77	175
Hiram J	40	m	w	AL	Fresno	Millerton P O	72	192
John G	45	m	w	VA	Fresno	Kings Rvr P O	72	204
Peter	28	m	w	PRUS	Alameda	Oakland	68	180
R R	38	m	w	VA	Amador	Ione City P O	69	358
William	21	m	w	TX	Los Angeles	Los Nietos Twp	73	589
CRUMPTON								
Hezekiah	41	m	w	SC	Placer	Bath P O	76	427
CRUMRY								
Alice	21	f	w	FL	San Francisco	San Francisco P O	80	374
CRUMUELL								
Margaret	14	f	w	KS	Calaveras	San Andreas P O	70	197
CRUNCH								
Geo A	36	m	w	NY	Butte	Chico Twp	70	25
John	38	m	w	OH	Sacramento	Brighton Twp	77	76
CRUNEY								
A	12	f	w	CA	Alameda	Oakland	68	192
CRUNLANDER								
John C	25	m	w	SHOL	San Mateo	Half Moon Bay P O	87	405
CRUNY								
Thomas	26	m	w	IREL	Los Angeles	Los Angeles	73	566
CRUS								
Eugenia	40	f	w	CA	San Diego	San Luis Rey	78	515
CRUSE								
C	40	m	w	MO	Alameda	Oakland	68	164
G	30	m	w	IL	Tehama	Hunters Twp	92	187
Geo	30	m	w	HANO	San Francisco	2-Wd San Francisco	79	222
Henry	46	m	w	PRUS	Calaveras	Copperopolis P O	70	241
John	35	m	w	IREL	Santa Clara	Fremont Twp	88	59
John	35	m	w	PRUS	Yuba	Rose Bar Twp	93	661
John	32	m	w	BADE	Yuba	Rose Bar Twp	93	656
Matherana	63	f	w	CHIL	Yuba	Marysville	93	600
Olean	18	m	i	MEXI	Inyo	Cerro Gordo Twp	73	323
CRUSEN								
J	29	m	w	IN	Alameda	Oakland	68	261
William J	19	m	w	AR	Calaveras	San Andreas P O	70	192
Wm	40	m	w	OH	Yuba	Marysville	93	592

© 2001 by Heritage Quest. All rights reserved.

Name	Age	S	R	B-PL	County	Locale	Series M593 Roll	Pg
CRUSEY								
Adolph	35	m	w	FRAN	San Francisco	11-Wd San Francisc	84	449
CRUSHER								
Henry	31	m	w	PA	Nevada	Meadow Lake Twp	75	259
CRUSINS								
Lewis	48	m	w	BAVA	Del Norte	Crescent	71	464
CRUSMAN								
John	38	m	w	PA	San Joaquin	Tulare Twp	86	251
CRUSO								
---	56	m	w	FRAN	Yuba	Marysville	93	613
Christopher	40	m	w	HANO	Amador	Jackson P O	69	345
CRUSON								
Henry	9	f	w	CA	Sutter	Nicolaus Twp	92	115
Thomas	67	m	w	KY	El Dorado	Placerville Twp	72	99
CRUSSELL								
F R	40	m	w	ENGL	San Francisco	3-Wd San Francisco	79	313
CRUST								
John	9	m	w	CA	El Dorado	Placerville Twp	72	101
CRUTCHELL								
Rebecca	26	f	w	MA	San Francisco	11-Wd San Francisc	84	611
CRUTCHER								
William M	41	m	w	KY	Placer	Auburn P O	76	366
CRUTCHFIELD								
Jos	50	m	w	KY	Shasta	Fort Crook P O	89	477
CRUTCHPORT								
John	20	m	w	GERM	San Luis Obispo	San Luis Obispo Tw	87	300
CRUTHER								
Jessie	37	m	w	IL	Trinity	Indian Crk	92	200
CRUTHERS								
Frank	29	m	w	OH	Solano	Vallejo	90	160
Harmon	60	m	w	NY	San Francisco	San Francisco P O	83	283
Thomas	25	m	w	NY	Sonoma	Petaluma Twp	91	321
Wm	17	m	w	CA	San Joaquin	Douglas Twp	86	40
CRUZ								
Antone	40	m	w	CHIL	Marin	San Rafael Twp	74	32
Aquin	53	m	w	CHIL	El Dorado	Mud Springs Twp	72	73
Catarina	4	f	i	CA	Los Angeles	Los Angeles	73	501
D	30	m	w	CHIL	Alameda	Oakland	68	252
Feliz	50	m	w	MEXI	Fresno	Millerton P O	72	160
Florentine	28	m	w	MEXI	Mariposa	Mariposa P O	74	94
Francisco	20	m	w	MEXI	Los Angeles	Los Angeles Twp	73	486
Francisco	16	m	w	CA	Marin	San Rafael Twp	74	46
Jose La	15	m	w	CA	Los Angeles	Los Angeles	73	519
Juan	18	m	w	MEXI	Los Angeles	Los Angeles	73	515
Manuel	60	m	w	SAME	Los Angeles	Los Angeles	73	510
Mary	38	f	w	CHIL	San Francisco	2-Wd San Francisco	79	147
Ramon	30	m	w	MEXI	Kern	Bakersfield P O	73	364
Vacunda	38	f	w	CA	Los Angeles	Los Angeles	73	561
CRUZE								
Elizabeth	35	f	w	IREL	San Francisco	2-Wd San Francisco	79	243
CRUZON								
Geo S	50	m	w	MA	Santa Barbara	Santa Barbara P O	87	501
CRWLEY								
John D	34	m	w	IREL	San Francisco	San Francisco P O	83	404
CRY								
Ah	26	m	c	CHIN	Mariposa	Mariposa P O	74	102
CRYAN								
Thos	38	m	w	IREL	Solano	Vallejo	90	173
CRYDEN								
Patrick	32	m	w	IREL	Nevada	Eureka Twp	75	130
CRYDENWISE								
Clark S	41	m	w	NY	Santa Clara	2-Wd San Jose	88	325
CRYDERMAN								
Joseph	46	m	w	NY	San Francisco	San Francisco P O	85	746
CRYER								
Charles	47	m	w	ENGL	San Francisco	San Francisco P O	83	285
Robert	40	m	w	ENGL	Nevada	Grass Valley Twp	75	188
CRYLER								
Sirves	35	m	w	MO	Colusa	Monroe Twp	71	311
CRYS								
Ah	30	m	c	CHIN	Butte	Chico Twp	70	31
CRYSTAL								
James	16	m	w	CA	Plumas	Quartz Twp	77	42
Thomas	34	m	w	SCOT	Marin	San Rafael Twp	74	39
CU								
Ah	30	m	c	CHIN	Nevada	Grass Valley Twp	75	219
Chin	35	m	c	CHIN	Nevada	Little York Twp	75	242
Chock	35	m	c	CHIN	Trinity	Junction City Pct	92	206
Cum	40	m	c	CHIN	Calaveras	San Andreas P O	70	199
Lok	34	m	c	CHIN	Fresno	Millerton P O	72	202
CUANDO								
David	34	m	w	MEXI	Calaveras	Copperopolis P O	70	259
CUARTE								
Maria	36	f	w	CA	Los Angeles	El Monte Twp	73	452
Rafaela	28	f	w	CA	Los Angeles	San Gabriel Twp	73	597
CUASER								
G	41	m	w	VT	Sierra	Butte Twp	89	512
CUBASO								
Leonardo	20	m	w	MEXI	Kern	Bakersfield P O	73	365
CUBB								
George	40	m	w	SWED	San Francisco	3-Wd San Francisco	79	295
CUBBAGE								
Tilford	29	m	w	IL	Los Angeles	El Monte Twp	73	448
CUBBERLY								
Daniel	51	m	w	NJ	Placer	Auburn P O	76	367
CUBBERTSON								
Clark	29	m	w	OH	Santa Clara	Santa Clara Twp	88	139
CUBELO								
Rodolph	28	m	w	SWED	Santa Clara	San Jose Twp	88	208
CUBERY								
Wm M	35	m	w	MA	San Francisco	San Francisco P O	83	132
CUBRAL								
H	30	m	w	WIND	Alameda	Alameda	68	7
CUBULA								
M	25	f	w	MEXI	Santa Clara	Gilroy Twp	88	77
CUCHETH								
James	27	m	w	ENGL	San Francisco	1-Wd San Francisco	79	118
CUCUEL								
George	41	m	w	FRAN	San Francisco	8-Wd San Francisco	82	445
CUCUS								
James	50	m	w	FRAN	San Francisco	11-Wd San Francisc	84	566
CUCY								
Wm	37	m	w	MD	Yuba	Marysville	93	589
CUDD								
Eliza J	15	f	w	MO	Butte	Kimshew Tpw	70	78
Jack	41	m	w	MO	Butte	Oregon Twp	70	130
Jas	40	m	w	KY	Butte	Kimshew Tpw	70	78
CUDDABACK								
Jon W	24	m	w	IL	Butte	Chico Twp	70	21
CUDDEBACK								
Frank	50	m	w	NY	Kern	Tehachapi P O	73	353
CUDDEHEY								
Thomas	40	m	w	IREL	Nevada	Grass Valley Twp	75	220
CUDDERBACK								
Henry	45	m	w	OH	Humboldt	Eel Rvr Twp	72	247
CUDDIEBACK								
C	32	m	w	IL	Yuba	Linda Twp	93	554
CUDDIHY								
Martin	40	m	c	IREL	Del Norte	Happy Camp Twp	71	470
CUDDINGTON								
Harley S	39	m	w	NY	San Francisco	8-Wd San Francisco	82	424
CUDDY								
Cathine	44	f	w	IREL	San Francisco	San Francisco P O	85	834
Francis	32	m	w	MO	Solano	Suisun Twp	90	104
James	40	m	w	IREL	San Mateo	Menlo Park P O	87	377
James	37	m	w	IREL	San Mateo	Menlo Park P O	87	377
John	30	m	w	PA	San Francisco	5-Wd San Francisco	81	18
John	26	m	w	CANA	San Francisco	San Francisco P O	85	790
L	23	f	w	IREL	San Francisco	San Francisco P O	85	791
Martin	35	m	w	IREL	Butte	Ophir Twp	70	117
Wm	27	m	w	NY	Solano	Vallejo	90	139
CUDIHEY								
Mortis	23	m	w	IREL	San Francisco	11-Wd San Francisc	84	694
CUDOGAN								
Joseph	26	m	w	IREL	San Francisco	3-Wd San Francisco	79	300
CUDWELL								
Mary	13	f	w	ENGL	San Francisco	6-Wd San Francisco	81	132
CUDWIG								
Chas	28	m	w	DENM	Butte	Chico Twp	70	26
CUDWITH								
Wallace	47	m	w	VT	San Francisco	6-Wd San Francisco	81	124
CUE								
Ah	42	m	c	CHIN	Butte	Kimshew Tpw	70	84
Ah	40	m	c	CHIN	Placer	Bath P O	76	423
Ah	38	m	c	CHIN	Placer	Newcastle Twp	76	477
Ah	32	m	c	CHIN	Alameda	Oakland	68	223
Ah	32	m	c	CHIN	Plumas	Goodwin Twp	77	2
Ah	30	m	c	CHIN	Solano	Suisun Twp	90	105
Ah	3	f	c	CA	Nevada	Grass Valley Twp	75	168
Ah	26	m	c	CHIN	Placer	Dutch Flat P O	76	410
Ah	24	m	c	CHIN	Plumas	Goodwin Twp	77	4
Ah	23	m	c	CHIN	Sacramento	1-Wd Sacramento	77	198
Ah	23	m	c	CHIN	Calaveras	Copperopolis P O	70	258
Ah	22	m	c	CHIN	San Diego	San Diego	78	499
Ah	18	m	c	CHIN	Plumas	Goodwin Twp	77	2
Ah	17	m	c	CHIN	Placer	Colfax P O	76	387
Ah	13	m	c	CHIN	San Francisco	1-Wd San Francisco	79	114
Ang	36	m	c	CHIN	Plumas	Seneca Twp	77	48
Hung	26	m	c	CHIN	Yuba	Marysville	93	630
Meng	41	m	c	CHIN	Yuba	Marysville	93	630
William	50	m	w	IREL	San Francisco	7-Wd San Francisco	81	200
William	18	m	w	NY	San Francisco	7-Wd San Francisco	81	200
Yo	25	m	c	CHIN	Yuba	Marysville	93	630
CUELLA								
Crecencia	50	f	w	MEXI	Los Angeles	Santa Ana Twp	73	607
Rogue	40	m	w	MEXI	Monterey	Monterey	74	361
Serafina	29	f	w	MEXI	Los Angeles	Santa Ana Twp	73	607
CUELLAS								
Tomas	42	m	w	MEXI	Los Angeles	Santa Ana Twp	73	606
CUEN								
Bee	22	f	c	CHIN	Fresno	Millerton P O	72	201
CUERAS								
Antonio	40	m	w	MEXI	Los Angeles	San Juan Twp	73	625
CUEROTE								
John	40	m	w	CHIL	Calaveras	San Andreas P O	70	219
CUERVO								
Susan	27	f	w	CA	San Francisco	San Francisco P O	80	409
CUEVES								
Rosa	24	f	w	MEXI	San Francisco	2-Wd San Francisco	79	252
CUEVO								
John	32	m	w	MO	Colusa	Colusa Twp	71	274
CUEY								
Ah	27	m	c	CHIN	San Francisco	3-Wd San Francisco	79	301

© 2001 by Heritage Quest. All rights reserved.

California 1870 Census

Name	Age	S	R	B-PL	County	Series M593 Locale	Roll	Pg
CUFF								
Dennis	45	m	w	MA	San Francisco	San Francisco P O	83	1
Frances	24	f	w	ENGL	San Francisco	8-Wd San Francisco	82	441
Mary	18	f	w	IREL	San Francisco	San Francisco P O	83	40
Paul	50	m	w	MA	San Diego	San Diego	78	503
Thomas	29	m	w	ENGL	Solano	Suisun Twp	90	111
CUFFEY								
Antonie	52	m	w	FRAN	San Francisco	3-Wd San Francisco	79	319
CUFFMANN								
Alxn	38	m	w	PERS	Monterey	Alisal Twp	74	291
CUFFY								
Thos	32	m	w	IREL	Sonoma	Santa Rosa	91	407
CUFKIN								
D T	52	m	w	ME	Sacramento	Franklin Twp	77	108
CUGNEIF								
Teodore	36	m	w	FRAN	Santa Barbara	San Buenaventura P	87	444
CUHN								
Charles	40	m	w	GERM	Santa Barbara	San Buenaventura P	87	428
CUIER								
Lewis	38	m	w	PRUS	Santa Cruz	Soquel Twp	89	444
CUILLES								
Manuel	30	m	w	CA	San Diego	Temecula Dist	78	527
CUILLS								
John	4	m	w	CA	San Francisco	11-Wd San Francisc	84	629
CUIM								
Ah	26	m	c	CHIN	Solano	Suisun Twp	90	106
CUISICK								
Delia	25	f	w	CA	Sacramento	4-Wd Sacramento	77	348
CULAMORE								
Isaac	24	m	w	ME	Yuba	East Bear Rvr Twp	93	544
CULBERG								
Isaac	47	m	w	SWED	Humboldt	Arcata Twp	72	235
CULBERT								
A D	62	m	w	NY	Sacramento	3-Wd Sacramento	77	289
Charles	38	m	w	IREL	San Joaquin	2-Wd Stockton	86	166
David	23	m	w	CANA	Mendocino	Sanel Twp	74	227
M M	38	m	w	MO	Amador	Drytown P O	69	419
T L	34	m	w	MO	Amador	Amador City P O	69	393
William	14	m	w	CANA	Contra Costa	Martinez P O	71	445
CULBERTSEN								
G F	42	m	w	MA	Tuolumne	Big Oak Flat P O	93	391
John	26	m	w	PA	San Francisco	11-Wd San Francisc	84	686
CULBERTSON								
A J	22	m	w	OH	Calaveras	Copperopolis P O	70	226
Alfred	44	m	w	OH	Monterey	Pajaro Twp	74	372
Elizabeth	54	f	w	TN	Nevada	Little York Twp	75	238
James	41	m	w	TX	Nevada	Meadow Lake Twp	75	270
John	38	m	w	MD	Santa Cruz	Pajaro Twp	89	350
John	37	m	w	VA	San Bernardino	San Bernardino Twp	78	429
Saml	10	m	w	CA	Sonoma	Santa Rosa	91	404
Wilm	52	m	w	NC	Monterey	Pajaro Twp	74	375
CULBERY								
Andrew	28	m	w	SWED	Sonoma	Petaluma Twp	91	360
CULBRETH								
John	48	m	w	IREL	San Francisco	1-Wd San Francisco	79	2
CULBRSON								
Henry C	43	m	w	NC	Sonoma	Sonoma Twp	91	444
CULBURT								
William	25	m	w	IREL	Nevada	Bridgeport Twp	75	105
CULCAN								
Jas	26	m	w	NY	Solano	Vallejo	90	145
CULCHETH								
William	35	m	w	ENGL	San Francisco	3-Wd San Francisco	79	316
CULFER								
Bridget	36	f	w	IREL	San Francisco	8-Wd San Francisco	82	305
CULINAN								
James	65	m	w	IREL	San Francisco	San Francisco P O	85	846
CULKINS								
Bedlia	34	f	w	IREL	El Dorado	Placerville	72	124
CULL								
Henry	29	m	w	CANA	Nevada	Bridgeport Twp	75	106
Michael	35	m	w	NY	Alameda	Washington Twp	68	283
William	41	m	w	KY	Alameda	Eden Twp	68	69
CULLAGHAN								
Owen	35	m	w	IREL	San Francisco	11-Wd San Francisc	84	592
Patrick	34	m	w	IREL	San Francisco	11-Wd San Francisc	84	523
CULLAN								
Margaret	40	f	w	IREL	San Francisco	7-Wd San Francisco	81	252
CULLEB								
G	48	m	w	FRAN	Sierra	Lincoln Twp	89	545
CULLEGAN								
Michl	47	m	w	IREL	San Francisco	San Francisco P O	83	66
CULLEMBER								
Joseph	18	m	w	TX	Santa Cruz	Pajaro Twp	89	355
CULLEN								
Andrew	25	m	w	IREL	San Francisco	11-Wd San Francisc	84	642
Bridget	28	f	w	IREL	Alameda	Oakland	68	198
Catherine	55	f	w	IREL	San Francisco	8-Wd San Francisco	82	483
Cathrine	15	f	w	NY	San Francisco	1-Wd San Francisco	79	116
Charles	40	m	w	IREL	El Dorado	Mud Springs Twp	72	81
Charles	31	m	w	IREL	San Francisco	San Francisco P O	83	374
Chas	32	m	w	PA	Tehama	Tehama Twp	92	192
Dennis	37	m	w	IREL	Santa Clara	Milpitas Twp	88	113
Edward	29	m	w	IREL	San Francisco	11-Wd San Francisc	84	438
Ellen	42	f	w	IREL	San Francisco	San Francisco P O	83	297
Henriette	26	f	w	NY	Tehama	Red Bluff	92	173
J	41	m	w	ENGL	Alameda	Oakland	68	150
J Wallace	33	m	w	RI	San Diego	San Diego	78	500
James	40	m	w	IREL	San Francisco	11-Wd San Francisc	84	601
James	38	m	w	IREL	San Francisco	San Francisco P O	83	350
John	55	m	w	IREL	Solano	Vallejo	90	157
John	42	m	w	IREL	San Francisco	San Francisco P O	80	353
John	37	m	w	IREL	San Francisco	1-Wd San Francisco	79	30
John	36	m	w	PA	San Francisco	11-Wd San Francisc	84	563
John	35	m	w	IREL	San Francisco	San Francisco P O	83	413
John	18	m	w	CA	San Francisco	11-Wd San Francisc	84	592
Kate	30	f	w	IREL	San Francisco	8-Wd San Francisco	82	306
Lawrence	39	m	w	IREL	San Francisco	San Francisco P O	80	332
Margaret	20	f	w	IREL	San Francisco	San Francisco P O	83	207
Maria	30	f	w	IREL	San Francisco	San Francisco P O	83	99
Mary	30	f	w	IREL	San Francisco	1-Wd San Francisco	79	114
Mary	23	f	w	IREL	San Francisco	San Francisco P O	83	97
Mary	23	f	w	NY	San Francisco	San Francisco P O	83	112
Michael	28	m	w	IREL	Yuba	Linda Twp	93	556
Michael	25	m	w	IREL	San Francisco	3-Wd San Francisco	79	295
Nellie A	17	f	w	NY	San Francisco	8-Wd San Francisco	82	333
Patric	45	m	w	IREL	Trinity	Junction City Pct	92	205
Patrick	40	m	w	IREL	San Mateo	Redwood Twp	87	361
Patrick	38	m	w	IREL	Monterey	San Juan Twp	74	393
Patrick	23	m	w	CANA	Santa Clara	Alviso Twp	88	26
Paul	12	m	w	CA	San Francisco	11-Wd San Francisc	84	592
Peter	48	m	w	IREL	Siskiyou	Scott Valley Twp	89	614
Peter	28	m	w	IREL	Colusa	Colusa Twp	71	284
Phillip	43	m	w	IREL	San Francisco	7-Wd San Francisco	81	198
Stephen	31	m	w	PA	Tehama	Red Bluff	92	173
Thomas	45	m	w	ENGL	San Francisco	3-Wd San Francisco	79	313
Thomas	37	m	w	IREL	San Mateo	Redwood Twp	87	361
Thos	29	m	w	IREL	Alameda	Oakland	68	214
Thos	25	m	w	IREL	Alameda	Oakland	68	260
Thos	14	m	w	CA	San Francisco	11-Wd San Francisc	84	592
Wm	49	m	w	IREL	Shasta	Shasta P O	89	455
CULLENS								
Patk	28	m	w	IREL	San Francisco	1-Wd San Francisco	79	44
CULLER								
Reuben	40	m	w	NH	Sacramento	Sutter Twp	77	390
CULLERY								
Ann	35	f	w	IREL	San Francisco	San Francisco P O	83	181
CULLETON								
Jas	36	m	w	IREL	Sacramento	1-Wd Sacramento	77	178
Morris	28	m	w	IREL	Yolo	Cache Crk Twp	93	436
CULLEVER								
D	35	m	w	MEXI	Alameda	Oakland	68	135
CULLEW								
Thomas	33	m	w	IREL	Yuba	Linda Twp	93	556
CULLEY								
James	45	m	w	IREL	Plumas	Mineral Twp	77	20
John	16	m	w	NY	San Francisco	7-Wd San Francisco	81	178
CULLIGAN								
James	37	m	w	IREL	Sonoma	Petaluma Twp	91	323
John	35	m	w	IREL	San Francisco	San Francisco P O	85	734
CULLIN								
Ben	48	m	w	AR	Butte	Chico Twp	70	58
Gerrard	47	m	w	IREL	San Francisco	2-Wd San Francisco	79	250
Mike	45	m	w	IREL	San Francisco	San Francisco P O	85	795
Robt	33	m	w	OH	Sacramento	3-Wd Sacramento	77	259
Thomas	27	m	w	IREL	San Francisco	11-Wd San Francisc	84	490
Thos M	36	m	w	KY	Sierra	Table Rock Twp	89	571
CULLINAN								
Bridget	30	f	w	IREL	San Francisco	6-Wd San Francisco	81	129
Julia	28	f	w	IREL	San Francisco	6-Wd San Francisco	81	96
CULLINS								
David	35	m	w	IREL	Sacramento	Dry Crk Twp	77	101
Isaac	42	m	w	SCOT	Alameda	Eden Twp	68	71
Mary	70	f	w	IREL	San Francisco	11-Wd San Francisc	84	431
CULLITON								
M	36	m	w	IREL	Sacramento	1-Wd Sacramento	77	178
CULLITY								
Eugene	28	m	w	IL	Santa Clara	1-Wd San Jose	88	230
CULLOM								
Frank	41	m	w	IREL	San Francisco	San Francisco P O	83	284
George	68	m	w	OH	Placer	Lincoln P O	76	486
CULLOUGH								
John	52	m	w	GERM	San Francisco	San Francisco P O	83	151
CULLOVIN								
James	32	m	w	IREL	Nevada	Eureka Twp	75	130
CULLUM								
A	15	m	w	KY	Solano	Benicia	90	21
A C	47	m	w	OH	San Francisco	San Francisco P O	83	63
William	40	m	w	NY	San Francisco	7-Wd San Francisco	81	208
CULLUN								
Anna	29	f	w	IREL	San Francisco	7-Wd San Francisco	81	161
Edward	29	m	w	IREL	San Francisco	San Francisco P O	85	861
H	60	m	w	NY	Solano	Vallejo	90	188
CULLY								
Anna	16	f	w	NY	Solano	Vallejo	90	182
James	44	m	w	IREL	Butte	Ophir Twp	70	115
James	35	m	w	IREL	San Francisco	San Francisco P O	83	244
Wm L	30	m	w	NY	Solano	Vallejo	90	195
CULMAN								
Ann	25	f	w	IREL	Alameda	Alameda	68	18
CULNER								
Mary	45	f	w	IREL	San Francisco	San Francisco P O	80	340
CULONELL								
Pat	33	m	w	IREL	San Francisco	11-Wd San Francisc	84	686

© 2001 by Heritage Quest. All rights reserved.

Series M593

Name	Age	S	R	B-PL	County	Locale	Roll	Pg
CULP								
Alexander W	28	m	w	MO	Tulare	Tule Rvr Twp	92	261
Amos	36	m	w	OH	Amador	Drytown P O	69	418
Bell	17	f	b	MO	Colusa	Colusa Twp	71	287
Ben F	39	m	w	KY	San Luis Obispo	San Luis Obispo Tw	87	301
Daniel	38	m	w	PA	Alameda	Eden Twp	68	65
Elizabeth M	27	f	w	MO	Nevada	Grass Valley Twp	75	207
Francis	31	m	w	TN	Sonoma	Santa Rosa	91	401
Henry	46	m	w	KY	Colusa	Colusa	71	289
Jas D	30	m	w	NY	Santa Clara	Gilroy Twp	88	70
John Armstrong	42	m	w	PA	Plumas	Rich Bar Twp	77	8
John M	43	m	w	KY	Colusa	Colusa Twp	71	287
Maria	57	f	w	NY	Santa Clara	San Jose Twp	88	181
Thomas	45	m	w	PA	Nevada	Nevada Twp	75	316
CULTEE								
F T	44	m	m	VT	Solano	Benicia	90	2
Jane	36	f	w	IREL	Solano	Benicia	90	2
CULTER								
Theadore	30	m	w	IL	Humboldt	Mattole Twp	72	285
CULVER								
Amelia	46	f	w	OH	Yuba	New York Twp	93	638
Andrew I	50	m	w	CT	Placer	Colfax P O	76	387
Benjamin	69	m	w	NY	Butte	Bidwell Twp	70	1
C Boliver	34	m	w	VT	San Diego	San Diego	78	509
C F	40	m	w	NY	San Francisco	3-Wd San Francisco	79	314
Calvin	33	m	w	CANA	El Dorado	Placerville Twp	72	102
Cornelius	69	m	w	NJ	Solano	Benicia	90	7
Edgar	47	m	w	CT	Placer	Newcastle Twp	76	475
Edward	45	m	w	NY	Yolo	Cottonwood Twp	93	472
Ella	14	f	w	CA	Nevada	Grass Valley Twp	75	150
Elsie	56	f	w	NY	San Francisco	11-Wd San Francisc	84	495
Ezra	39	m	w	NY	Plumas	Quartz Twp	77	36
Frank	37	m	w	NY	San Joaquin	2-Wd Stockton	86	193
Harvey	9	m	w	CA	Butte	Ophir Twp	70	116
Henry	41	m	w	PRUS	Marin	Bolinas Twp	74	5
Henry	40	m	w	NY	Solano	Tremont Twp	90	35
Henry	35	m	w	NY	Solano	Silveyville Twp	90	72
James	40	m	w	NY	San Francisco	5-Wd San Francisco	81	14
James H	34	m	w	NY	San Francisco	San Francisco P O	83	343
John	23	m	w	IL	Colusa	Monroe Twp	71	319
Kate	25	f	w	TX	San Joaquin	2-Wd Stockton	86	163
Lin	20	m	c	CHIN	Colusa	Monroe Twp	71	319
Linda C	15	f	w	WI	Butte	Bidwell Twp	70	2
Samuel	20	m	w	CA	Colusa	Monroe Twp	71	319
Stephen	42	m	w	NY	San Mateo	Half Moon Bay P O	87	408
Willett	57	m	w	NY	San Francisco	San Francisco P O	85	872
William	45	m	w	NY	Solano	Tremont Twp	90	35
William	43	m	w	NY	San Francisco	San Francisco P O	80	479
William H	45	m	w	MA	San Francisco	6-Wd San Francisco	81	37
CULVERHOUSE								
Jerry	38	m	w	TN	Shasta	Shasta P O	89	462
CULVERSON								
William	40	m	w	OH	Solano	Vacaville Twp	90	131
CULVERWELL								
Chas	30	m	w	MO	San Joaquin	1-Wd Stockton	86	152
J E	32	m	w	DC	San Francisco	San Francisco P O	85	842
Solomon S	42	m	w	MD	San Diego	San Diego	78	509
CULVIN								
Wm	26	m	w	IREL	Solano	Vallejo	90	217
CUM								
Ah	68	m	c	CHIN	Placer	Auburn P O	76	358
Ah	55	m	c	CHIN	Sierra	Eureka Twp	89	526
Ah	52	m	c	CHIN	San Francisco	San Francisco P O	80	445
Ah	50	m	c	CHIN	Tuolumne	Chinese Camp P O	93	375
Ah	50	m	c	CHIN	Butte	Kimshew Tpw	70	86
Ah	49	m	c	CHIN	Butte	Ophir Twp	70	103
Ah	45	m	c	CHIN	Placer	Newcastle Twp	76	477
Ah	45	m	c	CHIN	Nevada	Grass Valley Twp	75	171
Ah	43	m	c	CHIN	San Francisco	San Francisco P O	80	494
Ah	40	m	c	CHIN	Mariposa	Mariposa P O	74	133
Ah	40	f	c	CHIN	Mariposa	Mariposa P O	74	114
Ah	40	f	c	CHIN	Mariposa	Mariposa P O	74	132
Ah	40	m	c	CHIN	San Francisco	San Francisco P O	80	499
Ah	39	m	c	CHIN	San Francisco	San Francisco P O	80	498
Ah	37	m	c	CHIN	Fresno	Millerton P O	72	155
Ah	35	m	c	CHIN	Stanislaus	Emory Twp	92	20
Ah	33	f	c	CHIN	Amador	Jackson P O	69	344
Ah	33	m	c	CHIN	Solano	Suisun Twp	90	105
Ah	33	m	c	CHIN	San Francisco	San Francisco P O	80	510
Ah	32	m	c	CHIN	Butte	Chico Twp	70	27
Ah	32	m	c	CHIN	San Francisco	San Francisco P O	80	489
Ah	31	m	c	CHIN	Calaveras	San Andreas P O	70	179
Ah	31	m	c	CHIN	Placer	Auburn P O	76	383
Ah	30	m	c	CHIN	Solano	Suisun Twp	90	104
Ah	30	m	c	CHIN	Stanislaus	Emory Twp	92	23
Ah	30	m	c	CHIN	Nevada	Grass Valley Twp	75	144
Ah	30	m	c	CHIN	Fresno	Millerton P O	72	191
Ah	30	m	c	CHIN	Amador	Volcano P O	69	387
Ah	30	m	c	CHIN	San Francisco	San Francisco P O	80	507
Ah	30	m	c	CHIN	San Francisco	San Francisco P O	80	506
Ah	29	m	c	CHIN	Tuolumne	Chinese Camp P O	93	370
Ah	27	m	c	CHIN	Mariposa	Maxwell Crk P O	74	147
Ah	27	f	c	CHIN	Calaveras	San Andreas P O	70	181
Ah	26	m	c	CHIN	Calaveras	San Andreas P O	70	171
Ah	26	m	c	CHIN	Placer	Auburn P O	76	362
Ah	25	m	c	CHIN	San Mateo	Pescadero P O	87	416
Ah	24	m	c	CHIN	Solano	Vacaville Twp	90	131
Ah	24	f	c	CHIN	Butte	Ophir Twp	70	104
Ah	22	m	c	CHIN	Solano	Suisun Twp	90	106
Ah	22	f	c	CHIN	Mariposa	Mariposa P O	74	133
Ah	21	m	c	CHIN	San Francisco	San Francisco P O	80	336
Ah	20	f	c	CHIN	San Francisco	San Francisco P O	80	434
Ah	19	m	c	CHIN	Butte	Hamilton Twp	70	67
Ah	19	m	c	CHIN	San Francisco	San Francisco P O	80	413
Ah	19	m	c	CHIN	San Francisco	San Francisco P O	80	456
Ah	16	f	c	CHIN	Mariposa	Mariposa P O	74	114
Ah	12	m	c	CHIN	San Francisco	San Francisco P O	80	352
Ah	---	m	c	CHIN	Fresno	Millerton P O	72	199
An	17	f	c	CHIN	Placer	Bath P O	76	429
Charley	33	m	c	CHIN	Placer	Colfax P O	76	384
Chaw	29	f	c	CHIN	Marin	San Rafael Twp	74	40
Chi	20	m	c	CHIN	Sacramento	2-Wd Sacramento	77	245
Chung	48	m	c	CHIN	Yuba	Marysville	93	620
Cloy	18	f	c	CHIN	San Francisco	6-Wd San Francisco	81	60
Com	30	m	c	CHIN	Calaveras	San Andreas P O	70	169
Coo	25	m	c	CHIN	Yuba	Marysville	93	631
Enge	27	m	c	CHIN	Mariposa	Maxwell Crk P O	74	145
Fok	32	m	c	CHIN	Fresno	Millerton P O	72	202
Foo	48	m	c	CHIN	Tuolumne	Chinese Camp P O	93	379
Fow	28	m	c	CHIN	Tuolumne	Columbia P O	93	361
Gee	41	m	c	CHIN	Tuolumne	Chinese Camp P O	93	385
How	24	f	c	CHIN	Nevada	Grass Valley Twp	75	205
I	34	f	c	CHIN	Stanislaus	Emory Twp	92	22
Kee	28	f	c	CHIN	Tuolumne	Chinese Camp P O	93	379
Lee	31	m	c	CHIN	Placer	Newcastle Twp	76	478
Lic	19	m	c	CHIN	Calaveras	Copperopolis P O	70	264
Ling	28	m	c	CHIN	Fresno	Millerton P O	72	202
Loi	15	m	c	CHIN	Butte	Kimshew Tpw	70	85
Loo	30	m	c	CHIN	Tuolumne	Chinese Camp P O	93	382
Luan	33	m	c	CHIN	Calaveras	San Andreas P O	70	190
Me	31	m	c	CHIN	Yuba	Marysville	93	630
Moi	8	f	c	CA	Mariposa	Maxwell Crk P O	74	138
Moy	17	f	c	CHIN	San Francisco	6-Wd San Francisco	81	60
Ni	28	m	c	CHIN	Sonoma	Vallejo Twp	91	450
Sang	40	f	c	CHIN	San Francisco	6-Wd San Francisco	81	75
See	60	m	c	CHIN	Amador	Jackson P O	69	344
See	18	m	c	CHIN	Amador	Jackson P O	69	331
Shong	30	m	c	CHIN	Mariposa	Maxwell Crk P O	74	142
Si	28	m	c	CHIN	San Francisco	6-Wd San Francisco	81	52
Sig	45	m	c	CHIN	Calaveras	San Andreas P O	70	190
Sing	40	f	c	CHIN	Placer	Colfax P O	76	388
Sing	22	f	c	CHIN	Placer	Colfax P O	76	384
Sing	19	m	c	CHIN	Butte	Hamilton Twp	70	67
Tung	24	f	c	CHIN	Mariposa	Mariposa P O	74	103
Wick	19	m	c	CHIN	Solano	Silveyville Twp	90	85
Yea	35	m	c	CHIN	Fresno	Millerton P O	72	201
Yo	31	f	c	CHIN	Mariposa	Mariposa P O	74	132
Yung	33	m	c	CHIN	Calaveras	San Andreas P O	70	171
CUMBERFORD								
Chas	24	m	w	NY	Sacramento	4-Wd Sacramento	77	340
CUMBERLAND								
John	58	m	w	NY	San Francisco	San Francisco P O	85	742
CUMBERSON								
A J	49	m	w	NY	Yuba	Marysville	93	578
Sam	32	m	w	TN	Butte	Chico Twp	70	54
CUMBRA								
Manuel	30	m	w	PORT	Alameda	Eden Twp	68	72
CUMBRLAND								
Mary	28	f	w	IREL	San Francisco	11-Wd San Francisc	84	422
CUMER								
Patrick	21	m	w	IREL	El Dorado	Diamond Springs Tw	72	33
CUMERFORD								
A D	30	m	w	PA	San Mateo	Schoolhouse Statio	87	331
CUMINGHAM								
Joseph	31	m	w	IREL	San Francisco	11-Wd San Francisc	84	613
CUMINGS								
Anthony	25	m	w	IREL	Solano	Maine Prairie Twp	90	52
Edward	43	m	w	IREL	Nevada	Bloomfield Twp	75	93
James	40	m	w	ENGL	Trinity	Minersville Pct	92	215
James H	37	m	w	IREL	Sacramento	Cosumnes Twp	77	89
L S	60	m	w	MD	Nevada	Nevada Twp	75	279
Pat	28	m	w	IREL	San Francisco	11-Wd San Francisc	84	595
Thomas	39	m	w	ENGL	Trinity	Minersville Pct	92	203
William	52	m	w	IREL	Nevada	Washington Twp	75	344
CUMINSKEY								
Ella	38	f	w	NY	San Francisco	8-Wd San Francisco	82	347
Terence	26	m	w	RI	San Francisco	San Francisco P O	83	188
CUMISKY								
Cornelius	40	m	w	IREL	Nevada	Rough & Ready Twp	75	327
Henry	44	m	w	IREL	San Francisco	San Francisco P O	80	380
CUMMENS								
Edward	40	m	w	IREL	San Mateo	San Mateo P O	87	352
CUMMER								
Wm A	36	m	w	TN	Trinity	Minersville Pct	92	215
CUMMIGS								
Douglas W	35	m	w	CANA	Santa Cruz	Soquel Twp	89	442
CUMMING								
Anna W	30	f	w	OH	Santa Cruz	Santa Cruz	89	409
D H	39	m	w	PA	San Francisco	San Francisco P O	83	107
David J	30	m	w	CANA	Santa Cruz	Soquel Twp	89	441
Geo	45	m	w	SCOT	San Francisco	San Francisco P O	83	106
John	50	m	w	PA	Placer	Lincoln P O	76	492
John	40	m	w	CANA	Mendocino	Navarro & Big Rvr	74	176
Nancy	70	f	w	IREL	San Francisco	2-Wd San Francisco	79	278

© 2001 by Heritage Quest. All rights reserved.

California 1870 Census

Name	Age	S	R	B-PL	County	Locale	Roll	Pg
						Series M593		
Richard	31	m	w	CANA	San Francisco	3-Wd San Francisco	79	289
Thos	35	m	w	IREL	San Francisco	7-Wd San Francisco	81	257
Wm	23	m	w	IREL	Santa Clara	Gilroy Twp	88	89
CUMMINGHAM								
J	58	m	w	IREL	Sierra	Downieville Twp	89	517
J S	52	m	w	RI	Santa Clara	Gilroy Twp	88	80
Margaret	18	f	w	CA	San Francisco	11-Wd San Francisc	84	710
CUMMINGS								
A	39	m	w	NY	Alameda	Oakland	68	211
A E	40	f	w	MD	Alameda	Oakland	68	211
A H	35	m	w	NY	Sacramento	3-Wd Sacramento	77	312
A H	20	m	w	IL	Sacramento	4-Wd Sacramento	77	372
A M	56	m	w	OH	Siskiyou	Callahan P O	89	632
Abel	35	m	w	NY	San Francisco	5-Wd San Francisco	81	19
Albert	42	m	w	KY	Tulare	White Rvr Twp	92	301
Alfred	24	m	w	MO	Kern	Tehachapi P O	73	354
Amelia	59	f	w	MA	Marin	San Rafael	74	58
Andrew	65	m	w	IREL	Marin	San Rafael Twp	74	36
Ann	35	f	w	ME	Solano	Vacaville Twp	90	129
Cecilia	53	f	w	IREL	Santa Clara	2-Wd San Jose	88	313
Charles	29	m	w	CANA	Santa Cruz	Santa Cruz Twp	89	379
Charles O	30	m	w	ME	Santa Cruz	Watsonville	89	369
Chas	15	m	w	NY	San Francisco	1-Wd San Francisco	79	95
Cyrus	51	m	w	ME	Marin	San Rafael Twp	74	36
Daniel	66	m	w	KY	Los Angeles	Santa Ana Twp	73	603
E C	32	m	w	NY	Humboldt	Pacific Twp	72	297
Eli R	38	m	w	NC	Sonoma	Washington Twp	91	470
Elizh	30	f	w	VA	Sonoma	Petaluma Twp	91	366
Elmore	39	m	w	ME	Stanislaus	Empire Twp	92	51
Elon	40	m	w	NY	Contra Costa	Martinez P O	71	431
F	22	m	w	NY	San Joaquin	2-Wd Stockton	86	162
Francis	2	m	w	IA	Los Angeles	Los Angeles Twp	73	473
Frank	38	m	w	AUST	Placer	Newcastle Twp	76	476
Frank	26	m	w	MA	Sacramento	1-Wd Sacramento	77	172
G W	35	m	w	ENGL	Sierra	Sears Twp	89	558
George	46	m	w	SWED	Los Angeles	San Jose Twp	73	619
George	36	m	w	AUST	Kern	Tehachapi P O	73	354
H	59	m	w	VT	Placer	Dutch Flat P O	76	405
H P K	43	m	w	VT	San Francisco	San Francisco P O	83	94
Harrison	35	m	w	NY	San Francisco	San Francisco P O	83	189
Henry	43	m	w	MA	San Francisco	7-Wd San Francisco	81	246
Henry	24	m	w	OH	Sonoma	Analy Twp	91	230
Herman B	39	m	w	NY	Santa Cruz	Soquel Twp	89	447
Horatio	44	m	w	MA	Yolo	Washington Twp	93	531
Horton	42	m	w	PA	San Francisco	5-Wd San Francisco	81	33
J	57	m	w	TN	Amador	Ione City P O	69	352
J F	35	m	m	IREL	Humboldt	Eureka Twp	72	277
J H	40	m	w	ME	Sacramento	3-Wd Sacramento	77	256
J S	45	m	w	NC	Lake	Big Valley	73	399
James	58	m	w	CANA	San Francisco	2-Wd San Francisco	79	251
James	41	m	w	IREL	Marin	Sausalito Twp	74	69
James	40	m	w	ME	San Francisco	7-Wd San Francisco	81	172
James	40	m	w	IREL	San Francisco	8-Wd San Francisco	82	398
James	33	m	w	IREL	Los Angeles	Los Angeles	73	559
James	32	m	w	ENGL	Fresno	Kingston P O	72	219
James B	24	m	w	MA	Los Angeles	Santa Ana Twp	73	601
James M	34	m	w	NC	Sonoma	Washington Twp	91	470
Jane	60	f	w	IREL	San Francisco	1-Wd San Francisco	79	35
Jane	48	f	w	MO	Kern	Kernville P O	73	367
Jas	46	m	w	MO	Fresno	Kingston P O	72	221
Jas	20	m	w	TX	San Diego	Warners Rancho Dis	78	530
Jno F	34	m	w	OH	Butte	Ophir Twp	70	112
Jno S	57	m	w	PA	Sonoma	Mendocino Twp	91	299
Johana	70	f	w	IREL	San Francisco	San Francisco P O	80	375
John	47	m	w	MA	San Francisco	San Francisco P O	83	94
John	40	m	w	IREL	Tuolumne	Chinese Camp P O	93	335
John	40	m	w	RUSS	Alpine	Monitor P O	69	313
John	34	m	w	IREL	San Francisco	8-Wd San Francisco	82	490
John	33	m	w	MI	Yolo	Cache Crk Twp	93	452
John	30	m	w	CANA	Mendocino	Casper & Big Rvr	74	163
John	30	m	w	IREL	San Francisco	San Francisco P O	83	372
John M	33	m	w	IN	Los Angeles	Santa Ana Twp	73	603
John Oliver	36	m	w	PA	Plumas	Plumas Twp	77	27
Jonathan	37	m	w	ME	Alameda	Brooklyn	68	26
Joseph	45	m	w	MA	Stanislaus	Empire Twp	92	35
Joseph	40	m	m	NJ	San Francisco	2-Wd San Francisco	79	234
Joseph	28	m	w	MA	Marin	San Rafael	74	58
Joseph	25	m	w	IREL	San Francisco	San Francisco P O	85	758
Joseph	23	m	w	MO	Calaveras	San Andreas P O	70	220
Judson	33	m	w	NY	San Mateo	Pescadero P O	87	416
Kate	70	f	w	IREL	Sacramento	4-Wd Sacramento	77	367
L	28	m	w	IREL	Humboldt	Eureka Twp	72	273
L J	40	m	w	IN	Humboldt	Mattole Twp	72	286
Laurence	34	m	w	IREL	San Francisco	11-Wd San Francisc	84	450
Luis	21	m	w	PA	Sacramento	1-Wd Sacramento	77	176
M J	36	m	w	IREL	San Francisco	San Francisco P O	83	271
Mary	29	f	w	TN	Monterey	Pajaro Twp	74	368
Mary	24	f	w	IREL	San Francisco	7-Wd San Francisco	81	259
Mary	21	f	w	IREL	San Francisco	7-Wd San Francisco	81	185
Michael	45	m	w	IREL	San Francisco	San Francisco P O	85	755
Michael	25	m	w	IREL	Nevada	Grass Valley Twp	75	214
Noah	30	m	w	KY	Los Angeles	El Monte Twp	73	456
Orson N	36	m	w	NY	San Francisco	San Francisco P O	83	170
Patk	35	m	w	IREL	San Francisco	San Francisco P O	85	852
Patrick	40	m	w	IREL	San Francisco	8-Wd San Francisco	82	319
Patrick	39	m	w	IREL	San Francisco	San Francisco P O	85	755
Peter	48	m	w	IREL	Stanislaus	San Joaquin Twp	92	79
Polly	40	f	w	KY	Calaveras	Copperopolis P O	70	262
Quincy	20	m	w	NY	Sacramento	4-Wd Sacramento	77	372
Richd	28	m	w	IREL	San Francisco	1-Wd San Francisco	79	63
Robert	39	m	w	IA	Los Angeles	Santa Ana Twp	73	603
Robert	28	m	w	IREL	San Mateo	San Mateo P O	87	356
Rose	52	f	w	NY	San Francisco	7-Wd San Francisco	81	159
S	43	m	w	MO	Yuba	Marysville	93	604
Samuel	38	m	w	CANA	Stanislaus	Empire Twp	92	43
Samuel	25	m	w	CANA	Alpine	Monitor P O	69	317
Seth	54	m	w	MA	Butte	Chico Twp	70	37
Silas	47	m	w	ENGL	San Francisco	7-Wd San Francisco	81	274
Soloman	23	m	w	MO	Calaveras	Copperopolis P O	70	261
T R	36	m	w	PA	Siskiyou	Callahan P O	89	625
Theodor	49	m	w	NY	San Francisco	San Francisco P O	83	401
Thomas	42	m	w	PA	Calaveras	San Andreas P O	70	173
Thomas	36	m	w	IREL	San Francisco	11-Wd San Francisc	84	529
Thomas	29	m	w	CANA	San Francisco	San Francisco P O	85	745
Thomas	29	m	w	PA	Humboldt	Eureka Twp	72	256
Thomas M	22	m	w	IN	Los Angeles	Santa Ana Twp	73	603
Thos	38	m	w	AL	Marin	San Rafael Twp	74	42
Walt	70	m	w	IREL	Sacramento	4-Wd Sacramento	77	367
Wiley	23	m	w	TX	Fresno	Kings Rvr P O	72	212
Will	51	m	w	IREL	San Francisco	6-Wd San Francisco	81	95
William	45	m	w	LA	Kern	Linns Valley P O	73	344
William	32	m	w	MO	Solano	Tremont Twp	90	28
William	30	m	w	NY	San Francisco	San Francisco P O	83	361
Willm	40	m	w	NY	Sonoma	Mendocino Twp	91	292
Wm	49	m	w	PA	Sacramento	3-Wd Sacramento	77	315
Wm	46	m	w	AL	Siskiyou	Scott Valley Twp	89	617
Wm	45	m	w	MA	San Francisco	1-Wd San Francisco	79	13
Wm	23	m	w	IREL	San Francisco	3-Wd San Francisco	79	319
Wm H	53	m	w	NY	San Francisco	8-Wd San Francisco	82	332
Wm M	40	m	w	CANA	Santa Cruz	Santa Cruz	89	433
CUMMINS								
Alexander	51	m	w	PA	Mendocino	Anderson Twp	74	156
C	45	m	w	ENGL	Santa Clara	Gilroy Twp	88	87
Charles	30	m	w	LA	Sacramento	2-Wd Sacramento	77	243
Chas H	47	m	w	MA	Sacramento	4-Wd Sacramento	77	345
Christian	50	m	w	NY	Sacramento	2-Wd Sacramento	77	247
Daniel F	32	m	w	IREL	Sacramento	2-Wd Sacramento	77	210
Edward	39	m	w	IREL	San Francisco	11-Wd San Francisc	84	510
Edward	34	m	w	IREL	Santa Clara	Redwood Twp	88	123
Francis	23	m	w	SWED	Inyo	Bishop Crk Twp	73	317
Gordon P	41	m	w	NY	Sacramento	2-Wd Sacramento	77	248
Harriet	38	f	w	OH	Alameda	Washington Twp	68	289
James	40	m	w	IREL	Santa Clara	Santa Clara Twp	88	162
James H	25	m	w	MO	Santa Cruz	Santa Cruz Twp	89	400
Jas	30	m	w	NH	San Francisco	San Francisco P O	83	292
John	29	m	w	IREL	San Francisco	San Francisco P O	80	531
John	27	m	w	OH	Solano	Vallejo	90	197
John	20	m	w	IREL	Sacramento	2-Wd Sacramento	77	215
Julia	41	f	b	LA	Sacramento	2-Wd Sacramento	77	236
Larence	43	m	w	IREL	San Francisco	San Francisco P O	83	13
M J	25	m	w	IREL	Solano	Vallejo	90	203
Marshall	41	m	w	NY	San Mateo	Pescadero P O	87	417
Mary	50	f	w	IREL	Contra Costa	Martinez P O	71	383
Mary	46	f	w	IREL	Calaveras	San Andreas P O	70	188
Mary	36	f	w	NY	San Joaquin	Liberty Twp	86	83
Mayberry	25	f	w	IREL	San Francisco	San Francisco P O	83	312
Thomas	31	m	w	IL	Colusa	Colusa Twp	71	273
Thomas	29	m	w	CANA	Sacramento	2-Wd Sacramento	77	244
Thos	63	m	w	IREL	San Francisco	11-Wd San Francisc	84	579
William	45	m	w	PA	Monterey	Pajaro Twp	74	373
William H	26	m	w	NY	Inyo	Bishop Crk Twp	73	315
CUMPLEY								
Patrick	47	m	w	IREL	Monterey	San Benito Twp	74	381
CUMTON								
M T	30	m	w	IREL	Alameda	Alameda	68	5
CUN								
Ah	48	m	c	CHIN	Trinity	Lewiston Pct	92	214
Ah	42	m	c	CHIN	Tuolumne	Big Oak Flat P O	93	394
Ah	40	m	c	CHIN	Tuolumne	Chinese Camp P O	93	370
Ah	36	m	c	CHIN	Stanislaus	Emory Twp	92	20
Ah	30	m	c	CHIN	Napa	Napa	75	51
Ah	29	m	c	CHIN	San Francisco	San Francisco P O	80	492
Ah	27	m	c	CHIN	Tuolumne	Chinese Camp P O	93	388
Ah	19	f	c	CHIN	San Francisco	San Francisco P O	80	526
Fo	33	m	c	CHIN	El Dorado	Diamond Springs Tw	72	33
I	20	f	c	CHIN	Stanislaus	Emory Twp	92	23
Ly	32	m	c	CHIN	Calaveras	San Andreas P O	70	171
Ti Lee	20	f	c	CHIN	Amador	Drytown P O	69	419
CUNA								
Trinidad	30	m	w	MEXI	San Diego	Julian Dist	78	474
CUNAN								
Bridget	22	f	w	IREL	San Francisco	San Francisco P O	83	130
Jerome	25	m	w	NY	San Francisco	5-Wd San Francisco	81	13
Maggie	16	f	w	IREL	Sacramento	4-Wd Sacramento	77	324
Mary	70	f	w	IREL	Monterey	San Benito Twp	74	384
Mary A	37	f	w	IREL	Sacramento	4-Wd Sacramento	77	345
Michael	35	m	w	IREL	San Francisco	San Francisco P O	83	15
Michael Jr	28	m	w	IREL	Monterey	San Benito Twp	74	384
Thomas	35	m	w	IREL	Monterey	San Benito Twp	74	384
CUNCO								
Antonio	28	m	w	ITAL	Amador	Volcano P O	69	383
Joseph	30	m	w	ITAL	Amador	Jackson P O	69	337
CUNDEL								
Robt	33	m	w	WURT	San Francisco	2-Wd San Francisco	79	229

© 2001 by Heritage Quest. All rights reserved.

Name	Age	S	R	B-PL	County	Locale	Roll	Pg
						Series M593		
CUNDON								
James	45	m	w	ME	Placer	Gold Run Twp	76	398
CUNDY								
Arthur	22	m	w	ENGL	Mariposa	Mariposa P O	74	98
David	42	m	w	ENGL	Nevada	Grass Valley Twp	75	232
David	23	m	w	ENGL	Nevada	Grass Valley Twp	75	153
Joseph	34	m	w	ENGL	Nevada	Grass Valley Twp	75	199
CUNE								
Ah	35	f	c	CHIN	Nevada	Bridgeport Twp	75	110
Ah	20	f	c	CHIN	Amador	Jackson P O	69	344
Frank M	56	m	w	VA	Butte	Oregon Twp	70	127
Jno	24	m	w	FL	Sacramento	1-Wd Sacramento	77	182
CUNEO								
Andrew	58	m	w	ITAL	San Francisco	2-Wd San Francisco	79	165
Andrew	38	m	w	ITAL	Amador	Jackson P O	69	322
Appolyte	8	m	w	CA	Calaveras	Copperopolis P O	70	246
August	35	m	w	ITAL	San Francisco	2-Wd San Francisco	79	164
Charles	38	m	w	ENGL	Calaveras	San Andreas P O	70	180
Charles	30	m	w	ITAL	Merced	Snelling P O	74	277
Charles	16	m	w	ITAL	San Francisco	2-Wd San Francisco	79	232
Frank	29	m	w	ENGL	Calaveras	San Andreas P O	70	180
J B	35	m	w	ITAL	Amador	Jackson P O	69	335
J P	26	m	w	ITAL	Tuolumne	Big Oak Flat P O	93	392
John	30	m	w	ITAL	Amador	Jackson P O	69	339
John	29	m	w	ITAL	San Francisco	2-Wd San Francisco	79	200
John	23	m	w	ITAL	San Francisco	2-Wd San Francisco	79	164
Joseph	36	m	w	ITAL	Amador	Volcano P O	69	373
Joseph B	37	m	w	ITAL	Amador	Volcano P O	69	386
Louis	41	m	w	ITAL	Amador	Sutter Crk P O	69	412
Louis	30	m	w	ITAL	San Francisco	1-Wd San Francisco	79	111
Louis	22	m	w	ITAL	Amador	Jackson P O	69	339
CUNETHERS								
William	40	m	w	LA	Los Angeles	Los Nietos Twp	73	575
CUNEW								
John	49	m	w	ENGL	Tuolumne	Columbia P O	93	344
CUNEY								
Robert	31	m	w	SCOT	San Francisco	3-Wd San Francisco	79	293
CUNG								
Ah	47	m	c	CHIN	Tuolumne	Big Oak Flat P O	93	394
Ah	41	m	c	CHIN	Amador	Sutter Crk P O	69	411
Ah	40	m	c	CHIN	Amador	Drytown P O	69	419
Ah	35	m	c	CHIN	San Francisco	11-Wd San Francisc	84	695
Ah	30	m	c	CHIN	Nevada	Grass Valley Twp	75	171
Ah	28	m	c	CHIN	Alameda	Oakland	68	158
Ah	24	m	c	CHIN	San Diego	San Diego	78	494
Ah	22	m	c	CHIN	Alameda	Alameda	68	2
Ah	22	m	c	CHIN	Alameda	Eden Twp	68	62
Ah	19	m	c	CHIN	Tuolumne	Chinese Camp P O	93	374
I	33	f	c	CHIN	Stanislaus	Emory Twp	92	22
Wong	40	m	c	CHIN	Butte	Ophir Twp	70	106
CUNIER								
Albert	31	m	w	NH	San Francisco	San Francisco P O	83	158
Benj S	59	m	w	ME	San Francisco	San Francisco P O	83	71
CUNIFF								
B	19	m	w	LA	San Francisco	San Francisco P O	85	786
Edward	41	m	w	IREL	Santa Clara	San Jose Twp	88	195
CUNIN								
Mary	30	f	w	IREL	San Francisco	San Francisco P O	83	372
CUNING								
Frank	30	m	w	IN	Santa Clara	San Jose Twp	88	186
CUNINGHAM								
Benjamin	39	m	w	AL	Trinity	Lewiston Pct	92	211
George	33	m	w	IREL	San Francisco	7-Wd San Francisco	81	202
James	43	m	w	IREL	San Francisco	7-Wd San Francisco	81	192
John	35	m	w	IREL	San Francisco	11-Wd San Francisc	84	673
Mary	35	f	w	IREL	San Francisco	7-Wd San Francisco	81	202
Robt	47	m	w	VA	Sutter	Vernon Twp	92	136
W	53	m	w	ME	Sierra	Forest Twp	89	531
W J	39	m	w	OH	Lake	Big Valley	73	399
CUNINGHAN								
Jones	38	m	w	PA	Yuba	North East Twp	93	646
CUNINGS								
Agness	71	f	w	SCOT	Trinity	Minersville Pct	92	203
John	75	m	w	SCOT	Trinity	Minersville Pct	92	203
CUNIO								
Andrea	40	m	w	ITAL	Amador	Volcano P O	69	377
H B	24	m	w	ITAL	Tuolumne	Chinese Camp P O	93	371
John	30	m	w	ITAL	Tuolumne	Chinese Camp P O	93	371
Michael	34	m	w	ITAL	San Francisco	2-Wd San Francisco	79	210
CUNIS								
Joseph	28	m	w	ITAL	Mariposa	Maxwell Crk P O	74	141
CUNN								
Ah	35	m	c	CHIN	San Francisco	11-Wd San Francisc	84	695
Ah	18	m	c	CHIN	Alameda	Alvarado	68	303
C	25	m	w	NY	Sacramento	3-Wd Sacramento	77	316
CUNNAN								
Ellen	24	f	w	IREL	Santa Clara	2-Wd San Jose	88	292
CUNNER								
Simeon	25	m	w	CANA	Nevada	Nevada Twp	75	322
CUNNIFF								
Mary A	12	f	w	MA	San Francisco	San Francisco P O	83	7
Wm	33	m	w	IREL	San Francisco	San Francisco P O	83	67
CUNNIGHAM								
Thos	28	m	w	IREL	San Francisco	3-Wd San Francisco	79	313
CUNNING								
B	47	m	w	IREL	Yuba	Rose Bar Twp	93	664
Jas	25	m	w	SCOT	San Luis Obispo	Arroyo Grande Twp	87	271
CUNNINGHAM								
A	35	m	w	NY	San Francisco	8-Wd San Francisco	82	346
A	25	m	w	ME	Humboldt	Eel Rvr Twp	72	251
A	25	m	w	IREL	San Francisco	7-Wd San Francisco	81	218
A A	23	m	w	MA	Tuolumne	Big Oak Flat P O	93	400
Alex	40	m	w	IREL	San Francisco	7-Wd San Francisco	81	256
Alfred	16	m	w	MEXI	San Francisco	6-Wd San Francisco	81	96
Andw	25	m	w	IN	Fresno	Millerton P O	72	149
Ann	55	f	w	VA	San Francisco	8-Wd San Francisco	82	480
Ann	28	f	w	IREL	San Francisco	San Francisco P O	80	390
Anne	35	f	w	IREL	San Francisco	6-Wd San Francisco	81	151
Anne	19	f	w	IREL	San Francisco	8-Wd San Francisco	82	384
Annie	25	f	w	ENGL	San Francisco	San Francisco P O	83	209
Arthur	35	m	w	VA	San Francisco	San Francisco P O	83	64
Brgt	24	f	w	IREL	San Francisco	8-Wd San Francisco	82	315
Bridget	67	f	w	IREL	San Francisco	San Francisco P O	85	872
Bridget	6	f	w	MA	San Francisco	San Francisco P O	85	772
Bridget	35	f	w	IREL	San Francisco	6-Wd San Francisco	81	146
Bridget	24	f	w	IREL	Solano	Vallejo	90	198
C C	77	m	w	VA	San Bernardino	San Bernardino Twp	78	446
Cathe	32	f	w	IREL	San Mateo	Menlo Park P O	87	377
Chas	35	m	w	ME	San Francisco	5-Wd San Francisco	81	27
Chas	30	m	w	NY	San Francisco	8-Wd San Francisco	82	294
Chas	28	m	w	IREL	Solano	Vallejo	90	158
Daniel	35	m	w	IREL	San Francisco	San Francisco P O	83	417
David	40	m	w	IREL	Contra Costa	Martinez P O	71	450
David	28	m	w	IREL	Los Angeles	Los Angeles	73	502
Dennis	30	m	w	IREL	Colusa	Spring Valley Twp	71	341
E	22	m	w	ENGL	San Francisco	8-Wd San Francisco	82	359
Ed	38	m	w	IREL	San Francisco	2-Wd San Francisco	79	213
Ed	10	m	w	CANA	Humboldt	Eureka Twp	72	257
Edwd	28	m	w	IREL	San Francisco	San Francisco P O	83	127
Elen	48	f	w	MA	San Francisco	8-Wd San Francisco	82	291
Ellen	55	f	w	IREL	San Francisco	San Francisco P O	83	251
Ellen	25	f	w	CANA	Alameda	Oakland	68	232
Enoch	54	m	w	VA	Placer	Bath P O	76	447
F	37	m	w	MA	Yuba	Marysville	93	615
F	25	m	w	VT	Solano	Vallejo	90	157
F M	45	m	w	IL	Tuolumne	Columbia P O	93	353
Francis	32	m	w	MO	Sonoma	Salt Point	91	381
Frank	38	m	w	IREL	San Francisco	San Francisco P O	85	747
Frank	37	m	w	PA	Yolo	Grafton Twp	93	493
Frank	15	m	w	ME	Stanislaus	Empire Twp	92	41
Geo	42	m	w	MA	San Francisco	7-Wd San Francisco	81	280
Geo	34	m	w	NY	Nevada	Eureka Twp	75	138
Geo H	30	m	w	ME	Nevada	Nevada Twp	75	310
Geo W	40	m	w	TN	Nevada	Grass Valley Twp	75	218
George	35	m	w	ME	Placer	Summit P O	76	496
George	24	m	w	NY	San Francisco	San Francisco P O	80	474
George W	43	m	w	PA	Los Angeles	Santa Ana Twp	73	615
Gussie	15	f	w	ME	Santa Cruz	Soquel Twp	89	446
H	30	m	w	IREL	Solano	Vallejo	90	194
Henry	28	m	w	OH	Solano	Silveyville Twp	90	79
Howard	22	m	w	MO	Solano	Vacaville Twp	90	120
J	69	m	w	IREL	Sacramento	3-Wd Sacramento	77	302
J	66	f	w	PA	Sonoma	Russian Rvr	91	372
J	47	m	w	OH	Yuba	Marysville	93	574
J	38	m	w	ME	Sierra	Downieville Twp	89	519
J	38	m	w	IREL	San Francisco	1-Wd San Francisco	79	52
J	34	f	w	IREL	Alameda	Oakland	68	194
J A	6	m	w	CA	Tehama	Battle Crk Twp	92	158
J A	50	m	w	IREL	San Francisco	San Francisco P O	83	331
J H	3	m	w	CA	Solano	Vallejo	90	158
J R	40	m	w	IREL	Tehama	Red Bluff	92	183
Jacob	26	m	w	PA	Yolo	Grafton Twp	93	482
James	54	m	w	IREL	Solano	Denverton Twp	90	27
James	50	m	w	IREL	Calaveras	San Andreas P O	70	180
James	49	m	w	SCOT	Marin	Point Reyes Twp	74	23
James	43	m	w	IREL	Plumas	Goodwin Twp	77	4
James	41	m	w	IREL	Marin	Sausalito Twp	74	72
James	39	m	w	IREL	San Francisco	San Francisco P O	83	383
James	38	m	w	MD	Mendocino	Ten Mile Rvr Twp	74	172
James	37	m	w	IA	Calaveras	San Andreas P O	70	211
James	36	m	w	PA	San Francisco	San Francisco P O	85	757
James	35	m	w	IREL	San Francisco	11-Wd San Francisc	84	654
James	30	m	w	IREL	Yolo	Washington Twp	93	537
James	30	m	w	IREL	Sacramento	2-Wd Sacramento	77	240
James	27	m	w	IREL	Sacramento	2-Wd Sacramento	77	240
James	25	m	w	IREL	Napa	Napa	75	57
Jane	22	f	w	NY	San Francisco	6-Wd San Francisco	81	95
Jas	50	m	w	IREL	San Diego	San Diego	78	507
Jas	40	m	w	SCOT	San Francisco	1-Wd San Francisco	79	68
Jas	40	m	w	IREL	San Francisco	1-Wd San Francisco	79	94
Jas	32	m	w	IREL	Solano	Vallejo	90	187
Jas	21	m	w	SCOT	San Francisco	1-Wd San Francisco	79	111
Jesse	15	f	w	MO	Sacramento	3-Wd Sacramento	77	262
Jessee	56	m	w	VA	Solano	Vacaville Twp	90	119
Jno	42	m	w	VT	Butte	Chico Twp	70	22
Jno	42	m	w	OH	San Francisco	5-Wd San Francisco	81	29
Jno	32	m	w	IREL	Sacramento	1-Wd Sacramento	77	186
Jno	28	m	w	NY	Sacramento	3-Wd Sacramento	77	300
Jno A	38	m	w	OH	Nevada	Grass Valley Twp	75	182
John	65	m	w	MD	Nevada	Nevada Twp	75	271
John	49	m	w	IREL	Merced	Snelling P O	74	255
John	49	m	w	ITAL	San Francisco	San Francisco P O	85	836
John	46	m	w	IREL	Tehama	Tehama Twp	92	192
John	45	m	w	IREL	San Francisco	San Francisco P O	83	154

© 2001 by Heritage Quest. All rights reserved.

Series M593

Name	Age	S	R	B-PL	County	Locale	Roll	Pg
John	45	m	w	OH	San Francisco	11-Wd San Francisc	84	555
John	43	m	w	SCOT	San Francisco	San Francisco P O	83	122
John	42	m	w	NY	San Francisco	San Francisco P O	85	822
John	40	m	w	CANA	Yolo	Putah Twp	93	520
John	37	m	w	IREL	San Francisco	7-Wd San Francisco	81	279
John	37	m	w	IREL	San Francisco	11-Wd San Francisc	84	683
John	35	m	w	IN	Santa Clara	Redwood Twp	88	129
John	34	m	w	IREL	San Francisco	San Francisco P O	83	245
John	34	m	w	CANA	San Francisco	San Francisco P O	83	210
John	32	m	w	IREL	San Francisco	7-Wd San Francisco	81	238
John	30	m	w	IREL	San Francisco	San Francisco P O	83	389
John	3	m	w	NY	Solano	Vallejo	90	158
John	28	m	w	IREL	San Francisco	1-Wd San Francisco	79	114
John	21	m	w	NY	Yolo	Cottonwood Twp	93	461
John	20	m	w	NY	Sonoma	Sonoma Twp	91	438
John J	35	m	w	KY	Yolo	Fremont Twp	93	476
Jos A	39	m	w	NY	San Francisco	San Francisco P O	83	71
Jos C	21	m	w	MO	Solano	Vacaville Twp	90	125
Joseph	50	m	w	TN	Solano	Green Valley Twp	90	38
Joseph	36	m	w	IREL	Butte	Oroville Twp	70	140
Joseph	29	m	w	MO	Sonoma	Petaluma Twp	91	322
Js	41	m	w	IREL	Merced	Snelling P O	74	255
Julia	38	f	w	IREL	Santa Clara	Fremont Twp	88	61
Kate	40	f	w	CA	San Francisco	6-Wd San Francisco	81	131
Leander	38	m	w	VT	Sonoma	Analy Twp	91	225
Leander	38	m	w	OH	Stanislaus	Empire Twp	92	36
Lewis	51	m	w	NY	San Francisco	San Francisco P O	83	147
M	42	f	w	IREL	San Francisco	San Francisco P O	85	779
M	34	f	w	IREL	Alameda	Oakland	68	187
M	28	f	w	IREL	Alameda	Oakland	68	132
M	25	f	w	IREL	Solano	Vallejo	90	158
M	23	f	w	IREL	Sacramento	3-Wd Sacramento	77	258
Margaret L	12	f	w	CA	Los Angeles	Los Angeles Twp	73	494
Mary	41	f	w	NY	Napa	Napa	75	5
Mary	31	f	w	NY	San Francisco	11-Wd San Francisc	84	480
Mary	28	f	w	CANA	Solano	Silveyville Twp	90	75
Mary	20	f	w	IREL	Solano	Suisun Twp	90	111
Mary	18	f	w	MA	San Francisco	11-Wd San Francisc	84	498
Mary E	30	f	w	IREL	San Francisco	8-Wd San Francisco	82	322
Michael	39	m	w	IREL	Yolo	Putah Twp	93	509
Michael J	24	m	w	NY	Yuba	Slate Range Bar Tw	93	671
Michl	25	m	w	IREL	San Francisco	San Francisco P O	83	14
Michl	21	m	w	IREL	San Francisco	1-Wd San Francisco	79	85
Mike	41	m	w	IREL	Sacramento	Granite Twp	77	139
Moses	25	m	w	IREL	San Francisco	5-Wd San Francisco	81	32
P	40	m	w	IREL	San Francisco	San Francisco P O	83	309
Pat	41	m	w	IREL	San Francisco	1-Wd San Francisco	79	102
Pat	36	m	w	IREL	Sonoma	Russian Rvr	91	376
Pat	23	m	w	IREL	San Francisco	11-Wd San Francisc	84	683
Patk	39	m	w	IREL	San Francisco	1-Wd San Francisco	79	72
Patk	26	m	w	IREL	San Francisco	1-Wd San Francisco	79	76
Patrick	47	m	w	IREL	Plumas	Goodwin Twp	77	4
Patrick	30	m	w	IREL	San Francisco	San Francisco P O	83	396
Peter	78	m	w	IREL	Santa Clara	1-Wd San Jose	88	260
Peter	40	m	w	ME	San Francisco	San Francisco P O	83	231
Peter	36	m	w	IREL	San Francisco	1-Wd San Francisco	79	62
Peter	29	m	w	IREL	San Francisco	3-Wd San Francisco	79	302
Peter	25	m	w	MA	San Francisco	5-Wd San Francisco	81	18
Rich	42	m	w	IREL	San Mateo	Schoolhouse Statio	87	341
Robert	39	m	w	MA	San Francisco	8-Wd San Francisco	82	488
Robert	35	m	w	MN	Tulare	Tule Rvr Twp	92	260
Robt	35	m	w	IREL	San Francisco	1-Wd San Francisco	79	107
S D	60	m	w	MA	San Francisco	6-Wd San Francisco	81	133
S M	25	f	w	VA	Sacramento	3-Wd Sacramento	77	294
Saml	45	m	w	SCOT	San Francisco	San Francisco P O	83	49
Saml	28	m	w	IREL	Marin	San Rafael	74	57
Samuel	15	m	w	PA	Sonoma	Bodega Twp	91	257
Sarah	30	f	w	PA	Alameda	Eden Twp	68	68
Steven	21	m	w	IREL	San Francisco	7-Wd San Francisco	81	262
T	45	m	w	IREL	Napa	Napa Twp	75	30
T	26	m	w	IREL	Sacramento	3-Wd Sacramento	77	318
T N	45	m	w	OH	San Francisco	6-Wd San Francisco	81	112
Thos	45	m	w	IREL	Sierra	Sears Twp	89	558
Thos	38	m	w	IREL	San Francisco	7-Wd San Francisco	81	239
Thos	37	m	w	IREL	San Francisco	San Francisco P O	83	272
Thos	35	m	w	MO	Solano	Vacaville Twp	90	128
Thos	34	m	w	PA	Alameda	Hayward	68	75
Thos	32	m	w	IREL	San Joaquin	1-Wd Stockton	86	131
Thos	32	m	w	MO	Solano	Vacaville Twp	90	125
Thos	31	m	w	IREL	Sonoma	Bodega Twp	91	252
Thos	28	m	w	IREL	San Francisco	11-Wd San Francisc	84	567
Thos J	41	m	w	IREL	Santa Clara	Milpitas Twp	88	114
W	43	m	w	PA	Amador	Ione City P O	69	359
W	19	m	w	IREL	San Francisco	San Francisco P O	83	281
W J	45	m	w	OH	Napa	Yountville Twp	75	77
W W	48	m	w	TN	Mendocino	Ukiah Twp	74	235
Will	4	m	w	RI	San Mateo	San Mateo P O	87	354
William	49	m	w	VA	El Dorado	Diamond Springs Tw	72	30
William	42	m	w	TN	Siskiyou	Yreka Twp	89	669
William	34	m	w	OH	Tulare	Visalia	92	297
William	29	m	w	IREL	San Francisco	8-Wd San Francisco	82	451
William	21	m	w	OH	Colusa	Colusa Twp	71	286
William	15	m	w	WI	Sonoma	Petaluma Twp	91	349
William E	23	m	w	CANA	Santa Cruz	Santa Cruz Twp	89	394
Wm	45	m	w	IREL	San Francisco	San Francisco P O	83	181
Wm	43	m	w	AL	Sonoma	Sonoma Twp	91	445
Wm	35	m	w	MA	Napa	Napa	75	45
Wm	29	m	w	CANA	San Francisco	San Francisco P O	83	179
Wm	22	m	w	MA	Solano	Benicia	90	18
Z H	38	m	w	ME	San Francisco	San Francisco P O	85	855
CUNNINGHAME								
David	27	m	w	IREL	Sonoma	Bodega Twp	91	254
John	41	m	w	IREL	Sonoma	Bodega Twp	91	252
Wm	30	m	w	IREL	Sonoma	Bodega Twp	91	254
CUNNINGS								
Geo D	21	m	w	CANA	Sacramento	Sutter Twp	77	382
Robert	63	m	w	KY	Los Angeles	El Monte Twp	73	455
W P	20	m	w	MA	Merced	Snelling P O	74	271
Williard	36	m	w	PA	Nevada	Bloomfield Twp	75	92
CUNNINGTON								
Joseph	17	m	w	LA	San Francisco	San Francisco P O	83	179
CUNNINGWORTH								
J B	49	m	w	ENGL	San Francisco	1-Wd San Francisco	79	111
CUNNINS								
Frank H	24	m	w	NY	Sacramento	American Twp	77	65
CUNSALVA								
Manuel	26	m	w	AZOR	San Francisco	1-Wd San Francisco	79	118
CUON								
Ah	17	m	c	CHIN	Sacramento	3-Wd Sacramento	77	283
CUONG								
Ah	28	m	c	CHIN	Trinity	Weaverville Pct	92	231
Ah	20	m	c	CHIN	Napa	Napa Twp	75	32
CUPE								
Tobias	35	m	w	IN	San Joaquin	Dent Twp	86	20
CUPELE								
Jos	45	m	w	MEXI	Alameda	Murray Twp	68	101
CUPID								
M M	36	f	w	IREL	Sacramento	3-Wd Sacramento	77	272
Margaret	20	f	w	MS	Monterey	Pajaro Twp	74	373
CUPIDO								
Samuel	29	m	w	IREL	Contra Costa	Martinez P O	71	432
CUPRERO								
John	34	m	w	ITAL	El Dorado	Diamond Springs Tw	72	29
CURA								
Ah	23	f	c	CHIN	Monterey	Monterey Twp	74	351
CURALAGAL								
Manuel	25	m	w	CA	Monterey	San Antonio Twp	74	316
CURAN								
Michael	50	m	w	CANA	Stanislaus	Empire Twp	92	36
CURB								
Robert A	42	m	w	MO	Yuba	New York Twp	93	637
CURBY								
Albert	16	m	w	CA	San Diego	San Diego	78	506
CURDRAN								
M	50	m	w	FRAN	Siskiyou	Scott Rvr Twp	89	603
CURDTS								
Charles	40	m	w	PRUS	Santa Clara	1-Wd San Jose	88	266
CURDY								
Geo A	24	m	w	CANA	Merced	Snelling P O	74	258
Julia	30	f	w	FRAN	San Francisco	2-Wd San Francisco	79	195
S	35	m	w	IL	San Joaquin	Liberty Twp	86	88
CURE								
Emil	41	m	w	FRAN	Tuolumne	Sonora P O	93	318
Mary E	40	f	w	ENGL	Mendocino	Point Arena Twp	74	211
CURENDE								
John	22	m	w	OH	Monterey	Castroville Twp	74	340
CURESES								
Jose	27	m	w	MEXI	Stanislaus	Emory Twp	92	25
CURETON								
A S	22	m	w	MO	Mendocino	Calpella Twp	74	183
Sarah Ann	78	f	w	MO	Mendocino	Anderson Twp	74	156
Thomas M	30	m	w	MO	Mendocino	Anderson Twp	74	157
Wm H	28	m	w	MO	Mendocino	Ukiah Twp	74	233
CUREY								
Montgomery	24	m	w	NY	Solano	Silveyville Twp	90	74
CURIAS								
Loreta	8	f	w	CA	Los Angeles	Los Angeles	73	509
CURICK								
James	28	m	w	ITAL	Amador	Volcano P O	69	377
CURIUX								
C	32	m	w	GERM	Sierra	Alleghany & Forest	89	533
CURKEN								
J	35	m	w	SWIT	Sierra	Butte Twp	89	512
CURL								
George W	45	m	w	PA	Placer	Rocklin Twp	76	463
James T	46	m	w	KY	Yolo	Cache Crk Twp	93	430
Lewis	40	m	w	PA	Placer	Colfax P O	76	390
Lewis	40	m	w	PA	Nevada	Meadow Lake Twp	75	250
CURLAY								
D	31	m	w	IREL	Sacramento	3-Wd Sacramento	77	311
CURLBURT								
A D	63	m	w	NY	Sacramento	3-Wd Sacramento	77	298
CURLE								
Amanda A	24	f	w	MO	Yuba	New York Twp	93	638
Ellen	15	f	w	AUST	Sacramento	2-Wd Sacramento	77	212
Joseph	35	m	w	ENGL	San Francisco	2-Wd San Francisco	79	169
CURLESS								
Charles	32	m	w	OH	Kern	Havilah P O	73	340
James	40	m	w	IREL	Santa Clara	Fremont Twp	88	63
CURLEW								
William L	46	m	w	MO	Stanislaus	Empire Twp	92	34
William M	26	m	w	MO	Los Angeles	Los Nietos Twp	73	579
CURLEY								
Bernard	36	m	w	NY	San Francisco	1-Wd San Francisco	79	132

© 2001 by Heritage Quest. All rights reserved.

Series M593

Name	Age	S	R	B-PL	County	Locale	Roll	Pg
Bridget	26	f	w	IREL	San Francisco	San Francisco P O	85	807
Catharine	63	f	w	IREL	San Francisco	11-Wd San Francisc	84	621
Cathe	28	f	w	IREL	San Francisco	San Francisco P O	83	134
Charles M	26	m	w	CANA	Mendocino	Point Arena Twp	74	212
Cornelius	50	m	w	IREL	San Francisco	San Francisco P O	83	409
Delia	35	f	w	IREL	San Francisco	San Francisco P O	83	111
James	28	m	w	CANA	Mendocino	Point Arena Twp	74	212
James	19	m	w	MA	San Francisco	7-Wd San Francisco	81	186
John	54	m	w	MD	Calaveras	San Andreas P O	70	156
John	32	m	w	IREL	Santa Clara	2-Wd San Jose	88	312
John	24	m	w	IREL	Stanislaus	Empire Twp	92	52
John M	50	m	w	IREL	San Francisco	2-Wd San Francisco	79	252
M	45	m	w	IREL	Sierra	Forest Twp	89	531
Margaret	60	f	w	IREL	San Francisco	7-Wd San Francisco	81	187
Mark	55	m	w	IREL	San Francisco	8-Wd San Francisco	82	423
Maryanne	24	f	w	NY	San Francisco	San Francisco P O	83	282
Mathew	28	m	w	ENGL	Humboldt	Eureka Twp	72	279
Michael	40	m	w	MA	Placer	Pino Twp	76	472
Michael	35	m	w	IREL	San Francisco	San Francisco P O	85	730
Michael	26	m	w	IREL	San Francisco	San Francisco P O	83	229
Pat	40	m	w	IREL	Solano	Benicia	90	15
Patrick	40	m	w	IREL	San Francisco	1-Wd San Francisco	79	87
Patrick	39	m	w	IREL	Alameda	Eden Twp	68	90
Patrick	36	m	w	IREL	Nevada	Nevada Twp	75	273
Patrick	34	m	w	IREL	San Francisco	San Francisco P O	85	801
Thomas	34	m	w	NY	Placer	Colfax P O	76	387
Thomas	28	m	w	IREL	San Francisco	7-Wd San Francisco	81	202
Thomas	19	m	w	IREL	San Francisco	11-Wd San Francisc	84	551
Thomas B	32	m	w	LA	Santa Barbara	Santa Barbara P O	87	475
Tim	40	m	w	IREL	Alameda	Oakland	68	250
William	32	m	w	IREL	San Francisco	San Francisco P O	83	227
Wm	50	m	w	IREL	San Francisco	San Francisco P O	85	761
CURLI								
Henry	20	m	w	PRUS	Mendocino	Big Rvr Twp	74	171
CURLIER								
Charles	24	m	w	LA	San Francisco	San Francisco P O	80	333
CURLS								
John B	41	m	w	PA	Amador	Sutter Crk P O	69	414
CURLY								
Ah	28	m	c	CHIN	Sacramento	Franklin Twp	77	109
Cornelius	35	m	w	OH	Butte	Mountain Spring Tw	70	88
Delia	30	f	w	IREL	San Francisco	San Francisco P O	80	485
John	40	m	w	IREL	Tuolumne	Chinese Camp P O	93	371
M	50	m	w	IREL	Solano	Vallejo	90	196
CURM								
Foo	25	f	w	CHIN	Tuolumne	Columbia P O	93	336
CURN								
Daniel	36	m	w	IREL	San Francisco	San Francisco P O	85	874
John	21	m	w	IREL	San Mateo	San Mateo P O	87	356
Joseph	38	m	w	NY	San Francisco	11-Wd San Francisc	84	467
Julia	40	f	w	IREL	Alameda	Oakland	68	176
Patrick	25	m	w	IREL	Mariposa	Mariposa P O	74	114
Yon	28	f	c	CHIN	San Francisco	2-Wd San Francisco	79	216
CURNER								
John	38	m	w	PRUS	Alameda	Brooklyn	68	22
CURNEY								
Robert	21	m	w	NY	Solano	Vacaville Twp	90	133
William	46	m	w	PA	Inyo	Lone Pine Twp	73	334
CURNOW								
Wm	24	m	w	ENGL	Tuolumne	Sonora P O	93	320
CURNS								
Edward M	21	m	w	NY	Los Angeles	Los Angeles	73	527
J F	40	m	w	WALE	Sierra	Downieville Twp	89	519
CURNY								
Daniel	50	m	w	MO	Sutter	Vernon Twp	92	131
CURO								
William	30	m	w	FRAN	Santa Clara	2-Wd San Jose	88	316
CURPEN								
Peter	19	m	w	MO	Monterey	San Juan Twp	74	406
CURRACCO								
D	50	m	w	SWIT	Amador	Jackson P O	69	338
CURRAGH								
Henry	50	m	w	IREL	Alameda	Alvarado	68	305
CURRAH								
John	26	m	w	ENGL	Nevada	Grass Valley Twp	75	215
CURRAN								
Anne	60	f	w	IREL	San Francisco	7-Wd San Francisco	81	236
Bella	17	f	w	CANA	Stanislaus	Washington Twp	92	85
Bernard	45	m	w	IREL	San Francisco	San Francisco P O	83	210
Bridget	28	f	w	IREL	San Francisco	8-Wd San Francisco	82	441
Catherine	39	f	w	IREL	San Francisco	San Francisco P O	83	227
D A	24	m	w	MA	Solano	Vallejo	90	140
Ellen	21	f	w	IREL	San Francisco	San Francisco P O	80	484
Francis John	24	m	w	CANA	Plumas	Goodwin Twp	77	58
Hannah	31	f	w	IREL	San Francisco	San Francisco P O	83	297
Helen	33	f	w	CANA	Santa Clara	Santa Clara Twp	88	155
Hugh	44	m	w	IREL	San Francisco	1-Wd San Francisco	79	62
Hugh	38	m	w	NJ	Sacramento	Granite Twp	77	148
Hugh	35	m	w	IREL	San Francisco	1-Wd San Francisco	79	135
Hugh [Rev]	30	m	w	IREL	Monterey	Castroville Twp	74	328
James	50	m	w	IREL	San Francisco	5-Wd San Francisco	81	7
James	40	m	w	IREL	Sonoma	Analy Twp	91	233
James	20	m	w	NH	Sacramento	2-Wd Sacramento	77	245
Jas	29	m	w	IREL	San Joaquin	Dent Twp	86	17
John	40	m	w	IREL	San Francisco	1-Wd San Francisco	79	113
John	38	m	w	IREL	Sacramento	Cosumnes Twp	77	93
John	35	m	w	IREL	Santa Barbara	Santa Barbara P O	87	496

Series M593

Name	Age	S	R	B-PL	County	Locale	Roll	Pg
John	16	m	w	ME	Marin	San Rafael Twp	74	43
Joseph	40	m	w	FRAN	San Francisco	11-Wd San Francisc	84	489
Laurence	37	m	w	MA	San Francisco	1-Wd San Francisco	79	133
M J	23	m	w	MA	Santa Clara	Gilroy Twp	88	83
Magie	13	f	w	CA	Solano	Benicia	90	16
Mark	52	m	w	IREL	Yuba	Rose Bar Twp	93	652
Michael	48	m	w	IREL	Stanislaus	San Joaquin Twp	92	81
Michl	31	m	w	IREL	San Francisco	1-Wd San Francisco	79	8
P H	45	m	w	IREL	San Francisco	San Francisco P O	85	818
Pat	29	m	w	IREL	San Joaquin	Dent Twp	86	18
Patrick	30	m	w	IREL	San Francisco	1-Wd San Francisco	79	93
Robert	35	m	w	IREL	Amador	Jackson P O	69	329
Rosey	22	f	w	IREL	San Francisco	1-Wd San Francisco	79	136
Samuel	32	m	w	NY	Siskiyou	Yreka Twp	89	665
Thomas	56	m	w	IREL	San Francisco	San Francisco P O	83	149
Valentine	44	m	w	IREL	Nevada	Little York Twp	75	240
W J	28	m	w	KY	Tehama	Tehama Twp	92	193
William	7	m	w	CA	Marin	San Rafael Twp	74	28
CURRANE								
Thomas	30	m	w	IREL	Humboldt	Eureka Twp	72	277
CURRANS								
James	12	m	w	CA	Marin	San Rafael Twp	74	27
CURRANT								
Michael	35	m	w	IREL	Sacramento	Cosumnes Twp	77	89
CURRAO								
Frank	7	m	w	CA	San Francisco	2-Wd San Francisco	79	147
CURRATTO								
B	30	m	w	ITAL	Amador	Sutter Crk P O	69	410
CURRAY								
G	4	f	w	CA	San Francisco	San Francisco P O	85	799
CURRELL								
Robert	21	m	w	OH	Placer	Bath P O	76	443
Spencer	47	m	w	NC	Alameda	Eden Twp	68	66
CURREN								
Alice	22	f	w	IREL	San Francisco	8-Wd San Francisco	82	425
Annie	17	f	w	MA	Calaveras	Copperopolis P O	70	253
Ellen	20	f	w	IREL	San Francisco	San Francisco P O	83	226
J	37	m	w	OH	Sierra	Butte Twp	89	512
James	38	m	w	IREL	San Francisco	San Francisco P O	83	133
Jas	28	m	w	IREL	Butte	Chico Twp	70	55
John	46	m	w	IREL	Placer	Bath P O	76	441
John	32	m	w	IREL	Solano	Vallejo	90	198
John	30	m	w	IREL	Contra Costa	Martinez P O	71	368
Maggie	26	f	w	IREL	San Francisco	8-Wd San Francisco	82	344
Martin	25	m	w	NY	Alameda	Alvarado	68	304
Mike	27	m	w	IREL	Sierra	Gibson Twp	89	538
Thomas	28	m	w	IREL	San Francisco	11-Wd San Francisc	84	707
Thomas	22	m	w	IREL	Monterey	Castroville Twp	74	340
Wm	23	m	w	CANA	Solano	Vallejo	90	198
CURRENT								
Hugh C	28	m	w	CANA	El Dorado	Georgetown Twp	72	43
CURREY								
Chas	25	m	w	MA	San Francisco	7-Wd San Francisco	81	229
J	25	m	w	MO	Lassen	Susanville Twp	73	444
John	55	m	w	NY	San Francisco	San Francisco P O	83	147
John	39	m	w	IREL	Santa Cruz	Santa Cruz	89	430
John	35	m	w	IREL	Santa Clara	2-Wd San Jose	88	292
Margaret	71	f	w	KY	Santa Clara	1-Wd San Jose	88	229
Mettie	21	f	w	OH	Mendocino	Ukiah Twp	74	239
Patrick	53	m	w	IREL	San Francisco	San Francisco P O	83	190
Patrick	43	m	w	IREL	Sonoma	Analy Twp	91	222
Thomas	17	m	w	IREL	Placer	Cisco P O	76	494
Thos	36	m	w	IREL	San Francisco	7-Wd San Francisco	81	271
William	21	m	w	TX	Merced	Snelling P O	74	273
Xaiver	23	m	w	PA	Merced	Snelling P O	74	276
CURRIAN								
Mary	25	f	w	IREL	San Francisco	8-Wd San Francisco	82	294
CURRIE								
Belle	22	f	w	NY	San Francisco	San Francisco P O	83	263
David H	40	m	w	SCOT	San Francisco	3-Wd San Francisco	79	315
Ellack	30	m	w	CANA	Solano	Rio Vista Twp	90	60
James	40	m	w	CANA	Mendocino	Casper & Big Rvr	74	163
James	27	m	w	FRAN	San Joaquin	Elliott Twp	86	71
John	78	m	w	SCOT	Solano	Rio Vista Twp	90	60
John	35	m	w	MA	San Francisco	1-Wd San Francisco	79	129
L D	47	m	w	PA	Tuolumne	Chinese Camp P O	93	389
Robt K	44	m	w	SCOT	San Francisco	San Francisco P O	83	76
Thomas	29	m	w	CANA	Placer	Summit P O	76	495
William	32	m	w	NY	San Francisco	7-Wd San Francisco	81	214
CURRIEN								
James	70	m	w	VT	Santa Clara	San Jose Twp	88	219
CURRIER								
Albion	32	m	w	ME	Calaveras	San Andreas P O	70	220
Anos	33	m	w	CANA	San Francisco	8-Wd San Francisco	82	462
Charles J	28	m	w	NH	San Francisco	6-Wd San Francisco	81	146
Danel	60	m	w	NY	Trinity	North Fork Twp	92	218
E L	46	m	w	NH	Sacramento	Granite Twp	77	147
F R	40	m	w	ME	Solano	Vallejo	90	177
Frank	40	m	w	CANA	Solano	Vallejo	90	147
Frank W	30	m	w	IREL	Nevada	Meadow Lake Twp	75	250
George	21	m	w	MA	Colusa	Colusa Twp	71	275
Jno B	55	m	w	NH	San Francisco	San Francisco P O	83	314
John H	52	m	w	NY	Santa Clara	2-Wd San Jose	88	324
John M	27	m	w	MA	Nevada	Bloomfield Twp	75	94
M L	28	f	w	MA	Solano	Vallejo	90	168
Nath	40	m	w	CANA	Sacramento	3-Wd Sacramento	77	291
S O	43	f	w	MA	Solano	Vallejo	90	199

© 2001 by Heritage Quest. All rights reserved.

California 1870 Census

Name	Age	S	R	B-PL	County	Locale	Series M593 Roll	Pg
Seth	36	m	w	ME	Inyo	Bishop Crk Twp	73	310
Susan	44	f	w	MA	Sonoma	Healdsburg	91	274
CURRIN								
Alvina	50	f	w	NH	San Diego	San Diego	78	510
Chas	43	m	w	CANA	San Francisco	11-Wd San Francisc	84	495
Daniel	17	m	w	CA	Yolo	Putah Twp	93	513
E A	16	m	w	MO	San Joaquin	2-Wd Stockton	86	163
George W	32	m	w	MN	Sonoma	Salt Point	91	388
James	32	m	w	NH	San Diego	San Diego	78	510
Joseph	44	m	w	NY	San Francisco	11-Wd San Francisc	84	537
P W	36	m	w	IREL	Alameda	Oakland	68	262
Saml	51	m	w	NY	San Francisco	2-Wd San Francisco	79	205
CURRY								
Austin	23	m	w	CANA	Solano	Vacaville Twp	90	134
C M	21	m	w	AR	Lake	Coyote Valley	73	401
Cathan	26	f	w	IREL	Tehama	Red Bluff	92	177
Edwd	50	m	w	IREL	Solano	Vallejo	90	177
Elias	54	m	w	IN	Sacramento	4-Wd Sacramento	77	319
Eliza A	42	f	w	MO	Placer	Roseville P O	76	352
Ellen	2	f	w	CA	Marin	Nicasio Twp	74	16
Enoch	43	m	w	AL	Kern	Linns Valley P O	73	347
F I C	28	m	w	NY	San Francisco	San Francisco P O	85	838
Francis M	28	m	w	IN	Yolo	Grafton Twp	93	500
G A	17	m	w	CA	Alameda	Oakland	68	243
H C	37	m	w	IN	Tehama	Red Bluff	92	181
Harrison	25	m	b	VA	Marin	Sausalito Twp	74	72
Harrison	25	m	b	DC	San Francisco	San Francisco P O	80	334
Henry	35	m	w	CANA	Solano	Vacaville Twp	90	130
Hugh	40	m	w	IREL	San Francisco	11-Wd San Francisc	84	646
J B	45	m	w	CANA	Yuba	Marysville	93	606
James	54	m	w	IREL	Shasta	Horsetown P O	89	503
James	36	m	w	TN	Contra Costa	Martinez P O	71	443
James	28	m	w	NY	Sonoma	Santa Rosa	91	407
James	19	m	w	NY	San Francisco	7-Wd San Francisco	81	185
James C	40	m	w	KY	Placer	Newcastle Twp	76	479
Jas	38	m	w	SCOT	Solano	Vallejo	90	178
Jas	35	m	w	PA	Solano	Vallejo	90	166
Jas	23	m	w	IREL	San Francisco	7-Wd San Francisco	81	258
Jno	43	m	w	IREL	San Joaquin	2-Wd Stockton	86	187
Johana	28	f	w	IREL	San Francisco	San Francisco P O	80	340
John	43	m	w	IREL	San Francisco	San Francisco P O	83	102
John	42	m	w	IREL	Amador	Volcano P O	69	385
John	4	m	w	NY	San Francisco	San Francisco P O	83	180
John	36	m	w	NY	Sacramento	2-Wd Sacramento	77	246
John	33	m	w	ENGL	Nevada	Grass Valley Twp	75	183
John	32	m	w	NY	San Francisco	11-Wd San Francisc	84	592
John	30	m	w	NY	Yuba	Marysville	93	581
John	28	m	w	AL	Yuba	Marysville	93	583
John	27	m	w	IREL	San Francisco	11-Wd San Francisc	84	440
John L	59	m	w	IREL	Mariposa	Maxwell Crk P O	74	145
John M	35	m	w	VA	Yolo	Grafton Twp	93	498
Jos	37	m	w	NH	Sacramento	3-Wd Sacramento	77	269
Joseph H	56	m	w	KY	Sonoma	Analy Twp	91	240
Julia	20	f	w	CT	San Francisco	11-Wd San Francisc	84	618
Kate	12	f	w	NY	San Francisco	San Francisco P O	85	730
Mary	55	f	w	IREL	San Francisco	7-Wd San Francisco	81	213
Mary	39	f	w	IREL	San Francisco	11-Wd San Francisc	84	688
Mary	25	f	w	IREL	San Francisco	8-Wd San Francisco	82	345
Michael	45	m	w	IREL	San Francisco	11-Wd San Francisc	84	512
Michael	19	m	w	NY	Santa Clara	Gilroy Twp	88	93
Nathaniel	45	m	w	IREL	San Francisco	San Francisco P O	83	22
Robert	19	m	w	CANA	Solano	Vacaville Twp	90	134
Roger	35	m	w	IREL	San Francisco	San Francisco P O	85	735
S P	39	m	w	KY	Merced	Snelling P O	74	254
Samuel	24	m	w	TX	Santa Cruz	Santa Cruz Twp	89	394
Samuel T	27	m	w	PA	Santa Clara	2-Wd San Jose	88	330
Thomas	35	m	w	IREL	San Diego	San Diego	78	488
Thomas	24	m	w	PA	San Francisco	7-Wd San Francisco	81	177
Thomas	24	m	w	NY	San Francisco	8-Wd San Francisco	82	321
Thos	45	m	w	IREL	Yuba	W Bear Rvr Twp	93	680
Thos	32	m	w	IREL	San Joaquin	2-Wd Stockton	86	186
Thos	18	m	w	ENGL	San Francisco	1-Wd San Francisco	79	91
Virgil	32	m	w	IN	Yuba	Rose Bar Twp	93	657
William	32	m	w	IREL	San Francisco	5-Wd San Francisco	81	32
William	25	m	w	ME	San Francisco	7-Wd San Francisco	81	221
CURRYL								
Chas	49	m	w	IREL	Alameda	Oakland	68	146
CURSAN								
P	40	m	w	CANA	Alameda	Oakland	68	247
CURSON								
Saul	31	m	w	NJ	Tehama	Tehama Twp	92	192
Wm R	37	m	w	VA	Mariposa	Mariposa P O	74	91
CURT								
George	31	m	w	BADE	Santa Clara	2-Wd San Jose	88	320
Wesly B	41	m	w	TN	Shasta	Stillwater P O	89	478
CURTAIN								
Chatherine	11	f	w	CA	Amador	Jackson P O	69	322
Mar	56	m	w	FRAN	Tuolumne	Sonora P O	93	322
Mary	12	f	w	IREL	San Francisco	11-Wd San Francisc	84	422
Patrick	35	m	w	IREL	San Mateo	Schoolhouse Statio	87	335
CURTAT								
Lon	19	m	w	FRAN	San Francisco	San Francisco P O	80	416
CURTAZ								
Benjamin	37	m	w	BAVA	San Francisco	8-Wd San Francisco	82	429
CURTCHLEY								
Mary	27	f	w	LA	San Francisco	11-Wd San Francisc	84	496

Name	Age	S	R	B-PL	County	Locale	Series M593 Roll	Pg
CURTELL								
Thomas	36	m	w	IREL	Alameda	Murray Twp	68	121
CURTEN								
Jeremiah	26	m	w	IREL	San Francisco	1-Wd San Francisco	79	50
Wm	28	m	w	IREL	San Francisco	1-Wd San Francisco	79	50
CURTER								
Chas	47	m	w	IREL	San Francisco	7-Wd San Francisco	81	237
G	51	m	w	PA	Sacramento	Granite Twp	77	147
Jas	30	m	w	ENGL	Sacramento	1-Wd Sacramento	77	188
Jo	30	m	w	MA	Sacramento	3-Wd Sacramento	77	291
John	50	m	w	PA	Solano	Vallejo	90	213
Louisa	15	f	b	MD	San Joaquin	2-Wd Stockton	86	176
Wm	23	m	w	OH	San Joaquin	Tulare Twp	86	259
CURTES								
Bradley	46	m	w	NY	San Joaquin	2-Wd Stockton	86	209
CURTESS								
Gilbert	25	m	w	MI	Colusa	Monroe Twp	71	313
CURTICE								
Daniel B	41	m	w	CT	Inyo	Bishop Crk Twp	73	310
Louiza	14	f	b	VA	Inyo	Independence Twp	73	327
Samuel	45	m	w	NH	San Francisco	2-Wd San Francisco	79	256
CURTIER								
Chris	42	m	w	IREL	Sacramento	3-Wd Sacramento	77	304
CURTIN								
Annie	34	f	w	MA	San Francisco	San Francisco P O	85	808
Bridget	37	f	w	IREL	Alameda	Washington Twp	68	280
Bridget	30	f	w	IREL	San Francisco	2-Wd San Francisco	79	283
Bridget	20	f	w	IREL	San Francisco	San Francisco P O	85	715
Bridget	18	f	w	IREL	San Francisco	San Francisco P O	83	312
Carohan	43	m	w	IREL	San Francisco	8-Wd San Francisco	82	419
Catherine	30	f	w	ENGL	San Francisco	San Francisco P O	83	208
Chas	28	m	w	IREL	San Francisco	7-Wd San Francisco	81	275
Ellen	28	f	w	IREL	San Francisco	San Francisco P O	83	324
George	9	m	w	CA	Marin	San Rafael Twp	74	28
James	51	m	w	IREL	San Francisco	San Francisco P O	80	381
James	38	m	w	IREL	San Francisco	1-Wd San Francisco	79	103
John	38	m	w	IREL	Tuolumne	Columbia P O	93	344
John	29	m	w	IREL	San Francisco	11-Wd San Francisc	84	451
M	38	m	w	IREL	San Francisco	San Francisco P O	85	794
Martin	21	m	w	IREL	San Francisco	1-Wd San Francisco	79	104
Michael	13	m	w	MA	Calaveras	Copperopolis P O	70	226
William	5	m	w	CA	Amador	Jackson P O	69	346
William	43	m	w	IREL	Santa Clara	San Jose Twp	88	204
CURTINER								
Henry	45	m	w	IN	Alameda	Washington Twp	68	286
CURTING								
George	84	m	w	PA	Placer	Dutch Flat P O	76	414
CURTIS								
---	23	m	w	WI	Yuba	East Bear Rvr Twp	93	539
A B	26	f	w	NJ	Yuba	Rose Bar Twp	93	663
Abigail	65	f	w	NY	Plumas	Plumas Twp	77	29
Ann	19	f	w	CT	San Francisco	San Francisco P O	83	124
Anna C	39	f	w	MA	Sacramento	2-Wd Sacramento	77	248
Annie	27	f	w	IREL	San Francisco	11-Wd San Francisc	84	458
B M	28	m	w	VA	Nevada	Meadow Lake Twp	75	253
Benjamin	39	m	w	ME	Mendocino	Gualala Twp	74	225
Buchannan	43	m	w	OH	San Mateo	Schoolhouse Statio	87	340
C H	30	m	w	ME	Alameda	Oakland	68	221
C W	46	m	w	NY	San Francisco	3-Wd San Francisco	79	312
Carleton	26	m	w	NY	Santa Cruz	Santa Cruz	89	411
Carlos	40	m	w	VT	Yuba	East Bear Rvr Twp	93	539
Catharine	50	f	w	IREL	San Francisco	San Francisco P O	83	37
Cathrine	20	f	w	NY	San Francisco	1-Wd San Francisco	79	99
Charles	44	m	w	ME	Calaveras	Copperopolis P O	70	252
Charles	36	m	w	IN	Mariposa	Mariposa P O	74	114
Charles	34	m	w	NH	San Francisco	San Francisco P O	80	472
Charles	31	m	w	NY	San Francisco	San Francisco P O	80	471
Charles	30	m	w	VT	Mariposa	Mariposa P O	74	99
Charles H	60	m	w	NY	Santa Clara	2-Wd San Jose	88	295
Charles H	21	m	w	PA	Stanislaus	Empire Twp	92	29
Charles S	24	m	w	CT	San Francisco	8-Wd San Francisco	82	426
Charles W	32	m	w	NY	Santa Clara	2-Wd San Jose	88	295
Chas	39	m	w	MA	San Francisco	8-Wd San Francisco	82	310
Chas S	62	m	w	ME	Butte	Oregon Twp	70	133
Clarence S	12	m	w	CA	Sacramento	San Joaquin Twp	77	398
David T	26	m	w	PA	Stanislaus	Empire Twp	92	29
Dennis	30	m	w	MA	San Francisco	8-Wd San Francisco	82	351
Dennis	29	m	w	IREL	San Francisco	San Francisco P O	83	93
Drayton P	20	m	w	OH	Yolo	Washington Twp	93	535
E D	24	m	w	OH	El Dorado	Georgetown Twp	72	38
Edw B	37	m	w	NY	Alameda	Oakland	68	234
Edward	60	m	w	ENGL	Sonoma	Petaluma Twp	91	354
Edward	47	m	w	IREL	San Francisco	8-Wd San Francisco	82	372
Edward	30	m	w	TN	Yolo	Merritt Twp	93	506
Edward	24	m	w	NY	San Francisco	San Francisco P O	80	425
Edward E	22	m	w	ME	Santa Cruz	Soquel Twp	89	442
Edward H	39	m	w	OH	Yolo	Grafton Twp	93	498
Eli	39	m	w	PA	Tulare	Venice Twp	92	274
Elija S	50	m	w	MA	Humboldt	Mattole Twp	72	283
Elizabeth	26	f	w	SCOT	San Francisco	San Francisco P O	83	220
Emma	48	f	w	OH	El Dorado	Greenwood Twp	72	53
Frank	16	m	w	IL	San Francisco	6-Wd San Francisco	81	113
Geo H	32	m	w	VA	San Francisco	5-Wd San Francisco	81	18
Geo W	46	m	w	MA	San Francisco	7-Wd San Francisco	81	270
George	20	m	w	NY	Sacramento	2-Wd Sacramento	77	223
Greenleaf	34	m	w	ME	Del Norte	Crescent Twp	71	454
H K	35	m	w	PA	San Francisco	8-Wd San Francisco	82	363

© 2001 by Heritage Quest. All rights reserved.

Name	Age	S	R	B-PL	County	Locale	Series M593 Roll	Pg
Hanna	37	f	w	IREL	San Francisco	7-Wd San Francisco	81	277
Hanora	40	f	w	IREL	San Francisco	San Francisco P O	83	257
Harmantt	43	m	w	NY	Santa Clara	1-Wd San Jose	88	231
Harvey S	58	m	w	MA	San Francisco	1-Wd San Francisco	79	85
Henrietta	19	f	w	AUSL	San Francisco	11-Wd San Francisc	84	446
Henry	70	m	w	CANA	San Francisco	1-Wd San Francisco	79	91
Henry	63	m	w	VT	Santa Barbara	San Buenaventura P	87	439
Hiram	40	m	w	OH	Alameda	Oakland	68	170
Israel C	51	m	w	MS	Los Angeles	Los Angeles Twp	73	493
J A	45	m	w	ME	Humboldt	Eureka Twp	72	268
J B	46	m	w	IL	Amador	Sutter Crk P O	69	413
J C	23	m	w	ME	Napa	Yountville Twp	75	89
J M	68	m	w	CT	San Francisco	7-Wd San Francisco	81	287
J M	33	m	w	IN	Alameda	Oakland	68	181
J W	37	m	w	NJ	Napa	Yountville Twp	75	77
James	56	m	w	NY	Stanislaus	Empire Twp	92	29
James	40	m	w	IREL	San Francisco	2-Wd San Francisco	79	148
James	39	m	w	NY	San Joaquin	Oneal Twp	86	107
James	36	m	w	MA	San Francisco	7-Wd San Francisco	81	222
James	25	m	w	NY	Marin	San Rafael Twp	74	42
James	24	m	w	US	San Francisco	11-Wd San Francisc	84	435
James	23	m	w	ENGL	Tuolumne	Columbia P O	93	336
James H	21	m	w	IL	Sonoma	Bodega Twp	91	256
Janette	14	f	w	CA	Calaveras	Copperopolis P O	70	258
Jas E	30	m	w	CT	Tehama	Red Bluff	92	179
Jeramiah	23	m	w	IN	Sonoma	Cloverdale Twp	91	268
Jeremiah	41	m	w	IREL	San Francisco	3-Wd San Francisco	79	291
Jesse G	56	m	w	VA	Yolo	Merritt Twp	93	503
Jno	38	m	w	NY	San Joaquin	Douglas Twp	86	44
Job Ms	18	f	w	NY	San Francisco	5-Wd San Francisco	81	13
John	42	m	w	MA	San Francisco	7-Wd San Francisco	81	284
John	41	m	w	ME	Colusa	Stony Crk Twp	71	331
John	40	m	w	IREL	San Francisco	San Francisco P O	83	380
John	38	m	w	MA	Yuba	Marysville	93	587
John	37	m	w	ENGL	Nevada	Nevada Twp	75	301
John	35	m	w	IL	San Francisco	5-Wd San Francisco	81	13
John	33	m	w	IREL	Alameda	Eden Twp	68	86
John	30	m	w	IREL	San Francisco	8-Wd San Francisco	82	485
John	24	m	w	POLA	Solano	Vallejo	90	210
Joseph	45	m	w	LA	San Francisco	San Francisco P O	83	327
Joseph	45	m	w	ME	Amador	Sutter Crk P O	69	409
Joshua F	31	m	w	IN	Yolo	Cache Crk Twp	93	438
Joshua F	29	m	w	IN	Yolo	Washington Twp	93	534
Joshua S	63	m	w	NC	Yolo	Washington Twp	93	536
Kate	30	f	w	OH	San Francisco	8-Wd San Francisco	82	445
Kate	29	f	w	OH	Alameda	Oakland	68	170
Leonard	55	m	w	MA	Yolo	Cache Crk Twp	93	457
Leonard	46	m	w	VT	Santa Cruz	Santa Cruz	89	431
Loomes	40	m	w	NY	Contra Costa	Martinez P O	71	450
Lucien	50	m	w	CT	San Francisco	7-Wd San Francisco	81	269
Lyman	58	m	w	NY	Colusa	Butte Twp	71	271
Lyman	40	m	w	ENGL	Yuba	New York Twp	93	639
M	71	f	w	ENGL	Alameda	Oakland	68	234
M	60	m	w	MA	Alameda	Oakland	68	179
M	51	m	w	ME	San Joaquin	Oneal Twp	86	102
M	43	m	w	IL	Amador	Sutter Crk P O	69	413
Margaret	44	f	w	ENGL	Placer	Roseville P O	76	353
Margaret	32	f	w	IREL	Solano	Suisun Twp	90	112
Mary	22	f	w	IREL	San Francisco	San Francisco P O	83	323
Mary E	20	f	w	IL	Sonoma	Bodega Twp	91	257
Meta	18	f	w	PRUS	San Francisco	San Francisco P O	85	847
Mich	44	m	w	IREL	Alameda	Oakland	68	252
Michael	32	m	w	IREL	San Francisco	San Francisco P O	83	389
Murry	38	m	w	MA	Alameda	Oakland	68	205
Peter	5	m	w	CA	San Francisco	San Francisco P O	85	848
Richard	37	m	w	IREL	San Francisco	11-Wd San Francisc	84	627
Richard	28	m	w	ENGL	Nevada	Grass Valley Twp	75	163
S M	26	f	w	NJ	Yuba	Marysville	93	597
Saml	29	m	w	NY	Sacramento	1-Wd Sacramento	77	177
Saml F	36	m	w	NY	San Francisco	1-Wd San Francisco	79	88
Sarah	17	f	w	CA	Monterey	Monterey	74	362
Stephen	48	m	w	PA	Tulare	Venice Twp	92	274
Thales	40	m	w	MA	Nevada	Nevada Twp	75	283
Thomas	48	m	w	TN	El Dorado	Salmon Falls Twp	72	131
Thomas	15	m	w	MI	Yolo	Cache Crk Twp	93	439
Thos	42	m	w	ENGL	Nevada	Nevada Twp	75	292
Tylo	40	m	w	VA	San Francisco	San Francisco P O	85	788
W	31	m	w	MA	Alameda	Oakland	68	179
Wilbur	65	m	w	MA	San Francisco	3-Wd San Francisco	79	318
Wilbur	63	m	w	NY	Santa Barbara	Santa Barbara P O	87	456
William	52	m	w	NJ	Mariposa	Maxwell Crk P O	74	141
William	44	m	w	MI	San Bernardino	San Bernardino Twp	78	440
William	42	m	w	KY	Monterey	Monterey	74	355
William	35	m	w	ENGL	Inyo	Cerro Gordo Twp	73	323
William	32	m	w	IN	San Bernardino	San Bernardino Twp	78	423
William C	20	m	w	MI	Yolo	Cache Crk Twp	93	457
Wm	39	m	w	ME	Butte	Concow Twp	70	12
Wm	39	m	w	MA	Sacramento	Sutter Twp	77	380
Wm	30	m	w	ENGL	Nevada	Nevada Twp	75	301
Wm R	33	m	w	MA	Solano	Vallejo	90	159
Wm R	21	m	w	NJ	Humboldt	Pacific Twp	72	291
CURTISE								
Joseph F	37	m	w	NY	Amador	Ione City P O	69	357
CURTISS								
A C	36	f	w	MA	Sacramento	3-Wd Sacramento	77	317
Alice	26	f	w	MO	San Diego	San Diego	78	502
Andrew	34	m	w	NY	Shasta	Fort Crook P O	89	473

Name	Age	S	R	B-PL	County	Locale	Series M593 Roll	Pg
David	34	m	w	MI	Shasta	Shasta P O	89	452
Francis	27	m	w	NY	San Francisco	11-Wd San Francisc	84	532
George	61	m	w	MA	San Diego	San Diego	78	502
Greene	44	m	w	SC	Sacramento	3-Wd Sacramento	77	289
James	27	m	w	CANA	Alameda	Washington Twp	68	291
Jas H	44	m	w	CT	Sonoma	Mendocino Twp	91	294
Louis A	31	m	w	WI	San Diego	San Diego	78	500
N Greene	45	m	w	SC	Sacramento	4-Wd Sacramento	77	375
N P	58	m	w	MA	Santa Clara	Gilroy Twp	88	92
Nettie	14	f	w	MI	Sacramento	4-Wd Sacramento	77	373
Saml	41	m	w	LA	San Francisco	1-Wd San Francisco	79	108
Saml S	29	m	w	NY	Fresno	Millerton P O	72	158
Samuel	25	m	w	GA	Fresno	Millerton P O	72	158
Thos	57	m	w	IREL	Sacramento	4-Wd Sacramento	77	359
CURTLEY								
Charles	47	m	w	ENGL	Sonoma	Salt Point	91	389
CURTLY								
George W	28	m	w	MO	Yolo	Grafton Twp	93	501
CURTS								
Henry	34	m	w	CANA	Santa Clara	Fremont Twp	88	60
John	45	m	w	ENGL	San Francisco	8-Wd San Francisco	82	288
John F	52	m	w	PA	Placer	Auburn P O	76	493
Peter	31	m	w	CANA	Alpine	Markleeville P O	69	316
Thomas H	78	m	w	PA	Solano	Suisun Twp	90	107
CURWIN								
John	29	m	w	IA	San Francisco	6-Wd San Francisco	81	88
CURY								
Howard	46	m	w	ME	Butte	Oregon Twp	70	136
John	38	m	w	ENGL	El Dorado	White Oak Twp	72	138
John	27	m	w	IREL	San Francisco	7-Wd San Francisco	81	209
CURZIE								
William	21	m	w	SHOL	San Francisco	2-Wd San Francisco	79	216
CUSACK								
Danl	30	m	w	IREL	San Francisco	1-Wd San Francisco	79	87
Paul	54	m	w	SC	Kern	Havilah P O	73	338
CUSE								
Robert D	27	m	w	IA	San Diego	San Diego	78	500
Torres M S Jr	20	m	w	CA	San Diego	San Diego	78	500
CUSEBIO								
Fortunatus	44	m	w	SWIT	Plumas	Seneca Twp	77	47
CUSECK								
Thomas	29	m	w	IREL	San Francisco	San Francisco P O	85	779
CUSEY								
Thos	39	m	w	IREL	Sacramento	1-Wd Sacramento	77	204
CUSHAM								
Patrick	26	m	w	IREL	Santa Clara	Fremont Twp	88	41
CUSHEON								
Ellen	30	f	w	IREL	San Francisco	San Francisco P O	83	240
Mary	23	f	w	IREL	San Francisco	6-Wd San Francisco	81	86
Volney	43	m	w	MA	San Francisco	6-Wd San Francisco	81	122
CUSHIM								
C	29	m	w	IL	Alameda	Oakland	68	149
CUSHING								
Benjn F	38	m	w	MA	San Francisco	San Francisco P O	83	118
Charles	38	m	w	MA	Solano	Maine Prairie Twp	90	48
Charles A	42	m	w	MA	San Francisco	San Francisco P O	85	714
Chris	25	m	w	MA	San Francisco	6-Wd San Francisco	81	95
E S	47	m	w	MA	Tehama	Battle Crk Twp	92	157
Edward	25	m	w	CANA	Nevada	Grass Valley Twp	75	199
Edward	24	m	w	CANA	Nevada	Bridgeport Twp	75	113
F W	27	m	w	IL	Solano	Vallejo	90	143
Frank	28	m	w	MA	Sacramento	2-Wd Sacramento	77	247
G H	38	m	w	ME	Sierra	Lincoln Twp	89	551
Henry	36	m	w	MA	Alameda	Eden Twp	68	92
J W	35	m	w	IREL	Alameda	Oakland	68	265
James	26	m	w	MA	Contra Costa	Martinez P O	71	396
John	50	m	w	KY	Nevada	Meadow Lake Twp	75	250
John	44	m	w	VT	Solano	Maine Prairie Twp	90	53
John	42	m	w	MA	Monterey	San Antonio Twp	74	320
John	40	m	w	IREL	Humboldt	Eureka Twp	72	273
John	37	m	w	VT	Shasta	Horsetown P O	89	506
John	28	m	w	IREL	Stanislaus	Empire Twp	92	59
John	26	m	w	IN	Tehama	Red Bluff	92	177
John F	48	m	w	CANA	San Luis Obispo	Santa Rosa Twp	87	324
John J	48	m	w	RI	San Francisco	8-Wd San Francisco	82	387
Joshua	22	m	w	MA	San Francisco	San Francisco P O	85	840
M T	40	m	w	IN	Mariposa	Maxwell Crk P O	74	145
Nicholas	54	m	w	RI	Santa Cruz	Santa Cruz Twp	89	400
Rebecca	30	f	w	ME	San Francisco	8-Wd San Francisco	82	308
Robert	34	m	w	MA	Marin	San Rafael Twp	74	42
Robert	30	m	w	IREL	San Francisco	8-Wd San Francisco	82	433
Simeon	37	m	w	MA	San Francisco	San Francisco P O	83	78
Stephen	36	m	w	MA	Butte	Chico Twp	70	14
Thomas	35	m	w	VT	Mariposa	Mariposa P O	74	96
Thos	34	m	w	IREL	San Francisco	11-Wd San Francisc	84	568
CUSHINGHAM								
Sarah	19	f	w	NY	Sonoma	Petaluma Twp	91	354
CUSHION								
John D	40	m	w	IREL	San Francisco	San Francisco P O	83	201
O C	23	m	w	NY	San Francisco	San Francisco P O	85	785
Thos	28	m	w	IREL	Alameda	Oakland	68	146
CUSHLEY								
John	40	m	w	IREL	Trinity	Indian Crk	92	200
CUSHMAN								
A C	56	m	w	MA	Tuolumne	Columbia P O	93	356
Abed	44	m	w	NY	Butte	Ophir Twp	70	113
Alfred	23	m	w	MA	Santa Clara	1-Wd San Jose	88	245

© 2001 by Heritage Quest. All rights reserved.

Name	Age	S	R	B-PL	County	Locale	Series M593 Roll	Pg
Daniel	42	m	w	ME	Solano	Denverton Twp	90	24
George	38	m	w	ME	San Diego	Temecula Dist	78	527
Hypolite	34	m	w	CANA	San Francisco	2-Wd San Francisco	79	179
J W	35	m	w	CANA	Amador	Drytown P O	69	418
J W	35	m	w	NY	Amador	Drytown P O	69	415
Jas	27	m	w	ME	Shasta	Horsetown P O	89	501
John	41	m	w	IREL	Santa Clara	Fremont Twp	88	41
John	39	m	w	ENGL	Alameda	Oakland	68	265
Leonidas	40	m	w	OH	Nevada	Bloomfield Twp	75	97
Lucien	40	m	w	MA	Colusa	Stony Crk Twp	71	332
M S	58	m	w	MA	Sacramento	3-Wd Sacramento	77	306
Mary	7	f	w	NY	Trinity	Weaverville Pct	92	224
Michael	37	m	w	IREL	Alameda	Washington Twp	68	271
R S	26	m	w	ME	Nevada	Meadow Lake Twp	75	248
Robt	42	m	w	MA	El Dorado	Georgetown Twp	72	45
Rosco	26	m	w	ME	Placer	Bath P O	76	460
W	44	m	w	OH	Del Norte	Smith Rvr Twp	71	477
Walter	34	m	w	NJ	San Francisco	5-Wd San Francisco	81	27
William	35	m	w	MA	Colusa	Stony Crk Twp	71	333
William	29	m	w	KY	Santa Clara	Fremont Twp	88	43
CUSHNEY								
John	60	m	w	NY	Placer	Dutch Flat P O	76	414
CUSHON								
Thomas	30	m	w	IREL	Alameda	Washington Twp	68	281
CUSIC								
Thos	31	m	w	IREL	San Francisco	11-Wd San Francisc	84	667
CUSICH								
Michael	28	m	w	NY	San Mateo	Schoolhouse Statio	87	342
CUSICK								
Andrew	33	m	w	IREL	Shasta	Shasta P O	89	458
Anne	35	f	w	IREL	San Francisco	6-Wd San Francisco	81	149
Charles	37	m	w	ENGL	Sacramento	2-Wd Sacramento	77	234
Charles	27	m	w	VT	Solano	Montezuma Twp	90	66
Jane	28	f	w	IREL	San Francisco	San Francisco P O	80	395
John	33	m	w	IREL	San Francisco	San Francisco P O	83	387
John	30	m	w	IREL	Solano	Vallejo	90	163
John	29	m	w	IREL	San Francisco	1-Wd San Francisco	79	94
Michael	1	m	w	NY	San Francisco	San Francisco P O	85	768
Patrick	33	m	w	IREL	San Francisco	1-Wd San Francisco	79	134
Patrick	25	m	w	IREL	Santa Clara	Alviso Twp	88	29
Rosa	26	f	w	IREL	San Francisco	San Francisco P O	85	724
Solomon	65	m	w	NY	Shasta	Fort Crook P O	89	475
Wm	36	m	w	ENGL	San Francisco	7-Wd San Francisco	81	267
CUSIT								
Francis	32	m	w	MEXI	San Francisco	11-Wd San Francisc	84	504
CUSKER								
Ellen	24	f	w	IREL	San Francisco	San Francisco P O	80	360
Mary	39	f	w	IREL	San Francisco	8-Wd San Francisco	82	450
CUSKEY								
Thomas	24	m	w	IREL	Solano	Vacaville Twp	90	122
CUSLER								
Daniel	36	m	w	BADE	Placer	Dutch Flat P O	76	415
John	13	m	w	MO	Siskiyou	Callahan P O	89	629
Nanny	10	f	w	MD	San Francisco	7-Wd San Francisco	81	233
CUSPARD								
Joseph	50	m	b	GA	Siskiyou	Yreka	89	657
CUSSAS								
Andrea	37	m	w	ITAL	Calaveras	Copperopolis P O	70	228
CUSSICK								
James	30	m	w	MA	San Francisco	7-Wd San Francisco	81	204
Jane	25	f	w	IREL	San Francisco	7-Wd San Francisco	81	204
CUSSING								
P J	40	m	w	IN	Alameda	Oakland	68	259
P J	30	m	w	NY	Alameda	Oakland	68	247
CUSSIS								
Frank	38	m	w	FRAN	Stanislaus	Empire Twp	92	60
CUST								
Peter	47	m	w	FRAN	El Dorado	Mud Springs Twp	72	83
CUSTAR								
John	30	m	w	SWIT	Yuba	East Bear Rvr Twp	93	539
Lucilia	32	f	w	OH	Yuba	Long Bar Twp	93	563
CUSTARD								
Ezra	54	m	w	IN	Santa Clara	Gilroy Twp	88	104
CUSTELL								
Guido	54	m	w	HUNG	San Francisco	San Francisco P O	83	24
CUSTER								
Benjamin	60	m	w	PA	Colusa	Monroe Twp	71	318
Chas	18	m	w	CA	San Francisco	5-Wd San Francisco	81	9
James	19	m	w	OH	Inyo	Cerro Gordo Twp	73	318
John	49	m	w	KY	Napa	Yountville Twp	75	91
Joseph	25	m	w	PORT	Alameda	Washington Twp	68	286
Louis	35	m	w	PRUS	San Francisco	San Francisco P O	85	845
Mahedda	62	f	w	SC	Napa	Napa	75	2
CUSTIN								
Mathew	26	m	w	IREL	Solano	Rio Vista Twp	90	62
CUSTWAITE								
Philip	45	m	w	IREL	San Diego	San Diego	78	483
CUT								
Ah	46	m	c	CHIN	Amador	Fiddletown P O	69	429
Ah	42	m	c	CHIN	Nevada	Nevada Twp	75	313
Ah	30	m	c	CHIN	Stanislaus	Buena Vista Twp	92	13
Hong	33	m	c	CHIN	Placer	Blue Canyon P O	76	417
Sing	34	m	c	CHIN	Mariposa	Maxwell Crk P O	74	147
CUTBERTH								
George K	43	m	w	IA	Sonoma	Petaluma Twp	91	334
CUTBERTSON								
Robert	29	m	w	SCOT	Mendocino	Gualala Twp	74	226
CUTE								
Robert	37	m	w	IREL	Nevada	Grass Valley Twp	75	158
CUTER								
Tuffler	26	m	w	CANA	Sierra	Sears Twp	89	558
CUTHBERT								
Abel	21	m	w	VA	Stanislaus	Emory Twp	92	16
Ellen	23	f	w	IREL	Santa Cruz	Santa Cruz	89	433
George	21	m	b	JAMA	Yolo	Cache Crk Twp	93	457
Margaret A	34	f	b	NY	Sacramento	2-Wd Sacramento	77	243
CUTIES								
Antoine	41	m	w	GREE	Plumas	Quartz Twp	77	35
CUTLER								
B B	39	m	w	NH	Sacramento	4-Wd Sacramento	77	336
James	23	m	w	PA	Klamath	Trinidad Twp	73	392
James M	47	m	w	MA	Santa Clara	1-Wd San Jose	88	246
Jane	47	f	w	OH	Santa Clara	2-Wd San Jose	88	283
John	50	m	w	IN	Tulare	Venice Twp	92	278
Jonathan P	34	m	w	TN	Santa Barbara	San Buenaventura P	87	447
Luther C	51	m	w	ME	El Dorado	Diamond Springs Tw	72	33
Mary	42	f	w	MD	San Francisco	San Francisco P O	83	24
Nathan	48	m	w	CANA	Napa	Yountville Twp	75	86
R	30	m	w	SC	Alameda	Alameda	68	18
Richd	31	m	w	MS	San Francisco	8-Wd San Francisco	82	371
Silas P	20	m	w	NH	Yolo	Grafton Twp	93	494
Tho J	44	m	w	ME	El Dorado	Georgetown Twp	72	36
Thomas	44	m	w	CT	Humboldt	Eureka Twp	72	263
William	15	m	w	NY	San Francisco	San Francisco P O	83	303
CUTLIN								
H	40	m	w	FRAN	Alameda	Oakland	68	170
CUTRELL								
Thos	25	m	w	NY	Alameda	Oakland	68	222
CUTS								
Marion H	37	m	w	NY	Sacramento	Georgianna Twp	77	122
CUTT								
Ah	20	m	c	CHIN	Yuba	Marysville	93	619
CUTTER								
Alfred	26	m	w	IREL	San Francisco	San Francisco P O	85	735
Catharine	77	f	w	NY	Solano	Green Valley Twp	90	44
Daniel	34	m	w	ME	San Francisco	San Francisco P O	83	403
David	33	m	w	NY	San Francisco	7-Wd San Francisco	81	175
E P	35	m	w	MA	Sonoma	Sonoma Twp	91	447
Edwd O	35	m	w	PRUS	San Francisco	San Francisco P O	83	15
H W	23	m	w	OH	Mendocino	Calpella Twp	74	182
Henry	27	m	w	ME	Marin	Sausalito Twp	74	68
Henry	23	m	w	CANA	San Mateo	Menlo Park P O	87	379
Hobert	30	m	w	NY	Santa Clara	Redwood Twp	88	126
Horace F	48	m	w	NY	San Francisco	8-Wd San Francisco	82	474
Jacob	77	m	w	NY	Solano	Green Valley Twp	90	44
Jas	25	m	w	CANA	Humboldt	Eureka Twp	72	269
Jas	23	m	w	ME	Humboldt	Eureka Twp	72	258
Jas H	50	m	w	NY	San Francisco	8-Wd San Francisco	82	296
Jennie	30	f	w	OH	San Francisco	7-Wd San Francisco	81	175
John	35	m	w	OH	Solano	Silveyville Twp	90	88
Jos W	29	m	w	LA	San Francisco	8-Wd San Francisco	82	357
Joseph S	47	m	w	MA	Sonoma	Petaluma Twp	91	311
Lillie	11	f	w	WI	San Francisco	7-Wd San Francisco	81	175
Mildred S	34	f	w	VA	San Francisco	6-Wd San Francisco	81	121
Mollie	21	f	w	IL	Humboldt	Pacific Twp	72	292
Patrick	40	m	w	IREL	San Francisco	8-Wd San Francisco	82	288
Robert	35	m	w	NY	Fresno	Millerton P O	72	158
Samuel	38	m	w	MA	San Francisco	3-Wd San Francisco	79	310
Sarah	29	f	w	MA	Contra Costa	Martinez Twp	71	347
Thomas A	40	m	w	MA	Inyo	Bishop Crk Twp	73	317
Thos	60	m	w	CANA	Santa Clara	Gilroy Twp	88	93
Thos	31	m	w	CT	San Francisco	11-Wd San Francisc	84	426
CUTTIN								
Ed	31	m	w	CANA	Humboldt	Eureka Twp	72	273
CUTTING								
C B	34	m	w	MA	Tuolumne	Chinese Camp P O	93	386
Calvin	25	m	w	NY	San Francisco	11-Wd San Francisc	84	565
David C	29	m	w	VT	Sonoma	Bodega Twp	91	254
Edward	63	m	w	MA	San Francisco	San Francisco P O	83	193
Ephrain	59	m	w	MA	Calaveras	Copperopolis P O	70	252
Hiram E	50	m	w	VT	El Dorado	Placerville Twp	72	100
James	29	m	w	OH	Alameda	Washington Twp	68	289
L M	38	m	w	MA	San Joaquin	2-Wd Stockton	86	158
Louis	65	m	w	MA	San Francisco	San Francisco P O	83	113
Page	30	m	w	NH	Calaveras	Copperopolis P O	70	256
R M	48	m	w	MA	Tuolumne	Chinese Camp P O	93	389
Robert C	61	m	w	MA	Calaveras	Copperopolis P O	70	252
Water B	32	m	w	NY	Placer	Auburn P O	76	383
CUTTLE								
Mathias	25	m	w	NY	San Francisco	8-Wd San Francisco	82	421
CUTTON								
David	21	m	w	CANA	Humboldt	Eureka Twp	72	279
Robert	63	m	w	CANA	Humboldt	Eureka Twp	72	267
CUTTS								
A W	55	m	w	ME	Yuba	Marysville	93	587
F M	32	m	w	IREL	Sonoma	Santa Rosa	91	401
CUVILLA								
William	40	m	w	ENGL	Nevada	Little York Twp	75	238
CUYAS								
Antonio	50	m	w	SPAI	Los Angeles	Los Angeles	73	568
CUYEL								
E	24	m	w	GERM	Sacramento	1-Wd Sacramento	77	177
CUYLER								
Henry	27	m	w	IREL	Solano	Silveyville Twp	90	74

© 2001 by Heritage Quest. All rights reserved.

Name	Age	S	R	B-PL	County	Locale	Series M593 Roll	Pg
CUZNER								
Mary A	18	f	w	ENGL	San Francisco	6-Wd San Francisco	81	134
CY								
Ah	25	m	c	CHIN	Amador	Jackson P O	69	331
Hap	40	m	c	CHIN	Inyo	Cerro Gordo Twp	73	319
CYE								
Ah	30	m	c	CHIN	San Joaquin	1-Wd Stockton	86	151
Ah	20	m	c	CHIN	Sacramento	1-Wd Sacramento	77	198
CYLNIAR								
Augustine	43	m	w	FRAN	Calaveras	San Andreas P O	70	177
CYLVEAS								
Encarnacion	37	f	w	CA	Contra Costa	Martinez P O	71	439
CYNPHER								
Jacob	21	m	w	ME	San Mateo	Pescadero P O	87	415
CYPHERS								
Theodore	31	m	w	NY	San Francisco	1-Wd San Francisco	79	57
CYPRAU								
L	40	m	w	LA	San Joaquin	3-Wd Stockton	86	225
CYPRIAN								
Isadore	51	m	w	CA	Contra Costa	Martinez P O	71	438
CYRAS								
Rebecca	73	f	w	NC	Napa	Napa	75	15
CYRENIUS								
Louis	23	m	w	MA	San Francisco	7-Wd San Francisco	81	177
CYRENS								
Joseph	39	m	w	KY	Placer	Lincoln P O	76	492
CYRUS								
John	39	m	w	IL	Napa	Napa	75	15
William	25	m	w	MO	Lake	Scotts Crk	73	426
CZAMECKI								
Frances	46	m	w	POLA	Alameda	Hayward	68	78
DA								
Ah	35	m	c	CHIN	Trinity	Weaverville Pct	92	228
Hu	20	m	c	CHIN	San Francisco	8-Wd San Francisco	82	465
DAAKE								
Charles	32	m	w	CANA	Colusa	Butte Twp	71	272
DABADIE								
Jean B	55	m	w	FRAN	Santa Cruz	Santa Cruz	89	416
DABALA								
Bebian	35	m	w	MEXI	Mariposa	Mariposa P O	74	93
DABANELLO								
Giuseppi	32	m	w	ITAL	San Francisco	3-Wd San Francisco	79	289
DABB								
James	30	m	w	ENGL	Nevada	Bloomfield Twp	75	92
DABIGNE								
Edward	41	m	w	FRAN	Santa Clara	2-Wd San Jose	88	317
DABIS								
Agnes	15	f	w	CA	Santa Clara	Santa Clara Twp	88	149
DABLE								
Charles	21	m	w	AUST	Inyo	Independence Twp	73	327
William	22	m	w	ENGL	Inyo	Cerro Gordo Twp	73	320
DABNER								
John	40	m	w	PORT	Alameda	Eden Twp	68	90
DABNEY								
Garland A	58	m	w	VA	Santa Clara	2-Wd San Jose	88	285
William E	41	m	w	VA	Placer	Colfax P O	76	389
DABORNA								
August	30	m	w	PRUS	Sutter	Sutter Twp	92	116
DABOVICH								
Charles	47	m	w	RUSS	San Francisco	6-Wd San Francisco	81	101
Michael	50	m	w	AUST	San Francisco	2-Wd San Francisco	79	186
DABOWICH								
George	28	m	w	AUST	San Francisco	3-Wd San Francisco	79	288
DABOYCE								
Samuel	53	m	w	NY	Contra Costa	Martinez P O	71	438
DABRUNTEE								
Ant	37	m	w	CANA	Sierra	Sears Twp	89	557
DABULE								
Charles	35	m	w	FRAN	Stanislaus	Branch Twp	92	7
DABY								
Wm	35	m	w	NY	Sonoma	Salt Point Twp	91	382
DAC								
Ah	39	m	c	CHIN	Placer	Dutch Flat P O	76	408
Ah	30	m	c	CHIN	Placer	Clipper Gap P O	76	392
DACE								
Manuel J	29	m	w	AZOR	Shasta	American Ranch P O	89	498
DACER								
Frances	51	m	w	SCOT	Contra Costa	Martinez P O	71	423
DACEY								
Daniel	70	m	w	IREL	San Francisco	San Francisco P O	83	395
John	34	m	w	IREL	San Joaquin	Tulare Twp	86	251
Timothy	20	m	w	IREL	Nevada	Bridgeport Twp	75	120
William	42	m	w	IREL	San Francisco	San Francisco P O	83	395
DACHES								
S	40	m	w	BAVA	San Joaquin	Tulare Twp	86	261
DACHOW								
Geo W	21	m	w	MA	San Joaquin	3-Wd Stockton	86	229
DACIN								
William J	38	m	w	ME	Calaveras	San Andreas P O	70	163
DACK								
Ah	32	m	c	CHIN	Kern	Tehachapi P O	73	353
George	22	m	w	ENGL	Siskiyou	Scott Valley Twp	89	615
John	29	m	c	CHIN	Tulare	Tule Rvr Twp	92	259
Yung	54	m	c	CHIN	Fresno	Millerton P O	72	202
DACKERY								
John	63	m	w	IREL	Trinity	Weaverville Pct	92	225
Patric	46	m	w	IREL	Trinity	Weaverville Pct	92	225
DACKWEILER								
Christian	37	m	w	BAVA	Inyo	Cerro Gordo Twp	73	319
DACLIN								
Charles	40	m	w	FRAN	Calaveras	San Andreas P O	70	186
DACON								
Joseph	42	m	w	PORT	Alameda	Washington Twp	68	275
DACOOMAN								
Bautiste	22	m	w	FRAN	Santa Clara	2-Wd San Jose	88	302
DACOT								
Peter	31	m	w	FRAN	Stanislaus	Branch Twp	92	7
DACOTA								
John	14	m	w	ITAL	Amador	Volcano P O	69	375
DACRE								
Joseph	58	m	w	FRAN	San Francisco	San Francisco P O	80	347
DACRUZ								
Jos Furtado	31	m	w	AZOR	Shasta	Horsetown P O	89	507
Manuel F	40	m	w	AZOR	Shasta	Horsetown P O	89	507
DACUMON								
August	26	m	w	FRAN	Los Angeles	Los Angeles	73	567
Charles L	49	m	w	SWIT	Los Angeles	Los Angeles	73	567
DACY								
Daniel D	30	m	w	ITAL	Yolo	Grafton Twp	93	478
Jerrymire	40	m	w	IREL	Trinity	Junction City Pct	92	209
DAD								
Ah	50	m	c	CHIN	El Dorado	Mud Springs Twp	72	74
DADAN								
Peter	42	m	w	SWIT	Marin	San Antonio Twp	74	60
DADD								
William	32	m	w	IL	Inyo	Bishop Crk Twp	73	311
DADDES								
Andrew	40	m	w	IREL	Sacramento	2-Wd Sacramento	77	243
DADE								
Henry	22	m	w	ENGL	San Joaquin	2-Wd Stockton	86	174
Henry C	29	m	w	ENGL	Nevada	Bridgeport Twp	75	106
DADEN								
Calvin W	32	m	w	OH	El Dorado	Mud Springs Twp	72	71
DADGE								
John G	33	m	w	TN	San Luis Obispo	Morro Twp	87	285
DADLAY								
P	37	m	w	FRAN	Sierra	Butte Twp	89	511
DADO								
Celestine	23	m	w	SWIT	Sonoma	Santa Rosa	91	396
Palo	30	m	w	SWIT	Marin	Tomales Twp	74	76
Palo	22	m	w	SWIT	Marin	Tomales Twp	74	76
DADSON								
S	61	m	w	NY	Sierra	Butte Twp	89	510
DAE								
Ah	37	m	c	CHIN	El Dorado	Coloma Twp	72	1
DAEGENER								
William	49	m	w	PRUS	Tuolumne	Columbia P O	93	336
DAEL								
Henry	28	m	w	NORW	Nevada	Grass Valley Twp	75	222
DAELY								
Jno	35	m	w	IREL	Sacramento	1-Wd Sacramento	77	173
DAFFY								
John	8	m	w	CA	Alameda	Brooklyn	68	36
Wm	13	m	w	CA	San Francisco	11-Wd San Francisc	84	593
DAFOR								
Edward	31	m	w	CANA	Sonoma	Analy Twp	91	229
DAGAN								
Patrick H	27	m	w	IREL	Mariposa	Mariposa P O	74	108
DAGANY								
Eugene	27	m	w	FRAN	Santa Clara	Fremont Twp	88	56
Jules	23	m	w	FRAN	Santa Clara	Fremont Twp	88	56
DAGENAIS								
Getta	36	m	w	CANA	Santa Clara	2-Wd San Jose	88	313
DAGER								
Joseph	49	m	w	MA	Alameda	Brooklyn Twp	68	40
DAGERT								
Jacob F	43	m	w	SWED	Santa Clara	Fremont Twp	88	60
Joseph A	17	m	w	IN	Santa Clara	2-Wd San Jose	88	309
DAGETT								
George	39	m	w	MA	Klamath	Liberty Twp	73	374
DAGGARD								
Henry	25	m	w	MI	Sonoma	Analy Twp	91	237
DAGGER								
Aleck	48	m	w	FRAN	Calaveras	Copperopolis P O	70	247
DAGGET								
Eliza	68	f	w	NY	Klamath	South Fork Twp	73	385
Henry	28	m	w	MI	Sonoma	Mendocino Twp	91	302
Hiram	64	m	w	ME	Alameda	Brooklyn	68	25
Wesley	29	m	w	ME	Alameda	Brooklyn	68	24
DAGGETT								
D F	45	m	w	MA	San Joaquin	2-Wd Stockton	86	184
Daniel O	39	m	w	ME	Yuba	New York Twp	93	638
Eben	50	m	w	NY	Del Norte	Happy Camp Twp	71	471
Elizabeth T	22	f	w	NY	Klamath	South Fork Twp	73	385
Enos	63	m	w	ME	El Dorado	Placerville	72	125
George	30	m	w	MI	Contra Costa	Martinez P O	71	379
H	28	m	w	ME	Solano	Vallejo	90	190
Henry	78	m	w	CA	Marin	Tomales Twp	74	84
James	44	m	w	ME	Tulare	Farmersville Twp	92	243
Johana	54	f	w	OH	San Joaquin	2-Wd Stockton	86	213
John	37	m	w	NY	Klamath	South Fork Twp	73	385
John	27	m	w	ME	Solano	Vallejo	90	165
Jos M	41	m	w	NH	Butte	Kimshew Tpw	70	81
Kate	23	f	w	PRUS	San Joaquin	2-Wd Stockton	86	201

© 2001 by Heritage Quest. All rights reserved.

California 1870 Census

Name	Age	S	R	B-PL	County	Locale	Roll	Pg
R	56	m	w	ME	San Joaquin	2-Wd Stockton	86	197
Samuel W	30	m	w	ME	Placer	Bath P O	76	436
Susan	24	f	w	NORW	Butte	Chico Twp	70	41
Wm	28	m	w	MA	San Joaquin	2-Wd Stockton	86	184
Wm L	43	m	w	ME	Sonoma	Petaluma Twp	91	318
DAGGS								
George W	52	m	w	VA	Tulare	Kings Rvr Twp	92	252
Harry	23	m	w	MO	Tulare	Kings Rvr Twp	92	252
Martha J	9	f	w	MO	Tulare	Kings Rvr Twp	92	252
DAGLLAS								
John	37	m	w	ENGL	Santa Cruz	Santa Cruz Twp	89	386
DAGMAN								
Edd	8	m	w	CA	Butte	Ophir Twp	70	117
DAGNALL								
James	41	m	w	IREL	San Francisco	11-Wd San Francisc	84	424
DAGNAN								
Michael	25	m	w	IREL	Yuba	Rose Bar Twp	93	662
DAGNER								
William	40	m	w	PRUS	Monterey	San Juan Twp	74	400
DAGOLIA								
Judson W	39	m	w	NY	Nevada	Grass Valley Twp	75	225
DAGUD								
William	29	m	w	SCOT	Contra Costa	Martinez P O	71	419
DAH								
Ah	19	m	c	CHIN	Solano	Vallejo	90	209
Loo	17	m	c	CHIN	Solano	Vallejo	90	209
DAHA								
Jean H	41	m	w	FRAN	Calaveras	San Andreas P O	70	176
DAHAL								
Fred	26	m	w	DENM	Alameda	Oakland	68	174
DAHAN								
John	34	m	w	IREL	San Francisco	7-Wd San Francisco	81	257
DAHL								
Allen	40	m	w	GERM	Stanislaus	Empire Twp	92	31
Christopher	31	m	w	PRUS	San Francisco	San Francisco P O	80	392
Frederick	26	m	w	BAVA	San Francisco	San Francisco P O	83	195
Frederick	26	m	w	BAVA	San Francisco	San Francisco P O	83	165
Geo	50	m	w	PRUS	San Joaquin	3-Wd Stockton	86	215
Peter	39	m	w	DENM	San Francisco	3-Wd San Francisco	79	288
William	23	m	w	DENM	Alameda	Oakland	68	168
DAHLBERG								
Alex	41	m	w	SWED	Yuba	Rose Bar Twp	93	654
Margaret	40	f	w	SWED	Butte	Bidwell Twp	70	3
DAHLE								
Olive	8	f	w	CA	Nevada	Rough & Ready Twp	75	328
DAHLEM								
J	25	m	w	GERM	Sonoma	Sonoma Twp	91	447
DAHLEN								
David	50	m	w	PRUS	Tulare	Tule Rvr Twp	92	261
Francis	42	m	w	PRUS	San Francisco	2-Wd San Francisco	79	280
DAHLGREEN								
David	22	m	w	MEXI	San Francisco	San Francisco P O	80	471
DAHLGREN								
Chas	28	m	w	SWED	San Francisco	San Francisco P O	83	93
Ed	25	m	w	DENM	San Joaquin	2-Wd Stockton	86	209
DAHLKE								
Charles	36	m	w	PRUS	San Luis Obispo	Santa Rosa Twp	87	324
DAHLMAN								
Caroline	70	f	w	BAVA	San Francisco	8-Wd San Francisco	82	402
Charles	40	m	w	FRAN	San Francisco	8-Wd San Francisco	82	390
Mary	13	f	w	CA	Sonoma	Petaluma Twp	91	339
DAHMKA								
Fred	42	m	w	PRUS	San Francisco	San Francisco P O	85	811
DAHN								
Charles	43	m	w	PRUS	San Francisco	8-Wd San Francisco	82	387
DAHONEY								
William	36	m	w	IREL	San Francisco	11-Wd San Francisc	84	480
DAI								
Chow	29	m	c	CHIN	Plumas	Mineral Twp	77	24
DAICY								
Cyrus A	37	m	w	CANA	San Francisco	San Francisco P O	83	347
DAID								
Edward	22	m	w	CANA	Contra Costa	San Pablo Twp	71	360
DAIDJIRO								
---	46	m	j	JAPA	El Dorado	Coloma Twp	72	4
DAIE								
Ong	18	m	c	CHIN	Nevada	Washington Twp	75	342
DAIGER								
John	57	m	w	MD	Amador	Volcano P O	69	373
DAIGH								
John M	27	m	w	FRAN	San Francisco	1-Wd San Francisco	79	47
DAIGNEAU								
Euzebe	39	m	w	CANA	Marin	Tomales Twp	74	78
DAIGNEE								
Delia	23	f	w	IREL	San Francisco	San Francisco P O	83	140
DAILEY								
Andrew	41	m	w	VA	Solano	Silveyville Twp	90	72
Andrew	34	m	w	NY	San Francisco	San Francisco P O	83	245
Anna A	35	f	w	CANA	Santa Clara	Santa Clara Twp	88	155
Bridget	19	f	w	IREL	San Francisco	San Francisco P O	83	207
Catherine	22	f	w	IREL	Alameda	Hayward	68	76
Charles	8	m	w	MA	Marin	San Rafael Twp	74	29
Enos	44	m	w	IREL	San Francisco	2-Wd San Francisco	79	267
Heber C	24	m	w	MO	Colusa	Spring Valley Twp	71	336
Henry	33	m	w	NY	Contra Costa	Martinez Twp	71	347
James	42	m	w	IREL	Sacramento	Natomas Twp	77	167
Jeremiah	42	m	w	IREL	Monterey	Castroville Twp	74	327
John	38	m	w	IREL	Colusa	Spring Valley Twp	71	340
John	28	m	w	IREL	Tuolumne	Chinese Camp P O	93	375
John	27	m	w	IREL	Inyo	Bishop Crk Twp	73	315
John W	53	m	w	MD	El Dorado	Georgetown Twp	72	47
John W	40	m	w	IREL	Tulare	Visalia	92	296
Laurence	26	m	w	IREL	Contra Costa	San Pablo Twp	71	363
Lawrence	35	m	w	IREL	San Francisco	San Francisco P O	83	223
Lewis	32	m	w	IN	Colusa	Spring Valley Twp	71	336
Margrett	27	f	w	IREL	San Francisco	1-Wd San Francisco	79	4
Michael	65	m	w	IREL	San Mateo	Belmont P O	87	372
Michael	35	m	w	IREL	Solano	Green Valley Twp	90	42
Owens	33	m	w	MO	Colusa	Colusa Twp	71	279
Parius C	50	m	w	CANA	Tulare	Tule Rvr Twp	92	261
Patrick	26	m	w	IREL	Tuolumne	Chinese Camp P O	93	375
Robert	33	m	w	IREL	San Francisco	San Francisco P O	83	240
Robert	32	m	w	IREL	San Francisco	1-Wd San Francisco	79	63
Thomas	27	m	w	IREL	Inyo	Independence Twp	73	325
Timothy	23	m	w	IREL	Contra Costa	San Pablo Twp	71	363
William T	40	m	w	IREL	Yolo	Washington Twp	93	531
Wm	50	m	w	SCOT	Butte	Kimshew Tpw	70	81
Wm	35	m	w	MA	San Francisco	San Francisco P O	83	80
DAILS								
Michael	38	m	w	IREL	San Francisco	11-Wd San Francisc	84	659
DAILY								
Anna	24	f	w	IREL	San Francisco	8-Wd San Francisco	82	329
Bartholemew	38	m	w	IREL	Sonoma	Petaluma Twp	91	320
Bridget	25	f	w	IREL	San Francisco	8-Wd San Francisco	82	292
Bridget	19	f	w	MI	Sierra	Gibson Twp	89	543
Catherine	40	f	w	IREL	San Mateo	Redwood Twp	87	369
Catherine	39	f	w	IREL	San Francisco	8-Wd San Francisco	82	339
Clinton	10	m	w	NY	San Francisco	8-Wd San Francisco	82	313
Cornelius	20	m	b	MO	Colusa	Colusa	71	290
David	37	m	w	IREL	San Francisco	San Francisco P O	83	69
Delia	24	f	w	IREL	San Francisco	San Francisco P O	85	812
Dennis	66	m	w	IREL	Sutter	Vernon Twp	92	132
Edward	49	m	w	IREL	San Francisco	San Francisco P O	85	759
Edward	45	m	w	NY	San Bernardino	San Bernardino Twp	78	424
Edward	31	m	w	IREL	Sutter	Yuba Twp	92	149
Emund	25	m	w	IREL	San Mateo	Half Moon Bay P O	87	405
Francis	34	m	w	IREL	San Francisco	11-Wd San Francisc	84	653
Honora	25	f	w	IREL	San Francisco	11-Wd San Francisc	84	616
Honora	22	f	w	IREL	San Francisco	8-Wd San Francisco	82	289
I W	23	m	w	IREL	San Francisco	San Francisco P O	85	845
J	26	m	w	MO	Sierra	Butte Twp	89	508
James	50	m	w	IREL	San Francisco	8-Wd San Francisco	82	324
James	50	m	w	IREL	Butte	Chico Twp	70	42
James	38	m	w	IREL	San Francisco	11-Wd San Francisc	84	655
James	13	m	w	CA	Butte	Hamilton Twp	70	63
Jno	26	m	w	IREL	Sacramento	1-Wd Sacramento	77	188
Jno S	36	m	w	IREL	Sacramento	1-Wd Sacramento	77	178
John	35	m	w	IREL	San Francisco	San Francisco P O	85	845
John	33	m	w	IREL	San Francisco	8-Wd San Francisco	82	345
John	32	m	w	IREL	San Francisco	8-Wd San Francisco	82	374
John	31	m	w	IREL	San Francisco	San Francisco P O	80	482
John	30	m	w	MA	San Francisco	7-Wd San Francisco	81	221
John D	65	m	w	MD	Yolo	Cache Crk Twp	93	446
Joseph R	38	m	w	SWED	Alpine	Woodfords P O	69	315
Maggie	27	f	w	IREL	San Francisco	2-Wd San Francisco	79	248
Mary	28	f	w	IREL	San Francisco	8-Wd San Francisco	82	289
Patrick	39	m	w	IREL	Sierra	Eureka Twp	89	524
Patrick	33	m	w	IREL	Sierra	Gibson Twp	89	541
Robert	39	m	w	MA	Tulare	Visalia	92	290
Robert	29	m	w	MA	San Diego	San Pasqual	78	520
Rosa	40	f	w	IREL	San Francisco	8-Wd San Francisco	82	351
Thomas	35	m	w	IREL	San Francisco	11-Wd San Francisc	84	545
Thomas	24	m	w	IREL	San Mateo	Schoolhouse Statio	87	337
Thos	27	m	w	IREL	Sierra	Gibson Twp	89	543
Tim	50	m	w	IREL	Sacramento	1-Wd Sacramento	77	184
Timothy	38	m	w	IREL	San Mateo	Woodside P O	87	386
Wm H	21	m	w	NY	San Francisco	1-Wd San Francisco	79	82
DAIN								
---	18	m	c	CHIN	Siskiyou	Yreka	89	659
Adam	40	m	w	ME	Placer	Colfax P O	76	392
Ah	23	m	c	CHIN	Plumas	Quartz Twp	77	43
DAINE								
Thomas H	41	m	w	MA	Santa Cruz	Santa Cruz	89	425
DAINGERFIELD								
Wm	46	m	w	VA	San Francisco	8-Wd San Francisco	82	299
DAINS								
Henry M	41	m	w	NY	El Dorado	Georgetown Twp	72	40
DAIR								
Simon	22	m	w	CA	Fresno	Millerton P O	72	153
DAIRING								
Geo	29	m	w	HCAS	San Francisco	11-Wd San Francisc	84	650
DAIRY								
Catherine	30	f	w	IREL	San Mateo	San Mateo P O	87	357
DAIS								
Alree	28	m	w	MEXI	Fresno	Millerton P O	72	151
DAISEY								
F	60	f	w	IREL	Amador	Jackson P O	69	346
DAISY								
Bell	2	f	w	CA	Yuba	East Bear Rvr Twp	93	540
Celia	33	f	w	NY	San Francisco	San Francisco P O	83	352
DAIT								
Augustus	49	m	w	GERM	Santa Clara	Fremont Twp	88	62
DAKAN								
Elmer	37	m	w	OH	Santa Cruz	Santa Cruz	89	411

© 2001 by Heritage Quest. All rights reserved.

Name	Age	S	R	B-PL	County	Locale	Series M593 Roll	Pg
DAKE								
Ah	30	m	c	CHIN	Alameda	Eden Twp	68	62
Alonzo H	38	m	w	NY	Placer	Auburn P O	76	382
Charles W	40	m	w	NY	Alpine	Monitor P O	69	313
Frank	40	m	w	IREL	San Joaquin	3-Wd Stockton	86	244
Henry H	39	m	w	NY	Plumas	Plumas Twp	77	33
James	59	m	w	IL	Sacramento	Georgianna Twp	77	124
John	34	m	w	CA	Sacramento	Cosumnes Twp	77	90
Theo	26	m	w	NY	Sacramento	1-Wd Sacramento	77	176
DAKEN								
Frank	24	m	w	ME	Yolo	Cottonwood Twp	93	463
DAKIN								
Edwd	29	m	w	NY	San Francisco	San Francisco P O	83	20
George H	49	m	w	NY	Los Angeles	Los Angeles	73	541
H	27	m	w	MI	Lassen	Janesville Twp	73	433
Isaac	49	m	w	CANA	Stanislaus	Emory Twp	92	22
W H	28	m	w	MI	Lassen	Janesville Twp	73	433
William	35	m	w	ENGL	San Francisco	San Francisco P O	83	356
DAL								
Ab	42	m	c	CHIN	San Joaquin	1-Wd Stockton	86	142
DALACIA								
Sylvester	22	m	w	SWIT	Marin	San Antonio Twp	74	64
DALAN								
James	36	m	w	IREL	Tuolumne	Big Oak Flat P O	93	406
Patrick	35	m	w	IREL	San Joaquin	3-Wd Stockton	86	234
DALARCON								
Calisto	26	m	w	MEXI	Santa Cruz	Santa Cruz	89	404
DALAVEGE								
Ignacio	68	m	w	CHIL	Calaveras	San Andreas P O	70	216
DALBERG								
Charles	38	m	w	SWED	San Francisco	3-Wd San Francisco	79	292
John	48	m	w	SWED	Plumas	Mineral Twp	77	22
Josephine	15	f	w	OH	Plumas	Plumas Twp	77	27
DALBEY								
Franklin	59	m	w	PA	Placer	Lincoln P O	76	490
DALBSY								
Henry	38	m	w	PRUS	Santa Clara	Redwood Twp	88	118
DALBY								
A A	35	m	w	NY	Nevada	Meadow Lake Twp	75	260
Joel B	35	m	w	OH	Siskiyou	Scott Valley Twp	89	614
DALCIDO								
Victorio	30	m	w	MEXI	Los Angeles	Los Angeles	73	554
DALE								
A C	39	m	w	MO	El Dorado	Lake Valley Twp	72	63
Charles	7	m	w	CA	San Francisco	San Francisco P O	85	828
Edward	59	m	w	TN	Santa Clara	Fremont Twp	88	64
Evan	36	m	w	ENGL	San Francisco	1-Wd San Francisco	79	89
Frederick	32	m	w	TN	Siskiyou	Butte Twp	89	585
James	59	m	w	AR	Fresno	Millerton P O	72	147
James W	48	m	w	MO	Stanislaus	Empire Twp	92	64
Jeremiah	35	m	w	PA	Humboldt	Eel Rvr Twp	72	247
John	60	m	w	ENGL	Butte	Mountain Spring Tw	70	88
John	41	m	w	PA	Humboldt	South Fork Twp	72	302
M E	26	f	w	MO	Santa Clara	Gilroy Twp	88	74
Milton	38	m	w	MO	Yolo	Grafton Twp	93	491
Philip	50	m	w	PA	Yuba	East Bear Rvr Twp	93	543
Philip A	49	m	w	MA	El Dorado	Cosumnes Twp	72	18
R K	50	m	w	NY	Nevada	Nevada Twp	75	273
Richd	44	m	w	ENGL	Sacramento	3-Wd Sacramento	77	281
Sarah	38	f	w	IL	Santa Clara	Redwood Twp	88	121
Stephen	22	m	w	MO	Yolo	Cottonwood Twp	93	460
Vincent B	36	m	w	GA	Stanislaus	Empire Twp	92	62
William	34	m	w	MO	Santa Clara	Fremont Twp	88	63
William	30	m	w	MO	Siskiyou	Big Valley Twp	89	582
William	25	m	w	SCOT	Santa Clara	2-Wd San Jose	88	305
William C	38	m	w	GA	Stanislaus	Empire Twp	92	32
William N	28	m	w	IL	Siskiyou	Butte Twp	89	585
Wm	9	m	w	IL	San Francisco	San Francisco P O	85	828
DALEFIELD								
Henry	45	m	w	NY	San Francisco	San Francisco P O	83	31
DALEMAN								
Mary	40	f	w	PRUS	San Francisco	5-Wd San Francisco	81	13
DALEY								
Aeneas	34	m	w	IREL	San Francisco	San Francisco P O	85	745
Anna	20	f	w	IREL	San Francisco	8-Wd San Francisco	82	454
Anne	5	f	w	IREL	San Francisco	1-Wd San Francisco	79	67
Bridget	50	f	w	IREL	San Francisco	San Francisco P O	80	379
Bridget	30	f	w	IREL	San Francisco	San Francisco P O	83	312
Bridget	25	f	w	IREL	San Francisco	1-Wd San Francisco	79	56
Bridget	25	f	w	IREL	San Francisco	San Francisco P O	83	325
Catharine	60	f	w	IREL	Yuba	Slate Range Bar Tw	93	675
Catherine	32	f	w	IREL	Santa Clara	1-Wd San Jose	88	241
Charles H	28	m	w	AUST	San Francisco	8-Wd San Francisco	82	495
Cornelius	35	m	w	IREL	San Francisco	8-Wd San Francisco	82	433
Cornelius	32	m	w	IREL	San Francisco	San Francisco P O	83	410
Daniel	53	m	w	MO	Tehama	Tehama Twp	92	194
Dennis	41	m	w	IREL	San Francisco	8-Wd San Francisco	82	423
Edward	30	m	w	IREL	San Francisco	San Francisco P O	83	266
Edward	23	m	w	IREL	San Francisco	1-Wd San Francisco	79	64
Elisha	49	m	w	PA	Sacramento	Center Twp	77	84
Eliza	20	f	w	IREL	San Francisco	San Francisco P O	83	343
Ellen	30	f	w	IREL	San Francisco	San Francisco P O	85	718
Eugene	35	m	w	MA	San Francisco	San Francisco P O	83	335
Frank	8	m	w	NY	Marin	San Rafael Twp	74	29
Frank	30	m	w	IREL	Santa Clara	2-Wd San Jose	88	322
Geo	26	m	w	AUSL	San Francisco	1-Wd San Francisco	79	22
George	30	m	w	IREL	Mariposa	Mariposa P O	74	98
H	30	m	w	IREL	Lake	Morgan Valley	73	425
Hannah	30	f	w	IREL	San Francisco	8-Wd San Francisco	82	429
Hugh	31	m	w	CANA	San Francisco	1-Wd San Francisco	79	62
Hugh	26	m	w	NY	Solano	Vallejo	90	206
Hugh	24	m	w	NY	Solano	Vallejo	90	175
James	6	m	w	IREL	Marin	San Rafael Twp	74	29
James	50	m	w	MO	Napa	Napa Twp	75	69
James	39	m	w	IREL	San Francisco	San Francisco P O	83	288
James	39	m	w	IREL	Nevada	Bloomfield Twp	75	95
James	31	m	w	WI	Tulare	Packwood Twp	92	255
James	30	m	w	PA	Yuba	Rose Bar Twp	93	662
James	27	m	w	IREL	Marin	Sausalito Twp	74	68
James	23	m	w	MA	San Francisco	7-Wd San Francisco	81	173
Joanna	42	f	w	NY	San Francisco	San Francisco P O	83	79
John	41	m	w	IREL	Santa Clara	San Jose Twp	88	188
John	36	m	w	IREL	Santa Clara	San Jose Twp	88	204
John	35	m	w	IREL	Nevada	Bridgeport Twp	75	108
John	30	m	w	IREL	Marin	Nicasio Twp	74	19
John	30	m	w	MD	Solano	Vallejo	90	203
John	29	m	w	ENGL	San Francisco	3-Wd San Francisco	79	291
John	26	m	w	IREL	Marin	San Rafael Twp	74	43
John	26	m	w	IREL	Kern	Havilah P O	73	337
John	22	m	w	NJ	Los Angeles	Santa Ana Twp	73	599
John	22	m	w	IREL	San Francisco	San Francisco P O	83	312
John H	37	m	w	NY	San Francisco	6-Wd San Francisco	81	37
Joseph	38	m	w	ENGL	San Francisco	7-Wd San Francisco	81	221
Joseph	28	m	w	IREL	Santa Clara	Milpitas Twp	88	115
Julia	23	f	w	IREL	San Francisco	8-Wd San Francisco	82	425
Kate	36	f	w	IREL	Santa Clara	1-Wd San Jose	88	230
Kate	23	f	w	IREL	San Francisco	8-Wd San Francisco	82	474
M	3	f	w	CA	Los Angeles	Los Angeles	73	569
M B	37	m	w	OH	Yuba	Marysville	93	613
Maggie	27	f	w	IREL	San Francisco	San Francisco P O	80	408
Maria	33	f	w	IREL	San Francisco	8-Wd San Francisco	82	465
Mary	44	f	w	IREL	San Francisco	7-Wd San Francisco	81	210
Mary	34	f	w	IREL	San Francisco	11-Wd San Francisc	84	666
Mary	30	f	w	IREL	Nevada	Meadow Lake Twp	75	263
Mary	25	f	w	IREL	San Francisco	1-Wd San Francisco	79	67
Mary	22	f	w	NY	San Francisco	7-Wd San Francisco	81	173
Michael	31	m	w	IREL	San Francisco	San Francisco P O	83	306
Michael	26	m	w	IREL	San Francisco	8-Wd San Francisco	82	433
Michl	36	m	w	IREL	San Francisco	1-Wd San Francisco	79	78
Nellie	3	f	w	IREL	San Francisco	1-Wd San Francisco	79	67
Patrick	49	m	w	IREL	El Dorado	Placerville Twp	72	97
Patrick	40	m	w	IREL	Yuba	Rose Bar Twp	93	660
Patrick	36	m	w	IREL	San Francisco	6-Wd San Francisco	81	81
Patrick	35	m	w	IREL	Santa Clara	Burnett Twp	88	31
Patrick	35	m	w	IREL	Marin	Sausalito Twp	74	70
Patrick	30	m	w	IREL	San Francisco	11-Wd San Francisc	84	480
Patrick	20	m	w	IREL	San Francisco	8-Wd San Francisco	82	463
Patrick	19	m	w	IREL	San Francisco	San Francisco P O	83	312
Peter	45	m	w	IREL	San Francisco	1-Wd San Francisco	79	42
Peter	36	m	w	IREL	Placer	Lincoln P O	76	492
Peter	35	m	w	IREL	Yuba	Slate Range Bar Tw	93	674
Peter	33	m	w	IREL	San Francisco	6-Wd San Francisco	81	118
Peter	21	m	w	IREL	San Francisco	7-Wd San Francisco	81	176
Samuel	11	m	w	NY	San Francisco	11-Wd San Francisc	84	587
Sarah	36	f	w	IREL	Los Angeles	Los Angeles	73	524
T	38	m	w	IREL	Lake	Knoxville Mines	73	404
Thomas	40	m	w	IREL	San Francisco	11-Wd San Francisc	84	699
Thomas	40	m	w	IREL	San Francisco	San Francisco P O	85	868
W K	28	m	w	IL	Merced	Snelling P O	74	275
William	28	m	w	IREL	San Francisco	1-Wd San Francisco	79	46
William	23	m	w	IREL	San Francisco	1-Wd San Francisco	79	67
Wm	33	m	w	IREL	San Francisco	1-Wd San Francisco	79	136
DALGADO								
M	33	m	w	MEXI	San Joaquin	3-Wd Stockton	86	221
DALGAS								
A F	11	m	w	MI	Sacramento	3-Wd Sacramento	77	276
DALGREEN								
Fernando	45	m	w	SWED	Nevada	Rough & Ready Twp	75	327
DALILY								
Edward	25	m	w	IREL	Mendocino	Navarro & Big Rvr	74	174
DALIS								
Chas	11	m	w	CA	Alameda	Oakland	68	153
Pelzo	29	m	w	MEXI	Nevada	Meadow Lake Twp	75	269
DALL								
Abbott	38	m	w	OH	Stanislaus	San Joaquin Twp	92	80
Christopher	39	m	w	NY	San Francisco	San Francisco P O	80	421
G W	32	m	w	PA	Santa Clara	Gilroy Twp	88	105
H L	20	m	w	BAVA	San Francisco	San Francisco P O	83	300
Henry J	33	m	w	IN	Los Angeles	Soledad Twp	73	630
John	47	m	w	NY	San Francisco	San Francisco P O	80	532
Lucinda	43	f	w	WURT	Tuolumne	Sonora P O	93	331
P	35	m	w	IREL	Lake	Knoxville Mines	73	405
William	50	m	w	SC	San Francisco	San Francisco P O	83	274
DALLACHI								
Joaquin	52	m	w	ITAL	Tuolumne	Columbia P O	93	340
DALLAM								
Richard	40	m	w	KY	San Francisco	2-Wd San Francisco	79	216
DALLARD								
Wm	33	m	w	IREL	Calaveras	Copperopolis P O	70	235
DALLAS								
Alexander	33	m	w	AL	Los Angeles	Los Nietos Twp	73	574
Charles	55	m	w	SCOT	Stanislaus	Branch Twp	92	5
Emma	26	f	w	PRUS	San Francisco	8-Wd San Francisco	82	428
Evaline	29	f	b	MO	Napa	Napa	75	37

© 2001 by Heritage Quest. All rights reserved.

California 1870 Census

Name	Age	S	R	B-PL	County	Locale	Series M593 Roll	Pg
George	40	m	w	FRAN	San Francisco	San Francisco P O	80	422
Henry	35	m	w	TX	San Joaquin	Douglas Twp	86	45
J L	28	m	w	SCOT	Alameda	Oakland	68	174
James	39	m	w	OH	Napa	Yountville Twp	75	86
John	23	m	w	IA	Stanislaus	Branch Twp	92	5
Robert	29	m	w	IA	Stanislaus	Branch Twp	92	5
Sarah	18	f	w	US	San Joaquin	2-Wd Stockton	86	176
Sarah	16	f	w	OH	Sacramento	2-Wd Sacramento	77	212
Simon	21	m	w	NY	San Francisco	1-Wd San Francisco	79	65
Thomas	38	m	w	IL	Sacramento	2-Wd Sacramento	77	254
William	27	m	w	IA	Stanislaus	Branch Twp	92	5
DALLEN								
C	21	m	w	ENGL	San Joaquin	2-Wd Stockton	86	187
William	38	m	w	SWED	San Francisco	8-Wd San Francisco	82	411
DALLES								
Thomas	38	m	w	IL	Sacramento	2-Wd Sacramento	77	249
DALLEY								
Ferdinand	34	m	w	PRUS	Napa	Napa	75	4
John	30	m	w	IREL	Butte	Kimshew Tpw	70	83
Willm	58	m	w	ENGL	Santa Barbara	San Buenaventura P	87	444
DALLIDET								
Hepolito	47	m	w	FRAN	San Luis Obispo	San Luis Obispo Tw	87	312
DALLING								
Josaphine	30	f	w	IREL	Sacramento	2-Wd Sacramento	77	225
DALLIS								
William	38	m	w	SC	Placer	Bath P O	76	425
DALLIVAN								
The	42	m	w	NY	Butte	Ophir Twp	70	97
DALLIVON								
Jacob	46	m	w	KY	Butte	Ophir Twp	70	102
DALLMAN								
Clara	8	f	w	CA	Sonoma	Petaluma Twp	91	318
Joseph	30	m	w	BAVA	Placer	Lincoln P O	76	485
Louis	31	m	w	BAVA	Placer	Auburn P O	76	368
Salig	23	m	w	BAVA	Placer	Lincoln P O	76	486
DALLON								
George	45	m	w	NY	San Francisco	5-Wd San Francisco	81	13
George	37	m	w	IREL	Los Angeles	Los Angeles Twp	73	489
John G	34	m	w	ENGL	Los Angeles	Los Angeles Twp	73	466
DALLY								
Alexr	25	m	w	NY	San Francisco	5-Wd San Francisco	81	28
Henry J	53	m	w	NY	Santa Barbara	Santa Barbara P O	87	459
James	37	m	w	IREL	Santa Barbara	San Buenaventura P	87	438
John S	50	m	w	NY	San Francisco	5-Wd San Francisco	81	28
Laurence	28	m	w	IREL	San Francisco	5-Wd San Francisco	81	32
Richard	30	m	w	ENGL	Nevada	Grass Valley Twp	75	144
William M	35	m	w	NY	Solano	Silveyville Twp	90	77
DALLYN								
Richard	40	m	w	IREL	Sonoma	Petaluma Twp	91	311
DALMARCENI								
Joseph	22	m	w	ITAL	Santa Clara	2-Wd San Jose	88	315
DALMER								
Chas H	40	m	w	NY	Sonoma	Analy Twp	91	220
DALMUS								
J	14	f	w	CA	Alameda	Oakland	68	242
DALO								
Peter	20	m	w	SWIT	Marin	Tomales Twp	74	76
DALON								
James	28	m	w	IREL	Alameda	Oakland	68	239
DALONE								
Michael	22	m	w	IREL	Inyo	Cerro Gordo Twp	73	319
DALRYMPLE								
Henry	42	m	w	PA	Sacramento	Franklin Twp	77	111
Thos	28	m	w	NY	San Francisco	3-Wd San Francisco	79	310
DALSIG								
Joseph	41	m	w	PRUS	Placer	Rocklin Twp	76	464
DALSON								
Theophalus	35	m	w	IA	Sacramento	Sutter Twp	77	382
DALSTON								
Erasmus	35	m	w	SWED	Marin	Sausalito Twp	74	68
DALTON								
Alfred	46	m	w	ENGL	Solano	Benicia	90	3
Anne	20	f	w	IREL	San Francisco	6-Wd San Francisco	81	146
Christopher	44	m	w	NY	Placer	Pino Twp	76	471
Daniel	40	m	w	IREL	San Francisco	San Francisco P O	85	770
Daniel	12	m	w	CA	Marin	San Rafael Twp	74	29
Daniel	10	m	w	CA	Marin	San Rafael Twp	74	28
Edward	32	m	w	ENGL	San Francisco	5-Wd San Francisco	81	32
Edward	28	m	w	IREL	San Francisco	8-Wd San Francisco	82	434
Elizabeth	70	f	w	ENGL	San Francisco	7-Wd San Francisco	81	156
Eugene	43	m	w	IREL	San Francisco	San Francisco P O	85	763
Eugene	14	m	w	CA	Marin	San Rafael Twp	74	27
Frank	25	m	w	MO	San Francisco	2-Wd San Francisco	79	250
Frank	24	m	w	IN	San Francisco	San Francisco P O	83	317
George	39	m	w	WALE	Nevada	Bridgeport Twp	75	124
Henry	66	m	w	ENGL	Los Angeles	El Monte Twp	73	460
Henry	40	m	w	NY	Contra Costa	Martinez P O	71	434
Henry	26	m	w	IREL	Marin	San Rafael Twp	74	40
Henry C	43	m	w	KY	Fresno	Millerton P O	72	145
Hero	35	m	w	LA	Marin	San Rafael Twp	74	36
James	48	m	w	IREL	San Francisco	San Francisco P O	83	284
James	22	m	w	IREL	San Francisco	7-Wd San Francisco	81	202
Jno	30	m	w	CANA	Santa Clara	Gilroy Twp	88	97
John	64	m	b	MD	Tuolumne	Big Oak Flat P O	93	391
John	52	m	w	PA	El Dorado	Placerville Twp	72	101
John	42	m	w	IREL	Mariposa	Mariposa P O	74	133
John	41	m	w	IREL	San Francisco	San Francisco P O	83	116
John	40	m	w	IL	Tehama	Tehama Twp	92	186
John	33	m	w	LA	Solano	Vallejo	90	183
John	23	m	w	IREL	Alameda	Oakland	68	182
Jos	28	m	w	IREL	Sacramento	3-Wd Sacramento	77	278
Joseph	42	m	w	NY	San Francisco	1-Wd San Francisco	79	106
Joseph	28	m	w	NY	San Francisco	1-Wd San Francisco	79	123
Julia	28	f	w	IREL	San Francisco	San Francisco P O	83	278
Julia	21	f	w	IREL	Sonoma	Petaluma Twp	91	350
L	6	f	w	CA	Los Angeles	Los Angeles	73	569
L	15	f	w	CA	Los Angeles	Los Angeles	73	569
Louisa	30	f	w	AR	Stanislaus	Branch Twp	92	1
Margaret	8	f	w	CA	San Francisco	11-Wd San Francisc	84	711
Mat	25	m	w	CANA	Santa Clara	Gilroy Twp	88	97
Michael	38	m	w	IREL	San Francisco	San Francisco P O	85	859
Michael	35	m	w	IREL	San Francisco	San Francisco P O	83	235
Micheal	35	m	w	IREL	San Francisco	7-Wd San Francisco	81	201
Micheal	22	m	w	IREL	San Francisco	7-Wd San Francisco	81	172
Nancy	77	f	w	KY	Colusa	Stony Crk Twp	71	328
Nelly	24	f	w	IN	San Francisco	7-Wd San Francisco	81	247
Oliver	30	m	w	SWED	San Francisco	11-Wd San Francisc	84	525
Patrick	40	m	w	IREL	Mariposa	Mariposa P O	74	108
Paul E	32	m	w	TN	San Francisco	5-Wd San Francisco	81	18
Peter	29	m	w	IREL	Marin	San Rafael Twp	74	41
Peter	26	m	w	ENGL	Santa Clara	San Jose Twp	88	202
Richard W	29	m	w	ME	Placer	Dutch Flat P O	76	415
Richd	60	m	w	IREL	San Francisco	1-Wd San Francisco	79	79
Robert	32	m	w	IL	Siskiyou	Surprise Valley Tw	89	641
Robert	32	m	w	IL	Siskiyou	Surprise Valley Tw	89	643
S W	43	m	w	ENGL	Solano	Benicia	90	6
Thomas	26	m	w	MO	San Bernardino	San Bernardino Twp	78	417
Thomas J	43	m	w	IREL	Nevada	Grass Valley Twp	75	160
Tim	36	m	w	IREL	San Francisco	5-Wd San Francisco	81	24
Timothy	33	m	w	IREL	Nevada	Grass Valley Twp	75	182
William	7	m	w	CA	Marin	San Rafael Twp	74	28
William	48	m	w	KY	Sonoma	Petaluma Twp	91	353
DALUCHI								
Antonio	28	m	w	ITAL	Amador	Volcano P O	69	385
Giovani	35	m	w	ITAL	Amador	Volcano P O	69	384
DALY								
Asa	70	m	w	NY	Butte	Wyandotte Twp	70	150
Bernard	35	m	w	IREL	San Francisco	San Francisco P O	80	355
Bridget	70	f	w	IREL	San Francisco	7-Wd San Francisco	81	237
Bridget	60	f	w	IREL	San Joaquin	3-Wd Stockton	86	220
Catherine	65	f	w	IREL	San Francisco	6-Wd San Francisco	81	83
Catherine	26	f	w	AUST	Solano	Vallejo	90	182
Cecelia	65	f	w	IREL	San Francisco	San Francisco P O	85	842
Charles	29	m	w	IREL	San Francisco	San Francisco P O	85	745
Chas	30	m	w	NY	Solano	Vallejo	90	179
Cornelious	39	m	w	IREL	San Francisco	11-Wd San Francisc	84	505
Daniel	24	m	w	IREL	Santa Clara	2-Wd San Jose	88	312
Dennis	44	m	w	IREL	San Joaquin	2-Wd Stockton	86	162
Dennis	26	m	w	IREL	San Francisco	11-Wd San Francisc	84	449
Donald	40	m	w	IREL	San Francisco	7-Wd San Francisco	81	270
Edwards	23	m	w	IREL	Sutter	Sutter Twp	92	129
Edwd	34	m	w	ME	Solano	Vallejo	90	209
Edwin	31	m	w	IREL	San Francisco	11-Wd San Francisc	84	523
Ellen C	37	f	w	IREL	Solano	Vallejo	90	150
Elmira	70	f	w	MO	San Bernardino	San Bernardino Twp	78	421
Francis	36	m	w	IREL	San Francisco	San Francisco P O	85	785
Hugh	42	m	w	IREL	Santa Cruz	Santa Cruz Twp	89	391
Isabel	21	f	w	MA	San Francisco	6-Wd San Francisco	81	131
James	50	m	w	IREL	San Francisco	San Francisco P O	83	381
James	39	m	w	IREL	San Francisco	11-Wd San Francisc	84	436
James	35	m	w	IREL	San Francisco	1-Wd San Francisco	79	37
James	30	m	w	IREL	Los Angeles	Wilmington Twp	73	640
James	30	m	w	IREL	Contra Costa	Martinez P O	71	382
James	30	m	w	IREL	Sierra	Gibson Twp	89	543
James	25	m	w	MA	San Francisco	San Francisco P O	83	22
James	24	m	w	IL	Contra Costa	Martinez P O	71	378
James	23	m	w	IREL	San Francisco	1-Wd San Francisco	79	67
Jas	41	m	w	IREL	San Francisco	7-Wd San Francisco	81	270
Jas	28	m	w	IREL	San Joaquin	1-Wd Stockton	86	157
Jeremiah	30	m	w	IREL	San Francisco	San Francisco P O	83	29
John	55	m	w	KY	Monterey	San Juan Twp	74	418
John	47	m	w	IREL	San Joaquin	2-Wd Stockton	86	189
John	45	m	w	IREL	San Francisco	7-Wd San Francisco	81	260
John	45	m	w	PA	San Francisco	1-Wd San Francisco	79	103
John	35	m	w	IREL	San Francisco	San Francisco P O	83	151
John	35	m	w	IREL	Fresno	Millerton P O	72	165
John	35	m	w	IREL	Monterey	San Juan Twp	74	396
John	34	m	w	IREL	San Francisco	3-Wd San Francisco	79	292
John	32	m	w	IREL	San Francisco	6-Wd San Francisco	81	70
John	32	m	w	NY	San Joaquin	2-Wd Stockton	86	158
John	30	m	w	IREL	Sierra	Gibson Twp	89	543
John	23	m	w	IREL	San Francisco	7-Wd San Francisco	81	234
John	23	m	w	IREL	Plumas	Quartz Twp	77	38
John D	30	m	w	MA	San Mateo	San Mateo P O	87	349
John T	48	m	w	MO	Yolo	Cache Crk Twp	93	454
Kate	24	f	w	IREL	San Francisco	3-Wd San Francisco	79	320
Kate	22	f	w	IREL	Santa Clara	Fremont Twp	88	44
Kate	20	f	w	IREL	Santa Cruz	Watsonville	89	366
Lawrence	38	m	w	IREL	Yuba	Rose Bar Twp	93	658
Lawrence	3	m	w	CA	Solano	Suisun Twp	90	116
Linvilla	44	m	w	KY	Sacramento	Dry Crk Twp	77	99
Louisa	56	f	w	IREL	San Francisco	2-Wd San Francisco	79	234
Margaret	18	f	w	CANA	San Joaquin	3-Wd Stockton	86	220
Martin	35	m	w	NY	San Francisco	San Francisco P O	85	736

© 2001 by Heritage Quest. All rights reserved.

Name	Age	S	R	B-PL	County	Locale	Roll	Pg
Mary	37	f	w	NY	Humboldt	Eureka Twp	72	267
Mary	35	f	w	IREL	San Francisco	San Francisco P O	83	166
Mary	26	f	w	IREL	San Francisco	11-Wd San Francisc	84	434
Mary	20	f	w	IREL	Santa Cruz	Watsonville	89	365
Mary	19	f	w	MA	San Francisco	11-Wd San Francisc	84	517
Michael	44	m	w	IREL	San Francisco	1-Wd San Francisco	79	78
Michael	23	m	w	IREL	Santa Cruz	Watsonville	89	366
Michael H	35	m	w	IREL	Sacramento	2-Wd Sacramento	77	234
Michl A	30	m	w	IREL	San Francisco	1-Wd San Francisco	79	74
Moses	43	m	w	OH	San Bernardino	San Bernardino Twp	78	421
Nicholas	35	m	w	IREL	Sacramento	Granite Twp	77	144
Pat	40	m	w	IREL	San Francisco	7-Wd San Francisco	81	260
Pat	25	m	w	IREL	Solano	Vallejo	90	214
Patk	31	m	w	IREL	San Francisco	San Francisco P O	83	133
Patrick	48	m	w	IREL	Santa Cruz	Santa Cruz	89	415
Patrick	36	m	w	PA	Nevada	Grass Valley Twp	75	198
Patrick	35	m	w	IREL	Plumas	Quartz Twp	77	34
Patrick	30	m	w	IREL	Solano	Vallejo	90	158
Patrick	29	m	w	IREL	Plumas	Quartz Twp	77	34
Patrick	27	m	w	IREL	Sacramento	2-Wd Sacramento	77	216
Peter	38	m	w	ENGL	San Francisco	San Francisco P O	83	185
Phineas	44	m	w	OH	San Bernardino	San Bernardino Twp	78	438
Richard H	54	m	w	VA	Mariposa	Mariposa P O	74	116
Robt	30	m	w	CANA	Solano	Vallejo	90	171
Simon	40	m	w	IREL	Solano	Vallejo	90	186
Simon	25	m	w	IREL	Yolo	Cache Crk Twp	93	431
Simon	23	m	w	IREL	Yolo	Cache Crk Twp	93	425
Stephen	32	m	w	CA	San Joaquin	Union Twp	86	266
Thomas	41	m	w	CANA	San Francisco	11-Wd San Francisc	84	471
Thomas	33	m	w	IREL	San Francisco	San Francisco P O	83	189
Thomas	28	m	w	IREL	San Francisco	11-Wd San Francisc	84	456
Thomas	13	m	m	CA	Mariposa	Maxwell Crk P O	74	145
Thos W	40	m	w	IREL	Solano	Vallejo	90	192
Timothy	45	m	w	IREL	Santa Clara	Fremont Twp	88	50
Timothy	30	m	w	IREL	San Francisco	11-Wd San Francisc	84	503
Timothy	24	m	w	IREL	San Francisco	San Francisco P O	83	198
William	41	m	w	IREL	Santa Clara	Fremont Twp	88	54
William	40	m	w	IREL	Santa Cruz	Pajaro Twp	89	362
William	37	m	w	IREL	San Francisco	San Francisco P O	80	472
DALYN								
Thos	40	m	w	IREL	Alameda	Oakland	68	247
DALZELL								
William	23	m	w	MA	Monterey	San Juan Twp	74	386
DALZIEL								
James	39	m	w	SCOT	Alameda	Oakland	68	153
R D	32	m	w	SCOT	Alameda	Oakland	68	207
DAM								
Ah	30	m	c	CHIN	Trinity	Indian Crk	92	199
Ah	24	m	c	CHIN	Mariposa	Maxwell Crk P O	74	145
Alphonso	44	m	w	ME	San Francisco	San Francisco P O	85	749
Andrew	27	m	w	DENM	Alameda	Eden Twp	68	57
Benj	29	m	w	MA	Yuba	East Bear Rvr Twp	93	541
Geo W	56	m	w	ME	Alameda	Oakland	68	235
Thomas	25	m	w	ENGL	Tuolumne	Sonora P O	93	310
DAMAINO								
C	35	m	w	ITAL	San Joaquin	2-Wd Stockton	86	164
DAMAN								
Andrew	52	m	w	HAMB	San Francisco	San Francisco P O	83	84
DAMANA								
Louis	27	m	w	ITAL	San Francisco	11-Wd San Francisc	84	710
DAMANTIN								
Jas	28	m	w	ITAL	San Francisco	11-Wd San Francisc	84	710
DAMARES								
Ambrosio	20	m	w	MEXI	Los Angeles	Los Nietos Twp	73	587
Gertrudes	34	f	w	MEXI	Los Angeles	Los Nietos Twp	73	587
DAMARTINI								
Guadalupe	19	m	w	ITAL	Santa Clara	2-Wd San Jose	88	316
DAMAS								
Jose	20	m	w	CA	Santa Barbara	Santa Barbara P O	87	501
DAMATI								
Frank	39	m	w	ITAL	Tuolumne	Big Oak Flat P O	93	398
DAMAUGH								
Frank	27	m	w	RI	San Francisco	2-Wd San Francisco	79	213
DAMAVE								
Henry	28	m	w	PRUS	San Francisco	7-Wd San Francisco	81	221
DAMBAR								
Andrew	25	m	w	CANA	Solano	Maine Prairie Twp	90	51
DAMBERCHER								
John	45	m	w	GERM	Tuolumne	Columbia P O	93	350
DAME								
David	36	m	w	IREL	Solano	Vacaville Twp	90	133
DAMER								
Joseph	30	m	w	IA	Colusa	Colusa	71	294
Martin	32	m	w	WI	San Francisco	11-Wd San Francisc	84	463
DAMERAL								
Henry	35	m	w	HANO	Los Angeles	Los Angeles	73	525
DAMERON								
Green M	37	m	w	TN	Yolo	Buckeye Twp	93	408
James	23	m	w	MO	Sonoma	Santa Rosa	91	412
John S	53	m	w	TN	San Bernardino	San Salvador Twp	78	457
DAMES								
Wm	50	m	w	PRUS	San Francisco	San Francisco P O	83	97
DAMESEN								
C C	24	m	w	ME	Sierra	Lincoln Twp	89	545
DAMESON								
Willis M	38	m	w	MO	Solano	Rio Vista Twp	90	56
DAMFORDE								
Lew E	40	f	w	NY	Placer	Gold Run Twp	76	397
DAMIEN								
Emille	30	m	w	FRAN	Sacramento	2-Wd Sacramento	77	248
DAMINT								
Giddion S	27	m	w	IA	Amador	Volcano P O	69	388
DAMIS								
Charles	31	m	w	SCOT	Alameda	Oakland	68	264
DAMKROGER								
Gotleib	39	m	w	PRUS	San Francisco	San Francisco P O	80	392
DAMM								
Chas	47	m	w	DENM	San Francisco	11-Wd San Francisc	84	611
Cyrus	35	m	w	ME	Alameda	Oakland	68	265
Lewey	48	m	w	HDAR	Trinity	Weaverville Pct	92	223
DAMMAN								
Andw	44	m	w	PRUS	San Francisco	San Francisco P O	83	81
DAMMER								
Fred	33	m	w	PRUS	San Francisco	8-Wd San Francisco	82	374
DAMMES								
Ernest	32	m	w	PRUS	San Francisco	8-Wd San Francisco	82	400
DAMON								
Arther D	36	m	w	IREL	Colusa	Spring Valley Twp	71	340
Benjamin	20	m	w	ME	Humboldt	Eureka Twp	72	282
Caroline	21	f	w	MA	Nevada	Grass Valley Twp	75	154
Charles	35	m	w	IN	Los Angeles	El Monte Twp	73	455
Charles	33	m	w	MA	Alameda	Alameda	68	20
Charles	23	m	w	MA	Marin	Tomales Twp	74	81
Charles W	30	m	w	MA	San Francisco	San Francisco P O	83	346
Dexter	68	m	w	MA	San Francisco	6-Wd San Francisco	81	127
E C	25	m	w	IN	Humboldt	Pacific Twp	72	294
Geo D	47	m	w	MA	San Francisco	7-Wd San Francisco	81	270
Jacob	40	m	w	ME	Nevada	Nevada Twp	75	296
John N	54	m	w	MA	Placer	Gold Run Twp	76	396
Luke	53	m	w	VT	Santa Clara	Gilroy Twp	88	74
Nathaniel	40	m	w	MA	Alameda	Brooklyn Twp	68	43
Newton	32	m	w	MA	San Francisco	11-Wd San Francisc	84	467
Peter	31	m	w	MA	Solano	Vacaville Twp	90	127
Seth T	28	m	w	MA	San Francisco	6-Wd San Francisco	81	137
Stephen	48	m	w	ME	Yolo	Cottonwood Twp	93	465
William	24	m	w	NH	Marin	Sausalito Twp	74	73
William C	28	m	w	OH	Yolo	Cache Crk Twp	93	428
DAMORA								
Eljinio	40	m	w	MEXI	Fresno	Millerton P O	72	165
DAMOS								
Stephen	19	m	w	CA	Sacramento	2-Wd Sacramento	77	215
DAMP								
Joseph E	24	m	w	ENGL	Yolo	Grafton Twp	93	480
DAMPIER								
William	46	m	w	FRAN	Marin	Novato Twp	74	12
DAMPMAN								
William D	26	m	w	PA	Contra Costa	Martinez P O	71	383
DAMPNER								
Jacob	56	m	w	PA	Kern	Linns Valley P O	73	348
DAMPSAY								
Thomas	35	m	w	IREL	Santa Clara	Redwood Twp	88	125
DAMRELL								
Danl	44	m	w	ME	Marin	San Rafael	74	48
Frank	19	m	w	ME	San Francisco	11-Wd San Francisc	84	559
Jas	42	m	w	IREL	San Joaquin	Douglas Twp	86	49
DAMRON								
William	38	m	w	TN	San Bernardino	San Salvador Twp	78	457
DAMS								
Henry	40	m	w	PRUS	San Francisco	San Francisco P O	80	360
DAMSEL								
Jeremeh	43	m	w	ENGL	Tehama	Antelope Twp	92	155
DAMSGARD								
John	46	m	w	NORW	Placer	Dutch Flat P O	76	414
DAN								
Ah	30	m	c	CHIN	Placer	Alta P O	76	413
Ah	30	m	c	CHIN	Santa Clara	Santa Clara Twp	88	171
Ah	30	m	c	CHIN	Santa Cruz	Soquel Twp	89	443
Ah	23	m	c	CHIN	San Francisco	8-Wd San Francisco	82	341
Ah	22	m	c	CHIN	Santa Clara	Santa Clara Twp	88	159
Ah	15	m	c	CHIN	Santa Cruz	Pajaro Twp	89	341
Ah	14	m	c	CHIN	Alameda	Washington Twp	68	291
Carles	30	m	w	CA	Sacramento	Georgianna Twp	77	129
L H	15	m	w	NH	Sierra	Lincoln Twp	89	549
Lee	34	m	c	CHIN	San Joaquin	1-Wd Stockton	86	144
Sing	34	m	c	CHIN	Nevada	Grass Valley Twp	75	209
Won	48	m	c	CHIN	Sierra	Downieville Twp	89	520
DANA								
A	28	m	w	SCOT	Alameda	Oakland	68	265
Adam	23	m	w	PRUS	Sacramento	4-Wd Sacramento	77	372
Chas W	33	m	w	CA	San Luis Obispo	San Luis Obispo Tw	87	309
Elma	34	f	w	NY	Placer	Pino Twp	76	471
George S	40	m	w	NY	San Francisco	San Francisco P O	85	751
Henery	46	m	w	NY	San Francisco	7-Wd San Francisco	81	156
Henry C	31	m	w	CA	San Luis Obispo	Arroyo Grande Twp	87	270
James	33	m	w	MA	Butte	Concow Twp	70	9
John	62	m	w	NH	Amador	Volcano P O	69	379
John	55	m	w	NJ	San Francisco	5-Wd San Francisco	81	26
John F	32	m	w	CA	San Luis Obispo	Arroyo Grande Twp	87	270
Julia	25	f	w	IN	Placer	Rocklin Twp	76	465
Kate	16	f	w	CA	San Joaquin	1-Wd Stockton	86	120
Lorin	44	m	w	NY	Shasta	Fort Crook P O	89	474
Paul	37	m	w	CANA	Santa Clara	San Jose Twp	88	181
Peter	44	m	w	MA	San Francisco	5-Wd San Francisco	81	26

© 2001 by Heritage Quest. All rights reserved.

Name	Age	S	R	B-PL	County	Locale	Series M593 Roll	Pg
Ralswell	33	m	w	NY	Alameda	Washington Twp	68	295
Smiley	45	m	w	KY	Placer	Roseville P O	76	352
Wm C	34	m	w	CA	San Luis Obispo	Arroyo Grande Twp	87	270
DANAGHE								
Danial	30	m	w	IREL	San Francisco	7-Wd San Francisco	81	210
DANAHAVE								
M J	16	f	w	CA	Los Angeles	Los Angeles	73	569
DANAHER								
John	29	m	w	IREL	San Francisco	11-Wd San Francisc	84	605
DANAHEY								
William	30	m	w	IREL	San Francisco	San Francisco P O	83	192
DANALIE								
Joseph	35	m	w	ITAL	Monterey	Alisal Twp	74	304
DANALS								
Wm	30	m	w	TN	San Joaquin	2-Wd Stockton	86	193
DANAN								
John	28	m	w	ITAL	Mariposa	Mariposa P O	74	131
DANARIO								
John B	40	m	w	ITAL	Inyo	Lone Pine Twp	73	332
DANBAR								
A F	44	m	w	NH	Tuolumne	Chinese Camp P O	93	378
Wm C	33	m	w	MO	Santa Cruz	Santa Cruz Twp	89	396
DANBER								
Jacob	53	m	w	HAMB	Sacramento	Franklin Twp	77	117
John	56	m	w	SCOT	Monterey	San Antonio Twp	74	318
DANBERY								
Geo	47	m	w	ENGL	San Joaquin	1-Wd Stockton	86	131
DANBY								
Geo	54	m	w	ENGL	Yuba	East Bear Rvr Twp	93	539
DANCE								
Henry D	45	m	w	ENGL	Santa Clara	2-Wd San Jose	88	295
Thomas	40	m	w	MO	Santa Clara	2-Wd San Jose	88	315
DANCKER								
J H	33	m	w	SHOL	Merced	Snelling P O	74	277
DANCONA								
David	34	m	w	FRAN	San Francisco	San Francisco P O	83	409
DANCOX								
Alex	30	m	b	AL	Butte	Chico Twp	70	30
DAND								
John	42	m	w	ENGL	Alameda	Oakland	68	229
DANDARO								
M	24	m	w	ITAL	Tuolumne	Big Oak Flat P O	93	395
DANDERS								
Claud	30	m	w	PRUS	Stanislaus	Empire Twp	92	65
William	25	m	w	MA	San Francisco	San Francisco P O	83	400
DANDI								
Peter	42	m	w	CHIL	El Dorado	Placerville Twp	72	103
DANDLE								
David T	49	m	w	AL	San Luis Obispo	Santa Rosa Twp	87	328
DANDOM								
Thomas	35	m	w	IREL	Sonoma	Vallejo Twp	91	453
DANDREW								
William	83	m	w	IREL	San Francisco	7-Wd San Francisco	81	207
DANDRIDGE								
Robert	38	m	w	VA	Nevada	Little York Twp	75	240
DANDY								
Michael	70	m	w	IREL	San Luis Obispo	Arroyo Grande Twp	87	272
DANE								
Augustus	32	m	w	DENM	Sacramento	Sutter Twp	77	385
Ewa	42	m	w	MA	Tuolumne	Big Oak Flat P O	93	405
James H	39	m	w	ENGL	San Francisco	San Francisco P O	85	742
John	48	m	w	GERM	Contra Costa	Martinez P O	71	411
Peter	23	m	w	DENM	Sacramento	Center Twp	77	84
S S	50	m	w	IL	Sacramento	American Twp	77	66
DANELIA								
Elizabeth	50	f	w	IREL	San Joaquin	2-Wd Stockton	86	197
DANELL								
A	27	m	w	IREL	Humboldt	Eureka Twp	72	270
DANELS								
Benjain	37	m	w	ENGL	Nevada	Nevada Twp	75	309
C M	35	m	w	CT	Merced	Snelling P O	74	246
DANELY								
Alfred M	28	m	w	IN	Sonoma	Healdsburg & Mendo	91	283
DANERI								
Andrea	19	m	w	ITAL	San Francisco	11-Wd San Francisc	84	642
Antonio	31	m	w	ITAL	San Francisco	2-Wd San Francisco	79	284
Francis	50	m	w	ITAL	San Francisco	San Francisco P O	80	424
Louis	36	m	w	ITAL	San Francisco	1-Wd San Francisco	79	79
Luigi	34	m	w	ITAL	San Francisco	1-Wd San Francisco	79	110
DANERIE								
Miguel	25	m	w	ITAL	San Francisco	11-Wd San Francisc	84	476
DANEWOOD								
Melvin	36	m	w	IN	Colusa	Colusa Twp	71	277
DANEY								
---	45	m	w	VT	San Mateo	Belmont P O	87	373
Adam	53	m	w	PRUS	San Joaquin	3-Wd Stockton	86	243
Catherine	25	f	w	IREL	San Mateo	Schoolhouse Statio	87	341
Cathrine	26	f	w	IREL	San Francisco	7-Wd San Francisco	81	162
Edwd M	40	m	w	FRAN	San Francisco	1-Wd San Francisco	79	83
Jacob	37	m	w	IL	Marin	San Rafael Twp	74	42
Jerry	32	m	w	ME	San Francisco	San Francisco P O	83	267
Joseph	3M	m	w	CA	San Francisco	7-Wd San Francisco	81	162
Leonard	52	m	w	VT	Contra Costa	Martinez P O	71	403
DANFFEY								
Robert	18	m	w	PA	San Francisco	San Francisco P O	80	368
DANFORD								
Chas	25	m	w	ME	San Francisco	1-Wd San Francisco	79	70
Geo	18	m	w	OR	Butte	Chico Twp	70	49
George	40	m	w	ENGL	Yolo	Grafton Twp	93	499
Henry L	21	m	w	MA	San Francisco	1-Wd San Francisco	79	126
DANFORTH								
David	49	m	w	PA	Mendocino	Ukiah Twp	74	240
David	32	m	w	NY	San Francisco	San Francisco P O	85	745
E	30	m	w	NY	Alameda	Oakland	68	202
Ed	35	m	w	NH	Sierra	Sears Twp	89	555
Edmon	40	m	w	MA	San Francisco	8-Wd San Francisco	82	326
Enoch	45	m	w	MA	San Francisco	11-Wd San Francisc	84	658
George	40	m	w	NH	San Francisco	6-Wd San Francisco	81	154
Lena	15	f	w	CA	San Francisco	8-Wd San Francisco	82	466
M J	40	f	w	NH	Alameda	Oakland	68	162
M Y	26	m	w	NY	Alameda	Oakland	68	202
W G	40	m	w	MA	Alameda	Oakland	68	182
Wm	48	m	w	VT	Butte	Ophir Twp	70	94
DANG								
Ah	41	m	c	CHIN	Plumas	Mineral Twp	77	24
DANGER								
Cathrine	48	f	w	HDAR	San Francisco	1-Wd San Francisco	79	52
Henry	25	m	w	ENGL	San Francisco	7-Wd San Francisco	81	218
DANGERFIELD								
Amelia	25	f	b	PA	San Francisco	6-Wd San Francisco	81	101
Edwin	41	m	w	VA	Santa Clara	Gilroy Twp	88	83
Elizabeth	45	f	m	DE	San Francisco	San Francisco P O	80	415
James	40	m	b	VA	San Francisco	San Francisco P O	80	415
DANGLADA								
Antonia	43	f	w	CA	Monterey	Monterey	74	366
DANGLADE								
Manuela	46	f	w	MEXI	San Francisco	11-Wd San Francisc	84	521
DANGLADO								
Ignacia	24	m	w	MEXI	San Francisco	San Francisco P O	83	201
DANGLISE								
Julian	35	m	w	CANA	San Francisco	San Francisco P O	83	170
DANGMAN								
John	33	m	w	IREL	San Joaquin	Tulare Twp	86	258
Joseph	30	m	w	ENGL	San Luis Obispo	Salinas Twp	87	293
DANGOT								
Herman	50	m	w	FRAN	Sacramento	San Joaquin Twp	77	404
DANGUENGER								
Alfred	21	m	w	FRAN	San Francisco	11-Wd San Francisc	84	554
DANHAUSER								
Moritz	52	m	w	WURT	San Francisco	2-Wd San Francisco	79	160
DANI								
John	55	m	w	OH	Sacramento	Center Twp	77	87
DANIEL								
A E	26	m	w	ENGL	Monterey	Alisal Twp	74	303
Barton	36	m	w	IL	Sacramento	Alabama Twp	77	61
Dougherty	38	m	w	IREL	Yuba	Rose Bar Twp	93	659
Francis	54	m	w	PRUS	San Francisco	11-Wd San Francisc	84	520
George	15	m	w	MEXI	Los Angeles	Los Angeles Twp	73	483
Hector S	48	m	w	ME	San Francisco	5-Wd San Francisco	81	12
James	29	m	w	BELG	San Francisco	11-Wd San Francisc	84	519
Jas	28	m	w	CA	Santa Clara	Almaden Twp	88	7
Jesse	29	m	w	MO	Yolo	Buckeye Twp	93	409
Jesus	19	m	w	MEXI	Los Angeles	Los Angeles Twp	73	486
John	63	m	w	PA	Santa Clara	San Jose Twp	88	217
John	35	m	w	CANA	San Francisco	8-Wd San Francisco	82	487
John H	45	m	w	HANO	San Francisco	1-Wd San Francisco	79	27
Joseph	35	m	w	CT	Sacramento	4-Wd Sacramento	77	372
Joseph	20	m	w	SWIT	San Francisco	11-Wd San Francisc	84	659
Jule	48	m	w	FRAN	Santa Clara	Fremont Twp	88	50
L	39	m	w	IREL	Solano	Benicia	90	9
Lewis	41	m	w	WALE	Sierra	Sears Twp	89	559
Manuel	15	m	w	CA	San Luis Obispo	San Luis Obispo Tw	87	306
Nathan	38	m	w	OH	Mendocino	Bourns Landing Twp	74	223
Peter	40	m	w	FRAN	San Francisco	1-Wd San Francisco	79	52
Romulo	30	m	w	MEXI	Fresno	Millerton P O	72	153
Saul S	24	m	w	ENGL	San Francisco	5-Wd San Francisco	81	11
Thomas	31	m	w	ENGL	Nevada	Washington Twp	75	344
William	36	m	w	SCOT	San Francisco	11-Wd San Francisc	84	531
William	31	m	w	HCAS	Contra Costa	Martinez P O	71	383
DANIELEWITZ								
Joseph	39	m	w	POLA	San Francisco	San Francisco P O	83	353
DANIELL								
S D	50	m	w	KY	Humboldt	Pacific Twp	72	293
Thomas	43	m	w	ME	San Francisco	2-Wd San Francisco	79	271
DANIELOVITZ								
G	42	m	w	PRUS	Amador	Sutter Crk P O	69	399
DANIELS								
Alice	35	f	w	IREL	Yuba	Marysville	93	632
Auguste	14	m	w	MA	San Francisco	11-Wd San Francisc	84	588
Austin	62	m	w	TN	Trinity	Trinity Center Pct	92	205
Benj	46	m	w	ENGL	San Francisco	San Francisco P O	85	821
Benjamin	40	m	w	PA	Santa Clara	Redwood Twp	88	129
Bridget	37	f	w	IREL	Nevada	Grass Valley Twp	75	226
Catharine	19	f	i	CA	El Dorado	Diamond Springs Tw	72	32
Chas	57	m	w	NY	Siskiyou	Surprise Valley Tw	89	639
Cornelius	37	m	w	NY	Yolo	Washington Twp	93	530
David	33	m	w	WALE	Butte	Oregon Twp	70	125
E G	55	m	w	NY	Placer	Pino Twp	76	470
Earl	56	m	w	VA	Marin	Tomales Twp	74	77
Emanuel	48	m	w	MEXI	Fresno	Millerton P O	72	161
Emil	25	m	w	PRUS	San Francisco	San Francisco P O	80	532
Ephriam	44	m	w	NY	Nevada	Rough & Ready Twp	75	330
Eugene	42	m	w	FRAN	Trinity	Lewiston Pct	92	214
Fayette	25	m	w	NY	San Diego	Julian Dist	78	469

© 2001 by Heritage Quest. All rights reserved.

Name	Age	S	R	B-PL	County	Locale	Series M593 Roll	Pg
Franklin	26	m	w	MO	El Dorado	Diamond Springs Tw	72	25
Geo F	48	m	w	SCOT	Butte	Bidwell Twp	70	3
George	40	m	w	PA	San Francisco	San Francisco P O	80	415
George W	58	m	w	PA	Stanislaus	San Joaquin Twp	92	74
Gertrude	68	f	w	MEXI	Fresno	Millerton P O	72	146
Greenleaf	44	m	w	ME	Solano	Denverton Twp	90	24
H S	54	m	w	NH	Humboldt	Arcata Twp	72	232
Henry	37	m	w	MA	San Mateo	San Mateo P O	87	358
Henry	17	m	w	BREM	San Francisco	2-Wd San Francisco	79	160
J B	49	m	w	ME	San Francisco	San Francisco P O	83	275
J M	55	m	w	NY	San Francisco	San Francisco P O	85	876
J M	44	m	w	CT	San Joaquin	1-Wd Stockton	86	128
James	53	m	w	SCOT	Nevada	Rough & Ready Twp	75	332
James	42	m	w	ENGL	San Francisco	San Francisco P O	83	339
James	38	m	w	CT	Mariposa	Maxwell Crk P O	74	145
James	36	m	w	IREL	San Francisco	1-Wd San Francisco	79	76
James	30	m	w	TN	Trinity	Lewiston Pct	92	213
Jno R	41	m	w	WALE	Butte	Oregon Twp	70	125
John	56	m	w	SCOT	El Dorado	Greenwood Twp	72	54
John	45	m	w	WI	Sacramento	San Joaquin Twp	77	397
John	35	m	w	WALE	Contra Costa	Martinez P O	71	428
John	35	m	w	WALE	Nevada	Bridgeport Twp	75	107
John	33	m	w	IREL	Marin	San Rafael Twp	74	27
John	28	m	w	ENGL	Amador	Jackson P O	69	321
Joseph	40	m	w	ENGL	Sacramento	2-Wd Sacramento	77	244
Joseph	35	m	w	IREL	Sacramento	2-Wd Sacramento	77	216
Jus H	37	m	w	KY	Butte	Oregon Twp	70	136
M	40	f	w	AR	Yuba	Marysville	93	633
Milan	36	m	w	OH	Sutter	Butte Twp	92	102
Nancy	63	f	w	NC	Sacramento	1-Wd Sacramento	77	203
Peter	63	m	w	PA	Stanislaus	Empire Twp	92	57
Pillear	14	f	w	CA	Fresno	Millerton P O	72	167
R	29	m	w	IL	San Joaquin	Elkhorn Twp	86	63
Robert A	55	m	w	KY	Yolo	Buckeye Twp	93	415
Russell B	42	m	w	NY	El Dorado	Cosumnes Twp	72	14
Sam L	36	m	w	NY	Butte	Chico Twp	70	13
Saml	40	m	w	OH	Butte	Hamilton Twp	70	70
Samuel	44	m	w	NY	Tuolumne	Chinese Camp P O	93	370
Samuel	41	m	w	ENGL	Marin	Sausalito Twp	74	73
Samuel	35	m	w	ENGL	Nevada	Nevada Twp	75	301
Seneca	43	m	w	NY	Sonoma	Vallejo Twp	91	452
Seth	50	m	w	NY	Kern	Havilah P O	73	350
Stephen	40	m	w	IL	Marin	Tomales Twp	74	78
Stephen R	35	m	w	MO	El Dorado	Diamond Springs Tw	72	31
T H	46	m	w	MO	Yuba	Marysville	93	591
Thomas	35	m	w	IREL	Stanislaus	Branch Twp	92	2
Thomas	33	m	w	MA	San Francisco	San Francisco P O	83	389
William	68	m	w	ENGL	Santa Clara	2-Wd San Jose	88	298
William	32	m	w	NY	Alameda	Washington Twp	68	284
William	24	m	w	NH	San Mateo	Pescadero P O	87	413
Wm	28	m	w	NY	San Francisco	1-Wd San Francisco	79	125
Wm	26	m	w	VA	San Francisco	8-Wd San Francisco	82	366
Wm J	37	m	w	TN	Butte	Ophir Twp	70	109
DANIELSON								
Erick	22	m	w	NORW	San Francisco	3-Wd San Francisco	79	293
John	30	m	w	SWED	San Francisco	5-Wd San Francisco	81	20
DANIELWICZ								
Samuel	28	m	w	PRUS	San Francisco	San Francisco P O	83	219
DANIGAN								
Bernard	65	m	w	IREL	Alameda	Washington Twp	68	292
John	45	m	w	IREL	San Francisco	San Francisco P O	83	87
Pat	75	m	w	IREL	Alameda	Oakland	68	248
Patrick	64	m	w	IREL	Santa Clara	2-Wd San Jose	88	334
DANINO								
Ramon	37	m	w	MEXI	Tulare	White Rvr Twp	92	302
DANIRADAN								
Gertrude	10	f	m	MA	San Francisco	San Francisco P O	80	420
DANIRAL								
A H	39	m	w	NY	Sierra	Downieville Twp	89	518
DANIVAN								
Patrick	47	m	w	IREL	Sacramento	Granite Twp	77	154
DANJIN								
Charles	64	m	w	FRAN	San Francisco	2-Wd San Francisco	79	156
DANK								
James	41	m	w	MI	Nevada	Meadow Lake Twp	75	267
DANKEN								
Louis	26	m	w	GERM	Contra Costa	Martinez P O	71	396
DANKER								
Fredrick	43	m	w	OLDE	Sonoma	Petaluma Twp	91	332
Jane	50	f	w	OH	Sonoma	Petaluma Twp	91	365
John	40	m	w	BAVA	Calaveras	San Andreas P O	70	206
DANKERTZ								
C	28	m	w	PRUS	San Francisco	8-Wd San Francisco	82	360
DANKIN								
Joseph F	26	m	w	ENGL	Stanislaus	San Joaquin Twp	92	72
DANKINS								
Tho	10	m	b	SC	Yuba	Marysville	93	590
DANKMEYER								
Henry	46	m	w	PRUS	San Francisco	San Francisco P O	83	420
DANLEY								
James	25	m	w	AR	Colusa	Colusa Twp	71	278
DANLY								
Micheal	31	m	w	IREL	San Francisco	8-Wd San Francisco	82	369
DANN								
Edwd	31	m	w	NY	San Francisco	1-Wd San Francisco	79	98
Fredrick	34	m	w	NY	San Francisco	San Francisco P O	80	488
Michael	26	m	w	GERM	Contra Costa	San Pablo Twp	71	364
Timothy	40	m	w	IREL	San Francisco	8-Wd San Francisco	82	319
DANNAHER								
Edward	9	m	w	CA	San Francisco	11-Wd San Francisc	84	593
Henry	12	m	w	CA	San Francisco	11-Wd San Francisc	84	593
DANNALS								
C W	46	m	w	NY	Nevada	Bridgeport Twp	75	113
Francis	47	m	w	ENGL	Yuba	North East Twp	93	644
Henry	53	m	w	IN	Nevada	Bridgeport Twp	75	106
DANNANBAUM								
J	31	m	w	PRUS	Santa Clara	Gilroy Twp	88	75
DANNAWAY								
Elias	31	m	w	TN	Tuolumne	Sonora P O	93	326
DANNE								
John	69	m	w	IREL	Sonoma	Healdsburg & Mendo	91	278
DANNELLY								
Ellen	30	f	w	IREL	Sierra	Eureka Twp	89	526
DANNENFELETTER								
Ted P	39	m	w	PRUS	San Francisco	San Francisco P O	83	34
DANNER								
F	44	m	w	NC	Merced	Snelling P O	74	254
Fredk	26	m	w	PRUS	San Francisco	San Francisco P O	83	194
Nathan	47	m	w	NC	Merced	Snelling P O	74	253
DANNES								
Mary A	16	f	w	CA	Santa Clara	2-Wd San Jose	88	337
DANNEY								
John	30	m	w	IREL	San Francisco	San Francisco P O	83	133
Jos	41	m	w	FRAN	San Joaquin	2-Wd Stockton	86	213
Samuel	33	m	w	PA	Inyo	Bishop Crk Twp	73	310
DANNIELL								
Saml	50	m	w	IL	Butte	Ophir Twp	70	111
DANNIELS								
C H	40	m	w	CT	Alameda	Oakland	68	197
DANNING								
John	31	m	w	IREL	Sacramento	4-Wd Sacramento	77	370
DANNO								
Mary	22	f	w	ITAL	San Francisco	11-Wd San Francisc	84	710
DANOKE								
W A	38	m	w	SCOT	Alameda	Oakland	68	264
DANON								
Jules	29	m	w	SPAI	San Francisco	11-Wd San Francisc	84	661
DANSEN								
Philip	30	m	w	PRUS	San Francisco	San Francisco P O	80	539
DANSFORTH								
W A	27	m	w	PA	Sacramento	3-Wd Sacramento	77	273
DANSIE								
Patrick	26	m	w	IREL	Sonoma	Bodega Twp	91	260
DANSKIN								
George	66	m	w	SCOT	San Luis Obispo	Santa Rosa Twp	87	318
George	40	m	w	CANA	Contra Costa	Martinez P O	71	437
Jas S	36	m	w	NY	Humboldt	Eel Rvr Twp	72	250
DANSON								
Edward G	50	m	w	IN	Nevada	Nevada Twp	75	310
James	35	m	w	CANA	Contra Costa	Martinez P O	71	447
William	49	m	w	NY	Contra Costa	Martinez P O	71	413
William	29	m	w	TN	Kern	Tehachapi P O	73	353
DANT								
Casper	40	m	w	WURT	Trinity	North Fork Twp	92	216
Maggy	34	f	w	IREL	Sonoma	Bodega Twp	91	248
DANTON								
Gilbert	50	m	w	NY	Alameda	Washington Twp	68	296
Solomon	36	m	w	OH	Solano	Maine Prairie Twp	90	47
DANTZ								
Jno	35	m	w	DENM	Butte	Oregon Twp	70	135
DANUN								
Thomas	50	m	w	MA	Santa Cruz	Santa Cruz Twp	89	396
DANUSON								
Math	39	m	w	SWIT	Sierra	Eureka Twp	89	525
DANY								
John	41	m	w	ENGL	Mariposa	Maxwell Crk P O	74	142
Susan	39	f	w	SWIT	Santa Clara	2-Wd San Jose	88	309
DANZIENO								
Chs	65	m	w	FRAN	San Francisco	2-Wd San Francisco	79	188
DANZIGER								
Henry	42	m	w	PRUS	San Francisco	11-Wd San Francisc	84	493
DANZY								
Julia	2	f	w	CA	Yolo	Grafton Twp	93	492
DAONEY								
John	46	m	w	IREL	San Francisco	11-Wd San Francisc	84	581
DAPER								
Cyrus	41	m	w	MA	San Francisco	5-Wd San Francisco	81	23
DAR								
Lee	36	m	c	CHIN	Yuba	Marysville	93	629
DARAH								
Patrick	37	m	w	CANA	Yuba	New York Twp	93	639
DARATT								
Edwd J	39	m	w	NY	Shasta	Portugese Flat P O	89	471
DARAWN								
Peter	24	m	w	DENM	Santa Cruz	Pajaro Twp	89	346
DARBEAU								
Alphonso	60	m	w	SWIT	Siskiyou	Callahan P O	89	628
DARBEY								
Andrew	64	m	w	SC	Contra Costa	Martinez P O	71	411
George	29	m	w	MO	Contra Costa	Martinez P O	71	403
DARBIN								
Thomas	30	m	w	VT	Santa Clara	Fremont Twp	88	47
DARBLIEX								
Arnot	61	m	w	FRAN	Amador	Volcano P O	69	384

© 2001 by Heritage Quest. All rights reserved.

Name	Age	S	R	B-PL	County	Locale	Series M593 Roll	Pg
DARBY								
Charles A	19	m	w	NY	Napa	Napa	75	36
Elizabeth	34	f	w	IREL	San Francisco	San Francisco P O	85	726
John	58	m	w	IREL	Fresno	Millerton P O	72	187
Loyd	39	m	w	OH	Solano	Vacaville Twp	90	117
Marion	23	m	w	MO	Sutter	Vernon Twp	92	135
Peter	46	m	w	IREL	Del Norte	Crescent	71	466
Robert R	42	m	w	AL	Yolo	Cottonwood Twp	93	469
Thomas	35	m	w	IN	Siskiyou	Surprise Valley Tw	89	639
Timothy	60	m	w	IREL	Santa Clara	2-Wd San Jose	88	291
DARBYSHIRE								
D K	48	m	w	PA	Napa	Napa	75	17
Fannie E	30	f	w	PA	Napa	Napa	75	17
DARCEY								
Chas B	26	m	w	SWIT	San Francisco	San Francisco P O	85	873
James	38	m	w	IREL	San Francisco	San Francisco P O	83	218
Peter	23	m	w	IREL	San Joaquin	1-Wd Stockton	86	134
DARCY								
Arthurine	17	f	w	IREL	San Joaquin	2-Wd Stockton	86	169
Charles	31	m	w	IA	Inyo	Bishop Crk Twp	73	310
Edward	50	m	w	IREL	San Francisco	7-Wd San Francisco	81	264
Edward	24	m	w	IREL	Santa Clara	2-Wd San Jose	88	313
Hannah	20	f	w	IREL	San Francisco	1-Wd San Francisco	79	67
James	23	m	w	IREL	Santa Clara	Santa Clara Twp	88	147
John	35	m	w	IREL	San Francisco	San Francisco P O	83	51
Mary	40	f	w	IREL	San Joaquin	2-Wd Stockton	86	177
Patrick	34	m	w	IREL	San Francisco	San Francisco P O	83	203
Wm	37	m	w	CANA	San Francisco	7-Wd San Francisco	81	277
DARDE								
Theofield	50	m	w	FRAN	Yuba	Bullards Bar P O	93	553
DARDEN								
George	50	m	w	TN	Sonoma	Santa Rosa	91	425
W W	25	m	w	MO	Sonoma	Santa Rosa	91	425
Wm C	40	m	w	IL	Napa	Yountville Twp	75	85
DARDES								
Andrew	27	m	w	NY	Sonoma	Petaluma Twp	91	322
DARDIS								
John	38	m	w	IREL	Alpine	Bullion P O	69	314
DARE								
J F	30	m	w	NY	Solano	Vallejo	90	209
L	32	m	w	BADE	San Joaquin	2-Wd Stockton	86	193
DARELSON								
John	41	m	w	SCOT	El Dorado	Placerville Twp	72	101
DARES								
Isaac N	32	m	w	IL	Nevada	Meadow Lake Twp	75	251
Solomon	28	m	w	MO	Contra Costa	Martinez P O	71	406
DARETY								
James	37	m	w	ENGL	Contra Costa	Martinez P O	71	411
DAREY								
James	37	m	w	IREL	San Joaquin	1-Wd Stockton	86	128
William	37	m	w	NY	Nevada	Meadow Lake Twp	75	267
DARFIAS								
Mexeum	24	m	w	FRAN	Los Angeles	Los Angeles	73	523
DARGAN								
Daniel	42	m	w	IREL	Santa Clara	Santa Clara Twp	88	136
M K	30	m	w	IREL	Sonoma	Vallejo Twp	91	459
Mary	25	f	w	VT	San Francisco	8-Wd San Francisco	82	455
Moro	26	m	w	AL	San Francisco	8-Wd San Francisco	82	450
DARGE								
William W	21	m	w	PA	Colusa	Butte Twp	71	268
DARGELCH								
Charles	21	m	w	HANO	Santa Clara	Fremont Twp	88	42
DARGLE								
Joseph	40	m	w	CANA	Tuolumne	Chinese Camp P O	93	372
DARGON								
John	52	m	w	IREL	Amador	Volcano P O	69	388
DARHAM								
Geo	26	m	w	PRUS	Butte	Kimshew Tpw	70	80
John	38	m	w	NY	Tuolumne	Big Oak Flat P O	93	399
John H	45	m	w	TN	Stanislaus	Branch Twp	92	6
William	30	m	w	KY	Colusa	Colusa Twp	71	276
DARIANO								
Jose	20	m	w	CA	Santa Clara	Almaden Twp	88	19
DARIGAN								
John	50	m	w	IREL	Amador	Jackson P O	69	339
DARIGER								
I	34	m	w	NY	Sacramento	3-Wd Sacramento	77	311
DARILA								
Jose M	11	m	w	CA	Santa Cruz	Pajaro Twp	89	343
DARING								
Clarence	17	m	w	CA	Napa	Napa	75	35
DARIUS								
Adam	51	m	w	OH	Stanislaus	Empire Twp	92	54
Chris	33	m	w	FRAN	Yuba	Marysville	93	615
Mich	35	m	w	IREL	Alameda	Oakland	68	163
Peter	56	m	w	FRAN	San Francisco	San Francisco P O	80	535
DARK								
Albert	38	m	w	NY	San Francisco	3-Wd San Francisco	79	316
Levi J	28	m	w	CANA	Mendocino	Albion & Big Rvr T	74	166
Robert	20	m	w	CANA	Mendocino	Albion & Big Rvr T	74	166
Samuel	32	m	w	ENGL	Placer	Bath P O	76	459
DARKE								
Fred E	24	m	w	PA	San Luis Obispo	Santa Rosa Twp	87	325
John G	44	m	w	MS	Solano	Silveyville Twp	90	83
DARKEY								
Louis	31	m	w	FRAN	Los Angeles	Los Angeles	73	571
DARKIS								
Samuel	32	m	w	CANA	Nevada	Grass Valley Twp	75	184
DARLACH								
Leo	34	m	w	BADE	Stanislaus	San Joaquin Twp	92	72
DARLEY								
Michael	14	m	w	CA	Santa Clara	San Jose Twp	88	194
Patrick	29	m	w	IREL	Contra Costa	Martinez P O	71	422
Patrick	28	m	w	IREL	Contra Costa	Martinez P O	71	421
Wm	24	m	w	IREL	San Francisco	1-Wd San Francisco	79	106
DARLIN								
John	44	m	b	KY	Tehama	Tehama Twp	92	190
DARLING								
Abram F	30	m	w	NY	Santa Cruz	Soquel Twp	89	442
Alfred	47	m	w	MA	El Dorado	Georgetown Twp	72	47
Alvida	25	f	w	NY	Marin	San Rafael Twp	74	33
Annie	19	f	w	IREL	Sacramento	3-Wd Sacramento	77	262
Aracena	50	m	w	FRAN	Sacramento	2-Wd Sacramento	77	212
Barber	38	m	w	NY	Santa Cruz	Soquel Twp	89	448
Benj A	41	m	w	NY	Napa	Yountville Twp	75	84
C C	43	m	w	CANA	Sierra	Downieville Twp	89	519
Charles P	36	m	w	MA	Nevada	Little York Twp	75	243
Dick	25	m	i	CA	Fresno	Kings Rvr P O	72	216
Eben	41	m	w	VT	San Francisco	8-Wd San Francisco	82	319
Ebner O	31	m	w	VT	Mariposa	Mariposa P O	74	111
Eleazer T	40	m	w	NH	Placer	Bath P O	76	457
Elhanan W	36	m	w	CA	Santa Clara	Milpitas Twp	88	108
Gashum	45	m	w	NY	Humboldt	Mattole Twp	72	285
Gee	45	m	w	ENGL	Sacramento	Mississippi Twp	77	162
Geo	33	m	w	SWED	San Francisco	11-Wd San Francisc	84	676
Grace	27	f	w	IREL	San Francisco	3-Wd San Francisco	79	325
Henry	28	m	w	CANA	Solano	Vallejo	90	147
Jas C	30	m	w	RI	Butte	Chico Twp	70	60
John	46	m	w	ENGL	San Diego	San Diego	78	487
John	23	m	w	SHOL	Marin	Sausalito Twp	74	67
John	23	m	w	NY	Napa	Napa	75	6
L W	28	m	w	NY	San Francisco	San Francisco P O	85	846
Lewes W	36	m	w	CANA	Trinity	Lewiston Pct	92	211
Mary	23	f	w	NY	San Francisco	San Francisco P O	83	221
Otis	50	m	w	IA	Nevada	Bridgeport Twp	75	125
Patrick	40	m	w	OH	Solano	Tremont Twp	90	29
Peter	43	m	w	ENGL	Inyo	Bishop Crk Twp	73	316
Richard	40	m	w	IREL	San Francisco	San Francisco P O	83	280
Samuel	38	m	w	OH	Placer	Bath P O	76	446
T G	43	m	w	PA	Sierra	Sierra Twp	89	568
T W	18	m	w	NY	Alameda	Oakland	68	146
Thos	22	m	w	NY	San Francisco	8-Wd San Francisco	82	366
William	30	m	w	NY	Sutter	Sutter Twp	92	125
William R	33	m	w	MA	Santa Cruz	Santa Cruz Twp	89	387
DARLINGTON								
Abraham	49	m	w	NJ	El Dorado	Placerville Twp	72	94
DARLISON								
Thomas F	32	m	w	ENGL	Yolo	Cottonwood Twp	93	470
DARLY								
Hugh	60	m	w	ENGL	Colusa	Colusa Twp	71	286
James	40	m	w	IREL	San Francisco	San Francisco P O	85	877
Wm	39	m	w	IREL	Sacramento	American Twp	77	66
DARMAN								
James	26	m	w	IREL	Sonoma	Petaluma Twp	91	328
Lawrence	27	m	w	SHOL	Santa Cruz	Pajaro Twp	89	346
William	30	m	w	BREM	Sonoma	Sonoma Twp	91	438
DARMOND								
T	26	f	w	SAME	San Joaquin	1-Wd Stockton	86	133
DARMONT								
Norman	30	m	w	NORW	Yolo	Buckeye Twp	93	413
DARN								
Daniel	35	m	w	ENGL	Contra Costa	Martinez P O	71	421
DARNA								
W J	32	m	w	ENGL	Tuolumne	Big Oak Flat P O	93	402
DARNEAL								
Edward M	37	m	w	KY	Yuba	Slate Range Bar Tw	93	675
DARNEILLE								
Fielding	55	m	w	KY	Yuba	Parks Bar Twp	93	650
DARNEL								
John	36	m	w	IL	Santa Barbara	San Buenaventura P	87	424
DARNELL								
Cale B	60	m	w	IL	Calaveras	San Andreas P O	70	175
Thomas	50	m	w	MD	Calaveras	San Andreas P O	70	152
Walter D	34	m	w	ENGL	Calaveras	San Andreas P O	70	218
DARNES								
C W	62	m	w	VA	Amador	Drytown P O	69	416
DARNEY								
William	53	m	w	VA	Contra Costa	Martinez P O	71	400
William	45	m	w	PRUS	San Francisco	6-Wd San Francisco	81	81
DARNLEY								
Theo	50	m	w	CANA	Tuolumne	Sonora P O	93	325
DARNO								
John	30	m	w	GERM	San Joaquin	2-Wd Stockton	86	169
DARO								
Jared	14	m	w	CA	San Francisco	San Francisco P O	85	764
DAROSH								
Joseph	33	m	w	CANA	Sonoma	Vallejo Twp	91	454
DAROUX								
Pierre	36	m	w	FRAN	Sacramento	2-Wd Sacramento	77	233
DARPEL								
Caroline	16	f	w	CA	Yuba	Marysville	93	609
DARPLE								
Caroline	14	f	w	CA	Sutter	Butte Twp	92	89

© 2001 by Heritage Quest. All rights reserved.

Series M593

Name	Age	S	R	B-PL	County	Locale	Roll	Pg
DARR								
Caroline	19	f	w	PRUS	San Francisco	1-Wd San Francisco	79	24
Caroline	18	f	w	CA	San Francisco	San Francisco P O	80	532
George	36	m	w	MO	Shasta	Millville P O	89	486
J C	38	m	w	ME	Trinity	Trinity Center Pct	92	205
John	28	m	w	IREL	Stanislaus	Branch Twp	92	3
Juan	35	m	w	AZOR	San Francisco	1-Wd San Francisco	79	130
Robert M	34	m	w	VA	Mendocino	Point Arena Twp	74	213
DARRAH								
Caroline	40	f	w	NY	San Francisco	7-Wd San Francisco	81	204
Jno H	38	m	w	VA	Shasta	Millville P O	89	486
Joseph	42	m	w	OH	Inyo	Cerro Gordo Twp	73	318
Lucy	44	f	w	PRUS	San Francisco	7-Wd San Francisco	81	207
Lucy	27	f	w	MA	San Francisco	San Francisco P O	83	333
Simon H	33	m	w	VA	Shasta	Millville P O	89	484
DARRER								
Maurice	33	m	w	CANA	Alpine	Monitor P O	69	317
DARRIA								
Frederika	22	f	w	HANO	San Francisco	6-Wd San Francisco	81	72
DARRINGTON								
Lon	27	m	w	ENGL	El Dorado	Salmon Falls Twp	72	132
DARRION								
J C	44	m	w	OH	San Joaquin	2-Wd Stockton	86	198
DARRON								
G H	27	m	w	CT	Tuolumne	Chinese Camp P O	93	375
DARROW								
Carrie	30	f	w	IN	Stanislaus	Buena Vista Twp	92	14
G A	58	m	w	NY	Tuolumne	Columbia P O	93	351
Thos	40	m	w	PA	Santa Clara	Gilroy Twp	88	75
W L	42	m	w	NY	Humboldt	Mattole Twp	72	283
William	31	m	w	NY	Stanislaus	Emory Twp	92	21
DARRY								
James	32	m	w	SCOT	San Francisco	1-Wd San Francisco	79	82
DARSEY								
Thos	25	m	w	IREL	Tehama	Tehama Twp	92	192
DARSON								
S	23	m	w	FINL	Lake	Lower Lake	73	415
DARSONS								
Lewis N	31	m	w	CANA	Sonoma	Petaluma Twp	91	327
DARSTO								
John	36	m	w	ITAL	Amador	Sutter Crk P O	69	414
DART								
Arthur E	15	m	w	CA	Santa Cruz	Soquel Twp	89	440
George	28	m	w	NY	San Francisco	7-Wd San Francisco	81	221
Harrison	51	m	w	NY	Santa Cruz	Soquel Twp	89	440
Henry	47	m	w	NY	Sacramento	2-Wd Sacramento	77	243
John S	40	m	w	OH	Tuolumne	Sonora P O	93	322
Livey	25	m	w	MA	Sacramento	San Joaquin Twp	77	395
Martin	59	m	w	CT	Sacramento	San Joaquin Twp	77	397
Mary	10	f	w	CA	Santa Clara	San Jose Twp	88	219
P C	45	m	w	NY	Alameda	Oakland	68	196
Thomas	40	m	w	CT	Humboldt	Eureka Twp	72	273
Wm	7	m	w	CANA	Sacramento	Alabama Twp	77	60
DARTMAN								
H	30	m	w	HANO	Sierra	Butte Twp	89	509
DARTNELL								
Gustave	44	m	w	FRAN	San Francisco	8-Wd San Francisco	82	288
DARTOIS								
Gustave	43	m	w	FRAN	Sacramento	4-Wd Sacramento	77	362
DARUS								
Louis	53	m	w	FRAN	Shasta	Shasta P O	89	457
DARVES								
Julia	41	f	w	FRAN	San Francisco	2-Wd San Francisco	79	194
Richard	33	m	w	MA	Alameda	Brooklyn	68	24
DARVILLA								
Antone	35	m	w	PORT	Sacramento	Sutter Twp	77	387
DARVILLE								
Clarence	45	m	w	IREL	Butte	Ophir Twp	70	111
DARVIS								
Julia	14	f	w	ENGL	Alameda	Oakland	68	251
DARVOLA								
Lawrence	35	m	w	ITAL	San Francisco	San Francisco P O	80	533
DARWICK								
Michael	45	m	w	IREL	San Francisco	San Francisco P O	83	384
DARWIN								
Andw M	49	m	w	TN	Fresno	Millerton P O	72	185
Henry	20	m	w	NY	Humboldt	Eel Rvr Twp	72	252
Odaac	32	m	w	CANA	Merced	Snelling P O	74	248
Patrick	36	m	w	IREL	Yolo	Washington Twp	93	533
Thomas	27	m	w	IREL	Siskiyou	Scott Valley Twp	89	619
DARY								
James	39	m	w	NY	Stanislaus	Buena Vista Twp	92	15
Jessie	25	m	w	ME	Mendocino	Navarro & Big Rvr	74	174
John	39	m	w	AUST	Plumas	Washington Twp	77	52
DASARO								
Manuel	22	m	w	MEXI	San Diego	San Pasqual	78	520
DASCEY								
John	32	m	w	IREL	Santa Clara	Fremont Twp	88	50
DASCOMB								
C	26	m	w	MA	Alameda	Oakland	68	161
DASE								
Anna	51	f	w	HAMB	San Francisco	2-Wd San Francisco	79	185
Henry	34	m	w	GERM	Tuolumne	Big Oak Flat P O	93	405
DASEY								
D C	35	m	w	NH	San Francisco	7-Wd San Francisco	81	167
Michael	25	m	w	IREL	San Francisco	San Francisco P O	83	415
DASH								
George J	29	m	w	NY	Santa Clara	2-Wd San Jose	88	318
DASHA								
John	40	m	w	MA	San Francisco	San Francisco P O	83	351
DASHIEL								
T W	32	m	w	MD	Mendocino	Calpella Twp	74	187
DASHIELL								
F S	37	m	w	MD	Mendocino	Round Valley Twp	74	218
William	45	m	w	MD	Solano	Silveyville Twp	90	82
DASHO								
Fred	23	m	w	HAMB	Monterey	Alisal Twp	74	288
DASON								
Anna	23	f	w	IREL	San Francisco	2-Wd San Francisco	79	140
DASSO								
John	31	m	w	ITAL	Calaveras	San Andreas P O	70	182
DASSOLA								
Josepha	26	m	w	ITAL	Santa Clara	Santa Clara Twp	88	175
DASSONVILLE								
Chas	20	m	w	NY	San Francisco	11-Wd San Francisc	84	674
Fred	27	m	w	MA	Sacramento	4-Wd Sacramento	77	331
Thomas	51	m	w	FRAN	Los Angeles	Santa Ana Twp	73	609
DASTA								
Jespah	35	m	w	ITAL	San Francisco	11-Wd San Francisc	84	701
DASY								
Timothy	32	m	w	IREL	Marin	San Rafael	74	49
DATA								
Adda O	7	f	w	WI	Trinity	Lewiston Pct	92	213
DATCH								
Albert	27	m	w	FRAN	Los Angeles	Wilmington Twp	73	642
DATE								
Edward	40	m	w	ITAL	Solano	Rio Vista Twp	90	63
DATER								
Robert	52	m	w	NY	El Dorado	Placerville	72	107
DATO								
Paul	28	m	w	GERM	San Francisco	8-Wd San Francisco	82	373
DATRA								
M S	34	m	w	SCOT	Siskiyou	Scott Valley Twp	89	611
DATRICK								
T	25	m	w	MEXI	San Joaquin	1-Wd Stockton	86	133
DATTER								
John C	32	m	w	BAVA	Los Angeles	Los Angeles	73	525
DATTOLBAUM								
Phil	24	m	w	PRUS	San Francisco	8-Wd San Francisco	82	345
DATTON								
Ellen	23	f	w	IREL	San Francisco	2-Wd San Francisco	79	262
George	64	m	w	ENGL	Los Angeles	Los Angeles	73	508
Michail	30	m	w	IREL	Humboldt	Eureka Twp	72	273
Thomas	48	m	w	IREL	Colusa	Colusa Twp	71	284
Wm H	28	m	w	IREL	San Francisco	San Francisco P O	83	31
DATTY								
Pablo	25	m	w	SPAI	Los Angeles	Los Angeles	73	570
DAUB								
Edmond A	63	m	w	PA	Plumas	Washington Twp	77	25
DAUBENBISS								
Henry	41	m	w	BAVA	Santa Cruz	Soquel Twp	89	441
DAUBENDISS								
John	54	m	w	BAVA	Santa Cruz	Soquel Twp	89	443
DAUD								
Aaron	38	m	w	NY	San Francisco	11-Wd San Francisc	84	566
DAUDON								
Alex	30	m	w	FRAN	San Francisco	5-Wd San Francisco	81	32
DAUGAN								
William	37	m	w	VA	El Dorado	Mud Springs Twp	72	85
DAUGHERTY								
Anna	50	f	w	IREL	Sacramento	2-Wd Sacramento	77	215
Anna	30	f	w	IREL	Sacramento	2-Wd Sacramento	77	226
C K	45	m	w	ME	Sacramento	1-Wd Sacramento	77	189
Chris	20	f	w	IREL	San Joaquin	3-Wd Stockton	86	218
Dan	28	m	w	IREL	Sacramento	2-Wd Sacramento	77	246
Frances	37	f	w	ENGL	Napa	Napa Twp	75	69
Geo	45	m	w	IREL	San Francisco	1-Wd San Francisco	79	61
Geo	41	m	w	IREL	San Joaquin	Elkhorn Twp	86	58
Geo	27	m	w	IA	San Joaquin	Elkhorn Twp	86	60
Hile C	24	m	w	AR	Butte	Chico Twp	70	48
J F	53	m	w	MD	San Joaquin	Elkhorn Twp	86	52
Jas	42	m	w	NY	San Joaquin	Elliott Twp	86	76
John	35	m	w	PA	San Joaquin	2-Wd Stockton	86	166
Kate	25	f	w	IL	San Joaquin	Elkhorn Twp	86	61
L J	49	m	w	MD	San Joaquin	Elkhorn Twp	86	52
Martin	50	m	w	IREL	Calaveras	San Andreas P O	70	159
DAUGHTER								
Nedzer	64	m	w	SWIT	Calaveras	Copperopolis P O	70	243
DAUGHTERS								
Joseph	47	m	w	DE	Solano	Denverton Twp	90	22
DAUGLER								
James	41	m	w	PRUS	San Francisco	San Francisco P O	80	474
DAUGTH								
Jno H	34	m	w	BADE	San Francisco	San Francisco P O	83	315
DAUM								
Charles	35	m	w	SAXO	Colusa	Spring Valley Twp	71	342
DAUMEN								
Joseph	39	m	w	IREL	San Luis Obispo	Salinas Twp	87	293
DAUNET								
Auguste	29	m	w	FRAN	San Francisco	11-Wd San Francisc	84	556
DAUPHIN								
A	40	m	w	FRAN	Sierra	Sears Twp	89	560

© 2001 by Heritage Quest. All rights reserved.

California 1870 Census

Name	Age	S	R	B-PL	County	Locale	Roll	Pg
DAUPHINOT								
Paul	22	m	w	FRAN	San Francisco	San Francisco P O	80	470
DAUR								
Fredrick	36	m	w	BAVA	San Luis Obispo	San Luis Obispo Tw	87	314
John	40	m	w	ENGL	Contra Costa	Martinez P O	71	423
DAUS								
Isadore	26	m	w	PRUS	San Francisco	2-Wd San Francisco	79	147
Jane	20	f	w	PA	Sacramento	3-Wd Sacramento	77	306
DAUSCHER								
Peter	38	m	w	FRAN	Nevada	Bridgeport Twp	75	115
DAUSETT								
George	40	m	w	NY	San Francisco	San Francisco P O	80	420
DAUSON								
John	25	m	w	IREL	Contra Costa	San Pablo Twp	71	363
Saml	30	m	w	ENGL	Contra Costa	San Pablo Twp	71	363
DAUT								
Frederick	34	m	w	HDAR	Mariposa	Mariposa P O	74	121
DAUTERMAN								
Wm	32	m	w	BAVA	San Francisco	San Francisco P O	85	843
DAVA								
H	36	m	w	NJ	Nevada	Meadow Lake Twp	75	252
DAVAILA								
Augustus	53	m	w	MEXI	Contra Costa	San Pablo Twp	71	357
DAVAL								
Caroline	58	f	w	FRAN	San Francisco	11-Wd San Francisc	84	557
DAVALA								
Josephine	31	f	w	MEXI	San Francisco	San Francisco P O	85	845
DAVAN								
P E P	54	m	w	FRAN	San Francisco	6-Wd San Francisco	81	79
DAVANAY								
Hugh	56	m	w	TN	Mariposa	Mariposa P O	74	120
Manuel	47	m	w	TN	Mariposa	Mariposa P O	74	120
DAVANER								
Manuel	30	m	w	AZOR	Contra Costa	Martinez P O	71	394
DAVARADE								
John	42	m	w	FRAN	Los Angeles	Los Angeles	73	508
DAVE								
James	54	m	w	SCOT	Tuolumne	Columbia P O	93	342
Joseph	22	m	w	FRAN	Santa Clara	Fremont Twp	88	62
William E	28	m	w	OH	Inyo	Independence Twp	73	328
DAVEGA								
Benj	48	m	w	SC	San Francisco	2-Wd San Francisco	79	173
DAVEGIO								
Stephen	45	m	w	ITAL	Santa Clara	2-Wd San Jose	88	314
DAVENCI								
Lorenzo	23	m	w	ITAL	Santa Clara	2-Wd San Jose	88	315
DAVENESS								
A	58	m	w	PORT	Sacramento	4-Wd Sacramento	77	376
DAVENPORT								
A	18	f	w	NY	Sacramento	3-Wd Sacramento	77	317
A C	29	m	w	CANA	San Joaquin	1-Wd Stockton	86	135
A J	40	m	w	ME	San Francisco	8-Wd San Francisco	82	315
B M	54	m	w	MO	Los Angeles	Los Nietos Twp	73	583
Curtis	51	m	w	OH	Santa Cruz	Soquel Twp	89	450
David	27	m	w	OH	Santa Cruz	Soquel Twp	89	442
Edward	55	m	w	NY	Placer	Colfax P O	76	385
Edward	40	m	w	MA	Sacramento	2-Wd Sacramento	77	248
Estella	13	f	w	IN	Santa Cruz	Watsonville	89	375
Ezekiel V	37	m	w	SC	El Dorado	Diamond Springs Tw	72	21
Frances M	17	f	w	IL	Tulare	Visalia	92	293
Frank	16	m	w	MA	Mariposa	Mariposa P O	74	123
H C	19	m	w	MI	Tehama	Red Bluff	92	184
Harriet	45	f	w	NY	Solano	Silveyville Twp	90	72
Henry S	46	m	w	OH	Santa Barbara	San Buenaventura P	87	426
Horace	60	m	w	NY	Placer	Newcastle Twp	76	475
Jacob	28	m	w	MO	Los Angeles	Los Nietos Twp	73	584
Jacob P	35	m	w	NJ	Los Angeles	Los Angeles	73	543
Jeffeson	31	m	w	NY	Contra Costa	Martinez P O	71	373
Jesse	51	m	w	OH	Santa Cruz	Soquel Twp	89	450
Joel	51	m	w	NY	Solano	Silveyville Twp	90	82
John	52	m	w	NY	Solano	Silveyville Twp	90	87
John	40	m	w	ENGL	San Francisco	San Francisco P O	83	155
John	25	m	w	NY	San Francisco	2-Wd San Francisco	79	141
John P	52	m	w	RI	Santa Cruz	Santa Cruz Twp	89	398
John R	30	m	w	KY	Solano	Maine Prairie Twp	90	51
Joseph	21	m	w	OH	Santa Barbara	San Buenaventura P	87	426
Leman W	31	m	w	NY	Inyo	Bishop Crk Twp	73	310
Lucinda	38	f	w	MA	Santa Clara	San Jose Twp	88	208
M H	34	f	w	PA	Santa Clara	Gilroy Twp	88	83
Marshal	35	m	w	IL	Tulare	Visalia Twp	92	286
Martin	54	m	w	OH	Tulare	Visalia	92	297
Mary	29	f	w	IREL	Santa Clara	2-Wd San Jose	88	327
Mary	25	f	w	VA	San Francisco	7-Wd San Francisco	81	249
Newell	22	m	w	AL	San Francisco	San Francisco P O	80	418
R J	70	m	w	KY	Napa	Napa	75	23
R N	29	m	w	CANA	San Joaquin	Oneal Twp	86	110
Richard	39	m	b	LA	San Francisco	San Francisco P O	80	417
Rufus	68	m	w	ME	Sacramento	Brighton Twp	77	70
S B	51	m	w	CT	Nevada	Nevada Twp	75	285
Stephn	52	m	w	KY	San Francisco	San Francisco P O	85	787
T T	40	m	w	MA	Nevada	Nevada Twp	75	275
Thomas	45	m	w	ENGL	Alameda	Alameda	68	16
Thomas	40	m	w	MA	San Diego	Julian Dist	78	469
Thomas	36	m	w	IREL	San Francisco	2-Wd San Francisco	79	263
W A	36	m	w	CANA	San Joaquin	Douglas Twp	86	33
William	28	m	w	MA	San Mateo	Woodside P O	87	386
William H	28	m	w	MO	Tulare	Visalia Twp	92	287
DAVER								
Danl	26	m	w	IREL	Sierra	Table Rock Twp	89	576
DAVERKOZEN								
Peter	53	m	w	PRUS	San Francisco	San Francisco P O	85	769
DAVERONE								
Louis	30	m	w	FRAN	San Mateo	San Mateo P O	87	349
DAVERS								
James	50	m	w	MO	Los Angeles	Los Angeles	73	518
DAVERSON								
J N	47	m	w	CANA	Alameda	Alameda	68	17
DAVEY								
Edward	25	m	w	IREL	Mendocino	Albion & Big Rvr T	74	167
George	28	m	w	ENGL	San Francisco	1-Wd San Francisco	79	62
Henry	35	m	w	PA	San Francisco	San Francisco P O	83	217
James	37	m	w	IREL	San Francisco	7-Wd San Francisco	81	197
Peter	40	m	w	IREL	San Francisco	1-Wd San Francisco	79	92
Richard	75	m	w	ENGL	Sonoma	Analy Twp	91	245
Richard	36	m	w	ENGL	Nevada	Grass Valley Twp	75	223
Stephen	32	m	w	ENGL	Sonoma	Analy Twp	91	245
Thomas	26	m	w	PA	Mariposa	Mariposa P O	74	131
W	22	m	w	ENGL	Sierra	Butte Twp	89	508
William	35	m	w	ENGL	Mariposa	Mariposa P O	74	127
William	25	m	w	ENGL	Yuba	Rose Bar Twp	93	659
Wm	42	m	w	TN	Lake	Lower Lake	73	420
Wm	42	m	w	ENGL	El Dorado	Georgetown Twp	72	38
DAVID								
August	35	m	w	FRAN	San Francisco	San Francisco P O	80	484
Benjn	35	m	w	NY	San Francisco	5-Wd San Francisco	81	9
Charles	39	m	w	FRAN	Sutter	Nicolaus Twp	92	115
David	32	m	w	POLA	San Francisco	11-Wd San Francisc	84	569
David	27	m	w	ENGL	Sonoma	Petaluma Twp	91	323
David	15	m	w	CANA	Contra Costa	San Pablo Twp	71	356
F L	17	m	w	PA	Lassen	Susanville Twp	73	441
Frances	38	m	w	CANA	Contra Costa	Martinez P O	71	367
Francis	46	m	w	FRAN	Santa Clara	San Jose Twp	88	196
Francisco	29	f	w	HAMB	San Francisco	11-Wd San Francisc	84	473
Gabriel	38	m	w	VT	Los Angeles	Wilmington Twp	73	641
Geo	37	m	w	ENGL	Sonoma	Santa Rosa	91	405
Henry	29	m	w	MI	Monterey	San Juan Twp	74	386
Henry	28	m	w	TN	Sonoma	Salt Point	91	381
James	41	m	w	IREL	El Dorado	Georgetown Twp	72	42
James	28	m	w	IREL	Inyo	Bishop Crk Twp	73	316
Jane	72	f	w	SWIT	Alameda	Washington Twp	68	286
John	35	m	w	IREL	El Dorado	Greenwood Twp	72	50
John	26	m	w	PA	San Francisco	San Francisco P O	80	471
John	15	m	w	CA	Sacramento	Brighton Twp	77	77
Jose	40	m	w	CHIL	Santa Barbara	Arroyo Burro P O	87	509
Josevina	9	f	w	CA	Humboldt	Arcata Twp	72	227
Levi	24	m	w	ENGL	Yuba	Rose Bar Twp	93	662
Louis	60	m	w	FRAN	Mariposa	Mariposa P O	74	104
Peter	40	m	w	FRAN	Amador	Jackson P O	69	325
Richard	50	m	w	TN	Stanislaus	Empire Twp	92	58
Silas	44	m	w	IREL	San Francisco	11-Wd San Francisc	84	612
Thomas	37	m	w	MD	Calaveras	San Andreas P O	70	209
Virginia	11	f	w	CANA	Yolo	Cache Crk Twp	93	425
William	26	m	w	AR	Tulare	Tule Rvr Twp	92	268
Willis	60	m	w	MO	Santa Clara	Santa Clara Twp	88	148
DAVIDE								
Luigi	41	m	w	ITAL	San Francisco	11-Wd San Francisc	84	594
DAVIDMAI								
Chas	39	m	w	FRAN	San Francisco	1-Wd San Francisco	79	50
DAVIDS								
Abram	31	m	w	OH	Solano	Vacaville Twp	90	127
Charles	44	m	w	NY	San Francisco	11-Wd San Francisc	84	486
David	29	m	w	PRUS	Solano	Vacaville Twp	90	126
H S	30	m	w	VA	Solano	Vallejo	90	200
Thomas	30	m	w	ENGL	Nevada	Grass Valley Twp	75	203
DAVIDSON								
A	37	m	w	NY	Monterey	San Juan Twp	74	405
A	28	m	w	CANA	San Francisco	San Francisco P O	83	287
Abe	52	m	w	NORW	San Francisco	San Francisco P O	83	187
Adam	30	m	w	CANA	Marin	San Antonio Twp	74	60
Adam	30	m	w	CANA	Marin	San Antonio Twp	74	61
Alex	40	m	w	IL	San Francisco	7-Wd San Francisco	81	199
Allen	31	m	w	OH	Sonoma	Cloverdale Twp	91	273
Allen	26	m	w	NY	Marin	Tomales Twp	74	85
Amy	13	f	w	CA	Santa Cruz	Santa Cruz	89	406
Amy	12	f	w	CA	Santa Cruz	Santa Cruz	89	432
Andrew	41	m	w	NY	Placer	Gold Run Twp	76	396
Andrew	36	m	w	VA	Colusa	Monroe Twp	71	324
Bridget	38	f	w	IREL	San Francisco	1-Wd San Francisco	79	121
Carlton	43	m	w	NC	Mariposa	Maxwell Crk P O	74	145
Charles	36	m	w	ENGL	Santa Clara	Fremont Twp	88	44
Charles	19	m	w	NY	San Mateo	Redwood City P O	87	375
D	39	m	w	CANA	Alameda	Oakland	68	226
D C	56	m	w	VT	Yuba	Marysville	93	618
Daniel	52	m	w	SCOT	Alpine	Silver Mtn P O	69	307
Daniel D	30	m	w	IN	Sonoma	Sonoma Twp	91	448
Danl	37	m	w	SWED	San Francisco	1-Wd San Francisco	79	121
David	45	m	w	CANA	San Francisco	11-Wd San Francisc	84	572
Douglas	11	m	b	CA	Santa Clara	1-Wd San Jose	88	241
Elizabeth W	32	f	w	ENGL	Los Angeles	Los Angeles	73	536
Ester	42	f	w	PRUS	Colusa	Stony Crk Twp	71	331
Esther	31	f	w	CANA	Yolo	Cache Crk Twp	93	446
F W	29	m	w	MO	Mendocino	Ukiah Twp	74	242
Fleming	42	m	w	VA	Siskiyou	Scott Valley Twp	89	621
Geo W	27	m	w	MI	Sacramento	Cosumnes Twp	77	93

Series M593

© 2001 by Heritage Quest. All rights reserved.

Name	Age	S	R	B-PL	County	Locale	Series M593 Roll	Pg
George	40	m	w	KS	Sutter	Butte Twp	92	91
George	30	m	w	OH	Santa Cruz	Santa Cruz Twp	89	393
George	27	m	w	ENGL	San Francisco	San Francisco P O	83	196
Harrison	32	m	w	VA	Plumas	Quartz Twp	77	43
Henry	33	m	w	SCOT	San Joaquin	2-Wd Stockton	86	169
Henry	25	m	w	CANA	Marin	San Antonio Twp	74	61
Henry	11	m	w	CA	San Francisco	San Francisco P O	83	360
Henry B	39	m	w	TN	Santa Barbara	Santa Barbara P O	87	466
I	27	m	w	CANA	Sierra	Sierra Twp	89	569
J	47	m	w	PRUS	San Francisco	San Francisco P O	85	784
J E	69	m	w	KY	Sonoma	Santa Rosa	91	394
J M	50	m	w	SCOT	San Francisco	1-Wd San Francisco	79	70
J W	41	m	w	TN	Nevada	Bridgeport Twp	75	101
Jacob	33	m	w	CANA	Sutter	Sutter Twp	92	120
James	57	m	w	VA	Siskiyou	Scott Valley Twp	89	621
James	45	m	w	VA	Siskiyou	Callahan P O	89	632
James	39	m	w	OH	San Bernardino	San Bernardino Twp	78	428
James	36	m	w	CANA	Humboldt	Table Bluff Twp	72	306
James	35	m	w	NY	Monterey	Alisal Twp	74	301
James	31	m	w	IN	Siskiyou	Scott Valley Twp	89	613
James	28	m	w	CANA	Marin	San Antonio Twp	74	61
James	26	m	w	SCOT	San Francisco	11-Wd San Francisc	84	526
James	24	m	w	SCOT	San Francisco	7-Wd San Francisco	81	171
Jno D	38	m	w	SC	Sonoma	Mendocino Twp	91	287
John	78	m	w	NY	Solano	Vallejo	90	197
John	63	m	w	IREL	Sierra	Eureka Twp	89	524
John	50	m	w	IREL	Fresno	Millerton P O	72	152
John	45	m	w	SCOT	San Francisco	11-Wd San Francisc	84	518
John	32	m	w	CANA	Sonoma	Petaluma Twp	91	329
John	27	m	w	CANA	Placer	Dutch Flat P O	76	415
John	22	m	w	CANA	Marin	San Antonio Twp	74	65
John A	76	m	w	CA	Santa Clara	Santa Clara Twp	88	157
John A	34	m	w	DC	Fresno	Kingston P O	72	217
John H	32	m	w	NY	Placer	Dutch Flat P O	76	407
John P	52	m	w	NC	Siskiyou	Yreka	89	658
Joseph	42	m	w	KY	Nevada	Bloomfield Twp	75	98
Joseph	32	m	w	IL	Sonoma	Washington Twp	91	469
Joseph	22	m	w	CANA	Marin	San Antonio Twp	74	60
Julia	62	f	w	IREL	El Dorado	Mud Springs Twp	72	84
Julia	33	f	w	CANA	San Francisco	San Francisco P O	83	217
Keneth	68	m	w	US	Sacramento	Cosumnes Twp	77	93
L	45	f	w	NY	San Francisco	San Francisco P O	83	107
L	25	m	w	POLA	Sacramento	1-Wd Sacramento	77	188
Leander	39	m	w	CANA	Monterey	San Benito Twp	74	379
Louis	40	m	w	PRUS	Yolo	Cache Crk Twp	93	434
Louis	39	m	w	PRUS	Calaveras	San Andreas P O	70	193
Louis	29	m	w	PRUS	Solano	Vacaville Twp	90	117
M A	40	m	w	VT	Tuolumne	Columbia P O	93	343
Margaret	53	f	w	ENGL	San Francisco	6-Wd San Francisco	81	140
Mary	18	f	w	NY	San Francisco	6-Wd San Francisco	81	129
Meyer	35	m	w	PRUS	San Francisco	San Francisco P O	83	272
Milton C	24	m	w	IA	El Dorado	Placerville	72	124
Morris	40	m	w	PRUS	Yolo	Cache Crk Twp	93	434
Moses	45	m	w	POLA	San Francisco	San Francisco P O	83	354
Nathan	31	m	w	OH	Sutter	Sutter Twp	92	119
Ophelia	6	f	w	CA	San Francisco	San Francisco P O	85	738
Orpha	74	f	w	VA	Siskiyou	Scott Valley Twp	89	613
Peter	55	m	w	GREE	Santa Clara	2-Wd San Jose	88	302
Peter	41	m	w	NORW	Mendocino	Casper & Big Rvr	74	163
R N	41	m	w	NH	Trinity	Weaverville Pct	92	230
Robert	42	m	w	IREL	Sonoma	Petaluma Twp	91	335
Robert	29	m	w	AR	Sacramento	Sutter Twp	77	391
Robert P	30	m	w	IL	Yolo	Cache Crk Twp	93	425
Rosa	20	f	w	PRUS	San Francisco	San Francisco P O	83	395
Rowland C	32	m	w	ENGL	Los Angeles	Los Angeles	73	535
S B	49	m	w	NY	Sierra	Downieville Twp	89	522
S B	49	m	w	CANA	Sierra	Downieville Twp	89	522
Saml M	40	m	w	TN	San Luis Obispo	Santa Rosa Twp	87	327
Samuel	24	m	w	NY	Marin	San Rafael	74	50
Sara	35	m	w	PRUS	Yolo	Cache Crk Twp	93	434
Sarah	42	f	w	NY	Santa Cruz	Watsonville	89	368
Sarah	12	f	w	CA	Sierra	Eureka Twp	89	524
Saul	25	m	w	PRUS	San Francisco	San Francisco P O	83	177
Soloma	44	m	w	PRUS	Calaveras	San Andreas P O	70	198
Solomon	16	m	w	PRUS	Colusa	Stony Crk Twp	71	331
T H	30	m	w	IN	San Joaquin	2-Wd Stockton	86	171
Thomas	70	m	w	MA	El Dorado	White Oak Twp	72	137
Thomas	52	m	w	MO	Monterey	San Juan Twp	74	409
Thomas	50	m	w	IREL	San Francisco	11-Wd San Francisc	84	527
Thomas	42	m	w	IREL	El Dorado	Mud Springs Twp	72	90
Thos	40	m	w	ENGL	Nevada	Nevada Twp	75	289
V	69	m	w	KY	Siskiyou	Callahan P O	89	624
W	35	m	w	CANA	Alameda	Alameda	68	4
W H	39	m	w	CANA	Nevada	Nevada Twp	75	272
W J	44	m	w	OH	Napa	Napa	75	10
W P	37	m	w	SCOT	San Francisco	San Francisco P O	85	781
Walter	34	m	w	MA	San Francisco	San Francisco P O	85	816
Wilbert	25	m	w	CANA	San Francisco	San Francisco P O	83	358
William	47	m	w	OH	Yolo	Cache Crk Twp	93	440
William	38	m	w	IN	El Dorado	Mud Springs Twp	72	90
William	29	m	w	SCOT	Contra Costa	Martinez P O	71	419
William J	25	m	w	CANA	Mendocino	Point Arena Twp	74	206
Wm	41	m	w	VA	Siskiyou	Scott Valley Twp	89	609
DAVIDWICH								
Rosa	35	f	w	IREL	Yuba	Slate Range Bar Tw	93	673
DAVIES								
Douglas	42	m	w	EIND	San Francisco	San Francisco P O	80	377
Edwin H	45	m	w	ME	Santa Clara	Santa Clara Twp	88	142
Elisha L	41	m	w	AL	Sonoma	Santa Rosa	91	398
F A	43	m	w	NY	San Joaquin	2-Wd Stockton	86	200
J D	39	m	w	CANA	Amador	Jackson P O	69	325
J T	43	m	w	HANO	Tuolumne	Chinese Camp P O	93	381
John	42	m	w	GERM	San Francisco	8-Wd San Francisco	82	376
John	37	m	w	WALE	Butte	Wyandotte Twp	70	146
John	27	m	w	ENGL	Nevada	Grass Valley Twp	75	203
Richard	35	m	w	ENGL	Nevada	Grass Valley Twp	75	231
Sol W	52	m	w	NC	Sonoma	Healdsburg	91	274
Stephen L	36	m	w	ENGL	San Francisco	8-Wd San Francisco	82	488
William	39	m	w	ENGL	San Bernardino	San Bernardino Twp	78	438
William H	37	m	w	CANA	San Francisco	8-Wd San Francisco	82	439
Wm J	30	m	w	WALE	Tuolumne	Big Oak Flat P O	93	405
DAVIGRO								
Bartolo	52	m	w	ITAL	Calaveras	San Andreas P O	70	219
DAVILA								
Manuel	45	m	w	PORT	Los Angeles	San Juan Twp	73	629
Sylva	26	m	w	PORT	Monterey	Pajaro Twp	74	368
DAVILL								
W	48	m	w	TX	Sierra	Butte Twp	89	509
DAVILLA								
Antonio	56	m	w	MEXI	Los Angeles	Los Angeles	73	556
DAVINE								
John	37	m	w	IREL	San Francisco	1-Wd San Francisco	79	136
DAVINER								
Frank	20	m	w	SCOT	Alameda	Brooklyn Twp	68	45
DAVINI								
Luigi	30	m	w	ITAL	San Francisco	1-Wd San Francisco	79	110
DAVIS								
---	46	m	w	KY	Monterey	Alisal Twp	74	299
---	40	m	w	NY	Sacramento	4-Wd Sacramento	77	373
--- [Capt]	27	m	w	SCOT	San Francisco	7-Wd San Francisco	81	257
A	68	m	w	NC	Lake	Lower Lake	73	422
A	57	m	w	NJ	Sierra	Sierra Twp	89	564
A	21	m	w	IL	Lake	Lower Lake	73	419
A A	35	m	w	MA	Alameda	Oakland	68	155
A F	14	f	w	MO	Amador	Sutter Crk P O	69	409
A H	35	m	w	NH	Solano	Vallejo	90	177
A James	39	m	w	KY	San Diego	San Diego	78	491
A M	40	m	w	NY	San Joaquin	2-Wd Stockton	86	189
A P	35	f	w	CANA	San Francisco	San Francisco P O	83	270
Aaron	27	m	w	ME	Solano	Vacaville Twp	90	123
Abbe	40	m	w	NORW	San Joaquin	2-Wd Stockton	86	167
Abraham	56	m	w	POLA	San Francisco	11-Wd San Francisc	84	629
Abraham	40	m	w	PRUS	San Francisco	San Francisco P O	83	163
Ada	10	f	w	CA	El Dorado	Coloma Twp	72	7
Adam	52	m	w	MO	Mendocino	Big Rvr Twp	74	171
Albert	41	m	w	OH	Sonoma	Petaluma Twp	91	332
Albert	38	m	w	IREL	San Francisco	San Francisco P O	83	167
Albert	21	m	w	MO	Sutter	Butte Twp	92	103
Albert R	38	m	w	NY	Los Angeles	El Monte Twp	73	459
Alexander P	43	m	w	PA	Santa Cruz	Santa Cruz Twp	89	391
Alfred	45	m	w	NJ	San Francisco	6-Wd San Francisco	81	95
Alfred	29	m	w	ENGL	Santa Barbara	Santa Barbara P O	87	455
Alfred E	41	m	w	NJ	Nevada	Grass Valley Twp	75	151
Alfred J	42	m	w	ME	El Dorado	Mountain Twp	72	68
Alfred P	40	m	w	KY	Stanislaus	Empire Twp	92	57
Allen	32	m	w	MO	Trinity	Trinity Center Pct	92	204
Allen B	32	m	w	IL	Inyo	Independence Twp	73	325
Alonzo	17	m	w	NY	Marin	San Rafael	74	52
Alpheus	25	m	w	MA	San Mateo	Half Moon Bay P O	87	407
Ama L	68	f	w	NC	Alameda	Oakland	68	209
America	51	f	w	KY	Placer	Pino Twp	76	471
America	29	f	w	IN	Colusa	Grand Island Twp	71	304
Amos	35	m	w	CANA	San Francisco	11-Wd San Francisc	84	582
Andrew	50	m	w	MD	Kern	Linns Valley P O	73	343
Andrew	45	m	w	WALE	Butte	Oregon Twp	70	122
Andrew	33	m	w	NY	Stanislaus	Branch Twp	92	7
Andrew	17	m	w	MA	Colusa	Monroe Twp	71	311
Andrew J	41	m	w	CANA	Siskiyou	Yreka Twp	89	673
Andrew J	38	m	w	OH	San Diego	San Diego	78	495
Andrew J	36	m	w	TN	Tulare	Farmersville Twp	92	243
Ann	51	f	w	ENGL	Monterey	Pajaro Twp	74	368
Ann	26	f	w	WALE	San Francisco	6-Wd San Francisco	81	72
Annie	26	f	w	NY	San Francisco	San Francisco P O	80	474
Ansel	42	m	w	ME	Calaveras	Copperopolis P O	70	258
Antone	39	m	w	PORT	Marin	Nicasio Twp	74	20
Antonio	22	m	w	PORT	San Mateo	Half Moon Bay P O	87	391
Argen	69	f	w	NC	Solano	Silveyville Twp	90	86
Artemus L	24	m	w	IL	Colusa	Butte Twp	71	267
Aug S	26	m	w	ME	Siskiyou	Big Valley Twp	89	580
Augustus	30	m	w	IREL	Santa Clara	Milpitas Twp	88	111
Ausley	18	m	w	OH	San Francisco	7-Wd San Francisco	81	281
B	43	m	w	PA	Sierra	Lincoln Twp	89	552
B F	48	m	w	ME	Yuba	Marysville	93	603
B J	32	m	w	VA	Sonoma	Russian Rvr	91	368
Balam	35	m	w	GA	Solano	Silveyville Twp	90	87
Barbra	72	f	w	PA	San Joaquin	2-Wd Stockton	86	211
Barney	30	m	w	IREL	Colusa	Spring Valley Twp	71	340
Barton	34	m	w	VA	Solano	Vacaville Twp	90	136
Benj	15	m	w	CA	Yuba	Marysville	93	597
Benj B	45	m	w	NY	Mariposa	Mariposa P O	74	108
Benjaman	28	m	w	NY	San Francisco	3-Wd San Francisco	79	323
Benjamin	49	m	w	CANA	Santa Clara	Gilroy Twp	88	81
Benjamin	38	m	w	POLA	San Francisco	San Francisco P O	83	367
Benjamin	29	m	w	WALE	Contra Costa	Martinez P O	71	426

© 2001 by Heritage Quest. All rights reserved.

Name	Age	S	R	B-PL	County	Locale	Roll	Pg
Bridget	33	f	w	IREL	San Francisco	8-Wd San Francisco	82	395
Budd	52	m	w	TN	Stanislaus	Empire Twp	92	59
C	20	m	w	WI	Sierra	Sierra Twp	89	564
C E	37	m	w	NJ	Napa	Napa	75	21
C M	30	m	w	MI	Monterey	Alisal Twp	74	298
Caleb S	43	m	w	OH	Fresno	Kings Rvr P O	72	203
Calvin	41	m	w	MA	San Francisco	11-Wd San Francisc	84	622
Caroline	40	f	w	NY	San Francisco	8-Wd San Francisco	82	464
Catharine	28	f	w	PA	Sacramento	1-Wd Sacramento	77	204
Catharine A	59	f	w	PA	Amador	Fiddletown P O	69	438
Catherine	45	f	w	MA	San Francisco	7-Wd San Francisco	81	177
Celvin P	43	m	w	MA	Sonoma	Analy Twp	91	245
Charles	56	m	w	KY	Marin	San Rafael Twp	74	40
Charles	48	m	w	FRAN	Alameda	Alvarado	68	305
Charles	48	m	w	MA	Placer	Auburn P O	76	383
Charles	42	m	w	MA	San Francisco	11-Wd San Francisc	84	603
Charles	40	m	b	KY	San Francisco	6-Wd San Francisco	81	110
Charles	40	m	b	KY	San Francisco	6-Wd San Francisco	81	107
Charles	40	m	w	NY	San Francisco	8-Wd San Francisco	82	376
Charles	37	m	w	IREL	Trinity	Minersville Pct	92	203
Charles	34	m	w	NY	El Dorado	Lake Valley Twp	72	64
Charles	33	m	w	OH	Butte	Wyandotte Twp	70	147
Charles	32	m	w	ENGL	Solano	Rio Vista Twp	90	59
Charles	31	m	w	NY	San Francisco	San Francisco P O	83	397
Charles	28	m	w	OH	Santa Clara	Redwood Twp	88	132
Charles	26	m	w	NY	Yolo	Cache Crk Twp	93	423
Charles	20	m	w	IL	San Bernardino	San Bernardino Twp	78	427
Charles	20	m	w	ME	Sacramento	Brighton Twp	77	70
Charles	19	m	w	CA	San Francisco	San Francisco P O	80	472
Charles	18	m	w	CA	San Joaquin	2-Wd Stockton	86	161
Charles	17	m	w	OH	San Francisco	San Francisco P O	83	297
Charles	17	m	w	CA	El Dorado	Mud Springs Twp	72	75
Charles	14	m	w	CA	Contra Costa	Martinez P O	71	437
Charles H	45	m	w	ME	Yolo	Cottonwood Twp	93	474
Chas	40	m	w	DENM	San Francisco	San Francisco P O	85	845
Chas	37	m	w	TN	Solano	Vallejo	90	185
Chas	32	m	w	IA	Tehama	Tehama Twp	92	192
Chas	25	m	w	WALE	Solano	Benicia	90	21
Chas	22	m	w	MO	San Joaquin	Tulare Twp	86	261
Chas A	29	m	m	MO	Solano	Vallejo	90	164
Chas M	51	m	w	OH	Nevada	Bridgeport Twp	75	113
Chas M	25	m	w	OH	Humboldt	Arcata Twp	72	231
Chas M	25	m	w	OH	Humboldt	Eureka Twp	72	275
Chas W	24	m	w	ME	Nevada	Meadow Lake Twp	75	267
Clinton C	26	m	w	IL	Colusa	Butte Twp	71	267
D A	41	m	w	MO	Santa Clara	Gilroy Twp	88	105
D L	43	m	w	OH	Sacramento	Dry Crk Twp	77	97
D M	36	m	w	IL	Alameda	Murray Twp	68	114
D W	37	m	w	IL	San Francisco	8-Wd San Francisco	82	369
D W	24	m	w	DC	Solano	Vallejo	90	202
Dan	40	m	w	MA	Alameda	Oakland	68	263
Daniel	50	m	w	NY	El Dorado	Georgetown Twp	72	43
Daniel	50	m	w	OH	Santa Clara	Redwood Twp	88	117
Daniel	46	m	w	PA	Siskiyou	Callahan P O	89	631
Daniel	40	m	w	PA	San Francisco	San Francisco P O	83	213
Daniel	36	m	w	NY	San Francisco	San Francisco P O	80	539
Daniel	34	m	w	WALE	Contra Costa	Martinez P O	71	427
Daniel	22	m	w	PRUS	San Francisco	5-Wd San Francisco	81	5
Daniel E	37	m	w	NY	San Francisco	1-Wd San Francisco	79	98
Danil	35	m	w	IL	Humboldt	Arcata Twp	72	226
Danl	27	m	w	WALE	Butte	Concow Twp	70	6
David	66	m	w	ME	El Dorado	Placerville	72	109
David	51	m	w	WALE	Butte	Oregon Twp	70	130
David	49	m	w	WALE	Contra Costa	Martinez P O	71	425
David	43	m	w	WALE	Nevada	Bridgeport Twp	75	112
David	39	m	w	WALE	San Francisco	1-Wd San Francisco	79	45
David	39	m	w	WALE	Contra Costa	Martinez P O	71	431
David	37	m	w	OH	San Joaquin	Oneal Twp	86	100
David	36	m	w	NY	San Francisco	5-Wd San Francisco	81	21
David	36	m	w	WALE	Sierra	Sears Twp	89	556
David	35	m	w	WALE	Nevada	Bridgeport Twp	75	124
David	34	m	w	OH	Sonoma	Russian Rvr	91	370
David	32	m	w	VA	San Francisco	1-Wd San Francisco	79	107
David	23	m	w	OH	Placer	Pino Twp	76	471
David	21	m	w	PRUS	Sacramento	2-Wd Sacramento	77	245
David	20	m	w	WI	Butte	Chico Twp	70	29
David	20	m	w	PRUS	San Francisco	San Francisco P O	83	403
David D	28	m	w	WALE	San Francisco	8-Wd San Francisco	82	381
David H	35	m	w	WALE	El Dorado	Placerville	72	110
David N	26	m	w	OH	Placer	Pino Twp	76	470
David P	48	m	w	WALE	Calaveras	Copperopolis P O	70	248
David R	35	m	w	WALE	Nevada	Bloomfield Twp	75	93
David S	42	m	w	WALE	Sierra	Sears Twp	89	561
David T	29	m	w	PA	Amador	Sutter Crk P O	69	409
Delia	26	f	w	LA	San Francisco	11-Wd San Francisc	84	603
Devoto	40	m	w	ITAL	Amador	Sutter Crk P O	69	400
Dexter A	37	m	w	RI	Stanislaus	Empire Twp	92	28
E	35	f	w	NY	Sacramento	3-Wd Sacramento	77	258
E	31	m	w	OH	Alameda	Murray Twp	68	108
E	31	m	w	PRUS	Sacramento	1-Wd Sacramento	77	179
E	30	m	w	MD	San Joaquin	Oneal Twp	86	102
E	14	m	w	CA	Napa	Napa Twp	75	63
E A	31	m	w	NY	Yuba	Marysville	93	581
Eben	40	m	w	ENGL	Butte	Oregon Twp	70	127
Ebenezer	40	m	w	OH	Plumas	Rich Bar Twp	77	46
Ed P	48	m	w	MA	Mono	Bridgeport P O	74	283
Edward	65	m	w	TN	Stanislaus	Buena Vista Twp	92	13

Name	Age	S	R	B-PL	County	Locale	Roll	Pg
Edward	52	m	w	IN	Shasta	Fort Crook P O	89	477
Edward	38	m	w	ENGL	El Dorado	Salmon Falls Twp	72	131
Edward	36	m	w	CT	Calaveras	San Andreas P O	70	213
Edward	33	m	w	NH	Calaveras	San Andreas P O	70	177
Edward	26	m	w	TN	Mendocino	Anderson Twp	74	151
Edward	20	m	w	ENGL	Monterey	San Antonio Twp	74	320
Edward H	46	m	w	ENGL	Nevada	Grass Valley Twp	75	206
Edward N	39	m	w	ENGL	Los Angeles	Los Nietos Twp	73	587
Edwd	48	m	w	WALE	Solano	Vallejo	90	148
Edwd	39	m	w	NY	Solano	Vallejo	90	143
Edwd	34	m	w	PA	Yuba	Rose Bar Twp	93	666
Edwd H	29	m	w	WALE	San Francisco	1-Wd San Francisco	79	61
Edwd J	39	m	w	OH	Butte	Oregon Twp	70	132
Edwin	42	m	w	MO	Tulare	Farmersville Twp	92	249
Edwin	31	m	w	NY	Yuba	Marysville	93	574
Edwin	23	m	w	IREL	Solano	Silveyville Twp	90	79
Eli	40	m	w	OH	Sutter	Yuba Twp	92	147
Eli	36	m	w	AL	Sonoma	Santa Rosa	91	401
Elijah	40	m	w	MO	Colusa	Grand Island Twp	71	302
Elinor	40	m	w	OH	Sutter	Butte Twp	92	92
Elisha	40	m	w	MA	Stanislaus	Emory Twp	92	24
Elisha	38	m	w	ME	Calaveras	San Andreas P O	70	203
Elisha M	35	m	w	VA	Yuba	North East Twp	93	644
Eliza	59	f	w	NC	San Joaquin	2-Wd Stockton	86	166
Elizabeth	70	f	w	ENGL	Calaveras	Copperopolis P O	70	241
Elizabeth	67	f	w	PA	Santa Clara	Gilroy Twp	88	91
Elizabeth	62	f	w	ENGL	Los Angeles	Los Angeles Twp	73	469
Ellen	49	f	w	ENGL	Sacramento	3-Wd Sacramento	77	274
Ellen	14	f	w	CA	Siskiyou	Callahan P O	89	632
Elmira	35	f	w	OH	Sonoma	Washington Twp	91	465
Elvira	12	f	w	CA	San Diego	Julian Dist	78	470
Elwin	28	m	w	MA	Santa Clara	2-Wd San Jose	88	284
Emma	39	f	w	SWED	Mendocino	Big Rvr Twp	74	159
Emma	15	f	w	CA	San Joaquin	2-Wd Stockton	86	178
Emma	13	f	w	ENGL	Nevada	Grass Valley Twp	75	204
Emogen	31	f	w	NY	Yuba	Marysville	93	581
Enoch	47	m	w	OH	Yolo	Grafton Twp	93	496
Esther	52	f	b	MD	San Francisco	8-Wd San Francisco	82	438
Evan W	38	m	w	WALE	Siskiyou	Cottonwood Twp	89	591
Evans	63	m	w	WALE	Mendocino	Point Arena Twp	74	205
Evans S	29	m	w	MO	Yolo	Buckeye Twp	93	415
Ezekiel	36	m	w	ME	Marin	Novato Twp	74	11
Ezra	19	m	w	CANA	Sonoma	Petaluma Twp	91	350
F	36	m	w	ENGL	Sierra	Butte Twp	89	511
F	34	m	w	IREL	Humboldt	Eureka Twp	72	272
Fanny	26	f	w	PA	San Francisco	San Francisco P O	80	359
Francis C	35	m	w	VA	Santa Barbara	San Buenaventura P	87	429
Francis E	22	m	w	MN	San Francisco	San Francisco P O	85	745
Francis Marion	40	m	w	ME	Plumas	Mineral Twp	77	20
Francisco	51	m	w	AZOR	Monterey	Monterey	74	365
Frank	45	m	w	CANA	Sacramento	Sutter Twp	77	385
Frank	40	m	b	HI	Siskiyou	Cottonwood Twp	89	590
Frank	35	m	w	IL	Yuba	Marysville	93	592
Frank	31	m	w	MO	San Joaquin	Union Twp	86	267
Frank	24	m	w	NY	Santa Clara	1-Wd San Jose	88	254
Frank	23	m	w	NY	Santa Clara	2-Wd San Jose	88	335
Frank	22	m	w	PA	Merced	Snelling P O	74	267
Frank	18	m	w	MO	Colusa	Stony Crk Twp	71	329
Frank C	32	m	w	AR	Stanislaus	Empire Twp	92	30
Franklin	24	m	w	MO	Sonoma	Mendocino Twp	91	292
G	30	m	w	NH	Alameda	Oakland	68	186
G R	33	m	w	CANA	Sierra	Butte Twp	89	508
G W	37	m	w	PA	Sierra	Butte Twp	89	511
G W	32	m	w	IL	Lake	Big Valley	73	398
G W	28	m	w	ME	Humboldt	Bucksport Twp	72	243
Geo	40	m	w	VA	Butte	Kimshew Tpw	70	76
Geo	38	m	w	PA	Sierra	Gibson Twp	89	540
Geo	34	m	w	MS	San Joaquin	Union Twp	86	267
Geo	30	m	w	FL	San Joaquin	Elkhorn Twp	86	66
Geo	28	m	w	PA	Solano	Vallejo	90	200
Geo	27	m	w	DENM	San Francisco	1-Wd San Francisco	79	77
Geo	26	m	w	VT	Sacramento	3-Wd Sacramento	77	278
Geo	14	m	w	CA	San Francisco	11-Wd San Francisc	84	588
Geo C	14	m	w	CA	Sacramento	San Joaquin Twp	77	395
Geo L	42	m	w	WALE	Klamath	Liberty Twp	73	375
Geo M	---	m	w	VA	San Joaquin	Oneal Twp	86	103
Geo W	56	m	w	NC	San Francisco	San Francisco P O	83	284
Geo W	51	m	w	OH	Sonoma	Santa Rosa	91	417
Geo W	35	m	w	PA	Santa Cruz	Santa Cruz Twp	89	381
Geo W	22	m	w	WI	San Joaquin	Douglas Twp	86	39
George	53	m	w	NY	Monterey	San Antonio Twp	74	320
George	49	m	w	NY	Sutter	Nicolaus Twp	92	107
George	48	m	w	NY	Yuba	Marysville	93	588
George	45	m	w	PA	Nevada	Nevada Twp	75	302
George	45	m	w	WALE	Solano	Montezuma Twp	90	69
George	42	m	w	NY	Stanislaus	Branch Twp	92	9
George	38	m	w	IN	Placer	Alta P O	76	411
George	38	m	w	NY	Alameda	Alameda	68	16
George	37	m	w	VT	San Diego	Julian Dist	78	474
George	35	m	w	PA	San Diego	San Pasqual	78	522
George	32	m	w	ENGL	San Francisco	7-Wd San Francisco	81	209
George	28	m	w	PA	Sacramento	San Joaquin Twp	77	401
George	27	m	w	IREL	Sonoma	Analy Twp	91	222
George	24	m	w	ME	Marin	San Rafael	74	53
George	20	m	w	MA	San Francisco	6-Wd San Francisco	81	147
George	2	m	b	CA	Los Angeles	Los Angeles	73	534
George	15	m	w	CA	San Francisco	San Francisco P O	80	333

Series M593

© 2001 by Heritage Quest. All rights reserved.

Name	Age	S	R	B-PL	County	Locale	Series M593 Roll	Pg
George B	46	m	w	VT	San Francisco	6-Wd San Francisco	81	122
George E	45	m	w	ENGL	San Francisco	11-Wd San Francisc	84	702
George G	47	m	w	ENGL	Nevada	Nevada Twp	75	315
George G	40	m	w	OH	Nevada	Bridgeport Twp	75	109
George L	32	m	w	CANA	Monterey	Alisal Twp	74	304
George P	43	m	w	ENGL	Alameda	Alameda	68	4
George V	36	m	w	VA	Santa Barbara	San Buenaventura P	87	445
George W	49	m	w	TN	Yolo	Putah Twp	93	511
George W	43	m	w	KY	San Francisco	6-Wd San Francisco	81	90
George W	41	m	w	VA	Santa Cruz	Soquel Twp	89	447
George W	38	m	w	ME	San Luis Obispo	Santa Rosa Twp	87	326
George W	38	m	w	MO	Trinity	Lewiston Pct	92	213
George W	28	m	w	OH	Santa Clara	Fremont Twp	88	44
George W	17	m	w	AR	Stanislaus	Branch Twp	92	10
Gertrude	45	f	w	PRUS	Alameda	Oakland	68	148
Gilman	52	m	w	CANA	Shasta	Shasta P O	89	463
Gilman	34	m	w	NH	San Diego	San Diego	78	508
Griffith	45	m	w	ENGL	San Francisco	2-Wd San Francisco	79	226
Gustave	31	m	w	PRUS	Los Angeles	Santa Ana Twp	73	611
H	51	m	w	KY	Nevada	Meadow Lake Twp	75	248
H	30	m	w	MO	San Joaquin	Oneal Twp	86	103
H J	55	m	w	DE	Humboldt	Mattole Twp	72	284
Hannah	62	f	w	VA	San Joaquin	Oneal Twp	86	103
Hannah	16	f	w	CA	San Francisco	8-Wd San Francisco	82	459
Hans	42	m	w	DENM	Marin	Bolinas Twp	74	4
Harris	50	m	w	RUSS	San Francisco	San Francisco P O	83	378
Harris	45	m	w	RUSS	San Francisco	1-Wd San Francisco	79	56
Harrison	34	m	w	WALE	Santa Cruz	Santa Cruz Twp	89	387
Harrison	27	m	w	IL	Humboldt	Eel Rvr Twp	72	248
Harvey	52	m	w	IN	Stanislaus	Branch Twp	92	4
Harvey G	44	m	w	VT	Calaveras	Copperopolis P O	70	244
Helen	47	f	w	NY	San Francisco	San Francisco P O	83	102
Helena	36	f	w	DENM	Mariposa	Maxwell Crk P O	74	146
Henery	19	m	w	ENGL	San Francisco	7-Wd San Francisco	81	191
Henry	54	m	w	WALE	San Francisco	1-Wd San Francisco	79	67
Henry	52	m	w	NY	Nevada	Grass Valley Twp	75	146
Henry	49	m	w	ENGL	San Francisco	San Francisco P O	83	388
Henry	45	m	w	ENGL	Humboldt	Eel Rvr Twp	72	250
Henry	41	m	w	ENGL	San Francisco	San Francisco P O	80	456
Henry	40	m	w	ENGL	Nevada	Rough & Ready Twp	75	336
Henry	38	m	w	WALE	Calaveras	San Andreas P O	70	209
Henry	35	m	w	ME	Tuolumne	Sonora P O	93	329
Henry	34	m	w	AR	Santa Clara	Burnett Twp	88	31
Henry	31	m	w	IL	Stanislaus	Empire Twp	92	42
Henry	30	m	w	IREL	Mendocino	Albion & Big Rvr T	74	166
Henry	29	m	w	IL	Solano	Vacaville Twp	90	133
Henry	28	m	w	ME	San Francisco	5-Wd San Francisco	81	27
Henry	27	m	w	NH	Yolo	Putah Twp	93	511
Henry	27	m	w	NY	San Francisco	11-Wd San Francisc	84	478
Henry	26	m	w	WALE	San Francisco	7-Wd San Francisco	81	264
Henry	18	m	w	OH	Yuba	Slate Range Bar Tw	93	675
Henry	16	m	w	NY	San Francisco	1-Wd San Francisco	79	95
Henry A	45	m	w	MA	San Francisco	6-Wd San Francisco	81	94
Henry A	34	m	w	IN	Placer	Pino Twp	76	470
Henry E	28	m	w	CT	San Francisco	1-Wd San Francisco	79	111
Henry H	44	m	w	KY	Stanislaus	Empire Twp	92	57
Henry L	42	m	w	RI	San Francisco	6-Wd San Francisco	81	133
Henry L	38	m	w	OH	Siskiyou	Table Rock Twp	89	648
Henry O	39	m	w	OH	Placer	Colfax P O	76	390
Heny	9	m	w	MO	San Joaquin	Oneal Twp	86	103
Hiram	46	m	w	VT	Calaveras	Copperopolis P O	70	222
Hiram	40	m	w	NY	Alameda	Washington Twp	68	298
Hiram F	40	m	w	OH	Placer	Roseville P O	76	354
Horace	40	m	w	MA	San Francisco	San Francisco P O	80	484
Horace T	52	m	w	VT	Stanislaus	Empire Twp	92	61
Howell	38	m	w	PA	Colusa	Grand Island Twp	71	302
Hugh	38	m	w	CANA	Sacramento	Georgianna Twp	77	126
Hugh	26	m	w	IA	Siskiyou	Surprise Valley Tw	89	636
I	35	m	w	OH	Sierra	Downieville Twp	89	515
Ida	1	f	w	CA	San Francisco	San Francisco P O	83	76
Ira H	33	m	w	OH	Sonoma	Vallejo Twp	91	461
Ira W	40	m	w	MA	Tulare	Visalia	92	297
Irwin	39	m	w	CT	San Francisco	6-Wd San Francisco	81	113
Isaac	61	m	w	TN	Solano	Green Valley Twp	90	42
Isaac E	47	m	w	MA	San Francisco	San Francisco P O	83	99
Isaac N	24	m	w	ENGL	Santa Cruz	Pajaro Twp	89	349
Isidor	31	m	w	POLA	San Francisco	San Francisco P O	83	51
Israel	58	m	w	MO	San Joaquin	1-Wd Stockton	86	123
Isreal W	45	m	w	MA	Tulare	Visalia	92	292
J	38	m	w	WALE	Sierra	Forest Twp	89	531
J D	34	m	w	OH	Amador	Drytown P O	69	415
J E	24	m	w	IA	Sacramento	Franklin Twp	77	121
J H	24	m	w	ENGL	Sierra	Butte Twp	89	511
J H	24	m	w	IL	Sutter	Sutter Twp	92	125
J J	39	m	w	MS	San Joaquin	Tulare Twp	86	259
J K	40	m	w	MS	San Joaquin	3-Wd Stockton	86	239
J L	45	m	w	PA	Yuba	W Bear Rvr Twp	93	684
J M	54	m	w	VA	San Joaquin	Oneal Twp	86	103
J M	40	m	w	WI	Alameda	Murray Twp	68	118
J M	35	m	w	KY	Lake	Coyote Valley	73	417
J N	37	m	w	MO	Tuolumne	Columbia P O	93	340
J P	40	m	w	KY	San Joaquin	2-Wd Stockton	86	182
J R	47	m	w	NY	San Joaquin	2-Wd Stockton	86	161
J R	33	m	w	IN	San Joaquin	2-Wd Stockton	86	211
J S	38	m	w	PA	Merced	Snelling P O	74	261
J W	51	m	w	MA	El Dorado	Greenwood Twp	72	52
J W	47	m	w	NH	Alameda	Oakland	68	230

Name	Age	S	R	B-PL	County	Locale	Series M593 Roll	Pg
J W	28	m	w	SWED	Solano	Vallejo	90	201
Jacob	37	m	w	BAVA	San Francisco	3-Wd San Francisco	79	315
Jacob Z	50	m	w	PA	San Francisco	1-Wd San Francisco	79	18
James	9	m	w	CA	Humboldt	Bucksport Twp	72	244
James	60	m	w	WALE	San Francisco	6-Wd San Francisco	81	105
James	55	m	w	NC	Stanislaus	Branch Twp	92	1
James	50	m	w	IN	Colusa	Colusa Twp	71	273
James	48	m	w	NY	Amador	Volcano P O	69	374
James	45	m	w	AUST	Fresno	Millerton P O	72	158
James	45	m	w	WALE	Mariposa	Mariposa P O	74	113
James	45	m	w	ENGL	Nevada	Washington Twp	75	343
James	44	m	w	IREL	Colusa	Colusa	71	292
James	44	m	w	ENGL	Placer	Alta P O	76	411
James	40	m	w	IN	Marin	San Rafael Twp	74	38
James	40	m	w	ENGL	Nevada	Grass Valley Twp	75	201
James	39	m	w	OH	Sutter	Vernon Twp	92	130
James	38	m	w	NC	Amador	Fiddletown P O	69	440
James	38	m	w	WI	Sutter	Nicolaus Twp	92	110
James	38	m	w	IREL	Alameda	Oakland	68	226
James	38	m	w	IREL	Alameda	Oakland	68	233
James	38	m	w	WALE	Butte	Kimshew Tpw	70	80
James	38	m	w	KY	Monterey	Salinas Twp	74	310
James	36	m	w	NY	Sacramento	4-Wd Sacramento	77	324
James	36	m	w	IN	Plumas	Quartz Twp	77	36
James	36	m	w	NC	Amador	Fiddletown P O	69	426
James	36	m	w	NY	Tehama	Red Bluff	92	183
James	36	m	w	TN	Sacramento	2-Wd Sacramento	77	207
James	35	m	w	ENGL	Marin	Bolinas Twp	74	6
James	35	m	w	KY	Sutter	Sutter Twp	92	119
James	34	m	w	IREL	San Diego	San Pasqual	78	522
James	33	m	w	AUST	San Francisco	3-Wd San Francisco	79	293
James	33	m	w	NY	Sacramento	2-Wd Sacramento	77	224
James	30	m	w	MO	Tehama	Antelope Twp	92	156
James	28	m	w	PA	San Francisco	San Francisco P O	83	47
James	28	m	w	NY	San Francisco	San Francisco P O	80	539
James	25	m	w	IL	Colusa	Butte Twp	71	268
James	25	m	w	ENGL	Colusa	Monroe Twp	71	322
James	23	m	w	MO	San Francisco	San Francisco P O	80	335
James	19	m	w	IL	Sacramento	2-Wd Sacramento	77	241
James C	50	m	w	MA	Los Angeles	San Gabriel Twp	73	594
James H	48	m	w	NY	Los Angeles	Los Nietos Twp	73	585
James H	31	m	w	IL	Alameda	Eden Twp	68	69
James Jr	51	m	w	ME	Humboldt	Eureka Twp	72	265
James L	40	m	w	MO	Los Angeles	San Gabriel Twp	73	597
James N	17	m	w	NV	Sonoma	Salt Point	91	389
James S	35	m	w	NORW	Sonoma	Sonoma Twp	91	443
James S	28	m	w	MA	Solano	Maine Prairie Twp	90	50
Jas	22	m	w	WALE	Sierra	Sears Twp	89	557
Jas H	40	m	w	MD	San Francisco	San Francisco P O	83	304
Jas T	26	m	w	MO	San Joaquin	1-Wd Stockton	86	139
Jeff	7	m	i	CA	Siskiyou	Table Rock Twp	89	647
Jeff	12	m	i	MO	Yolo	Grafton Twp	93	489
Jefferson	51	m	w	TN	Napa	Yountville Twp	75	87
Jefferson	30	m	w	MO	Sacramento	Lee Twp	77	159
Jefferson	15	m	b	AFRI	Santa Clara	Alviso Twp	88	22
Jefferson F	41	m	w	NY	Mendocino	Anderson Twp	74	157
Jenny	18	f	w	NY	San Francisco	6-Wd San Francisco	81	72
Jerome	27	m	w	OH	Sutter	Butte Twp	92	100
Jesse	36	m	w	OH	Siskiyou	Table Rock Twp	89	648
Jesse	33	m	w	IL	San Joaquin	Douglas Twp	86	39
Jesse S	35	m	w	NC	Shasta	Stillwater P O	89	478
Jno	24	m	w	AL	Santa Clara	Burnett Twp	88	30
Jno K	39	m	w	WALE	Sierra	Table Rock Twp	89	576
Jno S	32	m	w	TX	Butte	Chico Twp	70	54
Jno W	24	m	w	IL	Butte	Kimshew Tpw	70	79
Joe	46	m	w	PORT	Sacramento	Sutter Twp	77	386
Joe	30	m	w	MO	Lake	Lower Lake	73	422
Joe	23	m	w	BADE	Alameda	Oakland	68	194
Joe H	35	m	w	MA	Sacramento	3-Wd Sacramento	77	282
Joel	68	m	w	KY	Tulare	Kings Rvr Twp	92	252
Joel M	14	m	w	CA	Siskiyou	Callahan P O	89	632
John	70	m	w	MO	Santa Clara	Redwood Twp	88	117
John	66	m	w	IREL	Sonoma	Cloverdale Twp	91	267
John	62	m	w	NC	Nevada	Grass Valley Twp	75	218
John	61	m	w	ENGL	Stanislaus	Empire Twp	92	61
John	54	m	w	WALE	Mariposa	Mariposa P O	74	111
John	52	m	w	WALE	Nevada	Bridgeport Twp	75	107
John	50	m	w	ENGL	Humboldt	Table Bluff Twp	72	304
John	50	m	w	SWIT	San Francisco	5-Wd San Francisco	81	9
John	5	m	b	CA	Sutter	Vernon Twp	92	133
John	48	m	w	PRUS	San Francisco	San Francisco P O	85	739
John	47	m	w	WALE	El Dorado	Placerville Twp	72	102
John	45	m	w	MO	Siskiyou	Yreka	89	655
John	45	m	b	VA	San Francisco	San Francisco P O	80	414
John	45	m	w	AUST	Contra Costa	San Pablo Twp	71	364
John	45	m	w	ENGL	San Francisco	San Francisco P O	83	10
John	44	m	w	IN	Mendocino	Ukiah Twp	74	244
John	44	m	w	PRUS	Lassen	Susanville Twp	73	440
John	42	m	w	WALE	Nevada	Nevada Twp	75	307
John	41	m	w	PA	Placer	Bath P O	76	436
John	41	m	b	TN	Butte	Chico Twp	70	14
John	41	m	w	MA	Solano	Vacaville Twp	90	135
John	40	m	w	NY	Monterey	San Antonio Twp	74	319
John	40	m	w	NY	Solano	Vacaville Twp	90	122
John	40	m	w	MA	San Francisco	11-Wd San Francisc	84	637
John	40	m	w	MA	San Francisco	7-Wd San Francisco	81	177
John	39	m	w	AL	Los Angeles	El Monte Twp	73	448

© 2001 by Heritage Quest. All rights reserved.

Name	Age	S	R	B-PL	County	Locale	Roll	Pg
						Series M593		
John	39	m	w	IREL	San Francisco	2-Wd San Francisco	79	215
John	38	m	b	RI	San Francisco	1-Wd San Francisco	79	95
John	37	m	w	ME	Stanislaus	Empire Twp	92	34
John	37	m	w	WALE	Nevada	Bridgeport Twp	75	117
John	37	m	w	MA	Humboldt	Table Bluff Twp	72	307
John	36	m	w	IREL	Nevada	Eureka Twp	75	126
John	35	m	w	CT	Sacramento	4-Wd Sacramento	77	372
John	35	m	w	WALE	San Francisco	1-Wd San Francisco	79	91
John	35	m	w	ME	Del Norte	Happy Camp Twp	71	472
John	35	m	w	HOLL	Solano	Vallejo	90	200
John	35	m	w	ME	Santa Clara	Redwood Twp	88	133
John	35	m	b	RI	San Francisco	11-Wd San Francisc	84	520
John	34	m	w	VA	Shasta	Fort Crook P O	89	476
John	34	m	w	IREL	San Francisco	San Francisco P O	80	533
John	33	m	w	WALE	Plumas	Indian Twp	77	9
John	32	m	w	IREL	Alameda	Oakland	68	245
John	32	m	w	ITAL	Contra Costa	Martinez P O	71	427
John	31	m	w	IREL	Solano	Silveyville Twp	90	85
John	31	m	w	PA	Yuba	Rose Bar Twp	93	654
John	30	m	w	AR	Sutter	Nicolaus Twp	92	111
John	30	m	w	IREL	Sacramento	American Twp	77	66
John	30	m	w	MO	Nevada	Nevada Twp	75	310
John	30	m	w	IREL	San Francisco	1-Wd San Francisco	79	80
John	29	m	w	ENGL	Contra Costa	Martinez P O	71	424
John	28	m	w	IREL	Solano	Vallejo	90	181
John	28	m	b	WIND	San Francisco	San Francisco P O	80	409
John	28	m	w	SWED	Mendocino	Point Arena Twp	74	204
John	28	m	w	NY	San Francisco	7-Wd San Francisco	81	218
John	28	m	w	PA	Yuba	Rose Bar Twp	93	655
John	27	m	w	ENGL	Nevada	Grass Valley Twp	75	232
John	27	m	w	WALE	San Francisco	8-Wd San Francisco	82	292
John	26	m	w	MO	Amador	Ione City P O	69	370
John	25	m	w	CHIL	San Francisco	San Francisco P O	85	824
John	25	m	w	ENGL	San Francisco	2-Wd San Francisco	79	270
John	25	m	w	MD	Placer	Cisco P O	76	494
John	25	m	w	NY	Solano	Vallejo	90	157
John	24	m	w	ENGL	Solano	Rio Vista Twp	90	63
John	23	m	w	TX	Calaveras	Copperopolis P O	70	255
John	22	m	w	IREL	San Francisco	1-Wd San Francisco	79	43
John	20	m	w	NY	Los Angeles	Los Angeles	73	541
John	18	m	w	IL	San Bernardino	San Bernardino Twp	78	440
John	17	m	w	MA	Marin	San Rafael	74	48
John	15	m	w	CA	San Francisco	11-Wd San Francisc	84	591
John A	39	m	w	WALE	Sierra	Sears Twp	89	558
John B	43	m	w	OH	Humboldt	Eel Rvr Twp	72	254
John C	42	m	b	PA	Nevada	Nevada Twp	75	274
John C	37	m	w	NH	San Francisco	8-Wd San Francisco	82	365
John C	21	m	w	CA	Napa	Yountville Twp	75	78
John E	20	m	w	VT	San Francisco	3-Wd San Francisco	79	315
John F	36	m	w	IL	Stanislaus	Empire Twp	92	45
John H	42	m	w	MO	San Francisco	San Francisco P O	83	347
John J	44	m	w	IN	Amador	Fiddletown P O	69	439
John L	35	m	w	WALE	Alpine	Monitor P O	69	314
John M	29	m	w	ENGL	San Francisco	3-Wd San Francisco	79	328
John R	40	m	w	WALE	San Francisco	6-Wd San Francisco	81	151
John S	68	m	w	VA	Nevada	Rough & Ready Twp	75	328
John S	40	m	w	NY	San Mateo	San Mateo P O	87	371
John S	39	m	w	VA	Sacramento	4-Wd Sacramento	77	356
John S C	48	m	w	IL	Calaveras	San Andreas P O	70	165
John T	25	m	w	PA	Amador	Sutter Crk P O	69	410
John V	32	m	w	WI	Stanislaus	Empire Twp	92	61
Jos	21	m	w	OR	Solano	Benicia	90	20
Jos N	25	m	w	IL	Solano	Benicia	90	13
Jos P	32	m	w	IL	Mono	Bridgeport P O	74	287
Joseph	60	m	w	ENGL	Los Angeles	San Gabriel Twp	73	595
Joseph	45	m	w	UT	Alameda	Eden Twp	68	67
Joseph	43	m	w	IN	Amador	Fiddletown P O	69	430
Joseph	42	m	w	WALE	Plumas	Washington Twp	77	56
Joseph	38	m	w	KY	Solano	Maine Prairie Twp	90	51
Joseph	37	m	w	OH	Napa	Yountville Twp	75	84
Joseph	35	m	w	MEXI	Los Angeles	El Monte Twp	73	454
Joseph	3	m	m	CA	San Francisco	11-Wd San Francisc	84	611
Joseph	26	m	w	IL	Amador	Ione City P O	69	369
Joseph	25	m	w	MO	Napa	Napa	75	18
Joseph	25	m	w	MA	San Francisco	5-Wd San Francisco	81	11
Joseph	25	m	w	OH	Yolo	Grafton Twp	93	496
Joseph	24	m	w	IREL	San Francisco	8-Wd San Francisco	82	496
Joseph	22	m	w	MO	Solano	Vacaville Twp	90	133
Joseph D	42	m	w	WALE	Placer	Bath P O	76	435
Joseph Stillman	34	m	w	RI	Plumas	Washington Twp	77	55
Joshua	34	m	w	IN	Mariposa	Mariposa P O	74	107
Joshua	25	m	w	ENGL	San Francisco	3-Wd San Francisco	79	302
Josiah P W	34	m	w	OH	Sonoma	Healdsburg & Mendo	91	283
Josias	50	m	w	VA	Humboldt	Arcata Twp	72	231
Julia	25	f	w	IL	Alameda	Oakland	68	147
Kate	18	f	w	NY	San Francisco	5-Wd San Francisco	81	25
L D	29	m	w	IL	Amador	Ione City P O	69	357
L F	35	m	w	OH	Napa	Napa	75	56
L F	22	m	w	MO	San Joaquin	2-Wd Stockton	86	161
L P	38	m	w	ME	Sacramento	1-Wd Sacramento	77	184
Laura I	2	f	w	CA	Sacramento	4-Wd Sacramento	77	362
Lavinia	30	f	w	MA	Marin	San Rafael	74	52
Lee	31	m	w	PA	Placer	Auburn P O	76	363
Lena	20	f	w	PRUS	San Francisco	San Francisco P O	85	847
Letcher	43	m	w	MO	Napa	Napa Twp	75	58
Levi	48	m	w	IN	Sonoma	Analy Twp	91	240
Levi	28	m	w	AUST	Merced	Snelling P O	74	265
Levi P	34	m	w	OH	Sacramento	San Joaquin Twp	77	405
Lewis	48	m	w	WALE	Sierra	Table Rock Twp	89	578
Lewis	40	m	w	WALE	Siskiyou	Scott Valley Twp	89	612
Lewis M	43	m	w	ME	El Dorado	Mud Springs Twp	72	80
Lilly	22	f	w	PA	San Francisco	6-Wd San Francisco	81	86
Lissie	29	f	w	ME	San Francisco	11-Wd San Francisc	84	645
Lizzie	24	f	w	AL	Solano	Silveyville Twp	90	81
Lizzie	1	f	w	CA	San Francisco	San Francisco P O	83	162
Louis	12	m	w	CA	Alameda	Oakland	68	258
Louis	12	m	w	CA	Siskiyou	Callahan P O	89	624
Louisa	34	f	w	MO	Solano	Vacaville Twp	90	125
M	30	f	w	MO	Sacramento	3-Wd Sacramento	77	281
M A	17	f	w	US	Yuba	Marysville	93	609
M B	24	m	w	IN	Sacramento	1-Wd Sacramento	77	175
M H	46	m	w	OH	Sacramento	4-Wd Sacramento	77	354
M H	26	f	w	MO	San Francisco	8-Wd San Francisco	82	362
M M	6	f	w	MO	Alameda	Oakland	68	244
Maberry Jr	30	m	w	IL	Colusa	Butte Twp	71	267
Mabery Sr	46	m	w	IL	Colusa	Butte Twp	71	272
Manuel	25	m	b	WIND	Solano	Vallejo	90	203
Margaret	34	f	w	PA	Nevada	Bridgeport Twp	75	107
Margret	49	f	w	WALE	San Francisco	1-Wd San Francisco	79	45
Maria	26	f	w	OH	Tulare	Farmersville Twp	92	249
Mark	27	m	w	PRUS	San Francisco	San Francisco P O	83	232
Marks	44	m	w	RUSS	San Francisco	1-Wd San Francisco	79	46
Marks	30	m	w	PRUS	San Francisco	San Francisco P O	83	194
Marks	21	m	w	POLA	San Francisco	8-Wd San Francisco	82	359
Martha	10	f	w	CA	Amador	Amador City P O	69	395
Marx	21	m	w	NY	San Francisco	8-Wd San Francisco	82	498
Mary	55	f	w	IREL	Sierra	Table Rock Twp	89	575
Mary	35	f	w	IREL	San Francisco	San Francisco P O	83	14
Mary	35	f	w	NY	San Francisco	11-Wd San Francisc	84	520
Mary	28	f	w	IREL	Contra Costa	Martinez P O	71	426
Mary	16	f	w	CA	San Francisco	11-Wd San Francisc	84	630
Mary A	50	f	w	KY	Mendocino	Ukiah Twp	74	242
Mary Ann	30	f	b	PA	Nevada	Nevada Twp	75	280
Mary E	14	f	w	CA	San Francisco	6-Wd San Francisco	81	94
Matilda	9	f	i	CA	Del Norte	Crescent	71	466
Matilda	10	f	w	CA	Contra Costa	Martinez P O	71	450
Michael	42	m	w	NY	San Francisco	San Francisco P O	83	216
Milton	46	m	w	KY	Solano	Vacaville Twp	90	121
Minna	42	f	w	BADE	San Francisco	5-Wd San Francisco	81	10
Mish	46	m	b	HI	Siskiyou	Cottonwood Twp	89	590
Morgan	36	m	w	WALE	Sierra	Table Rock Twp	89	571
Morris	27	m	w	WI	San Francisco	San Francisco P O	83	396
Moses	45	m	w	VT	Santa Clara	Santa Clara Twp	88	144
Moses	43	m	w	TN	Monterey	Alisal Twp	74	298
Moses	40	m	w	WALE	Nevada	Bridgeport Twp	75	107
Moses	34	m	w	VA	Solano	Silveyville Twp	90	91
Moses	28	m	w	AL	Marin	San Rafael Twp	74	43
Moses C	45	m	w	MA	San Francisco	San Francisco P O	83	84
N Russell	28	m	w	IREL	San Francisco	San Francisco P O	83	60
Nancy	12	f	w	IA	Monterey	Salinas Twp	74	310
Nancy A	5	f	w	TX	San Diego	Milquaty Dist	78	476
Nancy E	47	f	w	IL	Shasta	American Ranch P O	89	500
Nathan	69	m	w	NY	Santa Clara	Redwood Twp	88	124
Nathaniel	51	m	w	PA	Mendocino	Navarro & Big Rvr	74	177
Nathaniel	45	m	w	NY	San Francisco	11-Wd San Francisc	84	520
Nehemiah	70	m	w	DE	Monterey	Pajaro Twp	74	368
Nelly	13	f	w	US	Yuba	Marysville	93	609
Nelson H	22	m	w	OH	Sutter	Vernon Twp	92	138
Nero	35	m	w	TN	Yuba	East Bear Rvr Twp	93	539
Nicolas	25	m	w	AUST	Monterey	San Juan Twp	74	410
Norman	33	m	w	PA	Placer	Lincoln P O	76	492
Norman	20	m	w	GA	Yuba	Marysville	93	604
Norman	19	m	w	GA	Butte	Ophir Twp	70	96
O S	49	m	w	VT	Tuolumne	Sonora P O	93	334
Oran W	36	m	w	NY	Calaveras	Copperopolis P O	70	251
Orlina	8	f	w	OH	Sierra	Sears Twp	89	559
Owen	50	m	w	WALE	Sacramento	Brighton Twp	77	70
P	32	m	w	IREL	Butte	Bidwell Twp	70	3
Perry	45	m	w	NY	Sacramento	4-Wd Sacramento	77	378
Peter	9	m	w	CA	Humboldt	Eel Rvr Twp	72	249
Peter	45	m	w	NJ	Amador	Volcano P O	69	383
Peter	44	m	w	NY	Calaveras	San Andreas P O	70	173
Peter	44	m	w	ENGL	Santa Barbara	Santa Barbara P O	87	478
Peter	40	m	w	AUST	Contra Costa	San Pablo Twp	71	353
Peter	35	m	w	PRUS	San Francisco	San Francisco P O	80	540
Philip	43	m	w	PRUS	Los Angeles	Santa Ana Twp	73	611
Phillip	22	m	w	WALE	Contra Costa	Martinez P O	71	425
Phillips	45	m	w	WALE	Contra Costa	Martinez P O	71	425
Preston	26	m	w	OH	Humboldt	Arcata Twp	72	231
R	45	m	w	NY	Sacramento	3-Wd Sacramento	77	280
R	28	m	w	ENGL	Tuolumne	Big Oak Flat P O	93	396
R A	40	m	w	VT	Tuolumne	Big Oak Flat P O	93	399
R A	29	m	w	MA	San Francisco	San Francisco P O	85	854
R C	25	m	w	IN	Tuolumne	Columbia P O	93	348
R J	24	m	w	NY	Solano	Vallejo	90	199
Rachael	41	f	b	NJ	Sacramento	4-Wd Sacramento	77	329
Reason	39	m	w	TN	Contra Costa	Martinez P O	71	433
Reseda	35	f	w	PRUS	San Francisco	San Francisco P O	83	377
Reuben	70	m	w	ME	Sonoma	Analy Twp	91	245
Reuben	34	m	w	CANA	Yuba	Rose Bar Twp	93	661
Richard	6	m	w	CA	Santa Clara	Santa Clara Twp	88	154
Richard	50	m	w	NY	San Francisco	8-Wd San Francisco	82	311
Richard	21	m	w	CA	Placer	Bath P O	76	436
Richard P	31	m	w	ENGL	Santa Barbara	San Buenaventura P	87	448

© 2001 by Heritage Quest. All rights reserved.

Name	Age	S	R	B-PL	County	Locale	Series M593 Roll	Pg
Riley	40	m	w	IREL	Stanislaus	Branch Twp	92	2
Rita	31	f	w	CA	Santa Barbara	Santa Barbara P O	87	463
Robert	55	m	w	IREL	Santa Clara	Santa Clara Twp	88	163
Robert	50	m	w	IREL	Santa Clara	Santa Clara Twp	88	157
Robert	48	m	w	PA	San Francisco	5-Wd San Francisco	81	24
Robert	45	m	w	NY	Yuba	Marysville	93	581
Robert	42	m	w	ENGL	Placer	Auburn P O	76	380
Robert	35	m	w	CANA	Stanislaus	Emory Twp	92	25
Robert	27	m	w	CANA	San Francisco	San Francisco P O	83	405
Robert M	21	m	w	SC	Marin	Tomales Twp	74	85
Robinson	47	m	w	ME	San Bernardino	San Bernardino Twp	78	415
Robt	42	m	w	IREL	Alameda	Oakland	68	225
Robt	17	m	w	NY	San Francisco	11-Wd San Francisc	84	593
Roscoe	37	m	w	WI	Yolo	Putah Twp	93	509
Rufus	37	m	w	AL	Santa Clara	Burnett Twp	88	31
Russel	63	m	b	SC	San Francisco	2-Wd San Francisco	79	249
S	44	m	w	NY	Sierra	Downieville Twp	89	518
S Amanda A	25	f	w	MD	San Francisco	5-Wd San Francisco	81	1
S I	24	m	w	VT	Sacramento	3-Wd Sacramento	77	311
S T	53	m	w	OH	Sutter	Butte Twp	92	97
Salem	36	m	w	ME	San Francisco	2-Wd San Francisco	79	248
Sam	38	m	w	IREL	Alameda	Oakland	68	267
Sam	29	m	w	MO	San Joaquin	Tulare Twp	86	263
Saml	60	m	w	IREL	Tuolumne	Big Oak Flat P O	93	404
Saml	38	m	w	NY	San Francisco	8-Wd San Francisco	82	373
Saml	32	m	w	MS	Sacramento	3-Wd Sacramento	77	278
Saml	25	m	w	NJ	San Francisco	1-Wd San Francisco	79	41
Saml B	24	m	w	PA	Siskiyou	Butte Twp	89	584
Samuel	64	m	w	ME	Sonoma	Salt Point	91	387
Samuel	55	m	w	SWED	El Dorado	Mud Springs Twp	72	83
Samuel	49	m	w	VT	Stanislaus	Empire Twp	92	51
Samuel	49	m	b	VA	San Francisco	San Francisco P O	80	396
Samuel	45	m	w	NY	San Francisco	5-Wd San Francisco	81	18
Samuel	44	m	w	KY	Sacramento	Granite Twp	77	143
Samuel	27	m	w	UT	Marin	San Rafael Twp	74	38
Samuel	18	m	w	AR	Stanislaus	Buena Vista Twp	92	12
Samuel H	23	m	w	NJ	Nevada	Grass Valley Twp	75	214
Samuel J	44	m	w	NY	Los Angeles	Santa Ana Twp	73	610
Samuel J	37	m	w	KY	Colusa	Monroe Twp	71	324
Samuel P	35	m	w	OH	Colusa	Colusa	71	297
Samuel R	20	m	w	ME	Sonoma	Salt Point	91	386
Samuel W	38	m	w	MO	Nevada	Grass Valley Twp	75	216
Sande	20	f	w	MO	San Joaquin	Douglas Twp	86	33
Sarah	39	f	w	HDAR	San Francisco	8-Wd San Francisco	82	400
Sarah	18	f	w	IL	El Dorado	Diamond Springs Tw	72	24
Sarah	18	f	w	IL	Mono	Bridgeport P O	74	286
Schuyler B	44	m	w	SC	Santa Clara	Santa Clara Twp	88	171
Selim	52	m	w	ENGL	Sacramento	2-Wd Sacramento	77	236
Seneca	36	m	w	VT	El Dorado	Placerville	72	119
Shephard	64	m	w	ME	Nevada	Rough & Ready Twp	75	323
Solomon	40	m	w	AR	Mendocino	Ukiah Twp	74	237
Solomon	34	m	w	BAVA	San Francisco	San Francisco P O	80	540
Solomon	33	m	w	MA	San Francisco	San Francisco P O	83	254
Stanton	1	m	w	CA	Alameda	Oakland	68	147
Stephen	82	m	w	PA	Calaveras	Copperopolis P O	70	241
Studley	40	m	w	NY	San Francisco	8-Wd San Francisco	82	387
Susanna	31	f	w	ENGL	Sierra	Sears Twp	89	558
Susie	10	f	w	CA	Alameda	Oakland	68	242
Sylvester C	35	m	w	NH	Sonoma	Sonoma Twp	91	446
T J	39	m	w	ME	Nevada	Eureka Twp	75	139
Tanner	55	m	w	AL	Santa Clara	Burnett Twp	88	30
Thadious	59	m	w	NY	Monterey	Alisal Twp	74	291
Theodore	15	m	w	MO	Yuba	Bullards Bar P O	93	549
Theodrick	27	m	w	IN	Mendocino	Ukiah Twp	74	242
Thomas	70	m	w	WALE	Santa Cruz	Pajaro Twp	89	344
Thomas	70	m	w	WALE	Santa Cruz	Santa Cruz Twp	89	399
Thomas	61	m	w	IREL	Tuolumne	Chinese Camp P O	93	390
Thomas	60	m	w	DC	Monterey	San Juan Twp	74	387
Thomas	53	m	w	IREL	Marin	Nicasio Twp	74	19
Thomas	52	m	w	WALE	Nevada	Bridgeport Twp	75	124
Thomas	49	m	w	WALE	Contra Costa	Martinez P O	71	428
Thomas	40	m	w	IREL	Tuolumne	Chinese Camp P O	93	375
Thomas	39	m	w	PA	Sonoma	Bodega Twp	91	260
Thomas	38	m	w	WALE	Siskiyou	Cottonwood Twp	89	590
Thomas	36	m	w	IREL	Marin	Sausalito Twp	74	74
Thomas	35	m	w	ENGL	Sutter	Sutter Twp	92	124
Thomas	35	m	w	WALE	Contra Costa	Martinez P O	71	426
Thomas	34	m	w	WALE	Contra Costa	Martinez P O	71	426
Thomas	31	m	w	MO	Sutter	Butte Twp	92	104
Thomas	31	m	w	IREL	Marin	San Rafael Twp	74	26
Thomas	28	m	w	ME	San Francisco	6-Wd San Francisco	81	104
Thomas	26	m	w	IREL	Marin	Sausalito Twp	74	72
Thomas	23	m	w	PA	Solano	Montezuma Twp	90	65
Thomas	19	m	w	CA	Placer	Bath P O	76	436
Thomas F	46	m	w	NH	San Mateo	Redwood Twp	87	363
Thomas H	40	m	w	SC	Tulare	Venice Twp	92	275
Thomas S S	48	m	w	IN	El Dorado	Mud Springs Twp	72	83
Thompson	38	m	w	MO	Tulare	Farmersville Twp	92	249
Thos	45	m	w	OH	San Joaquin	Elkhorn Twp	86	60
Thos	41	m	w	WALE	Sierra	Sears Twp	89	561
Thos	36	m	w	ENGL	San Francisco	1-Wd San Francisco	79	70
Thos	33	m	w	PRUS	San Francisco	1-Wd San Francisco	79	57
Thos A	50	m	w	ME	Calaveras	Copperopolis P O	70	229
Thos E	27	m	w	WALE	Sierra	Table Rock Twp	89	576
Thos F	46	m	w	NH	San Francisco	San Francisco P O	83	77
Thos F	35	m	w	TN	Butte	Chico Twp	70	54
Thos R	23	m	w	WALE	Sierra	Sears Twp	89	557
Thos T	40	m	w	WALE	Sierra	Sears Twp	89	556
Timothy	40	m	w	NY	Calaveras	Copperopolis P O	70	250
V P	60	m	w	DENM	Monterey	San Juan Twp	74	409
Vain E	27	m	w	CANA	Sonoma	Russian Rvr	91	370
W	36	m	w	IREL	Lake	Lower Lake	73	418
W A	32	m	w	TN	Monterey	Monterey Twp	74	348
W B	23	m	w	WI	Sierra	Sierra Twp	89	568
W C	30	m	w	FRAN	Sierra	Butte Twp	89	508
W E	37	m	w	PA	Sierra	Downieville Twp	89	517
W F	33	m	w	ME	Humboldt	Eureka Twp	72	263
W G	41	m	w	NY	San Francisco	3-Wd San Francisco	79	319
W H	60	m	w	VA	Sacramento	4-Wd Sacramento	77	373
W H	43	m	w	ENGL	Tuolumne	Chinese Camp P O	93	363
W J	45	m	w	VA	Siskiyou	Callahan P O	89	627
W R	40	m	w	MA	El Dorado	Greenwood Twp	72	56
W W	52	m	w	NC	Amador	Drytown P O	69	423
W W	47	m	w	NY	Sacramento	1-Wd Sacramento	77	178
Walter	5	m	w	CA	Humboldt	Eel Rvr Twp	72	246
Washington	57	m	w	TN	Calaveras	Copperopolis P O	70	249
Wesley	42	m	w	MA	San Joaquin	1-Wd Stockton	86	132
White	47	m	w	AUST	Merced	Snelling P O	74	246
William	66	m	w	SCOT	Contra Costa	Martinez P O	71	422
William	57	m	w	OH	Solano	Suisun Twp	90	114
William	56	m	w	KY	Placer	Bath P O	76	457
William	55	m	w	ENGL	San Francisco	7-Wd San Francisco	81	208
William	53	m	w	ENGL	Contra Costa	Martinez P O	71	424
William	52	m	w	PA	San Diego	Warners Rancho Dis	78	530
William	52	m	w	PA	Sonoma	Petaluma Twp	91	312
William	50	m	w	WI	Nevada	Bridgeport Twp	75	119
William	50	m	w	NC	Napa	Napa	75	18
William	50	m	w	MA	San Francisco	6-Wd San Francisco	81	155
William	48	m	w	HI	San Francisco	11-Wd San Francisc	84	500
William	46	m	b	NY	Mariposa	Mariposa P O	74	97
William	45	m	w	ENGL	Monterey	San Juan Twp	74	415
William	45	m	w	WALE	Nevada	Eureka Twp	75	129
William	45	m	w	NY	San Francisco	7-Wd San Francisco	81	206
William	43	m	w	CANA	San Francisco	San Francisco P O	80	336
William	42	m	w	KY	Lake	Coyote Valley	73	400
William	42	m	w	PA	Calaveras	Copperopolis P O	70	254
William	42	m	w	NY	San Francisco	3-Wd San Francisco	79	315
William	40	m	w	MA	Inyo	Independence Twp	73	325
William	40	m	w	ENGL	Contra Costa	Martinez P O	71	424
William	39	m	w	MO	Marin	San Rafael Twp	74	31
William	38	m	w	IREL	San Francisco	1-Wd San Francisco	79	81
William	36	m	w	ENGL	Marin	San Rafael Twp	74	36
William	35	m	w	VA	Stanislaus	San Joaquin Twp	92	81
William	35	m	w	WALE	Contra Costa	Martinez P O	71	427
William	33	m	w	ENGL	San Francisco	San Francisco P O	83	222
William	33	m	w	PA	Sonoma	Vallejo Twp	91	451
William	32	m	w	TN	Lake	Big Valley	73	394
William	32	m	w	NETH	San Mateo	Half Moon Bay P O	87	394
William	32	m	w	PRUS	San Mateo	Half Moon Bay P O	87	391
William	30	m	b	VA	San Francisco	San Francisco P O	80	385
William	29	m	w	LA	San Francisco	1-Wd San Francisco	79	90
William	26	m	w	WALE	Contra Costa	Martinez P O	71	427
William	26	m	w	WALE	Santa Clara	1-Wd San Jose	88	232
William	25	m	w	IREL	Santa Clara	Milpitas Twp	88	111
William	24	m	w	HI	San Francisco	11-Wd San Francisc	84	501
William	24	m	w	OH	Solano	Silveyville Twp	90	80
William	24	m	w	IA	Sutter	Vernon Twp	92	131
William	20	m	w	ENGL	San Francisco	San Francisco P O	80	420
William	18	m	w	IN	San Francisco	11-Wd San Francisc	84	526
William	17	m	w	MO	Placer	Pino Twp	76	470
William A	18	m	w	UT	San Bernardino	San Bernardino Twp	78	417
William B	54	m	w	MA	San Francisco	San Francisco P O	83	240
William B	42	m	w	KY	Solano	Vacaville Twp	90	124
William E	30	m	w	OH	San Mateo	San Mateo P O	87	355
William F	53	m	w	NC	Stanislaus	Branch Twp	92	1
William F	34	m	w	MO	Colusa	Colusa Twp	71	277
William F	21	m	w	WALE	Stanislaus	Empire Twp	92	52
William H	64	m	w	KY	Stanislaus	Empire Twp	92	57
William H	50	m	b	VA	Santa Clara	2-Wd San Jose	88	336
William H	42	m	w	ME	Placer	Bath P O	76	447
William H	40	m	w	WALE	El Dorado	Placerville	72	127
William J	35	m	w	WALE	Placer	Bath P O	76	441
William L	50	m	w	WALE	Placer	Bath P O	76	437
William M	38	m	w	WALE	Nevada	Bridgeport Twp	75	104
William M	35	m	w	PA	Placer	Lincoln P O	76	489
William P	62	m	w	NY	Butte	Oregon Twp	70	126
William W	54	m	w	ME	Placer	Rocklin Twp	76	468
William W	54	m	w	NC	El Dorado	Cosumnes Twp	72	16
William W	37	m	w	KY	Santa Clara	Santa Clara Twp	88	151
Williams A	31	m	w	PA	Inyo	Cerro Gordo Twp	73	321
Willis	4	m	w	CA	Santa Clara	Santa Clara Twp	88	154
Wilson	48	m	m	MO	Placer	Pino Twp	76	470
Wilson	46	m	w	MS	Sacramento	Sutter Twp	77	389
Wilson	42	m	w	MO	Placer	Pino Twp	76	471
Wilson	38	m	w	TN	Nevada	Little York Twp	75	245
Wm	50	m	w	MS	San Francisco	8-Wd San Francisco	82	314
Wm	48	m	w	WALE	Sacramento	4-Wd Sacramento	77	364
Wm	44	m	w	WALE	Sierra	Table Rock Twp	89	572
Wm	43	m	w	NY	San Francisco	1-Wd San Francisco	79	93
Wm	42	m	w	KY	Shasta	Millville P O	89	485
Wm	41	m	w	WALE	San Francisco	1-Wd San Francisco	79	71
Wm	38	m	w	KY	Fresno	Millerton P O	72	189
Wm	38	m	w	IREL	Del Norte	Crescent	71	466
Wm	36	m	w	US	San Joaquin	2-Wd Stockton	86	162

© 2001 by Heritage Quest. All rights reserved.

California 1870 Census

Name	Age	S	R	B-PL	County	Locale	Series M593 Roll	Pg
Wm	35	m	w	PA	Butte	Ophir Twp	70	107
Wm	30	m	w	ENGL	San Francisco	1-Wd San Francisco	79	70
Wm	28	m	w	KY	San Joaquin	3-Wd Stockton	86	247
Wm	27	m	w	ENGL	Butte	Kimshew Tpw	70	80
Wm	23	m	w	MO	San Joaquin	Oneal Twp	86	104
Wm	21	m	w	PA	Santa Barbara	San Buenaventura P	87	420
Wm	15	m	w	CA	San Francisco	11-Wd San Francisc	84	593
Wm A	25	m	w	MA	San Francisco	San Francisco P O	83	162
Wm B	37	m	w	PA	San Francisco	5-Wd San Francisco	81	24
Wm B	36	m	m	PA	Sacramento	1-Wd Sacramento	77	204
Wm D	21	m	w	MO	Santa Barbara	San Buenaventura P	87	436
Wm F	41	m	w	OH	Butte	Oregon Twp	70	132
Wm H	40	m	w	TN	Fresno	Kings Rvr P O	72	203
Wm I	35	m	w	US	Nevada	Grass Valley Twp	75	232
Wm O	39	m	w	TN	Sacramento	Natomas Twp	77	168
Wm W	50	m	w	VA	Butte	Chico Twp	70	41
Wm W	39	m	w	ME	San Francisco	7-Wd San Francisco	81	248
Wm W	19	m	w	NY	Shasta	Millville P O	89	484
Wolf	37	m	w	POLA	San Francisco	San Francisco P O	85	864
Zeno P	51	m	w	IN	Nevada	Nevada Twp	75	272
DAVISON								
B	26	m	w	CANA	Alameda	Alameda	68	17
Charles	43	m	w	ENGL	San Francisco	San Francisco P O	83	226
Charles	19	m	w	SCOT	Solano	Silveyville Twp	90	89
E F	32	f	w	ME	Alameda	Alameda	68	1
Elizabeth	45	f	w	NY	San Francisco	8-Wd San Francisco	82	465
George	30	m	w	SCOT	Sonoma	Salt Point	91	384
Gustavus	37	m	w	OH	Solano	Suisun Twp	90	108
Henry B	47	m	w	IREL	Colusa	Colusa	71	300
Israel	31	m	w	RUSS	Inyo	Independence Twp	73	324
James	48	m	w	IREL	Stanislaus	Empire Twp	92	44
Jane	26	f	w	MS	San Francisco	8-Wd San Francisco	82	314
Jenny	3	m	w	CA	Sacramento	Cosumnes Twp	77	93
John	39	m	w	SCOT	Sonoma	Salt Point	91	392
John	28	m	w	IREL	Colusa	Spring Valley Twp	71	344
Moses	40	m	w	SWED	San Francisco	8-Wd San Francisco	82	292
Simon P	53	m	w	ENGL	Inyo	Bishop Crk Twp	73	317
W F	32	m	w	PA	Amador	Amador City P O	69	391
William	23	m	w	SCOT	Colusa	Grand Island Twp	71	303
DAVISSON								
Constance	62	f	w	ENGL	San Francisco	2-Wd San Francisco	79	259
Hugh	30	m	w	SCOT	San Francisco	8-Wd San Francisco	82	441
James E	43	m	w	IREL	Colusa	Colusa	71	297
Obediah	59	m	w	OH	Solano	Suisun Twp	90	103
Robt G	35	m	w	NY	San Francisco	2-Wd San Francisco	79	262
William G	38	m	w	OH	Solano	Suisun Twp	90	102
DAVIT								
James	50	m	w	FRAN	Contra Costa	Martinez P O	71	381
DAVITCH								
Mark	40	m	w	AUST	Santa Clara	2-Wd San Jose	88	317
DAVITT								
Jules	47	m	w	LA	San Francisco	San Francisco P O	83	325
DAVOCK								
M J	37	m	w	NY	Monterey	Salinas Twp	74	308
DAVOE								
Alfred	35	m	w	NY	Sacramento	Lee Twp	77	158
DAVONPORT								
Peter	43	m	w	PA	Calaveras	San Andreas P O	70	185
DAVY								
B	24	m	w	ENGL	Sierra	Butte Twp	89	509
Catherine	35	f	w	ENGL	San Joaquin	Douglas Twp	86	33
F	24	m	w	ENGL	Sierra	Butte Twp	89	509
Henry	26	m	w	NY	Solano	Silveyville Twp	90	92
Henry	23	m	w	MA	Solano	Silveyville Twp	90	91
James	27	m	w	ENGL	Butte	Wyandotte Twp	70	146
Jane	23	f	w	CANA	Solano	Silveyville Twp	90	91
Mary	30	f	w	IREL	Napa	Yountville Twp	75	77
S	24	m	w	NY	Sierra	Butte Twp	89	509
Villa	12	f	w	CA	Alameda	Brooklyn Twp	68	53
William H	47	m	w	NORW	Yuba	North East Twp	93	643
DAW								
Edwrd	38	m	w	ENGL	San Francisco	7-Wd San Francisco	81	269
J W	48	m	w	NC	Mendocino	Sanel Twp	74	230
DAWBINS								
Willis	53	m	b	VA	El Dorado	Mud Springs Twp	72	87
DAWDEN								
Samuel	36	m	w	ENGL	Sacramento	Granite Twp	77	136
DAWE								
Silas	25	m	w	ENGL	Nevada	Grass Valley Twp	75	178
DAWES								
Edward	21	m	w	MO	Santa Clara	San Jose Twp	88	213
Elizabeth	42	f	w	NY	Alameda	Oakland	68	191
Evaline	31	f	w	VA	Solano	Maine Prairie Twp	90	52
James	43	m	w	ENGL	San Francisco	San Francisco P O	85	716
James	27	m	w	IREL	Marin	Sausalito Twp	74	73
John H	33	m	w	IL	Santa Clara	San Jose Twp	88	186
Michael	37	m	w	IREL	Sacramento	2-Wd Sacramento	77	225
William	47	m	w	ENGL	Sacramento	2-Wd Sacramento	77	238
William H	37	m	w	IREL	San Francisco	2-Wd San Francisco	79	261
DAWGET								
Bridget	33	f	w	IREL	San Joaquin	2-Wd Stockton	86	169
DAWKING								
Wm	40	m	w	ENGL	Humboldt	Eureka Twp	72	261
DAWLEY								
Hank	42	m	w	NY	Nevada	Nevada Twp	75	284
Nathan W	50	m	w	NY	San Mateo	Woodside P O	87	381
Timothy	33	m	w	IREL	San Mateo	Schoolhouse Statio	87	342
DAWLING								
Ann	57	f	w	IREL	San Francisco	San Francisco P O	83	153
DAWN								
George	35	m	w	HCAS	San Francisco	11-Wd San Francisc	84	570
DAWS								
A B	36	m	w	CANA	Sacramento	Brighton Twp	77	80
Edwin	36	m	w	ENGL	Nevada	Grass Valley Twp	75	199
John	30	m	w	ENGL	Nevada	Grass Valley Twp	75	224
John B	40	m	w	ENGL	Nevada	Grass Valley Twp	75	165
Mary A	39	f	w	ENGL	Sonoma	Santa Rosa	91	428
Peter	23	m	w	ENGL	Nevada	Grass Valley Twp	75	148
William	45	m	w	ENGL	Nevada	Grass Valley Twp	75	144
DAWSON								
Alexander	42	m	w	NY	Tuolumne	Chinese Camp P O	93	380
Ames	37	m	w	ME	Mendocino	Anderson Twp	74	156
Anna	35	f	w	IREL	San Mateo	Redwood City P O	87	376
Annie	12	f	w	NY	San Francisco	11-Wd San Francisc	84	608
C	34	m	w	ME	Yuba	Marysville	93	595
Cabbott	31	m	w	IN	Stanislaus	Branch Twp	92	4
E G	50	m	w	IN	Nevada	Nevada Twp	75	283
Edward	9	m	w	CA	Siskiyou	Callahan P O	89	624
Elie	6	f	w	CA	Siskiyou	Callahan P O	89	631
Ellen	14	f	w	CA	Alameda	Oakland	68	246
Eva	12	f	w	CA	Siskiyou	Callahan P O	89	625
George	36	m	w	SCOT	San Francisco	8-Wd San Francisco	82	394
George	32	m	w	ENGL	San Francisco	San Francisco P O	83	35
George	30	m	w	ENGL	San Francisco	San Francisco P O	83	32
Hatty	12	f	w	CA	Siskiyou	Callahan P O	89	630
Henry	36	m	w	IREL	Sutter	Vernon Twp	92	131
Henry	31	m	w	IREL	San Francisco	San Francisco P O	83	197
Hezekiah	30	m	w	IN	San Francisco	1-Wd San Francisco	79	88
J	39	m	w	IREL	Lake	Knoxville Mines	73	404
J	38	m	w	GA	Amador	Ione City P O	69	363
J M	20	m	w	WI	Sutter	Butte Twp	92	92
J T	43	m	w	KY	Sonoma	Santa Rosa	91	427
J V	40	m	w	NY	San Francisco	8-Wd San Francisco	82	373
Jacob W	38	m	w	ME	San Mateo	Half Moon Bay P O	87	402
James M	62	m	w	MD	Santa Clara	1-Wd San Jose	88	254
Jas A	45	m	w	CANA	Humboldt	Eureka Twp	72	273
Jno	34	m	w	ENGL	Sacramento	3-Wd Sacramento	77	306
Jno	22	m	w	NY	Sacramento	1-Wd Sacramento	77	180
John	45	m	w	IREL	Mono	Bridgeport P O	74	282
John	36	m	w	IREL	San Francisco	San Francisco P O	83	82
John	35	m	w	IREL	Solano	Vallejo	90	170
Jos	46	m	w	ENGL	Sacramento	1-Wd Sacramento	77	178
Joseph	38	m	w	MO	Amador	Jackson P O	69	340
Joseph	34	m	w	ENGL	Napa	Napa	75	24
Lorenzo	27	m	w	MA	Stanislaus	Emory Twp	92	25
Michael	60	m	w	IREL	Santa Clara	Santa Clara Twp	88	144
Nathan	40	m	w	IREL	Santa Clara	Fremont Twp	88	55
Noble	40	m	w	IREL	Stanislaus	Buena Vista Twp	92	12
Olivia	39	f	w	NY	San Francisco	11-Wd San Francisc	84	596
Patrick	32	m	w	IREL	Sacramento	Brighton Twp	77	70
R H N	32	m	w	MO	Tehama	Merrill	92	197
Reily S	32	m	w	AR	Plumas	Quartz Twp	77	34
Robert	40	m	w	ENGL	Mendocino	Little Lake Twp	74	197
Robt	35	m	w	ENGL	Sacramento	4-Wd Sacramento	77	356
Rose	26	f	w	CT	San Francisco	7-Wd San Francisco	81	156
Rose	20	f	w	IREL	San Francisco	8-Wd San Francisco	82	475
Saml	30	m	w	OH	San Diego	San Diego	78	495
Sarah	67	f	w	TN	Stanislaus	Branch Twp	92	3
Thomas	46	m	w	OH	Trinity	Junction City Pct	92	210
Thorn	50	m	w	OH	San Diego	Warners Rancho Dis	78	528
W	53	m	w	NY	Amador	Ione City P O	69	360
William	51	m	w	IA	Stanislaus	Emory Twp	92	21
William	40	m	w	IREL	Santa Clara	Santa Clara Twp	88	155
William	22	m	w	IA	Stanislaus	Emory Twp	92	21
Willy	20	f	w	NY	San Francisco	6-Wd San Francisco	81	108
Wm	60	m	w	IREL	San Francisco	1-Wd San Francisco	79	20
Wm	36	m	w	NY	San Francisco	8-Wd San Francisco	82	373
Wm	28	m	w	IREL	San Joaquin	Douglas Twp	86	45
Wm	14	m	w	CA	Siskiyou	Scott Valley Twp	89	615
Wm J	55	m	w	IREL	Sonoma	Analy Twp	91	223
DAY								
Abner	22	m	w	MO	Colusa	Monroe Twp	71	318
Ah	25	m	c	CHIN	San Francisco	6-Wd San Francisco	81	90
Ah	25	m	c	CHIN	Alameda	Oakland	68	220
Ah	18	f	c	CHIN	San Francisco	6-Wd San Francisco	81	74
Ah	15	m	c	CHIN	San Francisco	5-Wd San Francisco	81	17
Allen	27	m	w	ME	Monterey	Alisal Twp	74	295
Amelia	12	f	w	CAME	San Mateo	San Mateo P O	87	357
Andrew	44	m	w	OH	Butte	Chico Twp	70	56
Andrew	41	m	w	KY	San Joaquin	2-Wd Stockton	86	168
Andrew J	47	m	w	TN	Stanislaus	Empire Twp	92	65
Anna J Sr	54	f	w	CA	San Diego	San Diego	78	493
Annie M	55	f	w	NY	Yolo	Cache Crk Twp	93	450
B O	53	m	w	NY	Tuolumne	Chinese Camp P O	93	378
Bernhard	54	m	w	SWIT	San Francisco	2-Wd San Francisco	79	172
Carrie L	19	f	w	WI	Calaveras	San Andreas P O	70	156
Catherine	30	f	w	IREL	San Mateo	San Mateo P O	87	357
Charles	42	m	w	MO	Yolo	Cache Crk Twp	93	444
Charles	30	m	w	NY	Tulare	White Rvr Twp	92	301
Charles	25	m	w	NY	Tulare	Tule Rvr Twp	92	270
Charles G	41	m	w	KY	Yolo	Cache Crk Twp	93	441
Charles W	35	m	w	IL	Trinity	Junction City Pct	92	209
Christopher	46	m	w	IL	San Francisco	5-Wd San Francisco	81	22
Daniel	26	m	w	OH	Santa Clara	Gilroy Twp	88	101

© 2001 by Heritage Quest. All rights reserved.

Name	Age	S	R	B-PL	County	Locale	Series M593 Roll	Pg
Daniel C	39	m	w	VT	Santa Clara	1-Wd San Jose	88	250
Darius W	42	m	w	NY	Santa Cruz	Pajaro Twp	89	348
Dewitt C	44	m	w	OH	Butte	Wyandotte Twp	70	147
Dorance	37	m	w	ME	El Dorado	Salmon Falls Twp	72	132
E A	38	m	w	IL	Lassen	Long Valley Twp	73	436
E M	46	m	w	NY	Lake	Lower Lake	73	420
E W	41	m	w	MA	Butte	Mountain Spring Tw	70	87
Ed	19	m	w	CANA	Humboldt	Bucksport Twp	72	243
Edward	42	m	w	MD	Solano	Vacaville Twp	90	121
Edward	35	m	w	MD	Solano	Vacaville Twp	90	133
Edwd	62	m	w	IREL	San Francisco	1-Wd San Francisco	79	106
Eli	62	m	w	VT	Mendocino	Ukiah Twp	74	240
Elizabeth	18	f	w	AUSL	San Francisco	1-Wd San Francisco	79	106
Erastus M	46	m	w	NY	Santa Clara	1-Wd San Jose	88	261
F H	43	m	w	NY	San Francisco	3-Wd San Francisco	79	311
Frances	40	f	w	IREL	Solano	Vallejo	90	199
Francis	59	m	w	FRAN	Calaveras	San Andreas P O	70	195
Francis	31	m	w	ME	Santa Cruz	Watsonville	89	378
Frank W	44	m	w	NY	Butte	Ophir Twp	70	91
Franklin	21	m	w	NY	Sonoma	Petaluma Twp	91	313
Georg	40	m	w	MA	Calaveras	San Andreas P O	70	210
George	53	m	w	ENGL	San Francisco	11-Wd San Francisc	84	652
George	47	m	w	ENGL	Sonoma	Mendocino Twp	91	291
George	34	m	w	ENGL	San Bernardino	Chino Twp	78	412
George	29	m	w	NY	Colusa	Butte Twp	71	266
George	22	m	w	MA	Nevada	Eureka Twp	75	135
George	21	m	w	MO	Stanislaus	San Joaquin Twp	92	77
George	19	m	w	CT	San Francisco	8-Wd San Francisco	82	362
George B	29	m	w	NY	Mono	Bridgeport P O	74	282
George M	35	m	w	ME	Santa Cruz	Santa Cruz Twp	89	392
Gilman	41	m	w	ME	Placer	Summit P O	76	496
H L	36	m	w	ME	Nevada	Meadow Lake Twp	75	251
Henry	70	m	w	MA	El Dorado	Coloma Twp	72	8
Henry	24	m	w	ENGL	El Dorado	Placerville Twp	72	98
Heny G	30	m	w	ME	Butte	Kimshew Tpw	70	83
Ira	34	m	w	VA	Siskiyou	Yreka Twp	89	672
J	22	m	w	IREL	Sacramento	1-Wd Sacramento	77	182
J	22	m	w	NY	Alameda	Oakland	68	212
J J	27	m	w	KY	Los Angeles	Los Angeles	73	571
J R	36	m	w	NY	Monterey	San Juan Twp	74	388
James	44	m	w	KY	Mendocino	Calpella Twp	74	190
James	30	m	m	MD	San Francisco	San Francisco P O	80	384
James	26	m	w	IREL	San Mateo	Schoolhouse Statio	87	335
James A	39	m	b	MD	San Francisco	6-Wd San Francisco	81	78
James C	33	m	w	VA	Butte	Chico Twp	70	57
James F	35	m	w	MO	Stanislaus	San Joaquin Twp	92	77
James P	42	m	w	ME	Butte	Bidwell Twp	70	2
James S	22	m	w	OH	Yolo	Putah Twp	93	519
James T	47	m	w	TN	Sacramento	Brighton Twp	77	73
Jerry	42	m	w	IREL	Sacramento	4-Wd Sacramento	77	359
John	40	m	w	ENGL	Santa Clara	2-Wd San Jose	88	322
John	34	m	w	OH	Sonoma	Vallejo Twp	91	454
John	30	m	m	GA	San Francisco	San Francisco P O	80	423
John	30	m	w	IREL	San Francisco	7-Wd San Francisco	81	160
John	28	m	w	IREL	San Francisco	7-Wd San Francisco	81	221
John	27	m	w	ENGL	San Francisco	1-Wd San Francisco	79	106
John	24	m	w	IREL	Solano	Denverton Twp	90	23
John C	37	m	w	OH	El Dorado	Kelsey Twp	72	60
John R	37	m	w	IREL	San Francisco	6-Wd San Francisco	81	121
John R	37	m	w	IREL	San Francisco	San Francisco P O	83	249
John W	30	m	w	ENGL	San Francisco	6-Wd San Francisco	81	105
Joseph	36	m	w	OH	Sonoma	Santa Rosa	91	395
Julia	28	f	w	ENGL	San Francisco	6-Wd San Francisco	81	124
Lot	75	m	w	NJ	Yolo	Cache Crk Twp	93	448
Louis V	29	m	w	OH	Santa Clara	Gilroy Twp	88	101
Luly	16	f	w	MA	San Francisco	1-Wd San Francisco	79	106
Margaret	35	f	w	IREL	San Francisco	San Francisco P O	83	3
Mariana Mrs	33	f	w	CA	Monterey	Monterey	74	367
Mary	38	f	w	IREL	Contra Costa	Martinez P O	71	435
Mary	30	f	w	MA	Sacramento	2-Wd Sacramento	77	253
Mary E	26	f	m	MD	San Francisco	6-Wd San Francisco	81	78
Michael	40	m	w	IREL	San Francisco	San Francisco P O	83	391
Michael	30	m	w	IREL	San Mateo	Belmont P O	87	388
Nathaniel	36	m	w	ME	Butte	Bidwell Twp	70	3
Nathaniel T	64	m	w	ME	Colusa	Butte Twp	71	272
Orrin	50	m	w	NY	Placer	Dutch Flat P O	76	410
P L	20	m	w	OH	Monterey	San Juan Twp	74	393
P O	27	m	w	IREL	Alameda	Oakland	68	154
Patrick	55	m	w	IREL	San Francisco	1-Wd San Francisco	79	4
Paul	43	m	w	NY	Santa Cruz	Watsonville	89	366
Peter	38	m	w	MO	Plumas	Plumas Twp	77	26
Q A	42	m	w	OH	Butte	Wyandotte Twp	70	147
R	39	m	w	ME	Lassen	Susanville Twp	73	443
Rachel M	46	f	w	IL	San Francisco	6-Wd San Francisco	81	92
Richard	22	m	w	IREL	San Francisco	11-Wd San Francisc	84	661
Robert	21	m	w	IREL	San Francisco	8-Wd San Francisco	82	430
Roger S	30	m	w	MA	Sacramento	Granite Twp	77	143
Royal W	29	m	w	IA	Sacramento	Dry Crk Twp	77	101
Russell	54	m	w	NY	Yolo	Cache Crk Twp	93	446
S Thomas	31	m	w	NH	San Francisco	8-Wd San Francisco	82	369
Samuel	42	m	w	IREL	Santa Clara	Santa Clara Twp	88	155
Sherman	61	m	w	CT	Alameda	Oakland	68	187
Thomas	54	m	w	IREL	Calaveras	Copperopolis P O	70	253
Thomas	52	m	w	VA	San Joaquin	Oneal Twp	86	107
Thomas	48	m	w	MA	San Francisco	San Francisco P O	83	256
Thomas	39	m	w	ME	San Francisco	11-Wd San Francisc	84	568
Thomas	39	m	w	TN	Colusa	Butte Twp	71	267

Name	Age	S	R	B-PL	County	Locale	Series M593 Roll	Pg
Thomas	37	m	w	IL	San Joaquin	Tulare Twp	86	258
Thomas	35	m	w	IREL	San Francisco	San Francisco P O	83	2
Thomas	30	m	w	NY	Nevada	Meadow Lake Twp	75	270
Thomas S	27	m	w	NY	San Francisco	8-Wd San Francisco	82	453
Thos	43	m	w	IL	San Joaquin	Dent Twp	86	29
Timothy	35	m	w	MA	San Francisco	5-Wd San Francisco	81	23
Timothy	34	m	w	IREL	Marin	San Rafael Twp	74	35
W H	26	m	w	OH	San Francisco	8-Wd San Francisco	82	376
Willard	41	m	w	ME	Marin	Sausalito Twp	74	67
William	42	m	w	KY	Mendocino	Calpella Twp	74	190
William	39	m	w	OH	San Francisco	11-Wd San Francisc	84	469
William	35	m	w	NY	San Francisco	San Francisco P O	83	297
William	26	m	w	ENGL	Solano	Silveyville Twp	90	81
William	25	m	w	IREL	San Francisco	6-Wd San Francisco	81	100
William A	40	m	w	ME	Santa Cruz	Santa Cruz Twp	89	395
William E	30	m	w	ME	Santa Cruz	Santa Cruz Twp	89	392
William S	52	m	w	NY	El Dorado	Diamond Springs Tw	72	35
Willis A	40	m	w	OH	San Mateo	Woodside P O	87	385
Wm	40	m	w	MO	San Joaquin	Tulare Twp	86	250
Wm	27	m	w	ENGL	San Francisco	1-Wd San Francisco	79	80
Zebulon	35	m	w	OH	Placer	Bath P O	76	446
DAYBALL								
Martin	30	m	w	NY	San Francisco	11-Wd San Francisc	84	482
DAYLEY								
E W	32	m	w	VT	Sacramento	3-Wd Sacramento	77	316
Georgenia	22	f	w	MA	San Francisco	11-Wd San Francisc	84	506
DAYLY								
Agnes C	21	f	w	IREL	Yuba	Slate Range Bar Tw	93	673
DAYMAN								
John	32	m	w	TX	Kern	Tehachapi P O	73	354
DAYO								
Yip	26	m	c	CHIN	Solano	Vallejo	90	208
DAYS								
Antone	45	m	w	PORT	Napa	Napa	75	25
John M	36	m	w	ENGL	Nevada	Grass Valley Twp	75	160
Wolverton	60	m	w	MD	Nevada	Grass Valley Twp	75	222
DAYTON								
Alex	33	m	w	MO	San Joaquin	2-Wd Stockton	86	165
Alexander	36	m	w	MO	Sonoma	Salt Point	91	380
C W	22	m	w	OH	San Joaquin	2-Wd Stockton	86	165
Calvin	26	m	w	MI	Merced	Snelling P O	74	253
Elija [Dr]	56	m	w	CT	San Joaquin	Elkhorn Twp	86	57
Franklin	40	m	w	ME	Yolo	Cottonwood Twp	93	465
Geo	40	m	w	NH	San Francisco	San Francisco P O	85	867
H B	31	m	w	MD	Humboldt	Eureka Twp	72	281
J B	41	m	w	NJ	San Francisco	San Francisco P O	83	324
John E	30	m	w	NY	Alameda	Washington Twp	68	282
Ransom	35	m	w	NY	San Joaquin	Oneal Twp	86	102
Samuel	32	m	w	OH	Nevada	Nevada Twp	75	296
William	36	m	w	NY	Monterey	Pajaro Twp	74	372
DAYWOLD								
Geo	59	m	w	PA	El Dorado	Cosumnes Twp	72	14
DAZY								
John B	43	m	w	FRAN	San Francisco	2-Wd San Francisco	79	215
DAZZA								
Maria	51	m	w	FRAN	San Mateo	Half Moon Bay P O	87	390
DE								
Caw	19	m	c	CHIN	Yuba	Marysville	93	622
DEA								
Aleck	38	m	w	MEXI	El Dorado	Mud Springs Twp	72	76
Gon	45	m	c	CHIN	Yuba	Marysville	93	622
DEABAT								
John	56	m	w	FRAN	Nevada	Rough & Ready Twp	75	328
DEABLE								
W A	38	m	w	ENGL	Sierra	Sierra Twp	89	562
DEACON								
Edwin	35	m	w	ENGL	San Francisco	1-Wd San Francisco	79	96
George	32	m	w	ME	Nevada	Grass Valley Twp	75	217
Hiram	32	m	w	ENGL	Amador	Sutter Crk P O	69	410
Thomas	46	m	w	MO	Siskiyou	Big Valley Twp	89	582
William	39	m	w	OH	El Dorado	Placerville Twp	72	94
Wm	35	m	w	IREL	San Francisco	San Francisco P O	85	782
DEACY								
Cornelius	37	m	w	IREL	San Francisco	1-Wd San Francisco	79	31
Martin	22	m	w	ENGL	San Francisco	11-Wd San Francisc	84	548
DEADMAN								
Andrew	38	m	w	GA	Placer	Auburn P O	76	365
Dudley	38	m	w	MO	Nevada	Grass Valley Twp	75	228
William	31	m	w	MO	Nevada	Grass Valley Twp	75	218
DEADY								
D C	59	m	w	MD	San Joaquin	Elkhorn Twp	86	54
E N	16	m	w	OR	Solano	Benicia	90	21
Edward	37	m	w	IREL	San Francisco	San Francisco P O	85	811
Frank	8	m	w	MEXI	San Francisco	1-Wd San Francisco	79	23
George	32	m	w	NH	Yolo	Cottonwood Twp	93	459
Mary	54	f	w	IREL	San Francisco	San Francisco P O	83	198
DEAF								
Henry	43	m	w	DENM	Butte	Oregon Twp	70	125
DEAFIELD								
Bernard	31	m	w	PRUS	San Francisco	8-Wd San Francisco	82	491
DEAGALON								
Casimer	66	m	w	BELG	San Francisco	1-Wd San Francisco	79	34
DEAGAN								
William	28	m	w	IREL	Santa Clara	Fremont Twp	88	41
DEAKIN								
Edward	32	m	w	CA	San Francisco	11-Wd San Francisc	84	654
Robert	56	m	w	ENGL	San Francisco	11-Wd San Francisc	84	653

© 2001 by Heritage Quest. All rights reserved.

California 1870 Census

Name	Age	S	R	B-PL	County	Locale	Series M593 Roll	Pg
Wm	42	m	w	ENGL	Fresno	Kings Rvr P O	72	206
DEAL								
Abe	27	m	w	OH	Santa Barbara	San Buenaventura P	87	421
David	50	m	w	ENGL	San Francisco	11-Wd San Francisc	84	691
Ephram	29	m	w	OH	El Dorado	Georgetown Twp	72	42
George	48	m	w	PA	Del Norte	Mountain Twp	71	474
George	37	m	w	PA	Siskiyou	Cottonwood Twp	89	590
Janetta S	60	f	w	MD	Nevada	Nevada Twp	75	281
John	43	m	w	PRUS	San Francisco	San Francisco P O	80	339
John	30	m	w	MA	San Francisco	San Francisco P O	85	785
John E	40	m	w	NC	Yuba	Slate Range Bar Tw	93	671
Julia	32	f	w	IREL	San Francisco	7-Wd San Francisco	81	203
M S	31	m	w	MD	Nevada	Nevada Twp	75	281
Matti A	20	f	w	MD	Nevada	Nevada Twp	75	283
Simon	48	m	w	PA	Sacramento	4-Wd Sacramento	77	319
Thos	54	m	w	VA	San Francisco	11-Wd San Francisc	84	610
DEALDEVENDA								
Nudor A	27	f	w	MEXI	Sonoma	Mendocino Twp	91	287
DEALER								
Carson	27	m	w	DENM	Mendocino	Gualala Twp	74	226
DEALING								
Orestes W	48	m	w	CT	Sacramento	2-Wd Sacramento	77	232
DEALOGRES								
Coman	20	m	w	MEXI	Los Angeles	Los Angeles	73	508
DEALY								
Samuel	50	m	w	NJ	Tuolumne	Columbia P O	93	337
DEAM								
Ah	21	m	c	CHIN	Trinity	Weaverville Pct	92	231
H Mercer	36	m	w	AR	Humboldt	Pacific Twp	72	294
M H	27	m	w	AR	Humboldt	Pacific Twp	72	291
William	30	m	b	FL	Sacramento	2-Wd Sacramento	77	211
DEAMAN								
Jacob	39	m	w	WURT	Nevada	Rough & Ready Twp	75	332
DEAMER								
Wm E	38	m	w	ENGL	Nevada	Grass Valley Twp	75	186
DEAMON								
Jas	26	m	w	IREL	San Joaquin	Douglas Twp	86	36
DEAN								
---	20	m	c	CHIN	Siskiyou	Butte Twp	89	584
Alfred	38	m	w	ENGL	Amador	Volcano P O	69	385
Amanda	32	f	w	CT	Marin	Sausalito Twp	74	72
Amos	31	m	w	CANA	Alpine	Woodfords P O	69	316
Andrew	33	m	w	NY	Yolo	Cache Crk Twp	93	449
B	26	m	w	NY	San Francisco	San Francisco P O	83	67
Benjamin D	50	m	w	MA	San Francisco	8-Wd San Francisco	82	380
Charles	30	m	w	MA	Nevada	Eureka Twp	75	131
Charles F	40	m	w	NY	San Francisco	6-Wd San Francisco	81	89
Chas	45	m	w	NY	Butte	Chico Twp	70	34
Christian	60	m	w	HANO	San Francisco	1-Wd San Francisco	79	127
Daniel	28	m	w	VT	Kern	Bakersfield P O	73	365
Daniel W	30	m	w	OH	Solano	Suisun Twp	90	108
David	43	m	w	WALE	Calaveras	San Andreas P O	70	203
David	35	m	w	US	Contra Costa	Martinez P O	71	368
Davis H	43	m	w	OH	Butte	Oregon Twp	70	126
E D	43	m	w	NY	Nevada	Nevada Twp	75	290
Edward	29	m	w	NY	San Francisco	8-Wd San Francisco	82	426
Eliza	40	f	b	NY	Sacramento	2-Wd Sacramento	77	218
Elizabett	6	f	w	CA	Humboldt	Eel Rvr Twp	72	253
Emma	49	f	w	ENGL	San Joaquin	2-Wd Stockton	86	171
Eunice	68	f	w	CT	Napa	Napa Twp	75	67
F M	31	m	w	ENGL	San Francisco	San Francisco P O	85	857
Frederick	63	m	w	CT	Nevada	Nevada Twp	75	283
Geo A	34	m	w	MA	San Francisco	7-Wd San Francisco	81	245
George	31	m	w	TX	Tulare	Venice Twp	92	273
George C	53	m	w	NY	Tulare	Farmersville Twp	92	250
George E	31	m	w	NY	Tulare	Farmersville Twp	92	250
George W	43	m	w	GA	Humboldt	Pacific Twp	72	290
Gilbert M	10	m	w	MI	Alpine	Monitor P O	69	313
Gilbert S	29	m	w	TX	Tulare	Visalia	92	289
Harry	22	m	w	NY	Marin	Sausalito Twp	74	73
Henery	29	m	w	HANO	San Francisco	7-Wd San Francisco	81	164
Henry	40	m	w	IREL	San Francisco	7-Wd San Francisco	81	241
Henry	31	m	w	VT	Kern	Bakersfield P O	73	359
Henry K	40	m	w	CT	San Mateo	San Mateo P O	87	348
Horace F	53	m	w	NY	San Francisco	San Francisco P O	83	87
Hugh E	29	m	w	IREL	San Francisco	San Francisco P O	83	201
Ira	60	m	w	VA	Merced	Snelling P O	74	246
Isaac I	46	m	w	KY	Santa Clara	San Jose Twp	88	214
Jacob	50	m	w	GERM	Yolo	Putah Twp	93	515
James	50	m	w	IREL	San Francisco	6-Wd San Francisco	81	144
James	50	m	w	NY	San Francisco	11-Wd San Francisc	84	644
James	24	m	w	ENGL	Los Angeles	Wilmington Twp	73	641
James E	33	m	w	RI	El Dorado	Placerville	72	117
James Francis	35	m	w	IREL	Plumas	Seneca Twp	77	48
James M	53	m	w	PA	Calaveras	San Andreas P O	70	170
Jas F	63	m	w	NY	San Francisco	San Francisco P O	83	195
Job G	55	m	w	MA	Sacramento	Dry Crk Twp	77	100
Job G	55	m	w	MA	El Dorado	Mud Springs Twp	72	71
John	45	m	w	IREL	San Francisco	6-Wd San Francisco	81	147
John	40	m	w	IREL	Alameda	Brooklyn Twp	68	53
John	40	m	w	PA	Tehama	Deer Crk Twp	92	171
John	38	m	w	ENGL	Calaveras	Copperopolis P O	70	261
John	29	m	w	VA	Solano	Vacaville Twp	90	119
John	27	m	w	MA	Santa Cruz	Soquel Twp	89	441
John	26	m	w	CANA	Humboldt	Eureka Twp	72	281
John	21	m	w	IREL	Solano	Suisun Twp	90	112
John	21	m	w	PA	Solano	Suisun Twp	90	113
John J	40	m	w	OH	El Dorado	Mud Springs Twp	72	80
Julia	22	f	w	IREL	Sutter	Vernon Twp	92	136
Kate	26	f	w	IREL	San Francisco	San Francisco P O	83	311
Kate A	34	f	w	OH	Sacramento	1-Wd Sacramento	77	182
L V	27	f	b	VA	Alameda	Oakland	68	217
Louis	45	m	w	SWED	Calaveras	San Andreas P O	70	176
Lucretia	57	f	w	MA	San Francisco	11-Wd San Francisc	84	665
Lucy	40	f	w	VT	San Francisco	San Francisco P O	83	260
M J	52	f	w	TN	Humboldt	Pacific Twp	72	291
Mary	40	f	w	ENGL	San Francisco	11-Wd San Francisc	84	552
Michael	39	m	w	OH	El Dorado	Greenwood Twp	72	56
Minturn	61	m	w	VT	San Diego	San Diego	78	493
Myra	30	f	w	OH	Santa Clara	1-Wd San Jose	88	246
P A	29	m	w	SWED	San Francisco	San Francisco P O	85	829
Peter	41	m	w	WALE	San Francisco	6-Wd San Francisco	81	148
Platt	30	m	w	NY	San Francisco	2-Wd San Francisco	79	269
Portius F	46	m	w	NY	Santa Cruz	Pajaro Twp	89	359
Ransom	43	m	w	NY	Calaveras	Copperopolis P O	70	263
Richard S	46	m	w	IREL	Los Angeles	Los Angeles	73	567
Rosetta	17	f	w	LA	San Francisco	8-Wd San Francisco	82	326
Samuel	33	m	w	ME	Sacramento	Mississippi Twp	77	163
T	43	m	w	IL	San Joaquin	Tulare Twp	86	256
T C	44	m	w	KY	Merced	Snelling P O	74	277
Theodore	22	m	w	NY	Sutter	Butte Twp	92	89
Thomas	60	m	w	ME	Humboldt	Eureka Twp	72	280
Thomas	17	m	w	OH	Sonoma	Bodega Twp	91	258
Thos	23	m	w	NY	Sacramento	Franklin Twp	77	114
Victoria	30	f	w	NY	San Francisco	8-Wd San Francisco	82	428
Victoria	30	f	w	MA	San Francisco	8-Wd San Francisco	82	488
William	62	m	w	ENGL	Sutter	Butte Twp	92	89
William	39	m	w	MS	Kern	Havilah P O	73	339
William	35	m	w	IREL	San Francisco	11-Wd San Francisc	84	707
William	35	m	w	CANA	Sacramento	4-Wd Sacramento	77	338
William	26	m	w	MO	Inyo	Independence Twp	73	325
Wilson S	40	m	w	OH	Plumas	Plumas Twp	77	26
Wm	23	m	w	MO	Sacramento	Brighton Twp	77	78
Wm H	42	m	w	ME	Napa	Napa	75	57
Wm Smith	37	m	w	IN	Plumas	Seneca Twp	77	51
DEANDRIES								
Beagio	47	m	w	ITAL	San Francisco	San Francisco P O	83	57
DEANE								
Bernard	26	m	w	HANO	San Francisco	1-Wd San Francisco	79	101
Charles	12	m	w	CA	Stanislaus	Empire Twp	92	47
Coll	35	m	w	IREL	San Francisco	San Francisco P O	83	136
G B	39	m	w	NY	Sacramento	3-Wd Sacramento	77	270
George	15	m	w	NY	Sutter	Yuba Twp	92	147
Henry	45	m	w	MA	Stanislaus	Empire Twp	92	48
Joseph	49	m	w	PA	San Francisco	1-Wd San Francisco	79	25
Nannie	17	f	w	CA	Solano	Benicia	90	16
W D	38	m	w	ENGL	San Francisco	San Francisco P O	85	841
William	28	m	w	LA	San Francisco	San Francisco P O	80	364
William	20	m	w	ENGL	San Francisco	3-Wd San Francisco	79	313
Wm	21	m	w	MA	San Francisco	1-Wd San Francisco	79	85
DEANER								
Marry	28	m	w	MO	Yolo	Cache Crk Twp	93	446
Samuel	35	m	w	MD	Sutter	Vernon Twp	92	139
DEANGELIS								
John	36	m	w	NY	San Francisco	San Francisco P O	80	353
DEANHARD								
John	28	m	w	PRUS	San Francisco	San Francisco P O	83	389
DEANOR								
Harry J	27	m	w	MD	Yolo	Cache Crk Twp	93	425
DEANS								
Thos	21	m	w	IREL	San Joaquin	Tulare Twp	86	261
William	15	m	w	NJ	Marin	Sausalito Twp	74	72
DEANY								
Mary	30	f	w	MA	San Francisco	7-Wd San Francisco	81	220
DEAR								
Yee	37	m	c	CHIN	Yuba	Marysville	93	629
DEARBORN								
Elias	36	m	w	ME	Los Angeles	Los Angeles	73	506
J	50	m	w	NH	San Francisco	8-Wd San Francisco	82	369
J B	65	m	w	NH	Solano	Vallejo	90	214
S S	50	m	w	MA	Alameda	Oakland	68	163
DEARCE								
Ponter	38	m	w	HANO	Alameda	Oakland	68	169
S	21	m	w	CA	Alameda	Oakland	68	159
DEARCY								
Sarah	36	f	w	IREL	Napa	Napa	75	40
DEARDEN								
Robert	37	m	w	CANA	Placer	Bath P O	76	453
DEARDOFF								
S F	44	m	w	IN	Merced	Snelling P O	74	259
DEARDORFF								
John R	42	m	w	PA	San Francisco	San Francisco P O	83	345
DEAREN								
Duncan	27	m	w	CANA	Sonoma	Vallejo Twp	91	454
DEAREY								
Abbie	19	f	w	IREL	San Francisco	San Francisco P O	83	18
DEARING								
Annie	49	f	w	PA	San Francisco	San Francisco P O	83	336
George	46	m	w	IREL	Humboldt	Table Bluff Twp	72	305
Henry	25	m	w	MO	Lake	Coyote Valley	73	400
J A	26	m	w	MO	Lake	Morgan Valley	73	424
J H	31	m	w	NC	Lake	Morgan Valley	73	424
John	33	m	w	NC	Lake	Morgan Valley	73	424
Orin A	25	m	w	ME	San Francisco	8-Wd San Francisco	82	340

© 2001 by Heritage Quest. All rights reserved.

Series M593

Name	Age	S	R	B-PL	County	Locale	Roll	Pg
Richard N	57	m	w	NY	San Francisco	3-Wd San Francisco	79	302
Wm	38	m	w	MI	Humboldt	Table Bluff Twp	72	305
DEARLOVE								
Wainte	46	f	w	NGRA	San Francisco	San Francisco P O	80	347
DEARMAN								
James	24	m	w	CANA	Solano	Vacaville Twp	90	125
James R	21	m	w	CANA	Santa Clara	San Jose Twp	88	195
DEARNY								
Henry	36	m	w	BAVA	Alameda	Oakland	68	153
DEARON								
Solomon	50	m	w	NY	Santa Clara	2-Wd San Jose	88	335
DEARRING								
Eldin C	22	m	w	ME	Placer	Colfax P O	76	391
DEARTH								
Gilbert	56	m	w	VT	Monterey	Pajaro Twp	74	373
DEARTNEY								
Eugene	13	m	w	IL	Colusa	Spring Valley Twp	71	343
Thom	51	m	w	US	Yuba	Marysville	93	576
DEARY								
Anna	43	f	w	IREL	San Francisco	8-Wd San Francisco	82	341
Henry	14	m	w	ME	Humboldt	Table Bluff Twp	72	305
DEAS								
Celestina	15	f	w	CA	Los Angeles	Los Angeles	73	528
John	39	m	w	ENGL	San Francisco	7-Wd San Francisco	81	217
DEASCOTSTCH								
M	47	m	w	AUST	San Joaquin	1-Wd Stockton	86	130
DEASER								
George W	28	m	w	MD	Los Angeles	Wilmington Twp	73	636
DEASOR								
Simon	22	m	w	CA	Fresno	Millerton P O	72	146
DEASSER								
Frank	31	m	w	CA	San Luis Obispo	San Luis Obispo Tw	87	297
DEASY								
James	40	m	w	IREL	Alameda	Eden Twp	68	87
John	45	m	w	IREL	San Francisco	1-Wd San Francisco	79	99
John	33	m	w	IREL	San Francisco	San Francisco P O	85	795
Maggie	27	f	w	IREL	Sonoma	Healdsburg & Mendo	91	278
DEAUCH								
Charles	52	m	w	PRUS	Amador	Volcano P O	69	376
DEAUGUSTINA								
Mathias	30	m	w	SWIT	Plumas	Seneca Twp	77	47
DEAVEN								
Mary	16	f	w	MA	San Francisco	San Francisco P O	83	195
DEAVENPORT								
John	45	m	w	MA	San Francisco	8-Wd San Francisco	82	336
DEAVERS								
George	36	m	w	MD	Los Angeles	Los Angeles Twp	73	494
DEAVILA								
Antonio	38	m	w	PORT	San Francisco	1-Wd San Francisco	79	130
DEAVIS								
Edwin	52	m	w	PA	San Francisco	2-Wd San Francisco	79	235
DEAVITT								
Wm	38	m	w	PA	Amador	Volcano P O	69	377
DEAY								
Bryan	22	m	w	IREL	San Francisco	1-Wd San Francisco	79	69
DEAZ								
Hosea	34	m	w	MEXI	Yuba	Marysville	93	611
Manuel	31	m	w	CHIL	Santa Clara	2-Wd San Jose	88	312
Nicklas	8	m	i	CA	Inyo	Lone Pine Twp	73	333
Thuteris	35	m	i	CHIL	Inyo	Lone Pine Twp	73	333
DEB								
Ah	35	m	c	CHIN	Butte	Kimshew Tpw	70	85
DEBACK								
Josias	41	m	w	HOLL	Santa Cruz	Pajaro Twp	89	355
DEBANARD								
John	33	m	w	SWIT	El Dorado	Lake Valley Twp	72	65
DEBAR								
John	50	m	w	FRAN	Contra Costa	Martinez P O	71	406
DEBARD								
Francis	36	m	w	TX	Monterey	Monterey	74	360
DEBARDELABEN								
A	29	f	w	IL	San Joaquin	2-Wd Stockton	86	185
DEBASE								
Michael	34	m	w	IREL	Stanislaus	Emory Twp	92	25
DEBAST								
Amand F C	50	m	w	BELG	Contra Costa	Martinez P O	71	375
DEBBLESS								
Arnold	28	m	w	IN	Butte	Chico Twp	70	43
DEBELLOCQ								
Alfred	49	m	w	FRAN	Nevada	Grass Valley Twp	75	146
DEBERA								
Marie T	28	f	w	FRAN	San Francisco	8-Wd San Francisco	82	449
DEBERCY								
Fred	63	m	w	FRAN	San Francisco	3-Wd San Francisco	79	322
DEBERKLEY								
Eugene	26	m	w	FRAN	Plumas	Plumas Twp	77	31
DEBERMAND								
Patri	29	m	w	SWIT	San Francisco	San Francisco P O	80	478
DEBERNAL								
Carmel	67	f	w	CA	San Francisco	11-Wd San Francisc	84	573
Jeronima	30	f	w	ARGE	San Francisco	11-Wd San Francisc	84	573
DEBERNARDI								
Jos	39	m	w	SWIT	Nevada	Nevada Twp	75	283
Julius	28	m	w	ITAL	Nevada	Meadow Lake Twp	75	259
Saml	40	m	w	SWIT	San Francisco	5-Wd San Francisco	81	16
DEBERNER								
John	42	m	w	FRAN	San Francisco	6-Wd San Francisco	81	88

Series M593

Name	Age	S	R	B-PL	County	Locale	Roll	Pg
DEBERNORDI								
Martin	50	m	w	SWIT	El Dorado	Placerville Twp	72	104
DEBERTRAND								
E	47	m	w	LA	Klamath	Trinidad Twp	73	390
DEBETT								
Minnie	12	f	w	OR	Alameda	Oakland	68	209
DEBIAS								
Pedro	36	m	w	CHIL	Santa Clara	Almaden Twp	88	11
DEBINGER								
Jas M	40	m	w	BADE	Mono	Bridgeport P O	74	282
DEBLAIS								
Geo L	45	m	w	RI	San Francisco	San Francisco P O	83	22
DEBLE								
C	35	m	w	ENGL	Sierra	Sierra Twp	89	569
Joseph	64	m	w	FRAN	San Francisco	San Francisco P O	80	345
Sampson	37	m	w	ENGL	Yuba	Rose Bar Twp	93	663
W	39	m	w	OH	Sierra	Sierra Twp	89	569
DEBLOIS								
Silas	19	m	w	RI	San Francisco	2-Wd San Francisco	79	269
DEBNAM								
Franklin Pitts	37	m	w	TN	Plumas	Plumas Twp	77	28
M	32	f	w	OH	San Joaquin	2-Wd Stockton	86	208
DEBNARDO								
Charles	26	m	w	SWIT	San Francisco	2-Wd San Francisco	79	150
DEBNEY								
Gerard	31	m	w	ENGL	Santa Cruz	Pajaro Twp	89	340
DEBO								
John F	38	m	w	OH	Nevada	Bloomfield Twp	75	94
DEBOIS								
A	8	m	w	CA	Lassen	Janesville Twp	73	433
Charles P	36	m	w	PA	Yolo	Grafton Twp	93	500
G	39	m	w	NY	Lassen	Janesville Twp	73	432
Jos	40	m	w	FRAN	San Francisco	8-Wd San Francisco	82	375
Thomas	32	m	b	NY	Los Angeles	Los Angeles	73	528
DEBONARDI								
John	19	m	w	SWIT	Yolo	Putah Twp	93	517
DEBONE								
Chas	10	m	w	CA	San Francisco	San Francisco P O	85	800
DEBONEY								
Franklin	37	m	m	PORT	Inyo	Lone Pine Twp	73	332
DEBONS								
Louis	40	m	w	FRAN	Tuolumne	Columbia P O	93	353
DEBOOTS								
John	62	m	w	FRAN	Mariposa	Mariposa P O	74	91
DEBOR								
Peter	50	m	w	FRAN	Los Angeles	Los Angeles	73	568
DEBORE								
Eugene E	36	m	w	IOFC	San Francisco	1-Wd San Francisco	79	49
DEBORNOLL								
J	45	m	w	SWIT	Sierra	Butte Twp	89	510
DEBOSS								
L	25	m	w	ITAL	Alameda	Oakland	68	221
DEBOTT								
G W	37	m	w	OH	Sutter	Vernon Twp	92	139
DEBOURNE								
Joseph	32	m	w	HANO	San Francisco	7-Wd San Francisco	81	224
DEBOVAL								
Eugene	32	m	w	FRAN	San Francisco	2-Wd San Francisco	79	197
DEBOVICH								
C	29	m	w	AUST	Amador	Amador City P O	69	392
DEBOVITCH								
Peter	29	m	w	AUST	Amador	Amador City P O	69	392
DEBOW								
Samuel	58	m	w	VA	Nevada	Eureka Twp	75	135
DEBOYCE								
Wm P	62	m	w	MD	Napa	Napa	75	19
DEBRASSEL								
Manuel	20	m	w	PORT	Marin	Point Reyes Twp	74	22
DEBRAY								
J	25	m	w	FRAN	San Joaquin	Tulare Twp	86	258
DEBRE								
Jacob	39	m	w	AUSL	San Francisco	1-Wd San Francisco	79	93
Susan	33	f	w	AUSL	San Francisco	1-Wd San Francisco	79	93
DEBREDIER								
Abel	47	m	w	FRAN	Shasta	Horsetown P O	89	504
DEBRIES								
Wm	38	m	w	MD	San Joaquin	Elkhorn Twp	86	52
DEBRIGE								
Francois	60	m	w	FRAN	San Francisco	11-Wd San Francisc	84	583
DEBRIS								
Frank	40	m	w	ITAL	San Joaquin	1-Wd Stockton	86	123
Wm	44	m	w	BELG	San Francisco	7-Wd San Francisco	81	248
DEBROW								
Slayback	30	m	w	IREL	San Francisco	San Francisco P O	83	256
DEBSLEY								
Chas	34	m	w	NY	Alameda	Murray Twp	68	108
DEBUE								
Ernest	49	m	w	HAMB	Placer	Auburn P O	76	359
John D	60	m	w	CANA	El Dorado	White Oak Twp	72	144
DEBURCK								
Louis	55	m	w	BELG	San Francisco	San Francisco P O	80	339
DEBUS								
Jane	24	f	w	ENGL	San Francisco	8-Wd San Francisco	82	292
DEBUSTHE								
D	29	m	w	CANA	Nevada	Eureka Twp	75	138
DECAMP								
C	37	m	w	NJ	Sutter	Butte Twp	92	97

© 2001 by Heritage Quest. All rights reserved.

Series M593

Name	Age	S	R	B-PL	County	Locale	Roll	Pg
Charles	32	m	w	BELG	Sonoma	Sonoma Twp	91	432
DECAMPS								
Joseph	35	m	w	PORT	San Francisco	8-Wd San Francisco	82	295
DECARFANS								
John	30	m	w	CUBA	San Francisco	San Francisco P O	83	180
DECARLO								
Francis	46	m	w	SPAI	Solano	Green Valley Twp	90	41
DECARTER								
Fred	30	m	w	ENGL	San Francisco	7-Wd San Francisco	81	256
DECASTELLO								
Carlos	11	m	w	CUBA	Alameda	Hayward	68	76
DECASTRO								
Tomasa	60	f	w	MEXI	San Francisco	1-Wd San Francisco	79	20
DECATER								
Martin	39	m	w	NH	San Francisco	7-Wd San Francisco	81	207
DECENT								
Edward	62	m	w	SCOT	El Dorado	Placerville Twp	72	104
DECHANG								
Charles	35	m	w	PRUS	San Francisco	6-Wd San Francisco	81	155
DECHEMME								
Juste M	46	m	w	CANA	Yolo	Cache Crk Twp	93	453
DECHENDI								
Louis	40	m	w	ITAL	Santa Clara	2-Wd San Jose	88	316
DECHENE								
John	35	m	w	CANA	Nevada	Nevada Twp	75	309
DECHESNE								
H	48	m	w	CANA	San Francisco	San Francisco P O	83	135
DECHMAN								
James W	40	m	w	MA	Santa Barbara	Santa Barbara P O	87	464
DECILEYEE								
John C	30	m	w	PORT	San Luis Obispo	Salinas Twp	87	293
DECIMA								
Lolita	11	f	w	CA	Santa Clara	2-Wd San Jose	88	338
DECIOUS								
J	24	m	w	OH	Lassen	Janesville Twp	73	431
Mary	15	f	w	IA	Lassen	Milford Twp	73	438
DECK								
Ah	27	m	c	CHIN	Nevada	Nevada Twp	75	312
Alexander	34	m	w	MO	Sutter	Nicolaus Twp	92	111
Eli	36	m	w	OH	Sutter	Vernon Twp	92	133
John	28	m	w	HANO	Alameda	Eden Twp	68	86
Louisa	17	f	w	WURT	San Francisco	San Francisco P O	80	408
Virginia	19	f	w	CA	San Francisco	San Francisco P O	83	48
Yung	30	m	c	CHIN	San Francisco	8-Wd San Francisco	82	384
DECKER								
Barbara	46	f	w	BAVA	San Francisco	11-Wd San Francisc	84	495
Bella	30	f	w	IN	San Francisco	11-Wd San Francisc	84	497
Chas	34	m	w	OH	Butte	Chico Twp	70	21
Chas H	37	m	w	ME	Santa Barbara	San Buenaventura P	87	429
Christian	43	m	w	PRUS	San Francisco	11-Wd San Francisc	84	457
Delia	12	f	w	NY	San Francisco	San Francisco P O	85	798
Esther	36	f	w	CANA	Sacramento	Mississippi Twp	77	163
F G	43	m	w	NY	Sierra	Sears Twp	89	558
Frank	45	m	w	HOLL	Mariposa	Mariposa P O	74	105
Fredk	2	m	w	CA	San Francisco	San Francisco P O	85	799
George	34	m	w	CANA	Siskiyou	Butte Twp	89	586
Harry	50	m	w	NY	San Francisco	11-Wd San Francisc	84	554
Henry	55	m	w	HANO	San Francisco	7-Wd San Francisco	81	250
Isaac	41	m	w	OH	Solano	Vacaville Twp	90	129
J	42	m	w	OH	Sierra	Lincoln Twp	89	550
J M	36	m	w	OH	Sutter	Butte Twp	92	93
Jacob	49	m	w	BAVA	San Francisco	San Francisco P O	85	870
Jas	49	m	w	PA	Tehama	Antelope Twp	92	156
Jas M	35	m	w	IN	Tehama	Toomes & Grant	92	169
John	31	m	w	BREM	San Francisco	11-Wd San Francisc	84	423
John	27	m	w	ENGL	Marin	San Rafael Twp	74	26
John H	22	m	w	PRUS	San Francisco	6-Wd San Francisco	81	149
Joseph	43	m	w	GERM	Butte	Oroville Twp	70	139
Josephah	55	m	w	IN	Colusa	Grand Island Twp	71	304
Louis	32	m	w	BAVA	San Francisco	San Francisco P O	80	535
Louisa	16	f	w	KY	San Francisco	11-Wd San Francisc	84	495
M	30	m	w	KY	San Joaquin	Douglas Twp	86	47
Richard	50	m	w	PRUS	San Francisco	6-Wd San Francisco	81	149
Rosa	4	f	w	CA	San Francisco	San Francisco P O	85	798
Sarah	42	f	w	ENGL	Sacramento	2-Wd Sacramento	77	209
Solomon	44	m	w	OH	Solano	Vacaville Twp	90	130
Thomas	42	m	w	PA	Sutter	Sutter Twp	92	127
Thos	28	m	w	PA	Butte	Oregon Twp	70	129
Wm	22	m	w	IL	San Francisco	8-Wd San Francisco	82	358
Wm W	41	m	w	OH	Mariposa	Maxwell Crk P O	74	140
DECKES								
Holles	12	m	w	GERM	Sacramento	Sutter Twp	77	388
DECKLER								
Frank	25	m	w	FRAN	Stanislaus	Empire Twp	92	52
DECLEMENTA								
Peter	28	m	w	ITAL	Mariposa	Mariposa P O	74	111
DECLERG								
H A	37	m	w	FRAN	San Francisco	8-Wd San Francisco	82	373
DECLOUT								
Julia	10	f	w	HI	Alameda	Oakland	68	197
DECO								
Antoine	17	m	w	PORT	Santa Cruz	Santa Cruz	89	410
DECOCK								
Fredk A	46	m	w	SHOL	San Francisco	San Francisco P O	83	74
DECOE								
Florence	11	f	w	NY	Marin	San Rafael	74	57
DECON								
William	35	m	w	OH	El Dorado	Placerville Twp	72	96
DECOR								
Oliver	37	m	w	FRAN	San Mateo	San Mateo P O	87	349
DECORDA								
Mary	19	f	w	NY	San Francisco	8-Wd San Francisco	82	385
Thomas	19	m	w	NY	Santa Clara	Fremont Twp	88	56
DECOSH								
Antoine	46	m	w	FRAN	Shasta	Shasta P O	89	455
DECOSTA								
Antonio	40	m	w	AZOR	Placer	Newcastle Twp	76	473
Frank	38	m	w	PORT	Sacramento	Franklin Twp	77	106
John W	60	m	w	ENGL	San Francisco	San Francisco P O	85	736
Manuel E	38	m	w	PORT	Sacramento	Franklin Twp	77	106
Mary	40	f	w	ENGL	Marin	Sausalito Twp	74	66
N	32	m	w	ENGL	San Joaquin	2-Wd Stockton	86	203
DECOSTO								
David	35	m	w	PORT	San Luis Obispo	Salinas Twp	87	293
DECOSTY								
Jane	44	f	w	IREL	San Francisco	11-Wd San Francisc	84	475
DECOTE								
Frank	28	m	w	FRAN	San Francisco	2-Wd San Francisco	79	189
DECOTO								
Adolpha	43	m	w	CANA	Alameda	Washington Twp	68	300
Ezra	35	m	w	CANA	Alameda	Washington Twp	68	300
DECOURCI								
John	58	m	w	IREL	Solano	Benicia	90	10
DECOURCY								
Frank	29	m	w	ENGL	Yolo	Cache Crk Twp	93	434
DECOURSIE								
Jaques	34	m	w	IREL	San Francisco	11-Wd San Francisc	84	548
DECRAY								
Augustus	39	m	w	PRUS	Yuba	Slate Range Bar Tw	93	675
DECRESCONER								
Hans	29	m	w	DENM	San Francisco	1-Wd San Francisco	79	122
DECROE								
Isaac	35	m	w	OH	San Bernardino	San Bernardino Twp	78	448
DECROISE								
Miguel	31	m	w	MEXI	San Bernardino	Chino Twp	78	412
DECROWNA								
Edmon G	28	m	w	SWIT	San Francisco	8-Wd San Francisco	82	327
DECUDIES								
Stephen	50	m	w	NY	Stanislaus	Empire Twp	92	60
DECUNHA								
Manuel	36	m	w	AZOR	Placer	Newcastle Twp	76	473
DEDANCOURT								
Mendon	27	f	w	FRAN	San Francisco	3-Wd San Francisco	79	321
DEDASOWER								
C	36	f	b	TN	Alameda	Oakland	68	132
DEDE								
Geo W	14	m	w	CA	San Joaquin	2-Wd Stockton	86	162
DEDEN								
Mary	35	f	w	FRAN	Yuba	Marysville	93	613
DEDENBACK								
Jas	45	m	w	BAVA	San Francisco	8-Wd San Francisco	82	359
DEDERICH								
Edington	30	m	w	MD	San Francisco	8-Wd San Francisco	82	405
DEDERKY								
Henry	36	m	w	PRUS	San Francisco	5-Wd San Francisco	81	8
DEDGARD								
Frank	10	m	w	CA	Marin	San Rafael Twp	74	27
DEDIA								
Pattie	36	f	w	FRAN	Siskiyou	Yreka Twp	89	669
DEDICAN								
Charles	35	m	w	FRAN	San Francisco	San Francisco P O	80	462
DEDIER								
Emiele	50	m	w	FRAN	Amador	Sutter Crk P O	69	413
Jean	31	m	w	FRAN	San Francisco	San Francisco P O	80	334
DEDIOS								
Francis	38	m	w	SPAI	Calaveras	San Andreas P O	70	160
DEDLEY								
George S	36	m	w	NY	Solano	Silveyville Twp	90	86
DEDMAN								
Chas	40	m	w	DENM	Marin	San Rafael Twp	74	36
John Washington	33	m	w	MO	Plumas	Quartz Twp	77	38
DEDMIN								
Jas A	36	m	w	SC	Placer	Bath P O	76	429
DEDOT								
Marie	21	f	w	FRAN	San Francisco	6-Wd San Francisco	81	72
DEDOW								
Stephen W	45	m	w	NY	Los Angeles	Los Angeles Twp	73	491
DEDRICK								
Kate	24	f	w	PA	San Francisco	6-Wd San Francisco	81	112
Richard	29	m	w	NY	Santa Clara	1-Wd San Jose	88	226
DEDRICKSON								
Charles	43	m	w	SHOL	San Francisco	6-Wd San Francisco	81	147
DEDRO								
Derius	30	m	w	MEXI	Stanislaus	Emory Twp	92	25
Rapheal	70	m	w	MEXI	Tulare	Tule Rvr Twp	92	258
DEE								
A S	19	f	w	IREL	San Francisco	San Francisco P O	85	863
Ah	8	m	c	CHIN	San Francisco	San Francisco P O	80	443
Ah	46	m	c	CHIN	San Francisco	San Francisco P O	80	503
Ah	46	m	c	CHIN	San Francisco	San Francisco P O	80	506
Ah	46	m	c	CHIN	Placer	Dutch Flat P O	76	407
Ah	45	m	c	CHIN	San Francisco	San Francisco P O	80	442
Ah	41	m	c	CHIN	San Francisco	San Francisco P O	80	514

© 2001 by Heritage Quest. All rights reserved.

Name	Age	S	R	B-PL	County	Locale	Series M593 Roll	Pg
Ah	37	m	c	CHIN	San Francisco	San Francisco P O	80	447
Ah	37	m	c	CHIN	San Francisco	San Francisco P O	80	512
Ah	36	m	c	CHIN	San Francisco	San Francisco P O	80	511
Ah	34	m	c	CHIN	San Francisco	San Francisco P O	80	441
Ah	34	m	c	CHIN	San Francisco	San Francisco P O	80	443
Ah	3	f	c	CA	San Francisco	San Francisco P O	80	438
Ah	29	m	c	CHIN	San Francisco	San Francisco P O	80	436
Ah	28	m	c	CHIN	San Francisco	San Francisco P O	80	503
Ah	26	m	c	CHIN	Alameda	Murray Twp	68	120
Ah	26	m	c	CHIN	San Francisco	San Francisco P O	80	516
Ah	26	f	c	CHIN	San Francisco	San Francisco P O	80	506
Ah	24	m	c	CHIN	Santa Barbara	Las Cruces P O	87	504
Ah	22	m	c	CHIN	San Francisco	San Francisco P O	80	511
Ah	19	f	c	CHIN	San Francisco	San Francisco P O	80	505
Ah	19	m	c	CHIN	Santa Clara	1-Wd San Jose	88	273
Ah	17	f	c	CHIN	San Francisco	San Francisco P O	80	432
Alexander	12	m	w	PA	Contra Costa	Martinez P O	71	426
Daniel	36	m	w	OH	Solano	Tremont Twp	90	29
Daniel J	3	m	w	CA	Calaveras	San Andreas P O	70	181
George	27	m	w	ENGL	Sonoma	Salt Point	91	389
Isabella	28	f	w	CANA	San Francisco	7-Wd San Francisco	81	244
John	36	m	w	IREL	Mariposa	Mariposa P O	74	131
Laurence	50	m	w	IREL	Monterey	Castroville Twp	74	339
Margaret	22	f	m	IREL	Yolo	Putah Twp	93	519
Mary	27	f	w	IREL	San Francisco	2-Wd San Francisco	79	142
W	26	m	w	IREL	Lake	Knoxville Mines	73	405
DEEBLE								
Daniel	32	m	w	ENGL	Nevada	Grass Valley Twp	75	203
John	40	m	w	ENGL	Nevada	Grass Valley Twp	75	184
Sampson	36	m	w	ENGL	Nevada	Grass Valley Twp	75	165
Sampson	33	m	w	ENGL	Calaveras	Copperopolis P O	70	262
Thomas	36	m	w	ENGL	Calaveras	Copperopolis P O	70	262
DEEDE								
Alexander	40	m	w	HANO	San Francisco	2-Wd San Francisco	79	228
DEEDLAR								
Charles	34	m	w	SWED	San Francisco	8-Wd San Francisco	82	427
DEEDON								
Juana	60	f	w	CA	Los Angeles	Los Angeles Twp	73	478
DEEDRICH								
Conrad	29	m	w	PRUS	San Francisco	11-Wd San Francisc	84	530
DEEDS								
George	40	m	w	PA	Nevada	Rough & Ready Twp	75	336
John	38	m	w	PA	Nevada	Rough & Ready Twp	75	325
Wesley B	37	m	w	TN	Sonoma	Santa Rosa	91	406
DEEF								
John	57	m	w	PRUS	Solano	Tremont Twp	90	34
DEEFER								
Nathan	42	m	w	GA	Tuolumne	Chinese Camp P O	93	378
DEEFOUR								
Mary	20	f	w	NY	Placer	Dutch Flat P O	76	404
DEEGAN								
Jeremiah	42	m	w	IREL	Calaveras	Copperopolis P O	70	245
Peter	35	m	w	IREL	San Francisco	1-Wd San Francisco	79	62
DEEHER								
Charles	25	m	w	HANO	Sonoma	Petaluma Twp	91	357
DEEK								
Ah	29	m	c	CHIN	San Francisco	6-Wd San Francisco	81	69
DEEKER								
John	38	m	w	ME	Tuolumne	Columbia P O	93	339
Milton	37	m	w	HAMB	San Francisco	6-Wd San Francisco	81	111
DEELELMAFF								
Jacob	27	m	w	PRUS	San Francisco	5-Wd San Francisco	81	9
DEELMAN								
Jacob	27	m	w	MO	Butte	Chico Twp	70	26
DEELY								
Wm	14	m	w	CA	Sacramento	Cosumnes Twp	77	88
DEEMER								
John	30	m	w	PRUS	Contra Costa	Martinez P O	71	443
DEEN								
Ah	40	m	c	CHIN	San Francisco	6-Wd San Francisco	81	61
Ah	15	m	c	CHIN	San Francisco	6-Wd San Francisco	81	60
E W	21	m	w	CANA	Humboldt	Mattole Twp	72	285
Ebenezer	60	m	w	NY	Humboldt	South Fork Twp	72	301
George	45	m	w	NY	Alameda	Oakland	68	185
Isaac	39	m	w	IN	San Luis Obispo	Santa Rosa Twp	87	318
James	56	m	w	NY	San Francisco	San Francisco P O	80	479
James S	56	m	w	NY	San Francisco	6-Wd San Francisco	81	37
Thos	34	m	w	IREL	Sierra	Table Rock Twp	89	575
DEENY								
Julia	21	f	w	IREL	San Francisco	San Francisco P O	83	91
Patrick	39	m	w	IREL	San Mateo	Schoolhouse Statio	87	335
William	30	m	w	IREL	San Francisco	San Francisco P O	83	142
DEEP								
Ah	23	m	c	CHIN	Colusa	Spring Valley Twp	71	339
DEER								
Lee	24	m	c	CHIN	San Francisco	6-Wd San Francisco	81	75
Mary	19	f	w	NY	San Francisco	2-Wd San Francisco	79	246
DEERBON								
John	53	m	w	NH	Alameda	Oakland	68	246
DEERE								
Henry	16	m	w	HANO	San Francisco	2-Wd San Francisco	79	229
DEERING								
Alex	38	m	w	ME	Mariposa	Mariposa P O	74	117
Ambrose	47	m	w	VA	Stanislaus	Empire Twp	92	32
Chas J	39	m	w	ME	San Francisco	San Francisco P O	83	203
Fred C	22	m	w	MO	Napa	Napa	75	17
Henry	40	m	w	ME	Sacramento	1-Wd Sacramento	77	184
James	51	m	w	IREL	Humboldt	Bucksport Twp	72	245
James H	47	m	w	ME	San Francisco	6-Wd San Francisco	81	113
John	38	m	w	IREL	Solano	Suisun Twp	90	102
Mary	38	f	w	IREL	San Francisco	11-Wd San Francisc	84	440
Robert	55	m	w	ME	Alameda	Brooklyn	68	30
Thomas	38	m	w	IREL	San Francisco	San Francisco P O	83	339
William	22	m	w	KY	Los Angeles	Los Nietos Twp	73	577
DEERY								
Catherine	22	f	w	IREL	San Francisco	6-Wd San Francisco	81	143
Ellen	24	f	w	IREL	Napa	Napa Twp	75	46
Eugene	25	m	w	IREL	San Francisco	San Francisco P O	85	753
Francis	38	m	w	IREL	San Francisco	San Francisco P O	83	189
James	40	m	w	IREL	San Francisco	San Francisco P O	83	262
John N	35	m	w	ME	San Francisco	San Francisco P O	83	216
Thomas	35	m	w	IREL	San Francisco	San Francisco P O	83	37
DEES								
Daniel R	63	m	w	SC	Calaveras	Copperopolis P O	70	260
J	50	f	w	SC	Sierra	Lincoln Twp	89	547
Lewis	32	m	w	WURT	San Francisco	San Francisco P O	83	86
Louis	36	m	w	HOLL	San Francisco	San Francisco P O	80	382
William R	39	m	w	GA	Calaveras	Copperopolis P O	70	263
DEESE								
Isabel	36	f	w	CHIL	Yuba	Marysville	93	614
DEETH								
Edward	21	m	w	IREL	Solano	Silveyville Twp	90	72
Henry	32	m	w	IREL	Solano	Tremont Twp	90	31
Henry	25	m	w	MO	Solano	Silveyville Twp	90	73
Jacob	55	m	w	PA	San Francisco	11-Wd San Francisc	84	606
William	37	m	w	OH	Solano	Rio Vista Twp	90	64
DEETKEN								
Charles	36	m	w	BADE	San Francisco	San Francisco P O	83	217
DEETKIN								
A H	40	m	w	HANO	Nevada	Washington Twp	75	344
Gustavus F	34	m	w	BADE	Nevada	Grass Valley Twp	75	189
Manuel	36	m	w	IREL	Nevada	Meadow Lake Twp	75	267
DEETZ								
Antone	38	m	w	SWIT	Amador	Volcano P O	69	381
DEFAUR								
Frank	36	m	w	MO	Butte	Kimshew Tpw	70	79
DEFELIZ								
Vicente	64	m	w	ITAL	Santa Barbara	Santa Barbara P O	87	464
DEFERADA								
Jacob	40	m	w	ITAL	Calaveras	Copperopolis P O	70	247
DEFERARI								
John	27	m	w	ITAL	San Francisco	San Francisco P O	80	466
DEFERE								
Francis	21	m	w	IREL	Marin	San Rafael	74	57
DEFERIMIO								
Giovanni	31	m	w	SWIT	San Francisco	1-Wd San Francisco	79	105
DEFERIONIO								
Joseph	42	m	w	SWIT	San Francisco	1-Wd San Francisco	79	105
DEFFARARO								
Lewis	22	m	w	ITAL	San Francisco	2-Wd San Francisco	79	164
DEFFEBACH								
Thos B	43	m	w	PA	Marin	Sausalito Twp	74	71
DEFFENBECKER								
Henry	35	m	w	PA	San Bernardino	San Bernardino Twp	78	453
DEFFENER								
George	42	m	w	BAVA	San Luis Obispo	San Luis Obispo Tw	87	314
DEFFIN								
John	35	m	w	NY	Contra Costa	Martinez P O	71	411
DEFFNER								
George	61	m	w	ENGL	San Francisco	San Francisco P O	83	200
DEFFOAT								
Charles	65	m	w	FRAN	Yuba	Long Bar Twp	93	561
DEFIENNES								
Hy	30	m	w	BELG	San Francisco	San Francisco P O	83	128
DEFIEZ								
George	43	m	w	MA	San Francisco	San Francisco P O	83	125
DEFLAYKE								
John G	20	m	w	ENGL	San Francisco	San Francisco P O	83	201
DEFLY								
Jacob	32	m	w	ENGL	Yuba	Marysville	93	584
DEFOE								
Franklin	24	m	w	NY	Colusa	Grand Island Twp	71	306
Joseph	48	m	w	FRAN	Placer	Auburn P O	76	380
William	30	m	w	FRAN	Calaveras	San Andreas P O	70	205
DEFORD								
J L	35	m	w	MO	Merced	Snelling P O	74	257
DEFOREST								
C	49	m	w	NY	Lassen	Susanville Twp	73	440
Charles L	44	m	w	VT	Placer	Auburn P O	76	361
Louis	28	m	w	NY	Butte	Kimshew Tpw	70	78
W F	30	m	w	NY	San Francisco	7-Wd San Francisco	81	182
DEFORSA								
John	39	m	w	BELG	Calaveras	San Andreas P O	70	214
DEFOSSEY								
Henry	64	m	w	FRAN	San Francisco	San Francisco P O	80	409
DEFRAGA								
Antone	21	m	w	SCOT	Alameda	San Leandro	68	95
Joseph	41	m	w	PORT	Alameda	Eden Twp	68	89
DEFRATES								
John	20	m	w	PORT	Marin	San Rafael Twp	74	59
Joseph	22	m	w	PORT	Marin	San Rafael Twp	74	25
DEFREMERY								
Wm	37	m	w	HOLL	Alameda	Oakland	68	169

© 2001 by Heritage Quest. All rights reserved.

California 1870 Census

Name	Age	S	R	B-PL	County	Locale	Series M593 Roll	Pg
DEFRESE								
Jean	25	m	w	FRAN	Mendocino	Albion & Big Rvr T	74	167
DEFRIES								
Augustus	15	m	w	CA	Marin	Novato Twp	74	11
John	16	m	w	CA	Marin	Tomales Twp	74	76
DEFRIESE								
Gertrude	40	f	w	MEXI	San Francisco	1-Wd San Francisco	79	48
Josh	31	m	w	IN	San Francisco	1-Wd San Francisco	79	53
DEFROY								
Joseph	22	m	w	CT	San Francisco	6-Wd San Francisco	81	90
DEFUSA								
Henri	50	m	w	FRAN	Calaveras	San Andreas P O	70	205
DEGAGNOR								
Godfrey	29	m	w	CANA	Yolo	Cache Crk Twp	93	425
DEGALAVI								
Gugeppi	29	m	w	ITAL	Santa Clara	San Jose Twp	88	221
DEGAN								
Franklin	42	m	w	SWIT	Placer	Bath P O	76	437
Pat	35	m	w	IREL	Alameda	Murray Twp	68	124
Philip	44	m	w	HANO	San Francisco	11-Wd San Francisc	84	617
DEGANT								
Joseph	51	m	w	PA	Sacramento	2-Wd Sacramento	77	248
DEGARA								
Auguipito	38	m	w	MEXI	San Luis Obispo	Salinas Twp	87	291
DEGARMO								
John	42	m	w	NY	Siskiyou	Surprise Valley Tw	89	642
DEGARNETT								
B	36	m	w	PA	Lake	Knoxville Mines	73	404
DEGAY								
Henry	32	m	w	BADE	Solano	Silveyville Twp	90	92
DEGEAR								
Geo W	40	m	w	NY	San Francisco	San Francisco P O	83	10
DEGEIN								
Marie	40	f	w	FRAN	Santa Clara	Fremont Twp	88	52
DEGELMAN								
John	36	m	w	BAVA	El Dorado	Placerville	72	113
DEGENNE								
Pedro	60	m	w	FRAN	Santa Barbara	Santa Barbara P O	87	476
DEGERE								
Spotswood	58	m	b	VA	Yuba	Linda Twp	93	554
DEGERICKS								
T	24	m	w	BREM	Solano	Vallejo	90	185
DEGGERT								
Albert	35	m	w	NY	San Francisco	1-Wd San Francisco	79	103
DEGLE								
John	29	m	w	FRAN	San Francisco	San Francisco P O	80	461
DEGMAN								
Thomas	38	m	w	ENGL	Kern	Havilah P O	73	339
DEGMEN								
Michael	23	m	w	IREL	San Francisco	7-Wd San Francisco	81	264
DEGNAN								
Susan	18	f	w	ME	Humboldt	Table Bluff Twp	72	305
DEGNEY								
Danl	25	m	w	SAXO	Butte	Kimshew Tpw	70	82
DEGO								
Lane	35	m	w	ENGL	Alameda	Murray Twp	68	104
DEGOLIA								
Darwin	52	m	w	NY	El Dorado	Placerville	72	107
DEGONT								
Maria	40	f	w	FRAN	Marin	San Rafael	74	51
DEGRATH								
W H	18	m	w	NY	San Francisco	San Francisco P O	85	821
DEGRAY								
Edwin	35	m	w	OH	Mendocino	Round Valley Twp	74	217
Frances	31	f	w	FRAN	San Francisco	6-Wd San Francisco	81	87
Francis	49	m	w	UNKN	San Joaquin	2-Wd Stockton	86	168
DEGREGARIL								
L	29	m	w	ITAL	Alameda	Oakland	68	212
DEGRODELLO								
Maria	40	f	w	CA	Los Angeles	Los Nietos Twp	73	585
DEGROFF								
Chas	33	m	w	NY	Solano	Vallejo	90	165
DEGROOT								
Edward	35	m	w	NY	Santa Clara	Fremont Twp	88	57
Eliza	45	f	w	NY	San Francisco	San Francisco P O	85	738
Henry	47	m	w	NY	San Francisco	11-Wd San Francisc	84	581
John	52	m	w	NY	Amador	Jackson P O	69	341
William	38	m	w	NY	Marin	San Rafael Twp	74	31
DEGROSS								
Daniel	51	m	w	MD	Yolo	Merritt Twp	93	503
DEGROTE								
David	30	m	w	IREL	San Francisco	7-Wd San Francisco	81	204
DEGRUTE								
Ellen	25	f	w	HOLL	San Francisco	San Francisco P O	85	768
DEGUERRE								
Norman	43	m	w	OH	Santa Clara	Gilroy Twp	88	94
DEGUFF								
Charles	33	m	w	NY	Yolo	Grafton Twp	93	498
DEGUIRE								
Lewis	40	m	w	MO	Butte	Chico Twp	70	17
Mary J	13	f	i	CA	Butte	Wyandotte Twp	70	141
DEGURMO								
Ezra	35	m	w	VA	Amador	Volcano P O	69	387
DEHAN								
Mary	29	f	w	IREL	San Francisco	11-Wd San Francisc	84	483
DEHARRO								
Alonzo	25	m	w	CA	Alameda	Eden Twp	68	64
DEHART								
Edward P	34	m	w	NJ	San Francisco	San Francisco P O	83	147
Saml	44	m	b	NC	Yuba	Rose Bar Twp	93	662
Samuel	30	m	b	NY	Nevada	Eureka Twp	75	128
DEHAVEN								
---	16	m	w	CA	Humboldt	Pacific Twp	72	289
Abrahm	26	m	w	MO	Humboldt	Eel Rvr Twp	72	252
David	38	m	w	KY	Tehama	Paskenta Twp	92	166
Geo	34	m	w	IN	Tehama	Bell Mills Twp	92	159
Henry	32	m	w	MD	Nevada	Meadow Lake Twp	75	255
T F	29	f	w	IL	Mendocino	Calpella Twp	74	186
Wm	69	m	w	KY	Tehama	Paskenta Twp	92	165
Wm N	50	m	w	PA	Butte	Chico Twp	70	19
DEHENRY								
Paul	56	m	w	FRAN	Santa Clara	2-Wd San Jose	88	297
DEHOFF								
Henry	41	m	w	OH	Placer	Lincoln P O	76	489
DEHON								
Frank	45	m	w	NY	San Francisco	5-Wd San Francisco	81	14
DEHONDT								
Francois	64	m	w	BELG	Sacramento	2-Wd Sacramento	77	249
DEHORN								
John	37	m	w	HOLL	San Francisco	1-Wd San Francisco	79	2
DEHOSE								
John	35	m	w	NY	Yolo	Grafton Twp	93	494
DEHOUSE								
Wm W	38	m	w	LA	Santa Clara	Gilroy Twp	88	80
DEI								
Ah	36	m	c	CHIN	San Francisco	San Francisco P O	80	496
DEIAS								
William	20	m	w	HANO	San Francisco	7-Wd San Francisco	81	224
DEIBACK								
Gustave	26	m	w	GERM	San Francisco	8-Wd San Francisco	82	375
DEIBLE								
Thos	25	m	w	ENGL	Fresno	Millerton P O	72	165
DEICE								
Edmond	27	m	w	BADE	San Francisco	San Francisco P O	85	762
DEICHERT								
Jos	62	m	w	BAVA	Sutter	Butte Twp	92	89
DEICHL								
Thomas R	39	m	w	PA	Plumas	Quartz Twp	77	40
DEICHMANN								
Peter	42	m	w	PRUS	San Francisco	San Francisco P O	83	8
DEICK								
Manuel	35	m	w	HI	Yolo	Merritt Twp	93	505
DEIDELL								
F H	41	m	w	PRUS	Sierra	Forest	89	536
DEIDERHEIMER								
J	41	m	w	PRUS	Alameda	Alameda	68	5
DEIDERHEMER								
Peter	35	m	w	PRUS	San Francisco	5-Wd San Francisco	81	31
DEIDLE								
John	39	m	w	GERM	Yuba	Linda Twp	93	557
DEIDRICH								
Louise	32	f	w	PRUS	San Joaquin	2-Wd Stockton	86	191
DEIFERNDORFF								
Cornelius	56	m	w	NY	Colusa	Grand Island Twp	71	303
DEIFFENDORFF								
W	27	m	w	CANA	Sutter	Sutter Twp	92	122
DEIGARD								
Peter	50	m	w	ENGL	Klamath	Klamath Twp	73	370
DEIGO								
Juan	30	m	w	CA	Santa Clara	Gilroy Twp	88	93
Lobatto	80	m	w	MEXI	San Bernardino	San Bernardino Twp	78	443
DEIHI								
John	30	m	w	BADE	San Francisco	2-Wd San Francisco	79	206
DEIHL								
Jos	41	m	w	BADE	Shasta	Horsetown P O	89	504
DEIN								
Louis	40	m	w	BAVA	Los Angeles	Santa Ana Twp	73	615
DEINGAR								
Lizzie	14	f	w	KY	Solano	Benicia	90	16
DEIRS								
John	56	m	w	HAMB	San Francisco	1-Wd San Francisco	79	96
DEIS								
Edward	40	m	w	MEXI	Merced	Snelling P O	74	251
DEISER								
Philip	23	m	w	BAVA	San Francisco	San Francisco P O	85	837
DEISSINGER								
Chas	40	m	w	PRUS	San Francisco	5-Wd San Francisco	81	8
DEITCHMAN								
John	42	m	w	GERM	Tuolumne	Columbia P O	93	345
Sand	39	m	w	GERM	Tuolumne	Columbia P O	93	345
DEITSLER								
Magdaline	7	f	w	CA	Sierra	Gibson Twp	89	540
DEITZ								
Jacob	44	m	w	OH	Siskiyou	Butte Twp	89	584
Louis	40	m	w	BAVA	Yolo	Cache Crk Twp	93	428
DEITZLER								
Michael	39	m	w	PRUS	Butte	Hamilton Twp	70	62
DEITZMAN								
Ellen	10	f	w	CA	Santa Clara	Santa Clara Twp	88	170
Francis	6	m	w	CA	Santa Clara	Santa Clara Twp	88	170
John	8	m	w	CA	Santa Clara	Santa Clara Twp	88	170
Levy J	12	f	w	CA	Santa Clara	Santa Clara Twp	88	170
DEJARNETT								
Burriss	24	m	w	KY	Colusa	Colusa	71	295

© 2001 by Heritage Quest. All rights reserved.

Name	Age	S	R	B-PL	County	Locale	Series M593 Roll	Pg
William H	51	m	w	KY	Colusa	Colusa	71	295
DEJOHN								
John	35	m	w	CANA	Contra Costa	San Pablo Twp	71	359
Perrin	60	m	w	FRAN	El Dorado	Georgetown Twp	72	48
DEJUNE								
Eugene	19	m	w	FRAN	Santa Clara	1-Wd San Jose	88	258
DEKALB								
B	40	m	w	ME	Alameda	Oakland	68	160
DEKAY								
Seeley	45	m	w	NJ	Sacramento	Center Twp	77	83
DEKIND								
Solomon	37	m	w	POLA	Sacramento	1-Wd Sacramento	77	175
DEKOY								
Charles	45	m	w	FRAN	San Francisco	6-Wd San Francisco	81	90
DEKRUSE								
Rudolph	44	m	w	HANO	Placer	Bath P O	76	451
DEKUFFOR								
Agnes	40	f	w	FRAN	San Francisco	San Francisco P O	83	181
DEL								
Ah	37	m	c	CHIN	Kern	Kernville P O	73	368
DELA								
Gueria Jose A	43	m	w	CA	San Luis Obispo	San Luis Obispo Tw	87	308
Tom Antonio	23	m	w	MEXI	San Francisco	San Francisco P O	83	75
Torre Jose	41	m	w	MEXI	San Francisco	San Francisco P O	80	470
DELABORA								
Alexander	52	m	w	FRAN	Yolo	Merritt Twp	93	503
DELACRUZ								
Edward	17	m	w	CA	Mariposa	Mariposa P O	74	96
Victor	48	m	b	PHIL	Mariposa	Mariposa P O	74	96
DELACUESTA								
Ramon	44	m	w	SPAI	Santa Barbara	Las Cruces P O	87	515
DELACY								
Chas	34	m	w	LA	San Joaquin	Union Twp	86	265
Chas	26	m	w	DENM	San Francisco	8-Wd San Francisco	82	345
Giuseppi	16	m	w	SWIT	Marin	Tomales Twp	74	76
Hugh	23	m	w	LA	Santa Clara	2-Wd San Jose	88	327
Stephen D	27	m	w	LA	Santa Clara	2-Wd San Jose	88	333
DELADESAGUNA								
Antonio	49	m	w	FRAN	San Francisco	2-Wd San Francisco	79	252
DELAFARE								
Blanche	18	f	w	IL	San Francisco	8-Wd San Francisco	82	384
DELAFIELD								
Alexr	39	m	w	NY	San Francisco	5-Wd San Francisco	81	21
Alfred	35	m	w	NY	San Francisco	5-Wd San Francisco	81	30
DELAFONTAIN								
Joseph	37	m	w	BELG	San Francisco	11-Wd San Francisc	84	454
Victor	31	m	w	BELG	San Francisco	San Francisco P O	83	246
DELAFONTAINE								
Chs	47	m	w	BELG	San Francisco	2-Wd San Francisco	79	181
DELAGUERA								
Charles	18	m	w	CA	Los Angeles	Los Angeles	73	570
Jose K	34	m	w	CA	San Luis Obispo	San Luis Obispo Tw	87	309
DELAGUERRA								
Antonio M	45	m	w	CA	Santa Barbara	Santa Barbara P O	87	456
Francisco	52	m	w	CA	Santa Barbara	Santa Barbara P O	87	457
Jose A	65	m	w	CA	Santa Barbara	Santa Maria P O	87	514
Pablo	50	m	w	CA	Santa Barbara	Santa Barbara P O	87	456
Santiago	20	m	w	CA	Santa Barbara	San Buenaventura P	87	427
Wm	32	m	w	CA	Santa Barbara	Santa Maria P O	87	514
DELAGUIRRA								
Miguel	46	m	w	CA	Santa Barbara	Santa Barbara P O	87	457
DELAHANNTY								
Ellen	29	f	w	IREL	Sierra	Gibson Twp	89	538
Thos	38	m	w	IREL	Sierra	Gibson Twp	89	538
DELAHANTE								
Henry	43	m	w	LA	Shasta	Horsetown P O	89	504
DELAHANTY								
Annie	17	f	w	NY	San Francisco	San Francisco P O	83	22
Edward	40	m	w	IREL	Solano	Denverton Twp	90	26
James	48	m	w	IREL	Sonoma	Bodega Twp	91	255
John	30	m	w	CANA	San Luis Obispo	Arroyo Grande Twp	87	279
M	38	m	w	IREL	Sonoma	Santa Rosa	91	414
Micheal	46	m	w	IREL	San Francisco	7-Wd San Francisco	81	177
DELAHENTY								
Richard	32	m	w	CANA	San Francisco	7-Wd San Francisco	81	268
DELAHEY								
James	35	m	w	MD	San Francisco	San Francisco P O	83	191
DELAHORTA								
Patrick	48	m	w	IREL	Sonoma	Petaluma Twp	91	347
DELAHOYDE								
Thomas	42	m	w	IREL	Del Norte	Smith Rvr Twp	71	479
DELAI								
J L	62	m	w	CANA	Tuolumne	Columbia P O	93	357
DELAITI								
Victor	21	m	w	SWIT	Santa Clara	Santa Clara Twp	88	176
DELALA								
Francis	8	f	w	CA	El Dorado	Greenwood Twp	72	53
DELALAND								
Quistser	49	m	w	FRAN	Nevada	Bridgeport Twp	75	117
DELAMATER								
Mary A	42	f	w	IREL	San Francisco	8-Wd San Francisco	82	435
DELAMATES								
Guysbert B V	43	m	w	NY	Santa Cruz	Santa Cruz	89	418
DELAMER								
Rose	55	f	w	IREL	San Francisco	San Francisco P O	83	145
DELAMETER								
John	45	m	w	NY	Solano	Green Valley Twp	90	37

Name	Age	S	R	B-PL	County	Locale	Series M593 Roll	Pg
Theodore C	37	m	w	NY	San Francisco	San Francisco P O	85	755
DELAMONTAGUE								
John	44	m	w	NY	San Francisco	6-Wd San Francisco	81	95
DELAMONTANYA								
James	50	m	w	NY	San Francisco	San Francisco P O	80	396
M	41	m	w	NY	San Francisco	1-Wd San Francisco	79	35
DELAMOT								
Frank	27	m	w	MA	San Francisco	San Francisco P O	80	337
DELANA								
Anna G	28	f	w	MO	Sonoma	Petaluma Twp	91	341
DELANCE								
James	32	m	w	IREL	Alameda	Oakland	68	135
DELANCEY								
Julia	21	f	w	IREL	Napa	Napa	75	53
DELANCIE								
Richard	31	m	w	ENGL	Butte	Wyandotte Twp	70	148
DELANCY								
Gertrude	16	f	w	CA	San Francisco	8-Wd San Francisco	82	336
James	36	m	w	IREL	El Dorado	White Oak Twp	72	142
Oliver	40	m	w	NY	Contra Costa	Martinez P O	71	379
DELAND								
Alford	50	m	w	NY	San Francisco	8-Wd San Francisco	82	429
Laure	18	f	w	MA	Alameda	Oakland	68	185
Michael	48	m	w	IREL	Sutter	Vernon Twp	92	135
DELANE								
Thomas	30	m	w	IREL	Sonoma	Bodega Twp	91	261
DELANEY								
Ah	44	m	w	MI	San Francisco	San Francisco P O	85	755
Bridget	40	f	w	IREL	San Francisco	8-Wd San Francisco	82	427
Clay	25	m	w	TN	Tehama	Tehama Twp	92	192
Daniel	37	m	w	MA	San Francisco	8-Wd San Francisco	82	314
Danl J	41	m	w	TN	Tehama	Deer Crk Twp	92	170
Edward	22	m	w	MD	San Francisco	8-Wd San Francisco	82	403
Elizabeth	27	f	w	MO	Sonoma	Analy Twp	91	231
Francis W	41	m	w	MO	Colusa	Butte Twp	71	268
Frank	21	m	w	MO	Butte	Chico Twp	70	57
Hannah	25	f	w	IREL	San Francisco	1-Wd San Francisco	79	30
James	55	m	w	IREL	Plumas	Quartz Twp	77	43
James	51	m	w	DE	Sonoma	Analy Twp	91	231
James	24	m	w	IREL	Sonoma	Salt Point	91	388
John	40	m	w	NY	Nevada	Grass Valley Twp	75	223
John	32	m	b	NY	San Francisco	San Francisco P O	80	481
John	31	m	w	IREL	Kern	Bakersfield P O	73	357
John	26	m	w	IREL	San Francisco	7-Wd San Francisco	81	173
John G	39	m	w	NY	Nevada	Grass Valley Twp	75	176
Kate	25	f	w	IREL	Napa	Napa	75	44
M	26	m	w	NY	Nevada	Nevada Twp	75	277
Mary	62	f	w	ENGL	San Francisco	San Francisco P O	85	768
Mary	36	f	w	CANA	San Francisco	San Francisco P O	83	289
Mary	13	f	w	CA	Butte	Wyandotte Twp	70	145
Mgt	45	f	w	IREL	San Francisco	San Francisco P O	83	271
Michael	24	m	w	IREL	San Francisco	San Francisco P O	83	335
Nicholas	38	m	w	IREL	Solano	Vallejo	90	211
P	53	m	w	PA	Sierra	Butte Twp	89	511
P H	30	m	w	IREL	Amador	Amador City P O	69	391
Pat	19	m	w	MA	San Francisco	7-Wd San Francisco	81	259
Patrick	54	m	w	IREL	San Francisco	San Francisco P O	83	167
Patrick	52	m	w	IREL	Stanislaus	Branch Twp	92	7
Richard	43	m	w	TN	San Francisco	11-Wd San Francisc	84	648
Russell	12	m	w	CA	Tehama	Deer Crk Twp	92	170
Samuel	67	m	w	PA	Yuba	Parks Bar Twp	93	649
Sarah	69	f	w	KY	Tehama	Deer Crk Twp	92	171
Thomas	40	m	w	IREL	San Francisco	San Francisco P O	83	267
Thos	42	m	w	IREL	San Francisco	San Francisco P O	85	824
Thos	40	m	w	PA	Tehama	Cottonwood Twp	92	162
Thos J	17	m	w	MO	Tehama	Tehama Twp	92	192
W	40	m	w	MO	Siskiyou	Scott Rvr Twp	89	604
W D	35	m	w	NY	San Francisco	San Francisco P O	83	42
W G	50	m	w	TN	Tehama	Deer Crk Twp	92	170
William	21	m	w	IREL	Napa	Yountville Twp	75	81
William	12	m	w	NY	Sonoma	Petaluma Twp	91	361
Wm	48	m	w	IREL	San Francisco	San Francisco P O	83	36
Wm	39	m	w	IREL	Butte	Ophir Twp	70	107
DELANG								
Wm L	37	m	w	CANA	Plumas	Washington Twp	77	25
DELANGE								
Conradas	50	m	w	NORW	Sonoma	Santa Rosa	91	418
Jacob	60	m	w	FRAN	San Francisco	2-Wd San Francisco	79	148
Louis	40	m	w	FRAN	San Francisco	6-Wd San Francisco	81	78
DELANO								
Alonzo	63	m	w	NY	Nevada	Grass Valley Twp	75	146
Annie	24	f	w	IREL	San Francisco	7-Wd San Francisco	81	245
Chas	40	m	w	NH	San Francisco	San Francisco P O	83	110
George	25	m	w	ENGL	Fresno	Millerton P O	72	164
J W	46	m	w	NY	San Francisco	8-Wd San Francisco	82	363
John	38	m	w	SCOT	Alameda	Oakland	68	261
John	28	m	w	MA	Solano	Vallejo	90	160
Maria	14	f	w	CA	Sonoma	Petaluma Twp	91	322
Mathew	35	m	w	SCOT	San Francisco	7-Wd San Francisco	81	254
Michael	34	m	w	IREL	Sutter	Butte Twp	92	103
Michael	29	m	w	IREL	Kern	Kernville P O	73	368
N S	27	m	w	MI	Nevada	Eureka Twp	75	139
Nathaniel S	43	m	w	MA	Nevada	Grass Valley Twp	75	159
Robt T	39	m	w	MA	San Francisco	San Francisco P O	83	117
Silvas D	37	m	w	MA	Los Angeles	Wilmington Twp	73	638
Thomas	40	m	w	MO	Los Angeles	Los Angeles	73	506
Wm	13	m	w	CA	Santa Barbara	San Buenaventura P	87	418

© 2001 by Heritage Quest. All rights reserved.

Name	Age	S	R	B-PL	County	Locale	Series M593 Roll	Pg
DELANTY								
William	40	m	w	IREL	San Francisco	7-Wd San Francisco	81	210
DELANY								
Charles	23	m	i	CA	Sacramento	Lee Twp	77	157
D	25	m	w	NY	San Joaquin	Elkhorn Twp	86	62
George	44	m	w	ENGL	Trinity	Hayfork Valley	92	239
James	35	m	w	IREL	Sacramento	Granite Twp	77	143
James	35	m	w	IREL	San Francisco	11-Wd San Francisc	84	655
James	29	m	w	IREL	San Francisco	11-Wd San Francisc	84	548
John	30	m	w	IREL	San Francisco	8-Wd San Francisco	82	330
M	42	m	w	IREL	Sacramento	1-Wd Sacramento	77	189
Martin	24	m	w	IREL	San Francisco	1-Wd San Francisco	79	94
Mary	38	f	w	IREL	San Francisco	8-Wd San Francisco	82	453
Patrick	39	m	w	IREL	San Francisco	11-Wd San Francisc	84	583
Patrick	30	m	w	NY	Sacramento	1-Wd Sacramento	77	188
Susan	60	f	i	CA	Trinity	Hayfork Valley	92	239
William	47	m	w	ENGL	Mendocino	Little Lake Twp	74	196
William	28	m	w	IREL	Santa Cruz	Santa Cruz	89	415
William	26	m	w	IREL	San Francisco	11-Wd San Francisc	84	454
DELANZY								
Frank	29	m	w	NY	San Francisco	5-Wd San Francisco	81	27
DELAOZA								
Juan	22	m	w	MEXI	Monterey	San Juan Twp	74	385
DELAPEIR								
Henry	31	m	w	FRAN	San Luis Obispo	San Luis Obispo Tw	87	307
DELAPERIERE								
Louis	63	m	w	FRAN	San Francisco	11-Wd San Francisc	84	575
DELAPP								
John	41	m	w	MO	Plumas	Mineral Twp	77	20
DELARGY								
John	50	m	w	IREL	Sacramento	American Twp	77	67
DELARMER								
A N	29	m	w	CANA	Del Norte	Crescent Twp	71	455
DELAROACH								
Frank	27	m	w	FRAN	Contra Costa	San Pablo Twp	71	357
DELARONA								
John	76	m	w	MEXI	Contra Costa	Martinez Twp	71	347
DELARUELLE								
Gustave	40	m	w	FRAN	San Francisco	2-Wd San Francisco	79	172
DELARUP								
Jno	60	m	w	NY	Santa Clara	Almaden Twp	88	19
DELARY								
Caroline	14	f	w	MO	Butte	Chico Twp	70	13
DELAS								
Frank	23	m	w	AFRI	Alameda	Alameda	68	13
DELASHMAN								
William	35	m	w	IA	Yolo	Grafton Twp	93	499
DELASHMEET								
Ranard	36	m	w	MO	Colusa	Monroe Twp	71	312
DELASHMUTT								
B	40	m	w	MO	Merced	Snelling P O	74	277
DELASSAUX								
James	40	m	w	ENGL	Humboldt	Pacific Twp	72	296
DELATE								
Wm	37	m	w	ME	Sierra	Table Rock Twp	89	573
DELATON								
August	36	m	w	FRAN	San Francisco	San Francisco P O	80	342
DELATORE								
Joaquin	23	m	w	CA	Monterey	Alisal Twp	74	298
DELATORES								
Gabrell	65	m	w	CA	Monterey	Monterey	74	356
DELATOUR								
Alex	49	m	w	NY	Alameda	Oakland	68	212
DELATREZ								
Franklin	40	m	w	CHIL	Kern	Bakersfield P O	73	366
DELAVAN								
Lewis T	52	m	w	NY	Nevada	Grass Valley Twp	75	168
DELAVEGA								
Geo	15	m	w	MEXI	San Francisco	11-Wd San Francisc	84	591
Juan	13	m	w	MEXI	San Francisco	11-Wd San Francisc	84	591
Manuel	11	m	w	MEXI	San Francisco	11-Wd San Francisc	84	591
DELAVEGER								
Ignatius	52	m	w	MEXI	San Francisco	8-Wd San Francisco	82	450
DELAVEN								
John	58	m	w	PA	San Francisco	2-Wd San Francisco	79	254
DELAVERA								
Manuel	51	m	w	AZOR	San Francisco	1-Wd San Francisco	79	24
DELAVIA								
Dennis	20	m	w	IREL	Placer	Summit P O	76	497
DELAVINE								
Chas	37	m	w	NY	Butte	Ophir Twp	70	120
DELAY								
Daniel	25	m	w	ME	San Francisco	11-Wd San Francisc	84	518
Daniel	24	m	w	ME	San Francisco	11-Wd San Francisc	84	564
Edward	56	m	w	IREL	Nevada	Grass Valley Twp	75	212
Margaret	18	f	w	MA	San Francisco	7-Wd San Francisco	81	215
Mary	26	f	w	IREL	San Francisco	8-Wd San Francisco	82	426
Timothy	30	m	w	IREL	Yuba	Marysville	93	607
Timothy	17	m	w	ME	Nevada	Grass Valley Twp	75	143
DELAYNEY								
Jas M	44	m	w	OH	Butte	Ophir Twp	70	117
DELAZO								
Frank	28	m	w	ITAL	Solano	Montezuma Twp	90	67
DELAZOREZ								
Theo	37	m	w	CA	Monterey	Monterey	74	358
DELBANCO								
J	62	m	w	HAMB	San Francisco	San Francisco P O	83	134

Name	Age	S	R	B-PL	County	Locale	Series M593 Roll	Pg
DELBART								
Louis	55	m	w	FRAN	Plumas	Washington Twp	77	56
DELBEFREY								
M	25	m	w	GERM	Santa Clara	Gilroy Twp	88	72
DELBOND								
Margaret	40	f	w	FRAN	San Francisco	6-Wd San Francisco	81	70
Victor	47	m	w	FRAN	San Francisco	6-Wd San Francisco	81	70
DELBRIDGE								
Wm H	30	m	w	ENGL	El Dorado	Mountain Twp	72	70
DELCAMPO								
Flavio	24	m	w	CHIL	Sacramento	2-Wd Sacramento	77	254
DELCARNEM								
Rohemo	38	m	w	PHIL	San Mateo	Half Moon Bay P O	87	393
DELCIA								
Juan	38	m	w	MEXI	Kern	Bakersfield P O	73	365
DELCISCO								
Peter	72	m	w	FRAN	San Mateo	San Mateo P O	87	348
DELCONTE								
Joseph	43	m	w	ITAL	Santa Clara	1-Wd San Jose	88	257
DELEAMERA								
Antonio	57	m	w	SPAI	Inyo	Cerro Gordo Twp	73	323
DELEAN								
Jos	21	m	w	FRAN	San Francisco	San Francisco P O	83	135
DELECENY								
Juan	21	m	w	CA	San Diego	Coronado	78	466
DELEG								
Jean	52	m	w	FRAN	Calaveras	San Andreas P O	70	190
DELEHANT								
Michael	33	m	w	IREL	San Francisco	San Francisco P O	83	152
DELEHANTY								
D	24	m	w	NY	Solano	Vallejo	90	202
Eliza	40	f	w	IREL	San Francisco	2-Wd San Francisco	79	216
Pat	27	m	w	IREL	Solano	Vallejo	90	171
Thomas	28	m	w	IREL	San Francisco	San Francisco P O	83	256
DELEMANY								
Nicholas	48	m	w	GREE	Marin	Sausalito Twp	74	69
DELEMSTER								
James	37	m	w	NY	Los Angeles	Los Angeles	73	507
DELENG								
Jno M	46	m	w	NY	San Joaquin	2-Wd Stockton	86	209
DELEON								
Maria	18	f	w	NY	San Mateo	Redwood Twp	87	365
Ponce F	32	m	w	CA	San Luis Obispo	San Luis Obispo Tw	87	309
DELEPLANIE								
Charles	44	m	w	VA	San Diego	Julian Dist	78	469
DELERO								
Jose	28	m	w	MEXI	Stanislaus	Branch Twp	92	5
DELERTRO								
Pete	35	m	w	ITAL	Sacramento	Georgianna Twp	77	129
DELERY								
Joseph	23	m	w	SWIT	Amador	Volcano P O	69	388
DELESKY								
John	35	m	w	HANO	San Joaquin	Dent Twp	86	19
DELEVAL								
Charles	38	m	w	FRAN	Santa Clara	2-Wd San Jose	88	284
DELEVAN								
F H	37	m	w	IREL	Nevada	Meadow Lake Twp	75	267
James L	60	m	w	PA	El Dorado	White Oak Twp	72	143
Lewis	27	m	w	TN	Butte	Oregon Twp	70	129
Martin	48	m	w	IREL	San Joaquin	3-Wd Stockton	86	230
DELEVECHIO								
Jean	47	m	w	ITAL	Marin	Novato Twp	74	10
DELEX								
Ellen	35	f	w	IREL	San Francisco	11-Wd San Francisc	84	553
DELEY								
D	25	m	w	IREL	Alameda	Oakland	68	245
DELFOCH								
Barnard	33	m	w	SWIT	El Dorado	Diamond Springs Tw	72	29
DELFS								
Henry	38	m	w	SHOL	Humboldt	Arcata Twp	72	235
DELGADILLO								
Santo	33	m	w	CHIL	Mariposa	Mariposa P O	74	110
DELGADO								
Antone	35	m	w	MEXI	Santa Clara	Gilroy Twp	88	77
Pedro	68	m	w	SPAI	Santa Barbara	Las Cruces P O	87	515
DELGARA								
Mary	23	f	w	MEXI	Alameda	Eden Twp	68	93
Quartin	69	m	w	MEXI	Tuolumne	Sonora P O	93	330
DELGARDO								
Manuel	15	m	w	MEXI	San Francisco	2-Wd San Francisco	79	183
DELGER								
Anna	15	f	w	CA	San Mateo	San Mateo P O	87	357
DELGIER								
Alex	40	m	w	BRAN	San Francisco	8-Wd San Francisco	82	305
DELGRASSA								
Antonio	25	m	w	ITAL	Nevada	Grass Valley Twp	75	204
DELHARREGUY								
Louis	43	m	w	FRAN	Calaveras	San Andreas P O	70	211
DELIA								
Wilhelmina	23	f	w	SWED	San Francisco	San Francisco P O	80	466
DELIALDO								
Pasqual	34	m	w	ITAL	San Francisco	1-Wd San Francisco	79	39
DELIARD								
August	33	m	w	FRAN	Siskiyou	Surprise Valley Tw	89	637
DELICAT								
Frederick	45	m	w	HANO	Nevada	Little York Twp	75	235
John F	2	m	w	CA	Nevada	Little York Twp	75	235

© 2001 by Heritage Quest. All rights reserved.

Name	Age	S	R	B-PL	County	Locale	Series M593 Roll	Pg
DELICATE								
Annie	14	f	w	GERM	Nevada	Nevada Twp	75	281
DELIGNA								
Letta	24	f	w	IN	Colusa	Colusa	71	294
DELILLE								
Edw	40	m	w	CANA	San Joaquin	Dent Twp	86	24
DELINOT								
Lewis	45	m	w	FRAN	Los Angeles	Wilmington Twp	73	634
DELIOS								
Cornelius	30	m	w	PRUS	San Francisco	11-Wd San Francisc	84	685
DELIX								
Augustus	11	m	w	CA	Marin	San Rafael Twp	74	29
Edward	10	m	w	CA	Marin	San Rafael Twp	74	27
DELL								
Charles	28	m	w	IREL	Napa	Napa Twp	75	67
Christopher	53	m	w	ENGL	San Joaquin	3-Wd Stockton	86	225
Henry	23	m	w	BAVA	Solano	Vallejo	90	168
John E	30	m	w	NY	San Francisco	7-Wd San Francisco	81	231
Louis	35	m	w	BADE	Nevada	Meadow Lake Twp	75	246
DELLACELLI								
Gerardo	43	m	w	ITAL	Los Angeles	Wilmington Twp	73	641
DELLAFANT								
Max	28	m	w	WURT	Sierra	Table Rock Twp	89	578
DELLAMAR								
Armand	45	m	w	FRAN	San Francisco	1-Wd San Francisco	79	50
DELLAN								
Michael	28	m	w	IREL	Humboldt	Bucksport Twp	72	243
W G	42	m	w	PRUS	Tuolumne	Columbia P O	93	340
DELLATARRA								
Giuseppi	35	m	w	SWIT	Marin	Nicasio Twp	74	17
DELLAVEDORA								
Marco	35	m	w	SWIT	Sonoma	Sonoma Twp	91	431
DELLEGHER								
Isabella	18	f	w	SCOT	San Francisco	San Francisco P O	83	195
DELLEN								
Jeramiah	26	m	w	IA	Los Angeles	Los Angeles	73	566
DELLEX								
John V	52	m	w	PA	San Mateo	Redwood Twp	87	366
DELLEY								
Charles	29	m	w	ENGL	San Francisco	San Francisco P O	83	273
DELLIHANTY								
John	48	m	w	IREL	Solano	Vallejo	90	159
DELLIMORE								
Ed	42	m	w	ENGL	San Francisco	2-Wd San Francisco	79	213
DELLINAS								
John	24	m	w	IREL	San Francisco	8-Wd San Francisco	82	302
DELLINGHAM								
Jno	30	m	w	ME	Butte	Chico Twp	70	29
DELLINS								
Paul	54	m	w	FRAN	San Francisco	San Francisco P O	80	338
DELLON								
George	46	m	w	IREL	Marin	Tomales Twp	74	79
Kate	40	f	w	IREL	San Francisco	11-Wd San Francisc	84	422
DELLWIG								
Augusta	21	f	w	PRUS	San Francisco	San Francisco P O	83	349
Theodore	36	m	w	HANO	San Francisco	San Francisco P O	83	176
DELMAESTRO								
William	33	m	w	SWIT	Santa Clara	2-Wd San Jose	88	317
DELMAR								
Edward	24	m	w	NY	Santa Clara	San Jose Twp	88	221
Giuseppe	18	m	w	SWIT	Santa Cruz	Santa Cruz Twp	89	397
Hanry	29	m	w	PRUS	San Francisco	San Francisco P O	80	460
Sylvester	20	m	w	SWIT	Santa Cruz	Santa Cruz Twp	89	397
DELMARCO								
Domenico	20	m	w	ITAL	San Francisco	11-Wd San Francisc	84	594
DELMARE								
W	40	m	w	NJ	Alameda	Oakland	68	225
DELMAS								
Antonio	52	m	w	FRAN	Santa Clara	2-Wd San Jose	88	331
Delphon M	26	m	w	FRAN	Santa Clara	2-Wd San Jose	88	331
Philomel	37	m	w	FRAN	Mariposa	Mariposa P O	74	128
DELMON								
Auther	39	m	w	MA	Butte	Oregon Twp	70	131
DELMONLY								
Antonio	46	m	w	FRAN	Santa Clara	2-Wd San Jose	88	309
Disera	5	f	w	CA	Santa Clara	2-Wd San Jose	88	302
DELMONT								
F	29	m	w	FRAN	Lake	Lower Lake	73	428
DELMORE								
Margaret	48	f	w	IREL	San Francisco	11-Wd San Francisc	84	467
DELMUS								
Gustav	12	m	w	CA	San Francisco	8-Wd San Francisco	82	429
DELNEY								
Julia	21	f	w	OH	San Francisco	San Francisco P O	83	263
DELNO								
Josiah	31	m	w	MA	Sonoma	Healdsburg	91	274
DELOCA								
Francisco	50	m	w	ITAL	Sacramento	Cosumnes Twp	77	90
DELOCABE								
R	16	m	w	MEXI	Alameda	Oakland	68	159
DELOGE								
Julia	48	f	w	FRAN	San Francisco	6-Wd San Francisco	81	95
DELOGURE								
O	24	m	w	CANA	Nevada	Eureka Twp	75	138
DELOHERY								
Thos	52	m	w	IREL	San Francisco	San Francisco P O	83	69
DELOKI								
Angelo	19	m	w	ITAL	El Dorado	Mountain Twp	72	69
DELON								
Mary	45	f	w	ASEA	Yolo	Cottonwood Twp	93	463
DELONG								
Albert A	36	m	w	NY	Yolo	Cache Crk Twp	93	434
Alexander	36	m	w	NY	Santa Clara	2-Wd San Jose	88	289
Alva	42	m	w	VT	El Dorado	Georgetown Twp	72	45
Archy	27	m	w	TN	Butte	Chico Twp	70	34
Chas W	28	m	w	MI	Mariposa	Mariposa P O	74	97
Edmond	40	m	w	MA	El Dorado	Coloma Twp	72	9
Francis	62	m	w	VT	Marin	Novato Twp	74	12
Frank	26	m	w	NY	San Francisco	8-Wd San Francisco	82	327
H R	24	m	w	NY	San Joaquin	Liberty Twp	86	82
Joseph	45	m	w	IREL	Sacramento	Granite Twp	77	146
Marka	14	f	w	CA	San Joaquin	Oneal Twp	86	105
Mary	17	f	w	CA	San Joaquin	Oneal Twp	86	105
Nicholas	45	m	w	FRAN	Stanislaus	North Twp	92	67
Pary	54	m	w	IL	San Joaquin	Elkhorn Twp	86	54
Robt	34	m	w	MS	San Joaquin	Oneal Twp	86	105
Thomas	52	m	w	IREL	San Francisco	7-Wd San Francisco	81	194
Thomas G	62	m	w	NY	Mariposa	Mariposa P O	74	134
W L	40	m	w	OH	Sutter	Sutter Twp	92	126
DELONGENAY								
Daniel	31	m	w	VT	Stanislaus	Washington Twp	92	84
DELONGY								
Gabriel	67	m	w	CANA	Monterey	Monterey	74	362
DELONIE								
V	46	m	w	ITAL	Sierra	Downieville Twp	89	517
DELONY								
James	51	m	w	OH	Siskiyou	Table Rock Twp	89	646
DELOP								
Alexander	24	m	w	IL	Sacramento	Lee Twp	77	160
DELORAS								
Santa	45	f	w	CHIL	Amador	Jackson P O	69	322
DELORME								
G D	26	m	w	NH	San Francisco	7-Wd San Francisco	81	274
G O	49	m	w	CANA	San Francisco	San Francisco P O	83	135
Victor	20	m	w	CANA	Nevada	Grass Valley Twp	75	156
DELOSEY								
Peter	39	m	w	CANA	San Francisco	San Francisco P O	80	457
DELOUNE								
Wm	40	m	w	FRAN	San Francisco	2-Wd San Francisco	79	286
DELOVAN								
W	33	m	w	NY	Nevada	Nevada Twp	75	279
DELPH								
Willm	38	m	w	PRUS	Alameda	Murray Twp	68	111
DELPLACE								
Ernest	30	m	w	SWIT	Contra Costa	Martinez Twp	71	347
DELPODIO								
Peter	45	m	w	FRAN	San Francisco	8-Wd San Francisco	82	295
DELPORT								
Fostena	35	m	w	ITAL	Amador	Jackson P O	69	328
DELPRAT								
George	33	m	w	NY	San Francisco	San Francisco P O	80	373
DELREAL								
Marcus	38	m	w	MEXI	Calaveras	San Andreas P O	70	208
DELSE								
Antonia	24	f	w	MEXI	Los Angeles	Los Angeles	73	515
DELSESCAUX								
Remy	40	m	w	FRAN	Sacramento	2-Wd Sacramento	77	248
DELSESCEANG								
Bartholomew	40	m	w	FRAN	Sacramento	2-Wd Sacramento	77	242
DELSEY								
Gus	44	m	w	CANA	Contra Costa	San Pablo Twp	71	356
DELSOL								
Augt	34	m	w	PRUS	San Francisco	8-Wd San Francisco	82	373
August	34	m	w	FRAN	San Francisco	San Francisco P O	83	267
DELT								
L B	49	m	w	NY	San Joaquin	1-Wd Stockton	86	126
DELUCA								
Sophia	18	f	w	BELG	Solano	Benicia	90	16
DELUCHE								
John	44	m	w	FRAN	San Francisco	San Francisco P O	83	243
DELUCHI								
Lorenzo	30	m	w	ITAL	Amador	Volcano P O	69	372
Lorenzo	29	m	w	ITAL	Amador	Volcano P O	69	386
Luigi	30	m	w	ITAL	San Francisco	11-Wd San Francisc	84	594
Martino	30	m	w	ITAL	Amador	Volcano P O	69	384
P N	50	m	w	FRAN	Tuolumne	Chinese Camp P O	93	368
DELUCHIO								
Dominica	29	m	w	ITAL	Amador	Volcano P O	69	384
Gaetano	37	m	w	ITAL	Sacramento	3-Wd Sacramento	77	289
DELUCY								
---	31	m	w	IA	San Joaquin	Elkhorn Twp	86	68
Moses	30	m	w	DENM	San Francisco	5-Wd San Francisco	81	15
DELUKE								
Ansi	30	m	w	ITAL	San Francisco	San Francisco P O	85	859
John	36	m	w	ITAL	San Francisco	San Francisco P O	85	859
Joseph	33	m	w	ITAL	San Francisco	San Francisco P O	85	859
Louis	32	m	w	ITAL	San Francisco	San Francisco P O	85	859
DELUME								
Antonio	28	m	w	SWIT	Santa Cruz	Santa Cruz	89	412
DELUMOND								
M	35	m	w	PORT	Sonoma	Sonoma Twp	91	435
DELUOSA								
Tabucis	29	m	w	CA	Los Angeles	Los Angeles Twp	73	479

© 2001 by Heritage Quest. All rights reserved.

Name	Age	S	R	B-PL	County	Locale	Series M593 Roll	Pg
DELURPI								
Mark	31	m	w	ITAL	Santa Clara	2-Wd San Jose	88	316
DELURY								
George	38	m	w	IREL	Nevada	Grass Valley Twp	75	201
DELVECCHIO								
Chas H	49	m	b	NY	Tehama	Red Bluff	92	177
DELVENTHALL								
John	28	m	w	HAMB	San Francisco	6-Wd San Francisco	81	89
DELVIN								
Henry	38	m	w	MA	Siskiyou	Yreka	89	657
Rosanna	25	f	w	PA	San Francisco	San Francisco P O	83	52
DELVINE								
Wm	55	m	w	BELG	Sutter	Sutter Twp	92	118
DELVITT								
William M	29	m	w	KY	Santa Cruz	Santa Cruz	89	426
DELWARD								
Marg	50	f	w	FRAN	San Francisco	2-Wd San Francisco	79	162
DELWATER								
Walter	28	m	w	NY	Fresno	Millerton P O	72	146
DELWICK								
Henry F	42	m	w	OLDE	El Dorado	Georgetown Twp	72	49
DELZER								
Fredk	18	m	w	SC	Santa Clara	Gilroy Twp	88	81
DEMACK								
John	25	m	w	CANA	San Francisco	7-Wd San Francisco	81	205
DEMAGE								
Henry	31	m	w	IREL	Santa Clara	Almaden Twp	88	9
DEMAIN								
John	30	m	w	ENGL	Tuolumne	Chinese Camp P O	93	365
DEMAJERY								
Adele	40	f	b	VA	San Francisco	6-Wd San Francisco	81	72
DEMAN								
Charles	13	m	w	CA	Inyo	Bishop Crk Twp	73	313
DEMANGON								
Aug	43	m	w	FRAN	San Francisco	8-Wd San Francisco	82	303
DEMANIEL								
Geo	27	m	w	IREL	Sonoma	Salt Point	91	386
DEMANS								
Roy	24	m	w	CANA	Placer	Bath P O	76	460
DEMANTI								
Francis	51	m	w	ITAL	San Francisco	San Francisco P O	80	466
DEMAR								
Mary	27	f	w	PRUS	San Francisco	3-Wd San Francisco	79	320
DEMARCE								
Luie	55	m	w	CANA	Alameda	Brooklyn	68	38
DEMAREE								
Isaac N	41	m	w	PA	Plumas	Washington Twp	77	53
DEMARERO								
Louisa	26	f	w	ITAL	San Francisco	2-Wd San Francisco	79	142
DEMARSH								
A	30	m	w	IREL	Sacramento	4-Wd Sacramento	77	373
DEMARTANA								
Apollo	30	m	w	ITAL	San Francisco	11-Wd San Francisc	84	614
DEMARTEN								
Antonio	30	m	w	ITAL	San Francisco	1-Wd San Francisco	79	42
DEMARTENA								
Antonio	40	m	w	ITAL	Calaveras	San Andreas P O	70	179
DEMARTENO								
Olive	22	f	w	ITAL	San Francisco	2-Wd San Francisco	79	150
DEMARTIN								
Andrew	39	m	w	SWIT	Marin	San Antonio Twp	74	62
Antone	29	m	w	ITAL	Calaveras	San Andreas P O	70	179
Charles	40	m	w	ITAL	Sonoma	Vallejo Twp	91	463
Jno	20	m	w	ITAL	San Francisco	11-Wd San Francisc	84	710
John	36	m	w	SWIT	Marin	Tomales Twp	74	76
John	28	m	w	ITAL	Calaveras	San Andreas P O	70	173
John	28	m	w	ITAL	Calaveras	San Andreas P O	70	179
Lewis	31	m	w	SWIT	Sonoma	Petaluma Twp	91	337
Lin	22	m	w	ITAL	Calaveras	San Andreas P O	70	173
Louis	37	m	w	ITAL	Calaveras	San Andreas P O	70	179
Michael	48	m	w	SWIT	Marin	Bolinas Twp	74	1
Peter	27	m	w	ITAL	Calaveras	San Andreas P O	70	179
DEMARTINA								
P	36	m	w	ITAL	Calaveras	Copperopolis P O	70	232
Paul	24	m	w	ITAL	Calaveras	San Andreas P O	70	179
DEMARTINE								
Angelo	31	m	w	ITAL	Calaveras	Copperopolis P O	70	239
G	27	m	w	ITAL	Calaveras	Copperopolis P O	70	231
Giovanni	33	m	w	ITAL	Calaveras	San Andreas P O	70	179
J	50	m	w	ITAL	Calaveras	Copperopolis P O	70	231
J	45	m	w	ITAL	Calaveras	Copperopolis P O	70	230
J	25	m	w	ITAL	Calaveras	Copperopolis P O	70	231
Jac	29	m	w	ITAL	Calaveras	San Andreas P O	70	180
Jerome	35	m	w	AUST	Calaveras	San Andreas P O	70	205
Jovanie	27	m	w	ITAL	Calaveras	Copperopolis P O	70	251
DEMARTINI								
Alexander	40	m	w	ITAL	San Francisco	2-Wd San Francisco	79	237
August	25	m	w	ITAL	San Francisco	2-Wd San Francisco	79	180
Frank	38	m	w	ITAL	San Francisco	2-Wd San Francisco	79	161
Joseph	48	m	w	ITAL	San Francisco	2-Wd San Francisco	79	180
Paul	44	m	w	ITAL	San Francisco	2-Wd San Francisco	79	180
Paul	36	m	w	ITAL	San Francisco	2-Wd San Francisco	79	176
Paul	25	m	w	ITAL	San Francisco	2-Wd San Francisco	79	237
DEMARTINO								
Paulo	33	m	w	ITAL	San Francisco	11-Wd San Francisc	84	456
DEMARTON								
Bernard	53	m	w	FRAN	San Francisco	2-Wd San Francisco	79	281

Name	Age	S	R	B-PL	County	Locale	Series M593 Roll	Pg
DEMAS								
Joseph	30	m	w	SCOT	Siskiyou	Yreka Twp	89	668
DEMASINI								
Velchohhs	47	m	w	ITAL	San Francisco	San Francisco P O	83	311
DEMATINI								
Joseph	44	m	w	ITAL	San Francisco	2-Wd San Francisco	79	149
DEMATS								
Jose Antonio	20	m	w	AZOR	San Francisco	1-Wd San Francisco	79	130
DEMBA								
Dennis	77	m	w	IREL	El Dorado	Cosumnes Twp	72	19
DEMBLING								
Daniel	52	m	w	SCOT	San Francisco	3-Wd San Francisco	79	310
DEME								
August	30	m	w	MEXI	San Francisco	San Francisco P O	80	424
DEMEEHY								
Dennis	51	m	w	IREL	Sonoma	Healdsburg & Mendo	91	277
DEMELLS								
Joseph	28	m	w	PORT	San Francisco	San Francisco P O	83	358
DEMENS								
Louis	70	m	w	CANA	Siskiyou	Callahan P O	89	631
Peter	69	m	w	NY	Santa Barbara	San Buenaventura P	87	446
DEMENT								
George	19	m	w	IA	Amador	Ione City P O	69	353
John	46	m	w	MD	San Francisco	11-Wd San Francisc	84	619
DEMENY								
Joseph	20	m	w	SWIT	Marin	San Antonio Twp	74	61
DEMERAL								
Frank	23	m	w	AZOR	Monterey	Castroville Twp	74	334
DEMEREST								
James	51	m	w	RI	San Francisco	San Francisco P O	80	363
DEMERITT								
Chas	30	m	w	NH	San Francisco	8-Wd San Francisco	82	364
Elbridge	39	m	w	ME	Alameda	Eden Twp	68	68
G C	30	m	w	ME	San Joaquin	2-Wd Stockton	86	175
DEMERNEAU								
Rosalie	38	f	w	FRAN	San Francisco	6-Wd San Francisco	81	72
DEMERRER								
P	54	m	w	FRAN	Alameda	Murray Twp	68	109
DEMERRIE								
Lorenzo	38	m	w	SWIT	Placer	Bath P O	76	425
DEMERRITT								
D A	40	m	w	NH	Humboldt	Bucksport Twp	72	241
DEMERRITTE								
Chas J	24	m	w	NH	Tulare	Visalia	92	297
DEMETREUS								
John	59	m	w	GREE	San Francisco	11-Wd San Francisc	84	612
DEMETZ								
Henry	29	m	w	BAVA	San Francisco	8-Wd San Francisco	82	455
DEMIAN								
Daniel	37	m	w	IREL	Trinity	Junction City Pct	92	205
DEMICHELLI								
Giovanni	26	m	w	ITAL	San Francisco	11-Wd San Francisc	84	594
DEMICK								
George	38	m	w	BAVA	Del Norte	Mountain Twp	71	474
Joseph	28	m	w	IL	Sonoma	Russian Rvr	91	376
Wm	38	m	w	PA	San Joaquin	2-Wd Stockton	86	189
DEMID								
Joseph	27	m	w	FRAN	San Joaquin	1-Wd Stockton	86	138
DEMING								
Charlotte	17	f	w	CA	San Francisco	San Francisco P O	80	419
George	24	m	w	ME	San Francisco	8-Wd San Francisco	82	368
H C	40	m	w	IREL	Tuolumne	Big Oak Flat P O	93	402
Hariet	24	f	w	NY	Tulare	Visalia	92	289
Henry V	33	m	w	IN	San Francisco	3-Wd San Francisco	79	298
Horace A	36	m	w	VT	San Francisco	8-Wd San Francisco	82	321
James G	39	m	w	IN	San Francisco	3-Wd San Francisco	79	298
John F	46	m	w	NY	Solano	Benicia	90	15
Rufus	71	m	w	MA	Napa	Napa Twp	75	66
Theodore	34	m	w	IN	Yolo	Cache Crk Twp	93	437
DEMINT								
G S	27	m	w	IA	Amador	Ione City P O	69	357
William	64	m	w	KY	Amador	Ione City P O	69	357
DEMIS								
Tim	42	m	w	IREL	San Joaquin	1-Wd Stockton	86	157
DEMITT								
Rheuben	44	m	w	PA	El Dorado	Kelsey Twp	72	60
DEMLING								
Chas	42	m	w	HANO	San Francisco	1-Wd San Francisco	79	135
DEMMAN								
James	44	m	w	OH	San Luis Obispo	Salinas Twp	87	292
DEMMERY								
Harrison	30	m	w	ME	San Joaquin	3-Wd Stockton	86	231
DEMMETT								
John H	36	m	w	ME	Santa Cruz	Santa Cruz Twp	89	388
William F	32	m	w	ME	Santa Cruz	Santa Cruz Twp	89	388
DEMMICK								
Henry	41	m	w	PA	San Francisco	San Francisco P O	83	27
DEMMINCY								
Joseph	44	m	w	HAMB	Stanislaus	Branch Twp	92	6
William	39	m	w	HAMB	Stanislaus	Branch Twp	92	6
DEMMING								
Hiram M	30	m	w	MO	Santa Barbara	San Buenaventura P	87	423
J D	41	m	w	CT	Alameda	Oakland	68	198
Oliver	45	m	w	NY	San Francisco	8-Wd San Francisco	82	330
DEMMOND								
M	33	m	w	IREL	Lake	Knoxville Mines	73	405

© 2001 by Heritage Quest. All rights reserved.

Name	Age	S	R	B-PL	County	Locale	Series M593 Roll	Pg
DEMNER								
Henry	25	m	w	NJ	San Francisco	5-Wd San Francisco	81	31
DEMO								
Frank	40	m	w	VA	Tehama	Tehama Twp	92	186
DEMON								
Nathan S	54	m	w	MA	Placer	Gold Run Twp	76	398
DEMONE								
Jno	29	m	w	PA	San Joaquin	Elliott Twp	86	81
DEMONG								
Sarah	19	f	w	OH	Monterey	San Juan Twp	74	406
DEMONPLAS								
Catherine	21	f	w	FRAN	San Francisco	6-Wd San Francisco	81	62
DEMONS								
Francis	19	m	w	CA	Marin	Tomales Twp	74	79
DEMONT								
Joseph	53	m	w	NY	Alameda	Eden Twp	68	89
DEMONTE								
Bernandina	68	f	w	ITAL	San Francisco	2-Wd San Francisco	79	182
Lorenzo	34	m	w	ITAL	San Francisco	2-Wd San Francisco	79	182
DEMONTPREVILLE								
Cyrill	52	m	w	FRAN	San Francisco	1-Wd San Francisco	79	108
DEMORAY								
Arson	44	m	w	NY	Colusa	Colusa Twp	71	281
Cleat	18	m	c	CHIN	Colusa	Colusa Twp	71	281
DEMORE								
T	37	m	w	CANA	Amador	Sutter Crk P O	69	413
DEMOREST								
David	45	m	w	NJ	Calaveras	Copperopolis P O	70	240
DEMORETT								
Jacob	43	m	w	NY	San Francisco	11-Wd San Francisc	84	618
DEMORO								
Francisco	38	m	w	HANO	San Francisco	2-Wd San Francisco	79	189
DEMORY								
Timothy	28	m	w	IREL	San Francisco	7-Wd San Francisco	81	266
DEMOS								
Rem	24	m	w	KY	Solano	Tremont Twp	90	28
DEMOSS								
Jacob	15	m	w	UT	Stanislaus	Empire Twp	92	61
DEMOTE								
Wm	32	m	w	MI	Butte	Ophir Twp	70	107
DEMOTT								
George	24	m	w	MI	Contra Costa	Martinez P O	71	407
Henry	44	m	w	NJ	Colusa	Colusa	71	295
John	40	m	w	ITAL	San Francisco	1-Wd San Francisco	79	3
DEMOURNEY								
Jean	19	f	w	FRAN	San Francisco	6-Wd San Francisco	81	71
DEMPEY								
Peter	28	m	w	IREL	San Francisco	1-Wd San Francisco	79	44
Peter	20	m	w	OH	Butte	Chico Twp	70	29
DEMPSEY								
Andrew	26	m	w	IREL	Santa Clara	Santa Clara Twp	88	165
Arthur	22	m	w	CANA	Plumas	Indian Twp	77	9
C F	33	f	w	IREL	Solano	Vallejo	90	145
Catherine	29	f	w	NY	Solano	Vallejo	90	139
Cathrin	37	f	w	IREL	San Francisco	8-Wd San Francisco	82	377
Dan	34	m	w	MI	Santa Barbara	San Buenaventura P	87	436
Daniel	30	m	w	IREL	San Francisco	San Francisco P O	83	357
Danl	25	m	w	ENGL	San Francisco	7-Wd San Francisco	81	267
Dennis F	32	m	w	IREL	San Mateo	San Mateo P O	87	355
E	25	f	w	IREL	San Francisco	San Francisco P O	85	825
Edward	45	m	w	IREL	Placer	Rocklin P O	76	462
James	44	m	w	IREL	San Francisco	1-Wd San Francisco	79	101
James	33	m	w	CANA	San Mateo	Redwood City P O	87	375
James	24	m	w	CANA	Plumas	Plumas Twp	77	30
Jeremiah	35	m	w	IREL	San Francisco	8-Wd San Francisco	82	490
Johanna	25	f	w	IREL	San Francisco	San Francisco P O	83	343
John	36	m	w	IREL	Nevada	Bridgeport Twp	75	115
John	33	m	w	IREL	Santa Clara	Alviso Twp	88	28
John	30	m	w	IREL	San Francisco	8-Wd San Francisco	82	433
John	30	m	w	IREL	San Francisco	San Francisco P O	83	198
John	28	m	w	NY	Solano	Vallejo	90	165
John	20	m	w	LA	Yolo	Grafton Twp	93	479
John G	30	m	w	IREL	San Francisco	San Francisco P O	83	248
John H	25	m	w	IREL	Santa Barbara	San Buenaventura P	87	427
Mary	53	f	w	IREL	San Francisco	San Francisco P O	83	298
Michael	25	m	w	NY	San Francisco	San Francisco P O	83	248
Patk	23	m	w	IREL	San Francisco	1-Wd San Francisco	79	61
Patrick	35	m	w	IREL	San Francisco	San Francisco P O	83	198
Peter	39	m	w	IREL	San Francisco	San Francisco P O	83	32
Peter	39	m	w	IREL	San Francisco	1-Wd San Francisco	79	89
William	20	m	w	MA	Nevada	Grass Valley Twp	75	149
Wm	38	m	w	IREL	San Joaquin	Dent Twp	86	16
Wm	35	m	w	IREL	San Luis Obispo	San Luis Obispo Tw	87	303
Wm	30	m	w	IREL	Solano	Vallejo	90	215
DEMPSTER								
Alexr	48	m	w	SCOT	San Francisco	San Francisco P O	85	747
James	42	m	w	IREL	Plumas	Plumas Twp	77	26
Mary	22	f	w	ENGL	Santa Clara	1-Wd San Jose	88	226
William	28	m	w	CANA	Solano	Silveyville Twp	90	92
DEMPSY								
John	31	m	w	IREL	Yuba	Rose Bar Twp	93	652
Patrick	35	m	w	IREL	Sacramento	Granite Twp	77	154
Saml	40	m	w	CANA	Butte	Ophir Twp	70	117
Wm	51	m	w	TN	Butte	Oregon Twp	70	130
DEMSEY								
Ellen	14	f	w	FL	San Francisco	7-Wd San Francisco	81	265
Maggie	28	f	w	NY	San Francisco	5-Wd San Francisco	81	33
DEMSPEY								
Catharinna	36	f	w	IREL	Nevada	Bridgeport Twp	75	100
DEMSTER								
Evo	30	m	w	PORT	Sacramento	Granite Twp	77	147
DEN								
Ah	26	m	c	CHIN	Nevada	Grass Valley Twp	75	218
Alfred	17	m	w	CA	Santa Clara	Santa Clara Twp	88	177
Alphonso	14	m	w	CA	Santa Barbara	Santa Barbara P O	87	492
Alphonso	14	m	w	CA	Santa Barbara	Santa Barbara P O	87	500
Augustus	12	m	w	CA	Santa Barbara	Santa Barbara P O	87	492
Catherine	24	f	w	CA	Santa Barbara	Santa Barbara P O	87	502
Emanuel R	24	m	w	CA	Santa Barbara	Santa Barbara P O	87	466
How	21	f	c	CHIN	Los Angeles	Santa Ana Twp	73	613
Joseph	12	m	w	NJ	San Francisco	5-Wd San Francisco	81	25
Kate M	20	f	w	ENGL	San Francisco	5-Wd San Francisco	81	25
Nicholas C	22	m	w	CA	Santa Barbara	Santa Barbara P O	87	500
Pauline	50	f	w	FRAN	Santa Clara	2-Wd San Jose	88	326
William	19	m	w	CA	Santa Clara	Santa Clara Twp	88	177
William	10	m	w	NJ	San Francisco	5-Wd San Francisco	81	25
Wm	20	m	w	MEXI	San Francisco	11-Wd San Francisc	84	593
DENA								
Antonio	22	m	w	PORT	San Francisco	2-Wd San Francisco	79	282
DENADIE								
Peter	4	m	w	FRAN	Santa Cruz	Soquel Twp	89	437
DENAGRO								
Jack	40	m	w	ITAL	Napa	Napa	75	43
DENAHAN								
Ellen	40	f	w	IREL	Sacramento	3-Wd Sacramento	77	290
DENANNY								
John	30	m	w	NY	Solano	Vallejo	90	172
DENASO								
Pedro	40	m	w	CHIL	El Dorado	Georgetown Twp	72	40
DENAVEAUX								
Martin	40	m	w	FRAN	San Francisco	1-Wd San Francisco	79	82
DENAY								
Joseph	56	m	w	NY	San Mateo	Half Moon Bay P O	87	398
DENBY								
Isaac	33	m	w	ENGL	Solano	Suisun Twp	90	109
DENCE								
Wm W	47	m	w	NY	Monterey	Salinas Twp	74	306
DENCH								
John W	32	m	w	OH	El Dorado	Placerville	72	111
DENCHEL								
Jeremiah	28	m	w	IREL	San Mateo	Schoolhouse Statio	87	341
DENCHER								
Augt	27	m	w	RUSS	San Francisco	3-Wd San Francisco	79	310
DENDARO								
John	40	m	w	ITAL	San Francisco	2-Wd San Francisco	79	231
Mary	50	f	w	ITAL	San Francisco	2-Wd San Francisco	79	149
DENDEN								
Eleaser	41	m	w	FRAN	Kern	Bakersfield P O	73	358
DENDRIOS								
Fernando	38	m	w	CA	Fresno	Millerton P O	72	160
DENEAULIS								
Michl	38	m	w	ITAL	San Francisco	1-Wd San Francisco	79	106
DENECKEN								
Geo	35	m	w	SAXO	San Francisco	11-Wd San Francisc	84	613
DENEGRE								
Joseph	21	m	w	ENGL	San Francisco	San Francisco P O	80	362
DENEHAN								
Hank	31	f	w	IREL	Sacramento	1-Wd Sacramento	77	186
DENEHY								
John	35	m	w	IREL	San Francisco	7-Wd San Francisco	81	173
DENEKER								
Fredk	27	m	w	HAMB	San Francisco	1-Wd San Francisco	79	104
DENELSON								
Barbara	75	f	w	IREL	San Mateo	San Mateo P O	87	371
Wm	80	m	w	IREL	San Mateo	San Mateo P O	87	371
DENELTA								
Joseph	30	m	w	ITAL	Monterey	San Antonio Twp	74	323
DENENBRINK								
C	47	m	w	HANO	Trinity	Canyon City Pct	92	202
DENER								
Michael	40	m	w	IREL	Kern	Havilah P O	73	339
DENERIO								
Manwell	23	m	w	ITAL	San Mateo	Searsville P O	87	382
DENERY								
John	50	m	w	IREL	Sonoma	Vallejo Twp	91	459
Leon	37	m	w	FRAN	San Francisco	2-Wd San Francisco	79	137
DENEVAUX								
Martin	48	m	w	FRAN	San Francisco	San Francisco P O	80	356
DENEVILLE								
Paul	52	m	w	IL	Sacramento	4-Wd Sacramento	77	362
DENEY								
Adolph	65	m	w	FRAN	San Francisco	1-Wd San Francisco	79	111
Joseph J	55	m	w	KY	Santa Clara	1-Wd San Jose	88	227
DENG								
Ah	31	m	w	CHIN	Plumas	Mineral Twp	77	24
Ah	30	m	c	CHIN	Sacramento	Georgianna Twp	77	127
Ah	14	m	c	CHIN	Contra Costa	Martinez P O	71	430
DENGER								
Louisa	18	f	w	NY	Sacramento	2-Wd Sacramento	77	249
Margaret	40	f	w	IREL	San Francisco	2-Wd San Francisco	79	203
Mary	25	f	w	IREL	San Francisco	2-Wd San Francisco	79	170
Michael	45	m	w	BAVA	Yolo	Putah Twp	93	512
DENGIN								
Russion	33	m	w	AK	San Francisco	2-Wd San Francisco	79	272

© 2001 by Heritage Quest. All rights reserved.

Name	Age	S	R	B-PL	County	Locale	Series M593 Roll	Pg
DENGLE								
James	24	m	w	ENGL	Amador	Sutter Crk P O	69	410
DENGLER								
Adam	51	m	w	BAVA	Yolo	Putah Twp	93	511
Philip	35	m	w	BAVA	San Francisco	San Francisco P O	83	195
Philip	35	m	w	BAVA	San Francisco	San Francisco P O	83	165
DENGWER								
Wm	35	m	w	POLA	San Francisco	2-Wd San Francisco	79	254
DENHALTER								
Henry	39	m	w	HANO	San Joaquin	1-Wd Stockton	86	138
DENHAM								
Oswold	11	m	w	CA	San Francisco	San Francisco P O	80	539
Pocahontos	25	f	m	PA	San Francisco	2-Wd San Francisco	79	141
Wm	47	m	w	PRUS	San Francisco	2-Wd San Francisco	79	199
DENIAS								
William H	41	m	w	NY	Santa Clara	2-Wd San Jose	88	336
DENICE								
Percosper	38	m	w	NY	Inyo	Cerro Gordo Twp	73	323
R C	57	m	w	NY	Sutter	Nicolaus Twp	92	115
DENICKE								
Fredrick	68	f	w	HANO	San Francisco	11-Wd San Francisc	84	447
DENIEN								
John	40	m	w	FRAN	San Francisco	1-Wd San Francisco	79	99
DENIGAN								
Stancil	42	m	w	IN	Sacramento	Granite Twp	77	136
Thomas	32	m	w	IREL	San Francisco	11-Wd San Francisc	84	637
DENIGER								
John	40	m	w	SHOL	Alameda	Eden Twp	68	85
DENIKE								
William	40	m	w	IREL	San Francisco	San Francisco P O	80	367
DENIN								
A M	34	m	w	ME	Alameda	Oakland	68	217
John	38	m	w	IREL	Alameda	Oakland	68	258
Mary	40	f	w	MA	San Francisco	11-Wd San Francisc	84	653
William	24	m	w	IREL	Marin	San Rafael	74	56
DENINE								
Daniel	42	m	w	IREL	San Francisco	San Francisco P O	83	331
DENING								
John	21	m	w	ENGL	San Francisco	2-Wd San Francisco	79	252
DENINI								
Paul	40	m	w	SWIT	Marin	San Antonio Twp	74	62
DENIO								
C B	51	m	w	NY	Solano	Vallejo	90	191
John	46	m	w	VT	El Dorado	Mountain Twp	72	70
John	43	m	w	NY	San Francisco	San Francisco P O	83	64
Joseph	40	m	w	PA	Sutter	Butte Twp	92	100
Thomas	25	m	w	HAMB	Sacramento	Franklin Twp	77	110
DENIS								
Benjamin	32	m	b	NGRA	San Francisco	1-Wd San Francisco	79	96
Frank	55	m	w	IREL	Fresno	Millerton P O	72	164
J	35	m	w	IREL	Sierra	Butte Twp	89	509
John	61	m	w	GA	Yolo	Cottonwood Twp	93	470
Joseph	38	m	w	PORT	Alameda	Eden Twp	68	57
Joseph	23	m	w	PORT	Alameda	Eden Twp	68	64
Napoleon	38	m	w	FRAN	Calaveras	Copperopolis P O	70	246
DENISE								
Michael	26	m	w	IREL	Kern	Havilah P O	73	339
DENISON								
Eugene	46	m	w	FRAN	Trinity	Lewiston Pct	92	214
H	43	m	w	OH	Alameda	Oakland	68	260
J N	51	m	w	OH	Lake	Upper Lake	73	409
John	22	m	w	ENGL	San Francisco	7-Wd San Francisco	81	218
Precilla	50	f	w	PA	Yolo	Cache Crk Twp	93	428
DENIZOTT								
Jules	32	m	w	FRAN	San Francisco	6-Wd San Francisco	81	104
DENKE								
Steven	35	m	w	HOLL	San Francisco	1-Wd San Francisco	79	133
DENKER								
Andrew	29	m	w	CANA	Kern	Havilah P O	73	336
Henry	24	m	w	PRUS	Tulare	Visalia	92	296
Jacob	38	m	w	BAVA	Butte	Kimshew Tpw	70	83
John A	34	m	w	BAVA	Sonoma	Petaluma Twp	91	365
DENKIN								
Fred	35	m	w	PRUS	Contra Costa	Martinez P O	71	396
DENKINS								
William H	34	m	w	TN	El Dorado	Mud Springs Twp	72	81
DENKNER								
John	40	m	w	WURT	Contra Costa	Martinez P O	71	446
DENLIN								
Timothy	48	m	w	IREL	Placer	Bath P O	76	424
DENLY								
Henry	33	m	w	NY	San Francisco	San Francisco P O	83	85
DENMAN								
Chas	36	m	w	OH	Marin	San Rafael Twp	74	36
Eliza	18	f	w	NC	San Francisco	11-Wd San Francisc	84	618
Emma E	40	f	w	ENGL	San Francisco	San Francisco P O	85	768
Ezekiel	42	m	w	NY	Sonoma	Petaluma Twp	91	340
James	41	m	w	NY	San Francisco	San Francisco P O	83	147
Martin	30	m	w	NY	Mendocino	Point Arena Twp	74	205
DENMANN								
Andrew	38	m	w	OH	Humboldt	Pacific Twp	72	291
DENMARK								
Charles	42	m	w	NY	Mendocino	Anderson Twp	74	156
G J	41	m	w	NY	Monterey	Castroville Twp	74	326
Joseph	46	m	w	NY	Alameda	Washington Twp	68	289
DENMEAD								
Daniel	74	m	w	ENGL	Placer	Newcastle Twp	76	477
DENN								
A	56	m	w	KY	Sierra	Sierra Twp	89	566
Alex	63	m	w	KY	Merced	Snelling P O	74	279
John	52	m	w	NJ	San Francisco	San Francisco P O	83	224
John	28	m	w	ENGL	Nevada	Grass Valley Twp	75	228
O C	33	m	w	OH	Merced	Snelling P O	74	279
Thos A	32	m	w	NY	San Joaquin	1-Wd Stockton	86	131
DENNAN								
Patrick	46	m	w	IREL	San Francisco	11-Wd San Francisc	84	573
DENNAR								
Sarah	27	f	w	LA	Tulare	Farmersville Twp	92	244
DENNE								
M H	45	f	w	IREL	Alameda	Oakland	68	177
DENNEFF								
John	34	m	w	HANO	Stanislaus	San Joaquin Twp	92	76
DENNELLY								
Bridget	22	f	w	IREL	San Francisco	2-Wd San Francisco	79	231
Pat	41	m	w	IREL	San Francisco	2-Wd San Francisco	79	283
Thomas	70	m	w	IREL	San Francisco	2-Wd San Francisco	79	247
DENNEN								
John	31	m	w	TN	Nevada	Grass Valley Twp	75	176
William	20	m	w	MA	Amador	Drytown P O	69	415
DENNER								
Eph	38	m	w	OH	Tehama	Paskenta Twp	92	166
James	42	m	w	IN	Alameda	Washington Twp	68	290
John B	52	m	w	FRAN	Shasta	Dog Crk P O	89	471
Peter	38	m	w	HDAR	San Francisco	11-Wd San Francisc	84	455
DENNERY								
W C	40	m	w	IREL	Sacramento	1-Wd Sacramento	77	188
DENNESON								
Richard	18	m	w	HOLL	Plumas	Goodwin Twp	77	5
William	42	m	w	IREL	Sonoma	Petaluma Twp	91	353
DENNETT								
A G	39	m	w	NY	Nevada	Bloomfield Twp	75	96
Wm B	40	m	w	AL	Fresno	Millerton P O	72	152
DENNEY								
Bridget	31	f	w	IREL	San Francisco	San Francisco P O	83	243
Edwin	58	m	w	NY	San Francisco	7-Wd San Francisco	81	168
Ellen	27	f	w	IREL	Alameda	Oakland	68	132
J P	37	m	w	IL	Lake	Upper Lake	73	413
John	34	m	w	VA	Stanislaus	Washington Twp	92	87
John B	60	m	w	FRAN	Placer	Colfax P O	76	387
W C	57	m	w	SC	Nevada	Eureka Twp	75	135
DENNIAS								
Carl	15	m	w	CA	Stanislaus	Emory Twp	92	16
DENNICO								
F	70	m	w	FRAN	Santa Clara	Almaden Twp	88	20
DENNIE								
James	34	m	w	IREL	San Francisco	1-Wd San Francisco	79	93
William	42	m	w	NJ	Santa Clara	2-Wd San Jose	88	288
DENNIGAN								
Ellen	60	f	w	IREL	San Francisco	San Francisco P O	83	390
James	26	m	w	ENGL	San Francisco	San Francisco P O	83	155
Thomas	33	m	w	IREL	San Francisco	11-Wd San Francisc	84	502
DENNIN								
Charles	19	m	w	IREL	San Francisco	San Francisco P O	85	873
Hugh	30	m	w	IREL	Napa	Napa Twp	75	74
John	25	m	w	IREL	San Francisco	San Francisco P O	85	864
John	24	m	w	IREL	San Francisco	7-Wd San Francisco	81	236
DENNING								
E O	37	m	w	IN	San Francisco	San Francisco P O	85	831
Edward	25	m	w	CANA	Solano	Silveyville Twp	90	81
Geo D	39	m	w	HANO	Butte	Concow Twp	70	9
George	19	m	w	MO	Stanislaus	Empire Twp	92	66
J C	41	m	w	MA	Nevada	Meadow Lake Twp	75	246
James	33	m	w	ME	Placer	Dutch Flat P O	76	405
James M	23	m	w	LA	Santa Cruz	Soquel Twp	89	448
Johanna	24	f	w	IREL	Yolo	Cottonwood Twp	93	471
Margaret	30	f	w	ME	San Francisco	San Francisco P O	83	210
Otis	52	m	w	ME	Butte	Chico Twp	70	58
Pete	35	m	w	IREL	Santa Clara	Almaden Twp	88	12
Thos	21	m	w	OH	San Joaquin	Dent Twp	86	16
William	40	m	w	TN	Napa	Napa	75	2
DENNIS								
A	48	m	w	FRAN	Alameda	Oakland	68	132
A J	38	m	w	IL	Amador	Drytown P O	69	419
Alexander	42	m	w	ENGL	Calaveras	Copperopolis P O	70	261
Alx J	37	m	w	CANA	Sacramento	4-Wd Sacramento	77	336
Amos	30	m	w	NY	San Mateo	Redwood Twp	87	367
Baldwin	35	m	w	PA	Colusa	Colusa	71	291
Benjamin	51	m	w	IL	Yolo	Cache Crk Twp	93	438
C T	29	m	w	MA	San Francisco	San Francisco P O	85	787
Calvin	38	m	w	TN	Sutter	Yuba Twp	92	148
Calvin	31	m	w	IN	Sutter	Butte Twp	92	98
Carre	52	m	w	IREL	San Joaquin	2-Wd Stockton	86	200
Clara	16	f	w	CA	San Francisco	11-Wd San Francisc	84	505
D H Mrs	45	f	w	NJ	San Francisco	8-Wd San Francisco	82	347
D S	41	m	w	SCOT	Alameda	Oakland	68	157
David C	53	m	w	PA	Yuba	Slate Range Bar Tw	93	669
Delfornia	34	m	w	ME	Calaveras	Copperopolis P O	70	260
E	6	m	w	CA	San Joaquin	2-Wd Stockton	86	200
Edward	46	m	w	ENGL	San Bernardino	San Bernardino Twp	78	419
Edward	39	m	w	IN	Fresno	Millerton P O	72	148
Edwd	39	m	w	NY	San Francisco	1-Wd San Francisco	79	100
Elizabeth	35	f	w	CANA	Amador	Jackson P O	69	345
Ely	34	m	w	PA	Sutter	Yuba Twp	92	151
Francis	8	f	w	CA	Yolo	Cottonwood Twp	93	474

© 2001 by Heritage Quest. All rights reserved.

Name	Age	S	R	B-PL	County	Locale	Series M593 Roll	Pg
Frank B	27	m	w	MA	Santa Barbara	San Buenaventura P	87	437
Franklin	39	m	w	MO	Fresno	Millerton P O	72	148
Gabriel	36	m	w	ME	Santa Clara	Fremont Twp	88	55
George	42	m	m	AL	San Francisco	2-Wd San Francisco	79	230
George	36	m	w	TN	Sutter	Yuba Twp	92	148
George	30	m	w	IREL	San Francisco	7-Wd San Francisco	81	163
Henry	53	m	w	BAVA	Yuba	Marysville	93	580
Henry	50	m	w	PRUS	Alameda	Alameda	68	7
J M	53	m	w	MO	Amador	Sutter Crk P O	69	399
Jacob	37	m	w	BAVA	San Francisco	San Francisco P O	80	467
James	40	m	w	NJ	San Francisco	San Francisco P O	83	211
James	10	m	w	CA	Marin	San Rafael Twp	74	27
James M	41	m	w	OH	Placer	Auburn P O	76	359
James W	29	m	w	TN	Solano	Suisun Twp	90	108
Jane	25	f	w	IREL	San Francisco	7-Wd San Francisco	81	238
John	7	m	w	CA	Marin	San Rafael Twp	74	28
John	60	m	w	MO	Yolo	Cottonwood Twp	93	468
John	55	m	w	FRAN	San Francisco	San Francisco P O	80	476
John	50	m	w	ENGL	San Francisco	11-Wd San Francisc	84	503
John	40	m	w	IREL	San Francisco	San Francisco P O	80	417
John	37	m	w	IA	Santa Clara	2-Wd San Jose	88	329
John	35	m	w	IREL	Solano	Vallejo	90	215
John	25	m	w	MO	Mono	Bridgeport P O	74	285
Joseph	36	m	w	IREL	San Francisco	2-Wd San Francisco	79	144
Joseph	35	m	w	IREL	Santa Clara	2-Wd San Jose	88	333
Joseph	35	m	w	NY	San Francisco	5-Wd San Francisco	81	18
Joseph	32	m	w	IREL	Klamath	Trinidad Twp	73	391
Joseph	30	m	w	IREL	San Francisco	7-Wd San Francisco	81	263
Large	23	m	c	CHIN	Sutter	Yuba Twp	92	148
Leroy	28	m	w	IL	Fresno	Millerton P O	72	147
M A	50	f	w	NY	Sacramento	1-Wd Sacramento	77	175
Mary	55	f	w	IREL	San Francisco	San Francisco P O	83	378
Matthew L	41	m	w	KY	El Dorado	Placerville Twp	72	102
Michael	35	m	w	IREL	San Francisco	San Francisco P O	80	340
Nelson	43	m	w	OH	Santa Clara	2-Wd San Jose	88	298
Orrin	41	m	w	ME	Santa Clara	Fremont Twp	88	49
Patrick	31	m	w	IREL	Sutter	Butte Twp	92	102
Peter	64	m	w	CANA	Del Norte	Crescent	71	464
Peter	51	m	w	RI	San Francisco	2-Wd San Francisco	79	179
Richd	51	m	w	MA	Solano	Vallejo	90	201
Rodman	44	m	w	CT	San Francisco	5-Wd San Francisco	81	21
Roxana	9	f	w	CA	Santa Clara	Fremont Twp	88	49
Saml	42	m	w	TN	Fresno	Millerton P O	72	148
Saml	34	m	w	ME	San Francisco	11-Wd San Francisc	84	601
Saml	33	m	w	IREL	San Francisco	San Francisco P O	83	306
Samuel W	34	m	w	ME	San Francisco	8-Wd San Francisco	82	380
Sarah	59	f	w	NJ	Humboldt	Eureka Twp	72	258
Sullivan	30	m	w	IREL	Monterey	Pajaro Twp	74	375
Sylvia	65	f	b	SC	San Francisco	San Francisco P O	80	380
Sylvia	50	f	b	VA	San Francisco	San Francisco P O	80	386
T T	37	m	w	TN	San Joaquin	Elliott Twp	86	76
Thomas W	25	m	w	IREL	San Francisco	8-Wd San Francisco	82	460
Thos J	55	m	w	MA	San Francisco	8-Wd San Francisco	82	296
Valentin	40	m	w	GERM	Yolo	Merritt Twp	93	507
Vincent	38	m	w	PORT	San Francisco	6-Wd San Francisco	81	153
W H	30	m	w	ME	San Francisco	7-Wd San Francisco	81	220
W H	20	m	w	ME	Sierra	Gibson Twp	89	541
Walter	39	m	w	NY	Siskiyou	Scott Valley Twp	89	608
William	38	m	w	NY	San Francisco	7-Wd San Francisco	81	222
William	37	m	w	PA	Plumas	Quartz Twp	77	34
William A	33	m	w	ENGL	Santa Clara	Santa Clara Twp	88	135
William H	38	m	w	LA	Yolo	Cache Crk Twp	93	423
Wiseman	31	m	w	IREL	Sonoma	Sonoma Twp	91	438
Wm	61	m	w	NJ	San Joaquin	1-Wd Stockton	86	120
Wm	17	m	w	IREL	San Joaquin	Tulare Twp	86	259
DENNISON								
Alex	44	m	w	PA	Tehama	Battle Crk Twp	92	172
B T	26	m	w	VA	San Francisco	San Francisco P O	83	322
Celia	21	f	w	NY	Sonoma	Analy Twp	91	231
Chas H	50	m	w	ENGL	Nevada	Grass Valley Twp	75	168
D	39	m	w	IREL	Sacramento	3-Wd Sacramento	77	279
Edgar	51	m	w	PA	San Francisco	5-Wd San Francisco	81	22
Eira	53	m	w	IL	San Francisco	11-Wd San Francisc	84	527
Frank	34	m	w	PA	San Francisco	2-Wd San Francisco	79	181
George	33	m	w	PA	Santa Cruz	Santa Cruz	89	411
Harry	41	m	w	NY	Sacramento	2-Wd Sacramento	77	208
Isaac	42	m	w	NJ	San Francisco	11-Wd San Francisc	84	566
James	30	m	m	LA	Sacramento	2-Wd Sacramento	77	211
Jas	28	m	w	PA	Sierra	Sears Twp	89	558
Joseph L	40	m	w	NY	Sacramento	2-Wd Sacramento	77	208
Josepha	45	f	w	MEXI	San Francisco	11-Wd San Francisc	84	568
Margaret	55	f	w	SCOT	San Bernardino	Chino Twp	78	411
Maria T	50	f	w	NY	San Francisco	San Francisco P O	83	47
Mary	35	f	w	IREL	San Francisco	8-Wd San Francisco	82	498
Mary	21	f	w	NY	San Joaquin	1-Wd Stockton	86	135
Merrett	23	m	w	MO	Solano	Silveyville Twp	90	85
Mitchel	28	m	w	IREL	San Francisco	8-Wd San Francisco	82	345
Thomas	33	m	w	IREL	San Francisco	11-Wd San Francisc	84	485
Thomas	30	m	w	IREL	San Francisco	11-Wd San Francisc	84	653
W B	49	m	w	IN	Sonoma	Santa Rosa	91	417
William	30	m	w	IREL	Santa Clara	1-Wd San Jose	88	225
William	25	m	w	OH	San Francisco	7-Wd San Francisco	81	185
William H	40	m	w	NY	Los Angeles	Los Angeles	73	510
Wm	30	m	w	IREL	San Francisco	11-Wd San Francisc	84	614
Wm E	21	m	w	NY	San Francisco	7-Wd San Francisco	81	236
DENNISSON								
John K	37	m	w	CT	Mono	Bridgeport P O	74	283
DENNISTER								
Merritt	23	m	w	IA	Solano	Silveyville Twp	90	88
DENNISTON								
Benj	32	m	w	PA	San Francisco	1-Wd San Francisco	79	65
E George	37	m	w	NY	San Francisco	San Francisco P O	83	200
Isaac	66	m	w	NJ	San Mateo	Half Moon Bay P O	87	389
Joseph	45	m	w	IREL	Marin	San Rafael Twp	74	31
Richard	42	m	w	IREL	San Francisco	San Francisco P O	85	720
Sarah	57	f	w	VA	San Francisco	2-Wd San Francisco	79	219
DENNLER								
Jacob	40	m	w	SWIT	Nevada	Nevada Twp	75	297
DENNOND								
John	35	m	w	IREL	Solano	Vallejo	90	215
DENNY								
A H	35	m	w	WI	Siskiyou	Callahan P O	89	627
Charles	32	m	w	KY	Santa Clara	1-Wd San Jose	88	241
Edward	41	m	w	DE	San Francisco	11-Wd San Francisc	84	623
Hugh	57	m	w	IREL	Yolo	Washington Twp	93	531
James	38	m	w	MO	Humboldt	Arcata Twp	72	234
James E	34	m	w	IL	Tulare	Visalia	92	296
John	37	m	w	IREL	Sacramento	Dry Crk Twp	77	99
John	34	m	w	IREL	San Francisco	11-Wd San Francisc	84	531
John	26	m	w	IREL	San Francisco	5-Wd San Francisco	81	29
John N	33	m	w	KY	Merced	Snelling P O	74	248
John W	50	m	w	CANA	San Francisco	San Francisco P O	83	190
Margarett	80	f	w	IREL	Sacramento	Dry Crk Twp	77	99
Mary	45	f	w	IREL	San Francisco	San Francisco P O	80	340
Oliver	32	m	w	CANA	Yuba	Marysville	93	593
P A	41	m	w	KY	Tuolumne	Columbia P O	93	350
Patk	34	m	w	IREL	San Francisco	San Francisco P O	83	114
Patrick	40	m	w	IREL	Yolo	Washington Twp	93	529
Philip	35	m	w	IREL	Sacramento	2-Wd Sacramento	77	223
Porter	43	m	w	IL	Tehama	Bell Mills Twp	92	159
S S	40	m	w	IN	Mendocino	Little Lake Twp	74	196
Timothy	43	m	w	IREL	San Francisco	San Francisco P O	83	293
William	52	m	w	IREL	Plumas	Washington Twp	77	52
Wm	44	m	w	IN	Santa Clara	Gilroy Twp	88	102
DENO								
William	30	m	w	CANA	Santa Cruz	Santa Cruz Twp	89	390
DENOCHI								
Fredrino	31	m	w	ITAL	Sonoma	Analy Twp	91	236
DENOGEANT								
Caspar	45	m	w	FRAN	San Francisco	6-Wd San Francisco	81	40
DENOIN								
John	33	m	w	BREM	San Francisco	San Francisco P O	83	17
DENOK								
Deloris	38	m	w	MEXI	Tulare	Visalia	92	298
DENON								
Frank	35	m	w	ITAL	Calaveras	San Andreas P O	70	178
DENORE								
Chas	44	m	w	MEXI	Napa	Napa	75	55
DENOS								
Louis	50	m	w	FRAN	Marin	Sausalito Twp	74	69
DENOVAN								
Patrick	27	m	w	IREL	San Francisco	11-Wd San Francisc	84	495
DENOZO								
J M D	53	m	w	CA	El Dorado	Greenwood Twp	72	55
DENS								
Gustavus	36	m	w	FRAN	Trinity	North Fork Twp	92	219
Joseph	48	m	w	PORT	Trinity	Indian Crk	92	200
R C	45	m	w	MEXI	Tuolumne	Sonora P O	93	314
DENSBURY								
Bella	25	f	w	SCOT	San Francisco	6-Wd San Francisco	81	70
DENSEMORE								
John	34	m	w	MA	Sonoma	Salt Point	91	384
DENSEN								
Sam C	30	m	w	IL	Sacramento	4-Wd Sacramento	77	336
DENSLER								
Adam	51	m	w	BAVA	Solano	Tremont Twp	90	29
DENSMORE								
Hugh	35	m	w	NY	Solano	Tremont Twp	90	28
Jesse N	39	m	w	MA	Placer	Bath P O	76	459
John	48	m	w	NY	Santa Clara	Santa Clara Twp	88	178
John E	28	m	w	CANA	Sonoma	Vallejo Twp	91	458
Sanford	30	m	w	ME	Inyo	Independence Twp	73	326
Thos	40	m	w	IREL	San Francisco	1-Wd San Francisco	79	85
William	28	m	w	IA	Inyo	Bishop Crk Twp	73	310
DENSON								
Edward	32	m	w	IREL	San Francisco	7-Wd San Francisco	81	224
Eunice	22	f	w	LA	Yuba	Marysville	93	606
Fredk	24	m	w	SWED	San Francisco	1-Wd San Francisco	79	122
Thos A	32	m	w	IA	Tehama	Paynes Crk Twp	92	160
DENSTOFF								
Peter	22	m	w	PRUS	San Francisco	8-Wd San Francisco	82	356
DENSTORF								
Emil	23	m	w	HANO	San Francisco	San Francisco P O	83	176
DENSWORTH								
Chas	37	m	w	NY	San Francisco	1-Wd San Francisco	79	86
Edwd E	60	m	w	NY	San Francisco	1-Wd San Francisco	79	86
DENT								
D E	26	m	w	NJ	Santa Clara	Gilroy Twp	88	82
F	31	m	w	SCOT	Alameda	Oakland	68	265
F E	38	m	w	PRUS	Alameda	Oakland	68	263
F S	23	m	w	CANA	Alameda	Oakland	68	214
Fred	23	m	w	MS	San Francisco	San Francisco P O	83	107
G W	50	m	w	MO	San Francisco	San Francisco P O	85	809
George	28	m	w	IREL	Santa Barbara	San Buenaventura P	87	418

© 2001 by Heritage Quest. All rights reserved.

Name	Age	S	R	B-PL	County	Locale	Series M593 Roll	Pg
Henry	24	m	w	MO	San Francisco	11-Wd San Francisc	84	525
John	49	m	w	IREL	San Francisco	6-Wd San Francisco	81	133
Mary	28	f	w	MA	San Francisco	8-Wd San Francisco	82	349
Patrick	30	m	w	IREL	San Francisco	11-Wd San Francisc	84	455
Samuel	47	m	w	MO	Amador	Fiddletown P O	69	426
DENTAL								
Charles	49	m	w	FRAN	Marin	San Rafael Twp	74	38
DENTAN								
A A	51	m	w	NY	Alameda	Oakland	68	149
DENTNER								
Geo	22	m	w	FRAN	San Francisco	2-Wd San Francisco	79	229
DENTON								
Anna	35	f	w	NY	San Francisco	8-Wd San Francisco	82	392
Arnold	65	m	w	KY	Placer	Lincoln P O	76	489
Cynthie L	28	f	w	IL	Sacramento	Franklin Twp	77	114
Ebenezer	40	m	w	MA	Santa Clara	Fremont Twp	88	41
Edward M	50	m	w	NY	Nevada	Rough & Ready Twp	75	336
Harris	32	m	w	TN	Los Angeles	Los Nietos Twp	73	580
John	44	m	w	NY	Yuba	Rose Bar Twp	93	655
John	30	m	w	NY	San Francisco	11-Wd San Francisc	84	541
John F	37	m	w	ENGL	Inyo	Independence Twp	73	328
Patrick	28	m	w	IREL	Inyo	Independence Twp	73	328
Salomon	52	m	w	NY	Sacramento	4-Wd Sacramento	77	353
W A	48	m	w	NJ	Tuolumne	Columbia P O	93	362
W H	42	m	w	IL	Yuba	Marysville	93	608
Wm	32	m	w	KY	Yuba	East Bear Rvr Twp	93	543
DENTS								
John	77	m	w	SWED	Contra Costa	Martinez Twp	71	348
DENUKER								
Henry	38	m	w	HANO	Nevada	Bridgeport Twp	75	105
DENUNE								
J P	40	m	w	CANA	Sierra	Gibson Twp	89	540
DENVER								
William	34	m	w	IREL	San Francisco	8-Wd San Francisco	82	409
DENWORTH								
Peter	28	m	w	IREL	San Francisco	San Francisco P O	83	8
DENYON								
Clemence	20	f	w	FRAN	San Francisco	6-Wd San Francisco	81	72
DENZELL								
Robert	31	m	w	CANA	Sonoma	Salt Point	91	380
DENZELMAN								
Frederick	25	m	w	PRUS	San Francisco	8-Wd San Francisco	82	388
DENZER								
Peter	47	m	w	BAVA	Amador	Volcano P O	69	385
DENZLER								
Jacob	42	m	w	SWIT	San Francisco	8-Wd San Francisco	82	398
DEO								
Ah	27	f	c	CHIN	Santa Clara	1-Wd San Jose	88	272
DEOIT								
Felix	40	m	w	IREL	Santa Cruz	Pajaro Twp	89	345
DEOKER								
William	59	m	w	NY	Sonoma	Petaluma Twp	91	364
DEOLIN								
Edwd	36	m	w	NY	San Francisco	1-Wd San Francisco	79	125
Thomas	36	m	w	CANA	Humboldt	Arcata Twp	72	232
DEOLOQUES								
Maria	15	f	w	CA	Los Angeles	Los Angeles	73	508
DEON								
Fred	42	m	w	NY	San Joaquin	Castoria Twp	86	7
Gee	25	m	c	CHIN	Plumas	Mineral Twp	77	24
DEOR								
Henry	37	m	w	OH	Sacramento	Franklin Twp	77	121
DEORSAY								
Jos W	26	m	w	FRAN	San Francisco	San Francisco P O	83	173
DEOS								
Manuel	49	m	w	MEXI	Calaveras	San Andreas P O	70	197
DEP								
Ah	43	m	c	CHIN	Plumas	Plumas Twp	77	31
Ah	18	m	c	CHIN	Shasta	American Ranch P O	89	497
DEPAS								
Chas Birg	24	m	w	LA	San Francisco	San Francisco P O	83	44
F	40	m	w	FRAN	San Joaquin	Tulare Twp	86	263
William	28	m	w	NY	San Francisco	8-Wd San Francisco	82	458
DEPASS								
Alexander	28	m	m	WIND	San Francisco	San Francisco P O	80	371
DEPAUL								
Joseph	8	m	w	CA	Marin	San Rafael Twp	74	28
DEPAULA								
Dominica	22	m	w	ITAL	Amador	Volcano P O	69	384
Vinzenea	30	m	w	ITAL	Amador	Volcano P O	69	384
DEPAULI								
Antonio	36	m	w	ITAL	Mariposa	Mariposa P O	74	108
Antonio	25	m	w	ITAL	Mariposa	Mariposa P O	74	91
DEPEE								
Thomas	52	m	b	PA	San Francisco	San Francisco P O	80	415
DEPENCIER								
John	26	m	w	CANA	Sonoma	Analy Twp	91	234
DEPERE								
Paul	38	m	w	CANA	Sacramento	4-Wd Sacramento	77	333
DEPERRY								
Herter	45	f	w	NY	Contra Costa	Martinez P O	71	407
DEPETING								
Teronato	52	m	w	ITAL	Amador	Jackson P O	69	339
DEPEW								
Isaac	45	m	w	NY	Nevada	Rough & Ready Twp	75	337
DEPHOLZ								
George	40	m	w	HANO	Amador	Volcano P O	69	385
DEPINETT								
Joseph	43	m	w	FRAN	Trinity	Canyon City Pct	92	201
DEPKIN								
Gerard	26	m	w	PRUS	San Francisco	6-Wd San Francisco	81	91
DEPME								
T	39	m	w	NY	Alameda	Oakland	68	202
DEPO								
John	30	m	w	CANA	Yuba	East Bear Rvr Twp	93	540
DEPONT								
John	37	m	w	FRAN	Alameda	Murray Twp	68	108
DEPOSIER								
Frank	38	m	w	OH	Colusa	Monroe Twp	71	311
DEPOW								
William	40	m	w	NY	Calaveras	San Andreas P O	70	198
DEPOWDI								
Gilman	22	m	w	ITAL	San Francisco	11-Wd San Francisc	84	701
DEPP								
John	48	m	w	KY	Mendocino	Little Lake Twp	74	193
DEPPEN								
Annie	12	f	w	PRUS	San Francisco	San Francisco P O	85	718
DEPPOLD								
Hunrich	27	m	w	BAVA	San Francisco	San Francisco P O	85	759
DEPRAY								
Celestine	32	m	w	PA	Contra Costa	Martinez P O	71	380
Paul	51	m	w	LA	Shasta	American Ranch P O	89	496
DEPREFONTAINE								
J R	28	m	w	MO	San Francisco	San Francisco P O	83	296
Mary	58	f	w	DE	San Francisco	San Francisco P O	83	339
DEPREY								
Joseph	39	m	w	CANA	San Francisco	11-Wd San Francisc	84	612
Julian	27	m	w	CANA	Contra Costa	San Pablo Twp	71	365
DEPRIES								
Joseph	28	m	w	PRUS	San Francisco	7-Wd San Francisco	81	224
DEPUE								
Spencer	26	m	w	OH	Yuba	Marysville	93	603
DEPUIS								
Francois	39	m	w	FRAN	San Francisco	11-Wd San Francisc	84	568
DEPULAH								
Johose	20	m	w	ITAL	San Francisco	11-Wd San Francisc	84	712
DEPUTRON								
Jacob	56	m	w	FRAN	San Francisco	2-Wd San Francisco	79	202
DEPUY								
James	35	m	w	NY	Yolo	Buckeye Twp	93	417
Sylvanus H	53	m	w	NY	Yolo	Buckeye Twp	93	416
DEQUAY								
James	40	m	w	FRAN	San Francisco	San Francisco P O	80	455
DEQUEANT								
Not	54	m	w	SCOT	San Joaquin	Douglas Twp	86	51
DEQUIRE								
P W	44	m	w	MO	San Joaquin	2-Wd Stockton	86	199
DERAS								
Sylvera	36	m	w	MEXI	Santa Clara	Almaden Twp	88	12
DERAY								
Edward	25	m	w	FRAN	Santa Clara	2-Wd San Jose	88	324
Jean	76	m	w	FRAN	Santa Clara	Alviso Twp	88	26
DERBIN								
Adolphus	40	m	w	VT	Santa Clara	Fremont Twp	88	57
John	24	m	w	IREL	Solano	Silveyville Twp	90	75
Theressa	78	f	w	KY	Solano	Green Valley Twp	90	41
Warren P	45	m	w	MO	Solano	Green Valley Twp	90	41
DERBORAUGH								
Danel	34	m	w	NJ	Sacramento	Brighton Twp	77	73
DERBY								
Andrew B	39	m	w	MA	Sonoma	Petaluma Twp	91	326
Charles	9	m	w	ASEA	San Francisco	San Francisco P O	85	754
Charles	26	m	w	MA	San Francisco	11-Wd San Francisc	84	548
Charles B	26	m	w	NY	Sacramento	2-Wd Sacramento	77	248
Charles L	42	m	w	VT	El Dorado	Diamond Springs Tw	72	25
Chas	27	m	w	MA	San Francisco	San Francisco P O	83	284
Chas B	38	m	w	IL	Sacramento	1-Wd Sacramento	77	173
E Mrs	52	f	w	VT	Napa	Napa Twp	75	28
Edward	41	m	w	MA	Alameda	Brooklyn Twp	68	40
Emma	23	f	w	OH	San Francisco	2-Wd San Francisco	79	248
George	22	m	w	MA	Santa Clara	Alviso Twp	88	23
George H	57	m	w	VT	Sonoma	Analy Twp	91	226
Joseph	40	m	w	ENGL	San Francisco	5-Wd San Francisco	81	36
Laura A	43	f	w	MA	Santa Clara	2-Wd San Jose	88	330
Thomas	27	m	w	NY	San Francisco	San Francisco P O	83	393
Thos	32	m	w	CANA	Sacramento	Granite Twp	77	144
Warren H	41	m	w	MA	Napa	Yountville Twp	75	90
DERCKS								
Ludwig	25	m	w	SHOL	Sonoma	Bodega Twp	91	260
DEREAMER								
D	41	m	w	NY	Napa	Napa	75	56
DEREITER								
Chas	89	m	w	PRUS	San Francisco	11-Wd San Francisc	84	649
DEREMA								
Susan	25	f	w	MA	San Francisco	1-Wd San Francisco	79	110
DERENG								
Jno	25	m	w	IREL	Sacramento	3-Wd Sacramento	77	260
DERENTINGER								
Joseph	28	m	w	FRAN	Alameda	Washington Twp	68	292
DERETCALE								
Charles	30	m	w	SWED	Sacramento	Brighton Twp	77	73
DERGAN								
Jas	39	m	w	PA	Sacramento	4-Wd Sacramento	77	376

© 2001 by Heritage Quest. All rights reserved.

Name	Age	S	R	B-PL	County	Locale	Series M593 Roll	Pg
DERHAM								
Anna	22	f	w	NY	San Francisco	2-Wd San Francisco	79	255
B	53	m	w	IREL	San Francisco	San Francisco P O	85	795
Charles J	32	m	w	ENGL	Sonoma	Salt Point Twp	91	384
D	40	m	w	IREL	Solano	Benicia	90	9
Edward	47	m	w	IREL	Nevada	Grass Valley Twp	75	149
Edward B	45	m	w	MA	San Francisco	5-Wd San Francisco	81	19
James	60	m	w	IREL	San Francisco	2-Wd San Francisco	79	255
DERHY								
John	31	m	w	VT	San Joaquin	1-Wd Stockton	86	123
DERIAS								
Sixto	32	m	w	PORT	Monterey	San Juan Twp	74	396
DERICK								
Augustus	50	m	b	AL	Mariposa	Mariposa P O	74	97
DERIDER								
Peter	40	m	w	HOLL	San Francisco	San Francisco P O	83	77
DERIEMER								
Mary	17	f	w	HOLL	San Francisco	San Francisco P O	85	768
DERIJIAH								
Frank	40	m	w	FRAN	San Joaquin	1-Wd Stockton	86	122
DERIN								
Joseph F	41	m	w	IREL	Los Angeles	San Gabriel Twp	73	597
DERK								
Frank	52	m	w	BAVA	Mariposa	Mariposa P O	74	90
DERKIN								
William	25	m	w	MO	Colusa	Colusa	71	289
DERLER								
John	52	m	w	FRAN	Sacramento	Natomas Twp	77	165
DERLEY								
Michael	38	m	w	IREL	Colusa	Colusa	71	290
DERLIN								
Mark	35	m	w	IREL	San Mateo	Schoolhouse Statio	87	339
Mathew	36	m	w	IREL	San Francisco	11-Wd San Francisc	84	434
DERMAN								
Wm	57	m	w	PA	Sonoma	Russian Rvr	91	370
DERMER								
Mc Chas	22	m	w	OR	Santa Clara	Gilroy Twp	88	97
DERMETT								
George H	36	m	w	ME	Santa Cruz	Santa Cruz Twp	89	387
DERMODY								
Edd	46	m	w	IREL	Yuba	Bullards Bar P O	93	547
Jas W	31	m	w	NY	San Francisco	San Francisco P O	83	330
Kate	25	f	w	IREL	San Francisco	San Francisco P O	83	113
Maggy	24	f	w	NY	Solano	Vallejo	90	139
Mich	56	m	w	IREL	San Francisco	San Francisco P O	85	840
DERMOE								
Elizabeth	48	f	w	ENGL	San Francisco	San Francisco P O	85	853
DERMOND								
Dennis	35	m	w	IREL	San Francisco	San Francisco P O	83	296
Jerry	23	m	w	IREL	Placer	Summit P O	76	495
Patrick	40	m	w	IREL	Kern	Havilah P O	73	350
DERMOT								
John	42	m	w	MA	Alameda	Oakland	68	149
DERMOTT								
Jane	36	f	w	IREL	San Francisco	1-Wd San Francisco	79	35
Jos	40	m	w	IREL	San Joaquin	Elkhorn Twp	86	66
Kate	28	f	w	IREL	Contra Costa	Martinez P O	71	415
Patk	24	m	w	IREL	San Francisco	1-Wd San Francisco	79	76
DERMOTTY								
Kate	40	f	w	IREL	San Francisco	8-Wd San Francisco	82	403
DERNER								
Geo A	43	m	w	WURT	Solano	Benicia	90	6
John	28	m	w	IREL	Solano	Vallejo	90	213
DERNEY								
P J	40	m	w	IREL	Tuolumne	Big Oak Flat P O	93	405
DERNHAM								
Henry	25	m	w	PRUS	San Francisco	6-Wd San Francisco	81	87
DERNICK								
John	23	m	w	IREL	Mendocino	Navarro & Big Rvr	74	174
DERNITZSKI								
Ch	45	m	w	POLA	San Francisco	8-Wd San Francisco	82	306
DERNON								
Pete	25	m	w	SCOT	Sacramento	1-Wd Sacramento	77	203
DERNSIA								
Susan	23	f	w	ME	Placer	Bath P O	76	426
DERNY								
William S	60	m	w	DE	Los Angeles	El Monte Twp	73	460
DERO								
Chas	55	m	w	NY	San Francisco	San Francisco P O	83	100
DEROCHBUNE								
Alfred	52	m	w	FRAN	Santa Clara	2-Wd San Jose	88	331
DEROIN								
Frank	40	m	w	MO	Sonoma	Sonoma Twp	91	442
DEROIS								
Fred	30	m	w	GA	Sacramento	1-Wd Sacramento	77	172
DEROLMAN								
Duse	32	m	w	ITAL	San Francisco	11-Wd San Francisc	84	709
DERON								
William	25	m	w	CANA	San Francisco	11-Wd San Francisc	84	500
DEROQUET								
Louis	33	m	w	FRAN	San Francisco	San Francisco P O	80	354
DEROSA								
Jane	37	f	w	FRAN	San Joaquin	1-Wd Stockton	86	123
DEROSEAR								
Joseph	24	m	w	CANA	Nevada	Grass Valley Twp	75	225
DEROSI								
Pierre	46	m	w	CANA	Sacramento	4-Wd Sacramento	77	343

Name	Age	S	R	B-PL	County	Locale	Series M593 Roll	Pg
DEROSSI								
Albert	31	m	w	ITAL	San Francisco	1-Wd San Francisco	79	41
DEROY								
John	34	m	w	IREL	San Mateo	Schoolhouse Statio	87	337
DERPRES								
Phillip F	40	m	w	FRAN	San Francisco	11-Wd San Francisc	84	699
DERR								
Peter	58	m	w	PA	Humboldt	Eel Rvr Twp	72	246
DERRAGETTA								
Peter	28	m	w	SWIT	Amador	Volcano P O	69	386
DERRAGH								
Pat	37	m	w	IREL	San Francisco	7-Wd San Francisco	81	276
DERRENAY								
Antoine	44	m	w	ME	San Francisco	San Francisco P O	83	189
DERRICK								
Alexander	22	m	w	AL	Kern	Bakersfield P O	73	360
Alonzo	46	m	w	ME	Butte	Ophir Twp	70	114
Annie	10	f	w	CA	San Francisco	San Francisco P O	85	827
Anthony	46	m	w	FRAN	Alpine	Woodfords P O	69	315
Edwin S	25	m	w	WI	Butte	Oroville Twp	70	138
Frouzee	34	m	w	HOLL	Yolo	Cache Crk Twp	93	445
George	9	m	w	CA	San Francisco	San Francisco P O	85	827
George W	23	m	w	MO	Placer	Pino Twp	76	470
Henry	29	m	w	HANO	San Francisco	11-Wd San Francisc	84	476
Honora	65	f	w	IREL	San Francisco	San Francisco P O	83	378
John	45	m	w	TN	Placer	Pino Twp	76	470
John	40	m	m	AR	Santa Cruz	Watsonville	89	376
Joseph	42	m	w	TN	Sonoma	Mendocino Twp	91	295
Marian	22	m	w	TX	San Bernardino	Chino Twp	78	411
Peter	80	m	w	IREL	San Francisco	San Francisco P O	83	378
T F	27	m	w	TN	Sonoma	Bodega Twp	91	259
Walter	19	m	w	MO	Mendocino	Big Rvr Twp	74	171
Wm H	22	m	w	MO	Sonoma	Bodega Twp	91	264
DERRICKE								
C F N	33	m	w	NORW	San Francisco	8-Wd San Francisco	82	364
DERRICKSON								
--- [Dr]	35	m	w	NY	Yuba	Marysville	93	588
B F	40	m	w	KY	Nevada	Bridgeport Twp	75	104
Dvd	51	m	w	DE	Contra Costa	Martinez P O	71	446
DERRING								
Delia	19	f	w	IREL	Sacramento	2-Wd Sacramento	77	227
Elden	26	m	w	MA	Nevada	Grass Valley Twp	75	228
George	49	m	w	CANA	San Diego	Julian Dist	78	468
DERRINGER								
Jeru	38	m	w	TN	San Francisco	11-Wd San Francisc	84	429
W C	30	m	w	GERM	Marin	San Rafael Twp	74	40
DERRIS								
John	25	m	w	NY	Alameda	Oakland	68	261
Santa	50	m	w	SPAI	Butte	Oregon Twp	70	124
DERRIVAN								
M	50	m	w	IREL	Yuba	Rose Bar Twp	93	660
DERROLIN								
John	31	m	w	ITAL	Amador	Fiddletown P O	69	433
DERRY								
August	33	m	w	BELG	San Francisco	2-Wd San Francisco	79	184
Thos	46	m	w	OH	Butte	Kimshew Tpw	70	82
Thos	37	m	w	ENGL	Solano	Vallejo	90	195
William	40	m	b	PA	San Francisco	8-Wd San Francisco	82	431
DERSCH								
George	39	m	w	BAVA	Shasta	Millville P O	89	489
DERSOM								
G S	33	m	w	NJ	Sierra	Eureka Twp	89	523
DERTH								
Irving	37	m	w	OH	Sacramento	Cosumnes Twp	77	89
DERTHESON								
David	34	m	w	TN	Monterey	Pajaro Twp	74	374
DERTRIG								
Eugone	51	m	w	SWIT	Placer	Blue Canyon P O	76	419
DERUSSY								
Helen A	37	f	w	VA	San Francisco	San Francisco P O	83	96
Linda	21	f	w	KY	San Francisco	San Francisco P O	85	746
Rene E	27	m	w	VA	San Francisco	San Francisco P O	85	745
DERUTH								
Thoph	17	m	w	CA	Alameda	Oakland	68	257
DERUTTE								
Wm	31	m	w	FRAN	San Francisco	8-Wd San Francisco	82	375
DERVAN								
John	31	m	w	IREL	San Francisco	2-Wd San Francisco	79	156
DERVIN								
John	50	m	w	IREL	Yuba	Rose Bar Twp	93	662
Theresa	16	f	w	NY	Alameda	Washington Twp	68	271
DERVY								
Jahio	43	m	w	NY	Sacramento	Sutter Twp	77	386
DERWA								
John	40	m	w	IREL	Monterey	Castroville Twp	74	333
DERWE								
De Pillers	30	m	w	CANA	Sierra	Sears Twp	89	556
DERWIN								
Anne	20	f	w	IREL	San Francisco	8-Wd San Francisco	82	483
John	41	m	w	IREL	Sonoma	Analy Twp	91	244
Louis	33	m	w	IN	Monterey	Pajaro Twp	74	377
M S	50	m	w	IREL	Solano	Vallejo	90	165
DERWITT								
Daniel	19	m	w	CANA	Sonoma	Sonoma Twp	91	431
DERY								
Louis	39	m	w	FRAN	San Francisco	San Francisco P O	80	479

© 2001 by Heritage Quest. All rights reserved.

Name	Age	S	R	B-PL	County	Locale	Series M593 Roll	Pg
DESADA								
Justa	27	f	w	SPAI	San Francisco	8-Wd San Francisco	82	467
DESAINT								
Denis Jules	36	m	w	FRAN	San Francisco	11-Wd San Francisc	84	568
DESALLA								
Jacob	52	m	w	HOLL	San Francisco	2-Wd San Francisco	79	143
DESALLAS								
Envalla	45	f	w	MEXI	San Francisco	San Francisco P O	83	398
DESALME								
John	43	m	w	FRAN	El Dorado	Placerville Twp	72	102
DESANGE								
Jacques	67	m	w	FRAN	San Francisco	2-Wd San Francisco	79	146
DESANOZ								
Steven	67	m	w	NH	San Francisco	3-Wd San Francisco	79	300
DESANY								
Bridget	40	f	w	IREL	San Francisco	2-Wd San Francisco	79	138
DESAULIS								
James	33	m	w	FRAN	San Francisco	1-Wd San Francisco	79	50
DESAULUS								
Norbert	34	m	w	CANA	Los Angeles	Los Angeles	73	567
DESBOCK								
John	24	m	w	NY	San Francisco	2-Wd San Francisco	79	182
DESCALSO								
Mary	38	f	w	IREL	San Francisco	San Francisco P O	85	782
DESCAMPS								
Bernard	70	m	w	BELG	San Francisco	11-Wd San Francisc	84	476
DESCHAMPS								
Gustave	36	m	w	FRAN	San Francisco	San Francisco P O	80	483
DESCHANET								
Martin	61	m	w	FRAN	Santa Clara	2-Wd San Jose	88	328
DESCHE								
John	35	m	w	CANA	Nevada	Nevada Twp	75	276
DESCON								
Henry St J	27	m	w	MS	Fresno	Millerton P O	72	156
DESEBROCK								
Fred	47	m	w	HANO	San Francisco	San Francisco P O	83	78
DESELBROCK								
C	38	m	w	HANO	Alameda	Oakland	68	229
DESENFANTS								
Eugene	39	m	w	FRAN	Santa Clara	1-Wd San Jose	88	233
DESERALE								
Among	53	m	w	FRAN	Calaveras	Copperopolis P O	70	244
DESERT								
Arcola	50	m	w	ITAL	El Dorado	Diamond Springs Tw	72	27
DESEVE								
J B	50	m	w	CANA	Sacramento	4-Wd Sacramento	77	348
DESEVILLE								
George	34	m	m	FL	Nevada	Grass Valley Twp	75	167
DESGARDEN								
Alex	37	m	w	CANA	Sierra	Sears Twp	89	557
DESGRIPPEE								
E	39	m	w	FRAN	Solano	Benicia	90	14
DESHAM								
James	24	m	w	NY	San Francisco	San Francisco P O	80	421
DESHEAR								
J	24	m	w	IA	Lassen	Janesville Twp	73	431
DESHIELDS								
Brit	27	m	w	LA	Tehama	Red Bluff	92	173
DESHLET								
Louis	63	m	w	FRAN	El Dorado	White Oak Twp	72	141
DESIDERO								
Anto	18	m	w	CA	San Diego	San Luis Rey	78	513
DESIGER								
John	29	m	w	BADE	Marin	San Rafael Twp	74	34
DESILLER								
Constant	44	m	w	AZOR	Marin	Sausalito Twp	74	69
DESILVA								
Pascal	44	m	w	ITAL	Nevada	Grass Valley Twp	75	168
DESILVER								
J	40	m	w	PORT	Alameda	Murray Twp	68	104
DESIMONE								
Joseph	40	m	w	ITAL	Santa Clara	1-Wd San Jose	88	224
DESINAL								
Danl	64	m	w	ENGL	Sonoma	Santa Rosa	91	409
DESINE								
Bridget	27	f	w	IREL	San Francisco	San Francisco P O	83	148
DESIRCH								
Christopher	40	m	w	ITAL	San Francisco	2-Wd San Francisco	79	180
DESIRE								
Lafafa	62	f	w	FRAN	San Francisco	2-Wd San Francisco	79	226
DESLANDES								
David	55	m	w	FRAN	Mariposa	Mariposa P O	74	133
Emile	43	f	w	FRAN	Mariposa	Mariposa P O	74	117
DESLLEMO								
Peter	53	m	w	FRAN	Inyo	Cerro Gordo Twp	73	320
DESMACLAIR								
S	44	m	w	CANA	El Dorado	Greenwood Twp	72	53
DESMARTIN								
John	26	m	w	SWIT	Marin	San Antonio Twp	74	62
DESMEBON								
Adelaide	34	f	w	FRAN	San Francisco	6-Wd San Francisco	81	89
DESMEE								
Joseph	49	m	w	FRAN	San Francisco	San Francisco P O	80	348
Joseph	49	m	w	FRAN	San Francisco	San Francisco P O	80	347
DESMON								
Anne	40	f	w	IREL	San Francisco	11-Wd San Francisc	84	609
J	11	m	w	MA	Yuba	Linda Twp	93	556
DESMOND								
Amon	43	m	w	FRAN	Trinity	Lewiston Pct	92	212
Ann	48	f	w	IREL	San Francisco	San Francisco P O	83	122
Arthur	34	m	w	IREL	Sutter	Sutter Twp	92	129
Bridget	30	f	w	IREL	San Francisco	8-Wd San Francisco	82	470
C	44	m	w	IREL	San Francisco	San Francisco P O	83	297
Cathrine	70	f	w	IREL	San Francisco	1-Wd San Francisco	79	38
Cornelius	29	m	w	IREL	Marin	San Rafael	74	58
D	44	m	w	IREL	Sacramento	4-Wd Sacramento	77	373
Dan	37	m	w	IREL	San Francisco	11-Wd San Francisc	84	653
Daniel	40	m	w	IREL	San Francisco	San Francisco P O	83	59
Daniel	38	m	w	IREL	San Francisco	San Francisco P O	83	77
Daniel	36	m	w	IREL	Los Angeles	Los Angeles	73	546
Daniel	28	m	w	IREL	San Francisco	San Francisco P O	85	734
Dennis	46	m	w	IREL	Shasta	French Gulch P O	89	467
Edwd	40	m	w	IREL	San Francisco	San Francisco P O	83	39
Felix	15	m	w	CA	San Francisco	11-Wd San Francisc	84	451
James	40	m	w	IREL	San Francisco	11-Wd San Francisc	84	550
Jeremh	42	m	w	IREL	Monterey	Pajaro Twp	74	368
Jeremiah	27	m	w	IREL	San Francisco	San Francisco P O	83	149
Johann	32	m	w	IREL	Trinity	Weaverville Pct	92	224
John	40	m	w	IREL	San Francisco	2-Wd San Francisco	79	244
John	35	m	w	IREL	San Francisco	San Francisco P O	83	8
John	19	m	w	NY	Marin	Nicasio Twp	74	16
M E	16	f	w	MA	San Francisco	San Francisco P O	85	854
Margaret	30	f	w	IREL	San Francisco	8-Wd San Francisco	82	399
Margaret	27	f	w	IREL	Marin	San Rafael	74	58
Mary	60	f	w	IREL	Marin	San Rafael	74	58
Michael	42	m	w	IREL	Nevada	Grass Valley Twp	75	166
Michl	30	m	w	IREL	San Francisco	1-Wd San Francisco	79	38
Pat	26	m	w	IREL	Sacramento	1-Wd Sacramento	77	185
Patk	35	m	w	IREL	Sacramento	1-Wd Sacramento	77	178
Patrick	40	m	w	IREL	San Francisco	8-Wd San Francisco	82	396
Patrick	24	m	w	IREL	San Francisco	San Francisco P O	83	305
Patrick	23	m	w	IREL	San Francisco	San Francisco P O	80	339
Rosetta	70	f	w	ITAL	Santa Clara	1-Wd San Jose	88	235
T S	28	m	w	IN	Nevada	Meadow Lake Twp	75	268
Thomas	31	m	w	IREL	San Mateo	San Mateo P O	87	355
Timothy	45	m	w	IREL	Calaveras	San Andreas P O	70	170
Willie	14	m	w	CA	Marin	San Rafael Twp	74	33
Wm	39	m	w	IREL	San Francisco	San Francisco P O	83	92
Wm	35	m	w	IREL	San Francisco	San Francisco P O	83	20
Wm K	50	m	w	IREL	Placer	Bath P O	76	425
DESMORNES								
Jean	27	m	w	FRAN	San Francisco	6-Wd San Francisco	81	72
DESNAY								
P	39	m	w	IREL	San Joaquin	2-Wd Stockton	86	173
DESOLA								
Pierre	42	m	w	CHIL	San Francisco	San Francisco P O	80	537
DESON								
Frank	34	m	w	ITAL	Calaveras	San Andreas P O	70	183
DESONJE								
Gabriel	52	m	w	CANA	Monterey	Monterey Twp	74	347
DESORMAND								
Charles	40	m	w	CANA	San Francisco	San Francisco P O	83	249
DESOTO								
Antonio	32	m	w	AZOR	Contra Costa	San Pablo Twp	71	359
DESOUZA								
Thos M	35	m	m	JAMA	San Francisco	San Francisco P O	83	113
DESOZA								
John	33	m	w	SCOT	Siskiyou	Yreka Twp	89	669
DESPAIN								
Thomas	35	m	w	TN	Kern	Linns Valley P O	73	344
DESPALOTROVITCH								
M	34	m	w	AUST	Sierra	Gibson Twp	89	541
DESPEUX								
Mary	35	f	w	MA	San Francisco	San Francisco P O	83	102
DESPIUS								
Constant	60	m	w	FRAN	San Francisco	11-Wd San Francisc	84	461
DESPLAS								
John	44	m	w	FRAN	Calaveras	San Andreas P O	70	157
John	42	m	w	FRAN	Tuolumne	Big Oak Flat P O	93	400
John	38	m	w	BAVA	Tuolumne	Chinese Camp P O	93	365
DESPONNER								
Claude	22	m	w	FRAN	San Francisco	San Francisco P O	83	135
DESPOSI								
Blass	40	m	w	FRAN	Monterey	San Antonio Twp	74	321
DESPREZ								
Adolphe Hyp	59	m	w	FRAN	San Francisco	San Francisco P O	83	135
DESRAD								
Jane	34	f	w	IREL	Alameda	Oakland	68	150
DESROCHES								
Moses	44	m	w	NH	Plumas	Indian Twp	77	18
DESROSIERS								
Andr	30	m	w	CANA	Sierra	Sears Twp	89	558
DESROSSIER								
Huarly	40	m	w	CANA	San Francisco	11-Wd San Francisc	84	703
DESSAUTEL								
Joseph	29	m	w	CANA	Marin	Tomales Twp	74	83
DESSE								
Wm	32	m	w	PRUS	San Francisco	San Francisco P O	83	81
DESSENAN								
H H	73	m	w	HANO	Amador	Jackson P O	69	324
DESSENBURY								
John	40	m	w	ENGL	Monterey	San Juan Twp	74	408
DESSLER								
Isaac	47	m	w	OH	Tuolumne	Big Oak Flat P O	93	397

© 2001 by Heritage Quest. All rights reserved.

Name	Age	S	R	B-PL	County	Locale	Series M593 Roll	Pg
DESSOL								
Emil	31	m	w	FRAN	San Francisco	6-Wd San Francisco	81	86
DESSON								
Jas	25	m	w	IREL	San Francisco	8-Wd San Francisco	82	364
DESTANG								
Alfred	25	m	w	FRAN	San Francisco	6-Wd San Francisco	81	137
DESTIHAM								
H A	31	m	w	DENM	Alameda	Oakland	68	265
DESTOP								
John	40	m	w	FRAN	Los Angeles	Los Angeles Twp	73	473
DESTOUELLE								
R O	33	m	w	NY	Nevada	Eureka Twp	75	136
DESTUGUE								
Victor	31	m	w	FRAN	San Francisco	1-Wd San Francisco	79	54
DESTY								
Charles	35	m	w	FRAN	San Bernardino	San Bernardino Twp	78	453
Robert	47	m	w	CANA	San Francisco	7-Wd San Francisco	81	206
Robert	43	m	w	CANA	San Francisco	7-Wd San Francisco	81	156
Robert	37	m	w	NY	San Francisco	1-Wd San Francisco	79	95
DESUNUS								
M	25	m	w	PORT	San Francisco	San Francisco P O	83	265
DESURGY								
Lewis	55	m	w	CANA	Alameda	Brooklyn Twp	68	48
DESY								
Conlin	35	m	w	IREL	San Francisco	San Francisco P O	83	99
DETAVEL								
Achille	37	m	w	FRAN	San Francisco	San Francisco P O	83	345
DETEAU								
Ellen	72	f	w	IREL	San Francisco	11-Wd San Francisc	84	673
DETEL								
Enrico	25	m	w	CHIL	Calaveras	San Andreas P O	70	205
DETELS								
Dora	29	f	w	HANO	San Francisco	San Francisco P O	83	191
Henry	29	m	w	PRUS	San Francisco	San Francisco P O	83	117
Henry	10	m	w	CA	San Francisco	San Francisco P O	85	828
John	8	m	w	CA	San Francisco	San Francisco P O	85	828
Martin	31	m	w	PRUS	San Francisco	San Francisco P O	83	117
Wm	6	m	w	CA	San Francisco	San Francisco P O	85	828
DETER								
David	57	m	w	PA	Siskiyou	Table Rock Twp	89	648
George	24	m	w	OH	Siskiyou	Table Rock Twp	89	647
John	44	m	w	PA	Colusa	Colusa Twp	71	281
Westley	21	m	w	MD	Solano	Suisun Twp	90	111
DETERDING								
Chas	15	m	w	CA	Sacramento	4-Wd Sacramento	77	344
DETERS								
B F	40	m	w	WI	San Joaquin	Dent Twp	86	26
David	34	m	w	PRUS	San Francisco	5-Wd San Francisco	81	9
DETGEN								
John	50	m	w	ENGL	San Francisco	8-Wd San Francisco	82	349
DETHLEFSEN								
George	34	m	w	SHOL	San Francisco	3-Wd San Francisco	79	287
DETHLEFSON								
Nis	31	m	w	SHOL	Santa Cruz	Pajaro Twp	89	357
DETILEBACH								
Julius	36	m	w	PRUS	Stanislaus	Empire Twp	92	35
DETMAN								
Charles	22	m	w	PRUS	Marin	Bolinas Twp	74	7
DETNER								
George	34	m	w	HDAR	San Francisco	8-Wd San Francisco	82	431
DETON								
John	42	m	w	SPAI	San Francisco	8-Wd San Francisco	82	304
DETONES								
Longina	60	f	w	MEXI	San Francisco	6-Wd San Francisco	81	91
DETREMERY								
J L	13	m	w	CA	Alameda	Oakland	68	243
DETREY								
Carrie	10	f	w	CA	San Francisco	7-Wd San Francisco	81	277
DETRICH								
Fred	39	m	w	BADE	Butte	Ophir Twp	70	120
DETRICK								
John	32	m	w	WURT	Sierra	Eureka Twp	89	523
DETRIDGE								
M	36	m	w	OH	Yuba	Marysville	93	604
DETRO								
John	27	m	w	OH	Butte	Kimshew Tpw	70	78
Marcus	40	m	w	NY	San Luis Obispo	Santa Rosa Twp	87	323
DETROY								
Geo	34	m	w	BAVA	Santa Barbara	San Buenaventura P	87	434
DETSON								
Martin	35	m	w	PRUS	San Francisco	1-Wd San Francisco	79	60
DETTEN								
C	45	m	w	PRUS	San Joaquin	Oneal Twp	86	110
DETTERDING								
Wm	51	m	w	HANO	Sacramento	Brighton Twp	77	75
DETTERLBACH								
E	33	m	w	RUSS	San Francisco	7-Wd San Francisco	81	179
DETTMAN								
Henry	45	m	w	PRUS	San Francisco	San Francisco P O	83	63
DETTMER								
Mary	16	f	w	CA	San Francisco	San Francisco P O	85	816
DETTSLER								
Charles	26	m	w	SHOL	San Joaquin	Castoria Twp	86	4
DETURK								
Isaac	35	m	w	PA	Sonoma	Santa Rosa	91	422
DETURNIEL								
Paul	10	m	w	MEXI	San Francisco	8-Wd San Francisco	82	394
DETZ								
Andrew	80	m	w	PRUS	San Joaquin	2-Wd Stockton	86	187
Geo	40	m	w	PRUS	San Joaquin	2-Wd Stockton	86	187
DEUBELL								
Lewis G	38	m	w	SWIT	Yolo	Cottonwood Twp	93	475
DEUCHER								
Alfonse	65	m	w	SWIT	San Francisco	7-Wd San Francisco	81	248
DEUCOT								
Samuel	37	m	w	ENGL	Los Angeles	Santa Ana Twp	73	604
DEUEL								
J F	44	m	w	NY	Butte	Oroville Twp	70	137
S J	39	m	w	CANA	Sacramento	3-Wd Sacramento	77	262
Wm H	39	m	w	NY	Yuba	Marysville	93	604
DEUGAN								
John	60	m	w	TN	San Luis Obispo	Salinas Twp	87	293
DEUMAN								
Chas E	19	m	w	MO	San Luis Obispo	San Luis Obispo Tw	87	312
DEUMBO								
Fred	36	m	w	FRAN	Contra Costa	Martinez P O	71	397
DEUN								
Isaac	34	m	w	NY	El Dorado	Mud Springs Twp	72	78
DEUNG								
Tape	49	m	c	CHIN	Placer	Bath P O	76	439
DEUS								
Francisco	27	m	w	MEXI	Yuba	Marysville	93	614
Hosea	65	m	w	MEXI	Yuba	Marysville	93	611
Wallupi	15	f	w	CA	Calaveras	Copperopolis P O	70	245
DEUSTCH								
Gustave	32	m	w	PRUS	Marin	Sausalito Twp	74	72
DEUTCH								
Andrew	48	m	w	HDAR	San Francisco	San Francisco P O	80	533
Andrew	41	m	w	BAVA	San Francisco	1-Wd San Francisco	79	52
DEUTSCH								
Jacob	35	m	w	HUNG	San Francisco	San Francisco P O	80	534
Michael	35	m	w	PRUS	San Francisco	8-Wd San Francisco	82	397
DEUXHEIMER								
E	46	f	w	PRUS	Yuba	Marysville	93	614
DEVA								
Alpha	14	f	w	OR	San Joaquin	Elkhorn Twp	86	53
DEVACHIO								
G	35	m	w	ITAL	Amador	Jackson P O	69	327
DEVAGE								
Louis	29	m	w	ITAL	Calaveras	Copperopolis P O	70	247
DEVAL								
Charles	36	m	w	NY	Inyo	Cerro Gordo Twp	73	319
Jose	25	m	w	MEXI	San Diego	Fort Yuma Dist	78	464
DEVALCOURT								
Cornelius	40	m	w	NY	San Francisco	11-Wd San Francisc	84	612
DEVALGO								
Reno	40	m	w	MEXI	Tulare	Visalia	92	299
DEVALIN								
William	45	m	w	MD	Sacramento	2-Wd Sacramento	77	210
DEVALL								
Thos H	37	m	w	ENGL	Santa Clara	Gilroy Twp	88	86
DEVALLERS								
O	35	m	w	FRAN	San Joaquin	1-Wd Stockton	86	135
DEVALOYS								
John	32	m	w	HOLL	Alameda	Eden Twp	68	59
DEVAN								
Anne	43	f	w	IREL	San Francisco	11-Wd San Francisc	84	655
Pauline	34	f	w	FRAN	San Francisco	San Francisco P O	80	467
Peter	40	m	w	DENM	San Francisco	San Francisco P O	80	540
Thomas	38	m	w	IREL	San Francisco	San Francisco P O	85	736
William	37	m	w	IREL	Calaveras	San Andreas P O	70	192
DEVANEY								
John	39	m	w	IREL	San Francisco	San Francisco P O	85	764
John	24	m	w	IREL	San Francisco	5-Wd San Francisco	81	32
Margaret	47	f	w	IREL	San Francisco	7-Wd San Francisco	81	283
DEVANNEY								
John	38	m	w	IREL	San Francisco	San Francisco P O	83	314
DEVANY								
Michl	58	m	w	IREL	Alameda	Murray Twp	68	99
Terence	47	m	w	IREL	San Francisco	San Francisco P O	83	165
DEVARA								
F	49	m	w	MEXI	Santa Clara	Almaden Twp	88	1
DEVARETOWSKY								
John	36	m	w	POLA	San Diego	San Diego	78	489
DEVARRE								
Florence	40	f	w	MEXI	Mariposa	Mariposa P O	74	104
DEVARY								
Delia	16	f	w	IREL	Sacramento	2-Wd Sacramento	77	217
DEVATRE								
George	21	m	w	AL	San Francisco	8-Wd San Francisco	82	363
DEVAUX								
Celia	60	f	w	FRAN	Sacramento	2-Wd Sacramento	77	234
DEVEAN								
Pauline	20	f	w	FRAN	San Francisco	San Francisco P O	83	52
DEVEE								
Sarah	69	f	w	VA	Sonoma	Russian Rvr	91	378
DEVEGGIO								
Antonio	29	m	w	ITAL	San Francisco	1-Wd San Francisco	79	114
John	28	m	w	AUST	Calaveras	San Andreas P O	70	203
DEVELBIS								
George	18	m	w	MO	Yolo	Buckeye Twp	93	411
John	64	m	w	MD	Yolo	Buckeye Twp	93	411
John A	28	m	w	MO	Solano	Silveyville Twp	90	74

© 2001 by Heritage Quest. All rights reserved.

California 1870 Census

Name	Age	S	R	B-PL	County	Locale	Series M593 Roll	Pg
DEVELIN								
B	45	f	w	IREL	San Francisco	San Francisco P O	83	281
Bernard	24	m	w	NY	San Francisco	San Francisco P O	83	61
Jas H	29	m	w	PA	Solano	Vallejo	90	217
Mary	32	f	w	IREL	San Francisco	3-Wd San Francisco	79	294
Sarah	67	f	w	IREL	San Francisco	San Francisco P O	83	146
DEVELL								
George E	46	m	b	VA	San Francisco	San Francisco P O	83	246
DEVEN								
Charles	46	m	w	BADE	Alameda	Murray Twp	68	104
Peter	47	m	w	BELG	Mariposa	Mariposa P O	74	128
DEVENAUX								
Victorine	40	f	w	FRAN	San Francisco	San Francisco P O	80	538
DEVENDORF								
G M	34	m	w	NY	Tehama	Bell Mills Twp	92	159
DEVENING								
Stephen	34	m	w	IN	Colusa	Colusa Twp	71	276
DEVENNEY								
Robert	50	m	w	PA	Mendocino	Point Arena Twp	74	207
DEVENPORT								
E	41	m	w	MA	San Joaquin	Dent Twp	86	20
Geo	25	m	w	IN	San Joaquin	2-Wd Stockton	86	164
John	28	m	w	MO	Solano	Silveyville Twp	90	75
Thomas	31	m	w	ENGL	Humboldt	Eureka Twp	72	256
DEVENY								
James	40	m	w	IN	El Dorado	Georgetown Twp	72	41
DEVER								
John	39	m	w	IREL	San Francisco	11-Wd San Francisc	84	576
Michael	38	m	w	IREL	Yuba	Marysville	93	606
Richard M	42	m	w	KY	San Luis Obispo	Morro Twp	87	285
Rose	46	f	w	IREL	San Francisco	San Francisco P O	83	398
Zach	52	m	w	IN	Lake	Big Valley	73	398
DEVERAUGH								
Noel	35	m	w	IREL	Sonoma	Vallejo Twp	91	452
DEVERAUX								
Peter	25	m	w	IREL	Humboldt	Table Bluff Twp	72	306
DEVERE								
Chas	31	m	w	LA	Sacramento	1-Wd Sacramento	77	179
Louisa	17	f	w	CA	Sacramento	4-Wd Sacramento	77	340
Viletta	19	f	w	IA	San Francisco	8-Wd San Francisco	82	348
DEVEREAUX								
John	31	m	w	IREL	San Francisco	1-Wd San Francisco	79	82
Simeon	36	m	w	FRAN	San Francisco	1-Wd San Francisco	79	55
DEVEREUX								
James	26	m	w	IREL	Santa Cruz	Pajaro Twp	89	342
Nicholas	38	m	w	CANA	Santa Clara	Fremont Twp	88	61
Thos P	25	m	w	NC	Fresno	Millerton P O	72	146
DEVERICK								
Wm	40	m	w	CANA	Alameda	Murray Twp	68	99
DEVERNE								
Alphonse	31	m	w	FRAN	San Francisco	1-Wd San Francisco	79	109
DEVERS								
Andrew	39	m	b	VA	Yuba	Long Bar Twp	93	560
James	29	m	w	IREL	Solano	Suisun Twp	90	111
Jason M	51	m	w	SC	Amador	Fiddletown P O	69	438
Michael	35	m	w	FRAN	San Mateo	Belmont P O	87	374
Susan	67	f	w	IREL	Yuba	Marysville	93	607
DEVERY								
Francis	24	f	w	IREL	San Francisco	San Francisco P O	80	533
DEVES								
Henry	37	m	w	FRAN	Colusa	Monroe Twp	71	313
DEVEVEY								
Louis	35	m	w	FRAN	Tulare	Kings Rvr Twp	92	253
DEVIA								
Francesco	47	m	w	CHIL	Calaveras	Copperopolis P O	70	246
DEVICCIO								
Joseph	41	m	w	ITAL	San Francisco	2-Wd San Francisco	79	232
DEVIGNE								
Aline	29	m	w	FRAN	San Francisco	2-Wd San Francisco	79	253
DEVIL								
Samuel	20	m	w	MO	Sutter	Yuba Twp	92	148
DEVILAN								
Henry	41	m	w	IREL	Nevada	Nevada Twp	75	302
DEVILL								
Geo	32	m	w	MA	San Joaquin	1-Wd Stockton	86	127
DEVILLARSON								
Adele	38	f	w	FRAN	San Francisco	San Francisco P O	83	135
Oscar	44	m	w	WIND	San Francisco	San Francisco P O	83	135
DEVILLAS								
Arthur	23	m	w	ITAL	San Francisco	1-Wd San Francisco	79	21
DEVILLE								
Jacob	36	m	w	FRAN	Santa Clara	2-Wd San Jose	88	281
Josephine	29	f	w	FRAN	San Francisco	San Francisco P O	80	484
DEVILY								
Henry K	35	m	w	SWIT	Placer	Bath P O	76	454
DEVIN								
Edward	45	m	w	IREL	Sacramento	4-Wd Sacramento	77	340
James	42	m	w	MD	Stanislaus	Empire Twp	92	53
John	35	m	w	FRAN	Los Angeles	Los Angeles Twp	73	478
John A	37	m	w	PA	Stanislaus	San Joaquin Twp	92	80
Susan	17	f	w	MO	Sacramento	San Joaquin Twp	77	403
DEVINCHIS								
Dominnio	21	m	w	ITAL	El Dorado	Mountain Twp	72	69
DEVINE								
Adolfus	40	m	w	SWED	Contra Costa	Martinez P O	71	422
Ann	23	f	w	IREL	Santa Clara	Gilroy Twp	88	86
Annie	26	f	w	ENGL	San Francisco	San Francisco P O	83	255
Benjamin	27	m	w	IREL	San Francisco	San Francisco P O	85	762
Benjn	27	m	w	IREL	San Francisco	San Francisco P O	85	724
Bridget	25	f	w	IREL	Sacramento	4-Wd Sacramento	77	327
Catharine	35	f	w	IREL	San Francisco	San Francisco P O	83	274
Charles	28	m	w	ENGL	Nevada	Grass Valley Twp	75	161
Danial	50	m	w	IREL	San Francisco	7-Wd San Francisco	81	198
David	40	m	w	SCOT	San Francisco	San Francisco P O	83	236
Dennis	41	m	w	IREL	Mariposa	Mariposa P O	74	109
Edward	65	m	w	IREL	Sacramento	4-Wd Sacramento	77	355
Edward	43	m	w	IREL	San Bernardino	Belleville Twp	78	408
Ellen	31	f	w	IREL	San Francisco	San Francisco P O	85	769
Francis	40	m	w	IREL	Stanislaus	Emory Twp	92	17
Francis	27	m	w	IREL	San Francisco	8-Wd San Francisco	82	391
Frank	30	m	w	IREL	San Francisco	1-Wd San Francisco	79	44
H	18	f	w	NH	Sierra	Butte Twp	89	509
Henry	36	m	w	NY	San Francisco	San Francisco P O	80	342
Henry	29	m	w	PA	Mono	Bridgeport P O	74	284
James	28	m	w	IREL	San Francisco	San Francisco P O	83	299
James	25	m	w	IREL	Sacramento	4-Wd Sacramento	77	340
James	16	m	w	CA	San Francisco	11-Wd San Francisc	84	587
Johanna	45	f	w	IREL	San Francisco	7-Wd San Francisco	81	263
John	44	m	w	IREL	Placer	Bath P O	76	427
John	35	m	w	IREL	Santa Clara	2-Wd San Jose	88	306
John	33	m	w	IREL	San Francisco	5-Wd San Francisco	81	7
John	28	m	w	IREL	Nevada	Meadow Lake Twp	75	258
John	28	m	w	IREL	San Francisco	San Francisco P O	80	336
John Chas	33	m	w	IREL	Sacramento	4-Wd Sacramento	77	340
Kate	25	f	w	LA	San Francisco	San Francisco P O	83	271
Kate	25	f	w	IREL	San Francisco	San Francisco P O	83	149
Kate	20	f	w	IREL	San Francisco	San Francisco P O	85	777
Laura	14	f	w	MA	Solano	Benicia	90	16
Louis	27	m	w	IREL	San Francisco	2-Wd San Francisco	79	214
Martin	34	m	w	IREL	Sacramento	4-Wd Sacramento	77	324
Martin	32	m	w	IREL	San Francisco	11-Wd San Francisc	84	460
Martin	26	m	w	IREL	Santa Clara	Gilroy Twp	88	68
Mary	63	f	w	IREL	San Francisco	San Francisco P O	85	843
Mary	35	f	w	AUSL	San Francisco	2-Wd San Francisco	79	208
Mary	24	f	w	IREL	San Francisco	7-Wd San Francisco	81	239
Mat	30	m	w	MS	Napa	Napa	75	26
Michael	37	m	w	IREL	Sacramento	2-Wd Sacramento	77	234
Nattie	23	f	w	IREL	Sonoma	Petaluma Twp	91	311
Nicholas	32	m	w	IREL	Plumas	Quartz Twp	77	34
Pat	30	m	w	IREL	San Francisco	7-Wd San Francisco	81	239
Patrick	57	m	w	IREL	San Luis Obispo	Salinas Twp	87	295
Patrick	30	m	w	DENM	San Francisco	7-Wd San Francisco	81	194
Patrick	30	m	w	IREL	San Francisco	7-Wd San Francisco	81	181
Sylvester	43	m	w	ENGL	San Francisco	San Francisco P O	85	856
Thomas	48	m	w	IREL	Alameda	Washington Twp	68	294
Thomas	42	m	w	IREL	San Francisco	8-Wd San Francisco	82	378
Thomas	24	m	w	IREL	Marin	San Rafael Twp	74	32
Thos	33	m	w	IREL	San Francisco	1-Wd San Francisco	79	37
William	30	m	w	IREL	Nevada	Meadow Lake Twp	75	255
William	27	m	w	PA	San Francisco	11-Wd San Francisc	84	519
DEVINER								
William	26	m	w	PORT	Alameda	Washington Twp	68	281
DEVINEY								
Hugh	35	m	w	IREL	San Francisco	8-Wd San Francisco	82	417
DEVINISH								
John	49	m	w	IN	Humboldt	Table Bluff Twp	72	305
DEVINNEY								
James	28	m	w	OH	Yolo	Grafton Twp	93	493
Jos L	45	m	w	PA	San Francisco	San Francisco P O	83	128
DEVINS								
Charles	25	m	w	ENGL	Colusa	Grand Island Twp	71	308
F	27	m	w	IREL	Sierra	Butte Twp	89	511
Mark	28	m	w	MD	Santa Cruz	Pajaro Twp	89	350
DEVINY								
Wm	40	m	w	PA	Sacramento	Center Twp	77	83
DEVIRE								
Joseph	40	m	w	PA	Los Angeles	Wilmington Twp	73	645
DEVIS								
Manuel	23	m	w	PORT	Mendocino	Big Rvr Twp	74	159
DEVISO								
Wm	50	m	w	NY	Alameda	Murray Twp	68	120
DEVIT								
Peter	24	m	w	OH	Solano	Silveyville Twp	90	80
DEVITT								
A M	31	m	w	MI	Alameda	Oakland	68	263
Catherine	52	f	w	HOLL	San Francisco	11-Wd San Francisc	84	522
Cathrine	36	f	w	IREL	San Francisco	1-Wd San Francisco	79	14
DEVLIN								
Archi	67	m	w	IREL	Butte	Ophir Twp	70	107
Fannie	25	f	w	IREL	San Francisco	7-Wd San Francisco	81	167
James	47	m	w	IREL	San Francisco	San Francisco P O	83	292
James	23	m	w	NY	San Francisco	11-Wd San Francisc	84	454
John	42	m	w	IREL	Solano	Suisun Twp	90	100
John	40	m	w	IREL	San Francisco	San Francisco P O	80	375
John A	32	m	w	NY	San Francisco	San Francisco P O	83	342
Layden	27	m	w	IREL	Humboldt	Eureka Twp	72	270
Mary	36	f	w	IREL	San Francisco	San Francisco P O	83	332
Mary	36	f	w	IREL	San Francisco	San Francisco P O	83	133
Patrick	26	m	w	IREL	Humboldt	Bucksport Twp	72	242
Patrick	26	m	w	IREL	Inyo	Cerro Gordo Twp	73	321
Robert	46	m	w	IREL	Sacramento	2-Wd Sacramento	77	235
Sarah	29	f	w	IREL	San Francisco	8-Wd San Francisco	82	475
Thos	39	m	w	ENGL	San Francisco	7-Wd San Francisco	81	263
Wm	30	m	w	IREL	San Francisco	1-Wd San Francisco	79	39

© 2001 by Heritage Quest. All rights reserved.

Name	Age	S	R	B-PL	County	Locale	Roll	Pg
DEVOE								
Benjamin	45	m	w	FRAN	San Francisco	6-Wd San Francisco	81	106
C W	24	m	w	NY	Sacramento	Dry Crk Twp	77	102
Henry	50	m	w	MECK	Placer	Bath P O	76	427
James	38	m	w	PRUS	San Francisco	San Francisco P O	80	346
James	37	m	w	CANA	San Francisco	San Francisco P O	80	429
Louisa	40	f	w	CANA	San Francisco	6-Wd San Francisco	81	46
Sam	35	m	w	OH	San Joaquin	Douglas Twp	86	45
DEVOER								
James	17	m	w	IREL	Sacramento	4-Wd Sacramento	77	347
Sarah	17	m	w	FRAN	Contra Costa	San Pablo Twp	71	353
DEVOL								
Norman	30	m	w	VT	Butte	Wyandotte Twp	70	149
DEVOLA								
Joseph	26	m	w	ITAL	Calaveras	San Andreas P O	70	168
DEVOLCKI								
Henry	43	m	w	HOLL	San Francisco	1-Wd San Francisco	79	115
DEVOLL								
Henry	28	m	w	MA	San Joaquin	1-Wd Stockton	86	140
Phillip	60	m	w	MA	San Joaquin	1-Wd Stockton	86	141
DEVOLLI								
J G	39	m	w	VT	Tuolumne	Sonora P O	93	307
DEVOLT								
James	45	m	w	MD	Yuba	Marysville	93	583
Peter	40	m	w	MO	Del Norte	Crescent Twp	71	457
DEVON								
Elizabeth	60	f	w	NJ	Solano	Vallejo	90	159
DEVONE								
Bernard	31	m	w	IREL	San Francisco	1-Wd San Francisco	79	33
Clotilda	40	f	w	FRAN	San Francisco	2-Wd San Francisco	79	169
Lizzie	40	f	w	IREL	San Francisco	1-Wd San Francisco	79	66
DEVONGLAS								
Joseph	52	m	w	FRAN	Siskiyou	Table Rock Twp	89	648
DEVORE								
Gideon	39	m	w	OH	Amador	Drytown P O	69	422
DEVORTI								
Antonio	30	m	w	ITAL	San Francisco	San Francisco P O	80	344
DEVOTE								
Ante	37	m	w	SPAI	San Francisco	8-Wd San Francisco	82	373
Bendetto	40	m	w	ITAL	Calaveras	San Andreas P O	70	217
DEVOTED								
James	25	m	w	NY	Butte	Chico Twp	70	42
DEVOTIE								
El Louise	27	m	w	NY	Plumas	Seneca Twp	77	49
DEVOTO								
Antoni	40	m	w	ITAL	El Dorado	Diamond Springs Tw	72	34
Charles	36	m	w	ITAL	San Luis Obispo	Arroyo Grande Twp	87	276
Paul	37	m	w	ITAL	Amador	Jackson P O	69	327
Ternice	12	f	w	CA	Amador	Jackson P O	69	325
DEVOW								
Alfred	38	m	w	NY	Monterey	Castroville Twp	74	326
DEVOY								
Henry	22	m	w	CANA	Humboldt	Bucksport Twp	72	244
John C	34	m	w	IREL	San Francisco	San Francisco P O	83	8
DEVRIES								
Emily	6	f	w	CA	San Francisco	San Francisco P O	85	827
Eugine	28	m	w	FRAN	Colusa	Monroe Twp	71	325
Gertrude	41	f	w	MEXI	San Francisco	San Francisco P O	85	847
Joseph	30	m	w	HOLL	Placer	Newcastle Twp	76	478
DEVROE								
Peter	24	m	w	NY	San Joaquin	Elkhorn Twp	86	66
DEW								
Ah	16	m	c	CHIN	Yuba	Marysville	93	619
Frank	27	m	w	CANA	Placer	Summit P O	76	496
William T	42	m	w	NH	Sonoma	Salt Point	91	381
DEWAL								
Etienne	39	m	w	FRAN	San Francisco	11-Wd San Francisc	84	643
John	10	m	w	CA	Alameda	Alvarado	68	302
DEWALL								
Felix A	47	m	w	HOLL	Sonoma	Salt Point	91	381
S N	41	m	w	TN	Napa	Napa	75	23
Wm	69	m	w	TN	Napa	Napa	75	23
DEWAN								
James	11	m	w	CT	San Mateo	Half Moon Bay P O	87	394
Patrick	40	m	w	IREL	San Mateo	Belmont P O	87	388
DEWANS								
Micheal	23	m	w	FRAN	San Francisco	7-Wd San Francisco	81	207
DEWAR								
Donald M	35	m	w	SCOT	Santa Clara	2-Wd San Jose	88	283
Jno	25	m	w	CANA	Sierra	Table Rock Twp	89	574
Wm	19	m	w	BREM	San Francisco	San Francisco P O	83	68
DEWARE								
Robt	29	m	w	IREL	Solano	Vallejo	90	215
Thos	24	m	w	IREL	San Francisco	1-Wd San Francisco	79	82
DEWDERT								
Stephen	56	m	w	AUST	Contra Costa	Martinez P O	71	450
DEWEBER								
Isaiah	60	m	w	NY	Stanislaus	Branch Twp	92	1
William	30	m	w	IREL	Contra Costa	Martinez P O	71	367
DEWEES								
G W	52	m	w	KY	Napa	Napa Twp	75	67
DEWEESE								
William	33	m	w	KY	San Francisco	3-Wd San Francisco	79	328
DEWEL								
B	47	m	w	OH	Lake	Upper Lake	73	412
C C	24	m	w	MO	Monterey	Alisal Twp	74	302
Elmira	25	f	w	IL	Butte	Hamilton Twp	70	65
John C	43	m	w	NY	Nevada	Grass Valley Twp	75	151
Wm	59	m	w	OH	Monterey	Alisal Twp	74	302
DEWELL								
Edward	38	m	w	IREL	Placer	Alta P O	76	412
DEWER								
John	42	m	w	NY	San Diego	Julian Dist	78	470
John D	22	m	w	WI	Alameda	Washington Twp	68	282
DEWES								
Benjiman A	18	m	w	AR	Los Angeles	Los Angeles	73	542
DEWEY								
B F	33	m	w	IL	Tehama	Stony Crk	92	166
Blueford	30	m	w	TN	Stanislaus	Emory Twp	92	24
Edward	42	m	w	MA	San Francisco	11-Wd San Francisc	84	599
Eugene	27	m	w	NY	San Francisco	2-Wd San Francisco	79	246
Hannah	33	f	w	IREL	San Joaquin	1-Wd Stockton	86	129
Henry	46	m	w	CANA	San Joaquin	Elkhorn Twp	86	57
Henry	45	m	w	MA	San Joaquin	Elkhorn Twp	86	54
J F	31	m	w	NY	Nevada	Meadow Lake Twp	75	253
James	55	m	w	CANA	San Francisco	San Francisco P O	83	78
Jane	30	f	w	IREL	Santa Clara	2-Wd San Jose	88	325
Jehiel	36	m	w	PA	Placer	Roseville P O	76	354
John	40	m	w	IREL	San Francisco	11-Wd San Francisc	84	513
John	36	m	w	IREL	Butte	Chico Twp	70	16
John H	38	m	w	NY	Nevada	Grass Valley Twp	75	172
Levi H	40	m	w	NY	Colusa	Colusa	71	291
Louis	28	m	w	NY	San Francisco	3-Wd San Francisco	79	289
Olando F	39	m	w	NY	Yolo	Cache Crk Twp	93	438
Richard	28	m	w	IREL	San Francisco	8-Wd San Francisco	82	353
Saml L	50	m	w	NY	Butte	Kimshew Tpw	70	80
Thomas	45	m	w	IREL	San Francisco	8-Wd San Francisco	82	338
Wm	46	m	w	PA	Sacramento	1-Wd Sacramento	77	189
DEWING								
Alonso	15	m	w	NY	San Mateo	Woodside P O	87	385
Charles S	29	m	w	PA	Mendocino	Big Rvr Twp	74	158
Francis	31	m	w	CT	San Francisco	6-Wd San Francisco	81	116
DEWIRE								
Thomas	38	m	w	IREL	Sacramento	2-Wd Sacramento	77	224
DEWIS								
Jacob	44	m	w	BADE	Inyo	Cerro Gordo Twp	73	323
DEWISE								
Riley W	14	m	w	TN	Shasta	Millville P O	89	485
DEWIT								
Emma J	18	f	w	OH	Mono	Bridgeport P O	74	285
DEWITT								
Allen W	49	m	w	KY	Colusa	Colusa Twp	71	274
Alonzo	35	m	w	NY	Sacramento	Natomas Twp	77	166
Andrew	47	m	w	PA	San Francisco	San Francisco P O	83	6
Charles	30	m	w	NY	Sacramento	Natomas Twp	77	166
Chas	14	m	w	MO	Sonoma	Washington Twp	91	468
Cora	24	f	w	AUSL	San Francisco	3-Wd San Francisco	79	320
Cornelius	16	m	w	HOLL	San Francisco	11-Wd San Francisc	84	478
Duncan	30	m	w	MA	San Francisco	6-Wd San Francisco	81	94
Elezar	26	m	w	KY	Colusa	Colusa Twp	71	274
Hugh	56	m	w	PA	Amador	Sutter Crk P O	69	412
James	58	m	w	KY	Siskiyou	Yreka	89	655
John	30	m	w	NY	Kern	Tehachapi P O	73	355
John	24	m	w	NY	San Francisco	San Francisco P O	80	473
Lemuel	32	m	w	OH	El Dorado	Placerville Twp	72	103
M L	30	f	w	ME	Lassen	Janesville Twp	73	430
Monroe	52	m	w	TN	Santa Cruz	Santa Cruz Twp	89	397
Mortimore	34	m	w	NJ	San Francisco	San Francisco P O	83	231
Reuben	43	m	w	IN	San Bernardino	San Bernardino Twp	78	437
Robert O	38	m	w	KY	Siskiyou	Yreka	89	660
Sykes	41	m	w	NY	San Francisco	San Francisco P O	80	475
Washington	26	m	w	MO	Solano	Green Valley Twp	90	39
William	38	m	w	TN	San Francisco	7-Wd San Francisco	81	218
Wm T	37	m	w	IL	Napa	Napa Twp	75	68
DEWITTE								
J J	36	m	w	HOLL	San Francisco	3-Wd San Francisco	79	319
DEWLANEY								
Wm	39	m	w	TN	Santa Barbara	Santa Barbara P O	87	498
DEWLEY								
M	40	m	w	CANA	Alameda	Murray Twp	68	113
DEWOLF								
Armise	3	m	w	CA	Alameda	Brooklyn Twp	68	42
Benjamin R	51	m	w	CANA	Santa Cruz	Santa Cruz Twp	89	387
Eliza	30	f	w	MA	San Francisco	11-Wd San Francisc	84	620
John	18	m	w	ME	Santa Cruz	Santa Cruz	89	408
Sidney	25	m	w	CANA	Santa Clara	San Jose Twp	88	216
DEWOODY								
T J	45	m	w	AL	Napa	Napa Twp	75	71
DEWOULFE								
Eluisa	35	f	w	TN	Alameda	Oakland	68	193
DEWS								
Samuel K	49	m	w	TN	Yuba	Long Bar Twp	93	566
DEWULF								
Bernard	45	m	w	BELG	San Francisco	San Francisco P O	83	219
DEWY								
Edward	37	m	w	IREL	San Mateo	Schoolhouse Statio	87	342
Lemuel	53	m	w	MA	Amador	Drytown P O	69	421
DEXLER								
Geo	22	m	w	MD	Merced	Snelling P O	74	256
DEXTER								
Albert	61	m	w	MA	Santa Clara	Gilroy Twp	88	91
Albert G	53	m	w	RI	San Francisco	8-Wd San Francisco	82	321
Alonzo	36	m	w	ME	Mariposa	Maxwell Crk P O	74	143
C H	46	m	w	RI	San Francisco	San Francisco P O	85	875

© 2001 by Heritage Quest. All rights reserved.

Name	Age	S	R	B-PL	County	Locale	Series M593 Roll	Pg
Celia	45	f	w	CT	San Francisco	8-Wd San Francisco	82	367
Chas	26	m	w	NY	San Francisco	5-Wd San Francisco	81	7
Chas H	45	m	w	RI	San Francisco	8-Wd San Francisco	82	345
Edward	33	m	w	RI	Mono	Bridgeport P O	74	284
Frank	36	m	w	MA	San Francisco	San Francisco P O	80	411
Fredrick	28	m	w	NY	San Francisco	7-Wd San Francisco	81	186
George	24	m	w	PRUS	Tulare	Tule Rvr Twp	92	271
Granville	32	m	w	ME	Alameda	Eden Twp	68	66
H C	7	m	w	IL	Alameda	Oakland	68	149
Henry	44	m	w	CANA	Solano	Vallejo	90	189
Henry	43	m	w	MA	Tuolumne	Sonora P O	93	323
Henry S	59	m	w	CT	San Francisco	San Francisco P O	83	111
Homer	43	m	w	NY	Yolo	Cottonwood Twp	93	459
Joseph	62	m	w	MA	Mariposa	Maxwell Crk P O	74	145
Leonard	29	m	w	MA	Santa Clara	Redwood Twp	88	131
Lorenzo	55	m	w	NY	Yolo	Buckeye Twp	93	410
Obed	40	m	w	MA	Santa Clara	Fremont Twp	88	62
R	53	m	w	MA	San Joaquin	2-Wd Stockton	86	197
Rebecca	59	f	w	ME	Santa Clara	Redwood Twp	88	131
Sam	40	m	w	MA	Tehama	Paskenta Twp	92	165
Thomas J	39	m	w	CANA	Yolo	Cache Crk Twp	93	445
Thomas W	31	m	w	RI	Mono	Bridgeport P O	74	284
Tuttle	37	m	w	NY	Colusa	Grand Island Twp	71	305
W A	28	m	w	IL	Tehama	Tehama Twp	92	194
DEXTON								
James	36	m	w	MA	San Francisco	11-Wd San Francisc	84	686
DEYAERT								
P	52	m	w	BELG	Napa	Napa	75	56
DEYDEN								
Edward	40	m	w	IREL	Contra Costa	San Pablo Twp	71	357
DEYLL								
Nanete	33	f	w	WURT	San Francisco	San Francisco P O	85	821
DEYONG								
Cornelius	38	m	w	FRAN	Butte	Ophir Twp	70	120
DEYOR								
S P	46	m	w	NY	Sierra	Alleghany & Forest	89	534
W A	42	m	w	NY	Sierra	Alleghany & Forest	89	535
DEYOUNG								
Amanda	23	f	w	NY	San Francisco	San Francisco P O	83	311
Henry	33	m	w	PA	Sacramento	1-Wd Sacramento	77	175
M H	71	m	w	ENGL	San Francisco	San Francisco P O	83	300
DEYS								
Warren B	57	m	w	NH	Nevada	Grass Valley Twp	75	227
DEZALDO								
Joseph	25	m	w	NY	Santa Clara	Fremont Twp	88	49
Ramon	65	m	w	SPAI	Santa Clara	Fremont Twp	88	49
DEZELL								
James	31	m	w	NY	Yuba	Rose Bar Twp	93	657
DEZERILLE								
Christopher	40	m	w	ITAL	San Francisco	2-Wd San Francisco	79	181
DEZOHN								
John	38	m	w	CANA	San Francisco	8-Wd San Francisco	82	485
DEZOMBRA								
John	46	m	w	PRUS	Plumas	Indian Twp	77	18
DEZOSAS								
Manuel	25	m	w	AZOR	San Francisco	1-Wd San Francisco	79	118
DGERGOWSKY								
N	42	m	w	POLA	Butte	Ophir Twp	70	94
DGORGIN								
Joseph	30	m	w	ITAL	Calaveras	San Andreas P O	70	194
DHAH								
Moa	19	m	c	CHIN	San Francisco	1-Wd San Francisco	79	118
DHEEM								
Shelah	21	m	c	CHIN	San Francisco	1-Wd San Francisco	79	60
DHELICH								
Jacob	40	m	w	BAVA	Calaveras	San Andreas P O	70	166
DHERTY								
Celia	28	f	w	IREL	Alameda	Oakland	68	145
DHESMER								
Louis	22	m	w	PRUS	San Francisco	8-Wd San Francisco	82	381
DHEW								
Ah	28	m	c	CHIN	El Dorado	White Oak Twp	72	142
DHIEST								
August	35	m	w	PRUS	Yolo	Putah Twp	93	515
DHILING								
Fred	33	m	w	GERM	Sutter	Yuba Twp	92	146
DHLEN								
Jno A	26	m	w	PRUS	San Francisco	5-Wd San Francisco	81	9
DHU								
Roderick	32	m	w	SCOT	Santa Clara	2-Wd San Jose	88	287
DI								
Ah	35	m	c	CHIN	El Dorado	White Oak Twp	72	140
Ah	29	m	c	CHIN	Butte	Chico Twp	70	54
Lee	19	m	c	CHIN	Santa Clara	1-Wd San Jose	88	265
See	31	m	c	CHIN	Calaveras	San Andreas P O	70	191
DIABLO								
Peter	55	m	w	CHIL	Amador	Jackson P O	69	338
DIAGO								
John	68	m	i	CA	San Mateo	San Mateo P O	87	348
DIAL								
Hastin J	34	m	w	GA	Amador	Volcano P O	69	383
John	40	m	w	IREL	San Joaquin	3-Wd Stockton	86	235
DIAM								
Ah	18	m	c	CHIN	San Francisco	7-Wd San Francisco	81	243
DIAMOND								
Chas	30	m	w	PA	San Francisco	11-Wd San Francisc	84	554
Henry	33	m	w	IREL	San Mateo	San Mateo P O	87	350
Hugh	39	m	w	IREL	Alameda	Brooklyn Twp	68	53
James	26	m	w	IREL	Butte	Oregon Twp	70	127
John	50	m	w	NY	San Francisco	1-Wd San Francisco	79	106
John	40	m	w	IREL	San Francisco	San Francisco P O	83	402
Pat	49	m	w	IREL	San Mateo	San Mateo P O	87	359
Susie I	28	f	w	NY	Sonoma	Petaluma Twp	91	330
Wm A	52	m	w	US	Nevada	Rough & Ready Twp	75	336
DIAR								
William G	26	m	w	ENGL	San Francisco	San Francisco P O	83	247
DIARD								
Joseph	34	m	w	FRAN	Alameda	Brooklyn Twp	68	54
DIARY								
Abraham	56	m	w	WIND	San Francisco	11-Wd San Francisc	84	524
Thomas	51	m	w	CHIL	San Francisco	11-Wd San Francisc	84	520
DIAS								
Allejo	40	m	w	MEXI	Los Angeles	Los Angeles	73	550
Ambrosio	10	m	w	CA	Los Angeles	Los Angeles Twp	73	496
Antonio	30	m	w	PORT	Marin	Nicasio Twp	74	20
Benito	54	m	w	CA	Monterey	Monterey	74	363
Bonifacio	35	m	w	CHIL	Fresno	Millerton P O	72	153
Carmen	50	f	w	CHIL	San Francisco	1-Wd San Francisco	79	3
Edward	36	m	w	NY	San Francisco	1-Wd San Francisco	79	89
Emanuel	30	m	w	PORT	Alameda	Washington Twp	68	276
Ester	56	f	w	WIND	San Francisco	8-Wd San Francisco	82	346
Esther L	54	f	w	WI	Sonoma	Petaluma Twp	91	364
Francisco	31	m	w	PORT	Marin	Nicasio Twp	74	20
Jesus	33	m	w	MEXI	Sierra	Sears Twp	89	559
Joseph	53	m	w	SHOL	Siskiyou	Callahan P O	89	632
Joseph	47	m	w	IREL	San Joaquin	2-Wd Stockton	86	183
Joseph	23	m	w	WIND	Sacramento	2-Wd Sacramento	77	223
Juan	50	m	i	CA	Santa Barbara	Las Cruces P O	87	505
Justo	61	m	w	MEXI	Los Angeles	Los Angeles	73	551
Lorenzo	45	m	w	MEXI	Fresno	Millerton P O	72	164
Luciano	51	m	w	MEXI	Monterey	Monterey Twp	74	345
Luisa E	47	f	w	CA	Monterey	Monterey	74	367
M	24	m	w	MEXI	Santa Clara	Almaden Twp	88	13
Manuel	50	m	w	SPAI	San Bernardino	San Bernardino Twp	78	442
Manuel	20	m	w	AZOR	Marin	Sausalito Twp	74	71
Maria	11	f	w	CA	Monterey	Monterey Twp	74	345
Marthando	52	f	w	MEXI	Los Angeles	Los Angeles	73	529
Miguel	46	m	w	MEXI	Fresno	Millerton P O	72	155
Pancho	28	m	w	CA	Santa Clara	Burnett Twp	88	39
Papi	60	m	w	FRAN	Santa Clara	Burnett Twp	88	39
Santiago	65	m	w	MEXI	Los Angeles	Los Angeles	73	558
Tablo	50	m	w	MEXI	Santa Clara	Almaden Twp	88	3
Thos	49	m	w	CHIL	San Francisco	San Francisco P O	83	44
DIAZ								
Adolph	13	m	w	CA	San Bernardino	San Bernardino Twp	78	416
Andres	48	m	w	CHIL	Placer	Auburn P O	76	382
Antonio	34	m	w	MEXI	Los Angeles	Los Angeles Twp	73	481
Felina	32	f	w	MEXI	San Francisco	2-Wd San Francisco	79	242
Ignaius	29	m	w	MEXI	San Francisco	2-Wd San Francisco	79	147
Jesus	43	m	i	MEXI	Inyo	Cerro Gordo Twp	73	322
Jose	36	m	w	SPAI	San Francisco	San Francisco P O	80	415
Jose	33	m	w	PORT	Marin	San Rafael	74	58
Loretto	22	f	w	MEXI	San Francisco	San Francisco P O	80	331
Lotario	33	m	w	CHIL	Santa Clara	Alviso Twp	88	24
Lowriana	30	m	w	MEXI	San Francisco	San Francisco P O	80	343
Manuel	38	m	w	PORT	Marin	San Rafael Twp	74	35
Prudencio	44	m	w	MEXI	Santa Clara	1-Wd San Jose	88	255
Rafael	42	m	w	CHIL	Santa Clara	Alviso Twp	88	24
Roman	24	m	w	MEXI	San Diego	Coronado	78	465
DIAZZOTTIE								
Johan	25	m	w	ITAL	Sonoma	Salt Point	91	391
DIBBEN								
Henry	50	m	w	HAMB	San Francisco	2-Wd San Francisco	79	185
DIBBERN								
Joseph	43	m	w	PRUS	Nevada	Nevada Twp	75	320
DIBBINS								
Jane	45	f	w	ENGL	Trinity	Weaverville Pct	92	230
DIBBLE								
Albert	48	m	w	NY	San Francisco	8-Wd San Francisco	82	316
Alfred B	40	m	w	NY	Nevada	Grass Valley Twp	75	146
Edwin	33	m	w	NY	Monterey	Pajaro Twp	74	375
J C	25	m	w	MI	Shasta	Shasta P O	89	454
Jenny	11	f	w	NV	Santa Clara	Santa Clara Twp	88	146
Jerome	49	m	w	CT	Mendocino	Ukiah Twp	74	233
Jno C	23	m	w	MI	Butte	Chico Twp	70	20
John	30	m	w	SHOL	Alameda	Eden Twp	68	65
John H	51	m	w	PA	Santa Clara	Santa Clara Twp	88	146
Milo B	27	m	w	NY	Alameda	Brooklyn	68	37
Nathan	14	m	w	MI	Butte	Chico Twp	70	40
Philander	66	m	w	MA	Santa Cruz	Santa Cruz Twp	89	385
Robert	57	m	w	OH	Santa Clara	Santa Clara Twp	88	151
William	38	m	w	NY	San Francisco	San Francisco P O	83	328
Wm	22	m	w	ME	Sonoma	Salt Point	91	392
DIBBLEE								
Nelson P	32	m	w	NY	Amador	Volcano P O	69	388
Thos B	43	m	w	NY	Santa Barbara	Las Cruces P O	87	506
Walter	22	m	w	ME	Sonoma	Salt Point	91	392
DIBBORN								
Hugh	41	m	w	SHOL	Nevada	Nevada Twp	75	313
DIBECHIE								
Stephen	22	m	w	ITAL	San Francisco	2-Wd San Francisco	79	147
DIBLE								
Danl	34	m	w	ENGL	Sierra	Table Rock Twp	89	575

© 2001 by Heritage Quest. All rights reserved.

Name	Age	S	R	B-PL	County	Locale	Series M593 Roll	Pg
DIBLEY								
Alexdr	31	m	w	ME	Stanislaus	Branch Twp	92	5
DICE								
Henry	32	m	w	WALD	San Joaquin	Elkhorn Twp	86	53
DICH								
Jno	37	m	w	GERM	San Joaquin	2-Wd Stockton	86	213
DICHEY								
Mary J	22	f	w	OH	Klamath	Orleans Twp	73	379
DICHMAN								
Ed	40	m	w	WURT	San Joaquin	Tulare Twp	86	254
George	33	m	w	PRUS	San Francisco	San Francisco P O	83	9
DICK								
Ah	50	m	c	CHIN	Placer	Auburn P O	76	364
Ah	49	m	c	CHIN	Nevada	Nevada Twp	75	311
Ah	40	m	c	CHIN	Nevada	Meadow Lake Twp	75	256
Ah	37	m	c	CHIN	Butte	Hamilton Twp	70	68
Ah	35	m	c	CHIN	Butte	Chico Twp	70	27
Ah	30	m	c	CHIN	Nevada	Nevada Twp	75	311
Ah	28	m	c	CHIN	Monterey	Castroville Twp	74	341
Ah	27	m	c	CHIN	Amador	Fiddletown P O	69	428
Ah	27	m	c	CHIN	Nevada	Nevada Twp	75	312
Ah	19	m	c	CHIN	Butte	Hamilton Twp	70	68
Ah	16	m	c	CHIN	Nevada	Meadow Lake Twp	75	265
Alex	35	m	w	SCOT	Butte	Hamilton Twp	70	62
Charles	42	m	w	SCOT	Yuba	Marysville	93	597
John	57	m	w	CT	Butte	Ophir Twp	70	96
John	48	m	w	SCOT	Plumas	Indian Twp	77	15
John	36	m	c	CHIN	Stanislaus	Branch Twp	92	5
Joseph	29	m	w	VA	Mariposa	Mariposa P O	74	134
Lewis F	37	m	w	VA	El Dorado	Placerville Twp	72	98
Morris	34	m	w	VA	Mono	Bridgeport P O	74	286
Robert	46	m	w	SCOT	San Francisco	11-Wd San Francisc	84	449
Robert	37	m	w	IREL	Stanislaus	San Joaquin Twp	92	80
Roberts	48	m	w	IREL	Butte	Kimshew Tpw	70	85
S W	47	m	w	IN	San Francisco	San Francisco P O	85	804
Samuel	47	m	w	PA	Tuolumne	Chinese Camp P O	93	378
Theodore	1	m	w	CA	San Francisco	San Francisco P O	83	32
Thomas	29	m	w	FRAN	San Francisco	7-Wd San Francisco	81	179
Tim	33	m	c	CHIN	Nevada	Nevada Twp	75	311
William	42	m	w	NY	San Francisco	11-Wd San Francisc	84	630
DICKELT								
Henry	33	m	w	BREM	San Francisco	3-Wd San Francisco	79	314
DICKENS								
Calvin J	31	m	w	NC	Amador	Volcano P O	69	382
Henry	34	m	w	ENGL	Calaveras	San Andreas P O	70	204
Johnathan	38	m	w	ENGL	Alpine	Silver Mtn P O	69	306
Richd	50	m	w	IREL	Marin	Tomales Twp	74	84
Samuel	44	m	w	US	Santa Cruz	Soquel Twp	89	444
Thos W	60	m	w	ENGL	San Francisco	San Francisco P O	83	109
William	37	m	w	TN	Santa Clara	2-Wd San Jose	88	325
DICKENSON								
A C	40	m	w	TN	Sonoma	Santa Rosa	91	428
Alonzo	27	m	w	NH	Marin	Novato Twp	74	10
Asa E	34	m	w	VT	Plumas	Plumas Twp	77	29
Charles	25	m	w	HANO	Mariposa	Mariposa P O	74	130
Elisha	32	m	w	TN	Siskiyou	Surprise Valley Tw	89	643
Francis	50	m	b	MD	San Francisco	San Francisco P O	80	396
H	23	m	w	NY	Siskiyou	Surprise Valley Tw	89	637
H C	36	m	w	VT	Sierra	Table Rock Twp	89	578
Henry	47	m	w	MA	San Francisco	2-Wd San Francisco	79	159
Henry	27	m	w	MO	Siskiyou	Surprise Valley Tw	89	643
J P	48	m	w	TN	Los Angeles	Los Nietos Twp	73	584
Jas W	30	m	w	NY	Siskiyou	Surprise Valley Tw	89	643
Joel	44	m	w	GA	Siskiyou	Surprise Valley Tw	89	643
John	47	m	w	NH	Marin	Novato Twp	74	10
John	40	m	w	ENGL	Sonoma	Sonoma Twp	91	443
John	37	m	w	ENGL	El Dorado	Diamond Springs Tw	72	28
John	25	m	w	DENM	Alameda	Eden Twp	68	82
Joseph	41	m	w	VA	Yolo	Grafton Twp	93	486
Napoleon	38	m	w	VA	Stanislaus	Empire Twp	92	61
Obadiah	42	m	w	MA	San Francisco	San Francisco P O	80	539
S J	44	m	w	CT	Sierra	Table Rock Twp	89	571
William	58	m	w	NY	Alameda	Washington Twp	68	290
DICKER								
Peter	36	m	w	HAMB	San Francisco	2-Wd San Francisco	79	208
DICKERHOFF								
Fred M	26	m	w	MD	El Dorado	Placerville Twp	72	94
Henrietta	40	f	w	ME	Sacramento	2-Wd Sacramento	77	245
DICKERMAN								
B	31	m	w	OH	Humboldt	Eureka Twp	72	264
H	9	m	w	CA	Amador	Ione City P O	69	359
Hank	40	m	w	OH	Amador	Ione City P O	69	357
Herbert	31	m	w	OH	San Diego	Julian Dist	78	470
J C	49	m	w	VT	Nevada	Nevada Twp	75	288
DICKERS								
Charles	35	m	w	IREL	Los Angeles	Wilmington Twp	73	642
DICKERSON								
Charles	36	m	w	AR	Sonoma	Petaluma Twp	91	354
G F	31	m	w	RI	Sacramento	3-Wd Sacramento	77	316
H B	60	m	w	NY	Del Norte	Crescent	71	467
Hart	28	f	w	ENGL	Alameda	Oakland	68	220
Harvey F	40	m	w	TN	Shasta	Millville P O	89	492
Hiram	20	m	w	ME	San Diego	Fort Yuma Dist	78	463
Horace F	36	m	w	GA	Shasta	Horsetown P O	89	504
Isabel F	14	f	w	CA	San Luis Obispo	Arroyo Grande Twp	87	270
J	56	m	w	NJ	Sacramento	3-Wd Sacramento	77	279
Jas H	40	m	w	GA	Shasta	Horsetown P O	89	504
Jas W	43	m	w	IL	Placer	Bath P O	76	421
Jno	39	m	w	KY	Santa Clara	Gilroy Twp	88	102
John M	24	m	w	IL	Yolo	Cache Crk Twp	93	426
Marshall	35	m	w	KY	San Mateo	Woodside P O	87	381
Marshall	35	m	w	MO	San Mateo	Woodside P O	87	386
Oliver E	23	m	w	IL	Yolo	Putah Twp	93	515
Thomas	31	m	w	LA	San Luis Obispo	Arroyo Grande Twp	87	270
Thomas	30	m	w	OH	Santa Barbara	Arroyo Grande P O	87	508
Wiley	39	m	w	IL	Solano	Benicia	90	19
William	33	m	w	TN	Plumas	Indian Twp	77	16
William	24	m	w	NJ	San Francisco	11-Wd San Francisc	84	554
DICKEY								
A	41	m	w	NY	Sierra	Sierra Twp	89	568
Amos	55	m	w	ME	Nevada	Meadow Lake Twp	75	261
Archebald R	28	m	w	MO	Santa Cruz	Watsonville	89	366
Calvin	37	m	w	ME	Santa Clara	Gilroy Twp	88	86
Charles	28	m	w	IL	Alameda	Alameda	68	1
Charles W	9	m	w	ME	San Francisco	3-Wd San Francisco	79	320
David	35	m	w	CANA	Solano	Rio Vista Twp	90	59
David W	61	m	w	KY	Stanislaus	Empire Twp	92	28
Fred M	28	m	w	MO	San Luis Obispo	Santa Rosa Twp	87	326
George S	40	m	w	MD	San Francisco	8-Wd San Francisco	82	441
Horation	26	m	w	ME	Santa Cruz	Santa Cruz Twp	89	386
J H	45	m	w	TN	Sierra	Eureka Twp	89	523
J R	44	m	w	NY	San Francisco	San Francisco P O	85	874
James	50	m	w	VA	Yuba	Marysville	93	616
James	40	m	w	PA	San Mateo	Woodside P O	87	381
James	38	m	w	CANA	Yuba	Marysville	93	614
Jane	40	f	w	ENGL	Sacramento	Dry Crk Twp	77	103
John	47	m	w	PA	El Dorado	Mud Springs Twp	72	84
John	40	m	w	NY	Solano	Vallejo	90	211
John G	32	m	w	NY	Nevada	Little York Twp	75	237
La Fayette	30	m	w	MO	Stanislaus	Empire Twp	92	28
Sanford	37	m	w	IN	Sacramento	Franklin Twp	77	113
Sebastion	48	m	w	IN	Sonoma	Petaluma Twp	91	356
Thomas	32	m	w	IN	Yolo	Cottonwood Twp	93	459
William	64	m	w	SCOT	San Francisco	7-Wd San Francisco	81	197
DICKIE								
Albert A	29	m	w	CANA	Solano	Denverton Twp	90	22
DICKIESON								
W R	26	m	w	CANA	Nevada	Eureka Twp	75	134
DICKINS								
E F	22	m	w	DC	Humboldt	Eureka Twp	72	258
DICKINSON								
---	45	m	w	NY	Sacramento	1-Wd Sacramento	77	182
Augusta	32	f	w	NY	Shasta	French Gulch P O	89	468
Barny H	48	m	w	NY	Yuba	Slate Range Bar Tw	93	677
D P	47	m	w	MA	El Dorado	Kelsey Twp	72	61
E S	51	m	w	MD	Butte	Mountain Spring Tw	70	89
Ellen	19	f	w	WI	Nevada	Grass Valley Twp	75	208
Erastus	48	m	w	NY	Shasta	French Gulch P O	89	467
Frank H	20	m	w	NY	Placer	Auburn P O	76	368
G W	30	m	w	MO	Merced	Snelling P O	74	267
George D	24	m	w	NY	San Luis Obispo	Arroyo Grande Twp	87	271
H S	36	m	w	MD	Marin	San Rafael Twp	74	40
Hiram	22	m	w	AR	Monterey	Pajaro Twp	74	372
Isaac	52	m	w	NY	Tuolumne	Columbia P O	93	358
J	59	f	w	TN	Merced	Snelling P O	74	264
J	26	m	w	ENGL	Alameda	Murray Twp	68	124
J B	37	m	w	NY	Tuolumne	Columbia P O	93	358
J H	21	m	w	NY	Solano	Benicia	90	20
J J	44	m	w	PA	Del Norte	Crescent	71	463
J M	39	m	w	NY	Nevada	Bridgeport Twp	75	121
James	37	m	w	TN	Mariposa	Maxwell Crk P O	74	142
James H	22	m	w	MD	Colusa	Colusa	71	295
John	30	m	w	MO	Butte	Mountain Spring Tw	70	87
Joseph	30	m	w	NY	Santa Clara	Fremont Twp	88	60
Joseph W	48	m	w	ENGL	Nevada	Grass Valley Twp	75	162
Lawrence	31	m	w	NY	Nevada	Nevada Twp	75	316
Leonora	18	f	w	WI	Placer	Auburn P O	76	368
M	30	f	w	PA	Alameda	Oakland	68	186
Mansfield	38	m	w	TN	Butte	Wyandotte Twp	70	146
Mary	42	f	w	IN	Placer	Auburn P O	76	374
Mary	39	f	w	MA	San Francisco	San Francisco P O	83	278
May	26	f	w	WI	San Joaquin	2-Wd Stockton	86	211
Myrtle J	7	f	w	CA	Amador	Volcano P O	69	383
N	67	f	w	TN	Sonoma	Russian Rvr	91	368
Obadiah	42	m	w	MA	San Francisco	San Francisco P O	83	203
Richerson	41	m	w	TN	Butte	Mountain Spring Tw	70	87
Sam	33	m	w	MO	Merced	Snelling P O	74	256
Susan P	48	f	w	MA	Sonoma	Healdsburg & Mendo	91	279
Thadeus	40	m	w	CANA	Sonoma	Salt Point	91	392
Theo	38	m	w	NY	Shasta	French Gulch P O	89	466
Thomas	38	m	w	ENGL	Stanislaus	Emory Twp	92	24
Thos H	29	m	w	CANA	Placer	Newcastle Twp	76	478
William	36	m	w	MO	Sonoma	Healdsburg	91	275
William F	23	m	w	AL	Yolo	Cache Crk Twp	93	426
Wilson	63	m	w	VA	Butte	Wyandotte Twp	70	146
Wm H	52	m	w	NY	Tuolumne	Sonora P O	93	322
DICKISON								
Chas	35	m	w	NY	San Joaquin	2-Wd Stockton	86	164
DICKMAN								
Bodie	11	m	w	CA	Calaveras	San Andreas P O	70	162
Carle	40	m	w	DENM	Calaveras	San Andreas P O	70	189
Charles	33	m	w	WI	Sacramento	Brighton Twp	77	80
Charles	28	m	w	PRUS	San Francisco	San Francisco P O	83	242
Elmon	46	m	w	NJ	Sacramento	Granite Twp	77	140

© 2001 by Heritage Quest. All rights reserved.

Name	Age	S	R	B-PL	County	Locale	Roll	Pg
Ferdinand	50	m	w	SWIT	Calaveras	San Andreas P O	70	201
Henry	35	m	w	SHOL	Alameda	Eden Twp	68	58
Henry	23	m	w	SHOL	Alameda	Eden Twp	68	63
Mary E	43	f	w	HANO	Sacramento	4-Wd Sacramento	77	341
N	21	m	w	PRUS	Sierra	Table Rock Twp	89	576
DICKMANN								
Hirman	24	m	w	PRUS	San Francisco	11-Wd San Francisc	84	703
DICKS								
Rebecca	70	f	w	OH	El Dorado	Mud Springs Twp	72	83
DICKSON								
Abby M	23	f	w	CANA	Sacramento	3-Wd Sacramento	77	283
Calvin	35	m	w	VT	Marin	Nicasio Twp	74	20
Charles	52	m	w	BRUN	Sacramento	San Joaquin Twp	77	400
Charles	45	m	w	NORW	Trinity	Douglas	92	233
Chas	28	m	w	CANA	Humboldt	Table Bluff Twp	72	307
Chas	25	m	w	ENGL	San Joaquin	Dent Twp	86	20
Chas B	41	m	w	MS	Sonoma	Petaluma Twp	91	322
Chilan	28	m	w	IN	Inyo	Bishop Crk Twp	73	316
David	46	m	w	SCOT	Humboldt	South Fork Twp	72	300
David S	43	m	w	VT	Sonoma	Vallejo Twp	91	462
Davies	59	m	w	CANA	San Diego	San Jacinto Dist	78	517
Eliza	22	f	w	ENGL	Alameda	Oakland	68	196
Francis	28	m	w	SCOT	San Francisco	San Francisco P O	83	133
George	28	m	w	VT	Marin	Nicasio Twp	74	20
Henry	25	m	w	ENGL	San Francisco	3-Wd San Francisco	79	294
J	48	m	w	ENGL	Sierra	Sierra Twp	89	570
J L	28	m	w	OH	Alameda	Oakland	68	176
J P	49	m	w	MA	Sacramento	3-Wd Sacramento	77	281
James	24	m	w	MA	San Francisco	San Francisco P O	83	222
James	21	m	w	NY	Napa	Napa	75	16
James C	30	m	w	NY	Yolo	Cache Crk Twp	93	431
Jas	33	m	w	IREL	Sonoma	Santa Rosa	91	427
Jno H	53	m	w	TN	Nevada	Nevada Twp	75	279
John	39	m	w	IREL	San Francisco	San Francisco P O	83	140
John	28	m	w	ENGL	San Francisco	San Francisco P O	83	248
John C	42	m	w	TN	Placer	Rocklin Twp	76	464
John K	40	m	w	TN	Los Angeles	Los Nietos Twp	73	580
John W B	41	m	w	PA	El Dorado	Placerville Twp	72	93
Joseph	50	m	w	TN	Nevada	Bridgeport Twp	75	100
Levi	40	m	w	MI	Stanislaus	Washington Twp	92	84
R	25	m	w	SCOT	Alameda	Oakland	68	179
Robert	50	m	w	IREL	Stanislaus	Washington Twp	92	86
Thomas	68	m	w	SCOT	San Francisco	San Francisco P O	83	140
Thos	23	m	w	ENGL	San Francisco	7-Wd San Francisco	81	246
William	43	m	w	SCOT	Humboldt	South Fork Twp	72	300
Wm J	41	m	w	VT	Marin	Nicasio Twp	74	20
DICKY								
Rupert	30	m	w	CANA	Kern	Havilah P O	73	340
Thomas	71	m	w	OH	San Bernardino	San Bernardino Twp	78	417
DICROW								
John	62	m	w	FRAN	Mariposa	Mariposa P O	74	91
DICUS								
S C	52	m	w	TN	Tehama	Deer Crk Twp	92	170
DIDAMI								
Bernardo	26	m	w	SWIT	Marin	Tomales Twp	74	76
DIDAWICK								
Stephen	39	m	w	VA	Humboldt	Eel Rvr Twp	72	248
DIDIER								
Jose	26	m	w	FRAN	Santa Clara	2-Wd San Jose	88	323
DIDONCUS								
John	20	m	w	FRAN	Sacramento	Georgianna Twp	77	128
DIDRICH								
Julius	37	m	w	POLA	San Francisco	San Francisco P O	83	161
DIE								
Ah	46	m	c	CHIN	Fresno	Millerton P O	72	199
Ah	45	m	c	CHIN	Siskiyou	Yreka	89	657
Ah	42	m	c	CHIN	Fresno	Millerton P O	72	200
Ah	40	m	c	CHIN	Butte	Hamilton Twp	70	68
Ah	29	m	c	CHIN	Sacramento	Georgianna Twp	77	122
Ah	22	m	c	CHIN	Alameda	Eden Twp	68	92
Ah	18	m	c	CHIN	San Francisco	San Francisco P O	80	507
Albert	16	m	w	CA	Santa Cruz	Pajaro Twp	89	360
Ar	20	m	c	CHIN	Sonoma	Petaluma Twp	91	363
Ki	32	m	c	CHIN	Nevada	Nevada Twp	75	313
Yon	31	f	c	CHIN	Yuba	Marysville	93	627
DIEAS								
Frank	29	m	w	PORT	Alameda	Eden Twp	68	80
Joseph	40	m	w	PORT	Alameda	Washington Twp	68	269
Manuel	24	m	w	PORT	Alameda	Brooklyn Twp	68	49
DIEATCH								
Franklin	50	m	w	NY	San Mateo	San Mateo P O	87	357
DIEAUD								
Josephine	36	f	w	FRAN	San Francisco	San Francisco P O	80	347
DIEBEL								
Theodore	23	m	w	NJ	Tulare	Tule Rvr Twp	92	262
DIEBOLD								
C G	36	m	w	PA	Amador	Ione City P O	69	367
DIECE								
Jeone Vieont	55	m	w	FRAN	Yuba	Long Bar Twp	93	560
DIECKMAN								
Peter	37	m	w	SHOL	Placer	Alta P O	76	411
DIEDAICH								
Waltzan	32	m	w	PRUS	Monterey	Castroville Twp	74	332
DIEDER								
Henry	46	m	w	FRNK	San Francisco	San Francisco P O	80	333
DIEDERICK								
Herman	21	m	w	HAMB	Santa Clara	1-Wd San Jose	88	232
DIEDERICKSON								
William	50	m	w	DENM	San Francisco	San Francisco P O	83	255
DIEDRICH								
Jacob	35	m	w	PRUS	Calaveras	Copperopolis P O	70	241
Kate	14	f	w	HDAR	San Francisco	2-Wd San Francisco	79	273
DIEDRICK								
Hy	29	m	w	SHOL	San Francisco	11-Wd San Francisc	84	617
Richard R	29	m	w	NY	Santa Clara	1-Wd San Jose	88	249
DIEGIN								
Patrick	30	m	w	IREL	San Francisco	San Francisco P O	85	768
DIEGO								
Cocoro	54	m	w	CA	San Diego	Warners Rancho Dis	78	528
Ignacio	34	m	w	CA	San Diego	Warners Rancho Dis	78	528
Jose	62	m	w	CA	San Diego	Warners Rancho Dis	78	528
Juan	43	m	w	CA	San Diego	Warners Rancho Dis	78	528
Ortega	43	m	w	CA	Santa Barbara	Santa Barbara P O	87	463
DIEHL								
Conrad	40	m	w	PRUS	San Francisco	San Francisco P O	80	456
George	27	m	w	PRUS	San Francisco	San Francisco P O	80	460
Henry W	30	m	w	PA	Yolo	Cache Crk Twp	93	425
Jacob	44	m	w	GERM	Nevada	Nevada Twp	75	271
James	43	m	w	PRUS	San Francisco	San Francisco P O	80	477
DIEL								
Valentine	50	m	w	HDAR	Santa Clara	Fremont Twp	88	58
DIELBAL								
Fred	26	m	w	SWIT	El Dorado	Coloma Twp	72	4
DIELGEN								
Ludary	23	m	w	HANO	San Francisco	11-Wd San Francisc	84	478
DIELL								
George	30	m	w	WI	Sutter	Butte Twp	92	94
DIEM								
Ah	27	m	c	CHIN	Placer	Bath P O	76	446
DIEN								
Eliza	38	f	w	BREM	Sacramento	3-Wd Sacramento	77	284
DIENER								
J F	51	m	w	WURT	Trinity	Minersville Pct	92	215
DIERCE								
Sophonia	35	m	m	SC	San Francisco	8-Wd San Francisco	82	494
DIERCKS								
Eliza	37	f	w	PRUS	San Francisco	San Francisco P O	83	293
Henry	46	m	w	PRUS	San Francisco	San Francisco P O	80	402
John	30	m	w	HANO	Mendocino	Round Valley Twp	74	217
DIERDOFF								
W P	40	m	w	IA	San Joaquin	3-Wd Stockton	86	236
DIEREN								
Edward	41	m	w	PRUS	San Francisco	San Francisco P O	85	762
DIERGO								
Rafael	23	m	w	SWIT	Marin	Tomales Twp	74	77
DIERHAM								
Johana	21	f	w	FRAN	San Francisco	San Francisco P O	80	455
DIERNEY								
George	60	m	w	FRAN	Marin	San Rafael Twp	74	25
DIERS								
William	21	m	w	HANO	San Francisco	San Francisco P O	83	176
DIERSSREN								
Dick	18	m	w	BREM	Sacramento	4-Wd Sacramento	77	339
DIERSTIEN								
W	35	m	w	PRUS	Sierra	Forest	89	537
DIES								
Jose	26	m	w	CA	Marin	San Rafael Twp	74	41
Nicholes	39	f	w	SAME	San Joaquin	1-Wd Stockton	86	133
DIESBACH								
Chris	49	m	w	PRUS	Sacramento	3-Wd Sacramento	77	303
DIESBOURG								
Chas	41	m	w	MA	San Francisco	San Francisco P O	83	138
DIESCHLER								
Frederik	48	m	w	BAVA	San Francisco	2-Wd San Francisco	79	244
DIESEN								
Chas	48	m	w	PRUS	San Francisco	1-Wd San Francisco	79	51
DIESING								
Reynold O	40	m	w	BRUN	Santa Cruz	Santa Cruz	89	411
DIESON								
Thos	34	m	w	ENGL	San Francisco	11-Wd San Francisc	84	675
DIESSER								
Benjamin	49	m	w	ME	San Francisco	2-Wd San Francisco	79	263
DIESTELHORST								
George	49	m	w	HANO	Shasta	Shasta P O	89	452
DIESTON								
Henry	21	m	w	PRUS	San Francisco	San Francisco P O	85	870
DIETCHE								
Car	17	f	w	BADE	Sacramento	3-Wd Sacramento	77	307
DIETERMAN								
H	34	m	w	PRUS	San Francisco	San Francisco P O	85	803
DIETLEDGE								
Detrich	37	m	w	PRUS	San Francisco	San Francisco P O	83	400
DIETRELL								
John	41	m	w	FRAN	Solano	Denverton Twp	90	27
DIETRICH								
Chas	25	m	w	BADE	Sacramento	3-Wd Sacramento	77	287
Chris	51	m	w	WURT	San Francisco	11-Wd San Francisc	84	680
Ferdinand	35	m	w	SWIT	San Francisco	3-Wd San Francisco	79	324
Isral W	37	m	w	PA	Del Norte	Crescent Twp	71	456
Pauline	29	f	w	SAXO	San Francisco	San Francisco P O	83	134
T	55	m	w	GERM	Yuba	Marysville	93	612
William	38	m	w	PA	San Francisco	6-Wd San Francisco	81	155
DIETRICK								
John	28	m	w	PRUS	San Francisco	San Francisco P O	83	232

© 2001 by Heritage Quest. All rights reserved.

Name	Age	S	R	B-PL	County	Locale	Roll	Pg
DIETS								
Chas	25	m	w	PRUS	San Francisco	San Francisco P O	85	866
DIETTERLE								
Helena	35	f	w	AUST	San Francisco	11-Wd San Francisc	84	626
DIETTRIECH								
Hans	20	m	w	PRUS	San Francisco	San Francisco P O	80	458
DIETZ								
Bertha	16	f	w	CA	San Francisco	San Francisco P O	80	415
Pedro	43	m	w	MEXI	Mariposa	Mariposa P O	74	94
Phillip	42	m	w	SAXO	San Francisco	San Francisco P O	80	476
DIETZER								
William	36	m	w	PRUS	San Francisco	San Francisco P O	80	532
DIEVENDORFF								
Henry	43	m	w	NY	San Diego	San Diego	78	497
DIEWALD								
Matthias	47	m	w	PRUS	El Dorado	Diamond Springs Tw	72	26
DIEZ								
Benjamin	17	m	w	CA	Santa Cruz	Soquel Twp	89	437
DIFFCACH								
Lew	33	m	w	PRUS	Alameda	Oakland	68	176
DIFFER								
Adison	55	m	w	FRAN	Calaveras	San Andreas P O	70	157
James	50	m	w	IREL	Stanislaus	Emory Twp	92	25
DIFFINDERFFER								
B W	33	m	w	MD	Napa	Napa	75	19
DIFFING								
Isaac	35	m	w	PA	San Francisco	San Francisco P O	83	133
DIFFLEY								
Peter	55	m	w	IREL	San Francisco	8-Wd San Francisco	82	409
DIFFRANDINO								
Angel	35	m	w	ITAL	San Francisco	San Francisco P O	83	311
DIFFRETH								
Francis	22	m	w	IREL	Marin	San Rafael	74	55
DIG								
Lo	36	m	c	CHIN	Sacramento	1-Wd Sacramento	77	173
DIGGER								
Herbert	24	m	w	CANA	Solano	Vacaville Twp	90	117
DIGGINS								
Charles	36	m	w	VT	Mendocino	Round Valley Twp	74	220
Wesley	63	m	w	VT	San Francisco	San Francisco P O	85	867
DIGGLES								
Henry J	35	m	w	MA	Siskiyou	Scott Valley Twp	89	608
J	37	m	w	MA	Siskiyou	Callahan P O	89	630
DIGGS								
David	42	m	w	MO	Yolo	Cache Crk Twp	93	456
Henry	27	m	w	MO	Tulare	Packwood Twp	92	257
Montgomery	36	m	w	IREL	San Mateo	Half Moon Bay P O	87	392
DIGMAN								
Chris	34	m	w	IREL	Klamath	Liberty Twp	73	375
John	29	m	w	IREL	San Francisco	8-Wd San Francisco	82	315
DIGNALL								
David	35	m	w	SCOT	Butte	Kimshew Tpw	70	78
DIGNAN								
Francis	28	m	w	IREL	San Francisco	7-Wd San Francisco	81	279
DIGNARD								
Joseph	20	m	w	CANA	Santa Cruz	Santa Cruz Twp	89	396
DIGNER								
Ann	25	f	w	IREL	Sacramento	2-Wd Sacramento	77	223
DIGNON								
Thomas J	38	m	w	IREL	Humboldt	Eel Rvr Twp	72	251
DIGNOT								
Thos	30	m	w	IREL	Alameda	Oakland	68	228
DIGON								
Jno	27	m	w	BAVA	Sacramento	1-Wd Sacramento	77	176
DIGONS								
Alford	28	m	w	ENGL	San Francisco	7-Wd San Francisco	81	209
DIJEAU								
Peter	51	m	w	FRAN	Santa Clara	Fremont Twp	88	56
DIK								
Ah	29	m	c	CHIN	San Francisco	San Francisco P O	85	748
Ah	24	m	c	CHIN	San Francisco	6-Wd San Francisco	81	63
Ah	20	m	c	CHIN	San Francisco	6-Wd San Francisco	81	59
DIKE								
Ato	25	m	w	PRUS	Solano	Vallejo	90	170
Edmund C	35	m	w	NY	San Francisco	8-Wd San Francisco	82	446
John	24	m	w	IREL	Solano	Rio Vista Twp	90	70
Owen	35	m	w	NY	Calaveras	San Andreas P O	70	159
DIKEMAN								
Charles	35	m	w	SWED	Colusa	Spring Valley Twp	71	344
Eliza	76	f	w	NY	Yuba	Marysville	93	578
H	27	m	w	PA	Siskiyou	Callahan P O	89	631
Saml H	45	m	w	PRUS	Nevada	Rough & Ready Twp	75	323
Vincent	12	m	w	CA	Sacramento	4-Wd Sacramento	77	378
DIKEN								
Joshua	18	m	w	OH	Sonoma	Salt Point	91	387
DIKENS								
Louis	32	m	w	MA	San Francisco	6-Wd San Francisco	81	73
DIKSON								
Joseph M	39	m	w	TN	Yuba	Bullards Bar P O	93	553
DILAURD								
John	35	m	w	ITAL	San Joaquin	2-Wd Stockton	86	188
DILDER								
John	22	m	w	ME	San Francisco	San Francisco P O	83	88
DILGES								
Jacob	32	m	w	HDAR	San Francisco	San Francisco P O	83	30
DILHS								
William	35	m	w	PA	San Diego	Julian Dist	78	470

Name	Age	S	R	B-PL	County	Locale	Roll	Pg
DILKE								
John	28	m	w	NY	San Francisco	7-Wd San Francisco	81	227
DILKS								
Wm Lewley	40	m	w	PA	Plumas	Washington Twp	77	58
DILL								
A G	48	m	w	OH	Butte	Wyandotte Twp	70	149
Armstrong	48	m	w	OH	Plumas	Indian Twp	77	10
George	43	m	w	IL	San Joaquin	Tulare Twp	86	254
Henry	42	m	w	GERM	Yolo	Grafton Twp	93	492
Henry	36	m	w	MO	Nevada	Eureka Twp	75	133
John	41	m	w	IL	Nevada	Washington Twp	75	346
John	23	m	w	OR	Mendocino	Little Lake Twp	74	194
Joseph	25	m	w	CANA	San Mateo	Woodside P O	87	385
Nelson	19	m	w	CANA	San Joaquin	Oneal Twp	86	114
DILLAN								
James	36	m	w	IREL	San Francisco	San Francisco P O	80	360
James	35	m	w	IREL	Sacramento	2-Wd Sacramento	77	209
DILLARD								
Caleb J	53	m	w	IL	Sacramento	Dry Crk Twp	77	97
Lewis	37	m	w	OH	Santa Cruz	Pajaro Twp	89	350
Robt M	30	m	w	KY	Santa Barbara	Santa Barbara P O	87	453
DILLAS								
William	39	m	w	HDAR	Solano	Green Valley Twp	90	39
DILLE								
Daniel K	40	m	w	OH	Napa	Napa	75	22
J T	38	m	w	OH	Alameda	Oakland	68	157
Samuel H	41	m	w	OH	Nevada	Grass Valley Twp	75	150
DILLEN								
---	16	f	w	CA	Los Angeles	Los Angeles	73	569
Patric	37	m	w	IREL	Humboldt	Eureka Twp	72	270
DILLER								
Chris	39	m	w	WURT	Los Angeles	Los Angeles	73	528
George	58	m	w	PA	Tuolumne	Sonora P O	93	327
DILLEY								
Cyrus	22	m	w	IL	Sacramento	Dry Crk Twp	77	102
D M	35	m	w	MI	Humboldt	Arcata Twp	72	227
George	38	m	w	MI	Los Angeles	Los Angeles Twp	73	489
James	54	m	w	OH	Santa Clara	Santa Clara Twp	88	139
John B	26	m	w	WI	San Francisco	San Francisco P O	83	205
DILLI								
Joseph B	37	m	w	OH	El Dorado	Cosumnes Twp	72	13
DILLIAN								
Francis	39	m	w	MO	Amador	Volcano P O	69	388
Henry	30	m	w	IA	Amador	Ione City P O	69	352
Wm E	35	m	w	IA	Amador	Volcano P O	69	372
DILLIN								
Johnana	12	f	w	NY	San Francisco	7-Wd San Francisco	81	180
William	30	m	w	IREL	Placer	Emigrant Gap P O	76	416
DILLING								
John	26	m	w	PRUS	Stanislaus	Emory Twp	92	19
Otto	23	m	w	PRUS	Stanislaus	Emory Twp	92	21
DILLINGER								
Mary	61	f	w	SC	Santa Clara	Fremont Twp	88	46
DILLINGHAM								
Henry	33	m	w	SCOT	Contra Costa	Martinez P O	71	419
Henry	33	m	w	ME	Contra Costa	Martinez P O	71	419
W E	37	m	w	MD	Amador	Volcano P O	69	386
Wm K	20	m	w	MO	Sonoma	Mendocino Twp	91	293
DILLINGHAN								
W W	34	m	w	MA	Solano	Benicia	90	3
DILLION								
Henry	42	m	w	IREL	San Francisco	7-Wd San Francisco	81	221
Micheal	40	m	w	IREL	San Francisco	7-Wd San Francisco	81	191
Patrick	37	m	w	IREL	San Francisco	7-Wd San Francisco	81	216
Peter	35	m	w	IREL	San Francisco	7-Wd San Francisco	81	221
DILLMAN								
Elijah	43	m	w	KY	Stanislaus	Empire Twp	92	40
George	42	m	w	BAVA	San Francisco	San Francisco P O	80	533
George	21	m	w	IL	Stanislaus	Empire Twp	92	63
DILLMORE								
John W	31	m	w	OH	Santa Clara	2-Wd San Jose	88	320
DILLON								
Albert	31	m	w	MO	San Joaquin	Elliott Twp	86	75
Andrew	39	m	w	PRUS	Mendocino	Point Arena Twp	74	204
Annie	16	f	w	CA	San Francisco	San Francisco P O	85	765
Bernard	28	m	w	IREL	San Francisco	8-Wd San Francisco	82	490
Bridget	47	f	w	IREL	San Francisco	San Francisco P O	83	309
Calvin	62	m	w	VA	Amador	Ione City P O	69	361
Catherin	27	f	w	IREL	Alameda	Eden Twp	68	92
Charles H	37	m	w	MO	Sonoma	Sonoma Twp	91	439
Chas	17	m	w	IREL	San Francisco	1-Wd San Francisco	79	25
Daniel	26	m	w	IREL	San Francisco	1-Wd San Francisco	79	62
Dennis	50	m	w	IREL	San Mateo	Redwood Twp	87	361
E	40	f	w	IREL	San Francisco	San Francisco P O	85	789
Edward	50	m	w	IREL	San Francisco	2-Wd San Francisco	79	248
Edward	30	m	w	OH	San Luis Obispo	Morro Twp	87	287
Elizabeth	10	f	w	CA	Amador	Fiddletown P O	69	439
Ellen	33	f	w	IREL	San Francisco	San Francisco P O	83	187
Frank	25	m	w	PRUS	Placer	Dutch Flat P O	76	415
Geo L	50	m	w	IREL	San Francisco	1-Wd San Francisco	79	1
George	6	m	w	CA	San Francisco	San Francisco P O	83	74
Henry	38	m	w	IREL	San Francisco	San Francisco P O	83	130
Ira P	45	m	w	NC	Tulare	Farmersville Twp	92	248
J E	53	m	w	IREL	Nevada	Eureka Twp	75	135
J M	46	m	w	NY	Alameda	Oakland	68	144
James	39	m	w	IREL	Plumas	Indian Twp	77	14
James	29	m	w	IREL	San Francisco	San Francisco P O	83	155

© 2001 by Heritage Quest. All rights reserved.

California 1870 Census

Series M593

Name	Age	S	R	B-PL	County	Locale	Roll	Pg
James	25	m	w	IREL	San Francisco	San Francisco P O	83	206
Jas Patrick	10	m	w	NC	San Francisco	San Francisco P O	83	202
Johanna	30	f	w	IREL	San Francisco	San Francisco P O	85	802
Johanna	26	f	w	IREL	San Francisco	7-Wd San Francisco	81	278
John	48	m	w	NY	Colusa	Colusa Twp	71	277
John	42	m	w	IREL	Placer	Clipper Gap P O	76	376
John	40	m	w	IREL	San Joaquin	Oneal Twp	86	107
John	34	m	w	IREL	San Francisco	8-Wd San Francisco	82	404
John	34	m	w	IREL	Mendocino	Round Valley Twp	74	217
John	33	m	w	CANA	Plumas	Washington Twp	77	55
John B	51	m	w	IREL	Colusa	Colusa Twp	71	281
John R	40	m	w	VA	Humboldt	Arcata Twp	72	235
Jos	38	m	w	IREL	San Francisco	11-Wd San Francisc	84	425
Jos	35	m	w	IREL	San Francisco	7-Wd San Francisco	81	257
Joseph A	41	m	w	MO	Butte	Chico Twp	70	58
K	12	f	w	CA	Alameda	Oakland	68	241
Kate	40	f	w	IREL	San Francisco	6-Wd San Francisco	81	155
L B	39	m	w	KY	Merced	Snelling P O	74	260
Larkin W	45	m	w	VA	El Dorado	Mud Springs Twp	72	84
Loton H	41	m	w	NC	San Francisco	1-Wd San Francisco	79	133
Lotten H	40	m	w	NC	Sacramento	2-Wd Sacramento	77	249
Luke	50	m	w	IREL	San Francisco	San Francisco P O	85	869
M	38	m	w	IREL	Lassen	Milford Twp	73	438
Margaret	45	f	w	MA	San Francisco	San Francisco P O	80	486
Margaret	35	f	w	IREL	San Francisco	7-Wd San Francisco	81	283
Martha Ann	60	f	w	NJ	Santa Clara	Santa Clara Twp	88	137
Mary	24	f	w	IREL	San Francisco	San Francisco P O	83	280
Mary	24	f	w	IREL	Alameda	Oakland	68	147
Mary E	19	f	w	PA	San Francisco	San Francisco P O	83	197
Mary Joseph	36	f	w	IREL	San Francisco	San Francisco P O	83	129
Maurice	40	m	w	IREL	Del Norte	Mountain Twp	71	475
Michael	31	m	w	IREL	Sacramento	2-Wd Sacramento	77	250
Michl	55	m	w	IREL	San Francisco	1-Wd San Francisco	79	17
Nathan	50	m	w	NC	Tulare	Farmersville Twp	92	244
Nathaniel	52	m	w	NY	Tulare	Tule Rvr Twp	92	263
Nicolas	60	m	w	IREL	San Francisco	San Francisco P O	83	387
P F	58	m	w	IREL	Nevada	Bloomfield Twp	75	96
P W	50	m	w	IREL	Solano	Benicia	90	1
Pat	45	m	w	IREL	Santa Clara	Gilroy Twp	88	93
Pat	24	m	w	IREL	Sacramento	3-Wd Sacramento	77	311
Patrick	60	m	w	IREL	Santa Clara	San Jose Twp	88	185
Patrick	32	m	w	IREL	Sutter	Butte Twp	92	95
Patrick	30	m	w	IREL	Nevada	Grass Valley Twp	75	197
Patrick	23	m	w	IREL	San Francisco	San Francisco P O	83	387
Peter	48	m	w	IREL	Alameda	Murray Twp	68	122
Richard	34	m	w	IREL	Nevada	Eureka Twp	75	134
Robt	35	m	w	IREL	Solano	Vallejo	90	188
Ruben	36	m	w	KY	Amador	Fiddletown P O	69	435
S J	38	m	w	NY	Sacramento	Franklin Twp	77	114
Sarah	24	f	w	CHIL	Los Angeles	Los Angeles	73	523
Theresa	25	f	w	IREL	San Francisco	8-Wd San Francisco	82	432
Thomas	53	m	w	IREL	Alameda	Washington Twp	68	290
Thomas	39	m	w	ENGL	San Francisco	1-Wd San Francisco	79	19
Thomas	21	m	w	IREL	San Francisco	San Francisco P O	83	155
Thos H	35	m	w	IREL	San Francisco	San Francisco P O	83	267
Warren	6M	m	w	CA	Tehama	Merrill	92	198
William	40	m	w	IREL	Marin	Tomales Twp	74	83
William H	24	m	w	IN	Santa Clara	Santa Clara Twp	88	137
Wm	43	m	w	IREL	Yuba	Marysville	93	595
Wm	26	m	w	CANA	Humboldt	Pacific Twp	72	289
Wm	19	m	w	LA	San Francisco	1-Wd San Francisco	79	41
DILLY								
Abraham	55	m	w	NJ	Santa Clara	Santa Clara Twp	88	144
Cyrus	21	m	w	MA	Sacramento	Natomas Twp	77	169
John	41	m	w	NY	Alameda	San Leandro	68	96
DILMAN								
F W	39	m	w	BAVA	Sacramento	4-Wd Sacramento	77	367
DILSEAUX								
Virginia	40	f	w	BELG	Alameda	Brooklyn Twp	68	40
DILSLINN								
A	38	m	w	SWED	Siskiyou	Scott Valley Twp	89	611
DILSTRUM								
Helen	38	f	w	SWED	Siskiyou	Scott Valley Twp	89	613
DILTON								
G H	33	m	w	HAMB	Nevada	Meadow Lake Twp	75	259
James	58	m	w	IL	Amador	Volcano P O	69	385
DILTS								
Daniel C S	45	m	w	NJ	San Diego	San Diego	78	492
DILWOOD								
John	50	m	w	MO	Contra Costa	Martinez P O	71	404
DILWORTH								
Jane	35	f	w	NY	San Francisco	11-Wd San Francisc	84	530
DIM								
---	19	m	c	CHIN	San Francisco	6-Wd San Francisco	81	64
Chs	49	m	w	PA	Sierra	Forest Twp	89	531
John	19	m	w	IL	Contra Costa	Martinez P O	71	396
DIMAN								
Joseph	53	m	w	FRAN	Placer	Auburn P O	76	379
DIMEEN								
Julia	25	f	w	MA	Solano	Benicia	90	16
DIMICK								
C A	40	m	w	VT	Napa	Napa	75	17
DIMING								
Bynn	43	m	w	VT	Humboldt	Arcata Twp	72	230
DIMMICK								
Jno	25	m	w	IL	Sonoma	Russian Rvr	91	378
DIMMON								
Pat	26	m	w	IREL	Alameda	Murray Twp	68	124
DIMOCK								
Daniel	38	m	w	IREL	Nevada	Meadow Lake Twp	75	250
David Wo	44	m	w	NY	Los Angeles	Santa Ana Twp	73	612
Jos	30	m	w	CANA	Santa Clara	Gilroy Twp	88	85
R B	35	m	w	IREL	Nevada	Meadow Lake Twp	75	250
R V	28	m	w	CANA	Nevada	Meadow Lake Twp	75	258
DIMON								
Charles L	47	m	w	NY	Nevada	Grass Valley Twp	75	173
Jacob	45	m	w	NY	San Francisco	11-Wd San Francisc	84	557
John	34	m	w	NY	El Dorado	Placerville Twp	72	95
DIMOND								
Chas	25	m	w	NY	San Francisco	5-Wd San Francisco	81	31
Chas	24	m	w	PA	San Francisco	5-Wd San Francisco	81	36
Daniel	48	m	w	IREL	Tuolumne	Columbia P O	93	346
James	38	m	w	IREL	Yuba	Slate Range Bar Tw	93	672
Martin	40	m	w	IREL	San Francisco	5-Wd San Francisco	81	3
Robt	30	m	w	MD	Alameda	Oakland	68	165
William	31	m	w	HI	San Francisco	8-Wd San Francisco	82	472
Wm M	52	m	w	PA	Nevada	Grass Valley Twp	75	203
DIMONS								
Henry	28	m	w	CANA	Nevada	Grass Valley Twp	75	229
DIMOTH								
Ira J	29	m	w	PA	Sonoma	Petaluma Twp	91	319
DIMPFEL								
Geo L	64	m	w	FRAN	Solano	Benicia	90	16
DIN								
Ah	40	m	c	CHIN	Yolo	Grafton Twp	93	482
Ah	37	m	c	CHIN	San Francisco	San Francisco P O	80	514
Ah	34	m	c	CHIN	San Francisco	San Francisco P O	80	512
Ah	30	m	c	CHIN	San Francisco	San Francisco P O	80	519
Ah	27	m	c	CHIN	San Francisco	San Francisco P O	80	500
Ah	25	m	c	CHIN	Placer	Summit P O	76	496
Ah	24	m	c	CHIN	San Francisco	San Francisco P O	80	505
Ah	24	m	c	CHIN	San Francisco	San Francisco P O	80	524
Ah	20	m	c	CHIN	San Francisco	San Francisco P O	80	497
Ah	13	m	c	CHIN	Napa	Napa	75	57
Che	24	m	c	CHIN	Trinity	North Fork Twp	92	216
Gelon	32	m	c	CHIN	Yuba	Marysville	93	622
Him	30	m	c	CHIN	Trinity	North Fork Twp	92	216
Jeen	26	m	c	CHIN	San Francisco	6-Wd San Francisco	81	52
Yov	35	m	c	CHIN	Placer	Bath P O	76	429
DINAN								
D J	19	m	w	MA	San Francisco	3-Wd San Francisco	79	318
Dennis	36	m	w	IREL	Siskiyou	Yreka Twp	89	670
Frank	38	m	w	IREL	San Francisco	6-Wd San Francisco	81	80
James B	46	m	w	IREL	San Francisco	6-Wd San Francisco	81	118
Jeremiah	50	m	w	IREL	Nevada	Grass Valley Twp	75	213
DINCUTT								
H P	50	m	w	VT	Sierra	Sierra Twp	89	562
DIND								
John F	22	m	w	NY	Placer	Gold Run Twp	76	395
DINEEN								
John	22	m	w	AUST	Sierra	Table Rock Twp	89	578
Nova	40	f	w	IREL	San Francisco	11-Wd San Francisc	84	501
DINEGAN								
John	55	m	w	IREL	Santa Clara	Santa Clara Twp	88	144
DINEHOUGH								
Mary	4	f	w	ME	Humboldt	Eureka Twp	72	260
DINELEY								
Emmeline A	5	f	w	CA	Santa Cruz	Santa Cruz Twp	89	385
Samuel	39	m	w	ENGL	Tulare	Visalia	92	292
DINELY								
John	17	m	w	NY	San Francisco	11-Wd San Francisc	84	593
DINEN								
John	28	m	w	IREL	San Francisco	San Francisco P O	83	153
DINER								
Frederick	42	m	w	PRUS	Sacramento	Natomas Twp	77	169
Henry	45	m	w	PRUS	Placer	Bath P O	76	428
DINESDEM								
John	37	m	w	SHOL	San Francisco	2-Wd San Francisco	79	273
DING								
Ah	51	m	c	CHIN	Sacramento	Granite Twp	77	137
Ah	40	m	c	CHIN	San Francisco	San Francisco P O	80	513
Ah	40	m	c	CHIN	San Francisco	San Francisco P O	80	505
Ah	38	m	c	CHIN	Placer	Dutch Flat P O	76	408
Ah	36	m	c	CHIN	San Francisco	San Francisco P O	80	454
Ah	36	m	c	CHIN	Sacramento	Granite Twp	77	139
Ah	34	m	c	CHIN	San Francisco	San Francisco P O	80	514
Ah	34	m	c	CHIN	San Francisco	San Francisco P O	80	509
Ah	34	m	c	CHIN	San Francisco	San Francisco P O	80	504
Ah	34	m	c	CHIN	Sierra	Alleghany & Forest	89	535
Ah	32	m	c	CHIN	San Francisco	San Francisco P O	80	501
Ah	32	m	c	CHIN	San Francisco	San Francisco P O	80	497
Ah	31	m	c	CHIN	San Bernardino	San Bernardino Twp	78	433
Ah	31	m	c	CHIN	Trinity	Douglas	92	233
Ah	31	m	c	CHIN	Fresno	Millerton P O	72	199
Ah	30	m	c	CHIN	Placer	Colfax P O	76	386
Ah	29	m	c	CHIN	San Francisco	San Francisco P O	80	502
Ah	28	m	c	CHIN	San Francisco	6-Wd San Francisco	81	65
Ah	27	m	c	CHIN	Nevada	Nevada Twp	75	311
Ah	27	m	c	CHIN	Santa Clara	Fremont Twp	88	58
Ah	27	m	c	CHIN	Fresno	Millerton P O	72	202
Ah	25	f	c	CHIN	San Francisco	San Francisco P O	80	503
Ah	24	m	c	CHIN	San Francisco	6-Wd San Francisco	81	59
Ah	21	m	c	CHIN	San Francisco	San Francisco P O	80	499

© 2001 by Heritage Quest. All rights reserved.

Name	Age	S	R	B-PL	County	Locale	Roll	Pg
						Series M593		
Ah	21	m	c	CHIN	Calaveras	San Andreas P O	70	204
Ah	20	m	c	CHIN	Alameda	Oakland	68	194
Ah	20	m	c	CHIN	El Dorado	Coloma Twp	72	8
Ah	19	m	c	CHIN	San Francisco	San Francisco P O	80	504
Ah	19	m	c	CHIN	San Francisco	San Francisco P O	80	497
Gee	46	m	c	CHIN	Plumas	Mineral Twp	77	24
Man	70	m	c	CHIN	Calaveras	San Andreas P O	70	219
Ti	20	m	c	CHIN	San Joaquin	1-Wd Stockton	86	144
Yee	30	m	c	CHIN	Yuba	Marysville	93	623
Yuen	24	m	c	CHIN	Calaveras	San Andreas P O	70	203
DINGBERG								
John	28	m	w	PRUS	Santa Cruz	Santa Cruz	89	432
DINGEL								
George	28	m	w	FRAN	San Francisco	2-Wd San Francisco	79	145
DINGENS								
Frances	37	m	w	FRAN	Yolo	Grafton Twp	93	485
DINGEON								
Leo	45	m	w	FRAN	San Francisco	8-Wd San Francisco	82	363
DINGERALD								
Thomas	25	m	w	VT	Santa Cruz	Santa Cruz Twp	89	400
DINGHAM								
Henry L	48	m	w	CA	El Dorado	Placerville Twp	72	99
DINGLE								
George	45	m	w	ME	San Francisco	2-Wd San Francisco	79	172
James	29	m	w	ENGL	Amador	Sutter Crk P O	69	396
Jno	60	m	w	BADE	Butte	Kimshew Tpw	70	76
Joseph	36	m	w	BADE	Siskiyou	Scott Valley Twp	89	619
Nelson	32	m	w	NY	San Francisco	San Francisco P O	83	404
Richard	38	m	w	ENGL	San Francisco	11-Wd San Francisc	84	439
DINGLEY								
Charles V	40	m	w	ME	Mariposa	Mariposa P O	74	125
Chas L	41	m	w	ME	San Francisco	7-Wd San Francisco	81	273
Samuel	50	m	w	ME	Stanislaus	Buena Vista Twp	92	15
Wm	40	m	w	ME	San Francisco	San Francisco P O	85	820
DINGMAN								
Geo	30	m	w	PRUS	San Joaquin	Tulare Twp	86	264
George	32	m	w	NY	San Francisco	6-Wd San Francisco	81	105
George	29	m	w	CANA	San Mateo	Schoolhouse Statio	87	331
J W	42	m	w	OH	Sutter	Butte Twp	92	90
Mary	55	f	w	ENGL	San Mateo	Schoolhouse Statio	87	331
Sylvester W	45	m	w	NY	Yuba	Bullards Bar P O	93	549
DINGURA								
M	41	m	w	ME	Alameda	Oakland	68	261
DININE								
Danl	20	m	w	MA	San Francisco	7-Wd San Francisco	81	270
DINING								
Jeremiah	35	m	w	IREL	San Francisco	7-Wd San Francisco	81	235
DININGHER								
John	9	m	w	CA	San Francisco	11-Wd San Francisc	84	577
DINK								
Ah	40	m	c	CHIN	Kern	Havilah P O	73	338
DINKELSPIEL								
Adolph	22	m	w	BADE	Solano	Silveyville Twp	90	91
Lazenis	46	m	w	BADE	San Francisco	8-Wd San Francisco	82	401
DINKENSPIEL								
Moses	44	m	w	BADE	Solano	Suisun Twp	90	96
DINKHAM								
Marg	60	f	w	IREL	San Joaquin	2-Wd Stockton	86	163
DINKIN								
John	20	m	w	ENGL	San Francisco	1-Wd San Francisco	79	68
DINKINS								
James	26	m	w	IREL	Monterey	Alisal Twp	74	294
DINKINSON								
Geo	32	m	w	ENGL	Contra Costa	Martinez P O	71	419
DINKLE								
Jno	65	m	w	BAVA	Butte	Kimshew Tpw	70	82
Manuel	19	m	w	CA	San Diego	Temecula Dist	78	526
DINKLEGE								
Herman D	13	m	w	CA	San Francisco	San Francisco P O	83	57
DINKLESPEIL								
Samuel B	34	m	w	BADE	San Francisco	8-Wd San Francisco	82	294
DINMAN								
Chas	18	m	w	IL	Humboldt	Arcata Twp	72	228
DINMORE								
L	28	m	w	OH	Solano	Vallejo	90	209
Samuel	43	m	w	NH	San Francisco	San Francisco P O	83	279
DINN								
John	28	m	w	IREL	Plumas	Plumas Twp	77	28
Margaret	40	f	w	IREL	Colusa	Stony Crk Twp	71	331
DINNAN								
Con	35	m	w	IREL	Solano	Vallejo	90	162
Mary	55	f	w	IREL	Sacramento	Granite Twp	77	142
DINNEEN								
Margaret	28	f	w	IREL	San Francisco	San Francisco P O	83	28
DINNEN								
Patrick	31	m	w	IREL	Santa Cruz	Santa Cruz	89	410
DINNENN								
W	23	m	w	ITAL	Amador	Jackson P O	69	330
DINNER								
Robert	11	m	w	MO	Mendocino	Sanel Twp	74	229
DINNEY								
Thomas	24	m	w	IREL	Amador	Amador City P O	69	392
DINNIN								
P	34	m	w	IREL	Lake	Knoxville Mines	73	404
DINNY								
Mary	46	f	w	IREL	San Francisco	San Francisco P O	83	281
DINON								
Clara	20	f	w	NY	San Francisco	11-Wd San Francisc	84	611
DINSDALE								
Owen	56	m	w	ENGL	Yolo	Cache Crk Twp	93	450
DINSMAN								
Wm	36	m	w	IREL	San Joaquin	Elliott Twp	86	81
DINSMORE								
Augustus	34	m	w	ME	Santa Barbara	Santa Barbara P O	87	488
Bradbury T	59	m	w	ME	Santa Barbara	Santa Barbara P O	87	488
J O	44	m	w	ME	Humboldt	Eel Rvr Twp	72	251
James P	52	m	w	NH	San Francisco	8-Wd San Francisco	82	430
John	60	m	w	KY	Shasta	Shasta P O	89	452
John	34	m	w	CT	Sacramento	2-Wd Sacramento	77	248
Robert B	37	m	w	OH	Yolo	Cache Crk Twp	93	423
Theodore	46	m	w	PA	Sacramento	2-Wd Sacramento	77	245
W G	49	m	w	ME	Alameda	Oakland	68	196
Walter	45	m	w	OH	San Joaquin	Elliott Twp	86	78
DINVEY								
James M	32	m	w	IN	Santa Clara	San Jose Twp	88	197
DINWIDDI								
James W	26	m	w	MO	Yolo	Grafton Twp	93	479
John	54	m	w	KY	Yolo	Grafton Twp	93	482
DINWIDDIE								
Columbus B	35	m	w	MO	Yolo	Grafton Twp	93	491
James L	36	m	w	MO	Sonoma	Petaluma Twp	91	322
John	59	m	w	VA	Sonoma	Analy Twp	91	245
John F	30	m	w	MO	Yolo	Grafton Twp	93	491
William	28	m	w	MO	Yolo	Cottonwood Twp	93	463
DINWITTY								
A K	53	m	w	OH	Lassen	Long Valley Twp	73	436
DINWOODIE								
William	33	m	w	CANA	Solano	Vacaville Twp	90	135
DIOGA								
John	47	m	w	PORT	Alameda	Washington Twp	68	274
DION								
C	19	m	w	CANA	Alameda	Oakland	68	225
Chas	24	m	w	CANA	Alameda	Oakland	68	231
DIONNE								
Augustine	44	m	w	CANA	Siskiyou	Yreka	89	661
DIOREZ								
Jose	24	m	w	MEXI	San Francisco	San Francisco P O	80	342
DIOS								
Antone Donay	22	m	w	PORT	Mendocino	Casper & Big Rvr	74	164
Benantia	54	f	w	CHIL	Santa Clara	Santa Clara Twp	88	158
Carlos	32	m	b	CHIL	Mariposa	Maxwell Crk P O	74	139
Henry	18	m	w	HANO	Marin	Novato Twp	74	13
Ulalia	5	f	w	CA	Santa Clara	Santa Clara Twp	88	157
DIOZ								
Carmilita	24	f	w	MEXI	San Francisco	2-Wd San Francisco	79	174
DIPHEIMER								
John	44	m	w	DENM	Marin	San Rafael	74	50
DIPLER								
John W	35	m	w	BAVA	Nevada	Grass Valley Twp	75	227
DIPPEL								
William G	36	m	w	SAXO	San Francisco	8-Wd San Francisco	82	381
DIPPENDEENER								
Fred	42	m	w	PRUS	Placer	Auburn P O	76	381
DIPPLE								
William	47	m	w	BADE	Inyo	Bishop Crk Twp	73	311
DIRFO								
Juan	44	m	w	CA	San Diego	San Pasqual	78	519
DIRIEUX								
Jas L	32	m	w	TN	Sonoma	Cloverdale Twp	91	268
DIRKIN								
Mary	27	f	w	IREL	Alameda	Oakland	68	203
DIRKING								
August	50	m	w	SWIT	San Francisco	3-Wd San Francisco	79	320
Fritz	20	m	w	SWIT	San Francisco	7-Wd San Francisco	81	248
DIRKS								
F C	21	m	w	BREM	San Francisco	San Francisco P O	83	334
DISARAGO								
Francisco	30	m	w	MEXI	Yuba	Linda Twp	93	558
DISBROW								
Frank	19	m	w	NJ	Marin	San Rafael Twp	74	26
Hiram	40	m	w	NY	Calaveras	San Andreas P O	70	195
DISCH								
Charles	57	m	w	BADE	Amador	Jackson P O	69	320
Joseph	29	m	w	SWIT	Amador	Sutter Crk P O	69	400
Martin	32	m	w	NY	Butte	Ophir Twp	70	116
Philip	55	m	w	WURT	Amador	Sutter Crk P O	69	412
DISCOLL								
Jared	27	m	w	IREL	Colusa	Colusa Twp	71	283
DISCOLZO								
G	45	m	w	ITAL	Yuba	Marysville	93	614
DISCON								
David	25	m	w	NY	Fresno	Millerton P O	72	162
Robert	43	m	w	IREL	San Francisco	San Francisco P O	83	342
DISCONIA								
Louisa	18	f	w	ITAL	San Francisco	2-Wd San Francisco	79	259
DISCOO								
Daniel	36	m	w	IREL	San Francisco	11-Wd San Francisc	84	705
DISELSHIRE								
Henry	25	m	w	PA	Butte	Hamilton Twp	70	64
DISH								
Joseph	28	m	w	BADE	Amador	Sutter Crk P O	69	402
DISHER								
Chas	40	m	w	PRUS	Shasta	American Ranch P O	89	499

© 2001 by Heritage Quest. All rights reserved.

Series M593

Name	Age	S	R	B-PL	County	Locale	Roll	Pg
Joseph	26	m	w	IN	Solano	Rio Vista Twp	90	61
DISHITO								
Louis	55	m	w	FRAN	Mariposa	Mariposa P O	74	101
DISKELL								
Timothy	23	m	w	IREL	Colusa	Spring Valley Twp	71	344
DISNEY								
Mary	44	f	w	IREL	San Francisco	8-Wd San Francisco	82	489
Mordecai	46	m	w	MD	Contra Costa	Martinez P O	71	374
Thomas	49	m	w	MD	Tuolumne	Chinese Camp P O	93	382
DISON								
Nathaniel	21	m	w	WI	Sutter	Sutter Twp	92	129
DISS								
Franklin J	35	m	w	LA	San Francisco	San Francisco P O	83	139
Paul	44	m	w	FRAN	El Dorado	Diamond Springs Tw	72	26
DISSABELL								
A H	42	m	w	NY	Siskiyou	Surprise Valley Tw	89	639
DISSANTA								
Jose	39	m	i	CA	Yolo	Cache Crk Twp	93	427
DISSENTI								
Hosapath	30	f	i	CA	Yolo	Cache Crk Twp	93	428
DISSOSWAY								
Ham	35	m	w	NY	Alameda	Oakland	68	178
DISTAN								
Mary	26	f	w	WURT	San Francisco	San Francisco P O	80	482
DISTEL								
Francis	28	m	w	FRAN	Santa Clara	Fremont Twp	88	51
Frank	30	m	w	FRAN	Santa Clara	Fremont Twp	88	53
Leonard	25	m	w	FRAN	Santa Clara	Fremont Twp	88	53
DIT								
Ah	21	m	c	CHIN	San Joaquin	1-Wd Stockton	86	144
DITE								
Ah	32	m	c	CHIN	Nevada	Nevada Twp	75	312
DITHMARR								
Christ A	37	m	w	PA	San Francisco	San Francisco P O	83	46
DITMAN								
Charles	46	m	w	PRUS	Santa Barbara	Santa Barbara P O	87	450
Charles	21	m	w	CA	Santa Barbara	Santa Barbara P O	87	450
Wm	27	m	w	OH	Santa Clara	Almaden Twp	88	20
DITMAR								
Charles	29	m	w	PRUS	San Francisco	8-Wd San Francisco	82	383
DITMERR								
Elizabeth	40	f	w	NY	Contra Costa	Martinez P O	71	415
DITMUS								
Thomas T	50	m	w	NY	San Mateo	Half Moon Bay P O	87	405
William	36	m	w	PRUS	Solano	Tremont Twp	90	30
DITRICH								
A H	39	m	w	GERM	Marin	San Rafael Twp	74	40
Nicholas	57	m	w	FRAN	El Dorado	Mud Springs Twp	72	82
DITSLER								
Magdl	45	f	w	BAVA	Sierra	Gibson Twp	89	539
DITSON								
Merritt S	32	m	w	MA	Sacramento	2-Wd Sacramento	77	222
DITTA								
Edward	32	m	w	AL	Santa Clara	Redwood Twp	88	125
DITTAMORE								
Elizth	78	f	w	PA	Sonoma	Mendocino Twp	91	289
J Wallace	51	m	w	IN	Sonoma	Mendocino Twp	91	289
Jno W	25	m	w	MO	Sonoma	Mendocino Twp	91	289
Lewis	21	m	w	MO	Sonoma	Mendocino Twp	91	289
Theo	46	m	w	IN	Sonoma	Mendocino Twp	91	289
DITTEVESIN								
J	40	m	w	DENM	Sierra	Table Rock Twp	89	576
DITTLE								
Ambrose	57	m	w	NY	Butte	Chico Twp	70	39
DITTMAN								
Henry	43	m	w	HDAR	San Francisco	8-Wd San Francisco	82	355
DITTMAR								
Edward	44	m	w	HANO	Santa Clara	2-Wd San Jose	88	290
DITTMER								
Frederick	34	m	w	HANO	San Francisco	San Francisco P O	83	189
Henry	49	m	w	SHOL	Alameda	Eden Twp	68	58
Hermann	31	m	w	SHOL	San Francisco	8-Wd San Francisco	82	294
John	39	m	w	HANO	Yuba	Rose Bar Twp	93	652
DITTON								
Henry	23	m	w	NY	San Francisco	1-Wd San Francisco	79	63
DITTY								
John S	50	m	w	WV	Mariposa	Mariposa P O	74	134
Mary	15	f	w	CA	Napa	Napa Twp	75	69
DITWORTH								
J W	37	m	w	TX	Alameda	Oakland	68	202
DITZEMAN								
Emma	10	f	w	CA	Santa Clara	2-Wd San Jose	88	282
DIVALE								
Leronzo	23	m	i	MEXI	San Luis Obispo	Salinas Twp	87	290
DIVELLO								
Forsenera	52	m	w	MEXI	Tulare	Tule Rvr Twp	92	266
DIVELY								
Garland	37	m	w	MO	Butte	Chico Twp	70	15
DIVENEY								
Thomas	28	m	w	IREL	Amador	Amador City P O	69	392
DIVENS								
John O	42	m	w	TN	Sacramento	San Joaquin Twp	77	404
DIVENY								
Michael	46	m	w	IREL	Nevada	Grass Valley Twp	75	214
DIVER								
A T	47	m	w	VA	Amador	Fiddletown P O	69	430
Charles	48	m	w	SWED	Calaveras	San Andreas P O	70	204
Charles	37	m	w	IREL	Yuba	Bullards Bar P O	93	549
John	39	m	w	IREL	Calaveras	San Andreas P O	70	154
John	35	m	w	IREL	San Francisco	7-Wd San Francisco	81	237
Mary	45	f	w	IREL	Colusa	Monroe Twp	71	321
R A	29	m	w	NY	Nevada	Nevada Twp	75	322
DIVERS								
Fannie	17	f	w	NY	Yuba	Marysville	93	602
DIVIL								
Otto	27	m	w	PRUS	San Francisco	11-Wd San Francisc	84	477
DIVINE								
Davis	62	m	w	NY	Santa Clara	2-Wd San Jose	88	338
John	29	m	w	VA	Colusa	Colusa	71	292
John	23	m	w	MA	San Francisco	11-Wd San Francisc	84	558
Patrick	24	m	w	IREL	Santa Clara	2-Wd San Jose	88	329
William	34	m	w	IREL	San Francisco	2-Wd San Francisco	79	204
DIVINELL								
Hellen	33	f	w	NH	Solano	Vallejo	90	199
DIVINY								
James	28	m	w	OH	Yolo	Grafton Twp	93	494
DIVIS								
Cosmo	38	m	w	MO	Los Angeles	San Gabriel Twp	73	598
DIVOLL								
Franklin	35	m	w	NH	Alameda	Hayward	68	75
DIVOLLI								
George	70	m	w	VT	Tuolumne	Sonora P O	93	307
DIX								
Anna	35	f	w	ENGL	Sierra	Table Rock Twp	89	575
Caspar	33	m	w	PRUS	San Francisco	San Francisco P O	85	737
Edwd W	10	m	i	CA	Shasta	Buckeye P O	89	482
Henry	38	m	w	MA	Humboldt	Pacific Twp	72	290
Henry	37	m	w	MA	Humboldt	Mattole Twp	72	283
John R	39	m	w	OH	Amador	Jackson P O	69	334
Maria C	13	f	i	CA	Shasta	Shasta P O	89	457
Mary A	14	f	m	CA	Shasta	Stillwater P O	89	478
Thomas H	40	m	w	MA	Humboldt	Pacific Twp	72	291
DIXEN								
John	30	m	w	GREE	San Francisco	San Francisco P O	85	863
DIXEY								
Frank	50	m	w	PA	San Francisco	San Francisco P O	85	731
DIXON								
A B	42	m	w	NJ	Alameda	Oakland	68	250
Agnes	72	f	w	SCOT	Alameda	Brooklyn	68	27
Albert	37	m	w	MA	San Francisco	3-Wd San Francisco	79	301
Alexander	35	m	w	SCOT	Amador	Volcano P O	69	386
Alfred	49	m	w	CANA	Sacramento	San Joaquin Twp	77	400
Alfred	46	m	w	ENGL	Yuba	Bullards Bar P O	93	552
Alfred	30	m	w	IL	San Francisco	11-Wd San Francisc	84	522
Anna	38	f	w	PA	Napa	Napa	75	4
Benjamin	30	m	b	NC	Siskiyou	Yreka	89	655
Clement	43	m	w	ENGL	San Francisco	2-Wd San Francisco	79	209
Daniel	35	m	w	NJ	San Diego	Julian Dist	78	474
Ed	24	m	w	IREL	Alameda	Oakland	68	204
Eda	13	f	w	CA	Sacramento	4-Wd Sacramento	77	363
Edwin T	22	m	w	MS	Fresno	Millerton P O	72	152
Elijah M	39	m	w	OH	Shasta	Horsetown P O	89	502
Eliza	18	f	w	PA	Marin	San Rafael	74	54
Fanny	23	f	m	NY	San Francisco	2-Wd San Francisco	79	137
Geo R	27	m	w	SCOT	San Francisco	San Francisco P O	83	104
Geo W	43	m	w	ENGL	Shasta	Horsetown P O	89	505
George	50	m	w	ENGL	Santa Clara	Santa Clara Twp	88	143
George	50	m	w	IN	Tuolumne	Sonora P O	93	318
George	40	m	w	IREL	San Francisco	San Francisco P O	83	38
George	36	m	w	ENGL	Alameda	Brooklyn	68	29
George W	29	m	w	NY	Nevada	Grass Valley Twp	75	146
Gideon B	34	m	w	MA	San Francisco	3-Wd San Francisco	79	301
Gr	32	m	w	MO	Sierra	Downieville Twp	89	521
H	29	m	w	TN	San Joaquin	Elkhorn Twp	86	64
H E	43	f	w	NY	Sacramento	1-Wd Sacramento	77	175
Harriet	70	f	w	NC	Shasta	Horsetown P O	89	502
Henry	44	m	w	ENGL	Amador	Fiddletown P O	69	438
Henry G	49	m	w	SCOT	El Dorado	Lake Valley Twp	72	64
I W	34	m	w	IL	Siskiyou	Big Valley Twp	89	580
Isaac	42	m	w	CANA	Santa Clara	San Jose Twp	88	219
J	61	m	w	CANA	Humboldt	Bucksport Twp	72	242
J	45	m	w	NY	Sierra	Lincoln Twp	89	545
J F	33	m	w	ME	Sacramento	3-Wd Sacramento	77	271
J F	22	m	w	MA	Sacramento	4-Wd Sacramento	77	360
J G	41	m	w	LA	Tuolumne	Chinese Camp P O	93	372
James	45	m	w	IREL	Trinity	Douglas	92	236
James	40	m	w	IREL	Sonoma	Salt Point	91	392
James	35	m	w	AUSL	Alameda	Oakland	68	240
James	29	m	w	BADE	Placer	Blue Canyon P O	76	418
James	28	m	b	PA	San Francisco	2-Wd San Francisco	79	137
James	28	m	w	IL	Santa Clara	Fremont Twp	88	49
James	26	m	w	CANA	Colusa	Butte Twp	71	267
Jas	40	m	b	MS	Sacramento	3-Wd Sacramento	77	274
Jas	10	m	m	CA	Sacramento	3-Wd Sacramento	77	266
Jas P	23	m	w	MS	Fresno	Millerton P O	72	152
Jno E	38	m	w	NJ	San Francisco	5-Wd San Francisco	81	26
Joel	36	m	w	IL	San Bernardino	San Bernardino Twp	78	437
John	70	m	w	ENGL	Santa Clara	San Jose Twp	88	219
John	52	m	w	SCOT	Santa Clara	Santa Clara Twp	88	146
John	40	m	w	MO	Sonoma	Cloverdale Twp	91	269
John	38	m	b	NC	San Joaquin	1-Wd Stockton	86	150
John	38	m	w	ME	Placer	Gold Run Twp	76	399
John	37	m	w	IREL	San Francisco	3-Wd San Francisco	79	319
John	36	m	w	IREL	Solano	Vallejo	90	187

© 2001 by Heritage Quest. All rights reserved.

Name	Age	S	R	B-PL	County	Locale	Roll	Pg
John	35	m	w	CANA	Alameda	Brooklyn	68	35
John	32	m	w	SCOT	San Francisco	San Francisco P O	83	413
John	28	m	w	IREL	Alameda	San Leandro	68	98
John	26	m	w	IREL	Solano	Vallejo	90	164
John	23	m	w	NY	San Mateo	Pescadero P O	87	413
Joseph	54	m	w	ENGL	Yuba	Bullards Bar P O	93	549
Joseph	40	m	w	OH	San Francisco	San Francisco P O	83	297
Joseph	39	m	w	TN	Napa	Napa	75	6
Joshua	40	m	w	IL	Shasta	Fort Crook P O	89	473
Julius	39	m	w	CT	San Francisco	1-Wd San Francisco	79	127
Lotte A	11	f	w	ME	Sacramento	4-Wd Sacramento	77	365
M A Mrs	59	f	w	MO	Sonoma	Petaluma Twp	91	338
Maggie	30	f	w	IREL	San Francisco	San Francisco P O	83	26
Mary	30	f	w	AUSL	Alameda	Brooklyn	68	27
Mary	25	f	i	CA	Siskiyou	Yreka	89	655
Matthew	40	m	w	VA	Alameda	Washington Twp	68	286
Michael P	25	m	w	ENGL	Sacramento	Lee Twp	77	159
Nathan	38	m	w	IN	Placer	Bath P O	76	453
Paul	57	m	w	IREL	Tehama	Cottonwood Twp	92	161
R J	41	m	w	ENGL	San Francisco	San Francisco P O	85	786
Richard	55	m	w	PA	Placer	Dutch Flat P O	76	415
Richard	45	m	w	IREL	San Francisco	San Francisco P O	80	388
Richd L	55	m	w	VA	Fresno	Millerton P O	72	152
Robert	45	m	w	IREL	Tuolumne	Sonora P O	93	332
Rose	25	f	w	OH	Sacramento	Sutter Twp	77	390
T L	27	m	w	IL	San Joaquin	Oneal Twp	86	110
Thomas	70	m	w	PA	Solano	Silveyville Twp	90	86
Thomas	42	m	w	PA	Amador	Fiddletown P O	69	438
Thomas	30	m	w	NY	San Francisco	1-Wd San Francisco	79	70
Thos	28	m	w	MA	Solano	Vallejo	90	185
Thos	28	m	w	CANA	Solano	Vallejo	90	197
W S	41	m	w	ME	Alameda	Oakland	68	263
William	56	m	m	VA	Amador	Fiddletown P O	69	438
William	36	m	w	SCOT	Colusa	Butte Twp	71	269
William	28	m	w	SCOT	San Mateo	Belmont P O	87	372
Wilson	50	m	m	VA	Solano	Vallejo	90	168
Wm	37	m	w	IREL	Alameda	Oakland	68	211
Wm	27	m	w	AR	San Joaquin	Castoria Twp	86	15
Wm F	26	m	w	AR	Santa Barbara	Santa Barbara P O	87	502
Wm H	36	m	w	ENGL	Sacramento	Lee Twp	77	159
DIXTER								
Dennis	40	m	w	MA	San Joaquin	Tulare Twp	86	253
DLASUIS								
Marie	58	f	w	MEXI	San Bernardino	San Salvador Twp	78	456
DMARTENE								
H	40	m	w	ITAL	San Francisco	San Francisco P O	85	849
DO								
Ah	36	m	c	CHIN	Nevada	Nevada Twp	75	299
Ah	14	m	c	CHIN	Yuba	Marysville	93	596
Lee	16	m	c	CHIN	San Joaquin	1-Wd Stockton	86	147
Lu	29	m	c	CHIN	Solano	Suisun Twp	90	105
DOAG								
James	52	m	w	KY	Santa Cruz	Santa Cruz Twp	89	395
DOAK								
J K	42	m	w	PA	San Joaquin	2-Wd Stockton	86	202
Phillip	23	m	w	CA	Santa Clara	Gilroy Twp	88	87
DOAKE								
Charlotte	51	f	b	KY	Contra Costa	Martinez P O	71	437
David	36	m	w	IREL	Napa	Yountville Twp	75	79
Saml	42	m	w	PA	San Francisco	5-Wd San Francisco	81	6
DOAL								
John	36	m	w	PRUS	Colusa	Colusa Twp	71	273
DOALE								
C E	28	m	w	ME	Sacramento	1-Wd Sacramento	77	176
DOALMEYER								
Henry	52	m	w	HANO	Calaveras	Copperopolis P O	70	241
DOAN								
A C	32	m	w	ME	Solano	Vallejo	90	211
Alice	18	f	w	CA	Sonoma	Healdsburg & Mendo	91	284
Alonzo	23	m	w	MO	Colusa	Colusa Twp	71	281
Eli	42	m	w	CANA	Sonoma	Mendocino Twp	91	290
Frank	38	m	w	MD	Colusa	Monroe Twp	71	325
Geo W	29	m	w	MO	Sonoma	Healdsburg & Mendo	91	277
J S	28	m	w	ME	Nevada	Meadow Lake Twp	75	267
Jacob	60	m	w	KY	Sonoma	Healdsburg & Mendo	91	277
Jacob	42	m	w	OH	Santa Clara	Gilroy Twp	88	91
John	50	m	w	PA	Amador	Fiddletown P O	69	429
John	39	m	w	IREL	San Francisco	2-Wd San Francisco	79	213
L E	37	m	w	ME	Nevada	Meadow Lake Twp	75	267
Orrin	26	m	w	US	Solano	Vallejo	90	144
Robt	36	m	w	CANA	El Dorado	Lake Valley Twp	72	66
Speryhin	22	m	w	CANA	Yolo	Grafton Twp	93	481
W J	37	m	w	ME	Solano	Vallejo	90	174
Wallace	27	m	w	MI	Solano	Vallejo	90	162
William	41	m	w	IREL	Solano	Silveyville Twp	90	81
Wm S	29	m	w	MI	Solano	Vallejo	90	162
DOANE								
Chloe	66	f	w	NY	San Francisco	San Francisco P O	83	37
Daniel	29	m	w	CANA	San Joaquin	Oneal Twp	86	101
Geo W	49	m	w	MA	San Francisco	7-Wd San Francisco	81	239
J G	38	m	w	MA	San Francisco	San Francisco P O	85	847
J O	31	m	w	CANA	San Francisco	San Francisco P O	85	859
James	2	m	w	CA	San Francisco	1-Wd San Francisco	79	19
James A	23	m	w	OR	Contra Costa	Martinez P O	71	380
Marshall	42	m	w	MA	San Francisco	11-Wd San Francisc	84	598
Mary	16	f	w	NY	San Francisco	San Francisco P O	83	291
Michael	34	m	w	MA	San Francisco	San Francisco P O	85	767
Mortimer	19	m	w	MI	Placer	Lincoln P O	76	488
Nancy	53	f	w	PA	Contra Costa	Martinez P O	71	381
Nathan A	39	m	w	MA	Napa	Yountville Twp	75	84
Orson	63	m	w	VT	Marin	Bolinas Twp	74	4
Phillip	50	m	w	PRUS	Sacramento	4-Wd Sacramento	77	374
Riley	45	m	w	NY	El Dorado	Diamond Springs Tw	72	34
Robert	70	m	w	NY	Colusa	Butte Twp	71	272
Robt	50	m	w	IREL	San Francisco	5-Wd San Francisco	81	13
Sarah ?	15	f	w	MA	Nevada	Grass Valley Twp	75	177
Sharon P	43	m	w	MA	San Francisco	6-Wd San Francisco	81	127
William	60	m	w	IREL	Plumas	Seneca Twp	77	51
DOBAS								
---	21	m	w	SWIT	Santa Clara	Gilroy Twp	88	102
Peter	35	m	w	FRAN	Yuba	Bullards Bar P O	93	553
DOBBAS								
Elija	37	m	w	SWIT	El Dorado	Georgetown Twp	72	36
DOBBELER								
Joseph	38	m	w	HOLL	San Francisco	11-Wd San Francisc	84	650
DOBBES								
James	30	m	w	SWIT	El Dorado	Georgetown Twp	72	42
DOBBIE								
E B	42	f	w	CT	Tuolumne	Columbia P O	93	348
Thomas	31	m	w	CANA	Placer	Bath P O	76	460
DOBBIN								
Adam	37	m	w	IREL	Contra Costa	Martinez P O	71	390
George	32	m	w	CANA	Mariposa	Mariposa P O	74	114
DOBBINS								
D	32	m	w	MO	Lake	Lower Lake	73	416
George	40	m	w	CANA	Monterey	San Juan Twp	74	409
Hugh H	37	m	w	OH	Santa Barbara	Santa Barbara P O	87	481
J W W	55	m	w	KY	Sierra	Forest	89	537
James	40	m	w	ENGL	Solano	Rio Vista Twp	90	59
James H	21	m	w	MD	Nevada	Grass Valley Twp	75	202
John	28	m	w	NY	Solano	Rio Vista Twp	90	70
Oscar	15	m	w	CA	Santa Clara	Santa Clara Twp	88	177
Sarah E	52	f	w	VA	Nevada	Grass Valley Twp	75	183
Theophilis	30	m	w	MS	Yolo	Cache Crk Twp	93	453
Thomas	35	m	w	AL	Sutter	Yuba Twp	92	140
William J	43	m	w	KY	Solano	Vacaville Twp	90	125
DOBBS								
Enoch	29	m	w	TN	Yolo	Putah Twp	93	518
Henry	28	m	w	IREL	Solano	Silveyville Twp	90	84
Lard	37	f	w	MEXI	San Joaquin	3-Wd Stockton	86	224
Nancy	14	f	w	MO	San Francisco	San Francisco P O	85	798
Peter	41	m	w	MA	Solano	Silveyville Twp	90	81
Wm	50	m	w	GA	Santa Cruz	Pajaro Twp	89	347
Wm	33	m	w	NY	Solano	Vallejo	90	170
DOBBYN								
William B	38	m	w	MD	Humboldt	South Fork Twp	72	301
DOBE								
John	26	m	w	PRUS	Sacramento	4-Wd Sacramento	77	373
DOBER								
Francis	47	m	w	PA	San Francisco	San Francisco P O	83	401
Joseph	44	m	w	PA	San Francisco	San Francisco P O	83	368
DOBERER								
Henry	32	m	w	ITAL	San Francisco	1-Wd San Francisco	79	54
DOBIE								
Donald	54	m	w	SCOT	Los Angeles	Los Angeles Twp	73	494
John	25	m	w	SCOT	Mariposa	Mariposa P O	74	114
DOBINO								
Lewis	50	m	w	CHIL	Butte	Concow Twp	70	7
DOBINS								
M A	43	f	w	IL	Lassen	Susanville Twp	73	439
DOBINSPECK								
James	55	m	w	KY	Napa	Napa	75	20
DOBKINS								
Margaret	54	f	w	VA	Shasta	Portugese Flat P O	89	471
DOBLE								
Abner	41	m	w	IN	San Francisco	San Francisco P O	85	725
Henry	41	m	w	SHOL	San Mateo	Half Moon Bay P O	87	403
Jno	34	m	w	ENGL	Santa Clara	Almaden Twp	88	10
Phil	38	m	w	ENGL	Santa Clara	Almaden Twp	88	9
DOBLER								
C L	13	m	w	CA	Yuba	Marysville Twp	93	571
Christian	34	m	w	AUST	San Diego	San Diego	78	500
DOBLOW								
Fred	30	m	w	PRUS	Alameda	Washington Twp	68	293
DOBNER								
Morris	24	m	w	PRUS	San Francisco	San Francisco P O	80	355
DOBNEY								
Geo	44	m	w	ENGL	San Joaquin	2-Wd Stockton	86	180
DOBOVICH								
Peter	33	m	w	AUST	Amador	Amador City P O	69	394
DOBRIEQ								
John	40	m	w	FRAN	San Francisco	San Francisco P O	80	413
DOBROWSKY								
Adolph	38	m	w	BOHE	Shasta	Shasta P O	89	459
Ernest	32	m	w	BOHE	Shasta	Shasta P O	89	459
DOBRZENSKY								
Morris	50	m	w	PRUS	San Francisco	8-Wd San Francisco	82	478
DOBSON								
Abel	47	m	w	ENGL	Nevada	Grass Valley Twp	75	156
Andrea	40	m	w	CA	Santa Cruz	Pajaro Twp	89	361
Anna	9	f	w	CA	Contra Costa	Martinez P O	71	392
Chas H	32	m	w	NY	San Francisco	San Francisco P O	83	38
Fances	25	m	w	NJ	Merced	Snelling P O	74	267
Geo	47	m	w	IREL	San Francisco	San Francisco P O	83	126

© 2001 by Heritage Quest. All rights reserved.

California 1870 Census

Name	Age	S	R	B-PL	County	Locale	Roll	Pg
						Series M593		
Henry	42	m	w	NY	San Francisco	San Francisco P O	83	168
James	37	m	w	IREL	San Francisco	3-Wd San Francisco	79	317
Jessie	31	f	w	PA	San Francisco	5-Wd San Francisco	81	24
Jno	19	m	w	MO	San Joaquin	Dent Twp	86	20
John	35	m	w	NY	Merced	Snelling P O	74	267
John	28	m	w	ENGL	San Francisco	San Francisco P O	80	464
John	26	m	w	CANA	Napa	Napa	75	20
Marcelles M	50	m	w	AL	Yolo	Cache Crk Twp	93	441
Monroe	27	m	w	TN	Yolo	Cache Crk Twp	93	444
Patrick	44	m	w	IREL	San Francisco	7-Wd San Francisco	81	212
Richard	38	m	w	NJ	San Francisco	11-Wd San Francisc	84	690
Robert	44	m	w	VA	Los Angeles	Los Angeles	73	539
Thomas H	28	m	w	KY	Yolo	Cache Crk Twp	93	456
William	50	m	w	ENGL	Los Angeles	El Monte Twp	73	452
Zackeriah	24	m	w	PA	Inyo	Independence Twp	73	328
DOBZELE								
Frank	27	m	w	PRUS	San Francisco	San Francisco P O	83	81
DOBZINSKI								
Soloman	44	m	w	HAMB	San Francisco	7-Wd San Francisco	81	178
DOC								
Ah	42	m	c	CHIN	El Dorado	Diamond Springs Tw	72	24
Ah	35	m	c	CHIN	El Dorado	Mud Springs Twp	72	79
Ah	30	m	c	CHIN	El Dorado	Mud Springs Twp	72	76
Ah	30	m	c	CHIN	Mariposa	Maxwell Crk P O	74	147
Ah	16	m	c	CHIN	Placer	Auburn P O	76	379
Hang	40	m	c	CHIN	Amador	Jackson P O	69	332
DOCERY								
Edward	35	m	w	IREL	Trinity	Weaverville Pct	92	225
DOCHERTY								
Mary	24	f	w	IREL	Solano	Silveyville Twp	90	91
Pat	31	m	w	IREL	San Joaquin	3-Wd Stockton	86	247
DOCHMAN								
Joseph	54	m	w	PRUS	Amador	Drytown P O	69	417
DOCK								
Ah	30	m	c	CHIN	Sacramento	Sutter Twp	77	383
Ah	23	m	c	CHIN	Sacramento	Granite Twp	77	137
Henry S G	38	m	w	VT	Solano	Denverton Twp	90	22
Kick	38	m	w	CANA	Alameda	Murray Twp	68	125
Man	34	m	c	CHIN	San Francisco	3-Wd San Francisco	79	320
Sam	22	m	c	CA	Colusa	Colusa	71	289
Soon	30	m	c	CHIN	Shasta	Shasta P O	89	453
DOCKENDORF								
George	35	m	w	HAMB	San Francisco	8-Wd San Francisco	82	437
DOCKER								
P	40	m	w	OH	Yuba	Marysville	93	595
DOCKERTY								
James	31	m	w	ENGL	Sacramento	2-Wd Sacramento	77	245
DOCKERY								
Delia	24	f	w	IREL	San Francisco	San Francisco P O	83	162
Edward	23	m	w	ENGL	San Francisco	San Francisco P O	80	375
R F	33	m	w	GA	Amador	Jackson P O	69	334
DOCKET								
John	39	m	w	NH	Mendocino	Bourns Landing Twp	74	223
DOCKHAM								
Daniel	65	m	w	NH	San Francisco	11-Wd San Francisc	84	502
John M	39	m	w	ME	San Mateo	Woodside P O	87	385
Phobe	70	f	w	MA	San Francisco	11-Wd San Francisc	84	502
DOCKHAN								
Henry	44	m	w	ME	San Francisco	2-Wd San Francisco	79	168
DOCKING								
Joel	30	m	w	ENGL	San Francisco	1-Wd San Francisco	79	8
DOCKNY								
James	27	m	w	IREL	San Mateo	Woodside P O	87	386
DOCKRAY								
Ann	29	f	w	IREL	San Francisco	5-Wd San Francisco	81	10
John A	41	m	w	ENGL	Santa Cruz	Pajaro Twp	89	348
DOCKS								
Jacob M	38	m	w	NY	San Francisco	1-Wd San Francisco	79	62
DOCKSON								
Francis	30	m	w	SCOT	San Francisco	1-Wd San Francisco	79	59
DOCKSTEADER								
George	34	m	w	CANA	El Dorado	Mud Springs Twp	72	77
DOCKUNG								
Charles	30	m	w	PRUS	San Francisco	2-Wd San Francisco	79	145
DOCKURDORF								
John	30	m	w	HANO	San Francisco	11-Wd San Francisc	84	649
DOCKWIELER								
Heny	43	m	w	GERM	Los Angeles	Los Angeles	73	518
DOCTOR								
Bingham	28	m	w	PA	Alameda	Oakland	68	196
DOD								
Ah	19	m	c	CHIN	San Francisco	6-Wd San Francisco	81	52
DODD								
Alx B	32	m	w	NY	El Dorado	Lake Valley Twp	72	65
Ann	20	f	w	IREL	Santa Clara	Gilroy Twp	88	76
Benjaman	48	m	w	MA	San Francisco	3-Wd San Francisco	79	314
Edward	32	m	w	SCOT	San Francisco	San Francisco P O	85	746
Elbert N	22	m	w	IL	Plumas	Quartz Twp	77	40
Henry	24	m	w	ENGL	Santa Clara	Almaden Twp	88	19
Hiram	34	m	w	MO	Solano	Vacaville Twp	90	124
James	30	m	w	NY	San Francisco	5-Wd San Francisco	81	35
James	26	m	w	IREL	Alameda	Oakland	68	182
Jas W	31	m	w	IL	Calaveras	Copperopolis P O	70	238
John	44	m	w	VA	Contra Costa	San Pablo Twp	71	366
John	38	m	w	NJ	El Dorado	Kelsey Twp	72	61
Lydia	20	f	w	CA	San Bernardino	San Bernardino Twp	78	443
Orin	24	m	w	ME	San Francisco	8-Wd San Francisco	82	446

Name	Age	S	R	B-PL	County	Locale	Roll	Pg
						Series M593		
Samuel	56	m	w	IREL	Placer	Lincoln P O	76	487
Solomon	52	m	w	NC	Santa Clara	1-Wd San Jose	88	238
Taswell	25	m	w	IL	Inyo	Cerro Gordo Twp	73	321
Thomas	48	m	w	ENGL	San Francisco	11-Wd San Francisc	84	519
W A	26	m	w	NY	Solano	Vallejo	90	186
W W	45	m	w	IREL	Monterey	Salinas Twp	74	307
William	32	m	w	IREL	San Francisco	San Francisco P O	83	400
William	26	m	w	MO	Solano	Silveyville Twp	90	75
William	24	m	w	IREL	Solano	Silveyville Twp	90	89
William	17	m	w	CA	Santa Clara	San Jose Twp	88	222
DODDINS								
Jno	28	m	w	IREL	Sacramento	1-Wd Sacramento	77	188
DODDS								
Henry H	31	m	w	GA	Mariposa	Mariposa P O	74	96
McCray	38	m	w	SCOT	Sonoma	Mendocino Twp	91	287
Thomas	54	m	w	SCOT	Placer	Bath P O	76	421
William	9	m	w	CA	San Francisco	8-Wd San Francisco	82	357
William	27	m	w	ENGL	Los Angeles	Soledad Twp	73	633
DODDY								
James	34	m	w	IREL	San Francisco	1-Wd San Francisco	79	88
DODE								
William	24	m	w	PRUS	San Luis Obispo	Salinas Twp	87	293
DODEN								
Jesus	36	m	w	CA	Santa Clara	Almaden Twp	88	3
DODERO								
Josefa	55	f	w	CA	Santa Cruz	Santa Cruz	89	415
Juan	39	m	w	CA	Santa Clara	Burnett Twp	88	39
Juan	29	m	w	CA	Santa Clara	Gilroy Twp	88	106
DODEWORTH								
M	40	m	w	ENGL	Sacramento	3-Wd Sacramento	77	315
DODGE								
---	40	m	w	IL	El Dorado	Mud Springs Twp	72	83
Albert C	36	m	w	ME	Sonoma	Mendocino Twp	91	294
Ansel H	33	m	w	NY	Sacramento	2-Wd Sacramento	77	226
Antoinette	13	f	w	CA	Santa Cruz	Watsonville	89	365
Augustus	38	m	w	NH	San Diego	Julian Dist	78	468
Benj	33	m	w	NY	San Joaquin	Douglas Twp	86	44
Benj	21	m	w	OH	Solano	Vallejo	90	209
Benjamin S	19	m	w	NY	Yolo	Putah Twp	93	515
Charles	54	m	w	MA	San Francisco	11-Wd San Francisc	84	485
Charles L	39	m	w	ME	Los Angeles	Los Nietos Twp	73	590
Clara	30	f	w	PA	San Francisco	San Francisco P O	80	465
D D	54	m	w	NY	Alameda	Oakland	68	157
Daniel	42	m	w	MA	San Francisco	San Francisco P O	83	222
Daniel D	54	m	w	VT	Santa Cruz	Santa Cruz	89	434
David	41	m	w	NY	San Joaquin	Elliott Twp	86	80
David	38	m	w	IL	Stanislaus	Empire Twp	92	39
David	38	m	w	ME	San Francisco	11-Wd San Francisc	84	704
David	31	m	w	NY	Nevada	Meadow Lake Twp	75	247
David F	44	m	w	MA	Nevada	Grass Valley Twp	75	157
E A	26	m	w	ME	Tuolumne	Big Oak Flat P O	93	396
E J	33	m	w	NH	Humboldt	Pacific Twp	72	292
E L	33	f	w	VT	Tuolumne	Sonora P O	93	307
Ebenezer R	54	m	w	NH	Sacramento	2-Wd Sacramento	77	247
Edward	44	m	w	ME	Amador	Volcano P O	69	381
Edward	22	m	w	NY	Placer	Summit P O	76	495
Edward E	25	m	w	TN	Los Angeles	Wilmington Twp	73	634
Edward K	57	m	w	VT	Los Angeles	Wilmington Twp	73	634
Elbridge	38	m	w	VT	Butte	Oregon Twp	70	134
Eleasar	47	m	w	VT	San Francisco	11-Wd San Francisc	84	513
Elijah	41	m	w	ME	Siskiyou	Surprise Valley Tw	89	641
Eliphalet	28	m	w	ME	Humboldt	Eureka Twp	72	275
Elizabeth	50	f	w	PA	Santa Clara	2-Wd San Jose	88	292
Elizabeth	40	f	w	IL	San Francisco	7-Wd San Francisco	81	172
Elizabeth	25	f	w	IL	Santa Cruz	Santa Cruz	89	421
Elsley	22	m	w	NY	Sacramento	2-Wd Sacramento	77	221
Eunice	69	f	w	ME	Santa Cruz	Santa Cruz	89	432
Francis	56	m	w	ME	Humboldt	Arcata Twp	72	228
Francis	48	m	w	OH	San Francisco	2-Wd San Francisco	79	221
Francis	43	m	w	ME	San Francisco	San Francisco P O	85	835
Francis	19	m	w	ME	San Francisco	2-Wd San Francisco	79	284
Geo	26	m	w	IL	San Joaquin	Oneal Twp	86	102
George	40	m	w	ME	Contra Costa	Martinez P O	71	397
George	40	m	w	IL	Mendocino	Round Valley Twp	74	218
Gideon O	40	m	w	RI	Mendocino	Noyo & Big Rvr Twp	74	173
Harriet	44	f	w	KY	Placer	Bath P O	76	455
Henry	37	m	w	CANA	San Joaquin	Douglas Twp	86	51
Henry L	45	m	w	VT	San Francisco	San Francisco P O	83	147
Henry W	35	m	w	IL	Santa Clara	Santa Clara Twp	88	145
Horace F	20	m	w	MA	Sonoma	Petaluma Twp	91	331
J H	50	m	w	VT	San Joaquin	Douglas Twp	86	45
James	40	m	w	ENGL	Stanislaus	Empire Twp	92	61
James	14	m	w	IA	Butte	Chico Twp	70	26
Jennie	6	f	w	CA	Nevada	Nevada Twp	75	283
John	43	m	w	RI	San Francisco	San Francisco P O	80	395
John	24	m	w	IL	Mendocino	Round Valley Twp	74	216
John D	45	m	w	ENGL	Sonoma	Petaluma Twp	91	356
John D	45	m	w	NH	Placer	Colfax P O	76	389
John J	37	m	w	NH	Humboldt	Eureka Twp	72	264
Joseph	42	m	w	ME	Amador	Volcano P O	69	381
Josiah	43	m	w	TN	Nevada	Grass Valley Twp	75	218
Josiah G	33	m	w	TN	San Luis Obispo	Arroyo Grande Twp	87	278
Julia	28	f	w	VA	Monterey	San Juan Twp	74	387
Julia	26	f	w	LA	San Francisco	5-Wd San Francisco	81	10
L I	35	m	w	NH	Solano	Vallejo	90	183
Laura	13	f	w	IL	Solano	Benicia	90	16
Leonard	32	m	w	ME	Mendocino	Ten Mile Rvr Twp	74	172

© 2001 by Heritage Quest. All rights reserved.

Name	Age	S	R	B-PL	County	Locale	Roll	Pg
						Series M593		
Mary	54	f	w	MA	San Francisco	7-Wd San Francisco	81	240
Mary E	16	f	w	CA	Santa Clara	2-Wd San Jose	88	290
Moses C	51	m	w	ME	San Mateo	Pescadero P O	87	417
Nathan	36	m	w	ME	San Francisco	San Francisco P O	85	781
Nicholas	30	m	w	ME	Santa Clara	2-Wd San Jose	88	332
O J	45	m	w	NH	Sacramento	3-Wd Sacramento	77	269
O R	27	m	w	VT	Sacramento	3-Wd Sacramento	77	273
P M	60	m	w	NY	Humboldt	Eureka Twp	72	276
Robert	22	m	w	NY	Mendocino	Albion & Big Rvr T	74	167
Royal L	32	m	w	ME	Humboldt	Arcata Twp	72	229
S K	40	m	w	ME	Sacramento	3-Wd Sacramento	77	288
Sarah	14	f	w	JAMA	Nevada	Nevada Twp	75	278
Seymour	60	m	w	NY	Sacramento	2-Wd Sacramento	77	247
Susan	60	f	w	OH	Sonoma	Healdsburg & Mendo	91	280
W M	55	m	w	NH	Humboldt	Eureka Twp	72	264
Wilbur S	43	m	w	ME	Shasta	French Gulch P O	89	466
William	44	m	w	ENGL	Stanislaus	Empire Twp	92	63
William	40	m	w	NY	San Francisco	8-Wd San Francisco	82	464
William J	26	m	w	ME	Los Angeles	Wilmington Twp	73	641
William W	7	m	w	CA	Nevada	Grass Valley Twp	75	209
Wm C	54	m	w	NY	Alameda	Oakland	68	185
Wm R	65	m	w	ENGL	Sonoma	Cloverdale Twp	91	269
Wm R	53	m	w	OH	Butte	Bidwell Twp	70	2
DODGER								
Benjamin	33	m	b	KY	Amador	Ione City P O	69	357
DODGO								
Thomas	24	m	w	ENGL	Nevada	Grass Valley Twp	75	227
DODON								
Antonio	27	m	w	ITAL	San Mateo	Half Moon Bay P O	87	390
DODS								
Henry	30	m	w	NJ	Placer	Bath P O	76	436
James	42	m	w	NJ	Placer	Bath P O	76	455
DODSEN								
W Y	26	m	w	NY	Sierra	Sierra Twp	89	568
DODSON								
Benjamin	39	m	w	ENGL	Colusa	Monroe Twp	71	324
Beverly	25	m	b	VA	San Francisco	San Francisco P O	80	416
Doctor [Dr]	41	m	w	KY	Lake	Kelsey Crk	73	402
Elias	30	m	w	MO	Colusa	Colusa Twp	71	279
Elijah	34	m	w	IL	San Bernardino	San Bernardino Twp	78	426
Elizabeth	53	f	w	NC	Los Angeles	Los Angeles	73	536
Henry C	36	m	w	KY	San Bernardino	San Bernardino Twp	78	426
James	33	m	w	OH	Kern	Bakersfield P O	73	357
James	15	m	w	MO	El Dorado	Lake Valley Twp	72	64
James	11	m	w	CA	Los Angeles	Los Angeles	73	554
Jasper	44	m	w	PA	Kern	Havilah P O	73	340
Jerusha	47	f	w	OH	Stanislaus	Empire Twp	92	42
Jess	35	m	w	IN	Mendocino	Point Arena Twp	74	215
Jethro	33	m	w	KY	Marin	San Antonio Twp	74	61
John	38	m	w	IREL	Santa Barbara	Santa Barbara P O	87	501
John	37	m	w	MO	Los Angeles	El Monte Twp	73	463
John	37	m	b	MD	San Francisco	1-Wd San Francisco	79	95
John	37	m	w	IN	Contra Costa	Martinez P O	71	406
John	33	m	w	TN	Siskiyou	Surprise Valley Tw	89	642
Joseph	42	m	w	KY	Marin	San Antonio Twp	74	61
Marcus H	39	m	w	KY	El Dorado	Mud Springs Twp	72	73
Nancy	4	f	w	CA	Siskiyou	Surprise Valley Tw	89	640
Otto M	51	m	w	PA	Los Angeles	Los Angeles	73	551
Rachael	51	f	w	KY	Yolo	Grafton Twp	93	486
Ritner	34	m	w	PA	San Luis Obispo	Santa Rosa Twp	87	319
S P	36	m	w	TN	Mariposa	Mariposa P O	74	128
Seraphine	20	f	w	CA	Santa Cruz	Pajaro Twp	89	348
V	39	m	w	PA	Sierra	Downieville Twp	89	519
Walter	35	m	b	VA	San Francisco	San Francisco P O	80	405
William	34	m	w	TN	Siskiyou	Surprise Valley Tw	89	640
DODSWORTH								
James	25	m	w	NY	Yolo	Putah Twp	93	519
Jno	54	m	w	ENGL	Sacramento	3-Wd Sacramento	77	272
John	44	m	w	NY	San Francisco	5-Wd San Francisco	81	33
Martin	35	m	w	NY	San Francisco	5-Wd San Francisco	81	33
DODYE								
Wm	32	m	w	MA	San Diego	San Diego	78	483
DODYS								
B F	26	m	w	NY	Alameda	Oakland	68	265
DOE								
Ah	50	m	c	CHIN	Butte	Concow Twp	70	11
Ah	50	m	c	CHIN	Sacramento	American Twp	77	68
Ah	47	m	c	CHIN	Yuba	Marysville	93	630
Ah	40	m	c	CHIN	Nevada	Nevada Twp	75	311
Ah	36	m	c	CHIN	Nevada	Nevada Twp	75	311
Ah	32	m	c	CHIN	San Francisco	San Francisco P O	80	487
Ah	28	m	c	CHIN	Placer	Auburn P O	76	378
Ah	20	m	c	CHIN	Placer	Dutch Flat P O	76	410
Anna	30	f	w	ITAL	Santa Clara	San Jose Twp	88	206
Charles A	31	m	w	ME	Humboldt	Mattole Twp	72	285
Chas	30	m	w	GERM	Santa Clara	Gilroy Twp	88	100
E	40	m	w	VT	Alameda	Oakland	68	240
Elizabeth	45	f	w	VT	San Francisco	San Francisco P O	83	401
Fannie	14	f	w	MA	San Francisco	7-Wd San Francisco	81	286
Fred	31	m	w	OH	Santa Clara	Burnett Twp	88	31
Harrison	22	m	w	ME	Humboldt	Eureka Twp	72	278
Henry D	38	m	w	US	Nevada	Grass Valley Twp	75	213
Herman	20	m	w	ME	Humboldt	Eureka Twp	72	278
Jenny	27	f	w	HAMB	San Francisco	6-Wd San Francisco	81	72
John	32	m	w	PRUS	Santa Clara	San Jose Twp	88	209
John	30	m	w	SWED	Sacramento	4-Wd Sacramento	77	367
John	30	m	w	BADE	San Joaquin	2-Wd Stockton	86	160
John	20	m	w	ITAL	Santa Clara	Gilroy Twp	88	88
John	12	m	w	NY	San Francisco	San Francisco P O	85	742
Joseph	32	m	w	ENGL	Santa Cruz	Soquel Twp	89	442
Joseph	27	m	w	NY	San Francisco	8-Wd San Francisco	82	362
Kee	11	m	c	CHIN	Yuba	Marysville	93	628
Otis	60	m	w	ME	Placer	Auburn P O	76	357
Otto	24	m	w	NH	San Francisco	7-Wd San Francisco	81	213
Richard	43	m	w	WI	Calaveras	San Andreas P O	70	212
Stephen	44	m	w	ME	Nevada	Grass Valley Twp	75	191
DOEBELIN								
John	58	m	w	BADE	Shasta	Shasta P O	89	455
DOEHN								
Albert	10	m	w	LA	San Francisco	San Francisco P O	85	827
Sophia	7	f	w	LA	San Francisco	San Francisco P O	85	827
DOEMER								
Charles	37	m	w	FRAN	San Francisco	San Francisco P O	83	197
DOENGER								
Henry	29	m	w	HESS	Los Angeles	Wilmington Twp	73	641
DOENIS								
B	19	m	w	SWIT	Monterey	Alisal Twp	74	304
DOEPLITZ								
A	22	m	w	POLA	San Francisco	8-Wd San Francisco	82	375
DOER								
Ah	18	m	c	CHIN	San Francisco	6-Wd San Francisco	81	75
DOERCHER								
John	37	m	w	SWIT	San Francisco	San Francisco P O	80	480
DOERER								
Charles	30	m	w	HDAR	Santa Clara	1-Wd San Jose	88	232
DOERGER								
Charles	40	m	w	PRUS	San Francisco	San Francisco P O	80	401
DOERMER								
N	38	m	w	PRUS	Sacramento	3-Wd Sacramento	77	303
DOERN								
Anthon	37	m	w	PRUS	Monterey	San Juan Twp	74	390
DOERR								
Henry	25	m	w	PRUS	San Francisco	San Francisco P O	85	745
Philip	42	m	w	HDAR	Santa Clara	1-Wd San Jose	88	232
DOESCHER								
Christiana	30	f	w	HANO	San Francisco	San Francisco P O	83	85
DOEY								
Ah	25	m	c	CHIN	San Francisco	6-Wd San Francisco	81	62
Young	24	m	c	CHIN	Placer	Lincoln P O	76	491
DOFANNY								
Geo	38	m	w	CANA	Humboldt	Eureka Twp	72	273
DOFFERTY								
Michael	43	m	w	IREL	Placer	Bath P O	76	432
DOFFY								
John	22	m	w	IREL	Los Angeles	Los Angeles	73	571
DOFIELD								
Isaac	37	m	w	MO	Nevada	Eureka Twp	75	138
DOGE								
James	33	m	w	CANA	San Mateo	San Mateo P O	87	355
DOGERTY								
Harry	29	m	w	IREL	San Francisco	5-Wd San Francisco	81	19
DOGET								
John	34	m	w	IREL	Santa Clara	Fremont Twp	88	54
DOGGETT								
Bolivar	15	m	w	CA	San Francisco	1-Wd San Francisco	79	110
Emily	28	f	w	ENGL	San Francisco	6-Wd San Francisco	81	99
John	40	m	w	MO	Siskiyou	Scott Rvr Twp	89	604
Saml W	45	m	w	VA	San Francisco	1-Wd San Francisco	79	110
Samuel	44	m	w	MA	San Francisco	San Francisco P O	80	427
W J	27	m	w	AR	Napa	Napa Twp	75	61
W T	31	m	w	AR	Napa	Napa Twp	75	61
DOGHERTY								
John	37	m	w	IREL	Santa Clara	2-Wd San Jose	88	304
Rosanna	30	f	w	IREL	Nevada	Grass Valley Twp	75	160
William	55	m	w	IREL	San Francisco	6-Wd San Francisco	81	126
DOGMAN								
Pat	55	m	w	IREL	Mariposa	Maxwell Crk P O	74	143
DOH								
Ah	23	m	c	CHIN	Butte	Oregon Twp	70	133
DOHAHUE								
P	32	m	w	IREL	Lake	Knoxville Mines	73	404
DOHAM								
J J	35	m	w	MO	Humboldt	Eureka Twp	72	274
DOHARTY								
Thos	38	m	w	IREL	Sutter	Nicolaus Twp	92	110
DOHEN								
Daniel	25	m	w	NY	San Francisco	San Francisco P O	83	166
DOHENEY								
James	33	m	w	IREL	San Francisco	11-Wd San Francisc	84	481
DOHENY								
John	44	m	w	IREL	San Francisco	San Francisco P O	83	402
Wm	35	m	w	IREL	San Francisco	11-Wd San Francisc	84	583
DOHERTY								
Agnes	30	f	w	IREL	Sacramento	3-Wd Sacramento	77	307
Ann	40	f	w	IREL	San Francisco	San Francisco P O	85	861
Anne	34	f	w	IREL	San Francisco	11-Wd San Francisc	84	523
Annie	20	f	w	IREL	San Francisco	San Francisco P O	80	412
Barnaba	35	m	w	ENGL	San Francisco	San Francisco P O	83	154
Barnes	36	m	w	IREL	Contra Costa	Martinez P O	71	419
Benj	55	m	w	KY	Mendocino	Little Lake Twp	74	200
Bennett	26	m	w	IREL	San Francisco	San Francisco P O	83	121
Bernard	33	m	w	IREL	San Francisco	San Francisco P O	85	753
Bridget	30	f	w	IREL	San Francisco	San Francisco P O	83	94
C	41	m	w	IREL	Alameda	Oakland	68	261

© 2001 by Heritage Quest. All rights reserved.

California 1870 Census

Name	Age	S	R	B-PL	County	Locale	Series M593 Roll	Pg
Catharine	40	f	w	IREL	San Francisco	San Francisco P O	83	324
Cathine	63	f	w	IREL	San Francisco	San Francisco P O	85	856
Daniel	40	m	w	IREL	San Francisco	San Francisco P O	83	271
Danl	32	m	w	IREL	San Francisco	San Francisco P O	83	122
Dennis	37	m	w	IREL	San Francisco	San Francisco P O	85	836
Edwd	39	m	w	IREL	San Francisco	1-Wd San Francisco	79	95
Edwd	31	m	w	IREL	San Francisco	1-Wd San Francisco	79	67
Elisa	37	f	w	SCOT	San Francisco	11-Wd San Francisc	84	542
Francis	60	m	w	IREL	San Francisco	San Francisco P O	80	370
George	64	m	w	IREL	Stanislaus	Empire Twp	92	30
George	37	m	w	IREL	Sonoma	Petaluma Twp	91	353
George	16	m	w	MA	Stanislaus	Empire Twp	92	30
Hannah	25	f	w	IREL	Alameda	Oakland	68	199
Hannah	22	f	w	IREL	San Francisco	8-Wd San Francisco	82	378
I	23	m	w	MA	Alameda	Oakland	68	164
James	40	m	w	IREL	Sacramento	3-Wd Sacramento	77	305
James	32	m	w	IREL	San Francisco	1-Wd San Francisco	79	72
James	30	m	w	IREL	San Francisco	1-Wd San Francisco	79	82
Jas	23	m	w	IREL	Sacramento	1-Wd Sacramento	77	188
John	45	m	w	IREL	Santa Cruz	Santa Cruz Twp	89	379
John	44	m	w	IREL	Santa Clara	2-Wd San Jose	88	292
John	40	m	w	IREL	Santa Barbara	Santa Maria P O	87	514
John	37	m	w	IREL	Nevada	Grass Valley Twp	75	147
John	34	m	w	IREL	Santa Clara	1-Wd San Jose	88	243
John	30	m	w	IREL	San Francisco	1-Wd San Francisco	79	65
John	2M	m	w	CA	San Francisco	1-Wd San Francisco	79	40
John	28	m	w	IREL	San Francisco	San Francisco P O	83	127
John	28	m	w	IREL	San Francisco	San Francisco P O	83	114
John	24	m	w	AUST	Mendocino	Cuffeys Cove Twp	74	168
John H	45	m	w	NY	San Francisco	8-Wd San Francisco	82	348
Kate	23	f	w	IREL	Siskiyou	Yreka	89	653
Kate	16	f	w	IREL	San Francisco	San Francisco P O	83	117
Lizzie	27	f	w	IREL	Sacramento	1-Wd Sacramento	77	172
Lizzie	18	f	w	MA	San Francisco	8-Wd San Francisco	82	334
Margery	20	f	w	IREL	San Francisco	11-Wd San Francisc	84	620
Margret	30	f	w	IREL	San Francisco	1-Wd San Francisco	79	89
Mary	20	f	w	IREL	Sacramento	3-Wd Sacramento	77	305
Matthew	26	m	w	CANA	Inyo	Bishop Crk Twp	73	310
Michael	43	m	w	IREL	Calaveras	San Andreas P O	70	203
Michael	35	m	w	IREL	San Mateo	San Mateo P O	87	355
Michael	35	m	w	IREL	San Francisco	San Francisco P O	85	768
Michael G	33	m	w	IREL	Sacramento	2-Wd Sacramento	77	244
Patrick	56	m	w	IREL	San Francisco	11-Wd San Francisc	84	646
Patrick	24	m	w	IREL	Santa Clara	Fremont Twp	88	46
Richard	37	m	w	MA	San Mateo	Half Moon Bay P O	87	404
Richard	37	m	w	IREL	Del Norte	Mountain Twp	71	474
Roger G	42	m	w	IREL	San Francisco	San Francisco P O	83	72
Rosa	40	f	w	IREL	Sacramento	3-Wd Sacramento	77	265
Sarah	28	f	w	IREL	Nevada	Grass Valley Twp	75	149
Thomas	40	m	w	IREL	Sutter	Sutter Twp	92	129
Thomas	36	m	w	IREL	Kern	Havilah P O	73	340
Thos	35	m	w	IREL	San Francisco	1-Wd San Francisco	79	41
W K	39	m	w	IREL	San Francisco	San Francisco P O	83	290
William	22	m	w	AR	San Bernardino	San Bernardino Twp	78	453
Wm	18	m	w	NY	Sacramento	3-Wd Sacramento	77	255
DOHIMAN								
Fred	29	m	w	PRUS	San Francisco	2-Wd San Francisco	79	207
DOHLEN								
Neno	35	m	w	PRUS	San Francisco	1-Wd San Francisco	79	52
DOHMAN								
J	51	m	w	PRUS	Alameda	Oakland	68	230
DOHN								
Chas	40	m	w	BADE	Sacramento	3-Wd Sacramento	77	310
Ph	42	m	w	BAVA	San Francisco	San Francisco P O	83	134
DOHNE								
D	30	m	w	DENM	Sonoma	Sonoma Twp	91	447
DOHREEN								
Peter	18	m	w	PRUS	San Francisco	5-Wd San Francisco	81	15
DOHRMAN								
Chas	24	m	w	PRUS	San Joaquin	2-Wd Stockton	86	185
Maria	34	f	w	CHIL	San Francisco	11-Wd San Francisc	84	444
DOHRR								
H C	52	m	w	RUSS	Alameda	Oakland	68	231
DOHRWALDT								
Fred	40	m	w	SHOL	San Francisco	3-Wd San Francisco	79	287
DOHS								
Chas Fredk	42	m	w	PRUS	San Francisco	San Francisco P O	83	28
Christian	26	m	w	PRUS	San Francisco	San Francisco P O	80	412
Frank	13	m	w	NY	San Francisco	San Francisco P O	85	828
Fred	23	m	w	GERM	Los Angeles	Los Angeles	73	526
George	11	m	w	NY	San Francisco	San Francisco P O	85	828
John	18	m	w	NY	Los Angeles	Los Angeles	73	526
DOHYASABAL								
Gervase	18	m	w	FRAN	Los Angeles	Santa Ana Twp	73	606
DOI								
Ah	25	f	c	CHIN	San Francisco	6-Wd San Francisco	81	77
Ah	25	m	c	CHIN	San Francisco	6-Wd San Francisco	81	51
Ah	18	m	c	CHIN	San Francisco	6-Wd San Francisco	81	54
Ah	17	m	c	CHIN	San Francisco	6-Wd San Francisco	81	63
Ann	22	m	c	CHIN	San Francisco	6-Wd San Francisco	81	44
Ham	25	m	c	CHIN	San Francisco	6-Wd San Francisco	81	40
DOILE								
Thomas	30	m	w	IREL	San Francisco	11-Wd San Francisc	84	543
DOISY								
Caroline	55	f	w	FRAN	Santa Clara	1-Wd San Jose	88	268
DOJORKES								
Julian	32	m	w	MEXI	Yuba	Linda Twp	93	558

Name	Age	S	R	B-PL	County	Locale	Series M593 Roll	Pg
DOK								
Ah	40	m	c	CHIN	San Francisco	6-Wd San Francisco	81	38
Ah	32	m	c	CHIN	San Francisco	11-Wd San Francisc	84	503
Ah	30	m	c	CHIN	Nevada	Little York Twp	75	234
Ah	25	m	c	CHIN	Sierra	Lincoln Twp	89	550
DOKE								
Henry	26	m	b	MO	Contra Costa	Martinez P O	71	448
DOKEN								
Michael	48	m	w	PRUS	Mendocino	Anderson Twp	74	152
DOKENDOFF								
Emel	25	m	w	HAMB	San Mateo	San Mateo P O	87	348
DOL								
Ah	40	m	c	CHIN	Butte	Hamilton Twp	70	72
DOLA								
Joseph	43	m	w	SWIT	Calaveras	San Andreas P O	70	214
DOLALDA								
Ascencion	11	f	w	CA	Santa Barbara	Santa Barbara P O	87	502
DOLAM								
T	51	m	w	IREL	Sierra	Downieville Twp	89	522
DOLAN								
Alfred	50	m	w	KY	Tulare	Packwood Twp	92	257
Andrew	26	m	w	CANA	Humboldt	Eureka Twp	72	267
Anna	22	f	w	IREL	San Francisco	2-Wd San Francisco	79	234
Annie	19	f	w	IREL	San Francisco	2-Wd San Francisco	79	192
Bridget	5M	f	w	IREL	San Francisco	San Francisco P O	83	406
Bridget	42	f	w	IREL	San Francisco	San Francisco P O	83	145
Bridget	36	f	w	IREL	San Francisco	San Francisco P O	85	744
Bridget	30	f	w	IREL	San Francisco	8-Wd San Francisco	82	449
Bridget	24	f	w	IREL	San Francisco	8-Wd San Francisco	82	325
Catherine	67	f	w	IREL	Sacramento	4-Wd Sacramento	77	369
Cathrina	30	f	w	IREL	San Francisco	San Francisco P O	83	378
Cecelia	30	f	m	LA	San Francisco	8-Wd San Francisco	82	389
Delia	38	f	w	IREL	Alameda	Alameda	68	19
Dorothy	40	f	w	AUSL	Marin	Sausalito Twp	74	66
Ed	48	m	w	IREL	San Francisco	San Francisco P O	85	794
Edward B	27	m	w	IREL	Sacramento	4-Wd Sacramento	77	319
Edwd	25	m	w	IREL	Solano	Vallejo	90	156
Elen	40	f	w	IREL	Alameda	Alameda	68	6
Elizabeth	27	f	w	MA	San Francisco	8-Wd San Francisco	82	321
Ellen	26	f	w	IREL	San Joaquin	2-Wd Stockton	86	172
Geneveve(Sister)	25	f	w	AUSL	Sonoma	Petaluma Twp	91	339
George	8	m	w	CA	Marin	San Rafael Twp	74	28
H A	23	m	w	PA	Yuba	Marysville	93	616
H P	33	m	w	IREL	Humboldt	Table Bluff Twp	72	309
Henry	30	m	w	NJ	San Francisco	5-Wd San Francisco	81	4
J J	35	m	w	IREL	San Francisco	8-Wd San Francisco	82	358
James	48	m	w	IREL	Amador	Ione City P O	69	364
James	35	m	w	CANA	Nevada	Meadow Lake Twp	75	269
James	35	m	w	IREL	San Francisco	5-Wd San Francisco	81	7
James	33	m	w	IREL	Mariposa	Mariposa P O	74	111
James	32	m	w	IREL	San Francisco	1-Wd San Francisco	79	55
James	23	m	w	IREL	San Francisco	11-Wd San Francisc	84	701
James P	35	m	w	IREL	San Mateo	Redwood City P O	87	376
Jas F	32	m	w	IREL	Solano	Vallejo	90	148
John	57	m	w	IREL	Solano	Vacaville Twp	90	131
John	5	m	w	CA	Marin	San Rafael Twp	74	28
John	43	m	w	NY	San Francisco	11-Wd San Francisc	84	534
John	40	m	w	IREL	San Francisco	San Francisco P O	83	8
John	32	m	w	IREL	San Francisco	11-Wd San Francisc	84	581
John	30	m	w	IREL	Sonoma	Petaluma Twp	91	350
John	29	m	w	IREL	San Francisco	San Francisco P O	83	335
John	25	m	w	CANA	Solano	Vallejo	90	171
Jos	25	m	w	NY	Solano	Vallejo	90	165
Julia	27	f	w	VA	San Francisco	San Francisco P O	83	396
Kate	28	f	w	IREL	Santa Cruz	Santa Cruz Twp	89	388
Lee	46	m	w	KY	Amador	Fiddletown P O	69	426
M	40	f	w	IREL	San Francisco	San Francisco P O	83	287
M	27	m	w	IREL	Lake	Big Valley	73	395
Maggie	17	f	w	IREL	Solano	Vallejo	90	188
Malachi	37	m	w	IREL	Contra Costa	Martinez P O	71	398
Margaret	70	f	w	IREL	San Mateo	Redwood City P O	87	376
Margt	34	f	w	IREL	San Francisco	8-Wd San Francisco	82	365
Mark	36	m	w	NJ	Tuolumne	Columbia P O	93	339
Martin	44	m	w	IREL	Santa Clara	1-Wd San Jose	88	237
Martin	43	m	w	IREL	Santa Clara	2-Wd San Jose	88	316
Martin	33	m	w	IREL	San Francisco	San Francisco P O	85	809
Mary	50	f	w	IREL	Placer	Blue Canyon P O	76	418
Mary	40	f	w	IREL	Solano	Benicia	90	16
Mary	35	f	w	IREL	San Francisco	1-Wd San Francisco	79	113
Mary	30	f	w	IREL	San Francisco	7-Wd San Francisco	81	286
Mary	30	f	w	IREL	Alameda	Oakland	68	154
Mary	30	f	w	IREL	San Francisco	San Francisco P O	80	337
Mary	29	f	w	CANA	San Francisco	San Francisco P O	83	312
Mary	28	f	w	IREL	Alameda	Oakland	68	242
Mary	27	f	w	IREL	Marin	San Rafael Twp	74	30
Mary	25	f	w	IREL	Santa Cruz	Santa Cruz	89	413
Mary	23	f	w	MA	Solano	Benicia	90	16
Mary	18	f	w	MA	Marin	Tomales Twp	74	85
Mary	14	f	w	NY	San Francisco	San Francisco P O	83	151
Mary	13	f	w	NY	San Francisco	11-Wd San Francisc	84	611
Mary A	31	f	w	CANA	San Francisco	8-Wd San Francisco	82	393
Mary J	5	f	w	CA	Nevada	Grass Valley Twp	75	158
Mary T	56	f	w	ENGL	Sacramento	4-Wd Sacramento	77	358
Maurice	30	m	w	IREL	Monterey	San Juan Twp	74	406
Michael	40	m	w	IREL	Santa Clara	Fremont Twp	88	41
Michael	33	m	w	IREL	San Francisco	San Francisco P O	85	823
Michael	32	m	w	IREL	San Francisco	11-Wd San Francisc	84	474

© 2001 by Heritage Quest. All rights reserved.

Series M593

Name	Age	S	R	B-PL	County	Locale	Roll	Pg
Micheal	40	m	w	IREL	San Francisco	7-Wd San Francisco	81	202
Mike	50	m	w	IREL	Alameda	Murray Twp	68	121
Mike	24	m	w	IREL	Alameda	Murray Twp	68	122
P	27	m	w	IREL	Sacramento	3-Wd Sacramento	77	317
P F	29	m	w	IREL	Sacramento	4-Wd Sacramento	77	344
Pat	60	m	w	IREL	San Francisco	11-Wd San Francisc	84	673
Patrick	75	m	w	IREL	San Francisco	11-Wd San Francisc	84	569
Patrick	40	m	w	IREL	San Francisco	11-Wd San Francisc	84	440
Patrick	38	m	w	IREL	San Francisco	1-Wd San Francisco	79	94
Patrick	23	m	w	IREL	San Francisco	11-Wd San Francisc	84	595
Peter	40	m	w	IREL	San Francisco	San Francisco P O	80	401
Peter	28	m	w	IREL	Sutter	Nicolaus Twp	92	110
Peter	26	m	w	IREL	Sonoma	Bodega Twp	91	261
Phelix	38	m	w	IREL	Sacramento	Franklin Twp	77	118
Phil	26	m	w	IREL	Santa Clara	Gilroy Twp	88	97
Richard	33	m	w	IREL	San Francisco	San Francisco P O	83	267
Richard	16	m	w	CA	Marin	Sausalito Twp	74	66
Rosa	50	f	w	IREL	San Francisco	2-Wd San Francisco	79	234
Rosana	50	f	w	IREL	San Francisco	San Francisco P O	80	374
Thomas	97	m	w	IREL	Sacramento	2-Wd Sacramento	77	240
Thomas	40	m	w	IREL	San Francisco	San Francisco P O	83	155
Thomas	38	m	w	IREL	Placer	Pino Twp	76	472
Thomas	33	m	w	IREL	San Francisco	7-Wd San Francisco	81	173
Thomas	32	m	w	IREL	San Francisco	5-Wd San Francisco	81	28
Thomas	31	m	w	IREL	San Francisco	San Francisco P O	83	1
Thomas B	32	m	w	IREL	San Francisco	San Francisco P O	85	744
Thos	39	m	w	IREL	San Francisco	8-Wd San Francisco	82	371
Thos	21	m	w	MA	San Francisco	11-Wd San Francisc	84	478
Thos J	37	m	w	IREL	San Francisco	8-Wd San Francisco	82	373
Timothy	45	m	w	IREL	Monterey	San Juan Twp	74	406
William	32	m	w	IREL	San Francisco	8-Wd San Francisco	82	319
DOLAND								
Andrew	29	m	w	CANA	Sonoma	Vallejo Twp	91	454
Eliza	23	f	w	IREL	Sacramento	4-Wd Sacramento	77	346
Frank	35	m	w	IREL	Sacramento	San Joaquin Twp	77	399
Frank F	32	m	w	NY	Sacramento	4-Wd Sacramento	77	326
J	44	m	w	IREL	Lake	Knoxville Mines	73	405
John	40	m	w	IREL	San Mateo	Schoolhouse Statio	87	341
John	32	m	w	IREL	Los Angeles	Los Nietos Twp	73	577
Margaret	22	f	w	IREL	Sacramento	4-Wd Sacramento	77	344
Maria	28	f	w	IREL	Santa Clara	Gilroy Twp	88	104
Mary	48	f	w	IREL	Alameda	Oakland	68	146
Michael	35	m	w	IREL	San Francisco	San Francisco P O	83	52
Michael	30	m	w	IREL	San Mateo	Half Moon Bay P O	87	389
Patrick	61	m	w	IREL	Alameda	Eden Twp	68	66
DOLANEY								
Pat	31	m	w	IREL	San Joaquin	1-Wd Stockton	86	150
DOLANS								
Mary A	27	f	w	MA	San Francisco	San Francisco P O	85	798
DOLARD								
Joseph	36	m	w	SICI	Monterey	San Juan Twp	74	406
DOLARE								
Baptiste	48	m	w	FRAN	Calaveras	San Andreas P O	70	200
DOLBEARE								
Frank	62	m	w	CT	San Joaquin	Oneal Twp	86	107
DOLBEER								
Jno	35	m	w	NY	San Francisco	5-Wd San Francisco	81	18
DOLBEGUY								
G	52	m	w	FRAN	Monterey	San Juan Twp	74	408
DOLCHER								
Henry	48	m	w	SWIT	Humboldt	Table Bluff Twp	72	307
DOLCHY								
Henrietta	43	f	w	HAMB	San Francisco	11-Wd San Francisc	84	484
John L	49	m	w	PRUS	Placer	Rocklin Twp	76	468
DOLCIATO								
Louis	65	m	w	FRAN	Calaveras	San Andreas P O	70	156
DOLCINI								
Giuseppi	27	m	w	SWIT	Santa Cruz	Santa Cruz Twp	89	399
DOLD								
Valentine	68	m	w	BADE	Sacramento	3-Wd Sacramento	77	289
William	27	m	w	NY	Marin	Tomales Twp	74	85
DOLE								
David	35	m	w	NY	San Francisco	7-Wd San Francisco	81	274
Elbridge	47	m	w	ME	Contra Costa	Martinez P O	71	387
F A	30	m	w	ME	Sacramento	1-Wd Sacramento	77	180
Jas	28	m	w	MO	Santa Clara	Gilroy Twp	88	98
John	30	m	w	GERM	Yolo	Cottonwood Twp	93	462
John	30	m	w	GERM	Yolo	Cottonwood Twp	93	460
Joseph	43	m	w	FRAN	Tehama	Red Bluff	92	177
W	36	m	w	ENGL	Sierra	Alleghany & Forest	89	535
Wm	13	m	w	CA	Butte	Chico Twp	70	45
DOLEN								
Catherin	24	f	w	IREL	Contra Costa	Martinez P O	71	368
J	38	m	w	IREL	Sierra	Sierra Twp	89	569
J	29	m	w	IREL	Alameda	Oakland	68	184
John	36	m	w	IREL	San Francisco	San Francisco P O	85	794
William	40	m	w	IREL	San Francisco	11-Wd San Francisc	84	510
DOLENSON								
Daniel	41	m	w	NY	Santa Clara	Santa Clara Twp	88	147
DOLET								
August	53	m	w	FRAN	San Francisco	2-Wd San Francisco	79	204
Frank	34	m	w	IREL	San Francisco	San Francisco P O	80	474
G B	37	m	w	FRAN	San Francisco	San Francisco P O	83	63
DOLEY								
Chas	19	m	w	CANA	Solano	Vallejo	90	150
Michael	42	m	w	IREL	Alameda	Brooklyn Twp	68	50
Patrick	30	m	w	IREL	Alameda	Hayward	68	79
Patrick	30	m	w	IREL	Nevada	Grass Valley Twp	75	224
DOLFINO								
Philips	23	m	w	SWIT	Monterey	Monterey Twp	74	344
DOLHEGUY								
Adolph	45	m	w	FRAN	San Francisco	8-Wd San Francisco	82	311
DOLING								
A	12	f	w	CA	Alameda	Oakland	68	242
DOLINGER								
Ambrose	35	m	w	MO	Solano	Vacaville Twp	90	133
DOLINS								
Maria	45	f	w	CA	San Diego	San Luis Rey	78	514
DOLITTLE								
Wm	34	m	w	NY	San Francisco	8-Wd San Francisco	82	376
DOLIVER								
Alonzo	24	m	w	OH	Butte	Chico Twp	70	25
Edward	39	m	w	ME	Nevada	Washington Twp	75	345
DOLIVERA								
Louis	45	m	w	FRAN	San Francisco	San Francisco P O	80	538
DOLL								
Ferdinand	35	m	w	BADE	Shasta	Horsetown P O	89	503
Hulda	35	f	w	MO	San Mateo	San Mateo P O	87	358
James	35	m	w	ENGL	San Bernardino	Chino Twp	78	412
Jos	30	m	w	GERM	Solano	Vallejo	90	193
Josiah	41	m	w	OH	Siskiyou	Callahan P O	89	629
Michael	38	m	w	PRUS	Sacramento	Granite Twp	77	144
Valentine	33	m	w	BADE	Shasta	Horsetown P O	89	503
DOLLAR								
J	37	m	w	KY	Lake	Lower Lake	73	423
James	40	m	w	MO	Lake	Big Valley	73	394
John	32	m	w	IL	Mendocino	Gualala Twp	74	226
Julia	15	f	w	CA	Mendocino	Little Lake Twp	74	192
William	31	m	w	MO	Mendocino	Gualala Twp	74	226
William	30	m	w	ME	Mendocino	Big Rvr Twp	74	171
DOLLARD								
Mary	41	f	w	CHIL	Sacramento	2-Wd Sacramento	77	238
DOLLARHIDE								
A J	35	m	w	IN	Napa	Napa	75	26
Edward	19	m	w	IREL	Stanislaus	Emory Twp	92	25
Even	65	m	w	SC	Yolo	Cache Crk Twp	93	423
Lucy	49	f	w	OH	Stanislaus	Empire Twp	92	32
DOLLE								
Edman	48	m	w	ME	Alameda	Hayward	68	73
DOLLEGHY								
B	46	m	w	FRAN	San Francisco	8-Wd San Francisco	82	305
DOLLER								
Andrew	59	m	w	BAVA	El Dorado	Greenwood Twp	72	55
Wm R	34	m	w	IL	Sonoma	Cloverdale Twp	91	270
DOLLET								
Bridget	31	f	w	IREL	Sacramento	2-Wd Sacramento	77	243
DOLLEY								
E P	28	m	w	ME	Sierra	Sierra Twp	89	567
O B	38	m	w	ME	Sierra	Sierra Twp	89	567
Samuel	24	m	w	MA	Stanislaus	Empire Twp	92	38
DOLLIF								
J F	42	m	w	ME	Trinity	Douglas	92	234
DOLLINA								
Henry	35	m	w	MA	San Francisco	San Francisco P O	83	190
DOLLING								
Otto	22	m	w	PRUS	Calaveras	Copperopolis P O	70	222
DOLLISON								
J R	46	m	w	PA	Humboldt	Eureka Twp	72	268
DOLLIVER								
Emma	21	f	w	OH	San Francisco	San Francisco P O	85	774
Fannie	30	f	w	MA	San Francisco	San Francisco P O	85	826
John L	37	m	w	MA	San Francisco	2-Wd San Francisco	79	202
Mary	70	f	w	MA	San Francisco	San Francisco P O	83	48
Saml	46	m	w	MA	San Francisco	8-Wd San Francisco	82	314
DOLLOLA								
Ygnacio	35	m	b	PHIL	Mariposa	Mariposa P O	74	104
DOLLOROS								
Madrea	40	m	w	MEXI	Merced	Snelling P O	74	259
DOLLY								
Geo	40	m	w	ME	El Dorado	Greenwood Twp	72	51
DOLMAN								
Martin	20	m	w	IREL	Stanislaus	Emory Twp	92	26
DOLOFF								
Jerome B	38	m	w	NH	San Mateo	Half Moon Bay P O	87	398
DOLOLING								
Elmira	30	f	w	ME	San Diego	San Diego	78	492
DOLOMDIER								
Peter D	50	m	w	FRAN	Yuba	Bullards Bar P O	93	550
DOLON								
Daniel	45	m	w	IREL	Monterey	San Juan Twp	74	395
F	26	m	w	IREL	Alameda	Oakland	68	266
Hannah	28	f	w	IREL	Alameda	Oakland	68	208
DOLONY								
Jacob M	22	m	w	IL	Butte	Oregon Twp	70	133
DOLORAES								
Juan	32	m	i	CA	San Luis Obispo	Morro Twp	87	281
DOLORES								
Aquia	34	m	w	MEXI	San Francisco	San Francisco P O	80	471
Carlos	24	m	w	MEXI	San Francisco	San Francisco P O	80	470
Henri	40	m	w	MEXI	San Bernardino	Chino Twp	78	413
Jose	40	m	w	CA	San Diego	San Pasqual	78	521
Jose	30	m	w	NM	Fresno	Millerton P O	72	148
Jose	15	m	i	CA	Los Angeles	Los Angeles	73	501
Juan	31	m	w	CA	Santa Clara	Burnett Twp	88	39

© 2001 by Heritage Quest. All rights reserved.

Name	Age	S	R	B-PL	County	Locale	Roll	Pg
						Series M593		
Letta	37	f	w	SAME	Nevada	Nevada Twp	75	281
Maria	50	f	w	MEXI	Santa Clara	Santa Clara Twp	88	154
Maria	45	f	w	CA	San Diego	San Pasqual	78	521
Urice	15	f	w	MEXI	San Francisco	San Francisco P O	83	211
DOLOREZ								
Joseph	35	m	w	AZOR	Contra Costa	San Pablo Twp	71	362
DOLORS								
O	36	f	w	MEXI	Sierra	Forest Twp	89	531
DOLOVER								
Alonzo	27	m	w	MO	Butte	Chico Twp	70	49
DOLOZZES								
Miguel	35	m	w	CA	Monterey	Pajaro Twp	74	373
DOLPHIN								
I	40	m	w	FRAN	Alameda	Oakland	68	166
Saml	28	m	w	KY	Tehama	Tehama Twp	92	192
DOLSENO								
M	24	m	w	CANA	Alameda	Murray Twp	68	122
DOLSON								
Dewitt	50	m	w	NY	San Francisco	11-Wd San Francisc	84	492
Harriett	28	f	w	NY	San Francisco	6-Wd San Francisco	81	142
Henry	30	m	w	MA	San Francisco	8-Wd San Francisco	82	348
John C	46	m	w	NY	Sacramento	San Joaquin Twp	77	400
Mary A	26	f	w	IREL	Santa Clara	Santa Clara Twp	88	155
Sarah	112	f	b	NC	San Francisco	8-Wd San Francisco	82	355
DOLT								
Alexander	28	m	w	PRUS	Nevada	Little York Twp	75	241
DOLTON								
Jackson	35	m	w	OH	Butte	Chico Twp	70	29
John	28	m	w	CANA	Humboldt	Eureka Twp	72	267
M	26	m	w	IREL	Alameda	Oakland	68	182
Mary	23	f	w	IREL	San Francisco	8-Wd San Francisco	82	313
DOLZER								
Jennie	29	f	w	PA	San Francisco	11-Wd San Francisc	84	445
DOMA								
Ratols	25	m	w	ITAL	San Francisco	11-Wd San Francisc	84	709
DOMALAN								
Peter	38	m	w	FRAN	El Dorado	White Oak Twp	72	144
DOMALDO								
Francisco	21	m	w	PORT	San Mateo	Schoolhouse Statio	87	339
DOMAN								
Joseph	65	m	w	FRAN	El Dorado	Cosumnes Twp	72	19
DOMANE								
Margaret	27	f	w	NY	San Francisco	7-Wd San Francisco	81	217
DOMANS								
James	37	m	w	IREL	Marin	San Rafael	74	53
DOMANSKY								
William	29	m	w	PRUS	Contra Costa	Martinez P O	71	437
DOMANY								
Joseph	43	m	w	CANA	Mariposa	Mariposa P O	74	124
DOMARICHE								
Charles	38	m	w	ITAL	San Luis Obispo	Santa Rosa Twp	87	327
DOMBERGER								
Lambert	43	m	w	FRAN	Santa Clara	Fremont Twp	88	51
DOMBUSH								
Fred	54	m	w	GERM	Sacramento	4-Wd Sacramento	77	321
DOMCLIFF								
Thomas	35	m	w	PA	San Francisco	San Francisco P O	83	242
DOME								
Ah	35	m	c	CHIN	Yolo	Putah Twp	93	510
DOMEGAN								
M	15	f	w	IL	Sonoma	Russian Rvr	91	371
DOMENIC								
Wm	21	m	w	FRAN	Butte	Kimshew Tpw	70	80
DOMENICK								
F	16	f	w	CA	Los Angeles	Los Angeles	73	569
DOMENY								
Ellis W	42	m	w	PA	Del Norte	Crescent Twp	71	456
DOMEO								
San	40	m	w	ITAL	San Francisco	11-Wd San Francisc	84	712
DOMESTIC								
Joseph	30	m	w	ITAL	Amador	Volcano P O	69	373
DOMETRE								
George	24	m	w	GREE	Santa Clara	2-Wd San Jose	88	330
DOMEY								
Andrew	38	m	w	SWED	San Francisco	San Francisco P O	85	789
DOMIC								
Peter	45	m	w	FRAN	Los Angeles	Los Angeles	73	567
DOMICK								
Remo	25	m	w	FRAN	San Francisco	11-Wd San Francisc	84	710
DOMICO								
Jean	36	m	w	FRAN	San Francisco	1-Wd San Francisco	79	50
DOMIGUES								
Maria	20	f	w	CA	Los Angeles	Los Angeles Twp	73	490
DOMIN								
Felomeno	16	f	w	MEXI	Los Angeles	Los Angeles	73	509
DOMINGAS								
A S	31	m	w	PORT	Tuolumne	Columbia P O	93	356
Lozero	39	m	w	PHIL	San Mateo	Half Moon Bay P O	87	393
DOMINGE								
Jose	20	m	w	PORT	Contra Costa	Martinez P O	71	368
DOMINGO								
C C	21	m	w	CHIL	Tuolumne	Chinese Camp P O	93	383
F	40	f	w	CAME	San Joaquin	1-Wd Stockton	86	133
H	20	m	w	MEXI	San Joaquin	1-Wd Stockton	86	133
Hortago	37	m	b	MEXI	Yuba	Marysville Twp	93	568
Ja	35	m	w	ITAL	Sacramento	Georgianna Twp	77	129
John	30	m	w	FRAN	San Francisco	San Francisco P O	80	535

Name	Age	S	R	B-PL	County	Locale	Roll	Pg
						Series M593		
Jose	45	m	w	POLY	Santa Barbara	Las Cruces P O	87	516
Jose	15	m	w	CA	Marin	San Rafael Twp	74	26
Joseph	30	m	w	AZOR	Marin	Sausalito Twp	74	68
Joseph	30	m	w	CHIL	El Dorado	Georgetown Twp	72	40
Juan	41	m	w	MEXI	San Francisco	San Francisco P O	80	470
L	28	m	w	ITAL	Santa Clara	Gilroy Twp	88	100
Lora	27	m	w	ITAL	San Joaquin	1-Wd Stockton	86	141
Manuel	38	m	w	MEXI	Amador	Sutter Crk P O	69	412
Pauline	26	f	w	MEXI	San Francisco	San Francisco P O	80	476
Pedro	45	m	w	FRAN	Los Angeles	Los Nietos Twp	73	589
Ramon	33	m	w	CA	Santa Barbara	Las Cruces P O	87	516
Ramond	40	m	w	MEXI	Kern	Tehachapi P O	73	355
Rosa	27	f	w	CA	Santa Barbara	Las Cruces P O	87	516
DOMINGOS								
Jose	25	m	w	CA	Kern	Bakersfield P O	73	362
DOMINGUES								
Anton	38	m	w	SPAI	San Francisco	1-Wd San Francisco	79	30
Antonio	32	m	w	SPAI	San Francisco	1-Wd San Francisco	79	132
Arminta	20	f	w	CA	San Diego	San Diego	78	503
Elenor	36	f	w	CA	Los Angeles	Los Angeles	73	514
Feliciano	24	m	w	CA	Santa Barbara	Santa Barbara P O	87	479
Francisco	40	m	w	CA	Santa Barbara	Santa Barbara P O	87	479
Isabel	40	f	w	CA	Santa Barbara	Santa Barbara P O	87	464
Jago	36	m	w	CA	San Francisco	1-Wd San Francisco	79	57
John	40	m	w	GA	Sacramento	2-Wd Sacramento	77	227
Jose	29	m	w	MEXI	Marin	San Rafael Twp	74	39
Jose	23	m	i	CA	Santa Barbara	San Buenaventura P	87	439
Jose	22	m	w	MEXI	San Luis Obispo	San Luis Obispo Tw	87	304
Jose M	50	m	w	CA	Santa Barbara	Santa Barbara P O	87	471
Martino	42	m	w	CA	Santa Barbara	Santa Barbara P O	87	464
Pedro	45	m	w	CA	Santa Barbara	Santa Barbara P O	87	462
Ricardo	10	m	w	MEXI	San Francisco	8-Wd San Francisco	82	448
Rosario	29	m	w	MEXI	Los Angeles	Los Angeles	73	560
Tomas	40	m	w	CA	Los Angeles	Los Nietos Twp	73	588
DOMINGUEZ								
Adelaida	27	f	w	CA	Los Angeles	Los Angeles	73	561
Andrea	46	f	w	CA	Los Angeles	Los Angeles	73	561
Augustine	45	m	w	MEXI	San Luis Obispo	Arroyo Grande Twp	87	271
Candelara	48	f	w	CA	Santa Barbara	San Buenaventura P	87	437
Carlos	18	m	w	MEXI	Los Angeles	Los Angeles	73	515
Carnen	12	f	w	CA	Los Angeles	San Gabriel Twp	73	598
Cristiana	12	f	w	CA	Los Angeles	Santa Ana Twp	73	607
Dolores	25	m	w	CA	Los Angeles	Los Angeles	73	561
Domecio	97	m	w	CA	Santa Barbara	Santa Barbara P O	87	488
Estefan	21	m	w	CA	Los Angeles	Los Angeles Twp	73	490
Francisco	46	m	w	CA	Santa Barbara	Santa Barbara P O	87	488
Francisco	40	f	w	CA	Los Angeles	Los Angeles	73	563
Frederick	25	m	w	CA	Los Angeles	Los Angeles Twp	73	489
Ignacio	4	m	w	CA	Los Angeles	Los Angeles Twp	73	474
Isabel	11	f	w	CA	Santa Barbara	Santa Barbara P O	87	474
Jesus	45	m	w	MEXI	Los Angeles	El Monte Twp	73	451
Jose	78	m	w	CA	Santa Barbara	Santa Barbara P O	87	489
Jose	40	m	w	CA	Los Angeles	Los Angeles Twp	73	478
Jose	18	m	w	CA	Santa Barbara	Santa Barbara P O	87	489
Jose C	28	m	w	CA	Los Angeles	San Jose Twp	73	618
Jose M	49	m	w	CA	Santa Barbara	Santa Barbara P O	87	491
Josefa	47	f	w	CA	Los Angeles	Los Angeles	73	566
Juan	56	m	w	MEXI	Los Angeles	Los Nietos Twp	73	583
Juan	23	m	w	MEXI	Santa Barbara	San Buenaventura P	87	428
Juana	31	f	w	CA	Los Angeles	Los Angeles	73	523
Luisa	54	f	w	CA	Santa Barbara	Santa Barbara P O	87	489
Manuel	67	m	w	CA	Los Angeles	Wilmington Twp	73	638
Manuel	19	m	w	CA	Santa Barbara	San Buenaventura P	87	426
Manuela	20	f	w	CA	Los Angeles	Los Angeles	73	552
Maria A	52	f	w	MEXI	Los Angeles	Los Angeles	73	561
Maria V	75	f	w	CA	Santa Barbara	Santa Barbara P O	87	488
Mateo	13	m	w	CA	Los Angeles	Los Angeles	73	552
Matias	11	m	w	CA	Santa Barbara	Santa Barbara P O	87	491
Palomo	54	m	w	CA	Los Angeles	Los Angeles Twp	73	478
Paula	50	f	w	CA	Los Angeles	Santa Ana Twp	73	607
Pedro	55	m	w	CA	Los Angeles	Wilmington Twp	73	638
Pedro	11	m	w	CA	Los Angeles	Los Angeles Twp	73	489
Pedro S	43	m	w	CA	Los Angeles	Los Angeles Twp	73	487
Prudencia	35	m	w	CA	Santa Barbara	San Buenaventura P	87	428
Roberto	48	m	w	NY	Santa Barbara	San Buenaventura P	87	423
Santiago	54	m	w	MEXI	Santa Barbara	San Buenaventura P	87	428
Susana	25	f	w	CA	Los Angeles	Los Angeles	73	522
Tomas	51	m	w	MEXI	Los Angeles	San Juan Twp	73	626
DOMINI								
Martin	32	m	w	SWIT	San Francisco	2-Wd San Francisco	79	198
DOMINIC								
Petesta	27	m	w	ITAL	Mariposa	Mariposa P O	74	113
DOMINICK								
Connell	50	m	w	FRAN	Sutter	Vernon Twp	92	139
Peter	35	m	w	ITAL	San Francisco	1-Wd San Francisco	79	36
DOMINICO								
Feca	35	m	w	ITAL	San Francisco	3-Wd San Francisco	79	289
Francis	18	m	w	ITAL	San Mateo	Schoolhouse Statio	87	346
John	32	m	w	ITAL	San Mateo	Schoolhouse Statio	87	346
DOMINIK								
Bertrand	49	m	w	FRAN	San Francisco	6-Wd San Francisco	81	70
DOMINIO								
Francisco	23	m	w	ITAL	San Mateo	Schoolhouse Statio	87	334
DOMINIQUE								
Bellagorry	38	m	w	FRAN	San Diego	Julian Dist	78	470
DOMINO								
Jane	26	m	w	SWIT	El Dorado	Lake Valley Twp	72	64

© 2001 by Heritage Quest. All rights reserved.

Series M593

Name	Age	S	R	B-PL	County	Locale	Roll	Pg
Morris	38	m	w	SWIT	San Francisco	San Francisco P O	80	429
DOMION								
Maria	44	f	w	IREL	San Francisco	2-Wd San Francisco	79	173
DOMON								
Jos	25	m	w	PA	Solano	Vallejo	90	201
DOMOT								
Charles H	44	m	w	VA	Los Angeles	San Jose Twp	73	623
DOMOTT								
William E	46	m	w	MA	San Francisco	8-Wd San Francisco	82	415
DON								
Agnes	14	f	w	CA	San Joaquin	1-Wd Stockton	86	137
Ah	40	m	c	CHIN	Contra Costa	Martinez P O	71	398
George	50	m	w	SCOT	San Francisco	San Francisco P O	83	154
Lo	25	m	c	CHIN	Colusa	Butte Twp	71	269
On	40	m	c	CHIN	Butte	Kimshew Tpw	70	84
Ramon	45	m	w	FRAN	Santa Clara	Santa Clara Twp	88	157
Thomas J	28	m	w	IL	Colusa	Colusa Twp	71	283
Thos H	38	m	w	NY	Butte	Ophir Twp	70	97
William	24	m	w	MA	Solano	Maine Prairie Twp	90	51
DONACA								
John	35	m	w	IL	Humboldt	Mattole Twp	72	285
DONAGAN								
M	45	m	w	IREL	Sierra	Gibson Twp	89	540
DONAGHEE								
James	25	m	w	IREL	San Francisco	6-Wd San Francisco	81	79
DONAGHUE								
Phillip	35	m	w	IREL	San Francisco	6-Wd San Francisco	81	96
DONAGHY								
Edward	39	m	w	IREL	Siskiyou	Cottonwood Twp	89	592
John	28	m	w	IREL	Santa Cruz	Santa Cruz Twp	89	393
Michael	25	m	w	IREL	Santa Cruz	Santa Cruz Twp	89	394
DONAHAN								
Alexander	20	m	w	BAVA	Sonoma	Sonoma Twp	91	446
Timothy	69	m	w	IREL	Shasta	Shasta P O	89	453
DONAHEY								
Mike	42	m	w	IREL	Alameda	Oakland	68	233
DONAHO								
Mary	30	f	w	IREL	Alameda	Oakland	68	186
Michl	23	m	w	IREL	San Francisco	1-Wd San Francisco	79	41
DONAHOE								
C	28	f	w	IREL	San Francisco	San Francisco P O	85	784
Cornelius	40	m	w	IREL	Sacramento	Center Twp	77	84
Jane	39	f	w	IREL	San Francisco	11-Wd San Francisc	84	685
John	38	m	w	CANA	San Joaquin	Dent Twp	86	19
Michl	42	m	w	IREL	Sierra	Eureka Twp	89	523
Thoms	48	m	w	IREL	San Francisco	2-Wd San Francisco	79	184
Thos	37	m	w	IREL	San Francisco	2-Wd San Francisco	79	187
W	38	m	w	IREL	Alameda	Murray Twp	68	102
DONAHOO								
John H	40	m	w	IREL	Sierra	Sears Twp	89	556
Pat	42	m	w	IREL	Sierra	Sears Twp	89	558
Timothy	40	m	w	IREL	Sierra	Sears Twp	89	561
DONAHU								
Thos	44	m	w	IA	Santa Clara	Gilroy Twp	88	103
DONAHUE								
Albert	36	m	w	MA	Alameda	Oakland	68	265
Ann	25	f	w	IREL	San Francisco	San Francisco P O	83	97
Anna	27	f	w	IREL	Santa Clara	2-Wd San Jose	88	298
Barnard	40	m	w	IREL	Sacramento	2-Wd Sacramento	77	229
Bridget	39	f	w	IREL	Nevada	Grass Valley Twp	75	178
C	55	f	w	IREL	San Francisco	San Francisco P O	85	786
Calvin	60	m	w	AR	Sutter	Yuba Twp	92	150
Catharine	50	f	w	IREL	Alameda	Brooklyn Twp	68	50
Chas W	11	m	w	CA	San Francisco	San Francisco P O	83	161
Cornel	27	m	w	IREL	Yuba	Rose Bar Twp	93	659
D	45	m	w	IREL	Alameda	Oakland	68	258
D W	21	m	w	CANA	Alameda	Oakland	68	157
Ed	20	m	w	CANA	Alameda	Oakland	68	253
Eliza	26	f	w	IREL	San Francisco	11-Wd San Francisc	84	550
Ellen	50	f	w	IREL	Nevada	Nevada Twp	75	299
Ellen	34	f	w	IN	El Dorado	Mud Springs Twp	72	78
F M	34	m	w	IN	Klamath	Orleans Twp	73	380
Frank	45	m	w	IREL	Sacramento	2-Wd Sacramento	77	241
H	25	f	w	IREL	Alameda	Alameda	68	10
J	19	m	w	CANA	Alameda	Oakland	68	253
J C	43	m	w	IREL	Sutter	Butte Twp	92	103
James	51	m	w	IREL	Tuolumne	Big Oak Flat P O	93	403
James	38	m	w	IREL	Sonoma	Petaluma Twp	91	360
James	30	m	w	IREL	Trinity	Junction City Pct	92	207
James	28	m	w	SCOT	San Francisco	1-Wd San Francisco	79	112
James	24	m	w	ME	Colusa	Colusa	71	292
James	13	m	w	CA	San Francisco	11-Wd San Francisc	84	592
Jane	29	f	w	PA	El Dorado	Placerville	72	125
Jeremiah	35	m	w	IREL	Mendocino	Anderson Twp	74	152
Jeremiah	24	m	w	IREL	San Francisco	11-Wd San Francisc	84	614
Jno	38	m	w	IREL	San Joaquin	Tulare Twp	86	259
John	53	m	w	IREL	Napa	Yountville Twp	75	86
John	39	m	w	IREL	Sacramento	2-Wd Sacramento	77	240
John	14	m	w	CA	San Francisco	11-Wd San Francisc	84	593
Josephine	2	f	w	CA	San Francisco	11-Wd San Francisc	84	608
Kate	22	f	w	IREL	San Francisco	11-Wd San Francisc	84	506
M J	18	f	w	NY	Sacramento	3-Wd Sacramento	77	265
Mamie	15	f	w	CA	Santa Clara	2-Wd San Jose	88	337
Martin	41	m	w	IREL	San Francisco	1-Wd San Francisco	79	93
Mary	65	f	w	IREL	San Joaquin	3-Wd Stockton	86	223
Mary	20	f	w	IREL	San Francisco	11-Wd San Francisc	84	608
Mary	---	f	w	CA	Santa Clara	Santa Clara Twp	88	157
Meroyn	11	m	w	CA	Santa Clara	Santa Clara Twp	88	177
Michael	65	m	w	IREL	Tuolumne	Sonora P O	93	332
Michael	60	m	w	IREL	Alameda	Brooklyn Twp	68	53
Michael	50	m	w	IREL	Stanislaus	Washington Twp	92	84
Michael	43	m	w	IREL	Mendocino	Cuffeys Cove Twp	74	169
Michael	25	m	w	IREL	Colusa	Monroe Twp	71	325
Micheal	32	m	w	CANA	Sonoma	Vallejo Twp	91	452
Mikiel	40	m	w	IREL	Sonoma	Sonoma Twp	91	442
Owen	36	m	w	IREL	Tuolumne	Sonora P O	93	318
P	42	m	w	IREL	Mariposa	Maxwell Crk P O	74	144
Pat	43	m	w	IREL	San Joaquin	2-Wd Stockton	86	162
Pat	30	m	w	IREL	Humboldt	Eureka Twp	72	277
Patrick	39	m	w	IREL	Los Angeles	Wilmington Twp	73	642
Patrick	28	m	w	IREL	Alameda	Washington Twp	68	282
Patrick	21	m	w	CANA	Napa	Yountville Twp	75	88
Patrk	53	m	w	IREL	Sacramento	4-Wd Sacramento	77	345
R	13	f	w	US	Yuba	Marysville	93	609
Robt	47	m	w	IREL	Mariposa	Maxwell Crk P O	74	144
Thomas G	42	m	w	NY	Nevada	Grass Valley Twp	75	159
Timothy	35	m	w	IREL	San Francisco	San Francisco P O	83	152
Tissa	48	f	w	KY	El Dorado	White Oak Twp	72	142
Tymothy	38	m	w	IREL	San Francisco	San Francisco P O	85	804
Waller	48	m	w	AR	Sutter	Yuba Twp	92	150
William	35	m	w	NY	El Dorado	Mud Springs Twp	72	81
William J	31	m	w	IREL	Klamath	Camp Gaston	73	372
William M	40	m	w	IREL	El Dorado	Placerville	72	113
Wm	27	m	w	IREL	San Joaquin	1-Wd Stockton	86	157
DONAHUGH								
Mary A	4	f	w	ME	Humboldt	Eureka Twp	72	279
DONAKE								
Anne	30	f	w	BREM	San Francisco	6-Wd San Francisco	81	109
DONAKER								
Jacob	52	m	w	PRUS	Sierra	Table Rock Twp	89	574
DONAL								
Mc Chas	32	m	w	ENGL	Santa Clara	Gilroy Twp	88	98
Mc Chas	32	m	w	ENGL	Santa Clara	Gilroy Twp	88	98
DONALD								
Albert E	1	m	w	CA	San Francisco	San Francisco P O	83	3
C	40	m	w	IREL	Yuba	Marysville	93	588
D W	30	m	w	IREL	Alameda	Oakland	68	264
James	26	m	w	CANA	Plumas	Indian Twp	77	14
James	25	m	w	SCOT	San Francisco	1-Wd San Francisco	79	112
James	23	m	w	IREL	Sacramento	Georgianna Twp	77	128
Jno	43	m	w	SCOT	Santa Clara	Gilroy Twp	88	93
Jno	27	m	w	SCOT	Santa Clara	Gilroy Twp	88	95
John	60	m	w	ENGL	San Mateo	San Mateo P O	87	358
John	42	m	w	IREL	Los Angeles	Los Angeles Twp	73	477
Kate	26	f	w	ENGL	San Francisco	11-Wd San Francisc	84	688
Mary	42	f	w	MO	San Francisco	11-Wd San Francisc	84	674
Patrick	29	m	w	IREL	San Francisco	7-Wd San Francisco	81	233
Sarah	28	f	w	IREL	San Francisco	11-Wd San Francisc	84	676
Sarah J	38	f	w	CANA	San Francisco	8-Wd San Francisco	82	289
Thos	27	m	w	ENGL	Nevada	Nevada Twp	75	301
DONALDSON								
A B	46	m	w	VA	Lake	Lower Lake	73	418
A S	27	m	w	OH	Sutter	Butte Twp	92	100
Alex	77	m	w	VA	Alameda	Brooklyn Twp	68	53
Alex	38	m	w	OH	Sutter	Nicolaus Twp	92	113
Alex	33	m	w	SCOT	Sierra	Table Rock Twp	89	579
Alexander	26	m	w	IL	Colusa	Spring Valley Twp	71	345
Alfred	43	m	w	NY	Tulare	White Rvr Twp	92	301
Andrew	60	m	w	IREL	Alameda	Eden Twp	68	83
Charles	34	m	w	NY	San Francisco	11-Wd San Francisc	84	515
D S	54	m	w	PA	Napa	Napa	75	9
Dan	35	m	w	IREL	Santa Clara	Gilroy Twp	88	76
Daniel	40	m	w	SWED	Napa	Napa Twp	75	29
David	29	m	w	SCOT	Santa Clara	2-Wd San Jose	88	329
Jacob	35	m	w	OH	Solano	Vacaville Twp	90	133
James	38	m	w	SCOT	Klamath	Klamath Twp	73	371
James W	47	m	w	VA	Solano	Suisun Twp	90	114
Jas	29	m	w	IREL	San Francisco	1-Wd San Francisco	79	93
John	64	m	w	NY	Sonoma	Petaluma Twp	91	357
John	37	m	w	KY	Mendocino	Little Lake Twp	74	192
John	37	m	w	KY	Mendocino	Little Lake Twp	74	203
John	35	m	w	IREL	San Francisco	1-Wd San Francisco	79	66
Joshua	40	m	w	OH	Solano	Vacaville Twp	90	133
L H	17	m	w	OH	San Francisco	San Francisco P O	85	830
Oscar	43	m	w	NORW	Napa	Napa Twp	75	33
Philip	28	m	w	VT	Klamath	Camp Gaston	73	372
Robert	48	m	w	MA	Stanislaus	Branch Twp	92	4
S	41	m	w	PA	Yuba	Marysville	93	595
Stewart	23	m	w	ENGL	San Francisco	San Francisco P O	83	82
Wm	35	m	w	SCOT	San Francisco	1-Wd San Francisco	79	76
Wm	32	m	w	OH	Napa	Napa Twp	75	28
DONALLAN								
B C	47	m	w	OH	San Francisco	San Francisco P O	83	299
DONALLY								
James	27	m	w	NY	Alameda	Oakland	68	148
Lizzie	15	f	w	MA	Alameda	Oakland	68	139
Mary	19	f	w	NY	Sacramento	4-Wd Sacramento	77	322
DONALSON								
Gus	23	m	w	SWED	Alpine	Markleeville P O	69	312
John	18	m	w	WI	Colusa	Spring Valley Twp	71	344
Robt	39	m	w	MO	Shasta	Millville P O	89	485
Wm	36	m	w	CT	Sacramento	4-Wd Sacramento	77	349
DONALY								
Owen	40	m	w	IREL	Sonoma	Petaluma Twp	91	321

© 2001 by Heritage Quest. All rights reserved.

Name	Age	S	R	B-PL	County	Locale	Series M593 Roll	Pg
DONARI								
Bartolomew	55	m	w	ITAL	San Francisco	1-Wd San Francisco	79	36
DONARIO								
Mercedes	37	f	w	CHIL	San Francisco	San Francisco P O	83	98
DONASON								
Peter B	33	m	w	IREL	San Francisco	San Francisco P O	83	156
DONAVAN								
Charles	32	m	w	IREL	San Francisco	San Francisco P O	83	243
Cornelius	30	m	w	IREL	San Francisco	3-Wd San Francisco	79	315
D	45	m	w	IREL	Lake	Scotts Crk	73	428
Dan	8	m	w	CA	Alameda	Oakland	68	233
Daniel	50	m	w	IREL	Nevada	Grass Valley Twp	75	212
Frank	17	m	w	MO	Butte	Chico Twp	70	31
James	36	m	w	IREL	Monterey	Alisal Twp	74	292
Jerry	40	m	w	IREL	Nevada	Bridgeport Twp	75	120
John	44	m	w	IREL	Colusa	Colusa	71	292
John	40	m	w	IREL	Nevada	Grass Valley Twp	75	211
John	35	m	w	IREL	San Francisco	3-Wd San Francisco	79	316
Michael	42	m	w	IREL	El Dorado	Mud Springs Twp	72	84
Michel	32	m	w	IREL	Sutter	Yuba Twp	92	144
Patrick	45	m	w	IREL	Nevada	Grass Valley Twp	75	211
Thos	35	m	w	IREL	San Joaquin	Oneal Twp	86	104
DONAVIN								
Michael	30	m	w	CANA	San Francisco	San Francisco P O	83	144
DONBROKE								
S	66	f	w	GERM	Alameda	Oakland	68	191
DONBUCHER								
Joseph	22	m	w	ITAL	San Mateo	San Mateo P O	87	358
DONCASTER								
Saml	36	m	w	PA	El Dorado	Georgetown Twp	72	46
DONCHU								
Theodore	49	m	w	DC	Los Angeles	Los Angeles	73	526
DONCHUE								
John	25	m	w	CANA	San Mateo	Woodside P O	87	386
DONCKS								
B H	49	m	w	PRUS	San Francisco	San Francisco P O	85	809
DOND								
Ellen	35	f	w	IREL	Alameda	Eden Twp	68	80
DONDAR								
Nicholas	28	m	w	ITAL	Sonoma	Sonoma Twp	91	441
DONDARO								
Mary	68	f	w	ITAL	San Francisco	2-Wd San Francisco	79	165
DONDEE								
Maurice	47	m	w	FRAN	Plumas	Rich Bar Twp	77	45
DONDELL								
James	27	m	w	IREL	Napa	Napa	75	21
DONDERO								
Stefano	36	m	w	ITAL	San Francisco	11-Wd San Francisc	84	642
DONDIN								
Frederick	50	m	w	FRAN	Los Angeles	Los Angeles	73	509
DONDON								
Thomas	55	m	w	KY	San Francisco	11-Wd San Francisc	84	712
DONDORA								
F	28	m	w	ITAL	Calaveras	Copperopolis P O	70	232
DONE								
Ah	52	m	c	CHIN	El Dorado	Mud Springs Twp	72	76
Ah	32	m	c	CHIN	San Joaquin	1-Wd Stockton	86	149
Ah	30	m	c	CHIN	Placer	Auburn P O	76	367
Joseph H	42	m	w	NY	Stanislaus	Branch Twp	92	4
DONEANACHO								
Dolores	35	f	w	MEXI	Los Angeles	Los Angeles	73	516
DONECHAND								
John	47	m	w	FRAN	San Francisco	San Francisco P O	85	792
DONEGAN								
Daniel	30	m	w	IREL	San Francisco	11-Wd San Francisc	84	518
Eliza	25	f	w	IREL	Napa	Napa	75	18
J E	39	m	w	IREL	Sacramento	3-Wd Sacramento	77	271
Mary	36	f	w	IREL	San Francisco	6-Wd San Francisco	81	117
Patrick	37	m	w	IREL	San Francisco	6-Wd San Francisco	81	142
Patrick	30	m	w	CANA	Humboldt	Eureka Twp	72	267
Sarah	12	f	w	MO	Sonoma	Healdsburg & Mendo	91	279
DONEGAY								
Michl	27	m	w	IREL	San Francisco	1-Wd San Francisco	79	77
DONEGON								
Owen	48	m	w	IREL	Tuolumne	Columbia P O	93	344
DONEHEE								
James	25	m	w	LA	San Francisco	2-Wd San Francisco	79	214
DONEHOE								
Hannah	26	f	w	IREL	San Francisco	8-Wd San Francisco	82	331
Mary	38	f	w	IREL	San Francisco	8-Wd San Francisco	82	342
Mary	24	f	w	IREL	San Francisco	8-Wd San Francisco	82	365
DONEHOUGH								
P	32	m	w	IREL	Humboldt	Eureka Twp	72	268
DONEHUE								
Eugene	24	m	w	NY	San Mateo	Schoolhouse Statio	87	342
James	29	m	w	IREL	San Mateo	Schoolhouse Statio	87	342
Julius	23	f	w	IREL	Alameda	Oakland	68	133
Kate	30	f	w	IREL	Alameda	Oakland	68	227
Peter	47	m	w	SCOT	San Francisco	8-Wd San Francisco	82	299
Tenneis	40	m	w	IREL	San Francisco	11-Wd San Francisc	84	430
William	27	m	w	CANA	San Mateo	Woodside P O	87	386
DONEL								
Patrick	45	m	w	IREL	San Francisco	11-Wd San Francisc	84	492
DONELAN								
Chs	29	m	w	IREL	Santa Clara	Gilroy Twp	88	95
DONELECHA								
Mary	13	f	w	FRAN	Santa Barbara	Santa Barbara P O	87	502

Name	Age	S	R	B-PL	County	Locale	Series M593 Roll	Pg
DONELLE								
John	50	m	w	SWIT	San Francisco	2-Wd San Francisco	79	235
DONELLEY								
Michael	45	m	w	IREL	San Mateo	Half Moon Bay P O	87	390
DONELLY								
Bernard	38	m	w	IREL	San Francisco	1-Wd San Francisco	79	123
Danl	35	m	w	IREL	San Francisco	1-Wd San Francisco	79	69
David	34	m	w	IREL	San Francisco	1-Wd San Francisco	79	123
John	47	m	w	IREL	San Francisco	1-Wd San Francisco	79	123
John	24	m	w	AUSL	San Francisco	1-Wd San Francisco	79	96
Josh	25	m	w	NY	San Francisco	1-Wd San Francisco	79	69
Margaret	13	f	w	OH	Santa Clara	2-Wd San Jose	88	321
Mary	21	f	w	IREL	San Francisco	7-Wd San Francisco	81	287
T	45	m	w	IREL	Alameda	Oakland	68	133
DONELMAN								
Philip	34	m	w	FRAN	San Francisco	San Francisco P O	83	137
DONELSON								
Daniel	40	m	w	PRUS	San Francisco	San Francisco P O	80	462
David	39	m	w	SCOT	San Francisco	San Francisco P O	83	32
Edwin M	39	m	w	SC	Placer	Bath P O	76	448
DONELTON								
Frank	25	m	w	NICA	San Francisco	1-Wd San Francisco	79	124
DONELY								
Edward	18	m	w	MA	Alameda	Brooklyn	68	32
James	35	m	w	IREL	Los Angeles	Soledad Twp	73	631
DONER								
Leonard	20	m	w	PRUS	El Dorado	Coloma Twp	72	3
DONERLEY								
John	25	m	w	NJ	San Francisco	7-Wd San Francisco	81	188
DONET								
Andrew	44	m	w	FRAN	Amador	Jackson P O	69	336
DONEVAN								
Daniel	38	m	w	IREL	San Mateo	Woodside P O	87	386
Danl	33	m	w	IREL	Butte	Oregon Twp	70	126
Dave	27	m	w	IREL	Butte	Hamilton Twp	70	71
Dennis	30	m	w	IREL	San Mateo	San Mateo P O	87	357
Ellen	19	f	w	ME	Sacramento	2-Wd Sacramento	77	214
Hannah	13	f	w	NY	Sacramento	2-Wd Sacramento	77	231
Saml	30	m	w	IREL	Butte	Chico Twp	70	47
DONEY								
John	34	m	w	ENGL	Placer	Bath P O	76	437
Semantha	15	f	w	CA	Santa Clara	San Jose Twp	88	182
DONEYO								
Peter	41	m	w	ARGE	Sacramento	1-Wd Sacramento	77	176
DONFEE								
James	35	m	w	IREL	Los Angeles	El Monte Twp	73	456
DONG								
---	22	m	c	CHIN	Siskiyou	Yreka Twp	89	667
Ah	38	m	c	CHIN	San Francisco	6-Wd San Francisco	81	59
Ah	32	m	c	CHIN	San Francisco	6-Wd San Francisco	81	69
Ah	31	m	c	CHIN	Nevada	Eureka Twp	75	141
Ah	29	m	c	CHIN	San Francisco	6-Wd San Francisco	81	57
Ah	28	m	c	CHIN	Mendocino	Gualala Twp	74	223
Ah	27	m	c	CHIN	San Joaquin	1-Wd Stockton	86	142
Ah	12	m	c	CHIN	San Francisco	6-Wd San Francisco	81	119
Benjamin	19	m	b	CA	Sutter	Nicolaus Twp	92	115
Gong	20	m	c	CHIN	San Francisco	5-Wd San Francisco	81	1
DONGAN								
John	28	m	w	IREL	San Mateo	Menlo Park P O	87	378
DONGEL								
Samuel	22	m	w	LA	San Francisco	San Francisco P O	83	218
DONGERS								
Dedrick	20	m	w	PRUS	San Francisco	6-Wd San Francisco	81	97
DONGHUE								
James	23	m	w	IREL	Siskiyou	Surprise Valley Tw	89	642
DONGTOO								
Ah	18	m	c	CHIN	San Joaquin	Castoria Twp	86	13
DONHAN								
S	40	m	w	MA	San Joaquin	Douglas Twp	86	50
DONHOE								
Owen	40	m	w	IREL	Yuba	Slate Range Bar Tw	93	672
DONIGAN								
Barnett	34	m	w	IREL	Alameda	Washington Twp	68	291
Edward	26	m	w	IREL	San Francisco	San Francisco P O	83	385
Ellen	25	f	w	NY	San Francisco	8-Wd San Francisco	82	484
Thomas	32	m	w	IREL	San Francisco	San Francisco P O	83	279
DONIHOE								
James	39	m	w	IREL	San Francisco	8-Wd San Francisco	82	376
DONILLAN								
E E	16	f	w	CA	Alameda	Oakland	68	237
DONIM								
Bertoli	40	m	w	ITAL	Los Angeles	Los Angeles	73	504
DONIVAN								
---	58	m	w	WALE	San Joaquin	2-Wd Stockton	86	167
E	39	m	w	ME	Amador	Sutter Crk P O	69	400
J	42	m	w	IREL	Amador	Sutter Crk P O	69	402
John	39	m	w	IREL	Amador	Sutter Crk P O	69	402
Mary	32	f	w	IREL	San Francisco	8-Wd San Francisco	82	296
Mary	11	f	w	DC	San Francisco	8-Wd San Francisco	82	296
Timothy	40	m	w	IREL	San Mateo	Redwood Twp	87	362
DONKLIN								
Emely	16	f	w	NY	Alameda	Oakland	68	245
DONLAN								
Bridget	47	f	w	IREL	Sacramento	4-Wd Sacramento	77	328
Constantia	40	f	w	IREL	Santa Barbara	Santa Barbara P O	87	501
Edward	52	m	w	IREL	Santa Clara	2-Wd San Jose	88	283
Michael	35	m	w	IREL	San Francisco	San Francisco P O	83	203

© 2001 by Heritage Quest. All rights reserved.

Name	Age	S	R	B-PL	County	Locale (Series M593)	Roll	Pg
Peter	22	m	w	IREL	San Francisco	San Francisco P O	83	130
Thomas	42	m	w	IREL	San Francisco	8-Wd San Francisco	82	428
DONLEN								
James	30	m	w	IREL	San Francisco	San Francisco P O	83	308
DONLEVY								
Peter	34	m	w	IREL	Klamath	Sawyers Bar	73	377
DONLEY								
D M	38	m	w	IREL	Alameda	Oakland	68	262
Jno	31	m	w	IREL	Butte	Chico Twp	70	31
John	40	m	w	IREL	Del Norte	Mountain Twp	71	474
John	40	m	w	IREL	Sonoma	Petaluma Twp	91	339
Martin	26	m	w	IREL	Colusa	Colusa Twp	71	282
Mary A	30	f	w	IREL	Santa Clara	2-Wd San Jose	88	325
Mickey	30	m	w	IREL	Colusa	Colusa Twp	71	282
Peter	32	m	w	IREL	San Mateo	San Mateo P O	87	357
Rachael	40	f	w	IREL	San Francisco	8-Wd San Francisco	82	343
Simon	22	m	w	CANA	Humboldt	Bucksport Twp	72	243
Thomas	44	m	w	IREL	Colusa	Colusa Twp	71	287
William	49	m	w	IREL	Stanislaus	Branch Twp	92	4
DONLIN								
Michael	24	m	w	IREL	San Francisco	San Francisco P O	83	335
Michel	45	m	w	IREL	Napa	Napa Twp	75	69
DONLITY								
Patrick	25	m	w	NY	Alameda	Eden Twp	68	85
DONLON								
Bernard	26	m	w	IREL	San Francisco	1-Wd San Francisco	79	46
Bridget	45	f	w	IREL	Sacramento	4-Wd Sacramento	77	321
John	38	m	w	IREL	Alameda	Murray Twp	68	99
Joseph	34	m	w	IREL	San Francisco	San Francisco P O	83	336
DONLUN								
Thomas	32	m	w	IREL	San Francisco	11-Wd San Francisc	84	441
DONLY								
Lizzie	20	f	w	IREL	Alameda	Oakland	68	232
Maria	22	f	w	IREL	San Francisco	8-Wd San Francisco	82	327
Richard	37	m	w	ENGL	Alameda	Oakland	68	205
Thomas	37	m	w	IREL	Sonoma	Petaluma Twp	91	315
Wm	58	m	w	ME	Alameda	Oakland	68	256
DONNAHUE								
Henry	33	m	w	IREL	San Francisco	7-Wd San Francisco	81	162
Thomas	40	m	w	IREL	San Francisco	7-Wd San Francisco	81	221
Wm	27	m	w	IN	Marin	Point Reyes Twp	74	23
Wm	21	m	w	ME	Marin	San Rafael Twp	74	38
DONNALLAN								
John	41	m	w	IREL	Calaveras	San Andreas P O	70	174
DONNALLY								
Hugh	44	m	w	IREL	Calaveras	San Andreas P O	70	163
James	42	m	w	IREL	Nevada	Bloomfield Twp	75	98
Peter	45	m	w	IREL	Nevada	Bloomfield Twp	75	97
DONNALY								
P W	23	m	w	VT	Alameda	Oakland	68	214
DONNAN								
Wm	42	m	w	CANA	Solano	Benicia	90	18
DONNAT								
Peter	63	m	w	FRAN	San Francisco	2-Wd San Francisco	79	149
DONNAVAN								
Jerry	55	m	w	IREL	San Francisco	11-Wd San Francisc	84	613
John	23	m	w	IREL	Calaveras	San Andreas P O	70	162
Mary	33	f	w	IREL	San Francisco	San Francisco P O	83	199
DONNAY								
Micheal	38	m	w	IREL	San Francisco	7-Wd San Francisco	81	209
DONNE								
Richard	33	m	w	IREL	San Francisco	San Francisco P O	85	848
DONNEAU								
Thomas	56	m	w	SC	Marin	Tomales Twp	74	88
DONNEBERK								
Anna	23	f	w	PRUS	San Mateo	Redwood City P O	87	376
DONNEGAN								
C A	40	m	w	IREL	Tuolumne	Big Oak Flat P O	93	396
Chas	47	m	w	IREL	San Joaquin	Tulare Twp	86	261
Saml	35	m	w	TN	Humboldt	Arcata Twp	72	225
DONNEL								
Randolph	46	m	w	KY	Kern	Linns Valley P O	73	347
DONNELIN								
Frances	25	f	w	IREL	San Francisco	7-Wd San Francisco	81	256
DONNELL								
Henry	24	m	w	ME	Sonoma	Bodega Twp	91	254
Jim	24	m	w	MO	San Joaquin	Elliott Twp	86	75
John	50	m	w	IREL	Tuolumne	Chinese Camp P O	93	370
John	29	m	w	IREL	Santa Cruz	Santa Cruz Twp	89	394
M E	13	f	w	MA	Solano	Vallejo	90	186
Mary G	47	f	w	OH	Nevada	Nevada Twp	75	319
Michael	35	m	w	IREL	Yolo	Cache Crk Twp	93	421
R O	45	m	w	IREL	Tuolumne	Chinese Camp P O	93	372
William	36	m	w	IA	Solano	Denverton Twp	90	25
Wm M	41	m	w	ME	Calaveras	Copperopolis P O	70	256
DONNELLE								
Michael	34	m	w	IREL	Contra Costa	San Pablo Twp	71	357
DONNELLEY								
Daniel	31	m	w	IREL	Amador	Sutter Crk P O	69	407
John	40	m	w	CANA	San Francisco	San Francisco P O	83	328
DONNELLI								
David	37	m	w	VA	Marin	San Rafael Twp	74	36
DONNELLS								
St Sam	46	m	w	ME	San Diego	San Diego	78	489
DONNELLY								
A	35	m	w	IREL	Sacramento	1-Wd Sacramento	77	186
And J	38	m	w	IREL	San Francisco	6-Wd San Francisco	81	78
Andrew	55	m	w	IREL	San Francisco	San Francisco P O	83	306
Andrew	26	m	w	IREL	Marin	Sausalito Twp	74	74
Ann	36	f	w	IREL	San Francisco	San Francisco P O	80	467
Ann	35	f	w	IREL	San Francisco	San Francisco P O	83	113
Annie	37	f	w	IREL	San Francisco	11-Wd San Francisc	84	503
Annie	26	f	w	IREL	San Francisco	11-Wd San Francisc	84	430
Bernard	50	m	w	IREL	San Francisco	11-Wd San Francisc	84	573
Bernard	46	m	w	IREL	Alameda	Hayward	68	77
Bernard	31	m	w	IREL	San Francisco	11-Wd San Francisc	84	520
Brian	35	m	w	IREL	San Francisco	11-Wd San Francisc	84	436
Bridget	27	f	w	IREL	Yolo	Grafton Twp	93	480
Bridget	25	f	w	IREL	San Francisco	11-Wd San Francisc	84	512
Bridget	25	f	w	IREL	Alameda	Oakland	68	180
Catherine	60	f	w	IREL	San Francisco	8-Wd San Francisco	82	395
Catherine	38	f	w	IREL	San Francisco	8-Wd San Francisco	82	469
Chas B	29	m	w	CANA	Mono	Bridgeport P O	74	283
Delia	24	f	w	IREL	San Francisco	San Francisco P O	83	108
E W	31	m	w	ME	Nevada	Nevada Twp	75	283
Edward	43	m	w	IREL	San Francisco	2-Wd San Francisco	79	270
Edward T	24	m	w	IREL	Monterey	San Benito Twp	74	381
Effie	17	f	w	PA	Tehama	Merrill	92	197
Eliza	27	f	w	IREL	San Francisco	2-Wd San Francisco	79	282
Elizabeth	18	f	w	NY	Marin	San Rafael	74	54
George	35	m	w	IREL	San Mateo	Half Moon Bay P O	87	392
Hector	58	m	w	IREL	Amador	Jackson P O	69	324
Hugh	40	m	w	IREL	Sacramento	2-Wd Sacramento	77	220
J	50	m	w	IREL	Solano	Vallejo	90	164
James	40	m	w	IREL	San Francisco	San Francisco P O	80	424
James	40	m	w	IREL	Santa Clara	Gilroy Twp	88	103
James	35	m	w	IREL	Klamath	Trinidad Twp	73	390
James	25	m	w	IREL	San Francisco	5-Wd San Francisco	81	2
James H	28	m	w	NY	San Mateo	Half Moon Bay P O	87	401
Jane	32	f	w	IREL	San Francisco	San Francisco P O	83	110
Jas	41	m	w	IREL	San Francisco	7-Wd San Francisco	81	237
Jas E	40	m	w	PA	Solano	Vallejo	90	171
John	53	m	w	OH	San Francisco	5-Wd San Francisco	81	10
John	51	m	w	IREL	Sonoma	Petaluma Twp	91	322
John	40	m	w	IREL	San Francisco	8-Wd San Francisco	82	420
John	40	m	w	IREL	San Francisco	2-Wd San Francisco	79	285
John	40	m	w	IREL	Napa	Napa	75	47
John	38	m	w	IREL	Nevada	Nevada Twp	75	286
John	35	m	w	IREL	San Francisco	San Francisco P O	83	399
John	35	m	w	IREL	Monterey	Monterey Twp	74	346
John	33	m	w	NY	San Francisco	8-Wd San Francisco	82	436
John	30	m	w	IREL	San Francisco	San Francisco P O	83	120
John	30	m	w	IREL	San Francisco	San Francisco P O	80	369
John	29	m	w	IREL	Contra Costa	Martinez Twp	71	346
John	23	m	w	IREL	San Francisco	San Francisco P O	83	224
John F	27	m	w	IREL	Santa Clara	2-Wd San Jose	88	288
John Z	39	m	w	IREL	San Francisco	San Francisco P O	83	2
Joseph	30	m	w	IREL	Solano	Suisun Twp	90	115
Luke	45	m	w	IREL	San Francisco	San Francisco P O	85	861
Luke	35	m	w	IREL	San Francisco	San Francisco P O	85	753
Mark	31	m	w	IREL	Santa Cruz	Pajaro Twp	89	342
Martha	22	m	w	CANA	San Mateo	Redwood City P O	87	375
Martin	16	m	w	RI	Marin	Nicasio Twp	74	15
Mary	41	f	w	PA	Nevada	Grass Valley Twp	75	163
Mary	40	f	w	IREL	Tehama	Red Bluff	92	184
Mary	35	f	w	IREL	San Francisco	San Francisco P O	85	831
Mary	28	f	w	IREL	Napa	Napa	75	48
Mary	21	f	w	IREL	San Francisco	11-Wd San Francisc	84	649
Michael	39	m	w	IREL	San Francisco	San Francisco P O	83	382
Michael	38	m	w	NY	Placer	Bath P O	76	426
Michael	37	m	w	IREL	Placer	Lincoln P O	76	488
Michael	36	m	w	IREL	Marin	San Rafael Twp	74	39
Michl	27	m	w	IREL	San Francisco	1-Wd San Francisco	79	62
P	45	m	w	IREL	San Joaquin	Oneal Twp	86	115
Pat	40	m	w	IREL	Butte	Ophir Twp	70	118
Patrick	75	m	w	IREL	San Francisco	11-Wd San Francisc	84	436
Patrick	40	m	w	IREL	San Francisco	San Francisco P O	83	132
Patrick	35	m	w	IREL	San Francisco	San Francisco P O	85	831
Patrick	29	m	w	IREL	San Francisco	San Francisco P O	83	224
Patrick	25	m	w	IREL	San Francisco	San Francisco P O	83	192
Peter	24	m	w	IREL	Contra Costa	Martinez P O	71	399
Peter	21	m	w	IREL	Santa Clara	Gilroy Twp	88	103
Peter	12	m	w	CA	Santa Barbara	Santa Barbara P O	87	492
Robt	28	m	w	MA	San Francisco	San Francisco P O	85	785
Saml	40	m	w	IREL	Solano	Vallejo	90	141
Sarah	32	f	w	PA	Tehama	Red Bluff	92	184
Terence	44	m	w	IREL	Marin	Nicasio Twp	74	17
Terrance	24	m	w	IREL	Napa	Napa	75	48
Theresa	13	f	w	MA	San Francisco	San Francisco P O	83	348
Thomas	30	m	w	IREL	San Francisco	San Francisco P O	83	16
Thomas	30	m	w	IREL	San Francisco	11-Wd San Francisc	84	701
Thomas	29	m	w	IREL	Contra Costa	San Pablo Twp	71	360
Thos	50	m	w	IREL	San Francisco	1-Wd San Francisco	79	21
Thos	15	m	w	MA	Alameda	Oakland	68	177
Thos J	25	m	w	IREL	San Francisco	San Francisco P O	83	53
Walter	30	m	w	IREL	San Francisco	5-Wd San Francisco	81	28
William	30	m	w	IREL	San Francisco	8-Wd San Francisco	82	438
Wm	54	m	w	IREL	Tehama	Merrill	92	197
Wm	27	m	w	IREL	San Francisco	5-Wd San Francisco	81	27
Wm	22	m	w	NY	San Francisco	11-Wd San Francisc	84	663
DONNELS								
Thomas	51	m	w	PA	Santa Cruz	Santa Cruz	89	408
DONNELSON								
J D	31	m	w	NY	Solano	Vallejo	90	203

© 2001 by Heritage Quest. All rights reserved.

Name	Age	S	R	B-PL	County	Locale	Roll	Pg
						Series M593		
William	38	m	w	MO	Inyo	Cerro Gordo Twp	73	321
DONNELY								
J F	47	m	w	IREL	San Francisco	7-Wd San Francisco	81	181
James	33	m	w	IREL	San Francisco	7-Wd San Francisco	81	171
John	25	m	w	IREL	San Francisco	7-Wd San Francisco	81	218
Martin	35	m	w	IREL	San Francisco	7-Wd San Francisco	81	196
Mary A	30	f	w	MA	San Francisco	San Francisco P O	83	152
Mat	40	m	w	NY	Sacramento	3-Wd Sacramento	77	300
Pat	40	m	w	IREL	San Joaquin	2-Wd Stockton	86	192
Patrick	48	m	w	IREL	Mendocino	Anderson Twp	74	152
Polk	45	m	w	IREL	Solano	Silveyville Twp	90	78
DONNER								
E K	24	m	w	NJ	Sierra	Downieville Twp	89	518
Fredk	57	m	w	BADE	San Francisco	San Francisco P O	83	34
G H	38	m	w	WURT	Napa	Yountville Twp	75	85
George	33	m	w	IL	Santa Clara	Fremont Twp	88	62
H	46	m	w	PRUS	Calaveras	Copperopolis P O	70	224
James	12	m	w	CA	Yuba	North East Twp	93	643
Louisa	21	f	w	NY	San Francisco	3-Wd San Francisco	79	288
Thomas	31	m	w	IREL	San Francisco	8-Wd San Francisco	82	372
DONNERY								
Wm H	45	m	w	ENGL	Tuolumne	Chinese Camp P O	93	369
DONNES								
G B	45	m	w	FRAN	Shasta	American Ranch P O	89	496
DONNEVAN								
James	22	m	w	IREL	Butte	Oregon Twp	70	126
DONNEY								
Dennis	35	m	w	IREL	Solano	Suisun Twp	90	111
James	36	m	w	IREL	San Francisco	11-Wd San Francisc	84	470
John	40	m	w	IREL	San Francisco	7-Wd San Francisco	81	276
Joseph	11	m	w	CA	San Francisco	11-Wd San Francisc	84	587
Michael	21	m	w	IREL	Solano	Denverton Twp	90	27
DONNIE								
Henry	29	m	w	SCOT	San Francisco	San Francisco P O	83	122
William	33	m	w	VT	Marin	Point Reyes Twp	74	21
DONNIGBURG								
M	30	m	w	AUST	San Francisco	8-Wd San Francisco	82	358
DONNIN								
Geo	39	m	w	NY	Alameda	Oakland	68	192
DONNIVAN								
Dennis	30	m	w	IREL	Yolo	Cache Crk Twp	93	421
Dennis	30	m	w	IREL	Yolo	Cache Crk Twp	93	454
Eugene	24	m	w	MI	Yolo	Cache Crk Twp	93	440
Jerem	40	m	w	IREL	Alameda	Eden Twp	68	91
DONNNOVAN								
James	44	m	w	IREL	Marin	San Rafael Twp	74	59
DONNOHUE								
J H	27	m	w	IREL	Solano	Benicia	90	13
Jas	30	m	w	IREL	Solano	Vallejo	90	176
John	38	m	w	IREL	Alameda	Brooklyn Twp	68	51
John	30	m	w	IREL	San Francisco	7-Wd San Francisco	81	205
M	27	m	w	KY	Solano	Vallejo	90	204
Patrick	28	m	w	IREL	Alameda	Washington Twp	68	300
DONNOLEY								
Edward	26	m	w	ME	San Francisco	7-Wd San Francisco	81	168
John	27	m	w	MA	San Francisco	7-Wd San Francisco	81	186
DONNOLIN								
Thomas	29	m	w	IREL	San Francisco	7-Wd San Francisco	81	170
DONNOLLY								
Thomas	24	m	w	IREL	Kern	Havilah P O	73	350
DONNOLY								
Honora	35	f	w	IREL	San Francisco	San Francisco P O	83	118
DONNOR								
Patrick	32	m	w	IREL	Santa Clara	Gilroy Twp	88	83
DONNOVAN								
A	28	f	w	IREL	Yuba	Marysville	93	595
Bridget	44	f	w	IREL	San Francisco	San Francisco P O	83	164
Catherine	18	f	w	IREL	Marin	San Antonio Twp	74	61
Danl	51	m	w	IREL	Solano	Vallejo	90	146
Danl	26	m	w	IREL	Marin	Sausalito Twp	74	74
George	18	m	w	CANA	El Dorado	Mud Springs Twp	72	71
J B	30	m	w	IREL	Alameda	Oakland	68	212
John	30	m	w	IREL	San Francisco	7-Wd San Francisco	81	182
John	21	m	w	IREL	San Francisco	7-Wd San Francisco	81	180
John	21	m	w	IREL	Marin	San Antonio Twp	74	62
Margt	23	f	w	IREL	San Francisco	San Francisco P O	83	111
Mary	35	f	w	IREL	San Francisco	7-Wd San Francisco	81	171
Mary	35	f	w	IREL	San Francisco	7-Wd San Francisco	81	177
Michael	28	m	w	IREL	San Francisco	11-Wd San Francisc	84	541
Michael	23	m	w	IREL	Santa Cruz	Santa Cruz Twp	89	387
Michael	10	m	w	IREL	Marin	San Rafael Twp	74	29
Micheal	34	m	w	ENGL	San Francisco	7-Wd San Francisco	81	193
Patk	45	m	w	ENGL	Solano	Vallejo	90	154
Peter	23	m	w	IREL	San Francisco	San Francisco P O	83	172
W	35	m	w	IREL	San Francisco	San Francisco P O	85	864
DONNUTTI								
Joseph	32	m	w	SWIT	Marin	San Rafael Twp	74	32
DONNYBURGH								
Frank	41	m	w	GERM	Alameda	Washington Twp	68	289
DONODALL								
John	55	m	w	IREL	Sonoma	Sonoma Twp	91	431
DONOHOE								
Annie	23	f	w	IREL	San Francisco	San Francisco P O	80	408
Catharine	27	f	w	IREL	San Francisco	San Francisco P O	85	754
Daniel	26	m	w	IREL	Yolo	Cache Crk Twp	93	421
Denis	26	m	w	IREL	San Francisco	1-Wd San Francisco	79	94
Edwd	21	m	w	NY	San Francisco	1-Wd San Francisco	79	90
Ellen	18	f	w	IREL	Yolo	Cache Crk Twp	93	421
James	43	m	w	IREL	El Dorado	Kelsey Twp	72	58
James	30	m	w	IREL	San Francisco	5-Wd San Francisco	81	32
James E	39	m	w	IREL	San Francisco	1-Wd San Francisco	79	97
Jane	44	m	w	IREL	Santa Cruz	Santa Cruz	89	425
Johanna	60	f	w	IREL	San Francisco	1-Wd San Francisco	79	28
John	37	m	w	IREL	Merced	Snelling P O	74	269
John	33	m	w	MA	San Francisco	1-Wd San Francisco	79	47
John	28	m	w	CANA	San Francisco	1-Wd San Francisco	79	104
John	27	m	w	IREL	San Francisco	San Francisco P O	85	773
John	26	m	w	IREL	San Francisco	1-Wd San Francisco	79	71
John	23	m	w	IREL	San Francisco	San Francisco P O	85	773
John	21	m	w	IREL	San Francisco	San Francisco P O	80	473
Kate	22	f	w	IREL	San Francisco	8-Wd San Francisco	82	413
Martin	31	m	w	IREL	Yolo	Cache Crk Twp	93	449
Michl	26	m	w	NY	San Francisco	5-Wd San Francisco	81	33
Owen	42	m	w	IREL	San Francisco	San Francisco P O	85	861
P	35	m	w	IREL	San Francisco	San Francisco P O	85	820
Thos	30	m	w	IREL	Butte	Chico Twp	70	29
DONOHUE								
Anne	18	f	w	MA	San Francisco	8-Wd San Francisco	82	440
Bernard	35	m	w	IREL	San Francisco	11-Wd San Francisc	84	475
Catharine	28	f	w	IREL	San Francisco	7-Wd San Francisco	81	235
Catherine	15	f	w	NV	Santa Cruz	Santa Cruz	89	417
Cornelious	27	m	w	IREL	San Francisco	San Francisco P O	83	269
Cornelus	22	m	w	IREL	Mariposa	Mariposa P O	74	109
Dennis	36	m	w	IREL	San Francisco	7-Wd San Francisco	81	167
Edmund	38	m	w	NY	Sonoma	Analy Twp	91	225
Edward	40	m	w	IREL	San Francisco	8-Wd San Francisco	82	397
Edward	28	m	w	IREL	Santa Clara	1-Wd San Jose	88	225
Eliza	49	f	w	IREL	San Francisco	11-Wd San Francisc	84	427
Elizabeth	20	f	w	IREL	San Francisco	8-Wd San Francisco	82	446
Ellen	30	f	w	IREL	San Francisco	7-Wd San Francisco	81	270
Ellen	19	f	w	IREL	San Francisco	11-Wd San Francisc	84	448
Eugene	24	m	w	IREL	San Francisco	San Francisco P O	83	30
Francis	47	m	w	IREL	San Francisco	11-Wd San Francisc	84	641
Frank	28	m	w	IREL	San Francisco	San Francisco P O	83	349
Henry	19	m	w	NY	San Francisco	5-Wd San Francisco	81	7
Hugh	31	m	w	IREL	San Francisco	San Francisco P O	83	286
James	49	m	w	IREL	San Francisco	San Francisco P O	85	838
James	42	m	w	IREL	San Francisco	7-Wd San Francisco	81	195
James	41	m	w	IREL	San Francisco	San Francisco P O	83	314
James	34	m	w	IREL	San Francisco	San Francisco P O	83	317
James	28	m	w	IREL	San Francisco	3-Wd San Francisco	79	320
James	27	m	w	IREL	San Francisco	3-Wd San Francisco	79	316
Jeff	31	m	w	IL	Fresno	Millerton P O	72	181
Jeffrey	35	m	w	IREL	San Francisco	San Francisco P O	83	15
Jeremiah	40	m	w	IREL	San Francisco	8-Wd San Francisco	82	484
Jerry	38	m	w	IREL	San Francisco	1-Wd San Francisco	79	85
Jerry	35	m	w	IREL	San Francisco	11-Wd San Francisc	84	442
Jerry	28	m	w	IREL	Sacramento	1-Wd Sacramento	77	204
John	48	m	w	IREL	San Francisco	11-Wd San Francisc	84	478
John	39	m	w	IREL	Siskiyou	Yreka	89	661
John	38	m	w	IREL	San Francisco	11-Wd San Francisc	84	516
John	37	m	w	IREL	Santa Cruz	Pajaro Twp	89	347
John	35	m	w	IREL	San Francisco	7-Wd San Francisco	81	187
John	35	m	w	IREL	Santa Clara	Redwood Twp	88	118
John	27	m	w	IREL	Sacramento	4-Wd Sacramento	77	354
John	26	m	w	IREL	San Francisco	San Francisco P O	85	785
Joseph	43	m	w	NY	San Francisco	7-Wd San Francisco	81	287
Julia	19	f	w	IREL	San Francisco	San Francisco P O	83	259
Kate	35	f	w	IREL	San Francisco	8-Wd San Francisco	82	487
Kate	20	f	w	IREL	San Francisco	8-Wd San Francisco	82	421
Kate	16	f	w	NY	Monterey	San Juan Twp	74	416
Lissie	24	f	w	IREL	San Francisco	11-Wd San Francisc	84	541
Margaret	28	f	w	IREL	San Francisco	11-Wd San Francisc	84	537
Maria	24	f	w	NY	San Francisco	8-Wd San Francisco	82	384
Mary	22	f	w	IREL	San Francisco	San Francisco P O	80	462
Mary	14	f	w	NY	San Francisco	San Francisco P O	80	487
Michael	49	m	w	IREL	San Francisco	8-Wd San Francisco	82	399
Michael	40	m	w	IREL	San Francisco	San Francisco P O	83	329
Michael	37	m	w	IREL	San Francisco	San Francisco P O	85	819
Neal	25	m	w	IREL	Plumas	Goodwin Twp	77	7
P	36	m	w	IREL	Sacramento	1-Wd Sacramento	77	183
Pat K	45	m	w	IREL	San Francisco	San Francisco P O	83	27
Patrick	45	m	w	IREL	San Francisco	San Francisco P O	83	335
Patrick	40	m	w	IREL	Alameda	Washington Twp	68	293
Patrick	37	m	w	IREL	San Francisco	San Francisco P O	83	291
Patrick	36	m	w	IREL	San Francisco	11-Wd San Francisc	84	508
Patrick	35	m	w	IREL	Santa Clara	1-Wd San Jose	88	240
Patrick	33	m	w	IREL	San Luis Obispo	San Luis Obispo Tw	87	311
Peter	40	m	w	IREL	San Francisco	San Francisco P O	83	16
Peter Jas	12	m	w	NJ	San Francisco	7-Wd San Francisco	81	287
Robert	4	m	w	NY	San Francisco	8-Wd San Francisco	82	384
Roger	24	m	w	IREL	El Dorado	Georgetown Twp	72	37
Rose	25	f	w	IREL	San Francisco	8-Wd San Francisco	82	495
Thomas	34	m	w	IREL	San Francisco	San Francisco P O	83	185
Thos	26	m	w	PA	San Francisco	7-Wd San Francisco	81	242
Wm W	42	m	w	NC	El Dorado	Salmon Falls Twp	72	132
DONOLDSON								
W T	24	m	w	MD	Humboldt	Eel Rvr Twp	72	252
DONOLEY								
Henry	35	m	w	IREL	Sacramento	Granite Twp	77	148
Robert	28	m	w	IREL	San Francisco	7-Wd San Francisco	81	221
DONOLLY								
C	28	f	w	IREL	Alameda	Oakland	68	150
J S	38	m	w	CANA	Alameda	Oakland	68	158

© 2001 by Heritage Quest. All rights reserved.

Name	Age	S	R	B-PL	County	Locale	Series M593 Roll	Pg
Michael	32	m	w	IREL	Santa Clara	2-Wd San Jose	88	315
DONOMAN								
Christ	41	m	w	FRAN	Santa Clara	Almaden Twp	88	13
DONOTHAN								
J R	33	m	w	IREL	Alameda	Oakland	68	260
DONOUGH								
John	32	m	w	IL	Sacramento	2-Wd Sacramento	77	245
P	23	m	w	IREL	Alameda	Oakland	68	132
DONOUGHEN								
David	27	m	w	IREL	San Francisco	7-Wd San Francisco	81	182
DONOUGHUE								
M	30	m	w	IREL	Solano	Vallejo	90	192
Mary	33	f	w	IREL	San Francisco	7-Wd San Francisco	81	177
DONOVAN								
Ada	30	f	w	IREL	Alameda	Oakland	68	150
Albert	37	m	w	BAVA	San Francisco	San Francisco P O	83	211
Ann	60	f	w	IREL	San Francisco	8-Wd San Francisco	82	481
Ann	51	f	w	IREL	Yuba	Marysville	93	633
Ann	35	f	w	IREL	San Francisco	8-Wd San Francisco	82	436
Anne	40	f	w	IREL	San Francisco	San Francisco P O	83	329
Anne	36	f	w	IREL	San Francisco	1-Wd San Francisco	79	91
Annie	27	f	w	IREL	San Francisco	San Francisco P O	85	774
Bartholomew	36	m	w	IREL	San Francisco	11-Wd San Francisc	84	521
Bridget	30	f	w	IREL	San Francisco	San Francisco P O	80	411
Bridget	24	f	w	IREL	Santa Clara	Redwood Twp	88	127
Catherine	66	f	w	IREL	Santa Clara	San Jose Twp	88	195
Chas	31	m	w	MA	San Francisco	San Francisco P O	83	283
Chas	19	m	w	IN	Sacramento	1-Wd Sacramento	77	188
Con	22	m	w	IREL	San Francisco	San Francisco P O	83	318
Corneleus	36	m	w	IREL	Contra Costa	Martinez P O	71	419
Cornelius	30	m	w	IREL	San Francisco	8-Wd San Francisco	82	391
Damiel	32	m	w	IREL	San Francisco	2-Wd San Francisco	79	190
Dan	53	m	w	IREL	San Francisco	11-Wd San Francisc	84	667
Danial	28	m	w	IREL	San Francisco	7-Wd San Francisco	81	221
Daniel	40	m	w	IREL	Alameda	Oakland	68	142
Daniel	36	m	w	IREL	Monterey	Castroville Twp	74	325
Daniel	36	m	w	IREL	San Francisco	San Francisco P O	83	267
Daniel	33	m	w	IREL	San Francisco	San Francisco P O	85	814
Daniel	26	m	w	IREL	San Mateo	Schoolhouse Statio	87	342
Danl	30	m	w	IREL	San Francisco	1-Wd San Francisco	79	24
Danl	29	m	w	IREL	San Francisco	1-Wd San Francisco	79	103
Donald	42	m	w	IREL	San Mateo	Schoolhouse Statio	87	338
E S	29	m	w	IREL	Sacramento	1-Wd Sacramento	77	172
Edward	36	m	w	ME	Amador	Sutter Crk P O	69	398
Ellen	50	f	w	IREL	San Francisco	8-Wd San Francisco	82	462
Ellen	40	f	w	IREL	San Francisco	San Francisco P O	80	532
Ellen	38	f	w	CANA	Santa Clara	2-Wd San Jose	88	307
Ellen	27	f	w	IREL	San Francisco	8-Wd San Francisco	82	404
Ellen	22	f	w	IREL	San Francisco	San Francisco P O	80	390
Eugene	42	m	w	IREL	Monterey	San Juan Twp	74	396
Geo	40	m	w	IREL	Alameda	Oakland	68	233
Hannah	35	f	w	IREL	San Francisco	San Francisco P O	83	401
Hannah	15	f	w	CA	Monterey	Pajaro Twp	74	373
James	48	m	w	IREL	Yuba	New York Twp	93	642
James	45	m	w	NY	San Francisco	8-Wd San Francisco	82	482
James	40	m	w	MA	San Francisco	6-Wd San Francisco	81	144
James	39	m	w	IREL	San Francisco	San Francisco P O	83	303
James	30	m	w	NH	Solano	Rio Vista Twp	90	57
James	24	m	w	IREL	Santa Clara	2-Wd San Jose	88	318
James H	22	m	w	MA	San Francisco	San Francisco P O	83	142
Jeremiah	45	m	w	IREL	San Francisco	11-Wd San Francisc	84	461
Jeremiah	35	m	w	IREL	San Francisco	San Francisco P O	85	817
Jerry	60	m	w	IREL	San Francisco	7-Wd San Francisco	81	235
Jerry	35	m	w	IREL	San Francisco	1-Wd San Francisco	79	91
Jerry	25	m	w	IREL	San Francisco	1-Wd San Francisco	79	88
Jno	34	m	w	IREL	Sacramento	1-Wd Sacramento	77	187
Johana	35	f	w	IREL	San Francisco	San Francisco P O	80	460
Johanna	25	f	w	IREL	San Francisco	2-Wd San Francisco	79	194
Johanna	19	f	w	IREL	San Francisco	1-Wd San Francisco	79	105
John	74	m	w	IREL	San Francisco	8-Wd San Francisco	82	482
John	7	m	w	CA	San Francisco	San Francisco P O	83	142
John	49	m	w	IREL	Tehama	Cottonwood Twp	92	161
John	46	m	w	IREL	Yuba	Marysville	93	595
John	38	m	w	ENGL	San Francisco	San Francisco P O	83	215
John	37	m	w	IREL	San Francisco	San Francisco P O	80	472
John	35	m	w	IREL	San Francisco	7-Wd San Francisco	81	264
John	35	m	w	IREL	San Francisco	1-Wd San Francisco	79	134
John	32	m	w	IREL	San Francisco	San Francisco P O	83	357
John	31	m	w	ENGL	San Francisco	8-Wd San Francisco	82	482
John	31	m	w	IREL	San Francisco	1-Wd San Francisco	79	106
John	28	m	w	CT	Humboldt	Bucksport Twp	72	242
John	27	m	w	NY	San Francisco	7-Wd San Francisco	81	190
John	26	m	w	IREL	San Francisco	7-Wd San Francisco	81	218
John	26	m	w	MA	San Francisco	6-Wd San Francisco	81	80
John	25	m	w	IREL	San Francisco	1-Wd San Francisco	79	15
John	24	m	w	IREL	San Francisco	11-Wd San Francisc	84	532
John	23	m	w	IREL	Santa Clara	Santa Clara Twp	88	137
John	19	m	w	IREL	Santa Clara	Santa Clara Twp	88	176
John	15	m	w	CA	Alameda	Oakland	68	138
John	14	m	w	CA	San Francisco	11-Wd San Francisc	84	593
Joseph	37	m	w	IREL	San Francisco	San Francisco P O	85	852
Justis E	26	m	w	NY	San Francisco	1-Wd San Francisco	79	91
Kate	24	f	w	IREL	San Francisco	8-Wd San Francisco	82	299
Lizzie	36	f	w	IREL	San Francisco	San Francisco P O	80	488
M	40	m	w	IREL	Yuba	Marysville	93	589
Maggie	28	f	w	IREL	San Francisco	San Francisco P O	83	134
Margaret	40	f	w	IREL	San Francisco	8-Wd San Francisco	82	400
Margaret	20	f	w	IREL	San Francisco	7-Wd San Francisco	81	230
Margaret	18	f	w	IREL	San Francisco	2-Wd San Francisco	79	210
Margaret	13	f	w	NY	San Francisco	San Francisco P O	83	130
Margret	56	f	w	IREL	Tuolumne	Chinese Camp P O	93	372
Mari	22	f	w	IREL	Monterey	Salinas Twp	74	306
Maria	26	f	w	IREL	San Francisco	8-Wd San Francisco	82	419
Martin	36	m	w	IREL	San Francisco	11-Wd San Francisc	84	494
Mary	50	f	w	IREL	San Francisco	San Francisco P O	85	728
Mary	35	f	w	IREL	San Francisco	2-Wd San Francisco	79	284
Mary	35	f	w	IREL	San Francisco	6-Wd San Francisco	81	141
Mary	30	f	w	IREL	San Francisco	San Francisco P O	83	181
Mary	21	f	w	IREL	San Francisco	8-Wd San Francisco	82	338
Michael	50	m	w	IREL	Alameda	Eden Twp	68	89
Michael	46	m	w	IREL	San Francisco	San Francisco P O	85	802
Michael	45	m	w	IREL	San Francisco	11-Wd San Francisc	84	658
Michael	38	m	w	CANA	San Francisco	11-Wd San Francisc	84	636
Mike	40	m	w	IREL	Sacramento	1-Wd Sacramento	77	179
Mike	38	m	w	IREL	San Francisco	11-Wd San Francisc	84	531
Mike	24	m	w	IREL	San Francisco	11-Wd San Francisc	84	438
Mort	40	m	w	IREL	Mariposa	Mariposa P O	74	107
Nancy	53	f	w	IREL	San Francisco	San Francisco P O	83	68
P	40	m	w	IREL	Sacramento	1-Wd Sacramento	77	187
Pat	38	m	w	IREL	San Francisco	11-Wd San Francisc	84	438
Pat	28	m	w	CANA	Humboldt	Eureka Twp	72	271
Patrick	36	m	w	IREL	San Francisco	San Francisco P O	83	252
Patrick	30	m	w	IREL	Sonoma	Mendocino Twp	91	302
Paul	30	m	w	IREL	San Francisco	1-Wd San Francisco	79	71
R	46	f	w	IREL	San Francisco	San Francisco P O	85	859
Richard	60	m	w	IREL	Alameda	Eden Twp	68	89
Robert B	47	m	w	DE	Santa Clara	Santa Clara Twp	88	148
Rodger	35	m	w	IREL	San Francisco	11-Wd San Francisc	84	669
Russel	41	m	w	IL	Sacramento	4-Wd Sacramento	77	336
Thomas	40	m	w	IREL	San Diego	Julian Dist	78	471
Timothy	40	m	w	IREL	San Francisco	1-Wd San Francisco	79	80
Timothy	30	m	w	NY	San Francisco	2-Wd San Francisco	79	283
Timothy	30	m	w	MA	San Francisco	San Francisco P O	83	70
William	59	m	w	IREL	Santa Clara	2-Wd San Jose	88	291
William	36	m	w	NY	Stanislaus	Empire Twp	92	47
Wm	37	m	w	IREL	San Francisco	San Francisco P O	85	810
DONOVANT								
Elbert T	40	m	w	TN	Amador	Fiddletown P O	69	430
DONOVEN								
Wm	34	m	w	IREL	Sierra	Table Rock Twp	89	574
DONOVON								
John	60	m	w	IREL	Butte	Wyandotte Twp	70	149
DONRAY								
John	42	m	w	FRAN	San Francisco	San Francisco P O	80	456
DONSEY								
Caleb	45	m	w	MD	Tuolumne	Sonora P O	93	308
DONSHERTY								
Hannah	21	f	w	IREL	San Francisco	San Francisco P O	83	195
DONTRAY								
King	49	m	w	AZOR	San Francisco	1-Wd San Francisco	79	13
DONVAN								
Dennis	30	m	w	IREL	San Francisco	8-Wd San Francisco	82	423
DONWELL								
William	36	m	w	IREL	Solano	Denverton Twp	90	24
DONWORTH								
James Jr	23	m	w	ME	Sonoma	Bodega Twp	91	260
DONY								
Maggie	14	f	w	OR	Santa Clara	Santa Clara Twp	88	156
DONZEL								
Aimi	43	m	w	SWIT	San Francisco	2-Wd San Francisco	79	262
DONZIETTA								
Gabriel	34	m	w	ITAL	San Francisco	San Francisco P O	80	426
DOO								
Ah	25	m	c	CHIN	Amador	Fiddletown P O	69	437
Ah	22	m	c	CHIN	San Francisco	San Francisco P O	80	481
Ah	22	m	c	CHIN	San Francisco	6-Wd San Francisco	81	70
Ah	18	f	c	CHIN	San Francisco	6-Wd San Francisco	81	77
Ah	15	m	c	CHIN	San Francisco	San Francisco P O	83	58
Ah	12	m	c	CHIN	Shasta	American Ranch P O	89	497
Gee	32	m	c	CHIN	Plumas	Mineral Twp	77	24
Hong	24	m	c	CHIN	Yuba	Marysville	93	622
John	37	m	w	IREL	San Joaquin	3-Wd Stockton	86	231
Le	40	m	c	CHIN	San Joaquin	1-Wd Stockton	86	156
Le	31	m	c	CHIN	San Joaquin	1-Wd Stockton	86	156
Lee	29	m	c	CHIN	Yuba	Marysville	93	622
DOOD								
Robert	38	m	w	VA	Lassen	Long Valley Twp	73	437
DOODY								
Annie	28	f	w	IREL	Napa	Napa	75	50
Bridget	25	f	w	IREL	San Francisco	8-Wd San Francisco	82	471
Edward	27	m	w	MI	Plumas	Quartz Twp	77	34
Honora	25	f	w	IREL	San Francisco	1-Wd San Francisco	79	132
Jas	35	m	w	IREL	Sierra	Sears Twp	89	561
Josephine	17	f	w	NY	Sacramento	3-Wd Sacramento	77	306
Kate	20	f	w	IREL	Santa Clara	1-Wd San Jose	88	267
M	31	m	w	IREL	Alameda	Oakland	68	177
Mary	60	f	w	IREL	San Mateo	Schoolhouse Statio	87	333
Mathew	47	m	w	IREL	Sacramento	3-Wd Sacramento	77	271
Michael	35	m	w	IREL	San Francisco	11-Wd San Francisc	84	465
Peter	22	m	w	IREL	Alameda	Oakland	68	144
Thomas	27	m	w	IREL	San Francisco	11-Wd San Francisc	84	646
Thomas	25	m	w	CANA	Solano	Silveyville Twp	90	85
Thos	35	m	w	IREL	Alameda	Oakland	68	231

© 2001 by Heritage Quest. All rights reserved.

Name	Age	S	R	B-PL	County	Locale	Roll	Pg
						Series M593		
DOOGAN								
Daniel	28	m	w	IREL	San Francisco	1-Wd San Francisco	79	130
John	32	m	w	IREL	San Francisco	1-Wd San Francisco	79	126
DOOGEAT								
John	55	m	w	FRAN	Santa Cruz	Watsonville	89	367
DOOI								
An	12	m	c	CHIN	San Francisco	11-Wd San Francisc	84	448
DOOIN								
Michael	38	m	w	IREL	San Luis Obispo	Salinas Twp	87	292
DOOL								
Deliton	60	m	w	MD	San Joaquin	1-Wd Stockton	86	126
DOOLA								
Eva	2	f	w	CA	Lassen	Milford Twp	73	438
DOOLAN								
Daniel	24	m	w	IREL	Santa Clara	2-Wd San Jose	88	312
Dennis	38	m	w	IREL	Nevada	Rough & Ready Twp	75	327
Dennis	37	m	w	IREL	San Francisco	San Francisco P O	83	69
J C	34	m	w	OH	Siskiyou	Callahan P O	89	631
Jerry	41	m	w	IREL	San Francisco	San Francisco P O	83	311
Martin W	30	m	w	NJ	San Francisco	6-Wd San Francisco	81	89
Mary	22	f	w	IREL	San Francisco	2-Wd San Francisco	79	256
Mary A	33	f	w	NY	San Francisco	San Francisco P O	83	158
Micheal	40	m	w	IREL	San Francisco	7-Wd San Francisco	81	195
Morris	20	m	w	IREL	Colusa	Colusa Twp	71	278
Patrick	50	m	w	IREL	Colusa	Colusa Twp	71	278
Patrick	30	m	w	IREL	San Francisco	7-Wd San Francisco	81	202
Patrick	28	m	w	IREL	Nevada	Little York Twp	75	238
Patrick	27	m	w	IREL	San Francisco	11-Wd San Francisc	84	701
Sargent	40	m	w	ME	Siskiyou	Callahan P O	89	631
DOOLAY								
Patrick G	25	m	w	IREL	Sonoma	Salt Point	91	380
DOOLEN								
Thomas	72	m	w	IREL	San Francisco	7-Wd San Francisco	81	185
DOOLETTE								
John	22	m	w	PA	Tehama	Red Bluff	92	182
DOOLEY								
Cathrain	41	f	w	IREL	San Francisco	San Francisco P O	80	357
Clement	65	m	w	GA	Nevada	Little York Twp	75	243
Elijah	35	m	w	TN	Mendocino	Sanel Twp	74	230
Ephraim	40	m	w	KY	Placer	Bath P O	76	439
George W	28	m	w	IA	Santa Clara	Milpitas Twp	88	116
J E	25	m	w	IL	Nevada	Meadow Lake Twp	75	258
James	33	m	w	IREL	San Francisco	San Francisco P O	83	99
James L	26	m	w	IA	Stanislaus	Empire Twp	92	60
John	33	m	w	IREL	San Francisco	San Francisco P O	85	844
John	32	m	w	IREL	Amador	Ione City P O	69	357
John S	54	m	w	KY	Stanislaus	Empire Twp	92	60
Joseph	18	m	w	IA	Amador	Ione City P O	69	358
Julia	40	f	w	IL	Amador	Sutter Crk P O	69	411
Michael	14	m	w	CA	San Francisco	11-Wd San Francisc	84	591
Mike	18	m	w	IREL	Nevada	Eureka Twp	75	138
Nora	23	m	w	IREL	San Francisco	2-Wd San Francisco	79	205
Obid	35	m	w	MO	Kern	Linns Valley P O	73	346
Patrick	33	m	w	IREL	San Francisco	1-Wd San Francisco	79	69
William	56	m	w	IREL	San Francisco	San Francisco P O	83	244
William	32	m	w	IREL	San Francisco	San Francisco P O	83	175
DOOLIN								
Archibald	67	m	w	IREL	San Francisco	2-Wd San Francisco	79	213
James	29	m	w	IREL	San Francisco	San Francisco P O	83	406
John	28	m	w	IREL	Nevada	Eureka Twp	75	126
Morris	50	m	w	IREL	Nevada	Eureka Twp	75	126
Thomas	21	m	w	IREL	Nevada	Meadow Lake Twp	75	267
DOOLING								
Ellen	24	f	w	IREL	San Francisco	7-Wd San Francisco	81	171
Patrick	29	m	w	IREL	Nevada	Nevada Twp	75	277
Timothy	24	m	w	IREL	Santa Clara	Alviso Twp	88	27
DOOLINGER								
Geo	36	m	w	PRUS	El Dorado	Lake Valley Twp	72	65
DOOLITTE								
Andrew J	48	m	w	VT	Nevada	Washington Twp	75	340
DOOLITTLE								
Albert	46	m	w	NH	Del Norte	Happy Camp Twp	71	470
Alphonzo	40	m	w	NH	Del Norte	Happy Camp Twp	71	470
Forest	57	m	w	OH	Monterey	San Juan Twp	74	406
Geo W	38	m	w	NY	San Francisco	San Francisco P O	83	266
Henry	43	m	w	NH	Del Norte	Happy Camp Twp	71	472
Ira R	44	m	w	NH	Santa Clara	Gilroy Twp	88	83
L	35	f	w	NY	San Francisco	San Francisco P O	83	276
Louis	30	m	w	FRAN	San Francisco	1-Wd San Francisco	79	135
Nancy	37	f	w	NY	Santa Cruz	Santa Cruz	89	403
DOOLY								
Andrew	42	m	w	IREL	San Francisco	11-Wd San Francisc	84	508
Charles	50	m	w	VA	Sutter	Nicolaus Twp	92	107
Ellen	79	f	w	VA	Sutter	Nicolaus Twp	92	108
Emily	9	f	w	IA	Sutter	Nicolaus Twp	92	108
Greenville	43	m	w	VA	Sutter	Nicolaus Twp	92	107
J	34	m	w	CANA	Sierra	Sierra Twp	89	565
J Wm	55	m	w	VA	Sutter	Nicolaus Twp	92	108
Maria	46	f	w	MEXI	San Francisco	2-Wd San Francisco	79	182
Maria J	49	f	w	IREL	San Mateo	Menlo Park P O	87	377
Mary	50	f	w	IREL	San Mateo	Half Moon Bay P O	87	389
Michael	27	m	w	IREL	Santa Clara	1-Wd San Jose	88	277
Patrick	40	m	w	IREL	San Francisco	2-Wd San Francisco	79	262
Riel	35	m	w	CANA	Humboldt	Eureka Twp	72	279
Robert	34	m	w	VA	Lassen	Milford Twp	73	438
Thomas	40	m	w	IREL	Sutter	Yuba Twp	92	146

Name	Age	S	R	B-PL	County	Locale	Roll	Pg
						Series M593		
DOOMAS								
James	36	m	w	IN	Yuba	Linda Twp	93	554
DOOME								
Carson	42	m	w	HANO	Yuba	Linda Twp	93	555
DOOMOYN								
Wm	50	m	w	IREL	Alameda	Oakland	68	235
DOON								
Ah	28	m	c	CHIN	Klamath	South Fork Twp	73	382
Ah	22	m	c	CHIN	San Francisco	6-Wd San Francisco	81	55
Chas	19	m	w	ME	Butte	Chico Twp	70	50
Mike	29	m	w	VT	Butte	Kimshew Tpw	70	81
Nun	38	m	c	CHIN	San Francisco	3-Wd San Francisco	79	307
DOONAN								
John	30	m	w	IREL	Colusa	Spring Valley Twp	71	336
Lizzie	24	f	w	IREL	San Francisco	3-Wd San Francisco	79	322
DOONE								
Fanny	15	f	w	CA	San Francisco	11-Wd San Francisc	84	517
DOONOHOE								
Peter	21	m	w	IREL	San Francisco	1-Wd San Francisco	79	125
DOOR								
Theo	46	m	w	IREL	Butte	Kimshew Tpw	70	80
DOORE								
Peter	47	m	w	SHOL	San Francisco	2-Wd San Francisco	79	214
DOORMALEN								
John	26	m	w	HOLL	Santa Clara	1-Wd San Jose	88	229
DOOSE								
Frederick	41	m	w	SHOL	Nevada	Washington Twp	75	346
DOOTRILL								
Manual	32	m	w	AZOR	Yuba	Parks Bar Twp	93	649
DOOY								
---	24	m	c	CHIN	Shasta	American Ranch P O	89	496
DOPEZ								
Joseph D	19	m	w	MEXI	Colusa	Colusa	71	295
DOPKING								
Daniel	69	m	w	NY	Yolo	Cache Crk Twp	93	446
Ira E	24	m	w	CANA	Yolo	Cache Crk Twp	93	438
Joseph H	26	m	w	CANA	Yolo	Cache Crk Twp	93	446
Theodore F	42	f	w	NY	Yolo	Cache Crk Twp	93	446
DOPKINS								
Emma	19	f	w	IN	Yolo	Cache Crk Twp	93	444
DOPTE								
Louis	23	m	w	SWIT	San Mateo	Pescadero P O	87	413
DOR								
C	42	m	w	FRAN	San Francisco	San Francisco P O	85	855
John	40	m	w	PRUS	Sonoma	Salt Point	91	392
John	25	m	w	PRUS	Sonoma	Salt Point	91	392
DORA								
John	28	m	w	OH	Solano	Silveyville Twp	90	74
DORACINO								
Garcia	21	m	w	MEXI	Merced	Snelling P O	74	276
DORAHARTY								
Mary A	15	f	w	CA	Santa Clara	San Jose Twp	88	182
DORAINE								
Daniel	30	m	w	PRUS	San Francisco	San Francisco P O	80	338
DORAL								
Antonio	37	m	w	ITAL	Stanislaus	Branch Twp	92	8
DORAMA								
Pomacino	40	m	w	MEXI	Contra Costa	Martinez P O	71	385
DORAMI								
Hilario	35	m	w	MEXI	Santa Clara	Fremont Twp	88	48
DORAMIE								
Max	35	m	w	MEXI	Los Angeles	Wilmington Twp	73	641
DORAN								
Abram	40	m	w	ENGL	Contra Costa	Martinez Twp	71	352
Alexander	46	m	w	IREL	San Francisco	6-Wd San Francisco	81	105
Bridget	35	f	w	IREL	San Francisco	San Francisco P O	83	143
Chas A	27	m	w	IREL	San Francisco	San Francisco P O	83	16
Dan	23	m	w	CANA	San Joaquin	Douglas Twp	86	37
Delia	27	f	w	IREL	Sonoma	Bodega Twp	91	248
E C	49	m	w	PA	Solano	Vallejo	90	199
Edward	28	m	w	IREL	Mendocino	Navarro & Big Rvr	74	177
Ella	10	f	w	MA	San Francisco	8-Wd San Francisco	82	493
Ellen	40	f	w	IREL	Sacramento	1-Wd Sacramento	77	200
Frank	30	m	w	CANA	San Joaquin	Douglas Twp	86	37
Geo	43	m	w	ME	San Francisco	8-Wd San Francisco	82	315
J Thomas	58	m	w	IREL	San Francisco	San Francisco P O	83	178
James	45	m	w	IREL	San Francisco	San Francisco P O	80	415
James	37	m	w	IREL	San Francisco	San Francisco P O	83	45
Jas	38	m	w	IREL	Sacramento	1-Wd Sacramento	77	187
John	49	m	w	IREL	Nevada	Grass Valley Twp	75	211
John	40	m	w	IREL	San Francisco	11-Wd San Francisc	84	649
Joseph	40	m	w	IREL	Sacramento	2-Wd Sacramento	77	231
Julia	37	f	w	IREL	San Francisco	San Francisco P O	83	376
Mary	35	f	w	IREL	Sacramento	2-Wd Sacramento	77	234
Mary	33	f	w	IREL	San Francisco	San Francisco P O	83	151
Mary	24	f	w	ENGL	Marin	San Rafael	74	55
Max	37	m	w	BAVA	Sierra	Eureka Twp	89	524
Michael	30	m	w	IREL	San Francisco	3-Wd San Francisco	79	320
Mike	52	m	w	IREL	San Francisco	11-Wd San Francisc	84	612
Morris	30	m	w	IREL	Alameda	San Leandro	68	96
Nicholas	38	m	w	IREL	Santa Barbara	Las Cruces P O	87	515
Patrick	38	m	w	IREL	Mariposa	Mariposa P O	74	112
Peter W	35	m	w	VT	Butte	Kimshew Tpw	70	78
Phillip	37	m	w	MEXI	Santa Clara	Almaden Twp	88	9
Richard	34	m	w	IREL	Klamath	Sawyers Bar	73	377
Richard	32	m	w	PA	San Francisco	11-Wd San Francisc	84	618
Robert	34	m	w	IREL	Yuba	Rose Bar Twp	93	655

© 2001 by Heritage Quest. All rights reserved.

Series M593

Name	Age	S	R	B-PL	County	Locale	Roll	Pg
Robt	45	m	w	CANA	El Dorado	Kelsey Twp	72	59
Sarah J	43	f	w	OH	Butte	Oregon Twp	70	133
Tim	50	m	w	IREL	Solano	Vallejo	90	180
William	44	m	w	IREL	San Francisco	San Francisco P O	80	403
Wm M	44	m	w	TN	Sonoma	Bodega Twp	91	254
DORAS								
Francisco	55	m	w	PA	San Francisco	San Francisco P O	80	362
DORATO								
Don	30	m	w	MEXI	Yuba	Marysville	93	588
DORATY								
George	17	m	w	MA	Stanislaus	San Joaquin Twp	92	70
William	44	m	w	IREL	Stanislaus	Washington Twp	92	86
DORAY								
Masel	26	m	w	CANA	Nevada	Meadow Lake Twp	75	248
DORBERT								
Frederick	40	m	w	FRAN	Los Angeles	Los Angeles	73	529
DORBEY								
Samuel	29	m	w	MA	Stanislaus	San Joaquin Twp	92	83
DORBY								
George L	36	m	w	NH	El Dorado	Mud Springs Twp	72	78
DORCAN								
J	34	f	w	IREL	Alameda	Oakland	68	226
DORCEY								
Patrick	32	m	w	IREL	San Francisco	San Francisco P O	85	758
Tom	35	m	w	IREL	San Joaquin	Oneal Twp	86	114
DORCHER								
Hermann	41	m	w	HANO	San Francisco	San Francisco P O	83	192
Morris	37	m	w	BAVA	Santa Clara	San Jose Twp	88	215
DORCY								
James	34	m	w	CANA	San Joaquin	Union Twp	86	267
John	42	m	w	IREL	San Joaquin	Oneal Twp	86	111
John	26	m	w	IREL	San Joaquin	1-Wd Stockton	86	130
May	37	f	w	IREL	San Joaquin	Elliott Twp	86	81
DORDWICK								
D P	22	m	w	OH	Klamath	South Fork Twp	73	385
DORE								
Albert	35	m	w	PA	Butte	Ophir Twp	70	97
Anna M	32	f	w	ME	San Francisco	2-Wd San Francisco	79	284
Benjamin	44	m	w	ME	San Francisco	2-Wd San Francisco	79	189
C	26	m	w	IREL	Solano	Vallejo	90	216
Cornillas	30	m	w	IREL	San Luis Obispo	Salinas Twp	87	294
Honora	15	f	w	NY	San Francisco	8-Wd San Francisco	82	291
Mary	35	f	w	IREL	San Francisco	San Francisco P O	80	426
Maurice	42	m	w	IREL	San Francisco	8-Wd San Francisco	82	318
Olivar	34	m	w	CANA	Sierra	Sears Twp	89	556
Thos	24	m	w	MA	San Francisco	8-Wd San Francisco	82	371
DOREEN								
Patrick	25	m	w	IREL	Sacramento	Granite Twp	77	144
DOREM								
Antone	37	m	w	MEXI	Contra Costa	Martinez P O	71	367
DOREMAN								
Hans	38	m	w	NORW	San Francisco	7-Wd San Francisco	81	274
DOREME								
Jose	50	m	w	MEXI	San Luis Obispo	Arroyo Grande Twp	87	273
DOREMEN								
John J	43	m	w	NY	Placer	Dutch Flat P O	76	407
DOREN								
John	63	m	w	GERM	Los Angeles	Los Angeles	73	517
Patrick	38	m	w	IREL	Contra Costa	San Pablo Twp	71	355
Patrick	27	m	w	IREL	San Francisco	San Francisco P O	85	753
DORENTI								
N E	23	m	w	CA	San Francisco	San Francisco P O	85	839
DORER								
Leopold	39	m	w	BADE	Placer	Bath P O	76	454
Richard	42	m	w	BADE	Placer	Bath P O	76	454
DORES								
Antonie	41	f	w	MEXI	Calaveras	San Andreas P O	70	177
John	52	m	w	SCOT	Contra Costa	Martinez P O	71	427
DORESEY								
Elisabeth	15	f	w	CA	Trinity	Weaverville Pct	92	227
DORETHY								
Samuel	43	m	w	VA	Butte	Ophir Twp	70	113
DORETTO								
Jose	40	m	b	CHIL	Mariposa	Maxwell Crk P O	74	139
DORETY								
James	40	m	w	IREL	Santa Clara	Santa Clara Twp	88	172
Matthew	44	m	w	IREL	San Francisco	San Francisco P O	83	130
DOREY								
Ah	24	m	c	CHIN	Plumas	Quartz Twp	77	43
C L	35	m	w	CANA	Sierra	Sierra Twp	89	564
DORFE								
Michael	33	m	w	IREL	Tuolumne	Sonora P O	93	310
DORFLE								
Henry	42	m	w	HANO	Sacramento	1-Wd Sacramento	77	182
DORGAN								
Bridget	29	f	w	IREL	Santa Clara	1-Wd San Jose	88	251
Daniel	27	m	w	IREL	Santa Clara	Redwood Twp	88	128
John	30	m	w	IREL	Yolo	Grafton Twp	93	489
Patk	37	m	w	IREL	Marin	Tomales Twp	74	77
Thomas	49	m	w	IREL	San Francisco	San Francisco P O	83	239
William	40	m	w	IREL	San Francisco	7-Wd San Francisco	81	167
Wm	41	m	w	IREL	San Francisco	11-Wd San Francisc	84	427
Wm	35	m	w	IREL	San Francisco	San Francisco P O	85	747
DORGE								
Henery	43	m	w	SCOT	San Francisco	7-Wd San Francisco	81	184
William	16	m	w	CA	San Francisco	7-Wd San Francisco	81	184
DORGEN								
T	35	m	w	IREL	Alameda	Oakland	68	226
DORGER								
Mary	28	f	w	PRUS	San Francisco	San Francisco P O	83	375
DORHERTY								
James	31	m	w	IREL	San Mateo	Schoolhouse Statio	87	337
Mary	28	f	w	IREL	Alameda	Eden Twp	68	82
DORHETY								
James	13	m	w	IREL	San Francisco	San Francisco P O	85	828
DORHM								
John	55	m	w	IREL	Yolo	Grafton Twp	93	479
DORHMAN								
C	24	m	w	SHOL	San Joaquin	1-Wd Stockton	86	138
Heny	63	m	w	HANO	Contra Costa	San Pablo Twp	71	356
DORIAN								
John W	26	m	w	IREL	Amador	Volcano P O	69	388
Patrick	22	m	w	IREL	Amador	Volcano P O	69	388
DORIGA								
Feliz	26	m	w	MEXI	Fresno	Millerton P O	72	166
DORIMON								
Leonce	34	m	w	FRAN	San Francisco	11-Wd San Francisc	84	640
DORING								
F	36	m	w	PRUS	Yuba	Marysville	93	586
Lorenzo	48	m	w	SHOL	Tehama	Tehama Twp	92	196
DORIOT								
Adele	63	f	w	SWIT	San Francisco	San Francisco P O	80	421
DORIS								
Dasida	37	m	w	MEXI	Fresno	Millerton P O	72	157
DORITY								
P	31	m	w	IREL	Sierra	Butte Twp	89	509
R	60	m	w	MEXI	Alameda	Murray Twp	68	110
DORKHORN								
Fredk	26	m	w	PRUS	Santa Barbara	Santa Barbara P O	87	500
DORLAN								
Christa	65	f	w	CANA	Sacramento	4-Wd Sacramento	77	344
DORLAND								
Henry	30	m	w	CANA	San Francisco	11-Wd San Francisc	84	572
J J	42	m	w	CANA	Santa Clara	Gilroy Twp	88	73
James	36	m	w	CANA	San Francisco	11-Wd San Francisc	84	569
P S	50	m	w	CANA	Butte	Oroville Twp	70	140
Robt	28	m	w	CANA	San Francisco	11-Wd San Francisc	84	567
Thos	26	m	w	CANA	San Francisco	11-Wd San Francisc	84	566
William	39	m	w	IREL	Solano	Silveyville Twp	90	78
DORLETT								
L	33	m	w	CANA	Lake	Lower Lake	73	416
DORLING								
Chas	27	m	w	NY	San Francisco	San Francisco P O	83	295
DORMAN								
Austin E	38	m	w	PA	Contra Costa	Martinez P O	71	389
Chas	40	m	w	MA	Solano	Vallejo	90	209
Claus	40	m	w	HANO	San Francisco	11-Wd San Francisc	84	457
D C	39	m	w	NY	Mendocino	Round Valley Twp	74	216
Elizabeth	38	f	w	CANA	San Francisco	San Francisco P O	80	354
George	25	m	w	ME	Yuba	New York Twp	93	640
H G S	36	m	w	BADE	Alameda	Oakland	68	148
Henny	40	m	w	PRUS	San Francisco	San Francisco P O	80	338
Isaac N	46	m	w	OH	Sonoma	Mendocino Twp	91	299
Mary	60	f	w	IREL	San Francisco	San Francisco P O	83	28
Richerd	30	m	w	NY	San Francisco	11-Wd San Francisc	84	522
William	55	m	w	BRAN	San Francisco	11-Wd San Francisc	84	541
DORMAR								
Julia	62	f	w	IREL	San Francisco	San Francisco P O	83	174
DORMER								
James E	35	m	w	NY	Yuba	Slate Range Bar Tw	93	671
Thomas	35	m	w	IREL	San Francisco	San Francisco P O	80	478
DORMO								
Manuel	58	m	w	MEXI	Mariposa	Mariposa P O	74	99
DORMODY								
William	74	m	w	IREL	El Dorado	White Oak Twp	72	135
DORMURE								
Wm	40	m	w	CANA	Solano	Benicia	90	18
DORN								
Andrew	44	m	w	HDAR	Amador	Drytown P O	69	417
Geo W	33	m	w	OH	Alameda	Oakland	68	142
Jacob	48	m	w	HDAR	Mariposa	Mariposa P O	74	122
Louisa	16	f	w	CA	San Francisco	San Francisco P O	83	281
Myran	26	m	w	OH	Contra Costa	Martinez P O	71	407
Nicodemus A J	40	m	w	KY	Santa Cruz	Pajaro Twp	89	350
Rosea	16	f	w	MN	Alameda	Eden Twp	68	89
Samuel W	23	m	w	NY	Stanislaus	Branch Twp	92	1
DORNALECH								
Juan	56	m	w	SPAI	Santa Barbara	Santa Barbara P O	87	452
DORNAN								
Andrew	32	m	w	CANA	Contra Costa	Martinez P O	71	394
George	27	m	w	PRUS	San Francisco	San Francisco P O	80	536
Robert	38	m	w	PA	Tuolumne	Columbia P O	93	347
DORNBURK								
E	20	m	w	ENGL	San Joaquin	1-Wd Stockton	86	138
DORNE								
Lizzie	15	f	w	CA	San Francisco	8-Wd San Francisco	82	387
DORNER								
Henry	45	m	w	HANO	San Francisco	11-Wd San Francisc	84	505
DORNEY								
Patrick S	27	m	w	IREL	Yolo	Buckeye Twp	93	416
DORNICK								
Peter	24	m	w	FRAN	San Francisco	11-Wd San Francisc	84	710

© 2001 by Heritage Quest. All rights reserved.

Name	Age	S	R	B-PL	County	Locale (Series M593)	Roll	Pg
DORNIN								
Samuel	17	m	w	IN	Santa Barbara	San Buenaventura P	87	440
Wm H	38	m	w	NY	San Francisco	San Francisco P O	83	111
DORNON								
William	38	m	w	ENGL	Alameda	San Leandro	68	94
DORNOR								
P	28	m	w	CANA	Sierra	Butte Twp	89	508
DOROCHERS								
Charles	45	m	w	FRAN	Alameda	Oakland	68	200
DOROHAN								
Jas	28	m	w	ME	Alameda	Oakland	68	262
DOROTHY								
Ann	39	f	w	IREL	San Francisco	San Francisco P O	83	189
Jacob	43	m	w	PA	Sacramento	2-Wd Sacramento	77	231
Joseph	25	m	w	MA	San Francisco	San Francisco P O	83	198
Michael	50	m	w	IREL	San Francisco	San Francisco P O	83	120
DOROUGH								
Daniel	31	m	w	IREL	Yuba	Long Bar Twp	93	565
DOROUGHTY								
James	20	m	w	IREL	Yolo	Cache Crk Twp	93	431
DORPOWFSKY								
Wm	43	m	w	PRUS	San Francisco	1-Wd San Francisco	79	106
DORR								
Arthur W	42	m	w	ME	El Dorado	Lake Valley Twp	72	64
Arthur W	40	m	w	ME	El Dorado	Lake Valley Twp	72	66
E W	38	m	w	MD	San Francisco	San Francisco P O	83	28
Edward	31	m	w	ME	Alameda	Alvarado	68	302
Edward	25	m	w	HANO	San Francisco	7-Wd San Francisco	81	218
Edwin	45	m	w	FRAN	San Francisco	San Francisco P O	80	538
Eliza A	47	f	w	KY	San Francisco	San Francisco P O	83	65
George	29	m	w	WURT	Santa Clara	Gilroy Twp	88	80
Henry	44	m	w	PRUS	Shasta	French Gulch P O	89	468
Henry	38	m	w	HDAR	Placer	Bath P O	76	420
J B	45	m	w	VT	San Francisco	8-Wd San Francisco	82	369
James	40	m	w	PRUS	Alameda	Oakland	68	247
James C	23	m	w	MA	San Francisco	San Francisco P O	83	36
John	55	m	w	HANO	Nevada	Rough & Ready Twp	75	331
Martin	14	m	w	IREL	San Francisco	11-Wd San Francisc	84	592
Mathias	40	m	w	PRUS	Napa	Napa	75	41
Michael	26	m	w	IREL	San Mateo	Redwood City P O	87	375
Michael	25	m	w	IREL	Santa Clara	Santa Clara Twp	88	154
Ralph	30	m	w	KY	San Francisco	8-Wd San Francisco	82	459
William	49	m	w	NY	Amador	Volcano P O	69	373
William	26	m	w	IA	Solano	Silveyville Twp	90	79
DORRA								
Antoine	18	m	w	FRAN	San Francisco	San Francisco P O	85	831
DORRAIN								
Morris	25	m	w	IREL	Marin	Tomales Twp	74	88
DORRANCE								
Benton	46	m	w	VT	Tuolumne	Big Oak Flat P O	93	402
H T	30	m	w	VT	San Joaquin	2-Wd Stockton	86	160
Wm	30	m	w	SCOT	San Francisco	11-Wd San Francisc	84	432
Wm F	38	m	w	CT	San Francisco	3-Wd San Francisco	79	320
DORREICH								
M H	49	m	w	PA	Butte	Ophir Twp	70	95
DORREL								
Jno	46	m	w	PA	Butte	Concow Twp	70	7
DORRELL								
George	35	m	w	IL	Mendocino	Round Valley Twp	74	216
John	28	m	w	PRUS	San Francisco	San Francisco P O	80	343
DORRENTES								
Joseph	32	m	w	CANA	San Francisco	San Francisco P O	80	345
DORRETY								
Ellen	30	f	w	IREL	San Francisco	San Francisco P O	83	115
DORRICK								
Lizzie	23	f	w	PA	San Francisco	8-Wd San Francisco	82	335
DORRIDAN								
Maggie	20	f	w	IREL	San Francisco	8-Wd San Francisco	82	294
DORRILL								
J G	26	m	w	IREL	San Francisco	San Francisco P O	83	130
DORRIS								
C G	38	m	w	IL	Solano	Benicia	90	20
Carlos J	44	m	w	TN	Siskiyou	Table Rock Twp	89	646
Columbus	32	m	w	IL	Solano	Benicia	90	20
Corrie	29	m	w	IREL	San Francisco	5-Wd San Francisco	81	20
Elizabeth	18	f	w	NY	San Francisco	8-Wd San Francisco	82	403
Henry	26	m	w	MA	San Francisco	8-Wd San Francisco	82	381
Jonah	73	m	w	TN	Solano	Benicia	90	20
Lucy	73	f	w	VA	Solano	Benicia	90	20
Preston A	46	m	w	TN	Siskiyou	Table Rock Twp	89	646
Watson	20	m	b	AR	Los Angeles	San Jose Twp	73	621
DORRLARD								
Mary	19	f	w	MA	Sacramento	3-Wd Sacramento	77	291
DORSAN								
J	28	m	w	ENGL	San Francisco	8-Wd San Francisco	82	367
James	19	m	w	NY	Colusa	Spring Valley Twp	71	344
DORSAY								
Ferdinand	10	m	w	NV	San Francisco	11-Wd San Francisc	84	593
DORSCH								
Christ F	28	m	w	WURT	Sonoma	Sonoma Twp	91	447
Sophia	19	f	w	PRUS	Santa Cruz	Santa Cruz	89	424
DORSCHER								
Geo H	34	m	w	PRUS	San Francisco	San Francisco P O	83	67
Kate	27	f	w	BAVA	San Francisco	8-Wd San Francisco	82	402
DORSEY								
A	18	m	w	IN	Santa Clara	Gilroy Twp	88	82
A D	1	m	w	IL	Humboldt	Arcata Twp	72	225
Alex	41	m	w	IREL	Sierra	Table Rock Twp	89	579
B J	38	m	w	FL	San Francisco	8-Wd San Francisco	82	377
Benjamin	20	m	w	CA	Sutter	Nicolaus Twp	92	115
C	16	m	w	CA	Solano	Benicia	90	21
Caleb	32	m	w	MD	Stanislaus	Emory Twp	92	16
Carry	3	f	w	OR	Amador	Ione City P O	69	356
Cornelius	35	m	w	IREL	San Francisco	11-Wd San Francisc	84	479
Danl	12	m	w	CA	Humboldt	Pacific Twp	72	299
Delia	35	f	w	IREL	San Francisco	8-Wd San Francisco	82	409
George	35	m	w	MA	San Francisco	San Francisco P O	83	329
George	20	m	w	NY	Tuolumne	Chinese Camp P O	93	371
Gustavus Y	56	m	w	IN	Nevada	Grass Valley Twp	75	186
Henry	40	m	b	DC	Nevada	Nevada Twp	75	290
Jane	32	f	m	JAMA	Sacramento	2-Wd Sacramento	77	218
John	33	m	w	IREL	Napa	Yountville Twp	75	79
John	30	m	w	ENGL	San Francisco	San Francisco P O	83	185
John J	45	m	w	IN	Nevada	Grass Valley Twp	75	186
John W	40	m	w	MD	Stanislaus	Emory Twp	92	16
Kate	25	f	w	IREL	San Francisco	1-Wd San Francisco	79	18
Kate	24	f	w	IREL	San Francisco	11-Wd San Francisc	84	504
Kevren	12	m	w	CA	Los Angeles	San Gabriel Twp	73	597
L P	21	m	w	AR	Nevada	Nevada Twp	75	279
Lloyd	59	m	b	MD	Napa	Napa Twp	75	28
Mary	30	f	w	IREL	San Francisco	2-Wd San Francisco	79	193
Mary	30	f	w	IREL	San Francisco	San Francisco P O	83	407
Mary	29	f	w	IREL	Santa Clara	1-Wd San Jose	88	269
Mary A	16	f	w	LA	Napa	Napa	75	21
Mary P	70	f	w	KY	Amador	Ione City P O	69	352
Mat	40	m	w	IREL	San Joaquin	Tulare Twp	86	254
Mathew	27	m	w	ENGL	San Francisco	San Francisco P O	83	115
Michael	29	m	w	IREL	San Francisco	San Francisco P O	85	746
Michael	27	m	w	IREL	San Francisco	San Francisco P O	83	312
Mike	37	m	w	IREL	San Joaquin	3-Wd Stockton	86	231
Pat	30	m	w	IREL	Sierra	Gibson Twp	89	543
Patrick	63	m	w	IREL	Amador	Jackson P O	69	345
Patrick	40	m	w	IREL	San Francisco	11-Wd San Francisc	84	520
Patrick	33	m	w	IREL	Santa Cruz	Santa Cruz	89	428
Patrick	27	m	w	IREL	San Francisco	7-Wd San Francisco	81	167
Richard	30	m	w	MD	Kern	Linns Valley P O	73	345
Samuel P	42	m	w	LA	Nevada	Grass Valley Twp	75	149
Susan	25	f	w	IREL	Sacramento	3-Wd Sacramento	77	265
T	61	m	w	IREL	Lassen	Janesville Twp	73	431
Thomas	32	m	w	IREL	Nevada	Grass Valley Twp	75	224
DORSON								
Chs	20	m	w	TN	Merced	Snelling P O	74	261
John	26	m	w	IREL	San Francisco	11-Wd San Francisc	84	610
DORSOR								
Charles N	39	m	w	IN	Placer	Rocklin Twp	76	463
DORSY								
P M	30	m	w	IREL	San Joaquin	Tulare Twp	86	254
DORT								
Henry	26	m	w	NY	San Joaquin	Elkhorn Twp	86	57
DORTHY								
Thomas	50	m	w	IREL	Yolo	Buckeye Twp	93	411
DORTUA								
Jose	30	m	w	CA	Stanislaus	Buena Vista Twp	92	12
DORVA								
Manwell	35	m	w	PORT	San Mateo	Half Moon Bay P O	87	393
DORWIN								
Jos	28	m	w	PORT	Butte	Ophir Twp	70	117
Lizzie	28	f	w	IREL	San Francisco	8-Wd San Francisco	82	335
DORY								
John	26	m	w	CANA	Plumas	Goodwin Twp	77	7
Philip	34	m	w	CANA	Sierra	Sears Twp	89	558
DORZIE								
Bridget	36	f	w	IREL	San Francisco	11-Wd San Francisc	84	492
DOSANTOS								
Domingos	35	m	w	PORT	San Francisco	3-Wd San Francisco	79	288
DOSCHER								
Benjn	21	m	w	HANO	San Francisco	San Francisco P O	83	87
Charles	35	m	w	HANO	Sacramento	2-Wd Sacramento	77	230
Chas Hy	33	m	w	HANO	San Francisco	San Francisco P O	83	14
Henry	35	m	w	PRUS	Marin	San Rafael Twp	74	32
Henry	29	m	w	PRUS	San Francisco	8-Wd San Francisco	82	323
John D	36	m	w	HANO	San Francisco	1-Wd San Francisco	79	103
DOSE								
Christian	26	m	w	PRUS	San Francisco	2-Wd San Francisco	79	186
J	38	m	b	MEXI	Alameda	Murray Twp	68	107
Seth B	5	m	w	CA	Monterey	Castroville Twp	74	335
Wm	25	m	w	PRUS	San Francisco	San Francisco P O	85	871
DOSETTA								
Joseph	36	m	w	ITAL	Los Angeles	Los Angeles	73	522
DOSEY								
Henry	69	m	w	ENGL	Santa Cruz	Santa Cruz	89	421
DOSH								
Charles	43	m	w	FRNK	Amador	Ione City P O	69	351
Edward	37	m	w	HCAS	Sacramento	4-Wd Sacramento	77	371
Peter	37	m	w	MD	Shasta	Shasta P O	89	455
DOSHE								
E Miss	20	f	w	BREM	San Francisco	8-Wd San Francisco	82	300
DOSHER								
Annie	20	f	w	PRUS	San Francisco	San Francisco P O	80	422
Fredk	20	m	w	HANO	San Francisco	San Francisco P O	83	191
Henry	29	m	w	HANO	San Francisco	11-Wd San Francisc	84	428
John	43	m	w	HANO	San Francisco	7-Wd San Francisco	81	208
John	42	m	w	HANO	Klamath	Klamath Twp	73	370

© 2001 by Heritage Quest. All rights reserved.

Name	Age	S	R	B-PL	County	Locale	Series M593 Roll	Pg
DOSHIER								
John	36	m	w	TN	Kern	Tehachapi P O	73	353
Robert C	33	m	w	IL	Mariposa	Mariposa P O	74	124
DOSIER								
George	29	m	w	IL	Monterey	San Antonio Twp	74	320
George	26	m	w	TX	Santa Barbara	San Buenaventura P	87	419
John	31	m	w	KY	Monterey	Castroville Twp	74	336
DOSS								
Charles	60	m	w	PRUS	Nevada	Grass Valley Twp	75	225
Edward	40	m	w	KY	Los Angeles	Los Angeles	73	502
Edward W	40	m	w	KY	Los Angeles	Los Angeles Twp	73	476
G W	37	m	w	IN	Monterey	Castroville Twp	74	334
Hugh F	32	m	w	AR	Fresno	Millerton P O	72	182
Joel W	36	m	w	IN	Sonoma	Petaluma Twp	91	354
John F	41	m	w	IN	Amador	Fiddletown P O	69	427
John R	32	m	w	IL	Sonoma	Petaluma Twp	91	351
S W	44	m	w	MS	Calaveras	Copperopolis P O	70	226
DOSSANO								
Margaret	41	f	w	FRAN	San Joaquin	2-Wd Stockton	86	169
DOSSE								
Louis	30	m	w	PRUS	Santa Clara	2-Wd San Jose	88	329
DOST								
Jacob D	35	m	w	IL	Santa Clara	San Jose Twp	88	208
DOSWELL								
C E A	17	m	w	CA	Alameda	Oakland	68	159
DOT								
Ah	40	m	c	CHIN	San Francisco	San Francisco P O	80	495
Ah	37	m	c	CHIN	Butte	Kimshew Tpw	70	86
Ah	36	m	c	CHIN	Placer	Auburn P O	76	361
Ah	30	m	c	CHIN	San Francisco	San Francisco P O	85	748
Ah	29	m	c	CHIN	Butte	Hamilton Twp	70	74
Ah	21	f	c	CHIN	San Francisco	San Francisco P O	80	496
Gee	41	m	c	CHIN	Butte	Concow Twp	70	11
Gee	36	m	c	CHIN	Butte	Hamilton Twp	70	74
DOTA								
Samuel	47	m	w	IN	Placer	Summit P O	76	496
DOTE								
Ah	27	m	c	CHIN	Butte	Hamilton Twp	70	72
DOTEN								
John F	41	m	w	ME	Siskiyou	Yreka	89	657
DOTEY								
Daniel	61	m	w	NY	Tehama	Red Bluff	92	180
Geo W	37	m	w	NY	Tehama	Red Bluff	92	180
DOTRA								
Joseph	19	m	w	PORT	Alameda	Washington Twp	68	288
DOTT								
Annie	34	f	w	SCOT	San Francisco	San Francisco P O	85	810
DOTTA								
Antoine	32	m	w	SWIT	Plumas	Seneca Twp	77	49
Charles	26	m	w	SWIT	Plumas	Seneca Twp	77	49
Florain	33	m	w	SWIT	Plumas	Seneca Twp	77	47
Francis	24	m	w	SWIT	Plumas	Indian Twp	77	19
James	38	m	w	FRAN	Amador	Jackson P O	69	338
DOTTO								
Genoeffa	76	f	w	SWIT	Amador	Jackson P O	69	336
Martin	46	m	w	SWIT	Amador	Jackson P O	69	336
DOTY								
A J	32	m	w	IL	Lake	Upper Lake	73	409
Abel	39	m	w	NY	Los Angeles	Los Nietos Twp	73	574
Albert	61	m	w	NY	Santa Barbara	Santa Barbara P O	87	485
Albert	31	m	w	VT	Sonoma	Vallejo Twp	91	460
B F	37	m	w	IN	Sacramento	Franklin Twp	77	112
Clark	69	m	w	NY	Los Angeles	Santa Ana Twp	73	605
Dennis	26	m	w	NY	Sutter	Sutter Twp	92	122
Edward	50	m	w	NY	Santa Clara	San Jose Twp	88	188
Edward	20	m	w	PA	Napa	Napa Twp	75	32
Edward	20	m	w	OH	Contra Costa	Martinez P O	71	415
Elizabeth	56	f	w	NY	Mendocino	Ukiah Twp	74	233
Fawn	35	m	w	MO	Santa Clara	1-Wd San Jose	88	232
Gillis	34	m	w	PA	Sacramento	San Joaquin Twp	77	406
H	45	m	w	NY	Santa Clara	Gilroy Twp	88	88
Henry	27	m	w	NY	Marin	San Rafael Twp	74	45
Hiram W	37	m	w	NY	Klamath	Liberty Twp	73	376
I I	38	m	w	NY	Amador	Drytown P O	69	422
J	37	m	w	MO	Lake	Upper Lake	73	412
Jacob	33	m	w	NY	Sutter	Butte Twp	92	92
James	51	m	w	VA	Tulare	Kings Rvr Twp	92	253
James	19	m	w	IL	Sonoma	Bodega Twp	91	262
James R	56	m	w	MA	San Francisco	San Francisco P O	83	376
John	56	m	w	OH	Santa Cruz	Santa Cruz Twp	89	394
John	24	m	w	IL	Sonoma	Bodega Twp	91	261
John J	30	m	w	ENGL	San Francisco	5-Wd San Francisco	81	18
Lewis	38	m	w	NY	Colusa	Spring Valley Twp	71	335
Martin	51	m	w	NY	Monterey	San Juan Twp	74	404
Nimrod	38	m	w	NY	San Francisco	1-Wd San Francisco	79	107
William	42	m	w	NY	Sutter	Butte Twp	92	92
William R	53	m	w	NY	Sonoma	Sonoma Twp	91	435
DOU								
Ah	17	m	c	CHIN	Solano	Benicia	90	2
Joseph	37	m	w	FRAN	Mariposa	Mariposa P O	74	117
DOUB								
Valentine	38	m	w	MD	Marin	San Rafael	74	57
DOUBERRY								
Marshall	39	m	w	FRAN	San Mateo	Belmont P O	87	374
DOUBLAN								
Jane	42	f	w	FRAN	San Francisco	San Francisco P O	83	392

Name	Age	S	R	B-PL	County	Locale	Series M593 Roll	Pg
DOUBLE								
John	50	m	w	OH	Stanislaus	Washington Twp	92	86
DOUBLEDAY								
C F	47	m	w	NY	San Joaquin	3-Wd Stockton	86	229
Frank	30	m	w	MI	Contra Costa	Martinez P O	71	416
James	65	m	w	NJ	San Francisco	5-Wd San Francisco	81	26
DOUBT								
John	37	m	w	ENGL	Yuba	Rose Bar Twp	93	661
Joseph	28	m	w	ENGL	Yuba	Rose Bar Twp	93	658
DOUCET								
Frances	40	f	w	FRAN	Amador	Jackson P O	69	327
H	51	m	w	FRAN	Amador	Jackson P O	69	327
DOUCHERTY								
Patrick	46	m	w	IREL	Santa Clara	San Jose Twp	88	220
DOUD								
Bernard	29	m	w	IREL	San Francisco	11-Wd San Francisc	84	425
Berney	37	m	w	IREL	San Francisco	San Francisco P O	85	773
Bridget	70	f	w	IREL	Mendocino	Point Arena Twp	74	205
Edward	40	m	w	IREL	Sonoma	Vallejo Twp	91	450
Elder S	34	m	w	PA	Placer	Colfax P O	76	389
Francis	90	m	w	IREL	Mendocino	Point Arena Twp	74	205
Francis	48	m	w	IREL	Monterey	Monterey	74	365
Hannah	40	f	w	IREL	San Francisco	San Francisco P O	83	201
James	34	m	w	IREL	San Francisco	San Francisco P O	80	539
Owen	31	m	w	OH	Sierra	Eureka Twp	89	524
Patrick	41	m	w	IREL	Calaveras	San Andreas P O	70	185
Patrick	30	m	w	IREL	Santa Clara	Fremont Twp	88	60
Peter	37	m	w	IREL	San Francisco	11-Wd San Francisc	84	579
Richard	42	m	w	IREL	San Francisco	7-Wd San Francisco	81	199
Thomas	23	m	w	IREL	Stanislaus	Emory Twp	92	21
Truman	23	m	w	CT	Santa Clara	1-Wd San Jose	88	244
W D	41	m	w	OH	Sierra	Eureka Twp	89	524
DOUDE								
Amalia	12	f	w	CA	Santa Clara	2-Wd San Jose	88	337
DOUDEBES								
John	41	m	w	FRAN	San Francisco	San Francisco P O	80	539
DOUDER								
George W	25	m	w	GA	Stanislaus	Emory Twp	92	17
DOUDS								
James	30	m	w	IREL	San Francisco	7-Wd San Francisco	81	199
Mary	35	f	w	IREL	San Francisco	7-Wd San Francisco	81	199
DOUDY								
Sarah	18	f	w	TN	El Dorado	Georgetown Twp	72	43
DOUFORD								
Patrick	42	m	w	IREL	Nevada	Eureka Twp	75	128
Patrick	40	m	w	IREL	Nevada	Eureka Twp	75	126
DOUG								
Ah	25	m	c	CHIN	Placer	Auburn P O	76	383
DOUGAL								
Anne	18	f	w	ENGL	Yuba	Marysville	93	586
Thomas	36	m	w	SCOT	Yuba	Marysville	93	586
William	35	m	w	NY	San Francisco	6-Wd San Francisco	81	127
DOUGALL								
John	60	m	w	SCOT	San Francisco	San Francisco P O	83	336
Robert	40	m	w	CANA	Sonoma	Salt Point	91	380
DOUGAN								
James	30	m	w	OH	Sutter	Vernon Twp	92	135
Jeremiah	40	m	w	IREL	San Francisco	7-Wd San Francisco	81	231
Michael	31	m	w	IREL	San Francisco	11-Wd San Francisc	84	540
Thomas	37	m	w	IREL	San Mateo	Redwood Twp	87	363
DOUGART								
John I	40	m	w	FRAN	San Francisco	San Francisco P O	85	769
DOUGELL								
Louis	10	m	w	CA	Santa Cruz	Santa Cruz	89	420
DOUGHARTY								
Jas	30	m	w	IREL	Sierra	Table Rock Twp	89	575
John	61	m	w	PA	Sonoma	Analy Twp	91	232
Joseph	25	m	w	MD	Sonoma	Analy Twp	91	232
Michael	59	m	w	IREL	Sacramento	Sutter Twp	77	385
DOUGHERITY								
R	15	f	w	US	Yuba	Marysville	93	609
DOUGHERT								
John	38	m	w	IREL	Nevada	Nevada Twp	75	280
DOUGHERTY								
Abner R	38	m	w	NJ	Santa Clara	1-Wd San Jose	88	231
Alexander	27	m	w	MO	Yuba	Long Bar Twp	93	564
Ann	38	f	w	IREL	San Francisco	San Francisco P O	83	261
Anna	32	f	w	IREL	San Francisco	2-Wd San Francisco	79	276
Arthur	36	m	w	IREL	Klamath	Trinidad Twp	73	390
B	35	m	w	CA	San Francisco	San Francisco P O	85	817
Barney	17	m	w	MA	Plumas	Goodwin Twp	77	7
Benj G	51	m	w	PA	Sonoma	Analy Twp	91	232
Bernard	34	m	w	IREL	San Francisco	11-Wd San Francisc	84	429
Charles	33	m	w	IREL	Kern	Bakersfield P O	73	366
Chas	49	m	w	IREL	Sonoma	Petaluma Twp	91	326
Chas	31	m	w	OH	San Joaquin	Tulare Twp	86	261
Chas	13	m	w	CA	San Francisco	11-Wd San Francisc	84	587
Clara L	35	f	w	NJ	Sonoma	Bodega Twp	91	256
Daniel	50	m	w	IREL	Sacramento	4-Wd Sacramento	77	323
Daniel	40	m	w	IREL	Trinity	North Fork Twp	92	218
Danl	19	m	w	CANA	Solano	Vallejo	90	202
Delia	38	f	w	IREL	San Francisco	San Francisco P O	83	236
Delia	31	f	w	IREL	Solano	Vallejo	90	152
Dennis	25	m	w	IREL	San Francisco	San Francisco P O	85	745
Dominick	42	m	w	IREL	Santa Clara	Santa Clara Twp	88	135
E	20	f	w	IREL	Solano	Vallejo	90	210
E C	69	m	w	VA	Yuba	Rose Bar Twp	93	664

© 2001 by Heritage Quest. All rights reserved.

Name	Age	S	R	B-PL	County	Locale	Roll	Pg
						Series M593		
Edward	27	m	w	CANA	San Francisco	7-Wd San Francisco	81	279
Edwart	39	m	w	IREL	San Francisco	2-Wd San Francisco	79	265
Eliza	35	f	w	IREL	San Francisco	San Francisco P O	83	372
Elizabeth	39	f	w	IREL	San Francisco	8-Wd San Francisco	82	493
Frank	30	m	w	PA	Santa Clara	2-Wd San Jose	88	319
Franklin	5	m	w	CA	Humboldt	Pacific Twp	72	299
G	30	m	w	IREL	Sierra	Sears Twp	89	557
Geo	20	m	w	IREL	Solano	Benicia	90	17
George	60	m	w	IREL	San Francisco	San Francisco P O	83	396
George	45	m	w	IREL	San Francisco	2-Wd San Francisco	79	283
George	41	m	w	IREL	Marin	Nicasio Twp	74	15
George	35	m	w	IREL	San Francisco	7-Wd San Francisco	81	218
Harry	37	m	w	CANA	San Diego	San Diego	78	498
Henry	45	m	w	IREL	San Francisco	San Francisco P O	83	383
Henry	32	m	w	ME	Sacramento	Georgianna Twp	77	128
Henry	25	m	w	IREL	San Francisco	11-Wd San Francisc	84	463
Henry	23	m	w	IA	San Diego	San Diego	78	503
Hugh	38	m	w	IREL	San Francisco	7-Wd San Francisco	81	250
Hugh	30	m	w	IREL	San Francisco	7-Wd San Francisco	81	221
Hugh	26	m	w	IREL	Santa Clara	1-Wd San Jose	88	230
Isabel	21	f	b	MD	San Francisco	San Francisco P O	80	424
J	30	m	w	IREL	Yuba	Marysville	93	583
J	26	m	w	IREL	Solano	Vallejo	90	197
J	21	m	w	CA	Yuba	Marysville	93	617
James	42	m	w	IREL	Sacramento	4-Wd Sacramento	77	360
James	40	m	w	IREL	San Francisco	1-Wd San Francisco	79	28
James	39	m	w	IREL	Humboldt	Arcata Twp	72	231
James	35	m	w	IREL	San Francisco	2-Wd San Francisco	79	242
James	32	m	w	IREL	Nevada	Bridgeport Twp	75	120
James	30	m	w	IREL	Sonoma	Vallejo Twp	91	459
James	28	m	w	IREL	Yuba	Rose Bar Twp	93	662
James	25	m	w	IREL	San Francisco	2-Wd San Francisco	79	283
James	22	m	w	MA	San Francisco	1-Wd San Francisco	79	88
James	11	m	w	CA	San Francisco	11-Wd San Francisc	84	587
Jas	57	m	w	TN	Alameda	Murray Twp	68	99
Jas	40	m	w	IREL	Sierra	Eureka Twp	89	526
Jas	35	m	w	IREL	San Diego	San Diego	78	496
Jno	21	m	w	IREL	San Joaquin	2-Wd Stockton	86	212
John	72	m	w	IREL	Sacramento	Georgianna Twp	77	126
John	59	m	w	SCOT	San Francisco	San Francisco P O	83	347
John	49	m	w	IREL	Mendocino	Big Rvr Twp	74	160
John	48	m	w	IREL	San Francisco	7-Wd San Francisco	81	159
John	40	m	w	ME	Mendocino	Anderson Twp	74	154
John	40	m	w	IREL	Solano	Vallejo	90	170
John	39	m	w	IREL	Nevada	Bloomfield Twp	75	99
John	37	m	w	NY	San Francisco	7-Wd San Francisco	81	232
John	36	m	w	IREL	San Francisco	San Francisco P O	83	346
John	35	m	w	IREL	San Francisco	2-Wd San Francisco	79	245
John	35	m	w	IREL	Plumas	Goodwin Twp	77	6
John	35	m	w	IREL	Sierra	Table Rock Twp	89	544
John	32	m	w	IREL	San Francisco	2-Wd San Francisco	79	244
John	30	m	w	IREL	Fresno	Millerton P O	72	157
John	28	m	w	NY	Santa Clara	Santa Clara Twp	88	154
John	27	m	w	IREL	San Francisco	San Francisco P O	80	484
John	25	m	w	IREL	San Francisco	San Francisco P O	83	249
John	23	m	w	MA	San Francisco	San Francisco P O	83	288
John	22	m	w	IREL	San Francisco	2-Wd San Francisco	79	203
John	16	m	w	PA	Santa Clara	Santa Clara Twp	88	135
Josephine	12	f	w	MA	Sonoma	Petaluma Twp	91	339
Leonard	18	f	w	IL	Contra Costa	Martinez P O	71	373
Lizzie	23	f	w	IREL	San Francisco	San Francisco P O	83	133
Lizzie	21	f	w	NY	San Francisco	San Francisco P O	83	146
M L	44	m	w	IREL	Tuolumne	Columbia P O	93	348
Margaret	24	f	w	IREL	San Francisco	San Francisco P O	83	156
Margaret	15	f	w	MA	San Francisco	6-Wd San Francisco	81	150
Mary	48	f	w	IREL	Alameda	Oakland	68	177
Mary	40	f	w	IREL	San Joaquin	3-Wd Stockton	86	219
Mary	40	f	w	IN	San Diego	San Diego	78	498
Mary	30	f	w	IREL	San Francisco	San Francisco P O	83	84
Mary	25	f	w	NY	San Francisco	San Francisco P O	80	396
Mary	16	f	w	PA	Santa Clara	2-Wd San Jose	88	319
Mat	40	m	w	IREL	Solano	Vallejo	90	171
Mc Maley	26	m	w	OH	Tulare	White Rvr Twp	92	302
Michael	53	m	w	IREL	Solano	Benicia	90	7
Michael	45	m	w	KY	Mendocino	Ten Mile Rvr Twp	74	172
Michael	45	m	w	IREL	Yuba	Rose Bar Twp	93	660
Michael	40	m	w	IREL	Fresno	Millerton P O	72	168
Michael	33	m	w	IREL	San Diego	San Diego	78	494
Nathan	50	m	w	IN	Napa	Napa	75	2
Ned	36	m	w	IREL	San Diego	San Diego	78	494
Neil	30	m	w	IREL	San Francisco	11-Wd San Francisc	84	541
Neller	16	m	w	CA	Contra Costa	Martinez Twp	71	347
Niel	38	m	w	IREL	Los Angeles	Los Angeles	73	541
Pat	28	m	w	IREL	Solano	Vallejo	90	203
Patk	45	m	w	IREL	San Francisco	1-Wd San Francisco	79	76
Patk	35	m	w	IREL	San Francisco	San Francisco P O	83	82
Patrick	70	m	w	IREL	San Francisco	8-Wd San Francisco	82	461
Patrick	48	m	w	IREL	San Francisco	2-Wd San Francisco	79	283
Patrick	40	m	w	IREL	Sonoma	Analy Twp	91	243
Patrick	34	m	w	IREL	San Francisco	7-Wd San Francisco	81	176
Patrick	34	m	w	IREL	Marin	Sausalito Twp	74	73
Patrick	32	m	w	ENGL	Nevada	Grass Valley Twp	75	231
Patrick	21	m	w	SCOT	San Francisco	San Francisco P O	83	343
Philip	58	m	w	IREL	Nevada	Grass Valley Twp	75	181
Phillip	40	m	w	IREL	Amador	Ione City P O	69	362
Rebecca	33	f	w	IREL	Nevada	Rough & Ready Twp	75	336
Richard	26	m	w	IREL	Sierra	Gibson Twp	89	540

Name	Age	S	R	B-PL	County	Locale	Roll	Pg
						Series M593		
Robert	28	m	w	MA	Stanislaus	San Joaquin Twp	92	80
Rose	46	f	w	IREL	San Francisco	11-Wd San Francisc	84	630
Samuel	43	m	w	TN	San Diego	Milquaty Dist	78	478
Samuel	23	m	w	MA	San Francisco	7-Wd San Francisco	81	176
Sarah	18	f	w	MA	San Francisco	8-Wd San Francisco	82	397
Susan	12	m	w	CA	Contra Costa	Martinez P O	71	380
T L	44	m	w	IN	Santa Clara	Gilroy Twp	88	67
Tho	39	m	w	IREL	El Dorado	Coloma Twp	72	2
Thomas	41	m	w	PA	San Francisco	8-Wd San Francisco	82	472
Thomas	36	m	w	IREL	Placer	Cisco P O	76	494
Thos	40	m	w	NY	San Francisco	3-Wd San Francisco	79	326
W	39	m	w	IREL	San Joaquin	2-Wd Stockton	86	182
W F	23	m	w	NY	Solano	Vallejo	90	202
William	45	m	w	IN	Kern	Kernville P O	73	367
William	45	m	w	NY	San Francisco	San Francisco P O	80	405
William	44	m	w	IREL	San Francisco	San Francisco P O	83	252
William P	35	m	w	IREL	Santa Clara	1-Wd San Jose	88	258
Wm	46	m	w	MI	Merced	Snelling P O	74	274
Wm	45	m	w	IREL	Mariposa	Mariposa P O	74	125
Wm	43	m	w	IREL	Calaveras	Copperopolis P O	70	236
Wm	40	m	w	VT	Tuolumne	Sonora P O	93	318
Wm	34	m	w	OH	Santa Clara	Gilroy Twp	88	93
Wm	26	m	w	IREL	San Francisco	1-Wd San Francisco	79	57
Wm	12	m	w	CA	San Francisco	11-Wd San Francisc	84	598
Young	52	m	w	PA	Placer	Lincoln P O	76	492
DOUGHIN								
Mary	30	f	w	IREL	San Francisco	6-Wd San Francisco	81	99
DOUGHLAS								
James A	43	m	w	VA	Yolo	Cache Crk Twp	93	434
T A	28	m	w	ENGL	Solano	Vallejo	90	190
DOUGHLASS								
Robt C	34	m	w	ENGL	Calaveras	Copperopolis P O	70	241
William	42	m	w	MA	San Mateo	Woodside P O	87	381
DOUGHTERTY								
Alex	34	m	w	CANA	San Francisco	3-Wd San Francisco	79	294
Maggie	23	f	w	MA	San Francisco	3-Wd San Francisco	79	296
DOUGHTY								
Jacob V	47	m	w	NY	San Francisco	3-Wd San Francisco	79	314
John	45	m	w	NY	San Francisco	San Francisco P O	80	388
DOUGINE								
James	28	m	w	CT	San Francisco	11-Wd San Francisc	84	486
DOUGLAS								
A C	28	m	w	ME	San Francisco	San Francisco P O	85	776
Ann	12	f	w	PRUS	San Francisco	11-Wd San Francisc	84	689
Charles	16	m	w	CANA	San Francisco	San Francisco P O	80	477
Chas	38	m	w	NY	San Francisco	5-Wd San Francisco	81	26
Cora	15	f	w	CA	Alameda	Oakland	68	258
Cyrus	40	m	w	MO	Solano	Vacaville Twp	90	128
Daniel	30	m	w	NY	San Francisco	8-Wd San Francisco	82	437
David R	56	m	w	NY	Tulare	Visalia	92	297
Edward	26	m	w	IREL	San Francisco	San Francisco P O	80	427
Frdk	38	m	w	SWIT	San Francisco	San Francisco P O	83	271
Fredk	40	m	w	NY	San Francisco	5-Wd San Francisco	81	26
Guerdon	43	m	w	CA	Mariposa	Mariposa P O	74	111
Guy	55	m	w	CT	Santa Clara	1-Wd San Jose	88	247
Hellen	19	f	w	PA	San Francisco	5-Wd San Francisco	81	8
Henrietta	8	f	w	NY	Colusa	Grand Island Twp	71	302
Henry	24	m	w	CANA	Solano	Green Valley Twp	90	39
James	34	m	w	NY	Nevada	Rough & Ready Twp	75	323
Jno A	46	m	w	NJ	San Francisco	5-Wd San Francisco	81	22
John	54	m	w	ENGL	Placer	Bath P O	76	453
John	50	m	w	IREL	San Francisco	San Francisco P O	83	17
John	40	m	w	NY	San Francisco	7-Wd San Francisco	81	233
John	38	m	w	SCOT	San Francisco	11-Wd San Francisc	84	482
John	32	m	w	NY	Santa Cruz	Soquel Twp	89	446
John A	10	m	w	CA	Butte	Wyandotte Twp	70	149
John H	45	m	w	HAMB	Placer	Bath P O	76	426
John W	36	m	w	OH	Placer	Rocklin P O	76	462
Joseph	43	m	w	PA	Calaveras	San Andreas P O	70	196
Josephine	6	f	w	CA	Butte	Ophir Twp	70	116
M	75	f	b	MA	Sacramento	3-Wd Sacramento	77	296
Maggie	17	f	w	OH	San Francisco	11-Wd San Francisc	84	689
Margaret	40	f	w	OH	San Francisco	6-Wd San Francisco	81	147
Mary	19	f	w	IREL	San Francisco	San Francisco P O	85	789
Oliver	32	m	w	SCOT	Placer	Roseville P O	76	353
Oliver P	59	m	w	CT	Mariposa	Mariposa P O	74	106
Percy	31	m	w	ENGL	San Francisco	San Francisco P O	85	787
Phil	27	m	w	ENGL	Sacramento	3-Wd Sacramento	77	270
Robert	47	m	w	ME	Sonoma	Bodega Twp	91	262
Spencer	48	m	w	NY	Sacramento	San Joaquin Twp	77	398
Thomas	63	m	w	CT	Santa Clara	1-Wd San Jose	88	278
Thomas	18	m	w	NY	San Francisco	San Francisco P O	83	381
Thomas	12	m	w	NY	Alameda	Alameda	68	16
Thos	47	m	w	SCOT	San Francisco	1-Wd San Francisco	79	103
Thos	30	m	w	NY	Solano	Vallejo	90	141
W A	35	m	w	VT	Sonoma	Santa Rosa	91	402
William	48	m	w	MD	Santa Cruz	Watsonville	89	374
William	38	m	b	GA	Sacramento	2-Wd Sacramento	77	253
William	27	m	w	ME	Mendocino	Point Arena Twp	74	224
William A	45	m	w	VA	San Francisco	8-Wd San Francisco	82	428
Wm	40	m	w	CANA	San Joaquin	Douglas Twp	86	50
Wm	32	m	w	VT	Sonoma	Santa Rosa	91	411
Wm J F	41	m	w	KY	San Francisco	1-Wd San Francisco	79	100
DOUGLASS								
Anne	69	f	w	IREL	San Francisco	11-Wd San Francisc	84	611
Annie	24	f	w	IL	Santa Cruz	Watsonville	89	372
Benjamin	24	m	w	MO	Santa Clara	2-Wd San Jose	88	329

© 2001 by Heritage Quest. All rights reserved.

Name	Age	S	R	B-PL	County	Locale	Series M593 Roll	Pg
Benjm	31	m	w	CT	Tuolumne	Columbia P O	93	338
C	61	f	w	NY	Alameda	Oakland	68	138
Charles	53	m	w	SWED	San Francisco	3-Wd San Francisco	79	292
Charles	21	m	m	DC	Santa Clara	Redwood Twp	88	132
Chas	36	m	w	SCOT	San Francisco	11-Wd San Francisc	84	497
Coffin	24	m	w	IREL	Contra Costa	Martinez P O	71	368
D F	49	m	w	TN	San Joaquin	Douglas Twp	86	36
Edwd	40	m	w	IREL	Tuolumne	Chinese Camp P O	93	374
Ellen A	52	f	w	IREL	San Francisco	San Francisco P O	85	724
Frank	36	m	w	NY	Plumas	Indian Twp	77	15
Freeman	42	m	b	ME	San Joaquin	2-Wd Stockton	86	162
G S	33	m	w	NY	Solano	Vallejo	90	202
George	25	m	w	ME	San Mateo	Woodside P O	87	386
George N	55	m	w	TN	Santa Cruz	Watsonville	89	375
Gilbert	47	m	w	VT	Mariposa	Maxwell Crk P O	74	143
H A	41	m	w	IREL	Tuolumne	Chinese Camp P O	93	373
Hamer	26	m	w	ME	Humboldt	Arcata Twp	72	227
Hugh	52	m	w	PA	Plumas	Quartz Twp	77	43
J E	25	m	w	ME	San Francisco	3-Wd San Francisco	79	314
J M	37	m	w	TN	San Joaquin	Oneal Twp	86	98
James	54	m	w	SCOT	Marin	San Rafael Twp	74	40
James	44	m	w	NY	Butte	Bidwell Twp	70	3
James	38	m	w	IL	Solano	Vacaville Twp	90	129
James	34	m	w	IL	Solano	Vacaville Twp	90	118
James	26	m	w	IREL	San Francisco	7-Wd San Francisco	81	177
James	26	m	w	FRAN	San Francisco	2-Wd San Francisco	79	214
James A	42	m	w	VA	Yolo	Cache Crk Twp	93	448
Jane	35	f	w	ENGL	San Mateo	Redwood Twp	87	368
Jesse	40	m	w	DENM	Placer	Colfax P O	76	389
Jno	31	m	w	CANA	Sierra	Gibson Twp	89	541
John	55	m	w	PA	Sacramento	Granite Twp	77	136
John	50	m	w	SCOT	Del Norte	Happy Camp Twp	71	471
John	50	m	w	MO	Sacramento	2-Wd Sacramento	77	234
John	40	m	w	NY	San Joaquin	3-Wd Stockton	86	217
John	40	m	w	IREL	Trinity	Weaverville Pct	92	229
John	35	m	m	SC	Los Angeles	Los Angeles Twp	73	470
John	34	m	w	IREL	San Francisco	San Francisco P O	83	417
John	32	m	w	IREL	San Francisco	San Francisco P O	80	389
John	16	m	w	CA	Sonoma	Sonoma Twp	91	444
John A	49	m	w	TN	Monterey	Alisal Twp	74	291
John N	30	m	w	MO	Plumas	Mineral Twp	77	22
John W	52	m	w	SCOT	Los Angeles	Los Angeles Twp	73	471
L	43	m	w	OH	Nevada	Eureka Twp	75	135
Low	20	m	w	IL	Tehama	Antelope Twp	92	153
Mabel	15	f	w	CA	Los Angeles	Los Angeles	73	522
Maria	36	f	w	IREL	San Francisco	San Francisco P O	85	821
Mary	37	f	w	IREL	San Joaquin	2-Wd Stockton	86	167
Norial	47	m	w	TN	Merced	Snelling P O	74	260
O	50	m	w	PA	Alameda	Alameda	68	18
Peres	37	m	w	ME	San Joaquin	2-Wd Stockton	86	162
R J	3	m	w	CA	San Francisco	San Francisco P O	85	821
Rose	39	f	w	IREL	Los Angeles	Los Angeles Twp	73	483
Stephen	18	m	w	CA	Siskiyou	Table Rock Twp	89	646
T E	42	m	w	NY	Yuba	Marysville	93	611
Thomas	66	m	w	VA	Sutter	Butte Twp	92	103
Thomas	50	m	w	SCOT	San Francisco	San Francisco P O	83	165
Thos	37	m	w	UNKN	San Joaquin	2-Wd Stockton	86	172
Thos	30	m	b	WIND	San Joaquin	2-Wd Stockton	86	163
Thos H	39	m	w	NY	San Francisco	8-Wd San Francisco	82	341
W J	33	m	w	CANA	Solano	Benicia	90	2
William	44	m	w	SCOT	San Mateo	San Mateo P O	87	352
William	42	m	w	KY	San Francisco	11-Wd San Francisc	84	516
William	36	m	w	WI	Nevada	Grass Valley Twp	75	168
William	35	m	w	US	Nevada	Grass Valley Twp	75	221
William	26	m	w	IREL	Nevada	Grass Valley Twp	75	184
Wm	40	m	w	NY	San Francisco	2-Wd San Francisco	79	197
Wm	27	m	w	SCOT	Sutter	Sutter Twp	92	129
Wm	27	m	w	AZOR	Monterey	San Antonio Twp	74	321
DOULAN								
James	30	m	w	IREL	Santa Clara	Fremont Twp	88	58
DOULEY								
P J	47	m	w	IREL	Humboldt	Eureka Twp	72	265
DOULIN								
James	30	m	w	IREL	Placer	Newcastle Twp	76	476
DOULON								
Anna	21	f	w	IREL	Santa Clara	1-Wd San Jose	88	240
DOUN								
Anna	30	f	w	IREL	Contra Costa	Martinez P O	71	433
DOUNBECK								
Christopher	73	f	w	PRUS	Placer	Dutch Flat P O	76	406
DOUNET								
Henry	35	m	w	FRAN	San Francisco	2-Wd San Francisco	79	203
DOUNING								
Theodore	44	m	w	MI	Contra Costa	Martinez P O	71	436
DOUNLEY								
John	43	m	w	NH	San Francisco	11-Wd San Francisc	84	689
DOUNS								
James	40	m	w	IREL	Contra Costa	Martinez P O	71	433
John	25	m	w	OH	Contra Costa	Martinez P O	71	446
DOUNTE								
Stephen	19	m	w	SWIT	Yolo	Cache Crk Twp	93	452
DOUR								
Mary	29	f	w	FRAN	Nevada	Grass Valley Twp	75	151
DOUSELMAN								
J H	42	m	w	HANO	Alameda	Oakland	68	194
DOUSER								
Mark	30	m	w	PRUS	San Joaquin	2-Wd Stockton	86	181
DOUSHAN								
J	25	m	w	SCOT	Alameda	Oakland	68	264
DOUSMAN								
Henry	49	m	w	FRAN	Sonoma	Salt Point Twp	91	382
DOUTHITT								
D W	40	m	w	TN	San Francisco	San Francisco P O	83	327
DOUTON								
Robt	55	m	w	VA	San Joaquin	3-Wd Stockton	86	226
DOUTRICK								
Frank	24	m	w	PA	San Mateo	Redwood Twp	87	366
John	27	m	w	PA	San Mateo	Redwood Twp	87	366
DOUTY								
P R	38	m	w	ME	Calaveras	Copperopolis P O	70	237
DOUVILL								
G H	28	m	w	WI	Sutter	Butte Twp	92	104
DOV								
Luke	45	m	w	ME	Solano	Vallejo	90	209
Meng	33	m	c	CHIN	Yuba	Marysville	93	629
DOVE								
Ezra	36	m	w	MA	Solano	Rio Vista Twp	90	70
Jane	35	f	b	PA	San Francisco	San Francisco P O	80	369
John	33	m	w	NY	Butte	Ophir Twp	70	118
John	16	m	w	CANA	San Francisco	11-Wd San Francisc	84	588
Ulysses	19	m	w	FRAN	San Francisco	1-Wd San Francisco	79	83
William	23	m	w	MO	San Bernardino	San Bernardino Twp	78	445
William H	37	m	w	NY	San Francisco	8-Wd San Francisco	82	427
DOVEE								
Elizabeth	20	f	w	KY	Stanislaus	Empire Twp	92	29
DOVELL								
Henry	29	m	w	KY	Nevada	Meadow Lake Twp	75	268
DOVEN								
Richard	39	m	w	NY	San Francisco	5-Wd San Francisco	81	24
DOVENECK								
Chas	42	m	w	HANO	San Francisco	11-Wd San Francisc	84	567
DOVER								
Bolin G	43	m	w	KY	Placer	Newcastle Twp	76	474
Charles D	15	m	w	NV	El Dorado	Diamond Springs Tw	72	31
Jessie	30	m	w	TN	Santa Clara	Gilroy Twp	88	97
John M	36	m	w	TN	San Luis Obispo	Morro Twp	87	282
Levi P	33	m	w	MO	Butte	Chico Twp	70	17
William	49	m	w	ENGL	Santa Barbara	Santa Barbara P O	87	480
DOVETON								
C J G	40	m	w	AFRI	Amador	Amador City P O	69	395
DOVGAN								
Bridget	20	f	w	IREL	San Francisco	San Francisco P O	83	371
DOVIGO								
John	25	m	w	SPAI	San Francisco	1-Wd San Francisco	79	123
DOVIL								
Louis	30	m	w	CANA	San Francisco	San Francisco P O	80	463
DOVILA								
Edwd	35	m	w	FRAN	Butte	Ophir Twp	70	119
DOW								
Aaron	70	m	w	NH	Nevada	Grass Valley Twp	75	149
Ah	50	m	c	CHIN	Trinity	Weaverville Pct	92	231
Ah	45	m	c	CHIN	San Mateo	San Mateo P O	87	356
Ah	41	m	c	CHIN	El Dorado	Placerville	72	115
Ah	32	m	c	CHIN	Placer	Auburn P O	76	364
Ah	26	m	c	CHIN	Trinity	Douglas	92	235
Ah	20	m	c	CHIN	San Francisco	San Francisco P O	80	496
Ah	17	m	c	CHIN	San Francisco	San Francisco P O	83	398
Brown	60	m	w	SCOT	Contra Costa	Martinez P O	71	446
C C	26	m	w	NH	San Francisco	San Francisco P O	85	795
C E	35	m	w	ENGL	San Francisco	7-Wd San Francisco	81	221
Cyrus E	37	m	w	ME	Mendocino	Noyo & Big Rvr Twp	74	173
E B	36	m	w	ME	San Francisco	8-Wd San Francisco	82	345
Foo	25	f	c	CHIN	Butte	Hamilton Twp	70	73
Frank	22	m	w	ME	Humboldt	Arcata Twp	72	234
Frank	22	m	w	CA	Santa Clara	Almaden Twp	88	19
Franklin W	40	m	w	ME	Santa Cruz	Santa Cruz Twp	89	388
Geo	29	m	w	VT	Alameda	Oakland	68	247
Geo P	25	m	w	NH	Humboldt	Arcata Twp	72	230
Henry	25	m	w	IREL	Solano	Suisun Twp	90	102
Henry W	37	m	w	ME	Sutter	Yuba Twp	92	140
Jacob	30	m	w	MA	San Francisco	8-Wd San Francisco	82	364
James	54	m	w	IREL	Marin	Nicasio Twp	74	16
James	49	m	w	IREL	Sutter	Butte Twp	92	100
Jno	32	m	w	VT	Santa Clara	Gilroy Twp	88	97
John	60	m	w	NC	Stanislaus	Buena Vista Twp	92	11
John	45	m	w	IREL	Calaveras	San Andreas P O	70	178
John	24	m	w	IREL	Solano	Vacaville Twp	90	133
John B	53	m	w	NH	San Francisco	6-Wd San Francisco	81	129
John B	43	m	w	ME	San Diego	Coronado	78	465
John Lyman	32	m	w	NH	Plumas	Plumas Twp	77	26
Joseph	24	m	w	ME	Santa Clara	Gilroy Twp	88	98
Joseph G	45	m	w	NH	Sonoma	Mendocino Twp	91	307
Lo	20	m	c	CHIN	Placer	Colfax P O	76	386
Lorenzo	55	m	w	ME	Contra Costa	Martinez P O	71	393
Lorenzo	26	m	w	CANA	Santa Clara	2-Wd San Jose	88	284
Louis C	56	m	w	NY	Contra Costa	Martinez P O	71	386
Louisa S	63	f	w	NY	Santa Clara	2-Wd San Jose	88	281
Low	20	m	c	CHIN	Colusa	Colusa	71	299
Lucinda	26	f	w	NY	San Francisco	8-Wd San Francisco	82	345
Luis	36	m	w	MECK	Los Angeles	Santa Ana Twp	73	612
Martin	37	m	w	ME	San Francisco	7-Wd San Francisco	81	175
Mary	25	f	w	IL	San Francisco	San Francisco P O	80	401
New	30	m	c	CHIN	Santa Clara	Santa Clara Twp	88	158
Perron P	50	m	w	NH	Inyo	Independence Twp	73	327

© 2001 by Heritage Quest. All rights reserved.

Name	Age	S	R	B-PL	County	Locale	Series M593 Roll	Pg
Peter	44	m	w	FRAN	Siskiyou	Callahan P O	89	625
Peter	41	m	w	IREL	Solano	Rio Vista Twp	90	62
Philip	41	m	w	IREL	Solano	Silveyville Twp	90	74
Robert S	32	m	w	ME	Placer	Alta P O	76	412
S L	40	m	w	MA	Alameda	Oakland	68	260
Thomas	50	m	i	CANA	Shasta	Dog Crk P O	89	471
Thomas	40	m	w	SCOT	Alameda	Oakland	68	262
Thomas	36	m	w	CANA	Plumas	Plumas Twp	77	31
William	54	m	w	ME	Santa Cruz	Pajaro Twp	89	352
William	43	m	w	NJ	Lassen	Janesville Twp	73	434
William	43	m	w	SCOT	San Mateo	San Mateo P O	87	352
William	33	m	w	ME	San Mateo	Pescadero P O	87	415
William	28	m	w	IREL	Solano	Green Valley Twp	90	37
William	26	m	w	OH	Solano	Denverton Twp	90	25
William	25	m	w	ME	Mendocino	Point Arena Twp	74	209
William	18	m	w	CA	Sonoma	Mendocino Twp	91	291
Wm	44	m	w	ME	San Francisco	11-Wd San Francisc	84	604
DOWANE								
M D	45	m	w	NY	Yuba	East Bear Rvr Twp	93	544
DOWBY								
James B	39	m	w	WI	Sacramento	2-Wd Sacramento	77	245
DOWD								
Catherine	30	f	w	IREL	San Francisco	8-Wd San Francisco	82	430
Cleophas	12	m	w	CA	San Francisco	11-Wd San Francisc	84	592
Edward	53	m	w	PA	Alpine	Markleeville P O	69	311
Eleanor	60	f	w	IREL	Marin	San Rafael	74	52
Ellen	39	f	w	IREL	San Joaquin	1-Wd Stockton	86	126
Frank	24	m	w	IL	Merced	Snelling P O	74	269
Henery	29	m	w	NY	San Francisco	7-Wd San Francisco	81	179
Honora	50	f	w	IREL	San Francisco	8-Wd San Francisco	82	486
James	32	m	w	IREL	San Francisco	1-Wd San Francisco	79	84
James	30	m	w	IREL	Alameda	Oakland	68	232
Mary	5	f	w	CA	Klamath	Orleans Twp	73	379
Mary	30	f	w	IREL	San Francisco	8-Wd San Francisco	82	476
Mary	27	f	w	IREL	San Francisco	11-Wd San Francisc	84	553
Matilda	33	f	w	IREL	Marin	Sausalito Twp	74	66
Matthew	45	m	w	IREL	Kern	Kernville P O	73	368
Patrick	37	m	w	IREL	San Francisco	San Francisco P O	83	76
Philo	51	m	w	NY	San Francisco	8-Wd San Francisco	82	325
Thomas	28	m	w	IREL	Placer	Lincoln P O	76	492
Thos	23	m	w	IREL	San Joaquin	Douglas Twp	86	32
DOWDA								
Michael	50	m	w	IREL	Santa Clara	San Jose Twp	88	220
DOWDALL								
Richard	60	m	w	IREL	Sonoma	Petaluma Twp	91	356
DOWDELL								
Grace	36	f	w	IREL	San Francisco	San Francisco P O	83	262
Robert	24	m	w	NY	San Francisco	7-Wd San Francisco	81	174
DOWDEN								
James	41	m	w	PA	Marin	Novato Twp	74	11
Joseph	44	m	w	ME	Plumas	Mineral Twp	77	20
Joseph	37	m	w	IN	San Joaquin	Elliott Twp	86	75
Julia	30	f	w	IREL	San Francisco	8-Wd San Francisco	82	409
Sophie	13	f	w	CA	Sonoma	Russian Rvr	91	369
DOWDING								
Henry	25	m	w	IREL	San Francisco	1-Wd San Francisco	79	62
DOWDLE								
Mark	30	m	w	NY	Colusa	Spring Valley Twp	71	337
DOWDS								
Charles	47	m	w	CANA	Klamath	Orleans Twp	73	380
David	26	m	w	IL	Colusa	Colusa Twp	71	280
James	41	m	w	IREL	Placer	Lincoln P O	76	487
James	38	m	w	CANA	Klamath	Orleans Twp	73	379
James	30	m	w	NY	San Francisco	7-Wd San Francisco	81	193
DOWDY								
Hanson	34	m	w	NC	Santa Clara	Gilroy Twp	88	99
Hayden	30	m	w	IN	Santa Clara	Gilroy Twp	88	95
Hiram	38	m	w	KY	El Dorado	Coloma Twp	72	2
Isaac	63	m	w	CT	Santa Clara	Redwood Twp	88	124
Jno	31	m	w	NC	Santa Clara	Gilroy Twp	88	99
John	40	m	w	LA	San Mateo	Woodside P O	87	386
Perry	41	m	w	IN	Santa Clara	Gilroy Twp	88	101
Phebe J	29	f	w	CT	Santa Clara	Redwood Twp	88	124
DOWE								
David	43	m	w	NY	Contra Costa	Martinez P O	71	437
Edw	30	m	w	MA	Alameda	Oakland	68	211
Lo	45	f	c	CHIN	Placer	Colfax P O	76	388
Thos	41	m	w	ME	Alameda	Oakland	68	259
Thos	29	m	w	ENGL	Alameda	Oakland	68	214
DOWEL								
J W	40	m	w	VA	Lake	Upper Lake	73	410
DOWELL								
Chas	45	m	w	WI	Yuba	Marysville	93	604
James	35	m	w	ENGL	Butte	Oroville Twp	70	138
John	30	m	w	ENGL	Yuba	New York Twp	93	641
Martha E	39	f	w	OH	Contra Costa	Martinez P O	71	386
Nicholas	56	m	w	KY	Santa Cruz	Watsonville	89	372
Richard	26	m	w	ENGL	Santa Barbara	Santa Barbara P O	87	478
DOWELLE								
Mary	30	f	w	IREL	Alameda	Alameda	68	4
DOWER								
John	42	m	w	ENGL	Nevada	Eureka Twp	75	138
Lizzie	23	f	w	IREL	San Francisco	San Francisco P O	85	778
William	45	m	w	ENGL	Nevada	Nevada Twp	75	315
DOWERS								
Edward	37	m	w	IREL	Sonoma	Analy Twp	91	224
DOWHANTY								
J	33	m	w	IREL	Yuba	Marysville Twp	93	569
DOWING								
Charles W	20	m	w	MA	San Francisco	7-Wd San Francisco	81	173
G B	23	m	w	IL	San Joaquin	Castoria Twp	86	6
Mary	19	f	w	WI	Nevada	Nevada Twp	75	273
DOWKINS								
Wm	40	m	w	ENGL	Humboldt	Bald Hills	72	237
DOWLAN								
Ellen	23	f	w	IREL	San Francisco	8-Wd San Francisco	82	406
DOWLAND								
Andw	35	m	w	CANA	San Francisco	San Francisco P O	83	9
Kate	30	f	w	IREL	San Francisco	San Francisco P O	83	102
DOWLER								
Thos	55	m	w	IREL	San Francisco	San Francisco P O	83	280
DOWLEY								
George	45	m	w	OH	Mendocino	Casper & Big Rvr	74	162
DOWLIN								
Frank	32	m	w	BAVA	San Francisco	3-Wd San Francisco	79	327
George W	33	m	w	NH	Santa Clara	Fremont Twp	88	49
DOWLING								
Albert	14	m	w	CA	Calaveras	San Andreas P O	70	206
Ann	64	f	w	IREL	Alameda	Brooklyn Twp	68	47
Bridget	42	f	w	IREL	San Francisco	San Francisco P O	80	400
Daniel	20	m	w	IREL	San Francisco	8-Wd San Francisco	82	395
Ed	27	m	w	IREL	San Francisco	2-Wd San Francisco	79	234
Eugene	35	m	w	IREL	San Francisco	San Francisco P O	83	132
Frederick	48	m	w	AUSL	Santa Clara	2-Wd San Jose	88	334
Gustave	22	m	w	MA	San Francisco	7-Wd San Francisco	81	175
Helena	22	f	w	CANA	Solano	Silveyville Twp	90	91
Henry	48	m	w	HAMB	San Francisco	2-Wd San Francisco	79	268
James	52	m	w	ME	San Francisco	1-Wd San Francisco	79	42
James	38	m	w	IREL	San Francisco	11-Wd San Francisc	84	647
James	17	m	w	IREL	San Francisco	San Francisco P O	83	385
Jno	48	m	w	OH	San Joaquin	Douglas Twp	86	50
John	65	m	w	IREL	San Francisco	San Francisco P O	83	276
John	50	m	w	NY	Humboldt	Mattole Twp	72	285
John	37	m	w	IREL	Sacramento	4-Wd Sacramento	77	327
John	35	m	w	IREL	Solano	Vallejo	90	142
John	30	m	w	IREL	San Francisco	San Francisco P O	83	290
John	25	m	w	IREL	San Francisco	San Francisco P O	85	753
John	18	m	w	CA	Sacramento	2-Wd Sacramento	77	234
John E	32	m	w	ENGL	Humboldt	Table Bluff Twp	72	304
Joseph	20	m	w	IREL	San Francisco	7-Wd San Francisco	81	221
Julia	40	f	w	IREL	San Francisco	11-Wd San Francisc	84	472
Kate	21	f	w	IREL	San Francisco	8-Wd San Francisco	82	475
Madison	45	m	w	NY	San Francisco	7-Wd San Francisco	81	278
Mary	32	f	w	IREL	San Francisco	7-Wd San Francisco	81	159
Mary	29	f	w	IREL	San Francisco	San Francisco P O	85	791
Micheal	36	m	w	IREL	San Francisco	11-Wd San Francisc	84	424
Pat	46	m	w	IREL	San Francisco	2-Wd San Francisco	79	258
Pat	35	m	w	IREL	Sonoma	Santa Rosa	91	401
Pat F	23	m	w	IREL	Sonoma	Santa Rosa	91	408
Peter	40	m	w	IREL	San Francisco	San Francisco P O	83	394
Richard	43	m	w	IREL	Alameda	Brooklyn Twp	68	43
Richard	40	m	w	MA	San Francisco	7-Wd San Francisco	81	229
Thos	26	m	w	IREL	San Francisco	San Francisco P O	83	271
Victor	41	m	w	OH	Stanislaus	Emory Twp	92	21
Wm M	50	m	w	IREL	San Francisco	San Francisco P O	85	869
DOWLONG								
John	40	m	w	IREL	Siskiyou	Yreka	89	657
DOWLY								
Pat	35	m	w	IREL	San Joaquin	2-Wd Stockton	86	174
DOWMAN								
J	19	m	w	MO	Amador	Drytown P O	69	417
Jerry	38	m	w	IREL	Contra Costa	Martinez P O	71	451
DOWN								
Adolphus	21	m	w	WI	Siskiyou	Table Rock Twp	89	647
Albert S	32	m	w	ENGL	Sonoma	Analy Twp	91	236
Dominic	23	m	w	IREL	Contra Costa	San Pablo Twp	71	356
John	35	m	w	ENGL	Sierra	Sears Twp	89	554
Wm	27	m	w	ENGL	San Joaquin	2-Wd Stockton	86	164
DOWNARD								
Robert	40	m	m	KY	Placer	Alta P O	76	412
Thomas	30	m	w	PA	Santa Clara	Redwood Twp	88	123
William	41	m	w	ENGL	San Bernardino	San Bernardino Twp	78	452
William	33	m	w	WI	Placer	Bath P O	76	436
DOWNE								
Patrick	33	m	w	IREL	Sutter	Sutter Twp	92	128
DOWNER								
Almer L	62	m	w	NY	Shasta	Shasta P O	89	458
Dewitt C	53	m	w	NY	Butte	Kimshew Tpw	70	77
E	39	m	w	IREL	Nevada	Meadow Lake Twp	75	260
Elijah G	36	m	w	MI	Sacramento	Franklin Twp	77	108
Elijah H	42	m	w	PA	Nevada	Meadow Lake Twp	75	247
Ellen	45	f	w	IREL	Santa Clara	Santa Clara Twp	88	152
Harrison	21	m	w	NY	Butte	Ophir Twp	70	107
Herman P	26	m	w	NY	Butte	Ophir Twp	70	91
Hugh H	51	m	w	PA	Santa Clara	San Jose Twp	88	199
John	27	m	w	IREL	Solano	Vallejo	90	190
Thomas	56	m	w	MA	San Francisco	8-Wd San Francisco	82	413
DOWNES								
Delia	23	f	w	IREL	San Francisco	San Francisco P O	80	352
H	40	m	w	ME	Alameda	Oakland	68	238
John	36	m	w	MI	Butte	Chico Twp	70	59
Mary	28	f	w	IREL	Sacramento	4-Wd Sacramento	77	343
William	32	m	w	NJ	San Francisco	San Francisco P O	80	425

© 2001 by Heritage Quest. All rights reserved.

Name	Age	S	R	B-PL	County	Locale	Series M593 Roll	Pg
DOWNEY								
Alex	66	m	w	IREL	Sonoma	Russian Rvr	91	377
Alvah	40	m	w	CANA	San Bernardino	San Bernardino Twp	78	423
Andrew	38	m	w	ENGL	San Francisco	3-Wd San Francisco	79	301
Anne	38	f	w	IREL	Alameda	Oakland	68	173
Batt	22	m	w	IREL	Yuba	Rose Bar Twp	93	662
Danl M	33	m	w	PA	Solano	Vacaville Twp	90	134
Dennis	38	m	w	IREL	Napa	Yountville Twp	75	78
E J	21	f	w	IL	Nevada	Bridgeport Twp	75	104
Edward	32	m	w	IREL	San Francisco	2-Wd San Francisco	79	283
Eliza	24	f	w	IREL	Alameda	Alameda	68	8
Ellen	24	f	w	ENGL	San Francisco	11-Wd San Francisc	84	457
Francis W	12	m	w	AUSL	San Francisco	8-Wd San Francisco	82	311
George	38	m	w	SCOT	Yuba	Marysville	93	598
Henry	21	m	w	OH	Solano	Silveyville Twp	90	91
James	42	m	w	IREL	Sacramento	Franklin Twp	77	119
James	35	m	w	IREL	Sonoma	Vallejo Twp	91	459
James R	36	m	w	IN	Nevada	Rough & Ready Twp	75	334
Jane	34	f	w	IREL	Alameda	Alameda	68	11
John	39	m	w	OH	Nevada	Bridgeport Twp	75	105
John	35	m	w	IREL	San Francisco	11-Wd San Francisc	84	668
John	28	m	w	IREL	Solano	Vallejo	90	201
John	24	m	w	IREL	San Francisco	3-Wd San Francisco	79	312
John	22	m	w	NY	Los Angeles	Los Angeles	73	541
John G	45	m	w	IREL	Los Angeles	Los Angeles	73	543
John H	36	m	w	MD	Siskiyou	Scott Valley Twp	89	608
Josiah	45	m	w	IN	Napa	Napa	75	15
Kate	14	f	w	CA	Stanislaus	Emory Twp	92	21
Lawrence	32	m	w	IREL	Los Angeles	Los Angeles Twp	73	496
M	30	m	w	IREL	Sierra	Butte Twp	89	511
Major	32	m	w	NY	San Francisco	5-Wd San Francisco	81	28
Margaret	40	f	w	IREL	San Francisco	7-Wd San Francisco	81	194
Mary	21	f	w	IREL	San Francisco	11-Wd San Francisc	84	655
Mary	11	f	w	IREL	Los Angeles	Los Nietos Twp	73	574
Michael	27	m	w	IREL	San Francisco	San Francisco P O	85	806
Patrick	50	m	w	IREL	San Francisco	San Francisco P O	83	153
Patrick	43	m	w	IREL	Los Angeles	Los Angeles	73	571
Phillip	9	m	w	NY	San Mateo	Woodside P O	87	381
Prudence	18	f	w	IREL	San Francisco	8-Wd San Francisco	82	329
Saml	32	m	w	IREL	Butte	Ophir Twp	70	97
Thomas	25	m	w	NY	San Francisco	San Francisco P O	83	411
Timothy	70	m	w	IREL	San Francisco	San Francisco P O	83	300
William	59	m	w	VT	Contra Costa	Martinez P O	71	367
William	30	m	w	PA	Contra Costa	Martinez Twp	71	347
Winfred	47	m	w	MA	Solano	Silveyville Twp	90	83
Wm K	40	m	w	NY	Siskiyou	Callahan P O	89	630
DOWNIE								
John	39	m	w	SCOT	Nevada	Nevada Twp	75	306
Saml	9	m	w	CA	Yuba	Linda Twp	93	556
Thos H	32	m	w	IREL	Tuolumne	Columbia P O	93	341
W J	4	m	w	CANA	Sierra	Downieville Twp	89	514
Wm	50	m	w	SCOT	Sierra	Downieville Twp	89	515
Wm C	35	m	w	ENGL	Solano	Vallejo	90	151
DOWNIG								
Chas	55	m	w	NJ	Yuba	East Bear Rvr Twp	93	542
DOWNING								
A	44	m	w	ENGL	San Joaquin	Douglas Twp	86	50
A	28	m	w	MA	Santa Clara	Gilroy Twp	88	101
Alex	15	m	w	PA	Yuba	W Bear Rvr Twp	93	680
Andrew I	37	m	w	IN	San Luis Obispo	San Luis Obispo Tw	87	302
Anna	45	f	w	IREL	Butte	Ophir Twp	70	98
August	45	m	w	SPAI	Nevada	Eureka Twp	75	130
Edward	35	m	w	IREL	Placer	Roseville P O	76	348
Ellen	33	f	w	MD	Santa Barbara	Santa Barbara P O	87	501
Frances	31	f	w	OH	Sonoma	Analy Twp	91	234
Geo	35	m	w	PA	Yuba	Marysville	93	604
George	28	m	w	IN	San Francisco	San Francisco P O	83	402
Gerome	25	m	w	ME	Monterey	Castroville Twp	74	325
Henry	40	m	w	MD	San Francisco	San Francisco P O	85	856
Henry	18	m	w	PA	Plumas	Plumas Twp	77	31
Henry	17	m	w	MA	San Francisco	11-Wd San Francisc	84	443
J M	32	f	w	IREL	San Francisco	San Francisco P O	85	784
Jackson R	39	m	w	IL	Tulare	Visalia	92	293
Jerome	35	m	w	US	Santa Cruz	Watsonville	89	365
John	48	m	w	PA	Tuolumne	Sonora P O	93	318
John	48	m	w	IREL	Nevada	Nevada Twp	75	273
John	40	m	w	IREL	San Francisco	11-Wd San Francisc	84	707
John C	61	m	w	NH	Sonoma	Healdsburg & Mendo	91	279
John S	41	m	w	TN	Alpine	Woodfords P O	69	310
John W	51	m	w	IREL	Nevada	Nevada Twp	75	278
Joseph	46	m	w	MO	Stanislaus	Empire Twp	92	43
Joshua	50	m	w	VT	San Francisco	San Francisco P O	80	382
Lizzie	22	f	w	NY	Yuba	Marysville	93	587
Madison J	15	m	w	MO	Shasta	Horsetown P O	89	505
Margaret	33	f	w	IREL	San Francisco	7-Wd San Francisco	81	285
Mary	35	f	w	SWIT	Alameda	Oakland	68	175
Oliver	19	m	w	VT	San Mateo	Menlo Park P O	87	379
Pat	24	m	w	IREL	Alameda	Oakland	68	242
Patrick B	46	m	w	IREL	San Francisco	San Francisco P O	83	190
Patrick D H	37	m	w	IREL	Los Angeles	Wilmington Twp	73	638
Peter	25	m	w	CANA	Contra Costa	Martinez P O	71	428
Philander	42	m	w	IA	Siskiyou	Butte Twp	89	587
Saml	34	m	w	IREL	Butte	Oregon Twp	70	126
Stephen	32	m	w	IN	Calaveras	San Andreas P O	70	151
Sylvester	34	m	w	IREL	San Francisco	2-Wd San Francisco	79	202
Thomas	50	m	w	IREL	Butte	Ophir Twp	70	95
W A	64	f	w	VT	Alameda	Oakland	68	180
W D	67	m	w	OH	Humboldt	Eel Rvr Twp	72	249
Wm	42	m	w	TN	San Joaquin	Liberty Twp	86	88
Wm	28	m	w	NY	Solano	Vallejo	90	160
Wm	23	m	w	CA	San Joaquin	Elkhorn Twp	86	62
DOWNINGS								
Thos	34	m	w	CANA	San Francisco	11-Wd San Francisc	84	675
DOWNNING								
Jacob	48	m	w	NY	San Mateo	Half Moon Bay P O	87	407
Michael	45	m	w	IREL	San Francisco	San Francisco P O	83	257
DOWNS								
Alvah	42	m	w	VT	San Francisco	8-Wd San Francisco	82	398
Ames	37	m	w	IL	Mendocino	Point Arena Twp	74	224
Andrew J	46	m	w	KY	Yolo	Cottonwood Twp	93	466
Andrew J	44	m	w	KY	Yolo	Grafton Twp	93	492
Annie	23	f	w	IREL	San Francisco	San Francisco P O	85	861
Charles	20	m	w	NH	Yolo	Grafton Twp	93	493
Daniel	63	m	w	NC	Placer	Dutch Flat P O	76	410
Dennis	40	m	w	IREL	Yuba	New York Twp	93	635
Dr	40	m	w	NH	Lake	Lakeport	73	407
Edward	27	m	w	IREL	San Francisco	San Francisco P O	83	223
Geo	40	m	w	NY	Butte	Ophir Twp	70	120
George	66	m	w	FRAN	Placer	Bath P O	76	422
George	40	m	w	NY	Butte	Wyandotte Twp	70	141
H	35	m	w	MA	Alameda	Oakland	68	256
H P	52	m	w	ME	Sacramento	3-Wd Sacramento	77	297
Horace	44	m	w	NH	San Francisco	San Francisco P O	83	248
James	38	m	w	IREL	Santa Cruz	Pajaro Twp	89	347
Jas	30	m	w	IREL	Sierra	Gibson Twp	89	543
Joshua	40	m	w	ME	Santa Clara	San Jose Twp	88	189
Kate	30	f	w	IREL	San Joaquin	2-Wd Stockton	86	160
Leondas	30	m	w	IN	San Francisco	San Francisco P O	83	220
Michael	35	m	w	IREL	San Francisco	2-Wd San Francisco	79	268
Patrick	30	m	w	IREL	San Francisco	7-Wd San Francisco	81	172
R C	42	m	w	CT	Amador	Sutter Crk P O	69	397
Samuel	24	m	w	ENGL	Mendocino	Little Rvr Twp	74	171
Vernon	42	m	w	OH	Sonoma	Santa Rosa	91	417
W W	30	m	w	CT	Amador	Sutter Crk P O	69	402
William	33	m	w	IREL	San Francisco	11-Wd San Francisc	84	455
Winniford	46	f	w	IREL	Alameda	Eden Twp	68	91
Wm	41	m	w	IREL	Monterey	Alisal Twp	74	292
Zack R	23	m	w	MEXI	Placer	Alta P O	76	413
DOWRAY								
Henry	36	m	w	FRAN	Nevada	Meadow Lake Twp	75	267
DOWS								
James	63	m	w	NY	San Francisco	San Francisco P O	83	147
Lorenzo	40	m	w	CHIL	Amador	Jackson P O	69	346
Samuel	42	m	w	NY	Sonoma	Analy Twp	91	236
DOWSETT								
George	40	m	w	ENGL	San Francisco	San Francisco P O	83	46
DOWTHET								
Sarah A	46	f	w	PA	Tehama	Red Bluff	92	183
DOWTY								
Wm	39	m	w	ENGL	San Joaquin	3-Wd Stockton	86	219
DOXY								
Beverly M	40	m	w	TN	Calaveras	Copperopolis P O	70	245
DOY								
Ah	22	m	c	CHIN	San Francisco	6-Wd San Francisco	81	56
Cum	3	f	c	CHIN	Butte	Kimshew Tpw	70	84
David R	33	m	w	NY	Nevada	Eureka Twp	75	129
Ty	19	m	c	CHIN	Butte	Hamilton Twp	70	67
DOYCE								
Ellen	30	f	w	IREL	San Francisco	8-Wd San Francisco	82	433
DOYCHERT								
J J	28	m	w	PRUS	Sonoma	Santa Rosa	91	401
DOYD								
James	36	m	w	MO	Solano	Vacaville Twp	90	123
DOYE								
John	47	m	w	IREL	San Mateo	Redwood City P O	87	375
Mary	75	f	w	IREL	San Mateo	Redwood City P O	87	375
Morris	75	m	w	IREL	San Mateo	Redwood City P O	87	375
Morris	36	m	w	IREL	San Mateo	Belmont P O	87	374
Ton	25	m	c	CHIN	Placer	Clipper Gap P O	76	376
DOYER								
Peter	33	m	w	FRAN	El Dorado	White Oak Twp	72	142
DOYL								
John	38	m	w	ME	Lassen	Long Valley Twp	73	437
DOYLE								
Alexander	53	m	w	IREL	Yuba	Rose Bar Twp	93	657
Andrew	38	m	w	IREL	Marin	Tomales Twp	74	83
Andrew	35	m	w	IREL	San Francisco	11-Wd San Francisc	84	477
Andrew J	32	m	w	IL	Plumas	Indian Twp	77	18
Aneta	11	f	w	MS	Solano	Silveyville Twp	90	84
Bertha	35	f	w	IREL	San Francisco	2-Wd San Francisco	79	240
Bridget	75	f	w	IREL	San Francisco	San Francisco P O	85	775
Bryan	39	m	w	IREL	San Francisco	1-Wd San Francisco	79	112
C W	41	m	w	OH	Sonoma	Santa Rosa	91	423
Catharine	31	f	w	IREL	San Francisco	San Francisco P O	85	759
Catherin	41	f	w	IREL	Sacramento	Granite Twp	77	146
Catherine	24	f	w	ME	Napa	Napa	75	35
Charles	46	m	w	IREL	Santa Cruz	Pajaro Twp	89	349
Charles	30	m	w	IREL	Colusa	Spring Valley Twp	71	341
Charles	22	m	w	ENGL	San Francisco	San Francisco P O	85	745
Charles	20	m	w	IN	Colusa	Butte Twp	71	267
D B	50	m	w	IREL	San Francisco	San Francisco P O	85	820
Danl	39	m	w	IREL	San Francisco	1-Wd San Francisco	79	102
Danl	37	m	w	IREL	Yuba	Marysville	93	613
Demis	41	m	w	IREL	Tuolumne	Columbia P O	93	344

© 2001 by Heritage Quest. All rights reserved.

Name	Age	S	R	B-PL	County	Locale	Series M593 Roll	Pg
Edgar	24	m	w	NY	San Francisco	5-Wd San Francisco	81	31
Edward	40	m	w	ME	San Francisco	11-Wd San Francisc	84	632
Edward	40	m	w	IREL	Tuolumne	Columbia P O	93	348
Edward	40	m	w	CANA	San Francisco	11-Wd San Francisc	84	581
Edwd	46	m	w	IREL	San Francisco	San Francisco P O	83	7
Edwd	40	m	w	IREL	San Francisco	1-Wd San Francisco	79	100
Edwin	36	m	w	IREL	San Francisco	11-Wd San Francisc	84	532
Elizabeth	14	f	w	NY	Santa Clara	2-Wd San Jose	88	314
Elizebeth	17	f	w	MS	Tehama	Red Bluff	92	182
Ellen	40	f	w	IREL	San Francisco	1-Wd San Francisco	79	19
Ellen	35	f	w	IREL	San Francisco	7-Wd San Francisco	81	239
Ellen	25	f	w	IREL	San Francisco	8-Wd San Francisco	82	428
Eugene	48	m	w	PA	San Francisco	7-Wd San Francisco	81	271
Francis	35	m	w	IREL	Santa Clara	Fremont Twp	88	61
Garret	30	m	w	IREL	San Francisco	11-Wd San Francisc	84	496
George	4	m	w	CA	Stanislaus	San Joaquin Twp	92	71
George	34	m	w	IN	Sacramento	Granite Twp	77	142
H	60	m	w	VT	San Joaquin	Elkhorn Twp	86	61
H M	47	m	w	VA	Tuolumne	Chinese Camp P O	93	381
Hannah	20	f	w	IREL	San Francisco	7-Wd San Francisco	81	275
Henry	33	m	w	OH	Solano	Vacaville Twp	90	135
Hewit	30	m	w	IREL	Solano	Suisun Twp	90	103
Hugh	35	m	w	IREL	San Francisco	1-Wd San Francisco	79	5
Jacob	33	m	w	TN	Mariposa	Mariposa P O	74	124
Jacob	32	m	w	TN	Mariposa	Mariposa P O	74	131
Jacob	31	m	w	IREL	Solano	Silveyville Twp	90	75
James	47	m	w	IREL	San Francisco	11-Wd San Francisc	84	540
James	44	m	w	GA	San Francisco	8-Wd San Francisco	82	368
James	43	m	w	IREL	Los Angeles	Los Angeles	73	519
James	42	m	w	IREL	San Francisco	7-Wd San Francisco	81	161
James	40	m	w	IREL	San Francisco	2-Wd San Francisco	79	172
James	38	m	w	IREL	San Francisco	San Francisco P O	83	235
James	38	m	w	IREL	San Diego	San Diego	78	510
James	36	m	w	IREL	Plumas	Goodwin Twp	77	6
James	35	m	w	IREL	Sonoma	Russian Rvr	91	377
James	35	m	w	IREL	Nevada	Eureka Twp	75	131
James	32	m	w	IREL	Yuba	Rose Bar Twp	93	659
James	30	m	w	IREL	San Francisco	San Francisco P O	83	106
James	29	m	w	IREL	San Francisco	7-Wd San Francisco	81	162
James	23	m	w	AUST	San Francisco	11-Wd San Francisc	84	529
James F	41	m	w	IREL	Sonoma	Vallejo Twp	91	450
James J	40	m	w	IREL	San Francisco	2-Wd San Francisco	79	192
James Jr	26	m	w	IREL	San Francisco	San Francisco P O	85	850
Jas	41	m	w	CANA	Solano	Vallejo	90	185
Jno	49	m	w	IREL	Sacramento	3-Wd Sacramento	77	278
Jno	35	m	w	IREL	Sacramento	3-Wd Sacramento	77	258
Jno	28	m	w	NY	Santa Clara	Burnett Twp	88	38
Jno J	27	m	w	IN	Sonoma	Santa Rosa	91	423
John	48	m	w	MO	Solano	Montezuma Twp	90	65
John	45	m	w	IREL	Alameda	Oakland	68	248
John	44	m	w	IREL	San Francisco	San Francisco P O	85	873
John	42	m	w	ME	Siskiyou	Butte Twp	89	586
John	41	m	w	IREL	Santa Cruz	Soquel Twp	89	449
John	40	m	w	NY	San Francisco	1-Wd San Francisco	79	88
John	39	m	w	IREL	Lassen	Milford Twp	73	438
John	38	m	w	IREL	San Francisco	11-Wd San Francisc	84	473
John	38	m	w	IREL	San Francisco	2-Wd San Francisco	79	214
John	38	m	w	IREL	Mendocino	Casper & Big Rvr	74	162
John	35	m	w	IREL	Solano	Maine Prairie Twp	90	49
John	35	m	w	IREL	San Francisco	San Francisco P O	83	379
John	35	m	w	IREL	San Francisco	11-Wd San Francisc	84	629
John	32	m	w	IREL	Santa Clara	1-Wd San Jose	88	240
John	32	m	w	IREL	Napa	Napa	75	19
John	32	m	w	MO	Solano	Silveyville Twp	90	74
John	31	m	w	IREL	Solano	Suisun Twp	90	102
John	30	m	w	IREL	San Francisco	1-Wd San Francisco	79	42
John	29	m	w	OH	Solano	Vacaville Twp	90	124
John	29	m	w	NY	San Francisco	San Francisco P O	83	276
John	28	m	w	CANA	Placer	Roseville P O	76	354
John	28	m	w	IREL	Solano	Silveyville Twp	90	75
John	28	m	w	IREL	San Francisco	San Francisco P O	83	218
John	27	m	w	IL	Merced	Snelling P O	74	275
John	27	m	w	IREL	Solano	Silveyville Twp	90	81
John	25	m	w	NY	San Francisco	San Francisco P O	83	140
John	25	m	w	IREL	Mono	Bridgeport P O	74	282
John	23	m	w	IREL	San Francisco	7-Wd San Francisco	81	167
John	22	m	w	IREL	San Francisco	5-Wd San Francisco	81	32
John	19	m	w	IREL	Marin	San Antonio Twp	74	61
John T	50	m	w	NY	San Francisco	San Francisco P O	83	102
John T	5	m	w	CA	San Francisco	San Francisco P O	83	102
John T	41	m	w	IREL	San Francisco	1-Wd San Francisco	79	112
Kate	45	f	w	IREL	San Francisco	7-Wd San Francisco	81	232
Lawrence	68	m	w	IREL	Calaveras	Copperopolis P O	70	255
Lawrence	35	m	w	IREL	San Francisco	11-Wd San Francisc	84	517
Lizzie	25	f	w	AL	San Joaquin	Tulare Twp	86	250
Luke D	43	m	w	IREL	San Francisco	San Francisco P O	85	770
M	57	m	w	NJ	Santa Clara	Gilroy Twp	88	68
M J	42	m	w	IREL	Napa	Napa	75	36
M J	29	m	w	IREL	Sacramento	1-Wd Sacramento	77	178
Maggie	30	f	w	IREL	San Francisco	8-Wd San Francisco	82	293
Maggie	25	f	w	IREL	Alameda	Alameda	68	20
Manville	39	m	w	IL	Sonoma	Petaluma Twp	91	329
Manville	39	m	w	IL	Sonoma	Petaluma Twp	91	365
Margaret	30	f	w	IREL	San Francisco	8-Wd San Francisco	82	440
Margaret	25	f	w	IREL	Santa Clara	San Jose Twp	88	219
Margaret	25	f	w	IREL	Santa Clara	San Jose Twp	88	199
Margaret	19	f	w	IREL	San Francisco	San Francisco P O	80	409
Martin	36	m	w	IREL	San Francisco	San Francisco P O	83	381
Martin	35	m	w	IREL	San Francisco	San Francisco P O	83	108
Mary	66	f	w	IREL	San Mateo	Redwood Twp	87	364
Mary	52	f	w	IREL	Placer	Rocklin Twp	76	465
Mary	39	f	w	IREL	San Francisco	11-Wd San Francisc	84	507
Mary	34	f	w	IREL	San Francisco	San Francisco P O	80	536
Mary	30	f	w	ME	San Francisco	8-Wd San Francisco	82	441
Mary	25	f	w	IREL	San Francisco	8-Wd San Francisco	82	429
Mary Ann	30	f	w	ENGL	San Francisco	San Francisco P O	83	139
Mary E	11	f	w	CA	Sacramento	3-Wd Sacramento	77	292
Matthew	26	m	w	CANA	Santa Clara	Milpitas Twp	88	111
Michael	41	m	w	IREL	Calaveras	San Andreas P O	70	206
Michael	35	m	w	IREL	San Francisco	San Francisco P O	83	32
Michael	30	m	w	IREL	Tuolumne	Sonora P O	93	326
Michael K	36	m	w	ME	San Mateo	Woodside P O	87	384
Michal	36	m	w	IREL	San Francisco	7-Wd San Francisco	81	167
Michl	38	m	w	IREL	San Francisco	1-Wd San Francisco	79	78
Miriam	40	f	w	PA	San Francisco	San Francisco P O	80	371
Morris	38	m	w	IREL	San Francisco	11-Wd San Francisc	84	621
Morris	26	m	w	IREL	San Francisco	San Francisco P O	83	2
Nicholas	42	m	w	IREL	Nevada	Bridgeport Twp	75	123
Patrick	37	m	w	IREL	Sacramento	4-Wd Sacramento	77	323
Patrick	34	m	w	IREL	San Francisco	San Francisco P O	83	276
Patrick	33	m	w	IREL	Santa Clara	1-Wd San Jose	88	250
Peter	40	m	w	IREL	Sacramento	Franklin Twp	77	119
Peter	35	m	w	IREL	Santa Clara	1-Wd San Jose	88	235
Peter J	32	m	w	IREL	Solano	Vacaville Twp	90	135
Phoebe	26	f	w	IREL	San Francisco	San Francisco P O	85	717
Richard	45	m	w	IREL	San Francisco	11-Wd San Francisc	84	622
Richard	37	m	w	IREL	San Francisco	3-Wd San Francisco	79	320
Richard	32	m	w	IREL	San Francisco	7-Wd San Francisco	81	271
Robert E	41	m	w	NY	San Mateo	Menlo Park P O	87	379
Rodey	39	m	w	IREL	San Francisco	11-Wd San Francisc	84	605
Rose	6	f	w	CA	San Francisco	San Francisco P O	85	827
S H	33	m	w	ME	Lassen	Long Valley Twp	73	437
Saml	24	m	w	IN	Sonoma	Santa Rosa	91	405
Thomas	62	m	w	IREL	San Francisco	San Francisco P O	83	19
Thomas	48	m	w	IREL	Nevada	Grass Valley Twp	75	204
Thomas	35	m	w	IREL	San Francisco	San Francisco P O	85	870
Thomas	31	m	w	IREL	San Francisco	San Francisco P O	83	15
Thomas	16	m	w	CA	San Francisco	San Francisco P O	83	369
Thos	35	m	w	IREL	San Francisco	7-Wd San Francisco	81	242
William	40	m	w	IREL	Kern	Havilah P O	73	340
William	40	m	w	IREL	Kern	Bakersfield P O	73	358
William	38	m	w	IREL	San Francisco	11-Wd San Francisc	84	534
William	32	m	w	MO	Amador	Ione City P O	69	360
William	31	m	w	IREL	Solano	Silveyville Twp	90	90
William	27	m	w	IREL	Contra Costa	Martinez P O	71	425
William	26	m	w	MO	Solano	Silveyville Twp	90	80
William	22	m	w	IREL	Solano	Silveyville Twp	90	89
William	22	m	w	IREL	Solano	Silveyville Twp	90	77
Wm	47	m	w	IREL	Sacramento	3-Wd Sacramento	77	258
Wm	45	m	w	IREL	Sacramento	3-Wd Sacramento	77	292
Wm	38	m	w	IREL	San Francisco	1-Wd San Francisco	79	88
Wm	36	m	w	CANA	Butte	Oroville Twp	70	140
Wm	36	m	w	MO	Sacramento	Alabama Twp	77	60
Wm	30	m	w	NY	San Francisco	7-Wd San Francisco	81	236
Wm	30	m	w	IREL	San Joaquin	3-Wd Stockton	86	217
Wm	29	m	w	IREL	San Francisco	11-Wd San Francisc	84	675
DOZIER								
Edward C	24	m	w	SC	Solano	Rio Vista Twp	90	56
Edward F	38	m	w	NC	Los Angeles	Wilmington Twp	73	638
Malvina	20	f	w	TX	Monterey	Pajaro Twp	74	371
Washington	65	m	m	MA	Sacramento	2-Wd Sacramento	77	212
William E	37	m	w	SC	Solano	Rio Vista Twp	90	58
DRACE								
Edward	26	m	w	MO	Stanislaus	North Twp	92	67
DRACHENFELS								
George	41	m	w	AUST	Siskiyou	Scott Rvr Twp	89	603
DRACKE								
James	34	m	w	BADE	El Dorado	Greenwood Twp	72	52
DRACKWELL								
Christine	73	f	w	ENGL	San Joaquin	2-Wd Stockton	86	192
Wm	75	m	w	ENGL	San Joaquin	2-Wd Stockton	86	192
DRACO								
Jesus	34	m	w	MEXI	Tulare	Tule Rvr Twp	92	271
DRADDY								
Mary	53	f	w	IREL	San Francisco	8-Wd San Francisco	82	400
DRADY								
John	28	m	w	IREL	San Francisco	San Francisco P O	83	119
DRAFFIN								
John	40	m	w	IREL	Sonoma	Bodega Twp	91	265
DRAGER								
John	28	m	w	HAMB	San Francisco	1-Wd San Francisco	79	60
DRAGO								
Nelson	36	m	w	CANA	Sonoma	Analy Twp	91	246
DRAGONVITCH								
J	38	m	w	AUST	Amador	Jackson P O	69	329
DRAGOO								
Mary	42	f	w	PA	Contra Costa	Martinez P O	71	391
DRAHAM								
Minna	32	f	w	PRUS	San Francisco	2-Wd San Francisco	79	283
DRAIMER								
Charles	40	m	w	NY	San Francisco	San Francisco P O	80	463
DRAIN								
David	35	m	w	PA	San Francisco	7-Wd San Francisco	81	276

© 2001 by Heritage Quest. All rights reserved.

Name	Age	S	R	B-PL	County	Locale	Roll	Pg
						Series M593		
DRAIS								
A S	22	m	w	MO	San Joaquin	Douglas Twp	86	46
Jas	35	m	w	MO	San Joaquin	Douglas Twp	86	35
M J	50	m	w	NY	San Joaquin	Douglas Twp	86	47
DRAKE								
C	34	m	w	ME	Yuba	Marysville	93	595
C P	42	m	w	NH	San Francisco	8-Wd San Francisco	82	362
Chas	47	m	w	DE	Solano	Vallejo	90	182
Curtis	44	m	w	OH	Solano	Suisun Twp	90	102
Ebner	23	m	w	OH	Santa Barbara	San Buenaventura P	87	425
Edward R	39	m	w	ME	Plumas	Seneca Twp	77	48
Ellis	24	m	w	NY	San Francisco	8-Wd San Francisco	82	368
Enos R	49	m	w	NJ	Yolo	Putah Twp	93	517
Eugene	16	m	w	CA	Butte	Chico Twp	70	55
Eugene B	40	m	w	NC	San Francisco	8-Wd San Francisco	82	454
Frank	36	m	w	NY	Sonoma	Salt Point	91	385
Frank	25	m	w	BAVA	Calaveras	San Andreas P O	70	189
George	25	m	w	IL	Inyo	Independence Twp	73	327
George W	40	m	w	NH	San Francisco	6-Wd San Francisco	81	122
H A	40	f	w	CANA	San Francisco	1-Wd San Francisco	79	54
H B	26	m	w	NY	San Francisco	San Francisco P O	83	67
Harriet	21	f	w	ME	Solano	Benicia	90	3
Hiram	65	m	w	VA	Shasta	Stillwater P O	89	478
Horace	50	m	w	NY	Humboldt	Eel Rvr Twp	72	251
J	32	m	w	WI	Sacramento	1-Wd Sacramento	77	181
J F	52	m	w	NH	Siskiyou	Scott Valley Twp	89	615
J S	25	m	w	CANA	Alameda	Oakland	68	165
Jacob	39	m	w	OH	Stanislaus	Empire Twp	92	40
James	47	m	w	NY	Butte	Wyandotte Twp	70	146
James	12	m	w	CA	San Francisco	San Francisco P O	83	408
James H	43	m	w	NY	Yuba	North East Twp	93	644
James L	20	m	w	OH	Solano	Suisun Twp	90	108
Korsus	47	f	w	MEXI	Tehama	Deer Crk Twp	92	172
Louisa	13	f	w	CA	Sacramento	4-Wd Sacramento	77	326
Mary	21	f	w	MI	Santa Clara	Redwood Twp	88	131
S D	50	m	w	NH	San Francisco	8-Wd San Francisco	82	364
Samuel	50	m	w	VT	Solano	Vacaville Twp	90	132
Samuel	44	m	w	NY	San Francisco	San Francisco P O	80	409
Samuel	34	m	w	NH	San Francisco	8-Wd San Francisco	82	376
Simon	38	m	w	NH	Solano	Vallejo	90	215
Simon	30	m	w	OH	Siskiyou	Yreka	89	662
Simpson	48	m	w	OH	Stanislaus	Empire Twp	92	40
W K	29	m	w	ME	Sierra	Table Rock Twp	89	577
William	55	m	w	NJ	Solano	Vacaville Twp	90	138
William	23	m	w	NY	Solano	Suisun Twp	90	111
Willis	34	m	w	NY	Alameda	Washington Twp	68	295
Willis	29	m	w	NY	Alameda	Washington Twp	68	295
DRAKLA								
Monja	39	m	w	MEXI	Tulare	Tule Rvr Twp	92	271
DRAKMAN								
Emma	18	f	w	WURT	San Francisco	San Francisco P O	83	43
DRAMAN								
John	36	m	w	NY	San Francisco	1-Wd San Francisco	79	67
DRAN								
John	21	m	w	NY	Alameda	Oakland	68	230
DRANDY								
Robert	24	m	w	CANA	Santa Clara	2-Wd San Jose	88	290
DRANNAN								
Catherine	26	f	w	IREL	Alameda	Brooklyn	68	25
J C	27	m	w	MO	Tehama	Deer Crk Twp	92	170
DRAPER								
Benjamin	45	m	w	ENGL	Santa Clara	San Jose Twp	88	214
Christina	67	f	w	NC	Sonoma	Petaluma Twp	91	359
Ed	33	m	w	NY	Alameda	Murray Twp	68	116
Edward	24	m	w	ME	San Francisco	San Francisco P O	85	753
Emerson H	40	m	w	MA	El Dorado	White Oak Twp	72	136
James	21	m	w	IL	Plumas	Quartz Twp	77	38
John	38	m	w	MS	Fresno	Kingston P O	72	224
Mary	18	f	w	IREL	Yuba	Linda Twp	93	555
Nelson	36	m	w	CT	Amador	Jackson P O	69	325
R C	47	m	w	PA	Tehama	Paskenta Twp	92	165
Richd	33	m	w	MA	San Francisco	San Francisco P O	85	811
Saml	21	m	w	OH	San Joaquin	2-Wd Stockton	86	164
Samuel	68	m	w	VA	Placer	Auburn P O	76	382
Thomas	39	m	w	NY	Trinity	Minersville Pct	92	215
William	36	m	w	NY	Nevada	Nevada Twp	75	272
Wm	50	m	w	TN	Shasta	Stillwater P O	89	480
DRAPP								
Mary	19	f	w	BADE	San Francisco	8-Wd San Francisco	82	481
DRASCOVITCH								
N	23	m	w	AUST	San Joaquin	1-Wd Stockton	86	135
DRATHEN								
Peter	26	m	w	SHOL	Santa Clara	1-Wd San Jose	88	232
DRATHMAN								
Ferdinand W	36	m	w	BREM	San Francisco	8-Wd San Francisco	82	479
DRATT								
Andrew	46	m	w	NY	Sonoma	Mendocino Twp	91	306
DRAUT								
Nicholas	26	m	w	LUXE	Contra Costa	Martinez P O	71	387
DRAVEDER								
Ferdinand	26	m	w	SWIT	Los Angeles	Los Nietos Twp	73	588
DRAVERO								
David	48	m	w	FRAN	San Francisco	1-Wd San Francisco	79	50
DRAY								
F R	35	m	w	PA	Sacramento	3-Wd Sacramento	77	263
James	26	m	w	IREL	Sacramento	2-Wd Sacramento	77	237

Name	Age	S	R	B-PL	County	Locale	Roll	Pg
						Series M593		
DRAYS								
John W	49	m	w	MO	San Francisco	1-Wd San Francisco	79	53
DRAZA								
Phillip	35	m	w	PRUS	San Joaquin	1-Wd Stockton	86	135
DREADMAN								
Edward	32	m	w	IREL	San Francisco	San Francisco P O	83	391
DREARS								
Chs	33	m	w	PERS	Monterey	Alisal Twp	74	294
DREBBIESBY								
Louis	55	m	w	PA	Marin	San Rafael Twp	74	41
DREEMAN								
J F	41	m	w	GERM	Sacramento	1-Wd Sacramento	77	187
DREEN								
Albert	25	m	w	IL	Los Angeles	Santa Ana Twp	73	605
Daniel	24	m	w	CANA	San Francisco	San Francisco P O	85	746
DREESE								
Henry A	43	m	w	RUSS	Sonoma	Petaluma Twp	91	332
DREGAN								
Kate	33	f	w	IREL	San Francisco	1-Wd San Francisco	79	5
DREGNAT								
Joseph	61	m	w	FRAN	San Francisco	San Francisco P O	83	135
DREHER								
Catherine	40	f	w	BADE	Santa Cruz	Santa Cruz	89	412
DREHOUS								
Fred	26	m	w	GERM	Yuba	W Bear Rvr Twp	93	684
DREIBER								
Francois Ant	39	m	w	FRAN	San Francisco	San Francisco P O	83	135
DREILING								
Jos	41	m	w	PRUS	Shasta	American Ranch P O	89	498
DREITHOFF								
M	27	m	w	PRUS	San Francisco	8-Wd San Francisco	82	376
DREIYFUS								
Evard	28	m	w	BAVA	Sonoma	Petaluma Twp	91	321
DREKMAN								
Henry	35	m	w	PRUS	Sacramento	San Joaquin Twp	77	406
DREMAS								
John	28	m	w	PRUS	San Francisco	1-Wd San Francisco	79	49
DREMSON								
T H	26	m	w	NY	Santa Clara	Gilroy Twp	88	100
DREN								
James H	29	m	w	CANA	San Francisco	San Francisco P O	83	176
DRENE								
Nerene	19	m	w	ME	Merced	Snelling P O	74	264
DRENNAN								
James	46	m	w	IREL	Tuolumne	Sonora P O	93	308
M	28	m	w	IREL	Solano	Vallejo	90	165
Samuel	40	m	w	IL	Santa Cruz	Santa Cruz	89	418
T J	41	m	w	TN	Sonoma	Santa Rosa	91	428
DRENNEN								
Wm F	37	m	w	TN	Santa Barbara	Santa Barbara P O	87	474
DRENNON								
John	39	m	w	OH	Napa	Napa Twp	75	30
DRENTAL								
Julius M	22	m	w	FRAN	San Francisco	7-Wd San Francisco	81	241
DRENTWEHL								
C	30	m	w	HANO	Monterey	Alisal Twp	74	301
DREPER								
A R	30	m	w	IL	Sutter	Yuba Twp	92	142
Anna	35	f	w	IREL	San Francisco	2-Wd San Francisco	79	171
Ching	14	m	c	CHIN	Sutter	Yuba Twp	92	142
William	24	m	w	IL	Sacramento	2-Wd Sacramento	77	242
DRESBACK								
William	36	m	w	PRUS	Yolo	Putah Twp	93	511
DRESCALL								
Timothy	27	m	w	IREL	Placer	Alta P O	76	412
DRESCHFELD								
Fannie	17	f	w	BAVA	San Francisco	8-Wd San Francisco	82	403
DRESCHFIELD								
Sophie	38	f	w	HAMB	San Francisco	8-Wd San Francisco	82	400
DRESCHMEYER								
Samuel	38	m	w	GERM	Santa Clara	1-Wd San Jose	88	276
DRESCHMEZER								
Fredk	20	m	w	GERM	Santa Clara	Gilroy Twp	88	68
DRESCHWAGON								
James	50	m	w	PRUS	San Francisco	5-Wd San Francisco	81	13
DRESCO								
Lorenzo	43	m	w	ITAL	Mariposa	Mariposa P O	74	109
DRESCOLL								
Chas	34	m	w	IREL	San Francisco	1-Wd San Francisco	79	29
Denis	33	m	w	IREL	Calaveras	San Andreas P O	70	181
J	26	m	w	NY	Lake	Morgan Valley	73	425
Jerremiah	39	m	w	IREL	Calaveras	Copperopolis P O	70	239
DRESDEN								
Walter	42	m	w	ENGL	San Francisco	San Francisco P O	83	232
DRESEL								
Julius	53	m	w	GERM	Sonoma	Sonoma Twp	91	446
DRESHER								
Phil E	51	m	w	GERM	Sutter	Nicolaus Twp	92	107
DRESHMEYER								
C	29	m	w	GERM	Santa Clara	Gilroy Twp	88	100
DRESKER								
W H	32	m	w	OH	Sutter	Butte Twp	92	88
DRESS								
Dedrich C	45	m	w	OLDE	Sonoma	Petaluma Twp	91	350
DRESSELL								
A	26	m	w	SWIT	Alameda	Oakland	68	182

© 2001 by Heritage Quest. All rights reserved.

California 1870 Census

Name	Age	S	R	B-PL	County	Locale	Roll	Pg
						Series M593		
DRESSENGSON								
Chas	34	m	w	DENM	San Francisco	11-Wd San Francisc	84	694
DRESSER								
Albertina	23	f	w	MA	Nevada	Grass Valley Twp	75	177
Albertina	20	f	w	MA	Nevada	Grass Valley Twp	75	222
C C	39	m	w	HANO	Tuolumne	Chinese Camp P O	93	369
Charles	25	m	w	IL	Yolo	Grafton Twp	93	494
Francis	55	m	w	MA	Santa Clara	Redwood Twp	88	125
Jessie	47	m	w	PA	Sacramento	Granite Twp	77	143
John	34	m	w	MO	Sutter	Butte Twp	92	101
Mary I	40	f	w	NY	Sacramento	Granite Twp	77	146
Peter O	45	m	w	ME	Sonoma	Salt Point	91	389
Rufus	55	m	w	MA	El Dorado	Mountain Twp	72	70
Thomas	47	m	w	ME	Santa Clara	1-Wd San Jose	88	230
William	55	m	w	IL	Yolo	Grafton Twp	93	493
William O	33	m	w	IL	Yolo	Grafton Twp	93	494
DRESSLER								
Mary	14	f	w	NY	Santa Clara	1-Wd San Jose	88	243
DRESTUHEFT								
Prebley	17	f	w	PRUS	Monterey	Monterey	74	367
DREVANE								
Thos	23	m	w	ENGL	Sierra	Table Rock Twp	89	577
DREVDONNE								
Augustus	24	m	w	FRAN	Yolo	Grafton Twp	93	486
DREVER								
David	40	m	w	SCOT	Sonoma	Salt Point Twp	91	383
DREVES								
Christopher	47	m	w	HANO	Calaveras	Copperopolis P O	70	221
DREW								
A B	34	m	w	VT	Tuolumne	Big Oak Flat P O	93	391
Albert B	34	m	w	MA	Santa Cruz	Santa Cruz	89	416
Allen Waldron	35	m	w	NH	Plumas	Seneca Twp	77	51
C C	32	m	w	VT	Tuolumne	Big Oak Flat P O	93	391
Charles	25	m	w	MA	Sonoma	Analy Twp	91	233
Charles C	40	m	w	NH	Napa	Yountville Twp	75	82
Christina	20	f	w	AUST	Amador	Sutter Crk P O	69	399
Cornelius	40	m	w	IREL	Santa Clara	1-Wd San Jose	88	246
David	35	m	w	MA	Calaveras	Copperopolis P O	70	226
Doc	24	m	w	ME	Santa Clara	Gilroy Twp	88	82
E	44	m	w	NY	Solano	Vallejo	90	207
Edward	33	m	w	FRAN	San Francisco	11-Wd San Francisc	84	678
Edward	32	m	w	IREL	San Francisco	11-Wd San Francisc	84	670
Edward	19	m	w	ME	Sacramento	4-Wd Sacramento	77	335
Edwin	51	m	w	ENGL	Amador	Fiddletown P O	69	431
Edwin	28	m	w	ENGL	Nevada	Grass Valley Twp	75	177
Fanny	24	f	w	PA	San Francisco	5-Wd San Francisco	81	29
Frank	35	m	m	WIND	San Francisco	1-Wd San Francisco	79	95
Frank	34	m	w	ME	Santa Cruz	Santa Cruz	89	429
George	50	m	w	IREL	Butte	Hamilton Twp	70	64
George	36	m	w	NY	Monterey	San Benito Twp	74	383
H L	33	m	w	VT	San Francisco	San Francisco P O	85	804
Henry	38	m	w	ME	Santa Clara	1-Wd San Jose	88	240
Henry	23	m	w	ME	Santa Clara	Gilroy Twp	88	97
Henry P	58	m	w	ME	San Francisco	7-Wd San Francisco	81	240
Hiram	27	m	w	CANA	El Dorado	White Oak Twp	72	141
James	36	m	w	NH	Shasta	Horsetown P O	89	505
James	35	m	w	MA	Stanislaus	Buena Vista Twp	92	11
James	24	m	w	NY	Santa Barbara	San Buenaventura P	87	440
Jobe	30	m	w	ME	San Joaquin	2-Wd Stockton	86	170
John	38	m	w	NY	Humboldt	Eel Rvr Twp	72	253
John R	33	m	w	IREL	San Francisco	San Francisco P O	83	267
Johnathan	58	m	w	VT	Sonoma	Analy Twp	91	229
Joshua C	39	m	w	NY	Santa Cruz	Pajaro Twp	89	362
L B	43	m	w	NH	San Francisco	San Francisco P O	85	852
Lewis	27	m	w	NY	San Francisco	8-Wd San Francisco	82	370
M A	17	f	w	CA	Amador	Sutter Crk P O	69	397
Margaret	40	f	w	ENGL	San Francisco	6-Wd San Francisco	81	128
Martin	40	m	w	ENGL	El Dorado	Mud Springs Twp	72	78
Mary	27	f	w	IREL	San Francisco	San Francisco P O	83	141
Mary M	29	f	w	ME	Santa Clara	1-Wd San Jose	88	230
N M	39	m	w	ME	Sacramento	1-Wd Sacramento	77	187
Nathaniel L	45	m	w	NH	Sacramento	2-Wd Sacramento	77	253
Pat	36	m	w	IREL	San Francisco	11-Wd San Francisc	84	674
Patk	40	m	w	IREL	Yuba	Rose Bar Twp	93	663
R D	26	m	w	KY	Sutter	Yuba Twp	92	148
Simon	27	m	w	IREL	San Francisco	San Francisco P O	85	785
Sophia	29	f	w	ME	Santa Cruz	Santa Cruz	89	430
Thomas	68	m	w	ENGL	Nevada	Grass Valley Twp	75	177
Thomas	53	m	w	HI	Los Angeles	Wilmington Twp	73	635
Wallace	30	m	w	ME	Santa Clara	Gilroy Twp	88	97
William	37	m	w	CANA	Mendocino	Ukiah Twp	74	237
William	35	m	w	ENGL	Nevada	Grass Valley Twp	75	177
Willis	24	m	w	IN	Sutter	Yuba Twp	92	148
DREWERY								
George	34	m	w	CANA	Alameda	Hayward	68	74
John W	64	m	w	VA	Placer	Bath P O	76	454
DREWES								
John	25	m	w	HANO	San Francisco	7-Wd San Francisco	81	217
DREWS								
Frank	42	m	w	PRUS	Santa Clara	2-Wd San Jose	88	320
Louis	42	m	w	POLA	San Francisco	San Francisco P O	83	179
DREXIL								
Harrison	25	m	w	ENGL	Colusa	Grand Island Twp	71	307
DREYDENIE								
Pierre	43	m	w	FRAN	San Francisco	San Francisco P O	83	135
DREYER								
John H	31	m	w	HANO	Merced	Snelling P O	74	272

Name	Age	S	R	B-PL	County	Locale	Roll	Pg
						Series M593		
DREYFOUS								
Jules	54	m	w	FRAN	San Francisco	San Francisco P O	83	323
DREYFUS								
Alex	30	m	w	FRAN	Sacramento	3-Wd Sacramento	77	302
DREYFUSE								
Benjamin	45	m	w	BAVA	Los Angeles	Santa Ana Twp	73	615
DREYFUSS								
Julius	39	m	w	GERM	Nevada	Nevada Twp	75	273
Lewis W	46	m	w	GERM	Nevada	Nevada Twp	75	281
DREYPOELCHER								
F	35	m	w	NY	San Francisco	San Francisco P O	85	844
DRIAS								
Francisco	37	m	w	MEXI	Santa Clara	Almaden Twp	88	5
DRIBBLE								
Henry	28	m	w	AL	Tulare	Venice Twp	92	276
DRICKER								
John	49	m	w	HANO	San Joaquin	2-Wd Stockton	86	193
DRICKS								
John J	45	m	w	HOLL	San Francisco	11-Wd San Francisc	84	697
DRIER								
James	40	m	w	AR	Sacramento	Franklin Twp	77	119
Martin	28	m	w	BADE	Placer	Bath P O	76	420
DRIFFLE								
Wm	22	m	w	IREL	Butte	Chico Twp	70	21
DRIGGS								
Elizabeth	66	f	w	NY	San Francisco	San Francisco P O	80	488
Geo R	32	m	w	NY	San Francisco	1-Wd San Francisco	79	133
DRIGS								
Richard	44	m	w	BAVA	Sonoma	Petaluma Twp	91	315
DRIK								
William	22	m	w	CANA	Humboldt	Eureka Twp	72	274
DRILL								
Jacob	30	m	w	MA	San Francisco	11-Wd San Francisc	84	463
DRINKHOUSE								
Jno A	40	m	w	PA	San Francisco	San Francisco P O	83	96
DRINKLE								
F	48	m	w	PA	Yuba	Marysville	93	586
DRINKWATER								
A M	20	m	w	MA	San Francisco	San Francisco P O	85	863
Addison	47	m	w	ME	El Dorado	Salmon Falls Twp	72	131
David	9	m	w	CA	San Francisco	San Francisco P O	85	827
E	8	f	w	CA	San Francisco	San Francisco P O	85	827
Eliza	18	f	w	CA	San Francisco	San Francisco P O	83	284
Geo M	29	m	w	ENGL	Butte	Oregon Twp	70	127
L H	49	m	w	ME	Alameda	Oakland	68	203
Thos	60	m	w	ENGL	San Francisco	8-Wd San Francisco	82	364
W C	40	m	w	ME	Trinity	Hayfork Valley	92	238
DRINNEN								
John	54	m	w	IREL	Solano	Vallejo	90	143
DRIPS								
William A	32	m	w	OH	Yolo	Cottonwood Twp	93	460
DRIRE								
Jerry	35	m	w	IREL	Sonoma	Vallejo Twp	91	459
DRISCAL								
John	35	m	w	IREL	Alameda	Brooklyn Twp	68	50
DRISCALL								
James	22	m	w	MA	San Francisco	11-Wd San Francisc	84	519
DRISCO								
F	19	m	w	CA	Santa Clara	Gilroy Twp	88	106
Jose	26	m	w	CA	Santa Clara	Gilroy Twp	88	106
DRISCOL								
Cornelius	46	m	w	IREL	San Francisco	8-Wd San Francisco	82	301
D	24	m	w	IREL	San Francisco	San Francisco P O	83	314
Daniel	25	m	w	IREL	Yolo	Putah Twp	93	510
Daniel	22	m	w	ENGL	Sacramento	Georgianna Twp	77	123
Danl	40	m	w	IREL	Sacramento	1-Wd Sacramento	77	187
Dennis	20	m	w	IREL	San Francisco	San Francisco P O	83	314
Geo	21	m	w	IA	San Joaquin	Liberty Twp	86	93
James	25	m	w	MA	Humboldt	Eureka Twp	72	282
Jas	40	m	w	IREL	Sacramento	1-Wd Sacramento	77	179
John	38	m	w	IREL	Sacramento	2-Wd Sacramento	77	219
John	28	m	w	IREL	San Francisco	7-Wd San Francisco	81	230
Margaret	30	f	w	IREL	San Francisco	San Francisco P O	83	379
Margt	22	f	w	IREL	San Francisco	8-Wd San Francisco	82	305
Neeley	11	m	w	CA	Sacramento	2-Wd Sacramento	77	252
Reed	45	m	w	MA	Sonoma	Cloverdale Twp	91	270
Samuel	40	m	w	IREL	San Francisco	San Francisco P O	83	313
Thos	30	m	w	IREL	San Joaquin	2-Wd Stockton	86	171
DRISCOLL								
Anna	23	f	w	IREL	San Francisco	8-Wd San Francisco	82	492
Catharine	35	f	w	IREL	San Francisco	San Francisco P O	83	57
Cathrine	55	f	w	IREL	San Francisco	San Francisco P O	85	823
Con	30	m	w	IREL	Solano	Vallejo	90	186
Cornelius	39	m	w	ENGL	San Francisco	2-Wd San Francisco	79	211
Daniel	36	m	w	MA	San Francisco	11-Wd San Francisc	84	521
Daniel	34	m	w	MO	San Francisco	San Francisco P O	85	746
Daniel	23	m	w	IREL	San Francisco	San Francisco P O	83	93
Dennis	46	m	w	IREL	Solano	Vallejo	90	146
Dennis	45	m	w	IREL	San Francisco	8-Wd San Francisco	82	407
Dennis	38	m	w	IREL	San Francisco	11-Wd San Francisc	84	472
Dennis	35	m	w	IREL	San Francisco	San Francisco P O	83	381
Dennis	27	m	w	IREL	Marin	San Antonio Twp	74	62
Dennis	27	m	w	IREL	Marin	Nicasio Twp	74	15
Dennis	19	m	w	IREL	Nevada	Nevada Twp	75	286
Dennis	17	m	w	NY	San Francisco	11-Wd San Francisc	84	591
Edward	28	m	w	IREL	Placer	Rocklin Twp	76	465
Elizabeth	22	f	w	IREL	Tulare	Visalia	92	296

© 2001 by Heritage Quest. All rights reserved.

Name	Age	S	R	B-PL	County	Locale	Series M593 Roll	Pg
Ellen	18	f	w	MA	San Francisco	San Francisco P O	83	148
Ellen	16	f	w	ENGL	San Francisco	San Francisco P O	83	196
Ellen T	26	f	w	IREL	San Francisco	San Francisco P O	83	202
Frank	39	m	w	IREL	San Francisco	11-Wd San Francisc	84	669
Henry	37	m	w	IREL	Solano	Green Valley Twp	90	38
J	43	m	w	IN	San Joaquin	Liberty Twp	86	84
J	39	m	w	IREL	San Francisco	7-Wd San Francisco	81	196
J	23	m	w	ME	San Joaquin	Castoria Twp	86	9
James	43	m	w	IREL	Tulare	Visalia Twp	92	288
James	42	m	w	KY	Santa Cruz	Pajaro Twp	89	354
James	32	m	w	IREL	San Francisco	San Francisco P O	80	345
James	30	m	w	IREL	San Francisco	5-Wd San Francisco	81	17
James	25	m	w	IREL	San Francisco	1-Wd San Francisco	79	126
James	18	m	w	NY	San Francisco	3-Wd San Francisco	79	316
James H	47	m	w	IREL	Tulare	Kings Rvr Twp	92	253
Jeramiah	36	m	w	IREL	Marin	Nicasio Twp	74	17
Jeremiah	39	m	w	IREL	Santa Cruz	Pajaro Twp	89	341
Jeremiah	30	m	w	IREL	San Francisco	San Francisco P O	85	875
Jeremiah	20	m	w	MA	Santa Clara	Santa Clara Twp	88	175
Jerry	35	m	w	IREL	San Francisco	1-Wd San Francisco	79	132
Jerry	30	m	w	IREL	Marin	San Antonio Twp	74	62
Jno	38	m	w	IREL	Sonoma	Santa Rosa	91	423
Johannah	35	f	w	IREL	Alameda	Hayward	68	76
Johanne	48	f	w	IREL	Solano	Benicia	90	9
John	50	m	w	IREL	Santa Cruz	Santa Cruz	89	415
John	43	m	w	IREL	Tuolumne	Big Oak Flat P O	93	406
John	43	m	w	IREL	Sacramento	Cosumnes Twp	77	88
John	43	m	w	IREL	Nevada	Rough & Ready Twp	75	331
John	42	m	w	IREL	Marin	San Rafael Twp	74	45
John	40	m	w	IREL	Nevada	Bridgeport Twp	75	120
John	35	m	w	IREL	Nevada	Grass Valley Twp	75	227
John	34	m	w	PA	San Francisco	11-Wd San Francisc	84	694
John	34	m	w	IREL	San Francisco	San Francisco P O	83	29
John	33	m	w	IREL	Mendocino	Big Rvr Twp	74	159
John	30	m	w	IREL	San Francisco	1-Wd San Francisco	79	67
John	30	m	w	IREL	San Francisco	San Francisco P O	83	357
John	20	m	w	IREL	San Francisco	1-Wd San Francisco	79	15
John	15	m	w	NY	San Francisco	11-Wd San Francisc	84	588
Joseph	38	m	w	OH	Siskiyou	Yreka	89	661
Julia	19	f	w	NY	San Francisco	San Francisco P O	83	265
Kate	25	f	w	MA	Solano	Tremont Twp	90	34
M	29	m	w	NY	San Joaquin	2-Wd Stockton	86	184
Margaret	23	f	w	MA	San Francisco	8-Wd San Francisco	82	457
Maria	27	f	w	CT	Nevada	Grass Valley Twp	75	144
Maria	22	f	w	ME	Nevada	Grass Valley Twp	75	211
Mary	64	f	w	IREL	San Francisco	San Francisco P O	85	836
Mary	39	f	w	IREL	San Joaquin	1-Wd Stockton	86	140
Mary	32	f	w	IREL	San Francisco	8-Wd San Francisco	82	434
Mary	30	f	w	IREL	San Francisco	San Francisco P O	83	125
Mary	26	f	w	WURT	San Francisco	6-Wd San Francisco	81	71
Mary	14	f	w	IREL	San Francisco	7-Wd San Francisco	81	273
Maryett	15	f	w	CA	San Francisco	11-Wd San Francisc	84	710
Michael	38	m	w	IREL	Solano	Suisun Twp	90	114
Michael	25	m	w	IREL	San Francisco	7-Wd San Francisco	81	252
Michael J	16	m	w	MA	San Francisco	8-Wd San Francisco	82	303
Michl	26	m	w	IREL	San Francisco	San Francisco P O	83	32
Mike	32	m	w	IREL	Solano	Vallejo	90	203
Mike	32	m	w	IREL	Solano	Vallejo	90	215
Moses	42	m	w	TN	San Francisco	11-Wd San Francisc	84	639
Murty	30	m	w	IREL	Solano	Benicia	90	19
Nellie	14	f	w	CA	San Francisco	11-Wd San Francisc	84	710
Patrick	37	m	w	IREL	San Diego	Julian Dist	78	469
Thomas	35	m	w	IREL	Placer	Rocklin Twp	76	466
Timothy	8	m	w	ME	El Dorado	Diamond Springs Tw	72	31
Timothy	49	m	w	IREL	Shasta	Buckeye P O	89	482
Timothy	45	m	w	IREL	San Francisco	11-Wd San Francisc	84	513
Timothy	31	m	w	IREL	Nevada	Grass Valley Twp	75	210
William	21	m	w	NY	San Francisco	7-Wd San Francisco	81	176
William H	29	m	w	IREL	San Francisco	6-Wd San Francisco	81	86
Wm	38	m	w	IREL	Sacramento	4-Wd Sacramento	77	359
DRISDEN								
Murphy	28	m	w	IREL	Stanislaus	Emory Twp	92	22
Sally	44	f	b	MO	Amador	Sutter Crk P O	69	402
W	9	m	b	CA	Amador	Amador City P O	69	395
DRISDON								
Joseph	16	m	b	CA	Amador	Amador City P O	69	395
DRISKEL								
John	45	m	w	IREL	Santa Clara	Santa Clara Twp	88	178
DRISTAL								
Catherine	26	f	w	IREL	San Francisco	7-Wd San Francisco	81	205
DRITZ								
Ambrose	32	m	w	LA	Sacramento	4-Wd Sacramento	77	361
DRIVER								
Annie	24	f	w	CANA	Contra Costa	San Pablo Twp	71	357
E S	40	m	w	IN	Sacramento	Center Twp	77	82
John	50	m	w	PA	Nevada	Nevada Twp	75	288
John	35	m	b	KY	El Dorado	Mud Springs Twp	72	91
Mary	28	f	w	CA	Nevada	Nevada Twp	75	289
Sam H	56	m	w	TN	Trinity	Weaverville Pct	92	231
Thos	59	m	w	ENGL	San Joaquin	1-Wd Stockton	86	137
Thos	49	m	w	SCOT	Yuba	Marysville	93	598
Thos	45	m	w	SCOT	Yuba	Marysville	93	583
DRIZA								
J R	52	m	w	VA	San Joaquin	Tulare Twp	86	250
DROBATZ								
Annie	27	f	w	IREL	San Francisco	1-Wd San Francisco	79	120
Matteo	38	m	w	AUST	San Francisco	1-Wd San Francisco	79	120

Name	Age	S	R	B-PL	County	Locale	Series M593 Roll	Pg
DROGE								
Adam	35	m	w	PRUS	Plumas	Indian Twp	77	12
Frederick	38	m	w	HANO	San Francisco	7-Wd San Francisco	81	158
Henry	35	m	w	HANO	San Francisco	1-Wd San Francisco	79	81
John C	29	m	w	PRUS	San Francisco	6-Wd San Francisco	81	99
DROHAN								
Ellen	25	f	w	IREL	San Francisco	8-Wd San Francisco	82	468
DROHE								
J H	46	m	w	HANO	Alameda	Oakland	68	154
DROIG								
George	26	m	w	SCOT	San Francisco	San Francisco P O	83	243
DROIGHT								
T F	24	m	w	NJ	San Francisco	5-Wd San Francisco	81	36
DROKE								
S P	53	m	w	MA	Monterey	San Juan Twp	74	396
DROKET								
John	36	m	w	CHIL	San Francisco	2-Wd San Francisco	79	279
DROLINGER								
S D	48	m	w	IN	Yuba	East Bear Rvr Twp	93	540
DROMIE								
Constance	42	f	w	FRAN	San Francisco	6-Wd San Francisco	81	78
DRONAN								
Annie	19	f	w	VT	San Francisco	San Francisco P O	83	364
Martin	51	m	w	IREL	San Francisco	1-Wd San Francisco	79	94
DRONARLLETT								
Gustav	43	m	w	FRAN	San Francisco	1-Wd San Francisco	79	106
DRONER								
V S	54	m	w	SWIT	Tuolumne	Chinese Camp P O	93	387
DRONETTE								
Hippolite	56	m	w	FRAN	San Francisco	8-Wd San Francisco	82	387
DRONT								
John V D	29	m	w	NJ	Santa Cruz	Pajaro Twp	89	352
DRONZE								
George	59	m	w	FRAN	Plumas	Washington Twp	77	53
DROSIER								
Peter	27	m	w	CANA	Sierra	Sears Twp	89	557
DROSSER								
Joseph	30	m	w	PRUS	San Francisco	San Francisco P O	80	384
DROST								
B	30	m	w	PRUS	Alameda	Oakland	68	265
William	25	m	w	PRUS	San Francisco	11-Wd San Francisc	84	530
DROSTE								
Henry	24	m	w	GERM	Los Angeles	Los Angeles	73	565
Herman	29	m	w	HANO	San Francisco	San Francisco P O	85	833
DROUDORD								
John	49	m	w	FRAN	Yuba	Parks Bar Twp	93	648
DROUGER								
Peter	35	m	w	WURT	San Francisco	San Francisco P O	83	217
DROUILHAT								
J	45	m	w	FRAN	San Francisco	San Francisco P O	85	797
DROUILLARD								
Joseph	20	m	w	IA	Sacramento	Franklin Twp	77	109
Wm	44	m	w	OH	Sacramento	Franklin Twp	77	120
DROVER								
Jas	28	m	w	CT	Contra Costa	San Pablo Twp	71	365
DROVES								
Addeline	25	f	w	MEXI	Yuba	Marysville	93	600
DROWN								
Albert N	31	m	w	RI	San Francisco	San Francisco P O	85	749
Geo	42	m	w	NY	Butte	Mountain Spring Tw	70	89
Isabella	15	f	w	CA	Santa Barbara	Santa Barbara P O	87	502
Joseph W	17	m	w	CA	Santa Clara	Santa Clara Twp	88	177
DRUCHER								
Herman	21	m	w	HANO	San Mateo	Schoolhouse Statio	87	331
DRUCKEN								
John	31	m	w	HANO	San Francisco	San Francisco P O	83	45
DRUCKER								
August	42	m	w	BRUN	San Francisco	1-Wd San Francisco	79	51
Elial	41	m	w	HANO	San Francisco	11-Wd San Francisc	84	444
DRUCKESATER								
Melville	34	m	w	ME	Santa Clara	San Jose Twp	88	212
DRUDGEN								
John Pearrl	26	m	w	ENGL	Plumas	Indian Twp	77	9
DRUELL								
Wm	20	m	w	IN	Sacramento	American Twp	77	64
DRUGAN								
Jas	31	m	w	IREL	San Joaquin	Tulare Twp	86	258
John	29	m	w	IREL	Alameda	Oakland	68	137
DRUILER								
Charles	12	m	w	NY	Trinity	Weaverville Pct	92	224
DRUILLARD								
Edward	49	m	w	OH	Tulare	Visalia Twp	92	287
DRUKE								
George	52	m	w	IREL	Trinity	Weaverville Pct	92	222
DRULAND								
John	40	m	w	NY	Solano	Vallejo	90	216
DRULEY								
Peter	37	m	w	IREL	San Francisco	7-Wd San Francisco	81	180
DRULLAND								
A	38	m	w	CANA	San Joaquin	Oneal Twp	86	102
DRULLESTON								
John R	59	m	w	WALE	Mono	Bridgeport P O	74	282
DRUM								
Jane	40	f	w	IREL	San Francisco	6-Wd San Francisco	81	147
P D	36	m	w	NY	Sutter	Yuba Twp	92	140
Patrick	43	m	w	IREL	Calaveras	San Andreas P O	70	201
Peter	47	m	w	PA	Yuba	Marysville	93	618

© 2001 by Heritage Quest. All rights reserved.

Name	Age	S	R	B-PL	County	Locale	Roll	Pg
						Series M593		
Thomas	26	m	w	IL	San Francisco	11-Wd San Francisc	84	660
Thomas J	27	m	w	MO	San Francisco	6-Wd San Francisco	81	120
Wm	57	m	w	NY	Yuba	Marysville Twp	93	570
DRUMAN								
William	27	m	w	CANA	Solano	Vacaville Twp	90	124
DRUMAND								
Donald	36	m	w	CANA	Sonoma	Petaluma Twp	91	352
DRUMLETS								
Paul	32	m	w	PRUS	San Francisco	San Francisco P O	80	479
DRUMM								
Benj	53	m	w	MO	Monterey	Castroville Twp	74	340
Chas	23	m	w	BAVA	Napa	Napa Twp	75	70
J S	40	m	w	IL	Alameda	Oakland	68	211
DRUMMER								
Henry	50	m	w	BAVA	San Francisco	1-Wd San Francisco	79	39
DRUMMOND								
A J	40	m	w	TN	Santa Clara	Gilroy Twp	88	72
B	43	m	w	OH	Sacramento	3-Wd Sacramento	77	269
Eliza	39	f	w	SCOT	San Francisco	7-Wd San Francisco	81	258
Elizebeth	40	f	w	SCOT	San Francisco	7-Wd San Francisco	81	281
Hugh	67	m	w	IREL	Nevada	Nevada Twp	75	321
J B	27	m	w	WI	Nevada	Nevada Twp	75	280
James	60	m	w	ENGL	Marin	Novato Twp	74	11
Jane	25	m	w	IL	Yolo	Cache Crk Twp	93	447
Jas	45	m	w	ME	Sacramento	3-Wd Sacramento	77	257
John	9	m	w	MA	San Francisco	7-Wd San Francisco	81	245
Jonathan G	40	m	w	IL	Yolo	Putah Twp	93	512
Joseph	32	m	w	RI	Contra Costa	Martinez P O	71	444
Richard	40	m	w	DC	San Francisco	11-Wd San Francisc	84	544
DRUMOND								
A N	63	m	w	KY	El Dorado	Georgetown Twp	72	47
DRUMUND								
J B	28	m	w	WI	Nevada	Nevada Twp	75	297
DRUNZER								
Peter	39	m	w	BAVA	Nevada	Little York Twp	75	238
DRURY								
A J	43	m	w	NH	Marin	San Rafael Twp	74	39
Bridget	42	f	w	IREL	Sacramento	3-Wd Sacramento	77	257
Clara	19	f	w	PA	Sacramento	3-Wd Sacramento	77	259
Ella	12	f	w	CANA	San Francisco	San Francisco P O	83	311
Frederick S	34	m	w	NY	San Francisco	8-Wd San Francisco	82	436
Gardner	29	m	b	MS	San Francisco	San Francisco P O	80	411
Gerd	40	m	w	NY	San Joaquin	Castoria Twp	86	11
James	52	m	w	MA	Sacramento	Sutter Twp	77	393
James	43	m	w	CANA	San Francisco	San Francisco P O	85	859
John Reynolds	44	m	w	IN	Plumas	Indian Twp	77	15
Owen J	50	m	w	IREL	Calaveras	San Andreas P O	70	179
Patk	35	m	w	IREL	Yuba	Rose Bar Twp	93	660
Peter	36	m	w	IREL	San Francisco	1-Wd San Francisco	79	1
Rafael	63	m	w	US	El Dorado	Diamond Springs Tw	72	24
Robert	65	m	w	VA	Placer	Bath P O	76	441
Sol	38	m	w	NY	San Joaquin	Castoria Twp	86	11
Wm	49	m	w	PA	San Francisco	11-Wd San Francisc	84	572
DRUS								
Christina	19	f	w	AUST	Amador	Fiddletown P O	69	432
DRUSSELL								
Daniel	36	m	w	PRUS	San Francisco	San Francisco P O	83	290
DRY								
Nathan	44	m	w	PA	Siskiyou	Surprise Valley Tw	89	640
DRYBER								
Frank	39	m	w	FRAN	Yolo	Putah Twp	93	524
DRYBREAD								
Hess	21	m	w	IN	Siskiyou	Callahan P O	89	632
DRYDEN								
Anita	32	f	w	CA	Los Angeles	Los Angeles	73	512
Cornelius	45	m	w	PA	Solano	Maine Prairie Twp	90	46
Dan A	46	m	w	VA	San Diego	San Diego	78	501
David	44	m	w	MA	Placer	Rocklin Twp	76	468
Michael	35	m	w	IREL	Contra Costa	Martinez Twp	71	350
Nathan B	37	m	w	MO	El Dorado	Kelsey Twp	72	60
O D	48	m	w	MO	Santa Clara	Gilroy Twp	88	99
Richard	35	m	w	ENGL	Nevada	Grass Valley Twp	75	221
Solidad	38	f	w	CA	Los Angeles	Los Angeles	73	530
Thos L	50	m	w	KY	Monterey	San Juan Twp	74	393
William	35	m	w	NY	Los Angeles	Los Angeles Twp	73	491
DRYDON								
R A	35	m	w	VA	Sierra	Sierra Twp	89	563
DRYE								
John	29	m	w	KY	San Diego	Warners Rancho Dis	78	530
DRYER								
Charles	35	m	w	NY	San Francisco	San Francisco P O	80	343
Henry	42	m	w	PRUS	El Dorado	White Oak Twp	72	139
John	39	m	w	HANO	San Francisco	3-Wd San Francisco	79	290
Patrick	37	m	w	IREL	San Francisco	11-Wd San Francisc	84	525
Wm F	36	m	w	LA	San Francisco	1-Wd San Francisco	79	54
DRYNAN								
Alexander	19	m	w	CANA	Nevada	Little York Twp	75	237
Catherine	40	f	w	CANA	Nevada	Little York Twp	75	241
John	44	m	w	MA	Alameda	Oakland	68	150
Robert	58	m	w	SCOT	Nevada	Little York Twp	75	243
DRYNE								
Julia	40	f	w	IREL	San Francisco	San Francisco P O	83	324
DRYRY								
John	24	m	w	NY	San Francisco	8-Wd San Francisco	82	430
DRYSDALE								
James	21	m	w	NY	San Francisco	3-Wd San Francisco	79	296

Name	Age	S	R	B-PL	County	Locale	Roll	Pg
						Series M593		
DRYSON								
Israel	39	m	w	ENGL	Nevada	Meadow Lake Twp	75	270
DSOIS								
Adam N	29	m	w	IL	Placer	Emigrant Gap P O	76	416
DU								
Ah	18	m	c	CHIN	Sierra	Eureka Twp	89	523
Gee	27	m	c	CHIN	Yuba	Marysville	93	624
High	24	m	c	CHIN	Tehama	Antelope Twp	92	155
DUANE								
C B	40	m	w	IREL	San Francisco	San Francisco P O	85	869
Edward	60	m	w	IREL	San Francisco	San Francisco P O	83	315
Henry L	40	m	w	CT	Sonoma	Petaluma Twp	91	317
Johanna	25	f	w	IREL	San Francisco	5-Wd San Francisco	81	27
John	32	m	w	IREL	San Francisco	2-Wd San Francisco	79	282
John	28	m	w	IREL	Solano	Vallejo	90	187
John	25	m	w	MO	San Francisco	6-Wd San Francisco	81	92
Mary	42	f	w	IREL	Napa	Napa Twp	75	65
Timothy	33	m	w	IREL	San Francisco	San Francisco P O	83	8
DUANN								
Mary	6	f	w	NY	San Francisco	11-Wd San Francisc	84	606
DUARD								
J	24	m	w	NY	Sacramento	1-Wd Sacramento	77	188
DUART								
Cruz	40	m	w	MEXI	Kern	Bakersfield P O	73	357
Jesse	25	m	w	PORT	Monterey	San Juan Twp	74	397
Joseph	36	m	w	PORT	Monterey	San Juan Twp	74	397
DUARTA								
Domingo	27	m	w	PORT	Alameda	Washington Twp	68	268
DUARTE								
Andres	35	m	w	CA	Los Angeles	San Jose Twp	73	623
Angel	40	m	w	MEXI	Los Angeles	Los Angeles	73	515
Cayetano	38	m	w	CA	Los Angeles	San Gabriel Twp	73	597
Domnic	28	m	w	MEXI	Calaveras	Copperopolis P O	70	261
Francisca	51	f	w	CA	Los Angeles	Los Angeles	73	555
Jose	46	m	w	CA	Los Angeles	Santa Ana Twp	73	612
Jose A	15	m	w	CA	Los Angeles	San Gabriel Twp	73	593
Juana	60	f	w	MEXI	Los Angeles	Los Angeles Twp	73	467
Lorette	28	m	m	MEXI	Mariposa	Maxwell Crk P O	74	143
Luis	40	m	w	MEXI	Los Angeles	San Gabriel Twp	73	594
Manuel	65	m	w	PORT	Los Angeles	Wilmington Twp	73	640
Manuel	35	m	w	MEXI	Los Angeles	Los Angeles Twp	73	467
Manul	26	m	w	CA	Los Angeles	El Monte Twp	73	459
Mayo	65	m	w	CA	Los Angeles	San Jose Twp	73	623
Paula	18	f	w	CA	Los Angeles	San Jose Twp	73	620
Ramon	30	f	w	CA	Los Angeles	Santa Ana Twp	73	614
Rosario	20	m	w	MEXI	Los Angeles	Los Angeles	73	516
DUARTO								
Guadaloup	33	m	w	MEXI	Fresno	Millerton P O	72	166
Joan	38	m	w	MEXI	Fresno	Millerton P O	72	157
Romaldo	38	m	i	MEXI	Inyo	Cerro Gordo Twp	73	323
Satiago	60	m	w	CA	Santa Clara	Almaden Twp	88	18
DUARTY								
Francis	37	m	w	MEXI	San Joaquin	2-Wd Stockton	86	171
Francisco	35	m	w	MEXI	Fresno	Millerton P O	72	155
DUAS								
Joseph	37	m	w	PORT	Contra Costa	Martinez P O	71	437
DUBACKER								
Caspar	28	m	w	SWIT	Shasta	American Ranch P O	89	499
DUBAKER								
H	30	m	w	SWIT	Tehama	Antelope Twp	92	154
DUBB								
Jas	21	m	w	CANA	Solano	Vallejo	90	139
DUBBERS								
Henry	50	m	w	GERM	Santa Barbara	San Buenaventura P	87	433
DUBBS								
Michael	43	m	w	FRAN	San Mateo	Woodside P O	87	387
DUBEAU								
Harmon	50	m	w	BADE	Calaveras	San Andreas P O	70	178
John	38	m	w	FRAN	Marin	Nicasio Twp	74	18
Joseph	53	m	w	FRAN	Plumas	Goodwin Twp	77	8
DUBEC								
Julien	26	m	w	CANA	Plumas	Washington Twp	77	25
DUBECKER								
Frank	24	m	w	SWED	Sacramento	Franklin Twp	77	119
DUBEE								
Pierre	50	m	w	FRAN	Santa Clara	San Jose Twp	88	188
DUBES								
Adon	50	m	w	FRAN	El Dorado	Salmon Falls Twp	72	131
DUBEY								
George	40	m	w	CANA	El Dorado	Placerville	72	121
DUBIES								
Francis	16	m	w	CA	San Francisco	11-Wd San Francisc	84	673
DUBLER								
Anna	37	f	w	SWIT	Sacramento	4-Wd Sacramento	77	331
DUBOIS								
Abraham C	65	m	w	NY	Placer	Auburn P O	76	368
Amos S	42	m	w	NY	Placer	Auburn P O	76	367
Annie E	36	f	w	NY	San Francisco	8-Wd San Francisco	82	301
Cyrus	47	m	w	NY	Santa Cruz	Watsonville	89	367
Edme	71	m	w	FRAN	San Francisco	San Francisco P O	83	135
Elijah	37	m	w	OH	Marin	San Rafael	74	58
George	22	m	w	GERM	San Luis Obispo	San Luis Obispo Tw	87	309
Henriquez	44	m	w	FRAN	Los Angeles	Los Angeles	73	553
Henry A	30	m	w	NY	Marin	San Rafael	74	54
James	32	m	w	NY	San Francisco	San Francisco P O	80	539
James	13	m	w	CA	Santa Clara	Gilroy Twp	88	102
John	36	m	w	AL	Los Angeles	Santa Ana Twp	73	617

© 2001 by Heritage Quest. All rights reserved.

Name	Age	S	R	B-PL	County	Locale	Roll	Pg
John B	33	m	w	OH	Los Angeles	Los Angeles	73	529
Julia	48	f	w	FRAN	San Francisco	11-Wd San Francisc	84	652
Julius	26	m	w	SWIT	Napa	Napa	75	22
Leon	24	m	w	FRAN	Sierra	Sears Twp	89	556
Lida	16	f	w	NY	San Francisco	San Francisco P O	83	130
Manuel	46	m	w	FRAN	Sacramento	4-Wd Sacramento	77	337
Mary	28	f	w	OH	Marin	Bolinas Twp	74	7
Orrin	51	m	w	NY	Santa Clara	San Jose Twp	88	205
Phillip	30	m	w	FRAN	San Francisco	San Francisco P O	83	330
Thomas L	43	m	w	AL	Yolo	Merritt Twp	93	507
Victor	40	m	w	FRAN	San Francisco	San Francisco P O	80	350
Virginie	55	f	w	FRAN	San Francisco	San Francisco P O	80	455
W C	33	m	w	OH	Alameda	Oakland	68	174
William	14	m	w	IL	Yolo	Cache Crk Twp	93	440
Wm	39	m	w	NY	San Diego	San Diego	78	497
DUBOISE								
Alfred	41	m	w	FRAN	San Francisco	1-Wd San Francisco	79	50
Felipe	60	m	w	FRAN	Calaveras	San Andreas P O	70	184
Franquin	53	m	w	ITAL	Calaveras	San Andreas P O	70	174
DUBOKE								
J	45	m	w	FRAN	Alameda	Alameda	68	19
DUBOSA								
William	48	m	w	FRAN	Mariposa	Mariposa P O	74	129
DUBOURDINE								
B	46	m	w	FRAN	Los Angeles	Los Angeles	73	558
DUBRIALDO								
Frank	31	m	w	ITAL	Sacramento	Sutter Twp	77	386
DUBRICE								
James	40	m	w	NY	Alameda	Oakland	68	129
DUBRUTZ								
Frank C M	24	m	w	AL	San Francisco	6-Wd San Francisco	81	73
DUBUREAU								
Leopold	40	m	w	FRAN	San Francisco	1-Wd San Francisco	79	50
DUBURTZ								
Fred	24	m	w	AL	San Francisco	8-Wd San Francisco	82	333
DUBUSSE								
Felix	48	m	w	FRAN	Calaveras	San Andreas P O	70	155
DUC								
Ah	30	m	c	CHIN	Sacramento	1-Wd Sacramento	77	204
DUCA								
Philip	37	m	w	ITAL	Nevada	Nevada Twp	75	273
DUCAN								
Mary	22	f	w	IREL	Sacramento	3-Wd Sacramento	77	318
William	55	m	w	SCOT	San Francisco	San Francisco P O	83	359
DUCAT								
Mad	36	f	w	FRAN	San Joaquin	2-Wd Stockton	86	172
DUCATO								
Joseph	33	m	w	ITAL	Alameda	Eden Twp	68	60
DUCETT								
Charles M	26	m	w	ME	San Mateo	Pescadero P O	87	412
DUCH								
Ah	38	m	c	CHIN	El Dorado	Coloma Twp	72	10
DUCHAM								
Alfred	33	m	w	CANA	Marin	Novato Twp	74	13
DUCHANGE								
Henry	45	m	w	FRAN	San Francisco	San Francisco P O	80	465
DUCHENE								
Paul	32	m	w	FRAN	San Francisco	1-Wd San Francisco	79	50
DUCHENNE								
Albert	60	m	w	FRAN	Trinity	North Fork Twp	92	217
DUCHESNE								
Henri	43	m	w	FRAN	San Francisco	5-Wd San Francisco	81	30
DUCHESNEAU								
John C	38	m	w	CANA	Santa Clara	Fremont Twp	88	52
DUCHINE								
Vincent	40	m	w	FRAN	San Francisco	1-Wd San Francisco	79	49
DUCHOW								
J C	39	m	w	MA	Tuolumne	Columbia P O	93	342
M C	23	m	w	MA	Tuolumne	Columbia P O	93	338
DUCHSTEIN								
Fredk	56	m	w	PRUS	Placer	Newcastle Twp	76	473
DUCIN								
August	24	m	w	FRAN	Los Angeles	Los Angeles Twp	73	478
DUCK								
Ah	45	m	c	CHIN	Placer	Bath P O	76	429
Ah	40	m	c	CHIN	Stanislaus	Emory Twp	92	23
Ah	35	m	c	CHIN	Fresno	Millerton P O	72	201
Ah	31	m	c	CHIN	Trinity	North Fork Twp	92	216
Ah	31	m	c	CHIN	Kern	Bakersfield P O	73	357
Ah	30	m	c	CHIN	Sacramento	Granite Twp	77	141
Ah	30	m	c	CHIN	Stanislaus	Emory Twp	92	23
Ah	25	m	c	CHIN	Plumas	Goodwin Twp	77	4
Elisha	18	m	w	WI	Trinity	Lewiston Pct	92	211
Gee	16	m	c	CHIN	Plumas	Mineral Twp	77	24
John	48	m	w	ENGL	Trinity	Lewiston Pct	92	213
John A	40	m	w	PA	Alameda	Brooklyn	68	32
Kim	36	m	c	CHIN	Placer	Dutch Flat P O	76	402
DUCKATEL								
Frank	30	m	w	FRAN	Sacramento	Granite Twp	77	148
DUCKEL								
Michael	36	m	w	NY	San Francisco	2-Wd San Francisco	79	246
DUCKER								
Albert	35	m	w	PRUS	San Francisco	San Francisco P O	83	208
Benj	27	m	w	MO	Fresno	Kings Rvr P O	72	213
Charles	38	m	w	PRUS	San Francisco	San Francisco P O	83	395
Christopher	27	m	w	HANO	Santa Clara	Fremont Twp	88	53
Frederick	32	m	w	HANO	San Francisco	San Francisco P O	83	143
Henry	30	m	w	HANO	Santa Clara	Fremont Twp	88	53
John	40	m	w	IREL	Mendocino	Point Arena Twp	74	205
John	35	m	w	PRUS	San Francisco	San Francisco P O	83	395
DUCKERT								
John	48	m	w	HDAR	San Francisco	San Francisco P O	80	532
Theodore	35	m	w	SHOL	San Francisco	1-Wd San Francisco	79	51
Wm	75	m	w	KY	Sonoma	Santa Rosa	91	417
DUCKET								
Joseph	22	m	w	NC	Sonoma	Analy Twp	91	238
DUCKETT								
Edward	63	m	w	ENGL	San Francisco	11-Wd San Francisc	84	509
John	31	m	w	MI	Humboldt	Pacific Twp	72	290
Rachel	57	f	w	IREL	San Francisco	1-Wd San Francisco	79	31
William	33	m	w	MI	Humboldt	Pacific Twp	72	290
DUCKIN								
Thos	35	m	w	IREL	San Francisco	11-Wd San Francisc	84	666
DUCKMANTIN								
Saml	28	m	w	ENGL	Alameda	Washington Twp	68	295
DUCKWALL								
D D	27	m	w	IL	Tuolumne	Sonora P O	93	324
W L	38	m	w	OH	Tuolumne	Sonora P O	93	324
Wm J	62	m	w	VA	Tuolumne	Sonora P O	93	324
DUCKWORTH								
Edward	44	m	w	ENGL	El Dorado	Mud Springs Twp	72	77
Erania	12	f	w	CA	Monterey	Monterey Twp	74	348
Sanpego	39	m	w	CA	Monterey	Monterey Twp	74	348
W	42	m	w	CA	Monterey	Monterey	74	358
DUCOING								
Clara	15	f	w	CA	San Francisco	3-Wd San Francisco	79	317
DUCOMMERA								
Mary	32	f	w	OH	San Francisco	San Francisco P O	83	348
DUCOMMON								
E	19	f	w	SWIT	Solano	Vallejo	90	199
DUCOMON								
Eugene	22	m	w	NY	San Francisco	3-Wd San Francisco	79	321
DUCORRIN								
Jane	37	f	w	ENGL	San Francisco	San Francisco P O	80	380
DUCORRON								
Chs	30	m	w	ENGL	San Francisco	2-Wd San Francisco	79	193
DUCOTEY								
Jane	55	f	w	FRAN	Nevada	Grass Valley Twp	75	223
DUCRAY								
John	37	m	w	FRAN	Nevada	Nevada Twp	75	305
John B	45	m	w	FRAN	Nevada	Nevada Twp	75	287
DUCRUET								
Gustine	48	f	w	FRAN	San Francisco	San Francisco P O	83	259
DUCY								
Patrick	50	m	w	IREL	Alameda	Brooklyn	68	21
DUDAES								
John	57	m	w	FRAN	Inyo	Lone Pine Twp	73	334
DUDDING								
Richard	58	m	w	ENGL	Napa	Napa	75	42
DUDDLEY								
Morris	25	m	w	IREL	San Francisco	11-Wd San Francisc	84	705
DUDDY								
James	29	m	w	IREL	San Francisco	San Francisco P O	83	307
DUDE								
Conrad	25	m	w	DENM	San Francisco	1-Wd San Francisco	79	74
DUDEN								
Geo E	38	m	w	PA	Sacramento	Sutter Twp	77	388
George	58	m	w	PA	San Francisco	San Francisco P O	83	312
DUDENI								
Jackims	38	m	w	SWIT	Napa	Napa Twp	75	28
DUDERICK								
Henry	26	m	w	PRUS	San Francisco	8-Wd San Francisco	82	331
DUDERKIRK								
Isaac	28	m	w	CANA	Monterey	San Juan Twp	74	413
DUDEY								
Woah	24	f	w	IREL	San Francisco	San Francisco P O	83	329
DUDFIELD								
James	33	m	w	ENGL	Santa Clara	1-Wd San Jose	88	252
DUDGEON								
Eneas	55	m	w	SCOT	San Francisco	11-Wd San Francisc	84	449
DUDINE								
Ferdinand	68	m	w	ITAL	Calaveras	San Andreas P O	70	206
DUDLES								
Thomas	36	m	w	ENGL	San Francisco	3-Wd San Francisco	79	301
DUDLEY								
A A	37	m	w	PA	San Joaquin	Castoria Twp	86	3
A K	34	m	w	ME	Amador	Sutter Crk P O	69	398
Albert	40	m	w	IREL	San Joaquin	1-Wd Stockton	86	123
Allen P	50	m	w	NH	San Francisco	2-Wd San Francisco	79	257
Benjamin	40	m	w	NY	Mendocino	Cuffeys Cove Twp	74	168
C P	48	m	w	NH	San Francisco	San Francisco P O	85	844
Charles	32	m	w	VT	Alpine	Markleeville P O	69	312
Chas	26	m	w	MA	San Francisco	8-Wd San Francisco	82	354
Chas S	44	m	w	ME	Shasta	French Gulch P O	89	469
D D	29	m	w	ME	Humboldt	Pacific Twp	72	293
E G	40	m	w	MA	Solano	Vallejo	90	209
Evan	42	m	w	WALE	Siskiyou	Yreka	89	659
George	60	m	w	TN	Siskiyou	Yreka Twp	89	672
George	35	m	w	IREL	San Francisco	11-Wd San Francisc	84	523
Greengrove	42	m	w	ME	Humboldt	Pacific Twp	72	296
H E	47	m	w	ME	Mariposa	Maxwell Crk P O	74	143
Henry	53	m	w	NY	Sonoma	Healdsburg & Mendo	91	277
Henry H	32	m	w	CT	San Francisco	1-Wd San Francisco	79	88
James	37	m	w	IL	Humboldt	Mattole Twp	72	287

© 2001 by Heritage Quest. All rights reserved.

California 1870 Census

Series M593

Name	Age	S	R	B-PL	County	Locale	Roll	Pg
James	25	m	w	NY	Marin	San Rafael Twp	74	45
Jane	40	f	w	NY	Monterey	San Juan Twp	74	411
John	45	m	w	MA	San Diego	Fort Yuma Dist	78	463
John	30	m	w	IREL	Alameda	Oakland	68	264
Johnathan	39	m	w	NY	Solano	Silveyville Twp	90	88
L F	28	m	w	ME	Mariposa	Maxwell Crk P O	74	143
Mary	31	f	w	TN	Napa	Napa	75	1
Owen	36	m	w	ME	Humboldt	Pacific Twp	72	295
P W	27	m	w	KY	San Joaquin	2-Wd Stockton	86	188
S J	38	m	w	NC	Sacramento	1-Wd Sacramento	77	191
Solomon	60	m	b	VA	Nevada	Bloomfield Twp	75	94
Theron C	24	m	w	NY	El Dorado	Placerville	72	108
Thomas	49	m	w	MA	Placer	Roseville P O	76	351
Thomas	46	m	w	KY	Santa Cruz	Soquel Twp	89	441
Thomas	45	m	w	FRAN	San Francisco	5-Wd San Francisco	81	16
V E	27	m	w	ME	Mariposa	Maxwell Crk P O	74	143
W L	42	m	w	NY	San Joaquin	2-Wd Stockton	86	196
Wilberforce	38	m	w	ENGL	Solano	Vallejo	90	158
DUDLY								
Joseph F	32	m	w	ME	Yuba	Slate Range Bar Tw	93	674
Lewis	32	m	w	ME	Nevada	Nevada Twp	75	308
Martin	35	m	w	IREL	Alameda	Oakland	68	149
DUDMAN								
Wm	25	m	w	ENGL	Humboldt	Arcata Twp	72	235
DUDVIT								
Ann	45	f	w	ENGL	Alameda	Oakland	68	197
DUDY								
William	48	m	w	IREL	Yolo	Cache Crk Twp	93	422
DUE								
Ah	30	m	c	CHIN	Sacramento	1-Wd Sacramento	77	197
Ah	14	m	c	CHIN	Placer	Colfax P O	76	390
E H	36	m	w	DENM	San Joaquin	Tulare Twp	86	253
Geo	50	m	w	ENGL	Calaveras	Copperopolis P O	70	230
Who	20	m	c	CHIN	Yuba	Marysville	93	622
William	58	m	w	TN	Calaveras	Copperopolis P O	70	222
William	42	m	w	NJ	Contra Costa	Martinez P O	71	435
DUEAZEIN								
Jean	28	m	w	FRAN	Los Angeles	Wilmington Twp	73	644
DUEGAN								
Samuel	35	m	w	IREL	San Francisco	San Francisco P O	83	347
DUEGER								
Alice	42	f	w	IREL	San Francisco	San Francisco P O	80	534
DUEGLEHUTH								
C	44	m	w	HDAR	San Francisco	11-Wd San Francisc	84	448
DUEL								
Calritra	40	m	w	PORT	Santa Clara	Almaden Twp	88	8
Edmond	34	m	w	NY	Humboldt	Arcata Twp	72	231
Elmina	7	f	w	CA	Yuba	Parks Bar Twp	93	649
J B	44	m	w	MO	Mendocino	Little Lake Twp	74	193
Joseph	44	m	w	ENGL	Marin	San Rafael Twp	74	47
DUELL								
Joseph	50	m	w	FRAN	San Francisco	2-Wd San Francisco	79	243
Joseph	35	m	w	NY	San Francisco	1-Wd San Francisco	79	93
Philip	40	m	w	NY	Mendocino	Round Valley India	74	180
DUELY								
A [Capt]	55	m	w	NY	San Francisco	8-Wd San Francisco	82	364
DUENALD								
Frank	41	m	w	PRUS	San Francisco	2-Wd San Francisco	79	178
DUENKEL								
Herman	46	m	w	PRUS	Siskiyou	Yreka	89	654
Willm	35	m	w	PRUS	Siskiyou	Yreka	89	656
DUENSING								
Adolf	20	m	w	HANO	Butte	Oregon Twp	70	123
Conrad	64	m	w	HANO	Butte	Kimshew Tpw	70	82
Earnest	45	m	w	HANO	Butte	Kimshew Tpw	70	82
Edwd	6	m	w	CA	Butte	Concow Twp	70	9
Geo	40	m	w	BADE	Butte	Oregon Twp	70	131
Robt	80	m	w	BADE	Butte	Oregon Twp	70	131
Wm	22	m	w	HANO	Butte	Hamilton Twp	70	66
DUER								
Chas A	20	m	w	MO	San Francisco	San Francisco P O	83	202
Jerry	18	m	w	SHOL	Alameda	Eden Twp	68	68
DUERDEN								
Lizzie	12	f	w	ME	San Francisco	San Francisco P O	85	798
DUEROQUET								
August	36	m	w	FRAN	San Francisco	San Francisco P O	80	468
DUERRING								
John	50	m	w	VA	San Francisco	2-Wd San Francisco	79	253
DUERTA								
Martina	10	f	w	CA	Monterey	Monterey	74	359
DUERTE								
Albino	50	m	w	CA	Mendocino	Sanel Twp	74	228
Rosario	42	m	w	CA	Monterey	Monterey	74	354
DUESLER								
James Wm	55	m	w	NY	Plumas	Plumas Twp	77	28
DUEY								
Ah	28	m	c	CHIN	Yuba	Marysville	93	619
Ah	24	m	c	CHIN	Nevada	Little York Twp	75	234
DUFAAN								
Charles	45	m	w	FRAN	San Francisco	San Francisco P O	80	350
DUFAN								
John T	26	m	w	NY	Nevada	Meadow Lake Twp	75	250
DUFF								
Abraham	51	m	w	VA	Merced	Snelling P O	74	247
Adel	45	f	m	DC	Mariposa	Mariposa P O	74	119
Alice	8	f	w	CA	Santa Clara	Santa Clara Twp	88	151
Alice	35	f	w	IREL	San Francisco	San Francisco P O	85	759

Series M593

Name	Age	S	R	B-PL	County	Locale	Roll	Pg
Andrew	38	m	w	IREL	San Francisco	San Francisco P O	83	13
Caltha	17	f	w	MO	Contra Costa	Martinez P O	71	375
Charles	22	m	w	NY	Sacramento	Natomas Twp	77	165
Chas	23	m	w	NY	San Joaquin	Douglas Twp	86	35
Eliza R	72	f	w	CANA	Humboldt	Eureka Twp	72	256
Ferris B C	44	m	w	AL	Fresno	Millerton P O	72	181
George	28	m	w	OH	Placer	Bath P O	76	460
Green	39	m	w	IL	Santa Clara	Santa Clara Twp	88	169
J E	27	m	w	IREL	San Joaquin	3-Wd Stockton	86	218
James	49	m	b	FL	Mariposa	Mariposa P O	74	119
James	41	m	w	NY	San Francisco	San Francisco P O	83	359
James	39	m	w	TN	Placer	Lincoln P O	76	488
James	36	m	w	SCOT	San Francisco	1-Wd San Francisco	79	125
James	31	m	w	SCOT	San Francisco	2-Wd San Francisco	79	166
James	28	m	w	CANA	Mendocino	Point Arena Twp	74	213
James R	47	m	w	CANA	Humboldt	Eureka Twp	72	268
John	48	m	w	NY	San Francisco	11-Wd San Francisc	84	609
John	20	m	w	SCOT	San Francisco	3-Wd San Francisco	79	323
Louise V	16	f	w	CA	San Francisco	San Francisco P O	83	96
M H	22	m	w	CT	Solano	Vallejo	90	146
Mary	37	f	w	IREL	San Francisco	6-Wd San Francisco	81	153
Mary	30	f	b	MD	San Francisco	6-Wd San Francisco	81	79
Mary Ann	68	f	w	IREL	Napa	Napa Twp	75	30
Mary E	15	f	w	DC	Mariposa	Mariposa P O	74	119
Michael	27	m	w	IREL	San Francisco	San Francisco P O	83	156
Milton	22	m	w	OH	Tulare	White Rvr Twp	92	301
Richard	74	m	w	ENGL	Humboldt	Eureka Twp	72	256
Robert	28	m	w	PA	San Francisco	5-Wd San Francisco	81	24
S A	37	m	w	TN	Siskiyou	Scott Valley Twp	89	613
Simon	45	m	w	IREL	Sacramento	1-Wd Sacramento	77	188
Thomas	32	m	w	NY	San Francisco	2-Wd San Francisco	79	271
Thos G	35	m	w	DC	San Francisco	San Francisco P O	83	42
William	23	m	w	CANA	Nevada	Grass Valley Twp	75	229
Wm	30	m	w	ENGL	San Francisco	1-Wd San Francisco	79	6
DUFFE								
John	40	m	w	IREL	San Francisco	2-Wd San Francisco	79	213
Michael	35	m	w	IREL	Merced	Snelling P O	74	272
DUFFEE								
Dennis	35	m	w	MA	Placer	Pino Twp	76	472
James	43	m	w	PA	Yolo	Washington Twp	93	534
James	42	m	w	PA	Yolo	Washington Twp	93	528
James	37	m	w	PA	Placer	Roseville P O	76	355
James	25	m	w	IREL	Placer	Pino Twp	76	472
Jas J	25	m	w	CANA	Nevada	Eureka Twp	75	138
John	60	m	w	IREL	Sonoma	Petaluma Twp	91	360
John	22	m	w	NY	Sacramento	San Joaquin Twp	77	397
Kate	10	f	w	CA	Alameda	Oakland	68	242
Martin	45	m	w	IREL	Calaveras	San Andreas P O	70	160
Mary	57	f	w	IREL	Solano	Benicia	90	6
DUFFEN								
Joseph	28	m	w	FRAN	San Francisco	2-Wd San Francisco	79	247
DUFFEY								
Anne	35	f	w	IREL	San Francisco	San Francisco P O	83	329
B C	35	m	w	IREL	San Francisco	San Francisco P O	83	325
Catherine	11	f	w	CA	Yuba	New York Twp	93	641
Dennis	63	m	w	IREL	Marin	San Antonio Twp	74	62
Edward	42	m	w	ENGL	Nevada	Little York Twp	75	239
Edward	25	m	w	IREL	San Francisco	3-Wd San Francisco	79	323
G A	43	m	w	VA	Tehama	Antelope Twp	92	155
George	23	m	w	ENGL	Nevada	Little York Twp	75	241
Henry	33	m	w	IREL	San Francisco	San Francisco P O	83	331
Hugh	31	m	w	NY	Contra Costa	Martinez P O	71	427
James	40	m	w	IREL	San Francisco	San Francisco P O	85	846
James	39	m	w	IREL	Yuba	Slate Range Bar Tw	93	668
James	27	m	w	IREL	San Francisco	San Francisco P O	83	219
James	23	m	w	IREL	Alameda	Oakland	68	132
John	45	m	w	PRUS	San Francisco	11-Wd San Francisc	84	533
John	40	m	w	IREL	Alameda	Murray Twp	68	119
John	40	m	w	IREL	San Francisco	11-Wd San Francisc	84	613
John P	24	m	w	PA	San Francisco	San Francisco P O	83	370
Pat	43	m	w	IREL	Alameda	Oakland	68	249
Patrick	40	m	w	IREL	San Francisco	San Francisco P O	83	245
Patrick	27	m	w	IREL	San Francisco	7-Wd San Francisco	81	172
Peter	30	m	w	IREL	Contra Costa	San Pablo Twp	71	360
Rogers	32	m	w	IREL	San Joaquin	1-Wd Stockton	86	125
Thomas	25	m	w	IREL	San Luis Obispo	Salinas Twp	87	295
William	28	m	w	CANA	Yolo	Cache Crk Twp	93	424
Wm P	30	m	w	IREL	San Francisco	3-Wd San Francisco	79	302
DUFFICY								
Alicia	55	f	w	IREL	Santa Clara	Gilroy Twp	88	72
Dennis	25	m	w	IREL	Yuba	Marysville	93	582
M C	30	m	w	IREL	Yuba	Marysville	93	582
DUFFIE								
A	28	m	w	WI	Humboldt	Eureka Twp	72	260
Mary	15	f	w	CA	El Dorado	Salmon Falls Twp	72	131
DUFFIELD								
Alexander	48	m	w	IL	Nevada	Grass Valley Twp	75	225
Christopher	43	m	w	VA	Solano	Silveyville Twp	90	85
Geo W	41	m	w	ENGL	San Francisco	1-Wd San Francisco	79	29
Jesse H	27	m	w	IL	Colusa	Grand Island Twp	71	303
DUFFIN								
James	72	m	w	IREL	Sacramento	3-Wd Sacramento	77	283
John	28	m	w	IREL	San Francisco	7-Wd San Francisco	81	178
Wm	30	m	w	ENGL	Sacramento	3-Wd Sacramento	77	297
DUFFING								
William	22	m	w	CANA	Nevada	Grass Valley Twp	75	157

© 2001 by Heritage Quest. All rights reserved.

Name	Age	S	R	B-PL	County	Locale	Series M593 Roll	Pg
DUFFIT								
Frank	51	m	w	FRAN	Alameda	Oakland	68	130
DUFFLEY								
C	60	m	w	IREL	Solano	Vallejo	90	195
Thos	35	m	w	IREL	San Francisco	San Francisco P O	85	835
DUFFMAN								
Jac	46	m	w	US	San Joaquin	3-Wd Stockton	86	218
DUFFOURG								
Charles	57	m	w	FRAN	Nevada	Grass Valley Twp	75	213
DUFFUZET								
Cloud	46	m	w	FRAN	Yuba	Bullards Bar P O	93	550
DUFFY								
Allice	15	f	w	CA	Sacramento	3-Wd Sacramento	77	264
Andrew	15	m	w	CA	San Francisco	11-Wd San Francisc	84	593
Ann	52	f	w	IREL	San Joaquin	1-Wd Stockton	86	140
Ann	50	f	w	IREL	San Joaquin	2-Wd Stockton	86	175
Ann	37	f	w	IREL	San Francisco	5-Wd San Francisco	81	29
Bessie	34	f	w	IREL	Santa Cruz	Soquel Twp	89	448
Bridget	42	f	w	IREL	San Francisco	11-Wd San Francisc	84	467
Bridget	38	f	w	IREL	Sacramento	2-Wd Sacramento	77	217
Catharine	14	f	w	CA	San Francisco	7-Wd San Francisco	81	241
Catherin	55	f	w	IREL	San Francisco	11-Wd San Francisc	84	488
Catherine	40	f	w	IREL	Santa Clara	Alviso Twp	88	23
D N	38	m	w	IREL	San Joaquin	2-Wd Stockton	86	174
Daniel	31	m	w	IREL	San Francisco	San Francisco P O	83	108
Daniel	23	m	w	MA	San Francisco	San Francisco P O	83	18
David	21	m	w	MA	San Joaquin	Castoria Twp	86	7
Edward	48	m	w	IREL	San Francisco	2-Wd San Francisco	79	201
Edward	39	m	w	NY	Sacramento	2-Wd Sacramento	77	222
Edward	38	m	w	IREL	Sacramento	2-Wd Sacramento	77	254
Edward	23	m	w	IREL	San Francisco	2-Wd San Francisco	79	213
Edward	23	m	w	IREL	Inyo	Cerro Gordo Twp	73	318
Edward	23	m	w	IREL	San Francisco	11-Wd San Francisc	84	612
Edwd	44	m	w	IREL	San Francisco	1-Wd San Francisco	79	92
Edwd C	18	m	w	MA	Sonoma	Petaluma Twp	91	343
Ferdinand	33	m	w	KY	Calaveras	Copperopolis P O	70	240
Francis	30	m	w	IREL	Nevada	Grass Valley Twp	75	221
George	25	m	w	ENGL	Santa Clara	Gilroy Twp	88	80
Henry	30	m	w	NY	San Francisco	11-Wd San Francisc	84	480
Hugh	45	m	w	IREL	San Francisco	San Francisco P O	80	351
Hugh	23	m	w	IREL	Sacramento	2-Wd Sacramento	77	252
Hyacinthe	57	m	w	IREL	San Francisco	San Francisco P O	80	368
James	52	m	w	IREL	Butte	Oregon Twp	70	132
James	45	m	w	IREL	San Francisco	1-Wd San Francisco	79	57
James	44	m	w	SCOT	Tuolumne	Sonora P O	93	330
James	40	m	w	IREL	Los Angeles	Los Angeles	73	504
James	35	m	w	IREL	Yuba	Rose Bar Twp	93	659
James	34	m	w	IREL	Calaveras	San Andreas P O	70	181
James	29	m	w	NY	San Francisco	11-Wd San Francisc	84	553
James	26	m	w	IREL	Sonoma	Santa Rosa	91	408
James	24	m	w	NY	San Diego	Julian Dist	78	472
James H	38	m	w	IREL	Sacramento	2-Wd Sacramento	77	249
James T	25	m	w	IREL	San Francisco	San Francisco P O	83	188
Jane	55	f	w	IREL	Amador	Ione City P O	69	360
Jane	49	f	w	IREL	San Francisco	11-Wd San Francisc	84	553
Jas	45	m	w	IREL	Solano	Vallejo	90	157
Jas	36	m	w	IREL	Sacramento	3-Wd Sacramento	77	267
Jas	30	m	w	IREL	Sierra	Table Rock Twp	89	571
Jerry	17	m	w	NY	Del Norte	Crescent Twp	71	454
Jno	38	m	w	IREL	San Joaquin	Elkhorn Twp	86	68
Johanna	30	f	w	IREL	San Mateo	San Mateo P O	87	350
John	50	m	w	IREL	Placer	Bath P O	76	430
John	40	m	w	IREL	Sonoma	Vallejo Twp	91	461
John	38	m	w	IREL	San Francisco	San Francisco P O	85	811
John	38	m	w	IREL	Marin	San Rafael Twp	74	42
John	36	m	w	IREL	San Joaquin	Union Twp	86	265
John	33	m	w	IREL	San Francisco	11-Wd San Francisc	84	600
John	29	m	w	IREL	San Francisco	11-Wd San Francisc	84	427
John	28	m	w	MA	San Francisco	San Francisco P O	80	408
John	27	m	w	IREL	Santa Barbara	San Buenaventura P	87	430
John	23	m	w	IL	San Francisco	1-Wd San Francisco	79	113
John	20	m	w	IREL	San Francisco	San Francisco P O	83	326
John	14	m	w	CA	Del Norte	Crescent	71	467
John H	26	m	w	NY	Placer	Rocklin Twp	76	466
Kate	30	f	w	IREL	San Francisco	6-Wd San Francisco	81	99
Lizzie	17	f	w	CA	San Francisco	San Francisco P O	83	158
Martin	36	m	w	IREL	Tuolumne	Chinese Camp P O	93	374
Martin	30	m	w	IREL	San Francisco	1-Wd San Francisco	79	59
Mary	35	f	w	IREL	San Francisco	8-Wd San Francisco	82	453
Mary	27	f	w	IREL	Santa Clara	2-Wd San Jose	88	330
Mary	26	f	w	IREL	San Francisco	8-Wd San Francisco	82	302
Mary	13	f	w	CA	Sonoma	Petaluma Twp	91	315
Michael	40	m	w	IREL	Monterey	San Juan Twp	74	387
Michael	26	m	w	IREL	San Francisco	San Francisco P O	85	773
Michael	23	m	w	IREL	Marin	San Rafael Twp	74	46
Michl	45	m	w	IREL	San Francisco	1-Wd San Francisco	79	113
Michl	43	m	w	IREL	San Francisco	1-Wd San Francisco	79	53
Nellie	7	f	w	CA	Nevada	Grass Valley Twp	75	230
Owen	25	m	w	IREL	Del Norte	Crescent Twp	71	454
Pat	32	m	w	IREL	San Joaquin	3-Wd Stockton	86	226
Patrick	47	m	w	IREL	San Francisco	1-Wd San Francisco	79	76
Patrick	45	m	w	IREL	San Francisco	San Francisco P O	83	45
Patrick	40	m	w	IREL	Sacramento	Sutter Twp	77	388
Patrick	39	m	w	IREL	San Francisco	11-Wd San Francisc	84	471
Patrick	38	m	w	IREL	San Francisco	11-Wd San Francisc	84	476
Patrick	37	m	w	ENGL	Nevada	Nevada Twp	75	281
Patrick	35	m	w	IREL	San Francisco	San Francisco P O	83	203

Name	Age	S	R	B-PL	County	Locale	Series M593 Roll	Pg
Patrick	22	m	w	IREL	San Francisco	San Francisco P O	85	773
Patrick	20	m	w	IREL	Sacramento	2-Wd Sacramento	77	245
Peter	40	m	w	IREL	San Francisco	San Francisco P O	83	133
Peter	30	m	w	IREL	San Diego	Julian Dist	78	468
Phillip	25	m	w	IREL	San Francisco	6-Wd San Francisco	81	116
Sarah	34	f	w	IREL	San Joaquin	2-Wd Stockton	86	165
Susan	16	f	w	CA	Alameda	Oakland	68	180
Terrance	27	m	w	IREL	San Francisco	San Francisco P O	83	144
Thomas	45	m	w	IREL	Tuolumne	Chinese Camp P O	93	374
Thomas	44	m	w	IREL	Klamath	Salmon Twp	73	388
Thomas	41	m	w	IREL	San Francisco	San Francisco P O	85	743
Thomas	40	m	w	IREL	San Francisco	1-Wd San Francisco	79	41
Thomas	37	m	w	IREL	Santa Clara	2-Wd San Jose	88	316
Thomas	32	m	w	IREL	Santa Clara	2-Wd San Jose	88	325
Thomas	27	m	w	IREL	Solano	Maine Prairie Twp	90	52
Thos	38	m	w	IREL	Sacramento	4-Wd Sacramento	77	343
Thos	28	m	w	IREL	San Francisco	1-Wd San Francisco	79	13
Thos	14	m	w	IREL	Butte	Ophir Twp	70	99
Timothy	28	m	w	IREL	San Francisco	7-Wd San Francisco	81	200
William	54	m	w	IREL	Santa Cruz	Soquel Twp	89	449
William	40	m	w	IREL	San Francisco	11-Wd San Francisc	84	490
William	36	m	w	IREL	San Francisco	8-Wd San Francisco	82	414
William	30	m	w	OH	San Francisco	San Francisco P O	83	170
William C	60	m	w	IREL	Contra Costa	Martinez P O	71	380
Winifred	22	f	w	ENGL	San Francisco	2-Wd San Francisco	79	245
DUFIE								
Jules	42	m	w	FRAN	Santa Clara	1-Wd San Jose	88	267
DUFORSEE								
Charles	32	m	w	ENGL	Alameda	Washington Twp	68	295
DUFREE								
John	21	m	w	FRAN	Fresno	Millerton P O	72	158
DUFRESNE								
J	45	m	w	FRAN	San Joaquin	2-Wd Stockton	86	174
DUFRIEN								
Charles	42	m	w	FRAN	Amador	Ione City P O	69	369
H	34	f	w	ENGL	Amador	Ione City P O	69	369
DUFRIEND								
Delphis	27	m	w	CANA	Santa Cruz	Santa Cruz Twp	89	390
DUGA								
Lewis	26	m	w	CANA	Sonoma	Bodega Twp	91	264
DUGAL								
John C	38	m	w	SWED	Santa Clara	Santa Clara Twp	88	137
Patrick	20	m	w	IREL	Santa Clara	2-Wd San Jose	88	334
DUGAN								
Alice	42	f	w	IREL	Inyo	Independence Twp	73	326
Anasstasia	70	f	w	IREL	Del Norte	Crescent	71	466
Andrew	21	m	w	NY	Sacramento	4-Wd Sacramento	77	325
Ann	12	f	w	AUSL	Solano	Maine Prairie Twp	90	52
Arthur	9	m	w	IREL	Solano	Silveyville Twp	90	73
Barny	60	m	w	IREL	San Francisco	8-Wd San Francisco	82	361
Bernard	32	m	w	IREL	San Francisco	San Francisco P O	85	739
Charles	40	m	w	IREL	Sacramento	2-Wd Sacramento	77	251
Charles	30	m	w	DENM	San Francisco	7-Wd San Francisco	81	218
Chas	60	m	w	MA	San Francisco	San Francisco P O	83	88
Daniel	30	m	w	IREL	San Francisco	San Francisco P O	85	856
Edward	38	m	w	VT	Stanislaus	Empire Twp	92	34
Edward	32	m	w	IREL	San Francisco	7-Wd San Francisco	81	214
Edward	32	m	w	IREL	San Francisco	7-Wd San Francisco	81	279
Edward	23	m	w	LA	Nevada	Bridgeport Twp	75	121
Elizabeth	35	f	w	IREL	San Francisco	San Francisco P O	83	315
Ellen	67	f	w	IREL	San Francisco	San Francisco P O	83	315
Ellen	24	f	w	LA	Nevada	Bloomfield Twp	75	97
Ellen	19	f	w	CA	San Francisco	San Francisco P O	83	95
Frank	45	m	w	IREL	Stanislaus	Emory Twp	92	22
Hagan	30	m	w	IREL	San Francisco	11-Wd San Francisc	84	694
Hugh	35	m	w	IREL	San Francisco	8-Wd San Francisco	82	422
James	45	m	w	IREL	Yuba	Rose Bar Twp	93	664
James	40	m	w	PA	Sacramento	Granite Twp	77	139
James	23	m	w	IREL	Stanislaus	Emory Twp	92	19
James	12	m	w	CA	Placer	Roseville P O	76	348
Jeremiah	31	m	w	MA	San Francisco	1-Wd San Francisco	79	84
Jno	28	m	w	IL	Santa Clara	Burnett Twp	88	36
John	56	m	w	PA	San Francisco	11-Wd San Francisc	84	684
John	48	m	w	IREL	San Francisco	7-Wd San Francisco	81	266
John	37	m	w	IREL	San Francisco	San Francisco P O	80	369
John	32	m	w	IREL	San Francisco	11-Wd San Francisc	84	559
John	26	m	w	IREL	San Francisco	San Francisco P O	83	130
John	25	m	w	IL	Inyo	Bishop Crk Twp	73	315
Joseph	44	m	w	IREL	Inyo	Cerro Gordo Twp	73	321
Julia	32	f	w	IREL	San Francisco	8-Wd San Francisco	82	322
Kate	30	f	w	IREL	San Joaquin	2-Wd Stockton	86	171
Maggie	54	f	w	IREL	San Francisco	San Francisco P O	83	313
Maggie	22	f	w	IREL	San Joaquin	1-Wd Stockton	86	139
Margaret	23	f	w	IREL	San Francisco	San Francisco P O	80	488
Margaret	23	f	w	IREL	San Joaquin	3-Wd Stockton	86	225
Margt	27	f	w	IREL	San Francisco	8-Wd San Francisco	82	297
Maria	19	f	w	AUST	San Francisco	8-Wd San Francisco	82	475
Mark	40	m	w	IREL	San Francisco	7-Wd San Francisco	81	243
Mark M	46	m	w	CANA	San Francisco	8-Wd San Francisco	82	422
Martin	28	m	w	IREL	San Joaquin	1-Wd Stockton	86	141
Mary	87	f	w	IREL	San Francisco	San Francisco P O	83	315
Mary	68	f	w	IREL	San Francisco	San Francisco P O	83	22
Mary	48	f	w	OH	El Dorado	Mud Springs Twp	72	83
Mary	25	f	w	NY	San Francisco	8-Wd San Francisco	82	435
Mary	23	f	w	IREL	Nevada	Grass Valley Twp	75	156
Mary	20	f	w	IREL	San Francisco	6-Wd San Francisco	81	116
Mary	17	f	w	IREL	San Francisco	8-Wd San Francisco	82	428

© 2001 by Heritage Quest. All rights reserved.

Name	Age	S	R	B-PL	County	Locale (Series M593)	Roll	Pg
Mich	35	m	w	IREL	Merced	Snelling P O	74	261
Michael	40	m	w	IREL	Santa Clara	Milpitas Twp	88	113
Owen	38	m	w	IREL	San Francisco	11-Wd San Francisc	84	532
Patrick	60	m	w	IREL	San Francisco	San Francisco P O	83	315
Patrick	44	m	w	IREL	San Francisco	2-Wd San Francisco	79	249
Patrick	39	m	w	IREL	San Francisco	11-Wd San Francisc	84	524
Patrick	24	m	w	IREL	Fresno	Millerton P O	72	163
Richard	42	m	w	NY	Del Norte	Crescent	71	466
Sinson	42	m	w	IREL	San Francisco	7-Wd San Francisco	81	215
Theodore	22	m	w	OH	El Dorado	Mud Springs Twp	72	83
Thos	30	m	w	IREL	Sacramento	Brighton Twp	77	70
Tim	28	m	w	IREL	Alameda	Alameda	68	20
Timothy	35	m	w	PA	Nevada	Grass Valley Twp	75	226
William	44	m	w	IREL	San Francisco	San Francisco P O	83	369
William	42	m	w	IREL	Santa Clara	Fremont Twp	88	65
William	32	m	w	PA	San Francisco	San Francisco P O	83	402
William	22	m	w	IREL	San Francisco	8-Wd San Francisco	82	351
Wm	60	m	w	IREL	San Joaquin	2-Wd Stockton	86	165
DUGANNE								
George	11	m	w	CA	San Francisco	8-Wd San Francisco	82	441
DUGARDIN								
Julius	21	m	w	FRAN	San Francisco	1-Wd San Francisco	79	47
DUGEE								
Bartola	31	m	w	ITAL	Calaveras	San Andreas P O	70	217
John	19	m	w	ITAL	Calaveras	San Andreas P O	70	217
DUGEN								
Johanna	46	f	w	IREL	Sacramento	4-Wd Sacramento	77	369
DUGER								
Patrick	45	m	w	IREL	Amador	Jackson P O	69	341
DUGGAN								
Charles	33	m	w	IREL	Santa Cruz	Santa Cruz Twp	89	402
James	28	m	w	IREL	San Francisco	San Francisco P O	83	314
John	36	m	w	IREL	Santa Cruz	Santa Cruz Twp	89	402
Mary	22	f	w	IREL	San Francisco	San Francisco P O	83	226
Patrick	46	m	w	IREL	San Francisco	11-Wd San Francisc	84	469
Thomas H	30	m	w	IREL	Nevada	Eureka Twp	75	137
Wm	22	m	w	IREL	San Francisco	1-Wd San Francisco	79	64
DUGGELL								
Fred G	42	m	w	ENGL	Butte	Ophir Twp	70	107
DUGGIN								
Daniel	40	m	w	IREL	San Francisco	San Francisco P O	85	865
Margaret	30	f	w	IREL	San Francisco	San Francisco P O	83	353
Moses	49	m	w	KY	Colusa	Colusa Twp	71	279
DUGGINS								
John	55	m	w	WALE	El Dorado	Mud Springs Twp	72	86
DUGGON								
Patrick	37	m	w	IREL	San Francisco	11-Wd San Francisc	84	464
DUGH								
John	36	m	w	IREL	San Francisco	San Francisco P O	83	414
DUGHE								
Govachino	32	m	w	ITAL	San Luis Obispo	Arroyo Grande Twp	87	276
DUGIN								
John	35	m	w	IREL	Santa Clara	Santa Clara Twp	88	141
Martha	44	f	w	ENGL	El Dorado	Mountain Twp	72	68
DUGLAS								
Joseph	26	m	w	ENGL	Humboldt	Arcata Twp	72	235
DUGLASS								
Peres	49	m	w	MA	Sonoma	Sonoma Twp	91	449
Wallace	38	m	w	MO	Sonoma	Mendocino Twp	91	307
DUGLE								
James E	29	m	w	OH	San Diego	San Diego	78	498
DUGNELL								
James C	33	m	w	ME	Tulare	Tule Rvr Twp	92	271
DUGUENSE								
Danl	36	m	w	BELG	Tuolumne	Sonora P O	93	309
DUHAIN								
Chas	38	m	w	VA	Yuba	Rose Bar Twp	93	661
DUHARD								
John	30	m	w	FRAN	Trinity	Junction City Pct	92	210
DUHART								
Celesta	33	f	w	FRAN	San Francisco	San Francisco P O	83	229
DUHIG								
Dennis D	33	m	w	MA	Santa Barbara	San Buenaventura P	87	423
James	46	m	w	MA	Napa	Napa Twp	75	28
John	32	m	w	IREL	San Francisco	2-Wd San Francisco	79	213
DUHNE								
Herman	34	m	w	HANO	San Francisco	8-Wd San Francisco	82	359
DUHU								
F W	40	f	w	PRUS	San Francisco	San Francisco P O	85	826
DUHUNG								
Fredk	44	m	w	GERM	Sonoma	Sonoma Twp	91	439
DUIFFY								
Patrick	32	m	w	IREL	San Francisco	11-Wd San Francisc	84	610
DUIMONES								
Lorenzo	28	m	w	MEXI	Monterey	San Juan Twp	74	385
DUING								
John	36	m	w	NY	Los Angeles	San Juan Twp	73	628
DUISENBERG								
Chs A C	42	m	w	BREM	San Francisco	San Francisco P O	83	18
DUJARDIN								
F	34	m	w	BELG	San Francisco	San Francisco P O	85	823
DUJEE								
Jean	46	m	w	FRAN	Santa Clara	Fremont Twp	88	58
DUJLEY								
Thos F	40	m	w	ME	Nevada	Nevada Twp	75	314
DUJOINE								
John	29	m	w	NY	San Diego	Julian Dist	78	471

Name	Age	S	R	B-PL	County	Locale (Series M593)	Roll	Pg
DUK								
Yum	30	m	c	CHIN	San Francisco	6-Wd San Francisco	81	43
DUKE								
Addie	33	f	w	TN	Los Angeles	Santa Ana Twp	73	599
Ah	16	m	c	CHIN	Trinity	Douglas	92	235
Alexr	58	m	b	DE	San Francisco	11-Wd San Francisc	84	612
Catherine	40	f	w	IREL	San Francisco	San Francisco P O	83	212
D A	18	m	w	MS	Tehama	Red Bluff	92	182
James	36	m	w	IL	Contra Costa	Martinez P O	71	412
John	40	m	w	CANA	San Francisco	San Francisco P O	83	38
John	30	m	w	IL	San Joaquin	2-Wd Stockton	86	174
Lucretia	12	f	w	CA	Sacramento	4-Wd Sacramento	77	378
Mary	48	f	w	IREL	Amador	Sutter Crk P O	69	409
Mary J	36	f	w	ENGL	Sacramento	4-Wd Sacramento	77	339
Mary J	10	f	w	CA	Sacramento	4-Wd Sacramento	77	378
Robt W	30	m	w	CANA	San Francisco	San Francisco P O	83	124
Susan	35	f	w	NY	Yuba	Marysville	93	582
Wm	30	m	w	MA	San Francisco	San Francisco P O	83	132
DUKES								
H	22	m	w	MO	Mendocino	Ukiah Twp	74	242
Wm H	38	m	w	TN	Contra Costa	Martinez P O	71	372
DULAC								
John	39	m	w	FRAN	San Francisco	San Francisco P O	80	458
Lewis	50	m	w	FRAN	Nevada	Washington Twp	75	344
Lewis	50	m	w	FRAN	Nevada	Washington Twp	75	345
DULAN								
Kate	30	f	w	IREL	San Francisco	8-Wd San Francisco	82	368
Micheil	62	m	w	IREL	San Francisco	8-Wd San Francisco	82	361
Patrick	24	m	w	IREL	San Francisco	8-Wd San Francisco	82	376
DULAND								
John	29	m	w	NY	San Francisco	11-Wd San Francisc	84	670
DULAY								
Dennis	35	m	w	IREL	San Francisco	11-Wd San Francisc	84	550
Mary	40	f	w	IREL	San Francisco	11-Wd San Francisc	84	686
DULEN								
E	38	m	w	IREL	Sacramento	3-Wd Sacramento	77	317
DULETORES								
Esteven	53	m	w	CA	Monterey	Castroville Twp	74	331
DULEY								
Ann	28	f	w	ENGL	Contra Costa	Martinez Twp	71	349
John	30	m	w	IREL	San Francisco	11-Wd San Francisc	84	519
W H	52	m	w	NY	El Dorado	Lake Valley Twp	72	64
DULIA								
Maria	30	f	w	MEXI	Los Angeles	Los Angeles	73	563
DULIAN								
Leon	26	m	w	FRAN	San Francisco	San Francisco P O	80	536
DULIN								
Ed	34	m	w	IREL	Alameda	Oakland	68	251
Joseph M	31	m	w	SC	Stanislaus	Emory Twp	92	21
DULING								
Patrick	25	m	w	IREL	San Francisco	11-Wd San Francisc	84	703
DULINS								
Sam C	33	m	w	IL	San Joaquin	Tulare Twp	86	262
DULION								
J P	56	m	w	FRAN	San Francisco	8-Wd San Francisco	82	366
DULIP								
John	40	m	w	FRAN	San Francisco	San Francisco P O	80	340
DULL								
John	23	m	w	IREL	Marin	Sausalito Twp	74	73
DULLEA								
Charles	40	m	w	IREL	San Francisco	11-Wd San Francisc	84	502
Chas	62	m	w	IREL	San Francisco	San Francisco P O	85	815
DULLEY								
Martin	37	m	w	IREL	Alameda	Oakland	68	150
DULLIAN								
Paul	42	m	w	FRAN	San Francisco	San Francisco P O	80	464
DULLIVAN								
Elijah	42	m	w	CANA	Butte	Chico Twp	70	50
DULLMAS								
Joseph	56	m	w	FRAN	Alameda	Brooklyn	68	34
DULLUGHN								
Thomas	34	m	w	IREL	San Francisco	7-Wd San Francisco	81	161
DULMAN								
Alex	60	m	w	SCOT	Alameda	Oakland	68	220
DULON								
Arnold	27	m	w	RUSS	Sacramento	3-Wd Sacramento	77	255
DULORA								
Frances	30	f	w	SWIT	Santa Barbara	Santa Barbara P O	87	465
DULTON								
Margaret	15	f	w	IREL	Yuba	Marysville	93	599
Samuel E	27	m	w	ME	San Francisco	San Francisco P O	83	196
DULTZEN								
Margret	22	f	w	IREL	Monterey	Castroville Twp	74	333
DUMAN								
C V	42	m	w	KY	Monterey	Castroville Twp	74	338
John	24	m	w	IREL	Sacramento	Franklin Twp	77	108
DUMAR								
Henry	16	m	w	IL	Butte	Ophir Twp	70	105
DUMARC								
Paul	52	m	w	FRAN	Calaveras	San Andreas P O	70	167
DUMART								
H	40	m	w	CANA	Alameda	Oakland	68	259
DUMAS								
Caroline A	35	f	w	PA	San Francisco	San Francisco P O	83	97
Francis	43	m	w	CANA	Siskiyou	Yreka Twp	89	664
Jeone	50	m	w	FRAN	Yuba	Bullards Bar P O	93	551
Joseph	48	m	w	FRAN	Plumas	Rich Bar Twp	77	45

© 2001 by Heritage Quest. All rights reserved.

Name	Age	S	R	B-PL	County	Locale	Series M593 Roll	Pg
Lewis	34	m	w	CANA	Sierra	Sears Twp	89	555
Lucian	36	m	w	FRAN	San Francisco	6-Wd San Francisco	81	97
Shem	36	m	w	CANA	Sierra	Sears Twp	89	557
DUMBLE								
Ephraim	32	m	w	PA	Kern	Havilah P O	73	336
DUMBRELL								
James H	34	m	w	ENGL	San Francisco	San Francisco P O	85	770
DUME								
James	31	m	w	IREL	San Francisco	7-Wd San Francisco	81	193
DUMET								
August	33	m	w	FRAN	Santa Clara	2-Wd San Jose	88	306
DUMEY								
Julia	40	f	w	OH	Monterey	San Juan Twp	74	393
Phil	20	m	w	IREL	Butte	Oregon Twp	70	129
DUMFORD								
Margarete	33	f	w	IREL	Humboldt	Eureka Twp	72	261
Margarete	33	f	w	IREL	Humboldt	Eureka Twp	72	262
Thomes	30	m	w	CANA	Humboldt	Eureka Twp	72	277
W T	13	m	w	CANA	Humboldt	Eureka Twp	72	262
Wm T	13	m	w	CANA	Humboldt	Eureka Twp	72	261
DUMFREES								
Jordan	41	m	b	VA	Tulare	Visalia Twp	92	287
DUMING								
Catherine	45	f	w	IREL	Sacramento	Granite Twp	77	147
DUMINO								
Ali	19	f	w	MEXI	San Joaquin	1-Wd Stockton	86	133
DUMLIN								
John	40	m	w	IREL	San Francisco	11-Wd San Francisc	84	693
DUMMOND								
John	30	m	w	SCOT	Monterey	San Benito Twp	74	381
DUMOD								
Norma	20	f	w	PRUS	San Francisco	8-Wd San Francisco	82	380
DUMOND								
Jas	42	m	b	DE	San Francisco	8-Wd San Francisco	82	361
John	56	m	w	FRAN	Solano	Benicia	90	21
DUMONT								
Adolphe	72	m	w	FRAN	San Francisco	11-Wd San Francisc	84	557
Frank	28	m	w	AL	San Francisco	8-Wd San Francisco	82	423
Mary	11	f	w	CA	Yolo	Cache Crk Twp	93	419
Victor	40	m	w	FRAN	San Francisco	2-Wd San Francisco	79	283
William R	7	m	w	CA	Yolo	Cache Crk Twp	93	419
DUMONTFER								
Reinard	60	m	w	FRAN	San Francisco	2-Wd San Francisco	79	215
DUMPHERY								
Wm	35	m	w	IREL	Sonoma	Salt Point	91	392
DUMPHEY								
Dexter	36	m	w	OH	Yolo	Cache Crk Twp	93	435
Samuel	28	m	w	IREL	San Francisco	San Francisco P O	83	335
DUMPHRY								
Jennie	14	f	w	CA	Sacramento	4-Wd Sacramento	77	335
DUMPHY								
Henry	29	m	w	MS	Butte	Chico Twp	70	31
Jas	33	m	w	IREL	Sierra	Gibson Twp	89	538
Luke	40	m	w	IREL	San Francisco	San Francisco P O	85	758
M	35	m	w	ME	Klamath	Trinidad Twp	73	389
Mary	24	f	w	IREL	San Francisco	San Francisco P O	85	759
Patk	25	m	w	IREL	Sacramento	4-Wd Sacramento	77	370
DUMPSEY								
Pat	33	m	w	IREL	San Joaquin	Dent Twp	86	17
DUN								
Ah	27	m	c	CHIN	Placer	Newcastle Twp	76	475
Ah	27	m	c	CHIN	Placer	Auburn P O	76	364
Ah	25	m	c	CHIN	San Francisco	San Francisco P O	80	498
Ah	24	m	c	CHIN	San Francisco	2-Wd San Francisco	79	261
Ah	24	m	c	CHIN	El Dorado	Diamond Springs Tw	72	35
Ah	22	m	c	CHIN	Placer	Alta P O	76	413
C	34	m	w	ME	Alameda	Oakland	68	235
David	24	m	m	MA	Sacramento	2-Wd Sacramento	77	225
David	18	m	w	IREL	San Francisco	7-Wd San Francisco	81	196
Dee	40	m	c	CHIN	San Francisco	San Francisco P O	83	380
Edward	45	m	w	ENGL	El Dorado	Mud Springs Twp	72	77
Hop	22	m	c	CHIN	Tehama	Tehama Twp	92	189
James	28	m	c	CHIN	Colusa	Colusa	71	300
John W	19	m	w	NY	San Francisco	7-Wd San Francisco	81	206
Kate	28	f	w	IREL	Colusa	Monroe Twp	71	315
Lip	22	m	c	CHIN	San Joaquin	1-Wd Stockton	86	144
Thomas	25	m	w	RI	San Francisco	8-Wd San Francisco	82	319
DUNAGAN								
Bridget	22	f	w	IREL	San Francisco	San Francisco P O	85	753
DUNAN								
Margaret	28	f	w	IREL	San Francisco	11-Wd San Francisc	84	539
DUNAND								
Louis	20	m	w	LA	San Francisco	6-Wd San Francisco	81	73
Mark A	69	m	w	FRAN	San Francisco	6-Wd San Francisco	81	73
DUNAVAN								
C	24	m	w	IREL	San Francisco	7-Wd San Francisco	81	167
Can	48	m	w	IREL	San Joaquin	2-Wd Stockton	86	164
Margaret	36	f	w	IREL	Sierra	Sears Twp	89	561
DUNAY								
Catharine	35	f	w	IREL	Colusa	Monroe Twp	71	313
DUNBAR								
Alexan	68	m	w	TN	San Luis Obispo	San Luis Obispo Tw	87	302
Amos T	50	m	w	NH	Marin	Bolinas Twp	74	2
Elizabeth	50	f	w	IREL	San Francisco	San Francisco P O	83	358
Fred	37	m	w	GERM	Nevada	Nevada Twp	75	282
Freeman	54	m	w	NH	Calaveras	Copperopolis P O	70	253
Geo F	28	m	w	NY	San Francisco	3-Wd San Francisco	79	314
Henry N	34	m	w	MI	El Dorado	Placerville Twp	72	96
J W	34	m	w	PA	Alameda	Oakland	68	175
James	33	m	w	CANA	Sonoma	Analy Twp	91	218
James H	27	m	w	IL	Santa Cruz	Santa Cruz Twp	89	396
Jno	27	m	w	PA	San Joaquin	Elkhorn Twp	86	69
John	25	m	w	ENGL	San Joaquin	Elkhorn Twp	86	67
Jos	33	m	w	CANA	Solano	Vallejo	90	147
Jos	30	m	w	IREL	Alameda	Oakland	68	182
L	35	m	w	MA	Sierra	Table Rock Twp	89	575
L S L	27	m	w	ME	San Joaquin	3-Wd Stockton	86	217
Mark	30	m	w	ENGL	San Francisco	7-Wd San Francisco	81	258
Mary H	27	f	w	ME	Nevada	Grass Valley Twp	75	185
Nicholas	22	m	w	MO	Sonoma	Sonoma Twp	91	438
Noah	36	m	w	NY	Shasta	Portugese Flat P O	89	471
Peter	38	m	w	NH	Tuolumne	Sonora P O	93	327
Peter G	39	m	w	NH	Tuolumne	Sonora P O	93	327
Phoebe	63	f	w	ME	San Joaquin	3-Wd Stockton	86	241
Samuel	55	m	w	NY	Tulare	Farmersville Twp	92	248
Sarah	52	f	w	ENGL	San Francisco	1-Wd San Francisco	79	22
Stan G	35	m	w	IL	Sutter	Yuba Twp	92	141
Thos	49	m	w	SCOT	San Francisco	1-Wd San Francisco	79	98
Thos	41	m	w	NY	San Francisco	1-Wd San Francisco	79	111
W A	41	m	w	MA	San Francisco	San Francisco P O	83	289
William	35	m	w	OH	San Francisco	San Francisco P O	83	330
William	29	m	w	NY	San Francisco	San Francisco P O	80	378
Willis	34	m	w	NH	Calaveras	Copperopolis P O	70	253
Wm Henry	29	m	w	MA	Plumas	Indian Twp	77	9
DUNBARR								
Allen	30	m	w	CANA	Mendocino	Point Arena Twp	74	214
DUNBAULD								
Geo	36	m	w	PA	Merced	Snelling P O	74	265
DUNBESTON								
Augustin	25	m	w	SPAI	Fresno	Millerton P O	72	168
DUNCAN								
Adam	37	m	w	SCOT	Placer	Bath P O	76	423
Addison C	30	m	w	KY	Colusa	Monroe Twp	71	320
Alexander	54	m	w	IREL	Placer	Dutch Flat P O	76	406
Alx	48	m	w	IREL	Sonoma	Bodega Twp	91	260
Andrew	28	m	w	MO	Stanislaus	Empire Twp	92	55
Andrew J	43	m	w	PA	Mariposa	Mariposa P O	74	98
Benj	48	m	w	VA	El Dorado	Kelsey Twp	72	60
Benjamin	36	m	w	TN	Calaveras	Copperopolis P O	70	261
Benjamin	30	m	w	IN	Yolo	Cottonwood Twp	93	469
Betsy	30	f	i	CA	Calaveras	Copperopolis P O	70	250
C S	57	m	w	VA	San Joaquin	2-Wd Stockton	86	162
Catherine	58	f	w	ENGL	San Francisco	11-Wd San Francisc	84	460
Charles	50	m	w	TN	Tulare	Tule Rvr Twp	92	259
Cornelius	16	m	w	IREL	San Francisco	San Francisco P O	83	360
Cyrus	19	m	w	IL	Yolo	Cottonwood Twp	93	469
D	38	m	w	MO	Merced	Snelling P O	74	278
E	24	f	w	CHIL	Alameda	Oakland	68	229
E H	45	m	w	TN	Mendocino	Sanel Twp	74	228
Ed	27	m	w	IREL	Sacramento	3-Wd Sacramento	77	318
Emma	9	f	w	CA	Yolo	Buckeye Twp	93	416
F M	34	m	w	MO	Napa	Napa Twp	75	32
Flora	13	f	w	CA	Mariposa	Mariposa P O	74	92
Frank	30	m	w	NC	Mendocino	Little Lake Twp	74	198
Franklin	32	m	w	IN	Yolo	Cottonwood Twp	93	460
G H	32	m	w	SCOT	San Francisco	San Francisco P O	85	840
Geo	42	m	w	SCOT	Sierra	Lincoln Twp	89	551
Geo	30	m	w	SCOT	Sacramento	3-Wd Sacramento	77	314
Geo	29	m	m	PA	San Francisco	San Francisco P O	83	39
George	67	m	b	KY	Yuba	Rose Bar Twp	93	654
George	50	m	w	ENGL	Santa Clara	Milpitas Twp	88	110
George	36	m	w	CT	Colusa	Stony Crk Twp	71	333
George	32	m	w	WI	San Francisco	8-Wd San Francisco	82	436
George	31	m	w	SCOT	San Mateo	Half Moon Bay P O	87	403
George	25	m	w	IREL	Mendocino	Little Rvr Twp	74	170
George E	59	m	w	MA	El Dorado	Diamond Springs Tw	72	26
George W	37	m	w	IL	Tulare	Tule Rvr Twp	92	271
Henery	41	m	w	SCOT	San Francisco	7-Wd San Francisco	81	201
Henry	45	m	b	VA	Mariposa	Mariposa P O	74	113
Henry	22	m	w	IL	Yolo	Putah Twp	93	521
Henry	20	m	w	NY	San Francisco	8-Wd San Francisco	82	386
Hilarion	39	m	w	CHIL	Contra Costa	Martinez P O	71	425
Hiram	71	m	w	KY	San Joaquin	Douglas Twp	86	41
Hiram	39	m	w	MO	Mendocino	Albion & Big Rvr T	74	167
Isabella	43	f	w	ENGL	San Francisco	San Francisco P O	80	344
Isabella	33	f	w	IREL	San Francisco	San Francisco P O	83	47
J A	36	m	w	KY	Sacramento	3-Wd Sacramento	77	299
J T	35	m	w	TN	Sierra	Sears Twp	89	556
Ja	36	m	w	KY	Sacramento	3-Wd Sacramento	77	311
Jacob	42	m	w	VA	Mendocino	Ukiah Twp	74	244
Jame	46	m	w	SCOT	Humboldt	Bald Hills	72	237
James	54	m	w	ENGL	Shasta	French Gulch P O	89	466
James	49	m	w	SCOT	San Francisco	11-Wd San Francisc	84	477
James	48	m	w	KY	Marin	San Rafael Twp	74	35
James	47	m	b	PA	San Francisco	6-Wd San Francisco	81	100
James	45	m	w	SCOT	San Francisco	San Francisco P O	83	61
James	44	m	w	ENGL	Sacramento	Granite Twp	77	150
James	44	m	w	CANA	Santa Clara	Gilroy Twp	88	95
James	38	m	w	KY	San Francisco	San Francisco P O	83	227
James	32	m	w	SCOT	Tehama	Red Bluff	92	175
James	26	m	w	IREL	Yolo	Merritt Twp	93	503
James	23	m	w	ARGE	Marin	San Rafael	74	57
James	15	m	w	CA	El Dorado	Salmon Falls Twp	72	132
James E	35	m	w	IREL	San Francisco	8-Wd San Francisco	82	493

© 2001 by Heritage Quest. All rights reserved.

California 1870 Census

Series M593

Name	Age	S	R	B-PL	County	Locale	Roll	Pg
James H	36	m	w	WI	Mariposa	Mariposa P O	74	137
James S	41	m	w	IN	Colusa	Colusa Twp	71	278
James W	45	m	w	IN	San Francisco	6-Wd San Francisco	81	149
Jane	41	f	w	SCOT	San Francisco	San Francisco P O	80	457
Jane	31	f	w	SCOT	Contra Costa	Martinez P O	71	446
Jim	40	m	w	IREL	San Joaquin	Oneal Twp	86	100
Jno	38	m	w	TN	San Joaquin	Douglas Twp	86	40
John	53	m	w	TN	Colusa	Spring Valley Twp	71	339
John	46	m	w	KY	Merced	Snelling P O	74	264
John	43	m	w	KY	Yolo	Washington Twp	93	533
John	43	m	w	RI	El Dorado	Salmon Falls Twp	72	132
John	42	m	w	BELG	Placer	Bath P O	76	431
John	42	m	w	ENGL	Sacramento	Granite Twp	77	148
John	40	m	w	CANA	Placer	Auburn P O	76	374
John	40	m	w	PA	Placer	Auburn P O	76	378
John	38	m	w	NJ	San Francisco	San Francisco P O	80	412
John	36	m	w	SCOT	Sutter	Sutter Twp	92	125
John	21	m	w	SCOT	San Francisco	San Francisco P O	80	458
John A	33	m	b	PA	Santa Clara	1-Wd San Jose	88	239
John F	53	m	w	SHOL	Humboldt	Table Bluff Twp	72	304
John G	59	m	w	NH	El Dorado	Salmon Falls Twp	72	129
Jos W	60	m	w	PA	San Francisco	8-Wd San Francisco	82	293
Joseph	42	m	w	KY	Tulare	Tule Rvr Twp	92	267
Joseph C	45	m	w	PA	San Francisco	8-Wd San Francisco	82	397
Joshua	39	m	w	VA	San Francisco	11-Wd San Francisc	84	453
Julia	18	f	w	MO	Santa Clara	Gilroy Twp	88	70
Jus	19	m	w	IN	Butte	Chico Twp	70	50
Kate	51	f	w	IREL	Santa Clara	Redwood Twp	88	122
Lareson	24	m	w	CT	Sacramento	1-Wd Sacramento	77	172
Lawrence	30	m	w	OH	Sonoma	Vallejo Twp	91	451
Luis	20	m	w	ENGL	Santa Clara	Santa Clara Twp	88	147
Margurite	50	f	w	SCOT	Contra Costa	Martinez P O	71	442
Mary	40	f	w	IREL	Santa Clara	Fremont Twp	88	41
May	15	f	w	CA	Placer	Alta P O	76	411
Nancy	40	f	w	IREL	Santa Clara	1-Wd San Jose	88	276
Nellie	22	f	w	IA	San Francisco	11-Wd San Francisc	84	498
Noel	24	m	w	MO	Sonoma	Healdsburg & Mendo	91	281
Oliver	38	m	w	IN	Tulare	Kings Rvr Twp	92	253
Peter	51	m	w	SCOT	Plumas	Quartz Twp	77	42
Peter	41	m	w	IREL	Sacramento	1-Wd Sacramento	77	180
Phil	32	m	w	IL	Butte	Ophir Twp	70	118
R L	32	m	w	PA	Solano	Vallejo	90	181
Richard H	46	m	w	VA	El Dorado	Mud Springs Twp	72	75
Robert	47	m	w	IREL	Yolo	Grafton Twp	93	478
Robert	44	m	w	CANA	San Francisco	San Francisco P O	85	732
Robert	37	m	w	AUSL	San Francisco	San Francisco P O	80	362
Robert	30	m	w	IN	Santa Barbara	San Buenaventura P	87	418
Robert	21	m	w	NJ	Contra Costa	Martinez P O	71	377
Robt	35	m	w	GA	San Francisco	11-Wd San Francisc	84	643
S A	34	m	w	ME	Tuolumne	Big Oak Flat P O	93	405
Sam	55	m	w	MO	Sonoma	Mendocino Twp	91	308
Sam	40	m	w	TN	Mendocino	Ukiah Twp	74	234
Saml	21	m	w	MA	San Francisco	5-Wd San Francisco	81	9
Saml C	44	m	w	PA	Tehama	Tehama Twp	92	195
Samson	30	m	w	SCOT	Monterey	San Juan Twp	74	390
Samuel M	46	m	w	IREL	Sonoma	Bodega Twp	91	260
Sarah	65	f	w	NY	Butte	Chico Twp	70	39
Stafford	30	m	w	IREL	Marin	Tomales Twp	74	77
Stephen	30	m	w	LA	San Francisco	6-Wd San Francisco	81	108
Tall	51	m	w	KY	Sonoma	Mendocino Twp	91	306
Thomas	50	m	w	KY	Calaveras	Copperopolis P O	70	250
Thomas	42	m	w	PA	Tuolumne	Chinese Camp P O	93	380
Thomas	35	m	w	TN	Stanislaus	Empire Twp	92	55
Thomas	30	m	w	IREL	Los Angeles	Santa Ana Twp	73	602
Thomas	21	m	w	ENGL	Santa Clara	Santa Clara Twp	88	145
Thomas	19	m	w	OH	Mariposa	Mariposa P O	74	99
Thomas L	34	m	w	ENGL	Nevada	Grass Valley Twp	75	229
Thomas W	34	m	w	AR	Plumas	Indian Twp	77	11
Thos	27	m	w	MA	San Joaquin	2-Wd Stockton	86	161
William	42	m	w	TN	Los Angeles	Los Angeles Twp	73	469
William	39	m	w	IL	Tulare	Tule Rvr Twp	92	271
William	29	m	w	SCOT	San Francisco	San Francisco P O	80	480
William	28	m	w	IL	Yolo	Grafton Twp	93	479
William	26	m	w	IL	Yolo	Grafton Twp	93	491
William K	45	m	w	TN	Stanislaus	Empire Twp	92	55
Wm	46	m	w	KY	Mono	Bridgeport P O	74	287
Wm L	45	m	w	MD	San Francisco	San Francisco P O	83	99
Wm T	20	m	w	CA	Marin	Novato Twp	74	11
Wyat G	40	m	w	VA	Yolo	Cottonwood Twp	93	469
DUNCE								
John	28	m	w	SWIT	San Joaquin	1-Wd Stockton	86	132
DUNCER								
Julius	40	m	w	PRUS	San Francisco	8-Wd San Francisco	82	355
DUNCH								
Conrad	39	m	w	BAVA	Mariposa	Mariposa P O	74	90
Jno	37	m	w	NY	San Joaquin	Elliott Twp	86	72
DUNCHA								
David	36	m	w	OH	Sonoma	Petaluma Twp	91	346
DUNCHIN								
Louis	40	m	w	FRAN	Napa	Napa	75	47
DUNCING								
William	40	m	w	HANO	San Francisco	7-Wd San Francisco	81	171
DUNCKEN								
C W	44	m	w	HAMB	Sacramento	3-Wd Sacramento	77	317
DUNDARO								
Nicho	35	m	w	ITAL	El Dorado	Placerville Twp	72	101
DUNDAS								
William	28	m	w	NY	Nevada	Eureka Twp	75	130
DUNDE								
Betta	32	f	w	HAMB	Placer	Colfax P O	76	391
DUNDIN								
Chas	25	m	w	MA	San Francisco	San Francisco P O	83	328
DUNDON								
H	30	m	w	NY	Nevada	Eureka Twp	75	135
Hugh	30	m	w	NY	Nevada	Eureka Twp	75	135
John	35	m	w	IREL	San Francisco	San Francisco P O	83	317
Patk	25	m	w	IREL	Solano	Vallejo	90	196
DUNDRAT								
Monell	26	m	w	PORT	Solano	Benicia	90	6
DUNDUE								
Louis	39	m	w	ITAL	Tuolumne	Columbia P O	93	345
DUNDUS								
Luzi	34	m	w	ITAL	Tuolumne	Columbia P O	93	350
DUNDY								
Joseph	28	m	w	ITAL	Amador	Amador City P O	69	390
DUNEEN								
Ellen	23	f	w	IREL	San Francisco	6-Wd San Francisco	81	148
DUNEKE								
David	35	m	w	IREL	San Francisco	7-Wd San Francisco	81	266
DUNEVANT								
D	55	m	w	NY	San Francisco	San Francisco P O	83	332
DUNEWAR								
D	40	m	w	IREL	San Francisco	San Francisco P O	85	786
DUNEY								
Louis J	20	m	w	MO	Los Angeles	Santa Ana Twp	73	601
DUNEYVAN								
Jno	28	m	w	IREL	Alameda	Oakland	68	252
DUNFORD								
Bridget	26	f	w	IREL	San Francisco	San Francisco P O	83	104
Thomas	35	m	w	ENGL	Humboldt	Eureka Twp	72	263
DUNG								
Yen	32	m	c	CHIN	Nevada	Bridgeport Twp	75	111
DUNGAN								
Ezra	34	m	w	IREL	Solano	Rio Vista Twp	90	59
G A	41	m	w	KY	Humboldt	Pacific Twp	72	291
James	26	m	w	ENGL	Alameda	Eden Twp	68	57
John	43	m	w	KY	Humboldt	Pacific Twp	72	292
John B	30	m	w	VA	Yolo	Grafton Twp	93	500
Julius	42	m	w	NY	San Francisco	5-Wd San Francisco	81	30
Robert	33	m	w	IL	Humboldt	Pacific Twp	72	293
Thomas	70	m	w	MD	Humboldt	Pacific Twp	72	293
DUNGANON								
Maggie	19	f	w	NY	San Francisco	11-Wd San Francisc	84	688
DUNGAY								
Henry	40	m	w	ENGL	San Francisco	1-Wd San Francisco	79	44
DUNGLADA								
Albert	26	m	w	MEXI	San Francisco	6-Wd San Francisco	81	103
DUNHAGAN								
Thos	44	m	w	KY	Sutter	Vernon Twp	92	138
DUNHAM								
Almond N	24	m	w	OH	Shasta	Millville P O	89	486
C	64	f	w	NY	Alameda	Oakland	68	174
Chas P	28	m	w	OH	Shasta	American Ranch P O	89	498
Columbus	42	m	w	NY	San Diego	San Diego	78	500
Davis I	45	m	w	VT	Nevada	Rough & Ready Twp	75	334
Edgar	48	m	w	NY	Plumas	Seneca Twp	77	49
G	28	m	w	CANA	Solano	Vallejo	90	172
Geo A	50	m	w	MA	Solano	Vallejo	90	183
George	20	m	w	NY	Sacramento	2-Wd Sacramento	77	245
George L	29	m	w	KY	Colusa	Colusa Twp	71	276
H	42	m	w	MO	Santa Clara	Gilroy Twp	88	67
H A	37	f	w	VT	San Francisco	8-Wd San Francisco	82	362
Hiram	36	m	w	ME	Colusa	Spring Valley Twp	71	336
Isaac	44	m	w	MA	Santa Clara	San Jose Twp	88	189
J F	40	m	w	FRAN	Sierra	Downieville Twp	89	514
James A	26	m	w	OH	Tehama	Battle Crk Twp	92	172
John B	40	m	w	PA	Colusa	Monroe Twp	71	321
Jonathan	57	m	w	OH	Shasta	Millville P O	89	491
M	32	m	w	ME	Solano	Vallejo	90	165
O S	46	m	w	NY	Alameda	Oakland	68	135
Seth	42	m	w	ME	Lake	Lower Lake	73	414
Thomas	46	m	w	MA	Colusa	Spring Valley Twp	71	344
Warren	33	m	w	CANA	Shasta	Horsetown P O	89	505
DUNHAN								
A A	35	m	w	OH	San Francisco	3-Wd San Francisco	79	306
Jas	48	m	w	ME	San Joaquin	Dent Twp	86	29
Joseph C	29	m	w	MA	Solano	Rio Vista Twp	90	59
Robt	52	m	w	VA	Butte	Chico Twp	70	40
Wm	26	m	w	MO	Butte	Chico Twp	70	40
DUNICAN								
Edwin	20	m	w	NJ	San Francisco	San Francisco P O	83	293
Sarah	50	f	w	IREL	San Francisco	San Francisco P O	83	29
DUNICK								
Margaret	23	f	w	IL	Santa Clara	Redwood Twp	88	130
DUNIGAN								
Annie	45	f	w	PA	San Francisco	San Francisco P O	83	258
Bridget	30	m	w	IREL	San Francisco	San Francisco P O	83	260
Frank	55	m	w	IREL	San Francisco	San Francisco P O	83	383
Frank	50	m	w	IREL	Solano	Benicia	90	7
John	45	m	w	IREL	San Francisco	1-Wd San Francisco	79	113
John	42	m	w	IREL	San Francisco	1-Wd San Francisco	79	55
John	38	m	w	IREL	San Francisco	San Francisco P O	83	374
John	33	m	w	IREL	San Francisco	1-Wd San Francisco	79	113

© 2001 by Heritage Quest. All rights reserved.

Name	Age	S	R	B-PL	County	Locale	Roll (Series M593)	Pg
Michael	50	m	w	IREL	San Francisco	San Francisco P O	80	366
Michl	32	m	w	IREL	San Francisco	San Francisco P O	83	8
DUNION								
Mathew	37	m	w	IREL	San Francisco	San Francisco P O	83	23
William H	42	m	w	NH	Santa Cruz	Pajaro Twp	89	350
DUNIVAN								
Dennis	40	m	w	IREL	San Francisco	8-Wd San Francisco	82	298
James	35	m	w	IREL	Sacramento	Alabama Twp	77	63
Jane	8M	f	w	CA	Sutter	Yuba Twp	92	145
Richard	38	m	w	IREL	Sutter	Vernon Twp	92	136
DUNKEE								
W A	27	m	w	PA	Alameda	Oakland	68	202
DUNKEL								
Oscar	41	m	w	PRUS	Placer	Colfax P O	76	386
DUNKER								
Christopher	27	m	w	HANO	San Francisco	San Francisco P O	83	115
Ernest	53	m	w	LUEB	San Francisco	San Francisco P O	83	186
Henry	30	m	w	FRAN	San Francisco	5-Wd San Francisco	81	19
Herman	44	m	w	HANO	El Dorado	White Oak Twp	72	138
S	40	m	w	SHOL	San Joaquin	Tulare Twp	86	256
DUNKERLEY								
A	27	m	w	OH	Solano	Benicia	90	12
DUNKERLY								
Joseph	50	m	w	ENGL	San Francisco	2-Wd San Francisco	79	261
DUNKIL								
Edward	47	m	w	PRUS	Placer	Colfax P O	76	385
DUNKIN								
Caleb	43	m	w	GA	Trinity	Hayfork Valley	92	239
Matherson	46	m	w	SCOT	Trinity	Minersville Pct	92	215
R	46	m	w	ENGL	Sierra	Forest Twp	89	531
DUNKLE								
Henry	46	m	w	PA	Tuolumne	Columbia P O	93	354
DUNKLEE								
John	43	m	w	SCOT	Siskiyou	Klamath Twp	89	600
DUNKUM								
Charley	55	m	w	VA	Plumas	Quartz Twp	77	43
DUNLAP								
A G	34	m	w	ME	Monterey	Castroville Twp	74	340
A W	39	m	w	ME	San Francisco	8-Wd San Francisco	82	306
Albert	37	m	w	IL	Stanislaus	Empire Twp	92	40
Albert	19	m	w	TX	San Bernardino	Belleville Twp	78	408
Alexander	32	m	w	SCOT	El Dorado	Placerville Twp	72	94
Andrew	67	m	w	NY	San Francisco	11-Wd San Francisc	84	484
Andrew	63	m	w	NY	San Francisco	11-Wd San Francisc	84	446
Augusta	25	f	w	NY	San Francisco	11-Wd San Francisc	84	446
Chas V	21	m	w	CT	San Francisco	1-Wd San Francisco	79	63
Danl	49	m	w	AUSL	San Francisco	San Francisco P O	85	795
David	25	m	w	PA	San Francisco	San Francisco P O	83	256
Delia	24	f	w	IREL	San Francisco	San Francisco P O	80	404
E K	43	m	w	NY	Santa Clara	Gilroy Twp	88	92
Edw	21	m	w	OH	Tehama	Tehama Twp	92	193
Edward	35	m	w	ME	Tuolumne	Sonora P O	93	321
Elmer	21	m	w	OH	Tehama	Cottonwood Twp	92	162
Elon	40	m	w	NY	El Dorado	Diamond Springs Tw	72	22
Eva	10	f	w	MO	Colusa	Grand Island Twp	71	310
Frank	26	m	w	NH	Colusa	Colusa	71	288
H	35	m	w	NY	Alameda	Oakland	68	171
Hannah	40	f	w	ME	San Francisco	San Francisco P O	80	347
Henry	36	m	w	ME	Humboldt	Bucksport Twp	72	244
Henry	24	m	w	WI	Sacramento	San Joaquin Twp	77	406
Houston	22	m	w	TX	San Bernardino	San Bernardino Twp	78	444
Isaiah	31	m	b	VA	Sacramento	2-Wd Sacramento	77	216
J R	24	m	w	PA	Amador	Jackson P O	69	329
James	32	m	w	TX	Kern	Linns Valley P O	73	348
James L	26	m	w	MI	Sonoma	Mendocino Twp	91	298
James M	36	m	w	OH	Yolo	Cache Crk Twp	93	430
Jane	39	f	w	IL	Colusa	Colusa	71	293
John	60	m	w	TN	Tuolumne	Chinese Camp P O	93	384
John	56	m	w	KY	Placer	Roseville P O	76	356
John	56	m	w	MO	Kern	Linns Valley P O	73	348
John	40	m	w	ENGL	Merced	Snelling P O	74	272
John	34	m	w	SCOT	San Francisco	San Francisco P O	80	362
John	33	m	w	KY	Placer	Bath P O	76	441
John	30	m	w	IREL	San Francisco	7-Wd San Francisco	81	201
John	26	m	w	IREL	Monterey	Castroville Twp	74	337
John	26	m	w	OH	Nevada	Meadow Lake Twp	75	248
Jonathan D	42	m	w	NH	Los Angeles	Los Angeles	73	572
Joseph	40	m	w	OH	Colusa	Butte Twp	71	272
Leml S	41	m	w	MO	Colusa	Grand Island Twp	71	309
M	22	m	w	CANA	Solano	Vallejo	90	167
Martin	28	m	w	NH	Colusa	Colusa	71	293
Mary	15	f	w	NY	San Francisco	11-Wd San Francisc	84	626
Mary A	64	f	w	VA	Santa Cruz	Pajaro Twp	89	343
Pres	53	m	w	PA	Sacramento	3-Wd Sacramento	77	275
Robert R	47	m	w	PA	Santa Barbara	San Buenaventura P	87	446
Sam	40	m	w	PA	Amador	Jackson P O	69	345
Samuel	40	m	w	VA	Santa Clara	Redwood Twp	88	128
Sarah	14	f	w	MO	Stanislaus	Empire Twp	92	41
Thomas	38	m	w	OH	Amador	Sutter Crk P O	69	396
Thos J	42	m	w	MO	Fresno	Millerton P O	72	149
W C	47	m	w	NJ	Solano	Vallejo	90	147
W R	39	m	w	NY	Santa Clara	Gilroy Twp	88	92
William	40	m	w	IREL	Plumas	Washington Twp	77	54
William B	42	m	w	VA	Placer	Roseville P O	76	356
William B	36	m	w	OH	Placer	Lincoln P O	76	489
Wm	37	m	w	IL	San Joaquin	2-Wd Stockton	86	165
Wm M	12	m	w	CA	Plumas	Indian Twp	77	12
DUNLAPP								
J	38	m	w	PA	San Joaquin	Elkhorn Twp	86	56
James	69	m	w	IREL	Inyo	Lone Pine Twp	73	331
DUNLAVY								
Jas	35	m	w	BRAN	Tehama	Tehama Twp	92	193
John	60	m	w	IREL	San Francisco	7-Wd San Francisco	81	186
DUNLAY								
Edward	27	m	w	IREL	San Francisco	7-Wd San Francisco	81	176
John	34	m	w	IREL	Humboldt	Eureka Twp	72	256
DUNLEARY								
Andrew	40	m	w	IREL	San Francisco	8-Wd San Francisco	82	426
DUNLEAVY								
Jeremiah	30	m	w	IREL	San Francisco	8-Wd San Francisco	82	380
DUNLEVY								
Andrew	38	m	w	IREL	San Francisco	San Francisco P O	83	419
John	23	m	w	MD	Placer	Auburn P O	76	383
Robert W	40	m	w	PA	Sacramento	2-Wd Sacramento	77	216
DUNLEY								
John	47	m	w	IREL	San Francisco	7-Wd San Francisco	81	254
DUNLOP								
Frank	25	m	w	IN	Yolo	Putah Twp	93	519
John	40	m	w	OH	Santa Cruz	Pajaro Twp	89	356
Samuel	41	m	w	VA	Monterey	San Juan Twp	74	387
DUNLY								
Jno	36	m	w	IREL	Alameda	Oakland	68	215
DUNMASTER								
E	30	f	w	HANO	Sierra	Lincoln Twp	89	545
DUNN								
Acinthe	32	f	w	MI	Contra Costa	Martinez P O	71	447
Ah	53	m	c	CHIN	Sacramento	1-Wd Sacramento	77	188
Alex	29	m	w	MO	Mendocino	Ukiah Twp	74	235
Alexander	39	m	w	IL	Siskiyou	Scott Valley Twp	89	621
Andrew	61	m	w	PA	San Joaquin	2-Wd Stockton	86	201
Andrew	52	m	w	IREL	Solano	Vallejo	90	196
Andrew	37	m	w	ENGL	Nevada	Grass Valley Twp	75	231
Andrew	30	m	w	IREL	San Francisco	8-Wd San Francisco	82	388
Andrew	22	m	w	ME	Mendocino	Point Arena Twp	74	214
Andrew B	28	m	w	NY	Mendocino	Point Arena Twp	74	211
Ann	70	f	w	IREL	San Francisco	San Francisco P O	85	814
Ann	29	f	w	IREL	San Francisco	San Francisco P O	80	418
Anna	20	f	w	IREL	San Francisco	6-Wd San Francisco	81	113
Annie	50	f	w	IREL	San Francisco	11-Wd San Francisc	84	630
B	40	f	w	IREL	Sonoma	Santa Rosa	91	410
Ballard	40	m	w	VA	Alameda	Oakland	68	161
Bernard	50	m	w	IREL	San Francisco	1-Wd San Francisco	79	22
Bernard	28	m	w	IREL	San Francisco	8-Wd San Francisco	82	430
Bridget	35	f	w	IREL	San Francisco	6-Wd San Francisco	81	102
Catherine	40	f	w	IREL	Yuba	Marysville	93	585
Celia	40	f	w	IREL	Santa Clara	1-Wd San Jose	88	243
Charles	42	m	w	SWED	Contra Costa	Martinez P O	71	417
Charles	33	m	w	KY	Nevada	Meadow Lake Twp	75	266
Charles	30	m	w	NY	San Francisco	San Francisco P O	83	222
Charles	30	m	w	ENGL	Contra Costa	Martinez P O	71	419
Charles	27	m	w	MA	Los Angeles	San Gabriel Twp	73	594
Charles	24	m	w	ME	Los Angeles	Wilmington Twp	73	634
Charles	21	m	w	IN	Marin	San Rafael Twp	74	40
Chas	31	m	w	SCOT	San Joaquin	3-Wd Stockton	86	221
Chas	21	m	w	ME	San Francisco	8-Wd San Francisco	82	368
Christopher	38	m	w	IREL	San Francisco	11-Wd San Francisc	84	459
Cornelious	27	m	w	AUST	San Francisco	11-Wd San Francisc	84	632
Cornelius	50	m	w	IREL	San Francisco	San Francisco P O	83	370
Cornelius	45	m	w	IREL	Sacramento	2-Wd Sacramento	77	209
Daniel	30	m	w	IREL	El Dorado	Placerville	72	108
Danl	46	m	w	IREL	Solano	Vallejo	90	183
David	48	m	w	NY	Placer	Gold Run Twp	76	400
David G	26	m	w	IN	Placer	Dutch Flat P O	76	414
Dennis	56	m	w	IREL	Mariposa	Mariposa P O	74	113
Dennis	36	m	w	IREL	San Francisco	San Francisco P O	83	313
Dennis C	40	m	w	IREL	San Francisco	San Francisco P O	83	125
Dennis H	55	m	w	IREL	Shasta	Shasta P O	89	462
E R	20	f	w	WI	Amador	Drytown P O	69	423
E S	38	m	w	OH	Alameda	Oakland	68	197
Ed	29	m	w	IA	San Joaquin	Douglas Twp	86	31
Edward	50	m	w	IREL	Sacramento	2-Wd Sacramento	77	228
Edward	38	m	w	IREL	San Francisco	San Francisco P O	83	62
Edward	38	m	w	KY	Contra Costa	Martinez P O	71	389
Edward	38	m	w	IREL	Monterey	Alisal Twp	74	294
Edward	23	m	w	MA	Inyo	Bishop Crk Twp	73	313
Edward F	27	m	w	OH	San Francisco	San Francisco P O	83	240
Edwd	34	m	w	NY	San Francisco	1-Wd San Francisco	79	125
Elizabeth	43	f	w	IREL	San Francisco	2-Wd San Francisco	79	238
Ellen	24	f	w	IREL	Santa Clara	Gilroy Twp	88	70
Elnathan D	30	m	w	OH	Mendocino	Point Arena Twp	74	206
Ervin	33	m	w	NY	Sacramento	San Joaquin Twp	77	399
Esquire	60	m	w	TN	Tulare	Visalia Twp	92	282
Esquire la F	4	m	w	CA	Tulare	Venice Twp	92	273
France	67	m	m	IL	Nevada	Nevada Twp	75	320
Frances	5	f	w	CA	San Francisco	11-Wd San Francisc	84	711
Frank	50	m	w	IREL	San Francisco	2-Wd San Francisco	79	160
Frank	31	m	w	BREM	San Francisco	1-Wd San Francisco	79	124
Frank	31	m	w	IREL	San Francisco	5-Wd San Francisco	81	28
Frederick	39	m	w	IREL	San Mateo	San Mateo P O	87	355
Geo W	56	m	w	PA	Butte	Chico Twp	70	20
George M	18	m	w	PA	Sonoma	Salt Point	91	385
George W	48	m	w	NJ	San Francisco	3-Wd San Francisco	79	314
Georgiana	23	f	w	ME	Humboldt	Eureka Twp	72	271
H C	26	m	w	MI	Calaveras	Copperopolis P O	70	255

© 2001 by Heritage Quest. All rights reserved.

Name	Age	S	R	B-PL	County	Locale	Roll	Pg
Harriet	22	f	w	MO	Sacramento	1-Wd Sacramento	77	172
Henry	52	m	w	IREL	Nevada	Rough & Ready Twp	75	335
Henry	20	m	w	CANA	Sierra	Gibson Twp	89	542
Horace D	40	m	w	NY	San Francisco	San Francisco P O	83	103
Hy	16	m	w	CA	San Francisco	11-Wd San Francisc	84	592
Isaac	32	m	w	ENGL	Mendocino	Albion & Big Rvr T	74	166
J	20	m	w	OH	Sacramento	1-Wd Sacramento	77	177
J F	52	m	w	KY	Lassen	Janesville Twp	73	432
J H	25	m	w	NY	Solano	Vallejo	90	142
J R	35	m	w	KY	Lassen	Janesville Twp	73	432
J R	30	m	w	KY	Lassen	Janesville Twp	73	431
J S	60	m	w	NY	Nevada	Nevada Twp	75	307
J T	48	m	w	MA	Merced	Snelling P O	74	269
Jacob	49	m	w	PRUS	Solano	Tremont Twp	90	29
Jame	63	m	w	CANA	Lassen	Janesville Twp	73	431
James	70	m	w	IREL	San Francisco	San Francisco P O	85	814
James	65	m	w	IREL	San Francisco	11-Wd San Francisc	84	613
James	49	m	w	IREL	San Francisco	11-Wd San Francisc	84	431
James	48	m	w	MS	Los Angeles	San Jose Twp	73	621
James	47	m	w	IREL	Santa Clara	Gilroy Twp	88	92
James	40	m	w	IREL	Sacramento	4-Wd Sacramento	77	373
James	36	m	w	IREL	Alameda	Oakland	68	264
James	35	m	w	IREL	San Francisco	San Francisco P O	80	410
James	33	m	w	IREL	San Diego	Coronado	78	466
James	25	m	w	IREL	Humboldt	Eureka Twp	72	277
James	24	m	w	IN	San Francisco	2-Wd San Francisco	79	145
James	24	m	w	IREL	Nevada	Grass Valley Twp	75	215
James	22	m	w	MA	San Francisco	11-Wd San Francisc	84	550
James	21	m	w	MA	Marin	San Rafael Twp	74	35
James M	51	m	w	VA	Sonoma	Petaluma Twp	91	361
Jane	27	f	w	WALE	Sierra	Sears Twp	89	558
Jane	25	f	w	IREL	Alameda	San Leandro	68	94
Jas	40	m	w	PA	Sacramento	1-Wd Sacramento	77	172
Jas	29	m	w	AUSL	San Francisco	7-Wd San Francisco	81	279
Jas	25	m	w	CANA	Humboldt	Eureka Twp	72	260
Jas	17	m	w	CA	Sonoma	Cloverdale Twp	91	270
John	54	m	w	IREL	San Francisco	San Francisco P O	83	157
John	52	m	w	IREL	Yuba	Long Bar Twp	93	562
John	48	m	w	IREL	Sonoma	Vallejo Twp	91	457
John	46	m	w	ENGL	Santa Clara	Almaden Twp	88	3
John	44	m	w	IREL	San Francisco	San Francisco P O	83	123
John	40	m	w	ENGL	San Francisco	8-Wd San Francisco	82	472
John	39	m	w	IREL	San Francisco	6-Wd San Francisco	81	136
John	38	m	w	CANA	San Francisco	San Francisco P O	83	391
John	36	m	w	IREL	Alameda	Brooklyn Twp	68	41
John	34	m	w	ENGL	Nevada	Grass Valley Twp	75	182
John	32	m	w	NY	San Francisco	7-Wd San Francisco	81	176
John	30	m	w	IREL	San Francisco	San Francisco P O	85	861
John	30	m	w	IREL	Stanislaus	Branch Twp	92	2
John	30	m	w	IREL	San Francisco	7-Wd San Francisco	81	251
John	29	m	w	CANA	San Francisco	3-Wd San Francisco	79	319
John	27	m	w	CANA	Solano	Vallejo	90	203
John	24	m	w	IREL	San Francisco	11-Wd San Francisc	84	447
John	22	m	w	AUSL	Solano	Vallejo	90	145
John	18	m	w	IREL	San Francisco	San Francisco P O	83	170
John	14	m	w	CA	Sutter	Vernon Twp	92	135
John A	46	m	w	GA	Los Angeles	Los Nietos Twp	73	573
Joseph	45	m	w	IREL	San Francisco	San Francisco P O	80	396
Joseph	41	m	w	VA	El Dorado	Cosumnes Twp	72	16
Joseph	26	m	w	IREL	San Francisco	San Francisco P O	80	337
Joseph	23	m	w	IN	Santa Clara	Santa Clara Twp	88	136
Joseph	19	m	w	CANA	Klamath	Trinidad Twp	73	392
Julia	26	f	w	IREL	Solano	Vallejo	90	168
Kate	30	f	w	IREL	Sacramento	3-Wd Sacramento	77	298
Kate	26	f	w	IREL	Santa Clara	Gilroy Twp	88	77
Lawrence	30	m	w	IREL	San Francisco	8-Wd San Francisco	82	393
Lewis	31	m	w	PA	Nevada	Bridgeport Twp	75	108
Louisa	68	f	w	NY	San Francisco	San Francisco P O	83	418
Lucy	30	f	w	IREL	San Francisco	San Francisco P O	83	102
M	41	m	w	IREL	Alameda	Oakland	68	229
M A	21	f	w	AUST	Tuolumne	Columbia P O	93	360
Margaret	43	f	w	IREL	Nevada	Grass Valley Twp	75	157
Margaret	42	f	w	IREL	San Francisco	San Francisco P O	83	158
Martin	45	m	w	IREL	San Francisco	8-Wd San Francisco	82	480
Martin	30	m	w	IREL	San Francisco	6-Wd San Francisco	81	102
Martin	25	m	w	IREL	Sacramento	Dry Crk Twp	77	101
Mary	88	f	w	IREL	San Francisco	San Francisco P O	83	70
Mary	50	f	w	IREL	San Francisco	2-Wd San Francisco	79	165
Mary	43	f	w	IREL	El Dorado	Placerville	72	111
Mary	43	f	w	IREL	San Francisco	11-Wd San Francisc	84	456
Mary	40	f	w	IREL	San Francisco	11-Wd San Francisc	84	543
Mary	36	f	w	IREL	San Francisco	San Francisco P O	85	738
Mary	21	f	w	IREL	San Francisco	San Francisco P O	85	721
Mathew	50	m	w	IREL	San Francisco	11-Wd San Francisc	84	442
Mathew	30	m	w	IREL	San Francisco	8-Wd San Francisco	82	443
Mathew	26	m	w	IREL	Sonoma	Vallejo Twp	91	451
Mathew	25	m	w	NY	San Francisco	7-Wd San Francisco	81	188
Michael	36	m	w	IREL	Sacramento	2-Wd Sacramento	77	233
Michael	31	m	w	IREL	Siskiyou	Yreka	89	651
Michael	30	m	w	IREL	Santa Clara	Fremont Twp	88	59
Michael	25	m	w	IREL	San Francisco	3-Wd San Francisco	79	312
Michael	16	m	w	PA	San Francisco	San Francisco P O	83	165
Michel	40	m	w	IREL	Napa	Napa Twp	75	68
Nelson	40	m	w	CANA	El Dorado	Placerville	72	121
Nicholas R	46	m	w	MA	Shasta	Stillwater P O	89	479
Owen	24	m	w	IREL	San Francisco	San Francisco P O	83	184
Pat	30	m	w	IREL	Sierra	Gibson Twp	89	542
Patrick	52	m	w	ME	Mendocino	Point Arena Twp	74	214
Patrick	50	m	w	IREL	San Francisco	San Francisco P O	83	229
Patrick	50	m	w	NY	San Francisco	San Francisco P O	85	801
Patrick	47	m	w	IREL	Santa Clara	1-Wd San Jose	88	244
Patrick	47	m	w	IREL	San Francisco	San Francisco P O	83	165
Patrick	45	m	w	IREL	San Joaquin	Castoria Twp	86	1
Patrick	38	m	w	IREL	Klamath	Klamath Twp	73	371
Patrick	24	m	w	IREL	San Francisco	11-Wd San Francisc	84	430
Patrick	17	m	w	CA	Santa Clara	Santa Clara Twp	88	177
Peter	43	m	w	HANO	Butte	Kimshew Tpw	70	81
Peter	35	m	w	IREL	Santa Clara	Gilroy Twp	88	104
Peter	30	m	w	MA	San Francisco	11-Wd San Francisc	84	677
Philip	35	m	w	IREL	San Francisco	San Francisco P O	83	184
Phillip	33	m	w	NY	Alameda	Oakland	68	222
Richard	23	m	w	IREL	Solano	Vallejo	90	160
Robb H D	45	m	w	IREL	San Francisco	6-Wd San Francisco	81	91
Robert	38	m	w	IREL	Los Angeles	Santa Ana Twp	73	613
Robert B	28	m	w	PA	San Francisco	1-Wd San Francisco	79	65
Robt	23	m	w	PA	Solano	Vallejo	90	140
Roscoe	37	m	w	CANA	Yolo	Cache Crk Twp	93	455
Rufus K	23	m	w	KY	Tulare	Venice Twp	92	274
Samuel	52	m	w	ME	Santa Cruz	Santa Cruz Twp	89	381
Simeon	32	m	w	NJ	San Francisco	San Francisco P O	83	156
Susan	19	f	w	MO	San Francisco	San Francisco P O	80	399
Thomas	55	m	w	IREL	El Dorado	Placerville	72	108
Thomas	48	m	w	MI	Yolo	Grafton Twp	93	498
Thomas	46	m	w	NORW	Los Angeles	Wilmington Twp	73	640
Thomas	46	m	w	NY	Sonoma	Sonoma Twp	91	436
Thomas	39	m	w	IREL	San Francisco	7-Wd San Francisco	81	210
Thomas	39	m	w	IREL	Nevada	Bridgeport Twp	75	118
Thomas	30	m	w	IREL	Los Angeles	Soledad Twp	73	633
Thomas	30	m	w	IREL	San Francisco	7-Wd San Francisco	81	173
Thomas	26	m	w	IREL	Yolo	Cache Crk Twp	93	440
Thomas	26	m	w	IREL	Yolo	Grafton Twp	93	481
Thomas	26	m	w	IREL	San Francisco	7-Wd San Francisco	81	167
Thomas	26	m	w	IREL	Sutter	Sutter Twp	92	129
Thomas	25	m	w	IREL	San Francisco	San Francisco P O	85	763
Thomas	25	m	w	CANA	San Francisco	7-Wd San Francisco	81	164
Thos	50	m	w	NY	Nevada	Nevada Twp	75	307
Thos	35	m	w	IREL	San Joaquin	2-Wd Stockton	86	173
Thos	29	m	w	NY	Sierra	Sears Twp	89	559
Thos	27	m	w	IREL	Butte	Chico Twp	70	42
Thos	25	m	w	KY	San Francisco	1-Wd San Francisco	79	64
Thos	14	m	w	CA	San Francisco	11-Wd San Francisc	84	592
W B	37	m	w	VA	Yuba	East Bear Rvr Twp	93	542
W E	17	m	w	CA	Alameda	Oakland	68	242
W L	58	m	w	NC	Lassen	Janesville Twp	73	433
Walter	30	m	w	NY	San Francisco	San Francisco P O	83	387
William	55	m	w	IREL	San Francisco	11-Wd San Francisc	84	526
William	49	m	w	IREL	Los Angeles	Los Angeles Twp	73	492
William	47	m	w	NY	San Francisco	2-Wd San Francisco	79	169
William	36	m	w	ENGL	San Francisco	San Francisco P O	85	744
William	34	m	w	IREL	Marin	San Rafael Twp	74	45
William	30	m	w	OH	Monterey	Pajaro Twp	74	371
William A	60	m	w	KY	Solano	Vacaville Twp	90	133
William H	27	m	w	ME	Mendocino	Point Arena Twp	74	206
William W	37	m	w	MO	Placer	Gold Run Twp	76	396
Wm	90	m	w	IREL	San Francisco	San Francisco P O	83	70
Wm	35	m	w	OH	San Joaquin	2-Wd Stockton	86	165
Wm H	25	m	w	NY	Shasta	Shasta P O	89	462
Wm Henry	50	m	w	KY	Plumas	Mineral Twp	77	22
DUNNAGAN								
Thomas	35	m	w	IL	Contra Costa	Martinez P O	71	373
DUNNAGIN								
David	49	m	w	IREL	Merced	Snelling P O	74	272
DUNNAM								
Benjamin D	43	m	w	AL	Placer	Auburn P O	76	367
DUNNAS								
Alfred	28	m	w	CANA	San Francisco	2-Wd San Francisco	79	229
DUNNE								
Annie	45	f	w	IREL	San Francisco	11-Wd San Francisc	84	429
Geo L	35	m	w	IREL	Solano	Benicia	90	14
Harry	30	m	w	ENGL	Nevada	Grass Valley Twp	75	145
James	55	m	w	IREL	San Francisco	11-Wd San Francisc	84	429
James	45	m	w	IREL	San Francisco	11-Wd San Francisc	84	512
James	19	m	w	NY	Santa Clara	Alviso Twp	88	28
James	15	m	w	CA	Santa Clara	Santa Clara Twp	88	177
John	40	m	w	IREL	San Francisco	11-Wd San Francisc	84	512
John	35	m	w	NY	Solano	Vallejo	90	140
John	31	m	w	IREL	San Francisco	1-Wd San Francisco	79	79
John L	16	m	w	CA	Santa Barbara	Santa Barbara P O	87	451
Joseph	24	m	w	IREL	San Francisco	San Francisco P O	83	152
Michl	35	m	w	IREL	San Francisco	1-Wd San Francisco	79	80
Patk	39	m	w	IREL	Solano	Vallejo	90	201
Patk	35	m	w	IREL	San Francisco	1-Wd San Francisco	79	44
Patrick F	37	m	w	IREL	San Francisco	6-Wd San Francisco	81	140
Peter	26	m	w	IREL	San Francisco	11-Wd San Francisc	84	505
Theo	35	m	w	HAMB	Sacramento	3-Wd Sacramento	77	317
Timothy	30	m	w	IREL	San Francisco	1-Wd San Francisco	79	105
William	49	m	w	IREL	San Francisco	San Francisco P O	80	377
William	34	m	w	IREL	San Francisco	11-Wd San Francisc	84	454
DUNNEGAN								
Danl C	38	m	w	GA	Fresno	Kings Rvr P O	72	213
James	24	m	w	CANA	Napa	Napa Twp	75	62
Nicholas	30	m	w	TN	Kern	Linns Valley P O	73	347
DUNNEGAR								
Anna	25	f	w	IREL	San Francisco	5-Wd San Francisco	81	27

© 2001 by Heritage Quest. All rights reserved.

Name	Age	S	R	B-PL	County	Locale	Series M593 Roll	Pg
DUNNELL								
Eldridge	51	m	w	NY	Siskiyou	Cottonwood Twp	89	593
DUNNELS								
James F	33	m	w	PA	Trinity	Lewiston Pct	92	211
DUNNEN								
John	30	m	w	IREL	Alameda	Oakland	68	205
DUNNICLIFF								
John	40	m	w	ENGL	Nevada	Nevada Twp	75	280
DUNNIER								
Robert	28	m	w	CANA	Klamath	Trinidad Twp	73	392
DUNNIGAN								
Anthony W	58	m	w	VA	Yolo	Grafton Twp	93	495
Edward	35	m	w	IREL	San Francisco	San Francisco P O	83	352
George	21	m	w	NJ	Marin	San Rafael Twp	74	30
Hugh	23	m	w	IREL	San Francisco	11-Wd San Francisc	84	459
J R	22	m	w	NY	Solano	Vallejo	90	203
James	24	m	w	CANA	Napa	Napa	75	35
Jerry	37	m	w	IREL	Marin	Tomales Twp	74	82
Michael	39	m	w	CA	San Francisco	San Francisco P O	83	406
W	40	m	w	IREL	Tehama	Tehama Twp	92	156
DUNNIGER								
Anne	25	f	w	IREL	San Francisco	San Francisco P O	83	110
DUNNING								
A	14	f	w	CA	Alameda	Oakland	68	258
Benjamin P	43	m	w	ME	Yuba	Slate Range Bar Tw	93	675
Charles	46	m	w	ME	Calaveras	San Andreas P O	70	201
Charles	45	m	w	SCOT	San Francisco	6-Wd San Francisco	81	83
Christopher	44	m	w	ME	Calaveras	San Andreas P O	70	210
Climena	44	f	w	ME	Sonoma	Cloverdale Twp	91	266
E B	39	m	w	VT	Alameda	Oakland	68	203
E B	30	m	w	NY	San Francisco	5-Wd San Francisco	81	33
F M	38	m	w	KY	Santa Clara	Gilroy Twp	88	97
Frank	19	m	w	RI	Marin	Tomales Twp	74	85
Georgiana	21	f	w	NY	San Francisco	6-Wd San Francisco	81	71
Hattie	30	f	w	VT	San Francisco	6-Wd San Francisco	81	84
Henry	45	m	w	VT	El Dorado	Diamond Springs Tw	72	31
Hiram A	44	m	w	ME	Yuba	Slate Range Bar Tw	93	675
James	40	m	w	ME	Placer	Gold Run Twp	76	400
James	28	m	w	IREL	San Francisco	San Francisco P O	83	396
John	42	m	w	IREL	Santa Clara	San Jose Twp	88	205
John	26	m	w	OH	Yolo	Grafton Twp	93	478
Joseph	38	m	w	ME	Monterey	San Juan Twp	74	411
Julia	55	f	w	TN	Sonoma	Healdsburg & Mendo	91	279
Kate	26	f	w	IREL	San Francisco	San Francisco P O	83	299
Lorenzo	37	m	w	OH	Yolo	Grafton Twp	93	478
Marcus	35	m	w	NY	El Dorado	Cosumnes Twp	72	18
Mary	70	f	w	ENGL	San Francisco	San Francisco P O	85	822
Mary	35	f	w	IREL	Alameda	Oakland	68	187
Michail	32	m	w	IREL	San Francisco	11-Wd San Francisc	84	464
O	30	m	w	MA	Alameda	Oakland	68	263
Robert	37	m	w	WI	Calaveras	San Andreas P O	70	201
Robert	22	m	w	LA	Monterey	Pajaro Twp	74	376
T	44	m	w	ME	Nevada	Nevada Twp	75	281
Terrence	23	m	w	IREL	San Francisco	11-Wd San Francisc	84	464
Thomas	35	m	w	MA	Colusa	Spring Valley Twp	71	342
Thomas	35	m	w	IREL	San Francisco	San Francisco P O	83	396
Thomas	19	m	w	NY	San Francisco	6-Wd San Francisco	81	83
Thos	35	m	w	IREL	San Francisco	San Francisco P O	83	39
W S	47	m	w	ME	Amador	Jackson P O	69	320
William	53	m	w	AL	Monterey	Pajaro Twp	74	376
William	35	m	w	ME	Nevada	Bridgeport Twp	75	101
Z	44	m	w	ME	Yuba	Marysville	93	608
DUNNLER								
M B	35	m	w	BAVA	Nevada	Nevada Twp	75	321
DUNNON								
James	53	m	w	OH	Alameda	Brooklyn	68	24
DUNNUM								
John	40	m	w	IREL	Placer	Bath P O	76	428
DUNOON								
Mary	22	f	w	IREL	San Francisco	11-Wd San Francisc	84	514
DUNOS								
G B	44	m	w	FRAN	San Francisco	San Francisco P O	85	825
DUNPHY								
Edward	40	m	w	IREL	San Francisco	11-Wd San Francisc	84	469
James	10	m	w	CA	San Francisco	11-Wd San Francisc	84	593
Jannes	42	m	w	PA	San Francisco	8-Wd San Francisco	82	492
John	24	m	w	ENGL	San Francisco	San Francisco P O	80	335
P	40	m	w	IREL	San Francisco	San Francisco P O	85	790
P F	41	m	w	ME	Klamath	Trinidad Twp	73	393
Richd D	30	m	w	IREL	San Francisco	1-Wd San Francisco	79	136
William	40	m	w	NY	San Francisco	6-Wd San Francisco	81	78
DUNRIPPLE								
Wm	40	m	w	MD	San Francisco	8-Wd San Francisco	82	323
DUNROE								
George	30	m	w	IREL	San Francisco	8-Wd San Francisco	82	350
DUNS								
Antthony	26	m	w	DENM	San Francisco	2-Wd San Francisco	79	219
DUNSCAN								
Thos	27	m	w	IREL	Sacramento	Alabama Twp	77	60
DUNSCAP								
Thomas	30	m	w	IREL	Amador	Ione City P O	69	356
DUNSCOMB								
J	36	m	w	NY	Mariposa	Maxwell Crk P O	74	141
James R	40	m	w	NY	Plumas	Seneca Twp	77	50
DUNSCOMBE								
C	46	m	w	NY	Sacramento	3-Wd Sacramento	77	318
Robt	29	m	w	ENGL	San Luis Obispo	Salinas Twp	87	293
DUNSEAUSE								
Jean	50	m	w	FRAN	Calaveras	San Andreas P O	70	168
DUNSFORD								
John	25	m	w	CANA	San Francisco	7-Wd San Francisco	81	194
DUNSHEE								
Cornelius	35	m	w	MI	San Francisco	11-Wd San Francisc	84	705
John	46	m	w	VT	Santa Barbara	Santa Barbara P O	87	477
DUNSON								
Theodore	35	m	w	DENM	San Francisco	San Francisco P O	83	208
DUNSTAN								
Jno	35	m	w	ENGL	Santa Clara	Almaden Twp	88	10
Joseph	46	m	w	ENGL	Nevada	Grass Valley Twp	75	200
DUNSTER								
A J	34	m	w	NJ	Tuolumne	Columbia P O	93	335
Geo Wm	25	m	w	IN	Placer	Rocklin Twp	76	463
Isaac	57	m	w	ENGL	Solano	Vallejo	90	197
John H	19	m	w	NY	Napa	Napa Twp	75	64
Joseph	18	m	w	NY	Stanislaus	Empire Twp	92	53
DUNSTON								
John	40	m	w	ENGL	Fresno	Millerton P O	72	165
William	40	m	w	ENGL	Nevada	Grass Valley Twp	75	217
William	39	m	w	ENGL	Nevada	Eureka Twp	75	138
DUNSTONE								
John	47	m	w	ENGL	Butte	Wyandotte Twp	70	143
Thomas	44	m	w	ENGL	Santa Cruz	Santa Cruz Twp	89	391
William	42	m	w	ENGL	Butte	Wyandotte Twp	70	143
William	35	m	w	ENGL	Nevada	Grass Valley Twp	75	208
William	29	m	w	ENGL	Nevada	Grass Valley Twp	75	145
DUNT								
David	40	m	w	SWIT	Yolo	Cottonwood Twp	93	465
DUNTIN								
Squire	34	m	w	MO	Napa	Napa Twp	75	32
DUNTON								
E H	24	m	w	NY	San Francisco	3-Wd San Francisco	79	319
Edwd	25	m	w	MI	San Francisco	1-Wd San Francisco	79	79
Franklin	41	m	w	ME	Nevada	Grass Valley Twp	75	199
James	25	m	w	ME	Trinity	Hayfork Valley	92	239
Timothy	36	m	w	ME	Tuolumne	Sonora P O	93	320
DUNTONI								
Domingo	46	m	w	ITAL	Tuolumne	Sonora P O	93	317
DUNTSON								
W	22	m	w	ENGL	Sierra	Butte Twp	89	508
DUNUN								
James	30	m	w	IREL	San Francisco	San Francisco P O	83	197
Patrick	60	m	w	IREL	San Francisco	San Francisco P O	83	197
DUNWALD								
Chas F	33	m	w	PRUS	San Francisco	San Francisco P O	83	197
DUNWIDDIE								
Alex	56	m	w	PA	Sonoma	Santa Rosa	91	425
G W	24	m	w	IA	Sonoma	Santa Rosa	91	425
Z	19	m	w	IA	Sonoma	Santa Rosa	91	410
DUNWIDY								
Geo W	28	m	w	IA	Sonoma	Santa Rosa	91	422
DUNWORTH								
John	29	m	w	IREL	San Mateo	Half Moon Bay P O	87	389
Mosey	20	m	w	CT	Sacramento	2-Wd Sacramento	77	236
W M	38	m	w	TN	San Joaquin	Liberty Twp	86	93
DUNY								
Edgar	39	m	w	NY	Siskiyou	Callahan P O	89	625
S A	32	f	w	NY	Siskiyou	Callahan P O	89	625
DUNZ								
Chas J	55	m	w	SWIT	Nevada	Nevada Twp	75	279
DUNZLEMAN								
Harry	45	m	w	HOLL	Tulare	Tule Rvr Twp	92	265
DUONG								
Ah	48	m	c	CHIN	Amador	Fiddletown P O	69	441
DUOYN								
Edward	40	m	w	FRAN	Santa Clara	2-Wd San Jose	88	313
DUPAR								
John	32	m	w	MA	San Francisco	San Francisco P O	83	234
DUPARIS								
Victor	24	m	w	BELG	Santa Cruz	Pajaro Twp	89	343
DUPARK								
Francis	55	m	w	FRAN	Calaveras	San Andreas P O	70	206
DUPARON								
Bertrand	60	m	w	FRAN	Santa Clara	2-Wd San Jose	88	306
DUPAS								
John	35	m	w	MA	San Francisco	8-Wd San Francisco	82	415
DUPASS								
Benjamin	24	m	w	LA	San Francisco	6-Wd San Francisco	81	80
DUPEE								
Alzico	34	m	w	CANA	Placer	Bath P O	76	454
Antoni	51	m	w	HI	Yolo	Merritt Twp	93	505
DUPERU								
Numa	54	m	w	VA	San Francisco	San Francisco P O	83	113
DUPING								
Edward	49	m	w	ENGL	San Bernardino	San Bernardino Twp	78	452
DUPINS								
Chas	33	m	w	SWIT	San Joaquin	2-Wd Stockton	86	161
Harvey	20	m	w	OR	Sonoma	Analy Twp	91	225
J B	23	m	w	IL	San Joaquin	1-Wd Stockton	86	141
DUPLEX								
E P	39	m	m	VA	Yuba	Marysville	93	634
DUPLISSIS								
Narcisso	27	m	w	FRAN	Siskiyou	Scott Valley Twp	89	609
DUPOND								
Baptiste	44	m	w	CANA	Nevada	Grass Valley Twp	75	228

© 2001 by Heritage Quest. All rights reserved.

Series M593

Name	Age	S	R	B-PL	County	Locale	Roll	Pg
Joseph	43	m	w	CANA	Nevada	Grass Valley Twp	75	156
DUPONG								
Vallieve	25	f	w	FRAN	San Francisco	6-Wd San Francisco	81	78
DUPONT								
Alpheus	44	m	w	FRAN	Santa Clara	San Jose Twp	88	195
E L	51	m	w	FRAN	Amador	Jackson P O	69	321
John	61	m	w	SC	San Francisco	7-Wd San Francisco	81	242
Justin	25	m	w	FRAN	Contra Costa	Martinez P O	71	442
Mary	13	f	w	CA	Sonoma	Salt Point	91	393
Rht	25	m	w	LUXE	Merced	Snelling P O	74	262
Rosella	45	f	w	FRAN	Sonoma	Salt Point	91	393
DUPOQUE								
Lewis	50	m	w	FRAN	San Francisco	San Francisco P O	83	268
DUPORE								
Harry	22	m	w	NY	Sonoma	Analy Twp	91	230
DUPORT								
Charles	49	m	w	FRAN	San Francisco	San Francisco P O	85	751
DUPPE								
Perre	60	m	w	FRAN	Butte	Kimshew Tpw	70	81
DUPPIE								
Edward	61	m	w	IREL	Yuba	Slate Range Bar Tw	93	674
DUPRAT								
Joseph	46	m	w	NY	San Francisco	8-Wd San Francisco	82	426
DUPRAY								
Elizabeth	43	f	w	IREL	San Francisco	8-Wd San Francisco	82	446
Frank	42	m	w	FRAN	Shasta	Shasta P O	89	457
DUPRE								
Charles	12	m	w	CA	San Francisco	2-Wd San Francisco	79	170
Eugene	57	m	w	FRAN	San Francisco	11-Wd San Francisc	84	567
Felix	36	m	w	FRAN	San Francisco	San Francisco P O	80	477
DUPREE								
John L	28	m	w	MO	Colusa	Spring Valley Twp	71	345
Louis	38	m	w	FRAN	San Joaquin	2-Wd Stockton	86	171
William	30	m	w	CT	Santa Clara	2-Wd San Jose	88	324
DUPRET								
Frank	40	m	w	FRAN	Inyo	Cerro Gordo Twp	73	319
DUPREY								
Alexander	26	m	w	FRAN	Sacramento	2-Wd Sacramento	77	242
August	46	m	w	FRAN	San Francisco	11-Wd San Francisc	84	643
Charles	21	m	w	FRAN	San Francisco	2-Wd San Francisco	79	142
Chas	71	m	w	FRAN	San Francisco	1-Wd San Francisco	79	43
George	40	m	w	FRAN	Sacramento	2-Wd Sacramento	77	248
John D	29	m	w	NY	Humboldt	Eureka Twp	72	272
Joseph	33	m	w	NY	San Diego	San Diego	78	491
Mates	27	m	w	FRAN	Santa Barbara	Santa Barbara P O	87	452
Perry	32	m	w	FRAN	Fresno	Millerton P O	72	193
DUPUIS								
E	33	m	w	CANA	Sierra	Sears Twp	89	556
DUPUY								
John	34	m	w	FRAN	San Francisco	San Francisco P O	80	340
Justin	26	m	w	FRAN	San Francisco	San Francisco P O	80	350
Maria	16	f	w	FRAN	Santa Clara	2-Wd San Jose	88	331
Paul	41	m	w	FRAN	San Francisco	3-Wd San Francisco	79	321
DUPY								
Ernest	49	m	w	FRAN	Los Angeles	Los Angeles	73	550
DUQUESNAY								
Chas	37	m	w	FRAN	San Francisco	11-Wd San Francisc	84	554
DURAL								
Charles H	52	m	w	FRAN	El Dorado	Mud Springs Twp	72	76
Francisco	47	m	w	MEXI	Los Angeles	Los Angeles Twp	73	473
James	23	m	w	AL	San Francisco	11-Wd San Francisc	84	700
Wm	27	m	w	NY	San Francisco	San Francisco P O	83	108
DURALDE								
Arthur	37	m	w	US	Nevada	Rough & Ready Twp	75	336
DURALL								
Charles	52	m	w	FRAN	El Dorado	Mud Springs Twp	72	76
DURAN								
Ancension	20	m	w	MEXI	Los Angeles	Los Nietos Twp	73	585
Franco	30	m	w	CHIL	Placer	Auburn P O	76	382
Frank	31	m	w	FRAN	Santa Clara	Redwood Twp	88	123
Joseph	33	m	w	IREL	Sacramento	4-Wd Sacramento	77	319
Juan	49	m	w	SPAI	Los Angeles	Wilmington Twp	73	639
Martin	35	m	w	IREL	Alameda	Murray Twp	68	126
Patrick	35	m	w	CHIL	San Francisco	San Francisco P O	83	44
Pedro	50	m	w	FRAN	San Francisco	1-Wd San Francisco	79	34
DURAND								
Adrian	58	m	w	FRAN	Santa Clara	2-Wd San Jose	88	323
Adrian	23	m	w	FRAN	San Francisco	San Francisco P O	80	348
Alphonso	36	m	w	FRAN	Nevada	Bloomfield Twp	75	92
Edward	38	m	w	IREL	San Francisco	San Francisco P O	83	171
Francis	29	m	m	FRAN	San Francisco	2-Wd San Francisco	79	241
Frank	17	m	w	MEXI	San Francisco	San Francisco P O	80	476
Henry	29	m	w	FRAN	Santa Clara	Fremont Twp	88	57
Henry	28	m	w	FRAN	Santa Clara	Fremont Twp	88	51
Horace	40	m	w	NY	San Diego	San Diego	78	483
Jacque	30	m	w	FRAN	San Francisco	San Francisco P O	80	408
John	53	m	w	IREL	San Francisco	San Francisco P O	80	460
Joseph	37	m	w	NJ	Butte	Bidwell Twp	70	3
Miguel O	45	m	w	SPAI	San Diego	San Luis Rey	78	512
Robt	34	m	w	IREL	Yuba	Rose Bar Twp	93	652
Saml	60	m	w	ENGL	Yuba	Rose Bar Twp	93	666
Samuel M	35	m	w	NY	Plumas	Washington Twp	77	52
DURANG								
Christian	30	m	w	PRUS	Yolo	Cache Crk Twp	93	443
DURANI								
Lucat	21	m	w	ITAL	Amador	Jackson P O	69	339
DURANT								
A	41	m	w	MA	San Joaquin	2-Wd Stockton	86	185
Frank	35	m	w	IL	San Francisco	5-Wd San Francisco	81	23
Henry	68	m	w	MA	Alameda	Oakland	68	156
Horace	35	m	w	NY	San Diego	Temecula Dist	78	527
Philip	29	m	w	FRAN	San Francisco	San Francisco P O	80	535
Victor	33	m	w	PRUS	San Francisco	11-Wd San Francisc	84	476
DURAS								
Arceas	38	m	w	MEXI	Fresno	Millerton P O	72	155
Francisco	38	m	w	MEXI	Fresno	Millerton P O	72	155
Ramon	25	m	w	MEXI	Fresno	Millerton P O	72	157
DURASSA								
Jesus	30	m	w	MEXI	San Luis Obispo	San Luis Obispo Tw	87	307
DURAT								
Emanuel	31	m	w	PORT	Alameda	Washington Twp	68	290
DURATE								
Francisco	26	m	w	CA	Santa Cruz	Pajaro Twp	89	342
DURAZ								
Ramon	40	m	w	MEXI	Santa Barbara	Santa Barbara P O	87	469
DURAZA								
Ephemia	8	f	w	CA	Santa Barbara	Santa Barbara P O	87	465
DURBAN								
Chas L	50	m	w	ENGL	Butte	Oregon Twp	70	132
DURBIN								
Daniel	34	m	w	MO	Napa	Napa	75	26
John	13	m	w	CA	San Francisco	11-Wd San Francisc	84	587
Leon	30	m	w	VT	Nevada	Grass Valley Twp	75	225
Peter	37	m	w	VT	Nevada	Grass Valley Twp	75	154
DURBROW								
Alfo K	32	m	w	NY	San Francisco	San Francisco P O	85	727
Joseph	60	m	w	NY	San Francisco	8-Wd San Francisco	82	427
DURBY								
Mitton P	43	m	w	IN	Yuba	New York Twp	93	636
DURCEY								
Joseph	24	m	w	SWIT	Nevada	Nevada Twp	75	313
DURCHE								
Phillip F	43	m	w	FRAN	San Francisco	6-Wd San Francisco	81	100
DURCHLOUB								
Hans	30	m	w	GERM	Marin	San Rafael Twp	74	26
DURDELA								
Madelena	19	f	w	CA	San Bernardino	San Salvador Twp	78	462
DURDEN								
Chas	12	m	w	ME	San Francisco	San Francisco P O	85	799
Florence A	18	f	w	AL	Sacramento	2-Wd Sacramento	77	254
DURELL								
Thos	40	m	w	ENGL	San Francisco	8-Wd San Francisco	82	355
DUREN								
George H	8	m	w	CA	Butte	Chico Twp	70	20
DURESS								
Joseph	55	m	w	PRUS	Alameda	Oakland	68	147
DURETEA								
Manuel	45	f	w	CHIL	Monterey	San Juan Twp	74	407
DURETT								
Chas N	43	m	w	NY	Butte	Oregon Twp	70	123
DURFEE								
George W	47	m	w	OH	Los Angeles	El Monte Twp	73	449
James	31	m	w	IL	Los Angeles	El Monte Twp	73	449
Jno	20	m	w	IA	Santa Clara	Gilroy Twp	88	95
Joseph	25	m	w	IL	Santa Barbara	Arroyo Grande P O	87	508
W H	37	m	w	MA	Solano	Vallejo	90	179
DURFFEE								
Sylvester	27	m	w	IL	Monterey	San Benito Twp	74	384
DURFIEN								
M	70	m	w	FRAN	Amador	Ione City P O	69	369
DURFOR								
Edwin	42	m	w	PA	Shasta	Shasta P O	89	462
DURGAN								
James	55	m	w	MA	El Dorado	Georgetown Twp	72	38
John	50	m	w	IREL	Solano	Vallejo	90	158
P	49	m	w	NH	El Dorado	Greenwood Twp	72	55
Patrick	45	m	w	IREL	San Francisco	San Francisco P O	83	368
Patrick	18	m	w	CA	Santa Clara	San Jose Twp	88	216
DURGIN								
John	49	m	w	NH	San Francisco	San Francisco P O	85	778
DURHAM								
Benjamin	72	m	w	TN	Contra Costa	Martinez P O	71	447
E W	16	m	w	ME	Alameda	Oakland	68	135
Frank	36	m	w	IREL	San Francisco	1-Wd San Francisco	79	8
George	41	m	w	KY	Amador	Jackson P O	69	324
James	48	m	b	PA	Sacramento	2-Wd Sacramento	77	221
James H	57	m	w	KY	Colusa	Colusa Twp	71	275
Joshua	40	m	w	TN	Contra Costa	Martinez P O	71	447
Kate	60	f	w	IREL	Marin	San Antonio Twp	74	62
Ott	28	m	w	OH	San Mateo	Woodside P O	87	385
P J	38	m	w	VT	Tuolumne	Columbia P O	93	355
Renzee	24	m	w	TX	Contra Costa	Martinez P O	71	448
Thomas J	37	m	w	NJ	San Mateo	Woodside P O	87	385
W	19	m	w	ENGL	Amador	Ione City P O	69	371
William	43	m	w	IREL	Nevada	Little York Twp	75	242
William	39	m	w	NJ	San Mateo	Woodside P O	87	385
DURIA								
Manuel	25	m	w	PRUS	San Luis Obispo	Salinas Twp	87	295
DURIE								
Pauline	40	f	w	PRUS	Sonoma	Vallejo Twp	91	455
DURIN								
Segisbert	51	m	w	FRAN	Monterey	San Juan Twp	74	401

© 2001 by Heritage Quest. All rights reserved.

Name	Age	S	R	B-PL	County	Locale	Series M593 Roll	Pg
DURINE								
John	41	m	w	PRUS	Alameda	Alameda	68	5
DURING								
Chas	22	m	w	MO	San Joaquin	Liberty Twp	86	96
DURKE								
F D	35	m	w	MI	San Francisco	7-Wd San Francisco	81	168
DURKEE								
George	39	m	w	CANA	Alameda	Washington Twp	68	284
Jefferson	38	m	w	CANA	Alameda	Washington Twp	68	287
John L	43	m	w	MD	San Francisco	6-Wd San Francisco	81	130
Oscar	43	m	w	NY	Sutter	Butte Twp	92	96
Roswall	23	m	w	MO	Nevada	Rough & Ready Twp	75	331
W W	45	m	w	MI	Sutter	Vernon Twp	92	131
DURKEN								
James	44	m	w	IREL	San Francisco	11-Wd San Francisc	84	483
Mary	14	f	w	CA	Santa Clara	1-Wd San Jose	88	246
DURKEY								
Ellen	9	f	w	CA	Santa Clara	1-Wd San Jose	88	249
DURKIN								
Anthony	39	m	w	IREL	Contra Costa	Martinez P O	71	431
Edward	39	m	w	IREL	San Francisco	San Francisco P O	83	364
Eliza	22	f	w	IREL	San Francisco	2-Wd San Francisco	79	180
J M	30	m	w	IREL	San Francisco	3-Wd San Francisco	79	315
James	19	m	w	IREL	San Francisco	5-Wd San Francisco	81	35
John	32	m	w	ME	Alameda	Oakland	68	263
John	16	m	w	CA	Monterey	Castroville Twp	74	336
Mark	32	m	w	IREL	Contra Costa	Martinez P O	71	422
Michael	47	m	w	IREL	San Francisco	3-Wd San Francisco	79	299
Peter	30	m	w	IREL	San Francisco	1-Wd San Francisco	79	94
Thomas	34	m	w	IREL	San Francisco	San Francisco P O	83	335
DURM								
Jacob	33	m	w	BREM	Santa Cruz	Santa Cruz	89	429
DURMER								
John	18	m	w	NY	San Francisco	San Francisco P O	83	269
DURMIN								
Patrick	42	m	w	IREL	Sutter	Yuba Twp	92	151
DURMOND								
J	31	m	w	IREL	Alameda	Oakland	68	233
DURMOT								
R R	34	m	w	SCOT	Alameda	Oakland	68	264
DURN								
Richard W	20	m	w	NY	San Luis Obispo	San Luis Obispo Tw	87	309
DURNAN								
James	39	m	w	NY	Alameda	Eden Twp	68	88
DURNEY								
A F	42	m	w	PA	San Francisco	San Francisco P O	85	868
Geo	23	m	w	IREL	San Francisco	11-Wd San Francisc	84	694
DURNIN								
Edward	26	m	w	NY	Nevada	Grass Valley Twp	75	226
Edwd	26	m	w	IREL	San Francisco	1-Wd San Francisco	79	41
DURNING								
Charles	30	m	w	IREL	San Francisco	San Francisco P O	83	137
George Y	25	m	w	CANA	San Francisco	San Francisco P O	83	160
DURO								
Domingo	26	m	w	CA	San Diego	San Luis Rey	78	515
J B	42	m	w	ENGL	Alameda	Oakland	68	181
DUROC								
Joseph	50	m	w	FRAN	Marin	Nicasio Twp	74	17
DUROSIO								
Emil	26	m	w	MEXI	Los Angeles	Los Angeles	73	568
DUROSS								
Francis	49	m	w	ENGL	San Francisco	San Francisco P O	80	374
DURPHY								
Cate	18	f	w	NY	Humboldt	Eureka Twp	72	280
Eliza	45	f	w	MA	Yuba	Marysville Twp	93	571
DURR								
Jacob	26	m	w	BAVA	Monterey	Monterey Twp	74	352
John	38	f	w	IREL	San Francisco	8-Wd San Francisco	82	478
John M	19	m	w	PA	Monterey	Monterey Twp	74	346
John Michel	50	m	w	BAVA	Monterey	Monterey Twp	74	352
Julius	25	m	w	CA	Santa Barbara	San Buenaventura P	87	442
Julius	22	m	w	OH	Santa Barbara	San Buenaventura P	87	426
DURRAND								
Geo	49	m	w	SCOT	Siskiyou	Callahan P O	89	631
DURRELL								
David M	70	m	w	ME	Los Angeles	Los Angeles Twp	73	470
Josiah F	43	m	w	ME	Los Angeles	Los Angeles Twp	73	470
Kate	26	f	w	MA	Solano	Vallejo	90	160
Orrin	35	m	w	ME	Plumas	Washington Twp	77	53
DURRICOTT								
Thomas	21	m	w	ENGL	Santa Barbara	Santa Barbara P O	87	456
DURST								
D P	44	m	w	PA	Yuba	East Bear Rvr Twp	93	542
Frank	43	m	w	SWIT	Solano	Vallejo	90	204
John	45	m	w	SWIT	Lake	Big Valley	73	395
DURY								
Cornelius G	44	m	w	NY	Placer	Auburn P O	76	357
DURYEA								
Peter	36	m	w	FRAN	Mariposa	Maxwell Crk P O	74	146
Wm H	41	m	w	NY	Nevada	Little York Twp	75	236
DUSAN								
Acinto	21	m	w	MEXI	Los Angeles	Los Angeles Twp	73	477
DUSCOING								
Clara	15	f	w	SC	San Francisco	San Francisco P O	85	789
DUSCOMB								
Jas	36	m	w	NY	Butte	Chico Twp	70	14
Richard	39	m	w	ENGL	San Luis Obispo	Santa Rosa Twp	87	329
DUSENBERG								
Isidore	38	m	w	PRUS	San Francisco	8-Wd San Francisco	82	403
Nath	36	m	w	POLA	San Francisco	11-Wd San Francisc	84	422
DUSENBERRY								
G W	57	m	w	NY	Sacramento	Granite Twp	77	136
J	30	m	w	NY	Sacramento	Brighton Twp	77	74
DUSENBURG								
Chs	31	m	w	NY	San Francisco	8-Wd San Francisco	82	350
DUSENBURY								
Adolphus	28	m	w	CANA	Inyo	Bishop Crk Twp	73	311
Charles	32	m	w	NY	San Francisco	San Francisco P O	80	535
D E	22	m	w	NY	Sacramento	Cosumnes Twp	77	89
M T	31	m	w	NY	Alameda	Oakland	68	129
DUSH								
Annie D	12	f	w	CA	San Francisco	San Francisco P O	83	408
DUSHAM								
Jno	38	m	w	KY	San Joaquin	Oneal Twp	86	115
DUSHER								
Joseph	24	m	w	AZOR	San Francisco	1-Wd San Francisco	79	133
DUSING								
Caroline	62	f	w	PRUS	San Francisco	San Francisco P O	80	483
Fred	38	m	w	GERM	San Joaquin	Elkhorn Twp	86	69
Titus	24	m	w	PRUS	San Francisco	San Francisco P O	80	483
DUSKEY								
A V	37	m	w	KY	Klamath	Klamath Twp	73	371
DUSKIN								
Thomas	24	m	w	IREL	Marin	Point Reyes Twp	74	23
DUSSAULT								
Jacques	35	m	w	WURT	San Francisco	11-Wd San Francisc	84	631
DUSSOL								
Charles	23	m	w	NY	San Francisco	San Francisco P O	80	353
Gustave	40	m	w	FRAN	San Francisco	8-Wd San Francisco	82	322
DUSSONE								
Frank	50	m	w	FRAN	Nevada	Nevada Twp	75	296
DUSSTON								
Jas	24	m	w	ENGL	Sierra	Table Rock Twp	89	576
DUSSUGE								
Edward	53	m	w	FRAN	Amador	Jackson P O	69	325
DUSTER								
Thomas	38	m	w	ENGL	Calaveras	San Andreas P O	70	193
DUSTERBERRY								
Henry	39	m	w	HAMB	Alameda	Washington Twp	68	278
DUSTES								
Mitchell	40	m	w	GERM	Los Angeles	Los Angeles	73	529
DUSTIN								
Alexander	33	m	w	SCOT	San Francisco	San Francisco P O	80	338
C H	50	m	w	VT	Santa Clara	Gilroy Twp	88	79
Jane	36	f	b	NY	San Francisco	San Francisco P O	83	185
Peter	48	m	w	CANA	Santa Clara	Gilroy Twp	88	73
DUSTON								
Joseph	23	m	w	IL	San Bernardino	San Bernardino Twp	78	442
Julia	26	f	w	IL	Yolo	Cache Crk Twp	93	453
Oscar	20	m	w	US	Sacramento	Sutter Twp	77	390
DUTARD								
Eugene	25	m	w	CHIL	San Francisco	5-Wd San Francisco	81	6
Hypolite	27	m	w	FRAN	San Francisco	11-Wd San Francisc	84	608
DUTARTE								
Baptiste	37	m	w	FRAN	San Francisco	San Francisco P O	80	341
DUTAT								
Johanna	50	f	w	SPAI	San Francisco	2-Wd San Francisco	79	279
DUTCH								
Alex	30	m	w	CANA	Humboldt	Bucksport Twp	72	244
Fred	30	m	w	PRUS	Sutter	Butte Twp	92	102
Fritz	50	m	w	BADE	San Joaquin	1-Wd Stockton	86	138
John	40	m	w	HANO	Monterey	San Benito Twp	74	380
William	38	m	w	NY	San Francisco	8-Wd San Francisco	82	422
DUTCHER								
Elisabeth	45	f	w	NY	Alameda	Hayward	68	76
Geo N	38	m	w	ENGL	San Francisco	1-Wd San Francisco	79	59
H	36	m	w	CANA	Yuba	Marysville	93	604
J M	33	m	w	NY	San Francisco	San Francisco P O	85	862
Lyman	45	m	w	NY	Sonoma	Mendocino Twp	91	299
Moses	20	m	w	MA	San Joaquin	1-Wd Stockton	86	135
Newton	40	m	w	CT	Los Angeles	El Monte Twp	73	463
DUTCHES								
Camberes	21	m	w	PA	Santa Clara	Santa Clara Twp	88	160
DUTE								
John	30	m	w	PORT	Tuolumne	Columbia P O	93	357
DUTER								
Charles	35	m	w	FRAN	San Francisco	San Francisco P O	80	420
DUTERTE								
John	57	m	w	FRAN	San Francisco	San Francisco P O	80	539
John	2	m	w	CA	San Francisco	San Francisco P O	80	541
DUTESH								
Joseph	53	m	w	FRAN	Santa Clara	2-Wd San Jose	88	302
DUTIL								
Lorenzo	51	m	w	FRAN	Contra Costa	Martinez Twp	71	348
DUTLAN								
Jane	60	f	w	MA	Alameda	Oakland	68	201
DUTON								
Antone	26	m	w	PORT	El Dorado	Greenwood Twp	72	52
DUTRA								
Antonio	35	m	w	PORT	Santa Cruz	Santa Cruz Twp	89	383
Frank	33	m	w	PORT	Santa Clara	San Jose Twp	88	195
Frank	18	m	w	AZOR	Marin	Sausalito Twp	74	71
Juan	30	m	w	CA	Monterey	Castroville Twp	74	334
Manuel	23	m	w	CA	Monterey	Monterey	74	358

© 2001 by Heritage Quest. All rights reserved.

California 1870 Census

Name	Age	S	R	B-PL	County	Locale	Series M593 Roll	Pg
Manuel	19	m	w	PORT	Alameda	Washington Twp	68	268
Wm	46	m	w	AZOR	Monterey	Monterey Twp	74	344
DUTRE								
Manuel	80	m	w	PORT	San Francisco	San Francisco P O	80	430
Milton	24	m	w	SCOT	San Luis Obispo	Santa Rosa Twp	87	329
DUTREUX								
Josephine	40	f	w	PRUS	San Francisco	3-Wd San Francisco	79	325
DUTRIE								
Antone	48	m	w	HI	Yolo	Merritt Twp	93	505
DUTRO								
Estacio	21	m	w	AZOR	Santa Cruz	Santa Cruz	89	429
DUTROU								
Sebast	40	m	w	FRAN	San Joaquin	2-Wd Stockton	86	196
DUTRY								
James	22	m	w	IREL	Placer	Rocklin Twp	76	468
DUTSCH								
Golliup	42	m	w	SAXO	San Francisco	11-Wd San Francisc	84	644
DUTSCKK								
Herman	35	m	w	SAXO	Amador	Ione City P O	69	358
DUTTON								
Albert	35	m	w	NY	Contra Costa	Martinez P O	71	445
Alfred	40	m	w	CANA	Contra Costa	Martinez P O	71	450
Alsina	15	f	w	IL	Sonoma	Vallejo Twp	91	457
B J	47	m	w	NY	Amador	Drytown P O	69	424
Charlotte	1	f	w	CA	San Francisco	San Francisco P O	83	196
Chas	27	m	w	NY	San Francisco	8-Wd San Francisco	82	376
Cyrous H	55	m	m	PA	San Francisco	San Francisco P O	83	50
David	54	m	w	TX	Solano	Vacaville Twp	90	129
Ella	13	f	w	CA	Santa Clara	2-Wd San Jose	88	338
Evelyn	32	m	w	MI	Santa Cruz	Santa Cruz Twp	89	388
Geo	37	m	w	ENGL	Yuba	Marysville	93	613
Geo W	44	m	w	VT	Marin	Tomales Twp	74	88
Geo W	42	m	w	TN	Siskiyou	Callahan P O	89	629
George	44	m	w	CT	Santa Cruz	Santa Cruz Twp	89	402
George	42	m	w	US	Santa Cruz	Santa Cruz Twp	89	387
Henry	60	m	w	ME	San Francisco	San Francisco P O	85	862
Henry	39	m	w	CT	Santa Cruz	Santa Cruz	89	404
Henry Jr	30	m	w	ME	San Francisco	San Francisco P O	83	226
James M	40	m	w	ME	Yolo	Grafton Twp	93	500
Jno C	27	m	w	IL	Sonoma	Santa Rosa	91	422
John	42	m	w	VT	El Dorado	Placerville Twp	72	105
Joseph	34	m	w	IREL	San Francisco	San Francisco P O	85	849
Oscer	34	m	w	IN	Yolo	Cache Crk Twp	93	454
P	33	m	w	NY	Butte	Wyandotte Twp	70	141
Reed	35	m	w	NY	Marin	Tomales Twp	74	80
Warren	47	m	w	NY	Marin	Tomales Twp	74	86
Wm P	18	m	w	VT	San Francisco	3-Wd San Francisco	79	328
DUTY								
A C	35	m	w	NY	Alameda	Oakland	68	232
Manuel	36	m	w	AZOR	Nevada	Nevada Twp	75	294
William	68	m	w	TN	Kern	Tehachapi P O	73	354
DUVAIN								
Maria	17	f	w	FRAN	San Francisco	8-Wd San Francisco	82	317
DUVAL								
Alexr	36	m	w	VT	Sonoma	Washington Twp	91	469
Giles	30	m	w	FRAN	San Mateo	Schoolhouse Statio	87	338
J F	50	m	w	MA	Sacramento	Granite Twp	77	147
Richard	35	m	w	LA	Yolo	Cache Crk Twp	93	421
William	30	m	w	CANA	San Francisco	7-Wd San Francisco	81	185
DUVALL								
Charles T	34	m	w	KY	Nevada	Grass Valley Twp	75	229
Norman	33	m	w	US	Nevada	Rough & Ready Twp	75	336
Wm Henry	40	m	w	KY	Nevada	Grass Valley Twp	75	180
DUVAN								
David	29	m	w	IREL	San Francisco	San Francisco P O	83	154
DUVE								
Frederick H	40	m	w	BAVA	Sacramento	2-Wd Sacramento	77	244
DUVER								
Andy	27	m	w	NY	San Joaquin	3-Wd Stockton	86	236
DUWALL								
Gee W	65	m	w	MD	El Dorado	Kelsey Twp	72	59
DUXBURY								
John	60	m	w	MA	San Francisco	San Francisco P O	80	414
DUYAN								
Jesse	45	m	w	KY	Humboldt	Table Bluff Twp	72	309
DUYER								
Michl	50	m	w	IREL	Alameda	Murray Twp	68	117
William	31	m	w	IREL	San Francisco	11-Wd San Francisc	84	518
DUZENBERY								
James	51	m	w	OH	Siskiyou	Surprise Valley Tw	89	643
DWANE								
William R	42	m	w	KY	San Francisco	2-Wd San Francisco	79	167
DWARES								
Manuel	18	m	w	AZOR	Contra Costa	San Pablo Twp	71	359
DWARGASDUTRE								
Jose	21	m	w	PORT	Marin	Tomales Twp	74	79
DWARTHY								
M	32	m	w	NY	Santa Clara	Gilroy Twp	88	104
DWELLE								
John	27	m	w	NY	San Francisco	8-Wd San Francisco	82	455
DWELLEY								
Elisha S	30	m	w	ME	Mendocino	Cuffeys Cove Twp	74	168
Rebecca	35	f	w	MA	Santa Clara	1-Wd San Jose	88	235
DWER								
Edward	47	m	w	IREL	Plumas	Goodwin Twp	77	6
Theresa	24	f	w	IREL	San Francisco	San Francisco P O	83	360
DWEY								
Ah	42	m	c	CHIN	Plumas	Plumas Twp	77	31
DWIER								
Anne	38	f	w	IREL	San Francisco	11-Wd San Francisc	84	491
Geo	42	m	w	PA	Solano	Vallejo	90	148
Patrick	22	m	w	IREL	Sacramento	Cosumnes Twp	77	88
DWIGHT								
Geo	39	m	w	MA	San Francisco	11-Wd San Francisc	84	574
George	55	m	w	MA	San Francisco	3-Wd San Francisco	79	324
Hiram L	45	m	w	NY	Plumas	Goodwin Twp	77	8
James	23	m	w	NY	San Francisco	San Francisco P O	83	50
Lorenzo	36	m	w	MA	Sonoma	Santa Rosa	91	419
DWINE								
E F	21	f	w	IREL	Sierra	Sears Twp	89	555
John	16	m	w	NY	San Francisco	San Francisco P O	83	31
Joseph	32	m	w	IL	Butte	Ophir Twp	70	112
DWINELE								
Theodore	40	m	w	FRAN	Mariposa	Mariposa P O	74	130
DWINELL								
I W	49	m	w	VT	Sacramento	4-Wd Sacramento	77	326
DWINELLE								
A J	22	m	w	NY	Butte	Mountain Spring Tw	70	89
Aaron	31	m	w	ME	Plumas	Plumas Twp	77	32
Henry	13	m	w	CA	Santa Clara	Santa Clara Twp	88	177
John W	54	m	w	NY	Alameda	Oakland	68	192
M H	14	m	w	CA	Alameda	Oakland	68	243
DWING								
John	31	m	w	ENGL	Napa	Napa Twp	75	73
DWINNELLE								
Samuel H	46	m	w	NY	San Francisco	8-Wd San Francisco	82	475
DWIRE								
Ellen	28	f	w	IREL	San Francisco	San Francisco P O	83	33
John	39	m	w	IREL	Mariposa	Mariposa P O	74	99
John	19	m	w	IREL	Mendocino	Gualala Twp	74	226
Thos	24	m	w	MA	Yuba	Marysville	93	611
DWISLEY								
Lewis	43	m	w	FRAN	Sierra	Sears Twp	89	556
DWITT								
Elon	38	m	w	OH	San Francisco	11-Wd San Francisc	84	498
DWONER								
Thomas	38	m	w	IREL	Sutter	Vernon Twp	92	136
DWORTE								
Alexander	10	m	w	CA	San Diego	Temecula Dist	78	527
DWOYAZOK								
Benedict	41	m	w	AUST	San Francisco	6-Wd San Francisco	81	154
DWYER								
Ann	30	f	w	IREL	Alameda	Oakland	68	233
Anna	26	f	w	IREL	San Francisco	1-Wd San Francisco	79	98
C	45	m	w	IREL	Alameda	Oakland	68	140
Cathrine	42	f	w	IREL	San Francisco	7-Wd San Francisco	81	167
Edward	35	m	w	IREL	Del Norte	Smith Rvr Twp	71	477
Edward	15	m	w	NY	San Francisco	7-Wd San Francisco	81	246
Ellen	18	f	w	IREL	San Francisco	11-Wd San Francisc	84	611
Ellen	16	f	w	CA	Alameda	Oakland	68	195
Frank	40	m	w	IREL	Sacramento	3-Wd Sacramento	77	257
Fritz	16	m	w	HANO	San Francisco	San Francisco P O	83	173
Geo	24	m	w	AUSL	Alameda	Oakland	68	182
H H	55	m	w	VT	Solano	Vallejo	90	165
Henry	32	m	w	PRUS	Colusa	Grand Island Twp	71	306
J	50	m	w	IREL	Sierra	Butte Twp	89	510
J M	27	m	w	IREL	Sierra	Butte Twp	89	512
James	54	m	w	IREL	Santa Clara	Almaden Twp	88	13
James	45	m	w	IREL	Santa Clara	Almaden Twp	88	2
James	42	m	w	IN	Contra Costa	Martinez P O	71	415
James	40	m	w	NY	San Diego	Julian Dist	78	471
James	36	m	w	IREL	San Francisco	San Francisco P O	83	265
James	19	m	w	IREL	San Francisco	7-Wd San Francisco	81	189
John	48	m	w	IREL	Santa Clara	2-Wd San Jose	88	326
John	40	m	w	HANO	San Francisco	7-Wd San Francisco	81	215
John	37	m	w	MA	Humboldt	Eureka Twp	72	257
John	36	m	w	IREL	Placer	Cisco P O	76	494
John	34	m	w	NY	Solano	Silveyville Twp	90	74
John	32	m	w	IREL	San Francisco	San Francisco P O	80	404
John	31	m	w	IREL	San Francisco	11-Wd San Francisc	84	488
John	28	m	w	MO	Solano	Silveyville Twp	90	74
John	27	m	w	IREL	San Francisco	San Francisco P O	83	417
John	25	m	w	IREL	San Francisco	San Francisco P O	83	155
John P	31	m	w	NY	San Francisco	San Francisco P O	83	43
Julia	40	f	w	CT	San Francisco	8-Wd San Francisco	82	444
Kate	36	f	w	NY	San Francisco	7-Wd San Francisco	81	168
Lion	40	m	w	IREL	San Francisco	11-Wd San Francisc	84	668
Lizzie	18	f	w	IREL	San Francisco	11-Wd San Francisc	84	556
Margaret	35	f	w	IREL	San Francisco	San Francisco P O	83	134
Mary	28	f	w	IREL	Alameda	Oakland	68	231
Mary	25	f	w	IREL	San Francisco	2-Wd San Francisco	79	246
Mary	20	f	w	LA	San Francisco	San Francisco P O	80	410
Michael	40	m	w	IREL	San Francisco	San Francisco P O	83	362
Michael	29	m	w	IREL	San Francisco	San Francisco P O	83	310
Michael	18	m	w	IL	Santa Clara	Almaden Twp	88	17
Patrick	71	m	w	IREL	Klamath	Sawyers Bar	73	377
Patrick	21	m	w	IREL	Contra Costa	Martinez P O	71	379
Patrick R	32	m	w	IREL	San Bernardino	San Bernardino Twp	78	418
Stephen	38	m	w	IREL	Placer	Auburn P O	76	370
T G	42	m	w	IREL	Sacramento	3-Wd Sacramento	77	317
Thomas	36	m	w	IREL	San Francisco	San Francisco P O	83	295
Thomas	35	m	w	IREL	San Francisco	San Francisco P O	85	749
Thomas J	30	m	w	IREL	San Francisco	3-Wd San Francisco	79	308

© 2001 by Heritage Quest. All rights reserved.

Name	Age	S	R	B-PL	County	Locale	Roll	Pg
						Series M593		
Thos	36	m	w	IREL	San Francisco	11-Wd San Francisc	84	616
Timothy	31	m	w	IREL	San Francisco	San Francisco P O	83	153
Timothy	21	m	w	IREL	Alameda	Brooklyn Twp	68	43
William	55	m	w	IREL	Solano	Vacaville Twp	90	133
William	45	m	w	IREL	Santa Clara	2-Wd San Jose	88	314
William	35	m	w	ME	San Bernardino	San Bernardino Twp	78	453
Wm	53	m	w	IREL	Sacramento	3-Wd Sacramento	77	275
Wm	35	m	w	IREL	San Francisco	1-Wd San Francisco	79	69
Wm	25	m	w	IREL	San Francisco	1-Wd San Francisco	79	69
DWYRE								
Anthony	42	m	w	IREL	San Francisco	San Francisco P O	85	808
DY								
Isaac	40	m	w	MO	Butte	Chico Twp	70	40
DYAR								
John	50	m	w	IREL	San Francisco	San Francisco P O	83	307
DYAS								
Edward	38	m	w	KY	Amador	Jackson P O	69	337
DYBALL								
James	50	m	w	ENGL	El Dorado	Georgetown Twp	72	47
DYBERG								
Alfred	33	m	w	SWED	San Francisco	San Francisco P O	83	40
DYBURG								
Victor A	32	m	w	SWED	San Francisco	3-Wd San Francisco	79	313
DYCHE								
George	46	m	w	VA	San Diego	Warners Rancho Dis	78	529
DYE								
Charles	73	m	w	MA	San Francisco	San Francisco P O	85	769
D S	48	m	w	OH	San Joaquin	Elkhorn Twp	86	63
Daniel	46	m	w	IN	Siskiyou	Butte Twp	89	584
George W	46	m	w	MO	Los Angeles	Los Angeles Twp	73	491
Isaac	39	m	w	OH	San Joaquin	Castoria Twp	86	8
James M	61	m	w	KY	San Diego	Warners Rancho Dis	78	530
Jonathan	38	m	w	NY	San Francisco	San Francisco P O	80	474
Joseph	38	m	w	MO	Los Angeles	Los Angeles	73	541
P E	39	m	w	NY	Alameda	Oakland	68	252
Sperry	25	m	w	IA	Sacramento	Franklin Twp	77	113
Sung	33	f	c	CHIN	Yuba	Marysville	93	627
Tray	27	m	w	IA	Sacramento	Franklin Twp	77	113
William M	33	m	w	NY	San Francisco	6-Wd San Francisco	81	123
DYEN								
Joseph	20	m	w	CT	San Joaquin	1-Wd Stockton	86	157
DYER								
A M	16	f	w	CA	Alameda	Oakland	68	237
A O	35	m	w	MO	Sacramento	Dry Crk Twp	77	98
A S	17	m	w	NY	Santa Clara	Gilroy Twp	88	72
Aaron	51	m	w	RI	Contra Costa	San Pablo Twp	71	358
Atkins	60	m	w	MA	Placer	Bath P O	76	439
Barlow	50	m	w	ME	Calaveras	Copperopolis P O	70	229
Cathrine	50	f	w	IREL	San Francisco	1-Wd San Francisco	79	82
Charles	50	m	w	ME	Placer	Colfax P O	76	385
Chas	45	m	w	KY	Nevada	Nevada Twp	75	304
Chas	25	m	w	NY	San Francisco	1-Wd San Francisco	79	18
Chas A	43	m	w	IN	Nevada	Nevada Twp	75	322
Columbia	44	m	w	ME	San Francisco	11-Wd San Francisc	84	705
Columbian	45	m	w	ME	Solano	Vallejo	90	141
D A	34	m	w	CANA	Monterey	Salinas Twp	74	306
D N	34	m	w	NH	Amador	Drytown P O	69	416
David	38	m	w	MA	Humboldt	Arcata Twp	72	225
Ebenezer	45	m	w	ME	Alameda	Washington Twp	68	299
Edward	62	m	w	ENGL	Yolo	Grafton Twp	93	483
Emerson	35	m	w	ME	Yolo	Grafton Twp	93	481
Ephriam	42	m	w	ME	Alameda	Alvarado	68	304
Geo W	39	m	w	ME	Butte	Ophir Twp	70	119
George	39	m	w	ME	Santa Cruz	Santa Cruz Twp	89	382
Grace	45	f	w	IREL	San Francisco	7-Wd San Francisco	81	243
Gregory	33	m	w	CANA	Sacramento	Sutter Twp	77	381
H M	26	f	w	VT	Mariposa	Maxwell Crk P O	74	143
Henry	62	m	w	ME	Sacramento	Mississippi Twp	77	163
J	34	m	w	MO	San Joaquin	3-Wd Stockton	86	247
J F	35	m	w	MA	Solano	Vallejo	90	209
James	50	m	w	IREL	Placer	Colfax P O	76	390
James	40	m	w	IREL	Alameda	Oakland	68	252
James J	25	m	w	IREL	Santa Cruz	Santa Cruz	89	414
James S	32	m	w	NY	San Francisco	San Francisco P O	85	714
James W	45	m	w	VA	Placer	Roseville P O	76	355
John	45	m	w	ME	Tuolumne	Big Oak Flat P O	93	397
John	28	m	w	SCOT	San Francisco	11-Wd San Francisc	84	519
John C	30	m	w	TN	Yolo	Buckeye Twp	93	416
John R	36	m	w	MO	Placer	Roseville P O	76	355
Joseph	48	m	w	VA	Lassen	Long Valley Twp	73	436
Joseph P	43	m	w	ME	Mariposa	Mariposa P O	74	98
Louisa	32	f	w	ME	San Francisco	5-Wd San Francisco	81	16
M	46	m	w	US	San Joaquin	3-Wd Stockton	86	218
Major	70	m	w	KY	Santa Clara	Gilroy Twp	88	79
Margaret	37	f	w	NY	San Francisco	11-Wd San Francisc	84	523
Mary	70	f	w	MA	Alameda	Oakland	68	228
Michael	37	m	w	MA	Sacramento	4-Wd Sacramento	77	339
N M	28	m	w	MA	Solano	Vallejo	90	200
Orson	38	m	w	NY	Monterey	San Juan Twp	74	406
R E	32	m	w	CANA	Monterey	Salinas Twp	74	306
Richard	38	m	w	PRUS	San Francisco	San Francisco P O	85	844
Robt D	30	m	w	VA	Sonoma	Santa Rosa	91	410
Rodolphus C	36	m	w	NY	San Francisco	6-Wd San Francisco	81	155
Samuel	50	m	w	NY	San Francisco	11-Wd San Francisc	84	595
Samuel H	34	m	w	ME	Los Angeles	Santa Ana Twp	73	616
Thomas	40	m	w	ENGL	Yolo	Washington Twp	93	533
W I	34	m	w	NY	Sierra	Table Rock Twp	89	576

Name	Age	S	R	B-PL	County	Locale	Roll	Pg
						Series M593		
William	56	m	w	IREL	San Francisco	3-Wd San Francisco	79	319
William	50	m	w	IREL	Santa Clara	Redwood Twp	88	118
William	45	m	w	IREL	San Francisco	1-Wd San Francisco	79	40
William	40	m	w	PA	Contra Costa	Martinez Twp	71	347
William	36	m	w	VT	Marin	San Rafael	74	52
William	27	m	w	AR	Merced	Snelling P O	74	264
Wm	38	m	w	NY	San Francisco	5-Wd San Francisco	81	25
Wm	32	m	w	IREL	Alameda	Oakland	68	165
DYHEMAN								
Joseph	50	m	w	MI	Los Angeles	Los Angeles Twp	73	496
DYKE								
Silas	35	m	w	IL	Sonoma	Santa Rosa	91	427
DYKEMAN								
Owen	33	m	w	IREL	San Francisco	6-Wd San Francisco	81	117
Robt	44	m	w	NY	San Joaquin	1-Wd Stockton	86	138
DYKERS								
Arminta	16	f	w	IA	Sonoma	Salt Point	91	388
Priscilla	45	f	w	OH	Sonoma	Salt Point	91	388
DYKES								
Thos J	36	m	w	MD	Nevada	Nevada Twp	75	317
DYKMAN								
John	63	m	w	NY	San Francisco	San Francisco P O	83	327
DYLE								
Elizabeth	42	f	w	IREL	San Francisco	San Francisco P O	85	817
DYLLON								
Thomas	38	m	w	IREL	San Francisco	San Francisco P O	83	166
DYNAN								
M	44	m	w	ENGL	Amador	Drytown P O	69	419
DYNE								
H F	20	m	w	MO	San Joaquin	Tulare Twp	86	252
DYONS								
Hannah	30	f	w	AUSL	San Francisco	11-Wd San Francisc	84	663
DYRE								
Ann	69	f	w	NY	San Francisco	San Francisco P O	85	851
Clayburn	48	m	w	TN	Sonoma	Sonoma Twp	91	438
D E	24	m	w	ME	San Francisco	San Francisco P O	85	805
J E	36	m	w	MA	San Francisco	3-Wd San Francisco	79	314
Michael	57	m	w	IREL	San Francisco	San Francisco P O	85	787
DYRER								
Fred	40	m	w	HANO	San Francisco	11-Wd San Francisc	84	687
John	23	m	w	HAMB	San Francisco	11-Wd San Francisc	84	687
DYRES								
O S	45	m	w	NY	Trinity	North Fork Twp	92	218
DYSART								
James	34	m	w	NY	Mendocino	Ukiah Twp	74	243
John	38	m	w	SCOT	Nevada	Meadow Lake Twp	75	251
Joseph	19	m	w	MI	San Luis Obispo	Salinas Twp	87	293
DYSER								
Harvey	45	m	w	TN	Colusa	Spring Valley Twp	71	335
DYSERT								
Aaron	41	m	w	IL	Santa Cruz	Pajaro Twp	89	353
Joseph	18	m	w	IL	Nevada	Meadow Lake Twp	75	250
DYSON								
Isreal	35	m	w	ENGL	Nevada	Little York Twp	75	241
Joseph	24	m	w	MA	Plumas	Quartz Twp	77	41
DYSTONELL								
M	65	f	w	NY	Alameda	Oakland	68	177
EA								
Ah	44	m	c	CHIN	Calaveras	Copperopolis P O	70	243
Ah	41	m	c	CHIN	Placer	Roseville P O	76	348
EAC								
Ah	40	m	c	CHIN	Calaveras	Copperopolis P O	70	242
EACHEES								
Wm A	40	m	w	VA	Napa	Napa	75	12
EACHEW								
Eva	13	f	w	IA	Contra Costa	Martinez P O	71	408
EACHUS								
Bern D	45	m	w	VA	Tehama	Red Bluff	92	175
James	50	m	w	VA	Contra Costa	Martinez P O	71	409
EACKE								
John	46	m	w	PRUS	Placer	Bath P O	76	452
EADE								
William	39	m	w	ENGL	San Francisco	2-Wd San Francisco	79	206
EADES								
George	36	m	w	ENGL	Sonoma	Vallejo Twp	91	453
Isham	20	m	w	IA	Mendocino	Round Valley Twp	74	220
EADLE								
James	44	m	w	MEXI	Fresno	Millerton P O	72	167
EADS								
Richard	39	m	w	MO	Los Angeles	El Monte Twp	73	456
William	48	m	w	AUSL	San Francisco	7-Wd San Francisco	81	162
EAGAN								
Ann	69	f	w	IREL	San Francisco	8-Wd San Francisco	82	443
Anna	50	f	w	IREL	San Francisco	7-Wd San Francisco	81	170
Catherine	25	f	w	IREL	Marin	San Rafael Twp	74	27
Charles P	29	m	w	IREL	San Francisco	6-Wd San Francisco	81	141
Dillon T	40	m	w	IREL	San Francisco	8-Wd San Francisco	82	335
Edmond	39	m	w	IREL	San Francisco	2-Wd San Francisco	79	213
Edward	43	m	w	IREL	San Francisco	2-Wd San Francisco	79	260
Eliza	45	f	w	IREL	San Francisco	8-Wd San Francisco	82	468
Fredk	38	m	w	GERM	Marin	San Rafael Twp	74	45
Geo	35	m	w	OH	Yuba	Marysville	93	604
Henry	43	m	w	IREL	San Francisco	San Francisco P O	80	383
James	55	m	w	IREL	Solano	Green Valley Twp	90	38
James	45	m	w	IREL	Contra Costa	Martinez P O	71	431
James	30	m	w	IREL	San Francisco	San Francisco P O	83	170
James	26	m	w	IREL	Mariposa	Mariposa P O	74	113

© 2001 by Heritage Quest. All rights reserved.

California 1870 Census

Name	Age	S	R	B-PL	County	Locale	Series M593 Roll	Pg
Jane	30	f	w	AUSL	Marin	San Rafael Twp	74	30
Jennie	45	f	w	NY	San Francisco	8-Wd San Francisco	82	428
John	42	m	w	IREL	San Joaquin	Tulare Twp	86	263
John	41	m	w	IREL	Santa Clara	Santa Clara Twp	88	159
John	40	m	w	IREL	San Francisco	San Francisco P O	83	105
John	33	m	w	IREL	Santa Clara	Santa Clara Twp	88	147
John	26	m	w	IREL	Yuba	Rose Bar Twp	93	654
Julia	23	f	w	IREL	Sacramento	4-Wd Sacramento	77	327
Kate	23	f	w	IREL	San Joaquin	2-Wd Stockton	86	163
Kate	18	f	w	AUSL	San Francisco	7-Wd San Francisco	81	264
Kate	17	f	w	AUST	San Francisco	7-Wd San Francisco	81	245
Margaret	26	f	w	IREL	San Francisco	San Francisco P O	83	111
Mary	30	f	w	IREL	San Francisco	2-Wd San Francisco	79	218
Michael	48	m	w	IREL	Santa Cruz	Pajaro Twp	89	346
Michael	35	m	w	IREL	Santa Cruz	Santa Cruz	89	421
Michael	26	m	w	IREL	San Francisco	San Francisco P O	80	458
Mike	52	m	w	IREL	Solano	Benicia	90	10
P H	33	m	w	MI	Amador	Jackson P O	69	334
Patrick	27	m	w	IREL	San Francisco	San Francisco P O	83	193
Patrick	16	m	w	ENGL	San Francisco	11-Wd San Francisc	84	588
Peter	21	m	w	IREL	San Francisco	1-Wd San Francisco	79	64
Thomas	52	m	w	IREL	San Francisco	San Francisco P O	83	142
Thomas	45	m	w	IREL	Santa Clara	2-Wd San Jose	88	297
Thomas	35	m	w	IREL	San Francisco	5-Wd San Francisco	81	17
Thomas	35	m	w	IREL	San Francisco	8-Wd San Francisco	82	434
Thomas F	24	m	w	IREL	Contra Costa	Martinez P O	71	392
Thos	20	m	w	LA	San Francisco	2-Wd San Francisco	79	203
William	44	m	w	IN	Yolo	Cottonwood Twp	93	468
William	40	m	w	IREL	San Francisco	11-Wd San Francisc	84	647
William	34	m	w	IREL	Amador	Amador City P O	69	391
Wm	48	m	w	IREL	San Francisco	11-Wd San Francisc	84	564
Wm	26	m	w	IREL	San Francisco	San Francisco P O	83	81
EAGAR								
Thomas	40	m	w	NY	Alameda	Brooklyn	68	31
EAGEN								
Charles	28	m	w	MA	San Francisco	San Francisco P O	83	417
John	42	m	w	IREL	San Francisco	San Francisco P O	83	163
Pat	39	m	w	IREL	San Joaquin	2-Wd Stockton	86	187
EAGER								
John	30	m	w	IREL	San Francisco	6-Wd San Francisco	81	133
EAGIN								
Albert	17	m	w	CA	Solano	Vallejo	90	204
EAGLE								
Hunter	49	m	i	AR	Shasta	Shasta P O	89	452
Mary Ann	20	f	w	MO	Sutter	Vernon Twp	92	139
EAGLES								
Frank	26	m	b	MA	San Francisco	San Francisco P O	80	481
Henry	37	m	w	NY	San Francisco	San Francisco P O	83	300
John	28	m	w	ENGL	Solano	Vallejo	90	210
Marion	57	f	w	NJ	San Francisco	San Francisco P O	83	342
Minnie	21	f	w	NJ	San Francisco	San Francisco P O	83	342
EAGLESON								
Alexander	41	m	w	WI	Calaveras	San Andreas P O	70	152
Erastus	37	m	w	VA	Merced	Snelling P O	74	276
L	35	m	w	NY	San Joaquin	Castoria Twp	86	4
Thos	39	m	w	VA	Merced	Snelling P O	74	280
Thos	35	m	w	OH	Nevada	Nevada Twp	75	272
EAGLETON								
Ed	39	m	w	NY	San Joaquin	Dent Twp	86	23
H	35	m	w	IREL	Sacramento	3-Wd Sacramento	77	311
EAGON								
James	32	m	w	IREL	Mariposa	Mariposa P O	74	110
John A	41	m	w	VA	Amador	Sutter Crk P O	69	396
Mary	40	f	w	IREL	Alameda	Oakland	68	161
Michael	47	m	w	IREL	San Francisco	San Francisco P O	85	793
Michael	24	m	w	CHIL	San Francisco	San Francisco P O	85	872
Patrick	50	m	w	IREL	Santa Clara	Santa Clara Twp	88	141
Wm	41	m	w	IREL	San Francisco	San Francisco P O	85	764
EAGOS								
N	27	m	w	MEXI	San Joaquin	1-Wd Stockton	86	141
EAKEN								
Charles	50	m	w	SCOT	San Francisco	San Francisco P O	85	737
EAKIN								
Wm A	51	m	w	GA	Tuolumne	Columbia P O	93	348
EAKLE								
Christian	33	m	w	TN	Yolo	Cache Crk Twp	93	443
Henry P	37	m	w	TN	Colusa	Spring Valley Twp	71	337
J C	34	m	w	TN	Lake	Lakeport	73	407
EALBACK								
Anna E	47	f	w	FRNK	Sacramento	Franklin Twp	77	106
EAMANS								
John	30	m	w	NY	Solano	Vacaville Twp	90	118
EAMES								
Alfred	36	m	w	ME	Alameda	Eden Twp	68	72
Chas W	39	m	w	NY	Shasta	Shasta P O	89	460
Frank	15	m	w	CA	San Francisco	11-Wd San Francisc	84	593
Jonathan W	44	m	w	ME	Santa Barbara	Santa Barbara P O	87	495
Louisa	54	f	w	ME	San Francisco	7-Wd San Francisco	81	168
Nahum	45	m	w	ME	Nevada	Grass Valley Twp	75	216
Nathan	34	m	w	MN	Amador	Volcano P O	69	387
Nathan	34	m	w	ME	Solano	Maine Prairie Twp	90	45
Samuel L	50	m	w	ME	Los Angeles	Wilmington Twp	73	636
Wm	39	m	w	NH	Santa Clara	Gilroy Twp	88	76
EAMS								
Annie	19	f	w	ME	Contra Costa	Martinez P O	71	442
EAN								
Ah	35	m	c	CHIN	Trinity	Weaverville Pct	92	228

Name	Age	S	R	B-PL	County	Locale	Series M593 Roll	Pg
EANAS								
Monual	40	m	w	PORT	Yuba	Bullards Bar P O	93	551
EANERS								
Joseph	20	m	w	PORT	Alameda	Washington Twp	68	286
EANOS								
Antonio	30	m	w	AZOR	Monterey	Alisal Twp	74	292
Frank	30	m	w	AZOR	Monterey	Monterey Twp	74	343
EARCO								
Candila	40	f	w	CA	San Diego	San Pasqual	78	521
EARDLEY								
Jno R	32	m	w	ENGL	Santa Clara	Gilroy Twp	88	74
EARHARDT								
Henry	34	m	w	HCAS	Sacramento	Franklin Twp	77	117
John	33	m	w	HCAS	Sacramento	Franklin Twp	77	117
EARHARK								
Jacob	55	m	w	VA	Monterey	Pajaro Twp	74	373
EARHART								
Henry	50	m	w	PA	Siskiyou	Table Rock Twp	89	646
John W	41	m	w	VA	Sonoma	Petaluma Twp	91	341
Katie	12	f	w	CA	Santa Cruz	Watsonville	89	376
Thomas	22	m	w	MO	Monterey	Pajaro Twp	74	377
EARING								
Thos	39	m	w	ENGL	Contra Costa	Martinez P O	71	430
EARL								
A M Mrs	22	f	w	MO	Amador	Ione City P O	69	353
A R	50	m	w	NY	Trinity	Douglas	92	234
Asa C	60	m	w	NY	Yolo	Buckeye Twp	93	410
C A	25	m	w	PA	San Joaquin	2-Wd Stockton	86	175
D W	37	m	w	MI	Sacramento	4-Wd Sacramento	77	328
Daniel	30	m	w	MI	Sacramento	Sutter Twp	77	390
Emily H	23	f	w	NJ	San Francisco	8-Wd San Francisco	82	424
F A	38	m	w	ENGL	San Joaquin	2-Wd Stockton	86	193
Frederick	43	m	w	VT	El Dorado	Mountain Twp	72	70
John	64	m	w	OH	Contra Costa	San Pablo Twp	71	364
John	22	m	w	NY	Yuba	Marysville	93	586
John	20	m	w	IA	Yolo	Buckeye Twp	93	410
John M	57	m	w	MA	Yolo	Grafton Twp	93	498
John O	45	m	w	NJ	San Francisco	7-Wd San Francisco	81	285
Josiah	48	m	w	OH	Inyo	Independence Twp	73	327
Morris	67	m	w	NY	Sonoma	Analy Twp	91	247
Tarleton B	32	m	w	NY	San Francisco	San Francisco P O	83	123
Thomas	49	m	w	CANA	Napa	Napa	75	49
Thomas	28	m	w	ENGL	Nevada	Grass Valley Twp	75	183
W	18	m	w	ME	Nevada	Bridgeport Twp	75	100
William	38	m	w	OH	Placer	Bath P O	76	437
William	26	m	w	NY	San Diego	Temecula Dist	78	527
Wm	32	f	w	CANA	Nevada	Nevada Twp	75	282
EARLBAT								
George	29	m	w	WI	Santa Clara	Gilroy Twp	88	80
EARLE								
Alvin C	50	m	w	OH	San Francisco	San Francisco P O	85	876
David	24	m	w	MA	San Francisco	San Francisco P O	80	473
Edward	37	m	w	IREL	San Joaquin	3-Wd Stockton	86	222
George	67	m	w	VT	San Francisco	San Francisco P O	83	256
H W	37	m	w	ME	Sacramento	3-Wd Sacramento	77	316
Halfred	58	m	w	VT	San Francisco	San Francisco P O	85	774
Henry A	25	m	w	MA	San Francisco	San Francisco P O	83	292
John	38	m	w	NY	San Francisco	San Francisco P O	80	403
Joseph	33	m	w	WURT	San Francisco	11-Wd San Francisc	84	645
L M	52	m	w	MA	Amador	Ione City P O	69	363
Mary E	18	f	w	CA	Santa Cruz	Santa Cruz	89	417
S A	32	m	w	MA	San Francisco	San Francisco P O	85	829
Thomas	30	m	w	ENGL	Nevada	Grass Valley Twp	75	162
W H	34	m	w	VT	Sacramento	3-Wd Sacramento	77	300
William	63	m	w	NJ	Monterey	San Juan Twp	74	396
EARLES								
Anna	35	f	w	MA	San Francisco	7-Wd San Francisco	81	175
EARLEY								
Calvin D	36	m	w	IN	Sonoma	Mendocino Twp	91	294
John	36	m	w	IL	Monterey	Alisal Twp	74	292
S G	32	m	w	ME	Napa	Napa	75	12
Thomas	28	m	w	IREL	Placer	Cisco P O	76	495
EARLL								
Edward	40	m	w	NY	Yolo	Grafton Twp	93	495
William	37	m	w	NY	Yolo	Grafton Twp	93	495
EARLY								
Albert D	40	m	w	VA	Nevada	Rough & Ready Twp	75	323
All	63	m	w	NY	Sacramento	Sutter Twp	77	392
Anna	5	f	w	CA	San Mateo	Redwood Twp	87	369
Edward	42	m	w	IREL	Placer	Bath P O	76	445
James	34	m	w	IREL	San Francisco	11-Wd San Francisc	84	437
James D	38	m	w	IN	Nevada	Grass Valley Twp	75	185
John	30	m	w	IL	San Diego	Julian Dist	78	468
John	28	m	w	DC	Monterey	San Benito Twp	74	384
John	20	m	w	IREL	Los Angeles	Santa Ana Twp	73	602
Patrick	48	m	w	IREL	Plumas	Mineral Twp	77	20
Saml	39	m	w	NY	San Francisco	5-Wd San Francisco	81	26
Teddy	38	m	w	IREL	Yuba	Rose Bar Twp	93	654
Thomas	53	m	w	MO	Kern	Linns Valley P O	73	346
W S	28	m	w	ME	Napa	Napa	75	19
W T	23	m	w	MO	Sierra	Sears Twp	89	556
Wm Price	49	m	w	KY	Plumas	Plumas Twp	77	32
EARNES								
Antonio	38	m	w	PORT	Alameda	Washington Twp	68	275
Edward	25	m	w	NJ	San Francisco	8-Wd San Francisco	82	372
EARNEST								
Chas	22	m	w	IL	Nevada	Nevada Twp	75	282

© 2001 by Heritage Quest. All rights reserved.

Name	Age	S	R	B-PL	County	Locale	Roll	Pg
						Series M593		
Emma	13	f	w	OR	Butte	Chico Twp	70	42
Jesse S	40	m	w	TN	Nevada	Nevada Twp	75	316
Thompson	30	m	w	PA	Yolo	Grafton Twp	93	479
Willie	42	m	w	KY	Butte	Chico Twp	70	32
EARNEY								
Mary	14	f	w	CA	Calaveras	San Andreas P O	70	195
EARP								
Peter A	35	m	w	KY	Colusa	Grand Island Twp	71	302
EARRO								
Jesus	27	m	w	MEXI	Fresno	Millerton P O	72	160
EARRVILL								
J	25	m	w	ITAL	Sierra	Butte Twp	89	508
EASEL								
Charles	70	m	w	ITAL	San Francisco	11-Wd San Francisc	84	603
EASELY								
Woodson	36	m	w	MO	Santa Clara	San Jose Twp	88	179
EASEN								
Sarah	23	f	w	ENGL	San Francisco	8-Wd San Francisco	82	447
EASH								
John H	21	m	w	AR	Yuba	New York Twp	93	639
EASILY								
Benj	26	m	w	SWIT	San Francisco	7-Wd San Francisco	81	247
EASKOOT								
Alfred	47	m	w	MA	Marin	Bolinas Twp	74	6
EASLEY								
H E	32	f	w	IN	Sierra	Forest Twp	89	529
Pleasant	52	m	w	NC	Santa Clara	San Jose Twp	88	179
Stephen	76	m	w	VA	Santa Barbara	San Buenaventura P	87	430
Virginia	6	f	w	CA	Nevada	Grass Valley Twp	75	153
Warham	50	m	w	AL	Santa Barbara	San Buenaventura P	87	430
EASLY								
Harry	55	m	w	NY	El Dorado	Placerville	72	108
Wm	40	m	w	IREL	San Joaquin	Castoria Twp	86	2
EASMAN								
Francis H	33	m	w	NY	Santa Clara	Santa Clara Twp	88	137
EASON								
Charles N	27	m	w	NY	San Mateo	Menlo Park P O	87	377
EASSON								
Alexander	26	m	w	SCOT	Sacramento	Center Twp	77	85
EAST								
E J	44	m	w	GA	Tuolumne	Sonora P O	93	308
Jesse	33	m	w	MO	San Luis Obispo	Salinas Twp	87	293
John S	30	m	w	ENGL	Humboldt	Eel Rvr Twp	72	248
Thompson	26	m	w	MO	Stanislaus	San Joaquin Twp	92	80
William	37	m	w	CANA	Sonoma	Mendocino Twp	91	302
William	32	m	b	WIND	San Francisco	San Francisco P O	80	458
Wm T	39	m	w	MS	San Luis Obispo	Santa Rosa Twp	87	321
EASTABOO								
Mary	20	f	w	IL	Alameda	Oakland	68	166
EASTBRIS								
H W	29	m	w	PA	Alameda	Oakland	68	158
EASTBROOK								
John	30	m	w	NH	San Francisco	San Francisco P O	83	208
EASTEN								
Alexand	41	m	w	SCOT	El Dorado	Placerville Twp	72	94
EASTER								
Geo	23	m	w	OH	Sonoma	Analy Twp	91	240
J W	48	m	w	CANA	Sonoma	Petaluma Twp	91	345
John	40	m	w	VA	Santa Cruz	Santa Cruz Twp	89	398
EASTERBROOK								
Danl E	42	m	w	ENGL	San Francisco	San Francisco P O	83	202
G S	31	m	w	CANA	Sierra	Forest Twp	89	531
Samuel	40	m	w	ME	Placer	Roseville P O	76	352
Thos	25	m	w	MA	Alameda	Eden Twp	68	71
EASTERBROOKS								
Benj	49	m	w	NY	Sacramento	4-Wd Sacramento	77	359
EASTERBY								
Anthony T	52	m	w	ENGL	Napa	Napa	75	44
EASTERDAY								
Francis	48	m	w	KY	Santa Clara	Almaden Twp	88	15
W T	27	m	w	KY	Santa Clara	Almaden Twp	88	15
EASTERLY								
Jno	50	m	w	MO	Santa Clara	Almaden Twp	88	2
EASTERMAN								
William	44	m	w	PRUS	Santa Clara	San Jose Twp	88	186
EASTERN								
J W	19	m	w	IL	San Francisco	8-Wd San Francisco	82	365
James	40	m	w	KY	Merced	Snelling P O	74	268
Mathew	32	m	w	SCOT	San Bernardino	Chino Twp	78	411
EASTHAM								
Edwin H	39	m	w	ENGL	Yolo	Cache Crk Twp	93	455
Wm F	32	m	w	MA	Plumas	Quartz Twp	77	34
EASTHAN								
Henry F	58	m	w	NH	San Francisco	San Francisco P O	83	346
EASTIN								
Achilles	42	m	w	KY	Siskiyou	Yreka	89	657
Casus C	30	m	w	MO	Fresno	Millerton P O	72	160
James W	50	m	w	KY	Santa Clara	Redwood Twp	88	124
EASTING								
Bert	45	m	w	NY	Solano	Silveyville Twp	90	92
EASTLAKE								
Layfayette	36	m	w	PA	Siskiyou	Scott Valley Twp	89	616
Sylvester	44	m	w	OH	Siskiyou	Scott Valley Twp	89	615
Thomas	53	m	w	ENGL	Humboldt	Pacific Twp	72	293
EASTLAND								
Alfred	23	m	w	LA	San Francisco	San Francisco P O	85	722
George	30	m	w	ENGL	Napa	Napa	75	26
Joseph G	37	m	w	TN	San Francisco	8-Wd San Francisco	82	427
Rebecca	50	f	b	TN	San Francisco	8-Wd San Francisco	82	427
V	35	m	w	KY	Alameda	Oakland	68	165
EASTLES								
Manwell	46	m	w	MEXI	Yuba	Marysville	93	615
EASTLY								
John	30	m	w	PA	San Francisco	11-Wd San Francisc	84	490
EASTMAN								
Alonzo	44	m	w	ME	Plumas	Plumas Twp	77	27
Charles	55	m	w	NH	Trinity	Lewiston Pct	92	212
Charles	48	m	w	NH	San Francisco	San Francisco P O	83	260
Charles	14	m	w	NY	Sonoma	Bodega Twp	91	257
Charles S	32	m	w	ME	Santa Cruz	Santa Cruz	89	406
Chas	22	m	w	ME	Sonoma	Petaluma Twp	91	323
Edmund	39	m	w	NH	San Francisco	7-Wd San Francisco	81	228
Emily R	34	f	w	VT	San Francisco	San Francisco P O	83	159
Emma	20	f	w	PRUS	Los Angeles	Los Angeles	73	524
Frank	47	m	w	NH	San Francisco	6-Wd San Francisco	81	134
Geo	40	m	w	NY	San Francisco	5-Wd San Francisco	81	36
H H	42	m	w	CANA	Tehama	Mill Crk Twp	92	167
Harrison	57	m	w	NH	San Francisco	6-Wd San Francisco	81	125
Henry	34	m	w	ENGL	Alameda	Murray Twp	68	116
Henry	27	m	w	IN	Santa Clara	Almaden Twp	88	19
Isaac	45	m	w	FINL	Amador	Volcano P O	69	381
J Fred	37	m	w	ME	Yuba	Marysville	93	578
J G	30	m	w	NY	Yuba	Marysville	93	591
James	34	m	w	MO	Sutter	Butte Twp	92	99
Jas E	28	m	w	MA	San Francisco	1-Wd San Francisco	79	63
John	42	m	w	HOLL	Sonoma	Bodega Twp	91	256
Joseph C	36	m	w	PA	Nevada	Eureka Twp	75	126
Lewis D	30	m	w	KY	Butte	Chico Twp	70	26
Morse	39	m	w	VT	Alameda	Oakland	68	175
Moses	46	m	w	WI	Yuba	Slate Range Bar Tw	93	671
Oscar M	24	m	w	ME	Colusa	Monroe Twp	71	324
Peter	41	m	w	PRUS	Sonoma	Analy Twp	91	222
Robt K	60	m	w	NH	Santa Cruz	Santa Cruz	89	404
Sam E	59	m	w	NY	Butte	Chico Twp	70	40
Sarah M	40	f	w	ME	Nevada	Nevada Twp	75	300
Silas E	43	m	w	NH	San Francisco	6-Wd San Francisco	81	126
T S	49	m	w	NH	San Francisco	San Francisco P O	83	64
Theon H	39	m	w	VT	Placer	Rocklin P O	76	462
W W	32	m	w	VT	Sutter	Vernon Twp	92	139
William H	55	m	w	ME	San Francisco	6-Wd San Francisco	81	81
Wm	21	m	w	NY	Sonoma	Analy Twp	91	224
EASTMEAULPOR								
G J	32	m	w	NH	Los Angeles	Los Angeles	73	568
EASTON								
Adah	35	f	w	VT	San Mateo	San Mateo P O	87	359
Alice	15	f	w	CA	Santa Clara	Redwood Twp	88	134
Anderson	45	m	w	NY	San Joaquin	1-Wd Stockton	86	129
Ashahel	49	m	w	MA	San Francisco	8-Wd San Francisco	82	422
Charles	40	m	w	SCOT	San Francisco	San Francisco P O	85	808
Charles	36	m	w	MO	Placer	Auburn P O	76	365
Fredk	77	m	w	MA	San Francisco	San Francisco P O	85	733
Geo	35	m	w	LA	Yuba	Marysville	93	583
George	38	m	w	SCOT	San Francisco	2-Wd San Francisco	79	153
Giles A	41	m	w	NY	Santa Cruz	Santa Cruz	89	404
James	47	m	w	SCOT	Contra Costa	Martinez P O	71	414
James	44	m	w	MO	Los Angeles	Los Angeles	73	534
James	25	m	w	AL	Colusa	Spring Valley Twp	71	343
John	50	m	w	SCOT	Contra Costa	Martinez P O	71	409
John	22	m	w	MO	San Bernardino	San Bernardino Twp	78	449
John W	45	m	w	SCOT	San Francisco	San Francisco P O	83	253
Oliver W	54	m	w	MA	San Francisco	San Francisco P O	83	341
Pomeroy	57	m	w	VT	Tuolumne	Sonora P O	93	325
Robert	26	m	w	SCOT	Contra Costa	Martinez P O	71	419
Susan	45	f	m	CANA	San Francisco	San Francisco P O	80	464
Susanna	36	f	w	CANA	San Francisco	San Francisco P O	83	23
Tho W	46	m	w	ENGL	El Dorado	Cosumnes Twp	72	15
W W	44	m	w	KY	San Joaquin	3-Wd Stockton	86	237
William	29	m	w	OH	Solano	Maine Prairie Twp	90	47
EASTWOOD								
Gideon	59	m	w	OH	Calaveras	Copperopolis P O	70	229
J L	40	m	w	OH	Lassen	Janesville Twp	73	430
John	38	m	w	ENGL	Mendocino	Ukiah Twp	74	240
Morris S	38	m	w	OH	El Dorado	Diamond Springs Tw	72	31
Thomas	40	m	w	ENGL	San Francisco	7-Wd San Francisco	81	209
William	51	m	w	MO	San Diego	Julian Dist	78	468
Wm	39	m	w	OH	Calaveras	Copperopolis P O	70	229
EATON								
A S	35	m	w	NY	Alameda	Alameda	68	3
A W	24	m	w	IL	Sacramento	4-Wd Sacramento	77	350
Abby F	59	f	w	VT	Amador	Ione City P O	69	357
Albert	21	m	w	HANO	San Francisco	San Francisco P O	85	807
Benjamin	36	m	w	MA	Nevada	Grass Valley Twp	75	227
Benjamin S	46	m	w	CT	Los Angeles	San Gabriel Twp	73	594
Carey P	48	m	w	NY	Santa Clara	1-Wd San Jose	88	245
Charles	31	m	w	NH	San Francisco	San Francisco P O	80	410
Charles	23	m	w	VT	Colusa	Monroe Twp	71	316
Charles F	34	m	w	CANA	Placer	Auburn P O	76	360
Cornelius	45	m	w	VA	San Francisco	7-Wd San Francisco	81	277
Daniel	24	m	w	CT	Sutter	Nicolaus Twp	92	111
David	8	m	w	KS	Nevada	Grass Valley Twp	75	213
E A	33	m	w	MA	Solano	Vallejo	90	217
Edward	50	m	w	MA	El Dorado	Salmon Falls Twp	72	130
Edward	32	m	w	PA	Yuba	Slate Range Bar Tw	93	675
Edwin R	29	m	w	VT	San Francisco	San Francisco P O	83	195

© 2001 by Heritage Quest. All rights reserved.

California 1870 Census

Name	Age	S	R	B-PL	County	Locale	Roll	Pg
						Series M593		
Elmira	53	f	w	MA	San Francisco	7-Wd San Francisco	81	283
Fred W	25	m	w	MA	San Francisco	6-Wd San Francisco	81	149
Geo W	29	m	w	KY	Butte	Chico Twp	70	49
George	43	m	w	ME	Colusa	Spring Valley Twp	71	336
George	42	m	w	SCOT	Santa Clara	Gilroy Twp	88	99
George	40	m	w	OH	Humboldt	Bald Hills	72	239
George	18	m	w	MO	San Francisco	8-Wd San Francisco	82	318
George M	36	m	w	TN	Yolo	Cache Crk Twp	93	427
H F	49	m	w	MA	Solano	Vallejo	90	140
H P	30	m	w	OH	Santa Barbara	San Buenaventura P	87	444
Hannah	16	f	w	CA	San Joaquin	Douglas Twp	86	44
Henry	56	m	w	MD	Nevada	Meadow Lake Twp	75	265
Henry	48	m	w	ME	Santa Clara	Santa Clara Twp	88	168
Henry	40	m	w	VT	Contra Costa	Martinez P O	71	434
Ira A	47	m	w	NY	Nevada	Nevada Twp	75	278
Isacc F	38	m	w	NY	Sonoma	Petaluma Twp	91	357
J	17	f	w	CA	Alameda	Oakland	68	237
J A	31	m	w	ME	San Francisco	5-Wd San Francisco	81	2
James	56	m	w	MO	Amador	Volcano P O	69	382
James	31	m	w	MO	Sutter	Vernon Twp	92	131
James	23	m	w	NY	Alameda	Alameda	68	12
James G	36	m	w	CT	Nevada	Grass Valley Twp	75	180
James P	27	m	w	ME	Placer	Bath P O	76	440
Jas	27	m	w	IA	Butte	Chico Twp	70	26
Jas S	39	m	w	NY	Shasta	Stillwater P O	89	478
John	40	m	w	SWIT	Santa Clara	Gilroy Twp	88	94
John	35	m	w	IREL	Santa Cruz	Santa Cruz Twp	89	387
John	34	m	w	IREL	Mendocino	Navarro & Big Rvr	74	176
John	24	m	w	MO	Sutter	Sutter Twp	92	126
John H	62	m	w	NC	Yolo	Cache Crk Twp	93	434
Joseph	56	m	w	GA	El Dorado	Georgetown Twp	72	36
Joseph	22	m	w	ENGL	Alameda	Brooklyn Twp	68	39
Joseph Berry	36	m	w	GA	Plumas	Seneca Twp	77	48
L F	36	m	w	MO	Mendocino	Calpella Twp	74	183
Lotta	27	f	w	ENGL	Alameda	Oakland	68	161
M	14	f	w	IREL	Alameda	Oakland	68	169
Martha	43	f	w	ME	San Francisco	8-Wd San Francisco	82	424
Martha	25	f	w	NY	San Mateo	Schoolhouse Statio	87	340
Mary	32	f	w	NY	San Francisco	2-Wd San Francisco	79	274
Mathew	38	m	w	KY	Tulare	Packwood Twp	92	257
Monroe	40	m	w	KY	Yolo	Cache Crk Twp	93	446
Nathaniel	60	m	w	NH	Santa Clara	Fremont Twp	88	44
Posey	38	m	w	GA	Tuolumne	Sonora P O	93	324
Robert	33	m	w	IREL	Amador	Jackson P O	69	334
Saml	60	m	w	NY	Yuba	W Bear Rvr Twp	93	681
Sarah	34	f	w	ME	Alameda	Oakland	68	191
Stephen	46	m	w	NY	Yuba	Marysville Twp	93	571
Susan	39	f	w	KY	San Joaquin	Oneal Twp	86	109
Thomas	46	m	w	TN	San Francisco	7-Wd San Francisco	81	190
Thomas	22	m	w	CA	San Francisco	San Francisco P O	83	371
William	44	m	w	ME	San Francisco	San Francisco P O	80	361
William	38	m	w	ME	Inyo	Bishop Crk Twp	73	317
William	31	m	w	OH	Contra Costa	Martinez P O	71	406
Wm	35	m	w	KY	San Joaquin	Oneal Twp	86	109
Wm	34	m	w	NY	Plumas	Indian Twp	77	11
EATOUGH								
James	31	m	w	ENGL	Sacramento	Georgianna Twp	77	130
EATRASIE								
Antonio	56	m	w	MEXI	Inyo	Bishop Crk Twp	73	317
EAVES								
Ambrose	44	m	w	KY	Plumas	Indian Twp	77	11
John	40	m	w	ENGL	Contra Costa	Martinez P O	71	405
William	23	m	w	ENGL	San Francisco	7-Wd San Francisco	81	224
EB								
John	18	m	c	CHIN	San Joaquin	1-Wd Stockton	86	144
EBARESTO								
Martin	48	m	w	MEXI	Los Angeles	Santa Ana Twp	73	607
EBAT								
Victor	18	m	w	CA	Los Angeles	Los Angeles Twp	73	484
EBAUGH								
D B	40	m	w	MD	Nevada	Nevada Twp	75	319
James P	26	m	w	MO	Nevada	Nevada Twp	75	318
EBBECK								
Taylor	26	m	w	VA	San Joaquin	3-Wd Stockton	86	218
EBBERHARDT								
George	39	m	w	OH	Calaveras	San Andreas P O	70	195
EBBERLY								
Joseph	18	m	w	MO	Marin	San Rafael	74	50
EBBERT								
Geo	44	m	w	PA	Merced	Snelling P O	74	246
Pitts	28	m	w	TN	Napa	Napa	75	14
Samuel	22	m	w	CANA	Yolo	Cache Crk Twp	93	440
EBBETS								
Arthur	40	m	w	NY	San Francisco	San Francisco P O	80	541
Geo A	26	m	w	NY	San Francisco	San Francisco P O	83	202
EBBETTS								
Henry	27	m	w	MO	Solano	Silveyville Twp	90	80
EBBINGHAM								
Henry	30	m	w	PRUS	San Francisco	San Francisco P O	83	220
EBE								
David	28	m	w	OH	Plumas	Quartz Twp	77	38
David	25	m	w	TX	Tulare	Kings Rvr Twp	92	252
EBEL								
August	25	m	w	HAMB	Sacramento	2-Wd Sacramento	77	214
EBENHOUSER								
Frank	24	m	w	BREM	San Francisco	11-Wd San Francisc	84	687

Name	Age	S	R	B-PL	County	Locale	Roll	Pg
						Series M593		
EBENSTINE								
Charles	60	m	w	BAVA	El Dorado	Mud Springs Twp	72	74
EBER								
Herman	18	m	w	PRUS	San Francisco	3-Wd San Francisco	79	299
Lawrence	32	m	w	BAVA	San Francisco	8-Wd San Francisco	82	434
EBERENGER								
E A	50	m	w	ME	Alameda	Murray Twp	68	125
EBERHARD								
George	25	m	w	BADE	Santa Clara	Santa Clara Twp	88	175
Jacob	32	m	w	BADE	Santa Clara	Santa Clara Twp	88	175
John	30	m	w	BADE	Santa Clara	Santa Clara Twp	88	175
Michael	40	m	w	BADE	Santa Clara	Santa Clara Twp	88	175
EBERHARDT								
Conrad	26	m	w	PRUS	San Francisco	1-Wd San Francisco	79	95
D	31	m	w	PRUS	San Francisco	San Francisco P O	83	323
Henry	23	m	w	HANO	San Francisco	7-Wd San Francisco	81	207
William	50	m	w	PA	San Mateo	Schoolhouse Statio	87	341
EBERHART								
Adolph	42	m	w	SWIT	San Francisco	2-Wd San Francisco	79	188
James	40	m	w	MO	Stanislaus	Empire Twp	92	30
EBERL								
August	45	m	w	HDAR	San Francisco	2-Wd San Francisco	79	138
EBERLE								
Chas H	37	m	w	MA	Mendocino	Round Valley Twp	74	217
Francis A	31	m	w	WURT	Plumas	Goodwin Twp	77	6
John	37	m	w	WURT	Plumas	Goodwin Twp	77	6
John	36	m	w	WURT	Los Angeles	Los Angeles Twp	73	487
EBERLEE								
George	40	m	w	PRUS	Napa	Napa	75	6
EBERLEINE								
William	45	m	w	PA	Nevada	Rough & Ready Twp	75	337
EBERLY								
Ana	64	f	w	GERM	San Luis Obispo	Salinas Twp	87	288
EBERMAYER								
Frank	34	m	w	PRUS	San Francisco	San Francisco P O	80	531
EBERSOLE								
Henry	34	m	w	OH	Solano	Vacaville Twp	90	121
EBERSON								
Henry	38	m	w	DENM	Sonoma	Petaluma Twp	91	349
EBERT								
H	34	m	w	BREM	Sierra	Butte Twp	89	511
Howard	31	m	w	PA	Siskiyou	Surprise Valley Tw	89	636
Lewis	69	m	w	HDAR	Placer	Bath P O	76	457
V F	40	m	w	NY	Sacramento	1-Wd Sacramento	77	188
EBESO								
M	26	m	w	MEXI	Alameda	Murray Twp	68	116
EBI								
Elias D	26	m	w	IN	Yolo	Grafton Twp	93	479
Owen	21	m	w	MI	Yolo	Grafton Twp	93	481
EBINGER								
Louis	24	m	w	WURT	Santa Clara	2-Wd San Jose	88	281
EBLER								
William	36	m	w	GERM	Tuolumne	Columbia P O	93	335
EBLING								
Philip	30	m	w	HDAR	San Francisco	1-Wd San Francisco	79	7
EBNER								
Emma	14	f	w	CA	Santa Clara	2-Wd San Jose	88	337
Frank	40	m	w	BADE	Sacramento	3-Wd Sacramento	77	307
EBNORDRES								
Theodoric	65	m	w	MEXI	Calaveras	San Andreas P O	70	208
EBORLINE								
Wm	32	m	w	HAMB	Yuba	Marysville	93	582
EBRECK								
Thos	38	m	w	SCOT	Lake	Lower Lake	73	415
EBSAM								
Antona	50	f	w	MEXI	San Francisco	San Francisco P O	80	413
EBSEN								
Edward	28	m	w	PRUS	Solano	Montezuma Twp	90	67
EBSON								
Edwin	28	m	w	PRUS	Sacramento	Georgianna Twp	77	129
EBY								
Augustus	18	m	w	MI	Santa Clara	Milpitas Twp	88	112
David	24	m	w	MI	Monterey	San Juan Twp	74	396
L W	30	m	w	MO	Napa	Napa Twp	75	68
EC								
Toi	16	m	c	CHIN	San Francisco	11-Wd San Francisc	84	622
ECARDT								
Henry	39	m	w	OH	Sierra	Gibson Twp	89	540
ECASTAR								
J W	36	m	w	CHIL	Calaveras	Copperopolis P O	70	251
ECBERT								
Iquob	39	m	w	NY	San Francisco	8-Wd San Francisco	82	346
ECCARRES								
Edward	48	m	w	PRUS	Los Angeles	Los Angeles	73	526
ECCLES								
D G Jackson	38	m	w	ENGL	Monterey	San Antonio Twp	74	323
John	44	m	w	IREL	San Francisco	11-Wd San Francisc	84	579
Thomes	36	m	w	ENGL	Humboldt	Eureka Twp	72	280
W C	28	m	w	NY	Solano	Vallejo	90	172
William	11	m	w	CA	Alameda	Oakland	68	252
ECCLESON								
Asa	23	m	w	WI	Stanislaus	Empire Twp	92	61
ECCLESTON								
James	29	m	w	IL	Siskiyou	Surprise Valley Tw	89	639
Saml J	24	m	w	MO	Siskiyou	Surprise Valley Tw	89	640
ECCOMB								
Charles	30	m	w	SWED	Mendocino	Navarro & Big Rvr	74	177

© 2001 by Heritage Quest. All rights reserved.

Name	Age	S	R	B-PL	County	Locale	Series M593 Roll	Pg
ECE								
Ah	32	m	c	CHIN	San Joaquin	Oneal Twp	86	118
Say	28	m	c	CHIN	Contra Costa	Martinez P O	71	397
ECH								
Chew	25	m	c	CHIN	Amador	Volcano P O	69	387
Quah	47	m	c	CHIN	Amador	Volcano P O	69	387
Yow	45	m	c	CHIN	Amador	Volcano P O	69	387
ECHBAR								
S	32	m	w	BREM	Alameda	Oakland	68	142
ECHEAGARAY								
Juan	13	m	w	CHIL	San Francisco	11-Wd San Francisc	84	593
ECHEBERRE								
Martin	40	m	w	FRAN	Monterey	San Juan Twp	74	401
ECHERAGUY								
Bonita	32	f	w	SPAI	San Francisco	San Francisco P O	80	463
ECHERENN								
Francisco	43	m	w	MEXI	Marin	San Rafael Twp	74	38
ECHERT								
F M	50	m	w	PA	San Francisco	8-Wd San Francisco	82	371
Mary	18	f	w	HDAR	San Francisco	8-Wd San Francisco	82	352
ECHEVARIA								
Anglele	17	f	w	CA	Santa Clara	2-Wd San Jose	88	338
ECHEVARRIA								
Franco	46	m	w	MEXI	Monterey	San Juan Twp	74	416
ECHEVERRIA								
Jesus	41	m	w	MEXI	Alameda	Washington Twp	68	285
Refugio	37	m	w	MEXI	Monterey	San Juan Twp	74	413
ECHGELMEIR								
Hern	34	m	w	PRUS	San Francisco	1-Wd San Francisco	79	23
ECHI								
Campbell	30	m	w	CANA	El Dorado	Cosumnes Twp	72	13
ECHICK								
Christ	44	m	w	PRUS	San Francisco	2-Wd San Francisco	79	168
ECHODARO								
Francisco	75	m	c	CHIN	Santa Clara	1-Wd San Jose	88	270
ECHOLS								
John	71	m	w	OH	Santa Cruz	Watsonville	89	373
William	35	m	w	ENGL	San Francisco	1-Wd San Francisco	79	21
ECHRIVA								
Frances	40	m	w	FRAN	San Joaquin	2-Wd Stockton	86	162
ECHTER								
Frank	48	m	w	FRAN	San Francisco	San Francisco P O	80	344
ECHURT								
Henry	46	m	w	SAXO	San Francisco	1-Wd San Francisco	79	83
ECINA								
Manuel	30	m	w	MEXI	Plumas	Goodwin Twp	77	1
ECK								
Adam	48	m	w	BAVA	San Francisco	2-Wd San Francisco	79	226
Ah	64	m	c	CHIN	Calaveras	San Andreas P O	70	187
Ah	47	m	c	CHIN	Nevada	Nevada Twp	75	312
Ah	37	m	c	CHIN	Calaveras	Copperopolis P O	70	236
Ah	34	m	c	CHIN	Calaveras	San Andreas P O	70	183
Ah	32	m	c	CHIN	Calaveras	San Andreas P O	70	179
Ah	29	m	c	CHIN	Calaveras	San Andreas P O	70	190
Ah	29	m	c	CHIN	Monterey	Castroville Twp	74	340
Florence	50	m	w	FRAN	San Francisco	San Francisco P O	80	456
Frank	63	m	w	PRUS	San Joaquin	2-Wd Stockton	86	186
Henry	22	m	w	PRUS	Inyo	Cerro Gordo Twp	73	319
Que	27	f	c	CHIN	Butte	Ophir Twp	70	103
ECKAM								
Krank	18	m	w	LA	San Joaquin	3-Wd Stockton	86	217
ECKART								
Earnest	29	m	w	WI	Butte	Chico Twp	70	36
Hiram	42	m	w	NY	Butte	Ophir Twp	70	102
James	31	m	w	ME	Nevada	Meadow Lake Twp	75	267
ECKEL								
Henry	54	m	w	GERM	Tuolumne	Columbia P O	93	359
Jas	46	m	w	BAVA	San Francisco	8-Wd San Francisco	82	308
Otto	22	m	w	NY	San Francisco	11-Wd San Francisc	84	554
ECKELL								
Henry B	34	m	w	NJ	Marin	Tomales Twp	74	86
ECKELS								
Clement	44	m	w	DE	Los Angeles	Santa Ana Twp	73	613
ECKELSON								
Peter	38	m	w	HOLL	Butte	Concow Twp	70	8
ECKEMUTH								
Christina	24	f	w	LA	San Francisco	11-Wd San Francisc	84	603
ECKENROTH								
Joseph	45	m	w	PRUS	San Francisco	11-Wd San Francisc	84	492
ECKER								
Charles	55	m	w	NY	San Francisco	San Francisco P O	83	200
George	42	m	w	NY	San Francisco	8-Wd San Francisco	82	415
George	28	m	w	BAVA	San Francisco	San Francisco P O	83	238
ECKERMAN								
Fred	34	m	w	WURT	San Francisco	1-Wd San Francisco	79	56
ECKERT								
Henry	37	m	w	HCAS	Sacramento	3-Wd Sacramento	77	288
Henry	32	m	w	FRAN	Placer	Dutch Flat P O	76	405
Peter	33	m	w	FRAN	San Francisco	8-Wd San Francisco	82	432
Robt	22	m	w	WURT	Sacramento	3-Wd Sacramento	77	288
ECKFELDT								
Caroline	44	f	w	HCAS	San Francisco	1-Wd San Francisco	79	56
ECKFELLET								
J M	39	m	w	PA	Alameda	Oakland	68	194
ECKFORD								
Alexander	69	m	w	SCOT	Los Angeles	El Monte Twp	73	456
Charles	24	m	w	PRUS	San Francisco	San Francisco P O	80	531

Name	Age	S	R	B-PL	County	Locale	Series M593 Roll	Pg
ECKHARDT								
E	63	f	w	HCAS	San Francisco	San Francisco P O	85	786
Henny	34	m	w	HCAS	San Francisco	6-Wd San Francisco	81	149
Henry	36	m	w	HANO	San Francisco	11-Wd San Francisc	84	596
Louis	26	m	w	OH	San Francisco	2-Wd San Francisco	79	195
ECKHART								
A J	54	m	w	PA	Sutter	Vernon Twp	92	137
Henry	33	m	w	TN	Colusa	Colusa Twp	71	273
ECKHERT								
Willm	26	m	w	PRUS	Siskiyou	Yreka	89	655
ECKHOLM								
Thomas	62	m	w	RUSS	Marin	San Rafael Twp	74	41
William	38	m	w	PRUS	El Dorado	Cosumnes Twp	72	14
ECKLAN								
Charles	16	m	w	SWIT	Inyo	Lone Pine Twp	73	335
ECKLAND								
Chris	9	m	w	DENM	Sacramento	Granite Twp	77	148
Matilda	26	f	w	PRUS	Sacramento	2-Wd Sacramento	77	243
ECKLE								
Annie	57	f	w	TN	Yolo	Cache Crk Twp	93	450
Jacob	29	m	w	ITAL	San Francisco	5-Wd San Francisco	81	10
ECKLER								
Edward	47	m	w	ENGL	San Francisco	San Francisco P O	85	812
George	30	m	w	BAVA	San Francisco	2-Wd San Francisco	79	271
J C	23	m	w	OH	San Joaquin	Elkhorn Twp	86	56
ECKLEY								
John	40	m	w	MA	San Francisco	11-Wd San Francisc	84	687
ECKMAN								
Elias	36	m	w	MD	El Dorado	Diamond Springs Tw	72	31
John	25	m	w	PRUS	Sonoma	Russian Rvr	91	376
ECKMEYER								
Peter	32	m	w	HESS	Napa	Napa	75	57
ECKSTEIN								
John	30	m	w	PRUS	San Francisco	6-Wd San Francisco	81	111
Leopold	22	m	w	BOHE	San Francisco	1-Wd San Francisco	79	63
Samuel	25	m	w	NY	Alameda	Alvarado	68	303
Wm E	35	m	w	PRUS	San Francisco	1-Wd San Francisco	79	116
ECKSTROM								
Albert	30	m	w	SWED	San Joaquin	3-Wd Stockton	86	229
Albt	30	m	w	SWED	San Joaquin	2-Wd Stockton	86	194
Charles	42	m	w	SWED	San Francisco	San Francisco P O	80	466
Louise	20	f	w	SWED	San Francisco	San Francisco P O	83	202
Thos	35	m	w	SWED	San Joaquin	3-Wd Stockton	86	229
ECLAVA								
Joaquin	53	m	w	MEXI	Kern	Bakersfield P O	73	363
ECLO								
Veranus	43	m	w	MA	El Dorado	White Oak Twp	72	142
ECONNER								
Jane	30	f	w	IREL	Sonoma	Sonoma Twp	91	442
ECRITO								
David	39	m	w	ITAL	San Francisco	11-Wd San Francisc	84	521
ECTOR								
William	26	m	m	WIND	San Francisco	1-Wd San Francisco	79	83
ECUR								
James	22	m	w	IL	Sutter	Nicolaus Twp	92	107
EDALGO								
Becente	32	m	w	MEXI	Monterey	San Antonio Twp	74	317
Jesus	36	m	w	MEXI	Monterey	San Antonio Twp	74	318
EDD								
Cowan	40	m	w	NY	Klamath	Hoopa Valley India	73	386
EDDIE								
C H	19	m	w	IL	Mendocino	Calpella Twp	74	189
William	33	m	w	MO	Mendocino	Calpella Twp	74	189
EDDING								
Margaret	32	f	w	IREL	San Francisco	7-Wd San Francisco	81	287
William C	29	m	w	IA	Sacramento	2-Wd Sacramento	77	222
EDDINGS								
Frank	40	m	w	VA	Placer	Alta P O	76	413
Washington	55	m	w	LA	Placer	Pino Twp	76	471
EDDINGTON								
James	30	m	w	NY	San Francisco	1-Wd San Francisco	79	124
EDDLEKITTEL								
John C	39	m	w	HANO	Plumas	Washington Twp	77	56
EDDY								
A E	47	f	w	RI	Sierra	Forest Twp	89	531
A L	45	m	w	NY	San Joaquin	Elkhorn Twp	86	56
Alexr	29	m	w	IL	Siskiyou	Surprise Valley Tw	89	643
Amos	38	m	w	NY	Los Angeles	Wilmington Twp	73	634
Ann	45	f	w	ENGL	Yuba	Marysville	93	578
Belle	23	f	w	IREL	San Francisco	7-Wd San Francisco	81	278
Benjamin	29	m	w	ENGL	Nevada	Grass Valley Twp	75	212
C S	30	m	w	MA	Solano	Benicia	90	4
Clara	46	f	w	KY	Mendocino	Ukiah Twp	74	242
Dan	64	m	w	NY	San Joaquin	2-Wd Stockton	86	175
Ebenazer M	51	m	w	MA	Santa Cruz	Soquel Twp	89	447
Edward	26	m	w	ENGL	Plumas	Indian Twp	77	14
Elizabeth	55	f	w	ENGL	Nevada	Nevada Twp	75	288
Elsie A	30	f	w	MA	San Francisco	San Francisco P O	83	124
Enoch	48	m	w	MA	Sutter	Nicolaus Twp	92	114
Frank	28	m	w	MA	Mendocino	Albion & Big Rvr T	74	166
George	37	m	w	VT	Placer	Bath P O	76	427
George	14	m	w	MO	Sonoma	Washington Twp	91	464
Harriet	46	f	w	PA	Siskiyou	Butte Twp	89	588
Haven K	30	m	w	NY	Sacramento	2-Wd Sacramento	77	214
Henry W	37	m	w	CT	Sacramento	Sutter Twp	77	390
Isaac	40	m	w	IL	El Dorado	Placerville	72	118
James	32	m	w	ENGL	Nevada	Grass Valley Twp	75	195

© 2001 by Heritage Quest. All rights reserved.

Name	Age	S	R	B-PL	County	Locale	Series M593 Roll	Pg
James J	45	m	w	ENGL	San Francisco	1-Wd San Francisco	79	55
James L	52	m	w	CT	Los Angeles	Wilmington Twp	73	635
John	50	m	w	ENGL	Nevada	Nevada Twp	75	306
John	43	m	w	ENGL	Nevada	Grass Valley Twp	75	199
John	33	m	w	ENGL	Nevada	Bridgeport Twp	75	116
John	28	m	w	ENGL	Nevada	Grass Valley Twp	75	203
John C	35	m	w	ENGL	Fresno	Millerton P O	72	167
Jos	30	m	w	ENGL	Butte	Ophir Twp	70	101
Joseph	42	m	w	ENGL	Butte	Chico Twp	70	33
Joseph	34	m	w	IREL	Butte	Ophir Twp	70	94
Leonard	42	m	w	NY	Contra Costa	Martinez P O	71	393
Mathew	34	m	w	ENGL	Trinity	Weaverville Pct	92	229
Melvin	25	m	w	NY	Colusa	Grand Island Twp	71	309
Nathan H	39	m	w	NY	Siskiyou	Butte Twp	89	586
Nelson B	25	m	w	CT	San Francisco	8-Wd San Francisco	82	497
Olive	49	f	w	MA	San Francisco	7-Wd San Francisco	81	156
Peter M	22	m	w	ENGL	Placer	Auburn P O	76	357
Richard	31	m	w	ENGL	Nevada	Grass Valley Twp	75	232
Robt D	28	m	w	IL	Butte	Chico Twp	70	35
Russell	54	m	w	NY	Contra Costa	Martinez P O	71	396
Samuel	38	m	w	ENGL	Calaveras	Copperopolis P O	70	223
Samuel J	46	m	w	RI	Nevada	Nevada Twp	75	308
Stanly E	32	m	w	NY	Nevada	Bridgeport Twp	75	116
Thomas	51	m	w	NY	Colusa	Grand Island Twp	71	309
Thomas	50	m	w	NY	Tuolumne	Chinese Camp P O	93	371
W T	41	m	w	NV	Humboldt	Bald Hills	72	239
William	57	m	w	ENGL	Nevada	Nevada Twp	75	304
William	43	m	w	ENGL	Placer	Dutch Flat P O	76	403
William	38	m	w	ENGL	Placer	Colfax P O	76	391
William	30	m	w	ENGL	Nevada	Grass Valley Twp	75	211
William	30	m	w	ENGL	Trinity	Douglas	92	237
William C	31	m	w	WI	Siskiyou	Table Rock Twp	89	646
William M	44	m	w	NY	Nevada	Bridgeport Twp	75	116
Wm	37	m	w	ENGL	Nevada	Nevada Twp	75	281
Wm	36	m	w	MA	Plumas	Seneca Twp	77	47
Wm C	39	m	w	ENGL	Nevada	Grass Valley Twp	75	190
EDE								
Abraham	38	m	w	ENGL	Plumas	Quartz Twp	77	38
Hampton	48	m	w	ENGL	Plumas	Quartz Twp	77	38
Joseph	53	m	w	ENGL	Tuolumne	Sonora P O	93	310
P	60	m	w	ENGL	Sierra	Sierra Twp	89	566
Stephen	30	m	w	ENGL	Plumas	Quartz Twp	77	41
Walter	34	m	w	ENGL	Plumas	Quartz Twp	77	41
EDEL								
Geo H	29	m	w	IA	Butte	Ophir Twp	70	118
EDELEMAN								
Abram	40	m	w	RUSS	Los Angeles	Los Angeles	73	550
EDELEN								
L H	36	m	w	DC	Sacramento	3-Wd Sacramento	77	306
EDELINE								
William	58	m	w	PA	Humboldt	Eureka Twp	72	266
EDELKAMP								
Bernard	46	m	w	HANO	San Francisco	San Francisco P O	83	51
EDELMAN								
Jos	28	m	w	BAVA	San Francisco	2-Wd San Francisco	79	146
EDELMANN								
G W	45	m	w	HAMB	Sonoma	Petaluma Twp	91	311
EDEN								
Benjamin	36	m	w	OLDE	Alameda	Eden Twp	68	60
Edward	32	m	w	HOLL	Marin	San Rafael	74	50
Effie D	12	f	w	CA	San Francisco	8-Wd San Francisco	82	390
Henry	50	m	w	SAXO	Amador	Ione City P O	69	350
John	37	m	w	HANO	San Francisco	1-Wd San Francisco	79	29
John H	35	m	w	HANO	Nevada	Nevada Twp	75	308
William	30	m	w	ENGL	El Dorado	Mud Springs Twp	72	75
EDENBOTTLE								
Koler	24	m	w	PRUS	San Francisco	5-Wd San Francisco	81	20
EDEQUIST								
C V	47	m	w	FINL	San Francisco	3-Wd San Francisco	79	300
EDERLINE								
Frank	14	m	w	CA	El Dorado	Salmon Falls Twp	72	132
EDES								
Granville	48	m	w	KY	Shasta	Fort Crook P O	89	474
Granville G	21	m	w	IN	Shasta	Fort Crook P O	89	474
EDGAN								
James	33	m	w	CANA	Santa Clara	Santa Clara Twp	88	148
EDGAR								
A	47	m	w	IREL	Alameda	Oakland	68	226
Andrew J	41	m	w	KY	Yuba	Bullards Bar P O	93	548
Danl	37	m	w	MA	San Francisco	2-Wd San Francisco	79	236
Edward J	46	m	w	MD	Calaveras	San Andreas P O	70	164
Francis M	41	m	w	MO	San Bernardino	San Bernardino Twp	78	445
G G	33	m	w	KY	Humboldt	Arcata Twp	72	227
Geo	42	m	w	ENGL	Solano	Vallejo	90	176
Hannah	24	f	m	MO	Nevada	Grass Valley Twp	75	177
Hiram	45	m	w	NJ	Contra Costa	Martinez P O	71	368
James	45	m	w	CANA	Yolo	Cottonwood Twp	93	461
James	30	m	w	IREL	Alameda	Oakland	68	245
John	55	m	w	IREL	San Luis Obispo	Arroyo Grande Twp	87	279
John	40	m	w	SCOT	San Francisco	1-Wd San Francisco	79	30
John	38	m	w	KY	San Diego	San Diego	78	499
John	26	m	w	SCOT	Santa Barbara	Santa Maria P O	87	512
John C	36	m	w	IREL	San Mateo	Redwood Twp	87	365
John G	46	m	w	KY	Santa Barbara	Santa Barbara P O	87	478
Lydia	22	f	b	MO	Nevada	Grass Valley Twp	75	168
Michael	42	m	w	IREL	San Francisco	8-Wd San Francisco	82	487
Polly	56	f	w	IL	Fresno	Kingston P O	72	220
Silas C	27	m	w	NY	Mendocino	Point Arena Twp	74	210
Solomon W	48	m	w	KY	Yuba	Bullards Bar P O	93	548
Thomas	32	m	w	IREL	San Francisco	1-Wd San Francisco	79	41
Thomas	25	m	w	OH	Sonoma	Petaluma Twp	91	354
William	55	m	w	KY	Humboldt	Bald Hills	72	238
William	50	m	w	KY	Yolo	Buckeye Twp	93	417
William	49	m	w	PA	Yuba	Bullards Bar P O	93	548
William	30	m	w	SCOT	Plumas	Indian Twp	77	18
William A	19	m	w	CANA	San Francisco	3-Wd San Francisco	79	323
William E	4	m	m	CA	Nevada	Grass Valley Twp	75	177
William F	43	m	w	MO	San Bernardino	San Bernardino Twp	78	445
Wm	40	m	w	OH	Yuba	Linda Twp	93	555
EDGARTON								
Walter	28	m	w	MI	Sonoma	Petaluma Twp	91	363
EDGCOMB								
Chas Sumner	41	m	w	ME	San Francisco	1-Wd San Francisco	79	127
EDGCOMBE								
Lee	33	m	w	ME	Santa Cruz	Santa Cruz Twp	89	390
EDGE								
E R	37	m	w	ENGL	Sacramento	3-Wd Sacramento	77	303
Ellen	29	f	w	WI	Sacramento	3-Wd Sacramento	77	303
Henry F	25	m	w	MA	San Francisco	1-Wd San Francisco	79	97
Mathew	42	m	w	ENGL	Colusa	Butte Twp	71	266
Robert H	27	m	w	NH	San Joaquin	3-Wd Stockton	86	231
Thomas	28	m	w	WALE	Contra Costa	Martinez P O	71	430
EDGECOMB								
G V	53	m	w	ENGL	Solano	Vallejo	90	155
Jas	32	m	w	CANA	Solano	Vallejo	90	182
EDGECOMBE								
Wm W	30	m	w	ME	Santa Cruz	Santa Cruz Twp	89	389
EDGEMAN								
Silas	37	m	w	TX	Humboldt	Eel Rvr Twp	72	254
EDGEMON								
Silas	42	m	w	TN	Yuba	Parks Bar Twp	93	649
EDGER								
George	56	m	w	MA	San Francisco	8-Wd San Francisco	82	315
Jesse	36	m	w	TN	Fresno	Kings Rvr P O	72	212
EDGERLY								
Harry	8	m	w	MA	San Francisco	11-Wd San Francisc	84	577
Lafayette	44	m	w	NH	San Francisco	San Francisco P O	85	860
EDGERTON								
Calvin	31	m	w	VT	Siskiyou	Yreka	89	657
George H	42	m	w	VT	Santa Clara	2-Wd San Jose	88	288
Henry	38	m	w	VT	Sacramento	3-Wd Sacramento	77	318
Henry	38	m	w	MA	Sacramento	4-Wd Sacramento	77	350
EDGINGTON								
L C	45	m	w	OH	Sacramento	Sutter Twp	77	387
Wm	54	m	w	KY	Napa	Napa Twp	75	65
EDGWORTH								
Peter	56	m	w	CANA	Solano	Silveyville Twp	90	85
EDIE								
Edward	52	m	w	KY	Sonoma	Cloverdale Twp	91	273
EDIN								
George	30	m	w	ENGL	Monterey	Alisal Twp	74	297
EDINGER								
Jurgan	22	f	w	HANO	San Francisco	11-Wd San Francisc	84	478
Sarah P	29	f	w	NY	Placer	Bath P O	76	458
EDINGTON								
James S	31	m	w	MO	Napa	Yountville Twp	75	83
Luke	59	m	w	MO	Napa	Yountville Twp	75	83
Mary	14	f	i	CA	Napa	Yountville Twp	75	91
Nancy	25	f	w	MO	Napa	Yountville Twp	75	91
T B	30	m	w	MO	Napa	Yountville Twp	75	90
W R	32	m	w	MO	Napa	Yountville Twp	75	79
EDINS								
John	51	m	w	PA	San Joaquin	3-Wd Stockton	86	242
EDLAND								
J	25	m	w	WI	Yuba	Marysville	93	604
EDLE								
Henry	23	m	w	NY	Stanislaus	Empire Twp	92	45
EDLEMAN								
Henry	37	m	w	PA	Santa Cruz	Santa Cruz Twp	89	393
EDLER								
Charles	26	m	w	SWED	San Francisco	11-Wd San Francisc	84	705
EDLEY								
James	50	m	w	ENGL	San Francisco	7-Wd San Francisco	81	210
EDLIN								
F A	33	m	w	PRUS	Sacramento	Granite Twp	77	142
John	30	m	w	SWED	Alameda	Oakland	68	139
EDMAN								
John A	36	m	w	SWED	Plumas	Mineral Twp	77	20
Nels Peter	27	m	w	SWED	Plumas	Washington Twp	77	54
EDMER								
John	71	m	w	BAVA	Tuolumne	Sonora P O	93	307
EDMESTON								
George	22	m	w	SCOT	Humboldt	Mattole Twp	72	283
EDMINSTER								
Wm	23	m	w	VT	Sonoma	Analy Twp	91	226
EDMISTON								
Chas	14	m	w	IL	Napa	Napa Twp	75	30
J E	48	m	m	AR	Tuolumne	Sonora P O	93	306
EDMOND								
Adam	51	m	w	NC	Calaveras	San Andreas P O	70	163
Louis	50	m	w	FRAN	San Francisco	San Francisco P O	83	135
Marcas	42	m	w	VT	San Francisco	11-Wd San Francisc	84	626
Nick	48	m	w	FRAN	San Joaquin	2-Wd Stockton	86	166
Rachel	14	f	w	OR	Sonoma	Analy Twp	91	234

© 2001 by Heritage Quest. All rights reserved.

Name	Age	S	R	B-PL	County	Locale	Roll	Pg
						Series M593		
Thomas	24	m	w	FRAN	San Francisco	San Francisco P O	80	350
Walter	34	m	m	LA	Sacramento	2-Wd Sacramento	77	229
EDMONDS								
Charles	38	m	w	NY	San Francisco	San Francisco P O	80	380
Edward	25	m	w	OH	Sacramento	Franklin Twp	77	118
Edwin N	36	m	w	ENGL	Nevada	Grass Valley Twp	75	168
Frank	30	m	w	ENGL	San Joaquin	2-Wd Stockton	86	173
James	37	m	w	KY	Yolo	Cache Crk Twp	93	443
Jas M	33	m	w	MD	San Francisco	San Francisco P O	83	68
Jno L	44	m	w	NH	Sonoma	Mendocino Twp	91	303
Joseph E	30	m	w	KY	Yolo	Cache Crk Twp	93	450
Kris	30	m	w	NY	San Francisco	5-Wd San Francisco	81	10
Nicholas	38	m	w	IREL	Solano	Suisun Twp	90	100
Robert	29	m	w	ENGL	San Francisco	3-Wd San Francisco	79	314
Rubin	10	m	w	OR	Sonoma	Mendocino Twp	91	287
S	52	m	w	ENGL	Alameda	Oakland	68	245
Samuel	37	m	w	ENGL	Nevada	Grass Valley Twp	75	176
Stephen	25	m	w	ENGL	Nevada	Grass Valley Twp	75	224
Walter J	34	m	w	LA	Butte	Hamilton Twp	70	69
William	60	m	m	NY	San Francisco	San Francisco P O	80	381
William	44	m	w	ENGL	Nevada	Grass Valley Twp	75	165
William	35	m	w	MA	San Francisco	7-Wd San Francisco	81	158
Wm	46	m	m	LA	Solano	Vallejo	90	176
EDMONDSON								
Barker	37	m	w	ENGL	San Francisco	San Francisco P O	83	46
Bradley	28	m	w	NORW	Stanislaus	Empire Twp	92	61
James	50	m	w	AR	Stanislaus	San Joaquin Twp	92	75
Jonathan	39	m	w	OH	El Dorado	Cosumnes Twp	72	14
EDMONDSTON								
Brady	28	m	w	NORW	Stanislaus	Empire Twp	92	53
EDMONSON								
B	35	m	w	GA	Lake	Big Valley	73	395
Benjn B	46	m	w	MD	San Francisco	San Francisco P O	85	722
George	40	m	w	SCOT	San Francisco	6-Wd San Francisco	81	104
Robert	45	m	w	ENGL	San Mateo	Menlo Park P O	87	379
T J	26	m	w	IREL	Alameda	Hayward	68	79
EDMONSTON								
M	29	f	w	AR	Merced	Snelling P O	74	264
EDMUND								
Fredk	28	m	w	PRUS	Marin	Novato Twp	74	10
Henry	35	m	w	WALE	San Francisco	San Francisco P O	85	732
EDMUNDS								
H H	37	m	w	NH	San Francisco	San Francisco P O	85	812
Jefferson	50	m	w	NY	Alameda	Washington Twp	68	295
Joel	71	m	w	NY	Alameda	Washington Twp	68	295
Joseph	36	m	w	KY	Santa Clara	San Jose Twp	88	186
Levina	13	f	w	OR	Sonoma	Analy Twp	91	241
Pete	28	m	w	ENGL	Sacramento	1-Wd Sacramento	77	190
Warren	26	m	w	MI	Plumas	Indian Twp	77	14
Wm	62	m	w	NY	Butte	Ophir Twp	70	100
Wm	32	m	w	MI	Plumas	Plumas Twp	77	26
EDMUNDSON								
Albert	58	m	w	KY	Placer	Rocklin Twp	76	468
EDMUNSON								
Mary	38	f	w	CANA	San Diego	San Diego	78	511
EDNER								
Henry	56	m	w	MO	El Dorado	Cosumnes Twp	72	14
EDO								
Folkertz	40	m	w	HANO	San Francisco	7-Wd San Francisco	81	248
EDONNELLE								
Sarah	32	f	w	NY	San Francisco	2-Wd San Francisco	79	237
EDRINGTON								
B	62	m	w	KY	Sonoma	Russian Rvr	91	371
John	35	m	w	AUST	Monterey	San Juan Twp	74	395
Lilbon	53	m	w	KY	Monterey	Pajaro Twp	74	377
Philip	39	m	w	TN	Monterey	San Juan Twp	74	396
Zephaniah	28	m	w	KY	Monterey	Pajaro Twp	74	373
EDSALL								
Charles	41	m	w	VA	Mendocino	Round Valley Twp	74	220
Edwin	5	m	i	CA	Mendocino	Sanel Twp	74	228
Mary J	11	f	w	MO	Mendocino	Ukiah Twp	74	240
S B	41	m	w	OH	Mendocino	Ukiah Twp	74	240
EDSCOMB								
John	38	m	w	GERM	Nevada	Nevada Twp	75	308
EDSELL								
Jacob	25	m	w	IA	Solano	Tremont Twp	90	34
EDSON								
Agnes	32	f	w	NY	San Francisco	6-Wd San Francisco	81	80
C A	29	m	w	IL	Alameda	Alameda	68	16
Charles	50	m	w	CANA	Santa Clara	1-Wd San Jose	88	242
Daniel W	41	m	w	MA	Yolo	Grafton Twp	93	484
H B	60	m	w	NY	Santa Clara	Almaden Twp	88	19
Henry C	40	m	w	MA	Yolo	Grafton Twp	93	479
Jessie	28	m	w	NY	San Diego	San Diego	78	499
Josiah R	41	m	w	PA	Siskiyou	Butte Twp	89	588
EDSPERG								
Edward	25	m	w	DENM	Merced	Snelling P O	74	256
EDSTILL								
Wm W	41	m	w	MI	El Dorado	Kelsey Twp	72	62
EDSTON								
Thomas	45	m	w	CANA	San Francisco	6-Wd San Francisco	81	87
EDSTROM								
E C	55	m	w	NY	Humboldt	Pacific Twp	72	289
EDTHO								
Charles	49	m	w	FRAN	Calaveras	Copperopolis P O	70	244
EDWARD								
Charles	19	m	c	FRAN	San Francisco	11-Wd San Francisc	84	661

Name	Age	S	R	B-PL	County	Locale	Roll	Pg
						Series M593		
David	28	m	w	BADE	San Francisco	2-Wd San Francisco	79	138
Dudley	25	m	w	NY	Sacramento	4-Wd Sacramento	77	365
Edwin	18	m	w	MO	Colusa	Monroe Twp	71	313
G S	46	m	w	NY	Sacramento	Dry Crk Twp	77	100
Henry	50	m	w	ENGL	San Francisco	2-Wd San Francisco	79	215
J R	40	m	w	PORT	San Joaquin	2-Wd Stockton	86	173
Jack	36	m	b	HI	Siskiyou	Yreka Twp	89	668
James	40	m	w	ENGL	San Francisco	11-Wd San Francisc	84	697
James E	50	m	w	TN	Colusa	Butte Twp	71	268
John	58	m	w	WALE	Sacramento	American Twp	77	67
John	35	m	w	WALE	San Francisco	11-Wd San Francisc	84	680
Josh	32	m	w	WALE	San Francisco	1-Wd San Francisco	79	95
Juston L	40	m	w	ME	San Mateo	Pescadero P O	87	409
Mariah	50	f	w	IREL	Los Angeles	Los Angeles	73	545
R	38	m	w	WALE	Sierra	Butte Twp	89	512
Saml	42	m	w	ENGL	San Diego	San Diego	78	492
Thomas	59	m	w	FRAN	Los Angeles	Los Angeles	73	559
Thomas	42	m	w	NY	San Francisco	7-Wd San Francisco	81	221
EDWARDS								
A E	41	m	w	CT	Sacramento	1-Wd Sacramento	77	186
Alice	35	f	w	ENGL	San Francisco	8-Wd San Francisco	82	484
Allan	26	m	w	SCOT	Santa Barbara	San Buenaventura P	87	438
Amasa L	50	m	w	VT	Sonoma	Sonoma Twp	91	435
Amelia	47	f	w	MO	Nevada	Nevada Twp	75	288
Andrew	48	m	w	NY	Contra Costa	Martinez P O	71	453
Andrew	40	m	w	SWED	Marin	San Rafael Twp	74	34
Benj	40	m	w	----	El Dorado	Coloma Twp	72	1
Benj	26	m	w	MO	Marin	Tomales Twp	74	82
Benjamin	28	m	w	IL	Solano	Silveyville Twp	90	92
Brady	28	m	w	NORW	Stanislaus	Empire Twp	92	53
C John	40	m	w	NY	San Diego	San Diego	78	491
Carrie	27	f	w	NY	Yuba	Marysville	93	602
Catherin	34	f	w	WI	Nevada	Grass Valley Twp	75	159
Catherine	71	f	w	ENGL	Marin	Sausalito Twp	74	67
Charles	40	m	w	ENGL	Yuba	Parks Bar Twp	93	648
Charles	38	m	w	AL	Solano	Suisun Twp	90	93
Charles	35	m	w	MA	San Francisco	2-Wd San Francisco	79	153
Charles	28	m	w	CT	San Francisco	San Francisco P O	83	254
Charles	12	m	b	CA	Santa Clara	1-Wd San Jose	88	237
Charles W	40	m	w	ENGL	El Dorado	Mud Springs Twp	72	71
Chas	43	m	w	PA	Butte	Chico Twp	70	26
Chas B	50	m	w	ENGL	San Francisco	1-Wd San Francisco	79	34
Chas J	40	m	w	NY	San Diego	San Diego	78	495
Clara	15	f	w	NY	Alameda	Brooklyn	68	22
Cullen W	30	m	w	TX	Santa Barbara	San Buenaventura P	87	430
D A	56	m	w	MA	Lassen	Janesville Twp	73	430
Daniel P	35	m	w	IL	Yolo	Buckeye Twp	93	411
Danl	38	m	w	OH	Napa	Napa Twp	75	66
David	62	m	w	ENGL	Napa	Napa	75	10
David	42	m	w	ENGL	Sacramento	Franklin Twp	77	109
David	24	m	w	NY	Stanislaus	Emory Twp	92	20
E	24	m	w	IREL	Lake	Knoxville Mines	73	405
E	15	f	w	CA	Sierra	Sierra Twp	89	564
E A	24	m	w	NC	Santa Barbara	San Buenaventura P	87	434
E J	34	f	w	NY	Alameda	Oakland	68	180
Ed	35	m	w	IA	Santa Clara	Gilroy Twp	88	105
Edson	59	m	w	NY	Tuolumne	Sonora P O	93	303
Edward	57	m	w	ENGL	Nevada	Rough & Ready Twp	75	332
Edward	55	m	w	ENGL	Nevada	Grass Valley Twp	75	228
Edward	42	m	w	NY	San Francisco	11-Wd San Francisc	84	584
Edward	34	m	w	ENGL	Sonoma	Petaluma Twp	91	309
Edward	33	m	w	ENGL	San Francisco	San Francisco P O	83	157
Edward	30	m	w	BRAN	Sacramento	Sutter Twp	77	386
Edward	29	m	w	ME	San Francisco	11-Wd San Francisc	84	704
Edward	16	m	w	CA	Marin	San Rafael Twp	74	46
Edward J	55	m	w	KY	Los Angeles	Los Nietos Twp	73	574
Edwd	47	m	w	WALE	Butte	Kimshew Tpw	70	82
Edwd	32	m	w	ENGL	Sonoma	Petaluma Twp	91	340
Edwin	35	m	w	ENGL	Plumas	Indian Twp	77	17
Elias J	23	m	w	MO	Colusa	Colusa	71	300
Eliza	58	f	w	ENGL	San Francisco	7-Wd San Francisco	81	230
Eliza	42	f	w	PA	San Francisco	San Francisco P O	85	729
Eliza	30	f	w	CANA	San Francisco	San Francisco P O	83	288
Eliza	16	f	w	CA	San Francisco	San Francisco P O	83	72
Elizabeth	39	f	w	OH	San Francisco	San Francisco P O	83	262
Elizabeth	29	f	w	ENGL	Tuolumne	Sonora P O	93	320
Elizabeth J	53	f	w	WALE	El Dorado	Mud Springs Twp	72	90
Elizabeth J	46	f	w	ENGL	Nevada	Grass Valley Twp	75	187
Emma	22	f	w	PA	Santa Clara	2-Wd San Jose	88	314
Emma	17	f	w	NY	San Francisco	San Francisco P O	83	398
Ethelbert	27	m	w	TN	Placer	Bath P O	76	460
Etta	17	f	w	VT	Lassen	Janesville Twp	73	430
Frank G	46	m	w	ENGL	San Francisco	San Francisco P O	83	95
Frederick	26	m	w	ENGL	San Francisco	8-Wd San Francisco	82	451
G W	39	m	w	MO	Monterey	San Juan Twp	74	399
G W	22	m	w	CA	Alameda	Oakland	68	159
Geo	49	m	w	ENGL	San Francisco	11-Wd San Francisc	84	575
Geo	31	m	w	AL	Butte	Kimshew Tpw	70	83
Geo	21	m	w	NY	San Francisco	7-Wd San Francisco	81	278
Geo M	23	m	w	KY	Tulare	Visalia	92	296
Geo W	22	m	w	NY	Tuolumne	Sonora P O	93	328
George	46	m	w	DENM	Nevada	Eureka Twp	75	130
George	27	m	w	MI	Solano	Montezuma Twp	90	69
George	25	m	w	MO	Solano	Tremont Twp	90	30
George	24	m	w	PA	San Francisco	San Francisco P O	80	474
Griffith	20	m	w	ENGL	San Francisco	San Francisco P O	80	424
H C	30	m	w	NJ	San Francisco	San Francisco P O	85	797

© 2001 by Heritage Quest. All rights reserved.

Name	Age	S	R	B-PL	County	Locale	Roll	Pg
Hannah	48	f	w	NJ	Sonoma	Petaluma Twp	91	347
Hannah	25	f	w	WALE	Santa Clara	1-Wd San Jose	88	228
Hannibal	44	m	w	ENGL	Kern	Havilah P O	73	350
Hannibol	43	m	w	ENGL	Los Angeles	Los Angeles Twp	73	467
Henry	65	m	w	ENGL	Santa Clara	San Jose Twp	88	199
Henry	40	m	w	ENGL	San Francisco	San Francisco P O	85	792
Henry J	26	m	w	AL	Inyo	Cerro Gordo Twp	73	319
Isaac	38	m	w	ME	El Dorado	Mud Springs Twp	72	84
Isabele	19	f	w	OH	Butte	Chico Twp	70	45
J G	42	m	w	NC	Mendocino	Little Lake Twp	74	201
J L	52	m	w	MO	Napa	Napa	75	10
J T	35	m	w	AL	Napa	Napa	75	3
James	52	m	w	PA	San Francisco	8-Wd San Francisco	82	440
James	45	m	w	IL	Los Angeles	Los Angeles	73	521
James	45	m	w	MA	Mariposa	Mariposa P O	74	113
James	40	m	w	IREL	San Francisco	11-Wd San Francisc	84	712
James	40	m	w	IOFM	Placer	Bath P O	76	420
James	39	m	w	ENGL	Plumas	Indian Twp	77	17
James	36	m	w	CANA	Solano	Maine Prairie Twp	90	52
James	35	m	w	MO	Colusa	Monroe Twp	71	317
James	28	m	w	PA	Yuba	Marysville	93	602
James C	28	m	w	MO	Tulare	Visalia Twp	92	284
James Edwin	38	m	w	ENGL	Plumas	Plumas Twp	77	26
James G	48	m	w	KY	Solano	Suisun Twp	90	116
James J	43	m	w	ENGL	Nevada	Grass Valley Twp	75	173
Jas	49	m	w	NY	Solano	Vallejo	90	142
Jas	45	m	b	CANA	Alameda	Murray Twp	68	100
Jas	41	m	w	ENGL	San Joaquin	3-Wd Stockton	86	241
Jessua	35	m	w	ME	San Francisco	1-Wd San Francisco	79	37
Jno	32	m	w	IREL	Butte	Ophir Twp	70	101
Jno C	64	m	w	KY	San Joaquin	Oneal Twp	86	99
Jno T	36	m	w	OH	Shasta	Millville P O	89	486
John	56	m	w	ENGL	Santa Clara	Santa Clara Twp	88	153
John	55	m	w	ENGL	Mendocino	Sanel Twp	74	229
John	50	m	w	ENGL	Nevada	Meadow Lake Twp	75	269
John	50	m	w	IREL	Tuolumne	Columbia P O	93	357
John	48	m	w	WALE	Plumas	Quartz Twp	77	43
John	48	m	w	SWED	Santa Cruz	Pajaro Twp	89	349
John	47	m	w	VA	Santa Barbara	Las Cruces P O	87	506
John	45	m	w	ENGL	Plumas	Indian Twp	77	19
John	42	m	w	NY	Tulare	Visalia	92	293
John	41	m	w	WALE	Contra Costa	Martinez P O	71	426
John	41	m	w	ENGL	Santa Barbara	Santa Barbara P O	87	474
John	40	m	w	ENGL	Tuolumne	Chinese Camp P O	93	382
John	38	m	w	ENGL	Yuba	Rose Bar Twp	93	657
John	35	m	w	IREL	Napa	Napa Twp	75	74
John	35	m	w	FRAN	San Francisco	8-Wd San Francisco	82	308
John	33	m	w	ENGL	Alameda	Brooklyn Twp	68	54
John	30	m	w	ENGL	Tuolumne	Chinese Camp P O	93	378
John	29	m	w	IL	Solano	Vacaville Twp	90	117
John	28	m	w	KY	San Francisco	1-Wd San Francisco	79	65
John	25	m	w	AUSL	San Francisco	7-Wd San Francisco	81	218
John	22	m	w	IN	San Diego	Milquaty Dist	78	478
John	19	m	w	MEXI	San Francisco	San Francisco P O	80	337
John H	39	m	w	AR	San Francisco	San Francisco P O	85	720
John H	22	m	w	ENGL	San Francisco	1-Wd San Francisco	79	58
John L	45	m	w	WI	San Francisco	1-Wd San Francisco	79	79
John L	29	m	w	ENGL	Nevada	Grass Valley Twp	75	172
Jonathan	27	m	w	NY	San Francisco	1-Wd San Francisco	79	111
Jos	20	m	w	MO	Sacramento	1-Wd Sacramento	77	182
Joseph	53	m	w	IREL	El Dorado	Mud Springs Twp	72	82
Joseph	41	m	w	ENGL	Nevada	Grass Valley Twp	75	186
Joseph	25	m	w	NY	San Francisco	1-Wd San Francisco	79	95
Josh	30	m	w	WALE	San Francisco	1-Wd San Francisco	79	45
Joshua	42	m	w	OH	Butte	Chico Twp	70	25
L B	58	m	w	NY	San Francisco	8-Wd San Francisco	82	378
Lamb	40	m	w	ENGL	San Francisco	8-Wd San Francisco	82	360
Levi	35	m	w	OH	Napa	Napa Twp	75	30
Lizzie	14	f	w	CA	Yolo	Grafton Twp	93	487
Louis	47	m	w	MADE	Tuolumne	Sonora P O	93	330
M V	44	f	w	VA	Sacramento	3-Wd Sacramento	77	266
Maltby	35	m	w	NY	Yuba	Rose Bar Twp	93	653
Margaret	30	f	w	ENGL	San Francisco	7-Wd San Francisco	81	247
Martha	22	f	w	ENGL	Butte	Oregon Twp	70	127
Martin	25	m	w	WALE	Placer	Gold Run Twp	76	396
Martin	13	m	w	NY	San Francisco	11-Wd San Francisc	84	588
Martin	11	m	w	CA	Monterey	San Juan Twp	74	387
Mary	3	f	w	CA	Monterey	San Juan Twp	74	386
Mary	10	f	w	CA	Sonoma	Petaluma Twp	91	348
Mary A	13	f	w	CA	Santa Clara	2-Wd San Jose	88	298
Mathias	35	m	w	IREL	San Francisco	7-Wd San Francisco	81	235
Mathias	25	m	w	PORT	San Francisco	7-Wd San Francisco	81	235
Maze	35	m	w	MA	Sacramento	1-Wd Sacramento	77	184
Minus	41	m	w	TN	San Francisco	8-Wd San Francisco	82	367
Mitchell	36	m	w	PRUS	Sonoma	Analy Twp	91	232
Moses	55	m	w	IREL	Nevada	Bridgeport Twp	75	125
Mott	37	m	w	NY	San Francisco	5-Wd San Francisco	81	31
Nathan B	40	m	w	IREL	Santa Clara	1-Wd San Jose	88	251
Nellie	17	f	w	MO	San Joaquin	2-Wd Stockton	86	201
Paul P	1	m	w	CA	San Joaquin	Oneal Twp	86	114
Percy	7	m	w	CA	Santa Clara	San Jose Twp	88	182
Peter	41	m	w	NY	San Francisco	5-Wd San Francisco	81	26
Philander	52	m	w	MA	Placer	Newcastle Twp	76	476
Richard	43	m	w	WALE	Shasta	American Ranch P O	89	496
Richard	15	m	w	SCOT	San Bernardino	San Bernardino Twp	78	435
Richards	20	m	w	WA	Placer	Newcastle Twp	76	477
Richards W	39	m	w	WALE	Placer	Bath P O	76	453

Name	Age	S	R	B-PL	County	Locale	Roll	Pg
Robt	54	m	w	OH	Butte	Chico Twp	70	17
Rolland	40	m	w	ENGL	Alameda	Oakland	68	209
Rufus	56	m	w	NY	Marin	Bolinas Twp	74	1
Sam	37	m	w	ENGL	Butte	Ophir Twp	70	120
Sam	28	m	w	IREL	San Francisco	San Francisco P O	83	399
Samuel	50	m	w	MA	San Francisco	6-Wd San Francisco	81	82
Samuel	43	m	w	ENGL	Solano	Rio Vista Twp	90	60
Sol	20	m	w	CANA	Solano	Vallejo	90	202
Stephen	20	m	w	ENGL	Nevada	Grass Valley Twp	75	183
T	51	m	w	NC	Tuolumne	Big Oak Flat P O	93	402
T W	35	m	w	WALE	Sierra	Sears Twp	89	558
Theodore	51	m	w	MA	Santa Clara	2-Wd San Jose	88	286
Thomas	58	m	w	WALE	Contra Costa	Martinez P O	71	369
Thomas	49	m	w	ENGL	Sonoma	Petaluma Twp	91	314
Thomas	34	m	w	NY	San Francisco	San Francisco P O	80	485
Thomas	29	m	w	ENGL	Alameda	Washington Twp	68	280
Thomas Jr	8	m	w	WALE	Nevada	Bridgeport Twp	75	107
Thos	55	m	w	WALE	Sacramento	Sutter Twp	77	381
Thos	48	m	w	OH	Santa Clara	Gilroy Twp	88	71
Thos	41	m	w	WALE	San Francisco	7-Wd San Francisco	81	247
Thos H	44	m	w	ENGL	Mariposa	Mariposa P O	74	99
W D	29	m	w	GA	Tehama	Mill Crk Twp	92	167
William	52	m	w	KY	Amador	Fiddletown P O	69	426
William	47	m	w	ME	San Diego	Coronado	78	465
William	45	m	w	VA	San Mateo	Schoolhouse Statio	87	344
William	43	m	w	WALE	Nevada	Grass Valley Twp	75	228
William	36	m	w	WALE	Alpine	Monitor P O	69	314
William	32	m	w	ENGL	Contra Costa	Martinez P O	71	425
William	30	m	w	WALE	Contra Costa	Martinez P O	71	429
William	29	m	w	PA	Yolo	Cache Crk Twp	93	423
William	29	m	w	NY	San Francisco	3-Wd San Francisco	79	293
William	27	m	w	KY	Nevada	Nevada Twp	75	322
William	27	m	w	ME	Los Angeles	Los Nietos Twp	73	591
William	27	m	w	ENGL	Nevada	Grass Valley Twp	75	221
William	26	m	w	KY	Sonoma	Petaluma Twp	91	321
William A Z	47	m	w	ENGL	Santa Clara	San Jose Twp	88	192
William D	34	m	w	VA	Los Angeles	Los Angeles	73	524
William H	28	m	w	NY	Santa Clara	San Jose Twp	88	211
William H	26	m	w	MO	Yolo	Grafton Twp	93	491
Wm	45	m	w	IREL	Sutter	Sutter Twp	92	129
Wm	32	m	w	ENGL	Tuolumne	Sonora P O	93	319
Wm	30	m	w	NY	Tehama	Antelope Twp	92	158
Wm	28	m	w	WALE	San Francisco	1-Wd San Francisco	79	79
Wm	28	m	w	ENGL	Sacramento	1-Wd Sacramento	77	188
Wm	27	m	w	NY	San Francisco	7-Wd San Francisco	81	278
Wm	24	m	w	KY	San Joaquin	Douglas Twp	86	34
Wm	24	m	w	MA	Sacramento	1-Wd Sacramento	77	184
Wm	18	m	w	CA	Nevada	Nevada Twp	75	288
Wm	13	m	w	CA	Nevada	Bridgeport Twp	75	125
Wm H	32	m	w	MA	San Francisco	San Francisco P O	83	150
EDWARDSON								
Layard	39	m	w	SWED	Mendocino	Navarro & Big Rvr	74	174
EDWART								
Alexander	45	m	w	ENGL	San Francisco	8-Wd San Francisco	82	409
EDWIN								
Frank	33	m	w	PORT	Marin	San Rafael Twp	74	33
EDWINS								
Angeline	8	f	w	CA	Calaveras	San Andreas P O	70	196
EDZOF								
Thomas	35	m	w	ENGL	San Francisco	San Francisco P O	85	781
EE								
Hop	35	m	c	CHIN	Yuba	Marysville	93	632
EEAYER								
Peter	38	m	w	FRAN	Nevada	Bridgeport Twp	75	124
EED								
Leen	16	m	c	CHIN	San Francisco	8-Wd San Francisco	82	384
EEE								
Ay	25	m	c	CHIN	Marin	Tomales Twp	74	80
EEG								
Chong	38	m	c	CHIN	Nevada	Grass Valley Twp	75	206
EELLS								
John	39	m	w	NY	San Francisco	11-Wd San Francisc	84	619
Thomas	35	m	w	NY	San Francisco	11-Wd San Francisc	84	637
EEN								
Ah	20	m	c	CHIN	San Francisco	1-Wd San Francisco	79	50
EERL								
Robert	29	m	w	OH	Merced	Snelling P O	74	256
EERNESTERMILLER								
Chs	24	m	w	GERM	San Francisco	8-Wd San Francisco	82	368
EF								
Goom	18	m	c	CHIN	Yuba	Slate Range Bar Tw	93	677
EFEAL								
John	49	m	w	FRAN	Tuolumne	Columbia P O	93	352
EFFENDI								
Holland	18	m	b	ENGL	San Francisco	6-Wd San Francisco	81	109
EFFERANI								
Ernest	40	m	w	FRAN	San Francisco	2-Wd San Francisco	79	241
EFFINGER								
Custan	36	m	w	WURT	Sonoma	Petaluma Twp	91	327
Henry	28	m	w	IREL	Solano	Silveyville Twp	90	89
John	37	m	w	WURT	Calaveras	Copperopolis P O	70	249
John H	43	m	w	HANO	Nevada	Bridgeport Twp	75	108
EFFINGHAN								
Henry	30	m	w	ENGL	Monterey	San Antonio Twp	74	321
EFFMAN								
John	44	m	w	GREE	Del Norte	Happy Camp Twp	71	471

© 2001 by Heritage Quest. All rights reserved.

Name	Age	S	R	B-PL	County	Locale	Series M593 Roll	Pg
EFFNER								
Joseph	34	m	w	NY	Santa Barbara	Santa Barbara P O	87	460
EFFORD								
Noah	40	m	w	ENGL	San Francisco	2-Wd San Francisco	79	201
William	31	m	w	ENGL	Solano	Silveyville Twp	90	92
EFFORT								
Robert	36	m	w	DE	Solano	Vacaville Twp	90	124
EFFY								
Wm	42	m	w	PRUS	Santa Cruz	Santa Cruz	89	408
EFKIN								
Henry	44	m	w	HANO	Yuba	Marysville	93	576
EGAN								
Cornelius	24	m	w	IREL	San Francisco	1-Wd San Francisco	79	105
Cory	52	m	w	TN	Butte	Concow Twp	70	6
Danl	33	m	w	NY	Sonoma	Petaluma Twp	91	319
Edwd	46	m	w	IREL	San Francisco	1-Wd San Francisco	79	25
Edwd	32	m	w	IREL	San Francisco	1-Wd San Francisco	79	91
Frances	6	f	w	CA	El Dorado	White Oak Twp	72	136
Frederick	48	m	w	PRUS	San Francisco	8-Wd San Francisco	82	429
George	25	m	w	MO	Los Angeles	San Jose Twp	73	621
George L	11	m	w	CA	El Dorado	White Oak Twp	72	136
James	40	m	w	IREL	San Francisco	San Francisco P O	83	390
James	30	m	w	IREL	Alameda	Oakland	68	176
James	26	m	w	IREL	San Francisco	San Francisco P O	83	66
James F	34	m	w	IREL	Calaveras	Copperopolis P O	70	227
John	50	m	w	IREL	San Francisco	8-Wd San Francisco	82	369
John	35	m	w	IREL	Alameda	Washington Twp	68	296
John	30	m	w	IREL	San Francisco	San Francisco P O	85	758
John	30	m	w	IREL	Nevada	Eureka Twp	75	136
John	27	m	w	IREL	San Francisco	1-Wd San Francisco	79	94
John	27	m	w	IREL	San Francisco	11-Wd San Francisc	84	477
John	19	m	w	NY	San Francisco	San Francisco P O	83	237
John D	30	m	w	IREL	Yolo	Putah Twp	93	516
John F	36	m	w	IREL	San Francisco	San Francisco P O	83	286
John R	38	m	w	KY	Los Angeles	San Jose Twp	73	621
Kate	38	f	w	IREL	San Francisco	8-Wd San Francisco	82	297
Martin	42	m	w	IREL	San Joaquin	2-Wd Stockton	86	170
Mary E	23	f	w	AUSL	San Francisco	8-Wd San Francisco	82	295
Michael	30	m	w	IREL	San Mateo	San Mateo P O	87	359
Nora	20	f	w	IREL	San Francisco	San Francisco P O	85	802
Patrick	50	m	w	IREL	San Francisco	San Francisco P O	83	305
Patrick	40	m	w	IREL	San Francisco	San Francisco P O	83	291
Patrick	40	m	w	IREL	San Francisco	11-Wd San Francisc	84	481
Patrick	36	m	w	IREL	San Francisco	11-Wd San Francisc	84	505
R J	31	m	w	IREL	San Francisco	San Francisco P O	83	284
Richard	28	m	w	IREL	Los Angeles	San Juan Twp	73	627
Thomas	46	m	w	IREL	San Francisco	San Francisco P O	83	318
William	48	m	w	IREL	San Francisco	11-Wd San Francisc	84	518
William	35	m	w	IREL	San Francisco	8-Wd San Francisco	82	351
Wm	23	m	w	AUSL	San Francisco	San Francisco P O	83	130
EGAR								
Mark	29	m	w	NY	Alameda	Murray Twp	68	111
Mary	35	f	i	CA	Fresno	Millerton P O	72	180
William	35	m	w	GERM	Los Angeles	Los Angeles	73	542
EGARD								
Manuel	32	m	w	MEXI	Tuolumne	Chinese Camp P O	93	379
EGARIA								
Jesus	27	m	w	CA	Alameda	Washington Twp	68	290
EGAS								
Alexander	32	m	w	CA	San Luis Obispo	San Luis Obispo Tw	87	315
EGBERT								
Christopher M	34	m	w	MO	San Luis Obispo	Santa Rosa Twp	87	317
Enos	48	m	w	SWIT	Sierra	Gibson Twp	89	538
Henry	43	m	w	HANO	Siskiyou	Yreka Twp	89	673
Henry C	31	m	w	PA	Inyo	Independence Twp	73	328
John M	42	m	w	NY	Santa Barbara	San Buenaventura P	87	439
Louis H	36	m	w	PA	Solano	Rio Vista Twp	90	59
Oliver P	43	m	w	NY	Solano	Rio Vista Twp	90	55
Robert C	44	m	w	NY	Placer	Colfax P O	76	390
EGEE								
Henri	61	m	w	FRAN	San Francisco	6-Wd San Francisco	81	37
EGEI								
Henri	61	m	w	FRAN	San Francisco	San Francisco P O	80	480
EGELOW								
Peter	45	m	w	SWED	Los Angeles	Santa Ana Twp	73	599
EGELSON								
Benjamin	62	m	w	SCOT	Santa Clara	Redwood Twp	88	120
EGELSTINE								
Barns	26	m	w	POLA	San Francisco	8-Wd San Francisco	82	292
EGELSTON								
David	40	m	w	NY	Mendocino	Ukiah Twp	74	239
Joseph M	32	m	w	VT	El Dorado	Georgetown Twp	72	47
Theo	33	m	w	CANA	Butte	Ophir Twp	70	115
EGEN								
Elizabeth	25	f	w	IREL	Sacramento	2-Wd Sacramento	77	229
P	55	m	w	IREL	Sierra	Downieville Twp	89	518
EGENHOFF								
David	47	m	w	HANO	Mariposa	Mariposa P O	74	117
EGEO								
Victor	52	m	w	FRAN	San Joaquin	2-Wd Stockton	86	172
EGERA								
Juan	30	m	w	CA	San Luis Obispo	Santa Rosa Twp	87	328
EGERATH								
Jacob	43	m	w	SWIT	San Francisco	San Francisco P O	83	383
EGERMAN								
Christian	35	m	w	GERM	Los Angeles	Los Angeles Twp	73	486

Name	Age	S	R	B-PL	County	Locale	Series M593 Roll	Pg
EGERT								
George	22	m	w	NY	Los Angeles	Wilmington Twp	73	642
EGERY								
A J	55	m	w	MA	Solano	Vallejo	90	204
EGG								
Ah	28	m	c	CHIN	Plumas	Plumas Twp	77	29
EGGAN								
James	60	m	w	IREL	San Francisco	San Francisco P O	80	332
EGGELSON								
Chas	25	m	w	ENGL	San Francisco	8-Wd San Francisco	82	376
EGGER								
Jacob	35	m	w	SWIT	El Dorado	White Oak Twp	72	140
Jacob	30	m	w	PRUS	San Francisco	5-Wd San Francisco	81	8
EGGERLING								
Henry	25	m	w	PRUS	San Francisco	San Francisco P O	85	753
EGGERS								
Alexina	25	f	w	NY	Mono	Bridgeport P O	74	282
Fredrick	22	m	w	HAMB	San Mateo	San Mateo P O	87	352
George	50	m	w	HANO	San Francisco	11-Wd San Francisc	84	504
Hans F	39	m	w	PRUS	San Francisco	8-Wd San Francisco	82	412
Henry	39	m	w	HAMB	San Mateo	Schoolhouse Statio	87	340
Henry	18	m	w	HAMB	San Francisco	3-Wd San Francisco	79	293
Herman	47	m	w	PRUS	Alameda	Washington Twp	68	278
Jno F G	26	m	w	HANO	San Francisco	San Francisco P O	83	127
John C	32	m	w	HANO	San Francisco	San Francisco P O	83	97
Margaret	70	f	w	HANO	San Francisco	8-Wd San Francisco	82	294
EGGERT								
Hans	42	m	w	HANO	Siskiyou	Yreka	89	653
Henry	26	m	w	GERM	Yolo	Putah Twp	93	518
Herman C	28	m	w	PRUS	Nevada	Grass Valley Twp	75	153
Isabella	15	f	w	NY	Santa Cruz	Santa Cruz	89	409
William	27	m	w	PRUS	San Francisco	8-Wd San Francisco	82	319
Wm H	45	m	w	PA	San Francisco	2-Wd San Francisco	79	226
EGGLESON								
Sprague	64	m	w	NY	Fresno	Millerton P O	72	162
EGGLESTON								
Clark	55	m	w	NY	Mono	Bridgeport P O	74	286
H	29	m	w	OH	San Joaquin	Elliott Twp	86	80
Joseph	57	m	w	NY	Napa	Napa	75	42
Morris	43	m	w	NY	El Dorado	Coloma Twp	72	9
Theo	33	m	w	NY	Butte	Ophir Twp	70	113
EGGLETON								
Geo	47	m	w	KY	Tehama	Deer Crk Twp	92	170
Geo	40	m	w	ENGL	San Francisco	2-Wd San Francisco	79	204
EGGLING								
Ernest	31	m	w	HANO	Santa Clara	2-Wd San Jose	88	286
EGGSTORFF								
Henry	45	m	w	HANO	San Francisco	11-Wd San Francisc	84	554
EGHART								
Danl	44	m	w	GA	Mono	Bridgeport P O	74	286
EGIN								
S W	80	f	w	IREL	San Francisco	San Francisco P O	85	873
EGINTON								
William	25	m	w	IREL	San Francisco	3-Wd San Francisco	79	314
EGL								
A	50	m	w	AUSL	Sacramento	3-Wd Sacramento	77	289
EGLANHEART								
J	33	m	w	OH	Merced	Snelling P O	74	261
EGLESON								
S	32	m	w	OH	San Joaquin	Dent Twp	86	21
EGLI								
Anton	43	m	w	SWIT	Siskiyou	Yreka Twp	89	671
EGLIN								
Eugene	40	m	w	FRAN	Napa	Napa	75	48
EGLIND								
Wm	30	m	w	SWED	San Francisco	1-Wd San Francisco	79	71
EGLING								
Louis	38	m	w	BAVA	Tuolumne	Chinese Camp P O	93	389
EGLOFF								
John P	29	m	w	FRAN	San Diego	Coronado	78	467
EGMONT								
Jas F	36	m	w	KY	San Francisco	1-Wd San Francisco	79	3
EGNEISE								
Marie	25	f	w	MEXI	San Diego	Coronado	78	466
EGNER								
John	37	m	w	PRUS	San Francisco	8-Wd San Francisco	82	357
EGOE								
Mary	53	f	w	IREL	San Francisco	11-Wd San Francisc	84	676
EGUS								
D W	52	m	w	VA	Merced	Snelling P O	74	271
EH								
Ah	4	m	c	CHIN	El Dorado	Placerville Twp	72	97
Ah	35	m	c	CHIN	El Dorado	Mud Springs Twp	72	88
Chee	34	m	c	CHIN	Calaveras	San Andreas P O	70	199
Lo	23	m	c	CHIN	San Francisco	San Francisco P O	85	783
Quin	33	m	c	CHIN	El Dorado	Georgetown Twp	72	38
EHA								
Ah	25	m	c	CHIN	Trinity	Canyon City Pct	92	201
Ah	21	m	c	CHIN	Contra Costa	Martinez P O	71	413
EHALEN								
Mary	23	f	w	IREL	San Francisco	11-Wd San Francisc	84	579
EHAMENDO								
John	41	m	w	FRAN	Los Angeles	Los Angeles	73	523
EHART								
Marcus E	40	m	w	PA	Placer	Dutch Flat P O	76	414
EHAT								
Andrew A	17	m	w	WI	Amador	Fiddletown P O	69	430

© 2001 by Heritage Quest. All rights reserved.

Name	Age	S	R	B-PL	County	Locale	Series M593 Roll	Pg
Sophie	47	f	w	GERM	El Dorado	Diamond Springs Tw	72	23
EHBERLING								
Henry	38	m	w	HAMB	San Francisco	11-Wd San Francisc	84	440
EHELVE								
Peter	49	m	w	DENM	Placer	Gold Run Twp	76	399
EHENIO								
Jose	25	m	i	CA	Santa Barbara	San Buenaventura P	87	428
EHERHART								
Sophy	62	f	w	PRUS	San Joaquin	2-Wd Stockton	86	182
EHEWRE								
Treadon	45	m	w	CANA	Calaveras	Copperopolis P O	70	244
EHLART								
Robert	27	m	w	PRUS	San Francisco	1-Wd San Francisco	79	103
EHLBERG								
Frederika	60	f	w	PRUS	San Francisco	San Francisco P O	83	134
EHLER								
Fred	44	m	w	HANO	San Francisco	11-Wd San Francisc	84	671
EHLERS								
Hans J	43	m	w	SHOL	Siskiyou	Yreka	89	659
Herman	15	m	w	HANO	San Francisco	7-Wd San Francisco	81	211
EHLERT								
Ida	14	f	w	NY	San Francisco	San Francisco P O	85	817
EHLEY								
Berhard	26	m	w	HANO	Sacramento	2-Wd Sacramento	77	222
EHLIN								
Dick	17	m	w	HANO	San Francisco	7-Wd San Francisco	81	255
EHMANN								
Chris	36	m	w	WURT	Sacramento	2-Wd Sacramento	77	246
Henry	43	m	w	BADE	San Francisco	11-Wd San Francisc	84	484
Valentin	45	m	w	BADE	San Francisco	8-Wd San Francisco	82	307
EHMBURZ								
T	41	m	w	PRUS	Alameda	Alameda	68	9
EHN								
Gee	28	m	c	CHIN	Plumas	Rich Bar Twp	77	46
EHRENBERG								
Theo	41	m	w	PRUS	San Francisco	5-Wd San Francisco	81	2
EHRENFORT								
William	40	m	w	HANO	San Francisco	11-Wd San Francisc	84	556
EHRENPFORT								
Emma	61	f	w	PRUS	San Francisco	San Francisco P O	83	349
Frederika	35	m	w	PRUS	San Francisco	San Francisco P O	83	349
EHRENWORTH								
Jacob	20	m	w	PRUS	San Francisco	1-Wd San Francisco	79	72
EHRET								
Christian	27	m	w	BADE	Siskiyou	Yreka	89	655
John	36	m	w	GERM	San Francisco	7-Wd San Francisco	81	248
Michael	48	m	w	BADE	San Francisco	San Francisco P O	80	351
EHRHORN								
Adolph	43	m	w	HAMB	San Francisco	11-Wd San Francisc	84	501
Frank	16	m	w	CA	Santa Clara	Santa Clara Twp	88	177
EHRICHS								
Ernest	40	m	w	SHOL	Sacramento	2-Wd Sacramento	77	242
Fredrick	40	m	w	PRUS	San Francisco	San Francisco P O	80	417
EHRICKS								
John	30	m	w	HANO	San Francisco	11-Wd San Francisc	84	434
Richd	40	m	w	BREM	San Francisco	1-Wd San Francisco	79	73
EHRISER								
Matthew	62	m	w	BADE	Del Norte	Crescent	71	462
EHRKE								
Herman	45	m	w	PRUS	Sacramento	Granite Twp	77	144
EHRLICH								
Adelia	21	f	w	BAVA	San Francisco	2-Wd San Francisco	79	283
Fredinand	32	m	w	HAMB	Sonoma	Sonoma Twp	91	446
John	49	m	w	RUSS	Tehama	Tehama Twp	92	191
EHRLICK								
Herrman	27	m	w	PRUS	San Francisco	San Francisco P O	83	399
EHRMAN								
Geo	40	m	w	WURT	San Francisco	San Francisco P O	85	837
Henry	52	m	w	MD	Shasta	Millville P O	89	483
Henry	38	m	w	BAVA	Trinity	Junction City Pct	92	208
Joseph	22	m	w	NY	Contra Costa	Martinez P O	71	434
Joseph	18	m	w	MD	San Francisco	8-Wd San Francisco	82	482
Lena	23	f	w	BAVA	San Francisco	8-Wd San Francisco	82	486
Myer	28	m	w	MD	San Francisco	8-Wd San Francisco	82	481
Solomon	24	m	w	BAVA	Alameda	Washington Twp	68	291
EHRMANN								
Geo E	45	m	w	WURT	San Francisco	San Francisco P O	83	189
EIB								
Ida	23	m	w	PA	San Francisco	San Francisco P O	85	823
Peter	25	m	w	IL	Solano	Silveyville Twp	90	90
EIBES								
Mathias	53	m	w	VA	Yolo	Cache Crk Twp	93	457
EICH								
John	44	m	w	HDAR	Yuba	Parks Bar Twp	93	650
Wm	49	m	w	HESS	Napa	Napa Twp	75	66
EICHAR								
John	45	m	w	PA	Santa Clara	San Jose Twp	88	198
EICHEL								
Frederick	36	m	w	PRUS	Nevada	Grass Valley Twp	75	154
John F L	46	m	w	PRUS	Nevada	Bridgeport Twp	75	103
EICHELBERGER								
John C	32	m	w	PA	Monterey	San Antonio Twp	74	319
EICHERS								
John	49	m	w	PRUS	San Francisco	San Francisco P O	80	481
EICHLER								
Edward	48	m	w	AUST	Alameda	Eden Twp	68	60
Rudolf	41	m	w	MECK	Santa Clara	1-Wd San Jose	88	235
EICHMAN								
Jacob	19	m	w	PA	Amador	Amador City P O	69	391
EICHMANN								
Jacob	57	m	w	BAVA	Amador	Sutter Crk P O	69	401
EICKE								
Eleanor	53	f	w	HANO	Placer	Auburn P O	76	358
Elisabeth	28	f	w	HANO	Placer	Auburn P O	76	373
EICKENKOTTER								
Edward	18	m	w	CA	San Francisco	6-Wd San Francisco	81	83
EICKHOFF								
Wilhelmina	60	f	w	PRUS	Placer	Auburn P O	76	368
EICKLOOFF								
James H	25	m	w	BREM	Mariposa	Mariposa P O	74	118
EIDEL								
Martin	49	m	w	BAVA	Plumas	Seneca Twp	77	48
EIDENGER								
August	48	m	w	SAXO	El Dorado	Placerville	72	118
EIDENMULLER								
Chas	39	m	w	PRUS	San Francisco	6-Wd San Francisco	81	110
EIDLEMAN								
Jacob	32	m	w	SWIT	San Francisco	San Francisco P O	80	486
EIDNMELER								
Henry	14	m	w	CA	Alameda	Oakland	68	159
N C	16	m	w	CA	Alameda	Oakland	68	159
EIE								
Ah	21	m	c	CHIN	San Joaquin	Oneal Twp	86	118
EIGELBERRY								
Jno	55	m	w	OH	Santa Clara	Gilroy Twp	88	81
EIGENRAUCH								
Wm	41	m	w	PRUS	Siskiyou	Yreka	89	661
EIGENWILLING								
Charley	32	m	b	VA	San Joaquin	Elkhorn Twp	86	61
H	51	m	w	PRUS	San Joaquin	Elkhorn Twp	86	61
EIGERMAN								
F	27	f	w	US	Yuba	Marysville	93	609
EIGHAN								
Michl	49	m	w	IREL	San Francisco	1-Wd San Francisco	79	93
EIGLE								
Charlotte	61	f	w	SAXO	San Francisco	8-Wd San Francisco	82	422
Edward	25	m	w	CA	San Francisco	3-Wd San Francisco	79	325
EIGNOS								
Manuel	27	m	w	AZOR	Nevada	Eureka Twp	75	139
EIKENKOTTER								
August	53	m	w	PRUS	San Mateo	Searsville P O	87	382
Mary	19	f	w	LA	San Mateo	Searsville P O	87	382
EILBRALTO								
W R	59	m	w	PRUS	San Joaquin	1-Wd Stockton	86	155
EILER								
David	40	m	w	VA	Shasta	Millville P O	89	491
John	76	m	w	VA	Tehama	Red Bluff	92	179
Margaret	40	f	w	GERM	Yuba	Marysville	93	592
Peter	34	m	w	VA	Tehama	Red Bluff	92	179
EILERMAN								
B	38	m	w	BAVA	Yuba	Marysville	93	597
Frank	28	m	w	BREM	Nevada	Nevada Twp	75	276
H R	45	m	w	HANO	Yuba	Marysville	93	577
EILERS								
Detrick W	43	m	w	HANO	Sacramento	2-Wd Sacramento	77	216
Luppe	33	m	w	HANO	Shasta	Stillwater P O	89	481
EILMAN								
A	23	m	w	MI	Alameda	Oakland	68	240
EIM								
Ah	17	m	c	CHIN	San Francisco	8-Wd San Francisco	82	382
EIMER								
Henry	19	m	w	PRUS	San Francisco	7-Wd San Francisco	81	281
EIN								
Ling	30	m	c	CHIN	San Mateo	San Mateo P O	87	351
Won	40	m	c	CHIN	San Mateo	San Mateo P O	87	351
EINFELDT								
J	37	m	w	BAVA	Santa Clara	Gilroy Twp	88	71
EINFIELD								
Jacob	40	m	w	HANO	San Francisco	7-Wd San Francisco	81	179
EING								
Ah	25	m	c	CHIN	San Francisco	San Francisco P O	80	502
Erinel	40	m	w	PRUS	Sacramento	3-Wd Sacramento	77	258
EINH								
Ah	25	m	c	CHIN	San Francisco	1-Wd San Francisco	79	58
EINHAUS								
Henry	23	m	w	PRUS	Solano	Tremont Twp	90	32
EINI								
Bernard	28	m	w	SWIT	Plumas	Quartz Twp	77	38
EINOLF								
John	68	m	w	HANO	Sacramento	4-Wd Sacramento	77	376
EINSFELD								
Peter	29	m	w	HDAR	San Francisco	San Francisco P O	83	306
EINSTADTER								
Delia	30	f	w	SAXO	San Francisco	8-Wd San Francisco	82	460
EINSTEIN								
Jacob	42	m	w	BAVA	Santa Clara	Gilroy Twp	88	80
Morris	41	m	w	BAVA	Santa Clara	Gilroy Twp	88	80
EIPPER								
Thos	42	m	w	BAVA	San Francisco	1-Wd San Francisco	79	60
Wm	22	m	w	AL	Santa Clara	Gilroy Twp	88	80
EIRK								
Patrick F	48	m	w	IREL	Sacramento	1-Wd Sacramento	77	196
EIRO								
Antoine	46	m	w	FRAN	San Francisco	8-Wd San Francisco	82	398

© 2001 by Heritage Quest. All rights reserved.

Series M593

Name	Age	S	R	B-PL	County	Locale	Roll	Pg
EISEL								
John	40	m	w	PRUS	San Francisco	San Francisco P O	80	415
EISELEN								
Alfred	23	m	w	PRUS	San Francisco	San Francisco P O	83	149
EISEMAN								
Jacob	52	m	w	BADE	San Francisco	8-Wd San Francisco	82	395
EISEN								
A F	46	m	w	SWED	San Francisco	San Francisco P O	85	814
Francis E	40	m	w	SWED	San Francisco	San Francisco P O	83	103
James	35	m	w	CANA	San Francisco	7-Wd San Francisco	81	240
EISENBERG								
Chas	39	m	w	PRUS	San Francisco	1-Wd San Francisco	79	125
Isadore	38	m	w	AUST	San Francisco	2-Wd San Francisco	79	240
Simon	35	m	w	MO	Butte	Chico Twp	70	23
EISENHART								
Daniel	41	m	w	LA	Butte	Ophir Twp	70	96
Gotlieb	42	m	w	WURT	San Francisco	1-Wd San Francisco	79	56
John	31	m	w	WURT	San Francisco	1-Wd San Francisco	79	52
EISENHUER								
Adam	58	m	w	BADE	San Francisco	6-Wd San Francisco	81	126
EISENMENGER								
Barbary	42	f	w	BAVA	Sacramento	2-Wd Sacramento	77	246
EISENSTEIN								
Marcus	25	m	w	POLA	San Francisco	San Francisco P O	80	461
EISER								
Fredrick	44	m	w	PRUS	San Francisco	San Francisco P O	80	477
Lewis	35	m	w	SAXO	Yuba	W Bear Rvr Twp	93	684
EISERT								
Chas	31	m	w	SAXO	San Francisco	8-Wd San Francisco	82	348
EISFELDER								
Wm	32	m	w	BAVA	San Francisco	San Francisco P O	83	182
EISFELDT								
Thos	31	m	w	PRUS	San Francisco	1-Wd San Francisco	79	107
EISHER								
Christian	38	m	w	SAXO	San Francisco	San Francisco P O	83	189
EISLER								
Chas H	42	m	w	PRUS	San Francisco	1-Wd San Francisco	79	83
Harry	26	m	w	ENGL	San Francisco	1-Wd San Francisco	79	42
Moses	25	m	w	BOHE	San Francisco	1-Wd San Francisco	79	52
Saml	19	m	w	TX	Butte	Hamilton Twp	70	69
EISLEY								
Chas	30	m	w	PA	Santa Clara	Gilroy Twp	88	80
EISNER								
Jacob	38	m	w	PRUS	San Francisco	1-Wd San Francisco	79	97
EISON								
Samuel	46	m	w	PRUS	San Francisco	San Francisco P O	83	405
EISPIRAR								
Jane	45	f	w	MEXI	San Francisco	San Francisco P O	80	409
EISTE								
Victor	20	m	w	ITAL	Santa Clara	2-Wd San Jose	88	329
EISZLER								
Andrew	66	m	w	WURT	Placer	Bath P O	76	455
John H	1	m	w	CA	Placer	Bath P O	76	455
EITEL								
Amelia E	26	f	w	LA	San Francisco	San Francisco P O	83	330
C C	36	m	w	HAMB	Sierra	Lincoln Twp	89	552
Jno	35	m	w	BAVA	Sacramento	1-Wd Sacramento	77	175
EITHER								
Peter	35	m	w	CANA	Amador	Volcano P O	69	381
EITY								
Adam	60	m	w	PRUS	San Francisco	San Francisco P O	83	257
EIZAGA								
Florence	39	m	w	SPAI	San Francisco	8-Wd San Francisco	82	371
EJALU								
Joaquin	61	m	w	CHIL	Santa Clara	Alviso Twp	88	25
Juan	42	m	w	CHIL	Santa Clara	Alviso Twp	88	25
EJIOS								
Juana	30	f	w	MEXI	Los Angeles	Los Angeles Twp	73	473
EK								
Ah	20	m	c	CHIN	San Mateo	Pescadero P O	87	416
Ah	18	m	c	CHIN	Nevada	Rough & Ready Twp	75	338
EKEIN								
Kriegel	28	m	w	FRAN	Alameda	Washington Twp	68	292
EKEL								
E A	14	f	w	CA	Sacramento	3-Wd Sacramento	77	272
H S	31	m	w	PA	Sacramento	3-Wd Sacramento	77	272
John J	28	m	w	IL	El Dorado	Cosumnes Twp	72	14
EKELAND								
Eric	40	m	w	SWED	San Francisco	3-Wd San Francisco	79	321
EKENSTEEN								
August	40	m	w	SWED	San Francisco	2-Wd San Francisco	79	195
EKMAN								
William	25	m	w	FINL	Placer	Bath P O	76	457
EKMUN								
Mary	19	f	w	WURT	San Francisco	11-Wd San Francisc	84	431
EKOS								
Bartholomew	25	m	w	ENGL	Humboldt	Eureka Twp	72	270
EKOW								
---	25	m	c	CHIN	Sierra	Eureka Twp	89	525
ELAM								
Robert H	45	m	w	VA	San Francisco	8-Wd San Francisco	82	404
Sarah	50	f	w	NC	Tehama	Hunters Twp	92	187
Sarah A	45	f	w	VA	Mariposa	Mariposa P O	74	126
Thomas	36	m	w	TN	Stanislaus	Empire Twp	92	59
ELAN								
Aug M	29	m	w	TN	Butte	Chico Twp	70	55

Series M593

Name	Age	S	R	B-PL	County	Locale	Roll	Pg
ELANA								
Isabel	30	f	w	CA	San Diego	Warners Rancho Dis	78	530
ELAND								
Hann	22	f	w	MA	Alameda	Oakland	68	256
Jose	25	m	w	SPAI	Butte	Chico Twp	70	36
ELANDE								
Henry E	38	m	w	NY	San Francisco	8-Wd San Francisco	82	424
ELARD								
Walter	29	m	w	ME	San Francisco	11-Wd San Francisc	84	665
ELASA								
Monlore	45	m	m	CHIL	Placer	Bath P O	76	420
ELBE								
C B	27	m	w	PRUS	Sacramento	1-Wd Sacramento	77	174
ELBERT								
Henry	38	m	w	MECK	San Francisco	2-Wd San Francisco	79	281
ELBERY								
Robt	28	m	w	MA	San Francisco	8-Wd San Francisco	82	334
ELBRIDGE								
Pratt	32	m	w	ME	Mendocino	Navarro & Big Rvr	74	174
ELDARNO								
August	40	m	w	MEXI	San Francisco	2-Wd San Francisco	79	150
ELDEN								
Albert	22	m	w	PRUS	San Francisco	8-Wd San Francisco	82	348
John	36	m	w	SCOT	Alameda	Oakland	68	153
ELDER								
Abner B	37	m	w	OH	Inyo	Lone Pine Twp	73	335
Alexander	31	m	w	NY	San Francisco	11-Wd San Francisc	84	487
G W	22	m	w	MO	San Joaquin	Tulare Twp	86	250
George	23	m	w	CANA	San Mateo	Searsville P O	87	382
Hugh	32	m	w	IREL	Sacramento	Brighton Twp	77	72
Jacob	24	m	w	WI	Sutter	Vernon Twp	92	130
James	22	m	w	SCOT	San Francisco	11-Wd San Francisc	84	584
James A	44	m	w	MO	Sacramento	San Joaquin Twp	77	396
James A	43	m	w	MO	Sacramento	Lee Twp	77	157
James F	25	m	w	IN	Yolo	Grafton Twp	93	497
John	40	m	w	SCOT	San Francisco	San Francisco P O	85	721
Maria	39	f	w	NJ	Colusa	Spring Valley Twp	71	343
Maria	39	f	w	NJ	Yuba	Marysville	93	605
Martha	32	f	w	MS	San Francisco	San Francisco P O	83	339
Nathan	48	m	w	MA	San Joaquin	Douglas Twp	86	36
Orelia O	18	f	w	MO	Mendocino	Ukiah Twp	74	235
Silas R	46	m	w	NY	Placer	Auburn P O	76	364
T R	36	m	w	MD	Sierra	Butte Twp	89	513
William	58	m	m	SCOT	San Francisco	11-Wd San Francisc	84	487
Wm J	40	m	w	NY	San Francisco	7-Wd San Francisco	81	247
Wm Winzell	39	m	w	BREM	San Francisco	1-Wd San Francisco	79	85
ELDERMAN								
J J	28	m	w	IL	Monterey	Castroville Twp	74	325
ELDERTON								
Edwd	36	m	w	VA	Sacramento	1-Wd Sacramento	77	178
ELDERWOOD								
Edward	33	m	w	MA	Sacramento	2-Wd Sacramento	77	221
ELDRACHER								
Peter	38	m	w	BADE	San Francisco	San Francisco P O	83	317
ELDRALDI								
D	16	f	w	CA	Los Angeles	Los Angeles	73	569
ELDRECHT								
Michael	43	m	w	PRUS	San Francisco	8-Wd San Francisco	82	352
ELDRED								
Albert	50	m	w	MD	Alameda	Brooklyn Twp	68	51
H J	30	m	w	MI	Yuba	Marysville Twp	93	567
Horrace	45	m	w	NY	Sacramento	1-Wd Sacramento	77	183
James	19	m	w	UT	Placer	Lincoln P O	76	488
John J	35	m	w	NY	Sonoma	Analy Twp	91	238
Sidney	40	m	w	MI	Sacramento	4-Wd Sacramento	77	373
Stephen J	36	m	w	NY	Shasta	Millville P O	89	483
ELDREDGE								
Edward E	32	m	w	MA	Santa Clara	San Jose Twp	88	190
J E	41	m	w	NY	Del Norte	Crescent	71	464
James L	30	m	w	NY	San Francisco	San Francisco P O	85	738
ELDRID								
H P	30	m	w	NY	San Joaquin	Douglas Twp	86	31
ELDRIDGE								
Benjamin	31	m	w	NY	San Francisco	6-Wd San Francisco	81	103
Chas H	28	m	w	MA	San Francisco	San Francisco P O	83	109
Darias	38	m	w	ME	Yuba	Parks Bar Twp	93	650
E	30	m	w	NY	Alameda	Oakland	68	264
Ed	48	m	w	ENGL	Alameda	Oakland	68	171
Edwd D	40	m	w	NY	San Francisco	San Francisco P O	83	30
Ella	35	f	w	MA	San Joaquin	2-Wd Stockton	86	171
Fanny	22	f	w	MO	San Francisco	San Francisco P O	83	190
Flora	24	f	w	NY	Alpine	Monitor P O	69	313
G C	28	m	w	NY	Alameda	Oakland	68	163
George	30	m	w	NY	San Francisco	11-Wd San Francisc	84	494
George W	34	m	w	TN	Santa Cruz	Soquel Twp	89	442
H J	36	m	w	NY	Klamath	Sawyers Bar	73	377
H J	36	m	w	NY	Humboldt	Arcata Twp	72	230
James	32	m	w	NY	Alameda	Hayward	68	73
James T	35	m	w	ME	Mendocino	Navarro & Big Rvr	74	176
Jas P	30	m	w	TN	Tehama	Paynes Crk Twp	92	167
Jno	40	m	w	ENGL	San Joaquin	2-Wd Stockton	86	193
John	16	m	w	UT	El Dorado	Kelsey Twp	72	62
Kimball	41	m	w	MA	San Francisco	San Francisco P O	80	488
Livingston	40	m	w	PA	San Francisco	6-Wd San Francisco	81	90
Oliver	51	m	w	MA	San Francisco	8-Wd San Francisco	82	300
Oscar	42	m	w	NY	San Francisco	San Francisco P O	83	227
Sam	44	m	w	NY	San Joaquin	2-Wd Stockton	86	209

© 2001 by Heritage Quest. All rights reserved.

Name	Age	S	R	B-PL	County	Locale	Series M593 Roll	Pg
Thos R	40	m	w	LA	San Francisco	1-Wd San Francisco	79	3
W G	28	m	w	NY	Alameda	Oakland	68	163
William	50	m	w	SWED	Sonoma	Sonoma Twp	91	441
William	40	m	w	ME	San Francisco	San Francisco P O	83	143
Wm	45	m	w	MI	Butte	Chico Twp	70	34
ELDUAN								
Nelson	40	m	w	KY	Kern	Bakersfield P O	73	359
ELEAH								
Jacob	13	m	i	AK	San Francisco	6-Wd San Francisco	81	93
ELEAS								
Nicholas	30	m	w	MEXI	San Bernardino	San Salvador Twp	78	458
ELEERT								
Bonner	46	m	w	HANO	Butte	Oregon Twp	70	123
ELEHY								
Thomas	50	m	w	IREL	Sacramento	4-Wd Sacramento	77	321
ELEINCAMP								
Charles	34	m	w	SHOL	Alameda	Eden Twp	68	57
ELEKAMP								
Benjamin	35	m	w	PRUS	San Francisco	San Francisco P O	80	334
ELEMANS								
Emma	17	f	w	LA	Solano	Tremont Twp	90	34
ELENHART								
S	41	m	w	BADE	Sacramento	4-Wd Sacramento	77	359
ELENOR								
D	17	f	w	WI	Sonoma	Vallejo Twp	91	460
ELER								
Lewis	16	m	w	FRAN	Sutter	Yuba Twp	92	145
ELERBROOK								
Jachim	46	m	w	SHOL	Trinity	Weaverville Pct	92	231
ELERMAN								
Charles	27	m	w	HANO	Santa Clara	2-Wd San Jose	88	305
ELEVARD								
Micheal	35	m	w	IREL	San Francisco	7-Wd San Francisco	81	178
ELEY								
George	64	m	w	MD	Tuolumne	Chinese Camp P O	93	366
Heny	44	m	w	PA	San Joaquin	Tulare Twp	86	260
Jackson	39	m	w	OH	Tehama	Red Bank Twp	92	169
ELFELT								
Louis	36	m	w	PRUS	San Francisco	1-Wd San Francisco	79	120
ELFERS								
A D	46	m	w	HANO	Alameda	Oakland	68	211
ELFORD								
Alfred	35	m	w	ENGL	San Francisco	San Francisco P O	83	357
Henry E	26	m	w	ENGL	Santa Cruz	Santa Cruz Twp	89	398
ELFOSE								
Santo	36	m	w	MEXI	San Diego	Fort Yuma Dist	78	464
ELFSON								
Carl	47	m	w	NORW	San Francisco	1-Wd San Francisco	79	129
ELGEN								
Joseph	30	m	w	ITAL	San Francisco	1-Wd San Francisco	79	89
ELGIN								
George	38	m	w	KY	Lake	Little Borax	73	419
Wm A	41	m	w	VA	Napa	Napa	75	5
ELGORDO								
Francisco	72	m	i	OH	Inyo	Cerro Gordo Twp	73	320
ELHHOM								
Charles	32	m	w	IREL	San Mateo	Menlo Park P O	87	378
ELI								
G S	41	m	w	CT	Sutter	Butte Twp	92	88
ELIAS								
Andres	33	m	w	MEXI	Los Angeles	El Monte Twp	73	457
Anselm	40	m	w	PRUS	San Francisco	8-Wd San Francisco	82	454
Claus	30	m	w	PRUS	San Francisco	San Francisco P O	80	353
Edward	31	m	w	PRUS	Tuolumne	Columbia P O	93	336
Elijah	35	m	w	OH	Sacramento	Center Twp	77	83
Francisco	40	m	w	MEXI	San Francisco	1-Wd San Francisco	79	49
Frank	32	m	w	MEXI	Calaveras	San Andreas P O	70	181
Isaac	38	m	w	PRUS	Yuba	Slate Range Bar Tw	93	675
John	5	m	w	OH	Contra Costa	Martinez P O	71	427
John	36	m	w	HANO	Humboldt	Table Bluff Twp	72	304
Lipman	48	m	w	PRUS	San Francisco	2-Wd San Francisco	79	274
Morris	23	m	w	PRUS	San Francisco	San Francisco P O	80	348
Rafael	36	m	w	MEXI	Kern	Bakersfield P O	73	362
Simon	31	m	w	PRUS	Sacramento	San Joaquin Twp	77	396
Thomas	37	m	w	WALE	Contra Costa	Martinez P O	71	427
ELIASER								
Abram	50	m	w	AUST	San Francisco	7-Wd San Francisco	81	261
M	42	m	w	FRAN	Solano	Vallejo	90	214
ELIASON								
Ebenezer	55	m	w	VA	Calaveras	San Andreas P O	70	152
Sele	47	f	w	NORW	San Francisco	San Francisco P O	83	141
W A	48	m	w	VA	Sonoma	Santa Rosa	91	401
ELIASOR								
H D	15	m	w	MEXI	Alameda	Oakland	68	159
ELIDGE								
W D	58	m	w	KY	Amador	Ione City P O	69	363
ELIE								
Creton	40	m	w	FRAN	Calaveras	San Andreas P O	70	168
ELIGAR								
Albert	34	m	w	PRUS	San Francisco	2-Wd San Francisco	79	145
ELIKER								
Ellick	25	m	w	IL	Sacramento	Franklin Twp	77	112
ELIKINS								
David	37	m	w	VT	Amador	Jackson P O	69	347
ELIME								
B	22	m	w	GERM	Sacramento	1-Wd Sacramento	77	175

Name	Age	S	R	B-PL	County	Locale	Series M593 Roll	Pg
ELIN								
Charles	36	m	w	SWED	Santa Cruz	Watsonville	89	374
ELING								
Charles	50	m	w	SHOL	El Dorado	Greenwood Twp	72	56
ELINGSON								
Suran	36	m	w	NORW	San Francisco	7-Wd San Francisco	81	274
ELINO								
Megera	3	f	w	CA	Alameda	Murray Twp	68	104
ELIOR								
George	36	m	w	ENGL	San Bernardino	San Bernardino Twp	78	442
ELIOT								
James	34	m	w	TX	Los Angeles	El Monte Twp	73	456
Jno	27	m	w	TX	Butte	Chico Twp	70	20
Samuel	59	m	w	NY	Los Angeles	El Monte Twp	73	455
ELIOTT								
James	35	m	w	KY	Nevada	Bloomfield Twp	75	97
ELISALDE								
Francisco J	39	m	w	CA	Santa Barbara	Arroyo Burro P O	87	509
ELISALDI								
Francisco	30	m	w	CA	Los Angeles	Santa Ana Twp	73	611
Jose Anti	52	m	w	CA	Los Angeles	Santa Ana Twp	73	600
ELISHA								
George	36	m	w	MEXI	San Francisco	San Francisco P O	80	474
ELISIG								
Maria	33	f	w	IREL	Santa Clara	2-Wd San Jose	88	302
ELISON								
Lew	43	m	w	MO	Sonoma	Analy Twp	91	236
ELITCH								
John	48	m	w	AUST	Santa Clara	2-Wd San Jose	88	304
John	48	m	w	DALM	Santa Clara	2-Wd San Jose	88	319
ELITTAN								
Jon	22	m	w	CA	San Joaquin	Tulare Twp	86	251
ELIVENIA								
Esperito	51	m	w	SPAI	Calaveras	San Andreas P O	70	203
ELIZABETH								
J	38	f	w	NC	Sonoma	Washington Twp	91	468
ELIZALDA								
Jose M	16	m	w	CA	Santa Barbara	Santa Barbara P O	87	492
Maria A	60	f	w	CA	Santa Barbara	Santa Barbara P O	87	462
ELKELES								
Jacob	26	m	w	PRUS	San Francisco	1-Wd San Francisco	79	81
ELKEMA								
Proeder	37	m	w	RUSS	San Diego	San Jacinto Dist	78	517
ELKENS								
Peter R	34	m	w	TN	Butte	Kimshew Tpw	70	80
ELKIES								
Lewis	46	m	w	PRUS	Sacramento	2-Wd Sacramento	77	229
ELKIN								
C W	22	m	w	TX	San Joaquin	Douglas Twp	86	33
Frank E	32	m	w	NY	Colusa	Butte Twp	71	269
Wm	30	m	w	PRUS	San Joaquin	2-Wd Stockton	86	201
ELKINGTON								
James	40	m	w	ENGL	Napa	Napa Twp	75	58
ELKINS								
Adial	67	m	w	VT	Stanislaus	Emory Twp	92	22
Charles	40	m	w	NH	San Mateo	Half Moon Bay P O	87	402
David	36	m	w	VT	Amador	Jackson P O	69	342
David	31	m	w	AR	Mendocino	Anderson Twp	74	155
Erasmus	48	m	w	SC	Stanislaus	Empire Twp	92	47
J	39	m	w	VT	San Joaquin	Douglas Twp	86	34
Mathew W	34	m	w	VT	Alpine	Silver Mtn P O	69	307
ELKMAN								
Rudolph	49	m	w	PRUS	Shasta	Shasta P O	89	452
ELKUS								
H	42	m	w	PRUS	Sacramento	4-Wd Sacramento	77	322
ELLABARRIE								
Espirito	55	m	w	MEXI	Calaveras	San Andreas P O	70	208
ELLAND								
H	20	f	w	ME	Alameda	Oakland	68	238
Robt	37	m	w	ENGL	Alameda	Oakland	68	165
ELLARS								
Anna	38	f	w	FRAN	Contra Costa	San Pablo Twp	71	356
ELLAS								
Augustus	46	m	w	PRUS	Inyo	Lone Pine Twp	73	332
ELLEBROOT								
C	40	m	w	PRUS	Alameda	Murray Twp	68	123
ELLEDGE								
A D	43	m	w	IN	Yuba	Linda Twp	93	557
Anson	26	m	w	IL	Santa Clara	1-Wd San Jose	88	225
Joseph	33	m	w	TN	Mendocino	Ukiah Twp	74	241
Leonard	39	m	w	IL	Santa Clara	1-Wd San Jose	88	229
U L	29	m	w	IL	Amador	Ione City P O	69	361
William T	37	m	w	IL	Santa Clara	Redwood Twp	88	130
Wm C	42	m	w	TN	Mendocino	Ukiah Twp	74	240
ELLEE								
Englis	50	m	w	MEXI	Fresno	Millerton P O	72	163
ELLEGE								
Uriah F	29	m	w	IL	Alpine	Woodfords P O	69	309
ELLEIR								
Adolfo	25	m	w	AZ	Los Angeles	Soledad Twp	73	632
ELLEN								
Alfred	41	m	w	HANO	El Dorado	Mud Springs Twp	72	80
John	42	m	w	MO	Mariposa	Mariposa P O	74	135
John	36	m	w	GREE	Placer	Bath P O	76	442
P	25	m	w	MO	San Joaquin	Elkhorn Twp	86	59
ELLENBERGER								
Henry	41	m	w	AR	Contra Costa	Martinez P O	71	402

© 2001 by Heritage Quest. All rights reserved.

Series M593

Name	Age	S	R	B-PL	County	Locale	Roll	Pg
Jonus	37	m	w	IL	Contra Costa	Martinez P O	71	402
ELLENBURGER								
More	38	m	w	PA	San Joaquin	3-Wd Stockton	86	216
ELLENWOOD								
Jos	28	m	w	CANA	Santa Clara	Gilroy Twp	88	71
Phineas	34	m	w	NH	Stanislaus	Empire Twp	92	62
T	27	m	w	CANA	Santa Clara	Gilroy Twp	88	73
ELLER								
John	43	m	w	PRUS	Napa	Napa	75	44
John	24	m	w	SWED	San Francisco	11-Wd San Francisc	84	519
ELLERBROOK								
John	43	m	w	VT	San Joaquin	Tulare Twp	86	257
ELLERHORST								
Henry	49	m	w	HANO	Alameda	Eden Twp	68	64
ELLERMAN								
Charles	23	m	w	PRUS	Plumas	Washington Twp	77	56
ELLERT								
John	29	m	w	NY	Humboldt	Eureka Twp	72	268
Selena	17	f	w	ENGL	San Francisco	8-Wd San Francisco	82	392
ELLERY								
Epes	40	m	w	MA	Alameda	Alameda	68	14
Franklin	37	m	w	MA	Humboldt	Eureka Twp	72	264
H	32	m	w	NY	Sierra	Forest	89	537
James	34	m	w	ENGL	Trinity	Weaverville Pct	92	229
V	54	m	w	GERM	San Joaquin	2-Wd Stockton	86	174
William	45	m	w	RI	Contra Costa	Martinez P O	71	384
William	42	m	w	MA	Humboldt	Table Bluff Twp	72	308
ELLES								
George	44	m	w	ENGL	Contra Costa	San Pablo Twp	71	365
Jacob	36	m	w	SHOL	Contra Costa	San Pablo Twp	71	361
Jos	48	m	w	PA	Tehama	Tehama Twp	92	186
Theodore	28	m	w	NJ	Napa	Napa Twp	75	65
ELLET								
Annie	51	f	w	SCOT	Sacramento	4-Wd Sacramento	77	344
Louis	23	m	w	PRUS	San Francisco	5-Wd San Francisco	81	29
ELLETT								
William	50	m	w	TN	San Diego	Milquaty Dist	78	476
ELLEY								
George W	40	m	w	RI	Contra Costa	Martinez P O	71	384
ELLICE								
John	28	m	w	PA	Alameda	Oakland	68	164
ELLICH								
John	43	m	w	AUST	San Francisco	3-Wd San Francisco	79	293
ELLICOTT								
Andrew	45	m	w	NY	El Dorado	Placerville Twp	72	104
ELLIGOT								
Edmund	35	m	w	IREL	Monterey	San Benito Twp	74	384
ELLIKER								
John	20	m	w	SWIT	Sacramento	Franklin Twp	77	106
ELLING								
Betsey	82	m	w	CT	San Joaquin	Oneal Twp	86	114
ELLINGHOUSE								
August	41	m	w	BREM	Santa Clara	1-Wd San Jose	88	248
ELLINGS								
Worth R	33	m	w	PA	Sonoma	Mendocino Twp	91	295
ELLINGSWORTH								
A	38	m	w	PA	Amador	Drytown P O	69	419
Samuel	26	m	w	NY	Mendocino	Albion & Big Rvr T	74	167
Samuel	26	m	w	PRUS	Mendocino	Albion & Big Rvr T	74	166
ELLINGTON								
J W	23	m	w	VA	Solano	Vallejo	90	202
James	24	m	w	MO	Inyo	Lone Pine Twp	73	331
May	19	f	w	IL	Yuba	Marysville	93	577
ELLINGWOOD								
Giles W	39	m	w	ME	Santa Cruz	Santa Cruz	89	403
Isaac	32	m	w	ME	San Francisco	San Francisco P O	83	266
James	38	m	w	MD	Calaveras	San Andreas P O	70	184
ELLINWOOD								
Charles	36	m	w	VT	San Francisco	8-Wd San Francisco	82	422
ELLIOD								
John	20	m	w	IA	Mendocino	Navarro & Big Rvr	74	177
ELLIOT								
Angeline	39	f	w	CANA	Colusa	Butte Twp	71	266
C	43	m	w	VT	Alameda	Oakland	68	179
Charles	30	m	w	ME	San Francisco	7-Wd San Francisco	81	157
Chas	47	m	w	ENGL	Sacramento	3-Wd Sacramento	77	266
Chas	30	m	w	NY	San Francisco	7-Wd San Francisco	81	274
Chas	20	m	w	MA	San Francisco	8-Wd San Francisco	82	316
Edward	26	m	w	NH	San Diego	San Diego	78	488
Edwd	29	m	w	IL	Sacramento	1-Wd Sacramento	77	178
Ellen	22	f	w	DE	Solano	Benicia	90	14
Ellice	41	f	w	MO	Butte	Concow Twp	70	9
Emily	18	f	w	IL	San Francisco	8-Wd San Francisco	82	423
F	42	m	w	PRUS	Sacramento	4-Wd Sacramento	77	374
F H	31	m	w	MO	Lake	Upper Lake	73	410
Geo	30	m	w	PA	Yuba	Marysville	93	604
Geo	21	m	w	IREL	Sacramento	Sutter Twp	77	393
George	39	m	w	NY	Placer	Bath P O	76	460
George	31	m	w	IL	Monterey	San Juan Twp	74	413
George W	49	m	w	CA	Placer	Bath P O	76	420
Heman C	36	m	w	ME	San Francisco	8-Wd San Francisco	82	492
J	36	m	w	NH	Sierra	Downieville Twp	89	519
Jacob	38	m	w	MO	Butte	Concow Twp	70	9
James	57	m	w	KY	Tulare	Tule Rvr Twp	92	261
James	54	m	w	GA	Alameda	Murray Twp	68	110
James	45	m	w	MA	Sacramento	San Joaquin Twp	77	395
James	45	m	w	MO	Trinity	Hayfork Valley	92	238
James	30	m	w	OH	Yuba	East Bear Rvr Twp	93	543
James	27	m	w	SCOT	Yuba	North East Twp	93	645
James H	30	m	w	ENGL	Los Angeles	Santa Ana Twp	73	601
Jane	30	f	w	ENGL	Sacramento	San Joaquin Twp	77	395
John	34	m	b	HI	Tuolumne	Big Oak Flat P O	93	400
John Jr	50	m	w	PA	Santa Cruz	Santa Cruz Twp	89	379
Joshua	46	m	w	OH	Contra Costa	Martinez P O	71	385
L C	34	m	w	IREL	Tuolumne	Columbia P O	93	349
Leander	50	m	w	WI	Placer	Auburn P O	76	380
Margaret	20	f	w	NY	San Francisco	8-Wd San Francisco	82	428
Mark	44	m	w	OH	Contra Costa	Martinez P O	71	393
Robert	51	m	w	SCOT	Placer	Bath P O	76	458
Samuel	42	m	w	MA	San Francisco	San Francisco P O	80	488
Samuel	39	m	m	VA	Tuolumne	Sonora P O	93	311
Samuel	36	m	w	MA	Alameda	Brooklyn	68	24
Thomas	26	m	w	ENGL	Amador	Sutter Crk P O	69	410
W B	71	m	w	NC	Lake	Upper Lake	73	410
Washington L	45	m	w	PA	San Francisco	8-Wd San Francisco	82	467
ELLIOTT								
Albert	59	m	b	VA	San Francisco	San Francisco P O	83	259
Albert G	33	m	w	NY	Solano	Maine Prairie Twp	90	54
Alex M	41	m	w	IN	Butte	Kimshew Tpw	70	76
Alfred W	12	m	w	MO	Nevada	Rough & Ready Twp	75	334
Amy	10	f	w	CA	San Francisco	San Francisco P O	85	725
Andrew	30	m	w	IREL	Alameda	Murray Twp	68	122
Archibald	23	m	w	SCOT	Sacramento	2-Wd Sacramento	77	223
Benj	37	m	w	IREL	Marin	Tomales Twp	74	78
Benjn	43	m	w	MA	San Francisco	San Francisco P O	83	76
C	25	m	w	OH	Sierra	Sierra Twp	89	568
C W	33	m	w	ME	Sacramento	4-Wd Sacramento	77	364
Charles	50	m	w	VA	Kern	Linns Valley P O	73	348
Charles	40	m	w	NY	Kern	Havilah P O	73	336
Charles	32	m	w	SCOT	Yolo	Cache Crk Twp	93	430
Charles	22	m	w	ENGL	San Francisco	San Francisco P O	83	370
Charles E	28	m	w	ME	San Francisco	6-Wd San Francisco	81	146
Chas E	47	m	w	NY	Butte	Chico Twp	70	46
Chas T	24	m	w	IL	Mono	Bridgeport P O	74	282
Christopher	39	m	w	NY	Placer	Bath P O	76	423
Clark	35	m	w	NC	Yolo	Cache Crk Twp	93	429
Com F	39	m	w	VA	Tehama	Paynes Crk Twp	92	160
Delphina	24	f	w	AL	Sacramento	2-Wd Sacramento	77	238
Edmond	65	m	w	NH	San Joaquin	Oneal Twp	86	106
Edw	28	m	w	MA	Alameda	Oakland	68	216
Edward	34	m	w	OH	San Joaquin	Union Twp	86	265
Elias M	38	m	w	NC	Mariposa	Mariposa P O	74	131
Ella	20	f	w	ME	San Francisco	San Francisco P O	80	378
Erastus W	40	m	w	CT	Yuba	New York Twp	93	640
Fred	27	f	w	NY	San Francisco	11-Wd San Francisc	84	554
George	35	m	w	PA	Placer	Roseville P O	76	353
George	30	m	w	IL	Santa Clara	Gilroy Twp	88	82
George	25	m	w	ENGL	Nevada	Grass Valley Twp	75	230
George A	50	m	w	OH	Santa Clara	Santa Clara Twp	88	137
George T	35	m	w	NY	Solano	Maine Prairie Twp	90	50
Gillespie	43	m	w	OH	Alameda	San Leandro	68	96
H B	33	m	w	IL	San Joaquin	Elliott Twp	86	78
Henry	24	m	w	IREL	Mendocino	Navarro & Big Rvr	74	167
Hiram	28	m	w	CANA	San Joaquin	Douglas Twp	86	30
J C	35	m	w	VA	Napa	Napa	75	16
J M	50	m	w	KY	Mendocino	Round Valley Twp	74	219
Jacob	43	m	w	IN	Butte	Kimshew Tpw	70	76
Jacob	42	m	w	MO	Butte	Kimshew Tpw	70	80
James	41	m	w	OH	Solano	Suisun Twp	90	102
James	38	m	w	ME	San Joaquin	1-Wd Stockton	86	127
James	35	m	w	IREL	Alameda	Oakland	68	167
James	29	m	w	NY	San Bernardino	San Bernardino Twp	78	445
James	25	m	w	SCOT	Santa Clara	San Jose Twp	88	222
James F	35	m	w	PA	Yolo	Grafton Twp	93	494
Jennie	20	f	w	PA	San Francisco	San Francisco P O	85	840
Jeremiah	38	m	w	ENGL	Santa Clara	2-Wd San Jose	88	313
Jno P	24	m	w	IREL	Butte	Chico Twp	70	36
Joe	50	m	w	MA	Fresno	Kings Rvr P O	72	210
John	70	m	w	IREL	Yuba	Marysville	93	600
John	51	m	w	SC	Tehama	Stony Crk	92	166
John	48	m	w	ENGL	Merced	Snelling P O	74	272
John	42	m	w	ENGL	Sonoma	Petaluma Twp	91	352
John	39	m	w	IREL	San Francisco	11-Wd San Francisc	84	650
John	38	m	w	PA	El Dorado	Placerville Twp	72	93
John	38	m	w	NY	Solano	Denverton Twp	90	27
John	35	m	w	CANA	Alameda	Murray Twp	68	117
John	31	m	w	IREL	Amador	Amador City P O	69	393
John	28	m	w	IREL	San Francisco	11-Wd San Francisc	84	697
John	28	m	w	NY	Amador	Sutter Crk P O	69	400
John	22	m	w	ENGL	Nevada	Meadow Lake Twp	75	261
John M	25	m	w	SC	Santa Cruz	Santa Cruz	89	421
Josiah	43	m	w	OH	Butte	Oregon Twp	70	134
L W	37	m	w	IA	San Joaquin	2-Wd Stockton	86	184
Leander	50	m	w	ME	Placer	Roseville P O	76	355
Lee	80	m	i	CA	Yolo	Cache Crk Twp	93	427
Lorian	23	m	w	MO	Los Angeles	Los Angeles Twp	73	481
M	22	m	w	PA	Alameda	Oakland	68	175
Mary	40	f	b	MS	San Francisco	San Francisco P O	83	266
Mercy	10	f	w	CA	Sacramento	2-Wd Sacramento	77	249
N R	42	m	w	OH	San Joaquin	Elkhorn Twp	86	55
Nathan	36	m	w	IN	Yolo	Cache Crk Twp	93	423
Newton	32	m	w	IL	Yolo	Fremont Twp	93	477
Ormond	41	m	w	CANA	Sacramento	2-Wd Sacramento	77	238
Patrick	60	m	w	NY	San Joaquin	Douglas Twp	86	32

© 2001 by Heritage Quest. All rights reserved.

Name	Age	S	R	B-PL	County	Locale	Series M593 Roll	Pg
Paul M	55	m	w	OH	Fresno	Kings Rvr P O	72	204
Pony	25	f	i	CA	Klamath	Dillon Twp	73	369
Richard	40	m	w	IREL	San Francisco	11-Wd San Francisc	84	563
Richard	26	m	b	MO	Sacramento	Granite Twp	77	145
Robert	35	m	w	SCOT	Yuba	New York Twp	93	640
Robert W	43	m	w	PA	Klamath	Dillon Twp	73	369
Robt	28	m	w	ME	Alameda	Oakland	68	258
Robt	27	m	w	IREL	Alameda	Oakland	68	167
T L	39	m	w	ME	San Francisco	San Francisco P O	85	812
Thomas	50	m	w	IREL	San Francisco	San Francisco P O	83	143
Thomas	48	m	w	ENGL	San Francisco	San Francisco P O	83	3
Thomas E	41	m	w	MA	Nevada	Grass Valley Twp	75	151
Thomas E	25	m	w	NY	San Francisco	San Francisco P O	85	744
Thomas M	39	m	w	AL	Plumas	Plumas Twp	77	28
Walter M	45	m	w	NH	Tehama	Red Bluff	92	178
Walter M	44	m	w	CA	Butte	Ophir Twp	70	97
William	46	m	w	PA	Klamath	Dillon Twp	73	369
William	44	m	w	IN	Santa Cruz	Santa Cruz	89	407
William	39	m	w	NY	Solano	Rio Vista Twp	90	58
William	37	m	w	SCOT	Placer	Summit P O	76	495
William	34	m	w	ME	Mendocino	Point Arena Twp	74	213
William	23	m	w	MA	San Francisco	6-Wd San Francisco	81	81
William	21	m	w	MA	Sacramento	2-Wd Sacramento	77	239
Winfield S	20	m	w	IL	Yolo	Grafton Twp	93	480
Wm	40	m	w	MA	Butte	Chico Twp	70	45
Wm	35	m	w	IREL	Yuba	Marysville	93	600
Wm	24	m	w	IREL	Butte	Chico Twp	70	36
Wm T	31	m	w	IL	Mono	Bridgeport P O	74	282
ELLIS								
A G	40	m	w	NY	Mariposa	Maxwell Crk P O	74	140
A H	31	m	w	ME	Butte	Oroville Twp	70	137
A L	45	m	w	MA	Alameda	Oakland	68	260
A T	36	m	w	KY	Merced	Snelling P O	74	276
Ab	23	m	w	TN	San Joaquin	Elliott Twp	86	80
Alexander	41	m	w	IREL	San Joaquin	2-Wd Stockton	86	166
Alfred	53	m	w	ME	San Francisco	5-Wd San Francisco	81	16
Annie	34	f	w	IREL	San Francisco	San Francisco P O	80	352
Arden	42	m	w	ME	San Francisco	2-Wd San Francisco	79	277
Arthur	23	m	w	CANA	Santa Cruz	Soquel Twp	89	450
Asa	53	m	w	MO	Los Angeles	El Monte Twp	73	451
Augustus	45	m	w	MA	Shasta	Shasta P O	89	455
Benjam	54	m	w	MO	El Dorado	Placerville Twp	72	104
Benjamin F	38	m	w	ME	San Francisco	11-Wd San Francisc	84	704
Bennet	32	m	w	POLA	Sonoma	Russian Rvr	91	369
C	60	f	w	ME	Alameda	Oakland	68	169
Carrie	24	f	w	NY	San Francisco	8-Wd San Francisco	82	345
Celia	61	f	w	MS	Kern	Linns Valley P O	73	345
Charles	55	m	w	CANA	Alameda	Murray Twp	68	116
Charles	38	m	w	IL	Sutter	Sutter Twp	92	122
Charles	37	m	w	MA	San Francisco	6-Wd San Francisco	81	98
Charles	34	m	w	NORW	San Diego	Fort Yuma Dist	78	463
Charles	32	m	w	MA	San Francisco	San Francisco P O	83	165
Charles	30	m	w	NY	San Francisco	7-Wd San Francisco	81	221
Charles	25	m	w	MO	Sutter	Yuba Twp	92	145
Charles	24	m	w	IL	Amador	Fiddletown P O	69	433
Charles P	48	m	w	MA	Placer	Rocklin Twp	76	468
Chas P	50	m	w	MA	Butte	Chico Twp	70	42
D A	43	m	w	KY	El Dorado	Greenwood Twp	72	55
D W	49	m	w	CT	Santa Clara	Gilroy Twp	88	88
Dan	37	m	w	MA	San Francisco	11-Wd San Francisc	84	682
E	28	m	w	IL	Alameda	Oakland	68	221
Eben	50	m	w	IREL	Butte	Oregon Twp	70	124
Ebner	39	m	w	IA	San Diego	San Diego	78	494
Edmund	49	m	w	ENGL	Sacramento	2-Wd Sacramento	77	251
Eliza	19	f	w	WALE	San Francisco	8-Wd San Francisco	82	402
Evan	36	m	w	ENGL	Calaveras	San Andreas P O	70	173
F P	35	m	w	CT	Napa	Napa Twp	75	29
F W	29	m	w	NY	Napa	Yountville Twp	75	80
Fanny	22	f	w	IA	San Joaquin	2-Wd Stockton	86	189
Frank	35	m	w	IREL	Contra Costa	Martinez P O	71	369
Franklin	38	m	w	NY	Humboldt	Eel Rvr Twp	72	253
George	48	m	w	ME	San Francisco	5-Wd San Francisco	81	11
George	39	m	w	NY	San Francisco	San Francisco P O	80	409
George	26	m	w	ENGL	Nevada	Grass Valley Twp	75	163
George A	37	m	w	ME	Nevada	Eureka Twp	75	137
Guss	18	m	w	POLA	Mendocino	Calpella Twp	74	186
Harriet	40	f	w	IN	Tulare	Tule Rvr Twp	92	267
Harvey	40	m	w	IL	San Francisco	7-Wd San Francisco	81	274
Henry	37	m	w	NY	Sonoma	Salt Point Twp	91	382
Henry	29	m	w	POLA	Mendocino	Ukiah Twp	74	236
Henry	28	m	w	PRUS	Marin	Nicasio Twp	74	16
Henry C	24	m	w	IL	Santa Cruz	Santa Cruz	89	425
Henry H	40	m	w	ME	San Francisco	2-Wd San Francisco	79	284
I W	31	m	w	OH	Sutter	Vernon Twp	92	137
Isaac H	39	m	w	WALE	Siskiyou	Cottonwood Twp	89	590
J	40	m	w	MA	Alameda	Oakland	68	205
J	34	m	w	ENGL	Sierra	Butte Twp	89	509
J A	27	m	w	KY	San Francisco	3-Wd San Francisco	79	314
J D	35	m	w	MA	Solano	Vallejo	90	153
J H	40	m	w	IA	Santa Clara	Gilroy Twp	88	94
J S	20	f	w	MO	Alameda	Murray Twp	68	115
Jackson	41	m	w	VT	Kern	Bakersfield P O	73	361
Jacob M	40	m	w	MO	Sonoma	Santa Rosa	91	417
James	43	m	w	SCOT	San Francisco	8-Wd San Francisco	82	422
James	37	m	w	VT	Santa Clara	Redwood Twp	88	127
James	32	m	w	CANA	Santa Clara	1-Wd San Jose	88	254
James	30	m	w	ENGL	Nevada	Grass Valley Twp	75	203
James	28	m	w	MO	Solano	Silveyville Twp	90	74
James	25	m	w	ENGL	Nevada	Grass Valley Twp	75	231
James H	21	m	w	ENGL	Nevada	Grass Valley Twp	75	232
James M	33	m	w	OH	Placer	Roseville P O	76	351
James M	32	m	w	POLA	Mendocino	Round Valley Twp	74	216
James W	40	m	w	KY	Calaveras	Copperopolis P O	70	262
Jas H	33	m	w	ENGL	Sierra	Gibson Twp	89	542
Jeanett	19	f	w	POLA	Sonoma	Santa Rosa	91	402
Jennie	7	f	w	IA	Sacramento	3-Wd Sacramento	77	309
Jenny	20	f	w	MO	Santa Clara	Gilroy Twp	88	78
John	43	m	w	KY	Shasta	Millville P O	89	491
John	41	m	w	MO	Plumas	Indian Twp	77	15
John	40	m	w	ENGL	Klamath	Liberty Twp	73	374
John	34	m	w	NY	San Francisco	San Francisco P O	80	478
John	27	m	w	ENGL	San Francisco	1-Wd San Francisco	79	43
John	13	m	w	PA	San Francisco	11-Wd San Francisc	84	588
John F	27	m	w	MA	Los Angeles	Los Angeles	73	537
John J	45	m	w	KY	Santa Barbara	Santa Barbara P O	87	482
John Richard	34	m	w	ENGL	Nevada	Grass Valley Twp	75	174
John S	72	m	w	CANA	Nevada	Grass Valley Twp	75	171
Jonathan A	62	m	w	IREL	Amador	Volcano P O	69	387
Jos	36	m	w	MA	Solano	Vallejo	90	178
Jos	30	m	w	IREL	San Francisco	11-Wd San Francisc	84	692
Joseph	51	m	w	ENGL	San Francisco	San Francisco P O	80	476
Joseph	50	m	w	CT	San Francisco	11-Wd San Francisc	84	579
Joseph	34	m	m	CT	San Francisco	San Francisco P O	80	342
Joseph	23	m	w	IL	Mono	Bridgeport P O	74	286
Joseph F	32	m	w	WALE	Siskiyou	Cottonwood Twp	89	590
Joseph W	37	m	w	NY	Nevada	Grass Valley Twp	75	180
Josephus	13	m	w	CA	Plumas	Seneca Twp	77	51
Leander G	32	m	w	KY	Sonoma	Washington Twp	91	469
Leo	40	m	w	CANA	Sacramento	San Joaquin Twp	77	396
Levi	46	m	w	NY	Mendocino	Calpella Twp	74	184
M	21	m	w	ENGL	Sierra	Lincoln Twp	89	550
M A	47	f	m	MA	Tuolumne	Sonora P O	93	311
Martha	14	f	w	IA	Marin	Tomales Twp	74	85
Mary	9	f	w	CA	Sutter	Yuba Twp	92	145
Mary	40	f	w	NY	Contra Costa	Martinez P O	71	409
Mary	31	f	w	NY	San Francisco	6-Wd San Francisco	81	78
Mary B	29	f	w	PRUS	Sonoma	Russian Rvr	91	370
Michael	50	m	w	IREL	San Francisco	2-Wd San Francisco	79	151
Moses C	41	m	w	NY	Yuba	Marysville	93	634
Nathan	36	m	w	POLA	Mendocino	Ukiah Twp	74	236
Nathan R	34	m	w	GA	San Francisco	San Francisco P O	83	283
R A	40	m	w	IL	San Joaquin	1-Wd Stockton	86	126
R B	29	m	w	ENGL	San Joaquin	1-Wd Stockton	86	126
Ralph	57	m	w	NH	San Francisco	5-Wd San Francisco	81	13
Ralph	40	m	w	PA	Napa	Napa	75	51
Ralph J	25	m	w	MA	Los Angeles	San Gabriel Twp	73	594
Ransler	58	m	w	NY	Amador	Amador City P O	69	395
Richard	30	m	w	ENGL	San Francisco	San Francisco P O	83	319
Richard	28	m	w	ENGL	Mariposa	Mariposa P O	74	98
Robert	60	m	w	DE	Nevada	Meadow Lake Twp	75	264
Robt	27	m	w	ENGL	San Joaquin	3-Wd Stockton	86	236
Samuel	51	m	w	ENGL	San Francisco	11-Wd San Francisc	84	465
Samuel	35	m	w	IN	Merced	Snelling P O	74	273
Samuel	26	m	w	ROMA	San Bernardino	San Bernardino Twp	78	416
Sarah	18	f	w	WI	San Joaquin	Dent Twp	86	21
T H	24	m	w	NY	Amador	Amador City P O	69	395
Thomas	39	m	w	TN	Merced	Snelling P O	74	263
Thomas	27	m	w	MN	Colusa	Monroe Twp	71	319
Thomas	25	m	w	MO	Colusa	Colusa Twp	71	284
Thos	28	m	w	IA	Santa Clara	Almaden Twp	88	20
Thos J	27	m	w	IL	Los Angeles	San Jose Twp	73	623
Thos O	61	m	w	VA	Fresno	Kings Rvr P O	72	212
V E	32	m	w	NY	Amador	Sutter Crk P O	69	401
W T	45	m	w	MD	Yuba	Marysville	93	596
William	71	m	w	VA	Sonoma	Sonoma Twp	91	438
William	50	m	w	NY	Marin	San Rafael	74	57
William	45	m	w	ENGL	Los Angeles	El Monte Twp	73	451
William	42	m	w	MA	Sonoma	Petaluma Twp	91	316
William	39	m	w	NY	Solano	Vacaville Twp	90	133
William	32	m	w	IREL	Napa	Napa Twp	75	74
William	27	m	w	MO	Inyo	Bishop Crk Twp	73	317
William	27	m	w	ENGL	San Mateo	Menlo Park P O	87	378
William	27	m	w	WI	San Francisco	11-Wd San Francisc	84	540
William	26	m	w	NY	Santa Clara	2-Wd San Jose	88	336
William	22	m	w	NY	Sacramento	3-Wd Sacramento	77	296
William J	51	m	w	WALE	Sonoma	Sonoma Twp	91	446
William J	36	m	w	MO	Tulare	Tule Rvr Twp	92	262
Wm	60	m	w	VA	Sacramento	4-Wd Sacramento	77	354
Wm	53	m	w	IL	Sacramento	3-Wd Sacramento	77	275
Wm	47	m	w	ENGL	Butte	Wyandotte Twp	70	144
Wm	45	m	w	NJ	San Joaquin	Liberty Twp	86	91
Wm	30	m	w	CANA	San Joaquin	Douglas Twp	86	35
Wm	24	m	w	OH	San Joaquin	1-Wd Stockton	86	141
Wm	24	m	w	NY	Solano	Vallejo	90	200
Wm C	29	m	w	KY	Sonoma	Washington Twp	91	467
Wm H	40	m	w	KY	Sacramento	Brighton Twp	77	78
Wm J	24	m	w	WALE	Butte	Wyandotte Twp	70	146
Wm M	30	m	w	IL	Humboldt	Arcata Twp	72	228
ELLISE								
George	58	m	w	SCOT	San Francisco	7-Wd San Francisco	81	206
ELLISON								
Abram	54	m	w	NH	Yuba	Marysville	93	632
Chas	20	m	w	ENGL	Sutter	Sutter Twp	92	116
Daniel	30	m	w	MO	Yolo	Cache Crk Twp	93	451

© 2001 by Heritage Quest. All rights reserved.

Name	Age	S	R	B-PL	County	Locale	Series M593 Roll	Pg
Ed	25	m	w	SCOT	Alameda	Oakland	68	244
J	48	m	w	MO	San Joaquin	Liberty Twp	86	94
J	15	m	w	CA	Solano	Benicia	90	20
James	40	m	w	IREL	San Francisco	7-Wd San Francisco	81	245
James	34	m	w	ENGL	Yolo	Grafton Twp	93	481
John	39	m	w	NORW	Siskiyou	Butte Twp	89	587
John	24	m	w	CANA	Los Angeles	Los Angeles	73	542
John S	83	m	w	NY	Sacramento	2-Wd Sacramento	77	223
Joseph	35	m	w	NY	Nevada	Bridgeport Twp	75	116
William	39	m	b	GA	Merced	Snelling P O	74	276
Wm	40	m	w	ENGL	San Francisco	2-Wd San Francisco	79	206
ELLMAKER								
Frederick	57	m	w	PA	San Francisco	11-Wd San Francisc	84	569
ELLMORE								
Elizabeth	34	f	w	MA	San Francisco	San Francisco P O	83	236
Harvy	31	m	w	MI	Alameda	Washington Twp	68	293
ELLOTT								
John	36	m	w	IREL	San Francisco	11-Wd San Francisc	84	613
Wesley	42	m	w	NY	Butte	Chico Twp	70	58
ELLRICK								
Moses	35	m	w	NY	San Francisco	5-Wd San Francisco	81	33
ELLS								
Alan	70	m	w	NY	San Francisco	11-Wd San Francisc	84	621
George	40	m	w	VT	El Dorado	Diamond Springs Tw	72	25
ELLSBURY								
A J	41	m	w	MA	Tuolumne	Sonora P O	93	328
Jacob	40	m	w	IN	Napa	Napa	75	23
Wm	49	m	w	KY	Shasta	Shasta P O	89	453
ELLSON								
Edward	21	m	w	NJ	Stanislaus	Empire Twp	92	38
ELLSWORTH								
Albert	19	m	w	MI	Santa Clara	Milpitas Twp	88	115
Amos	35	m	w	NY	San Francisco	5-Wd San Francisco	81	19
Chas F	33	m	w	ME	Butte	Chico Twp	70	26
Henry	36	m	w	IN	Alameda	Washington Twp	68	291
Herman	41	m	w	IN	Calaveras	San Andreas P O	70	211
Jno C	30	m	w	ME	Butte	Oregon Twp	70	134
Jno H	45	m	w	CT	Butte	Kimshew Tpw	70	83
L	32	f	w	NY	Alameda	Oakland	68	199
L Stoten	30	m	w	CT	Alameda	Brooklyn Twp	68	43
Lee	42	m	w	NY	Sonoma	Petaluma Twp	91	314
Levi	37	m	w	NY	San Francisco	8-Wd San Francisco	82	368
Mary	50	f	w	NY	San Francisco	San Francisco P O	80	417
Orlando	24	m	w	NY	San Diego	Julian Dist	78	471
R S	39	m	w	OH	San Joaquin	3-Wd Stockton	86	221
Simon	35	m	w	ME	San Francisco	5-Wd San Francisco	81	19
Stephen	32	m	w	NH	Kern	Kernville P O	73	368
Stephen	25	m	w	CANA	Stanislaus	Empire Twp	92	53
Timothy	47	m	w	CT	San Francisco	San Francisco P O	83	96
William	60	m	w	CANA	Contra Costa	Martinez P O	71	411
Wm	39	m	w	CANA	Santa Barbara	Santa Barbara P O	87	473
Wm E	37	m	w	MA	Sacramento	Center Twp	77	87
ELLU								
Henry	19	m	w	IN	Siskiyou	Callahan P O	89	631
ELLUMS								
George	40	m	w	IREL	Santa Clara	Santa Clara Twp	88	143
ELLWELL								
Lot	63	m	w	MA	San Francisco	San Francisco P O	83	248
Y	12	m	w	CA	Alameda	Oakland	68	243
ELLWOOD								
E L	29	m	w	MI	Solano	Benicia	90	12
Thos	47	m	w	CANA	Solano	Vallejo	90	160
Tilden B	45	m	w	MA	El Dorado	Placerville Twp	72	94
ELLWORTH								
Fredk B	27	m	w	ENGL	Placer	Bath P O	76	439
ELLYSIOUS								
Mary	25	f	w	US	Nevada	Grass Valley Twp	75	230
ELMADO								
John	60	m	i	MEXI	Inyo	Cerro Gordo Twp	73	323
ELMANS								
Rose	24	f	w	MEXI	San Francisco	San Francisco P O	80	464
ELMAR								
Casper	23	m	w	SWIT	San Francisco	6-Wd San Francisco	81	155
ELMARES								
Frederick	57	m	w	FRAN	Mariposa	Mariposa P O	74	101
ELMENDORF								
Wm	34	m	w	NY	Santa Clara	Gilroy Twp	88	69
ELMER								
Edwd	44	m	w	AUST	Marin	San Rafael Twp	74	35
Marshal	38	m	w	MA	San Francisco	San Francisco P O	83	96
ELMES								
Henry	40	m	w	NORW	San Francisco	7-Wd San Francisco	81	281
ELMINGER								
Lee	40	m	w	SWIT	Sacramento	Sutter Twp	77	389
ELMISE								
Ellen	30	f	w	CA	San Francisco	11-Wd San Francisc	84	689
ELMOND								
Benjamin	24	m	w	MO	Stanislaus	Empire Twp	92	36
C	61	m	w	NY	Sonoma	Russian Rvr	91	369
ELMONDORF								
Damont	48	m	w	NJ	El Dorado	Placerville	72	108
ELMONDRON								
J W	43	m	w	IL	El Dorado	Georgetown Twp	72	47
ELMORE								
Abie C	45	f	w	ME	San Francisco	6-Wd San Francisco	81	124
Ambrose	24	m	w	MO	Stanislaus	Empire Twp	92	31
Anderson P	48	m	w	SC	Stanislaus	Empire Twp	92	31
Benj	45	m	b	TN	Santa Barbara	San Buenaventura P	87	432
Frederick	25	m	w	MA	San Francisco	6-Wd San Francisco	81	124
George	31	m	w	IL	Amador	Ione City P O	69	359
Hiram T	48	m	w	KY	Tehama	Red Bluff	92	173
J J	39	m	w	KY	Tehama	Stony Crk	92	198
James	27	m	w	MO	Stanislaus	Empire Twp	92	36
Jane	22	f	w	IREL	San Francisco	11-Wd San Francisc	84	609
M Gage	36	m	w	NY	San Francisco	8-Wd San Francisco	82	322
Mary	20	f	w	MO	Stanislaus	Empire Twp	92	36
Pat	40	m	w	IREL	Sierra	Gibson Twp	89	541
R H	22	m	w	MO	Tehama	Red Bluff	92	180
Samuel	57	m	w	NH	Sonoma	Vallejo Twp	91	450
Waldo	35	m	w	AR	Shasta	Dog Crk P O	89	471
Wm W	25	m	w	MO	Shasta	American Ranch P O	89	500
ELMS								
Annie	25	f	w	ENGL	San Francisco	San Francisco P O	80	483
J D	30	m	w	MEXI	Alameda	Oakland	68	159
ELOS								
Nicklas	22	m	i	MEXI	Inyo	Lone Pine Twp	73	332
ELOTZ								
Frederick	50	m	w	PRUS	Sacramento	2-Wd Sacramento	77	223
ELOYD								
W O	36	m	w	NY	San Francisco	San Francisco P O	85	821
ELPHIC								
Thomas	48	m	w	ENGL	Solano	Suisun Twp	90	108
ELPHICK								
Esther	65	f	w	ENGL	Marin	Bolinas Twp	74	8
George	36	m	w	ENGL	Marin	Bolinas Twp	74	7
Henry	30	m	w	ENGL	Marin	Tomales Twp	74	78
Thomas	70	m	w	ENGL	Marin	Tomales Twp	74	78
Thomas	26	m	w	ENGL	Marin	Bolinas Twp	74	5
ELROD								
Robt	68	m	w	NC	Santa Clara	Burnett Twp	88	39
S Noah	40	m	w	IN	Santa Clara	Gilroy Twp	88	101
ELROY								
Mack	48	m	w	NY	Calaveras	Copperopolis P O	70	240
Mary	37	f	w	IREL	San Francisco	8-Wd San Francisco	82	452
ELSASSER								
Charles	31	m	w	WURT	San Francisco	8-Wd San Francisco	82	431
Jonas	28	m	w	BAVA	San Francisco	8-Wd San Francisco	82	446
ELSCOSCOR								
F	26	m	w	PRUS	Sierra	Butte Twp	89	509
ELSEN								
John	41	m	w	PRUS	Placer	Bath P O	76	426
ELSER								
Louisa	34	f	w	PRUS	San Francisco	5-Wd San Francisco	81	8
ELSEY								
Charles	40	m	w	ENGL	Colusa	Spring Valley Twp	71	342
Henry	33	m	w	ENGL	Alameda	Brooklyn Twp	68	42
Henry	30	m	w	ENGL	Alameda	Oakland	68	182
Robert M	54	m	w	MO	Yolo	Buckeye Twp	93	415
Wiede	42	m	w	MA	Placer	Bath P O	76	433
ELSIE								
Fredk	46	m	w	HANO	Stanislaus	Empire Twp	92	54
ELSIM								
Maria	21	f	b	MEXI	San Joaquin	1-Wd Stockton	86	121
ELSINGER								
Leopold	33	m	w	PRUS	San Francisco	8-Wd San Francisco	82	356
ELSMORE								
Bery G	37	m	w	ME	Santa Cruz	Soquel Twp	89	448
ELSON								
Aca	36	m	w	OH	Shasta	Dog Crk P O	89	471
Edwd	35	m	w	IREL	San Francisco	1-Wd San Francisco	79	74
Elizabeth	20	f	w	CANA	San Luis Obispo	Salinas Twp	87	290
Wm	64	m	w	ENGL	Sonoma	Bodega Twp	91	255
Wm	60	m	w	WI	Butte	Oregon Twp	70	129
ELSOR								
Charles	25	m	w	PRUS	Stanislaus	San Joaquin Twp	92	80
ELSTEIN								
Henry	40	m	w	HANO	San Francisco	2-Wd San Francisco	79	140
ELSTER								
Alonzo	36	m	w	NY	Tulare	Venice Twp	92	275
ELSTON								
A	29	m	w	KY	Sacramento	4-Wd Sacramento	77	325
Charles	54	m	w	ENGL	Plumas	Seneca Twp	77	49
J B	34	m	w	OH	Merced	Snelling P O	74	274
Mary	35	f	w	IL	Merced	Snelling P O	74	274
ELSWORTH								
Daniel	31	m	w	NY	Yuba	Parks Bar Twp	93	649
Geo	48	m	w	ME	Humboldt	Arcata Twp	72	234
George	38	m	w	NY	Solano	Suisun Twp	90	99
George	35	m	w	NY	Solano	Green Valley Twp	90	37
Henry L	38	m	w	OH	Sacramento	Natomas Twp	77	170
J	50	m	w	IREL	Alameda	Murray Twp	68	124
John	10	m	w	WI	Sacramento	San Joaquin Twp	77	395
John H	35	m	w	ENGL	Placer	Bath P O	76	441
L	32	f	w	IL	Alameda	Oakland	68	173
ELTING								
David	44	m	w	NY	Siskiyou	Butte Twp	89	586
ELTON								
James	46	m	w	RI	Santa Cruz	Santa Cruz	89	408
Samuel N	34	m	w	CT	Nevada	Eureka Twp	75	135
ELTRINGHAM								
John	37	m	w	PA	Calaveras	Copperopolis P O	70	247
ELUM								
B W	60	m	w	MO	San Joaquin	Liberty Twp	86	87
W R	27	m	w	MO	San Joaquin	Liberty Twp	86	90

© 2001 by Heritage Quest. All rights reserved.

Name	Age	S	R	B-PL	County	Locale	Roll (Series M593)	Pg
ELUSE								
G	37	m	w	ITAL	Amador	Jackson P O	69	337
ELVERTON								
H S	28	m	w	NY	Sutter	Sutter Twp	92	126
ELVINS								
John	34	m	w	ENGL	San Mateo	Redwood Twp	87	368
ELVISH								
Robert	45	m	w	ENGL	Humboldt	Mattole Twp	72	285
ELWAGNER								
Herman	28	m	w	BAVA	Sacramento	2-Wd Sacramento	77	239
ELWELL								
Chas	51	m	w	MA	Tuolumne	Big Oak Flat P O	93	404
D T	26	m	w	PA	Sacramento	Lee Twp	77	161
David	38	m	w	MA	Alameda	Brooklyn Twp	68	40
Edward J	25	m	w	NY	San Francisco	6-Wd San Francisco	81	118
Frank	32	m	w	ME	Alameda	Hayward	68	79
Guadalupe	40	m	w	MA	Santa Barbara	San Buenaventura P	87	423
Henry	11	m	w	CA	Tuolumne	Big Oak Flat P O	93	402
J K P	24	m	w	DE	Sutter	Sutter Twp	92	124
John	46	m	w	MA	San Francisco	San Francisco P O	83	283
Juan	29	m	w	CA	Santa Barbara	San Buenaventura P	87	433
Sarah S	24	f	w	WI	Yuba	Slate Range Bar Tw	93	675
Stephen B	50	m	w	NH	Sacramento	2-Wd Sacramento	77	224
William	49	m	w	PA	Plumas	Quartz Twp	77	34
William	29	m	w	KY	Kern	Havilah P O	73	336
Willm	33	m	w	CA	Santa Barbara	San Buenaventura P	87	433
ELWELLS								
Louis	25	m	w	NY	San Francisco	5-Wd San Francisco	81	36
ELWICHO								
Pedro	26	m	w	MEXI	San Francisco	San Francisco P O	80	474
ELWIN								
David	20	m	w	IA	Tehama	Paskenta Twp	92	164
Thos	28	m	w	OH	Nevada	Bridgeport Twp	75	122
ELWIS								
Christopher	74	m	w	HANO	Placer	Bath P O	76	421
ELWOOD								
Ada	16	f	w	NY	Nevada	Eureka Twp	75	134
Fredrick	27	m	w	ENGL	San Francisco	San Francisco P O	83	209
G	28	m	w	IREL	Alameda	Murray Twp	68	112
Geo	22	m	w	NY	San Francisco	1-Wd San Francisco	79	64
John	48	m	w	CANA	Mariposa	Mariposa P O	74	135
Jonathan	30	m	w	IREL	Calaveras	San Andreas P O	70	203
Martin	28	m	w	IREL	Marin	Nicasio Twp	74	16
Matthew	35	m	w	IREL	Santa Clara	2-Wd San Jose	88	332
Thos	51	m	w	PA	Sacramento	Alabama Twp	77	62
ELWORTH								
Bernard	34	m	w	IREL	Santa Clara	San Jose Twp	88	186
Hans	35	m	w	NORW	San Francisco	7-Wd San Francisco	81	276
Henry	35	m	w	MECK	San Francisco	1-Wd San Francisco	79	110
ELWORTHY								
Fred C	26	m	w	ENGL	Sacramento	4-Wd Sacramento	77	349
ELY								
Aaron	45	m	w	NY	San Francisco	5-Wd San Francisco	81	7
Andrew	34	m	w	OH	Sacramento	2-Wd Sacramento	77	244
Anna	40	f	w	IREL	Alameda	Oakland	68	146
Benjamin	49	m	w	MO	Yolo	Buckeye Twp	93	415
Charles	38	m	w	BOHE	San Francisco	11-Wd San Francisc	84	658
David	59	m	w	OH	Humboldt	Eel Rvr Twp	72	253
David H	33	m	w	NY	San Luis Obispo	Santa Rosa Twp	87	324
Drury	32	m	w	MO	Yolo	Buckeye Twp	93	416
Elisha	44	m	w	NY	Sonoma	Washington Twp	91	470
Geo W	36	m	b	MO	Sonoma	Healdsburg & Mendo	91	283
Isaac J	32	m	w	MO	Yolo	Grafton Twp	93	486
James	46	m	w	MO	Solano	Denverton Twp	90	27
John	37	m	w	KY	Colusa	Colusa	71	292
John Heny	19	m	w	CT	San Francisco	8-Wd San Francisco	82	368
John James	50	m	w	IREL	Solano	Denverton Twp	90	27
John L	35	m	w	OH	Humboldt	Eel Rvr Twp	72	253
Margaret	76	f	w	KY	Yolo	Buckeye Twp	93	414
Marks	26	m	w	PRUS	Marin	San Rafael Twp	74	46
Nicholas	40	m	w	IREL	San Francisco	7-Wd San Francisco	81	239
Thomas	35	m	w	MO	El Dorado	Placerville	72	120
Thomas B	20	m	w	MO	Yolo	Buckeye Twp	93	414
William	45	m	w	PA	Siskiyou	Scott Valley Twp	89	610
William	41	m	w	NY	Santa Cruz	Santa Cruz	89	428
ELYBUR								
E S	42	m	w	PA	San Joaquin	3-Wd Stockton	86	215
ELYCOMB								
James	45	m	w	ME	Trinity	Weaverville Pct	92	222
EM								
You	30	m	c	CHIN	Yuba	Rose Bar Twp	93	656
EMAM								
Frank	37	m	w	FRAN	San Francisco	San Francisco P O	80	333
EMANDIS								
Florentina	60	f	w	MEXI	San Francisco	2-Wd San Francisco	79	178
EMANES								
Manuel	42	m	w	PA	Plumas	Washington Twp	77	52
EMANUEL								
Ellen	30	f	w	NY	Sacramento	2-Wd Sacramento	77	207
Harris	29	m	w	RUSS	San Francisco	1-Wd San Francisco	79	58
Isaac	50	m	w	ENGL	San Francisco	San Francisco P O	80	411
Lewis	41	m	w	ENGL	San Francisco	San Francisco P O	83	97
Marcus C	34	m	w	ENGL	San Francisco	6-Wd San Francisco	81	94
Peter	50	m	b	PORT	San Mateo	Half Moon Bay P O	87	405
Victor	42	m	w	FRAN	Marin	San Rafael Twp	74	47
EMAY								
Victor	30	m	w	CANA	Sacramento	3-Wd Sacramento	77	314
EMBAM								
E	32	m	w	SWED	Alameda	Oakland	68	172
EMBERRY								
Margret	23	f	w	IREL	San Francisco	1-Wd San Francisco	79	79
EMBERS								
Janie	24	f	b	AR	Los Angeles	Los Angeles	73	529
EMBERSON								
Chas	27	m	w	GA	Sonoma	Santa Rosa	91	422
EMBERTON								
John T	38	m	w	KY	Siskiyou	Cottonwood Twp	89	591
EMDEN								
John	28	m	w	PRUS	San Francisco	San Francisco P O	83	243
EMDY								
John	38	m	w	WURT	Amador	Sutter Crk P O	69	408
EMELE								
Gayin	17	m	w	MEXI	Stanislaus	Empire Twp	92	66
Loretta	37	m	w	FRAN	Stanislaus	Empire Twp	92	66
EMELIA								
Mary	19	f	w	PORT	Alameda	Hayward	68	74
EMELIN								
Ernest	21	m	w	FRAN	San Joaquin	1-Wd Stockton	86	134
EMELLO								
Jose	40	m	w	CA	Merced	Snelling P O	74	251
EMER								
Henry	39	m	w	NY	Sutter	Yuba Twp	92	151
EMERAGE								
John	40	m	w	PRUS	Santa Clara	San Jose Twp	88	181
EMEREA								
Bell	18	f	w	CA	Contra Costa	Martinez P O	71	434
EMERICK								
Joseph	54	m	w	FRAN	San Francisco	San Francisco P O	85	800
EMERINE								
C	17	f	w	IREL	Sacramento	3-Wd Sacramento	77	281
J	47	m	w	PRUS	Sierra	Forest	89	536
EMERS								
Ju	37	m	w	ITAL	San Joaquin	1-Wd Stockton	86	155
EMERSON								
Alfred	24	m	w	PA	San Francisco	1-Wd San Francisco	79	103
C	24	m	w	IL	Amador	Ione City P O	69	360
Calvin	38	m	w	ME	Sutter	Yuba Twp	92	149
Carlos B	46	m	w	ME	Santa Clara	Fremont Twp	88	61
Chas	61	m	w	MA	Colusa	Spring Valley Twp	71	337
Chas	29	m	w	VA	Sacramento	1-Wd Sacramento	77	202
Chester	15	m	w	CA	Stanislaus	Buena Vista Twp	92	13
D L	40	m	w	ME	Alameda	Oakland	68	162
David	47	m	w	OH	Napa	Napa	75	35
Donald B	48	m	w	NY	San Bernardino	San Bernardino Twp	78	445
Frank	26	m	w	ME	Los Angeles	Los Angeles	73	535
Geo	30	m	w	ME	Yuba	Rose Bar Twp	93	654
Geo	23	m	w	ME	Solano	Vallejo	90	169
George	35	m	w	MA	Santa Cruz	Santa Cruz	89	421
George	35	m	w	CANA	Alameda	Brooklyn Twp	68	42
Henry	63	m	w	KY	Sonoma	Analy Twp	91	234
Henry F	29	m	w	MO	Sonoma	Salt Point	91	381
Hiram S	36	m	w	MA	Los Angeles	Wilmington Twp	73	635
James	48	m	w	ENGL	Alameda	Washington Twp	68	282
James	39	m	w	MA	San Francisco	San Francisco P O	85	870
James	38	m	w	PA	San Francisco	1-Wd San Francisco	79	56
John	45	m	w	TN	Napa	Napa Twp	75	65
John	45	m	w	MA	San Francisco	San Francisco P O	80	346
John	32	m	w	TN	Sonoma	Healdsburg & Mendo	91	283
John Wm	30	m	w	MA	San Francisco	8-Wd San Francisco	82	295
Joice	42	m	w	SWED	Alameda	Washington Twp	68	298
L	40	m	w	OH	Alameda	Alameda	68	5
L G	37	m	w	ME	Solano	Vallejo	90	205
Levy	30	m	w	OH	Solano	Silveyville Twp	90	88
Lucy O	28	f	w	ME	Contra Costa	Martinez P O	71	373
Lulu	11	f	b	AFRI	Santa Clara	2-Wd San Jose	88	313
Lydia D	39	f	w	NH	San Francisco	8-Wd San Francisco	82	332
Mark	39	m	w	OH	San Mateo	Pescadero P O	87	409
Moses	48	m	w	NY	Amador	Fiddletown P O	69	426
Nehimiah	40	m	w	ME	San Francisco	San Francisco P O	80	410
Oliver	41	m	w	NORW	Sutter	Yuba Twp	92	148
Olof	38	m	w	SWED	San Francisco	San Francisco P O	83	348
Oscar	24	m	w	ME	Santa Clara	Alviso Twp	88	23
Philip	40	m	w	TN	San Francisco	5-Wd San Francisco	81	12
Richard	43	m	w	NH	Santa Cruz	Santa Cruz	89	420
S	38	f	w	IREL	Lassen	Susanville Twp	73	441
Silas B	49	m	w	ME	Santa Clara	Fremont Twp	88	61
W B	28	m	w	MO	Monterey	Monterey Twp	74	343
W H	43	m	w	MA	San Francisco	San Francisco P O	83	277
William	35	m	w	ME	San Francisco	San Francisco P O	80	355
Wm	46	m	w	NY	Solano	Vallejo	90	145
Zack	21	m	w	PA	Butte	Ophir Twp	70	108
EMERT								
D	30	m	w	OH	Alameda	Murray Twp	68	115
Joseph	36	m	w	IN	Alameda	Murray Twp	68	116
EMERY								
Allen	32	m	w	ME	Siskiyou	Callahan P O	89	629
August	22	m	w	PRUS	San Luis Obispo	Salinas Twp	87	291
Benj	42	m	w	ME	Nevada	Meadow Lake Twp	75	269
Chas	35	m	w	ME	San Francisco	San Francisco P O	85	863
E E	19	m	w	MA	Solano	Vallejo	90	201
E H	46	m	w	NH	Shasta	Horsetown P O	89	505
G W	48	m	w	ME	Del Norte	Crescent	71	464
Henry	41	m	w	ME	Solano	Vallejo	90	192
Henry	27	m	w	ME	San Diego	Milquaty Dist	78	476

© 2001 by Heritage Quest. All rights reserved.

Series M593

Name	Age	S	R	B-PL	County	Locale	Roll	Pg
J S	49	m	w	NH	Alameda	Oakland	68	231
Jesse	44	m	w	ME	San Joaquin	Douglas Twp	86	36
John	42	m	w	ME	Alameda	Eden Twp	68	72
John	42	m	w	AR	Alameda	Oakland	68	252
John	41	m	w	NY	Solano	Vacaville Twp	90	133
John	40	m	w	ENGL	Solano	Vacaville Twp	90	137
John G	40	m	w	ME	San Francisco	San Francisco P O	83	355
Joseph	50	m	w	ME	San Francisco	11-Wd San Francisc	84	516
Joseph	47	m	w	CANA	Yuba	East Bear Rvr Twp	93	544
Josiah	25	m	w	ME	San Francisco	11-Wd San Francisc	84	498
Josiah B	50	m	w	OH	Sonoma	Analy Twp	91	231
Josiah L	30	m	w	ME	San Francisco	San Francisco P O	83	86
M	14	f	w	MA	Alameda	Oakland	68	259
Maria	32	f	w	ENGL	Santa Clara	2-Wd San Jose	88	292
Thatcher	30	m	w	ME	San Francisco	San Francisco P O	85	801
Thos	47	m	w	MA	San Francisco	8-Wd San Francisco	82	367
W P	32	m	w	IL	Sacramento	4-Wd Sacramento	77	353
Webster	48	m	w	NY	Nevada	Rough & Ready Twp	75	326
William	28	m	w	ME	San Francisco	11-Wd San Francisc	84	498
William	23	m	w	ENGL	Santa Clara	1-Wd San Jose	88	252
William S	52	m	w	ME	San Diego	Milquaty Dist	78	476
EMEY								
Melissa	33	m	w	ME	Butte	Ophir Twp	70	100
EMHOFF								
Peter	56	m	w	BADE	Santa Clara	2-Wd San Jose	88	335
EMICH								
Charles N	47	m	w	MD	San Bernardino	San Bernardino Twp	78	416
EMILE								
Polita	38	m	w	FRAN	Marin	San Rafael Twp	74	34
Teresa	10	f	w	CA	Marin	San Rafael	74	53
EMILES								
Julius F	25	m	w	MA	San Francisco	San Francisco P O	83	195
EMILIA								
Marion	27	f	w	AZOR	Placer	Newcastle Twp	76	474
EMILLE								
Louis E	29	m	w	FRAN	San Francisco	1-Wd San Francisco	79	49
EMINAS								
Jose	18	m	w	MEXI	Fresno	Millerton P O	72	166
EMING								
Peter	38	m	w	BADE	Placer	Auburn P O	76	358
EMINGER								
Daniel	41	m	w	WURT	San Francisco	San Francisco P O	83	45
Jacob	57	m	w	PA	Amador	Volcano P O	69	387
EMINGTON								
F C	37	m	w	CT	San Joaquin	2-Wd Stockton	86	183
EMIS								
John	40	m	w	IL	San Joaquin	2-Wd Stockton	86	164
EMISGUES								
Olivares	38	m	w	CHIL	Calaveras	San Andreas P O	70	196
EMKEY								
Charles	46	m	w	PRUS	Contra Costa	Martinez P O	71	442
EMLAY								
Eli	40	m	w	CANA	Santa Clara	Gilroy Twp	88	69
EMMA								
Ah	28	f	c	CHIN	Amador	Fiddletown P O	69	427
Julia	11	f	i	CA	Solano	Green Valley Twp	90	41
EMMAL								
Jos B	55	m	w	NJ	San Francisco	8-Wd San Francisco	82	328
EMMANS								
Charles	38	m	w	PA	Santa Clara	1-Wd San Jose	88	255
EMME								
Claud	64	m	w	FRAN	Alameda	Oakland	68	220
Olim	35	m	w	CANA	Alameda	Oakland	68	251
EMMEL								
Catherine	56	f	w	IREL	Marin	San Rafael	74	54
EMMER								
Joseph	29	m	w	HESS	Sutter	Nicolaus Twp	92	107
EMMERIC								
Hattie B	39	f	w	DE	Yuba	Bullards Bar P O	93	551
EMMERICK								
George R	34	m	w	IL	Stanislaus	San Joaquin Twp	92	70
EMMERSON								
Anna	3	f	w	CA	San Joaquin	Elkhorn Twp	86	57
Bersvan E	41	m	w	NORW	Plumas	Quartz Twp	77	35
D W	38	m	w	MA	San Francisco	San Francisco P O	85	830
Daniel J	33	m	w	MA	Alpine	Silver Mtn P O	69	306
Edward S	37	m	w	MO	San Luis Obispo	San Luis Obispo Tw	87	304
Enoch A	51	m	w	ME	Yuba	North East Twp	93	643
Geo T	40	m	w	MA	San Francisco	7-Wd San Francisco	81	232
H G	38	m	w	VA	San Joaquin	Elkhorn Twp	86	62
Jerdon	27	m	w	PA	Santa Barbara	Santa Barbara P O	87	484
John H	33	m	w	IA	Fresno	Millerton P O	72	186
L A	23	f	w	NY	Santa Clara	Gilroy Twp	88	75
Levi	47	m	w	NH	San Bernardino	San Bernardino Twp	78	453
R	60	m	w	MA	Alameda	Oakland	68	196
Saml	40	m	w	ENGL	Butte	Oregon Twp	70	129
EMMERT								
Michael	24	m	w	MD	Yolo	Grafton Twp	93	490
EMMET								
Edwd	31	m	w	NY	San Francisco	1-Wd San Francisco	79	112
M	34	m	w	OH	Solano	Vallejo	90	210
Michael	24	m	w	MD	Yolo	Grafton Twp	93	496
EMMETT								
Temple	50	m	w	NY	San Francisco	6-Wd San Francisco	81	120
EMMONS								
Chas	38	m	w	MO	Butte	Chico Twp	70	38
Edd S	17	m	w	MA	San Francisco	San Francisco P O	83	203
Elisha	44	m	w	NH	Nevada	Grass Valley Twp	75	153
F W	38	m	w	NY	Alameda	Oakland	68	263
H C	39	m	w	NY	Alameda	Oakland	68	212
Horatio	42	m	w	NY	Plumas	Seneca Twp	77	49
Hosiah C	74	m	w	CT	Yolo	Buckeye Twp	93	413
J	27	m	w	WALE	Alameda	Murray Twp	68	108
J W	37	m	w	MA	San Joaquin	Elkhorn Twp	86	57
J W	26	m	w	MA	Sacramento	Sutter Twp	77	389
James	40	m	w	MO	Monterey	San Juan Twp	74	414
John	44	m	w	OH	Yuba	Marysville	93	602
Josiah	29	m	w	ME	San Francisco	1-Wd San Francisco	79	89
Lewis	38	m	w	CT	Nevada	Nevada Twp	75	290
Polly	52	f	w	NY	Sacramento	2-Wd Sacramento	77	228
S D	42	m	w	NY	Marin	San Rafael Twp	74	38
Samuel	40	m	w	OH	Amador	Volcano P O	69	387
Theodore F	40	m	w	NJ	Plumas	Indian Twp	77	13
Wm	42	m	w	PRUS	Sacramento	4-Wd Sacramento	77	337
EMMORDS								
D H	38	f	w	MI	Sacramento	1-Wd Sacramento	77	175
EMOND								
Henry	31	m	w	MI	Solano	Vacaville Twp	90	135
EMONOGLVI								
Deicaso	27	m	w	ITAL	San Francisco	1-Wd San Francisco	79	114
EMONS								
Samuel	38	m	w	NY	Amador	Jackson P O	69	348
EMORAY								
Rosa	47	f	w	MO	San Joaquin	2-Wd Stockton	86	202
EMOREY								
James	42	m	w	MO	San Bernardino	San Bernardino Twp	78	436
EMORY								
Augustus E	32	m	w	ME	Stanislaus	Buena Vista Twp	92	12
Charles	35	m	w	ME	Alameda	Oakland	68	182
Charles	17	m	w	CA	Santa Cruz	Santa Cruz	89	433
Chas G	34	m	w	ME	San Francisco	San Francisco P O	85	728
Edwd F	39	m	w	PA	San Francisco	1-Wd San Francisco	79	86
George	36	m	w	NY	San Francisco	5-Wd San Francisco	81	33
Gordon J	35	m	w	CANA	Santa Cruz	Watsonville	89	364
J	27	m	w	KY	Alameda	Oakland	68	240
Me	42	m	w	ME	Amador	Drytown P O	69	418
Ned	35	m	w	NY	Santa Clara	Almaden Twp	88	19
Nelson	30	m	w	MA	San Francisco	8-Wd San Francisco	82	441
Sherley	67	m	w	ME	Stanislaus	Buena Vista Twp	92	12
Simeon	31	m	b	PA	Sacramento	2-Wd Sacramento	77	238
EMPARO								
Bringus	18	f	w	CA	San Francisco	6-Wd San Francisco	81	97
EMPERO								
Victor	40	m	w	CHIL	Santa Clara	Fremont Twp	88	59
EMPEY								
Beak	32	m	w	CANA	Placer	Auburn P O	76	378
Charles	44	m	w	CANA	San Francisco	2-Wd San Francisco	79	176
William E	29	m	w	CANA	Santa Clara	1-Wd San Jose	88	238
EMPIE								
Joseph H	3	m	w	NY	Sacramento	Brighton Twp	77	71
Mary	76	f	w	NY	Sacramento	Brighton Twp	77	71
EMPY								
Geo	29	m	w	ENGL	Butte	Ophir Twp	70	95
John	30	m	w	CANA	Contra Costa	Martinez P O	71	450
EMRICK								
Geo E	19	m	w	PA	Mendocino	Little Lake Twp	74	193
John	32	m	w	GERM	San Luis Obispo	San Luis Obispo Tw	87	316
EMROP								
N	26	m	w	GERM	Solano	Vallejo	90	173
EMSBERY								
J J	50	m	w	SCOT	San Joaquin	Liberty Twp	86	90
EMSLY								
Martha	20	f	w	IREL	Los Angeles	Los Angeles	73	504
Oun	22	m	w	NY	Alpine	Silver Mtn P O	69	306
EMVELER								
Henry	35	m	w	PRUS	San Francisco	San Francisco P O	80	483
EN								
---	40	m	c	CHIN	Siskiyou	Cottonwood Twp	89	593
Ah	28	m	c	CHIN	Los Angeles	Los Angeles	73	566
Chee	28	m	c	CHIN	Butte	Wyandotte Twp	70	143
Chong	40	m	c	CHIN	Yuba	Slate Range Bar Tw	93	678
Fong	29	m	c	CHIN	Calaveras	San Andreas P O	70	211
Gow	31	m	c	CHIN	Inyo	Independence Twp	73	326
Lee	20	m	c	CHIN	San Mateo	Schoolhouse Statio	87	332
Lon	52	m	c	CHIN	Calaveras	San Andreas P O	70	162
Toy	18	m	c	CHIN	Butte	Wyandotte Twp	70	148
Yon Tong	67	m	c	CHIN	Sacramento	1-Wd Sacramento	77	196
ENANASS								
Angelo	36	m	w	AZOR	Monterey	Castroville Twp	74	334
ENAS								
George	28	m	w	MA	San Francisco	San Francisco P O	83	123
John	38	m	w	PORT	Butte	Ophir Twp	70	105
John	36	m	w	PORT	Alameda	Alvarado	68	305
John	35	m	w	PORT	Nevada	Rough & Ready Twp	75	336
John	21	m	w	PORT	Stanislaus	Empire Twp	92	37
Joseph	37	m	w	AZOR	Santa Cruz	Santa Cruz Twp	89	383
Joseph D	36	m	w	MA	San Francisco	6-Wd San Francisco	81	142
Lewis	37	m	w	PORT	Nevada	Grass Valley Twp	75	227
Maria	25	f	w	PORT	San Mateo	Half Moon Bay P O	87	400
ENASCIO								
Manuel	48	m	w	AZOR	Santa Cruz	Santa Cruz	89	429
ENASHIO								
Palas	48	m	w	MEXI	Yuba	Marysville	93	574

© 2001 by Heritage Quest. All rights reserved.

California 1870 Census

Series M593

Name	Age	S	R	B-PL	County	Locale	Roll	Pg
ENASTASIA								
Anna	25	f	w	IREL	San Francisco	8-Wd San Francisco	82	323
ENASTROM								
George	38	m	w	NORW	Mendocino	Casper & Big Rvr	74	164
John	31	m	w	SWED	Mendocino	Casper & Big Rvr	74	164
ENBORN								
Mary	12	f	w	CA	Sonoma	Petaluma Twp	91	336
ENCHOVE								
Thos J	40	m	w	OH	Butte	Hamilton Twp	70	62
ENCINA								
Augustine	30	m	w	MEXI	San Luis Obispo	Arroyo Grande Twp	87	272
Pasadez	19	m	w	MEXI	Los Angeles	Los Angeles Twp	73	473
ENCINAS								
Guadalupe	50	m	w	MEXI	Fresno	Millerton P O	72	155
Jesus	25	m	w	MEXI	Fresno	Millerton P O	72	154
Jose	18	m	w	MEXI	Santa Barbara	Santa Barbara P O	87	486
Juan	25	m	w	MEXI	San Luis Obispo	San Luis Obispo Tw	87	313
ENCINES								
Prudento	58	m	i	MEXI	Inyo	Cerro Gordo Twp	73	321
ENCK								
---	30	m	c	CHIN	Siskiyou	Cottonwood Twp	89	594
ENCO								
Vicorina	40	m	w	MEXI	Fresno	Millerton P O	72	153
END								
George	24	m	w	FRAN	San Mateo	San Mateo P O	87	349
ENDEAN								
William	34	m	w	ENGL	Placer	Dutch Flat P O	76	401
ENDERLEIN								
Wm	42	m	w	PRUS	Sierra	Eureka Twp	89	524
ENDERSON								
J	55	m	w	ENGL	Santa Clara	Almaden Twp	88	16
ENDEY								
Joseph	46	m	w	ENGL	Nevada	Grass Valley Twp	75	226
Richard	33	m	w	ENGL	El Dorado	Mud Springs Twp	72	77
ENDICOTT								
Chas	39	m	w	IN	Mendocino	Little Lake Twp	74	202
J B	55	m	w	KY	Mendocino	Calpella Twp	74	187
Margaret	25	f	w	IN	Mendocino	Little Lake Twp	74	203
ENDOZA								
James B	33	m	w	SPAI	Santa Cruz	Pajaro Twp	89	357
ENDRES								
Chas J	42	m	w	BAVA	Shasta	Horsetown P O	89	506
ENDRISS								
G D	41	m	w	WURT	El Dorado	Coloma Twp	72	2
Wm	33	m	w	WURT	San Francisco	8-Wd San Francisco	82	348
ENDS								
Henry	34	m	w	BAVA	San Francisco	San Francisco P O	83	332
ENDY								
Joseph	44	m	w	ENGL	Inyo	Cerro Gordo Twp	73	323
ENECIO								
James	37	m	w	FRAN	San Francisco	1-Wd San Francisco	79	50
ENEGREN								
William	30	m	w	SWED	San Francisco	3-Wd San Francisco	79	295
ENEMAN								
Saml	45	m	w	NY	San Francisco	1-Wd San Francisco	79	55
ENER								
Seneca	30	m	w	NY	Butte	Ophir Twp	70	108
ENERY								
C Lewis	25	m	w	HOLL	Los Angeles	Los Angeles	73	524
ENES								
John	22	m	w	PORT	Stanislaus	Washington Twp	92	84
ENESS								
Michael	45	m	w	IREL	Napa	Yountville Twp	75	83
ENEY								
Frederick	30	m	w	NY	San Francisco	San Francisco P O	83	279
ENFELD								
Fred	41	m	w	SHOL	San Francisco	2-Wd San Francisco	79	211
ENFIELD								
Charles	37	m	w	DENM	Nevada	Washington Twp	75	346
ENG								
Ah	61	m	c	CHIN	San Francisco	San Francisco P O	80	438
Ah	6	f	c	CA	San Francisco	San Francisco P O	80	444
Ah	50	m	c	CHIN	Los Angeles	Los Angeles	73	512
Ah	47	m	c	CHIN	San Francisco	San Francisco P O	80	436
Ah	45	m	c	CHIN	San Mateo	San Mateo P O	87	351
Ah	44	m	c	CHIN	San Francisco	San Francisco P O	80	432
Ah	42	m	c	CHIN	San Francisco	San Francisco P O	80	520
Ah	42	m	c	CHIN	San Francisco	San Francisco P O	80	495
Ah	40	m	c	CHIN	San Francisco	San Francisco P O	80	528
Ah	40	m	c	CHIN	San Francisco	San Francisco P O	80	520
Ah	40	m	c	CHIN	Tulare	Visalia	92	299
Ah	40	m	c	CHIN	San Francisco	San Francisco P O	80	448
Ah	40	m	c	CHIN	San Francisco	San Francisco P O	80	435
Ah	39	m	c	CHIN	San Francisco	San Francisco P O	80	512
Ah	39	m	c	CHIN	San Francisco	San Francisco P O	80	442
Ah	38	m	c	CHIN	San Francisco	San Francisco P O	80	454
Ah	38	m	c	CHIN	San Francisco	San Francisco P O	80	515
Ah	38	m	c	CHIN	San Francisco	San Francisco P O	80	519
Ah	38	m	c	CHIN	San Francisco	San Francisco P O	80	509
Ah	38	m	c	CHIN	San Joaquin	1-Wd Stockton	86	147
Ah	37	m	c	CHIN	San Francisco	San Francisco P O	80	527
Ah	37	m	c	CHIN	San Francisco	San Francisco P O	80	443
Ah	36	m	c	CHIN	San Francisco	San Francisco P O	80	530
Ah	36	m	c	CHIN	San Francisco	San Francisco P O	80	512
Ah	36	m	c	CHIN	San Francisco	San Francisco P O	80	514
Ah	36	m	c	CHIN	San Francisco	San Francisco P O	80	496
Ah	36	m	c	CHIN	San Francisco	San Francisco P O	80	491

Series M593

Name	Age	S	R	B-PL	County	Locale	Roll	Pg
Ah	35	m	c	CHIN	San Francisco	San Francisco P O	80	528
Ah	35	m	c	CHIN	San Francisco	San Francisco P O	80	518
Ah	35	m	c	CHIN	San Mateo	San Mateo P O	87	350
Ah	35	m	c	CHIN	San Francisco	San Francisco P O	80	453
Ah	35	m	c	CHIN	El Dorado	White Oak Twp	72	142
Ah	34	m	c	CHIN	San Francisco	San Francisco P O	80	518
Ah	34	m	c	CHIN	San Francisco	San Francisco P O	80	510
Ah	33	m	c	CHIN	San Francisco	San Francisco P O	80	513
Ah	32	m	c	CHIN	San Francisco	San Francisco P O	80	457
Ah	32	m	c	CHIN	San Francisco	San Francisco P O	80	522
Ah	32	m	c	CHIN	San Francisco	San Francisco P O	80	496
Ah	32	m	c	CHIN	San Francisco	San Francisco P O	80	445
Ah	30	m	c	CHIN	Sacramento	1-Wd Sacramento	77	200
Ah	30	m	c	CHIN	Sierra	Table Rock Twp	89	544
Ah	30	f	c	CHIN	San Francisco	San Francisco P O	80	434
Ah	29	f	c	CHIN	San Francisco	San Francisco P O	80	503
Ah	29	m	c	CHIN	San Francisco	San Francisco P O	80	436
Ah	27	m	c	CHIN	San Francisco	San Francisco P O	80	510
Ah	26	m	c	CHIN	San Francisco	San Francisco P O	80	530
Ah	26	f	c	CHIN	San Francisco	San Francisco P O	80	442
Ah	25	f	c	CHIN	San Francisco	San Francisco P O	80	491
Ah	24	m	c	CHIN	Sacramento	1-Wd Sacramento	77	193
Ah	23	m	c	CHIN	San Francisco	San Francisco P O	80	511
Ah	22	m	c	CHIN	San Francisco	San Francisco P O	80	504
Ah	21	m	c	CHIN	Sacramento	1-Wd Sacramento	77	197
Ah	21	f	c	CHIN	San Francisco	San Francisco P O	80	528
Ah	21	m	c	CHIN	San Francisco	San Francisco P O	80	466
Ah	21	m	c	CHIN	San Francisco	San Francisco P O	80	507
Ah	20	m	c	CHIN	Placer	Summit P O	76	495
Ah	20	m	c	CHIN	Sacramento	1-Wd Sacramento	77	193
Ah	20	m	c	CHIN	San Francisco	San Francisco P O	80	511
Ah	20	m	c	CHIN	Tuolumne	Chinese Camp P O	93	379
Ah	19	f	c	CHIN	San Francisco	San Francisco P O	80	496
Ah	19	f	c	CHIN	San Francisco	San Francisco P O	80	508
Ah	19	m	c	CHIN	San Francisco	San Francisco P O	80	499
Ah	19	m	c	CHIN	San Francisco	San Francisco P O	80	493
Ah	19	f	c	CHIN	San Francisco	San Francisco P O	80	447
Ah	19	f	c	CHIN	San Francisco	San Francisco P O	80	435
Ah	19	f	c	CHIN	San Francisco	San Francisco P O	80	437
Ah	19	m	c	CHIN	Butte	Hamilton Twp	70	68
Ah	17	f	c	CHIN	San Francisco	San Francisco P O	80	527
Ah	16	m	c	CHIN	San Francisco	11-Wd San Francisc	84	528
Ah	16	f	c	CHIN	San Francisco	San Francisco P O	80	432
Aml	20	m	c	CHIN	Sacramento	1-Wd Sacramento	77	200
Chee	46	m	c	CHIN	Butte	Wyandotte Twp	70	142
Gee	16	m	c	CHIN	San Francisco	2-Wd San Francisco	79	158
Hi	32	m	c	CHIN	Stanislaus	Empire Twp	92	40
Le	25	m	c	CHIN	San Joaquin	3-Wd Stockton	86	230
Leave	30	m	c	CHIN	Solano	Green Valley Twp	90	43
Ling	33	m	c	CHIN	Plumas	Mineral Twp	77	25
Song	37	m	c	CHIN	Sierra	Eureka Twp	89	525
We	28	m	c	CHIN	Plumas	Mineral Twp	77	25
ENGAPER								
Fullus	29	m	w	FRAN	Sutter	Vernon Twp	92	132
Michael	39	m	w	FRAN	Sutter	Vernon Twp	92	132
ENGEBERTSON								
Finkel	40	m	w	NORW	Napa	Napa	75	51
ENGEL								
B	57	m	w	HDAR	Calaveras	Copperopolis P O	70	221
Bathasa	35	m	w	SWIT	Calaveras	San Andreas P O	70	204
Ferdinand	38	m	w	GERM	Los Angeles	Wilmington Twp	73	642
Fred	29	m	w	HCAS	San Francisco	2-Wd San Francisco	79	216
George	35	m	w	PRUS	San Francisco	San Francisco P O	83	81
John	32	m	w	NY	San Francisco	5-Wd San Francisco	81	27
Meyer	39	m	w	NY	San Francisco	San Francisco P O	83	274
Nillie	19	f	w	NY	San Francisco	2-Wd San Francisco	79	216
ENGELBART								
F W	29	m	w	GERM	Tuolumne	Columbia P O	93	350
ENGELBARTH								
Christian	31	m	w	OLDE	San Francisco	11-Wd San Francisc	84	528
ENGELBRIGHT								
Virgil	32	m	w	AR	Calaveras	Copperopolis P O	70	238
ENGELER								
George	29	m	w	WURT	San Francisco	San Francisco P O	83	32
ENGELHARDT								
Geo	35	m	w	BAVA	San Francisco	1-Wd San Francisco	79	25
ENGELKE								
H	52	m	w	PRUS	San Francisco	San Francisco P O	83	134
ENGELKER								
F A	41	m	w	BADE	Tuolumne	Columbia P O	93	362
ENGELL								
John F	43	m	w	NY	Placer	Bath P O	76	420
Stephen	25	m	w	IA	Placer	Bath P O	76	422
ENGELMONSON								
Peter	46	m	w	NORW	Napa	Napa	75	36
ENGELS								
Henry A	60	m	w	PRUS	San Francisco	San Francisco P O	83	138
ENGER								
Rudolf	20	m	w	PA	San Francisco	3-Wd San Francisco	79	324
ENGERKEE								
Fred	26	m	w	BAVA	San Francisco	11-Wd San Francisc	84	495
ENGERT								
C J	34	m	w	ENGL	Sierra	Sierra Twp	89	570
Edward	42	m	w	PRUS	San Francisco	San Francisco P O	80	534
George	26	m	w	BAVA	San Francisco	1-Wd San Francisco	79	63
ENGERTA								
Anton	27	m	w	WURT	San Francisco	San Francisco P O	80	479

© 2001 by Heritage Quest. All rights reserved.

Name	Age	S	R	B-PL	County	Locale	Series M593 Roll	Pg
ENGESSER								
Frederick	38	m	w	WURT	El Dorado	White Oak Twp	72	136
ENGHRAM								
H	24	m	w	OH	Lassen	Long Valley Twp	73	437
Rob	27	m	w	IN	Lassen	Long Valley Twp	73	436
ENGIRK								
Heinrich	51	m	w	WURT	Calaveras	San Andreas P O	70	201
ENGLAND								
Barton	44	m	w	TN	Sonoma	Santa Rosa	91	411
Basha	15	f	w	MO	Sonoma	Salt Point	91	390
Beverly	28	m	w	MO	Santa Clara	Santa Clara Twp	88	170
Cyrus	21	m	w	MI	Colusa	Colusa	71	294
D C	40	m	w	IL	Lake	Coyote Valley	73	401
Honora	58	f	w	IREL	Sacramento	4-Wd Sacramento	77	374
J B	42	m	w	TN	Lake	Lower Lake	73	416
J C	45	m	w	TN	Lake	Big Valley	73	394
J W	42	m	w	ENGL	San Joaquin	1-Wd Stockton	86	132
John	59	m	w	DENM	Yuba	Rose Bar Twp	93	653
John	50	m	w	VA	Placer	Bath P O	76	443
Jose	33	m	w	IL	Merced	Snelling P O	74	275
Joseph	27	m	w	MO	Santa Clara	Santa Clara Twp	88	170
Julias	35	m	w	FINL	Contra Costa	Martinez P O	71	419
L	67	m	w	KY	Lake	Coyote Valley	73	401
Lucy	38	f	w	MO	Sacramento	Cosumnes Twp	77	91
Mary	29	f	w	PA	Placer	Auburn P O	76	367
R J	42	m	w	TN	Lake	Big Valley	73	394
Smith	35	m	w	TN	Napa	Napa Twp	75	62
William	38	m	w	NY	Los Angeles	Los Angeles Twp	73	471
ENGLANDER								
David	4	m	w	CA	San Francisco	11-Wd San Francisc	84	514
Emile	26	m	w	SILE	San Francisco	San Francisco P O	83	294
Gus	25	m	w	PRUS	San Francisco	San Francisco P O	83	421
Leopold	50	m	w	BAVA	San Francisco	8-Wd San Francisco	82	484
Marx	55	m	w	BAVA	San Francisco	8-Wd San Francisco	82	484
Wm	53	m	w	PRUS	San Francisco	San Francisco P O	83	294
ENGLE								
Alonzo	45	m	w	OH	Shasta	Horsetown P O	89	502
Christian	32	m	w	PA	Inyo	Lone Pine Twp	73	335
David	39	m	w	OH	Kern	Linns Valley P O	73	344
Epriam P	40	m	w	MD	Yuba	Long Bar Twp	93	562
Frederick	23	m	w	IREL	Solano	Maine Prairie Twp	90	51
Henry	46	m	w	BAVA	Trinity	North Fork Twp	92	217
J P	42	m	w	NY	San Francisco	San Francisco P O	85	754
Philip	33	m	w	GERM	Sonoma	Sonoma Twp	91	439
Samuel	23	m	w	POLA	San Francisco	7-Wd San Francisco	81	166
Volney	29	m	w	MI	Placer	Colfax P O	76	389
Wm Jackson	37	m	w	TN	Plumas	Indian Twp	77	9
ENGLEBERT								
Hagemeyer	27	m	w	PRUS	San Francisco	San Francisco P O	83	138
ENGLEBRECHT								
Stephen	38	m	w	PRUS	San Francisco	San Francisco P O	80	473
ENGLEBRIGHT								
E	16	m	w	MA	Solano	Vallejo	90	159
H	46	m	w	PRUS	Solano	Vallejo	90	187
ENGLEHARDT								
Fred	31	m	w	HAMB	Sacramento	1-Wd Sacramento	77	174
Hanah	42	f	w	PRUS	San Francisco	7-Wd San Francisco	81	223
Wm	30	m	w	PRUS	San Francisco	1-Wd San Francisco	79	30
ENGLEHART								
Albert	28	m	w	HANO	Stanislaus	Empire Twp	92	38
Edward	26	m	w	MO	Yolo	Buckeye Twp	93	411
Frits	24	m	w	HDAR	Sonoma	Petaluma Twp	91	316
George	21	m	w	HCAS	Los Angeles	Los Angeles Twp	73	475
James	49	m	w	OH	Sonoma	Healdsburg & Mendo	91	283
Phillip	34	m	w	PA	Stanislaus	Emory Twp	92	20
ENGLEKEY								
Louis	14	m	w	PA	Inyo	Bishop Crk Twp	73	314
ENGLEKIRK								
Annie	24	f	w	WURT	San Francisco	San Francisco P O	80	478
ENGLER								
Mathia	54	m	w	BADE	Sonoma	Sonoma Twp	91	437
Michael	36	m	w	BADE	Inyo	Independence Twp	73	328
ENGLES								
Katy	23	f	w	SCOT	San Francisco	8-Wd San Francisco	82	291
ENGLESBERG								
E A	49	m	w	SWED	San Francisco	5-Wd San Francisco	81	1
ENGLESMAN								
Hy	31	m	w	HOLL	San Francisco	San Francisco P O	83	127
ENGLEY								
Mathew C	25	m	w	ME	Sonoma	Salt Point	91	387
ENGLING								
John	40	m	w	ME	San Francisco	7-Wd San Francisco	81	224
ENGLIS								
Mike	35	m	w	HAMB	Sacramento	Franklin Twp	77	119
ENGLISH								
Alex	35	m	w	IL	Alameda	Alameda	68	2
Alice	50	f	w	IREL	San Francisco	2-Wd San Francisco	79	149
Alice	17	f	w	AUSL	San Francisco	2-Wd San Francisco	79	174
Amelia	15	f	w	CA	San Francisco	1-Wd San Francisco	79	47
Ann	21	f	w	IREL	San Francisco	San Francisco P O	83	251
Benj	27	m	w	ENGL	Sacramento	San Joaquin Twp	77	398
Benjamin F	55	m	w	MO	Solano	Green Valley Twp	90	41
C H	39	m	w	TN	Mendocino	Calpella Twp	74	182
C J	27	m	w	CANA	Sierra	Alleghany & Forest	89	533
Catharine	11	f	w	CA	San Francisco	11-Wd San Francisc	84	711
Catherine	60	f	w	IREL	San Francisco	2-Wd San Francisco	79	216
Catherine	28	f	w	IREL	Sacramento	Franklin Twp	77	114
Davd B	32	m	w	MO	Sonoma	Mendocino Twp	91	303
Elitie	22	f	w	CA	Alameda	Murray Twp	68	112
Eliza	66	f	w	IREL	San Francisco	8-Wd San Francisco	82	443
Eliza	23	f	w	ENGL	San Francisco	6-Wd San Francisco	81	108
Elizabeth	40	f	w	MA	San Francisco	San Francisco P O	83	223
Esther	21	f	w	MO	San Luis Obispo	Santa Rosa Twp	87	327
Geo	23	m	w	ENGL	Solano	Vallejo	90	165
George	25	m	w	ENGL	Sacramento	San Joaquin Twp	77	407
Harmon H	17	m	w	OR	Yolo	Cache Crk Twp	93	436
Hennan	16	m	w	OR	Yolo	Cache Crk Twp	93	435
Henry	40	m	w	IREL	Calaveras	San Andreas P O	70	173
J A	52	m	w	MA	San Francisco	San Francisco P O	85	805
J L	57	m	w	PA	Sacramento	3-Wd Sacramento	77	265
James	52	m	w	ENGL	Sacramento	Georgianna Twp	77	127
James	46	m	w	ME	San Francisco	11-Wd San Francisc	84	620
James	44	m	w	CANA	Sonoma	Analy Twp	91	237
James	30	m	w	ENGL	Monterey	San Juan Twp	74	402
John	53	m	w	ME	Sacramento	4-Wd Sacramento	77	347
John	50	m	w	ENGL	Sacramento	American Twp	77	68
John	43	m	w	IREL	Calaveras	Copperopolis P O	70	238
John	40	m	w	IREL	Yuba	Marysville	93	604
John	36	m	w	MD	Alameda	Murray Twp	68	112
John	35	m	w	IREL	San Francisco	San Francisco P O	85	822
John	30	m	w	NC	Santa Clara	1-Wd San Jose	88	227
John	24	m	w	MO	San Joaquin	2-Wd Stockton	86	173
John	21	m	w	NY	Yuba	Marysville	93	594
John	13	m	w	ENGL	Sacramento	San Joaquin Twp	77	406
John F	28	m	w	MA	San Francisco	8-Wd San Francisco	82	417
Jos	27	m	w	PA	Solano	Vallejo	90	209
Langton M	79	m	w	MD	San Diego	San Diego	78	499
Lawrence	61	m	w	ENGL	San Francisco	11-Wd San Francisc	84	613
M S	39	m	w	IREL	San Francisco	San Francisco P O	83	297
Margaret	27	f	w	IREL	Yuba	Marysville	93	605
Marshal M	30	m	w	VA	San Francisco	8-Wd San Francisco	82	384
Mary	58	f	w	LA	Tulare	Farmersville Twp	92	244
Mary	39	f	w	IREL	Sacramento	Cosumnes Twp	77	89
Mary A	28	f	w	PA	San Francisco	San Francisco P O	83	155
Pat	26	m	w	AUSL	San Francisco	2-Wd San Francisco	79	215
Patk	32	m	w	IREL	Sacramento	4-Wd Sacramento	77	356
Patrick	46	m	w	IREL	Nevada	Grass Valley Twp	75	152
Patrick	40	m	w	IREL	Sutter	Sutter Twp	92	121
Ralph M	27	m	w	IA	San Diego	San Diego	78	500
Richard	68	m	w	MO	Humboldt	South Fork Twp	72	300
Robert	54	m	w	MO	Los Angeles	Santa Ana Twp	73	604
Sam	35	m	w	ENGL	Sacramento	San Joaquin Twp	77	404
Saml	43	m	w	OH	Tehama	Red Bluff	92	173
Saml	40	m	w	IREL	Butte	Chico Twp	70	36
Thomas	21	m	w	IREL	Humboldt	Eureka Twp	72	267
W T	36	m	w	MO	Mendocino	Calpella Twp	74	185
Wiley	32	m	w	MO	Mendocino	Calpella Twp	74	185
William	45	m	w	IREL	San Francisco	11-Wd San Francisc	84	652
William	33	m	w	TX	Tulare	Tule Rvr Twp	92	264
Wm	37	m	w	VA	San Francisco	San Francisco P O	83	74
Wm G	51	m	w	NY	Sacramento	3-Wd Sacramento	77	291
Wm R	30	m	w	KY	Butte	Chico Twp	70	29
ENGLOR								
F	47	m	w	BADE	Sierra	Butte Twp	89	512
ENGOLDHEART								
Wm	44	m	w	OH	Sonoma	Analy Twp	91	228
ENGOR								
William	20	m	w	ENGL	San Francisco	6-Wd San Francisco	81	83
ENGRAM								
Christopher	30	m	w	IREL	San Mateo	Schoolhouse Statio	87	336
ENGRICH								
John	34	m	w	AUSL	San Francisco	2-Wd San Francisco	79	282
ENGST								
Antone	30	m	w	WURT	Alameda	Eden Twp	68	81
ENGTARN								
J	25	m	w	MO	Monterey	Alisal Twp	74	302
ENHART								
C	24	m	w	PA	Monterey	Alisal Twp	74	302
ENICH								
Frederick	42	m	w	PRUS	Kern	Havilah P O	73	338
ENICKS								
Cerges H	29	m	w	BAVA	San Francisco	San Francisco P O	83	283
ENIES								
Foster	22	m	w	PORT	Santa Barbara	Santa Barbara P O	87	497
ENING								
Josiah	24	m	w	OH	Sonoma	Petaluma Twp	91	354
William A	38	m	w	MD	San Diego	San Luis Rey	78	516
ENIS								
Antone	40	m	w	PORT	Alameda	Eden Twp	68	57
Antonio	40	m	w	PORT	Santa Cruz	Santa Cruz Twp	89	382
Jos	27	m	w	PORT	Sierra	Sears Twp	89	561
Joseph	25	m	w	PORT	Marin	San Rafael Twp	74	25
Mary	28	f	w	PORT	Alameda	Washington Twp	68	298
Matthew	28	m	w	PORT	Santa Cruz	Santa Cruz Twp	89	387
ENIST								
Antonio	45	m	i	PORT	Inyo	Cerro Gordo Twp	73	320
ENKLE								
Jacob	20	m	w	NY	San Francisco	2-Wd San Francisco	79	158
Morris	47	m	w	PRUS	San Francisco	2-Wd San Francisco	79	158
ENLO								
Joel	55	m	w	VA	Tulare	Venice Twp	92	278
John K	50	m	w	AR	Tulare	Venice Twp	92	273
Joseph	27	m	w	MO	Tulare	Venice Twp	92	278

© 2001 by Heritage Quest. All rights reserved.

Series M593

Name	Age	S	R	B-PL	County	Locale	Roll	Pg
ENLOW								
Hugh S	53	m	w	TN	Tulare	Tule Rvr Twp	92	271
ENMANIEL								
Silas	43	m	w	NM	Merced	Snelling P O	74	262
ENN								
---	24	m	c	CHIN	Siskiyou	Cottonwood Twp	89	594
Ah	21	m	c	CHIN	San Francisco	San Francisco P O	80	500
ENNARNY								
Pat	40	m	w	IREL	Solano	Benicia	90	4
ENNES								
A G	27	m	w	ME	Monterey	San Juan Twp	74	401
Joseph	51	m	w	ENGL	El Dorado	Placerville Twp	72	95
ENNIS								
Abraham	33	m	w	NJ	San Francisco	San Francisco P O	85	780
Corneilus	31	m	m	MD	San Francisco	San Francisco P O	80	477
Eliza	43	f	w	NY	Alameda	Brooklyn	68	36
Elizabeth	28	f	w	IREL	Solano	Vallejo	90	166
Ellen	65	f	w	IREL	San Francisco	1-Wd San Francisco	79	19
Frank	38	m	w	PORT	Monterey	Pajaro Twp	74	369
Frank	31	m	w	RI	Nevada	Little York Twp	75	236
Frank F	35	m	w	NY	Sonoma	Petaluma Twp	91	324
Geo	18	m	w	IREL	Solano	Vallejo	90	210
Henry	38	m	w	IREL	San Francisco	San Francisco P O	83	312
Henry	28	m	w	HCAS	San Francisco	1-Wd San Francisco	79	56
James	40	m	w	IREL	San Francisco	San Francisco P O	83	16
Jno	29	m	w	ENGL	Sacramento	1-Wd Sacramento	77	188
John	68	m	w	IREL	Alameda	Brooklyn	68	36
John	40	m	w	IREL	San Francisco	11-Wd San Francisc	84	519
John	35	m	w	IREL	San Francisco	5-Wd San Francisco	81	34
John	34	m	w	IREL	San Francisco	San Francisco P O	85	871
John H	47	m	w	NY	Solano	Vallejo	90	157
Joseph	44	m	w	IREL	San Francisco	1-Wd San Francisco	79	136
M J	20	m	w	NY	Solano	Vallejo	90	216
Manuel	34	m	w	PORT	Tuolumne	Sonora P O	93	329
Martin	37	m	w	IREL	San Francisco	11-Wd San Francisc	84	658
Mathew	26	m	w	IREL	San Francisco	8-Wd San Francisco	82	321
Nicholas	40	m	w	IREL	San Francisco	1-Wd San Francisco	79	10
Nicholas	21	m	w	IN	Solano	Vallejo	90	197
Norah	26	f	w	IREL	San Francisco	San Francisco P O	83	330
Peter	30	m	w	IREL	San Francisco	1-Wd San Francisco	79	19
R G	41	m	w	IREL	Tuolumne	Big Oak Flat P O	93	397
Robt	34	m	w	NY	Santa Clara	Gilroy Twp	88	105
William	45	m	w	IREL	San Francisco	11-Wd San Francisc	84	640
William	32	m	w	MO	San Mateo	Woodside P O	87	385
William	28	m	w	DC	San Francisco	11-Wd San Francisc	84	630
Wm	44	m	w	IREL	San Francisco	1-Wd San Francisco	79	91
ENNOCENTI								
Geo	37	m	w	SWIT	San Joaquin	2-Wd Stockton	86	188
ENNOE								
James	42	m	w	ENGL	Nevada	Rough & Ready Twp	75	333
ENNOR								
John	37	m	w	IL	Santa Cruz	Santa Cruz	89	419
ENO								
George	30	m	w	ENGL	Santa Cruz	Santa Cruz Twp	89	393
Henry	72	m	w	NY	San Francisco	3-Wd San Francisco	79	308
Joseph	25	m	w	CANA	Alameda	Brooklyn	68	38
Sense	30	m	w	CA	Alameda	Murray Twp	68	107
ENOCH								
Joseph	36	m	w	TN	Humboldt	Mattole Twp	72	284
ENOCHS								
John	35	m	w	VT	Sacramento	Center Twp	77	83
ENOE								
L H	26	f	w	WI	Sacramento	3-Wd Sacramento	77	259
ENOGADA								
Elaus	29	m	w	CA	San Diego	Warners Rancho Dis	78	528
ENOMIS								
Manuel D	40	m	w	PORT	San Luis Obispo	Santa Rosa Twp	87	323
ENON								
John	22	m	w	PORT	Trinity	Douglas	92	233
ENOO								
Frank	37	m	w	BADE	Solano	Suisun Twp	90	97
Joseph	38	m	w	SCOT	Alameda	Brooklyn Twp	68	48
ENORRIS								
Miguel	35	m	w	CA	Los Angeles	Los Angeles Twp	73	482
ENOS								
A	38	m	w	ENGL	Alameda	Oakland	68	264
Antoine	33	m	w	PORT	Shasta	Shasta P O	89	452
Anton	30	m	w	PORT	Sacramento	Granite Twp	77	149
Antone	40	m	w	PORT	Alameda	Washington Twp	68	298
Antone	40	m	w	PORT	Alameda	Eden Twp	68	88
Antone	28	m	w	PORT	Trinity	North Fork Twp	92	217
Charles	30	m	w	PORT	Siskiyou	Yreka Twp	89	666
Derias	37	m	w	ME	Sutter	Butte Twp	92	95
Eli	40	m	w	NY	San Francisco	5-Wd San Francisco	81	30
Elizabeth	45	f	w	NY	San Francisco	San Francisco P O	83	271
Emanuel	49	m	w	AZOR	Shasta	Shasta P O	89	453
Emanuel	48	m	w	SCOT	Siskiyou	Scott Valley Twp	89	612
Emanuel	25	m	w	PORT	Alameda	Washington Twp	68	269
Francis A	31	m	w	OH	Santa Clara	San Jose Twp	88	199
Frank	27	m	w	PORT	Alameda	Eden Twp	68	66
Frank	24	m	w	PORT	Solano	Suisun Twp	90	108
Frank	22	m	w	AZOR	Shasta	Shasta P O	89	453
Frank	18	m	w	PORT	Alameda	Eden Twp	68	87
George	30	m	w	PORT	Alameda	Eden Twp	68	67
J	21	m	w	CANA	Alameda	Oakland	68	240
J M	57	m	w	VT	Sacramento	3-Wd Sacramento	77	318
James	28	m	w	NY	Sutter	Sutter Twp	92	120
James M	57	m	w	VT	Sacramento	Brighton Twp	77	70
John	32	m	w	PORT	Alameda	Eden Twp	68	66
John	30	m	w	PORT	San Francisco	1-Wd San Francisco	79	12
John	20	m	w	SCOT	Alameda	Brooklyn Twp	68	55
Joseph	49	m	w	PORT	Calaveras	Copperopolis P O	70	255
Joseph	48	m	w	PORT	Sacramento	Georgianna Twp	77	124
Joseph	46	m	w	PORT	Santa Cruz	Santa Cruz Twp	89	401
Joseph	45	m	w	SCOT	San Luis Obispo	San Luis Obispo Tw	87	297
Joseph	40	m	w	PORT	Alameda	Washington Twp	68	299
Joseph	40	m	w	PORT	San Francisco	3-Wd San Francisco	79	294
Joseph	40	m	w	PORT	Butte	Wyandotte Twp	70	145
Joseph	38	m	w	AZOR	San Francisco	1-Wd San Francisco	79	134
Joseph	36	m	w	PORT	Santa Clara	Milpitas Twp	88	110
Joseph	35	m	w	PORT	Trinity	Douglas	92	236
Joseph	21	m	w	PORT	Alameda	Eden Twp	68	70
Joseph J	29	m	w	AZOR	San Francisco	1-Wd San Francisco	79	130
Lewis	41	m	w	PORT	Nevada	Rough & Ready Twp	75	328
Lewis	40	m	w	SCOT	San Luis Obispo	San Luis Obispo Tw	87	301
Manuel	60	m	w	PORT	Alameda	Eden Twp	68	90
Manuel	40	m	w	SCOT	Alameda	Brooklyn Twp	68	44
Manuel	38	m	w	PORT	Trinity	Douglas	92	234
Manuel	33	m	w	PORT	Trinity	Douglas	92	236
Manuel	25	m	w	PORT	Alameda	Washington Twp	68	291
Manuel	20	m	w	SCOT	Alameda	Brooklyn Twp	68	44
Mary	25	f	w	PORT	Trinity	Indian Crk	92	199
Mundere	35	m	w	PORT	Trinity	Douglas	92	233
Sarah	32	f	w	MO	Sutter	Yuba Twp	92	146
Saral	38	m	w	PORT	Placer	Bath P O	76	423
Thomas	27	m	w	PORT	Alameda	Washington Twp	68	292
William	38	m	w	MI	San Mateo	Redwood Twp	87	361
ENOSTROSA								
Trenedad	30	m	w	CHIL	Calaveras	San Andreas P O	70	177
ENOX								
Frank	23	m	w	PORT	Solano	Denverton Twp	90	25
ENQUITH								
August	44	m	w	SWED	San Francisco	3-Wd San Francisco	79	300
ENRICH								
Adam	54	m	w	WURT	Nevada	Bridgeport Twp	75	102
ENRICK								
Mary	45	f	w	IREL	Santa Clara	1-Wd San Jose	88	226
ENRIGHT								
Daniel	48	m	w	IREL	San Francisco	2-Wd San Francisco	79	153
Dennis	35	m	w	IREL	Napa	Napa	75	18
Edward	35	m	w	IREL	San Francisco	San Francisco P O	83	358
Fannie	15	f	w	CA	Santa Clara	2-Wd San Jose	88	337
George	34	m	w	MO	Nevada	Grass Valley Twp	75	199
George	28	m	w	ME	Nevada	Meadow Lake Twp	75	265
James	43	m	w	IREL	Santa Clara	Santa Clara Twp	88	168
Jno	45	m	w	IREL	Butte	Hamilton Twp	70	64
John	7	m	w	CA	Sacramento	3-Wd Sacramento	77	313
John	12	m	w	NY	Marin	San Rafael Twp	74	29
Joseph	34	m	w	IREL	Santa Clara	1-Wd San Jose	88	229
Margaret	6	f	w	CA	San Francisco	11-Wd San Francisc	84	711
Mary A	17	f	w	CA	Santa Clara	2-Wd San Jose	88	337
Michael	40	m	w	IREL	Nevada	Nevada Twp	75	303
Michael	28	m	w	IREL	Nevada	Little York Twp	75	240
Michael	11	m	w	CA	Marin	San Rafael Twp	74	29
Pat	35	m	w	IREL	San Francisco	11-Wd San Francisc	84	435
Robert	4	m	w	CA	San Francisco	11-Wd San Francisc	84	711
ENRRIQUES								
Manuel	30	m	w	CHIL	Contra Costa	San Pablo Twp	71	356
ENSBURY								
William	23	m	w	NY	San Francisco	11-Wd San Francisc	84	455
ENSCHUS								
Ramon	30	m	w	SPAI	San Francisco	1-Wd San Francisco	79	46
ENSCOR								
H	46	m	w	ENGL	Sierra	Sierra Twp	89	565
ENSEL								
Charles E	55	m	w	OH	Yolo	Putah Twp	93	522
ENSELMO								
Joan	33	m	w	ITAL	Fresno	Millerton P O	72	165
ENSEY								
A F	28	m	w	NY	San Francisco	3-Wd San Francisco	79	312
John C	60	m	w	MD	El Dorado	Mud Springs Twp	72	75
ENSIGN								
George	41	m	w	NY	San Francisco	San Francisco P O	80	485
Heman B	26	m	w	NY	Humboldt	Pacific Twp	72	298
J H	32	m	w	TN	Nevada	Meadow Lake Twp	75	247
Jas C	22	m	w	CT	Sonoma	Healdsburg & Mendo	91	280
Samuel	28	m	w	NY	San Francisco	3-Wd San Francisco	79	317
ENSIGNE								
Keente	30	m	w	MEXI	Monterey	San Juan Twp	74	401
ENSINE								
---	26	m	c	CHIN	San Francisco	11-Wd San Francisc	84	702
ENSING								
George	26	m	w	NY	Nevada	Meadow Lake Twp	75	266
Wm F	30	m	w	PA	San Francisco	5-Wd San Francisco	81	18
ENSINGER								
John	39	m	w	BAVA	Santa Cruz	Santa Cruz Twp	89	386
ENSKERCH								
Benj W	41	m	w	HOLL	Sonoma	Petaluma Twp	91	336
ENSLAY								
Allen	42	m	w	IL	Santa Clara	Almaden Twp	88	18
ENSLEY								
John	28	m	w	MO	Butte	Ophir Twp	70	94
Samuel	24	m	w	IN	Siskiyou	Yreka Twp	89	664

© 2001 by Heritage Quest. All rights reserved.

Name	Age	S	R	B-PL	County	Locale	Series M593 Roll	Pg
ENSLIN								
Henry	34	m	w	PA	Stanislaus	Buena Vista Twp	92	12
Henry	32	m	w	PA	Stanislaus	Emory Twp	92	22
ENSLOW								
G A	25	m	w	VA	Sonoma	Santa Rosa	91	409
Thos	49	m	w	OH	Butte	Wyandotte Twp	70	142
ENSLY								
Olive	66	f	w	NY	Butte	Ophir Twp	70	112
ENSMINGER								
Samuel J	55	m	w	VA	El Dorado	Placerville	72	120
ENSMORE								
David	21	m	w	ME	Stanislaus	Branch Twp	92	2
ENSON								
Edwd D	44	m	w	NY	San Francisco	1-Wd San Francisco	79	106
ENSTADT								
Anton	20	m	w	FRAN	San Francisco	11-Wd San Francisc	84	605
ENSUNSA								
Jno	45	m	w	CHIL	Alameda	Oakland	68	252
ENT								
Augustus	45	m	w	NY	Solano	Montezuma Twp	90	65
Caroline	32	f	w	MI	Santa Cruz	Santa Cruz	89	415
ENTEMAN								
George	25	m	w	WURT	San Francisco	San Francisco P O	83	176
ENTER								
Joseph F	25	m	w	VA	Santa Barbara	San Buenaventura P	87	431
ENTERIES								
Fabora	39	f	w	CA	Santa Clara	Almaden Twp	88	5
ENTREMONT								
Frank	22	m	w	FRAN	Napa	Napa Twp	75	46
ENTRICAN								
George	70	m	w	NY	Yolo	Grafton Twp	93	491
John	45	m	w	NY	Yolo	Grafton Twp	93	493
ENTRIGON								
George C	70	m	w	NY	Yolo	Washington Twp	93	535
ENTWISTLE								
Richd	33	m	w	IREL	Solano	Vallejo	90	198
S S	18	m	w	CA	Alameda	Oakland	68	159
Thomas	40	m	w	ENGL	Placer	Bath P O	76	450
ENWRIGHT								
C	25	m	w	IREL	Yuba	Rose Bar Twp	93	659
Edward	35	m	w	IREL	Trinity	Trinity Center Pct	92	204
Frank	24	m	w	NY	Solano	Vallejo	90	202
Geo	25	m	w	IREL	Solano	Vallejo	90	143
John	33	m	w	IREL	San Francisco	San Francisco P O	83	185
Margarett	39	f	w	IREL	Sonoma	Petaluma Twp	91	344
Margt	15	f	w	MA	San Francisco	1-Wd San Francisco	79	13
Thomas	22	m	w	IREL	Marin	San Rafael Twp	74	45
ENYART								
Milton	32	m	w	MO	Yolo	Putah Twp	93	522
EO								
Ah	42	m	c	CHIN	San Joaquin	1-Wd Stockton	86	142
Ah	39	m	c	CHIN	San Joaquin	1-Wd Stockton	86	142
EOFF								
John	48	m	w	OH	Sacramento	Granite Twp	77	143
Samuel	45	m	b	NJ	San Francisco	6-Wd San Francisco	81	71
EOGUNERI								
Demetrio	39	m	w	ITAL	Sonoma	Sonoma Twp	91	441
EOW								
Ah	31	m	c	CHIN	Siskiyou	Yreka	89	662
EP								
Ah	30	m	c	CHIN	Nevada	Little York Twp	75	242
Ah	22	m	c	CHIN	Placer	Dutch Flat P O	76	414
Christian	40	m	w	GERM	Alameda	Eden Twp	68	57
Ha	42	m	c	CHIN	Siskiyou	Yreka Twp	89	667
EPARASA								
Ross	32	m	w	ITAL	Calaveras	Copperopolis P O	70	247
EPATITA								
Josefa	72	f	w	MEXI	Monterey	Monterey	74	367
EPELINE								
Louis	21	m	w	PA	Sacramento	1-Wd Sacramento	77	173
EPENIO								
Casar	37	m	w	MEXI	Santa Clara	Almaden Twp	88	5
EPERLEE								
Leo	41	m	w	HESS	Santa Clara	Gilroy Twp	88	80
EPERLY								
Hawk W	39	m	w	MO	San Luis Obispo	Santa Rosa Twp	87	326
Mary	39	f	w	MO	San Luis Obispo	Morro Twp	87	283
Saml	67	m	w	NC	San Luis Obispo	Santa Rosa Twp	87	326
Thos S	52	m	w	KY	San Luis Obispo	Morro Twp	87	283
EPERSON								
Jacob	34	m	w	MO	Tulare	Farmersville Twp	92	246
Lewey	42	m	w	FRAN	Trinity	North Fork Twp	92	218
EPHRAIM								
A B	44	m	w	PRUS	San Francisco	San Francisco P O	83	272
Ferdinand	20	m	w	PRUS	San Francisco	8-Wd San Francisco	82	449
Julius	36	m	w	PRUS	San Francisco	3-Wd San Francisco	79	307
EPHRIAM								
Barnard	24	m	w	PRUS	Butte	Ophir Twp	70	91
EPIANDO								
Mary	30	f	w	MEXI	San Francisco	2-Wd San Francisco	79	165
EPIFAMA								
Maria	9	f	w	CA	San Diego	San Diego	78	487
EPIMARN								
John	45	m	w	BOHE	San Francisco	11-Wd San Francisc	84	645
EPINOUK								
Louis	35	m	w	FRAN	San Francisco	11-Wd San Francisc	84	592

Name	Age	S	R	B-PL	County	Locale	Series M593 Roll	Pg
EPLER								
G W	38	m	w	OH	Humboldt	Pacific Twp	72	292
EPLEY								
Dora	25	f	w	MI	Lassen	Janesville Twp	73	431
J W	46	m	w	PA	Lake	Lower Lake	73	418
T H	35	m	w	MI	Lassen	Janesville Twp	73	433
T R	27	m	w	MI	Lassen	Janesville Twp	73	433
EPLING								
Augustus	36	m	w	VA	Amador	Volcano P O	69	377
EPOLITE								
John	29	m	w	MEXI	Monterey	Alisal Twp	74	295
EPPENHEIMER								
William	35	m	w	PA	Santa Clara	Fremont Twp	88	45
EPPENSON								
Wm J	31	m	w	MO	Sacramento	Franklin Twp	77	120
EPPERLY								
Hiram F	29	m	w	MO	Santa Cruz	Santa Cruz Twp	89	393
EPPERSON								
Anthony	60	m	w	KY	Sacramento	Franklin Twp	77	120
Brutus C	39	m	w	KY	Colusa	Spring Valley Twp	71	335
Daniel	50	m	w	VA	Tehama	Red Bluff	92	174
Ephriam	29	m	w	OH	Plumas	Indian Twp	77	18
J	45	m	w	AL	San Joaquin	Douglas Twp	86	43
J	40	m	w	VT	San Joaquin	Douglas Twp	86	48
Jackson	22	m	w	AR	Alpine	Silver Mtn P O	69	306
John	27	m	w	MO	Sacramento	Franklin Twp	77	121
M M	55	m	w	VA	Lake	Scotts Crk	73	426
Mads	24	m	w	CANA	Sonoma	Petaluma Twp	91	316
Newton	14	m	w	VA	Tehama	Hunters Twp	92	187
EPPINGER								
Herman	29	m	w	BADE	Solano	Silveyville Twp	90	85
Jacob	32	m	w	BADE	El Dorado	Mud Springs Twp	72	84
Louis	39	m	w	PRUS	San Francisco	San Francisco P O	83	255
EPPISON								
Mads	24	m	w	DENM	Sonoma	Petaluma Twp	91	322
EPPLER								
Alfred	33	m	w	WURT	San Francisco	8-Wd San Francisco	82	359
EPPLERHEIMER								
William	28	m	w	BADE	San Francisco	San Francisco P O	83	244
EPPS								
Charles	40	m	b	LA	San Francisco	San Francisco P O	80	415
George	39	m	w	ENGL	San Francisco	7-Wd San Francisco	81	177
Mary	39	f	w	PA	San Francisco	7-Wd San Francisco	81	177
Nancy E	22	f	w	MO	Sonoma	Analy Twp	91	238
Tingley B	34	m	w	NC	El Dorado	Georgetown Twp	72	43
EPPSTEIN								
Joseph	34	m	w	PA	Lassen	Milford Twp	73	438
EPROSON								
Robert	45	m	w	AL	Calaveras	San Andreas P O	70	151
EPSTEIN								
David	19	m	w	NY	Napa	Napa	75	50
Henry	64	m	w	AUST	San Francisco	8-Wd San Francisco	82	477
Lena	21	f	w	WURT	San Francisco	8-Wd San Francisco	82	439
ERADE								
Maina	32	f	w	MEXI	San Joaquin	2-Wd Stockton	86	169
ERAMA								
Marie	18	f	w	CA	Los Angeles	Los Angeles	73	520
ERANMER								
J F	42	m	w	MD	San Francisco	San Francisco P O	85	841
ERAS								
J	30	m	w	WALE	Alameda	Oakland	68	213
ERASTS								
Thomas	38	m	w	MA	El Dorado	Placerville Twp	72	104
ERASTUS								
Peter	30	m	w	NY	Monterey	San Juan Twp	74	404
ERAVIS								
Marcelina	57	f	w	MEXI	Los Angeles	Los Angeles	73	523
ERAWOR								
Peter	53	m	w	BELG	Amador	Fiddletown P O	69	431
ERB								
John B	40	m	w	PA	Nevada	Eureka Twp	75	131
Julia	20	f	b	PA	Santa Clara	1-Wd San Jose	88	237
ERBACH								
Herman	21	m	w	PRUS	San Francisco	6-Wd San Francisco	81	80
ERBEN								
John H	41	m	w	NY	Santa Cruz	Santa Cruz Twp	89	397
Wm	32	m	w	HANO	San Francisco	San Francisco P O	85	877
ERBINE								
G	47	m	w	HCAS	Nevada	Meadow Lake Twp	75	246
ERBO								
Conrad	42	m	w	PRUS	Nevada	Little York Twp	75	235
ERBON								
Napoleon	55	m	w	FRAN	Monterey	San Juan Twp	74	410
ERBST								
Charles	57	m	w	SAXO	San Francisco	8-Wd San Francisco	82	482
ERCABAUTT								
Victoire	26	m	w	MEXI	San Diego	San Jacinto Dist	78	517
ERCANBACK								
Caleb K	46	m	w	NY	Santa Cruz	Watsonville	89	375
ERCEY								
Freman	18	m	w	MEXI	Fresno	Millerton P O	72	164
ERCH								
John	55	m	w	BADE	Sacramento	4-Wd Sacramento	77	376
ERCHBOCK								
Henry	46	m	w	SWIT	San Joaquin	2-Wd Stockton	86	179
ERCHOL								
Edmund	21	m	w	PA	San Francisco	5-Wd San Francisco	81	19

© 2001 by Heritage Quest. All rights reserved.

Name	Age	S	R	B-PL	County	Locale	Series M593 Roll	Pg
ERCISE								
Manuel	40	m	w	CHIL	El Dorado	Mountain Twp	72	67
ERCK								
Charles	40	m	w	HANO	Tuolumne	Chinese Camp P O	93	365
ERDIN								
Thomas	22	m	w	BADE	San Francisco	San Francisco P O	85	811
ERDMAN								
John M	40	m	w	PA	San Luis Obispo	Santa Rosa Twp	87	317
EREAGADO								
Luis	27	m	w	TX	Placer	Auburn P O	76	359
EREBIARA								
Gortancio	17	m	w	MEXI	Santa Clara	Almaden Twp	88	8
ERECKSON								
Erick	36	m	w	NORW	Alpine	Silver Mtn P O	69	307
EREGOG								
Coronel	24	m	w	MEXI	Los Angeles	Los Angeles	73	507
EREKINO								
Alexander	23	m	w	ME	Placer	Cisco P O	76	494
EREKSON								
Charles	32	m	w	SWED	San Francisco	San Francisco P O	83	40
ERENS								
David	53	m	w	WALE	Trinity	Junction City Pct	92	210
EREOVINS								
Charles	40	m	w	PRUS	San Francisco	11-Wd San Francisc	84	636
ERFORD								
John	25	m	w	OH	Santa Cruz	Santa Cruz	89	411
ERGOOD								
George	27	m	w	OH	Sacramento	2-Wd Sacramento	77	237
ERGUCHER								
Polita	42	f	w	MEXI	Santa Clara	Almaden Twp	88	5
ERGUIER								
Ignacio	55	m	w	MEXI	San Luis Obispo	San Luis Obispo Tw	87	313
ERHARDT								
David	45	m	w	BAVA	Calaveras	San Andreas P O	70	198
ERHART								
James	30	m	w	HDAR	Solano	Vacaville Twp	90	121
ERHEFENHTER								
Albert	19	m	w	BADE	Santa Clara	1-Wd San Jose	88	262
ERHENBERGER								
Maria	20	f	w	SWED	Santa Clara	San Jose Twp	88	193
ERHLIGH								
Joanna	70	f	w	GERM	Sonoma	Sonoma Twp	91	441
ERHRLICH								
Louis	24	m	w	GERM	Santa Clara	2-Wd San Jose	88	326
ERI								
Jose	52	m	i	MEXI	Los Angeles	Los Angeles Twp	73	498
ERICCSON								
John	28	m	w	SWED	San Francisco	7-Wd San Francisco	81	192
ERICH								
Carrie	21	f	w	PRUS	Tehama	Red Bluff	92	178
ERICHMAN								
C	11	f	w	CA	Amador	Sutter Crk P O	69	399
ERICHSEN								
Bena	26	f	w	SWED	San Francisco	11-Wd San Francisc	84	605
ERICISON								
William	22	m	w	SWED	Klamath	Trinidad Twp	73	391
ERICK								
Henery	33	m	w	ENGL	San Francisco	7-Wd San Francisco	81	171
John	27	m	w	SWED	Los Angeles	Los Angeles Twp	73	491
Julius	25	m	w	PRUS	Sutter	Sutter Twp	92	124
ERICKENSEN								
Henry	40	m	w	NY	San Francisco	7-Wd San Francisco	81	218
ERICKSON								
Alex	33	m	w	SWED	San Francisco	8-Wd San Francisco	82	304
Erick H	38	m	w	SWED	Alpine	Silver Mtn P O	69	307
Finger	27	m	w	NORW	Alpine	Silver Mtn P O	69	307
John	29	m	w	SWED	San Francisco	1-Wd San Francisco	79	121
John	28	m	w	SWED	San Francisco	1-Wd San Francisco	79	116
John	25	m	w	SWED	Mendocino	Little Rvr Twp	74	165
Lucy	30	f	w	GERM	San Francisco	2-Wd San Francisco	79	173
N	24	m	w	DENM	Lake	Lower Lake	73	420
Olock	25	m	w	SWED	Sutter	Sutter Twp	92	117
Oscar	25	m	w	SWED	San Francisco	1-Wd San Francisco	79	120
Peter	30	m	w	SWED	Sutter	Sutter Twp	92	119
Peter	27	m	w	NORW	Colusa	Spring Valley Twp	71	336
Stephen	44	m	w	NORW	San Francisco	1-Wd San Francisco	79	40
ERICSON								
Abraham	40	m	w	NORW	Stanislaus	Washington Twp	92	84
Ezra	73	m	w	SWED	Stanislaus	North Twp	92	68
Frederick	39	m	w	DENM	Santa Cruz	Pajaro Twp	89	355
M	25	m	w	SWED	Solano	Vallejo	90	204
ERIECKSEN								
Knuth	26	m	w	SILE	San Francisco	3-Wd San Francisco	79	287
ERING								
Christian	19	m	w	BAVA	Santa Clara	Santa Clara Twp	88	147
ERINS								
Geo W	53	m	w	GA	Merced	Snelling P O	74	249
ERISON								
John	52	m	w	PRUS	Alameda	Eden Twp	68	85
ERKE								
Harmon	33	m	w	PRUS	Sutter	Butte Twp	92	93
ERKEINE								
John	47	m	w	SWED	Plumas	Quartz Twp	77	35
ERKINS								
William	49	m	w	BELG	Santa Clara	1-Wd San Jose	88	269
ERKSON								
Alexander C	59	m	w	NY	Santa Clara	1-Wd San Jose	88	277

Name	Age	S	R	B-PL	County	Locale	Series M593 Roll	Pg
John	62	m	w	NY	Santa Clara	Santa Clara Twp	88	144
William	40	m	w	NY	Santa Clara	Alviso Twp	88	23
ERLANDERSON								
Ivers	46	m	w	NORW	Siskiyou	Callahan P O	89	627
ERLANGER								
Herman	42	m	w	WURT	San Francisco	San Francisco P O	85	722
ERLANSON								
E A	36	m	w	NORW	San Francisco	3-Wd San Francisco	79	318
ERLE								
Frederick	44	m	w	HCAS	Santa Clara	1-Wd San Jose	88	256
James	37	m	w	MA	Santa Barbara	Santa Barbara P O	87	500
Manuel	36	m	w	PRUS	San Francisco	San Francisco P O	80	351
ERLENWEIN								
John	37	m	w	BAVA	San Francisco	11-Wd San Francisc	84	553
ERLICH								
Chas	29	m	w	PRUS	Yuba	Rose Bar Twp	93	661
ERLIN								
George	27	m	w	SWED	San Francisco	San Francisco P O	83	72
ERMALINGER								
C	45	m	w	SWIT	Sierra	Sears Twp	89	527
ERN								
Ah	46	m	c	CHIN	Siskiyou	Cottonwood Twp	89	594
ERNART								
John	37	m	w	PA	Alameda	Washington Twp	68	281
ERNEST								
Alexr	20	m	w	PRUS	San Francisco	5-Wd San Francisco	81	29
Catharine	17	f	w	IL	Nevada	Nevada Twp	75	271
Frank C	46	m	w	FRAN	Stanislaus	Empire Twp	92	27
Henry B	47	m	w	HANO	Siskiyou	Cottonwood Twp	89	593
Herman	43	m	w	POLA	Los Angeles	Wilmington Twp	73	637
John	43	m	w	PRUS	Tuolumne	Chinese Camp P O	93	387
Joseph	45	m	w	ENGL	Stanislaus	Branch Twp	92	10
William	36	m	w	CANA	Stanislaus	Branch Twp	92	9
Wm	20	m	w	PRUS	San Francisco	8-Wd San Francisco	82	306
ERNESTEEN								
Chas	27	m	w	SWED	Sonoma	Vallejo Twp	91	455
ERNIN								
Georgiana	18	f	w	MA	San Francisco	San Francisco P O	83	187
ERNISTON								
Napoleon B	43	m	w	TN	Calaveras	Copperopolis P O	70	221
ERNSBY								
Margerett	17	f	w	RI	Los Angeles	Los Angeles	73	539
ERNSLEY								
Orren	20	m	w	TN	Calaveras	San Andreas P O	70	158
ERNSON								
Julius	20	m	w	PRUS	San Francisco	8-Wd San Francisco	82	356
ERNST								
Chas	40	m	w	PRUS	San Joaquin	3-Wd Stockton	86	215
Christ	20	m	w	DENM	Alameda	Eden Twp	68	63
Fred	19	m	w	HANO	San Francisco	11-Wd San Francisc	84	560
George	35	m	w	PRUS	Santa Clara	2-Wd San Jose	88	306
H	46	m	w	HAMB	Alameda	Alameda	68	19
Hermann	45	m	w	FRAN	Nevada	Nevada Twp	75	274
John	40	m	w	HANO	San Francisco	2-Wd San Francisco	79	235
Mathias	25	m	w	PRUS	Solano	Tremont Twp	90	36
P	25	m	w	BAVA	Nevada	Bridgeport Twp	75	104
Peter	44	m	w	BADE	San Francisco	11-Wd San Francisc	84	658
Peter	41	m	w	FRAN	Nevada	Eureka Twp	75	135
Rebecca	27	f	w	DENM	San Francisco	2-Wd San Francisco	79	174
ERNSTEIN								
Luis	30	m	w	BAVA	Los Angeles	El Monte Twp	73	459
ERNSTINE								
John	36	m	w	PRUS	Los Angeles	Los Angeles	73	549
ERNY								
Henrich	38	m	w	WURT	Calaveras	San Andreas P O	70	204
Mary	44	f	w	SWIT	Calaveras	San Andreas P O	70	202
EROLA								
Louis	30	m	w	ITAL	San Francisco	2-Wd San Francisco	79	284
ERRARA								
Wallaloupi	50	f	w	MEXI	Nevada	Grass Valley Twp	75	142
ERRARRA								
Louisa	26	m	w	CA	Fresno	Millerton P O	72	151
ERRERRAS								
Siriaco	57	m	w	MEXI	Fresno	Millerton P O	72	155
ERRICK								
Gustus	30	m	w	PRUS	Sutter	Sutter Twp	92	128
Realto	18	m	w	IA	Santa Clara	San Jose Twp	88	189
ERRICSON								
Andrew	32	m	w	SWED	Marin	Bolinas Twp	74	5
ERRINGTON								
Arthur	41	m	w	ENGL	Nevada	Grass Valley Twp	75	162
ERSGRABER								
Adolph	21	m	w	HANO	Sonoma	Sonoma Twp	91	440
ERSGRAEBER								
Charles	15	m	w	HANO	Sonoma	Sonoma Twp	91	439
ERSHERT								
Elfindohl	31	m	w	HANO	Placer	Bath P O	76	420
ERSIN								
Peter	26	m	w	BADE	San Francisco	1-Wd San Francisco	79	110
ERSINGER								
Eliza	25	f	w	SHOL	San Francisco	8-Wd San Francisco	82	358
Emily	70	f	w	SHOL	San Francisco	8-Wd San Francisco	82	358
ERSKINE								
Cyrus H	44	m	w	ME	Nevada	Little York Twp	75	234
David	24	m	w	CT	Contra Costa	Martinez P O	71	418
John A	27	m	w	CANA	Yolo	Cache Crk Twp	93	432
John B	30	m	m	BRAZ	San Francisco	2-Wd San Francisco	79	178

© 2001 by Heritage Quest. All rights reserved.

Series M593

Name	Age	S	R	B-PL	County	Locale	Roll	Pg
Melvill	35	m	w	NH	San Francisco	San Francisco P O	83	236
Peter	20	m	w	US	San Joaquin	Castoria Twp	86	9
Samuel	56	m	w	PA	Nevada	Nevada Twp	75	320
Sarah W	28	f	w	MA	San Francisco	San Francisco P O	83	175
William	48	m	w	ME	Placer	Auburn P O	76	359
William	35	m	w	OH	Nevada	Eureka Twp	75	138
William R	45	m	w	ME	Yuba	Bullards Bar P O	93	550
Wm	14	m	w	MEXI	Alameda	Oakland	68	159
ERSKINES								
John	51	m	w	ME	Nevada	Little York Twp	75	235
ERSKINS								
W	24	m	w	IREL	Sierra	Alleghany & Forest	89	533
ERTLE								
John	30	m	w	OH	Placer	Rocklin Twp	76	467
ERTRELLA								
Roman	16	m	w	MEXI	Alameda	Washington Twp	68	285
ERUP								
Trinidad	44	m	w	MEXI	Kern	Bakersfield P O	73	362
ERVAN								
Rose	28	f	w	IREL	Santa Clara	Santa Clara Twp	88	155
ERVELL								
Thomas	30	m	w	OH	Amador	Sutter Crk P O	69	396
ERVIN								
David	41	m	w	MO	Mendocino	Ukiah Twp	74	238
Harrison	33	m	w	IL	Santa Clara	Redwood Twp	88	128
James	27	m	b	NC	Siskiyou	Yreka	89	655
John	56	m	w	SCOT	San Joaquin	Douglas Twp	86	47
Lulu	20	f	i	CA	Siskiyou	Yreka	89	655
ERVINE								
W R	30	m	w	IREL	San Francisco	8-Wd San Francisco	82	313
ERVING								
George	37	m	w	CANA	San Francisco	San Francisco P O	85	867
Newton	35	m	w	IN	Kern	Tehachapi P O	73	355
Robt M	45	m	w	NY	Klamath	Dillon Twp	73	369
ERVINGS								
Geo	24	m	w	IL	Siskiyou	Surprise Valley Tw	89	639
Jas	44	m	w	ENGL	Solano	Benicia	90	2
Joseph	30	m	w	IL	Siskiyou	Surprise Valley Tw	89	639
ERVINS								
Mathew	19	m	w	PA	Placer	Colfax P O	76	389
ERVISO								
Francisco	35	m	w	MEXI	San Bernardino	Belleville Twp	78	408
ERWIN								
Anna	36	f	w	MI	Alameda	Washington Twp	68	276
C G	47	m	w	MO	San Francisco	San Francisco P O	83	36
Charles	38	m	w	BADE	San Francisco	San Francisco P O	80	335
Chas	21	m	w	MO	Colusa	Grand Island Twp	71	304
Elijah C	32	m	w	MS	Yolo	Merritt Twp	93	502
Emma	18	f	w	NY	San Francisco	8-Wd San Francisco	82	305
Francis	42	m	w	IL	Napa	Napa Twp	75	69
George T	29	m	w	VA	Yolo	Washington Twp	93	534
James	28	m	w	IREL	San Francisco	5-Wd San Francisco	81	32
John	38	m	w	KY	Yolo	Putah Twp	93	517
John W	19	m	w	IL	Napa	Napa Twp	75	28
Joseph	47	m	w	PA	Yuba	Slate Range Bar Tw	93	675
Nicholas	39	m	w	RI	Sonoma	Petaluma Twp	91	363
Samuel	26	m	w	IREL	Santa Clara	2-Wd San Jose	88	307
Sandy	25	m	w	IREL	Sutter	Vernon Twp	92	133
Sarah	32	f	w	MO	Yolo	Putah Twp	93	511
Thomas	57	m	w	KY	Santa Clara	Redwood Twp	88	128
William	47	m	w	PA	Contra Costa	Martinez P O	71	427
William	38	m	w	ENGL	San Francisco	11-Wd San Francisc	84	626
ERWING								
Otto	30	m	w	SWIT	San Francisco	11-Wd San Francisc	84	585
ERZGRABER								
Cathin	35	f	w	MA	San Francisco	San Francisco P O	85	855
Jul B	21	m	w	SAXO	San Francisco	San Francisco P O	83	134
Robt	32	m	w	DENM	Fresno	Millerton P O	72	189
ESADTO								
Sisto	45	m	i	MEXI	Merced	Snelling P O	74	251
ESALA								
Flora	47	f	w	MEXI	Calaveras	San Andreas P O	70	196
ESALOSA								
Jose	24	m	w	CA	Monterey	San Antonio Twp	74	321
ESAM								
Maria	28	f	w	IREL	San Francisco	6-Wd San Francisco	81	39
William	30	m	w	----	San Francisco	6-Wd San Francisco	81	39
ESAN								
Peter	48	m	w	PRUS	San Joaquin	2-Wd Stockton	86	161
ESANHERST								
H	66	m	w	PA	Merced	Snelling P O	74	247
ESARA								
Ramon	44	m	w	SPAI	Los Angeles	Los Angeles	73	523
ESARAMUS								
Emanuel	45	m	w	PORT	Alameda	Washington Twp	68	269
ESARCEGAR								
Manuel	34	m	w	PERU	Monterey	Monterey	74	363
ESARIN								
Juan H	70	m	w	MEXI	Los Angeles	Los Angeles Twp	73	477
ESAW								
Peter	30	m	w	HANO	Calaveras	Copperopolis P O	70	262
ESBERY								
Robt	27	m	w	DENM	Alameda	Oakland	68	250
ESBRIDGE								
Menford	22	m	w	ENGL	Los Angeles	Los Angeles	73	505
ESBY								
Mary	36	f	b	NY	San Francisco	8-Wd San Francisco	82	469

Series M593

Name	Age	S	R	B-PL	County	Locale	Roll	Pg
ESCAICH								
Francis	50	m	w	FRAN	Kern	Havilah P O	73	339
ESCAIG								
Jaques	32	m	w	FRAN	San Francisco	3-Wd San Francisco	79	316
ESCALANTA								
Incarnacion	25	m	w	CA	San Luis Obispo	Morro Twp	87	286
Perfecto	35	m	w	MEXI	Marin	San Rafael Twp	74	46
ESCALANTE								
Manuel	13	m	w	MEXI	San Luis Obispo	San Luis Obispo Tw	87	307
ESCALE								
Mary	73	f	w	FRAN	San Francisco	2-Wd San Francisco	79	286
ESCALENTA								
Mary	14	f	w	PORT	San Mateo	Half Moon Bay P O	87	395
ESCALET								
Ernest	32	m	w	FRAN	San Francisco	San Francisco P O	83	354
ESCALLA								
Joseph	22	m	w	FRAN	Marin	San Rafael Twp	74	32
ESCALLE								
Felix	65	m	w	FRAN	San Francisco	1-Wd San Francisco	79	46
ESCAMEIA								
Blaza	50	m	w	CA	Santa Cruz	Santa Cruz Twp	89	384
ESCAMILLA								
Joaquin	55	m	w	CA	Monterey	San Antonio Twp	74	324
ESCANDON								
Angel	37	m	w	SPAI	Santa Barbara	San Buenaventura P	87	434
ESCANILLA								
Francisco	38	m	w	CHIL	Los Angeles	San Juan Twp	73	629
ESCANTRARAS								
Gregorio	82	m	w	MEXI	Los Angeles	Los Angeles	73	523
ESCAPTA								
John	22	m	w	ITAL	San Mateo	Schoolhouse Statio	87	340
ESCARA								
Epomiseo	56	m	w	MEXI	Kern	Bakersfield P O	73	363
Gertrudes	35	f	w	MEXI	San Diego	Coronado	78	465
ESCARCE								
Luis	20	m	w	MEXI	Los Angeles	El Monte Twp	73	451
ESCAREIDO								
Antonio	59	m	w	MEXI	Mariposa	Mariposa P O	74	96
ESCARO								
Bonito	28	m	w	MEXI	Kern	Bakersfield P O	73	362
ESCASSEL								
Juan	43	m	w	MEXI	Santa Barbara	Santa Barbara P O	87	498
ESCAVAGE								
Manuel	42	m	w	MEXI	San Joaquin	3-Wd Stockton	86	227
ESCAVESS								
Mary	45	f	w	CHIL	Marin	Sausalito Twp	74	67
ESCHBACKER								
F A	44	m	w	BADE	Sierra	Downieville Twp	89	517
ESCHEN								
Jent	22	m	w	DENM	San Francisco	3-Wd San Francisco	79	287
ESCHENBACKER								
John	42	m	w	BADE	San Mateo	Pescadero P O	87	417
ESCHENBURG								
Eliza	70	f	w	DE	San Francisco	San Francisco P O	83	97
Rodny	38	m	w	DE	Santa Clara	Gilroy Twp	88	91
ESCHEVMON								
Chris	40	m	w	HANO	Butte	Oregon Twp	70	131
ESCOBAR								
Arsevo	32	m	w	CA	Monterey	Monterey Twp	74	346
Augustine	50	m	w	CA	Monterey	Monterey	74	365
Francisco	70	m	w	MEXI	Santa Clara	2-Wd San Jose	88	305
Franie	14	f	w	CA	Monterey	Monterey Twp	74	345
Jose	16	m	w	CA	San Francisco	11-Wd San Francisc	84	593
Jose M	22	m	w	CA	Monterey	Monterey Twp	74	345
Juan	49	m	w	CA	Monterey	Monterey	74	365
Nicolas	40	m	w	CA	Monterey	Monterey Twp	74	345
Tomasa	73	f	w	CA	Monterey	Monterey	74	358
ESCOBARDO								
Claro	40	m	w	MEXI	Amador	Jackson P O	69	327
ESCOL								
Henry	38	m	w	FRAN	Monterey	Monterey	74	361
ESCOLLE								
Julia	15	f	w	CA	Santa Cruz	Santa Cruz	89	417
ESCORES								
Jose	45	m	w	CHIL	Fresno	Millerton P O	72	159
ESCOVAL								
Antonio	45	m	w	MEXI	Solano	Vacaville Twp	90	138
Cavetana	26	m	w	MEXI	Solano	Vacaville Twp	90	138
ESCOVELLE								
Polenario	55	m	w	MEXI	Santa Barbara	San Buenaventura P	87	442
ESCUDERO								
Ignacio	12	m	w	MEXI	San Francisco	11-Wd San Francisc	84	593
ESCURA								
Guadalupe	60	f	w	CA	Santa Cruz	Santa Cruz	89	424
ESDEN								
A	35	m	w	VT	Alameda	Murray Twp	68	128
ESELE								
Henry	49	m	w	PRUS	San Francisco	2-Wd San Francisco	79	219
ESER								
Fredrick	37	m	w	SAXO	San Francisco	11-Wd San Francisc	84	455
ESFINORA								
Maria S	13	f	i	CA	Monterey	Monterey Twp	74	352
ESFINORO								
Abel	13	m	w	CA	Monterey	Monterey Twp	74	352
ESFINOS								
Manwel	47	m	w	CA	Monterey	Monterey Twp	74	352

© 2001 by Heritage Quest. All rights reserved.

California 1870 Census

Name	Age	S	R	B-PL	County	Locale	Series M593 Roll	Pg
ESH								
Geo W	38	m	w	NY	Mono	Bridgeport P O	74	283
ESHAD								
Joseph	60	m	w	FRAN	Calaveras	San Andreas P O	70	201
ESHADA								
Mariano	37	m	w	CA	San Luis Obispo	Santa Rosa Twp	87	324
ESHEL								
Frederick	37	m	w	FRAN	Mendocino	Big Rvr Twp	74	170
ESHER								
Minnie	25	f	w	SAXO	Yuba	Marysville	93	603
ESHINGER								
Michael	40	m	w	WURT	Sacramento	San Joaquin Twp	77	397
ESHINGTON								
Peter	45	m	w	OH	Mono	Bridgeport P O	74	283
ESHOM								
John	43	m	w	IL	Tulare	Tule Rvr Twp	92	269
ESICK								
Louis	47	m	w	BADE	San Francisco	7-Wd San Francisco	81	204
ESINHART								
---	39	m	w	PRUS	Alameda	Alameda	68	11
ESINVANI								
Maria	15	f	w	CA	Santa Cruz	Santa Cruz Twp	89	381
ESKRIDGE								
A W	40	m	w	VA	Sacramento	4-Wd Sacramento	77	347
ESLAIS								
Alfredo	30	m	w	MEXI	Santa Clara	Burnett Twp	88	35
ESLER								
Benjn	49	m	w	NJ	San Francisco	San Francisco P O	83	130
ESLES								
Robert	19	m	w	NY	San Francisco	1-Wd San Francisco	79	106
ESLEY								
John	36	m	w	SWIT	El Dorado	Georgetown Twp	72	37
ESLICK								
John	33	m	w	ENGL	Nevada	Grass Valley Twp	75	193
Joseph	7	m	w	CA	Mariposa	Mariposa P O	74	108
Joseph	34	m	w	ENGL	Mariposa	Mariposa P O	74	108
Thomas	29	m	w	ENGL	Santa Clara	Almaden Twp	88	10
ESLINGER								
George	45	m	w	WURT	Sutter	Sutter Twp	92	118
ESMOND								
D	55	m	w	NY	Alameda	Oakland	68	142
Edward	40	m	w	NY	Napa	Yountville Twp	75	79
Fred	26	m	w	WI	Sonoma	Russian Rvr	91	371
G H	33	m	w	IL	Sonoma	Russian Rvr	91	370
Hezekiah	38	m	w	NY	Solano	Maine Prairie Twp	90	49
Hezekiah	37	m	w	NY	Solano	Vacaville Twp	90	136
J A	38	m	w	NY	Sonoma	Russian Rvr	91	371
T B	35	m	w	NY	Nevada	Washington Twp	75	340
ESMULL								
Charles	35	m	w	NY	San Mateo	Half Moon Bay P O	87	390
ESNAULT								
Louis	24	m	w	FRAN	San Francisco	7-Wd San Francisco	81	241
ESORIS								
Jesus	40	f	w	MEXI	Los Angeles	Los Angeles	73	522
ESOTO								
Massa	41	m	w	MEXI	Tuolumne	Sonora P O	93	327
ESPAHO								
Augustine	26	m	w	MEXI	Alameda	Hayward	68	78
ESPAJO								
Augustine	29	m	w	PHIL	Santa Clara	Fremont Twp	88	48
ESPANERO								
Philomena	42	f	w	CA	Fresno	Millerton P O	72	157
ESPANNO								
M Y	40	m	w	MEXI	Tuolumne	Chinese Camp P O	93	389
ESPANOSA								
Jose Maria	50	m	w	CA	Monterey	Castroville Twp	74	332
Josefa B	40	f	w	CA	Monterey	Monterey	74	367
Milton	30	m	w	CA	Monterey	Salinas Twp	74	313
Namesia	43	m	w	MEXI	San Diego	San Pasqual	78	520
ESPARRE								
John	50	m	w	FRAN	San Francisco	San Francisco P O	80	484
ESPARSA								
Asento	50	m	w	MEXI	Los Angeles	Los Angeles	73	515
ESPARTERO								
Francisco	31	m	w	CHIL	Fresno	Millerton P O	72	158
ESPEE								
Mary	35	f	b	MO	Sonoma	Petaluma Twp	91	323
ESPEJO								
Ygnacia	40	f	w	MEXI	Los Angeles	Los Nietos Twp	73	586
ESPENAS								
Dolores	60	f	w	MEXI	Los Angeles	Los Angeles	73	512
ESPENASA								
Graveel	20	m	w	CA	Monterey	Monterey	74	364
ESPENOCA								
Gullena	34	m	w	CA	Monterey	Salinas Twp	74	313
ESPERANCE								
Victor	47	m	w	FRAN	San Francisco	San Francisco P O	80	356
ESPERG								
Matilda	34	f	w	NY	San Francisco	San Francisco P O	83	255
ESPERI								
Leon	10	m	w	CA	Los Angeles	Los Angeles	73	519
ESPERITE								
Jose	41	m	w	MEXI	Los Angeles	Los Angeles Twp	73	486
ESPERSON								
Espen P	49	m	w	DENM	San Francisco	3-Wd San Francisco	79	301
ESPEY								
George	16	m	m	CA	Sonoma	Santa Rosa	91	405
William	42	m	w	PA	Yolo	Buckeye Twp	93	413
ESPIE								
Wm	46	m	w	IREL	Humboldt	Eureka Twp	72	256
ESPINA								
Christiana	4	f	w	MEXI	Santa Clara	2-Wd San Jose	88	318
ESPINASSE								
P	32	m	w	ENGL	Sacramento	3-Wd Sacramento	77	264
ESPINDOLA								
Hypolita	42	m	w	MEXI	Santa Cruz	Pajaro Twp	89	359
Matthew	52	m	w	PORT	Santa Cruz	Santa Cruz Twp	89	382
ESPINELDO								
Jose	40	m	w	MEXI	San Francisco	San Francisco P O	80	472
ESPINOLA								
Braz	28	m	w	PORT	San Francisco	3-Wd San Francisco	79	313
Julius	30	m	w	PRUS	Santa Clara	San Jose Twp	88	204
ESPINOS								
Dolores	20	f	i	CA	Merced	Snelling P O	74	251
Josefa M	71	f	w	CA	Santa Barbara	Santa Barbara P O	87	480
ESPINOSA								
Adolfo	5	m	w	CA	Santa Cruz	Pajaro Twp	89	362
Albert	47	m	w	MEXI	Santa Barbara	Santa Barbara P O	87	483
Ana M	43	f	w	MEXI	Los Angeles	San Jose Twp	73	619
Anestacio	38	m	w	MEXI	Los Angeles	Los Angeles	73	568
Antonio	47	m	w	CA	San Mateo	Half Moon Bay P O	87	399
Carlos	24	m	w	MEXI	Los Angeles	Santa Ana Twp	73	602
Carmelia	28	f	w	CA	Los Angeles	Los Nietos Twp	73	583
Clemente	59	m	w	CA	Santa Barbara	Santa Barbara P O	87	466
Don Jose	19	m	w	CA	Yolo	Merritt Twp	93	508
Emanuel	40	m	w	MEXI	San Bernardino	San Salvador Twp	78	456
Fanny	33	f	w	CHIL	Sacramento	2-Wd Sacramento	77	238
Francisco	42	m	w	CA	Santa Barbara	Santa Barbara P O	87	471
Francisco	40	m	w	CA	Monterey	Castroville Twp	74	340
Francisco	36	m	w	CA	Santa Barbara	Santa Barbara P O	87	465
Gabriel	24	m	w	MEXI	Santa Clara	Burnett Twp	88	34
Gaspar	50	m	w	CA	Santa Barbara	Santa Barbara P O	87	463
Geniveia	13	f	w	CA	Santa Clara	Santa Clara Twp	88	157
Gregoria	56	f	w	CA	Los Angeles	Los Angeles	73	559
Guillermo	32	m	w	MEXI	Los Angeles	Los Nietos Twp	73	583
Hoorste	48	m	w	PHIL	San Mateo	Half Moon Bay P O	87	393
Jaquin	19	m	w	CA	Monterey	Monterey Twp	74	348
Jesus	46	m	w	MEXI	Plumas	Goodwin Twp	77	1
Jesus	35	m	w	MEXI	Monterey	San Juan Twp	74	407
Jose	45	m	w	CA	Monterey	Monterey Twp	74	348
Jose	36	m	w	MEXI	Los Angeles	Los Nietos Twp	73	586
Jose M	27	m	w	CA	Santa Cruz	Watsonville	89	373
Juan	34	m	w	MEXI	Los Angeles	Los Angeles	73	549
Juan	25	m	w	CA	Monterey	Alisal Twp	74	290
Leander	26	m	w	MEXI	Santa Clara	Almaden Twp	88	9
Lewis	22	m	w	CA	Monterey	Castroville Twp	74	327
Liandra	30	m	w	CHIL	Santa Clara	Almaden Twp	88	8
Luis	73	m	w	MEXI	Santa Barbara	San Buenaventura P	87	427
M	55	m	w	CA	Santa Clara	Gilroy Twp	88	87
M	26	m	w	CA	Santa Clara	Gilroy Twp	88	93
Manuel	38	m	w	CA	Marin	San Rafael Twp	74	39
Maria	40	f	i	CA	San Luis Obispo	Santa Rosa Twp	87	330
Mariano	53	m	w	CA	Monterey	San Juan Twp	74	417
Medora	44	f	w	CA	Santa Clara	Gilroy Twp	88	89
Miguel	46	m	w	CA	Santa Clara	Fremont Twp	88	49
Narcissa	38	f	w	MEXI	San Francisco	San Francisco P O	80	423
Nemesio	43	m	w	MEXI	San Diego	San Pasqual Valley	78	524
Prudencio	70	m	w	CA	Santa Clara	Fremont Twp	88	49
Ramon	30	m	w	CA	Santa Barbara	Santa Barbara P O	87	471
Romaldo	40	m	w	MEXI	Calaveras	San Andreas P O	70	156
Timothy	30	m	w	MEXI	San Francisco	San Francisco P O	80	430
Trinidad	33	m	w	CA	Santa Clara	Fremont Twp	88	49
ESPINOSO								
Jose	30	m	w	MEXI	Santa Clara	Almaden Twp	88	6
Patrio	32	m	w	MEXI	San Francisco	San Francisco P O	80	464
ESPINOZA								
Anatia	50	f	w	MEXI	San Francisco	San Francisco P O	80	331
Felip	34	m	w	MEXI	San Francisco	San Francisco P O	80	472
Gavina	24	f	w	MEXI	Santa Clara	2-Wd San Jose	88	311
Jose	34	m	w	MEXI	San Francisco	San Francisco P O	80	419
Jose	32	m	w	MEXI	San Francisco	San Francisco P O	80	395
M	57	f	w	CA	Santa Clara	Gilroy Twp	88	91
Prudence	31	f	w	MEXI	San Francisco	San Francisco P O	80	339
Ramon	37	m	w	CA	Santa Cruz	Pajaro Twp	89	352
ESPINZA								
Longuine	32	f	w	MEXI	San Francisco	2-Wd San Francisco	79	145
ESPOLLE								
George	41	m	w	FRAN	Merced	Snelling P O	74	266
ESPOSA								
Felix	47	m	w	MEXI	Kern	Bakersfield P O	73	362
ESPRADA								
M	40	m	w	MEXI	San Joaquin	3-Wd Stockton	86	227
ESPRIT								
J	47	m	w	FRAN	Amador	Fiddletown P O	69	429
ESPY								
Bowman	21	m	w	IL	Butte	Wyandotte Twp	70	149
David P	32	m	w	TN	Sonoma	Russian Rvr	91	367
Geo T	40	m	w	TN	Mendocino	Sanel Twp	74	231
Joseph B	21	m	w	PA	Butte	Ophir Twp	70	96
Mary	44	f	w	PA	Butte	Wyandotte Twp	70	149
Robt H	27	m	w	PA	Butte	Ophir Twp	70	115
ESQUEAVAL								
Mary	33	f	w	CRIC	Sacramento	2-Wd Sacramento	77	243

© 2001 by Heritage Quest. All rights reserved.

Name	Age	S	R	B-PL	County	Locale	Series M593 Roll	Pg
ESQUEMALD								
B C	40	m	w	MEXI	San Francisco	6-Wd San Francisco	81	73
ESQUIR								
Jesus	33	m	w	GUAD	San Joaquin	2-Wd Stockton	86	171
ESQUIVEL								
Eloise	14	f	w	CA	Santa Barbara	San Buenaventura P	87	433
ESQUON								
S	25	m	w	POLA	Alameda	Oakland	68	175
ESREY								
Hannah B	72	f	w	KY	Fresno	Kingston P O	72	220
John	42	m	w	IL	Fresno	Kingston P O	72	218
ESSARUDA								
John	19	m	w	PORT	Sutter	Sutter Twp	92	116
ESSARY								
David	49	m	w	TN	Butte	Chico Twp	70	20
ESSE								
Joseph	33	m	w	FRAN	San Mateo	Redwood Twp	87	363
ESSELSTROM								
Abraham	70	m	w	FINL	San Francisco	11-Wd San Francisc	84	652
ESSELSTYNE								
Jas H	57	m	w	NY	Sutter	Yuba Twp	92	152
ESSENMACHER								
J	25	m	w	PRUS	Santa Clara	Almaden Twp	88	20
ESSEX								
C	62	m	w	MO	Calaveras	Copperopolis P O	70	231
David	53	m	w	VA	Tehama	Cottonwood Twp	92	161
Geo W	23	m	w	IA	Tehama	Tehama Twp	92	193
ESSIG								
Bartholomew	46	m	w	HANO	Sacramento	2-Wd Sacramento	77	239
ESSINGER								
Marie	22	f	w	WURT	San Francisco	8-Wd San Francisco	82	447
ESSION								
Augustus	20	f	w	FRNK	San Francisco	11-Wd San Francisc	84	448
ESSLY								
Henry C	32	m	w	IN	Yolo	Grafton Twp	93	495
ESSMAN								
Ernest	38	m	w	PRUS	San Francisco	1-Wd San Francisco	79	108
ESSNER								
Peter	37	m	w	FRAN	Yuba	Rose Bar Twp	93	652
ESTABROOK								
Albion B	43	m	w	CANA	Santa Clara	1-Wd San Jose	88	255
Ambros	35	m	w	ENGL	Amador	Amador City P O	69	392
Mary	59	f	w	NH	Napa	Napa	75	40
ESTADILLO								
Juana	65	f	w	CA	Alameda	San Leandro	68	94
Salvador	33	m	w	CA	San Diego	San Jacinto Dist	78	518
ESTAIS								
Andros	38	m	w	CHIL	Marin	San Rafael Twp	74	32
ESTALETA								
Andreas	17	m	w	AZOR	San Francisco	1-Wd San Francisco	79	130
Joseph	31	m	w	AZOR	San Francisco	1-Wd San Francisco	79	130
ESTANOVICH								
Peter	30	m	w	AUST	San Francisco	1-Wd San Francisco	79	123
ESTAVA								
John	23	m	w	ITAL	San Mateo	Half Moon Bay P O	87	390
ESTE								
Amos	35	m	w	OH	Placer	Bath P O	76	422
Charles	50	m	w	CANA	Amador	Fiddletown P O	69	435
ESTEBER								
Serfino	45	m	w	ITAL	Monterey	San Antonio Twp	74	316
ESTEDELLO								
Louis	33	m	w	CA	Contra Costa	San Pablo Twp	71	353
ESTEE								
Morris M	35	m	w	PA	San Francisco	San Francisco P O	85	764
Stephen	37	m	w	NY	Yuba	Marysville	93	591
ESTEL								
Charles	41	m	w	LA	San Francisco	11-Wd San Francisc	84	455
Henry	32	m	w	LA	San Francisco	1-Wd San Francisco	79	96
ESTELE								
William K	49	m	w	MS	Colusa	Colusa	71	297
ESTELL								
Andrew H	43	m	w	NJ	Placer	Lincoln P O	76	485
ESTELLE								
Ida	13	f	w	CA	Santa Clara	Gilroy Twp	88	98
ESTEN								
John W	40	m	w	RI	San Francisco	San Francisco P O	83	236
ESTENAL								
Ashiel	44	m	w	FRAN	Amador	Volcano P O	69	384
ESTENEUR								
Danl	37	m	w	GERM	Solano	Vallejo	90	163
ESTEP								
Alfred	20	m	w	IA	Tehama	Antelope Twp	92	155
James	51	m	w	PA	Tehama	Red Bluff	92	174
ESTEPHE								
Charles	35	m	w	FRAN	Calaveras	San Andreas P O	70	204
ESTER								
Andrew	38	m	w	BAVA	San Joaquin	2-Wd Stockton	86	193
Charlotte	24	f	w	HCAS	Sacramento	4-Wd Sacramento	77	343
George	44	m	w	NY	Sonoma	Sonoma Twp	91	444
Isabell	37	f	w	CANA	Alameda	Eden Twp	68	85
Karl F	45	m	w	PA	San Francisco	5-Wd San Francisco	81	8
R C	15	m	w	CA	Alameda	Oakland	68	243
ESTERBROOK								
Charles	28	m	w	NH	San Francisco	7-Wd San Francisco	81	166
J K	55	m	w	ME	El Dorado	Greenwood Twp	72	55
James	44	m	w	CANA	Sacramento	Lee Twp	77	160
John	35	m	w	ENGL	Amador	Sutter Crk P O	69	399
Samuel	60	m	w	NH	Placer	Rocklin Twp	76	468
ESTERDAY								
Sol	34	m	w	MD	Santa Clara	2-Wd San Jose	88	310
ESTERLE								
Elizabeth	38	f	w	ME	San Francisco	San Francisco P O	83	219
ESTERLY								
Peter P	27	m	w	IL	Santa Cruz	Santa Cruz	89	410
Robt	22	m	w	NY	Alameda	Oakland	68	168
ESTERS								
Jackson	55	m	w	KY	Siskiyou	Big Valley Twp	89	582
Suphrain	38	m	w	VT	Sacramento	Brighton Twp	77	74
ESTES								
A L	26	m	w	WI	Nevada	Nevada Twp	75	271
Edw	65	m	w	VA	Tehama	Mill Crk Twp	92	168
G A	35	m	w	MO	Merced	Snelling P O	74	277
H	35	m	w	MO	Sonoma	Bodega Twp	91	257
J B	49	m	w	MO	Mendocino	Ukiah Twp	74	233
Jas H	17	m	w	IL	Tehama	Antelope Twp	92	155
Jesse L	31	m	w	MO	Siskiyou	Yreka	89	661
John M	37	m	w	MO	Trinity	Douglas	92	232
L C	46	m	w	NC	Tehama	Battle Crk Twp	92	157
W R	31	m	w	AR	Tehama	Merrill	92	197
Walter	36	m	w	KY	Stanislaus	Empire Twp	92	31
William C	59	m	w	KY	Trinity	Douglas	92	232
ESTEVAN								
Charles	33	m	w	CANA	Calaveras	San Andreas P O	70	205
ESTEY								
Charles L	40	m	w	MA	Marin	Novato Twp	74	12
Thomas	43	m	w	MA	Marin	Novato Twp	74	12
ESTILL								
Alf	40	m	w	VA	Sacramento	3-Wd Sacramento	77	291
ESTIMENT								
Bipaler	37	m	i	MEXI	Inyo	Cerro Gordo Twp	73	320
ESTLEN								
Saml	35	m	w	IL	Alameda	Murray Twp	68	127
ESTLEY								
Stephen	40	m	w	ENGL	Santa Clara	Almaden Twp	88	4
ESTLICK								
Stephen	39	m	w	ENGL	Santa Clara	Almaden Twp	88	10
ESTLITE								
Michl Antonio	32	m	w	PORT	San Francisco	1-Wd San Francisco	79	130
ESTOIO								
Victorio	40	f	w	MEXI	Mariposa	Mariposa P O	74	100
ESTON								
C H	26	m	w	IL	Yuba	Marysville	93	591
Stephen	40	m	w	RI	Marin	San Rafael	74	55
ESTORGA								
Manuel	17	m	w	MEXI	Santa Barbara	Santa Barbara P O	87	466
ESTOZA								
Guadolupe	32	f	w	MEXI	San Francisco	San Francisco P O	80	351
ESTRADA								
Antonio	59	m	w	CA	Santa Cruz	Pajaro Twp	89	351
Circeo	40	m	w	MEXI	Placer	Auburn P O	76	358
Dolores	34	f	w	MEXI	Monterey	Monterey	74	362
Domingo	15	m	w	CA	Santa Barbara	Santa Barbara P O	87	459
Entenira	25	f	w	MEXI	San Francisco	2-Wd San Francisco	79	282
Francisco	40	m	w	MEXI	Los Angeles	San Jose Twp	73	619
Gaudelara	8	f	w	CA	Santa Clara	2-Wd San Jose	88	309
Isadore	66	f	w	CA	Monterey	Pajaro Twp	74	368
Jaquin	52	m	w	CA	San Luis Obispo	San Luis Obispo Tw	87	311
Jose A	56	m	w	CA	Santa Barbara	Santa Maria P O	87	513
Jose A	30	m	w	CA	Santa Barbara	Las Cruces P O	87	506
Juan	24	m	w	MEXI	Los Angeles	Los Nietos Twp	73	573
Juan B	36	m	w	CA	San Francisco	1-Wd San Francisco	79	57
Julien	58	m	w	CA	San Luis Obispo	Santa Rosa Twp	87	327
Librada	36	f	w	MEXI	Los Angeles	Los Angeles	73	559
Lola	26	f	w	MEXI	San Francisco	6-Wd San Francisco	81	45
Pedro	46	m	w	CA	San Luis Obispo	San Luis Obispo Tw	87	310
Rafiel	50	m	w	CA	Monterey	Castroville Twp	74	341
ESTRADE								
Antone	43	m	w	MEXI	El Dorado	Placerville	72	117
ESTRADO								
Charles	57	m	w	FRAN	Calaveras	San Andreas P O	70	202
Cyrues	55	m	w	MEXI	San Diego	San Pasqual	78	522
Enipia	26	m	w	MEXI	Santa Clara	Burnett Twp	88	34
Juan	42	m	w	GA	Monterey	Castroville Twp	74	329
ESTRATA								
Jeremona	45	m	w	ITAL	San Francisco	1-Wd San Francisco	79	120
ESTRAZER								
Joachim	43	m	w	FRAN	San Francisco	1-Wd San Francisco	79	54
ESTREN								
Wm	31	m	w	HESS	San Joaquin	1-Wd Stockton	86	138
ESTRIDGE								
Mary	14	f	w	CA	Santa Clara	Gilroy Twp	88	93
ESTRODA								
Francisco	39	m	w	MEXI	Los Angeles	El Monte Twp	73	452
ESTS								
A E S	35	m	w	NC	San Francisco	San Francisco P O	85	775
ESTTOTO								
Dominico	34	m	w	SWIT	San Francisco	San Francisco P O	80	477
ESTUARDRO								
R	35	m	w	CHIL	Alameda	Oakland	68	252
ESTUDILLO								
Alejandro	38	m	w	ITAL	San Francisco	11-Wd San Francisc	84	660
Francisco	25	m	w	CA	San Diego	San Diego	78	487
Jose R	42	m	w	CA	Santa Barbara	Arroyo Grande P O	87	508
Jose V	36	m	w	CA	Santa Barbara	Arroyo Grande P O	87	508

© 2001 by Heritage Quest. All rights reserved.

Name	Age	S	R	B-PL	County	Locale	Series M593 Roll	Pg
ESTUDRAMIA								
Jesus	30	m	w	MEXI	Santa Clara	San Jose Twp	88	209
ESTURTILLO								
Jose A	30	m	w	CA	San Diego	Temecula Dist	78	526
ESTUS								
Ritlend H	26	m	w	ME	Inyo	Bishop Crk Twp	73	312
ESTWARDS								
J A	33	m	w	CHIL	Yuba	Marysville	93	632
ESTY								
Amos	37	m	w	OH	El Dorado	Placerville	72	124
David	47	m	w	TN	Butte	Chico Twp	70	44
Matilda	50	f	w	MO	Amador	Fiddletown P O	69	436
Sarah	40	f	w	IL	Amador	Fiddletown P O	69	436
William	26	m	w	KY	Yolo	Cache Crk Twp	93	449
ESVADO								
Manuel	23	m	w	PORT	Alameda	Washington Twp	68	293
ESWARO								
Luciano	30	m	w	MEXI	Kern	Bakersfield P O	73	366
ESWINE								
Matthew	46	m	w	HDAR	Del Norte	Crescent	71	463
ESWORTHY								
Edwin	43	m	w	ENGL	Santa Clara	Burnett Twp	88	38
ET								
Tem	40	m	c	CHIN	Yuba	Marysville	93	621
ETAN								
Wm H	36	m	w	NY	San Francisco	1-Wd San Francisco	79	113
ETCHBARNE								
Peter	30	m	w	FRAN	Santa Clara	1-Wd San Jose	88	264
ETCHEGOGAN								
Juan	37	m	w	FRAN	Santa Clara	Almaden Twp	88	13
ETCHELL								
Joseph	37	m	w	ENGL	Yolo	Washington Twp	93	533
ETCHELS								
Thomas	65	m	w	ENGL	Yolo	Washington Twp	93	533
ETCHEPAREZ								
Martin	38	m	w	FRAN	Los Angeles	Santa Ana Twp	73	606
ETELING								
Caroline	18	f	w	IL	Sacramento	3-Wd Sacramento	77	284
ETHELL								
George W	45	m	w	MO	Santa Clara	2-Wd San Jose	88	287
J A	40	m	w	MO	Yuba	Marysville	93	604
ETHERIDGE								
Benja	40	m	w	ENGL	Sutter	Nicolaus Twp	92	106
ETHRIDGE								
Darius	50	m	w	NY	San Francisco	San Francisco P O	83	143
ETIENE								
Paul	40	m	w	FRAN	San Francisco	San Francisco P O	80	342
ETIENNE								
Phillip	37	m	w	FRAN	San Francisco	San Francisco P O	80	349
ETIQUE								
John P	50	m	w	SWIT	San Francisco	7-Wd San Francisco	81	251
ETIS								
George	34	m	w	PA	Solano	Vacaville Twp	90	123
ETLAND								
Matilda	13	f	w	CA	Sacramento	San Joaquin Twp	77	404
ETLING								
Henry	22	m	w	NY	Sacramento	4-Wd Sacramento	77	319
ETOBEN								
Emanuel	75	m	w	CA	Fresno	Millerton P O	72	164
ETOROBLEUR								
A	40	m	w	PRUS	Alameda	Alameda	68	8
ETSON								
George B	2	m	w	CA	Yolo	Grafton Twp	93	478
ETTA								
Ah	45	m	c	CHIN	Santa Clara	Santa Clara Twp	88	158
ETTAMARIO								
Marie	45	f	w	MEXI	San Francisco	6-Wd San Francisco	81	111
ETTENGER								
Chas	30	m	w	GERM	San Francisco	8-Wd San Francisco	82	361
Montz	44	m	w	PRUS	San Francisco	8-Wd San Francisco	82	349
ETTER								
Benjamin	46	m	w	SWIT	El Dorado	Mud Springs Twp	72	74
Samuel	35	m	w	OH	Nevada	Bloomfield Twp	75	99
Samuel	28	m	w	IN	Nevada	Bloomfield Twp	75	95
ETTIG								
Henry	32	m	w	PA	San Francisco	San Francisco P O	83	359
ETTING								
Albert	20	m	w	NY	San Francisco	San Francisco P O	83	359
ETTINGHAUSER								
Wm	34	m	w	IA	Sonoma	Russian Rvr	91	376
ETTLEY								
Geo W	52	m	w	PA	Mariposa	Mariposa P O	74	118
ETTLINGER								
Benjamin	30	m	w	BADE	Solano	Silveyville Twp	90	85
ETUDILLO								
Guad	31	m	w	CA	San Diego	San Diego	78	483
ETZ								
Mortimer	50	m	w	OH	Calaveras	San Andreas P O	70	204
ETZEL								
Conrad	48	m	w	SAXO	El Dorado	White Oak Twp	72	139
ETZER								
Jacob	23	m	w	SAXO	El Dorado	White Oak Twp	72	135
ETZLER								
Martin	38	m	w	PA	Colusa	Monroe Twp	71	317
Sarah Jane	19	f	w	MO	Sacramento	Franklin Twp	77	110
EU								
---	28	m	c	CHIN	Siskiyou	Hamburg Twp	89	596
Ah	24	m	c	CHIN	Siskiyou	Hamburg Twp	89	596
Ah	18	m	c	CA	Stanislaus	Emory Twp	92	17
Ah	17	m	c	CHIN	San Francisco	San Francisco P O	80	497
EUBANKS								
David K	28	m	w	MO	Shasta	Millville P O	89	490
Isaiah	44	m	w	KY	Shasta	American Ranch P O	89	500
John	22	m	w	AR	Mendocino	Ukiah Twp	74	233
John S	41	m	w	IL	Siskiyou	Cottonwood Twp	89	591
EUBER								
John	32	m	w	FRAN	San Francisco	3-Wd San Francisco	79	321
EUCENIA								
Gregorio	41	m	w	CHIL	Amador	Fiddletown P O	69	440
EUDLITZ								
Maurice	25	m	w	FRAN	Monterey	San Juan Twp	74	404
EUGAN								
Elisha	40	m	w	MA	San Francisco	5-Wd San Francisco	81	26
William	35	m	w	SHOL	Sacramento	Franklin Twp	77	118
EUGENE								
David	25	m	w	FRAN	San Francisco	1-Wd San Francisco	79	34
Robin	44	m	w	FRAN	Sierra	Eureka Twp	89	527
EUGINE								
Lurand	30	f	w	FRAN	San Francisco	8-Wd San Francisco	82	364
EUH								
Ah	42	m	c	CHIN	Kern	Bakersfield P O	73	361
EUING								
Henry	14	m	w	CA	San Francisco	San Francisco P O	85	828
Richard	10	m	w	CA	San Francisco	San Francisco P O	85	828
EULARIO								
Dora	40	f	w	MEXI	Santa Clara	Almaden Twp	88	6
EULER								
Henry	44	m	w	SWIT	San Francisco	8-Wd San Francisco	82	298
EULES								
George	34	m	w	MO	Calaveras	San Andreas P O	70	175
EUNSTRO								
Manuel	29	m	w	MEXI	Monterey	San Antonio Twp	74	316
EURENAREBE								
G	32	m	i	CA	Alameda	Murray Twp	68	103
EUREVAS								
Carolina	13	f	w	CA	Santa Barbara	Santa Barbara P O	87	502
EURHART								
Mead	6	m	w	CA	Trinity	Weaverville Pct	92	222
EUSEBO								
J	29	m	w	MEXI	Alameda	Murray Twp	68	109
EUSELF								
William	28	m	w	NY	Colusa	Colusa Twp	71	284
EUSTACE								
George	30	m	w	NY	Solano	Montezuma Twp	90	66
James	32	m	w	CANA	San Francisco	11-Wd San Francisc	84	575
Jas	43	m	w	IREL	San Francisco	7-Wd San Francisco	81	261
EUSTACH								
Martial	40	m	w	FRAN	Santa Clara	Santa Clara Twp	88	149
EUSTAGO								
Morgan	18	m	w	SWIT	Sonoma	Bodega Twp	91	252
EUSTAN								
Edwd	30	m	w	IREL	San Francisco	1-Wd San Francisco	79	13
EUSTICE								
G	27	m	w	WI	Santa Clara	Gilroy Twp	88	71
James	25	m	w	IREL	San Francisco	11-Wd San Francisc	84	648
Wm	24	m	w	CANA	Solano	Vallejo	90	161
EUSTIS								
Edward W	24	m	w	MA	Santa Cruz	Santa Cruz Twp	89	399
EUTAW								
Mary	6	f	w	NE	Sacramento	Georgianna Twp	77	131
EVA								
James	32	m	w	ENGL	Alameda	Brooklyn Twp	68	40
Jim	40	m	i	CA	Colusa	Grand Island	71	310
John	44	m	w	ENGL	Nevada	Grass Valley Twp	75	201
Thomas	29	m	w	ENGL	Mariposa	Mariposa P O	74	98
EVAIN								
Louis	28	m	w	FRAN	Placer	Auburn P O	76	360
EVAL								
Jacob	16	m	w	CA	Los Angeles	Los Angeles Twp	73	489
EVAN								
Abijah	44	m	w	NY	Alameda	Alvarado	68	305
Emma A	29	f	w	NY	San Francisco	3-Wd San Francisco	79	328
Guadalupe	50	f	w	ITAL	Calaveras	San Andreas P O	70	174
J E	34	m	w	NY	San Francisco	3-Wd San Francisco	79	318
Wm F	29	m	w	RI	San Francisco	1-Wd San Francisco	79	118
EVANA								
Refugio	18	m	w	MEXI	Los Angeles	Los Angeles Twp	73	474
EVANCOVICH								
John	30	m	w	AUST	San Francisco	3-Wd San Francisco	79	325
EVANS								
A D	31	m	w	OH	Lassen	Long Valley Twp	73	437
A E	36	f	w	PA	Alameda	Oakland	68	171
A W	41	m	w	TN	Siskiyou	Scott Valley Twp	89	609
Aaron	33	m	w	ENGL	San Francisco	San Francisco P O	85	795
Alanson	39	m	w	OH	Santa Cruz	Pajaro Twp	89	346
Albert	38	m	w	NY	Napa	Napa Twp	75	63
Albert E	19	m	w	WALE	San Francisco	1-Wd San Francisco	79	95
Albert S	39	m	w	NH	San Francisco	2-Wd San Francisco	79	249
Albina S	40	f	w	NJ	Placer	Roseville P O	76	356
Alfred	40	m	w	WALE	Solano	Vallejo	90	155
Allen	36	m	w	OH	Los Angeles	Los Nietos Twp	73	573
Alorchan	40	m	w	BAVA	Sonoma	Petaluma Twp	91	363
Alvah	50	m	w	ME	Calaveras	Copperopolis P O	70	258
Ann	71	f	w	WALE	Tulare	Visalia Twp	92	284

© 2001 by Heritage Quest. All rights reserved.

California 1870 Census

Name	Age	S	R	B-PL	County	Locale	Series M593 Roll	Pg
Anna	18	f	w	CA	San Francisco	8-Wd San Francisco	82	329
Benjamin	53	m	w	WALE	Siskiyou	Hamburg Twp	89	597
Benjamin	38	m	w	WALE	Contra Costa	Martinez P O	71	427
Briget	40	f	w	IREL	San Francisco	7-Wd San Francisco	81	173
C	16	m	w	CA	Solano	Benicia	90	20
Catherine	34	f	w	NY	San Mateo	Half Moon Bay P O	87	407
Charles	51	m	w	PA	Santa Clara	Alviso Twp	88	24
Charles	47	m	w	GA	Alameda	Brooklyn	68	32
Charles	40	m	w	MA	San Francisco	6-Wd San Francisco	81	124
Charles	35	m	w	ENGL	San Francisco	7-Wd San Francisco	81	185
Charles	28	m	w	LA	Marin	San Rafael Twp	74	36
Charles	27	m	w	MI	San Francisco	7-Wd San Francisco	81	208
Charles P	46	m	w	ME	Sacramento	2-Wd Sacramento	77	236
Chas	33	m	w	FRAN	Sierra	Gibson Twp	89	539
Chas	3	m	w	CA	San Francisco	San Francisco P O	85	828
Clara	30	f	w	ENGL	Yolo	Cottonwood Twp	93	463
Daniel	39	m	w	ENGL	Contra Costa	Martinez P O	71	423
David	51	m	w	WALE	Mariposa	Mariposa P O	74	99
David	44	m	w	WALE	Contra Costa	Martinez P O	71	428
David	41	m	w	WALE	Yuba	New York Twp	93	639
David	35	m	w	WALE	Humboldt	Eureka Twp	72	267
David	22	m	w	WALE	Contra Costa	Martinez P O	71	427
Dudley	36	m	w	NY	Santa Clara	Alviso Twp	88	28
E	35	m	w	CANA	Solano	Vallejo	90	151
E C	37	f	w	AL	Sacramento	1-Wd Sacramento	77	185
Edward	41	m	w	SC	San Diego	San Diego	78	508
Edwd	34	m	w	WALE	San Francisco	1-Wd San Francisco	79	36
Eli	43	m	w	NY	Santa Clara	Redwood Twp	88	132
Ella	4	f	w	CA	San Francisco	San Francisco P O	85	799
Ellis	46	m	w	PA	Amador	Jackson P O	69	319
Emma	16	f	w	MA	San Francisco	8-Wd San Francisco	82	455
Emma G	27	f	w	MD	San Francisco	San Francisco P O	83	175
Eva	6	f	w	CA	Yolo	Washington Twp	93	533
Evan	50	m	w	WALE	Sierra	Table Rock Twp	89	571
Evan	40	m	w	OH	Sacramento	Alabama Twp	77	62
Evan	39	m	w	WALE	Nevada	Washington Twp	75	346
Evan	32	m	w	WALE	Nevada	Bridgeport Twp	75	107
Francis B	52	m	w	IREL	El Dorado	Placerville Twp	72	103
G R	38	m	w	IA	Yuba	Marysville	93	632
G R	23	m	w	IN	Amador	Jackson P O	69	324
Geo	49	m	w	OH	San Francisco	San Francisco P O	83	292
Geo A	40	m	w	WALE	San Francisco	7-Wd San Francisco	81	270
Geo E	31	m	w	IREL	San Francisco	1-Wd San Francisco	79	116
Geo S	44	m	w	MI	San Joaquin	2-Wd Stockton	86	182
Geo W	50	m	w	MD	Sonoma	Cloverdale Twp	91	271
George	42	m	w	ME	San Francisco	2-Wd San Francisco	79	266
George	39	m	w	MA	San Mateo	San Mateo P O	87	355
George	38	m	w	ENGL	Santa Clara	2-Wd San Jose	88	305
George	38	m	w	WALE	Amador	Sutter Crk P O	69	396
George	38	m	w	ENGL	San Bernardino	San Bernardino Twp	78	435
George	37	m	w	AL	Santa Cruz	Santa Cruz Twp	89	391
George	31	m	w	ENGL	San Francisco	San Francisco P O	83	253
George	29	m	w	IREL	Sacramento	Dry Crk Twp	77	104
George	26	m	w	ME	San Francisco	7-Wd San Francisco	81	204
George	26	m	w	ME	Mendocino	Anderson Twp	74	151
George	26	m	w	AUST	Tuolumne	Columbia P O	93	344
George H	42	m	w	TN	Solano	Silveyville Twp	90	86
George T	34	m	w	NY	San Francisco	San Francisco P O	83	255
George W	28	m	w	MD	Los Angeles	Wilmington Twp	73	641
Gertrude	1	f	w	CA	San Francisco	San Francisco P O	85	799
Griffith	26	m	w	WALE	Colusa	Spring Valley Twp	71	338
Hamet	24	f	i	CA	Klamath	Orleans Twp	73	379
Henry	80	f	w	SC	Colusa	Grand Island Twp	71	305
Henry	48	m	w	IREL	Marin	San Rafael Twp	74	26
Henry	36	m	w	MO	Colusa	Spring Valley Twp	71	341
Henry	30	m	w	NY	San Francisco	San Francisco P O	80	479
Henry	28	m	w	FRAN	San Francisco	7-Wd San Francisco	81	166
Henry	28	m	w	IREL	San Francisco	San Francisco P O	83	276
Henry	26	m	w	ENGL	Nevada	Grass Valley Twp	75	201
Henry J	47	m	w	WALE	Klamath	Orleans Twp	73	379
Henry P	24	m	w	NY	Butte	Oregon Twp	70	130
Henry W	46	m	w	TN	Los Angeles	Los Nietos Twp	73	584
Horace	20	m	w	AR	San Francisco	6-Wd San Francisco	81	109
Howell	38	m	w	WALE	Contra Costa	Martinez P O	71	427
I B	46	m	w	MA	El Dorado	Greenwood Twp	72	54
Ida	3	f	w	CA	San Francisco	San Francisco P O	85	799
J	60	m	w	OH	Siskiyou	Scott Valley Twp	89	613
J A	40	m	w	NY	Sacramento	Brighton Twp	77	74
J A	31	m	w	IL	Sutter	Butte Twp	92	102
J J	43	m	w	KY	San Joaquin	3-Wd Stockton	86	222
James	44	m	w	WALE	Contra Costa	Martinez P O	71	425
James	36	m	w	IL	Sonoma	Analy Twp	91	244
James	35	m	w	ME	Stanislaus	Empire Twp	92	30
James	31	m	w	IN	Santa Barbara	San Buenaventura P	87	424
James	31	m	w	OH	Del Norte	Crescent Twp	71	455
James	30	m	w	WALE	Placer	Bath P O	76	446
James	30	m	w	NY	San Diego	San Diego	78	511
James	27	m	w	ENGL	Contra Costa	Martinez P O	71	423
James	26	m	w	WALE	Tulare	Visalia Twp	92	284
James	25	m	w	WALE	Contra Costa	Martinez P O	71	425
James	24	m	w	ENGL	San Francisco	San Francisco P O	80	458
James	23	m	w	IA	Solano	Maine Prairie Twp	90	53
James A	40	m	w	OH	Nevada	Bridgeport Twp	75	105
James G	33	m	w	OH	Monterey	Alisal Twp	74	303
James L	48	m	w	MA	Sacramento	2-Wd Sacramento	77	232
James S	45	m	w	KY	Amador	Volcano P O	69	379
Jane	66	f	w	WALE	Placer	Bath P O	76	435

Name	Age	S	R	B-PL	County	Locale	Series M593 Roll	Pg
Jas A	37	m	w	IN	Siskiyou	Scott Valley Twp	89	620
Jehu	44	m	w	DE	El Dorado	Placerville	72	120
Jeremiah F	44	m	w	IL	Plumas	Indian Twp	77	12
Jerry	50	m	w	IREL	Sacramento	Granite Twp	77	140
Jesse	63	m	w	VA	Siskiyou	Scott Valley Twp	89	620
Jno F	21	m	w	GA	Butte	Oregon Twp	70	133
John	56	m	w	ENGL	Klamath	Salmon Twp	73	387
John	54	m	w	PA	Los Angeles	Los Angeles Twp	73	490
John	52	m	w	AUST	San Francisco	San Francisco P O	85	740
John	50	m	w	BADE	El Dorado	Placerville	72	116
John	40	m	w	IA	Stanislaus	Empire Twp	92	32
John	40	m	w	WALE	Contra Costa	Martinez P O	71	425
John	39	m	w	ENGL	Contra Costa	Martinez P O	71	422
John	37	m	w	ENGL	Contra Costa	Martinez P O	71	424
John	36	m	w	HOLL	Alpine	Markleeville P O	69	311
John	35	m	w	WALE	Sacramento	Granite Twp	77	149
John	34	m	w	ENGL	San Francisco	San Francisco P O	80	472
John	31	m	w	WALE	San Francisco	1-Wd San Francisco	79	71
John	28	m	w	ENGL	Nevada	Nevada Twp	75	315
John	28	m	w	ENGL	Contra Costa	Martinez P O	71	423
John	28	m	w	CA	Contra Costa	Martinez P O	71	425
John A	24	m	w	WALE	Placer	Bath P O	76	436
John D	30	m	w	WALE	Sierra	Sears Twp	89	557
John J	36	m	w	WALE	Sierra	Gibson Twp	89	543
John N	35	m	w	WALE	Sierra	Sears Twp	89	556
John R	45	m	w	ENGL	San Francisco	San Francisco P O	83	104
John R	38	m	w	ENGL	San Francisco	San Francisco P O	83	87
John W	40	m	w	IREL	Los Angeles	Wilmington Twp	73	639
Jonah	40	m	w	WALE	Monterey	Pajaro Twp	74	368
Joseph	66	m	w	TN	San Francisco	San Francisco P O	83	387
Joseph	35	m	w	MO	Colusa	Grand Island Twp	71	305
Joshua	23	m	w	NY	Yolo	Grafton Twp	93	500
Josiah	61	m	w	OH	Santa Clara	Milpitas Twp	88	111
Julia	36	f	w	VT	Placer	Bath P O	76	456
Julia	14	f	w	CA	Yuba	Marysville	93	576
Juliet	44	f	w	MO	Sonoma	Mendocino Twp	91	291
L	48	f	w	OH	Lassen	Long Valley Twp	73	436
Levi	9	m	w	IA	San Francisco	San Francisco P O	85	800
Lizzie	12	f	w	NY	Santa Clara	Gilroy Twp	88	95
Louis	34	m	w	FRAN	San Francisco	San Francisco P O	80	347
Louisa Mcgee	43	f	w	VA	Plumas	Indian Twp	77	11
Lucy	60	f	m	VA	San Francisco	6-Wd San Francisco	81	128
Maria	60	f	m	MD	San Francisco	2-Wd San Francisco	79	143
Mary	70	f	w	IREL	San Francisco	San Francisco P O	83	86
Mary	41	f	w	IN	Solano	Maine Prairie Twp	90	45
Mary	32	f	w	ENGL	San Francisco	7-Wd San Francisco	81	168
Mary	13	f	w	CA	Solano	Tremont Twp	90	35
Mary A	27	f	w	MA	San Francisco	San Francisco P O	83	202
Morgan D	61	m	w	WALE	San Francisco	1-Wd San Francisco	79	45
Morris	44	m	w	OH	Sierra	Gibson Twp	89	541
Nathan G	37	m	w	NY	Placer	Bath P O	76	434
Newton Bill	39	m	w	IN	Plumas	Mineral Twp	77	22
O H	41	m	w	WALE	Sierra	Sears Twp	89	553
O T	20	m	w	KY	Napa	Napa Twp	75	34
Ocar	44	m	w	NY	San Francisco	San Francisco P O	83	228
Orlando	52	m	w	OH	Nevada	Bridgeport Twp	75	105
Patrick	36	m	w	IREL	San Francisco	1-Wd San Francisco	79	98
Phil	56	m	w	NC	Butte	Kimshew Tpw	70	79
Richard	34	m	w	IREL	Calaveras	San Andreas P O	70	188
Richard	29	m	w	IL	Contra Costa	Martinez P O	71	369
Richd	76	m	w	VA	Butte	Kimshew Tpw	70	81
Richd	42	m	w	WALE	San Francisco	1-Wd San Francisco	79	45
Robert	30	m	w	ENGL	San Mateo	Pescadero P O	87	410
Robert	29	m	w	MA	Kern	Kernville P O	73	368
Robert	17	m	w	CANA	Contra Costa	Martinez P O	71	447
Roswell P	41	m	w	NY	Yolo	Grafton Twp	93	493
Ruth	39	f	w	TN	San Joaquin	2-Wd Stockton	86	175
Samuel	74	m	w	WALE	Tulare	Visalia Twp	92	284
Samuel	64	m	w	TN	Siskiyou	Scott Valley Twp	89	621
Susan	30	f	w	IA	Santa Clara	Milpitas Twp	88	108
Theodore	48	m	w	PORT	Contra Costa	Martinez P O	71	385
Theodore	23	m	w	ENGL	Sacramento	3-Wd Sacramento	77	288
Thomas	62	m	w	KY	Santa Barbara	San Buenaventura P	87	447
Thomas	45	m	w	WALE	San Francisco	3-Wd San Francisco	79	313
Thomas	35	m	w	IREL	Yuba	Marysville	93	583
Thomas	35	m	w	NY	Solano	Maine Prairie Twp	90	48
Thomas	28	m	w	ENGL	San Francisco	6-Wd San Francisco	81	83
Thomas	25	m	w	SCOT	San Francisco	1-Wd San Francisco	79	112
Thomas	25	m	w	NY	Yolo	Grafton Twp	93	481
Thomas	23	m	w	ENGL	Nevada	Grass Valley Twp	75	168
Thomas	23	m	w	IREL	Santa Clara	Gilroy Twp	88	84
Thomas C	33	m	w	OH	Solano	Silveyville Twp	90	80
Thomas Jr	60	m	w	ENGL	Calaveras	San Andreas P O	70	175
Thos	40	m	w	ME	Solano	Vallejo	90	161
Thos	29	m	w	CANA	Solano	Vallejo	90	178
Thos	26	m	w	IN	Sonoma	Washington Twp	91	466
Thos J	32	m	w	WALE	San Luis Obispo	Santa Rosa Twp	87	324
W A	40	m	w	VA	Mendocino	Ukiah Twp	74	237
W L	50	m	w	OH	Siskiyou	Klamath Twp	89	600
W S	34	m	w	WALE	Lassen	Long Valley Twp	73	437
W W	35	m	w	IL	Siskiyou	Callahan P O	89	626
Washington	36	m	w	IN	Monterey	Castroville Twp	74	328
Watkin	26	m	w	WALE	Amador	Sutter Crk P O	69	408
William	52	m	w	ENGL	San Diego	San Diego	78	486
William	47	m	w	WALE	Santa Cruz	Santa Cruz Twp	89	380
William	44	m	w	TN	Mariposa	Mariposa P O	74	110
William	40	m	w	ENGL	Stanislaus	Empire Twp	92	39

© 2001 by Heritage Quest. All rights reserved.

California 1870 Census

Series M593

Name	Age	S	R	B-PL	County	Locale	Roll	Pg
William	40	m	w	ENGL	Marin	San Rafael	74	50
William	38	m	w	ENGL	San Francisco	San Francisco P O	80	379
William	35	m	w	IN	Santa Barbara	San Buenaventura P	87	447
William	33	m	w	MA	Santa Clara	1-Wd San Jose	88	248
William	27	m	w	IREL	Siskiyou	Scott Valley Twp	89	614
William	26	m	w	CANA	Santa Barbara	Santa Barbara P O	87	455
William	21	m	w	MD	San Francisco	San Francisco P O	83	154
William	19	m	w	MO	Solano	Suisun Twp	90	99
William	19	m	w	ENGL	San Francisco	11-Wd San Francisc	84	468
William J	39	m	w	OH	Siskiyou	Table Rock Twp	89	648
Willie	10	m	w	OR	Santa Barbara	San Buenaventura P	87	438
Wm	50	m	w	IREL	Sacramento	Granite Twp	77	142
Wm	44	m	w	WALE	Butte	Wyandotte Twp	70	146
Wm	40	m	w	IREL	San Francisco	San Francisco P O	83	86
Wm	35	m	w	ENGL	San Francisco	1-Wd San Francisco	79	59
Wm	23	m	w	ENGL	San Francisco	1-Wd San Francisco	79	130
Wm F	40	m	w	NY	Nevada	Nevada Twp	75	275
Wm H	40	m	w	ENGL	San Francisco	San Francisco P O	83	109
Wm R	36	m	w	WALE	Plumas	Washington Twp	77	56
Wm S	42	m	w	WALE	Sierra	Sears Twp	89	555
Wm Washington	25	m	w	IL	Plumas	Indian Twp	77	11
EVANSBERG								
Wm	30	m	w	HANO	Mariposa	Mariposa P O	74	92
EVANSON								
Gunder	26	m	w	NORW	Marin	San Rafael Twp	74	26
Ole	30	m	w	NORW	El Dorado	Cosumnes Twp	72	14
EVANTS								
Wm C	33	m	w	AR	Monterey	Alisal Twp	74	290
EVARA								
Elario	50	m	w	CA	Los Angeles	Los Angeles	73	520
Francisca	23	f	w	CA	Los Angeles	Los Angeles	73	515
Francisco	28	m	w	MEXI	San Luis Obispo	Arroyo Grande Twp	87	273
Joanna	19	f	w	CA	Santa Clara	2-Wd San Jose	88	310
Jose	60	m	w	CA	Los Angeles	Los Angeles	73	520
Ramon	22	m	w	CA	Los Angeles	Los Angeles	73	520
EVARDO								
Elano	23	m	w	CA	Los Angeles	Los Angeles	73	519
Manuela	8	f	w	CA	Los Angeles	Los Angeles	73	556
EVARDRA								
Philomea	52	m	w	MEXI	Fresno	Millerton P O	72	154
EVARE								
Simon	37	m	w	CA	Monterey	Monterey Twp	74	349
EVARIA								
Margareta	16	f	w	CA	Los Angeles	Los Angeles Twp	73	485
EVARIO								
Pedro	46	m	w	CA	Los Angeles	Los Angeles	73	512
EVARRA								
Secundin	30	m	w	MEXI	Sonoma	Santa Rosa	91	429
EVART								
John	50	m	w	PRUS	Placer	Roseville P O	76	353
Robert	40	m	w	SCOT	San Francisco	7-Wd San Francisco	81	223
EVARTS								
Estelle	27	f	w	TN	San Francisco	6-Wd San Francisco	81	78
EVATT								
Daniel	36	m	w	MD	Sacramento	4-Wd Sacramento	77	320
Eleanore	71	f	w	IREL	San Francisco	San Francisco P O	83	55
Wm	33	m	w	MD	San Francisco	San Francisco P O	83	55
EVE								
Thos J	54	m	w	VA	Sierra	Table Rock Twp	89	571
EVEANS								
H W	41	m	w	ENGL	Lake	Lower Lake	73	418
John O	44	m	w	CANA	Sonoma	Petaluma Twp	91	354
EVEDO								
John	37	m	w	ITAL	San Francisco	1-Wd San Francisco	79	117
EVEHRSEN								
Chas	28	m	w	NORW	San Francisco	1-Wd San Francisco	79	120
EVEILS								
William	17	m	w	IREL	Solano	Silveyville Twp	90	72
EVELAND								
Joel	43	m	w	OH	Sierra	Sears Twp	89	560
Mary	26	f	w	OH	Tehama	Hunters Twp	92	187
EVELESTON								
Ransom	45	m	w	OH	Sacramento	4-Wd Sacramento	77	372
EVELETH								
John	25	m	w	VA	Kern	Tehachapi P O	73	356
Sarah	43	f	w	RI	San Francisco	San Francisco P O	85	714
EVELINE								
John	40	m	w	OH	San Francisco	7-Wd San Francisco	81	175
EVELITH								
Letica	47	f	w	IREL	Butte	Ophir Twp	70	92
EVEMIGHAM								
J W	21	m	w	IA	Napa	Napa	75	16
EVEN								
John	37	m	w	LUXE	Napa	Napa	75	40
EVENS								
A B	36	m	w	OH	Lassen	Long Valley Twp	73	436
Alexander	30	m	w	ENGL	Sonoma	Vallejo Twp	91	456
Chas	45	f	w	NY	San Joaquin	2-Wd Stockton	86	209
Cornelius	25	m	w	NY	Santa Clara	Redwood Twp	88	128
D P	33	m	w	OH	Monterey	Monterey Twp	74	350
Daniel	50	m	w	NY	San Francisco	8-Wd San Francisco	82	351
David	31	m	w	WALE	Humboldt	Eureka Twp	72	259
Esther	42	f	w	IREL	Alameda	Brooklyn	68	37
Ganes	42	m	w	NORW	Calaveras	San Andreas P O	70	164
George	33	m	w	IREL	San Francisco	San Francisco P O	85	759
J L	21	m	w	IA	Lassen	Susanville Twp	73	443
James	56	m	w	MD	Yuba	Parks Bar Twp	93	649
James	38	m	w	NJ	Calaveras	San Andreas P O	70	203
Magie	20	f	w	WI	Siskiyou	Callahan P O	89	626
Noah	39	m	w	WALE	Nevada	Bridgeport Twp	75	107
Owen	35	m	w	WALE	San Joaquin	2-Wd Stockton	86	165
Patrick H	36	m	w	IREL	Placer	Rocklin Twp	76	466
Peter Jr	40	m	w	SWED	San Francisco	2-Wd San Francisco	79	200
Richard	35	m	w	ENGL	Calaveras	Copperopolis P O	70	248
T J	34	m	w	RI	Tuolumne	Columbia P O	93	362
Tettus	70	m	w	WALE	Amador	Sutter Crk P O	69	412
W	57	m	w	WALE	Sierra	Forest Twp	89	532
William	57	m	w	SHOL	San Francisco	3-Wd San Francisco	79	321
EVENT								
Ed	40	m	w	IA	San Joaquin	Douglas Twp	86	50
Lort	47	m	w	CANA	San Joaquin	Elliott Twp	86	80
EVENTO								
John	40	m	w	IREL	Butte	Oregon Twp	70	125
EVER								
William	24	m	w	ENGL	Sacramento	Franklin Twp	77	113
EVERARD								
Elizabeth	56	f	w	NY	Amador	Jackson P O	69	324
James	54	m	w	NY	Alameda	Alameda	68	19
EVERBECK								
Charles	42	m	w	MA	Napa	Napa	75	42
EVERD								
E G	33	m	w	GERM	Sacramento	1-Wd Sacramento	77	176
EVERDING								
Chas	45	m	w	ROMA	Humboldt	Eureka Twp	72	270
Fred	40	m	w	PRUS	San Francisco	2-Wd San Francisco	79	220
John	40	m	w	CANA	San Francisco	1-Wd San Francisco	79	19
EVERET								
L	29	m	w	MI	San Joaquin	Oneal Twp	86	106
Phillip G	46	m	w	PA	Yolo	Cottonwood Twp	93	473
EVERETA								
Louis	9	m	w	CA	Los Angeles	Los Angeles	73	512
EVERETH								
C A	38	m	w	ME	Sacramento	American Twp	77	67
EVERETT								
A F	35	m	w	MA	San Francisco	San Francisco P O	85	860
Abija P	50	m	w	MA	San Francisco	San Francisco P O	83	89
Aratus	25	m	w	MI	Santa Barbara	San Buenaventura P	87	447
Charles	44	m	w	HOLL	El Dorado	Georgetown Twp	72	47
Chas	36	m	w	MA	Mono	Bridgeport P O	74	283
Edward	40	m	w	MA	San Francisco	8-Wd San Francisco	82	325
Edward A	30	m	w	MA	San Luis Obispo	Santa Rosa Twp	87	321
Geo	25	m	w	MA	Sacramento	1-Wd Sacramento	77	185
George	38	m	w	ENGL	Shasta	Horsetown P O	89	501
Harey S	49	m	w	MA	Yuba	Slate Range Bar Tw	93	675
Henry	43	m	w	NH	Nevada	Bridgeport Twp	75	123
Hiram	47	m	w	NJ	Santa Barbara	San Buenaventura P	87	447
J W	58	m	w	MI	Lake	Lower Lake	73	421
J W	44	m	w	TN	San Joaquin	Elkhorn Twp	86	61
John	28	m	w	MD	San Francisco	San Francisco P O	83	53
John	17	m	w	ENGL	Siskiyou	Scott Valley Twp	89	609
John T	40	m	w	ENGL	Siskiyou	Scott Rvr Twp	89	604
Joseph A	37	m	w	IL	Nevada	Grass Valley Twp	75	171
Julia	9	f	w	CA	El Dorado	Placerville Twp	72	102
Martin	50	m	w	IA	Yolo	Cottonwood Twp	93	473
Martin V	39	m	w	NY	San Francisco	San Francisco P O	85	731
Rufus	40	m	w	NH	San Francisco	11-Wd San Francisc	84	506
Samuel P	42	m	w	PA	Nevada	Grass Valley Twp	75	231
Thomas	34	m	w	VA	San Francisco	11-Wd San Francisc	84	462
W J	45	m	w	TN	San Joaquin	Elkhorn Twp	86	60
Warren	38	m	w	NY	Sacramento	2-Wd Sacramento	77	245
William	26	m	w	IREL	Solano	Silveyville Twp	90	74
Wm	29	m	w	IREL	San Francisco	1-Wd San Francisco	79	79
EVERETTS								
J	25	m	w	NORW	Lake	Knoxville Mines	73	405
EVERHARD								
George	53	m	w	CA	Placer	Gold Run Twp	76	400
James	55	m	w	NY	San Francisco	6-Wd San Francisco	81	96
Lander	45	m	w	OH	Placer	Gold Run Twp	76	400
EVERHART								
Amos C	33	m	w	PA	Calaveras	Copperopolis P O	70	248
William	39	m	w	OH	Trinity	Weaverville Pct	92	222
Wm	44	m	w	HCAS	Tuolumne	Chinese Camp P O	93	370
EVERINGHAM								
Elizabeth	49	f	w	NY	Santa Clara	2-Wd San Jose	88	287
Henry	50	m	w	NY	Yolo	Buckeye Twp	93	408
EVERLEE								
Geo	27	m	w	BRUN	San Francisco	1-Wd San Francisco	79	65
EVERLETH								
James	23	m	w	ME	Marin	Tomales Twp	74	84
EVERLING								
Charles	54	m	w	ME	Santa Cruz	Santa Cruz Twp	89	399
EVERLINS								
Joseph	25	m	w	PORT	Alameda	Eden Twp	68	71
EVERRAN								
G W	32	m	w	PA	Solano	Vallejo	90	179
EVERS								
Augustus	36	m	w	HANO	Sacramento	4-Wd Sacramento	77	350
Charles D	33	m	w	BREM	San Francisco	San Francisco P O	85	719
Deitrick H	36	m	w	HANO	Yuba	Parks Bar Twp	93	650
George	40	m	w	BREM	Alameda	Eden Twp	68	63
Henry	39	m	w	MO	Butte	Kimshew Tpw	70	79
Henry C	46	m	w	NORW	San Francisco	1-Wd San Francisco	79	36
Joseph	30	m	w	PRUS	Napa	Napa Twp	75	29
Otto	29	m	w	GERM	Los Angeles	Santa Ana Twp	73	599

© 2001 by Heritage Quest. All rights reserved.

Name	Age	S	R	B-PL	County	Locale	Series M593 Roll	Pg
William	45	m	w	PRUS	San Francisco	San Francisco P O	80	356
Williams	38	m	w	ENGL	San Francisco	1-Wd San Francisco	79	115
EVERSON								
Abram	53	m	w	NORW	Mendocino	Big Rvr Twp	74	158
Chas	35	m	w	NORW	San Francisco	1-Wd San Francisco	79	10
Edward E	31	m	w	NORW	Mendocino	Navarro & Big Rvr	74	174
George	45	m	w	FRAN	San Francisco	3-Wd San Francisco	79	319
Henry	22	m	w	NORW	Placer	Cisco P O	76	494
John	33	m	w	PRUS	San Francisco	7-Wd San Francisco	81	224
Julius	35	m	w	NY	Sacramento	San Joaquin Twp	77	395
Louis	37	m	w	DENM	Contra Costa	Martinez P O	71	401
Peter	27	m	w	DENM	Sonoma	Bodega Twp	91	260
Wallace	30	m	w	NY	San Francisco	8-Wd San Francisco	82	476
EVERSTEIN								
George	28	m	w	KY	Siskiyou	Butte Twp	89	587
EVERT								
Ebe	59	m	w	ME	San Joaquin	3-Wd Stockton	86	246
Ed	40	m	w	MA	San Joaquin	2-Wd Stockton	86	212
Jacob	43	m	w	BADE	Yuba	W Bear Rvr Twp	93	682
Marion E	6	f	w	CA	Placer	Bath P O	76	436
EVERTON								
Alfred	35	m	w	NY	Tulare	Farmersville Twp	92	248
EVERTS								
Alston W	25	m	w	IN	Napa	Napa	75	6
Ambrose	47	m	w	OH	San Bernardino	San Bernardino Twp	78	428
B	26	m	w	IREL	Alameda	Oakland	68	261
Chas N	21	m	w	IN	Napa	Napa	75	51
D Cheey	33	m	w	NY	Los Angeles	Los Angeles	73	524
Edward	15	m	w	TX	Napa	Napa	75	41
F D	41	m	w	IN	Napa	Napa	75	4
John H	48	m	w	OH	Yolo	Cache Crk Twp	93	421
Laura	36	f	w	IL	San Francisco	5-Wd San Francisco	81	23
Maria	61	f	w	OH	Napa	Napa	75	5
Mary	18	f	w	IL	San Francisco	5-Wd San Francisco	81	23
Melvina	25	f	w	MA	Placer	Gold Run Twp	76	398
Myron	40	m	w	NY	Kern	Tehachapi P O	73	356
EVERY								
Mary	12	f	w	MO	Santa Clara	Santa Clara Twp	88	166
EVES								
Henry	26	m	w	BREM	Alameda	Oakland	68	185
Jessie M	42	m	w	NY	Yolo	Cache Crk Twp	93	425
Morris W	46	m	w	KY	San Francisco	5-Wd San Francisco	81	12
EVET								
William	37	m	w	ENGL	Calaveras	San Andreas P O	70	163
EVEY								
Edward	57	m	w	MD	Los Angeles	Santa Ana Twp	73	602
Sarah M	38	f	w	MO	Napa	Napa	75	13
EVINS								
Emily	11	f	w	IA	San Francisco	San Francisco P O	85	798
Henry	38	m	w	WALE	Inyo	Bishop Crk Twp	73	314
EVIS								
Margaret	26	f	w	IREL	Colusa	Monroe Twp	71	315
EVONS								
Augustus	46	m	w	MO	Yuba	Bullards Bar P O	93	552
EVOY								
John	55	m	w	MO	Alameda	Oakland	68	247
EVRET								
Abner	65	m	w	NY	Sonoma	Petaluma Twp	91	355
EVRITH								
John	39	m	w	NY	Humboldt	Mattole Twp	72	286
EVVANS								
John	54	m	w	NY	Los Angeles	Los Angeles	73	536
EWALD								
Anton	72	m	w	PRUS	Trinity	Trinity Center Pct	92	204
Antonio	46	m	w	PRUS	San Francisco	San Francisco P O	80	426
Edward	38	m	w	HOLL	San Francisco	11-Wd San Francisc	84	509
Marcus	40	m	w	PRUS	San Francisco	San Francisco P O	80	464
EWATT								
Theodore	19	m	w	PRUS	San Francisco	San Francisco P O	80	455
EWE								
Ah	35	m	c	CHIN	Trinity	Douglas	92	237
Ah	32	m	c	CHIN	Trinity	Lewiston Pct	92	214
EWELL								
Charles A	40	m	w	MO	Tulare	White Rvr Twp	92	301
Eugene	19	m	w	FRAN	Contra Costa	Martinez Twp	71	350
John P	32	m	w	MO	Yolo	Grafton Twp	93	481
L J	41	m	w	NY	San Francisco	3-Wd San Francisco	79	313
Mary	38	f	w	TN	El Dorado	White Oak Twp	72	141
P B F	46	m	w	NY	Sonoma	Sonoma Twp	91	437
S C	36	f	w	NY	Alameda	Oakland	68	211
Susan H	27	f	w	ME	San Francisco	3-Wd San Francisco	79	314
EWEN								
Andrew	50	m	w	VA	Merced	Snelling P O	74	274
EWENS								
John	63	m	w	KY	Klamath	Dillon Twp	73	369
John	35	m	w	FRAN	Stanislaus	Branch Twp	92	7
EWER								
Charles	75	m	w	CHIL	San Francisco	San Francisco P O	80	462
David	60	m	w	OH	Butte	Wyandotte Twp	70	149
Elon E	64	m	w	VA	Butte	Wyandotte Twp	70	149
Frederika	26	f	w	BAVA	Sacramento	4-Wd Sacramento	77	353
Seneca	48	m	w	NY	Napa	Napa	75	11
Sofaro	30	m	w	NY	Sacramento	Natomas Twp	77	166
W D	35	m	w	ME	Sierra	Sierra Twp	89	563
Warren	56	m	w	VT	San Francisco	11-Wd San Francisc	84	620
EWERS								
George	22	m	w	OH	Santa Clara	Gilroy Twp	88	82
Nich	31	m	w	PRUS	Sacramento	3-Wd Sacramento	77	295
Nichols	38	m	w	ENGL	Sacramento	3-Wd Sacramento	77	261
EWIN								
J C	45	m	w	MO	Merced	Snelling P O	74	275
EWING								
Andrew	50	m	w	ENGL	San Francisco	3-Wd San Francisco	79	311
Edward	8	m	w	CA	San Francisco	2-Wd San Francisco	79	209
Etna	40	f	w	OH	San Francisco	6-Wd San Francisco	81	93
Francis	6	m	m	CA	San Francisco	San Francisco P O	80	475
Frank	34	m	b	MO	San Francisco	San Francisco P O	80	475
George	28	m	w	ENGL	Nevada	Grass Valley Twp	75	176
James	41	m	w	ENGL	Napa	Yountville Twp	75	79
James	40	m	w	VA	Contra Costa	Martinez P O	71	399
John	34	m	w	IREL	San Francisco	11-Wd San Francisc	84	469
Jos D	21	m	w	TN	Klamath	Trinidad Twp	73	392
Joseph	48	m	w	SCOT	Trinity	Hayfork Valley	92	238
Mary	37	f	w	IREL	San Francisco	San Francisco P O	80	475
Oliver	30	m	w	IREL	Sacramento	2-Wd Sacramento	77	240
Priscella	29	f	m	MO	San Francisco	6-Wd San Francisco	81	149
Robert	40	m	w	SCOT	San Francisco	San Francisco P O	85	809
Robt	30	m	w	CANA	San Francisco	5-Wd San Francisco	81	19
Samuel	50	m	w	OH	Sacramento	Alabama Twp	77	59
Sarah	67	f	w	PA	Del Norte	Smith Rvr Twp	71	478
Simon	44	m	w	OH	Santa Cruz	Soquel Twp	89	443
T	42	m	w	NY	Mariposa	Maxwell Crk P O	74	143
Titus	45	m	w	OH	Placer	Lincoln P O	76	485
W A D	40	m	w	TN	Marin	Bolinas Twp	74	5
William	49	m	w	VA	Solano	Rio Vista Twp	90	63
Wm	34	m	w	ENGL	Tuolumne	Sonora P O	93	328
EWINS								
Antone	52	m	w	IREL	Sacramento	2-Wd Sacramento	77	254
EWNIS								
Robert	32	m	w	SCOT	Napa	Napa Twp	75	61
EWRING								
Ira	30	m	w	CANA	San Mateo	Belmont P O	87	372
EX								
On	33	m	c	CHIN	Calaveras	San Andreas P O	70	184
Yee	29	m	c	CHIN	Calaveras	San Andreas P O	70	190
EXAN								
John S	19	m	w	IL	Los Angeles	Wilmington Twp	73	634
EXCELSIOR								
Indian	15	f	i	CA	Santa Barbara	San Buenaventura P	87	434
EXILIN								
Bernard	49	m	w	PA	San Luis Obispo	Salinas Twp	87	292
EXLER								
John	38	m	w	WURT	Sonoma	Santa Rosa	91	422
EXLEY								
Anna	43	f	w	ENGL	Shasta	Shasta P O	89	458
Fredrick	35	m	w	PA	Amador	Sutter Crk P O	69	406
EXLINE								
Levi	24	m	w	OH	El Dorado	Mountain Twp	72	68
EXMAN								
Ferdinand	35	m	w	BADE	San Francisco	San Francisco P O	80	464
EXODIUS								
Julia	40	f	w	BAVA	San Francisco	8-Wd San Francisco	82	437
EXPERT								
Marie	30	f	w	FRAN	San Francisco	San Francisco P O	80	455
Mary	60	f	w	FRAN	San Francisco	2-Wd San Francisco	79	138
EXTRAM								
Charles	42	m	w	SWED	San Francisco	San Francisco P O	80	466
EXTRON								
O	40	m	w	SWED	Alameda	Alameda	68	15
EXUM								
Richard	38	m	w	TN	Mendocino	Ukiah Twp	74	234
EYE								
---	26	m	c	CHIN	Siskiyou	Butte Twp	89	585
Ah	40	m	c	CHIN	Trinity	Lewiston Pct	92	214
Ah	35	m	c	CHIN	Trinity	Douglas	92	237
Ah	30	m	c	CHIN	Trinity	Douglas	92	237
Ah	26	m	c	CHIN	Trinity	Lewiston Pct	92	212
Ah	22	m	c	CHIN	Nevada	Nevada Twp	75	292
Ah	21	m	c	CHIN	Trinity	Indian Crk	92	199
Han	22	m	c	CHIN	Colusa	Butte Twp	71	269
Ling	42	m	c	CHIN	Siskiyou	Yreka	89	662
Toy	20	f	c	CHIN	Siskiyou	Yreka	89	662
Yen	25	m	c	CHIN	Klamath	Salmon Twp	73	387
EYERMAN								
Benj	38	m	w	BADE	Mendocino	Round Valley Twp	74	217
EYK								
Sin	25	m	c	CHIN	Calaveras	San Andreas P O	70	176
EYLER								
Louis	46	m	w	OH	Butte	Oregon Twp	70	128
EYLWARD								
A	50	m	w	IREL	Yuba	Rose Bar Twp	93	663
EYMANN								
Charles	42	m	w	PRUS	San Francisco	San Francisco P O	85	727
EYO								
Aurelian	70	m	w	MEXI	San Bernardino	San Salvador Twp	78	457
EYRE								
E E	44	m	w	PA	San Francisco	San Francisco P O	83	325
Johns	48	m	w	ENGL	San Francisco	11-Wd San Francisc	84	584
Manuel	28	m	w	PA	San Francisco	8-Wd San Francisco	82	410
Thomas T	41	m	w	ENGL	Mariposa	Mariposa P O	74	114
William	32	m	w	PA	San Francisco	3-Wd San Francisco	79	322
EYRICH								
William	40	m	w	PA	Alameda	Alameda	68	5

© 2001 by Heritage Quest. All rights reserved.

California 1870 Census

Name	Age	S	R	B-PL	County	Locale	Series M593 Roll	Pg
EYSEN								
Edward	24	m	w	PRUS	Shasta	Fort Crook P O	89	473
EYSLEE								
Albert	28	m	w	PRUS	Santa Clara	Gilroy Twp	88	76
EZALEDO								
Antonio J	46	m	w	AZOR	Monterey	Monterey	74	359
EZAR								
Bernardo	36	m	w	PERU	Los Angeles	Los Angeles	73	571
EZEKEIL								
Elizabeth	19	f	w	NY	Sacramento	1-Wd Sacramento	77	175
EZEKIEL								
Marks	24	m	w	NY	San Francisco	8-Wd San Francisco	82	341
Rebecca	34	f	w	AUSL	San Francisco	2-Wd San Francisco	79	194
FA								
Ah	48	m	c	CHIN	Tuolumne	Chinese Camp P O	93	388
Ah	32	m	c	CHIN	Mendocino	Point Arena Twp	74	215
Ah	21	f	c	CHIN	Santa Barbara	Santa Barbara P O	87	459
Ah	19	m	c	CHIN	Nevada	Eureka Twp	75	127
Mang	33	f	c	CHIN	Tulare	Visalia	92	299
Yen	19	m	c	CHIN	Solano	Vacaville Twp	90	136
FAA								
Ah	58	m	c	CHIN	Alameda	Oakland	68	245
FAAT								
Ah	33	m	c	CHIN	Amador	Ione City P O	69	355
FABA								
Ah	31	m	c	CHIN	Placer	Dutch Flat P O	76	411
FABAIM								
S G	38	m	w	FRAN	Tuolumne	Columbia P O	93	350
FABEL								
Lateber	40	f	w	MEXI	Calaveras	San Andreas P O	70	177
FABELA								
Cruz	53	m	w	MEXI	Santa Clara	Almaden Twp	88	5
FABEN								
Jules	40	m	w	FRAN	San Francisco	San Francisco P O	80	430
FABENS								
Francis	52	m	w	WURT	San Francisco	San Francisco P O	80	352
George	23	m	w	MA	Marin	Sausalito Twp	74	69
FABER								
Barbara	21	f	w	PRUS	San Francisco	San Francisco P O	83	351
Felix	65	m	w	FRAN	San Francisco	11-Wd San Francisc	84	612
Felix	27	m	w	LUXE	Marin	Nicasio Twp	74	20
Frederick	64	m	w	DENM	El Dorado	White Oak Twp	72	143
George	47	m	w	MA	Calaveras	San Andreas P O	70	201
George	39	m	w	FRAN	Santa Barbara	Santa Barbara P O	87	494
Hester	12	m	w	CA	Los Angeles	El Monte Twp	73	455
John S	60	m	w	VA	Santa Clara	2-Wd San Jose	88	283
Joseph	36	m	w	BADE	San Francisco	San Francisco P O	80	356
Martha A	16	f	w	CA	El Dorado	Mud Springs Twp	72	71
Mathew D	50	m	w	PRUS	Butte	Chico Twp	70	36
Michael	44	m	w	PRUS	Placer	Auburn P O	76	365
Orrin	29	m	w	NH	San Mateo	Schoolhouse Statio	87	333
FABERT								
Charles	30	m	w	CANA	San Francisco	3-Wd San Francisco	79	322
FABEY								
Thos I	28	m	w	IREL	San Francisco	San Francisco P O	83	103
FABIAN								
P	27	m	w	PRUS	San Joaquin	Tulare Twp	86	256
Sarah	28	f	w	RUSS	San Francisco	San Francisco P O	83	368
FABICAS								
John	58	m	w	CA	Tuolumne	Sonora P O	93	324
FABIEN								
John	30	m	w	PRUS	San Francisco	7-Wd San Francisco	81	217
FABING								
Henry W	35	m	w	FRAN	Santa Clara	Santa Clara Twp	88	144
FABINS								
William	28	m	w	IREL	Solano	Tremont Twp	90	31
FABO								
Joseph	31	m	b	NY	San Joaquin	1-Wd Stockton	86	138
FABOR								
Fredrick	32	m	w	NY	Amador	Jackson P O	69	318
Philip	23	m	w	PRUS	Santa Clara	Santa Clara Twp	88	168
Richard	26	m	w	NY	Stanislaus	Empire Twp	92	66
FABRE								
Benjamin C	23	m	w	PA	San Francisco	3-Wd San Francisco	79	319
Daniel	45	m	w	LA	Calaveras	San Andreas P O	70	205
FABRETTI								
Agostina	19	m	w	SWIT	Santa Cruz	Santa Cruz	89	426
FABRICO								
Poncho	35	m	i	MEXI	Inyo	Lone Pine Twp	73	335
FABRY								
L M	29	m	w	BADE	San Francisco	San Francisco P O	85	831
Labasline	26	m	w	BADE	San Francisco	11-Wd San Francisc	84	674
FABUN								
Clarks S	53	m	w	NY	San Bernardino	San Bernardino Twp	78	414
FACE								
Soloman	31	m	w	OH	Sonoma	Mendocino Twp	91	291
FACHLER								
John G	48	m	w	VA	San Francisco	8-Wd San Francisco	82	476
FACHS								
David	25	m	w	PRUS	Alameda	Murray Twp	68	125
FACK								
---	18	m	c	CHIN	Siskiyou	Cottonwood Twp	89	594
Ah	4	m	c	CHIN	Mariposa	Mariposa P O	74	132
Ah	30	m	c	CHIN	Calaveras	Copperopolis P O	70	264
Charles	55	m	w	FRAN	Inyo	Cerro Gordo Twp	73	319
Chong	19	m	c	CHIN	Santa Clara	2-Wd San Jose	88	311
Micheal	28	m	w	PRUS	San Francisco	7-Wd San Francisco	81	226

Name	Age	S	R	B-PL	County	Locale	Series M593 Roll	Pg
Su	27	m	c	CHIN	Solano	Suisun Twp	90	107
FACOON								
Antone	27	m	w	PORT	Alameda	Eden Twp	68	61
FACY								
Chas	40	m	w	ENGL	San Joaquin	3-Wd Stockton	86	224
Fanny	3	f	w	CA	San Joaquin	Liberty Twp	86	85
FADDEN								
Agnes	19	f	w	ENGL	San Francisco	San Francisco P O	83	245
Deliah	14	f	w	PA	Contra Costa	Martinez P O	71	422
Mary	16	f	w	PA	Contra Costa	Martinez P O	71	418
Thos	22	m	w	HANO	San Francisco	11-Wd San Francisc	84	640
FADDLE								
William	28	m	w	CANA	Santa Clara	Santa Clara Twp	88	168
FADDLER								
Jacob	42	m	w	BADE	Placer	Dutch Flat P O	76	402
FADDON								
James	30	m	w	ENGL	Tuolumne	Sonora P O	93	325
FADER								
Amos	25	m	w	CANA	Siskiyou	Callahan P O	89	625
C E	39	m	w	CANA	Trinity	Trinity Center Pct	92	205
Cornelous	30	m	w	CANA	Trinity	Trinity Center Pct	92	240
Isadore	36	m	w	PRUS	San Francisco	San Francisco P O	83	354
L J	28	m	w	CANA	Trinity	Trinity Center Pct	92	240
FADGGEN								
John	33	m	w	SCOT	Napa	Yountville Twp	75	88
FADING								
Joseph	24	m	w	CANA	Contra Costa	Martinez P O	71	440
FAEHRENBACH								
Geo	34	m	w	BADE	Shasta	Shasta P O	89	463
FAESSEN								
A J	30	m	w	HOLL	Merced	Snelling P O	74	273
FAFA								
Louis	43	m	w	FRAN	Siskiyou	Callahan P O	89	630
FAFFEY								
Willm	21	m	w	PA	Alameda	Murray Twp	68	108
FAFIANNO								
John	39	m	w	ITAL	Marin	Novato Twp	74	9
FAGAN								
Annie	25	f	w	IREL	San Francisco	11-Wd San Francisc	84	498
Bridget	33	f	w	IREL	San Francisco	San Francisco P O	83	216
Bridgett	29	f	w	IN	Napa	Napa Twp	75	32
Catharine	38	f	w	IREL	San Francisco	San Francisco P O	83	109
Chas	32	m	w	PA	San Joaquin	Douglas Twp	86	41
Chas A	23	m	w	PA	San Francisco	1-Wd San Francisco	79	65
Clarence E	20	m	w	IA	Santa Cruz	Soquel Twp	89	445
Edward	24	m	w	NY	Marin	San Rafael Twp	74	45
Eliza	49	f	w	NY	San Francisco	8-Wd San Francisco	82	490
Ellen	27	f	w	NY	San Francisco	San Francisco P O	83	48
Ellis	27	m	w	NY	Yuba	Marysville	93	583
Frank	21	m	w	MO	Stanislaus	Buena Vista Twp	92	15
Henry	53	m	w	PRUS	El Dorado	Diamond Springs Tw	72	33
Hugh	38	m	w	IREL	San Francisco	1-Wd San Francisco	79	106
Hugh	15	m	w	CANA	Colusa	Colusa	71	292
James	40	m	w	IREL	Plumas	Washington Twp	77	52
James	37	m	w	IREL	San Francisco	6-Wd San Francisco	81	80
James	35	m	w	IREL	Sonoma	Petaluma Twp	91	319
Jennie	15	f	w	CA	Solano	Benicia	90	16
John	45	m	w	IREL	San Francisco	8-Wd San Francisco	82	489
John	43	m	w	HDAR	San Francisco	1-Wd San Francisco	79	116
John	43	m	w	IREL	El Dorado	Placerville	72	111
John	41	m	w	MO	Stanislaus	Buena Vista Twp	92	15
John	33	m	w	ENGL	San Francisco	San Francisco P O	83	67
John	32	m	w	IREL	San Francisco	San Francisco P O	83	127
Jos	20	m	w	ENGL	San Francisco	San Francisco P O	83	84
M	24	m	w	CANA	Humboldt	Bucksport Twp	72	243
Margaret	45	f	w	IREL	San Francisco	8-Wd San Francisco	82	430
Mary	41	f	w	IREL	San Francisco	11-Wd San Francisc	84	441
Mary M	20	f	w	IL	Stanislaus	Buena Vista Twp	92	14
Michael	36	m	w	IREL	San Francisco	San Francisco P O	83	295
Michael	27	m	w	PA	Santa Barbara	San Buenaventura P	87	431
P B	27	m	w	IREL	Solano	Vallejo	90	175
P B [Dr]	52	m	w	US	Santa Cruz	Santa Cruz	89	406
Pat	40	m	w	IREL	Solano	Benicia	90	13
Patk	35	m	w	IREL	Sacramento	1-Wd Sacramento	77	180
Patrick	52	m	w	IREL	Mariposa	Mariposa P O	74	128
Patrick	39	m	w	IREL	San Francisco	1-Wd San Francisco	79	82
Peter	44	m	w	IREL	Napa	Napa Twp	75	30
Richard	38	m	w	MA	Tulare	Tule Rvr Twp	92	266
Terrence	35	m	w	IREL	San Francisco	San Francisco P O	83	53
Thomas	8	m	w	CA	Amador	Fiddletown P O	69	439
William	47	m	w	TN	Solano	Vacaville Twp	90	121
William M	40	m	w	OH	Placer	Bath P O	76	425
FAGEN								
Peter	35	m	w	CANA	Amador	Amador City P O	69	395
FAGER								
Daniel	32	m	w	IREL	Santa Clara	Redwood Twp	88	123
John	39	m	w	PRUS	San Francisco	San Francisco P O	80	478
FAGERBERG								
Fred	33	m	w	SWED	Solano	Maine Prairie Twp	90	47
Henry W	48	m	w	SWED	Nevada	Grass Valley Twp	75	185
FAGERLY								
Peter	35	m	w	GERM	Yolo	Cottonwood Twp	93	473
FAGERTY								
Thomas	40	m	w	IREL	Siskiyou	Yreka Twp	89	665
FAGG								
Gr	46	m	w	ENGL	Sierra	Sierra Twp	89	563
J	60	m	w	ENGL	Sierra	Sierra Twp	89	562

© 2001 by Heritage Quest. All rights reserved.

Name	Age	S	R	B-PL	County	Locale	Series M593 Roll	Pg
J D	44	m	w	ENGL	Sierra	Sierra Twp	89	566
Joseph	16	m	w	IN	Plumas	Quartz Twp	77	39
Nette	13	f	w	CA	Yuba	Marysville	93	598
FAGGAN								
P	22	m	w	NJ	Alameda	Oakland	68	226
FAGIN								
Elizabeth	53	f	w	NC	Stanislaus	Empire Twp	92	31
Thomas	29	m	w	IREL	San Francisco	6-Wd San Francisco	81	80
Thomas	26	m	w	PA	Los Angeles	Wilmington Twp	73	641
FAGIO								
Lorenzo	26	m	w	ITAL	San Francisco	11-Wd San Francisc	84	594
FAGLEDEE								
Mathias	25	m	w	DENM	San Mateo	San Mateo P O	87	355
FAGLEY								
Jos	35	m	w	KY	San Joaquin	Douglas Twp	86	31
FAGNER								
Antonio	25	m	w	ITAL	San Mateo	Schoolhouse Statio	87	334
FAGONIO								
Antonio	44	m	w	ITAL	Amador	Volcano P O	69	372
FAGOTTY								
John	46	m	w	FRAN	San Francisco	San Francisco P O	80	348
FAGUENAS								
Paul	52	m	w	SPAI	Marin	Bolinas Twp	74	3
FAGY								
Anna	25	f	w	IREL	San Francisco	San Francisco P O	85	729
FAH								
Ah	51	m	c	CHIN	Contra Costa	Martinez P O	71	436
Ah	35	m	c	CHIN	Santa Barbara	Santa Barbara P O	87	458
Ah	32	f	c	CHIN	Nevada	Nevada Twp	75	299
Ah	30	m	c	CHIN	San Francisco	3-Wd San Francisco	79	301
Ah	30	m	c	CHIN	Contra Costa	Martinez P O	71	436
Ah	29	m	c	CHIN	Calaveras	San Andreas P O	70	173
Foo	42	m	c	CHIN	Kern	Havilah P O	73	337
Ong	15	m	c	CHIN	Placer	Summit P O	76	497
FAHAY								
Ann	35	f	w	IREL	Amador	Jackson P O	69	318
FAHEY								
Ann	19	f	w	IREL	San Francisco	11-Wd San Francisc	84	423
Edward	45	m	w	IREL	Calaveras	San Andreas P O	70	193
John	42	m	w	IREL	Tuolumne	Sonora P O	93	333
John	38	m	w	IREL	Nevada	Grass Valley Twp	75	161
John	34	m	w	IREL	Marin	San Rafael Twp	74	36
John	26	m	w	IREL	San Francisco	San Francisco P O	83	272
Lawrence	38	m	w	IREL	Nevada	Grass Valley Twp	75	166
Lawrence	36	m	w	IREL	Placer	Cisco P O	76	495
Michael	50	m	w	IREL	Nevada	Grass Valley Twp	75	178
William	38	m	w	IREL	Tuolumne	Sonora P O	93	313
Winniford	5	f	w	CA	Tuolumne	Sonora P O	93	331
FAHIS								
John	32	m	w	SHOL	San Francisco	11-Wd San Francisc	84	528
FAHLO								
Henry	45	m	w	BREM	Placer	Newcastle Twp	76	474
FAHN								
Ah	17	m	c	CHIN	San Francisco	8-Wd San Francisco	82	447
John	20	m	w	IREL	Colusa	Monroe Twp	71	314
FAHRENBACH								
Wm	35	m	w	GERM	San Francisco	7-Wd San Francisco	81	230
FAHRENKRUG								
Christian	57	m	w	HANO	San Francisco	11-Wd San Francisc	84	604
FAHRITTER								
Gussep	34	m	w	AUST	Calaveras	San Andreas P O	70	205
FAHY								
Dennis	27	m	w	IREL	Tuolumne	Sonora P O	93	322
Michael	45	m	w	IREL	Tuolumne	Sonora P O	93	322
Patrick	25	m	w	IREL	San Francisco	1-Wd San Francisco	79	61
FAI								
Ah	29	m	c	CHIN	Butte	Chico Twp	70	51
Wie	23	m	c	CHIN	Solano	Vacaville Twp	90	132
FAILER								
Joseph	30	m	w	PRUS	San Francisco	San Francisco P O	85	758
FAILEY								
Andrew J	32	m	w	WIND	San Diego	Coronado	78	467
Fred E	24	m	w	IN	San Diego	San Diego	78	494
FAILING								
Dennis	53	m	w	IREL	Stanislaus	Branch Twp	92	6
FAILK								
Frederick	36	m	w	PRUS	Sacramento	2-Wd Sacramento	77	254
FAILOR								
M A	39	f	w	KY	Sacramento	1-Wd Sacramento	77	177
FAIN								
J C	50	m	w	IN	Humboldt	Bald Hills	72	237
Mary	35	f	w	IREL	San Francisco	5-Wd San Francisco	81	20
William	26	m	w	NY	Calaveras	San Andreas P O	70	177
William	25	m	w	MO	Klamath	South Fork Twp	73	384
FAINE								
Mary A	30	f	w	IREL	San Francisco	San Francisco P O	85	760
FAINER								
James	38	m	w	IREL	Sacramento	2-Wd Sacramento	77	228
FAINIGAN								
Susan	27	f	w	IREL	San Francisco	11-Wd San Francisc	84	556
FAIR								
David	34	m	w	SCOT	Marin	Point Reyes Twp	74	23
James	61	m	w	ENGL	Nevada	Grass Valley Twp	75	154
William	19	m	w	IREL	Santa Clara	San Jose Twp	88	212
Wm	62	m	w	SCOT	El Dorado	Georgetown Twp	72	40
FAIRBANK								
Martha	28	f	w	IA	Sonoma	Petaluma Twp	91	320
Melvin	9	m	w	CA	Sonoma	Analy Twp	91	229
FAIRBANKS								
A	30	m	w	TN	San Joaquin	Elkhorn Twp	86	65
Adam D	44	m	w	IN	San Luis Obispo	Salinas Twp	87	296
Albertine	16	f	w	CA	San Francisco	7-Wd San Francisco	81	270
Albt	45	m	w	VT	Butte	Concow Twp	70	7
Alex	46	m	w	NY	Butte	Chico Twp	70	49
Alphus	35	m	w	RI	San Joaquin	Elkhorn Twp	86	59
Alva	36	m	w	NY	Humboldt	Bald Hills	72	238
Austin	24	m	w	MI	Marin	Tomales Twp	74	82
B S	43	m	w	RI	San Joaquin	Elkhorn Twp	86	59
Benj	47	m	w	MA	Sonoma	Analy Twp	91	227
Geo	50	m	w	MO	El Dorado	Lake Valley Twp	72	63
Henry	45	m	w	NY	Mendocino	Point Arena Twp	74	207
Henry	40	m	w	NY	Butte	Concow Twp	70	6
Henry	35	m	w	VT	Butte	Oregon Twp	70	125
Hiram G	42	m	w	IN	Sonoma	Petaluma Twp	91	335
James	46	m	w	NY	Stanislaus	Empire Twp	92	54
John	59	m	w	ENGL	San Joaquin	3-Wd Stockton	86	234
John C	42	m	w	NH	Santa Barbara	Santa Barbara P O	87	473
M	20	f	w	MA	Alameda	Oakland	68	259
Mary A	33	f	w	MI	Nevada	Grass Valley Twp	75	166
Ophellia	9	f	w	CA	San Luis Obispo	Salinas Twp	87	296
Robert	29	m	w	NY	Sonoma	Salt Point	91	387
Rolandos	13	m	w	CA	El Dorado	Placerville	72	119
Thomas	60	m	w	NY	Santa Clara	1-Wd San Jose	88	227
Wm	31	m	w	NY	Sacramento	San Joaquin Twp	77	394
Wm R	32	m	w	VT	Marin	Tomales Twp	74	87
FAIRBEINS								
Wm	43	m	w	SCOT	Solano	Benicia	90	9
FAIRBROWN								
Fred	39	m	w	MA	San Francisco	11-Wd San Francisc	84	686
FAIRCHILD								
A	39	m	w	NC	Napa	Napa	75	22
Alfred	44	m	w	PA	Sonoma	Salt Point	91	380
Alice	18	f	w	NY	San Francisco	8-Wd San Francisco	82	449
Ben	38	m	w	VA	San Joaquin	Tulare Twp	86	258
Chas	38	m	w	BELG	San Joaquin	Tulare Twp	86	251
Chas	28	m	w	OH	Butte	Hamilton Twp	70	62
Chas	15	m	w	CA	Sacramento	1-Wd Sacramento	77	184
Ebenezer	47	m	w	IN	El Dorado	Salmon Falls Twp	72	129
Elizab	21	f	w	IN	El Dorado	Greenwood Twp	72	52
Elucus	52	m	w	PA	Sacramento	1-Wd Sacramento	77	202
George	45	m	w	PA	San Francisco	San Francisco P O	83	366
Henry	63	m	w	NY	San Francisco	6-Wd San Francisco	81	151
Isaac	38	m	w	OH	Butte	Hamilton Twp	70	61
John A	39	m	w	MS	Siskiyou	Yreka	89	655
John A	21	m	w	NY	Nevada	Nevada Twp	75	272
Judith	61	f	w	NY	Butte	Hamilton Twp	70	62
Nathan	38	m	w	IN	Siskiyou	Scott Valley Twp	89	614
S V	28	f	w	MO	Amador	Ione City P O	69	356
Saml D	67	m	w	NJ	San Francisco	7-Wd San Francisco	81	251
Step I	40	m	w	OH	Butte	Hamilton Twp	70	61
Susan	40	f	w	PA	San Francisco	San Francisco P O	83	384
T H	38	m	w	MA	Lassen	Milford Twp	73	438
Thomas	40	m	w	IREL	Placer	Lincoln P O	76	489
W	11	m	w	MO	Lassen	Milford Twp	73	438
William	30	m	w	OH	Solano	Vacaville Twp	90	129
FAIRCHILDS								
C	32	m	w	ME	Alameda	Oakland	68	261
G B	42	m	w	KY	Siskiyou	Surprise Valley Tw	89	641
Geo M	28	m	w	NY	Santa Barbara	Santa Barbara P O	87	455
George	28	m	w	NY	San Francisco	8-Wd San Francisco	82	322
J	19	m	w	CA	Alameda	Oakland	68	199
Joel	29	m	w	MI	Sonoma	Bodega Twp	91	248
Richard	39	m	w	OH	Sonoma	Petaluma Twp	91	309
W	50	m	w	PA	San Joaquin	Oneal Twp	86	112
W	5	m	w	CA	Klamath	South Fork Twp	73	382
Warren	35	m	w	NY	Inyo	Independence Twp	73	326
FAIRCLOUGH								
R	56	m	w	NJ	Solano	Vallejo	90	200
FAIRE								
Henry	35	m	w	SWIT	San Francisco	6-Wd San Francisco	81	113
FAIRFAX								
August	36	m	w	HANO	Santa Clara	Fremont Twp	88	45
Charles Mrs	40	f	w	MO	San Francisco	5-Wd San Francisco	81	33
Charles Mrs	35	f	w	OH	Sonoma	Salt Point	91	392
FAIRFIELD								
Annie	17	f	w	NY	Sacramento	1-Wd Sacramento	77	178
Chas	40	m	w	CT	Humboldt	Eureka Twp	72	273
D	40	m	w	CANA	Solano	Vallejo	90	208
Danial	40	m	w	CANA	San Francisco	7-Wd San Francisco	81	216
G C	55	m	w	MA	Humboldt	Eureka Twp	72	260
Hiram B	34	m	w	NY	Santa Clara	Alviso Twp	88	25
John	45	m	w	NY	Yolo	Grafton Twp	93	497
M	35	m	w	PRUS	San Francisco	San Francisco P O	85	807
Malcom	29	m	w	MI	Alameda	Washington Twp	68	298
Martin	53	m	w	NY	Contra Costa	Martinez P O	71	377
FAIRFILD								
David	41	m	w	CT	Napa	Napa	75	19
FAIRFOWL								
James	47	m	w	PA	San Francisco	11-Wd San Francisc	84	561
FAIRGROVE								
Emil	20	m	w	IL	San Francisco	1-Wd San Francisco	79	101
FAIRHURST								
George W	37	m	w	IN	Nevada	Grass Valley Twp	75	153

© 2001 by Heritage Quest. All rights reserved.

California 1870 Census

Name	Age	S	R	B-PL	County	Locale	Series M593 Roll	Pg
FAIRLEY								
Hettie	35	f	w	IREL	San Francisco	11-Wd San Francisc	84	445
FAIRMAN								
Edward	29	m	w	NY	San Francisco	San Francisco P O	80	532
T W	36	m	w	PA	Solano	Vallejo	90	194
Wm	34	m	w	PA	Sutter	Yuba Twp	92	143
FAIRVIEW								
John	42	m	w	IREL	San Francisco	11-Wd San Francisc	84	708
FAIRWEATHER								
A J	35	m	w	CANA	San Francisco	San Francisco P O	83	297
FAISCLOE								
George	25	m	w	NJ	Siskiyou	Butte Twp	89	585
FAIT								
John	40	m	w	SCOT	Tuolumne	Columbia P O	93	358
FAITE								
Elcie	41	f	w	PA	San Francisco	San Francisco P O	83	33
FAITH								
George	21	m	w	CANA	Santa Clara	San Jose Twp	88	188
FAITHFUL								
Edwin	37	m	w	ENGL	San Francisco	11-Wd San Francisc	84	507
FAITS								
William	43	m	w	BADE	San Francisco	2-Wd San Francisco	79	227
FAITT								
Ah	28	m	c	CHIN	Amador	Drytown P O	69	424
FAK								
Ah	63	m	c	CHIN	Calaveras	San Andreas P O	70	176
Ah	31	m	c	CHIN	San Francisco	San Francisco P O	80	494
Ah	25	f	c	CHIN	San Francisco	San Francisco P O	80	494
Ah	24	m	c	CHIN	San Francisco	San Francisco P O	80	496
FAKE								
Ah	39	m	c	CHIN	Mendocino	Anderson Twp	74	150
Ah	38	m	c	CHIN	Sierra	Butte Twp	89	512
Ah	30	m	c	CHIN	Trinity	Douglas	92	234
Ah	30	m	c	CHIN	Trinity	North Fork Twp	92	219
Ah	30	m	c	CHIN	Trinity	Weaverville Pct	92	230
Ah	23	m	c	CHIN	Trinity	Douglas	92	237
George S	70	m	w	NY	Amador	Volcano P O	69	381
War	50	m	c	CHIN	San Francisco	11-Wd San Francisc	84	528
FAKROENDO								
Emanuel	40	m	w	MEXI	Tulare	Visalia	92	294
FAL								
Ah	48	m	c	CHIN	Santa Barbara	Santa Barbara P O	87	452
Ah	42	m	c	CHIN	San Francisco	11-Wd San Francisc	84	478
Long	52	m	c	CHIN	Los Angeles	Los Angeles	73	516
FALANSBEE								
R S	26	m	w	ME	Tuolumne	Chinese Camp P O	93	374
W J	59	m	w	ME	Tuolumne	Chinese Camp P O	93	374
FALBY								
Edwd	22	m	w	IREL	San Francisco	1-Wd San Francisco	79	133
FALCH								
Valentine O	56	m	w	HDAR	El Dorado	White Oak Twp	72	139
FALCHER								
John	36	m	w	PRUS	San Francisco	San Francisco P O	83	416
FALCK								
Benhard	30	m	w	HAMB	San Francisco	7-Wd San Francisco	81	156
FALE								
Jacob A	43	m	w	FRAN	Inyo	Cerro Gordo Twp	73	319
Keng	37	m	c	CHIN	Solano	Vacaville Twp	90	129
Louis	18	m	w	CT	Sacramento	4-Wd Sacramento	77	370
FALENCIA								
Rafini	27	f	i	----	Marin	Sausalito Twp	74	89
FALES								
Alex	41	m	w	BELG	San Francisco	2-Wd San Francisco	79	169
Alexander	25	m	w	MI	Los Angeles	El Monte Twp	73	451
Arthur P	20	m	w	IL	Humboldt	Arcata Twp	72	234
Benj D	27	m	w	ME	Marin	Bolinas Twp	74	3
Burton	52	m	w	ME	Tuolumne	Columbia P O	93	359
Carlos	40	m	w	CA	Alameda	Washington Twp	68	285
David	28	m	w	CA	Santa Clara	Gilroy Twp	88	96
Edward	66	m	w	ME	San Francisco	11-Wd San Francisc	84	505
George	28	m	w	CA	Placer	Lincoln P O	76	488
Juan	33	m	w	MEXI	Los Angeles	Los Angeles	73	563
Juana	14	f	w	CA	Santa Clara	1-Wd San Jose	88	265
Milo J	49	m	w	OH	Humboldt	Arcata Twp	72	227
Nathaniel	60	m	w	ME	Tuolumne	Columbia P O	93	357
Orris	53	m	w	ME	Contra Costa	Martinez P O	71	379
Oscar	64	m	w	ME	Contra Costa	Martinez P O	71	379
Saml	38	m	w	MI	Mono	Bridgeport P O	74	286
Thomas	26	m	w	MI	Sutter	Yuba Twp	92	143
Tilman	55	m	w	MA	Placer	Roseville P O	76	355
FALEY								
Eliza	26	f	w	IREL	San Francisco	San Francisco P O	83	178
John	33	m	w	IREL	Marin	Tomales Twp	74	79
John	30	m	w	IREL	Napa	Yountville Twp	75	80
L	10	f	w	CA	Los Angeles	Los Angeles	73	569
Mary	50	f	w	IREL	Napa	Napa	75	5
Nathan	27	m	w	IREL	Napa	Napa	75	3
S	33	m	w	IREL	Del Norte	Crescent Twp	71	455
William	44	m	w	TN	Solano	Silveyville Twp	90	77
FALEZ								
L	12	f	w	CA	Los Angeles	Los Angeles	73	570
FALINE								
Margaret	36	f	w	IREL	San Francisco	San Francisco P O	83	171
FALING								
Byron C	26	m	w	MI	Santa Cruz	Santa Cruz	89	408
Horace	37	m	w	MI	Sacramento	Brighton Twp	77	71
FALIS								
Alcalada	41	m	w	CA	Santa Cruz	Santa Cruz	89	426
Antonio	37	m	w	CA	Santa Cruz	Santa Cruz	89	411
Bicenta	19	m	w	CA	San Luis Obispo	San Luis Obispo Tw	87	315
Carmela	38	f	w	CA	Santa Clara	1-Wd San Jose	88	262
Dilforma	34	f	w	MEXI	Placer	Emigrant Gap P O	76	416
Iago	45	m	w	CA	San Bernardino	San Bernardino Twp	78	447
Incarnacion	60	m	w	MEXI	San Luis Obispo	Santa Rosa Twp	87	324
Jose	48	m	w	SCOT	San Luis Obispo	Santa Rosa Twp	87	324
Jose N	56	m	w	CA	San Luis Obispo	San Luis Obispo Tw	87	305
Juan Jose	75	m	w	CA	Santa Cruz	Santa Cruz	89	411
Juaquin	27	m	w	CA	San Luis Obispo	San Luis Obispo Tw	87	315
Juaquin	27	m	w	CA	San Luis Obispo	San Luis Obispo Tw	87	315
Manuel	29	m	w	PORT	Tuolumne	Columbia P O	93	356
Maria A	80	f	w	CA	Santa Cruz	Santa Cruz	89	411
Miguel	49	m	w	CA	Santa Cruz	Santa Cruz	89	426
Phlomina	75	f	w	CA	San Luis Obispo	Morro Twp	87	286
Ramon	33	m	w	CA	San Luis Obispo	Morro Twp	87	286
Sacremento	26	m	w	MEXI	Los Angeles	Los Angeles	73	502
FALIZ								
Manuel	26	m	w	MEXI	Los Angeles	Soledad Twp	73	631
FALK								
Adolph	37	m	w	PRUS	San Francisco	8-Wd San Francisco	82	288
Ferdinand	27	m	w	BRAN	Sacramento	4-Wd Sacramento	77	319
John Christian	38	m	w	SWED	Plumas	Washington Twp	77	53
K	42	m	w	PRUS	San Francisco	San Francisco P O	83	294
Levy	48	m	w	POLA	San Francisco	7-Wd San Francisco	81	238
Philip	38	m	w	PRUS	San Francisco	San Francisco P O	85	784
Samuel	28	m	w	PRUS	San Francisco	8-Wd San Francisco	82	449
Solomon	33	m	w	PRUS	San Francisco	San Francisco P O	83	364
FALKE								
George	52	m	w	OH	Nevada	Eureka Twp	75	140
FALKENAU								
Louis	31	m	w	BOHE	San Francisco	11-Wd San Francisc	84	563
FALKENBURG								
Wm	28	m	w	FRAN	San Francisco	1-Wd San Francisco	79	52
FALKENBURGH								
Henry	48	m	w	NORW	San Francisco	San Francisco P O	83	142
Isabella	38	f	w	IREL	San Francisco	San Francisco P O	83	142
FALKENSTEIN								
---	40	m	w	PRUS	Sonoma	Salt Point	91	393
Gustave	39	m	w	PRUS	San Francisco	San Francisco P O	83	89
Jasper	33	m	w	VA	San Diego	San Jacinto Dist	78	518
Louis	40	m	w	FRNK	Siskiyou	Scott Rvr Twp	89	602
Robert	36	m	w	PRUS	San Mateo	Half Moon Bay P O	87	404
FALKENSTINE								
P	47	m	w	FRAN	San Joaquin	1-Wd Stockton	86	155
FALKER								
George	23	m	w	NH	Nevada	Grass Valley Twp	75	227
FALKERS								
Herman	35	m	w	OLDE	San Francisco	8-Wd San Francisco	82	402
FALKINGHAM								
Ed	34	m	w	ENGL	San Francisco	San Francisco P O	83	89
FALKINS								
Eliza	11	f	w	CA	Santa Clara	Santa Clara Twp	88	157
FALKMAN								
Henry	46	m	w	PRUS	San Joaquin	Liberty Twp	86	92
FALKNER								
A	46	m	w	NORW	Yuba	Marysville	93	604
Annie	19	f	w	NY	San Francisco	San Francisco P O	80	424
C A	18	m	w	CA	Alameda	Oakland	68	159
George	48	m	w	MA	San Francisco	8-Wd San Francisco	82	306
George	46	m	w	OH	Tulare	Packwood Twp	92	255
George	10	m	w	CA	Tulare	Packwood Twp	92	255
Henry	22	m	w	IL	Sonoma	Petaluma Twp	91	319
James	48	m	w	NJ	Santa Clara	1-Wd San Jose	88	232
John	50	m	w	NJ	San Francisco	5-Wd San Francisco	81	26
John F	38	m	w	IREL	Santa Clara	San Jose Twp	88	188
M C	33	m	w	MS	Yuba	Marysville	93	605
Mary	45	f	w	IREL	Santa Clara	2-Wd San Jose	88	308
Newton	23	m	w	MO	San Joaquin	Douglas Twp	86	31
Saml	76	m	w	NC	Butte	Oregon Twp	70	128
FALL								
Ah	24	m	c	CHIN	Nevada	Nevada Twp	75	311
Ah	20	m	c	CHIN	Sacramento	3-Wd Sacramento	77	265
Allice	34	f	w	AL	Los Angeles	Los Angeles	73	539
C	49	m	w	ENGL	Santa Clara	Almaden Twp	88	13
Charles	36	m	w	IN	Solano	Tremont Twp	90	30
George	35	m	w	BAVA	San Francisco	San Francisco P O	85	718
George M	27	m	w	OH	Los Angeles	Los Angeles	73	567
Henry	27	m	w	KY	Nevada	Meadow Lake Twp	75	252
John	35	m	w	SWIT	Siskiyou	Yreka	89	662
Richd	29	m	w	ENGL	Santa Clara	Almaden Twp	88	10
Stephen	48	m	w	BOHE	Sacramento	1-Wd Sacramento	77	172
Thomas	55	m	w	ENGL	Nevada	Grass Valley Twp	75	201
William B	28	m	w	WI	Santa Clara	2-Wd San Jose	88	284
FALLA								
M S	22	m	w	CANA	Tuolumne	Sonora P O	93	318
Marton	33	m	w	IREL	San Mateo	Schoolhouse Statio	87	334
Mowra	9	f	w	CA	Mariposa	Mariposa P O	74	94
FALLACE								
Elizabeth	60	f	w	IREL	San Francisco	8-Wd San Francisco	82	455
Johanna	19	f	w	IREL	San Francisco	8-Wd San Francisco	82	481
FALLAN								
Frank	28	m	w	IREL	Amador	Jackson P O	69	329
Kate	40	f	w	IREL	San Francisco	San Francisco P O	80	393
Patk	24	m	w	NY	Solano	Vallejo	90	160

© 2001 by Heritage Quest. All rights reserved.

Name	Age	S	R	B-PL	County	Locale	Series M593 Roll	Pg
FALLAR								
Thos	28	m	w	MO	Alameda	Murray Twp	68	126
FALLASO								
Frequandro	38	m	w	MEXI	Tulare	Visalia	92	298
FALLAY								
Bridget	70	f	w	IREL	Alameda	Brooklyn	68	32
FALLEN								
Annie	20	f	w	IREL	San Francisco	San Francisco P O	85	775
Hannah	26	f	w	IREL	San Francisco	8-Wd San Francisco	82	469
James	45	m	w	IREL	Alameda	Washington Twp	68	296
Joseph	58	m	w	IREL	Santa Cruz	Pajaro Twp	89	346
Margaret	8	f	w	CA	Santa Clara	Burnett Twp	88	33
Michael	39	m	w	IREL	San Francisco	San Francisco P O	83	419
Nicholas	66	m	w	ENGL	Placer	Lincoln P O	76	493
Peter J	27	m	w	IREL	San Francisco	San Francisco P O	83	230
Thomas	43	m	w	IREL	San Francisco	5-Wd San Francisco	81	25
Thomas	40	m	w	IREL	San Francisco	San Francisco P O	83	356
William	35	m	w	IREL	San Francisco	5-Wd San Francisco	81	25
FALLER								
Emil	27	m	w	WURT	San Francisco	1-Wd San Francisco	79	63
Robert	52	m	w	MA	Contra Costa	Martinez P O	71	403
FALLERO								
Gennaro	43	m	w	ITAL	San Francisco	San Francisco P O	80	468
FALLETO								
Emanuel	52	m	w	MEXI	Tulare	Tule Rvr Twp	92	266
FALLEY								
Mary J	4	f	w	CA	Alameda	Alameda	68	14
FALLIN								
Patrick	42	m	w	IREL	Contra Costa	San Pablo Twp	71	354
FALLNER								
M	36	m	w	SWIT	San Joaquin	1-Wd Stockton	86	132
FALLON								
Charls	26	m	w	PRUS	Alameda	Oakland	68	164
Ellen	57	f	w	IREL	Alameda	Murray Twp	68	101
Ellen	22	f	w	CANA	Alameda	Oakland	68	192
Hannah	40	f	w	IREL	Alameda	Hayward	68	79
James	42	m	w	IREL	Marin	Tomales Twp	74	85
James	15	m	w	CA	Alameda	Oakland	68	159
John	41	m	w	NY	Nevada	Little York Twp	75	241
John	40	m	w	IREL	Alameda	Oakland	68	206
John	38	m	w	IREL	San Francisco	11-Wd San Francisc	84	643
John	31	m	w	IREL	San Francisco	11-Wd San Francisc	84	429
Kate	30	f	w	IREL	San Francisco	San Francisco P O	83	274
Luke	36	m	w	IREL	Marin	Tomales Twp	74	83
Malichi	60	m	w	IREL	Alameda	Oakland	68	144
Mary	33	f	w	IREL	San Francisco	San Francisco P O	85	810
Mary	14	f	w	MA	Alameda	Oakland	68	129
Mary	14	f	w	MA	San Francisco	1-Wd San Francisco	79	43
Michiel	23	m	w	IA	Sonoma	Vallejo Twp	91	458
Mitchel	32	m	w	IREL	San Francisco	8-Wd San Francisco	82	302
Peter	16	m	w	IREL	San Francisco	San Francisco P O	85	808
Sempronius	17	m	w	CA	Santa Clara	2-Wd San Jose	88	306
Thomas	46	m	w	IREL	Santa Clara	2-Wd San Jose	88	301
William	14	m	w	CA	Santa Clara	Santa Clara Twp	88	177
FALLS								
Dollie	45	f	w	MA	San Francisco	San Francisco P O	83	413
Frederick	20	m	w	ENGL	San Mateo	Half Moon Bay P O	87	400
George C	40	m	w	NC	Los Angeles	San Jose Twp	73	621
James	55	m	w	ME	Alameda	Brooklyn	68	37
Jas	19	m	w	CA	Solano	Vallejo	90	178
John S	35	m	w	VA	Mendocino	Albion & Big Rvr T	74	167
Mary	22	f	w	IREL	San Francisco	6-Wd San Francisco	81	114
R J	50	m	w	NY	Solano	Vallejo	90	152
FALLTRICK								
Edwd	28	m	w	ENGL	Solano	Vallejo	90	202
FALMAR								
Rudolph	38	m	w	HAMB	San Francisco	11-Wd San Francisc	84	444
FALMOUTH								
George	12	m	w	CA	Amador	Drytown P O	69	417
FALON								
George	25	m	w	IREL	Santa Clara	Santa Clara Twp	88	175
Thos	53	m	w	IREL	Calaveras	Copperopolis P O	70	239
FALOR								
John	58	m	w	BADE	Monterey	Alisal Twp	74	300
Plinney	21	m	w	OH	Humboldt	Arcata Twp	72	234
FALQUE								
John	48	m	w	FRAN	Monterey	San Antonio Twp	74	319
John	39	m	w	FRAN	Santa Clara	Santa Clara Twp	88	157
FALSOM								
Myrick	42	m	w	ME	San Francisco	11-Wd San Francisc	84	706
FALTON								
Edward D	30	m	w	IREL	San Francisco	7-Wd San Francisco	81	251
FALTY								
Anna	48	f	w	IREL	San Francisco	7-Wd San Francisco	81	216
Peter	50	m	w	IREL	San Francisco	7-Wd San Francisco	81	202
FALTZ								
J B	31	m	w	PRUS	San Joaquin	Liberty Twp	86	87
FALVEY								
A	7	f	w	CA	Los Angeles	Los Angeles	73	570
Anna	18	f	w	RI	Sonoma	Petaluma Twp	91	324
Edward I	31	m	w	MA	Sacramento	2-Wd Sacramento	77	208
John	38	m	w	IREL	El Dorado	Lake Valley Twp	72	64
M T	10	f	w	CA	Los Angeles	Los Angeles	73	570
Margaret	50	f	w	IREL	Sonoma	Petaluma Twp	91	339
FALY								
Johanna	55	f	w	IREL	San Francisco	11-Wd San Francisc	84	424
FALZ								
Jose Agracia	35	m	w	CA	Los Angeles	Los Angeles	73	562
FAM								
Ah	38	m	c	CHIN	Tuolumne	Chinese Camp P O	93	363
Lin	34	m	c	CHIN	Placer	Bath P O	76	454
FAMBAN								
Gualo	43	m	w	SWIT	San Joaquin	2-Wd Stockton	86	170
FAMBRIM								
Motoer	35	m	w	ITAL	Sacramento	Sutter Twp	77	386
FAMLINER								
Geo	41	m	w	NY	San Joaquin	Tulare Twp	86	264
FAMMY								
William	23	m	w	IREL	Los Angeles	Los Angeles Twp	73	473
FAN								
Ah	56	m	c	CHIN	Tuolumne	Chinese Camp P O	93	363
Ah	45	m	c	CHIN	Sacramento	Granite Twp	77	151
Ah	45	m	c	CHIN	San Francisco	San Francisco P O	80	444
Ah	42	m	c	CHIN	San Francisco	San Francisco P O	80	496
Ah	42	m	c	CHIN	Sacramento	1-Wd Sacramento	77	197
Ah	40	m	c	CHIN	Butte	Concow Twp	70	10
Ah	40	m	c	CHIN	Sacramento	Granite Twp	77	138
Ah	40	m	c	CHIN	Nevada	Bridgeport Twp	75	110
Ah	40	m	c	CHIN	Tuolumne	Chinese Camp P O	93	364
Ah	40	f	c	CHIN	Placer	Auburn P O	76	372
Ah	37	m	c	CHIN	Nevada	Bridgeport Twp	75	110
Ah	37	m	c	CHIN	San Francisco	6-Wd San Francisco	81	63
Ah	36	m	c	CHIN	San Francisco	San Francisco P O	80	528
Ah	34	m	c	CHIN	San Francisco	San Francisco P O	80	518
Ah	34	m	c	CHIN	Tuolumne	Chinese Camp P O	93	370
Ah	34	f	c	CHIN	San Francisco	San Francisco P O	80	450
Ah	34	m	c	CHIN	San Francisco	San Francisco P O	80	446
Ah	32	f	c	CHIN	San Francisco	San Francisco P O	80	527
Ah	32	m	c	CHIN	Placer	Bath P O	76	428
Ah	32	f	c	CHIN	San Francisco	San Francisco P O	80	433
Ah	32	m	c	CHIN	Butte	Ophir Twp	70	103
Ah	31	m	c	CHIN	San Francisco	San Francisco P O	80	510
Ah	31	m	c	CHIN	Tuolumne	Chinese Camp P O	93	364
Ah	30	m	c	CHIN	Butte	Ophir Twp	70	103
Ah	30	f	c	CHIN	Placer	Bath P O	76	439
Ah	30	f	c	CHIN	San Francisco	San Francisco P O	80	440
Ah	30	m	c	CHIN	Del Norte	Crescent	71	464
Ah	29	m	c	CHIN	Nevada	Eureka Twp	75	135
Ah	28	f	c	CHIN	Tuolumne	Chinese Camp P O	93	388
Ah	28	m	c	CHIN	Tuolumne	Big Oak Flat P O	93	401
Ah	28	m	c	CHIN	Sonoma	Sonoma Twp	91	449
Ah	28	m	c	CHIN	Butte	Wyandotte Twp	70	146
Ah	27	f	c	CHIN	Sacramento	Granite Twp	77	151
Ah	27	m	c	CHIN	Placer	Bath P O	76	460
Ah	26	m	c	CHIN	Klamath	Liberty Twp	73	375
Ah	26	f	c	CHIN	San Francisco	San Francisco P O	80	431
Ah	25	m	c	CHIN	Klamath	Orleans Twp	73	380
Ah	25	m	c	CHIN	Butte	Ophir Twp	70	104
Ah	24	m	c	CHIN	Placer	Dutch Flat P O	76	410
Ah	24	m	c	CHIN	San Francisco	San Francisco P O	80	512
Ah	23	f	c	CHIN	San Francisco	San Francisco P O	80	431
Ah	22	f	c	CHIN	San Francisco	San Francisco P O	80	523
Ah	22	m	c	CHIN	Solano	Suisun Twp	90	105
Ah	21	f	c	CHIN	San Francisco	San Francisco P O	80	453
Ah	21	m	c	CHIN	San Francisco	San Francisco P O	80	516
Ah	21	f	c	CHIN	San Francisco	San Francisco P O	80	522
Ah	21	m	c	CHIN	Sacramento	2-Wd Sacramento	77	246
Ah	20	f	c	CHIN	San Francisco	San Francisco P O	80	529
Ah	20	f	c	CHIN	San Francisco	San Francisco P O	80	454
Ah	20	f	c	CHIN	Tuolumne	Chinese Camp P O	93	388
Ah	20	f	c	CHIN	San Francisco	San Francisco P O	80	432
Ah	20	f	c	CHIN	San Francisco	San Francisco P O	80	432
Ah	19	f	c	CHIN	San Francisco	San Francisco P O	80	527
Ah	19	f	c	CHIN	San Francisco	San Francisco P O	80	437
Ah	19	f	c	CHIN	San Francisco	San Francisco P O	80	451
Ah	18	m	c	CHIN	Butte	Wyandotte Twp	70	147
Ah	18	f	c	CHIN	San Francisco	San Francisco P O	80	526
Ah	18	f	c	CHIN	San Francisco	San Francisco P O	80	434
Ah	18	f	c	CHIN	San Francisco	San Francisco P O	80	440
Ah	17	m	c	CHIN	San Francisco	San Francisco P O	80	497
Ah	17	f	c	CHIN	San Francisco	San Francisco P O	80	434
Ah	16	m	c	CHIN	Placer	Emigrant Gap P O	76	416
Ah	---	m	c	CHIN	Fresno	Millerton P O	72	199
Awk	40	m	c	CHIN	Klamath	Sawyers Bar	73	378
Chas Mr	40	m	w	NY	San Francisco	5-Wd San Francisco	81	28
Chong	34	m	c	CHIN	Trinity	Weaverville Pct	92	229
Choo	41	m	c	CHIN	Tuolumne	Columbia P O	93	350
Fa	45	m	c	CHIN	Placer	Bath P O	76	428
G H	40	m	w	PA	San Joaquin	Douglas Twp	86	32
Goy	25	f	c	CHIN	Yuba	Marysville	93	627
Hoo	23	m	c	CHIN	Tuolumne	Big Oak Flat P O	93	406
I	16	f	c	CHIN	Stanislaus	Branch Twp	92	9
Len Ti	21	m	c	CHIN	San Francisco	11-Wd San Francisc	84	546
Lin	24	f	c	CHIN	Sacramento	1-Wd Sacramento	77	196
Mary E	33	f	w	WIND	San Francisco	8-Wd San Francisco	82	370
Mi	18	f	c	CHIN	Tuolumne	Big Oak Flat P O	93	397
Moie	28	f	c	CHIN	Sacramento	1-Wd Sacramento	77	194
Tung	40	m	c	CHIN	Sonoma	Sonoma Twp	91	447
FANAGAN								
Tynaio	32	m	w	MEXI	Inyo	Lone Pine Twp	73	331
FANANDIS								
Jesus	34	m	w	MEXI	Tuolumne	Columbia P O	93	344

© 2001 by Heritage Quest. All rights reserved.

Name	Age	S	R	B-PL	County	Locale (Series M593)	Roll	Pg
FANAR								
Albat	33	m	w	IREL	San Francisco	5-Wd San Francisco	81	11
FANBRISKIE								
George	42	m	w	PRUS	Tuolumne	Sonora P O	93	313
FANBROOK								
S	49	m	w	NORW	San Francisco	8-Wd San Francisco	82	355
FANCE								
Ricer	24	f	w	PRUS	San Francisco	San Francisco P O	83	9
FANCECANT								
Aug	45	m	w	FRAN	Sacramento	Brighton Twp	77	73
FANCES								
Jacob	21	m	w	FRAN	San Francisco	8-Wd San Francisco	82	351
FANCH								
J P	65	m	w	PRUS	San Joaquin	Douglas Twp	86	50
FANCHER								
Charles	46	m	w	DENM	Contra Costa	Martinez P O	71	403
Henry	30	m	w	FRAN	Marin	Bolinas Twp	74	1
Ira	27	m	w	NY	Contra Costa	Martinez P O	71	402
J W	68	m	w	NY	Merced	Snelling P O	74	254
Jennie M	19	f	w	IL	Santa Cruz	Santa Cruz	89	406
John	56	m	w	NY	Contra Costa	Martinez P O	71	402
Johnson	31	m	w	NY	Contra Costa	Martinez P O	71	403
FANCHIE								
Frank	30	m	w	FRAN	San Francisco	8-Wd San Francisco	82	376
FANCHILL								
Cyrus B	20	m	w	AL	Los Angeles	Los Angeles	73	549
FANCHON								
Rachael	11	f	w	CA	San Diego	San Diego	78	504
FANCI								
Augustine	32	m	m	CHIL	Placer	Bath P O	76	420
FANCUF								
E R	30	m	w	CANA	Monterey	Alisal Twp	74	300
FANCUK								
Henry	18	m	w	ITAL	San Mateo	Schoolhouse Statio	87	346
Jonal	22	m	w	ITAL	San Mateo	Schoolhouse Statio	87	346
FANCY								
Jack	31	m	c	CHIN	Nevada	Bridgeport Twp	75	111
Joseph	43	m	w	CANA	Humboldt	Arcata Twp	72	226
FANDER								
P W	45	m	w	NY	Alameda	Oakland	68	214
FANE								
Geo D	38	m	w	BAVA	San Francisco	1-Wd San Francisco	79	106
John	26	m	w	IREL	San Francisco	11-Wd San Francisc	84	678
FANEKE								
John	23	m	w	US	Contra Costa	Martinez P O	71	434
FANEL								
David	33	m	w	CANA	San Francisco	2-Wd San Francisco	79	138
Julia	53	f	w	IREL	San Francisco	2-Wd San Francisco	79	221
Thomas	34	m	w	IREL	San Francisco	San Francisco P O	83	362
Timothy	31	m	w	IREL	San Mateo	Schoolhouse Statio	87	342
FANELLO								
A M	28	m	w	ITAL	Tuolumne	Big Oak Flat P O	93	395
FANETTE								
Marion	27	m	w	OH	Contra Costa	Martinez P O	71	435
FANFERAN								
Termine	48	m	w	CHIL	San Mateo	Schoolhouse Statio	87	343
FANG								
---	25	m	c	CHIN	Siskiyou	Hamburg Twp	89	598
Ah	50	m	c	CHIN	Tuolumne	Chinese Camp P O	93	388
Ah	48	m	c	CHIN	Marin	Tomales Twp	74	84
Ah	45	m	c	CHIN	Tuolumne	Chinese Camp P O	93	364
Ah	44	m	c	CHIN	Mariposa	Maxwell Crk P O	74	142
Ah	44	m	c	CHIN	Siskiyou	Hamburg Twp	89	598
Ah	40	m	c	CHIN	Tuolumne	Big Oak Flat P O	93	399
Ah	40	m	c	CHIN	Placer	Auburn P O	76	372
Ah	39	m	c	CHIN	San Francisco	6-Wd San Francisco	81	84
Ah	39	m	c	CHIN	Amador	Sutter Crk P O	69	413
Ah	38	m	c	CHIN	Tuolumne	Chinese Camp P O	93	390
Ah	36	m	c	CHIN	San Francisco	San Francisco P O	80	524
Ah	32	m	c	CHIN	San Francisco	San Francisco P O	80	493
Ah	32	m	c	CHIN	San Francisco	San Francisco P O	80	525
Ah	31	m	c	CHIN	San Francisco	San Francisco P O	80	516
Ah	30	m	c	CHIN	Santa Clara	Santa Clara Twp	88	166
Ah	30	m	c	CHIN	San Francisco	San Francisco P O	80	502
Ah	29	m	c	CHIN	Amador	Drytown P O	69	423
Ah	29	m	c	CHIN	San Francisco	San Francisco P O	80	441
Ah	29	m	c	CHIN	Calaveras	San Andreas P O	70	178
Ah	28	m	c	CHIN	Solano	Suisun Twp	90	105
Ah	28	m	c	CHIN	El Dorado	Placerville Twp	72	105
Ah	27	m	c	CHIN	Santa Clara	1-Wd San Jose	88	277
Ah	26	f	c	CHIN	Los Angeles	Los Angeles	73	565
Ah	25	m	c	CHIN	Sonoma	Sonoma Twp	91	449
Ah	25	m	c	CHIN	Mariposa	Mariposa P O	74	102
Ah	25	m	c	CHIN	Plumas	Goodwin Twp	77	3
Ah	24	m	c	CHIN	Placer	Dutch Flat P O	76	410
Ah	23	m	c	CHIN	San Francisco	11-Wd San Francisc	84	559
Ah	22	m	c	CHIN	Stanislaus	Branch Twp	92	9
Ah	22	m	c	CHIN	Monterey	Castroville Twp	74	338
Ah	22	m	c	CHIN	San Francisco	San Francisco P O	80	436
Ah	22	m	c	CHIN	Placer	Bath P O	76	445
Ah	21	m	c	CHIN	San Francisco	San Francisco P O	80	509
Ah	20	m	c	CHIN	San Francisco	11-Wd San Francisc	84	557
Ah	20	f	c	CHIN	San Francisco	San Francisco P O	80	505
Ah	20	f	c	CHIN	El Dorado	Mud Springs Twp	72	79
Ah	19	m	c	CHIN	San Francisco	6-Wd San Francisco	81	48
Ah	19	m	c	CHIN	Napa	Napa Twp	75	71
Ah	18	m	c	CHIN	San Francisco	San Francisco P O	83	72
Ah	17	m	c	CHIN	San Francisco	6-Wd San Francisco	81	49
Ah	15	m	c	CHIN	San Luis Obispo	Arroyo Grande Twp	87	278
Ah	11	f	c	CHIN	San Francisco	San Francisco P O	80	452
Gee	41	m	w	CHIN	Plumas	Mineral Twp	77	24
Ho	30	m	c	CHIN	Sonoma	Sonoma Twp	91	445
In	15	m	c	CHIN	Santa Clara	Santa Clara Twp	88	161
La Nigh	17	m	c	CHIN	Amador	Ione City P O	69	366
Lee	35	m	c	CHIN	Nevada	Meadow Lake Twp	75	256
Ling	28	f	c	CHIN	Merced	Snelling P O	74	279
Sit	35	m	c	CHIN	San Francisco	11-Wd San Francisc	84	529
FANIES								
Jesus	43	m	w	MEXI	Calaveras	San Andreas P O	70	180
FANINE								
D	35	m	w	IREL	Sierra	Forest	89	536
FANING								
John	57	m	w	IREL	Amador	Drytown P O	69	417
FANINGER								
M S	40	m	w	IREL	Alameda	Oakland	68	177
FANINGTON								
Thomas	34	m	w	TN	Solano	Rio Vista Twp	90	62
FANIX								
John	44	m	w	PRUS	Tuolumne	Columbia P O	93	344
FANJOY								
William	19	m	w	CANA	San Francisco	San Francisco P O	83	297
FANK								
Ah	31	m	c	CHIN	Santa Clara	1-Wd San Jose	88	271
Ah	30	m	c	CHIN	San Joaquin	1-Wd Stockton	86	145
FANKEL								
Kate	30	f	w	PRUS	San Francisco	San Francisco P O	83	368
FANKLE								
George	38	m	w	OH	Alameda	Washington Twp	68	287
FANMAN								
E	35	m	w	ENGL	Alameda	Oakland	68	265
FANN								
Ah	33	m	c	CHIN	Napa	Napa	75	36
Ah	28	m	c	CHIN	Siskiyou	Yreka Twp	89	667
Frederick	26	m	w	ENGL	Marin	Novato Twp	74	12
Gabriel	44	m	w	MO	Santa Clara	Gilroy Twp	88	73
FANNAN								
Truman	69	m	w	NY	Santa Clara	Gilroy Twp	88	75
FANNARD								
James	35	m	w	IREL	San Francisco	San Francisco P O	83	187
Sarah	31	f	c	CHIN	El Dorado	Georgetown Twp	72	42
FANNELL								
Anna	13	f	w	CA	Alameda	Oakland	68	258
James	38	m	w	AL	San Joaquin	Douglas Twp	86	32
John	42	m	w	HAMB	Sacramento	4-Wd Sacramento	77	348
FANNER								
Frederick	33	m	w	MD	Santa Clara	Santa Clara Twp	88	165
Henry	28	m	w	NY	Alameda	Oakland	68	265
FANNEY								
Emily	37	f	w	FRAN	Alameda	Oakland	68	239
FANNI								
John P	42	m	w	SCOT	Amador	Ione City P O	69	349
FANNIGAN								
James	42	m	w	IREL	San Francisco	2-Wd San Francisco	79	266
FANNIN								
Mary	35	f	w	IREL	San Francisco	11-Wd San Francisc	84	525
Thomas	38	m	w	IREL	San Francisco	11-Wd San Francisc	84	655
FANNING								
Alexander	40	m	w	IREL	Butte	Wyandotte Twp	70	142
Augustus	38	m	w	DENM	San Francisco	2-Wd San Francisco	79	261
Barney	40	m	w	IREL	San Francisco	1-Wd San Francisco	79	44
D	43	m	w	NY	San Joaquin	Douglas Twp	86	36
Ed	38	m	w	IN	San Francisco	2-Wd San Francisco	79	212
Frederick	28	m	w	NY	Kern	Kernville P O	73	368
J	29	m	w	IREL	Yuba	Marysville Twp	93	567
J W	23	m	w	CANA	Solano	Benicia	90	6
James	40	m	w	IREL	Stanislaus	Branch Twp	92	7
James F	27	m	w	IREL	Yuba	Long Bar Twp	93	562
John	72	m	w	IREL	San Francisco	2-Wd San Francisco	79	247
John	39	m	w	CT	Kern	Havilah P O	73	336
John	30	m	w	IREL	San Francisco	2-Wd San Francisco	79	247
Joseph	40	m	w	OH	Sonoma	Salt Point	91	389
Lizzie	40	f	w	IREL	San Francisco	8-Wd San Francisco	82	299
Lucy	40	f	w	IREL	Napa	Napa	75	51
N S	51	m	w	IL	Mendocino	Ukiah Twp	74	237
Patrick	34	m	w	IREL	Solano	Maine Prairie Twp	90	49
Peter	45	m	w	IREL	Solano	Suisun Twp	90	115
Peter	32	m	w	OH	Solano	Tremont Twp	90	29
Thomas	45	m	w	IREL	San Francisco	San Francisco P O	83	396
Thomas	32	m	w	IREL	San Francisco	11-Wd San Francisc	84	709
FANNIS								
A J	47	m	w	NY	San Joaquin	Dent Twp	86	28
James	22	m	w	NY	San Francisco	8-Wd San Francisco	82	366
FANNO								
John	35	m	w	ITAL	San Mateo	Schoolhouse Statio	87	332
FANNON								
Luke	45	m	w	IREL	Placer	Bath P O	76	453
Michael	44	m	w	IREL	Placer	Bath P O	76	426
Saml D	21	m	w	IN	Butte	Oregon Twp	70	132
FANNY								
Christoph	31	m	w	SWIT	San Mateo	Half Moon Bay P O	87	408
Geo	28	m	w	GREE	Solano	Vallejo	90	200
H J	51	m	w	NY	San Joaquin	2-Wd Stockton	86	212
James	30	m	w	TN	Humboldt	Eureka Twp	72	276

© 2001 by Heritage Quest. All rights reserved.

Name	Age	S	R	B-PL	County	Locale	Series M593 Roll	Pg
FANONI								
George	36	m	w	MEXI	Tuolumne	Chinese Camp P O	93	383
FANORE								
Francis H	22	m	w	MS	Fresno	Millerton P O	72	152
FANSSTENN								
Gustave	52	m	w	HANO	Placer	Bath P O	76	420
FANSTON								
James	38	m	w	PA	Stanislaus	Buena Vista Twp	92	15
FANT								
Ah	45	m	c	CHIN	Sacramento	Franklin Twp	77	114
Ah	38	m	c	CHIN	Marin	San Rafael Twp	74	40
Ah	26	m	c	CHIN	Sierra	Eureka Twp	89	526
Thomas	36	m	w	IREL	Plumas	Indian Twp	77	11
Thos W	37	m	w	VA	Sierra	Table Rock Twp	89	571
FANTINE								
Antonio	22	m	w	SWIT	San Francisco	1-Wd San Francisco	79	105
FANTON								
George	23	m	w	CT	San Francisco	8-Wd San Francisco	82	325
FANTZ								
Fred	29	m	w	PRUS	San Francisco	2-Wd San Francisco	79	234
FANULT								
John A	31	m	w	NY	San Joaquin	1-Wd Stockton	86	126
FANY								
Ah	16	m	c	CHIN	Placer	Bath P O	76	442
FANYON								
Wm	35	m	w	ENGL	Mariposa	Maxwell Crk P O	74	144
FAO								
Ah	30	m	c	CHIN	Fresno	Millerton P O	72	202
FAPIANA								
Gabriel	33	m	w	ITAL	Amador	Volcano P O	69	382
FAQUIRO								
Antonis	38	m	w	ITAL	San Mateo	Schoolhouse Statio	87	346
FAR								
Ah	31	m	c	CHIN	Placer	Pino Twp	76	470
Ah	30	m	c	CHIN	San Mateo	Belmont P O	87	373
Ah	29	f	c	CHIN	Amador	Fiddletown P O	69	427
Ah	18	m	c	CHIN	Butte	Hamilton Twp	70	68
Choy	20	m	c	CHIN	Yuba	Marysville	93	631
Foo	30	m	c	CHIN	Yuba	Marysville	93	631
FARA								
Alonza	38	m	w	CANA	San Francisco	11-Wd San Francisc	84	712
Antonio	18	m	w	FRAN	Santa Clara	Redwood Twp	88	122
FARACCO								
Geanaro	34	m	w	ITAL	San Francisco	11-Wd San Francisc	84	591
FARADAY								
Joseph	17	m	w	ENGL	San Francisco	San Francisco P O	85	807
FARAL								
David	35	m	w	MO	Sacramento	Cosumnes Twp	77	90
FARARE								
Peter	33	m	w	ITAL	Amador	Jackson P O	69	336
FARARO								
Juan	33	m	w	CHIL	Amador	Fiddletown P O	69	432
FARAS								
Carlo	26	m	w	ITAL	San Mateo	Schoolhouse Statio	87	334
Dominica	17	m	w	ITAL	San Mateo	Schoolhouse Statio	87	346
John	22	m	w	ITAL	San Mateo	Schoolhouse Statio	87	346
FARBAUGH								
D	23	m	w	OH	Lassen	Susanville Twp	73	446
FARBER								
Horace	42	m	w	NY	Sierra	Gibson Twp	89	538
Wm	29	m	w	AUST	Sacramento	3-Wd Sacramento	77	261
FARCADA								
Baptist	39	m	w	FRAN	Calaveras	San Andreas P O	70	179
FARCELL								
Michael	21	m	w	IREL	Stanislaus	Emory Twp	92	22
FARCET								
George	14	m	w	TX	Tulare	Tule Rvr Twp	92	271
FARCIOT								
Anna	61	f	w	SWIT	San Francisco	8-Wd San Francisco	82	410
FARCOIT								
Charles	35	m	w	FRAN	San Francisco	7-Wd San Francisco	81	156
FARCYECO								
Richino	25	m	w	ITAL	San Francisco	11-Wd San Francisc	84	709
FARD								
J	40	m	w	IN	Alameda	Oakland	68	264
Patrick	31	m	w	IREL	Yuba	Rose Bar Twp	93	661
FARDELLA								
G	27	m	w	ITAL	Sonoma	Sonoma Twp	91	441
FARDEN								
James	21	m	w	ENGL	San Francisco	7-Wd San Francisco	81	224
Joseph	25	m	w	IREL	San Mateo	San Mateo P O	87	356
FARDLAW								
Ben R	56	m	w	VA	Sonoma	Mendocino Twp	91	288
FARE								
Ah	20	f	c	CHIN	Amador	Jackson P O	69	344
FAREA								
Frank	26	m	w	PORT	Alameda	Washington Twp	68	275
FAREBANKS								
John	30	m	w	NY	San Francisco	7-Wd San Francisco	81	161
FARECHILDS								
Daniel	33	m	w	VT	Calaveras	San Andreas P O	70	213
FAREL								
Jean	40	m	w	FRAN	Yuba	Slate Range Bar Tw	93	670
FARELL								
Ellen	49	f	w	IREL	Siskiyou	Callahan P O	89	628
FARELLY								
John	35	m	w	IREL	Alameda	Oakland	68	210

Name	Age	S	R	B-PL	County	Locale	Series M593 Roll	Pg
FAREN								
Salter	27	m	w	WI	Sonoma	Petaluma Twp	91	360
FARENBUCH								
Adam	19	m	w	HCAS	Sacramento	Granite Twp	77	136
FARENGER								
Geo	37	m	w	PA	San Joaquin	Liberty Twp	86	90
FAREO								
Maria L	28	f	w	CA	Los Angeles	Los Angeles Twp	73	485
FARER								
Louis	28	m	w	SWIT	San Mateo	Belmont P O	87	372
FARES								
August	55	m	w	FRAN	San Francisco	San Francisco P O	80	477
FARESH								
Lyman	50	m	w	NC	Contra Costa	Martinez P O	71	437
FARET								
Ah	27	m	c	CHIN	El Dorado	Coloma Twp	72	3
James	18	m	w	OH	Contra Costa	Martinez P O	71	441
FARETTO								
John	26	m	w	ITAL	El Dorado	Diamond Springs Tw	72	29
Louis	25	m	w	ITAL	El Dorado	Diamond Springs Tw	72	29
FAREWELL								
B E	52	m	w	NY	Alameda	Oakland	68	130
D	37	m	w	CANA	Alameda	Oakland	68	148
FARFAN								
Frank	26	m	w	ITAL	San Francisco	11-Wd San Francisc	84	710
FARGAI								
Joseph	20	m	w	PORT	Tuolumne	Columbia P O	93	356
FARGARSON								
A	40	m	w	IL	Monterey	Monterey Twp	74	347
FARGASON								
James F	43	m	w	TN	El Dorado	Diamond Springs Tw	72	32
John	36	m	w	IREL	El Dorado	Coloma Twp	72	11
FARGAY								
Nathaniel	30	m	w	MS	Plumas	Indian Twp	77	15
FARGEON								
Solomon	25	m	w	ENGL	Sacramento	Granite Twp	77	142
FARGICEN								
Wm H	25	m	w	PA	Sacramento	Dry Crk Twp	77	103
FARGO								
Darius C	51	m	w	NY	Santa Cruz	Santa Cruz	89	421
Earl	38	m	w	NY	San Francisco	11-Wd San Francisc	84	539
F S	33	m	w	PA	El Dorado	Greenwood Twp	72	53
Jerome	46	m	w	NY	San Francisco	11-Wd San Francisc	84	480
Lafayett	43	m	w	NY	Butte	Chico Twp	70	19
May	9	f	w	WI	San Francisco	San Francisco P O	83	185
Thomas	33	m	w	ENGL	Yuba	Rose Bar Twp	93	661
FARGUE								
John P	40	m	w	NY	San Francisco	2-Wd San Francisco	79	220
S S	37	m	w	IREL	San Joaquin	1-Wd Stockton	86	123
FARGUHAR								
G K	35	m	w	OH	Nevada	Nevada Twp	75	278
Mary	28	f	w	NY	Sonoma	Russian Rvr	91	375
FARGUHARSON								
Cas	21	m	w	NY	San Francisco	2-Wd San Francisco	79	147
D	42	m	w	SCOT	San Francisco	San Francisco P O	85	775
John	42	m	w	SCOT	Placer	Bath P O	76	444
FARHAM								
Juana	47	f	w	CHIL	Los Angeles	Los Angeles Twp	73	473
R	43	m	w	MA	San Joaquin	Castoria Twp	86	10
FARHANTO								
Sinto	45	m	w	MEXI	Tulare	Visalia	92	294
FARHILL								
Patrick	35	m	w	SCOT	San Francisco	1-Wd San Francisco	79	89
FARIA								
Ann	25	f	w	IREL	Placer	Bath P O	76	438
Candidas	31	m	w	PORT	San Francisco	1-Wd San Francisco	79	130
Feledonia	45	f	w	CA	Los Angeles	Los Angeles Twp	73	485
FARIBIN								
John	42	m	w	IREL	San Francisco	San Francisco P O	85	764
FARICH								
Adam T	59	m	w	NC	San Francisco	San Francisco P O	85	718
Lafayette	19	m	w	UT	Santa Clara	Gilroy Twp	88	92
FARILL								
J D	43	m	w	ME	Humboldt	Eureka Twp	72	275
William D	20	m	w	ME	Humboldt	Eureka Twp	72	275
FARING								
Mich	38	m	w	IREL	Alameda	Oakland	68	250
FARINGTON								
S	35	m	w	ME	Siskiyou	Callahan P O	89	625
FARINGTREW								
Henry	42	m	w	PRUS	Inyo	Bishop Crk Twp	73	310
FARINO								
Joseph	42	m	w	ITAL	San Francisco	San Francisco P O	80	468
FARIRI								
Jacaroni	42	m	w	ITAL	San Francisco	11-Wd San Francisc	84	603
FARIS								
Franklin	40	m	w	MO	Stanislaus	Empire Twp	92	53
Ponithar	50	m	w	KY	Humboldt	South Fork Twp	72	301
Urmacendo	49	f	w	MEXI	Kern	Havilah P O	73	337
FARISH								
Benjamin F	40	m	w	NC	Contra Costa	Martinez P O	71	379
FARISS								
Danl	36	m	w	BAVA	San Francisco	11-Wd San Francisc	84	605
Levi	25	m	w	BAVA	San Francisco	11-Wd San Francisc	84	659
FARKELLSON								
Lawrence	29	m	w	DENM	San Mateo	Redwood Twp	87	367

© 2001 by Heritage Quest. All rights reserved.

California 1870 Census

Series M593

Name	Age	S	R	B-PL	County	Locale	Roll	Pg
FARKILL								
Eveline	38	f	w	FRAN	Alameda	Alameda	68	13
FARL								
Mike	28	m	w	IREL	San Francisco	11-Wd San Francisc	84	694
FARLAND								
Dudley H	35	m	w	NY	Sacramento	2-Wd Sacramento	77	240
Henry	24	m	w	CANA	San Francisco	San Francisco P O	80	391
J	43	m	w	ENGL	Alameda	Murray Twp	68	102
J	40	m	w	IREL	Alameda	Oakland	68	266
James	50	m	w	IREL	San Francisco	2-Wd San Francisco	79	213
John	39	m	w	ENGL	San Francisco	2-Wd San Francisco	79	212
Louis	28	m	w	PRUS	Humboldt	Eureka Twp	72	280
Patrick	40	m	w	IREL	Butte	Oregon Twp	70	130
FARLEA								
Qui	28	f	c	CHIN	Tulare	Tule Rvr Twp	92	271
FARLEIGH								
John	46	m	w	SCOT	Tulare	Farmersville Twp	92	243
FARLEMAN								
John	60	m	w	PA	Nevada	Grass Valley Twp	75	185
FARLES								
Burton	50	m	w	IL	Stanislaus	Washington Twp	92	84
FARLEY								
A B	37	m	w	NJ	Tuolumne	Big Oak Flat P O	93	395
Anderson	47	m	w	VA	Napa	Napa Twp	75	62
Anthony	45	m	w	ENGL	Yolo	Putah Twp	93	510
Barney	32	m	w	IREL	San Joaquin	Oneal Twp	86	114
Barney	30	m	w	IREL	San Francisco	11-Wd San Francisc	84	615
Bill	15	m	i	CA	Napa	Napa Twp	75	62
C K	47	m	w	AL	Santa Clara	Gilroy Twp	88	85
Catherine	50	f	w	IREL	San Francisco	8-Wd San Francisco	82	413
Catherine	43	f	w	IREL	Nevada	Bridgeport Twp	75	117
Daniel	37	m	w	NY	San Francisco	1-Wd San Francisco	79	129
Dury	77	m	w	VA	San Diego	San Diego	78	497
Ebineezer	59	m	w	CANA	Alameda	Washington Twp	68	268
Ed	23	m	w	NY	Humboldt	Arcata Twp	72	236
Edward	38	m	w	IREL	San Francisco	11-Wd San Francisc	84	638
Edward	30	m	w	CANA	San Francisco	San Francisco P O	83	218
Frank	46	m	w	OH	Marin	Nicasio Twp	74	17
Fred	20	m	w	PRUS	San Joaquin	2-Wd Stockton	86	187
Frederick	38	m	w	IREL	San Francisco	San Francisco P O	83	168
Geo S [Dr]	45	m	w	AL	Monterey	Salinas Twp	74	312
George	34	m	w	ENGL	Sonoma	Washington Twp	91	468
George	24	m	w	NY	San Francisco	San Francisco P O	83	43
Gilbert W	37	m	w	IL	Shasta	Dog Crk P O	89	471
H D	48	m	w	NY	Yuba	Rose Bar Twp	93	658
Hugh	80	m	w	IREL	San Francisco	San Francisco P O	85	745
Hugh	28	m	w	IREL	Tuolumne	Columbia P O	93	348
J	28	m	w	OH	Alameda	Oakland	68	262
J H F	38	m	w	KY	Lake	Lakeport	73	406
Jackson	52	m	w	WV	Mendocino	Little Lake Twp	74	196
James	48	m	w	IREL	San Francisco	San Francisco P O	85	743
James	45	m	w	IREL	Siskiyou	Scott Valley Twp	89	617
James	42	m	w	IREL	San Francisco	11-Wd San Francisc	84	453
James	41	m	w	IREL	Santa Clara	San Jose Twp	88	202
James	40	m	w	IREL	San Francisco	2-Wd San Francisco	79	267
James	33	m	w	IREL	Merced	Snelling P O	74	255
James	31	m	w	IREL	Santa Barbara	Santa Barbara P O	87	482
James F	40	m	w	VA	Amador	Jackson P O	69	333
Jas	40	m	w	NY	San Diego	San Diego	78	509
John	48	m	w	MI	Alameda	Murray Twp	68	128
John	47	m	w	NY	San Joaquin	Oneal Twp	86	111
John	42	m	w	NY	Solano	Vacaville Twp	90	126
John	40	m	w	IREL	Amador	Ione City P O	69	358
John	35	m	w	IREL	Sacramento	Granite Twp	77	140
John	28	m	w	IREL	Klamath	Liberty Twp	73	374
Julia	56	f	w	IREL	San Francisco	7-Wd San Francisco	81	199
Kate	49	f	w	IREL	San Francisco	San Francisco P O	83	362
M J	52	f	w	VA	Tuolumne	Big Oak Flat P O	93	395
Margaret	31	f	w	IREL	San Francisco	11-Wd San Francisc	84	499
Martin	30	m	w	IREL	Santa Cruz	Soquel Twp	89	444
Mary	45	f	w	IREL	San Francisco	San Francisco P O	85	754
Mary	21	f	w	IREL	Monterey	Salinas Twp	74	314
Michael	60	m	w	IREL	Nevada	Bridgeport Twp	75	116
Michael	35	m	w	IREL	Monterey	Pajaro Twp	74	375
Michael	30	m	w	IREL	San Francisco	San Francisco P O	83	388
Michael	30	m	w	IREL	San Francisco	San Francisco P O	83	185
Michl	46	m	w	NY	Fresno	Millerton P O	72	160
Pat	45	m	w	IREL	Yuba	Marysville	93	598
Patrick	42	m	w	IREL	Alameda	Brooklyn	68	31
Patrick	34	m	w	IREL	San Francisco	San Francisco P O	85	861
Patrick	31	m	w	IREL	San Francisco	11-Wd San Francisc	84	526
Patrick	26	m	w	IREL	Santa Clara	Alviso Twp	88	28
Peter	45	m	w	IREL	Santa Clara	Gilroy Twp	88	104
Philip	53	m	w	IREL	Solano	Benicia	90	10
Philip	40	m	w	IREL	San Francisco	San Francisco P O	83	148
Philip	26	m	w	IREL	Los Angeles	San Gabriel Twp	73	593
Polly	70	f	w	NC	San Diego	San Diego	78	497
Porter	37	m	b	VA	Placer	Bath P O	76	435
R S	48	m	w	IN	San Joaquin	Tulare Twp	86	262
Robert	18	m	w	MO	Marin	Nicasio Twp	74	16
Thomas	46	m	w	IREL	San Francisco	1-Wd San Francisco	79	41
Thomas	42	m	w	IREL	San Francisco	San Francisco P O	85	744
Thomas	28	m	w	IREL	Plumas	Indian Twp	77	19
V B	31	m	w	VT	San Francisco	San Francisco P O	83	270
W T	33	m	w	TN	Monterey	Castroville Twp	74	325
William	35	m	w	IREL	Placer	Rocklin Twp	76	465
William	20	m	w	SWIT	Marin	Nicasio Twp	74	16
FARLIEN								
Achil	52	m	w	FRAN	San Francisco	San Francisco P O	83	43
FARLIN								
August	40	m	w	FRAN	Los Angeles	Soledad Twp	73	632
Charles	32	m	w	SWED	Yolo	Cottonwood Twp	93	462
Robert	36	m	w	IREL	Napa	Napa	75	19
FARLONG								
James	35	m	w	SCOT	Los Angeles	Soledad Twp	73	631
FARLOW								
George	50	m	w	OH	Yolo	Grafton Twp	93	491
Jonathan	51	m	w	NC	Shasta	Horsetown P O	89	506
FARLY								
Catherine	70	f	w	IREL	Tuolumne	Sonora P O	93	323
G W	63	m	w	OH	Sutter	Butte Twp	92	95
John	39	m	w	IREL	Sacramento	Georgianna Twp	77	124
Phillip	35	m	w	IREL	San Mateo	Schoolhouse Statio	87	337
Warren	22	m	w	OH	Sutter	Butte Twp	92	94
FARMAN								
Geo P	28	m	w	NY	Santa Clara	Gilroy Twp	88	89
Seth M	39	m	w	NY	San Bernardino	San Bernardino Twp	78	453
Thomas	38	m	w	PA	San Francisco	5-Wd San Francisco	81	23
FARMAR								
Fernando	29	m	w	NY	Santa Clara	Gilroy Twp	88	107
FARMER								
Ann	28	f	w	IREL	Santa Clara	1-Wd San Jose	88	246
Charles	19	m	w	CA	San Francisco	7-Wd San Francisco	81	165
Col	18	m	w	WI	Solano	Vallejo	90	216
E J	4	f	w	IL	Sonoma	Santa Rosa	91	410
E T	37	m	w	TN	Sonoma	Santa Rosa	91	410
Frank	50	m	w	MO	San Joaquin	Elkhorn Twp	86	54
Geo	45	m	w	OH	Sacramento	3-Wd Sacramento	77	278
Geo	20	m	w	WI	Solano	Vallejo	90	216
H A	33	m	w	ENGL	Alameda	Oakland	68	202
H M	24	m	w	NY	Solano	Vallejo	90	197
Hardin W	36	m	w	VA	Santa Cruz	Watsonville	89	364
Henry	24	m	w	PRUS	Solano	Tremont Twp	90	30
J W	52	m	w	NY	Solano	Vallejo	90	216
Jno H	42	m	w	TN	Sonoma	Santa Rosa	91	402
John	48	m	w	IL	Santa Clara	2-Wd San Jose	88	335
John	35	m	w	AR	Colusa	Colusa Twp	71	275
Kate	30	f	w	IREL	San Francisco	8-Wd San Francisco	82	299
L P	36	m	w	KY	Sutter	Yuba Twp	92	141
Leura	14	f	w	CA	San Joaquin	2-Wd Stockton	86	196
Life	56	m	w	MA	Mendocino	Calpella Twp	74	186
Mary	17	f	w	WI	Solano	Vallejo	90	216
Mary M	20	f	w	TN	El Dorado	Placerville	72	123
Napolian	23	m	w	DENM	Butte	Oregon Twp	70	135
Peter	17	m	w	IL	Butte	Ophir Twp	70	91
Richard	45	m	w	ENGL	San Francisco	2-Wd San Francisco	79	188
Robt	24	m	w	MO	San Luis Obispo	San Luis Obispo Tw	87	316
Rufus M	52	m	w	GA	Butte	Wyandotte Twp	70	142
Samuel	52	m	w	TN	Siskiyou	Surprise Valley Tw	89	639
Thomas	48	m	w	ENGL	Santa Cruz	Santa Cruz Twp	89	392
Thos	43	m	w	ENGL	San Francisco	11-Wd San Francisc	84	566
William	39	m	w	OH	Trinity	Weaverville Pct	92	225
William C	29	m	w	NY	Solano	Vacaville Twp	90	118
William T	39	m	w	KY	Contra Costa	Martinez P O	71	392
Wm	69	m	w	TN	Sonoma	Santa Rosa	91	417
Wm	46	m	w	KY	Lake	Coyote Valley	73	400
Wm	45	m	w	CANA	Sacramento	Granite Twp	77	145
Wm	13	m	w	CA	San Joaquin	Oneal Twp	86	110
Wm H	30	m	w	OH	Butte	Ophir Twp	70	98
Wm M	28	m	w	NY	San Mateo	San Mateo P O	87	359
FARMING								
James	5	m	w	CA	Marin	Bolinas Twp	74	5
FARN								
Ah	19	m	c	CHIN	San Francisco	3-Wd San Francisco	79	309
FARNALL								
F M	25	m	w	ME	Alameda	Oakland	68	189
FARNAM								
A	61	m	w	NY	Yuba	Marysville Twp	93	571
Joseph	37	m	w	IREL	Butte	Ophir Twp	70	112
FARNAN								
Lawrence	50	m	w	IREL	Shasta	Horsetown P O	89	503
FARNELL								
Albert	13	m	w	CA	Sacramento	4-Wd Sacramento	77	348
J H	40	m	w	NY	San Joaquin	Douglas Twp	86	51
Patrick	34	m	w	IREL	Nevada	Bloomfield Twp	75	99
FARNER								
Frank	47	m	w	PORT	Mendocino	Noyo & Big Rvr Twp	74	173
William	40	m	w	MA	Placer	Bath P O	76	438
FARNESS								
James	33	m	w	ENGL	Santa Cruz	Santa Cruz	89	411
FARNESWORTH								
Henry	27	m	w	CANA	Sonoma	Bodega Twp	91	252
John F	31	m	w	OH	El Dorado	Georgetown Twp	72	42
Junius	38	m	w	OH	Amador	Ione City P O	69	352
FARNETTE								
Luie	37	m	w	CANA	Alameda	Washington Twp	68	294
FARNEY								
Howard	48	m	w	TN	Mendocino	Anderson Twp	74	151
Jacob	53	m	w	FRAN	Los Angeles	Los Angeles	73	518
James	53	m	w	IREL	Santa Clara	Alviso Twp	88	28
Mark	45	m	w	IREL	Santa Clara	San Jose Twp	88	194
FARNHAM								
Alphonso	28	m	w	ME	Nevada	Bloomfield Twp	75	95
Apollos	40	m	w	ME	Santa Cruz	Santa Cruz	89	420

© 2001 by Heritage Quest. All rights reserved.

Name	Age	S	R	B-PL	County	Locale	Series M593 Roll	Pg
Daniel Jr	30	m	w	MI	Yolo	Cache Crk Twp	93	445
David	70	m	w	NH	Yolo	Cache Crk Twp	93	445
H	42	m	w	VT	Amador	Ione City P O	69	367
H L	27	m	w	ME	Nevada	Meadow Lake Twp	75	249
John	28	m	w	CANA	San Francisco	1-Wd San Francisco	79	41
John M	48	m	w	ME	San Francisco	San Francisco P O	83	114
Jon	30	m	w	ME	Solano	Vallejo	90	193
Julia	16	f	w	ME	San Francisco	San Francisco P O	83	418
Leona	50	m	w	NY	San Luis Obispo	San Luis Obispo Tw	87	308
Luther	61	m	w	VT	Santa Cruz	Santa Cruz	89	404
Mary	69	f	w	ME	San Francisco	11-Wd San Francisc	84	572
Moses P	32	m	w	NY	Trinity	Weaverville Pct	92	222
Rot	43	m	w	NY	San Joaquin	Castoria Twp	86	7
Wal	35	m	w	MA	Alameda	Oakland	68	178
William	30	m	w	CANA	Humboldt	Mattole Twp	72	287
FARNIA								
Florance	14	f	w	SWIT	El Dorado	Georgetown Twp	72	46
FARNIAH								
William	30	m	w	MO	Solano	Silveyville Twp	90	92
FARNIAM								
F	29	m	w	VA	San Joaquin	Castoria Twp	86	11
FARNINGTON								
Norton	35	m	w	IA	Colusa	Monroe Twp	71	320
FARNK								
Wm A	26	m	w	TN	San Francisco	San Francisco P O	85	720
FARNO								
August	28	m	w	ITAL	Santa Clara	San Jose Twp	88	187
FARNSWORTH								
Aaron	31	m	w	IN	Plumas	Quartz Twp	77	36
C B	66	m	w	OH	Sacramento	4-Wd Sacramento	77	366
Calvin E	36	m	w	WV	Mariposa	Mariposa P O	74	120
Charles C	38	m	w	MA	Santa Clara	1-Wd San Jose	88	247
D	44	m	w	MA	San Francisco	8-Wd San Francisco	82	365
David	36	m	w	NH	San Francisco	8-Wd San Francisco	82	368
David	31	m	w	NH	San Francisco	8-Wd San Francisco	82	464
Diantha	50	f	w	ME	San Francisco	8-Wd San Francisco	82	414
E S	48	m	w	VT	San Francisco	7-Wd San Francisco	81	283
Henry	26	m	w	NY	Sonoma	Analy Twp	91	227
J D	52	m	w	NY	San Francisco	San Francisco P O	85	843
J L	48	m	w	NY	San Francisco	8-Wd San Francisco	82	363
James	33	m	w	NY	San Diego	San Diego	78	506
James J	29	m	w	WV	Mariposa	Mariposa P O	74	118
Jno	36	m	w	VA	Santa Clara	Gilroy Twp	88	97
John	41	m	w	VT	El Dorado	Cosumnes Twp	72	18
Joseph	42	m	w	NY	Colusa	Grand Island Twp	71	309
Oliver W	43	m	w	MO	Santa Clara	San Jose Twp	88	206
Orin E	23	m	w	NH	San Francisco	8-Wd San Francisco	82	464
Richard	14	m	w	CA	Santa Cruz	Soquel Twp	89	449
Rosa	11	f	w	CA	Klamath	Trinidad Twp	73	391
Thomas	33	m	w	WV	Mariposa	Mariposa P O	74	119
Thomas H	45	m	w	MO	Santa Clara	San Jose Twp	88	215
William	54	m	w	OH	Inyo	Independence Twp	73	327
Wm C	41	m	w	WV	Sacramento	4-Wd Sacramento	77	366
Wm O	28	m	w	MA	San Francisco	San Francisco P O	85	716
FARNUM								
E P	36	m	w	ME	Butte	Bidwell Twp	70	3
H C	44	m	w	NY	Amador	Fiddletown P O	69	430
N T	35	m	w	ME	Solano	Vallejo	90	140
FARNWORTH								
Fredric	37	m	w	NY	Humboldt	Mattole Twp	72	285
FARNY								
Matilda	25	f	w	ITAL	Alameda	Oakland	68	169
FARO								
Anne E	20	f	w	PA	Tehama	Battle Crk Meadows	92	168
FAROL								
A	32	f	w	IREL	Alameda	Oakland	68	188
FARONI								
F	30	m	w	SWIT	San Joaquin	Oneal Twp	86	110
FAROR								
Terrie	21	m	w	MEXI	Tulare	Tule Rvr Twp	92	261
FAROT								
Peter	27	m	w	FRAN	Los Angeles	Los Angeles Twp	73	478
FARP								
Hanora	40	f	w	IREL	San Francisco	San Francisco P O	83	250
FARQUA								
Clara	66	f	w	FRAN	Butte	Oregon Twp	70	134
Geo	53	m	w	MD	Butte	Oregon Twp	70	134
FARQUAY								
Oliver	42	m	w	VA	Butte	Chico Twp	70	18
FARQUETTE								
Jane	30	f	w	ITAL	San Francisco	5-Wd San Francisco	81	35
FARQUHAR								
James	56	m	w	SCOT	Amador	Fiddletown P O	69	437
Wm	47	m	w	IN	San Francisco	8-Wd San Francisco	82	370
FARQUHARSON								
Chas	41	m	w	SCOT	San Francisco	8-Wd San Francisco	82	297
J	26	m	w	LA	San Francisco	8-Wd San Francisco	82	362
FARR								
Adam	40	m	w	BADE	Placer	Dutch Flat P O	76	402
Alonzo	48	m	w	OH	San Francisco	San Francisco P O	83	86
Annie	42	f	w	PRUS	Butte	Chico Twp	70	32
B A	45	m	w	NH	Sacramento	3-Wd Sacramento	77	257
Charles	38	m	w	ENGL	San Francisco	San Francisco P O	80	379
D T	59	m	w	NY	Sacramento	Sutter Twp	77	381
Franklin	53	m	w	NH	Calaveras	San Andreas P O	70	216
Geo	45	m	w	PRUS	Butte	Chico Twp	70	32
George	52	m	w	BAVA	Plumas	Seneca Twp	77	47
George	40	m	w	IL	San Francisco	San Francisco P O	83	19
Hellen	55	f	w	PRUS	Placer	Dutch Flat P O	76	404
Henry	42	m	w	PRUS	Santa Clara	Santa Clara Twp	88	165
Jim	14	m	c	CHIN	San Francisco	5-Wd San Francisco	81	10
Leonard	40	m	w	ME	San Mateo	Half Moon Bay P O	87	407
Philip	40	m	w	BAVA	Sierra	Sears Twp	89	559
William H	46	m	w	GA	Calaveras	San Andreas P O	70	202
Wolverson	55	m	w	KY	Calaveras	San Andreas P O	70	158
FARRA								
Bridget	60	f	w	IREL	Santa Clara	Santa Clara Twp	88	155
Oliver	42	m	w	PA	Plumas	Plumas Twp	77	31
FARRACY								
Michael	46	m	w	IREL	Santa Cruz	Santa Cruz	89	423
FARRAH								
George B	55	m	w	VA	Tulare	Tule Rvr Twp	92	260
John	27	m	w	IREL	San Francisco	11-Wd San Francisc	84	708
FARRAHAR								
Mary	40	f	w	IREL	Siskiyou	Butte Twp	89	588
FARRAL								
Bridget	40	f	w	IREL	San Francisco	San Francisco P O	85	779
Cecilia	20	f	w	IREL	San Francisco	2-Wd San Francisco	79	194
Hannah	40	f	w	ENGL	San Francisco	2-Wd San Francisco	79	193
FARRALD								
Anna	23	f	w	IREL	San Francisco	8-Wd San Francisco	82	300
Mary	25	f	w	IREL	San Francisco	8-Wd San Francisco	82	335
FARRALEY								
John	38	m	w	IREL	San Francisco	7-Wd San Francisco	81	194
FARRALL								
James	30	m	w	IREL	Butte	Chico Twp	70	42
FARRAN								
James	30	m	w	IREL	San Francisco	1-Wd San Francisco	79	31
John F	28	m	w	IREL	San Francisco	San Francisco P O	83	376
Robert	45	m	w	NY	Alameda	Brooklyn Twp	68	51
William	35	m	w	IREL	Plumas	Washington Twp	77	53
FARRANCE								
John	38	m	w	ENGL	Mendocino	Ukiah Twp	74	241
FARRAR								
Deliah	39	f	w	ME	San Joaquin	Dent Twp	86	16
Floyd	35	m	w	VA	Nevada	Grass Valley Twp	75	206
J G	52	m	w	PA	Amador	Jackson P O	69	328
Leonard	48	m	w	MO	Fresno	Kings Rvr P O	72	203
M C	39	m	w	VT	Humboldt	Pacific Twp	72	293
Monroe	58	m	w	MA	Alameda	Eden Twp	68	72
Thomas	48	m	w	ENGL	Calaveras	Copperopolis P O	70	227
FARRARIA								
Peter	34	m	w	ITAL	Amador	Jackson P O	69	333
FARRAS								
Castino	22	m	w	ITAL	San Mateo	Schoolhouse Statio	87	346
Dominico	30	m	w	ITAL	San Mateo	Schoolhouse Statio	87	334
FARRE								
Mary	65	f	w	FRAN	San Francisco	8-Wd San Francisco	82	344
FARREE								
Geo W	39	m	w	IN	El Dorado	Greenwood Twp	72	56
FARREL								
Anna	48	f	w	IREL	San Francisco	2-Wd San Francisco	79	244
Barney	40	m	w	IREL	San Mateo	San Mateo P O	87	358
Bernard	36	m	w	IREL	Santa Clara	2-Wd San Jose	88	307
Edward	41	m	w	DE	San Francisco	2-Wd San Francisco	79	254
James	30	m	w	IREL	Santa Clara	2-Wd San Jose	88	316
John	40	m	w	FRAN	Sierra	Sears Twp	89	560
John	36	m	w	IREL	Solano	Vallejo	90	171
John	26	m	w	PA	Yolo	Grafton Twp	93	486
Owen	30	m	w	IREL	San Mateo	Schoolhouse Statio	87	344
Pat	38	m	w	IREL	San Francisco	7-Wd San Francisco	81	229
Patrick	40	m	w	IREL	San Mateo	Schoolhouse Statio	87	343
Patrick	32	m	w	IREL	San Mateo	San Mateo P O	87	349
Robt	4M	m	w	CA	Sacramento	4-Wd Sacramento	77	345
Samuel	40	m	w	IL	Tulare	Tule Rvr Twp	92	261
Thos	23	m	w	IREL	San Francisco	7-Wd San Francisco	81	258
William	50	m	w	IREL	Tuolumne	Sonora P O	93	326
William	36	m	w	IREL	Solano	Silveyville Twp	90	79
William	29	m	w	IREL	San Mateo	Menlo Park P O	87	378
William	28	m	w	IREL	San Mateo	Menlo Park P O	87	378
Wm	24	m	w	IREL	San Francisco	7-Wd San Francisco	81	275
FARRELL								
A	18	m	w	IREL	San Joaquin	Tulare Twp	86	255
Alice	35	f	w	IREL	San Francisco	8-Wd San Francisco	82	476
Amanda	19	f	w	CANA	Santa Clara	Santa Clara Twp	88	138
Amy	45	f	w	IREL	Santa Clara	Redwood Twp	88	134
Ann	60	f	w	IREL	San Francisco	7-Wd San Francisco	81	173
Annie	43	f	b	VA	San Francisco	San Francisco P O	83	244
Catherine	42	f	w	IREL	Santa Clara	2-Wd San Jose	88	325
Cathrine	56	f	w	IREL	San Francisco	1-Wd San Francisco	79	8
Danl	23	m	w	IREL	Yuba	Marysville	93	595
David	42	m	w	IREL	San Joaquin	1-Wd Stockton	86	137
Delia	35	f	w	IREL	San Francisco	2-Wd San Francisco	79	195
Dominick	50	m	w	IREL	Marin	San Rafael	74	48
Dowd	31	m	w	IREL	Sierra	Sears Twp	89	554
E O	16	f	w	CA	Alameda	Oakland	68	242
Edward	42	m	w	IREL	San Francisco	San Francisco P O	85	745
Frank	55	m	w	IREL	San Francisco	San Francisco P O	80	534
Hannah	34	f	w	NY	San Francisco	8-Wd San Francisco	82	309
J J	43	m	w	IREL	Yuba	East Bear Rvr Twp	93	544
James	50	m	w	IREL	Tuolumne	Columbia P O	93	346
James	45	m	w	IREL	San Francisco	San Francisco P O	83	418
James	39	m	w	ENGL	San Francisco	San Francisco P O	85	745
James	38	m	w	IREL	San Francisco	San Francisco P O	83	87

© 2001 by Heritage Quest. All rights reserved.

Series M593

Name	Age	S	R	B-PL	County	Locale	Roll	Pg
James	38	m	w	IREL	San Francisco	San Francisco P O	83	294
James	37	m	w	ENGL	San Joaquin	2-Wd Stockton	86	171
James	35	m	w	IREL	San Francisco	1-Wd San Francisco	79	93
James	32	m	w	IREL	Alameda	Oakland	68	218
James	31	m	w	IREL	San Francisco	1-Wd San Francisco	79	113
James	30	m	w	ENGL	Nevada	Grass Valley Twp	75	183
James	28	m	w	IREL	San Francisco	7-Wd San Francisco	81	167
James A	43	m	w	IREL	Nevada	Grass Valley Twp	75	186
James M	29	m	w	IREL	San Francisco	San Francisco P O	85	870
Jaques	36	m	w	FRAN	Sierra	Sears Twp	89	560
John	56	m	w	IREL	San Francisco	San Francisco P O	83	268
John	46	m	w	IREL	San Francisco	1-Wd San Francisco	79	114
John	44	m	w	IREL	Los Angeles	Los Angeles	73	507
John	40	m	w	IREL	San Francisco	11-Wd San Francisc	84	488
John	39	m	w	IREL	San Francisco	8-Wd San Francisco	82	414
John	38	m	w	OH	Solano	Montezuma Twp	90	66
John	38	m	w	OH	Sacramento	Georgianna Twp	77	130
John	36	m	w	NY	Marin	San Rafael Twp	74	34
John	28	m	w	IREL	Solano	Tremont Twp	90	28
John	28	m	w	IREL	San Francisco	8-Wd San Francisco	82	396
John	27	m	w	IREL	Nevada	Grass Valley Twp	75	222
John	18	m	w	MA	Santa Clara	Fremont Twp	88	60
John M	38	m	w	IREL	San Francisco	San Francisco P O	83	394
John T	45	m	w	IREL	San Francisco	San Francisco P O	83	249
Kate	25	f	w	IREL	San Francisco	8-Wd San Francisco	82	411
Luke	38	m	w	IREL	Placer	Bath P O	76	448
M O	27	m	w	IA	Lassen	Long Valley Twp	73	436
Martha	25	f	w	IA	Santa Clara	2-Wd San Jose	88	325
Martin	34	m	w	IREL	Sonoma	Bodega Twp	91	258
Mary	32	f	w	KY	San Francisco	8-Wd San Francisco	82	453
Mary	28	f	w	IREL	San Francisco	San Francisco P O	83	56
Mary	27	f	w	IREL	San Francisco	8-Wd San Francisco	82	411
Mary S	40	f	w	IREL	San Francisco	1-Wd San Francisco	79	11
Mathew	24	m	w	NY	Yolo	Cache Crk Twp	93	429
Mgt	34	f	w	IREL	Yuba	Marysville	93	606
Michael	44	m	w	IREL	San Francisco	San Francisco P O	83	166
Michael	40	m	w	IREL	San Francisco	1-Wd San Francisco	79	102
Michael	34	m	w	IREL	Solano	Suisun Twp	90	113
Michael	32	m	w	IREL	San Francisco	San Francisco P O	83	264
Michael	30	m	w	IREL	Nevada	Grass Valley Twp	75	214
Michael	30	m	w	IREL	Nevada	Grass Valley Twp	75	196
Michael	25	m	w	IREL	Solano	Vacaville Twp	90	134
Michl	45	m	w	IREL	San Francisco	1-Wd San Francisco	79	105
Michl	37	m	w	CANA	San Francisco	1-Wd San Francisco	79	63
Mike	45	m	w	IREL	Solano	Vallejo	90	170
Milton	47	m	w	VA	Shasta	Millville P O	89	493
Owen	72	m	w	IREL	Nevada	Nevada Twp	75	302
Owen	37	m	w	IREL	Sacramento	2-Wd Sacramento	77	217
Patk	37	m	w	IREL	Solano	Vallejo	90	146
Patrick	65	m	w	IREL	San Francisco	7-Wd San Francisco	81	189
Patrick	61	m	w	IREL	Santa Clara	Santa Clara Twp	88	176
Patrick	44	m	w	IREL	San Francisco	11-Wd San Francisc	84	516
Patrick	35	m	w	NY	San Francisco	11-Wd San Francisc	84	558
Patrick F	18	m	w	MA	Placer	Roseville P O	76	348
Peter	40	m	w	IREL	Nevada	Grass Valley Twp	75	214
Peter	37	m	w	IREL	San Francisco	San Francisco P O	83	118
Placid	20	m	w	CHIL	Stanislaus	Empire Twp	92	66
Robert	37	m	w	IREL	Sacramento	Granite Twp	77	142
Robert	22	m	w	CA	Santa Clara	Santa Clara Twp	88	138
Saml	38	m	w	IREL	Alameda	Murray Twp	68	106
Samuel	39	m	w	IREL	San Francisco	San Francisco P O	83	386
Samuel B	33	m	w	IREL	San Francisco	6-Wd San Francisco	81	96
Thomas	41	m	w	IREL	Contra Costa	San Pablo Twp	71	364
Thomas	39	m	w	CANA	Santa Clara	San Jose Twp	88	200
Thomas	38	m	w	IREL	Yuba	Marysville	93	579
Thomas	36	m	w	IREL	San Francisco	San Francisco P O	83	205
Thomas	32	m	w	IREL	San Francisco	San Francisco P O	85	757
Thos	40	m	w	IREL	San Francisco	1-Wd San Francisco	79	43
Thos	24	m	w	PA	Butte	Kimshew Tpw	70	83
Thos	16	m	w	LA	San Francisco	11-Wd San Francisc	84	588
Timothy	32	m	w	IREL	San Francisco	8-Wd San Francisco	82	496
W B	23	m	w	IREL	Sacramento	1-Wd Sacramento	77	184
William	37	m	w	IREL	Sacramento	2-Wd Sacramento	77	231
William	37	m	w	IREL	Los Angeles	Los Angeles	73	566
William	29	m	w	NY	Santa Clara	San Jose Twp	88	194
William	27	m	w	IREL	San Francisco	San Francisco P O	80	336
William	27	m	w	IREL	San Francisco	San Francisco P O	83	144
William	25	m	w	CANA	San Francisco	San Francisco P O	83	166
William B	42	m	w	KY	El Dorado	Placerville	72	119
Wm	40	m	w	CANA	San Francisco	San Francisco P O	83	75
Wm	39	m	w	IREL	San Luis Obispo	Salinas Twp	87	288
Wm	35	m	w	IREL	San Francisco	11-Wd San Francisc	84	599
Wm	35	m	w	ENGL	San Joaquin	1-Wd Stockton	86	130
Wm	30	m	w	IREL	Solano	Benicia	90	4
FARRELLEY								
Chas	41	m	w	IREL	San Francisco	San Francisco P O	83	284
FARRELLY								
Patrick	40	m	w	IREL	San Francisco	1-Wd San Francisco	79	9
Robert	45	m	w	PA	Alameda	Brooklyn Twp	68	47
FARREN								
Bernard	36	m	w	IREL	Santa Clara	2-Wd San Jose	88	323
Celia	20	f	w	IREL	San Francisco	11-Wd San Francisc	84	657
Daniel	39	m	w	IREL	Sacramento	4-Wd Sacramento	77	327
Elisabeth	35	f	w	MA	Alameda	Brooklyn	68	34
Henry	33	m	w	IREL	San Francisco	San Francisco P O	83	391
John	48	m	w	IREL	Contra Costa	Martinez P O	71	389
John	43	m	w	NY	San Francisco	11-Wd San Francisc	84	458

Series M593

Name	Age	S	R	B-PL	County	Locale	Roll	Pg
John	36	m	w	IREL	San Francisco	7-Wd San Francisco	81	282
John	35	m	w	IREL	San Francisco	7-Wd San Francisco	81	198
John	35	m	w	IREL	Sacramento	4-Wd Sacramento	77	342
Joseph	29	m	w	KY	Butte	Ophir Twp	70	100
Joseph	28	m	w	IREL	Santa Clara	Redwood Twp	88	133
Kate	25	f	w	IREL	San Francisco	2-Wd San Francisco	79	248
Kate	20	f	w	IREL	Sonoma	Analy Twp	91	220
Mary	68	f	w	IREL	San Francisco	San Francisco P O	83	43
Mary	40	f	w	IREL	Santa Clara	2-Wd San Jose	88	307
Mary	35	f	w	IREL	San Francisco	San Francisco P O	83	38
Michl	30	m	w	IREL	San Francisco	San Francisco P O	83	88
Patrick	29	m	w	IREL	Santa Clara	2-Wd San Jose	88	305
Samuel	40	m	w	NY	San Francisco	San Francisco P O	85	765
Thomas	34	m	w	IREL	San Francisco	7-Wd San Francisco	81	210
Thomas J	28	m	w	NY	Siskiyou	Table Rock Twp	89	647
FARRENBAKER								
Andrew	45	m	w	BADE	Sacramento	Lee Twp	77	161
August	48	m	w	PRUS	Sacramento	Cosumnes Twp	77	93
Mike	40	m	w	BADE	Sacramento	Lee Twp	77	161
FARRERAS								
Rafael	55	m	w	MEXI	Mariposa	Mariposa P O	74	94
FARRETTI								
B	41	m	w	ITAL	Amador	Sutter Crk P O	69	400
B	40	m	w	ITAL	Amador	Jackson P O	69	329
FARRI								
John	45	m	w	AZOR	San Francisco	1-Wd San Francisco	79	102
Joseph	47	m	w	ITAL	San Francisco	1-Wd San Francisco	79	121
FARRIER								
Hiram	37	m	w	NY	Alameda	Brooklyn	68	25
Nancy	18	f	w	AR	Humboldt	Eel Rvr Twp	72	251
S N	20	m	w	NJ	Tuolumne	Chinese Camp P O	93	384
Wm	50	m	w	IOFM	Sacramento	Natomas Twp	77	165
FARRIGAN								
John	26	m	w	IREL	Solano	Montezuma Twp	90	65
FARRIGH								
Austin	35	m	w	TN	Butte	Oregon Twp	70	133
FARRILL								
John	25	m	w	IREL	San Francisco	2-Wd San Francisco	79	283
Jonathan	65	m	w	KY	Placer	Bath P O	76	433
FARRIN								
Geo	27	m	w	AR	Humboldt	Pacific Twp	72	296
Silas	59	m	w	TN	Humboldt	Pacific Twp	72	294
FARRING								
J B	30	m	w	NY	Sonoma	Santa Rosa	91	395
Louis	40	m	w	MA	San Francisco	7-Wd San Francisco	81	226
FARRINGTON								
A D	35	m	w	ME	Alameda	Oakland	68	194
Allen	26	m	w	ME	Plumas	Washington Twp	77	56
Bernard	40	m	w	IREL	San Francisco	7-Wd San Francisco	81	273
C J	21	m	w	NH	Siskiyou	Callahan P O	89	625
Charles L	45	m	w	ME	San Francisco	8-Wd San Francisco	82	448
George	40	m	w	ENGL	San Bernardino	San Bernardino Twp	78	417
Nathan C	50	m	w	NH	Shasta	Stillwater P O	89	478
Nelson	19	m	w	ME	Plumas	Washington Twp	77	52
Seth	34	m	w	ME	Plumas	Goodwin Twp	77	7
Thos A	35	m	w	MS	San Francisco	San Francisco P O	83	127
FARRIO								
Jacob	38	m	w	AUST	Amador	Amador City P O	69	392
FARRIS								
Allen	44	m	w	OH	Sonoma	Petaluma Twp	91	359
Andrew L	44	m	w	VA	Sonoma	Petaluma Twp	91	357
C O	40	m	w	NY	Solano	Vallejo	90	184
George	17	m	w	IA	Sonoma	Analy Twp	91	230
George B	37	m	w	KY	Los Angeles	Los Angeles Twp	73	465
George E	40	m	w	NY	Fresno	Millerton P O	72	183
James	43	m	w	IREL	Yolo	Putah Twp	93	515
Jordin	74	m	w	VA	Sonoma	Petaluma Twp	91	359
Joseph	17	m	w	CA	San Joaquin	Liberty Twp	86	84
Josie	42	f	w	MEXI	San Joaquin	2-Wd Stockton	86	170
M C	40	f	w	MO	San Joaquin	Liberty Twp	86	84
Marshal B	37	m	w	VA	Colusa	Colusa	71	289
N	32	m	w	MO	Lake	Lower Lake	73	418
Owen	45	m	w	IREL	San Francisco	San Francisco P O	83	142
Robt F	47	m	w	VA	Colusa	Colusa	71	290
William F	48	m	w	KY	Los Angeles	Los Nietos Twp	73	573
FARRISH								
John	27	m	w	PORT	Monterey	San Benito Twp	74	380
Thomas	33	m	w	TN	San Francisco	6-Wd San Francisco	81	141
FARRIT								
Thomas	46	m	w	IREL	Sonoma	Sonoma Twp	91	446
FARROH								
A L	24	m	w	TN	Monterey	San Juan Twp	74	399
FARROL								
James	34	m	w	IREL	Alameda	Eden Twp	68	65
FARROLD								
Wm M	26	m	w	IREL	San Francisco	8-Wd San Francisco	82	348
FARRON								
Jno	25	m	w	IREL	Sierra	Gibson Twp	89	542
William	50	m	w	ENGL	Amador	Fiddletown P O	69	441
FARROT								
John	25	m	w	ITAL	San Francisco	2-Wd San Francisco	79	237
FARROW								
Edward	34	m	w	WI	Contra Costa	Martinez Twp	71	352
Floyd	37	m	w	ENGL	Nevada	Grass Valley Twp	75	224
Isah	37	m	w	ME	San Joaquin	2-Wd Stockton	86	168
FARRY								
Daniel	9	m	w	CA	Marin	San Rafael Twp	74	29

© 2001 by Heritage Quest. All rights reserved.

Series M593

Name	Age	S	R	B-PL	County	Locale	Roll	Pg
Emma	45	f	w	ME	Alameda	Oakland	68	257
John	26	m	w	IREL	San Francisco	11-Wd San Francisc	84	650
John	25	m	w	ENGL	San Francisco	2-Wd San Francisco	79	214
Patrick	29	m	w	IREL	San Francisco	San Francisco P O	83	350
Richard	23	m	w	ENGL	Calaveras	San Andreas P O	70	204
FARSTER								
David	39	m	w	NY	Los Angeles	Los Angeles Twp	73	491
FARTA								
Manuel	20	m	w	PORT	Tuolumne	Columbia P O	93	356
FARTHING								
Martha	18	f	w	VA	San Francisco	San Francisco P O	85	759
Thomas	32	m	w	ME	Yolo	Grafton Twp	93	501
FARTHINHAM								
G	26	m	w	MO	Merced	Snelling P O	74	278
FARUM								
Isabella	11	f	m	CA	San Joaquin	1-Wd Stockton	86	129
FARVALL								
James	45	m	w	NY	Lake	Lower Lake	73	418
FARVAR								
Franklin	27	m	w	GA	Fresno	Millerton P O	72	193
FARVARE								
Chas	42	m	w	FRAN	Butte	Ophir Twp	70	98
FARVIS								
Jno H	23	m	w	IN	Santa Barbara	San Buenaventura P	87	418
Wm W	28	m	w	IN	Santa Barbara	San Buenaventura P	87	418
FARWELL								
Charlotte	71	f	w	MA	Solano	Suisun Twp	90	111
Ed	48	m	w	CT	San Joaquin	Castoria Twp	86	15
George	47	m	w	NH	San Diego	San Diego	78	491
J D	54	m	w	CA	Alameda	Alameda	68	2
J H	38	m	w	NH	San Joaquin	Oneal Twp	86	98
John	69	m	w	NH	Solano	Suisun Twp	90	111
Peter J	35	m	w	NY	Santa Clara	San Jose Twp	88	192
S O	42	m	w	OH	El Dorado	Coloma Twp	72	3
W H	33	m	w	ME	Alameda	Alameda	68	1
Wm	25	m	w	NY	Sonoma	Bodega Twp	91	265
FARY								
Ah	40	m	c	CHIN	Sacramento	Cosumnes Twp	77	92
Ah	27	m	c	CHIN	Sacramento	Cosumnes Twp	77	94
George	33	m	w	MA	Butte	Hamilton Twp	70	66
Hanah	25	f	w	IREL	Alameda	Oakland	68	235
Michael	37	m	w	IREL	Sacramento	Cosumnes Twp	77	88
FAS								
Ah	35	m	c	CHIN	Alameda	Alameda	68	6
Ah	12	m	c	CHIN	San Francisco	11-Wd San Francisc	84	538
FASANERO								
Dominick	35	m	w	ITAL	San Francisco	San Francisco P O	80	341
FASBIN								
Louis	55	m	w	PRUS	San Francisco	6-Wd San Francisco	81	99
FASCALINE								
F	25	m	w	CA	Alameda	Murray Twp	68	125
FASCAR								
Jas	39	m	w	SCOT	Solano	Vallejo	90	197
FASEN								
Banerat	32	m	w	PRUS	San Francisco	2-Wd San Francisco	79	143
Poidnes L	21	m	w	NY	Calaveras	San Andreas P O	70	192
FASH								
Ah	25	m	c	CHIN	Amador	Fiddletown P O	69	427
Thomas	33	m	w	IL	Santa Cruz	Watsonville	89	372
FASHT								
Mary	30	f	w	IREL	Alameda	Oakland	68	231
FASKER								
J F	51	m	w	VT	Shasta	Shasta P O	89	453
FASKING								
H	46	m	w	PRUS	Alameda	Alameda	68	15
Louis	53	m	w	PRUS	Alameda	Alameda	68	10
FASLER								
Oliver A	42	m	w	VT	Calaveras	San Andreas P O	70	218
FASNACH								
Anne	27	f	w	WURT	San Francisco	8-Wd San Francisco	82	413
FASON								
Fredk	47	m	w	MA	Tuolumne	Sonora P O	93	310
FASS								
Cynthia	20	f	w	NY	Butte	Hamilton Twp	70	71
Edmund	14	m	w	PA	Santa Clara	Milpitas Twp	88	108
Julius	19	m	w	PRUS	San Francisco	San Francisco P O	85	837
FASSAS								
Mc S	25	m	w	IA	Sonoma	Cloverdale Twp	91	268
FASSET								
John	30	m	w	MA	San Francisco	5-Wd San Francisco	81	33
FASSETT								
Alonzo	21	m	w	IA	Amador	Ione City P O	69	358
Augusta	18	f	w	IA	Amador	Amador City P O	69	390
Freeman W	63	m	w	VT	Sacramento	Franklin Twp	77	105
H H	38	m	w	OH	San Joaquin	Tulare Twp	86	252
Ira	52	m	w	NY	Amador	Ione City P O	69	355
Louis	35	m	w	PA	Sacramento	San Joaquin Twp	77	401
Thos	36	m	w	ME	Solano	Vallejo	90	202
Thos A	37	m	w	ME	Solano	Vallejo	90	159
FAST								
Ah	28	m	c	CHIN	Solano	Suisun Twp	90	106
George	52	m	w	OH	Mendocino	Sanel Twp	74	230
Henry	47	m	w	PRUS	San Francisco	11-Wd San Francisc	84	679
FASTEN								
M E	30	m	w	ME	Alameda	Oakland	68	211
William	49	m	w	VA	San Francisco	11-Wd San Francisc	84	493
FASTER								
C W	33	m	w	NY	Sierra	Sierra Twp	89	568
J A	45	m	w	NORW	Tuolumne	Columbia P O	93	354
O B	24	m	w	ME	Tuolumne	Columbia P O	93	352
Theodore	58	m	w	MA	Yolo	Putah Twp	93	516
Theodore	20	m	w	HAMB	Sacramento	Georgianna Twp	77	129
FASTERLING								
Louis	46	m	w	GERM	Tuolumne	Columbia P O	93	338
FASTINO								
Manwell	35	m	w	PORT	San Mateo	Half Moon Bay P O	87	390
Medina	29	m	w	CHIL	Sacramento	2-Wd Sacramento	77	223
FAT								
A	22	m	c	CHIN	Santa Clara	1-Wd San Jose	88	233
Ah	50	m	c	CHIN	El Dorado	Diamond Springs Tw	72	32
Ah	48	m	c	CHIN	Calaveras	San Andreas P O	70	169
Ah	46	m	c	CHIN	Calaveras	San Andreas P O	70	183
Ah	44	m	c	CHIN	Calaveras	San Andreas P O	70	190
Ah	42	m	c	CHIN	Sacramento	1-Wd Sacramento	77	193
Ah	40	m	c	CHIN	Amador	Drytown P O	69	419
Ah	40	m	c	CHIN	Tuolumne	Chinese Camp P O	93	388
Ah	40	m	c	CHIN	Mariposa	Mariposa P O	74	134
Ah	40	m	c	CHIN	El Dorado	Placerville	72	115
Ah	37	m	c	CHIN	San Francisco	6-Wd San Francisco	81	57
Ah	37	m	c	CHIN	Butte	Bidwell Twp	70	4
Ah	36	m	c	CHIN	Amador	Lancha Plana P O	69	369
Ah	35	m	c	CHIN	Placer	Auburn P O	76	372
Ah	35	m	c	CHIN	Butte	Chico Twp	70	28
Ah	34	m	c	CHIN	Santa Barbara	Santa Barbara P O	87	459
Ah	34	m	c	CHIN	Mono	Bridgeport P O	74	282
Ah	32	m	c	CHIN	Trinity	Canyon City Pct	92	202
Ah	32	m	c	CHIN	Nevada	Eureka Twp	75	141
Ah	32	m	c	CHIN	Butte	Hamilton Twp	70	67
Ah	32	f	c	CHIN	Butte	Chico Twp	70	27
Ah	32	m	c	CHIN	Calaveras	San Andreas P O	70	184
Ah	31	m	c	CHIN	Butte	Kimshew Tpw	70	84
Ah	30	m	c	CHIN	Sacramento	1-Wd Sacramento	77	205
Ah	30	m	c	CHIN	Nevada	Washington Twp	75	345
Ah	30	m	c	CHIN	Butte	Kimshew Tpw	70	86
Ah	29	m	c	CHIN	San Francisco	San Francisco P O	80	528
Ah	29	m	c	CHIN	Butte	Concow Twp	70	11
Ah	27	m	c	CHIN	Trinity	Junction City Pct	92	207
Ah	27	m	c	CHIN	Placer	Lincoln P O	76	483
Ah	27	m	c	CHIN	Butte	Ophir Twp	70	112
Ah	26	m	c	CHIN	Sacramento	2-Wd Sacramento	77	227
Ah	25	m	c	CHIN	Trinity	Lewiston Pct	92	214
Ah	25	m	c	CHIN	Tuolumne	Chinese Camp P O	93	388
Ah	24	m	c	CHIN	San Francisco	3-Wd San Francisco	79	309
Ah	23	m	c	CHIN	Sacramento	2-Wd Sacramento	77	208
Ah	23	m	c	CHIN	Nevada	Eureka Twp	75	140
Ah	23	m	c	CHIN	Calaveras	San Andreas P O	70	165
Ah	23	m	c	CHIN	Butte	Chico Twp	70	53
Ah	23	m	c	CHIN	Tuolumne	Chinese Camp P O	93	374
Ah	22	m	c	CHIN	Amador	Jackson P O	69	332
Ah	22	m	c	CHIN	Calaveras	San Andreas P O	70	171
Ah	22	m	c	CHIN	Tuolumne	Chinese Camp P O	93	363
Ah	21	m	c	CHIN	San Francisco	6-Wd San Francisco	81	69
Ah	21	m	c	CHIN	Sacramento	4-Wd Sacramento	77	321
Ah	21	m	c	CHIN	Placer	Emigrant Gap P O	76	416
Ah	20	m	c	CHIN	San Francisco	6-Wd San Francisco	81	48
Ah	2	f	c	CHIN	Butte	Chico Twp	70	30
Ah	18	m	c	CHIN	Placer	Alta P O	76	411
Ah	18	m	c	CHIN	Tuolumne	Chinese Camp P O	93	379
Ahs	22	m	c	CHIN	San Francisco	3-Wd San Francisco	79	329
Choy	34	m	c	CHIN	Tuolumne	Columbia P O	93	341
Chug	58	m	c	CHIN	Tuolumne	Columbia P O	93	349
Chung	50	m	c	CHIN	San Francisco	6-Wd San Francisco	81	39
Gee	41	m	c	CHIN	Plumas	Mineral Twp	77	24
Ha	20	m	c	CHIN	San Francisco	6-Wd San Francisco	81	43
Jan	46	m	c	CHIN	El Dorado	Diamond Springs Tw	72	33
Jno	30	m	c	CHIN	Sacramento	1-Wd Sacramento	77	189
Loo	47	m	c	CHIN	Marin	San Rafael Twp	74	59
Wing	22	m	c	CHIN	San Francisco	1-Wd San Francisco	79	120
Yo	20	m	c	CHIN	Yuba	Marysville	93	628
Yon	35	m	c	CHIN	San Mateo	San Mateo P O	87	351
FATAIS								
Thomas	38	m	w	MEXI	Tuolumne	Chinese Camp P O	93	369
FATE								
Albas	35	m	w	PRUS	Inyo	Lone Pine Twp	73	330
Alex	38	m	w	MI	Butte	Kimshew Tpw	70	78
FATER								
Nicolas	30	m	w	AZOR	Contra Costa	San Pablo Twp	71	359
FATH								
Adam	50	m	w	PRUS	Alameda	Murray Twp	68	124
Conrad	44	m	w	BAVA	Shasta	Horsetown P O	89	502
FATHES								
E	23	m	w	WI	Tehama	Cottonwood Twp	92	162
FATHUS								
Pedro	72	m	w	MEXI	Fresno	Millerton P O	72	158
FATHWAY								
Geo	24	m	w	ENGL	San Joaquin	Liberty Twp	86	89
John	50	m	w	ENGL	San Joaquin	Liberty Twp	86	89
FATJO								
Antonio	20	m	w	CHIL	Santa Clara	Santa Clara Twp	88	147
FATNONE								
Antino	20	m	w	ITAL	San Francisco	11-Wd San Francisc	84	709
FATT								
Ah	25	m	c	CHIN	Amador	Fiddletown P O	69	428

© 2001 by Heritage Quest. All rights reserved.

California 1870 Census

Name	Age	S	R	B-PL	County	Locale	Series M593 Roll	Pg
John	36	m	w	CHIN	Santa Cruz	Soquel Twp	89	440
Mathew	28	m	w	FRNK	San Francisco	San Francisco P O	80	339
Susan	21	f	w	PRUS	San Francisco	San Francisco P O	80	344
FATTEBERT								
Louis	38	m	w	SWIT	Nevada	Grass Valley Twp	75	219
FATZ								
John	37	m	w	NORW	San Francisco	1-Wd San Francisco	79	54
FAU								
Ah	28	m	c	CHIN	Los Angeles	Los Angeles	73	564
Ah	18	m	c	CHIN	Los Angeles	Los Angeles	73	565
FAUBERT								
Antone	28	m	w	FRAN	Nevada	Eureka Twp	75	139
Charles	48	m	w	PRUS	Alameda	Eden Twp	68	83
Phillip	34	m	w	HDAR	San Francisco	11-Wd San Francisc	84	504
FAUBLE								
Henry	21	m	w	CANA	San Francisco	11-Wd San Francisc	84	672
FAUBORG								
Baron	43	m	w	SWED	Marin	Bolinas Twp	74	8
FAUBROUGH								
Alexander	30	m	w	IREL	Stanislaus	San Joaquin Twp	92	81
FAUCETT								
James	27	m	w	ENGL	San Francisco	San Francisco P O	83	131
FAUDRE								
Steward W	54	m	w	KY	Sonoma	Analy Twp	91	239
Susan	13	m	w	CA	Sonoma	Analy Twp	91	240
FAUGHMAN								
John	40	m	w	ME	Tuolumne	Sonora P O	93	324
FAUGHT								
J M	35	m	w	IN	Mendocino	Ukiah Twp	74	241
Jabez	58	m	w	KY	Sonoma	Russian Rvr	91	368
T J	31	m	w	IN	Mendocino	Ukiah Twp	74	241
Willis	49	m	w	KY	Sonoma	Russian Rvr	91	372
Wm	68	m	w	KY	Mendocino	Ukiah Twp	74	244
FAUHART								
Jacob	24	m	w	SWIT	Los Angeles	Los Angeles	73	547
FAUKE								
Alfred	33	m	w	ENGL	Yolo	Buckeye Twp	93	407
FAULEY								
Adam	44	m	w	SCOT	Tuolumne	Columbia P O	93	337
FAULK								
G A	25	m	w	NORW	San Francisco	7-Wd San Francisco	81	218
John	37	m	w	GERM	San Joaquin	2-Wd Stockton	86	213
N H	33	m	w	PA	Humboldt	Eureka Twp	72	259
FAULKAER								
James	48	m	w	IREL	San Francisco	2-Wd San Francisco	79	156
FAULKENBERG								
Neilson	40	m	w	NJ	San Francisco	11-Wd San Francisc	84	447
FAULKENSTEIN								
Jno ?	30	m	w	PRUS	San Francisco	5-Wd San Francisco	81	9
FAULKMAN								
Jas	40	m	w	NJ	San Joaquin	1-Wd Stockton	86	157
FAULKNER								
Daniel	34	m	w	CANA	Alameda	Washington Twp	68	276
Harry	20	m	w	CANA	Yolo	Grafton Twp	93	492
Henry	48	m	w	OH	San Francisco	7-Wd San Francisco	81	166
Jacob H	39	m	w	SC	Santa Barbara	Santa Barbara P O	87	490
James	40	m	w	IREL	Alameda	Brooklyn	68	28
James	36	m	w	NY	Nevada	Grass Valley Twp	75	146
Jas	41	m	w	NY	San Francisco	1-Wd San Francisco	79	134
Jas	30	m	w	PA	Butte	Ophir Twp	70	108
John	44	m	w	NY	Santa Barbara	Santa Barbara P O	87	454
John	40	m	w	SWED	Solano	Vallejo	90	213
M F	33	m	w	IREL	Alameda	Murray Twp	68	122
Nelson	60	m	w	NY	Humboldt	Eureka Twp	72	257
S L	33	m	w	KY	San Joaquin	Elliott Twp	86	74
Thos	37	m	w	IREL	San Francisco	San Francisco P O	83	37
William	52	m	w	MA	Amador	Volcano P O	69	382
William	39	m	w	CT	San Francisco	8-Wd San Francisco	82	394
William E	35	m	w	NY	Mendocino	Albion & Big Rvr T	74	166
William S	54	m	w	IN	Calaveras	San Andreas P O	70	158
FAULKNERS								
Wm	62	m	w	CT	Alameda	Brooklyn	68	22
FAULL								
George	21	m	w	ENGL	Nevada	Grass Valley Twp	75	169
James	21	m	w	ENGL	Amador	Amador City P O	69	394
John	33	m	w	ENGL	Amador	Sutter Crk P O	69	408
John A	36	m	w	ENGL	Amador	Sutter Crk P O	69	408
M	35	m	w	SCOT	Alameda	Murray Twp	68	109
William	45	m	w	ENGL	Nevada	Bloomfield Twp	75	97
William	23	m	w	ENGL	Amador	Sutter Crk P O	69	397
FAULTON								
Edwd	35	m	w	NH	Butte	Kimshew Tpw	70	77
FAUN								
Ah	30	m	c	CHIN	Tuolumne	Columbia P O	93	341
Ah	29	m	c	CHIN	Plumas	Mineral Twp	77	21
FAUNJOY								
George A	26	m	w	VA	Marin	Bolinas Twp	74	8
FAUNKENBURG								
A	24	m	w	PRUS	San Francisco	8-Wd San Francisco	82	348
FAUNTLEROY								
W H	46	m	w	VA	Humboldt	Eel Rvr Twp	72	253
FAUPANT								
Joseph	19	m	w	CANA	Mendocino	Point Arena Twp	74	211
FAURE								
Camile	23	m	w	FRAN	Los Angeles	Los Angeles Twp	73	497
Moomie	17	f	w	FRAN	Solano	Benicia	90	5
Rosalie	29	f	w	FRAN	San Francisco	6-Wd San Francisco	81	45

Name	Age	S	R	B-PL	County	Locale	Series M593 Roll	Pg
Victor	55	m	w	FRAN	Sonoma	Sonoma Twp	91	440
Victor	15	m	w	FRAN	San Francisco	11-Wd San Francisc	84	556
FAURGERACE								
Jean	48	m	w	FRAN	Los Angeles	Los Angeles	73	528
FAUSOLADO								
Rays	36	m	w	CHIL	San Joaquin	2-Wd Stockton	86	173
FAUST								
Christian A	41	m	w	PRUS	Fresno	Millerton P O	72	151
Emil	36	m	w	PRUS	San Francisco	San Francisco P O	80	479
Ferdinand	20	m	w	PRUS	San Francisco	San Francisco P O	80	338
John	26	m	w	PRUS	San Francisco	San Francisco P O	83	419
Richd	29	m	w	PRUS	San Francisco	1-Wd San Francisco	79	126
Tobias	59	m	w	PRUS	San Francisco	San Francisco P O	83	415
FAUSTINA								
Torre	26	m	w	CA	Sacramento	2-Wd Sacramento	77	215
FAUSTINO								
Bargudo	35	m	w	CHIL	Santa Clara	San Jose Twp	88	209
FAUTH								
Mariah	22	f	w	HDAR	San Francisco	San Francisco P O	83	266
FAUVER								
Thomas	43	m	w	MD	Napa	Yountville Twp	75	77
FAUX								
Henry	41	m	w	HDAR	Santa Clara	Fremont Twp	88	48
Lean	16	m	c	CHIN	Napa	Napa	75	40
FAUZ								
Christopher	43	m	w	PRUS	San Francisco	San Francisco P O	85	765
FAVELL								
Chancey O	28	m	w	MA	San Francisco	San Francisco P O	83	75
FAVER								
M	38	m	w	NY	Sacramento	3-Wd Sacramento	77	268
FAVERIN								
Morse	38	m	w	PRUS	Fresno	Millerton P O	72	155
FAVI								
James	28	m	w	SCOT	San Francisco	1-Wd San Francisco	79	112
FAVIE								
Thomas	51	m	w	FRAN	San Francisco	2-Wd San Francisco	79	151
FAVIER								
Innocents	30	m	w	ITAL	San Francisco	San Francisco P O	80	400
FAVILLA								
Groacchino	45	m	w	ITAL	Santa Clara	Santa Clara Twp	88	176
FAVOR								
Frank	42	m	w	ME	Sacramento	Brighton Twp	77	74
John	32	m	w	CANA	Nevada	Eureka Twp	75	138
FAVRE								
John	45	m	w	FRAN	Calaveras	San Andreas P O	70	190
Kimball	54	m	w	NH	San Francisco	San Francisco P O	83	145
Salina	22	f	w	FRAN	San Francisco	San Francisco P O	83	147
Thomas	36	m	w	FRAN	San Francisco	San Francisco P O	80	472
FAVREIN								
Louis	45	m	w	CANA	Placer	Newcastle Twp	76	473
FAVRY								
Frank	53	m	w	FRAN	Humboldt	Arcata Twp	72	233
FAW								
Ah	50	m	c	CHIN	Calaveras	Copperopolis P O	70	243
Ah	39	m	c	CHIN	Yolo	Washington Twp	93	530
Ah	35	m	c	CHIN	Nevada	Meadow Lake Twp	75	254
Ah	35	m	c	CHIN	Kern	Havilah P O	73	337
Ah	29	f	c	CHIN	San Francisco	San Francisco P O	80	493
Ah	28	m	c	CHIN	Plumas	Plumas Twp	77	30
Ah	26	m	c	CHIN	Plumas	Plumas Twp	77	31
Ah	20	m	c	CHIN	San Francisco	San Francisco P O	80	522
Ah	15	m	c	CHIN	San Francisco	8-Wd San Francisco	82	308
Gee	35	m	c	CHIN	Plumas	Mineral Twp	77	24
Too	30	m	c	CHIN	Santa Clara	San Jose Twp	88	219
FAWCETT								
Alexander	22	m	w	IREL	Nevada	Grass Valley Twp	75	163
Edgar	28	m	w	MO	Solano	Tremont Twp	90	29
Frank	53	m	w	MA	Siskiyou	Yreka Twp	89	670
George	37	m	w	OH	Placer	Alta P O	76	413
Henry	23	m	w	LA	Santa Clara	2-Wd San Jose	88	330
Richard	40	m	w	ENGL	Nevada	Grass Valley Twp	75	166
Thomas	40	m	w	MO	Los Angeles	Los Nietos Twp	73	575
William	50	m	w	ENGL	San Francisco	San Francisco P O	83	274
William	28	m	w	IREL	Nevada	Grass Valley Twp	75	160
Wm	41	m	w	ENGL	Sacramento	Dry Crk Twp	77	99
FAWKE								
Alfred	33	m	w	ENGL	San Francisco	11-Wd San Francisc	84	458
FAWKS								
Guy	42	m	w	DENM	Yolo	Grafton Twp	93	479
FAWN								
Ah	31	m	c	CHIN	Butte	Concow Twp	70	8
Gee	31	m	c	CHIN	Plumas	Mineral Twp	77	23
FAWNSWORTH								
Charles	8	m	w	NY	San Francisco	5-Wd San Francisco	81	24
Chas	42	m	w	PA	San Francisco	5-Wd San Francisco	81	24
Chris Mrs	36	f	w	NY	San Francisco	5-Wd San Francisco	81	24
John	6	m	w	NY	San Francisco	5-Wd San Francisco	81	24
FAWRACK								
Charles	45	m	w	PRUS	San Francisco	7-Wd San Francisco	81	215
FAWSETT								
Geo H	37	m	w	MA	Placer	Colfax P O	76	385
FAXON								
Geo	51	m	w	OH	Humboldt	Eel Rvr Twp	72	249
J F	43	m	w	MA	Tuolumne	Sonora P O	93	308
FAY								
A	20	m	c	CHIN	Sacramento	3-Wd Sacramento	77	265
A C	24	f	w	MO	Sierra	Alleghany & Forest	89	533

© 2001 by Heritage Quest. All rights reserved.

Name	Age	S	R	B-PL	County	Locale	Roll	Pg
Ah	8	f	c	CHIN	Santa Clara	1-Wd San Jose	88	273
Ah	65	m	c	CHIN	Santa Clara	Fremont Twp	88	55
Ah	56	m	c	CHIN	Sacramento	Center Twp	77	86
Ah	45	m	c	CHIN	Siskiyou	Hamburg Twp	89	598
Ah	44	m	c	CHIN	Sacramento	Granite Twp	77	153
Ah	43	m	c	CHIN	Sacramento	Natomas Twp	77	171
Ah	41	m	c	CHIN	Sacramento	Natomas Twp	77	167
Ah	41	m	c	CHIN	Calaveras	Copperopolis P O	70	222
Ah	40	m	c	CHIN	Sacramento	Granite Twp	77	154
Ah	40	m	c	CHIN	Sacramento	Granite Twp	77	150
Ah	40	m	c	CHIN	Sacramento	Natomas Twp	77	171
Ah	37	m	c	CHIN	Trinity	Douglas	92	235
Ah	36	m	c	CHIN	Sacramento	Center Twp	77	86
Ah	36	m	c	CHIN	Shasta	French Gulch P O	89	466
Ah	36	m	c	CHIN	Siskiyou	Cottonwood Twp	89	591
Ah	35	m	c	CHIN	Sacramento	Cosumnes Twp	77	94
Ah	35	m	c	CHIN	Sacramento	Natomas Twp	77	171
Ah	34	m	c	CHIN	Sacramento	Granite Twp	77	155
Ah	34	m	c	CHIN	Sacramento	Center Twp	77	87
Ah	32	m	c	CHIN	Sacramento	Granite Twp	77	151
Ah	31	m	c	CHIN	Sacramento	1-Wd Sacramento	77	197
Ah	30	m	c	CHIN	Alameda	Eden Twp	68	58
Ah	30	m	c	CHIN	Sacramento	Cosumnes Twp	77	94
Ah	29	m	c	CHIN	Sacramento	American Twp	77	68
Ah	29	m	c	CHIN	Sacramento	Natomas Twp	77	167
Ah	28	m	c	CHIN	San Francisco	11-Wd San Francisc	84	631
Ah	28	m	c	CHIN	Sacramento	1-Wd Sacramento	77	205
Ah	27	m	c	CHIN	Alameda	Oakland	68	162
Ah	27	m	c	CHIN	Sacramento	Cosumnes Twp	77	93
Ah	26	m	c	CHIN	Placer	Bath P O	76	451
Ah	25	m	c	CHIN	Sacramento	Cosumnes Twp	77	94
Ah	25	m	c	CHIN	Sacramento	Cosumnes Twp	77	90
Ah	25	m	c	CHIN	Butte	Mountain Spring Tw	70	89
Ah	23	m	c	CHIN	Los Angeles	Los Angeles	73	565
Ah	23	m	c	CHIN	Siskiyou	Cottonwood Twp	89	594
Ah	22	f	c	CHIN	Calaveras	San Andreas P O	70	199
Ah	22	m	c	CHIN	Sacramento	Granite Twp	77	152
Ah	22	m	c	CHIN	Sacramento	San Joaquin Twp	77	405
Ah	21	m	c	CHIN	San Francisco	6-Wd San Francisco	81	124
Ah	20	m	c	CHIN	Sacramento	2-Wd Sacramento	77	218
Ah	19	m	c	CHIN	Alameda	Oakland	68	155
Ah	18	f	c	CHIN	Sacramento	Cosumnes Twp	77	94
Ah	18	m	c	CHIN	Alameda	Oakland	68	202
Ah	18	m	c	CHIN	Yolo	Cottonwood Twp	93	467
Ah	17	m	c	CHIN	Los Angeles	Los Angeles	73	546
Ah	16	m	c	CHIN	San Francisco	11-Wd San Francisc	84	539
Ah	12	m	c	CHIN	Sacramento	1-Wd Sacramento	77	191
Alfred	40	m	w	MO	San Mateo	Half Moon Bay P O	87	407
Andrew	24	m	w	IREL	San Francisco	6-Wd San Francisco	81	141
Andrew H	45	m	w	NY	Calaveras	Copperopolis P O	70	262
Ann	30	f	w	IREL	Alameda	Oakland	68	198
Charles	38	m	w	RI	Santa Clara	San Jose Twp	88	196
Daniel	41	m	w	IREL	Siskiyou	Callahan P O	89	629
David	48	m	w	VT	San Francisco	San Francisco P O	83	61
David	47	m	w	NY	San Francisco	2-Wd San Francisco	79	282
Edw	44	m	w	IREL	San Francisco	7-Wd San Francisco	81	236
Edward	35	m	w	IREL	San Francisco	8-Wd San Francisco	82	411
Eliza	28	f	w	NH	San Francisco	7-Wd San Francisco	81	277
Eliza	26	f	w	MO	Santa Clara	San Jose Twp	88	215
Enes C	36	m	w	VT	Sonoma	Bodega Twp	91	263
Frank	35	m	w	SAME	Sacramento	4-Wd Sacramento	77	332
Geo M	37	m	w	CT	Humboldt	Eureka Twp	72	279
George	51	m	w	NY	Kern	Havilah P O	73	350
George	47	m	w	PA	San Francisco	San Francisco P O	80	390
Goo	30	m	w	IREL	San Francisco	11-Wd San Francisc	84	695
J H	38	m	w	VT	Sierra	Alleghany & Forest	89	533
J M	47	m	w	PRUS	Sacramento	1-Wd Sacramento	77	174
James	34	m	w	IREL	San Francisco	San Francisco P O	80	474
James T	29	m	w	DE	Nevada	Grass Valley Twp	75	176
James T	25	m	w	IREL	Nevada	Grass Valley Twp	75	162
Jeremiah G	30	m	w	NY	Sonoma	Vallejo Twp	91	461
Jerome	29	m	w	VT	Siskiyou	Butte Twp	89	588
John	65	m	w	IREL	San Mateo	Half Moon Bay P O	87	407
John	42	m	w	NY	San Francisco	2-Wd San Francisco	79	217
John	37	m	w	NY	Sacramento	2-Wd Sacramento	77	222
John	35	m	w	NY	Mendocino	Cuffeys Cove Twp	74	168
John	30	m	w	ENGL	San Mateo	San Mateo P O	87	359
John	29	m	w	IREL	Yolo	Washington Twp	93	531
John	21	m	w	PRUS	San Francisco	7-Wd San Francisco	81	164
Joseph	30	m	w	IREL	San Francisco	San Francisco P O	83	155
Julius	23	m	w	FRAN	San Francisco	San Francisco P O	83	274
Laurence	40	m	w	IREL	San Francisco	San Francisco P O	83	16
Margaret	6	f	w	CA	Sacramento	Cosumnes Twp	77	89
Mary	30	f	w	IREL	San Francisco	8-Wd San Francisco	82	302
Mary	30	f	w	IREL	San Francisco	San Francisco P O	83	64
Mary	26	f	w	SCOT	San Francisco	11-Wd San Francisc	84	486
Michael	40	m	w	IREL	San Francisco	11-Wd San Francisc	84	586
Michael	38	m	w	IREL	Siskiyou	Callahan P O	89	624
Michael	33	m	w	IREL	San Mateo	Schoolhouse Statio	87	331
Michael	29	m	w	IREL	Santa Cruz	Pajaro Twp	89	341
Michael	28	m	w	IREL	San Francisco	San Francisco P O	83	250
Mike	30	m	w	IREL	San Francisco	11-Wd San Francisc	84	659
Monnan	47	m	w	NY	Sutter	Vernon Twp	92	131
Naham	50	m	w	MA	Humboldt	Eureka Twp	72	279
P S	28	m	w	NY	San Francisco	San Francisco P O	85	818
Patrick	40	m	w	IREL	San Francisco	San Francisco P O	83	267
Peter	44	m	w	IREL	San Francisco	2-Wd San Francisco	79	206

Name	Age	S	R	B-PL	County	Locale	Roll	Pg
Philip	48	m	w	IREL	Nevada	Eureka Twp	75	137
Roger	30	m	w	IREL	San Francisco	7-Wd San Francisco	81	161
Rosamond	37	f	w	VT	Napa	Napa	75	48
Sarah	25	f	w	IREL	San Francisco	San Francisco P O	83	415
Susan	22	f	w	IL	Yolo	Grafton Twp	93	484
Thomas	48	m	w	IREL	San Francisco	San Francisco P O	83	420
Thomas	45	m	w	IREL	San Francisco	San Francisco P O	83	78
Thomas	35	m	w	IREL	San Francisco	11-Wd San Francisc	84	550
Thos	24	m	w	IREL	San Joaquin	Tulare Twp	86	255
W	32	m	w	IREL	Sierra	Eureka Twp	89	526
William	66	m	w	IREL	Sonoma	Vallejo Twp	91	461
William	40	m	w	IREL	Contra Costa	Martinez P O	71	416
William	36	m	w	IREL	Santa Clara	2-Wd San Jose	88	315
William	24	m	w	NY	Solano	Maine Prairie Twp	90	51
William	19	m	w	IREL	Tuolumne	Sonora P O	93	325
William H	33	m	w	OH	Solano	Maine Prairie Twp	90	49
Wm	48	m	w	IREL	Sierra	Eureka Twp	89	527
FAYARD								
John B	37	m	w	FRAN	San Francisco	3-Wd San Francisco	79	322
FAYE								
---	20	f	c	CHIN	Siskiyou	Yreka	89	654
Alfred	30	m	w	ME	Santa Barbara	Santa Barbara P O	87	461
Marcia M	45	f	w	CT	Mariposa	Mariposa P O	74	116
FAYGAN								
Edward	30	m	w	CANA	Sacramento	Alabama Twp	77	60
FAYHEY								
Pat	23	m	w	IREL	Yuba	Marysville Twp	93	567
FAYLON								
George	75	m	w	OH	Calaveras	Copperopolis P O	70	252
James W	43	m	w	OH	Calaveras	Copperopolis P O	70	252
FAYLOR								
James	60	m	w	SCOT	San Luis Obispo	Santa Rosa Twp	87	328
John	30	m	w	IL	Sonoma	Analy Twp	91	245
John	20	m	w	MA	Placer	Rocklin Twp	76	466
W A	28	m	w	TX	Sacramento	3-Wd Sacramento	77	277
FAYMORVILLE								
Wm J	41	m	w	PRUS	Fresno	Millerton P O	72	145
FAZ								
Ah	21	m	c	CHIN	Butte	Hamilton Twp	70	68
FAZIER								
John	42	m	w	CANA	Tulare	Farmersville Twp	92	244
FAZINE								
Antonio	35	m	w	SWIT	Monterey	Alisal Twp	74	292
FAZUETA								
Jos M	60	m	w	MEXI	Santa Clara	Burnett Twp	88	35
FE								
Ah	26	m	c	CHIN	Sacramento	Georgianna Twp	77	125
FEAHOLTZ								
Nick J	60	m	w	PA	Butte	Oregon Twp	70	124
FEALY								
Frank	30	m	w	IREL	Monterey	San Benito Twp	74	380
FEANEY								
Robert	28	m	w	IREL	Napa	Napa	75	52
FEARN								
A C	38	f	w	MD	Sacramento	3-Wd Sacramento	77	297
FEARNE								
Frances	58	m	w	FRAN	Calaveras	Copperopolis P O	70	242
FEATHER								
Adolphus	36	m	w	NY	San Francisco	11-Wd San Francisc	84	665
FEATHERBY								
Sarah	52	f	w	NY	San Francisco	San Francisco P O	80	401
FEATHERSON								
Henry	23	m	w	SHOL	San Francisco	1-Wd San Francisco	79	129
FEATHERSTON								
George	24	m	w	ENGL	Santa Clara	San Jose Twp	88	222
George	23	m	w	ENGL	Santa Clara	1-Wd San Jose	88	237
John	36	m	w	VA	San Diego	Julian Dist	78	473
P	37	m	w	IREL	San Joaquin	1-Wd Stockton	86	132
William	24	m	w	IREL	San Francisco	San Francisco P O	80	477
FEATHERSTONE								
H	52	m	w	IREL	San Joaquin	Oneal Twp	86	106
Wm	40	m	w	ENGL	Butte	Ophir Twp	70	107
FEATHERTON								
Ann	72	f	w	IREL	San Joaquin	3-Wd Stockton	86	219
Hugh	84	m	w	IREL	San Joaquin	3-Wd Stockton	86	219
FEBARIA								
Sibastiana	60	f	w	CA	Monterey	Monterey	74	356
FEBECER								
Cutliss	60	m	w	PRUS	Santa Clara	Redwood Twp	88	124
FEBOR								
William H	33	m	w	KY	Inyo	Cerro Gordo Twp	73	319
FEBRE								
Joseph	21	m	w	CANA	Santa Clara	Almaden Twp	88	18
FEBUREA								
Elija	35	m	w	OH	San Francisco	2-Wd San Francisco	79	212
FEBY								
Henry	38	m	w	ENGL	El Dorado	Mud Springs Twp	72	75
FECHAN								
Kate	28	f	w	IREL	San Francisco	1-Wd San Francisco	79	30
FECHER								
Joseph	25	m	w	PRUS	San Francisco	2-Wd San Francisco	79	213
FECHTER								
Jacob	32	m	w	BAVA	Santa Cruz	Santa Cruz Twp	89	393
Louis	32	m	w	FRAN	San Francisco	San Francisco P O	80	334
FECK								
Joseph B	43	m	w	ITAL	San Mateo	Schoolhouse Statio	87	339
Nicholas	36	m	w	OH	San Francisco	11-Wd San Francisc	84	558

© 2001 by Heritage Quest. All rights reserved.

California 1870 Census

Name	Age	S	R	B-PL	County	Locale	Series M593 Roll	Pg
FECKLEY								
William	22	m	w	IL	Placer	Lincoln P O	76	487
FECUNDA								
Toledo	45	m	w	CHIL	Stanislaus	Empire Twp	92	29
FEDDERSON								
Louis	26	m	w	HAMB	Contra Costa	Martinez P O	71	390
FEDDY								
Hanon	13	f	w	CA	Alameda	Oakland	68	168
FEDER								
Leah	30	f	w	PRUS	San Francisco	11-Wd San Francisc	84	448
Robert	32	m	w	PRUS	San Francisco	11-Wd San Francisc	84	447
FEDERWITZ								
Dodger	44	m	w	HANO	El Dorado	Georgetown Twp	72	38
FEDESON								
Leon	35	m	w	MEXI	Kern	Bakersfield P O	73	364
FEDLER								
Louis	24	m	w	GERM	Yolo	Grafton Twp	93	496
FEE								
Ah	50	m	c	CHIN	Alameda	Oakland	68	254
Ah	45	m	c	CHIN	Tuolumne	Chinese Camp P O	93	386
Ah	42	m	c	CHIN	San Francisco	8-Wd San Francisco	82	336
Ah	40	m	c	CHIN	Alameda	Oakland	68	241
Ah	38	m	c	CHIN	San Francisco	San Francisco P O	80	491
Ah	37	m	c	CHIN	Alameda	Oakland	68	254
Ah	34	m	c	CHIN	Sonoma	Mendocino Twp	91	287
Ah	32	m	c	CHIN	Los Angeles	Los Angeles	73	524
Ah	30	m	c	CHIN	Alameda	Oakland	68	238
Ah	29	m	c	CHIN	Tuolumne	Big Oak Flat P O	93	394
Ah	28	m	c	CHIN	Tuolumne	Chinese Camp P O	93	375
Ah	28	m	c	CHIN	Tuolumne	Chinese Camp P O	93	374
Ah	28	m	c	CHIN	Alameda	Oakland	68	157
Ah	28	m	c	CHIN	Butte	Ophir Twp	70	103
Ah	24	m	c	CHIN	San Francisco	San Francisco P O	80	497
Ah	22	m	c	CHIN	Yuba	Marysville	93	580
Ah	22	m	c	CHIN	Tuolumne	Chinese Camp P O	93	388
Ah	22	m	c	CHIN	San Francisco	San Francisco P O	83	131
Ah	21	m	c	CHIN	Sonoma	Healdsburg & Mendo	91	278
Ah	20	m	c	CHIN	San Francisco	6-Wd San Francisco	81	50
Ah	19	m	c	CHIN	San Francisco	6-Wd San Francisco	81	63
Ah	18	m	c	CHIN	San Francisco	6-Wd San Francisco	81	66
Ah	17	m	c	CHIN	Alameda	Oakland	68	157
Ah	17	f	c	CHIN	San Francisco	6-Wd San Francisco	81	74
Ah	16	f	c	CHIN	San Francisco	San Francisco P O	80	507
Ah	12	m	c	CHIN	San Francisco	11-Wd San Francisc	84	577
Chow	40	m	c	CHIN	Placer	Lincoln P O	76	483
Chow	40	m	c	CHIN	Tuolumne	Big Oak Flat P O	93	394
George	36	m	w	IREL	San Francisco	5-Wd San Francisco	81	13
George W	32	m	w	MO	Santa Clara	2-Wd San Jose	88	330
Henry	30	m	w	IREL	Sacramento	Brighton Twp	77	73
Hop	32	m	c	CHIN	San Joaquin	1-Wd Stockton	86	156
James	30	m	w	IREL	Siskiyou	Surprise Valley Tw	89	637
James	25	m	w	IREL	San Francisco	5-Wd San Francisco	81	13
John	52	m	w	PA	Plumas	Washington Twp	77	52
John	30	m	w	IA	Lake	Scotts Crk	73	427
John	29	m	w	IREL	San Joaquin	3-Wd Stockton	86	243
Kate	35	f	w	IREL	San Francisco	11-Wd San Francisc	84	520
Kee	30	m	c	CHIN	San Francisco	6-Wd San Francisco	81	68
Kie	36	m	c	CHIN	Amador	Jackson P O	69	337
Koon	25	m	c	CHIN	Yuba	Marysville	93	632
L M	42	m	w	NY	Solano	Vallejo	90	209
Lee	24	m	c	CHIN	Yuba	Marysville	93	625
Lee	14	f	c	CHIN	San Francisco	6-Wd San Francisco	81	74
Loy	15	m	c	CHIN	Santa Clara	San Jose Twp	88	190
Mary	8	f	w	CA	Mendocino	Little Lake Twp	74	200
Mary	27	f	w	CANA	San Joaquin	1-Wd Stockton	86	150
Pat	25	m	w	IREL	Alameda	Oakland	68	226
Pat	19	m	w	IREL	Alameda	Oakland	68	175
Pat	18	m	w	IREL	Alameda	Oakland	68	234
Patrick	27	m	w	IREL	San Joaquin	3-Wd Stockton	86	220
Peter	51	m	w	NORW	Merced	Snelling P O	74	249
Susan	28	f	w	IREL	San Francisco	11-Wd San Francisc	84	520
Tung	30	f	c	CHIN	Yuba	Marysville	93	626
FEEBER								
Frederick	18	m	w	PRUS	San Diego	Julian Dist	78	469
FEECE								
William	29	m	w	IL	Sonoma	Healdsburg	91	274
FEECHAN								
Ellen	25	f	w	IREL	San Francisco	San Francisco P O	80	379
John	23	m	w	IREL	San Francisco	San Francisco P O	80	382
FEEDLER								
Julius	39	m	w	PRUS	Plumas	Goodwin Twp	77	8
FEEHAN								
John	42	m	w	IREL	San Francisco	San Francisco P O	85	806
Wm	37	m	w	IREL	Sonoma	Santa Rosa	91	400
FEEHERY								
Edward	30	m	w	IREL	San Francisco	San Francisco P O	85	754
FEEL								
Adam B	27	m	w	TX	Los Angeles	Santa Ana Twp	73	599
Josep J	50	m	w	POLA	Sacramento	Granite Twp	77	148
Owen	59	m	w	IREL	Solano	Green Valley Twp	90	38
FEELA								
Richrd	26	m	w	IREL	San Joaquin	2-Wd Stockton	86	163
FEELAN								
Margaret	19	f	w	IREL	Nevada	Bridgeport Twp	75	120
FEELER								
Archibald	52	m	w	VA	San Diego	San Luis Rey	78	515
Moses M	34	m	w	PRUS	Colusa	Stony Crk Twp	71	331

Name	Age	S	R	B-PL	County	Locale	Series M593 Roll	Pg
FEELEY								
Dennis	40	m	w	IREL	San Francisco	3-Wd San Francisco	79	316
Dennis C	42	m	w	IREL	Santa Cruz	Soquel Twp	89	444
John	40	m	w	IREL	Santa Clara	2-Wd San Jose	88	292
Michael	32	m	w	IREL	Nevada	Eureka Twp	75	136
Michael	30	m	w	IREL	Santa Clara	2-Wd San Jose	88	316
FEELON								
Richard	26	m	w	IREL	Marin	San Antonio Twp	74	62
FEELY								
John	29	m	w	IREL	San Joaquin	3-Wd Stockton	86	229
Joseph	28	m	w	NY	San Francisco	8-Wd San Francisco	82	339
Luke	24	m	w	IREL	Alameda	Eden Twp	68	87
FEEN								
Ah	23	m	c	CHIN	San Francisco	6-Wd San Francisco	81	65
Fa	30	m	c	CHIN	San Francisco	6-Wd San Francisco	81	52
Julia	35	f	w	IREL	San Francisco	San Francisco P O	83	202
FEENAN								
Michael	44	m	w	IREL	Amador	Sutter Crk P O	69	410
FEENEY								
Andria	29	m	w	IREL	San Francisco	San Francisco P O	85	861
Bridget	38	f	w	IREL	San Francisco	San Francisco P O	80	365
Bridget	31	f	w	IREL	Sacramento	2-Wd Sacramento	77	222
Ellen	20	f	w	NY	San Francisco	San Francisco P O	80	532
G W	60	f	w	NY	Alameda	Oakland	68	196
James	49	m	w	IREL	San Francisco	11-Wd San Francisc	84	469
James	35	m	w	IREL	Nevada	Grass Valley Twp	75	182
James	35	m	w	IREL	San Francisco	2-Wd San Francisco	79	266
James	35	m	w	IREL	San Francisco	San Francisco P O	85	766
John	44	m	w	IREL	Nevada	Grass Valley Twp	75	210
John	38	m	w	IREL	San Francisco	7-Wd San Francisco	81	196
John	26	m	w	IREL	San Francisco	11-Wd San Francisc	84	539
John	11	m	w	MA	San Francisco	San Francisco P O	85	864
Joseph	35	m	w	IREL	San Francisco	11-Wd San Francisc	84	435
Martin	35	m	w	IREL	San Francisco	7-Wd San Francisco	81	212
Mary	7	f	w	CA	Nevada	Grass Valley Twp	75	229
Mary	27	f	w	IREL	San Francisco	San Francisco P O	80	484
Michael	40	m	w	IREL	San Francisco	San Francisco P O	85	864
Michael	37	m	w	IREL	Alameda	Brooklyn Twp	68	42
Michael	15	m	w	ME	Contra Costa	Martinez P O	71	374
N	38	m	w	IREL	San Francisco	San Francisco P O	85	821
Patrick	40	m	w	IREL	Alameda	Brooklyn Twp	68	51
Richard	22	m	w	KY	San Diego	Julian Dist	78	469
Thomas	29	m	w	IREL	Nevada	Grass Valley Twp	75	213
FEENY								
Bartholomw	26	m	w	IREL	San Francisco	1-Wd San Francisco	79	133
Delia	23	f	w	IREL	Solano	Vallejo	90	163
Edward	26	m	w	IREL	San Francisco	5-Wd San Francisco	81	32
J C	42	m	w	IREL	San Francisco	7-Wd San Francisco	81	275
James	39	m	w	IREL	Plumas	Washington Twp	77	52
John	37	m	w	IREL	Plumas	Washington Twp	77	53
Mark	48	m	w	IREL	Alameda	Brooklyn Twp	68	50
Patrick	38	m	w	IREL	San Mateo	Schoolhouse Statio	87	337
Patrick	25	m	w	IREL	San Francisco	1-Wd San Francisco	79	62
Patrick	21	m	w	IN	San Francisco	8-Wd San Francisco	82	342
FEER								
Francis	40	m	w	HDAR	Solano	Vacaville Twp	90	117
FEERICK								
M	30	m	w	IREL	Solano	Vallejo	90	197
FEERINO								
Antoine	25	m	w	SWIT	Marin	San Antonio Twp	74	61
FEERY								
Wm	29	m	w	IREL	Nevada	Nevada Twp	75	280
FEFFREY								
Archibald	32	m	w	CANA	Santa Clara	Milpitas Twp	88	110
David	30	m	w	CANA	Santa Clara	Milpitas Twp	88	110
FEFOINDER								
Andrew	38	m	w	IL	San Bernardino	San Bernardino Twp	78	453
FEFUHIGO								
A	42	m	w	MEXI	Lake	Coyote Valley	73	401
FEGAN								
Andrew	44	m	w	IREL	San Francisco	2-Wd San Francisco	79	137
J J	53	m	w	IREL	Alameda	Oakland	68	129
Robt	38	m	w	HANO	Sacramento	Granite Twp	77	156
FEGARO								
Francisco	36	m	w	MEXI	Contra Costa	Martinez P O	71	440
FEGERSON								
M	44	m	w	IREL	San Joaquin	Oneal Twp	86	113
FEGLEY								
Jacob	51	m	w	PA	El Dorado	Placerville Twp	72	92
FEGO								
Andrew	55	m	w	ITAL	Amador	Jackson P O	69	337
FEHERTY								
Timothy	40	m	w	IREL	Nevada	Bridgeport Twp	75	102
FEHL								
Louis	30	m	w	PRUS	San Francisco	6-Wd San Francisco	81	90
FEHLMAN								
Charles	46	m	w	SWIT	San Francisco	6-Wd San Francisco	81	114
FEHN								
Henry	56	m	w	HESS	Sacramento	4-Wd Sacramento	77	330
FEHNER								
John	45	m	w	BAVA	Solano	Vallejo	90	172
FEHNING								
Mike	56	m	w	IREL	Calaveras	Copperopolis P O	70	228
FEHR								
Jacob	32	m	w	NY	San Francisco	San Francisco P O	83	144
FEI								
Henry	27	m	w	HDAR	San Francisco	San Francisco P O	85	765

© 2001 by Heritage Quest. All rights reserved.

Name	Age	S	R	B-PL	County	Locale	Series M593 Roll	Pg
FEICK								
Geo	33	m	w	HANO	Sierra	Forest Twp	89	530
FEIDLER								
Julius	59	m	w	PRUS	Sacramento	3-Wd Sacramento	77	303
FEIFER								
Phil	30	m	w	PRUS	Sacramento	4-Wd Sacramento	77	325
FEIG								
Alexander	34	m	w	PRUS	San Francisco	San Francisco P O	83	228
John H	33	m	w	SAXO	San Francisco	San Francisco P O	83	19
FEIGE								
R S	25	m	w	NY	Napa	Napa	75	16
FEIGENBAUM								
Chris	20	m	w	SHOL	San Mateo	Menlo Park P O	87	379
Joseph	37	m	w	BAVA	San Francisco	8-Wd San Francisco	82	490
FEIGER								
John	27	m	w	LA	San Francisco	8-Wd San Francisco	82	389
FEIKS								
Edward	12	m	w	CA	San Francisco	San Francisco P O	85	831
FEIL								
Herrman	30	m	w	PRUS	San Francisco	7-Wd San Francisco	81	273
FEILHAMER								
Joseph	42	m	w	WURT	San Diego	Temecula Dist	78	527
FEIMERAN								
Patrick	66	m	w	IREL	San Francisco	San Francisco P O	83	362
FEIN								
San	30	m	c	CHIN	Fresno	Millerton P O	72	202
FEINEY								
Eugene	42	m	w	IREL	San Francisco	San Francisco P O	83	379
FEIRARI								
Domenic	51	m	w	ITAL	San Francisco	1-Wd San Francisco	79	36
FEISEL								
Frederick	32	m	w	OH	San Francisco	San Francisco P O	85	843
FEIST								
Joseph	28	m	w	HDAR	Santa Clara	2-Wd San Jose	88	322
FEIT								
George C	40	m	w	MD	Shasta	French Gulch P O	89	465
FEITEL								
John	36	m	w	OH	Siskiyou	Scott Valley Twp	89	619
FEITEN								
Peter	45	m	w	ENGL	Nevada	Nevada Twp	75	296
FEITNER								
Annie	19	f	w	NY	San Francisco	11-Wd San Francisc	84	493
FEITO								
Fezzarini	26	m	w	SWIT	Marin	San Antonio Twp	74	63
FEITSEN								
Henery	36	m	w	HANO	San Francisco	7-Wd San Francisco	81	216
FEITTRO								
Joseph	40	m	w	OH	Solano	Rio Vista Twp	90	55
FEIX								
John	43	m	w	PRUS	San Francisco	San Francisco P O	85	809
FEKE								
Ah	28	m	c	CHIN	Trinity	Lewiston Pct	92	212
FELAX								
Joseph	35	m	w	ITAL	Calaveras	San Andreas P O	70	187
FELBURN								
Thomas	55	m	w	IREL	San Francisco	7-Wd San Francisco	81	211
FELCH								
C L	22	m	w	NY	Solano	Vallejo	90	202
Desire	35	m	w	FRAN	San Francisco	San Francisco P O	80	350
W C	47	m	w	VT	Sacramento	3-Wd Sacramento	77	313
FELDBUSH								
J D	35	m	w	HANO	San Francisco	San Francisco P O	85	787
John H	41	m	w	PRUS	San Francisco	8-Wd San Francisco	82	422
John H	37	m	w	HANO	San Francisco	San Francisco P O	85	725
FELDERWOOD								
John	38	m	w	PRUS	Del Norte	Smith Rvr Twp	71	476
FELDHAUS								
John	49	m	w	OLDE	Merced	Snelling P O	74	250
FELDHEIM								
N	28	m	w	BAVA	Sacramento	3-Wd Sacramento	77	282
FELDHEIMER								
Simon	24	m	w	NY	San Francisco	7-Wd San Francisco	81	241
FELDMAN								
Alther	37	m	w	POLA	Santa Clara	2-Wd San Jose	88	284
John	46	m	w	HANO	Nevada	Bridgeport Twp	75	104
FELDMANN								
Lewis	49	m	w	HANO	San Francisco	11-Wd San Francisc	84	609
FELDRO								
R C	44	m	w	MEXI	Alameda	Murray Twp	68	101
FELDSTEIN								
Mareus	43	m	w	PRUS	San Francisco	San Francisco P O	80	362
FELDTMAN								
Henry	26	m	w	HANO	San Francisco	2-Wd San Francisco	79	256
FELECEAN								
Antonio	25	m	w	AZOR	Monterey	Monterey	74	364
FELEIPE								
Francis	40	m	w	PORT	Nevada	Rough & Ready Twp	75	329
FELEPO								
J	24	m	w	ITAL	San Francisco	San Francisco P O	85	755
FELES								
Antonio	38	m	w	CA	Monterey	Castroville Twp	74	326
Frank	23	m	w	MEXI	Marin	San Rafael Twp	74	40
Gacinto	26	m	w	MEXI	Marin	San Rafael Twp	74	38
Jose	35	m	w	CA	Monterey	Castroville Twp	74	339
Julian	32	m	w	CA	Monterey	Castroville Twp	74	339
FELEY								
John	38	m	w	IREL	Solano	Benicia	90	9

Name	Age	S	R	B-PL	County	Locale	Series M593 Roll	Pg
FELEZ								
Manwell	14	m	w	CA	San Mateo	Schoolhouse Statio	87	343
Phillipe	21	m	w	MEXI	Kern	Tehachapi P O	73	354
FELHEIMER								
Bernard	36	m	w	BAVA	San Francisco	San Francisco P O	83	217
FELICE								
Jose	50	m	w	CA	Santa Barbara	Santa Barbara P O	87	464
Jose A	42	m	w	CA	Santa Barbara	Santa Maria P O	87	514
Thomas	70	m	b	CAME	Calaveras	Copperopolis P O	70	261
FELICIA								
Pedro	24	m	w	SWIT	Marin	Nicasio Twp	74	16
FELIEN								
Ferdinand	32	m	w	MEXI	Fresno	Millerton P O	72	167
FELIG								
Casmera	40	m	w	MEXI	San Diego	Coronado	78	467
FELING								
Tho J	45	m	w	IREL	Mono	Bridgeport P O	74	283
FELIP								
David	30	m	w	MEXI	Placer	Emigrant Gap P O	76	416
FELIPE								
Louis	40	m	w	FRAN	San Francisco	6-Wd San Francisco	81	83
Pietro	32	m	w	ITAL	San Francisco	1-Wd San Francisco	79	118
FELIS								
Adolfa	13	m	w	CA	Monterey	Monterey	74	362
Antone	40	m	w	CA	San Luis Obispo	Santa Rosa Twp	87	324
Felipe	20	m	w	CA	Santa Clara	Almaden Twp	88	7
George	29	m	w	CA	Colusa	Spring Valley Twp	71	341
James	44	m	w	SWIT	Marin	San Rafael Twp	74	32
Jesus	18	m	w	CA	Santa Clara	Almaden Twp	88	7
Jose	32	m	w	CA	San Luis Obispo	Morro Twp	87	283
Louis	46	m	w	CA	Santa Clara	Almaden Twp	88	14
Maria J	74	f	w	CA	Monterey	Monterey	74	359
FELISADO								
Flores	25	m	w	MEXI	San Francisco	3-Wd San Francisco	79	291
FELISSE								
Marie	58	f	w	PORT	Nevada	Rough & Ready Twp	75	333
FELIX								
Carmeo	30	f	w	MEXI	San Joaquin	3-Wd Stockton	86	222
David	35	m	w	WALE	San Francisco	San Francisco P O	83	187
David	33	m	w	MEXI	Calaveras	Copperopolis P O	70	259
George A	33	m	w	PRUS	San Francisco	6-Wd San Francisco	81	73
Jose	31	m	w	CA	Santa Clara	Fremont Twp	88	59
Louis	50	m	w	FRAN	San Francisco	6-Wd San Francisco	81	99
Paul	24	m	w	CHIL	San Francisco	San Francisco P O	80	333
FELIZ								
Americita	38	f	w	MEXI	Kern	Bakersfield P O	73	363
Anestacio	55	m	w	CA	Los Angeles	Los Angeles Twp	73	481
Ascencion	35	f	w	CA	Los Angeles	Santa Ana Twp	73	606
Cayetano	14	m	w	CA	Los Angeles	Los Angeles Twp	73	474
Cisto	27	m	w	CA	Mendocino	Sanel Twp	74	231
Clement	60	m	w	FRAN	Fresno	Millerton P O	72	160
Donaciana	17	m	w	CA	Contra Costa	Martinez P O	71	385
Franis	38	m	w	MEXI	Calaveras	San Andreas P O	70	168
Gumesindo	25	m	w	CA	Mendocino	Sanel Twp	74	231
Joaquin	45	m	w	MEXI	Contra Costa	Martinez P O	71	375
Jose	54	m	w	CA	Santa Barbara	Santa Barbara P O	87	495
Jose G	43	m	w	CA	Los Angeles	Los Angeles	73	563
Josephine	50	f	w	MEXI	Kern	Bakersfield P O	73	360
Manuel	53	m	w	CA	Los Angeles	Santa Ana Twp	73	607
Mariana	55	f	w	CA	Los Angeles	Los Angeles Twp	73	474
Raphael	36	m	w	CA	Mendocino	Sanel Twp	74	227
Refugia	50	f	w	CA	Los Angeles	Santa Ana Twp	73	606
Sefarosa	35	f	w	CA	Contra Costa	Martinez P O	71	385
Tomas	37	m	w	CA	Los Angeles	Los Angeles Twp	73	479
Urbano	44	m	w	CA	Contra Costa	Martinez P O	71	385
W	6	f	w	CA	Mendocino	Sanel Twp	74	227
FELKER								
Henry	37	m	w	ME	San Francisco	11-Wd San Francisc	84	563
Nicholus	62	m	w	TN	Santa Barbara	San Buenaventura P	87	423
Silas	47	m	w	ME	Santa Cruz	Santa Cruz	89	407
William	46	m	w	ME	Santa Cruz	Santa Cruz	89	431
William	30	m	w	WI	El Dorado	Cosumnes Twp	72	18
FELKNER								
Fred	35	m	w	GERM	Solano	Vallejo	90	161
FELL								
Annie H	18	f	w	PA	San Francisco	San Francisco P O	83	291
Christopher	68	f	w	PRUS	San Francisco	5-Wd San Francisco	81	10
Erastus	54	m	w	CANA	Sonoma	Petaluma Twp	91	344
George Wilson	39	m	w	PA	Plumas	Washington Twp	77	56
John	25	m	w	ENGL	Nevada	Grass Valley Twp	75	180
Jonathan	25	m	w	ENGL	Calaveras	Copperopolis P O	70	223
Wm	33	m	w	ENGL	San Francisco	San Francisco P O	83	1
FELLA								
Amilia	43	f	w	ENGL	San Francisco	7-Wd San Francisco	81	175
John	20	m	w	CA	San Francisco	8-Wd San Francisco	82	432
FELLENROTH								
Aug	45	m	w	FRAN	San Francisco	6-Wd San Francisco	81	102
FELLER								
Ellis	65	m	w	BADE	Nevada	Grass Valley Twp	75	218
Fred	34	m	w	ME	San Francisco	11-Wd San Francisc	84	628
Hattie	3	f	w	CA	San Joaquin	Tulare Twp	86	250
John	31	m	w	NY	San Francisco	11-Wd San Francisc	84	504
FELLERS								
Levina A	41	f	w	OH	Napa	Napa	75	39
FELLEY								
Alexander	35	m	w	FRAN	Santa Clara	2-Wd San Jose	88	318

© 2001 by Heritage Quest. All rights reserved.

California 1870 Census

Series M593

Name	Age	S	R	B-PL	County	Locale	Roll	Pg
FELLIN								
Lorenzo	32	m	w	PRUS	Napa	Napa	75	37
FELLING								
Edward	60	m	w	IREL	El Dorado	Kelsey Twp	72	60
FELLIS								
Barbera	21	f	w	CA	Napa	Napa	75	55
FELLITTA								
John	32	m	w	ITAL	San Francisco	San Francisco P O	80	472
FELLMAN								
Emma	21	f	w	SWIT	San Francisco	3-Wd San Francisco	79	324
John	23	m	w	HUNG	San Francisco	San Francisco P O	80	534
Matthies	28	m	w	PRUS	Tehama	Paskenta Twp	92	164
FELLOM								
Jno	30	m	w	CA	Santa Clara	Gilroy Twp	88	93
Pedro	14	m	w	CA	Santa Clara	Santa Clara Twp	88	177
FELLON								
John	37	m	w	PRUS	Sacramento	4-Wd Sacramento	77	333
Robert	34	m	w	IREL	Yuba	Linda Twp	93	554
Wm J	33	m	w	FRAN	Alameda	Oakland	68	170
FELLORES								
W	42	m	w	PA	Nevada	Meadow Lake Twp	75	247
FELLOW								
Chas T	51	m	w	FRAN	San Joaquin	2-Wd Stockton	86	170
Sinforino	17	m	w	CA	Santa Clara	Santa Clara Twp	88	177
FELLOWS								
Augustus	25	m	w	AR	Yolo	Cottonwood Twp	93	469
Charles	45	m	w	SCOT	Solano	Denverton Twp	90	27
Charles	32	m	w	SCOT	Solano	Green Valley Twp	90	38
David A	46	m	w	VT	San Francisco	San Francisco P O	85	763
David S	36	m	w	NH	Sonoma	Petaluma Twp	91	353
E C	36	m	w	NY	Alameda	Oakland	68	185
Eveline	13	f	w	CA	San Bernardino	San Bernardino Twp	78	450
Everitt P	22	m	w	MA	San Francisco	8-Wd San Francisco	82	303
George	45	m	w	NH	Napa	Napa	75	39
George W	41	m	w	NH	San Francisco	2-Wd San Francisco	79	261
Henry H	33	m	w	KY	Placer	Auburn P O	76	368
Hurt	70	m	w	MA	Sacramento	4-Wd Sacramento	77	358
James	34	m	w	NY	San Francisco	San Francisco P O	80	486
Joseph S	57	m	w	MA	Siskiyou	Butte Twp	89	585
Richard	25	m	w	KY	Marin	San Rafael Twp	74	45
Rufus	30	m	w	OH	Colusa	Stony Crk Twp	71	330
Thos	36	m	w	NY	San Francisco	2-Wd San Francisco	79	220
William	42	m	w	NH	Colusa	Grand Island Twp	71	304
William H H	27	m	w	IL	Placer	Auburn P O	76	367
FELLS								
J A	43	m	w	PORT	Tuolumne	Big Oak Flat P O	93	396
John	37	m	w	IREL	Sacramento	4-Wd Sacramento	77	370
William	44	m	w	PRUS	Yuba	Marysville	93	585
FELLUTI								
Patrici	30	m	w	ITAL	San Francisco	San Francisco P O	80	471
FELMA								
Magdalena	63	f	w	WURT	Santa Clara	Milpitas Twp	88	116
FELON								
Terreto	27	m	w	SWIT	Marin	San Antonio Twp	74	63
FELOS								
Peter	42	m	w	SWIT	Marin	San Rafael Twp	74	32
FELSENHELD								
David	27	m	w	BAVA	San Diego	San Diego	78	496
Max	28	m	w	BAVA	San Diego	San Diego	78	496
Rosa	18	f	w	BAVA	San Francisco	San Francisco P O	85	815
FELSENTHAL								
Caroline	44	f	w	HDAR	San Francisco	8-Wd San Francisco	82	419
FELSEY								
Lawrence	38	m	w	IREL	San Francisco	11-Wd San Francisc	84	673
FELT								
Cleney	52	m	w	NH	San Francisco	7-Wd San Francisco	81	165
Eliza	32	f	w	PRUS	San Francisco	San Francisco P O	83	192
Enos	32	m	w	MI	San Luis Obispo	Santa Rosa Twp	87	326
Jonathan	46	m	w	ME	Santa Clara	Fremont Twp	88	58
Josiah	48	m	w	MA	Amador	Volcano P O	69	375
T D	52	m	w	MA	Humboldt	Eel Rvr Twp	72	249
FELTCHOR								
William	37	m	w	IREL	Yuba	New York Twp	93	637
FELTEN								
A J	45	m	w	OH	Trinity	Weaverville Pct	92	226
FELTER								
Alfred	43	m	w	NY	Santa Clara	Milpitas Twp	88	113
Elam E	51	m	w	NY	Butte	Oregon Twp	70	134
J R	40	m	w	NY	Sacramento	3-Wd Sacramento	77	265
FELTERSON								
Augusta	30	f	w	PRUS	San Francisco	San Francisco P O	80	536
FELTHER								
Eliza	30	f	w	PRUS	San Francisco	6-Wd San Francisco	81	81
FELTHOUSE								
Gerhard	33	m	w	WURT	Colusa	Colusa Twp	71	277
FELTNER								
Lewis L	40	m	w	OH	Colusa	Stony Crk Twp	71	329
Rosa	16	f	w	PRUS	Mendocino	Big Rvr Twp	74	158
FELTON								
Bill	30	m	i	CA	Colusa	Stony Crk Twp	71	326
Charles	40	m	w	NY	San Francisco	11-Wd San Francisc	84	661
Chas	40	m	w	NY	San Francisco	8-Wd San Francisco	82	347
Chas N	40	m	w	NY	San Francisco	8-Wd San Francisco	82	372
Daniel	52	m	w	NY	Nevada	Nevada Twp	75	309
Ellen E	40	f	w	NY	Lake	Lower Lake	73	416
J H	31	m	w	OH	Mendocino	Little Lake Twp	74	201
James B	43	m	w	MA	Alameda	Oakland	68	208
John	34	m	w	SAXO	San Francisco	2-Wd San Francisco	79	260
John	32	m	w	PRUS	San Francisco	San Francisco P O	80	378
John	24	m	w	IREL	San Francisco	2-Wd San Francisco	79	216
Levi	55	m	w	PA	Mendocino	Little Lake Twp	74	201
Phineas	27	m	w	NY	Solano	Vacaville Twp	90	133
FELTS								
Christopher	34	m	w	GA	Colusa	Grand Island Twp	71	303
Marcus	26	m	w	MO	Colusa	Grand Island Twp	71	310
FELTUS								
Frank	23	m	w	OH	Solano	Suisun Twp	90	116
FELTY								
Cloyd	43	m	w	FRAN	San Francisco	2-Wd San Francisco	79	172
FELTZ								
Wm	39	m	w	PRUS	Humboldt	Eureka Twp	72	264
FELVY								
Bridget	39	f	w	IREL	San Francisco	11-Wd San Francisc	84	508
FEMBRES								
Manul	46	m	w	MEXI	El Dorado	Placerville Twp	72	92
FEMENTES								
Unofria	44	m	w	MEXI	Los Angeles	Los Angeles	73	562
FEMERON								
W	48	m	w	BADE	Alameda	Oakland	68	202
FEMERY								
James	44	m	w	HOLL	Alameda	Oakland	68	210
FEMING								
George	46	m	w	BAVA	Amador	Sutter Crk P O	69	405
FEMINUS								
Carlo	41	m	w	ITAL	Nevada	Grass Valley Twp	75	204
FEMMER								
Francisco	48	m	w	CANA	Alameda	San Leandro	68	94
Lucind	63	f	w	NY	Alameda	San Leandro	68	94
FEMORE								
Augustine	40	m	w	MEXI	Santa Barbara	Las Cruces P O	87	515
FEN								
Ah	32	m	c	CHIN	Trinity	Douglas	92	232
Ah	19	f	c	CHIN	San Francisco	San Francisco P O	80	494
Ah	17	m	c	CHIN	Solano	Benicia	90	18
Ching	35	m	c	CHIN	Sierra	Lincoln Twp	89	545
Julia	58	f	w	IREL	San Francisco	8-Wd San Francisco	82	320
Kin	28	m	c	CHIN	Trinity	Weaverville Pct	92	230
Mun	25	m	c	CHIN	Solano	Vacaville Twp	90	131
FENAESSY								
Joseph	17	m	w	NY	San Francisco	11-Wd San Francisc	84	593
FENALD								
H	35	m	w	SCOT	Alameda	Oakland	68	264
FENAR								
Juan	41	m	w	MEXI	Kern	Bakersfield P O	73	363
FENAUT								
Echin	61	m	w	FRAN	Calaveras	San Andreas P O	70	167
FENBACH								
Joseph	38	m	w	BADE	Inyo	Independence Twp	73	324
FENBRUMAN								
Albert	25	m	w	PRUS	San Francisco	5-Wd San Francisco	81	15
FENBURMAN								
John	22	m	w	PRUS	San Francisco	5-Wd San Francisco	81	15
FENBY								
Samuel	41	m	w	MA	Yuba	Bullards Bar P O	93	547
FENCH								
W R	38	m	w	NY	Humboldt	Eureka Twp	72	265
William	41	m	w	ME	Mono	Bridgeport P O	74	282
FENDER								
Aaron	56	m	w	NC	Shasta	Millville P O	89	490
Eli	23	m	w	IL	Shasta	Millville P O	89	490
Johnson	36	m	w	IL	Shasta	Millville P O	89	493
William	43	m	w	PRUS	Del Norte	Smith Rvr Twp	71	476
Wm H	32	m	w	IN	Shasta	Stillwater P O	89	481
FENDLEY								
Isabella	21	f	w	NY	Los Angeles	Los Angeles	73	545
FENDO								
John M	35	m	w	AUST	San Francisco	1-Wd San Francisco	79	89
FENDRAKE								
Mike	28	m	w	SWIT	Sacramento	4-Wd Sacramento	77	341
FENDRICK								
Nicholus	54	m	w	FRAN	Nevada	Bridgeport Twp	75	102
FENE								
Ah	21	m	c	CHIN	Solano	Benicia	90	14
Thos J	33	m	w	ME	Monterey	San Antonio Twp	74	322
FENELY								
James	33	m	w	IREL	Nevada	Grass Valley Twp	75	222
FENER								
Jose	28	m	w	SPAI	San Diego	San Diego	78	488
Manuel	8M	m	w	CA	San Diego	San Diego	78	493
Manuel	46	m	w	SPAI	San Diego	San Diego	78	493
FENETO								
John	25	m	w	ITAL	Tuolumne	Big Oak Flat P O	93	394
FENEY								
Ki	31	m	c	CHIN	Solano	Vacaville Twp	90	131
FENG								
Ah	44	m	c	CHIN	Calaveras	Copperopolis P O	70	222
Ah Hang	42	m	c	CHIN	Amador	Ione City P O	69	366
FENGER								
Chas	31	m	w	FRAN	San Francisco	1-Wd San Francisco	79	49
John	37	m	w	PRUS	Sonoma	Petaluma Twp	91	344
FENGIER								
Pierre	31	m	w	FRAN	San Francisco	8-Wd San Francisco	82	373
FENIS								
Charles	32	m	w	ENGL	Napa	Napa	75	18

© 2001 by Heritage Quest. All rights reserved.

Series M593

Name	Age	S	R	B-PL	County	Locale	Roll	Pg
FENISKYDE								
James	23	m	w	MO	Monterey	San Juan Twp	74	388
FENITA								
Jose	60	m	w	CA	San Diego	San Pasqual	78	521
Juan	21	m	w	CA	San Diego	San Pasqual	78	521
FENIX								
Nathaniel	25	m	w	NY	San Francisco	1-Wd San Francisco	79	73
FENKHAUSEN								
Amandus	45	m	w	PRUS	San Francisco	8-Wd San Francisco	82	484
FENLEY								
David	40	m	w	KY	Calaveras	Copperopolis P O	70	239
James	37	m	w	IREL	Los Angeles	Los Nietos Twp	73	581
Michael	37	m	w	IREL	Siskiyou	Scott Valley Twp	89	613
Richard	25	m	w	IREL	Santa Clara	Fremont Twp	88	50
Sam L	38	m	w	IL	Klamath	Sawyers Bar	73	378
W B	22	m	w	WI	Calaveras	Copperopolis P O	70	237
FENLOW								
James	38	m	w	IREL	Santa Barbara	San Buenaventura P	87	420
FENLY								
John	28	m	w	IREL	San Francisco	7-Wd San Francisco	81	218
FENN								
Abram	31	m	b	AL	Butte	Chico Twp	70	30
Andrew	23	m	w	BAVA	Solano	Vallejo	90	203
Frank	28	m	w	NY	San Francisco	5-Wd San Francisco	81	31
Fredrick	52	m	w	MD	San Francisco	San Francisco P O	83	10
Julia	18	f	w	NY	San Francisco	5-Wd San Francisco	81	31
Julius	34	m	w	IREL	San Francisco	7-Wd San Francisco	81	220
Mary T	23	f	w	IREL	Humboldt	Eureka Twp	72	259
Robert	35	m	w	MA	San Francisco	San Francisco P O	85	823
FENNALL								
Michael	57	m	w	IREL	San Francisco	11-Wd San Francisc	84	513
FENNAN								
James	33	m	w	IREL	Contra Costa	Martinez P O	71	388
FENNARTY								
John	60	m	w	IREL	Sonoma	Petaluma Twp	91	320
FENNAY								
John	33	m	w	IREL	San Francisco	7-Wd San Francisco	81	179
FENNEGAN								
John	36	m	w	NY	Calaveras	Copperopolis P O	70	232
Mary	38	f	w	IREL	San Francisco	8-Wd San Francisco	82	356
Patrk	38	m	w	IREL	Tuolumne	Columbia P O	93	349
FENNEL								
Edward	28	m	w	IREL	San Mateo	Schoolhouse Statio	87	335
Peter	26	m	w	IREL	Fresno	Millerton P O	72	155
FENNELL								
Catherine	32	f	w	IREL	San Francisco	San Francisco P O	83	249
Chas	24	m	w	ME	San Francisco	San Francisco P O	83	86
Dennis	30	m	w	IREL	San Francisco	8-Wd San Francisco	82	351
Henry	37	m	w	HCAS	San Francisco	11-Wd San Francisc	84	644
James	34	m	w	IREL	Santa Clara	Milpitas Twp	88	116
James	30	m	w	VA	San Francisco	San Francisco P O	83	99
John	40	m	w	KY	Napa	Yountville Twp	75	86
Martin	40	m	w	IREL	San Francisco	11-Wd San Francisc	84	580
Stephen	23	m	w	IREL	San Francisco	1-Wd San Francisco	79	135
Thos H	37	m	w	MA	Mariposa	Mariposa P O	74	135
William	25	m	w	CANA	Inyo	Cerro Gordo Twp	73	318
FENNER								
Geo D	39	m	w	NY	Yuba	New York Twp	93	642
Hardin C	38	m	w	MA	Yolo	Grafton Twp	93	497
Herman	72	m	w	WEST	Napa	Napa	75	7
James D	34	m	w	NY	Sacramento	2-Wd Sacramento	77	248
John	60	m	w	IL	Mendocino	Gualala Twp	74	225
Obadiah	45	m	w	RI	San Francisco	San Francisco P O	80	390
Philip	24	m	w	MD	San Francisco	3-Wd San Francisco	79	318
FENNESSAY								
Thomas	40	m	w	IREL	Calaveras	San Andreas P O	70	209
FENNESSEY								
John	22	m	w	IREL	San Francisco	San Francisco P O	85	852
FENNESSY								
Danil	45	m	w	IREL	San Francisco	8-Wd San Francisco	82	330
Hannah	23	f	w	IREL	San Francisco	3-Wd San Francisco	79	296
John	45	m	w	IREL	San Francisco	San Francisco P O	83	377
FENNETT								
James	26	m	w	IREL	San Joaquin	2-Wd Stockton	86	160
FENNEY								
James	27	m	w	IREL	Amador	Amador City P O	69	392
John	27	m	w	IREL	San Francisco	7-Wd San Francisco	81	180
FENNIGAN								
Mike	32	m	w	IREL	Alameda	Oakland	68	222
FENNING								
Wm	42	m	w	VA	Siskiyou	Yreka Twp	89	664
FENNINUS								
D	40	m	w	CHIL	Amador	Jackson P O	69	342
FENNO								
Charles	30	m	w	IREL	Sacramento	Granite Twp	77	140
Jas E	39	m	w	MA	Sonoma	Healdsburg & Mendo	91	278
FENNY								
Alex	35	m	w	SCOT	San Francisco	8-Wd San Francisco	82	341
George B	30	m	w	NY	Mendocino	Cuffeys Cove Twp	74	168
R H	48	m	w	IREL	Siskiyou	Callahan P O	89	628
FENONCHOW								
John B	30	m	w	ITAL	San Francisco	11-Wd San Francisc	84	701
FENSSIS								
Leopold	31	m	w	FRAN	San Francisco	1-Wd San Francisco	79	50
FENSTERMAKER								
---	52	f	w	VT	Sierra	Sierra Twp	89	569
FENSTERMAN								
Martin	44	m	w	PRUS	San Francisco	5-Wd San Francisco	81	8
FENT								
Thomas	54	m	w	IREL	Nevada	Bridgeport Twp	75	114
FENTEN								
Thomas	32	m	w	CANA	Nevada	Meadow Lake Twp	75	255
FENTHENEY								
J P	40	m	w	SWIT	San Francisco	7-Wd San Francisco	81	183
FENTO								
Julia A	31	f	w	ENGL	San Francisco	San Francisco P O	85	789
FENTON								
Benj	31	m	w	MO	Fresno	Millerton P O	72	155
Charles	50	m	w	DC	San Diego	San Pasqual Valley	78	525
Charles	46	m	w	VA	Mendocino	Round Valley Twp	74	218
Chas	43	m	w	KY	Butte	Oregon Twp	70	131
Clara B	11	f	w	OR	Merced	Snelling P O	74	259
D P	21	m	w	CA	San Francisco	San Francisco P O	85	877
Daniel	30	m	w	IREL	San Francisco	San Francisco P O	85	833
Edward	29	m	w	MA	San Francisco	7-Wd San Francisco	81	226
Edwin	40	m	w	IREL	San Francisco	7-Wd San Francisco	81	172
Ellen	8	f	w	CA	San Francisco	San Francisco P O	83	133
Ellen	15	f	w	CA	Santa Clara	2-Wd San Jose	88	337
Geo	35	m	w	NY	San Francisco	8-Wd San Francisco	82	371
Henry	41	m	w	NY	San Francisco	San Francisco P O	80	456
Henry W	26	m	w	CANA	Contra Costa	Martinez P O	71	373
J R	40	m	w	NJ	Amador	Amador City P O	69	395
James	42	m	w	SCOT	San Francisco	San Francisco P O	83	332
James	42	m	w	SCOT	Los Angeles	Los Angeles	73	524
James	42	m	w	SCOT	Stanislaus	Empire Twp	92	53
James	30	m	w	NY	San Luis Obispo	Salinas Twp	87	290
John	46	m	w	NY	San Francisco	2-Wd San Francisco	79	141
John	43	m	w	IREL	San Francisco	San Francisco P O	85	833
John	12	m	w	OR	San Joaquin	Liberty Twp	86	94
Josephine	14	f	w	OR	San Joaquin	Elkhorn Twp	86	54
Lizzie	15	f	w	MA	San Francisco	11-Wd San Francisc	84	643
Mary	13	f	w	MA	San Francisco	8-Wd San Francisco	82	408
Mary A	19	f	w	IREL	Nevada	Bridgeport Twp	75	124
Michal	36	m	w	IREL	Trinity	Weaverville Pct	92	223
Pat	34	m	w	IREL	San Francisco	7-Wd San Francisco	81	275
Patrick	57	m	w	IREL	Santa Clara	Santa Clara Twp	88	164
Patrick	39	m	w	IREL	San Francisco	San Francisco P O	85	831
R B	22	m	w	MO	San Joaquin	Oneal Twp	86	110
S F	26	m	w	NJ	San Francisco	8-Wd San Francisco	82	371
Susan	14	f	w	MA	San Francisco	San Francisco P O	83	264
Thomas	33	m	w	IREL	Sonoma	Analy Twp	91	232
William G	29	m	w	NY	Nevada	Bridgeport Twp	75	124
William H	48	m	w	NY	San Diego	San Pasqual	78	521
FENUS								
Annie	15	f	w	CA	San Francisco	San Francisco P O	83	413
FENY								
M	16	m	w	CA	Alameda	Oakland	68	159
Mathew	44	m	w	IREL	Marin	Bolinas Twp	74	6
FEON								
Ah	19	m	c	CHIN	San Francisco	1-Wd San Francisco	79	101
FEONG								
Ah	6	f	c	CHIN	San Francisco	6-Wd San Francisco	81	76
FEOUR								
John	24	m	w	ME	San Francisco	San Francisco P O	83	7
FERANBAUGH								
Henry	42	m	w	PRUS	Inyo	Cerro Gordo Twp	73	318
FERARI								
Andrew	35	m	w	ITAL	San Francisco	1-Wd San Francisco	79	105
FERARIS								
Mark	48	m	w	ITAL	Yuba	Slate Range Bar Tw	93	673
FERAULD								
Richard	38	m	w	PA	San Francisco	7-Wd San Francisco	81	175
FERBER								
E G	29	m	w	NH	San Joaquin	3-Wd Stockton	86	243
Wm	45	m	w	ME	Sonoma	Salt Point	91	388
FERBERD								
Nathan	58	m	b	DE	Del Norte	Happy Camp Twp	71	471
FERBES								
William H	25	m	w	NY	Stanislaus	Empire Twp	92	65
FERCADO								
Emile	28	m	w	CHIL	Marin	San Rafael Twp	74	33
FERCERNA								
Anna	40	f	w	MEXI	San Francisco	2-Wd San Francisco	79	144
FERCH								
Noah	51	m	w	IREL	Los Angeles	Los Angeles	73	547
FERDINAND								
John	25	m	w	SCOT	Siskiyou	Yreka Twp	89	666
FERDINANDES								
John	44	m	w	MEXI	San Francisco	San Francisco P O	83	420
FERDINANDO								
J	55	m	c	FRAN	Amador	Jackson P O	69	343
Louiza	27	m	w	ITAL	Amador	Volcano P O	69	372
FERDINDO								
M	50	m	w	CHIL	Amador	Jackson P O	69	342
FERDINO								
Emanuel	38	m	w	MEXI	Tulare	Packwood Twp	92	257
Peter	20	m	w	FRAN	Santa Clara	Fremont Twp	88	55
FERDMAIN								
Oscar	32	m	w	SWIT	San Francisco	San Francisco P O	80	535
FERDON								
William	41	m	w	VA	Calaveras	Copperopolis P O	70	259
FERDONIA								
Joseph	26	m	w	SWIT	Santa Clara	Fremont Twp	88	66

© 2001 by Heritage Quest. All rights reserved.

Series M593

Name	Age	S	R	B-PL	County	Locale	Roll	Pg
FEREA								
Mary	33	f	w	ITAL	Santa Clara	2-Wd San Jose	88	312
FEREIM								
Alberto	30	m	w	AZOR	San Francisco	3-Wd San Francisco	79	287
FERENCE								
Luigi	50	m	w	ITAL	Amador	Volcano P O	69	385
FERERE								
Mary	25	f	w	AUST	San Francisco	San Francisco P O	85	759
FERET								
Battiste	18	m	w	SWIT	Marin	San Antonio Twp	74	63
FERGERSON								
Eli	42	m	w	VA	Mendocino	Point Arena Twp	74	211
James	43	m	w	ENGL	San Francisco	San Francisco P O	80	370
Lewis	28	m	w	SHOL	Alameda	Eden Twp	68	67
FERGESON								
Archibald	25	m	w	CANA	Sacramento	Georgianna Twp	77	127
John	28	m	w	CANA	Sacramento	Georgianna Twp	77	128
T B	29	m	w	ME	Alameda	Murray Twp	68	106
FERGGA								
Fred	22	m	w	IOFM	San Francisco	1-Wd San Francisco	79	134
FERGISON								
Wm	30	m	w	IA	Sacramento	Lee Twp	77	157
FERGUESON								
Frank	25	m	w	TN	Marin	San Rafael Twp	74	45
George	24	m	w	WI	Sutter	Nicolaus Twp	92	113
Warren	23	m	b	IL	Marin	San Rafael Twp	74	43
FERGURSON								
John	49	m	w	IREL	San Joaquin	1-Wd Stockton	86	135
FERGUSEN								
John	28	m	w	SCOT	San Francisco	San Francisco P O	83	207
FERGUSON								
A W	10	m	w	CA	Solano	Benicia	90	14
Adam	39	m	w	LA	Placer	Dutch Flat P O	76	403
Alex	22	m	w	IL	Solano	Rio Vista Twp	90	55
Alexander	49	m	m	VA	San Francisco	San Francisco P O	80	486
Alexander	30	m	w	SCOT	San Francisco	San Francisco P O	80	378
Andrew	35	m	w	IN	San Francisco	2-Wd San Francisco	79	213
Andrew	21	m	w	SCOT	Contra Costa	Martinez P O	71	429
Andy	21	m	w	NY	Butte	Concow Twp	70	6
Anna	29	f	w	IREL	San Francisco	5-Wd San Francisco	81	35
C	40	m	w	CANA	Alameda	Oakland	68	142
C P	47	m	w	NY	San Francisco	3-Wd San Francisco	79	323
Candy	30	m	w	AR	Butte	Oregon Twp	70	133
Catherine	19	f	w	CANA	Solano	Silveyville Twp	90	77
Catherine	19	f	w	CANA	Solano	Rio Vista Twp	90	56
Charles	50	m	w	IREL	San Francisco	San Francisco P O	83	212
Charles	29	m	w	AR	San Diego	Julian Dist	78	473
Charles A	47	m	w	ME	Los Angeles	Santa Ana Twp	73	603
Chas	34	m	w	IA	Butte	Chico Twp	70	25
D	56	m	w	SCOT	El Dorado	Greenwood Twp	72	57
David	62	m	w	SCOT	Contra Costa	Martinez P O	71	429
Duncan	39	m	w	SCOT	Placer	Bath P O	76	457
E	34	m	w	IL	Alameda	Oakland	68	187
E J	66	m	w	NY	Tuolumne	Sonora P O	93	314
Ebenezer	20	m	w	CANA	Solano	Rio Vista Twp	90	57
Ed	39	m	w	TN	Fresno	Millerton P O	72	185
Emma	28	f	w	MEXI	Sacramento	4-Wd Sacramento	77	375
Frank	30	m	w	DENM	San Francisco	7-Wd San Francisco	81	184
Fredk	21	m	w	WI	Sacramento	4-Wd Sacramento	77	374
Geo	35	m	w	FRAN	San Joaquin	Douglas Twp	86	47
George	39	m	w	LA	Kern	Havilah P O	73	338
George	30	m	w	NY	San Francisco	San Francisco P O	80	384
George	25	m	w	SCOT	San Francisco	San Francisco P O	83	359
Helen	22	f	w	IREL	San Francisco	11-Wd San Francisc	84	607
Henry	45	m	w	MD	San Francisco	San Francisco P O	83	336
Henry O	32	m	w	IN	Sonoma	Mendocino Twp	91	289
Isaac	35	m	w	NY	Santa Barbara	Santa Barbara P O	87	453
Isabel	14	f	w	VA	Nevada	Bridgeport Twp	75	115
J	42	m	w	NY	Yuba	Marysville	93	586
J	37	m	w	OH	Sonoma	Santa Rosa	91	414
J	23	m	m	CANA	Sacramento	4-Wd Sacramento	77	321
James	60	m	w	LA	San Francisco	San Francisco P O	85	838
James	40	m	w	IL	Tehama	Paynes Crk Twp	92	167
James	36	m	w	NY	El Dorado	Coloma Twp	72	7
James	31	m	w	PA	San Francisco	1-Wd San Francisco	79	123
James	30	m	w	NY	Tuolumne	Sonora P O	93	314
James	22	m	m	PA	San Francisco	San Francisco P O	80	364
Jas P	40	m	w	IREL	San Francisco	San Francisco P O	83	93
Jno	75	m	w	NY	Sonoma	Santa Rosa	91	418
Jno	27	m	w	SCOT	San Joaquin	3-Wd Stockton	86	231
Jno W	34	m	w	IN	Sonoma	Mendocino Twp	91	289
John	56	m	b	VA	Calaveras	San Andreas P O	70	170
John	35	m	w	IREL	Solano	Silveyville Twp	90	75
John	35	m	w	CANA	Solano	Silveyville Twp	90	92
John	31	m	w	DENM	Solano	Silveyville Twp	90	82
John	31	m	w	SWED	San Francisco	3-Wd San Francisco	79	292
John	27	m	w	NY	Mendocino	Little Rvr Twp	74	171
John D	47	m	w	NY	Placer	Lincoln P O	76	491
John W	24	m	w	LA	Fresno	Millerton P O	72	145
L	34	m	w	SCOT	Nevada	Bridgeport Twp	75	115
Lewis B	29	m	w	KY	Butte	Chico Twp	70	15
Luke	36	m	w	SCOT	Nevada	Bridgeport Twp	75	106
Maggie	32	f	w	IREL	San Francisco	5-Wd San Francisco	81	20
Malcomb	45	m	w	SCOT	Santa Cruz	Santa Cruz Twp	89	395
Mary	35	f	w	IREL	Calaveras	San Andreas P O	70	194
Mary	10M	f	w	CA	Placer	Dutch Flat P O	76	402
Mary A	35	f	w	IREL	San Francisco	11-Wd San Francisc	84	710
Matthew	38	m	w	VA	Santa Barbara	San Buenaventura P	87	422
Max	16	m	w	CANA	Butte	Concow Twp	70	7
Michael	29	m	w	IREL	San Francisco	San Francisco P O	83	215
Nancy	65	f	w	VA	Santa Barbara	San Buenaventura P	87	422
P	41	m	w	PA	Yuba	Marysville	93	611
Paris J	25	m	w	IN	Sonoma	Mendocino Twp	91	292
Parker A	50	m	w	TN	Calaveras	San Andreas P O	70	218
Peter	30	m	w	IREL	San Mateo	Pescadero P O	87	413
Richard	51	m	w	PA	Calaveras	San Andreas P O	70	198
Robert	40	m	m	VA	Sacramento	2-Wd Sacramento	77	213
Robert	27	m	w	SCOT	San Mateo	San Mateo P O	87	357
Robert	12	m	b	MO	Santa Clara	2-Wd San Jose	88	326
Robert M	23	m	w	AR	Los Angeles	San Jose Twp	73	621
Robt G	17	m	w	AR	Shasta	Millville P O	89	494
Robt P	28	m	w	NY	Nevada	Meadow Lake Twp	75	260
Russel	48	m	w	TN	Sonoma	Santa Rosa	91	426
Thomas	27	m	w	PA	Santa Clara	2-Wd San Jose	88	313
Thos	40	m	w	IREL	San Francisco	San Francisco P O	83	69
Walter	41	m	w	OH	Sonoma	Santa Rosa	91	418
William	35	m	w	IREL	San Francisco	11-Wd San Francisc	84	701
William	31	m	w	CANA	San Mateo	Pescadero P O	87	409
William	16	m	w	CA	San Francisco	8-Wd San Francisco	82	391
William A	32	m	m	VA	San Francisco	6-Wd San Francisco	81	110
William F	53	m	w	OH	Placer	Bath P O	76	460
William R	43	m	w	GA	Solano	Silveyville Twp	90	86
William T	30	m	w	SCOT	Mendocino	Point Arena Twp	74	215
Willis	4	m	i	CA	Shasta	Horsetown P O	89	505
Wm W	59	m	w	NC	Sonoma	Mendocino Twp	91	292
FERGUSSON								
P	63	f	w	KY	Alameda	Oakland	68	231
William	18	m	w	CA	Santa Cruz	Watsonville	89	369
FERICH								
George N	42	m	w	ME	Fresno	Kings Rvr P O	72	204
FERICK								
Maggie	22	f	w	IREL	Solano	Vallejo	90	188
FERIER								
Felix	47	m	w	MEXI	Tulare	Visalia	92	298
FERIES								
W A	34	m	w	MA	Solano	Vallejo	90	202
FERIGGIONO								
Giamlutis M	35	m	w	ITAL	Yuba	Long Bar Twp	93	566
FERIN								
Daniel	38	m	w	IREL	Siskiyou	Callahan P O	89	628
FERING								
Ah	27	m	c	CHIN	El Dorado	Cosumnes Twp	72	19
Joseph	24	m	w	ENGL	Mendocino	Point Arena Twp	74	224
FERIRA								
Joseph	22	m	w	AZOR	Contra Costa	San Pablo Twp	71	362
FERIS								
Eva	19	f	w	WI	Plumas	Quartz Twp	77	40
John	43	m	w	CANA	San Bernardino	San Bernardino Twp	78	436
Margaret L	15	f	w	CA	Sacramento	1-Wd Sacramento	77	184
FERIVA								
Emanuel	36	m	w	PORT	Alameda	Washington Twp	68	269
FERK								
Michael	24	m	w	IREL	Inyo	Independence Twp	73	325
FERL								
Edward	30	m	w	PRUS	Santa Barbara	Santa Barbara P O	87	466
Wm	35	m	w	PRUS	Santa Barbara	Santa Barbara P O	87	502
FERLEY								
Dennis	35	m	w	IREL	San Francisco	San Francisco P O	83	92
FERM								
Thomas	34	m	w	IREL	Tuolumne	Columbia P O	93	348
FERMA								
Vernas	17	m	w	FRAN	San Mateo	Half Moon Bay P O	87	390
FERMAN								
Diego	17	m	w	MEXI	Santa Barbara	Santa Barbara P O	87	487
FERMEN								
August	50	m	w	FRAN	San Francisco	San Francisco P O	83	27
FERMER								
W C	41	m	w	NC	Merced	Snelling P O	74	266
FERMI								
Louis	55	m	w	FRAN	San Francisco	1-Wd San Francisco	79	108
FERMIER								
Solomon	35	m	w	FRAN	Santa Clara	2-Wd San Jose	88	313
FERMOURTY								
David	31	m	w	HANO	San Joaquin	Tulare Twp	86	259
FERN								
Elizabeth	33	f	w	IREL	Santa Clara	Redwood Twp	88	130
Elizabeth	32	f	w	IREL	Santa Clara	2-Wd San Jose	88	296
George	49	m	w	MA	San Francisco	8-Wd San Francisco	82	426
George	31	m	w	MA	Santa Barbara	Santa Barbara P O	87	455
James	44	m	w	IREL	Placer	Auburn P O	76	375
L	40	m	w	NY	Alameda	Oakland	68	167
W	54	m	w	MA	Sacramento	4-Wd Sacramento	77	361
Washington	54	m	w	MA	Sacramento	Sutter Twp	77	387
Wm	28	m	w	VA	San Francisco	1-Wd San Francisco	79	115
FERNALD								
Ann	13	f	w	MO	Sonoma	Mendocino Twp	91	300
Beck	23	m	w	AUST	San Francisco	San Francisco P O	80	342
Charles	42	m	w	ME	Santa Barbara	Santa Barbara P O	87	453
Johnson	47	m	w	ME	Sonoma	Petaluma Twp	91	318
R M	41	m	w	MD	Klamath	Trinidad Twp	73	389
Thomas	29	m	w	CANA	Santa Clara	2-Wd San Jose	88	330
FERNAN								
Gabriel	45	m	w	MEXI	San Joaquin	Douglas Twp	86	39

© 2001 by Heritage Quest. All rights reserved.

Name	Age	S	R	B-PL	County	Locale	Series M593 Roll	Pg
FERNANCE								
John	39	m	w	MADE	Alameda	Hayward	68	77
FERNAND								
Felix	34	m	w	FRAN	Sacramento	4-Wd Sacramento	77	370
Hendrick	46	m	w	AZOR	San Francisco	1-Wd San Francisco	79	133
FERNANDA								
Solomon	23	m	w	FRAN	San Luis Obispo	San Luis Obispo Tw	87	307
FERNANDAZ								
Aurilla	19	f	w	MEXI	San Francisco	2-Wd San Francisco	79	189
FERNANDES								
Alberto	57	m	b	PHIL	Mariposa	Mariposa P O	74	104
Ventura	42	m	w	CA	San Luis Obispo	San Luis Obispo Tw	87	314
FERNANDEZ								
--- Mrs	42	f	w	NGRA	San Francisco	San Francisco P O	83	318
A	75	m	w	MEXI	Santa Clara	Gilroy Twp	88	87
A	57	m	w	MEXI	Santa Clara	Almaden Twp	88	21
Alexander	50	m	w	MEXI	Los Angeles	Los Angeles Twp	73	477
Antone	23	m	w	SPAI	Marin	Sausalito Twp	74	67
Antonio	60	m	w	MEXI	Los Angeles	Los Angeles Twp	73	479
Bernard	45	m	w	PORT	Contra Costa	San Pablo Twp	71	366
Clorinda	11	f	w	CA	Santa Cruz	Pajaro Twp	89	360
F	36	m	w	MEXI	Santa Clara	Almaden Twp	88	10
Francis	36	m	w	MEXI	San Francisco	San Francisco P O	80	430
Francisco	24	m	w	MEXI	Santa Barbara	Santa Barbara P O	87	487
Hailard	30	m	w	MEXI	Fresno	Millerton P O	72	159
Incarnation	13	f	w	CA	San Francisco	1-Wd San Francisco	79	32
J	23	m	w	SPAI	Alameda	Oakland	68	135
Joaquin	30	m	w	SPAI	Santa Barbara	Santa Barbara P O	87	500
John	70	m	w	PORT	San Francisco	3-Wd San Francisco	79	290
Jose	71	m	w	SPAI	Santa Clara	Santa Clara Twp	88	163
Jose	65	m	w	SPAI	Santa Clara	Santa Clara Twp	88	158
Jose	34	m	w	SCOT	Siskiyou	Yreka Twp	89	669
Jose	28	m	w	PORT	Contra Costa	Martinez Twp	71	351
Juan	41	m	w	CA	Fresno	Kingston P O	72	222
Louis V	24	m	w	CA	Santa Cruz	Watsonville	89	373
Lucius	40	m	w	PHIL	Santa Clara	Santa Clara Twp	88	149
Manuel	25	m	w	PORT	San Francisco	3-Wd San Francisco	79	290
P	40	m	w	CA	Santa Clara	Gilroy Twp	88	87
Pedro	55	m	w	CHIL	Fresno	Millerton P O	72	167
Ricenta	45	m	w	CHIL	San Bernardino	Chino Twp	78	409
FERNANDO								
Patrice	36	m	w	ITAL	San Francisco	San Francisco P O	80	471
FERNARD								
Abby	80	f	w	ME	Alameda	Oakland	68	233
W H	48	m	w	ME	Alameda	Oakland	68	233
FERNARDE								
S	35	m	w	FRAN	Alameda	Oakland	68	233
FERNATER								
J	38	m	w	PRUS	Alameda	Murray Twp	68	126
FERNBACK								
Jonn	45	m	w	BADE	San Francisco	7-Wd San Francisco	81	183
FERNBERT								
Charles	20	m	w	CANA	San Diego	Julian Dist	78	469
FERNE								
Fanny	40	f	w	FRAN	Calaveras	San Andreas P O	70	196
Peter	43	m	w	NCOD	Nevada	Eureka Twp	75	131
FERNES								
Geo C	40	m	w	ENGL	San Francisco	5-Wd San Francisco	81	26
FERNEY								
Mary	12	f	w	SWIT	Amador	Sutter Crk P O	69	408
FERNIA								
Isadore	15	m	w	CA	Santa Clara	2-Wd San Jose	88	300
FERNICE								
Stafield	31	m	w	CANA	Inyo	Bishop Crk Twp	73	311
Theresa	27	f	w	SWIT	San Francisco	8-Wd San Francisco	82	352
FERNICH								
Eugenea	30	f	w	FRAN	Santa Clara	2-Wd San Jose	88	313
FERNIER								
Stephen	31	m	w	CANA	Nevada	Eureka Twp	75	138
FERNSMAN								
John	35	m	w	NORW	San Francisco	7-Wd San Francisco	81	274
FERO								
Juan	37	m	w	CHIL	Amador	Fiddletown P O	69	432
FEROLE								
Peter	48	m	w	ASEA	Siskiyou	Scott Valley Twp	89	614
FEROSO								
Leforoso	70	m	i	CA	Santa Barbara	San Buenaventura P	87	439
Mateo	70	m	i	CA	Santa Barbara	San Buenaventura P	87	439
FEROT								
Fredrick	28	m	w	FRAN	San Francisco	San Francisco P O	83	252
FEROZE								
Antonio	45	m	w	AZOR	Contra Costa	San Pablo Twp	71	354
FERRAIN								
Henry	45	m	w	NC	Yolo	Merritt Twp	93	504
FERRAL								
John	37	m	w	PA	Tuolumne	Sonora P O	93	329
FERRALL								
James	56	m	w	IREL	Placer	Bath P O	76	433
John	70	m	w	IREL	Sonoma	Santa Rosa	91	420
Lizzie	11	f	w	NY	San Francisco	San Francisco P O	83	97
Robt	29	m	w	PA	Sonoma	Santa Rosa	91	420
FERRAM								
C J	47	m	w	CANA	Trinity	Junction City Pct	92	209
FERRAN								
Charles	50	m	w	FRAN	Calaveras	Copperopolis P O	70	262
FERRAND								
Ch	45	m	w	FRAN	Nevada	Nevada Twp	75	273
Cipriano	32	m	w	FRAN	San Francisco	San Francisco P O	80	339
FERRANT								
Pauline	21	f	w	FRAN	San Francisco	6-Wd San Francisco	81	46
FERRAR								
Gregorio	23	m	w	SWIT	Los Angeles	Los Angeles	73	550
FERRARA								
Louis	45	m	w	ITAL	San Francisco	San Francisco P O	80	351
FERRARD								
A J	58	m	w	BAVA	San Francisco	8-Wd San Francisco	82	353
FERRARI								
Joseph	38	m	w	ITAL	Nevada	Grass Valley Twp	75	155
FERRARRO								
Carbin	42	m	w	SWIT	El Dorado	Diamond Springs Tw	72	31
FERRATE								
Angelo	25	m	w	ITAL	San Francisco	1-Wd San Francisco	79	114
FERRE								
Giddings H	40	m	w	MA	Nevada	Grass Valley Twp	75	199
FERREA								
Emanuel	24	m	w	PORT	Alameda	Washington Twp	68	274
FERREIR								
C F	42	m	w	MA	Tuolumne	Columbia P O	93	340
FERREL								
Robt	36	m	w	LA	Nevada	Nevada Twp	75	278
William	31	m	w	TX	Merced	Snelling P O	74	278
FERRELL								
Daniel	23	m	w	IA	Solano	Rio Vista Twp	90	58
David	35	m	w	IREL	Siskiyou	Scott Valley Twp	89	609
Henry C	37	m	w	OH	Shasta	Millville P O	89	494
James	46	m	w	IREL	Klamath	Liberty Twp	73	376
Michael	34	m	w	IREL	Solano	Denverton Twp	90	27
Sarah F	36	f	w	PA	Sacramento	2-Wd Sacramento	77	250
FERREN								
A E	70	m	w	CA	Sacramento	3-Wd Sacramento	77	262
Elliza	18	f	w	NY	Sacramento	3-Wd Sacramento	77	262
Patrick	29	m	w	IREL	Santa Clara	Milpitas Twp	88	113
FERRENBACH								
Hermann	42	m	w	PRUS	San Francisco	2-Wd San Francisco	79	141
FERRERA								
Manuel	18	m	w	AZOR	Marin	Sausalito Twp	74	71
FERRERE								
Joseph	28	m	w	PORT	Nevada	Grass Valley Twp	75	180
FERRERI								
Luigi	42	m	w	ITAL	San Francisco	San Francisco P O	85	757
FERRERO								
John	35	m	w	CUBA	San Francisco	1-Wd San Francisco	79	134
FERRESA								
Antone	44	m	w	AZOR	Marin	Sausalito Twp	74	69
FERRET								
Henrique	58	m	w	FRAN	Amador	Volcano P O	69	386
Jules	56	m	w	FRAN	Amador	Volcano P O	69	386
FERRETE								
Lorenzo	45	m	w	ITAL	Calaveras	Copperopolis P O	70	250
FERRETTO								
Joseph	34	m	w	ITAL	San Francisco	3-Wd San Francisco	79	317
FERREZ								
Pascuala	42	f	w	MEXI	Santa Barbara	Santa Barbara P O	87	466
FERRI								
Antone	40	m	w	PORT	Marin	Sausalito Twp	74	67
FERRIEN								
John S	32	m	w	SCOT	Trinity	Douglas	92	234
FERRIER								
---	46	m	w	IREL	Amador	Ione City P O	69	361
A J	40	m	w	OH	Del Norte	Crescent	71	463
Bona	52	m	w	FRAN	San Francisco	San Francisco P O	80	483
David	59	m	w	SCOT	Shasta	French Gulch P O	89	466
FERRIGAN								
Anne	61	f	w	IREL	San Francisco	San Francisco P O	83	271
FERRILL								
Thomas	36	m	w	KY	Stanislaus	Empire Twp	92	34
FERRIN								
Lawrence	36	m	w	IREL	Nevada	Washington Twp	75	339
Michael	28	m	w	SCOT	Humboldt	Eureka Twp	72	280
FERRINGTON								
George	20	m	w	MI	Santa Clara	2-Wd San Jose	88	305
FERRIS								
Abe	65	m	w	IL	San Joaquin	3-Wd Stockton	86	245
Almus	38	m	w	MI	Klamath	Orleans Twp	73	379
Andrew	34	m	w	IREL	Mono	Bridgeport P O	74	285
B F	65	m	w	NY	Alameda	Oakland	68	225
Camilla	21	f	w	FRAN	San Francisco	6-Wd San Francisco	81	78
Catharine	40	f	w	IREL	San Francisco	San Francisco P O	85	857
D C	38	m	w	NY	San Francisco	8-Wd San Francisco	82	346
David	42	m	w	IREL	San Francisco	6-Wd San Francisco	81	41
David	32	m	w	SCOT	Solano	Suisun Twp	90	97
Edgar	51	m	w	NY	Contra Costa	Martinez P O	71	436
Edwin	28	m	w	IL	Plumas	Quartz Twp	77	41
George	35	m	w	ITAL	San Francisco	3-Wd San Francisco	79	289
Grigoria	30	m	w	CHIL	Amador	Drytown P O	69	416
J H	41	m	w	NY	Amador	Ione City P O	69	352
J P	64	m	w	OH	Calaveras	Copperopolis P O	70	251
J R	40	m	w	VA	Alameda	Alameda	68	14
James	23	m	w	ENGL	Nevada	Grass Valley Twp	75	166
Jas	43	m	w	OH	Butte	Chico Twp	70	54
Jennie	29	f	w	IL	Placer	Auburn P O	76	383
John	35	m	w	ENGL	San Francisco	5-Wd San Francisco	81	28
John	32	m	w	MI	Placer	Roseville P O	76	351
John	27	m	w	MO	Amador	Volcano P O	69	385

© 2001 by Heritage Quest. All rights reserved.

Name	Age	S	R	B-PL	County	Locale	Roll	Pg
John	22	m	w	CANA	Nevada	Grass Valley Twp	75	220
John	21	m	w	NY	San Francisco	San Francisco P O	80	409
John	21	m	w	IREL	Santa Clara	Santa Clara Twp	88	162
Joseph	54	m	w	OH	Placer	Clipper Gap P O	76	376
Joseph	40	m	w	SCOT	Santa Clara	Santa Clara Twp	88	138
Joseph	23	m	w	IREL	San Francisco	11-Wd San Francisc	84	567
Joseph	21	m	w	PORT	Alameda	Eden Twp	68	61
Joseph	20	m	w	NY	San Francisco	San Francisco P O	83	206
Kate	25	f	w	IREL	San Francisco	San Francisco P O	83	99
Maria	40	f	w	IREL	San Francisco	San Francisco P O	83	144
Martha	17	f	w	NY	San Francisco	San Francisco P O	85	803
Mary	17	f	w	NY	San Francisco	7-Wd San Francisco	81	181
Micheal	31	m	w	IREL	San Francisco	7-Wd San Francisco	81	189
Nellie	35	f	w	IREL	San Francisco	8-Wd San Francisco	82	360
Nicholas	42	m	w	ITAL	Solano	Vallejo	90	213
P D	44	m	w	NH	San Joaquin	Douglas Twp	86	32
R D	33	m	w	NY	Sacramento	1-Wd Sacramento	77	183
S	70	m	w	CHIL	Amador	Drytown P O	69	416
S A	50	m	w	CT	San Francisco	3-Wd San Francisco	79	314
Thomas	40	m	w	IREL	San Francisco	7-Wd San Francisco	81	221
William	36	m	w	IREL	Solano	Silveyville Twp	90	77
William	23	m	w	LA	Mariposa	Mariposa P O	74	137
FERRISEE								
Cornelius	35	m	w	IREL	San Francisco	8-Wd San Francisco	82	486
FERRITT								
J W	50	m	w	NY	San Francisco	San Francisco P O	83	266
FERRO								
Domingo	45	m	w	ITAL	Santa Clara	2-Wd San Jose	88	315
FERROGIARRO								
Antonio	34	m	w	ITAL	San Francisco	11-Wd San Francisc	84	642
FERROR								
Manuel	38	m	w	CA	Napa	Napa	75	50
FERRUIT								
Jean	29	m	w	FRAN	Santa Barbara	Las Cruces P O	87	515
FERRY								
Abraham	60	m	w	ENGL	Santa Clara	Santa Clara Twp	88	144
Ana	50	f	w	IREL	Sacramento	3-Wd Sacramento	77	310
Antone	30	m	w	PORT	Sacramento	Granite Twp	77	149
Edward	33	m	w	IREL	Santa Clara	San Jose Twp	88	210
Edwd	24	m	w	IREL	San Francisco	1-Wd San Francisco	79	75
Francis	34	m	w	IL	Amador	Volcano P O	69	375
Frank	26	m	w	PORT	Alameda	Washington Twp	68	272
G F	36	m	w	NY	Humboldt	Eureka Twp	72	281
Grace	23	f	w	IREL	San Francisco	8-Wd San Francisco	82	494
Hugh	24	m	w	IREL	San Francisco	San Francisco P O	83	8
James	56	m	w	NORW	San Francisco	7-Wd San Francisco	81	276
Jerry	50	m	w	OH	Butte	Chico Twp	70	56
John	33	m	w	IREL	Marin	San Rafael Twp	74	26
Julett	50	m	w	FRAN	Alameda	Washington Twp	68	291
Margaret	21	f	w	IREL	San Francisco	San Francisco P O	83	178
Patrick	33	m	w	IREL	Nevada	Bridgeport Twp	75	117
FERSAULT								
Pedro	29	m	w	FRAN	Los Angeles	Los Angeles Twp	73	497
FERSON								
Geo L	25	m	w	MA	Sacramento	Sutter Twp	77	384
John A	24	m	w	ME	Marin	Tomales Twp	74	76
FERSTER								
Louisa	45	f	w	SWIT	San Francisco	8-Wd San Francisco	82	333
FERTAZ								
Joseph	30	m	w	AZOR	Marin	San Rafael Twp	74	32
FERTIG								
Valentine	43	m	w	OH	Siskiyou	Yreka	89	654
FERTON								
Wm	34	m	w	IL	Butte	Hamilton Twp	70	66
FERUGGIARE								
Gio Calto	18	m	w	ITAL	San Francisco	San Francisco P O	85	842
FERURA								
Gurine	18	m	w	ITAL	Yuba	Long Bar Twp	93	566
FESANFELD								
David	66	m	w	NY	Butte	Chico Twp	70	43
FESCHER								
Jacob	42	m	w	SWIT	Yuba	Long Bar Twp	93	561
FESLAR								
Frederick	18	m	w	BADE	San Francisco	8-Wd San Francisco	82	469
FESLER								
Isaac	51	m	w	KY	Santa Barbara	Santa Maria P O	87	510
FESS								
Paris	62	m	w	FRAN	Alameda	Oakland	68	168
FESSEL								
Rudolph	48	m	w	PRUS	Amador	Volcano P O	69	374
FESSENDEN								
Benjamin	35	m	w	RI	Santa Clara	Redwood Twp	88	131
Charles	51	m	w	MA	Contra Costa	Martinez P O	71	397
Louis	25	m	w	MA	San Francisco	7-Wd San Francisco	81	254
Mary C	46	f	w	VT	San Francisco	San Francisco P O	83	109
FESSLER								
Benjamin	33	m	w	PA	Placer	Lincoln P O	76	492
J	37	m	w	PA	Sierra	Alleghany & Forest	89	534
FESTER								
Silas W	21	m	w	CA	Santa Barbara	Arroyo Grande P O	87	508
FESTOE								
Dedrick	30	m	w	HANO	Alameda	Eden Twp	68	86
FESTRAIL								
Walter	25	m	w	ENGL	Fresno	Millerton P O	72	165
FESTUS								
Edwd	45	m	w	BAVA	Butte	Ophir Twp	70	99

Name	Age	S	R	B-PL	County	Locale	Roll	Pg
FET								
Ah	30	m	c	CHIN	San Francisco	San Francisco P O	80	498
FETCHER								
Chas	39	m	w	SALT	Siskiyou	Scott Rvr Twp	89	603
FETERO								
Metero	30	m	w	MEXI	Tulare	Visalia	92	298
FETHERBORG								
Peter	40	m	w	SWIT	Placer	Lincoln P O	76	482
FETHERSTON								
Michael	24	m	w	IREL	Sacramento	4-Wd Sacramento	77	320
FETICH								
Alis	20	m	w	AUST	San Francisco	3-Wd San Francisco	79	299
FETT								
Chas	37	m	w	PRUS	Placer	Bath P O	76	426
FETTEE								
Julius F	40	m	w	AL	Butte	Chico Twp	70	48
FETTER								
Benj	46	m	w	PA	Sonoma	Santa Rosa	91	428
Henry	34	m	w	PRUS	San Francisco	San Francisco P O	80	460
Paul	35	m	w	IN	Butte	Oregon Twp	70	129
FETTERLEY								
Amos	22	m	w	CANA	Sacramento	3-Wd Sacramento	77	257
Phillip	28	m	w	CANA	Sacramento	3-Wd Sacramento	77	308
FETTERLY								
Isah	22	m	w	CANA	Sacramento	Sutter Twp	77	385
FETTILL								
Chas	17	m	w	CA	El Dorado	Lake Valley Twp	72	65
FETTON								
Edward	23	m	w	ENGL	San Francisco	7-Wd San Francisco	81	226
Francis A	22	m	w	MA	Mendocino	Point Arena Twp	74	214
FETTULY								
Phillip	28	m	w	CANA	Yolo	Cache Crk Twp	93	423
FETTY								
Newton	32	m	w	WV	Mendocino	Round Valley Twp	74	218
FETZ								
Albert	40	m	w	OH	Butte	Oregon Twp	70	122
Joseph	24	m	w	PRUS	San Francisco	7-Wd San Francisco	81	226
FEUGE								
John	46	m	w	IREL	San Bernardino	San Bernardino Twp	78	433
FEUNER								
Anna	35	f	w	IREL	San Francisco	San Francisco P O	80	426
FEUNG								
Ah	28	m	c	CHIN	Stanislaus	Branch Twp	92	3
FEURE								
Edward	25	m	w	FRAN	San Francisco	6-Wd San Francisco	81	82
FEUSS								
Henry	30	m	w	BAVA	San Francisco	11-Wd San Francisc	84	597
Otto	33	m	w	BAVA	San Francisco	11-Wd San Francisc	84	597
FEVER								
Alfred	36	m	w	NY	San Francisco	5-Wd San Francisco	81	31
FEW								
Ah	40	m	c	CHIN	El Dorado	Cosumnes Twp	72	20
Ah	32	m	c	CHIN	Alameda	Oakland	68	202
Ah	28	m	c	CHIN	San Francisco	San Francisco P O	80	506
Ah	28	m	c	CHIN	Placer	Auburn P O	76	381
Ah	20	f	c	CHIN	Santa Clara	1-Wd San Jose	88	273
Gee	31	m	c	CHIN	Plumas	Mineral Twp	77	24
William A	59	m	w	GA	Amador	Jackson P O	69	338
FEWELL								
Jas	40	m	w	MO	Sonoma	Cloverdale Twp	91	270
FEWER								
James	26	m	w	ME	Trinity	Lewiston Pct	92	211
FEWINGS								
Sarah	37	f	w	AUST	Placer	Auburn P O	76	379
FEWLING								
H W	59	m	w	CANA	Humboldt	Mattole Twp	72	285
FEWY								
Ah	24	m	c	CHIN	San Francisco	1-Wd San Francisco	79	61
FEY								
Ah	21	m	c	CHIN	Placer	Colfax P O	76	386
Martin	45	m	w	GERM	Nevada	Bloomfield Twp	75	92
Mary	28	f	w	ENGL	San Francisco	3-Wd San Francisco	79	325
FEYGE								
Albert	47	m	w	BREM	San Francisco	11-Wd San Francisc	84	605
FEYHL								
Augustus	33	m	w	PRUS	Sacramento	2-Wd Sacramento	77	219
FEYN								
Ah	32	m	c	CHIN	Merced	Snelling P O	74	265
FEYNANI								
John	40	m	w	SWIT	Plumas	Seneca Twp	77	49
FEZACKLEY								
Jos	33	m	w	ENGL	San Francisco	San Francisco P O	83	69
FFLEMING								
Henry C	28	m	w	TN	Siskiyou	Cottonwood Twp	89	591
FHER								
William	24	m	w	IREL	Solano	Tremont Twp	90	29
FHRENKRUG								
William	32	m	w	PRUS	San Francisco	San Francisco P O	83	315
FI								
Ah	52	m	c	CHIN	El Dorado	Mud Springs Twp	72	91
Ah	51	m	c	CHIN	Tuolumne	Chinese Camp P O	93	379
Ah	50	m	c	CHIN	Tuolumne	Chinese Camp P O	93	371
Ah	50	f	c	CHIN	Placer	Blue Canyon P O	76	418
Ah	50	m	c	CHIN	Calaveras	San Andreas P O	70	190
Ah	43	m	c	CHIN	Tuolumne	Big Oak Flat P O	93	397
Ah	43	m	c	CHIN	Tuolumne	Big Oak Flat P O	93	399
Ah	40	m	c	CHIN	Tuolumne	Big Oak Flat P O	93	393

© 2001 by Heritage Quest. All rights reserved.

Name	Age	S	R	B-PL	County	Locale	Roll	Pg
						Series M593		
Ah	36	m	c	CHIN	Tuolumne	Chinese Camp P O	93	369
Ah	32	m	c	CHIN	Fresno	Millerton P O	72	200
Ah	29	m	c	CHIN	El Dorado	Mountain Twp	72	68
Ah	28	m	c	CHIN	Fresno	Millerton P O	72	199
Ah	25	m	c	CHIN	Tuolumne	Chinese Camp P O	93	388
Ah	24	m	c	CHIN	Tuolumne	Chinese Camp P O	93	382
Ah	24	m	c	CHIN	Yolo	Putah Twp	93	510
Ah	22	m	c	CHIN	San Francisco	11-Wd San Francisc	84	535
Ah	19	m	c	CHIN	Tuolumne	Big Oak Flat P O	93	404
Ah	19	m	c	CHIN	Tuolumne	Chinese Camp P O	93	382
Ah	18	m	c	CHIN	Tuolumne	Chinese Camp P O	93	383
Ah	16	f	c	CHIN	Tuolumne	Chinese Camp P O	93	388
Ah	16	m	c	CHIN	Sacramento	2-Wd Sacramento	77	212
Cam	48	m	c	CHIN	El Dorado	Cosumnes Twp	72	18
Chow	65	m	c	CHIN	Santa Clara	1-Wd San Jose	88	272
Loe	21	m	c	CHIN	Solano	Rio Vista Twp	90	64
Lun	35	m	c	CHIN	Fresno	Millerton P O	72	202
Yon	31	m	c	CHIN	Yuba	Marysville	93	632
FIA								
Long	18	m	c	CHIN	San Mateo	Schoolhouse Statio	87	336
FIADO								
Jose	21	m	w	MEXI	San Diego	Milquaty Dist	78	476
FIALLA								
Joseph	34	m	w	SWIT	Marin	San Rafael Twp	74	26
FIALLSE								
Manuel	30	m	w	AZOR	Monterey	Monterey	74	364
FIAME								
Thomas	39	m	w	IREL	San Francisco	San Francisco P O	83	155
FIARDO								
Jacomo	22	m	w	SWIT	Marin	Nicasio Twp	74	14
FIBER								
William	17	m	w	BADE	San Francisco	8-Wd San Francisco	82	436
FIBISH								
Rosana	25	f	w	PRUS	San Francisco	San Francisco P O	83	384
FICHTER								
Mary	20	f	w	BADE	San Francisco	6-Wd San Francisco	81	101
FICK								
Hattie	14	f	w	BREM	San Joaquin	2-Wd Stockton	86	207
Henry	38	m	w	PRUS	San Francisco	San Francisco P O	85	757
Louis	17	m	w	PRUS	Marin	Sausalito Twp	74	72
FICKAS								
Levi	47	m	w	IN	Santa Barbara	San Buenaventura P	87	425
FICKEN								
Christopher	24	m	w	NY	San Francisco	2-Wd San Francisco	79	246
Henry	40	m	w	HANO	Siskiyou	Hamburg Twp	89	596
Henry	21	m	w	BREM	San Francisco	San Francisco P O	83	171
John	34	m	w	HANO	San Francisco	3-Wd San Francisco	79	325
Louis	26	m	w	NY	San Francisco	8-Wd San Francisco	82	493
FICKERSON								
Charles	38	m	w	PRUS	Sacramento	2-Wd Sacramento	77	242
James	38	m	w	PRUS	Solano	Suisun Twp	90	114
FICKERT								
Frederick	39	m	w	PRUS	Kern	Tehachapi P O	73	355
Lewis	48	m	w	PRUS	Kern	Tehachapi P O	73	354
FICKET								
C W	43	m	w	BADE	Tehama	Red Bluff	92	179
John	41	m	w	ME	San Francisco	8-Wd San Francisco	82	486
Martha	66	f	w	PRUS	Tehama	Red Bluff	92	179
FICKETT								
Albus	45	m	w	ME	San Francisco	11-Wd San Francisc	84	705
C K	30	m	w	ME	Alameda	Oakland	68	158
FICKIES								
John	14	m	w	OH	San Francisco	2-Wd San Francisco	79	269
FICKLER								
J P	36	m	w	KY	Tehama	Tehama Twp	92	191
FICKLIN								
Emma	29	f	w	GA	San Francisco	7-Wd San Francisco	81	284
John	24	m	w	KY	San Francisco	11-Wd San Francisc	84	439
FICKS								
Leroy	50	m	w	TN	Trinity	Canyon City Pct	92	202
FICKTON								
George	50	m	w	BAVA	Trinity	Douglas	92	237
FICTO								
Peter	37	m	w	CANA	Trinity	Junction City Pct	92	210
FIDDER								
Johanna	33	f	w	MA	San Francisco	5-Wd San Francisco	81	26
FIDDICK								
James	39	m	w	ENGL	Nevada	Grass Valley Twp	75	223
FIDDLER								
Hercules	68	m	w	ME	Shasta	Horsetown P O	89	504
Nathan L	45	m	w	OH	Calaveras	Copperopolis P O	70	261
William K	55	m	w	OH	Placer	Gold Run Twp	76	396
FIDDYMENT								
Walter F	19	m	w	IL	Placer	Rocklin P O	76	462
FIDEL								
Roger	30	m	w	PRUS	San Francisco	2-Wd San Francisco	79	233
FIDELLO								
Joseph	20	m	w	SWIT	Marin	Point Reyes Twp	74	23
FIDESTER								
Samuel	38	m	w	AR	Tulare	Farmersville Twp	92	247
FIE								
Ah	65	m	c	CHIN	Mariposa	Mariposa P O	74	102
Ah	48	m	c	CHIN	Amador	Jackson P O	69	335
Ah	37	m	c	CHIN	San Joaquin	1-Wd Stockton	86	156
Ah	34	m	c	CHIN	San Joaquin	1-Wd Stockton	86	156
Ah	31	m	c	CHIN	San Francisco	6-Wd San Francisco	81	50
Ah	29	m	c	CHIN	Amador	Fiddletown P O	69	426
Ah	27	m	c	CHIN	San Joaquin	1-Wd Stockton	86	144
Ah	26	m	c	CHIN	San Joaquin	1-Wd Stockton	86	156
Ah	25	m	c	CHIN	Sacramento	Franklin Twp	77	116
Ah	17	m	c	CHIN	San Francisco	3-Wd San Francisco	79	309
Ah	14	m	c	CHIN	San Francisco	3-Wd San Francisco	79	306
Ah Mi	39	m	c	CHIN	Amador	Fiddletown P O	69	426
How	30	f	c	CHIN	Amador	Fiddletown P O	69	427
James	28	m	w	IREL	San Francisco	7-Wd San Francisco	81	181
Kee	29	m	c	CHIN	Amador	Jackson P O	69	338
Kie	24	m	c	CHIN	Solano	Vacaville Twp	90	130
Loe	21	m	c	CHIN	Alameda	Washington Twp	68	272
Oh	16	m	c	CHIN	Alameda	San Leandro	68	98
FIEBRA								
August	25	m	w	FRAN	Sacramento	4-Wd Sacramento	77	372
FIEGE								
Bernard	46	m	w	SARD	Marin	San Rafael Twp	74	45
FIELD								
Alfred H	40	m	w	ME	Mendocino	Point Arena Twp	74	204
Anne	63	f	w	ENGL	San Francisco	San Francisco P O	83	281
Annie	20	f	w	ENGL	Siskiyou	Butte Twp	89	588
Ansel L	34	m	w	ME	Mendocino	Point Arena Twp	74	204
Ben F	30	m	w	ME	Santa Cruz	Santa Cruz Twp	89	390
Charles	38	m	w	NY	San Francisco	San Francisco P O	83	86
Charles	25	m	w	IREL	San Francisco	San Francisco P O	83	169
Charles C	22	m	w	VT	Siskiyou	Butte Twp	89	586
Charles J	28	m	w	PA	Santa Clara	Fremont Twp	88	54
Chas	42	m	w	NY	San Francisco	San Francisco P O	83	46
Chas	28	m	w	IREL	San Francisco	7-Wd San Francisco	81	257
Chas	25	m	w	IREL	San Joaquin	Dent Twp	86	17
Chauncy	36	m	w	CT	Yolo	Buckeye Twp	93	416
Daniel M	43	m	w	ME	Mariposa	Maxwell Crk P O	74	143
E	48	m	w	RI	Sierra	Downieville Twp	89	516
E M	49	m	w	NY	Tuolumne	Columbia P O	93	349
Edward	40	m	w	IREL	San Joaquin	Dent Twp	86	20
Edwin Augustus	34	m	w	MA	Plumas	Washington Twp	77	58
Elias	41	m	w	ME	Calaveras	San Andreas P O	70	195
Ellen	25	f	w	IREL	San Francisco	San Francisco P O	83	240
Eugene	33	m	w	IREL	San Francisco	San Francisco P O	85	870
Fred	46	m	w	UNKN	San Joaquin	2-Wd Stockton	86	166
George	25	m	w	ENGL	San Mateo	Schoolhouse Statio	87	342
George E	53	m	w	VT	Los Angeles	Los Angeles	73	542
H E	32	m	w	HANO	San Francisco	7-Wd San Francisco	81	224
Hamlin	22	m	w	NY	San Francisco	8-Wd San Francisco	82	337
Hampton	53	m	w	MA	San Francisco	San Francisco P O	83	353
Happalonia	63	f	w	VT	Siskiyou	Butte Twp	89	586
James	33	m	w	CANA	Sonoma	Healdsburg & Mendo	91	278
James	30	m	w	DENM	Sacramento	Franklin Twp	77	115
Jasper	39	m	w	AL	Yuba	North East Twp	93	644
Jeremiah	48	m	w	IREL	San Francisco	11-Wd San Francisc	84	701
John	45	m	w	CANA	San Joaquin	3-Wd Stockton	86	223
John	39	m	w	KY	Sonoma	Cloverdale Twp	91	271
John W	78	m	w	PA	Santa Clara	Fremont Twp	88	53
Joseph	42	m	w	ENGL	Amador	Ione City P O	69	361
Joseph	38	m	w	NY	Humboldt	Arcata Twp	72	225
Joseph	26	m	w	PRUS	San Francisco	San Francisco P O	83	192
Joseph S	48	m	w	ME	Santa Cruz	Santa Cruz Twp	89	400
Josephine	4	f	w	WI	Yolo	Buckeye Twp	93	416
Matilda A	33	f	w	IN	Los Angeles	Santa Ana Twp	73	608
Mattie	32	f	w	NY	San Francisco	San Francisco P O	80	425
Merril	43	m	w	ME	Sacramento	Franklin Twp	77	108
Nouse Wm D	37	m	w	CANA	Yuba	North East Twp	93	644
Obediah	60	m	w	KY	Plumas	Seneca Twp	77	50
Olive B	10	f	w	MO	Sonoma	Cloverdale Twp	91	268
Patrick	33	m	w	IREL	Nevada	Grass Valley Twp	75	210
Peter C	37	m	w	ME	Mendocino	Point Arena Twp	74	204
Pleasant	64	m	w	KY	Placer	Clipper Gap P O	76	376
Richard	38	m	w	ENGL	Santa Cruz	Santa Cruz	89	427
Richard	33	m	w	VA	Fresno	Millerton P O	72	193
Samson	36	m	w	ME	Stanislaus	Branch Twp	92	6
Silas	60	m	w	NY	San Francisco	San Francisco P O	83	206
Stephen	23	m	w	MO	Sonoma	Washington Twp	91	467
Stover W	50	m	w	MA	Santa Cruz	Santa Cruz	89	404
Thomas	30	m	w	OH	Santa Clara	1-Wd San Jose	88	261
Thomas	24	m	w	NY	Santa Clara	Gilroy Twp	88	71
Thos	29	m	w	ENGL	Solano	Vallejo	90	194
Thos A	53	m	w	ME	Sonoma	Healdsburg & Mendo	91	281
Timothy	38	m	w	IREL	Nevada	Grass Valley Twp	75	212
W G	47	m	w	CANA	Sierra	Alleghany & Forest	89	534
Walter O	1	m	w	MO	Los Angeles	Santa Ana Twp	73	608
William	48	m	w	KY	Del Norte	Happy Camp Twp	71	471
William	33	m	w	IREL	Alameda	Brooklyn Twp	68	43
William A	36	m	w	NY	Santa Clara	Fremont Twp	88	53
Wm	43	m	w	NJ	Marin	San Rafael Twp	74	43
Zacariah	37	m	w	ME	Alpine	Woodfords P O	69	315
FIELDDEN								
Abraham	50	m	w	NJ	Del Norte	Happy Camp Twp	71	471
FIELDEN								
F	35	m	w	ENGL	San Francisco	San Francisco P O	85	796
M	26	m	w	IREL	San Joaquin	1-Wd Stockton	86	130
FIELDER								
Wm R	42	m	w	GA	Mono	Bridgeport P O	74	285
FIELDING								
Abraham	48	m	w	ENGL	San Francisco	8-Wd San Francisco	82	487
Frank	21	m	w	OH	Sutter	Yuba Twp	92	151
James	45	m	w	NY	San Francisco	San Francisco P O	80	540
Jas	41	m	w	ENGL	Shasta	French Gulch P O	89	467
John	45	m	w	SCOT	Alameda	San Leandro	68	93

© 2001 by Heritage Quest. All rights reserved.

California 1870 Census

Series M593

Name	Age	S	R	B-PL	County	Locale	Roll	Pg
Michl	26	m	w	IREL	San Francisco	1-Wd San Francisco	79	134
Rufus	14	m	w	CA	Kern	Tehachapi P O	73	353
Saml M	36	m	w	PA	San Francisco	San Francisco P O	83	292
Thomas	34	m	w	HOLL	Calaveras	San Andreas P O	70	186
FIELDMAN								
Mathew	30	m	w	PRUS	Contra Costa	Martinez P O	71	437
FIELDS								
Andrew	40	m	w	MA	Calaveras	San Andreas P O	70	206
Bridget	43	f	w	IREL	Sacramento	Brighton Twp	77	80
C	20	f	w	NC	Alameda	Oakland	68	162
Caroline	24	f	w	MA	San Francisco	6-Wd San Francisco	81	119
Charles	22	m	w	MA	Colusa	Colusa Twp	71	282
Chas	22	m	w	IL	Santa Clara	Almaden Twp	88	16
Chas B	28	m	w	VA	Sutter	Yuba Twp	92	146
Duvit	42	m	w	MO	Stanislaus	Buena Vista Twp	92	13
Edmond	40	m	w	IL	Colusa	Monroe Twp	71	315
Edward	23	m	w	IREL	San Francisco	San Francisco P O	85	852
Ellen	16	f	w	NY	Sonoma	Bodega Twp	91	255
Frank	41	m	w	SCOT	Alameda	Brooklyn Twp	68	44
George	20	m	w	IREL	San Francisco	7-Wd San Francisco	81	192
Green R	26	m	w	IL	El Dorado	Diamond Springs Tw	72	24
Isabella	9	f	w	CA	Humboldt	Pacific Twp	72	297
James	37	m	w	NY	Yuba	Marysville	93	633
James	36	m	w	NY	Placer	Colfax P O	76	388
James	30	m	w	IREL	Sonoma	Analy Twp	91	223
James	30	m	w	SCOT	San Francisco	San Francisco P O	83	206
James	20	m	w	NY	Sutter	Butte Twp	92	90
Jeremiah	58	m	w	NC	El Dorado	Diamond Springs Tw	72	24
John	66	m	w	IREL	Amador	Amador City P O	69	392
John	40	m	w	NY	San Francisco	San Francisco P O	83	339
John	35	m	w	IREL	Monterey	Castroville Twp	74	329
Joseph N	26	m	w	MO	Inyo	Cerro Gordo Twp	73	321
Lewis	28	m	w	ME	San Francisco	7-Wd San Francisco	81	235
Richard	45	m	w	NORW	Placer	Dutch Flat P O	76	414
Samuel	70	m	w	IREL	Sonoma	Analy Twp	91	223
Thos W	50	m	w	NY	Butte	Concow Twp	70	9
Timothy	49	m	i	GA	Siskiyou	Scott Valley Twp	89	618
Waterman	40	m	w	NY	Humboldt	Bucksport Twp	72	241
William	44	m	w	OH	Sutter	Vernon Twp	92	130
Wm	36	m	w	NY	San Francisco	7-Wd San Francisco	81	247
Wm H	49	m	w	PA	Tuolumne	Chinese Camp P O	93	381
Wm Jasper	36	m	w	TN	Shasta	Millville P O	89	489
FIELDSTEAD								
Christian	55	m	w	NORW	Santa Clara	San Jose Twp	88	222
FIELITZ								
Annie	68	f	w	PRUS	San Francisco	San Francisco P O	83	212
FIENE								
August	28	m	w	HANO	San Francisco	2-Wd San Francisco	79	225
FIENNE								
Henry	42	m	w	PRUS	Nevada	Rough & Ready Twp	75	331
Margaret	11	f	w	NY	Nevada	Rough & Ready Twp	75	331
FIEQUA								
John W	44	m	w	KY	Mariposa	Maxwell Crk P O	74	141
FIERANO								
Peter	19	m	w	SWIT	Marin	Point Reyes Twp	74	22
FIERKING								
Eliza	22	f	w	PRUS	San Francisco	8-Wd San Francisco	82	481
FIERNEY								
Peter	29	m	w	IREL	Solano	Benicia	90	15
FIERNO								
Jean	28	m	w	ITAL	San Francisco	San Francisco P O	80	469
William	36	m	w	ITAL	San Francisco	San Francisco P O	80	469
FIERO								
Leandro	32	m	w	MEXI	Marin	San Rafael Twp	74	36
Phillippe	41	m	w	CHIL	San Francisco	2-Wd San Francisco	79	180
FIEROT								
Chas	27	m	w	SWIT	San Francisco	8-Wd San Francisco	82	375
FIERRO								
Felipe	42	m	w	CHIL	San Francisco	1-Wd San Francisco	79	109
Juan	35	m	w	CHIL	Amador	Fiddletown P O	69	441
Julia	38	f	w	MEXI	Mariposa	Mariposa P O	74	94
FIES								
Chas John	29	m	w	LUXE	San Francisco	San Francisco P O	83	72
FIESE								
George J	24	m	w	GERM	Santa Cruz	Soquel Twp	89	451
FIEST								
Fannie	28	f	w	HDAR	Santa Clara	1-Wd San Jose	88	225
Felix	43	m	w	HDAR	Santa Clara	2-Wd San Jose	88	336
Lorenzo	50	m	w	BADE	Butte	Concow Twp	70	7
FIESTER								
Felix	43	m	w	OH	Santa Cruz	Santa Cruz	89	421
FIETH								
Thomas	48	m	w	CANA	Klamath	Trinidad Twp	73	390
FIETTE								
Frederick	26	m	w	CANA	Sonoma	Bodega Twp	91	260
FIFE								
Chas	32	m	m	KY	Shasta	Shasta P O	89	463
N	30	m	w	ME	San Francisco	San Francisco P O	83	10
Nelson	26	m	w	ME	San Francisco	San Francisco P O	83	417
FIFELY								
Frederick	33	m	w	PRUS	Monterey	San Juan Twp	74	390
FIFER								
Frederick	28	m	w	HANO	Nevada	Grass Valley Twp	75	143
William	18	m	w	PRUS	San Francisco	8-Wd San Francisco	82	434
FIFFER								
Theo	17	f	w	CA	Sacramento	3-Wd Sacramento	77	317
FIFFIELD								
A	22	m	w	ME	San Joaquin	Castoria Twp	86	8
Daniel	36	m	w	MA	Calaveras	San Andreas P O	70	213
FIFIELD								
A C	41	m	w	ME	San Joaquin	Douglas Twp	86	35
W E	43	m	w	ME	San Joaquin	Douglas Twp	86	33
Winthop J	38	m	w	NH	San Mateo	San Mateo P O	87	349
Wm H	27	m	w	MI	San Francisco	2-Wd San Francisco	79	265
FIFO								
Robert	27	m	w	SCOT	San Joaquin	1-Wd Stockton	86	124
FIG								
Ah	40	m	c	CHIN	San Francisco	San Francisco P O	80	522
Ah	38	m	c	CHIN	San Francisco	San Francisco P O	80	509
Ah	31	m	c	CHIN	San Francisco	San Francisco P O	80	455
Ah	22	m	c	CHIN	San Francisco	San Francisco P O	80	505
FIGADON								
Juan J	35	m	w	MEXI	San Diego	San Pasqual	78	519
FIGADOR								
Patricio	36	m	w	MEXI	San Luis Obispo	Arroyo Grande Twp	87	273
FIGARA								
Jesus	24	m	w	MEXI	San Joaquin	3-Wd Stockton	86	231
FIGARD								
Jose	52	m	w	MEXI	Stanislaus	Empire Twp	92	46
Louis	49	m	w	VA	San Francisco	2-Wd San Francisco	79	263
FIGARI								
Antonio	48	m	w	ITAL	San Francisco	11-Wd San Francisc	84	591
FIGARO								
Anton	55	m	w	ITAL	Calaveras	Copperopolis P O	70	233
Emanuel	45	m	w	CHIL	Fresno	Millerton P O	72	153
Frances	35	f	w	MEXI	San Francisco	2-Wd San Francisco	79	182
Jose	50	m	w	MEXI	Kern	Bakersfield P O	73	359
Martin	51	m	w	MEXI	Butte	Concow Twp	70	6
FIGAROA								
Antonio	27	m	w	MEXI	Kern	Bakersfield P O	73	362
Francisco	30	m	w	MEXI	Los Angeles	Los Angeles Twp	73	475
Jesus	42	m	w	MEXI	Fresno	Millerton P O	72	161
Jesus	30	m	w	MEXI	Los Angeles	Los Angeles	73	554
Ramon	60	m	w	MEXI	Los Angeles	Los Angeles Twp	73	468
Ynes	10	f	w	CA	Los Angeles	Los Angeles Twp	73	486
FIGARRA								
Giovanni	36	m	w	ITAL	San Francisco	11-Wd San Francisc	84	642
FIGEL								
Joseph	38	m	w	BOHE	San Francisco	11-Wd San Francisc	84	437
Louis	30	m	w	PRUS	San Francisco	San Francisco P O	80	461
Samuel	48	m	w	BOHE	San Francisco	8-Wd San Francisco	82	443
FIGER								
Benedict	43	m	w	PRUS	San Francisco	San Francisco P O	80	424
FIGERS								
Jesus	35	m	w	MEXI	Calaveras	San Andreas P O	70	175
FIGEST								
Jean	34	m	w	FRAN	San Francisco	San Francisco P O	80	468
FIGG								
Edward P	51	m	w	KY	Sacramento	2-Wd Sacramento	77	248
FIGHT								
Maria	25	f	w	MA	Alameda	Eden Twp	68	88
FIGIERO								
Matilda	35	f	w	ITAL	San Francisco	6-Wd San Francisco	81	101
FIGINER								
Silas	36	m	w	PRUS	San Francisco	San Francisco P O	83	214
FIGITT								
C C	42	m	w	MO	San Joaquin	Liberty Twp	86	82
FIGONE								
Augustus	24	m	w	ITAL	Amador	Amador City P O	69	390
FIGUERIA								
Jose	47	m	w	CHIL	Santa Barbara	San Buenaventura P	87	433
FIGUEROA								
Cuietan	30	m	w	CA	Santa Barbara	San Buenaventura P	87	434
Cyatana	36	m	w	CA	Santa Barbara	Santa Barbara P O	87	500
Jose	33	m	w	CHIL	Mariposa	Mariposa P O	74	110
Jose Maria	55	m	w	MEXI	Santa Clara	Milpitas Twp	88	113
Joseph	35	f	w	CA	Los Angeles	San Jose Twp	73	619
FIGUERRA								
Augustus	24	m	w	CA	Marin	San Rafael Twp	74	45
Matildo	20	m	w	MEXI	Los Angeles	El Monte Twp	73	460
Ramon	68	m	w	MEXI	Los Angeles	San Jose Twp	73	618
FIGUIERE								
Joseph	47	m	w	FRAN	Nevada	Nevada Twp	75	272
FII								
Ah	20	m	c	CHIN	San Francisco	San Francisco P O	80	499
Ah	19	f	c	CHIN	San Francisco	San Francisco P O	80	493
FIK								
Ah	26	f	c	CHIN	San Francisco	San Francisco P O	80	526
Ah	16	m	c	CHIN	Sacramento	1-Wd Sacramento	77	199
FIKE								
Abram	51	m	w	PA	Solano	Vallejo	90	183
Cena	20	m	w	OH	Marin	Tomales Twp	74	86
Edwd	28	m	w	IA	Santa Clara	Gilroy Twp	88	106
Henrietta	27	f	w	PRUS	San Francisco	San Francisco P O	83	210
Nathan	50	m	w	IL	Sonoma	Healdsburg & Mendo	91	284
Spencer	9	m	w	CA	Sonoma	Mendocino Twp	91	289
FIKENBAUM								
Jo	37	m	w	BADE	San Francisco	San Francisco P O	85	788
FIL								
Ah	33	m	c	CHIN	Shasta	French Gulch P O	89	469
FILANCK								
Peter	52	m	w	FRAN	San Bernardino	San Bernardino Twp	78	438

© 2001 by Heritage Quest. All rights reserved.

Series M593

Name	Age	S	R	B-PL	County	Locale	Roll	Pg
FILAND								
Ann	25	f	w	IREL	San Joaquin	2-Wd Stockton	86	193
Patrick	30	m	w	IREL	Sacramento	2-Wd Sacramento	77	206
FILBERT								
Bridget	23	f	w	IREL	San Francisco	11-Wd San Francisc	84	428
Henery	28	m	w	BADE	San Francisco	7-Wd San Francisco	81	176
L	45	f	w	MEXI	San Joaquin	1-Wd Stockton	86	133
FILBRICK								
Johana	42	f	w	NH	Alameda	Oakland	68	182
FILBY								
James	52	m	w	OH	Sonoma	Santa Rosa	91	427
FILCHER								
Thos J	58	m	w	ENGL	Yuba	W Bear Rvr Twp	93	683
FILE								
Andrew C	37	m	w	NC	Tehama	Antelope Twp	92	154
Fredrick	30	m	w	GERM	Yolo	Grafton Twp	93	499
FILEBROWN								
Charles	40	m	w	MA	Placer	Bath P O	76	438
FILECRANO								
E	30	m	w	AZOR	Monterey	Monterey	74	364
FILER								
Mason	61	m	w	VT	Yuba	Linda Twp	93	554
FILEY								
Hannah	22	f	w	IREL	San Francisco	San Francisco P O	83	25
William	37	m	w	OH	San Luis Obispo	Morro Twp	87	282
FILING								
Elizabeth	49	f	w	FRNK	Sutter	Butte Twp	92	94
FILIPO								
Jose	36	m	w	CA	Marin	San Rafael Twp	74	47
FILIPPI								
Jose	23	m	w	AZOR	Marin	Sausalito Twp	74	68
FILIPPINI								
Rind	29	m	w	SWIT	El Dorado	Georgetown Twp	72	36
FILIPPONA								
Conrad	27	m	w	SWIT	San Luis Obispo	Santa Rosa Twp	87	329
FILIZ								
Jesus	50	m	w	MEXI	Kern	Tehachapi P O	73	356
Patrick	47	m	w	IREL	San Francisco	11-Wd San Francisc	84	542
FILKINS								
C E	43	m	w	NY	Yuba	Marysville	93	591
Joseph	27	m	w	NY	Santa Clara	San Jose Twp	88	222
FILL								
Ah	39	m	c	CHIN	San Francisco	San Francisco P O	80	501
FILLEBROWN								
James	52	m	w	MA	San Francisco	San Francisco P O	83	364
FILLENUNO								
M	40	m	w	CHIL	Amador	Jackson P O	69	343
FILLER								
Jacob	50	m	w	MD	Colusa	Spring Valley Twp	71	342
Martha E	15	f	w	IA	Sacramento	Franklin Twp.	77	106
FILLET								
Antone	29	m	w	FRAN	Alameda	Brooklyn Twp	68	52
FILLEY								
William	36	m	w	MA	San Francisco	San Francisco P O	83	268
FILLIAT								
Frank	48	m	w	FRAN	San Francisco	2-Wd San Francisco	79	231
FILLIER								
Crosby	55	m	w	SWIT	El Dorado	Mud Springs Twp	72	82
FILLIGE								
Montoy	37	m	w	FRAN	San Francisco	San Francisco P O	80	535
FILLIO								
Nelson	52	m	w	NY	San Francisco	8-Wd San Francisco	82	492
FILLIPET								
Peter	45	m	w	ITAL	Marin	San Rafael Twp	74	30
FILLIPI								
Joseph	24	m	w	PORT	Marin	Sausalito Twp	74	71
FILLIPINI								
Carlo	22	m	w	SWIT	Marin	Nicasio Twp	74	14
Dennis	20	m	w	SWIT	Marin	Nicasio Twp	74	14
Joan	26	m	w	SWIT	Marin	San Antonio Twp	74	63
Louis	34	m	w	SWIT	Marin	Nicasio Twp	74	14
FILLIPPI								
Joseph	40	m	w	AZOR	Marin	Sausalito Twp	74	70
Paul	23	m	w	SWIT	Marin	Bolinas Twp	74	2
FILLIS								
Elhait	39	m	w	CANA	Stanislaus	Emory Twp	92	26
P	29	f	w	CAME	San Joaquin	1-Wd Stockton	86	133
FILLISON								
Joseph	35	m	w	NY	San Mateo	Pescadero P O	87	409
FILLKUN								
John	47	m	w	NY	Contra Costa	Martinez P O	71	412
FILLMORE								
Arnest	36	m	w	PRUS	Alameda	Eden Twp	68	86
James	27	m	w	MD	Solano	Suisun Twp	90	111
Josephine	50	f	w	SWED	San Francisco	San Francisco P O	80	427
Sarah	30	f	w	WURT	San Francisco	San Francisco P O	80	351
Thomas	42	m	b	NY	San Francisco	San Francisco P O	80	475
Wm	38	m	w	IREL	Santa Clara	Almaden Twp	88	11
FILLY								
John	32	m	w	IREL	San Joaquin	Douglas Twp	86	41
FILMER								
David	27	m	w	ENGL	Amador	Jackson P O	69	333
John	84	m	w	ENGL	Amador	Jackson P O	69	333
Thomas	49	m	w	ENGL	Amador	Jackson P O	69	333
Wm	42	m	w	ENGL	San Francisco	San Francisco P O	85	844
FILMORE								
Albert	25	m	w	NY	San Francisco	1-Wd San Francisco	79	70
Amelia	7	f	w	CA	San Francisco	San Francisco P O	85	799
Charles W	37	m	w	ME	Sonoma	Salt Point	91	386
Daniel	25	m	w	ENGL	Amador	Jackson P O	69	321
J	51	m	w	HANO	Amador	Jackson P O	69	327
John	83	m	w	ENGL	Amador	Jackson P O	69	321
John	36	m	w	IREL	Alameda	Oakland	68	152
Theo	40	m	w	IA	Butte	Oregon Twp	70	135
Thomas	45	m	w	ENGL	Amador	Jackson P O	69	321
Thos	---	m	b	NY	San Francisco	1-Wd San Francisco	79	97
FILODFUAET								
Philos	27	m	w	CANA	Sonoma	Petaluma Twp	91	322
FILOW								
Ah	36	m	c	CHIN	Trinity	Junction City Pct	92	206
FILSON								
Lorenza	20	f	w	CA	San Francisco	11-Wd San Francisc	84	573
FILTCH								
H S	40	m	w	IL	Alameda	Oakland	68	178
FILTEN								
Wayne	14	m	w	CA	Humboldt	Arcata Twp	72	234
FILTO								
Basile	37	m	w	CANA	Solano	Silveyville Twp	90	91
FILTZ								
Heine	25	m	w	HANO	Alameda	Alameda	68	5
FIM								
Ah	46	m	c	CHIN	Butte	Chico Twp	70	51
Ah	40	m	c	CHIN	Tuolumne	Columbia P O	93	341
Ah	40	m	c	CHIN	Sacramento	Center Twp	77	85
Ah	32	m	c	CHIN	Butte	Ophir Twp	70	109
Ah	30	m	c	CHIN	San Francisco	San Francisco P O	80	524
Ah	15	m	c	CHIN	San Francisco	11-Wd San Francisc	84	607
Chew	32	m	c	CHIN	Yuba	Slate Range Bar Tw	93	672
Cock	20	m	c	CHIN	Placer	Blue Canyon P O	76	417
FIMAR								
Rudolph	40	m	w	HAMB	San Francisco	11-Wd San Francisc	84	445
FIMISTZ								
John B	37	m	w	MA	Sacramento	Franklin Twp	77	117
FIMONS								
Maggie	23	f	w	IREL	Alameda	Brooklyn	68	28
FIMPLE								
Sam C	30	m	w	IL	Butte	Oregon Twp	70	129
FIN								
Ah	65	m	c	CHIN	Tuolumne	Chinese Camp P O	93	379
Ah	53	m	c	CHIN	Tuolumne	Big Oak Flat P O	93	402
Ah	50	m	c	CHIN	Tuolumne	Chinese Camp P O	93	366
Ah	46	m	c	CHIN	Tuolumne	Chinese Camp P O	93	364
Ah	46	m	c	CHIN	San Francisco	San Francisco P O	80	528
Ah	46	m	c	CHIN	Santa Clara	1-Wd San Jose	88	273
Ah	43	m	c	CHIN	Fresno	Millerton P O	72	201
Ah	43	m	c	CHIN	San Francisco	San Francisco P O	80	432
Ah	42	m	c	CHIN	San Francisco	San Francisco P O	80	435
Ah	41	m	c	CHIN	Placer	Newcastle Twp	76	477
Ah	40	m	c	CHIN	Placer	Dutch Flat P O	76	408
Ah	40	m	c	CHIN	San Francisco	San Francisco P O	80	517
Ah	39	m	c	CHIN	Butte	Chico Twp	70	52
Ah	38	m	c	CHIN	San Francisco	San Francisco P O	80	440
Ah	38	m	c	CHIN	San Francisco	San Francisco P O	80	512
Ah	38	m	c	CHIN	San Francisco	San Francisco P O	80	525
Ah	37	m	c	CHIN	San Francisco	San Francisco P O	80	446
Ah	37	m	c	CHIN	San Francisco	San Francisco P O	80	530
Ah	36	m	c	CHIN	San Francisco	San Francisco P O	80	447
Ah	36	m	c	CHIN	San Francisco	San Francisco P O	80	499
Ah	36	m	c	CHIN	San Francisco	San Francisco P O	80	526
Ah	35	m	c	CHIN	San Francisco	San Francisco P O	80	510
Ah	35	m	c	CHIN	San Francisco	San Francisco P O	80	529
Ah	34	m	c	CHIN	San Francisco	San Francisco P O	80	443
Ah	34	m	c	CHIN	Tuolumne	Chinese Camp P O	93	383
Ah	34	m	c	CHIN	San Francisco	San Francisco P O	80	502
Ah	34	m	c	CHIN	San Francisco	San Francisco P O	80	514
Ah	32	m	c	CHIN	San Francisco	San Francisco P O	80	509
Ah	31	m	c	CHIN	San Francisco	San Francisco P O	80	517
Ah	30	m	c	CHIN	San Francisco	San Francisco P O	80	518
Ah	28	m	c	CHIN	Fresno	Millerton P O	72	200
Ah	28	f	c	CHIN	San Francisco	San Francisco P O	80	442
Ah	28	m	c	CHIN	San Francisco	San Francisco P O	80	446
Ah	28	m	c	CHIN	San Francisco	6-Wd San Francisco	81	63
Ah	28	m	c	CHIN	Alameda	Oakland	68	239
Ah	27	m	c	CHIN	San Francisco	San Francisco P O	80	525
Ah	26	m	c	CHIN	San Francisco	San Francisco P O	80	503
Ah	26	m	c	CHIN	Placer	Blue Canyon P O	76	417
Ah	26	m	c	CHIN	San Francisco	San Francisco P O	80	517
Ah	26	m	c	CHIN	San Francisco	San Francisco P O	80	516
Ah	25	m	c	CHIN	San Francisco	San Francisco P O	80	510
Ah	25	m	c	CHIN	San Mateo	Belmont P O	87	371
Ah	24	f	c	CHIN	San Francisco	San Francisco P O	80	453
Ah	24	m	c	CHIN	San Francisco	San Francisco P O	80	514
Ah	24	m	c	CHIN	San Francisco	San Francisco P O	80	509
Ah	24	m	c	CHIN	San Francisco	San Francisco P O	80	520
Ah	23	f	c	CHIN	San Francisco	San Francisco P O	80	439
Ah	23	m	c	CHIN	Tuolumne	Chinese Camp P O	93	377
Ah	23	m	c	CHIN	San Mateo	Belmont P O	87	371
Ah	21	m	c	CHIN	Sacramento	2-Wd Sacramento	77	245
Ah	21	f	c	CHIN	San Francisco	San Francisco P O	80	449
Ah	21	m	c	CHIN	San Francisco	San Francisco P O	80	517
Ah	20	f	c	CHIN	San Francisco	San Francisco P O	80	433
Ah	20	f	c	CHIN	San Francisco	San Francisco P O	80	444
Ah	20	m	c	CHIN	Butte	Kimshew Tpw	70	85
Ah	20	m	c	CHIN	San Francisco	6-Wd San Francisco	81	50

© 2001 by Heritage Quest. All rights reserved.

Series M593

Name	Age	S	R	B-PL	County	Locale	Roll	Pg
Ah	19	f	c	CHIN	San Francisco	San Francisco P O	80	508
Ah	18	m	c	CHIN	Butte	Bidwell Twp	70	1
Ah	18	m	c	CHIN	Tuolumne	Chinese Camp P O	93	388
Ah	17	f	c	CHIN	San Francisco	San Francisco P O	80	507
Ah	16	m	c	CHIN	Butte	Kimshew Tpw	70	85
Ah	15	m	c	CHIN	San Francisco	6-Wd San Francisco	81	49
Ah	15	m	c	CHIN	Butte	Kimshew Tpw	70	84
Ah	12	f	c	CHIN	San Francisco	San Francisco P O	80	454
Foan	25	m	c	CHIN	San Francisco	11-Wd San Francisc	84	546
Hong Teng	15	m	c	CHIN	San Mateo	Schoolhouse Statio	87	336
Maria	29	f	w	IREL	Alameda	Oakland	68	208
Yon	39	m	c	CHIN	San Joaquin	1-Wd Stockton	86	143
FINA								
D	22	m	w	NY	Alameda	Oakland	68	213
FINAGAN								
James	44	m	w	IREL	Stanislaus	Emory Twp	92	25
FINANCE								
Louis	60	m	w	FRAN	San Francisco	San Francisco P O	80	535
FINARTY								
Thos	47	m	w	IREL	San Joaquin	2-Wd Stockton	86	167
FINAY								
John	15	m	w	CA	Sacramento	4-Wd Sacramento	77	326
FINBECK								
Louis	26	m	w	NY	San Francisco	6-Wd San Francisco	81	131
FINBERG								
Abraham	50	m	w	RUSS	San Francisco	San Francisco P O	80	457
FINCH								
Augusta	36	f	w	OH	Contra Costa	Martinez P O	71	424
Charles	55	m	w	ENGL	Colusa	Colusa Twp	71	280
Charles	17	m	w	MI	Marin	Bolinas Twp	74	2
Chs B	38	m	w	CT	Monterey	Monterey Twp	74	347
D	26	m	w	PRUS	El Dorado	Greenwood Twp	72	52
Dewitt	25	m	w	MA	Contra Costa	Martinez P O	71	401
Elizabeth	15	f	w	CA	Humboldt	Eel Rvr Twp	72	253
Geo	38	m	w	IL	Butte	Chico Twp	70	54
George	45	m	w	IN	Amador	Drytown P O	69	421
Henry	42	m	w	IL	Sonoma	Petaluma Twp	91	366
Henry P	35	m	w	MI	Yolo	Cache Crk Twp	93	440
J C	42	m	w	OH	Merced	Snelling P O	74	273
James B	40	m	w	NY	Santa Clara	1-Wd San Jose	88	247
John	43	m	w	NY	Solano	Benicia	90	16
John	36	m	w	ENGL	Tuolumne	Big Oak Flat P O	93	399
John S	38	m	w	NY	Alameda	Hayward	68	73
Julia Ann	72	f	w	CT	Monterey	Monterey	74	359
Kate	36	f	w	PRUS	Sacramento	3-Wd Sacramento	77	294
Maggie	4	f	w	CA	Mendocino	Little Lake Twp	74	201
Martin	43	m	w	NY	San Francisco	8-Wd San Francisco	82	352
Mary	72	f	w	HDAR	San Francisco	2-Wd San Francisco	79	267
Mary	27	f	w	IREL	Alameda	Brooklyn Twp	68	40
Mary	27	f	w	IREL	San Francisco	6-Wd San Francisco	81	103
Phebe	68	f	w	NY	Contra Costa	Martinez P O	71	377
Rawson R	27	m	w	MI	Yolo	Cache Crk Twp	93	440
Soloman	62	m	w	NY	Santa Clara	Santa Clara Twp	88	150
T J	63	m	w	VA	Humboldt	Table Bluff Twp	72	304
W	50	m	w	NY	San Joaquin	1-Wd Stockton	86	137
William	40	m	w	NY	San Francisco	San Francisco P O	83	297
William G	42	m	w	OH	San Francisco	8-Wd San Francisco	82	392
Wm	60	m	w	VA	San Joaquin	Dent Twp	86	18
Wm	44	m	w	ENGL	San Joaquin	3-Wd Stockton	86	228
Ziba	50	m	w	NY	Yolo	Cache Crk Twp	93	440
FINCHEL								
Cesar C	46	m	w	NY	Los Angeles	San Gabriel Twp	73	593
FINCHER								
Adam	60	m	w	GERM	Yolo	Buckeye Twp	93	411
John	34	m	w	AR	Tehama	Tehama Twp	92	192
Levi M	40	m	w	SC	Stanislaus	Empire Twp	92	41
Robert	40	m	w	MO	Sacramento	Alabama Twp	77	59
Susan	48	f	w	AL	Solano	Benicia	90	20
Susan	28	f	w	AR	Solano	Benicia	90	20
FINCHLEY								
Thomas F	59	m	w	CANA	Nevada	Grass Valley Twp	75	200
FINCHLY								
Percy E	50	f	w	MA	San Francisco	8-Wd San Francisco	82	347
FINCHY								
John	38	m	w	ENGL	San Joaquin	1-Wd Stockton	86	153
FINCK								
Inis	12	f	w	MI	Sacramento	Sutter Twp	77	388
Joe	25	m	i	CA	Fresno	Kings Rvr P O	72	216
Rebecca	50	f	w	BREM	San Francisco	San Francisco P O	83	160
Wm	44	m	w	NY	Sacramento	Sutter Twp	77	388
FINCKLE								
C C	46	m	m	BAHA	Sacramento	3-Wd Sacramento	77	260
FIND								
Henry	50	m	w	PRUS	San Francisco	8-Wd San Francisco	82	360
FINDESCIN								
Charles	50	m	w	SWED	Mendocino	Little Rvr Twp	74	171
FINDINGHAM								
P	40	m	w	PA	Sierra	Lincoln Twp	89	551
FINDLAY								
Joseph	59	m	w	KY	Alpine	Woodfords P O	69	315
Robert	45	m	w	SCOT	San Francisco	6-Wd San Francisco	81	135
FINDLEY								
Francis	50	m	w	IREL	San Francisco	2-Wd San Francisco	79	212
James	40	m	w	PA	San Francisco	2-Wd San Francisco	79	263
Jane	56	f	w	IN	Napa	Napa	75	42
John	60	m	w	TN	Tulare	Venice Twp	92	276
John	60	m	w	TN	San Luis Obispo	San Luis Obispo Tw	87	305
Sarah	15	f	w	CA	Nevada	Nevada Twp	75	273
Thomas	38	m	w	PA	Nevada	Grass Valley Twp	75	167
Venard J	34	m	w	TN	San Luis Obispo	Santa Rosa Twp	87	321
William	31	m	w	PA	San Francisco	2-Wd San Francisco	79	178
William	26	m	w	NY	San Francisco	San Francisco P O	85	744
William	19	m	w	TX	Tulare	Venice Twp	92	276
FINDLY								
--- Mrs	48	f	w	MS	Napa	Napa	75	21
FINDO								
Ramon	36	m	w	MEXI	Fresno	Millerton P O	72	166
FINDRA								
Savaro	35	m	w	MEXI	Los Angeles	Los Angeles	73	512
FINE								
Abraham	55	m	w	TN	Sonoma	Analy Twp	91	228
Abreham C	21	m	w	IL	Sonoma	Petaluma Twp	91	316
Ah	41	m	c	CHIN	Tuolumne	Chinese Camp P O	93	379
Ah	33	m	c	CHIN	San Francisco	San Francisco P O	80	495
Ah	19	m	c	CHIN	Santa Clara	Fremont Twp	88	57
Andrew	28	m	w	MO	Santa Cruz	Watsonville	89	365
Bincinto	45	f	w	ARGE	Santa Clara	Santa Clara Twp	88	164
Caroline	42	f	w	TN	Sonoma	Petaluma Twp	91	362
Charles	19	m	w	SAXO	Colusa	Colusa	71	296
David	50	m	w	MO	Stanislaus	Branch Twp	92	3
Dawson	28	m	w	WI	Stanislaus	Buena Vista Twp	92	12
Eduard E	32	m	w	MO	San Francisco	San Francisco P O	83	160
Elisha H	33	m	w	MO	Contra Costa	Martinez P O	71	376
Frank	50	m	w	FRAN	Siskiyou	Callahan P O	89	628
Fredrick	38	m	w	MO	Marin	San Antonio Twp	74	60
Holt	48	m	w	TN	San Francisco	11-Wd San Francisc	84	506
Hubbard	37	m	w	PRUS	Solano	Suisun Twp	90	104
Irbey H	49	m	w	TN	Sonoma	Petaluma Twp	91	345
James	45	m	w	MO	Tulare	Tule Rvr Twp	92	265
John	71	m	w	TN	Contra Costa	Martinez P O	71	375
John C	38	m	w	MO	Tulare	Tule Rvr Twp	92	265
Lewis	45	m	w	MO	Tulare	Tule Rvr Twp	92	264
Lidgerd	62	m	w	TN	Santa Clara	Gilroy Twp	88	91
Miller	32	m	w	MO	Contra Costa	Martinez P O	71	410
Morgan	70	m	w	TN	Santa Clara	Santa Clara Twp	88	159
S J	24	m	w	SCOT	Santa Clara	Gilroy Twp	88	97
Segard B	35	m	w	MO	Santa Clara	Santa Clara Twp	88	159
Smith	45	m	w	TX	Kern	Bakersfield P O	73	366
Smith H	47	m	w	MO	Tulare	Tule Rvr Twp	92	264
FINEGAN								
M	35	m	w	IREL	San Joaquin	2-Wd Stockton	86	199
Owen	52	m	w	IREL	Trinity	Weaverville Pct	92	226
FINEN								
Bartholomew	78	m	w	IREL	San Francisco	11-Wd San Francisc	84	607
FINER								
Martin	30	m	w	IREL	Sacramento	Granite Twp	77	139
Sarah	6	f	w	CA	San Francisco	8-Wd San Francisco	82	458
William J	38	m	w	GA	Placer	Bath P O	76	449
FINERTY								
James	40	m	w	IREL	Siskiyou	Butte Twp	89	588
James	38	m	w	IREL	San Mateo	San Mateo P O	87	360
John	28	m	w	ENGL	San Francisco	7-Wd San Francisco	81	182
Morton	26	m	w	IREL	Amador	Ione City P O	69	369
FINETE								
Hasley	33	m	w	OH	Nevada	Meadow Lake Twp	75	269
FINEY								
Joseph	16	m	w	SWIT	Alameda	Oakland	68	144
FING								
---	21	m	c	CHIN	San Francisco	6-Wd San Francisco	81	64
Ah	64	m	c	CHIN	Butte	Ophir Twp	70	103
Ah	60	m	c	CHIN	Tuolumne	Chinese Camp P O	93	380
Ah	53	m	c	CHIN	Tuolumne	Chinese Camp P O	93	383
Ah	50	m	c	CHIN	Calaveras	Copperopolis P O	70	242
Ah	4M	f	c	CA	San Francisco	San Francisco P O	80	492
Ah	48	m	c	CHIN	San Francisco	San Francisco P O	80	435
Ah	46	m	c	CHIN	San Francisco	San Francisco P O	80	501
Ah	45	m	c	CHIN	San Francisco	San Francisco P O	80	492
Ah	45	m	c	CHIN	San Francisco	San Francisco P O	80	513
Ah	44	m	c	CHIN	Butte	Ophir Twp	70	103
Ah	43	m	c	CHIN	San Francisco	San Francisco P O	80	527
Ah	43	m	c	CHIN	Sierra	Forest Twp	89	528
Ah	42	m	c	CHIN	Butte	Hamilton Twp	70	67
Ah	41	m	c	CHIN	Sierra	Lincoln Twp	89	549
Ah	41	m	c	CHIN	Amador	Jackson P O	69	347
Ah	41	m	c	CHIN	San Francisco	San Francisco P O	80	502
Ah	40	m	c	CHIN	San Francisco	San Francisco P O	80	493
Ah	40	m	c	CHIN	San Francisco	San Francisco P O	80	445
Ah	40	m	c	CHIN	San Francisco	San Francisco P O	80	450
Ah	40	m	c	CHIN	Sacramento	Granite Twp	77	155
Ah	40	m	c	CHIN	San Francisco	San Francisco P O	80	518
Ah	4	m	c	CA	San Francisco	San Francisco P O	80	452
Ah	39	m	c	CHIN	San Francisco	San Francisco P O	80	524
Ah	39	m	c	CHIN	San Francisco	San Francisco P O	80	523
Ah	39	m	c	CHIN	San Francisco	San Francisco P O	80	514
Ah	38	m	c	CHIN	Tuolumne	Chinese Camp P O	93	363
Ah	38	m	c	CHIN	San Francisco	San Francisco P O	80	519
Ah	38	m	c	CHIN	San Francisco	San Francisco P O	80	518
Ah	37	m	c	CHIN	Butte	Hamilton Twp	70	67
Ah	37	m	c	CHIN	San Francisco	San Francisco P O	80	526
Ah	37	m	c	CHIN	San Francisco	San Francisco P O	80	518
Ah	36	m	c	CHIN	Sierra	Lincoln Twp	89	552
Ah	36	m	c	CHIN	San Francisco	San Francisco P O	80	439
Ah	36	m	c	CHIN	San Francisco	San Francisco P O	80	529
Ah	36	m	c	CHIN	San Francisco	San Francisco P O	80	518

© 2001 by Heritage Quest. All rights reserved.

Series M593

Name	Age	S	R	B-PL	County	Locale	Roll	Pg
Ah	36	m	c	CHIN	San Francisco	San Francisco P O	80	526
Ah	36	m	c	CHIN	San Francisco	San Francisco P O	80	507
Ah	35	m	c	CHIN	San Francisco	San Francisco P O	80	518
Ah	34	m	c	CHIN	San Francisco	San Francisco P O	80	450
Ah	34	m	c	CHIN	San Francisco	San Francisco P O	80	443
Ah	34	m	c	CHIN	Amador	Jackson P O	69	347
Ah	34	m	c	CHIN	San Francisco	San Francisco P O	80	511
Ah	34	m	c	CHIN	San Francisco	San Francisco P O	80	501
Ah	34	m	c	CHIN	San Francisco	San Francisco P O	80	506
Ah	33	f	c	CHIN	San Francisco	San Francisco P O	80	433
Ah	32	m	c	CHIN	San Francisco	6-Wd San Francisco	81	67
Ah	32	m	c	CHIN	San Francisco	San Francisco P O	80	490
Ah	32	m	c	CHIN	San Francisco	San Francisco P O	80	520
Ah	31	m	c	CHIN	Amador	Ione City P O	69	354
Ah	31	m	c	CHIN	San Francisco	San Francisco P O	80	510
Ah	31	m	c	CHIN	San Francisco	San Francisco P O	80	513
Ah	30	f	c	CHIN	San Francisco	San Francisco P O	80	503
Ah	30	m	c	CHIN	San Mateo	San Mateo P O	87	354
Ah	30	m	c	CHIN	San Joaquin	Castoria Twp	86	12
Ah	30	m	c	CHIN	San Francisco	San Francisco P O	80	447
Ah	30	m	c	CHIN	Butte	Ophir Twp	70	99
Ah	30	m	c	CHIN	San Francisco	San Francisco P O	80	529
Ah	30	m	c	CHIN	San Francisco	San Francisco P O	80	499
Ah	3	f	c	CA	San Francisco	San Francisco P O	80	501
Ah	29	f	c	CHIN	San Francisco	San Francisco P O	80	495
Ah	29	m	c	CHIN	San Francisco	San Francisco P O	80	517
Ah	29	m	c	CHIN	San Francisco	San Francisco P O	80	503
Ah	28	m	c	CHIN	San Francisco	6-Wd San Francisco	81	68
Ah	28	m	c	CHIN	San Francisco	San Francisco P O	80	511
Ah	27	m	c	CHIN	San Francisco	San Francisco P O	80	511
Ah	27	m	c	CHIN	Santa Clara	San Jose Twp	88	190
Ah	26	m	c	CHIN	San Francisco	San Francisco P O	80	517
Ah	26	m	c	CHIN	San Francisco	San Francisco P O	80	509
Ah	25	m	c	CHIN	San Francisco	San Francisco P O	80	436
Ah	25	m	c	CHIN	Butte	Chico Twp	70	29
Ah	25	m	c	CHIN	San Francisco	San Francisco P O	80	523
Ah	24	m	c	CHIN	San Francisco	San Francisco P O	80	504
Ah	24	m	c	CHIN	Tuolumne	Chinese Camp P O	93	364
Ah	24	m	c	CHIN	Tuolumne	Chinese Camp P O	93	379
Ah	24	m	c	CHIN	San Francisco	San Francisco P O	80	507
Ah	23	f	c	CHIN	San Francisco	San Francisco P O	80	451
Ah	23	f	c	CHIN	San Francisco	San Francisco P O	80	506
Ah	21	f	c	CHIN	San Francisco	San Francisco P O	80	434
Ah	21	m	c	CHIN	San Francisco	San Francisco P O	80	528
Ah	20	f	c	CHIN	San Francisco	San Francisco P O	80	434
Ah	20	f	c	CHIN	San Francisco	San Francisco P O	80	448
Ah	20	f	c	CHIN	San Francisco	San Francisco P O	80	434
Ah	20	f	c	CHIN	San Francisco	San Francisco P O	80	435
Ah	18	m	c	CHIN	Tuolumne	Chinese Camp P O	93	388
Ah	18	f	c	CHIN	San Francisco	San Francisco P O	80	434
Ah	16	f	c	CHIN	San Francisco	San Francisco P O	80	526
Ah	11	f	c	CHIN	San Francisco	San Francisco P O	80	440
Ah	10	f	c	CHIN	San Francisco	San Francisco P O	80	491
Ah	1	m	c	CA	San Francisco	San Francisco P O	80	447
Can	26	m	c	CHIN	Tuolumne	Chinese Camp P O	93	388
Fen	49	m	c	CHIN	Tuolumne	Big Oak Flat P O	93	400
Gee	42	m	c	CHIN	El Dorado	Placerville Twp	72	92
Hip	51	m	c	CHIN	Tuolumne	Chinese Camp P O	93	379
Hoo	31	m	c	CHIN	Sierra	Forest	89	537
How	43	m	c	CHIN	Sierra	Lincoln Twp	89	548
How	24	m	c	CHIN	Santa Clara	San Jose Twp	88	193
John	23	m	c	CHIN	Sonoma	Santa Rosa	91	402
Ko	30	m	c	CHIN	San Francisco	6-Wd San Francisco	81	47
Par	20	m	c	CHIN	San Francisco	6-Wd San Francisco	81	69
Prue	31	m	c	CHIN	Plumas	Goodwin Twp	77	3
Si	23	f	c	CHIN	Sacramento	3-Wd Sacramento	77	300
Tee	30	m	c	CHIN	Placer	Bath P O	76	429
Tie	27	m	c	CHIN	Butte	Hamilton Twp	70	67
FINGAN								
Margaret	35	f	w	IREL	San Mateo	Pescadero P O	87	412
FINGER								
Augustus	63	m	w	PRUS	Santa Clara	Fremont Twp	88	62
Theodore	54	m	w	PRUS	San Mateo	Belmont P O	87	373
FINGERFIDDLER								
C F	52	m	w	GERM	San Joaquin	Liberty Twp	86	88
FINGLAND								
John	36	m	w	SCOT	Placer	Colfax P O	76	386
Robert	35	m	w	NY	San Francisco	7-Wd San Francisco	81	235
FINGLER								
Henry	53	m	w	HANO	San Francisco	1-Wd San Francisco	79	131
FINGLESTON								
John	35	m	w	SAXO	San Francisco	2-Wd San Francisco	79	274
FINGON								
Jos	53	m	w	ENGL	Butte	Concow Twp	70	6
FINIEL								
Eugene	68	m	w	FRAN	Placer	Bath P O	76	428
FINIGAN								
Ellen	27	f	w	IREL	San Francisco	San Francisco P O	80	457
Hanna	32	f	w	IREL	San Francisco	San Francisco P O	83	338
Holmes	52	m	w	FRAN	San Francisco	San Francisco P O	80	479
Owen	40	m	w	IREL	Sacramento	1-Wd Sacramento	77	188
Thomas	33	m	w	IREL	San Francisco	7-Wd San Francisco	81	203
FINITY								
Henry	34	m	w	NY	Trinity	Hayfork Valley	92	239
Thomas	23	m	w	IREL	Sonoma	Vallejo Twp	91	459
FINK								
Ah	34	m	c	CHIN	Sierra	Eureka Twp	89	525
Ah	31	m	c	CHIN	Sierra	Lincoln Twp	89	552
Ah	16	m	c	CHIN	San Francisco	San Francisco P O	80	497
Charles	33	m	w	BADE	El Dorado	Diamond Springs Tw	72	27
Christina	25	f	w	HANO	Sacramento	3-Wd Sacramento	77	305
Fred	23	m	w	WURT	Amador	Ione City P O	69	355
Fredrick	33	m	w	OH	Inyo	Cerro Gordo Twp	73	319
George	35	m	w	WURT	San Francisco	San Francisco P O	85	757
Harry	35	m	w	CANA	Kern	Kernville P O	73	368
Henry	25	m	w	HANO	San Francisco	San Francisco P O	83	193
Henry W	29	m	w	BREM	San Francisco	3-Wd San Francisco	79	295
James	29	m	w	NY	San Francisco	6-Wd San Francisco	81	84
John	38	m	w	BADE	El Dorado	Diamond Springs Tw	72	30
Joseph	24	m	w	ME	San Francisco	7-Wd San Francisco	81	226
Lewis	40	m	w	PRUS	Sacramento	San Joaquin Twp	77	396
Lewis	37	m	w	MA	San Francisco	5-Wd San Francisco	81	12
Nancy	60	f	w	NY	San Francisco	San Francisco P O	85	753
Peter	32	m	w	GERM	Yolo	Grafton Twp	93	482
Peter W	41	m	i	NY	Fresno	Kings Rvr P O	72	206
Stephen	41	m	w	BADE	Colusa	Monroe Twp	71	325
FINKBNER								
J	39	m	w	PRUS	San Joaquin	2-Wd Stockton	86	194
FINKE								
Alvis	39	m	w	AUST	San Francisco	2-Wd San Francisco	79	229
Henry	33	m	w	PRUS	San Francisco	2-Wd San Francisco	79	237
FINKELDAY								
Henry	43	m	w	PRUS	Alameda	Oakland	68	131
FINKELDY								
Werner	37	m	w	PRUS	Santa Cruz	Santa Cruz	89	413
FINKHAUS								
Henry	24	m	w	MA	San Joaquin	2-Wd Stockton	86	205
FINKING								
Richard	25	m	w	PRUS	San Francisco	2-Wd San Francisco	79	146
FINKNY								
George	38	m	w	IREL	San Francisco	11-Wd San Francisc	84	512
FINKS								
Almaria	39	m	w	NY	Inyo	Bishop Crk Twp	73	317
FINLAN								
Abijah	35	m	w	OH	Nevada	Rough & Ready Twp	75	336
FINLAND								
John	30	m	w	IREL	Marin	Nicasio Twp	74	17
FINLASON								
James	33	m	w	AUSL	San Francisco	2-Wd San Francisco	79	224
FINLAY								
Patrick	28	m	w	IREL	San Francisco	1-Wd San Francisco	79	30
Robt	23	m	w	ENGL	Sacramento	3-Wd Sacramento	77	318
FINLAYSON								
Daniel	38	m	w	CANA	Plumas	Plumas Twp	77	29
K	43	m	w	SCOT	Solano	Vallejo	90	203
FINLETTER								
Jas D	30	m	w	PA	Butte	Ophir Twp	70	117
FINLEY								
Bridget	39	f	w	IREL	El Dorado	Mud Springs Twp	72	74
C W	57	m	w	TN	Placer	Auburn P O	76	383
Charles C	40	m	w	MO	Solano	Maine Prairie Twp	90	50
Clara	19	f	w	CA	Alameda	Oakland	68	259
Cornelius	41	m	w	NY	Santa Clara	Gilroy Twp	88	86
David	33	m	w	CANA	San Francisco	San Francisco P O	83	41
Edwd	30	m	w	IREL	San Francisco	1-Wd San Francisco	79	60
Fred	29	m	w	CA	San Diego	San Diego	78	486
Geo	43	m	w	MO	Butte	Chico Twp	70	41
Geo	41	m	w	MA	Solano	Vallejo	90	207
Hamilton	45	m	w	IREL	Santa Clara	Redwood Twp	88	127
Harrison	33	m	w	MO	Contra Costa	Martinez P O	71	384
J M	49	m	w	KY	Lake	Coyote Valley	73	417
James	39	m	w	IREL	Nevada	Grass Valley Twp	75	199
Jeffison	19	m	w	MO	Sonoma	Petaluma Twp	91	356
John	50	m	b	KY	Yuba	Bullards Bar P O	93	553
John	45	m	w	IN	Sonoma	Bodega Twp	91	257
John	44	m	w	IREL	Sonoma	Salt Point	91	380
John	40	m	w	OH	Santa Clara	Santa Clara Twp	88	141
John	34	m	w	IREL	Solano	Vallejo	90	206
John	28	m	w	IREL	Nevada	Eureka Twp	75	133
John	28	m	w	NY	San Francisco	8-Wd San Francisco	82	465
John A	38	m	w	MO	Yolo	Buckeye Twp	93	408
John B	33	m	w	NY	San Francisco	7-Wd San Francisco	81	268
John C	40	m	w	NY	Yolo	Washington Twp	93	538
John J	24	m	w	AR	Sonoma	Analy Twp	91	247
John P	25	m	w	MO	Santa Clara	Santa Clara Twp	88	139
Joseph	29	m	w	NY	San Francisco	7-Wd San Francisco	81	182
Joseph J	44	m	w	MO	Sonoma	Bodega Twp	91	257
May	20	f	w	WI	Butte	Oregon Twp	70	129
N G	29	m	w	MO	Santa Clara	Burnett Twp	88	31
Newton	22	m	w	VA	Santa Clara	Burnett Twp	88	39
Rebecca	38	f	w	TN	Santa Clara	Santa Clara Twp	88	173
Richard	42	m	w	MA	San Francisco	San Francisco P O	83	358
Robert	32	m	w	CANA	Sonoma	Mendocino Twp	91	300
Samuel	45	m	w	IN	Sonoma	Bodega Twp	91	254
Thomas	35	m	w	NJ	Santa Clara	2-Wd San Jose	88	326
Thos C	39	m	w	NY	San Francisco	San Francisco P O	85	777
Victor	38	m	w	WURT	San Joaquin	Oneal Twp	86	119
William	38	m	w	OH	Contra Costa	Martinez P O	71	413
William	30	m	w	OH	Sonoma	Petaluma Twp	91	358
Wm	26	m	w	PA	Sacramento	American Twp	77	66
Wm A	25	m	w	IL	Yuba	East Bear Rvr Twp	93	539
FINLINSON								
Jacob H	47	m	w	PA	El Dorado	Placerville Twp	72	97

© 2001 by Heritage Quest. All rights reserved.

California 1870 Census

Name	Age	S	R	B-PL	County	Locale	Roll	Pg
FINLONG								
Kate	25	f	w	IREL	San Francisco	5-Wd San Francisco	81	20
FINLY								
Henry	10	m	w	CA	Marin	San Antonio Twp	74	61
Patrick	40	m	w	IREL	San Mateo	Schoolhouse Statio	87	342
William H	35	m	w	KY	Stanislaus	Empire Twp	92	52
FINN								
Ah	41	m	c	CHIN	San Francisco	San Francisco P O	80	491
Ah	28	m	c	CHIN	Tuolumne	Big Oak Flat P O	93	397
Ah	25	m	c	CHIN	Stanislaus	Emory Twp	92	23
Alva	46	m	w	PA	Santa Clara	Milpitas Twp	88	110
Ann	34	f	w	IREL	San Francisco	6-Wd San Francisco	81	72
Augustus	28	m	w	ME	San Francisco	San Francisco P O	80	425
Cal	31	m	w	MO	San Joaquin	Elliott Twp	86	80
Corwin	35	m	w	NY	Sonoma	Analy Twp	91	230
D	27	m	w	IREL	Amador	Jackson P O	69	330
David	55	m	w	IREL	San Francisco	San Francisco P O	80	411
David	40	m	w	ENGL	San Francisco	1-Wd San Francisco	79	98
David	25	m	w	IREL	Alameda	Eden Twp	68	82
Edward	38	m	w	IREL	San Francisco	7-Wd San Francisco	81	203
Ellen	27	f	w	IREL	Humboldt	Eureka Twp	72	277
Fredk	50	m	w	CT	Marin	Sausalito Twp	74	70
Hugh	42	m	w	IREL	El Dorado	Salmon Falls Twp	72	130
James	36	m	w	IREL	San Francisco	11-Wd San Francisc	84	533
James	32	m	w	IREL	San Francisco	11-Wd San Francisc	84	439
James	30	m	w	IREL	San Francisco	1-Wd San Francisco	79	78
Jas W	37	m	w	IREL	San Francisco	San Francisco P O	83	287
Jeremiah	48	m	w	IREL	San Francisco	11-Wd San Francisc	84	476
Johanna	22	f	w	IREL	San Francisco	San Francisco P O	83	406
John	45	m	w	IREL	San Joaquin	1-Wd Stockton	86	152
John	43	m	w	IREL	Napa	Napa	75	57
John	33	m	w	IREL	San Francisco	San Francisco P O	85	758
John	18	m	w	NY	Humboldt	Arcata Twp	72	225
Kate	26	f	w	IREL	San Francisco	2-Wd San Francisco	79	216
Kate	19	f	w	MA	San Francisco	11-Wd San Francisc	84	507
Lissie	24	f	w	MA	San Francisco	11-Wd San Francisc	84	516
Ma	28	f	c	CHIN	Tuolumne	Chinese Camp P O	93	381
Margaret	18	f	w	IREL	San Francisco	San Francisco P O	83	218
Mary	35	f	w	IREL	San Francisco	8-Wd San Francisco	82	338
Mary	14	f	w	MA	San Joaquin	1-Wd Stockton	86	141
Mary A	21	f	w	IREL	San Francisco	8-Wd San Francisco	82	491
Michael	50	m	w	IREL	San Francisco	11-Wd San Francisc	84	481
Michael	23	m	w	IREL	Alpine	Markleeville P O	69	312
Morris	25	m	w	IREL	Amador	Jackson P O	69	329
Nelly	11	f	w	MN	Amador	Amador City P O	69	391
Pat	45	m	w	IREL	San Francisco	7-Wd San Francisco	81	230
Rate	17	f	w	CA	San Joaquin	1-Wd Stockton	86	127
Stephen	40	m	w	IREL	Amador	Drytown P O	69	416
Thomas	7	m	w	CA	Amador	Drytown P O	69	415
Thomas	35	m	w	IREL	San Francisco	San Francisco P O	80	411
Timothy	32	m	w	IREL	San Francisco	San Francisco P O	83	76
Timothy	28	m	w	IREL	San Francisco	San Francisco P O	83	4
FINNAN								
John	33	m	w	IREL	Calaveras	San Andreas P O	70	171
FINNANAL								
Albert	44	m	w	HDAR	San Francisco	San Francisco P O	83	243
FINNBY								
Thomas J	33	m	w	VT	Placer	Bath P O	76	433
FINNE								
Thomas	30	m	w	IREL	Siskiyou	Callahan P O	89	631
FINNEGAN								
Ann	50	f	w	KY	Napa	Yountville Twp	75	82
Ann	40	f	w	IREL	Alameda	Oakland	68	238
Ann	22	f	w	IREL	San Francisco	8-Wd San Francisco	82	389
Barney	27	m	w	IREL	San Francisco	7-Wd San Francisco	81	215
Barney	26	m	w	IREL	Sonoma	Petaluma Twp	91	326
Bernard	35	m	w	IREL	Santa Cruz	Santa Cruz Twp	89	402
Bernard	26	m	w	OH	Sonoma	Healdsburg & Mendo	91	283
Bridget	30	f	w	IREL	San Francisco	8-Wd San Francisco	82	447
Bridget	30	f	w	IREL	San Francisco	2-Wd San Francisco	79	197
Cathe	40	f	w	IREL	San Francisco	San Francisco P O	83	71
Catherine	41	f	w	IREL	San Francisco	11-Wd San Francisc	84	436
Catherine	32	f	w	IREL	San Francisco	8-Wd San Francisco	82	469
David	55	m	w	IREL	Siskiyou	Callahan P O	89	631
Edward	30	m	w	IREL	San Francisco	San Francisco P O	83	357
Eliza	56	f	w	IREL	San Francisco	8-Wd San Francisco	82	326
Elizabeth	68	f	w	IREL	San Francisco	8-Wd San Francisco	82	292
Ellen	22	f	w	IREL	San Francisco	San Francisco P O	83	293
Johanna	27	f	w	IREL	San Francisco	1-Wd San Francisco	79	113
John	34	m	w	IREL	Santa Clara	2-Wd San Jose	88	316
John	32	m	w	IREL	Tehama	Red Bluff	92	182
Joseph	31	m	w	IREL	San Francisco	11-Wd San Francisc	84	613
Julia	23	f	w	IREL	San Francisco	8-Wd San Francisco	82	389
Maggie	28	f	w	IREL	Santa Clara	2-Wd San Jose	88	330
Margt	35	f	w	IREL	San Francisco	San Francisco P O	83	101
Michael	42	m	w	IREL	Nevada	Grass Valley Twp	75	197
Michl	25	m	w	IREL	San Francisco	1-Wd San Francisco	79	70
Pete	45	m	w	IREL	Sacramento	4-Wd Sacramento	77	369
Peter A	35	m	w	NY	San Francisco	8-Wd San Francisco	82	443
R S	36	m	w	IREL	Alameda	Oakland	68	261
Rosanna	14	f	w	NY	Nevada	Grass Valley Twp	75	159
Rose	26	f	w	IREL	San Francisco	8-Wd San Francisco	82	424
Stephen	31	m	w	NY	Alameda	Murray Twp	68	109
Thos	35	m	w	IREL	San Francisco	1-Wd San Francisco	79	95
FINNEJESS								
Henry	35	m	w	IREL	San Francisco	San Francisco P O	83	353
FINNEL								
Patrick	37	m	w	IREL	San Francisco	7-Wd San Francisco	81	239
FINNELL								
Martin	30	m	w	MO	Sacramento	3-Wd Sacramento	77	300
FINNEMORE								
Thos	30	m	w	NY	Sierra	Sears Twp	89	527
FINNER								
Robert	19	m	w	CANA	Santa Clara	Redwood Twp	88	133
FINNEREN								
Bridget	21	f	w	IREL	Alameda	Brooklyn Twp	68	39
FINNERTY								
Barthomw	24	m	w	NY	San Francisco	1-Wd San Francisco	79	52
Frank	21	m	w	MA	Calaveras	San Andreas P O	70	153
James	38	m	w	IREL	Yolo	Cottonwood Twp	93	459
James	30	m	w	IREL	San Francisco	3-Wd San Francisco	79	313
Jas	10	m	w	MA	San Francisco	7-Wd San Francisco	81	257
Margret	32	f	w	IREL	San Francisco	1-Wd San Francisco	79	98
Michl	37	m	w	IREL	Marin	San Rafael Twp	74	38
Michl	36	m	w	IREL	Fresno	Millerton P O	72	146
Peter	39	m	w	IREL	San Francisco	1-Wd San Francisco	79	93
Thomas	43	m	w	IREL	Calaveras	San Andreas P O	70	156
Thomas	38	m	w	PA	San Francisco	San Francisco P O	80	354
Thos	39	m	w	IREL	San Francisco	1-Wd San Francisco	79	116
FINNETONE								
Samuel	22	m	w	ENGL	Plumas	Indian Twp	77	17
FINNEY								
Anthony	29	m	w	MA	San Francisco	3-Wd San Francisco	79	294
Delia	35	f	w	IREL	San Francisco	San Francisco P O	83	91
Edward	47	m	w	IREL	Stanislaus	Emory Twp	92	18
Emma	1	f	w	CA	San Luis Obispo	Morro Twp	87	281
Frank	30	m	w	NY	Monterey	Monterey	74	354
Henry	30	m	w	ENGL	San Francisco	11-Wd San Francisc	84	460
Henry	28	m	w	IREL	Solano	Suisun Twp	90	115
I W	65	m	w	VA	Tuolumne	Sonora P O	93	314
J J	40	m	w	SCOT	Sierra	Butte Twp	89	509
James	40	m	w	IREL	Yuba	Rose Bar Twp	93	663
Jas	46	m	w	IL	Sacramento	1-Wd Sacramento	77	201
John	58	m	w	ENGL	Tuolumne	Big Oak Flat P O	93	402
John	47	m	w	PA	Tuolumne	Big Oak Flat P O	93	391
John	38	m	w	MA	Los Angeles	Wilmington Twp	73	635
John	24	m	w	CANA	Santa Clara	Redwood Twp	88	133
John	22	m	w	CANA	Solano	Vallejo	90	171
Joseph	58	m	w	MA	San Francisco	2-Wd San Francisco	79	246
Margaret	30	f	w	IREL	San Francisco	8-Wd San Francisco	82	404
Mary	38	f	w	IREL	San Francisco	San Francisco P O	83	100
Mary	18	f	w	PRUS	Alameda	Brooklyn Twp	68	47
Michael	37	m	w	IREL	Amador	Ione City P O	69	351
Nathaniel	53	m	w	MA	San Francisco	San Francisco P O	80	341
Peter	30	m	w	IREL	Santa Clara	Fremont Twp	88	52
Porter S	45	m	w	NY	San Luis Obispo	Arroyo Grande Twp	87	274
Samuel	37	m	w	PA	Los Angeles	Los Nietos Twp	73	579
Seldon J	42	m	w	NY	San Mateo	Pescadero P O	87	414
Thomas	62	m	w	VA	Contra Costa	Martinez P O	71	434
Thomas	45	m	w	IREL	Tuolumne	Chinese Camp P O	93	381
William	51	m	w	IL	Placer	Auburn P O	76	365
Wm	19	m	w	RI	Solano	Vallejo	90	203
FINNICER								
Harriett	59	f	w	KY	Tehama	Paynes Crk Twp	92	160
FINNICUM								
James	43	m	w	OH	Placer	Bath P O	76	432
FINNIE								
Edward	20	m	w	CANA	Santa Clara	Redwood Twp	88	131
Mary A	26	f	w	SCOT	Alameda	Oakland	68	225
Robert	39	m	w	SCOT	Nevada	Grass Valley Twp	75	152
FINNIG								
James	15	m	w	IA	Santa Barbara	Santa Barbara P O	87	492
FINNIGAN								
Daniel	35	m	w	IREL	San Francisco	11-Wd San Francisc	84	582
Hugh	34	m	w	IREL	San Francisco	San Francisco P O	85	785
James	49	m	w	IREL	San Francisco	7-Wd San Francisco	81	184
John	35	m	w	IREL	Santa Clara	San Jose Twp	88	208
Norah	20	f	w	IREL	San Francisco	San Francisco P O	85	718
Pat	40	m	w	IREL	Yuba	Rose Bar Twp	93	662
Pat	27	m	w	IREL	San Francisco	7-Wd San Francisco	81	281
Peter	46	m	w	NY	San Francisco	11-Wd San Francisc	84	578
Susie	24	f	w	IREL	San Francisco	11-Wd San Francisc	84	483
Thomas	45	m	w	IREL	Yolo	Putah Twp	93	515
Thos	35	m	w	IREL	San Francisco	7-Wd San Francisco	81	266
FINNIGEN								
John	33	m	w	IREL	San Francisco	11-Wd San Francisc	84	679
FINNIGHTY								
Anne	30	f	w	IREL	San Francisco	San Francisco P O	83	301
FINNIN								
Ellen	50	f	w	IREL	San Francisco	San Francisco P O	83	183
William W	46	m	w	MS	Inyo	Lone Pine Twp	73	331
FINNINGER								
R	45	m	w	SWIT	Nevada	Nevada Twp	75	273
FINNIS								
James	40	m	b	MD	San Francisco	San Francisco P O	80	483
FINNISSEE								
Jerry	35	m	w	IREL	Butte	Chico Twp	70	15
FINNK								
Geo	29	m	w	PA	Lassen	Susanville Twp	73	441
FINNURN								
John	26	m	w	IREL	San Mateo	San Mateo P O	87	359
FINNY								
Abraham	58	m	b	VA	Colusa	Colusa Twp	71	278

Series M593

© 2001 by Heritage Quest. All rights reserved.

Name	Age	S	R	B-PL	County	Locale	Roll	Pg
Bridget	35	f	w	IREL	San Mateo	San Mateo P O	87	357
Chas	20	m	w	IREL	Sierra	Gibson Twp	89	542
Clark W	33	m	w	MA	San Mateo	Woodside P O	87	380
James	28	m	w	IREL	Amador	Amador City P O	69	394
FINO								
Francisco	42	m	w	MEXI	Santa Barbara	San Buenaventura P	87	439
Luis	10	m	m	CA	Santa Barbara	San Buenaventura P	87	439
Marguerita	30	f	i	MEXI	Santa Barbara	San Buenaventura P	87	439
FINRICH								
Henry	29	f	w	IREL	San Mateo	Redwood Twp	87	366
FINSENT								
G C	38	m	w	ME	Humboldt	Eureka Twp	72	260
FINSLY								
Annie	25	f	w	IREL	San Francisco	7-Wd San Francisco	81	241
FINSTER								
Danial	52	m	w	CANA	San Francisco	7-Wd San Francisco	81	159
George	35	m	w	CANA	Yolo	Cache Crk Twp	93	425
Joseph	15	m	w	CANA	San Francisco	7-Wd San Francisco	81	159
William	24	m	w	PRUS	Yolo	Merritt Twp	93	507
FINSTERWALD								
Barber	51	f	w	SWIT	Nevada	Bridgeport Twp	75	113
FINT								
Ah	42	m	c	CHIN	Sierra	Eureka Twp	89	525
FINWICK								
J	8	f	w	CA	Sonoma	Santa Rosa	91	424
FIOD								
Laurence	30	m	w	SILE	San Francisco	2-Wd San Francisco	79	273
FIORATI								
William	28	m	w	ITAL	San Francisco	San Francisco P O	80	471
FIORATTI								
Charles	26	m	w	LA	San Francisco	San Francisco P O	80	461
FIORI								
Antoine	60	m	w	SWIT	Marin	San Antonio Twp	74	63
Antone	19	m	w	SWIT	Marin	San Antonio Twp	74	62
John	27	m	w	SWIT	Marin	San Antonio Twp	74	62
Joseph	44	m	w	SWIT	Marin	Bolinas Twp	74	2
FIP								
Ah	54	m	c	CHIN	San Francisco	San Francisco P O	80	508
Ah	29	m	c	CHIN	San Francisco	San Francisco P O	80	518
Ah	28	m	c	CHIN	Placer	Bath P O	76	425
Ah	22	m	c	CHIN	San Francisco	3-Wd San Francisco	79	310
Ah	22	m	c	CHIN	Sutter	Yuba Twp	92	147
Ah	22	m	c	CHIN	San Joaquin	Oneal Twp	86	117
FIPPPIN								
John	35	m	w	OH	Nevada	Rough & Ready Twp	75	323
FIPPS								
James	43	m	w	ENGL	Marin	San Rafael Twp	74	43
William	28	m	w	PA	Plumas	Quartz Twp	77	40
FIQUE								
---	30	m	w	ITAL	Sonoma	Salt Point	91	391
FIRCAR								
Louis	35	m	w	PRUS	San Francisco	6-Wd San Francisco	81	81
FIRCHER								
Emile	40	m	w	SAXO	San Francisco	2-Wd San Francisco	79	249
FIREBAUG								
James	25	m	w	VA	Tulare	Farmersville Twp	92	243
FIREBAUGH								
Andrew D T	49	m	w	VA	Fresno	Kings Rvr P O	72	203
Franklin	54	m	w	VA	Tulare	Farmersville Twp	92	243
FIRESTONE								
Levi	31	m	w	OH	Inyo	Independence Twp	73	324
FIRGANS								
Heney	25	m	w	DENM	San Francisco	7-Wd San Francisco	81	225
FIRK								
Ah	20	m	c	CHIN	San Francisco	1-Wd San Francisco	79	85
FIRMAN								
Jacob	19	m	w	WI	Marin	San Rafael Twp	74	26
John	23	m	w	ENGL	San Francisco	San Francisco P O	83	293
Maria A	65	f	w	NJ	El Dorado	Placerville	72	119
Mathew H	50	m	w	NY	San Francisco	6-Wd San Francisco	81	97
Peter	30	m	w	SCOT	Alameda	Oakland	68	259
FIRMERTY								
Jas	9	m	w	CA	Santa Barbara	Santa Barbara P O	87	492
FIRMSTONE								
Henry T	39	m	w	ENGL	Plumas	Indian Twp	77	18
James	36	m	w	ENGL	Plumas	Indian Twp	77	16
FIRNAGE								
Ferdinand	44	m	w	BAVA	Yuba	Long Bar Twp	93	560
FIRNEY								
Charles	38	m	w	SWIT	Calaveras	San Andreas P O	70	198
Joseph	18	m	w	SWIT	Calaveras	San Andreas P O	70	198
FIRT								
Ah	46	m	c	CHIN	Nevada	Eureka Twp	75	127
FIRTLE								
Joseph	43	m	w	ENGL	San Francisco	7-Wd San Francisco	81	282
FIS								
Richard	24	m	w	BREM	San Francisco	San Francisco P O	83	143
FISCHBECK								
J R	37	m	w	PRUS	San Francisco	San Francisco P O	83	291
FISCHER								
Bernard	42	m	w	PRUS	San Francisco	11-Wd San Francisc	84	631
Elanus	35	m	w	OLDE	Yuba	Linda Twp	93	554
Geo	33	m	w	SAXO	San Francisco	2-Wd San Francisco	79	214
George	23	m	w	BAVA	San Francisco	6-Wd San Francisco	81	82
Gotlip	58	m	w	BAVA	San Francisco	11-Wd San Francisc	84	636
John	53	m	w	HAMB	Los Angeles	Santa Ana Twp	73	610
John	20	m	w	GERM	Sonoma	Washington Twp	91	471
Jos	47	m	w	SWIT	Solano	Benicia	90	2
Karl	39	m	w	SAXO	San Francisco	11-Wd San Francisc	84	565
Pat	32	f	w	NY	San Joaquin	Castoria Twp	86	11
Saml	63	m	w	NY	San Joaquin	Castoria Twp	86	11
FISCHERMAN								
A	39	m	w	PRUS	Del Norte	Crescent	71	465
FISCHIRNER								
Max	35	m	w	PRUS	San Francisco	San Francisco P O	80	351
FISCK								
George	48	m	w	HAMB	Siskiyou	Yreka	89	660
FISCUS								
John	30	m	w	PA	Solano	Rio Vista Twp	90	63
FISH								
Almerin	63	m	w	VT	El Dorado	Placerville Twp	72	105
Barbara	25	f	w	NY	San Francisco	8-Wd San Francisco	82	443
Benjamin	38	m	w	IN	Mendocino	Little Lake Twp	74	193
Benjamin F	50	m	w	NY	Santa Clara	Santa Clara Twp	88	137
Charles	40	m	w	PA	Amador	Drytown P O	69	422
Charles	21	m	w	MA	San Francisco	3-Wd San Francisco	79	308
Chas	21	m	w	PA	San Francisco	1-Wd San Francisco	79	107
Chas E	28	m	w	ME	Sierra	Table Rock Twp	89	578
Daniel	49	m	w	PA	Yolo	Cache Crk Twp	93	444
Dora	71	f	w	HANO	San Francisco	2-Wd San Francisco	79	237
Edward P	33	m	w	NY	San Francisco	3-Wd San Francisco	79	317
Eliza	43	f	w	NY	San Francisco	San Francisco P O	85	856
Emma	10	f	w	CA	Santa Clara	Gilroy Twp	88	84
Erskine	40	m	w	NY	Tehama	Tehama Twp	92	186
Francis	38	m	w	IN	Mendocino	Point Arena Twp	74	206
G	60	m	w	PRUS	Sacramento	3-Wd Sacramento	77	263
George M	47	m	w	OH	San Francisco	1-Wd San Francisco	79	107
H W	36	m	w	ME	Nevada	Meadow Lake Twp	75	270
Harriet A	50	f	w	NY	Humboldt	Arcata Twp	72	230
Henry	40	m	w	CANA	Yolo	Cache Crk Twp	93	438
Henry	38	m	w	BELG	Sierra	Table Rock Twp	89	579
Horace G	45	m	w	MA	San Francisco	6-Wd San Francisco	81	116
Isaac B	46	m	w	OH	Santa Cruz	Watsonville	89	371
John	46	m	w	NY	Monterey	Castroville Twp	74	335
Joseph	60	m	w	NY	Contra Costa	Martinez Twp	71	351
Joseph	50	m	w	MA	Contra Costa	Martinez P O	71	438
Josh	23	m	w	AZOR	San Francisco	1-Wd San Francisco	79	97
Lafayette	43	m	w	NY	Tehama	Deer Crk Twp	92	172
Lena	65	f	w	FRNK	San Francisco	San Francisco P O	80	342
M W	45	m	w	NY	Solano	Benicia	90	13
N B	39	m	w	ME	Sierra	Table Rock Twp	89	573
Nathan	50	m	w	BAVA	San Francisco	San Francisco P O	83	18
Nathaniel	58	m	w	MA	Alameda	Brooklyn	68	37
P W	47	m	w	NY	Santa Clara	Gilroy Twp	88	81
Samuel J	26	m	w	ENGL	Yolo	Putah Twp	93	523
Thos	50	m	w	NY	Alameda	Oakland	68	255
W H	46	m	w	NY	Alameda	Oakland	68	186
FISHBACH								
James	22	m	w	IL	Yolo	Grafton Twp	93	497
FISHBACK								
Henry	26	m	w	PRUS	San Francisco	San Francisco P O	80	424
FISHBECK								
John	22	m	w	PRUS	San Francisco	San Francisco P O	80	402
FISHBOURNE								
Harry	28	m	w	OH	San Francisco	San Francisco P O	83	187
FISHBURN								
Eliza	45	f	w	SCOT	San Francisco	8-Wd San Francisco	82	492
FISHE								
Heny	17	m	w	HAMB	San Joaquin	Tulare Twp	86	250
John	37	m	w	BAVA	San Joaquin	Douglas Twp	86	31
FISHEL								
Henry	38	m	w	BOHE	San Francisco	8-Wd San Francisco	82	417
Maurice	35	m	w	AUST	San Francisco	3-Wd San Francisco	79	324
FISHELL								
J	49	m	w	NY	Lake	Big Valley	73	395
FISHEN								
John	35	m	w	PRUS	San Joaquin	Douglas Twp	86	31
FISHER								
---	26	m	w	CT	Yuba	Marysville	93	617
A	25	m	w	ENGL	Alameda	Oakland	68	144
A D	22	m	w	NY	San Francisco	7-Wd San Francisco	81	221
Abraham	29	m	w	OH	Nevada	Rough & Ready Twp	75	335
Albert C	23	m	w	MA	San Francisco	1-Wd San Francisco	79	88
Almond	52	m	w	VT	Contra Costa	Martinez P O	71	444
Amelia	8	f	w	CA	Santa Clara	1-Wd San Jose	88	243
Amelia	6	f	w	CA	San Francisco	San Francisco P O	85	799
Amos	39	m	w	PA	Yuba	Marysville	93	590
Andrew	45	m	w	WURT	Calaveras	San Andreas P O	70	157
Andrew	33	m	w	DENM	Marin	Tomales Twp	74	88
Arabella	35	f	w	PA	Yolo	Cache Crk Twp	93	424
Archy	35	m	b	TN	Nevada	Bridgeport Twp	75	105
Arthur	26	m	w	PRUS	San Francisco	5-Wd San Francisco	81	15
August	20	m	w	NY	San Francisco	7-Wd San Francisco	81	275
Augustus	30	m	w	VT	San Mateo	San Mateo P O	87	357
B	35	m	w	BADE	Amador	Drytown P O	69	422
B D	42	m	w	MO	San Joaquin	Tulare Twp	86	251
B H	35	m	w	MA	San Francisco	San Francisco P O	85	776
B P	48	m	w	MA	Alameda	Oakland	68	217
Benjamin	35	m	w	PA	Solano	Vacaville Twp	90	122
Bob	60	m	w	MA	Sacramento	Sutter Twp	77	385
C B	44	m	w	MO	San Joaquin	Douglas Twp	86	42
C E	40	m	w	MD	Sacramento	3-Wd Sacramento	77	276
Carrie	3	f	w	CA	San Francisco	2-Wd San Francisco	79	194
Charles	61	m	w	MA	Marin	Sausalito Twp	74	67

Series M593 (Roll, Pg)

© 2001 by Heritage Quest. All rights reserved.

Series M593

Name	Age	S	R	B-PL	County	Locale	Roll	Pg
Charles	55	m	w	AUST	San Francisco	2-Wd San Francisco	79	208
Charles	38	m	w	PRUS	Contra Costa	Martinez P O	71	412
Charles	38	m	m	NY	San Francisco	San Francisco P O	80	357
Charles	32	m	w	PRUS	San Francisco	2-Wd San Francisco	79	175
Charles	30	m	w	ENGL	Santa Clara	2-Wd San Jose	88	329
Charles	30	m	w	ENGL	San Francisco	2-Wd San Francisco	79	214
Charles	19	m	w	NY	Placer	Emigrant Gap P O	76	416
Charles	16	m	w	CA	San Francisco	11-Wd San Francisc	84	593
Charles F	16	m	w	PA	Alameda	Alameda	68	17
Charles H	34	m	w	PRUS	San Francisco	6-Wd San Francisco	81	128
Charles H	25	m	w	OH	Mendocino	Gualala Twp	74	225
Charles L	53	m	w	ENGL	Santa Clara	Santa Clara Twp	88	138
Charles S	37	m	w	ME	Los Angeles	Los Angeles	73	530
Charles W	53	m	w	MECK	Los Angeles	Wilmington Twp	73	641
Charles W	39	m	w	GERM	Los Angeles	Soledad Twp	73	630
Chas	39	m	w	HANO	San Francisco	11-Wd San Francisc	84	665
Chas	16	m	w	PA	San Francisco	11-Wd San Francisc	84	422
Chas A	38	m	w	NH	San Francisco	8-Wd San Francisco	82	340
Chas F	53	m	w	PORT	San Francisco	1-Wd San Francisco	79	10
Chas H	20	m	w	MO	Sacramento	1-Wd Sacramento	77	177
Clayburn	28	m	w	VA	Colusa	Butte Twp	71	265
Conrad	57	m	w	BAVA	Klamath	Liberty Twp	73	376
Daman A	68	m	w	VT	Nevada	Grass Valley Twp	75	206
Daniel	69	m	w	PRUS	Sacramento	Center Twp	77	84
Daniel	47	m	w	IL	Yolo	Cache Crk Twp	93	445
Daniel	38	m	w	SCOT	Sonoma	Salt Point	91	390
David	46	m	w	BADE	San Francisco	San Francisco P O	80	342
David	35	m	w	CANA	Sacramento	Alabama Twp	77	60
David	28	m	w	SCOT	Santa Clara	San Jose Twp	88	193
Dine	22	f	w	MO	San Joaquin	Liberty Twp	86	97
E D	30	m	w	MI	Sacramento	Franklin Twp	77	112
E W	26	m	w	MA	San Francisco	San Francisco P O	83	314
Edward	28	m	w	DENM	Sacramento	Dry Crk Twp	77	104
Edwd T	18	m	b	MD	San Francisco	1-Wd San Francisco	79	52
Elizabeth	76	f	w	PA	Butte	Chico Twp	70	33
Ellen	24	f	w	IREL	San Francisco	2-Wd San Francisco	79	277
Ellen F	24	f	w	MA	San Francisco	8-Wd San Francisco	82	441
Emily D	38	f	w	ME	San Francisco	8-Wd San Francisco	82	458
Emma	16	f	w	CA	Alameda	Oakland	68	182
Erasmus P	50	m	w	MA	Santa Clara	San Jose Twp	88	209
Eugene	24	m	w	MA	San Joaquin	Elkhorn Twp	86	55
F C	35	m	w	IREL	Solano	Benicia	90	10
Fannie	22	f	w	FRAN	San Francisco	San Francisco P O	83	191
Fayette	47	m	w	MA	Sutter	Butte Twp	92	98
Francis	40	m	w	TX	Stanislaus	Empire Twp	92	58
Frank	55	m	w	SWIT	El Dorado	Mud Springs Twp	72	87
Frank	31	m	w	NY	San Francisco	6-Wd San Francisco	81	94
Frank	29	m	w	MA	San Francisco	7-Wd San Francisco	81	278
Frank	27	m	w	PORT	Marin	Bolinas Twp	74	5
Frank H	44	m	w	NH	Nevada	Nevada Twp	75	284
Fred	42	m	w	HANO	Sacramento	3-Wd Sacramento	77	286
Fred	39	m	c	BADE	Sonoma	Sonoma Twp	91	440
Fred	29	m	w	MA	San Joaquin	Elkhorn Twp	86	55
Frederick	34	m	w	BADE	San Diego	Poway Dist	78	481
Fredk	37	m	w	PRUS	San Francisco	1-Wd San Francisco	79	52
French	60	m	w	FRAN	Sacramento	Natomas Twp	77	170
G A	54	m	w	BAVA	Tuolumne	Chinese Camp P O	93	370
G W	55	m	b	NJ	Placer	Auburn P O	76	373
G W	30	m	w	MA	Alameda	Oakland	68	227
Galen M	44	m	w	SAME	Napa	Napa	75	11
Geo	75	m	w	SWIT	Humboldt	Eureka Twp	72	278
Geo	37	m	w	NY	Sierra	Table Rock Twp	89	571
Geo	23	m	w	BADE	Sacramento	3-Wd Sacramento	77	278
George	78	m	w	GREE	San Francisco	5-Wd San Francisco	81	35
George	50	m	w	WURT	Amador	Jackson P O	69	333
George	48	m	w	HESS	El Dorado	White Oak Twp	72	138
George	47	m	w	TN	San Francisco	8-Wd San Francisco	82	368
George	45	m	w	NH	San Francisco	7-Wd San Francisco	81	227
George	43	m	w	PRUS	San Francisco	8-Wd San Francisco	82	307
George	38	m	w	HDAR	Mariposa	Maxwell Crk P O	74	145
George	37	m	w	PA	San Francisco	San Francisco P O	80	390
George	36	m	w	NY	San Francisco	San Francisco P O	80	380
George	28	m	w	BADE	Contra Costa	Martinez P O	71	396
George	28	m	w	NY	San Francisco	5-Wd San Francisco	81	22
George	22	m	w	IN	Napa	Napa	75	20
George H	31	m	w	PA	San Mateo	San Mateo P O	87	359
George S	23	m	w	NY	Santa Clara	Santa Clara Twp	88	145
Georgiana	14	f	w	LA	Sacramento	Franklin Twp	77	106
H	54	m	w	PA	San Joaquin	3-Wd Stockton	86	238
H	44	m	w	PRUS	Yuba	Marysville	93	586
H Jas	21	m	w	IA	Santa Clara	Gilroy Twp	88	95
Harry	50	m	w	PRUS	San Francisco	5-Wd San Francisco	81	10
Harry	11	m	w	NY	San Francisco	2-Wd San Francisco	79	253
Henry	42	m	w	AUSL	San Francisco	San Francisco P O	80	389
Henry	42	m	w	NETH	Sacramento	San Joaquin Twp	77	398
Henry	42	m	w	ENGL	San Francisco	8-Wd San Francisco	82	399
Henry	32	m	w	BELG	San Francisco	11-Wd San Francisc	84	611
Henry	24	m	w	PRUS	Los Angeles	Los Angeles	73	517
Henry	14	m	w	NY	San Francisco	11-Wd San Francisc	84	588
Isaac	41	m	w	PA	Yolo	Cache Crk Twp	93	444
Isaac B	38	m	w	NY	San Diego	San Diego	78	501
J H	49	m	w	SCOG	San Joaquin	Oneal Twp	86	111
J Z	66	m	w	CANA	Mendocino	Sanel Twp	74	228
Jacob	41	m	w	SWIT	Solano	Vallejo	90	204
Jacob B	34	m	w	VA	El Dorado	Mountain Twp	72	69
James	51	m	w	MA	San Joaquin	1-Wd Stockton	86	126
James	45	m	w	IL	Tulare	Visalia Twp	92	285

Series M593

Name	Age	S	R	B-PL	County	Locale	Roll	Pg
James	40	m	w	MO	Sutter	Sutter Twp	92	121
James	37	m	w	NY	Solano	Maine Prairie Twp	90	45
James	36	m	w	ENGL	Nevada	Grass Valley Twp	75	213
James	36	m	w	IREL	Yuba	Rose Bar Twp	93	663
James	35	m	w	NH	Solano	Maine Prairie Twp	90	48
James	27	m	w	NH	Placer	Gold Run Twp	76	396
James E	11	m	w	CA	Santa Clara	Gilroy Twp	88	69
Jas W	19	m	w	IREL	San Francisco	8-Wd San Francisco	82	346
John	8	m	w	CA	San Francisco	San Francisco P O	85	828
John	60	m	w	LA	San Francisco	7-Wd San Francisco	81	170
John	55	m	w	HI	Yolo	Merritt Twp	93	502
John	55	m	w	BADE	Amador	Ione City P O	69	355
John	49	m	w	PA	Trinity	Junction City Pct	92	206
John	46	m	w	GERM	San Diego	San Diego	78	494
John	44	m	w	HAMB	San Francisco	11-Wd San Francisc	84	693
John	41	m	w	DENM	Calaveras	Copperopolis P O	70	244
John	40	m	w	PRUS	San Francisco	5-Wd San Francisco	81	10
John	33	m	w	IREL	Nevada	Grass Valley Twp	75	182
John	32	m	w	OH	Solano	Denverton Twp	90	27
John	32	m	w	PA	Plumas	Indian Twp	77	17
John	31	m	w	IREL	Solano	Tremont Twp	90	29
John	30	m	w	MI	Alameda	Brooklyn	68	32
John	30	m	w	MO	Amador	Jackson P O	69	320
John	29	m	w	PORT	San Mateo	Half Moon Bay P O	87	400
John	29	m	w	SWIT	Los Angeles	Wilmington Twp	73	642
John	26	m	w	IA	Monterey	Alisal Twp	74	288
John	22	m	w	ME	Stanislaus	Empire Twp	92	45
John	13	m	w	CA	San Joaquin	1-Wd Stockton	86	139
John C	34	m	w	BAVA	Placer	Rocklin Twp	76	463
Jonathan	50	m	w	NH	Tulare	Visalia Twp	92	284
Jonathan	15	m	w	OH	Amador	Amador City P O	69	391
Jose	21	m	w	CA	Stanislaus	San Joaquin Twp	92	82
Joseph	45	m	w	BAVA	San Francisco	San Francisco P O	83	159
Joseph	30	m	w	NY	Monterey	San Antonio Twp	74	315
Joseph	23	m	w	PRUS	Placer	Auburn P O	76	368
Joseph	22	m	w	PORT	San Francisco	1-Wd San Francisco	79	89
Joseph F	49	m	w	GERM	El Dorado	Placerville	72	117
Joseph T	41	m	w	GERM	San Luis Obispo	San Luis Obispo Tw	87	309
Joshua K	33	m	w	PA	San Diego	San Diego	78	495
Juan	35	m	w	CA	Stanislaus	Emory Twp	92	20
Julius	24	m	w	SAXO	Butte	Kimshew Tpw	70	82
L G	45	m	w	MA	Trinity	Canyon City Pct	92	202
Lane	22	m	w	MA	San Francisco	11-Wd San Francisc	84	694
Leonard	36	m	w	MA	San Francisco	8-Wd San Francisco	82	415
Leonard	36	m	w	BAVA	Santa Clara	2-Wd San Jose	88	302
Levi	41	m	w	PA	Yolo	Cache Crk Twp	93	444
Lewis	50	m	w	PORT	Placer	Bath P O	76	425
Louis	35	m	w	SWIT	San Francisco	8-Wd San Francisco	82	435
Luis	39	m	w	NY	San Francisco	11-Wd San Francisc	84	616
Maria	46	f	w	BRAZ	San Francisco	San Francisco P O	83	288
Maria	30	f	w	NY	Stanislaus	Emory Twp	92	24
Martha	18	f	w	NY	San Francisco	8-Wd San Francisco	82	321
Martin	47	m	w	CANA	San Francisco	7-Wd San Francisco	81	182
Martin	27	m	w	PRUS	San Francisco	1-Wd San Francisco	79	103
Morris	46	m	w	PRUS	San Francisco	San Francisco P O	80	375
Nancy	25	f	w	MO	Trinity	North Fork Twp	92	217
Nichols	24	m	w	PRUS	San Francisco	7-Wd San Francisco	81	226
Oleguia	9	m	w	CA	Los Angeles	Los Angeles	73	556
Peter	42	m	w	PORT	San Luis Obispo	Salinas Twp	87	291
Peter	35	m	w	OH	Shasta	Millville P O	89	492
Peter	25	m	w	PRUS	Santa Clara	1-Wd San Jose	88	232
Philander	64	m	w	MA	San Francisco	San Francisco P O	83	170
Philip	36	m	w	BAVA	Yuba	Marysville	93	581
Philip	30	m	w	NY	San Francisco	2-Wd San Francisco	79	194
Philip H	41	m	w	MD	Sacramento	Brighton Twp	77	77
R	27	m	w	OH	Alameda	Oakland	68	216
R A	40	m	w	MA	Alameda	Oakland	68	260
R A	38	m	w	PA	Alameda	Oakland	68	193
R D	68	f	w	VA	Alameda	Oakland	68	244
Richd	50	m	w	PRUS	San Francisco	San Francisco P O	83	281
Robert	42	m	m	DC	Sacramento	2-Wd Sacramento	77	245
Robert	32	m	w	IREL	San Francisco	1-Wd San Francisco	79	92
Robert	30	m	w	ENGL	Los Angeles	Santa Ana Twp	73	601
S	33	m	w	ME	Sierra	Lincoln Twp	89	552
Saml	32	m	w	POLA	San Francisco	1-Wd San Francisco	79	108
Samuel	35	m	w	PA	Nevada	Grass Valley Twp	75	155
Sarah	32	f	w	MO	Amador	Volcano P O	69	385
Sarah	16	f	w	NY	San Francisco	San Francisco P O	80	378
Sidney A	28	m	w	OH	San Francisco	8-Wd San Francisco	82	328
Simon	32	m	w	PA	Solano	Vallejo	90	167
Simon	23	m	w	OH	San Joaquin	Union Twp	86	267
Susan C	58	f	w	MA	San Francisco	8-Wd San Francisco	82	325
Theodore	44	m	w	PRUS	Butte	Ophir Twp	70	102
Thomas	67	m	w	ENGL	Plumas	Quartz Twp	77	43
Thomas	42	m	w	ENGL	San Francisco	8-Wd San Francisco	82	408
Thomas	42	m	w	OH	Calaveras	San Andreas P O	70	173
Thomas	41	m	w	SCOT	Mendocino	Cuffeys Cove Twp	74	168
Thomas	26	m	w	MEXI	Santa Clara	Burnett Twp	88	37
Thos	61	m	w	MA	San Francisco	11-Wd San Francisc	84	693
Thos	46	m	w	MA	Sacramento	4-Wd Sacramento	77	344
Thos	40	m	w	OH	Butte	Ophir Twp	70	120
Thos	35	m	w	IN	Butte	Chico Twp	70	23
Upton	35	m	w	MD	Sacramento	Brighton Twp	77	80
W J	30	m	w	NY	San Francisco	5-Wd San Francisco	81	3
Wallace	30	m	w	MA	San Francisco	San Francisco P O	83	375
Wellington	21	m	w	NY	Sacramento	American Twp	77	66
William	39	m	w	CANA	Sacramento	American Twp	77	66

© 2001 by Heritage Quest. All rights reserved.

Name	Age	S	R	B-PL	County	Locale	Series M593 Roll	Pg
William	31	m	w	HANO	Santa Clara	2-Wd San Jose	88	294
William	31	m	w	WURT	San Francisco	6-Wd San Francisco	81	40
William	24	m	w	MEXI	Santa Clara	Burnett Twp	88	37
William	19	m	w	DC	Stanislaus	Empire Twp	92	43
William	18	m	w	WURT	Marin	San Rafael	74	48
William A	41	m	w	NY	Stanislaus	San Joaquin Twp	92	75
William G	35	m	w	GERM	Santa Clara	San Jose Twp	88	190
William J	35	m	w	PRUS	San Francisco	8-Wd San Francisco	82	440
Wm	33	m	w	IA	Santa Clara	Gilroy Twp	88	67
Wm	19	m	w	SCOT	San Francisco	San Francisco P O	85	859
Wm	10	m	w	CA	San Francisco	San Francisco P O	85	828
Wm A	50	m	w	SCOT	Napa	Napa Twp	75	65
Wm C	35	m	w	MA	San Francisco	1-Wd San Francisco	79	125
Wm F	37	m	w	PA	Napa	Napa	75	19
Wm J	38	m	w	MO	San Joaquin	Douglas Twp	86	36
Wm S	38	m	w	MO	Butte	Chico Twp	70	38
Wm T	23	m	w	MA	Yuba	Marysville	93	595
Wm V	45	m	w	KY	Shasta	Millville P O	89	488
FISHES								
Holmes C	24	m	w	MA	San Francisco	1-Wd San Francisco	79	55
FISHHER								
Herman C	33	m	w	PRUS	Monterey	Castroville Twp	74	336
FISK								
Abraham	56	m	w	NH	Tuolumne	Big Oak Flat P O	93	406
C H	28	m	w	ME	Mariposa	Maxwell Crk P O	74	144
Charles	57	m	w	VT	Calaveras	Copperopolis P O	70	254
Charles G	37	m	w	CANA	Santa Cruz	Santa Cruz Twp	89	385
Chas I	21	m	w	MA	San Francisco	San Francisco P O	85	873
Ed	31	m	w	NY	San Joaquin	3-Wd Stockton	86	233
Francisco	13	m	w	MN	Marin	Point Reyes Twp	74	21
Harry	21	m	w	HANO	San Francisco	11-Wd San Francisc	84	689
Henry	50	m	w	PRUS	San Joaquin	2-Wd Stockton	86	176
Ira A	56	m	w	OH	El Dorado	White Oak Twp	72	135
James	50	m	w	MA	San Francisco	6-Wd San Francisco	81	87
James	40	m	w	NY	San Francisco	San Francisco P O	83	328
John C	45	m	w	VT	Sonoma	Salt Point	91	389
Josia	35	m	w	VT	Marin	San Rafael Twp	74	33
Oliver	32	m	w	ME	Mariposa	Maxwell Crk P O	74	143
R A	32	m	w	ENGL	Sacramento	4-Wd Sacramento	77	349
Royal	60	m	w	MA	San Francisco	6-Wd San Francisco	81	132
Sherman	22	m	w	NY	Alameda	Alameda	68	8
William	51	m	w	NY	Contra Costa	Martinez P O	71	388
Wilson H	30	m	w	NH	Santa Barbara	San Buenaventura P	87	435
FISKE								
Albert W	21	m	w	MA	San Francisco	8-Wd San Francisco	82	346
Asa	51	m	w	MA	Solano	Maine Prairie Twp	90	53
Ezra	43	m	w	MA	San Joaquin	Elkhorn Twp	86	56
George D	42	m	w	MA	Yolo	Cache Crk Twp	93	435
H M	46	m	w	MA	Amador	Sutter Crk P O	69	408
John S	40	m	w	MA	Santa Clara	San Jose Twp	88	216
Lucius	56	m	w	MA	El Dorado	Placerville	72	127
FISKER								
Ellen	40	f	w	IREL	San Francisco	San Francisco P O	83	162
FISKLINGBURG								
Charles	30	m	w	PRUS	San Francisco	San Francisco P O	83	242
FISSEL								
Watson	37	m	w	OH	Solano	Silveyville Twp	90	88
FISSON								
Henry	32	m	w	BELG	Siskiyou	Surprise Valley Tw	89	641
FISTO								
Jumbo	27	m	w	ITAL	San Mateo	Belmont P O	87	374
FIT								
Ah	24	m	c	CHIN	San Francisco	1-Wd San Francisco	79	120
Ching	14	m	c	CHIN	San Francisco	2-Wd San Francisco	79	264
FITCH								
Alfred	21	m	w	NY	Santa Cruz	Soquel Twp	89	449
Amos	32	m	w	PRUS	San Francisco	5-Wd San Francisco	81	15
Asa	70	m	w	MA	Los Angeles	Santa Ana Twp	73	602
Casper	42	m	w	BADE	San Francisco	11-Wd San Francisc	84	703
Charles	28	m	w	CA	Sonoma	Russian Rvr	91	375
Charles A	49	m	w	NY	Santa Cruz	Santa Cruz	89	426
Charles H	65	m	w	CT	Stanislaus	Buena Vista Twp	92	11
Chas H	46	m	w	CT	Napa	Napa	75	6
Daniel	29	m	w	NY	San Francisco	San Francisco P O	83	266
Edwin	31	m	w	CT	Santa Cruz	Santa Cruz Twp	89	379
F B	80	m	w	OH	Sacramento	Brighton Twp	77	79
Geo A	26	m	w	VT	San Francisco	8-Wd San Francisco	82	362
George	33	m	w	BAVA	Colusa	Grand Island Twp	71	307
George C	46	m	w	OH	El Dorado	White Oak Twp	72	141
George K	44	m	w	NY	San Francisco	San Francisco P O	83	147
H Y	41	m	w	NY	Trinity	Trinity Center Pct	92	205
Hattie	3	f	w	CANA	Santa Clara	2-Wd San Jose	88	283
Henry	27	m	w	CANA	Santa Cruz	Pajaro Twp	89	350
Horace	22	m	w	OH	Santa Clara	Redwood Twp	88	133
Ida May	12	f	w	IA	Santa Clara	Gilroy Twp	88	74
Isaac	24	m	w	IL	Napa	Napa Twp	75	62
Ives J	42	m	w	NY	Placer	Auburn P O	76	368
J E	26	m	w	MI	Lassen	Milford Twp	73	438
J R	32	m	w	CANA	San Francisco	8-Wd San Francisco	82	300
John	50	m	b	NJ	San Francisco	San Francisco P O	80	422
John	24	m	w	MA	Solano	Vallejo	90	212
Josefa	63	f	w	CA	Sonoma	Russian Rvr	91	375
Joseph	34	m	w	CA	Sonoma	Russian Rvr	91	375
Lee Richmond	32	m	w	CANA	Santa Clara	Milpitas Twp	88	113
Lydia J	25	f	w	MO	Sonoma	Healdsburg & Mendo	91	282
Mary	46	f	w	NY	Alameda	Alameda	68	14
Mary	44	f	w	CT	San Francisco	San Francisco P O	83	261
Mary	41	f	w	LA	San Francisco	San Francisco P O	83	195
Oscar	29	m	w	NY	San Francisco	2-Wd San Francisco	79	256
Samuel	24	m	w	CT	Sacramento	3-Wd Sacramento	77	285
Walter	59	m	w	OH	Sacramento	Sutter Twp	77	383
William	50	m	w	OH	Mendocino	Little Lake Twp	74	197
William	45	m	w	NY	Solano	Suisun Twp	90	113
William	35	m	w	CA	Sonoma	Mendocino Twp	91	290
Wm	30	m	w	NY	Yuba	Rose Bar Twp	93	666
Wm S	35	m	w	PA	San Francisco	5-Wd San Francisco	81	18
Wm W	29	m	w	CANA	San Francisco	8-Wd San Francisco	82	365
FITCHER								
Jos	45	m	w	PRUS	San Francisco	San Francisco P O	83	105
FITCHET								
Jane	12	f	w	CA	Tehama	Red Bluff	92	183
FITCHNER								
Chas	52	m	w	PRUS	San Francisco	San Francisco P O	85	837
FITCHPATRICK								
Barny	35	m	w	IREL	Placer	Gold Run Twp	76	394
John	28	m	w	IREL	Placer	Dutch Flat P O	76	406
FITE								
George	32	m	w	PA	Kern	Linns Valley P O	73	343
John S	44	m	w	PA	San Francisco	8-Wd San Francisco	82	429
FITHIAN								
Amos	46	m	w	OH	Placer	Colfax P O	76	389
Ephraim	72	m	w	NJ	Los Angeles	Santa Ana Twp	73	612
James	53	m	w	KY	Los Angeles	Santa Ana Twp	73	613
Joseph C	44	m	w	OH	Amador	Ione City P O	69	371
S M	13	f	w	OH	Amador	Ione City P O	69	370
William	39	m	w	OH	Sonoma	Petaluma Twp	91	358
FITLOW								
Thomas	50	m	w	MD	Humboldt	Arcata Twp	72	229
FITO								
Otis	31	m	w	WI	Monterey	Castroville Twp	74	340
FITSCHAUD								
M	34	m	w	FRAN	Monterey	San Juan Twp	74	402
FITSGERALD								
Ellen	40	f	w	IREL	San Francisco	11-Wd San Francisc	84	653
Ellen	37	f	w	IREL	San Francisco	11-Wd San Francisc	84	700
Kate	60	f	w	IREL	San Francisco	11-Wd San Francisc	84	424
FITSGIBBON								
M	32	m	w	IREL	Sacramento	3-Wd Sacramento	77	281
FITSPATRIC								
Thos	40	m	w	MA	San Luis Obispo	Santa Rosa Twp	87	329
FITSPATRICK								
Rodgers	25	m	w	IREL	San Francisco	11-Wd San Francisc	84	534
Saml	53	m	w	IREL	Tuolumne	Columbia P O	93	355
Wm	28	m	w	CANA	San Francisco	11-Wd San Francisc	84	445
FITSSIMMONDS								
James	40	m	w	IREL	San Francisco	11-Wd San Francisc	84	453
FITSZGERALD								
Margt	22	f	w	IREL	San Francisco	11-Wd San Francisc	84	660
FITTER								
Eibe H	40	m	w	HANO	San Francisco	1-Wd San Francisco	79	119
John	34	m	w	HANO	Nevada	Bridgeport Twp	75	100
FITTIER								
Henry	32	m	w	SWIT	San Francisco	San Francisco P O	80	480
FITTIG								
Adele	22	f	w	PRUS	San Francisco	San Francisco P O	83	293
FITTON								
James	25	m	w	IREL	San Francisco	3-Wd San Francisco	79	312
Jeff	10	m	w	CA	Siskiyou	Scott Valley Twp	89	608
R B	18	m	w	IREL	San Francisco	3-Wd San Francisco	79	313
FITTS								
Austin	35	m	w	NY	Nevada	Eureka Twp	75	132
Elijah T	61	m	w	ME	Santa Clara	Santa Clara Twp	88	139
John	29	m	w	RI	San Francisco	1-Wd San Francisco	79	58
William	33	m	w	ME	Santa Clara	Milpitas Twp	88	112
FITTSON								
Semuel	48	m	w	ENGL	Placer	Bath P O	76	428
FITTZGIBBONS								
Daniel	35	m	w	IREL	Alameda	Washington Twp	68	271
FITZ								
Charles	24	m	w	BADE	San Francisco	7-Wd San Francisco	81	226
Gerald	35	m	w	IREL	San Francisco	San Francisco P O	85	811
Henry M	44	m	w	IREL	San Francisco	San Francisco P O	85	832
John Alfred	38	m	w	ENGL	Contra Costa	Martinez P O	71	414
Patrick Jas	45	m	w	IREL	San Francisco	1-Wd San Francisco	79	55
Patrick W	27	m	w	IREL	Sacramento	4-Wd Sacramento	77	338
Ruben R	33	m	w	NY	Yolo	Cache Crk Twp	93	441
Stephen C	48	m	w	NJ	Placer	Bath P O	76	447
Thos	35	m	w	IREL	Butte	Chico Twp	70	32
William Danl	44	m	w	IREL	Napa	Napa	75	7
FITZEARLS								
Thomas	79	m	w	IREL	Kern	Linns Valley P O	73	346
FITZEMERALD								
Alber	13	m	w	CA	Colusa	Colusa Twp	71	282
FITZENBERG								
Chs	36	m	w	BREM	San Francisco	2-Wd San Francisco	79	227
FITZERILL								
Mical	38	m	w	IREL	Humboldt	Bald Hills	72	239
FITZGERALD								
Adolph	28	m	w	NC	San Francisco	2-Wd San Francisco	79	279
And	40	m	w	IREL	Tuolumne	Sonora P O	93	325
Ann	57	f	w	IREL	Butte	Bidwell Twp	70	4
Annie	36	f	w	IREL	San Francisco	7-Wd San Francisco	81	284
Athin	2	f	w	CA	San Francisco	11-Wd San Francisc	84	711
Austin	40	m	w	IREL	San Francisco	6-Wd San Francisco	81	132

© 2001 by Heritage Quest. All rights reserved.

Name	Age	S	R	B-PL	County	Locale	Roll (Series M593)	Pg
Briget	45	f	w	IREL	San Francisco	7-Wd San Francisco	81	194
C	28	f	w	IL	Merced	Snelling P O	74	264
Charles	27	m	w	ME	Mendocino	Albion & Big Rvr T	74	166
Chas	30	m	w	IREL	Colusa	Spring Valley Twp	71	341
Chris	29	m	w	IREL	San Francisco	San Francisco P O	83	287
D	28	m	w	IREL	Alameda	Oakland	68	205
David	50	m	w	IREL	Nevada	Grass Valley Twp	75	213
Ed	30	m	w	IREL	Alameda	Oakland	68	143
Ed	25	m	w	MA	San Joaquin	Oneal Twp	86	102
Ed	23	m	w	NY	San Joaquin	Oneal Twp	86	102
Edward	40	m	w	IREL	Colusa	Butte Twp	71	268
Edward	27	m	w	NY	San Francisco	San Francisco P O	80	348
Eliza	50	f	w	IREL	San Francisco	San Francisco P O	83	302
Elizabeth	25	f	w	IREL	San Francisco	8-Wd San Francisco	82	447
Ellen	9	f	w	CA	Nevada	Grass Valley Twp	75	214
Ellen	28	f	w	IREL	San Francisco	8-Wd San Francisco	82	482
Ellen	22	f	w	IREL	Alameda	Eden Twp	68	57
Ester	26	f	w	IREL	Trinity	Weaverville Pct	92	222
Felix	47	m	w	IREL	Plumas	Plumas Twp	77	33
Frank	33	m	w	IREL	Sacramento	3-Wd Sacramento	77	257
G	32	m	w	IREL	Mendocino	Round Valley Twp	74	219
Geo R	45	m	w	MA	San Francisco	6-Wd San Francisco	81	155
George	32	m	w	IREL	Nevada	Grass Valley Twp	75	212
George C	55	m	w	IREL	Santa Clara	2-Wd San Jose	88	334
H	40	m	w	IREL	Alameda	Oakland	68	234
H E	56	f	w	VT	Sacramento	3-Wd Sacramento	77	301
H W	42	m	w	KY	Amador	Fiddletown P O	69	431
Henry	57	m	w	MA	Contra Costa	Martinez P O	71	384
I L	17	m	w	IL	Tehama	Tehama Twp	92	192
J	45	f	w	IREL	Santa Clara	Burnett Twp	88	30
J	30	m	w	IREL	Alameda	Oakland	68	217
J	25	m	w	IREL	Alameda	Oakland	68	261
J F	22	m	w	CANA	Sacramento	3-Wd Sacramento	77	317
J H	31	m	w	MO	San Francisco	3-Wd San Francisco	79	315
J T	34	m	w	MO	Merced	Snelling P O	74	272
Jacob	57	m	b	VA	San Francisco	San Francisco P O	80	423
Jacob	57	m	w	VA	Humboldt	Eureka Twp	72	269
James	43	m	w	CANA	Santa Clara	Burnett Twp	88	38
James	40	m	w	IREL	Santa Clara	2-Wd San Jose	88	316
James	40	m	w	IREL	San Francisco	8-Wd San Francisco	82	398
James	34	m	w	IREL	Alameda	Oakland	68	143
James	26	m	w	IREL	Placer	Emigrant Gap P O	76	416
James	25	m	w	IREL	San Francisco	1-Wd San Francisco	79	64
James E	35	m	w	MA	San Francisco	2-Wd San Francisco	79	188
Jane	29	f	w	IREL	San Francisco	7-Wd San Francisco	81	186
Jas	55	m	w	IREL	San Francisco	8-Wd San Francisco	82	318
Jas	42	m	w	IREL	San Francisco	1-Wd San Francisco	79	12
Jas	35	m	w	CANA	Solano	Vallejo	90	159
Jo	45	m	w	MO	San Joaquin	Liberty Twp	86	87
Johanna	74	f	w	IREL	Contra Costa	Martinez P O	71	372
John	47	m	w	ENGL	Placer	Emigrant Gap P O	76	416
John	41	m	w	IREL	San Francisco	San Francisco P O	85	869
John	34	m	w	IREL	San Francisco	11-Wd San Francisc	84	573
John	33	m	w	IREL	San Francisco	San Francisco P O	85	860
John	33	m	w	IL	Colusa	Grand Island Twp	71	304
John	30	m	w	IREL	San Francisco	San Francisco P O	85	755
John	30	m	w	CANA	Sonoma	Vallejo Twp	91	454
John	30	m	w	IREL	San Francisco	1-Wd San Francisco	79	134
John	27	m	w	IREL	San Francisco	1-Wd San Francisco	79	90
John	27	m	w	IREL	San Joaquin	Tulare Twp	86	255
John	25	m	w	IREL	Los Angeles	Wilmington Twp	73	642
John	25	m	w	IREL	San Francisco	1-Wd San Francisco	79	135
John	25	m	w	IREL	San Francisco	San Francisco P O	85	734
John	25	m	w	IREL	San Francisco	San Francisco P O	83	218
John	25	m	w	IREL	San Francisco	7-Wd San Francisco	81	186
John	14	m	w	CA	San Francisco	11-Wd San Francisc	84	588
John	10	m	w	CA	Marin	San Rafael Twp	74	27
John T	36	m	w	IREL	Stanislaus	Empire Twp	92	65
Jos	43	m	w	IREL	Sonoma	Bodega Twp	91	249
Joseph	7	m	w	CA	Marin	San Rafael Twp	74	28
Joseph E	40	m	w	MI	Sacramento	Granite Twp	77	136
Kate	40	f	w	IREL	Sonoma	Petaluma Twp	91	353
Kate	24	f	w	IREL	San Francisco	San Francisco P O	85	728
Kate	13	f	w	NY	Nevada	Bridgeport Twp	75	112
Katie	25	f	w	IREL	Sacramento	4-Wd Sacramento	77	350
Lawrence	29	m	w	IREL	Stanislaus	Empire Twp	92	49
Luke	20	m	w	IREL	Solano	Vallejo	90	214
Luke	20	m	w	IREL	Marin	San Rafael Twp	74	27
M	35	m	w	IREL	Yuba	Marysville	93	605
M	35	m	w	CANA	Santa Clara	Burnett Twp	88	38
M	29	f	w	IREL	Solano	Benicia	90	14
M	20	m	w	KY	Amador	Jackson P O	69	324
M	19	f	w	IREL	San Joaquin	2-Wd Stockton	86	162
M A	41	m	w	IREL	Tuolumne	Chinese Camp P O	93	366
M J	30	m	w	IREL	Solano	Vallejo	90	147
M O	42	m	w	IREL	Alameda	Oakland	68	222
Magt	35	f	w	IREL	San Francisco	1-Wd San Francisco	79	44
Magt	32	f	w	IREL	Sacramento	3-Wd Sacramento	77	318
Margaret	45	f	w	IREL	Yolo	Cache Crk Twp	93	448
Margaret	35	f	w	IREL	San Francisco	San Francisco P O	83	194
Margaret	30	f	w	IREL	Yolo	Cache Crk Twp	93	427
Margt	30	f	w	IREL	San Francisco	8-Wd San Francisco	82	334
Margt	18	f	w	MA	San Francisco	8-Wd San Francisco	82	325
Maria	27	f	w	IREL	Solano	Vallejo	90	167
Martin	65	m	w	IREL	Amador	Volcano P O	69	383
Mary	48	f	w	IREL	Nevada	Grass Valley Twp	75	160
Mary	36	f	w	IREL	Alameda	Oakland	68	157

Name	Age	S	R	B-PL	County	Locale	Roll (Series M593)	Pg
Mary	35	f	w	PA	San Francisco	San Francisco P O	83	101
Mary	33	f	w	KY	Los Angeles	Los Angeles	73	504
Mary	28	f	w	IREL	San Francisco	2-Wd San Francisco	79	176
Mary	18	f	w	MA	San Francisco	8-Wd San Francisco	82	294
Mary	17	f	w	IREL	San Francisco	San Francisco P O	83	192
Mary J	23	f	w	IREL	Alameda	Oakland	68	253
Mathew	26	m	w	IREL	Yolo	Grafton Twp	93	489
Maurice	33	m	w	IREL	San Francisco	1-Wd San Francisco	79	105
Michael	40	m	w	IREL	San Francisco	San Francisco P O	80	384
Michael	36	m	w	IREL	San Francisco	2-Wd San Francisco	79	176
Michael	34	m	w	IREL	Nevada	Grass Valley Twp	75	220
Michael	32	m	w	IREL	San Francisco	7-Wd San Francisco	81	229
Michael	25	m	w	NY	San Francisco	San Francisco P O	83	124
Michl	40	m	w	IREL	San Francisco	1-Wd San Francisco	79	60
Morris	35	m	w	IREL	San Francisco	San Francisco P O	83	143
N	29	m	w	VA	Butte	Oregon Twp	70	126
N D	54	m	w	NY	Tehama	Tehama Twp	92	156
Oscar P	41	m	w	NC	San Francisco	2-Wd San Francisco	79	262
P	41	m	w	OH	San Joaquin	1-Wd Stockton	86	157
Pat	40	m	w	IREL	San Francisco	7-Wd San Francisco	81	251
Pat	36	m	w	IREL	Solano	Vallejo	90	197
Pat	21	m	w	CANA	Solano	Vallejo	90	150
Patk	40	m	w	IREL	Sacramento	4-Wd Sacramento	77	349
Patrick	79	m	w	IREL	San Francisco	San Francisco P O	80	348
Patrick	58	m	w	IREL	San Francisco	San Francisco P O	83	367
Patrick	38	m	w	IREL	San Francisco	San Francisco P O	83	386
Patrick	37	m	w	IREL	Alameda	Brooklyn Twp	68	53
Patrick	36	m	w	IREL	San Francisco	San Francisco P O	85	848
Patrick	30	m	w	IREL	Solano	Vacaville Twp	90	117
Patrick	24	m	w	IREL	San Francisco	San Francisco P O	83	152
Peter	25	m	w	IREL	Yolo	Cache Crk Twp	93	424
Philemina	21	f	w	ENGL	San Francisco	11-Wd San Francisc	84	688
Phillip	40	m	w	NJ	San Joaquin	Oneal Twp	86	100
R	35	m	w	IREL	Santa Clara	Gilroy Twp	88	82
Rebecca	41	f	w	NY	San Francisco	7-Wd San Francisco	81	156
Richard	32	m	w	ENGL	San Francisco	San Francisco P O	83	358
Richard	30	m	w	IREL	San Francisco	7-Wd San Francisco	81	265
Richd	30	m	w	CANA	Santa Clara	Burnett Twp	88	38
S	22	f	w	IREL	San Joaquin	2-Wd Stockton	86	163
Stephen	42	m	w	IREL	San Francisco	San Francisco P O	83	55
Stephen	30	m	w	IREL	Stanislaus	Empire Twp	92	52
The J	48	m	w	IREL	El Dorado	Cosumnes Twp	72	17
Thomas	51	m	w	KY	Tulare	Kings Rvr Twp	92	252
Thomas	38	m	w	IREL	San Francisco	7-Wd San Francisco	81	194
Thomas	27	m	w	IREL	San Francisco	11-Wd San Francisc	84	466
Thos	47	m	w	IREL	San Joaquin	2-Wd Stockton	86	176
Thos	40	m	w	IREL	Sacramento	4-Wd Sacramento	77	371
Thos	39	m	w	IREL	San Francisco	San Francisco P O	83	327
Thos	33	m	w	IREL	San Francisco	1-Wd San Francisco	79	101
Thos	31	m	w	CANA	Santa Clara	Gilroy Twp	88	102
Thos	26	m	w	MD	San Francisco	2-Wd San Francisco	79	263
Thos	26	m	w	CANA	Solano	Benicia	90	15
Thos	25	m	w	IREL	Marin	Nicasio Twp	74	18
Timothy	33	m	w	IREL	Nevada	Little York Twp	75	239
Timothy W	30	m	w	MA	Contra Costa	Martinez P O	71	384
Tom	28	m	w	IREL	Solano	Vallejo	90	215
Walter	73	m	w	IREL	Santa Clara	Burnett Twp	88	38
Walter	29	m	w	IREL	San Francisco	San Francisco P O	83	408
William	72	m	w	IREL	San Francisco	San Francisco P O	83	252
William	45	m	w	PA	San Francisco	San Francisco P O	83	182
Wilson C	32	m	w	ME	Mendocino	Point Arena Twp	74	214
Wm	45	m	w	IREL	Napa	Napa	75	8
Wm	44	m	w	WI	San Francisco	San Francisco P O	83	201
Wm	42	m	w	IREL	Sonoma	Bodega Twp	91	248
Wm	40	m	w	IREL	San Francisco	8-Wd San Francisco	82	361
Wm	32	m	w	IREL	Butte	Chico Twp	70	21
Wm	14	m	w	CA	San Francisco	11-Wd San Francisc	84	593
Wm	14	m	w	CA	San Francisco	San Francisco P O	83	71
Wm F	50	m	w	KY	Fresno	Kingston P O	72	219
FITZGEROLD								
C C	26	m	w	PA	Humboldt	Eel Rvr Twp	72	252
J H	57	m	w	ENGL	San Joaquin	1-Wd Stockton	86	131
J P	29	m	w	PA	Humboldt	Pacific Twp	72	295
James W	34	m	w	KY	Yolo	Putah Twp	93	513
Sam	39	m	w	AL	San Joaquin	Castoria Twp	86	14
FITZGERRALD								
J	40	m	w	IREL	San Joaquin	Liberty Twp	86	90
Jno	34	m	w	IREL	San Joaquin	Douglas Twp	86	36
John	40	m	w	IREL	Contra Costa	San Pablo Twp	71	357
John	40	m	w	IREL	Contra Costa	San Pablo Twp	71	358
Mc	51	m	w	IREL	Alameda	Murray Twp	68	101
Thos	28	m	w	IREL	Sonoma	Petaluma Twp	91	326
FITZGIBBEN								
John M	35	m	w	IREL	San Francisco	7-Wd San Francisco	81	228
FITZGIBBON								
James	26	m	w	IREL	Napa	Napa Twp	75	33
M	25	m	w	IREL	Sacramento	1-Wd Sacramento	77	178
Mary	27	f	w	NY	San Francisco	San Francisco P O	85	732
Morris	40	m	w	IREL	Sacramento	4-Wd Sacramento	77	321
Sarah	13	f	w	NY	Santa Cruz	Santa Cruz	89	417
Thos	30	m	w	IREL	San Francisco	San Francisco P O	85	851
Thos	28	m	w	KY	Alameda	Oakland	68	178
Thos	27	m	w	IREL	Alameda	Brooklyn Twp	68	42
FITZGIBBONS								
Chas	24	m	w	IREL	Solano	Vallejo	90	200
David	38	m	w	US	San Francisco	San Francisco P O	83	172
Geralo	27	m	w	IREL	Los Angeles	Wilmington Twp	73	638

© 2001 by Heritage Quest. All rights reserved.

Name	Age	S	R	B-PL	County	Locale	Series M593 Roll	Pg
John	39	m	w	IREL	San Francisco	San Francisco P O	83	312
Mary A	30	f	w	IREL	San Francisco	6-Wd San Francisco	81	86
Thomas	34	m	w	MI	El Dorado	Mud Springs Twp	72	79
FITZGIBBONS								
Morris	39	m	w	IREL	Sacramento	Cosumnes Twp	77	93
FITZHARN								
Roulta	24	f	w	MO	San Joaquin	1-Wd Stockton	86	124
FITZHARRIS								
James	50	m	w	IREL	Santa Clara	2-Wd San Jose	88	309
FITZHAYT								
Patrick	27	m	w	IREL	Yolo	Cache Crk Twp	93	448
FITZHENRY								
E	49	m	w	PA	Sacramento	3-Wd Sacramento	77	280
Kette	72	f	w	KY	Sacramento	3-Wd Sacramento	77	280
Thos	70	m	w	KY	Sacramento	3-Wd Sacramento	77	280
FITZHUE								
Morris	42	m	w	IREL	Sacramento	1-Wd Sacramento	77	178
FITZHUGH								
Chas F	53	m	w	KY	Mariposa	Mariposa P O	74	90
Edward C	19	m	w	MO	Mariposa	Mariposa P O	74	137
Emma	20	f	w	MA	San Francisco	San Francisco P O	85	728
H	47	m	w	MO	Siskiyou	Big Valley Twp	89	582
J W	57	m	w	KY	Merced	Snelling P O	74	249
James	40	m	w	ENGL	Stanislaus	San Joaquin Twp	92	70
Samuel	49	m	w	MO	San Bernardino	San Bernardino Twp	78	437
Teresa	46	f	w	SWED	San Francisco	6-Wd San Francisco	81	86
William	50	m	w	KY	Stanislaus	Branch Twp	92	6
FITZIMMONS								
Patrick	39	m	w	IREL	Sacramento	2-Wd Sacramento	77	247
Thomas	28	m	w	IREL	San Francisco	San Francisco P O	83	206
FITZJAMES								
Henry	35	m	w	ENGL	San Francisco	3-Wd San Francisco	79	325
FITZJEARLD								
Michael	34	m	w	IREL	Alameda	Eden Twp	68	92
Morris	33	m	w	IREL	Alameda	Eden Twp	68	89
FITZJERALD								
A	14	f	w	NY	Yuba	Marysville	93	582
FITZMAURICE								
Lizzie	32	f	w	FRAN	San Francisco	1-Wd San Francisco	79	134
M	15	f	w	CA	Solano	Benicia	90	16
FITZMORAN								
J	40	m	w	IREL	San Joaquin	Elkhorn Twp	86	57
FITZMORRIS								
Annie	64	f	w	IREL	San Francisco	San Francisco P O	83	408
E	38	m	w	IREL	Solano	Vallejo	90	145
George	60	m	w	IREL	San Francisco	San Francisco P O	85	768
Wm	20	m	w	INDI	San Francisco	1-Wd San Francisco	79	132
FITZNOR								
Edman	31	m	w	GERM	Los Angeles	Los Angeles	73	557
FITZPARTICK								
John	6	m	w	CA	Marin	San Rafael Twp	74	28
FITZPATRICH								
Annie	78	f	w	IREL	San Francisco	7-Wd San Francisco	81	270
FITZPATRICK								
---	28	m	w	IREL	San Francisco	2-Wd San Francisco	79	210
Andrew	45	m	w	IREL	Sonoma	Bodega Twp	91	259
Ann	40	f	w	LA	San Francisco	San Francisco P O	80	338
Anna	22	f	w	IREL	San Francisco	8-Wd San Francisco	82	299
Arthur	34	m	w	CANA	San Francisco	11-Wd San Francisc	84	618
B	58	f	w	IREL	Yuba	Marysville	93	606
B	35	f	w	IREL	Solano	Benicia	90	12
Barney	23	m	w	IREL	San Francisco	San Francisco P O	83	32
Barny	28	m	w	IREL	San Francisco	5-Wd San Francisco	81	7
Barny	24	m	w	IREL	Sutter	Butte Twp	92	94
Bridget	35	f	w	IREL	Sacramento	4-Wd Sacramento	77	347
Bridget	33	f	w	IREL	San Francisco	San Francisco P O	83	170
Bridget	30	f	w	IREL	San Francisco	San Francisco P O	83	296
Bridget	27	f	w	IREL	San Francisco	San Francisco P O	83	340
Bridgt	27	f	w	IREL	San Francisco	1-Wd San Francisco	79	89
C S	37	m	w	KY	Amador	Sutter Crk P O	69	408
Dan	28	m	w	IREL	San Francisco	3-Wd San Francisco	79	316
Daniel	9	m	w	CA	Marin	San Rafael Twp	74	28
Daniel	44	m	w	IREL	Solano	Suisun Twp	90	110
Daniel	30	m	w	IREL	Mariposa	Mariposa P O	74	112
David	26	m	w	CANA	Contra Costa	Martinez P O	71	396
Delia	25	f	w	IREL	San Francisco	San Francisco P O	85	815
Dennis	36	m	w	IREL	Sutter	Butte Twp	92	98
Dennis	24	m	w	IREL	San Francisco	San Francisco P O	83	174
Dora	27	f	w	IREL	San Francisco	7-Wd San Francisco	81	238
Ed	46	m	w	IREL	Solano	Vallejo	90	182
Edward	44	m	w	IREL	San Francisco	3-Wd San Francisco	79	300
Edward	23	m	w	IREL	Inyo	Bishop Crk Twp	73	316
Edwd	9	m	w	CA	Marin	San Rafael Twp	74	28
Elen	19	f	w	IREL	San Francisco	8-Wd San Francisco	82	374
Elizth	28	f	w	IREL	San Francisco	San Francisco P O	83	13
F P	22	m	w	NY	Solano	Vallejo	90	201
Felix	28	m	w	IL	San Diego	San Diego	78	496
Fleming	30	m	w	IREL	San Francisco	1-Wd San Francisco	79	134
Hugh	35	m	w	IREL	San Francisco	San Francisco P O	83	18
J	26	m	w	IREL	Yuba	Marysville Twp	93	568
J	23	m	w	IREL	Alameda	Oakland	68	265
James	51	m	w	IREL	San Francisco	San Francisco P O	80	335
James	50	m	w	IREL	San Francisco	6-Wd San Francisco	81	79
James	50	m	w	ENGL	San Mateo	Schoolhouse Statio	87	331
James	40	m	w	IREL	San Francisco	San Francisco P O	85	738
James	36	m	w	IREL	San Francisco	San Francisco P O	83	239
Jas	50	m	w	PA	Sacramento	Alabama Twp	77	62
Jas	39	m	w	CANA	San Francisco	1-Wd San Francisco	79	105
John	40	m	w	MA	San Francisco	San Francisco P O	83	323
John	37	m	w	IREL	San Francisco	11-Wd San Francisc	84	482
John	35	m	w	ENGL	San Mateo	Menlo Park P O	87	377
John	33	m	w	IREL	Contra Costa	Martinez P O	71	403
John	30	m	w	IREL	Placer	Bath P O	76	448
John	29	m	w	IREL	San Francisco	2-Wd San Francisco	79	271
John	29	m	w	IREL	Solano	Maine Prairie Twp	90	52
John	27	m	w	IREL	San Francisco	7-Wd San Francisco	81	239
John	27	m	w	IREL	San Francisco	San Francisco P O	83	239
John	22	m	w	IREL	Stanislaus	Empire Twp	92	37
Kate	24	f	w	IREL	San Francisco	11-Wd San Francisc	84	650
Katy	15	f	w	CA	Santa Clara	1-Wd San Jose	88	267
L	30	m	w	IREL	Solano	Benicia	90	13
Lawrence	32	m	w	CANA	Mendocino	Point Arena Twp	74	206
M	34	m	w	IREL	Solano	Vallejo	90	186
M	29	m	w	IREL	San Francisco	San Francisco P O	83	277
M	20	f	w	NY	Yuba	Marysville	93	576
Mary	66	f	w	IREL	San Francisco	San Francisco P O	80	384
Mary	60	f	w	IREL	San Francisco	San Francisco P O	83	126
Mary	35	f	w	IREL	San Francisco	8-Wd San Francisco	82	476
Mary	22	f	w	IREL	San Francisco	11-Wd San Francisc	84	606
Mary	13	f	w	CA	San Francisco	2-Wd San Francisco	79	184
Mary	12	f	w	NY	San Francisco	7-Wd San Francisco	81	277
Michael	44	m	w	NY	San Francisco	2-Wd San Francisco	79	188
Michael	24	m	w	VT	San Francisco	San Francisco P O	85	764
Michl	32	m	w	IREL	San Francisco	1-Wd San Francisco	79	113
Mike	43	m	w	IREL	San Francisco	11-Wd San Francisc	84	619
Mike	40	m	w	IREL	Sacramento	4-Wd Sacramento	77	371
Mike	40	m	w	IREL	San Francisco	11-Wd San Francisc	84	613
Mike	30	m	w	IREL	Sacramento	4-Wd Sacramento	77	368
Nicholas	43	m	w	IREL	Nevada	Bloomfield Twp	75	97
Owen	45	m	w	IREL	Stanislaus	Empire Twp	92	27
Owen	18	m	w	IREL	San Francisco	7-Wd San Francisco	81	203
P	36	m	w	IREL	Yuba	Rose Bar Twp	93	662
Patk	23	m	w	IREL	San Francisco	1-Wd San Francisco	79	77
Patrick	58	m	w	IREL	San Francisco	7-Wd San Francisco	81	178
Patrick	50	m	w	IREL	Sacramento	Granite Twp	77	154
Peter	46	m	w	IREL	Shasta	Fort Crook P O	89	477
Peter	43	m	w	IREL	San Mateo	Redwood Twp	87	368
Peter	34	m	w	IREL	Yuba	Rose Bar Twp	93	657
R	24	m	w	NY	Yuba	Marysville	93	604
Simon	45	m	w	IREL	San Francisco	11-Wd San Francisc	84	573
Thomas	60	m	w	IREL	San Francisco	San Francisco P O	80	415
Thomas	43	m	w	IREL	San Francisco	San Francisco P O	83	364
Thomas	37	m	w	IREL	El Dorado	Mud Springs Twp	72	81
Thomas	31	m	w	DE	Contra Costa	Martinez P O	71	389
Thomas	25	m	w	IREL	Placer	Lincoln P O	76	493
Thomas C	32	m	w	IREL	El Dorado	White Oak Twp	72	143
Thos	18	m	w	MA	Sacramento	Granite Twp	77	154
Tim	38	m	w	IREL	San Francisco	San Francisco P O	83	319
Timothy	28	m	w	IREL	Mariposa	Mariposa P O	74	119
William	60	m	w	IREL	Santa Clara	2-Wd San Jose	88	289
Wm	56	m	w	IREL	San Francisco	11-Wd San Francisc	84	613
Wm H	32	m	w	CANA	Yuba	Long Bar Twp	93	563
FITZROY								
George	36	m	w	ENGL	Marin	San Rafael	74	52
FITZSICUNTS								
P	25	m	w	GERM	Alameda	Oakland	68	161
FITZSIMMONS								
B	60	f	w	IREL	Solano	Vallejo	90	156
Calvin	31	m	w	IREL	San Mateo	Schoolhouse Statio	87	342
Chs	50	m	w	IREL	San Francisco	8-Wd San Francisco	82	301
Dermot	37	m	w	IREL	Nevada	Grass Valley Twp	75	153
George	35	m	w	OH	San Diego	Fort Yuma Dist	78	464
Hugh	44	m	w	NY	Placer	Rocklin Twp	76	465
Hugh U	45	m	w	NY	Placer	Bath P O	76	427
James	34	m	w	ME	San Francisco	7-Wd San Francisco	81	214
John	50	m	w	NY	Amador	Ione City P O	69	361
John	24	m	w	IREL	San Francisco	11-Wd San Francisc	84	701
Jos	35	m	w	IREL	San Francisco	San Francisco P O	83	194
Joseph	29	m	w	NY	Mariposa	Mariposa P O	74	129
M	30	m	w	IREL	San Francisco	7-Wd San Francisco	81	194
Margt	37	f	w	IREL	San Francisco	1-Wd San Francisco	79	2
Mary	30	f	w	IREL	San Francisco	San Francisco P O	83	146
Michael	37	m	w	IREL	Humboldt	Table Bluff Twp	72	307
Pat	50	m	w	IREL	Solano	Vallejo	90	203
Peter	21	m	w	IREL	Klamath	Camp Gaston	73	373
S	42	m	w	IREL	Siskiyou	Callahan P O	89	629
Thomas	50	m	w	IREL	Yolo	Putah Twp	93	513
Thos	40	m	w	IREL	San Francisco	1-Wd San Francisco	79	2
Thos	30	m	w	IREL	San Francisco	1-Wd San Francisco	79	92
Thos	30	m	w	IREL	Klamath	Trinidad Twp	73	390
Wm	56	m	w	IREL	Solano	Vallejo	90	151
FITZSIMNONS								
Thos	58	m	w	IREL	Nevada	Bridgeport Twp	75	116
FITZSIMONDS								
John	40	m	w	SCOT	Sutter	Sutter Twp	92	124
Michael	46	m	w	IREL	Sutter	Vernon Twp	92	132
FITZSIMONS								
J	30	m	w	IREL	San Francisco	San Francisco P O	83	319
James	38	m	w	IA	Solano	Vacaville Twp	90	122
John	20	m	w	IREL	San Francisco	7-Wd San Francisco	81	176
FITZWATER								
Geo A	49	m	w	IN	Shasta	Millville P O	89	489
James	22	m	w	MO	Shasta	Millville P O	89	490

© 2001 by Heritage Quest. All rights reserved.

California 1870 Census

Series M593

Name	Age	S	R	B-PL	County	Locale	Roll	Pg
FITZWILLIAMS								
Jno	19	m	w	CANA	San Joaquin	Oneal Twp	86	99
FITZZIMONDS								
P	22	m	w	IREL	Sutter	Yuba Twp	92	145
FIVEY								
William	40	m	w	IREL	San Francisco	San Francisco P O	83	334
FIX								
Adam	28	m	w	FRAN	Sierra	Table Rock Twp	89	578
Charles	30	m	w	ME	San Francisco	San Francisco P O	83	323
Frarderic	47	m	w	HAMB	Placer	Bath P O	76	431
George T	20	m	w	WI	Sacramento	2-Wd Sacramento	77	236
Jesse K	50	m	w	IN	Sonoma	Analy Twp	91	236
FIZER								
Daniel	55	m	w	FRAN	Sutter	Vernon Twp	92	131
FIZGERALD								
Ellen	50	f	w	IREL	Placer	Emigrant Gap P O	76	417
Mary	36	f	w	IREL	Placer	Emigrant Gap P O	76	417
FIZZEL								
Joseph	40	m	w	FRAN	Los Angeles	El Monte Twp	73	458
FLAA								
Albert	25	m	w	SWED	Yolo	Putah Twp	93	520
FLACK								
John	39	m	w	ENGL	Sonoma	Mendocino Twp	91	307
John	31	m	w	PRUS	San Francisco	San Francisco P O	80	385
Joseph	42	m	w	NY	Nevada	Grass Valley Twp	75	217
Samuel	35	m	w	NY	San Francisco	San Francisco P O	83	306
Samuel	30	m	w	OH	Stanislaus	Branch Twp	92	9
Thomas	22	m	w	NY	Yolo	Cache Crk Twp	93	445
William	59	m	w	IREL	Tuolumne	Chinese Camp P O	93	381
FLACKLIN								
Albert	28	m	w	PA	Santa Clara	2-Wd San Jose	88	317
FLACRAINCE								
Alix	50	m	w	CANA	Trinity	Junction City Pct	92	209
FLADEN								
Eliza	40	f	w	IREL	San Francisco	San Francisco P O	83	391
FLAG								
Ah	14	m	c	CHIN	Placer	Colfax P O	76	392
N S	24	m	w	CANA	Merced	Snelling P O	74	260
William	38	m	w	IREL	San Francisco	7-Wd San Francisco	81	221
FLAGAN								
Charles	47	m	w	HCAS	Calaveras	Copperopolis P O	70	222
FLAGERTY								
John	33	m	w	IREL	San Luis Obispo	Salinas Twp	87	293
FLAGG								
Daniel S	59	m	w	MA	Santa Cruz	Santa Cruz	89	427
E W	30	m	w	ME	Sierra	Lincoln Twp	89	549
Edward Lank	37	m	w	ME	Plumas	Washington Twp	77	25
George	36	m	w	ME	Butte	Ophir Twp	70	114
Henry	48	m	w	NY	Tulare	Tule Rvr Twp	92	263
Jacob R	32	m	w	ME	Nevada	Little York Twp	75	238
Levy	45	m	w	MA	San Mateo	Belmont P O	87	373
Lucius F	51	m	w	MA	Santa Clara	Santa Clara Twp	88	144
Wm H	36	m	w	MA	Sonoma	Analy Twp	91	235
FLAGLAN								
Albert P	22	m	w	CANA	San Francisco	6-Wd San Francisco	81	78
FLAGLER								
Edwin	50	m	w	CANA	San Francisco	San Francisco P O	83	313
W H	38	m	w	NY	Lake	Lower Lake	73	418
William	52	m	w	ENGL	San Francisco	San Francisco P O	83	214
FLAGLEY								
Robert	29	m	w	SC	Monterey	San Antonio Twp	74	318
FLAGLOR								
Amasa	23	m	w	CANA	San Francisco	6-Wd San Francisco	81	145
FLAGOR								
Gilbert	80	m	w	ENGL	San Francisco	San Francisco P O	83	102
FLAHARTY								
Geo	51	m	w	IREL	San Joaquin	Elkhorn Twp	86	63
John	32	m	w	IREL	Amador	Jackson P O	69	318
Thos	35	m	w	ME	Tuolumne	Sonora P O	93	318
FLAHERITY								
Mary E	15	f	w	MA	San Francisco	2-Wd San Francisco	79	156
Michael	40	m	w	IREL	San Francisco	2-Wd San Francisco	79	228
FLAHERTY								
B	28	m	w	IREL	Solano	Vallejo	90	175
Bernard	40	m	w	IREL	San Francisco	11-Wd San Francisc	84	636
Bernard	35	m	w	IREL	Placer	Rocklin Twp	76	467
Bridget	65	f	w	IREL	San Francisco	8-Wd San Francisco	82	400
D	25	m	w	IREL	San Francisco	San Francisco P O	83	10
Daniel	30	m	w	IREL	San Mateo	San Mateo P O	87	353
Dennis	41	m	w	IREL	San Mateo	Redwood Twp	87	361
Dennis	35	m	w	IREL	San Mateo	San Mateo P O	87	353
Edward	33	m	w	NY	San Francisco	8-Wd San Francisco	82	405
Edwin	30	m	w	NY	San Francisco	3-Wd San Francisco	79	329
Elizabeth	24	f	w	IREL	Solano	Benicia	90	18
Ellen	20	f	w	IREL	San Joaquin	2-Wd Stockton	86	159
Hugh	28	m	w	IREL	San Francisco	3-Wd San Francisco	79	316
James	50	m	w	IREL	San Francisco	11-Wd San Francisc	84	596
John	40	m	w	IREL	San Francisco	8-Wd San Francisco	82	398
John	28	m	w	NY	San Francisco	1-Wd San Francisco	79	92
John	25	m	w	IREL	Placer	Pino Twp	76	472
Kate	27	f	w	IREL	San Francisco	7-Wd San Francisco	81	242
Kate	20	f	w	IREL	Solano	Vallejo	90	175
Margaret	26	f	w	IREL	Nevada	Grass Valley Twp	75	204
Margt	35	f	w	IREL	San Francisco	San Francisco P O	83	10
Martin	55	m	w	IREL	Placer	Auburn P O	76	375
Michael	22	m	w	IREL	San Francisco	San Francisco P O	80	333
Michl	24	m	w	IREL	San Francisco	1-Wd San Francisco	79	45
Owen	35	m	w	IREL	Contra Costa	Martinez P O	71	398
Pat	48	m	w	IREL	Sonoma	Mendocino Twp	91	308
Pat	31	m	w	IREL	San Francisco	11-Wd San Francisc	84	615
Pat	21	m	w	IREL	Solano	Vallejo	90	197
Patrick	37	m	w	IREL	San Francisco	San Francisco P O	83	389
Patrick	30	m	w	IREL	San Francisco	San Francisco P O	83	251
R	32	m	w	IREL	San Francisco	San Francisco P O	85	784
Roger	54	m	w	IREL	Alameda	Brooklyn Twp	68	55
Stephen	45	m	w	IREL	San Francisco	San Francisco P O	85	818
Thoms	45	m	w	IREL	San Francisco	San Francisco P O	83	17
FLAHIVE								
Mike	30	m	w	IREL	Solano	Vallejo	90	215
FLAHN								
John	43	m	w	HANO	San Francisco	11-Wd San Francisc	84	432
FLAHO								
Michael	43	m	w	IREL	Solano	Vacaville Twp	90	122
FLAHR								
Christian	34	m	w	GERM	Los Angeles	Los Angeles	73	565
FLAIG								
Martin	24	m	w	BAVA	San Francisco	San Francisco P O	83	232
FLAIS								
Jno	50	m	w	BADE	Butte	Oregon Twp	70	132
Leander	19	m	w	MEXI	Los Angeles	Wilmington Twp	73	635
FLAM								
Perry	30	m	w	OH	Sacramento	Lee Twp	77	160
FLANAGAN								
Andrew	45	m	w	IREL	San Francisco	San Francisco P O	85	726
Ann	51	f	w	PA	San Francisco	8-Wd San Francisco	82	483
Ann	25	f	w	IREL	San Francisco	8-Wd San Francisco	82	449
Anni	18	f	w	IREL	San Francisco	San Francisco P O	83	344
Annie	23	f	w	IREL	San Francisco	1-Wd San Francisco	79	75
Danl	34	m	w	IREL	Humboldt	Eureka Twp	72	277
Edward	27	m	w	IREL	San Francisco	3-Wd San Francisco	79	312
J	26	m	w	IREL	San Francisco	1-Wd San Francisco	79	67
James	54	m	w	IREL	Amador	Fiddletown P O	69	436
James	27	m	w	IREL	San Francisco	San Francisco P O	83	70
Jas	35	m	w	NY	Sacramento	1-Wd Sacramento	77	196
John	69	m	w	IREL	Mendocino	Big Rvr Twp	74	162
John	41	m	w	IREL	San Francisco	San Francisco P O	80	430
John	37	m	w	IREL	Fresno	Kings Rvr P O	72	214
John	30	m	w	IREL	San Francisco	San Francisco P O	85	874
John	23	m	w	IREL	Mendocino	Big Rvr Twp	74	158
Kate	39	f	w	IREL	Sacramento	3-Wd Sacramento	77	297
Lawrence	20	m	w	IREL	San Francisco	8-Wd San Francisco	82	397
Ligdia	30	f	w	IREL	San Francisco	8-Wd San Francisco	82	427
M	39	m	w	MA	Mariposa	Maxwell Crk P O	74	148
Mary	40	f	w	IREL	San Francisco	San Francisco P O	80	364
P	36	m	w	IREL	San Mateo	San Mateo P O	87	359
Peter	50	m	w	IREL	San Francisco	8-Wd San Francisco	82	435
Peter	36	m	w	IREL	San Francisco	1-Wd San Francisco	79	62
Sarah	35	f	w	IREL	Los Angeles	San Gabriel Twp	73	595
Ter	48	m	w	IREL	Merced	Snelling P O	74	262
Thomas	28	m	w	IREL	Napa	Napa Twp	75	28
FLANARY								
Susie	15	f	w	CA	Sonoma	Petaluma Twp	91	336
FLANDERS								
Alvan	45	m	w	NH	San Francisco	6-Wd San Francisco	81	136
Ann	26	f	w	ME	Solano	Montezuma Twp	90	66
C L	22	m	w	WI	San Joaquin	Elliott Twp	86	76
Charles A	30	m	w	MA	Alpine	Monitor P O	69	313
Daniel	48	m	w	MA	Santa Cruz	Santa Cruz Twp	89	398
I M	43	m	w	NY	Tuolumne	Columbia P O	93	338
Jackson	32	m	w	WI	Nevada	Bridgeport Twp	75	123
L C	60	m	w	KY	San Joaquin	Elliott Twp	86	77
L C	55	m	w	NY	San Joaquin	Elliott Twp	86	77
Lenas	64	m	w	NH	Nevada	Grass Valley Twp	75	189
Mary	50	f	w	CANA	Yolo	Washington Twp	93	529
Mary W	57	m	w	CT	Yolo	Washington Twp	93	534
Moses	51	m	w	MA	Calaveras	San Andreas P O	70	157
Nathan	57	m	w	NH	San Francisco	San Francisco P O	80	388
S B	58	m	w	NH	Amador	Drytown P O	69	416
Samuel	53	m	w	MA	Sacramento	Cosumnes Twp	77	92
Stephen C	67	m	w	NH	Nevada	Grass Valley Twp	75	157
Thomas	35	m	w	NY	San Francisco	5-Wd San Francisco	81	25
Thomas	30	m	w	ME	Trinity	Douglas	92	235
William	57	m	w	CANA	Yolo	Cache Crk Twp	93	429
Wm	22	f	w	MA	San Joaquin	Elkhorn Twp	86	65
FLANE								
Dennis	30	m	w	IREL	Marin	Tomales Twp	74	84
FLANEGAN								
Michl	34	m	w	IREL	San Francisco	5-Wd San Francisco	81	7
Richard	35	m	w	AL	Napa	Napa	75	12
FLANELLY								
Patrick	40	m	w	IREL	San Francisco	11-Wd San Francisc	84	583
FLANERTY								
Mary	28	f	w	NY	Alameda	Oakland	68	160
FLANERY								
Andrew	12	m	w	CA	Sonoma	Analy Twp	91	246
Ellen	20	f	w	IREL	Solano	Benicia	90	1
Patric	49	m	w	IREL	Trinity	Junction City Pct	92	208
Thomas	26	m	w	IREL	San Francisco	7-Wd San Francisco	81	173
FLANIGAN								
A	40	m	w	IREL	Alameda	Murray Twp	68	116
Alexander	30	m	w	SCOT	San Mateo	Half Moon Bay P O	87	396
Andrew	23	m	w	IREL	Sacramento	Granite Twp	77	138
Anne	25	f	w	IREL	Los Angeles	San Gabriel Twp	73	595
J R	38	m	w	GA	San Joaquin	Elkhorn Twp	86	65

© 2001 by Heritage Quest. All rights reserved.

Name	Age	S	R	B-PL	County	Locale (Series M593)	Roll	Pg
James	36	m	w	IREL	San Francisco	San Francisco P O	83	77
Jane	28	f	w	IREL	Alameda	Oakland	68	248
Jane	20	f	w	IREL	San Francisco	San Francisco P O	83	102
Jas B	30	m	w	MA	San Francisco	San Francisco P O	83	70
Jas M	37	m	w	MD	San Francisco	San Francisco P O	83	41
Linda	35	f	w	IREL	San Francisco	San Francisco P O	83	97
Mary	64	f	w	IREL	San Francisco	San Francisco P O	83	305
Mary	31	f	w	IREL	San Francisco	San Francisco P O	80	337
Mary	30	f	w	IREL	Sacramento	American Twp	77	67
Mary	25	f	w	CT	San Francisco	San Francisco P O	83	113
Maurice	32	m	w	IREL	Santa Clara	1-Wd San Jose	88	225
Michael	30	m	w	IREL	Santa Clara	2-Wd San Jose	88	306
Michl	32	m	w	IREL	San Francisco	1-Wd San Francisco	79	84
Patk	35	m	w	IREL	Sacramento	4-Wd Sacramento	77	333
Patk	25	m	w	IREL	Sacramento	4-Wd Sacramento	77	337
Rose	20	f	w	AUST	Tuolumne	Sonora P O	93	326
Thomas	18	m	w	CA	Tuolumne	Sonora P O	93	326
FLANIGHAN								
J	22	m	w	NY	Humboldt	Eureka Twp	72	279
FLANING								
Catherine	34	f	w	IREL	Sacramento	4-Wd Sacramento	77	333
FLANINGAN								
C C	45	m	w	IREL	Alameda	Oakland	68	236
John	41	m	w	IREL	Sonoma	Analy Twp	91	218
FLANNAGAN								
Biddy	60	f	w	IREL	San Francisco	San Francisco P O	83	402
J F	34	m	w	IREL	San Francisco	San Francisco P O	85	858
John	40	m	w	IREL	San Francisco	7-Wd San Francisco	81	242
John	32	m	w	IREL	San Francisco	San Francisco P O	85	773
Mary	38	f	w	IREL	San Francisco	San Francisco P O	83	65
Michael	30	m	w	IREL	Humboldt	Eureka Twp	72	275
Thos	45	m	w	IREL	Sacramento	4-Wd Sacramento	77	373
FLANNEGAN								
Catherine	14	f	w	NY	Nevada	Grass Valley Twp	75	223
John	24	m	w	IREL	Placer	Pino Twp	76	472
Pat	36	m	w	MA	Solano	Vallejo	90	208
Timothy	36	m	w	IREL	Kern	Tehachapi P O	73	354
William	38	m	w	IREL	San Francisco	11-Wd San Francisc	84	496
William	25	m	w	IREL	Kern	Havilah P O	73	339
FLANNELY								
Miles	37	m	w	IREL	San Francisco	7-Wd San Francisco	81	174
FLANNER								
John	40	m	w	TX	San Bernardino	San Bernardino Twp	78	453
Martin	21	m	w	ITAL	San Mateo	Schoolhouse Statio	87	344
FLANNERTY								
Rogers	32	m	w	IREL	Solano	Vallejo	90	197
FLANNERY								
Annie	20	f	w	IREL	San Francisco	San Francisco P O	83	255
Geo	35	m	w	IREL	San Francisco	2-Wd San Francisco	79	225
James	25	m	w	MO	Sonoma	Petaluma Twp	91	343
Jas	38	m	w	IREL	Solano	Benicia	90	11
John	38	m	w	IREL	Solano	Denverton Twp	90	26
Kate	58	f	w	IREL	San Francisco	1-Wd San Francisco	79	20
Patrick	44	m	w	IREL	Yuba	Parks Bar Twp	93	650
Patrick	27	m	w	IREL	Marin	Point Reyes Twp	74	22
Patrick J	33	m	w	IREL	Sacramento	2-Wd Sacramento	77	251
Philip	40	m	w	IREL	Sonoma	Petaluma Twp	91	337
Wm E	55	m	w	VA	Sonoma	Petaluma Twp	91	358
FLANNIGAN								
Ann	4	f	w	IREL	San Joaquin	Tulare Twp	86	261
Helen	50	f	w	IREL	San Francisco	11-Wd San Francisc	84	611
Herman	28	m	w	IREL	San Francisco	San Francisco P O	83	391
John	40	m	w	NY	San Francisco	7-Wd San Francisco	81	232
John	34	m	w	IREL	Napa	Napa Twp	75	33
John	25	m	w	IREL	San Francisco	San Francisco P O	83	169
Margaret	16	f	w	IREL	San Francisco	11-Wd San Francisc	84	637
Michal	26	m	w	IREL	San Francisco	San Francisco P O	83	203
Pat	35	m	w	IREL	San Francisco	11-Wd San Francisc	84	662
Peter	32	m	w	IREL	Nevada	Grass Valley Twp	75	224
Richard	30	m	w	MO	Solano	Suisun Twp	90	103
Robt	33	m	w	PA	San Francisco	1-Wd San Francisco	79	30
Rosa	36	f	w	IREL	Nevada	Grass Valley Twp	75	179
Thomas	33	m	w	IREL	San Francisco	San Francisco P O	83	237
Timothy	57	m	w	IREL	San Francisco	11-Wd San Francisc	84	615
FLANSBURGH								
Alonzo	37	m	w	NY	Shasta	Millville P O	89	492
Chas W	39	m	w	NY	Shasta	Millville P O	89	492
Francis	5	f	w	CA	Alameda	Eden Twp	68	66
FLANTRE								
John	55	m	w	FRAN	Calaveras	San Andreas P O	70	214
Pasqual	57	m	w	FRAN	Calaveras	San Andreas P O	70	214
FLANZBURG								
Harriet	21	f	w	IA	Placer	Alta P O	76	413
Phils	32	m	w	NY	Placer	Alta P O	76	413
FLAR								
Thomas	22	m	w	MA	Alameda	Oakland	68	182
FLARECCA								
Louis	24	m	w	ITAL	Calaveras	San Andreas P O	70	215
Tomaso V	22	m	w	ITAL	Calaveras	San Andreas P O	70	215
FLARETY								
David	24	m	w	IREL	San Francisco	San Francisco P O	83	370
Thomas	34	m	w	IREL	Santa Clara	San Jose Twp	88	222
FLARITY								
Mary	40	f	w	IREL	San Francisco	8-Wd San Francisco	82	288
FLARLEY								
Patrick	34	m	w	IREL	San Mateo	Schoolhouse Statio	87	338

Name	Age	S	R	B-PL	County	Locale (Series M593)	Roll	Pg
FLARRETY								
Patrick	22	m	w	IREL	San Francisco	7-Wd San Francisco	81	160
FLARRITY								
John	36	m	w	IREL	San Francisco	8-Wd San Francisco	82	369
Margt	37	f	w	IREL	San Francisco	8-Wd San Francisco	82	304
FLARTEY								
Patrick	20	m	w	IREL	San Diego	San Diego	78	490
FLARTY								
Patrick	33	m	w	IREL	Colusa	Spring Valley Twp	71	340
FLARY								
Thomas	17	m	w	NY	San Francisco	8-Wd San Francisco	82	433
FLASCHER								
Chas	29	m	w	PRUS	San Francisco	11-Wd San Francisc	84	618
FLASHMAN								
Charles	33	m	w	HCAS	San Mateo	Half Moon Bay P O	87	406
H	24	m	w	SC	Solano	Vallejo	90	209
Mary E	14	f	w	CA	Los Angeles	Los Angeles	73	570
FLASS								
Elen	25	f	w	CT	San Joaquin	2-Wd Stockton	86	163
FLATERBUSH								
D	30	m	w	NY	San Joaquin	Tulare Twp	86	249
FLATHERTY								
Bridget	27	f	w	IREL	Solano	Maine Prairie Twp	90	53
Edward	43	m	w	IREL	Klamath	Trinidad Twp	73	391
John	32	m	w	ME	Klamath	Trinidad Twp	73	392
John	30	m	w	IREL	San Francisco	7-Wd San Francisco	81	167
Thomas	30	m	w	IREL	San Francisco	7-Wd San Francisco	81	181
FLATHMAN								
J	38	m	w	GERM	Yuba	Marysville	93	614
FLATLEY								
John	40	m	w	IREL	San Francisco	San Francisco P O	83	267
FLATLY								
Wm	40	m	w	IREL	Sacramento	Granite Twp	77	154
FLATMAN								
Claus	30	m	w	PRUS	San Francisco	San Francisco P O	83	233
FLATREY								
James	26	m	w	NY	Sutter	Sutter Twp	92	122
FLATTERY								
Edward	22	m	w	IREL	Santa Clara	Fremont Twp	88	53
John	30	m	w	UNKN	San Joaquin	2-Wd Stockton	86	173
Margret	28	f	w	IREL	San Francisco	11-Wd San Francisc	84	710
FLAVA								
Antonio	18	m	w	FRAN	Santa Clara	Redwood Twp	88	119
FLAVEL								
George	42	m	w	ME	San Francisco	5-Wd San Francisco	81	18
FLAVER								
Jules	30	m	w	FRAN	Santa Clara	Fremont Twp	88	60
FLAVIA								
Bojorka	6M	f	w	CA	Yuba	Linda Twp	93	558
FLAVIER								
Martin	31	m	w	FRAN	San Francisco	1-Wd San Francisco	79	50
FLAVIL								
Francisca	22	f	w	CHIL	Santa Clara	2-Wd San Jose	88	335
FLAXMAN								
Thos	40	m	w	CANA	Sacramento	Franklin Twp	77	115
FLAY								
Byron	21	m	w	VT	San Francisco	11-Wd San Francisc	84	634
FLAYING								
Andrew	43	m	w	HCAS	Santa Barbara	Santa Barbara P O	87	450
Daniel	37	m	w	HCAS	Santa Barbara	Santa Barbara P O	87	450
FLAYTOR								
Pamelia	50	f	w	CANA	San Francisco	8-Wd San Francisco	82	315
FLEAK								
J R	28	m	w	MI	Shasta	Shasta P O	89	454
FLEANER								
Saml	18	m	w	OR	Humboldt	Pacific Twp	72	293
FLECHER								
Louisa	15	f	w	LA	Sacramento	American Twp	77	66
W J	50	m	w	ENGL	Sacramento	Alabama Twp	77	59
Wm	45	m	w	ENGL	Sacramento	Granite Twp	77	147
FLECK								
John	45	m	w	PA	Santa Cruz	Soquel Twp	89	441
Michael	45	m	w	PRUS	Placer	Gold Run Twp	76	400
Thomas	45	m	w	SCOT	Kern	Bakersfield P O	73	358
FLECOURT								
Edwd	27	m	w	FRAN	San Francisco	1-Wd San Francisco	79	54
FLEEHART								
A	66	m	w	OH	Amador	Sutter Crk P O	69	411
William	42	m	w	OH	Amador	Amador City P O	69	391
FLEEM								
Ah	34	m	c	CHIN	Placer	Bath P O	76	439
FLEENARY								
Pat	28	m	w	IREL	San Francisco	5-Wd San Francisco	81	7
FLEENER								
D D	22	m	w	MO	Lassen	Susanville Twp	73	443
Obanion	36	m	w	VA	Plumas	Seneca Twp	77	50
Simon	47	m	w	KY	Humboldt	Pacific Twp	72	293
FLEENY								
Catherine	65	f	w	IREL	San Mateo	Searsville P O	87	383
FLEETS								
Andrew	45	m	w	BAVA	Sacramento	1-Wd Sacramento	77	187
FLEGE								
Fred	12	m	w	CA	San Joaquin	2-Wd Stockton	86	162
FLEICHER								
Wm	42	m	w	ENGL	Yuba	Marysville	93	590
FLEICK								
Louis	24	m	w	FRAN	Plumas	Plumas Twp	77	31

© 2001 by Heritage Quest. All rights reserved.

Name	Age	S	R	B-PL	County	Locale	Roll	Pg
						Series M593		
FLEIN								
Adolph	38	m	w	HANO	San Francisco	11-Wd San Francisc	84	463
FLEIPSMAN								
John	33	m	w	FRAN	Santa Clara	2-Wd San Jose	88	322
FLEISCHER								
Bernard	10	m	w	NY	San Francisco	2-Wd San Francisco	79	188
FLEISCHMAN								
Benj	40	m	w	BADE	San Francisco	2-Wd San Francisco	79	140
Eliza	22	f	w	BOHE	San Francisco	8-Wd San Francisco	82	425
John	39	m	w	BAVA	San Francisco	San Francisco P O	83	159
Oscar	30	m	w	PRUS	San Mateo	Half Moon Bay P O	87	399
FLEISHER								
Wolf	51	m	w	AUST	San Bernardino	San Bernardino Twp	78	432
FLEISHMAN								
George	25	m	w	AUST	Los Angeles	El Monte Twp	73	451
Hermon	42	m	w	BAVA	Los Angeles	Los Angeles	73	539
Joseph	35	m	w	CA	San Diego	San Pasqual	78	522
L	22	f	w	BOHE	San Francisco	San Francisco P O	85	793
Martha	35	m	w	GERM	Yolo	Cache Crk Twp	93	452
Moses	24	m	w	AUST	Fresno	Kingston P O	72	217
FLEISMAN								
Eloisa	14	f	i	CA	Los Angeles	Los Angeles	73	500
FLEMEN								
Charles	25	m	w	IREL	Sonoma	Vallejo Twp	91	455
T I	47	m	w	OH	San Joaquin	Tulare Twp	86	263
FLEMIMG								
Patrick	35	m	w	IREL	Contra Costa	San Pablo Twp	71	364
FLEMIN								
Peter	35	m	w	CANA	Sonoma	Mendocino Twp	91	294
FLEMING								
Abigail	28	f	w	MA	San Francisco	8-Wd San Francisco	82	433
Alexander	31	m	w	SCOT	Amador	Jackson P O	69	340
Andrew	28	m	w	IL	Placer	Dutch Flat P O	76	415
Ann	22	f	w	IREL	San Francisco	San Francisco P O	83	22
Arthur	32	m	w	PA	Alameda	San Leandro	68	95
Charles	50	m	w	SWED	San Francisco	San Francisco P O	80	480
Charles	50	m	w	VT	Solano	Tremont Twp	90	35
Charles M	47	m	w	IREL	Santa Clara	San Jose Twp	88	220
David B	32	m	w	PA	Colusa	Monroe Twp	71	315
Edward	20	m	w	IREL	San Francisco	San Francisco P O	85	718
Ellen	40	f	w	WIND	San Francisco	San Francisco P O	80	405
Ellen	25	m	w	ENGL	San Francisco	San Francisco P O	85	755
F B	43	m	w	NY	Napa	Napa	75	22
Francis	40	m	w	IREL	San Francisco	San Francisco P O	83	65
Frank B	40	m	w	NY	Napa	Napa	75	2
Garrett	28	m	w	IREL	Santa Cruz	Santa Cruz Twp	89	398
George	30	m	b	TX	Santa Clara	1-Wd San Jose	88	235
George	26	m	w	OH	San Francisco	San Francisco P O	80	469
Horace	43	m	w	NY	Marin	San Rafael Twp	74	43
Horace J	35	m	w	MO	Tulare	Visalia Twp	92	285
J B	32	m	w	TN	Nevada	Nevada Twp	75	292
J F	36	m	w	IREL	Tuolumne	Big Oak Flat P O	93	400
James	61	m	w	IREL	Amador	Fiddletown P O	69	440
James	51	m	w	ITAL	Nevada	Nevada Twp	75	283
James	40	m	w	IREL	San Francisco	San Francisco P O	83	153
James	37	m	w	IREL	Amador	Jackson P O	69	337
James	37	m	w	IREL	San Francisco	7-Wd San Francisco	81	218
James	34	m	w	NY	San Francisco	1-Wd San Francisco	79	133
James	32	m	w	IREL	Yuba	Linda Twp	93	556
Jas	38	m	w	IREL	San Francisco	San Francisco P O	85	786
Jno	36	m	w	LA	San Joaquin	3-Wd Stockton	86	228
John	44	m	w	IREL	Yuba	East Bear Rvr Twp	93	546
John	43	m	w	IREL	Solano	Vallejo	90	211
John	41	m	w	PA	El Dorado	Diamond Springs Tw	72	33
John	36	m	w	IREL	Humboldt	Eureka Twp	72	271
John	35	m	w	IREL	San Francisco	7-Wd San Francisco	81	156
John	29	m	w	IREL	San Francisco	San Francisco P O	80	473
John	24	m	w	CANA	Sonoma	Sonoma Twp	91	431
John	23	m	w	LA	San Francisco	1-Wd San Francisco	79	100
John P	24	m	w	NC	Los Angeles	Los Nietos Twp	73	575
John W	23	m	w	IL	Placer	Dutch Flat P O	76	415
Kate	21	f	w	IREL	San Francisco	8-Wd San Francisco	82	464
Luke	38	m	w	IREL	El Dorado	Mud Springs Twp	72	81
M	50	m	w	IREL	Solano	Vallejo	90	190
Margt	63	f	w	PA	Alameda	San Leandro	68	95
Martin	44	m	w	IREL	El Dorado	Coloma Twp	72	8
Mary	50	f	w	IL	San Francisco	7-Wd San Francisco	81	156
Mary	23	f	w	IREL	San Francisco	8-Wd San Francisco	82	477
Mary	16	f	w	CA	Trinity	Hayfork Valley	92	239
Mary	11	f	w	CA	Mariposa	Maxwell Crk P O	74	142
Mary A	23	f	w	IREL	San Francisco	8-Wd San Francisco	82	405
Mike	51	m	w	IREL	Solano	Benicia	90	15
Nancy	75	f	w	NC	Tuolumne	Sonora P O	93	330
O C	19	m	w	IN	Tehama	Red Bluff	92	182
Patrick	39	m	w	IREL	San Francisco	11-Wd San Francisc	84	558
Peter	48	m	w	LUXE	El Dorado	White Oak Twp	72	138
Peter	33	m	w	IREL	San Francisco	San Francisco P O	83	66
Robert	20	m	w	CANA	Solano	Tremont Twp	90	28
Russel	37	m	w	PA	Fresno	Millerton P O	72	145
S C	36	m	w	NY	San Francisco	3-Wd San Francisco	79	301
S J	37	f	w	OH	Del Norte	Crescent Twp	71	454
Samuel	57	m	w	DE	El Dorado	Diamond Springs Tw	72	28
Thomas	40	m	w	IREL	San Francisco	San Francisco P O	80	336
Thomas R	31	m	w	NY	El Dorado	Mud Springs Twp	72	71
Thos W	50	m	w	ENGL	San Francisco	1-Wd San Francisco	79	71
W Ernest	30	m	w	MI	Mariposa	Mariposa P O	74	137
William	26	m	w	IREL	San Francisco	San Francisco P O	83	395
Wm	33	m	w	SCOT	San Francisco	1-Wd San Francisco	79	84
Wm	31	m	w	IREL	San Francisco	1-Wd San Francisco	79	84
FLEMMING								
August	48	m	w	FRNK	Calaveras	San Andreas P O	70	173
Bartholomew	45	m	w	IREL	San Francisco	2-Wd San Francisco	79	260
Bridget	28	f	w	IREL	San Francisco	San Francisco P O	83	257
Bridget	24	f	w	IREL	San Francisco	San Francisco P O	83	415
Chas	50	m	w	SWED	San Francisco	6-Wd San Francisco	81	37
Chris	56	m	w	HANO	San Francisco	11-Wd San Francisc	84	612
Coleman B	57	m	w	NJ	Yolo	Washington Twp	93	529
Ella	9	f	w	NE	Stanislaus	San Joaquin Twp	92	72
Fred	25	m	w	PRUS	San Francisco	6-Wd San Francisco	81	104
Isaac	39	m	w	OH	Nevada	Rough & Ready Twp	75	326
James	36	m	w	IREL	Yolo	Cache Crk Twp	93	449
James	36	m	w	CANA	San Diego	San Diego	78	511
John	46	m	w	PA	Yolo	Putah Twp	93	515
John	42	m	w	IREL	Shasta	Shasta P O	89	455
John	40	m	w	IREL	San Francisco	2-Wd San Francisco	79	225
John A	27	m	w	IREL	San Mateo	Half Moon Bay P O	87	389
Patrick	30	m	w	IREL	San Mateo	San Mateo P O	87	357
Patrick	28	m	w	IREL	Yolo	Grafton Twp	93	491
Robt	53	m	w	IREL	San Francisco	2-Wd San Francisco	79	268
Thomas	25	m	w	IREL	Marin	Point Reyes Twp	74	24
Thos	45	m	w	IREL	Yuba	Marysville	93	607
Thos	38	m	w	IREL	San Joaquin	2-Wd Stockton	86	164
William	25	m	w	OH	Los Angeles	Los Angeles	73	545
Wm	52	m	w	IREL	San Francisco	7-Wd San Francisco	81	243
Wm	40	m	w	IREL	Santa Clara	Almaden Twp	88	12
Wm	26	m	w	IREL	Sonoma	Bodega Twp	91	251
FLEMMISH								
Louis	50	m	w	IREL	Butte	Kimshew Tpw	70	80
FLEMONING								
Otto	25	m	w	PRUS	Contra Costa	Martinez P O	71	438
FLENCHE								
Augustus	40	m	w	HAMB	Mendocino	Ukiah Twp	74	233
FLENDELL								
John	31	m	w	UNKN	San Joaquin	2-Wd Stockton	86	173
FLENIGAN								
Charles	40	m	w	IREL	Los Angeles	Los Angeles	73	566
FLENN								
Benj F	70	m	w	CA	Monterey	Alisal Twp	74	296
George	30	m	w	IREL	Alameda	Alameda	68	13
John	34	m	w	IREL	Sonoma	Petaluma Twp	91	316
Peter	35	m	w	CANA	Alameda	Oakland	68	262
FLENNERY								
Howard	44	m	w	NY	San Joaquin	2-Wd Stockton	86	192
FLENNIKEN								
Thos	28	m	w	PA	San Francisco	1-Wd San Francisco	79	17
FLENNING								
Frank	20	m	w	IREL	Placer	Gold Run Twp	76	394
FLERICK								
Charles	34	m	w	WURT	San Francisco	11-Wd San Francisc	84	527
FLERKE								
Frank	23	m	w	IA	Sacramento	Sutter Twp	77	391
FLERNAY								
William	22	m	w	MO	Alameda	Eden Twp	68	68
FLERONG								
Mary	28	f	w	IREL	Alameda	Alameda	68	8
FLESHER								
William	29	m	w	SAXO	San Francisco	8-Wd San Francisco	82	421
FLESHMAN								
Francis	41	m	w	HDAR	Trinity	Lewiston Pct	92	213
FLESHNER								
Phillip	25	m	w	HUNG	Alameda	Oakland	68	181
FLETCHER								
A	62	m	w	ENGL	Calaveras	Copperopolis P O	70	236
A	40	m	w	IREL	Solano	Vallejo	90	184
Alford	30	m	w	LA	Colusa	Colusa	71	290
Almira	37	f	w	CANA	San Mateo	Redwood City P O	87	375
Andrew	56	m	w	SCOT	Santa Cruz	Santa Cruz Twp	89	401
Anne	18	f	w	NZEA	San Francisco	6-Wd San Francisco	81	41
Artemus T	56	m	w	MA	San Francisco	6-Wd San Francisco	81	140
Asa P	39	m	w	MA	San Francisco	San Francisco P O	83	124
Barney	49	m	b	MD	San Francisco	San Francisco P O	80	368
Berdan P	60	m	w	VA	Tulare	Farmersville Twp	92	249
Bernard	13	m	b	CA	San Francisco	11-Wd San Francisc	84	588
Charles	45	m	w	SCOT	Mendocino	Anderson Twp	74	154
Charles	40	m	i	RI	Monterey	Castroville Twp	74	327
Chas	30	m	w	NY	Butte	Chico Twp	70	20
Cyrus	67	m	w	ME	Lassen	Janesville Twp	73	430
Ed	29	m	w	PA	San Francisco	11-Wd San Francisc	84	687
Edward	45	m	w	MD	Klamath	Trinidad Twp	73	390
Edward	20	m	b	SC	San Francisco	San Francisco P O	83	209
Elias P	36	m	w	MI	Stanislaus	Empire Twp	92	61
Emma E	22	f	w	DC	Sacramento	2-Wd Sacramento	77	232
Francis	15	m	w	TX	Monterey	Monterey Twp	74	348
G W	17	m	w	MA	Sacramento	1-Wd Sacramento	77	200
Geo L	25	m	w	NY	Solano	Vallejo	90	212
George	35	m	w	IREL	Plumas	Quartz Twp	77	37
George	32	m	w	ENGL	Nevada	Grass Valley Twp	75	147
H D	41	m	w	NY	Monterey	San Juan Twp	74	391
Harriet	50	f	w	ENGL	San Francisco	San Francisco P O	83	78
Henry	41	m	w	ENGL	San Francisco	San Francisco P O	83	45
Henry E	60	m	w	VT	Sonoma	Analy Twp	91	245
J H	27	m	w	ME	Sierra	Sierra Twp	89	563
J H	25	m	w	PA	Sacramento	1-Wd Sacramento	77	183
J P	51	m	w	ENGL	Calaveras	Copperopolis P O	70	236

© 2001 by Heritage Quest. All rights reserved.

Name	Age	S	R	B-PL	County	Locale	Roll	Pg
J W	36	m	w	NY	San Joaquin	1-Wd Stockton	86	138
Jane	81	f	w	ENGL	San Francisco	1-Wd San Francisco	79	26
Jas H	33	m	w	ME	Siskiyou	Scott Valley Twp	89	616
John	40	m	w	NY	Solano	Vallejo	90	215
John	36	m	w	PA	Placer	Lincoln P O	76	488
John	30	m	w	ENGL	Colusa	Butte Twp	71	269
John	28	m	w	NY	Solano	Vallejo	90	217
John	21	m	w	PA	San Francisco	8-Wd San Francisco	82	370
John K	41	m	w	VA	San Luis Obispo	Morro Twp	87	282
John W	28	m	w	ENGL	San Bernardino	San Bernardino Twp	78	452
Joseph	39	m	w	IREL	Alameda	Washington Twp	68	268
L	37	m	w	ME	San Joaquin	3-Wd Stockton	86	219
Levinia	39	f	b	PA	San Francisco	2-Wd San Francisco	79	137
Lucinda	35	f	w	MO	Sonoma	Washington Twp	91	468
Lydia	30	f	w	CANA	San Francisco	8-Wd San Francisco	82	458
M	40	m	w	VA	Solano	Vallejo	90	199
Morris	38	m	w	NY	San Francisco	5-Wd San Francisco	81	31
Nancy	24	f	w	KY	Colusa	Colusa	71	290
Nathan	40	m	w	VA	Santa Barbara	Santa Barbara P O	87	498
Philander	48	m	w	PA	Colusa	Stony Crk Twp	71	331
Robert	27	m	b	DENM	Sacramento	2-Wd Sacramento	77	231
Robert	24	m	w	CANA	Solano	Silveyville Twp	90	81
Robert J	28	m	w	IL	Placer	Roseville P O	76	350
Saml J	37	m	w	ENGL	San Diego	San Diego	78	506
Samuel	26	m	w	IN	Stanislaus	Empire Twp	92	65
Sarah	28	f	w	OH	San Francisco	San Francisco P O	85	734
Seth H	34	m	w	ME	Santa Cruz	Santa Cruz	89	430
Stephen	46	m	w	ENGL	San Francisco	8-Wd San Francisco	82	336
Theodore M	45	m	w	NY	El Dorado	Placerville	72	113
Thomas	30	m	w	ENGL	San Francisco	3-Wd San Francisco	79	297
Thos	34	m	w	ENGL	San Francisco	7-Wd San Francisco	81	235
W C	32	m	w	OH	Nevada	Washington Twp	75	346
W F	35	m	w	ME	San Joaquin	1-Wd Stockton	86	134
Wesley D	36	m	w	CANA	Plumas	Seneca Twp	77	47
Wm	38	m	w	MA	San Francisco	2-Wd San Francisco	79	220
Y H	52	m	w	ME	Sierra	Sierra Twp	89	563
FLETHER								
Joshua	43	m	w	ENGL	San Francisco	8-Wd San Francisco	82	491
FLETT								
William	60	m	w	NY	Tuolumne	Sonora P O	93	303
FLETTE								
Pauline	24	f	w	FRAN	San Francisco	San Francisco P O	83	53
FLEUMETTE								
Jno	28	m	w	SWIT	San Francisco	5-Wd San Francisco	81	32
FLEURIER								
Louis	30	m	w	FRAN	San Francisco	7-Wd San Francisco	81	228
Mad	28	f	w	FRAN	San Francisco	7-Wd San Francisco	81	228
FLEURY								
Adolphe	46	m	w	FRAN	San Francisco	San Francisco P O	83	32
Desiret	62	f	w	FRAN	San Francisco	6-Wd San Francisco	81	91
Emil	32	m	w	FRAN	San Francisco	San Francisco P O	80	481
Henry	28	m	w	IL	Alameda	Hayward	68	77
Julius	34	m	w	FRAN	Solano	Vallejo	90	195
Mertin	50	m	w	FRAN	Yuba	Slate Range Bar Tw	93	670
P	50	m	w	FRAN	San Francisco	San Francisco P O	85	841
FLEWELLING								
C	23	m	w	CANA	Santa Clara	Gilroy Twp	88	86
J B	33	m	w	CANA	Sonoma	Petaluma Twp	91	330
Wm	39	m	w	CANA	Sonoma	Russian Rvr	91	371
FLEWRIS								
Leroy	60	m	w	FRAN	San Joaquin	2-Wd Stockton	86	166
FLEYE								
John	21	m	w	FRAN	Santa Clara	Redwood Twp	88	119
FLHEMING								
Patrick	24	m	w	IREL	Yolo	Grafton Twp	93	491
FLICK								
Conrad	59	m	w	PA	Placer	Bath P O	76	447
Elizabeth	53	f	w	NY	San Francisco	San Francisco P O	83	281
Fredrick	40	m	w	SAXO	San Francisco	San Francisco P O	80	398
Jacob	35	m	w	WURT	San Francisco	San Francisco P O	80	418
Jacob	30	m	w	BAVA	San Francisco	8-Wd San Francisco	82	381
James	34	m	w	IL	Plumas	Quartz Twp	77	34
William	50	m	w	PA	San Francisco	San Francisco P O	83	281
FLICKINGER								
Joseph H	40	m	w	PA	Santa Clara	1-Wd San Jose	88	252
FLIESHHAKER								
A	49	m	w	BAVA	San Francisco	San Francisco P O	85	775
FLIESS								
Pauline	22	f	w	NY	San Francisco	5-Wd San Francisco	81	8
FLIGGLE								
Jessie E	31	m	w	OH	Yolo	Putah Twp	93	514
FLIM								
Patrick	37	m	w	IREL	Yolo	Grafton Twp	93	495
FLIMIGER								
Clem	37	m	w	BADE	San Joaquin	2-Wd Stockton	86	168
FLIN								
Ah	34	m	c	CHIN	San Francisco	San Francisco P O	80	491
Ah	21	m	c	CHIN	Solano	Silveyville Twp	90	85
B F	51	m	w	KY	Trinity	North Fork Twp	92	216
Gone	53	m	c	CHIN	Sierra	Downieville Twp	89	520
FLINIGIN								
Michael	62	m	w	IREL	Colusa	Spring Valley Twp	71	344
FLINN								
Ah	44	m	c	CHIN	Placer	Auburn P O	76	371
Barney	35	m	w	IREL	San Francisco	7-Wd San Francisco	81	193
Bridget	18	f	w	IREL	Alameda	Oakland	68	248
David	25	m	w	IREL	San Francisco	7-Wd San Francisco	81	199

Name	Age	S	R	B-PL	County	Locale	Roll	Pg
Edward	37	m	w	IREL	Sonoma	Salt Point	91	388
Ellen	31	f	w	IREL	San Francisco	San Francisco P O	83	102
Elza	35	f	w	IREL	Alameda	Alameda	68	14
Geo	42	m	w	IREL	San Joaquin	Elliott Twp	86	77
Henry	39	m	w	SHOL	San Francisco	1-Wd San Francisco	79	26
James	38	m	w	IREL	San Francisco	7-Wd San Francisco	81	199
James	30	m	w	IREL	Yuba	Rose Bar Twp	93	661
Jno	44	m	w	IREL	Sierra	Table Rock Twp	89	571
Joel	38	m	w	ME	Butte	Bidwell Twp	70	2
John	35	m	w	IREL	Sacramento	Brighton Twp	77	70
John	30	m	w	IREL	San Francisco	7-Wd San Francisco	81	241
John	28	m	w	IREL	Marin	Point Reyes Twp	74	21
John	26	m	w	IREL	Colusa	Colusa Twp	71	284
Julia	24	f	w	IREL	Alameda	Oakland	68	199
Maggie	32	f	w	IREL	San Francisco	7-Wd San Francisco	81	278
Margaret	31	f	w	ENGL	Sacramento	Franklin Twp	77	108
Mary	30	f	w	IREL	San Francisco	7-Wd San Francisco	81	194
Mary	28	f	w	IREL	San Francisco	San Francisco P O	83	110
Mary	25	f	w	IREL	San Francisco	San Francisco P O	83	98
Mary	20	f	w	NY	San Francisco	San Francisco P O	83	114
Mary	18	f	w	IREL	Amador	Amador City P O	69	390
Michael	28	m	w	IREL	Marin	Sausalito Twp	74	73
Michael	24	m	w	IREL	Solano	Silveyville Twp	90	85
Michael	23	m	w	IREL	Del Norte	Crescent Twp	71	455
Morris	40	m	w	IREL	Sacramento	Cosumnes Twp	77	93
Patrick	40	m	w	IREL	Colusa	Spring Valley Twp	71	344
Patrick	34	m	w	IREL	Sacramento	Cosumnes Twp	77	92
Patrick	28	m	w	IREL	Napa	Napa Twp	75	65
Patrick	28	m	w	IREL	Alameda	San Leandro	68	96
Patrick	27	m	w	IREL	Placer	Cisco P O	76	494
Patsy	30	m	w	IREL	San Francisco	San Francisco P O	83	32
Rose	42	f	w	IREL	Alameda	Oakland	68	208
Thomas	35	m	w	IREL	Alameda	Oakland	68	257
W H	27	m	w	MA	Monterey	San Antonio Twp	74	321
William	36	m	w	IN	Colusa	Spring Valley Twp	71	336
William	25	m	w	IREL	Placer	Cisco P O	76	494
Wm	38	m	w	IREL	Napa	Napa	75	57
Wm	35	m	w	ENGL	San Francisco	7-Wd San Francisco	81	234
Wm E	52	m	w	NC	San Diego	San Diego	78	506
FLINSBURG								
Ernest	39	m	w	PRUS	San Francisco	8-Wd San Francisco	82	431
FLINT								
---	72	m	w	MO	Yuba	Marysville	93	614
---	22	m	w	VA	Yuba	Marysville	93	617
Addison A	38	m	w	MA	Sacramento	2-Wd Sacramento	77	247
B	20	m	w	SC	Yuba	Marysville	93	604
B P	27	m	w	ME	Monterey	San Juan Twp	74	415
Benj	43	m	w	ME	Monterey	San Juan Twp	74	415
Benjamin	44	m	w	ME	Humboldt	Mattole Twp	72	283
Bridget	30	f	w	IREL	San Francisco	8-Wd San Francisco	82	300
Catilla	17	f	w	NH	Humboldt	Eureka Twp	72	273
E P	35	m	w	MA	Alameda	Oakland	68	198
E P	34	f	w	PA	Alameda	Oakland	68	198
E S	20	m	w	MD	Yuba	Marysville	93	593
Elijah T	28	m	w	LA	Stanislaus	Emory Twp	92	23
Elijah T	27	m	w	LA	Alameda	Oakland	68	203
F	19	m	w	ME	Yuba	Marysville	93	617
F C	47	m	w	MA	San Francisco	San Francisco P O	85	813
F C	26	m	w	ME	Sacramento	Franklin Twp	77	120
George	55	m	w	ENGL	Nevada	Rough & Ready Twp	75	336
George B	24	m	w	MA	Alameda	Oakland	68	199
Hannah	19	f	w	IREL	San Francisco	8-Wd San Francisco	82	345
Hannibal	48	m	w	VA	Yolo	Cottonwood Twp	93	475
Henry	34	m	w	CT	Santa Barbara	San Buenaventura P	87	447
J H	20	m	w	CT	Yuba	Marysville	93	595
J P	67	m	w	MA	Alameda	Oakland	68	203
James	32	m	w	IREL	San Francisco	San Francisco P O	85	736
Jane	40	f	w	ENGL	San Francisco	San Francisco P O	80	426
John	45	m	w	ENGL	Yuba	Long Bar Twp	93	560
John	27	m	w	ME	Sacramento	San Joaquin Twp	77	398
John N	27	m	w	PA	Nevada	Rough & Ready Twp	75	324
John W	27	m	w	IL	San Luis Obispo	San Luis Obispo Tw	87	301
Joseph	29	m	w	NY	Yuba	Rose Bar Twp	93	656
Kate	12	f	w	US	Yuba	Marysville	93	609
L B	23	m	w	NH	Sacramento	Sutter Twp	77	386
L D	33	m	w	MA	Sierra	Butte Twp	89	510
L J	40	m	w	MA	Sierra	Sierra Twp	89	565
Levy	41	m	w	ENGL	Alameda	Oakland	68	216
Luna M	22	f	w	ME	Santa Barbara	Santa Barbara P O	87	500
M J	28	f	w	IREL	Yuba	Marysville	93	602
M J	10	f	w	US	Yuba	Marysville	93	609
M K	21	m	w	NY	Sonoma	Santa Rosa	91	407
Ralf H	25	m	w	OH	San Luis Obispo	San Luis Obispo Tw	87	301
Robert	26	m	w	ME	Tuolumne	Sonora P O	93	317
Robt G	53	m	w	ENGL	San Luis Obispo	Salinas Twp	87	290
Samuel	30	m	w	PA	Marin	Point Reyes Twp	74	23
T P	40	f	w	MA	San Francisco	San Francisco P O	83	282
W K	32	m	w	LA	Alameda	Oakland	68	203
William	34	m	w	ME	Santa Clara	Redwood Twp	88	133
FLINTALL								
Thomas	48	m	w	ENGL	San Francisco	San Francisco P O	83	186
FLINTON								
Henry	53	m	w	NY	Trinity	Trinity Center Pct	92	204
FLIP								
Ah	41	m	c	CHIN	San Francisco	San Francisco P O	80	505
Ah	34	m	c	CHIN	San Francisco	San Francisco P O	80	498
Mary	45	f	w	PORT	Santa Clara	Santa Clara Twp	88	159

Series M593

© 2001 by Heritage Quest. All rights reserved.

California 1870 Census

Name	Age	S	R	B-PL	County	Locale	Series M593 Roll	Pg
FLITERER								
Frederick	32	m	w	WURT	Santa Clara	Fremont Twp	88	57
FLITNER								
Edwin	43	m	w	ME	Siskiyou	Yreka	89	652
Frank	22	m	w	ME	Santa Cruz	Santa Cruz Twp	89	399
FLIYET								
Felix	30	m	w	FRAN	San Francisco	San Francisco P O	80	538
FLO								
Ah	30	m	c	CHIN	San Francisco	San Francisco P O	80	515
Ah	29	m	c	CHIN	Santa Clara	1-Wd San Jose	88	269
Ah	23	f	c	CHIN	San Francisco	San Francisco P O	80	494
FLOATER								
Christopher	37	m	w	PRUS	Tulare	Tule Rvr Twp	92	265
FLOBERG								
J P	40	m	w	SWED	Sacramento	1-Wd Sacramento	77	177
FLOCKHART								
Oliver J	35	m	w	SCOT	San Francisco	San Francisco P O	83	409
FLOES								
Mary F	34	f	w	HI	Yolo	Merritt Twp	93	508
FLOGG								
R B	42	m	w	VT	Sierra	Lincoln Twp	89	547
FLOHR								
A	55	m	w	BADE	Sacramento	3-Wd Sacramento	77	289
Martin H	22	m	w	PRUS	Sonoma	Analy Twp	91	225
FLOM								
Ah	21	m	c	CHIN	Placer	Lincoln P O	76	491
FLONI								
Saml	36	m	w	SWIT	El Dorado	Georgetown Twp	72	49
FLONK								
Ah	20	m	c	CHIN	Santa Clara	San Jose Twp	88	194
FLONSY								
Fierman	26	m	w	FRAN	Inyo	Lone Pine Twp	73	330
FLONZ								
Martin	18	m	w	ITAL	San Mateo	Schoolhouse Statio	87	344
FLOOD								
Alexr	25	m	w	IREL	San Francisco	San Francisco P O	83	72
Alice	50	f	w	IREL	San Francisco	8-Wd San Francisco	82	351
Alice	18	f	w	MA	San Francisco	8-Wd San Francisco	82	386
Andrew J	53	m	w	IN	Los Angeles	Wilmington Twp	73	644
Bernard	29	m	w	IREL	San Francisco	San Francisco P O	83	390
Bernard	26	m	w	IREL	San Francisco	San Francisco P O	83	357
Bridget	25	f	w	IREL	San Francisco	San Francisco P O	83	98
C B	34	m	w	ME	San Francisco	San Francisco P O	85	829
Christopher	42	m	w	IREL	San Francisco	7-Wd San Francisco	81	196
Christopher	31	m	w	IL	San Luis Obispo	Santa Rosa Twp	87	317
Daniel	30	m	w	IREL	San Francisco	1-Wd San Francisco	79	113
Edward	30	m	w	NY	San Francisco	San Francisco P O	83	290
Eliza	30	f	w	IREL	Sacramento	Dry Crk Twp	77	100
George	28	m	w	IA	Los Angeles	Wilmington Twp	73	645
Hannah	31	f	w	IREL	Alameda	Oakland	68	150
Henry I	31	m	w	IREL	San Francisco	8-Wd San Francisco	82	410
Hiram	21	m	w	DE	Solano	Denverton Twp	90	25
Hugh	42	m	w	IREL	San Francisco	San Francisco P O	83	156
Hugh	29	m	w	IREL	Yuba	Rose Bar Twp	93	663
Isaac	42	m	w	MA	San Luis Obispo	Morro Twp	87	284
James	38	m	w	NY	San Francisco	8-Wd San Francisco	82	296
James	37	m	w	IREL	San Francisco	San Francisco P O	83	254
James	33	m	w	IREL	Solano	Suisun Twp	90	113
James	32	m	w	IREL	San Francisco	San Francisco P O	83	117
James	27	m	w	NY	Nevada	Rough & Ready Twp	75	327
James	15	m	w	MA	Santa Cruz	Pajaro Twp	89	343
James	13	m	w	CA	Santa Clara	Santa Clara Twp	88	177
James A	9	m	w	IA	San Luis Obispo	Santa Rosa Twp	87	322
James C	43	m	w	NY	San Francisco	8-Wd San Francisco	82	463
Jennie	15	f	w	CA	Santa Clara	2-Wd San Jose	88	337
Jeremiah	43	m	w	NY	Contra Costa	Martinez P O	71	426
John	41	m	w	IREL	San Francisco	1-Wd San Francisco	79	57
John	36	m	w	IREL	Colusa	Stony Crk Twp	71	331
John	36	m	w	NY	San Francisco	6-Wd San Francisco	81	150
John	35	m	w	IREL	San Francisco	8-Wd San Francisco	82	355
John	30	m	w	US	Santa Cruz	Watsonville	89	369
John	28	m	w	MO	Solano	Vacaville Twp	90	124
John	26	m	w	NY	Colusa	Colusa Twp	71	284
John	22	m	w	IREL	San Francisco	2-Wd San Francisco	79	148
John	22	m	w	IREL	San Francisco	1-Wd San Francisco	79	82
John	13	m	w	CA	Santa Barbara	Santa Barbara P O	87	492
John W	45	m	w	IREL	San Francisco	San Francisco P O	83	254
John W	34	m	w	IREL	San Francisco	8-Wd San Francisco	82	470
Joseph	35	m	w	ME	Sonoma	Analy Twp	91	224
Joseph	35	m	w	ENGL	Sonoma	Petaluma Twp	91	360
Margaret	36	f	w	IREL	San Francisco	11-Wd San Francisc	84	583
Mary	40	f	w	IREL	San Francisco	11-Wd San Francisc	84	462
Mary	23	f	w	AR	Los Angeles	Wilmington Twp	73	645
Michael	64	m	w	IREL	Monterey	Pajaro Twp	74	375
Michael	50	m	w	IREL	San Francisco	11-Wd San Francisc	84	460
Michael	40	m	w	IREL	San Francisco	San Francisco P O	85	791
Michael J	20	m	w	CT	Sacramento	4-Wd Sacramento	77	326
Micheal	33	m	w	IREL	Sacramento	Dry Crk Twp	77	100
Noah	32	m	w	VA	San Francisco	San Francisco P O	80	538
Patrick	41	m	w	IREL	San Francisco	San Francisco P O	83	395
Patrick	23	m	w	IREL	San Francisco	1-Wd San Francisco	79	113
Purley O	4	m	w	NY	Santa Cruz	Santa Cruz	89	419
Richard	41	m	w	IREL	Butte	Wyandotte Twp	70	142
Richard	27	m	w	IA	San Francisco	San Francisco P O	83	330
T	35	m	w	IREL	Solano	Vallejo	90	140
Thos	35	m	w	IREL	San Joaquin	Douglas Twp	86	35
W A	46	m	w	CT	Alameda	Oakland	68	201
William	41	m	w	WI	Solano	Silveyville Twp	90	72
William	35	m	w	IREL	Solano	Rio Vista Twp	90	64
William	32	m	w	IREL	Santa Clara	Redwood Twp	88	124
William	24	m	w	MO	Solano	Denverton Twp	90	25
FLOP								
Ah	41	m	c	CHIN	San Francisco	San Francisco P O	80	491
Ah	34	m	c	CHIN	San Francisco	San Francisco P O	80	498
FLORA								
Andrew W	39	m	w	WI	El Dorado	Georgetown Twp	72	47
Joshua	26	m	w	IN	Butte	Chico Twp	70	23
Nichalous	50	m	w	CHIL	El Dorado	Placerville Twp	72	103
FLORANT								
Archibald	23	m	w	CANA	Nevada	Grass Valley Twp	75	157
FLORAS								
Guadalupe	55	f	i	MEXI	Inyo	Cerro Gordo Twp	73	318
Maryanne	16	f	w	MEXI	San Francisco	San Francisco P O	83	283
FLOREANCE								
Pablo	34	m	i	MEXI	Inyo	Cerro Gordo Twp	73	318
FLOREANSY								
Sarah	22	f	w	VA	Yolo	Putah Twp	93	519
FLOREN								
I	34	m	w	IREL	San Mateo	San Mateo P O	87	359
FLORENCE								
George	37	m	w	ENGL	San Francisco	2-Wd San Francisco	79	190
John	30	m	b	MO	Tehama	Red Bluff	92	182
Marshal	26	m	w	NC	Sonoma	Mendocino Twp	91	301
Robert	35	m	w	MO	Sacramento	San Joaquin Twp	77	394
S C	49	m	w	OH	Mendocino	Ukiah Twp	74	241
FLORENTI								
Joseph	17	m	w	FRAN	Marin	San Rafael Twp	74	34
FLORENTINE								
D	22	m	w	FRAN	Yuba	Marysville Twp	93	567
FLORES								
A C	60	f	w	MEXI	Tuolumne	Columbia P O	93	353
Anastacio	35	m	w	MEXI	Santa Barbara	Santa Barbara P O	87	494
Anastasia	50	m	w	MEXI	Santa Barbara	Santa Barbara P O	87	481
Anestacio	53	m	w	MEXI	Los Angeles	Los Angeles Twp	73	475
Ansarno	17	m	w	CA	Mariposa	Mariposa P O	74	135
Antone	50	m	w	FRAN	El Dorado	Diamond Springs Tw	72	26
Antone	35	m	w	PORT	Alameda	Hayward	68	75
Antonio	50	m	w	MEXI	Santa Clara	Almaden Twp	88	20
Antonio	50	m	w	MEXI	Santa Barbara	San Buenaventura P	87	447
Antonio	46	m	w	ITAL	San Francisco	San Francisco P O	80	408
Antonio	34	m	w	CA	Santa Clara	2-Wd San Jose	88	287
Avalarodo	34	m	w	MEXI	Los Angeles	Los Angeles	73	516
B	30	m	w	FRAN	Santa Clara	Almaden Twp	88	20
Candelaria	50	f	w	CA	Santa Cruz	Pajaro Twp	89	360
Catarina	50	f	w	OR	Los Angeles	San Gabriel Twp	73	593
Celedonia	25	f	i	CA	Sonoma	Bodega Twp	91	249
Charles	18	m	w	PORT	Alameda	Hayward	68	74
D	25	m	w	FRAN	Santa Clara	Almaden Twp	88	20
Dolores	22	f	w	MD	Sacramento	2-Wd Sacramento	77	249
Doloses	46	m	w	MEXI	Napa	Napa	75	55
Domingo	18	m	w	MEXI	Marin	San Rafael Twp	74	46
Dorothee	37	f	w	MEXI	San Francisco	San Francisco P O	80	460
Escoba	30	m	w	MEXI	San Francisco	San Francisco P O	80	342
Esther	47	f	w	CHIL	Calaveras	San Andreas P O	70	155
Eusebro	20	m	w	MEXI	Los Angeles	Wilmington Twp	73	640
Felicita	11	f	i	CA	San Luis Obispo	San Luis Obispo Tw	87	315
Fermina	28	f	w	MEXI	Los Angeles	Los Angeles	73	551
Fernando	65	m	w	CHIL	Santa Clara	San Jose Twp	88	209
Flores	47	f	w	CA	Santa Barbara	Santa Barbara P O	87	465
Francis	40	m	w	MEXI	Colusa	Colusa Twp	71	283
Francisco	50	f	w	MEXI	San Francisco	San Francisco P O	80	459
Francisco	46	f	w	MEXI	Los Angeles	Los Angeles	73	560
Francisco	45	m	w	MEXI	Santa Barbara	Santa Barbara P O	87	497
Francisco	40	m	w	CHIL	Fresno	Millerton P O	72	159
Frank	30	m	w	PORT	Alameda	Eden Twp	68	88
Frank	21	m	w	PORT	Tuolumne	Columbia P O	93	355
Gertrudes	25	f	w	MEXI	Los Angeles	Santa Ana Twp	73	604
Gregoria	18	f	w	MEXI	San Francisco	San Francisco P O	80	422
Guillermo	17	m	w	CA	Santa Cruz	Pajaro Twp	89	361
Hermone	20	m	w	MEXI	Santa Barbara	Las Cruces P O	87	504
Ignacia	39	m	w	MEXI	San Luis Obispo	San Luis Obispo Tw	87	313
Isabell	18	f	w	MEXI	Alameda	San Leandro	68	94
Jesus	40	m	w	MEXI	San Diego	Temecula Dist	78	526
Jesus	34	m	w	MEXI	San Francisco	San Francisco P O	80	470
Jesus	25	m	w	MEXI	Santa Clara	Almaden Twp	88	20
Joan	45	m	w	PERU	Fresno	Millerton P O	72	165
Jose L	41	m	w	MEXI	Mariposa	Mariposa P O	74	96
Jose M	46	m	w	CA	Santa Clara	Burnett Twp	88	37
Joseph A C	36	m	w	PORT	San Mateo	Half Moon Bay P O	87	394
Juan	41	m	w	CHIL	Santa Barbara	Santa Maria P O	87	512
Juan	36	m	w	MEXI	San Francisco	San Francisco P O	80	472
Juan	27	m	w	MEXI	Santa Barbara	San Buenaventura P	87	433
Juan	26	m	w	CA	Santa Barbara	San Buenaventura P	87	441
Juan	19	m	w	CA	Santa Barbara	Santa Barbara P O	87	450
Justo	35	m	w	MEXI	San Bernardino	San Bernardino Twp	78	415
Leandro	8	m	w	CA	Santa Clara	2-Wd San Jose	88	301
Leno	45	m	w	MEXI	Butte	Oroville Twp	70	137
Lorenzo	17	m	w	CA	Santa Barbara	Arroyo Grande P O	87	508
Louis	56	m	w	TX	Santa Cruz	Soquel Twp	89	436
Louis	32	m	w	MEXI	San Luis Obispo	San Luis Obispo Tw	87	303
Luis	19	m	w	CA	Santa Clara	Santa Clara Twp	88	158
M A	44	m	w	MEXI	Tuolumne	Big Oak Flat P O	93	392
Maria	20	f	i	CA	Calaveras	Copperopolis P O	70	253
Maria	16	f	w	CA	Santa Clara	Gilroy Twp	88	98

© 2001 by Heritage Quest. All rights reserved.

Series M593

Name	Age	S	R	B-PL	County	Locale	Roll	Pg
Martin	21	m	w	CA	Los Angeles	Los Angeles	73	561
Mary	9	f	w	CA	San Luis Obispo	San Luis Obispo Tw	87	300
Mary	50	f	w	PORT	Alameda	Eden Twp	68	89
Mary	42	f	w	MEXI	Tuolumne	Columbia P O	93	353
Meriano	50	m	b	PHIL	Mariposa	Mariposa P O	74	104
Miguel	62	m	w	MEXI	Placer	Auburn P O	76	360
Miguel	44	m	w	CA	Santa Clara	2-Wd San Jose	88	300
Morna	25	f	w	CA	Los Angeles	Los Angeles	73	509
Pabla	43	f	w	MEXI	Santa Clara	1-Wd San Jose	88	263
Pablo	33	m	w	MEXI	Santa Clara	Almaden Twp	88	10
Patricio	39	m	w	MEXI	Los Angeles	San Juan Twp	73	626
Paz	22	f	w	MEXI	San Francisco	San Francisco P O	80	341
Pedro	40	m	w	MEXI	Santa Barbara	San Buenaventura P	87	441
Pedro	17	m	w	MEXI	Los Angeles	Los Angeles	73	553
Refufie	30	f	w	MEXI	Napa	Napa	75	55
Refujia	48	f	w	MEXI	Fresno	Millerton P O	72	155
Rives	45	m	w	MEXI	Santa Clara	Almaden Twp	88	1
Santiago	25	m	w	CA	Los Angeles	San Gabriel Twp	73	593
Santos	39	m	w	MEXI	Kern	Bakersfield P O	73	364
Sefino	23	m	w	MEXI	Los Angeles	Los Angeles	73	551
Senovia	44	m	w	MEXI	Mariposa	Mariposa P O	74	95
Susan	15	f	w	CA	San Francisco	San Francisco P O	83	203
Tomas	29	m	w	MEXI	San Francisco	San Francisco P O	80	472
Trinidad	40	m	w	MEXI	San Francisco	1-Wd San Francisco	79	55
Valentine	27	m	w	MEXI	Fresno	Millerton P O	72	154
Valentine	26	m	w	MEXI	Santa Clara	Burnett Twp	88	37
Vicente	23	m	w	MEXI	Los Angeles	Los Angeles Twp	73	485
Vincelatho	34	m	w	CHIL	Santa Clara	Alviso Twp	88	23
FLORESCIO								
Marcus	32	m	w	MEXI	San Luis Obispo	Salinas Twp	87	295
FLOREZ								
Domenic	20	m	w	ITAL	San Mateo	Schoolhouse Statio	87	343
Frances	40	m	w	MEXI	Contra Costa	Martinez Twp	71	351
Francisco	68	m	w	MEXI	Contra Costa	Martinez P O	71	368
Gabriel	32	m	w	ITAL	San Mateo	Schoolhouse Statio	87	343
Gabriel	30	m	w	ITAL	San Mateo	Schoolhouse Statio	87	346
John	30	m	w	ITAL	San Mateo	Schoolhouse Statio	87	345
Joseph	27	m	w	MEXI	San Mateo	Half Moon Bay P O	87	389
Martin	31	m	w	ITAL	San Mateo	Schoolhouse Statio	87	345
Martin	17	m	w	ITAL	San Mateo	Schoolhouse Statio	87	343
Pedro	23	m	w	MEXI	Mariposa	Mariposa P O	74	110
Regino	32	m	w	MEXI	Mariposa	Mariposa P O	74	110
FLORICE								
Hora	45	m	i	MEXI	Inyo	Lone Pine Twp	73	333
FLORIDON								
Thomas	33	m	w	ENGL	Placer	Dutch Flat P O	76	406
FLORIN								
Batiste	71	m	w	BELG	San Francisco	11-Wd San Francisc	84	642
FLORINE								
John	40	m	w	PRUS	Santa Clara	Santa Clara Twp	88	159
Mariah	40	m	w	FRAN	San Joaquin	2-Wd Stockton	86	167
Olof	38	m	w	SWED	San Francisco	San Francisco P O	85	719
FLORIS								
Joe	32	m	w	MEXI	Alameda	Murray Twp	68	127
Ursula	34	f	w	CHIL	San Joaquin	2-Wd Stockton	86	174
FLORITA								
Dolores	60	f	w	MEXI	San Francisco	San Francisco P O	80	342
Dolores	50	f	w	BRAZ	San Francisco	San Francisco P O	80	349
William	28	m	w	ITAL	San Francisco	San Francisco P O	80	471
FLOROS								
Peter	26	m	w	ITAL	San Mateo	Schoolhouse Statio	87	344
FLORTON								
Eugene	38	m	w	SCOT	San Francisco	1-Wd San Francisco	79	98
FLOS								
Thomas	20	m	w	PORT	Marin	Tomales Twp	74	87
FLOTE								
William	39	m	w	HANO	Stanislaus	Branch Twp	92	8
FLOTO								
Eliza	10	f	w	CA	Mariposa	Mariposa P O	74	120
Herman	50	m	w	PRUS	San Francisco	5-Wd San Francisco	81	1
FLOUCAND								
Heny	57	m	w	FRAN	Mariposa	Maxwell Crk P O	74	139
FLOUR								
Christian	34	m	w	SWIT	San Francisco	11-Wd San Francisc	84	449
Henry	32	m	w	ITAL	San Mateo	Schoolhouse Statio	87	344
John	30	m	w	ITAL	San Mateo	Schoolhouse Statio	87	344
FLOURE								
Nathan	39	m	w	ME	San Francisco	5-Wd San Francisco	81	23
FLOURMOY								
William S	48	m	w	VA	Yolo	Grafton Twp	93	489
FLOURNEY								
Robt S	40	m	w	KY	Plumas	Indian Twp	77	9
FLOURNOY								
Daniel H	66	m	w	VA	Yolo	Grafton Twp	93	493
FLOUS								
Conrad	45	m	w	SWIT	Marin	San Antonio Twp	74	64
FLOVES								
N D	26	m	w	MEXI	Butte	Chico Twp	70	19
FLOVOR								
John	24	m	w	ITAL	San Mateo	Schoolhouse Statio	87	344
FLOW								
Ah	31	m	c	CHIN	San Francisco	San Francisco P O	80	500
Joseph	24	m	w	PORT	Alameda	Washington Twp	68	295
FLOWER								
Chas	42	m	w	ENGL	San Francisco	11-Wd San Francisc	84	677
Geo A	38	m	w	PA	San Diego	San Diego	78	496
George	21	m	m	LA	San Francisco	San Francisco P O	83	329
John	52	m	w	NY	Klamath	Klamath Twp	73	371
William	45	m	w	MI	San Francisco	2-Wd San Francisco	79	279
Wm G	40	m	w	IL	Sacramento	Franklin Twp	77	110
FLOWERDEW								
James	32	m	w	SCOT	Marin	San Rafael Twp	74	33
FLOWERS								
Ada	20	f	w	NY	San Francisco	2-Wd San Francisco	79	246
E D	11	f	w	CA	Alameda	Oakland	68	237
Ellen	37	f	w	MD	Sacramento	3-Wd Sacramento	77	262
Ellis	41	m	w	OH	Trinity	Canyon City Pct	92	201
James	42	m	w	IREL	San Francisco	San Francisco P O	80	406
James	15	m	w	CA	Alameda	Oakland	68	159
Joseph	38	m	b	GA	Butte	Chico Twp	70	18
Lonzo	47	m	w	NY	Sutter	Yuba Twp	92	149
Nathan M	42	m	w	NY	Stanislaus	Emory Twp	92	20
Roland	46	m	w	KY	Sutter	Butte Twp	92	89
Sarah	24	f	w	SPAI	Sacramento	2-Wd Sacramento	77	241
Thos W	42	m	w	ENGL	Nevada	Nevada Twp	75	274
Wm	42	m	w	VA	Sacramento	Alabama Twp	77	61
Wm A	47	m	w	ENGL	Humboldt	Pacific Twp	72	293
Wm P	41	m	w	OH	Butte	Ophir Twp	70	111
Zora	19	f	w	MI	San Francisco	11-Wd San Francisc	84	510
FLOWLER								
Gabriel	27	m	w	ITAL	San Mateo	Schoolhouse Statio	87	344
Henry	30	m	w	ITAL	San Mateo	Schoolhouse Statio	87	344
FLOWLES								
Go	14	m	w	ITAL	San Mateo	Schoolhouse Statio	87	345
FLOY								
Ah	47	m	c	CHIN	Santa Clara	San Jose Twp	88	190
Ah	39	m	c	CHIN	Santa Clara	1-Wd San Jose	88	270
Ah	32	m	c	CHIN	Santa Clara	1-Wd San Jose	88	271
Ah	27	m	c	CHIN	Santa Clara	1-Wd San Jose	88	271
Ah	20	m	c	CHIN	Trinity	Weaverville Pct	92	230
Ah	19	m	c	CHIN	Santa Clara	1-Wd San Jose	88	272
FLOYD								
Albert	31	m	w	MA	Yolo	Putah Twp	93	523
David	74	m	w	KY	Amador	Sutter Crk P O	69	413
Edmond	30	m	w	ME	San Francisco	San Francisco P O	83	93
Edward	54	m	w	WALE	Placer	Bath P O	76	438
Edwd	38	m	w	IREL	San Francisco	1-Wd San Francisco	79	133
James	45	m	b	MA	Santa Clara	1-Wd San Jose	88	236
James	31	m	w	ENGL	Nevada	Grass Valley Twp	75	168
Jennie	42	f	w	NY	Santa Clara	San Jose Twp	88	198
John	22	m	w	MA	San Francisco	3-Wd San Francisco	79	323
John M	21	m	w	NY	San Francisco	1-Wd San Francisco	79	16
M D	67	m	w	VA	Tehama	Stony Crk	92	166
Mary	45	f	w	ENGL	San Francisco	8-Wd San Francisco	82	370
R F	36	m	w	NY	Butte	Wyandotte Twp	70	145
Robert	50	m	w	NC	Los Angeles	El Monte Twp	73	452
Rose	21	f	w	VA	San Francisco	8-Wd San Francisco	82	387
Thomas P	36	m	w	ENGL	Mariposa	Mariposa P O	74	120
Thos	50	m	w	ENGL	San Francisco	7-Wd San Francisco	81	243
Thos	26	m	w	NY	San Francisco	San Francisco P O	83	48
W	22	m	w	ENGL	Sierra	Butte Twp	89	511
William	30	m	w	IREL	Santa Clara	Fremont Twp	88	65
William	30	m	w	ENGL	Nevada	Grass Valley Twp	75	207
William	26	m	w	ENGL	Tuolumne	Sonora P O	93	324
Wm	40	m	w	CA	San Joaquin	Union Twp	86	268
Wm	32	m	w	ENGL	Nevada	Nevada Twp	75	275
Zephus	30	m	w	ENGL	San Francisco	2-Wd San Francisco	79	196
FLOYDE								
George	35	m	w	ENGL	Amador	Drytown P O	69	425
FLRMAN								
Seth	35	m	w	NY	Kern	Linns Valley P O	73	344
FLU								
Kee	41	m	c	CHIN	Placer	Bath P O	76	430
FLUBACHER								
Emil	36	m	w	FRAN	San Francisco	1-Wd San Francisco	79	39
FLUDER								
J H	64	m	w	NY	Yuba	Marysville	93	617
FLUE								
Ah	16	m	c	CHIN	San Francisco	San Francisco P O	83	131
FLUEGGER								
Jno C	40	m	w	HANO	San Francisco	San Francisco P O	83	127
FLUELLEN								
James	33	m	w	CANA	Contra Costa	Martinez P O	71	419
FLUENIN								
Sarah J	15	f	w	CA	Humboldt	Pacific Twp	72	296
FLUENT								
James B	47	m	w	NY	Santa Clara	San Jose Twp	88	180
FLUERY								
Alexander	37	m	w	FRAN	San Francisco	6-Wd San Francisco	81	106
FLUGAL								
August	31	m	w	PRUS	San Francisco	6-Wd San Francisco	81	83
FLUGER								
Anthony	21	m	w	BREM	San Francisco	8-Wd San Francisco	82	336
FLUHART								
Creaton	23	m	w	IN	Amador	Amador City P O	69	390
FLUHR								
Charles	32	m	w	GERM	Los Angeles	Los Angeles	73	519
FLUKE								
J	44	m	w	PRUS	Sierra	Lincoln Twp	89	546
FLUKENSTINE								
C	34	m	w	PRUS	Sierra	Sierra Twp	89	568
FLUM								
Catherine	30	f	w	IREL	Alameda	Oakland	68	197
Sue	30	m	c	CHIN	Yuba	Marysville	93	626

© 2001 by Heritage Quest. All rights reserved.

California 1870 Census

Name	Age	S	R	B-PL	County	Locale	Series M593 Roll	Pg
William J	44	m	w	TN	El Dorado	Diamond Springs Tw	72	34
FLUMER								
George	16	m	w	CA	Sacramento	Alabama Twp	77	60
FLUMME								
Herman	20	m	w	PRUS	San Francisco	8-Wd San Francisco	82	307
FLUNG								
Anga	40	m	c	CHIN	Tulare	Visalia Twp	92	281
FLUORNOY								
Thomas	46	m	w	KY	Contra Costa	Martinez P O	71	383
FLUTOFF								
Joseph	41	m	w	IREL	Santa Cruz	Santa Cruz	89	407
FLY								
Ah	23	m	c	CHIN	San Francisco	San Francisco P O	80	511
James C	33	m	w	TN	Tulare	Farmersville Twp	92	244
John R	60	m	w	TN	Tulare	Farmersville Twp	92	243
John W	22	m	w	MO	Tulare	Farmersville Twp	92	244
Marion	42	m	w	TN	Tulare	Farmersville Twp	92	244
Mary Ann	59	f	w	ENGL	Napa	Napa Twp	75	29
Quintus	28	m	w	MO	Napa	Napa Twp	75	28
Reuben	38	m	w	ME	San Francisco	2-Wd San Francisco	79	159
Solomon	38	m	w	IREL	Contra Costa	Martinez P O	71	405
William M	26	m	w	TN	Tulare	Farmersville Twp	92	244
FLYE								
Egbert C	43	m	w	CANA	Siskiyou	Cottonwood Twp	89	592
Margaret	68	f	w	ME	Alameda	Brooklyn	68	30
FLYN								
Edward	35	m	w	IREL	Trinity	Junction City Pct	92	206
James	30	m	w	IREL	San Francisco	11-Wd San Francisc	84	662
John	60	m	w	IREL	San Francisco	11-Wd San Francisc	84	671
John	43	m	w	IREL	Napa	Yountville Twp	75	77
John H	40	m	w	IREL	San Francisco	San Francisco P O	83	224
Manuel	27	m	w	FRAN	San Francisco	2-Wd San Francisco	79	141
Thomas	31	m	w	IREL	San Francisco	San Francisco P O	83	250
Thos	52	m	w	IREL	San Francisco	11-Wd San Francisc	84	666
FLYNN								
Anthony	42	m	w	IREL	San Francisco	6-Wd San Francisco	81	137
Benjamin	30	m	w	IREL	Santa Clara	2-Wd San Jose	88	320
Bridget	50	f	w	IREL	San Francisco	San Francisco P O	83	336
Bridget	30	f	w	IREL	Alameda	Oakland	68	208
Bridget	28	f	w	IREL	San Francisco	San Francisco P O	80	405
Bridget	19	f	w	IREL	San Francisco	San Francisco P O	83	347
Cathrine	29	f	w	ENGL	San Francisco	2-Wd San Francisco	79	141
D	26	m	w	MO	San Joaquin	Oneal Twp	86	110
David	44	m	w	IREL	Placer	Bath P O	76	448
David	26	m	w	IREL	San Mateo	Redwood Twp	87	368
Edward	40	m	w	IREL	San Francisco	3-Wd San Francisco	79	319
Edward	38	m	w	IREL	San Francisco	8-Wd San Francisco	82	392
Edward	21	m	w	IREL	Santa Barbara	Santa Barbara P O	87	451
Ellen	40	f	w	IREL	San Francisco	5-Wd San Francisco	81	6
Evarista	31	f	w	IREL	Santa Barbara	Santa Barbara P O	87	501
Florence N	15	f	w	CA	Shasta	Shasta P O	89	457
George	23	m	w	IREL	San Francisco	11-Wd San Francisc	84	519
Hannah	52	f	w	IREL	San Francisco	2-Wd San Francisco	79	216
Hugh	52	m	w	IREL	Calaveras	San Andreas P O	70	215
Hugh	35	m	w	IREL	San Francisco	San Francisco P O	83	267
Ischam	40	m	w	TN	San Bernardino	San Bernardino Twp	78	437
James	40	m	w	IREL	San Joaquin	Liberty Twp	86	85
James	40	m	w	IREL	San Francisco	San Francisco P O	83	168
James	35	m	w	IREL	San Mateo	San Mateo P O	87	350
James	35	m	w	IREL	San Francisco	8-Wd San Francisco	82	323
James	31	m	w	IREL	Calaveras	San Andreas P O	70	201
James	30	m	w	IREL	San Francisco	1-Wd San Francisco	79	25
James	25	m	w	NY	San Francisco	11-Wd San Francisc	84	641
James C	34	m	w	IREL	Sutter	Nicolaus Twp	92	111
James F	37	m	w	NY	Santa Cruz	Santa Cruz	89	425
James H B	33	m	w	MA	Monterey	Monterey	74	365
Jas	27	m	w	IREL	San Francisco	7-Wd San Francisco	81	230
Jerry	40	m	w	IREL	San Joaquin	Liberty Twp	86	84
John	43	m	w	IREL	San Francisco	San Francisco P O	85	839
John	40	m	w	PA	San Francisco	1-Wd San Francisco	79	34
John	40	m	w	IREL	El Dorado	Georgetown Twp	72	39
John	37	m	w	IREL	Solano	Vallejo	90	196
John	35	m	w	IREL	Alameda	Murray Twp	68	120
John	30	m	w	IREL	San Francisco	1-Wd San Francisco	79	28
John	30	m	w	IREL	Los Angeles	Santa Ana Twp	73	601
John	30	m	w	IREL	Marin	San Rafael	74	56
John	30	m	w	IREL	Nevada	Grass Valley Twp	75	157
John	27	m	w	NJ	Sacramento	2-Wd Sacramento	77	226
John	26	m	w	MA	San Francisco	San Francisco P O	83	296
John	25	m	w	IREL	San Francisco	San Francisco P O	85	784
John	25	m	w	IREL	Alameda	Washington Twp	68	276
John	23	m	w	IREL	Alameda	Oakland	68	182
John M	27	m	w	IREL	Santa Clara	Santa Clara Twp	88	163
Julia	38	f	w	NY	Sacramento	3-Wd Sacramento	77	304
Kate	26	f	w	IREL	Santa Clara	Santa Clara Twp	88	167
Kate	25	f	w	IREL	San Francisco	8-Wd San Francisco	82	438
Kate	20	f	w	IREL	San Francisco	8-Wd San Francisco	82	469
Kate	11	f	w	NY	Solano	Vallejo	90	199
Kate	10	f	w	NY	Solano	Benicia	90	16
Kerrin	55	m	w	IREL	Yolo	Grafton Twp	93	500
Larrey	29	m	c	IREL	Santa Clara	Fremont Twp	88	65
Margaret	80	f	w	IREL	San Francisco	San Francisco P O	83	89
Martha	5	f	w	CA	San Francisco	11-Wd San Francisc	84	711
Martin	50	m	w	IREL	Contra Costa	Martinez P O	71	413
Martin	47	m	w	IREL	Calaveras	San Andreas P O	70	183
Martin	28	m	w	IREL	San Francisco	11-Wd San Francisc	84	475
Mary	8	f	w	CA	San Francisco	11-Wd San Francisc	84	711
Mary	60	f	w	IREL	San Francisco	1-Wd San Francisco	79	32
Mary	50	f	w	IREL	San Francisco	San Francisco P O	83	66
Mary	40	f	w	IREL	San Francisco	San Francisco P O	80	416
Mary	35	f	w	IREL	San Francisco	San Francisco P O	80	532
Mary	29	f	w	IREL	San Francisco	11-Wd San Francisc	84	660
Mary	28	f	w	MO	Contra Costa	Martinez P O	71	434
Mary	26	f	w	IREL	San Francisco	San Francisco P O	80	534
Mary	26	f	w	IREL	San Francisco	San Francisco P O	80	484
Mary	25	f	w	IREL	San Francisco	8-Wd San Francisco	82	335
Mary Jane	38	f	w	IREL	San Francisco	San Francisco P O	83	184
Mathew	27	m	w	IREL	Sacramento	2-Wd Sacramento	77	226
Matthew	27	m	w	IREL	Santa Clara	2-Wd San Jose	88	293
Michael	68	m	w	IREL	Calaveras	San Andreas P O	70	194
Michael	43	m	w	IREL	San Francisco	11-Wd San Francisc	84	618
Michael	38	m	w	IREL	San Francisco	San Francisco P O	85	810
Michael	30	m	w	IREL	Marin	Sausalito Twp	74	72
Michael	27	m	w	IREL	Santa Clara	Fremont Twp	88	48
Michael	25	m	w	IREL	San Francisco	San Francisco P O	83	360
Michael	24	m	w	IREL	Klamath	Camp Gaston	73	372
Michael	14	m	w	NY	San Francisco	11-Wd San Francisc	84	577
Michell	33	m	w	IREL	Los Angeles	Los Angeles	73	570
Michl	24	m	w	IREL	San Francisco	1-Wd San Francisco	79	136
Mike	30	m	w	IREL	San Joaquin	Elliott Twp	86	71
Miles	36	m	w	IREL	Yuba	Marysville	93	607
Morris	44	m	w	IREL	Santa Barbara	Santa Maria P O	87	511
Morris	42	m	w	IREL	San Francisco	11-Wd San Francisc	84	575
Morris	35	m	w	IREL	El Dorado	Cosumnes Twp	72	19
N	9	f	w	US	Yuba	Marysville	93	609
Nellie	20	f	w	CT	San Joaquin	2-Wd Stockton	86	183
Nelly	21	f	w	IREL	San Francisco	San Francisco P O	85	722
Nora	40	f	w	IREL	San Francisco	8-Wd San Francisco	82	482
P	37	m	w	IREL	San Joaquin	Elkhorn Twp	86	58
P H	34	m	w	IREL	San Joaquin	Liberty Twp	86	92
Pat	50	m	w	IREL	Monterey	San Juan Twp	74	396
Pat	35	m	w	IREL	San Joaquin	Tulare Twp	86	262
Pat	33	m	w	IREL	San Joaquin	Elkhorn Twp	86	69
Pat	30	m	w	IREL	Alameda	Oakland	68	262
Pat	25	m	w	IREL	Placer	Clipper Gap P O	76	393
Patrick	52	m	w	IREL	San Mateo	Half Moon Bay P O	87	404
Patrick	50	m	w	IREL	San Francisco	11-Wd San Francisc	84	428
Patrick	5	m	w	CA	Shasta	Shasta P O	89	453
Patrick	47	m	w	IREL	Nevada	Bridgeport Twp	75	123
Patrick	43	m	w	IREL	San Francisco	San Francisco P O	83	62
Patrick	40	m	w	IREL	San Francisco	2-Wd San Francisco	79	266
Patrick	40	m	w	IREL	Santa Cruz	Pajaro Twp	89	348
Patrick	37	m	w	IREL	San Joaquin	Elkhorn Twp	86	66
Patrick	37	m	w	IREL	Santa Clara	Fremont Twp	88	65
Patrick	35	m	w	IREL	Monterey	San Juan Twp	74	391
Richd L	37	m	w	CANA	San Francisco	1-Wd San Francisco	79	77
Stephen	8	m	w	CA	Marin	San Rafael Twp	74	29
T	39	m	w	IREL	Sierra	Sierra Twp	89	565
T	36	m	w	IREL	Sierra	Alleghany & Forest	89	535
Thomas	39	m	w	IREL	San Francisco	San Francisco P O	80	406
Thomas	36	m	w	IREL	San Francisco	San Francisco P O	83	238
Thomas	35	m	w	IREL	Santa Clara	2-Wd San Jose	88	311
Thomas	35	m	w	IREL	San Francisco	San Francisco P O	80	484
Thomas	23	m	w	MO	Yolo	Grafton Twp	93	501
Thomas	11	m	w	IREL	Yolo	Merritt Twp	93	503
Thomas	11	m	w	CA	Placer	Pino Twp	76	471
Timothy	40	m	w	IREL	San Francisco	San Francisco P O	83	380
Timothy	36	m	w	IREL	San Francisco	11-Wd San Francisc	84	572
Tymothy	35	m	w	IREL	San Francisco	San Francisco P O	85	756
W G	32	m	w	IREL	San Francisco	San Francisco P O	83	291
William	55	m	w	IREL	Santa Clara	Santa Clara Twp	88	176
William	37	m	w	NY	Santa Cruz	Pajaro Twp	89	362
William	28	m	w	IREL	San Mateo	Redwood Twp	87	368
William	19	m	w	NY	Alameda	Oakland	68	202
Wm	40	m	w	IREL	Solano	Vallejo	90	185
Wm	26	m	w	IREL	San Francisco	San Francisco P O	85	766
FLYNNE								
Edward	28	m	w	IREL	San Francisco	San Francisco P O	83	158
Morris	43	m	w	IREL	San Francisco	San Francisco P O	83	164
Patrick	30	m	w	IREL	San Francisco	1-Wd San Francisco	79	82
FLYZERO								
---	23	m	j	JAPA	El Dorado	Coloma Twp	72	4
FO								
Ah	70	m	c	CHIN	Sacramento	Granite Twp	77	152
Ah	48	m	c	CHIN	El Dorado	Mud Springs Twp	72	76
Ah	47	m	c	CHIN	Sacramento	Center Twp	77	87
Ah	45	m	c	CHIN	Sacramento	Center Twp	77	86
Ah	42	m	c	CHIN	Sacramento	Mississippi Twp	77	162
Ah	40	m	c	CHIN	San Francisco	2-Wd San Francisco	79	285
Ah	38	m	c	CHIN	Sacramento	Georgianna Twp	77	132
Ah	36	m	c	CHIN	El Dorado	Diamond Springs Tw	72	32
Ah	36	m	c	CHIN	Sacramento	Center Twp	77	87
Ah	36	m	c	CHIN	San Francisco	San Francisco P O	80	517
Ah	35	m	c	CHIN	Sacramento	Mississippi Twp	77	162
Ah	34	m	c	CHIN	El Dorado	Mud Springs Twp	72	89
Ah	34	m	c	CHIN	Sutter	Butte Twp	92	104
Ah	31	m	c	CHIN	San Joaquin	1-Wd Stockton	86	149
Ah	30	m	c	CHIN	El Dorado	Salmon Falls Twp	72	129
Ah	30	m	c	CHIN	Monterey	San Juan Twp	74	407
Ah	30	m	c	CHIN	Sacramento	Granite Twp	77	152
Ah	30	m	c	CHIN	Sacramento	Granite Twp	77	151
Ah	30	m	c	CHIN	Sacramento	Cosumnes Twp	77	94
Ah	30	m	c	CHIN	Sacramento	Center Twp	77	87
Ah	29	m	c	CHIN	El Dorado	Mud Springs Twp	72	79

© 2001 by Heritage Quest. All rights reserved.

Name	Age	S	R	B-PL	County	Locale	Roll	Pg
						Series M593		
Ah	29	m	c	CHIN	Placer	Roseville P O	76	348
Ah	28	m	c	CHIN	Sacramento	Georgianna Twp	77	129
Ah	28	m	c	CHIN	Sacramento	Granite Twp	77	154
Ah	28	m	c	CHIN	El Dorado	Placerville	72	114
Ah	27	m	c	CHIN	Sacramento	Center Twp	77	87
Ah	26	m	c	CHIN	Sacramento	Georgianna Twp	77	123
Ah	26	m	c	CHIN	Solano	Suisun Twp	90	106
Ah	25	m	c	CHIN	El Dorado	Diamond Springs Tw	72	24
Ah	25	m	c	CHIN	El Dorado	White Oak Twp	72	143
Ah	24	m	c	CHIN	El Dorado	Diamond Springs Tw	72	32
Chow	20	m	c	CHIN	San Francisco	8-Wd San Francisco	82	358
Chum	38	m	c	CHIN	El Dorado	Diamond Springs Tw	72	32
Ee	20	m	c	CHIN	San Francisco	11-Wd San Francisc	84	522
Gee	42	m	c	CHIN	Trinity	Indian Crk	92	199
Ling	37	m	c	CHIN	Calaveras	San Andreas P O	70	201
Lu	18	m	c	CHIN	Yuba	Marysville	93	632
Tap Loon	27	m	c	CHIN	San Francisco	11-Wd San Francisc	84	546
FOA								
Ah	41	m	c	CHIN	Kern	Tehachapi P O	73	356
Julius	45	m	w	FRAN	San Francisco	San Francisco P O	80	462
FOAK								
Ah	33	m	c	CHIN	Merced	Snelling P O	74	278
FOALE								
H J	31	m	w	ENGL	San Francisco	San Francisco P O	85	757
FOARD								
Bridget	25	f	w	IREL	Sacramento	3-Wd Sacramento	77	306
Edmund B	67	m	w	KY	Placer	Roseville P O	76	352
John M	38	m	w	MD	San Francisco	3-Wd San Francisco	79	327
FOBBS								
John Q	30	m	w	OH	El Dorado	Cosumnes Twp	72	18
FOBEAR								
Caroline	36	f	w	FRAN	San Francisco	San Francisco P O	80	475
FOBY								
Jessie	39	m	w	NY	Monterey	San Antonio Twp	74	323
FOC								
Tie	54	m	c	CHIN	Butte	Kimshew Tpw	70	84
FOCH								
John	48	m	w	FRAN	Siskiyou	Callahan P O	89	627
FOCHE								
Christopher	40	m	w	CANA	Yolo	Cache Crk Twp	93	456
FOCHT								
Joseph	42	m	w	PA	Tulare	Visalia Twp	92	280
FOCK								
Ah	45	m	c	CHIN	Placer	Alta P O	76	413
Ah	42	m	c	CHIN	Placer	Dutch Flat P O	76	408
Ah	40	m	c	CHIN	Placer	Dutch Flat P O	76	409
Ah	38	m	c	CHIN	Amador	Volcano P O	69	384
Ah	35	m	c	CHIN	Butte	Concow Twp	70	10
Ah	30	m	c	CHIN	Placer	Dutch Flat P O	76	408
Ah	29	m	c	CHIN	Butte	Hamilton Twp	70	72
Ah	24	m	c	CHIN	San Francisco	San Francisco P O	80	507
Ah	24	m	c	CHIN	Butte	Chico Twp	70	15
Gee	42	m	c	CHIN	Butte	Hamilton Twp	70	71
FODEN								
Charles	36	m	w	ENGL	Contra Costa	Martinez P O	71	383
FODGE								
John	25	m	w	NY	San Francisco	7-Wd San Francisco	81	234
FOE								
Ah	60	m	c	CHIN	Sacramento	Granite Twp	77	137
Ah	50	m	c	CHIN	Sacramento	Granite Twp	77	141
Ah	47	m	c	CHIN	Sacramento	Natomas Twp	77	171
Ah	46	m	c	CHIN	Sacramento	Granite Twp	77	138
Ah	45	m	c	CHIN	Sacramento	Granite Twp	77	138
Ah	42	m	c	CHIN	Sacramento	Granite Twp	77	151
Ah	42	m	c	CHIN	Alameda	Oakland	68	241
Ah	40	m	c	CHIN	Sacramento	Brighton Twp	77	71
Ah	40	m	c	CHIN	Sacramento	Franklin Twp	77	108
Ah	38	m	c	CHIN	Sacramento	San Joaquin Twp	77	399
Ah	33	m	c	CHIN	Sacramento	Granite Twp	77	138
Ah	32	m	c	CHIN	Sacramento	Georgianna Twp	77	128
Ah	32	m	c	CHIN	Sacramento	San Joaquin Twp	77	398
Ah	30	m	c	CHIN	Sacramento	Granite Twp	77	149
Ah	28	m	c	CHIN	Sacramento	Granite Twp	77	139
Ah	27	m	c	CHIN	Sacramento	Granite Twp	77	141
Ah	27	m	c	CHIN	Sacramento	Center Twp	77	86
Ah	27	m	c	CHIN	Shasta	French Gulch P O	89	469
Ah	26	m	c	CHIN	Sacramento	Granite Twp	77	152
Ah	25	f	c	CHIN	Sacramento	Granite Twp	77	151
Ah	22	m	c	CHIN	Sacramento	Granite Twp	77	155
Ah	22	m	c	CHIN	Sacramento	Brighton Twp	77	71
Ah	22	m	c	CHIN	Sacramento	Sutter Twp	77	391
Ah	20	f	c	CHIN	Sacramento	Granite Twp	77	153
Ah	19	m	c	CHIN	Shasta	American Ranch P O	89	497
Ah	18	m	c	CHIN	Sacramento	Granite Twp	77	137
Chay	56	m	c	CHIN	Butte	Chico Twp	70	51
Choy	28	m	c	CHIN	Butte	Chico Twp	70	52
FOEY								
Ah	30	m	c	CHIN	Solano	Suisun Twp	90	106
Wm	28	m	w	ENGL	Yuba	Marysville	93	611
FOG								
Ah	17	m	c	CHIN	Nevada	Rough & Ready Twp	75	331
FOGAL								
Caroline	30	f	w	HANO	San Francisco	7-Wd San Francisco	81	173
FOGAN								
Egmund	22	m	w	POLA	San Francisco	San Francisco P O	83	54
James	27	m	w	IREL	Placer	Summit P O	76	495
Mary	50	f	w	IREL	San Francisco	San Francisco P O	83	414
FOGARTH								
Florence	43	m	w	NORW	San Francisco	7-Wd San Francisco	81	281
FOGARTY								
Bartholemeo	40	m	w	IREL	Nevada	Grass Valley Twp	75	158
David	36	m	w	IREL	San Francisco	San Francisco P O	85	791
Edward	24	m	w	IREL	Santa Clara	Santa Clara Twp	88	156
Henry	38	m	w	NY	San Francisco	11-Wd San Francisc	84	567
James	38	m	w	IREL	San Francisco	San Francisco P O	83	289
James	37	m	w	IREL	Santa Clara	Alviso Twp	88	26
James	35	m	w	IREL	San Francisco	San Francisco P O	85	856
Jenney	42	f	w	MA	San Francisco	5-Wd San Francisco	81	2
Jennie	24	f	w	IREL	San Francisco	7-Wd San Francisco	81	285
John	49	m	w	IREL	San Francisco	San Francisco P O	85	869
John	38	m	w	IREL	Nevada	Bridgeport Twp	75	125
John	28	m	w	IREL	Sutter	Yuba Twp	92	143
Julia	19	f	w	IREL	Santa Clara	Gilroy Twp	88	71
Kate	13	f	w	CA	Sacramento	4-Wd Sacramento	77	331
Lizzie	25	f	w	IREL	San Francisco	1-Wd San Francisco	79	44
Lizzie	21	f	w	IREL	San Francisco	San Francisco P O	85	792
Maggie	25	f	w	IREL	San Francisco	San Francisco P O	83	113
Margret	28	f	w	IREL	San Francisco	1-Wd San Francisco	79	44
Martin	35	m	w	IREL	San Francisco	1-Wd San Francisco	79	43
Mary	45	f	w	IREL	San Francisco	8-Wd San Francisco	82	479
Michael	23	m	w	IREL	Nevada	Bridgeport Twp	75	125
P C	34	m	w	IREL	San Francisco	San Francisco P O	85	858
Patrick	45	m	w	IREL	Nevada	Eureka Twp	75	129
Thos	33	m	w	IREL	San Francisco	11-Wd San Francisc	84	583
William	29	m	w	IREL	Marin	San Rafael Twp	74	25
Wm	47	m	w	IREL	San Joaquin	1-Wd Stockton	86	120
Wm	40	m	w	IREL	Solano	Benicia	90	19
Wm	28	m	w	IREL	San Francisco	1-Wd San Francisco	79	63
FOGATA								
Peter	19	m	w	SWIT	Santa Clara	2-Wd San Jose	88	281
FOGE								
John	36	m	w	PRUS	San Francisco	San Francisco P O	83	290
William	26	m	w	PRUS	San Francisco	San Francisco P O	83	151
FOGEL								
George	28	m	w	POLA	San Francisco	3-Wd San Francisco	79	288
Jacob	32	m	w	AUST	San Francisco	San Francisco P O	83	219
John	35	m	w	FRAN	San Francisco	3-Wd San Francisco	79	300
FOGELI								
Casper	40	m	w	SWIT	Nevada	Nevada Twp	75	287
FOGERBY								
John	36	m	w	IREL	Solano	Maine Prairie Twp	90	50
FOGERTY								
Anne	70	f	w	IREL	San Francisco	San Francisco P O	83	325
C	28	f	w	IREL	San Francisco	San Francisco P O	83	132
John	39	m	w	IREL	Placer	Auburn P O	76	374
John	39	m	w	NJ	Plumas	Goodwin Twp	77	6
John	35	m	w	IREL	Alameda	Oakland	68	135
John	23	m	w	WALE	San Francisco	2-Wd San Francisco	79	261
Julius	36	m	w	ENGL	San Francisco	2-Wd San Francisco	79	283
Maggie	26	f	w	IREL	San Francisco	11-Wd San Francisc	84	443
Martin	46	m	w	IREL	Amador	Sutter Crk P O	69	404
Michael	40	m	w	IREL	San Francisco	11-Wd San Francisc	84	538
Michael	40	m	w	IREL	Yuba	Long Bar Twp	93	561
Mike	38	m	w	IREL	Sonoma	Healdsburg	91	274
Mitchell	28	m	w	OH	Solano	Green Valley Twp	90	39
Patrick	37	m	w	IREL	Napa	Napa Twp	75	33
Thomas	60	m	w	IREL	Solano	Vacaville Twp	90	133
Wm	60	m	w	IREL	San Francisco	8-Wd San Francisco	82	307
Wm	38	m	w	IREL	Sacramento	Center Twp	77	85
FOGESTEIN								
Joseph	32	m	w	BAVA	San Francisco	San Francisco P O	83	260
FOGETTA								
Antonia	20	f	w	ITAL	San Francisco	2-Wd San Francisco	79	182
FOGG								
Augusta	55	f	w	MA	San Francisco	San Francisco P O	85	816
Calvin	40	m	w	ME	San Diego	San Diego	78	487
David	36	m	w	PA	Solano	Vallejo	90	202
David	28	m	w	ENGL	Solano	Vallejo	90	198
Edmund W	20	m	w	ME	Butte	Ophir Twp	70	95
Ethan S	32	m	w	ME	Placer	Colfax P O	76	387
Geo W	40	m	w	NH	San Francisco	7-Wd San Francisco	81	228
George H	47	m	w	MA	Alameda	Oakland	68	163
J S	29	m	w	NH	Alameda	Oakland	68	207
John	40	m	w	IREL	San Joaquin	1-Wd Stockton	86	153
Nathaniel	64	m	w	MA	Sonoma	Santa Rosa	91	405
Putnam	25	m	w	MA	Marin	Bolinas Twp	74	1
Reuben T	42	m	w	NH	San Mateo	Redwood Twp	87	366
Royal W	24	m	w	ME	Santa Cruz	Santa Cruz Twp	89	400
Timothy	62	m	w	ME	Butte	Ophir Twp	70	95
William	21	m	w	IREL	Solano	Silveyville Twp	90	78
William A	25	m	w	MO	Santa Clara	2-Wd San Jose	88	330
William S	57	m	w	ME	Placer	Alta P O	76	413
FOGGERTY								
Cath	30	f	w	IREL	San Francisco	San Francisco P O	83	102
FOGGO								
Agnes	20	f	w	NY	San Francisco	8-Wd San Francisco	82	410
FOGLE								
Andrew	39	m	w	FRAN	Los Angeles	Los Angeles Twp	73	469
Anna Maria	10	f	w	AUST	Los Angeles	Los Angeles Twp	73	469
Henry	28	m	w	IL	Los Angeles	El Monte Twp	73	454
Joe	35	m	w	ENGL	San Joaquin	2-Wd Stockton	86	164
Lawrence	32	m	w	MA	Los Angeles	Los Angeles Twp	73	469
FOGLEBAUM								
H	40	m	w	GERM	Yuba	Rose Bar Twp	93	663

© 2001 by Heritage Quest. All rights reserved.

Name	Age	S	R	B-PL	County	Locale	Roll	Pg
FOGLER								
Benedict	59	m	w	BADE	Amador	Volcano P O	69	385
Joseph	39	m	w	FRAN	San Francisco	11-Wd San Francisc	84	490
Philip	66	m	w	HDAR	San Francisco	1-Wd San Francisco	79	101
FOGLESANG								
T	39	m	w	PA	Yuba	Marysville	93	613
FOGO								
Louis	50	m	w	FRAN	San Francisco	6-Wd San Francisco	81	100
FOGOS								
John	40	m	w	CA	San Joaquin	Oneal Twp	86	99
FOGOSSE								
Antoine	24	m	w	ITAL	San Francisco	San Francisco P O	85	860
FOGUL								
Elijah	36	m	w	MO	Nevada	Eureka Twp	75	137
FOH								
Ah	41	m	c	CHIN	San Francisco	San Francisco P O	80	505
Ah	40	m	c	CHIN	Solano	Vallejo	90	173
Ah	36	m	c	CHIN	San Francisco	San Francisco P O	80	496
Ah	28	m	c	CHIN	Santa Barbara	Santa Maria P O	87	514
Concepcion	8	f	i	CA	Santa Barbara	Santa Maria P O	87	514
Ka	25	f	c	CHIN	Napa	Napa Twp	75	58
Leroy	23	m	w	KY	Solano	Vallejo	90	200
FOHER								
John	35	m	w	FRAN	San Francisco	6-Wd San Francisco	81	73
FOHEY								
Catherine	75	f	w	IREL	Napa	Napa	75	5
FOHR								
Albert	33	m	w	SHOL	San Francisco	1-Wd San Francisco	79	116
FOI								
Ah	46	m	c	CHIN	San Francisco	San Francisco P O	80	529
Ah	41	m	c	CHIN	San Francisco	San Francisco P O	80	499
Ah	40	m	c	CHIN	San Francisco	San Francisco P O	80	496
Ah	40	m	c	CHIN	Santa Cruz	Watsonville	89	377
Ah	39	m	c	CHIN	San Francisco	San Francisco P O	80	519
Ah	38	m	c	CHIN	San Francisco	San Francisco P O	80	439
Ah	37	m	c	CHIN	San Francisco	San Francisco P O	80	493
Ah	36	m	c	CHIN	San Francisco	San Francisco P O	80	453
Ah	34	m	c	CHIN	San Francisco	San Francisco P O	80	530
Ah	33	m	c	CHIN	San Francisco	San Francisco P O	80	436
Ah	33	m	c	CHIN	San Francisco	San Francisco P O	80	515
Ah	31	m	c	CHIN	San Francisco	San Francisco P O	80	493
Ah	30	f	c	CHIN	San Francisco	San Francisco P O	80	494
Ah	30	m	c	CHIN	San Francisco	San Francisco P O	80	498
Ah	30	f	c	CHIN	San Francisco	San Francisco P O	80	508
Ah	30	m	c	CHIN	Butte	Ophir Twp	70	106
Ah	29	m	c	CHIN	San Francisco	San Francisco P O	80	515
Ah	25	f	c	CHIN	San Francisco	San Francisco P O	80	433
Ah	25	m	c	CHIN	San Francisco	San Francisco P O	80	494
Ah	21	f	c	CHIN	San Francisco	San Francisco P O	80	433
Ah	21	f	c	CHIN	San Francisco	San Francisco P O	80	500
Ah	20	f	c	CHIN	San Francisco	San Francisco P O	80	438
Ah	20	m	c	CHIN	San Francisco	San Francisco P O	80	525
Ah	18	m	c	CHIN	San Francisco	6-Wd San Francisco	81	59
Ah	18	f	c	CHIN	San Francisco	San Francisco P O	80	507
Ah	17	f	c	CHIN	San Francisco	San Francisco P O	80	437
Ah	11	f	c	CHIN	San Francisco	San Francisco P O	80	441
Choi	19	m	c	CHIN	Yuba	Marysville	93	630
Ti	30	m	c	CHIN	Yuba	Marysville	93	630
FOIBLE								
Henry	40	m	w	HDAR	Trinity	North Fork Twp	92	221
FOIE								
Ah	50	m	c	CHIN	Nevada	Nevada Twp	75	289
FOIERZONS								
Frank	28	m	w	FRAN	Yolo	Cache Crk Twp	93	422
FOIL								
Ah	41	m	c	CHIN	San Francisco	San Francisco P O	80	491
Edward	13	m	w	CANA	Napa	Napa	75	14
FOILEY								
Francis	32	m	w	IREL	San Francisco	San Francisco P O	83	346
FOIN								
Ah	30	m	c	CHIN	Nevada	Nevada Twp	75	298
FOIRY								
Thos	30	m	w	PA	San Diego	San Diego	78	507
FOISEY								
A M	60	m	w	CANA	Los Angeles	Los Angeles	73	543
FOISSIN								
August	29	m	w	ITAL	Calaveras	San Andreas P O	70	176
FOISSY								
Richd	40	m	w	ENGL	San Francisco	1-Wd San Francisco	79	18
FOIST								
Eliza	25	f	w	SHOL	San Francisco	San Francisco P O	83	63
FOIZELL								
Henry	26	m	w	MO	Sutter	Butte Twp	92	92
FOIZEY								
Olive	9	f	w	CA	Mariposa	Mariposa P O	74	110
Thomas E	14	m	w	CA	Mariposa	Mariposa P O	74	109
FOK								
---	30	m	c	CHIN	San Francisco	11-Wd San Francisc	84	503
---	18	m	c	CHIN	Sonoma	Bodega Twp	91	262
---	17	m	c	CHIN	San Francisco	6-Wd San Francisco	81	64
Ah	58	m	c	CHIN	San Francisco	6-Wd San Francisco	81	84
Ah	54	m	c	CHIN	Shasta	Shasta P O	89	456
Ah	48	m	c	CHIN	San Francisco	San Francisco P O	80	508
Ah	47	m	c	CHIN	San Francisco	6-Wd San Francisco	81	77
Ah	45	m	c	CHIN	San Francisco	6-Wd San Francisco	81	64
Ah	42	m	c	CHIN	San Francisco	6-Wd San Francisco	81	43
Ah	41	m	c	CHIN	San Francisco	San Francisco P O	80	528
Ah	41	m	c	CHIN	San Francisco	San Francisco P O	80	510
Ah	41	m	c	CHIN	San Francisco	6-Wd San Francisco	81	58
Ah	40	m	c	CHIN	San Francisco	11-Wd San Francisc	84	661
Ah	40	m	c	CHIN	San Francisco	San Francisco P O	80	524
Ah	39	m	c	CHIN	San Francisco	San Francisco P O	80	499
Ah	38	m	c	CHIN	San Francisco	San Francisco P O	80	520
Ah	38	m	c	CHIN	San Francisco	San Francisco P O	80	519
Ah	37	m	c	CHIN	San Francisco	San Francisco P O	80	519
Ah	37	m	c	CHIN	San Francisco	San Francisco P O	80	515
Ah	37	m	c	CHIN	San Francisco	San Francisco P O	80	515
Ah	37	m	c	CHIN	San Francisco	San Francisco P O	80	495
Ah	36	m	c	CHIN	San Francisco	San Francisco P O	80	518
Ah	35	m	c	CHIN	San Francisco	San Francisco P O	80	510
Ah	34	m	c	CHIN	San Francisco	San Francisco P O	80	496
Ah	34	m	c	CHIN	San Francisco	San Francisco P O	80	503
Ah	34	m	c	CHIN	Fresno	Millerton P O	72	199
Ah	32	m	c	CHIN	San Francisco	6-Wd San Francisco	81	47
Ah	31	m	c	CHIN	San Francisco	San Francisco P O	80	509
Ah	30	m	c	CHIN	San Francisco	6-Wd San Francisco	81	68
Ah	30	m	c	CHIN	San Francisco	6-Wd San Francisco	81	69
Ah	30	f	c	CHIN	San Francisco	6-Wd San Francisco	81	55
Ah	30	m	c	CHIN	El Dorado	White Oak Twp	72	136
Ah	30	f	c	CHIN	San Francisco	San Francisco P O	80	446
Ah	29	m	c	CHIN	San Francisco	San Francisco P O	80	522
Ah	29	f	c	CHIN	San Francisco	San Francisco P O	80	494
Ah	29	m	c	CHIN	San Francisco	San Francisco P O	80	435
Ah	28	m	c	CHIN	San Francisco	San Francisco P O	80	522
Ah	28	m	c	CHIN	San Francisco	6-Wd San Francisco	81	64
Ah	27	m	c	CHIN	San Francisco	6-Wd San Francisco	81	61
Ah	26	m	c	CHIN	San Francisco	San Francisco P O	80	509
Ah	26	m	c	CHIN	San Francisco	6-Wd San Francisco	81	59
Ah	25	m	c	CHIN	El Dorado	Mud Springs Twp	72	79
Ah	25	f	c	CHIN	San Francisco	San Francisco P O	80	447
Ah	24	f	c	CHIN	San Francisco	6-Wd San Francisco	81	76
Ah	24	m	c	CHIN	San Francisco	San Francisco P O	80	493
Ah	24	m	c	CHIN	San Francisco	6-Wd San Francisco	81	42
Ah	23	m	c	CHIN	San Francisco	6-Wd San Francisco	81	40
Ah	23	f	c	CHIN	San Francisco	San Francisco P O	80	453
Ah	22	m	c	CHIN	San Francisco	6-Wd San Francisco	81	67
Ah	22	f	c	CHIN	San Francisco	San Francisco P O	80	437
Ah	21	f	c	CHIN	San Francisco	San Francisco P O	80	506
Ah	21	f	c	CHIN	San Francisco	6-Wd San Francisco	81	77
Ah	21	f	c	CHIN	San Francisco	San Francisco P O	80	453
Ah	21	f	c	CHIN	San Francisco	San Francisco P O	80	444
Ah	21	f	c	CHIN	San Francisco	San Francisco P O	80	442
Ah	20	m	c	CHIN	San Francisco	San Francisco P O	80	511
Ah	20	m	c	CHIN	San Francisco	6-Wd San Francisco	81	66
Ah	20	m	c	CHIN	San Francisco	6-Wd San Francisco	81	85
Ah	20	m	c	CHIN	San Francisco	San Francisco P O	80	498
Ah	20	f	c	CHIN	San Francisco	San Francisco P O	80	501
Ah	20	m	c	CHIN	San Francisco	6-Wd San Francisco	81	46
Ah	20	f	c	CHIN	San Francisco	San Francisco P O	80	442
Ah	19	m	c	CHIN	San Francisco	San Francisco P O	80	516
Ah	19	f	c	CHIN	San Francisco	San Francisco P O	80	526
Ah	19	f	c	CHIN	San Francisco	San Francisco P O	80	508
Ah	19	m	c	CHIN	San Francisco	6-Wd San Francisco	81	69
Ah	19	m	c	CHIN	San Francisco	6-Wd San Francisco	81	63
Ah	19	f	c	CHIN	San Francisco	San Francisco P O	80	448
Ah	19	f	c	CHIN	San Francisco	San Francisco P O	80	445
Ah	18	m	c	CHIN	San Francisco	6-Wd San Francisco	81	68
Ah	18	f	c	CHIN	San Francisco	San Francisco P O	80	454
Ah	18	m	c	CHIN	San Francisco	3-Wd San Francisco	79	329
Ah	17	f	c	CHIN	San Francisco	6-Wd San Francisco	81	74
Ah	17	m	c	CHIN	San Francisco	6-Wd San Francisco	81	60
Ah	16	f	c	CHIN	San Francisco	San Francisco P O	80	492
Ah	16	m	c	CHIN	Nevada	Little York Twp	75	234
Ah	16	m	c	CHIN	San Francisco	6-Wd San Francisco	81	45
Ah	13	m	c	CHIN	San Francisco	6-Wd San Francisco	81	44
Ah	13	f	c	CHIN	San Francisco	San Francisco P O	80	436
Ah	1	m	c	CHIN	El Dorado	Placerville	72	114
Choy	40	f	c	CHIN	San Francisco	6-Wd San Francisco	81	73
La	16	m	c	CHIN	San Francisco	6-Wd San Francisco	81	66
Lee	20	m	c	CHIN	San Francisco	6-Wd San Francisco	81	65
Lee	17	m	c	CHIN	San Francisco	6-Wd San Francisco	81	69
Lee	16	m	c	CHIN	San Francisco	6-Wd San Francisco	81	51
Lee Ah	24	m	c	CHIN	San Francisco	6-Wd San Francisco	81	67
Leung	28	m	c	CHIN	Shasta	French Gulch P O	89	469
Linn	29	m	c	CHIN	San Francisco	6-Wd San Francisco	81	62
Loo	31	m	c	CHIN	San Francisco	6-Wd San Francisco	81	39
Sam	40	m	c	CHIN	San Francisco	6-Wd San Francisco	81	40
Soon	32	m	c	CHIN	San Francisco	3-Wd San Francisco	79	301
Wah	28	m	c	CHIN	Shasta	French Gulch P O	89	470
War	29	m	c	CHIN	San Francisco	6-Wd San Francisco	81	61
Wm	36	m	w	IREL	San Francisco	11-Wd San Francisc	84	617
FOKE								
Ah	48	m	c	CHIN	Trinity	Lewiston Pct	92	215
Ah	38	m	c	CHIN	Sierra	Downieville Twp	89	521
Ah	37	m	c	CHIN	Amador	Volcano P O	69	387
Ah	35	m	c	CHIN	Amador	Drytown P O	69	425
Ah	23	f	c	CHIN	Trinity	Weaverville Pct	92	229
Ah	15	m	c	CHIN	Solano	Vallejo	90	140
FOKEY								
Patrick	47	m	w	IREL	San Francisco	2-Wd San Francisco	79	143
FOKI								
Ah	27	m	c	CHIN	Sierra	Forest Twp	89	528
FOL								
Ah	32	m	c	CHIN	Sacramento	San Joaquin Twp	77	405

© 2001 by Heritage Quest. All rights reserved.

Name	Age	S	R	B-PL	County	Locale	Series M593 Roll	Pg
FOLAMAN								
Victoria	4	f	w	CA	Sacramento	4-Wd Sacramento	77	319
FOLAN								
Bridget	60	f	w	IREL	Sacramento	4-Wd Sacramento	77	333
FOLAND								
Jas	35	m	w	IREL	Solano	Vallejo	90	158
FOLANSBEE								
J	37	m	w	CT	Sacramento	4-Wd Sacramento	77	372
FOLAS								
Alviso	25	m	i	MEXI	Inyo	Cerro Gordo Twp	73	323
FOLCO								
Geo Batta	56	m	w	ITAL	Amador	Sutter Crk P O	69	404
FOLENS								
David	27	m	w	OH	Butte	Chico Twp	70	26
FOLES								
Becente	36	m	w	CA	Monterey	San Antonio Twp	74	322
FOLETTA								
Giuseppi	21	m	w	SWIT	Marin	Tomales Twp	74	76
FOLEY								
Andrew	31	m	w	MO	Solano	Silveyville Twp	90	74
Ann	30	f	w	IREL	San Francisco	8-Wd San Francisco	82	463
Ann M	35	f	w	IREL	Marin	Sausalito Twp	74	66
Bridget	37	f	w	IREL	San Francisco	San Francisco P O	80	359
Bridget	28	f	w	IREL	San Francisco	8-Wd San Francisco	82	472
Brina	40	m	w	IREL	Placer	Newcastle Twp	76	476
Catharine	76	f	w	IREL	El Dorado	Placerville	72	125
Charles	40	m	w	VA	Solano	Tremont Twp	90	35
Chrisn C	41	m	w	KY	San Francisco	1-Wd San Francisco	79	24
Cornelius	50	m	w	IREL	San Francisco	2-Wd San Francisco	79	277
Daniel	42	m	w	IREL	Trinity	Indian Crk	92	200
Daniel B	40	m	w	IREL	San Francisco	8-Wd San Francisco	82	391
Danl	36	m	w	IREL	San Francisco	11-Wd San Francisc	84	614
Danl	25	m	w	IREL	Solano	Benicia	90	18
Danl H	34	m	w	PRUS	Shasta	Shasta P O	89	452
Delia	22	f	w	IREL	San Francisco	2-Wd San Francisco	79	252
Dennis	35	m	w	IREL	Solano	Benicia	90	9
Dennis	35	m	w	IREL	San Francisco	11-Wd San Francisc	84	599
Dennis	34	m	w	IREL	Solano	Benicia	90	20
Dennis	25	m	w	IREL	Humboldt	Eureka Twp	72	276
Edmund	40	m	w	IREL	San Francisco	1-Wd San Francisco	79	10
Edward	76	m	w	IREL	San Francisco	8-Wd San Francisco	82	396
Edward	40	m	w	IREL	San Francisco	11-Wd San Francisc	84	531
Edward	30	m	w	IREL	Santa Clara	Alviso Twp	88	24
Edward	11	m	w	CA	Alameda	Alvarado	68	302
Edwd	36	m	w	IREL	San Francisco	1-Wd San Francisco	79	112
Ellen	32	f	w	IREL	San Francisco	San Francisco P O	83	347
Ellen	23	f	w	IREL	San Francisco	8-Wd San Francisco	82	485
Ellen	22	f	w	IREL	San Francisco	San Francisco P O	83	293
Francis	40	m	w	IREL	San Francisco	11-Wd San Francisc	84	425
Franklin	30	m	w	MO	Kern	Tehachapi P O	73	354
Garrett J	36	m	w	NY	Solano	Vallejo	90	156
George	25	m	w	IREL	San Francisco	San Francisco P O	80	335
Hannah	25	f	w	IREL	San Mateo	San Mateo P O	87	351
Hannah	17	f	w	IREL	San Francisco	11-Wd San Francisc	84	502
Helen E	11	f	w	CA	Nevada	Grass Valley Twp	75	164
Henrietta	19	f	w	CANA	San Francisco	San Francisco P O	83	115
Henry	66	m	w	IREL	San Mateo	Belmont P O	87	372
Henry	31	m	w	MO	Solano	Silveyville Twp	90	75
Henry	21	m	w	NH	Solano	Vacaville Twp	90	126
J J	59	m	w	VA	Alameda	Oakland	68	222
James	56	m	w	IREL	Siskiyou	Scott Rvr Twp	89	604
James	31	m	w	IREL	San Francisco	11-Wd San Francisc	84	572
James	27	m	w	IREL	San Francisco	1-Wd San Francisco	79	68
James	24	m	w	IREL	Marin	San Rafael	74	53
James M	36	m	w	KY	Amador	Volcano P O	69	385
Jeremiah M	34	m	w	IREL	Nevada	Grass Valley Twp	75	196
Jno	31	m	w	NY	Sacramento	1-Wd Sacramento	77	185
Jno	30	m	w	IREL	Sacramento	3-Wd Sacramento	77	272
John	55	m	w	IREL	Amador	Sutter Crk P O	69	400
John	55	m	w	IREL	San Francisco	7-Wd San Francisco	81	165
John	53	m	w	IREL	San Francisco	7-Wd San Francisco	81	252
John	50	m	w	IREL	San Francisco	San Francisco P O	83	381
John	48	m	w	IREL	Marin	Sausalito Twp	74	66
John	45	m	w	IREL	Nevada	Little York Twp	75	238
John	40	m	w	ENGL	Siskiyou	Yreka Twp	89	666
John	35	m	w	IREL	Sacramento	4-Wd Sacramento	77	320
John	35	m	w	IREL	San Francisco	8-Wd San Francisco	82	405
John	35	m	w	IREL	Santa Clara	1-Wd San Jose	88	251
John	34	m	w	NY	San Francisco	3-Wd San Francisco	79	315
John	33	m	w	IREL	San Francisco	11-Wd San Francisc	84	476
John	33	m	w	IREL	San Francisco	6-Wd San Francisco	81	114
John	30	m	w	IREL	San Francisco	1-Wd San Francisco	79	96
John	30	m	w	IREL	San Mateo	Schoolhouse Statio	87	331
John	28	m	w	CANA	Santa Cruz	Santa Cruz Twp	89	394
John	22	m	w	FRAN	San Francisco	San Francisco P O	85	852
John	21	m	w	IREL	Solano	Vallejo	90	214
John A	16	m	w	IREL	Santa Barbara	Santa Barbara P O	87	492
John G	35	m	w	IREL	San Francisco	8-Wd San Francisco	82	447
Julia	35	f	w	IREL	San Francisco	San Francisco P O	83	79
Julia	33	f	w	IREL	Sacramento	4-Wd Sacramento	77	351
Kate	24	f	w	VT	Santa Clara	Gilroy Twp	88	96
Kate	20	f	w	IREL	Santa Clara	2-Wd San Jose	88	297
Katie	19	f	w	IREL	Alameda	Washington Twp	68	278
Lizzie	30	f	w	IREL	San Francisco	7-Wd San Francisco	81	232
Louisa	23	f	w	NY	San Francisco	San Francisco P O	83	31
M	33	f	w	IREL	Alameda	Alameda	68	11
Margaret	40	f	w	IREL	San Francisco	8-Wd San Francisco	82	440
Margaret	26	f	w	IREL	San Francisco	6-Wd San Francisco	81	115
Margaret	21	f	w	NY	San Francisco	8-Wd San Francisco	82	481
Margaret	17	f	w	CA	Marin	Sausalito Twp	74	70
Martin	28	m	w	IREL	San Francisco	San Francisco P O	85	852
Mary	72	f	w	IREL	San Francisco	8-Wd San Francisco	82	396
Mary	62	f	w	IREL	San Francisco	11-Wd San Francisc	84	442
Mary	40	f	w	IREL	San Francisco	8-Wd San Francisco	82	483
Mary	35	f	w	IREL	Solano	Vallejo	90	150
Mary	30	f	w	IREL	San Francisco	San Francisco P O	80	405
Mary	25	f	w	IREL	Solano	Vallejo	90	200
Mary	21	f	w	IREL	San Joaquin	Dent Twp	86	28
Mary	14	f	w	NY	San Francisco	1-Wd San Francisco	79	118
Mary	14	f	w	CA	Nevada	Grass Valley Twp	75	149
Mary C	35	f	w	MO	Napa	Yountville Twp	75	79
Michael	45	m	w	IREL	Sacramento	American Twp	77	64
Michael	40	m	w	IREL	Sacramento	2-Wd Sacramento	77	240
Michael	36	m	w	IREL	Shasta	French Gulch P O	89	468
Michael	29	m	w	IREL	San Francisco	San Francisco P O	83	30
Michael	28	m	w	IREL	San Francisco	San Francisco P O	83	183
Michael C	47	m	w	NY	San Francisco	San Francisco P O	83	43
Micheal	38	m	w	IREL	San Francisco	11-Wd San Francisc	84	450
Michl	33	m	w	IREL	San Francisco	1-Wd San Francisco	79	112
Michl	21	m	w	CANA	San Francisco	1-Wd San Francisco	79	65
Mike	38	m	w	IREL	Solano	Benicia	90	19
Pat	23	m	w	IREL	San Francisco	5-Wd San Francisco	81	27
Patk	40	m	w	ENGL	Solano	Vallejo	90	196
Patk	19	m	w	NY	Solano	Vallejo	90	154
Patrick	58	m	w	IREL	Santa Cruz	Santa Cruz	89	417
Patrick	41	m	w	IREL	Calaveras	San Andreas P O	70	215
Patrick	40	m	w	IREL	San Francisco	11-Wd San Francisc	84	451
Patrick	38	m	w	IREL	San Francisco	7-Wd San Francisco	81	196
Patrick	35	m	w	IREL	San Francisco	San Francisco P O	85	825
Patrick	35	m	w	IREL	Nevada	Meadow Lake Twp	75	258
Patrick	31	m	w	IREL	Santa Cruz	Watsonville	89	369
Patrick	30	m	w	IREL	Napa	Napa	75	37
Patrick	27	m	w	IREL	Santa Clara	Santa Clara Twp	88	155
Patrick	26	m	w	VT	Sonoma	Salt Point	91	387
Patrick	24	m	w	IREL	Placer	Rocklin Twp	76	465
Peter	40	m	w	IREL	San Francisco	San Francisco P O	80	371
R J	40	m	w	IA	Del Norte	Happy Camp Twp	71	471
Richard	55	m	w	IREL	Sacramento	Granite Twp	77	147
Richard	33	m	w	IREL	Sacramento	Granite Twp	77	143
Richard	23	m	w	NY	San Francisco	San Francisco P O	80	368
Robt	40	m	w	IREL	San Francisco	San Francisco P O	83	311
Sarah F	9	f	w	CA	Sacramento	2-Wd Sacramento	77	211
Thomas	70	m	w	IREL	El Dorado	Placerville	72	125
Thomas	33	m	w	IREL	San Mateo	San Mateo P O	87	350
Thomas	33	m	w	IREL	Humboldt	Bald Hills	72	239
Thomas	29	m	w	IREL	San Francisco	San Francisco P O	83	159
Thomas	28	m	w	IREL	San Francisco	San Francisco P O	83	162
Thomas	28	m	w	MO	Solano	Silveyville Twp	90	80
Thomas	24	m	w	IREL	Solano	Vacaville Twp	90	127
Thomas	23	m	w	IREL	Solano	Silveyville Twp	90	89
Thomas	11	m	w	CA	San Francisco	San Francisco P O	85	738
Thomas J	37	m	w	IREL	Santa Cruz	Watsonville	89	376
Thos	51	m	w	IREL	San Francisco	1-Wd San Francisco	79	96
Thos	43	m	w	IREL	San Francisco	San Francisco P O	83	277
Thos	40	m	w	IREL	Santa Clara	Burnett Twp	88	31
Tim	45	m	w	IREL	Sacramento	4-Wd Sacramento	77	363
Timothy	65	m	w	IREL	San Francisco	11-Wd San Francisc	84	558
Timothy	53	m	w	IREL	Yolo	Cache Crk Twp	93	425
Timothy	36	m	w	IREL	San Francisco	11-Wd San Francisc	84	433
Timothy	36	m	w	IREL	Santa Barbara	Santa Barbara P O	87	484
Timothy	30	m	w	IREL	San Francisco	San Francisco P O	83	193
Timothy	28	m	w	IREL	Solano	Vacaville Twp	90	125
Timothy	25	m	w	IREL	Sacramento	Granite Twp	77	149
Timothy	19	m	w	NY	San Francisco	San Francisco P O	83	167
Walter	15	m	w	CANA	San Francisco	7-Wd San Francisco	81	282
William	29	m	w	IREL	Marin	Sausalito Twp	74	73
William	28	m	w	IREL	Humboldt	Eureka Twp	72	263
William	23	m	w	IREL	Solano	Silveyville Twp	90	75
Wm	32	m	w	IREL	San Francisco	1-Wd San Francisco	79	69
Wm Allison	45	m	w	KY	Plumas	Quartz Twp	77	36
Wm E	56	m	w	MD	Mariposa	Mariposa P O	74	128
Wm J	14	m	w	IREL	Santa Barbara	Santa Barbara P O	87	492
FOLGER								
A G	16	m	w	CA	Sutter	Vernon Twp	92	132
Alexander C	38	m	w	NY	Alpine	Silver Mtn P O	69	307
B F	20	m	w	MA	Monterey	San Juan Twp	74	415
Chas	50	m	w	NY	Sacramento	4-Wd Sacramento	77	362
Clarissa	40	f	w	NY	Sacramento	2-Wd Sacramento	77	252
D W	37	m	w	MA	San Francisco	San Francisco P O	85	791
Frank R	43	m	w	NY	Sacramento	2-Wd Sacramento	77	253
Fred	28	m	w	MA	San Francisco	11-Wd San Francisc	84	610
George	27	m	w	MA	Amador	Sutter Crk P O	69	412
Harvey	32	m	w	MA	Tehama	Tehama Twp	92	195
J P	39	m	w	MO	San Joaquin	Elkhorn Twp	86	64
James	33	m	w	NY	Alameda	Oakland	68	218
John M	53	m	w	MA	San Francisco	8-Wd San Francisco	82	471
Laura	27	f	w	NY	San Francisco	8-Wd San Francisco	82	371
Peter	46	m	w	MA	Santa Cruz	Watsonville	89	376
Robert M	49	m	w	NY	Alpine	Silver Mtn P O	69	307
S G	50	m	w	MA	Amador	Jackson P O	69	326
Sarah E	35	f	w	MA	San Francisco	San Francisco P O	85	780
Susan	58	f	w	MA	San Francisco	San Francisco P O	83	23
Timothy	39	m	w	MA	Contra Costa	Martinez Twp	71	348

© 2001 by Heritage Quest. All rights reserved.

California 1870 Census

Name	Age	S	R	B-PL	County	Locale	Series M593 Roll	Pg
FOLGERS								
James	27	m	w	SWIT	San Diego	San Diego	78	500
John	30	m	w	HOLL	San Francisco	1-Wd San Francisco	79	115
FOLIE								
David	36	m	w	IREL	Trinity	Weaverville Pct	92	229
James	29	m	w	NY	San Francisco	8-Wd San Francisco	82	372
Thomas	48	m	w	IREL	Trinity	Weaverville Pct	92	231
FOLINSBEE								
F A	48	m	w	ME	Klamath	Trinidad Twp	73	392
FOLK								
Abe	40	m	w	IL	Butte	Concow Twp	70	8
Adam	40	m	w	PRUS	San Francisco	San Francisco P O	83	328
Ah	18	m	c	CHIN	Sonoma	Salt Point	91	387
Charles	37	m	w	ENGL	Amador	Fiddletown P O	69	441
Solomon	45	m	w	POLA	San Francisco	San Francisco P O	83	25
Yee	25	m	c	CHIN	Klamath	Liberty Twp	73	375
FOLKELMYER								
Harmon	50	m	w	PRUS	El Dorado	Mud Springs Twp	72	74
FOLKENHEIMER								
B	27	m	w	NY	Butte	Hamilton Twp	70	71
FOLKERBERG								
Henry	29	m	w	PA	Monterey	San Juan Twp	74	399
FOLKES								
William	40	m	w	IREL	Sacramento	2-Wd Sacramento	77	224
FOLKINS								
Thomas	38	m	w	MA	San Francisco	1-Wd San Francisco	79	117
FOLKS								
I V	20	m	w	OH	Sutter	Yuba Twp	92	147
Jessie	63	m	w	MD	San Bernardino	San Bernardino Twp	78	426
John	34	m	w	OH	Sonoma	Bodega Twp	91	248
Samuel	32	m	w	AUST	San Francisco	San Francisco P O	83	363
FOLLAN								
Mike	33	m	w	IREL	Solano	Vallejo	90	179
Thomas	40	m	w	IREL	Sacramento	2-Wd Sacramento	77	228
FOLLAND								
Jeremiah	30	m	w	IREL	San Francisco	11-Wd San Francisc	84	491
FOLLANSBEE								
John S	47	m	w	MA	Shasta	Shasta P O	89	457
FOLLE								
John A	40	m	w	ME	Sutter	Butte Twp	92	96
FOLLEAU								
Peter	29	m	w	FRAN	San Francisco	San Francisco P O	80	470
FOLLET								
Abel D	64	m	w	VT	Santa Barbara	San Buenaventura P	87	444
FOLLETRO								
Peter	42	m	w	SWIT	Amador	Jackson P O	69	323
FOLLETT								
Ella	27	f	w	OH	Sacramento	3-Wd Sacramento	77	317
FOLLETTI								
A	30	m	w	SWIT	Amador	Jackson P O	69	347
FOLLEY								
Denis	40	m	w	IREL	San Francisco	8-Wd San Francisco	82	309
Isaac	23	m	w	WI	Trinity	Trinity Center Pct	92	204
John	57	m	w	IREL	San Francisco	7-Wd San Francisco	81	163
Maria A	20	f	w	NH	San Francisco	7-Wd San Francisco	81	228
Michael	24	m	w	IREL	San Francisco	7-Wd San Francisco	81	241
Peter	22	m	w	IREL	San Francisco	7-Wd San Francisco	81	241
Samuel	49	m	w	CT	San Francisco	3-Wd San Francisco	79	295
Wm	35	m	w	IREL	San Francisco	7-Wd San Francisco	81	241
FOLLI								
Carlo	48	m	w	FRAN	San Francisco	6-Wd San Francisco	81	86
FOLLIARD								
Michael	28	m	w	IREL	Marin	San Rafael Twp	74	27
FOLLIS								
Bridget	63	f	w	IREL	San Francisco	1-Wd San Francisco	79	78
Richd H	36	m	w	IREL	San Francisco	San Francisco P O	83	24
FOLLMER								
Chas	32	m	w	PRUS	San Francisco	5-Wd San Francisco	81	15
FOLMAN								
Chas A	23	m	w	SWED	San Joaquin	2-Wd Stockton	86	164
FOLNISER								
Alonso	18	m	w	NY	San Francisco	8-Wd San Francisco	82	445
FOLNY								
Mary	30	f	w	IREL	Humboldt	Eureka Twp	72	276
FOLSION								
Andrew	35	m	w	HAMB	Monterey	Monterey Twp	74	350
FOLSOM								
Albert	45	m	w	ME	San Francisco	6-Wd San Francisco	81	138
Annie	69	f	w	MA	San Francisco	San Francisco P O	83	222
Benj H	4M	m	w	CA	Mariposa	Mariposa P O	74	122
Cathers D	28	m	w	MA	Santa Cruz	Santa Cruz	89	431
Chas F V	37	m	w	MA	San Francisco	San Francisco P O	85	720
Daniel	36	m	w	MA	Mariposa	Mariposa P O	74	119
Daniel	27	m	w	ME	Plumas	Mineral Twp	77	22
George	40	m	w	NH	San Francisco	2-Wd San Francisco	79	151
George T	36	m	w	NY	San Francisco	San Francisco P O	85	714
Ira B	35	m	w	NY	Fresno	Kings Rvr P O	72	206
James W	45	m	w	NH	Santa Clara	Redwood Twp	88	119
Joseph B	49	m	w	MS	Fresno	Millerton P O	72	184
M J	33	m	w	ME	San Francisco	San Francisco P O	85	863
Wm	24	m	w	NY	San Francisco	8-Wd San Francisco	82	376
FOLSOME								
George	34	m	w	NH	Calaveras	San Andreas P O	70	187
Hiram	39	m	w	WI	Yuba	New York Twp	93	640
FOLSON								
Danial	22	m	w	NY	San Francisco	7-Wd San Francisco	81	164
Wm B	42	m	w	IN	Sonoma	Analy Twp	91	238
FOLSTEIN								
John	40	m	w	SWED	San Francisco	8-Wd San Francisco	82	306
FOLTING								
Fred	33	m	w	PRUS	San Francisco	3-Wd San Francisco	79	294
Simon	24	m	w	PRUS	San Francisco	3-Wd San Francisco	79	294
FOLTON								
Harry G	23	m	w	IA	Sacramento	1-Wd Sacramento	77	186
FOLTS								
Frederick	45	m	w	OH	Siskiyou	Scott Valley Twp	89	613
John	35	m	w	IREL	Humboldt	Eureka Twp	72	279
FOLTZ								
Amos	30	m	w	OH	Humboldt	Arcata Twp	72	229
Michael	48	m	w	FRAN	San Francisco	San Francisco P O	80	394
FOLY								
Daniel J	35	m	w	IREL	Mendocino	Navarro & Big Rvr	74	177
William	47	m	w	MO	El Dorado	Cosumnes Twp	72	15
FOLYER								
C	20	f	w	NY	Alameda	Oakland	68	197
Seth	45	m	w	MA	San Francisco	11-Wd San Francisc	84	459
FOM								
Ah	44	m	c	CHIN	El Dorado	Diamond Springs Tw	72	35
Ah	27	m	c	CHIN	Tuolumne	Chinese Camp P O	93	370
Ah	15	m	c	CHIN	San Francisco	San Francisco P O	80	388
FOMACITY								
L	29	f	w	MEXI	San Joaquin	1-Wd Stockton	86	133
FOMB								
Ah	52	m	c	CHIN	Monterey	Monterey Twp	74	351
FOMES								
Louis	25	m	w	ITAL	Amador	Jackson P O	69	329
FOMSTER								
John	37	m	w	MO	Solano	Vacaville Twp	90	135
FON								
Ah	62	m	c	CHIN	Trinity	Weaverville Pct	92	227
Ah	50	m	c	CHIN	Sacramento	Granite Twp	77	139
Ah	48	m	c	CHIN	Trinity	Weaverville Pct	92	229
Ah	44	m	c	CHIN	Trinity	Trinity Center Pct	92	240
Ah	44	m	c	CHIN	Calaveras	San Andreas P O	70	176
Ah	42	m	c	CHIN	San Joaquin	1-Wd Stockton	86	142
Ah	41	m	c	CHIN	Placer	Rocklin Twp	76	468
Ah	40	m	c	CHIN	Placer	Bath P O	76	452
Ah	40	m	c	CHIN	Tuolumne	Chinese Camp P O	93	370
Ah	39	m	c	CHIN	Tuolumne	Chinese Camp P O	93	375
Ah	37	m	c	CHIN	Placer	Rocklin Twp	76	463
Ah	36	m	c	CHIN	Trinity	Junction City Pct	92	206
Ah	36	m	c	CHIN	San Francisco	San Francisco P O	80	508
Ah	36	m	c	CHIN	Sierra	Lincoln Twp	89	548
Ah	35	m	c	CHIN	San Francisco	6-Wd San Francisco	81	45
Ah	34	m	c	CHIN	San Francisco	6-Wd San Francisco	81	40
Ah	33	m	c	CHIN	San Francisco	San Francisco P O	80	496
Ah	32	m	c	CHIN	Trinity	Douglas	92	232
Ah	30	m	c	CHIN	Nevada	Washington Twp	75	342
Ah	30	m	c	CHIN	Tuolumne	Chinese Camp P O	93	379
Ah	30	m	c	CHIN	Yuba	Linda Twp	93	558
Ah	29	m	c	CHIN	Alameda	Oakland	68	202
Ah	28	m	c	CHIN	Trinity	Junction City Pct	92	207
Ah	28	m	c	CHIN	Trinity	Lewiston Pct	92	214
Ah	26	m	c	CHIN	Placer	Blue Canyon P O	76	417
Ah	25	m	c	CHIN	Nevada	Grass Valley Twp	75	217
Ah	25	m	c	CHIN	Siskiyou	Yreka	89	650
Ah	24	m	c	CHIN	Trinity	North Fork Twp	92	221
Ah	24	m	c	CHIN	Placer	Dutch Flat P O	76	415
Ah	23	m	c	CHIN	San Mateo	Belmont P O	87	373
Ah	23	m	c	CHIN	El Dorado	Salmon Falls Twp	72	130
Ah	21	m	c	CHIN	San Francisco	San Francisco P O	80	496
Ah	21	m	c	CHIN	Sacramento	3-Wd Sacramento	77	266
Ah	20	m	c	CHIN	San Francisco	San Francisco P O	80	510
Ah	17	m	c	CHIN	Nevada	Nevada Twp	75	321
Ah	16	m	c	CHIN	San Francisco	3-Wd San Francisco	79	303
Ah	13	m	c	CHIN	Sacramento	1-Wd Sacramento	77	182
Ah	13	m	c	CHIN	Butte	Bidwell Twp	70	2
Ah	10	m	c	CHIN	Placer	Auburn P O	76	367
Braman Jr	21	f	w	BREM	San Francisco	San Francisco P O	85	815
Buck	17	m	c	CHIN	Santa Clara	Santa Clara Twp	88	164
Can	32	m	c	CHIN	El Dorado	Salmon Falls Twp	72	130
Chin	39	m	c	CHIN	Yuba	Marysville	93	622
Choo	27	m	c	CHIN	Tuolumne	Chinese Camp P O	93	382
Chow	27	m	c	CHIN	Butte	Ophir Twp	70	106
Fie	23	m	c	CHIN	Alameda	Washington Twp	68	272
Fook	30	m	c	CHIN	Butte	Chico Twp	70	27
Gan	36	m	c	CHIN	Fresno	Millerton P O	72	202
Joe	36	m	c	CHIN	San Joaquin	Oneal Twp	86	116
Ki	40	m	c	CHIN	Tuolumne	Chinese Camp P O	93	364
King	36	m	c	CHIN	Butte	Concow Twp	70	12
Lee	29	m	c	CHIN	Butte	Ophir Twp	70	119
Lee	22	m	c	CHIN	Alameda	Washington Twp	68	274
Long	35	m	c	CHIN	Butte	Hamilton Twp	70	75
Lun	39	m	c	CHIN	Butte	Hamilton Twp	70	72
Son	38	m	c	CHIN	Butte	Hamilton Twp	70	72
Sy	21	m	c	CHIN	Butte	Concow Twp	70	9
Tee	21	m	c	CHIN	San Francisco	6-Wd San Francisco	81	60
Ting	42	m	c	CHIN	San Francisco	6-Wd San Francisco	81	74
Ton	29	m	c	CHIN	Butte	Hamilton Twp	70	74
Ye	28	m	c	CHIN	Alameda	Washington Twp	68	301
Yon	38	m	c	CHIN	Sierra	Downieville Twp	89	521
FONA								
Philip	40	m	w	FRAN	San Joaquin	Castoria Twp	86	7

© 2001 by Heritage Quest. All rights reserved.

Name	Age	S	R	B-PL	County	Locale	Series M593 Roll	Pg
FONAGER								
Ah Yap	18	m	c	CHIN	San Francisco	1-Wd San Francisco	79	58
FONALI								
Joseph	33	m	w	ITAL	Yuba	Slate Range Bar Tw	93	673
FONBER								
Maria	27	f	w	AL	Los Angeles	Los Nietos Twp	73	588
FONCH								
John V	43	m	w	HOLL	Los Angeles	Los Angeles	73	534
FONCK								
Ah	20	m	c	CHIN	Marin	San Rafael	74	58
FOND								
Ah	40	m	c	CHIN	San Francisco	San Francisco P O	80	491
FONDA								
Alfred	45	m	w	NY	San Francisco	7-Wd San Francisco	81	284
Chas E	38	m	w	NY	Shasta	Millville P O	89	483
Chas E	38	m	w	NY	Tehama	Red Bluff	92	180
G D	34	m	w	NY	Tuolumne	Columbia P O	93	339
John S	44	m	w	NY	Sonoma	Petaluma Twp	91	340
Wm T	38	m	w	NY	San Francisco	San Francisco P O	85	772
Wm T	38	m	w	NY	San Francisco	San Francisco P O	85	772
FONDERBELL								
Conrad	45	m	w	PRUS	San Francisco	1-Wd San Francisco	79	93
FONDERS								
Placida	17	m	w	CA	Sacramento	Sutter Twp	77	384
FONE								
Ah	25	m	c	CHIN	Sonoma	Bodega Twp	91	261
Ah	25	m	c	CHIN	Santa Clara	Santa Clara Twp	88	165
FONERTHA								
Cobla	28	f	w	SWIT	Mendocino	Big Rvr Twp	74	159
FONESS								
F	35	m	w	NY	Alameda	Oakland	68	264
FONEY								
Ah	24	m	c	CHIN	Butte	Ophir Twp	70	103
FONG								
---	37	m	c	CHIN	San Francisco	6-Wd San Francisco	81	64
---	30	m	c	CHIN	Siskiyou	Cottonwood Twp	89	593
---	30	m	c	CHIN	San Francisco	11-Wd San Francisc	84	546
---	24	m	c	CHIN	Siskiyou	Yreka	89	660
A	37	m	c	CHIN	San Joaquin	2-Wd Stockton	86	181
Ah	7	f	c	CHIN	Placer	Dutch Flat P O	76	408
Ah	69	m	c	CHIN	Mariposa	Mariposa P O	74	127
Ah	64	m	c	CHIN	Shasta	French Gulch P O	89	470
Ah	64	m	c	CHIN	Tuolumne	Big Oak Flat P O	93	397
Ah	64	m	c	CHIN	Fresno	Millerton P O	72	199
Ah	54	m	c	CHIN	Placer	Auburn P O	76	371
Ah	50	m	c	CHIN	Trinity	Douglas	92	237
Ah	50	m	c	CHIN	Mariposa	Mariposa P O	74	126
Ah	50	m	c	CHIN	San Francisco	San Francisco P O	80	459
Ah	47	m	c	CHIN	Trinity	Douglas	92	233
Ah	46	m	c	CHIN	San Francisco	San Francisco P O	80	496
Ah	46	m	c	CHIN	Nevada	Meadow Lake Twp	75	259
Ah	45	m	c	CHIN	Los Angeles	Los Angeles	73	565
Ah	45	m	c	CHIN	Placer	Colfax P O	76	384
Ah	45	m	c	CHIN	Nevada	Bridgeport Twp	75	119
Ah	45	m	c	CHIN	Nevada	Rough & Ready Twp	75	329
Ah	44	m	c	CHIN	Mariposa	Mariposa P O	74	137
Ah	43	m	c	CHIN	Mariposa	Mariposa P O	74	133
Ah	43	m	c	CHIN	Mariposa	Mariposa P O	74	100
Ah	43	m	c	CHIN	San Francisco	San Francisco P O	80	491
Ah	43	m	c	CHIN	Placer	Bath P O	76	444
Ah	42	m	c	CHIN	San Joaquin	1-Wd Stockton	86	149
Ah	42	f	c	CHIN	Mariposa	Mariposa P O	74	114
Ah	42	m	c	CHIN	Nevada	Meadow Lake Twp	75	259
Ah	42	m	c	CHIN	San Francisco	San Francisco P O	80	508
Ah	41	m	c	CHIN	Tuolumne	Chinese Camp P O	93	374
Ah	41	m	c	CHIN	Nevada	Little York Twp	75	245
Ah	41	m	c	CHIN	San Francisco	San Francisco P O	80	510
Ah	40	m	c	CHIN	San Francisco	San Francisco P O	80	497
Ah	40	m	c	CHIN	San Francisco	6-Wd San Francisco	81	63
Ah	40	m	c	CHIN	Mariposa	Mariposa P O	74	127
Ah	40	m	c	CHIN	Placer	Colfax P O	76	388
Ah	40	m	c	CHIN	Placer	Colfax P O	76	388
Ah	40	m	c	CHIN	San Francisco	San Francisco P O	80	520
Ah	39	m	c	CHIN	Mariposa	Mariposa P O	74	115
Ah	39	m	c	CHIN	San Francisco	San Francisco P O	80	515
Ah	39	m	c	CHIN	Santa Clara	San Jose Twp	88	194
Ah	39	m	c	CHIN	Nevada	Grass Valley Twp	75	203
Ah	38	m	c	CHIN	Mariposa	Mariposa P O	74	134
Ah	38	m	c	CHIN	Sierra	Forest Twp	89	528
Ah	37	m	c	CHIN	Butte	Hamilton Twp	70	74
Ah	37	m	c	CHIN	El Dorado	Placerville	72	115
Ah	37	m	c	CHIN	Mariposa	Mariposa P O	74	106
Ah	37	m	c	CHIN	San Francisco	San Francisco P O	80	446
Ah	37	m	c	CHIN	Nevada	Meadow Lake Twp	75	257
Ah	36	m	c	CHIN	San Francisco	San Francisco P O	80	494
Ah	36	m	c	CHIN	Trinity	Trinity Center Pct	92	240
Ah	36	m	c	CHIN	Fresno	Millerton P O	72	201
Ah	36	m	c	CHIN	San Francisco	San Francisco P O	80	515
Ah	36	m	c	CHIN	San Francisco	San Francisco P O	80	512
Ah	36	f	c	CHIN	San Francisco	San Francisco P O	80	505
Ah	36	m	c	CHIN	San Francisco	San Francisco P O	80	524
Ah	35	m	c	CHIN	Sierra	Sears Twp	89	553
Ah	35	m	c	CHIN	Butte	Hamilton Twp	70	74
Ah	35	m	c	CHIN	Mariposa	Mariposa P O	74	105
Ah	35	m	c	CHIN	Placer	Auburn P O	76	379
Ah	35	m	c	CHIN	Fresno	Millerton P O	72	202
Ah	35	m	c	CHIN	Sacramento	Granite Twp	77	139

Name	Age	S	R	B-PL	County	Locale	Series M593 Roll	Pg
Ah	34	f	c	CHIN	San Francisco	San Francisco P O	80	494
Ah	34	m	c	CHIN	Tuolumne	Chinese Camp P O	93	379
Ah	34	m	c	CHIN	San Francisco	San Francisco P O	80	498
Ah	34	m	c	CHIN	San Francisco	San Francisco P O	80	516
Ah	34	m	c	CHIN	San Francisco	San Francisco P O	80	521
Ah	34	m	c	CHIN	San Mateo	San Mateo P O	87	351
Ah	34	m	c	CHIN	Nevada	Eureka Twp	75	127
Ah	33	m	c	CHIN	Sonoma	Salt Point	91	390
Ah	32	f	c	CHIN	San Francisco	San Francisco P O	80	499
Ah	32	m	c	CHIN	San Francisco	6-Wd San Francisco	81	43
Ah	32	m	c	CHIN	San Francisco	8-Wd San Francisco	82	361
Ah	32	m	c	CHIN	Placer	Auburn P O	76	365
Ah	32	m	c	CHIN	Nevada	Meadow Lake Twp	75	256
Ah	32	m	c	CHIN	Plumas	Plumas Twp	77	32
Ah	32	m	c	CHIN	San Francisco	San Francisco P O	80	455
Ah	32	m	c	CHIN	San Francisco	San Francisco P O	80	514
Ah	32	m	c	CHIN	San Francisco	San Francisco P O	80	509
Ah	32	m	c	CHIN	San Francisco	San Francisco P O	80	525
Ah	32	m	c	CHIN	Santa Barbara	Santa Barbara P O	87	458
Ah	32	m	c	CHIN	Nevada	Eureka Twp	75	127
Ah	32	m	c	CHIN	Placer	Auburn P O	76	364
Ah	31	m	c	CHIN	San Francisco	San Francisco P O	80	491
Ah	31	m	c	CHIN	Mariposa	Mariposa P O	74	93
Ah	31	m	c	CHIN	Nevada	Bridgeport Twp	75	119
Ah	30	m	c	CHIN	San Francisco	San Francisco P O	80	499
Ah	30	m	c	CHIN	Sierra	Gibson Twp	89	540
Ah	30	f	c	CHIN	Mariposa	Mariposa P O	74	113
Ah	30	m	c	CHIN	Placer	Clipper Gap P O	76	393
Ah	30	m	c	CHIN	Placer	Auburn P O	76	381
Ah	30	m	c	CHIN	San Francisco	6-Wd San Francisco	81	54
Ah	30	m	c	CHIN	San Francisco	San Francisco P O	80	519
Ah	30	m	c	CHIN	Sierra	Eureka Twp	89	527
Ah	3	m	c	CA	San Francisco	San Francisco P O	80	525
Ah	29	m	c	CHIN	Sierra	Sears Twp	89	554
Ah	29	m	c	CHIN	Calaveras	San Andreas P O	70	184
Ah	29	m	c	CHIN	Mariposa	Mariposa P O	74	128
Ah	29	m	c	CHIN	San Francisco	San Francisco P O	80	465
Ah	29	m	c	CHIN	San Francisco	San Francisco P O	80	514
Ah	29	m	c	CHIN	Nevada	Washington Twp	75	342
Ah	28	m	c	CHIN	San Francisco	San Francisco P O	80	499
Ah	28	m	c	CHIN	Sierra	Table Rock Twp	89	544
Ah	28	m	c	CHIN	Placer	Auburn P O	76	371
Ah	28	m	c	CHIN	Nevada	Washington Twp	75	347
Ah	28	m	c	CHIN	Mariposa	Mariposa P O	74	137
Ah	28	m	c	CHIN	Nevada	Eureka Twp	75	126
Ah	27	m	c	CHIN	Sierra	Table Rock Twp	89	574
Ah	27	m	c	CHIN	Sierra	Lincoln Twp	89	552
Ah	27	m	c	CHIN	San Francisco	San Francisco P O	80	487
Ah	27	m	c	CHIN	San Francisco	6-Wd San Francisco	81	77
Ah	27	m	c	CHIN	Trinity	Junction City Pct	92	207
Ah	27	m	c	CHIN	Nevada	Nevada Twp	75	311
Ah	26	m	c	CHIN	San Francisco	11-Wd San Francisc	84	694
Ah	26	m	c	CHIN	San Francisco	6-Wd San Francisco	81	64
Ah	26	m	c	CHIN	San Francisco	8-Wd San Francisco	82	328
Ah	26	m	c	CHIN	Yolo	Washington Twp	93	534
Ah	26	m	c	CHIN	Mariposa	Mariposa P O	74	134
Ah	26	m	c	CHIN	Mendocino	Point Arena Twp	74	205
Ah	26	m	c	CHIN	Placer	Blue Canyon P O	76	419
Ah	25	m	c	CHIN	Nevada	Rough & Ready Twp	75	323
Ah	25	m	c	CHIN	Nevada	Rough & Ready Twp	75	324
Ah	24	m	c	CHIN	San Francisco	8-Wd San Francisco	82	359
Ah	24	m	c	CHIN	Mariposa	Mariposa P O	74	114
Ah	24	m	c	CHIN	San Francisco	11-Wd San Francisc	84	629
Ah	24	m	c	CHIN	Solano	Benicia	90	15
Ah	24	m	c	CHIN	Trinity	Canyon City Pct	92	202
Ah	24	m	c	CHIN	Napa	Napa Twp	75	30
Ah	23	m	c	CHIN	San Francisco	6-Wd San Francisco	81	66
Ah	23	m	c	CHIN	San Francisco	6-Wd San Francisco	81	42
Ah	23	m	c	CHIN	San Francisco	11-Wd San Francisc	84	601
Ah	23	m	c	CHIN	Nevada	Rough & Ready Twp	75	335
Ah	23	m	c	CHIN	San Francisco	1-Wd San Francisco	79	118
Ah	22	f	c	CHIN	San Francisco	San Francisco P O	80	494
Ah	22	f	c	CHIN	San Francisco	San Francisco P O	80	439
Ah	22	m	c	CHIN	San Francisco	San Francisco P O	80	456
Ah	22	m	c	CHIN	Placer	Auburn P O	76	381
Ah	22	m	c	CHIN	San Francisco	6-Wd San Francisco	81	47
Ah	22	m	c	CHIN	San Francisco	San Francisco P O	80	504
Ah	22	m	c	CHIN	Calaveras	San Andreas P O	70	171
Ah	22	m	c	CHIN	Nevada	Nevada Twp	75	314
Ah	21	m	c	CHIN	San Francisco	6-Wd San Francisco	81	84
Ah	21	m	c	CHIN	San Francisco	San Francisco P O	80	500
Ah	21	m	c	CHIN	San Francisco	San Francisco P O	80	499
Ah	21	m	c	CHIN	San Francisco	San Francisco P O	80	505
Ah	21	m	c	CHIN	Trinity	Lewiston Pct	92	212
Ah	20	m	c	CHIN	San Francisco	San Francisco P O	80	497
Ah	20	m	c	CHIN	San Francisco	San Francisco P O	83	7
Ah	20	m	c	CHIN	Yolo	Buckeye Twp	93	408
Ah	20	m	c	CHIN	Yolo	Washington Twp	93	537
Ah	20	m	c	CHIN	San Francisco	San Francisco P O	80	421
Ah	20	m	c	CHIN	San Francisco	3-Wd San Francisco	79	309
Ah	20	m	c	CHIN	Nevada	Nevada Twp	75	299
Ah	20	f	c	CHIN	Nevada	Meadow Lake Twp	75	254
Ah	20	m	c	CHIN	Santa Clara	Redwood Twp	88	133
Ah	20	m	c	CHIN	Nevada	Little York Twp	75	234
Ah	19	m	c	CHIN	San Francisco	6-Wd San Francisco	81	85
Ah	19	m	c	CHIN	Tuolumne	Chinese Camp P O	93	364
Ah	19	m	c	CHIN	San Francisco	3-Wd San Francisco	79	307

© 2001 by Heritage Quest. All rights reserved.

Name	Age	S	R	B-PL	County	Locale	Series M593 Roll	Pg
Ah	19	m	c	CHIN	Napa	Napa	75	1
Ah	19	m	c	CHIN	Sacramento	1-Wd Sacramento	77	182
Ah	19	m	c	CHIN	Siskiyou	Yreka Twp	89	668
Ah	19	m	c	CHIN	Placer	Blue Canyon P O	76	417
Ah	19	m	c	CHIN	Placer	Emigrant Gap P O	76	417
Ah	18	f	c	CHIN	San Francisco	San Francisco P O	80	494
Ah	18	m	c	CHIN	Tuolumne	Columbia P O	93	349
Ah	18	m	c	CHIN	San Francisco	3-Wd San Francisco	79	304
Ah	18	m	c	CHIN	Sacramento	1-Wd Sacramento	77	185
Ah	18	m	c	CHIN	San Francisco	6-Wd San Francisco	81	119
Ah	18	m	c	CHIN	Mendocino	Anderson Twp	74	152
Ah	17	m	c	CHIN	San Francisco	San Francisco P O	80	359
Ah	16	m	c	CHIN	Yolo	Cottonwood Twp	93	467
Ah	16	m	c	CHIN	Nevada	Eureka Twp	75	126
Ah	16	m	c	CHIN	Yuba	Marysville	93	618
Ah	15	m	c	CHIN	Yolo	Cache Crk Twp	93	424
Ah	15	m	c	CHIN	San Francisco	3-Wd San Francisco	79	309
Ah	14	m	c	CHIN	San Francisco	6-Wd San Francisco	81	43
Ah	13	m	c	CHIN	San Francisco	8-Wd San Francisco	82	337
Ah	12	f	c	CHIN	San Francisco	6-Wd San Francisco	81	76
Ah	11	f	c	CHIN	San Francisco	San Francisco P O	80	494
Ah	10	f	c	CHIN	San Francisco	6-Wd San Francisco	81	77
Ah Mar	39	f	c	CHIN	Amador	Volcano P O	69	376
Ah Qu	24	m	c	CHIN	Amador	Ione City P O	69	366
Bong	18	m	c	CHIN	San Francisco	6-Wd San Francisco	81	51
Che	47	m	c	CHIN	Trinity	Trinity Center Pct	92	204
Cheung	35	m	c	CHIN	Calaveras	San Andreas P O	70	205
Chong	20	m	c	CHIN	San Francisco	6-Wd San Francisco	81	53
Cun	35	m	c	CHIN	Inyo	Lone Pine Twp	73	332
Doon	16	m	c	CHIN	San Francisco	6-Wd San Francisco	81	47
Fan Ah	19	m	c	CHIN	Santa Cruz	Santa Cruz	89	427
Faw	30	m	c	CHIN	Del Norte	Happy Camp Twp	71	469
Gee	32	m	c	CHIN	Plumas	Mineral Twp	77	24
Gue	41	m	c	CHIN	Alameda	Washington Twp	68	272
Hang	30	m	c	CHIN	San Francisco	11-Wd San Francisc	84	529
Hee	29	m	c	CHIN	Nevada	Bridgeport Twp	75	111
Hi	45	m	c	CHIN	Siskiyou	Hamburg Twp	89	598
Hi	40	m	c	CHIN	Tuolumne	Columbia P O	93	357
Ja En	30	m	c	CHIN	San Luis Obispo	San Luis Obispo Tw	87	303
Ka En	14	m	c	CHIN	San Luis Obispo	San Luis Obispo Tw	87	303
Ki	38	m	c	CHIN	Placer	Auburn P O	76	360
King	59	m	c	CHIN	Yuba	Marysville	93	621
Lee	40	f	c	CHIN	Nevada	Meadow Lake Twp	75	255
Lee	31	m	c	CHIN	Sacramento	1-Wd Sacramento	77	198
Lee	25	m	c	CHIN	Placer	Bath P O	76	439
Lee Ah	32	m	c	CHIN	Mendocino	Point Arena Twp	74	212
Lock	34	m	c	CHIN	Yuba	Marysville	93	631
Lung	29	m	c	CHIN	Butte	Concow Twp	70	11
Moi	20	m	c	CHIN	San Francisco	6-Wd San Francisco	81	52
Moon	28	m	c	CHIN	San Francisco	11-Wd San Francisc	84	703
Mow	39	m	c	CHIN	Butte	Chico Twp	70	53
Pee	22	m	c	CHIN	San Francisco	6-Wd San Francisco	81	61
Pun	45	m	c	CHIN	Nevada	Nevada Twp	75	298
Si	34	m	c	CHIN	Sacramento	3-Wd Sacramento	77	265
Si Koo	35	m	c	CHIN	San Francisco	11-Wd San Francisc	84	547
Sing	40	m	c	CHIN	Sierra	Downieville Twp	89	521
Tay	21	m	c	CHIN	San Francisco	6-Wd San Francisco	81	63
Wah	51	m	c	CHIN	Santa Clara	Santa Clara Twp	88	161
War	23	m	c	CHIN	San Francisco	6-Wd San Francisco	81	65
Wo	38	m	c	CHIN	Nevada	Grass Valley Twp	75	206
Woo	20	m	c	CHIN	San Francisco	6-Wd San Francisco	81	47
Ye	38	m	c	CHIN	Alameda	Washington Twp	68	272
Yick	40	m	c	CHIN	El Dorado	Mud Springs Twp	72	79
Young	30	m	c	CHIN	San Francisco	11-Wd San Francisc	84	703
FONILLOLL								
Emille	37	m	w	FRAN	Butte	Bidwell Twp	70	3
FONK								
---	36	m	c	CHIN	Siskiyou	Cottonwood Twp	89	595
Ah	41	m	c	CHIN	Amador	Drytown P O	69	425
Ah	37	m	c	CHIN	El Dorado	Diamond Springs Tw	72	32
Ah	32	m	c	CHIN	San Francisco	San Francisco P O	80	489
Ah	32	m	c	CHIN	Marin	San Rafael Twp	74	37
Ah	30	m	c	CHIN	Napa	Napa	75	57
Ah	28	m	c	CHIN	Sierra	Table Rock Twp	89	574
Ah	27	m	c	CHIN	Santa Clara	San Jose Twp	88	189
Ah	27	m	c	CHIN	Nevada	Nevada Twp	75	321
Ah	22	m	c	CHIN	Santa Clara	2-Wd San Jose	88	314
Ah	22	m	c	CHIN	Nevada	Rough & Ready Twp	75	329
Ah	20	m	c	CHIN	Sacramento	2-Wd Sacramento	77	236
Ah	18	m	c	CHIN	Santa Clara	San Jose Twp	88	192
Ah	18	m	c	CHIN	Sierra	Gibson Twp	89	538
Ah	16	f	c	CHIN	Santa Clara	1-Wd San Jose	88	273
Morris	29	m	w	IREL	Butte	Oregon Twp	70	129
FONONI								
G	28	m	w	ITAL	Alameda	Murray Twp	68	123
FONSECA								
Marijoldo	48	m	w	MEXI	San Luis Obispo	San Luis Obispo Tw	87	308
Santiago	60	m	w	MEXI	Los Angeles	Wilmington Twp	73	637
FONSETONI								
Gartani	19	m	w	ITAL	San Francisco	1-Wd San Francisco	79	45
FONT								
John	14	m	w	PA	Placer	Lincoln P O	76	491
Samuel	11	m	w	CA	Sonoma	Vallejo Twp	91	461
FONTAIN								
Roman	53	m	w	FRAN	Santa Barbara	Santa Barbara P O	87	465
FONTALEN								
John B	21	m	w	AL	Fresno	Millerton P O	72	151

Name	Age	S	R	B-PL	County	Locale	Series M593 Roll	Pg
FONTANA								
Andrew	44	m	w	ITAL	Calaveras	Copperopolis P O	70	228
Antonio	26	m	w	ITAL	San Francisco	1-Wd San Francisco	79	121
Bianca	50	f	w	ITAL	San Francisco	2-Wd San Francisco	79	182
D	35	m	w	ITAL	Alameda	Oakland	68	241
Joseph	60	m	w	AUST	Tuolumne	Chinese Camp P O	93	374
Joseph	24	m	w	ITAL	San Francisco	1-Wd San Francisco	79	109
Josh	21	m	w	ITAL	San Francisco	1-Wd San Francisco	79	28
Michael	20	m	w	ITAL	San Francisco	2-Wd San Francisco	79	182
Roderic	36	m	w	ITAL	San Francisco	1-Wd San Francisco	79	118
FONTANAROSA								
Louis	33	m	w	ITAL	San Francisco	1-Wd San Francisco	79	48
FONTANI								
Joseph	24	m	w	ITAL	San Francisco	San Francisco P O	80	466
Matthew	31	m	w	ITAL	San Francisco	1-Wd San Francisco	79	44
FONTAS								
Enoch	40	m	w	SCOT	San Luis Obispo	Santa Rosa Twp	87	323
FONTE								
Antonio	42	m	w	PORT	Alameda	Brooklyn	68	36
George	35	m	w	SCOT	Alameda	Brooklyn	68	38
FONTENAY								
Louis A	31	m	w	SWIT	San Francisco	1-Wd San Francisco	79	69
FONTENEAU								
Victor	52	m	w	FRAN	Sacramento	2-Wd Sacramento	77	247
FONTENER								
Louis	38	m	w	BAVA	Marin	San Antonio Twp	74	64
FONTENROSE								
James	44	m	w	ITAL	Amador	Sutter Crk P O	69	411
FONTES								
Dolores	20	f	w	MEXI	Yuba	Linda Twp	93	558
FONTICHILLO								
John	41	m	w	ITAL	Calaveras	San Andreas P O	70	215
FONTONE								
Frank	43	m	w	ITAL	San Francisco	2-Wd San Francisco	79	144
FONTS								
Benjamin L	46	m	w	IN	San Francisco	6-Wd San Francisco	81	118
Lewis	51	m	b	NC	El Dorado	Mud Springs Twp	72	89
FONTUS								
Frank	20	m	w	CA	Amador	Jackson P O	69	322
FONTY								
John	24	m	w	PORT	Marin	Sausalito Twp	74	71
FONZER								
Jacob	21	m	w	LA	San Francisco	San Francisco P O	83	181
FOO								
---	45	m	c	CHIN	Shasta	Shasta P O	89	454
Ah	9	m	c	CHIN	Nevada	Nevada Twp	75	322
Ah	69	m	c	CHIN	El Dorado	Mud Springs Twp	72	74
Ah	65	m	c	CHIN	Sacramento	Granite Twp	77	149
Ah	60	m	c	CHIN	San Francisco	San Francisco P O	80	498
Ah	58	m	c	CHIN	Tuolumne	Columbia P O	93	349
Ah	56	m	c	CHIN	Nevada	Nevada Twp	75	311
Ah	55	m	c	CHIN	Napa	Napa Twp	75	58
Ah	52	m	c	CHIN	San Francisco	San Francisco P O	80	519
Ah	50	m	c	CHIN	Siskiyou	Hamburg Twp	89	597
Ah	50	m	c	CHIN	Tuolumne	Chinese Camp P O	93	381
Ah	50	m	c	CHIN	Stanislaus	Empire Twp	92	63
Ah	50	m	c	CHIN	Mariposa	Mariposa P O	74	137
Ah	49	m	c	CHIN	Tuolumne	Chinese Camp P O	93	363
Ah	49	m	c	CHIN	Tuolumne	Sonora P O	93	323
Ah	48	m	c	CHIN	San Francisco	6-Wd San Francisco	81	62
Ah	48	m	c	CHIN	Calaveras	San Andreas P O	70	187
Ah	45	m	c	CHIN	Mariposa	Mariposa P O	74	108
Ah	45	m	c	CHIN	Mariposa	Mariposa P O	74	126
Ah	45	m	c	CHIN	Trinity	Lewiston Pct	92	215
Ah	44	m	c	CHIN	Tuolumne	Big Oak Flat P O	93	397
Ah	44	m	c	CHIN	Butte	Ophir Twp	70	103
Ah	43	m	c	CHIN	Tuolumne	Big Oak Flat P O	93	403
Ah	43	m	c	CHIN	Tuolumne	Columbia P O	93	348
Ah	43	m	c	CHIN	Mariposa	Mariposa P O	74	112
Ah	42	m	c	CHIN	Tuolumne	Chinese Camp P O	93	386
Ah	42	f	c	CHIN	Placer	Dutch Flat P O	76	414
Ah	42	m	c	CHIN	Sacramento	1-Wd Sacramento	77	201
Ah	42	m	c	CHIN	Kern	Havilah P O	73	337
Ah	41	m	c	CHIN	Alameda	Oakland	68	245
Ah	41	m	c	CHIN	Sacramento	Granite Twp	77	151
Ah	41	m	c	CHIN	San Francisco	San Francisco P O	80	512
Ah	40	m	c	CHIN	Tuolumne	Chinese Camp P O	93	382
Ah	40	m	c	CHIN	Tuolumne	Chinese Camp P O	93	364
Ah	40	m	c	CHIN	Tuolumne	Chinese Camp P O	93	363
Ah	40	m	c	CHIN	Tuolumne	Chinese Camp P O	93	379
Ah	40	m	c	CHIN	Tuolumne	Big Oak Flat P O	93	397
Ah	40	m	c	CHIN	Mariposa	Mariposa P O	74	128
Ah	40	m	c	CHIN	Mariposa	Maxwell Crk P O	74	144
Ah	40	m	c	CHIN	Alameda	Oakland	68	254
Ah	40	m	c	CHIN	Fresno	Millerton P O	72	201
Ah	40	m	c	CHIN	Nevada	Nevada Twp	75	279
Ah	40	m	c	CHIN	Nevada	Nevada Twp	75	315
Ah	40	m	c	CHIN	Placer	Newcastle Twp	76	479
Ah	40	m	c	CHIN	Nevada	Grass Valley Twp	75	217
Ah	40	m	c	CHIN	Alameda	San Leandro	68	96
Ah	40	m	c	CHIN	Alameda	Oakland	68	223
Ah	40	m	c	CHIN	Amador	Ione City P O	69	367
Ah	40	m	c	CHIN	Amador	Jackson P O	69	343
Ah	40	m	c	CHIN	San Francisco	San Francisco P O	80	520
Ah	40	m	c	CHIN	San Francisco	San Francisco P O	80	509
Ah	39	m	c	CHIN	Butte	Chico Twp	70	27
Ah	39	m	c	CHIN	Calaveras	Copperopolis P O	70	249

© 2001 by Heritage Quest. All rights reserved.

Name	Age	S	R	B-PL	County	Series M593 Locale	Roll	Pg
Ah	38	m	c	CHIN	Tuolumne	Big Oak Flat P O	93	391
Ah	38	m	c	CHIN	Mariposa	Mariposa P O	74	114
Ah	38	m	c	CHIN	Butte	Ophir Twp	70	104
Ah	38	m	c	CHIN	Amador	Fiddletown P O	69	435
Ah	38	m	c	CHIN	Alameda	Alameda	68	1
Ah	38	m	c	CHIN	Alameda	Eden Twp	68	61
Ah	38	m	c	CHIN	Alameda	Alameda	68	16
Ah	38	m	c	CHIN	Alameda	Washington Twp	68	271
Ah	38	m	c	CHIN	Butte	Kimshew Tpw	70	84
Ah	38	m	c	CHIN	San Francisco	San Francisco P O	80	516
Ah	37	m	c	CHIN	Sierra	Downieville Twp	89	521
Ah	37	m	c	CHIN	San Francisco	San Francisco P O	83	129
Ah	37	m	c	CHIN	San Francisco	San Francisco P O	80	517
Ah	36	m	c	CHIN	Sonoma	Salt Point Twp	91	384
Ah	36	m	c	CHIN	Tuolumne	Chinese Camp P O	93	364
Ah	36	m	c	CHIN	San Joaquin	1-Wd Stockton	86	147
Ah	36	m	c	CHIN	Mariposa	Mariposa P O	74	106
Ah	36	m	c	CHIN	Mariposa	Mariposa P O	74	128
Ah	36	m	c	CHIN	Nevada	Bridgeport Twp	75	110
Ah	36	m	c	CHIN	Placer	Lincoln P O	76	483
Ah	36	m	c	CHIN	San Francisco	San Francisco P O	80	517
Ah	36	m	c	CHIN	San Francisco	San Francisco P O	80	514
Ah	36	m	c	CHIN	Santa Clara	Fremont Twp	88	66
Ah	35	m	c	CHIN	Tuolumne	Sonora P O	93	311
Ah	35	m	c	CHIN	San Francisco	6-Wd San Francisco	81	40
Ah	35	m	c	CHIN	San Francisco	San Francisco P O	80	497
Ah	35	m	c	CHIN	Mariposa	Mariposa P O	74	100
Ah	35	m	c	CHIN	Placer	Auburn P O	76	373
Ah	35	m	c	CHIN	Alameda	Oakland	68	254
Ah	35	m	c	CHIN	Amador	Ione City P O	69	358
Ah	35	m	c	CHIN	San Francisco	San Francisco P O	80	512
Ah	34	m	c	CHIN	Tuolumne	Chinese Camp P O	93	388
Ah	34	f	c	CHIN	San Francisco	San Francisco P O	80	504
Ah	34	m	c	CHIN	San Francisco	San Francisco P O	80	495
Ah	34	m	c	CHIN	San Francisco	San Francisco P O	80	502
Ah	34	m	c	CHIN	San Joaquin	1-Wd Stockton	86	148
Ah	34	m	c	CHIN	Alameda	Oakland	68	245
Ah	34	m	c	CHIN	Amador	Sutter Crk P O	69	403
Ah	34	m	c	CHIN	San Francisco	San Francisco P O	80	516
Ah	34	m	c	CHIN	San Francisco	San Francisco P O	80	514
Ah	34	m	c	CHIN	San Francisco	San Francisco P O	80	524
Ah	34	m	c	CHIN	San Francisco	San Francisco P O	80	511
Ah	34	m	c	CHIN	San Francisco	San Francisco P O	80	510
Ah	33	m	c	CHIN	Alameda	Alameda	68	17
Ah	33	m	c	CHIN	Nevada	Rough & Ready Twp	75	337
Ah	33	m	c	CHIN	San Francisco	San Francisco P O	80	505
Ah	32	m	c	CHIN	Sierra	Lincoln Twp	89	548
Ah	32	m	c	CHIN	Fresno	Millerton P O	72	199
Ah	32	m	c	CHIN	Butte	Hamilton Twp	70	68
Ah	32	m	c	CHIN	Nevada	Nevada Twp	75	312
Ah	32	m	c	CHIN	Amador	Ione City P O	69	354
Ah	32	m	c	CHIN	San Francisco	San Francisco P O	80	508
Ah	32	m	c	CHIN	Shasta	American Ranch P O	89	497
Ah	31	m	c	CHIN	San Francisco	San Francisco P O	80	494
Ah	31	m	c	CHIN	Mariposa	Mariposa P O	74	105
Ah	31	m	c	CHIN	Mariposa	Mariposa P O	74	137
Ah	31	m	c	CHIN	Butte	Chico Twp	70	31
Ah	31	m	c	CHIN	Calaveras	San Andreas P O	70	171
Ah	31	m	c	CHIN	Alameda	Oakland	68	250
Ah	31	m	c	CHIN	San Francisco	San Francisco P O	80	501
Ah	31	m	c	CHIN	San Francisco	San Francisco P O	80	505
Ah	30	m	c	CHIN	Yuba	East Bear Rvr Twp	93	540
Ah	30	m	c	CHIN	Tuolumne	Big Oak Flat P O	93	397
Ah	30	m	c	CHIN	Tuolumne	Columbia P O	93	341
Ah	30	m	c	CHIN	San Francisco	San Francisco P O	80	492
Ah	30	m	c	CHIN	San Francisco	San Francisco P O	80	501
Ah	30	f	c	CHIN	San Francisco	San Francisco P O	80	493
Ah	30	m	c	CHIN	Merced	Snelling P O	74	251
Ah	30	m	c	CHIN	Butte	Chico Twp	70	28
Ah	30	m	c	CHIN	Butte	Ophir Twp	70	119
Ah	30	m	c	CHIN	Alameda	Oakland	68	250
Ah	30	m	c	CHIN	Alameda	Oakland	68	250
Ah	30	m	c	CHIN	Amador	Fiddletown P O	69	428
Ah	30	m	c	CHIN	San Francisco	3-Wd San Francisco	79	309
Ah	30	m	c	CHIN	Marin	San Rafael Twp	74	41
Ah	30	m	c	CHIN	Plumas	Washington Twp	77	56
Ah	30	m	c	CHIN	Sacramento	1-Wd Sacramento	77	196
Ah	30	m	c	CHIN	Sacramento	1-Wd Sacramento	77	192
Ah	30	m	c	CHIN	Alameda	Eden Twp	68	62
Ah	30	m	c	CHIN	Alameda	Eden Twp	68	66
Ah	30	m	c	CHIN	Alameda	Oakland	68	232
Ah	30	m	c	CHIN	Amador	Ione City P O	69	355
Ah	30	m	c	CHIN	Butte	Ophir Twp	70	106
Ah	30	m	c	CHIN	San Francisco	San Francisco P O	80	514
Ah	30	m	c	CHIN	San Francisco	11-Wd San Francisc	84	503
Ah	30	m	c	CHIN	Trinity	Junction City Pct	92	207
Ah	30	m	c	CHIN	Yuba	Marysville	93	624
Ah	29	m	c	CHIN	Tuolumne	Chinese Camp P O	93	389
Ah	29	m	c	CHIN	San Francisco	San Francisco P O	83	85
Ah	29	m	c	CHIN	Butte	Chico Twp	70	30
Ah	29	m	c	CHIN	Nevada	Meadow Lake Twp	75	259
Ah	29	m	c	CHIN	Nevada	Grass Valley Twp	75	202
Ah	29	m	c	CHIN	Nevada	Grass Valley Twp	75	205
Ah	29	m	c	CHIN	Sacramento	1-Wd Sacramento	77	205
Ah	29	m	c	CHIN	Alameda	Washington Twp	68	301
Ah	29	m	c	CHIN	Butte	Hamilton Twp	70	66
Ah	29	m	c	CHIN	San Francisco	San Francisco P O	80	513
Ah	28	m	c	CHIN	Amador	Fiddletown P O	69	436
Ah	28	m	c	CHIN	Sacramento	Natomas Twp	77	167
Ah	28	m	c	CHIN	Alameda	Alameda	68	6
Ah	28	m	c	CHIN	Alameda	Washington Twp	68	270
Ah	28	m	c	CHIN	Alameda	Oakland	68	224
Ah	28	m	c	CHIN	Alameda	Oakland	68	250
Ah	28	m	c	CHIN	Amador	Jackson P O	69	342
Ah	28	m	c	CHIN	San Francisco	San Francisco P O	80	513
Ah	28	m	c	CHIN	San Francisco	6-Wd San Francisco	81	54
Ah	27	m	c	CHIN	San Francisco	San Francisco P O	80	499
Ah	27	m	c	CHIN	Butte	Hamilton Twp	70	61
Ah	27	m	c	CHIN	Butte	Hamilton Twp	70	67
Ah	27	m	c	CHIN	San Francisco	3-Wd San Francisco	79	301
Ah	26	m	c	CHIN	Shasta	French Gulch P O	89	465
Ah	26	m	c	CHIN	Santa Clara	San Jose Twp	88	191
Ah	26	m	c	CHIN	Butte	Hamilton Twp	70	67
Ah	26	m	c	CHIN	Plumas	Plumas Twp	77	30
Ah	26	m	c	CHIN	Butte	Hamilton Twp	70	67
Ah	26	m	c	CHIN	San Francisco	San Francisco P O	80	522
Ah	26	m	c	CHIN	San Francisco	San Francisco P O	80	513
Ah	26	m	c	CHIN	Sierra	Table Rock Twp	89	571
Ah	25	m	c	CHIN	Santa Clara	Gilroy Twp	88	97
Ah	25	m	c	CHIN	Solano	Vallejo	90	210
Ah	25	m	c	CHIN	Yolo	Buckeye Twp	93	412
Ah	25	m	c	CHIN	Calaveras	Copperopolis P O	70	234
Ah	25	m	c	CHIN	El Dorado	Salmon Falls Twp	72	129
Ah	25	m	c	CHIN	Placer	Colfax P O	76	384
Ah	25	m	c	CHIN	Plumas	Goodwin Twp	77	5
Ah	25	m	c	CHIN	Alameda	Alameda	68	4
Ah	25	m	c	CHIN	Alameda	Brooklyn Twp	68	40
Ah	25	m	c	CHIN	Alameda	Washington Twp	68	270
Ah	25	m	c	CHIN	Klamath	Liberty Twp	73	376
Ah	25	m	c	CHIN	San Francisco	San Francisco P O	85	796
Ah	25	m	c	CHIN	Solano	Suisun Twp	90	104
Ah	24	m	c	CHIN	Solano	Vallejo	90	205
Ah	24	m	c	CHIN	Tuolumne	Chinese Camp P O	93	375
Ah	24	m	c	CHIN	Tuolumne	Chinese Camp P O	93	380
Ah	24	f	c	CHIN	Mariposa	Maxwell Crk P O	74	138
Ah	24	m	c	CHIN	Butte	Chico Twp	70	28
Ah	24	m	c	CHIN	San Francisco	1-Wd San Francisco	79	118
Ah	24	m	c	CHIN	San Francisco	3-Wd San Francisco	79	304
Ah	24	f	c	CHIN	Sacramento	Granite Twp	77	151
Ah	24	m	c	CHIN	Placer	Auburn P O	76	357
Ah	24	m	c	CHIN	Nevada	Eureka Twp	75	140
Ah	24	m	c	CHIN	Placer	Summit P O	76	497
Ah	24	m	c	CHIN	Sacramento	2-Wd Sacramento	77	219
Ah	24	m	c	CHIN	Alameda	Hayward	68	77
Ah	24	m	c	CHIN	San Francisco	San Francisco P O	80	506
Ah	24	m	c	CHIN	Sierra	Eureka Twp	89	527
Ah	24	m	c	CHIN	Trinity	Lewiston Pct	92	212
Ah	23	f	c	CHIN	San Francisco	San Francisco P O	80	503
Ah	23	m	c	CHIN	Fresno	Millerton P O	72	201
Ah	23	f	c	CHIN	Butte	Kimshew Tpw	70	77
Ah	23	m	c	CHIN	San Francisco	San Francisco P O	80	516
Ah	23	m	c	CHIN	San Francisco	San Francisco P O	80	516
Ah	23	m	c	CHIN	Siskiyou	Hamburg Twp	89	599
Ah	22	m	c	CHIN	Santa Barbara	Santa Barbara P O	87	458
Ah	22	f	c	CHIN	Butte	Chico Twp	70	28
Ah	22	f	c	CHIN	San Francisco	San Francisco P O	80	434
Ah	22	m	c	CHIN	San Francisco	San Francisco P O	80	360
Ah	22	m	c	CHIN	Plumas	Goodwin Twp	77	4
Ah	22	m	c	CHIN	Placer	Gold Run Twp	76	394
Ah	22	m	c	CHIN	Alameda	Washington Twp	68	294
Ah	22	m	c	CHIN	Alameda	Oakland	68	172
Ah	22	m	c	CHIN	San Francisco	11-Wd San Francisc	84	504
Ah	22	m	c	CHIN	San Mateo	San Mateo P O	87	351
Ah	22	m	c	CHIN	Shasta	American Ranch P O	89	499
Ah	21	m	c	CHIN	San Francisco	San Francisco P O	80	497
Ah	21	f	c	CHIN	San Francisco	San Francisco P O	80	441
Ah	21	m	c	CHIN	Plumas	Quartz Twp	77	35
Ah	21	m	c	CHIN	San Francisco	San Francisco P O	80	511
Ah	20	m	c	CHIN	Shasta	Shasta P O	89	457
Ah	20	m	c	CHIN	San Francisco	3-Wd San Francisco	79	310
Ah	20	m	c	CHIN	San Francisco	3-Wd San Francisco	79	329
Ah	20	m	c	CHIN	Plumas	Indian Twp	77	19
Ah	20	m	c	CHIN	Nevada	Eureka Twp	75	127
Ah	20	m	c	CHIN	Sacramento	Granite Twp	77	152
Ah	20	m	c	CHIN	Alameda	Alameda	68	1
Ah	20	m	c	CHIN	Alameda	Washington Twp	68	270
Ah	20	m	c	CHIN	Contra Costa	Martinez P O	71	406
Ah	20	f	c	CHIN	San Francisco	San Francisco P O	80	459
Ah	20	m	c	CHIN	San Francisco	San Francisco P O	80	506
Ah	19	m	c	CHIN	Solano	Vallejo	90	209
Ah	19	m	c	CHIN	Yolo	Buckeye Twp	93	408
Ah	19	f	c	CHIN	Butte	Chico Twp	70	28
Ah	19	m	c	CHIN	San Francisco	San Francisco P O	80	421
Ah	19	m	c	CHIN	Nevada	Rough & Ready Twp	75	337
Ah	19	m	c	CHIN	Alameda	Eden Twp	68	81
Ah	19	m	c	CHIN	Santa Clara	Gilroy Twp	88	75
Ah	18	f	c	CHIN	Solano	Vallejo	90	179
Ah	18	m	c	CHIN	Yolo	Grafton Twp	93	478
Ah	18	f	c	CHIN	Yolo	Buckeye Twp	93	416
Ah	18	m	c	CHIN	Tuolumne	Columbia P O	93	350
Ah	18	f	c	CHIN	San Francisco	San Francisco P O	80	503
Ah	18	m	c	CHIN	San Francisco	San Francisco P O	80	497
Ah	18	m	c	CHIN	San Mateo	San Mateo P O	87	352
Ah	18	m	c	CHIN	San Francisco	3-Wd San Francisco	79	304

© 2001 by Heritage Quest. All rights reserved.

California 1870 Census

Name	Age	S	R	B-PL	County	Locale	Roll (Series M593)	Pg
Ah	18	m	c	CHIN	San Francisco	San Francisco P O	80	408
Ah	18	m	c	CHIN	Sacramento	1-Wd Sacramento	77	199
Ah	18	m	c	CHIN	Alameda	Eden Twp	68	92
Ah	18	m	c	CHIN	San Francisco	San Francisco P O	80	503
Ah	18	m	c	CHIN	San Francisco	11-Wd San Francisc	84	554
Ah	18	m	c	CHIN	Stanislaus	Emory Twp	92	19
Ah	17	m	c	CHIN	San Francisco	11-Wd San Francisc	84	448
Ah	17	m	c	CHIN	Solano	Vallejo	90	161
Ah	16	f	c	CHIN	Tuolumne	Chinese Camp P O	93	388
Ah	16	m	c	CHIN	Alameda	Oakland	68	201
Ah	16	m	c	CHIN	Sacramento	1-Wd Sacramento	77	190
Ah	16	m	c	CHIN	Contra Costa	Martinez Twp	71	352
Ah	15	m	c	CHIN	San Francisco	2-Wd San Francisco	79	147
Ah	15	m	c	CHIN	San Francisco	2-Wd San Francisco	79	170
Ah	15	m	c	CHIN	Alameda	Brooklyn Twp	68	40
Ah	15	m	c	CHIN	San Mateo	San Mateo P O	87	354
Ah	15	m	c	CHIN	San Mateo	Woodside P O	87	387
Ah	14	m	c	CHIN	Yolo	Grafton Twp	93	492
Ah	14	m	c	CHIN	San Francisco	8-Wd San Francisco	82	361
Ah	14	m	c	CHIN	Butte	Chico Twp	70	27
Ah	14	m	c	CHIN	Alameda	Oakland	68	195
Ah	14	m	c	CHIN	San Francisco	3-Wd San Francisco	79	310
Ah	14	m	c	CA	Mariposa	Maxwell Crk P O	74	138
Ah	14	m	c	CHIN	Sacramento	2-Wd Sacramento	77	215
Ah	14	m	c	CHIN	San Francisco	6-Wd San Francisco	81	137
Ah	13	m	c	CHIN	Shasta	French Gulch P O	89	465
Ah	12	m	c	CHIN	Sacramento	2-Wd Sacramento	77	244
Ah	1	m	c	CA	San Francisco	San Francisco P O	80	492
Ah Low	43	m	c	CHIN	Amador	Sutter Crk P O	69	411
Ang	19	m	c	CHIN	Plumas	Seneca Twp	77	48
Boo	37	m	c	CHIN	Tuolumne	Columbia P O	93	342
Boock	29	m	c	CHIN	Yuba	Marysville	93	621
Bow	30	m	c	CHIN	Yuba	Marysville	93	632
Chee	28	m	c	CHIN	Mariposa	Maxwell Crk P O	74	145
Chee	15	m	c	CHIN	San Francisco	6-Wd San Francisco	81	62
Chi	25	m	c	CHIN	Alameda	Washington Twp	68	297
Chin	22	m	c	CHIN	Alameda	Washington Twp	68	297
Ching	40	m	c	CHIN	San Francisco	2-Wd San Francisco	79	285
Ching	33	m	c	CHIN	Placer	Bath P O	76	429
Choo	32	m	c	CHIN	Solano	Rio Vista Twp	90	64
Choo	26	m	c	CHIN	Tuolumne	Columbia P O	93	355
Chow	39	m	c	CHIN	Butte	Wyandotte Twp	70	143
Chow	30	m	c	CHIN	Sacramento	2-Wd Sacramento	77	246
Chow	17	m	c	CHIN	Santa Clara	2-Wd San Jose	88	333
Chun	19	f	c	CHIN	Placer	Colfax P O	76	384
Chung	22	f	c	CHIN	Placer	Colfax P O	76	388
Cling	48	m	c	CHIN	Trinity	Douglas	92	237
Cona	26	f	c	CHIN	Sierra	Downieville Twp	89	521
Fi	20	m	c	CHIN	Alameda	Washington Twp	68	276
Fung	23	m	c	CHIN	Yuba	Marysville	93	630
Fy	27	m	c	CHIN	Alameda	Washington Twp	68	274
Gan	35	m	c	CHIN	Yuba	Marysville	93	621
Gee	27	m	c	CHIN	Plumas	Mineral Twp	77	23
Gum	28	m	c	CHIN	Yuba	Marysville	93	628
Hang	45	m	c	CHIN	Placer	Dutch Flat P O	76	407
Hin	34	m	c	CHIN	Calaveras	San Andreas P O	70	211
Hing	27	m	c	CHIN	Solano	Vacaville Twp	90	122
Ho	42	m	c	CHIN	Butte	Chico Twp	70	52
Hon	19	m	c	CHIN	Yolo	Grafton Twp	93	484
Hoo	44	m	c	CHIN	Tuolumne	Columbia P O	93	348
Hop	42	m	c	CHIN	Yuba	Marysville	93	629
Jim	17	m	c	CHIN	Santa Clara	Redwood Twp	88	126
Joseph	18	m	c	CHIN	Los Angeles	Los Angeles	73	532
Kee	47	m	c	CHIN	Amador	Lancha Plana P O	69	369
Kee	47	m	c	CHIN	Amador	Fiddletown P O	69	428
Kee	44	m	c	CHIN	Amador	Drytown P O	69	425
Kee	38	m	c	CHIN	Amador	Jackson P O	69	347
Kee	28	m	c	CHIN	Amador	Drytown P O	69	418
Kee	20	m	c	CHIN	San Francisco	2-Wd San Francisco	79	141
Ken	45	m	c	CHIN	Shasta	French Gulch P O	89	470
King	61	m	c	CHIN	Mariposa	Mariposa P O	74	125
King	17	m	c	CHIN	Nevada	Nevada Twp	75	298
Lee	32	m	c	CHIN	San Joaquin	1-Wd Stockton	86	149
Lee	27	m	c	CHIN	San Joaquin	1-Wd Stockton	86	148
Lihusa	18	m	c	CHIN	Mendocino	Casper & Big Rvr	74	162
Lin	34	m	c	CHIN	Yuba	Marysville	93	631
Lo	27	m	c	CHIN	San Joaquin	Oneal Twp	86	117
Long	38	m	c	CHIN	Mariposa	Mariposa P O	74	128
Loy	29	m	c	CHIN	Butte	Ophir Twp	70	106
Loy	25	m	c	CHIN	San Francisco	San Francisco P O	85	765
Luk	33	m	c	CHIN	Calaveras	San Andreas P O	70	211
Lung	35	m	c	CHIN	Calaveras	San Andreas P O	70	167
Me	53	m	c	CHIN	Amador	Jackson P O	69	347
Ong	58	m	c	CHIN	Colusa	Colusa	71	298
Poo	42	m	c	CHIN	San Joaquin	1-Wd Stockton	86	147
Sat	25	m	c	CHIN	Yolo	Cache Crk Twp	93	455
Sin	20	m	c	CHIN	Solano	Vallejo	90	208
Sing	37	m	c	CHIN	Placer	Bath P O	76	439
Sing	33	m	c	CHIN	Butte	Hamilton Twp	70	72
Sing	30	m	c	CHIN	Amador	Jackson P O	69	330
Sing	17	m	c	CHIN	San Luis Obispo	Arroyo Grande Twp	87	279
So	40	m	c	CHIN	Tuolumne	Big Oak Flat P O	93	401
Thue	28	m	c	CHIN	Santa Clara	Santa Clara Twp	88	166
Ti	40	m	c	CHIN	Santa Clara	Fremont Twp	88	57
Toy	30	m	c	CHIN	Yuba	Rose Bar Twp	93	656
War	27	m	c	CHIN	Yuba	Marysville	93	623
Winy	55	m	c	CHIN	Yuba	Bullards Bar P O	93	553
You	62	m	c	CHIN	Shasta	Horsetown P O	89	506
FOOD								
Ah	20	f	c	CHIN	San Francisco	San Francisco P O	80	495
William	30	m	w	IREL	Marin	San Rafael Twp	74	36
FOOEY								
Ah	27	m	c	CHIN	Klamath	Dillon Twp	73	369
Ah	16	m	c	CHIN	Shasta	French Gulch P O	89	465
FOOG								
Ah	28	m	c	CHIN	Solano	Vallejo	90	174
FOOGARTY								
Micheal	40	m	w	IREL	San Joaquin	Castoria Twp	86	8
FOOH								
Ah	35	m	c	CHIN	San Francisco	3-Wd San Francisco	79	312
Ah	34	m	c	CHIN	Kern	Bakersfield P O	73	364
Ah	21	m	c	CHIN	Nevada	Meadow Lake Twp	75	254
Ah	20	m	c	CHIN	San Francisco	3-Wd San Francisco	79	329
FOOHY								
A V	33	m	w	IREL	San Joaquin	Dent Twp	86	19
FOOK								
Ah	9	m	c	CA	Amador	Fiddletown P O	69	438
Ah	55	m	c	CHIN	Plumas	Plumas Twp	77	31
Ah	55	m	c	CHIN	Nevada	Bridgeport Twp	75	111
Ah	55	m	c	CHIN	Shasta	American Ranch P O	89	500
Ah	50	m	c	CHIN	Tuolumne	Big Oak Flat P O	93	404
Ah	48	m	c	CHIN	Tuolumne	Big Oak Flat P O	93	397
Ah	48	m	c	CHIN	Tuolumne	Sonora P O	93	326
Ah	46	m	c	CHIN	Tuolumne	Chinese Camp P O	93	366
Ah	46	m	c	CHIN	Tuolumne	Columbia P O	93	350
Ah	45	m	c	CHIN	Tuolumne	Big Oak Flat P O	93	403
Ah	45	m	c	CHIN	Plumas	Washington Twp	77	57
Ah	44	m	c	CHIN	Tuolumne	Chinese Camp P O	93	363
Ah	44	m	c	CHIN	Sacramento	Granite Twp	77	137
Ah	43	m	c	CHIN	Sacramento	Cosumnes Twp	77	94
Ah	42	m	c	CHIN	Sacramento	Granite Twp	77	153
Ah	42	m	c	CHIN	Butte	Oregon Twp	70	135
Ah	42	m	c	CHIN	Amador	Drytown P O	69	421
Ah	42	m	c	CHIN	Sacramento	Cosumnes Twp	77	94
Ah	41	m	c	CHIN	Tuolumne	Columbia P O	93	350
Ah	41	m	c	CHIN	Tuolumne	Chinese Camp P O	93	364
Ah	41	m	c	CHIN	Butte	Wyandotte Twp	70	147
Ah	40	m	c	CHIN	Tuolumne	Big Oak Flat P O	93	391
Ah	40	m	c	CHIN	Tuolumne	Big Oak Flat P O	93	393
Ah	40	m	c	CHIN	Tuolumne	Chinese Camp P O	93	388
Ah	40	m	c	CHIN	Sacramento	Center Twp	77	85
Ah	40	m	c	CHIN	Nevada	Bridgeport Twp	75	111
Ah	40	m	c	CHIN	Sacramento	Georgianna Twp	77	129
Ah	40	m	c	CHIN	Sacramento	Granite Twp	77	141
Ah	39	m	c	CHIN	Nevada	Meadow Lake Twp	75	256
Ah	39	m	c	CHIN	Calaveras	San Andreas P O	70	173
Ah	39	m	c	CHIN	Amador	Volcano P O	69	378
Ah	38	m	c	CHIN	Butte	Chico Twp	70	27
Ah	37	m	c	CHIN	Tuolumne	Sonora P O	93	321
Ah	37	m	c	CHIN	Placer	Bath P O	76	452
Ah	37	m	c	CHIN	Sacramento	Granite Twp	77	138
Ah	37	m	c	CHIN	Sacramento	Center Twp	77	87
Ah	36	m	c	CHIN	El Dorado	Placerville	72	124
Ah	36	m	c	CHIN	Butte	Wyandotte Twp	70	143
Ah	35	m	c	CHIN	Nevada	Nevada Twp	75	289
Ah	35	m	c	CHIN	Sacramento	Granite Twp	77	155
Ah	35	m	c	CHIN	Sacramento	American Twp	77	67
Ah	35	f	c	CHIN	El Dorado	Placerville	72	116
Ah	34	m	c	CHIN	Nevada	Nevada Twp	75	311
Ah	33	m	c	CHIN	Placer	Auburn P O	76	379
Ah	33	m	c	CHIN	Klamath	South Fork Twp	73	382
Ah	32	m	c	CHIN	Mariposa	Mariposa P O	74	92
Ah	32	m	c	CHIN	El Dorado	White Oak Twp	72	136
Ah	32	m	c	CHIN	Plumas	Goodwin Twp	77	3
Ah	31	m	c	CHIN	Nevada	Bridgeport Twp	75	109
Ah	31	m	c	CHIN	Nevada	Nevada Twp	75	321
Ah	30	m	c	CHIN	Tuolumne	Big Oak Flat P O	93	396
Ah	30	m	c	CHIN	Tuolumne	Big Oak Flat P O	93	395
Ah	30	m	c	CHIN	Tuolumne	Chinese Camp P O	93	369
Ah	30	m	c	CHIN	San Francisco	1-Wd San Francisco	79	89
Ah	30	m	c	CHIN	Monterey	San Juan Twp	74	387
Ah	30	m	c	CHIN	Klamath	Liberty Twp	73	375
Ah	30	m	c	CHIN	Butte	Bidwell Twp	70	5
Ah	30	m	c	CHIN	Nevada	Bridgeport Twp	75	110
Ah	30	m	c	CHIN	Sacramento	Granite Twp	77	150
Ah	30	m	c	CHIN	Sacramento	Center Twp	77	86
Ah	30	m	c	CHIN	Sacramento	Center Twp	77	87
Ah	3	m	c	CHIN	Trinity	Weaverville Pct	92	228
Ah	29	m	c	CHIN	Calaveras	Copperopolis P O	70	264
Ah	29	m	c	CHIN	Sacramento	Georgianna Twp	77	133
Ah	29	m	c	CHIN	Sacramento	Cosumnes Twp	77	90
Ah	28	m	c	CHIN	Yolo	Grafton Twp	93	478
Ah	28	m	c	CHIN	Tuolumne	Sonora P O	93	327
Ah	28	m	c	CHIN	El Dorado	Placerville	72	120
Ah	28	m	c	CHIN	Plumas	Plumas Twp	77	31
Ah	27	m	c	CHIN	San Francisco	San Francisco P O	83	308
Ah	27	m	c	CHIN	Santa Cruz	Santa Cruz	89	434
Ah	27	m	c	CHIN	Placer	Auburn P O	76	362
Ah	27	m	c	CHIN	Sacramento	Georgianna Twp	77	132
Ah	27	m	c	CHIN	Sacramento	Georgianna Twp	77	132
Ah	27	m	c	CHIN	Sacramento	American Twp	77	68
Ah	26	m	c	CHIN	Placer	Colfax P O	76	386
Ah	26	m	c	CHIN	Placer	Auburn P O	76	378
Ah	26	m	c	CHIN	Sacramento	Mississippi Twp	77	162

© 2001 by Heritage Quest. All rights reserved.

Series M593

Name	Age	S	R	B-PL	County	Locale	Roll	Pg
Ah	26	m	c	CHIN	San Mateo	San Mateo P O	87	351
Ah	25	m	c	CHIN	San Mateo	Half Moon Bay P O	87	402
Ah	25	m	c	CHIN	Placer	Colfax P O	76	386
Ah	25	m	c	CHIN	Placer	Auburn P O	76	370
Ah	25	m	c	CHIN	Plumas	Plumas Twp	77	26
Ah	25	f	c	CHIN	Sacramento	Granite Twp	77	152
Ah	25	m	c	CHIN	Yuba	Marysville	93	591
Ah	25	m	c	CHIN	Butte	Mountain Spring Tw	70	89
Ah	25	m	c	CHIN	Calaveras	San Andreas P O	70	190
Ah	25	m	c	CHIN	Nevada	Eureka Twp	75	131
Ah	25	m	c	CHIN	Nevada	Bridgeport Twp	75	110
Ah	25	m	c	CHIN	Placer	Bath P O	76	423
Ah	24	m	c	CHIN	Amador	Ione City P O	69	367
Ah	24	m	c	CHIN	Placer	Auburn P O	76	361
Ah	23	m	c	CHIN	Fresno	Millerton P O	72	191
Ah	23	m	c	CHIN	Placer	Bath P O	76	445
Ah	22	m	c	CHIN	Plumas	Mineral Twp	77	25
Ah	22	f	c	CHIN	Sacramento	Granite Twp	77	153
Ah	22	m	c	CHIN	San Francisco	11-Wd San Francisc	84	528
Ah	21	m	c	CHIN	San Francisco	3-Wd San Francisco	79	307
Ah	21	m	c	CHIN	San Francisco	San Francisco P O	83	236
Ah	20	m	c	CHIN	San Francisco	1-Wd San Francisco	79	43
Ah	20	m	c	CHIN	San Francisco	1-Wd San Francisco	79	50
Ah	20	m	c	CHIN	San Francisco	San Francisco P O	80	335
Ah	20	f	c	CHIN	San Francisco	6-Wd San Francisco	81	75
Ah	19	m	c	CHIN	San Mateo	Redwood Twp	87	363
Ah	19	m	c	CHIN	Tuolumne	Chinese Camp P O	93	382
Ah	19	m	c	CHIN	Yolo	Cache Crk Twp	93	454
Ah	19	m	c	CHIN	San Francisco	1-Wd San Francisco	79	80
Ah	18	m	c	CHIN	San Francisco	11-Wd San Francisc	84	574
Ah	18	m	c	CHIN	San Francisco	3-Wd San Francisco	79	329
Ah	18	m	c	CHIN	Sacramento	Granite Twp	77	152
Ah	17	m	c	CHIN	El Dorado	Mud Springs Twp	72	76
Ah	17	m	c	CHIN	Butte	Wyandotte Twp	70	147
Ah	16	m	c	CHIN	San Francisco	1-Wd San Francisco	79	61
Ah	15	m	c	CHIN	San Francisco	6-Wd San Francisco	81	85
Ah	15	m	c	CHIN	San Francisco	San Francisco P O	83	279
Ah	14	m	c	CHIN	San Francisco	3-Wd San Francisco	79	305
Ah	14	m	c	CHIN	Butte	Oroville Twp	70	138
Chow	45	m	c	CHIN	Shasta	Shasta P O	89	461
Gee	38	m	c	CHIN	Plumas	Plumas Twp	77	30
Im	22	m	c	CHIN	San Francisco	3-Wd San Francisco	79	304
Kay	25	m	c	CHIN	Plumas	Washington Twp	77	57
Keu	20	m	c	CHIN	Shasta	American Ranch P O	89	499
Kim	23	m	c	CHIN	Placer	Dutch Flat P O	76	407
Lar	30	m	c	CHIN	San Francisco	6-Wd San Francisco	81	64
Lin	22	m	c	CHIN	San Francisco	San Francisco P O	83	83
Ling	45	m	c	CHIN	Nevada	Bridgeport Twp	75	110
Loy	16	f	c	CHIN	Placer	Auburn P O	76	371
On	42	m	c	CHIN	El Dorado	Diamond Springs Tw	72	32
Sam	31	m	c	CHIN	Placer	Bath P O	76	423
Sang	14	m	c	CHIN	Napa	Napa Twp	75	58
Sing	39	m	c	CHIN	San Francisco	11-Wd San Francisc	84	661
Sing	28	m	c	CHIN	Solano	Suisun Twp	90	105
Slin	29	m	c	CHIN	Shasta	American Ranch P O	89	499
Tick	27	m	c	CHIN	Calaveras	San Andreas P O	70	204
Tye	28	m	c	CHIN	San Francisco	1-Wd San Francisco	79	92
Tye	21	m	c	CHIN	San Francisco	1-Wd San Francisco	79	80
Yee	18	m	c	CHIN	Napa	Napa Twp	75	58
FOOKE								
Frank	22	m	w	PORT	San Mateo	Belmont P O	87	373
Joo	34	m	c	CHIN	Klamath	Salmon Twp	73	388
FOOKES								
Helen	70	f	w	IREL	San Francisco	11-Wd San Francisc	84	507
FOOKS								
William	25	m	w	ENGL	San Francisco	11-Wd San Francisc	84	447
FOOL								
Ah	50	m	c	CHIN	Tuolumne	Sonora P O	93	322
Ah	27	m	c	CHIN	Butte	Oregon Twp	70	131
FOOLER								
Simeon A	52	m	w	NY	Plumas	Washington Twp	77	56
FOOLEY								
Annie	30	f	w	IREL	San Francisco	San Francisco P O	83	240
Francis	35	m	w	IREL	San Francisco	San Francisco P O	83	207
John	23	m	w	IREL	Nevada	Meadow Lake Twp	75	250
Michael	50	m	w	IREL	San Francisco	San Francisco P O	83	251
Patrick	41	m	w	IREL	Nevada	Meadow Lake Twp	75	252
FOON								
Ah	7	m	c	CA	Placer	Dutch Flat P O	76	406
Ah	60	m	c	CHIN	Placer	Auburn P O	76	371
Ah	52	m	c	CHIN	Placer	Auburn P O	76	383
Ah	50	m	c	CHIN	Trinity	Indian Crk	92	199
Ah	45	m	c	CHIN	Placer	Dutch Flat P O	76	406
Ah	44	m	c	CHIN	Nevada	Meadow Lake Twp	75	254
Ah	44	m	c	CHIN	Trinity	Weaverville Pct	92	228
Ah	43	m	c	CHIN	Alameda	Oakland	68	135
Ah	40	m	c	CHIN	Sacramento	Natomas Twp	77	166
Ah	40	m	c	CHIN	Shasta	French Gulch P O	89	467
Ah	40	m	c	CHIN	Trinity	Indian Crk	92	199
Ah	38	m	c	CHIN	Butte	Ophir Twp	70	99
Ah	36	m	c	CHIN	Sierra	Downieville Twp	89	521
Ah	36	m	c	CHIN	San Mateo	San Mateo P O	87	350
Ah	35	m	c	CHIN	Contra Costa	Martinez P O	71	436
Ah	34	m	c	CHIN	Tuolumne	Chinese Camp P O	93	382
Ah	31	m	c	CHIN	Nevada	Nevada Twp	75	318
Ah	30	m	c	CHIN	Trinity	Weaverville Pct	92	228
Ah	30	m	c	CHIN	Plumas	Quartz Twp	77	43
Ah	30	m	c	CHIN	Placer	Lincoln P O	76	484
Ah	29	m	c	CHIN	Nevada	Nevada Twp	75	297
Ah	29	m	c	CHIN	Plumas	Goodwin Twp	77	5
Ah	27	m	c	CHIN	Placer	Dutch Flat P O	76	407
Ah	26	m	c	CHIN	Tuolumne	Chinese Camp P O	93	388
Ah	25	m	c	CHIN	Butte	Wyandotte Twp	70	143
Ah	25	m	c	CHIN	Contra Costa	Martinez P O	71	436
Ah	25	m	c	CHIN	Tuolumne	Chinese Camp P O	93	389
Ah	23	m	c	CHIN	San Francisco	6-Wd San Francisco	81	54
Ah	22	m	c	CHIN	San Mateo	San Mateo P O	87	351
Ah	21	m	c	CHIN	Nevada	Nevada Twp	75	321
Ah	21	m	c	CHIN	San Francisco	6-Wd San Francisco	81	43
Ah	20	m	c	CHIN	Tuolumne	Chinese Camp P O	93	380
Ah	20	m	c	CHIN	San Francisco	6-Wd San Francisco	81	54
Ah	20	m	c	CHIN	Plumas	Washington Twp	77	52
Ah	19	m	c	CHIN	San Francisco	6-Wd San Francisco	81	85
Ah	18	m	c	CHIN	San Francisco	3-Wd San Francisco	79	329
Ah	18	m	c	CHIN	Alameda	Eden Twp	68	61
Ah	16	m	c	CHIN	San Francisco	3-Wd San Francisco	79	310
Ah	16	m	c	CHIN	San Francisco	11-Wd San Francisc	84	522
Hay	21	f	c	CHIN	San Francisco	11-Wd San Francisc	84	574
Kem	34	m	c	CHIN	Yuba	Marysville	93	622
Long	32	m	c	CHIN	Nevada	Bridgeport Twp	75	107
Sung	31	m	c	CHIN	Placer	Auburn P O	76	371
Tee Yong	19	m	c	CHIN	San Francisco	11-Wd San Francisc	84	546
FOONE								
Ah	27	m	c	CHIN	Nevada	Nevada Twp	75	312
FOONEY								
Lewis	37	m	w	MS	San Joaquin	Douglas Twp	86	50
FOONG								
Ah	36	m	c	CHIN	San Francisco	3-Wd San Francisco	79	310
Ah	25	m	c	CHIN	San Francisco	6-Wd San Francisco	81	67
Ah	25	m	c	CHIN	Shasta	French Gulch P O	89	467
Ah	21	m	c	CHIN	San Francisco	6-Wd San Francisco	81	68
Ah	19	m	c	CHIN	San Francisco	3-Wd San Francisco	79	303
Ah	12	f	c	CHIN	San Francisco	6-Wd San Francisco	81	78
Hang	37	m	c	CHIN	Shasta	Horsetown P O	89	506
Hee	20	m	c	CHIN	San Francisco	11-Wd San Francisc	84	548
FOOP								
Ah	39	m	c	CHIN	Butte	Chico Twp	70	27
FOOR								
---	14	m	c	CHIN	Shasta	Shasta P O	89	454
Ah	27	m	c	CHIN	San Francisco	1-Wd San Francisco	79	58
Marcks	17	m	w	SWIT	San Francisco	San Francisco P O	85	756
FOORMAN								
Simon	45	m	w	BAVA	San Francisco	8-Wd San Francisco	82	448
FOOS								
Wm	35	m	w	SCOT	San Francisco	8-Wd San Francisco	82	306
FOOSTEL								
Andrew	43	m	w	MEXI	Fresno	Millerton P O	72	155
FOOSTER								
Anton	30	m	w	PORT	San Francisco	San Francisco P O	83	54
FOOT								
Ah	41	m	c	CHIN	Tuolumne	Chinese Camp P O	93	380
Ah	38	m	c	CHIN	Shasta	Horsetown P O	89	506
Ah	36	m	c	CHIN	Solano	Vallejo	90	161
Ah	30	m	c	CHIN	Tuolumne	Big Oak Flat P O	93	393
Ah	27	m	c	CHIN	Tuolumne	Chinese Camp P O	93	370
Ah	23	m	c	CHIN	Solano	Suisun Twp	90	107
Ah	22	m	c	CHIN	Yuba	Marysville	93	631
Albert C	35	m	w	MI	Nevada	Nevada Twp	75	310
Andrew	40	m	w	NY	Trinity	North Fork Twp	92	218
E N	51	m	w	NY	San Joaquin	Elliott Twp	86	72
Forrest	18	m	w	NY	Sacramento	Alabama Twp	77	61
Gee	60	m	w	ENGL	Alameda	Oakland	68	243
Henry	21	m	w	ENGL	Sonoma	Sonoma Twp	91	446
James	38	m	w	NY	San Diego	Julian Dist	78	471
James A	25	m	w	PA	Colusa	Colusa Twp	71	282
Joseph	50	m	w	PORT	Alameda	Washington Twp	68	298
L H	40	m	w	NY	Sacramento	1-Wd Sacramento	77	172
Leonard	24	m	w	ENGL	Yuba	Rose Bar Twp	93	659
Loman	50	m	w	PRUS	San Francisco	5-Wd San Francisco	81	20
M	11	f	w	CA	Los Angeles	Los Angeles	73	570
M C	41	m	w	NY	Tuolumne	Big Oak Flat P O	93	402
Milo	64	m	w	VT	Contra Costa	Martinez P O	71	438
Myron	55	m	w	NY	Nevada	Eureka Twp	75	133
Samuel S	23	m	w	CT	Sacramento	2-Wd Sacramento	77	225
Thomas	30	m	w	IREL	San Francisco	7-Wd San Francisco	81	201
Tung	23	m	c	CHIN	San Francisco	11-Wd San Francisc	84	661
V L	25	m	w	CANA	Alameda	Oakland	68	141
FOOTE								
Charles E	45	m	w	KY	Calaveras	San Andreas P O	70	158
Horace	28	m	w	IN	Santa Clara	1-Wd San Jose	88	227
Joseph	38	m	w	HOLL	San Francisco	San Francisco P O	83	303
Oliver	24	m	w	IN	Santa Clara	Fremont Twp	88	63
Oliver G	58	m	w	CT	Santa Clara	Redwood Twp	88	118
Storm R	28	m	w	OH	Santa Clara	1-Wd San Jose	88	242
W W	24	m	w	MS	Alameda	Oakland	68	181
William	44	m	w	NY	El Dorado	Diamond Springs Tw	72	24
Wm	38	m	w	NY	Sacramento	4-Wd Sacramento	77	369
FOOTHACHER								
L	37	m	w	ME	Solano	Vallejo	90	197
FOOTMAN								
Fredk	19	m	w	PRUS	San Francisco	5-Wd San Francisco	81	8
Henry	23	m	w	SC	Sacramento	Georgianna Twp	77	126
James	30	m	w	ME	San Mateo	Half Moon Bay P O	87	407
Jno	23	m	w	NY	San Francisco	5-Wd San Francisco	81	32

© 2001 by Heritage Quest. All rights reserved.

California 1870 Census

Name	Age	S	R	B-PL	County	Locale	Roll	Pg
John	30	m	w	NY	San Francisco	San Francisco P O	83	246
Orrin	17	m	w	ME	San Mateo	Woodside P O	87	385
Thos J	66	m	w	MA	Mariposa	Mariposa P O	74	131
FOOY								
Ah	17	f	c	CHIN	San Francisco	3-Wd San Francisco	79	307
Jo	21	m	c	CHIN	San Francisco	3-Wd San Francisco	79	307
Yan	19	m	c	CHIN	Shasta	Shasta P O	89	452
FOP								
Ah	40	f	c	CHIN	San Francisco	San Francisco P O	80	521
Ah	37	m	c	CHIN	Fresno	Millerton P O	72	201
Ah	36	m	c	CHIN	San Francisco	San Francisco P O	80	440
Ah	20	m	c	CHIN	Sacramento	1-Wd Sacramento	77	193
FOPIANA								
Frank	38	m	w	ITAL	Calaveras	Copperopolis P O	70	244
FOPIANO								
Antonio	62	m	w	ITAL	San Luis Obispo	San Luis Obispo Tw	87	310
FOPIANON								
Angelo	63	m	w	ITAL	Mariposa	Maxwell Crk P O	74	146
FOPLAN								
Francisco	24	m	w	ITAL	San Francisco	San Francisco P O	85	851
FOPLITZ								
Fabian	40	m	w	PRUS	San Francisco	8-Wd San Francisco	82	478
FOR								
Ah	6	f	c	CA	San Francisco	San Francisco P O	80	437
Ah	39	m	c	CHIN	San Francisco	San Francisco P O	80	456
Ah	36	m	c	CHIN	San Francisco	San Francisco P O	80	521
Ah	36	m	c	CHIN	San Francisco	San Francisco P O	80	519
Ah	36	m	c	CHIN	San Francisco	San Francisco P O	80	521
Ah	35	m	c	CHIN	San Francisco	San Francisco P O	80	520
Ah	33	m	c	CHIN	San Francisco	6-Wd San Francisco	81	47
Ah	32	m	c	CHIN	San Francisco	San Francisco P O	80	508
Ah	29	m	c	CHIN	San Francisco	San Francisco P O	80	512
Ah	26	m	c	CHIN	San Francisco	San Francisco P O	80	515
Ah	26	m	c	CHIN	San Francisco	San Francisco P O	80	508
Ah	25	m	c	CHIN	San Francisco	8-Wd San Francisco	82	459
Ah	25	f	c	CHIN	San Francisco	San Francisco P O	80	437
Ah	24	m	c	CHIN	San Francisco	San Francisco P O	80	514
Ah	18	m	c	CHIN	San Francisco	2-Wd San Francisco	79	282
Ah	16	f	c	CHIN	San Francisco	6-Wd San Francisco	81	74
Ah	12	m	c	CHIN	San Francisco	2-Wd San Francisco	79	259
Chee Ah	27	m	c	CHIN	San Francisco	3-Wd San Francisco	79	310
Chi	30	m	c	CHIN	Yuba	Marysville	93	628
See	45	m	c	CHIN	Yuba	Marysville	93	628
FORAM								
Wm	35	m	w	MA	Tehama	Red Bluff	92	182
FORAN								
James	48	m	w	IREL	Mariposa	Mariposa P O	74	124
M	58	m	w	IREL	San Joaquin	Douglas Twp	86	30
Timothy	32	m	w	IREL	Butte	Chico Twp	70	42
William A	18	m	w	PA	Mariposa	Mariposa P O	74	123
FORAY								
Frank	50	m	w	FRAN	San Mateo	Half Moon Bay P O	87	389
Pat	30	m	w	IREL	Mono	Bridgeport P O	74	284
FORBACH								
George	30	m	w	PRUS	San Francisco	San Francisco P O	80	479
William	36	m	w	FRAN	San Francisco	San Francisco P O	80	458
FORBES								
A F	22	f	w	AUSL	Sierra	Lincoln Twp	89	551
A M	45	m	w	ENGL	Klamath	Trinidad Twp	73	390
Aaron	32	m	w	MA	Solano	Vacaville Twp	90	126
Alex	40	m	w	MO	Humboldt	Pacific Twp	72	290
Alexander	48	m	w	SCOT	San Francisco	6-Wd San Francisco	81	148
Alexander R	43	m	w	CANA	Yuba	Parks Bar Twp	93	651
Andrew B	46	m	w	NJ	Alameda	Washington Twp	68	273
Andrew B	45	m	w	NJ	San Francisco	7-Wd San Francisco	81	286
Annie	35	f	w	MA	San Francisco	San Francisco P O	83	396
Archibald	41	m	w	SCOT	San Francisco	6-Wd San Francisco	81	88
Charles H	27	m	w	CA	Los Angeles	Los Angeles Twp	73	492
Chas	10	m	w	MI	Butte	Chico Twp	70	36
Christopher C	41	m	w	IN	El Dorado	Mountain Twp	72	69
Columbus C	38	m	w	IN	Amador	Fiddletown P O	69	439
David	65	m	w	NY	San Francisco	San Francisco P O	83	414
Geo	33	m	w	MO	San Joaquin	Dent Twp	86	28
George	55	m	w	OH	Sacramento	2-Wd Sacramento	77	225
George	36	m	w	PA	Alameda	Washington Twp	68	293
George	28	m	w	WI	Klamath	South Fork Twp	73	385
H	26	m	w	CANA	Sierra	Gibson Twp	89	544
J	46	m	w	SCOT	Sierra	Lincoln Twp	89	551
J F H	50	m	w	FRAN	Sierra	Alleghany & Forest	89	534
James	70	m	w	SCOT	Placer	Newcastle Twp	76	475
James	47	m	w	PA	Butte	Wyandotte Twp	70	145
James	41	m	w	GA	San Francisco	1-Wd San Francisco	79	116
James	34	m	w	IL	Klamath	South Fork Twp	73	382
James A	27	m	w	CA	Santa Clara	Santa Clara Twp	88	175
James Alex	65	m	w	SCOT	Santa Clara	Santa Clara Twp	88	146
Jane	14	f	w	ENGL	San Francisco	2-Wd San Francisco	79	240
Jas	42	m	w	SCOT	Solano	Vallejo	90	154
Jennie	23	f	w	MD	San Francisco	8-Wd San Francisco	82	335
John	43	m	w	SCOT	San Francisco	San Francisco P O	83	114
John	38	m	w	SCOT	San Francisco	1-Wd San Francisco	79	97
John	30	m	b	WIND	San Francisco	6-Wd San Francisco	81	99
John	27	m	w	MO	Yuba	Marysville Twp	93	567
John C	35	m	w	AR	Monterey	Castroville Twp	74	340
John E	39	m	w	ME	Yolo	Cache Crk Twp	93	454
John R	36	m	w	OH	San Bernardino	San Bernardino Twp	78	453
Louis	25	m	w	CA	Santa Clara	2-Wd San Jose	88	290
Margaret	26	f	w	SCOT	San Francisco	San Francisco P O	80	392

Name	Age	S	R	B-PL	County	Locale	Roll	Pg
Mary	10	f	w	MI	Butte	Chico Twp	70	35
Mary A	24	f	w	PA	Santa Cruz	Santa Cruz Twp	89	380
Peter	42	m	w	PA	Sierra	Gibson Twp	89	541
Peter	21	m	w	CANA	Inyo	Bishop Crk Twp	73	315
R	27	m	w	CANA	Sierra	Downieville Twp	89	514
Robert	58	m	w	NC	Merced	Snelling P O	74	276
Robt	37	m	w	ENGL	Sacramento	3-Wd Sacramento	77	273
Somerville	46	m	w	ENGL	Santa Clara	Fremont Twp	88	63
Thos	49	m	w	NY	Sierra	Gibson Twp	89	538
William	42	m	w	OH	Lake	Lakeport	73	406
William	39	m	w	NY	Santa Clara	Santa Clara Twp	88	150
William	26	m	w	IREL	Solano	Silveyville Twp	90	79
William	22	m	w	CANA	Humboldt	Arcata Twp	72	225
Wm	25	m	w	GA	San Luis Obispo	San Luis Obispo Tw	87	315
FORBS								
Andrew	41	m	w	IREL	Solano	Silveyville Twp	90	78
Eliza Jane	21	f	w	WI	Humboldt	Eel Rvr Twp	72	255
James O	56	m	w	VT	El Dorado	Georgetown Twp	72	45
William	27	m	w	PA	Inyo	Bishop Crk Twp	73	312
FORBUSH								
Cephas	51	m	w	MD	Los Angeles	Wilmington Twp	73	643
Josiah	29	m	w	ME	San Joaquin	Douglas Twp	86	37
Rosewell	49	m	w	NY	Santa Barbara	Santa Barbara P O	87	450
FORCADA								
Giuseppe	39	m	w	ITAL	San Francisco	11-Wd San Francisc	84	594
FORCADE								
F	18	f	w	PA	Solano	Vallejo	90	197
Joseph	60	m	w	FRAN	Fresno	Millerton P O	72	146
FORCADO								
Giuseppe	31	m	w	SPAI	San Francisco	11-Wd San Francisc	84	591
FORCAR								
Eliza	12	f	w	CA	Santa Clara	Gilroy Twp	88	87
FORCE								
Ah	24	m	c	CHIN	Amador	Fiddletown P O	69	427
William	40	m	w	CANA	Mendocino	Ukiah Twp	74	244
FORCEY								
Alfred	32	m	w	FRAN	San Francisco	8-Wd San Francisco	82	470
FORD								
A A	40	m	w	IA	Sacramento	4-Wd Sacramento	77	373
A J	36	m	w	KY	Merced	Snelling P O	74	261
A R	45	m	w	MA	Solano	Vallejo	90	209
Abram	35	m	w	VA	Yuba	Marysville	93	581
Albert	46	m	w	MA	Merced	Snelling P O	74	270
Alexander	28	m	w	IREL	San Francisco	San Francisco P O	83	294
Alexander	27	m	w	MO	Sonoma	Analy Twp	91	224
Andrew B	32	m	w	VT	Sonoma	Salt Point	91	389
Andrew Jackson	38	m	w	NH	Plumas	Indian Twp	77	12
Ann	46	f	w	IREL	San Joaquin	Oneal Twp	86	113
Anne	32	f	w	IREL	San Francisco	1-Wd San Francisco	79	23
Annie	13	f	w	OR	San Francisco	San Francisco P O	80	337
Anthony	35	m	w	IREL	Butte	Bidwell Twp	70	1
Anthony	32	m	w	IREL	San Francisco	San Francisco P O	80	376
Asa R	23	m	w	WI	Napa	Napa	75	51
B	50	f	w	IREL	San Joaquin	2-Wd Stockton	86	163
Barnard	42	m	w	IREL	Humboldt	Arcata Twp	72	232
Bartholimew	35	m	w	IREL	Trinity	Weaverville Pct	92	231
Benjamin F	33	m	w	MO	San Luis Obispo	Morro Twp	87	283
Bridget	65	f	w	IREL	San Francisco	2-Wd San Francisco	79	191
Byron	45	m	w	NY	San Francisco	San Francisco P O	83	292
C H	46	m	w	MA	Alameda	Oakland	68	202
Catherine	28	f	w	IREL	San Francisco	8-Wd San Francisco	82	421
Catherine	25	f	w	IREL	Marin	San Rafael	74	51
Chancey	53	m	w	CT	Nevada	Nevada Twp	75	289
Charles	46	m	w	NJ	Santa Cruz	Watsonville	89	364
Charles	40	m	w	MA	San Francisco	8-Wd San Francisco	82	479
Charles	37	m	w	INDI	San Francisco	San Francisco P O	83	68
Charles D	32	m	w	NY	Santa Cruz	Santa Cruz	89	413
Charles G	32	m	w	NY	Santa Cruz	Santa Cruz	89	408
Charlotte	70	f	w	SCOT	San Francisco	8-Wd San Francisco	82	362
Chas	15	m	w	NY	San Francisco	11-Wd San Francisc	84	588
Clara	33	f	w	MD	Butte	Ophir Twp	70	110
Cyrie	25	m	w	ME	San Francisco	1-Wd San Francisco	79	71
Daniel	54	m	w	SWED	San Mateo	Woodside P O	87	387
Daniel	47	m	w	IREL	San Mateo	Redwood Twp	87	367
Daniel	35	m	w	IREL	San Francisco	San Francisco P O	83	6
Daniel	35	m	w	MA	Santa Clara	Santa Clara Twp	88	175
Ebenezer	72	m	w	ME	Santa Clara	Redwood Twp	88	120
Ed	25	m	w	IREL	Santa Clara	Almaden Twp	88	9
Edward	55	m	w	SCOT	Placer	Gold Run Twp	76	397
Edward	40	m	w	IREL	Santa Clara	San Jose Twp	88	220
Edward	34	m	w	AUST	Sonoma	Bodega Twp	91	259
Elihue	50	m	w	NY	San Francisco	San Francisco P O	85	875
Ellen	30	f	w	IREL	San Francisco	8-Wd San Francisco	82	333
Erastus	41	m	w	MI	Contra Costa	Martinez P O	71	380
F	47	m	w	IREL	San Joaquin	2-Wd Stockton	86	162
Geo O	19	m	w	ME	Nevada	Meadow Lake Twp	75	248
Geo W	22	m	w	MO	Sonoma	Petaluma Twp	91	358
George	56	m	b	VA	Sacramento	2-Wd Sacramento	77	226
George	46	m	w	OH	El Dorado	Cosumnes Twp	72	16
George	30	m	w	NY	San Francisco	3-Wd San Francisco	79	314
George W	49	m	w	PA	Napa	Napa	75	43
George W	35	m	b	VA	Sacramento	2-Wd Sacramento	77	230
H C	50	m	w	MA	Sierra	Lincoln Twp	89	549
H D	35	m	w	KY	Amador	Jackson P O	69	320
Henrietta	30	f	w	PRUS	San Francisco	San Francisco P O	80	474
Henry	46	m	w	SCOT	San Francisco	3-Wd San Francisco	79	300
Henry	37	m	w	IREL	Placer	Bath P O	76	446

Series M593

© 2001 by Heritage Quest. All rights reserved.

Name	Age	S	R	B-PL	County	Locale	Roll	Pg
						Series M593		
Henry	26	m	w	VT	San Francisco	San Francisco P O	83	258
Henry E	15	m	w	CT	Tulare	Tule Rvr Twp	92	270
Henry P	40	m	w	OH	Butte	Kimshew Tpw	70	82
Honora	60	f	w	IREL	San Francisco	San Francisco P O	83	14
Isaac	39	m	w	ENGL	Sacramento	3-Wd Sacramento	77	257
J C	71	m	w	PRUS	Alameda	Oakland	68	171
J F	38	m	w	US	Sacramento	1-Wd Sacramento	77	182
James	52	m	w	NH	Plumas	Indian Twp	77	12
James	35	m	w	IREL	Santa Clara	San Jose Twp	88	210
James	33	m	w	IREL	San Francisco	6-Wd San Francisco	81	150
James	30	m	w	IREL	San Joaquin	Oneal Twp	86	115
James	29	m	w	ENGL	San Francisco	7-Wd San Francisco	81	206
James	28	m	w	ENGL	San Francisco	1-Wd San Francisco	79	88
James D	36	m	w	IL	Yolo	Putah Twp	93	514
James G	22	m	w	MO	Yolo	Cache Crk Twp	93	439
James M	6	m	w	CA	Napa	Napa Twp	75	72
Janes	40	f	w	IL	Alameda	Murray Twp	68	114
Jas	30	m	w	OH	Solano	Vallejo	90	151
Jasper	26	m	w	MO	Colusa	Colusa Twp	71	274
Jeremiah	61	m	w	MD	San Francisco	8-Wd San Francisco	82	486
Jeremiah	36	m	w	CT	San Francisco	11-Wd San Francisc	84	693
Jeremiah	23	m	w	IREL	Merced	Snelling P O	74	272
Jerome B	49	m	w	VT	Mendocino	Big Rvr Twp	74	158
Jerry	24	m	w	MO	Butte	Chico Twp	70	40
Jesse	24	m	w	MO	San Luis Obispo	Santa Rosa Twp	87	317
Johanna	24	f	w	IREL	San Francisco	11-Wd San Francisc	84	607
John	45	m	w	IREL	San Francisco	7-Wd San Francisco	81	192
John	40	m	w	IREL	Alameda	Eden Twp	68	63
John	40	m	w	IREL	Nevada	Meadow Lake Twp	75	258
John	40	m	w	NY	San Francisco	5-Wd San Francisco	81	9
John	40	m	b	KY	Yolo	Buckeye Twp	93	407
John	40	m	w	IREL	Tuolumne	Chinese Camp P O	93	370
John	40	m	w	IREL	San Francisco	1-Wd San Francisco	79	97
John	40	m	w	IREL	San Francisco	1-Wd San Francisco	79	3
John	38	m	w	NC	Tuolumne	Chinese Camp P O	93	385
John	38	m	w	IREL	Kern	Linns Valley P O	73	343
John	37	m	w	IREL	Nevada	Grass Valley Twp	75	213
John	37	m	w	IREL	San Francisco	2-Wd San Francisco	79	181
John	33	m	w	MD	Mendocino	Little Lake Twp	74	198
John	29	m	w	MA	Solano	Vallejo	90	207
John	28	m	w	ENGL	Alameda	Brooklyn	68	37
John	27	m	w	IREL	San Francisco	11-Wd San Francisc	84	650
John	26	m	w	IREL	Yuba	Linda Twp	93	557
John	24	m	w	LA	Santa Barbara	Santa Maria P O	87	514
John	21	m	w	PA	Los Angeles	Santa Ana Twp	73	601
John Henry	10	m	w	CA	Nevada	Grass Valley Twp	75	177
John L	34	m	w	CT	Calaveras	Copperopolis P O	70	227
John P	58	m	w	MA	Placer	Bath P O	76	438
John Q	35	m	b	OH	Yolo	Cottonwood Twp	93	459
Johnson P	45	m	w	NY	Santa Clara	Redwood Twp	88	120
Joseph A	29	m	w	MD	San Francisco	6-Wd San Francisco	81	93
Joseph C	28	m	w	NY	San Francisco	San Francisco P O	83	373
Josephine	27	f	w	PA	San Francisco	7-Wd San Francisco	81	238
Kate	28	f	w	IREL	San Francisco	8-Wd San Francisco	82	440
Kate	25	f	w	IREL	San Francisco	San Francisco P O	83	415
Katy	17	f	w	CA	Santa Clara	Gilroy Twp	88	83
Labin	33	m	w	MO	Santa Cruz	Santa Cruz Twp	89	393
Lila P	42	m	w	NY	San Francisco	2-Wd San Francisco	79	203
Louis	25	m	w	FRAN	Solano	Benicia	90	18
Lovel W	30	m	w	ENGL	San Francisco	6-Wd San Francisco	81	145
Maggie	29	f	w	IREL	San Francisco	San Francisco P O	83	399
Margaret	38	f	i	CA	Yolo	Buckeye Twp	93	407
Margaret	29	f	w	IREL	Nevada	Nevada Twp	75	286
Martha	34	f	w	OH	Alameda	Eden Twp	68	66
Martin	36	m	w	IREL	Nevada	Grass Valley Twp	75	178
Martin	30	m	w	IREL	Nevada	Grass Valley Twp	75	197
Mary	35	f	w	IREL	San Francisco	San Francisco P O	83	144
Mary	33	f	w	IREL	San Francisco	7-Wd San Francisco	81	164
Mary	29	f	w	IREL	San Francisco	7-Wd San Francisco	81	169
Mary	28	f	w	CANA	San Francisco	San Francisco P O	85	768
Mary	23	f	w	IREL	San Francisco	11-Wd San Francisc	84	631
Mary	16	f	w	CA	San Francisco	8-Wd San Francisco	82	470
Michael	36	m	w	IREL	San Francisco	San Francisco P O	85	780
Michael	35	m	w	IREL	San Francisco	7-Wd San Francisco	81	286
Michael	29	m	w	IREL	San Francisco	3-Wd San Francisco	79	308
Michael	24	m	w	MO	Klamath	Camp Gaston	73	373
Michael	14	m	w	MA	Santa Cruz	Santa Cruz	89	415
Michl	45	m	w	IREL	San Francisco	1-Wd San Francisco	79	78
Michl	35	m	w	IREL	San Francisco	1-Wd San Francisco	79	15
Michl	30	m	w	IREL	San Francisco	1-Wd San Francisco	79	59
Millon	45	m	w	VT	Sutter	Sutter Twp	92	125
Nat	43	m	b	NY	Nevada	Nevada Twp	75	278
Nathan	30	m	w	KY	San Francisco	11-Wd San Francisc	84	527
Nettie	22	f	w	GA	Tulare	Visalia	92	290
Pat	37	m	w	IREL	San Joaquin	3-Wd Stockton	86	236
Pat	35	m	w	IREL	San Francisco	7-Wd San Francisco	81	279
Pat	23	m	w	IREL	San Francisco	11-Wd San Francisc	84	662
Patrick	45	m	w	IREL	San Francisco	San Francisco P O	85	743
Patrick	40	m	w	IREL	Stanislaus	Emory Twp	92	17
Patrick	35	m	w	IREL	Santa Clara	Santa Clara Twp	88	157
Patrick	18	m	w	ME	Klamath	Camp Gaston	73	373
R M	44	m	w	MO	Amador	Drytown P O	69	419
R W	38	m	w	ME	Tuolumne	Big Oak Flat P O	93	406
Richard	48	m	w	ENGL	Nevada	Grass Valley Twp	75	231
Richard H	59	m	w	NH	Alpine	Silver Mtn P O	69	307
Robert	47	m	w	CT	Marin	Sausalito Twp	74	69
Robert	44	m	w	MD	San Francisco	11-Wd San Francisc	84	519
Saml	21	m	w	ENGL	San Francisco	1-Wd San Francisco	79	88
Samuel	28	m	w	IREL	Nevada	Nevada Twp	75	310
Samuel J	42	m	w	TN	El Dorado	Cosumnes Twp	72	14
Silva	63	f	w	NY	Nevada	Bridgeport Twp	75	119
Sylvester	33	m	w	IL	Placer	Summit P O	76	496
Sylvester	32	m	w	IREL	Nevada	Grass Valley Twp	75	199
T	40	m	w	IREL	Alameda	Oakland	68	220
Thomas	33	m	w	PRUS	San Francisco	6-Wd San Francisco	81	97
Thomas	32	m	w	IREL	Del Norte	Mountain Twp	71	474
Thomas	30	m	w	ENGL	San Francisco	1-Wd San Francisco	79	11
Thomas	28	m	w	CANA	San Francisco	8-Wd San Francisco	82	443
Thomas	28	m	w	IREL	Santa Clara	Fremont Twp	88	41
Timothy	40	m	w	IREL	San Francisco	8-Wd San Francisco	82	352
Timothy	40	m	w	IREL	San Francisco	8-Wd San Francisco	82	319
Timothy J	30	m	w	IREL	San Francisco	San Francisco P O	83	3
W B	40	m	w	NC	San Joaquin	Douglas Twp	86	46
Wallace	29	m	w	NY	San Francisco	7-Wd San Francisco	81	221
William	57	m	w	VA	Siskiyou	Surprise Valley Tw	89	639
William	45	m	w	NY	Contra Costa	Martinez Twp	71	352
William	43	m	w	SCOT	Monterey	Alisal Twp	74	303
William	40	m	w	ENGL	San Francisco	2-Wd San Francisco	79	212
William	39	m	w	IL	Mendocino	Ukiah Twp	74	240
William	35	m	w	ME	Los Angeles	Los Angeles	73	558
William	35	m	w	MD	San Francisco	8-Wd San Francisco	82	362
William	32	m	w	AR	Klamath	Liberty Twp	73	374
William	26	m	w	AL	Inyo	Cerro Gordo Twp	73	321
Winiford	66	f	w	IREL	Santa Clara	San Jose Twp	88	216
Wm	41	m	w	NY	Plumas	Quartz Twp	77	35
Wm	38	m	w	IREL	San Francisco	11-Wd San Francisc	84	685
Wm	34	m	w	ENGL	Santa Clara	Gilroy Twp	88	99
Wm H	40	m	w	NH	San Francisco	8-Wd San Francisco	82	324
Wm J	31	m	w	VT	Sacramento	4-Wd Sacramento	77	327
Wolcott	53	m	w	CT	Placer	Dutch Flat P O	76	401
FORDAHL								
James	54	m	w	NORW	San Francisco	2-Wd San Francisco	79	147
FORDE								
Mary	44	f	w	PA	San Francisco	San Francisco P O	80	485
FORDECILLO								
Jose	6M	m	w	CA	Santa Clara	1-Wd San Jose	88	256
FORDEM								
Saml	31	m	w	NY	San Joaquin	Elkhorn Twp	86	60
FORDER								
Joseph	36	m	w	NY	San Francisco	11-Wd San Francisc	84	430
FORDESILLA								
Bernardo	18	m	w	CHIL	Santa Clara	Alviso Twp	88	29
FORDHAM								
Fredk	72	m	w	NY	Shasta	Shasta P O	89	461
J	18	m	w	ENGL	Alameda	Oakland	68	183
Maria	72	f	w	CT	Siskiyou	Scott Valley Twp	89	615
P	32	m	w	PRUS	San Francisco	7-Wd San Francisco	81	226
Robert	42	m	w	NY	San Francisco	San Francisco P O	80	410
FORDMAN								
Dietrick	24	m	w	PRUS	San Francisco	3-Wd San Francisco	79	326
FORDO								
Joseph	26	m	w	IREL	Santa Clara	2-Wd San Jose	88	317
FORDON								
Rachael	20	f	w	PRUS	San Joaquin	2-Wd Stockton	86	179
FORDS								
Joseph	34	m	w	ENGL	Marin	San Rafael Twp	74	59
R	24	m	w	WURT	Sierra	Butte Twp	89	508
FORDSMAN								
James G	40	m	w	KY	Stanislaus	Empire Twp	92	52
FORDSON								
Polson	21	m	w	SWED	Santa Clara	Milpitas Twp	88	110
Wm	35	m	w	NH	San Joaquin	Elliott Twp	86	80
FORDU								
John	40	m	w	FRAN	San Francisco	San Francisco P O	80	468
FORDY								
Calhoun	37	m	w	MI	Calaveras	Copperopolis P O	70	263
FORDYCE								
James M	27	m	w	IREL	Marin	Sausalito Twp	74	72
FORE								
Edward	28	m	w	MO	Solano	Vacaville Twp	90	135
George	17	m	w	NY	Solano	Vacaville Twp	90	126
John	17	m	w	CA	Solano	Vacaville Twp	90	123
Thomas L	37	m	w	KY	Solano	Vacaville Twp	90	125
FOREE								
George	26	m	w	CA	San Francisco	7-Wd San Francisco	81	165
Henriette	13	f	w	CA	Solano	Vacaville Twp	90	121
FOREMAMAN								
George	20	m	w	PA	Alameda	Oakland	68	142
FOREMAN								
Antone	50	m	w	UNKN	San Joaquin	2-Wd Stockton	86	166
D F	56	m	w	OH	Mendocino	Ukiah Twp	74	244
George	42	m	w	PA	San Joaquin	Douglas Twp	86	34
Hugh	41	m	w	OH	Colusa	Monroe Twp	71	320
J L	42	m	w	KY	Merced	Snelling P O	74	247
J R	42	m	w	OH	Mendocino	Round Valley Twp	74	219
John	48	m	w	ENGL	San Francisco	San Francisco P O	80	408
John	44	m	w	PA	Sonoma	Mendocino Twp	91	300
John	37	m	w	MI	San Joaquin	2-Wd Stockton	86	205
Mary	40	f	w	MO	Merced	Snelling P O	74	250
Sam	43	m	w	PA	San Joaquin	Douglas Twp	86	33
Samuel	17	m	w	CA	Santa Cruz	Santa Cruz	89	419
Sands W	21	m	w	IL	San Francisco	6-Wd San Francisco	81	140
Solomon W	48	m	w	OH	Yolo	Cache Crk Twp	93	429
Stephen W	35	m	w	IL	Santa Cruz	Santa Cruz Twp	89	396

© 2001 by Heritage Quest. All rights reserved.

California 1870 Census

Name	Age	S	R	B-PL	County	Locale	Roll	Pg
Susannah	57	f	w	OH	Santa Cruz	Santa Cruz	89	433
William	49	m	w	MO	Contra Costa	Martinez P O	71	401
William	42	m	w	MO	Plumas	Indian Twp	77	10
Wm	44	m	w	OH	Butte	Bidwell Twp	70	1
Wm H	44	m	w	IL	Solano	Rio Vista Twp	90	61
FOREN								
Mary J	26	f	w	IL	Butte	Ophir Twp	70	118
Pat	51	m	w	IREL	San Francisco	7-Wd San Francisco	81	231
Peter	45	m	w	CANA	Nevada	Eureka Twp	75	126
FORES								
Rosalia	14	f	i	CA	Monterey	Monterey	74	361
FOREST								
Anna	45	f	w	US	Placer	Colfax P O	76	388
Edward	28	m	w	NH	Solano	Montezuma Twp	90	68
Edwin	30	m	w	NH	Solano	Rio Vista Twp	90	61
Isaac	22	m	w	TN	Shasta	Millville P O	89	486
John	39	m	w	PA	Monterey	San Antonio Twp	74	316
John	20	m	w	OH	Butte	Oregon Twp	70	129
Thos	32	m	w	IREL	Butte	Chico Twp	70	40
William	28	m	w	MS	San Francisco	San Francisco P O	80	531
FORESTER								
Andrew J	40	m	w	MO	Sonoma	Analy Twp	91	239
Eliza S	54	f	w	ENGL	San Francisco	San Francisco P O	83	170
G W	42	m	w	KY	Napa	Napa	75	22
James M	38	m	w	TN	Calaveras	Copperopolis P O	70	257
John	25	m	w	NY	San Francisco	1-Wd San Francisco	79	125
Lucius B	35	m	w	OH	Contra Costa	Martinez P O	71	378
Thomas	49	m	w	SCOT	Mendocino	Point Arena Twp	74	224
FORETTA								
L	38	m	w	CA	Alameda	Oakland	68	135
FOREY								
Chas	35	m	w	FRAN	Fresno	Millerton P O	72	158
Edmund	30	m	w	FRAN	San Francisco	San Francisco P O	80	461
William	28	m	w	IREL	Nevada	Grass Valley Twp	75	222
FORFAIR								
Herman	54	m	w	FRAN	Santa Clara	Fremont Twp	88	60
Jean	53	m	w	FRAN	Santa Clara	Fremont Twp	88	50
FORGART								
Wm	30	m	w	IREL	San Joaquin	1-Wd Stockton	86	157
FORGARTICEE								
A	46	m	w	ITAL	Amador	Jackson P O	69	339
FORGARTY								
John	37	m	w	IREL	San Francisco	7-Wd San Francisco	81	221
Patrick	47	m	w	IREL	San Francisco	7-Wd San Francisco	81	203
William	40	m	w	IREL	San Francisco	7-Wd San Francisco	81	181
FORGATE								
William N	44	m	w	NY	Santa Clara	Santa Clara Twp	88	142
FORGET								
John	24	m	w	FRAN	Nevada	Meadow Lake Twp	75	248
Noel	32	m	w	CANA	Contra Costa	Martinez P O	71	436
FORGEY								
Madison	45	m	w	OH	Klamath	Salmon Twp	73	388
Tommy	25	f	i	CA	Klamath	Salmon Twp	73	388
FORH								
Ah	3	m	c	CHIN	Placer	Dutch Flat P O	76	408
FORI								
Ah	21	f	c	CHIN	San Francisco	2-Wd San Francisco	79	216
FORIBIO								
Jose V	45	m	w	CHIL	Santa Barbara	Santa Barbara P O	87	492
FORIS								
Francisco	31	m	i	MEXI	Inyo	Cerro Gordo Twp	73	322
FORISS								
Manuel	28	m	i	MEXI	Inyo	Cerro Gordo Twp	73	322
FORK								
Ah	48	m	c	CHIN	Calaveras	San Andreas P O	70	169
Ah	35	m	c	CHIN	Alameda	Oakland	68	250
Ah	23	m	c	CHIN	Alameda	Oakland	68	250
Ah	20	m	c	CHIN	Alameda	Oakland	68	254
FORKAYER								
Carma	32	m	w	CHIL	Amador	Fiddletown P O	69	432
FORKE								
Franklin	40	m	w	NY	Nevada	Grass Valley Twp	75	232
Frederick	25	m	w	WALE	San Mateo	San Mateo P O	87	349
FORKEN								
James	24	m	w	IREL	Sutter	Sutter Twp	92	129
FORKER								
Aga	16	f	w	PA	Amador	Ione City P O	69	352
FORKINTO								
Jesus	38	m	w	MEXI	San Bernardino	San Salvador Twp	78	459
FORLAES								
John	33	m	w	CA	San Francisco	2-Wd San Francisco	79	190
FORLER								
Harriett	64	f	w	NY	San Francisco	San Francisco P O	83	286
FORLEY								
Frank	26	m	w	IREL	San Francisco	2-Wd San Francisco	79	215
Michael	43	m	w	AL	Monterey	Salinas Twp	74	306
FORLIO								
J	29	m	w	FRAN	Santa Clara	Almaden Twp	88	2
FORLLATI								
Urfula	45	m	w	ITAL	San Francisco	San Francisco P O	80	464
FORLY								
Joe	69	m	w	NY	Placer	Dutch Flat P O	76	415
John	34	m	w	VA	San Mateo	Woodside P O	87	387
FORM								
Ah	41	m	c	CHIN	Nevada	Eureka Twp	75	137
FORMAN								
Charles	18	m	w	CA	San Mateo	Redwood Twp	87	368
Henry	40	m	w	PRUS	Inyo	Lone Pine Twp	73	330
Herman	34	m	w	PRUS	San Francisco	San Francisco P O	80	468
John	43	m	w	PA	Monterey	Monterey Twp	74	346
John C	48	m	w	KY	Yolo	Buckeye Twp	93	415
Mary	26	f	w	KY	Los Angeles	El Monte Twp	73	459
Peter	50	m	w	BADE	San Joaquin	Elliott Twp	86	73
FORMANT								
Jean	30	m	w	FRAN	San Francisco	6-Wd San Francisco	81	40
FORMCALT								
Francis	47	m	w	FRAN	Calaveras	San Andreas P O	70	199
FORMELLA								
Bernard	58	m	w	SPAI	Contra Costa	Martinez P O	71	440
FORMSCHLAG								
John	32	m	w	PRUS	Sonoma	Vallejo Twp	91	457
FORNAH								
Jno	19	m	w	ITAL	San Francisco	11-Wd San Francisc	84	710
FORNAHURST								
John	35	m	w	HANO	San Francisco	1-Wd San Francisco	79	127
FORNCEUR								
---	69	m	w	FRAN	Alameda	Oakland	68	137
FORNEE								
Jean	38	f	w	FRAN	San Francisco	San Francisco P O	80	455
FORNER								
Eliza	85	f	w	VA	San Joaquin	2-Wd Stockton	86	211
Jacob R	42	m	w	BAVA	San Francisco	2-Wd San Francisco	79	156
Joseph C	45	m	w	PA	Humboldt	South Fork Twp	72	300
Wm	50	m	w	VA	San Joaquin	2-Wd Stockton	86	211
FORNET								
Pasqual	45	m	w	KY	Calaveras	San Andreas P O	70	220
FORNEY								
---	24	m	w	PA	Santa Barbara	Santa Barbara P O	87	466
Dennis	22	m	w	SWIT	El Dorado	Placerville	72	119
Jerry	40	m	b	NC	Amador	Ione City P O	69	365
John	50	m	b	TN	San Joaquin	Castoria Twp	86	3
John	35	m	w	IREL	San Francisco	1-Wd San Francisco	79	5
FORNIE								
Carlus	33	m	w	SWIT	El Dorado	Georgetown Twp	72	36
FORNIER								
Jacque	38	m	w	FRAN	San Francisco	San Francisco P O	80	347
Jacque	38	m	w	FRAN	San Francisco	San Francisco P O	80	348
Louis	46	m	w	MA	Amador	Sutter Crk P O	69	407
FOROSTENSOSI								
John	51	m	w	ITAL	Amador	Sutter Crk P O	69	403
FOROVER								
Mosses	17	m	w	SWIT	Monterey	Castroville Twp	74	335
FORRAS								
Bartholomew	39	m	w	ITAL	Amador	Jackson P O	69	347
FORRE								
Agostino	25	m	w	ITAL	San Francisco	11-Wd San Francisc	84	642
FORRELL								
Samuel	45	m	w	IREL	Trinity	Douglas	92	232
FORREN								
Livers	30	m	w	PORT	Sacramento	Sutter Twp	77	383
Louis	55	m	w	FRAN	Amador	Lancha Plana P O	69	369
FORRER								
Charles	45	m	w	MA	San Francisco	11-Wd San Francisc	84	459
Julius	32	m	w	HANO	San Francisco	San Francisco P O	83	271
FORRES								
Charles	34	m	w	FRAN	San Francisco	2-Wd San Francisco	79	145
FORREST								
Albert	61	m	w	SC	Nevada	Washington Twp	75	346
Charles	27	m	w	DENM	Marin	Sausalito Twp	74	69
Henry	24	m	w	NY	Kern	Bakersfield P O	73	361
James	40	m	w	IREL	San Francisco	San Francisco P O	85	829
James	36	m	w	SCOT	San Francisco	San Francisco P O	83	407
James	35	m	w	MA	San Francisco	11-Wd San Francisc	84	602
John	40	m	w	SCOT	San Francisco	7-Wd San Francisco	81	256
John	22	m	w	NY	Nevada	Meadow Lake Twp	75	250
Lilly	14	f	w	NH	San Mateo	Redwood Twp	87	362
Milton W	25	m	w	NY	Nevada	Meadow Lake Twp	75	250
Patrick	35	m	w	IREL	San Diego	San Diego	78	509
W G	43	m	w	KY	Monterey	Castroville Twp	74	326
William	30	m	w	NY	San Francisco	8-Wd San Francisco	82	465
Wm	34	m	w	WI	Fresno	Millerton P O	72	184
FORRESTELL								
Catharine	53	f	w	IREL	Sacramento	2-Wd Sacramento	77	223
FORRESTER								
E	24	m	w	LA	Solano	Vallejo	90	175
George H W	55	m	w	MA	El Dorado	Mud Springs Twp	72	84
Henry V	31	m	w	MI	San Francisco	6-Wd San Francisco	81	148
Hudael	45	m	w	IREL	Contra Costa	Martinez P O	71	453
James	23	m	w	PA	San Francisco	San Francisco P O	83	10
Jas D	31	m	w	ENGL	Alameda	Brooklyn Twp	68	50
John	36	m	w	SCOT	San Francisco	1-Wd San Francisco	79	112
Michael	40	m	w	IREL	Contra Costa	San Pablo Twp	71	357
Peter	74	m	w	IREL	San Luis Obispo	Santa Rosa Twp	87	325
Peter A	33	m	w	PA	San Luis Obispo	Santa Rosa Twp	87	317
Thos J	33	m	w	AR	Nevada	Washington Twp	75	346
Wm	26	m	w	NY	Marin	San Rafael Twp	74	47
FORREY								
Abraham	33	m	w	NY	Los Angeles	Wilmington Twp	73	640
Marcus	42	m	w	MA	Alameda	Washington Twp	68	282
FORREZ								
Frank	22	m	w	AZOR	San Francisco	1-Wd San Francisco	79	118
FORRMISS								
Wm	29	m	w	ENGL	San Francisco	San Francisco P O	83	2

© 2001 by Heritage Quest. All rights reserved.

Name	Age	S	R	B-PL	County	Locale	Series M593 Roll	Pg
FORROW								
Saml	28	m	w	PRUS	Butte	Chico Twp	70	18
FORRY								
William	45	m	w	PA	San Francisco	6-Wd San Francisco	81	126
FORSACK								
Bridget	56	f	w	IREL	San Joaquin	1-Wd Stockton	86	137
FORSAITH								
Edgar	35	m	w	MO	San Francisco	5-Wd San Francisco	81	33
Isabel B	27	f	w	RI	San Francisco	San Francisco P O	83	28
FORSCHLER								
Wm	40	m	w	HDAR	Shasta	Horsetown P O	89	502
FORSCYTHE								
James	26	m	w	SCOT	Sonoma	Bodega Twp	91	262
Wm	22	m	w	MA	Sonoma	Bodega Twp	91	255
FORSEE								
James	82	m	w	VA	San Bernardino	San Bernardino Twp	78	436
FORSEMAN								
Hugh	42	m	w	OH	Los Angeles	Los Nietos Twp	73	579
Jas	50	m	w	OH	Sonoma	Healdsburg & Mendo	91	280
FORSER								
Alexander	27	m	i	CA	Colusa	Stony Crk Twp	71	334
Maria	26	f	i	CA	Colusa	Stony Crk Twp	71	334
FORSEYTH								
William	22	m	w	AUSL	Sutter	Yuba Twp	92	147
FORSHEYA								
John	69	m	w	PA	Napa	Napa	75	25
FORSHNER								
John	50	m	w	CANA	Tuolumne	Sonora P O	93	321
FORSITH								
Bartholomew	36	m	w	ITAL	Sacramento	Sutter Twp	77	386
FORSMAN								
Thos	36	m	w	MO	San Joaquin	Douglas Twp	86	43
FORSOMA								
Frank	26	m	w	PORT	Tuolumne	Columbia P O	93	344
FORSSY								
Jule E	28	m	w	FRAN	San Francisco	1-Wd San Francisco	79	49
FORST								
G	40	m	w	ENGL	Alameda	Oakland	68	171
FORSTER								
Anna	35	f	w	CANA	Santa Cruz	Santa Cruz	89	419
Dolores	47	f	w	CA	Los Angeles	Los Angeles	73	536
Hugh	41	m	w	ENGL	San Diego	San Diego	78	487
Jacob	42	m	w	PRUS	Shasta	American Ranch P O	89	498
John	38	m	w	BAVA	Shasta	Shasta P O	89	457
Joseph	45	m	w	ENGL	Amador	Volcano P O	69	372
Laura	30	f	w	PA	San Francisco	11-Wd San Francisc	84	618
FORSYTH								
Briant	37	m	w	TN	Sonoma	Santa Rosa	91	409
David M	27	m	w	IREL	Sacramento	4-Wd Sacramento	77	325
Elijah	36	m	w	CANA	Santa Clara	Milpitas Twp	88	115
George	59	m	w	ME	Sacramento	Natomas Twp	77	169
George	35	m	w	NY	San Francisco	8-Wd San Francisco	82	430
Jas	29	m	w	CANA	Solano	Benicia	90	15
Milton	37	m	w	IL	Sacramento	Center Twp	77	82
Philo G	29	m	w	MI	Santa Barbara	Santa Barbara P O	87	472
Robert	27	m	w	CANA	Nevada	Grass Valley Twp	75	200
Robt	35	m	w	TN	Sonoma	Santa Rosa	91	410
S	77	f	w	NC	Sonoma	Santa Rosa	91	419
William	51	m	w	IREL	San Francisco	San Francisco P O	83	186
Wm C	25	m	w	CANA	San Francisco	San Francisco P O	83	42
FORSYTHE								
Alexander	32	m	w	IL	Kern	Kernville P O	73	367
Alexander S	31	m	w	CANA	Alpine	Silver Mtn P O	69	306
B F	50	m	w	PA	Mendocino	Calpella Twp	74	185
Chesterfield	45	m	w	KY	Colusa	Monroe Twp	71	312
Henry	28	m	w	PRUS	Sacramento	4-Wd Sacramento	77	340
James	29	m	w	IREL	Butte	Ophir Twp	70	120
Joseph	35	m	w	IREL	Merced	Snelling P O	74	252
Milton	29	m	w	TN	Placer	Roseville P O	76	355
Philip	56	m	w	TN	Placer	Roseville P O	76	355
Saml	46	m	w	IREL	San Francisco	11-Wd San Francisc	84	602
William	21	m	w	AUSL	Yuba	Long Bar Twp	93	561
FORT								
Abba	45	f	b	GA	Plumas	Indian Twp	77	9
Ah	30	m	c	CHIN	San Francisco	6-Wd San Francisco	81	45
Ah	29	m	c	CHIN	Alameda	Oakland	68	254
Ah	17	m	c	CHIN	Trinity	Douglas	92	237
Ah	15	m	c	CHIN	Butte	Bidwell Twp	70	1
Albert	34	m	w	BADE	Tuolumne	Chinese Camp P O	93	377
Frank	35	m	w	PORT	Santa Barbara	Santa Barbara P O	87	450
John A	58	m	w	AFRI	El Dorado	Salmon Falls Twp	72	130
FORTADO								
M S	48	m	w	SCOT	Siskiyou	Scott Valley Twp	89	612
FORTE								
Albert	37	m	w	FRAN	San Francisco	San Francisco P O	80	455
Leo	25	m	w	SWIT	San Francisco	San Francisco P O	85	753
FORTELLS								
Margret	40	f	w	FRAN	San Francisco	1-Wd San Francisco	79	54
FORTEN								
Alfonse N	53	m	w	FRAN	Butte	Ophir Twp	70	96
FORTENIL								
Honora	65	m	w	FRAN	Monterey	Pajaro Twp	74	368
FORTER								
Maggie	6	f	w	CA	San Joaquin	Douglas Twp	86	31
FORTES								
Joseph	26	m	w	SCOT	Siskiyou	Yreka Twp	89	667
FORTH								
Daniel	37	m	w	NY	San Francisco	6-Wd San Francisco	81	84
George	28	m	w	ENGL	Alameda	Eden Twp	68	62
FORTHER								
John	45	m	w	WI	Monterey	San Juan Twp	74	394
FORTHISE								
John	48	m	w	IREL	San Francisco	7-Wd San Francisco	81	173
FORTHMAN								
Droge S	28	m	w	SHOL	Monterey	Alisal Twp	74	294
FORTHMANN								
J D	28	m	w	PRUS	San Francisco	San Francisco P O	83	135
FORTIER								
C	43	m	w	CANA	Sierra	Forest Twp	89	529
Eucharíste	22	m	w	CANA	Yolo	Grafton Twp	93	487
Peter	50	m	w	CANA	Yuba	Bullards Bar P O	93	551
FORTIN								
Edward	26	m	w	CANA	Mariposa	Mariposa P O	74	112
Mary	29	f	w	OH	San Francisco	San Francisco P O	80	536
Pierce W	56	m	w	FRAN	San Francisco	5-Wd San Francisco	81	6
FORTINA								
Alfons	50	m	w	CHIL	Butte	Ophir Twp	70	107
FORTINER								
Theo	39	m	w	NJ	Butte	Chico Twp	70	19
FORTMAN								
Frank	21	m	w	HANO	San Francisco	6-Wd San Francisco	81	82
Henry	26	m	w	BRUN	San Francisco	San Francisco P O	83	139
John A	26	m	w	NCOD	San Mateo	Belmont P O	87	374
FORTNEY								
David	36	m	w	PA	Colusa	Grand Island Twp	71	304
Stephen	40	m	w	TN	Sutter	Yuba Twp	92	146
FORTRO								
Joseph	40	m	w	CANA	San Francisco	San Francisco P O	83	248
FORTS								
Joseph	24	m	w	OH	Placer	Bath P O	76	459
FORTSON								
John T	49	m	w	GA	Sonoma	Santa Rosa	91	406
FORTUNA								
Grabriela	30	f	i	CA	Los Angeles	Los Angeles	73	501
FORTUNATO								
Giuseppe	32	m	w	ITAL	San Francisco	11-Wd San Francisc	84	642
FORTUNE								
H W	30	m	w	IREL	San Francisco	San Francisco P O	85	775
James A	45	m	w	IREL	San Francisco	San Francisco P O	85	775
Joseph	50	m	w	IREL	Amador	Ione City P O	69	349
L J	23	m	w	IREL	Solano	Vallejo	90	163
Leonard S	31	m	w	MO	Contra Costa	Martinez P O	71	390
Martin	48	m	w	IREL	Yuba	Rose Bar Twp	93	656
Mary	66	f	w	IREL	San Francisco	8-Wd San Francisco	82	458
Mary	65	f	w	IREL	San Francisco	8-Wd San Francisco	82	382
Richd	27	m	w	NY	Solano	Vallejo	90	160
Wm	40	m	w	GA	El Dorado	Georgetown Twp	72	40
FORTUNTINA								
Pinquet	43	m	w	CHIL	Fresno	Millerton P O	72	162
FORTZ								
Peter	30	m	w	SWIT	Alameda	Oakland	68	263
FORVICE								
Levi	40	m	w	CANA	Butte	Chico Twp	70	21
FORWALT								
Enos	43	m	w	NJ	San Francisco	2-Wd San Francisco	79	264
FORWARD								
P	38	m	w	IA	San Joaquin	Elkhorn Twp	86	56
Walter	40	m	w	PA	Shasta	Millville P O	89	484
FORY								
David	48	m	w	VT	San Mateo	Pescadero P O	87	413
David	38	m	w	SCOT	San Francisco	8-Wd San Francisco	82	462
FORYE								
George	34	m	w	ENGL	Alameda	Oakland	68	197
FOS								
Paul	30	m	w	FRAN	San Francisco	3-Wd San Francisco	79	316
FOSBERRY								
Mary	40	f	w	IREL	San Francisco	San Francisco P O	85	798
FOSBERY								
William	38	m	w	IREL	San Francisco	11-Wd San Francisc	84	638
FOSC								
M E	43	f	w	ENGL	Sacramento	3-Wd Sacramento	77	314
FOSCELINE								
Geo	50	m	w	ITAL	Alameda	Murray Twp	68	116
FOSDICK								
Aaron	37	m	w	MI	Placer	Bath P O	76	433
FOSERTINA								
Fredk	16	m	w	SWIT	Marin	San Antonio Twp	74	60
FOSH								
Ah	40	m	c	CHIN	Sacramento	Georgianna Twp	77	128
FOSHAY								
Isaac	51	m	w	CANA	San Francisco	11-Wd San Francisc	84	650
FOSHEA								
Priscille	22	f	w	FRAN	San Francisco	San Francisco P O	80	455
FOSHEY								
J	30	m	w	OH	Lake	Zim Zim	73	417
FOSKER								
Daniel	22	m	w	NH	Sutter	Butte Twp	92	102
FOSKY								
Phil	39	m	w	FRAN	San Joaquin	Dent Twp	86	26
FOSS								
Aaron	24	m	w	PRUS	San Francisco	2-Wd San Francisco	79	148
August	34	m	w	HANO	San Francisco	1-Wd San Francisco	79	86
C J	44	m	w	ME	Sacramento	4-Wd Sacramento	77	374

© 2001 by Heritage Quest. All rights reserved.

California 1870 Census

Name	Age	S	R	B-PL	County	Locale	Roll	Pg
						Series M593		
Charles	37	m	w	DENM	San Francisco	2-Wd San Francisco	79	174
Charles L	30	m	w	ME	Yuba	New York Twp	93	637
Clark	50	m	w	NH	Sonoma	Healdsburg & Mendo	91	285
David R	36	m	w	NH	San Diego	San Luis Rey	78	513
Elizabeth	53	f	w	FRNK	San Francisco	11-Wd San Francisc	84	550
F A	13	f	w	CA	Alameda	Oakland	68	237
Frederick	21	m	w	ENGL	Sonoma	Salt Point	91	385
Hiram C	50	m	w	OH	San Francisco	3-Wd San Francisco	79	326
Isaac D	42	m	w	NH	Nevada	Eureka Twp	75	133
Ivory Lock	36	m	w	NH	Plumas	Mineral Twp	77	23
J C	34	m	w	ME	Humboldt	Table Bluff Twp	72	308
James B	34	m	w	ME	Mendocino	Point Arena Twp	74	224
L	47	m	w	NH	Yuba	W Bear Rvr Twp	93	684
Lemual	55	m	w	ME	Yuba	New York Twp	93	640
Mary	15	f	w	NY	San Francisco	San Francisco P O	83	126
Samuel B	30	m	w	ENGL	Sonoma	Salt Point	91	388
T H	42	m	w	ME	Humboldt	Eureka Twp	72	268
T H	40	m	w	ME	Humboldt	Pacific Twp	72	291
William	28	m	w	NORW	San Francisco	1-Wd San Francisco	79	74
FOSSAS								
Pedro	42	m	w	SPAI	San Francisco	6-Wd San Francisco	81	51
FOSSEN								
John	36	m	w	NORW	Tehama	Paskenta Twp	92	163
FOSSETT								
Horatio	29	m	w	ME	Marin	Point Reyes Twp	74	21
FOSSIAN								
John	40	m	w	ITAL	San Joaquin	Oneal Twp	86	118
FOSSUM								
Emily	40	f	w	DENM	San Francisco	3-Wd San Francisco	79	297
FOST								
Edward	50	m	w	SCOT	Sutter	Vernon Twp	92	133
FOSTENDEN								
T C	27	m	w	PRUS	San Joaquin	Dent Twp	86	28
FOSTER								
A	45	f	w	ENGL	Alameda	Oakland	68	173
A	37	m	w	MEXI	San Joaquin	1-Wd Stockton	86	141
A J	38	m	w	IL	Santa Clara	Almaden Twp	88	20
Adelaide	30	f	w	CT	Santa Clara	San Jose Twp	88	179
Adrian	45	m	w	SC	Sonoma	Russian Rvr	91	375
Adrian	17	m	w	OH	Amador	Ione City P O	69	351
Adrian	16	m	w	OH	Alpine	Woodfords P O	69	309
Albert T	33	m	w	NY	San Luis Obispo	Santa Rosa Twp	87	328
Alexander	15	m	w	OR	Solano	Tremont Twp	90	30
Allen	34	m	w	CANA	Monterey	Alisal Twp	74	297
Ambrose	23	m	w	AR	Fresno	Kingston P O	72	220
Andrew	30	m	w	MO	Mendocino	Round Valley Twp	74	218
Anna	5	f	w	CA	San Luis Obispo	Salinas Twp	87	290
Antone	38	m	w	PORT	Mendocino	Big Rvr Twp	74	159
August	52	m	w	PRUS	Plumas	Mineral Twp	77	20
Avery J	38	m	w	NY	Nevada	Grass Valley Twp	75	154
Ben	44	m	w	AL	San Joaquin	3-Wd Stockton	86	223
Benjamin	37	m	w	ME	Solano	Suisun Twp	90	108
C	39	m	w	ENGL	Santa Clara	Almaden Twp	88	20
C F	27	m	w	LA	Tehama	Bell Mills Twp	92	159
C H	40	m	w	OH	Sacramento	3-Wd Sacramento	77	287
Calvin	28	m	b	MO	Nevada	Nevada Twp	75	272
Catherine	68	f	w	KY	Solano	Tremont Twp	90	32
Charles	48	m	w	NY	Solano	Silveyville Twp	90	92
Charles	46	m	w	MO	Stanislaus	Empire Twp	92	65
Charles	45	m	m	NY	Sacramento	2-Wd Sacramento	77	210
Charles	38	m	w	ENGL	Nevada	Nevada Twp	75	320
Charles	33	m	w	DE	San Francisco	San Francisco P O	83	262
Charles	26	m	w	ME	Santa Clara	Redwood Twp	88	133
Charles R	27	m	w	ME	Mendocino	Point Arena Twp	74	204
Charles T	40	m	w	KY	El Dorado	Mud Springs Twp	72	89
Chas	38	m	w	PRUS	Sacramento	4-Wd Sacramento	77	367
Chas	32	m	w	MO	Sonoma	Mendocino Twp	91	303
Chas C	42	m	w	PA	San Francisco	1-Wd San Francisco	79	86
Chas E	34	m	w	NY	San Francisco	1-Wd San Francisco	79	35
Claiburn	58	m	w	VA	Amador	Volcano P O	69	385
Claus	25	m	w	PRUS	Marin	San Antonio Twp	74	62
Constantine	10	f	w	WI	San Francisco	11-Wd San Francisc	84	595
D	40	m	w	VA	Sacramento	1-Wd Sacramento	77	181
Danl	38	m	w	CANA	Solano	Vallejo	90	180
E	63	m	w	CANA	San Joaquin	Liberty Twp	86	86
E A	42	m	w	NY	Nevada	Washington Twp	75	345
E B F	35	m	w	KY	Marin	San Rafael Twp	74	41
E J	24	m	w	NY	San Francisco	San Francisco P O	85	874
Edward	37	m	w	NY	Calaveras	San Andreas P O	70	163
Edward	30	m	w	PRUS	Santa Cruz	Santa Cruz	89	412
Edward	21	m	w	IREL	Inyo	Cerro Gordo Twp	73	318
Edwd	35	m	w	ME	San Francisco	San Francisco P O	83	14
Elijah	41	m	w	ENGL	Alameda	Washington Twp	68	281
Elizabeth	22	f	w	AR	San Francisco	San Francisco P O	85	727
Ellen	22	f	w	CANA	Humboldt	Eel Rvr Twp	72	247
Emma	31	f	w	AUST	Alameda	Oakland	68	130
Emmetion	55	f	w	ME	Amador	Jackson P O	69	320
Eugene	22	m	w	IL	Santa Barbara	Santa Barbara P O	87	498
Ezra	42	m	w	VT	Sacramento	Sutter Twp	77	381
F P	28	m	w	NY	San Joaquin	Elkhorn Twp	86	56
Frances	38	m	w	IREL	Sacramento	3-Wd Sacramento	77	299
Frank	3	m	w	NY	San Francisco	5-Wd San Francisco	81	31
Frank	14	m	w	KY	Santa Barbara	Santa Barbara P O	87	499
Frederick	35	m	w	PRUS	Placer	Auburn P O	76	358
G W	29	m	w	OH	Humboldt	Bald Hills	72	237
Geo	40	m	w	MA	San Francisco	San Francisco P O	83	88
Geo	21	m	w	CANA	Yuba	Rose Bar Twp	93	664
Geo J	45	m	w	NH	San Francisco	San Francisco P O	85	793
Georgarett	9M	f	w	CA	San Francisco	San Francisco P O	83	16
George	55	m	w	AR	Inyo	Lone Pine Twp	73	331
George	40	m	w	NY	Sacramento	Dry Crk Twp	77	104
George	39	m	w	MO	Solano	Tremont Twp	90	31
George	35	m	w	ME	San Diego	San Diego	78	510
George	35	m	w	VT	Marin	San Rafael Twp	74	41
George	29	m	w	IL	Lake	Lower Lake	73	415
George	22	m	w	MO	Mendocino	Round Valley Twp	74	217
George G	37	m	w	NY	Sacramento	Dry Crk Twp	77	98
George M	73	m	w	ENGL	San Francisco	6-Wd San Francisco	81	112
George S	33	m	w	AL	Fresno	Kingston P O	72	218
George W	47	m	w	ME	San Luis Obispo	Santa Rosa Twp	87	323
George W	39	m	w	MO	Calaveras	San Andreas P O	70	158
George W	36	m	w	IL	Los Angeles	Los Nietos Twp	73	578
H C	20	m	w	CA	Alameda	Oakland	68	159
H E	37	m	w	NY	San Joaquin	Liberty Twp	86	91
Harris	23	m	w	MO	Merced	Snelling P O	74	263
Helen	46	f	w	NY	San Francisco	San Francisco P O	85	875
Henry A	48	m	w	MA	San Francisco	San Francisco P O	85	847
Herman	68	m	w	ME	San Mateo	Pescadero P O	87	417
Hiram	23	m	w	IL	Solano	Green Valley Twp	90	41
Honoria	40	f	w	ENGL	Santa Clara	Fremont Twp	88	64
Howard	29	m	w	CANA	Sonoma	Salt Point	91	388
Isaac G	48	m	w	NY	Santa Barbara	Santa Barbara P O	87	498
J B	35	m	w	GA	Sutter	Butte Twp	92	89
J E	33	m	w	MO	Alameda	Oakland	68	264
J M	37	m	w	OH	Nevada	Eureka Twp	75	138
J R	23	m	w	TN	Sacramento	3-Wd Sacramento	77	285
J W	34	m	w	NY	Nevada	Bloomfield Twp	75	98
Jac	48	m	w	CANA	Mendocino	Calpella Twp	74	189
Jacob	42	m	w	PA	San Francisco	8-Wd San Francisco	82	374
Jacob	38	m	w	BELG	Amador	Fiddletown P O	69	437
Jacob	36	m	w	PRUS	Monterey	Pajaro Twp	74	376
Jacob	23	m	w	BADE	Butte	Chico Twp	70	54
James	55	m	w	IN	Del Norte	Crescent Twp	71	456
James	45	m	w	ME	Contra Costa	Martinez P O	71	386
James	40	m	w	MA	Solano	Suisun Twp	90	103
James	34	m	w	PA	Amador	Sutter Crk P O	69	403
James	33	m	w	NY	San Francisco	1-Wd San Francisco	79	71
James	30	m	w	CANA	Placer	Gold Run Twp	76	395
James	25	m	w	MO	Nevada	Grass Valley Twp	75	206
James W	19	m	w	IL	Yolo	Grafton Twp	93	496
Jerome	45	m	w	NY	Butte	Ophir Twp	70	93
Jesse	25	m	w	MO	Mendocino	Round Valley Twp	74	219
Joel	70	m	w	GA	San Joaquin	Tulare Twp	86	253
Joel	41	m	w	MA	San Francisco	6-Wd San Francisco	81	150
John	44	m	w	IREL	Alameda	Alameda	68	12
John	40	m	w	MO	Kern	Tehachapi P O	73	353
John	40	m	w	NY	San Francisco	7-Wd San Francisco	81	226
John	33	m	w	SC	San Francisco	11-Wd San Francisc	84	485
John	28	m	w	ENGL	Yolo	Grafton Twp	93	499
John	27	m	w	KY	Marin	San Rafael Twp	74	36
John	23	m	w	IL	Santa Cruz	Santa Cruz Twp	89	381
John	1	m	w	NY	San Francisco	5-Wd San Francisco	81	31
John A	50	m	w	NH	Amador	Volcano P O	69	384
John A	15	m	w	NH	Amador	Volcano P O	69	374
John B	27	m	w	MA	Colusa	Colusa	71	290
John C	66	m	w	SC	Fresno	Kingston P O	72	218
John E	39	m	w	NH	Placer	Dutch Flat P O	76	414
John F	34	m	w	IN	Sonoma	Analy Twp	91	240
John R	34	m	w	SC	San Francisco	San Francisco P O	83	187
Johnson W	54	m	w	ME	El Dorado	Placerville	72	122
Jos	25	m	w	ENGL	Solano	Vallejo	90	202
Jose	25	m	w	SCOT	Siskiyou	Yreka Twp	89	666
Joseph	40	m	w	IL	Sonoma	Santa Rosa	91	427
Joseph	38	m	w	PORT	Mariposa	Mariposa P O	74	113
Joseph	32	m	w	PORT	Mariposa	Mariposa P O	74	111
Joseph	25	m	w	NORW	San Francisco	7-Wd San Francisco	81	218
Juan	57	m	w	ENGL	San Diego	San Luis Rey	78	514
Jubal A	39	m	w	NY	Calaveras	San Andreas P O	70	163
Junius G	47	m	w	CT	San Francisco	San Francisco P O	85	873
Justine	40	f	w	GERM	El Dorado	Placerville	72	111
King	20	m	w	MO	Sonoma	Salt Point	91	380
L D	37	m	w	IA	San Joaquin	Castoria Twp	86	14
Laura	27	f	w	KY	Solano	Benicia	90	5
Laura K	15	f	w	MI	Placer	Roseville P O	76	354
Lennard	40	m	w	ME	San Diego	San Luis Rey	78	516
Lewis	44	m	w	OH	Lake	Lower Lake	73	420
Lizzy	28	f	w	MS	San Francisco	6-Wd San Francisco	81	79
M	35	m	w	PORT	Alameda	Murray Twp	68	128
Maggie	20	f	w	IL	Butte	Chico Twp	70	21
Malcolm G	50	m	w	TN	Santa Barbara	Santa Maria P O	87	513
Marcus	30	m	w	CA	San Diego	San Luis Rey	78	514
Margaret	20	f	w	KY	Siskiyou	Yreka	89	652
Margret	17	f	w	IA	Alameda	Eden Twp	68	87
Marion	30	m	w	MO	Santa Barbara	Las Cruces P O	87	506
Mark	28	m	w	NY	Sacramento	4-Wd Sacramento	77	353
Martha	28	f	w	TX	Los Angeles	Los Nietos Twp	73	588
Mary J	20	f	w	NY	Nevada	Grass Valley Twp	75	204
Mercy T	76	f	w	MA	San Francisco	6-Wd San Francisco	81	117
Michael	23	m	w	IREL	Butte	Chico Twp	70	36
Minnie	16	f	w	CA	Yuba	Marysville	93	609
Moses G	36	m	w	ME	Calaveras	Copperopolis P O	70	239
N F	21	m	w	VT	Alameda	Oakland	68	215
Nettie F	23	f	w	KY	Solano	Benicia	90	5
Nimrod	39	m	w	TN	Amador	Ione City P O	69	367

© 2001 by Heritage Quest. All rights reserved.

Name	Age	S	R	B-PL	County	Locale	Roll	Pg
O	40	m	w	AR	San Joaquin	Tulare Twp	86	263
Octava	21	f	w	GA	Sacramento	Center Twp	77	82
Orlen	25	m	w	PORT	Alameda	Murray Twp	68	128
Overton	45	m	w	MO	Stanislaus	Empire Twp	92	63
Palatine	45	m	w	VA	Butte	Chico Twp	70	13
Parley S	43	m	w	NY	Stanislaus	Buena Vista Twp	92	15
Peter	31	m	w	IREL	San Francisco	7-Wd San Francisco	81	181
Phillip	25	m	w	IN	Tehama	Red Bluff	92	183
Phillip	25	m	w	ENGL	Yolo	Putah Twp	93	517
Phillip T	43	m	w	VA	Mariposa	Mariposa P O	74	134
Powell	44	m	w	PRUS	El Dorado	White Oak Twp	72	139
Ransom	39	m	w	SC	Butte	Wyandotte Twp	70	141
Rich E	70	m	w	NH	Humboldt	Bucksport Twp	72	244
Robert	64	m	w	SCOT	San Francisco	11-Wd San Francisc	84	625
Robert	56	m	w	IREL	Del Norte	Smith Rvr Twp	71	478
Robert	50	m	w	MO	Stanislaus	Empire Twp	92	53
Robert	25	m	w	MO	Sonoma	Mendocino Twp	91	300
Robt	43	m	w	LA	San Joaquin	3-Wd Stockton	86	236
Robt W	50	m	w	GA	Shasta	Portugese Flat P O	89	472
Rubie S	15	f	w	ENGL	Tulare	Farmersville Twp	92	246
S G	43	m	w	MA	Sacramento	Brighton Twp	77	72
S H	41	f	w	VT	Alameda	Oakland	68	227
S P	40	m	w	VT	San Joaquin	Dent Twp	86	16
Saml	28	m	w	MA	Alameda	Oakland	68	234
Samuel	30	m	w	IN	Contra Costa	Martinez P O	71	444
Squire	24	m	w	NY	Nevada	Grass Valley Twp	75	201
Stephen	32	m	w	NY	Sacramento	2-Wd Sacramento	77	237
Stephen C	54	m	w	ME	Los Angeles	Los Angeles	73	568
T J Capt	34	m	w	MA	Alameda	Oakland	68	201
Thomas	50	m	w	ENGL	San Diego	San Luis Rey	78	514
Thomas	50	m	w	ENGL	Santa Clara	Santa Clara Twp	88	178
Thomas	45	m	w	CT	San Francisco	5-Wd San Francisco	81	26
Thomas	40	m	w	SCOT	San Francisco	San Francisco P O	83	367
Thomas	32	m	w	KY	San Bernardino	San Bernardino Twp	78	448
Thomas	31	m	w	IREL	Mendocino	Round Valley Twp	74	219
Thomas	25	m	w	BREM	San Francisco	7-Wd San Francisco	81	184
Thomas	19	m	w	SCOT	San Francisco	San Francisco P O	80	458
Thurston	19	m	w	OR	Colusa	Colusa Twp	71	280
Vicenta	19	f	w	CA	Los Angeles	Wilmington Twp	73	636
Vinta	46	m	w	IL	Santa Clara	Almaden Twp	88	3
W G	28	m	w	ME	Tuolumne	Big Oak Flat P O	93	406
W H	45	m	w	ME	El Dorado	Kelsey Twp	72	59
Walter L	38	m	w	ME	San Diego	San Luis Rey	78	516
Warren R	49	m	w	KY	Yolo	Putah Twp	93	521
William	60	m	w	PA	El Dorado	Cosumnes Twp	72	16
William	55	m	w	PA	San Mateo	Pescadero P O	87	411
William	48	m	w	OH	Santa Barbara	Santa Barbara P O	87	490
William	37	m	w	VA	Placer	Auburn P O	76	383
William	32	m	w	MEXI	Yuba	New York Twp	93	641
William	18	m	w	CA	Mendocino	Ten Mile Rvr Twp	74	172
William	18	m	w	CA	Alameda	Oakland	68	159
William B	48	m	w	VA	Yolo	Merritt Twp	93	504
William T	33	m	w	NY	Nevada	Bridgeport Twp	75	112
William W	38	m	w	OH	San Francisco	San Francisco P O	83	199
Winthrop	48	m	w	ME	San Francisco	San Francisco P O	83	413
Wm	62	m	b	VA	Sacramento	1-Wd Sacramento	77	181
Wm	54	m	w	PA	San Francisco	11-Wd San Francisc	84	573
Wm	38	m	w	TN	Tehama	Battle Crk Twp	92	157
Wm	30	m	w	NY	San Francisco	1-Wd San Francisco	79	133
Wm	1	m	w	CA	San Francisco	San Francisco P O	85	799
Wm D	26	m	w	NY	San Diego	San Diego	78	495
Wm E	23	m	w	MO	Sonoma	Bodega Twp	91	252
Wm H	35	m	w	MA	San Francisco	7-Wd San Francisco	81	286
Wm H	22	m	w	CT	San Francisco	5-Wd San Francisco	81	30
Wm R	22	m	w	MO	Butte	Chico Twp	70	46
Wm W	34	m	w	AL	Fresno	Kingston P O	72	218
FOSTERN								
Chas	43	m	w	HOLL	Butte	Oregon Twp	70	122
Felix	40	m	w	PRUS	Butte	Oregon Twp	70	132
FOSTIN								
Clement	18	m	w	SWIT	Alameda	Oakland	68	239
FOSTINA								
Manuel	20	m	w	PORT	Marin	Nicasio Twp	74	18
FOSTING								
L	39	m	w	NY	Merced	Snelling P O	74	273
FOT								
Ah	45	m	c	CHIN	Nevada	Grass Valley Twp	75	217
Ah	40	m	c	CHIN	San Joaquin	1-Wd Stockton	86	151
Ah	40	m	c	CHIN	San Francisco	6-Wd San Francisco	81	66
Ah	27	m	c	CHIN	Nevada	Eureka Twp	75	127
Ah	20	m	c	CHIN	Nevada	Eureka Twp	75	140
Ah	20	m	c	CHIN	Marin	Novato Twp	74	12
Ah	19	m	c	CHIN	Nevada	Eureka Twp	75	129
Ah	13	m	c	CHIN	San Francisco	3-Wd San Francisco	79	329
Ling	35	m	c	CHIN	Butte	Chico Twp	70	51
Sue	35	m	c	CHIN	Yuba	Marysville	93	601
Tung	15	m	c	CHIN	San Francisco	San Francisco P O	85	806
FOTGTH								
Mateo	27	m	w	SWIT	San Francisco	San Francisco P O	85	754
FOTH								
William	42	m	w	PRUS	San Francisco	San Francisco P O	80	474
FOTHINGHAM								
George	21	m	w	SCOT	San Francisco	7-Wd San Francisco	81	205
FOTHRINGHAN								
George	56	m	w	SCOT	Sacramento	Dry Crk Twp	77	99
FOTT								
Ah	32	m	c	CHIN	San Joaquin	1-Wd Stockton	86	144
FOTTY								
John	35	m	w	GA	Kern	Havilah P O	73	340
FOU								
Ah	45	m	c	CHIN	Yuba	Marysville	93	623
Ah	40	m	c	CHIN	Alameda	Oakland	68	232
Ah	36	m	c	CHIN	Alameda	Oakland	68	157
Ah	30	m	c	CHIN	Alameda	Oakland	68	158
Ah	29	m	c	CHIN	Butte	Chico Twp	70	52
Ah	28	m	c	CHIN	Tehama	Tehama Twp	92	189
Ah	27	m	c	CHIN	Alameda	Oakland	68	158
Ah	23	m	c	CHIN	Yuba	Marysville	93	595
Ah	23	m	c	CHIN	Tehama	Tehama Twp	92	192
Ah	22	m	c	CHIN	Alameda	Oakland	68	216
Ah	22	m	c	CHIN	Tehama	Tehama Twp	92	188
Ah	20	m	c	CHIN	Alameda	Oakland	68	220
Ah	15	m	c	CHIN	San Francisco	7-Wd San Francisco	81	282
An	26	m	c	CHIN	Alameda	Washington Twp	68	299
Ching	22	m	c	CHIN	Tehama	Antelope Twp	92	158
Ching	18	m	c	CHIN	Tehama	Tehama Twp	92	189
Gung	19	m	c	CHIN	Yuba	Marysville	93	623
Ha	30	m	c	CHIN	Siskiyou	Yreka Twp	89	666
You	48	m	c	CHIN	Yuba	Rose Bar Twp	93	656
FOUBERT								
Eugene	50	m	w	FRAN	San Francisco	San Francisco P O	83	363
FOUCH								
Ah	40	m	c	CHIN	Tuolumne	Big Oak Flat P O	93	401
Ah	25	m	c	CHIN	Placer	Clipper Gap P O	76	392
Albert	37	m	w	OH	Napa	Yountville Twp	75	86
Annie	5	f	w	CA	Napa	Napa Twp	75	70
Fred	44	m	w	UNKN	San Joaquin	2-Wd Stockton	86	166
James	39	m	w	OH	Lake	Big Valley	73	395
FOUCHARD								
Rosalie	70	f	w	FRAN	San Francisco	San Francisco P O	80	339
FOUCHE								
Emeziah	22	m	w	OH	El Dorado	Diamond Springs Tw	72	33
FOUCHET								
John	22	m	w	FRAN	Santa Clara	Fremont Twp	88	66
FOUG								
Ah	40	m	c	CHIN	Solano	Benicia	90	2
Ah	38	m	c	CHIN	Kern	Havilah P O	73	337
FOUGARES								
Joseph	23	m	w	SWIT	San Francisco	San Francisco P O	80	426
FOUGERE								
Eugene	17	m	w	CA	San Francisco	San Francisco P O	83	63
FOUGERON								
Augustas	30	m	w	NY	Placer	Auburn P O	76	367
FOUGETT								
Albert	45	m	w	WURT	Sacramento	Granite Twp	77	143
FOUGNER								
Otto	27	m	w	NORW	Sonoma	Salt Point	91	387
FOUGREE								
Elisee	55	m	w	FRAN	San Francisco	San Francisco P O	80	347
FOUI								
Ah	28	m	c	CHIN	San Francisco	San Francisco P O	80	495
FOUIE								
Ah	21	m	c	CHIN	Nevada	Nevada Twp	75	315
FOUK								
---	20	m	c	CHIN	Siskiyou	Yreka Twp	89	673
Ah	45	m	c	CHIN	Marin	Tomales Twp	74	83
Ah	38	m	c	CHIN	Yuba	Marysville	93	620
Ah	13	m	c	CHIN	Yuba	Marysville	93	619
Que	19	m	c	CHIN	Yuba	Marysville	93	620
FOUL								
John	44	m	w	PRUS	Sutter	Nicolaus Twp	92	114
FOULDS								
Andrew	30	m	w	SCOT	San Francisco	7-Wd San Francisco	81	262
FOULER								
Albert	25	m	w	MO	San Luis Obispo	San Luis Obispo Tw	87	316
Henry C	36	m	w	OH	San Luis Obispo	Salinas Twp	87	293
Laura	6M	f	w	CA	San Luis Obispo	Salinas Twp	87	293
Lissie	17	f	w	MO	San Luis Obispo	San Luis Obispo Tw	87	316
FOULGER								
John	38	m	w	VT	San Francisco	San Francisco P O	83	206
FOULHEVER								
Margaret	60	f	w	FRAN	San Francisco	8-Wd San Francisco	82	390
FOULK								
Ah	40	m	c	CHIN	Placer	Bath P O	76	444
George A	39	m	w	PA	Colusa	Stony Crk Twp	71	330
FOULKES								
Jno	34	m	w	KY	Sacramento	3-Wd Sacramento	77	310
John	26	m	c	CHIN	Marin	San Rafael	74	58
Sarah	62	f	w	WALE	Nevada	Rough & Ready Twp	75	333
William	55	m	w	NORW	Nevada	Nevada Twp	75	321
FOULKS								
Edwd	24	m	w	WALE	San Francisco	1-Wd San Francisco	79	23
Effie	53	f	w	OH	Sacramento	San Joaquin Twp	77	396
Justinia	47	m	w	ENGL	Placer	Blue Canyon P O	76	418
Randolph	16	m	w	CA	Santa Barbara	San Buenaventura P	87	422
Thomas	35	m	w	ENGL	Tuolumne	Sonora P O	93	319
FOUN								
Han	24	m	c	CHIN	Sierra	Lincoln Twp	89	546
FOUNCE								
Granville	35	m	w	ENGL	Nevada	Washington Twp	75	345
FOUND								
Kit	28	f	c	CHIN	Calaveras	San Andreas P O	70	211
FOUNG								
Ah	45	m	c	CHIN	Calaveras	San Andreas P O	70	162

© 2001 by Heritage Quest. All rights reserved.

California 1870 Census

Name	Age	S	R	B-PL	County	Locale	Series M593 Roll	Pg
FOUNK								
John G	45	m	w	HOLL	Los Angeles	Los Angeles	73	524
FOUNTAIN								
Annie P	5	f	b	CA	Napa	Napa	75	56
Carolina	39	f	w	ENGL	Nevada	Meadow Lake Twp	75	246
Charles	25	m	w	ITAL	Plumas	Seneca Twp	77	51
Chester	27	m	w	NY	Sonoma	Salt Point	91	391
E	21	m	w	NY	San Joaquin	Dent Twp	86	16
Eliza	74	f	w	NY	Colusa	Colusa Twp	71	284
Eliza	17	f	w	MO	Sacramento	4-Wd Sacramento	77	362
Fred	20	m	w	CA	Solano	Vacaville Twp	90	138
G C	44	m	w	NY	Solano	Vallejo	90	214
Geo	43	m	w	NY	Alameda	Oakland	68	149
Geo W	48	m	w	NY	El Dorado	Lake Valley Twp	72	63
George	41	m	w	PORT	Los Angeles	San Juan Twp	73	629
George W	26	m	w	NY	Sacramento	2-Wd Sacramento	77	207
Guiatano	18	m	w	ITAL	Nevada	Nevada Twp	75	316
J	46	m	w	OH	Nevada	Meadow Lake Twp	75	265
James	32	m	w	PRUS	San Francisco	5-Wd San Francisco	81	9
John	46	m	w	OH	Nevada	Meadow Lake Twp	75	246
John	40	m	w	ME	Nevada	Meadow Lake Twp	75	262
Joseph	39	m	w	AR	Kern	Havilah P O	73	336
Joshua	50	m	w	MD	Sacramento	Franklin Twp	77	112
Lazarus	50	m	b	LA	San Francisco	San Francisco P O	80	398
Lewis	23	m	w	CANA	Placer	Dutch Flat P O	76	404
Mary	26	f	m	MA	San Francisco	San Francisco P O	80	383
R W	34	m	w	VA	Mendocino	Round Valley Twp	74	216
William	52	m	w	NY	Colusa	Colusa Twp	71	285
Wm A	32	m	w	MI	Sacramento	4-Wd Sacramento	77	363
FOUR								
Ah	35	m	c	CHIN	Fresno	Millerton P O	72	200
John	40	m	w	FRNK	Placer	Gold Run Twp	76	399
FOURACRE								
Wm Henry	26	m	w	ENGL	San Francisco	1-Wd San Francisco	79	86
FOURCADE								
Pierre	25	m	w	FRAN	San Francisco	San Francisco P O	80	460
FOURCADO								
Muguil	19	m	w	CA	San Luis Obispo	San Luis Obispo Tw	87	310
FOURER								
Charles	44	m	w	WURT	Placer	Summit P O	76	496
Jacob	50	m	w	SWIT	Calaveras	San Andreas P O	70	194
FOURETTE								
John R	45	m	w	NJ	San Francisco	1-Wd San Francisco	79	134
FOURGEAON								
Adam	28	m	w	SWIT	San Francisco	San Francisco P O	80	533
FOURGEAURD								
Victor	52	m	w	SC	San Francisco	8-Wd San Francisco	82	439
FOURIATT								
John	45	m	w	NJ	San Joaquin	1-Wd Stockton	86	157
FOURIER								
Victor	40	m	w	FRAN	San Francisco	San Francisco P O	80	345
FOURNESS								
Dyson	33	m	w	ENGL	San Francisco	11-Wd San Francisc	84	485
FOURNIER								
F	46	m	w	FRAN	Sierra	Butte Twp	89	513
Julius	60	m	w	FRAN	Yuba	New York Twp	93	636
FOUS								
Ah	49	m	c	CHIN	Sacramento	2-Wd Sacramento	77	250
FOUSBERG								
Mary	42	f	w	IREL	San Francisco	8-Wd San Francisco	82	320
FOUSEL								
John	19	m	w	CA	Solano	Silveyville Twp	90	72
FOUSEND								
G D	36	m	w	HANO	San Francisco	San Francisco P O	85	832
FOUSHER								
Edwin	34	m	w	MO	Sonoma	Santa Rosa	91	398
FOUST								
Lewis	43	m	w	OH	Yuba	Rose Bar Twp	93	653
FOUTE								
Fredk	25	m	w	PRUS	Sacramento	4-Wd Sacramento	77	352
FOUTENBAUGH								
Chas	23	m	w	NY	San Francisco	San Francisco P O	83	48
FOUTS								
Abraham	40	m	w	OH	Sonoma	Sonoma Twp	91	441
Andrew	39	m	w	IREL	Solano	Silveyville Twp	90	74
Charles	19	m	w	CA	Sonoma	Vallejo Twp	91	461
Edward	15	m	w	MO	Sonoma	Sonoma Twp	91	443
Emily T	44	f	w	NY	Sonoma	Cloverdale Twp	91	266
J F	41	m	w	OH	Sutter	Butte Twp	92	92
John	18	m	w	IL	Solano	Vacaville Twp	90	117
FOUTZ								
Edward	25	m	w	BADE	Placer	Auburn P O	76	373
Emery	20	m	w	MI	Monterey	Monterey Twp	74	346
FOUXCROUX								
Simon	27	m	w	CANA	Marin	San Rafael Twp	74	34
FOVEY								
William	28	m	w	ENGL	Colusa	Colusa	71	290
FOW								
Ah	53	m	c	CHIN	San Francisco	6-Wd San Francisco	81	58
Ah	50	m	c	CHIN	San Mateo	Half Moon Bay P O	87	402
Ah	46	m	c	CHIN	Plumas	Mineral Twp	77	25
Ah	46	m	c	CHIN	San Francisco	San Francisco P O	80	517
Ah	43	m	c	CHIN	Santa Barbara	Santa Barbara P O	87	452
Ah	40	m	c	CHIN	San Francisco	6-Wd San Francisco	81	47
Ah	40	m	c	CHIN	San Francisco	6-Wd San Francisco	81	130
Ah	40	m	c	CHIN	Amador	Volcano P O	69	377
Ah	39	m	c	CHIN	Placer	Dutch Flat P O	76	410

Name	Age	S	R	B-PL	County	Locale	Series M593 Roll	Pg
Ah	39	m	c	CHIN	San Francisco	San Francisco P O	80	515
Ah	39	m	c	CHIN	Alameda	Alameda	68	17
Ah	35	m	c	CHIN	Inyo	Cerro Gordo Twp	73	318
Ah	35	m	c	CHIN	San Francisco	6-Wd San Francisco	81	69
Ah	35	m	c	CHIN	Nevada	Nevada Twp	75	298
Ah	34	m	c	CHIN	San Francisco	San Francisco P O	80	495
Ah	34	m	c	CHIN	San Francisco	San Francisco P O	80	514
Ah	34	m	c	CHIN	San Francisco	San Francisco P O	80	521
Ah	32	m	c	CHIN	San Mateo	Pescadero P O	87	416
Ah	30	m	c	CHIN	El Dorado	Placerville	72	115
Ah	30	m	c	CHIN	Plumas	Plumas Twp	77	30
Ah	30	m	c	CHIN	Amador	Volcano P O	69	373
Ah	30	m	c	CHIL	Alameda	Brooklyn	68	27
Ah	30	m	c	CHIN	Alameda	Oakland	68	266
Ah	29	m	c	CHIN	El Dorado	Diamond Springs Tw	72	25
Ah	29	m	c	CHIN	Tuolumne	Chinese Camp P O	93	369
Ah	29	m	c	CHIN	Santa Barbara	Santa Maria P O	87	513
Ah	29	m	c	CHIN	Butte	Concow Twp	70	11
Ah	28	m	c	CHIN	San Francisco	San Francisco P O	80	518
Ah	28	m	c	CHIN	Nevada	Eureka Twp	75	136
Ah	28	m	c	CHIN	El Dorado	Diamond Springs Tw	72	32
Ah	24	m	c	CHIN	Marin	San Rafael Twp	74	39
Ah	22	m	c	CHIN	Tuolumne	Columbia P O	93	342
Ah	22	m	c	CHIN	Nevada	Little York Twp	75	245
Ah	22	m	c	CHIN	Alameda	Brooklyn Twp	68	41
Ah	21	f	c	CHIN	San Francisco	San Francisco P O	80	506
Ah	21	m	c	CHIN	San Francisco	San Francisco P O	80	513
Ah	20	m	c	CHIN	San Francisco	6-Wd San Francisco	81	58
Ah	20	m	c	CHIN	San Francisco	11-Wd San Francisc	84	477
Ah	20	m	c	CHIN	San Francisco	6-Wd San Francisco	81	85
Ah	19	m	c	CHIN	San Francisco	3-Wd San Francisco	79	310
Ah	19	m	c	CHIN	San Francisco	6-Wd San Francisco	81	40
Ah	18	m	c	CHIN	San Joaquin	Tulare Twp	86	251
Ah	18	m	c	CHIN	Nevada	Eureka Twp	75	140
Ah	16	m	c	CHIN	Mendocino	Point Arena Twp	74	224
Ah	16	m	c	CHIN	Placer	Bath P O	76	459
Ah	12	m	c	CHIN	San Francisco	6-Wd San Francisco	81	145
Ch	14	m	w	CHIN	Sacramento	Brighton Twp	77	78
Chew	29	m	c	CHIN	El Dorado	Greenwood Twp	72	56
Chim	10	f	c	CHIN	Placer	Auburn P O	76	370
Ching	16	m	c	CHIN	San Francisco	San Francisco P O	83	404
Chok	20	m	c	CHIN	San Francisco	6-Wd San Francisco	81	68
Chow	34	m	c	CHIN	Solano	Vacaville Twp	90	131
Choy	29	m	c	CHIN	Butte	Chico Twp	70	28
E	42	m	c	CHIN	El Dorado	Mud Springs Twp	72	75
Sin	62	m	c	CHIN	Yuba	Bullards Bar P O	93	552
FOWAR								
George	35	m	w	MEXI	Tuolumne	Big Oak Flat P O	93	392
FOWARD								
Waler	63	m	w	CT	Yolo	Buckeye Twp	93	411
FOWGUSHERM								
H	18	m	w	CA	Monterey	Castroville Twp	74	341
FOWKE								
William D	32	m	w	MD	Placer	Dutch Flat P O	76	415
FOWKES								
Richard	38	m	w	IREL	San Francisco	2-Wd San Francisco	79	251
FOWLE								
Elcho	5	m	w	MI	Yolo	Grafton Twp	93	494
Joseph	44	m	w	NY	Butte	Chico Twp	70	16
Noble	22	m	w	ITAL	Butte	Ophir Twp	70	102
FOWLER								
A C	58	m	w	VA	Sacramento	4-Wd Sacramento	77	325
Albert	60	m	w	NY	San Francisco	2-Wd San Francisco	79	236
Alex	30	m	w	CANA	Solano	Vallejo	90	212
Alex	30	m	w	CANA	Solano	Vallejo	90	213
Alexander	31	m	w	OH	San Francisco	11-Wd San Francisc	84	512
Allen	37	m	w	PA	San Francisco	5-Wd San Francisco	81	26
Alonzo	31	m	w	OH	Solano	Montezuma Twp	90	68
Andrew	35	m	b	MA	Santa Clara	2-Wd San Jose	88	319
Andrew J	45	m	w	DE	Colusa	Butte Twp	71	267
Ann	24	f	w	PA	San Francisco	8-Wd San Francisco	82	348
Benjamin F	45	m	w	MO	Stanislaus	San Joaquin Twp	92	73
C A	36	m	w	ME	Monterey	San Benito Twp	74	383
C A	32	f	w	NY	Solano	Vallejo	90	217
Charles	36	m	w	NY	Monterey	Pajaro Twp	74	374
Charles	36	m	w	MO	Monterey	San Juan Twp	74	390
Charles B	46	m	w	IN	Yolo	Cottonwood Twp	93	472
Chas	24	m	w	HAMB	San Francisco	1-Wd San Francisco	79	128
Douglas T	26	m	w	PA	Santa Barbara	Las Cruces P O	87	515
Edward	48	m	w	IN	Merced	Snelling P O	74	271
Edward	30	m	w	NY	Contra Costa	Martinez P O	71	379
Elsie	25	m	w	IREL	Solano	Vallejo	90	215
Emeson A	35	m	w	MA	Nevada	Bridgeport Twp	75	106
Eva	18	f	w	ME	Santa Clara	Gilroy Twp	88	80
F H	37	m	w	DC	San Joaquin	1-Wd Stockton	86	126
F M	28	m	w	MI	Alameda	Oakland	68	197
Filman	31	m	w	MO	Kern	Tehachapi P O	73	355
Frances L	43	f	w	MA	Calaveras	Copperopolis P O	70	254
Frank	44	m	w	OH	San Bernardino	Chino Twp	78	410
Frank	37	m	w	SCOT	Alameda	Oakland	68	265
Frank	22	m	w	OH	Solano	Vacaville Twp	90	134
Frank A	11	m	w	CA	Sacramento	3-Wd Sacramento	77	310
Fred J	24	m	w	ENGL	San Francisco	1-Wd San Francisco	79	11
George	19	m	w	TX	Los Angeles	Los Nietos Twp	73	589
Gertrude	70	f	w	CA	San Joaquin	Douglas Twp	86	48
H	40	f	w	VT	San Francisco	San Francisco P O	83	110
Hardwar D	38	m	w	NC	Los Angeles	Los Nietos Twp	73	573

© 2001 by Heritage Quest. All rights reserved.

Name	Age	S	R	B-PL	County	Locale	Roll (Series M593)	Pg
Henry	48	m	w	IL	Napa	Napa	75	43
Henry	36	m	w	WALE	Nevada	Bridgeport Twp	75	102
Henry P	40	m	w	AR	El Dorado	Mountain Twp	72	68
J B	28	m	w	NY	San Francisco	1-Wd San Francisco	79	26
J D	33	m	w	MO	Monterey	San Juan Twp	74	390
J G	57	m	w	CANA	Alameda	Oakland	68	233
J N	36	m	w	NH	Alameda	Oakland	68	164
Jackson	32	m	w	ME	Santa Cruz	Pajaro Twp	89	350
Jacob	29	m	w	BADE	Butte	Ophir Twp	70	112
James	39	m	w	IN	Stanislaus	San Joaquin Twp	92	77
James	33	m	w	NH	Alameda	Brooklyn	68	28
James	24	m	w	PA	Colusa	Grand Island Twp	71	307
James E	41	m	w	NY	Sonoma	Bodega Twp	91	248
James W	34	m	w	KY	Yolo	Cache Crk Twp	93	451
Jane	36	f	w	NY	Yuba	Marysville Twp	93	570
Jeremiah	65	m	w	MA	Sacramento	Sutter Twp	77	381
Jerusha G	50	f	w	MA	El Dorado	Diamond Springs Tw	72	23
John	63	m	w	TN	Merced	Snelling P O	74	271
John	44	m	w	ENGL	Alameda	Oakland	68	177
John	35	m	w	IREL	Stanislaus	Washington Twp	92	84
John	29	m	w	ENGL	Solano	Vallejo	90	198
John	28	m	w	ENGL	Nevada	Bridgeport Twp	75	124
John	27	m	w	MO	Napa	Napa	75	13
John	26	m	w	NJ	Sacramento	Sutter Twp	77	390
John	24	m	w	IREL	San Mateo	San Mateo P O	87	360
John E	35	m	w	IN	Yolo	Cache Crk Twp	93	447
John H	31	m	w	NY	Sonoma	Bodega Twp	91	248
John J	26	m	w	MA	El Dorado	Diamond Springs Tw	72	34
John K	33	m	w	NY	Siskiyou	Yreka	89	653
John T	36	m	w	IL	Stanislaus	San Joaquin Twp	92	77
John W	32	m	w	IREL	San Francisco	San Francisco P O	83	67
L C	35	m	w	OH	Solano	Vallejo	90	209
Laura	36	f	w	CT	San Francisco	11-Wd San Francisc	84	560
Lemuel	32	m	w	NY	San Francisco	5-Wd San Francisco	81	30
Martin	38	m	w	DENM	Butte	Chico Twp	70	45
Mary	30	f	w	ENGL	San Francisco	3-Wd San Francisco	79	317
Mary A	62	f	w	VA	San Francisco	San Francisco P O	83	144
Melina	24	m	w	MO	Yolo	Cache Crk Twp	93	444
Mortimer R	61	m	w	CT	Yolo	Cache Crk Twp	93	434
N	48	m	w	IN	San Joaquin	Douglas Twp	86	48
Nicholas	35	m	w	NY	San Francisco	5-Wd San Francisco	81	34
Patrick	25	m	w	IREL	Santa Clara	2-Wd San Jose	88	319
Peter	35	m	w	OH	Colusa	Grand Island Twp	71	302
Phebe E	35	f	w	NY	Sonoma	Bodega Twp	91	248
Prudence	42	f	w	MA	San Francisco	7-Wd San Francisco	81	158
Robert	51	m	w	ENGL	Sonoma	Sonoma Twp	91	437
S	35	m	w	NH	Alameda	Oakland	68	148
S B	29	m	w	ME	Nevada	Washington Twp	75	342
S T	32	m	w	ME	Solano	Vallejo	90	176
Sam	28	m	w	MO	San Joaquin	Liberty Twp	86	92
Saml	44	m	w	IN	Merced	Snelling P O	74	271
Saml S	58	m	w	OH	Plumas	Washington Twp	77	54
Sarah	11	f	w	CA	Sonoma	Petaluma Twp	91	319
Seven	34	m	w	OH	Solano	Suisun Twp	90	116
Stephen C	73	m	w	NY	Sonoma	Bodega Twp	91	248
T S	47	m	w	NY	Sacramento	3-Wd Sacramento	77	310
Theophilus	33	m	w	NY	Sonoma	Bodega Twp	91	253
Thomas	40	m	w	IREL	Tulare	Visalia	92	297
Thomas	13	m	w	CA	Napa	Yountville Twp	75	86
Thompson F	34	m	w	MO	Santa Clara	1-Wd San Jose	88	249
W L	35	m	w	OH	Yuba	W Bear Rvr Twp	93	684
W P	40	m	w	MA	Merced	Snelling P O	74	259
Welcom	51	m	w	TN	Merced	Snelling P O	74	271
Whitehead	36	m	w	NY	Sonoma	Bodega Twp	91	248
William	54	m	w	OH	San Francisco	11-Wd San Francisc	84	541
William	52	m	w	NY	Napa	Napa	75	19
William	40	m	w	ENGL	San Francisco	San Francisco P O	83	358
William	39	m	w	PRUS	San Francisco	1-Wd San Francisco	79	49
William B	56	m	w	CANA	Nevada	Grass Valley Twp	75	158
William B	28	m	w	ME	Nevada	Grass Valley Twp	75	214
William J	37	m	w	IN	Yolo	Cache Crk Twp	93	449
William L	65	m	w	TN	Yolo	Cache Crk Twp	93	441
Wm	56	m	w	MD	Sutter	Butte Twp	92	99
Wm	45	m	w	ENGL	El Dorado	Kelsey Twp	72	59
Wm	37	m	w	NY	San Joaquin	3-Wd Stockton	86	236
Wm H	9	m	w	CA	Shasta	Shasta P O	89	460
Wm K	48	m	w	WV	Tuolumne	Columbia P O	93	353
FOWLEY								
Ellen	22	f	w	NY	Nevada	Bridgeport Twp	75	102
Timothy	26	m	w	IREL	San Francisco	San Francisco P O	83	89
FOWN								
Ah	22	m	c	CHIN	Colusa	Grand Island Twp	71	306
Yi	45	m	c	CHIN	San Francisco	6-Wd San Francisco	81	84
FOWSER								
James	55	m	w	PA	Mendocino	Ukiah Twp	74	236
FOX								
Abraham D	43	m	w	PA	Alpine	Silver Mtn P O	69	306
Agnes	25	f	w	SAXO	San Francisco	8-Wd San Francisco	82	497
Ah	41	m	c	CHIN	San Francisco	San Francisco P O	80	466
Ah	34	m	c	CHIN	San Francisco	San Francisco P O	80	499
Ah	30	m	c	CHIN	Alameda	Oakland	68	224
Ah	17	m	c	CHIN	San Francisco	San Francisco P O	80	500
Alexander	47	m	w	ENGL	Napa	Napa	75	46
Ambross	11	m	w	CA	Monterey	Castroville Twp	74	334
Ann Elizabeth	59	f	w	ENGL	Plumas	Indian Twp	77	11
Anna	25	f	w	IREL	Alameda	Oakland	68	147
Annie	11	f	w	IREL	Santa Clara	2-Wd San Jose	88	337

Name	Age	S	R	B-PL	County	Locale	Roll (Series M593)	Pg
B	20	f	w	IREL	San Francisco	San Francisco P O	85	783
B B	35	m	w	OH	Mendocino	Sanel Twp	74	227
Bernard S	42	m	w	IREL	Santa Clara	San Jose Twp	88	194
Bridget	21	f	w	IREL	San Francisco	2-Wd San Francisco	79	139
Charles	45	m	w	OH	San Diego	Julian Dist	78	470
Charles	32	m	w	BADE	San Francisco	3-Wd San Francisco	79	328
Charles	28	m	w	IREL	San Francisco	San Francisco P O	83	213
Charles	25	m	w	CANA	Alameda	Oakland	68	253
Charles	24	m	w	ENGL	San Francisco	6-Wd San Francisco	81	153
Charles D	21	m	w	NY	San Francisco	6-Wd San Francisco	81	120
Charles F	48	m	w	CANA	Nevada	Little York Twp	75	238
Charles J	35	m	w	MA	San Diego	San Diego	78	507
Charles N	41	m	w	MI	San Mateo	Redwood Twp	87	369
Chas C	21	m	w	PRUS	Marin	San Rafael Twp	74	43
Chester P	29	m	w	MI	San Mateo	Redwood Twp	87	367
Conrad	20	m	w	HDAR	San Francisco	San Francisco P O	80	353
Daniel	39	m	w	OH	Yuba	Marysville Twp	93	570
Daniel W	45	m	w	CT	El Dorado	Georgetown Twp	72	36
David	27	m	w	MI	Contra Costa	Martinez P O	71	388
Elizabeth	40	f	w	IREL	Santa Clara	Gilroy Twp	88	67
Francis	24	m	w	IA	Colusa	Butte Twp	71	265
Frank Steers	39	m	w	ENGL	Plumas	Indian Twp	77	9
Frederick	35	m	w	PRUS	San Francisco	San Francisco P O	83	364
Geo	29	m	w	NY	San Joaquin	2-Wd Stockton	86	205
George	47	m	w	ENGL	Alameda	Alameda	68	7
George W	32	m	w	MI	San Mateo	Redwood Twp	87	365
Gustav	27	m	w	PRUS	Sacramento	3-Wd Sacramento	77	284
Harison	37	m	w	IL	Trinity	Lewiston Pct	92	213
Henry	37	m	w	FRAN	El Dorado	Greenwood Twp	72	51
Henry	23	m	w	NY	San Francisco	1-Wd San Francisco	79	39
Henry B	36	m	w	POLA	San Francisco	3-Wd San Francisco	79	299
Hiram	38	m	w	VT	San Francisco	San Francisco P O	80	486
Horace	45	m	w	MA	San Francisco	7-Wd San Francisco	81	164
Horton	32	m	w	NY	San Francisco	5-Wd San Francisco	81	34
Huldah	22	f	w	PRUS	San Francisco	San Francisco P O	83	177
J A	49	m	w	ENGL	Sacramento	3-Wd Sacramento	77	281
J M	33	m	w	KY	Lake	Lower Lake	73	416
Jacob	38	m	w	HANO	Yolo	Merritt Twp	93	506
James	57	m	w	WI	Yolo	Putah Twp	93	520
James	48	m	w	IREL	Calaveras	San Andreas P O	70	159
James	40	m	w	IREL	Contra Costa	San Pablo Twp	71	359
James	40	m	w	IREL	Placer	Lincoln P O	76	485
James	36	m	w	IREL	San Francisco	San Francisco P O	83	266
James	36	m	w	IREL	Alameda	Oakland	68	144
James	32	m	w	IREL	San Francisco	11-Wd San Francisc	84	571
James	30	m	w	ENGL	Monterey	Monterey Twp	74	349
James	25	m	w	IREL	Marin	Sausalito Twp	74	74
James	20	m	w	NY	San Francisco	2-Wd San Francisco	79	216
James W	39	m	w	VA	Siskiyou	Cottonwood Twp	89	592
Jerome B	36	m	w	NY	Santa Clara	Santa Clara Twp	88	178
Jesse	31	m	w	VA	Tulare	Visalia	92	291
John	50	m	w	IREL	Fresno	Millerton P O	72	150
John	50	m	w	IREL	San Francisco	7-Wd San Francisco	81	202
John	42	m	w	IREL	San Joaquin	3-Wd Stockton	86	236
John	41	m	w	IREL	Humboldt	Eureka Twp	72	260
John	41	m	w	OH	El Dorado	Placerville	72	127
John	40	m	w	IREL	Calaveras	San Andreas P O	70	183
John	38	m	w	ME	Stanislaus	Empire Twp	92	45
John	36	m	w	IREL	Sacramento	4-Wd Sacramento	77	357
John	32	m	w	IREL	San Francisco	San Francisco P O	83	202
John	32	m	w	IREL	Contra Costa	Martinez P O	71	376
John	30	m	w	IREL	San Francisco	8-Wd San Francisco	82	495
John	27	m	w	IREL	Solano	Vacaville Twp	90	117
John	22	m	w	NY	Los Angeles	Los Angeles Twp	73	485
John	17	m	w	CA	Sonoma	Vallejo Twp	91	455
John A	67	m	w	CT	Sutter	Yuba Twp	92	140
John J	30	m	w	IREL	Humboldt	Eureka Twp	72	256
John L	31	m	w	IREL	San Francisco	1-Wd San Francisco	79	7
John W	38	m	w	IREL	San Francisco	San Francisco P O	83	240
Joseph	45	m	w	IREL	San Francisco	San Francisco P O	83	231
Julia	50	f	b	VA	San Francisco	San Francisco P O	85	751
Kate	49	f	w	MO	Siskiyou	Yreka	89	658
Kate	29	f	w	IREL	Solano	Vallejo	90	177
La Fayette	45	m	w	NC	Stanislaus	Branch Twp	92	2
Lizzie	19	f	w	NY	San Francisco	San Francisco P O	80	472
Lizzie	14	f	w	CA	San Francisco	San Francisco P O	85	798
Louisa	32	f	w	OH	Plumas	Quartz Twp	77	40
Martin	29	m	w	FRAN	San Francisco	San Francisco P O	80	483
Martin	29	m	w	FRNK	San Francisco	San Francisco P O	80	356
Martin	28	m	w	CANA	Humboldt	Arcata Twp	72	231
Marx	26	m	w	POLA	Monterey	San Juan Twp	74	404
Mary	23	f	w	FRNK	San Francisco	San Francisco P O	80	356
Mary	16	f	w	NY	Contra Costa	Martinez P O	71	403
Mary S	41	f	w	IREL	Alameda	Oakland	68	190
Maurice	40	m	w	ENGL	San Francisco	2-Wd San Francisco	79	172
Michael	39	m	w	IREL	Monterey	Castroville Twp	74	334
Michael	28	m	w	IREL	Placer	Rocklin Twp	76	468
Morgan	34	m	w	OH	Sonoma	Petaluma Twp	91	338
N B	37	m	w	MA	Tuolumne	Big Oak Flat P O	93	394
Nicholas	28	m	w	MO	Colusa	Colusa Twp	71	274
Orson	45	m	w	CANA	Trinity	Weaverville Pct	92	224
Oskar	45	m	w	CT	Trinity	Weaverville Pct	92	227
Otis	20	m	w	NY	San Joaquin	Liberty Twp	86	96
P E	23	m	w	IREL	San Francisco	San Francisco P O	85	756
Patrick	46	m	w	IREL	Marin	Nicasio Twp	74	18
Patrick	30	m	w	IREL	Solano	Suisun Twp	90	114
Patrick	25	m	w	IREL	Solano	Vallejo	90	201

© 2001 by Heritage Quest. All rights reserved.

Name	Age	S	R	B-PL	County	Locale	Roll	Pg
Peter	27	m	w	RI	Solano	Vallejo	90	203
Philip	40	m	w	PRUS	San Francisco	San Francisco P O	83	377
Philliph	35	m	w	IREL	San Francisco	11-Wd San Francisc	84	441
Presley B	52	m	w	KY	Butte	Chico Twp	70	48
Richard	50	m	w	IREL	Sacramento	4-Wd Sacramento	77	371
Richard	35	m	w	IREL	San Francisco	7-Wd San Francisco	81	221
Robert	64	m	w	ENGL	Yolo	Grafton Twp	93	499
S	42	m	w	OH	Lake	Morgan Valley	73	424
Samuel	37	m	w	PRUS	San Francisco	11-Wd San Francisc	84	629
Sarah E	24	f	w	OH	Yolo	Cache Crk Twp	93	428
Sarah E	24	f	w	OH	San Francisco	San Francisco P O	83	275
T R	32	m	w	IL	Alameda	Oakland	68	172
Thomas	53	m	w	IREL	Butte	Wyandotte Twp	70	142
Thomas	47	m	w	IREL	San Diego	San Diego	78	483
Thomas	46	m	w	IREL	San Diego	San Pasqual Valley	78	525
Thomas	44	m	w	IREL	San Francisco	6-Wd San Francisco	81	134
Thomas	36	m	w	TN	Sutter	Yuba Twp	92	142
Thomas	32	m	w	IREL	Placer	Bath P O	76	430
Thomasene	15	f	w	IN	Santa Clara	2-Wd San Jose	88	337
Thos	26	m	w	MO	Sonoma	Analy Twp	91	240
Timothy	30	m	w	IREL	San Francisco	7-Wd San Francisco	81	189
William	54	m	w	NY	Marin	Nicasio Twp	74	18
William	38	m	w	PA	Alameda	Eden Twp	68	92
William	34	m	w	IREL	Alameda	Oakland	68	154
Wm	2	m	w	CA	San Francisco	11-Wd San Francisc	84	617
Wm A	26	m	w	PRUS	Santa Barbara	San Buenaventura P	87	433
Wm H	40	m	w	ENGL	Amador	Ione City P O	69	371
Wm R	37	m	w	OH	Butte	Ophir Twp	70	118
Woodford	25	m	w	ME	San Francisco	8-Wd San Francisco	82	382
FOXALL								
D	41	m	w	NC	Napa	Napa Twp	75	73
FOXEN								
Benjamin	72	m	w	ENGL	Santa Barbara	Santa Maria P O	87	513
Reyer	38	m	w	CA	Santa Barbara	Santa Barbara P O	87	490
Wm	37	m	w	CA	Santa Barbara	Santa Maria P O	87	513
FOXIPINS								
John	36	m	w	HOLL	Amador	Jackson P O	69	338
FOXWELL								
Geo W	27	m	w	MD	Sonoma	Analy Twp	91	245
Jonathan	39	m	m	IL	El Dorado	Placerville Twp	72	105
FOXWORTHY								
Jas	45	m	w	MO	Santa Clara	Almaden Twp	88	17
FOY								
Ah	70	m	c	CHIN	Santa Clara	1-Wd San Jose	88	271
Ah	60	m	c	CHIN	Sacramento	Center Twp	77	85
Ah	60	m	c	CHIN	Santa Clara	San Jose Twp	88	192
Ah	6	f	c	CA	San Francisco	San Francisco P O	80	525
Ah	50	m	c	CHIN	Nevada	Eureka Twp	75	141
Ah	50	m	c	CHIN	San Francisco	San Francisco P O	80	455
Ah	50	m	c	CHIN	San Francisco	San Francisco P O	80	497
Ah	49	m	c	CHIN	Sacramento	Granite Twp	77	149
Ah	49	m	c	CHIN	Sacramento	Granite Twp	77	138
Ah	48	m	c	CHIN	Sacramento	Cosumnes Twp	77	92
Ah	47	m	c	CHIN	Sacramento	Cosumnes Twp	77	95
Ah	46	m	c	CHIN	San Francisco	San Francisco P O	80	502
Ah	43	m	c	CHIN	San Francisco	San Francisco P O	80	503
Ah	42	m	c	CHIN	Fresno	Millerton P O	72	201
Ah	41	m	c	CHIN	San Francisco	San Francisco P O	80	501
Ah	41	m	c	CHIN	San Francisco	San Francisco P O	80	491
Ah	40	m	c	CHIN	Santa Clara	1-Wd San Jose	88	272
Ah	40	f	c	CHIN	El Dorado	Diamond Springs Tw	72	26
Ah	40	m	c	CHIN	Nevada	Nevada Twp	75	277
Ah	40	m	c	CHIN	Nevada	Meadow Lake Twp	75	256
Ah	40	m	c	CHIN	San Francisco	6-Wd San Francisco	81	66
Ah	39	m	c	CHIN	San Francisco	San Francisco P O	80	502
Ah	38	m	c	CHIN	Mariposa	Mariposa P O	74	137
Ah	37	m	c	CHIN	Nevada	Bridgeport Twp	75	106
Ah	37	m	c	CHIN	Sacramento	American Twp	77	68
Ah	37	m	c	CHIN	Sacramento	American Twp	77	67
Ah	36	m	c	CHIN	San Francisco	San Francisco P O	80	457
Ah	36	m	c	CHIN	San Francisco	San Francisco P O	80	524
Ah	36	m	c	CHIN	Amador	Fiddletown P O	69	438
Ah	36	m	c	CHIN	Mariposa	Mariposa P O	74	107
Ah	35	m	c	CHIN	Placer	Lincoln P O	76	484
Ah	34	m	c	CHIN	San Mateo	San Mateo P O	87	356
Ah	34	m	c	CHIN	San Francisco	San Francisco P O	80	513
Ah	34	m	c	CHIN	San Francisco	San Francisco P O	80	517
Ah	34	f	c	CHIN	San Francisco	San Francisco P O	80	523
Ah	34	m	c	CHIN	Amador	Ione City P O	69	369
Ah	34	m	c	CHIN	Alameda	Washington Twp	68	271
Ah	34	m	c	CHIN	Butte	Hamilton Twp	70	72
Ah	34	m	c	CHIN	Sacramento	Center Twp	77	87
Ah	32	m	c	CHIN	San Francisco	San Francisco P O	80	523
Ah	32	m	c	CHIN	Sacramento	Granite Twp	77	155
Ah	31	m	c	CHIN	Santa Clara	Fremont Twp	88	57
Ah	31	f	c	CHIN	San Francisco	San Francisco P O	80	521
Ah	31	m	c	CHIN	Santa Clara	San Jose Twp	88	194
Ah	31	m	c	CHIN	San Francisco	San Francisco P O	80	493
Ah	30	m	c	CHIN	San Francisco	San Francisco P O	80	500
Ah	30	m	c	CHIN	Colusa	Colusa	71	300
Ah	30	m	c	CHIN	Sacramento	Granite Twp	77	137
Ah	30	m	c	CHIN	San Francisco	San Francisco P O	80	435
Ah	30	m	c	CHIN	Yolo	Putah Twp	93	516
Ah	29	m	c	CHIN	San Francisco	San Francisco P O	80	513
Ah	29	m	c	CHIN	San Francisco	San Francisco P O	80	515
Ah	29	f	c	CHIN	San Francisco	San Francisco P O	80	524
Ah	29	m	c	CHIN	Nevada	Eureka Twp	75	127
Ah	29	m	c	CHIN	Butte	Chico Twp	70	29
Ah	29	m	c	CHIN	San Francisco	San Francisco P O	80	456
Ah	29	m	c	CHIN	San Francisco	San Francisco P O	80	500
Ah	28	m	c	CHIN	San Francisco	San Francisco P O	80	502
Ah	28	m	c	CHIN	San Francisco	San Francisco P O	80	502
Ah	28	m	c	CHIN	San Francisco	San Francisco P O	80	513
Ah	28	m	c	CHIN	El Dorado	Diamond Springs Tw	72	28
Ah	28	m	c	CHIN	Sacramento	Cosumnes Twp	77	94
Ah	28	m	c	CHIN	Sacramento	Center Twp	77	85
Ah	28	m	c	CHIN	Sacramento	Cosumnes Twp	77	92
Ah	28	m	c	CHIN	Placer	Bath P O	76	460
Ah	28	m	c	CHIN	Sacramento	4-Wd Sacramento	77	337
Ah	28	m	c	CHIN	Sacramento	Natomas Twp	77	168
Ah	28	m	c	CHIN	San Francisco	6-Wd San Francisco	81	65
Ah	27	m	c	CHIN	Santa Clara	1-Wd San Jose	88	271
Ah	27	m	c	CHIN	Yuba	Marysville	93	619
Ah	27	m	c	CHIN	Amador	Fiddletown P O	69	436
Ah	27	m	c	CHIN	Butte	Chico Twp	70	27
Ah	27	m	c	CHIN	Mariposa	Mariposa P O	74	114
Ah	26	f	c	CHIN	San Francisco	San Francisco P O	80	526
Ah	26	m	c	CHIN	Sacramento	Georgianna Twp	77	129
Ah	26	m	c	CHIN	Sacramento	Granite Twp	77	137
Ah	26	f	c	CHIN	Sacramento	Granite Twp	77	152
Ah	26	m	c	CHIN	San Francisco	San Francisco P O	80	498
Ah	26	m	c	CHIN	San Francisco	San Francisco P O	80	496
Ah	25	m	c	CHIN	Placer	Summit P O	76	497
Ah	25	m	c	CHIN	Sacramento	1-Wd Sacramento	77	195
Ah	25	m	c	CHIN	San Francisco	San Francisco P O	83	298
Ah	25	m	c	CHIN	San Francisco	6-Wd San Francisco	81	65
Ah	25	m	c	CHIN	Yolo	Grafton Twp	93	496
Ah	24	m	c	CHIN	Solano	Vallejo	90	142
Ah	24	f	c	CHIN	San Francisco	San Francisco P O	80	505
Ah	24	m	c	CHIN	San Francisco	San Francisco P O	80	516
Ah	24	m	c	CHIN	Placer	Newcastle Twp	76	479
Ah	24	m	c	CHIN	Nevada	Nevada Twp	75	322
Ah	24	m	c	CHIN	Placer	Summit P O	76	497
Ah	24	f	c	CHIN	San Francisco	San Francisco P O	80	435
Ah	24	m	c	CHIN	Yolo	Buckeye Twp	93	412
Ah	23	f	c	CHIN	San Francisco	San Francisco P O	80	530
Ah	23	m	c	CHIN	San Francisco	San Francisco P O	80	521
Ah	23	m	c	CHIN	Nevada	Eureka Twp	75	140
Ah	23	m	c	CHIN	Placer	Newcastle Twp	76	479
Ah	23	f	c	CHIN	Solano	Vallejo	90	179
Ah	22	m	c	CHIN	Santa Clara	2-Wd San Jose	88	297
Ah	22	m	c	CHIN	Santa Clara	2-Wd San Jose	88	297
Ah	22	m	c	CHIN	San Mateo	Belmont P O	87	371
Ah	22	m	c	CHIN	Solano	Benicia	90	14
Ah	22	m	c	CHIN	Nevada	Eureka Twp	75	136
Ah	22	m	c	CHIN	Nevada	Meadow Lake Twp	75	259
Ah	21	m	c	CHIN	Nevada	Bridgeport Twp	75	125
Ah	21	f	c	CHIN	Los Angeles	Santa Ana Twp	73	613
Ah	21	m	c	CHIN	Nevada	Meadow Lake Twp	75	259
Ah	21	m	c	CHIN	San Francisco	San Francisco P O	80	500
Ah	21	m	c	CHIN	Solano	Suisun Twp	90	105
Ah	20	m	c	CHIN	San Francisco	San Francisco P O	80	530
Ah	20	f	c	CHIN	Contra Costa	Martinez P O	71	398
Ah	20	f	c	CHIN	San Francisco	San Francisco P O	80	431
Ah	19	m	c	CHIN	Santa Clara	1-Wd San Jose	88	274
Ah	19	m	c	CHIN	Santa Clara	1-Wd San Jose	88	271
Ah	19	m	c	CHIN	Sacramento	3-Wd Sacramento	77	310
Ah	19	m	c	CHIN	Sacramento	2-Wd Sacramento	77	245
Ah	18	m	c	CHIN	Santa Clara	2-Wd San Jose	88	285
Ah	18	m	c	CHIN	Sacramento	Granite Twp	77	152
Ah	18	f	c	CHIN	Placer	Auburn P O	76	370
Ah	18	m	c	CHIN	San Francisco	San Francisco P O	80	499
Ah	17	m	c	CHIN	Santa Clara	San Jose Twp	88	192
Ah	16	f	c	CHIN	Contra Costa	Martinez P O	71	398
Ah	16	m	c	CHIN	San Francisco	San Francisco P O	85	749
Ah	15	m	c	CHIN	San Francisco	11-Wd San Francisc	84	624
Ah	15	m	c	CHIN	Napa	Napa	75	41
Ah	15	m	c	CHIN	San Francisco	8-Wd San Francisco	82	347
Ah Kee	53	m	c	CHIN	Amador	Jackson P O	69	347
Bridget	60	f	w	IREL	San Francisco	San Francisco P O	83	82
Charles	20	m	w	VT	San Mateo	Pescadero P O	87	413
Ching	21	m	c	CHIN	Nevada	Meadow Lake Twp	75	259
Christian	35	m	w	NORW	Humboldt	Table Bluff Twp	72	306
Daniel	40	m	w	PA	Plumas	Mineral Twp	77	20
Eliza P	54	f	w	NY	Santa Cruz	Santa Cruz	89	418
Fi	21	m	c	CHIN	Alameda	Washington Twp	68	297
Guss	28	m	c	CHIN	Yolo	Buckeye Twp	93	412
Henry M	19	m	w	ME	Mendocino	Little Rvr Twp	74	165
Hi	38	m	c	CHIN	Butte	Hamilton Twp	70	72
James E	27	m	w	PA	San Francisco	San Francisco P O	83	216
Jane R	64	f	w	NH	San Francisco	8-Wd San Francisco	82	393
John	54	m	w	IREL	Nevada	Bloomfield Twp	75	96
John	27	m	w	IREL	Merced	Snelling P O	74	274
John M	42	m	w	DC	San Bernardino	San Bernardino Twp	78	416
John W	27	m	w	ME	San Francisco	San Francisco P O	83	210
Jos	40	m	w	ME	Solano	Vallejo	90	142
Kee	28	m	c	CHIN	Amador	Ione City P O	69	364
Lee	27	m	c	CHIN	San Francisco	6-Wd San Francisco	81	49
Lee	25	m	c	CHIN	Santa Clara	San Jose Twp	88	183
Lee	21	f	c	CHIN	Mariposa	Mariposa P O	74	102
Lee My	34	m	c	CHIN	Amador	Jackson P O	69	344
Me	19	m	c	CHIN	Santa Clara	San Jose Twp	88	192
Me Kee	28	m	c	CHIN	Amador	Jackson P O	69	344
Michael	48	m	w	IREL	Sacramento	Granite Twp	77	150

(Series M593: Roll, Pg)

© 2001 by Heritage Quest. All rights reserved.

Name	Age	S	R	B-PL	County	Locale	Roll	Pg
						Series M593		
Micheal	40	m	w	IREL	San Francisco	7-Wd San Francisco	81	181
My	26	m	c	CHIN	Yolo	Merritt Twp	93	506
Peter	27	m	w	IREL	San Joaquin	2-Wd Stockton	86	203
Robert	30	m	w	PA	El Dorado	Cosumnes Twp	72	14
Samuel	38	m	w	ME	Los Angeles	Los Angeles	73	558
Sing	19	f	c	CHIN	Butte	Chico Twp	70	28
Sock	47	m	c	CHIN	Yuba	Marysville	93	622
Ti	26	m	c	CHIN	Santa Clara	2-Wd San Jose	88	297
Toy	27	f	c	CHIN	Nevada	Eureka Twp	75	136
William A	27	m	w	ME	Mendocino	Little Rvr Twp	74	170
William L	60	m	w	NC	Trinity	Lewiston Pct	92	213
Wm	50	m	w	CANA	Solano	Vallejo	90	172
Wo	41	m	c	CHIN	Santa Clara	San Jose Twp	88	191
Yang	29	m	c	CHIN	Solano	Suisun Twp	90	107
Yup	20	m	c	CHIN	Santa Clara	San Jose Twp	88	184
FOYD								
Antonie	13	f	w	CA	San Francisco	2-Wd San Francisco	79	233
FOYE								
Wm	36	m	w	CT	Sacramento	1-Wd Sacramento	77	172
Wm H	39	m	w	NH	San Francisco	8-Wd San Francisco	82	291
FOYL								
John	60	m	w	NH	Alameda	Brooklyn Twp	68	43
FOYLE								
Frederick	27	m	w	FRAN	Monterey	Castroville Twp	74	341
FOYLES								
M	50	m	w	RUSS	Alameda	Murray Twp	68	114
FRABRO								
Peter	51	m	w	FRAN	Mariposa	Mariposa P O	74	104
FRACH								
G Christian	43	m	w	WURT	San Francisco	San Francisco P O	83	176
FRACK								
Edward	45	m	w	MA	San Francisco	San Francisco P O	83	202
FRACY								
A	42	f	w	IREL	Sierra	Sierra Twp	89	569
FRADER								
Henry	27	m	w	HANO	San Francisco	2-Wd San Francisco	79	228
FRADING								
August	34	m	w	SWED	Mendocino	Big Rvr Twp	74	160
FRAEIHEIT								
Antone	32	m	w	BADE	Nevada	Bridgeport Twp	75	120
FRAGA								
Francisco	15	m	w	CA	San Luis Obispo	San Luis Obispo Tw	87	310
Joseph	26	m	w	PORT	Merced	Snelling P O	74	263
FRAGAY								
Henry	21	m	w	HANO	Sacramento	2-Wd Sacramento	77	248
FRAGEE								
Louis	28	m	w	CANA	Yolo	Cache Crk Twp	93	441
FRAGEL								
Hugo	26	m	w	PRUS	San Francisco	1-Wd San Francisco	79	128
FRAGELY								
Martin	32	m	w	IREL	San Francisco	San Francisco P O	83	410
FRAGENZA								
Thomas	35	f	w	ENGL	Sacramento	San Joaquin Twp	77	406
FRAGERA								
Refufio	19	m	w	MEXI	Santa Clara	Almaden Twp	88	5
FRAGINI								
David N	57	m	w	NY	Placer	Colfax P O	76	392
FRAGO								
Joseph	21	m	w	AZOR	Marin	Sausalito Twp	74	71
Moses	68	m	w	MA	Nevada	Nevada Twp	75	306
FRAHARTY								
Patk	50	m	w	IREL	Solano	Vallejo	90	213
FRAHLING								
Frank	22	m	w	PRUS	Los Angeles	Los Angeles	73	539
FRAHM								
Frank	44	m	w	GERM	Solano	Vallejo	90	151
Frank	16	m	w	MA	Solano	Vallejo	90	139
FRAIJO								
Gregorio	53	m	w	MEXI	Los Angeles	El Monte Twp	73	450
FRAIL								
James	35	m	w	PA	San Joaquin	Castoria Twp	86	6
Thos	43	m	w	IREL	San Francisco	11-Wd San Francisc	84	611
FRAIN								
John	43	m	w	MA	San Mateo	Redwood Twp	87	363
Martin R	35	m	w	MI	Siskiyou	Yreka Twp	89	664
Michael	45	m	w	IREL	San Francisco	San Francisco P O	85	758
FRAINA								
Frank	30	m	w	IREL	San Francisco	5-Wd San Francisco	81	35
FRAINER								
James	44	m	w	IREL	San Francisco	7-Wd San Francisco	81	223
John	36	m	w	IREL	Sacramento	4-Wd Sacramento	77	344
Thos	34	m	w	NY	Sacramento	4-Wd Sacramento	77	366
FRAISER								
Alex	38	m	w	CANA	Nevada	Washington Twp	75	346
Geo	24	m	w	NY	Sacramento	1-Wd Sacramento	77	185
FRAITES								
Joseph	35	m	w	PORT	Yuba	Parks Bar Twp	93	649
FRAIZE								
Matilda	18	f	w	PRUS	San Francisco	2-Wd San Francisco	79	175
FRAIZER								
M S	59	m	w	MD	El Dorado	Kelsey Twp	72	61
FRAJA								
Josefa	15	f	w	MEXI	Los Angeles	Los Nietos Twp	73	583
FRAKEN								
Zuleka	14	f	w	CA	San Joaquin	1-Wd Stockton	86	132
FRAKES								
John W	40	m	w	OH	Tulare	Visalia	92	298

Name	Age	S	R	B-PL	County	Locale	Roll	Pg
						Series M593		
L D	52	m	w	NY	Sacramento	4-Wd Sacramento	77	376
Saml H	37	m	w	IN	Fresno	Millerton P O	72	168
FRALER								
Chas	42	m	w	BAVA	Sierra	Sears Twp	89	559
Manuel	32	m	m	WIND	Tehama	Tehama Twp	92	193
FRALEY								
Danl	31	m	w	IREL	Klamath	South Fork Twp	73	385
John	56	m	w	BADE	El Dorado	Cosumnes Twp	72	17
FRALICH								
Mathias	44	m	w	FRAN	Plumas	Indian Twp	77	16
FRALICK								
Edwin	25	m	w	CANA	Nevada	Washington Twp	75	346
Hiram	28	m	w	CANA	Sacramento	4-Wd Sacramento	77	328
FRALLA								
Juan	11	m	w	CA	Santa Cruz	Soquel Twp	89	438
FRALSBURG								
Theodor	36	m	w	SPAI	San Joaquin	2-Wd Stockton	86	169
FRALY								
Jaana	19	m	w	SWIT	Santa Cruz	Santa Cruz Twp	89	397
James	43	m	w	VA	Sacramento	Lee Twp	77	161
FRAMBLEY								
M	32	m	w	CANA	Yuba	Marysville	93	593
FRAME								
Amos	38	m	w	PA	Humboldt	Eel Rvr Twp	72	252
Cornelius	35	m	w	IN	Sacramento	Sutter Twp	77	384
D F	51	m	w	OH	San Joaquin	Elliott Twp	86	72
David	60	m	w	KY	Sacramento	Sutter Twp	77	384
George	34	m	w	SCOT	Tuolumne	Chinese Camp P O	93	389
Joseph	35	m	w	NY	San Francisco	San Francisco P O	83	417
Josiah	37	m	w	OH	Tulare	Tule Rvr Twp	92	262
Mary E	16	f	w	CA	Del Norte	Smith Rvr Twp	71	476
Robert	45	m	w	IREL	San Francisco	San Francisco P O	83	168
Saml	36	m	w	PA	Siskiyou	Butte Twp	89	584
FRAMER								
Archibole	23	m	w	MO	Monterey	Monterey	74	354
John	41	m	w	DENM	San Francisco	2-Wd San Francisco	79	217
FRAMETTE								
John	32	m	w	AUST	San Francisco	1-Wd San Francisco	79	108
FRAMHAM								
Gilbert	38	m	w	ME	Los Angeles	Los Angeles Twp	73	491
FRANADA								
Mary	50	f	w	MEXI	San Joaquin	1-Wd Stockton	86	133
FRANAN								
Henry	26	m	w	HANO	San Francisco	San Francisco P O	83	81
FRANBEAU								
Frank	53	m	w	FRAN	Inyo	Cerro Gordo Twp	73	318
FRANBENHEIMER								
B	49	m	w	POLA	San Joaquin	2-Wd Stockton	86	179
FRANC								
Frank	40	m	w	FRAN	Sacramento	Sutter Twp	77	381
FRANCA								
John	40	m	w	PORT	Monterey	Pajaro Twp	74	373
Victoria	35	f	w	MEXI	Los Angeles	Santa Ana Twp	73	614
FRANCAIS								
George	30	m	w	CT	Sacramento	2-Wd Sacramento	77	208
FRANCALONA								
Joaquin	26	m	w	ITAL	San Francisco	1-Wd San Francisco	79	122
FRANCE								
Annie	21	f	w	NJ	Sacramento	1-Wd Sacramento	77	189
Bautista	21	m	w	CA	Santa Barbara	Las Cruces P O	87	516
Emanuel	40	m	w	AUST	Santa Barbara	San Buenaventura P	87	435
F	35	m	w	OH	Siskiyou	Scott Valley Twp	89	621
Geo W	39	m	w	MD	Santa Barbara	San Buenaventura P	87	438
Henry	55	m	w	ENGL	Sacramento	Sutter Twp	77	390
Henry	50	m	w	ENGL	Santa Clara	2-Wd San Jose	88	308
Jacob	28	m	w	VA	Los Angeles	Wilmington Twp	73	634
James	40	m	w	WURT	San Francisco	8-Wd San Francisco	82	416
Jas	32	m	w	SWIT	Sierra	Gibson Twp	89	540
Jerome	30	m	w	PRUS	San Francisco	5-Wd San Francisco	81	10
John R	45	m	w	VA	Butte	Hamilton Twp	70	70
John S	36	m	w	IN	Yolo	Cache Crk Twp	93	440
Olivica	99	m	w	CA	Santa Barbara	Las Cruces P O	87	516
P	31	m	w	PRUS	Alameda	Murray Twp	68	125
Peter	28	m	w	FRAN	Sacramento	Georgianna Twp	77	128
Polit	45	m	w	FRAN	Sacramento	Granite Twp	77	154
Sebastine	46	m	w	HESS	Alameda	Washington Twp	68	301
Secelia	30	f	w	DENM	Sonoma	Cloverdale Twp	91	269
William	22	m	w	KY	Santa Barbara	San Buenaventura P	87	427
William T	40	m	w	NJ	San Francisco	San Francisco P O	83	240
FRANCES								
Antone	46	m	w	PORT	Sacramento	Natomas Twp	77	169
Antone	25	m	w	PORT	Sacramento	Georgianna Twp	77	123
Antone	20	m	w	PORT	Alameda	Eden Twp	68	71
Antonio	30	m	w	AZOR	Monterey	Monterey Twp	74	344
C	37	m	b	WIND	Alameda	Oakland	68	129
Eben	38	m	w	MN	Butte	Chico Twp	70	29
Geo H	20	m	w	MA	Sacramento	3-Wd Sacramento	77	288
H A	49	m	w	MA	Alameda	Murray Twp	68	126
Henry	24	m	w	MO	Marin	San Rafael Twp	74	40
John	46	m	w	IREL	Humboldt	South Fork Twp	72	303
John	45	m	w	NY	San Francisco	11-Wd San Francisc	84	475
John	36	m	w	GERM	San Francisco	7-Wd San Francisco	81	262
John	33	m	w	PORT	San Francisco	1-Wd San Francisco	79	124
Joseph	62	m	w	PORT	San Francisco	1-Wd San Francisco	79	42
Joseph	25	m	w	PORT	Marin	San Rafael Twp	74	59
Joseph	25	m	w	AZOR	Marin	Nicasio Twp	74	20
Joseph	24	m	w	PORT	Alameda	Eden Twp	68	90

© 2001 by Heritage Quest. All rights reserved.

Name	Age	S	R	B-PL	County	Locale	Roll	Pg
Joseph	23	m	w	PORT	Alameda	Eden Twp	68	89
L	49	m	w	ENGL	San Francisco	San Francisco P O	85	795
Octove	27	m	w	CANA	San Mateo	Woodside P O	87	384
FRANCESCO								
Jackson	30	m	w	AZOR	San Francisco	1-Wd San Francisco	79	123
FRANCEY								
Victor	45	m	w	FRAN	Sacramento	Granite Twp	77	154
FRANCHI								
Tommisco	34	m	w	ITAL	San Francisco	11-Wd San Francisc	84	594
FRANCIS								
A A	26	m	w	ENGL	San Francisco	San Francisco P O	83	156
A J	37	m	w	NY	San Francisco	San Francisco P O	83	297
Ada	44	f	b	CT	San Joaquin	2-Wd Stockton	86	202
Albert	61	m	w	PORT	Solano	Montezuma Twp	90	66
Alexis	35	m	w	OH	Solano	Maine Prairie Twp	90	51
Allich A	43	m	w	PA	Yuba	North East Twp	93	647
Alx	22	m	w	SWIT	El Dorado	Georgetown Twp	72	42
Andrew	46	m	w	SWIT	Calaveras	San Andreas P O	70	209
Anton	35	m	w	PORT	Sacramento	Georgianna Twp	77	127
Antone	40	m	w	STHO	El Dorado	Salmon Falls Twp	72	130
Antone	40	m	w	SCOT	Alameda	Brooklyn Twp	68	45
Antone	40	m	w	PORT	Alameda	Washington Twp	68	282
Antone	35	m	w	PORT	Placer	Bath P O	76	460
Antonio	88	m	w	PORT	Santa Barbara	Santa Barbara P O	87	497
Caroline	23	f	w	MO	San Francisco	San Francisco P O	85	839
Charles	64	m	w	ENGL	Mariposa	Mariposa P O	74	137
Charles F	23	m	w	IL	Sonoma	Salt Point	91	385
Clara	17	f	w	MA	San Francisco	3-Wd San Francisco	79	325
Danl	63	m	w	MA	Sacramento	4-Wd Sacramento	77	376
David J	51	m	w	PA	El Dorado	Georgetown Twp	72	40
Elizabeth	23	f	w	MA	San Francisco	3-Wd San Francisco	79	325
Emanuel	29	m	w	PORT	Nevada	Rough & Ready Twp	75	328
Emanuel	20	m	w	PORT	Alameda	Washington Twp	68	272
Francis	52	m	w	WALE	Humboldt	Pacific Twp	72	298
G	49	m	w	ENGL	San Francisco	San Francisco P O	85	787
G	46	m	w	MA	Sacramento	4-Wd Sacramento	77	375
George	52	m	w	CT	Santa Clara	Fremont Twp	88	55
George	39	m	w	OH	Tulare	Visalia	92	289
George G	32	m	w	ME	San Francisco	8-Wd San Francisco	82	471
Harriet	22	f	w	MO	Yolo	Buckeye Twp	93	411
Henry	37	m	w	MI	San Luis Obispo	San Luis Obispo Tw	87	300
Henry M	24	m	w	IREL	San Francisco	8-Wd San Francisco	82	302
J F	39	m	w	MI	Alameda	Oakland	68	263
J G	32	m	w	NY	Napa	Napa	75	10
J P	38	m	w	ME	Sacramento	3-Wd Sacramento	77	258
J W	35	m	w	NY	San Francisco	8-Wd San Francisco	82	348
Jacob	65	m	w	SWED	El Dorado	Mud Springs Twp	72	88
Jacob	31	m	w	FRAN	San Francisco	1-Wd San Francisco	79	50
James	54	m	w	ENGL	Sacramento	Brighton Twp	77	78
James	54	m	w	ENGL	Inyo	Cerro Gordo Twp	73	323
James	30	m	w	CANA	Humboldt	Mattole Twp	72	287
James	25	m	b	WIND	San Francisco	San Francisco P O	80	368
James H	33	m	w	OH	Napa	Napa	75	4
James P	40	m	w	ENGL	Nevada	Grass Valley Twp	75	230
Jasper	17	m	w	TX	Santa Cruz	Santa Cruz Twp	89	391
Joaquin	45	m	w	PORT	Alameda	Washington Twp	68	298
Joe	29	m	w	PORT	Sacramento	Sutter Twp	77	387
John	55	m	w	WALE	Alameda	Brooklyn	68	27
John	51	m	b	PHIL	Mariposa	Mariposa P O	74	104
John	51	m	w	PA	Yuba	North East Twp	93	647
John	50	m	w	AZOR	Monterey	San Benito Twp	74	381
John	48	m	w	FRAN	Los Angeles	Wilmington Twp	73	640
John	40	m	w	CT	Butte	Chico Twp	70	33
John	40	m	w	PORT	Alameda	Washington Twp	68	274
John	39	m	w	PORT	San Francisco	7-Wd San Francisco	81	275
John	36	m	w	PORT	San Mateo	Pescadero P O	87	414
John	33	m	w	PORT	Nevada	Rough & Ready Twp	75	333
John	33	m	w	SCOT	Siskiyou	Yreka Twp	89	666
John	28	m	w	ENGL	Nevada	Grass Valley Twp	75	172
John	28	m	w	FRAN	San Francisco	7-Wd San Francisco	81	221
John	25	m	w	SCOT	Siskiyou	Yreka Twp	89	664
John F	25	m	w	IN	Mendocino	Anderson Twp	74	157
Jos	35	m	w	PORT	Sacramento	1-Wd Sacramento	77	179
Joseph	45	m	w	PORT	Alameda	Hayward	68	79
Joseph	45	m	w	PORT	Santa Cruz	Santa Cruz Twp	89	382
Joseph	45	m	m	BRAZ	San Francisco	11-Wd San Francisc	84	610
Joseph	40	m	w	PORT	Trinity	Lewiston Pct	92	213
Joseph	38	m	w	SCOT	Siskiyou	Yreka Twp	89	667
Joseph	37	m	w	PORT	San Mateo	Half Moon Bay P O	87	408
Joseph	32	m	w	SCOT	Alameda	Brooklyn Twp	68	50
Joseph	30	m	w	PORT	San Francisco	1-Wd San Francisco	79	101
Joseph	24	m	w	PORT	Plumas	Quartz Twp	77	34
Joseph	24	m	w	PORT	Alameda	Hayward	68	74
Joseph	23	m	w	PORT	San Mateo	Half Moon Bay P O	87	402
Joseph	22	m	w	SCOT	Siskiyou	Yreka Twp	89	664
Joseph	19	m	w	PORT	San Mateo	Half Moon Bay P O	87	390
Joshua	52	m	w	ENGL	Trinity	Canyon City Pct	92	201
Lewis	26	m	w	BELG	Nevada	Grass Valley Twp	75	218
Luis	20	m	w	FRAN	San Luis Obispo	San Luis Obispo Tw	87	310
Manuel	50	m	w	PORT	Alameda	Eden Twp	68	71
Manuel	37	m	w	PORT	Alameda	Hayward	68	78
Manuel	35	m	w	PORT	San Francisco	1-Wd San Francisco	79	95
Manuel	34	m	w	PORT	Marin	San Rafael Twp	74	33
Manuel	26	m	w	PORT	Santa Clara	Redwood Twp	88	121
Manul	32	m	w	PORT	San Francisco	San Francisco P O	80	533
Manwell	18	m	w	PORT	San Mateo	Half Moon Bay P O	87	390
Matthew	49	m	w	IREL	San Francisco	1-Wd San Francisco	79	93
Mirand	59	m	w	PHIL	San Mateo	Half Moon Bay P O	87	393
N J	40	m	w	ENGL	San Joaquin	2-Wd Stockton	86	166
Nicholas	40	m	w	FRAN	Solano	Rio Vista Twp	90	56
Patrick	21	m	w	IREL	Mendocino	Albion & Big Rvr T	74	167
Phillip	50	m	b	PHIL	Mariposa	Mariposa P O	74	104
Pierce	32	m	w	FRAN	San Francisco	5-Wd San Francisco	81	27
R	2	m	w	CA	Merced	Snelling P O	74	269
Robert	38	m	w	MA	San Francisco	11-Wd San Francisc	84	440
Robert C	46	m	w	PA	Santa Cruz	Santa Cruz	89	417
Ruanta	76	m	w	PHIL	San Mateo	Half Moon Bay P O	87	393
Samuel	42	m	b	PA	San Francisco	San Francisco P O	80	333
Samuel	41	m	w	RI	Mendocino	Point Arena Twp	74	224
Samuel	40	m	w	IREL	Sonoma	Bodega Twp	91	248
Samuel	36	m	w	ENGL	Tuolumne	Columbia P O	93	355
Samuel	22	m	w	IN	Santa Cruz	Soquel Twp	89	439
Samuel	19	m	i	CA	Yolo	Cache Crk Twp	93	427
Stephen	45	m	w	OH	Santa Barbara	San Buenaventura P	87	435
Stephen A	42	m	w	OH	Santa Barbara	San Buenaventura P	87	438
Thomas	37	m	w	ENGL	Calaveras	Copperopolis P O	70	247
Thomas J	36	m	w	ENGL	Yolo	Merritt Twp	93	505
Thos	36	m	w	PRUS	San Francisco	5-Wd San Francisco	81	20
William	39	m	w	ENGL	San Bernardino	San Bernardino Twp	78	452
William	37	m	w	VT	Plumas	Washington Twp	77	55
Willie O	38	m	w	ME	San Diego	San Diego	78	493
Wm	55	m	w	HAMB	San Francisco	San Francisco P O	83	120
Wm J	27	m	w	NY	Sonoma	Bodega Twp	91	250
FRANCISCA								
C	26	f	w	ITAL	San Francisco	San Francisco P O	85	789
FRANCISCO								
---	44	m	w	MEXI	Tehama	Mill Crk Twp	92	167
Adele	60	f	w	FRAN	San Francisco	6-Wd San Francisco	81	40
Antonio	54	m	w	BRAZ	Mendocino	Navarro & Big Rvr	74	167
Antonio	27	m	w	PORT	Alameda	Washington Twp	68	274
Brown	48	m	m	MEXI	Santa Barbara	Santa Barbara P O	87	455
C	46	m	w	MEXI	Sierra	Butte Twp	89	508
Clarence F	26	m	w	WI	San Diego	San Diego	78	492
Daniel	57	m	w	NY	Yolo	Buckeye Twp	93	408
De M	28	m	w	ITAL	Colusa	Grand Island Twp	71	308
Deist	40	m	w	MEXI	San Francisco	7-Wd San Francisco	81	162
Fortunat	43	m	w	ITAL	San Francisco	3-Wd San Francisco	79	289
G	32	m	w	MEXI	Sacramento	1-Wd Sacramento	77	195
Glandal	25	m	w	CHIL	Stanislaus	San Joaquin Twp	92	81
J	35	m	w	CA	Alameda	Murray Twp	68	107
John	40	m	w	PORT	Alameda	Alvarado	68	305
John	40	m	w	CHIL	El Dorado	Cosumnes Twp	72	16
John	39	m	w	SCOT	Siskiyou	Yreka Twp	89	666
John	28	m	w	SCOT	Siskiyou	Yreka Twp	89	669
Joseph	59	m	w	MEXI	Tuolumne	Sonora P O	93	315
Joseph	49	m	w	PORT	Klamath	Trinidad Twp	73	392
Joseph	44	m	w	PORT	Alameda	Washington Twp	68	269
Joseph	30	m	w	PORT	Alameda	Washington Twp	68	269
Justi	26	m	w	ITAL	Sonoma	Analy Twp	91	236
Leon	30	m	w	MEXI	Sacramento	2-Wd Sacramento	77	215
Leonardo	22	m	w	CUBA	San Francisco	2-Wd San Francisco	79	214
Lorenzo	38	f	c	CHIN	Mariposa	Mariposa P O	74	106
Louis	60	m	w	FRAN	San Francisco	6-Wd San Francisco	81	40
Manuel	39	m	w	AZOR	Yuba	Bullards Bar P O	93	547
Manuel	36	m	b	PHIL	Mariposa	Mariposa P O	74	106
Manuel	32	m	w	WIND	San Francisco	7-Wd San Francisco	81	223
Manuel	23	m	w	AZOR	Placer	Newcastle Twp	76	473
Manuel	20	m	w	PORT	Alameda	Eden Twp	68	85
Maria	9	m	w	CA	Santa Barbara	San Buenaventura P	87	441
Maria	30	m	w	CA	San Diego	San Pasqual	78	521
Martin	35	m	w	MEXI	Sonoma	Healdsburg & Mendo	91	283
Pedro	30	m	w	MEXI	Marin	Tomales Twp	74	85
Ramon	41	m	w	FRAN	Fresno	Millerton P O	72	193
FRANCISCOVICH								
John	38	m	w	AUST	Yuba	Marysville	93	614
Mattw	30	m	w	AUST	San Francisco	1-Wd San Francisco	79	127
FRANCK								
Fredk	44	m	w	BADE	Shasta	French Gulch P O	89	467
George C P	35	m	w	AUST	San Francisco	San Francisco P O	83	183
Ignatz	38	m	w	BADE	Shasta	French Gulch P O	89	468
John	19	m	w	MO	Shasta	Shasta P O	89	460
FRANCKLE								
Emil	46	m	w	BADE	San Francisco	San Francisco P O	83	200
FRANCO								
Charles	38	m	w	PRUS	Santa Clara	Fremont Twp	88	50
Pasqual	40	m	w	MEXI	Contra Costa	Martinez P O	71	385
FRANCOIS								
Chas	50	m	w	FRAN	Santa Clara	Gilroy Twp	88	99
Jane	31	f	w	FRAN	San Francisco	San Francisco P O	80	484
Noel	60	m	w	FRAN	Shasta	Stillwater P O	89	481
Papad	31	m	w	FRAN	San Francisco	1-Wd San Francisco	79	49
Pasqual	31	m	w	FRAN	San Francisco	1-Wd San Francisco	79	49
William	28	m	w	FRAN	San Francisco	San Francisco P O	80	535
FRANCOM								
Pierre	27	m	w	FRAN	San Francisco	San Francisco P O	80	458
FRANCONIA								
Giuseppi	21	m	w	SWIT	Santa Cruz	Santa Cruz	89	429
FRANCOUR								
G	36	m	w	CANA	San Francisco	San Francisco P O	85	842
FRANCUK								
Joval	17	m	w	ITAL	San Mateo	Schoolhouse Statio	87	333
FRANCWAY								
Bennett	45	m	w	VA	Contra Costa	San Pablo Twp	71	365

Series M593

© 2001 by Heritage Quest. All rights reserved.

Name	Age	S	R	B-PL	County	Locale	Series M593 Roll	Pg
FRAND								
Francois	50	m	w	FRAN	Santa Clara	Burnett Twp	88	37
FRANDERNES								
Cathe	44	f	w	IREL	San Francisco	San Francisco P O	83	87
FRANEN								
Peter	27	m	w	PRUS	San Francisco	8-Wd San Francisco	82	391
FRANENDEIMER								
Fred	28	m	w	WURT	San Francisco	1-Wd San Francisco	79	81
FRANENTHAL								
Isaac	66	m	w	BAVA	San Francisco	8-Wd San Francisco	82	453
FRANICISCO								
Manual	34	m	w	PORT	Yuba	Slate Range Bar Tw	93	672
FRANIEL								
Mary A	33	f	w	IREL	San Francisco	San Francisco P O	83	159
FRANK								
A B	40	m	w	PORT	Tuolumne	Columbia P O	93	351
Abram	35	m	w	POLA	San Francisco	1-Wd San Francisco	79	81
Ah	40	m	c	CHIN	Nevada	Nevada Twp	75	311
Ah	10	m	c	CHIN	Sacramento	1-Wd Sacramento	77	199
Ah	10	m	c	CHIN	Sacramento	1-Wd Sacramento	77	195
Antoine	26	m	w	FRAN	Santa Clara	2-Wd San Jose	88	313
Antonio	40	m	w	AUST	Del Norte	Mountain Twp	71	474
August	42	m	w	SAXO	San Francisco	San Francisco P O	85	794
August	33	m	w	PRUS	San Francisco	San Francisco P O	80	538
August	25	m	w	PRUS	San Francisco	San Francisco P O	80	407
Bernard	46	m	w	RUSS	Sacramento	4-Wd Sacramento	77	340
Bernard	21	m	w	PRUS	San Francisco	San Francisco P O	83	192
Charles	45	m	w	PRUS	Mariposa	Mariposa P O	74	129
Charles	32	m	w	BAVA	Amador	Volcano P O	69	388
Charles	31	m	w	HAMB	San Francisco	6-Wd San Francisco	81	102
Christ	25	m	w	OH	Placer	Colfax P O	76	387
David	36	m	w	OH	Shasta	Horsetown P O	89	502
David	23	m	w	IL	Kern	Havilah P O	73	341
E E	60	m	w	FRAN	Tuolumne	Chinese Camp P O	93	376
Eli	24	m	w	IREL	San Joaquin	1-Wd Stockton	86	139
Emily	28	f	w	FRNK	Sacramento	4-Wd Sacramento	77	351
Ephrain	38	m	w	POLA	San Francisco	San Francisco P O	80	408
Francis	40	m	w	OH	Santa Cruz	Pajaro Twp	89	348
Frank	28	m	w	PA	Sacramento	Dry Crk Twp	77	104
Fred	41	m	w	IN	Santa Clara	Gilroy Twp	88	100
Frederick	13	m	w	CA	San Francisco	8-Wd San Francisco	82	455
Frederick C	41	m	w	BAVA	Santa Clara	Santa Clara Twp	88	144
Geo	49	m	w	PRUS	Alameda	Oakland	68	213
George	33	m	w	SCOT	San Francisco	3-Wd San Francisco	79	291
H	25	m	w	CT	Sacramento	1-Wd Sacramento	77	185
Henri	50	m	w	ITAL	Sacramento	4-Wd Sacramento	77	321
Henry	45	m	w	PA	San Francisco	8-Wd San Francisco	82	458
Henry	40	m	w	PRUS	San Francisco	San Francisco P O	83	191
Henry	32	m	w	PRUS	San Francisco	3-Wd San Francisco	79	296
Henry	24	m	w	NY	Alameda	Oakland	68	257
Hinerd	44	m	w	PRUS	San Francisco	11-Wd San Francisc	84	699
Isaac	61	m	w	BAVA	San Francisco	8-Wd San Francisco	82	475
Isaac	42	m	w	FRAN	Solano	Vallejo	90	164
Isabella	20	f	w	NY	San Francisco	8-Wd San Francisco	82	290
Jacob	40	m	w	BAVA	Solano	Suisun Twp	90	96
Jacob	29	m	w	BAVA	San Francisco	11-Wd San Francisc	84	534
Jacob	25	m	w	ITAL	San Francisco	2-Wd San Francisco	79	141
James	30	m	w	PORT	Tuolumne	Columbia P O	93	357
Jas M	41	m	w	VA	Shasta	Horsetown P O	89	504
John	46	m	w	WURT	Nevada	Grass Valley Twp	75	144
John	43	m	w	IN	Sutter	Yuba Twp	92	141
John	41	m	w	PRUS	San Francisco	11-Wd San Francisc	84	700
John	40	m	w	SHOL	San Francisco	11-Wd San Francisc	84	466
John	40	m	w	PORT	Klamath	Liberty Twp	73	374
John	30	m	w	NJ	San Francisco	5-Wd San Francisco	81	22
John	28	m	w	SCOT	San Francisco	1-Wd San Francisco	79	57
John	26	m	w	ENGL	Placer	Summit P O	76	496
John	22	m	w	SWIT	San Francisco	3-Wd San Francisco	79	317
Joseph	57	m	w	AZOR	Marin	Sausalito Twp	74	71
Joseph	49	m	w	POLA	San Francisco	8-Wd San Francisco	82	297
Joseph	40	m	w	PORT	Marin	Sausalito Twp	74	68
Joseph	38	m	w	ENGL	San Francisco	1-Wd San Francisco	79	42
Joseph	35	m	w	PORT	San Francisco	1-Wd San Francisco	79	102
Joseph	35	m	w	WURT	Santa Clara	2-Wd San Jose	88	314
Joseph	32	m	w	PRUS	Santa Clara	2-Wd San Jose	88	329
Joseph	30	m	w	PORT	Mendocino	Noyo & Big Rvr Twp	74	173
Joseph	30	m	w	PORT	Alameda	Eden Twp	68	69
Joseph	27	m	w	GREE	San Joaquin	1-Wd Stockton	86	152
Julius	47	m	w	ENGL	San Francisco	San Francisco P O	83	253
Lean	25	m	w	FRAN	San Francisco	San Francisco P O	80	412
Lewis	45	m	w	ITAL	Santa Clara	Redwood Twp	88	119
Lewis	25	m	w	PA	San Francisco	5-Wd San Francisco	81	14
Lizzie	23	f	w	PRUS	Sacramento	4-Wd Sacramento	77	323
Louis	45	m	w	AUST	Tuolumne	Columbia P O	93	344
Louis	31	m	w	ITAL	Mariposa	Mariposa P O	74	131
Louis	30	m	w	ITAL	Tuolumne	Big Oak Flat P O	93	393
Louis P	39	m	w	BAVA	San Francisco	8-Wd San Francisco	82	438
Louisa	20	f	w	PRUS	San Francisco	San Francisco P O	80	386
M A	51	m	w	FRAN	Tuolumne	Chinese Camp P O	93	376
Manuel	40	m	w	AZOR	San Francisco	1-Wd San Francisco	79	102
Martinez	46	m	w	CA	San Bernardino	Chino Twp	78	411
Mary	8	f	w	CA	San Francisco	San Francisco P O	80	359
Mary	63	f	w	NY	Humboldt	Eel Rvr Twp	72	253
Mary E	47	f	w	CANA	El Dorado	Mud Springs Twp	72	85
Mattie	38	m	w	NY	San Joaquin	Douglas Twp	86	34
Morris	23	m	w	BAVA	San Francisco	8-Wd San Francisco	82	440
Mortin M	40	m	w	OH	El Dorado	Cosumnes Twp	72	15

Name	Age	S	R	B-PL	County	Locale	Series M593 Roll	Pg
Nichols	50	m	w	PRUS	San Francisco	8-Wd San Francisco	82	292
Phil	60	m	w	BAVA	Sacramento	3-Wd Sacramento	77	282
Phil	40	m	w	MEXI	Butte	Concow Twp	70	7
Phillip	26	m	w	AUST	San Francisco	San Francisco P O	80	331
Rossa	50	m	w	ITAL	San Francisco	1-Wd San Francisco	79	45
Rudolph	46	m	w	BAVA	San Francisco	8-Wd San Francisco	82	393
Sam F	44	m	w	SC	Tehama	Red Bluff	92	179
Sheridan	27	m	w	IREL	Merced	Snelling P O	74	246
Thomas	21	m	w	CANA	Humboldt	Arcata Twp	72	225
Thomas	14	m	w	NY	Monterey	Castroville Twp	74	329
Victor	42	m	w	FRAN	San Francisco	San Francisco P O	80	480
W M	38	m	w	OH	Yuba	Marysville Twp	93	567
William	45	m	w	NETH	Shasta	American Ranch P O	89	496
Wing	20	m	c	CHIN	San Francisco	1-Wd San Francisco	79	17
Wm	33	m	w	OH	Sierra	Eureka Twp	89	524
FRANKA								
Joseph	30	m	w	PORT	Marin	Sausalito Twp	74	67
Marie	60	f	w	MEXI	San Bernardino	San Salvador Twp	78	457
FRANKAEL								
Conrd	49	m	w	WURT	Inyo	Lone Pine Twp	73	331
FRANKANS								
Joseph	42	m	w	SWIT	Siskiyou	Yreka Twp	89	669
FRANKE								
Antonio	31	m	w	ITAL	Mariposa	Maxwell Crk P O	74	142
Chas	46	m	w	PRUS	Nevada	Eureka Twp	75	126
FRANKEIL								
Rosa	22	f	w	BOHE	San Francisco	San Francisco P O	83	419
FRANKEL								
Abraham	45	m	w	BAVA	San Francisco	San Francisco P O	83	332
David	24	m	w	FRAN	Solano	Vacaville Twp	90	120
Jacob	40	m	w	AUST	San Francisco	San Francisco P O	83	415
Samuel	30	m	w	BOHE	Los Angeles	Los Nietos Twp	73	576
Solomon	49	m	w	PRUS	San Francisco	San Francisco P O	85	866
FRANKEMAN								
Max	20	m	w	BAVA	San Francisco	8-Wd San Francisco	82	489
FRANKEN								
Edward	39	m	w	OH	Monterey	Alisal Twp	74	288
FRANKENBACH								
Valentine	55	m	w	BADE	San Francisco	San Francisco P O	83	157
FRANKENBURG								
Jos	37	m	w	PRUS	San Francisco	2-Wd San Francisco	79	158
Julius	44	m	w	SAXO	San Francisco	8-Wd San Francisco	82	302
FRANKENHEIMER								
Isaac	55	m	w	BAVA	San Francisco	8-Wd San Francisco	82	440
Joseph	48	m	w	BAVA	San Francisco	8-Wd San Francisco	82	440
FRANKENTHAL								
Louis	28	m	w	PRUS	San Francisco	8-Wd San Francisco	82	429
FRANKENTHAT								
Max	40	m	w	BAVA	San Francisco	San Francisco P O	85	815
FRANKER								
Walter	35	m	w	BREM	San Francisco	8-Wd San Francisco	82	389
FRANKEY								
Joseph	50	m	w	SWIT	Amador	Jackson P O	69	335
FRANKFORT								
Joseph	38	m	w	PA	Plumas	Indian Twp	77	18
FRANKLE								
Lazar B	38	m	w	BAVA	San Francisco	8-Wd San Francisco	82	468
FRANKLIN								
Abraham	36	m	w	PRUS	San Francisco	8-Wd San Francisco	82	389
Agoston	28	m	w	NY	Los Angeles	El Monte Twp	73	455
Ann	48	f	w	ENGL	Sonoma	Sonoma Twp	91	441
Anna	16	f	w	CA	Sonoma	Sonoma Twp	91	449
B O	45	m	w	VA	Santa Clara	Burnett Twp	88	39
Benj	53	m	b	MA	Siskiyou	Yreka	89	650
Benj	22	m	m	VA	Colusa	Monroe Twp	71	325
Benjamin	37	m	w	MD	San Francisco	San Francisco P O	80	362
Benjamin B	40	m	w	TN	Yolo	Cache Crk Twp	93	431
Cassia	13	f	b	CA	Los Angeles	Los Angeles	73	544
Catherine	14	f	b	CA	Los Angeles	Los Angeles	73	503
Chas	53	m	w	MA	San Joaquin	3-Wd Stockton	86	220
Chas	42	m	w	PRUS	San Francisco	1-Wd San Francisco	79	12
Chas	25	m	w	ME	San Francisco	1-Wd San Francisco	79	125
Dan	21	m	w	PRUS	San Francisco	San Francisco P O	83	49
David E	33	m	w	NY	San Francisco	San Francisco P O	83	75
Detvil	34	m	w	NJ	Los Angeles	Los Angeles Twp	73	490
E M	34	m	w	NY	Amador	Ione City P O	69	361
Edwin	34	m	w	NY	Amador	Ione City P O	69	349
F	42	m	w	IN	Santa Clara	Almaden Twp	88	20
Frances	24	f	w	MA	San Francisco	1-Wd San Francisco	79	95
Francis	40	m	w	MO	Yolo	Cache Crk Twp	93	451
Geo	32	m	w	PORT	Sacramento	Franklin Twp	77	107
Gilbert	40	m	w	MA	Solano	Vacaville Twp	90	118
Harris	35	m	w	RUSS	San Francisco	1-Wd San Francisco	79	50
Henry	45	m	w	ME	San Francisco	San Francisco P O	83	210
Isaac N	38	m	w	IN	Yolo	Grafton Twp	93	496
J	37	m	w	MA	San Francisco	8-Wd San Francisco	82	370
J J	64	m	w	TN	Tuolumne	Sonora P O	93	308
J S	48	m	w	PA	Merced	Snelling P O	74	274
James	63	m	w	IL	Contra Costa	Martinez P O	71	414
James	38	m	w	IREL	Santa Cruz	Santa Cruz Twp	89	399
James	35	m	w	MO	El Dorado	Mud Springs Twp	72	75
James	34	m	w	IREL	Stanislaus	Emory Twp	92	24
James	24	m	w	NC	Santa Barbara	Santa Barbara P O	87	484
Jas	29	m	w	BADE	San Francisco	San Francisco P O	83	55
Jas	27	m	w	MO	Siskiyou	Surprise Valley Tw	89	636
Jesse	34	m	w	ENGL	Siskiyou	Butte Twp	89	585
Jesse D	27	m	w	MS	Santa Barbara	Santa Barbara P O	87	485

© 2001 by Heritage Quest. All rights reserved.

California 1870 Census

Name	Age	S	R	B-PL	County	Locale	Roll	Pg
Jessee	50	m	w	VA	Solano	Vacaville Twp	90	121
Joachimo	18	m	w	SWIT	Santa Cruz	Santa Cruz Twp	89	397
John	50	m	w	PRUS	San Francisco	8-Wd San Francisco	82	389
John	40	m	w	CANA	San Mateo	Redwood City P O	87	375
John	39	m	w	CANA	Trinity	Junction City Pct	92	208
John	34	m	w	OH	Solano	Silveyville Twp	90	77
John	25	m	w	MO	Los Angeles	El Monte Twp	73	451
John H	36	m	w	LA	Santa Clara	San Jose Twp	88	198
John R	51	m	w	KY	Napa	Yountville Twp	75	81
Joseph	36	m	w	ENGL	El Dorado	Placerville Twp	72	94
Joseph	26	m	w	FRAN	San Francisco	1-Wd San Francisco	79	95
Josh	29	m	w	ENGL	San Francisco	1-Wd San Francisco	79	51
L A	65	f	w	KY	Mendocino	Ukiah Twp	74	239
L Mrs	63	f	w	OH	Lake	Lower Lake	73	421
Lambert	16	m	w	CA	Yolo	Grafton Twp	93	495
Laura	24	f	w	ENGL	Nevada	Grass Valley Twp	75	187
Leon	32	m	w	AUST	Santa Clara	2-Wd San Jose	88	317
M J	40	m	w	GERM	San Joaquin	3-Wd Stockton	86	235
M Mrs	36	f	w	NY	Lake	Scotts Crk	73	428
Manuel A	52	m	w	ENGL	San Bernardino	San Bernardino Twp	78	416
Marshall	28	m	m	VA	Los Angeles	Los Angeles	73	505
Martin	39	m	b	SC	Tulare	Visalia Twp	92	283
Max	25	m	w	PRUS	San Joaquin	1-Wd Stockton	86	135
Mildred	30	f	w	TN	Santa Barbara	Santa Barbara P O	87	484
Nancy	55	f	w	TN	Los Angeles	Los Angeles Twp	73	495
Paul	26	m	w	DENM	Sacramento	Georgianna Twp	77	129
Phil	36	m	w	HAMB	Sacramento	4-Wd Sacramento	77	329
Quincy L C	45	m	w	GA	El Dorado	Mud Springs Twp	72	82
Richd G	21	m	w	NC	Santa Barbara	Santa Barbara P O	87	485
Rodrick	40	m	w	CANA	San Francisco	7-Wd San Francisco	81	158
Rufus	34	m	w	AR	San Joaquin	Elkhorn Twp	86	55
S R	44	m	w	PA	Solano	Vallejo	90	199
Samuel	24	m	w	MO	Los Angeles	El Monte Twp	73	451
Thomas	22	m	w	MO	Los Angeles	El Monte Twp	73	451
W	42	m	w	PA	San Joaquin	Oneal Twp	86	112
W	30	m	w	AR	San Joaquin	Elkhorn Twp	86	60
W	28	m	w	MO	Santa Clara	Gilroy Twp	88	98
Washington	50	m	w	GA	Tulare	Venice Twp	92	277
William	46	m	w	NJ	Santa Clara	Redwood Twp	88	127
William	28	m	w	MI	Sacramento	Franklin Twp	77	109
William	28	m	w	ITAL	San Francisco	6-Wd San Francisco	81	71
William M	40	m	w	IREL	Placer	Lincoln P O	76	484
Wm A	60	m	w	NY	Santa Barbara	Santa Barbara P O	87	477
Wm F	52	m	w	ENGL	Sonoma	Santa Rosa	91	404
Wm H	29	m	w	NY	San Francisco	1-Wd San Francisco	79	69
Wm M	12	m	w	CA	Santa Barbara	Arroyo Burro P O	87	509
FRANKS								
Antone	25	m	w	AZOR	Nevada	Washington Twp	75	346
Chs	45	m	w	BAVA	San Francisco	2-Wd San Francisco	79	220
Edmund	26	m	w	TN	Placer	Roseville P O	76	354
Flora	20	f	w	HAMB	San Francisco	6-Wd San Francisco	81	71
Fred	33	m	w	ENGL	San Francisco	6-Wd San Francisco	81	80
H	30	m	w	PA	Sacramento	1-Wd Sacramento	77	181
Harriet	3	f	w	CA	San Francisco	11-Wd San Francisc	84	711
Henry	27	m	w	ME	San Francisco	3-Wd San Francisco	79	290
James	22	m	w	MO	Placer	Roseville P O	76	354
John	50	m	w	VA	Stanislaus	Empire Twp	92	43
Joseph H	49	m	w	PORT	Nevada	Little York Twp	75	243
Martin	39	m	w	HANO	Sacramento	2-Wd Sacramento	77	242
Thomas	36	m	w	OH	Amador	Sutter Crk P O	69	410
William M	67	m	w	SC	Placer	Roseville P O	76	351
FRANKY								
Frank	35	m	w	PORT	Sacramento	2-Wd Sacramento	77	212
FRANS								
John B	50	m	w	KY	Tulare	Venice Twp	92	277
Peter	32	m	w	FRAN	Plumas	Mineral Twp	77	20
FRANSEN								
Hans	36	m	w	PRUS	San Francisco	3-Wd San Francisco	79	295
FRANSWUA								
Lewis	30	m	w	PRUS	Sutter	Nicolaus Twp	92	111
FRANT								
B W	29	m	w	POLA	San Francisco	8-Wd San Francisco	82	305
Mary	49	f	w	IREL	San Francisco	San Francisco P O	85	775
FRANTIN								
Joseph	43	m	w	DENM	San Francisco	San Francisco P O	80	367
FRANTZ								
---	30	m	w	HAMB	San Mateo	Belmont P O	87	371
F J	41	m	w	PRUS	Del Norte	Crescent	71	462
John	19	m	w	BADE	Butte	Concow Twp	70	12
FRANZEN								
A B	27	m	w	PRUS	San Francisco	San Francisco P O	83	135
FRARCA								
Joseph	25	m	w	SCOT	Alameda	Brooklyn Twp	68	49
FRARIA								
Joseph	27	m	w	ITAL	Mariposa	Mariposa P O	74	91
Lawrence	32	m	w	ITAL	Mariposa	Mariposa P O	74	91
FRARK								
Peter	43	m	w	ME	Contra Costa	Martinez P O	71	371
FRARLEY								
Patrick	40	m	w	IREL	San Francisco	San Francisco P O	83	179
FRARO								
Louis	37	m	w	ITAL	San Francisco	2-Wd San Francisco	79	235
FRARRAT								
Octavia	25	m	w	CANA	Sierra	Table Rock Twp	89	578
FRARY								
A	19	m	w	PARA	Sierra	Butte Twp	89	511
Abraham P	43	m	w	OH	San Diego	Julian Dist	78	473
E Frank	49	m	w	VT	Placer	Colfax P O	76	391
Emma	9	f	w	CA	Nevada	Grass Valley Twp	75	207
FRASA								
Archibald	25	m	w	CANA	San Diego	San Diego	78	511
FRASCELLO								
Reyes	59	m	w	MEXI	Los Angeles	Los Nietos Twp	73	583
FRASE								
Frankie J	34	m	w	NY	Yolo	Grafton Twp	93	486
FRASER								
Alexander	22	m	w	SCOT	Nevada	Grass Valley Twp	75	192
Allen	39	m	w	MO	Mendocino	Gualala Twp	74	226
Cameron	15	m	w	ENGL	San Francisco	11-Wd San Francisc	84	593
Catherine	21	f	w	PRUS	San Francisco	8-Wd San Francisco	82	459
Daniel	43	m	w	CANA	Tuolumne	Chinese Camp P O	93	335
Daniel	40	m	w	CANA	San Francisco	8-Wd San Francisco	82	410
Daniel	34	m	w	CANA	San Francisco	3-Wd San Francisco	79	289
Davis	46	m	w	CANA	Sonoma	Analy Twp	91	219
Florence	13	f	w	CANA	San Francisco	8-Wd San Francisco	82	462
H R	44	m	w	CANA	San Francisco	San Francisco P O	83	7
Hugh	25	m	w	SCOT	San Francisco	San Francisco P O	83	188
James	40	m	w	NY	San Francisco	6-Wd San Francisco	81	80
James	37	m	w	CANA	San Diego	San Diego	78	510
James J	40	m	w	SCOT	San Francisco	6-Wd San Francisco	81	81
John	29	m	w	CANA	San Francisco	6-Wd San Francisco	81	114
Roderick	38	m	w	CANA	San Francisco	San Francisco P O	83	42
Sarah	16	f	w	NY	San Francisco	San Francisco P O	83	195
Thomas	60	m	w	NJ	San Francisco	San Francisco P O	83	62
Thomas	37	m	w	CANA	El Dorado	Placerville	72	119
Wm	36	m	w	CANA	San Francisco	San Francisco P O	85	838
FRASGUR								
Luis	45	m	w	SCOT	San Luis Obispo	San Luis Obispo Tw	87	313
FRASHOUR								
Andrew	61	m	w	NC	San Luis Obispo	Salinas Twp	87	294
Urith L	19	f	w	OH	San Luis Obispo	Salinas Twp	87	294
FRASIER								
Alexander	26	m	w	CANA	San Luis Obispo	Morro Twp	87	284
Allen	31	m	w	CANA	Sonoma	Petaluma Twp	91	321
Alxr	55	m	w	NY	Monterey	Monterey Twp	74	349
Benjamin	33	m	w	TN	Inyo	Independence Twp	73	326
Daniel S	31	m	w	NY	Sonoma	Petaluma Twp	91	349
David	39	m	w	ME	Marin	Bolinas Twp	74	1
F W	36	m	w	CANA	Alameda	Oakland	68	134
Fred	52	m	w	ME	Sonoma	Petaluma Twp	91	319
H H	29	m	w	OH	Sacramento	Lee Twp	77	160
James	37	m	w	NH	Marin	Novato Twp	74	10
John	43	m	w	CANA	Marin	Novato Twp	74	12
Joseph	30	m	w	PORT	Klamath	South Fork Twp	73	385
Luman	27	m	w	NY	Sonoma	Vallejo Twp	91	456
Marshall	27	m	w	IN	Stanislaus	Washington Twp	92	85
Patrick	42	m	w	IREL	Amador	Sutter Crk P O	69	402
FRASK								
Freeman	42	m	w	ME	San Francisco	San Francisco P O	83	43
Joseph	29	m	w	MA	Butte	Chico Twp	70	54
FRASLAVIMA								
Luiz	35	f	w	MEXI	Los Angeles	Los Nietos Twp	73	589
FRASSIER								
T	48	m	w	ENGL	Lake	Lower Lake	73	429
FRAST								
Josiah	50	m	w	ME	San Francisco	11-Wd San Francisc	84	624
FRASTEIL								
Walter	39	m	w	ENGL	Fresno	Millerton P O	72	168
FRATARDO								
Louis	37	m	w	PORT	Tuolumne	Columbia P O	93	342
FRATARO								
Joseph	40	m	w	SCOT	Alameda	San Leandro	68	95
FRATAS								
Abraham	23	m	w	PORT	Shasta	Shasta P O	89	452
Emanuel	32	m	w	AZOR	Shasta	Shasta P O	89	454
John	27	m	w	PORT	Tuolumne	Columbia P O	93	337
FRATEA								
Joseph	19	m	w	PORT	Alameda	Eden Twp	68	88
FRATER								
Domingo	30	m	w	AZOR	Marin	Sausalito Twp	74	70
Frank	25	m	w	AZOR	Sonoma	Analy Twp	91	222
Frank	24	m	w	SCOT	San Luis Obispo	Arroyo Grande Twp	87	278
Joseph	27	m	w	PORT	Marin	Bolinas Twp	74	4
Juan	22	m	w	PORT	Marin	Tomales Twp	74	85
FRATERZ								
John	35	m	w	MADE	San Francisco	San Francisco P O	83	358
FRATES								
A J	40	m	w	PORT	Tuolumne	Columbia P O	93	356
Antoine	44	m	w	SCOT	Siskiyou	Yreka Twp	89	666
Anton	29	m	w	PORT	Tuolumne	Columbia P O	93	356
Antone	31	m	w	PORT	Alameda	Eden Twp	68	90
Antonio	18	m	w	PORT	Mariposa	Mariposa P O	74	90
Catherine	25	f	w	SCOT	Alameda	Brooklyn Twp	68	44
Frank	60	m	w	PORT	San Francisco	3-Wd San Francisco	79	290
Frank	34	m	w	SCOT	Alameda	Brooklyn Twp	68	44
Frank	34	m	w	PORT	Monterey	Pajaro Twp	74	373
Frank	19	m	w	PORT	Tuolumne	Columbia P O	93	356
Fredk	40	m	w	PORT	Marin	Nicasio Twp	74	19
Joake	30	m	w	AZOR	Marin	Sausalito Twp	74	71
John	50	m	w	PORT	Solano	Rio Vista Twp	90	63
John	35	m	w	PORT	Alameda	Eden Twp	68	88
John	23	m	w	PORT	Marin	Sausalito Twp	74	69
John	19	m	w	PORT	Tuolumne	Columbia P O	93	356
Jose	36	m	w	AZOR	Marin	Sausalito Twp	74	71

Series M593

© 2001 by Heritage Quest. All rights reserved.

Name	Age	S	R	B-PL	County	Locale	Series M593 Roll	Pg
Josep	31	m	w	SCOT	Alameda	Brooklyn Twp	68	48
Joseph	48	m	w	PORT	Alameda	Washington Twp	68	286
Joseph	40	m	w	PORT	Marin	Nicasio Twp	74	20
Joseph	32	m	w	AZOR	Contra Costa	Martinez P O	71	394
Joseph	25	m	w	SCOT	Alameda	Brooklyn Twp	68	45
Joseph	21	m	w	PORT	Santa Cruz	Soquel Twp	89	437
Manuel	22	m	w	SCOT	Santa Clara	Santa Clara Twp	88	136
FRATINGER								
Anthony	28	m	w	OH	San Francisco	8-Wd San Francisco	82	461
FRATIS								
Thedore	55	m	w	PORT	Sacramento	Georgianna Twp	77	127
FRATO								
Matias	55	f	w	MEXI	Los Angeles	Los Angeles	73	551
FRATRES								
Frank	35	m	w	PORT	Alameda	Washington Twp	68	298
FRATRIE								
Caroline	22	f	w	WURT	Alameda	Oakland	68	173
FRATT								
Francis W	39	m	w	NY	Sacramento	2-Wd Sacramento	77	254
FRATTA								
Antonio	46	m	w	PORT	Santa Clara	Redwood Twp	88	124
FRATTER								
James	26	m	w	KY	Trinity	Weaverville Pct	92	223
FRATTEY								
Robert	35	m	w	NY	El Dorado	Mud Springs Twp	72	91
FRATUS								
John	30	m	w	PORT	Trinity	Douglas	92	234
John	29	m	w	DENM	San Francisco	1-Wd San Francisco	79	132
Joseph	33	m	w	PORT	Monterey	Pajaro Twp	74	373
Joseph	30	m	w	PORT	Trinity	Indian Crk	92	199
Manuel	25	m	w	PORT	Trinity	Indian Crk	92	199
FRAUENHOLT								
Phillip	39	m	w	BAVA	San Francisco	2-Wd San Francisco	79	144
FRAULSEN								
Fredk	34	m	w	PRUS	San Francisco	San Francisco P O	85	871
Otto J C	42	m	w	DENM	San Francisco	3-Wd San Francisco	79	292
FRAUNFELDER								
Frank	52	m	w	FRAN	Butte	Oregon Twp	70	135
FRAUNTZEE								
George	32	m	w	NY	San Francisco	3-Wd San Francisco	79	326
FRAVAL								
Nathan	35	m	w	VA	Nevada	Little York Twp	75	240
FRAVERS								
Michl	26	m	w	IREL	San Francisco	1-Wd San Francisco	79	64
FRAVIS								
John	35	m	w	CHIL	Placer	Bath P O	76	457
FRAVOSA								
Angelo	39	m	w	ITAL	Calaveras	San Andreas P O	70	176
FRAWLEY								
John	34	m	w	IREL	San Francisco	11-Wd San Francisc	84	585
M	27	m	w	IREL	San Joaquin	Liberty Twp	86	95
Patrick	44	m	w	IREL	Santa Clara	2-Wd San Jose	88	336
Richard	27	m	w	AUSL	San Francisco	San Francisco P O	83	410
William	42	m	w	IREL	San Francisco	11-Wd San Francisc	84	496
FRAYLOR								
William	44	m	w	MO	Tulare	Tule Rvr Twp	92	263
FRAZ								
Peter	51	m	w	FRAN	Marin	Novato Twp	74	9
FRAZEE								
F D	41	m	w	NY	Sonoma	Santa Rosa	91	420
Newton	12	m	w	CA	Sacramento	3-Wd Sacramento	77	309
Vitruvius	35	m	w	NY	San Francisco	San Francisco P O	85	806
FRAZER								
A	26	m	w	NY	Santa Clara	Gilroy Twp	88	91
Albert	55	m	w	NY	Sacramento	Brighton Twp	77	70
Alex	43	m	w	NY	Del Norte	Mountain Twp	71	474
Alexander	34	m	w	NY	San Francisco	1-Wd San Francisco	79	94
Alexander	31	m	w	SCOT	Mendocino	Bourns Landing Twp	74	223
Andrew	25	m	w	CANA	San Francisco	7-Wd San Francisco	81	208
Angus	32	m	w	CANA	Santa Cruz	Santa Cruz Twp	89	392
Benj	34	m	w	IL	Marin	San Rafael Twp	74	43
Chas D	41	m	w	NY	Sonoma	Santa Rosa	91	402
Christian	38	m	w	DENM	Marin	Novato Twp	74	9
Daniel	46	m	w	SCOT	Santa Cruz	Santa Cruz Twp	89	394
David	36	m	w	AL	Kern	Linns Valley P O	73	343
Donald	45	m	w	SCOT	Del Norte	Mountain Twp	71	474
Donald	33	m	w	SCOT	Yolo	Cache Crk Twp	93	428
Donald E	50	m	w	CHIN	Mendocino	Navarro & Big Rvr	74	174
George	50	m	w	SC	Kern	Bakersfield P O	73	360
George	32	m	w	IREL	Solano	Rio Vista Twp	90	58
George W	39	m	w	VA	Solano	Maine Prairie Twp	90	45
Henry	43	m	w	NY	Sutter	Butte Twp	92	104
Henry A	45	m	w	NY	San Francisco	6-Wd San Francisco	81	145
Hugh	38	m	w	SCOT	San Francisco	7-Wd San Francisco	81	208
James	48	m	w	SCOT	Nevada	Nevada Twp	75	307
Jane	44	f	w	SC	Monterey	Pajaro Twp	74	374
Job	40	m	w	MO	Del Norte	Happy Camp Twp	71	471
John	49	m	w	ENGL	San Francisco	San Francisco P O	85	769
John	41	m	w	SCOT	Santa Cruz	Santa Cruz Twp	89	379
John	39	m	w	PA	Placer	Colfax P O	76	391
John	37	m	w	RI	Lake	Upper Lake	73	409
John	19	m	w	IN	Marin	San Rafael Twp	74	45
John	17	m	w	ENGL	San Francisco	7-Wd San Francisco	81	170
John B	49	m	w	PRUS	San Francisco	1-Wd San Francisco	79	95
Joseph	28	m	w	IREL	Santa Cruz	Santa Cruz Twp	89	395
P B	29	m	w	CANA	San Joaquin	2-Wd Stockton	86	196
Robert J	42	m	w	CANA	Tulare	Visalia	92	291
Robt	35	m	w	CANA	San Francisco	San Francisco P O	83	104
S	29	m	w	DE	Lake	Big Valley	73	394
Sam	38	m	w	OH	Sacramento	3-Wd Sacramento	77	306
Thomas	38	m	w	ENGL	San Francisco	7-Wd San Francisco	81	168
Thomas	28	m	w	OH	Santa Clara	Santa Clara Twp	88	162
Thos	49	m	w	SCOT	Sonoma	Santa Rosa	91	413
Walter	56	m	w	MA	Calaveras	San Andreas P O	70	216
William G	24	m	w	SCOT	Mendocino	Albion & Big Rvr T	74	167
FRAZIER								
A J	26	f	w	WI	Alameda	Oakland	68	139
Abner	48	m	w	NC	Contra Costa	Martinez P O	71	453
Albert	25	m	w	MS	Sacramento	2-Wd Sacramento	77	241
Alexander	28	m	w	CANA	Solano	Maine Prairie Twp	90	51
Allen	50	m	w	NY	San Francisco	5-Wd San Francisco	81	29
Amos	25	m	w	NY	Butte	Oregon Twp	70	129
Benj	48	m	w	NY	Yuba	Rose Bar Twp	93	657
Benjamin	36	m	w	TN	Kern	Linns Valley P O	73	343
Charles	24	m	w	PA	Santa Clara	2-Wd San Jose	88	320
Chas	25	m	w	PA	Marin	San Rafael Twp	74	38
Chirt	25	m	w	PA	San Francisco	2-Wd San Francisco	79	213
Chs	29	m	w	OH	Yuba	Marysville	93	594
Daniel	36	m	w	CANA	Contra Costa	Martinez Twp	71	348
Daniel	33	m	w	CANA	Yuba	East Bear Rvr Twp	93	543
Dilia	38	f	w	TN	Contra Costa	Martinez Twp	71	350
G W	46	m	w	VA	Alameda	Oakland	68	155
George	18	m	w	AR	Stanislaus	Empire Twp	92	66
George W	59	m	w	KY	Santa Clara	Alviso Twp	88	24
Gilbert	29	m	w	SCOT	Alameda	Eden Twp	68	85
Irad	23	m	w	IL	Colusa	Grand Island Twp	71	304
Isaiah	36	m	w	PA	Calaveras	Copperopolis P O	70	256
J P	34	m	w	PA	Solano	Vallejo	90	167
James	40	m	w	CANA	Solano	Rio Vista Twp	90	63
James	39	m	w	KY	Sonoma	Washington Twp	91	465
James	38	m	w	OH	San Francisco	7-Wd San Francisco	81	208
James	27	m	w	SCOT	Contra Costa	Martinez P O	71	427
Jno	32	m	w	PA	Butte	Oregon Twp	70	131
John	28	m	w	CANA	Contra Costa	Martinez P O	71	367
John	25	m	w	AUSL	San Francisco	7-Wd San Francisco	81	164
John	22	m	w	CANA	Contra Costa	Martinez P O	71	367
Johns S	40	m	w	OH	Sacramento	2-Wd Sacramento	77	240
Maggie	25	f	w	IREL	Sacramento	4-Wd Sacramento	77	364
Magnes	48	m	w	SCOT	Humboldt	Table Bluff Twp	72	304
Martin	29	m	w	AZOR	Santa Cruz	Santa Cruz	89	429
Mary	18	f	w	NY	San Francisco	2-Wd San Francisco	79	263
Mary C	26	f	w	RI	San Francisco	6-Wd San Francisco	81	95
Newton	14	m	w	IA	Sacramento	San Joaquin Twp	77	395
Peter	52	m	w	TN	Yolo	Washington Twp	93	536
T L	30	m	w	OH	Mendocino	Ukiah Twp	74	243
W R	25	m	w	CANA	Yuba	Marysville	93	610
Wiley	41	m	w	KY	Sonoma	Bodega Twp	91	255
William	45	m	w	MA	Stanislaus	Empire Twp	92	57
William	32	m	w	TN	Mariposa	Mariposa P O	74	113
Wisely	11	m	w	CA	Yuba	East Bear Rvr Twp	93	543
Wm	45	m	w	IREL	Sacramento	4-Wd Sacramento	77	349
Wm	25	m	w	SC	San Joaquin	Oneal Twp	86	110
Wm	22	m	w	CANA	Solano	Vallejo	90	141
Wm M	39	m	w	OH	Sacramento	Dry Crk Twp	77	97
Wm S	37	m	w	TN	Shasta	Horsetown P O	89	507
FRAZIN								
John	39	m	w	IREL	San Francisco	8-Wd San Francisco	82	365
FRAZONE								
Luige	39	m	w	ITAL	Mariposa	Maxwell Crk P O	74	145
FREA								
Manuel	30	m	w	AZOR	Nevada	Washington Twp	75	339
FREACH								
Edward	40	m	w	SWED	San Francisco	7-Wd San Francisco	81	235
FREAGO								
Alonzo	32	m	w	SCOT	Alameda	Brooklyn Twp	68	45
FREAKS								
Lafayette	42	m	w	FRAN	Sacramento	Brighton Twp	77	70
FREAR								
Frank	23	m	w	SCOT	Alameda	Brooklyn Twp	68	48
Walter [Rev]	41	m	w	NY	Santa Cruz	Santa Cruz	89	412
FREARS								
Andrew	38	m	w	DENM	El Dorado	White Oak Twp	72	137
Henry H	50	m	w	HANO	El Dorado	White Oak Twp	72	139
FREASE								
J	28	m	w	BREM	Alameda	Oakland	68	213
FRECHET								
Eugene O	24	m	w	MI	San Francisco	San Francisco P O	85	757
FRECHLEAR								
Louis	40	m	w	GERM	Santa Clara	2-Wd San Jose	88	321
FRECK								
Francis	56	m	w	HANO	San Francisco	11-Wd San Francisc	84	612
Hem	15	m	c	CHIN	San Francisco	1-Wd San Francisco	79	43
FRED								
Frank	38	m	w	HAMB	Sonoma	Sonoma Twp	91	439
FREDBURGE								
James	35	m	w	IREL	Humboldt	Mattole Twp	72	284
FREDDER								
Christian	28	m	w	BADE	San Francisco	11-Wd San Francisc	84	454
FREDENBUE								
John	36	m	w	OH	Placer	Dutch Flat P O	76	404
FREDENBUER								
J B	40	m	w	OH	Tuolumne	Columbia P O	93	337
FREDERIC								
George A	25	m	w	BAVA	Los Angeles	Wilmington Twp	73	634

© 2001 by Heritage Quest. All rights reserved.

Series M593

Name	Age	S	R	B-PL	County	Locale	Roll	Pg
FREDERICA								
Andreas	42	m	w	MEXI	Fresno	Millerton P O	72	164
Francisco	62	m	w	MEXI	Kern	Bakersfield P O	73	364
Theodore	34	m	w	MEXI	Kern	Bakersfield P O	73	363
FREDERICH								
Chs	59	m	w	SAXO	San Francisco	2-Wd San Francisco	79	183
FREDERICHS								
Charles	33	m	w	PRUS	San Francisco	8-Wd San Francisco	82	430
FREDERICK								
Annie	18	f	w	KY	Sacramento	4-Wd Sacramento	77	373
C	30	m	w	DENM	Lake	Big Valley	73	395
Carl	26	m	w	POME	San Francisco	3-Wd San Francisco	79	287
Eugene	32	m	w	FRAN	Santa Clara	1-Wd San Jose	88	268
Frank	27	m	w	GERM	Sacramento	1-Wd Sacramento	77	172
George	31	m	w	CANA	Santa Clara	1-Wd San Jose	88	261
H	45	m	w	PRUS	San Joaquin	2-Wd Stockton	86	201
Hiram	50	m	w	PA	Sutter	Yuba Twp	92	152
Itty	15	m	w	ITAL	Sacramento	Sutter Twp	77	385
J	35	m	w	GERM	Alameda	Oakland	68	134
Jacques	60	m	w	FRAN	Plumas	Rich Bar Twp	77	45
Jno	28	m	w	CANA	Alameda	Oakland	68	261
John	41	m	w	CANA	Sacramento	2-Wd Sacramento	77	254
John	34	m	w	CANA	Sacramento	2-Wd Sacramento	77	254
John L	54	m	w	ITAL	Santa Cruz	Santa Cruz Twp	89	381
Johna	33	m	w	OH	San Francisco	San Francisco P O	83	263
Joseph	19	m	w	PRUS	Stanislaus	Buena Vista Twp	92	11
Levitte	18	m	w	PRUS	Sonoma	Analy Twp	91	225
Louis F	53	m	w	PRUS	Placer	Roseville P O	76	352
Margaret	59	f	w	PRUS	San Francisco	San Francisco P O	85	872
Phil	25	m	w	HANO	San Francisco	San Francisco P O	83	173
Vollon	26	m	w	FRAN	Los Angeles	Los Angeles Twp	73	478
FREDERICKS								
Albert	35	m	w	NY	San Francisco	1-Wd San Francisco	79	116
Alfred	36	m	w	NY	Humboldt	Table Bluff Twp	72	304
C W	63	m	w	HANO	El Dorado	Georgetown Twp	72	45
Danl	30	m	w	GERM	San Diego	San Diego	78	503
Fred	30	m	w	MA	Sacramento	Lee Twp	77	161
George	42	m	w	PRUS	Solano	Tremont Twp	90	30
Henry	50	m	w	BAVA	Amador	Volcano P O	69	375
J	38	m	w	PRUS	San Francisco	San Francisco P O	85	774
J	35	m	w	HANO	San Joaquin	Tulare Twp	86	249
J G	17	m	w	CA	Alameda	Oakland	68	159
James	30	m	w	PRUS	Sacramento	2-Wd Sacramento	77	229
John	38	m	w	HANO	San Francisco	San Francisco P O	85	856
Josep C	21	m	w	NY	Klamath	Camp Gaston	73	373
Phillip	25	m	w	PRUS	San Francisco	San Francisco P O	83	316
Wm	31	m	w	HANO	San Francisco	San Francisco P O	85	836
FREDERICKSON								
Antone	47	m	w	DENM	San Francisco	2-Wd San Francisco	79	154
Chas	29	m	w	DENM	San Francisco	1-Wd San Francisco	79	4
J P	41	m	w	DENM	Humboldt	Eureka Twp	72	281
Lawrence	24	m	w	SWED	San Francisco	1-Wd San Francisco	79	122
Nicholas	25	m	w	DENM	Alameda	Eden Twp	68	62
Sam	50	m	w	DENM	Nevada	Nevada Twp	75	313
Yance	58	m	w	SWED	Nevada	Nevada Twp	75	304
FREDERICO								
Roderep	52	m	w	MEXI	Kern	Bakersfield P O	73	362
FREDETT								
Thos	34	m	w	CANA	Sierra	Table Rock Twp	89	573
FREDINGER								
Atlas	43	m	w	NY	San Francisco	San Francisco P O	83	6
FREDLANDER								
Herman	30	m	w	PRUS	Monterey	Salinas Twp	74	306
FREDLE								
Lewis	19	m	w	PRUS	Sutter	Sutter Twp	92	124
FREDNES								
Otto	35	m	w	SWIT	Mendocino	Point Arena Twp	74	211
FREDRICH								
Chas	31	m	w	SAXO	San Francisco	11-Wd San Francisc	84	558
Devit	63	m	w	BADE	Placer	Dutch Flat P O	76	404
Elizabeth	72	f	w	SAXO	San Francisco	11-Wd San Francisc	84	558
FREDRICK								
Charles	30	m	w	PRUS	San Francisco	7-Wd San Francisco	81	218
Charles	28	m	w	PRUS	Yolo	Putah Twp	93	519
David	39	m	w	IN	San Joaquin	Oneal Twp	86	113
H	57	m	w	FRAN	Amador	Jackson P O	69	347
John	35	m	w	BAVA	Sacramento	Center Twp	77	83
John	30	m	w	PRUS	San Joaquin	Oneal Twp	86	118
Marie	54	f	w	FRAN	San Francisco	San Francisco P O	80	479
Robert	32	m	w	SAXO	Sonoma	Petaluma Twp	91	350
FREDRICKS								
Eliza	28	f	b	PA	San Francisco	San Francisco P O	80	475
Henry	48	m	w	GERM	Yolo	Buckeye Twp	93	408
J	45	m	w	HANO	San Joaquin	Tulare Twp	86	249
L	26	m	w	PRUS	Alameda	Murray Twp	68	113
Maria	35	f	w	PRUS	San Francisco	San Francisco P O	80	462
William	34	m	w	PRUS	San Francisco	11-Wd San Francisc	84	498
FREDRICKSON								
Chas	27	m	w	DENM	Alameda	Murray Twp	68	113
Harry	26	m	w	SHOL	Monterey	Pajaro Twp	74	371
FREDSON								
George	35	m	w	NH	Colusa	Monroe Twp	71	311
FREE								
Barney	24	m	w	OH	Sacramento	2-Wd Sacramento	77	235
George	14	m	w	MI	Alameda	Eden Twp	68	66
George	13	m	w	OH	Inyo	Bishop Crk Twp	73	315
Henry	62	m	w	OH	Sacramento	Georgianna Twp	77	128

Series M593

Name	Age	S	R	B-PL	County	Locale	Roll	Pg
Minor	15	m	w	MI	Alameda	Eden Twp	68	67
William	54	m	w	CANA	San Francisco	2-Wd San Francisco	79	278
FREEBORN								
Burtha	19	f	w	NJ	San Joaquin	2-Wd Stockton	86	164
Ella	45	f	w	MA	San Francisco	8-Wd San Francisco	82	341
Ellen	54	f	w	IREL	Solano	Green Valley Twp	90	41
Herleigh	35	f	w	SHOL	San Francisco	1-Wd San Francisco	79	106
Isaac S	50	m	w	RI	Inyo	Lone Pine Twp	73	331
James	43	m	w	CANA	San Francisco	8-Wd San Francisco	82	370
Jas Wm	2	m	w	CA	San Francisco	1-Wd San Francisco	79	106
John	43	m	w	NY	Sonoma	Mendocino Twp	91	303
Mary	15	f	w	MN	San Luis Obispo	San Luis Obispo Tw	87	298
Richard	28	m	w	IL	Yolo	Buckeye Twp	93	415
Wm	54	m	w	OH	San Luis Obispo	San Luis Obispo Tw	87	301
Wm Henry	39	m	w	NY	San Francisco	1-Wd San Francisco	79	106
FREEBURN								
Ellen	30	f	w	NY	San Francisco	8-Wd San Francisco	82	462
William	36	m	w	NY	San Francisco	San Francisco P O	80	404
Wm	24	m	w	SCOT	Sierra	Eureka Twp	89	524
FREED								
Barbara	19	f	w	BAVA	Solano	Benicia	90	16
Egnatz	32	m	w	BOHE	San Diego	San Diego	78	495
John B	36	m	w	OH	Santa Clara	San Jose Twp	88	211
FREEDEN								
Fredrick	39	m	w	BADE	San Francisco	7-Wd San Francisco	81	216
FREEDENBURG								
Martin	28	m	w	HANO	San Francisco	2-Wd San Francisco	79	256
FREEDLAND								
August	55	m	w	SAXO	Contra Costa	Martinez P O	71	405
FREEDLANDER								
M	30	m	w	PRUS	San Francisco	8-Wd San Francisco	82	359
FREEDMAN								
Kate	42	f	w	PRUS	San Francisco	5-Wd San Francisco	81	11
FREEDY								
Joseph	30	m	w	CANA	San Francisco	3-Wd San Francisco	79	295
FREEL								
Thomas	21	m	w	NY	San Francisco	San Francisco P O	80	333
FREELAND								
Benj	37	m	w	IN	San Francisco	San Francisco P O	83	262
Enoch	35	m	w	IN	San Francisco	San Francisco P O	83	262
John	58	m	w	NY	Shasta	Millville P O	89	485
John	18	m	w	IREL	Sacramento	2-Wd Sacramento	77	240
Mercy	63	f	w	MA	San Francisco	2-Wd San Francisco	79	229
Orlando B	35	m	w	NY	Sacramento	Franklin Twp	77	108
Sarah	53	f	w	WI	San Francisco	San Francisco P O	83	262
Thos	20	m	w	IL	Butte	Chico Twp	70	37
FREELANDER								
Saml	30	m	w	PRUS	San Francisco	8-Wd San Francisco	82	346
FREELANDS								
John	35	m	w	PERS	Monterey	Alisal Twp	74	293
FREELE								
James	36	m	w	IN	El Dorado	Lake Valley Twp	72	63
FREELING								
George	30	m	w	PRUS	San Francisco	San Francisco P O	85	756
Godfrey	33	m	w	RUSS	San Joaquin	2-Wd Stockton	86	162
FREELON								
John C	67	m	w	NY	Butte	Mountain Spring Tw	70	88
Thomas	25	m	w	ENGL	Amador	Amador City P O	69	392
FREELOUR								
William	32	m	w	IL	Solano	Tremont Twp	90	28
FREELOVE								
Thos W	43	m	w	VT	San Francisco	San Francisco P O	83	109
FREELS								
John	58	m	w	KY	Monterey	Pajaro Twp	74	375
FREELY								
Mary	19	f	w	IREL	San Francisco	San Francisco P O	83	205
FREEMAN								
A	30	m	w	MA	San Francisco	8-Wd San Francisco	82	346
A E	29	m	w	GA	Sacramento	4-Wd Sacramento	77	343
A J	39	m	w	NY	San Joaquin	1-Wd Stockton	86	141
A M	30	m	w	SWED	Nevada	Meadow Lake Twp	75	246
Ah	40	m	w	IL	El Dorado	Mud Springs Twp	72	90
Alfred	40	m	w	TX	San Diego	Warners Rancho Dis	78	529
Alice	19	f	b	MD	Sacramento	2-Wd Sacramento	77	232
Alice L	11	f	w	CA	Placer	Roseville P O	76	352
Andrew	37	m	w	NY	El Dorado	Lake Valley Twp	72	65
Ann	70	f	w	ENGL	Amador	Jackson P O	69	325
Ann	60	f	w	MA	San Joaquin	3-Wd Stockton	86	224
Benjn	35	m	w	OH	San Francisco	5-Wd San Francisco	81	18
Bernard	3M	m	w	CA	San Francisco	11-Wd San Francisc	84	711
Butler S	37	m	w	NY	Sonoma	Analy Twp	91	218
C C	27	m	w	IL	Sacramento	1-Wd Sacramento	77	187
C R	35	m	w	OH	El Dorado	Georgetown Twp	72	37
C R	32	m	w	NY	Sacramento	1-Wd Sacramento	77	178
C W	41	m	w	ME	San Francisco	San Francisco P O	85	797
Calvin	40	m	w	MA	San Francisco	2-Wd San Francisco	79	278
Charles	50	m	w	NY	San Francisco	San Francisco P O	80	414
Charles	35	m	w	SWED	San Francisco	6-Wd San Francisco	81	98
Charles	26	m	w	NY	San Francisco	7-Wd San Francisco	81	226
Charles	23	m	w	PRUS	San Francisco	San Francisco P O	83	394
Chas J	52	m	w	ENGL	Santa Barbara	Santa Barbara P O	87	459
Clarkson C	38	m	w	OH	Sacramento	Franklin Twp	77	110
David	25	m	i	CA	Tehama	Merrill	92	198
David M	39	m	w	NY	Santa Cruz	Pajaro Twp	89	360
E	38	m	w	NY	Sierra	Sierra Twp	89	570
E G	40	m	w	NY	Amador	Jackson P O	69	325
E J	26	f	w	MO	Amador	Sutter Crk P O	69	408

© 2001 by Heritage Quest. All rights reserved.

Name	Age	S	R	B-PL	County	Locale	Series M593 Roll	Pg
Edward	38	m	w	OH	Butte	Bidwell Twp	70	2
Edward	27	m	w	NY	San Francisco	San Francisco P O	83	169
Eli	65	m	w	OH	Santa Clara	Santa Clara Twp	88	172
Eliza	37	f	w	HANO	San Francisco	2-Wd San Francisco	79	148
Elizabeth	42	f	w	NY	Santa Clara	2-Wd San Jose	88	289
Franklin S	38	m	w	MO	Yolo	Cache Crk Twp	93	425
Fred	14	m	w	CA	San Francisco	2-Wd San Francisco	79	278
Frederick	59	m	w	NY	Nevada	Washington Twp	75	341
Frederick	39	m	w	VT	Butte	Wyandotte Twp	70	146
Frederick W	15	m	w	CA	Santa Clara	Santa Clara Twp	88	177
G	34	m	w	CT	Yuba	Marysville	93	604
Geo	30	m	w	NY	Siskiyou	Surprise Valley Tw	89	639
Geo F	3	m	w	CA	San Joaquin	Douglas Twp	86	34
George	3	m	w	CA	Solano	Green Valley Twp	90	40
George	25	m	w	IREL	Napa	Napa Twp	75	61
George	20	m	w	IA	Plumas	Quartz Twp	77	42
George M	39	m	w	NY	Sonoma	Petaluma Twp	91	351
George W	41	m	w	TN	Colusa	Monroe Twp	71	324
Gilbert	26	m	w	WI	Sacramento	Dry Crk Twp	77	100
H	50	m	b	RI	Sacramento	4-Wd Sacramento	77	329
H K	51	m	w	MO	San Joaquin	Douglas Twp	86	34
H T	45	m	w	MA	San Francisco	San Francisco P O	83	49
Harvey	45	m	w	PRUS	Sonoma	Salt Point	91	392
Henry	40	m	w	PRUS	San Francisco	San Francisco P O	83	71
Irvin I	30	m	w	PA	San Francisco	San Francisco P O	83	345
Isaac	56	m	w	OH	Sacramento	San Joaquin Twp	77	397
J A	32	m	w	TN	Sierra	Sierra Twp	89	567
J D	32	m	w	ME	Humboldt	Eureka Twp	72	276
J E	34	m	w	TN	Sierra	Sierra Twp	89	567
J F	39	m	w	NY	Santa Clara	Gilroy Twp	88	88
J S	28	m	w	OH	Humboldt	Pacific Twp	72	293
Jacob	48	m	w	BADE	San Francisco	11-Wd San Francisc	84	657
James	54	m	w	FRAN	Stanislaus	Branch Twp	92	8
James	50	m	w	NY	San Francisco	San Francisco P O	83	302
James	39	m	w	VA	Kern	Havilah P O	73	337
James F	39	m	w	OH	Nevada	Washington Twp	75	341
James R	42	m	w	MO	Alpine	Woodfords P O	69	310
Jas W	33	m	w	NY	Fresno	Millerton P O	72	158
Joel S	30	m	w	CANA	Plumas	Plumas Twp	77	26
John	51	m	w	ME	Sonoma	Petaluma Twp	91	324
John	44	m	w	MA	Butte	Wyandotte Twp	70	141
John	38	m	w	OH	Tehama	Merrill	92	198
John	35	m	w	SPAI	Placer	Rocklin Twp	76	465
John	35	m	w	IREL	Solano	Vallejo	90	198
John	32	m	w	DENM	San Francisco	7-Wd San Francisco	81	218
John	28	m	w	CANA	Sonoma	Bodega Twp	91	260
John	28	m	w	MS	Los Angeles	Los Nietos Twp	73	577
John	27	m	w	ENGL	San Mateo	Redwood Twp	87	365
John A	49	m	w	SC	Los Angeles	El Monte Twp	73	450
John E	41	m	w	NY	San Francisco	8-Wd San Francisco	82	305
John H	38	m	w	NH	San Francisco	San Francisco P O	83	261
John H	29	m	w	NY	Marin	Tomales Twp	74	81
John L	28	m	w	IA	San Luis Obispo	Morro Twp	87	282
John L	2	m	w	CA	San Francisco	11-Wd San Francisc	84	711
John M	47	m	w	CT	Sonoma	Petaluma Twp	91	351
John T	65	m	w	VA	Tehama	Merrill	92	198
John W	26	m	w	IA	Yolo	Cache Crk Twp	93	454
Joshua	42	m	w	NJ	San Francisco	1-Wd San Francisco	79	86
L W	54	f	w	NY	Solano	Benicia	90	18
Lizzie	27	f	w	ENGL	Santa Clara	San Jose Twp	88	185
Lorenzo	29	m	w	ME	Kern	Kernville P O	73	368
Loyal	42	m	w	MI	San Joaquin	Dent Twp	86	24
Lucy C	47	f	w	ME	San Joaquin	Castoria Twp	86	9
Lulu	1	f	w	CA	Santa Clara	1-Wd San Jose	88	250
Lydia	40	f	m	NY	Sacramento	2-Wd Sacramento	77	234
Margaret	28	f	w	IREL	San Francisco	2-Wd San Francisco	79	275
Mary	58	f	w	IREL	San Mateo	Half Moon Bay P O	87	401
Mary	32	f	w	CT	Alameda	Oakland	68	230
Matilda	34	f	w	IREL	San Francisco	San Francisco P O	83	401
Matilda	32	f	w	PRUS	San Francisco	San Francisco P O	83	384
Moses	37	m	w	NY	Stanislaus	Empire Twp	92	51
Moses	36	m	w	ME	Nevada	Meadow Lake Twp	75	258
N	47	m	w	IREL	Sierra	Eureka Twp	89	524
Nellie	25	f	w	MA	San Francisco	8-Wd San Francisco	82	326
O S	55	m	w	OH	Sacramento	San Joaquin Twp	77	397
Otis	24	m	w	MI	San Francisco	7-Wd San Francisco	81	284
Richard	34	m	w	ENGL	Inyo	Cerro Gordo Twp	73	323
Russell	38	m	w	TX	San Diego	Warners Rancho Dis	78	529
S A	28	m	w	MA	Mendocino	Round Valley Twp	74	219
S C	50	m	w	IL	San Joaquin	Dent Twp	86	28
S T	57	m	b	MA	El Dorado	Greenwood Twp	72	50
Samuel	53	m	w	NY	El Dorado	White Oak Twp	72	141
Samuel	35	m	w	NY	Santa Clara	San Jose Twp	88	212
Saul	48	m	b	MA	San Francisco	6-Wd San Francisco	81	114
Stephen	39	m	w	NY	Mariposa	Mariposa P O	74	101
Thos	42	m	w	ENGL	San Francisco	7-Wd San Francisco	81	252
Thos	40	m	w	AL	Tehama	Battle Crk Twp	92	157
W	54	m	w	TN	Sierra	Sierra Twp	89	566
W A	33	m	w	PA	Alameda	Oakland	68	210
W F	36	m	w	MA	San Joaquin	3-Wd Stockton	86	245
W R	39	m	w	NY	Sierra	Sierra Twp	89	565
Weller	21	m	w	IA	Sacramento	Franklin Twp	77	110
William	52	m	w	NY	Mendocino	Point Arena Twp	74	206
William	47	m	b	CT	San Francisco	San Francisco P O	80	422
William	25	m	m	NY	Sacramento	2-Wd Sacramento	77	217
William B	44	m	w	ENGL	Yolo	Washington Twp	93	531
Winsor L J	68	m	w	CANA	San Diego	San Diego	78	493
Wm	75	m	w	ENGL	San Francisco	11-Wd San Francisc	84	613
Wm	44	m	w	NY	Marin	Tomales Twp	74	82
Wm	37	m	w	MO	San Joaquin	Castoria Twp	86	12
Wm Edmund	44	m	w	ME	Plumas	Mineral Twp	77	20
FREEMON								
Edward	39	m	w	IREL	Contra Costa	San Pablo Twp	71	360
FREER								
Alexr	26	m	w	NY	San Francisco	1-Wd San Francisco	79	65
James	28	m	w	MO	Santa Barbara	San Buenaventura P	87	430
Peter	56	m	w	NY	Butte	Ophir Twp	70	91
Thomas	43	m	w	IN	Los Angeles	El Monte Twp	73	450
William H	56	m	w	OH	Santa Clara	San Jose Twp	88	206
FREES								
Thomas	60	m	w	SHOL	Butte	Wyandotte Twp	70	148
FREESE								
Albert	50	m	w	HANO	San Francisco	1-Wd San Francisco	79	128
Danial	35	m	w	PA	San Francisco	7-Wd San Francisco	81	188
Isaac	29	m	w	MD	San Joaquin	Elkhorn Twp	86	52
Jacob	25	m	w	HDAR	Sacramento	3-Wd Sacramento	77	317
John E	46	m	w	OH	San Francisco	San Francisco P O	85	862
John H	28	m	w	PRUS	Contra Costa	Martinez P O	71	393
Wm H	43	m	w	PA	El Dorado	Placerville Twp	72	99
FREESTONE								
Joshu	28	m	w	IN	Amador	Fiddletown P O	69	436
FREET								
Abrahan	37	m	w	POLA	San Francisco	7-Wd San Francisco	81	190
Alice	20	f	w	OH	Mono	Bridgeport P O	74	284
FREETBURG								
Adolph	40	m	w	PRUS	San Francisco	8-Wd San Francisco	82	328
FREEZE								
John	36	m	w	HOLL	San Francisco	1-Wd San Francisco	79	91
FREEZER								
Christian	30	m	w	DENM	San Francisco	2-Wd San Francisco	79	174
FREEZY								
Wm	22	m	w	ENGL	San Joaquin	2-Wd Stockton	86	170
FREHILL								
Edward	39	m	w	IREL	San Francisco	1-Wd San Francisco	79	89
FREHS								
Lewis	38	m	w	MO	Alameda	Murray Twp	68	106
FREI								
Andrew	36	m	w	SWIT	San Francisco	San Francisco P O	83	45
FREIDBURGER								
A	15	m	w	BADE	San Francisco	8-Wd San Francisco	82	358
FREIDEL								
Emma	22	f	w	PRUS	San Francisco	8-Wd San Francisco	82	294
FREIDER								
Heny	57	m	w	PRUS	San Francisco	8-Wd San Francisco	82	309
FREIDERIC								
Felix	37	m	w	FRAN	San Francisco	1-Wd San Francisco	79	49
FREIDERICH								
David	27	m	w	MD	San Francisco	San Francisco P O	83	201
FREIDEYER								
John	50	m	w	SWIT	Plumas	Indian Twp	77	17
FREIDIG								
Leander	28	m	w	SWIT	San Mateo	Half Moon Bay P O	87	402
FREIDMAN								
A	24	m	w	PRUS	Sutter	Butte Twp	92	94
Fred	46	m	w	PRUS	Fresno	Millerton P O	72	145
Henry	31	m	w	PRUS	San Francisco	1-Wd San Francisco	79	30
Louis	37	m	w	PRUS	San Francisco	7-Wd San Francisco	81	222
FREIDRING								
Carl	25	m	w	SWED	San Francisco	1-Wd San Francisco	79	51
Chas	31	m	w	BREM	San Francisco	1-Wd San Francisco	79	51
FREIE								
J H	42	m	w	PRUS	San Francisco	8-Wd San Francisco	82	305
FREIERMUTH								
G A	26	m	w	MA	San Francisco	San Francisco P O	85	853
George A	55	m	w	BAVA	Santa Cruz	Watsonville	89	365
FREIHE								
Bunner	34	m	w	SAXO	San Francisco	6-Wd San Francisco	81	109
FREIL								
James	25	m	w	IREL	San Francisco	7-Wd San Francisco	81	225
FREILBERGER								
Fred	30	m	w	GERM	Nevada	Nevada Twp	75	321
FREILING								
Peter	38	m	w	PRUS	San Francisco	San Francisco P O	83	121
FREISE								
Ellen	32	f	w	SCOT	Plumas	Quartz Twp	77	35
FREITAS								
Jas	30	m	w	AZOR	Shasta	Horsetown P O	89	504
FREITCHEN								
George	30	m	w	PRUS	San Francisco	8-Wd San Francisco	82	350
FREITES								
Joseph B	24	m	w	SPAI	San Francisco	San Francisco P O	83	232
FREITO								
Gregory	22	m	w	PORT	Mendocino	Big Rvr Twp	74	161
FREITSCH								
Joseph	38	m	w	BADE	Kern	Kernville P O	73	367
FREIZE								
Jonathan	50	m	w	ME	Humboldt	Eureka Twp	72	265
Luca	44	m	w	NY	San Joaquin	2-Wd Stockton	86	209
FREKLIN								
Leon	35	m	w	AUST	San Francisco	San Francisco P O	83	49
FRELETHE								
Herman	38	m	w	PRUS	San Francisco	5-Wd San Francisco	81	20
FRELEY								
Andrew	40	m	w	IREL	Santa Clara	Gilroy Twp	88	83

© 2001 by Heritage Quest. All rights reserved.

California 1870 Census

Name	Age	S	R	B-PL	County	Locale	Series M593 Roll	Pg
FRELICH								
Andrew	33	m	w	NY	San Francisco	11-Wd San Francisc	84	444
FRELLISH								
Charles	40	m	w	PRUS	Alpine	Woodfords P O	69	310
FREMAN								
Adam	50	m	w	NY	Calaveras	Copperopolis P O	70	259
Giles N	32	m	w	MO	Yolo	Cache Crk Twp	93	457
Peter	65	m	w	NY	Sutter	Sutter Twp	92	126
Richard	64	m	w	IREL	Sacramento	Lee Twp	77	157
Thomas	47	m	w	MD	Yuba	Slate Range Bar Tw	93	674
FREMONT								
L F	46	m	w	FRAN	Klamath	Liberty Twp	73	375
Otto	40	m	w	GERM	San Diego	San Diego	78	489
FREN								
Chooy	31	m	c	CHIN	Shasta	Shasta P O	89	453
John	44	m	w	IREL	Yuba	Marysville Twp	93	569
FRENANS								
Ed	40	m	w	IREL	Sacramento	4-Wd Sacramento	77	354
FRENCA								
James	30	m	w	SHOL	Humboldt	Eureka Twp	72	268
FRENCH								
A R	50	m	w	OH	Nevada	Bridgeport Twp	75	104
Abraham P	50	m	w	MI	San Diego	Fort Yuma Dist	78	463
Addison E	22	m	w	ME	Nevada	Nevada Twp	75	308
Alexander	47	m	w	NH	Monterey	Alisal Twp	74	288
Alfred	55	m	w	OH	Santa Clara	Milpitas Twp	88	108
Allen	41	m	w	MD	Calaveras	San Andreas P O	70	201
Amalia	60	f	w	KY	San Joaquin	Douglas Twp	86	41
Amelia	14	f	w	CA	Solano	Benicia	90	7
Amos	49	m	w	MA	Santa Clara	Fremont Twp	88	54
Annie	27	f	w	ME	San Francisco	San Francisco P O	83	217
Arthur	27	m	w	NY	Shasta	Fort Crook P O	89	474
Asa	25	m	w	IL	San Bernardino	San Bernardino Twp	78	438
Augustus	56	m	w	FRAN	Mariposa	Maxwell Crk P O	74	142
B T	35	m	w	IREL	San Francisco	7-Wd San Francisco	81	241
Benjamin	52	m	w	AR	Amador	Fiddletown P O	69	434
Benjamin	18	m	w	AR	San Diego	Julian Dist	78	472
C G M	48	m	w	MA	Sacramento	4-Wd Sacramento	77	348
C H	42	m	w	VT	Siskiyou	Callahan P O	89	628
C L	23	m	w	AR	Amador	Sutter Crk P O	69	413
Caroline	49	f	w	DE	San Francisco	San Francisco P O	85	759
Charles	38	m	w	VA	Santa Clara	1-Wd San Jose	88	226
Charles	25	m	w	IREL	San Francisco	6-Wd San Francisco	81	81
Charlotte H	28	m	w	ME	Santa Clara	Milpitas Twp	88	108
Chas	32	m	w	NH	San Francisco	5-Wd San Francisco	81	28
Chas	30	m	w	ME	Nevada	Bridgeport Twp	75	114
Conrad	20	m	w	NY	San Francisco	8-Wd San Francisco	82	444
Cyrus	36	m	w	ME	Yuba	Rose Bar Twp	93	653
Daniel	40	m	w	MA	Calaveras	San Andreas P O	70	212
Dora	16	f	w	IL	Sonoma	Petaluma Twp	91	361
Earl B	34	m	w	NY	Alameda	Hayward	68	80
Eliza	25	f	w	NH	San Francisco	8-Wd San Francisco	82	290
Elleck	60	m	w	FRAN	Sacramento	Franklin Twp	77	105
Emma	5	f	w	CA	Amador	Ione City P O	69	356
Eprahim	27	m	w	ENGL	San Diego	San Luis Rey	78	513
Erastus	47	m	w	NY	San Diego	San Diego	78	487
Ezekiel D	34	m	w	OH	Alpine	Monitor P O	69	314
F	39	m	w	NY	Amador	Jackson P O	69	339
Frank	24	m	w	MI	Sonoma	Healdsburg & Mendo	91	276
Frank	22	m	w	ME	San Francisco	8-Wd San Francisco	82	427
Frank J	32	m	w	ME	San Francisco	6-Wd San Francisco	81	117
G	24	m	w	MA	Humboldt	Eureka Twp	72	269
G C	43	m	w	NE	Trinity	Hayfork Valley	92	238
G P	60	m	w	CT	San Joaquin	Elkhorn Twp	86	60
Geo	25	m	w	NY	San Francisco	1-Wd San Francisco	79	54
George	58	m	w	TN	Amador	Fiddletown P O	69	440
George	42	m	w	ME	San Francisco	8-Wd San Francisco	82	456
George	34	m	w	NY	Yolo	Grafton Twp	93	491
George	33	m	w	KY	Humboldt	Mattole Twp	72	288
George S	32	m	w	NY	San Francisco	8-Wd San Francisco	82	393
George W	42	m	w	MA	Alameda	Brooklyn	68	38
Haden	30	m	w	MA	Merced	Snelling P O	74	258
Hanson	38	m	w	VT	Nevada	Bridgeport Twp	75	116
Harvey	40	m	w	NH	Alameda	Washington Twp	68	268
Henry	46	m	w	SCOT	Yuba	Slate Range Bar Tw	93	671
Henry	45	m	w	MA	San Francisco	8-Wd San Francisco	82	408
Henry	25	m	w	OH	San Bernardino	San Bernardino Twp	78	449
Isaac L	34	m	w	ENGL	El Dorado	Mud Springs Twp	72	71
J	44	m	w	NY	Alameda	Oakland	68	241
Jacob	37	m	w	MA	Santa Cruz	Santa Cruz Twp	89	384
James	33	m	w	MI	Placer	Lincoln P O	76	481
James	21	m	w	MA	Monterey	Pajaro Twp	74	369
James A	40	m	w	NH	San Francisco	6-Wd San Francisco	81	87
James H	28	m	w	ME	Nevada	Nevada Twp	75	321
Jane	54	f	w	NY	Santa Clara	Santa Clara Twp	88	140
Jas M	64	m	w	PA	Shasta	Stillwater P O	89	481
Jno	29	m	w	IL	Santa Clara	Gilroy Twp	88	100
John	50	m	w	IREL	San Francisco	San Francisco P O	83	124
John	45	m	w	NY	Stanislaus	San Joaquin Twp	92	78
John	38	m	w	SWIT	Tuolumne	Sonora P O	93	325
John	38	m	w	CANA	Solano	Vacaville Twp	90	125
John	32	m	w	EGYP	Butte	Ophir Twp	70	120
John	26	m	w	AR	San Diego	Julian Dist	78	472
John	23	m	w	OH	San Bernardino	San Bernardino Twp	78	454
John L	39	m	w	OH	Alpine	Bullion P O	69	314
Joseph	58	m	w	NY	San Francisco	3-Wd San Francisco	79	322
Joseph	43	m	w	VT	San Francisco	San Francisco P O	83	260
Joseph	34	m	w	FRAN	San Mateo	San Mateo P O	87	358
Josph	30	m	w	FRAN	Sacramento	San Joaquin Twp	77	404
Julia	29	f	w	IREL	Sacramento	Granite Twp	77	140
K	40	m	w	NY	Alameda	Oakland	68	241
Kilman	21	m	w	AR	El Dorado	Cosumnes Twp	72	13
Kinman	21	m	w	MO	Amador	Fiddletown P O	69	429
L W	37	m	w	GERM	San Joaquin	2-Wd Stockton	86	166
Larian	35	m	w	IN	Los Angeles	Los Angeles	73	508
Lee	23	m	w	AR	Amador	Fiddletown P O	69	432
Louis	44	m	w	NY	San Francisco	San Francisco P O	80	414
Louis	28	m	w	FRAN	San Francisco	San Francisco P O	80	346
M B	43	m	w	MO	Tehama	Red Bluff	92	174
M B	34	m	w	NH	San Francisco	San Francisco P O	83	326
M V	28	m	w	AR	Amador	Fiddletown P O	69	440
Martha	48	f	w	IREL	Sacramento	3-Wd Sacramento	77	303
Martin H	37	m	w	ME	Tulare	Visalia Twp	92	285
Mary	24	f	w	IL	San Francisco	San Francisco P O	83	67
Mary C	20	f	w	AR	Stanislaus	Empire Twp	92	35
Milton	35	m	w	MS	Colusa	Monroe Twp	71	318
Morris	50	m	w	FRAN	San Bernardino	San Bernardino Twp	78	419
Mortimer	30	m	w	NY	Santa Clara	Santa Clara Twp	88	140
N	58	m	w	IREL	Alameda	Oakland	68	207
Oliver G	49	m	w	CANA	Santa Cruz	Watsonville	89	375
Oscar	27	m	w	MD	San Francisco	8-Wd San Francisco	82	382
P	48	m	w	CT	Sacramento	1-Wd Sacramento	77	177
Peter	51	m	w	SWIT	San Francisco	San Francisco P O	80	425
Rachael	40	f	w	SCOT	Sacramento	Granite Twp	77	139
Richard	38	m	w	ENGL	Sonoma	Petaluma Twp	91	311
Richard	12	m	w	NY	San Francisco	11-Wd San Francisc	84	588
Robert	42	m	w	MD	San Diego	Julian Dist	78	471
Robert	36	m	w	CANA	San Francisco	7-Wd San Francisco	81	265
Rose	3	f	w	IL	Colusa	Colusa	71	295
Saml	52	m	w	VT	Shasta	Dog Crk P O	89	471
Samuel	53	m	w	MA	Sonoma	Petaluma Twp	91	353
Simon	52	m	w	MA	San Francisco	San Francisco P O	80	473
Simon P	45	m	w	KY	Colusa	Colusa	71	294
Stephen	40	m	w	MA	San Francisco	San Francisco P O	85	739
T H	26	m	w	MO	Monterey	San Antonio Twp	74	323
T J	30	m	w	MO	Lassen	Susanville Twp	73	446
Thomas	32	m	w	DC	San Francisco	San Francisco P O	83	68
Thomas	14	m	w	CA	Colusa	Colusa	71	294
Thomas D	33	m	w	AR	Amador	Fiddletown P O	69	440
Victor	40	m	w	FRAN	Sacramento	Granite Twp	77	154
Victor	38	m	w	FRAN	Sacramento	Granite Twp	77	156
Warren	30	m	w	NY	San Francisco	1-Wd San Francisco	79	71
William	35	m	w	ENGL	San Francisco	8-Wd San Francisco	82	457
William	21	m	w	NY	Alameda	Murray Twp	68	114
Wm	35	m	w	MA	San Francisco	San Francisco P O	85	854
Wm M	55	m	w	MD	San Francisco	San Francisco P O	85	757
FRENCHEL								
August	19	m	w	IA	Amador	Jackson P O	69	333
FRENCHMAN								
Pollie	28	m	w	FRAN	Sacramento	Sutter Twp	77	390
FRENERHAN								
George	26	m	w	IREL	San Francisco	San Francisco P O	80	427
FRENTIN								
Henry	32	m	w	PRUS	Placer	Dutch Flat P O	76	405
FRENTZ								
Fritz	27	m	w	PRUS	Sacramento	4-Wd Sacramento	77	344
John	40	m	w	PORT	Sacramento	Granite Twp	77	149
Theo	35	m	w	PRUS	Sacramento	4-Wd Sacramento	77	344
FRENZ								
Patrick	32	m	w	IREL	Sacramento	2-Wd Sacramento	77	209
FREOGOLA								
Domingo	56	m	w	ITAL	Amador	Jackson P O	69	336
FRERATHIN								
John	18	m	w	ENGL	Amador	Amador City P O	69	394
FRERES								
Emile	32	m	w	HAMB	San Francisco	3-Wd San Francisco	79	305
FRERICH								
Elizabeth	34	f	w	ENGL	San Francisco	2-Wd San Francisco	79	201
FRERY								
Elizabeth	35	f	w	NY	Contra Costa	Martinez P O	71	397
FRESE								
John	25	m	w	BREM	San Francisco	San Francisco P O	83	192
John H	12	m	w	CA	Santa Cruz	Santa Cruz Twp	89	381
FRESHER								
George	23	m	w	ENGL	Solano	Montezuma Twp	90	68
FRESHOUR								
C C	27	m	w	MO	Napa	Napa Twp	75	33
Joseph T	28	m	w	IN	Santa Cruz	Soquel Twp	89	446
William H	16	m	w	IN	Santa Cruz	Soquel Twp	89	447
FRESHOWER								
Antoinette	37	f	w	MO	San Joaquin	Douglas Twp	86	39
Elizabeth	84	f	w	PA	Santa Cruz	Soquel Twp	89	436
Martin	37	m	w	PA	San Joaquin	Douglas Twp	86	39
FRESIER								
Jane A	20	f	w	NY	Monterey	Monterey Twp	74	350
FRESLYN								
Francis	19	m	w	NJ	San Francisco	San Francisco P O	83	229
FRESONNE								
P	39	m	w	ITAL	Alameda	Oakland	68	241
FRESS								
Geovanier	24	m	w	SWIT	Sonoma	Santa Rosa	91	396
FRESSIUS								
Frederick	30	m	w	PRUS	San Francisco	6-Wd San Francisco	81	133

© 2001 by Heritage Quest. All rights reserved.

Series M593

Name	Age	S	R	B-PL	County	Locale	Roll	Pg
FRESSUS								
Antony	48	m	w	BADE	Santa Barbara	Santa Barbara P O	87	461
FRESTOBUS								
Lyman H	38	m	w	NC	San Luis Obispo	Morro Twp	87	282
FRESTYLE								
Geo	38	m	w	ENGL	Siskiyou	Scott Valley Twp	89	613
FRETA								
John	18	m	w	SCOT	Alameda	Brooklyn Twp	68	48
FRETAS								
Lunes	28	m	w	SCOT	San Luis Obispo	Santa Rosa Twp	87	323
FRETCHER								
Antoine	31	m	w	WIND	San Francisco	3-Wd San Francisco	79	317
FRETES								
Joseph	39	m	w	AZOR	Monterey	Castroville Twp	74	326
FRETEZ								
Manuel	35	m	w	AZOR	Monterey	Monterey	74	361
Manuel	24	m	w	AZOR	Monterey	Monterey Twp	74	343
FRETIGER								
Sam	35	m	w	SWIT	Amador	Drytown P O	69	422
FRETTY								
H R	31	m	w	IN	Lake	Upper Lake	73	410
FRETTYS								
Margaret	63	f	w	FRAN	San Francisco	San Francisco P O	83	49
FRETWEL								
Jas B	31	m	w	VA	Sonoma	Santa Rosa	91	400
FREUND								
Fred	24	m	w	PA	Merced	Snelling P O	74	261
Fredck	48	m	w	GERM	Tuolumne	Sonora P O	93	303
Fredk M	43	m	w	BADE	San Francisco	San Francisco P O	83	51
FREVILLE								
E	47	m	w	FRAN	San Francisco	San Francisco P O	85	819
FREW								
Samuel	45	m	w	PA	Butte	Wyandotte Twp	70	146
Thomas L	42	m	w	PA	Yuba	Bullards Bar P O	93	553
FREWIN								
M	27	m	w	MEXI	San Joaquin	2-Wd Stockton	86	184
FREY								
A T	31	m	w	NY	Nevada	Washington Twp	75	346
Ah	40	m	c	CHIN	Sacramento	Georgianna Twp	77	124
B	50	m	w	FRAN	Alameda	Oakland	68	180
Charles	43	m	w	PA	Yuba	North East Twp	93	643
Henry	79	m	w	SWIT	Yolo	Putah Twp	93	517
Henry	43	m	w	SWIT	Sacramento	4-Wd Sacramento	77	371
Henry	30	m	w	HANO	Sacramento	Franklin Twp	77	117
Jacob	25	m	w	BADE	San Francisco	San Francisco P O	80	429
John	40	m	w	WURT	Amador	Jackson P O	69	342
John	28	m	w	ME	Sacramento	2-Wd Sacramento	77	234
Joseph	45	m	w	FRAN	Santa Cruz	Santa Cruz	89	431
M A	40	m	w	PA	Sacramento	Lee Twp	77	161
Michael	62	m	w	IA	Sacramento	Lee Twp	77	161
Nicholes	28	m	w	PRUS	San Francisco	7-Wd San Francisco	81	226
Rosena	76	f	w	SWIT	Yolo	Putah Twp	93	517
William	27	m	w	ENGL	San Francisco	8-Wd San Francisco	82	331
William	22	m	w	SWIT	Yolo	Putah Twp	93	517
FREYSCHLHE								
Christian	44	m	w	BAVA	Santa Clara	2-Wd San Jose	88	294
FREYTE								
Joseph	37	m	w	FRAN	Butte	Oregon Twp	70	132
FREZE								
John B	40	m	w	HANO	Solano	Maine Prairie Twp	90	45
FREZELL								
Henry	26	m	w	MO	Sutter	Butte Twp	92	89
FRHM								
H F	55	m	w	----	El Dorado	Coloma Twp	72	1
FRIANT								
Alfred	45	m	w	FRAN	Santa Clara	2-Wd San Jose	88	331
John	35	m	w	FRAN	Santa Clara	2-Wd San Jose	88	309
FRIAR								
James	50	m	w	MA	Napa	Napa	75	20
FRIAS								
John B	23	m	w	MEXI	Mariposa	Mariposa P O	74	110
Nicholas	43	m	w	CA	Napa	Napa	75	53
FRIBBLE								
Andrew	36	m	w	ENGL	Amador	Sutter Crk P O	69	404
FRIBOO								
Saml	21	m	w	NY	Butte	Hamilton Twp	70	62
FRIBOR								
Ernest	43	f	w	PRUS	San Joaquin	2-Wd Stockton	86	165
FRICHO								
Guadelupe	30	f	w	MEXI	Los Angeles	Los Angeles	73	503
FRICHOT								
Battiste	55	m	w	FRAN	Placer	Lincoln P O	76	482
FRICK								
A	37	m	w	HESS	Alameda	Murray Twp	68	108
Abraham	45	m	w	BAVA	Placer	Rocklin Twp	76	468
Ah	16	m	c	CHIN	Sacramento	2-Wd Sacramento	77	223
Alfred	40	m	w	FRAN	San Francisco	San Francisco P O	83	59
Alice	16	f	w	IL	Alameda	Washington Twp	68	279
August	49	m	w	MECK	San Francisco	2-Wd San Francisco	79	258
Christian	50	m	w	NY	Trinity	Lewiston Pct	92	213
Christian	35	m	w	PRUS	San Francisco	San Francisco P O	83	179
Emily	26	m	w	FRAN	Alameda	Brooklyn	68	36
Ernest	46	m	w	GERM	Alameda	Washington Twp	68	281
Geo W	42	m	w	PA	Sonoma	Vallejo Twp	91	456
George A	40	m	w	NY	Nevada	Little York Twp	75	242
Henry F	7	m	w	CA	Sacramento	Franklin Twp	77	106
Isaac	24	m	w	OH	Solano	Maine Prairie Twp	90	45
James	23	m	w	SWIT	San Francisco	11-Wd San Francisc	84	529
James C	27	m	w	IL	Nevada	Grass Valley Twp	75	161
John	27	m	w	IL	Alameda	Murray Twp	68	108
Lin	30	m	c	CHIN	Sacramento	2-Wd Sacramento	77	223
FRICKE								
Charles	29	m	w	HAMB	Plumas	Goodwin Twp	77	8
FRICKEN								
Burchert	38	m	w	HANO	El Dorado	Mountain Twp	72	69
FRICKER								
Durst	39	m	w	SWIT	Placer	Auburn P O	76	373
Sophie	24	f	w	BELG	San Francisco	7-Wd San Francisco	81	248
FRICKETTE								
Peter	30	m	w	CANA	Placer	Lincoln P O	76	486
FRICKMYRE								
George	32	m	w	BAVA	Trinity	North Fork Twp	92	216
FRICKSON								
Joseph	54	m	w	FRAN	Shasta	Shasta P O	89	457
FRICOR								
John H	47	m	w	SWIT	San Francisco	6-Wd San Francisco	81	80
FRICOT								
John F	50	m	w	FRAN	Shasta	Shasta P O	89	454
FRIDATON								
Noses	30	m	w	SWIT	San Francisco	2-Wd San Francisco	79	190
FRIDAY								
Christine	46	f	w	PRUS	San Francisco	8-Wd San Francisco	82	428
F Amer	36	m	w	OH	San Bernardino	San Bernardino Twp	78	453
Fernon	40	m	w	PRUS	Sacramento	4-Wd Sacramento	77	360
Horman	28	m	w	PRUS	San Francisco	5-Wd San Francisco	81	32
FRIDEN								
Lansing	31	m	w	PRUS	San Francisco	San Francisco P O	80	471
FRIDERES								
Jacob	39	m	w	SWIT	Sonoma	Sonoma Twp	91	443
FRIDHOUS								
M H	25	m	w	CANA	Sutter	Sutter Twp	92	122
FRIDLER								
Jno	16	m	w	CA	Santa Clara	Almaden Twp	88	9
FRIDO								
Adolph	68	m	w	FRAN	San Francisco	San Francisco P O	80	342
FRIE								
Edward	48	m	w	FRAN	Amador	Jackson P O	69	342
FRIEBER								
Sarah	14	f	w	NY	San Francisco	San Francisco P O	85	816
FRIEBURG								
Godfrey	30	m	w	HANO	San Francisco	6-Wd San Francisco	81	81
FRIECHETTE								
Louis	33	m	w	CANA	San Francisco	11-Wd San Francisc	84	657
FRIED								
David	36	m	w	PRUS	San Francisco	San Francisco P O	83	9
Fred	23	m	w	BAVA	Solano	Benicia	90	2
George	41	m	w	BAVA	Siskiyou	Yreka	89	654
Henry	38	m	w	BAVA	Sonoma	Healdsburg & Mendo	91	277
Solomon	34	m	w	IN	Kern	Havilah P O	73	339
FRIEDBERG								
Ellis	19	m	w	RUSS	San Francisco	San Francisco P O	83	180
Morris	50	m	w	RUSS	San Francisco	San Francisco P O	83	199
FRIEDBERGHER								
A	40	m	w	WURT	San Joaquin	2-Wd Stockton	86	160
FRIEDDLER								
John	33	m	w	BAVA	El Dorado	Coloma Twp	72	2
FRIEDENBERGER								
A	40	m	w	PRUS	San Joaquin	2-Wd Stockton	86	181
FRIEDENBUR								
Wm	36	m	w	OH	Marin	Nicasio Twp	74	16
FRIEDLAND								
Alvis	35	m	w	HDAR	San Francisco	San Francisco P O	83	232
FRIEDLANDER								
Albert	5	m	w	CA	Santa Clara	1-Wd San Jose	88	265
Ernest	24	m	w	HAMB	San Francisco	8-Wd San Francisco	82	420
Ernesta	20	f	w	PRUS	San Francisco	San Francisco P O	83	135
Harriet	21	f	w	PRUS	Santa Clara	1-Wd San Jose	88	245
I	50	m	w	PRUS	San Francisco	San Francisco P O	83	102
Louis	26	m	w	NY	San Francisco	8-Wd San Francisco	82	423
P H	27	m	w	PRUS	San Francisco	San Francisco P O	83	328
Rose	20	f	w	MO	San Francisco	8-Wd San Francisco	82	490
Rose	20	f	w	MO	San Francisco	7-Wd San Francisco	81	184
Saml	23	m	w	HAMB	San Francisco	San Francisco P O	83	262
Saml	22	m	w	BAVA	San Francisco	San Francisco P O	83	271
William	32	m	w	PRUS	San Francisco	San Francisco P O	83	379
FRIEDLER								
F	38	m	w	PRUS	Santa Clara	Almaden Twp	88	12
Wm	29	m	w	BREM	San Francisco	1-Wd San Francisco	79	54
FRIEDMAN								
Chs	25	m	w	PRUS	San Francisco	2-Wd San Francisco	79	177
Conrad	38	m	w	POLA	San Francisco	San Francisco P O	80	531
Edward	42	m	w	BAVA	San Francisco	8-Wd San Francisco	82	402
Edward	34	m	w	BAVA	San Francisco	San Francisco P O	80	458
Fredinand	33	m	w	SWIT	San Luis Obispo	San Luis Obispo Tw	87	307
Isaac	35	m	w	POLA	San Francisco	San Francisco P O	80	371
J S	50	m	w	BAVA	San Francisco	San Francisco P O	85	787
Jacob	40	m	w	RUSS	San Francisco	1-Wd San Francisco	79	81
John	49	m	w	BADE	El Dorado	White Oak Twp	72	139
Myer	43	m	w	RUSS	Sacramento	2-Wd Sacramento	77	213
Sarah	35	f	w	PRUS	San Francisco	San Francisco P O	80	430
FRIEDN								
James	35	m	w	MO	Marin	Point Reyes Twp	74	23
FRIEDRICKS								
Hiram	56	m	w	IN	Sutter	Yuba Twp	92	146

© 2001 by Heritage Quest. All rights reserved.

Name	Age	S	R	B-PL	County	Locale	Series M593 Roll	Pg
FRIEDRICKSON								
F	50	m	w	SHOL	Alameda	Eden Twp	68	63
FRIEL								
Jeremiah	53	m	w	VA	Yolo	Grafton Twp	93	488
John	40	m	w	IREL	San Francisco	San Francisco P O	85	742
Niel	25	m	w	CANA	Humboldt	Bucksport Twp	72	242
Randolph	24	m	w	MO	Colusa	Spring Valley Twp	71	340
William	50	m	w	IREL	San Francisco	San Francisco P O	83	183
FRIELANDER								
Win	43	m	w	PRUS	Marin	Bolinas Twp	74	1
FRIEND								
A Jos	55	m	w	OH	Santa Clara	Gilroy Twp	88	91
Addi	35	f	w	NY	Santa Clara	Gilroy Twp	88	91
Augustus	24	m	w	MO	Humboldt	Bald Hills	72	237
Charles	70	m	w	SWED	Placer	Roseville P O	76	349
E S	16	m	w	OH	Sutter	Butte Twp	92	98
Ellis	28	m	w	ME	San Francisco	San Francisco P O	83	219
George	52	m	w	MO	Humboldt	Bald Hills	72	237
George	36	m	w	PRUS	San Francisco	1-Wd San Francisco	79	63
George V	39	m	w	NY	Santa Cruz	Santa Cruz Twp	89	387
Henry	22	m	w	HAMB	San Francisco	2-Wd San Francisco	79	261
Isaac	36	m	w	PRUS	Colusa	Spring Valley Twp	71	339
Isaac	33	m	w	OH	Butte	Oregon Twp	70	128
Israel	36	m	w	NH	San Francisco	San Francisco P O	83	254
James	55	m	w	MO	Butte	Chico Twp	70	40
Jno	65	m	w	VA	Butte	Oregon Twp	70	128
Jonah	53	m	w	MA	San Francisco	5-Wd San Francisco	81	23
Joseph	46	m	w	MA	Sacramento	2-Wd Sacramento	77	224
Joshua	37	m	w	NY	San Francisco	5-Wd San Francisco	81	12
T C	21	m	w	OH	Sutter	Butte Twp	92	88
William	42	m	w	OH	Alameda	Brooklyn	68	23
Wm A	18	m	w	OH	Sutter	Butte Twp	92	98
FRIENZZA								
John	25	m	w	ITAL	Sonoma	Vallejo Twp	91	454
FRIER								
George	28	m	w	SCOT	San Francisco	11-Wd San Francisc	84	559
John	34	m	w	WURT	Solano	Vallejo	90	193
Joseph	19	m	w	ENGL	Marin	Tomales Twp	74	77
FRIERK								
Peterson	55	m	w	HANO	Stanislaus	San Joaquin Twp	92	72
FRIERSON								
William J	60	m	w	SC	Yolo	Grafton Twp	93	485
FRIERY								
Patrick	55	m	w	IREL	Kern	Linns Valley P O	73	343
FRIES								
Charles	52	m	w	SWED	Marin	Bolinas Twp	74	6
Gr	36	m	w	PA	Sierra	Butte Twp	89	513
Jacob	39	m	w	PRUS	Siskiyou	Scott Valley Twp	89	620
Louis	35	m	w	BADE	San Francisco	San Francisco P O	80	356
Mary	21	f	w	BADE	San Francisco	3-Wd San Francisco	79	324
Otto	43	m	w	PRUS	San Francisco	San Francisco P O	83	232
FRIESBERG								
Abraham	31	m	w	PRUS	Napa	Napa	75	16
FRIESEKE								
Wm	49	m	w	PRUS	Sacramento	3-Wd Sacramento	77	273
FRIESENHAUSEN								
J	45	m	w	PRUS	San Francisco	San Francisco P O	85	864
FRIESLEBEN								
Danl	38	m	w	BOHE	Butte	Ophir Twp	70	94
FRIETAS								
Francis	4	m	w	CA	San Francisco	San Francisco P O	85	828
Nellie	4	f	w	CA	San Francisco	San Francisco P O	85	827
FRIEZE								
F	45	m	w	PRUS	Alameda	Oakland	68	240
George	42	m	w	NC	Kern	Tehachapi P O	73	354
FRIGERIO								
Giuseppe	48	m	w	ITAL	San Francisco	11-Wd San Francisc	84	594
FRIGGENS								
John F	30	m	w	ENGL	Yolo	Cache Crk Twp	93	435
FRIGGINS								
Job	23	m	w	ENGL	Nevada	Grass Valley Twp	75	172
John	24	m	w	ENGL	Yolo	Cache Crk Twp	93	429
FRIGOLA								
Antonio	40	m	w	ITAL	San Francisco	2-Wd San Francisco	79	205
FRIGOLO								
Antonio	27	m	w	ITAL	San Francisco	2-Wd San Francisco	79	232
FRIGORI								
Joseph	41	m	w	AUST	San Francisco	San Francisco P O	80	333
FRIHER								
Fredrick	41	m	w	PA	Inyo	Bishop Crk Twp	73	317
FRIMENTO								
John	27	m	w	PORT	Marin	Tomales Twp	74	87
FRINCHLE								
John	40	m	w	POLA	San Francisco	1-Wd San Francisco	79	101
FRINCK								
Horace	39	m	w	CT	San Bernardino	San Bernardino Twp	78	440
FRINDOFF								
Sarah	27	f	w	NY	San Francisco	San Francisco P O	80	465
FRING								
Ah	48	m	c	CHIN	Los Angeles	Los Angeles	73	540
Ah	46	m	c	CHIN	Fresno	Millerton P O	72	202
FRINGS								
Hugo	29	m	w	PRUS	San Francisco	1-Wd San Francisco	79	69
FRINK								
August	43	m	w	PRUS	San Francisco	2-Wd San Francisco	79	259
D B	37	m	w	NY	Nevada	Nevada Twp	75	272
Daniel	42	m	w	NY	Santa Clara	Fremont Twp	88	42
Edwin B	36	m	w	VT	Los Angeles	Los Angeles	73	565
Geo	43	m	w	NY	San Francisco	11-Wd San Francisc	84	423
John R	39	m	w	NY	San Bernardino	San Bernardino Twp	78	443
Joseph	25	m	w	PORT	San Mateo	Half Moon Bay P O	87	390
Ledyard	59	m	w	NY	Solano	Rio Vista Twp	90	57
Lewis	39	m	w	BAVA	San Francisco	8-Wd San Francisco	82	356
Rufus	38	m	w	RI	Siskiyou	Scott Rvr Twp	89	604
Russell	49	m	w	NY	Marin	San Rafael	74	57
T C	42	m	w	TN	San Joaquin	Castoria Twp	86	8
William	16	m	w	CA	Santa Clara	Santa Clara Twp	88	177
FRINS								
Frank	51	m	w	FRAN	San Mateo	Schoolhouse Statio	87	341
FRINTO								
Lewey	48	m	w	FRAN	Trinity	Junction City Pct	92	209
FRIOLBORG								
H	47	m	w	PRUS	Sierra	Forest Twp	89	532
FRIRORI								
Manuel	44	m	w	MEXI	San Diego	Coronado	78	466
FRISBEE								
E C	40	m	w	NY	Tuolumne	Chinese Camp P O	93	375
Heny	27	m	w	WI	Butte	Concow Twp	70	9
FRISBIE								
Edward	43	m	w	NY	Napa	Napa Twp	75	31
Eleazer	40	m	w	NY	Napa	Napa Twp	75	31
J N	27	m	w	MO	Solano	Vallejo	90	212
Jas	53	m	w	ME	Solano	Vallejo	90	171
John B	47	m	w	NY	Solano	Vallejo	90	180
Levi C	49	m	w	NY	Solano	Vallejo	90	179
M E	28	f	w	NY	Sonoma	Bodega Twp	91	257
Mary	64	f	w	CT	San Francisco	11-Wd San Francisc	84	602
Moses	25	m	w	MA	San Francisco	3-Wd San Francisco	79	325
W E	32	m	w	NY	Solano	Vallejo	90	205
Wallace	40	m	w	ME	Nevada	Bloomfield Twp	75	98
Wm	40	m	w	MA	San Francisco	San Francisco P O	83	81
FRISBY								
B F	32	m	w	NY	Sutter	Yuba Twp	92	149
Henry	29	m	w	OH	Contra Costa	Martinez P O	71	412
John	36	m	w	MO	Yolo	Buckeye Twp	93	413
Robe W	33	m	w	NY	Butte	Ophir Twp	70	110
FRISCH								
J W	44	m	w	PRUS	San Francisco	San Francisco P O	83	317
FRISEMONS								
Dennis	60	m	w	FRAN	San Mateo	San Mateo P O	87	349
FRISH								
V A	25	m	w	HUNG	San Francisco	7-Wd San Francisco	81	226
FRISHLOCK								
Antone	40	m	w	BADE	Sacramento	Franklin Twp	77	105
FRISHOLTZ								
Burney	34	m	w	PRUS	Butte	Hamilton Twp	70	62
Jno	36	m	w	BAVA	Butte	Ophir Twp	70	94
Mike	32	m	w	BAVA	Butte	Oregon Twp	70	132
FRISK								
John	30	m	w	SWED	San Francisco	1-Wd San Francisco	79	121
Thos	25	m	w	ENGL	Fresno	Millerton P O	72	165
FRISLE								
Walter	20	m	w	SCOT	Sonoma	Russian Rvr	91	370
FRISLEBEN								
Lena	31	f	w	BAVA	San Francisco	11-Wd San Francisc	84	513
FRIST								
Freeman	21	m	w	IL	Solano	Vacaville Twp	90	123
James	34	m	w	MD	San Francisco	San Francisco P O	83	335
Ransom	60	m	w	VT	Solano	Vacaville Twp	90	123
FRIT								
H	45	m	w	NY	Sierra	Lincoln Twp	89	547
FRITAG								
Charles	26	m	w	SAXO	Placer	Bath P O	76	443
FRITCH								
Charles	54	m	w	BADE	Nevada	Grass Valley Twp	75	187
Geo	41	m	w	CANA	San Francisco	1-Wd San Francisco	79	98
George	41	m	w	CANA	San Francisco	2-Wd San Francisco	79	248
John M	52	m	w	FRAN	Nevada	Grass Valley Twp	75	157
William	30	m	w	HANO	San Francisco	6-Wd San Francisco	81	41
FRITCHE								
Henry	31	m	w	PRUS	San Francisco	11-Wd San Francisc	84	681
John	28	m	w	SWIT	San Francisco	8-Wd San Francisco	82	387
FRITCHEY								
Ulrich	26	m	w	SWIT	San Francisco	11-Wd San Francisc	84	449
FRITER								
Wm	28	m	w	BADE	San Joaquin	Douglas Twp	86	35
FRITH								
Jacques	35	m	w	FRAN	Santa Clara	Almaden Twp	88	13
FRITSCH								
Charles	30	m	w	PRUS	San Francisco	San Francisco P O	83	343
Frederick	60	m	w	BADE	Alpine	Markleeville P O	69	311
George	36	m	w	HAMB	San Francisco	11-Wd San Francisc	84	462
Jacob	58	m	w	FRAN	Santa Cruz	Santa Cruz	89	428
John	41	m	w	FRAN	Sonoma	Petaluma Twp	91	329
John Baptiste	42	m	w	FRAN	Plumas	Indian Twp	77	18
John J	24	m	w	LA	Sacramento	4-Wd Sacramento	77	337
FRITSON								
Alonzo	23	m	w	ME	Sonoma	Santa Rosa	91	413
FRITTER								
George	40	m	w	SCOT	El Dorado	Kelsey Twp	72	60
John	36	m	w	OH	Butte	Chico Twp	70	36
FRITTON								
Eben	23	m	w	NORW	Solano	Denverton Twp	90	26

© 2001 by Heritage Quest. All rights reserved.

Series M593

Name	Age	S	R	B-PL	County	Locale	Roll	Pg
FRITTS								
John A	42	m	w	VA	Del Norte	Happy Camp Twp	71	470
FRITZ								
Chas	31	m	w	GERM	Solano	Vallejo	90	200
Christian	25	f	w	WURT	Los Angeles	Los Angeles	73	528
Clara B	15	f	w	NY	Yolo	Cache Crk Twp	93	443
Emerald J	44	m	w	MADE	Yuba	Marysville Twp	93	567
Fredk	48	m	w	HANO	Santa Clara	Gilroy Twp	88	82
G A	20	m	w	KY	Amador	Drytown P O	69	416
H	30	m	w	PRUS	San Francisco	San Francisco P O	83	328
Henry	30	m	w	NY	San Francisco	San Francisco P O	80	458
J M	38	m	w	FRAN	Sacramento	4-Wd Sacramento	77	362
James	32	m	w	SWIT	Santa Clara	Santa Clara Twp	88	174
James	28	m	w	POLA	Alameda	Murray Twp	68	108
John	45	m	w	FRAN	Sacramento	4-Wd Sacramento	77	376
John	45	m	w	PRUS	Colusa	Monroe Twp	71	311
John	45	m	w	WURT	Mariposa	Mariposa P O	74	118
John	45	m	w	WURT	San Francisco	8-Wd San Francisco	82	320
John	36	m	w	PORT	Santa Cruz	Santa Cruz Twp	89	387
John	35	m	w	AZOR	Santa Cruz	Santa Cruz	89	404
John	34	m	w	PRUS	Alameda	Murray Twp	68	105
John J	40	m	w	PRUS	Calaveras	San Andreas P O	70	198
Joseph	42	m	w	HDAR	Sacramento	4-Wd Sacramento	77	354
Josephine	60	f	w	FRAN	San Francisco	2-Wd San Francisco	79	167
Lawrence	48	m	w	FRAN	Siskiyou	Surprise Valley Tw	89	642
Manuel	26	m	w	PORT	Solano	Denverton Twp	90	25
Nora	26	f	w	NY	Alameda	Murray Twp	68	99
Ruben	19	m	w	GERM	Los Angeles	Los Angeles	73	571
William	26	m	w	PRUS	San Francisco	7-Wd San Francisco	81	197
FRITZEL								
Fred	20	m	w	WURT	Sacramento	4-Wd Sacramento	77	375
FRITZGERALD								
Thomas	45	m	w	IREL	Los Angeles	El Monte Twp	73	461
FRITZPATRICK								
Ellen	30	f	w	IREL	Alameda	Washington Twp	68	276
FRITZSIMMONS								
J	27	m	w	IREL	Lake	Knoxville Mines	73	405
FRIZE								
Conrad	50	m	w	PRUS	San Francisco	San Francisco P O	80	427
FRIZELL								
Joseph	40	m	w	CANA	Napa	Napa	75	57
Richard	40	m	w	IREL	San Francisco	3-Wd San Francisco	79	289
FRIZZELL								
David	19	m	w	MO	Sutter	Butte Twp	92	93
FRO								
Ah	46	m	c	CHIN	San Francisco	San Francisco P O	80	498
Ah	33	m	c	CHIN	San Francisco	San Francisco P O	80	509
Ah	10	m	c	CHIN	San Francisco	8-Wd San Francisco	82	310
FROBER								
Henry	26	m	w	PRUS	San Francisco	San Francisco P O	85	738
FROCAU								
Paul	45	m	w	FRAN	San Francisco	San Francisco P O	80	470
FROCHEAU								
Thomas	58	m	w	FRAN	Nevada	Bridgeport Twp	75	124
FROCHEU								
Selim	31	m	w	FRAN	San Francisco	San Francisco P O	80	468
FROD								
William H	49	m	w	ENGL	San Francisco	2-Wd San Francisco	79	281
FRODDEN								
Michael	26	m	w	IREL	San Francisco	11-Wd San Francisc	84	463
FRODINA								
Franseva	25	m	w	FRAN	Los Angeles	Los Angeles Twp	73	490
FRODSHAM								
Edward	31	m	w	ENGL	San Francisco	San Francisco P O	85	850
John	21	m	w	MO	San Francisco	2-Wd San Francisco	79	183
FROEDIT								
Matthew	40	m	w	PORT	Santa Cruz	Santa Cruz Twp	89	382
FROELICH								
George	45	m	w	HDAR	Santa Barbara	Santa Barbara P O	87	499
Gustave	43	m	w	PRUS	Amador	Jackson P O	69	318
Otto	36	m	w	DENM	Fresno	Millerton P O	72	145
Sine	32	f	w	DENM	Fresno	Millerton P O	72	145
FROEMAN								
Herrman	16	m	w	PRUS	San Francisco	San Francisco P O	83	384
FROES								
H C	46	m	w	HANO	Sierra	Butte Twp	89	510
FROGANI								
Stephen	52	m	w	ITAL	Calaveras	Copperopolis P O	70	245
FROHIN								
Henry	60	m	w	HAMB	Santa Clara	San Jose Twp	88	202
FROHLING								
Louis	50	m	w	GERM	Los Angeles	Los Angeles	73	510
FROHLINGER								
Theodore	26	m	w	PRUS	Los Angeles	Los Angeles	73	547
FROHLKING								
William	25	m	w	HAMB	Sonoma	Petaluma Twp	91	349
FROHMANN								
Susman	37	m	w	HESS	San Francisco	San Francisco P O	83	373
FROHME								
Louis	30	m	w	WURT	San Francisco	8-Wd San Francisco	82	383
FROLE								
Egan	28	m	w	MEXI	San Joaquin	2-Wd Stockton	86	172
FROLENCE								
Edwd	33	m	w	ITAL	San Francisco	1-Wd San Francisco	79	122
FROLING								
Ferosa	19	f	w	GERM	Los Angeles	Los Angeles	73	507
Maggie	28	f	w	IREL	San Francisco	San Francisco P O	83	110
FROM								
Ah	34	m	c	CHIN	San Francisco	San Francisco P O	80	455
Augustus	42	m	w	PRUS	Alameda	Alameda	68	15
FROMBERG								
A	30	m	w	PRUS	San Francisco	San Francisco P O	83	271
Chas	45	m	w	GERM	San Francisco	8-Wd San Francisco	82	371
FROMBERS								
Manuel	31	m	w	PORT	Alameda	Washington Twp	68	291
FROME								
Lewis	38	m	w	IREL	San Joaquin	2-Wd Stockton	86	174
FROMENSLAGER								
Jake	31	m	w	PRUS	Butte	Ophir Twp	70	108
FROMENT								
Eugene	55	m	w	FRAN	Santa Clara	2-Wd San Jose	88	331
FROMER								
Carl	29	m	w	PRUS	San Francisco	1-Wd San Francisco	79	51
George	26	m	w	WURT	Santa Clara	Fremont Twp	88	53
FROMET								
Frederica	49	f	w	PRUS	San Francisco	1-Wd San Francisco	79	49
FROMHEIMER								
James	25	m	w	PRUS	San Francisco	5-Wd San Francisco	81	15
FROMIER								
Gustave	40	m	w	SWED	Del Norte	Smith Rvr Twp	71	479
FROMKIEMN								
Wm	33	m	w	NY	San Francisco	11-Wd San Francisc	84	422
FROMLEY								
Isaac	38	m	w	POLA	San Francisco	San Francisco P O	83	273
FROMM								
Albert	17	m	w	PRUS	San Francisco	7-Wd San Francisco	81	250
FRONCO								
Charles	40	m	w	BELG	Santa Clara	2-Wd San Jose	88	324
FRONCUESWA								
Gerold	20	m	w	FRAN	Los Angeles	Los Angeles Twp	73	478
FRONEART								
J	53	m	w	FRAN	Sierra	Butte Twp	89	512
FRONENFELD								
Jacob	19	m	w	PA	San Francisco	8-Wd San Francisco	82	452
FRONINGTON								
F	67	m	w	FRAN	San Francisco	11-Wd San Francisc	84	613
FRONK								
George	39	m	w	MD	Yuba	Marysville	93	582
FRONTIER								
Peter	43	m	w	FRAN	San Francisco	8-Wd San Francisco	82	361
FROO								
Ah	36	m	c	CHIN	San Francisco	San Francisco P O	80	493
Ah	18	f	c	CHIN	San Francisco	San Francisco P O	80	492
Ah	17	m	c	CHIN	San Mateo	San Mateo P O	87	352
FROOM								
Amy	29	f	w	CANA	Sonoma	Bodega Twp	91	250
Anson	22	m	w	CANA	Marin	Tomales Twp	74	79
Eli	42	m	w	NY	San Diego	Julian Dist	78	468
James W	50	m	w	CANA	Solano	Silveyville Twp	90	89
Peter	55	m	w	NY	San Francisco	11-Wd San Francisc	84	707
Thornton	28	m	w	CANA	Sonoma	Analy Twp	91	220
FROPOLLO								
John B	48	m	w	SWIT	San Francisco	2-Wd San Francisco	79	253
FRORSIN								
Samuel B	35	m	w	GA	Placer	Bath P O	76	421
FROSHMAN								
C	36	m	w	GERM	San Joaquin	2-Wd Stockton	86	168
FROSS								
Caroline	38	f	w	GERM	Santa Clara	2-Wd San Jose	88	329
FROST								
A	44	m	w	SAXO	Humboldt	Table Bluff Twp	72	308
A	35	m	w	ME	Humboldt	Eureka Twp	72	268
Albert	41	m	w	MI	Siskiyou	Yreka	89	663
Amanda	50	f	w	MO	Sonoma	Mendocino Twp	91	300
Amanda	43	f	w	KY	Mendocino	Little Lake Twp	74	201
Amos L	45	m	w	NH	El Dorado	Placerville	72	127
Ann	63	f	w	RI	San Joaquin	Oneal Twp	86	106
Benj F	34	m	w	MO	Santa Barbara	San Buenaventura P	87	425
Bertha	24	f	w	MA	San Francisco	San Francisco P O	83	113
Bridget	30	f	w	IREL	San Francisco	San Francisco P O	83	176
Charles S	46	m	w	ME	Yolo	Cache Crk Twp	93	428
Chas B	29	m	w	ME	Nevada	Rough & Ready Twp	75	328
David	23	m	w	ENGL	San Francisco	1-Wd San Francisco	79	59
E M	20	m	w	IA	San Joaquin	Oneal Twp	86	110
Eleazer	52	m	w	MA	Santa Clara	San Jose Twp	88	211
Ellen	35	f	w	IREL	Napa	Yountville Twp	75	87
Ephram	58	m	w	MA	El Dorado	Coloma Twp	72	6
F F	48	m	w	MA	Solano	Vallejo	90	178
Frank W	36	m	w	ME	Santa Barbara	Santa Barbara P O	87	460
Geo F	37	m	w	ME	Butte	Chico Twp	70	19
George	76	m	w	ENGL	Calaveras	San Andreas P O	70	188
George A	36	m	w	ME	San Francisco	San Francisco P O	83	199
Gilbert	60	m	w	TN	Sonoma	Petaluma Twp	91	353
Hans	25	m	w	DENM	Alameda	Eden Twp	68	60
Henry	36	m	b	KY	Tehama	Red Bluff	92	182
Henry H	40	m	w	MA	Placer	Gold Run Twp	76	400
Hiram	26	m	w	IREL	Solano	Silveyville Twp	90	78
Horatio	47	m	w	NH	San Francisco	8-Wd San Francisco	82	380
Isham	24	m	w	MO	Mendocino	Little Lake Twp	74	200
J	38	m	w	IL	San Joaquin	Liberty Twp	86	89
J M	57	m	w	KY	San Joaquin	Elkhorn Twp	86	68
J M	41	m	w	CA	San Joaquin	Union Twp	86	265
J W	38	m	w	ME	Humboldt	Eureka Twp	72	277
James	48	m	w	ME	San Francisco	San Francisco P O	83	356

© 2001 by Heritage Quest. All rights reserved.

Series M593

Name	Age	S	R	B-PL	County	Locale	Roll	Pg
James H	37	m	w	ME	Butte	Chico Twp	70	49
Jas	33	m	w	NY	Solano	Vallejo	90	172
Jennie	32	f	w	MA	San Mateo	Redwood Twp	87	370
John	50	m	w	OH	Tehama	Red Bluff	92	182
John	36	m	w	WI	Tehama	Red Bluff	92	182
John	36	m	w	PA	Butte	Ophir Twp	70	102
John M	35	m	w	CANA	Santa Cruz	Soquel Twp	89	441
Joseph	39	m	w	ME	Humboldt	Eureka Twp	72	270
Leonard	47	m	w	NY	Sacramento	Granite Twp	77	147
Lowell Leland	44	m	w	MA	Plumas	Seneca Twp	77	51
M C	25	f	w	CANA	Santa Clara	Gilroy Twp	88	86
Martin	30	m	w	ME	Yolo	Fremont Twp	93	476
Mary	30	f	i	CA	Tehama	Red Bluff	92	182
Mary	27	f	w	IREL	San Joaquin	2-Wd Stockton	86	201
Mary Ann	36	f	w	IN	San Joaquin	2-Wd Stockton	86	169
Miner	26	m	w	WI	Santa Clara	San Jose Twp	88	211
Nathaniel	33	m	w	ME	Humboldt	Eureka Twp	72	277
Percy	22	m	w	MA	San Francisco	7-Wd San Francisco	81	188
Saml	44	m	w	MI	Mono	Bridgeport P O	74	285
Simeon	35	m	w	MI	Butte	Ophir Twp	70	111
Stephen	23	m	w	ME	Mendocino	Little Rvr Twp	74	170
W C	18	m	w	ME	Solano	Vallejo	90	203
Walter	18	m	w	ME	San Francisco	8-Wd San Francisco	82	399
William	38	m	w	VT	Sutter	Butte Twp	92	98
William	32	m	w	ENGL	San Francisco	San Francisco P O	83	191
FROSTUNE								
J	39	m	w	NY	Yuba	Marysville	93	616
FROTAN								
Archilles	27	m	w	FRAN	Napa	Napa	75	45
FROTHEN								
Robbert	38	m	w	SCOT	Alameda	Oakland	68	263
FROTHINGHAM								
Ann	72	f	w	NY	Sacramento	3-Wd Sacramento	77	296
Henry	34	m	w	IL	Solano	Denverton Twp	90	22
John	48	m	w	SCOT	Solano	Denverton Twp	90	26
FROW								
Ah	40	m	c	CHIN	San Francisco	San Francisco P O	80	491
Ah	36	m	c	CHIN	San Francisco	San Francisco P O	80	511
FROWANDANER								
Fred	26	m	w	WURT	San Francisco	1-Wd San Francisco	79	57
FROWD								
Laura	5	f	w	CA	Placer	Bath P O	76	421
FROY								
Joi	41	m	c	CHIN	Monterey	San Juan Twp	74	394
William	38	m	w	IREL	San Francisco	11-Wd San Francisc	84	649
FROYHA								
Mulleppa	70	f	w	NM	San Bernardino	San Salvador Twp	78	461
FROYIHA								
Dorata	43	m	w	NM	San Bernardino	San Salvador Twp	78	461
FRRISENKIR								
Anthony	31	m	w	GERM	San Diego	San Diego	78	501
FRUBURG								
Mary	47	f	w	BADE	Alameda	Oakland	68	145
FRUCHNICHT								
John	39	m	w	HANO	San Francisco	11-Wd San Francisc	84	620
FRUDENBERG								
J H	39	m	w	HANO	San Francisco	San Francisco P O	85	756
FRUELIN								
Joseph	24	m	w	ITAL	Santa Clara	San Jose Twp	88	204
FRUEN								
Chris	40	m	w	PRUS	Yuba	Marysville	93	600
Henry	12	m	w	IL	Yuba	Marysville	93	601
Julius	15	m	w	CA	San Francisco	San Francisco P O	83	102
FRUGANA								
Thomas	27	m	w	ENGL	Placer	Colfax P O	76	389
FRUGOLI								
Innocenzo	30	m	w	ITAL	San Francisco	11-Wd San Francisc	84	594
Vincenzo	30	m	w	ITAL	San Francisco	11-Wd San Francisc	84	594
FRUHLING								
William	40	m	w	PRUS	Santa Clara	1-Wd San Jose	88	250
FRUIT								
Arnold	14	m	w	MO	Solano	Vacaville Twp	90	129
FRUITA								
Tomas	30	m	w	CA	San Diego	San Pasqual	78	521
FRUITIGEN								
Jacob	45	m	w	SWIT	Trinity	North Fork Twp	92	217
FRUITS								
Frank	21	m	w	IN	Sonoma	Analy Twp	91	229
Jacob	64	m	w	IN	Sonoma	Analy Twp	91	228
FRUMER								
Anna	47	f	w	IREL	Alameda	Alameda	68	14
FRUNENHOLTS								
Hugo	25	m	w	PRUS	San Francisco	11-Wd San Francisc	84	481
FRUNK								
Ah	45	m	c	CHIN	Santa Clara	1-Wd San Jose	88	243
FRUNKE								
Christley	50	m	w	VA	Solano	Suisun Twp	90	109
FRURGMION								
William	36	m	w	AR	Los Angeles	Los Angeles	73	566
FRUSE								
E	8	f	w	CA	Sierra	Lincoln Twp	89	546
FRUST								
Andrew	45	m	w	HCAS	Santa Cruz	Santa Cruz	89	413
FRUTAS								
Lenis	31	f	w	MEXI	San Luis Obispo	San Luis Obispo Tw	87	311
FRUTH								
David	35	m	w	BAVA	El Dorado	Coloma Twp	72	4

Series M593

Name	Age	S	R	B-PL	County	Locale	Roll	Pg
Fred	49	m	w	BAVA	El Dorado	Coloma Twp	72	2
FRY								
Amos	36	m	w	OH	Stanislaus	Empire Twp	92	47
Catherine	35	f	w	IREL	San Francisco	8-Wd San Francisco	82	449
E M	35	m	w	IL	Sacramento	4-Wd Sacramento	77	350
Edward C	27	m	w	VA	San Francisco	7-Wd San Francisco	81	205
Fredric	43	m	w	WURT	Trinity	Lewiston Pct	92	211
G W	36	m	w	OH	Lassen	Janesville Twp	73	430
George	25	m	w	ENGL	Nevada	Grass Valley Twp	75	143
George	20	m	b	VA	Sacramento	2-Wd Sacramento	77	233
Henry	50	m	w	SHOL	San Mateo	Half Moon Bay P O	87	404
Henry	27	m	w	DENM	Contra Costa	Martinez P O	71	417
Isaac	46	m	w	PA	Siskiyou	Butte Twp	89	585
Isaac	34	m	w	IL	Stanislaus	Empire Twp	92	47
James	35	m	w	AR	San Joaquin	Castoria Twp	86	9
Jenny	26	f	w	MI	Sonoma	Santa Rosa	91	413
John	54	m	w	ENGL	Nevada	Grass Valley Twp	75	148
John	42	m	w	MA	San Francisco	6-Wd San Francisco	81	110
John	36	m	w	OH	Tehama	Red Bluff	92	176
John	35	m	w	ENGL	Tuolumne	Sonora P O	93	319
John	32	m	w	OH	Solano	Vallejo	90	154
John	30	m	w	MA	Solano	Silveyville Twp	90	92
John	24	m	w	PRUS	San Francisco	5-Wd San Francisco	81	13
John D	50	m	w	KY	San Francisco	8-Wd San Francisco	82	487
John H	33	m	w	RI	Solano	Silveyville Twp	90	88
Joseph	40	m	w	FRAN	Santa Cruz	Santa Cruz Twp	89	385
Joseph	20	m	w	IA	Sacramento	4-Wd Sacramento	77	353
Joseph J	33	m	w	MO	Butte	Ophir Twp	70	95
Martin	44	m	w	BADE	Shasta	American Ranch P O	89	499
Patrick	30	m	w	IREL	San Joaquin	Oneal Twp	86	114
Philip	30	m	w	IREL	San Francisco	8-Wd San Francisco	82	450
R A	49	f	w	ME	Humboldt	Eureka Twp	72	275
Robert B	39	m	w	MO	Butte	Oroville Twp	70	138
Thomas	50	m	w	IREL	Santa Clara	Redwood Twp	88	119
Thomas	30	m	w	KY	San Francisco	8-Wd San Francisco	82	488
William	38	m	w	MO	Sonoma	Mendocino Twp	91	301
William	31	m	w	ENGL	Nevada	Grass Valley Twp	75	148
Zilpha	52	f	w	KY	San Mateo	Belmont P O	87	372
FRYATT								
James	57	m	w	ENGL	Yolo	Grafton Twp	93	483
William	38	m	w	ENGL	Yolo	Grafton Twp	93	483
FRYDENALK								
Walter	35	m	w	NY	Stanislaus	San Joaquin Twp	92	71
FRYE								
Charles	30	m	w	SWIT	San Francisco	2-Wd San Francisco	79	187
Curtis	22	m	w	MO	Sacramento	Franklin Twp	77	116
Eliza	32	f	w	IN	Amador	Volcano P O	69	378
Henry	30	m	w	IREL	Solano	Vacaville Twp	90	122
John	38	m	w	HDAR	San Francisco	2-Wd San Francisco	79	147
Joseph W	42	m	w	MA	Mariposa	Mariposa P O	74	134
Robert A	55	m	w	VA	Mariposa	Mariposa P O	74	125
Ruben F	40	m	w	NY	Amador	Volcano P O	69	375
Wm	40	m	w	KY	Sacramento	Dry Crk Twp	77	98
Wm H	56	m	w	KY	Sacramento	Franklin Twp	77	116
FRYER								
Dicker F	27	m	w	NY	Butte	Oregon Twp	70	133
George	20	m	w	ENGL	San Francisco	11-Wd San Francisc	84	560
John W	28	m	w	AR	Los Angeles	San Jose Twp	73	623
Joseph	30	m	w	KY	Colusa	Spring Valley Twp	71	337
Mary R	14	f	w	AR	Los Angeles	Los Nietos Twp	73	575
FRYOR								
Jesus	21	m	w	AL	Los Angeles	San Jose Twp	73	621
Rich C	40	m	w	AL	Los Angeles	San Jose Twp	73	620
Thomas	35	m	w	ENGL	San Francisco	8-Wd San Francisco	82	323
FU								
Ah	26	m	c	CHIN	Alameda	Washington Twp	68	272
Lung	17	m	c	CHIN	Santa Clara	San Jose Twp	88	194
FUA								
Ah	3	m	c	CA	Monterey	Monterey Twp	74	343
FUACHONI								
Jaques	41	m	w	FRAN	Calaveras	San Andreas P O	70	176
FUAH								
A	33	m	c	CHIN	Santa Clara	San Jose Twp	88	219
Juan	38	m	c	CHIN	Sonoma	Salt Point	91	386
FUCH								
Ah	54	m	c	CHIN	Mariposa	Mariposa P O	74	114
Ah	45	m	c	CHIN	Amador	Drytown P O	69	419
Ah	24	m	c	CHIN	Mariposa	Mariposa P O	74	128
Henry	37	m	w	PRUS	San Francisco	5-Wd San Francisco	81	8
FUCHEREL								
Joseph	59	m	w	FRAN	Mariposa	Mariposa P O	74	97
FUCHS								
Adams	54	m	w	HDAR	Sacramento	3-Wd Sacramento	77	286
E	57	m	w	WURT	Sierra	Sierra Twp	89	564
Francis P	55	m	w	BAVA	Siskiyou	Yreka	89	655
George	44	m	w	PRUS	San Francisco	San Francisco P O	83	31
Henry	32	m	w	OH	Nevada	Grass Valley Twp	75	145
Louis	45	m	w	FRAN	San Francisco	1-Wd San Francisco	79	56
Martin	25	m	w	SWIT	San Mateo	San Mateo P O	87	350
Orchwald	41	m	w	BADE	Sacramento	3-Wd Sacramento	77	302
Peter	31	m	w	GERM	Sacramento	1-Wd Sacramento	77	180
FUDD								
Ephraim	26	m	w	TN	Colusa	Butte Twp	71	267
FUDGE								
Abraville	37	m	w	AR	Tulare	Venice Twp	92	275
Henry G	29	m	w	CANA	San Francisco	San Francisco P O	83	137
John	65	m	w	AR	Tulare	Venice Twp	92	275

© 2001 by Heritage Quest. All rights reserved.

Series M593

Name	Age	S	R	B-PL	County	Locale	Roll	Pg
John C	30	m	w	TN	Tulare	Visalia Twp	92	286
M A	28	m	w	AR	Santa Clara	Gilroy Twp	88	92
William	44	m	w	AR	Tulare	Venice Twp	92	275
FUE								
Ah	38	m	c	CHIN	Sacramento	1-Wd Sacramento	77	198
Ah	28	m	c	CHIN	Alameda	Alameda	68	4
Chick	42	m	c	CHIN	Plumas	Goodwin Twp	77	4
Chue	17	m	c	CHIN	San Francisco	8-Wd San Francisco	82	358
Gam	37	m	c	CHIN	Yuba	Marysville	93	631
Toy	26	m	c	CHIN	Trinity	Douglas	92	233
FUEG								
Jacob	34	m	w	SWIT	Yolo	Putah Twp	93	516
FUEL								
Henry	45	m	w	IN	Sonoma	Russian Rvr	91	376
FUEM								
Esau	40	m	w	ENGL	Santa Clara	2-Wd San Jose	88	284
FUENG								
Ah	27	m	c	CHIN	Sacramento	3-Wd Sacramento	77	309
FUENTA								
Frances	32	m	w	CHIL	Calaveras	Copperopolis P O	70	250
Patra	49	f	w	MEXI	Mariposa	Mariposa P O	74	93
FUENTE								
Antonio	30	m	w	MEXI	Los Angeles	Soledad Twp	73	632
FUENTEN								
Jose Maria	53	m	w	MEXI	Los Angeles	Los Angeles	73	517
FUENTES								
Manuel	44	m	w	CA	Monterey	Monterey	74	366
Octavio	30	m	w	MEXI	Fresno	Millerton P O	72	154
Perfecto	50	m	w	MEXI	Marin	San Rafael Twp	74	46
FUENTIS								
Perfecto	40	m	w	MEXI	Marin	San Rafael	74	53
FUENTOS								
Charles	24	m	w	MEXI	San Francisco	San Francisco P O	80	473
Joseph	40	m	w	CHIL	San Francisco	San Francisco P O	80	345
FUENTUS								
Stephen	58	m	w	MEXI	Mariposa	Mariposa P O	74	94
FUER								
George	30	m	w	ENGL	Santa Clara	San Jose Twp	88	214
John	50	m	w	IREL	Sacramento	Dry Crk Twp	77	97
FUERST								
George	40	m	w	WURT	San Diego	Coronado	78	467
FUES								
Thomas	46	m	w	PRUS	San Francisco	San Francisco P O	80	474
FUEY								
Fin	48	m	c	CHIN	San Francisco	6-Wd San Francisco	81	54
FUG								
Jas	40	m	w	MD	San Francisco	7-Wd San Francisco	81	287
FUGALE								
Rob C	38	m	w	VA	El Dorado	Coloma Twp	72	4
FUGAN								
Frank	34	m	w	IREL	Sacramento	4-Wd Sacramento	77	350
FUGATE								
Robert	39	m	w	VA	Sacramento	Sutter Twp	77	388
FUGAZZI								
John	32	m	w	ITAL	Sacramento	2-Wd Sacramento	77	210
FUGET								
S C	69	m	w	KY	Sacramento	Dry Crk Twp	77	101
FUGETT								
B	45	m	w	MO	San Joaquin	Liberty Twp	86	93
D C	37	m	w	MO	San Joaquin	Liberty Twp	86	89
F B	64	m	w	KY	San Joaquin	Liberty Twp	86	84
FUGGET								
William	21	m	w	KY	Colusa	Colusa	71	291
FUGITT								
Lyon L	31	m	w	MO	Marin	San Rafael Twp	74	45
William	43	m	w	MO	Kern	Linns Valley P O	73	345
FUGLER								
Francis	38	m	w	NY	Santa Barbara	Santa Maria P O	87	511
FUGNAY								
Franschi	46	m	w	IN	San Francisco	11-Wd San Francisc	84	645
FUGO								
Manuel	80	m	w	ITAL	Sacramento	American Twp	77	68
FUGOHA								
James	45	m	w	SWIT	Placer	Cisco P O	76	495
FUGOLDSBY								
Carrie	15	f	w	CA	San Francisco	San Francisco P O	80	364
FUGOLDSLY								
Alva	12	m	w	CA	San Francisco	San Francisco P O	80	361
FUGOSSE								
Lewis	40	m	w	ITAL	Merced	Snelling P O	74	267
FUGUA								
John	33	m	w	MO	San Joaquin	Liberty Twp	86	85
May	32	f	w	KY	San Joaquin	Liberty Twp	86	85
Wm	27	m	w	MO	San Joaquin	Liberty Twp	86	82
FUHE								
Patrick	22	m	w	IREL	San Francisco	San Francisco P O	85	773
FUHRMAN								
Henry	65	m	w	HAMB	San Francisco	8-Wd San Francisco	82	420
Nicholas	45	m	w	PRUS	Nevada	Little York Twp	75	241
FUHRST								
Frank	36	m	w	SHOL	San Francisco	1-Wd San Francisco	79	116
FUI								
Ah	17	m	c	CHIN	San Francisco	7-Wd San Francisco	81	287
FUICH								
William	36	m	w	ENGL	Santa Cruz	Santa Cruz Twp	89	387
FUIRIL								
Frederick	37	m	w	BAVA	Siskiyou	Scott Valley Twp	89	619

Series M593

Name	Age	S	R	B-PL	County	Locale	Roll	Pg
FUK								
Ah	40	m	c	CHIN	San Francisco	San Francisco P O	80	490
Ah	38	m	c	CHIN	San Francisco	San Francisco P O	80	503
Ah	34	f	c	CHIN	San Francisco	San Francisco P O	80	526
Ah	34	f	c	CHIN	San Francisco	San Francisco P O	80	438
Ah	32	f	c	CHIN	San Francisco	San Francisco P O	80	437
Ah	32	m	c	CHIN	Los Angeles	Santa Ana Twp	73	613
Ah	30	f	c	CHIN	San Francisco	San Francisco P O	80	492
Ah	30	m	c	CHIN	San Francisco	San Francisco P O	80	490
Ah	30	m	c	CHIN	San Francisco	San Francisco P O	80	501
Ah	3	m	c	CHIN	San Francisco	San Francisco P O	80	490
Ah	29	f	c	CHIN	San Francisco	San Francisco P O	80	439
Ah	27	m	c	CHIN	San Francisco	San Francisco P O	80	457
Ah	24	f	c	CHIN	San Francisco	San Francisco P O	80	433
Ah	22	m	c	CHIN	San Francisco	6-Wd San Francisco	81	63
Ah	21	f	c	CHIN	San Francisco	San Francisco P O	80	505
Ah	21	f	c	CHIN	San Francisco	San Francisco P O	80	504
Ah	20	f	c	CHIN	San Francisco	San Francisco P O	80	504
Ah	20	f	c	CHIN	San Francisco	San Francisco P O	80	507
Ah	20	f	c	CHIN	San Francisco	San Francisco P O	80	521
Ah	20	f	c	CHIN	San Francisco	San Francisco P O	80	431
Ah	19	f	c	CHIN	San Francisco	San Francisco P O	80	491
Ah	19	f	c	CHIN	San Francisco	San Francisco P O	80	459
Ah	19	f	c	CHIN	San Francisco	San Francisco P O	80	431
Ah	18	m	c	CHIN	San Francisco	San Francisco P O	80	504
Ah	17	f	c	CHIN	San Francisco	San Francisco P O	80	523
Ah	17	m	c	CHIN	San Francisco	San Francisco P O	83	138
Ah	16	m	c	CHIN	San Francisco	11-Wd San Francisc	84	559
Ah	12	m	c	CHIN	San Francisco	San Francisco P O	80	493
FUKE								
Ah	40	m	c	CHIN	Monterey	Monterey Twp	74	352
Ah	30	m	c	CHIN	Trinity	Douglas	92	235
Ah	24	m	c	CHIN	Sierra	Sears Twp	89	554
FUKES								
Matthias	23	m	w	BAVA	Colusa	Grand Island Twp	71	310
FUKI								
Ah	39	m	c	CHIN	Sierra	Forest Twp	89	532
FULCHER								
John	35	m	w	ENGL	San Francisco	11-Wd San Francisc	84	577
Mare	32	m	w	SHOL	Siskiyou	Surprise Valley Tw	89	638
Wm	46	m	w	MO	Yuba	W Bear Rvr Twp	93	684
FULDA								
Martin	62	m	w	RHIN	San Francisco	San Francisco P O	83	301
FULEY								
Michael	29	m	w	IREL	Yolo	Putah Twp	93	510
FULFORD								
Robert	27	m	w	MA	San Francisco	San Francisco P O	80	373
FULGER								
Susan	17	f	w	MO	San Joaquin	3-Wd Stockton	86	224
FULGHAM								
Benj	30	m	w	AL	San Bernardino	San Bernardino Twp	78	428
Geo F	55	m	w	GA	San Bernardino	San Bernardino Twp	78	421
John J	36	m	w	MS	Tulare	Packwood Twp	92	257
FULKERSON								
J S	62	m	w	KY	Sonoma	Santa Rosa	91	421
Jno	34	m	w	IN	Sonoma	Santa Rosa	91	406
Peter	37	m	w	VA	Santa Clara	Gilroy Twp	88	79
Rich	64	m	w	KY	Sonoma	Santa Rosa	91	406
S T	30	m	w	KY	Sonoma	Santa Rosa	91	425
FULKERTH								
A S	37	m	w	OH	San Joaquin	Oneal Twp	86	102
John	35	m	w	SWED	Stanislaus	Buena Vista Twp	92	11
Thomas	45	m	w	PA	Stanislaus	Empire Twp	92	48
William	40	m	w	PA	Stanislaus	Empire Twp	92	48
FULLAM								
Francis	44	m	w	NH	Santa Cruz	Santa Cruz	89	404
FULLAR								
Frank	32	m	w	BAVA	El Dorado	Georgetown Twp	72	38
Hiram H	40	m	w	NY	El Dorado	Georgetown Twp	72	42
FULLARD								
William	55	m	w	NY	San Francisco	7-Wd San Francisco	81	159
Wm	43	m	w	NH	San Francisco	7-Wd San Francisco	81	273
FULLEN								
Ed Aug	35	m	w	MA	San Francisco	7-Wd San Francisco	81	228
George	46	m	w	IREL	Amador	Jackson P O	69	318
James	45	m	w	IREL	Amador	Sutter Crk P O	69	411
James	45	m	w	IREL	Amador	Sutter Crk P O	69	405
John	54	m	w	IREL	Amador	Sutter Crk P O	69	405
Mary E	25	f	w	IREL	San Francisco	7-Wd San Francisco	81	228
Philip	89	m	w	BAVA	San Francisco	8-Wd San Francisco	82	432
FULLER								
A C	30	f	w	NY	Sacramento	3-Wd Sacramento	77	317
Addison	51	m	w	KY	San Diego	San Diego	78	495
Aldin W	23	m	w	ME	Trinity	North Fork Twp	92	221
Alonzo M	48	m	w	CT	Placer	Lincoln P O	76	492
Amos	35	m	w	MA	Alameda	Eden Twp	68	82
Andrew J	38	m	w	ENGL	Nevada	Washington Twp	75	345
Arnold	45	m	w	NY	San Francisco	San Francisco P O	85	716
Benjamin	81	m	w	MA	Yolo	Merritt Twp	93	507
Benjamin	61	m	w	NH	Solano	Maine Prairie Twp	90	46
C	35	m	w	PA	Humboldt	Eureka Twp	72	263
C H	36	m	w	MA	Calaveras	Copperopolis P O	70	229
Charles	54	m	w	PA	El Dorado	Diamond Springs Tw	72	26
Charles	38	m	w	NY	Placer	Auburn P O	76	383
Charles	28	m	w	ME	San Francisco	6-Wd San Francisco	81	86
Charles E	36	m	w	MA	Sonoma	Bodega Twp	91	258
Charles G	36	m	w	IL	Santa Clara	San Jose Twp	88	197

© 2001 by Heritage Quest. All rights reserved.

Series M593

Name	Age	S	R	B-PL	County	Locale	Roll	Pg
Chas	29	m	w	RI	San Joaquin	Elkhorn Twp	86	62
Daniel B	32	m	w	NY	Santa Clara	San Jose Twp	88	215
David	25	m	w	IN	Marin	San Antonio Twp	74	61
David	16	m	w	NY	San Francisco	San Francisco P O	80	380
Edgar C	52	m	w	NY	Butte	Concow Twp	70	7
Edward	45	m	w	MA	Placer	Pino Twp	76	471
Edward	38	m	w	NY	Santa Clara	Redwood Twp	88	129
Edwd	30	m	w	MA	Alameda	Oakland	68	182
Elizabeth	69	f	m	VA	Solano	Vallejo	90	164
Ellen	18	f	w	IREL	Nevada	Grass Valley Twp	75	163
Eugene	25	m	w	MA	Contra Costa	Martinez P O	71	397
Flora	30	f	w	NY	Yolo	Cache Crk Twp	93	457
Franklin B	34	m	w	CT	Santa Clara	San Jose Twp	88	189
Geo	39	m	w	NY	San Joaquin	2-Wd Stockton	86	192
Geo W	50	m	w	NY	San Francisco	5-Wd San Francisco	81	27
George A	44	m	w	MI	Amador	Fiddletown P O	69	431
Harry	30	m	w	NY	Placer	Emigrant Gap P O	76	417
Harry W	32	m	w	NY	Butte	Chico Twp	70	21
Henry S	40	m	w	NY	Sonoma	Healdsburg & Mendo	91	277
Horace	28	m	w	VA	Solano	Denverton Twp	90	23
Isaac	56	m	w	OH	Sonoma	Salt Point	91	381
J H	46	m	w	NY	San Joaquin	Tulare Twp	86	250
Jacob	29	m	w	PRUS	San Francisco	7-Wd San Francisco	81	170
Jacob W	59	m	w	CANA	Sacramento	4-Wd Sacramento	77	363
James	36	m	w	MA	Lake	Big Valley	73	395
James	29	m	w	RI	Amador	Jackson P O	69	329
James	25	m	w	CA	San Francisco	11-Wd San Francisc	84	571
James H	32	m	w	NY	Santa Clara	1-Wd San Jose	88	227
Jas	45	m	w	ME	Solano	Vallejo	90	189
John	38	m	w	NY	Sacramento	Center Twp	77	84
John	38	m	w	OH	Butte	Chico Twp	70	57
John	38	m	w	NY	Nevada	Little York Twp	75	242
John	25	m	w	MA	Yolo	Putah Twp	93	514
John E	38	m	w	OH	Yuba	Slate Range Bar Tw	93	673
John H	63	m	w	ME	San Francisco	San Francisco P O	83	311
John T	38	m	w	NY	Placer	Lincoln P O	76	481
Josep H	48	m	w	MA	Yuba	Slate Range Bar Tw	93	676
Josephine	5	f	w	CA	Santa Clara	San Jose Twp	88	198
Josiah	50	m	w	WI	San Francisco	3-Wd San Francisco	79	314
Kate	40	f	w	NY	San Francisco	8-Wd San Francisco	82	400
Kate M	24	f	w	NY	San Francisco	8-Wd San Francisco	82	347
Lewis H	28	m	w	ME	Sacramento	2-Wd Sacramento	77	235
Louisa Frances	45	f	w	ME	San Francisco	San Francisco P O	83	175
M	39	f	w	CANA	San Joaquin	Elkhorn Twp	86	56
M J	42	m	w	MA	Tuolumne	Columbia P O	93	337
Marcellus P	33	m	w	ME	Santa Cruz	Soquel Twp	89	441
Martin	17	m	w	NH	Sacramento	3-Wd Sacramento	77	282
Mary	44	f	w	MO	San Mateo	Pescadero P O	87	409
Mary A	47	m	w	MA	Yuba	Bullards Bar P O	93	551
Mason A	34	m	w	VT	Santa Clara	San Jose Twp	88	187
Melvina	32	f	w	IN	Marin	Nicasio Twp	74	16
N P	38	m	w	NY	Tehama	Red Bluff	92	176
Nancy	55	f	w	NY	Tehama	Antelope Twp	92	158
O	29	m	w	ME	San Francisco	San Francisco P O	85	811
O P	42	m	w	NY	Tehama	Antelope Twp	92	158
Oliver	24	m	w	OH	Sutter	Yuba Twp	92	151
Orlando	43	m	w	MA	San Francisco	San Francisco P O	83	92
Orlando	32	m	w	CANA	Alameda	Alvarado	68	303
Philo J	43	m	w	NY	Nevada	Grass Valley Twp	75	228
Ralph	19	m	w	MA	Placer	Colfax P O	76	390
Richard	55	m	w	NY	Placer	Lincoln P O	76	487
Ruben H	28	m	w	NY	Yolo	Cache Crk Twp	93	426
Russell	40	m	w	VT	Solano	Vallejo	90	197
S E	28	m	w	ME	San Francisco	7-Wd San Francisco	81	207
Sarah	54	f	w	PA	Sacramento	Sutter Twp	77	384
Stephen	37	m	w	NY	Tulare	Tule Rvr Twp	92	263
Theodore	40	m	w	NY	Sierra	Table Rock Twp	89	576
Thomas	59	m	w	CANA	Sonoma	Bodega Twp	91	252
Thomas	32	m	w	ENGL	Santa Cruz	Pajaro Twp	89	352
Thos	35	m	w	ENGL	San Francisco	1-Wd San Francisco	79	111
Thos	32	m	w	IA	Butte	Chico Twp	70	60
Tomas P	35	m	w	ENGL	Los Angeles	San Juan Twp	73	625
Wallace	21	m	w	PA	San Francisco	San Francisco P O	83	193
William	51	m	b	VA	San Francisco	San Francisco P O	80	430
William	35	m	w	MA	San Francisco	8-Wd San Francisco	82	484
William	34	m	w	IREL	Yolo	Putah Twp	93	513
William	20	m	w	WI	San Francisco	8-Wd San Francisco	82	485
Wm	28	m	w	NY	San Francisco	1-Wd San Francisco	79	126
Wm	24	m	w	NY	San Joaquin	2-Wd Stockton	86	165
FULLERTON								
J P	34	m	w	MO	San Joaquin	Douglas Twp	86	43
John	46	m	w	SCOT	San Francisco	San Francisco P O	83	115
Neal	45	m	w	IREL	San Francisco	1-Wd San Francisco	79	123
FULLMAN								
Annie	50	f	b	DE	San Francisco	San Francisco P O	80	481
Gus	38	m	w	PRUS	Solano	Vallejo	90	200
Jesse	23	m	w	CANA	Humboldt	Eureka Twp	72	257
FULLMORE								
Saml	39	m	w	CANA	Humboldt	Pacific Twp	72	293
Smith	36	m	w	CANA	Humboldt	Pacific Twp	72	293
FULLOM								
T	43	m	w	IREL	San Francisco	San Francisco P O	83	78
FULLON								
Patrick	30	m	w	IREL	Sutter	Butte Twp	92	90
Thos M	41	m	w	IREL	Merced	Snelling P O	74	255
FULLWILER								
Adam	54	m	w	OH	Tulare	Tule Rvr Twp	92	266

Series M593

Name	Age	S	R	B-PL	County	Locale	Roll	Pg
FULLY								
Jno A	40	m	w	KY	Butte	Ophir Twp	70	120
John	40	m	w	IREL	San Francisco	11-Wd San Francisc	84	629
Thomas	35	m	w	IREL	Napa	Yountville Twp	75	90
FULMAN								
Ledwick	31	m	w	BADE	Solano	Rio Vista Twp	90	59
Thomas	54	m	w	BAVA	Santa Clara	1-Wd San Jose	88	257
FULMER								
Amendus	30	m	w	HAMB	San Francisco	11-Wd San Francisc	84	694
James G	57	m	w	MD	Santa Clara	1-Wd San Jose	88	250
Josiah B	26	m	w	IN	Sonoma	Petaluma Twp	91	331
Nathaniel	28	m	w	MD	Placer	Cisco P O	76	494
FULTON								
Adonia	41	m	w	RI	San Francisco	11-Wd San Francisc	84	691
Albert	22	m	w	OH	Yolo	Cache Crk Twp	93	420
Alonzo	29	m	w	NY	San Francisco	7-Wd San Francisco	81	228
Ambrose	48	m	w	IN	Stanislaus	Empire Twp	92	65
Daniel	69	m	w	SCOT	San Francisco	6-Wd San Francisco	81	126
David	69	m	w	NC	Sonoma	Santa Rosa	91	419
David	46	m	w	VT	Napa	Napa	75	10
David	40	m	w	PA	Mariposa	Mariposa P O	74	100
Frank	38	m	w	NY	San Francisco	3-Wd San Francisco	79	311
Henry	20	m	w	IA	Yolo	Washington Twp	93	535
Horace	25	m	w	LA	San Francisco	8-Wd San Francisco	82	362
J M	25	m	w	NY	Sacramento	3-Wd Sacramento	77	270
James C	42	m	w	AL	Los Angeles	Los Nietos Twp	73	587
James M	56	m	w	NY	Sacramento	4-Wd Sacramento	77	360
John	46	m	w	IREL	San Francisco	11-Wd San Francisc	84	693
John	39	m	w	IREL	Yolo	Cottonwood Twp	93	471
John	36	m	w	NY	San Francisco	7-Wd San Francisco	81	259
John	33	m	w	MD	Marin	San Rafael Twp	74	37
John J	50	m	w	PA	San Francisco	San Francisco P O	83	92
Julia	18	f	b	CA	San Joaquin	Douglas Twp	86	36
L	39	m	w	MA	San Joaquin	2-Wd Stockton	86	203
Lizzie	35	f	w	MA	San Francisco	7-Wd San Francisco	81	231
Margaret	78	f	w	IREL	San Francisco	San Francisco P O	85	803
Margaret	42	f	w	IREL	San Francisco	8-Wd San Francisco	82	433
Margrett	49	f	w	IREL	Napa	Napa	75	47
Nellie	16	f	w	CA	San Francisco	2-Wd San Francisco	79	252
Pris	23	f	w	NY	Sacramento	3-Wd Sacramento	77	300
Ralph	51	m	w	ENGL	Nevada	Grass Valley Twp	75	162
Robert J	47	m	w	VT	Santa Clara	2-Wd San Jose	88	292
Robt J	34	m	w	SCOT	San Francisco	8-Wd San Francisco	82	355
Robt W	46	m	w	IL	Butte	Chico Twp	70	31
Thomas	50	m	w	NY	San Francisco	7-Wd San Francisco	81	231
Urias	28	m	w	CANA	Humboldt	Arcata Twp	72	232
William	45	m	w	OH	Yolo	Washington Twp	93	535
FULTS								
Sam J	32	m	w	VA	San Joaquin	Douglas Twp	86	32
FULTZ								
Matthew	46	m	w	VA	Siskiyou	Cottonwood Twp	89	591
FULWEILER								
Abraham	67	m	w	PA	Nevada	Rough & Ready Twp	75	330
John M	36	m	w	OH	Placer	Dutch Flat P O	76	407
FULWELL								
Horace	23	m	w	IL	Sacramento	Franklin Twp	77	112
FULWIELER								
Robt F	39	m	w	VA	Fresno	Kings Rvr P O	72	216
W C	38	m	w	VA	Mendocino	Little Lake Twp	74	201
FULWILER								
Andrew	51	m	w	VA	Placer	Bath P O	76	433
Horace	19	m	w	IL	Sacramento	2-Wd Sacramento	77	245
FULY								
James W	32	m	w	IREL	San Joaquin	1-Wd Stockton	86	130
FULZEA								
Henry	25	m	w	HANO	Los Angeles	Los Angeles	73	525
FUM								
Ah	33	m	c	CHIN	San Francisco	3-Wd San Francisco	79	290
Ah	28	m	c	CHIN	Solano	Suisun Twp	90	107
Ah	28	m	c	CHIN	Butte	Chico Twp	70	27
Ah	18	m	c	CHIN	Nevada	Little York Twp	75	234
Tas	24	m	c	CHIN	Solano	Vacaville Twp	90	130
FUMAGES								
Gusppa	50	m	m	CHIL	Placer	Bath P O	76	420
FUMAN								
Mary R	30	f	w	IREL	San Francisco	8-Wd San Francisco	82	371
FUMEX								
Antone	47	m	w	FRAN	Calaveras	San Andreas P O	70	167
Louis	33	m	w	FRAN	Calaveras	San Andreas P O	70	167
FUN								
Ah	60	m	c	CHIN	Tuolumne	Sonora P O	93	323
Ah	45	m	c	CHIN	Calaveras	San Andreas P O	70	181
Ah	45	m	c	CHIN	Nevada	Nevada Twp	75	311
Ah	42	m	c	CHIN	Sierra	Lincoln Twp	89	552
Ah	42	m	c	CHIN	Tuolumne	Chinese Camp P O	93	364
Ah	42	m	c	CHIN	San Francisco	6-Wd San Francisco	81	47
Ah	41	m	c	CHIN	Nevada	Nevada Twp	75	308
Ah	40	m	c	CHIN	Butte	Ophir Twp	70	116
Ah	39	m	c	CHIN	San Francisco	San Francisco P O	80	512
Ah	36	m	c	CHIN	Butte	Chico Twp	70	27
Ah	36	m	c	CHIN	Amador	Volcano P O	69	376
Ah	36	m	c	CHIN	Mariposa	Maxwell Crk P O	74	146
Ah	35	m	c	CHIN	Fresno	Kings Rvr P O	72	211
Ah	34	m	c	CHIN	Calaveras	San Andreas P O	70	218
Ah	32	m	c	CHIN	Santa Clara	1-Wd San Jose	88	277
Ah	31	m	c	CHIN	Tuolumne	Big Oak Flat P O	93	391
Ah	30	m	c	CHIN	Tuolumne	Big Oak Flat P O	93	398

© 2001 by Heritage Quest. All rights reserved.

Series M593

Name	Age	S	R	B-PL	County	Locale	Roll	Pg
Ah	29	m	c	CHIN	San Francisco	San Francisco P O	80	442
Ah	28	m	c	CHIN	Fresno	Millerton P O	72	200
Ah	28	m	c	CHIN	Solano	Suisun Twp	90	105
Ah	28	m	c	CHIN	Sacramento	Granite Twp	77	151
Ah	28	m	c	CHIN	Tehama	Tehama Twp	92	189
Ah	27	f	c	CHIN	Tuolumne	Columbia P O	93	341
Ah	27	m	c	CHIN	Nevada	Grass Valley Twp	75	208
Ah	26	m	c	CHIN	Amador	Ione City P O	69	367
Ah	25	f	c	CHIN	Placer	Auburn P O	76	372
Ah	25	m	c	CHIN	San Francisco	6-Wd San Francisco	81	40
Ah	24	m	c	CHIN	San Francisco	San Francisco P O	85	748
Ah	24	m	c	CHIN	Sacramento	3-Wd Sacramento	77	309
Ah	22	m	c	CHIN	El Dorado	White Oak Twp	72	138
Ah	22	m	c	CHIN	El Dorado	Diamond Springs Tw	72	25
Ah	21	f	c	CHIN	San Francisco	San Francisco P O	80	448
Ah	21	m	c	CHIN	San Francisco	8-Wd San Francisco	82	401
Ah	21	m	c	CHIN	San Mateo	Schoolhouse Statio	87	332
Ah	20	m	c	CHIN	Marin	San Rafael	74	55
Ah	20	m	c	CHIN	Sacramento	3-Wd Sacramento	77	316
Ah	19	m	c	CHIN	San Francisco	6-Wd San Francisco	81	62
Ah	19	m	c	CHIN	Nevada	Eureka Twp	75	141
Ah	18	m	c	CHIN	Santa Clara	San Jose Twp	88	196
Ah	17	m	c	CHIN	San Francisco	6-Wd San Francisco	81	85
Ah	16	m	c	CHIN	San Francisco	3-Wd San Francisco	79	310
Ah	16	m	c	CHIN	San Francisco	3-Wd San Francisco	79	304
Ah Chock	20	m	c	CHIN	Amador	Ione City P O	69	366
Chu	28	m	c	CHIN	Fresno	Millerton P O	72	202
Chung	42	m	c	CHIN	San Francisco	6-Wd San Francisco	81	43
Cun	29	m	c	CHIN	Yuba	Marysville	93	626
Foo	49	m	c	CHIN	Amador	Ione City P O	69	364
Gee	38	m	c	CHIN	Butte	Chico Twp	70	53
Ho	30	m	c	CHIN	San Joaquin	1-Wd Stockton	86	156
Ki	28	m	c	CHIN	Solano	Vacaville Twp	90	120
Kit	45	m	c	CHIN	Fresno	Millerton P O	72	201
Lac Coy	50	m	c	CHIN	Amador	Ione City P O	69	367
Lee	24	f	c	CHIN	Yuba	Marysville	93	627
Lee	23	m	c	CHIN	Yuba	Marysville	93	622
Lee	20	f	c	CHIN	Yuba	Marysville	93	627
Lim	28	m	c	CHIN	Yuba	Marysville	93	620
Mow	25	m	c	CHIN	Fresno	Millerton P O	72	202
Yen	48	m	c	CHIN	Siskiyou	Hamburg Twp	89	597
FUNEY								
Ah	21	m	c	CHIN	Butte	Hamilton Twp	70	68
FUNG								
---	28	m	c	CHIN	Siskiyou	Hamburg Twp	89	597
---	19	m	c	CHIN	San Francisco	6-Wd San Francisco	81	51
Ah	9	f	c	CHIN	San Francisco	San Francisco P O	80	443
Ah	62	m	c	CHIN	Tuolumne	Big Oak Flat P O	93	397
Ah	52	m	c	CHIN	El Dorado	Diamond Springs Tw	72	30
Ah	51	m	c	CHIN	Fresno	Millerton P O	72	152
Ah	50	m	c	CHIN	Siskiyou	Hamburg Twp	89	596
Ah	49	m	c	CHIN	San Francisco	San Francisco P O	80	438
Ah	48	f	c	CHIN	Nevada	Nevada Twp	75	299
Ah	47	m	c	CHIN	San Francisco	San Francisco P O	80	432
Ah	47	m	c	CHIN	Plumas	Plumas Twp	77	31
Ah	46	m	c	CHIN	San Francisco	San Francisco P O	80	436
Ah	46	m	c	CHIN	Placer	Alta P O	76	413
Ah	45	m	c	CHIN	Solano	Vallejo	90	174
Ah	45	m	c	CHIN	El Dorado	Placerville	72	116
Ah	45	m	c	CHIN	El Dorado	Diamond Springs Tw	72	32
Ah	45	m	c	CHIN	El Dorado	Mud Springs Twp	72	79
Ah	43	m	c	CHIN	Mariposa	Mariposa P O	74	106
Ah	43	m	c	CHIN	Plumas	Plumas Twp	77	31
Ah	43	m	c	CHIN	Butte	Kimshew Tpw	70	84
Ah	43	m	c	CHIN	Amador	Jackson P O	69	338
Ah	41	m	c	CHIN	San Francisco	San Francisco P O	80	453
Ah	41	m	c	CHIN	El Dorado	Placerville	72	114
Ah	40	m	c	CHIN	Santa Clara	San Jose Twp	88	190
Ah	40	m	c	CHIN	El Dorado	Placerville Twp	72	103
Ah	40	m	c	CHIN	Mariposa	Mariposa P O	74	107
Ah	40	m	c	CHIN	San Francisco	San Francisco P O	80	433
Ah	40	m	c	CHIN	San Francisco	San Francisco P O	80	440
Ah	38	m	c	CHIN	Tuolumne	Chinese Camp P O	93	363
Ah	38	m	c	CHIN	Stanislaus	San Joaquin Twp	92	78
Ah	38	m	c	CHIN	Merced	Snelling P O	74	279
Ah	38	m	c	CHIN	Kern	Bakersfield P O	73	357
Ah	38	m	c	CHIN	San Francisco	San Francisco P O	80	442
Ah	38	m	c	CHIN	San Francisco	3-Wd San Francisco	79	307
Ah	38	m	c	CHIN	San Francisco	San Francisco P O	80	520
Ah	37	m	c	CHIN	El Dorado	Diamond Springs Tw	72	28
Ah	37	m	c	CHIN	San Francisco	San Francisco P O	80	437
Ah	37	m	c	CHIN	San Francisco	San Francisco P O	80	454
Ah	37	m	c	CHIN	Trinity	North Fork Twp	92	219
Ah	37	m	c	CHIN	El Dorado	Diamond Springs Tw	72	32
Ah	36	m	c	CHIN	San Francisco	San Francisco P O	80	446
Ah	36	m	c	CHIN	San Francisco	San Francisco P O	80	521
Ah	36	m	c	CHIN	San Francisco	San Francisco P O	80	530
Ah	34	m	c	CHIN	San Francisco	San Francisco P O	80	494
Ah	34	m	c	CHIN	Plumas	Plumas Twp	77	31
Ah	34	m	c	CHIN	San Francisco	San Francisco P O	80	519
Ah	33	m	c	CHIN	Sierra	Lincoln Twp	89	548
Ah	33	m	c	CHIN	Santa Clara	1-Wd San Jose	88	273
Ah	33	m	c	CHIN	Butte	Chico Twp	70	51
Ah	33	m	c	CHIN	Plumas	Goodwin Twp	77	3
Ah	32	m	c	CHIN	San Francisco	San Francisco P O	80	436
Ah	32	m	c	CHIN	San Francisco	San Francisco P O	80	529
Ah	32	m	c	CHIN	El Dorado	Placerville Twp	72	92
Ah	31	m	c	CHIN	Santa Clara	San Jose Twp	88	195
Ah	31	m	c	CHIN	San Francisco	San Francisco P O	80	498
Ah	31	m	c	CHIN	Amador	Fiddletown P O	69	436
Ah	31	m	c	CHIN	Placer	Auburn P O	76	365
Ah	31	m	c	CHIN	Placer	Bath P O	76	461
Ah	30	m	c	CHIN	San Francisco	6-Wd San Francisco	81	43
Ah	30	m	c	CHIN	El Dorado	Placerville	72	115
Ah	30	m	c	CHIN	San Francisco	San Francisco P O	80	435
Ah	30	m	c	CHIN	San Francisco	San Francisco P O	80	443
Ah	30	m	c	CHIN	San Francisco	San Francisco P O	80	524
Ah	30	m	c	CHIN	Santa Clara	1-Wd San Jose	88	269
Ah	30	m	c	CHIN	Butte	Ophir Twp	70	98
Ah	30	m	c	CHIN	Plumas	Seneca Twp	77	49
Ah	29	m	c	CHIN	Tuolumne	Chinese Camp P O	93	379
Ah	29	m	c	CHIN	San Francisco	San Francisco P O	80	443
Ah	29	m	c	CHIN	San Francisco	San Francisco P O	80	501
Ah	29	m	c	CHIN	San Francisco	San Francisco P O	80	516
Ah	29	m	c	CHIN	Tehama	Tehama Twp	92	189
Ah	28	m	c	CHIN	Stanislaus	Buena Vista Twp	92	11
Ah	28	m	c	CHIN	Santa Clara	San Jose Twp	88	192
Ah	28	m	c	CHIN	El Dorado	Placerville	72	120
Ah	28	m	c	CHIN	Plumas	Goodwin Twp	77	4
Ah	28	m	c	CHIN	Plumas	Indian Twp	77	19
Ah	28	m	c	CHIN	San Francisco	San Francisco P O	80	516
Ah	28	m	c	CHIN	Tehama	Tehama Twp	92	189
Ah	27	m	c	CHIN	Santa Clara	San Jose Twp	88	192
Ah	27	m	c	CHIN	El Dorado	Placerville Twp	72	93
Ah	27	m	c	CHIN	Placer	Bath P O	76	430
Ah	27	m	c	CHIN	Santa Clara	1-Wd San Jose	88	272
Ah	26	m	c	CHIN	Tehama	Antelope Twp	92	153
Ah	26	f	c	CHIN	San Francisco	San Francisco P O	80	507
Ah	26	m	c	CHIN	San Francisco	San Francisco P O	80	518
Ah	26	m	c	CHIN	San Francisco	San Francisco P O	80	515
Ah	26	m	c	CHIN	Sacramento	Franklin Twp	77	118
Ah	25	m	c	CHIN	Amador	Fiddletown P O	69	426
Ah	25	f	c	CHIN	San Francisco	San Francisco P O	80	441
Ah	25	m	c	CHIN	San Francisco	1-Wd San Francisco	79	80
Ah	25	m	c	CHIN	Santa Clara	Santa Clara Twp	88	167
Ah	25	m	c	CHIN	El Dorado	Diamond Springs Tw	72	25
Ah	24	m	c	CHIN	Santa Barbara	Santa Barbara P O	87	458
Ah	24	m	c	CHIN	San Francisco	San Francisco P O	80	442
Ah	24	m	c	CHIN	Solano	Suisun Twp	90	105
Ah	24	m	c	CHIN	Santa Clara	2-Wd San Jose	88	297
Ah	24	m	c	CHIN	Plumas	Washington Twp	77	57
Ah	23	m	c	CHIN	Santa Clara	San Jose Twp	88	204
Ah	22	m	c	CHIN	Solano	Vallejo	90	174
Ah	22	m	c	CHIN	San Francisco	6-Wd San Francisco	81	44
Ah	22	m	c	CHIN	San Francisco	San Francisco P O	83	193
Ah	22	m	c	CHIN	Alameda	Oakland	68	158
Ah	21	m	c	CHIN	Santa Clara	San Jose Twp	88	194
Ah	21	m	c	CHIN	Santa Clara	San Jose Twp	88	191
Ah	21	f	c	CHIN	San Francisco	San Francisco P O	80	503
Ah	21	f	c	CHIN	San Francisco	San Francisco P O	80	433
Ah	21	m	c	CHIN	Santa Clara	2-Wd San Jose	88	307
Ah	21	m	c	CHIN	Santa Clara	1-Wd San Jose	88	271
Ah	20	m	c	CHIN	Solano	Suisun Twp	90	106
Ah	20	f	c	CHIN	Butte	Chico Twp	70	30
Ah	20	m	c	CHIN	San Francisco	San Francisco P O	80	441
Ah	20	m	c	CHIN	San Francisco	San Francisco P O	80	444
Ah	20	f	c	CHIN	San Francisco	San Francisco P O	80	439
Ah	2	f	c	CHIN	Placer	Bath P O	76	440
Ah	19	m	c	CHIN	San Francisco	8-Wd San Francisco	82	358
Ah	19	m	c	CHIN	Marin	San Rafael Twp	74	37
Ah	19	f	c	CHIN	San Francisco	San Francisco P O	80	432
Ah	19	m	c	CHIN	Santa Clara	1-Wd San Jose	88	272
Ah	19	m	c	CHIN	Plumas	Goodwin Twp	77	5
Ah	18	m	c	CHIN	San Francisco	6-Wd San Francisco	81	63
Ah	18	m	c	CHIN	Yuba	Marysville	93	602
Ah	18	m	c	CHIN	San Francisco	San Francisco P O	83	344
Ah	18	f	c	CHIN	Butte	Kimshew Tpw	70	84
Ah	18	m	c	CHIN	Sacramento	3-Wd Sacramento	77	300
Ah	18	m	c	CHIN	Plumas	Seneca Twp	77	47
Ah	17	f	c	CHIN	San Francisco	San Francisco P O	80	506
Ah	17	m	c	CHIN	Sacramento	3-Wd Sacramento	77	290
Ah	16	m	c	CHIN	San Francisco	San Francisco P O	80	502
Ah	16	m	c	CHIN	San Francisco	San Francisco P O	83	272
Ah	16	m	c	CHIN	San Francisco	3-Wd San Francisco	79	309
Ah	16	m	c	CHIN	Nevada	Rough & Ready Twp	75	335
Ah	16	m	c	CHIN	San Francisco	6-Wd San Francisco	81	146
Ah	16	m	c	CHIN	Solano	Benicia	90	15
Ah	16	f	c	CHIN	Santa Clara	1-Wd San Jose	88	273
Ah	16	m	c	CHIN	Sacramento	1-Wd Sacramento	77	195
Ah	15	m	c	CHIN	Placer	Colfax P O	76	388
Ah	14	m	c	CHIN	San Francisco	11-Wd San Francisc	84	510
Ah	14	m	c	CHIN	Santa Clara	Santa Clara Twp	88	163
Ah	12	m	c	CHIN	San Francisco	6-Wd San Francisco	81	44
Ah	11	m	c	CHIN	San Francisco	6-Wd San Francisco	81	125
Ah	10	m	c	CHIN	San Francisco	San Francisco P O	83	25
Chi	22	f	c	CHIN	Yuba	Marysville	93	601
Choo	41	m	c	CHIN	Mariposa	Maxwell Crk P O	74	142
Chow	53	m	c	CHIN	Plumas	Rich Bar Twp	77	45
Chow	24	m	c	CHIN	Santa Clara	1-Wd San Jose	88	277
Chow	22	m	c	CHIN	Santa Clara	San Jose Twp	88	194
Chung	40	m	c	CHIN	Nevada	Grass Valley Twp	75	217
Daei	19	m	c	CHIN	Sonoma	Petaluma Twp	91	342
Foo	17	m	c	CHIN	Solano	Vallejo	90	208
Ge	37	m	c	CHIN	El Dorado	Mud Springs Twp	72	75

© 2001 by Heritage Quest. All rights reserved.

Name	Age	S	R	B-PL	County	Locale	Series M593 Roll	Pg
Ge	35	m	c	CHIN	El Dorado	Diamond Springs Tw	72	25
Ge	32	m	c	CHIN	El Dorado	Mud Springs Twp	72	88
Gee	28	m	c	CHIN	Plumas	Mineral Twp	77	23
Gee	21	m	c	CHIN	San Francisco	6-Wd San Francisco	81	54
Goo	18	m	c	CHIN	Solano	Vallejo	90	209
He	31	m	c	CHIN	Tuolumne	Columbia P O	93	359
Hee	37	m	c	CHIN	Placer	Bath P O	76	430
Hen	32	m	c	CHIN	Siskiyou	Hamburg Twp	89	596
Him	41	m	c	CHIN	Plumas	Goodwin Twp	77	2
Ho	14	m	c	CHIN	Santa Cruz	Santa Cruz	89	423
Hon	25	m	c	CHIN	San Francisco	6-Wd San Francisco	81	46
Hoo	22	m	c	CHIN	Solano	Suisun Twp	90	106
Hung	30	m	c	CHIN	Yuba	Marysville	93	625
Ing	30	m	c	CHIN	San Francisco	6-Wd San Francisco	81	47
Jo	30	m	c	CHIN	San Francisco	3-Wd San Francisco	79	307
Joseph	44	m	w	SWIT	Plumas	Seneca Twp	77	47
Kan	40	m	c	CHIN	Siskiyou	Hamburg Twp	89	597
Kee	19	m	c	CHIN	Santa Clara	San Jose Twp	88	190
Kit	32	m	c	CHIN	Santa Clara	Gilroy Twp	88	96
Kit	24	m	c	CHIN	San Francisco	6-Wd San Francisco	81	64
Kum	15	f	c	CHIN	San Francisco	6-Wd San Francisco	81	61
Lah	25	m	c	CHIN	Marin	Tomales Twp	74	86
Lee	26	m	c	CHIN	Santa Clara	San Jose Twp	88	194
Lee	24	m	c	CHIN	Santa Clara	1-Wd San Jose	88	273
Leong	20	m	c	CHIN	San Francisco	6-Wd San Francisco	81	46
Lip	35	m	c	CHIN	Yuba	Marysville	93	626
Loo	22	m	c	CHIN	Solano	Vallejo	90	217
Moo	27	m	c	CHIN	Yuba	Marysville	93	620
Pak	24	m	c	CHIN	San Francisco	6-Wd San Francisco	81	47
Pow	45	m	c	CHIN	Plumas	Goodwin Twp	77	2
Quok	14	m	c	CHIN	San Francisco	6-Wd San Francisco	81	47
Sam	28	m	c	CHIN	Marin	San Rafael Twp	74	59
See	25	m	c	CHIN	El Dorado	Cosumnes Twp	72	20
Sung	43	m	c	CHIN	Yuba	Marysville	93	628
Sy	15	m	c	CHIN	San Francisco	1-Wd San Francisco	79	131
Tang	30	m	c	CHIN	San Francisco	6-Wd San Francisco	81	47
Ten Loy	33	m	c	CHIN	Amador	Ione City P O	69	366
Ti	40	m	c	CHIN	Santa Clara	1-Wd San Jose	88	273
Tie	20	f	c	CHIN	Los Angeles	Los Angeles	73	524
Tie	19	f	c	CHIN	Los Angeles	Los Angeles	73	524
Toy	21	f	c	CHIN	Plumas	Goodwin Twp	77	2
Ty	27	m	c	CHIN	Butte	Hamilton Twp	70	68
We	23	m	c	CHIN	Santa Clara	San Jose Twp	88	192
Wen	40	m	c	CHIN	Butte	Kimshew Tpw	70	84
Wey	35	m	c	CHIN	Plumas	Mineral Twp	77	25
Yaw	40	m	c	CHIN	Plumas	Plumas Twp	77	31
Ye	33	m	c	CHIN	Amador	Jackson P O	69	331
Yee	52	m	c	CHIN	San Francisco	6-Wd San Francisco	81	66
Yee	25	f	c	CHIN	Yuba	Marysville	93	627
Yn	41	m	c	CHIN	Amador	Fiddletown P O	69	438
Yo	25	m	c	CHIN	Tuolumne	Columbia P O	93	348
Yon	40	m	c	CHIN	Plumas	Plumas Twp	77	31
Young At	72	m	c	CHIN	Amador	Ione City P O	69	366
FUNK								
Ah	39	m	c	CHIN	San Francisco	San Francisco P O	80	435
Ah	30	m	c	CHIN	Santa Clara	1-Wd San Jose	88	271
Ann R	26	f	w	MO	Yolo	Cottonwood Twp	93	467
Chee	32	m	c	CHIN	Tuolumne	Big Oak Flat P O	93	392
Clara	13	f	w	IA	Siskiyou	Scott Valley Twp	89	608
Henry	54	m	w	DENM	San Francisco	11-Wd San Francisc	84	611
Henry	18	m	w	HAMB	San Francisco	San Francisco P O	85	785
Him	34	m	c	CHIN	Tuolumne	Chinese Camp P O	93	364
John	56	m	w	BADE	Shasta	Shasta P O	89	454
John	35	m	w	MO	Kern	Bakersfield P O	73	358
Julius	42	m	w	PRUS	San Francisco	San Francisco P O	80	532
Lewis	41	m	w	HANO	Sierra	Eureka Twp	89	524
Martin M	39	m	w	OH	El Dorado	Cosumnes Twp	72	14
Newson Danel	37	m	w	IN	Trinity	Minersville Pct	92	203
Nicholas	40	m	w	PRUS	San Francisco	1-Wd San Francisco	79	60
Samuel	51	m	w	PA	Tuolumne	Sonora P O	93	316
FUNKE								
Fredk	39	m	w	PRUS	San Francisco	San Francisco P O	83	27
L	41	m	w	PRUS	Sierra	Lincoln Twp	89	545
FUNKENSTEIN								
Julius	35	m	w	PRUS	San Francisco	8-Wd San Francisco	82	437
FUNKINSTEIN								
Peter	34	m	w	HANO	San Francisco	6-Wd San Francisco	81	154
FUNN								
Ah	33	m	c	CHIN	San Francisco	6-Wd San Francisco	81	42
FUNNALL								
Joseph	46	m	w	ENGL	Alameda	Eden Twp	68	80
FUNSTON								
James	60	m	w	IREL	Sacramento	4-Wd Sacramento	77	378
Mathew H	42	m	w	IREL	Nevada	Grass Valley Twp	75	154
FUNT								
Fannie	18	f	w	NY	San Francisco	2-Wd San Francisco	79	231
FUNY								
L	43	m	w	PA	San Joaquin	2-Wd Stockton	86	212
FUON								
Fok	48	m	c	CHIN	Butte	Concow Twp	70	12
Hiss	29	m	c	CHIN	Butte	Hamilton Twp	70	71
FUQUA								
Margaret	56	f	w	KY	Butte	Oroville Twp	70	137
FUQUAY								
Thomas B	33	m	w	AR	Inyo	Lone Pine Twp	73	335
FUR								
Anne	25	f	w	IREL	San Francisco	8-Wd San Francisco	82	475

Name	Age	S	R	B-PL	County	Locale	Series M593 Roll	Pg
FURBACH								
Joseph	25	m	w	PRUS	San Francisco	5-Wd San Francisco	81	9
FURBER								
Geo C	52	m	w	MA	Siskiyou	Callahan P O	89	631
FURBISH								
Moses	66	m	w	ME	San Francisco	2-Wd San Francisco	79	275
FURBOSH								
Orrin	44	m	w	ME	Nevada	Grass Valley Twp	75	217
FURBUSH								
C	31	m	w	PA	Yuba	Marysville	93	595
Chs	26	m	w	ME	Yuba	Marysville	93	581
Ezra	27	m	w	WI	Butte	Chico Twp	70	17
Jack	14	m	w	MA	Butte	Chico Twp	70	54
FURCK								
Jane	54	f	w	PRUS	San Francisco	San Francisco P O	80	469
FURDON								
Agnes	40	f	w	IREL	San Francisco	7-Wd San Francisco	81	286
FURGASON								
George	40	m	w	IREL	Amador	Drytown P O	69	422
H	36	m	w	VA	Amador	Jackson P O	69	334
Mary	18	f	w	OH	San Joaquin	2-Wd Stockton	86	172
Tho	32	m	w	MO	El Dorado	Greenwood Twp	72	50
Wm	26	m	i	CA	Merced	Snelling P O	74	269
FURGELON								
Wm	50	m	w	GERM	San Francisco	8-Wd San Francisco	82	367
FURGER								
Mary	46	f	w	SWIT	Mariposa	Maxwell Crk P O	74	146
Mary A	49	f	w	PRUS	San Francisco	San Francisco P O	83	420
FURGERSON								
Alfred Hall	48	m	w	NC	Plumas	Plumas Twp	77	26
Benjamin M	40	m	w	PA	Plumas	Seneca Twp	77	48
Ella	13	f	w	CA	Santa Clara	Santa Clara Twp	88	151
John	18	m	w	WI	Yolo	Washington Twp	93	536
Marcus	25	m	w	DENM	San Francisco	7-Wd San Francisco	81	218
Mary	35	f	w	IREL	San Francisco	8-Wd San Francisco	82	341
Robert	23	m	w	SCOT	Yolo	Putah Twp	93	517
William	45	m	w	IREL	San Francisco	7-Wd San Francisco	81	223
FURGERSUN								
Christena	59	f	w	SCOT	Solano	Denverton Twp	90	25
FURGESON								
David	50	m	w	SCOT	Mariposa	Mariposa P O	74	93
Diadema	73	f	w	KY	Sonoma	Analy Twp	91	237
Duncan	30	m	w	NY	Sonoma	Salt Point	91	387
Edward	25	m	w	DENM	Los Angeles	Los Angeles	73	571
Geo	65	m	w	MA	San Francisco	2-Wd San Francisco	79	243
Jas	29	m	w	IREL	Mariposa	Mariposa P O	74	130
John	37	m	w	NY	Inyo	Independence Twp	73	327
John	30	m	w	NY	Sacramento	Georgianna Twp	77	135
Joseph	5	m	w	CA	Marin	San Rafael Twp	74	29
Joseph	27	m	w	IREL	Marin	San Rafael Twp	74	26
M A	40	m	c	TN	Del Norte	Happy Camp Twp	71	470
M S	31	m	w	IA	Nevada	Eureka Twp	75	139
Mary	38	f	w	IREL	San Francisco	2-Wd San Francisco	79	206
Newton J	42	m	w	OH	Sonoma	Salt Point	91	387
FURGISON								
Daniel H	54	m	w	NY	Inyo	Cerro Gordo Twp	73	318
Wm	32	m	w	WI	Sacramento	Brighton Twp	77	78
FURGUESON								
J H	33	m	w	ENGL	Sutter	Nicolaus Twp	92	106
FURGURSON								
J L	40	m	w	IN	Santa Clara	Gilroy Twp	88	88
Tho	77	m	w	PA	El Dorado	Greenwood Twp	72	51
FURGUSON								
Amelia	35	f	w	MEXI	San Joaquin	2-Wd Stockton	86	168
Edward	35	m	w	NY	Solano	Suisun Twp	90	114
Eugene	39	m	w	NY	Santa Cruz	Pajaro Twp	89	349
Fred	39	m	w	IREL	San Joaquin	2-Wd Stockton	86	168
George	62	m	w	IREL	Santa Clara	Santa Clara Twp	88	153
George	61	m	w	NH	San Mateo	Schoolhouse Statio	87	341
Henry	33	m	w	SCOT	Monterey	Pajaro Twp	74	368
Henry	30	m	w	IREL	San Francisco	7-Wd San Francisco	81	192
Jackson	48	m	w	US	San Joaquin	2-Wd Stockton	86	168
James	39	m	w	NY	Nevada	Grass Valley Twp	75	149
James	37	m	w	NY	Santa Clara	Santa Clara Twp	88	154
Maria	43	f	w	MEXI	San Joaquin	2-Wd Stockton	86	168
Peter	50	m	w	SCOT	Sonoma	Analy Twp	91	223
Reuben	30	m	w	IL	Colusa	Colusa	71	290
Robert	30	m	w	CANA	Solano	Denverton Twp	90	26
William	33	m	w	IREL	Nevada	Grass Valley Twp	75	228
William	30	m	w	CANA	Nevada	Little York Twp	75	244
William J	37	m	w	DC	Nevada	Grass Valley Twp	75	144
William P	36	m	w	IL	Nevada	Rough & Ready Twp	75	331
William S	46	m	w	KY	El Dorado	Mud Springs Twp	72	72
FURHOPPE								
Jno	28	m	w	SHOL	Sacramento	3-Wd Sacramento	77	317
FURIS								
G	43	m	w	NY	San Joaquin	1-Wd Stockton	86	141
FURLAH								
Mary	28	f	w	IREL	Marin	Point Reyes Twp	74	23
FURLEY								
Asa	47	m	w	MO	Kern	Linns Valley P O	73	346
John	39	m	w	NY	San Francisco	6-Wd San Francisco	81	109
John F	40	m	w	NY	San Francisco	6-Wd San Francisco	81	82
Mary J	50	f	w	NY	San Francisco	6-Wd San Francisco	81	101
Wm H	56	m	w	TN	Butte	Concow Twp	70	6
FURLING								
Thos	28	m	w	IREL	San Francisco	1-Wd San Francisco	79	13

© 2001 by Heritage Quest. All rights reserved.

Series M593

Name	Age	S	R	B-PL	County	Locale	Roll	Pg
FURLL								
Lee	29	m	c	CHIN	San Francisco	5-Wd San Francisco	81	3
FURLON								
J T	32	m	w	NORW	Sierra	Lincoln Twp	89	545
FURLONG								
Andrew	56	m	w	IREL	Contra Costa	Martinez P O	71	382
Ann	28	f	w	PRUS	San Francisco	11-Wd San Francisc	84	689
Edward	36	m	w	IREL	Santa Clara	Santa Clara Twp	88	167
Ellen	24	f	w	IREL	San Francisco	11-Wd San Francisc	84	577
Geo	24	m	w	IREL	San Francisco	11-Wd San Francisc	84	586
James	29	m	w	IREL	Sonoma	Bodega Twp	91	263
John	38	m	w	IREL	Sierra	Eureka Twp	89	524
John	34	m	w	IREL	Alameda	Eden Twp	68	64
John	27	m	w	IREL	Alameda	San Leandro	68	98
John	25	m	w	IREL	San Francisco	7-Wd San Francisco	81	173
John	23	m	w	CANA	Sutter	Sutter Twp	92	117
Joseph	43	m	w	IREL	San Francisco	8-Wd San Francisco	82	415
Luke	42	m	w	IREL	Los Angeles	Los Nietos Twp	73	581
Nicholas	29	m	w	IREL	Santa Clara	2-Wd San Jose	88	294
Pat	40	m	w	IREL	San Francisco	11-Wd San Francisc	84	610
Patrick	45	m	w	IREL	Nevada	Grass Valley Twp	75	231
R	28	m	w	IREL	Yuba	Marysville	93	611
Thomas	38	m	w	WALE	Mendocino	Navarro & Big Rvr	74	176
Thos	21	m	w	IREL	Sonoma	Bodega Twp	91	257
William	36	m	w	IREL	Yolo	Putah Twp	93	522
William	35	m	w	IREL	Yolo	Cache Crk Twp	93	430
William	34	m	w	IREL	Yolo	Buckeye Twp	93	417
Wm H	35	m	w	NJ	Santa Clara	Gilroy Twp	88	86
FURMAN								
A W	31	m	w	OH	Merced	Snelling P O	74	263
Arthur	29	m	w	OH	Merced	Snelling P O	74	259
George R	34	m	w	OH	Los Angeles	Wilmington Twp	73	637
J S	25	m	w	OH	Merced	Snelling P O	74	263
Noah	30	m	w	NY	Marin	San Rafael Twp	74	26
T	15	f	w	CA	Alameda	Oakland	68	242
William	28	m	w	OH	Merced	Snelling P O	74	263
William	11	m	w	CA	Marin	San Rafael Twp	74	27
FURMISH								
G B	36	m	w	MO	Amador	Amador City P O	69	395
FURN								
Ah	60	m	c	CHIN	Trinity	Weaverville Pct	92	229
Charles	25	m	w	IL	Alameda	Oakland	68	265
FURNA								
Jesus	33	m	w	MEXI	Kern	Bakersfield P O	73	362
FURNACE								
L	31	m	w	MI	San Joaquin	Elkhorn Twp	86	65
FURNALD								
Thomas	31	m	w	CANA	Santa Clara	2-Wd San Jose	88	329
FURNAN								
Richard	35	m	w	NY	San Francisco	11-Wd San Francisc	84	514
FURNANCE								
Manwell	20	m	w	PORT	Sacramento	Franklin Twp	77	106
FURNAS								
Nichs	46	m	w	CHIL	Sierra	Table Rock Twp	89	573
FURNAY								
Chas F	23	m	w	ENGL	San Francisco	6-Wd San Francisco	81	104
FURNEIS								
Grenville	33	m	w	MO	Fresno	Kings Rvr P O	72	214
FURNER								
Chas	40	m	w	FRAN	Butte	Chico Twp	70	54
Jacob	50	m	w	SWIT	San Francisco	6-Wd San Francisco	81	83
M	60	f	w	ENGL	Alameda	Oakland	68	245
FURNES								
Nick J	45	m	w	MO	Butte	Oregon Twp	70	124
FURNESS								
Catharine	30	f	w	IREL	Santa Clara	1-Wd San Jose	88	254
George	31	m	w	ENGL	Los Angeles	San Jose Twp	73	623
FURNETT								
John	30	m	w	IREL	San Francisco	San Francisco P O	83	139
FURNEY								
John	46	m	w	MD	San Bernardino	San Bernardino Twp	78	414
Jos	25	m	w	ENGL	Solano	Vallejo	90	149
Peter	39	m	w	US	Nevada	Grass Valley Twp	75	230
FURNHAM								
Bridget	43	f	w	IREL	San Francisco	11-Wd San Francisc	84	631
FURNIS								
Tom	30	m	w	IREL	San Joaquin	Oneal Twp	86	107
FURNISH								
J B	49	m	w	MO	San Joaquin	Liberty Twp	86	82
FURNISS								
Miles	36	m	w	NY	Yolo	Cache Crk Twp	93	426
FURREY								
William	29	m	w	NY	San Francisco	8-Wd San Francisco	82	325
FURROW								
William	50	m	w	ENGL	El Dorado	Cosumnes Twp	72	13
FURROWS								
Isaac	34	m	w	NY	San Bernardino	San Bernardino Twp	78	452
FURRY								
Henry	39	m	w	OH	Yolo	Cache Crk Twp	93	433
FURSON								
William	30	m	w	CANA	San Francisco	7-Wd San Francisco	81	224
FURST								
Henry	44	m	w	NY	San Francisco	1-Wd San Francisco	79	131
Martin J	66	m	w	POLA	Santa Barbara	Santa Barbara P O	87	450
FURSTENFELD								
M	29	m	w	GERM	Solano	Vallejo	90	174
FURT								
Charles	35	m	w	BOHE	San Francisco	2-Wd San Francisco	79	194
Tie	39	m	c	CHIN	Placer	Bath P O	76	443
Wm Henry	46	m	w	VA	Nevada	Little York Twp	75	234
FURTARZOSA								
Frank	24	m	w	AZOR	Shasta	American Ranch P O	89	498
FURTH								
Catharine	32	f	w	GERM	Nevada	Nevada Twp	75	280
Daniel	38	m	w	BOHE	Nevada	Bridgeport Twp	75	100
Jacob	30	m	w	BOHE	Colusa	Colusa	71	301
Samuel	37	m	w	AUST	San Francisco	San Francisco P O	80	482
Simon	45	m	w	BOHE	Nevada	Bridgeport Twp	75	100
FURTNEY								
Wm	38	m	w	MA	San Joaquin	Castoria Twp	86	8
FURZE								
William	50	m	w	PA	Marin	San Rafael Twp	74	59
FUS								
George J	24	m	w	BADE	Santa Cruz	Soquel Twp	89	446
FUSAH								
Taro	21	m	j	JAPA	San Francisco	San Francisco P O	85	784
FUSALIER								
John	37	m	w	HANO	San Francisco	2-Wd San Francisco	79	227
FUSCHINSCHI								
John	53	m	w	PRUS	San Francisco	2-Wd San Francisco	79	138
FUSE								
Sabastian	15	m	w	CA	Los Angeles	Los Angeles Twp	73	495
FUSENTHILE								
H	47	m	w	PRUS	San Francisco	San Francisco P O	83	330
FUSEY								
Ferdinant	21	m	w	NY	San Joaquin	1-Wd Stockton	86	126
FUSIER								
Henry	62	m	w	FRAN	San Francisco	2-Wd San Francisco	79	141
FUSS								
Mary	19	f	w	WURT	El Dorado	Placerville	72	109
FUSSE								
Annie	19	f	w	HANO	San Francisco	11-Wd San Francisc	84	422
FUT								
Ah	25	m	c	CHIN	Sacramento	1-Wd Sacramento	77	198
Ah	18	m	c	CHIN	San Francisco	6-Wd San Francisco	81	49
FUTCH								
George M	20	m	w	CANA	Santa Cruz	Santa Cruz Twp	89	400
John	23	m	w	CANA	Santa Cruz	Santa Cruz Twp	89	400
FUTCHER								
Joseph	20	m	w	MO	Amador	Sutter Crk P O	69	413
FUTEY								
Louis	30	m	w	PRUS	Siskiyou	Callahan P O	89	632
FUTITSON								
Charles	18	m	w	SWED	San Mateo	Schoolhouse Statio	87	334
FUTT								
Ah	25	m	c	CHIN	San Francisco	6-Wd San Francisco	81	68
Loon	27	m	c	CHIN	Sacramento	1-Wd Sacramento	77	181
FUTTON								
Henriette	9	f	w	CA	Sonoma	Santa Rosa	91	427
James	43	m	w	IN	Sonoma	Santa Rosa	91	427
Thomas	40	m	w	IN	Sonoma	Santa Rosa	91	427
FUTTZ								
Geo W	43	m	w	NY	San Joaquin	Oneal Twp	86	115
FUYAT								
J B	66	m	w	VA	Sacramento	3-Wd Sacramento	77	267
FUZENOT								
Annise	30	f	w	FRAN	San Francisco	11-Wd San Francisc	84	700
FUZLIER								
Sarah	13	f	w	CA	San Francisco	8-Wd San Francisco	82	398
FWA								
Gee	55	m	c	CHIN	Plumas	Mineral Twp	77	23
FWE								
Ah	40	m	c	CHIN	Plumas	Goodwin Twp	77	2
Ah	30	m	c	CHIN	Plumas	Goodwin Twp	77	4
Ah	29	m	c	CHIN	Plumas	Goodwin Twp	77	2
Ah	20	m	c	CHIN	Plumas	Goodwin Twp	77	4
FWOK								
Ah	29	m	c	CHIN	Plumas	Goodwin Twp	77	2
FY								
Ah	44	m	c	CHIN	Amador	Jackson P O	69	347
Ah	42	m	c	CHIN	San Francisco	San Francisco P O	80	524
Ah	42	m	c	CHIN	Calaveras	Copperopolis P O	70	256
Ah	40	m	c	CHIN	Yolo	Washington Twp	93	537
Ah	39	m	c	CHIN	San Francisco	San Francisco P O	80	336
Ah	38	m	c	CHIN	Amador	Ione City P O	69	370
Ah	31	m	c	CHIN	Alameda	Eden Twp	68	61
Ah	28	m	c	CHIN	Sacramento	Cosumnes Twp	77	94
Ah	28	m	c	CHIN	Butte	Bidwell Twp	70	4
Ah	28	m	c	CHIN	Yolo	Cache Crk Twp	93	455
Ah	25	m	c	CHIN	Sacramento	4-Wd Sacramento	77	355
Ah	22	m	c	CHIN	San Francisco	San Francisco P O	80	381
Ah	14	m	c	CHIN	Nevada	Eureka Twp	75	141
Ah	11	m	c	CHIN	Sacramento	2-Wd Sacramento	77	237
Chong	20	f	c	CHIN	Butte	Ophir Twp	70	109
I	27	f	c	CHIN	Stanislaus	Emory Twp	92	17
Kee Yok	35	m	c	CHIN	Amador	Volcano P O	69	378
Lee	56	m	c	CHIN	Butte	Kimshew Tpw	70	85
Sho	18	m	c	CHIN	Sacramento	2-Wd Sacramento	77	251
Yan	35	m	c	CHIN	Butte	Chico Twp	70	51
FYE								
Ah	30	m	c	CHIN	Sacramento	Granite Twp	77	152
FYLER								
Harriet	16	f	w	IL	Siskiyou	Scott Rvr Twp	89	603

© 2001 by Heritage Quest. All rights reserved.

Name	Age	S	R	B-PL	County	Locale	Series M593 Roll	Pg
FYON								
Dominic	29	m	w	ITAL	Calaveras	San Andreas P O	70	175
GA								
Ah	32	m	c	CHIN	Sacramento	1-Wd Sacramento	77	201
Woh	46	m	c	CHIN	Calaveras	Copperopolis P O	70	264
Yin	47	m	c	CHIN	Calaveras	Copperopolis P O	70	264
GAAFTS								
Thomas	44	m	w	ME	Amador	Volcano P O	69	380
GAAL								
Wm C	24	m	w	IL	San Francisco	2-Wd San Francisco	79	190
GAAZEDER								
Jack	30	m	w	FRAN	Los Angeles	Los Angeles Twp	73	476
GABAI								
Mary	80	f	w	MEXI	Tuolumne	Sonora P O	93	316
GABARINO								
Andrew	25	m	w	ITAL	San Francisco	1-Wd San Francisco	79	33
GABAS								
Hosea	45	m	w	CHIL	El Dorado	Kelsey Twp	72	58
Thomas	50	m	w	CHIL	El Dorado	Kelsey Twp	72	58
GABAY								
William	24	m	w	MO	Siskiyou	Surprise Valley Tw	89	641
GABB								
Frederick	10	m	w	NY	San Francisco	San Francisco P O	85	828
George	8	m	w	NY	San Francisco	San Francisco P O	85	828
John	29	m	w	MO	Solano	Silveyville Twp	90	87
GABBART								
John	57	m	w	KY	Calaveras	San Andreas P O	70	152
GABBRYETT								
R	39	m	w	IL	Sierra	Downieville Twp	89	517
GABBS								
Wm	69	m	w	ENGL	San Francisco	San Francisco P O	85	825
GABEL								
Henry	35	m	w	OH	San Francisco	8-Wd San Francisco	82	381
Jacob	50	m	w	HDAR	San Francisco	2-Wd San Francisco	79	273
Thomas	47	m	w	MO	Los Angeles	Los Nietos Twp	73	589
GABELAN								
Pablo	37	m	w	CHIL	Santa Clara	Alviso Twp	88	27
GABELE								
August	44	m	w	HCAS	San Francisco	San Francisco P O	85	840
GABENGO								
Ticon	18	m	w	SWIT	Fresno	Millerton P O	72	164
GABERS								
Wm	34	m	w	MO	Santa Clara	Almaden Twp	88	11
GABEY								
David	41	m	w	NY	Yuba	Rose Bar Twp	93	666
GABIEL								
Waver	44	m	w	SWIT	Sacramento	Alabama Twp	77	62
GABLE								
Amos W	36	m	w	OH	Yolo	Grafton Twp	93	498
Fred	21	m	w	IL	San Francisco	2-Wd San Francisco	79	280
Harvey C	34	m	w	OH	Yolo	Grafton Twp	93	498
Jacob	39	m	w	PRUS	Sacramento	Granite Twp	77	142
William	37	m	w	PRUS	Calaveras	Copperopolis P O	70	222
William	36	m	w	OH	Placer	Colfax P O	76	391
William	18	m	w	IA	Amador	Ione City P O	69	359
GABLES								
Sylvester A	32	m	w	OH	Yolo	Grafton Twp	93	498
GABOTHE								
John	45	m	w	CANA	Yolo	Cache Crk Twp	93	426
GABOUR								
Charles	36	m	w	PRUS	Contra Costa	Martinez P O	71	370
GABRAIEL								
Mexican	45	m	w	MEXI	El Dorado	Mud Springs Twp	72	76
GABRIALDO								
Pacrien	21	m	w	ITAL	Sacramento	Sutter Twp	77	386
GABRIEL								
Alfred	12	m	w	CA	Santa Clara	1-Wd San Jose	88	224
Andrew	14	m	w	CA	Santa Clara	1-Wd San Jose	88	233
August	33	m	w	PRUS	Santa Clara	Santa Clara Twp	88	156
C	30	m	w	MEXI	Napa	Napa Twp	75	31
Fentun	34	m	w	FRAN	San Francisco	11-Wd San Francisc	84	433
Frank	23	m	w	NY	San Francisco	8-Wd San Francisco	82	318
Henry	42	m	w	SWIT	Butte	Oregon Twp	70	132
Henry	11	m	w	CA	Santa Clara	2-Wd San Jose	88	328
Jacob	59	m	w	PRUS	San Francisco	8-Wd San Francisco	82	401
Jno	50	m	w	FRAN	Santa Clara	Gilroy Twp	88	93
Jose	30	m	w	MEXI	Santa Barbara	San Buenaventura P	87	428
Maria	25	f	w	OR	Los Angeles	Los Angeles	73	541
Mary	16	f	w	NY	Santa Clara	1-Wd San Jose	88	263
Ralph	56	m	w	ENGL	Santa Clara	1-Wd San Jose	88	235
William	34	m	w	PRUS	Santa Clara	Santa Clara Twp	88	140
GABRIELDS								
Refucio	35	m	w	MEXI	Santa Clara	Almaden Twp	88	5
GABRIL								
John	43	m	w	PORT	Trinity	Indian Crk	92	200
GABY								
Elijah	55	m	w	PA	Solano	Vallejo	90	152
GACHOONE								
Jote	25	m	w	EIND	San Francisco	11-Wd San Francisc	84	520
GACIA								
Louisa	12	f	w	CA	San Luis Obispo	Arroyo Grande Twp	87	272
GACIO								
Lucie	33	m	w	MEXI	Tulare	Tule Rvr Twp	92	258
GACY								
Ah	35	m	c	CHIN	Trinity	Douglas	92	235
Ah	30	m	c	CHIN	Trinity	North Fork Twp	92	220
Ah	29	m	c	CHIN	Trinity	Douglas	92	233
Ah	25	m	c	CHIN	Trinity	Junction City Pct	92	207
Chung	51	m	c	CHIN	Trinity	North Fork Twp	92	219
GAD								
Bernard	38	m	w	PRUS	Nevada	Grass Valley Twp	75	148
GADAUS								
Simon	29	m	w	CANA	Alameda	Brooklyn	68	38
GADBERY								
Ellen A	15	f	w	UT	Stanislaus	Empire Twp	92	64
GADBURY								
John W	47	m	w	TN	El Dorado	Mountain Twp	72	67
GADD								
Bell	19	f	w	CA	Amador	Sutter Crk P O	69	401
Browd	25	m	w	OH	El Dorado	Cosumnes Twp	72	13
Thomas	51	m	w	OH	Amador	Sutter Crk P O	69	412
GADDES								
Andrew	25	m	w	MA	Plumas	Quartz Twp	77	34
GADDI								
Albino	14	m	w	ITAL	Santa Clara	Santa Clara Twp	88	176
Ludovico	46	m	w	ITAL	Santa Clara	Santa Clara Twp	88	176
Luigi	19	m	w	ITAL	San Francisco	1-Wd San Francisco	79	114
Stephen	21	m	w	ITAL	Santa Clara	Santa Clara Twp	88	176
GADDIE								
Felix M C	27	m	w	AL	Tulare	Visalia	92	297
GADDIS								
Alex	21	m	w	CANA	Humboldt	Arcata Twp	72	231
Annie	43	f	w	NY	Yolo	Grafton Twp	93	489
GADDY								
Martin R	41	m	w	IN	Los Angeles	Los Nietos Twp	73	589
R	37	m	w	TN	Lake	Big Valley	73	394
Thomas	38	m	w	KY	Butte	Wyandotte Twp	70	149
GADEANDE								
Antonio	52	m	w	FRAN	Calaveras	San Andreas P O	70	214
GADEAU								
Eugene	35	m	w	FRAN	San Francisco	San Francisco P O	80	341
GADEN								
Sophia	25	f	w	NY	Marin	San Rafael	74	55
GADFONI								
Joseph	16	m	w	SWIT	Marin	Nicasio Twp	74	17
GADIA								
Jake	33	m	w	PRUS	San Joaquin	2-Wd Stockton	86	190
GADICKE								
Elliott	50	m	w	HANO	Yuba	Linda Twp	93	554
GADING								
Justus	33	m	w	BREM	Alameda	Eden Twp	68	59
Nicholas	46	m	w	BREM	Alameda	Eden Twp	68	58
GADJONI								
Amadio	27	m	w	SWIT	Marin	Nicasio Twp	74	14
GADSBY								
Ben C	27	m	w	ENGL	Santa Cruz	Santa Cruz	89	427
Elijah	33	m	w	ENGL	San Francisco	11-Wd San Francisc	84	566
GAE								
Lei	34	m	c	CHIN	Solano	Green Valley Twp	90	43
On	50	m	c	CHIN	Trinity	Douglas	92	237
GAEMLICH								
Chs	45	m	w	SAXO	Siskiyou	Yreka Twp	89	665
GAERA								
Batista	43	m	w	CA	Santa Barbara	San Buenaventura P	87	427
GAESHLIN								
Frank	45	m	w	SWIT	San Francisco	8-Wd San Francisco	82	421
GAET								
Ah	40	m	c	CHIN	Trinity	Douglas	92	234
GAETANO								
Fadricca	25	m	w	SWIT	San Francisco	1-Wd San Francisco	79	105
GAEYHAM								
John	13	m	w	CA	Marin	San Rafael Twp	74	29
GAFF								
John	27	m	w	NY	Inyo	Bishop Crk Twp	73	317
GAFFANI								
Edward	33	m	w	SWIT	Santa Clara	San Jose Twp	88	204
GAFFANISCH								
A	41	m	w	FRAN	Sacramento	3-Wd Sacramento	77	279
GAFFANY								
James	24	m	w	IREL	San Francisco	7-Wd San Francisco	81	167
GAFFENEY								
Augusta	40	f	w	CA	Santa Barbara	Santa Barbara P O	87	468
C H	23	m	w	MA	Merced	Snelling P O	74	257
GAFFENY								
Hugh	46	m	w	IREL	Tuolumne	Columbia P O	93	346
James	40	m	w	PA	Santa Barbara	Las Cruces P O	87	515
Thos	36	m	w	IREL	Butte	Ophir Twp	70	109
GAFFEREY								
Peter	40	m	w	IREL	Marin	San Rafael Twp	74	40
GAFFERNY								
James	30	m	w	IREL	San Francisco	8-Wd San Francisco	82	351
GAFFERT								
Nancy	60	f	w	SC	Sacramento	Cosumnes Twp	77	93
GAFFEY								
Pat	34	m	w	IREL	San Francisco	5-Wd San Francisco	81	32
GAFFIGAN								
Mary	35	f	w	IREL	San Francisco	San Francisco P O	83	398
Thomas	28	m	w	IREL	San Francisco	San Francisco P O	80	401
GAFFINO								
James	58	m	w	MALT	San Francisco	San Francisco P O	80	342
GAFFNER								
George	36	m	w	MA	San Luis Obispo	Morro Twp	87	287
GAFFNEY								
B	36	m	w	IREL	Solano	Vallejo	90	170

© 2001 by Heritage Quest. All rights reserved.

Series M593

Name	Age	S	R	B-PL	County	Locale	Roll	Pg
James	54	m	w	IREL	San Francisco	San Francisco P O	83	395
James	45	m	w	IREL	San Francisco	San Francisco P O	80	387
James	40	m	w	IREL	San Francisco	San Francisco P O	83	341
James	38	m	w	IREL	El Dorado	Mud Springs Twp	72	86
James	19	m	w	IREL	San Francisco	San Francisco P O	83	335
Jane	69	f	w	IREL	El Dorado	Mud Springs Twp	72	90
Jane	30	f	w	ENGL	San Francisco	6-Wd San Francisco	81	71
John	35	m	w	IREL	San Joaquin	1-Wd Stockton	86	131
John	30	m	w	IREL	San Francisco	7-Wd San Francisco	81	237
John	30	m	w	NY	Amador	Ione City P O	69	359
John	28	m	w	OH	Solano	Tremont Twp	90	29
John	13	m	w	CA	San Francisco	11-Wd San Francisc	84	593
Jos	9	m	w	NY	Solano	Vallejo	90	173
Kate	22	f	w	IREL	San Francisco	7-Wd San Francisco	81	244
Maria	7	f	m	CA	San Francisco	San Francisco P O	80	464
Mary	10	f	w	MA	San Francisco	San Francisco P O	83	320
Michael	41	m	w	IREL	Sacramento	Cosumnes Twp	77	89
Michael	28	m	w	IREL	San Francisco	San Francisco P O	83	398
Owen	39	m	w	IREL	San Francisco	3-Wd San Francisco	79	325
Patrick	29	m	w	IREL	Sacramento	Cosumnes Twp	77	91
Thos	30	m	w	IREL	San Francisco	7-Wd San Francisco	81	242
Wm	29	m	w	IREL	San Francisco	1-Wd San Francisco	79	69
GAFFORD								
William C	76	m	w	VA	El Dorado	Mud Springs Twp	72	83
GAFFRAY								
Rose	25	f	w	IREL	San Francisco	5-Wd San Francisco	81	33
GAFFREY								
John	19	m	w	IREL	San Francisco	11-Wd San Francisc	84	512
GAFFY								
Ann E	48	f	w	IREL	Santa Cruz	Pajaro Twp	89	346
John	40	m	w	IREL	Santa Cruz	Pajaro Twp	89	345
GAFNEY								
Annie	35	f	w	IREL	Sacramento	3-Wd Sacramento	77	262
John	55	m	w	IREL	Sacramento	Cosumnes Twp	77	91
John	29	m	w	IREL	Sonoma	Sonoma Twp	91	443
Maria	25	f	w	IREL	San Francisco	8-Wd San Francisco	82	491
Michael	35	m	w	NY	San Francisco	6-Wd San Francisco	81	155
Miles	40	m	w	IREL	Sonoma	Bodega Twp	91	256
William	56	m	w	PA	San Mateo	Half Moon Bay P O	87	398
GAFNY								
Mary E	20	f	w	NY	Alameda	Oakland	68	161
GAFORTH								
Jasper	26	m	w	MO	Santa Clara	Almaden Twp	88	16
GAFT								
C A	41	m	w	PA	Tuolumne	Big Oak Flat P O	93	405
GAGAN								
Edward	30	m	w	IREL	Nevada	Nevada Twp	75	319
Frances	15	f	w	NY	Santa Clara	2-Wd San Jose	88	321
J	50	m	w	FRAN	Alameda	Oakland	68	131
John	27	m	w	MD	Contra Costa	Martinez P O	71	416
Julia	21	f	w	NY	San Francisco	5-Wd San Francisco	81	10
Luke	17	m	w	NY	San Francisco	11-Wd San Francisc	84	553
Thomas	36	m	w	IREL	San Francisco	11-Wd San Francisc	84	439
Wm	37	m	w	IREL	Alameda	Oakland	68	191
Wm	33	m	w	IREL	San Francisco	1-Wd San Francisco	79	66
GAGE								
A S	50	m	w	OH	Tuolumne	Chinese Camp P O	93	389
Aaron	44	m	w	MA	San Francisco	San Francisco P O	80	351
Albert	38	m	w	NY	Sacramento	3-Wd Sacramento	77	303
Alexander	52	m	w	ME	Placer	Newcastle Twp	76	477
Anna T	74	f	w	NH	San Francisco	6-Wd San Francisco	81	131
C	13	f	w	CA	Alameda	Oakland	68	259
Chas C	48	m	w	MA	San Francisco	8-Wd San Francisco	82	370
Daniel W	39	m	w	NY	Los Angeles	Los Angeles	73	571
David	39	m	w	NH	Butte	Oregon Twp	70	126
Delos	35	m	w	NY	Sacramento	San Joaquin Twp	77	399
Edgar	11	m	w	CA	San Francisco	San Francisco P O	85	828
Edward	16	m	w	CA	Sonoma	Petaluma Twp	91	336
Ellen	40	f	w	ENGL	Sacramento	4-Wd Sacramento	77	339
Ferdinand	31	m	w	HAMB	San Francisco	6-Wd San Francisco	81	91
Frank P	24	m	w	MA	Shasta	Shasta P O	89	452
George	21	m	w	NY	San Francisco	5-Wd San Francisco	81	7
H K	36	m	w	MA	Nevada	Meadow Lake Twp	75	262
Henry	23	m	w	MA	Sutter	Yuba Twp	92	146
Isabella	14	f	w	CA	Stanislaus	Empire Twp	92	48
J C	41	m	w	NY	San Joaquin	3-Wd Stockton	86	235
Jannette	34	f	w	OH	Sacramento	4-Wd Sacramento	77	319
John	56	m	w	NY	San Francisco	8-Wd San Francisco	82	430
John D	44	m	w	NH	Colusa	Colusa	71	300
John F	60	m	w	NH	Shasta	Shasta P O	89	454
Julia	56	f	w	NY	Shasta	Horsetown P O	89	501
Nancy	34	f	w	NY	San Francisco	7-Wd San Francisco	81	245
Sybol A	28	f	w	NH	Butte	Oregon Twp	70	124
T C	22	m	w	MA	Solano	Vallejo	90	210
T W	34	m	w	NY	San Francisco	8-Wd San Francisco	82	371
Waltern	24	m	w	NY	Santa Clara	Alviso Twp	88	23
GAGEN								
Bridget	37	f	w	IREL	San Francisco	8-Wd San Francisco	82	305
Jane	40	f	w	IREL	San Francisco	San Francisco P O	83	140
GAGER								
C	53	m	w	CT	Sierra	Downieville Twp	89	518
George	40	m	w	GERM	Santa Clara	San Jose Twp	88	196
George G	44	m	w	CT	Sonoma	Bodega Twp	91	258
James	58	m	w	NY	San Francisco	11-Wd San Francisc	84	581
Mary	42	f	w	IREL	San Francisco	5-Wd San Francisco	81	7
Rosy	40	f	w	IREL	San Francisco	5-Wd San Francisco	81	7
GAGIN								
James	24	m	w	IREL	San Francisco	11-Wd San Francisc	84	659
GAGIRE								
Joseph	48	m	w	SARD	Tuolumne	Columbia P O	93	360
GAGIS								
Elizabeth	35	f	w	IREL	Alameda	Oakland	68	167
GAGLE								
J	65	m	w	PA	Sierra	Sierra Twp	89	569
GAGLIARDO								
Andrew	36	m	w	ITAL	Mariposa	Mariposa P O	74	101
Anton	40	m	w	GERM	Tuolumne	Chinese Camp P O	93	386
Anton	20	m	w	ITAL	Tuolumne	Columbia P O	93	342
Antonio	27	m	w	ITAL	Calaveras	Copperopolis P O	70	248
Bartholomew	30	m	w	ITAL	San Francisco	2-Wd San Francisco	79	179
Bartolomy	34	m	w	ITAL	San Francisco	11-Wd San Francisc	84	591
Francis	45	m	w	ITAL	San Francisco	2-Wd San Francisco	79	210
Giuseppe	33	m	w	ITAL	Mariposa	Mariposa P O	74	100
GAGNER								
A	35	m	w	CANA	Sacramento	4-Wd Sacramento	77	326
GAGNON								
Michael	43	m	w	CANA	Santa Cruz	Pajaro Twp	89	345
GAGNOR								
P W	36	m	w	IREL	Nevada	Bridgeport Twp	75	100
GAGUN								
M	17	m	w	CA	Alameda	Oakland	68	257
GAGUS								
Manuel	32	m	w	SPAI	Tuolumne	Sonora P O	93	329
GAH								
Ah	42	m	c	CHIN	Shasta	French Gulch P O	89	470
Ah	40	m	c	CHIN	Plumas	Mineral Twp	77	23
GAHAGAN								
Thomas	38	m	w	IREL	Sonoma	Petaluma Twp	91	331
GAHAGEN								
Peter	55	m	w	IREL	Solano	Silveyville Twp	90	75
GAHAN								
Eliza	57	f	w	IREL	San Francisco	San Francisco P O	83	351
John	40	m	w	IREL	San Francisco	San Francisco P O	83	29
John	40	m	w	IREL	San Joaquin	2-Wd Stockton	86	182
Mary	28	f	w	IREL	Sonoma	Petaluma Twp	91	313
GAHARDT								
Peter	26	m	w	PRUS	Santa Clara	1-Wd San Jose	88	258
GAHART								
Margaret	26	f	w	IOFW	Sonoma	Petaluma Twp	91	314
GAHEGAN								
Thomas	27	m	w	IREL	Marin	San Rafael Twp	74	31
GAHEGEN								
Michael	39	m	w	IREL	San Francisco	San Francisco P O	80	378
GAHER								
A J	32	m	w	MO	San Joaquin	Douglas Twp	86	46
GAHL								
Ah	20	m	c	CHIN	Santa Cruz	Santa Cruz Twp	89	388
GAHN								
John	40	m	w	FRAN	San Joaquin	Oneal Twp	86	118
John	32	m	w	IA	San Joaquin	Liberty Twp	86	84
William	25	m	w	IREL	Stanislaus	San Joaquin Twp	92	82
GAHON								
Mary	15	f	w	CA	Alameda	Oakland	68	242
GAHRET								
Charles	29	m	w	SWIT	San Francisco	6-Wd San Francisco	81	90
GAI								
Ah	19	m	c	CHIN	Santa Clara	Gilroy Twp	88	83
GAIERBACK								
George	36	m	w	PRUS	Amador	Volcano P O	69	380
GAIFERATO								
Antonio	29	m	w	ITAL	San Francisco	11-Wd San Francisc	84	709
GAIFFY								
Ezekiel	38	m	w	GA	San Luis Obispo	Salinas Twp	87	293
GAIGE								
Patrick	24	m	w	IREL	Inyo	Independence Twp	73	328
GAILER								
John	30	m	w	PORT	Stanislaus	San Joaquin Twp	92	81
Wm	39	m	w	NY	Sacramento	Lee Twp	77	158
GAILHARD								
Chas	40	m	w	FRAN	San Francisco	8-Wd San Francisco	82	373
GAILLARD								
I C	41	m	w	SC	Monterey	San Juan Twp	74	415
Jean	22	m	w	BELG	San Francisco	1-Wd San Francisco	79	50
Joseph	32	m	w	BELG	San Francisco	San Francisco P O	83	334
GAILLARDI								
Chas	46	m	w	ITAL	San Francisco	11-Wd San Francisc	84	660
GAILY								
John	30	m	w	IREL	San Francisco	11-Wd San Francisc	84	694
GAIN								
Ah	31	m	c	CHIN	Merced	Snelling P O	74	255
Ah	19	m	c	CHIN	Mendocino	Point Arena Twp	74	208
Lo	37	m	c	CHIN	San Joaquin	Liberty Twp	86	97
GAINERD								
Mary	19	f	w	MA	San Francisco	8-Wd San Francisco	82	441
GAINES								
Bud	18	m	w	CA	Los Angeles	Los Angeles Twp	73	469
Crocket	37	m	w	TN	Sonoma	Russian Rvr	91	368
Effi	8	f	w	OH	Yuba	East Bear Rvr Twp	93	542
George	19	m	w	NY	Nevada	Bloomfield Twp	75	96
James H	21	m	w	IN	Solano	Rio Vista Twp	90	61
John	55	m	w	VA	Placer	Auburn P O	76	378
John W	44	m	w	ENGL	El Dorado	Salmon Falls Twp	72	130
Michael	45	m	w	IREL	Santa Clara	Redwood Twp	88	128

© 2001 by Heritage Quest. All rights reserved.

Name	Age	S	R	B-PL	County	Locale	Roll	Pg
						Series M593		
Michael	26	m	w	IREL	San Francisco	San Francisco P O	80	369
R M	45	m	m	MD	Nevada	Meadow Lake Twp	75	249
Richd	43	m	w	VA	Sonoma	Santa Rosa	91	419
Robert	57	m	w	PA	Los Angeles	Los Angeles Twp	73	492
Samuel	18	m	w	MS	Los Angeles	San Gabriel Twp	73	595
Thomas	40	m	b	NY	Napa	Napa	75	56
William	40	m	m	MD	San Francisco	6-Wd San Francisco	81	125
William S	46	m	w	KY	Santa Clara	Milpitas Twp	88	115
Wm H	36	m	w	NY	Sierra	Gibson Twp	89	540
GAINEY								
Elizabeth	42	f	w	IREL	San Francisco	San Francisco P O	83	174
GAINIE								
Amelia	21	f	w	NY	San Francisco	San Francisco P O	80	392
GAINO								
Thos	33	m	w	CANA	Santa Clara	Gilroy Twp	88	98
GAINOR								
Wm	30	m	w	IREL	Tuolumne	Columbia P O	93	347
GAIRNAUD								
Louis	36	m	w	FRAN	Santa Clara	Santa Clara Twp	88	148
GAIRR								
M F	62	m	w	VA	Sutter	Sutter Twp	92	126
GAIS								
Manuella	55	f	w	CA	Marin	San Rafael	74	48
GAISEAU								
Frank	55	m	w	FRAN	Sacramento	Granite Twp	77	145
GAJAOLO								
Jesus	26	m	w	MEXI	Los Angeles	Los Angeles	73	560
GAJAR								
Annetta	60	f	w	BRUN	San Francisco	San Francisco P O	83	342
GAJIOLA								
Amelia	14	f	w	CA	San Luis Obispo	San Luis Obispo Tw	87	299
Guadelupe	36	m	w	CA	San Luis Obispo	Santa Rosa Twp	87	328
Jose	35	m	w	CA	San Luis Obispo	Salinas Twp	87	295
Peter	18	m	w	CA	San Luis Obispo	Santa Rosa Twp	87	330
Philipe	39	m	w	CA	San Luis Obispo	San Luis Obispo Tw	87	309
Valentine	45	m	w	CA	San Luis Obispo	San Luis Obispo Tw	87	306
GALA								
Julia A	30	f	w	MD	San Francisco	2-Wd San Francisco	79	188
GALAGHER								
Daniel	75	m	w	IREL	Sacramento	2-Wd Sacramento	77	212
Daniel	27	m	w	IREL	Alameda	Washington Twp	68	284
Hugh	48	m	w	IREL	Calaveras	San Andreas P O	70	217
GALAIT								
Edward	41	m	w	FRAN	Santa Clara	2-Wd San Jose	88	311
GALAND								
Geo	27	m	w	OH	San Francisco	11-Wd San Francisc	84	686
GALANY								
S F	27	m	w	IN	San Joaquin	2-Wd Stockton	86	198
GALARDO								
Ella	16	f	w	CA	San Francisco	2-Wd San Francisco	79	229
GALASAN								
Juan	37	m	w	MEXI	Santa Clara	Burnett Twp	88	35
GALAVAN								
Michael	30	m	w	IREL	San Francisco	7-Wd San Francisco	81	266
GALAVICE								
Miguil	30	m	w	MEXI	San Luis Obispo	San Luis Obispo Tw	87	304
GALAVIDO								
Josephe	48	m	w	MEXI	Fresno	Millerton P O	72	156
GALAVIZ								
Pedro	56	m	w	MEXI	Mariposa	Mariposa P O	74	110
GALAVOTTI								
Theodore	65	m	w	ITAL	San Francisco	8-Wd San Francisco	82	463
GALAWAY								
Mary	67	f	w	NH	Sonoma	Analy Twp	91	245
Robt	42	m	w	SCOT	Humboldt	Pacific Twp	72	289
GALBERT								
Robert	22	m	w	MO	Santa Clara	Redwood Twp	88	132
GALBOA								
Pedro	30	m	w	MEXI	San Luis Obispo	Arroyo Grande Twp	87	274
GALBRAITH								
Geo	36	m	w	SCOT	Merced	Snelling P O	74	263
James	54	m	w	KY	Santa Clara	1-Wd San Jose	88	251
John	36	m	w	IREL	San Francisco	San Francisco P O	83	14
Samuel	63	m	w	PA	Nevada	Rough & Ready Twp	75	330
Wm	30	m	w	IREL	San Francisco	San Francisco P O	83	41
GALBRATH								
Frank W	19	m	w	OH	Colusa	Stony Crk Twp	71	328
GALBREATH								
Alexander	53	m	w	KY	Yolo	Cache Crk Twp	93	427
James	37	m	w	SCOT	Butte	Hamilton Twp	70	66
James E	26	m	w	MO	Santa Clara	San Jose Twp	88	199
Milton	58	m	w	KY	Yolo	Cache Crk Twp	93	427
Robert	22	m	w	MO	Santa Clara	Redwood Twp	88	132
GALBRETH								
C H	22	m	w	PA	Sonoma	Vallejo Twp	91	454
Eline	12	f	w	CA	San Joaquin	3-Wd Stockton	86	229
GALBRIETH								
James	45	m	w	OH	Solano	Montezuma Twp	90	65
GALBRINTH								
Joe	50	m	w	OH	San Joaquin	Elkhorn Twp	86	62
GALDATIN								
A	28	m	w	BADE	Alameda	Oakland	68	192
GALDEN								
J	37	m	w	NY	San Joaquin	Elliott Twp	86	75
S A	43	m	w	BAVA	Sacramento	3-Wd Sacramento	77	279
GALDING								
George	40	m	w	ENGL	Colusa	Butte Twp	71	266

Name	Age	S	R	B-PL	County	Locale	Roll	Pg
						Series M593		
GALE								
Adelbert	21	m	w	MA	Nevada	Rough & Ready Twp	75	327
Algernon C	51	m	w	VA	Placer	Auburn P O	76	383
Andrew	25	m	w	PA	San Francisco	5-Wd San Francisco	81	28
Charles	38	m	w	ENGL	Plumas	Rich Bar Twp	77	46
Charles	34	m	w	ME	Sacramento	2-Wd Sacramento	77	210
Charles O	44	m	w	MA	Yuba	North East Twp	93	644
Dennis	40	m	w	OH	Sonoma	Petaluma Twp	91	360
Edd H	31	m	w	VT	Yuba	Slate Range Bar Tw	93	678
Edward	28	m	w	MA	San Francisco	San Francisco P O	83	223
Edward H	39	m	w	MA	Plumas	Goodwin Twp	77	2
Geo	45	m	w	PA	Solano	Vallejo	90	170
George	45	m	w	NY	Placer	Auburn P O	76	383
George	39	m	w	ENGL	El Dorado	Coloma Twp	72	11
George	27	m	b	TX	Tuolumne	Columbia P O	93	339
George	18	m	w	CA	Yolo	Cache Crk Twp	93	423
George	17	m	w	CA	Yolo	Cache Crk Twp	93	456
George W	26	m	w	CANA	San Francisco	San Francisco P O	83	360
H	31	m	w	MO	Nevada	Meadow Lake Twp	75	252
Henry	43	m	w	DENM	San Francisco	2-Wd San Francisco	79	221
James	40	m	w	MA	Alameda	Oakland	68	263
James	23	m	w	ENGL	Nevada	Grass Valley Twp	75	161
Jennetta	49	f	w	SCOT	Napa	Napa	75	56
Jno	45	m	b	MD	Sacramento	3-Wd Sacramento	77	308
John	40	m	w	VT	El Dorado	Lake Valley Twp	72	63
John	35	m	w	VT	Sierra	Downieville Twp	89	522
John	27	m	w	CANA	San Francisco	San Francisco P O	83	189
John W	52	m	w	VT	San Diego	San Diego	78	501
Joseph	33	m	b	MD	San Francisco	2-Wd San Francisco	79	154
Josiah	73	m	w	NH	Calaveras	San Andreas P O	70	197
Lester	32	m	w	NY	Sonoma	Healdsburg & Mendo	91	284
Lorenzo	42	m	w	OH	Sonoma	Santa Rosa	91	395
Louisa Anna	64	f	w	VT	Nevada	Grass Valley Twp	75	151
Lucy	32	f	w	NY	Los Angeles	Los Angeles	73	539
Mary	45	f	w	NY	Sacramento	4-Wd Sacramento	77	358
Minnie T	14	f	w	CT	Santa Cruz	Watsonville	89	364
O	37	m	w	OH	Sonoma	Santa Rosa	91	395
O P	56	m	w	MA	Tuolumne	Columbia P O	93	354
Otis S	21	m	w	MO	Sonoma	Bodega Twp	91	254
Richard	43	m	w	NH	Sacramento	3-Wd Sacramento	77	299
Stevens	37	m	w	MA	San Diego	Temecula Dist	78	526
Thomas	28	m	w	NY	San Francisco	San Francisco P O	83	275
GALEAZZI								
Antonio	34	m	w	IREL	San Francisco	11-Wd San Francisc	84	594
GALEDEBT								
James	40	m	w	NY	San Francisco	San Francisco P O	83	79
GALEGA								
Dotta	36	m	w	SWIT	San Francisco	San Francisco P O	80	477
GALEGER								
Amstace	47	m	w	MEXI	Amador	Ione City P O	69	351
GALEHOUSE								
Scott	19	m	w	OH	Sutter	Yuba Twp	92	149
GALEN								
Mary	35	f	w	IREL	San Francisco	San Francisco P O	83	111
GALENDA								
Augustine	40	m	w	CA	Contra Costa	Martinez P O	71	451
GALENDO								
Aralada	7	m	w	CA	Napa	Napa	75	55
GALENO								
Jack	36	m	w	ITAL	Sonoma	Petaluma Twp	91	327
GALEPPE								
William	32	m	w	SWIT	San Mateo	Pescadero P O	87	413
GALERO								
Bernardo	40	m	w	ITAL	Monterey	San Juan Twp	74	402
GALERON								
Hyppolite	31	m	w	FRAN	Calaveras	San Andreas P O	70	176
GALES								
J H	29	m	w	IREL	San Joaquin	2-Wd Stockton	86	186
GALESATE								
W	17	m	w	CA	Alameda	Oakland	68	229
GALEWSKY								
D	34	m	w	PRUS	Napa	Napa	75	3
Rebecca	29	f	w	POLA	Napa	Napa	75	4
GALEY								
Ellen	60	f	w	IREL	Alameda	Oakland	68	204
GALGANI								
Louis	44	m	w	ITAL	Tuolumne	Columbia P O	93	362
GALGIANI								
T	47	m	w	ITAL	San Joaquin	1-Wd Stockton	86	154
GALGONA								
M	53	m	w	SWIT	San Joaquin	Oneal Twp	86	110
GALGUM								
H	37	m	w	SWIT	San Joaquin	2-Wd Stockton	86	190
GALIAS								
Jean	55	m	w	FRAN	Los Angeles	El Monte Twp	73	461
V S	46	m	w	MEXI	Tuolumne	Columbia P O	93	344
GALIGAN								
A	25	m	w	IREL	Alameda	Oakland	68	257
Mary	29	f	w	IREL	Alameda	Alameda	68	2
GALIGER								
John	44	m	w	IREL	Sonoma	Petaluma Twp	91	348
GALIGHER								
Saml	35	m	w	IREL	Humboldt	Eureka Twp	72	275
GALIMBERTI								
Carlo	31	m	w	ITAL	San Francisco	11-Wd San Francisc	84	594
GALINDA								
Antonio	35	m	w	CHIL	Sacramento	2-Wd Sacramento	77	222

© 2001 by Heritage Quest. All rights reserved.

Name	Age	S	R	B-PL	County	Locale	Series M593 Roll	Pg
Banadito	24	m	w	CA	San Mateo	San Mateo P O	87	348
David	26	m	w	US	San Mateo	Half Moon Bay P O	87	389
Eurena	50	f	w	MEXI	San Francisco	San Francisco P O	80	341
Madeleine	60	f	w	CA	Santa Clara	2-Wd San Jose	88	311
Mary A	25	f	w	CA	Santa Clara	2-Wd San Jose	88	310
Marya	16	f	w	MEXI	Santa Clara	Burnett Twp	88	35
Romana	15	f	w	CA	Santa Clara	2-Wd San Jose	88	309
GALINDO								
Albert	16	m	w	CA	Santa Clara	Almaden Twp	88	14
Francisco	50	m	w	CA	Marin	San Rafael Twp	74	39
Frank	15	m	w	CA	Santa Clara	Milpitas Twp	88	112
Fransico	46	m	w	CA	Contra Costa	Martinez P O	71	440
Guadalupe	12	f	w	CA	San Francisco	2-Wd San Francisco	79	282
Jose	60	m	w	CA	Santa Clara	Santa Clara Twp	88	138
Jose	29	m	w	CA	Santa Clara	San Jose Twp	88	184
Jose	28	m	w	CA	Marin	Point Reyes Twp	74	23
Juana	65	f	w	CA	Santa Clara	1-Wd San Jose	88	262
Manuel	33	m	w	MEXI	Santa Clara	1-Wd San Jose	88	275
Maria	15	f	w	CA	Alameda	Washington Twp	68	272
Pablo	30	m	w	MEXI	Santa Clara	Almaden Twp	88	1
Raphael	38	m	w	CA	Santa Cruz	Watsonville	89	373
GALINGER								
Abram	47	m	w	BAVA	Butte	Ophir Twp	70	91
GALISPIE								
James	38	m	w	PA	Yuba	Marysville	93	611
GALIVAN								
Michael	33	m	w	IREL	Stanislaus	San Joaquin Twp	92	72
GALKEY								
Mary	65	f	w	IREL	San Francisco	7-Wd San Francisco	81	201
GALL								
? J	55	m	w	FRAN	Humboldt	Eureka Twp	72	279
A	45	m	w	SCOT	San Joaquin	2-Wd Stockton	86	158
Archi	33	m	w	PRUS	San Francisco	San Francisco P O	83	384
Clinton	42	m	w	MO	Stanislaus	North Twp	92	68
George	57	m	w	SCOT	San Joaquin	1-Wd Stockton	86	129
Julius	20	m	w	PRUS	San Francisco	San Francisco P O	83	149
Maggie	13	f	w	SCOT	San Joaquin	2-Wd Stockton	86	158
Maria	17	f	w	IREL	San Francisco	11-Wd San Francisc	84	649
William	32	m	w	OH	Sonoma	Russian Rvr	91	371
William	20	m	w	WURT	San Francisco	3-Wd San Francisco	79	315
GALLABERTO								
Frank	28	m	w	ITAL	Calaveras	San Andreas P O	70	175
GALLADO								
Jesus	40	m	w	MEXI	Calaveras	San Andreas P O	70	175
GALLAGAN								
Mary	40	f	w	IREL	Alameda	Oakland	68	153
Mathew	45	m	w	IREL	Yuba	East Bear Rvr Twp	93	539
Thos	33	m	w	IREL	Sierra	Table Rock Twp	89	573
GALLAGAR								
Peter	45	m	w	IREL	San Francisco	San Francisco P O	85	814
GALLAGER								
Frank	47	m	w	IREL	El Dorado	Coloma Twp	72	1
John	38	m	w	NJ	Siskiyou	Surprise Valley Tw	89	638
Patrick	38	m	w	IREL	Tuolumne	Sonora P O	93	331
Thomas	30	m	w	IREL	Placer	Dutch Flat P O	76	414
GALLAGHAN								
James	38	m	w	IREL	Yuba	Rose Bar Twp	93	661
John	40	m	w	IREL	Sacramento	2-Wd Sacramento	77	212
GALLAGHER								
---	50	m	w	IREL	San Joaquin	Tulare Twp	86	254
Alice	23	f	w	PRUS	San Francisco	San Francisco P O	83	405
Ann	65	f	w	IREL	San Francisco	San Francisco P O	80	419
Ann	28	f	w	IREL	San Francisco	2-Wd San Francisco	79	149
Anne	35	f	w	IREL	San Francisco	1-Wd San Francisco	79	7
Antony	54	m	w	IREL	Santa Barbara	Santa Barbara P O	87	492
B C	55	f	w	IREL	Alameda	Murray Twp	68	99
Bennett	35	m	w	IREL	San Francisco	San Francisco P O	83	105
Bernard	39	m	w	IREL	San Francisco	San Francisco P O	83	125
Bridget	65	f	w	IREL	San Francisco	San Francisco P O	83	36
Bridget	40	m	w	IREL	Solano	Vallejo	90	141
Bridget	37	f	w	IREL	San Francisco	San Francisco P O	85	746
Charlot	36	m	w	IREL	San Francisco	San Francisco P O	83	348
Charls	18	m	w	CA	El Dorado	Kelsey Twp	72	61
Chas	33	m	w	IREL	San Francisco	11-Wd San Francisc	84	556
Christiana	39	f	w	FRAN	Nevada	Nevada Twp	75	305
Daniel	32	m	w	IREL	Stanislaus	Empire Twp	92	48
Daniel	14	m	w	CA	San Francisco	11-Wd San Francisc	84	593
Danl	60	m	w	IREL	San Francisco	11-Wd San Francisc	84	642
Danl	30	m	w	IREL	San Francisco	San Francisco P O	83	11
Dom	31	m	w	IREL	Alameda	Washington Twp	68	285
Dominic	27	m	w	IREL	Marin	San Rafael Twp	74	47
Ed	40	m	w	IREL	San Francisco	San Francisco P O	83	337
Edw	25	m	w	MA	Tehama	Merrill	92	198
Edward	38	m	w	IREL	Marin	Nicasio Twp	74	15
Elizabeth	72	f	w	IREL	San Francisco	San Francisco P O	83	337
Elizabeth	35	f	w	IREL	San Francisco	San Francisco P O	83	167
Ellen	52	f	w	IREL	San Francisco	San Francisco P O	83	381
Ellen	38	f	w	IREL	San Francisco	San Francisco P O	80	485
Ellen	26	f	w	IREL	Santa Clara	2-Wd San Jose	88	308
Ellen	25	f	w	MA	San Francisco	San Francisco P O	83	145
Ellen	12	f	w	PA	San Francisco	2-Wd San Francisco	79	263
Farrell	86	m	w	IREL	San Francisco	San Francisco P O	83	105
Farrell	80	m	w	IREL	San Joaquin	2-Wd Stockton	86	174
Francis	40	m	w	IREL	San Francisco	1-Wd San Francisco	79	59
Francis	29	m	w	IREL	San Francisco	San Francisco P O	85	871
Frank	45	m	w	MD	San Francisco	1-Wd San Francisco	79	4
Frank	35	m	w	IREL	Yuba	Linda Twp	93	554
Gertrude	16	f	w	CA	San Francisco	San Francisco P O	83	97
Grove	45	m	w	OH	Placer	Roseville P O	76	348
H A	25	m	w	NY	San Francisco	San Francisco P O	83	87
Henry	31	m	w	ME	Contra Costa	Martinez P O	71	406
Henry	30	m	w	NY	San Francisco	San Francisco P O	83	272
Hugh	60	m	w	IREL	El Dorado	Coloma Twp	72	11
Hugh	55	m	w	IREL	San Francisco	11-Wd San Francisc	84	642
Hugh	39	m	w	MA	San Francisco	11-Wd San Francisc	84	662
Hugh	39	m	w	IREL	San Francisco	7-Wd San Francisco	81	162
Hugh	36	m	w	IREL	San Francisco	7-Wd San Francisco	81	191
Hugh	35	m	w	IREL	San Mateo	San Mateo P O	87	360
Hugh	32	m	w	IREL	San Francisco	7-Wd San Francisco	81	232
Hugh	16	m	w	CA	San Francisco	11-Wd San Francisc	84	593
Humphry	9	m	w	MA	San Francisco	11-Wd San Francisc	84	507
Humphry	45	m	w	IREL	San Francisco	11-Wd San Francisc	84	507
Isaac	58	m	b	WIND	Sacramento	2-Wd Sacramento	77	233
J	48	m	w	AL	Yuba	Marysville	93	578
J B	42	m	w	OH	Yuba	Linda Twp	93	554
James	58	m	w	IREL	San Francisco	11-Wd San Francisc	84	613
James	45	m	w	IREL	San Francisco	1-Wd San Francisco	79	76
James	45	m	w	IREL	El Dorado	Cosumnes Twp	72	13
James	43	m	w	IREL	Calaveras	San Andreas P O	70	154
James	41	m	w	IREL	San Francisco	11-Wd San Francisc	84	639
James	40	m	w	IREL	Calaveras	San Andreas P O	70	188
James	37	m	w	IREL	San Francisco	5-Wd San Francisco	81	32
James	35	m	w	IREL	San Francisco	San Francisco P O	83	207
James	35	m	w	ME	Calaveras	San Andreas P O	70	175
James	33	m	w	IREL	San Francisco	11-Wd San Francisc	84	451
James	33	m	w	IREL	Yuba	Rose Bar Twp	93	663
James	30	m	w	IREL	San Francisco	8-Wd San Francisco	82	436
James	26	m	w	IREL	San Francisco	San Francisco P O	83	379
James	26	m	w	IL	Solano	Tremont Twp	90	35
James	26	m	w	IREL	Yuba	Marysville	93	611
Jas L	43	m	w	MI	San Francisco	San Francisco P O	83	33
Jas P	24	m	w	NY	San Francisco	1-Wd San Francisco	79	113
Jinnie	17	f	w	MA	San Francisco	11-Wd San Francisc	84	541
Jno A	36	m	w	IREL	San Francisco	San Francisco P O	83	333
Jno B	35	m	w	NY	San Francisco	6-Wd San Francisco	81	104
John	9	m	w	CA	San Francisco	8-Wd San Francisco	82	460
John	50	m	w	IREL	El Dorado	Georgetown Twp	72	37
John	49	m	w	IREL	Tuolumne	Chinese Camp P O	93	373
John	42	m	w	NY	San Francisco	7-Wd San Francisco	81	268
John	41	m	w	IREL	San Mateo	San Mateo P O	87	360
John	40	m	w	IREL	San Francisco	San Francisco P O	80	531
John	39	m	w	IREL	Calaveras	San Andreas P O	70	164
John	32	m	w	IREL	San Francisco	San Francisco P O	83	133
John	32	m	w	IREL	Nevada	Nevada Twp	75	296
John	32	m	w	CANA	Marin	San Rafael Twp	74	46
John	30	m	w	IREL	San Francisco	San Francisco P O	83	254
John	30	m	w	IREL	Nevada	Meadow Lake Twp	75	248
John	30	m	w	IREL	San Joaquin	Dent Twp	86	25
John	30	m	w	IREL	San Francisco	San Francisco P O	85	873
John	30	m	w	FL	San Francisco	3-Wd San Francisco	79	312
John	27	m	w	IREL	San Francisco	1-Wd San Francisco	79	81
John	21	m	w	SCOT	San Francisco	San Francisco P O	83	146
John	10	m	w	CA	San Francisco	11-Wd San Francisc	84	593
Joseph	60	m	w	PA	San Francisco	1-Wd San Francisco	79	85
Julia	25	f	w	IREL	San Francisco	8-Wd San Francisco	82	404
Kate	30	f	w	IREL	San Francisco	San Francisco P O	80	390
Lawrenc	47	m	w	IREL	San Joaquin	Castoria Twp	86	2
M	28	m	w	IREL	Amador	Jackson P O	69	329
Margaret	50	f	w	IREL	San Francisco	San Francisco P O	83	197
Maria	25	f	w	IREL	Santa Clara	2-Wd San Jose	88	300
Martin	28	m	w	IREL	Santa Clara	1-Wd San Jose	88	253
Martin	11	m	w	CA	San Francisco	San Francisco P O	83	306
Mary	7	f	w	CA	Calaveras	San Andreas P O	70	174
Mary	65	f	w	IREL	San Francisco	7-Wd San Francisco	81	229
Mary	60	f	w	IREL	San Francisco	11-Wd San Francisc	84	642
Mary	35	f	w	NY	San Francisco	2-Wd San Francisco	79	263
Mary	27	f	w	IREL	San Joaquin	2-Wd Stockton	86	206
Mary	25	f	w	IREL	San Francisco	San Francisco P O	83	113
Michael	50	m	w	IREL	San Francisco	2-Wd San Francisco	79	183
Michael	35	m	w	IREL	San Francisco	San Francisco P O	80	535
Michael	34	m	w	IREL	San Francisco	3-Wd San Francisco	79	321
Michael	31	m	w	IREL	Calaveras	San Andreas P O	70	170
Michael	31	m	w	NY	Nevada	Grass Valley Twp	75	223
Michael	30	m	w	IREL	Santa Clara	2-Wd San Jose	88	288
Michael	26	m	w	IREL	Contra Costa	Martinez P O	71	428
Micheal	45	m	w	IREL	San Francisco	11-Wd San Francisc	84	463
Michl	26	m	w	IREL	San Francisco	San Francisco P O	83	75
Michl	20	m	w	IREL	San Francisco	1-Wd San Francisco	79	100
Nancy	30	f	w	IREL	San Francisco	San Francisco P O	83	145
Noel	58	m	w	IREL	El Dorado	Kelsey Twp	72	58
Pat	30	m	w	IREL	Yuba	Rose Bar Twp	93	661
Patk	33	m	w	IREL	Solano	Vallejo	90	171
Patrick	42	m	w	IREL	Solano	Denverton Twp	90	26
Patrick	42	m	w	IREL	Sonoma	Analy Twp	91	246
Patrick	38	m	w	IREL	San Francisco	11-Wd San Francisc	84	454
Patrick	37	m	w	IREL	Monterey	San Juan Twp	74	387
Patrick	37	m	w	IREL	Yuba	Rose Bar Twp	93	661
Patrick	35	m	w	CANA	San Francisco	San Francisco P O	83	397
Patrick	30	m	w	IREL	Contra Costa	Martinez P O	71	424
Patrick	27	m	w	IREL	Marin	San Rafael Twp	74	27
Patrick	25	m	w	IREL	San Francisco	1-Wd San Francisco	79	63
Patrick	23	m	w	IREL	Contra Costa	Martinez P O	71	424
Peter	45	m	w	IREL	Nevada	Rough & Ready Twp	75	328
Peter	40	m	w	IREL	San Francisco	8-Wd San Francisco	82	460

© 2001 by Heritage Quest. All rights reserved.

Name	Age	S	R	B-PL	County	Locale	Roll	Pg
Peter	36	m	w	DE	San Francisco	San Francisco P O	83	233
Peter	31	m	w	IREL	San Francisco	1-Wd San Francisco	79	76
Peter	28	m	w	IREL	San Francisco	5-Wd San Francisco	81	32
Peter	24	m	w	IREL	San Francisco	1-Wd San Francisco	79	96
Robert T	37	m	w	IREL	Santa Cruz	Pajaro Twp	89	339
Rose I	34	f	w	NY	Solano	Benicia	90	16
Sarah	65	f	w	IREL	San Francisco	11-Wd San Francisc	84	611
Susan	82	f	w	IREL	San Francisco	San Francisco P O	83	105
Susan	21	f	w	MA	Santa Clara	2-Wd San Jose	88	304
Thomas	9	m	w	CA	Monterey	San Juan Twp	74	388
Thomas	48	m	w	IREL	Los Angeles	Wilmington Twp	73	643
Thomas	45	m	w	IREL	Los Angeles	Wilmington Twp	73	640
Thomas	45	m	w	IREL	Santa Clara	1-Wd San Jose	88	250
Thomas	42	m	w	IREL	Santa Clara	Santa Clara Twp	88	165
Thomas	41	m	w	IREL	El Dorado	Salmon Falls Twp	72	131
Thomas	35	m	w	IREL	San Francisco	San Francisco P O	80	374
Thos	84	m	w	IREL	San Francisco	San Francisco P O	83	113
Thos	35	m	w	IREL	Yuba	Rose Bar Twp	93	661
Thos Jr	42	m	w	IREL	San Francisco	San Francisco P O	83	113
Timothy	35	m	w	IREL	Contra Costa	Martinez P O	71	368
William	43	m	w	IREL	San Francisco	San Francisco P O	83	343
William	35	m	w	IREL	Calaveras	San Andreas P O	70	188
Winifred	55	f	w	IREL	San Francisco	6-Wd San Francisco	81	143
GALLAGHIER								
John	34	m	w	IREL	Sacramento	2-Wd Sacramento	77	233
GALLAGLY								
James	40	m	w	IREL	Sacramento	Cosumnes Twp	77	92
GALLAHAN								
John	29	m	w	IREL	Colusa	Monroe Twp	71	313
John A	44	m	w	OH	El Dorado	Diamond Springs Tw	72	21
Minna	40	f	w	IREL	San Francisco	8-Wd San Francisco	82	349
Nancy	63	f	w	TN	San Joaquin	1-Wd Stockton	86	137
GALLAHER								
James	40	m	w	CANA	San Francisco	San Francisco P O	83	375
John A	38	m	w	TN	Santa Cruz	Pajaro Twp	89	350
GALLAM								
Aaron	32	m	w	PRUS	Colusa	Monroe Twp	71	313
GALLAN								
James	35	m	w	ENGL	San Francisco	1-Wd San Francisco	79	126
Sophia	16	f	w	CA	San Francisco	1-Wd San Francisco	79	90
GALLAND								
Benj	40	m	w	PRUS	Tehama	Red Bluff	92	177
Bennie	30	m	w	PRUS	San Francisco	San Francisco P O	83	361
Jos B	39	m	w	PRUS	Tehama	Red Bluff	92	177
L B	40	m	w	PRUS	Tehama	Red Bluff	92	180
GALLAP								
Edmond	33	m	w	CT	Yolo	Cache Crk Twp	93	445
GALLARD								
Beny	43	m	w	POLA	San Francisco	7-Wd San Francisco	81	276
GALLARDO								
Alewin	52	m	w	CHIL	Fresno	Millerton P O	72	153
Decelano	40	m	w	CA	Los Angeles	Los Angeles Twp	73	481
Ejenio	36	m	w	MEXI	Los Angeles	Los Angeles Twp	73	465
Fernando	40	m	w	MEXI	Santa Barbara	Santa Barbara P O	87	471
Francisco	30	m	w	MEXI	Los Angeles	San Jose Twp	73	619
GALLASPIE								
J C	45	m	w	KY	Napa	Napa Twp	75	33
GALLAT								
Louis	36	m	w	FRAN	San Francisco	11-Wd San Francisc	84	449
Paul	56	m	w	FRAN	Tuolumne	Chinese Camp P O	93	365
GALLATIN								
Albert	35	m	w	NY	Sacramento	2-Wd Sacramento	77	253
Louis	24	m	w	PA	San Francisco	San Francisco P O	80	385
GALLAWAY								
Amanda	28	f	w	KY	San Francisco	San Francisco P O	80	408
James	65	m	w	DE	Yolo	Cottonwood Twp	93	460
Jas	34	m	w	IREL	San Francisco	1-Wd San Francisco	79	134
John	45	m	w	SCOT	Mendocino	Point Arena Twp	74	214
John	27	m	w	CANA	Alameda	Murray Twp	68	112
Morris	30	m	w	IREL	Alameda	Oakland	68	227
GALLDATO								
Emanuel	37	m	w	CHIL	Fresno	Millerton P O	72	159
GALLEGER								
Wm	30	m	w	IREL	San Joaquin	2-Wd Stockton	86	193
GALLEGHER								
Bridget	55	f	w	IREL	San Francisco	8-Wd San Francisco	82	303
Bridget	30	f	w	IREL	San Francisco	8-Wd San Francisco	82	336
James	25	m	w	IREL	Napa	Napa	75	42
Thomas	36	m	w	ME	Mendocino	Noyo & Big Rvr Twp	74	173
Thomas	30	m	w	IREL	San Francisco	7-Wd San Francisco	81	160
Thos J	28	m	w	MI	San Francisco	8-Wd San Francisco	82	328
Tom	55	m	w	IREL	San Francisco	8-Wd San Francisco	82	356
GALLEGO								
A	35	m	w	MEXI	Alameda	Murray Twp	68	104
Brigeta	40	f	w	CA	Santa Barbara	Las Cruces P O	87	516
Jose	27	m	w	CA	Santa Barbara	Las Cruces P O	87	516
GALLEJO								
Greyoria	50	m	w	MEXI	San Diego	San Pasqual	78	522
Romulus	28	m	w	MD	San Francisco	8-Wd San Francisco	82	494
GALLEN								
Elias	30	m	w	NC	Stanislaus	Empire Twp	92	37
James	36	m	w	ME	Monterey	Castroville Twp	74	337
GALLENGER								
O	38	m	w	IREL	Lake	Knoxville Mines	73	404
GALLERT								
E M	40	f	w	NY	Tuolumne	Sonora P O	93	309

Name	Age	S	R	B-PL	County	Locale	Roll	Pg
GALLES								
Vincent	36	m	w	ITAL	San Francisco	San Francisco P O	80	463
GALLET								
Andre	38	m	w	FRAN	San Francisco	San Francisco P O	83	135
GALLETO								
Deuderro	37	m	w	MEXI	Fresno	Millerton P O	72	159
GALLEY								
Frank	40	m	w	ITAL	Solano	Montezuma Twp	90	67
James	33	m	w	CANA	Alameda	Murray Twp	68	109
Louis	62	m	w	CANA	Tuolumne	Sonora P O	93	321
William	40	m	w	IL	Tulare	Tule Rvr Twp	92	263
GALLI								
Allen	20	m	w	SCOT	Tuolumne	Chinese Camp P O	93	385
Carlo	29	m	w	ITAL	San Francisco	1-Wd San Francisco	79	105
Felix	32	m	w	SWIT	San Francisco	2-Wd San Francisco	79	235
GALLIANO								
Antonio	56	m	w	ITAL	San Francisco	1-Wd San Francisco	79	68
John	33	m	w	ITAL	Mariposa	Mariposa P O	74	101
GALLIARD								
Peter	68	m	w	FRAN	Santa Clara	1-Wd San Jose	88	276
GALLIAVA								
Esteran	25	m	w	MEXI	Fresno	Millerton P O	72	166
GALLIBERT								
Francis	40	m	w	FRAN	Calaveras	Copperopolis P O	70	262
GALLICHAN								
Mathew	58	m	w	ENGL	San Francisco	11-Wd San Francisc	84	642
GALLIEZ								
Fernando	35	m	w	MEXI	Tulare	White Rvr Twp	92	301
GALLIFORD								
William	24	m	w	IREL	Solano	Maine Prairie Twp	90	52
GALLIGAN								
Bartholw	42	m	w	IREL	Santa Cruz	Pajaro Twp	89	348
Charles	60	m	w	IREL	Placer	Summit P O	76	496
John	20	m	w	IREL	Sutter	Yuba Twp	92	143
Mary	20	f	w	IREL	San Joaquin	Oneal Twp	86	106
GALLIGER								
Bridget	28	f	w	IREL	San Mateo	Menlo Park P O	87	377
Silas	41	m	w	ME	Butte	Kimshew Tpw	70	78
Wm	35	m	w	IREL	Butte	Chico Twp	70	56
GALLIGHER								
Andrew	39	m	w	NY	Santa Clara	Santa Clara Twp	88	164
Anna	37	f	w	IREL	Napa	Yountville Twp	75	80
Charles	24	m	w	IREL	Alpine	Monitor P O	69	313
Chas	35	m	w	IREL	San Francisco	11-Wd San Francisc	84	676
Thos	36	m	w	IREL	San Francisco	8-Wd San Francisco	82	375
GALLIGILLO								
R	30	m	w	CHIL	Napa	Napa	75	54
GALLIJOS								
Isabel	35	m	w	MEXI	San Diego	Coronado	78	465
GALLIMER								
Nicholas	35	m	w	IA	El Dorado	Placerville Twp	72	94
GALLIMORE								
Welsey	47	m	w	NC	Santa Clara	Fremont Twp	88	41
GALLINGER								
Joseph	33	m	w	BAVA	San Francisco	8-Wd San Francisco	82	479
Nancy	18	f	w	BAVA	San Francisco	San Francisco P O	85	722
GALLIO								
Christiana	28	f	w	CANA	San Francisco	7-Wd San Francisco	81	163
GALLIPPI								
Feliz	38	m	w	SWIT	Plumas	Quartz Twp	77	38
GALLIRA								
Andrew	31	m	w	ITAL	Amador	Volcano P O	69	372
Joseph	19	m	w	ITAL	Amador	Volcano P O	69	377
GALLISON								
Winslow	44	m	w	ME	Mariposa	Mariposa P O	74	117
GALLIVAN								
Cornelius	36	m	w	IREL	San Francisco	San Francisco P O	83	180
Mary	16	f	w	DC	San Mateo	Half Moon Bay P O	87	394
GALLMAN								
Trustin	66	m	w	CANA	San Francisco	1-Wd San Francisco	79	32
GALLO								
Nestor	40	m	w	CHIL	Calaveras	San Andreas P O	70	180
GALLOGH								
Peter	48	m	w	IREL	Nevada	Bridgeport Twp	75	122
GALLOGHER								
W R	35	m	w	VA	El Dorado	Coloma Twp	72	9
GALLON								
Mary	38	f	w	IREL	San Francisco	8-Wd San Francisco	82	345
GALLOP								
James	42	m	w	MA	Inyo	Independence Twp	73	324
William	20	m	w	HAMB	San Mateo	Woodside P O	87	384
GALLOSBY								
M	40	m	w	IREL	Sierra	Butte Twp	89	510
GALLOUP								
Edward	17	m	w	MA	Alameda	Brooklyn	68	33
GALLOVER								
Thos	50	m	w	ENGL	Butte	Kimshew Tpw	70	80
GALLOW								
Francis	24	m	w	CANA	Calaveras	San Andreas P O	70	204
GALLOWAY								
Andrew J	50	m	w	TN	Sonoma	Mendocino Twp	91	304
C V A	45	m	w	SCOT	Merced	Snelling P O	74	248
James	43	m	w	NY	San Francisco	San Francisco P O	80	391
James	37	m	w	PA	Santa Clara	San Jose Twp	88	179
John	17	m	w	TN	Contra Costa	Martinez P O	71	452
Joseph	58	m	w	NY	San Francisco	San Francisco P O	80	362
Joseph	28	m	w	NY	Contra Costa	Martinez P O	71	398

© 2001 by Heritage Quest. All rights reserved.

Name	Age	S	R	B-PL	County	Locale	Roll	Pg
						Series M593		
Nicholas	30	m	w	ENGL	San Francisco	7-Wd San Francisco	81	257
William	52	m	w	PA	San Francisco	8-Wd San Francisco	82	392
William	14	m	w	MA	Contra Costa	Martinez P O	71	390
William H	34	m	w	MO	Placer	Newcastle Twp	76	477
GALLOWS								
Fred	40	m	w	SWEE	San Joaquin	2-Wd Stockton	86	158
GALLS								
Frank	39	m	w	ITAL	Solano	Montezuma Twp	90	67
GALLUGHER								
J	29	m	w	IREL	Napa	Napa Twp	75	75
GALLUP								
B H	30	m	w	CT	Sacramento	3-Wd Sacramento	77	314
Benj C	34	m	w	ITAL	Mendocino	Round Valley Twp	74	217
Isaac	43	m	w	NY	Stanislaus	Branch Twp	92	6
John	30	m	w	ME	San Francisco	5-Wd San Francisco	81	35
Timothy A	41	m	w	CT	Yolo	Grafton Twp	93	500
W R	42	m	w	CT	Sacramento	3-Wd Sacramento	77	292
GALLUPI								
Agnes	35	f	w	FRAN	San Francisco	6-Wd San Francisco	81	98
GALLUSIA								
David A	43	m	w	VT	Monterey	San Antonio Twp	74	315
GALLUT								
Victor	39	m	w	FRAN	Tuolumne	Sonora P O	93	309
GALLVAN								
Patrick	38	m	w	IREL	San Francisco	11-Wd San Francisc	84	541
GALLY								
Sebastian	55	m	w	FRAN	Calaveras	San Andreas P O	70	190
GALLYER								
Francisco	30	m	w	MEXI	San Diego	Coronado	78	465
GALOINI								
A P	36	m	w	SARD	Tuolumne	Big Oak Flat P O	93	395
GALON								
Martin	47	m	w	FRAN	Siskiyou	Yreka Twp	89	668
GALONEY								
Edwin	36	m	w	MI	San Luis Obispo	Arroyo Grande Twp	87	274
GALONI								
Barney	41	m	w	IREL	Tuolumne	Columbia P O	93	354
John	34	m	w	IREL	Sacramento	4-Wd Sacramento	77	369
GALOON								
Patrick	43	m	w	IREL	Siskiyou	Scott Rvr Twp	89	602
GALOUR								
John	50	m	w	IREL	Contra Costa	San Pablo Twp	71	359
GALOVAN								
Ellen	30	f	w	IREL	San Francisco	7-Wd San Francisco	81	179
GALPEN								
Wm	16	m	w	CA	San Francisco	5-Wd San Francisco	81	5
GALPIN								
Curtis	43	m	w	OH	Amador	Volcano P O	69	388
Fannie	7	f	w	CA	Sacramento	4-Wd Sacramento	77	346
GALPINE								
Lucy	15	f	w	WI	El Dorado	Cosumnes Twp	72	15
GALT								
Mary	49	f	w	FRAN	San Francisco	San Francisco P O	80	356
Thomas A	40	m	w	SC	El Dorado	Mud Springs Twp	72	80
Thos L	42	m	w	NY	Sonoma	Santa Rosa	91	401
William	46	m	m	VA	Sacramento	2-Wd Sacramento	77	230
GALUSHA								
N H	45	m	w	VT	Sonoma	Petaluma Twp	91	365
GALVA								
S	41	m	b	HI	Sutter	Butte Twp	92	97
GALVAREZ								
Lucia	18	f	w	MEXI	Los Angeles	San Gabriel Twp	73	593
GALVEZ								
Benigno	46	m	w	MEXI	Monterey	San Juan Twp	74	414
Guadolupe	10	f	w	CA	Monterey	San Juan Twp	74	407
GALVIN								
Annie	35	f	w	IREL	San Francisco	San Francisco P O	83	411
Barbara	35	f	w	IREL	San Francisco	San Francisco P O	83	197
Briget	21	f	w	IREL	San Francisco	7-Wd San Francisco	81	179
D J	47	m	w	MD	Tehama	Antelope Twp	92	153
Garrett	40	m	w	CANA	San Francisco	San Francisco P O	80	361
Garrett	40	m	w	CANA	San Francisco	San Francisco P O	83	247
Hugh	48	m	w	IREL	San Francisco	5-Wd San Francisco	81	32
James	52	m	w	IREL	Solano	Suisun Twp	90	114
James	36	m	w	IREL	San Francisco	11-Wd San Francisc	84	543
James	34	m	w	IREL	San Francisco	11-Wd San Francisc	84	610
James S	47	m	w	AUSL	Sonoma	Petaluma Twp	91	338
Jeremiah	37	m	w	IREL	San Francisco	San Francisco P O	83	180
John	40	m	w	IREL	San Francisco	7-Wd San Francisco	81	275
John	36	m	w	IREL	Sacramento	4-Wd Sacramento	77	332
John	35	m	w	NY	Stanislaus	San Joaquin Twp	92	81
John	24	m	w	IREL	Alameda	Washington Twp	68	296
John	20	m	w	IREL	San Francisco	San Francisco P O	85	753
Mary	24	f	w	ENGL	San Francisco	7-Wd San Francisco	81	185
Mich J C	29	m	w	PA	Mendocino	Navarro & Big Rvr	74	174
Michael	25	m	w	IREL	San Francisco	San Francisco P O	85	823
Morris	35	m	w	MA	San Francisco	6-Wd San Francisco	81	124
Moses	30	m	w	IL	San Joaquin	Elkhorn Twp	86	66
Nelly	26	f	w	MA	San Francisco	San Francisco P O	85	764
Patrick	25	m	w	IREL	Alameda	Washington Twp	68	296
William	52	m	w	IREL	Contra Costa	San Pablo Twp	71	360
William	41	m	w	IREL	Placer	Rocklin Twp	76	465
William	30	m	w	IREL	San Francisco	11-Wd San Francisc	84	535
GALVINS								
Francesco	52	m	w	FRAN	Butte	Ophir Twp	70	117
GALWAY								
Chas	35	m	w	IREL	Napa	Napa Twp	75	61
James	35	m	w	IREL	Santa Clara	Santa Clara Twp	88	139
Mary	47	f	b	AR	Santa Clara	Fremont Twp	88	64
GALWITH								
Gabriel	44	m	w	MD	El Dorado	Mud Springs Twp	72	75
GALYON								
Abraham J	42	m	w	TN	Tulare	Farmersville Twp	92	242
GAM								
Ah	41	m	c	CHIN	Trinity	North Fork Twp	92	221
Ah	32	m	c	CHIN	San Francisco	11-Wd San Francisc	84	522
Ah	31	m	c	CHIN	Nevada	Meadow Lake Twp	75	259
Ah	27	m	c	CHIN	Amador	Jackson P O	69	332
Ah	27	m	c	CHIN	Nevada	Nevada Twp	75	307
Ah	25	f	c	CHIN	Mariposa	Mariposa P O	74	113
Ah	25	m	c	CHIN	Nevada	Nevada Twp	75	311
Ah	21	m	c	CHIN	Nevada	Eureka Twp	75	129
Ah	20	m	c	CHIN	Placer	Alta P O	76	413
Ah	18	m	c	CHIN	Alameda	Oakland	68	198
Ah	14	m	c	CHIN	San Francisco	8-Wd San Francisco	82	350
Samuel	35	m	w	PRUS	San Francisco	San Francisco P O	83	291
GAMA								
Domineca	42	m	w	CHIL	Calaveras	San Andreas P O	70	197
GAMACHE								
Joseph	24	m	w	CANA	Amador	Jackson P O	69	326
M	44	m	w	CANA	Amador	Jackson P O	69	325
GAMAS								
Buerta	44	m	w	ITAL	San Mateo	Schoolhouse Statio	87	340
GAMBA								
Louis	42	m	w	ITAL	San Francisco	8-Wd San Francisco	82	471
GAMBACH								
Christian	50	m	w	HESS	Shasta	Millville P O	89	486
GAMBATISTA								
J	27	m	w	ITAL	San Francisco	San Francisco P O	85	865
GAMBELL								
Andrew	53	m	w	TN	San Francisco	2-Wd San Francisco	79	279
Bertha	11	f	w	CA	Santa Clara	2-Wd San Jose	88	321
Blanche	11	f	w	CA	Santa Clara	2-Wd San Jose	88	338
Samuel	26	m	w	PRUS	Placer	Lincoln P O	76	492
GAMBER								
William	43	m	w	NY	Sonoma	Petaluma Twp	91	362
GAMBERT								
Emma	8	f	w	CA	Santa Clara	2-Wd San Jose	88	338
Frank	36	m	w	HDAR	Siskiyou	Scott Valley Twp	89	618
Leonie	10	f	w	CA	Santa Clara	2-Wd San Jose	88	338
GAMBETA								
Josefa	48	f	w	CHIL	Placer	Newcastle Twp	76	473
GAMBETT								
Christopher	25	m	w	PRUS	Placer	Gold Run Twp	76	394
GAMBETTA								
J A	25	m	w	ITAL	San Joaquin	3-Wd Stockton	86	232
John	24	m	w	ITAL	San Joaquin	1-Wd Stockton	86	139
GAMBETTI								
Ed	47	m	w	ITAL	San Joaquin	1-Wd Stockton	86	155
GAMBITZ								
Chas	24	m	w	PRUS	San Francisco	1-Wd San Francisco	79	97
K	40	m	w	PRUS	San Francisco	San Francisco P O	83	324
GAMBLE								
Abram	44	m	w	OH	Solano	Green Valley Twp	90	41
Alexr	46	m	w	ME	San Francisco	San Francisco P O	83	110
Andrew	47	m	w	PA	Solano	Green Valley Twp	90	41
Andrew J	33	m	w	IL	El Dorado	Placerville Twp	72	105
George	66	m	w	IREL	Solano	Vacaville Twp	90	134
George	16	m	w	IREL	San Francisco	8-Wd San Francisco	82	359
Henriette	21	f	w	SCOT	San Joaquin	1-Wd Stockton	86	121
Isaac	39	m	w	OH	Santa Barbara	Santa Maria P O	87	511
Isaac K	33	m	w	ME	Nevada	Nevada Twp	75	303
J C	38	m	w	PA	Santa Clara	Gilroy Twp	88	75
J L	40	m	w	NY	Solano	Vallejo	90	159
James	45	m	w	IL	Yolo	Cache Crk Twp	93	447
John	35	m	w	ENGL	San Francisco	5-Wd San Francisco	81	10
John	29	m	w	IREL	San Francisco	11-Wd San Francisc	84	648
John F	23	m	w	AL	Yolo	Cottonwood Twp	93	462
Joseph	30	m	w	KY	Santa Clara	San Jose Twp	88	207
Micheal	42	m	w	IREL	San Francisco	8-Wd San Francisco	82	356
Rees	30	m	w	AR	Kern	Bakersfield P O	73	358
Richard	40	m	w	AL	Siskiyou	Scott Valley Twp	89	620
Robert	69	m	w	PA	Solano	Green Valley Twp	90	41
Robert	40	m	w	CANA	Solano	Rio Vista Twp	90	63
Robert	28	m	w	PA	San Francisco	San Francisco P O	80	531
Samuel	24	m	w	US	Sacramento	Lee Twp	77	160
W P	27	m	w	CANA	Sonoma	Santa Rosa	91	395
William	42	m	w	NY	Calaveras	San Andreas P O	70	211
William H	28	m	w	ENGL	San Francisco	3-Wd San Francisco	79	328
GAMBLETON								
James	31	m	w	MD	Contra Costa	Martinez P O	71	417
GAMBLIN								
Josiah	43	m	w	GA	El Dorado	Cosumnes Twp	72	15
Wm Y	35	m	w	KY	Plumas	Indian Twp	77	12
GAMBLING								
J	34	m	w	ENGL	San Joaquin	Tulare Twp	86	252
GAMBOA								
Rey	17	m	w	MEXI	Santa Clara	San Jose Twp	88	222
GAMBONI								
Battiste	28	m	w	SWIT	Marin	Bolinas Twp	74	1
Frank N	33	m	w	NY	Butte	Ophir Twp	70	93
Joseph	50	m	w	SWIT	El Dorado	Placerville	72	108
Natal	25	m	w	SWIT	San Francisco	6-Wd San Francisco	81	129

© 2001 by Heritage Quest. All rights reserved.

California 1870 Census

Name	Age	S	R	B-PL	County	Locale	Series M593 Roll	Pg
GAMBONINI								
Battiste	23	m	w	SWIT	Marin	Nicasio Twp	74	18
GAMBREL								
S W	39	m	w	VA	Mendocino	Round Valley Twp	74	218
GAMBRETTI								
Jacomo	23	m	w	SWIT	Marin	Bolinas Twp	74	1
GAMBS								
Ferdinand	30	m	w	GERM	San Francisco	11-Wd San Francisc	84	542
John	42	m	w	HDAR	Contra Costa	Martinez P O	71	437
GAMBURG								
Henry	40	m	w	HAMB	Alameda	Eden Twp	68	86
GAMCE								
Leonard	45	m	w	CANA	San Francisco	8-Wd San Francisco	82	456
GAME								
Ah	24	m	c	CHIN	Plumas	Plumas Twp	77	30
GAMER								
J	50	m	w	KY	San Joaquin	Liberty Twp	86	90
J W	58	m	w	KY	Tuolumne	Chinese Camp P O	93	379
Saul	36	m	w	OH	San Joaquin	3-Wd Stockton	86	247
GAMERDON								
John	50	m	w	ENGL	San Francisco	11-Wd San Francisc	84	618
GAMES								
E	35	m	w	ITAL	Sierra	Lincoln Twp	89	551
GAMETT								
Eliza	67	f	w	VA	Solano	Vacaville Twp	90	125
GAMEY								
Charles	37	m	w	MA	San Francisco	6-Wd San Francisco	81	104
GAMING								
Jacques	65	m	w	FRAN	San Francisco	San Francisco P O	80	334
James	25	m	w	IREL	San Francisco	1-Wd San Francisco	79	24
GAMLOE								
Pedro	40	m	w	MEXI	Plumas	Goodwin Twp	77	1
GAMMELL								
Dora	35	f	w	PRUS	San Francisco	6-Wd San Francisco	81	103
GAMMON								
Harvey	25	m	w	MI	Humboldt	Pacific Twp	72	294
Jane	21	f	w	IREL	San Francisco	San Francisco P O	83	211
Mary	16	f	w	CA	Santa Barbara	Santa Barbara P O	87	460
GAMMONS								
George B	43	m	w	MA	San Francisco	6-Wd San Francisco	81	95
GAMON								
Drusilla	39	f	w	MI	Sacramento	Franklin Twp	77	113
Lawrence	25	m	w	IREL	Solano	Vallejo	90	213
GAMTILY								
Alphonso	33	m	w	FRAN	San Francisco	2-Wd San Francisco	79	162
GAMUS								
Philip	38	m	w	MEXI	Sierra	Table Rock Twp	89	579
GAN								
---	24	m	c	CHIN	Siskiyou	Cottonwood Twp	89	592
---	15	m	c	CHIN	Siskiyou	Yreka Twp	89	668
Ah	46	m	c	CHIN	Sacramento	Georgianna Twp	77	131
Ah	40	m	c	CHIN	Stanislaus	Emory Twp	92	17
Ah	38	m	c	CHIN	Mariposa	Mariposa P O	74	98
Ah	35	m	c	CHIN	Butte	Kimshew Tpw	70	85
Ah	30	m	c	CHIN	Shasta	French Gulch P O	89	467
Ah	30	m	c	CHIN	Sacramento	Franklin Twp	77	112
Ah	30	m	c	CHIN	Placer	Dutch Flat P O	76	407
Ah	28	m	c	CHIN	Stanislaus	Empire Twp	92	59
Ah	28	m	c	CHIN	Sacramento	Georgianna Twp	77	132
Ah	25	m	c	CHIN	Sacramento	Georgianna Twp	77	122
Ah	24	m	c	CHIN	Sierra	Eureka Twp	89	525
Ah	24	m	c	CHIN	Trinity	Junction City Pct	92	209
Ah	23	m	c	CHIN	Plumas	Washington Twp	77	58
Ah	22	m	c	CHIN	Sonoma	Sonoma Twp	91	447
Ah	21	m	c	CHIN	Santa Cruz	Santa Cruz Twp	89	388
Ah	21	m	c	CHIN	Santa Cruz	Santa Cruz	89	434
Ah	20	m	c	CHIN	Placer	Dutch Flat P O	76	415
Ah	17	m	c	CHIN	Santa Barbara	Santa Barbara P O	87	500
Ah	12	m	c	CHIN	San Francisco	8-Wd San Francisco	82	293
Gee	22	m	c	CHIN	Yuba	Marysville	93	629
He	23	m	c	CHIN	San Francisco	6-Wd San Francisco	81	52
How	23	m	c	CHIN	Yuba	Marysville	93	628
Jim	18	m	c	CHIN	Monterey	San Juan Twp	74	394
Ka	38	m	c	CHIN	Tuolumne	Big Oak Flat P O	93	398
Long	33	m	c	CHIN	San Joaquin	1-Wd Stockton	86	151
Matias	12	m	i	CA	Santa Barbara	Santa Barbara P O	87	500
Pen	53	m	c	CHIN	Mariposa	Mariposa P O	74	128
Pen	35	m	c	CHIN	Calaveras	San Andreas P O	70	177
Pew	52	m	c	CHIN	Calaveras	San Andreas P O	70	155
Quee	30	f	c	CHIN	Shasta	American Ranch P O	89	499
Sing	26	m	c	CHIN	Solano	Suisun Twp	90	106
Sun Lung	60	m	c	CHIN	Siskiyou	Yreka	89	650
Yee	30	m	c	CHIN	Yuba	Marysville	93	629
Youn	36	m	c	CHIN	Fresno	Millerton P O	72	202
GANAHL								
Frank	34	m	w	GA	Los Angeles	Los Angeles	73	546
GANANRING								
J O	28	m	w	MI	Humboldt	Arcata Twp	72	228
GANATY								
James	45	m	w	IREL	Sacramento	4-Wd Sacramento	77	369
GANAUGH								
G	28	m	w	IL	Yuba	East Bear Rvr Twp	93	539
GANAZLE								
Jacob	28	m	w	MD	San Francisco	San Francisco P O	83	296
GANBERDISA								
Joseph	20	m	w	SWIT	Monterey	Alisal Twp	74	292
GANBET								
Viola	43	f	w	FRAN	San Francisco	6-Wd San Francisco	81	70
GANCEY								
Joseph	42	m	w	TN	San Diego	Warners Rancho Dis	78	528
GANDARA								
Pedro	39	m	w	MEXI	Santa Clara	2-Wd San Jose	88	305
Thomas	31	m	w	MEXI	Santa Clara	2-Wd San Jose	88	334
GANDEESS								
Frank	45	m	w	FRAN	San Francisco	7-Wd San Francisco	81	200
GANDELL								
I M	34	m	w	ME	San Joaquin	2-Wd Stockton	86	191
GANDERSON								
Andrew	65	m	w	LA	Sacramento	American Twp	77	65
GANDO								
E A	16	m	w	CA	Alameda	Oakland	68	159
GANDOLPHO								
John	33	m	w	ITAL	Amador	Volcano P O	69	376
GANDON								
Alfred	42	m	w	FRAN	Del Norte	Mountain Twp	71	474
GANDRY								
Joseph	37	m	w	ENGL	Yuba	Long Bar Twp	93	562
GANDS								
Chas	33	m	w	PRUS	San Francisco	11-Wd San Francisc	84	693
GANDUFF								
A H	36	m	w	PRUS	Alameda	Alameda	68	9
GANDY								
Ed	36	m	w	KY	San Joaquin	Elkhorn Twp	86	62
Horace	12	m	w	ENGL	San Francisco	1-Wd San Francisco	79	11
Isaac	33	m	w	ENGL	Alpine	Woodfords P O	69	315
Job	47	m	w	KY	Yolo	Cache Crk Twp	93	438
Job L	47	m	w	KY	Yolo	Cache Crk Twp	93	454
GANE								
Geo W	43	m	w	MO	Nevada	Bridgeport Twp	75	112
GANELLI								
Jacob	37	m	w	ITAL	Calaveras	Copperopolis P O	70	247
GANER								
James Wm	36	m	w	IREL	Plumas	Quartz Twp	77	34
GANERO								
Antonio	40	m	w	AUST	Tuolumne	Sonora P O	93	329
GANES								
Mary	23	f	w	MO	Los Angeles	Los Angeles	73	571
GANESLEY								
Seth	38	m	w	ENGL	Yolo	Washington Twp	93	528
GANET								
Calvin	53	m	w	VT	Santa Cruz	Santa Cruz Twp	89	381
GANETT								
Mary	11	f	w	CA	San Francisco	San Francisco P O	85	827
Melissa	55	f	w	TN	Los Angeles	Wilmington Twp	73	636
Robert O	45	m	w	KY	Los Angeles	Los Nietos Twp	73	585
Samuel	13	m	w	CA	San Francisco	San Francisco P O	85	827
GANETTY								
John	38	m	w	FRAN	San Francisco	San Francisco P O	85	822
GANEY								
Catherine	37	f	w	IREL	San Francisco	8-Wd San Francisco	82	391
Patrick	30	m	w	IREL	San Mateo	San Mateo P O	87	354
Peter	70	m	w	IREL	San Francisco	8-Wd San Francisco	82	433
GANG								
---	63	m	c	CHIN	Shasta	American Ranch P O	89	496
Ah	40	m	c	CHIN	Santa Clara	Santa Clara Twp	88	166
Ah	40	m	c	CHIN	San Joaquin	1-Wd Stockton	86	145
Ah	40	m	c	CHIN	Tuolumne	Big Oak Flat P O	93	394
Ah	39	m	c	CHIN	San Francisco	San Francisco P O	80	494
Ah	35	m	c	CHIN	Shasta	French Gulch P O	89	466
Ah	34	m	c	CHIN	San Francisco	San Francisco P O	80	440
Ah	33	m	c	CHIN	Shasta	French Gulch P O	89	469
Ah	29	m	c	CHIN	Butte	Bidwell Twp	70	5
Ah	26	m	c	CHIN	Placer	Alta P O	76	413
Ah	26	m	c	CHIN	San Francisco	San Francisco P O	80	453
Ah	22	m	c	CHIN	San Francisco	San Francisco P O	83	131
Ah	20	m	c	CHIN	Santa Clara	Gilroy Twp	88	75
Benjamin	25	m	w	OH	Alameda	Brooklyn	68	32
Ho	50	m	c	CHIN	Yuba	Bullards Bar P O	93	552
Jim	19	m	c	CHIN	San Bernardino	San Bernardino Twp	78	433
Quon	24	m	c	CHIN	Shasta	French Gulch P O	89	464
Sophia	23	f	w	BADE	San Francisco	2-Wd San Francisco	79	241
Whoa	45	m	c	CHIN	San Francisco	11-Wd San Francisc	84	631
Woo	41	m	c	CHIN	Tuolumne	Columbia P O	93	361
GANGAS								
Jove	40	m	w	CHIL	Contra Costa	Martinez P O	71	367
GANGLOFF								
Joseph	46	m	w	FRAN	San Francisco	San Francisco P O	83	319
Theresa	48	f	w	SAXO	San Francisco	8-Wd San Francisco	82	399
GANGOS								
John	51	m	w	FRAN	Santa Clara	1-Wd San Jose	88	256
GANIM								
Louis	37	m	w	ITAL	Alameda	Oakland	68	144
GANIN								
Mary	24	f	w	NY	San Francisco	San Francisco P O	83	51
GANION								
Louis	48	m	w	FRAN	San Francisco	San Francisco P O	80	350
GANKUS								
Justin	31	m	w	FRAN	San Francisco	6-Wd San Francisco	81	86
GANL								
Ah	16	m	c	CHIN	San Francisco	11-Wd San Francisc	84	427
GANLAY								
Mary	19	f	w	IREL	Mendocino	Point Arena Twp	74	206

© 2001 by Heritage Quest. All rights reserved.

Name	Age	S	R	B-PL	County	Locale	Series M593 Roll	Pg
GANLEE								
James	48	m	w	IREL	San Francisco	11-Wd San Francisc	84	610
GANLEY								
Edwd	36	m	w	IREL	Alameda	Oakland	68	172
John	35	m	w	IREL	San Francisco	7-Wd San Francisco	81	242
GANLY								
Robt	21	m	w	CA	Monterey	Alisal Twp	74	292
GANN								
Adam	45	m	w	TN	Calaveras	Copperopolis P O	70	262
Ah	45	m	c	CHIN	Placer	Auburn P O	76	374
Andrew	60	m	w	TN	Mariposa	Mariposa P O	74	90
Ann	39	f	w	IREL	San Joaquin	3-Wd Stockton	86	232
John	56	m	w	TN	Calaveras	Copperopolis P O	70	263
John	37	m	w	MO	San Joaquin	1-Wd Stockton	86	129
Samuel C	32	m	w	TN	Mariposa	Mariposa P O	74	91
Sarah	17	f	w	CA	Mariposa	Mariposa P O	74	91
Susan	9	f	w	CA	Klamath	Orleans Twp	73	380
Thomas	34	m	w	LA	Mariposa	Mariposa P O	74	91
Thomas	28	m	w	IREL	Solano	Tremont Twp	90	29
Wm	21	m	w	CA	Santa Clara	Gilroy Twp	88	97
Wm H	29	m	w	MO	Mariposa	Mariposa P O	74	128
GANNAN								
Geo	35	m	w	IREL	Humboldt	Arcata Twp	72	226
Mary	30	f	w	IREL	San Francisco	San Francisco P O	80	360
GANNAR								
Paul	25	m	w	PA	Contra Costa	Martinez P O	71	382
GANNDIN								
W W	30	m	w	MO	Sonoma	Santa Rosa	91	415
GANNER								
Andrew	25	m	w	MO	Sonoma	Salt Point	91	393
GANNIA								
Santos	26	m	w	CA	Santa Cruz	Watsonville	89	370
GANNON								
Abram	45	m	w	SCOT	San Francisco	San Francisco P O	80	531
Ann	56	f	w	IREL	Alameda	San Leandro	68	95
Anthony	31	m	w	IL	Shasta	Millville P O	89	488
Bridget	33	f	w	IREL	San Francisco	11-Wd San Francisc	84	570
Fredk	55	m	w	IREL	Amador	Ione City P O	69	349
Irena	18	f	w	MA	Amador	Ione City P O	69	350
James	40	m	w	NY	San Francisco	6-Wd San Francisco	81	150
James	33	m	w	NY	Sonoma	Analy Twp	91	235
James	30	m	w	IREL	Alameda	San Leandro	68	96
James	25	m	w	IREL	Yuba	Marysville	93	588
John	40	m	w	NY	Marin	San Rafael	74	56
John	36	m	w	IREL	San Francisco	San Francisco P O	83	8
John	36	m	w	IREL	Solano	Vallejo	90	215
John	31	m	w	IREL	San Francisco	11-Wd San Francisc	84	681
John	26	m	m	JAMA	Solano	Vallejo	90	198
L	35	m	w	IREL	Amador	Sutter Crk P O	69	398
Lewis	27	m	w	IREL	Solano	Vallejo	90	215
Margaret	35	f	w	IREL	San Francisco	6-Wd San Francisco	81	108
Margret	3	f	w	NY	San Francisco	11-Wd San Francisc	84	711
Martin	37	m	w	ME	San Francisco	7-Wd San Francisco	81	228
Michael	70	m	w	IREL	Alameda	San Leandro	68	96
Michael	54	m	w	IREL	Alameda	Washington Twp	68	290
Michael	35	m	w	IREL	Marin	San Rafael Twp	74	30
Peter	33	m	w	IREL	San Francisco	11-Wd San Francisc	84	681
Peter T	30	m	w	NY	San Francisco	San Francisco P O	83	201
Thomas	55	m	w	IREL	Solano	Green Valley Twp	90	38
Thomas	29	m	w	IREL	Santa Clara	2-Wd San Jose	88	281
Thos	40	m	w	IREL	Solano	Vallejo	90	163
GANNY								
George	41	m	c	CHIN	Marin	San Rafael Twp	74	41
GANON								
Edward	38	m	w	IREL	San Francisco	San Francisco P O	83	299
GANONG								
Joseph L	18	m	w	CA	Santa Clara	San Jose Twp	88	218
O T	35	m	w	NY	Sacramento	3-Wd Sacramento	77	258
Wm	46	m	w	MI	El Dorado	Coloma Twp	72	2
GANOR								
R B	82	m	w	VA	Santa Clara	Burnett Twp	88	39
Victor	37	m	w	FRAN	San Joaquin	2-Wd Stockton	86	169
GANORICH								
G	35	m	w	ITAL	Santa Clara	Burnett Twp	88	38
GANOTIA								
Dan	28	m	w	ITAL	Calaveras	San Andreas P O	70	178
GANS								
Arthur	45	m	w	PRUS	San Luis Obispo	Santa Rosa Twp	87	317
Bernhard	23	m	w	GERM	San Francisco	8-Wd San Francisco	82	373
C A	40	m	w	AUST	San Francisco	8-Wd San Francisco	82	302
Isadore	27	m	w	PRUS	San Francisco	San Francisco P O	83	273
GANSAS								
George	28	m	w	PORT	Tuolumne	Columbia P O	93	356
GANSBERGER								
John X	45	m	w	HANO	Alameda	Eden Twp	68	84
GANSBERRG								
Jno	30	m	w	PRUS	San Francisco	5-Wd San Francisco	81	20
GANSLER								
Christopher	64	m	w	HUNG	San Francisco	San Francisco P O	80	535
GANSNER								
Benjamin	37	m	w	SWIT	Plumas	Rich Bar Twp	77	45
GANSOLAS								
W H	31	m	w	CANA	Sierra	Butte Twp	89	508
GANSON								
Eliza E	30	f	w	TN	Butte	Chico Twp	70	60
H	40	m	w	SWED	San Joaquin	2-Wd Stockton	86	175

Name	Age	S	R	B-PL	County	Locale	Series M593 Roll	Pg
GANT								
Daniel B	28	m	w	KY	Colusa	Butte Twp	71	268
Gant	53	m	w	VA	Placer	Bath P O	76	458
Henry	27	m	w	MD	Los Angeles	El Monte Twp	73	460
M	77	f	w	FRAN	Alameda	Alameda	68	19
Mary	27	f	w	IREL	Tulare	Visalia Twp	92	287
Obediah	38	m	w	OH	Tulare	Visalia Twp	92	285
Peter	34	m	w	KY	San Joaquin	Dent Twp	86	23
Richard	52	m	w	PA	Colusa	Grand Island Twp	71	302
Sylvester	38	m	w	KY	Contra Costa	Martinez P O	71	407
GANTHAM								
John	25	m	w	SWED	San Francisco	1-Wd San Francisco	79	119
GANTHER								
Julia	51	f	w	WURT	Santa Clara	1-Wd San Jose	88	259
GANTLAND								
James	32	m	w	IREL	San Mateo	Schoolhouse Statio	87	342
GANTLETT								
Joseph	46	m	w	ENGL	Alameda	Alvarado	68	304
GANTLEY								
Am	40	f	w	IREL	San Francisco	7-Wd San Francisco	81	201
Margaret	13	f	w	NY	San Francisco	San Francisco P O	85	822
GANTNER								
John	46	m	w	SWIT	San Francisco	11-Wd San Francisc	84	516
Richd	35	m	w	WURT	San Francisco	1-Wd San Francisco	79	47
GANTRY								
Mary	20	f	w	IREL	San Francisco	San Francisco P O	83	343
GANY								
Hon	41	m	c	CHIN	San Joaquin	1-Wd Stockton	86	145
GANYAN								
Joseph	60	m	w	CANA	Placer	Summit P O	76	496
GANYARD								
Peter	41	m	w	NY	Humboldt	Eureka Twp	72	261
GANYOR								
B	37	m	w	IREL	Solano	Benicia	90	9
GANZERT								
Jacob	38	m	w	HDAR	San Francisco	San Francisco P O	85	757
GANZHORN								
Chris	38	m	w	WURT	San Francisco	1-Wd San Francisco	79	52
GANZIR								
Heli	32	m	w	PRUS	Plumas	Indian Twp	77	14
GAOGKEGAN								
Bernard	38	m	w	IREL	San Francisco	11-Wd San Francisc	84	701
GAOHEHEN								
John	28	m	w	IREL	Santa Cruz	Santa Cruz	89	415
GAP								
Ah	35	m	c	CHIN	Kern	Havilah P O	73	338
Ah	27	m	c	CHIN	Sacramento	Georgianna Twp	77	123
GAPEN								
John	42	m	w	PA	Solano	Suisun Twp	90	102
GAPHOFF								
Frederik	49	m	w	PRUS	San Francisco	2-Wd San Francisco	79	139
GAPP								
Ah	28	m	c	CHIN	San Francisco	11-Wd San Francisc	84	560
GAPPKE								
Henry	40	m	w	PRUS	San Francisco	2-Wd San Francisco	79	238
GAR								
Ah	55	m	c	CHIN	Butte	Kimshew Tpw	70	85
Ah	39	m	c	CHIN	Mono	Bridgeport P O	74	283
Ginn	27	m	c	CHIN	Sonoma	Salt Point	91	386
GARA								
Maria A	20	f	w	CA	San Diego	San Pasqual	78	520
Merced	24	f	w	CA	Los Angeles	Los Angeles	73	555
Pancho	38	m	w	MEXI	San Luis Obispo	San Luis Obispo Tw	87	302
GARABALDI								
A	33	m	w	ITAL	Calaveras	Copperopolis P O	70	237
Anton	40	m	w	ITAL	Amador	Jackson P O	69	335
Frank	45	m	w	ITAL	San Francisco	2-Wd San Francisco	79	161
John	47	m	w	ITAL	Tuolumne	Columbia P O	93	345
John	34	m	w	ITAL	San Francisco	2-Wd San Francisco	79	235
Josemulius	36	m	w	ITAL	San Francisco	2-Wd San Francisco	79	245
Joseph	35	m	w	ITAL	San Francisco	2-Wd San Francisco	79	157
S	32	m	w	ITAL	Calaveras	Copperopolis P O	70	237
Tomaso	45	m	w	ITAL	Calaveras	San Andreas P O	70	204
GARABEE								
Sam	30	m	w	IN	Alameda	Oakland	68	264
GARABLE								
Jos	30	m	w	PA	Tehama	Red Bluff	92	182
GARACIA								
Joaquin	70	m	w	MEXI	Los Angeles	Los Angeles	73	551
GARADI								
Joseph	22	m	w	ITAL	Tuolumne	Columbia P O	93	344
GARADY								
Mary	60	f	w	IREL	Alameda	Washington Twp	68	290
GARAER								
M	50	m	w	WIND	Alameda	Oakland	68	240
GARAFALI								
Henry	41	m	w	ITAL	Solano	Montezuma Twp	90	67
GARAGAN								
Patrick	40	m	w	IREL	San Francisco	7-Wd San Francisco	81	194
GARAGHAN								
Patrick	48	m	w	IREL	San Francisco	6-Wd San Francisco	81	143
GARAGHER								
John	40	m	w	IREL	Sacramento	2-Wd Sacramento	77	240
GARAGHTY								
John	30	m	w	ENGL	San Francisco	7-Wd San Francisco	81	167
GARAITTLE								
Lunch	21	m	w	IREL	Los Angeles	Los Angeles Twp	73	497

© 2001 by Heritage Quest. All rights reserved.

Name	Age	S	R	B-PL	County	Locale	Roll	Pg
						Series M593		
GARALANO								
Jessie	36	m	w	SWIT	Calaveras	San Andreas P O	70	198
GARALD								
Dora	28	f	w	PRUS	San Francisco	2-Wd San Francisco	79	157
GARARIA								
Francisco	32	m	w	MEXI	San Luis Obispo	Salinas Twp	87	295
GARARO								
Ignacio	46	m	w	MEXI	San Luis Obispo	San Luis Obispo Tw	87	305
Joseph	19	m	w	CA	Los Angeles	Los Angeles	73	567
GARATE								
John	51	m	w	ITAL	Calaveras	Copperopolis P O	70	240
GARAVES								
William	21	m	w	IL	Santa Clara	Santa Clara Twp	88	159
GARAVINTI								
Dominico	32	m	w	ITAL	San Francisco	1-Wd San Francisco	79	114
GARAYZAR								
Jose	14	m	w	MEXI	San Francisco	11-Wd San Francisc	84	593
GARBARDI								
Fredrick	29	m	w	NORW	Calaveras	San Andreas P O	70	205
GARBARENO								
Joseph	19	m	w	ITAL	Amador	Jackson P O	69	328
GARBER								
Charles	22	m	w	LA	Nevada	Grass Valley Twp	75	152
Christian	62	m	w	SWIT	Siskiyou	Callahan P O	89	629
Henry	45	m	w	BADE	El Dorado	Mud Springs Twp	72	89
Henry	37	m	w	MECK	Mariposa	Mariposa P O	74	120
Jacob	42	m	w	VA	Humboldt	South Fork Twp	72	300
Saml	40	m	w	OH	Yuba	Marysville	93	587
GARBETTI								
John	24	m	w	ITAL	El Dorado	Mountain Twp	72	69
GARBINE								
Antonio	36	m	w	ITAL	San Francisco	2-Wd San Francisco	79	232
GARBINI								
J S	25	m	w	ITAL	Tuolumne	Big Oak Flat P O	93	395
GARBINNER								
Rich	50	m	w	ITAL	San Mateo	Searsville P O	87	383
GARBINO								
G	33	m	w	ITAL	Amador	Ione City P O	69	371
GARBNAR								
Peanu	33	m	w	ITAL	Amador	Amador City P O	69	393
GARBOLINA								
Mattie	35	m	w	ITAL	Los Angeles	Los Angeles	73	512
GARBOTTI								
Joseph	30	m	w	ITAL	Santa Clara	San Jose Twp	88	185
Louis	28	m	w	ITAL	Santa Clara	2-Wd San Jose	88	312
GARBOU								
Hiram	57	m	w	ENGL	Butte	Ophir Twp	70	113
GARBURNES								
J A	40	m	w	ITAL	Amador	Jackson P O	69	336
GARBY								
Anles	38	m	w	HANO	Placer	Bath P O	76	430
GARCE								
Chas	36	m	w	PA	Alameda	Oakland	68	262
GARCEAU								
John	29	m	w	CANA	Marin	Novato Twp	74	9
GARCELON								
Catherine	53	f	w	ME	Alameda	Oakland	68	160
Harris	47	m	w	ME	San Francisco	11-Wd San Francisc	84	581
Harvey	42	m	w	ME	San Francisco	11-Wd San Francisc	84	441
S	63	m	w	ME	Alameda	Oakland	68	160
GARCHNIR								
Amelia	44	f	w	HANO	Yuba	Bullards Bar P O	93	550
GARCIA								
Alcario	20	m	w	MEXI	San Bernardino	San Salvador Twp	78	456
Alfred	9	m	w	CA	San Francisco	San Francisco P O	80	343
Alta G	51	f	w	CA	Santa Barbara	Santa Barbara P O	87	465
Angel	30	f	w	MEXI	Napa	Napa	75	54
Angel	23	m	w	CA	San Luis Obispo	Salinas Twp	87	295
Anita	54	f	w	MEXI	Los Angeles	Santa Ana Twp	73	616
Anselmo	52	m	w	MEXI	Los Angeles	Los Angeles	73	552
Anton	36	m	w	PORT	San Francisco	San Francisco P O	80	469
Antone	36	m	w	NCOD	Santa Cruz	Santa Cruz Twp	89	390
Antone	26	m	w	MEXI	San Luis Obispo	Morro Twp	87	285
Antonio	60	m	w	MEXI	Los Angeles	San Juan Twp	73	628
Antonio	53	m	w	MEXI	San Joaquin	Dent Twp	86	24
Antonio	40	m	w	TX	Napa	Napa Twp	75	34
Antonio	40	m	w	CA	Los Angeles	San Jose Twp	73	623
Antonio	37	m	w	CA	Santa Barbara	Santa Barbara P O	87	484
Antonio	31	m	w	CA	Marin	San Rafael Twp	74	40
Antonio	30	m	w	TX	Solano	Vallejo	90	212
Antonio	29	m	w	CA	Monterey	San Antonio Twp	74	315
Antonio	28	m	w	CA	Marin	Bolinas Twp	74	6
Antonio	26	m	w	CA	Solano	Benicia	90	19
Armada	12	f	w	CA	Los Angeles	Los Angeles Twp	73	484
Babara	60	f	w	MEXI	Los Angeles	Santa Ana Twp	73	615
Caezar	6	m	w	CA	Santa Barbara	San Buenaventura P	87	427
Camilla	20	f	w	CA	San Luis Obispo	San Luis Obispo Tw	87	303
Carlos	24	m	w	CA	Santa Barbara	Santa Barbara P O	87	466
Castaneo	55	m	w	MEXI	San Bernardino	San Bernardino Twp	78	449
Christoval	33	m	w	CA	Santa Cruz	Santa Cruz Twp	89	383
Corazno	45	m	w	FRAN	Los Angeles	Wilmington Twp	73	640
Crus	51	m	w	CHIL	Sacramento	2-Wd Sacramento	77	242
David	22	m	w	CA	San Luis Obispo	Salinas Twp	87	289
Dolores	65	m	w	MEXI	Los Angeles	Los Angeles Twp	73	489
Dolores	48	m	w	CA	Santa Barbara	Santa Barbara P O	87	462
Dolores	40	m	w	MEXI	Los Angeles	Los Angeles	73	555
Dolores	39	f	w	MEXI	San Francisco	San Francisco P O	80	430
Dolores	36	m	w	MEXI	Los Angeles	Santa Ana Twp	73	605
Dolores	35	m	w	CA	Fresno	Millerton P O	72	151
Dolores	31	m	w	MEXI	Los Angeles	Los Angeles	73	556
Domingo	46	m	w	SPAI	Los Angeles	Los Angeles	73	572
Domingo	29	m	w	MEXI	Calaveras	Copperopolis P O	70	263
Domingo	19	m	w	MEXI	Los Angeles	San Jose Twp	73	618
Dominguez	40	m	w	CA	Santa Barbara	San Buenaventura P	87	448
Emanuel	6	m	w	MA	Alameda	Washington Twp	68	298
Emanuel	30	m	w	MEXI	Fresno	Millerton P O	72	167
Emanuel	30	m	w	PORT	Alameda	Washington Twp	68	291
Emily	24	f	w	CHIL	Santa Clara	2-Wd San Jose	88	302
Esperado	25	m	w	MEXI	Los Angeles	Los Angeles	73	556
Eugenio	62	m	w	CA	Santa Barbara	Santa Barbara P O	87	460
F	37	m	w	CA	Santa Clara	Almaden Twp	88	10
Felicita	40	f	w	CA	Santa Clara	2-Wd San Jose	88	300
Femia	98	m	w	MEXI	San Diego	San Diego	78	506
Francis	40	m	w	SCOT	Siskiyou	Yreka Twp	89	668
Francis	40	m	w	CA	Los Angeles	Santa Ana Twp	73	614
Francisco	50	f	w	MEXI	Los Angeles	Los Nietos Twp	73	589
Francisco	38	m	w	SPAI	San Francisco	San Francisco P O	83	413
Francisco	35	f	w	MEXI	Los Angeles	Los Angeles	73	565
Francisco	30	m	w	MEXI	Fresno	Millerton P O	72	166
Francisco	25	m	w	MEXI	Los Angeles	San Gabriel Twp	73	593
Francisco	20	m	w	CA	Monterey	San Antonio Twp	74	315
Francisco	12	m	w	CA	Los Angeles	Wilmington Twp	73	635
Francisco	10	f	w	CA	Los Angeles	Wilmington Twp	73	636
Frank	29	m	w	PORT	Alameda	Washington Twp	68	300
Frank	25	m	i	MEXI	Merced	Snelling P O	74	259
G	28	m	w	CA	Alameda	Oakland	68	251
Gabriel	60	m	w	MEXI	San Bernardino	San Salvador Twp	78	455
Gabriel	45	m	w	MEXI	Siskiyou	Scott Valley Twp	89	612
Gaudelup	19	m	w	MEXI	San Bernardino	Belleville Twp	78	408
Genera	7	f	w	CA	Santa Clara	Fremont Twp	88	60
Hayaten	18	m	w	CA	Marin	San Rafael Twp	74	37
Ignacia	98	f	w	MEXI	San Bernardino	San Salvador Twp	78	455
Ignacio	75	f	w	MEXI	San Mateo	Half Moon Bay P O	87	393
Ignacio	43	m	w	MEXI	Los Angeles	Los Angeles	73	528
Ignacio	24	m	w	CA	Los Angeles	San Jose Twp	73	621
Incarnacion	44	f	w	CA	Santa Cruz	Soquel Twp	89	438
Inocenta	81	m	w	CA	San Luis Obispo	San Luis Obispo Tw	87	300
Jacinto	17	m	w	CA	Marin	San Antonio Twp	74	63
Jesus	40	f	w	MEXI	Los Angeles	Los Angeles Twp	73	480
Jesus	38	m	w	MEXI	Plumas	Goodwin Twp	77	1
Jesus	35	m	w	CA	Santa Clara	Fremont Twp	88	60
Jesus	33	m	w	MEXI	Los Angeles	San Gabriel Twp	73	596
Jesus	27	m	w	MEXI	Los Angeles	Los Angeles	73	503
Jesus	25	m	w	MEXI	San Diego	Julian Dist	78	474
John	50	m	w	MEXI	San Bernardino	Belleville Twp	78	408
John	37	m	w	PORT	Contra Costa	Martinez P O	71	437
John	24	m	w	PORT	San Mateo	Half Moon Bay P O	87	401
Jonaquin	30	m	w	MEXI	San Diego	Coronado	78	465
Jose	58	m	w	MEXI	Los Angeles	San Jose Twp	73	623
Jose	50	m	w	MEXI	Los Angeles	Los Angeles	73	550
Jose	46	m	w	MEXI	San Bernardino	San Bernardino Twp	78	424
Jose	44	m	w	CA	Santa Barbara	Santa Barbara P O	87	488
Jose	42	m	w	TX	Los Angeles	Los Angeles	73	510
Jose	40	m	w	MEXI	Sacramento	Lee Twp	77	160
Jose	35	m	w	MEXI	San Francisco	San Francisco P O	80	341
Jose	35	m	w	CA	Los Angeles	San Jose Twp	73	621
Jose	34	m	w	MEXI	Santa Clara	1-Wd San Jose	88	255
Jose	30	m	w	PORT	Contra Costa	Martinez P O	71	366
Jose	30	m	w	MEXI	Santa Barbara	San Buenaventura P	87	442
Jose	25	m	w	PORT	Contra Costa	Martinez P O	71	367
Jose A	40	m	w	CA	Monterey	Monterey	74	359
Jose Anto	50	m	w	MEXI	Los Angeles	San Juan Twp	73	626
Jose D	38	m	w	CA	Los Angeles	San Juan Twp	73	625
Jose J	26	m	w	MEXI	Santa Barbara	Santa Barbara P O	87	465
Jose Jesus	24	m	w	CA	Monterey	San Antonio Twp	74	315
Jose L	30	m	w	CA	Los Angeles	San Jose Twp	73	623
Jose M	40	m	w	CA	Contra Costa	Martinez P O	71	381
Jose M	26	m	w	CA	San Luis Obispo	San Luis Obispo Tw	87	303
Jose Maria	40	m	w	MEXI	Napa	Yountville Twp	75	80
Jose P	35	m	w	CA	San Bernardino	San Salvador Twp	78	457
Joseph	35	m	w	MEXI	San Bernardino	San Bernardino Twp	78	418
Joseph	26	m	w	CA	San Francisco	6-Wd San Francisco	81	45
Joseph	24	m	w	SCOT	Siskiyou	Yreka Twp	89	667
Joseph S	47	m	w	MEXI	San Bernardino	Chino Twp	78	412
Juan	61	m	w	MEXI	Monterey	San Juan Twp	74	417
Juan	48	m	w	MEXI	Los Angeles	Los Angeles Twp	73	467
Juan	38	m	w	CA	Los Angeles	San Jose Twp	73	620
Juan	35	m	w	MEXI	Los Angeles	Wilmington Twp	73	640
Juan	34	m	w	MEXI	San Francisco	San Francisco P O	80	466
Juan	34	m	w	CA	Marin	Bolinas Twp	74	2
Julien	37	m	w	NM	San Luis Obispo	Salinas Twp	87	289
Lauriano	45	m	w	CA	Los Angeles	Santa Ana Twp	73	608
Leandro	30	m	w	MEXI	Los Angeles	Los Angeles Twp	73	475
Leonardo	26	m	w	MEXI	Los Angeles	Santa Ana Twp	73	608
Leonora	5	f	w	MEXI	Solano	Green Valley Twp	90	38
Loreta	25	f	w	MEXI	Los Angeles	San Gabriel Twp	73	593
Lorreta	55	f	w	CA	Marin	Bolinas Twp	74	2
Louis	39	m	w	MEXI	Santa Clara	2-Wd San Jose	88	301
Louisa	35	f	w	CA	San Bernardino	San Salvador Twp	78	462
Lucas	38	m	w	MEXI	Santa Barbara	San Buenaventura P	87	429
Lucio	30	m	w	MEXI	Los Angeles	San Gabriel Twp	73	595
M L	24	f	w	MEXI	Napa	Napa	75	55
Madalina	30	f	w	CA	Los Angeles	Los Angeles	73	548
Magdelina	19	f	w	CA	Santa Barbara	San Buenaventura P	87	428

© 2001 by Heritage Quest. All rights reserved.

Name	Age	S	R	B-PL	County	Locale	Roll	Pg
						Series M593		
Magill	40	m	w	MEXI	San Bernardino	San Salvador Twp	78	455
Manuel	40	m	w	MEXI	Santa Barbara	Santa Barbara P O	87	492
Manuel	36	m	w	MEXI	Plumas	Mineral Twp	77	22
Manuel	30	m	w	CA	Santa Barbara	Santa Maria P O	87	512
Manuel	27	m	w	ITAL	Sacramento	1-Wd Sacramento	77	190
Manuel	27	m	w	CA	Los Angeles	San Jose Twp	73	620
Manuela	7	f	w	CA	Los Angeles	Wilmington Twp	73	639
Mara	14	f	w	CA	Los Angeles	Los Angeles	73	566
Maria J	61	f	w	MEXI	Monterey	Monterey	74	359
Maria L	14	f	w	CA	Los Angeles	San Juan Twp	73	626
Mariah	45	f	i	MEXI	San Luis Obispo	San Luis Obispo Tw	87	313
Mariana	14	m	w	CA	Santa Barbara	San Buenaventura P	87	427
Marsellus	44	m	w	MEXI	Shasta	Shasta P O	89	456
Mary	40	f	w	MEXI	San Francisco	San Francisco P O	80	428
Mattes	25	m	w	MEXI	Fresno	Millerton P O	72	154
Morene	45	m	w	MEXI	Los Angeles	Los Angeles Twp	73	480
Nicasio	20	m	w	CA	Santa Clara	1-Wd San Jose	88	261
Nicholas	29	m	w	MEXI	Santa Clara	2-Wd San Jose	88	334
Nicolasa	22	f	w	MEXI	Los Angeles	Los Angeles Twp	73	465
Nicolasa	22	f	w	MEXI	Los Angeles	Los Angeles Twp	73	491
Nievas	37	m	w	MEXI	Placer	Auburn P O	76	358
Pablo	75	m	w	NM	Santa Cruz	Pajaro Twp	89	344
Pablo	18	m	w	MEXI	Santa Barbara	Santa Barbara P O	87	501
Pasqual	35	m	w	MEXI	Fresno	Kingston P O	72	217
Pedro	53	m	w	NM	San Luis Obispo	San Luis Obispo Tw	87	303
Pedro	40	m	w	FRAN	Los Angeles	Los Nietos Twp	73	589
Pedro	30	m	w	CA	Monterey	San Benito Twp	74	378
Pelnon	43	m	w	MEXI	Monterey	San Antonio Twp	74	315
Phil	13	m	w	CA	Santa Clara	Burnett Twp	88	30
Pretoneta	14	f	w	CA	Santa Clara	2-Wd San Jose	88	315
Prosalis R	27	m	i	MEXI	Inyo	Lone Pine Twp	73	332
Prudencia	28	m	w	CA	Sacramento	2-Wd Sacramento	77	253
R	23	m	w	CA	Monterey	Monterey	74	359
Rafael	60	m	w	MEXI	San Diego	Fort Yuma Dist	78	463
Rafaul	45	m	w	MEXI	Los Angeles	San Gabriel Twp	73	593
Rafel	27	m	w	MEXI	Fresno	Millerton P O	72	167
Ramon	50	m	w	MEXI	Los Angeles	Los Angeles Twp	73	475
Refugia	26	f	m	CA	Santa Barbara	Santa Barbara P O	87	455
Salvador	19	m	w	CA	Santa Cruz	Pajaro Twp	89	362
Sanchez	34	m	w	MEXI	Calaveras	Copperopolis P O	70	263
Santiago	37	m	w	MEXI	Los Angeles	Soledad Twp	73	631
Santiago	33	m	w	CA	Santa Clara	Milpitas Twp	88	112
Santiago	25	m	w	MEXI	Los Angeles	El Monte Twp	73	449
Seraphira	18	f	w	MEXI	Santa Clara	Santa Clara Twp	88	135
Tanophanes	23	m	w	MEXI	San Diego	San Pasqual Valley	78	525
Thos	18	m	w	CA	Alameda	Oakland	68	159
Tomas	50	m	w	MEXI	Los Angeles	Los Angeles Twp	73	484
Tomasa	18	f	w	MEXI	Solano	Benicia	90	17
Trinidad	29	m	w	MEXI	Fresno	Millerton P O	72	167
Trinidad	26	m	w	CA	Monterey	San Benito Twp	74	380
Trinidad	19	f	w	CA	Santa Clara	Almaden Twp	88	18
Ujinio	22	m	w	NM	Los Angeles	Los Angeles Twp	73	496
Veviana	50	f	w	CA	Santa Clara	2-Wd San Jose	88	309
Vicente	28	m	w	CA	Santa Barbara	Santa Barbara P O	87	497
Vincente	38	m	w	MEXI	Fresno	Kings Rvr P O	72	214
Ygnacio	26	m	w	CA	Monterey	Monterey Twp	74	347
GARCIER								
Anna	36	f	w	SCOT	Alameda	Brooklyn Twp	68	47
Antone	40	m	w	SCOT	Alameda	Brooklyn Twp	68	48
Emanuel	30	m	w	PORT	Alameda	Eden Twp	68	66
Emanuel	29	m	w	CA	San Joaquin	Tulare Twp	86	259
Frances	32	m	w	PORT	Alameda	Eden Twp	68	64
Joseph	43	m	w	SCOT	Alameda	Brooklyn Twp	68	47
Manuel	34	m	w	PORT	Alameda	Eden Twp	68	67
GARCIN								
Leopold	45	m	w	NY	San Francisco	11-Wd San Francisc	84	509
GARCIO								
Francisco	40	m	w	SPAI	Santa Clara	Almaden Twp	88	1
Juan J	40	m	w	CA	Santa Cruz	Pajaro Twp	89	357
Tomas	50	m	w	CA	Los Angeles	Santa Ana Twp	73	609
GARCIS								
Manuel	55	m	w	PORT	Los Angeles	San Juan Twp	73	625
Miguel	30	m	w	MEXI	Los Angeles	Soledad Twp	73	632
GARCISSE								
Trinidad	48	f	w	MEXI	Yuba	New York Twp	93	641
GARD								
Alex	37	m	w	NH	San Joaquin	Elliott Twp	86	81
Charles W [Adopted]	7	m	w	CANA	Lake	Big Valley	73	397
David	38	m	w	OH	Lake	Big Valley	73	394
Francis	23	m	w	ENGL	Nevada	Grass Valley Twp	75	189
John	38	m	w	CANA	San Francisco	San Francisco P O	80	348
Louisa	60	f	w	FRAN	San Francisco	San Francisco P O	80	463
Richard	43	m	w	PRUS	Plumas	Goodwin Twp	77	7
Roswell D	35	m	w	IN	Santa Clara	San Jose Twp	88	196
S W	44	m	w	OH	Lake	Big Valley	73	397
GARDDUWERTT								
Staford	28	m	w	ITAL	San Francisco	11-Wd San Francisc	84	709
GARDE								
Arthur	28	m	w	FRAN	Santa Clara	1-Wd San Jose	88	267
John	40	m	w	IREL	San Francisco	11-Wd San Francisc	84	482
Q	37	m	w	ITAL	Alameda	Oakland	68	241
GARDEL								
Bartholow	30	m	w	ITAL	San Francisco	2-Wd San Francisco	79	150
GARDELA								
Julius	40	m	w	ITAL	San Mateo	Schoolhouse Statio	87	333
GARDELL								
K	32	m	w	FRAN	Alameda	Murray Twp	68	128
GARDELLA								
Charles	33	m	w	ITAL	Amador	Jackson P O	69	335
Charles	32	m	w	ITAL	Sonoma	Analy Twp	91	234
Francisco	35	m	w	ITAL	Monterey	San Juan Twp	74	416
John	28	m	w	ITAL	Sonoma	Analy Twp	91	234
Joseph	30	m	w	ITAL	Butte	Ophir Twp	70	100
Loro	29	m	w	ITAL	Sonoma	Analy Twp	91	234
Louise	33	m	w	ITAL	Sonoma	Analy Twp	91	234
Maria	50	f	w	ITAL	Monterey	San Juan Twp	74	416
GARDELLI								
Charles	50	m	w	ITAL	Tuolumne	Chinese Camp P O	93	371
George	58	m	w	ITAL	Tuolumne	Chinese Camp P O	93	371
John	26	m	w	ITAL	San Francisco	1-Wd San Francisco	79	114
GARDELLO								
Augustino	33	m	w	ITAL	El Dorado	Diamond Springs Tw	72	29
Frank	23	m	w	ITAL	El Dorado	Diamond Springs Tw	72	29
John	23	m	w	ITAL	El Dorado	Diamond Springs Tw	72	29
Lawrence	26	m	w	ITAL	El Dorado	Diamond Springs Tw	72	30
GARDEN								
Beatrice	29	f	w	CHIL	Sacramento	2-Wd Sacramento	77	215
Edwin	10	m	w	SAME	San Francisco	San Francisco P O	85	827
Ellen	6	f	w	SAME	San Francisco	San Francisco P O	85	827
Emma	8	f	w	SAME	San Francisco	San Francisco P O	85	827
James	50	m	w	IN	Alameda	Eden Twp	68	68
Jno W	48	m	w	PA	Shasta	Horsetown P O	89	507
Lewis B	30	m	w	IL	Colusa	Grand Island Twp	71	302
Robert	42	m	w	IN	Alameda	Eden Twp	68	68
Timothy	48	m	w	MEXI	San Joaquin	3-Wd Stockton	86	243
Wm	40	m	w	GA	San Joaquin	3-Wd Stockton	86	246
GARDENARO								
J	22	m	w	ITAL	Mariposa	Maxwell Crk P O	74	148
GARDENAU								
Henry	18	m	w	ITAL	San Francisco	11-Wd San Francisc	84	709
GARDENER								
Bart S	28	m	w	IN	Sonoma	Healdsburg	91	275
Benjamin	41	m	w	ENGL	Placer	Bath P O	76	424
Ed	37	m	w	GA	Sierra	Table Rock Twp	89	578
Ellen	29	f	w	ME	Amador	Sutter Crk P O	69	401
Enoch	34	m	w	IA	Sutter	Butte Twp	92	89
Francis B	37	m	w	ME	San Francisco	San Francisco P O	83	183
Frederick	35	m	w	ENGL	Mariposa	Mariposa P O	74	130
Henry	48	m	w	PRUS	Sutter	Butte Twp	92	96
J	38	m	w	ME	Sierra	Sierra Twp	89	567
James	60	m	w	SC	Marin	Sausalito Twp	74	70
Levi	27	m	w	CANA	Colusa	Grand Island Twp	71	307
Lizzie	22	f	w	LA	San Francisco	San Francisco P O	83	350
Lydia	35	f	w	WI	San Francisco	11-Wd San Francisc	84	447
Martin	43	m	w	NY	San Francisco	8-Wd San Francisco	82	456
Peter	34	m	w	NY	Marin	Sausalito Twp	74	66
Samuel	50	m	w	PA	San Francisco	3-Wd San Francisco	79	327
Silas	46	m	w	KY	Stanislaus	Buena Vista Twp	92	12
Wm	19	m	w	IN	Marin	San Rafael Twp	74	46
GARDENHIER								
Archibald	24	m	w	AR	Stanislaus	Washington Twp	92	87
Frederick	38	m	w	TN	Stanislaus	Empire Twp	92	66
J	55	m	w	TN	San Joaquin	Tulare Twp	86	254
GARDENHIRE								
Sarah	34	f	w	TN	Stanislaus	Branch Twp	92	1
GARDENIER								
Chris W	40	m	w	CANA	Shasta	Shasta P O	89	457
Henry	40	m	w	NJ	San Francisco	San Francisco P O	85	847
GARDENS								
J	44	m	w	CANA	Lake	Lakeport	73	407
GARDENSOSKY								
Emil	28	m	w	PRUS	San Francisco	San Francisco P O	83	279
GARDER								
Peter	50	m	w	MEXI	San Joaquin	1-Wd Stockton	86	141
GARDERE								
Jean	39	m	w	FRAN	San Francisco	11-Wd San Francisc	84	552
GARDILA								
Julius	18	m	w	ITAL	San Mateo	Schoolhouse Statio	87	346
GARDINER								
Baldwin	31	m	w	NY	San Francisco	San Francisco P O	80	396
Benjamin A	53	m	w	MA	El Dorado	White Oak Twp	72	136
Charles	58	m	w	TN	Placer	Auburn P O	76	374
Charles	40	m	w	NY	Los Angeles	Wilmington Twp	73	639
Charles	38	m	w	NY	Stanislaus	Emory Twp	92	23
Charles	30	m	w	NY	Contra Costa	Martinez P O	71	435
Edward	38	m	w	NY	Placer	Auburn P O	76	368
Geo	28	m	w	ME	Solano	Vallejo	90	166
George	39	m	w	AR	Solano	Vacaville Twp	90	119
H H	34	m	w	NY	Alameda	Oakland	68	194
Harry	63	m	w	ENGL	Contra Costa	Martinez P O	71	400
Henry	45	m	w	CANA	San Francisco	San Francisco P O	83	408
Henry	22	m	w	ME	Stanislaus	Emory Twp	92	26
J G	47	m	w	VA	Solano	Vallejo	90	140
J H	33	m	w	VA	Mendocino	Little Lake Twp	74	197
J J	57	m	w	VA	Alameda	Oakland	68	227
James J	40	m	w	NY	San Francisco	2-Wd San Francisco	79	264
Jno	65	m	w	MA	Sacramento	1-Wd Sacramento	77	189
Jno H	52	m	w	NJ	San Francisco	5-Wd San Francisco	81	6
Jno P	40	m	w	ENGL	San Francisco	5-Wd San Francisco	81	19
John	13	m	w	CA	Solano	Vallejo	90	185
Jonathan	27	m	w	ENGL	Santa Barbara	San Buenaventura P	87	427
Jonathan W	40	m	w	NC	Plumas	Washington Twp	77	56
Joseph	34	m	w	IL	Nevada	Eureka Twp	75	135
Joseph	27	m	w	WI	Nevada	Bloomfield Twp	75	99

© 2001 by Heritage Quest. All rights reserved.

Name	Age	S	R	B-PL	County	Locale	Roll	Pg
						Series M593		
M S	55	m	w	ME	Placer	Dutch Flat P O	76	405
Mary	15	f	w	CA	Yuba	Bullards Bar P O	93	547
R E	43	m	w	NY	Tuolumne	Sonora P O	93	308
Robt	28	m	w	IREL	San Bernardino	San Bernardino Twp	78	426
Stephen B	53	m	w	RI	El Dorado	Mud Springs Twp	72	79
Thos	42	m	w	SCOT	Sacramento	4-Wd Sacramento	77	346
W A	43	m	w	NY	Tuolumne	Columbia P O	93	340
W J	53	m	w	SCOT	San Francisco	3-Wd San Francisco	79	311
Wm	23	m	w	SCOT	San Francisco	1-Wd San Francisco	79	135
GARDINI								
Andrew	43	m	w	ITAL	Tuolumne	Chinese Camp P O	93	371
GARDINIER								
Thomas	40	m	w	NY	Plumas	Goodwin Twp	77	2
Thomas	24	m	w	ENGL	San Francisco	San Francisco P O	83	417
GARDINOT								
Louis	35	m	w	FRAN	San Francisco	San Francisco P O	80	535
GARDISER								
Jacob	32	m	w	ALSA	Santa Clara	1-Wd San Jose	88	224
GARDNER								
---	37	m	w	SCOT	Humboldt	Eureka Twp	72	273
A	37	m	w	PRUS	San Francisco	3-Wd San Francisco	79	315
A	31	m	w	CANA	Klamath	Trinidad Twp	73	392
A C	40	m	w	RI	Tuolumne	Columbia P O	93	348
A H	40	m	w	KY	Sierra	Forest Twp	89	529
Abraham	24	m	w	CANA	Monterey	Pajaro Twp	74	371
Alfred	41	m	w	NY	Tuolumne	Sonora P O	93	318
Andrew	52	m	w	PA	Stanislaus	Washington Twp	92	85
Bartol	43	m	w	IREL	San Francisco	San Francisco P O	80	356
Bridget	50	f	b	NY	San Francisco	6-Wd San Francisco	81	110
Byron	32	m	w	NY	Santa Cruz	Pajaro Twp	89	349
C H	38	m	w	LA	Monterey	Salinas Twp	74	307
C H	34	m	w	MA	Del Norte	Crescent	71	465
Charles	7	m	w	CA	Yolo	Buckeye Twp	93	408
Charles	34	m	w	NY	Santa Cruz	Santa Cruz Twp	89	392
Charles A	42	m	w	CT	El Dorado	Placerville	72	119
Chas	43	m	w	MA	Humboldt	Eureka Twp	72	271
Chas	25	m	w	ENGL	San Francisco	11-Wd San Francisc	84	584
Daniel	40	m	w	OH	Santa Clara	Santa Clara Twp	88	170
Daniel F	51	m	w	ME	Santa Cruz	Soquel Twp	89	448
Danl	37	m	w	MA	Sacramento	4-Wd Sacramento	77	325
David	45	m	w	OH	Amador	Amador City P O	69	391
David	30	m	w	IREL	San Francisco	7-Wd San Francisco	81	221
Dayton P	33	m	w	NY	Santa Cruz	Pajaro Twp	89	356
Ebenezer	52	m	w	IL	Colusa	Colusa	71	291
Edward	48	m	w	OH	San Joaquin	Union Twp	86	268
Edwin	39	m	w	NY	Marin	San Rafael Twp	74	31
Eli	39	m	w	IL	Amador	Jackson P O	69	341
Fanny	11	f	w	CA	San Francisco	2-Wd San Francisco	79	224
Francis	28	m	w	IREL	San Francisco	San Francisco P O	83	220
Frank A	9	m	w	CA	Sacramento	Dry Crk Twp	77	102
Fredk	48	m	w	PA	Shasta	Horsetown P O	89	502
G G	50	m	w	RI	Calaveras	Copperopolis P O	70	225
Geo D	25	m	w	RI	San Francisco	2-Wd San Francisco	79	276
Geo E	45	m	w	NY	San Francisco	1-Wd San Francisco	79	53
Geo M	43	m	w	NJ	San Francisco	1-Wd San Francisco	79	42
Geo T	43	m	w	KY	Butte	Bidwell Twp	70	4
George	35	m	w	IREL	Butte	Wyandotte Twp	70	144
George	24	m	w	IL	Stanislaus	North Twp	92	69
George D B	28	m	w	ME	Placer	Gold Run Twp	76	396
George H	49	m	w	NJ	Solano	Rio Vista Twp	90	56
Gr A	25	m	w	ENGL	Monterey	Alisal Twp	74	288
Harriet	42	f	w	ME	San Francisco	7-Wd San Francisco	81	277
Harriet	41	f	w	ENGL	Humboldt	Eureka Twp	72	271
Harry	16	m	w	SWED	Sacramento	2-Wd Sacramento	77	241
Henry	38	m	w	NJ	Solano	Rio Vista Twp	90	56
Henry	26	m	w	SWIT	Siskiyou	Scott Valley Twp	89	621
Isaac	45	m	w	ME	Stanislaus	San Joaquin Twp	92	80
J	40	m	w	PA	El Dorado	Lake Valley Twp	72	63
J C	23	m	w	WI	San Joaquin	Dent Twp	86	22
J H	30	m	w	NY	Santa Clara	Gilroy Twp	88	70
Jacob	58	m	w	PRUS	Stanislaus	North Twp	92	69
Jacob	29	m	w	ME	Humboldt	Eureka Twp	72	280
Jacob	24	m	w	MA	Marin	Sausalito Twp	74	71
James	64	m	w	VA	Humboldt	Eel Rvr Twp	72	249
James	62	m	w	ENGL	Sacramento	Franklin Twp	77	110
James	36	m	w	NJ	San Francisco	8-Wd San Francisco	82	378
James A	48	m	w	ENGL	San Francisco	San Francisco P O	85	761
Jemima	14	f	w	ENGL	Santa Cruz	Soquel Twp	89	436
Joel	38	m	w	MA	Sacramento	Center Twp	77	82
John	50	m	w	IREL	San Francisco	11-Wd San Francisc	84	565
John	50	m	w	PRUS	Humboldt	Bucksport Twp	72	244
John	48	m	w	SCOT	Calaveras	Copperopolis P O	70	257
John	46	m	w	OH	San Francisco	San Francisco P O	83	206
John	40	m	w	PA	San Francisco	11-Wd San Francisc	84	708
John	30	m	w	ME	Stanislaus	Emory Twp	92	26
John	30	m	w	OH	San Francisco	5-Wd San Francisco	81	21
John	22	m	w	CT	San Francisco	7-Wd San Francisco	81	204
John	18	m	w	PA	San Diego	San Pasqual	78	520
John H	56	m	w	RI	San Francisco	6-Wd San Francisco	81	139
Johnson	39	m	w	IN	Humboldt	Eureka Twp	72	276
Jonathan	40	m	w	NC	Mendocino	Little Lake Twp	74	193
Joseph	35	m	w	NJ	San Francisco	San Francisco P O	80	380
L M	50	m	w	NY	Sacramento	3-Wd Sacramento	77	301
Leander E	27	m	w	ME	Santa Clara	Santa Clara Twp	88	169
Leonard B	36	m	w	NY	Santa Cruz	Watsonville	89	371
Louis	50	m	w	PRUS	Santa Clara	Santa Clara Twp	88	150
Luke	60	m	w	IREL	Tehama	Antelope Twp	92	153
Lyon	34	m	w	ME	Placer	Gold Run Twp	76	400
Maria	28	f	w	IREL	San Mateo	Redwood Twp	87	364
Martha	35	f	w	CA	Sacramento	3-Wd Sacramento	77	286
May	33	f	w	CANA	Humboldt	Arcata Twp	72	229
Moody	21	m	w	MO	Santa Clara	Redwood Twp	88	126
N B	36	m	w	UNKN	San Joaquin	2-Wd Stockton	86	166
Nathan	47	m	w	NY	Placer	Colfax P O	76	390
Orren G	48	m	w	MA	Sonoma	Salt Point	91	386
P G	47	m	w	NY	Tuolumne	Chinese Camp P O	93	365
Patric	50	m	w	IREL	San Luis Obispo	San Luis Obispo Tw	87	316
Pliny F	40	m	w	MA	Stanislaus	Branch Twp	92	1
Rhodes	31	m	w	OH	Fresno	Millerton P O	72	158
Robert	36	m	w	CANA	Humboldt	Eureka Twp	72	266
Robt	72	m	w	IREL	San Francisco	11-Wd San Francisc	84	613
Robt	29	m	w	MA	Humboldt	Eureka Twp	72	277
S J	64	m	w	NY	Calaveras	Copperopolis P O	70	235
Taylor M	31	m	w	NY	Santa Cruz	Pajaro Twp	89	356
Thaddeus	39	m	w	OH	Colusa	Butte Twp	71	268
Thomas	66	m	w	CAPE	Santa Clara	Fremont Twp	88	42
Thomas	50	m	w	MA	Tuolumne	Sonora P O	93	331
Thomas	30	m	w	NY	Sacramento	2-Wd Sacramento	77	219
Thos	40	m	w	ENGL	San Francisco	11-Wd San Francisc	84	577
Thos	40	m	w	NY	San Joaquin	Castoria Twp	86	4
Thos	38	m	w	OH	San Joaquin	Tulare Twp	86	258
Thos	29	m	w	NY	San Francisco	11-Wd San Francisc	84	709
Vienna	43	m	w	MI	Sacramento	Brighton Twp	77	70
William	4	m	w	CA	Sacramento	3-Wd Sacramento	77	289
William	34	m	w	IREL	El Dorado	Cosumnes Twp	72	16
William	27	m	w	VT	Santa Clara	Fremont Twp	88	65
William	26	m	w	SCOT	San Francisco	7-Wd San Francisco	81	199
William	24	m	w	NY	Sonoma	Petaluma Twp	91	351
William H	40	m	w	VA	Placer	Bath P O	76	441
William H	38	m	w	RI	San Mateo	Pescadero P O	87	410
Wm	54	m	w	NY	San Joaquin	Tulare Twp	86	262
Wm	53	m	w	ME	Yuba	Rose Bar Twp	93	666
Wm C	52	m	w	NY	Shasta	Horsetown P O	89	505
GARDNEY								
John M	56	m	w	SAXO	San Francisco	2-Wd San Francisco	79	223
GARDO								
Nicholas	42	m	w	ITAL	Tuolumne	Columbia P O	93	341
GARDSON								
Phillip J	63	m	w	FRAN	El Dorado	Placerville	72	118
GARECT								
John O	63	m	w	CT	Sacramento	4-Wd Sacramento	77	371
GAREGAS								
Thomas	40	m	w	IREL	Sonoma	Petaluma Twp	91	318
GAREGG								
Allen	27	m	w	CANA	Colusa	Colusa Twp	71	286
GAREGO								
Jose	33	m	w	CHIL	Santa Cruz	Pajaro Twp	89	346
GAREN								
L G	46	m	w	CANA	Alameda	Oakland	68	196
Thomas	31	m	w	AL	Kern	Kernville P O	73	368
GARET								
Patrick	17	m	w	CA	San Francisco	11-Wd San Francisc	84	593
GARETH								
Claus	38	m	w	SHOL	Siskiyou	Scott Valley Twp	89	615
GARETY								
Thomas	10	m	w	CA	Trinity	Junction City Pct	92	210
GAREY								
Kirke W	20	m	w	MA	Alameda	Washington Twp	68	292
Thomas A	40	m	w	OH	Los Angeles	Los Angeles	73	506
GARFIAS								
Henruque	21	m	w	CA	Los Angeles	Santa Ana Twp	73	610
GARFIELD								
Alfred	40	m	w	MA	Siskiyou	Yreka	89	662
Charles E	29	m	w	OH	Solano	Denverton Twp	90	22
Fredk	63	m	w	ME	Butte	Bidwell Twp	70	2
Hattie N	15	f	w	CA	Sacramento	2-Wd Sacramento	77	224
Henry	38	m	w	NY	San Francisco	5-Wd San Francisco	81	10
John Q	32	m	w	NH	San Francisco	6-Wd San Francisco	81	148
Louisa	19	f	w	CA	Solano	Vacaville Twp	90	120
Maynard	47	m	w	MA	San Francisco	11-Wd San Francisc	84	511
Maynard J	47	m	w	MA	Santa Clara	Santa Clara Twp	88	137
Seth	38	m	w	MA	Sacramento	2-Wd Sacramento	77	226
GARGERY								
A M	30	m	w	MA	San Francisco	San Francisco P O	83	88
GARGIN								
Jane	41	f	w	IREL	San Francisco	7-Wd San Francisco	81	247
GARGNARD								
Elzab	45	f	w	SWIT	Sacramento	4-Wd Sacramento	77	347
GARGNENDO								
Alexis	40	m	w	FRAN	Calaveras	San Andreas P O	70	167
GARGRAVE								
Geo	32	m	w	OH	Sacramento	1-Wd Sacramento	77	183
GARHAM								
F A	38	m	w	PA	Solano	Vallejo	90	200
GARIA								
Jose	37	m	w	MEXI	Butte	Mountain Spring Tw	70	87
GARIBALDI								
Giuseppi	45	m	w	ITAL	Amador	Volcano P O	69	373
Jacob	25	m	w	ITAL	Mariposa	Mariposa P O	74	129
John	62	m	w	ITAL	Los Angeles	Los Angeles	73	570
John	47	m	w	ITAL	Los Angeles	Los Angeles	73	555
Juan	50	m	w	ITAL	Los Angeles	Los Angeles Twp	73	466
Juan B	38	m	w	ITAL	Los Angeles	Los Angeles	73	558
Lorencio	35	m	w	ITAL	Los Angeles	Los Angeles	73	555

© 2001 by Heritage Quest. All rights reserved.

Name	Age	S	R	B-PL	County	Locale	Series M593 Roll	Pg
GARIBOLDI								
A	50	m	w	ITAL	Sierra	Downieville Twp	89	517
GARIEPHY								
L L	36	m	w	CANA	Siskiyou	Scott Rvr Twp	89	603
GARIETY								
Michl	26	m	w	IREL	San Francisco	1-Wd San Francisco	79	135
GARIGAN								
Mary	53	f	w	IREL	San Francisco	San Francisco P O	83	251
GARILOTTA								
Piedro	26	m	w	ITAL	San Francisco	11-Wd San Francisc	84	642
GARIN								
Ah	32	m	c	CHIN	Solano	Vallejo	90	173
GARINET								
Marie	50	f	w	FRAN	Santa Clara	1-Wd San Jose	88	275
GARING								
Joseph	23	m	w	PRUS	Los Angeles	Wilmington Twp	73	642
Tim	30	m	w	IREL	Alameda	Alameda	68	10
GARIOTO								
Jno	30	m	w	PA	Butte	Chico Twp	70	46
GARISSON								
Emma	40	f	w	BADE	San Francisco	7-Wd San Francisco	81	204
GARITY								
Owen	45	m	w	IREL	Placer	Bath P O	76	447
Thomas	40	m	w	IREL	Placer	Bath P O	76	447
GARIVENTO								
John	28	m	w	ITAL	Amador	Volcano P O	69	376
GARK								
Michael	46	m	w	IREL	Sacramento	Natomas Twp	77	168
GARKIN								
Denis	14	m	w	CA	San Francisco	11-Wd San Francisc	84	593
GARLACH								
Rhinart	40	m	w	TX	San Francisco	San Francisco P O	83	225
GARLAND								
Betsey	53	f	w	NH	San Francisco	San Francisco P O	83	346
Catherine	64	f	w	IREL	San Francisco	2-Wd San Francisco	79	261
Chas	25	m	w	NH	Fresno	Millerton P O	72	181
Cornelius	50	m	w	ME	Calaveras	San Andreas P O	70	189
E O	65	m	w	NH	Tehama	Paskenta Twp	92	166
Eaton	20	m	w	IREL	Contra Costa	Martinez P O	71	420
Elbridge A	44	m	w	NH	El Dorado	Salmon Falls Twp	72	129
Frank	42	m	w	MA	Solano	Vallejo	90	202
Harry	38	m	w	ENGL	Yuba	Rose Bar Twp	93	663
Harry	35	m	w	CANA	San Francisco	7-Wd San Francisco	81	272
Hattie	10	f	w	CA	San Francisco	San Francisco P O	85	720
Henry	33	m	w	ENGL	Yuba	Rose Bar Twp	93	657
Hiram	23	m	w	IREL	Solano	Silveyville Twp	90	78
Jacob	40	m	w	PRUS	Mendocino	Albion & Big Rvr T	74	166
James	45	m	w	MA	San Francisco	6-Wd San Francisco	81	109
James	43	m	w	IL	San Francisco	5-Wd San Francisco	81	23
James	20	m	w	NY	San Francisco	8-Wd San Francisco	82	455
John	39	m	w	ME	Calaveras	Copperopolis P O	70	254
John	29	m	w	ENGL	Alameda	Washington Twp	68	272
John C	46	m	w	NY	Sacramento	4-Wd Sacramento	77	346
John W	40	m	w	MA	Shasta	Shasta P O	89	453
Louisa	17	f	w	VT	San Francisco	5-Wd San Francisco	81	24
Mary	19	f	w	VT	San Francisco	5-Wd San Francisco	81	24
Mary B	60	f	w	NH	Tehama	Paskenta Twp	92	166
Milton	37	m	w	ME	San Francisco	8-Wd San Francisco	82	451
Richard	39	m	w	CANA	Plumas	Plumas Twp	77	28
S L	54	m	w	NH	Solano	Vallejo	90	207
Samul	24	m	w	ENGL	San Francisco	8-Wd San Francisco	82	392
Thomas	71	m	w	IREL	El Dorado	Mountain Twp	72	69
William D	43	m	w	ME	San Francisco	6-Wd San Francisco	81	117
Wm	36	m	w	ENGL	San Diego	San Diego	78	504
Wm	23	m	w	ENGL	San Francisco	3-Wd San Francisco	79	308
GARLANDS								
Miller	20	m	w	MA	Calaveras	San Andreas P O	70	213
GARLE								
Ida	27	f	w	IREL	Sacramento	1-Wd Sacramento	77	200
GARLENO								
Frank	32	m	w	MEXI	Alameda	Hayward	68	78
GARLENS								
Jo	35	m	w	MEXI	Alameda	Alameda	68	8
GARLENTENA								
Joseph	30	m	w	ITAL	Calaveras	San Andreas P O	70	189
GARLEY								
Charles	27	m	w	ENGL	Mariposa	Mariposa P O	74	134
George	45	m	w	IL	Santa Clara	2-Wd San Jose	88	297
GARLICK								
Aaron	51	m	w	ENGL	Sacramento	2-Wd Sacramento	77	220
J P	33	m	w	IL	Butte	Bidwell Twp	70	3
James	65	m	w	ENGL	Humboldt	Pacific Twp	72	299
GARLOCK								
Jerome	30	m	w	NY	Amador	Drytown P O	69	421
GARLOPK								
Walter	22	m	w	PRUS	San Francisco	5-Wd San Francisco	81	16
GARLOTTI								
Carlo	50	m	w	ITAL	San Francisco	San Francisco P O	80	418
GARLY								
Richd	51	m	w	CHIL	Butte	Kimshew Tpw	70	82
Thos C	33	m	w	OH	Butte	Chico Twp	70	47
GARMAC								
Jose	60	m	w	CA	Santa Clara	Burnett Twp	88	33
GARMAN								
David	30	m	w	OH	San Francisco	7-Wd San Francisco	81	225
Hannah	18	f	w	IREL	San Francisco	San Francisco P O	83	215
Mike	27	m	w	IREL	Placer	Alta P O	76	419
W F	30	m	w	BADE	Tuolumne	Chinese Camp P O	93	376
William	53	m	w	PA	Monterey	San Benito Twp	74	380
GARMEN								
Patrin	38	f	w	MEXI	Yuba	New York Twp	93	641
GARMER								
Eugene	27	m	w	FRAN	Los Angeles	Los Angeles Twp	73	478
GARMON								
John	17	m	w	MA	Sacramento	2-Wd Sacramento	77	223
Michael	30	m	w	IREL	San Francisco	San Francisco P O	83	235
Thomas	11M	m	w	NY	San Francisco	11-Wd San Francisc	84	711
GARN								
Isaac	33	m	w	MO	Contra Costa	Martinez P O	71	405
William	40	m	w	POLA	San Francisco	7-Wd San Francisco	81	190
GARNEAU								
G	40	m	w	CANA	San Francisco	San Francisco P O	83	299
GARNER								
Abraham	33	m	b	MO	El Dorado	Cosumnes Twp	72	14
B	29	m	w	TN	San Joaquin	Elkhorn Twp	86	65
Benj	35	m	w	IL	San Bernardino	San Bernardino Twp	78	445
C N	50	m	w	IL	Tehama	Deer Crk Twp	92	170
Charles W	48	m	w	IL	Stanislaus	Empire Twp	92	42
Elizabeth	12	f	w	CA	Sierra	Gibson Twp	89	541
Ellen	8	f	w	CA	Alameda	Oakland	68	135
Francisco	56	f	w	CA	Monterey	Monterey	74	360
Gerard	33	m	w	VT	Inyo	Bishop Crk Twp	73	315
Guadalupe	32	m	w	CA	Monterey	Alisal Twp	74	295
H A	52	m	w	SC	Tuolumne	Big Oak Flat P O	93	402
Ignasio	26	m	w	CA	Monterey	Monterey	74	359
J F	37	m	w	MO	San Joaquin	3-Wd Stockton	86	239
James	34	m	w	IL	Stanislaus	Empire Twp	92	42
Jesse	50	m	w	VA	Tulare	Tule Rvr Twp	92	261
John	50	m	w	NC	San Bernardino	San Bernardino Twp	78	419
John	38	m	w	PORT	Alameda	Eden Twp	68	67
John R	30	m	w	OH	Napa	Yountville Twp	75	80
Joseph	16	m	w	CA	Yolo	Cache Crk Twp	93	451
Lewis	37	m	w	SAXO	Butte	Kimshew Tpw	70	82
Mariano	14	m	w	CA	Monterey	Monterey Twp	74	347
Martin	68	m	w	IREL	Alameda	Brooklyn	68	33
Monroe L	38	m	w	PA	Stanislaus	San Joaquin Twp	92	70
Moses	40	m	w	IL	San Bernardino	San Bernardino Twp	78	454
Ransom	49	m	w	PA	Stanislaus	San Joaquin Twp	92	72
Squire	56	m	w	IL	Butte	Chico Twp	70	59
Valentine	34	m	w	IL	Monterey	San Benito Twp	74	382
Watson	10	m	w	CA	San Diego	Milquaty Dist	78	475
William	42	m	w	IL	Stanislaus	Empire Twp	92	42
Wm	45	m	w	MO	San Joaquin	3-Wd Stockton	86	245
Wm P	64	m	w	VA	El Dorado	Georgetown Twp	72	48
GARNET								
Edwin	35	m	w	ME	Stanislaus	San Joaquin Twp	92	83
John M	39	m	w	OH	Colusa	Colusa	71	297
R A	24	m	w	NY	Sacramento	San Joaquin Twp	77	401
GARNETT								
Frank	50	m	w	CA	Fresno	Millerton P O	72	193
George	52	m	w	SCOT	Amador	Jackson P O	69	334
Harriet	35	f	w	IREL	San Francisco	8-Wd San Francisco	82	463
James S	39	m	w	MO	Solano	Silveyville Twp	90	84
Jas S	29	m	w	IL	San Joaquin	2-Wd Stockton	86	184
John	55	m	w	ENGL	Yuba	Slate Range Bar Tw	93	671
L	12	m	w	CA	Solano	Benicia	90	21
Louis A	40	m	w	VA	San Francisco	7-Wd San Francisco	81	284
Peter	18	m	w	CA	Fresno	Millerton P O	72	193
Richd	46	m	w	KY	Napa	Napa	75	14
W	34	m	w	CANA	Alameda	Oakland	68	195
GARNEY								
Alfred	25	m	w	ME	Tuolumne	Sonora P O	93	318
Frk K	32	m	w	ME	Tuolumne	Sonora P O	93	318
John A	34	m	w	AL	Santa Cruz	Soquel Twp	89	445
Manuel	53	m	w	MEXI	Mariposa	Mariposa P O	74	120
Mary	18	f	w	CA	San Francisco	San Francisco P O	83	197
GARNHER								
Henry	35	m	w	SCOT	Contra Costa	Martinez P O	71	420
GARNHERT								
Felix	36	m	w	FRAN	Santa Clara	1-Wd San Jose	88	265
GARNIER								
Albert	27	m	w	FRAN	Kern	Havilah P O	73	337
Alexr	66	m	w	FRAN	Sacramento	4-Wd Sacramento	77	376
Cumlo	21	m	w	FRAN	Los Angeles	Los Angeles Twp	73	477
Florentin	18	m	w	FRAN	San Francisco	San Francisco P O	85	752
Louis	40	m	w	FRAN	San Francisco	6-Wd San Francisco	81	73
GARNIS								
Peter	23	m	w	HANO	San Francisco	2-Wd San Francisco	79	151
GARNISS								
Henry	29	m	w	ENGL	San Francisco	San Francisco P O	83	129
James R	40	m	w	NJ	San Francisco	6-Wd San Francisco	81	140
GARNO								
Francis F	37	m	w	IL	Yuba	North East Twp	93	644
GARNOT								
Halarie	49	m	w	FRAN	San Mateo	San Mateo P O	87	348
GARNSIA								
Antonia	33	f	w	MEXI	Placer	Bath P O	76	426
GARONNE								
Felix	52	m	w	ITAL	San Francisco	6-Wd San Francisco	81	96
GAROUCHETE								
Eugene	59	m	w	FRAN	San Francisco	11-Wd San Francisc	84	642
GAROUTTE								
Jerry M	42	m	w	OH	Yolo	Cache Crk Twp	93	426

© 2001 by Heritage Quest. All rights reserved.

California 1870 Census

Series M593

Name	Age	S	R	B-PL	County	Locale	Roll	Pg
GARR								
Martha	31	f	w	VA	Sutter	Butte Twp	92	98
Peter	44	m	w	SHOL	Marin	Sausalito Twp	74	68
William	40	m	w	IREL	Nevada	Eureka Twp	75	130
GARRACES								
Noricsa	44	m	w	MEXI	Alameda	Washington Twp	68	286
GARRAH								
Wm W	65	m	w	SC	Sacramento	Alabama Twp	77	59
GARRAISINO								
Stephano	42	m	w	ITAL	San Francisco	11-Wd San Francisc	84	517
GARRANT								
Justina	23	f	w	NY	San Francisco	6-Wd San Francisco	81	122
GARRARD								
Mary	16	f	w	CA	Santa Clara	2-Wd San Jose	88	337
GARRASINO								
Vincenzio	31	m	w	ITAL	San Francisco	11-Wd San Francisc	84	517
GARRASO								
Ramon	53	m	w	CHIL	Tuolumne	Sonora P O	93	326
GARRATT								
Henry	51	m	w	ME	Calaveras	Copperopolis P O	70	261
Joseph	63	m	w	ENGL	San Francisco	11-Wd San Francisc	84	606
Joseph	12	m	w	MA	San Francisco	11-Wd San Francisc	84	606
Richard	26	m	w	ENGL	Santa Clara	2-Wd San Jose	88	298
Wm T	40	m	w	CT	San Francisco	San Francisco P O	83	23
GARREA								
Becenta	9	m	w	CA	Alameda	Washington Twp	68	286
GARRECHT								
David	32	m	w	BAVA	Shasta	American Ranch P O	89	498
Lawrence	34	m	w	BAVA	Shasta	Shasta P O	89	460
Theobald	72	m	w	BAVA	Shasta	Shasta P O	89	460
GARREDET								
Alfred	32	m	w	FRAN	Santa Clara	2-Wd San Jose	88	288
GARREN								
Louis	35	m	w	POLA	San Francisco	7-Wd San Francisco	81	171
Margrate	18	f	w	CA	San Francisco	7-Wd San Francisco	81	164
GARRENBERG								
Gustave	24	m	w	HAMB	San Francisco	San Francisco P O	83	195
GARRET								
Cathrine	72	f	w	NY	Sacramento	San Joaquin Twp	77	404
David	17	m	w	SWIT	Yolo	Grafton Twp	93	491
J R	33	m	w	NY	Yuba	Marysville	93	596
Mathew	57	m	w	IREL	San Bernardino	San Bernardino Twp	78	416
Robert	6	m	w	CA	San Francisco	San Francisco P O	85	817
Sheldon	47	m	w	NY	Santa Clara	1-Wd San Jose	88	228
T J	53	m	w	KY	Lake	Lower Lake	73	418
GARRETSON								
Fannie	23	f	w	WI	San Francisco	7-Wd San Francisco	81	284
John	31	m	w	NJ	San Mateo	Pescadero P O	87	412
Joseph M	34	m	w	IN	Santa Barbara	Santa Barbara P O	87	483
Patric	55	m	w	IREL	Sacramento	Sutter Twp	77	384
GARRETT								
Albert W	45	m	w	OH	Sonoma	Healdsburg & Mendo	91	278
Alex C	37	m	w	ENGL	San Francisco	8-Wd San Francisco	82	330
Annis	26	f	w	IL	Sacramento	Sutter Twp	77	380
Benj F	40	m	w	AR	Shasta	Portugese Flat P O	89	472
Cuyler	23	m	w	OH	Shasta	Millville P O	89	490
Edward	50	m	w	ENGL	San Francisco	5-Wd San Francisco	81	28
Edwin	26	m	w	IL	Yuba	Marysville	93	580
Elizabeth	30	f	w	IREL	San Francisco	San Francisco P O	83	281
Francis	39	m	w	ENGL	San Francisco	1-Wd San Francisco	79	114
H M	38	m	w	MO	Napa	Napa	75	16
Harmon	57	m	w	NY	Alameda	Washington Twp	68	278
Henry	34	m	w	ENGL	Plumas	Mineral Twp	77	23
Hiram	30	m	w	OH	Sacramento	4-Wd Sacramento	77	333
Hiram	2	m	w	CA	Sacramento	4-Wd Sacramento	77	333
Isaac	45	m	w	GA	Stanislaus	San Joaquin Twp	92	82
J P	37	m	w	KY	Lassen	Janesville Twp	73	435
James	54	m	w	IREL	San Francisco	1-Wd San Francisco	79	31
James	47	m	w	VA	San Joaquin	Castoria Twp	86	7
James H	35	m	w	IREL	San Francisco	8-Wd San Francisco	82	492
Jerry	40	m	w	IREL	Sacramento	San Joaquin Twp	77	398
Jno	40	m	w	IL	Santa Clara	Gilroy Twp	88	98
John	50	m	w	FRAN	San Francisco	8-Wd San Francisco	82	400
John	37	m	w	ENGL	Nevada	Meadow Lake Twp	75	246
John	30	m	w	ENGL	Yolo	Cottonwood Twp	93	472
John	25	m	w	IL	Sonoma	Washington Twp	91	466
Joseph	45	m	w	SC	Kern	Tehachapi P O	73	352
Mark	29	m	w	NY	San Diego	Julian Dist	78	469
Mike	26	m	w	IREL	San Francisco	San Francisco P O	83	360
Mike	16	m	w	CA	Amador	Drytown P O	69	418
Rebecca	16	f	w	CA	Humboldt	Eureka Twp	72	259
Samuel	43	m	w	CANA	Sacramento	San Joaquin Twp	77	403
T P	45	m	w	SC	Klamath	Klamath Twp	73	371
Thos H	42	m	w	IL	Siskiyou	Surprise Valley Tw	89	640
William	29	m	w	PA	San Francisco	7-Wd San Francisco	81	226
William	24	m	w	MO	Yolo	Grafton Twp	93	487
Wm	38	m	w	TN	Sierra	Lincoln Twp	89	550
Wm C	40	m	w	SC	Napa	Yountville Twp	75	79
GARRETTY								
Mary	20	f	w	NY	San Francisco	San Francisco P O	83	192
GARRETY								
Cornelius	62	m	w	IREL	Contra Costa	San Pablo Twp	71	363
John	31	m	w	IREL	Contra Costa	San Pablo Twp	71	357
Patrick	26	m	w	IREL	Contra Costa	San Pablo Twp	71	364
Thomas	45	m	w	IREL	San Mateo	Belmont P O	87	373
GARREY								
J B	36	m	w	PA	San Joaquin	Douglas Twp	86	36
Maxwell	45	m	w	PORT	Sacramento	Georgianna Twp	77	122
GARRIBALDI								
Jo	38	m	w	ITAL	San Francisco	5-Wd San Francisco	81	16
GARRICK								
Wm H	48	m	w	CANA	San Francisco	8-Wd San Francisco	82	317
GARRIDO								
Antonio	53	m	w	CHIL	Contra Costa	Martinez P O	71	387
GARRIGA								
Andrew	28	m	w	SPAI	San Francisco	2-Wd San Francisco	79	142
GARRIGAN								
F	35	m	w	IREL	Alameda	Oakland	68	263
John	31	m	w	IREL	San Francisco	1-Wd San Francisco	79	72
Laughlin	45	m	w	IREL	San Francisco	1-Wd San Francisco	79	9
Mathew	42	m	w	IREL	San Mateo	Half Moon Bay P O	87	407
Patk	30	m	w	SWED	San Francisco	1-Wd San Francisco	79	36
GARRIGUS								
Finley	50	m	w	OH	Santa Clara	Santa Clara Twp	88	156
GARRIN								
Sylvester	23	m	w	IL	Santa Clara	Almaden Twp	88	15
GARRINO								
Victor	34	m	w	FRAN	Marin	Sausalito Twp	74	69
GARRIOCH								
Margaret	40	f	w	SCOT	San Francisco	8-Wd San Francisco	82	395
GARRIOT								
J	44	m	w	FRAN	Alameda	Oakland	68	180
GARRIS								
John	40	m	w	ITAL	San Francisco	San Francisco P O	80	486
GARRISERE								
Frank	40	m	w	FRAN	San Francisco	San Francisco P O	80	538
GARRISON								
A	55	m	w	NY	San Joaquin	Castoria Twp	86	11
Adelaide	9	f	m	CA	Butte	Mountain Spring Tw	70	87
Alfred	28	m	m	CT	San Francisco	2-Wd San Francisco	79	143
Ambrose	46	m	b	NY	Butte	Mountain Spring Tw	70	87
Andrew	38	m	w	PA	Solano	Silveyville Twp	90	75
Anna	57	f	w	VT	Humboldt	South Fork Twp	72	302
Cal M	30	m	w	IL	Sonoma	Mendocino Twp	91	297
Christ	28	m	w	TN	San Joaquin	Dent Twp	86	18
Elizabeth	25	f	w	ME	San Francisco	7-Wd San Francisco	81	172
Enoch	66	m	w	OH	Siskiyou	Big Valley Twp	89	580
Henry A	47	m	w	NY	San Francisco	San Francisco P O	83	81
Jane	30	f	m	MA	San Francisco	6-Wd San Francisco	81	112
Jno	60	m	w	NJ	Santa Clara	Burnett Twp	88	33
John	59	m	w	NY	Mendocino	Sanel Twp	74	228
John G	38	m	w	ME	Placer	Bath P O	76	427
Joseph	34	m	w	NJ	Siskiyou	Scott Rvr Twp	89	602
Joseph L	45	m	w	NY	Inyo	Bishop Crk Twp	73	315
L B	40	m	w	NY	San Francisco	San Francisco P O	83	84
Lizzie	31	f	w	NJ	San Bernardino	San Bernardino Twp	78	436
Mary L	20	f	w	WI	Sacramento	Brighton Twp	77	73
Oscar	26	m	w	NJ	Stanislaus	Washington Twp	92	84
S J	30	m	w	AL	Sierra	Downieville Twp	89	518
Susan	25	f	i	CA	Butte	Mountain Spring Tw	70	87
William E	38	m	w	TN	Tulare	White Rvr Twp	92	301
Wm T	38	m	w	IN	Sonoma	Mendocino Twp	91	296
GARRITAN								
Mary	22	f	w	CANA	Marin	Bolinas Twp	74	1
GARRITSON								
N H	58	m	w	PA	Solano	Benicia	90	7
Sally	21	f	w	WI	Solano	Benicia	90	19
GARRITY								
Edward	23	m	w	NY	Klamath	Camp Gaston	73	372
Ellen	17	f	w	MO	Santa Clara	2-Wd San Jose	88	321
John	55	m	w	IREL	Mariposa	Mariposa P O	74	116
John	35	m	w	IREL	Plumas	Plumas Twp	77	32
Julia	26	f	w	IREL	San Francisco	San Francisco P O	80	418
Lawrence	29	m	w	IREL	Tuolumne	Sonora P O	93	309
Mariah	20	f	w	IREL	San Francisco	San Francisco P O	83	366
Mary	27	f	w	IREL	San Francisco	1-Wd San Francisco	79	103
Mary	22	f	w	IREL	San Francisco	San Francisco P O	85	746
Mathew	24	m	w	NY	Solano	Montezuma Twp	90	65
Michael	42	m	w	IREL	San Francisco	2-Wd San Francisco	79	271
Patrick	32	m	w	IREL	San Francisco	3-Wd San Francisco	79	312
Peter	25	m	w	MA	San Francisco	San Francisco P O	80	383
GARRON								
Mary	37	f	w	IN	Santa Cruz	Watsonville	89	375
GARRONE								
William	35	m	w	IREL	Marin	San Rafael	74	57
GARROT								
Louisa	43	f	w	FRAN	Calaveras	San Andreas P O	70	160
Samuel	46	m	w	NJ	Colusa	Colusa Twp	71	282
GARROTT								
A	39	m	w	NY	Amador	Lancha Plana P O	69	368
James	63	m	w	VA	Amador	Sutter Crk P O	69	398
L	40	m	w	CANA	Lake	Upper Lake	73	408
William	38	m	w	IREL	Amador	Drytown P O	69	424
GARROTTE								
William	27	m	w	MO	Yolo	Grafton Twp	93	491
GARRPI								
John	35	m	w	SWIT	Marin	Nicasio Twp	74	16
GARRY								
Edward	42	m	w	IREL	El Dorado	Mountain Twp	72	68
Edward	17	m	w	MA	San Francisco	7-Wd San Francisco	81	233
Mary	7	f	w	MA	Alameda	Washington Twp	68	298
Michael	45	m	w	IREL	Calaveras	San Andreas P O	70	164
Michael Mr	43	m	w	IREL	Calaveras	San Andreas P O	70	168
Wm	28	m	w	PRUS	Humboldt	Arcata Twp	72	234

© 2001 by Heritage Quest. All rights reserved.

Series M593

Name	Age	S	R	B-PL	County	Locale	Roll	Pg
GARS								
Mary	52	f	w	FRAN	San Francisco	2-Wd San Francisco	79	152
GARSER								
Dora	40	f	w	PRUS	San Francisco	7-Wd San Francisco	81	207
GARSHAN								
H J	25	f	w	PORT	San Joaquin	2-Wd Stockton	86	174
GARSIA								
Antona	12	f	w	CA	Monterey	Castroville Twp	74	334
Antonio	25	m	w	AZOR	San Francisco	1-Wd San Francisco	79	102
Felipe	37	m	w	CA	Monterey	Monterey Twp	74	349
Magdalena	40	f	w	MEXI	Yuba	Marysville	93	617
Manuel	19	m	w	AZOR	San Francisco	1-Wd San Francisco	79	118
GARSIDE								
George	22	m	w	ENGL	San Francisco	11-Wd San Francisc	84	513
Hugh	61	m	w	ENGL	Santa Clara	Santa Clara Twp	88	141
John	26	m	w	ENGL	Yolo	Grafton Twp	93	491
Thomas	49	m	w	ENGL	Monterey	Alisal Twp	74	302
GARSON								
James	29	m	w	SCOT	San Francisco	San Francisco P O	83	94
James	29	m	w	SCOT	San Francisco	2-Wd San Francisco	79	157
GARST								
Joel	59	m	w	VA	Butte	Bidwell Twp	70	3
GARSTNER								
Anton	56	m	w	BADE	San Francisco	San Francisco P O	83	249
GARTEN								
Oliver P	41	m	w	OH	Placer	Gold Run Twp	76	395
GARTENBURG								
Edward	45	m	w	AUST	San Francisco	8-Wd San Francisco	82	452
GARTER								
Chas A	40	m	w	VT	San Francisco	5-Wd San Francisco	81	11
Chas A	27	m	w	NY	Sacramento	3-Wd Sacramento	77	291
Ephraim	61	m	w	NY	Sacramento	2-Wd Sacramento	77	253
William	49	m	w	NY	Marin	Novato Twp	74	12
GARTHAFNAR								
C	33	m	w	MO	Yuba	Marysville	93	632
GARTHE								
Leopold	46	m	w	GERM	Nevada	Nevada Twp	75	278
GARTHIN								
Cathine	22	f	w	IREL	San Francisco	San Francisco P O	85	859
GARTHOM								
William A	16	m	w	CA	San Mateo	Half Moon Bay P O	87	402
GARTHORNE								
Elias	49	m	w	ENGL	San Francisco	11-Wd San Francisc	84	492
GARTHWAITE								
Henry	43	m	w	ENGL	San Francisco	8-Wd San Francisco	82	409
GARTIKE								
Manuel	40	m	w	CHIL	Santa Clara	Fremont Twp	88	62
GARTLAN								
Ann	29	f	w	IREL	San Francisco	6-Wd San Francisco	81	155
GARTLAND								
Bernard	45	m	w	IREL	Shasta	French Gulch P O	89	467
John	43	m	w	IREL	San Francisco	San Francisco P O	83	232
P	40	m	w	IREL	Amador	Drytown P O	69	425
GARTLEMAN								
Herman	33	m	w	HANO	Plumas	Washington Twp	77	56
John	30	m	w	BREM	San Francisco	6-Wd San Francisco	81	70
GARTLEY								
Albert	27	m	w	OH	Contra Costa	Martinez Twp	71	349
GARTMAN								
Daniel	40	m	w	BREM	Santa Clara	Fremont Twp	88	63
Henry	50	m	w	HANO	Klamath	Trinidad Twp	73	389
GARTNER								
Nekolaus	43	m	w	PRUS	Amador	Volcano P O	69	376
GARTONI								
Z	40	m	w	ITAL	Sierra	Butte Twp	89	512
GARTRELL								
Mortimor	35	m	w	CA	Yolo	Cache Crk Twp	93	445
GARTSFIELD								
Louis	45	m	w	PRUS	San Francisco	San Francisco P O	80	349
GARTSTEIN								
Alex	24	m	w	CANA	San Joaquin	Douglas Twp	86	51
GARTTINO								
Francisco	63	m	w	SPAI	Yolo	Grafton Twp	93	480
GARTY								
George	42	m	w	MO	Mariposa	Maxwell Crk P O	74	147
GARUCHT								
Thomas	67	m	w	CANA	Sacramento	4-Wd Sacramento	77	376
GARUS								
Elias	24	m	w	MO	Fresno	Millerton P O	72	148
GARVAN								
Ellen	25	f	w	IREL	San Francisco	7-Wd San Francisco	81	242
GARVEN								
William	38	m	w	IREL	San Francisco	8-Wd San Francisco	82	319
GARVENTO								
Gerodda	21	m	w	ITAL	San Mateo	Schoolhouse Statio	87	340
GARVER								
Abram B	22	m	w	PA	Santa Cruz	Santa Cruz Twp	89	381
Jacob	26	m	w	KY	Butte	Oregon Twp	70	126
Michael	45	m	w	OH	Nevada	Nevada Twp	75	284
Simeon	26	m	w	OH	Butte	Oregon Twp	70	126
GARVEY								
Catherine	55	f	w	IREL	San Francisco	San Francisco P O	83	360
Chris	24	m	w	MO	San Francisco	San Francisco P O	83	366
David	22	m	w	IREL	San Francisco	11-Wd San Francisc	84	449
Ellen	44	f	w	IREL	San Francisco	7-Wd San Francisco	81	197
James	28	m	w	CANA	San Francisco	8-Wd San Francisco	82	435
James	27	m	w	IREL	San Francisco	San Francisco P O	83	71
James P	30	m	w	MO	San Francisco	8-Wd San Francisco	82	424
John	52	m	w	IREL	Siskiyou	Yreka Twp	89	671
John	35	m	w	MA	Nevada	Bloomfield Twp	75	92
Josephine	23	f	w	IREL	Nevada	Grass Valley Twp	75	153
Katharine	29	f	w	NY	San Francisco	San Francisco P O	83	161
Martin	38	m	w	IREL	San Francisco	San Francisco P O	85	745
Mary	29	f	w	IREL	Alameda	Hayward	68	76
Mary A	36	f	w	IREL	San Mateo	Half Moon Bay P O	87	404
Michael	35	m	w	IREL	Nevada	Grass Valley Twp	75	173
Michael	21	m	w	VT	Siskiyou	Table Rock Twp	89	648
Peter	36	m	w	IREL	San Francisco	2-Wd San Francisco	79	185
Peter	25	m	w	WI	Mariposa	Mariposa P O	74	125
Richard	33	m	w	NY	San Francisco	5-Wd San Francisco	81	31
Richard	32	m	w	IREL	San Bernardino	Belleville Twp	78	408
Saml	26	m	w	ME	Tehama	Tehama Twp	92	187
Timothy	32	m	w	MA	Santa Clara	Redwood Twp	88	128
Timothy	26	m	w	MA	Santa Clara	2-Wd San Jose	88	312
William	35	m	w	KY	San Francisco	1-Wd San Francisco	79	17
GARVIA								
Nicholas	60	m	w	CA	San Diego	San Pasqual	78	521
GARVIN								
James	24	m	w	IREL	Sacramento	2-Wd Sacramento	77	228
John	38	m	w	IREL	San Joaquin	2-Wd Stockton	86	200
Lillie	20	f	w	VT	Sacramento	Sutter Twp	77	384
M J	35	m	w	IREL	San Joaquin	2-Wd Stockton	86	198
Margaret	72	f	w	IREL	San Francisco	San Francisco P O	80	375
Mary	20	f	w	IREL	San Francisco	8-Wd San Francisco	82	469
Mary	11	f	w	CA	San Francisco	8-Wd San Francisco	82	436
Michael	30	m	w	IREL	San Francisco	8-Wd San Francisco	82	451
Thomas	35	m	w	IREL	San Francisco	San Francisco P O	80	375
GARVINA								
Caroline	22	f	w	WI	San Francisco	8-Wd San Francisco	82	293
GARVINE								
Peter	40	m	w	BADE	San Joaquin	Oneal Twp	86	101
GARVITT								
Elijah W	61	m	w	CT	El Dorado	Placerville Twp	72	96
GARVY								
William	45	m	w	CHIL	Amador	Jackson P O	69	336
Wm	33	m	w	IREL	San Mateo	San Mateo P O	87	360
GARWIN								
John	23	m	w	IREL	Sacramento	4-Wd Sacramento	77	370
Margaret	51	f	w	IREL	San Francisco	San Francisco P O	85	782
Wm	47	m	w	IREL	San Joaquin	1-Wd Stockton	86	124
GARWOOD								
Harriet	30	f	w	NY	San Francisco	San Francisco P O	83	93
J M	45	m	w	TN	San Joaquin	Castoria Twp	86	5
Laura	10	f	w	CA	San Joaquin	Douglas Twp	86	30
S S	43	m	w	OH	Trinity	Canyon City Pct	92	202
V J	20	m	w	AR	San Joaquin	Tulare Twp	86	254
Wm T	32	m	w	PA	San Francisco	3-Wd San Francisco	79	328
Zemri	52	m	w	OH	Santa Clara	Santa Clara Twp	88	161
GARY								
Calvin C	34	m	w	IL	Colusa	Butte Twp	71	268
Henry	60	m	w	IREL	Alameda	Hayward	68	73
Henry	48	m	w	FRAN	Shasta	Horsetown P O	89	504
John	41	m	w	IREL	San Joaquin	2-Wd Stockton	86	167
John	22	m	w	MS	Solano	Silveyville Twp	90	84
Louis	32	m	w	WI	Sacramento	4-Wd Sacramento	77	349
Robert	24	m	w	AR	Kern	Bakersfield P O	73	358
GARYAM								
Jas	45	m	w	ITAL	San Joaquin	Oneal Twp	86	118
GARYLORD								
Enna	10	f	w	CA	Calaveras	Copperopolis P O	70	257
GARZA								
Jose	65	m	w	ITAL	Los Angeles	Los Angeles	73	554
GARZOLI								
Basil	17	m	w	SWIT	Marin	Tomales Twp	74	77
Jacomo	30	m	w	SWIT	Marin	Bolinas Twp	74	2
Morris	31	m	w	SWIT	Marin	San Antonio Twp	74	62
Peter	24	m	w	SWIT	Marin	Tomales Twp	74	77
Placido	30	m	w	SWIT	Marin	Nicasio Twp	74	17
GASAGAN								
John	55	m	w	IREL	Stanislaus	Branch Twp	92	1
GASBAD								
Charles	35	m	w	HOLL	San Francisco	San Francisco P O	80	462
GASBERY								
Joseph F	45	m	w	CANA	Santa Clara	Santa Clara Twp	88	142
GASBO								
John	30	m	w	PORT	Alameda	Alameda	68	10
GASCHWIND								
Risne	42	m	w	SWIT	San Francisco	11-Wd San Francisc	84	554
GASCIA								
Manuel	30	m	w	MEXI	Santa Barbara	Santa Barbara P O	87	473
GASEALL								
Silas	35	m	w	MI	San Diego	Milquaty Dist	78	477
Simon	26	m	w	MI	San Diego	Milquaty Dist	78	477
GASELY								
Mary	40	f	w	IREL	San Francisco	11-Wd San Francisc	84	662
GASEVITCH								
Mark	53	m	w	AUST	Santa Clara	2-Wd San Jose	88	301
GASEY								
W S	38	m	w	WURT	Nevada	Nevada Twp	75	321
GASHIRN								
Rebecca J	70	f	w	NY	Yuba	Bullards Bar P O	93	548
Richard J	32	m	w	NY	Yuba	Bullards Bar P O	93	548
GASHKY								
Frederick	25	m	w	GERM	Yolo	Cache Crk Twp	93	452

© 2001 by Heritage Quest. All rights reserved.

California 1870 Census

Series M593

Name	Age	S	R	B-PL	County	Locale	Roll	Pg
GASHNER								
Wm	59	m	w	BADE	San Francisco	8-Wd San Francisco	82	350
GASHNILER								
John	37	m	w	MO	San Francisco	11-Wd San Francisc	84	539
GASHO								
Jacob	31	m	w	HAMB	San Francisco	San Francisco P O	85	758
GASIN								
John	42	m	w	CANA	Alameda	Oakland	68	187
GASKELL								
Colet	58	m	w	PA	Plumas	Quartz Twp	77	34
G W	53	m	w	PA	Yuba	Marysville	93	606
GASKEN								
Charles W	44	m	w	NY	San Francisco	3-Wd San Francisco	79	306
GASKER								
John	27	m	w	CA	San Diego	San Diego	78	508
GASKIL								
Thomas	22	m	w	ENGL	San Mateo	Schoolhouse Statio	87	340
GASKILL								
Courtland	66	m	w	NY	Sonoma	Petaluma Twp	91	354
D W C	44	m	w	VT	Butte	Oroville Twp	70	137
Laura	50	f	w	NY	San Francisco	8-Wd San Francisco	82	444
Rollin	37	m	w	VT	San Francisco	7-Wd San Francisco	81	283
GASKIN								
Henrietta	32	f	w	ENGL	Plumas	Goodwin Twp	77	58
GASKINS								
James	28	m	w	VA	Mendocino	Navarro & Big Rvr	74	176
GASLIN								
Charles	32	m	w	HANO	San Francisco	2-Wd San Francisco	79	137
Samuel	43	m	w	ME	San Mateo	Redwood Twp	87	366
GASNE								
Francis	46	m	w	FRAN	Los Angeles	Los Angeles	73	520
GASNEY								
Jacob	39	m	w	NY	Solano	Rio Vista Twp	90	58
GASOLE								
Juan	31	m	w	NM	San Luis Obispo	San Luis Obispo Tw	87	311
GASOLO								
Bartolomew	23	m	w	ITAL	Amador	Sutter Crk P O	69	405
GASPAR								
Wm	15	m	w	NJ	San Francisco	11-Wd San Francisc	84	588
GASPER								
Andrew	40	m	w	PRUS	San Francisco	7-Wd San Francisco	81	203
Anne	18	f	w	US	Yuba	Marysville	93	609
Eugene	38	m	w	FRAN	San Francisco	San Francisco P O	80	341
Henery	19	m	w	NY	San Francisco	7-Wd San Francisco	81	177
James	43	m	w	PORT	Nevada	Rough & Ready Twp	75	333
Thomas	25	m	w	HANO	Sacramento	3-Wd Sacramento	77	314
GASPITCH								
John	37	m	w	AUST	Santa Clara	2-Wd San Jose	88	317
GASQUET								
Horace	42	m	w	FRAN	Del Norte	Mountain Twp	71	474
GASS								
Andrew	28	m	w	SWED	Mariposa	Maxwell Crk P O	74	139
Augustus M	39	m	w	TN	San Diego	Milquaty Dist	78	477
Emma	22	f	w	AR	Butte	Kimshew Tpw	70	80
George	29	m	w	CANA	San Francisco	11-Wd San Francisc	84	489
Henry	31	m	w	CANA	Sonoma	Santa Rosa	91	394
James	23	m	w	IREL	Sacramento	Dry Crk Twp	77	104
John	41	m	w	ENGL	San Francisco	5-Wd San Francisco	81	11
John M	29	m	w	WI	San Francisco	San Francisco P O	83	67
Peter	48	m	w	LA	Calaveras	San Andreas P O	70	201
Susan	47	f	w	NY	Butte	Chico Twp	70	43
GASSALUPE								
John	30	m	w	ITAL	Calaveras	San Andreas P O	70	187
Jose	28	m	w	ITAL	Calaveras	San Andreas P O	70	187
GASSAWAY								
Charles	24	m	w	MO	Contra Costa	Martinez P O	71	386
Chas D	43	m	w	KY	Nevada	Rough & Ready Twp	75	327
James E	38	m	w	KY	Nevada	Grass Valley Twp	75	219
T	40	m	m	VA	Yuba	Marysville	93	597
Upton S	63	m	w	KY	Nevada	Grass Valley Twp	75	166
William	31	m	w	MO	Colusa	Colusa Twp	71	276
Wm W	41	m	w	KY	Nevada	Rough & Ready Twp	75	327
GASSEL								
William	52	m	w	PA	San Francisco	11-Wd San Francisc	84	491
GASSELL								
William	40	m	w	VA	San Francisco	6-Wd San Francisco	81	108
GASSELO								
Henry	30	m	w	HAMB	Monterey	Alisal Twp	74	292
GASSER								
Chas	33	m	w	GERM	San Diego	San Diego	78	496
GASSETINO								
Conjang	49	m	w	SWIT	San Francisco	San Francisco P O	80	477
GASSETT								
Abrah	72	m	w	TN	Sonoma	Santa Rosa	91	414
GASSEY								
Ah	35	m	c	CHIN	Amador	Drytown P O	69	423
GASSIAN								
Louis	31	m	w	ENGL	Butte	Ophir Twp	70	96
GASSIM								
Harriett	65	f	w	FRAN	Alameda	Oakland	68	129
GASSITI								
William	55	m	w	ENGL	Santa Clara	Santa Clara Twp	88	162
GASSMAN								
Cart	26	m	w	PRUS	Solano	Benicia	90	2
Joseph	33	m	w	FRAN	San Francisco	1-Wd San Francisco	79	35
GASSMUS								
Chas	27	m	w	PRUS	San Francisco	5-Wd San Francisco	81	3

Series M593

Name	Age	S	R	B-PL	County	Locale	Roll	Pg
GASSNER								
J	46	m	w	HANO	Sierra	Lincoln Twp	89	549
Rachel	28	f	w	NY	San Francisco	8-Wd San Francisco	82	470
GASSON								
Francis	35	m	w	FRAN	Yuba	Slate Range Bar Tw	93	671
GASSOWAY								
U T	29	m	w	MO	Marin	San Rafael Twp	74	41
GAST								
August	34	m	w	PRUS	San Francisco	11-Wd San Francisc	84	648
August	34	m	w	PRUS	San Francisco	1-Wd San Francisco	79	47
GASTA								
Paul	36	m	w	CHIL	Tuolumne	Chinese Camp P O	93	380
GASTELL								
Javier	50	m	w	BELG	San Francisco	8-Wd San Francisco	82	470
GASTEN								
Hester A	32	m	w	TX	Santa Cruz	Watsonville	89	375
GASTENART								
P	38	m	w	CHIL	El Dorado	Greenwood Twp	72	50
GASTERNLES								
Salvador	37	m	w	FRAN	Monterey	San Antonio Twp	74	315
GASTIN								
Martin	44	m	w	OH	Sonoma	Petaluma Twp	91	353
GASTON								
Hamilton	46	m	w	OH	Sonoma	Petaluma Twp	91	352
Henry	30	m	w	PRUS	San Francisco	8-Wd San Francisco	82	431
Hugh	37	m	w	OH	Sonoma	Petaluma Twp	91	353
Jane	54	f	b	NY	Sacramento	3-Wd Sacramento	77	296
John	45	m	w	IL	Del Norte	Mountain Twp	71	474
Mooney	20	f	i	CA	Del Norte	Mountain Twp	71	474
Octavius	35	m	w	MO	Stanislaus	San Joaquin Twp	92	83
Simeon F	60	m	w	PA	Shasta	Shasta P O	89	452
Wm F	30	m	w	OH	Butte	Chico Twp	70	44
GASTRA								
L L	50	m	w	CHIL	Tuolumne	Chinese Camp P O	93	373
GASTRESE								
Joseph	66	m	w	IREL	San Joaquin	1-Wd Stockton	86	132
GASUR								
Rosana	73	f	w	PA	Humboldt	Mattole Twp	72	285
GAT								
---	26	m	c	CHIN	Siskiyou	Yreka Twp	89	673
---	14	m	c	CHIN	Siskiyou	Yreka Twp	89	668
Ah	45	m	c	CHIN	Butte	Bidwell Twp	70	5
Ah	44	m	c	CHIN	Mono	Bridgeport P O	74	283
Ah	28	m	c	CHIN	Sierra	Lincoln Twp	89	546
GATCLEY								
Thomas B	36	m	w	IREL	San Francisco	San Francisco P O	85	766
GATE								
Ah	23	m	c	CHIN	Shasta	Horsetown P O	89	503
G W	54	m	b	NC	Tuolumne	Chinese Camp P O	93	377
GATELEY								
Patrick	42	m	w	IREL	San Francisco	San Francisco P O	85	737
GATELY								
Annie	28	f	w	IREL	San Francisco	7-Wd San Francisco	81	231
Henry	31	m	w	LA	Santa Clara	Redwood Twp	88	120
John	42	m	w	IREL	Contra Costa	San Pablo Twp	71	362
Margaret	35	m	w	IREL	Yuba	East Bear Rvr Twp	93	543
Mary B	33	f	w	IREL	San Francisco	8-Wd San Francisco	82	409
Michael	49	m	w	IREL	Santa Clara	Santa Clara Twp	88	154
Michael	35	m	w	NY	San Francisco	San Francisco P O	85	818
Minnie	16	f	w	MA	Santa Clara	2-Wd San Jose	88	318
Patk	26	m	w	IREL	San Francisco	1-Wd San Francisco	79	99
Patrick	37	m	w	IREL	San Francisco	San Francisco P O	85	845
Thos	50	m	w	IREL	Solano	Vallejo	90	213
William	36	m	w	IREL	Calaveras	Copperopolis P O	70	248
GATEMAN								
Zoe	20	f	w	NY	San Francisco	6-Wd San Francisco	81	86
GATEN								
John	50	m	w	IREL	San Francisco	7-Wd San Francisco	81	256
GATERMAN								
Hans H	44	m	w	SHOL	El Dorado	Placerville	72	113
GATES								
A	33	m	w	MO	Sierra	Lincoln Twp	89	551
Adda	13	f	w	CA	Los Angeles	Los Angeles	73	537
Albert	23	m	w	IL	San Francisco	San Francisco P O	83	242
Alfred	39	m	w	NY	San Francisco	San Francisco P O	83	22
Asa H	43	m	w	MA	Placer	Lincoln P O	76	493
Bryant	49	m	w	ME	Kern	Tehachapi P O	73	356
C E	20	m	w	MA	San Francisco	San Francisco P O	85	855
Charles	29	m	w	IL	Santa Clara	Gilroy Twp	88	89
Corybin	50	m	w	MA	El Dorado	Placerville	72	120
D	50	m	w	FRAN	San Joaquin	1-Wd Stockton	86	133
Dwight	23	m	w	NY	Alameda	Hayward	68	76
E	53	m	w	NY	Sierra	Sierra Twp	89	562
E H	43	m	w	CANA	Sonoma	Bodega Twp	91	261
Edmond	29	m	w	CANA	Alameda	Brooklyn Twp	68	43
Elijah	48	m	m	KY	Mariposa	Maxwell Crk P O	74	141
Elijah H	54	m	w	NY	Sacramento	Cosumnes Twp	77	93
Emma	24	f	w	NY	San Francisco	San Francisco P O	83	207
Fanny	23	f	w	MI	Sutter	Butte Twp	92	98
Frank A	55	m	w	MA	Los Angeles	Santa Ana Twp	73	602
Garland	38	m	w	MO	Solano	Vacaville Twp	90	122
Geo	22	m	w	TN	Nevada	Meadow Lake Twp	75	252
Geo	13	m	w	CA	San Francisco	11-Wd San Francisc	84	587
George A	24	m	w	ME	San Mateo	Pescadero P O	87	416
H S	60	m	w	NY	San Francisco	San Francisco P O	85	857
Hamilton	35	m	w	KY	Solano	Suisun Twp	90	100
Horace	50	m	w	MA	San Francisco	San Francisco P O	83	344

© 2001 by Heritage Quest. All rights reserved.

Series M593

Name	Age	S	R	B-PL	County	Locale	Roll	Pg
Horace	41	m	w	TN	Stanislaus	Branch Twp	92	7
I N	65	m	w	KY	Tehama	Paynes Crk Twp	92	160
James	40	m	w	TN	Solano	Vacaville Twp	90	128
James B	50	m	w	NY	Sacramento	Dry Crk Twp	77	103
James H	33	m	w	NY	San Francisco	San Francisco P O	83	58
Johanna	31	f	w	IREL	Nevada	Grass Valley Twp	75	219
John	41	m	w	CT	El Dorado	Georgetown Twp	72	40
John	37	m	w	SWED	Mendocino	Albion & Big Rvr T	74	166
John	29	m	w	PA	San Francisco	San Francisco P O	83	306
Justin	45	m	w	NJ	Sacramento	3-Wd Sacramento	77	305
Luther	41	m	w	NY	Nevada	Grass Valley Twp	75	170
Melinda	37	f	w	VA	San Diego	San Diego	78	492
Messenger E	26	m	w	MA	Sacramento	2-Wd Sacramento	77	254
O J	40	m	w	NY	Trinity	Weaverville Pct	92	223
Samuel	37	m	w	CANA	Stanislaus	Empire Twp	92	28
Solomon	33	m	w	CANA	Mendocino	Little Lake Twp	74	197
Wallace	40	m	w	NY	Kern	Bakersfield P O	73	365
William	58	m	w	CANA	San Diego	San Diego	78	492
GATEWOOD								
Jeff	40	m	w	IL	San Diego	San Diego	78	483
Napoleon	21	m	w	TX	San Bernardino	San Salvador Twp	78	457
Silas	42	m	w	VA	Solano	Vacaville Twp	90	136
GATHER								
James W	40	m	w	KY	Colusa	Stony Crk Twp	71	329
GATHRIE								
Dexter	52	m	w	NY	Napa	Napa	75	22
Richd	21	m	w	IREL	Napa	Napa	75	14
Robert B	37	m	w	MO	Los Angeles	Los Nietos Twp	73	592
GATHSENOR								
Annette	27	f	w	FRAN	San Francisco	6-Wd San Francisco	81	45
GATKE								
John	26	m	w	HANO	San Francisco	11-Wd San Francisc	84	471
GATLEN								
E H	35	m	w	CA	Alameda	Oakland	68	159
GATLIN								
C	60	f	w	FRAN	Alameda	Oakland	68	214
Ephraim	43	m	w	KY	Butte	Ophir Twp	70	92
GATMER								
M	23	m	w	PRUS	Sacramento	San Joaquin Twp	77	396
GATO								
Pedro	46	m	w	MEXI	Tuolumne	Columbia P O	93	353
GATOS								
Jose	35	m	w	MEXI	Santa Clara	Almaden Twp	88	15
GATOSKY								
Morris	30	m	w	POLA	Napa	Yountville Twp	75	89
GATRALL								
Albert	25	m	w	OH	Siskiyou	Surprise Valley Tw	89	636
GATRICK								
Obed	28	m	w	NORW	Sacramento	Sutter Twp	77	382
GATRO								
Peter	22	m	w	CANA	Sonoma	Vallejo Twp	91	454
GATRON								
H	38	m	w	DENM	Sierra	Butte Twp	89	513
GATTELY								
John	38	m	w	IREL	San Francisco	San Francisco P O	83	166
GATTIE								
Antone	31	m	w	ITAL	Calaveras	San Andreas P O	70	179
Michael	31	m	w	ITAL	Calaveras	San Andreas P O	70	179
GATTIGAN								
Michael	45	m	w	IREL	San Francisco	San Francisco P O	83	410
GATTMAN								
J	8	m	w	HUNG	Sacramento	3-Wd Sacramento	77	281
GATTNEY								
T J	45	m	w	GERM	Sacramento	1-Wd Sacramento	77	179
GATTRELL								
P	32	m	w	RI	Sacramento	3-Wd Sacramento	77	316
GATTS								
Frances	10	f	w	CA	Monterey	Castroville Twp	74	326
GATZMAN								
Thos	45	m	w	BADE	Calaveras	Copperopolis P O	70	221
GAU								
Ah	25	m	c	CHIN	Amador	Ione City P O	69	367
GAUB								
John	49	m	w	BADE	Butte	Chico Twp	70	46
GAUBEL								
Martin	41	m	w	HDAR	San Francisco	11-Wd San Francisc	84	628
GAUBER								
Chas	49	m	w	HAMB	Butte	Kimshew Tpw	70	82
Joseph	36	m	w	FRAN	San Mateo	Pescadero P O	87	410
GAUCH								
Cathrine	55	f	w	IREL	San Francisco	1-Wd San Francisco	79	43
GAUCHET								
Ferdinand	69	m	w	FRAN	Sacramento	4-Wd Sacramento	77	376
Henri	60	m	w	FRAN	San Francisco	San Francisco P O	83	292
GAUCKER								
Asa	22	m	w	MI	San Joaquin	Liberty Twp	86	91
GAUDALUPE								
Joseph	38	m	w	ITAL	Mariposa	Mariposa P O	74	113
GAUDELUPE								
M	50	f	w	CA	San Bernardino	San Salvador Twp	78	455
GAUDIN								
J Maria	46	m	w	FRAN	San Francisco	6-Wd San Francisco	81	45
John	38	m	w	FRAN	San Francisco	San Francisco P O	85	804
GAUGE								
Jo	20	m	c	CHIN	Sonoma	Mendocino Twp	91	287
GAUGHAN								
Melinda	29	f	w	IREL	San Francisco	San Francisco P O	83	201
GAUGHEGAN								
Thomas	50	m	w	IREL	San Francisco	11-Wd San Francisc	84	452
GAUGHER								
Dolathea	40	f	w	PRUS	San Francisco	San Francisco P O	85	760
GAUINS								
Sery	38	m	w	SWIT	El Dorado	Georgetown Twp	72	36
GAUL								
Margaret	55	f	w	MI	Sacramento	4-Wd Sacramento	77	363
Margt	17	f	w	NJ	San Francisco	8-Wd San Francisco	82	317
Mary	43	f	w	IREL	San Francisco	San Francisco P O	83	28
Wm	41	m	w	ENGL	San Francisco	San Francisco P O	85	828
GAULDER								
George W	55	m	w	ME	Calaveras	San Andreas P O	70	201
GAULDIN								
B F	26	m	w	MO	Monterey	Alisal Twp	74	297
Laura	7	f	w	CA	Sonoma	Analy Twp	91	228
Mary	24	f	w	MO	Sonoma	Analy Twp	91	226
GAULEE								
James	48	m	w	IREL	San Francisco	11-Wd San Francisc	84	613
GAULETBERG								
Grace	20	f	w	PRUS	San Francisco	11-Wd San Francisc	84	688
GAULEY								
Wm H	51	m	w	NY	San Francisco	San Francisco P O	83	115
GAULOSE								
John	28	m	w	FRAN	San Francisco	San Francisco P O	80	472
GAULSON								
John	55	m	w	ENGL	San Mateo	Pescadero P O	87	416
GAULT								
Alex	40	m	w	IREL	Nevada	Nevada Twp	75	273
Elizabeth	30	f	w	IREL	San Francisco	San Francisco P O	83	170
John	49	m	w	NH	Placer	Auburn P O	76	360
Thomas	32	m	w	OH	Monterey	Alisal Twp	74	291
GAULY								
Francis	19	m	w	IREL	Sonoma	Petaluma Twp	91	351
GAUM								
Magdelin	33	f	w	BADE	Trinity	Weaverville Pct	92	225
GAUNDBERT								
Peter	54	m	w	FRAN	Santa Clara	1-Wd San Jose	88	232
GAUNT								
Charles	35	m	w	NY	Nevada	Meadow Lake Twp	75	248
GAUNTIC								
John	43	m	w	FRAN	San Francisco	San Francisco P O	80	332
GAUP								
Samuel	22	m	w	MA	Butte	Hamilton Twp	70	65
GAUSBAUGH								
George	40	m	w	PRUS	San Francisco	San Francisco P O	83	376
GAUSETT								
Samuel	40	m	w	SWIT	Marin	San Antonio Twp	74	60
GAUSNER								
Flinn	41	m	w	SWIT	Plumas	Plumas Twp	77	32
GAUSSAIL								
Bernard	46	m	w	FRAN	San Francisco	San Francisco P O	80	423
GAUSSETT								
Jefferson	18	m	w	GA	Marin	Point Reyes Twp	74	23
GAUTHEIR								
Ferdinand	38	m	w	CANA	Los Angeles	Los Angeles	73	528
GAUTHER								
Jean N	58	m	w	FRAN	Plumas	Rich Bar Twp	77	45
GAUTHIER								
Appolinaire	35	m	w	FRAN	Nevada	Grass Valley Twp	75	189
Joseph	23	m	w	CANA	Amador	Sutter Crk P O	69	408
Louis	37	m	w	CANA	Yolo	Grafton Twp	93	492
GAUTHUR								
Joseph	51	m	w	FRAN	Yuba	Bullards Bar P O	93	547
GAUTIER								
Adelia	37	f	w	FRAN	San Francisco	2-Wd San Francisco	79	170
Gustave	37	m	w	FRAN	Plumas	Rich Bar Twp	77	45
James W	44	m	w	KY	Nevada	Grass Valley Twp	75	219
Leon P	48	m	w	FRAN	San Francisco	8-Wd San Francisco	82	483
Maria M	68	f	w	FRAN	Santa Clara	Alviso Twp	88	23
Theodore	60	m	w	FRAN	Santa Cruz	Pajaro Twp	89	351
GAUVERSEAU								
Evner	37	m	w	CANA	San Mateo	Redwood Twp	87	364
GAUVIANA								
Gergona	20	m	w	ITAL	Calaveras	San Andreas P O	70	184
Nicolas	48	m	w	ITAL	Calaveras	San Andreas P O	70	184
GAUZEN								
Henry	45	m	w	FRAN	San Francisco	San Francisco P O	83	166
GAVAGAN								
Thos	38	m	w	IREL	San Francisco	San Francisco P O	85	859
GAVAN								
Francis	34	m	w	MEXI	Calaveras	Copperopolis P O	70	259
James	22	m	w	IREL	San Francisco	San Francisco P O	80	336
GAVE								
John	49	m	w	ENGL	San Francisco	1-Wd San Francisco	79	33
S	38	m	w	VT	Sierra	Butte Twp	89	511
GAVEN								
Edward S	40	m	w	OH	San Francisco	6-Wd San Francisco	81	129
Ellen	13	f	w	NY	San Francisco	San Francisco P O	83	51
George	37	m	w	CANA	Contra Costa	Martinez P O	71	438
John	50	m	w	IREL	Yuba	Marysville	93	617
John	32	m	w	IREL	Santa Clara	San Jose Twp	88	187
John	30	m	w	IREL	San Francisco	San Francisco P O	85	874
Mary	55	f	w	IREL	Solano	Vallejo	90	206
Patk	22	m	w	KY	Solano	Vallejo	90	212
Sarah	27	f	w	NJ	San Francisco	8-Wd San Francisco	82	469

© 2001 by Heritage Quest. All rights reserved.

California 1870 Census

Series M593

Name	Age	S	R	B-PL	County	Locale	Roll	Pg
GAVENIS								
J	40	m	w	ITAL	San Joaquin	1-Wd Stockton	86	155
Wm	37	m	w	ITAL	San Joaquin	1-Wd Stockton	86	155
GAVENS								
Manuel	31	m	w	PORT	Santa Clara	Santa Clara Twp	88	159
GAVER								
Henry	55	m	w	MD	Napa	Napa	75	2
John	47	m	w	PA	Amador	Sutter Crk P O	69	400
John	44	m	w	MD	San Francisco	San Francisco P O	80	367
GAVERENA								
Oliver	57	m	w	CANA	San Francisco	San Francisco P O	80	364
GAVIGAIN								
William	42	m	w	IREL	San Francisco	San Francisco P O	83	405
GAVIGAN								
Martin	42	m	w	IREL	San Francisco	7-Wd San Francisco	81	280
Mary	39	f	w	IREL	Mariposa	Mariposa P O	74	112
GAVILAND								
Francis	36	f	w	PRUS	San Francisco	San Francisco P O	83	200
GAVILLE								
Lorenzo D	44	m	w	RI	Los Angeles	Los Angeles Twp	73	481
GAVIN								
Barney	30	m	w	IREL	El Dorado	Mud Springs Twp	72	77
Edward	38	m	w	IREL	Napa	Napa	75	39
John	50	m	w	IREL	San Francisco	San Francisco P O	80	377
Lawrence	39	m	w	IREL	San Francisco	1-Wd San Francisco	79	88
Samuel	45	m	w	IREL	San Francisco	San Francisco P O	85	765
Thomas	28	m	w	IREL	Placer	Alta P O	76	419
Thomas	18	m	w	CANA	Santa Cruz	Santa Cruz	89	409
GAVINAH								
Sista	8	f	w	CA	Fresno	Millerton P O	72	162
GAW								
Ah	36	m	c	CHIN	San Bernardino	San Bernardino Twp	78	433
Ah	27	m	c	CHIN	San Joaquin	1-Wd Stockton	86	156
Ah	23	m	c	CHIN	San Francisco	San Francisco P O	83	286
In	28	m	c	CHIN	San Francisco	San Francisco P O	83	82
Robert	21	m	w	PRUS	Colusa	Monroe Twp	71	312
GAWB								
Jacob	40	m	w	FRAN	Butte	Ophir Twp	70	118
GAWDIS								
J	24	m	w	FRAN	Alameda	Alameda	68	7
GAWEY								
James	38	m	w	NY	San Francisco	San Francisco P O	83	160
GAWIN								
Daniel	33	m	w	CANA	San Francisco	11-Wd San Francisc	84	702
John	31	m	w	IREL	San Francisco	7-Wd San Francisco	81	157
GAWLEY								
Anne S	45	f	w	NY	San Francisco	6-Wd San Francisco	81	91
GAWNE								
John	40	m	w	ENGL	San Joaquin	3-Wd Stockton	86	229
GAXIOLA								
Nicolas	35	m	w	MEXI	San Francisco	San Francisco P O	83	99
GAY								
Abram	36	m	w	MO	Solano	Tremont Twp	90	31
Ah	42	m	c	CHIN	Trinity	Canyon City Pct	92	201
Ah	30	m	c	CHIN	Alameda	Hayward	68	77
Ah	30	m	c	CHIN	Alameda	Brooklyn Twp	68	40
Ah	30	m	c	CHIN	Sacramento	1-Wd Sacramento	77	202
Ah	30	m	c	CHIN	Nevada	Bridgeport Twp	75	119
Ah	27	m	c	CHIN	Nevada	Washington Twp	75	347
Ah	26	m	c	CHIN	Santa Clara	Santa Clara Twp	88	165
Ah	26	m	c	CHIN	Nevada	Washington Twp	75	344
Ah	24	m	c	CHIN	Solano	Vallejo	90	173
Ah	23	m	c	CHIN	Plumas	Quartz Twp	77	41
Ah	18	m	c	CHIN	Placer	Clipper Gap P O	76	393
Ah	15	m	c	CHIN	San Francisco	San Francisco P O	83	91
Ambrose C	52	m	w	CT	El Dorado	Placerville	72	110
Andrew	26	m	w	IL	Solano	Silveyville Twp	90	79
Ang	40	m	c	CHIN	Plumas	Seneca Twp	77	48
C H	38	m	w	ME	Alameda	Oakland	68	260
Charles	30	m	w	CT	San Francisco	7-Wd San Francisco	81	226
Charles J	11	m	w	CA	Solano	Suisun Twp	90	112
Dan C	43	m	w	OH	San Francisco	1-Wd San Francisco	79	134
Daniel M	69	m	w	VA	Yolo	Buckeye Twp	93	416
David	42	m	w	ME	Solano	Vallejo	90	181
David	36	m	w	LA	Calaveras	San Andreas P O	70	163
Davis	29	m	w	IREL	Solano	Silveyville Twp	90	81
Francois C	45	m	w	FRAN	Santa Cruz	Watsonville	89	367
Frank	41	m	w	VT	Del Norte	Crescent Twp	71	456
George	9	m	w	CA	Colusa	Monroe Twp	71	318
Gilbert L	36	m	w	NY	Mariposa	Maxwell Crk P O	74	145
Gilbert L	35	m	w	ME	Mariposa	Mariposa P O	74	135
Hannah	23	f	w	PA	Santa Clara	San Jose Twp	88	198
Hial H	45	m	w	NC	Sonoma	Vallejo Twp	91	458
Hing	40	m	c	CHIN	Placer	Auburn P O	76	371
Hop	25	m	c	CHIN	Alameda	Washington Twp	68	272
Hop	24	m	c	CHIN	Alameda	Washington Twp	68	297
J	32	m	w	ENGL	Sierra	Forest Twp	89	531
J	30	f	w	SCOT	San Francisco	San Francisco P O	85	830
James	52	m	w	ME	Calaveras	San Andreas P O	70	218
James	40	m	w	SCOT	Contra Costa	Martinez P O	71	445
James	21	m	w	MO	Solano	Silveyville Twp	90	75
Jane	49	f	w	HANO	Calaveras	San Andreas P O	70	195
Jannett	78	f	w	SCOT	Napa	Napa	75	19
John	33	m	w	NY	San Francisco	1-Wd San Francisco	79	134
John M	46	m	w	FRAN	San Francisco	2-Wd San Francisco	79	204
Lewis	55	m	w	ME	Monterey	San Juan Twp	74	389
M	65	m	w	NY	Alameda	Oakland	68	147

Series M593

Name	Age	S	R	B-PL	County	Locale	Roll	Pg
Marian	14	f	w	NE	San Francisco	8-Wd San Francisco	82	418
Mary	3	f	w	CA	Solano	Maine Prairie Twp	90	47
Michael	35	m	w	IREL	Placer	Pino Twp	76	472
Miles	52	m	w	NC	Santa Clara	San Jose Twp	88	205
Minop	35	m	w	OH	Mendocino	Point Arena Twp	74	207
Peter A	36	m	w	OH	Placer	Dutch Flat P O	76	410
Sin	34	m	c	CHIN	Alameda	Washington Twp	68	276
Sin	32	m	c	CHIN	Alameda	Washington Twp	68	288
Sin	31	m	c	CHIN	Alameda	Eden Twp	68	58
Sin	30	m	c	CHIN	Alameda	Eden Twp	68	58
Sin	30	m	c	CHIN	Alameda	Eden Twp	68	71
Sin	28	m	c	CHIN	Alameda	Alvarado	68	304
Sin	27	m	c	CHIN	Alameda	Washington Twp	68	270
Sin	26	m	c	CHIN	Alameda	Washington Twp	68	272
Sin	22	m	c	CHIN	Alameda	Washington Twp	68	271
Sin	21	m	c	CHIN	Alameda	Washington Twp	68	271
Sin	19	m	c	CHIN	Alameda	Washington Twp	68	301
Sin	16	m	c	CHIN	Alameda	Washington Twp	68	279
William	40	m	w	IN	Nevada	Rough & Ready Twp	75	334
William	40	m	w	OH	Yuba	Rose Bar Twp	93	666
William	35	m	w	IREL	Nevada	Eureka Twp	75	137
William C	37	m	w	VT	Solano	Maine Prairie Twp	90	51
Willie	13	m	w	CA	Solano	Silveyville Twp	90	84
GAYBEYS								
Felix	40	m	w	BELG	San Francisco	San Francisco P O	83	86
GAYEGO								
Incarnacion	18	m	w	CA	San Luis Obispo	San Luis Obispo Tw	87	304
GAYETTE								
Abraham	23	m	w	CANA	Contra Costa	Martinez P O	71	383
John	29	m	w	CANA	Alameda	Alvarado	68	304
GAYETTY								
I C	53	m	w	NH	Merced	Snelling P O	74	266
GAYLAND								
Abram	21	m	w	MO	Solano	Vacaville Twp	90	124
R	50	m	w	FRAN	Siskiyou	Callahan P O	89	627
GAYLE								
Samuel	28	m	w	IREL	Solano	Silveyville Twp	90	72
GAYLOR								
Albert	27	m	w	SAXO	San Diego	Julian Dist	78	468
GAYLORD								
Andrew	21	m	w	IREL	Solano	Silveyville Twp	90	76
E H	39	m	w	NY	Nevada	Meadow Lake Twp	75	262
John W	56	m	w	NC	San Luis Obispo	Santa Rosa Twp	87	328
Mary A	22	f	w	IA	Placer	Roseville P O	76	349
Samuel	69	m	w	CT	Santa Barbara	Santa Barbara P O	87	477
Sarah	51	f	w	NY	Placer	Rocklin Twp	76	465
William	42	m	w	CT	El Dorado	White Oak Twp	72	140
William	40	m	w	NY	San Francisco	11-Wd San Francisc	84	705
GAYNARD								
Chas	37	m	w	IREL	Napa	Napa	75	52
Edward	40	m	w	IREL	San Francisco	San Francisco P O	83	146
Ellen	11	f	w	MA	San Francisco	San Francisco P O	83	192
GAYNAS								
Kate	25	f	w	IREL	Napa	Napa	75	6
GAYNER								
Catherine	24	f	w	MD	Nevada	Grass Valley Twp	75	155
Chas	36	m	w	IREL	San Francisco	7-Wd San Francisco	81	254
GAYNOR								
Archibald	14	m	w	CA	San Francisco	11-Wd San Francisc	84	588
G B	43	m	w	CANA	Alameda	Oakland	68	129
Hugh	52	m	w	IREL	Alameda	Oakland	68	175
John	36	m	w	IREL	San Francisco	11-Wd San Francisc	84	633
John P	45	m	w	ME	San Francisco	San Francisco P O	83	108
Kate	18	f	w	IREL	Solano	Vallejo	90	141
Margaret	38	f	w	IREL	San Francisco	2-Wd San Francisco	79	155
Michael	40	m	w	IREL	Shasta	French Gulch P O	89	465
GAYON								
Athaune	50	m	w	FRAN	Santa Barbara	San Buenaventura P	87	432
GAYS								
John	2	m	w	CA	Fresno	Millerton P O	72	168
GAYTON								
Mary F	20	f	w	ENGL	San Francisco	6-Wd San Francisco	81	71
GAZA								
P T	31	m	w	PRUS	Siskiyou	Callahan P O	89	624
GAZANARY								
John	27	m	w	AR	San Diego	Julian Dist	78	474
GAZOLA								
Lazzaro	35	m	w	ITAL	Amador	Volcano P O	69	383
GAZOLLA								
Joseph	18	m	w	ITAL	Amador	Sutter Crk P O	69	411
GAZZLE								
Martin	60	m	b	KY	Nevada	Rough & Ready Twp	75	332
GAZZOLO								
John	25	m	w	ITAL	Fresno	Millerton P O	72	168
GE								
Ah	58	m	c	CHIN	Nevada	Nevada Twp	75	312
Ah	45	m	c	CHIN	El Dorado	Placerville Twp	72	93
Ah	43	m	c	CHIN	Yuba	Marysville	93	599
Ah	40	m	c	CHIN	El Dorado	Mud Springs Twp	72	87
Ah	40	m	c	CHIN	Sacramento	Granite Twp	77	141
Ah	39	m	c	CHIN	Sacramento	Granite Twp	77	151
Ah	33	m	c	CHIN	Mariposa	Mariposa P O	74	128
Ah	31	m	c	CHIN	Sacramento	1-Wd Sacramento	77	205
Ah	28	m	c	CHIN	Sacramento	Granite Twp	77	138
Ho	20	m	c	CHIN	Sacramento	1-Wd Sacramento	77	183
Hop	35	m	c	CHIN	Butte	Kimshew Tpw	70	77
Hum	35	m	c	CHIN	Yuba	Marysville	93	631

© 2001 by Heritage Quest. All rights reserved.

Name	Age	S	R	B-PL	County	Series M593 Locale	Roll	Pg
Kee	19	m	c	CHIN	Santa Clara	1-Wd San Jose	88	272
Lon	30	m	c	CHIN	Yuba	Marysville	93	628
Ming	40	m	c	CHIN	Butte	Wyandotte Twp	70	147
Ong	34	m	c	CHIN	Klamath	Liberty Twp	73	375
Ton	40	m	c	CHIN	Butte	Kimshew Tpw	70	85
Wang	32	m	c	CHIN	El Dorado	Diamond Springs Tw	72	32
Yat	21	m	c	CHIN	Santa Clara	Alviso Twp	88	25
GEA								
Ah	20	m	c	CHIN	Placer	Clipper Gap P O	76	392
GEACH								
Wm	50	m	w	ENGL	Santa Clara	Almaden Twp	88	11
GEACONINI								
James	18	m	w	SWIT	Sonoma	Petaluma Twp	91	316
GEAGAN								
Hugh	40	m	w	IREL	Contra Costa	Martinez P O	71	388
GEAGHEART								
Phoeba	29	f	w	IN	Yolo	Cottonwood Twp	93	474
GEAH								
Ah	19	m	c	CHIN	Shasta	Shasta P O	89	454
GEALER								
Henry	35	m	w	SAXO	Monterey	San Benito Twp	74	384
GEAM								
Ellen	20	f	w	IREL	Alameda	Alameda	68	14
GEAMEAN								
Yves	66	m	w	FRAN	Plumas	Rich Bar Twp	77	45
GEAMNA								
Dennis	30	m	w	IREL	San Mateo	Schoolhouse Statio	87	342
GEAN								
---	12	m	c	CHIN	Shasta	American Ranch P O	89	500
Sanac	33	m	w	FRAN	Alameda	Washington Twp	68	292
GEANNETTI								
Vittorio	28	m	w	ITAL	Alameda	Washington Twp	68	287
GEAR								
Alexander T	48	m	w	PA	Stanislaus	San Joaquin Twp	92	73
C L	17	f	w	ME	Tuolumne	Columbia P O	93	345
Hiram Lewis	27	m	w	OH	Plumas	Plumas Twp	77	28
John	48	m	w	NY	Shasta	Shasta P O	89	453
Levi R	36	m	w	NY	Colusa	Grand Island Twp	71	308
Philo	62	m	w	CT	Shasta	Millville P O	89	491
S A	43	m	w	MA	Tuolumne	Columbia P O	93	358
GEARDEN								
James	30	m	w	IREL	San Mateo	Belmont P O	87	374
GEAREY								
Edward	46	m	w	IREL	San Diego	San Diego	78	510
James	26	m	w	IREL	San Francisco	11-Wd San Francisc	84	519
GEARHEART								
John	49	m	w	MO	Humboldt	Bald Hills	72	239
Phillip	20	m	w	CA	Colusa	Colusa Twp	71	277
GEARHEISER								
Risina	43	f	w	WURT	San Francisco	1-Wd San Francisco	79	41
GEARHITY								
John	60	m	w	IREL	San Francisco	San Francisco P O	80	398
GEARING								
A	21	m	w	CA	Solano	Vallejo	90	179
Charles	42	m	w	PRUS	Sonoma	Analy Twp	91	235
GEARMAN								
Mary	14	f	w	CA	San Francisco	11-Wd San Francisc	84	484
GEARN								
Patrick	30	m	w	IREL	San Francisco	San Francisco P O	85	824
GEARONO								
G	21	m	w	SWIT	Monterey	Alisal Twp	74	292
GEARRY								
Michael	34	m	w	IREL	San Francisco	2-Wd San Francisco	79	213
GEARS								
George	45	m	m	VA	Sacramento	4-Wd Sacramento	77	347
GEART								
Ah	30	m	c	CHIN	Calaveras	San Andreas P O	70	162
GEARY								
Abraham	28	m	w	ENGL	Mariposa	Mariposa P O	74	113
Danl	40	m	w	IREL	San Francisco	1-Wd San Francisco	79	14
Denis	36	m	w	IREL	San Francisco	7-Wd San Francisco	81	250
Eugene	27	m	w	IREL	San Mateo	Schoolhouse Statio	87	342
Ferdinand	35	m	w	MA	San Francisco	San Francisco P O	83	186
Fredk	37	m	w	BADE	San Francisco	San Francisco P O	85	868
George	36	m	w	MO	Mendocino	Round Valley Twp	74	218
George	30	m	w	WI	Yolo	Cottonwood Twp	93	459
Henry	40	m	w	IREL	San Francisco	8-Wd San Francisco	82	396
Honora	42	f	w	IREL	San Francisco	San Francisco P O	85	846
James	25	m	w	IREL	San Francisco	7-Wd San Francisco	81	223
James	23	m	w	NY	San Francisco	1-Wd San Francisco	79	49
Jas	35	m	w	IREL	Solano	Vallejo	90	196
Jno Francis	24	m	w	IREL	San Francisco	San Francisco P O	83	25
John	50	m	w	IREL	San Mateo	Schoolhouse Statio	87	342
John	47	m	w	IREL	Mariposa	Mariposa P O	74	128
John	37	m	w	IREL	San Francisco	7-Wd San Francisco	81	263
John F	56	m	w	IREL	San Francisco	San Francisco P O	83	143
Mary Ann	22	f	w	IREL	Santa Cruz	Santa Cruz	89	410
Michael	33	m	w	IREL	Solano	Vallejo	90	184
Morris	42	m	w	IREL	San Francisco	San Francisco P O	85	736
Pat	37	m	w	IREL	Alameda	Oakland	68	183
Patrick	31	m	w	IREL	San Francisco	11-Wd San Francisc	84	586
Peter	5	m	w	CA	San Francisco	11-Wd San Francisc	84	593
William	68	m	w	VA	Yolo	Cottonwood Twp	93	459
William	15	m	w	CA	Santa Clara	Santa Clara Twp	88	177
Wm	36	m	w	PRUS	San Francisco	7-Wd San Francisco	81	256
GEASON								
Henry	26	m	w	DENM	Contra Costa	Martinez P O	71	393
Jos	32	m	w	ENGL	Mono	Bridgeport P O	74	284
GEAT								
Ah	32	m	c	CHIN	Calaveras	San Andreas P O	70	162
GEATEOT								
Lewis	31	m	w	WI	Yolo	Grafton Twp	93	489
GEATO								
Domingo	33	m	w	ITAL	Calaveras	Copperopolis P O	70	244
GEAUCHAT								
Frederick	30	m	w	SWIT	Marin	San Rafael Twp	74	25
GEBARRA								
F	48	m	w	MEXI	Santa Clara	Almaden Twp	88	9
GEBBS								
Lester	39	m	w	MA	Klamath	South Fork Twp	73	383
GEBBY								
John	35	m	w	ENGL	San Francisco	7-Wd San Francisco	81	204
GEBERD								
Jacob	24	m	w	SWIT	Sacramento	4-Wd Sacramento	77	377
GEBERS								
Henry	58	m	w	HANO	Alameda	Eden Twp	68	61
GEBERSON								
John	35	m	w	OH	Yolo	Washington Twp	93	535
GEBHARD								
William	48	m	w	BADE	Amador	Sutter Crk P O	69	405
William	44	m	w	HDAR	San Francisco	8-Wd San Francisco	82	337
GEBHARDT								
Emile	22	m	w	NY	San Francisco	San Francisco P O	83	168
Fred	29	m	w	HAMB	San Francisco	3-Wd San Francisco	79	287
Margart	40	f	w	SWIT	Calaveras	San Andreas P O	70	194
Wentel	42	m	w	HDAR	San Francisco	6-Wd San Francisco	81	95
GEBHART								
Fred	42	m	w	PRUS	San Francisco	San Francisco P O	83	304
George A	44	m	w	BADE	San Francisco	6-Wd San Francisco	81	83
Jacob	32	m	w	BAVA	Yolo	Merritt Twp	93	508
Theodore	12	m	w	CA	Calaveras	Copperopolis P O	70	257
GEBNEY								
John	38	m	w	IREL	Contra Costa	Martinez P O	71	427
GEBRIRO								
Rofufa	35	m	i	MEXI	Inyo	Cerro Gordo Twp	73	320
GECHELL								
Con	40	m	w	PRUS	San Joaquin	2-Wd Stockton	86	188
GECK								
Ah	37	m	c	CHIN	Butte	Hamilton Twp	70	67
Ah	27	m	c	CHIN	Plumas	Plumas Twp	77	32
Ah	19	m	c	CHIN	Placer	Clipper Gap P O	76	393
Catherine	30	f	w	HESS	Yolo	Cache Crk Twp	93	434
Gee	26	m	c	CHIN	Plumas	Seneca Twp	77	51
GECKLER								
Ed	45	m	w	DENM	Sacramento	3-Wd Sacramento	77	299
GECOBIE								
P C	36	m	w	PA	San Francisco	7-Wd San Francisco	81	206
Sarah	32	f	w	PA	San Francisco	7-Wd San Francisco	81	206
GEDDEN								
John	23	m	w	IREL	Humboldt	Eureka Twp	72	279
GEDDES								
Alexander	37	m	w	IA	San Francisco	2-Wd San Francisco	79	214
Alexander	32	m	w	SCOT	San Francisco	11-Wd San Francisc	84	482
Brown	28	m	w	HANO	San Francisco	San Francisco P O	83	30
Chas	49	m	w	CANA	San Francisco	11-Wd San Francisc	84	440
Hannah	28	f	w	IREL	San Francisco	11-Wd San Francisc	84	540
James	40	m	w	SCOT	San Francisco	1-Wd San Francisco	79	107
James	20	m	w	OH	Stanislaus	Empire Twp	92	65
John	36	m	w	PA	Stanislaus	Empire Twp	92	63
John	32	m	w	CANA	Stanislaus	Empire Twp	92	59
Jonathan	35	m	w	OH	Stanislaus	San Joaquin Twp	92	72
Nicholas	29	m	w	PRUS	San Francisco	San Francisco P O	80	334
GEDDIS								
Cecelia	28	f	w	IA	San Joaquin	Elkhorn Twp	86	52
Emma S	11	f	w	IA	Stanislaus	Empire Twp	92	33
GEDERHOLM								
Wm	25	m	w	SWED	San Francisco	1-Wd San Francisco	79	119
GEDERSON								
Joseph	40	m	w	NJ	Mendocino	Point Arena Twp	74	205
GEDGE								
George	50	m	w	ENGL	San Francisco	6-Wd San Francisco	81	154
John	17	m	w	LA	Contra Costa	Martinez Twp	71	352
GEDIS								
Chas	3M	m	w	CA	San Francisco	11-Wd San Francisc	84	665
GEDNEY								
Allen M	32	m	w	CANA	Shasta	Fort Crook P O	89	477
Jas E	40	m	w	IN	Sonoma	Healdsburg & Mendo	91	283
Robert	49	m	w	NY	Tulare	Visalia	92	297
GEDRYE								
Henry	21	m	w	IL	Solano	Rio Vista Twp	90	58
GEE								
---	41	m	c	CHIN	Siskiyou	Cottonwood Twp	89	595
---	22	m	c	CHIN	Shasta	Shasta P O	89	454
---	22	m	c	CHIN	Siskiyou	Butte Twp	89	586
Ah	9	m	c	CHIN	San Francisco	2-Wd San Francisco	79	158
Ah	60	m	c	CHIN	Mariposa	Mariposa P O	74	100
Ah	60	m	c	CHIN	Sacramento	Georgianna Twp	77	127
Ah	6	f	c	CA	Santa Clara	1-Wd San Jose	88	273
Ah	57	m	c	CHIN	Marin	San Rafael Twp	74	37
Ah	56	m	c	CHIN	El Dorado	Mud Springs Twp	72	73
Ah	54	m	c	CHIN	Mariposa	Mariposa P O	74	126
Ah	52	m	c	CHIN	Nevada	Rough & Ready Twp	75	331
Ah	52	m	c	CHIN	Placer	Dutch Flat P O	76	408
Ah	51	m	c	CHIN	Santa Clara	San Jose Twp	88	183

© 2001 by Heritage Quest. All rights reserved.

California 1870 Census

Name	Age	S	R	B-PL	County	Locale	Series M593 Roll	Pg
Ah	50	m	c	CHIN	Sacramento	Dry Crk Twp	77	101
Ah	50	m	c	CHIN	Amador	Drytown P O	69	419
Ah	50	m	c	CHIN	Sacramento	Dry Crk Twp	77	101
Ah	48	m	c	CHIN	Mariposa	Mariposa P O	74	113
Ah	47	m	c	CHIN	Trinity	Lewiston Pct	92	215
Ah	46	m	c	CHIN	San Francisco	San Francisco P O	80	503
Ah	45	m	c	CHIN	Shasta	Shasta P O	89	461
Ah	45	m	c	CHIN	San Francisco	6-Wd San Francisco	81	42
Ah	45	m	c	CHIN	Plumas	Mineral Twp	77	25
Ah	45	m	c	CHIN	Fresno	Millerton P O	72	199
Ah	45	m	c	CHIN	Sacramento	Granite Twp	77	138
Ah	44	m	c	CHIN	Sacramento	Granite Twp	77	155
Ah	43	m	c	CHIN	El Dorado	Salmon Falls Twp	72	132
Ah	43	m	c	CHIN	Yuba	Marysville	93	618
Ah	42	m	c	CHIN	Sierra	Eureka Twp	89	526
Ah	42	m	c	CHIN	Placer	Colfax P O	76	384
Ah	42	m	c	CHIN	Sacramento	Georgianna Twp	77	128
Ah	42	m	c	CHIN	Kern	Linns Valley P O	73	343
Ah	42	m	c	CHIN	Mariposa	Mariposa P O	74	102
Ah	42	m	c	CHIN	Butte	Hamilton Twp	70	67
Ah	42	m	c	CHIN	San Francisco	San Francisco P O	80	493
Ah	42	m	c	CHIN	Nevada	Grass Valley Twp	75	206
Ah	41	m	c	CHIN	Yolo	Merritt Twp	93	503
Ah	41	m	c	CHIN	Mariposa	Mariposa P O	74	132
Ah	41	m	c	CHIN	San Francisco	San Francisco P O	80	504
Ah	41	m	c	CHIN	El Dorado	Greenwood Twp	72	56
Ah	40	m	c	CHIN	Sierra	Sears Twp	89	554
Ah	40	m	c	CHIN	Trinity	Douglas	92	234
Ah	40	m	c	CHIN	San Mateo	San Mateo P O	87	352
Ah	40	m	c	CHIN	San Francisco	San Francisco P O	80	498
Ah	40	m	c	CHIN	Placer	Clipper Gap P O	76	393
Ah	40	m	c	CHIN	Mariposa	Mariposa P O	74	121
Ah	40	m	c	CHIN	Mariposa	Mariposa P O	74	126
Ah	40	m	c	CHIN	Mariposa	Mariposa P O	74	106
Ah	40	m	c	CHIN	San Francisco	San Francisco P O	83	31
Ah	40	m	c	CHIN	El Dorado	Cosumnes Twp	72	15
Ah	40	m	c	CHIN	Alameda	Alameda	68	17
Ah	40	m	c	CHIN	Sacramento	1-Wd Sacramento	77	194
Ah	40	m	c	CHIN	Placer	Dutch Flat P O	76	409
Ah	39	m	c	CHIN	Fresno	Millerton P O	72	199
Ah	39	m	c	CHIN	Alameda	Oakland	68	254
Ah	39	m	c	CHIN	Alameda	Murray Twp	68	114
Ah	38	m	c	CHIN	Solano	Suisun Twp	90	98
Ah	38	m	c	CHIN	San Mateo	Half Moon Bay P O	87	396
Ah	38	m	c	CHIN	San Francisco	San Francisco P O	80	494
Ah	38	m	c	CHIN	Mariposa	Mariposa P O	74	107
Ah	38	m	c	CHIN	Mariposa	Mariposa P O	74	133
Ah	38	m	c	CHIN	Fresno	Millerton P O	72	200
Ah	38	m	c	CHIN	Trinity	Junction City Pct	92	209
Ah	37	m	c	CHIN	Mariposa	Mariposa P O	74	122
Ah	37	m	c	CHIN	Butte	Ophir Twp	70	106
Ah	37	m	c	CHIN	San Francisco	San Francisco P O	80	503
Ah	37	m	c	CHIN	San Francisco	San Francisco P O	80	512
Ah	37	m	c	CHIN	Sacramento	Georgianna Twp	77	131
Ah	36	m	c	CHIN	Stanislaus	Empire Twp	92	64
Ah	36	m	c	CHIN	San Joaquin	1-Wd Stockton	86	156
Ah	36	m	c	CHIN	San Joaquin	Oneal Twp	86	116
Ah	36	m	c	CHIN	Mariposa	Mariposa P O	74	132
Ah	36	m	c	CHIN	Humboldt	Eureka Twp	72	266
Ah	35	m	c	CHIN	Shasta	French Gulch P O	89	465
Ah	35	m	c	CHIN	Sacramento	Franklin Twp	77	116
Ah	35	m	c	CHIN	Mariposa	Mariposa P O	74	106
Ah	35	m	c	CHIN	Colusa	Spring Valley Twp	71	336
Ah	35	m	c	CHIN	Alameda	Oakland	68	210
Ah	35	m	c	CHIN	Alameda	Oakland	68	232
Ah	35	m	c	CHIN	Alameda	Oakland	68	254
Ah	35	m	c	CHIN	El Dorado	White Oak Twp	72	136
Ah	35	m	c	CHIN	El Dorado	Mud Springs Twp	72	74
Ah	35	m	c	CHIN	El Dorado	Mud Springs Twp	72	76
Ah	35	m	c	CHIN	Calaveras	Copperopolis P O	70	222
Ah	35	m	c	CHIN	Alameda	Oakland	68	238
Ah	35	m	c	CHIN	Yuba	Marysville	93	619
Ah	34	m	c	CHIN	Kern	Bakersfield P O	73	357
Ah	34	m	c	CHIN	San Francisco	San Francisco P O	80	516
Ah	34	m	c	CHIN	Nevada	Eureka Twp	75	127
Ah	34	m	c	CHIN	Sacramento	San Joaquin Twp	77	405
Ah	34	m	c	CHIN	Sacramento	Granite Twp	77	137
Ah	34	m	c	CHIN	Sacramento	Georgianna Twp	77	125
Ah	33	m	c	CHIN	Solano	Vallejo	90	174
Ah	33	m	c	CHIN	Santa Clara	San Jose Twp	88	194
Ah	33	m	c	CHIN	Sacramento	1-Wd Sacramento	77	193
Ah	33	m	c	CHIN	Alameda	Oakland	68	158
Ah	33	m	c	CHIN	San Francisco	2-Wd San Francisco	79	184
Ah	32	f	c	CHIN	San Francisco	San Francisco P O	80	441
Ah	32	m	c	CHIN	Sacramento	Georgianna Twp	77	123
Ah	32	m	c	CHIN	Mariposa	Mariposa P O	74	126
Ah	32	m	c	CHIN	Santa Clara	Alviso Twp	88	25
Ah	32	m	c	CHIN	Fresno	Millerton P O	72	199
Ah	32	m	c	CHIN	Nevada	Eureka Twp	75	127
Ah	32	m	c	CHIN	Sacramento	Georgianna Twp	77	127
Ah	32	m	c	CHIN	Yuba	Marysville	93	619
Ah	31	m	c	CHIN	San Francisco	San Francisco P O	80	500
Ah	31	m	c	CHIN	Butte	Hamilton Twp	70	74
Ah	31	m	c	CHIN	Trinity	Lewiston Pct	92	211
Ah	31	m	c	CHIN	Nevada	Eureka Twp	75	140
Ah	31	m	c	CHIN	Sacramento	Georgianna Twp	77	133
Ah	30	m	c	CHIN	Nevada	Nevada Twp	75	318
Ah	30	m	c	CHIN	Sacramento	Georgianna Twp	77	124
Ah	30	m	c	CHIN	Butte	Chico Twp	70	28
Ah	30	m	c	CHIN	Alameda	Oakland	68	245
Ah	30	m	c	CHIN	Trinity	Minersville Pct	92	203
Ah	30	m	c	CHIN	San Mateo	Schoolhouse Statio	87	341
Ah	30	m	c	CHIN	Alameda	Oakland	68	254
Ah	30	m	c	CHIN	Nevada	Eureka Twp	75	136
Ah	30	m	c	CHIN	Yuba	W Bear Rvr Twp	93	681
Ah	29	m	c	CHIN	Santa Barbara	San Buenaventura P	87	438
Ah	29	m	c	CHIN	Butte	Ophir Twp	70	121
Ah	29	m	c	CHIN	Sierra	Eureka Twp	89	525
Ah	29	m	c	CHIN	San Francisco	San Francisco P O	80	510
Ah	29	m	c	CHIN	Alameda	Eden Twp	68	61
Ah	28	m	c	CHIN	Tuolumne	Big Oak Flat P O	93	392
Ah	28	m	c	CHIN	Yolo	Putah Twp	93	510
Ah	28	m	c	CHIN	Nevada	Rough & Ready Twp	75	329
Ah	28	m	c	CHIN	Sacramento	Georgianna Twp	77	125
Ah	28	m	c	CHIN	Sacramento	Georgianna Twp	77	124
Ah	28	m	c	CHIN	Sacramento	Georgianna Twp	77	123
Ah	28	m	c	CHIN	Santa Clara	Alviso Twp	88	25
Ah	28	m	c	CHIN	San Francisco	7-Wd San Francisco	81	158
Ah	28	m	c	CHIN	Alameda	Oakland	68	172
Ah	28	m	c	CHIN	Placer	Gold Run Twp	76	400
Ah	27	m	c	CHIN	San Joaquin	2-Wd Stockton	86	162
Ah	27	m	c	CHIN	Sacramento	San Joaquin Twp	77	405
Ah	27	m	c	CHIN	Mariposa	Mariposa P O	74	126
Ah	27	m	c	CHIN	Sacramento	Granite Twp	77	150
Ah	27	m	c	CHIN	Sacramento	Georgianna Twp	77	124
Ah	26	m	c	CHIN	Sierra	Gibson Twp	89	538
Ah	26	m	c	CHIN	San Francisco	San Francisco P O	80	514
Ah	26	m	c	CHIN	Nevada	Washington Twp	75	346
Ah	26	m	c	CHIN	Sacramento	Granite Twp	77	138
Ah	26	m	c	CHIN	Sacramento	Georgianna Twp	77	128
Ah	26	m	c	CHIN	Sacramento	Georgianna Twp	77	135
Ah	25	m	c	CHIN	Solano	Suisun Twp	90	105
Ah	25	m	c	CHIN	Tuolumne	Chinese Camp P O	93	382
Ah	25	m	c	CHIN	Tuolumne	Chinese Camp P O	93	389
Ah	25	m	c	CHIN	San Francisco	6-Wd San Francisco	81	46
Ah	25	m	c	CHIN	San Francisco	6-Wd San Francisco	81	60
Ah	25	m	c	CHIN	San Francisco	6-Wd San Francisco	81	61
Ah	25	m	c	CHIN	Placer	Clipper Gap P O	76	393
Ah	25	m	c	CHIN	Mariposa	Mariposa P O	74	102
Ah	25	m	c	CHIN	San Francisco	San Francisco P O	85	835
Ah	25	m	c	CHIN	San Francisco	San Francisco P O	80	509
Ah	25	m	c	CHIN	San Francisco	7-Wd San Francisco	81	174
Ah	25	m	c	CHIN	Amador	Ione City P O	69	354
Ah	25	m	c	CHIN	Alameda	Oakland	68	223
Ah	25	m	c	CHIN	Sacramento	Georgianna Twp	77	135
Ah	25	m	c	CHIN	Sacramento	Georgianna Twp	77	133
Ah	25	m	c	CHIN	Sacramento	Georgianna Twp	77	129
Ah	25	m	c	CHIN	Yuba	Marysville	93	620
Ah	24	m	c	CHIN	Sonoma	Sonoma Twp	91	449
Ah	24	m	c	CHIN	San Francisco	San Francisco P O	80	447
Ah	24	m	c	CHIN	Sacramento	Dry Crk Twp	77	101
Ah	24	m	c	CHIN	Alameda	Oakland	68	202
Ah	24	m	c	CHIN	San Francisco	San Francisco P O	80	539
Ah	24	m	c	CHIN	Amador	Volcano P O	69	383
Ah	24	m	c	CHIN	Mariposa	Mariposa P O	74	98
Ah	24	m	c	CHIN	Nevada	Nevada Twp	75	316
Ah	22	m	c	CHIN	San Francisco	2-Wd San Francisco	79	256
Ah	22	m	c	CHIN	Placer	Emigrant Gap P O	76	417
Ah	22	m	c	CHIN	Sonoma	Salt Point	91	393
Ah	22	m	c	CHIN	San Francisco	7-Wd San Francisco	81	176
Ah	22	m	c	CHIN	San Francisco	San Francisco P O	80	510
Ah	22	m	c	CHIN	Calaveras	San Andreas P O	70	187
Ah	22	m	c	CHIN	Alameda	Oakland	68	181
Ah	22	m	c	CHIN	Nevada	Eureka Twp	75	141
Ah	22	f	c	CHIN	Placer	Dutch Flat P O	76	408
Ah	22	m	c	CHIN	Placer	Auburn P O	76	374
Ah	22	m	c	CHIN	Sacramento	Georgianna Twp	77	133
Ah	21	m	c	CHIN	Solano	Suisun Twp	90	105
Ah	21	m	c	CHIN	Butte	Chico Twp	70	27
Ah	21	m	c	CHIN	San Francisco	San Francisco P O	83	238
Ah	21	m	c	CHIN	Amador	Ione City P O	69	371
Ah	20	m	c	CHIN	Shasta	French Gulch P O	89	469
Ah	20	m	c	CHIN	San Francisco	6-Wd San Francisco	81	42
Ah	20	m	c	CHIN	San Francisco	2-Wd San Francisco	79	196
Ah	20	m	c	CHIN	Trinity	North Fork Twp	92	216
Ah	20	m	c	CHIN	Shasta	American Ranch P O	89	497
Ah	20	m	c	CHIN	Santa Clara	Santa Clara Twp	88	148
Ah	20	m	c	CHIN	El Dorado	White Oak Twp	72	141
Ah	20	m	c	CHIN	Butte	Bidwell Twp	70	1
Ah	20	m	c	CHIN	Alameda	Oakland	68	256
Ah	20	m	c	CHIN	Alameda	Oakland	68	255
Ah	20	m	c	CHIN	Sacramento	Georgianna Twp	77	130
Ah	19	m	c	CHIN	Sutter	Sutter Twp	92	127
Ah	19	m	c	CHIN	San Francisco	6-Wd San Francisco	81	60
Ah	19	f	c	CHIN	Butte	Chico Twp	70	28
Ah	19	m	c	CHIN	Alameda	Oakland	68	216
Ah	19	m	c	CHIN	Tehama	Tehama Twp	92	188
Ah	19	m	c	CHIN	Solano	Suisun Twp	90	105
Ah	19	m	c	CHIN	Contra Costa	Martinez P O	71	404
Ah	19	m	c	CHIN	Calaveras	San Andreas P O	70	176
Ah	19	m	c	CHIN	Alameda	Oakland	68	135
Ah	19	m	c	CHIN	Sacramento	1-Wd Sacramento	77	189
Ah	18	f	c	CHIN	San Francisco	San Francisco P O	80	503
Ah	18	m	c	CHIN	San Francisco	San Francisco P O	80	336

© 2001 by Heritage Quest. All rights reserved.

Name	Age	S	R	B-PL	County	Locale	Roll	Pg
Ah	18	m	c	CHIN	Placer	Auburn P O	76	379
Ah	18	m	c	CHIN	Sacramento	San Joaquin Twp	77	398
Ah	18	m	c	CHIN	Alameda	Oakland	68	152
Ah	18	f	c	CHIN	Colusa	Colusa	71	299
Ah	17	m	c	CHIN	Nevada	Rough & Ready Twp	75	329
Ah	17	m	c	CHIN	San Francisco	6-Wd San Francisco	81	97
Ah	17	m	c	CHIN	Nevada	Grass Valley Twp	75	197
Ah	17	m	c	CHIN	Placer	Cisco P O	76	494
Ah	16	m	c	CHIN	San Joaquin	Castoria Twp	86	12
Ah	16	m	c	CHIN	San Joaquin	Oneal Twp	86	111
Ah	16	m	c	CHIN	Yuba	Marysville	93	596
Ah	16	m	c	CHIN	Santa Cruz	Pajaro Twp	89	342
Ah	16	m	c	CHIN	San Francisco	San Francisco P O	83	225
Ah	16	m	c	CHIN	San Francisco	7-Wd San Francisco	81	157
Ah	16	m	c	CHIN	San Francisco	7-Wd San Francisco	81	205
Ah	15	m	c	CHIN	San Francisco	2-Wd San Francisco	79	283
Ah	15	m	c	CHIN	Butte	Ophir Twp	70	104
Ah	15	m	c	CHIN	Alameda	Oakland	68	136
Ah	14	m	c	CHIN	San Francisco	1-Wd San Francisco	79	55
Ah	14	m	c	CHIN	Sacramento	3-Wd Sacramento	77	310
Ah	14	f	c	CHIN	Butte	Chico Twp	70	27
Ah	14	m	c	CHIN	San Francisco	San Francisco P O	83	160
Ah	13	m	c	CHIN	Alameda	Oakland	68	188
Ah	12	m	c	CHIN	San Francisco	8-Wd San Francisco	82	447
Ah	12	m	c	CHIN	Nevada	Eureka Twp	75	127
An	45	m	c	CHIN	Calaveras	San Andreas P O	70	199
An	39	m	c	CHIN	El Dorado	Mud Springs Twp	72	75
An	27	f	c	CHIN	Amador	Drytown P O	69	419
An	22	m	c	CHIN	El Dorado	Placerville	72	115
Ar	25	m	c	CHIN	Sonoma	Petaluma Twp	91	363
Charles	27	m	w	ENGL	Placer	Lincoln P O	76	489
Chin	13	m	c	CHIN	San Francisco	8-Wd San Francisco	82	387
Chit	20	m	c	CHIN	Yuba	Marysville	93	622
Chung	45	m	c	CHIN	Yuba	Marysville	93	621
Chung	30	m	c	CHIN	Alameda	Oakland	68	202
Cow	26	m	c	CHIN	Yuba	Marysville	93	622
Cull	34	m	c	CHIN	Yuba	Marysville	93	630
Edward	28	m	w	IREL	Solano	Silveyville Twp	90	75
Ferdinann	39	m	w	PRUS	San Francisco	San Francisco P O	83	52
Fong	40	m	c	CHIN	Nevada	Eureka Twp	75	127
Fong Ah	15	m	c	CHIN	San Francisco	2-Wd San Francisco	79	184
Foy	23	m	c	CHIN	Yolo	Washington Twp	93	536
Fung	38	m	c	CHIN	Nevada	Rough & Ready Twp	75	331
Gam	29	m	c	CHIN	Yuba	Marysville	93	623
Geo G	25	m	w	MA	Sacramento	3-Wd Sacramento	77	281
Gin	45	m	c	CHIN	Yuba	Marysville	93	620
Gin	35	f	c	CHIN	Yuba	Marysville	93	627
Han	32	m	c	CHIN	Yuba	Marysville	93	629
He	19	m	c	CHIN	Placer	Summit P O	76	497
Hem	42	m	c	CHIN	Yuba	Marysville	93	629
Heng	30	m	c	CHIN	Yuba	Marysville	93	629
Hi	29	m	c	CHIN	Yolo	Washington Twp	93	537
Hi	20	m	c	CHIN	San Francisco	1-Wd San Francisco	79	84
Hin	40	m	c	CHIN	Marin	San Rafael Twp	74	39
Ho	14	m	c	CHIN	San Francisco	8-Wd San Francisco	82	385
Hop	32	m	c	CHIN	Nevada	Eureka Twp	75	136
Hop	32	m	c	CHIN	Butte	Wyandotte Twp	70	142
Hop	31	m	c	CHIN	Butte	Chico Twp	70	49
Hop	27	m	c	CHIN	Butte	Chico Twp	70	27
Hop	24	m	c	CHIN	Yolo	Merritt Twp	93	506
Hop	20	m	c	CHIN	San Francisco	San Francisco P O	83	270
Hop	17	m	c	CHIN	Butte	Chico Twp	70	27
Hoy	30	m	c	CHIN	Yuba	Marysville	93	626
Hoy	29	m	c	CHIN	San Francisco	6-Wd San Francisco	81	64
Hoy	13	m	c	CHIN	Yuba	Marysville	93	628
Jim	17	m	c	CHIN	San Francisco	8-Wd San Francisco	82	494
John	33	m	w	IREL	San Francisco	7-Wd San Francisco	81	259
John	30	m	c	CHIN	Colusa	Colusa	71	299
Kin	17	m	c	CHIN	San Francisco	11-Wd San Francisc	84	664
Kong	45	m	c	CHIN	Siskiyou	Cottonwood Twp	89	594
La	21	m	c	CHIN	Santa Clara	Alviso Twp	88	25
Lam	24	m	c	CHIN	San Joaquin	Elkhorn Twp	86	69
Lan	32	m	c	CHIN	San Joaquin	Elkhorn Twp	86	69
Lang	17	m	c	CA	San Francisco	6-Wd San Francisco	81	44
Lay	29	m	c	CHIN	Butte	Ophir Twp	70	121
Le	30	m	c	CHIN	Stanislaus	Emory Twp	92	25
Lee	42	m	c	CHIN	Calaveras	San Andreas P O	70	171
Lee	33	m	c	CHIN	Nevada	Washington Twp	75	342
Lee	29	m	c	CHIN	San Joaquin	3-Wd Stockton	86	230
Lee	21	m	c	CHIN	San Francisco	6-Wd San Francisco	81	64
Len	41	m	c	CHIN	Butte	Chico Twp	70	27
Li	28	m	c	CHIN	San Joaquin	Oneal Twp	86	116
Ling	24	f	c	CHIN	Butte	Chico Twp	70	27
Long	47	m	c	CHIN	Siskiyou	Yreka Twp	89	673
Long	25	m	c	CHIN	San Francisco	1-Wd San Francisco	79	84
Long	25	m	c	CHIN	Yuba	Marysville	93	624
Look	24	m	c	CHIN	Yuba	Marysville	93	626
Louin	35	m	c	CHIN	Shasta	American Ranch P O	89	496
Low	18	m	c	CHIN	Yuba	Marysville	93	624
Loy	39	m	c	CHIN	Yuba	Marysville	93	622
Luck	34	m	c	CHIN	Yuba	Marysville	93	630
Lue	39	m	c	CHIN	Yuba	Marysville	93	624
Lun	18	m	c	CHIN	Yuba	Marysville	93	629
Lung	35	m	c	CHIN	Yuba	Marysville	93	621
Margt	19	f	w	IREL	Sacramento	3-Wd Sacramento	77	301
Nar	28	f	c	CHIN	Yuba	Marysville	93	627
Nathaniel	6	m	w	MO	Colusa	Grand Island Twp	71	302
Nuie	30	m	c	CHIN	Nevada	Nevada Twp	75	298
On	22	m	c	CHIN	Solano	Suisun Twp	90	107
On	20	m	c	CHIN	Placer	Clipper Gap P O	76	392
On	10	m	c	CHIN	San Francisco	8-Wd San Francisco	82	349
Ong	52	m	c	CHIN	Santa Clara	San Jose Twp	88	190
Ong	25	m	c	CHIN	San Francisco	3-Wd San Francisco	79	309
Pet	35	m	c	CHIN	Yuba	Marysville	93	631
Poy	35	m	c	CHIN	Yuba	Marysville	93	629
S J	45	m	w	OH	Siskiyou	Surprise Valley Tw	89	643
Sam	37	m	c	CHIN	Calaveras	San Andreas P O	70	216
Sam	27	m	c	CHIN	San Joaquin	3-Wd Stockton	86	230
Sam	17	m	c	CHIN	Santa Clara	1-Wd San Jose	88	272
Shang	29	m	c	CHIN	Nevada	Meadow Lake Twp	75	256
Show	40	m	c	CHIN	San Francisco	6-Wd San Francisco	81	42
Sin	30	f	c	CHIN	El Dorado	Placerville	72	114
Sing	30	m	c	CHIN	Yuba	Marysville	93	629
Sing	20	m	c	CHIN	Sonoma	Santa Rosa	91	409
Sum	14	m	c	CHIN	Yuba	Marysville	93	621
Sung	26	m	c	CHIN	Placer	Bath P O	76	445
Tang	19	m	c	CHIN	San Francisco	8-Wd San Francisco	82	387
Ti	33	m	c	CHIN	Nevada	Rough & Ready Twp	75	327
Tung	29	m	c	CHIN	Klamath	Dillon Twp	73	369
Up	51	m	c	CHIN	Santa Clara	Alviso Twp	88	25
Up	30	m	c	CHIN	Siskiyou	Hamburg Twp	89	598
Up	19	m	c	CHIN	Solano	Vallejo	90	209
Up Ah	36	m	c	CHIN	Santa Clara	San Jose Twp	88	194
Wa	23	m	c	CHIN	Solano	Suisun Twp	90	106
Wah	28	m	c	CHIN	San Francisco	11-Wd San Francisc	84	527
Wah	15	m	c	CHIN	Solano	Suisun Twp	90	94
Wing	40	m	c	CHIN	Butte	Chico Twp	70	28
Wo	38	m	c	CHIN	Mariposa	Mariposa P O	74	103
Wo	30	m	c	CHIN	Stanislaus	Empire Twp	92	62
Won	35	m	c	CHIN	Yolo	Cache Crk Twp	93	428
Wop	25	m	c	CHIN	Stanislaus	Empire Twp	92	64
Wy	50	m	c	CHIN	Siskiyou	Hamburg Twp	89	596
Y	37	m	c	CHIN	Yuba	Marysville	93	629
Yee	43	m	c	CHIN	Yuba	Marysville	93	630
Yee	25	m	c	CHIN	Klamath	Liberty Twp	73	375
Yip	42	m	c	CHIN	San Francisco	3-Wd San Francisco	79	322
Yon Ding	24	m	c	CHIN	Plumas	Rich Bar Twp	77	46
Yuen	25	m	c	CHIN	Yuba	Marysville	93	624
Yung	24	m	c	CHIN	Kern	Bakersfield P O	73	364
Yup	47	m	c	CHIN	Santa Clara	1-Wd San Jose	88	272
GEED								
Christian	28	m	w	WURT	Monterey	San Juan Twp	74	407
GEEGORY								
U S	21	m	w	TX	El Dorado	Cosumnes Twp	72	13
GEELHOLD								
Peter	26	m	w	HOLL	Mono	Bridgeport P O	74	284
GEELMON								
J H	47	m	w	IREL	Alameda	Oakland	68	233
GEEN								
---	28	m	c	CHIN	Siskiyou	Cottonwood Twp	89	594
Ah	30	f	c	CHIN	El Dorado	Georgetown Twp	72	44
Ah	23	m	c	CHIN	Placer	Dutch Flat P O	76	410
Ah	19	m	c	CHIN	Napa	Yountville Twp	75	84
Ah	19	m	c	CHIN	San Francisco	6-Wd San Francisco	81	43
GEENE								
Eloise	21	f	w	NY	San Francisco	San Francisco P O	83	114
GEENTLEY								
Andrew	41	m	w	SWIT	Mendocino	Anderson Twp	74	150
GEER								
Joseph	33	m	w	SWIT	San Francisco	2-Wd San Francisco	79	215
Richard	51	m	w	ENGL	Sacramento	Granite Twp	77	150
GEEREIN								
Margaret	40	f	w	IREL	San Francisco	2-Wd San Francisco	79	200
GEESAE								
Ah	45	m	c	CHIN	San Joaquin	Castoria Twp	86	12
GEESE								
Adam	45	m	w	PRUS	San Francisco	San Francisco P O	85	808
GEESER								
Louise	65	f	w	BADE	San Francisco	San Francisco P O	83	143
GEESLIN								
T	53	m	w	NC	Sierra	Forest Twp	89	529
GEET								
Goo	14	m	c	CHIN	San Francisco	3-Wd San Francisco	79	304
GEEUP								
Ah	32	m	c	CHIN	Yuba	Marysville	93	620
GEFFKE								
Henry	37	m	w	HANO	San Francisco	11-Wd San Francisc	84	478
GEFKIN								
Chas	28	m	w	PRUS	San Francisco	San Francisco P O	83	317
GEFT								
William M	37	m	w	VA	Nevada	Meadow Lake Twp	75	262
GEGAN								
Michael	29	m	w	IREL	Amador	Amador City P O	69	391
Winnefred	26	f	w	IREL	San Francisco	8-Wd San Francisco	82	475
GEGEL								
Higenus	42	m	w	BADE	Napa	Napa	75	19
GEGGEN								
John	55	m	w	GERM	Trinity	Weaverville Pct	92	226
GEGGUS								
Wm	13	m	w	CA	San Francisco	11-Wd San Francisc	84	593
GEGHAGAN								
Margaret	35	f	w	IREL	San Francisco	San Francisco P O	83	419
GEGOW								
Ah	14	m	c	CHIN	Nevada	Nevada Twp	75	314

Series M593

© 2001 by Heritage Quest. All rights reserved.

California 1870 Census

Name	Age	S	R	B-PL	County	Locale	Series M593 Roll	Pg
GEGRAN								
Wm	21	m	w	MD	San Francisco	8-Wd San Francisco	82	364
GEH								
Ah	19	m	c	CHIN	Nevada	Bridgeport Twp	75	119
Gee	33	m	c	CHIN	Plumas	Mineral Twp	77	23
GEHAKEN								
Ann	16	f	w	HAMB	San Francisco	8-Wd San Francisco	82	468
GEHAM								
Charles	35	m	w	CT	San Francisco	11-Wd San Francisc	84	518
GEHAN								
John	25	m	w	IREL	San Francisco	1-Wd San Francisco	79	67
Michael	50	m	w	IREL	San Francisco	San Francisco P O	83	307
GEHEGAN								
Michael	39	m	w	IREL	Mariposa	Mariposa P O	74	114
GEHMAN								
John	38	m	w	GERM	Solano	Vallejo	90	193
GEHNE								
William	28	m	w	POME	San Francisco	3-Wd San Francisco	79	287
GEHRICK								
O F	46	m	w	PRUS	San Francisco	San Francisco P O	83	50
GEHRING								
Fred	28	m	w	BADE	Sacramento	3-Wd Sacramento	77	303
John B	45	m	w	BADE	Santa Cruz	Santa Cruz	89	406
GEHRINGER								
And	47	m	w	GERM	Contra Costa	Martinez P O	71	451
GEHRS								
Jacob	34	m	w	PRUS	San Francisco	San Francisco P O	80	536
GEI								
Ah	16	f	c	CHIN	San Francisco	San Francisco P O	80	490
Yap	40	m	w	PRUS	San Francisco	11-Wd San Francisc	84	483
GEIB								
Jessie	40	m	w	OH	San Francisco	San Francisco P O	83	284
GEIGER								
Antoine	46	m	w	SWIT	Butte	Bidwell Twp	70	4
Eliza	30	f	w	BADE	San Francisco	2-Wd San Francisco	79	244
Ferdinand	23	m	w	WURT	San Francisco	1-Wd San Francisco	79	57
Frank	54	m	w	BAVA	Shasta	Horsetown P O	89	502
Frank	35	m	w	PRUS	San Francisco	San Francisco P O	80	423
Ingolby	27	m	w	WURT	Santa Clara	2-Wd San Jose	88	320
John L	39	m	w	MO	Butte	Oroville Twp	70	138
Joseph	35	m	w	PRUS	San Francisco	5-Wd San Francisco	81	20
Peter	24	m	w	HDAR	San Francisco	San Francisco P O	83	212
William C	42	m	w	IL	Santa Clara	San Jose Twp	88	189
GEIGERMAN								
Hannah	19	f	w	PRUS	San Francisco	8-Wd San Francisco	82	412
GEIL								
Mary	32	f	w	IREL	Yuba	Linda Twp	93	556
Sam F	28	m	w	PA	Monterey	Monterey	74	362
GEILES								
Fredrick	26	m	w	HANO	San Francisco	7-Wd San Francisco	81	210
GEILS								
Henry H	37	m	w	HANO	San Francisco	San Francisco P O	85	716
GEIM								
Ah	32	m	c	CHIN	Nevada	Eureka Twp	75	140
Ah	26	m	c	CHIN	Sierra	Sears Twp	89	561
GEIMAN								
Peter	30	m	w	NY	San Mateo	Schoolhouse Statio	87	342
William	40	m	w	BADE	San Francisco	San Francisco P O	80	408
GEIN								
Ong	25	m	c	CHIN	Nevada	Eureka Twp	75	126
Wm	21	m	w	WIND	Merced	Snelling P O	74	259
GEINE								
Ah	20	m	c	CHIN	Nevada	Eureka Twp	75	126
GEIRRINE								
Chas	23	m	w	NY	San Francisco	1-Wd San Francisco	79	30
GEISCHEN								
Henry	39	m	w	HANO	Klamath	Liberty Twp	73	375
GEISE								
Jacob	11	m	w	CA	Plumas	Indian Twp	77	18
GEISEL								
Henry	39	m	w	GERM	Sacramento	Sutter Twp	77	388
GEISENDORFER								
George	43	m	w	PRUS	Placer	Auburn P O	76	382
GEISER								
Frank J	29	m	w	IN	San Francisco	8-Wd San Francisco	82	491
Jno	32	m	w	GERM	Sacramento	1-Wd Sacramento	77	181
GEISHAKER								
Andw	34	m	w	PRUS	San Francisco	San Francisco P O	83	101
GEISICKER								
Henry	47	m	w	BREM	Fresno	Millerton P O	72	147
GEISLER								
Vitalia	42	m	w	BELG	Fresno	Kingston P O	72	217
GEISSENDORFER								
F	42	m	w	BAVA	San Francisco	San Francisco P O	83	56
GEISSMAN								
Caspar	46	m	w	SWIT	Santa Clara	San Jose Twp	88	200
GEIST								
William	38	m	w	AUST	San Francisco	3-Wd San Francisco	79	326
GEITNER								
Franklin J	50	m	w	NY	Yolo	Fremont Twp	93	476
Fredk H	40	m	w	WURT	San Luis Obispo	Santa Rosa Twp	87	324
Lewis S	22	m	w	OH	Yolo	Fremont Twp	93	476
GEIZER								
Henry	38	m	w	SWIT	El Dorado	Georgetown Twp	72	43
GEK								
Ah	19	m	c	CHIN	Sonoma	Salt Point	91	386

Name	Age	S	R	B-PL	County	Locale	Series M593 Roll	Pg
GELA								
Ah	19	m	c	CHIN	Santa Clara	Alviso Twp	88	25
GELACK								
John	37	m	w	BADE	San Joaquin	Tulare Twp	86	254
GELALIA								
John	52	m	w	AUST	San Francisco	1-Wd San Francisco	79	129
GELANEY								
Josephine	18	f	w	PA	San Francisco	San Francisco P O	85	835
Mary E	9M	f	w	CA	San Francisco	11-Wd San Francisc	84	711
GELATT								
Richard D	29	m	w	PA	Alpine	Monitor P O	69	313
GELCHELL								
Remington	30	m	w	ME	Santa Cruz	Santa Cruz Twp	89	389
GELCISH								
Vincent	42	m	w	DALM	Los Angeles	Los Angeles	73	523
GELERES								
James	27	m	w	TX	Stanislaus	San Joaquin Twp	92	70
GELERO								
Bartolo	20	m	w	ITAL	Amador	Volcano P O	69	377
John B	38	m	w	ITAL	Amador	Volcano P O	69	377
GELES								
Carter	18	m	c	CHIN	San Joaquin	Dent Twp	86	18
GELESKY								
Socrates	38	m	w	POLA	Yolo	Cache Crk Twp	93	453
GELGICK								
Peter G	33	m	w	AUST	Inyo	Cerro Gordo Twp	73	320
GELIEN								
Robert G	52	m	w	HAMB	San Francisco	6-Wd San Francisco	81	83
GELIN								
Dora	23	f	w	PRUS	San Francisco	1-Wd San Francisco	79	40
GELINES								
John	48	m	w	CANA	San Francisco	11-Wd San Francisc	84	562
GELISPE								
Cornelius	18	m	w	NY	Butte	Chico Twp	70	42
GELKEY								
H	29	m	w	ME	San Joaquin	Dent Twp	86	16
GELL								
John	3	m	w	CA	Los Angeles	El Monte Twp	73	448
GELLAIRLY								
Richard	33	m	w	SCOT	Monterey	San Juan Twp	74	400
GELLAN								
Andrew	40	m	w	PA	San Joaquin	Oneal Twp	86	112
H	24	f	w	IL	Alameda	Murray Twp	68	118
GELLATY								
Peter	31	m	w	IREL	Nevada	Grass Valley Twp	75	199
GELLEN								
Edward	35	m	w	MD	Sonoma	Sonoma Twp	91	443
GELLICK								
Mike	33	m	w	IREL	San Francisco	11-Wd San Francisc	84	689
GELLIN								
Catherine	55	f	w	IREL	Santa Clara	Santa Clara Twp	88	153
GELLIS								
Edward	29	m	w	PRUS	San Francisco	5-Wd San Francisco	81	35
Joseph	60	m	w	PORT	San Francisco	11-Wd San Francisc	84	612
GELLMAN								
Henry	56	m	w	OH	Calaveras	San Andreas P O	70	151
GELLOT								
Paul	56	m	w	FRAN	Tuolumne	Chinese Camp P O	93	368
GELLY								
Mathew	23	m	w	NJ	Solano	Montezuma Twp	90	65
GELMAN								
L	29	m	w	MA	San Francisco	7-Wd San Francisco	81	226
GELO								
Lewis	40	m	w	FRAN	Stanislaus	Branch Twp	92	7
GELROY								
Urvan	10	m	w	CA	Monterey	Monterey	74	366
GELTHAUSER								
John	40	m	w	HESS	Sutter	Yuba Twp	92	142
GELWICKS								
D W	45	m	w	MD	Sacramento	3-Wd Sacramento	77	301
GELZERDEMAN								
Ezra	42	m	w	DC	San Bernardino	San Bernardino Twp	78	452
GEM								
Ah	42	m	c	CHIN	Nevada	Eureka Twp	75	141
Ah	42	m	c	CHIN	Nevada	Meadow Lake Twp	75	257
Ah	37	m	c	CHIN	Nevada	Washington Twp	75	342
Ah	23	m	c	CHIN	Tuolumne	Sonora P O	93	311
Ah	22	m	c	CHIN	Nevada	Bridgeport Twp	75	119
Ah	21	m	c	CHIN	San Francisco	6-Wd San Francisco	81	116
Ah	14	m	c	CHIN	Nevada	Meadow Lake Twp	75	266
Lem	1	f	c	CA	Yuba	Marysville	93	627
GEMAR								
Peter	37	m	w	BAVA	San Francisco	11-Wd San Francisc	84	467
GEMBERT								
Leon	47	m	w	FRAN	Santa Clara	2-Wd San Jose	88	300
Mariana	78	f	w	FRAN	Santa Clara	2-Wd San Jose	88	300
GEN								
---	24	m	c	CHIN	Siskiyou	Yreka	89	661
A Ka	34	m	c	CHIN	Sonoma	Sonoma Twp	91	447
Ah	50	m	c	CHIN	Calaveras	San Andreas P O	70	179
Ah	45	m	c	CHIN	Butte	Kimshew Tpw	70	84
Ah	40	m	c	CHIN	Nevada	Eureka Twp	75	136
Ah	37	m	c	CHIN	Placer	Cisco P O	76	495
Ah	34	m	c	CHIN	Butte	Oregon Twp	70	124
Ah	32	m	c	CHIN	Sacramento	Georgianna Twp	77	122
Ah	31	m	c	CHIN	Butte	Ophir Twp	70	121
Ah	30	m	c	CHIN	El Dorado	Diamond Springs Tw	72	22

© 2001 by Heritage Quest. All rights reserved.

Name	Age	S	R	B-PL	County	Locale	Series M593 Roll	Pg
Ah	29	m	c	CHIN	San Francisco	6-Wd San Francisco	81	61
Ah	28	m	c	CHIN	Sacramento	1-Wd Sacramento	77	196
Ah	27	m	c	CHIN	Placer	Auburn P O	76	365
Ah	25	m	c	CHIN	Solano	Suisun Twp	90	106
Ah	25	m	c	CHIN	Placer	Newcastle Twp	76	478
Ah	25	m	c	CHIN	Nevada	Eureka Twp	75	129
Ah	24	m	c	CHIN	Sierra	Eureka Twp	89	525
Ah	23	m	c	CHIN	Nevada	Eureka Twp	75	134
Ah	22	m	c	CHIN	Sacramento	Georgianna Twp	77	125
Ah	22	m	c	CHIN	Sierra	Eureka Twp	89	525
Ah	20	m	c	CHIN	San Francisco	6-Wd San Francisco	81	57
Ah	17	m	c	CHIN	Sonoma	Salt Point	91	387
Ah	17	m	c	CHIN	San Francisco	6-Wd San Francisco	81	53
Ah	17	m	c	CHIN	Placer	Blue Canyon P O	76	417
Ah	13	m	c	CHIN	Sacramento	2-Wd Sacramento	77	215
Amable	50	m	w	FRAN	Tuolumne	Columbia P O	93	362
Aug	21	m	c	CHIN	Placer	Dutch Flat P O	76	406
Chung	29	m	c	CHIN	Solano	Suisun Twp	90	107
Heng	20	m	c	CHIN	San Francisco	6-Wd San Francisco	81	55
How	54	m	c	CHIN	Marin	San Rafael Twp	74	40
Kit	18	m	c	CHIN	Placer	Dutch Flat P O	76	411
Lung	42	m	c	CHIN	Yuba	Marysville	93	630
Mow	31	m	c	CHIN	Yuba	Marysville	93	628
On	30	m	c	CHIN	Butte	Ophir Twp	70	103
Pra	23	m	c	CHIN	Calaveras	San Andreas P O	70	166
Quing	45	m	c	CHIN	El Dorado	Placerville	72	114
Teung	34	m	c	CHIN	Yuba	East Bear Rvr Twp	93	545
Toy	6	m	c	CA	Yuba	Marysville	93	627
Wing	30	m	c	CHIN	San Francisco	6-Wd San Francisco	81	54
Wood	15	m	c	CHIN	San Francisco	8-Wd San Francisco	82	395
GENA								
Lu	25	f	c	CHIN	Del Norte	Crescent	71	464
GENACIA								
Charles	38	m	w	SWIT	Nevada	Nevada Twp	75	313
GENAN								
Daniel	28	m	w	IREL	Nevada	Bloomfield Twp	75	95
GENANO								
Fales	44	m	w	MEXI	Los Angeles	Los Angeles	73	508
GENARRO								
Angeline	37	f	w	ITAL	Amador	Jackson P O	69	326
GENASCI								
Antoine	34	m	w	SWIT	Plumas	Seneca Twp	77	49
GENATZI								
Louis	19	m	w	SWIT	Marin	Nicasio Twp	74	17
Thomas	34	m	w	SWIT	Marin	Bolinas Twp	74	6
GENAU								
Hanri	29	m	w	FRAN	San Francisco	San Francisco P O	80	470
GENCKER								
Theodore	45	m	w	CANA	Nevada	Meadow Lake Twp	75	265
GENCY								
Blair	38	m	w	GA	El Dorado	Georgetown Twp	72	40
GENDAR								
E F	53	m	w	NY	San Francisco	San Francisco P O	83	330
John	23	m	w	NY	San Francisco	San Francisco P O	83	332
GENDER								
W A	22	m	w	NY	Yuba	Marysville	93	605
GENDICE								
Alexander	24	m	w	SWIT	El Dorado	Diamond Springs Tw	72	28
Dominic	24	m	w	ITAL	Monterey	San Juan Twp	74	402
GENDOTTI								
Louis	35	m	w	SWIT	Calaveras	Copperopolis P O	70	224
GENE								
Chas	31	m	c	CHIN	Santa Barbara	Santa Barbara P O	87	501
George	15	m	c	CHIN	Santa Barbara	Santa Barbara P O	87	501
Thos	18	m	c	CHIN	Santa Barbara	Santa Barbara P O	87	501
GENEAR								
Granell	25	m	w	CA	San Luis Obispo	Salinas Twp	87	294
GENECCIO								
Joseph	49	m	w	ITAL	San Francisco	2-Wd San Francisco	79	179
GENEMIE								
Clementee	32	m	w	SWIT	Nevada	Nevada Twp	75	313
GENENAN								
Lee	21	m	c	CHIN	Tulare	White Rvr Twp	92	301
GENER								
S J	38	m	w	ENGL	San Joaquin	Dent Twp	86	29
GENERICH								
Julius	36	m	w	BADE	San Francisco	8-Wd San Francisco	82	304
GENEST								
Ephriam	43	m	w	CANA	El Dorado	Placerville Twp	72	97
GENESY								
G	49	m	w	SWIT	Amador	Sutter Crk P O	69	404
GENET								
Andrew	40	m	w	FRAN	San Francisco	3-Wd San Francisco	79	320
GENETTAL								
Louis	47	m	w	FRAN	Los Angeles	Los Angeles	73	526
GENEVA								
Louis	32	m	w	FRAN	San Francisco	6-Wd San Francisco	81	93
GENEY								
Henry	35	m	w	FRAN	Siskiyou	Callahan P O	89	630
GENG								
Ah	34	m	c	CHIN	San Francisco	San Francisco P O	80	431
Ah	31	m	c	CHIN	Sierra	Sears Twp	89	553
Ah	30	m	c	CHIN	Plumas	Plumas Twp	77	31
Ah	28	m	c	CHIN	Sierra	Sears Twp	89	554
Ah	25	m	c	CHIN	Trinity	Canyon City Pct	92	201
Ah	22	m	c	CHIN	Sierra	Sears Twp	89	554
Ah	21	m	c	CHIN	San Francisco	6-Wd San Francisco	81	69
Ah	20	m	c	CHIN	San Francisco	6-Wd San Francisco	81	48
Gee	24	m	c	CHIN	San Francisco	6-Wd San Francisco	81	45
San	18	m	c	CHIN	Colusa	Colusa	71	294
GENGUE								
Leander	51	m	w	CANA	El Dorado	Placerville Twp	72	92
GENILIA								
Fortunat	45	m	w	FRAN	Los Angeles	Wilmington Twp	73	635
GENIS								
P	26	m	w	SWIT	Sierra	Downieville Twp	89	516
GENIZ								
Henry	38	m	w	PRUS	San Francisco	San Francisco P O	83	213
GENKE								
Ah	65	m	c	CHIN	Santa Cruz	Santa Cruz	89	434
Job	23	m	w	ITAL	Inyo	Cerro Gordo Twp	73	320
GENN								
Ah	14	f	c	CHIN	Placer	Dutch Flat P O	76	409
Henry	34	m	w	ME	Calaveras	Copperopolis P O	70	233
GENNAN								
John	24	m	w	NY	San Francisco	3-Wd San Francisco	79	319
GENNARD								
Adrian	35	m	w	FRAN	Nevada	Grass Valley Twp	75	230
GENNELLA								
V	19	m	w	SWIT	Yuba	Marysville Twp	93	568
GENNENI								
G	36	m	w	ITAL	Amador	Jackson P O	69	333
GENNEY								
Julia	23	f	w	IREL	San Francisco	8-Wd San Francisco	82	410
GENNIE								
Wm	35	m	w	SWIT	El Dorado	Lake Valley Twp	72	64
GENNINE								
Josephine	28	f	w	SWIT	San Francisco	8-Wd San Francisco	82	307
GENNING								
Norton	50	m	w	IREL	San Francisco	San Francisco P O	83	411
GENNUNI								
Dorn	30	m	w	ITAL	Amador	Jackson P O	69	333
GENOCCHIO								
B	44	m	w	ITAL	Amador	Jackson P O	69	333
GENOCHE								
Antonio	50	m	w	ITAL	Calaveras	San Andreas P O	70	179
GENOCHEO								
Antonio	41	m	w	ITAL	Los Angeles	Los Angeles	73	516
GENOCHIO								
Dominico	34	m	w	ITAL	Amador	Volcano P O	69	384
GENONO								
Sebastine	38	m	w	ITAL	San Francisco	2-Wd San Francisco	79	180
GENOSHO								
John	17	m	w	CA	Mendocino	Calpella Twp	74	190
GENOT								
Moses	35	m	w	CA	Colusa	Stony Crk Twp	71	331
GENRY								
Jeremiah	49	m	w	IREL	San Francisco	11-Wd San Francisc	84	520
GENS								
Lorenzo W	27	m	w	IREL	Nevada	Eureka Twp	75	137
GENSKI								
---	20	m	j	JAPA	San Francisco	8-Wd San Francisco	82	466
GENSLER								
Julius	29	m	w	PRUS	San Francisco	San Francisco P O	83	419
Michael	38	m	w	PRUS	San Francisco	San Francisco P O	83	347
GENSOUL								
Adrian	46	m	w	FRAN	San Francisco	8-Wd San Francisco	82	390
GENSVINE								
Elizabeth	27	f	w	WURT	Santa Clara	1-Wd San Jose	88	237
GENSWINDT								
Margaret	31	f	w	IREL	Marin	San Rafael	74	55
GENT								
William	35	m	w	ENGL	Sacramento	2-Wd Sacramento	77	206
GENTCHER								
Chris	29	m	w	DENM	San Joaquin	Castoria Twp	86	9
GENTERAND								
August	34	m	w	ITAL	San Francisco	2-Wd San Francisco	79	149
GENTLEMAN								
Wm	28	m	w	ENGL	San Francisco	8-Wd San Francisco	82	326
GENTNER								
Horace	35	m	w	ME	Amador	Volcano P O	69	381
GENTOSIA								
Louis	20	m	w	ITAL	San Francisco	11-Wd San Francisc	84	614
GENTRY								
Abmea	32	m	w	MO	San Francisco	5-Wd San Francisco	81	9
Al K	40	m	w	MO	Nevada	Nevada Twp	75	284
Albert W	42	m	w	VA	Yuba	Parks Bar Twp	93	649
Ann	50	f	w	IREL	San Francisco	8-Wd San Francisco	82	411
Calvin	36	m	w	TN	San Diego	San Diego	78	509
J	53	m	w	KY	Lake	Morgan Valley	73	424
James C	41	m	w	KY	Plumas	Plumas Twp	77	30
James C	35	m	w	KY	Sonoma	Analy Twp	91	226
R B	28	m	w	WI	Nevada	Nevada Twp	75	275
Sanderson	47	m	w	KY	San Bernardino	San Bernardino Twp	78	448
Thomas	34	m	w	KY	El Dorado	Diamond Springs Tw	72	34
Timothy	---	m	w	SCOT	Yuba	Marysville Twp	93	567
Wm O	37	m	w	MO	Sonoma	Santa Rosa	91	400
GENTY								
Ann	30	f	w	IREL	San Francisco	San Francisco P O	83	28
John	47	m	w	IREL	Mono	Bridgeport P O	74	283
GENTZEN								
Otto	48	m	w	PRUS	San Francisco	San Francisco P O	85	843
GEO								
Ah	38	m	c	CHIN	Tuolumne	Chinese Camp P O	93	364

© 2001 by Heritage Quest. All rights reserved.

California 1870 Census

Name	Age	S	R	B-PL	County	Locale	Roll	Pg
Ah	38	m	c	CHIN	Sacramento	Sutter Twp	77	382
Ah	32	m	c	CHIN	Sacramento	Granite Twp	77	136
Ah	21	m	c	CHIN	Solano	Suisun Twp	90	105
Finch	38	m	w	IL	Butte	Chico Twp	70	54
John	52	m	w	ITAL	Calaveras	Copperopolis P O	70	244
GEOMONI								
Gehelistsa	25	m	w	ITAL	San Francisco	1-Wd San Francisco	79	114
GEON								
---	40	m	c	CHIN	Shasta	American Ranch P O	89	496
Ah	24	m	c	CHIN	Santa Cruz	Santa Cruz Twp	89	388
Ah	24	m	c	CHIN	San Joaquin	1-Wd Stockton	86	139
GEONG								
Sam	30	m	c	CHIN	Sacramento	3-Wd Sacramento	77	265
GEORG								
James	30	m	w	SCOT	San Francisco	San Francisco P O	80	392
GEORGE								
A C	40	m	w	PA	Trinity	Junction City Pct	92	210
Adams	40	m	w	NY	Butte	Chico Twp	70	18
Ah	41	m	c	CHIN	Placer	Dutch Flat P O	76	409
Ah	40	m	c	CHIN	Santa Cruz	Watsonville	89	377
Ah	40	m	c	CHIN	Napa	Yountville Twp	75	88
Ah	40	m	c	CHIN	Napa	Napa Twp	75	71
Ah	30	m	c	CHIN	Napa	Napa Twp	75	67
Ah	29	m	c	CHIN	Placer	Dutch Flat P O	76	411
Ah	22	m	c	CHIN	San Francisco	San Francisco P O	80	428
Ah	22	m	c	CHIN	San Francisco	San Francisco P O	80	498
Ah	22	m	c	CHIN	Placer	Dutch Flat P O	76	411
Ah	22	m	c	CHIN	Placer	Dutch Flat P O	76	414
Ah	21	m	c	CHIN	Placer	Gold Run Twp	76	397
Ah	19	m	c	CHIN	Placer	Auburn P O	76	379
Ah	18	m	c	CHIN	Santa Clara	Alviso Twp	88	25
Ah	17	m	c	CHIN	Santa Cruz	Santa Cruz Twp	89	400
Ah	14	m	c	CHIN	Nevada	Bloomfield Twp	75	94
Alex	35	m	w	CANA	Sacramento	3-Wd Sacramento	77	303
Alfred	36	m	w	US	Nevada	Little York Twp	75	238
Andrew	36	m	w	KY	Nevada	Eureka Twp	75	132
Anton	34	m	w	PORT	San Francisco	1-Wd San Francisco	79	89
Antone	19	m	w	SWIT	Santa Clara	Gilroy Twp	88	90
Antonio	67	m	w	PORT	Alameda	Washington Twp	68	275
B	11	m	w	KY	Lake	Coyote Valley	73	401
B F	50	m	w	CANA	Solano	Vallejo	90	209
B M	59	m	w	VT	Trinity	Hayfork Valley	92	238
Benjamin	21	m	w	KY	Nevada	Washington Twp	75	344
Constantine	26	m	w	GREE	Placer	Bath P O	76	442
Cyrus	45	m	w	SHOL	Del Norte	Crescent	71	465
David	64	m	w	PRUS	San Francisco	San Francisco P O	80	421
David	23	m	w	NY	San Bernardino	San Bernardino Twp	78	419
David W	43	m	w	MA	Santa Clara	2-Wd San Jose	88	330
Ducus S	18	m	w	PA	Los Angeles	Los Angeles	73	568
Edward	22	m	w	NZEA	San Francisco	San Francisco P O	80	473
Ether	30	m	w	IL	San Francisco	3-Wd San Francisco	79	323
Evan	35	m	w	NY	San Francisco	San Francisco P O	83	152
Francis S	24	m	w	ENGL	Shasta	French Gulch P O	89	466
Frank	30	m	w	PORT	Alameda	Washington Twp	68	270
Frank S	18	m	w	PA	San Francisco	San Francisco P O	83	202
Frank S	17	m	w	PA	San Francisco	San Francisco P O	83	196
Fred	40	m	w	PRUS	Solano	Vallejo	90	214
George	29	m	w	ENGL	San Francisco	San Francisco P O	85	777
George	23	m	w	ENGL	El Dorado	Placerville Twp	72	104
George	23	m	w	ENGL	El Dorado	Placerville Twp	72	100
H Bigg	35	m	w	ITAL	Amador	Sutter Crk P O	69	405
Henry	36	m	w	ME	San Francisco	San Francisco P O	80	485
Henry	30	m	w	PA	Sacramento	4-Wd Sacramento	77	332
Henry	25	m	w	CANA	San Francisco	San Francisco P O	83	360
Henry D	45	m	w	VA	Los Angeles	San Juan Twp	73	625
I L	42	m	w	NY	Tuolumne	Columbia P O	93	347
Isaac B	36	m	w	ME	San Diego	San Jacinto Dist	78	517
J D	25	m	w	VA	Solano	Vallejo	90	201
Jacob G	36	m	w	PA	Yolo	Putah Twp	93	511
James	50	m	w	FRAN	Tuolumne	Sonora P O	93	331
James	45	m	w	PA	Sacramento	3-Wd Sacramento	77	309
Jas W	21	m	w	KY	Butte	Hamilton Twp	70	66
John	59	m	w	ENGL	Tuolumne	Big Oak Flat P O	93	398
John	50	m	w	PA	Alameda	Washington Twp	68	292
John	50	m	w	IREL	El Dorado	Placerville Twp	72	98
John	43	m	w	FRAN	Yolo	Grafton Twp	93	496
John	41	m	w	PA	Shasta	Shasta P O	89	461
John	40	m	w	FRAN	Los Angeles	Los Angeles Twp	73	489
John	37	m	w	POLA	San Francisco	8-Wd San Francisco	82	361
John	37	m	w	OH	San Francisco	San Francisco P O	83	257
John	32	m	w	US	Del Norte	Crescent Twp	71	455
John	16	m	w	PORT	Alameda	Alvarado	68	305
John S	47	m	w	MA	Sacramento	2-Wd Sacramento	77	219
Joseph	42	m	w	OH	Mariposa	Mariposa P O	74	106
Joseph	37	m	w	NH	Trinity	Weaverville Pct	92	227
Joseph	35	m	w	AZOR	San Francisco	1-Wd San Francisco	79	26
Joseph	15	m	w	CA	Fresno	Millerton P O	72	165
Julius	37	m	w	GERM	San Francisco	8-Wd San Francisco	82	297
Laura	21	f	w	ENGL	San Joaquin	2-Wd Stockton	86	211
Lawrence M	60	m	w	VA	El Dorado	Diamond Springs Tw	72	21
Leet	26	m	w	NY	Sutter	Nicolaus Twp	92	114
Levi	35	m	w	WALE	Napa	Napa Twp	75	30
Louis	58	m	w	FRAN	San Francisco	6-Wd San Francisco	81	82
Louis F	58	m	w	ME	San Francisco	6-Wd San Francisco	81	89
Louisa	45	f	w	HANO	San Francisco	11-Wd San Francisc	84	659
Louisa	1M	f	w	CA	San Francisco	7-Wd San Francisco	81	157
Manuel	35	m	w	AZOR	Marin	San Rafael Twp	74	32

Name	Age	S	R	B-PL	County	Locale	Roll	Pg
Manuel	31	m	w	PORT	Nevada	Rough & Ready Twp	75	331
Manuel	24	m	w	AZOR	Monterey	Monterey	74	362
Mary	45	f	w	OH	Sacramento	Franklin Twp	77	111
Oliver	19	m	w	OH	Sutter	Yuba Twp	92	149
Oscar	37	m	w	VA	Los Angeles	Santa Ana Twp	73	611
Otto	24	m	w	GERM	Los Angeles	Wilmington Twp	73	642
Peter	36	m	w	HAMB	San Bernardino	San Bernardino Twp	78	439
Richard	26	m	w	ENGL	Nevada	Grass Valley Twp	75	184
Robert	45	m	w	MD	San Francisco	San Francisco P O	85	731
S B	47	m	w	ME	Solano	Vallejo	90	209
Saml	42	m	w	DE	San Francisco	5-Wd San Francisco	81	29
Samuel	57	m	w	ENGL	Placer	Newcastle Twp	76	474
Samuel	56	m	w	OH	Tulare	Visalia	92	294
Samuel	51	m	w	ENGL	Nevada	Grass Valley Twp	75	172
Samuel	42	m	w	CANA	San Francisco	2-Wd San Francisco	79	251
Theo	47	m	w	BAVA	Sacramento	3-Wd Sacramento	77	310
Thomas	52	m	w	KY	Yuba	Rose Bar Twp	93	666
Thomas	49	m	w	ENGL	Nevada	Grass Valley Twp	75	231
Thomas	37	m	w	KY	Nevada	Grass Valley Twp	75	187
Thomas	27	m	w	ENGL	Nevada	Eureka Twp	75	138
Thomas A	50	m	w	KY	Amador	Fiddletown P O	69	437
Thomas D	24	m	w	WALE	San Francisco	3-Wd San Francisco	79	322
Thos	36	m	w	KY	Tehama	Red Bluff	92	182
W H	41	m	w	ME	Nevada	Meadow Lake Twp	75	267
W L	7	m	w	CA	San Mateo	San Mateo P O	87	371
William	40	m	w	VA	Inyo	Independence Twp	73	325
William	30	m	w	ENGL	San Francisco	7-Wd San Francisco	81	157
William	30	m	w	ENGL	Nevada	Grass Valley Twp	75	172
William	27	m	w	IREL	El Dorado	Placerville Twp	72	95
William	27	m	w	IREL	El Dorado	Placerville Twp	72	101
William	22	m	w	ENGL	Nevada	Washington Twp	75	343
William J	26	m	w	KY	Nevada	Grass Valley Twp	75	214
Wm	55	m	w	ENGL	San Francisco	1-Wd San Francisco	79	77
Wm	29	m	w	FRAN	San Francisco	8-Wd San Francisco	82	350
Wm George	29	m	w	ENGL	Plumas	Indian Twp	77	15
GEORGENS								
Martin V	36	m	w	SHOL	Sacramento	4-Wd Sacramento	77	339
GEORGENSON								
Closs	22	m	w	DENM	Sacramento	Granite Twp	77	136
GEORGES								
Hypolite	36	m	w	FRAN	San Francisco	San Francisco P O	80	535
Mary	22	f	w	ENGL	San Francisco	San Francisco P O	80	531
Robert	30	m	w	AUST	San Francisco	San Francisco P O	80	460
GEORGESON								
Marks	24	m	w	DENM	San Francisco	7-Wd San Francisco	81	218
GEORGIANNI								
Anthony	45	m	w	ITAL	San Francisco	6-Wd San Francisco	81	107
GEORGOT								
Hortense	30	f	w	BAVA	San Francisco	6-Wd San Francisco	81	72
GEORING								
Charles	13	m	w	HAMB	Trinity	Junction City Pct	92	210
Louisey	37	f	w	SHOL	Trinity	Weaverville Pct	92	222
GEORNANER								
Ruffett	27	m	w	SWIT	Trinity	North Fork Twp	92	221
GEOTZ								
Nicolas	26	m	w	SHOL	San Francisco	1-Wd San Francisco	79	103
GEOVUNARA								
Peter	43	m	w	SWIT	Sonoma	Sonoma Twp	91	437
GEOY								
Ah	38	m	c	CHIN	Butte	Oregon Twp	70	135
GEP								
Ah	43	m	c	CHIN	Butte	Ophir Twp	70	121
Ah	41	m	c	CHIN	Nevada	Meadow Lake Twp	75	259
Ah	41	m	c	CHIN	Nevada	Meadow Lake Twp	75	255
Ah	30	m	c	CHIN	Nevada	Eureka Twp	75	127
Ah	29	m	c	CHIN	Nevada	Washington Twp	75	344
Ah	29	m	c	CHIN	Butte	Kimshew Tpw	70	85
Ah	24	m	c	CHIN	Nevada	Meadow Lake Twp	75	259
Ah	23	m	c	CHIN	Plumas	Indian Twp	77	18
Ah	19	m	c	CHIN	Nevada	Eureka Twp	75	140
Sing	44	m	c	CHIN	Tuolumne	Chinese Camp P O	93	385
GEPHARD								
George	47	m	w	CANA	Sacramento	2-Wd Sacramento	77	253
George	41	m	w	GERM	Nevada	Grass Valley Twp	75	189
Levi	39	m	w	OH	Butte	Kimshew Tpw	70	78
GEPHART								
John	47	m	w	OH	Sacramento	American Twp	77	66
Lowe	21	f	w	MI	Nevada	Nevada Twp	75	293
GER								
Ah	21	m	c	CHIN	El Dorado	Diamond Springs Tw	72	27
Ah	21	m	c	CHIN	Sacramento	1-Wd Sacramento	77	197
Hop	40	m	c	CHIN	Butte	Chico Twp	70	28
GERA								
Jose	66	m	w	CHIL	Santa Clara	Fremont Twp	88	57
GERACEA								
Henri	30	m	w	FRAN	Monterey	San Juan Twp	74	414
GERAGHTY								
Annie	22	f	w	IREL	San Francisco	1-Wd San Francisco	79	84
Bernard	45	m	w	IREL	San Francisco	8-Wd San Francisco	82	482
Ellen	16	f	w	CA	Santa Clara	2-Wd San Jose	88	337
Mich	35	m	w	IREL	San Francisco	11-Wd San Francisc	84	446
Patrick	44	m	w	IREL	San Francisco	1-Wd San Francisco	79	103
Patrick	41	m	w	IREL	San Francisco	1-Wd San Francisco	79	93
GERALD								
Chas	23	m	w	ME	Butte	Chico Twp	70	58
David D	29	m	w	RI	San Francisco	San Francisco P O	83	94
John	40	m	w	IL	San Joaquin	Oneal Twp	86	101

© 2001 by Heritage Quest. All rights reserved.

Series M593

Name	Age	S	R	B-PL	County	Locale	Roll	Pg
GERALDSON								
Hans	40	m	w	NORW	Placer	Auburn P O	76	357
GERAND								
Grande	26	m	w	FRAN	Santa Barbara	Santa Barbara P O	87	474
GERAOLDA								
Charles	39	m	w	SWIT	Amador	Volcano P O	69	378
GERARD								
Andrew	68	m	w	PA	San Joaquin	Castoria Twp	86	7
Chas	43	m	w	FRAN	Sacramento	4-Wd Sacramento	77	353
Edward	27	m	w	FRAN	San Francisco	8-Wd San Francisco	82	292
Emma	21	f	w	MO	San Joaquin	2-Wd Stockton	86	161
James	29	m	w	ENGL	San Francisco	San Francisco P O	83	139
Janions	61	m	w	FRAN	San Mateo	Half Moon Bay P O	87	390
John	45	m	w	ENGL	San Joaquin	Elkhorn Twp	86	64
John	34	m	w	FRAN	Tuolumne	Chinese Camp P O	93	376
Joseph	36	m	w	FRAN	Tuolumne	Chinese Camp P O	93	376
Martin	48	m	w	FRAN	San Francisco	1-Wd San Francisco	79	50
GERARDIN								
Emil	30	m	w	FRAN	San Francisco	San Francisco P O	80	341
GERAUX								
David	33	m	w	CANA	Alameda	Brooklyn	68	38
GERBACIO								
Robira	45	m	w	PHIL	Santa Clara	Almaden Twp	88	9
GERBACK								
Lewis	32	m	w	IL	Mendocino	Anderson Twp	74	154
GERBEN								
Robert	32	m	b	PA	San Francisco	San Francisco P O	80	475
GERBER								
Adam	51	m	w	GERM	Tuolumne	Columbia P O	93	345
Agatka	48	f	w	BADE	San Francisco	2-Wd San Francisco	79	144
E	39	m	w	BADE	Yuba	Marysville	93	602
Jabella	56	f	w	BADE	Sacramento	Sutter Twp	77	390
Joseph	50	m	w	AUST	San Francisco	San Francisco P O	85	766
Max	35	m	w	BRUN	San Francisco	1-Wd San Francisco	79	51
Phillip	44	m	w	PRUS	Amador	Sutter Crk P O	69	413
Stephen	38	m	w	BADE	Sacramento	4-Wd Sacramento	77	367
Wilhelmina	40	f	w	PRUS	San Francisco	8-Wd San Francisco	82	421
William	17	m	w	NY	Colusa	Spring Valley Twp	71	342
GERBERDING								
Mary J	50	f	w	VA	San Francisco	6-Wd San Francisco	81	134
GERBERGER								
John	60	m	w	SWIT	Contra Costa	San Pablo Twp	71	362
GERBET								
Noter	52	m	w	FRAN	Monterey	San Juan Twp	74	410
GERBY								
Oren	35	m	w	OH	Butte	Chico Twp	70	50
GERCEA								
John	30	m	w	AZOR	Contra Costa	San Pablo Twp	71	361
GERCIAE								
A S	48	m	w	ITAL	Alameda	Oakland	68	168
GERCKEN								
Ellis	32	m	w	PRUS	San Francisco	2-Wd San Francisco	79	154
GERDE								
Friedrick	31	m	w	OLDE	San Francisco	1-Wd San Francisco	79	127
GERDEN								
Carra	4	f	w	CA	Humboldt	Eureka Twp	72	263
Henry	24	m	w	NY	Contra Costa	Martinez P O	71	415
GERDENBUCH								
Geo	37	m	w	GERM	San Joaquin	2-Wd Stockton	86	213
GERDENS								
Geo	30	m	w	SHOL	San Mateo	Half Moon Bay P O	87	403
GERDES								
Alexander	40	m	w	OLDE	San Francisco	San Francisco P O	83	181
Christian J	36	m	w	HANO	Santa Clara	1-Wd San Jose	88	255
Louis	9	m	w	CA	Santa Clara	2-Wd San Jose	88	290
Richard	38	m	w	PRUS	Santa Clara	1-Wd San Jose	88	235
GERDIN								
August	28	m	w	PRUS	Santa Clara	San Jose Twp	88	183
GERDIS								
John M	33	m	w	HANO	San Francisco	2-Wd San Francisco	79	143
GERDO								
Proto	30	m	w	MEXI	Santa Clara	Burnett Twp	88	34
GERDON								
James	35	m	w	ME	San Mateo	Half Moon Bay P O	87	407
John	25	m	w	NY	Los Angeles	Soledad Twp	73	631
GERDRENG								
Joseph P	35	m	w	BADE	Placer	Colfax P O	76	388
GERDY								
Thos	50	m	w	ME	San Joaquin	Liberty Twp	86	85
GERE								
Cung	48	m	c	CHIN	Placer	Gold Run Twp	76	400
GERECHE								
Francis	21	m	w	ITAL	San Mateo	Schoolhouse Statio	87	346
John	16	m	w	ITAL	San Mateo	Schoolhouse Statio	87	346
GEREGHEE								
James	22	m	w	AUST	Amador	Sutter Crk P O	69	408
GERELICKI								
Giovanni	22	m	w	ITAL	San Francisco	1-Wd San Francisco	79	114
GEREMA								
Chas	46	m	w	ITAL	San Francisco	8-Wd San Francisco	82	362
GERENEEI								
Charles	19	m	w	SWIT	Plumas	Quartz Twp	77	38
GERETA								
H	26	m	w	ITAL	San Francisco	San Francisco P O	85	755
GERGAN								
Edward	36	m	w	IREL	San Francisco	San Francisco P O	83	15
GERGHEN								
Henry	46	m	w	HANO	San Francisco	San Francisco P O	85	804
GERGLEY								
Patrick	30	m	w	IREL	San Francisco	1-Wd San Francisco	79	56
GERGORY								
E D	48	m	w	NY	San Joaquin	Dent Twp	86	28
Walter	32	m	w	ENGL	Mendocino	Big Rvr Twp	74	161
GERGUSON								
Lucy	40	f	w	ME	San Joaquin	Douglas Twp	86	34
GERHALT								
Lucy	54	f	w	WURT	San Francisco	6-Wd San Francisco	81	111
GERHARD								
Azes	28	m	w	PRUS	San Francisco	San Francisco P O	80	478
Berthold	42	m	w	SAXO	San Francisco	San Francisco P O	80	466
Canhape	42	m	w	FRAN	San Diego	Fort Yuma Dist	78	463
Simon	30	m	w	PRUS	San Francisco	1-Wd San Francisco	79	51
GERHARDT								
Jacob	40	m	w	PRUS	Mendocino	Anderson Twp	74	155
T	41	m	w	LA	San Francisco	1-Wd San Francisco	79	52
GERHARDY								
Chas	34	m	w	HANO	San Francisco	1-Wd San Francisco	79	30
GERHOKE								
George	40	m	w	PRUS	San Francisco	7-Wd San Francisco	81	199
GERHOW								
Fred	39	m	w	PRUS	San Francisco	7-Wd San Francisco	81	255
GERICH								
Henry	22	m	w	SWIT	San Francisco	11-Wd San Francisc	84	584
GERICHTEN								
Charles	35	m	w	PRUS	San Francisco	8-Wd San Francisco	82	476
Conrad	32	m	w	HAMB	San Francisco	San Francisco P O	85	725
GERICKE								
Adolph	39	m	w	HANO	Marin	Tomales Twp	74	86
GERIDELLA								
John	45	m	w	ITAL	Amador	Jackson P O	69	335
GERIE								
Rosa	28	f	w	ITAL	San Francisco	6-Wd San Francisco	81	57
GERIHOLET								
John	29	m	w	ITAL	San Francisco	San Francisco P O	80	469
GERIKEEN								
Wm	27	m	w	SHOL	San Francisco	1-Wd San Francisco	79	24
GERIMER								
Casper	40	m	w	PRUS	Yuba	Slate Range Bar Tw	93	675
GERIN								
Joseph	32	m	w	FRAN	San Francisco	San Francisco P O	80	348
William	45	m	w	MEXI	Tuolumne	Sonora P O	93	324
GERINGER								
Jno	26	m	w	WURT	Sierra	Table Rock Twp	89	574
GERIOUX								
Andrew	30	m	w	CANA	San Francisco	1-Wd San Francisco	79	94
GERISH								
Christopher	28	m	w	OH	Solano	Silveyville Twp	90	91
GERIZES								
Margaret	60	f	w	BREM	San Francisco	San Francisco P O	80	429
GERK								
Edwd D	68	m	w	IREL	Butte	Oregon Twp	70	124
Frederick	33	m	w	PRUS	El Dorado	Greenwood Twp	72	51
GERKE								
Henry	50	m	w	HANO	Tehama	Tehama Twp	92	191
Henry	48	m	w	FRNK	Tehama	Deer Crk Twp	92	170
L A	21	m	w	CA	Tehama	Tehama Twp	92	192
Nelly	14	f	w	CA	San Francisco	11-Wd San Francisc	84	551
GERKEY								
Michael	43	m	w	IREL	San Francisco	San Francisco P O	83	77
GERKHARDT								
Heny F	49	m	w	HANO	Sonoma	Cloverdale Twp	91	270
GERKIN								
Richd	28	m	w	HANO	San Francisco	1-Wd San Francisco	79	34
Rose	32	f	w	IREL	San Francisco	11-Wd San Francisc	84	496
GERKINS								
Charles	27	m	w	HANO	San Francisco	7-Wd San Francisco	81	211
Henry	32	m	w	SHOL	Sonoma	Vallejo Twp	91	457
GERKY								
Hosmond	42	m	w	HANO	Butte	Hamilton Twp	70	70
GERL								
Charles	43	m	w	HANO	Sonoma	Salt Point Twp	91	383
GERLACH								
G	44	m	w	PRUS	Calaveras	Copperopolis P O	70	230
Geo	25	m	w	BELG	San Francisco	1-Wd San Francisco	79	109
George	24	m	w	PRUS	San Francisco	San Francisco P O	80	409
H	45	m	w	PRUS	Calaveras	Copperopolis P O	70	224
L	43	f	w	PRUS	Calaveras	Copperopolis P O	70	236
L	34	m	w	PRUS	San Joaquin	2-Wd Stockton	86	205
L	14	f	w	CA	Calaveras	Copperopolis P O	70	235
R	18	m	w	PA	Calaveras	Copperopolis P O	70	235
GERLACK								
Andrew	40	m	w	GERM	Tuolumne	Sonora P O	93	333
Henry	37	m	w	PRUS	Placer	Auburn P O	76	370
GERLEY								
Robert	38	m	w	SCOT	Inyo	Cerro Gordo Twp	73	321
GERLICK								
John H	38	m	w	HANO	San Francisco	7-Wd San Francisco	81	250
GERM								
Ti	35	m	c	CHIN	Sacramento	1-Wd Sacramento	77	195
GERMA								
John	36	m	w	SWED	Sacramento	Natomas Twp	77	169
GERMAIN								
Henry	60	m	w	IREL	San Francisco	8-Wd San Francisco	82	418

© 2001 by Heritage Quest. All rights reserved.

Name	Age	S	R	B-PL	County	Locale	Series M593 Roll	Pg
Louis	44	m	w	FRAN	Tulare	Visalia	92	298
Mary	46	f	w	MO	Sonoma	Santa Rosa	91	410
Parker	54	m	w	NY	Contra Costa	Martinez P O	71	434
Virgin	20	m	w	OH	Santa Clara	2-Wd San Jose	88	296
GERMAN								
Andrew	47	m	w	CANA	Contra Costa	Martinez P O	71	451
Antonio	50	m	w	CA	Monterey	San Juan Twp	74	418
Cayetano	43	m	w	CA	Santa Barbara	Santa Barbara P O	87	454
David	24	m	w	IREL	San Francisco	7-Wd San Francisco	81	181
Faustino	80	m	w	CA	Monterey	San Juan Twp	74	414
Frederick	47	m	w	PRUS	Plumas	Mineral Twp	77	20
Gordon G	27	m	w	CANA	Santa Clara	San Jose Twp	88	214
Henry	30	m	w	HAMB	Sacramento	Sutter Twp	77	393
Isaac	45	m	w	MO	Sacramento	Cosumnes Twp	77	96
J	30	m	w	IREL	Siskiyou	Scott Valley Twp	89	617
James	35	m	w	CA	Sacramento	4-Wd Sacramento	77	355
John	30	m	w	PRUS	Sacramento	Center Twp	77	84
John	27	m	w	AUST	El Dorado	Salmon Falls Twp	72	131
Jose	23	m	w	CA	Monterey	San Benito Twp	74	380
Joseph	47	m	w	TN	San Bernardino	San Bernardino Twp	78	446
Joseph	32	m	w	FRAN	Calaveras	Copperopolis P O	70	242
Joseph	31	m	w	SWIT	San Francisco	San Francisco P O	85	754
Juan	50	m	w	CA	Monterey	San Juan Twp	74	416
Juana	37	f	i	CA	Santa Barbara	Santa Barbara P O	87	472
Louis	47	m	w	CA	Monterey	San Juan Twp	74	404
Manuel	45	m	w	CA	Santa Barbara	Santa Barbara P O	87	472
Manuel	34	m	w	MEXI	Santa Barbara	Santa Barbara P O	87	502
Maria A	79	f	w	CA	Monterey	San Juan Twp	74	414
Peter	42	m	w	BAVA	Los Angeles	Los Angeles Twp	73	488
S	31	m	w	CANA	San Joaquin	1-Wd Stockton	86	138
Samuel	32	m	w	MO	Sutter	Butte Twp	92	101
Smith	32	m	w	CANA	Alameda	Brooklyn	68	35
Theodore	35	m	w	PRUS	Sacramento	Brighton Twp	77	72
Thos	30	m	w	NJ	Marin	San Rafael Twp	74	39
William H	36	m	w	OH	Santa Clara	2-Wd San Jose	88	291
Wm	30	m	w	HAMB	Sacramento	Brighton Twp	77	74
GERMANATTI								
Franz	43	m	w	ITAL	San Francisco	6-Wd San Francisco	81	51
GERMEAU								
Thos	34	m	w	CANA	San Joaquin	Douglas Twp	86	37
GERMEN								
Joe	22	m	w	SWED	Sacramento	Sutter Twp	77	388
GERMERHOUSEN								
Barnard	38	m	w	PRUS	Yolo	Putah Twp	93	526
Joseph	35	m	w	PRUS	Yolo	Putah Twp	93	526
GERMIER								
William	40	m	w	PRUS	Sacramento	Natomas Twp	77	168
GERMMAN								
John	38	m	w	HDAR	Nevada	Bridgeport Twp	75	101
GERMON								
Andrew	57	m	w	MA	San Francisco	7-Wd San Francisco	81	213
Louis	66	m	w	FRAN	Stanislaus	Empire Twp	92	52
GERMOND								
Geo W	3	m	w	ME	Sacramento	Georgianna Twp	77	130
Wm	23	m	w	ME	Sacramento	Georgianna Twp	77	130
GERMURIGUE								
Mary M	44	m	w	FRAN	Yuba	Bullards Bar P O	93	551
GERN								
Ah	42	m	c	CHIN	Sacramento	Georgianna Twp	77	124
Ah	28	m	c	CHIN	Nevada	Bridgeport Twp	75	122
GERNAZO								
Francis	20	m	w	MEXI	Fresno	Millerton P O	72	164
GERNDOTTE								
Andrew	27	m	w	SWIT	Calaveras	San Andreas P O	70	208
Louis	31	m	w	SWIT	Calaveras	San Andreas P O	70	208
GERNED								
J G	40	m	w	SWIT	Tuolumne	Columbia P O	93	361
GERNELLA								
Charles	28	m	w	ITAL	Calaveras	San Andreas P O	70	189
Joseph	39	m	w	ITAL	Calaveras	San Andreas P O	70	189
GERNER								
George	19	m	w	HESS	Mariposa	Mariposa P O	74	133
GERNERRI								
John	29	m	w	ITAL	El Dorado	Diamond Springs Tw	72	29
GERNEY								
Hannah	24	f	w	IREL	San Francisco	8-Wd San Francisco	82	345
John	49	m	w	HUNG	Alameda	Eden Twp	68	58
GERNICH								
August	45	m	w	PRUS	San Francisco	San Francisco P O	83	183
GERNION								
John	46	m	w	GERM	Santa Clara	Fremont Twp	88	63
GERNIS								
Eleizer	41	m	w	KY	Merced	Snelling P O	74	263
GERNSEY								
A A	27	m	w	OH	San Joaquin	1-Wd Stockton	86	138
GERNY								
H J	30	m	w	MO	Lake	Coyote Valley	73	417
GERO								
Eso	52	m	w	CA	Alameda	Murray Twp	68	104
Lucaso	67	m	w	CA	Alameda	Murray Twp	68	115
GERODER								
Lon	25	m	w	FRAN	San Francisco	11-Wd San Francisc	84	700
GEROLD								
Augustine	52	m	w	ITAL	Monterey	San Juan Twp	74	410
Henry	38	m	w	ME	Butte	Ophir Twp	70	120
Henry	37	m	w	NY	Solano	Montezuma Twp	90	68
Henry	36	m	w	PRUS	San Francisco	7-Wd San Francisco	81	269
GEROLOMO								
Paula	25	m	w	ITAL	Amador	Volcano P O	69	384
GEROSLOMO								
Bartholomew	28	m	w	SWIT	San Francisco	2-Wd San Francisco	79	235
GEROUX								
David	26	m	w	CANA	Santa Barbara	Santa Barbara P O	87	455
GERRAINA								
Antone	47	m	w	SPAI	Calaveras	San Andreas P O	70	209
GERRAM								
Theador	50	m	w	MEXI	Calaveras	San Andreas P O	70	175
GERRAND								
Martin	21	m	w	FRAN	Los Angeles	Los Angeles	73	541
GERRANI								
Antone	32	m	c	ITAL	Nevada	Washington Twp	75	347
GERRANS								
Jeremiah	51	m	w	ENGL	El Dorado	Mud Springs Twp	72	75
John	22	m	w	ENGL	El Dorado	Mud Springs Twp	72	75
GERRARD								
Elise	25	f	w	FRAN	San Francisco	6-Wd San Francisco	81	71
Seona	50	m	w	FRAN	Mariposa	Mariposa P O	74	90
Thomas	35	m	w	IREL	San Francisco	11-Wd San Francisc	84	701
GERRARO								
Diego	38	m	w	SPAI	Merced	Snelling P O	74	274
GERRATY								
Patrick	30	m	w	IREL	San Francisco	11-Wd San Francisc	84	477
GERRELL								
Charles	38	m	w	MO	Placer	Bath P O	76	443
GERRERD								
Henry	62	m	w	FRAN	Yuba	Bullards Bar P O	93	550
GERRICHTON								
Fredk	40	m	w	BADE	San Francisco	8-Wd San Francisco	82	330
GERRICK								
Chas	32	m	w	SWIT	Napa	Napa Twp	75	60
William	22	m	w	PRUS	Solano	Rio Vista Twp	90	64
GERRIEN								
Harman	35	m	w	PRUS	San Francisco	7-Wd San Francisco	81	234
GERRIS								
Dora	32	f	w	HOLL	San Francisco	8-Wd San Francisco	82	391
GERRISH								
J A	33	m	w	NH	Sacramento	3-Wd Sacramento	77	263
Mary E	38	f	w	MA	San Francisco	San Francisco P O	83	274
Pables Patrick	32	m	w	ME	Los Angeles	Los Angeles Twp	73	490
S H	66	m	w	NH	Sacramento	3-Wd Sacramento	77	263
S H	36	m	w	NH	Sacramento	3-Wd Sacramento	77	264
GERRITEY								
Catharine	80	f	w	IREL	San Francisco	San Francisco P O	83	320
GERRITY								
Ann	45	f	w	IREL	San Francisco	2-Wd San Francisco	79	216
Cornelius	13	m	w	CA	San Francisco	11-Wd San Francisc	84	593
John	29	m	w	IREL	San Francisco	San Francisco P O	83	389
Patrick	30	m	w	IREL	San Francisco	San Francisco P O	83	400
Patrick B	43	m	w	IREL	Los Angeles	Los Angeles Twp	73	494
GERRY								
Antone	36	m	w	SWIT	San Francisco	11-Wd San Francisc	84	576
Bartler	17	m	w	FRAN	San Francisco	11-Wd San Francisc	84	679
Frank	30	m	w	SWIT	San Francisco	11-Wd San Francisc	84	570
R C	28	m	w	ENGL	Sierra	Butte Twp	89	512
Samuel	54	m	w	MA	San Francisco	San Francisco P O	80	538
GERSBACH								
Chas	30	m	w	PRUS	Alameda	Murray Twp	68	125
GERSCHUNSKEY								
John	27	m	w	POLA	San Francisco	San Francisco P O	83	210
GERSEN								
Christ	13	m	w	PRUS	Butte	Chico Twp	70	42
GERSER								
John	30	m	w	SWED	Mendocino	Big Rvr Twp	74	171
GERSHON								
Thomas	40	m	w	IREL	Nevada	Bloomfield Twp	75	97
GERSON								
Caroline	30	f	w	GERM	Los Angeles	Los Angeles	73	530
Charles	40	m	w	FRAN	San Diego	Coronado	78	465
H	44	m	w	PRUS	Sierra	Alleghany & Forest	89	534
Mary	36	f	w	PRUS	San Francisco	8-Wd San Francisco	82	312
S	19	m	w	OH	Sacramento	1-Wd Sacramento	77	176
GERSTENBERG								
Anna	22	f	w	PRUS	San Francisco	San Francisco P O	85	820
Fred	24	m	w	DENM	Alameda	Eden Twp	68	85
H	29	m	w	HCAS	San Francisco	San Francisco P O	85	819
GERSTINE								
Willie	8	m	w	OH	San Francisco	5-Wd San Francisco	81	21
GERSTMAYER								
Albert	43	m	w	BAVA	Santa Clara	1-Wd San Jose	88	266
GERTER								
Antonio	31	m	w	ITAL	San Francisco	2-Wd San Francisco	79	142
GERTHESON								
Ferdinand	38	m	w	NY	San Francisco	2-Wd San Francisco	79	215
GERTHEVIT								
Chas	51	m	w	NJ	Alameda	Murray Twp	68	104
GERTONINI								
Bernard	26	m	w	SWIT	San Francisco	San Francisco P O	85	751
GERTREIN								
Peter	38	m	w	FRAN	San Francisco	San Francisco P O	80	335
GERTS								
Neil C	33	m	w	MA	San Francisco	San Francisco P O	85	738
GERTY								
Jacob	38	m	w	GERM	Marin	San Rafael Twp	74	46

© 2001 by Heritage Quest. All rights reserved.

Name	Age	S	R	B-PL	County	Locale	Series M593 Roll	Pg
GERTZ								
Launcelot	21	m	w	CA	Fresno	Kingston P O	72	217
GERUSAL								
Peter	26	m	w	ITAL	San Francisco	2-Wd San Francisco	79	223
GERVAN								
Charles	50	m	w	NY	Contra Costa	Martinez P O	71	396
GERVCOPOLO								
Constantine	29	m	w	TURK	Placer	Bath P O	76	437
GERVELL								
E F	39	m	w	IL	Monterey	San Juan Twp	74	406
James	27	m	w	OH	Monterey	San Juan Twp	74	406
GERVIN								
Jane	22	f	w	NY	Contra Costa	Martinez P O	71	399
GERWAN								
Jose	45	m	w	CA	Monterey	San Juan Twp	74	385
GERZABECK								
Oscar	35	m	w	PRUS	San Francisco	3-Wd San Francisco	79	326
GESAW								
Ah	17	m	c	CHIN	San Joaquin	Castoria Twp	86	13
Jim	19	m	c	CHIN	San Joaquin	Castoria Twp	86	10
GESCHE								
Frederick	48	m	w	WURT	San Mateo	Schoolhouse Statio	87	334
GESFORD								
Prestons	50	m	w	KY	Napa	Napa	75	57
GESHKE								
Charles	24	m	w	GERM	Yolo	Cache Crk Twp	93	453
GESNER								
Henry	19	m	w	PA	Plumas	Quartz Twp	77	43
GESSEL								
Jos	25	m	w	FRAN	San Francisco	11-Wd San Francisc	84	688
GESSELL								
John	28	m	w	GERM	Marin	Sausalito Twp	74	74
GESSEN								
Mathew	53	m	w	PRUS	San Francisco	San Francisco P O	85	821
GESSLEN								
Archie	18	m	w	CANA	Nevada	Grass Valley Twp	75	154
GESSLER								
Joseph	27	m	w	BADE	Sonoma	Sonoma Twp	91	446
Julio A	42	m	w	PA	Amador	Drytown P O	69	416
GESSMESS								
Edwd	22	m	w	SAXO	San Francisco	1-Wd San Francisco	79	110
GESSNER								
Wm	47	m	w	GERM	Lake	Upper Lake	73	408
GEST								
William M	40	m	w	IL	Santa Cruz	Santa Cruz Twp	89	396
GESTEL								
Louis	24	m	w	ME	San Francisco	7-Wd San Francisco	81	285
GESTIE								
Cristoval	30	m	w	GERM	Los Angeles	Los Angeles	73	508
GESU								
Delmarine	18	m	w	ITAL	San Francisco	1-Wd San Francisco	79	114
GET								
Ah	50	m	c	CHIN	Placer	Colfax P O	76	388
Ah	42	m	c	CHIN	Nevada	Little York Twp	75	234
Ah	41	m	c	CHIN	El Dorado	Placerville Twp	72	98
Ah	40	m	c	CHIN	Placer	Auburn P O	76	364
Ah	40	m	c	CHIN	El Dorado	White Oak Twp	72	142
Ah	35	m	c	CHIN	Butte	Hamilton Twp	70	74
Ah	35	m	c	CHIN	Placer	Alta P O	76	413
Ah	34	m	c	CHIN	Placer	Bath P O	76	442
Ah	34	m	c	CHIN	San Francisco	San Francisco P O	80	491
Ah	34	m	c	CHIN	San Francisco	San Francisco P O	80	504
Ah	33	m	c	CHIN	San Francisco	San Francisco P O	80	499
Ah	32	m	c	CHIN	Sierra	Lincoln Twp	89	550
Ah	30	m	c	CHIN	Plumas	Washington Twp	77	58
Ah	30	m	c	CHIN	Placer	Clipper Gap P O	76	392
Ah	30	m	c	CHIN	Placer	Auburn P O	76	363
Ah	28	m	c	CHIN	Sacramento	Georgianna Twp	77	123
Ah	28	m	c	CHIN	Nevada	Eureka Twp	75	140
Ah	26	m	c	CHIN	Tehama	Tehama Twp	92	189
Ah	25	f	c	CHIN	San Francisco	San Francisco P O	80	490
Ah	25	m	c	CHIN	San Francisco	San Francisco P O	80	512
Ah	24	m	c	CHIN	Solano	Suisun Twp	90	104
Ah	23	m	c	CHIN	Solano	Suisun Twp	90	107
Ah	22	f	c	CHIN	San Francisco	San Francisco P O	80	494
Ah	21	m	c	CHIN	San Francisco	San Francisco P O	80	511
Ah	21	m	c	CHIN	San Francisco	San Francisco P O	80	497
Ah	19	m	c	CHIN	Placer	Colfax P O	76	387
Ah	18	f	c	CHIN	San Francisco	San Francisco P O	80	492
Ah	18	m	c	CHIN	Santa Clara	Santa Clara Twp	88	163
Ah	18	m	c	CHIN	Tehama	Tehama Twp	92	188
Ah	17	m	c	CHIN	Trinity	Lewiston Pct	92	214
Chun	54	m	c	CHIN	El Dorado	Mountain Twp	72	67
Maw	30	m	c	CHIN	Nevada	Nevada Twp	75	311
Sap	29	m	c	CHIN	Yuba	Marysville	93	630
Sing	40	m	c	CHIN	Placer	Bath P O	76	439
Suing	37	m	c	CHIN	Placer	Bath P O	76	442
Tock	37	m	c	CHIN	Amador	Jackson P O	69	332
Took	41	m	c	CHIN	Klamath	Sawyers Bar	73	378
GETANIA								
Joseph	28	m	w	ITAL	San Francisco	1-Wd San Francisco	79	34
GETANIO								
John	24	m	w	ITAL	San Mateo	Schoolhouse Statio	87	346
GETANO								
Thedore	38	m	w	ITAL	San Mateo	Schoolhouse Statio	87	346
GETASH								
James	24	m	w	MEXI	Stanislaus	San Joaquin Twp	92	80
GETCHEL								
Otis	54	m	w	ME	Sonoma	Petaluma Twp	91	339
GETCHELL								
Anna	23	f	w	WI	El Dorado	Georgetown Twp	72	43
Dana B	24	m	w	ME	Nevada	Nevada Twp	75	280
G S S	50	m	w	ME	Nevada	Nevada Twp	75	317
Geo	36	m	w	MA	San Francisco	San Francisco P O	83	284
Hiram	27	m	w	MI	Yuba	North East Twp	93	646
James	39	m	w	ME	San Francisco	San Francisco P O	83	108
Joseph	39	m	w	OH	Calaveras	San Andreas P O	70	211
Osgood	24	m	w	ME	Mendocino	Gualala Twp	74	225
W D	44	m	w	ME	Solano	Vallejo	90	192
GETEMERE								
John	51	m	w	PRUS	Yolo	Putah Twp	93	515
GETENDINA								
Mary	60	f	w	MD	Sonoma	Petaluma Twp	91	309
GETHARD								
Adolphe	45	m	w	HANO	San Diego	Julian Dist	78	473
Henri	35	m	w	FRAN	San Francisco	San Francisco P O	80	412
GETHE								
August	56	m	w	SAXO	Sonoma	Petaluma Twp	91	317
GETHER								
Johose	27	m	w	ITAL	San Francisco	11-Wd San Francisc	84	709
GETHINGS								
James	31	m	w	IREL	San Francisco	San Francisco P O	83	359
GETLESON								
Bernard	42	m	w	PRUS	San Francisco	2-Wd San Francisco	79	195
Henry	40	m	w	HAMB	Napa	Napa	75	16
GETLIEF								
Chas J	31	m	w	ENGL	San Francisco	8-Wd San Francisco	82	364
GETMAN								
Oscar	33	m	w	IL	Nevada	Rough & Ready Twp	75	325
Oscar	29	m	w	IL	Napa	Yountville Twp	75	89
GETO								
Joseph	43	m	w	ITAL	El Dorado	Salmon Falls Twp	72	131
GETOM								
Earnest	40	m	w	NY	Monterey	Castroville Twp	74	335
GETS								
Come	24	f	c	CHIN	Colusa	Colusa	71	300
GETT								
W A	53	m	w	KY	Sacramento	4-Wd Sacramento	77	373
GETTEL								
Jacob	33	m	w	OH	Colusa	Monroe Twp	71	320
GETTEN								
Oliver J	44	m	w	NY	San Francisco	1-Wd San Francisco	79	78
GETTER								
Charles	39	m	w	BADE	San Francisco	11-Wd San Francisc	84	562
Henrietta H	20	f	w	PRUS	Butte	Ophir Twp	70	94
GETTES								
Robert	25	m	w	VA	Klamath	Liberty Twp	73	374
GETTIGAN								
Mary	28	f	w	IREL	San Francisco	San Francisco P O	83	148
GETTINGS								
Benjamin T	38	m	w	KY	Placer	Dutch Flat P O	76	409
Norah	40	f	w	IREL	San Francisco	7-Wd San Francisco	81	277
GETTINS								
Daniel	38	m	w	IREL	Yuba	Bullards Bar P O	93	549
GETTRELL								
J	40	m	w	MD	Lake	Big Valley	73	398
GETTRILL								
Annie	18	f	w	MD	Yolo	Cache Crk Twp	93	448
Mortimer	30	m	w	MD	Yolo	Cache Crk Twp	93	448
GETTS								
Edwd	38	m	w	FRAN	Butte	Ophir Twp	70	117
GETTY								
James	31	m	w	IREL	San Francisco	San Francisco P O	85	731
GETZ								
Abraham	62	m	w	PRUS	San Francisco	San Francisco P O	83	367
Joseph	31	m	w	PRUS	Lake	Lower Lake	73	421
Louisa	21	f	w	HDAR	Sacramento	4-Wd Sacramento	77	374
Meta	48	f	w	PRUS	San Joaquin	2-Wd Stockton	86	186
Soloman	20	m	w	PRUS	Sonoma	Cloverdale Twp	91	268
GETZELMAN								
John	35	m	w	BAVA	Sonoma	Cloverdale Twp	91	268
GETZMAN								
Alex	50	m	w	PRUS	Santa Cruz	Santa Cruz Twp	89	380
GETZS								
Marcus	35	m	w	PRUS	Lake	Coyote Valley	73	400
Maurice	25	m	w	PRUS	Sonoma	Analy Twp	91	232
GEU								
---	45	m	c	CHIN	Shasta	American Ranch P O	89	496
Ah	19	m	c	CHIN	Yuba	Marysville	93	595
GEUBO								
Albert	42	m	w	CANA	Placer	Bath P O	76	458
GEUNG								
---	30	m	c	CHIN	Siskiyou	Hamburg Twp	89	597
Ah	28	m	c	CHIN	Trinity	Douglas	92	233
GEUP								
---	53	m	c	CHIN	Shasta	Shasta P O	89	454
GEURRER								
Angel	26	m	w	AZ	San Bernardino	Belleville Twp	78	408
GEVARA								
Bentura	64	m	w	MEXI	Monterey	Castroville Twp	74	332
GEVERA								
Antonio	36	m	w	MEXI	Santa Barbara	San Buenaventura P	87	423
GEVERIN								
Sebastian	22	m	w	NY	San Francisco	San Francisco P O	80	364

© 2001 by Heritage Quest. All rights reserved.

Name	Age	S	R	B-PL	County	Locale	Roll	Pg
						Series M593		
GEVLIN								
Delia	20	f	w	IREL	San Francisco	San Francisco P O	85	801
GEVRIA								
China	25	m	c	CHIN	Santa Clara	Santa Clara Twp	88	147
GEW								
Ah	47	m	c	CHIN	Placer	Dutch Flat P O	76	406
Ah	16	m	c	CHIN	Placer	Colfax P O	76	388
GEWATZI								
Louis	26	m	w	SWIT	Marin	Tomales Twp	74	77
GEWAY								
Eugene	23	m	w	IREL	San Francisco	7-Wd San Francisco	81	176
GEWIS								
Martin B	66	m	w	VA	Fresno	Millerton P O	72	149
GEY								
Ah	30	m	c	CHIN	Sierra	Downieville Twp	89	521
Ah	30	m	c	CHIN	Sacramento	Georgianna Twp	77	123
Ah	24	m	c	CHIN	Sacramento	Georgianna Twp	77	124
GEYER								
Philip	32	m	w	FRNK	Santa Clara	Fremont Twp	88	53
Philip	31	m	w	FRNK	Santa Clara	Fremont Twp	88	55
Rosana	27	f	w	BADE	San Francisco	San Francisco P O	80	392
GEYSER								
William	35	m	w	PA	San Francisco	8-Wd San Francisco	82	488
GEZARDO								
Joseph	32	m	w	CHIL	San Mateo	Half Moon Bay P O	87	397
GHAIR								
N C	40	m	w	NY	Napa	Napa	75	2
GHALLIGER								
Danl	40	m	w	IREL	Sutter	Sutter Twp	92	116
GHARADELLI								
Andrew	26	m	w	ITAL	Calaveras	Copperopolis P O	70	239
Antonio	38	m	w	ITAL	Calaveras	Copperopolis P O	70	244
B	37	m	w	ITAL	Calaveras	Copperopolis P O	70	237
Joseph	20	m	w	ITAL	Calaveras	Copperopolis P O	70	239
Joseph	17	m	w	ITAL	Calaveras	Copperopolis P O	70	244
GHARAOLLA								
A	28	m	w	ITAL	Calaveras	Copperopolis P O	70	231
Antone	26	m	w	ITAL	Calaveras	Copperopolis P O	70	231
D	29	m	w	ITAL	Calaveras	Copperopolis P O	70	231
GHARKY								
David	64	m	w	OH	Santa Cruz	Santa Cruz	89	426
David J	32	m	w	OH	Santa Cruz	Santa Cruz	89	433
GHARRITY								
Mary	25	f	w	IREL	San Francisco	8-Wd San Francisco	82	334
GHASTANO								
Batasti	14	m	w	ITAL	San Francisco	11-Wd San Francisc	84	594
GHE								
Ah	20	m	c	CHIN	San Francisco	8-Wd San Francisco	82	326
Caroline	11	f	w	CA	San Francisco	San Francisco P O	83	363
GHEE								
Ah	14	m	c	CHIN	San Francisco	8-Wd San Francisco	82	294
GHEO								
Babtiste	30	m	w	ITAL	San Luis Obispo	Arroyo Grande Twp	87	276
GHET								
Ah	19	m	c	CHIN	Yolo	Washington Twp	93	536
GHI								
Ah	26	m	c	CHIN	Solano	Vallejo	90	140
GHIE								
Ching	41	m	c	CHIN	San Francisco	2-Wd San Francisco	79	285
GHIM								
Young	41	m	c	CHIN	Yolo	Putah Twp	93	516
GHIN								
Ah	25	m	c	CHIN	Calaveras	Copperopolis P O	70	226
GHIO								
James	45	m	w	ITAL	Amador	Volcano P O	69	372
GHIRADELLI								
G B	23	m	w	ITAL	Amador	Drytown P O	69	420
GHIRARDELLI								
Giovanni	43	m	w	ITAL	San Francisco	11-Wd San Francisc	84	591
Joseph	17	m	w	ITAL	Santa Clara	Santa Clara Twp	88	177
GHISELIN								
Thos A	26	m	w	MD	San Luis Obispo	Santa Rosa Twp	87	317
GHISLER								
Peter	25	m	w	SWIT	San Francisco	6-Wd San Francisco	81	89
GHIT								
Ah	30	m	c	CHIN	Amador	Jackson P O	69	332
GHODE								
William	49	m	w	HANO	Plumas	Washington Twp	77	56
GHRDTO								
Antonio	41	m	w	ITAL	San Francisco	11-Wd San Francisc	84	613
GHRET								
Christian	28	m	w	WURT	San Francisco	6-Wd San Francisco	81	41
GI								
Ah	28	m	c	CHIN	Tuolumne	Chinese Camp P O	93	364
Oh	15	m	c	CHIN	San Francisco	7-Wd San Francisco	81	248
GIACAMAGGI								
Paul	26	m	w	ITAL	Santa Clara	2-Wd San Jose	88	316
GIACOMAZZI								
Antonio	39	m	w	SWIT	Santa Cruz	Pajaro Twp	89	345
Constant	21	m	w	SWIT	Santa Cruz	Pajaro Twp	89	346
Jno P	27	m	w	SWIT	Santa Cruz	Pajaro Twp	89	342
Joseph	21	m	w	SWIT	Santa Cruz	Pajaro Twp	89	343
Louis	18	m	w	SWIT	Santa Cruz	Pajaro Twp	89	342
GIACOMETTI								
Philip	18	m	w	SWIT	Monterey	Pajaro Twp	74	370
GIACOMEZZI								
Fredk	14	m	w	SWIT	Santa Cruz	Pajaro Twp	89	347

Name	Age	S	R	B-PL	County	Locale	Roll	Pg
						Series M593		
GIACOMINI								
Antone	30	m	w	SWIT	Marin	Tomales Twp	74	77
Battiste	34	m	w	CA	Marin	San Antonio Twp	74	62
Dominco	17	m	w	SWIT	Marin	Tomales Twp	74	76
Domingo	35	m	w	SWIT	Marin	Bolinas Twp	74	2
John	14	m	w	SWIT	Marin	San Antonio Twp	74	63
Julio	49	m	w	SWIT	Marin	Nicasio Twp	74	15
Natale	28	m	w	SWIT	Marin	San Antonio Twp	74	60
GIACOMIO								
Silagie	28	m	w	SWIT	San Francisco	San Francisco P O	80	477
GIACOMMAZZI								
Jesse	30	m	w	SWIT	Santa Cruz	Pajaro Twp	89	358
GIACOMMEZZI								
Juan	21	m	w	SWIT	Santa Cruz	Pajaro Twp	89	346
GIACOMMOZZI								
Giacomi	22	m	w	SWIT	Santa Cruz	Pajaro Twp	89	345
GIACOMO								
Lucca	32	m	w	SWIT	San Francisco	San Francisco P O	80	478
GIADO								
Juan	35	m	w	CHIL	Marin	Bolinas Twp	74	2
GIAGO								
L	16	f	w	CA	Los Angeles	Los Angeles	73	570
GIAIHETINI								
Thos	35	m	w	ITAL	Alameda	Eden Twp	68	59
GIALIS								
Antonio	39	m	w	MEXI	Santa Clara	Almaden Twp	88	15
GIAMELLA								
L	44	m	w	SWIT	Yuba	Marysville Twp	93	570
GIANANTONICO								
Antonio	25	m	w	ITAL	San Francisco	11-Wd San Francisc	84	591
GIANDI								
Magini	21	m	w	SWIT	Humboldt	Mattole Twp	72	283
GIANETTE								
Francisco	25	m	w	ITAL	San Francisco	3-Wd San Francisco	79	305
GIANINI								
Ambrose	41	m	w	SWIT	Santa Clara	Fremont Twp	88	45
GIANINNI								
Henry	47	m	w	SWIT	San Francisco	San Francisco P O	83	299
GIANNI								
Pietro	45	m	w	ITAL	San Francisco	11-Wd San Francisc	84	594
GIANNINI								
Joshua	55	m	w	SWIT	San Francisco	7-Wd San Francisco	81	245
P A	41	m	w	SWIT	San Francisco	3-Wd San Francisco	79	321
GIARDO								
Incarnation	40	m	w	MEXI	Mariposa	Mariposa P O	74	94
GIARNESE								
Frank	44	m	w	NCOD	San Joaquin	3-Wd Stockton	86	218
John	35	m	w	NCOD	San Joaquin	3-Wd Stockton	86	218
GIARRA								
Felice	62	m	w	ITAL	San Francisco	11-Wd San Francisc	84	642
GIASALES								
Matteo	45	m	i	MEXI	Tuolumne	Sonora P O	93	331
GIASH								
S Jno	21	m	w	ENGL	Santa Clara	Almaden Twp	88	9
GIAUGUE								
Louis N	40	m	w	SWIT	Napa	Napa	75	1
T A	46	m	w	SWIT	Napa	Napa	75	1
GIBAL								
Eugene	51	m	w	FRAN	Santa Clara	Burnett Twp	88	39
GIBARDO								
Antony	26	m	w	ITAL	San Francisco	San Francisco P O	85	752
GIBB								
James	30	m	w	SCOT	San Francisco	San Francisco P O	83	218
William N	22	m	w	MO	Los Angeles	Los Nietos Twp	73	591
GIBBE								
C D	56	m	w	SC	San Francisco	3-Wd San Francisco	79	318
GIBBELS								
Nicholas	40	m	w	PRUS	San Francisco	San Francisco P O	83	409
GIBBENS								
Abram	38	m	w	NY	Plumas	Washington Twp	77	54
M A	15	f	w	CA	Tuolumne	Chinese Camp P O	93	386
GIBBENSON								
Julia	40	f	w	IREL	Alameda	Oakland	68	218
GIBBERT								
Geo	29	m	w	NY	Sacramento	1-Wd Sacramento	77	182
Thos	30	m	w	ENGL	Nevada	Nevada Twp	75	301
GIBBIN								
Pat	34	m	w	IREL	San Francisco	7-Wd San Francisco	81	274
Timothy	45	m	w	IREL	San Francisco	7-Wd San Francisco	81	264
GIBBINS								
Frances	39	f	w	AR	Colusa	Colusa Twp	71	273
Lewis G	41	m	w	NY	Placer	Auburn P O	76	368
Wm	25	m	w	CANA	Humboldt	Table Bluff Twp	72	306
GIBBON								
George	40	m	w	ENGL	Alameda	Brooklyn Twp	68	43
John	40	m	w	ENGL	San Francisco	2-Wd San Francisco	79	281
W	19	f	w	OH	Alameda	Oakland	68	242
GIBBONS								
Alexander	30	m	w	IREL	San Francisco	San Francisco P O	85	771
Alfred	33	m	w	NC	Napa	Yountville Twp	75	80
Austin	40	m	w	IREL	Santa Cruz	Santa Cruz Twp	89	394
Charles	35	m	w	CANA	Inyo	Bishop Crk Twp	73	310
Charles	27	m	w	IREL	San Francisco	11-Wd San Francisc	84	634
Charles	25	m	w	NY	San Bernardino	Chino Twp	78	410
Chas	40	m	w	IL	Tehama	Red Bluff	92	183
Chas	40	m	w	IREL	Tehama	Paskenta Twp	92	164
David	43	m	w	IREL	San Francisco	2-Wd San Francisco	79	254

© 2001 by Heritage Quest. All rights reserved.

Series M593

Name	Age	S	R	B-PL	County	Locale	Roll	Pg
David	40	m	w	IREL	Tuolumne	Columbia P O	93	346
David	40	m	w	IREL	San Joaquin	Oneal Twp	86	99
Deming	48	m	w	NY	Tulare	Tule Rvr Twp	92	260
Edwd	21	m	w	IL	Marin	Sausalito Twp	74	73
Elisha	47	m	w	IN	Santa Clara	Gilroy Twp	88	101
Elizabeth	22	f	w	IREL	San Francisco	8-Wd San Francisco	82	382
F W	52	m	w	IREL	San Francisco	San Francisco P O	83	328
George	44	m	b	KY	Colusa	Colusa	71	290
Henry	61	m	w	DE	San Francisco	San Francisco P O	85	777
Henry	34	m	w	IL	Solano	Denverton Twp	90	23
Henry	15	m	w	CA	Napa	Napa Twp	75	31
I W	40	m	w	AR	Mendocino	Sanel Twp	74	229
J R	36	m	w	AR	Mendocino	Sanel Twp	74	229
James	45	m	w	IREL	Santa Clara	2-Wd San Jose	88	313
James	30	m	w	IREL	Alameda	Oakland	68	266
James	25	m	w	IREL	San Francisco	1-Wd San Francisco	79	61
James	17	m	w	MA	San Francisco	San Francisco P O	83	181
Jane	55	f	w	ENGL	San Francisco	11-Wd San Francisc	84	637
Jane	50	f	w	IREL	Marin	San Rafael	74	57
Jane	30	f	w	IREL	Santa Clara	1-Wd San Jose	88	263
John	39	m	w	IREL	San Francisco	San Francisco P O	80	409
John	34	m	w	IREL	Tuolumne	Columbia P O	93	347
John	31	m	w	MO	Los Angeles	Los Angeles	73	517
John	30	m	w	IREL	San Francisco	8-Wd San Francisco	82	328
John	26	m	w	IREL	Solano	Vallejo	90	215
John	25	m	w	WALE	Contra Costa	Martinez P O	71	428
John H	45	m	w	IREL	Inyo	Cerro Gordo Twp	73	319
Joseph	22	m	w	TN	Siskiyou	Callahan P O	89	630
Kate	18	f	w	NY	San Francisco	5-Wd San Francisco	81	4
L	37	m	w	AL	Sutter	Vernon Twp	92	133
Louis	32	m	w	WALE	Santa Cruz	Soquel Twp	89	445
M W	14	f	w	CA	Mendocino	Sanel Twp	74	229
Maryanne	40	f	w	NY	San Francisco	San Francisco P O	83	304
Patrick	41	m	w	IREL	San Francisco	3-Wd San Francisco	79	313
R	5	f	w	CA	Los Angeles	Los Angeles	73	569
Rebecca	35	f	w	IREL	Los Angeles	Soledad Twp	73	633
Rodman	48	m	w	MD	Alameda	Oakland	68	144
Thomas	43	m	w	IREL	San Francisco	11-Wd San Francisc	84	513
W P	59	m	w	DE	Alameda	Alameda	68	5
William	40	m	w	IREL	Alameda	Washington Twp	68	292
Wm	34	m	w	IREL	Sacramento	Dry Crk Twp	77	104
GIBBORS								
John	35	m	w	ENGL	Napa	Napa	75	6
GIBBS								
Andrea	34	f	w	IREL	Santa Cruz	Santa Cruz	89	417
Andrew	15	f	w	CA	Alameda	Oakland	68	175
Charles	37	m	w	RI	San Francisco	11-Wd San Francisc	84	539
Charles E	27	m	w	ME	San Francisco	6-Wd San Francisco	81	119
Chas E	47	m	w	MA	San Francisco	1-Wd San Francisco	79	53
Clara	33	f	w	MA	San Francisco	San Francisco P O	83	202
Cornelius V	46	m	w	RI	San Francisco	8-Wd San Francisco	82	470
Cynthia	18	f	w	IL	El Dorado	White Oak Twp	72	137
Danl	45	m	w	IREL	Solano	Benicia	90	18
David A	32	m	w	NC	El Dorado	Placerville	72	127
E G	27	m	w	MA	Amador	Jackson P O	69	319
F A	41	m	w	RI	Sacramento	1-Wd Sacramento	77	182
Fullon	43	m	w	MO	Tehama	Tehama Twp	92	186
G I	25	m	w	SC	Sacramento	Georgianna Twp	77	124
Geo W	40	m	w	MA	San Francisco	5-Wd San Francisco	81	30
Geo W	39	m	w	NY	Shasta	Stillwater P O	89	478
George	48	m	w	WI	Sacramento	Cosumnes Twp	77	88
George	24	m	w	MA	Contra Costa	Martinez P O	71	386
Henry	55	m	w	NY	Sonoma	Petaluma Twp	91	354
James	48	m	w	GA	Mariposa	Mariposa P O	74	131
James	32	m	w	IREL	Alameda	Murray Twp	68	99
Jane R	36	f	w	CUBA	Sacramento	1-Wd Sacramento	77	205
Jauk	35	m	w	VT	Nevada	Bridgeport Twp	75	100
Jennie	22	f	w	VT	San Francisco	11-Wd San Francisc	84	503
Jennie S	40	f	w	NY	San Francisco	San Francisco P O	83	171
Jerry	35	m	w	GA	Mariposa	Mariposa P O	74	131
John W	16	m	w	OH	Sacramento	Brighton Twp	77	80
Joseph	30	m	b	MA	Sacramento	2-Wd Sacramento	77	236
Joseph S	55	m	w	ME	San Francisco	5-Wd San Francisco	81	19
Josiah H	39	m	w	MA	San Francisco	1-Wd San Francisco	79	111
Oscar	9	m	w	CA	Santa Clara	San Jose Twp	88	213
Patrick	40	m	w	IREL	San Francisco	11-Wd San Francisc	84	488
Reuben	35	m	w	VT	San Francisco	7-Wd San Francisco	81	204
Rose B	42	f	w	NY	Alpine	Woodfords P O	69	315
Sarah A	45	f	b	PA	San Francisco	6-Wd San Francisco	81	101
Serano C	29	m	w	NY	Santa Clara	2-Wd San Jose	88	298
Susan	22	f	w	IL	Sacramento	2-Wd Sacramento	77	229
Sylvester S	32	m	w	NY	Yolo	Grafton Twp	93	497
T T	45	m	w	MO	Tehama	Tehama Twp	92	195
W C	44	m	w	AL	Tuolumne	Sonora P O	93	332
William	42	m	w	IN	Napa	Yountville Twp	75	77
William	33	m	w	ME	Mendocino	Big Rvr Twp	74	160
Wm	28	m	w	NY	San Joaquin	Oneal Twp	86	105
Wm T	40	m	w	MO	El Dorado	Georgetown Twp	72	37
GIBBY								
Hannah	55	f	w	MA	Sacramento	2-Wd Sacramento	77	208
Wm	50	m	w	SCOT	San Francisco	1-Wd San Francisco	79	133
GIBENS								
George F	52	m	w	KY	Los Angeles	Los Angeles Twp	73	491
GIBERANA								
Miguel	28	m	w	MEXI	Los Angeles	Los Angeles	73	542
GIBERSON								
John	40	m	w	NJ	Marin	Tomales Twp	74	81

Series M593

Name	Age	S	R	B-PL	County	Locale	Roll	Pg
GIBERT								
Isaac	28	m	w	IREL	San Francisco	5-Wd San Francisco	81	27
GIBLE								
Wm	40	m	w	SCOT	San Francisco	2-Wd San Francisco	79	206
GIBLER								
Elizebeth	56	f	w	PA	Tehama	Cottonwood Twp	92	162
James	39	m	w	IREL	San Francisco	7-Wd San Francisco	81	166
GIBLIN								
Chas M	21	m	w	NY	San Francisco	1-Wd San Francisco	79	64
James	35	m	w	IREL	Plumas	Quartz Twp	77	37
Margaret	40	f	w	IREL	Sutter	Butte Twp	92	101
Margarett	40	f	w	IREL	Sutter	Yuba Twp	92	151
Michael	27	m	w	IREL	Marin	San Rafael Twp	74	31
Thomas	45	m	w	IREL	San Francisco	San Francisco P O	80	419
Wm	47	m	w	IREL	Sacramento	Granite Twp	77	142
GIBNEY								
George	32	m	w	MA	Sonoma	Cloverdale Twp	91	266
John	33	m	w	MO	Napa	Napa	75	25
John	31	m	w	IREL	San Francisco	1-Wd San Francisco	79	77
Margaret	43	f	w	IREL	San Francisco	San Francisco P O	83	65
Mary	54	f	w	IREL	Mendocino	Anderson Twp	74	155
Nicholas	40	m	w	IREL	San Francisco	San Francisco P O	83	366
Owen	24	m	w	IREL	Los Angeles	Wilmington Twp	73	639
Thomas	31	m	w	IREL	Sacramento	3-Wd Sacramento	77	287
GIBON								
James	45	m	w	IREL	Contra Costa	Martinez P O	71	451
Marie	52	f	w	FRAN	San Francisco	6-Wd San Francisco	81	73
GIBSOM								
Swit	41	m	w	NORW	San Francisco	11-Wd San Francisc	84	691
GIBSON								
A C	29	m	w	OH	Nevada	Nevada Twp	75	280
A J	47	m	w	TN	Mendocino	Ukiah Twp	74	240
Adrastus	23	m	w	AL	Alameda	Brooklyn Twp	68	42
Alex	43	m	w	IREL	San Francisco	11-Wd San Francisc	84	437
Almos	37	m	w	TN	Shasta	Stillwater P O	89	480
Andrew	38	m	w	IL	Solano	Maine Prairie Twp	90	54
Andrew	21	m	w	SCOT	Santa Cruz	Santa Cruz Twp	89	402
Annie	37	f	w	CANA	Solano	Silveyville Twp	90	85
Annie	19	f	w	MA	Solano	Maine Prairie Twp	90	47
Carry	26	f	w	ENGL	Sacramento	4-Wd Sacramento	77	378
Catherine	9	f	w	CA	Alameda	Oakland	68	137
Charles	58	m	w	NH	Calaveras	Copperopolis P O	70	246
Charles	39	m	w	VA	Los Angeles	Los Angeles	73	558
Charles	37	m	w	SCOT	San Francisco	2-Wd San Francisco	79	256
Charles	36	m	m	PA	Sacramento	2-Wd Sacramento	77	217
Charles	28	m	b	MO	Santa Clara	Redwood Twp	88	119
Charles A	30	m	w	VA	Solano	Suisun Twp	90	97
Chas	47	m	w	ENGL	Alameda	Oakland	68	137
Claud S	28	m	w	VT	Sonoma	Vallejo Twp	91	460
Crien R	42	m	w	KY	Solano	Vacaville Twp	90	122
Danl	37	m	w	ENGL	San Francisco	1-Wd San Francisco	79	107
David	39	m	w	NY	Stanislaus	Emory Twp	92	25
David	38	m	w	CANA	Humboldt	Bald Hills	72	238
David	38	m	w	MO	Colusa	Monroe Twp	71	325
Dorsey	16	m	w	US	Santa Cruz	Watsonville	89	369
E G	37	m	w	VA	Mendocino	Round Valley Twp	74	221
Edward	39	m	w	CANA	Mono	Bridgeport P O	74	286
Edward A	43	m	w	NY	Placer	Gold Run Twp	76	395
Edwin F	33	m	w	ME	Alpine	Silver Mtn P O	69	307
Elizabeth	33	f	w	IREL	San Francisco	8-Wd San Francisco	82	472
Enoch	37	m	w	VA	Mendocino	Round Valley Twp	74	220
Fielding W	56	m	w	MS	Los Angeles	El Monte Twp	73	458
Francis	33	m	w	ENGL	Sutter	Vernon Twp	92	132
Francis M	45	m	w	KY	San Luis Obispo	Santa Rosa Twp	87	319
G M	41	m	w	VT	Napa	Napa	75	7
Geo W	41	m	w	TN	Mendocino	Ukiah Twp	74	235
George	40	m	w	NY	Stanislaus	Emory Twp	92	26
George	32	m	w	NC	Marin	Sausalito Twp	74	74
George	28	m	w	ME	San Francisco	7-Wd San Francisco	81	221
George	26	m	w	CANA	Humboldt	Bucksport Twp	72	244
George	21	m	w	MO	Butte	Oregon Twp	70	127
George	15	m	w	CANA	Yolo	Washington Twp	93	528
H B	4M	m	w	CA	Alameda	Oakland	68	221
Henry	48	m	w	IREL	Sonoma	Petaluma Twp	91	345
Henry	44	m	b	MD	Sacramento	Granite Twp	77	145
Henry	37	m	w	OH	Los Angeles	Wilmington Twp	73	636
Henry	35	m	w	PRUS	San Francisco	8-Wd San Francisco	82	386
Henry	28	m	w	SCOT	Santa Clara	Redwood Twp	88	119
Hugh	57	m	w	PA	Santa Clara	Redwood Twp	88	129
J	25	m	w	HDAR	San Francisco	8-Wd San Francisco	82	374
J	22	m	w	SCOT	Alameda	Oakland	68	221
J C	35	m	w	MS	Sacramento	4-Wd Sacramento	77	319
J W	25	m	w	OH	Yuba	Marysville Twp	93	569
James	64	m	w	IREL	Mariposa	Mariposa P O	74	133
James	48	m	w	MD	San Francisco	3-Wd San Francisco	79	323
James	22	m	w	MD	Alameda	Washington Twp	68	296
James	21	m	w	NY	Santa Clara	Santa Clara Twp	88	163
James L	48	m	w	CANA	Yuba	North East Twp	93	644
Jane	19	f	w	OH	Yolo	Cache Crk Twp	93	456
Jas	41	m	w	KY	Butte	Chico Twp	70	55
Jas	21	m	w	ME	Butte	Chico Twp	70	55
Jno G	35	m	w	NY	San Francisco	San Francisco P O	83	124
Jno R	54	m	w	KY	Sonoma	Mendocino Twp	91	294
John	55	m	w	ENGL	Sonoma	Sonoma Twp	91	434
John	53	m	w	WALE	Calaveras	Copperopolis P O	70	239
John	44	m	w	NY	San Luis Obispo	Santa Rosa Twp	87	323
John	38	m	w	MO	Contra Costa	Martinez P O	71	442

© 2001 by Heritage Quest. All rights reserved.

California 1870 Census

Name	Age	S	R	B-PL	County	Locale (Series M593)	Roll	Pg
John	32	m	w	DENM	San Francisco	San Francisco P O	83	35
John	31	m	w	PA	Calaveras	Copperopolis P O	70	240
John	30	m	w	MO	Solano	Tremont Twp	90	36
John	27	m	w	NY	San Francisco	San Francisco P O	83	414
John	25	m	w	NY	Sonoma	Sonoma Twp	91	431
John	23	m	w	IREL	Los Angeles	Los Nietos Twp	73	582
John	20	m	w	SHOL	San Francisco	11-Wd San Francisc	84	569
John	18	m	w	IREL	Marin	Tomales Twp	74	76
John A	51	m	w	ENGL	Sierra	Sears Twp	89	559
John C	42	m	w	CANA	Yuba	North East Twp	93	644
John D	25	m	w	KY	Colusa	Colusa Twp	71	277
John H	50	m	w	CANA	Merced	Snelling P O	74	274
John W	43	m	w	MO	Siskiyou	Yreka	89	661
John W	35	m	w	IL	Santa Clara	Redwood Twp	88	118
Jos	37	m	w	CANA	Sierra	Sears Twp	89	553
Joseph	39	m	w	MO	Los Angeles	Santa Ana Twp	73	603
Joseph	28	m	w	MO	Yolo	Cache Crk Twp	93	439
Joseph	14	m	w	CA	Solano	Maine Prairie Twp	90	54
Joseph L	42	m	w	MO	Colusa	Colusa Twp	71	274
Laura B Mrs	38	f	w	NY	San Diego	San Diego	78	491
Lucy	40	f	w	MO	Amador	Fiddletown P O	69	429
Lucy J	6	f	w	CA	San Luis Obispo	Santa Rosa Twp	87	321
Luther	35	m	w	OH	Los Angeles	Los Nietos Twp	73	575
M L	71	m	w	NC	Mendocino	Ukiah Twp	74	234
Mary	36	f	w	NY	San Francisco	1-Wd San Francisco	79	34
Mary	35	f	w	SCOT	Sacramento	1-Wd Sacramento	77	200
Mary	26	f	w	IREL	San Francisco	7-Wd San Francisco	81	263
Mathew	40	m	w	KY	Inyo	Cerro Gordo Twp	73	320
Mathew M	32	m	w	PA	San Francisco	6-Wd San Francisco	81	117
Miles	41	m	w	VA	Mendocino	Little Lake Twp	74	199
Moses	40	m	b	DC	Sacramento	2-Wd Sacramento	77	246
Otis	43	m	w	NY	San Francisco	San Francisco P O	83	299
P S	34	m	w	MO	Napa	Yountville Twp	75	87
Patrick	42	m	w	IREL	Fresno	Kings Rvr P O	72	215
Peter	45	m	w	DENM	San Francisco	San Francisco P O	80	536
Peter	33	m	w	DENM	Placer	Lincoln P O	76	488
Phoebe	44	f	w	ENGL	San Francisco	2-Wd San Francisco	79	208
R J	43	m	w	TN	Mendocino	Ukiah Twp	74	238
Reuben P	44	m	w	MA	Shasta	Portugese Flat P O	89	471
Robbert	43	m	w	SCOT	Trinity	Indian Crk	92	200
Robert	45	m	w	IREL	Marin	Tomales Twp	74	78
Robert	36	m	w	ENGL	San Francisco	7-Wd San Francisco	81	260
Saml	36	m	w	ME	Sacramento	3-Wd Sacramento	77	300
Samuel	38	m	w	IN	Merced	Snelling P O	74	269
Samuel	35	m	w	MO	Stanislaus	Empire Twp	92	27
Sarah	78	f	w	TN	Yolo	Grafton Twp	93	498
Sarah	73	f	w	NC	Yolo	Grafton Twp	93	494
Scott	22	m	w	OH	Santa Barbara	San Buenaventura P	87	448
Seth	22	m	w	OH	Santa Barbara	San Buenaventura P	87	446
Stephen A	30	m	w	ME	Mendocino	Cuffeys Cove Twp	74	168
T W John	37	m	w	OH	Klamath	South Fork Twp	73	385
Thomas	14	m	w	CA	Solano	Maine Prairie Twp	90	54
Thos	28	m	w	PA	San Francisco	San Francisco P O	83	124
Thos	27	m	w	ENGL	San Francisco	1-Wd San Francisco	79	70
W J	29	m	w	KY	Humboldt	Bald Hills	72	238
W L	45	m	w	TN	San Joaquin	1-Wd Stockton	86	128
W S	28	m	w	MI	San Joaquin	1-Wd Stockton	86	153
W T	48	m	w	KY	San Joaquin	2-Wd Stockton	86	161
W T	35	m	w	MA	Alameda	Oakland	68	182
William	66	m	w	SCOT	San Francisco	San Francisco P O	83	238
William	61	m	w	TN	Marin	San Rafael Twp	74	36
William	41	m	w	VT	Calaveras	Copperopolis P O	70	257
William	40	m	w	TN	Sonoma	Washington Twp	91	466
William	39	m	w	OH	Monterey	Pajaro Twp	74	370
William	30	m	w	SCOT	San Francisco	7-Wd San Francisco	81	218
William	27	m	w	NY	Napa	Napa	75	47
William	19	m	w	KY	San Francisco	11-Wd San Francisc	84	648
William B	38	m	w	VA	Yolo	Cache Crk Twp	93	441
William C	53	m	w	PA	Santa Clara	1-Wd San Jose	88	245
Wm W	43	m	w	IL	Plumas	Goodwin Twp	77	8
Young	56	m	w	DENM	Del Norte	Happy Camp Twp	71	468
GIBZHAUSER								
John	13	m	w	CA	Santa Barbara	Santa Barbara P O	87	492
GICHANNI								
Michael	39	m	w	ITAL	Santa Clara	2-Wd San Jose	88	316
GICK								
Ah	44	m	c	CHIN	Placer	Dutch Flat P O	76	406
Ong	40	m	c	CHIN	Nevada	Nevada Twp	75	313
GICKER								
J K	28	m	w	PA	Sierra	Sierra Twp	89	566
GID								
Ah	35	m	c	CHIN	Mariposa	Mariposa P O	74	131
GIDALGO								
Manuel	22	m	w	MEXI	San Francisco	San Francisco P O	80	343
GIDDING								
Charles	17	m	w	CA	Los Angeles	Los Angeles	73	566
GIDDINGS								
August	35	m	w	SWED	San Francisco	1-Wd San Francisco	79	126
Austin	40	m	w	MA	Calaveras	San Andreas P O	70	153
Claude J	26	m	w	OH	Yolo	Cache Crk Twp	93	430
Elisha E	40	m	w	CT	Stanislaus	Empire Twp	92	45
H	26	m	w	IL	Alameda	Oakland	68	261
Henry	32	m	w	IL	Solano	Suisun Twp	90	104
John	36	m	w	CT	El Dorado	Mud Springs Twp	72	81
Moses	34	m	w	PA	Solano	Denverton Twp	90	25
GIDDINS								
Edwin	51	m	w	OH	Yolo	Cache Crk Twp	93	428

Name	Age	S	R	B-PL	County	Locale (Series M593)	Roll	Pg
GIDDIS								
A	29	m	w	WI	Sierra	Sierra Twp	89	568
W	26	m	w	WI	Sierra	Sierra Twp	89	568
GIDDLE								
J H	40	m	w	NY	Sutter	Yuba Twp	92	148
GIDDONS								
Henry	38	m	w	NY	Solano	Montezuma Twp	90	65
GIDEON								
Joseph	26	m	w	TX	San Bernardino	San Bernardino Twp	78	453
GIDER								
Adam	32	m	w	HDAR	Placer	Lincoln P O	76	493
GIDLEY								
Mary J	16	f	w	CA	Nevada	Grass Valley Twp	75	158
GIDLEYE								
William	27	m	w	ENGL	Mariposa	Mariposa P O	74	120
GIDLEZ								
William	65	m	w	ENGL	Mariposa	Mariposa P O	74	120
GIE								
Ah	40	m	c	CHIN	Sacramento	Dry Crk Twp	77	101
Ah	30	m	c	CHIN	San Francisco	6-Wd San Francisco	81	64
Ah	26	m	c	CHIN	San Joaquin	Oneal Twp	86	116
Ah	22	m	c	CHIN	Placer	Dutch Flat P O	76	414
GIECOMINI								
Antonio	50	m	w	SWIT	Marin	Point Reyes Twp	74	23
GIEDER								
Henry	26	m	w	HANO	Sacramento	Franklin Twp	77	117
GIEGLINGEN								
Arthur	40	m	w	WURT	San Francisco	San Francisco P O	83	177
GIELER								
Antonio	52	m	w	BADE	Amador	Jackson P O	69	322
GIELOW								
Chas	34	m	w	DENM	San Francisco	San Francisco P O	83	123
GIEMER								
Drederick	25	m	w	HANO	San Francisco	San Francisco P O	83	176
GIER								
Fabian	20	m	w	FRAN	San Francisco	11-Wd San Francisc	84	593
GIERHARTA								
Prudencia	45	m	w	MEXI	Alameda	Washington Twp	68	294
GIERLOW								
Clara	45	f	w	MA	San Francisco	8-Wd San Francisco	82	430
GIERSON								
Mary	60	f	w	IREL	Los Angeles	Los Angeles	73	533
GIERST								
Catharine	20	f	w	OH	Sacramento	2-Wd Sacramento	77	239
GIERSZOSKI								
Felix	31	m	w	POLA	San Francisco	11-Wd San Francisc	84	592
GIERZ								
Jacob	34	m	w	PRUS	San Francisco	San Francisco P O	80	478
GIES								
Killian	42	m	w	PRUS	San Francisco	1-Wd San Francisco	79	51
GIESE								
John	26	m	w	SALT	Santa Cruz	Santa Cruz Twp	89	401
GIESEMAN								
Henry	52	m	w	HANO	Santa Clara	2-Wd San Jose	88	323
GIESENKIRCHEN								
Adam	48	m	w	PRUS	San Francisco	San Francisco P O	83	33
GIESMANN								
Charles	41	m	w	SAXO	San Francisco	3-Wd San Francisco	79	302
GIFF								
Ah	24	m	c	CHIN	San Francisco	San Francisco P O	83	48
GIFFERD								
Robert	41	m	w	ENGL	Placer	Dutch Flat P O	76	402
GIFFIN								
Ann	24	f	w	NY	San Francisco	2-Wd San Francisco	79	234
G W	38	m	w	IL	Nevada	Meadow Lake Twp	75	248
GIFFORD								
Albert G	33	m	w	PA	Colusa	Colusa	71	296
Alford	24	m	w	ME	Colusa	Stony Crk Twp	71	327
Amaida	25	f	w	SAXO	Colusa	Monroe Twp	71	325
Annie M	17	f	w	MA	El Dorado	Placerville	72	122
Asal	37	m	w	MA	Santa Clara	Almaden Twp	88	16
C	32	m	w	IL	Alameda	Murray Twp	68	112
Charles B	35	m	w	MA	Santa Clara	2-Wd San Jose	88	282
Charles P	54	m	w	PA	Colusa	Colusa	71	289
Daniel	56	m	w	ME	Marin	Bolinas Twp	74	6
Daniel T	33	m	w	MA	Yolo	Cottonwood Twp	93	465
Edwin	35	m	w	NY	Butte	Chico Twp	70	25
Ellen G	34	f	w	MA	San Francisco	San Francisco P O	83	346
Francis	26	m	w	OH	Sonoma	Analy Twp	91	246
Fred	35	m	w	NY	Santa Clara	Redwood Twp	88	131
Henry	36	m	w	HDAR	Solano	Silveyville Twp	90	91
Henry	29	m	w	IL	Santa Cruz	Pajaro Twp	89	354
Jno	39	m	w	MA	Santa Clara	Almaden Twp	88	16
John	60	m	w	IREL	San Francisco	2-Wd San Francisco	79	142
John	34	m	w	MA	Kern	Linns Valley P O	73	348
John	22	m	w	OH	San Diego	San Diego	78	495
John P	43	m	w	NY	Solano	Montezuma Twp	90	68
Josephus	40	m	w	NY	Contra Costa	Martinez P O	71	423
Julia	49	f	w	IREL	San Joaquin	2-Wd Stockton	86	166
Saml	66	m	w	DE	Colusa	Spring Valley Twp	71	335
Thomas	50	m	w	ME	Placer	Bath P O	76	457
Thomas	49	m	w	MA	Sonoma	Bodega Twp	91	251
GIFLIN								
Francis	10	m	w	CA	San Francisco	11-Wd San Francisc	84	588
GIFT								
Albert	22	m	w	WI	Humboldt	Eureka Twp	72	257
Hariet E	26	f	w	IA	Yolo	Fremont Twp	93	476

© 2001 by Heritage Quest. All rights reserved.

Name	Age	S	R	B-PL	County	Locale	Series M593 Roll	Pg
Harry	11	m	w	CA	Sacramento	San Joaquin Twp	77	396
Isaac	49	m	w	PA	Humboldt	Bald Hills	72	239
Joseph	19	m	w	ME	Humboldt	Eureka Twp	72	278
Josp	13	m	w	CA	San Francisco	2-Wd San Francisco	79	197
William	73	m	w	TN	Contra Costa	Martinez Twp	71	346
William	47	m	w	TN	Contra Costa	Martinez Twp	71	346
William R	33	m	w	TN	Santa Barbara	Santa Barbara P O	87	467
GIGEER								
Fabian	35	m	w	CANA	Yolo	Cache Crk Twp	93	456
GIGER								
William	42	m	w	MO	Stanislaus	San Joaquin Twp	92	79
GIGI								
Luca	36	m	w	ITAL	Solano	Montezuma Twp	90	67
GIGLIN								
Antonio	47	m	w	BADE	Monterey	Castroville Twp	74	339
Valentine	42	m	w	BADE	Monterey	Castroville Twp	74	339
GIGNAT								
Peter	29	m	w	FRAN	San Francisco	1-Wd San Francisco	79	83
GIGNEY								
Ann	35	f	w	IREL	San Francisco	8-Wd San Francisco	82	472
GIHI								
Ferdinand	32	m	w	ITAL	San Francisco	3-Wd San Francisco	79	317
GIHON								
Kate	47	f	w	IREL	San Francisco	San Francisco P O	83	190
Thos	40	m	w	IREL	San Francisco	San Francisco P O	83	102
GIJON								
Nicolas	40	m	w	ITAL	Calaveras	San Andreas P O	70	205
GIKA								
Nicholas	29	m	w	GREE	San Francisco	San Francisco P O	83	175
GIL								
Elizabeth	43	f	w	ENGL	Inyo	Independence Twp	73	324
Jose M	14	m	w	CA	San Luis Obispo	Arroyo Grande Twp	87	276
GILA								
Annitta	50	f	w	FRAN	Los Angeles	Los Angeles	73	561
GILAHURT								
Jas	38	m	w	SPAI	San Joaquin	3-Wd Stockton	86	231
GILARDEN								
Eugene	31	m	w	IL	Alameda	Brooklyn Twp	68	49
Joseph	65	m	w	BELG	Alameda	Brooklyn Twp	68	49
GILARDIA								
D	41	m	w	SWIT	Amador	Drytown P O	69	415
GILARDO								
Raphael	28	m	w	SPAI	San Francisco	San Francisco P O	83	30
GILARIO								
Jumbo	26	m	w	ITAL	San Mateo	Schoolhouse Statio	87	346
GILAS								
John B	39	m	w	MA	Santa Barbara	San Buenaventura P	87	423
GILBATE								
R	29	m	w	ITAL	San Joaquin	2-Wd Stockton	86	172
GILBERT								
---	3	m	w	CA	Lake	Lower Lake	73	414
A	1	m	w	CA	Amador	Drytown P O	69	422
A B	32	m	w	NY	San Francisco	8-Wd San Francisco	82	333
A J	38	m	w	IL	Shasta	Horsetown P O	89	506
Aaron	38	m	w	NY	Napa	Napa Twp	75	30
Abraham	54	m	w	MA	Sacramento	2-Wd Sacramento	77	236
Alice C	65	f	w	CANA	Santa Barbara	Santa Barbara P O	87	501
Attesbert	37	m	w	VT	San Diego	San Diego	78	497
August	50	m	w	FRAN	San Francisco	San Francisco P O	83	139
Benjamin F	41	m	w	KY	Placer	Bath P O	76	425
C W	42	m	w	NY	Sierra	Downieville Twp	89	517
Caroline	35	f	w	WURT	San Francisco	2-Wd San Francisco	79	208
Charles	26	m	w	ENGL	Nevada	Nevada Twp	75	309
Charles	25	m	w	FRAN	Amador	Jackson P O	69	321
Charles	23	m	w	ME	Del Norte	Crescent Twp	71	455
Chas	40	m	w	IL	San Francisco	San Francisco P O	85	872
Chas	18	m	i	CA	Shasta	Shasta P O	89	455
Chester C	37	m	w	MI	El Dorado	Diamond Springs Tw	72	30
Christopher	26	m	w	LA	San Francisco	San Francisco P O	83	158
D	35	m	w	NC	El Dorado	Mud Springs Twp	72	82
D E	40	m	w	IN	Monterey	San Juan Twp	74	401
Daton	49	m	w	CANA	Marin	Novato Twp	74	13
David	47	m	w	NY	Santa Cruz	Santa Cruz	89	404
David W	27	m	w	OH	Santa Barbara	San Buenaventura P	87	423
Eckbert	36	m	w	PRUS	San Francisco	1-Wd San Francisco	79	120
Edward	41	m	w	CANA	San Francisco	San Francisco P O	83	305
Edward	40	m	w	NY	San Francisco	3-Wd San Francisco	79	313
Edward	37	m	w	LA	San Francisco	San Francisco P O	83	355
Elijah	52	m	w	ALOR	San Francisco	11-Wd San Francisc	84	427
Emil	22	m	w	GERM	Solano	Vallejo	90	203
Ephraim	59	m	w	KY	San Diego	Julian Dist	78	470
Ernest	30	m	w	LA	San Francisco	5-Wd San Francisco	81	20
Francis	35	m	w	IREL	Sonoma	Analy Twp	91	219
Franlin C	33	m	w	MI	San Mateo	Woodside P O	87	385
Fred	31	m	w	SWED	San Francisco	1-Wd San Francisco	79	70
G G	25	m	w	MA	Solano	Vallejo	90	211
G I W	42	m	w	PA	San Francisco	San Francisco P O	85	846
Geo	25	m	w	NH	Butte	Chico Twp	70	16
Geo S	48	m	w	ENGL	Santa Barbara	San Buenaventura P	87	441
Geo W	44	m	w	NY	San Francisco	5-Wd San Francisco	81	21
George	60	m	w	NY	Amador	Drytown P O	69	423
George	32	m	w	PA	Siskiyou	Surprise Valley Tw	89	640
George	27	m	w	MI	Amador	Drytown P O	69	422
George	21	m	w	NY	Santa Barbara	San Buenaventura P	87	437
George H	46	m	w	NY	El Dorado	Placerville	72	111
H	14	m	w	CA	Alameda	Oakland	68	257
Harlow	31	m	w	NY	San Diego	San Pasqual	78	523
Harriett	34	f	w	TN	Kern	Bakersfield P O	73	361
Harvey	58	m	w	NY	Marin	San Rafael	74	52
Henery	40	m	w	FRAN	San Francisco	7-Wd San Francisco	81	224
Henora	52	f	w	FRAN	San Francisco	2-Wd San Francisco	79	279
Henry	39	m	w	PA	Santa Clara	Gilroy Twp	88	85
Henry D	36	m	w	MI	Sonoma	Petaluma Twp	91	365
Hiram	34	m	w	IN	San Diego	Julian Dist	78	471
Hypolite	18	m	w	FRAN	San Francisco	11-Wd San Francisc	84	611
Isaac	34	m	w	PRUS	San Mateo	Pescadero P O	87	417
J	48	m	w	OH	Lake	Upper Lake	73	412
J	40	m	w	ENGL	Sierra	Butte Twp	89	509
J B	51	m	w	NY	Sacramento	Brighton Twp	77	71
Jacob	70	m	w	NY	Sonoma	Petaluma Twp	91	326
James	40	m	w	IN	Sacramento	Sutter Twp	77	382
James	36	m	w	US	El Dorado	Mud Springs Twp	72	85
James C	53	m	w	LA	Marin	San Rafael Twp	74	45
James T	68	m	w	LA	Placer	Auburn P O	76	381
James T	68	m	w	LA	Placer	Auburn P O	76	380
Jane	30	f	w	NY	San Francisco	5-Wd San Francisco	81	28
John	38	m	w	ENGL	San Mateo	Woodside P O	87	386
John	38	m	w	MO	Sonoma	Mendocino Twp	91	301
John	33	m	w	TN	Tuolumne	Chinese Camp P O	93	386
John	31	m	w	ENGL	Nevada	Grass Valley Twp	75	184
John	30	m	w	ENGL	Nevada	Grass Valley Twp	75	164
John	29	m	w	ENGL	Nevada	Grass Valley Twp	75	211
John	26	m	w	ENGL	El Dorado	Mud Springs Twp	72	77
John	24	m	w	SWIT	San Francisco	6-Wd San Francisco	81	105
John E	36	m	w	ENGL	San Francisco	1-Wd San Francisco	79	95
John W	48	m	w	ENGL	Sacramento	2-Wd Sacramento	77	227
Jonathan R	64	m	w	VT	Shasta	Millville P O	89	495
Joseph	38	m	w	VT	Del Norte	Smith Rvr Twp	71	476
Joseph	33	m	w	ENGL	Nevada	Grass Valley Twp	75	144
Joseph	32	m	w	NY	San Bernardino	San Bernardino Twp	78	419
Josiah	33	m	w	ENGL	Nevada	Grass Valley Twp	75	143
Josiah	30	m	w	ENGL	Plumas	Indian Twp	77	17
Julius	30	m	w	IL	San Francisco	San Francisco P O	85	872
Kirk	22	m	w	CA	Napa	Yountville Twp	75	78
M	45	f	w	CA	Alameda	Murray Twp	68	128
M E	15	f	w	LA	San Francisco	San Francisco P O	85	792
Martin S	38	m	w	NY	El Dorado	Diamond Springs Tw	72	30
Mary Ann	19	f	w	NY	San Francisco	San Francisco P O	83	149
Mary E	16	f	w	CA	Humboldt	Table Bluff Twp	72	305
Michael	48	m	w	PRUS	San Francisco	San Francisco P O	83	154
Miguel	37	m	w	CA	Santa Barbara	San Buenaventura P	87	437
Minerva	12	f	w	CA	Tuolumne	Sonora P O	93	318
Morton K	51	m	w	PA	Shasta	Shasta P O	89	459
Nat C	55	m	w	NY	Sonoma	Mendocino Twp	91	293
Phillip	48	m	w	BAVA	Amador	Sutter Crk P O	69	413
Refugia O	35	f	w	CA	Santa Barbara	Santa Barbara P O	87	466
Robert	42	m	w	TN	Kern	Bakersfield P O	73	361
Robert	31	m	w	MI	Stanislaus	Empire Twp	92	63
S C	53	m	w	NY	Amador	Fiddletown P O	69	426
Saml J R	23	m	w	OH	Shasta	Millville P O	89	495
Saml W	62	m	w	CT	Napa	Napa	75	48
Sarah	30	f	w	KY	Sacramento	4-Wd Sacramento	77	328
Stephen	36	m	w	ECUA	San Francisco	11-Wd San Francisc	84	592
Stephen B	45	m	w	NY	San Mateo	Woodside P O	87	380
Thomas	44	m	w	ENGL	Inyo	Cerro Gordo Twp	73	323
Thomas	40	m	w	NY	Sonoma	Petaluma Twp	91	328
Thomas	35	m	w	ENGL	Nevada	Grass Valley Twp	75	190
Thomas	27	m	w	ENGL	Nevada	Grass Valley Twp	75	198
Thos	45	m	w	ME	San Joaquin	Dent Twp	86	21
Thos	27	m	w	ENGL	San Francisco	7-Wd San Francisco	81	235
V	16	f	w	CA	Alameda	Murray Twp	68	128
W R	52	m	w	TN	Merced	Snelling P O	74	253
W S	20	m	w	AR	Tehama	Paskenta Twp	92	164
William	20	m	w	MO	Colusa	Spring Valley Twp	71	341
William	20	m	w	AR	Tehama	Tehama Twp	92	193
William	17	m	w	ENGL	Inyo	Cerro Gordo Twp	73	323
Wm	57	m	w	SPAI	San Joaquin	2-Wd Stockton	86	212
Wm	47	m	w	SPAI	San Joaquin	1-Wd Stockton	86	139
Wm H	35	m	w	ENGL	Tuolumne	Sonora P O	93	323
Zachariah	12	m	w	CA	Tulare	Venice Twp	92	278
GILBERTSON								
Emma	26	f	w	IREL	San Francisco	6-Wd San Francisco	81	111
W	27	m	w	MO	Lassen	Susanville Twp	73	446
GILBETSON								
John	25	m	w	CA	San Francisco	11-Wd San Francisc	84	694
GILBIN								
Jos	24	m	w	CANA	Alameda	Oakland	68	248
GILBRAITH								
B H	54	m	w	ME	Solano	Benicia	90	12
James	41	m	w	IREL	San Francisco	11-Wd San Francisc	84	573
John	10	m	w	CANA	Alameda	Oakland	68	251
GILBREATH								
John	38	m	w	OH	Monterey	San Antonio Twp	74	316
GILBRIDE								
Owen	21	m	w	IREL	San Francisco	1-Wd San Francisco	79	82
Patrick	49	m	w	IREL	Sonoma	Mendocino Twp	91	290
Rodger	37	m	w	IREL	Sonoma	Mendocino Twp	91	293
GILBS								
James	27	m	w	ITAL	Los Angeles	Los Angeles	73	565
GILCHARD								
Ransom	25	m	w	NY	Marin	San Antonio Twp	74	64
GILCHRIST								
Alexander	50	m	w	IREL	Solano	Suisun Twp	90	109
Andrew	27	m	w	SCOT	Sonoma	Petaluma Twp	91	349

© 2001 by Heritage Quest. All rights reserved.

California 1870 Census

Series M593

Name	Age	S	R	B-PL	County	Locale	Roll	Pg
Andrew	21	m	w	SCOT	San Francisco	San Francisco P O	80	337
Charles	40	m	w	NH	Santa Barbara	Santa Barbara P O	87	454
David	19	m	w	NY	Solano	Denverton Twp	90	26
Ira	43	m	w	SCOT	Solano	Vallejo	90	153
James	49	m	w	PA	San Francisco	3-Wd San Francisco	79	312
James	29	m	w	IREL	San Francisco	1-Wd San Francisco	79	125
John G	40	m	w	SCOT	San Francisco	6-Wd San Francisco	81	107
Maria	40	f	w	MO	San Francisco	San Francisco P O	83	263
Patrick	57	m	w	IREL	Nevada	Nevada Twp	75	292
Robert C	43	m	w	PA	Marin	San Rafael Twp	74	35
GILCREST								
John B	46	m	w	PA	San Mateo	Half Moon Bay P O	87	395
GILCRIST								
James	41	m	w	PA	Colusa	Colusa Twp	71	274
S F	50	m	w	PA	Alameda	Oakland	68	131
GILD								
Mary	27	f	w	IREL	San Francisco	San Francisco P O	85	863
GILDAY								
Anne	19	f	w	IREL	San Francisco	San Francisco P O	83	301
Bridget	30	f	w	IREL	Santa Clara	2-Wd San Jose	88	329
Charles	55	m	w	IREL	Sacramento	2-Wd Sacramento	77	225
Chas	23	m	w	IREL	Contra Costa	Martinez P O	71	424
Edward	30	m	w	MA	Sacramento	4-Wd Sacramento	77	349
James	38	m	w	PA	Los Angeles	Los Angeles	73	546
GILDEMESTER								
Kate	9	f	w	CA	Alameda	Oakland	68	210
GILDEN								
Charles	33	m	w	IREL	El Dorado	Placerville	72	127
GILDERMEISTER								
Henry	30	m	w	PRUS	San Francisco	2-Wd San Francisco	79	209
J P H	46	m	w	HOLL	San Francisco	3-Wd San Francisco	79	318
GILDERNS								
Henry Von	54	m	w	HANO	Yuba	Slate Range Bar Tw	93	672
GILDERSLEEVE								
G B	42	m	w	NY	Alameda	Oakland	68	239
George	41	m	w	NY	San Francisco	11-Wd San Francisc	84	634
Richard	42	m	w	NY	Placer	Newcastle Twp	76	478
Smith	44	m	w	NY	San Francisco	11-Wd San Francisc	84	634
GILDESATINE								
George	68	m	w	NY	Inyo	Lone Pine Twp	73	331
GILDMACHER								
Melchior	30	m	w	PRUS	Butte	Oroville Twp	70	139
GILDMAKER								
Dan	27	m	w	PRUS	Butte	Ophir Twp	70	102
GILDMEISTER								
Frank	6	m	w	CA	San Francisco	San Francisco P O	80	411
Napoleon	2	m	w	CA	San Francisco	San Francisco P O	80	411
GILDY								
John	27	m	w	NY	Napa	Napa Twp	75	67
GILE								
Andrew	40	m	w	IREL	Butte	Chico Twp	70	56
E T	40	m	w	ME	San Francisco	San Francisco P O	85	779
Henry	29	m	w	PRUS	Butte	Chico Twp	70	15
GILEBERT								
James	37	m	w	HANO	San Joaquin	Castoria Twp	86	9
GILERON								
Eliza	39	f	w	MD	San Francisco	San Francisco P O	83	264
GILES								
Abraham	37	m	b	MD	Sacramento	4-Wd Sacramento	77	366
Albert L	28	m	w	NH	Butte	Chico Twp	70	17
Anna	39	f	w	MD	Sacramento	4-Wd Sacramento	77	366
Annie	42	f	b	MD	Sacramento	4-Wd Sacramento	77	334
D	26	m	w	OH	Lassen	Susanville Twp	73	442
Fredrick	37	m	w	MA	Napa	Yountville Twp	75	79
Geo W	74	m	w	NH	Sonoma	Analy Twp	91	237
George W	36	m	w	OH	Santa Cruz	Soquel Twp	89	442
Harrison	32	m	w	CANA	Sonoma	Analy Twp	91	229
Henry	35	m	w	ENGL	Inyo	Bishop Crk Twp	73	316
Isaac	57	m	w	ENGL	Butte	Chico Twp	70	38
J K	48	m	w	MA	Tehama	Stony Crk	92	198
James	47	m	w	MA	Napa	Napa	75	45
James W	23	m	w	NY	San Francisco	7-Wd San Francisco	81	241
Jo H	37	m	w	NY	San Joaquin	1-Wd Stockton	86	130
John	41	m	w	NY	Calaveras	San Andreas P O	70	207
John	28	m	w	ENGL	San Diego	San Diego	78	500
John W S	45	m	w	NY	El Dorado	White Oak Twp	72	142
Joseph	38	m	w	MA	Alpine	Silver Mtn P O	69	306
Joseph S	20	m	w	MA	Santa Clara	2-Wd San Jose	88	304
Laura M	24	f	w	ENGL	Monterey	Alisal Twp	74	291
Lewis R	49	m	w	ENGL	Sonoma	Healdsburg	91	275
Mary	27	f	w	NY	San Joaquin	1-Wd Stockton	86	130
Melvin	31	m	w	MI	Santa Barbara	San Buenaventura P	87	424
Moel	33	m	w	MA	Contra Costa	Martinez P O	71	397
Oliver	24	m	w	OH	Santa Clara	Gilroy Twp	88	74
Richard	30	m	w	ENGL	Alameda	Murray Twp	68	101
Robert	51	m	w	IREL	San Francisco	7-Wd San Francisco	81	270
Samuel	36	m	w	MA	Monterey	San Antonio Twp	74	319
Thomas	23	m	w	CANA	San Mateo	Pescadero P O	87	412
Timothy	47	m	w	ENGL	Nevada	Nevada Twp	75	284
William	40	m	b	VA	Amador	Sutter Crk P O	69	412
William	37	m	w	NY	Sutter	Butte Twp	92	92
William A	31	m	w	IL	Sonoma	Mendocino Twp	91	297
Wm H	35	m	w	MA	Yuba	Marysville	93	574
GILESPI								
John	23	m	w	IREL	Yolo	Grafton Twp	93	497
GILESPIE								
A	14	f	w	CA	Alameda	Oakland	68	236
D	12	f	w	CA	Alameda	Oakland	68	236
James	15	m	w	NY	San Francisco	San Francisco P O	83	353
GILFEATHER								
Frances	35	m	w	MA	Contra Costa	Martinez P O	71	438
James	61	m	w	IREL	San Francisco	San Francisco P O	80	393
Owen	30	m	w	MA	San Francisco	1-Wd San Francisco	79	25
GILFELLOW								
Daniel	67	m	w	IREL	San Francisco	8-Wd San Francisco	82	423
GILFILLAN								
Jonah	26	m	w	VT	San Francisco	San Francisco P O	80	404
GILFILLEN								
Gilbert	30	m	w	VT	San Francisco	11-Wd San Francisc	84	645
GILFIN								
William	40	m	w	IREL	Contra Costa	San Pablo Twp	71	354
GILFINNREY								
Gilbert	30	m	w	NY	Marin	San Rafael Twp	74	33
GILFOIL								
John	34	m	w	IREL	San Francisco	7-Wd San Francisco	81	180
John	34	m	w	IREL	San Francisco	7-Wd San Francisco	81	183
Patrick	58	m	w	IREL	Sonoma	Vallejo Twp	91	455
GILFORD								
Mary	18	f	w	MD	San Francisco	San Francisco P O	83	213
GILFOY								
William	45	m	w	IREL	Contra Costa	San Pablo Twp	71	363
GILGER								
Charles	32	m	w	PA	Stanislaus	Emory Twp	92	25
Charles	32	m	w	PA	Stanislaus	Emory Twp	92	25
GILGORDON								
John	23	m	w	MEXI	Trinity	Weaverville Pct	92	225
GILGORE								
James	26	m	w	CANA	San Francisco	2-Wd San Francisco	79	230
William	36	m	w	US	Nevada	Rough & Ready Twp	75	336
GILHAM								
Frank	15	m	w	OH	San Francisco	7-Wd San Francisco	81	282
John	40	m	w	IL	Sonoma	Analy Twp	91	244
Lewis	39	m	w	IL	Merced	Snelling P O	74	269
Mitchell	55	m	w	VA	Sonoma	Analy Twp	91	243
William B	50	m	w	IL	Nevada	Rough & Ready Twp	75	326
Wm W	37	m	w	VA	Sonoma	Petaluma Twp	91	342
GILHARDI								
George	42	m	w	ITAL	San Francisco	San Francisco P O	80	479
GILHOOLEY								
Thos	19	m	w	NY	San Francisco	7-Wd San Francisco	81	264
GILIERE								
Antonio	45	m	w	ITAL	San Francisco	1-Wd San Francisco	79	105
GILIGORN								
Catherine	30	f	w	IREL	San Francisco	2-Wd San Francisco	79	249
GILIN								
Wm	25	m	w	IREL	Sierra	Sears Twp	89	557
GILISPEE								
Joseph L	43	m	w	CT	Mendocino	Navarro & Big Rvr	74	177
GILISPIE								
Catherine	32	f	w	NY	Alameda	Alameda	68	7
James	19	m	w	NC	Solano	Maine Prairie Twp	90	46
Thomas	27	m	w	SCOT	Yuba	New York Twp	93	639
GILKE								
Riley	45	m	w	NY	Tuolumne	Sonora P O	93	321
GILKESON								
Frank	31	m	w	KY	Siskiyou	Surprise Valley Tw	89	639
GILKEY								
Edward	25	m	w	ME	Stanislaus	Empire Twp	92	47
John	32	m	w	MI	Monterey	San Juan Twp	74	418
Justus	68	m	w	NY	Monterey	San Juan Twp	74	418
L B	46	m	w	ME	Siskiyou	Scott Valley Twp	89	608
Melvin J	46	m	w	NY	Santa Cruz	Watsonville	89	377
William	49	m	w	NY	Monterey	Pajaro Twp	74	372
GILKIE								
Ransom	24	m	w	ME	Siskiyou	Callahan P O	89	626
GILKY								
H A	40	m	w	MI	Alameda	Oakland	68	253
GILKYSON								
Jno W	42	m	w	PA	Butte	Chico Twp	70	19
GILL								
Ah	20	m	c	CHIN	San Francisco	San Francisco P O	80	496
Ah	18	m	c	CHIN	Butte	Bidwell Twp	70	1
Ah	18	m	c	CHIN	San Joaquin	1-Wd Stockton	86	142
Albin	31	m	w	CANA	Humboldt	Pacific Twp	72	298
Alexander	22	m	w	CANA	Mendocino	Ten Mile Rvr Twp	74	172
Amasa	22	m	w	CANA	Humboldt	Pacific Twp	72	291
Benjamin	27	m	w	NY	Nevada	Meadow Lake Twp	75	250
C Wesley	23	m	w	CANA	Humboldt	Eel Rvr Twp	72	253
Catharine	48	f	w	IREL	San Francisco	San Francisco P O	83	22
Charles	28	m	w	PA	Marin	San Rafael Twp	74	38
Charles	23	m	w	ENGL	Sacramento	2-Wd Sacramento	77	245
Danial	30	m	w	IREL	San Francisco	7-Wd San Francisco	81	173
Danil	21	m	w	CANA	Mendocino	Casper & Big Rvr	74	163
Edw	30	m	w	IREL	Alameda	Oakland	68	245
Elizabeth	8	f	w	CA	Alameda	Oakland	68	164
Francis	28	m	w	IREL	San Francisco	7-Wd San Francisco	81	193
Frederick	30	m	w	PA	Marin	Sausalito Twp	74	73
G	40	m	w	ENGL	Yuba	Marysville	93	604
George	59	m	w	KY	Sonoma	Petaluma Twp	91	345
Hannah	24	m	w	IREL	Solano	Benicia	90	2
Harriet	60	f	w	ENGL	Yolo	Cottonwood Twp	93	462
Hendson	31	m	w	KY	Sonoma	Washington Twp	91	470
Henry	33	m	w	IREL	Humboldt	Eureka Twp	72	278
Henry	30	m	w	ENGL	Nevada	Nevada Twp	75	315

© 2001 by Heritage Quest. All rights reserved.

Name	Age	S	R	B-PL	County	Locale (Series M593)	Roll	Pg
Henry	28	m	w	ENGL	Yolo	Cottonwood Twp	93	462
Henry	27	m	w	ENGL	Nevada	Nevada Twp	75	309
Henry	20	m	w	PRUS	San Francisco	8-Wd San Francisco	82	369
Henry	10	m	w	IL	Santa Cruz	Soquel Twp	89	443
Ho	44	m	c	CHIN	San Joaquin	1-Wd Stockton	86	144
Isaac N	37	m	w	TN	Yolo	Washington Twp	93	531
James	52	m	w	CANA	Humboldt	Pacific Twp	72	297
James	47	m	w	MA	Contra Costa	Martinez Twp	71	350
James	40	m	w	ME	Contra Costa	San Pablo Twp	71	353
James	29	m	w	IREL	San Francisco	5-Wd San Francisco	81	19
James	28	m	w	ENGL	Nevada	Grass Valley Twp	75	224
James F	32	m	w	NY	San Francisco	1-Wd San Francisco	79	88
James W	38	m	w	VA	Yolo	Grafton Twp	93	478
John	62	m	w	ENGL	Tuolumne	Chinese Camp P O	93	375
John	42	m	w	IREL	Yuba	Marysville	93	586
John	40	m	w	IREL	Santa Clara	1-Wd San Jose	88	228
John	39	m	w	OH	Kern	Linns Valley P O	73	344
John	35	m	w	IREL	Nevada	Grass Valley Twp	75	218
John	35	m	w	IREL	Nevada	Grass Valley Twp	75	178
John	32	m	w	IREL	San Francisco	8-Wd San Francisco	82	436
John	31	m	w	AZOR	Monterey	Castroville Twp	74	337
John	23	m	w	KY	Colusa	Colusa	71	294
Jose Maria	49	m	w	MEXI	Monterey	San Antonio Twp	74	316
Joseph	51	m	w	ENGL	Amador	Amador City P O	69	391
Joseph	35	m	w	ENGL	Amador	Amador City P O	69	392
Joseph	16	m	w	NY	Placer	Rocklin Twp	76	468
Joseph E	21	m	w	IA	Inyo	Independence Twp	73	328
Layfayette	18	m	w	IA	Inyo	Independence Twp	73	326
Lydia	10	f	w	MO	Sonoma	Washington Twp	91	470
Martin	67	m	w	IREL	Nevada	Nevada Twp	75	296
Mary	35	f	w	IREL	San Francisco	San Francisco P O	83	252
Mary	24	f	w	IREL	San Francisco	San Francisco P O	83	72
My	25	m	c	CHIN	Marin	Sausalito Twp	74	71
N B	31	m	w	IA	San Joaquin	Liberty Twp	86	96
Owen	34	m	w	IREL	San Francisco	1-Wd San Francisco	79	81
Owen	34	m	w	IREL	San Francisco	7-Wd San Francisco	81	167
Perese	17	f	w	NY	San Francisco	San Francisco P O	85	846
Robert A	39	m	w	OH	Napa	Yountville Twp	75	81
T A	31	m	w	TN	San Joaquin	Elliott Twp	86	76
Thomas	45	m	w	ENGL	Nevada	Bridgeport Twp	75	118
Thomas	38	m	w	IREL	Alameda	San Leandro	68	94
Thomas	35	m	w	IREL	Sonoma	Petaluma Twp	91	331
Waa	40	m	c	CHIN	Humboldt	Eureka Twp	72	280
William	40	m	w	IREL	Alameda	Oakland	68	186
William	32	m	w	ENGL	Nevada	Grass Valley Twp	75	166
William	27	m	w	OH	Inyo	Bishop Crk Twp	73	313
William	17	m	w	PA	Colusa	Colusa	71	294
William A	29	m	w	MA	Santa Clara	2-Wd San Jose	88	294
Wm	50	m	w	IREL	San Joaquin	Tulare Twp	86	255
Wm	30	m	w	IREL	San Luis Obispo	Salinas Twp	87	292
Wm	19	m	w	MA	San Francisco	7-Wd San Francisco	81	258
GILLAGAN								
Hugh	46	m	w	IREL	Tulare	Tule Rvr Twp	92	265
GILLAM								
Cornelius	30	m	w	MO	Mendocino	Little Lake Twp	74	200
John	40	m	w	PA	Napa	Napa	75	8
Michael	39	m	w	IREL	Calaveras	San Andreas P O	70	182
Samuel T	42	m	w	MO	Tulare	Tule Rvr Twp	92	268
GILLAN								
Bridget	40	f	w	IREL	San Francisco	6-Wd San Francisco	81	89
Daniel	25	m	w	IREL	Napa	Yountville Twp	75	81
Delia	29	f	w	IREL	San Francisco	6-Wd San Francisco	81	103
George	35	m	w	MO	San Joaquin	1-Wd Stockton	86	123
Henry	28	m	w	IREL	Napa	Yountville Twp	75	76
James S	42	m	w	VA	San Francisco	6-Wd San Francisco	81	107
John	43	m	w	KY	Tuolumne	Columbia P O	93	354
John	34	m	w	IREL	San Francisco	11-Wd San Francisc	84	616
Julia	36	f	w	IREL	San Francisco	San Francisco P O	85	723
Kate	14	f	w	CA	Solano	Vallejo	90	206
Mark	37	m	w	IREL	Solano	Vallejo	90	167
Mathew	41	m	w	IREL	San Francisco	San Francisco P O	80	340
Neal	35	m	w	IREL	Napa	Napa	75	53
Pat	50	m	w	IREL	Alameda	Murray Twp	68	106
Patk	45	m	w	IREL	Solano	Vallejo	90	175
Patrick	50	m	w	IREL	Calaveras	San Andreas P O	70	156
Thomas	35	m	w	IREL	San Francisco	6-Wd San Francisco	81	148
Tom	36	m	w	IREL	Alameda	Murray Twp	68	106
Wm	36	m	w	NY	Sacramento	3-Wd Sacramento	77	311
GILLAND								
M Mrs	45	f	w	NY	Amador	Jackson P O	69	325
William E	62	m	w	OH	Santa Clara	Redwood Twp	88	131
GILLANDES								
Mary	28	f	w	NJ	San Francisco	8-Wd San Francisco	82	434
GILLAR								
M	35	m	w	IREL	Monterey	Alisal Twp	74	299
GILLARD								
Delia	22	f	w	IREL	San Francisco	11-Wd San Francisc	84	560
Mary	29	f	w	IREL	San Francisco	11-Wd San Francisc	84	552
Thomas	45	m	w	IREL	San Mateo	San Mateo P O	87	357
GILLARDO								
Rafael	38	m	w	MEXI	Kern	Bakersfield P O	73	357
GILLAREN								
Patrick	28	m	w	IREL	Santa Clara	2-Wd San Jose	88	290
GILLASBY								
Joseph	45	m	w	CT	San Francisco	8-Wd San Francisco	82	336
GILLASPY								
Robt C	40	m	w	KY	Napa	Yountville Twp	75	87

Name	Age	S	R	B-PL	County	Locale (Series M593)	Roll	Pg
GILLCASE								
Owen	30	m	w	IREL	Nevada	Little York Twp	75	243
GILLCHRIST								
Patrick	36	m	w	IREL	Calaveras	San Andreas P O	70	168
GILLDAY								
Anna	19	f	w	NY	Solano	Vallejo	90	205
GILLEAN								
Frank	50	m	w	IREL	Tuolumne	Columbia P O	93	359
GILLEIT								
Henry	19	m	w	NY	Santa Cruz	Watsonville	89	377
GILLELAND								
J M	35	m	w	PA	El Dorado	Greenwood Twp	72	55
William	39	m	w	IREL	San Francisco	11-Wd San Francisc	84	540
GILLELEA								
John	25	m	w	IREL	San Francisco	1-Wd San Francisco	79	129
GILLEM								
Hiram	53	m	w	OH	San Francisco	San Francisco P O	83	419
William	32	m	w	MEXI	Mariposa	Mariposa P O	74	104
GILLEN								
Bartholomew	40	m	w	IREL	San Francisco	1-Wd San Francisco	79	31
Bernard	44	m	w	IREL	San Francisco	San Francisco P O	80	422
Chas	23	m	w	NY	San Francisco	11-Wd San Francisc	84	434
Eliza	56	f	w	VA	Sacramento	Franklin Twp	77	112
Eliza	50	f	w	NY	Contra Costa	Martinez P O	71	394
Isabella I	33	f	w	IREL	San Francisco	1-Wd San Francisco	79	19
John	11	m	w	CA	San Francisco	11-Wd San Francisc	84	588
Patrick	39	m	w	IREL	San Francisco	11-Wd San Francisc	84	468
Patrick	12	m	w	CA	San Francisco	11-Wd San Francisc	84	588
Phillip	28	m	w	FRAN	San Bernardino	San Bernardino Twp	78	430
GILLENER								
Anna	22	f	w	IREL	Alameda	Oakland	68	227
GILLENI								
Joseph	27	m	w	ITAL	San Francisco	San Francisco P O	80	400
GILLENS								
Francis	50	m	w	FRAN	Inyo	Lone Pine Twp	73	334
GILLENWATER								
Calvin	51	m	w	TN	Sutter	Sutter Twp	92	118
J H	36	m	w	IN	Sutter	Sutter Twp	92	118
GILLENWATERS								
Mary A	39	f	w	KY	El Dorado	Placerville	72	125
GILLEPSIE								
William	21	m	w	ENGL	San Mateo	Half Moon Bay P O	87	394
GILLER								
E	30	m	w	ME	Alameda	Oakland	68	263
John	36	m	w	PRUS	San Francisco	San Francisco P O	80	471
GILLERMO								
De Paula	32	m	w	ITAL	Amador	Volcano P O	69	384
GILLERO								
Giuseppe	46	m	w	ITAL	Amador	Volcano P O	69	383
GILLES								
George	29	m	w	NY	San Diego	San Luis Rey	78	515
James	40	m	w	NY	San Joaquin	Oneal Twp	86	98
Margaret	58	f	w	GA	Sonoma	Petaluma Twp	91	350
GILLESPI								
Thomas	30	m	w	IREL	San Francisco	San Francisco P O	85	773
GILLESPIE								
A H	57	m	w	NY	San Francisco	3-Wd San Francisco	79	319
Asa	50	m	w	OH	Nevada	Nevada Twp	75	300
Benjamin	12	m	w	MO	Mendocino	Calpella Twp	74	191
Chs B	60	m	w	NY	San Francisco	2-Wd San Francisco	79	202
Dominic	23	m	w	WALE	Contra Costa	Martinez P O	71	429
Edward F	48	m	w	NY	Solano	Suisun Twp	90	95
Ellen	35	f	w	SCOT	San Francisco	8-Wd San Francisco	82	446
Ellen	25	f	w	IREL	San Francisco	8-Wd San Francisco	82	386
Ellen	15	f	w	MA	San Francisco	6-Wd San Francisco	81	117
George	9	m	w	CA	Sacramento	3-Wd Sacramento	77	299
George A	38	m	w	MO	Solano	Suisun Twp	90	94
George W	39	m	w	PA	Calaveras	Copperopolis P O	70	223
Henry N	30	m	w	MA	San Francisco	6-Wd San Francisco	81	119
Heny	28	m	w	IREL	Placer	Cisco P O	76	494
James	50	m	w	IREL	San Francisco	San Francisco P O	80	341
James	21	m	w	IL	Mendocino	Calpella Twp	74	191
James S	36	m	w	OH	San Francisco	5-Wd San Francisco	81	6
Jas	30	m	w	MA	San Francisco	San Francisco P O	85	805
Jean	50	f	w	IN	San Francisco	San Francisco P O	80	427
Jerry	44	m	w	KY	Solano	Green Valley Twp	90	39
John	39	m	w	IREL	Santa Clara	San Jose Twp	88	196
John	36	m	w	PRUS	San Francisco	1-Wd San Francisco	79	47
John	35	m	w	IREL	Solano	Vallejo	90	157
Kate	35	f	w	IREL	San Francisco	San Francisco P O	85	726
Lafayette	13	m	w	MO	Mendocino	Calpella Twp	74	191
Nathaniel	10	m	w	CA	Mendocino	Calpella Twp	74	191
Pat	41	m	w	NY	San Francisco	7-Wd San Francisco	81	275
Patk	40	m	w	IREL	San Francisco	1-Wd San Francisco	79	93
Patrick	60	m	w	IREL	El Dorado	Mud Springs Twp	72	87
Patrick	45	m	w	IREL	San Francisco	1-Wd San Francisco	79	23
Robert	30	m	w	NY	Siskiyou	Table Rock Twp	89	648
Samuel	27	m	w	OH	Nevada	Grass Valley Twp	75	151
Samuel	18	m	w	IA	Solano	Suisun Twp	90	94
Thomas	36	m	w	NY	San Francisco	San Francisco P O	83	72
Thomas	33	m	w	MA	San Francisco	6-Wd San Francisco	81	115
Thos	50	m	w	TN	Mendocino	Calpella Twp	74	191
W E	32	m	w	KY	Mendocino	Little Lake Twp	74	203
William	41	m	w	CANA	Placer	Bath P O	76	424
William	32	m	w	IREL	San Francisco	San Francisco P O	80	379
William	28	m	w	IREL	Contra Costa	Martinez P O	71	412
Wm J	60	m	w	AL	San Diego	San Diego	78	508

© 2001 by Heritage Quest. All rights reserved.

California 1870 Census

Series M593

Name	Age	S	R	B-PL	County	Locale	Roll	Pg
Wm M	43	m	w	VA	San Luis Obispo	Santa Rosa Twp	87	325
GILLESPY								
William	47	m	w	IREL	San Francisco	11-Wd San Francisc	84	712
GILLET								
Edward	24	m	w	OH	Marin	Point Reyes Twp	74	23
Mary	67	f	w	CT	Solano	Vacaville Twp	90	121
GILLETT								
Daniel	35	m	w	MO	Nevada	Eureka Twp	75	138
Edward	53	m	w	OH	Monterey	Castroville Twp	74	331
Frederick	25	m	w	ENGL	San Francisco	San Francisco P O	83	141
Geo	30	m	w	VT	Yuba	East Bear Rvr Twp	93	539
George	45	m	w	ENGL	Santa Cruz	Santa Cruz	89	430
H H	32	m	w	OH	Humboldt	Mattole Twp	72	284
Henry	25	m	w	CT	Sonoma	Bodega Twp	91	261
Isaac C	30	m	w	NY	San Francisco	San Francisco P O	83	242
Jacques	32	m	w	FRAN	San Francisco	San Francisco P O	80	458
James O	22	m	w	OR	Santa Cruz	Santa Cruz Twp	89	380
Joseph	36	m	w	ENGL	Sacramento	3-Wd Sacramento	77	300
Lewis	41	m	w	OH	Humboldt	Mattole Twp	72	285
Thomas E	31	m	w	MI	El Dorado	Placerville	72	127
Thomas J	64	m	w	CT	El Dorado	Placerville	72	127
Thomas J	64	m	w	NY	El Dorado	Placerville	72	117
William	66	m	w	ENGL	Contra Costa	San Pablo Twp	71	356
GILLETTE								
Columbus	54	m	w	OH	Los Angeles	Los Nietos Twp	73	576
Emma	26	f	w	NY	San Francisco	San Francisco P O	80	393
Jackson	23	m	w	WI	Monterey	Castroville Twp	74	333
Jery W	34	m	w	NY	Los Angeles	Los Angeles	73	546
Julia	28	f	w	WI	San Francisco	8-Wd San Francisco	82	309
Thomas	56	m	w	NY	Monterey	San Antonio Twp	74	323
Thomas	23	m	w	LA	Los Angeles	Los Angeles Twp	73	470
W A	26	m	w	OH	Alameda	Alameda	68	5
GILLEWAY								
Bridget	63	f	w	IREL	San Francisco	San Francisco P O	83	287
GILLEY								
I H	49	m	b	MD	Merced	Snelling P O	74	247
Michael	22	m	w	MA	San Joaquin	1-Wd Stockton	86	140
GILLFEATHER								
Thos	24	m	w	IREL	Alameda	Washington Twp	68	285
GILLFIELD								
Mary	25	f	w	NJ	San Francisco	8-Wd San Francisco	82	322
GILLFILLAN								
Alex	41	m	w	PA	Colusa	Colusa	71	295
John	40	m	w	SCOT	San Francisco	11-Wd San Francisc	84	460
GILLFILLEUN								
Walter	22	m	w	VT	San Francisco	11-Wd San Francisc	84	646
GILLHAM								
Chas	52	m	w	OH	Humboldt	Pacific Twp	72	295
James H	76	m	w	IL	Nevada	Rough & Ready Twp	75	324
GILLHOULEY								
Ellen	37	f	w	IREL	San Francisco	7-Wd San Francisco	81	277
GILLIAM								
Robert	54	m	w	NC	Tulare	Tule Rvr Twp	92	263
GILLIAN								
James	38	m	w	IREL	Placer	Emigrant Gap P O	76	416
James	37	m	w	IREL	San Francisco	7-Wd San Francisco	81	225
John	45	m	w	IREL	Tuolumne	Columbia P O	93	352
John	38	m	w	IREL	Tuolumne	Columbia P O	93	347
Mike	41	m	w	IREL	San Joaquin	Tulare Twp	86	254
Patrick	45	m	w	IREL	San Francisco	2-Wd San Francisco	79	283
GILLIAND								
R	42	m	w	AR	Amador	Jackson P O	69	345
Thomas	26	m	w	ENGL	San Francisco	11-Wd San Francisc	84	638
GILLIARD								
Jane	34	f	b	DE	San Francisco	San Francisco P O	80	418
GILLIARDO								
John	31	m	w	ITAL	Mariposa	Maxwell Crk P O	74	143
GILLIARSA								
Juan	44	m	w	ITAL	San Francisco	11-Wd San Francisc	84	642
GILLIAS								
F	35	m	w	ITAL	San Joaquin	3-Wd Stockton	86	232
GILLICH								
George	40	m	w	HDAR	Amador	Drytown P O	69	424
GILLIGAN								
Annie	20	f	w	IREL	San Francisco	San Francisco P O	80	408
Edward	45	m	w	IREL	Santa Clara	Santa Clara Twp	88	155
Honora	19	f	w	IREL	San Francisco	11-Wd San Francisc	84	450
James	48	m	w	IREL	Alameda	Oakland	68	143
James	40	m	w	IREL	San Francisco	San Francisco P O	85	730
John	29	m	w	IREL	San Joaquin	2-Wd Stockton	86	167
Kate	45	f	w	IREL	San Francisco	11-Wd San Francisc	84	644
Kate	27	f	w	IREL	San Francisco	San Francisco P O	83	296
Kate	26	f	w	IREL	San Francisco	San Francisco P O	83	151
Kate	19	f	w	IREL	Yuba	Marysville	93	597
Lewis	22	m	w	CANA	Placer	Gold Run Twp	76	395
Martin	25	m	w	IREL	San Francisco	11-Wd San Francisc	84	428
Mathew	28	m	w	IREL	Marin	San Rafael	74	54
Michl	45	m	w	IREL	San Francisco	1-Wd San Francisco	79	44
Owen	28	m	w	IREL	San Francisco	San Francisco P O	83	159
S	26	m	w	NY	Yuba	Marysville	93	595
GILLILAND								
John R	40	m	w	MO	Napa	Napa	75	39
GILLIN								
Alexander	39	m	w	IREL	San Francisco	11-Wd San Francisc	84	467
Eliza	34	f	w	IREL	Sierra	Sears Twp	89	555
George	55	m	w	VA	Sacramento	Franklin Twp	77	111
John H M	54	m	w	PA	San Joaquin	2-Wd Stockton	86	202
GILLING								
Henry	29	m	w	HANO	Santa Cruz	Santa Cruz Twp	89	393
GILLINGHAM								
Charles	35	m	w	ENGL	San Francisco	San Francisco P O	83	218
H C	39	m	w	PA	San Joaquin	Elkhorn Twp	86	57
Jas	56	m	w	IREL	San Francisco	San Francisco P O	83	137
John	25	m	w	ENGL	San Diego	San Diego	78	492
GILLINGHAN								
C A	56	m	w	PA	San Joaquin	1-Wd Stockton	86	134
GILLION								
Phillip	45	m	w	PRUS	Trinity	North Fork Twp	92	218
GILLIPIE								
F	16	m	w	MEXI	Alameda	Oakland	68	159
GILLIRO								
Gaspard	24	m	w	ITAL	Amador	Volcano P O	69	377
GILLIRRO								
John B	28	m	w	ITAL	Amador	Volcano P O	69	377
GILLIS								
Alex	36	m	w	CANA	Amador	Ione City P O	69	352
Charles	50	m	w	NY	Santa Clara	2-Wd San Jose	88	332
D	42	m	w	IREL	San Joaquin	Elliott Twp	86	76
D	40	m	w	OH	San Joaquin	Oneal Twp	86	112
David W	46	m	w	OH	Stanislaus	Emory Twp	92	22
Dougald	35	m	w	VT	Sacramento	3-Wd Sacramento	77	292
Duncan	32	m	w	SCOT	Nevada	Grass Valley Twp	75	147
Edw	24	m	w	CANA	Alameda	Oakland	68	214
Frank	30	m	w	OH	Butte	Ophir Twp	70	100
Frank	23	m	w	CA	San Luis Obispo	Santa Rosa Twp	87	324
George	26	m	w	MI	San Diego	Warners Rancho Dis	78	528
H M	14	m	w	CA	Alameda	Oakland	68	243
Hudson B	33	m	w	VT	Siskiyou	Yreka	89	663
Hugh	50	m	w	SCOT	San Luis Obispo	Salinas Twp	87	292
J N	39	m	w	GA	Tuolumne	Columbia P O	93	354
James	40	m	w	IREL	Alameda	Murray Twp	68	112
James	26	m	w	ME	Alameda	Oakland	68	255
James L	45	m	w	IREL	Sonoma	Petaluma Twp	91	320
John	27	m	w	MO	Solano	Silveyville Twp	90	74
John H	45	m	w	NC	San Francisco	8-Wd San Francisco	82	336
Joseph	50	m	w	NY	Yolo	Washington Twp	93	538
Mary	27	f	w	IREL	Santa Clara	Gilroy Twp	88	73
N A	42	m	w	GA	Tuolumne	Chinese Camp P O	93	383
Newton B	21	m	w	IA	San Luis Obispo	Santa Rosa Twp	87	324
Norman	32	m	w	CANA	Amador	Ione City P O	69	352
Peter	33	m	w	IA	San Luis Obispo	Santa Rosa Twp	87	324
Peter S	61	m	w	MO	San Luis Obispo	Santa Rosa Twp	87	324
Polk	27	m	w	MO	Solano	Silveyville Twp	90	72
R C	35	m	w	ENGL	Mariposa	Mariposa P O	74	134
Robert	35	m	w	NY	San Francisco	7-Wd San Francisco	81	188
Wm	16	m	w	CA	San Francisco	San Francisco P O	85	840
GILLISH								
John	30	m	w	ME	Stanislaus	Empire Twp	92	66
GILLISPI								
Henry	39	m	w	NY	Sonoma	Healdsburg & Mendo	91	281
GILLISPIE								
Julia	27	f	w	IREL	San Francisco	7-Wd San Francisco	81	233
Mary	14	m	w	PA	San Joaquin	Tulare Twp	86	256
Needham	34	m	w	OH	San Luis Obispo	Santa Rosa Twp	87	318
Owen	62	m	w	IREL	Klamath	South Fork Twp	73	385
Robert	53	m	w	VA	Amador	Volcano P O	69	383
Simon H	49	m	w	IN	Placer	Bath P O	76	456
GILLMAN								
A M	31	m	w	NH	San Francisco	7-Wd San Francisco	81	250
Chas	32	m	w	IREL	Sonoma	Salt Point	91	388
Frank	42	m	w	ME	Klamath	Trinidad Twp	73	390
Frank	37	m	w	KY	Alameda	Washington Twp	68	272
H	24	m	w	MA	San Francisco	8-Wd San Francisco	82	370
Henry	23	m	w	RI	San Francisco	8-Wd San Francisco	82	374
J W	22	m	w	NY	San Francisco	8-Wd San Francisco	82	363
John	64	m	w	ME	San Francisco	7-Wd San Francisco	81	164
John	40	m	w	ME	Stanislaus	Branch Twp	92	8
Nicholas	60	m	w	NH	Solano	Vallejo	90	145
S J	46	m	w	NH	San Francisco	San Francisco P O	83	281
Sacremento	21	f	w	CA	Los Angeles	Los Angeles	73	513
William	32	m	w	IREL	Humboldt	Bucksport Twp	72	242
GILLME								
Charles H	36	m	w	ME	Inyo	Independence Twp	73	327
GILLMEISTER								
Edwd	30	m	w	MECK	San Francisco	1-Wd San Francisco	79	108
GILLMER								
Charles	18	m	w	GERM	Los Angeles	Los Angeles	73	550
GILLMORE								
Armon	29	m	w	IREL	Contra Costa	Martinez P O	71	435
Geo W	38	m	w	KY	Calaveras	Copperopolis P O	70	229
John	38	m	w	CANA	Mariposa	Mariposa P O	74	122
M E	32	m	w	ME	Yuba	Marysville	93	608
Nell	30	f	w	NY	San Francisco	11-Wd San Francisc	84	548
R N	39	m	w	ME	Amador	Amador City P O	69	390
Robert	64	m	w	IREL	Alameda	Eden Twp	68	85
Stephen D	52	m	w	NH	San Francisco	7-Wd San Francisco	81	249
William	31	m	w	IREL	Contra Costa	Martinez P O	71	431
GILLNORO								
Bistisa	14	m	w	CA	Santa Clara	Almaden Twp	88	8
GILLOCK								
Terrence	30	m	w	IREL	Amador	Volcano P O	69	378
GILLON								
Charles	46	m	w	PA	Calaveras	Copperopolis P O	70	255
George	28	m	w	PA	Merced	Snelling P O	74	253

© 2001 by Heritage Quest. All rights reserved.

California 1870 Census

Series M593

Name	Age	S	R	B-PL	County	Locale	Roll	Pg
J J	18	m	w	NY	Merced	Snelling P O	74	253
John	25	m	w	LA	San Francisco	11-Wd San Francisc	84	467
GILLONS								
John	24	m	w	ENGL	Butte	Chico Twp	70	56
GILLOOLY								
Lawrence	35	m	w	IREL	Santa Clara	2-Wd San Jose	88	293
Patrick	41	m	w	IREL	Shasta	Shasta P O	89	461
GILLOOTS								
John	30	m	w	FRAN	San Francisco	6-Wd San Francisco	81	96
GILLORY								
Alfred	47	m	w	FRAN	Los Angeles	Los Angeles	73	519
GILLOTT								
Louis	10	m	w	CA	Marin	San Rafael Twp	74	27
GILLOTTE								
B	38	m	w	ITAL	Alameda	Oakland	68	167
GILLOW								
Ellen	45	f	w	IREL	San Francisco	San Francisco P O	83	281
Wm	30	m	w	SCOT	San Joaquin	3-Wd Stockton	86	217
GILLROY								
B	46	m	w	IREL	San Joaquin	2-Wd Stockton	86	174
GILLS								
---	22	m	w	CANA	Mendocino	Ten Mile Rvr Twp	74	172
E W	30	m	w	ME	San Joaquin	Oneal Twp	86	111
George C	25	m	w	NY	San Francisco	3-Wd San Francisco	79	328
GILLSON								
C B	29	m	w	NY	Sierra	Gibson Twp	89	539
Eleazor	57	m	w	NY	Shasta	Horsetown P O	89	504
John	40	m	w	MI	Marin	Bolinas Twp	74	6
GILLSPIE								
Ellen	25	f	w	IREL	San Francisco	11-Wd San Francisc	84	423
GILLUM								
Benjamin	44	m	w	IA	San Mateo	Half Moon Bay P O	87	406
Burill	55	m	b	LA	Sacramento	Granite Twp	77	145
John	50	m	w	VA	San Mateo	Redwood Twp	87	367
John	22	m	w	OR	Kern	Linns Valley P O	73	344
Jonathon	32	m	w	MO	Yolo	Buckeye Twp	93	408
Roulson	48	m	w	KY	Sutter	Yuba Twp	92	145
GILLY								
Joseph	28	m	w	FRAN	San Francisco	2-Wd San Francisco	79	162
GILMAM								
A	45	m	w	NH	Santa Clara	Gilroy Twp	88	77
GILMAN								
Alexr	45	m	w	ME	San Francisco	5-Wd San Francisco	81	30
Andrew J	35	m	w	ME	Yolo	Cottonwood Twp	93	461
Benj F	39	m	w	ME	San Francisco	7-Wd San Francisco	81	230
Benjn	30	m	w	KY	San Francisco	5-Wd San Francisco	81	26
C H	33	m	w	NH	Solano	Vallejo	90	178
C H	23	m	w	NH	Sacramento	3-Wd Sacramento	77	284
Cassy	23	f	w	MA	San Francisco	6-Wd San Francisco	81	62
Charles H	26	m	w	CANA	Yolo	Grafton Twp	93	479
Chas	10	m	w	CA	Shasta	American Ranch P O	89	496
Elbridge G	52	m	w	NH	Yuba	Long Bar Twp	93	562
Frances	42	f	w	AUST	San Francisco	San Francisco P O	83	171
Frank L	29	m	w	NH	San Francisco	3-Wd San Francisco	79	330
J T	48	m	w	NH	Alameda	Alameda	68	12
James	27	m	w	PA	Sacramento	2-Wd Sacramento	77	221
James M	28	m	w	NH	San Bernardino	San Bernardino Twp	78	445
Jerome A	26	m	w	NY	Butte	Ophir Twp	70	96
Jno	36	m	w	NY	San Joaquin	Douglas Twp	86	41
John	40	m	w	VT	Sacramento	4-Wd Sacramento	77	376
John	22	m	w	NJ	Kern	Bakersfield P O	73	362
John	20	m	w	IREL	Stanislaus	Empire Twp	92	64
Joseph	32	m	w	MO	San Joaquin	Castoria Twp	86	6
Joseph C	27	m	w	ME	Santa Cruz	Watsonville	89	364
Lyman	24	m	w	ME	Calaveras	San Andreas P O	70	191
Lyman P	26	m	w	PA	Sacramento	2-Wd Sacramento	77	225
M	14	m	w	MO	Alameda	Oakland	68	255
Martha A	29	f	w	ME	Santa Cruz	Watsonville	89	375
Mary	28	f	w	IREL	San Francisco	San Francisco P O	83	15
Mary H	64	f	w	NH	Sonoma	Healdsburg	91	275
Mat	50	m	w	NH	San Francisco	5-Wd San Francisco	81	24
Mercy A	10	f	w	CA	El Dorado	Diamond Springs Tw	72	23
Morris	36	m	w	PA	Sacramento	2-Wd Sacramento	77	225
Orlando W	28	m	w	ME	Alpine	Silver Mtn P O	69	307
Peter	31	m	w	NY	Santa Clara	Gilroy Twp	88	90
Roscoe	29	m	w	ME	Solano	Vallejo	90	177
S S	40	m	w	PA	Tehama	Red Bluff	92	183
Saml	48	m	w	VA	Calaveras	Copperopolis P O	70	239
Sewell	31	m	w	ME	San Diego	Julian Dist	78	470
Thomas	38	m	b	TN	Tuolumne	Columbia P O	93	351
Thomas	35	m	w	IREL	Sacramento	2-Wd Sacramento	77	233
William	38	m	w	ME	El Dorado	Cosumnes Twp	72	13
GILMAND								
Joseph	63	m	w	FRAN	San Francisco	San Francisco P O	80	465
GILMARTIN								
Danl	27	m	w	IREL	Alameda	Murray Twp	68	106
F	24	m	w	IREL	Alameda	Murray Twp	68	106
GILMEN								
Avery	38	m	w	ME	Calaveras	San Andreas P O	70	192
GILMENIA								
Cerise	24	m	w	SWIT	Calaveras	San Andreas P O	70	198
GILMER								
Abranher	42	m	w	CANA	Humboldt	Eureka Twp	72	274
Andrew	48	m	w	IREL	El Dorado	Mud Springs Twp	72	91
Jos	60	m	w	NY	Solano	Benicia	90	5
Peter	33	m	w	FRAN	Colusa	Grand Island Twp	71	302
Rufus	45	m	w	MO	Tulare	Farmersville Twp	92	243

Series M593

Name	Age	S	R	B-PL	County	Locale	Roll	Pg
T W	57	m	w	IREL	Sacramento	3-Wd Sacramento	77	302
GILMON								
George D	40	m	w	SCOT	San Francisco	San Francisco P O	83	21
GILMORE								
Alice	26	f	w	ME	El Dorado	Mud Springs Twp	72	75
Catherine	30	f	w	IREL	Solano	Vallejo	90	156
Charles	38	m	w	NY	San Francisco	San Francisco P O	85	745
Charles	25	m	w	NY	San Francisco	8-Wd San Francisco	82	382
David	24	m	w	IREL	Contra Costa	Martinez P O	71	369
Elijah	40	m	w	OH	San Francisco	11-Wd San Francisc	84	638
F G	33	m	w	NY	Solano	Vallejo	90	203
G W	39	m	w	ME	San Francisco	San Francisco P O	83	325
George	24	m	w	ENGL	San Francisco	San Francisco P O	80	336
Henry	30	m	w	MA	San Francisco	11-Wd San Francisc	84	524
Henry	28	m	w	WI	Siskiyou	Butte Twp	89	586
Hewie	46	m	w	IREL	Sacramento	3-Wd Sacramento	77	278
Hiram	43	m	w	NY	Mendocino	Anderson Twp	74	157
Isaah	58	m	w	MO	San Joaquin	Elkhorn Twp	86	52
James	54	m	w	IREL	Tuolumne	Sonora P O	93	308
James	52	m	w	MA	Nevada	Nevada Twp	75	272
James	49	m	w	VA	Solano	Green Valley Twp	90	44
James	41	m	w	NH	Los Angeles	El Monte Twp	73	456
James	38	m	w	IREL	Santa Cruz	Pajaro Twp	89	343
James	29	m	w	KY	Siskiyou	Butte Twp	89	588
James	23	m	w	IA	Napa	Napa	75	45
Jas	41	m	w	IREL	San Francisco	7-Wd San Francisco	81	279
John	35	m	w	IREL	San Francisco	7-Wd San Francisco	81	167
John	35	m	w	PA	San Francisco	11-Wd San Francisc	84	505
John	33	m	w	CANA	Colusa	Colusa	71	290
John	33	m	w	PA	Tehama	Antelope Twp	92	155
John	31	m	w	MA	San Francisco	11-Wd San Francisc	84	635
John	21	m	w	IREL	San Francisco	San Francisco P O	83	309
John W	20	m	w	IL	Fresno	Millerton P O	72	149
Joseph	38	m	w	IN	El Dorado	Cosumnes Twp	72	17
Josephine	40	f	w	ENGL	San Francisco	6-Wd San Francisco	81	105
Julia	40	f	w	IREL	Napa	Napa Twp	75	33
Lide	21	f	w	IL	Yolo	Cache Crk Twp	93	428
Maria	31	f	w	IREL	San Francisco	7-Wd San Francisco	81	167
Martin	57	m	w	IREL	San Joaquin	Castoria Twp	86	8
Mary	38	f	w	FRAN	San Francisco	2-Wd San Francisco	79	198
Mary	25	f	w	IREL	San Francisco	11-Wd San Francisc	84	432
Mary	20	f	w	IREL	San Francisco	8-Wd San Francisco	82	444
Michael	60	m	w	IREL	Napa	Napa Twp	75	31
Michel	60	m	w	IREL	Napa	Napa Twp	75	33
Michl	30	m	w	IREL	Alameda	Oakland	68	178
Nathan	40	m	w	OH	El Dorado	Mud Springs Twp	72	81
Nellie	37	f	w	ME	Mariposa	Mariposa P O	74	120
Robert	44	m	w	NH	El Dorado	Placerville	72	114
Robert M	32	m	w	PA	El Dorado	Mud Springs Twp	72	75
Robt	28	m	w	OH	San Francisco	11-Wd San Francisc	84	424
Royal F	53	m	w	KY	Sonoma	Healdsburg & Mendo	91	281
Samuel	45	m	w	CANA	San Francisco	2-Wd San Francisco	79	256
Samuel	27	m	w	CANA	Colusa	Colusa	71	290
Thomas	28	m	w	TN	Los Angeles	Los Nietos Twp	73	577
William	31	m	w	IREL	Sacramento	3-Wd Sacramento	77	305
Wm	42	m	w	ENGL	Sacramento	1-Wd Sacramento	77	173
Wm	35	m	w	ENGL	Sacramento	1-Wd Sacramento	77	173
GILMORES								
W	40	m	w	ME	Amador	Sutter Crk P O	69	411
GILMOUR								
Thomas	47	m	w	SCOT	San Francisco	San Francisco P O	85	833
Thomas	36	m	w	ENGL	San Francisco	San Francisco P O	80	473
GILNACK								
Charles	30	m	w	CT	Yolo	Washington Twp	93	535
GILOOLY								
Hugh	35	m	w	IREL	San Francisco	San Francisco P O	83	396
GILOTTE								
Gault	36	m	w	SWIT	San Francisco	San Francisco P O	80	533
GILOWARD								
Leon	35	m	w	CANA	Siskiyou	Hamburg Twp	89	598
GILPATRICK								
E	40	m	w	ME	Calaveras	Copperopolis P O	70	230
Edwin	28	m	w	ME	Sonoma	Salt Point	91	388
Frank	4	m	w	CA	Sutter	Sutter Twp	92	123
G A	38	m	w	ME	Sutter	Butte Twp	92	94
George	36	m	w	ME	Sutter	Butte Twp	92	97
Hellen	21	f	w	OH	Sutter	Butte Twp	92	90
J T	40	m	w	ME	Sutter	Butte Twp	92	94
James	29	m	w	ME	Calaveras	San Andreas P O	70	175
N	40	m	w	ME	El Dorado	Greenwood Twp	72	51
P	31	m	w	ME	Yuba	Marysville Twp	93	571
GILPAY								
Jas	42	m	w	IREL	Sacramento	1-Wd Sacramento	77	190
GILPIN								
Susan	60	f	w	PA	Sacramento	3-Wd Sacramento	77	294
GILREATH								
Noah	48	m	w	KY	Nevada	Grass Valley Twp	75	159
GILRORY								
Michael	40	m	w	ME	San Francisco	San Francisco P O	83	239
GILROY								
C	30	m	w	CA	Santa Clara	Gilroy Twp	88	89
James	40	m	w	IREL	Yuba	Long Bar Twp	93	561
James	28	m	w	IREL	Napa	Napa Twp	75	29
John	33	m	w	IREL	Nevada	Grass Valley Twp	75	193
John	25	m	w	IREL	Plumas	Indian Twp	77	17
Jose	25	m	w	CA	Santa Clara	Gilroy Twp	88	87
Manuel	18	m	w	CA	Santa Clara	Gilroy Twp	88	91

© 2001 by Heritage Quest. All rights reserved.

Name	Age	S	R	B-PL	County	Locale	Roll	Pg
Margt	33	f	w	IREL	San Francisco	8-Wd San Francisco	82	331
Mary	25	f	w	IREL	San Francisco	6-Wd San Francisco	81	107
Neofita	41	m	w	CA	Santa Clara	Gilroy Twp	88	87
P G	37	m	w	IREL	Tuolumne	Columbia P O	93	341
Patrick	37	m	w	IREL	San Francisco	San Francisco P O	83	209
Patrick	30	m	w	IREL	San Francisco	San Francisco P O	85	848
S	13	m	w	CA	Santa Clara	Gilroy Twp	88	104
Thomas	33	m	w	IREL	San Francisco	1-Wd San Francisco	79	104
Thomas	30	m	w	IREL	San Francisco	San Francisco P O	83	255
GILS								
Peter	37	m	w	PRUS	Santa Cruz	Pajaro Twp	89	348
GILSEN								
John	34	m	w	DENM	San Francisco	San Francisco P O	80	470
Robert	36	m	w	DENM	San Francisco	San Francisco P O	80	538
GILSON								
A	28	f	w	WALE	Sierra	Butte Twp	89	510
Alferd	17	m	w	IL	Colusa	Grand Island Twp	71	302
Edward	44	m	w	IREL	San Francisco	2-Wd San Francisco	79	254
Emma	44	f	w	NY	Colusa	Colusa	71	297
Geo	45	m	w	ENGL	San Francisco	1-Wd San Francisco	79	134
George E	35	m	w	VT	San Francisco	San Francisco P O	85	758
J	37	m	w	IREL	Sierra	Butte Twp	89	510
J C	30	m	w	PA	Alameda	Washington Twp	68	283
James	45	m	w	KY	San Francisco	2-Wd San Francisco	79	215
James	34	m	w	NY	Mendocino	Cuffeys Cove Twp	74	168
Lyman	38	m	w	NY	Tuolumne	Big Oak Flat P O	93	406
Margaret	75	f	w	SCOT	San Francisco	11-Wd San Francisc	84	564
Susan	35	f	w	IREL	San Francisco	8-Wd San Francisco	82	340
Thomas	36	m	w	IL	Tehama	Red Bluff	92	180
W D	40	m	w	NY	Napa	Napa Twp	75	63
W K	43	m	w	OH	Klamath	Klamath Twp	73	371
Wm	35	m	w	PA	Sacramento	Brighton Twp	77	78
Wm	20	m	w	IREL	Sacramento	1-Wd Sacramento	77	172
GILSTON								
Wm	42	m	w	SCOT	Butte	Ophir Twp	70	108
GILTNER								
J P	28	m	w	IN	Monterey	Monterey Twp	74	349
Michael	53	m	w	IN	Santa Barbara	Santa Maria P O	87	511
GILUM								
Thos E	37	m	w	VA	Sacramento	Franklin Twp	77	120
GILUS								
Henery	27	m	w	MA	San Francisco	7-Wd San Francisco	81	199
GILVIA								
John	50	m	w	HI	Yolo	Merritt Twp	93	505
GILWORTH								
Joseph	52	m	w	ENGL	Del Norte	Crescent	71	466
GILYERMO								
William	52	m	w	CHIL	Calaveras	Copperopolis P O	70	246
GILZENE								
James	55	m	w	SCOT	Trinity	Canyon City Pct	92	201
GIM								
A	32	m	c	CHIN	Placer	Bath P O	76	443
Ah	55	m	c	CHIN	Shasta	American Ranch P O	89	499
Ah	50	m	c	CHIN	Sacramento	Franklin Twp	77	115
Ah	43	m	c	CHIN	Sacramento	Granite Twp	77	138
Ah	43	m	c	CHIN	Amador	Jackson P O	69	332
Ah	40	m	c	CHIN	Sacramento	Granite Twp	77	137
Ah	40	m	c	CHIN	Sierra	Eureka Twp	89	526
Ah	40	m	c	CHIN	Butte	Wyandotte Twp	70	142
Ah	40	m	c	CHIN	Alameda	Oakland	68	254
Ah	37	m	c	CHIN	Nevada	Nevada Twp	75	316
Ah	35	m	c	CHIN	Nevada	Meadow Lake Twp	75	254
Ah	35	m	c	CHIN	Trinity	North Fork Twp	92	216
Ah	35	m	c	CHIN	Alameda	Oakland	68	241
Ah	35	m	c	CHIN	Fresno	Millerton P O	72	201
Ah	34	m	c	CHIN	El Dorado	Georgetown Twp	72	44
Ah	32	m	c	CHIN	Sierra	Eureka Twp	89	525
Ah	31	m	c	CHIN	Butte	Wyandotte Twp	70	146
Ah	30	m	c	CHIN	Alameda	Oakland	68	254
Ah	30	m	c	CHIN	Shasta	French Gulch P O	89	465
Ah	29	m	c	CHIN	Placer	Newcastle Twp	76	479
Ah	28	m	c	CHIN	Alameda	Oakland	68	232
Ah	28	m	c	CHIN	San Mateo	Schoolhouse Statio	87	338
Ah	27	m	c	CHIN	Sacramento	1-Wd Sacramento	77	201
Ah	27	m	c	CHIN	Solano	Suisun Twp	90	98
Ah	26	m	c	CHIN	San Francisco	San Francisco P O	80	498
Ah	25	m	c	CHIN	Sacramento	1-Wd Sacramento	77	202
Ah	25	m	c	CHIN	Sierra	Table Rock Twp	89	574
Ah	25	m	c	CHIN	Alameda	Oakland	68	254
Ah	25	m	c	CHIN	Sacramento	Franklin Twp	77	115
Ah	24	m	c	CHIN	San Mateo	Schoolhouse Statio	87	335
Ah	24	m	c	CHIN	Nevada	Meadow Lake Twp	75	257
Ah	23	m	c	CHIN	El Dorado	Salmon Falls Twp	72	134
Ah	23	m	c	CHIN	Alameda	Oakland	68	245
Ah	21	m	c	CHIN	Nevada	Little York Twp	75	237
Ah	20	f	c	CHIN	Sacramento	Cosumnes Twp	77	94
Ah	20	m	c	CHIN	Nevada	Nevada Twp	75	314
Ah	20	f	c	CHIN	Siskiyou	Yreka	89	650
Ah	2	m	c	CA	San Francisco	San Francisco P O	80	438
Ah	19	m	c	CHIN	Nevada	Bloomfield Twp	75	94
Ah	19	m	c	CHIN	Butte	Bidwell Twp	70	2
Ah	19	m	c	CHIN	Sonoma	Salt Point	91	386
Ah	18	m	c	CHIN	Placer	Auburn P O	76	362
Ah	18	m	c	CHIN	Santa Clara	Alviso Twp	88	26
Ah	18	m	c	CHIN	Alameda	Oakland	68	249
Ah	18	m	c	CHIN	San Francisco	3-Wd San Francisco	79	329
Ah	18	f	c	CHIN	San Francisco	San Francisco P O	80	437

Name	Age	S	R	B-PL	County	Locale	Roll	Pg
Ah	17	m	c	CHIN	San Francisco	San Francisco P O	80	403
Ah	16	m	c	CHIN	San Francisco	3-Wd San Francisco	79	297
Ah	12	m	c	CHIN	San Francisco	San Francisco P O	83	311
Ah Tai	13	m	c	CHIN	San Francisco	San Francisco P O	83	136
Chong	45	m	c	CHIN	Tuolumne	Columbia P O	93	341
Doo	42	m	c	CHIN	Plumas	Seneca Twp	77	49
Gim	19	m	c	CHIN	San Francisco	3-Wd San Francisco	79	307
Henry	30	m	c	CHIN	Sacramento	Sutter Twp	77	384
Heung	39	m	c	CHIN	Yuba	Marysville	93	620
Him	30	f	c	CHIN	Sacramento	1-Wd Sacramento	77	177
Hong	18	m	c	CHIN	San Francisco	3-Wd San Francisco	79	307
Hu	18	m	c	CHIN	Placer	Dutch Flat P O	76	402
Lee	34	m	c	CHIN	San Francisco	San Francisco P O	80	403
Nam	20	m	c	CHIN	Contra Costa	Martinez P O	71	378
Set	21	m	c	CHIN	Nevada	Meadow Lake Twp	75	257
Shang	12	m	c	CHIN	San Francisco	8-Wd San Francisco	82	442
Un	32	m	c	CHIN	San Francisco	San Francisco P O	83	131
Yon	25	m	c	CHIN	San Mateo	Schoolhouse Statio	87	335
GIMAN								
Patrick	46	m	w	HDAR	Solano	Silveyville Twp	90	91
GIMBALL								
Catharine	23	f	w	PRUS	San Francisco	San Francisco P O	85	819
GIMBEL								
Geo	35	m	w	US	Sacramento	1-Wd Sacramento	77	177
George	32	m	w	PRUS	San Francisco	5-Wd San Francisco	81	20
Henrietta	24	f	w	HDAR	San Francisco	7-Wd San Francisco	81	239
Henry	29	m	w	PRUS	San Francisco	7-Wd San Francisco	81	239
GIMBLE								
Christian	17	f	w	PRUS	San Francisco	San Francisco P O	83	117
GIME								
Ah	28	m	c	CHIN	San Francisco	6-Wd San Francisco	81	61
GIMENES								
Simon	17	m	w	MEXI	San Francisco	San Francisco P O	80	399
GIMLAY								
William	40	m	w	ME	San Diego	San Diego	78	484
GIMMELL								
John	43	m	w	PA	Tehama	Toomes & Grant	92	169
GIMMEY								
John G	46	m	w	WURT	Napa	Yountville Twp	75	85
GIMO								
Ah	27	m	c	CHIN	San Joaquin	Oneal Twp	86	116
GIMPLE								
Geo W	34	m	w	MD	Siskiyou	Scott Valley Twp	89	616
Morris	30	m	w	HAMB	San Francisco	11-Wd San Francisc	84	645
GIN								
---	30	m	c	CHIN	Shasta	Shasta P O	89	454
---	29	m	c	CHIN	Siskiyou	Cottonwood Twp	89	594
Ack	25	m	c	CHIN	Klamath	Liberty Twp	73	375
Ah	64	m	c	CHIN	El Dorado	Mud Springs Twp	72	75
Ah	60	m	c	CHIN	Trinity	Lewiston Pct	92	211
Ah	55	m	c	CHIN	El Dorado	Diamond Springs Tw	72	35
Ah	55	m	c	CHIN	Placer	Auburn P O	76	379
Ah	50	m	c	CHIN	Mariposa	Mariposa P O	74	134
Ah	48	m	c	CHIN	Trinity	Douglas	92	234
Ah	45	m	c	CHIN	Trinity	Lewiston Pct	92	212
Ah	45	m	c	CHIN	Tuolumne	Chinese Camp P O	93	370
Ah	45	m	c	CHIN	San Francisco	San Francisco P O	80	447
Ah	45	m	c	CHIN	El Dorado	Placerville	72	123
Ah	45	m	c	CHIN	El Dorado	Diamond Springs Tw	72	26
Ah	44	m	c	CHIN	El Dorado	Diamond Springs Tw	72	27
Ah	43	m	c	CHIN	San Francisco	San Francisco P O	80	436
Ah	43	m	c	CHIN	Mariposa	Mariposa P O	74	111
Ah	43	m	c	CHIN	Mono	Bridgeport P O	74	282
Ah	42	m	c	CHIN	Sacramento	American Twp	77	68
Ah	42	m	c	CHIN	Napa	Napa Twp	75	58
Ah	42	m	c	CHIN	Calaveras	Copperopolis P O	70	259
Ah	41	m	c	CHIN	Solano	Vacaville Twp	90	130
Ah	40	m	c	CHIN	San Francisco	San Francisco P O	80	529
Ah	40	m	c	CHIN	Shasta	French Gulch P O	89	469
Ah	40	m	c	CHIN	San Francisco	San Francisco P O	80	441
Ah	40	f	c	CHIN	San Francisco	San Francisco P O	80	450
Ah	40	m	c	CHIN	Placer	Auburn P O	76	371
Ah	40	m	c	CHIN	Placer	Rocklin Twp	76	464
Ah	40	m	c	CHIN	Placer	Blue Canyon P O	76	419
Ah	40	m	c	CHIN	Butte	Concow Twp	70	10
Ah	40	m	c	CHIN	Mariposa	Mariposa P O	74	130
Ah	40	m	c	CHIN	El Dorado	Mud Springs Twp	72	89
Ah	38	m	c	CHIN	El Dorado	White Oak Twp	72	141
Ah	38	m	c	CHIN	Amador	Ione City P O	69	370
Ah	38	m	c	CHIN	Mariposa	Mariposa P O	74	127
Ah	37	m	c	CHIN	El Dorado	White Oak Twp	72	135
Ah	37	m	c	CHIN	San Francisco	San Francisco P O	80	454
Ah	37	m	c	CHIN	San Francisco	San Francisco P O	80	443
Ah	37	m	c	CHIN	Placer	Rocklin P O	76	462
Ah	36	m	c	CHIN	San Francisco	San Francisco P O	80	512
Ah	36	m	c	CHIN	San Francisco	San Francisco P O	80	524
Ah	36	m	c	CHIN	San Joaquin	1-Wd Stockton	86	144
Ah	36	m	c	CHIN	San Francisco	San Francisco P O	80	498
Ah	36	m	c	CHIN	San Francisco	3-Wd San Francisco	79	303
Ah	36	m	c	CHIN	Mariposa	Mariposa P O	74	102
Ah	36	f	c	CHIN	Mariposa	Mariposa P O	74	103
Ah	35	m	c	CHIN	San Francisco	San Francisco P O	80	509
Ah	35	m	c	CHIN	Trinity	Junction City Pct	92	209
Ah	35	m	c	CHIN	El Dorado	Mud Springs Twp	72	90
Ah	34	m	c	CHIN	Nevada	Grass Valley Twp	75	202
Ah	34	m	c	CHIN	San Francisco	San Francisco P O	80	433
Ah	33	m	c	CHIN	San Francisco	San Francisco P O	80	437

Series M593

© 2001 by Heritage Quest. All rights reserved.

Name	Age	S	R	B-PL	County	Locale	Roll	Pg
						Series M593		
Ah	33	m	c	CHIN	Butte	Hamilton Twp	70	68
Ah	33	m	c	CHIN	Mariposa	Mariposa P O	74	106
Ah	32	m	c	CHIN	Placer	Colfax P O	76	388
Ah	32	m	c	CHIN	Mariposa	Mariposa P O	74	102
Ah	31	m	c	CHIN	Mariposa	Mariposa P O	74	106
Ah	30	m	c	CHIN	Alameda	Alameda	68	18
Ah	30	m	c	CHIN	Calaveras	San Andreas P O	70	202
Ah	30	m	c	CHIN	Sacramento	Granite Twp	77	138
Ah	30	m	c	CHIN	Placer	Lincoln P O	76	484
Ah	30	m	c	CHIN	San Francisco	San Francisco P O	80	519
Ah	30	m	c	CHIN	San Francisco	San Francisco P O	80	525
Ah	30	m	c	CHIN	Alameda	Oakland	68	238
Ah	30	m	c	CHIN	Mariposa	Mariposa P O	74	126
Ah	29	m	c	CHIN	Sacramento	Granite Twp	77	138
Ah	29	m	c	CHIN	Solano	Suisun Twp	90	98
Ah	29	m	c	CHIN	Tuolumne	Chinese Camp P O	93	380
Ah	29	f	c	CHIN	San Francisco	San Francisco P O	80	433
Ah	28	m	c	CHIN	Plumas	Goodwin Twp	77	3
Ah	28	m	c	CHIN	Sacramento	Georgianna Twp	77	125
Ah	28	m	c	CHIN	Sacramento	Georgianna Twp	77	124
Ah	28	m	c	CHIN	Placer	Dutch Flat P O	76	406
Ah	28	m	c	CHIN	Trinity	Lewiston Pct	92	214
Ah	27	m	c	CHIN	Fresno	Millerton P O	72	188
Ah	27	m	c	CHIN	El Dorado	Coloma Twp	72	1
Ah	26	m	c	CHIN	Placer	Roseville P O	76	350
Ah	26	m	c	CHIN	San Francisco	San Francisco P O	83	85
Ah	25	m	c	CHIN	El Dorado	White Oak Twp	72	138
Ah	25	m	c	CHIN	Sacramento	Georgianna Twp	77	123
Ah	25	m	c	CHIN	Shasta	French Gulch P O	89	469
Ah	25	m	c	CHIN	Trinity	Junction City Pct	92	207
Ah	25	m	c	CHIN	Tuolumne	Chinese Camp P O	93	363
Ah	25	m	c	CHIN	San Francisco	San Francisco P O	80	494
Ah	25	f	c	CHIN	San Francisco	San Francisco P O	80	444
Ah	25	m	c	CHIN	Mariposa	Mariposa P O	74	92
Ah	25	m	c	CHIN	Placer	Auburn P O	76	379
Ah	25	m	c	CHIN	Alameda	Murray Twp	68	110
Ah	24	m	c	CHIN	Solano	Suisun Twp	90	104
Ah	24	m	c	CHIN	Solano	Suisun Twp	90	107
Ah	24	m	c	CHIN	San Francisco	San Francisco P O	80	335
Ah	24	m	c	CHIN	San Francisco	3-Wd San Francisco	79	329
Ah	23	m	c	CHIN	Amador	Fiddletown P O	69	429
Ah	23	f	c	CHIN	San Francisco	San Francisco P O	80	506
Ah	23	m	c	CHIN	Yuba	Marysville	93	619
Ah	22	m	c	CHIN	San Francisco	San Francisco P O	80	496
Ah	22	m	c	CHIN	San Francisco	San Francisco P O	83	82
Ah	22	m	c	CHIN	Sacramento	Georgianna Twp	77	124
Ah	22	m	c	CHIN	El Dorado	Placerville Twp	72	101
Ah	21	f	c	CHIN	San Francisco	San Francisco P O	80	439
Ah	21	f	c	CHIN	San Francisco	San Francisco P O	80	446
Ah	20	m	c	CHIN	Los Angeles	Los Angeles	73	526
Ah	20	m	c	CHIN	Placer	Roseville P O	76	353
Ah	20	m	c	CHIN	Sacramento	3-Wd Sacramento	77	315
Ah	20	m	c	CHIN	San Francisco	7-Wd San Francisco	81	206
Ah	20	m	c	CHIN	San Francisco	San Francisco P O	80	491
Ah	20	m	c	CHIN	Siskiyou	Butte Twp	89	587
Ah	20	m	c	CHIN	Solano	Vallejo	90	139
Ah	20	m	c	CHIN	Santa Cruz	Santa Cruz Twp	89	388
Ah	20	f	c	CHIN	San Francisco	San Francisco P O	80	434
Ah	20	m	c	CHIN	Mariposa	Mariposa P O	74	113
Ah	19	m	c	CHIN	San Francisco	7-Wd San Francisco	81	182
Ah	19	m	c	CHIN	Nevada	Nevada Twp	75	278
Ah	19	m	c	CHIN	Placer	Colfax P O	76	391
Ah	18	m	c	CHIN	San Francisco	San Francisco P O	83	131
Ah	18	m	c	CHIN	San Francisco	San Francisco P O	83	170
Ah	18	m	c	CHIN	San Francisco	7-Wd San Francisco	81	208
Ah	18	f	c	CHIN	San Francisco	San Francisco P O	80	529
Ah	18	m	c	CHIN	Solano	Suisun Twp	90	98
Ah	18	m	c	CHIN	Santa Clara	Santa Clara Twp	88	147
Ah	18	m	c	CHIN	Alameda	Alameda	68	15
Ah	17	m	c	CHIN	San Francisco	7-Wd San Francisco	81	174
Ah	17	m	c	CHIN	Shasta	American Ranch P O	89	497
Ah	17	m	c	CHIN	San Francisco	1-Wd San Francisco	79	80
Ah	16	m	c	CHIN	Nevada	Grass Valley Twp	75	227
Ah	16	m	c	CHIN	San Francisco	8-Wd San Francisco	82	334
Ah	16	m	c	CHIN	Placer	Colfax P O	76	387
Ah	15	m	c	CHIN	Alameda	Brooklyn Twp	68	54
Ah	15	m	c	CHIN	San Francisco	7-Wd San Francisco	81	206
Ah	15	m	c	CHIN	San Francisco	8-Wd San Francisco	82	330
Ah	15	m	c	CHIN	Napa	Napa	75	56
Ah	14	m	c	CHIN	San Francisco	11-Wd San Francisc	84	578
Ah	14	m	c	CHIN	San Francisco	8-Wd San Francisco	82	332
Ah	12	m	c	CHIN	San Francisco	San Francisco P O	80	485
Ah	12	m	c	CHIN	Santa Clara	Alviso Twp	88	26
Ah	12	m	c	CHIN	San Francisco	3-Wd San Francisco	79	307
Ah	10	m	c	CHIN	Santa Clara	Santa Clara Twp	88	158
An	34	m	c	CHIN	Sonoma	Vallejo Twp	91	457
An	25	m	c	CHIN	El Dorado	Mud Springs Twp	72	88
An	17	m	c	CHIN	San Francisco	8-Wd San Francisco	82	456
Aw	10	m	c	CHIN	San Francisco	8-Wd San Francisco	82	463
Bon	34	m	c	CHIN	Marin	San Rafael Twp	74	39
Chong	31	m	c	CHIN	Siskiyou	Hamburg Twp	89	597
Choon Lim	22	m	c	CHIN	Siskiyou	Hamburg Twp	89	597
Con	24	m	c	CHIN	Inyo	Independence Twp	73	327
Gee	42	m	c	CHIN	San Joaquin	Oneal Twp	86	116
Goo	17	f	c	CHIN	Tuolumne	Sonora P O	93	312
Hee	24	m	c	CHIN	San Francisco	7-Wd San Francisco	81	183
Ho	32	f	c	CHIN	Nevada	Grass Valley Twp	75	205

Name	Age	S	R	B-PL	County	Locale	Roll	Pg
						Series M593		
Ho	22	m	c	CHIN	San Joaquin	1-Wd Stockton	86	144
Hong	30	m	c	CHIN	Calaveras	San Andreas P O	70	204
Hong	20	m	c	CHIN	Placer	Dutch Flat P O	76	414
Hoy	44	m	c	CHIN	Klamath	South Fork Twp	73	384
Hung	36	m	c	CHIN	Yuba	Marysville	93	623
Lea	38	m	c	CHIN	Siskiyou	Yreka	89	658
Lee	40	m	c	CHIN	Siskiyou	Hamburg Twp	89	598
Lee	24	m	c	CHIN	Butte	Concow Twp	70	10
Lee	18	m	c	CHIN	San Francisco	7-Wd San Francisco	81	174
Lee	17	m	c	CHIN	San Francisco	San Francisco P O	83	404
Ley	29	m	c	CHIN	Yuba	Marysville	93	625
Lin Eck	59	m	c	CHIN	Calaveras	San Andreas P O	70	202
Ling	30	f	c	CHIN	Merced	Snelling P O	74	279
Lock	18	m	c	CHIN	Yuba	Marysville	93	620
Loo	34	m	c	CHIN	Tulare	Visalia	92	297
Lop	37	m	c	CHIN	San Joaquin	Oneal Twp	86	116
Loy	25	m	c	CHIN	Plumas	Washington Twp	77	57
Men	20	m	c	CHIN	Del Norte	Happy Camp Twp	71	471
On	36	m	c	CHIN	Tuolumne	Big Oak Flat P O	93	406
On	19	m	c	CHIN	Amador	Jackson P O	69	332
Robt	27	m	w	ME	San Joaquin	Liberty Twp	86	85
San	30	m	c	CHIN	Shasta	Horsetown P O	89	503
Shee	32	m	c	CHIN	Plumas	Plumas Twp	77	31
Sin	33	m	c	CHIN	El Dorado	Placerville	72	115
Song	55	m	c	CHIN	Shasta	American Ranch P O	89	497
Tel	16	m	c	CHIN	Yuba	Marysville	93	597
Toy	26	f	c	CHIN	Yuba	Marysville	93	626
Twi	30	m	c	CHIN	San Francisco	11-Wd San Francisc	84	661
Yee	28	m	c	CHIN	Yuba	Marysville	93	620
GINANE								
Kate	22	f	w	IREL	San Francisco	11-Wd San Francisc	84	498
GINCHARD								
Frank	39	m	w	FRAN	Nevada	Meadow Lake Twp	75	268
GINCOSTA								
Antony	65	m	w	ITAL	Alameda	Brooklyn	68	31
GINDER								
Ellen	19	f	w	IREL	San Francisco	8-Wd San Francisco	82	460
Mary	38	f	w	HANO	San Francisco	11-Wd San Francisc	84	616
GINE								
Ah	33	m	c	CHIN	Placer	Colfax P O	76	388
Ah	31	m	c	CHIN	Nevada	Nevada Twp	75	316
Ah	31	m	c	CHIN	Nevada	Eureka Twp	75	136
Ah	27	m	c	CHIN	Nevada	Washington Twp	75	340
Ah	25	m	c	CHIN	San Francisco	San Francisco P O	83	132
Ah	24	m	c	CHIN	Plumas	Plumas Twp	77	31
Lu	17	m	c	CHIN	San Francisco	8-Wd San Francisco	82	389
GINEAR								
Sallie	19	f	w	OH	Contra Costa	Martinez P O	71	399
GINET								
Peter	29	m	w	FRAN	San Francisco	San Francisco P O	80	356
GING								
Ah	60	m	c	CHIN	Placer	Roseville P O	76	356
Ah	60	m	c	CHIN	Nevada	Bridgeport Twp	75	110
Ah	50	m	c	CHIN	San Francisco	San Francisco P O	80	525
Ah	41	m	c	CHIN	Calaveras	Copperopolis P O	70	233
Ah	41	m	c	CHIN	San Francisco	San Francisco P O	80	527
Ah	40	m	c	CHIN	Tuolumne	Chinese Camp P O	93	377
Ah	39	m	c	CHIN	San Francisco	San Francisco P O	80	438
Ah	39	m	c	CHIN	Tuolumne	Chinese Camp P O	93	363
Ah	39	m	c	CHIN	San Francisco	San Francisco P O	80	517
Ah	38	m	c	CHIN	San Francisco	San Francisco P O	80	501
Ah	38	m	c	CHIN	Sierra	Forest Twp	89	528
Ah	37	m	c	CHIN	San Francisco	3-Wd San Francisco	79	303
Ah	36	m	c	CHIN	San Francisco	San Francisco P O	80	529
Ah	33	m	c	CHIN	San Francisco	San Francisco P O	80	449
Ah	33	m	c	CHIN	Nevada	Rough & Ready Twp	75	329
Ah	33	m	c	CHIN	San Francisco	San Francisco P O	80	524
Ah	32	m	c	CHIN	San Francisco	3-Wd San Francisco	79	317
Ah	32	m	c	CHIN	Nevada	Meadow Lake Twp	75	254
Ah	32	m	c	CHIN	Nevada	Meadow Lake Twp	75	256
Ah	32	m	c	CHIN	San Francisco	San Francisco P O	80	521
Ah	31	m	c	CHIN	Placer	Clipper Gap P O	76	393
Ah	31	m	c	CHIN	San Francisco	San Francisco P O	80	505
Ah	30	m	c	CHIN	San Francisco	6-Wd San Francisco	81	42
Ah	30	m	c	CHIN	Sacramento	Georgianna Twp	77	131
Ah	30	m	c	CHIN	Sacramento	Sutter Twp	77	382
Ah	30	m	c	CHIN	San Francisco	San Francisco P O	80	513
Ah	30	m	c	CHIN	San Francisco	San Francisco P O	80	501
Ah	30	m	c	CHIN	San Francisco	San Francisco P O	80	512
Ah	29	m	c	CHIN	San Francisco	San Francisco P O	80	515
Ah	29	m	c	CHIN	Solano	Suisun Twp	90	106
Ah	27	m	c	CHIN	San Francisco	San Francisco P O	80	431
Ah	26	f	c	CHIN	San Francisco	San Francisco P O	80	513
Ah	26	m	c	CHIN	Sacramento	Georgianna Twp	77	122
Ah	25	m	c	CHIN	Nevada	Nevada Twp	75	297
Ah	25	m	c	CHIN	San Francisco	San Francisco P O	80	519
Ah	24	m	c	CHIN	San Francisco	San Francisco P O	80	504
Ah	24	f	c	CHIN	Santa Clara	Santa Clara Twp	88	164
Ah	22	m	c	CHIN	Tuolumne	Chinese Camp P O	93	379
Ah	20	m	c	CHIN	San Francisco	San Francisco P O	80	433
Ah	18	f	c	CHIN	San Francisco	3-Wd San Francisco	79	309
Ah	18	m	c	CHIN	San Francisco	San Francisco P O	80	489
Ah	18	f	c	CHIN	San Francisco	6-Wd San Francisco	81	55
Ah	18	m	c	CHIN	San Francisco	San Francisco P O	80	510
Ah	18	m	c	CHIN	San Francisco	6-Wd San Francisco	81	85
Ah	16	m	c	CHIN	San Francisco	6-Wd San Francisco	81	63
Ah	16	m	c	CHIN	Sacramento	2-Wd Sacramento	77	215
Ah	15	m	c	CHIN				

© 2001 by Heritage Quest. All rights reserved.

Name	Age	S	R	B-PL	County	Series M593 Locale	Roll	Pg
Christopher	52	m	w	IREL	San Francisco	San Francisco P O	83	186
Fang	23	m	c	CHIN	Plumas	Mineral Twp	77	25
Gee	40	m	c	CHIN	Butte	Chico Twp	70	28
He	20	m	c	CHIN	San Francisco	8-Wd San Francisco	82	442
Jon	29	m	c	CHIN	Nevada	Bridgeport Twp	75	111
Lee	30	m	c	CHIN	Yuba	Marysville	93	620
Leo	45	m	c	CHIN	San Francisco	11-Wd San Francisc	84	695
Lim	40	m	c	CHIN	Yuba	Marysville	93	622
Long	28	m	c	CHIN	San Francisco	2-Wd San Francisco	79	229
Low	34	m	c	CHIN	Plumas	Rich Bar Twp	77	46
Low	34	m	c	CHIN	Plumas	Washington Twp	77	52
Lun	20	m	c	CHIN	San Joaquin	1-Wd Stockton	86	139
Mon	15	m	c	CHIN	Napa	Napa Twp	75	58
GINGER								
Charles	34	m	w	WURT	San Francisco	San Francisco P O	83	224
GINGEY								
Daniel	36	m	w	PA	Siskiyou	Butte Twp	89	584
GINGG								
Jacob	34	m	w	SWIT	San Francisco	San Francisco P O	80	479
John	36	m	w	SWIT	San Francisco	San Francisco P O	80	479
GINGHER								
A K	42	m	w	PA	Siskiyou	Callahan P O	89	632
GINGLE								
Jacob	55	m	w	ENGL	Yuba	Marysville	93	581
GINGRA								
Thomas	35	m	w	CANA	Calaveras	San Andreas P O	70	160
GINGRICK								
Emma	22	f	w	PA	San Francisco	11-Wd San Francisc	84	496
GINLEY								
Daniel	30	m	w	IREL	Santa Clara	2-Wd San Jose	88	298
GINLIO								
Parelo	28	m	w	ITAL	San Francisco	1-Wd San Francisco	79	110
GINLOW								
John	49	m	w	DENM	Humboldt	Eureka Twp	72	269
GINLY								
H S	33	m	w	HAMB	Alameda	Oakland	68	158
GINN								
Ah	58	m	c	CHIN	Nevada	Nevada Twp	75	311
Ah	40	m	c	CHIN	San Francisco	11-Wd San Francisc	84	528
Ah	29	m	c	CHIN	Sacramento	Dry Crk Twp	77	101
Ah	28	m	c	CHIN	Nevada	Meadow Lake Twp	75	256
Ar	48	m	c	CHIN	Sonoma	Petaluma Twp	91	363
James J	36	m	w	OH	Los Angeles	Santa Ana Twp	73	603
GINNANI								
Giacomo	25	m	w	SWIT	Amador	Jackson P O	69	338
Joseph	38	m	w	SWIT	Amador	Jackson P O	69	338
GINNENIAN								
James	58	m	w	IREL	San Francisco	2-Wd San Francisco	79	265
GINNETT								
Hattie	17	f	w	MI	Sonoma	Santa Rosa	91	425
GINNIS								
Jas	24	m	w	IREL	Solano	Vallejo	90	211
W C	33	m	w	IL	Alameda	Oakland	68	247
GINNOCHIO								
A	23	m	w	ITAL	Amador	Jackson P O	69	325
E	34	m	w	ITAL	Amador	Jackson P O	69	325
GINNONG								
Henry	23	m	w	NJ	Santa Barbara	Santa Maria P O	87	514
GINNY								
A	28	m	w	SCOT	Alameda	Oakland	68	226
Ah	32	m	c	CHIN	Sacramento	Dry Crk Twp	77	101
GINOCHIO								
Andrew	28	m	w	ITAL	Amador	Volcano P O	69	384
Stefano	28	m	w	ITAL	Amador	Volcano P O	69	384
GINON								
Lu	30	m	c	CHIN	Solano	Suisun Twp	90	105
GINOU								
A E	42	f	w	CANA	San Francisco	San Francisco P O	83	286
GINOUNG								
Arthur W	45	m	w	PA	San Francisco	8-Wd San Francisco	82	382
GINS								
Ah	37	m	c	CHIN	Sacramento	Georgianna Twp	77	132
Joseph	24	m	w	ME	Solano	Montezuma Twp	90	67
GINSBURG								
Archer	40	m	w	RUSS	San Francisco	3-Wd San Francisco	79	297
GINSLEY								
Ah	25	m	c	CHIN	Fresno	Kingston P O	72	217
GINSON								
James	26	m	b	SC	San Francisco	San Francisco P O	83	277
GINSTER								
Frank	37	m	w	ITAL	San Francisco	San Francisco P O	85	812
GINTER								
J	38	m	w	ENGL	Calaveras	Copperopolis P O	70	233
John H	52	m	w	PA	Santa Clara	Fremont Twp	88	45
Joseph	43	m	w	PRUS	Amador	Drytown P O	69	415
Michael	27	m	w	PRUS	Santa Clara	San Jose Twp	88	208
GINTHER								
Edward	33	m	w	PA	Sacramento	Sutter Twp	77	385
Martha	14	f	w	WURT	Santa Clara	1-Wd San Jose	88	246
GINTTAR								
Flemming	36	m	w	MO	Yolo	Grafton Twp	93	478
GINTY								
Eliza	24	f	w	IREL	San Francisco	7-Wd San Francisco	81	228
James	27	m	w	IREL	San Francisco	7-Wd San Francisco	81	228
John	34	m	w	CANA	Sacramento	Dry Crk Twp	77	100
GINZARDI								
John	17	m	w	NY	Marin	Sausalito Twp	74	72

Name	Age	S	R	B-PL	County	Series M593 Locale	Roll	Pg
Peter	55	m	w	ITAL	Marin	Sausalito Twp	74	72
GIO								
Kim	21	m	c	CHIN	San Luis Obispo	Arroyo Grande Twp	87	279
GIOBATTA								
Leon	33	m	w	ITAL	San Francisco	3-Wd San Francisco	79	287
GIODCO								
Joseph	43	m	w	ITAL	San Francisco	3-Wd San Francisco	79	289
GIOLE								
Joseph	40	m	w	ITAL	San Francisco	11-Wd San Francisc	84	544
GION								
John	25	m	w	FRAN	Placer	Cisco P O	76	495
GIONINO								
Giovani	39	m	w	ITAL	San Francisco	2-Wd San Francisco	79	179
GIORGI								
Domenico	39	m	w	ITAL	San Francisco	11-Wd San Francisc	84	594
GIORIAMO								
Poche	40	m	w	ITAL	San Joaquin	Oneal Twp	86	99
GIOVANINI								
Daniel	37	m	w	ITAL	San Francisco	San Francisco P O	80	426
GIOVANNI								
Arrati	56	m	w	ITAL	San Francisco	1-Wd San Francisco	79	45
Batista	30	m	w	ITAL	San Francisco	1-Wd San Francisco	79	110
David	20	m	w	ITAL	Humboldt	Pacific Twp	72	296
GIOVANOH								
Joseph	35	m	w	ITAL	Amador	Sutter Crk P O	69	405
GIOVAPINO								
Joseph	22	m	w	ITAL	Santa Clara	2-Wd San Jose	88	316
GIOVENO								
Joseph	48	m	w	ITAL	Calaveras	Copperopolis P O	70	247
GIOVICH								
Martin	34	m	w	AUST	San Francisco	San Francisco P O	83	87
GIP								
Ah	51	m	c	CHIN	Placer	Auburn P O	76	363
Ah	50	m	c	CHIN	Shasta	French Gulch P O	89	469
Ah	37	m	c	CHIN	Butte	Oregon Twp	70	133
Ah	37	m	c	CHIN	Nevada	Bloomfield Twp	75	96
Ah	36	m	c	CHIN	San Joaquin	1-Wd Stockton	86	142
Ah	32	m	c	CHIN	Butte	Hamilton Twp	70	67
Ah	30	m	c	CHIN	Tuolumne	Chinese Camp P O	93	377
Ah	29	m	c	CHIN	Butte	Kimshew Tpw	70	86
Ah	26	m	c	CHIN	Nevada	Meadow Lake Twp	75	259
Ah	25	m	c	CHIN	Placer	Dutch Flat P O	76	408
Ah	24	m	c	CHIN	Nevada	Meadow Lake Twp	75	257
Ah	22	m	c	CHIN	Trinity	Douglas	92	235
Ah	22	m	c	CHIN	San Francisco	San Francisco P O	85	777
Chock	42	m	c	CHIN	Placer	Bath P O	76	439
Gee	39	m	c	CHIN	Tuolumne	Chinese Camp P O	93	390
Go	40	m	c	CHIN	San Joaquin	1-Wd Stockton	86	142
Han	37	m	c	CHIN	San Mateo	Schoolhouse Statio	87	332
Kee	32	m	c	CHIN	Tuolumne	Chinese Camp P O	93	377
Kee	28	m	c	CHIN	Tuolumne	Columbia P O	93	349
Lue	36	m	c	CHIN	San Joaquin	1-Wd Stockton	86	142
Poy	49	m	c	CHIN	Amador	Jackson P O	69	332
Thung	34	m	c	CHIN	San Francisco	San Francisco P O	85	866
Tom	28	m	c	CHIN	Colusa	Colusa	71	298
Wing	45	m	c	CHIN	Placer	Dutch Flat P O	76	407
Yin	49	m	c	CHIN	Placer	Dutch Flat P O	76	407
GIPE								
David W	40	m	w	PA	El Dorado	Diamond Springs Tw	72	25
GIPP								
Ah	42	m	c	CHIN	San Francisco	6-Wd San Francisco	81	66
Henry	24	m	w	PRUS	Colusa	Spring Valley Twp	71	342
Sum	46	m	c	CHIN	Klamath	Dillon Twp	73	369
GIPSON								
Edwd	39	m	w	TN	Shasta	Millville P O	89	485
Percy	34	m	w	ENGL	San Francisco	San Francisco P O	85	856
GIRA								
Ah	26	m	c	CHIN	San Mateo	San Mateo P O	87	356
GIRADO								
Jesus	46	m	w	MEXI	Los Angeles	San Juan Twp	73	624
Louis	42	m	w	FRAN	Siskiyou	Scott Valley Twp	89	618
GIRAND								
Joseph	50	m	w	FRAN	Siskiyou	Table Rock Twp	89	645
Jules	38	m	w	FRAN	San Francisco	11-Wd San Francisc	84	660
Philippe	40	m	w	FRAN	San Francisco	San Francisco P O	83	135
Virgil	28	m	w	FRAN	Butte	Bidwell Twp	70	3
GIRARD								
A	60	m	w	FRAN	Nevada	Bridgeport Twp	75	104
A	25	m	w	CANA	Sacramento	3-Wd Sacramento	77	314
Cathine	33	f	w	FRAN	San Francisco	San Francisco P O	85	851
Francis	25	m	w	FRAN	Monterey	Monterey	74	361
George	34	m	w	FRAN	San Francisco	San Francisco P O	80	348
George	34	m	w	FRAN	San Francisco	San Francisco P O	80	347
Isaac C	27	m	w	ENGL	Butte	Ophir Twp	70	96
Jean	37	m	w	ITAL	San Francisco	San Francisco P O	85	851
Joseph	55	m	w	CANA	Nevada	Eureka Twp	75	132
Joseph	45	m	w	CANA	Nevada	Eureka Twp	75	132
Joseph	45	m	w	SICI	San Francisco	11-Wd San Francisc	84	661
Leonard	50	m	w	FRAN	San Francisco	3-Wd San Francisco	79	327
Louis	60	m	m	FRAN	Mariposa	Maxwell Crk P O	74	139
Louis	40	m	w	FRAN	Solano	Denverton Twp	90	26
Philip	26	m	w	FRAN	San Francisco	San Francisco P O	80	470
GIRARDO								
Jesus	55	m	w	MEXI	San Diego	San Luis Rey	78	515
GIRAUD								
Antonio	43	m	w	FRAN	San Francisco	San Francisco P O	80	464
Eugene	30	m	w	FRAN	San Francisco	San Francisco P O	80	476

© 2001 by Heritage Quest. All rights reserved.

Name	Age	S	R	B-PL	County	Locale	Series M593 Roll	Pg
GIRAUDOU								
Justin	57	m	w	FRAN	Sierra	Table Rock Twp	89	544
GIRAUE								
Ernest	40	m	w	FRAN	Plumas	Rich Bar Twp	77	45
GIRD								
Henry H	44	m	w	NY	Los Angeles	Los Angeles Twp	73	488
Henry S	40	m	w	NY	Sonoma	Washington Twp	91	468
Mary	36	f	w	NY	San Francisco	San Francisco P O	83	290
GIRDEAU								
Jacque	39	m	w	FRAN	San Francisco	San Francisco P O	80	430
GIRDES								
Caston	34	m	w	HANO	San Francisco	11-Wd San Francisc	84	597
GIRDNER								
Joseph	41	m	w	KY	Sutter	Sutter Twp	92	118
GIRENGHETTI								
Lewis	28	m	w	SWIT	Calaveras	San Andreas P O	70	216
Martin	30	m	w	SWIT	Calaveras	San Andreas P O	70	216
GIRENS								
W C	39	m	w	ME	Trinity	Junction City Pct	92	209
GIRESPIE								
Thomas	20	m	w	SCOT	Sutter	Sutter Twp	92	122
GIRIA								
Tamancia	33	m	w	MEXI	Santa Clara	Burnett Twp	88	35
GIRKEN								
Julian	46	m	w	PRUS	San Francisco	5-Wd San Francisco	81	15
GIRLEY								
Jacob	40	m	w	NJ	San Francisco	5-Wd San Francisco	81	29
GIRNDT								
Gottlob	34	m	w	PRUS	Marin	San Rafael	74	49
GIROCHO								
Lazaro	17	m	w	ITAL	Amador	Volcano P O	69	373
GIROD								
Emily	27	f	w	NY	San Francisco	6-Wd San Francisco	81	97
GIRONI								
John	30	m	w	ITAL	San Francisco	11-Wd San Francisc	84	603
Joseph	33	m	w	ITAL	San Francisco	11-Wd San Francisc	84	603
GIROT								
Delia	36	f	w	IREL	San Francisco	San Francisco P O	80	400
Salie	56	f	w	FRAN	Santa Clara	2-Wd San Jose	88	302
Stephen	51	m	w	FRAN	San Francisco	San Francisco P O	83	236
GIROUX								
A L	20	m	w	ME	Sacramento	3-Wd Sacramento	77	303
Isaac	21	m	w	CANA	San Francisco	San Francisco P O	80	336
GIRRARD								
Allert H	36	m	w	SWIT	Yuba	Bullards Bar P O	93	547
GIRT								
James	35	m	w	CANA	Tehama	Tehama Twp	92	196
GIRTY								
Mary	60	f	w	IREL	Alameda	Washington Twp	68	291
GIRZONSKY								
William	27	m	w	HUNG	San Francisco	San Francisco P O	80	333
GIS								
Ah	42	m	c	CHIN	Merced	Snelling P O	74	264
GISANI								
William	35	m	w	ITAL	San Francisco	San Francisco P O	80	460
GISEN								
John	28	m	w	IREL	San Francisco	San Francisco P O	85	837
GISER								
Charles	38	m	w	BADE	San Francisco	2-Wd San Francisco	79	234
GISERE								
Peter	42	m	w	FRAN	San Francisco	11-Wd San Francisc	84	688
GISH								
David E	40	m	w	IN	Santa Clara	San Jose Twp	88	192
Mary	36	f	w	OH	San Francisco	San Francisco P O	83	152
Mary M	25	f	w	IL	Yolo	Cache Crk Twp	93	422
GISHELL								
George	49	m	w	ME	Mendocino	Navarro & Big Rvr	74	177
GISHER								
John	43	m	w	DENM	Contra Costa	Martinez P O	71	413
GISIN								
Chas G	2	m	w	CA	San Luis Obispo	Santa Rosa Twp	87	325
GIST								
David	30	m	w	OH	Trinity	Trinity Center Pct	92	204
James	23	m	w	AR	Fresno	Kings Rvr P O	72	214
William	34	m	w	KY	Santa Clara	Redwood Twp	88	131
Wm T	40	m	w	IL	Sacramento	4-Wd Sacramento	77	325
GIT								
Ah	40	m	c	CHIN	Mono	Bridgeport P O	74	283
Ah	38	m	c	CHIN	Tuolumne	Big Oak Flat P O	93	401
Ah	25	m	c	CHIN	Plumas	Seneca Twp	77	48
Ah	25	m	c	CHIN	Nevada	Rough & Ready Twp	75	331
Ah	22	f	c	CHIN	El Dorado	Placerville	72	116
Ah	20	m	c	CHIN	Shasta	American Ranch P O	89	497
Ah	14	m	c	CHIN	Sacramento	3-Wd Sacramento	77	300
Bore	17	m	c	CHIN	Sacramento	3-Wd Sacramento	77	306
Chow	24	m	c	CHIN	Marin	San Rafael	74	57
Chung	40	m	c	CHIN	Placer	Bath P O	76	441
John	54	m	c	CHIN	El Dorado	Diamond Springs Tw	72	22
Quoy	26	f	c	CHIN	San Francisco	6-Wd San Francisco	81	60
Slin	25	m	c	CHIN	Shasta	American Ranch P O	89	499
GITARIO								
Jumbo	20	m	w	ITAL	San Mateo	Schoolhouse Statio	87	334
GITCHEL								
Francis	33	f	w	ME	Monterey	San Juan Twp	74	415
GITCHELL								
Fred E	28	m	w	CANA	Humboldt	Arcata Twp	72	231
George W	37	m	w	ME	Calaveras	San Andreas P O	70	168
James	45	m	w	OH	San Francisco	11-Wd San Francisc	84	606
S	38	m	w	ME	Alameda	Oakland	68	215
GITH								
D H	75	m	w	VA	Humboldt	Pacific Twp	72	292
GITOURI								
Mirander	25	m	w	SWIT	Marin	San Rafael Twp	74	33
GITURANI								
Benecita	21	m	w	SWIT	Marin	San Antonio Twp	74	61
GITY								
James	27	m	w	IREL	San Francisco	7-Wd San Francisco	81	218
GITZLER								
Edward	7	m	w	CA	Alameda	Oakland	68	159
GIUSEPPE								
Kinio	30	m	w	SWIT	San Francisco	San Francisco P O	80	477
Lotti	27	m	w	ITAL	San Francisco	11-Wd San Francisc	84	617
GIUSEPPI								
Maria	34	f	w	SWIT	San Francisco	San Francisco P O	80	477
GIUSETTI								
Joachim	18	m	w	ITAL	San Francisco	San Francisco P O	80	464
GIUSTE								
Alfonzo	30	m	w	ITAL	Sutter	Butte Twp	92	104
GIUSTI								
Natale	28	m	w	ITAL	San Francisco	11-Wd San Francisc	84	594
GIVAN								
Charles	27	m	w	FRAN	San Francisco	San Francisco P O	80	429
GIVANS								
Chas C	75	m	w	NC	Monterey	Alisal Twp	74	291
Chs Thos	33	m	w	IN	Monterey	Alisal Twp	74	291
GIVE								
Yu	27	f	c	CHIN	Siskiyou	Yreka	89	662
GIVEN								
George	31	m	w	VA	Tulare	Tule Rvr Twp	92	271
John	42	m	w	IREL	Sacramento	2-Wd Sacramento	77	242
John	30	m	w	SCOT	San Francisco	San Francisco P O	80	473
Wm	21	m	w	MO	Sacramento	Alabama Twp	77	60
GIVENS								
A W	29	m	w	NY	Sacramento	3-Wd Sacramento	77	300
Catharine	65	f	w	KY	Mariposa	Mariposa P O	74	100
Charles	39	m	w	PA	Nevada	Rough & Ready Twp	75	331
Eleazor	52	m	w	IN	Santa Clara	1-Wd San Jose	88	247
Fleming	17	m	w	IN	Siskiyou	Scott Valley Twp	89	613
George	39	m	w	MO	Santa Clara	2-Wd San Jose	88	325
Jabe Dale	36	m	w	KY	Butte	Ophir Twp	70	92
James	5	m	w	CA	Santa Clara	2-Wd San Jose	88	306
Jas	29	m	w	IREL	Solano	Benicia	90	18
Jeremiah C	40	m	w	IN	Placer	Roseville P O	76	352
John E	27	m	w	NY	Sacramento	Lee Twp	77	158
John H	32	m	w	KY	Mariposa	Mariposa P O	74	100
M L	31	f	b	PA	Sacramento	3-Wd Sacramento	77	308
R R	43	m	w	KY	San Francisco	San Francisco P O	83	323
Sarah	70	f	w	NY	San Francisco	8-Wd San Francisco	82	350
Thomas	35	m	w	KY	Mariposa	Mariposa P O	74	100
Wm	24	m	w	MO	Solano	Vallejo	90	198
GIVERDIN								
Juan	49	m	w	SWIT	Monterey	Monterey	74	363
GIVI								
A	16	m	c	CHIN	San Francisco	San Francisco P O	85	815
GIVINS								
William	30	m	w	IREL	Solano	Suisun Twp	90	101
GIVRE								
Thos	30	m	w	IREL	San Francisco	11-Wd San Francisc	84	680
GLACIER								
R	37	m	w	PRUS	San Joaquin	2-Wd Stockton	86	174
GLACKEN								
Andrew	10	m	w	CA	Sacramento	4-Wd Sacramento	77	363
GLADDING								
A J	54	m	w	RI	Alameda	Oakland	68	227
C B	48	m	w	RI	Alameda	Oakland	68	236
Lydia H	25	f	w	RI	Yolo	Cottonwood Twp	93	470
GLADEWITZ								
Christian	37	m	w	PRUS	Santa Clara	2-Wd San Jose	88	335
GLADIN								
John	25	m	w	HDAR	Solano	Silveyville Twp	90	87
GLADSTONE								
Saml	41	m	w	PA	Solano	Vallejo	90	195
GLADWIN								
Geo	43	m	w	NY	San Francisco	11-Wd San Francisc	84	602
GLADWORTHY								
F	24	m	w	WI	Santa Clara	Gilroy Twp	88	104
GLAER								
Jane	38	f	b	MS	Sacramento	1-Wd Sacramento	77	179
GLAISTER								
D S	49	m	w	ENGL	Sonoma	Sonoma Twp	91	446
William	45	m	w	ENGL	Nevada	Bridgeport Twp	75	114
GLAMWELL								
Flora	20	f	w	IL	Yolo	Merritt Twp	93	505
GLANCEY								
Hugh	40	m	w	IREL	San Francisco	San Francisco P O	85	865
Wm	35	m	w	IREL	San Francisco	San Francisco P O	85	865
GLANCY								
Barnard	30	m	w	IREL	Alameda	Eden Twp	68	86
John	35	m	w	IREL	San Francisco	7-Wd San Francisco	81	177
John	31	m	w	IREL	Yolo	Washington Twp	93	535
Pat	28	m	w	IREL	Solano	Benicia	90	21
GLAND								
Wm	26	m	w	MO	San Francisco	San Francisco P O	85	864

© 2001 by Heritage Quest. All rights reserved.

Name	Age	S	R	B-PL	County	Locale	Roll	Pg
						Series M593		
GLANDING								
Charles A	20	m	w	PA	San Francisco	San Francisco P O	85	757
GLANIS								
Antone	40	m	w	ITAL	Calaveras	San Andreas P O	70	203
GLANNEN								
Edward	54	m	w	IREL	Placer	Pino Twp	76	472
John	34	m	w	MI	Alameda	Oakland	68	205
GLANNON								
James	60	m	w	IREL	Calaveras	San Andreas P O	70	219
GLANSEY								
Peter	50	m	w	IREL	San Francisco	11-Wd San Francisc	84	533
GLANVILL								
James	30	m	w	IREL	San Francisco	7-Wd San Francisco	81	218
GLANVILLE								
W J	28	m	w	ENGL	Amador	Sutter Crk P O	69	409
GLAP								
Mary M	11	f	w	CA	Santa Clara	Gilroy Twp	88	92
GLAROVITCH								
N	30	m	w	AUST	Amador	Jackson P O	69	329
GLARY								
Patrick	36	m	w	IREL	San Francisco	11-Wd San Francisc	84	639
William	38	m	b	NY	San Francisco	San Francisco P O	80	486
William	30	m	b	PA	San Francisco	2-Wd San Francisco	79	177
GLASAR								
Sebastian	18	m	w	BAVA	San Francisco	11-Wd San Francisc	84	551
GLASBY								
Barbara	31	f	w	IREL	San Francisco	8-Wd San Francisco	82	331
Daniel	23	m	w	CANA	Santa Clara	Redwood Twp	88	131
GLASCO								
Thos	48	m	w	PA	Shasta	Shasta P O	89	463
GLASCOCK								
W H	49	m	w	VA	Alameda	Oakland	68	139
GLASE								
Mary	40	f	w	FRNK	Sacramento	4-Wd Sacramento	77	353
GLASER								
Andrew	48	m	w	BAVA	Solano	Rio Vista Twp	90	62
Chas	40	m	w	POLA	San Francisco	San Francisco P O	83	268
Max	19	m	w	AUST	San Luis Obispo	San Luis Obispo Tw	87	309
Mike	32	m	w	PORT	San Mateo	Schoolhouse Statio	87	339
GLASFORD								
J E	22	f	w	CT	San Francisco	San Francisco P O	85	774
Peter S	38	m	w	CANA	San Francisco	8-Wd San Francisco	82	448
GLASGOW								
James	44	m	w	SCOT	San Francisco	11-Wd San Francisc	84	615
James	24	m	w	IREL	Stanislaus	San Joaquin Twp	92	80
Mary V	19	f	w	DC	San Francisco	San Francisco P O	83	339
Richard	39	m	w	PA	Klamath	Sawyers Bar	73	377
GLASHEEN								
Edmond	29	m	w	IREL	Yolo	Cache Crk Twp	93	421
GLASKE								
Adolphe	24	m	w	AUST	San Francisco	6-Wd San Francisco	81	73
GLASKIN								
A B	37	f	w	KY	San Joaquin	2-Wd Stockton	86	181
John	46	m	w	IREL	Santa Clara	Santa Clara Twp	88	150
Thos	40	m	w	ENGL	Alameda	Murray Twp	68	125
GLASLY								
Hanna	25	f	w	IREL	San Francisco	8-Wd San Francisco	82	308
GLASS								
A H	12	f	w	CA	Santa Clara	Gilroy Twp	88	92
Alice	14	f	w	CA	Contra Costa	Martinez P O	71	379
David	51	m	w	PA	Contra Costa	Martinez P O	71	392
F P	31	m	w	BAVA	Tehama	Cottonwood Twp	92	162
Frank	33	m	w	PRUS	Alameda	Alameda	68	19
Frank	23	m	w	FRAN	San Francisco	5-Wd San Francisco	81	1
Henry	38	m	w	MD	Fresno	Millerton P O	72	150
James	26	m	w	MI	Contra Costa	Martinez P O	71	444
James R	30	m	w	NY	Yolo	Cache Crk Twp	93	453
Jas	28	m	w	CANA	Solano	Vallejo	90	139
John	59	m	w	IL	El Dorado	Georgetown Twp	72	39
John	31	m	w	NY	Santa Cruz	Santa Cruz	89	429
John	27	m	w	IREL	Alameda	Oakland	68	257
Joseph P	28	m	w	BAVA	Tehama	Antelope Twp	92	160
Julius	25	m	w	PRUS	San Francisco	San Francisco P O	80	476
Louis	24	m	w	DE	Santa Barbara	San Buenaventura P	87	433
Mark	28	m	w	PRUS	San Francisco	6-Wd San Francisco	81	70
Richard C	25	m	w	TX	Tulare	Farmersville Twp	92	250
Robe P	34	m	w	KY	Colusa	Spring Valley Twp	71	340
Robert	64	m	w	TN	Tulare	Farmersville Twp	92	249
Samuel	69	m	w	OH	Butte	Oregon Twp	70	123
Schenck	41	m	w	NY	Nevada	Grass Valley Twp	75	166
Thomas	36	m	w	PA	Placer	Auburn P O	76	362
William	38	m	w	ME	Alameda	Brooklyn	68	27
GLASSBURNER								
Andre	39	m	w	PA	Tehama	Antelope Twp	92	154
F	66	m	w	BAVA	El Dorado	Greenwood Twp	72	56
GLASSCOCK								
A B	38	m	w	MO	Placer	Dutch Flat P O	76	404
Affred H	34	m	w	IL	Tulare	Visalia	92	290
Clinton	30	m	w	MO	Colusa	Spring Valley Twp	71	338
Felix B	22	m	w	MO	Tehama	Deer Crk Twp	92	170
G W	33	m	w	MO	Lassen	Milford Twp	73	438
George	56	m	w	VA	Yolo	Grafton Twp	93	489
George	37	m	w	AR	Kern	Kernville P O	73	368
Granville	42	m	w	ENGL	Nevada	Grass Valley Twp	75	230
I H	65	m	w	VA	Lassen	Milford Twp	73	438
Marshall	38	m	w	VA	Colusa	Spring Valley Twp	71	340
Martha	16	f	w	OR	Colusa	Spring Valley Twp	71	336

Name	Age	S	R	B-PL	County	Locale	Roll	Pg
						Series M593		
Peter S	36	m	w	MO	Yolo	Grafton Twp	93	480
Spencer	60	m	w	VA	Yolo	Cottonwood Twp	93	474
Thomas	30	m	w	VA	Yolo	Cache Crk Twp	93	448
GLASSELL								
Andrew	76	m	w	VA	Los Angeles	Los Angeles	73	530
GLASSEN								
Eliza	30	f	w	SWIT	San Francisco	San Francisco P O	83	45
James	41	m	w	ENGL	Nevada	Grass Valley Twp	75	184
James	39	m	w	ENGL	Nevada	Grass Valley Twp	75	159
Joseph	25	m	w	ENGL	Nevada	Grass Valley Twp	75	168
GLASSER								
Fredk	33	m	w	PA	Shasta	Horsetown P O	89	506
George	26	m	w	WURT	Santa Clara	2-Wd San Jose	88	319
GLASSETT								
John	42	m	w	IREL	Nevada	Bridgeport Twp	75	122
GLASSEY								
Rose	40	f	w	IREL	Santa Clara	Fremont Twp	88	57
GLASSFORD								
Elizabeth	54	f	w	IREL	San Francisco	San Francisco P O	83	71
Joseph	31	m	w	IL	El Dorado	Diamond Springs Tw	72	26
R B	56	m	w	IREL	Sacramento	3-Wd Sacramento	77	294
GLASSLY								
Jesse R	51	m	w	PA	San Francisco	8-Wd San Francisco	82	461
GLASSMAN								
Jacob	38	m	w	FRAN	San Francisco	8-Wd San Francisco	82	466
Kris	36	m	w	POLA	San Francisco	5-Wd San Francisco	81	6
GLASSON								
James	30	m	w	ENGL	Trinity	Weaverville Pct	92	231
John	25	m	w	PRUS	San Francisco	11-Wd San Francisc	84	530
John	25	m	w	ENGL	Contra Costa	Martinez P O	71	389
Jos	23	m	w	ENGL	Solano	Vallejo	90	149
Josiah	51	m	w	ENGL	Nevada	Nevada Twp	75	287
Josiah	29	m	w	ENGL	Nevada	Eureka Twp	75	139
Wm	25	m	w	ENGL	Tuolumne	Sonora P O	93	325
GLATT								
B	36	m	w	BADE	Humboldt	Eureka Twp	72	265
B	36	m	w	CA	Humboldt	Eureka Twp	72	265
GLATZ								
Frederick	52	m	w	PRUS	Sacramento	2-Wd Sacramento	77	233
GLAUN								
Edward	40	m	w	IREL	San Francisco	San Francisco P O	83	420
Thomas	32	m	w	IREL	San Francisco	San Francisco P O	83	420
GLAVIN								
John	67	m	w	IREL	Sacramento	2-Wd Sacramento	77	212
Robert	31	m	w	IREL	San Francisco	1-Wd San Francisco	79	71
Thomas	22	m	w	IREL	Los Angeles	Los Angeles	73	541
Wm	38	m	w	IREL	Sacramento	Granite Twp	77	154
GLAYAS								
John	36	m	w	ENGL	El Dorado	Placerville	72	116
GLAZE								
D N	44	m	w	VA	Amador	Ione City P O	69	355
J W	48	m	w	VA	Amador	Ione City P O	69	355
J W	22	m	w	MO	Amador	Ione City P O	69	355
Martin	55	m	w	TN	Mendocino	Round Valley Twp	74	221
GLAZIER								
Charles	40	m	w	PRUS	Sonoma	Salt Point	91	392
Isaac	40	m	w	AUST	San Francisco	8-Wd San Francisco	82	424
Jas	36	m	w	ME	Mendocino	Ukiah Twp	74	241
Samuel	32	m	w	PRUS	Butte	Oregon Twp	70	129
Simon W	35	m	w	PRUS	San Francisco	8-Wd San Francisco	82	306
GLEAMES								
L	67	m	w	NY	Alameda	Oakland	68	244
GLEAN								
Silas C	27	m	w	TN	Los Angeles	El Monte Twp	73	448
GLEASE								
Pat	35	m	w	IREL	Alameda	Murray Twp	68	111
GLEASEN								
John	59	m	w	NH	San Francisco	11-Wd San Francisc	84	612
GLEASER								
John	36	m	w	PRUS	San Francisco	San Francisco P O	83	232
GLEASON								
Alex	53	m	w	IREL	Santa Cruz	Santa Cruz	89	428
Ann	25	f	w	IREL	San Francisco	8-Wd San Francisco	82	293
Catherine	17	f	w	WI	Plumas	Quartz Twp	77	41
Charles	44	m	w	NH	Alameda	Washington Twp	68	278
Chas	39	m	w	PA	Yuba	Marysville Twp	93	571
Cyrus	35	m	w	MA	Butte	Oroville Twp	70	140
David	33	m	w	MA	Sutter	Vernon Twp	92	132
Dennis	55	m	w	IREL	Butte	Ophir Twp	70	95
Dennis	40	m	w	IREL	San Francisco	8-Wd San Francisco	82	313
Dennis	40	m	w	IREL	Sacramento	3-Wd Sacramento	77	273
Dennis	31	m	w	NY	Alameda	San Leandro	68	95
Edward	22	m	w	IREL	San Francisco	8-Wd San Francisco	82	361
Eliza	24	f	w	IREL	San Francisco	8-Wd San Francisco	82	443
Finis D	39	m	w	OH	Colusa	Grand Island Twp	71	310
G M	34	m	w	PRUS	Tehama	Tehama Twp	92	194
George	40	m	w	ENGL	Alameda	Oakland	68	153
George	40	m	w	ENGL	San Francisco	3-Wd San Francisco	79	300
George	26	m	w	CT	Los Angeles	Soledad Twp	73	630
George A	38	m	w	NY	Santa Clara	Fremont Twp	88	61
Henry	39	m	w	PRUS	Klamath	Camp Gaston	73	373
Henry	18	m	w	CA	Santa Cruz	Watsonville	89	368
J J	29	m	w	NY	Sacramento	4-Wd Sacramento	77	335
James	44	m	w	IREL	Placer	Bath P O	76	449
James	40	m	w	IREL	Calaveras	San Andreas P O	70	188
James	37	m	w	IREL	San Diego	Julian Dist	78	469
James	32	m	w	MA	San Francisco	11-Wd San Francisc	84	445

© 2001 by Heritage Quest. All rights reserved.

Name	Age	S	R	B-PL	County	Locale	Series M593 Roll	Pg
James	28	m	w	IREL	San Mateo	San Mateo P O	87	371
Jasper	34	m	w	PA	San Diego	San Diego	78	509
John	60	m	w	IREL	San Joaquin	2-Wd Stockton	86	210
John	54	m	w	MD	Sutter	Vernon Twp	92	138
John	40	m	w	IREL	Amador	Volcano P O	69	376
John	40	m	w	IREL	Shasta	Horsetown P O	89	503
John	37	m	w	PRUS	Tehama	Paskenta Twp	92	164
John	34	m	w	IREL	San Francisco	San Francisco P O	83	387
John	33	m	w	IREL	San Francisco	San Francisco P O	83	400
John A	30	m	w	NH	Plumas	Plumas Twp	77	27
John M	51	m	w	NY	Sacramento	Georgianna Twp	77	123
Joseph	25	m	w	IREL	San Diego	San Diego	78	505
Kate	20	f	w	CANA	Sonoma	Santa Rosa	91	420
Lucy G	18	f	w	CA	Monterey	Monterey Twp	74	351
Mariana	17	f	w	CA	Monterey	Monterey	74	357
Marks	21	m	w	SHOL	San Francisco	11-Wd San Francisc	84	617
Martin	31	m	w	IREL	San Francisco	11-Wd San Francisc	84	470
Mary	50	f	w	IREL	San Francisco	11-Wd San Francisc	84	470
Mary	27	f	w	IREL	San Joaquin	Oneal Twp	86	114
Mary	19	f	w	IREL	San Francisco	8-Wd San Francisco	82	403
Matthew	32	m	w	IREL	Santa Clara	2-Wd San Jose	88	322
Michael	64	m	w	IREL	Placer	Bath P O	76	450
Michael	27	m	w	IREL	San Francisco	San Francisco P O	80	398
Nellie	4	f	w	NY	Alameda	Oakland	68	153
P	22	m	w	IL	San Joaquin	2-Wd Stockton	86	193
Pat	39	m	w	IREL	San Francisco	2-Wd San Francisco	79	218
Pat	39	m	w	IREL	San Joaquin	3-Wd Stockton	86	225
Pat	37	m	w	IREL	San Joaquin	3-Wd Stockton	86	223
Pat	32	m	w	IREL	San Joaquin	2-Wd Stockton	86	210
Patk	33	m	w	IREL	Sacramento	4-Wd Sacramento	77	345
Patrick	34	m	w	IREL	San Francisco	8-Wd San Francisco	82	487
Patrick	31	m	w	CANA	Stanislaus	Empire Twp	92	65
Patrick	28	m	w	IREL	San Mateo	San Mateo P O	87	360
Patrick	24	m	w	IREL	Santa Clara	Fremont Twp	88	55
Sarah	36	f	w	POLA	San Francisco	San Francisco P O	83	294
T	22	m	w	NY	Calaveras	Copperopolis P O	70	235
T C	39	m	w	NY	Sutter	Sutter Twp	92	125
Thomas	44	m	w	IREL	San Francisco	San Francisco P O	80	366
Thomas	26	m	w	IREL	Los Angeles	Los Angeles Twp	73	489
Thos	31	m	w	IREL	Yuba	Rose Bar Twp	93	663
Tim	42	m	w	IREL	San Francisco	San Francisco P O	83	396
Timothy	28	m	w	IREL	San Francisco	11-Wd San Francisc	84	517
W A	36	m	w	ENGL	Alameda	Oakland	68	263
William	61	m	w	MA	El Dorado	Mud Springs Twp	72	87
William	34	m	w	NY	San Francisco	8-Wd San Francisco	82	423
William	26	m	w	CANA	San Diego	Julian Dist	78	472
Wm	38	m	w	IREL	San Francisco	5-Wd San Francisco	81	35
Wm	25	m	w	IREL	Sonoma	Bodega Twp	91	260
Wm H	35	m	w	IREL	San Francisco	8-Wd San Francisco	82	324
GLEAVES								
Saml	21	m	w	OH	San Francisco	1-Wd San Francisco	79	64
GLEESING								
Henry	30	m	w	SWED	San Francisco	1-Wd San Francisco	79	71
GLEESON								
F	35	m	w	IREL	Sacramento	3-Wd Sacramento	77	317
James	25	m	w	IREL	San Francisco	5-Wd San Francisco	81	32
Mary	30	f	w	IREL	San Francisco	1-Wd San Francisco	79	75
Michl	36	m	w	IREL	San Francisco	1-Wd San Francisco	79	93
Michl J	30	m	w	IREL	San Francisco	San Francisco P O	83	15
Peter	30	m	w	IREL	San Francisco	1-Wd San Francisco	79	99
Stephen	32	m	w	IREL	San Francisco	San Francisco P O	83	74
Thos	40	m	w	NY	San Francisco	1-Wd San Francisco	79	43
Wm	43	m	w	IREL	San Francisco	11-Wd San Francisc	84	592
Wm	40	m	w	IREL	San Francisco	1-Wd San Francisco	79	33
Wm	37	m	w	IREL	San Francisco	San Francisco P O	85	840
GLEIN								
Caroline	63	f	w	HCAS	Santa Clara	2-Wd San Jose	88	327
Philip	51	m	w	PRUS	Santa Clara	1-Wd San Jose	88	265
Samuel	62	m	w	IREL	Tuolumne	Chinese Camp P O	93	374
GLEINS								
Erick	48	m	w	NH	Marin	San Rafael Twp	74	38
Henry	33	m	w	SWED	San Francisco	1-Wd San Francisco	79	120
GLEINTHROOT								
S	42	m	w	BADE	San Francisco	8-Wd San Francisco	82	355
GLEISTER								
Salvato	25	m	w	SWIT	San Francisco	San Francisco P O	80	343
GLEIZES								
Benj	48	m	w	FRAN	San Francisco	2-Wd San Francisco	79	160
GLEMMON								
John	42	m	w	IREL	Alameda	Alameda	68	4
GLEN								
Alexander	38	m	w	SCOT	Nevada	Grass Valley Twp	75	204
David	38	m	w	MO	Solano	Vacaville Twp	90	127
Glen	60	m	w	MO	San Bernardino	San Bernardino Twp	78	447
James	37	m	w	NY	Stanislaus	Buena Vista Twp	92	15
Jas	25	m	w	ME	Solano	Vallejo	90	209
Mary	49	f	w	SCOT	San Joaquin	2-Wd Stockton	86	184
Patrick	29	m	w	IREL	San Francisco	11-Wd San Francisc	84	496
Robert	27	m	w	IL	San Joaquin	2-Wd Stockton	86	184
Robt	28	m	w	NY	San Joaquin	2-Wd Stockton	86	184
William	21	m	w	ENGL	Nevada	Meadow Lake Twp	75	252
Wm H	30	m	w	MO	Nevada	Meadow Lake Twp	75	259
GLENCAMP								
John	25	m	w	TN	Sacramento	Mississippi Twp	77	163
GLENCE								
Patrick	32	m	w	IREL	Mendocino	Point Arena Twp	74	205

Name	Age	S	R	B-PL	County	Locale	Series M593 Roll	Pg
GLENDALE								
Carl	24	m	w	SAXO	San Francisco	1-Wd San Francisco	79	63
GLENDENNING								
William	35	m	w	SCOT	Kern	Bakersfield P O	73	357
GLENDON								
John	42	m	w	IREL	Solano	Benicia	90	9
GLENFORD								
Alice	9	f	w	CA	Yolo	Cache Crk Twp	93	445
GLENN								
A C	37	m	w	CANA	Monterey	San Juan Twp	74	405
A C	36	m	w	CANA	Monterey	San Juan Twp	74	398
Alexander	42	m	w	OH	Stanislaus	San Joaquin Twp	92	83
Alexander	40	m	w	TN	Kern	Linns Valley P O	73	347
Alphonso	18	m	w	CA	Santa Clara	Santa Clara Twp	88	177
Amos	40	m	w	OH	Fresno	Millerton P O	72	158
C D	24	m	w	MO	Sutter	Nicolaus Twp	92	112
Daniel	37	m	w	OH	Sacramento	Franklin Twp	77	119
Dennis	35	m	w	IREL	San Joaquin	2-Wd Stockton	86	163
Edward	53	m	w	IREL	Santa Clara	2-Wd San Jose	88	286
Hugh	26	m	w	NY	Santa Clara	2-Wd San Jose	88	286
Hugh J	45	m	w	VA	Colusa	Monroe Twp	71	313
James	50	m	w	TN	Kern	Linns Valley P O	73	346
James	39	m	w	MO	Siskiyou	Scott Valley Twp	89	610
James	24	m	w	SCOT	Santa Clara	Fremont Twp	88	51
Jeremiah	28	m	w	MO	Kern	Tehachapi P O	73	352
John	27	m	w	IREL	Los Angeles	Los Angeles Twp	73	479
John	25	m	w	MO	Sutter	Nicolaus Twp	92	112
Joseph	50	m	w	TX	Kern	Linns Valley P O	73	344
Laurence	15	m	w	CA	Santa Clara	Santa Clara Twp	88	177
M C	56	m	w	MA	Tuolumne	Big Oak Flat P O	93	394
Peter	26	m	w	OH	Sacramento	Franklin Twp	77	119
Rebecca	71	f	w	NC	Kern	Linns Valley P O	73	346
Richard	23	m	w	NY	Yolo	Putah Twp	93	515
Richd M	42	m	w	AL	Fresno	Kings Rvr P O	72	213
Robert	27	m	w	MO	Siskiyou	Scott Valley Twp	89	621
Robt	31	m	w	MO	Sonoma	Santa Rosa	91	412
Silas C	25	m	w	AL	Los Angeles	San Gabriel Twp	73	595
Thomas	30	m	w	IREL	San Francisco	San Francisco P O	83	412
Thos	36	m	w	AR	Tehama	Tehama Twp	92	186
Thos W	27	m	w	MO	Sutter	Sutter Twp	92	118
Timothy	35	m	w	IREL	San Francisco	San Francisco P O	83	236
Vincent	45	m	w	NJ	Sacramento	Franklin Twp	77	119
William	36	m	w	KY	Siskiyou	Surprise Valley Tw	89	641
William	30	m	w	NH	Tehama	Merrill	92	198
William	15	m	w	MO	Colusa	Colusa Twp	71	280
William J	46	m	w	MO	Solano	Montezuma Twp	90	68
William P	14	m	w	TN	Santa Cruz	Watsonville	89	368
Wm	40	m	w	AL	Fresno	Kings Rvr P O	72	213
GLENNAN								
Ann	40	f	w	IREL	San Francisco	San Francisco P O	85	720
Lawrence	26	m	w	IREL	San Francisco	8-Wd San Francisco	82	397
Martin	25	m	w	IREL	San Francisco	8-Wd San Francisco	82	415
Micheal	25	m	w	DENM	San Francisco	7-Wd San Francisco	81	221
GLENNE								
John	27	m	w	IREL	Alameda	San Leandro	68	96
GLENNEN								
John W	29	m	w	ENGL	San Mateo	Redwood Twp	87	365
GLENNIN								
Thomas	35	m	w	IREL	Placer	Auburn P O	76	375
GLENNON								
Eliza	60	f	w	IREL	San Francisco	San Francisco P O	83	280
James	36	m	w	IREL	Monterey	San Juan Twp	74	408
James P	39	m	w	IREL	Sacramento	2-Wd Sacramento	77	241
Jas	34	m	w	IREL	Solano	Vallejo	90	182
Patrick	50	m	w	IREL	Nevada	Bloomfield Twp	75	98
Richard	33	m	w	IREL	Kern	Havilah P O	73	350
GLENNY								
James	18	m	w	SCOT	San Mateo	Redwood City P O	87	375
GLENS								
Charles	20	m	w	MA	Marin	San Rafael Twp	74	46
Ralph	19	m	w	MA	Marin	San Rafael Twp	74	46
GLENSHY								
Jane	29	f	w	IREL	San Francisco	6-Wd San Francisco	81	147
GLENSON								
Michael	26	m	w	IREL	San Joaquin	1-Wd Stockton	86	121
GLESHON								
Peter	35	m	w	GERM	Contra Costa	Martinez P O	71	446
GLESON								
Patrick	36	m	w	IREL	Placer	Roseville P O	76	355
GLEW								
William	37	m	w	MO	Sonoma	Vallejo Twp	91	458
William	26	m	w	IN	Nevada	Meadow Lake Twp	75	264
GLICK								
Gustave	20	m	w	WURT	San Francisco	2-Wd San Francisco	79	206
Kolman	37	m	w	BADE	San Francisco	San Francisco P O	83	208
GLICKAUF								
Jos	53	m	w	BOHE	Butte	Ophir Twp	70	116
GLICKMAN								
David	16	m	w	PRUS	San Francisco	2-Wd San Francisco	79	239
GLIDDEN								
Albert	50	m	w	ME	Santa Clara	Fremont Twp	88	58
Benj	35	m	w	ME	Yuba	Rose Bar Twp	93	653
Benja	65	m	w	ME	Mariposa	Mariposa P O	74	134
Charles	34	m	w	MA	Sutter	Sutter Twp	92	122
James	29	m	w	MA	Los Angeles	San Gabriel Twp	73	596
John F	40	m	w	NH	Placer	Auburn P O	76	364
John S	25	m	w	ME	Mendocino	Navarro & Big Rvr	74	177

© 2001 by Heritage Quest. All rights reserved.

Name	Age	S	R	B-PL	County	Locale	Series M593 Roll	Pg
Lorenzo R	29	m	w	ME	Yuba	Slate Range Bar Tw	93	674
Mary	35	f	w	CHIL	San Francisco	11-Wd San Francisc	84	610
W J	19	m	w	ME	Sacramento	Franklin Twp	77	109
GLIDDON								
Albert	25	m	w	NH	San Joaquin	Dent Twp	86	20
Hattie	18	f	w	WI	San Joaquin	Dent Twp	86	20
Louisa	39	f	w	OH	San Francisco	11-Wd San Francisc	84	620
Simon	45	m	w	ENGL	Nevada	Grass Valley Twp	75	192
GLIDE								
Joseph H	40	m	w	ENGL	Colusa	Monroe Twp	71	322
GLIDEN								
Charles	23	m	w	ME	San Joaquin	Elkhorn Twp	86	54
William	25	m	w	ME	Inyo	Bishop Crk Twp	73	316
GLIN								
Ah	37	m	c	CHIN	Sacramento	Georgianna Twp	77	123
Hanah	25	f	w	IREL	Alameda	Oakland	68	132
Kate	21	f	w	IREL	Solano	Rio Vista Twp	90	55
GLINCHEY								
Patrick	40	m	w	IREL	San Francisco	3-Wd San Francisco	79	300
GLINE								
A	35	m	w	IL	El Dorado	Greenwood Twp	72	52
Rudolph	60	m	w	NY	San Bernardino	Chino Twp	78	411
GLINES								
Abraham	40	m	w	OH	Nevada	Little York Twp	75	243
John	38	m	w	CANA	Stanislaus	Empire Twp	92	58
Joseph	55	m	w	OH	Nevada	Rough & Ready Twp	75	332
Joshua	36	m	w	TX	Stanislaus	Empire Twp	92	64
Sumner	34	m	w	NH	El Dorado	Mud Springs Twp	72	88
GLINN								
A	39	m	w	NH	El Dorado	Greenwood Twp	72	52
J H	18	m	w	IA	El Dorado	Lake Valley Twp	72	64
Owen	44	m	w	IREL	Sacramento	Granite Twp	77	154
T A	24	m	w	NY	Lake	Lower Lake	73	419
GLINNEN								
Bridget	33	f	w	IREL	San Francisco	7-Wd San Francisco	81	233
GLINSON								
Wm	30	m	w	IREL	San Francisco	San Francisco P O	85	852
GLISE								
Nathaniel	47	m	w	OH	Nevada	Grass Valley Twp	75	225
GLISLOPIE								
E	25	f	w	WI	Sierra	Sierra Twp	89	564
GLISON								
Pat	29	m	w	IREL	San Joaquin	1-Wd Stockton	86	154
GLISTENER								
C F	30	m	w	VA	San Joaquin	2-Wd Stockton	86	173
GLITZ								
Chas	35	m	w	GERM	Solano	Vallejo	90	169
GLOB								
James	24	m	w	PRUS	San Francisco	5-Wd San Francisco	81	22
GLOCKER								
Frederick R	34	m	w	WURT	Santa Clara	2-Wd San Jose	88	326
GLOCKLER								
Charles	38	m	w	BADE	Yolo	Putah Twp	93	525
GLOCKLIN								
A G	23	m	w	WURT	Placer	Dutch Flat P O	76	405
GLOGLEY								
James	19	m	w	NY	Marin	San Rafael Twp	74	26
GLORE								
Michael	36	m	w	WI	Solano	Silveyville Twp	90	82
GLORIA								
Sadina	21	f	w	PORT	Alameda	Eden Twp	68	84
GLORIAS								
William	19	m	c	CHIN	Marin	San Rafael Twp	74	46
GLORIE								
James	19	m	w	IL	San Francisco	San Francisco P O	83	268
GLOSBY								
John C	43	m	w	NY	Inyo	Independence Twp	73	325
GLOSS								
Ah	25	m	c	CHIN	Sacramento	Georgianna Twp	77	124
C	59	m	w	SWIT	Alameda	Oakland	68	147
Margaret	18	f	w	BAVA	San Francisco	8-Wd San Francisco	82	416
GLOSSETT								
D	28	m	w	IREL	Sierra	Forest Twp	89	530
GLOSSIN								
Margaret	28	f	w	IREL	San Joaquin	2-Wd Stockton	86	175
GLOSSON								
John	37	m	w	IREL	Solano	Silveyville Twp	90	87
GLOTEBACK								
Sebartian	41	m	w	SAXO	Monterey	Monterey	74	357
GLOTSBACH								
Narcus	19	m	w	CA	Monterey	Monterey	74	364
Valentin	18	m	w	CA	Monterey	Monterey	74	360
GLOTZ								
Catharine	50	f	w	PRUS	Calaveras	Copperopolis P O	70	236
GLOUBER								
Herman	48	m	w	BOHE	Sonoma	Petaluma Twp	91	364
Herman	47	m	w	AUST	San Francisco	8-Wd San Francisco	82	345
GLOVEN								
Edmund	26	m	w	IREL	Yolo	Buckeye Twp	93	410
GLOVER								
A J	37	m	w	NY	Solano	Benicia	90	2
Andrew	34	m	w	AUST	San Francisco	1-Wd San Francisco	79	28
B	35	m	w	MI	Alameda	Oakland	68	262
B C	32	m	w	CANA	Alameda	Oakland	68	214
B S	58	m	w	NH	Tuolumne	Chinese Camp P O	93	381
Chas G	23	m	w	MO	San Francisco	1-Wd San Francisco	79	63
Ed	48	m	w	MA	Sacramento	4-Wd Sacramento	77	325
Edmond	56	m	w	IN	El Dorado	White Oak Twp	72	140
Esau	59	m	w	NH	Santa Cruz	Santa Cruz	89	414
George	29	m	w	MA	San Francisco	11-Wd San Francisc	84	571
J	35	m	w	IN	Alameda	Oakland	68	265
J E	29	m	w	MD	San Francisco	7-Wd San Francisco	81	226
James	36	m	w	SCOT	Alameda	Brooklyn	68	28
James	30	m	w	ENGL	San Francisco	8-Wd San Francisco	82	484
James	28	m	w	ENGL	San Francisco	San Francisco P O	83	156
James	28	m	w	MO	San Bernardino	San Bernardino Twp	78	451
James F	20	m	w	CA	Santa Clara	1-Wd San Jose	88	235
James F	20	m	w	CA	Santa Clara	San Jose Twp	88	193
James R	44	m	w	ME	Placer	Bath P O	76	431
Jas	37	m	w	NY	Sacramento	1-Wd Sacramento	77	174
Jasper	22	m	w	MO	Mendocino	Ukiah Twp	74	236
Jenny	37	f	w	IN	Sonoma	Analy Twp	91	222
John	50	m	w	IREL	San Francisco	11-Wd San Francisc	84	548
John	30	m	w	AUST	San Francisco	7-Wd San Francisco	81	178
Joseph	33	m	w	CT	San Francisco	1-Wd San Francisco	79	89
Margaret	36	f	w	IREL	San Francisco	7-Wd San Francisco	81	178
Milton W	56	m	w	KY	San Bernardino	San Bernardino Twp	78	421
Osmond	31	m	w	CANA	Inyo	Independence Twp	73	326
Robbert	43	m	w	IN	Trinity	Junction City Pct	92	206
Robbert	31	m	w	MD	Alameda	Oakland	68	197
S M	45	f	w	CT	Solano	Benicia	90	14
William	48	m	w	IN	Mendocino	Point Arena Twp	74	213
William	44	m	w	IL	Placer	Newcastle Twp	76	478
GLOVERI								
Andres	36	m	w	ITAL	San Francisco	San Francisco P O	80	426
GLOVIN								
A	22	m	w	MO	Sierra	Forest Twp	89	531
D	34	m	w	MO	Sierra	Forest Twp	89	531
GLOWER								
Godlip G	42	m	w	PA	Santa Barbara	San Buenaventura P	87	423
GLOYD								
D J	52	m	w	VA	Lake	Lower Lake	73	429
GLUCK								
George	25	m	w	BADE	San Francisco	San Francisco P O	80	392
John F	47	m	w	WURT	San Francisco	8-Wd San Francisco	82	416
GLUCKAN								
John	22	m	w	PA	Sacramento	4-Wd Sacramento	77	324
GLUCKSMAN								
Isaac	35	m	w	PRUS	San Francisco	San Francisco P O	83	415
GLUESSING								
Geo	33	m	w	PRUS	San Francisco	San Francisco P O	83	313
GLUM								
Daniel	45	m	w	OH	Sacramento	San Joaquin Twp	77	398
GLUMAZ								
Jno	29	m	w	AUST	Sierra	Table Rock Twp	89	575
GLUNLEE								
Jacob	50	m	w	WURT	Sacramento	3-Wd Sacramento	77	283
GLUNOVITCH								
L	41	m	w	AUST	Amador	Sutter Crk P O	69	401
GLUSKIN								
A	39	m	w	IL	San Joaquin	Castoria Twp	86	11
GLUTZ								
John	24	m	w	HDAR	San Francisco	San Francisco P O	80	460
GLUYAS								
George	65	m	w	ENGL	San Francisco	5-Wd San Francisco	81	26
George Mrs	60	f	w	ENGL	San Francisco	5-Wd San Francisco	81	26
James	42	m	w	ENGL	Nevada	Grass Valley Twp	75	191
Reese	28	m	w	PA	San Francisco	11-Wd San Francisc	84	505
Richard	34	m	w	ENGL	Nevada	Grass Valley Twp	75	192
GLYDEN								
Henry	26	m	w	MO	Solano	Silveyville Twp	90	73
GLYN								
Sarah	22	f	w	IREL	San Francisco	1-Wd San Francisco	79	62
Wm G	36	m	w	PA	Tuolumne	Columbia P O	93	357
GLYNN								
Ann	60	f	w	IREL	Solano	Vallejo	90	195
Anne M	20	f	w	MA	Santa Clara	2-Wd San Jose	88	281
Dennis	37	m	w	IREL	San Francisco	San Francisco P O	83	384
Edward	55	m	w	IREL	San Francisco	San Francisco P O	83	384
Ignatius	14	m	w	CA	Santa Barbara	Santa Barbara P O	87	492
Ira	72	m	w	VT	El Dorado	Placerville	72	109
James	42	m	w	IREL	San Francisco	2-Wd San Francisco	79	271
James	37	m	w	IREL	San Francisco	San Francisco P O	83	412
John	36	m	w	IREL	Nevada	Grass Valley Twp	75	211
John	33	m	w	IREL	San Francisco	San Francisco P O	85	723
John	25	m	w	IREL	San Francisco	8-Wd San Francisco	82	434
Louisa	72	f	w	IREL	Santa Clara	Fremont Twp	88	59
Mary	23	f	w	IREL	San Francisco	San Francisco P O	80	386
Michael	48	m	w	IREL	Nevada	Grass Valley Twp	75	197
Michael	22	m	w	IREL	Amador	Amador City P O	69	392
Michiel	34	m	w	IREL	Sonoma	Sonoma Twp	91	441
Theresa	25	f	w	IREL	San Francisco	8-Wd San Francisco	82	397
Thomas	55	m	w	MA	Santa Cruz	Santa Cruz Twp	89	393
Thos	45	m	w	IREL	San Francisco	11-Wd San Francisc	84	613
Thos	25	m	w	MA	Butte	Chico Twp	70	31
Thos S	24	m	w	LA	San Francisco	8-Wd San Francisco	82	303
GNEKOW								
Rudolph	35	m	w	PRUS	San Joaquin	3-Wd Stockton	86	216
GNESS								
John	40	m	w	AR	Los Angeles	El Monte Twp	73	451
GNO								
Ley	20	m	c	CHIN	Colusa	Butte Twp	71	266
GO								
Ah	61	m	c	CHIN	Sacramento	Granite Twp	77	140

© 2001 by Heritage Quest. All rights reserved.

California 1870 Census

Series M593

Name	Age	S	R	B-PL	County	Locale	Roll	Pg
Ah	60	m	c	CHIN	Sacramento	Granite Twp	77	141
Ah	55	m	c	CHIN	Sacramento	Natomas Twp	77	171
Ah	50	m	c	CHIN	Nevada	Meadow Lake Twp	75	259
Ah	47	m	c	CHIN	Sacramento	Georgianna Twp	77	133
Ah	44	m	c	CHIN	Sacramento	Granite Twp	77	138
Ah	40	m	c	CHIN	Sacramento	Natomas Twp	77	166
Ah	40	m	c	CHIN	San Francisco	San Francisco P O	80	522
Ah	38	m	c	CHIN	Stanislaus	Empire Twp	92	65
Ah	38	m	c	CHIN	Sacramento	Georgianna Twp	77	132
Ah	37	m	c	CHIN	San Joaquin	Oneal Twp	86	116
Ah	37	m	c	CHIN	Sacramento	Granite Twp	77	141
Ah	35	m	c	CHIN	Alameda	Oakland	68	158
Ah	35	m	c	CHIN	Sacramento	Granite Twp	77	138
Ah	35	m	c	CHIN	Sacramento	Granite Twp	77	137
Ah	34	m	c	CHIN	El Dorado	Cosumnes Twp	72	20
Ah	34	m	c	CHIN	San Francisco	San Francisco P O	80	510
Ah	34	m	c	CHIN	Sacramento	Granite Twp	77	140
Ah	32	m	c	CHIN	Nevada	Meadow Lake Twp	75	257
Ah	32	m	c	CHIN	Sacramento	Georgianna Twp	77	123
Ah	32	m	c	CHIN	Sacramento	Cosumnes Twp	77	95
Ah	30	f	c	CHIN	Sacramento	Granite Twp	77	151
Ah	28	m	c	CHIN	Sacramento	Granite Twp	77	138
Ah	27	m	c	CHIN	San Joaquin	1-Wd Stockton	86	156
Ah	25	m	c	CHIN	San Francisco	6-Wd San Francisco	81	66
Ah	25	m	c	CHIN	Sacramento	Georgianna Twp	77	123
Ah	24	m	c	CHIN	San Francisco	San Francisco P O	80	509
Ah	21	m	c	CHIN	San Joaquin	1-Wd Stockton	86	143
Ah	21	f	c	CHIN	San Francisco	San Francisco P O	80	495
Ah	21	m	c	CHIN	San Francisco	San Francisco P O	80	499
Ah	21	m	c	CHIN	Sacramento	Granite Twp	77	137
Ah	16	m	c	CHIN	Siskiyou	Yreka	89	650
Ah	12	m	c	CHIN	Placer	Summit P O	76	497
Chong	27	m	c	CHIN	San Joaquin	1-Wd Stockton	86	139
Cum	30	m	c	CHIN	Fresno	Millerton P O	72	188
Hal	33	m	c	CHIN	San Joaquin	1-Wd Stockton	86	156
Han	18	f	c	CHIN	San Joaquin	1-Wd Stockton	86	153
Ho	40	m	c	CHIN	San Joaquin	Oneal Twp	86	116
Joon	28	m	c	CHIN	San Joaquin	1-Wd Stockton	86	151
Lip	35	m	c	CHIN	San Joaquin	1-Wd Stockton	86	145
Lo	38	m	c	CHIN	San Joaquin	1-Wd Stockton	86	144
Lo	14	m	c	CHIN	San Joaquin	1-Wd Stockton	86	143
Lue	27	m	c	CHIN	San Joaquin	1-Wd Stockton	86	144
Mun	39	m	c	CHIN	San Joaquin	1-Wd Stockton	86	156
On	26	m	c	CHIN	Calaveras	San Andreas P O	70	169
Up	27	m	c	CHIN	Del Norte	Happy Camp Twp	71	469
GOA								
Ah	23	m	c	CHIN	Calaveras	Copperopolis P O	70	253
GOACH								
Fred	20	m	w	ME	Placer	Summit P O	76	496
GOAD								
Frank W	38	m	w	KY	Colusa	Colusa	71	292
James W	31	m	w	KY	Colusa	Colusa	71	297
John C	38	m	w	KY	Nevada	Grass Valley Twp	75	190
GOAK								
Ah	35	m	c	CHIN	Mariposa	Mariposa P O	74	137
GOALMEDA								
Frank	28	m	w	PORT	San Francisco	3-Wd San Francisco	79	291
GOAMBOA								
Jesus	46	f	w	MEXI	San Francisco	2-Wd San Francisco	79	244
GOAN								
Ah	36	m	c	CHIN	Nevada	Little York Twp	75	236
Ann	25	f	w	FRAN	San Francisco	11-Wd San Francisc	84	688
Peter	51	m	w	IREL	Sonoma	Salt Point	91	392
GOAR								
Charles	40	m	w	MA	San Francisco	6-Wd San Francisco	81	94
James	23	m	w	IL	Butte	Chico Twp	70	44
Lucinda	50	f	w	IL	Butte	Chico Twp	70	57
Richd B	39	m	w	WI	Butte	Chico Twp	70	29
GOARD								
Geo	40	m	w	ENGL	Sierra	Sears Twp	89	558
GOATCHY								
Wm	25	m	w	SWED	San Francisco	1-Wd San Francisco	79	71
GOATLEY								
Armsted	40	m	w	KY	Sonoma	Petaluma Twp	91	362
GOB								
Ah	35	f	c	CHIN	Nevada	Grass Valley Twp	75	205
GOBB								
Susan	45	f	w	GERM	San Joaquin	2-Wd Stockton	86	165
GOBBEE								
Joseph	56	m	w	FRAN	San Francisco	7-Wd San Francisco	81	283
GOBBIE								
Daniel	45	m	w	ITAL	Mendocino	Ukiah Twp	74	239
Helena	14	f	w	ITAL	Mendocino	Ukiah Twp	74	233
GOBBLE								
Geo	57	m	w	PA	Sierra	Gibson Twp	89	542
GOBER								
W R	46	m	w	KY	Sacramento	3-Wd Sacramento	77	314
GOBERT								
Francis	42	m	w	FRAN	San Francisco	2-Wd San Francisco	79	233
Francisco	45	m	w	MEXI	Monterey	San Juan Twp	74	401
GOBIEL								
Louis	32	m	w	CANA	Alameda	Oakland	68	164
GOBIN								
E C	6	m	w	CA	Tuolumne	Big Oak Flat P O	93	402
S D	54	m	w	PA	Tuolumne	Big Oak Flat P O	93	396
William	51	m	w	PA	Stanislaus	Buena Vista Twp	92	14
GOBLE								
Elenuser	57	m	w	PA	Yuba	North East Twp	93	643
Isaac	47	m	w	IN	Santa Clara	Redwood Twp	88	124
Jacob	47	m	w	PA	San Bernardino	San Bernardino Twp	78	433
James	37	m	w	NY	Plumas	Quartz Twp	77	40
John	30	m	w	ENGL	San Francisco	San Francisco P O	83	87
GOBLEY								
Josephine	31	f	w	MD	San Francisco	2-Wd San Francisco	79	188
GOBRECK								
Phillip	38	m	w	PRUS	San Francisco	San Francisco P O	83	230
GOBY								
Mary	28	f	w	IREL	Alameda	Oakland	68	235
GOCH								
Martin	25	m	w	SHOL	Napa	Napa Twp	75	71
GOCHEY								
Thomas	43	m	w	VT	Contra Costa	Martinez P O	71	411
GOCK								
Ah	42	m	c	CHIN	Placer	Dutch Flat P O	76	409
James	26	m	w	NJ	Nevada	Eureka Twp	75	139
GOCKANHAUMER								
Marks	30	m	w	HDAR	San Francisco	8-Wd San Francisco	82	319
GOCY								
Ah	30	m	c	CHIN	Yolo	Putah Twp	93	519
GOD								
Ah	39	m	c	CHIN	Placer	Blue Canyon P O	76	417
GODANO								
John B	35	m	w	ITAL	Mariposa	Mariposa P O	74	132
GODARA								
Francis	26	f	w	MEXI	San Francisco	2-Wd San Francisco	79	231
GODARD								
A F	47	m	w	ENGL	Sacramento	3-Wd Sacramento	77	261
Geo	24	m	w	MA	Sacramento	1-Wd Sacramento	77	185
Henry L	31	m	w	MO	Sonoma	Healdsburg & Mendo	91	280
John	43	m	w	AR	El Dorado	Mud Springs Twp	72	73
Loid L	41	m	w	NY	Yolo	Grafton Twp	93	500
GODARE								
Henry	53	m	m	IL	Nevada	Nevada Twp	75	320
GODART								
Albert	40	m	w	FRAN	San Francisco	2-Wd San Francisco	79	223
GODAUT								
Henry	52	m	w	FRAN	San Francisco	San Francisco P O	80	350
GODAY								
Adrian	41	m	w	CHIL	Marin	San Antonio Twp	74	63
GODBEIT								
John	48	m	w	FRAN	Amador	Jackson P O	69	338
GODBERG								
Francis	40	m	w	SWED	Shasta	French Gulch P O	89	466
GODCHAIN								
J	26	m	w	FRAN	San Joaquin	Tulare Twp	86	251
GODCHAN								
L	43	m	w	FRAN	San Joaquin	Tulare Twp	86	252
GODCHAUX								
Lazar	40	m	w	LA	San Francisco	8-Wd San Francisco	82	444
Louis	20	m	w	WI	Sacramento	3-Wd Sacramento	77	287
Sozanes	42	m	w	FRAN	Monterey	San Antonio Twp	74	322
GODCHEAUX								
Jacques	55	m	w	FRAN	San Francisco	San Francisco P O	80	334
GODDALL								
Wm	34	m	w	ENGL	Shasta	Horsetown P O	89	502
GODDARD								
Aug G	40	m	w	ENGL	Sacramento	3-Wd Sacramento	77	295
Jane	44	f	w	OH	Sonoma	Mendocino Twp	91	300
Joseph	40	m	w	ENGL	Nevada	Grass Valley Twp	75	185
Joseph	26	m	w	WI	Nevada	Grass Valley Twp	75	228
Robt R	44	m	w	GA	Sacramento	Mississippi Twp	77	162
S H	23	m	w	ME	Alameda	Oakland	68	201
S R	42	m	w	NY	Nevada	Meadow Lake Twp	75	248
Squire B	37	m	w	NY	San Francisco	San Francisco P O	83	113
Thomas	13	m	w	OH	Nevada	Grass Valley Twp	75	145
William	45	m	w	HDAR	Sacramento	2-Wd Sacramento	77	213
Wm H	55	m	w	VT	Sonoma	Healdsburg & Mendo	91	282
GODDEN								
Richard	18	m	w	FL	San Francisco	San Francisco P O	85	755
GODEFROY								
Alfred	46	m	w	HAMB	San Francisco	San Francisco P O	80	360
GODELL								
Elizabeth	36	f	w	NY	Santa Clara	San Jose Twp	88	186
GODER								
Thomas J	37	m	w	MO	Placer	Gold Run Twp	76	395
GODERIS								
John D	36	m	w	HOLL	San Francisco	11-Wd San Francisc	84	699
GODET								
Louis	45	m	w	FRAN	San Francisco	San Francisco P O	83	286
GODEY								
Alexis	50	m	w	MO	Kern	Bakersfield P O	73	358
Henry	23	m	w	IREL	Sonoma	Bodega Twp	91	249
Joseph	42	m	w	FRAN	Monterey	Monterey Twp	74	351
Julia	50	f	w	OH	San Francisco	5-Wd San Francisco	81	18
Louis	25	m	w	CANA	San Francisco	San Francisco P O	83	166
William	40	m	w	IREL	Solano	Vacaville Twp	90	123
GODFIELD								
Wm	42	m	w	BOHE	San Diego	San Diego	78	495
GODFINKER								
Aaron	46	m	w	POLA	San Francisco	San Francisco P O	80	463
GODFRAY								
Charles W	15	m	w	ME	Yuba	Slate Range Bar Tw	93	672

© 2001 by Heritage Quest. All rights reserved.

California 1870 Census

Series M593

Name	Age	S	R	B-PL	County	Locale	Roll	Pg
GODFREY								
Augustus	45	m	w	MA	San Francisco	8-Wd San Francisco	82	382
B A	43	m	w	NY	Siskiyou	Scott Valley Twp	89	609
Cyrus P	36	m	w	VT	Yuba	Slate Range Bar Tw	93	670
Dennis	53	m	w	IREL	San Francisco	7-Wd San Francisco	81	185
Edward	38	m	w	PA	Santa Clara	Milpitas Twp	88	113
Edward	30	m	m	MA	San Francisco	San Francisco P O	80	404
Geo	50	m	w	ENGL	Alameda	Oakland	68	211
George	28	m	w	OH	Contra Costa	San Pablo Twp	71	354
George	25	m	w	ENGL	San Francisco	San Francisco P O	83	83
Grove K	45	m	w	NY	Siskiyou	Yreka	89	659
Henry	37	m	w	ENGL	San Luis Obispo	San Luis Obispo Tw	87	311
Henry A	40	m	w	TN	Tulare	Kings Rvr Twp	92	253
Ira	30	m	w	NY	San Francisco	San Francisco P O	83	322
J T	44	m	w	CT	San Francisco	San Francisco P O	83	290
Jas	33	m	w	CANA	Sacramento	3-Wd Sacramento	77	272
Jeremiah	58	m	w	IREL	Nevada	Grass Valley Twp	75	173
John	51	m	w	MO	Tehama	Paskenta Twp	92	163
John	31	m	w	IREL	San Francisco	San Francisco P O	83	111
John	25	m	w	CANA	Santa Clara	1-Wd San Jose	88	225
Joseph	46	m	w	FRAN	San Francisco	2-Wd San Francisco	79	180
L	50	m	w	VA	Yuba	East Bear Rvr Twp	93	539
Levi S	35	m	w	CT	San Diego	San Diego	78	510
M	40	f	w	ENGL	San Joaquin	1-Wd Stockton	86	139
Michael	40	m	w	IREL	Santa Clara	1-Wd San Jose	88	242
Nathanil	40	m	m	MA	San Francisco	San Francisco P O	80	398
Thomas	25	m	w	CANA	Santa Clara	2-Wd San Jose	88	317
Thomas B	24	m	w	CANA	Santa Clara	2-Wd San Jose	88	329
Thomas J	37	m	w	IREL	Sonoma	Petaluma Twp	91	316
William	42	m	w	BAVA	San Diego	San Pasqual	78	519
William	35	m	w	NY	San Bernardino	San Bernardino Twp	78	417
Wm H	25	m	w	ME	San Francisco	1-Wd San Francisco	79	106
GODFRIED								
Pat	45	m	w	IREL	San Francisco	7-Wd San Francisco	81	251
GODFRITZ								
Jacob	37	m	w	PRUS	Calaveras	Copperopolis P O	70	257
GODFRY								
Charles	44	m	w	CANA	Yuba	Slate Range Bar Tw	93	674
F G	48	m	w	CT	Santa Clara	Gilroy Twp	88	104
James P	65	m	w	VT	Yuba	Slate Range Bar Tw	93	668
GODIA								
Manuel	36	m	w	CA	San Francisco	San Francisco P O	80	466
GODICK								
Charles	31	m	w	PRUS	Siskiyou	Yreka	89	651
GODIN								
Patrick	37	m	w	IREL	San Francisco	8-Wd San Francisco	82	417
GODINEZ								
Jesus	40	m	w	MEXI	Los Angeles	San Juan Twp	73	624
GODKIM								
Thomas	40	m	w	IREL	San Francisco	San Francisco P O	80	346
GODLER								
Henry	32	m	w	PRUS	Marin	Sausalito Twp	74	72
GODLEY								
Montgomery	42	m	w	PA	San Francisco	San Francisco P O	83	189
GODLUP								
Dedrick	42	m	w	WURT	Sonoma	Analy Twp	91	232
GODORD								
Jno	35	m	w	CANA	Butte	Chico Twp	70	26
GODOY								
Amelia	18	f	w	CA	San Luis Obispo	San Luis Obispo Tw	87	310
Bartola	50	f	w	CHIL	San Francisco	1-Wd San Francisco	79	55
GODRAY								
Conrad	35	m	w	DENM	Tehama	Red Bluff	92	176
GODSCHAUX								
Jos	38	m	w	FRAN	San Francisco	2-Wd San Francisco	79	171
GODSIL								
James	27	m	w	IREL	San Francisco	San Francisco P O	83	334
John	36	m	w	IREL	San Francisco	San Francisco P O	83	300
GODTHALL								
Carohal	60	f	w	PRUS	Sacramento	4-Wd Sacramento	77	358
GODWIN								
A C	41	m	w	VA	San Joaquin	Dent Twp	86	29
Absolom	43	m	w	NC	Humboldt	Mattole Twp	72	286
Dan	48	m	w	WI	San Joaquin	Elliott Twp	86	78
Thomas	30	m	w	VA	Kern	Tehachapi P O	73	354
GODWOOD								
John	32	m	w	ENGL	Humboldt	Bucksport Twp	72	244
GODYOL								
Joseph	40	m	w	SPAI	Santa Barbara	Santa Barbara P O	87	492
GODZIN								
Annie	21	f	w	HANO	San Francisco	San Francisco P O	85	804
GOE								
Ah	42	m	c	CHIN	Mariposa	Mariposa P O	74	102
Ah	35	m	c	CHIN	Sacramento	Georgianna Twp	77	124
Ah	35	m	c	CHIN	Placer	Lincoln P O	76	483
Ah	32	m	c	CHIN	Placer	Dutch Flat P O	76	408
Ah	30	m	c	CHIN	Sacramento	1-Wd Sacramento	77	198
Ah	20	m	c	CHIN	Sacramento	Granite Twp	77	152
Ah	2	f	c	CA	Sacramento	1-Wd Sacramento	77	192
Ah	13	m	c	CHIN	San Mateo	Half Moon Bay P O	87	402
Sing	40	m	c	CHIN	Placer	Dutch Flat P O	76	407
GOEDELL								
Mary	40	f	w	IN	Santa Clara	1-Wd San Jose	88	240
GOEFFER								
Hermon	50	m	w	BADE	Santa Clara	Santa Clara Twp	88	175
GOEGER								
James	34	m	w	HOLL	San Francisco	San Francisco P O	80	456
GOEHLER								
Chas	40	m	w	WURT	Nevada	Nevada Twp	75	308
GOEINS								
Edwd	55	m	w	PA	Solano	Benicia	90	6
GOEMAERE								
Mary	63	f	w	BELG	Solano	Benicia	90	16
GOEN								
Ah	24	m	c	CHIN	Santa Clara	San Jose Twp	88	190
Emanuel	35	m	w	PA	Yolo	Merritt Twp	93	504
Ming	20	m	c	CHIN	Santa Clara	San Jose Twp	88	190
Sing	40	m	c	CHIN	Marin	San Rafael Twp	74	59
GOEPEL								
H	45	m	w	PRUS	Sacramento	3-Wd Sacramento	77	285
GOERERO								
Augustine	21	m	w	CA	Monterey	Castroville Twp	74	329
GOERS								
Charles	25	m	w	OH	Solano	Silveyville Twp	90	91
GOERTZHIEM								
Herman	25	m	w	PRUS	San Francisco	6-Wd San Francisco	81	154
GOESS								
George A	49	m	w	BAVA	Sonoma	Sonoma Twp	91	435
GOETCHINS								
Wm	40	m	w	NY	Shasta	Horsetown P O	89	504
GOETHE								
Matthias	43	m	w	PRUS	Sacramento	4-Wd Sacramento	77	347
GOETJE								
Honorie	40	m	w	FRAN	Nevada	Grass Valley Twp	75	194
GOETSCHINS								
John M	59	m	w	OH	Sacramento	Brighton Twp	77	75
GOETTE								
Henry	50	m	w	SWIT	Yuba	Parks Bar Twp	93	648
GOETYEN								
H	31	m	w	PRUS	Alameda	Murray Twp	68	125
GOETZ								
Beltzer	32	m	w	HDAR	San Francisco	2-Wd San Francisco	79	187
Cathrain	27	f	w	FRAN	San Francisco	San Francisco P O	80	346
Leopold	38	m	w	BADE	San Francisco	2-Wd San Francisco	79	158
Manuel	38	m	w	PRUS	San Francisco	6-Wd San Francisco	81	70
GOETZEN								
Charles	22	m	w	HANO	San Francisco	2-Wd San Francisco	79	227
GOEWEY								
James A	41	m	w	NY	San Francisco	8-Wd San Francisco	82	481
GOEY								
---	19	m	c	CHIN	San Francisco	6-Wd San Francisco	81	64
---	16	m	c	CHIN	Shasta	American Ranch P O	89	500
Ah	43	m	c	CHIN	El Dorado	Mud Springs Twp	72	77
Ah	37	m	c	CHIN	Trinity	Minersville Pct	92	215
Ah	34	m	c	CHIN	San Francisco	San Francisco P O	80	487
Ah	34	m	c	CHIN	San Francisco	3-Wd San Francisco	79	300
Ah	25	m	c	CHIN	El Dorado	Placerville	72	107
Ah	24	m	c	CHIN	San Francisco	11-Wd San Francisc	84	681
Ah	20	m	c	CHIN	San Francisco	San Francisco P O	80	493
Ah	15	m	c	CHIN	Sacramento	2-Wd Sacramento	77	233
Gim	29	f	c	CHIN	Yuba	Rose Bar Twp	93	656
Yee	24	m	c	CHIN	Yuba	Marysville	93	621
GOFER								
Leonard	39	m	w	ME	San Joaquin	2-Wd Stockton	86	206
GOFF								
A M	42	m	w	NY	Yuba	Marysville	93	603
Abner W	42	m	w	OH	Placer	Bath P O	76	454
Almon	37	m	w	NY	San Francisco	San Francisco P O	83	71
Catherine	50	f	w	IREL	San Francisco	San Francisco P O	83	6
Charles P	49	m	w	VT	Alpine	Markleeville P O	69	311
Dwight	42	m	w	CT	San Francisco	1-Wd San Francisco	79	22
Eliza	4	f	m	CA	Mariposa	Maxwell Crk P O	74	147
Frank	36	m	w	RI	Mariposa	Maxwell Crk P O	74	147
Ged	41	m	w	CANA	Santa Clara	Gilroy Twp	88	74
H G	38	m	w	MD	Alameda	Oakland	68	246
Hugh	40	m	w	IREL	Kern	Kernville P O	73	368
James	62	m	w	IREL	Santa Cruz	Santa Cruz Twp	89	393
James	40	m	w	IREL	Yuba	Rose Bar Twp	93	660
James	30	m	w	IL	Santa Clara	Santa Clara Twp	88	139
James H	26	m	w	IL	Humboldt	Mattole Twp	72	285
Jno	40	m	w	NY	San Joaquin	3-Wd Stockton	86	228
John	26	m	w	IREL	San Francisco	San Francisco P O	83	6
Joseph	39	m	w	NY	San Francisco	San Francisco P O	80	535
Leslie	14	m	w	MI	Sacramento	Brighton Twp	77	70
Lewis	35	m	w	FRAN	San Mateo	Redwood City P O	87	375
Marion G	24	m	w	IREL	Colusa	Monroe Twp	71	319
Martin L	39	m	w	OH	Alpine	Monitor P O	69	314
Mary Mrs	48	f	w	IREL	Amador	Fiddletown P O	69	430
Michael	32	m	w	IREL	San Mateo	Redwood City P O	87	375
North Star	17	f	i	CA	Mariposa	Maxwell Crk P O	74	147
P	40	m	w	IREL	Sierra	Butte Twp	89	509
Patience W	23	f	w	RI	San Francisco	8-Wd San Francisco	82	380
Patrick	25	m	w	IREL	San Francisco	8-Wd San Francisco	82	367
Richard	24	m	w	IREL	Yuba	Rose Bar Twp	93	662
S Taylor	23	m	w	IL	Humboldt	Mattole Twp	72	287
Silus M	24	m	w	IL	Humboldt	Mattole Twp	72	287
Stephen	59	m	w	NC	Humboldt	Mattole Twp	72	287
William	25	m	w	POLA	San Francisco	San Francisco P O	83	214
Wm	59	m	b	NY	Butte	Oregon Twp	70	124
GOFFCOTT								
Mary	52	f	w	IREL	San Francisco	2-Wd San Francisco	79	252
GOFFEN								
Wm	44	m	w	IREL	San Francisco	5-Wd San Francisco	81	10

© 2001 by Heritage Quest. All rights reserved.

Name	Age	S	R	B-PL	County	Locale	Series M593 Roll	Pg
GOFFENEY								
Mike	50	m	w	IREL	Butte	Chico Twp	70	42
GOFFENY								
John	31	m	w	NY	Amador	Ione City P O	69	349
GOFFIN								
Cyrus	70	m	b	GA	El Dorado	Salmon Falls Twp	72	131
GOFFING								
John	22	m	w	ME	Mendocino	Little Rvr Twp	74	171
GOFFNEY								
Elizabeth	25	f	w	TN	San Francisco	8-Wd San Francisco	82	405
GOFFOHERD								
Albert	45	m	w	PRUS	San Francisco	San Francisco P O	83	81
GOFFOITT								
Joseph M	29	m	w	TN	Yolo	Cottonwood Twp	93	464
GOFNEY								
Owen	35	m	w	CANA	Santa Clara	Redwood Twp	88	133
GOFORTH								
Angeline	27	f	w	MO	Sonoma	Petaluma Twp	91	323
George	40	m	w	MO	Fresno	Kings Rvr P O	72	213
Levina	67	f	w	TN	Sonoma	Bodega Twp	91	248
Milton P	36	m	w	NC	Sonoma	Vallejo Twp	91	456
William	38	m	w	ENGL	Alameda	Eden Twp	68	83
GOG								
Ah	28	m	c	CHIN	Sacramento	Franklin Twp	77	108
GOGA								
Lucy	38	f	w	WI	Yolo	Cottonwood Twp	93	459
GOGAN								
Bridget	40	f	w	IREL	San Francisco	6-Wd San Francisco	81	92
Catherine	28	f	w	IREL	San Francisco	8-Wd San Francisco	82	468
Cornelia	50	f	w	BADE	San Francisco	San Francisco P O	83	301
Minna	22	f	w	IREL	San Francisco	2-Wd San Francisco	79	169
GOGE								
Elder F	22	m	w	IA	Fresno	Kings Rvr P O	72	206
GOGEL								
Gottlieb	26	m	w	WURT	Stanislaus	Emory Twp	92	23
GOGELIA								
Claude	18	m	w	CA	Stanislaus	Empire Twp	92	65
GOGER								
S	62	m	w	NY	Sierra	Sierra Twp	89	563
GOGERTY								
Owen	50	m	w	IREL	San Francisco	7-Wd San Francisco	81	235
GOGESHALL								
Josias	50	m	w	MA	San Francisco	7-Wd San Francisco	81	282
GOGGIN								
David	24	m	w	IREL	San Mateo	Pescadero P O	87	409
Edwin	33	m	w	IREL	Mendocino	Round Valley Twp	74	219
GOGGINS								
David	30	m	w	IREL	San Francisco	San Francisco P O	83	182
John	30	m	w	IREL	Sacramento	Center Twp	77	85
Patrick	35	m	w	IREL	San Francisco	7-Wd San Francisco	81	163
Richard	52	m	w	MD	Sacramento	2-Wd Sacramento	77	210
Richard	40	m	w	MO	Sacramento	2-Wd Sacramento	77	252
Wm	54	m	w	IREL	Sacramento	4-Wd Sacramento	77	376
GOGHGEN								
Martin	33	m	w	IREL	Santa Clara	Fremont Twp	88	54
GOGHILL								
John	51	m	w	PA	San Francisco	San Francisco P O	80	351
GOGO								
Martin	34	m	w	FRAN	Napa	Napa	75	40
GOGRE								
Geo	19	m	w	NORW	San Francisco	1-Wd San Francisco	79	119
GOH								
Ah	33	m	c	CHIN	San Francisco	7-Wd San Francisco	81	236
Ah	26	m	c	CHIN	San Joaquin	Oneal Twp	86	116
Ah	24	m	c	CHIN	Santa Clara	Santa Clara Twp	88	178
Ang	26	m	c	CHIN	Merced	Snelling P O	74	279
GOHAN								
Edward	36	m	w	CANA	Mono	Bridgeport P O	74	282
GOHD								
Ellen	27	f	w	MO	San Joaquin	1-Wd Stockton	86	122
GOHENE								
Vorstine	27	f	w	OLDE	San Mateo	Redwood City P O	87	375
GOHRANSON								
Oscar F	34	m	w	SWED	Santa Clara	San Jose Twp	88	204
GOHSEN								
Chas	33	m	w	PRUS	Alameda	Oakland	68	214
GOHUN								
Banner G	33	m	w	OH	Santa Cruz	Soquel Twp	89	445
GOI								
---	24	m	c	CHIN	Siskiyou	Cottonwood Twp	89	594
GOIA								
Ah	18	m	c	CHIN	San Francisco	San Francisco P O	80	499
GOIAN								
Frank	36	m	w	ENGL	El Dorado	Placerville Twp	72	100
GOILLEE								
Nicholas	52	m	w	FRAN	San Francisco	San Francisco P O	80	349
GOIN								
Ah	35	m	c	CHIN	San Francisco	San Francisco P O	80	350
Ah	25	m	c	CHIN	Placer	Roseville P O	76	353
Ah	25	m	c	CHIN	Nevada	Nevada Twp	75	298
Ah	25	m	c	CHIN	Sacramento	Georgianna Twp	77	126
Thomas J	27	m	w	KY	Stanislaus	San Joaquin Twp	92	73
GOINE								
Ah	18	m	c	CHIN	Alameda	Oakland	68	161
GOING								
Ah	6	f	c	CA	Trinity	Weaverville Pct	92	228
Benj L	48	m	w	PA	Sacramento	Alabama Twp	77	61
Edward	52	m	w	MD	Sacramento	Alabama Twp	77	61
GOINGS								
Elisha	37	m	w	IL	Sacramento	Alabama Twp	77	61
GOINS								
Elijah	35	m	w	TN	Stanislaus	San Joaquin Twp	92	74
Percy	49	m	w	TN	Stanislaus	San Joaquin Twp	92	74
GOINTLACH								
Fred	25	m	w	PRUS	San Francisco	1-Wd San Francisco	79	60
GOINTZ								
Robert	28	m	w	PRUS	San Francisco	San Francisco P O	80	467
GOIST								
John	38	m	w	WURT	San Francisco	11-Wd San Francisc	84	677
GOK								
Ah	30	m	c	CHIN	Sacramento	Georgianna Twp	77	122
Ah	24	m	c	CHIN	Napa	Napa	75	8
GOKE								
Ah	38	m	c	CHIN	Santa Cruz	Santa Cruz	89	434
Ah	25	m	c	CHIN	Santa Cruz	Pajaro Twp	89	348
Ah	25	m	c	CHIN	Sonoma	Bodega Twp	91	262
GOKEN								
Bermard	33	m	w	HANO	Placer	Bath P O	76	437
GOKEY								
Alexander	32	m	w	MO	Plumas	Indian Twp	77	9
John	29	m	w	CANA	Napa	Napa	75	42
GOL								
Ah	40	m	c	CHIN	San Joaquin	1-Wd Stockton	86	145
Ah	39	m	c	CHIN	San Joaquin	1-Wd Stockton	86	143
Ah	38	m	c	CHIN	Marin	Bolinas Twp	74	1
GOLAY								
Andrew	33	m	w	IREL	Alameda	Washington Twp	68	296
GOLBELS								
Hugo	46	m	w	SAXO	Placer	Bath P O	76	426
GOLD								
Ann	30	f	w	IREL	San Francisco	8-Wd San Francisco	82	468
August	31	m	w	GERM	Sonoma	Sonoma Twp	91	433
Chas	14	m	w	MA	San Francisco	San Francisco P O	85	810
Francis E	42	m	w	PA	Calaveras	San Andreas P O	70	166
Hannah	58	f	w	PRUS	San Francisco	San Francisco P O	83	268
Henry	39	m	w	ENGL	Sacramento	4-Wd Sacramento	77	350
Joseph	35	m	w	NH	San Francisco	San Francisco P O	83	144
William	34	m	w	IREL	Marin	Tomales Twp	74	80
GOLDALDA								
P	37	m	w	ITAL	Calaveras	Copperopolis P O	70	231
GOLDARACIMA								
Miguel	46	m	w	SPAI	Los Angeles	Los Angeles	73	518
GOLDBAUM								
A	25	m	w	PRUS	Los Angeles	Soledad Twp	73	631
Louis	38	m	w	PRUS	San Francisco	3-Wd San Francisco	79	322
Simon	21	m	w	PRUS	Los Angeles	Los Angeles	73	525
GOLDBEAUM								
Henry	45	m	w	PRUS	Plumas	Washington Twp	77	56
GOLDBERG								
Adolph	26	m	w	PRUS	San Francisco	8-Wd San Francisco	82	368
Alaxander	38	m	w	PRUS	Sacramento	San Joaquin Twp	77	406
Augusta	35	f	w	RUSS	San Bernardino	San Bernardino Twp	78	421
Charles	31	m	w	DENM	San Francisco	7-Wd San Francisco	81	168
Daniel	40	m	w	POLA	San Francisco	San Francisco P O	80	409
Ezekiel	45	m	w	POLA	San Francisco	San Francisco P O	83	369
H	36	m	w	PRUS	Sacramento	1-Wd Sacramento	77	177
Rebecca	17	f	w	CA	Sonoma	Petaluma Twp	91	339
Samuel	22	m	w	PRUS	San Francisco	San Francisco P O	85	757
Solomon	48	m	w	PRUS	San Francisco	San Francisco P O	83	234
GOLDEN								
Anne	20	f	w	ENGL	San Francisco	8-Wd San Francisco	82	452
Benj	22	m	b	GA	Nevada	Nevada Twp	75	274
Danl	42	m	w	IREL	San Francisco	7-Wd San Francisco	81	233
Darby	50	m	w	IREL	Alameda	Eden Twp	68	67
Ellen	55	f	w	IREL	San Francisco	San Francisco P O	83	413
Ellen	25	f	w	IREL	San Francisco	San Francisco P O	83	363
Eva	24	f	w	NY	San Francisco	6-Wd San Francisco	81	51
Genevive	28	f	w	NY	Solano	Benicia	90	17
Gertrude	20	f	w	BAVA	San Francisco	San Francisco P O	80	427
James	44	m	w	IREL	Marin	Bolinas Twp	74	4
John	50	m	w	ENGL	Contra Costa	Martinez P O	71	411
John	40	m	w	FRAN	San Francisco	San Francisco P O	83	163
John	35	m	w	IREL	Sacramento	San Joaquin Twp	77	394
John	34	m	w	IREL	San Francisco	2-Wd San Francisco	79	283
Julia	41	f	w	IREL	El Dorado	Kelsey Twp	72	62
Julia	26	f	w	IREL	Nevada	Grass Valley Twp	75	166
Margaret	29	f	w	NY	Solano	Benicia	90	16
Martin J	31	m	w	IREL	Los Angeles	Los Angeles Twp	73	491
Michael	27	m	w	IREL	San Francisco	San Francisco P O	83	195
Michael	24	m	w	IREL	San Francisco	San Francisco P O	83	166
Pat	28	m	w	IREL	San Francisco	7-Wd San Francisco	81	275
Patrick	33	m	w	IREL	San Luis Obispo	Salinas Twp	87	293
Robert	31	m	w	IREL	Sonoma	Bodega Twp	91	263
Saml	29	m	w	NH	San Joaquin	Elliott Twp	86	70
Thomas	50	m	w	IREL	San Francisco	8-Wd San Francisco	82	483
Thos	32	m	w	IREL	Sacramento	3-Wd Sacramento	77	270
Vinnie	15	f	w	CA	Solano	Benicia	90	16
W	34	m	w	OH	San Joaquin	Tulare Twp	86	263
William	37	m	w	MO	Nevada	Meadow Lake Twp	75	261
GOLDER								
Field	60	m	w	TN	Contra Costa	Martinez P O	71	395
Louis	43	m	w	WURT	San Mateo	Redwood City P O	87	376
GOLDERAN								
Marie	50	f	w	MEXI	San Diego	Temecula Dist	78	527

© 2001 by Heritage Quest. All rights reserved.

California 1870 Census

Name	Age	S	R	B-PL	County	Locale	Series M593 Roll	Pg
GOLDETTI								
Jack	35	m	w	ITAL	Calaveras	Copperopolis P O	70	244
GOLDFISH								
B	35	m	w	PRUS	Sonoma	Santa Rosa	91	420
Joseph	30	m	w	PRUS	Monterey	San Juan Twp	74	401
GOLDIE								
Robert	68	m	w	SCOT	Sacramento	Franklin Twp	77	107
GOLDIN								
J	70	m	w	PA	Sierra	Forest Twp	89	529
GOLDING								
Ann	28	f	w	IREL	Solano	Vallejo	90	200
James	30	m	w	ENGL	San Francisco	San Francisco P O	85	718
James	28	m	w	NY	San Francisco	5-Wd San Francisco	81	15
Thomas	50	m	w	IREL	Sonoma	Vallejo Twp	91	460
Thomas	22	m	w	IREL	San Francisco	3-Wd San Francisco	79	294
Wm	38	m	w	CT	Solano	Vallejo	90	200
GOLDKOFER								
William	42	m	w	WURT	Santa Cruz	Watsonville	89	366
GOLDMAN								
Abram	30	m	w	RUSS	San Francisco	1-Wd San Francisco	79	60
Adolph	20	m	w	BAVA	Yolo	Cache Crk Twp	93	427
Alexander	27	m	w	PRUS	Yolo	Grafton Twp	93	481
Bertha	20	f	w	BAVA	San Francisco	8-Wd San Francisco	82	425
Charles	39	m	w	DENM	Sacramento	Franklin Twp	77	119
Charles	26	m	w	BAVA	Yolo	Cache Crk Twp	93	422
Isaac	47	m	w	BAVA	San Francisco	11-Wd San Francisc	84	510
Isaac W	34	m	w	BAVA	San Francisco	8-Wd San Francisco	82	485
Joseph	46	m	w	PRUS	San Francisco	8-Wd San Francisco	82	454
Lewis	23	m	w	POLA	Merced	Snelling P O	74	277
Max	26	m	w	BAVA	San Francisco	San Francisco P O	80	537
Rebecca	21	f	w	POLA	San Francisco	San Francisco P O	80	351
Samuel	55	m	w	POLA	San Francisco	7-Wd San Francisco	81	179
Simon	22	m	w	PRUS	Marin	Bolinas Twp	74	1
Tilly	14	f	w	PA	Sacramento	2-Wd Sacramento	77	217
GOLDMEYER								
Louis	48	m	w	HDAR	San Francisco	11-Wd San Francisc	84	459
GOLDNER								
C	65	m	w	PRUS	Alameda	Oakland	68	175
H	43	m	w	PRUS	Amador	Jackson P O	69	320
Julius	40	m	w	PRUS	El Dorado	Placerville	72	108
GOLDONI								
Aleander	25	m	w	SWIT	Placer	Bath P O	76	444
GOLDRICH								
Ann	18	f	w	IREL	San Francisco	11-Wd San Francisc	84	489
GOLDRIN								
Jose	20	m	w	PORT	Marin	Bolinas Twp	74	4
GOLDS								
Wm H	33	m	w	PRUS	Sutter	Sutter Twp	92	121
GOLDSBERRY								
William	26	m	w	IN	Placer	Auburn P O	76	374
GOLDSBORO								
Martha	50	f	b	VA	San Francisco	6-Wd San Francisco	81	106
GOLDSBOROUGH								
J R	59	m	w	DC	Solano	Vallejo	90	199
GOLDSBROW								
Margt	47	f	w	CANA	San Francisco	6-Wd San Francisco	81	136
GOLDSBY								
Adaline	26	f	b	MS	Placer	Pino Twp	76	470
Joseph L	43	m	w	GA	Placer	Pino Twp	76	470
GOLDSCHMIDT								
Henry	29	m	w	PRUS	San Diego	San Pasqual Valley	78	524
GOLDSCHMITH								
Henry	42	m	w	PRUS	San Francisco	3-Wd San Francisco	79	326
GOLDSINE								
Mary	60	f	w	PRUS	San Francisco	7-Wd San Francisco	81	192
GOLDSMIDT								
A	34	m	w	CT	Yuba	Marysville	93	634
GOLDSMITH								
A	38	m	w	PRUS	Nevada	Nevada Twp	75	276
A M	26	m	w	RUSS	San Francisco	San Francisco P O	83	282
Anson	28	m	w	PRUS	San Francisco	San Francisco P O	83	110
Ed	26	m	w	PRUS	Nevada	Nevada Twp	75	276
Geo	40	m	w	IREL	San Francisco	1-Wd San Francisco	79	95
Gustave	36	m	w	PRUS	San Francisco	San Francisco P O	83	280
Henry	31	m	w	BAVA	San Francisco	8-Wd San Francisco	82	441
Henry	29	m	w	PRUS	San Diego	San Pasqual	78	519
Isaac	53	m	w	PRUS	San Francisco	8-Wd San Francisco	82	452
J G	55	m	w	OH	San Francisco	San Francisco P O	83	118
Joe	26	m	w	PRUS	Merced	Snelling P O	74	247
John	29	m	w	IL	Lake	Lower Lake	73	421
Joseph	54	m	w	MA	San Francisco	8-Wd San Francisco	82	454
L	39	m	w	HESS	San Joaquin	3-Wd Stockton	86	229
Leon	43	m	w	FRAN	Sacramento	2-Wd Sacramento	77	229
Levi	27	m	w	GERM	San Joaquin	2-Wd Stockton	86	164
Louisa	10	f	w	CA	San Francisco	1-Wd San Francisco	79	43
Mary	40	f	w	IREL	San Francisco	2-Wd San Francisco	79	267
N	35	m	w	PRUS	San Francisco	San Francisco P O	83	302
Sam	36	m	w	KY	Butte	Chico Twp	70	15
Samuel	27	m	w	PRUS	Los Angeles	Wilmington Twp	73	645
Sarah	24	f	w	NY	San Francisco	San Francisco P O	83	144
Saul	35	m	w	BAVA	San Francisco	8-Wd San Francisco	82	446
Simon	41	m	w	HDAR	San Francisco	San Francisco P O	83	229
Simon	25	m	w	NY	San Francisco	8-Wd San Francisco	82	356
W C	40	m	w	IN	Lake	Lower Lake	73	422
William E	45	m	w	MA	Santa Clara	Santa Clara Twp	88	156
Wilson P	63	m	w	NJ	Yolo	Cottonwood Twp	93	460

Name	Age	S	R	B-PL	County	Locale	Series M593 Roll	Pg
GOLDSTEEN								
D	30	m	w	PRUS	Lassen	Susanville Twp	73	441
GOLDSTEIN								
Dora	25	f	w	AUSL	San Francisco	8-Wd San Francisco	82	460
Emanuel	49	m	w	PRUS	San Francisco	8-Wd San Francisco	82	452
Eva	30	f	w	GERM	San Francisco	San Francisco P O	83	140
Henry	31	m	w	PRUS	San Francisco	San Francisco P O	83	253
Israel	45	m	w	BAVA	San Francisco	San Francisco P O	80	531
Jacob	39	m	w	RUSS	San Francisco	San Francisco P O	80	532
Jacob	31	m	w	GERM	San Francisco	San Francisco P O	83	137
Leon	21	m	w	LA	San Francisco	San Francisco P O	83	368
Morris	55	m	w	PRUS	San Francisco	San Francisco P O	83	179
Nathan	36	m	w	PRUS	Butte	Ophir Twp	70	94
Peter	57	m	w	PRUS	San Francisco	2-Wd San Francisco	79	242
Samuel	41	m	w	POLA	Los Angeles	Santa Ana Twp	73	610
Sophia	37	f	w	PRUS	Los Angeles	Los Angeles	73	550
Therese	38	f	w	BAVA	Santa Clara	1-Wd San Jose	88	245
William	31	m	w	RUSS	San Francisco	11-Wd San Francisc	84	551
William	30	m	w	PRUS	San Francisco	8-Wd San Francisco	82	328
GOLDSTEN								
Jacob	28	m	w	PRUS	San Francisco	5-Wd San Francisco	81	13
James G	43	m	w	TN	Yuba	North East Twp	93	646
GOLDSTIEN								
Henry	50	m	w	POLA	Sonoma	Petaluma Twp	91	319
Isaac	26	m	w	BAVA	Tulare	Visalia	92	298
GOLDSTINE								
Ester	40	f	w	PRUS	San Francisco	7-Wd San Francisco	81	191
Fred	26	m	w	WURT	Sacramento	Granite Twp	77	143
James	25	m	w	ENGL	San Francisco	7-Wd San Francisco	81	182
Samuel	35	m	w	PRUS	Solano	Silveyville Twp	90	83
GOLDSTON								
Mitchel	50	m	w	PRUS	San Francisco	8-Wd San Francisco	82	450
GOLDSTONE								
Charles	39	m	w	PRUS	San Francisco	San Francisco P O	83	52
Harris	48	m	w	PRUS	Sonoma	Petaluma Twp	91	334
Samuel	38	m	w	PRUS	San Francisco	San Francisco P O	83	201
Sarah S	18	f	w	NC	San Francisco	San Francisco P O	83	201
GOLDSTORIO								
James	45	m	w	ENGL	Sacramento	2-Wd Sacramento	77	233
GOLDSWORTHY								
Collen	37	m	w	ENGL	Nevada	Grass Valley Twp	75	183
James	40	m	w	ENGL	Los Angeles	Los Angeles	73	571
Jane	45	f	w	ENGL	Sonoma	Petaluma Twp	91	319
John	56	m	w	ENGL	Santa Clara	Redwood Twp	88	129
John	29	m	w	ENGL	Los Angeles	Los Angeles	73	507
John	29	m	m	ENGL	Alpine	Monitor P O	69	313
John	28	m	w	WI	Santa Clara	Redwood Twp	88	129
John	23	m	w	ENGL	Nevada	Grass Valley Twp	75	176
Joseph	31	m	w	ENGL	Trinity	Weaverville Pct	92	230
Josiah	37	m	w	ENGL	Mariposa	Mariposa P O	74	117
Paul	18	m	w	WI	Santa Clara	Santa Clara Twp	88	135
R	22	m	w	WI	Del Norte	Mountain Twp	71	474
Richard	25	m	w	ENGL	Nevada	Grass Valley Twp	75	162
Richard	22	m	w	WI	Santa Clara	Redwood Twp	88	129
Stephen	30	m	w	ENGL	Nevada	Grass Valley Twp	75	183
T	41	m	w	ENGL	Amador	Amador City P O	69	395
Thomas	24	m	w	WI	Santa Clara	Redwood Twp	88	129
Wesley	20	m	w	WI	Santa Clara	Redwood Twp	88	129
William	30	m	w	ENGL	Nevada	Grass Valley Twp	75	162
Wm	44	m	w	ENGL	Santa Clara	Almaden Twp	88	9
GOLDTHWAIT								
Arnold	47	m	w	NH	Sacramento	Franklin Twp	77	105
J	31	m	w	ME	San Joaquin	2-Wd Stockton	86	163
S B	36	m	w	ME	Sierra	Lincoln Twp	89	549
GOLDTREE								
Morris	21	m	w	PRUS	San Luis Obispo	San Luis Obispo Tw	87	310
Ne	23	m	w	PRUS	Monterey	Monterey	74	355
GOLDWATER								
Joseph	38	m	w	PRUS	San Francisco	San Francisco P O	83	201
Michael	48	m	w	RUSS	San Francisco	San Francisco P O	83	301
GOLDWORTHY								
J	35	m	w	ENGL	Sierra	Butte Twp	89	508
J	30	m	w	ENGL	Sierra	Butte Twp	89	508
T	58	m	w	ENGL	Merced	Snelling P O	74	250
W	27	m	w	ENGL	Merced	Snelling P O	74	250
GOLDY								
James	9	m	w	CA	El Dorado	Placerville	72	126
M	1	f	w	ME	Santa Clara	Gilroy Twp	88	77
GOLE								
Julia	42	f	w	MD	Sacramento	2-Wd Sacramento	77	219
Samuel	53	m	m	MD	Sacramento	2-Wd Sacramento	77	219
GOLEHOUSE								
Fred	40	m	w	KY	San Francisco	11-Wd San Francisc	84	606
GOLET								
Nelson	38	m	w	CANA	Sonoma	Bodega Twp	91	250
GOLEY								
Anne	40	f	w	IREL	Alameda	Oakland	68	201
GOLEYHER								
Pat	40	m	w	IREL	Los Angeles	Los Angeles Twp	73	478
GOLGERT								
Fredrick	30	m	w	PRUS	Mendocino	Point Arena Twp	74	213
GOLIN								
Frank W	30	m	w	IL	Santa Clara	Redwood Twp	88	120
GOLINDA								
Antonio	30	m	w	CA	Santa Clara	San Jose Twp	88	184
Juan	93	m	w	CA	Santa Clara	San Jose Twp	88	184
Maria	25	f	w	CA	Santa Clara	1-Wd San Jose	88	240

© 2001 by Heritage Quest. All rights reserved.

Name	Age	S	R	B-PL	County	Locale	Roll	Pg
Narcissio	68	m	w	CA	Santa Clara	San Jose Twp	88	184
GOLL								
Francis	70	m	w	HOLL	Los Angeles	Los Angeles Twp	73	471
GOLLAHER								
Allen	32	m	w	VA	Yuba	Rose Bar Twp	93	665
GOLLAIS								
Luco	29	m	i	CA	Los Angeles	Los Angeles	73	500
GOLLASEN								
Henry	24	m	w	SWED	San Francisco	San Francisco P O	83	306
GOLLEGO								
Romaldo	26	m	w	CA	Marin	Novato Twp	74	10
GOLLER								
John	35	m	w	WURT	San Francisco	2-Wd San Francisco	79	185
GOLLEY								
John	60	m	w	FRAN	San Francisco	2-Wd San Francisco	79	186
GOLLINDO								
Rafael	40	m	w	MEXI	Los Angeles	Los Angeles	73	571
GOLLINS								
James	45	m	w	IREL	Sacramento	Franklin Twp	77	118
GOLLOR								
John	43	m	w	BAVA	Los Angeles	Los Angeles	73	550
GOLM								
Wm	26	m	w	ME	Butte	Kimshew Tpw	70	80
GOLMER								
John	30	m	w	WURT	Los Angeles	Los Angeles	73	538
GOLOTE								
Mand F	25	m	w	AZOR	Monterey	Castroville Twp	74	333
GOLPHIN								
Cyrus	84	m	b	SC	El Dorado	Salmon Falls Twp	72	130
GOLSIDES								
H	34	m	w	CHIL	Alameda	Oakland	68	166
GOLSIER								
H M	40	m	w	MEXI	Amador	Sutter Crk P O	69	397
GOLSTONE								
J B	30	m	w	PRUS	San Francisco	San Francisco P O	83	314
GOLSUDA								
Antonio	17	m	w	ITAL	San Mateo	Schoolhouse Statio	87	340
GOLTES								
Pablo	25	m	w	SPAI	Los Angeles	Los Angeles	73	568
GOLVAN								
Stephen	60	m	i	MEXI	Inyo	Lone Pine Twp	73	334
GOLVER								
Albert	30	m	w	MA	Sonoma	Analy Twp	91	222
GOLVIN								
J	55	m	w	IREL	San Francisco	San Francisco P O	85	795
James	35	m	w	IREL	Merced	Snelling P O	74	267
GOLVIS								
Charles	35	m	w	CHIL	Yolo	Buckeye Twp	93	409
GOM								
Ah	56	m	c	CHIN	Nevada	Eureka Twp	75	141
Ah	42	m	c	CHIN	Placer	Auburn P O	76	374
Ah	39	m	c	CHIN	Nevada	Eureka Twp	75	127
Ah	32	m	c	CHIN	Placer	Newcastle Twp	76	477
Ah	28	m	c	CHIN	Nevada	Meadow Lake Twp	75	257
Ah	28	m	c	CHIN	Nevada	Meadow Lake Twp	75	256
Ah	24	m	c	CHIN	Nevada	Meadow Lake Twp	75	255
Chas	33	m	w	MI	San Joaquin	Tulare Twp	86	258
Han	25	m	c	CHIN	Sacramento	1-Wd Sacramento	77	191
GOMACH								
Michel	33	m	w	CANA	Yolo	Grafton Twp	93	487
GOMAN								
Santiago	59	m	m	MEXI	Placer	Auburn P O	76	383
GOMAS								
H M	50	m	w	MEXI	Amador	Sutter Crk P O	69	407
Joseph	26	m	w	PORT	Mendocino	Big Rvr Twp	74	162
Julian	39	m	w	MEXI	Marin	San Rafael Twp	74	46
Santas	48	m	w	MEXI	Tuolumne	Columbia P O	93	349
GOMBEFER								
John	37	m	w	WURT	Yolo	Putah Twp	93	516
GOMBERT								
Augustus	40	m	w	HCAS	Amador	Fiddletown P O	69	430
GOMBS								
Frank	38	m	w	CANA	Nevada	Eureka Twp	75	139
GOMBURG								
Ferdinand	47	m	w	GERM	San Joaquin	2-Wd Stockton	86	213
GOMEN								
J	25	m	w	ITAL	Santa Clara	Almaden Twp	88	19
GOMER								
J	22	m	w	IREL	Lake	Morgan Valley	73	425
Julius	38	m	w	IL	San Francisco	San Francisco P O	80	456
Percey	26	m	w	IL	Contra Costa	Martinez P O	71	409
GOMERS								
Frank	43	m	w	ITAL	Calaveras	San Andreas P O	70	175
GOMERTO								
Jean	27	m	w	FRAN	Santa Clara	Almaden Twp	88	13
GOMES								
Frank	50	m	w	AZOR	Nevada	Washington Twp	75	346
Merced	18	f	w	CA	Santa Clara	Almaden Twp	88	20
Saturine	13	m	w	CA	Santa Clara	Gilroy Twp	88	98
Thomas	15	m	w	CA	Alameda	Murray Twp	68	126
GOMEZ								
Aliya	50	f	w	MEXI	Calaveras	San Andreas P O	70	210
Anson	55	m	w	MEXI	San Mateo	Half Moon Bay P O	87	394
Antone	40	m	w	AZOR	Marin	San Rafael Twp	74	32
Antone	30	m	w	PORT	Siskiyou	Hamburg Twp	89	597
Antonio	45	m	w	MEXI	Santa Barbara	Santa Barbara P O	87	477
Antonio	26	m	w	CA	Santa Clara	1-Wd San Jose	88	277
Antonio	23	m	w	CA	Santa Clara	Milpitas Twp	88	112
Chis	55	m	w	CHIL	El Dorado	Kelsey Twp	72	58
Feriz	34	m	w	CHIL	Fresno	Millerton P O	72	165
Florencia	40	m	w	CHIL	Santa Clara	2-Wd San Jose	88	302
Frances	40	m	w	PORT	Contra Costa	Martinez P O	71	438
Francis	31	m	w	PORT	Nevada	Rough & Ready Twp	75	329
Frank	40	m	w	PORT	San Francisco	1-Wd San Francisco	79	118
Frank	32	m	w	INDI	San Francisco	8-Wd San Francisco	82	423
Frank	22	m	w	PORT	Solano	Montezuma Twp	90	66
Ignatio	14	m	w	CA	Santa Clara	Santa Clara Twp	88	177
Jesus	50	m	w	MEXI	Calaveras	San Andreas P O	70	182
Jesus	24	m	w	MEXI	Fresno	Millerton P O	72	156
Jose	30	m	w	CHIL	Los Angeles	Wilmington Twp	73	641
Jose	30	m	w	CHIL	Los Angeles	Los Angeles	73	523
Jose J	23	m	w	CA	Santa Barbara	Santa Barbara P O	87	471
Jose M	49	m	w	MEXI	Monterey	San Juan Twp	74	393
Joseph	23	m	w	AZOR	Contra Costa	Martinez P O	71	394
Joseph F	48	m	w	SPAI	Santa Barbara	San Buenaventura P	87	436
Juan	22	m	w	MEXI	Kern	Bakersfield P O	73	363
Juan E	35	m	w	CA	Monterey	Monterey Twp	74	351
Julian	62	m	w	MEXI	Santa Barbara	San Buenaventura P	87	440
L	22	m	b	INDI	Lake	Lower Lake	73	418
Manual	48	m	w	MEXI	Yuba	New York Twp	93	642
Manual	34	m	w	PORT	Yuba	New York Twp	93	641
Manuel	43	m	w	ARGE	Santa Clara	1-Wd San Jose	88	256
Manuel	42	m	w	PORT	Marin	Nicasio Twp	74	19
Manuel	29	m	w	AZOR	Marin	Novato Twp	74	9
Manuel	19	m	w	PORT	Marin	San Rafael Twp	74	33
Maria	35	f	w	MEXI	San Joaquin	2-Wd Stockton	86	167
Mary	45	f	w	MEXI	San Francisco	2-Wd San Francisco	79	223
Mary	33	f	w	MEXI	San Francisco	San Francisco P O	83	211
Maxim	37	m	w	MEXI	Fresno	Millerton P O	72	159
Nestor	25	m	w	OH	Sonoma	Santa Rosa	91	429
Rafiel	36	m	w	CA	Monterey	Monterey Twp	74	350
Resereto	38	m	w	MEXI	San Mateo	Half Moon Bay P O	87	393
Sylvester	37	m	w	CA	San Diego	San Pasqual	78	522
Sylvester	36	m	w	CA	San Diego	Pala Valley Reserv	78	480
Thomas	15	m	w	PERU	San Francisco	11-Wd San Francisc	84	593
Tomas	55	m	w	MEXI	Kern	Tehachapi P O	73	356
GOMLEY								
Jennie	22	f	w	MA	Sacramento	4-Wd Sacramento	77	333
GOMLIN								
Lafayette	34	m	w	KY	Sacramento	2-Wd Sacramento	77	210
GOMM								
John	25	m	w	ENGL	Marin	Tomales Twp	74	87
GOMO								
John A	43	m	w	FRAN	Solano	Benicia	90	8
GOMON								
Glous	35	m	w	SWIT	San Francisco	San Francisco P O	85	756
GOMPH								
John	25	m	w	CANA	San Mateo	Redwood Twp	87	361
GON								
Ah	65	m	c	CHIN	Mariposa	Mariposa P O	74	102
Ah	60	m	c	CHIN	Placer	Colfax P O	76	390
Ah	56	m	c	CHIN	Sacramento	Georgianna Twp	77	123
Ah	42	m	c	CHIN	Sacramento	Georgianna Twp	77	133
Ah	42	m	c	CHIN	Calaveras	San Andreas P O	70	199
Ah	40	m	c	CHIN	Sacramento	Georgianna Twp	77	128
Ah	38	m	c	CHIN	Alameda	Oakland	68	158
Ah	37	m	c	CHIN	San Francisco	San Francisco P O	80	446
Ah	37	m	c	CHIN	Placer	Lincoln P O	76	484
Ah	36	m	c	CHIN	Placer	Clipper Gap P O	76	393
Ah	36	m	c	CHIN	San Francisco	San Francisco P O	80	516
Ah	36	m	c	CHIN	San Francisco	San Francisco P O	80	520
Ah	36	m	c	CHIN	Sierra	Table Rock Twp	89	577
Ah	34	m	c	CHIN	Sacramento	Franklin Twp	77	116
Ah	33	m	c	CHIN	Sierra	Sears Twp	89	554
Ah	32	m	c	CHIN	Sacramento	Franklin Twp	77	118
Ah	31	m	c	CHIN	San Francisco	San Francisco P O	80	519
Ah	30	m	c	CHIN	Sierra	Sears Twp	89	553
Ah	30	m	c	CHIN	Tuolumne	Chinese Camp P O	93	364
Ah	30	f	c	CHIN	San Francisco	San Francisco P O	80	441
Ah	30	m	c	CHIN	Sacramento	Georgianna Twp	77	125
Ah	29	m	c	CHIN	Sacramento	Granite Twp	77	141
Ah	28	m	c	CHIN	Alameda	Oakland	68	158
Ah	27	m	c	CHIN	Sacramento	Georgianna Twp	77	123
Ah	26	m	c	CHIN	Sacramento	Franklin Twp	77	119
Ah	26	m	c	CHIN	Butte	Chico Twp	70	51
Ah	25	m	c	CHIN	Sacramento	Georgianna Twp	77	125
Ah	25	m	c	CHIN	Sacramento	Franklin Twp	77	119
Ah	25	f	c	CHIN	Sacramento	1-Wd Sacramento	77	197
Ah	24	m	c	CHIN	Sacramento	1-Wd Sacramento	77	195
Ah	24	m	c	CHIN	Sacramento	Georgianna Twp	77	133
Ah	22	m	c	CHIN	Siskiyou	Cottonwood Twp	89	594
Ah	22	m	c	CHIN	Sierra	Gibson Twp	89	538
Ah	21	m	c	CHIN	San Francisco	8-Wd San Francisco	82	357
Ah	21	m	c	CHIN	Solano	Suisun Twp	90	98
Ah	21	m	c	CHIN	Sacramento	Georgianna Twp	77	123
Ah	20	m	c	CHIN	Sierra	Sears Twp	89	554
Ah	20	m	c	CHIN	Trinity	Douglas	92	237
Ah	20	m	c	CHIN	San Francisco	San Francisco P O	80	436
Ah	20	f	c	CHIN	Butte	Hamilton Twp	70	75
Ah	19	m	c	CHIN	San Francisco	8-Wd San Francisco	82	310
Ah	18	m	c	CHIN	Sacramento	Georgianna Twp	77	134
Ah	16	m	c	CHIN	Santa Clara	Gilroy Twp	88	83
Ah	15	m	c	CHIN	Solano	Vallejo	90	173
An	31	m	c	CHIN	Amador	Ione City P O	69	366

© 2001 by Heritage Quest. All rights reserved.

California 1870 Census

Series M593

Name	Age	S	R	B-PL	County	Locale	Roll	Pg
Ash	15	m	c	CHIN	Yolo	Cache Crk Twp	93	446
Charley	28	m	c	CHIN	Lake	Lower Lake	73	416
Chee	38	m	c	CHIN	Napa	Napa Twp	75	58
Die	32	f	c	CHIN	Kern	Havilah P O	73	338
Fon	25	m	c	CHIN	Del Norte	Happy Camp Twp	71	469
Han	27	f	c	CHIN	Placer	Bath P O	76	439
Hong	15	m	c	CHIN	Trinity	North Fork Twp	92	219
John	43	m	w	TN	Inyo	Lone Pine Twp	73	334
Lo	27	m	c	CHIN	San Joaquin	Oneal Twp	86	117
Lon	12	m	c	CHIN	Sacramento	4-Wd Sacramento	77	375
Nack	32	m	c	CHIN	Yuba	Marysville	93	622
Own	21	m	c	CHIN	Nevada	Nevada Twp	75	313
Sun	21	f	c	CHIN	Placer	Colfax P O	76	388
Tey	24	m	c	CHIN	Trinity	Junction City Pct	92	208
Tip	30	m	c	CHIN	Santa Clara	Gilroy Twp	88	83
Wong	45	m	c	CHIN	Sierra	Sears Twp	89	554
Yon	15	m	c	CHIN	San Francisco	2-Wd San Francisco	79	228
GONA								
Ah	30	m	c	CHIN	Santa Clara	1-Wd San Jose	88	266
GONANELLA								
Peter	42	m	w	FRAN	San Francisco	San Francisco P O	80	464
GONAVER								
Geo	40	m	w	OH	Butte	Ophir Twp	70	120
GONCALVES								
Antone	40	m	w	PORT	Alameda	Washington Twp	68	288
Moses	28	m	w	PORT	San Francisco	8-Wd San Francisco	82	288
GONCH								
Harriet	78	f	w	MA	Los Angeles	San Gabriel Twp	73	598
GONCIN								
Pedro	55	m	w	MEXI	Calaveras	Copperopolis P O	70	260
GONCY								
F M	63	m	w	NY	Santa Clara	Gilroy Twp	88	87
GONDY								
Elizabeth	31	f	w	MO	San Diego	San Diego	78	501
GONE								
Ah	41	m	c	CHIN	San Francisco	San Francisco P O	80	443
Ah	36	m	c	CHIN	San Francisco	San Francisco P O	80	491
Ah	31	m	c	CHIN	Nevada	Rough & Ready Twp	75	338
Ah	26	m	c	CHIN	San Francisco	San Francisco P O	80	360
Ah	24	m	c	CHIN	Trinity	Weaverville Pct	92	230
Ah	24	m	c	CHIN	San Francisco	San Francisco P O	80	442
Ah	22	m	c	CHIN	San Francisco	6-Wd San Francisco	81	62
Ah	17	m	c	CHIN	Trinity	Junction City Pct	92	210
Ah	13	m	c	CHIN	Trinity	Lewiston Pct	92	211
Ah	13	m	c	CHIN	Trinity	Douglas	92	235
Hon	30	m	c	CHIN	Trinity	Junction City Pct	92	206
GONEAS								
H	43	m	w	MEXI	Alameda	Murray Twp	68	104
Jesus	32	m	i	MEXI	Inyo	Cerro Gordo Twp	73	322
GONEL								
Henry	25	m	w	FRAN	Amador	Jackson P O	69	325
Henry	24	m	w	FRAN	Amador	Volcano P O	69	388
GONEMARI								
Peter	50	m	w	FRAN	San Francisco	1-Wd San Francisco	79	54
GONETZ								
Davis	42	m	w	CT	San Francisco	5-Wd San Francisco	81	10
GONEY								
Ah	14	m	c	CHIN	San Francisco	San Francisco P O	85	814
GONG								
---	26	m	c	CHIN	Siskiyou	Yreka	89	661
---	24	m	c	CHIN	Siskiyou	Hamburg Twp	89	597
---	21	m	c	CHIN	Siskiyou	Yreka Twp	89	668
Ah	52	m	c	CHIN	Placer	Auburn P O	76	374
Ah	50	f	c	CHIN	San Francisco	San Francisco P O	80	506
Ah	50	m	c	CHIN	Placer	Blue Canyon P O	76	419
Ah	46	m	c	CHIN	San Francisco	San Francisco P O	80	502
Ah	45	m	c	CHIN	Sierra	Lincoln Twp	89	546
Ah	45	m	c	CHIN	Trinity	Douglas	92	237
Ah	44	m	c	CHIN	Trinity	Lewiston Pct	92	211
Ah	44	m	c	CHIN	Santa Clara	Santa Clara Twp	88	168
Ah	43	m	c	CHIN	San Francisco	San Francisco P O	80	527
Ah	42	m	c	CHIN	Trinity	Minersville Pct	92	203
Ah	41	m	c	CHIN	San Francisco	San Francisco P O	80	436
Ah	41	m	c	CHIN	San Francisco	San Francisco P O	80	526
Ah	41	m	c	CHIN	San Francisco	San Francisco P O	80	523
Ah	40	m	c	CHIN	San Francisco	San Francisco P O	80	502
Ah	40	m	c	CHIN	San Francisco	San Francisco P O	80	449
Ah	40	m	c	CHIN	San Francisco	San Francisco P O	80	454
Ah	40	m	c	CHIN	San Francisco	San Francisco P O	80	455
Ah	40	m	c	CHIN	Sacramento	1-Wd Sacramento	77	196
Ah	39	m	c	CHIN	San Francisco	San Francisco P O	80	495
Ah	39	m	c	CHIN	San Francisco	San Francisco P O	80	450
Ah	39	m	c	CHIN	San Francisco	San Francisco P O	80	443
Ah	38	m	c	CHIN	Placer	Colfax P O	76	384
Ah	38	m	c	CHIN	San Francisco	San Francisco P O	80	508
Ah	38	m	c	CHIN	San Francisco	San Francisco P O	80	511
Ah	37	m	c	CHIN	San Francisco	San Francisco P O	80	447
Ah	37	m	c	CHIN	San Francisco	San Francisco P O	80	435
Ah	37	m	c	CHIN	San Francisco	San Francisco P O	80	437
Ah	37	m	c	CHIN	San Francisco	San Francisco P O	80	520
Ah	36	m	c	CHIN	Tuolumne	Chinese Camp P O	93	363
Ah	36	m	c	CHIN	San Francisco	San Francisco P O	80	445
Ah	36	m	c	CHIN	San Francisco	San Francisco P O	80	441
Ah	36	m	c	CHIN	San Francisco	San Francisco P O	80	517
Ah	36	m	c	CHIN	San Francisco	San Francisco P O	80	528
Ah	36	m	c	CHIN	San Francisco	San Francisco P O	80	510
Ah	35	m	c	CHIN	San Francisco	San Francisco P O	80	501
Ah	35	m	c	CHIN	El Dorado	Greenwood Twp	72	50
Ah	34	m	c	CHIN	San Francisco	San Francisco P O	80	530
Ah	34	m	c	CHIN	San Francisco	San Francisco P O	80	496
Ah	32	m	c	CHIN	Sierra	Table Rock Twp	89	579
Ah	32	m	c	CHIN	Placer	Auburn P O	76	377
Ah	31	m	c	CHIN	San Francisco	3-Wd San Francisco	79	329
Ah	30	m	c	CHIN	Solano	Suisun Twp	90	104
Ah	30	m	c	CHIN	Nevada	Meadow Lake Twp	75	255
Ah	30	m	c	CHIN	San Francisco	San Francisco P O	80	452
Ah	30	m	c	CHIN	Nevada	Bridgeport Twp	75	110
Ah	29	m	c	CHIN	San Francisco	San Francisco P O	80	497
Ah	29	m	c	CHIN	San Francisco	San Francisco P O	80	450
Ah	29	m	c	CHIN	San Francisco	San Francisco P O	80	439
Ah	29	m	c	CHIN	San Francisco	San Francisco P O	80	454
Ah	29	m	c	CHIN	San Francisco	San Francisco P O	80	516
Ah	29	m	c	CHIN	San Francisco	San Francisco P O	80	522
Ah	29	m	c	CHIN	San Francisco	San Francisco P O	80	525
Ah	28	m	c	CHIN	Trinity	Lewiston Pct	92	212
Ah	28	m	c	CHIN	Santa Clara	1-Wd San Jose	88	277
Ah	27	m	c	CHIN	Alameda	Oakland	68	152
Ah	26	m	c	CHIN	El Dorado	Mud Springs Twp	72	76
Ah	25	m	c	CHIN	Shasta	Shasta P O	89	460
Ah	25	m	c	CHIN	San Francisco	6-Wd San Francisco	81	60
Ah	25	m	c	CHIN	Trinity	Canyon City Pct	92	201
Ah	25	m	c	CHIN	San Francisco	San Francisco P O	80	509
Ah	24	m	c	CHIN	Trinity	Douglas	92	236
Ah	24	m	c	CHIN	San Francisco	6-Wd San Francisco	81	61
Ah	24	m	c	CHIN	Sacramento	Franklin Twp	77	108
Ah	24	f	c	CHIN	San Francisco	San Francisco P O	80	454
Ah	23	m	c	CHIN	San Francisco	San Francisco P O	80	507
Ah	23	m	c	CHIN	San Francisco	6-Wd San Francisco	81	47
Ah	22	m	c	CHIN	San Francisco	San Francisco P O	80	500
Ah	22	f	c	CHIN	San Francisco	San Francisco P O	80	446
Ah	22	m	c	CHIN	Alameda	Oakland	68	210
Ah	22	m	c	CHIN	Shasta	American Ranch P O	89	497
Ah	21	m	c	CHIN	Sierra	Downieville Twp	89	521
Ah	21	m	c	CHIN	San Francisco	San Francisco P O	80	497
Ah	21	m	c	CHIN	Santa Clara	San Jose Twp	88	189
Ah	20	f	c	CHIN	San Francisco	San Francisco P O	80	439
Ah	20	f	c	CHIN	San Francisco	San Francisco P O	80	435
Ah	20	f	c	CHIN	San Francisco	San Francisco P O	80	444
Ah	20	f	c	CHIN	San Francisco	San Francisco P O	80	444
Ah	20	m	c	CHIN	Placer	Emigrant Gap P O	76	417
Ah	20	m	c	CHIN	Santa Clara	Alviso Twp	88	25
Ah	20	m	c	CHIN	San Francisco	San Francisco P O	80	521
Ah	20	f	c	CHIN	San Francisco	San Francisco P O	80	528
Ah	20	m	c	CHIN	Placer	Dutch Flat P O	76	414
Ah	19	f	c	CHIN	San Francisco	San Francisco P O	80	528
Ah	19	m	c	CHIN	San Francisco	San Francisco P O	80	466
Ah	19	m	c	CHIN	Nevada	Eureka Twp	75	136
Ah	18	m	c	CHIN	Santa Clara	San Jose Twp	88	191
Ah	18	m	c	CHIN	San Francisco	San Francisco P O	80	359
Ah	18	f	c	CHIN	San Francisco	San Francisco P O	80	525
Ah	17	m	c	CHIN	Santa Clara	Santa Clara Twp	88	166
Ah	16	f	c	CHIN	San Francisco	San Francisco P O	80	440
Ah	16	m	c	CHIN	Placer	Clipper Gap P O	76	393
Ah	16	m	c	CHIN	Santa Clara	Fremont Twp	88	52
Ah	14	m	c	CHIN	San Francisco	8-Wd San Francisco	82	358
Ah	14	f	c	CHIN	Trinity	Weaverville Pct	92	228
Ah	13	m	c	CHIN	San Francisco	11-Wd San Francisc	84	560
Ang	17	m	c	CHIN	San Francisco	7-Wd San Francisco	81	283
Foo	51	m	c	CHIN	Klamath	Sawyers Bar	73	378
Han	22	m	c	CHIN	San Francisco	6-Wd San Francisco	81	46
Ho	27	m	c	CHIN	San Joaquin	1-Wd Stockton	86	143
James	44	m	m	VA	Colusa	Spring Valley Twp	71	345
Lee	12	m	c	CHIN	San Francisco	San Francisco P O	83	298
Lee	11	m	c	CHIN	San Francisco	San Francisco P O	83	298
Oah	14	m	c	CHIN	San Francisco	San Francisco P O	85	876
Tay	22	m	c	CHIN	Yuba	North East Twp	93	645
Ti	23	m	c	CHIN	San Francisco	6-Wd San Francisco	81	43
Woo	27	m	c	CHIN	Klamath	Liberty Twp	73	374
GONGE								
C	60	m	w	FRAN	San Francisco	San Francisco P O	83	135
GONGGOW								
Ah	22	m	c	CHIN	Yuba	Marysville	93	601
GONILLSMETTE								
J B	26	m	w	FRAN	San Francisco	1-Wd San Francisco	79	49
GONIN								
Frank	32	m	w	FRAN	San Francisco	San Francisco P O	80	535
Louis	36	m	w	FRAN	San Francisco	San Francisco P O	80	535
GONITA								
Ano	41	m	w	FRAN	Santa Clara	Almaden Twp	88	18
GONLER								
David C	37	m	w	PRUS	Los Angeles	Santa Ana Twp	73	600
GONLET								
S	11	m	w	CA	Alameda	Oakland	68	159
W H	11	m	w	CA	Alameda	Oakland	68	159
GONLEY								
Chas	33	m	w	CANA	Alameda	Oakland	68	158
Ellen	40	f	w	IREL	San Francisco	San Francisco P O	80	382
GONN								
Ah	18	m	c	CHIN	Nevada	Nevada Twp	75	298
J W	34	m	w	GERM	San Joaquin	Dent Twp	86	23
GONNAN								
Eugene	25	m	w	NJ	San Francisco	San Francisco P O	83	346
Mary	33	f	w	IREL	Amador	Sutter Crk P O	69	405

© 2001 by Heritage Quest. All rights reserved.

Name	Age	S	R	B-PL	County	Locale	Roll	Pg
GONNELLY								
James	40	m	w	IREL	San Francisco	11-Wd San Francisc	84	453
GONNER								
David	45	m	w	NY	Sonoma	Petaluma Twp	91	354
GONORIER								
Antonio	33	m	w	ITAL	Solano	Vallejo	90	213
GONS								
John B	65	m	w	FRAN	San Francisco	8-Wd San Francisco	82	433
GONSAL								
Joseph	47	m	w	PORT	Trinity	Minersville Pct	92	203
Manuel	47	m	w	PORT	Trinity	Minersville Pct	92	203
GONSALAS								
Jesus	40	m	w	MEXI	Inyo	Bishop Crk Twp	73	310
Jesus	36	m	i	MEXI	Inyo	Cerro Gordo Twp	73	322
GONSALES								
Anton	42	m	w	MEXI	Tuolumne	Chinese Camp P O	93	377
Francisco	43	m	w	CA	San Mateo	Half Moon Bay P O	87	397
Geo	16	m	w	CA	Humboldt	Pacific Twp	72	295
Jesus	44	m	w	CHIL	Calaveras	San Andreas P O	70	180
John	40	m	w	CHIL	San Mateo	Menlo Park P O	87	378
Joseph	34	m	w	MEXI	Tuolumne	Sonora P O	93	306
M	54	m	w	CHIL	Amador	Jackson P O	69	338
M G	40	m	w	ME	Tuolumne	Columbia P O	93	350
M J	51	m	w	MEXI	Tuolumne	Sonora P O	93	314
Ricards	13	m	w	CA	Tuolumne	Sonora P O	93	325
GONSALEZ								
Antonia	23	f	w	MEXI	San Francisco	San Francisco P O	80	476
August	31	m	w	MEXI	San Francisco	San Francisco P O	80	464
Carmelita	15	f	w	MEXI	San Francisco	San Francisco P O	80	383
Elizabeth	23	f	w	NY	San Francisco	San Francisco P O	80	409
Gregiorio	45	f	w	CHIL	San Francisco	San Francisco P O	80	348
Maria	11	f	w	MEXI	San Francisco	San Francisco P O	80	347
Marie	40	f	w	SPAI	San Francisco	San Francisco P O	80	459
Mary	36	f	w	CHIL	San Francisco	San Francisco P O	80	370
Pedro	43	m	w	MEXI	San Francisco	San Francisco P O	80	464
Sylvana	14	m	w	MEXI	San Francisco	San Francisco P O	80	422
GONSALIAES								
F F	29	m	w	PORT	Tuolumne	Columbia P O	93	337
GONSALVES								
Emanuel	27	m	w	PORT	Alameda	Washington Twp	68	275
Thomas	22	m	w	SWIT	Santa Cruz	Santa Cruz Twp	89	382
GONSARES								
Manuel M	30	m	w	AZOR	Monterey	Monterey	74	360
GONSER								
Edward	31	m	w	OH	Alpine	Monitor P O	69	317
GONSILDIO								
Christos	38	m	w	PORT	Tuolumne	Sonora P O	93	331
GONSOLIS								
W G	54	m	w	MEXI	Tuolumne	Sonora P O	93	306
GONSTIAUX								
Augt	28	m	w	FRAN	San Francisco	San Francisco P O	83	135
GONSULIS								
Joseph	68	m	w	SPAI	Tuolumne	Sonora P O	93	314
GONT								
Ah	28	m	c	CHIN	Plumas	Goodwin Twp	77	3
Saml	50	m	w	ENGL	Shasta	American Ranch P O	89	498
GONTOOD								
Louis	43	m	w	FRAN	Plumas	Washington Twp	77	56
GONUS								
Criswanes	45	m	i	MEXI	Inyo	Lone Pine Twp	73	333
Jose de Jesus	23	m	w	CA	Monterey	Monterey	74	363
GONY								
Ah	26	m	c	CHIN	San Francisco	San Francisco P O	83	128
GONZ								
John	39	m	w	MI	San Joaquin	2-Wd Stockton	86	206
GONZALAS								
Antone	40	m	w	CHIL	Amador	Fiddletown P O	69	440
GONZALES								
Alex	49	m	b	PHIL	Mariposa	Mariposa P O	74	104
Annie	26	f	w	NY	Santa Cruz	Santa Cruz	89	413
Anton	30	m	w	CHIL	Calaveras	Copperopolis P O	70	255
Antonio	55	m	w	MEXI	San Francisco	1-Wd San Francisco	79	55
Antonio	46	m	w	CHIL	Santa Barbara	Santa Barbara P O	87	477
Antonio	35	m	w	CHIL	Contra Costa	San Pablo Twp	71	363
Antonio	30	m	w	PORT	Marin	Nicasio Twp	74	19
Antonio	24	m	w	PORT	Marin	Nicasio Twp	74	20
Antonio	23	m	w	MEXI	Marin	San Rafael Twp	74	41
Ayandro	32	m	w	MEXI	Santa Barbara	Santa Barbara P O	87	489
Bersabe	17	f	w	CA	Santa Cruz	Santa Cruz	89	417
Bueneventura	28	m	w	CA	Monterey	Monterey	74	365
C	49	m	w	MEXI	Santa Clara	Almaden Twp	88	10
Cassino	40	m	w	MEXI	Fresno	Kingston P O	72	220
Cherinda	5	f	w	CA	Los Angeles	Los Angeles	73	514
Domingo	59	m	w	MEXI	Santa Clara	Gilroy Twp	88	93
Elentena	10	f	w	CA	Los Angeles	San Juan Twp	73	627
Elizabeth	31	f	w	ENGL	Los Angeles	San Gabriel Twp	73	593
Emanuel	15	m	w	CA	Fresno	Millerton P O	72	159
Emanuel	10	m	w	CA	Fresno	Millerton P O	72	165
Eugenio	45	m	w	MEXI	Los Angeles	Santa Ana Twp	73	612
Euregui	47	m	w	CA	Santa Barbara	Santa Barbara P O	87	470
Felipe	47	m	w	CA	Santa Cruz	Watsonville	89	373
Felipe	42	m	w	CA	Santa Barbara	Santa Barbara P O	87	468
Felix	30	m	w	MEXI	Los Angeles	Los Nietos Twp	73	582
Feliz	38	m	w	MEXI	Los Angeles	El Monte Twp	73	453
Francis	36	m	w	MEXI	Marin	San Rafael Twp	74	41
Francisca	37	f	w	CA	Santa Barbara	Santa Barbara P O	87	452
Francisco	56	m	w	CHIL	Fresno	Millerton P O	72	146

Name	Age	S	R	B-PL	County	Locale	Roll	Pg
Francisco	46	m	w	CA	Los Angeles	Los Angeles	73	515
Francisco	42	m	w	ARGE	Santa Clara	Milpitas Twp	88	109
Francisco	39	m	i	MEXI	Inyo	Cerro Gordo Twp	73	318
Francisco	36	m	w	CA	Santa Barbara	San Buenaventura P	87	438
Francisco	10	m	w	CA	Santa Barbara	Santa Barbara P O	87	468
Fred	22	m	w	PORT	San Francisco	2-Wd San Francisco	79	214
Gandalupe	26	f	w	MEXI	Napa	Napa	75	55
Guadalupe	38	f	i	CA	Monterey	Castroville Twp	74	335
Hasses	50	m	w	MEXI	Yuba	Linda Twp	93	558
Hosea	38	m	w	CHIL	Fresno	Millerton P O	72	146
Incarnacion	38	m	w	MEXI	San Bernardino	Chino Twp	78	412
Javan	45	m	w	MEXI	Santa Clara	San Jose Twp	88	209
Jesus	38	m	w	MEXI	San Bernardino	Belleville Twp	78	408
Jesus	35	m	w	MEXI	Fresno	Millerton P O	72	155
John	30	m	w	MEXI	San Francisco	2-Wd San Francisco	79	182
Jose	60	m	w	CHIL	Calaveras	San Andreas P O	70	177
Jose	46	m	w	CA	Fresno	Millerton P O	72	162
Jose	45	m	w	CHIL	Monterey	San Juan Twp	74	407
Jose	40	m	w	CHIL	Santa Clara	Alviso Twp	88	27
Jose	35	m	w	SPAI	Marin	San Rafael Twp	74	41
Jose	31	m	w	MEXI	Fresno	Millerton P O	72	154
Jose	22	m	w	CAME	Placer	Bath P O	76	427
Jose A	32	m	w	CA	Santa Barbara	Santa Barbara P O	87	469
Jose Mide	64	m	w	MEXI	Santa Barbara	Santa Barbara P O	87	492
Josefa	34	f	w	NGRA	Santa Clara	1-Wd San Jose	88	255
Josefa	32	f	w	MEXI	San Francisco	San Francisco P O	80	349
Joseph	28	m	w	CA	Santa Clara	Fremont Twp	88	50
Joseph	18	m	w	NY	Santa Clara	Santa Clara Twp	88	175
Josepha	35	f	w	MEXI	San Diego	San Pasqual Valley	78	525
Juan	42	m	w	MEXI	Santa Clara	1-Wd San Jose	88	262
Juan	36	m	w	MEXI	Santa Clara	Gilroy Twp	88	82
Juana	40	f	w	MEXI	Santa Clara	Almaden Twp	88	20
Juanner	38	f	w	MEXI	Napa	Napa	75	55
Louis	40	m	w	CA	Santa Cruz	Watsonville	89	375
M	30	m	w	MEXI	Santa Clara	Gilroy Twp	88	90
Malaga	42	f	w	MEXI	San Francisco	San Francisco P O	80	424
Manuel	28	m	w	PORT	Mariposa	Mariposa P O	74	111
Manuel	14	m	w	SPAI	San Francisco	2-Wd San Francisco	79	170
Manuel	11	m	w	CA	Santa Barbara	San Buenaventura P	87	441
Maria	60	f	w	MEXI	Santa Clara	Santa Clara Twp	88	158
Maria	38	m	w	MEXI	Plumas	Goodwin Twp	77	5
Maria	27	f	w	CA	Santa Barbara	San Buenaventura P	87	440
Mariano	50	m	w	CHIL	San Luis Obispo	Santa Rosa Twp	87	324
Mercy	45	f	w	CHIL	Calaveras	Copperopolis P O	70	245
Miguel	14	m	w	CA	San Francisco	11-Wd San Francisc	84	588
Minar	54	m	w	MEXI	Fresno	Millerton P O	72	159
Morga	35	m	w	MEXI	Santa Clara	Almaden Twp	88	1
Nicholas	35	m	w	CA	Santa Clara	Almaden Twp	88	6
Nichols	30	m	w	CA	Santa Clara	Almaden Twp	88	13
Pare	24	m	w	MEXI	San Francisco	San Francisco P O	80	476
Pascual	42	m	w	MEXI	Los Angeles	Los Nietos Twp	73	573
Pascual	35	m	w	MEXI	Plumas	Goodwin Twp	77	5
Pasqual	37	m	w	MEXI	Calaveras	San Andreas P O	70	208
Pasqual	33	m	w	CA	Fresno	Millerton P O	72	155
Pedro	50	m	w	MEXI	San Francisco	1-Wd San Francisco	79	39
Pedro	42	m	w	NM	Fresno	Millerton P O	72	152
Pedro	33	m	w	MEXI	Fresno	Millerton P O	72	154
Pedro	25	m	w	MEXI	Kern	Bakersfield P O	73	357
Philip	10	m	w	CA	Placer	Auburn P O	76	383
Rafael	74	m	w	CA	Santa Barbara	Santa Barbara P O	87	469
Rafael	65	m	w	CA	Santa Barbara	San Buenaventura P	87	441
Rafael	34	m	w	MEXI	Los Angeles	El Monte Twp	73	462
Rafiel	37	m	w	WIND	Monterey	Castroville Twp	74	335
Ramales	2	f	w	CA	San Bernardino	Chino Twp	78	412
Ramon	42	m	w	CA	Santa Barbara	Santa Barbara P O	87	462
Ramon	35	m	w	MEXI	Calaveras	San Andreas P O	70	208
Ramon	34	m	w	MEXI	Monterey	San Juan Twp	74	408
Refugia	30	f	w	CA	Santa Barbara	San Buenaventura P	87	439
Rosario	3	f	w	CA	San Bernardino	Chino Twp	78	412
Sabina	61	m	w	MEXI	Tuolumne	Sonora P O	93	327
Sacria	40	m	w	MEXI	Mariposa	Mariposa P O	74	105
Santiago	22	m	i	MEXI	Inyo	Cerro Gordo Twp	73	322
Santiago	20	m	w	CA	Santa Clara	Fremont Twp	88	50
Simeon	20	m	w	CA	Santa Clara	San Jose Twp	88	184
Theodore	14	m	w	CA	Santa Clara	1-Wd San Jose	88	261
Trafino	40	m	w	MEXI	Santa Cruz	Pajaro Twp	89	354
Ventura	30	m	w	CA	Monterey	San Antonio Twp	74	317
Vicente	40	m	w	CHIL	Contra Costa	San Pablo Twp	71	362
GONZALEZ								
Adolfo	14	m	w	CA	Contra Costa	Martinez P O	71	438
Alfredo	23	m	w	CA	Monterey	Monterey	74	356
Antonio	40	m	w	MEXI	Los Angeles	Los Angeles	73	554
Antonio	35	m	w	MEXI	Los Angeles	Los Angeles	73	521
Carlos	24	m	w	MEXI	San Francisco	8-Wd San Francisco	82	373
Concepcion	20	m	w	CA	San Diego	San Luis Rey	78	515
Domineck	40	m	w	SPAI	San Francisco	San Francisco P O	83	341
Eduardo	35	m	w	MEXI	Los Angeles	Los Angeles Twp	73	484
Estefan	44	m	w	TX	Los Angeles	Los Angeles	73	532
Felipe	66	m	w	MEXI	Los Angeles	Los Angeles	73	554
Francisco	15	m	w	CA	Los Angeles	Los Angeles	73	538
Gregorio	48	m	w	MEXI	Los Angeles	Los Angeles	73	557
Jose	36	m	w	CHIL	Fresno	Millerton P O	72	165
Jose	18	m	w	MEXI	Monterey	Alisal Twp	74	295
Juan	45	m	w	CHIL	Los Angeles	Los Angeles	73	523
Juan	42	m	w	NY	Santa Barbara	San Buenaventura P	87	422
Juan	36	m	w	MEXI	Kern	Bakersfield P O	73	362
Libeau	39	m	w	MEXI	Marin	San Rafael Twp	74	42

© 2001 by Heritage Quest. All rights reserved.

Name	Age	S	R	B-PL	County	Locale	Roll	Pg
Lorenzo	42	f	w	CHIL	Monterey	Monterey	74	364
Martenos	35	m	w	NM	Monterey	San Antonio Twp	74	321
Merida	16	f	w	CA	Los Angeles	Los Angeles	73	560
Mouricio	60	m	w	MEXI	Monterey	Monterey	74	355
Perfecto	30	m	w	MEXI	Los Angeles	Los Angeles	73	536
Ramon	25	m	w	MEXI	Kern	Tehachapi P O	73	354
Ramon	18	m	w	CA	Los Angeles	Los Angeles Twp	73	484
Refufio	40	m	w	MEXI	Kern	Havilah P O	73	338
Romero	44	m	w	MEXI	Los Angeles	Los Angeles	73	555
Sylvestre	41	m	w	MEXI	Santa Cruz	Pajaro Twp	89	357
Theodoro	67	m	w	MEXI	Monterey	Monterey	74	356
Vijinio	45	m	w	MEXI	Los Angeles	Los Angeles	73	523
GONZALIS								
Jose	46	m	w	MEXI	Napa	Napa Twp	75	59
GONZZALES								
Martin	30	m	w	MEXI	San Francisco	2-Wd San Francisco	79	145
GOO								
Ah	41	m	c	CHIN	San Francisco	San Francisco P O	80	446
Ah	40	m	c	CHIN	Alameda	Oakland	68	254
Ah	40	m	c	CHIN	Alameda	Oakland	68	224
Ah	39	m	c	CHIN	San Joaquin	Oneal Twp	86	117
Ah	39	m	c	CHIN	Alameda	Oakland	68	232
Ah	38	m	c	CHIN	San Joaquin	Oneal Twp	86	117
Ah	37	m	c	CHIN	Alameda	Oakland	68	250
Ah	37	m	c	CHIN	San Joaquin	1-Wd Stockton	86	143
Ah	36	m	c	CHIN	San Joaquin	Oneal Twp	86	117
Ah	36	m	c	CHIN	San Joaquin	1-Wd Stockton	86	145
Ah	34	m	c	CHIN	Yuba	Marysville	93	594
Ah	34	m	c	CHIN	San Francisco	San Francisco P O	80	503
Ah	32	m	c	CHIN	Alameda	Oakland	68	223
Ah	31	m	c	CHIN	Solano	Suisun Twp	90	98
Ah	31	m	c	CHIN	Nevada	Washington Twp	75	347
Ah	30	m	c	CHIN	San Joaquin	Castoria Twp	86	12
Ah	30	m	c	CHIN	San Francisco	San Francisco P O	80	515
Ah	29	m	c	CHIN	San Joaquin	2-Wd Stockton	86	212
Ah	28	m	c	CHIN	Alameda	Alameda	68	1
Ah	28	m	c	CHIN	Alameda	Oakland	68	202
Ah	28	m	c	CHIN	Alameda	Oakland	68	254
Ah	27	m	c	CHIN	Klamath	South Fork Twp	73	384
Ah	26	m	c	CHIN	San Francisco	San Francisco P O	80	525
Ah	25	m	c	CHIN	Alameda	Oakland	68	223
Ah	24	m	c	CHIN	San Francisco	San Francisco P O	80	523
Ah	19	m	c	CHIN	Alameda	Oakland	68	164
Ah	19	m	c	CHIN	San Francisco	San Francisco P O	80	501
Chan	42	m	c	CHIN	Siskiyou	Yreka	89	657
Chong	25	m	c	CHIN	San Francisco	6-Wd San Francisco	81	38
Chuch	22	m	c	CHIN	San Joaquin	Oneal Twp	86	102
Gee	32	m	c	CHIN	Tuolumne	Columbia P O	93	352
Hi	25	m	c	CHIN	San Joaquin	1-Wd Stockton	86	146
Lee	24	m	c	CHIN	San Joaquin	1-Wd Stockton	86	146
Nee	27	m	c	CHIN	Tuolumne	Columbia P O	93	352
Oon	13	m	c	CHIN	San Francisco	11-Wd San Francisc	84	494
Sam	38	m	c	CHIN	San Joaquin	Oneal Twp	86	117
Toy	30	m	c	CHIN	San Francisco	11-Wd San Francisc	84	574
GOOBY								
John	35	m	w	ENGL	Alameda	Brooklyn Twp	68	42
GOOCH								
A J	40	m	w	MA	Tehama	Tehama Twp	92	196
C J	34	m	w	MA	Tehama	Tehama Twp	92	196
Jas H	41	m	w	MA	San Luis Obispo	Santa Rosa Twp	87	317
Jerry	46	m	w	ME	San Joaquin	Dent Twp	86	21
John	73	m	w	MA	Tehama	Tehama Twp	92	196
Nancy	55	f	b	MO	El Dorado	Coloma Twp	72	9
Oscar	24	m	w	ME	Placer	Summit P O	76	496
Richard S	37	m	w	ENGL	Stanislaus	Empire Twp	92	66
Thomas L	22	m	w	NC	Los Angeles	Los Nietos Twp	73	581
Wm H	42	m	w	MA	Shasta	Dog Crk P O	89	471
GOOD								
Abraham	38	m	w	PA	Mono	Bridgeport P O	74	286
Ah	32	m	c	CHIN	Yuba	Marysville	93	619
Ah	30	m	c	CHIN	San Joaquin	1-Wd Stockton	86	151
Ah	27	m	c	CHIN	Butte	Bidwell Twp	70	1
Ah	15	m	c	CHIN	Sacramento	Granite Twp	77	136
Andrew	36	m	w	PA	Nevada	Meadow Lake Twp	75	263
Anna	30	f	w	CANA	Sacramento	2-Wd Sacramento	77	220
Annie	40	f	w	PA	San Francisco	San Francisco P O	83	274
Bye	52	m	c	CHIN	Klamath	Orleans Twp	73	380
Christian	52	m	w	SWIT	Sonoma	Sonoma Twp	91	435
Cyrus	26	m	w	IREL	Solano	Silveyville Twp	90	89
Edward	69	m	w	ENGL	Tuolumne	Chinese Camp P O	93	373
Eliza	14	f	w	MO	Stanislaus	Emory Twp	92	21
Henry	31	m	w	MO	Solano	Silveyville Twp	90	86
Henry	30	m	w	MA	San Francisco	San Francisco P O	83	130
Henry	30	m	w	SWIT	Sacramento	Granite Twp	77	145
James M	30	m	w	MO	Sutter	Vernon Twp	92	139
John	34	m	w	TN	Yolo	Cache Crk Twp	93	441
John	32	m	w	IREL	San Joaquin	2-Wd Stockton	86	196
John	32	m	w	PRUS	San Francisco	6-Wd San Francisco	81	119
John	30	m	w	NH	San Francisco	San Francisco P O	83	206
Joseph W	41	m	w	IL	San Bernardino	San Bernardino Twp	78	452
Levi	44	m	w	PA	Trinity	Hayfork Valley	92	239
Lizzie	17	f	w	NY	San Francisco	San Francisco P O	83	111
M E	16	f	w	IL	Calaveras	Copperopolis P O	70	224
Minerva	1	f	w	CA	Sutter	Vernon Twp	92	139
Simon	18	m	w	IL	Yolo	Cottonwood Twp	93	464
Stephen	23	m	w	OH	Solano	Silveyville Twp	90	80
Volney	50	m	w	KY	Butte	Concow Twp	70	7

Name	Age	S	R	B-PL	County	Locale	Roll	Pg
Widow M	66	f	w	PA	Lake	Big Valley	73	395
William	51	m	w	KY	Stanislaus	Emory Twp	92	19
Wm M	58	m	w	VA	Amador	Ione City P O	69	349
GOODAIR								
Edward	37	m	w	ENGL	Solano	Suisun Twp	90	97
GOODAL								
Robert	23	m	w	IL	Sutter	Yuba Twp	92	152
GOODALE								
Adelade	47	f	w	MO	San Joaquin	2-Wd Stockton	86	168
David	52	m	w	NH	Contra Costa	San Pablo Twp	71	358
Deveroe	54	m	w	NY	Yolo	Cottonwood Twp	93	474
Frederick	46	m	w	MA	Kern	Havilah P O	73	338
Joseph	38	m	w	ME	Merced	Snelling P O	74	260
Justin	32	m	w	VT	Contra Costa	Martinez P O	71	439
Lyman	39	m	w	OH	Yolo	Buckeye Twp	93	407
Oliver	38	m	w	NY	Siskiyou	Scott Valley Twp	89	620
Thomas J	37	m	w	CT	Inyo	Independence Twp	73	325
GOODALL								
Abraham	36	m	w	ENGL	San Diego	San Diego	78	498
Albert	63	m	w	VT	Humboldt	Eel Rvr Twp	72	250
Edwin	26	m	w	ENGL	San Francisco	San Francisco P O	83	10
Frederick	22	m	w	IL	Nevada	Little York Twp	75	242
John E	42	m	w	KY	Mono	Bridgeport P O	74	287
Joseph	45	m	w	ENGL	Amador	Volcano P O	69	372
GOODAN								
H G W	34	m	w	PRUS	Klamath	Trinidad Twp	73	390
Mary	28	f	w	IREL	San Francisco	8-Wd San Francisco	82	497
GOODARD								
Joseph	40	m	w	MA	San Mateo	Woodside P O	87	386
GOODART								
William	38	m	w	OH	Amador	Fiddletown P O	69	434
GOODAY								
Lewis	39	m	w	PRUS	Butte	Oregon Twp	70	126
Max	25	m	w	PRUS	Butte	Chico Twp	70	13
GOODBAN								
Henry	17	m	w	NY	San Francisco	San Francisco P O	83	350
GOODCHALK								
Betsy	40	f	w	MA	Solano	Suisun Twp	90	103
GOODCHILD								
Cecil	23	m	w	ENGL	San Luis Obispo	Arroyo Grande Twp	87	271
Mary	50	f	w	NY	San Francisco	2-Wd San Francisco	79	188
GOODE								
Anderson	25	m	w	IL	Stanislaus	North Twp	92	69
Daniel B	54	m	w	KY	Yolo	Cache Crk Twp	93	435
John	35	m	w	PA	San Francisco	11-Wd San Francisc	84	496
Joseph	45	m	w	ENGL	Klamath	Orleans Twp	73	379
Joseph	35	m	w	OH	Amador	Volcano P O	69	378
GOODELL								
Council	28	m	w	ME	Calaveras	Copperopolis P O	70	257
G	43	m	w	OH	Sierra	Sears Twp	89	556
G W	43	m	w	ME	San Joaquin	3-Wd Stockton	86	241
George	36	m	w	ME	Alameda	Hayward	68	77
Katie C	20	f	w	MA	Calaveras	Copperopolis P O	70	248
Nathanel	60	m	w	MA	Sacramento	4-Wd Sacramento	77	352
GOODEN								
Eliza V	56	f	w	CANA	Santa Clara	1-Wd San Jose	88	276
GOODENOE								
A J	39	m	w	NY	Siskiyou	Scott Valley Twp	89	609
GOODENOUGH								
Albert	49	m	w	MA	San Francisco	San Francisco P O	83	376
Jos	40	m	w	PRUS	San Francisco	San Francisco P O	83	15
Mary	16	f	w	BADE	San Francisco	San Francisco P O	83	253
GOODENOW								
Mary	16	f	w	NY	Mendocino	Ukiah Twp	74	236
GOODEY								
Thomas	32	m	w	ENGL	San Francisco	7-Wd San Francisco	81	158
GOODFELLOW								
C	30	m	w	IL	Sacramento	1-Wd Sacramento	77	185
Chas	38	m	w	IREL	Nevada	Eureka Twp	75	132
J E	21	m	w	WI	Solano	Vallejo	90	203
James	62	m	w	NY	Merced	Snelling P O	74	266
James	61	m	w	MO	Merced	Snelling P O	74	280
Jos	50	m	w	PRUS	Amador	Volcano P O	69	388
Michael	35	m	w	IREL	San Francisco	8-Wd San Francisco	82	413
Sam	55	m	w	ME	San Joaquin	2-Wd Stockton	86	162
Thos	32	m	w	ENGL	San Francisco	8-Wd San Francisco	82	292
Wm Dickerson	25	m	w	CANA	Plumas	Indian Twp	77	19
GOODFREUND								
Chas	33	m	w	DENM	San Francisco	1-Wd San Francisco	79	108
GOODFRIEND								
Aaron	21	m	w	POLA	San Francisco	1-Wd San Francisco	79	104
Eliza	21	f	w	GERM	San Joaquin	2-Wd Stockton	86	163
Fredk	30	m	w	BAVA	San Francisco	San Francisco P O	83	194
GOODHALL								
John	23	m	w	IREL	San Francisco	11-Wd San Francisc	84	427
GOODHART								
Geo	56	m	w	NY	Tuolumne	Big Oak Flat P O	93	396
J	39	m	w	MS	San Joaquin	3-Wd Stockton	86	246
GOODHEART								
William	40	m	w	OH	Amador	Fiddletown P O	69	426
GOODHEN								
Oliver	30	m	w	VT	Sacramento	4-Wd Sacramento	77	329
GOODHOUSE								
Fred	29	m	w	BREM	San Francisco	8-Wd San Francisco	82	353
GOODHUE								
A R	41	m	w	MO	Lassen	Susanville Twp	73	446
Charles	38	m	w	NH	Santa Clara	2-Wd San Jose	88	322

© 2001 by Heritage Quest. All rights reserved.

Name	Age	S	R	B-PL	County	Locale	Series M593 Roll	Pg
James H	48	m	w	NY	Colusa	Grand Island Twp	71	303
John	71	m	w	MA	San Joaquin	2-Wd Stockton	86	160
Joseph	30	m	w	ME	Sonoma	Vallejo Twp	91	462
Langdon	35	m	w	NH	Santa Clara	Redwood Twp	88	119
Peter	58	m	w	MA	Tulare	Visalia	92	296
Samuel G	34	m	w	NH	San Mateo	San Mateo P O	87	352
GOODIE								
Nelson	36	m	w	ME	San Francisco	San Francisco P O	80	540
GOODIN								
E J	52	m	w	NC	Tuolumne	Columbia P O	93	354
George	30	m	w	MI	Los Angeles	Santa Ana Twp	73	601
J B	41	m	w	MO	Lake	Upper Lake	73	409
Sarah L	8	f	w	CA	Tulare	Farmersville Twp	92	243
William	39	m	w	TN	Tulare	Tule Rvr Twp	92	267
William L	4	m	w	CA	Tulare	Venice Twp	92	273
William M	46	m	w	MO	Yolo	Cache Crk Twp	93	437
GOODING								
A	30	m	w	MO	Amador	Ione City P O	69	367
J A	38	m	w	MO	Amador	Ione City P O	69	367
Jenny	70	f	w	KY	Amador	Ione City P O	69	367
GOODJON								
Mary	25	f	w	NY	Sonoma	Petaluma Twp	91	366
GOODKIND								
Henry	31	m	w	BADE	San Francisco	8-Wd San Francisco	82	475
GOODLESS								
John	34	m	w	MEXI	Sacramento	2-Wd Sacramento	77	215
GOODLEY								
George W	24	m	w	NY	Placer	Blue Canyon P O	76	418
GOODLING								
James	36	m	w	PA	Del Norte	Smith Rvr Twp	71	477
GOODMAN								
Aaron	12	m	w	CA	Sacramento	Brighton Twp	77	80
Allen	23	m	w	MO	San Luis Obispo	San Luis Obispo Tw	87	302
Allice	18	f	w	CA	Humboldt	Eel Rvr Twp	72	249
Benj	30	m	w	MO	Solano	Vallejo	90	214
C	43	m	w	PRUS	Sierra	Forest Twp	89	529
David	35	m	w	WURT	San Francisco	8-Wd San Francisco	82	440
Dennis	13	m	w	CA	San Francisco	11-Wd San Francisc	84	588
Fred	41	m	w	FRAN	San Francisco	8-Wd San Francisco	82	291
G	43	m	w	BOHE	San Francisco	San Francisco P O	85	804
Geo	41	m	w	AUST	El Dorado	Cosumnes Twp	72	14
George	16	m	w	ENGL	San Francisco	7-Wd San Francisco	81	175
George E	45	m	w	NY	Napa	Napa	75	38
H	30	m	w	CT	Solano	Vallejo	90	193
Harris	40	m	w	POLA	San Francisco	San Francisco P O	85	864
Harris	37	m	w	PRUS	Plumas	Goodwin Twp	77	58
Henry	34	m	w	ENGL	San Francisco	3-Wd San Francisco	79	322
Isaac	45	m	w	PRUS	San Francisco	San Francisco P O	85	849
Isaac	30	m	w	AL	San Luis Obispo	Salinas Twp	87	290
Isidore	24	m	w	PRUS	San Francisco	8-Wd San Francisco	82	289
James	35	m	w	MO	Yuba	Linda Twp	93	558
James	28	m	w	IREL	San Francisco	San Francisco P O	83	244
James	11	m	w	CA	San Francisco	11-Wd San Francisc	84	588
James H	46	m	w	NY	Napa	Napa	75	41
Jas	6	m	w	MO	Sonoma	Russian Rvr	91	376
Jas W	30	m	w	KY	Sonoma	Russian Rvr	91	376
John	40	m	w	VA	Yuba	Bullards Bar P O	93	549
John	40	m	w	NY	San Joaquin	2-Wd Stockton	86	172
John F	33	m	w	WURT	Santa Clara	1-Wd San Jose	88	253
John R	45	m	w	PA	Nevada	Nevada Twp	75	284
Jos M	38	m	w	PA	Butte	Hamilton Twp	70	70
Joseph	39	m	w	IREL	San Francisco	San Francisco P O	83	407
Julio	42	m	w	NC	Butte	Ophir Twp	70	117
L S	33	m	w	BAVA	Sonoma	Bodega Twp	91	251
Leah	21	f	w	PA	San Francisco	San Francisco P O	83	337
Libby	7	m	w	CA	Monterey	San Antonio Twp	74	322
Louis	53	m	w	NH	Tuolumne	Big Oak Flat P O	93	393
Louis	30	m	w	WURT	San Francisco	8-Wd San Francisco	82	425
Martin	34	m	w	GERM	Yolo	Cache Crk Twp	93	452
Mary	40	f	w	IREL	San Francisco	San Francisco P O	85	838
Mary	40	f	w	IREL	San Francisco	7-Wd San Francisco	81	284
Mathew R	25	m	w	IA	Shasta	Millville P O	89	485
Merritt	49	m	w	NY	Siskiyou	Yreka	89	654
Milas	53	m	w	NC	Shasta	Fort Crook P O	89	474
Pauline	25	f	w	ENGL	San Francisco	6-Wd San Francisco	81	95
Peter	41	m	w	AL	San Joaquin	Tulare Twp	86	259
Sallie	16	f	w	LA	San Joaquin	Elliott Twp	86	70
Sarah	36	f	w	PRUS	San Francisco	San Francisco P O	83	105
Simon	40	m	w	PRUS	San Francisco	8-Wd San Francisco	82	289
Susan	47	f	b	NJ	San Francisco	6-Wd San Francisco	81	110
Theo H	40	m	w	NY	Sacramento	1-Wd Sacramento	77	172
Thos	8	m	w	CA	San Francisco	11-Wd San Francisc	84	588
Thos	34	m	w	IREL	Alameda	Eden Twp	68	90
W	4	m	w	CA	Sonoma	Russian Rvr	91	367
William	39	m	w	ENGL	El Dorado	Mountain Twp	72	70
Willis	38	m	w	KY	Sonoma	Sonoma Twp	91	438
Wm	24	m	w	MO	Humboldt	Bald Hills	72	238
GOODMANSON								
Bertha	30	f	w	NORW	Napa	Napa	75	45
GOODNIGHT								
Thomas	32	m	w	MO	Los Angeles	Los Angeles Twp	73	482
GOODNOE								
H	31	m	w	NH	Solano	Vallejo	90	205
GOODNOW								
Geo V	35	m	w	NY	Sacramento	Georgianna Twp	77	132
John P	36	m	w	NY	Yolo	Grafton Twp	93	499
Lloyd	50	m	w	NH	Mono	Bridgeport P O	74	286
GOODPUSTUN								
Amos	55	m	w	OH	El Dorado	Mud Springs Twp	72	90
GOODRICH								
A	39	m	w	VT	San Joaquin	Tulare Twp	86	252
Adam H	50	m	w	NY	Placer	Colfax P O	76	388
Adolph	21	m	w	IL	San Francisco	8-Wd San Francisco	82	390
C	48	m	w	VT	Sierra	Downieville Twp	89	516
C	31	m	w	ME	Amador	Volcano P O	69	381
C C	52	m	w	NY	Lassen	Susanville Twp	73	442
C F	43	m	w	NY	San Joaquin	1-Wd Stockton	86	122
Carle	19	m	w	WI	Butte	Chico Twp	70	17
Chas	42	m	w	ME	Solano	Vallejo	90	165
Chas	35	m	w	IL	Sutter	Nicolaus Twp	92	112
Chas C	28	m	w	NY	Napa	Napa	75	38
Chauncy	42	m	w	CA	Los Angeles	Los Angeles Twp	73	470
Chs	32	m	w	ME	Monterey	San Juan Twp	74	416
E E	38	f	w	IN	San Joaquin	1-Wd Stockton	86	122
Edwin C	20	m	w	CA	Siskiyou	Butte Twp	89	586
Elisha	38	m	w	MO	Placer	Newcastle Twp	76	473
Etta	16	f	w	ME	Siskiyou	Yreka	89	660
Foster	25	m	w	MA	San Francisco	1-Wd San Francisco	79	70
Geo	40	m	w	HAMB	Sacramento	Sutter Twp	77	382
George C	32	m	w	IL	Santa Clara	Redwood Twp	88	128
Halston	28	m	w	IL	Los Angeles	Los Nietos Twp	73	582
Hiram	56	m	w	NY	Napa	Napa Twp	75	29
Hugh M	38	m	w	NH	Humboldt	Arcata Twp	72	232
J B V	34	m	w	NY	Alameda	Oakland	68	204
Jane E	40	f	w	ENGL	Stanislaus	Empire Twp	92	33
Johan	21	m	w	WI	Solano	Tremont Twp	90	31
John	63	m	w	ME	Humboldt	Arcata Twp	72	232
John	55	m	w	TN	Santa Clara	San Jose Twp	88	199
John	43	m	w	NH	Amador	Sutter Crk P O	69	399
John	34	m	w	ME	Amador	Volcano P O	69	380
Joseph	45	m	w	ENGL	Santa Cruz	Soquel Twp	89	439
Layman	25	m	w	MI	Solano	Maine Prairie Twp	90	45
Louis H	34	m	w	NY	Santa Clara	2-Wd San Jose	88	328
Mary	50	f	w	IREL	San Mateo	Pescadero P O	87	413
Myron S	26	m	w	NY	Los Angeles	Los Angeles	73	533
Richd	35	m	w	IREL	San Francisco	San Francisco P O	83	4
S D	53	m	w	NY	Napa	Napa Twp	75	73
Susanna	26	f	w	CA	Los Angeles	Santa Ana Twp	73	611
Thomas A	32	m	w	MA	Los Angeles	Santa Ana Twp	73	610
William	45	m	w	MA	San Mateo	Woodside P O	87	387
William	42	m	w	KY	Siskiyou	Cottonwood Twp	89	590
Wm P	42	m	w	NY	Butte	Chico Twp	70	20
GOODRICK								
O C	44	m	w	ME	Nevada	Washington Twp	75	340
GOODRID								
William	40	m	w	ENGL	Colusa	Grand Island Twp	71	306
GOODRIDGE								
Augustus	45	m	w	ME	Inyo	Bishop Crk Twp	73	314
Ed	19	m	w	CANA	Mendocino	Little Lake Twp	74	196
George	41	m	w	MA	Inyo	Cerro Gordo Twp	73	323
James	65	m	w	TN	Colusa	Stony Crk Twp	71	333
James S	36	m	w	ME	El Dorado	Diamond Springs Tw	72	34
Joseph	52	m	w	VT	San Francisco	San Francisco P O	83	341
GOODRO								
Philix	23	m	w	NJ	San Mateo	Woodside P O	87	385
GOODRUM								
George	53	m	w	ENGL	San Francisco	11-Wd San Francisc	84	536
GOODS								
Astoria C	27	f	w	MO	Santa Clara	Santa Clara Twp	88	141
Christian	47	m	w	FRAN	San Francisco	San Francisco P O	80	380
Levis	40	m	w	TN	Yolo	Cache Crk Twp	93	434
William	26	m	w	KY	Sutter	Vernon Twp	92	135
GOODSALE								
Thomas	30	m	w	IREL	San Francisco	San Francisco P O	83	17
GOODSEL								
Thomas	47	m	w	NY	Mariposa	Mariposa P O	74	111
GOODSELL								
David	24	m	w	OH	Santa Clara	2-Wd San Jose	88	325
Decorey	48	m	w	NY	San Francisco	11-Wd San Francisc	84	700
GOODSILE								
Ezra M	41	m	w	CT	Inyo	Bishop Crk Twp	73	310
GOODSON								
John	24	m	w	IL	Yolo	Cottonwood Twp	93	474
Thomas	41	m	w	MO	Yolo	Cache Crk Twp	93	451
Wm P	32	m	w	US	Nevada	Grass Valley Twp	75	231
GOODSPEAD								
Isaac R	39	m	w	ME	San Mateo	Pescadero P O	87	413
Robt	29	m	w	VT	Butte	Chico Twp	70	45
GOODSPEED								
Alvin G	28	m	w	ME	Nevada	Little York Twp	75	235
Anson	56	m	w	MA	Stanislaus	Empire Twp	92	28
Gilson G	28	m	w	ME	Placer	Dutch Flat P O	76	414
Myer H	32	m	w	ME	Nevada	Little York Twp	75	244
Pembroke S	36	m	w	ME	Nevada	Little York Twp	75	235
Wm	30	m	w	ME	Nevada	Eureka Twp	75	133
GOODSTEIN								
Chas	13	m	w	POLA	San Francisco	San Francisco P O	85	777
GOODTREE								
John	65	m	w	FRAN	Stanislaus	Branch Twp	92	8
GOODWHAL								
Myer	46	m	w	FRAN	Calaveras	San Andreas P O	70	192
GOODWILLER								
Joseph	30	m	w	MA	San Francisco	5-Wd San Francisco	81	23

© 2001 by Heritage Quest. All rights reserved.

California 1870 Census

Name	Age	S	R	B-PL	County	Series M593 Locale	Roll	Pg
GOODWIN								
A C	46	m	w	NY	San Joaquin	Elliott Twp	86	79
A D	49	m	w	NY	San Joaquin	Oneal Twp	86	106
A F	47	m	w	MO	Napa	Yountville Twp	75	87
A S	46	m	w	ME	Sierra	Lincoln Twp	89	545
Adolph	27	m	w	DENM	San Francisco	San Francisco P O	85	739
Alonzo A	35	m	w	VT	Santa Cruz	Santa Cruz	89	434
Andrew	51	m	w	OH	Humboldt	Pacific Twp	72	295
B F	35	m	w	KY	Sonoma	Santa Rosa	91	397
Benjamin H	40	m	w	ME	Solano	Suisun Twp	90	114
C A	30	m	w	MO	San Joaquin	2-Wd Stockton	86	164
C H	46	m	w	ME	Humboldt	Eureka Twp	72	273
Chas	54	m	w	NY	Lake	Big Valley	73	398
Clarence	36	m	w	NY	Mendocino	Noyo & Big Rvr Twp	74	173
Cyrus	38	m	w	ME	San Francisco	1-Wd San Francisco	79	78
Darius	63	m	w	VT	San Joaquin	Castoria Twp	86	2
Erwin C	39	m	w	MA	Klamath	Dillon Twp	73	369
Francis	51	m	w	ME	Plumas	Washington Twp	77	52
Francis	27	m	w	IREL	Humboldt	Bucksport Twp	72	245
Francis	26	m	w	MA	Fresno	Kings Rvr P O	72	212
Frank	36	m	w	NY	Plumas	Indian Twp	77	15
Frank	22	m	w	NH	Mono	Bridgeport P O	74	285
Fredrick	40	m	w	ME	Sonoma	Petaluma Twp	91	359
George	62	m	w	ME	Mariposa	Mariposa P O	74	106
George	36	m	w	MD	Amador	Fiddletown P O	69	433
H E	35	m	w	CT	Santa Clara	Almaden Twp	88	16
H W	26	f	w	NH	Solano	Benicia	90	12
Hermen	42	m	w	PRUS	Butte	Ophir Twp	70	106
J A	45	m	w	ENGL	Tuolumne	Chinese Camp P O	93	378
J O	45	m	w	NY	Yuba	Marysville	93	595
James	54	m	w	RI	San Francisco	San Francisco P O	80	390
James	31	m	w	RI	San Francisco	San Francisco P O	80	389
Jesse	37	m	w	GA	San Joaquin	Liberty Twp	86	94
John	56	m	w	MA	Merced	Snelling P O	74	272
John	34	m	w	ENGL	San Francisco	11-Wd San Francisc	84	520
John	29	m	w	ME	San Bernardino	San Salvador Twp	78	458
John	26	m	w	IREL	San Francisco	3-Wd San Francisco	79	320
John	25	m	w	IREL	San Bernardino	San Bernardino Twp	78	444
John	21	m	w	SCOT	Mariposa	Mariposa P O	74	111
John	20	m	w	ENGL	Los Angeles	Los Nietos Twp	73	590
John Daniel	40	m	w	SC	Plumas	Plumas Twp	77	28
John W	40	m	w	NY	Santa Barbara	San Buenaventura P	87	435
Jonah	44	m	w	CT	Kern	Linns Valley P O	73	344
Joseph	38	m	w	OH	El Dorado	Coloma Twp	72	4
Landale	39	m	w	GA	Los Angeles	Los Angeles	73	541
Lem W	44	m	w	ME	Calaveras	San Andreas P O	70	194
Major	39	m	w	NY	Butte	Ophir Twp	70	110
Martha	16	f	w	PA	Mariposa	Maxwell Crk P O	74	138
Mary	28	f	w	IL	San Mateo	Redwood Twp	87	366
Mary	25	f	w	MA	Sonoma	Vallejo Twp	91	457
Michl	36	m	w	IREL	San Francisco	San Francisco P O	83	87
Olive	57	f	w	CT	Nevada	Grass Valley Twp	75	171
Patrick	34	m	w	IREL	Humboldt	Eureka Twp	72	279
Ransom	35	m	w	NY	Butte	Ophir Twp	70	92
Robert	62	m	w	NH	Amador	Volcano P O	69	387
Saml B	55	m	w	MA	Santa Clara	Fremont Twp	88	48
Samuel	36	m	w	SC	Plumas	Plumas Twp	77	27
Solomon	46	m	w	NY	Butte	Oroville Twp	70	137
T	32	m	w	IREL	Lake	Knoxville Mines	73	405
Thomas	40	m	w	ENGL	San Francisco	3-Wd San Francisco	79	320
Thomas	20	m	w	SCOT	Mariposa	Mariposa P O	74	114
Thomas A	36	m	w	ME	Santa Clara	Santa Clara Twp	88	147
Thos	54	m	w	ME	San Joaquin	1-Wd Stockton	86	150
Thos	31	m	w	SCOT	San Francisco	7-Wd San Francisco	81	235
V L B	30	m	w	KY	Solano	Vallejo	90	161
W B	39	m	w	ME	Tuolumne	Columbia P O	93	359
William A	33	m	w	CT	Placer	Bath P O	76	455
William P	41	m	w	NY	Santa Cruz	Watsonville	89	370
Willis C	40	m	w	ENGL	San Diego	San Diego	78	500
Wm	28	m	w	ME	Butte	Chico Twp	70	58
Wm	25	m	w	CANA	Monterey	Alisal Twp	74	298
Wm E	40	m	w	ENGL	San Francisco	11-Wd San Francisc	84	642
GOODY								
Saml B	40	m	w	NH	San Francisco	6-Wd San Francisco	81	84
GOODYEAR								
Andrew	49	m	w	CT	Solano	Benicia	90	19
Saml	30	m	w	NY	San Francisco	5-Wd San Francisco	81	36
GOOE								
Ah	26	m	c	CHIN	Placer	Lincoln P O	76	484
GOOEY								
Ah	32	m	c	CHIN	Plumas	Plumas Twp	77	32
Ah	21	m	c	CHIN	Shasta	Millville P O	89	490
GOOF								
Mike	22	m	w	IREL	San Joaquin	3-Wd Stockton	86	218
GOOGIN								
John	44	m	w	MA	Sacramento	Sutter Twp	77	390
GOOGINS								
Ansel B	32	m	w	ME	Santa Cruz	Santa Cruz Twp	89	394
Michael	16	m	w	CA	El Dorado	Lake Valley Twp	72	64
GOOGLE								
Chris	29	m	w	NY	Sacramento	3-Wd Sacramento	77	301
GOOGLESBEER								
Andrew	34	m	w	HDAR	San Francisco	2-Wd San Francisco	79	155
GOOING								
Han	30	m	c	CHIN	San Francisco	6-Wd San Francisco	81	46
Pan	32	m	c	CHIN	San Francisco	6-Wd San Francisco	81	46

Name	Age	S	R	B-PL	County	Series M593 Locale	Roll	Pg
GOOK								
Ah	38	m	c	CHIN	Plumas	Plumas Twp	77	32
Ah	24	m	c	CHIN	Nevada	Meadow Lake Twp	75	259
Ah	20	m	c	CHIN	Nevada	Nevada Twp	75	297
Ah	18	m	c	CHIN	Santa Cruz	Santa Cruz	89	434
Lun	14	m	c	CHIN	Nevada	Nevada Twp	75	293
Ong	26	m	c	CHIN	Nevada	Meadow Lake Twp	75	256
Ong	22	m	c	CHIN	Nevada	Meadow Lake Twp	75	254
Quong	46	m	c	CHIN	Shasta	Shasta P O	89	461
GOOKIE								
T P	46	m	w	NH	Solano	Vallejo	90	139
GOOKIN								
Brower	11	m	w	CA	Butte	Wyandotte Twp	70	149
G D	42	m	w	MA	Tuolumne	Chinese Camp P O	93	375
John B	41	m	w	MA	Butte	Wyandotte Twp	70	149
GOOKY								
David	48	m	w	SCOT	Solano	Rio Vista Twp	90	64
GOOLD								
Gardner	53	m	w	ME	Contra Costa	Martinez P O	71	383
GOOM								
Ah	29	m	c	CHIN	Nevada	Nevada Twp	75	318
GOON								
---	40	m	c	CHIN	Shasta	Horsetown P O	89	507
---	14	m	c	CHIN	Siskiyou	Cottonwood Twp	89	593
Ah	60	m	c	CHIN	Placer	Auburn P O	76	364
Ah	60	m	c	CHIN	Placer	Clipper Gap P O	76	393
Ah	52	m	c	CHIN	Placer	Auburn P O	76	364
Ah	46	m	c	CHIN	Placer	Auburn P O	76	375
Ah	42	m	c	CHIN	Placer	Dutch Flat P O	76	410
Ah	40	m	c	CHIN	Siskiyou	Hamburg Twp	89	598
Ah	36	m	c	CHIN	Nevada	Nevada Twp	75	311
Ah	35	m	c	CHIN	Alameda	Eden Twp	68	62
Ah	35	m	c	CHIN	Plumas	Seneca Twp	77	49
Ah	34	m	c	CHIN	Plumas	Mineral Twp	77	23
Ah	31	m	c	CHIN	Butte	Chico Twp	70	53
Ah	31	m	c	CHIN	Butte	Chico Twp	70	54
Ah	31	m	c	CHIN	Placer	Lincoln P O	76	484
Ah	30	m	c	CHIN	Placer	Clipper Gap P O	76	393
Ah	30	m	c	CHIN	Sacramento	Georgianna Twp	77	124
Ah	30	m	c	CHIN	Nevada	Nevada Twp	75	311
Ah	30	m	c	CHIN	Placer	Auburn P O	76	360
Ah	29	m	c	CHIN	Placer	Auburn P O	76	373
Ah	29	m	c	CHIN	Siskiyou	Yreka Twp	89	666
Ah	28	m	c	CHIN	San Francisco	6-Wd San Francisco	81	58
Ah	27	m	c	CHIN	Placer	Auburn P O	76	378
Ah	27	m	c	CHIN	Nevada	Eureka Twp	75	140
Ah	26	m	c	CHIN	Placer	Emigrant Gap P O	76	416
Ah	26	m	c	CHIN	Sacramento	Granite Twp	77	150
Ah	25	m	c	CHIN	Placer	Colfax P O	76	384
Ah	25	m	c	CHIN	Sacramento	Georgianna Twp	77	126
Ah	24	m	c	CHIN	Sacramento	Georgianna Twp	77	132
Ah	20	m	c	CHIN	San Francisco	8-Wd San Francisco	82	380
Ah	20	m	c	CHIN	San Francisco	3-Wd San Francisco	79	309
Ah	19	m	c	CHIN	San Francisco	3-Wd San Francisco	79	330
Ah	18	m	c	CHIN	San Francisco	3-Wd San Francisco	79	328
Ah	16	m	c	CHIN	Placer	Dutch Flat P O	76	411
Ah	15	m	c	CHIN	Placer	Colfax P O	76	391
Ah	15	m	c	CHIN	Napa	Napa	75	9
Ah	15	m	c	CHIN	Placer	Dutch Flat P O	76	411
Ah	14	m	c	CHIN	San Francisco	San Francisco P O	83	131
Ah	14	m	c	CHIN	San Francisco	3-Wd San Francisco	79	322
Al	12	m	c	CHIN	San Francisco	1-Wd San Francisco	79	17
Ang	40	m	c	CHIN	Plumas	Seneca Twp	77	48
Daniel	33	m	w	IN	Nevada	Little York Twp	75	243
Gung	57	m	c	CHIN	Placer	Auburn P O	76	373
Hoo	34	m	c	CHIN	Butte	Kimshew Tpw	70	84
Hu	22	m	c	CHIN	Placer	Dutch Flat P O	76	402
John	22	m	w	PORT	Mendocino	Noyo & Big Rvr Twp	74	173
Lee	25	m	c	CHIN	San Francisco	6-Wd San Francisco	81	128
Linn	16	m	c	CHIN	San Francisco	6-Wd San Francisco	81	128
Sang	22	m	c	CHIN	Shasta	French Gulch P O	89	464
Sue	36	m	c	CHIN	Butte	Ophir Twp	70	103
Un	40	m	c	CHIN	Shasta	Horsetown P O	89	506
Wah	38	m	c	CHIN	Yuba	North East Twp	93	643
Wing Ung	24	m	c	CHIN	San Francisco	San Francisco P O	83	408
Yang	20	m	c	CHIN	Plumas	Goodwin Twp	77	4
Yong	29	m	c	CHIN	Plumas	Goodwin Twp	77	3
GOONAN								
Chars	25	m	w	PRUS	Butte	Oregon Twp	70	136
Edward	21	m	w	IREL	San Francisco	6-Wd San Francisco	81	141
Margaret	47	f	w	IREL	San Francisco	San Francisco P O	83	383
GOONER								
Julius	39	m	w	IREL	Mendocino	Point Arena Twp	74	204
GOONG								
Ah	30	m	c	CHIN	Shasta	American Ranch P O	89	497
Ah	22	m	c	CHIN	San Francisco	6-Wd San Francisco	81	43
Ah	17	m	c	CHIN	San Francisco	3-Wd San Francisco	79	309
Whan	25	m	c	CHIN	Butte	Bidwell Twp	70	1
GOOPEL								
Robert	33	m	w	PRUS	San Francisco	8-Wd San Francisco	82	354
GOOR								
Jacob	61	m	w	GERM	San Bernardino	San Bernardino Twp	78	444
GOORY								
W H	25	m	w	NY	Tuolumne	Chinese Camp P O	93	381
GOOS								
Peter	38	m	w	HAMB	San Francisco	1-Wd San Francisco	79	96

© 2001 by Heritage Quest. All rights reserved.

Name	Age	S	R	B-PL	County	Locale	Roll	Pg
GOOSBY								
Sarah	40	f	w	ENGL	Amador	Volcano P O	69	374
GOOSE								
Abraham	48	m	w	SHOL	Siskiyou	Surprise Valley Tw	89	638
Henry C N	45	m	w	SHOL	Placer	Bath P O	76	449
Levi S	31	m	w	SHOL	Placer	Bath P O	76	449
GOOSEN								
Fred	60	m	w	PRUS	Solano	Green Valley Twp	90	42
GOOT								
Ah	31	m	c	CHIN	Butte	Mountain Spring Tw	70	90
GOOTCHKIE								
Allen	40	m	w	POLA	Marin	San Rafael Twp	74	40
GOOTH								
Addam	39	m	w	BAVA	Trinity	North Fork Twp	92	216
Joseph	38	m	w	FRAN	Sacramento	San Joaquin Twp	77	404
GOOY								
Lee	55	m	c	CHIN	Yuba	Marysville	93	631
GOOZELIER								
Louis	71	m	w	FRAN	Santa Clara	2-Wd San Jose	88	331
GOPINCHI								
Francis	30	m	w	MEXI	El Dorado	Mud Springs Twp	72	76
GOPP								
Horace O	36	m	w	OH	Siskiyou	Surprise Valley Tw	89	638
GOR								
Ah	20	m	c	CHIN	Yolo	Cache Crk Twp	93	448
Chee	36	m	c	CHIN	Shasta	American Ranch P O	89	496
Fat	28	m	c	CHIN	Sacramento	1-Wd Sacramento	77	197
GORAM								
Geo R	45	m	w	MA	Humboldt	Bucksport Twp	72	243
GORARBACH								
Francis	36	m	w	AUST	San Francisco	5-Wd San Francisco	81	10
GORARONDNID								
August	41	m	w	FRAN	Plumas	Rich Bar Twp	77	8
GORBET								
Clara	10	f	w	CA	Yuba	Marysville	93	576
William W	40	m	w	OH	Yuba	New York Twp	93	637
GORBONNA								
Rosa	40	f	w	ITAL	San Mateo	Searsville P O	87	383
GORCIGLIA								
Antone	43	m	w	MEXI	Calaveras	Copperopolis P O	70	259
GORCKAN								
John	26	m	w	HANO	San Francisco	San Francisco P O	83	81
GORDANA								
Jo	31	m	w	FRAN	Butte	Ophir Twp	70	101
GORDANO								
Giovanni	26	m	w	ITAL	San Francisco	11-Wd San Francisc	84	586
GORDELLA								
Angello	35	m	w	FRAN	Butte	Ophir Twp	70	119
GORDEN								
A B	44	m	w	MO	Tuolumne	Big Oak Flat P O	93	393
A D	41	m	w	OH	Humboldt	Bald Hills	72	239
Andrew J	46	m	w	MO	Sonoma	Mendocino Twp	91	304
Annette	20	f	w	IN	San Diego	San Diego	78	501
Edwin H	25	m	w	MO	Sonoma	Mendocino Twp	91	304
Geo W	33	m	w	NH	Monterey	Monterey Twp	74	347
Hans	35	m	w	PRUS	Solano	Silveyville Twp	90	79
Henry	28	m	w	KY	Placer	Bath P O	76	460
Henry	21	m	w	NY	San Mateo	San Mateo P O	87	359
J H	42	m	w	CT	Alameda	Oakland	68	190
J P	24	m	w	CA	Alameda	Oakland	68	176
James	67	m	w	SCOT	Santa Clara	Santa Clara Twp	88	164
James	37	m	w	NY	San Diego	San Diego	78	488
Jno E H	41	m	w	MO	Sonoma	Mendocino Twp	91	299
Joseph H	61	m	w	PA	Sonoma	Bodega Twp	91	263
Mary	24	f	w	MA	Alameda	Oakland	68	236
Pricilla	75	f	b	VA	Colusa	Colusa	71	290
S B	42	m	w	SC	Monterey	Monterey Twp	74	347
S Simon	38	m	w	NY	San Diego	San Diego	78	489
S W	32	m	w	MA	Monterey	Salinas Twp	74	312
GORDER								
F	65	m	w	PRUS	Solano	Vallejo	90	139
GORDION								
Endellan	26	m	i	MEXI	Santa Clara	Almaden Twp	88	6
GORDO								
Jesus	32	m	w	CHIL	Amador	Volcano P O	69	384
GORDOM								
M A	50	f	w	PA	Solano	Vallejo	90	191
GORDON								
Abraham	27	m	w	MO	Solano	Silveyville Twp	90	81
Aenias B	55	m	w	SCOT	Los Angeles	Soledad Twp	73	633
Alex	54	m	w	IN	Del Norte	Crescent Twp	71	456
Alex	27	m	w	VA	Marin	Novato Twp	74	10
Alex	26	m	w	CANA	Sierra	Gibson Twp	89	544
Alexander	43	m	w	CANA	Mendocino	Casper & Big Rvr	74	162
Alexander	43	m	w	NY	San Mateo	Pescadero P O	87	409
Alexander	23	m	w	CANA	Contra Costa	Martinez P O	71	434
Alexander	21	m	w	VA	San Francisco	11-Wd San Francisc	84	626
Amelia	44	f	w	AFRI	San Francisco	2-Wd San Francisco	79	236
Amos W	22	m	w	MI	Nevada	Grass Valley Twp	75	190
Asher	28	m	w	FRAN	San Francisco	6-Wd San Francisco	81	71
B	27	m	w	IREL	Humboldt	Eureka Twp	72	270
Ben	42	m	w	MO	Santa Clara	Burnett Twp	88	36
Betsey	36	f	w	IREL	Santa Clara	Santa Clara Twp	88	150
C	36	m	w	VA	Alameda	Oakland	68	129
Catherine	21	f	w	IREL	San Francisco	San Francisco P O	83	205
Charles	29	m	w	ME	Contra Costa	Martinez P O	71	419
Charles	26	m	w	NY	San Diego	Julian Dist	78	469

Name	Age	S	R	B-PL	County	Locale	Roll	Pg
Charles B	48	m	w	TN	Yolo	Cottonwood Twp	93	471
Chas	33	m	w	CANA	Sierra	Sears Twp	89	561
Chas	30	m	w	NY	San Francisco	8-Wd San Francisco	82	347
Chas H	37	m	w	SCOT	San Francisco	3-Wd San Francisco	79	327
D P	41	m	w	IL	Humboldt	Eureka Twp	72	256
Daniel	59	m	w	NY	Siskiyou	Scott Valley Twp	89	618
David	31	m	w	CANA	Mendocino	Point Arena Twp	74	205
Donald	44	m	w	SCOT	San Francisco	San Francisco P O	85	745
Edsie E	35	m	w	NY	Yolo	Grafton Twp	93	498
Edward	9	m	w	CA	Colusa	Monroe Twp	71	312
Edward	42	m	w	IREL	Solano	Silveyville Twp	90	85
Edwards	20	m	w	CANA	Contra Costa	Martinez P O	71	429
Elizabeth	45	f	w	ENGL	Santa Clara	Fremont Twp	88	57
Elizabeth	17	f	w	CA	Yolo	Cottonwood Twp	93	462
Frank	31	m	w	IREL	Placer	Blue Canyon P O	76	418
Frank	12	m	w	NY	Yuba	Marysville	93	594
G R	52	m	w	OH	Mendocino	Calpella Twp	74	190
Geo	50	m	w	NY	Solano	Vallejo	90	187
Geo	23	m	w	NJ	Sacramento	4-Wd Sacramento	77	371
George	49	m	w	NY	San Francisco	8-Wd San Francisco	82	384
George	39	m	w	CANA	Tehama	Battle Crk Twp	92	157
Henry	38	m	w	NY	Sacramento	Cosumnes Twp	77	88
Heny G	24	m	w	PA	San Francisco	7-Wd San Francisco	81	262
J	40	m	w	NY	San Francisco	San Francisco P O	85	779
J D	51	m	w	OH	Nevada	Eureka Twp	75	133
J E C	40	m	w	MA	San Francisco	6-Wd San Francisco	81	100
J G V	34	m	w	NH	Alameda	Oakland	68	156
J W	30	m	w	ME	San Joaquin	Douglas Twp	86	45
James	41	m	w	MO	Contra Costa	Martinez P O	71	399
James	40	m	w	IREL	San Francisco	11-Wd San Francisc	84	452
James	36	m	w	CANA	Mendocino	Point Arena Twp	74	208
James	35	m	w	IREL	San Francisco	7-Wd San Francisco	81	214
James	25	m	w	NY	San Francisco	7-Wd San Francisco	81	218
James	24	m	w	IREL	Los Angeles	Los Angeles	73	566
James	23	m	w	CANA	Mendocino	Anderson Twp	74	151
James	22	m	w	CANA	San Mateo	Woodside P O	87	386
James A	26	m	w	MI	Yolo	Buckeye Twp	93	414
Jas	35	m	w	NY	Sonoma	Santa Rosa	91	405
Jesse	23	f	w	ENGL	San Francisco	11-Wd San Francisc	84	688
Jo	28	m	w	IREL	San Francisco	5-Wd San Francisco	81	13
John	67	m	w	ENGL	Santa Clara	2-Wd San Jose	88	295
John	64	m	w	IREL	San Francisco	San Francisco P O	80	380
John	64	m	w	ME	Klamath	Trinidad Twp	73	392
John	63	m	w	ME	Mendocino	Point Arena Twp	74	209
John	56	m	w	FRAN	Contra Costa	Martinez P O	71	374
John	53	m	w	NJ	Santa Clara	Santa Clara Twp	88	163
John	50	m	w	AR	Mariposa	Mariposa P O	74	136
John	42	m	w	MA	San Francisco	6-Wd San Francisco	81	81
John	42	m	w	IREL	Marin	Sausalito Twp	74	72
John	40	m	w	SCOT	San Francisco	7-Wd San Francisco	81	188
John	40	m	w	MD	Kern	Kernville P O	73	368
John	38	m	w	NM	Yolo	Cottonwood Twp	93	474
John	35	m	w	IREL	San Joaquin	Oneal Twp	86	107
John	33	m	w	NY	Sutter	Sutter Twp	92	122
John	32	m	w	NY	San Francisco	San Francisco P O	80	473
John	22	m	w	SHOL	Santa Barbara	Las Cruces P O	87	515
John	22	m	w	IREL	Solano	Silveyville Twp	90	74
John F	30	m	w	OH	Los Angeles	Santa Ana Twp	73	603
John H	42	m	w	ENGL	Santa Clara	2-Wd San Jose	88	294
Joseph	45	m	w	IREL	San Joaquin	2-Wd Stockton	86	174
Joseph	42	m	w	IREL	Sonoma	Analy Twp	91	223
Joseph	40	m	w	IREL	Marin	Tomales Twp	74	78
Joseph	34	m	w	MO	Amador	Jackson P O	69	322
Joseph	32	m	w	MEXI	Yolo	Cottonwood Twp	93	467
Joseph	17	m	w	CA	Mendocino	Ukiah Twp	74	243
Julia	45	f	w	CUBA	San Francisco	San Francisco P O	83	99
Louis	32	m	w	CANA	Marin	Bolinas Twp	74	5
Louisa	32	f	w	IREL	San Francisco	San Francisco P O	83	249
Luke	24	m	w	IREL	San Francisco	1-Wd San Francisco	79	93
M W	58	m	w	TN	Amador	Jackson P O	69	320
Manly	30	m	w	MI	Butte	Oregon Twp	70	131
Margaret	58	f	w	OH	Sacramento	Franklin Twp	77	117
Margaret	38	f	w	IREL	San Francisco	San Francisco P O	83	208
Maria	33	f	w	MA	San Francisco	San Francisco P O	85	729
Mary	40	f	w	IL	Santa Clara	Burnett Twp	88	36
Mary	11	f	w	CA	Santa Cruz	Santa Cruz	89	430
Mary A	43	f	w	TN	Yuba	New York Twp	93	636
Maryett	12	m	w	CA	Napa	Yountville Twp	75	77
Mathew	27	m	w	CANA	Nevada	Meadow Lake Twp	75	259
Mattie	3	f	w	CA	Santa Clara	Burnett Twp	88	36
Mell B	42	m	w	VT	Yolo	Putah Twp	93	518
Micheal	70	m	w	IREL	San Francisco	7-Wd San Francisco	81	162
Montgomery G	28	m	w	CANA	Sonoma	Salt Point	91	388
Oscar L	40	m	w	ME	Santa Cruz	Santa Cruz	89	418
P	39	m	w	IREL	Sierra	Butte Twp	89	508
P H	50	m	w	VA	Siskiyou	Big Valley Twp	89	581
Patrick	29	m	w	IREL	San Francisco	11-Wd San Francisc	84	525
Peter	56	m	w	TN	Butte	Chico Twp	70	57
Peter	40	m	w	IREL	Shasta	Shasta P O	89	458
Peter	35	m	w	NY	Mariposa	Mariposa P O	74	135
Peter Y	38	m	w	ME	Mendocino	Point Arena Twp	74	224
Richmond	43	m	w	NY	Solano	Maine Prairie Twp	90	51
Robert	47	m	w	IREL	Placer	Auburn P O	76	368
Robert	44	m	w	IREL	Sonoma	Analy Twp	91	223
Robert	28	m	w	SCOT	Los Angeles	Soledad Twp	73	630
Robert	25	m	w	IREL	San Francisco	11-Wd San Francisc	84	432
Robert A	38	m	w	VT	Siskiyou	Butte Twp	89	587

© 2001 by Heritage Quest. All rights reserved.

California 1870 Census

Name	Age	S	R	B-PL	County	Locale	Roll	Pg
						Series M593		
Robt	54	m	w	NY	Yuba	East Bear Rvr Twp	93	543
Robt	29	m	w	IREL	Tehama	Deer Crk Twp	92	170
Robt	25	m	w	TN	Sonoma	Santa Rosa	91	423
S	30	m	w	VA	Lassen	Susanville Twp	73	439
S J	37	m	w	MD	Lake	Big Valley	73	397
S L	22	m	w	MA	Solano	Vallejo	90	164
Sam B	37	m	w	IREL	Butte	Ophir Twp	70	92
Saml	58	m	w	IREL	San Francisco	7-Wd San Francisco	81	244
Samuel	49	m	w	SC	Los Angeles	Los Nietos Twp	73	578
Samuel	28	m	w	ENGL	San Francisco	San Francisco P O	83	151
Stephen	25	m	w	SCOT	Merced	Snelling P O	74	259
Thomas	50	m	w	IREL	Marin	San Rafael Twp	74	34
Thomas	35	m	w	IREL	Marin	San Rafael	74	49
Thomas	24	m	w	CANA	Santa Clara	1-Wd San Jose	88	278
Thoms	47	m	w	IREL	San Francisco	5-Wd San Francisco	81	29
Tomy	34	m	w	FRAN	San Francisco	6-Wd San Francisco	81	71
Upton	38	m	w	PA	Marin	San Rafael	74	49
Virginia	36	f	w	VA	Del Norte	Crescent	71	463
W A	18	m	w	VA	San Francisco	San Francisco P O	85	785
W M	20	m	w	NY	San Francisco	3-Wd San Francisco	79	312
Wellington	57	m	w	VA	San Francisco	8-Wd San Francisco	82	486
William	27	m	w	ME	Del Norte	Smith Rvr Twp	71	476
William	23	m	w	NY	San Mateo	Half Moon Bay P O	87	391
William H	36	m	w	IREL	Calaveras	Copperopolis P O	70	244
William Y	38	m	w	VT	Yolo	Putah Twp	93	518
Willm A	30	m	w	NY	Santa Barbara	San Buenaventura P	87	444
Wm	69	m	w	OH	Lake	Lower Lake	73	429
Wm	40	m	w	KY	San Joaquin	Elliott Twp	86	80
Wm	30	m	w	NY	El Dorado	Greenwood Twp	72	57
Wm H	31	m	w	NY	Sacramento	1-Wd Sacramento	77	172
Wm Jr	34	m	w	NM	Napa	Napa Twp	75	60
GORDUNA								
Torivia	40	m	w	NM	San Luis Obispo	San Luis Obispo Tw	87	313
GORE								
Ah	42	m	c	CHIN	Tuolumne	Big Oak Flat P O	93	395
Benjamin B	46	m	w	ME	San Francisco	San Francisco P O	83	409
Gardiner	45	m	w	ME	Yuba	Bullards Bar P O	93	550
James	11	m	w	CA	Sacramento	Brighton Twp	77	73
John	40	m	w	CT	Santa Clara	Milpitas Twp	88	109
John	33	m	w	IREL	Solano	Vallejo	90	217
Mary	22	f	w	KY	Sacramento	Brighton Twp	77	73
Michael	33	m	w	IREL	Marin	San Rafael	74	51
Peter	40	m	w	NY	Sierra	Lincoln Twp	89	547
Peter	35	m	w	CANA	Contra Costa	Martinez P O	71	440
R D	59	m	w	TN	Sonoma	Bodega Twp	91	253
Robert R	41	m	w	NY	San Francisco	1-Wd San Francisco	79	86
Robt	28	m	w	IREL	Solano	Vallejo	90	216
Wm F	28	m	w	KY	Sonoma	Bodega Twp	91	253
GORELL								
Mary	13	f	w	NY	San Francisco	San Francisco P O	85	803
GOREMAN								
Frank	40	m	w	PORT	Sacramento	Franklin Twp	77	106
John	34	m	w	IREL	San Francisco	San Francisco P O	85	785
GORENA								
Margaret	42	f	w	MEXI	San Francisco	San Francisco P O	80	343
GORET								
Marie	22	f	w	FRAN	San Francisco	6-Wd San Francisco	81	82
Marie	21	f	w	FRAN	San Francisco	6-Wd San Francisco	81	45
GOREVAN								
James	51	m	w	IREL	San Francisco	6-Wd San Francisco	81	120
GORG								
Better	60	m	w	PRUS	San Francisco	1-Wd San Francisco	79	52
GORGAN								
Alexr	25	m	w	IREL	San Francisco	1-Wd San Francisco	79	39
GORGANUS								
Wm	36	m	w	IREL	San Francisco	San Francisco P O	83	79
GORGAS								
F G	56	m	w	POLA	Tuolumne	Columbia P O	93	351
GORGES								
Ferdinand	40	m	w	FRAN	San Francisco	San Francisco P O	80	350
GORGHON								
John	19	m	c	CHIN	San Francisco	8-Wd San Francisco	82	383
GORHAM								
A	43	m	w	ENGL	Solano	Vallejo	90	177
Bartley	26	m	w	IREL	Sacramento	2-Wd Sacramento	77	240
Chas	44	m	w	MA	San Francisco	11-Wd San Francisc	84	602
Chas	39	m	w	CT	Yuba	Marysville	93	634
Daniel	32	m	w	NY	San Francisco	6-Wd San Francisco	81	117
Emily A	57	f	w	NY	San Francisco	San Francisco P O	83	360
Hannah C	94	f	w	VA	Nevada	Grass Valley Twp	75	167
Henry H	24	m	w	WI	Calaveras	Copperopolis P O	70	229
Isabella	43	f	w	IREL	San Francisco	11-Wd San Francisc	84	670
James H	66	m	w	NY	Contra Costa	Martinez P O	71	377
John	38	m	w	MA	Amador	Volcano P O	69	373
John	34	m	w	VA	San Francisco	2-Wd San Francisco	79	199
John J	25	m	w	WI	Contra Costa	Martinez P O	71	376
Joseph	50	m	w	NY	San Francisco	5-Wd San Francisco	81	16
Rachel	60	f	b	MD	Placer	Auburn P O	76	380
Robert	56	m	w	NY	Calaveras	Copperopolis P O	70	259
S P	56	m	w	ME	San Joaquin	2-Wd Stockton	86	159
Sarah	16	f	w	MA	San Francisco	San Francisco P O	83	196
Thos	30	m	w	IREL	San Francisco	11-Wd San Francisc	84	671
Valentine	30	m	w	IREL	San Francisco	8-Wd San Francisco	82	419
W J	33	m	w	CANA	Tuolumne	Columbia P O	93	338
William	39	m	w	IL	Calaveras	Copperopolis P O	70	221
William M	44	m	w	IL	Contra Costa	Martinez P O	71	377

Name	Age	S	R	B-PL	County	Locale	Roll	Pg
						Series M593		
GORHARD								
Joeth	40	m	w	GERM	San Joaquin	2-Wd Stockton	86	165
GORHMAN								
Dries	38	m	w	IREL	San Francisco	11-Wd San Francisc	84	663
GORI								
Lorenzo	34	m	w	ITAL	San Francisco	1-Wd San Francisco	79	110
GORIA								
Antonio	32	m	w	ITAL	Santa Barbara	Santa Barbara P O	87	503
GORIE								
James	32	m	w	SCOT	San Francisco	San Francisco P O	80	344
GORILLA								
Frank	30	m	w	MEXI	San Francisco	2-Wd San Francisco	79	150
GORINI								
Andros	50	m	w	ITAL	San Francisco	3-Wd San Francisco	79	310
GORK								
Han	40	m	c	CHIN	San Francisco	6-Wd San Francisco	81	42
GORKER								
Mary	18	f	w	PA	San Francisco	5-Wd San Francisco	81	21
W Mrs	30	f	w	PA	San Francisco	5-Wd San Francisco	81	21
Walter	50	m	w	PA	San Francisco	5-Wd San Francisco	81	21
GORLAND								
David	38	m	w	MO	Inyo	Bishop Crk Twp	73	312
GORLEY								
Hugh	35	m	w	PA	San Francisco	San Francisco P O	80	407
Jas	38	m	w	TN	Tehama	Paskenta Twp	92	165
Samuel	23	m	w	CANA	Santa Cruz	Soquel Twp	89	445
GORLIER								
Marshall	30	m	w	ITAL	San Francisco	2-Wd San Francisco	79	179
GORLIN								
Fred	43	m	w	BADE	San Joaquin	Dent Twp	86	27
GORMAN								
Anne	23	f	w	CA	San Francisco	11-Wd San Francisc	84	535
Barney	37	m	w	IREL	Alameda	Eden Twp	68	85
Barney	35	m	w	IREL	Sacramento	3-Wd Sacramento	77	297
Barny	35	m	w	IREL	San Francisco	8-Wd San Francisco	82	358
Bernard	31	m	w	IREL	San Francisco	San Francisco P O	83	142
Bessie	30	f	w	IREL	Stanislaus	Empire Twp	92	57
Bridget	25	f	w	IREL	San Francisco	11-Wd San Francisc	84	622
Catharine	8	f	w	IREL	Sutter	Vernon Twp	92	136
Catherine	51	f	w	IREL	San Francisco	2-Wd San Francisco	79	244
Catherine	50	f	w	IREL	Santa Clara	Redwood Twp	88	122
Charles	33	m	w	IREL	San Francisco	San Francisco P O	83	221
David	40	m	w	IREL	Solano	Benicia	90	11
Dennis	26	m	w	IREL	Alameda	Brooklyn Twp	68	42
Dennis L	43	m	w	OH	Placer	Bath P O	76	443
Dorinda	18	f	w	CA	Calaveras	Copperopolis P O	70	227
Edward	3	m	w	CA	Los Angeles	Soledad Twp	73	633
Evaline	10	f	w	CA	Calaveras	San Andreas P O	70	166
Frederick	18	m	w	PORT	Stanislaus	Emory Twp	92	25
George	35	m	w	IREL	Contra Costa	Martinez P O	71	417
James	48	m	w	MA	Calaveras	San Andreas P O	70	170
James	45	m	w	IREL	Los Angeles	Soledad Twp	73	632
James	32	m	w	MA	San Francisco	San Francisco P O	83	361
James	31	m	w	IREL	Napa	Napa Twp	75	67
James	28	m	w	CT	Napa	Yountville Twp	75	82
James	28	m	w	IREL	Sacramento	4-Wd Sacramento	77	346
Jas	24	m	w	IREL	San Francisco	11-Wd San Francisc	84	615
Jas W	24	m	w	NY	San Francisco	San Francisco P O	83	68
Johanna	27	f	w	IREL	San Francisco	San Francisco P O	83	227
John	6	m	w	CA	San Francisco	11-Wd San Francisc	84	593
John	49	m	w	PA	San Francisco	San Francisco P O	83	202
John	43	m	w	IREL	San Francisco	11-Wd San Francisc	84	650
John	41	m	w	IREL	Sacramento	Granite Twp	77	139
John	40	m	w	IREL	San Francisco	2-Wd San Francisco	79	255
John	34	m	w	IREL	Alameda	Eden Twp	68	86
John	32	m	w	IREL	San Francisco	San Francisco P O	83	77
John	30	m	w	IREL	San Francisco	11-Wd San Francisc	84	458
Joseph	37	m	w	AUSL	San Francisco	1-Wd San Francisco	79	112
Josephin	28	f	w	MN	San Francisco	8-Wd San Francisco	82	327
Josephine	10	f	w	CA	Nevada	Nevada Twp	75	318
Kate	19	f	w	IREL	San Francisco	8-Wd San Francisco	82	428
Lawrence	42	m	w	IREL	San Francisco	San Francisco P O	80	337
Lawrence	39	m	w	IREL	San Francisco	11-Wd San Francisc	84	535
Lazarus	56	m	w	IREL	Napa	Napa Twp	75	31
M	30	m	w	IREL	Amador	Sutter Crk P O	69	397
M F	32	m	w	IREL	Amador	Sutter Crk P O	69	397
Maggie	22	f	w	IREL	San Francisco	San Francisco P O	80	387
Margaret	35	f	w	IREL	San Francisco	San Francisco P O	83	310
Margaret	30	f	w	IREL	San Francisco	San Francisco P O	80	355
Margaret	29	f	w	IREL	San Francisco	11-Wd San Francisc	84	548
Margaret	16	f	w	IREL	San Francisco	San Francisco P O	83	260
Martin	32	m	w	IREL	Tuolumne	Chinese Camp P O	93	370
Mary	39	f	w	IREL	San Francisco	11-Wd San Francisc	84	660
Mary	25	f	w	IREL	San Francisco	San Francisco P O	80	422
Mary	22	f	w	IREL	San Francisco	5-Wd San Francisco	81	29
Mary	19	f	w	MA	San Francisco	San Francisco P O	83	201
Mary	18	f	w	MA	Santa Clara	Fremont Twp	88	56
Michael	40	m	w	IREL	San Francisco	San Francisco P O	83	287
Michael	39	m	w	IREL	San Francisco	San Francisco P O	83	391
Michael	35	m	w	IREL	San Francisco	San Francisco P O	83	35
Michael	34	m	w	IREL	San Francisco	San Francisco P O	83	318
Michael	29	m	w	IREL	Amador	Sutter Crk P O	69	409
Michael	25	m	w	IREL	Placer	Dutch Flat P O	76	406
Michel	35	m	w	IREL	Sacramento	4-Wd Sacramento	77	356
P	43	m	w	IREL	San Francisco	San Francisco P O	85	793
Patk	32	m	w	IREL	San Francisco	1-Wd San Francisco	79	42
Patrick	40	m	w	IREL	San Francisco	8-Wd San Francisco	82	388

© 2001 by Heritage Quest. All rights reserved.

Name	Age	S	R	B-PL	County	Locale	Series M593 Roll	Pg
Patrick	35	m	w	IREL	San Francisco	San Francisco P O	83	241
Patrick	35	m	w	IREL	San Francisco	San Francisco P O	83	227
Patrick	28	m	w	IREL	San Francisco	San Francisco P O	83	187
Peter	41	m	w	NY	San Francisco	San Francisco P O	83	324
Peter	25	m	w	IREL	San Francisco	San Francisco P O	83	206
R	25	m	w	MI	San Joaquin	Elkhorn Twp	86	63
Remora	40	m	w	IREL	San Mateo	Redwood City P O	87	376
Richard	29	m	w	IREL	San Bernardino	Belleville Twp	78	408
Richd	49	m	w	NY	El Dorado	Georgetown Twp	72	43
Richd	36	m	w	IREL	San Francisco	1-Wd San Francisco	79	62
S P	25	m	w	IREL	San Francisco	1-Wd San Francisco	79	59
Sarah	40	f	w	IREL	San Francisco	San Francisco P O	85	768
Thomas	40	m	w	IREL	Plumas	Quartz Twp	77	34
Thomas	36	m	w	MA	San Francisco	8-Wd San Francisco	82	445
Thomas	28	m	w	IREL	Sacramento	2-Wd Sacramento	77	241
Thos	57	m	w	IREL	Calaveras	Copperopolis P O	70	229
Thos	33	m	w	NY	San Francisco	1-Wd San Francisco	79	115
Thos	31	m	w	IREL	Sacramento	3-Wd Sacramento	77	299
Thos	30	m	w	IREL	San Francisco	11-Wd San Francisc	84	616
W G	29	m	w	IREL	Tuolumne	Big Oak Flat P O	93	391
William	40	m	w	IREL	Santa Cruz	Santa Cruz	89	407
William	14	m	w	CA	Nevada	Bridgeport Twp	75	122
William G	40	m	w	DC	Los Angeles	Los Angeles	73	540
Wm	47	m	w	IREL	San Joaquin	Tulare Twp	86	255
GORMAND								
Simon	35	m	w	IREL	San Francisco	7-Wd San Francisco	81	272
GORMER								
James	53	m	w	IREL	Nevada	Bridgeport Twp	75	115
Mary	21	f	w	NY	Sacramento	Sutter Twp	77	381
GORMERLY								
Thos	40	m	w	IREL	Santa Barbara	Santa Maria P O	87	511
GORMEZ								
Antone	47	m	w	PORT	Butte	Kimshew Tpw	70	83
GORMIN								
H	14	f	w	IREL	Alameda	Oakland	68	241
GORMLAY								
Patk	46	m	w	IREL	Solano	Vallejo	90	173
GORMLEY								
James	28	m	w	IREL	Nevada	Little York Twp	75	240
Jas L	51	m	w	IREL	Solano	Vallejo	90	164
Patrick	48	m	w	IREL	Santa Cruz	Soquel Twp	89	447
GORMLY								
James	30	m	w	IREL	Alameda	Oakland	68	182
John	45	m	w	MA	San Francisco	1-Wd San Francisco	79	113
John Jr	14	m	w	NY	San Francisco	1-Wd San Francisco	79	113
GORMON								
Barnard	40	m	w	IREL	Butte	Ophir Twp	70	98
Ellen	40	f	w	IREL	San Francisco	11-Wd San Francisc	84	658
P	35	m	w	IREL	Sierra	Forest Twp	89	530
GORMOS								
Carlo	50	m	w	MEXI	Stanislaus	Washington Twp	92	87
GORN								
Ah	30	m	c	CHIN	Sacramento	Georgianna Twp	77	124
Ah	26	m	c	CHIN	Sierra	Sears Twp	89	553
Ah	19	m	c	CHIN	Placer	Clipper Gap P O	76	393
Bridget	26	f	w	IREL	San Francisco	San Francisco P O	83	365
Charles	48	m	w	BADE	San Francisco	San Francisco P O	83	285
GORNA								
Joaquin	23	m	w	CA	Los Angeles	Los Angeles	73	525
GORNE								
John	29	m	w	PRUS	Santa Barbara	Santa Barbara P O	87	483
GORNELIO								
Pedro	20	m	w	MEXI	San Diego	San Diego	78	507
GORNELL								
Mary	36	f	w	IREL	San Joaquin	2-Wd Stockton	86	171
GORNER								
John G	49	m	w	ME	Los Angeles	Los Angeles Twp	73	482
GORNEY								
Ah	20	m	c	CHIN	Trinity	Indian Crk	92	200
GORNOSSET								
C	40	f	w	CANA	Sierra	Downieville Twp	89	515
GORNOW								
John	41	m	w	VA	Solano	Silveyville Twp	90	75
GORO								
Mary F	58	f	w	ME	San Francisco	8-Wd San Francisco	82	330
GOROW								
Edward	40	m	w	MO	Monterey	Castroville Twp	74	335
GORRELL								
Margrett	13	f	w	NY	San Francisco	1-Wd San Francisco	79	3
Robert	47	m	w	WV	Monterey	Monterey	74	362
Wm	53	m	w	IREL	Nevada	Nevada Twp	75	304
GORREMY								
Sarah	37	f	w	IREL	San Francisco	San Francisco P O	83	272
GORRILL								
William H	29	m	w	OH	Stanislaus	Emory Twp	92	23
GORRINGE								
John	50	m	w	ENGL	San Francisco	2-Wd San Francisco	79	170
GORRY								
Mary	25	f	w	IREL	San Francisco	8-Wd San Francisco	82	371
GORSEER								
Joseph	30	m	w	SPAI	San Francisco	8-Wd San Francisco	82	463
GORSHA								
Perry	34	m	w	AR	San Luis Obispo	Morro Twp	87	287
GORSIG								
Henry	44	m	w	PRUS	Calaveras	Copperopolis P O	70	228
GORSS								
Joseph	60	m	w	FRAN	Plumas	Washington Twp	77	56
GORSY								
Ang	20	m	c	CHIN	Plumas	Seneca Twp	77	48
GORTEMAN								
A	35	m	w	PRUS	Sierra	Butte Twp	89	508
GORTERIA								
Marcus	38	m	w	MEXI	San Diego	Coronado	78	467
GORTIN								
Jose	27	m	w	CHIL	Stanislaus	San Joaquin Twp	92	80
GORTON								
Albert S	49	m	w	ME	San Francisco	San Francisco P O	83	117
Barton H	40	m	w	OH	Napa	Napa	75	38
C H	38	m	w	NY	Alameda	Oakland	68	153
John	53	m	w	ME	Amador	Amador City P O	69	395
GORYEGO								
Gregorio	56	m	w	MEXI	San Diego	Pala Valley Reserv	78	480
GORZAN								
Joseph	35	m	w	PRUS	San Bernardino	San Bernardino Twp	78	447
GOS								
Chow	17	m	c	CHIN	San Joaquin	Oneal Twp	86	115
GOSCH								
Peter	44	m	w	HDAR	El Dorado	Diamond Springs Tw	72	34
GOSDELL								
George B	60	m	w	PRUS	San Francisco	6-Wd San Francisco	81	115
GOSE								
James	35	m	w	VA	Yolo	Cottonwood Twp	93	460
GOSEA								
Lorilla	36	f	w	MEXI	San Francisco	San Francisco P O	80	346
GOSEL								
Robert	32	m	w	GERM	Los Angeles	Los Angeles	73	546
GOSELL								
Mitchell	20	m	w	IREL	San Francisco	11-Wd San Francisc	84	457
GOSEMAN								
Thomas	26	m	w	SCOT	San Francisco	7-Wd San Francisco	81	159
GOSEN								
Henry	39	m	w	HAMB	San Francisco	6-Wd San Francisco	81	37
GOSENER								
Richard	55	m	w	MO	Fresno	Millerton P O	72	160
GOSENOVITCH								
John	40	m	w	AUST	Amador	Sutter Crk P O	69	402
GOSERET								
David	15	m	w	AR	Mariposa	Mariposa P O	74	106
GOSEY								
Lewis	45	m	w	MO	Plumas	Goodwin Twp	77	7
GOSHAM								
John	41	m	w	VT	Yolo	Cottonwood Twp	93	465
Silas	32	m	w	SCOT	Yolo	Buckeye Twp	93	413
GOSHEN								
Geo	30	m	w	NY	San Joaquin	Douglas Twp	86	49
Marcus	40	m	w	VA	Marin	Nicasio Twp	74	16
GOSHER								
Joshua	45	m	w	CANA	Yolo	Grafton Twp	93	499
GOSHETTA								
Jacomano	34	m	w	SWIT	Amador	Jackson P O	69	333
GOSHINE								
Lewis	55	m	w	NY	El Dorado	Kelsey Twp	72	59
GOSHNEL								
Harry	36	m	w	NY	San Joaquin	2-Wd Stockton	86	190
GOSHORN								
J M	33	m	w	IN	Sierra	Butte Twp	89	508
GOSIAS								
Antonio	42	m	w	AZOR	San Francisco	1-Wd San Francisco	79	19
GOSLAND								
Andrew	28	m	w	CANA	Nevada	Grass Valley Twp	75	204
Thomas	38	m	w	SCOT	San Francisco	San Francisco P O	83	142
GOSLIN								
John	26	m	w	MD	San Francisco	San Francisco P O	83	364
Maggie	25	f	w	NY	San Francisco	5-Wd San Francisco	81	33
V	22	m	w	CANA	Los Angeles	Los Angeles	73	566
GOSLINER								
Jos	20	m	w	PRUS	San Francisco	7-Wd San Francisco	81	260
Julius	31	m	w	PRUS	Colusa	Grand Island Twp	71	302
Simon	28	m	w	PRUS	San Francisco	San Francisco P O	83	127
GOSLING								
Caleb	40	m	w	ENGL	Napa	Yountville Twp	75	85
James	50	m	w	NY	San Francisco	San Francisco P O	83	388
John	37	m	w	ENGL	Sacramento	Sutter Twp	77	380
Joseph	36	m	w	ENGL	Sacramento	Franklin Twp	77	105
Lucy	28	f	w	IREL	San Francisco	San Francisco P O	80	473
GOSLINSKI								
Elias	34	m	w	PRUS	San Francisco	8-Wd San Francisco	82	454
GOSNELL								
Edmond H	56	m	w	MD	Plumas	Rich Bar Twp	77	45
GOSONEY								
James	30	m	w	ENGL	Santa Barbara	Las Cruces P O	87	507
GOSPIPI								
Costa	31	m	w	ITAL	Santa Clara	San Jose Twp	88	221
GOSS								
A B	47	m	w	VT	Trinity	Hayfork Valley	92	238
Alexander	60	m	w	MI	Santa Clara	2-Wd San Jose	88	325
David	41	m	w	IN	Marin	Bolinas Twp	74	1
E A	15	m	w	CA	Alameda	Oakland	68	243
G	41	m	w	NY	Sierra	Sierra Twp	89	568
Geo M	55	m	w	TN	Butte	Ophir Twp	70	110
Jacob	42	m	w	OH	San Francisco	11-Wd San Francisc	84	599
John	33	m	w	NC	Los Angeles	Los Nietos Twp	73	590
Joseph H	39	m	w	KY	Tuolumne	Sonora P O	93	326
Leonard	52	m	w	ME	Sacramento	3-Wd Sacramento	77	265

© 2001 by Heritage Quest. All rights reserved.

Name	Age	S	R	B-PL	County	Locale	Roll	Pg
Levy	43	m	w	ME	Amador	Ione City P O	69	359
Margaret	28	f	w	IREL	Contra Costa	Martinez P O	71	374
Michael	35	m	w	MALT	San Francisco	San Francisco P O	80	331
Norman D	34	m	w	VT	Santa Cruz	Santa Cruz	89	410
O S	38	m	w	MA	Tuolumne	Columbia P O	93	349
Peter	45	m	w	MA	San Francisco	8-Wd San Francisco	82	343
Rebecca	19	f	w	KY	Sonoma	Analy Twp	91	233
Richard J	42	m	w	ENGL	Yuba	Long Bar Twp	93	561
Thomas	32	m	w	ENGL	Santa Barbara	San Buenaventura P	87	437
Wilts G	46	m	w	AL	Los Angeles	Los Angeles Twp	73	472
Wm F M	42	m	w	MA	Santa Barbara	Santa Barbara P O	87	454
GOSSAGE								
Jerome	44	m	w	OH	Sonoma	Petaluma Twp	91	356
Joseph	41	m	w	OH	Sonoma	Analy Twp	91	230
Wm	55	m	w	OH	Sonoma	Analy Twp	91	245
Yeph	46	m	w	OH	Sonoma	Analy Twp	91	230
GOSSE								
Geo	37	m	w	PRUS	San Francisco	1-Wd San Francisco	79	85
GOSSEAP								
Carlos	22	m	w	CA	Stanislaus	San Joaquin Twp	92	81
GOSSECHACK								
Augustus	52	m	w	GERM	Sonoma	Sonoma Twp	91	447
GOSSETT								
Clay W	8	m	w	CA	Tehama	Cottonwood Twp	92	162
GOSSIER								
Raphael	60	m	w	MEXI	San Joaquin	Douglas Twp	86	38
GOSSILLUS								
Antone	36	m	w	MEXI	Sacramento	Center Twp	77	85
GOSSMAR								
John	60	m	w	SWIT	Mendocino	Anderson Twp	74	152
GOSSNER								
Bart	46	m	w	BAVA	Sacramento	3-Wd Sacramento	77	289
Joseph	48	m	w	WURT	Mariposa	Mariposa P O	74	100
GOSSOM								
Calvin	53	m	w	ME	Amador	Ione City P O	69	356
GOSTER								
Albert	43	m	w	ME	San Francisco	2-Wd San Francisco	79	212
GOSTICK								
Abram	30	m	w	ENGL	Yolo	Cottonwood Twp	93	463
GOSTIL								
Rufino	45	m	w	MEXI	Calaveras	San Andreas P O	70	208
GOT								
Ah	40	m	c	CHIN	San Joaquin	1-Wd Stockton	86	156
Ah	38	m	c	CHIN	San Joaquin	Oneal Twp	86	117
Ah	30	m	c	CHIN	Amador	Ione City P O	69	364
Ah	26	m	c	CHIN	San Joaquin	Oneal Twp	86	116
Meim	29	f	c	CHIN	Nevada	Eureka Twp	75	136
Sam	27	m	c	CHIN	San Joaquin	1-Wd Stockton	86	145
GOTAI								
Anton	89	m	w	MEXI	Tuolumne	Sonora P O	93	316
GOTAIS								
Ramon	54	m	w	MEXI	Tuolumne	Sonora P O	93	306
GOTALIE								
Julius	25	m	w	ITAL	San Francisco	8-Wd San Francisco	82	388
GOTARDO								
Corona	23	m	w	SWIT	Santa Cruz	Santa Cruz	89	429
GOTARIES								
Felicita	24	f	w	MEXI	Santa Clara	1-Wd San Jose	88	232
GOTCH								
John	34	m	w	PRUS	Solano	Silveyville Twp	90	73
GOTCHE								
Joseph	52	m	w	RUSS	Stanislaus	Empire Twp	92	45
GOTCHER								
Mary C	31	f	w	MI	Santa Clara	Santa Clara Twp	88	143
GOTCHET								
John	33	m	w	SWIT	Yuba	Marysville	93	578
GOTELOT								
Herman	50	m	w	PRUS	San Francisco	6-Wd San Francisco	81	105
GOTERA								
Manuel	43	m	w	CA	San Diego	Warners Rancho Dis	78	529
GOTERES								
Faboria	30	f	w	MEXI	Santa Clara	Almaden Twp	88	6
GOTEREZ								
Loanno	49	m	w	MEXI	Napa	Napa Twp	75	60
GOTFRIED								
Herman	40	m	w	PRUS	San Francisco	6-Wd San Francisco	81	89
GOTGE								
John	27	m	w	SHOL	Colusa	Spring Valley Twp	71	344
GOTH								
Charles	43	m	w	MECK	Santa Clara	Fremont Twp	88	42
GOTHE								
Louis	22	m	w	FRAN	San Francisco	7-Wd San Francisco	81	241
GOTHEY								
J W	21	m	w	PA	Amador	Sutter Crk P O	69	407
GOTHIE								
William	50	m	w	PRUS	Amador	Sutter Crk P O	69	408
GOTHMANN								
Julia	42	f	w	BREM	San Francisco	2-Wd San Francisco	79	218
GOTHOLD								
Augustus	24	m	w	BELG	Sacramento	2-Wd Sacramento	77	252
GOTHORN								
J	31	m	w	HAMB	Sierra	Butte Twp	89	508
GOTHSCHALK								
Charles	36	m	w	PRUS	San Francisco	San Francisco P O	83	369
GOTIE								
Charles	44	m	w	SWIT	Calaveras	San Andreas P O	70	200

Name	Age	S	R	B-PL	County	Locale	Roll	Pg
GOTLIEB								
Frost	44	m	w	PRUS	San Francisco	2-Wd San Francisco	79	170
GOTLIG								
Lawrence	43	m	w	SHOL	San Francisco	2-Wd San Francisco	79	253
GOTSCHALK								
Charles	36	m	w	WALD	San Francisco	6-Wd San Francisco	81	119
GOTSLEY								
William	24	m	w	GERM	Yolo	Cache Crk Twp	93	452
GOTSWALL								
Conrad	47	m	w	HDAR	Sutter	Sutter Twp	92	123
GOTT								
Ah	30	m	c	CHIN	Plumas	Goodwin Twp	77	5
Ah	14	m	c	CHIN	San Francisco	11-Wd San Francisc	84	562
Robert	33	m	w	IL	Plumas	Indian Twp	77	16
William	62	m	w	KY	Placer	Rocklin Twp	76	464
GOTTCHER								
Marcel	32	m	w	FRAN	San Francisco	8-Wd San Francisco	82	431
GOTTE								
Henry	27	m	w	BREM	San Francisco	11-Wd San Francisc	84	499
GOTTENBERG								
Hans	34	m	w	ME	Solano	Tremont Twp	90	32
John	23	m	w	NY	Contra Costa	Martinez P O	71	409
GOTTHELF								
Bertha	42	f	w	PRUS	Santa Clara	1-Wd San Jose	88	244
GOTTHIL								
S	35	m	w	BAVA	Sacramento	4-Wd Sacramento	77	328
GOTTHOLD								
A	56	f	w	PRUS	Sacramento	3-Wd Sacramento	77	309
G A	24	m	w	PRUS	Sacramento	3-Wd Sacramento	77	288
GOTTING								
Chas W	52	m	w	PRUS	San Francisco	7-Wd San Francisco	81	255
GOTTLEIB								
Maenbressa	44	f	w	PRUS	San Francisco	San Francisco P O	83	22
GOTTLIEB								
Davideo	46	m	w	PRUS	San Francisco	San Francisco P O	83	17
GOTTRIALS								
Mary	14	f	w	CA	Yolo	Cache Crk Twp	93	452
GOTTRIL								
Henry	45	m	w	GERM	Yolo	Cache Crk Twp	93	452
GOTTSCH								
Claus	50	m	w	SHOL	El Dorado	Mud Springs Twp	72	91
GOTTSCHALK								
Chris	37	m	w	PRUS	San Francisco	5-Wd San Francisco	81	24
John	50	m	w	SHOL	San Francisco	1-Wd San Francisco	79	4
GOTZ								
Andreas	28	m	w	AUST	San Francisco	2-Wd San Francisco	79	229
GOTZE								
Fritz	44	m	w	PRUS	Placer	Newcastle Twp	76	473
GOTZEN								
Ahrendt	18	m	w	HANO	San Francisco	San Francisco P O	85	870
GOU								
Ah	32	m	c	CHIN	Alameda	Oakland	68	152
Ah	30	m	c	CHIN	San Francisco	1-Wd San Francisco	79	118
Ah	28	m	c	CHIN	Alameda	Oakland	68	158
Ah	18	m	c	CHIN	Alameda	Eden Twp	68	62
Hung	19	m	c	CHIN	Alameda	Oakland	68	158
GOUCH								
Henri	35	m	w	PRUS	San Francisco	San Francisco P O	80	408
John	34	m	w	IREL	Mendocino	Anderson Twp	74	153
GOUCHIER								
Frank	45	m	w	FRAN	San Francisco	San Francisco P O	83	7
GOUDET								
Charles	29	m	w	FRAN	San Francisco	11-Wd San Francisc	84	660
GOUDETTE								
Peter	44	m	w	PRUS	Kern	Linns Valley P O	73	344
GOUDY								
George	50	m	w	CANA	San Diego	San Diego	78	503
Henry	33	m	w	IN	Santa Clara	Fremont Twp	88	63
Washington	24	m	w	IN	Santa Clara	Redwood Twp	88	121
GOUED								
Isaac	23	m	w	CANA	Sierra	Gibson Twp	89	540
GOUET								
Robert	38	m	w	PA	San Francisco	1-Wd San Francisco	79	133
GOUGAR								
Eli	23	m	w	CANA	Nevada	Grass Valley Twp	75	154
GOUGER								
James	47	m	w	VA	Napa	Yountville Twp	75	82
GOUGH								
Chas H	40	m	w	MD	San Francisco	8-Wd San Francisco	82	323
David	54	m	w	OH	Sacramento	4-Wd Sacramento	77	376
Francis	18	m	w	LA	San Francisco	11-Wd San Francisc	84	686
James	28	m	w	GERM	Los Angeles	Wilmington Twp	73	642
James	19	m	w	MA	San Francisco	San Francisco P O	83	157
John	50	m	w	CT	Alameda	Murray Twp	68	128
John	25	m	w	IREL	Marin	San Rafael Twp	74	34
Margaret	35	f	w	IREL	San Francisco	8-Wd San Francisco	82	424
Michael	26	m	w	CANA	Solano	Benicia	90	5
Patk	35	m	w	IREL	San Francisco	San Francisco P O	83	118
Richard	27	m	w	IREL	Nevada	Grass Valley Twp	75	176
Slevellyn	29	m	w	ENGL	San Diego	San Diego	78	485
GOUGHLAN								
Peter	33	m	w	IREL	Santa Clara	2-Wd San Jose	88	321
GOUIE								
Ah	20	f	c	CHIN	Nevada	Meadow Lake Twp	75	255
Ong	32	m	c	CHIN	Nevada	Nevada Twp	75	298
GOUIG								
Ah	15	m	c	CHIN	San Francisco	11-Wd San Francisc	84	559

© 2001 by Heritage Quest. All rights reserved.

Name	Age	S	R	B-PL	County	Locale	Series M593 Roll	Pg
GOULD								
Aaron	66	m	w	VT	Yolo	Buckeye Twp	93	407
Abner	41	m	w	NY	Solano	Vacaville Twp	90	126
Andrew J	44	m	w	IL	Inyo	Cerro Gordo Twp	73	319
Annie	30	f	w	IREL	Marin	San Rafael Twp	74	30
Asa	45	m	w	VT	Colusa	Grand Island Twp	71	309
C B	33	m	w	ME	Santa Clara	Gilroy Twp	88	85
C W	11	m	w	CA	San Francisco	San Francisco P O	85	799
Caroline	51	f	w	VA	Santa Clara	Gilroy Twp	88	83
Celia	36	f	w	IL	Alpine	Markleeville P O	69	316
Charles	45	m	w	ME	Alameda	Murray Twp	68	118
Charles	43	m	w	FRAN	Placer	Newcastle Twp	76	475
Charles	32	m	w	MA	Yolo	Putah Twp	93	512
Charles W	31	m	w	KY	Los Angeles	Los Angeles	73	546
Chas	32	m	w	VT	Sierra	Table Rock Twp	89	577
Chas G	33	m	w	PA	San Francisco	1-Wd San Francisco	79	80
Eleanor	33	f	w	NY	San Francisco	8-Wd San Francisco	82	465
Elisabeth	38	f	w	VA	Alameda	Alvarado	68	304
Elmore H	45	m	w	VA	Butte	Ophir Twp	70	94
Emily	4	f	w	CA	Sonoma	Russian Rvr	91	370
F	45	m	w	NH	Alameda	Oakland	68	266
F	40	m	w	NY	Alameda	Oakland	68	190
F C	9	m	w	CA	San Francisco	San Francisco P O	85	799
Fred Peter	40	m	w	RUSS	San Francisco	1-Wd San Francisco	79	68
G F	19	m	w	MA	Merced	Snelling P O	74	252
Geo	17	m	w	CT	Santa Clara	Burnett Twp	88	32
Gillman	43	m	w	ME	Amador	Drytown P O	69	422
Hanson W	51	m	w	ME	Inyo	Cerro Gordo Twp	73	318
Henry	44	m	w	MD	Tuolumne	Sonora P O	93	318
Henry	38	m	w	CT	Contra Costa	San Pablo Twp	71	353
Henry	36	m	w	MI	El Dorado	Mud Springs Twp	72	83
Henry	34	m	w	MO	Solano	Montezuma Twp	90	65
Henry	24	m	w	MO	Solano	Silveyville Twp	90	90
I D	47	m	w	MA	San Francisco	3-Wd San Francisco	79	319
J B	46	m	w	ME	Humboldt	Pacific Twp	72	295
J F	45	m	w	MD	Amador	Jackson P O	69	333
Jame L	32	m	w	ME	Placer	Dutch Flat P O	76	409
James	45	m	w	MA	San Francisco	San Francisco P O	80	464
James	43	m	w	NY	San Francisco	3-Wd San Francisco	79	317
James	33	m	w	IREL	Klamath	South Fork Twp	73	385
James	24	m	w	MA	Solano	Denverton Twp	90	25
James C	38	m	w	MA	Santa Clara	Milpitas Twp	88	110
Jas	47	m	w	PA	Sierra	Table Rock Twp	89	577
John	60	m	w	IREL	Santa Clara	2-Wd San Jose	88	316
John	49	m	w	NH	Sacramento	Granite Twp	77	142
John	45	m	w	NY	Sacramento	Natomas Twp	77	166
John	34	m	w	ENGL	Tuolumne	Sonora P O	93	310
John	34	m	w	CT	San Diego	San Diego	78	486
John	30	m	w	IREL	San Francisco	7-Wd San Francisco	81	251
John	21	m	w	IL	Humboldt	Mattole Twp	72	286
John P	48	m	w	MD	Yolo	Putah Twp	93	515
Joseph	50	m	w	ARGE	San Francisco	2-Wd San Francisco	79	165
Josiah G	49	m	w	NY	Placer	Roseville P O	76	354
L F	63	m	w	MA	Sacramento	1-Wd Sacramento	77	178
Levi A	48	m	w	ME	Santa Clara	Santa Clara Twp	88	161
M	31	f	w	IREL	Alameda	Oakland	68	147
M P	41	m	w	MD	Tuolumne	Columbia P O	93	348
Michael	28	m	w	IREL	Santa Clara	2-Wd San Jose	88	316
Nancy A	42	f	w	NH	San Francisco	San Francisco P O	85	722
Nelson Chas	35	m	w	NY	San Francisco	San Francisco P O	83	58
Richd	23	m	w	WURT	Butte	Chico Twp	70	42
Robert S	23	m	w	NY	Santa Cruz	Santa Cruz Twp	89	390
Robt	28	m	w	ME	Solano	Benicia	90	18
Saml	43	m	w	NY	San Francisco	5-Wd San Francisco	81	26
Simeon	50	m	w	ME	Yolo	Cache Crk Twp	93	440
T J	40	m	w	IN	Mendocino	Sanel Twp	74	229
Thomas	40	m	w	OH	Solano	Vacaville Twp	90	127
Thos	50	m	w	NH	San Joaquin	1-Wd Stockton	86	153
Warren	35	m	w	ME	Plumas	Quartz Twp	77	39
William	40	m	w	MO	Solano	Denverton Twp	90	25
William	36	m	w	MI	Calaveras	Copperopolis P O	70	257
William F	35	m	w	ME	Placer	Bath P O	76	448
Wm	28	m	w	CT	San Diego	San Diego	78	486
Wm	19	m	w	AUSL	San Joaquin	1-Wd Stockton	86	130
GOULDEN								
Ella	50	f	w	IREL	Alameda	Oakland	68	208
John	60	m	w	IREL	San Francisco	2-Wd San Francisco	79	222
John	25	m	w	IREL	San Francisco	2-Wd San Francisco	79	222
GOULDING								
Geo	12	m	w	MA	San Francisco	San Francisco P O	85	849
Saml	35	m	w	OH	Colusa	Spring Valley Twp	71	336
GOULE								
Jacob S	36	m	w	NY	Sierra	Gibson Twp	89	538
GOULER								
Herman	40	m	w	PRUS	San Francisco	San Francisco P O	80	462
GOULET								
Isador	39	m	w	CANA	San Francisco	San Francisco P O	83	328
Samuel P	41	m	w	MI	Yolo	Cache Crk Twp	93	435
GOULETT								
Clara	8	f	w	CA	Alameda	Oakland	68	259
GOULIHARD								
Bernard	51	m	w	FRAN	Plumas	Goodwin Twp	77	6
GOULINSKY								
David	59	m	w	PRUS	Yolo	Grafton Twp	93	485
GOULON								
Wm	45	m	w	VA	Sacramento	1-Wd Sacramento	77	180
GOULY								
Chas	40	m	w	NY	San Joaquin	Tulare Twp	86	253
GOUMAZ								
P J	25	m	w	SWIT	Lassen	Susanville Twp	73	439
GOUN								
Ah	36	m	c	CHIN	Nevada	Meadow Lake Twp	75	259
GOUNG								
Ah	30	m	c	CHIN	Sierra	Sears Twp	89	553
GOUNT								
John	57	m	w	OH	Placer	Dutch Flat P O	76	415
GOURGESON								
Lena	16	f	w	NORW	San Francisco	2-Wd San Francisco	79	166
GOURGRIET								
Albert	18	m	w	CA	Mariposa	Mariposa P O	74	121
GOURGUET								
Dennis	50	m	w	FRAN	Mariposa	Mariposa P O	74	133
GOURIS								
Alex	34	m	w	ENGL	Merced	Snelling P O	74	274
GOURL								
George	23	m	w	IREL	Nevada	Nevada Twp	75	304
Mary	38	f	w	IREL	Nevada	Nevada Twp	75	293
GOURLEY								
David	24	m	w	NY	Solano	Rio Vista Twp	90	70
Eliakim	27	m	w	CANA	Santa Barbara	Santa Barbara P O	87	451
Fitz William	29	m	w	CANA	Sierra	Table Rock Twp	89	571
Joseph	53	m	w	PA	Sonoma	Analy Twp	91	238
Thos B	36	m	w	OH	Sonoma	Analy Twp	91	241
GOURMET								
Andre	53	m	w	FRAN	El Dorado	Salmon Falls Twp	72	131
GOURMEY								
Silas	40	m	w	NY	Butte	Ophir Twp	70	100
GOURNEY								
Leonard	55	m	w	FRAN	Butte	Ophir Twp	70	91
GOUSETTE								
Vincent	35	m	w	SWIT	Calaveras	San Andreas P O	70	210
GOUSIE								
Joseph	20	m	w	SPAI	San Francisco	7-Wd San Francisco	81	188
GOUSLIN								
Arthur	18	m	w	FRAN	Nevada	Grass Valley Twp	75	194
GOUTCHIER								
Natalie	40	f	w	FRAN	San Francisco	6-Wd San Francisco	81	51
GOUTHEY								
Prosper	47	m	w	FRAN	Yuba	Long Bar Twp	93	560
GOUTIER								
Louis M	47	m	w	FRAN	San Francisco	6-Wd San Francisco	81	100
GOUTON								
Alexan	26	m	w	SCOT	Napa	Napa	75	1
GOUX								
Emile J	36	m	w	FRAN	Santa Barbara	Santa Barbara P O	87	450
GOUY								
Ah	22	m	c	CHIN	Placer	Bath P O	76	446
Ah	18	m	c	CHIN	Santa Cruz	Santa Cruz	89	427
GOV								
Ah	42	m	c	CHIN	Butte	Kimshew Tpw	70	84
Ah	41	m	c	CHIN	Placer	Auburn P O	76	364
GOVAN								
Frank	50	m	w	CANA	Nevada	Meadow Lake Twp	75	260
Jas	52	m	w	SCOT	Sacramento	4-Wd Sacramento	77	330
John	20	m	w	IREL	Yolo	Grafton Twp	93	486
GOVE								
Albion C	44	m	w	ME	San Francisco	8-Wd San Francisco	82	415
Andrew	37	m	w	NH	San Francisco	San Francisco P O	80	362
Aquila	25	m	w	ME	San Francisco	San Francisco P O	83	123
Austin J	38	m	w	ME	Yuba	Bullards Bar P O	93	548
Gardner	50	m	w	TN	Nevada	Bridgeport Twp	75	116
H L	42	m	w	ME	Nevada	Nevada Twp	75	293
J E	33	m	w	ME	Nevada	Nevada Twp	75	283
GOVER								
Andrew F	34	m	w	OH	Sonoma	Analy Twp	91	218
Chas F	35	m	w	TN	Shasta	Millville P O	89	490
David	49	m	w	SCOT	San Francisco	7-Wd San Francisco	81	269
James	38	m	w	KY	Yolo	Cache Crk Twp	93	434
Jus	21	m	w	AUSL	San Joaquin	2-Wd Stockton	86	211
GOVERAIN								
Philip	45	m	w	IREL	Santa Clara	Fremont Twp	88	44
GOVERN								
James	61	m	w	IREL	Placer	Rocklin Twp	76	468
Mc Jas	27	m	w	IREL	Santa Clara	Gilroy Twp	88	95
Michael	25	m	w	IREL	Contra Costa	Martinez P O	71	367
GOVERNLOCK								
W	38	m	w	SCOT	Yuba	Marysville Twp	93	567
GOVERNOR								
Charles	29	m	w	POLA	Marin	San Rafael Twp	74	37
GOVERSON								
Charles	40	m	w	PRUS	Santa Clara	2-Wd San Jose	88	314
GOVERSTON								
Charles	30	m	w	NORW	Santa Clara	2-Wd San Jose	88	302
GOVIN								
Wm M	65	m	w	TN	San Francisco	San Francisco P O	83	113
GOVINANNI								
Rokatilla	21	m	w	ITAL	San Francisco	6-Wd San Francisco	81	124
GOVSY								
Jas	39	m	w	SPAI	Sierra	Gibson Twp	89	543
GOVY								
Ah	16	m	c	CHIN	Yolo	Buckeye Twp	93	413
GOW								
Ah	7	f	c	CA	Mariposa	Mariposa P O	74	125

© 2001 by Heritage Quest. All rights reserved.

California 1870 Census

Series M593

Name	Age	S	R	B-PL	County	Locale	Roll	Pg
Ah	60	m	c	CHIN	Trinity	Indian Crk	92	199
Ah	58	m	c	CHIN	Trinity	Lewiston Pct	92	211
Ah	49	m	c	CHIN	Placer	Roseville P O	76	356
Ah	48	m	c	CHIN	Siskiyou	Cottonwood Twp	89	592
Ah	48	m	c	CHIN	El Dorado	Georgetown Twp	72	44
Ah	45	m	c	CHIN	El Dorado	Mud Springs Twp	72	79
Ah	43	m	c	CHIN	Mono	Bridgeport P O	74	283
Ah	42	m	c	CHIN	El Dorado	Mountain Twp	72	70
Ah	40	m	c	CHIN	El Dorado	Salmon Falls Twp	72	133
Ah	40	m	c	CHIN	El Dorado	Georgetown Twp	72	41
Ah	39	m	c	CHIN	Plumas	Plumas Twp	77	32
Ah	39	m	c	CHIN	El Dorado	Greenwood Twp	72	56
Ah	37	m	c	CHIN	Nevada	Eureka Twp	75	141
Ah	35	m	c	CHIN	Plumas	Plumas Twp	77	31
Ah	35	m	c	CHIN	Santa Cruz	Watsonville	89	369
Ah	35	m	c	CHIN	El Dorado	Coloma Twp	72	3
Ah	35	m	c	CHIN	Butte	Concow Twp	70	12
Ah	35	m	c	CHIN	Nevada	Bridgeport Twp	75	110
Ah	35	m	c	CHIN	Mariposa	Mariposa P O	74	92
Ah	33	m	c	CHIN	Sacramento	Georgianna Twp	77	125
Ah	32	m	c	CHIN	Mariposa	Mariposa P O	74	127
Ah	32	m	c	CHIN	El Dorado	Coloma Twp	72	1
Ah	32	m	c	CHIN	Butte	Kimshew Tpw	70	85
Ah	32	m	c	CHIN	Nevada	Grass Valley Twp	75	228
Ah	30	m	c	CHIN	Shasta	French Gulch P O	89	464
Ah	30	m	c	CHIN	Nevada	Nevada Twp	75	277
Ah	30	m	c	CHIN	Butte	Chico Twp	70	51
Ah	29	m	c	CHIN	Amador	Volcano P O	69	387
Ah	28	m	c	CHIN	Placer	Blue Canyon P O	76	419
Ah	28	m	c	CHIN	El Dorado	Georgetown Twp	72	44
Ah	28	m	c	CHIN	Nevada	Nevada Twp	75	312
Ah	27	m	c	CHIN	Santa Barbara	Las Cruces P O	87	505
Ah	27	m	c	CHIN	Butte	Chico Twp	70	51
Ah	27	m	c	CHIN	Calaveras	Copperopolis P O	70	233
Ah	27	m	c	CHIN	Nevada	Nevada Twp	75	311
Ah	27	m	c	CHIN	Napa	Napa	75	9
Ah	26	m	c	CHIN	Butte	Chico Twp	70	52
Ah	26	m	c	CHIN	Butte	Chico Twp	70	53
Ah	26	m	c	CHIN	Alameda	Oakland	68	140
Ah	26	m	c	CHIN	Nevada	Eureka Twp	75	136
Ah	26	m	c	CHIN	Yuba	Rose Bar Twp	93	656
Ah	25	m	c	CHIN	El Dorado	Salmon Falls Twp	72	132
Ah	25	m	c	CHIN	Amador	Volcano P O	69	387
Ah	25	m	c	CHIN	Nevada	Nevada Twp	75	299
Ah	24	m	c	CHIN	Trinity	Douglas	92	233
Ah	24	m	c	CHIN	Shasta	French Gulch P O	89	469
Ah	24	m	c	CHIN	El Dorado	Salmon Falls Twp	72	134
Ah	23	m	c	CHIN	Nevada	Eureka Twp	75	140
Ah	22	m	c	CHIN	San Joaquin	1-Wd Stockton	86	148
Ah	21	m	c	CHIN	Alameda	Washington Twp	68	301
Ah	21	m	c	CHIN	Alameda	Washington Twp	68	297
Ah	20	m	c	CHIN	Trinity	Weaverville Pct	92	230
Ah	20	m	c	CHIN	Trinity	Douglas	92	237
Ah	20	m	c	CHIN	Shasta	French Gulch P O	89	470
Ah	20	m	c	CHIN	San Francisco	6-Wd San Francisco	81	66
Ah	20	m	c	CHIN	Placer	Blue Canyon P O	76	417
Ah	20	m	c	CHIN	Placer	Auburn P O	76	362
Ah	20	m	c	CHIN	Nevada	Grass Valley Twp	75	210
Ah	18	m	c	CHIN	Yolo	Putah Twp	93	519
Ah	18	m	c	CHIN	San Francisco	3-Wd San Francisco	79	309
Ah	18	m	c	CHIN	Alameda	Washington Twp	68	288
Ah	17	m	c	CHIN	Plumas	Goodwin Twp	77	3
Ah	15	m	c	CHIN	Nevada	Nevada Twp	75	279
Ah	14	m	c	CHIN	Solano	Vallejo	90	179
Ah	14	m	c	CHIN	Placer	Clipper Gap P O	76	393
Ah	13	m	c	CHIN	Siskiyou	Yreka	89	656
Ah	12	m	c	CHIN	Trinity	Lewiston Pct	92	211
Ah	10	m	c	CHIN	Yolo	Putah Twp	93	517
Daniel	44	m	w	NY	Sonoma	Petaluma Twp	91	355
Finn	22	m	c	CHIN	San Francisco	6-Wd San Francisco	81	103
Frank	38	m	w	ITAL	Sacramento	Georgianna Twp	77	130
Gee	30	m	c	CHIN	Yuba	Marysville	93	628
Hock	40	m	c	CHIN	Colusa	Colusa	71	299
Mi	52	m	c	CHIN	El Dorado	Placerville Twp	72	92
Tong	45	m	c	CHIN	El Dorado	Coloma Twp	72	3
Un	28	f	c	CHIN	El Dorado	Placerville	72	115
Wee	40	m	c	CHIN	Sacramento	1-Wd Sacramento	77	196
GOWAN								
David	34	m	w	IREL	Amador	Jackson P O	69	326
Edward	40	m	w	IREL	Amador	Jackson P O	69	318
Frank	48	m	w	CANA	Nevada	Meadow Lake Twp	75	265
James	23	m	w	IREL	San Francisco	1-Wd San Francisco	79	67
John	42	m	w	CANA	San Joaquin	1-Wd Stockton	86	121
John	30	m	w	WI	Nevada	Grass Valley Twp	75	220
Katharina	37	f	w	IREL	San Francisco	San Francisco P O	83	165
R W	26	m	w	MI	Santa Clara	Almaden Twp	88	20
GOWANOSK								
J	23	m	w	NY	Monterey	Alisal Twp	74	300
GOWAY								
Eugene	62	m	w	FRAN	Sierra	Eureka Twp	89	524
GOWDY								
James	25	m	w	CANA	Colusa	Butte Twp	71	267
GOWE								
An	18	m	c	CHIN	Sierra	Eureka Twp	89	527
GOWELL								
Orrin	44	m	w	ME	Plumas	Goodwin Twp	77	8
Samuel	40	m	w	ME	Plumas	Goodwin Twp	77	1
GOWEN								
Lee	46	m	w	TN	Santa Clara	Santa Clara Twp	88	142
GOWENLECK								
Reuben	65	m	w	ENGL	San Francisco	2-Wd San Francisco	79	280
GOWER								
George	16	m	w	HI	Alameda	Eden Twp	68	84
Hattie	8	f	w	HI	Alameda	Brooklyn	68	28
GOWES								
J	24	m	w	AFRI	Alameda	Alameda	68	13
GOWEY								
Frank	21	m	w	NY	Santa Clara	Gilroy Twp	88	86
Manuel	38	m	w	PORT	Butte	Ophir Twp	70	119
Pierre	42	m	w	FRAN	Butte	Ophir Twp	70	117
GOWING								
Martin	66	m	w	MA	Santa Barbara	San Buenaventura P	87	425
GOWN								
Ah	12	m	c	CHIN	San Francisco	1-Wd San Francisco	79	18
GOWSI								
Jose	33	m	w	FRAN	San Joaquin	2-Wd Stockton	86	165
GOWTTLIP								
Mack	24	m	w	GERM	Humboldt	Mattole Twp	72	285
GOY								
Ah	60	m	c	CHIN	Amador	Ione City P O	69	356
Ah	39	m	c	CHIN	Nevada	Meadow Lake Twp	75	259
Ah	37	m	c	CHIN	Butte	Hamilton Twp	70	74
Ah	28	m	c	CHIN	Sonoma	Bodega Twp	91	251
Ah	22	m	c	CHIN	Sierra	Eureka Twp	89	525
Ah	21	m	c	CHIN	Sacramento	San Joaquin Twp	77	398
Ah	14	m	c	CHIN	Placer	Dutch Flat P O	76	414
An	55	m	c	CHIN	Amador	Ione City P O	69	352
Au	30	f	c	CHIN	San Francisco	6-Wd San Francisco	81	45
Bock	26	m	c	CHIN	Trinity	Junction City Pct	92	206
Chim	33	m	c	CHIN	Alameda	Washington Twp	68	297
Kin	16	m	c	CHIN	Alameda	Washington Twp	68	298
R S	67	m	w	VT	Sierra	Sierra Twp	89	568
Ye	17	m	c	CHIN	Sonoma	Petaluma Twp	91	352
GOYEN								
John	32	m	w	ENGL	Sierra	Gibson Twp	89	540
Richard	41	m	w	ENGL	El Dorado	Mud Springs Twp	72	75
William	29	m	w	ENGL	Alpine	Monitor P O	69	313
GOYENECKE								
T B	48	m	w	SPAI	San Francisco	San Francisco P O	83	283
GOYET								
Lazdt	32	m	w	CANA	Alpine	Monitor P O	69	317
GOYNE								
John	38	m	w	ENGL	Nevada	Washington Twp	75	345
Richard	37	m	w	ENGL	Nevada	Washington Twp	75	344
GOZALES								
Manuel	18	m	w	MEXI	San Francisco	6-Wd San Francisco	81	133
GOZEY								
John	32	m	w	FRAN	Sierra	Gibson Twp	89	540
GOZOLA								
G	43	m	w	ITAL	Mariposa	Maxwell Crk P O	74	139
GOZZENS								
Andre	28	m	w	FRAN	San Francisco	San Francisco P O	80	350
Fredrick	27	m	w	FRAN	San Francisco	San Francisco P O	80	350
Joseph	30	m	w	FRAN	San Francisco	San Francisco P O	80	350
GRAAD								
Martin	24	m	w	PRUS	San Francisco	8-Wd San Francisco	82	434
GRAAF								
George	36	m	w	BAVA	San Francisco	8-Wd San Francisco	82	434
Mary	15	f	w	CA	Sacramento	3-Wd Sacramento	77	315
Peter	43	m	w	BADE	Contra Costa	San Pablo Twp	71	363
GRAAFF								
Samuel	41	m	w	PRUS	San Francisco	San Francisco P O	80	466
GRAAFFE								
Geo	32	m	w	ENGL	San Francisco	1-Wd San Francisco	79	107
GRAB								
Conrad	49	m	w	HDAR	San Francisco	San Francisco P O	83	21
GRABB								
Stephen	40	m	w	MO	Solano	Silveyville Twp	90	75
GRABBLE								
Paul	59	m	w	PA	Placer	Alta P O	76	419
GRABE								
Emma	16	f	w	KY	Santa Clara	1-Wd San Jose	88	250
Frank	28	m	w	PRUS	San Francisco	3-Wd San Francisco	79	297
GRABENA								
Baptiste	40	m	w	ITAL	San Francisco	2-Wd San Francisco	79	164
GRABER								
Chas B	35	m	w	HDAR	Butte	Bidwell Twp	70	3
Lissette	21	f	w	PRUS	San Francisco	San Francisco P O	85	774
GRABHER								
William	35	m	w	PRUS	Trinity	North Fork Twp	92	218
GRABILL								
George G	46	m	w	MD	Plumas	Indian Twp	77	12
GRABLE								
Henry W	27	m	w	IN	Santa Cruz	Santa Cruz	89	404
GRABO								
Jane	70	f	w	HANO	Sacramento	3-Wd Sacramento	77	276
Lissie	35	f	w	BADE	Sacramento	3-Wd Sacramento	77	317
GRABOUSKY								
Frantz	47	m	w	PALA	Colusa	Stony Crk Twp	71	333
GRABY								
Louis	40	m	w	IL	Tuolumne	Chinese Camp P O	93	368
Saml	42	m	w	HUNG	Solano	Benicia	90	17
GRACE								
Bridget	37	f	w	IREL	San Francisco	8-Wd San Francisco	82	471

© 2001 by Heritage Quest. All rights reserved.

Name	Age	S	R	B-PL	County	Locale	Series M593 Roll	Pg
Edwd	36	m	w	MA	Solano	Vallejo	90	157
Emlie	42	f	w	BAVA	San Francisco	San Francisco P O	83	248
George	40	m	w	PA	Tulare	Venice Twp	92	274
Henry	23	m	w	IA	Nevada	Grass Valley Twp	75	207
John	25	m	w	IREL	San Mateo	Belmont P O	87	372
John	24	m	w	IREL	San Francisco	San Francisco P O	85	734
John	19	m	w	IREL	Solano	Silveyville Twp	90	74
Joseph	42	m	w	PORT	Placer	Auburn P O	76	372
M W	36	m	w	ME	Alameda	Oakland	68	261
Mary	24	f	w	IREL	Fresno	Millerton P O	72	147
Mary	24	f	w	IREL	San Francisco	San Francisco P O	83	64
Mary	23	f	w	IREL	Alameda	Hayward	68	79
Patrick	38	m	w	IREL	Fresno	Millerton P O	72	147
Peter	34	m	w	PRUS	Solano	Rio Vista Twp	90	55
Robert	50	m	w	IN	Sonoma	Santa Rosa	91	427
Robert	33	m	w	CANA	Plumas	Mineral Twp	77	22
Timothy	50	m	w	VA	Placer	Bath P O	76	427
Wm	38	m	w	IREL	San Francisco	San Francisco P O	83	40
GRACEA								
Antonio	44	m	w	AZOR	Contra Costa	San Pablo Twp	71	360
Manuel	60	m	w	PORT	Contra Costa	San Pablo Twp	71	354
Manuel	46	m	w	AZOR	Contra Costa	San Pablo Twp	71	362
GRACEY								
E W	13	m	m	MO	Del Norte	Smith Rvr Twp	71	479
GRACIA								
Ann	50	f	w	ME	Yuba	W Bear Rvr Twp	93	684
Anton	65	m	w	MEXI	Tuolumne	Chinese Camp P O	93	369
Anton	54	m	w	CHIL	Tuolumne	Sonora P O	93	306
Blas	60	m	w	MEXI	Los Angeles	Los Angeles	73	556
Frank	42	m	w	SCOT	Siskiyou	Yreka Twp	89	669
J M	24	m	w	CA	Alameda	Murray Twp	68	111
James	30	m	w	SWIT	Marin	Tomales Twp	74	76
Jose	25	m	w	MEXI	Los Angeles	Los Angeles	73	504
Jose F	36	m	w	AZOR	Placer	Newcastle Twp	76	473
Joseph	70	m	w	MEXI	Tuolumne	Chinese Camp P O	93	369
Lemuel	17	m	w	CA	San Francisco	San Francisco P O	80	472
Manuel	35	m	w	PORT	Alameda	Eden Twp	68	90
Paulita	7	f	w	CA	Napa	Napa	75	55
Richd	40	m	w	AZOR	San Francisco	1-Wd San Francisco	79	102
Simon	19	m	w	CA	San Francisco	San Francisco P O	80	472
GRACIANO								
E	50	m	w	CA	Santa Clara	Almaden Twp	88	20
GRACIE								
Joseph	48	m	w	PORT	Sonoma	Mendocino Twp	91	306
GRACIER								
Francisco	25	m	w	AZOR	San Francisco	1-Wd San Francisco	79	130
Frank	40	m	w	ME	San Francisco	11-Wd San Francisc	84	645
Frank	33	m	w	PORT	San Francisco	San Francisco P O	80	420
GRACIO								
David	48	m	w	FRAN	Shasta	Shasta P O	89	457
Foustens	48	m	w	MEXI	Yuba	Linda Twp	93	558
Jose	30	m	w	PORT	Trinity	Indian Crk	92	199
GRACY								
John	24	m	w	OH	Solano	Tremont Twp	90	31
Samuel	63	m	w	PA	Alameda	Brooklyn	68	23
GRADES								
Edwin	32	m	w	DENM	Klamath	Camp Gaston	73	372
GRADILLA								
Leonor	25	f	w	CA	Los Angeles	San Gabriel Twp	73	597
GRADIOS								
Josepha	30	f	w	CA	San Diego	San Luis Rey	78	514
Rifill	50	m	w	MEXI	San Diego	San Luis Rey	78	513
GRADOS								
Antone	50	m	w	FRAN	El Dorado	Diamond Springs Tw	72	26
GRADWALL								
Morris	11	m	w	CA	San Francisco	8-Wd San Francisco	82	448
GRADWOHL								
Abraham	28	m	w	LA	San Francisco	2-Wd San Francisco	79	221
GRADY								
Andrew	41	m	w	IREL	Butte	Ophir Twp	70	100
Andrew	38	m	w	IREL	Butte	Ophir Twp	70	93
Danl	29	m	w	IREL	San Francisco	1-Wd San Francisco	79	135
Dennis	58	m	w	IREL	San Francisco	San Francisco P O	83	12
Edw	22	m	w	NY	San Francisco	7-Wd San Francisco	81	236
James	47	m	w	ENGL	San Francisco	7-Wd San Francisco	81	198
James	31	m	w	IREL	Sacramento	Georgianna Twp	77	130
James	28	m	w	IREL	San Francisco	San Francisco P O	80	483
James	26	m	w	NY	San Francisco	San Francisco P O	80	425
James D	8	m	w	CA	San Luis Obispo	Salinas Twp	87	294
James H	48	m	w	IREL	San Francisco	8-Wd San Francisco	82	295
Jane	25	f	w	IREL	San Francisco	8-Wd San Francisco	82	437
John	44	m	w	PA	Napa	Napa Twp	75	34
John	40	m	w	IREL	San Francisco	San Francisco P O	83	310
John	40	m	w	IREL	Solano	Vallejo	90	141
John	35	m	w	IREL	San Francisco	11-Wd San Francisc	84	595
John	35	m	w	IREL	San Francisco	7-Wd San Francisco	81	279
John	26	m	w	IREL	San Francisco	San Francisco P O	80	483
John	26	m	w	IREL	Santa Cruz	Santa Cruz Twp	89	399
John	24	m	w	IREL	Solano	Benicia	90	20
John	24	m	w	CANA	Monterey	San Juan Twp	74	415
John	23	m	w	IREL	Solano	Vallejo	90	217
Julia	24	f	w	ENGL	San Francisco	2-Wd San Francisco	79	283
Martin	23	m	w	PA	San Francisco	1-Wd San Francisco	79	64
Mary	25	f	w	IREL	San Francisco	8-Wd San Francisco	82	498
Michael	53	m	w	IREL	San Francisco	San Francisco P O	83	85
Michael	44	m	w	IREL	Solano	Vacaville Twp	90	128
Michael	27	m	w	IREL	San Francisco	8-Wd San Francisco	82	392
Michael	25	m	w	PA	Los Angeles	San Gabriel Twp	73	597
Michael	22	m	w	PA	Amador	Ione City P O	69	357
Michael	21	m	w	IREL	San Mateo	Pescadero P O	87	414
Mike	25	m	w	IREL	Solano	Vallejo	90	197
Nicke	22	m	w	IREL	San Joaquin	Dent Twp	86	18
Patrick	45	m	w	IREL	Santa Cruz	Pajaro Twp	89	349
Patrick	45	m	w	IREL	Amador	Sutter Crk P O	69	404
Patrick	37	m	w	MA	San Francisco	7-Wd San Francisco	81	271
Patrick	32	m	w	IREL	Nevada	Grass Valley Twp	75	214
Patrick	20	m	w	IREL	Mendocino	Navarro & Big Rvr	74	177
Phillip	24	m	w	IREL	San Francisco	San Francisco P O	83	246
Rodger	50	m	w	IREL	Amador	Ione City P O	69	355
Theodr	10	m	w	CA	Alameda	Oakland	68	257
Thomas	36	m	w	IREL	Amador	Sutter Crk P O	69	408
Thos	23	m	w	IREL	Alameda	Oakland	68	253
GRAE								
William	28	m	w	SCOT	San Francisco	11-Wd San Francisc	84	707
GRAEBE								
Augustus	46	m	w	HDAR	Santa Clara	1-Wd San Jose	88	236
Herman	44	m	w	PRUS	Calaveras	Copperopolis P O	70	245
GRAEF								
Mary	22	f	w	SWIT	San Francisco	San Francisco P O	85	794
Rudolph	30	m	w	PRUS	Santa Clara	Gilroy Twp	88	73
GRAEFEN								
Charles	33	m	w	BRAN	San Francisco	6-Wd San Francisco	81	84
GRAEFNER								
Mark	45	m	w	PRUS	San Francisco	San Francisco P O	83	47
GRAEHWOHL								
Heny	39	m	w	BADE	Tuolumne	Big Oak Flat P O	93	393
GRAELLIGER								
E	36	m	w	BAVA	Sacramento	4-Wd Sacramento	77	340
GRAEVERSON								
George	31	m	w	FRNK	Fresno	Millerton P O	72	146
GRAF								
A	55	m	w	SWIT	Sacramento	4-Wd Sacramento	77	355
Chas	36	m	w	HANO	Nevada	Nevada Twp	75	275
Henry	21	m	w	HAMB	Sonoma	Sonoma Twp	91	449
Jacob	36	m	w	SWIT	San Francisco	San Francisco P O	83	335
M	41	m	w	BADE	Sacramento	1-Wd Sacramento	77	186
Minna	25	f	w	HAMB	San Francisco	San Francisco P O	83	315
Robert	22	m	w	SWIT	San Francisco	3-Wd San Francisco	79	324
William N	46	m	w	NY	Placer	Gold Run Twp	76	396
GRAFELMAN								
Peter	45	m	w	PRUS	Alameda	Oakland	68	256
GRAFF								
George	36	m	w	BADE	Amador	Jackson P O	69	338
Herman	37	m	w	BADE	Los Angeles	Los Angeles	73	531
J J	40	m	w	SWIT	San Francisco	San Francisco P O	85	857
Jacob	39	m	w	WURT	Yuba	Marysville	93	617
John	45	m	w	BADE	Los Angeles	Los Angeles Twp	73	489
Justin	11	m	w	NY	San Francisco	11-Wd San Francisc	84	588
Louisa	40	f	w	GERM	San Joaquin	2-Wd Stockton	86	162
Paul	24	m	w	BADE	Sacramento	4-Wd Sacramento	77	325
William	50	m	w	PRUS	San Francisco	San Francisco P O	83	206
GRAFFAM								
Ben	23	m	w	ME	San Francisco	11-Wd San Francisc	84	685
GRAFFARN								
J H	26	m	w	ME	Solano	Vallejo	90	187
GRAFFE								
Napoleon	30	m	w	PRUS	Alpine	Monitor P O	69	313
GRAFFINO								
John Bn	28	m	w	ITAL	Amador	Volcano P O	69	384
GRAFFMILLER								
John	47	m	w	BADE	Placer	Auburn P O	76	382
GRAFIUS								
John	29	m	w	NY	San Luis Obispo	San Luis Obispo Tw	87	297
GRAFMILLER								
A	49	m	w	BADE	Sacramento	3-Wd Sacramento	77	292
GRAFT								
C	10	f	w	CA	San Francisco	San Francisco P O	85	798
Dora	7	f	w	CA	San Francisco	San Francisco P O	85	798
John	26	m	w	HESS	Colusa	Colusa Twp	71	275
Trenia	55	f	w	HESS	Colusa	Colusa Twp	71	275
GRAFTON								
Harker M	34	m	w	OH	Contra Costa	Martinez P O	71	387
Joel	25	m	w	IL	Yolo	Buckeye Twp	93	408
John	33	m	w	CANA	Monterey	Pajaro Twp	74	377
Joseph	25	m	w	IL	Yolo	Cottonwood Twp	93	461
M E	30	f	w	MA	Alameda	Oakland	68	237
William	50	m	w	OH	Yolo	Cottonwood Twp	93	460
GRAGADO								
Ambrose	36	m	w	MEXI	Marin	San Rafael Twp	74	41
GRAGG								
Abel W	44	m	w	NY	Alameda	Alvarado	68	304
Amos P	9	m	w	MO	Shasta	Stillwater P O	89	481
Jacob	64	m	w	PA	Yuba	New York Twp	93	638
GRAGGAN								
D	33	m	w	IREL	Alameda	Oakland	68	240
GRAGORIO								
Gornie	42	m	w	CHIL	El Dorado	Placerville	72	117
GRAGSBY								
B M	53	m	w	TN	Sacramento	Sutter Twp	77	388
GRAHAM								
---	40	m	w	US	Amador	Sutter Crk P O	69	396
A J	44	m	w	NY	Sacramento	Brighton Twp	77	70
Adam	26	m	w	IREL	San Francisco	San Francisco P O	83	218
Albert	43	m	w	HANO	Mariposa	Mariposa P O	74	119

© 2001 by Heritage Quest. All rights reserved.

California 1870 Census

Name	Age	S	R	B-PL	County	Locale	Roll	Pg
Alex	24	m	w	CANA	Humboldt	Eureka Twp	72	266
Andrew	38	m	w	TN	Tulare	Visalia Twp	92	288
Andrew	33	m	w	CANA	Alpine	Silver Mtn P O	69	307
Andrew J	40	m	w	NY	El Dorado	Mountain Twp	72	67
Andrew W	60	m	w	KY	Yolo	Merritt Twp	93	505
Angus	37	m	w	SCOT	Tuolumne	Columbia P O	93	345
Ann	30	f	w	IREL	Sonoma	Petaluma Twp	91	361
Anna	25	f	w	PA	San Francisco	8-Wd San Francisco	82	348
Anna	19	f	w	IREL	San Francisco	2-Wd San Francisco	79	248
Annie	25	f	w	IREL	San Francisco	San Francisco P O	83	23
Arthur	45	m	w	OH	Trinity	Hayfork Valley	92	239
Arthur	40	m	w	IREL	Plumas	Goodwin Twp	77	4
Asa S	38	m	w	CT	Placer	Cisco P O	76	494
B F	32	m	w	IREL	San Joaquin	1-Wd Stockton	86	141
Benjamin	32	m	w	CANA	Alameda	Brooklyn	68	34
Benjamin F	34	m	w	NY	Santa Clara	2-Wd San Jose	88	325
Bjn	74	m	w	ENGL	San Francisco	11-Wd San Francisc	84	613
Burnett	28	m	w	IREL	Solano	Vallejo	90	207
C B	23	m	w	CANA	Tuolumne	Chinese Camp P O	93	384
Carey	34	f	i	CA	Klamath	Orleans Twp	73	379
Caroline	34	f	w	NY	Plumas	Washington Twp	77	56
Catherine	30	f	w	IREL	San Francisco	11-Wd San Francisc	84	646
Charles	44	m	w	PA	Santa Barbara	Santa Barbara P O	87	461
Chas	31	m	w	IREL	San Francisco	11-Wd San Francisc	84	582
Chas	31	m	w	ENGL	Shasta	Shasta P O	89	454
Christopher	28	m	w	PA	Sacramento	American Twp	77	66
Daniel	60	m	w	IREL	Santa Clara	Santa Clara Twp	88	176
Danl	34	m	w	NY	San Francisco	11-Wd San Francisc	84	631
David	56	m	w	SCOT	El Dorado	Placerville Twp	72	95
David	36	m	w	TN	Amador	Sutter Crk P O	69	397
Dennis	28	m	w	MO	Butte	Ophir Twp	70	115
Donald	59	m	w	SCOT	Tuolumne	Big Oak Flat P O	93	405
Ebenezer	37	m	w	CANA	Solano	Vacaville Twp	90	128
Edward	45	m	w	ENGL	San Francisco	8-Wd San Francisco	82	436
Edwin R	42	m	w	OH	Colusa	Grand Island Twp	71	303
Elijah	35	m	w	OH	Butte	Chico Twp	70	58
Elisha	19	m	w	TX	San Diego	Milquaty Dist	78	475
Ellen	53	f	w	IREL	San Francisco	San Francisco P O	83	335
Eugene	22	m	w	IN	Solano	Vacaville Twp	90	134
Francis	29	m	w	AR	San Bernardino	San Bernardino Twp	78	433
Francis	12	f	w	CA	Colusa	Grand Island Twp	71	309
Frank	33	m	w	OH	Alpine	Monitor P O	69	317
Franklin	42	m	w	MO	Colusa	Colusa Twp	71	276
Freend	37	m	w	NY	Mono	Bridgeport P O	74	286
Geo	52	m	w	VA	Humboldt	Eureka Twp	72	278
Geo	51	m	w	NY	Butte	Chico Twp	70	57
Geo	47	m	w	CANA	Solano	Vallejo	90	154
Geo	40	m	w	ENGL	San Francisco	5-Wd San Francisco	81	9
Geo	33	m	w	SCOT	San Francisco	1-Wd San Francisco	79	59
Geo	28	m	w	NY	San Francisco	1-Wd San Francisco	79	127
Geo	28	m	w	IREL	San Francisco	7-Wd San Francisco	81	265
Geo	15	m	w	MA	San Francisco	11-Wd San Francisc	84	588
Geo F	45	m	w	NY	San Francisco	1-Wd San Francisco	79	127
George	55	m	w	VA	Humboldt	Bald Hills	72	238
George	45	m	w	NY	Yolo	Cache Crk Twp	93	457
George	38	m	w	IREL	Santa Cruz	Santa Cruz Twp	89	386
George	30	m	w	NY	Colusa	Butte Twp	71	266
George	27	m	w	IREL	Sonoma	Salt Point	91	380
George	24	m	w	IA	Alpine	Markleeville P O	69	316
H	9	f	w	CA	San Joaquin	2-Wd Stockton	86	164
Hannah	26	f	w	CANA	Sonoma	Russian Rvr	91	369
Herbert	19	m	w	CA	San Francisco	San Francisco P O	85	749
Hillmer L	27	m	w	IN	Los Angeles	Los Angeles	73	529
Hiram	45	m	w	OH	Colusa	Colusa Twp	71	279
Hugh	52	m	w	VT	Fresno	Millerton P O	72	149
Irwin	19	m	w	IREL	San Francisco	8-Wd San Francisco	82	408
Isaac	47	m	w	KY	Santa Clara	Fremont Twp	88	48
Isaac	40	m	w	IL	Kern	Linns Valley P O	73	344
Isaac	33	m	w	PA	Tehama	Antelope Twp	92	155
J	15	f	w	US	Yuba	Marysville	93	609
J J	46	m	w	TX	Merced	Snelling P O	74	277
J W	35	m	w	ENGL	Sonoma	Russian Rvr	91	369
James	45	m	w	CANA	San Francisco	11-Wd San Francisc	84	604
James	44	m	w	VA	Klamath	Orleans Twp	73	379
James	40	m	w	LA	Stanislaus	Empire Twp	92	35
James	39	m	w	SCOT	Marin	Tomales Twp	74	84
James	35	m	w	NY	Contra Costa	San Pablo Twp	71	366
James	35	m	w	IREL	Nevada	Nevada Twp	75	306
James	32	m	w	IREL	San Francisco	7-Wd San Francisco	81	282
James	31	m	w	IREL	San Francisco	8-Wd San Francisco	82	408
James	27	m	w	IREL	Yolo	Putah Twp	93	517
James	24	m	w	CANA	Marin	Point Reyes Twp	74	23
James	19	m	w	IREL	Sacramento	San Joaquin Twp	77	394
James	16	m	w	CA	Monterey	San Benito Twp	74	379
James E	40	m	w	IREL	San Francisco	San Francisco P O	83	239
James F	24	m	w	MO	Stanislaus	Empire Twp	92	49
James R	44	m	w	IREL	Yuba	Slate Range Bar Tw	93	676
Jane	59	f	w	MD	Yolo	Putah Twp	93	525
Jas	38	m	w	SCOT	Solano	Vallejo	90	198
Jas	37	m	w	IREL	San Francisco	7-Wd San Francisco	81	265
Jas B	42	m	w	GA	Shasta	Shasta P O	89	453
Jeanette	38	f	w	SCOT	San Francisco	1-Wd San Francisco	79	127
Jennie	19	f	w	NY	Tulare	Visalia	92	295
Jesse J	35	m	w	IA	Stanislaus	Empire Twp	92	33
Jno	18	m	w	IL	San Joaquin	Oneal Twp	86	99
John	55	m	w	IREL	El Dorado	White Oak Twp	72	143
John	40	m	w	ME	Calaveras	San Andreas P O	70	153
John	35	m	w	CANA	San Francisco	11-Wd San Francisc	84	604
John	28	m	w	CANA	Humboldt	Arcata Twp	72	232
John	27	m	w	NC	Mono	Bridgeport P O	74	283
John	27	m	w	IREL	Alameda	Brooklyn Twp	68	42
John	26	m	w	IREL	Marin	San Rafael	74	56
John	22	m	w	IREL	San Francisco	2-Wd San Francisco	79	215
John	11	m	w	CA	Tulare	Farmersville Twp	92	245
John	10	m	w	CA	San Francisco	1-Wd San Francisco	79	127
John H	25	m	w	MO	San Francisco	1-Wd San Francisco	79	134
John M	28	m	w	PA	Placer	Colfax P O	76	390
John S	50	m	w	OH	Plumas	Quartz Twp	77	36
Jos	5	m	w	VA	Sacramento	3-Wd Sacramento	77	258
Jose	40	m	w	MEXI	Los Angeles	Los Angeles	73	519
Joseph	40	m	w	CANA	Solano	Denverton Twp	90	22
Joseph	40	m	w	CANA	Solano	Silveyville Twp	90	89
Joseph	39	m	w	OH	Alameda	Hayward	68	79
Joseph	30	m	w	IREL	San Francisco	2-Wd San Francisco	79	162
Joseph	29	m	w	PA	Yolo	Putah Twp	93	509
Joseph	27	m	w	AR	Tulare	Tule Rvr Twp	92	262
Juan	14	m	w	CA	Santa Clara	San Jose Twp	88	217
Julia	25	f	w	ENGL	San Francisco	5-Wd San Francisco	81	9
L	14	f	w	CA	Sacramento	3-Wd Sacramento	77	317
Levi A	34	m	w	CANA	El Dorado	Diamond Springs Tw	72	33
Levy S	70	m	w	MD	Sacramento	2-Wd Sacramento	77	251
Lillie	15	f	w	CA	San Francisco	11-Wd San Francisc	84	621
M	50	f	w	US	Sacramento	1-Wd Sacramento	77	183
M	46	m	w	NY	Merced	Snelling P O	74	247
Mariah	27	f	w	NY	Sacramento	San Joaquin Twp	77	398
Marshall	61	m	w	MA	San Francisco	San Francisco P O	83	143
Martha	53	f	w	IN	Sacramento	3-Wd Sacramento	77	257
Martha	53	f	w	IN	Solano	Silveyville Twp	90	82
Mary	44	f	w	NY	Alameda	Oakland	68	163
Mary	38	f	w	IREL	San Francisco	San Francisco P O	83	227
Mary	25	f	w	IREL	San Francisco	8-Wd San Francisco	82	466
Mary E	32	f	w	NY	San Francisco	1-Wd San Francisco	79	86
Mary H	60	f	w	IREL	San Francisco	6-Wd San Francisco	81	125
Mary Jane	16	f	w	CA	San Francisco	1-Wd San Francisco	79	126
Matilda	54	f	w	KY	Yolo	Washington Twp	93	529
Michael	43	m	w	IREL	Kern	Havilah P O	73	337
Michael	25	m	w	IREL	San Francisco	San Francisco P O	83	143
Micheal	28	m	w	IREL	San Francisco	7-Wd San Francisco	81	225
Morris	35	m	w	OH	Sacramento	Georgianna Twp	77	126
Nelson	47	m	w	ENGL	San Francisco	11-Wd San Francisc	84	596
P R	31	m	w	NY	San Francisco	8-Wd San Francisco	82	370
Patrick	35	m	w	IREL	Santa Clara	Santa Clara Twp	88	156
Patrick	30	m	w	IREL	Santa Clara	Santa Clara Twp	88	163
Patrick	23	m	w	IREL	San Diego	San Luis Rey	78	513
Peter	36	m	w	IREL	Nevada	Bridgeport Twp	75	113
Peter	21	m	w	IREL	San Francisco	3-Wd San Francisco	79	315
Peter	18	m	w	ENGL	San Francisco	1-Wd San Francisco	79	124
R	60	m	w	MD	San Joaquin	3-Wd Stockton	86	240
R L	43	m	w	KY	San Joaquin	Elkhorn Twp	86	60
R W	37	m	w	MS	Alameda	Murray Twp	68	125
Richd	28	m	w	ENGL	San Francisco	1-Wd San Francisco	79	101
Robert	49	m	w	CANA	Nevada	Nevada Twp	75	274
Robert	40	m	w	IREL	San Francisco	San Francisco P O	85	736
Robert	37	m	w	SCOT	San Francisco	8-Wd San Francisco	82	451
Robert	29	m	w	IREL	San Francisco	3-Wd San Francisco	79	293
Robert	23	m	w	IL	Yolo	Grafton Twp	93	499
Robt	25	m	w	NY	San Francisco	San Francisco P O	83	268
Robt	22	m	w	IREL	San Francisco	5-Wd San Francisco	81	32
Robt T	24	m	w	AUSL	San Francisco	San Francisco P O	85	740
Samuel	44	m	w	KY	Klamath	South Fork Twp	73	383
Sarah A	15	f	w	CA	Sacramento	American Twp	77	69
Sarah J	28	f	w	ENGL	Yolo	Cache Crk Twp	93	420
Sophia	4	f	w	CA	Nevada	Bridgeport Twp	75	112
Thomas	44	m	w	MO	Siskiyou	Yreka Twp	89	670
Thomas	39	m	w	IREL	San Francisco	8-Wd San Francisco	82	496
Thomas J	56	m	w	NY	Sonoma	Petaluma Twp	91	331
Thomas W	37	m	w	ENGL	San Diego	San Diego	78	492
Thos	46	m	w	VA	San Francisco	San Francisco P O	83	42
Thos	40	m	w	IREL	San Francisco	7-Wd San Francisco	81	275
Thos	36	m	w	NY	Butte	Chico Twp	70	31
Thos	26	m	w	IREL	San Francisco	San Francisco P O	83	22
V M	28	m	w	WI	Sacramento	Brighton Twp	77	79
W	59	m	w	PA	Alameda	Oakland	68	155
W	40	m	w	IREL	San Francisco	3-Wd San Francisco	79	323
Walter	80	m	w	SCOT	Colusa	Spring Valley Twp	71	340
Washington	48	m	w	OH	Mendocino	Point Arena Twp	74	204
Willard	20	m	w	IN	Solano	Vacaville Twp	90	134
William	48	m	w	SCOT	Mariposa	Mariposa P O	74	128
William	39	m	w	KY	Stanislaus	Empire Twp	92	27
William	35	m	w	SCOT	San Francisco	11-Wd San Francisc	84	635
William	32	m	w	PA	Sacramento	2-Wd Sacramento	77	251
William	27	m	w	CANA	Mendocino	Anderson Twp	74	152
William	25	m	w	IREL	Santa Clara	San Jose Twp	88	209
William	22	m	w	NJ	San Francisco	San Francisco P O	83	139
Wm	45	m	w	MD	San Joaquin	2-Wd Stockton	86	211
Wm	36	m	w	MO	San Joaquin	Union Twp	86	265
Wm	35	m	w	SCOT	San Francisco	1-Wd San Francisco	79	59
Wm	34	m	w	CANA	Sonoma	Salt Point	91	386
Wm	30	m	w	IREL	Yuba	Marysville	93	590
Wm	25	m	w	MO	Yuba	East Bear Rvr Twp	93	544
Wm	25	m	w	MO	San Joaquin	Elkhorn Twp	86	55
Wm	23	m	w	MO	San Joaquin	Elkhorn Twp	86	68
Wm	22	m	w	CANA	Humboldt	Bucksport Twp	72	243

Series M593

© 2001 by Heritage Quest. All rights reserved.

Series M593

Name	Age	S	R	B-PL	County	Locale	Roll	Pg
GRAHAME								
Alexander	32	m	w	NY	San Francisco	San Francisco P O	83	339
George	35	m	w	IL	Solano	Vacaville Twp	90	136
GRAHAMS								
William	33	m	w	IREL	Mendocino	Navarro & Big Rvr	74	174
GRAHAN								
Angus	21	m	w	IL	San Joaquin	Oneal Twp	86	99
Jas	26	m	w	PA	Butte	Chico Twp	70	32
Louis	32	m	w	KY	Calaveras	Copperopolis P O	70	238
Thos	49	m	w	IREL	Solano	Vallejo	90	161
William G	37	m	w	NJ	Tulare	Visalia	92	296
GRAHER								
Charles	28	m	w	PRUS	Santa Clara	1-Wd San Jose	88	224
GRAHL								
John	40	m	w	PRUS	Tuolumne	Sonora P O	93	318
GRAHM								
Annie	38	f	w	ME	San Francisco	San Francisco P O	80	337
John	40	m	w	SCOT	San Francisco	San Francisco P O	80	427
William	26	m	w	SCOT	San Francisco	San Francisco P O	80	540
GRAIG								
John	35	m	w	KY	Placer	Alta P O	76	412
Stephen G	39	m	w	OH	Inyo	Bishop Crk Twp	73	311
Worthington	16	m	w	IN	Alameda	Brooklyn Twp	68	51
GRAINER								
Charles	42	m	w	MA	Tuolumne	Chinese Camp P O	93	374
GRAINOR								
Fred	45	m	w	MA	Tuolumne	Big Oak Flat P O	93	404
GRAINY								
John	6	m	w	CA	Marin	San Rafael Twp	74	29
Thomas	10	m	w	CA	Marin	San Rafael Twp	74	29
GRAIZARD								
Frank	28	m	w	GERM	San Francisco	8-Wd San Francisco	82	292
GRAJEDA								
Felipe	57	m	w	MEXI	Santa Barbara	Santa Barbara P O	87	468
GRALEN								
M	34	m	w	PRUS	San Joaquin	2-Wd Stockton	86	192
GRALEY								
Annie	37	f	w	IREL	San Francisco	San Francisco P O	83	6
GRALLIS								
Ann	30	f	w	IREL	San Francisco	San Francisco P O	80	372
GRAM								
Chas	28	m	w	ENGL	San Francisco	1-Wd San Francisco	79	121
Henry	45	m	w	NY	San Bernardino	San Bernardino Twp	78	450
GRAMANN								
L	16	m	w	PRUS	San Joaquin	Tulare Twp	86	256
GRAMARGEN								
Geo	48	m	w	PRUS	Fresno	Millerton P O	72	164
GRAMBERT								
John	39	m	w	BREM	Amador	Drytown P O	69	420
GRAMBLE								
John	47	m	w	IREL	Tuolumne	Big Oak Flat P O	93	395
GRAME								
George	24	m	w	HANO	Sutter	Nicolaus Twp	92	106
GRAMER								
Jesus	30	m	w	MEXI	Los Angeles	Los Angeles	73	505
GRAMES								
David	30	m	w	HANO	Sutter	Nicolaus Twp	92	107
Mike	35	m	w	IREL	Solano	Vallejo	90	203
GRAMETT								
John	42	m	w	ENGL	Stanislaus	San Joaquin Twp	92	70
GRAMIRES								
Dolores	26	f	w	MEXI	San Francisco	San Francisco P O	80	466
GRAMMAR								
O S	14	m	w	MO	Sierra	Gibson Twp	89	544
GRAMMONT								
Adolph H	51	m	w	CANA	Mendocino	Point Arena Twp	74	224
GRAMOR								
Lewis B	30	m	w	PA	Santa Cruz	Soquel Twp	89	444
GRAMP								
Fred	30	m	w	GERM	Tuolumne	Columbia P O	93	339
GRAN								
Geo	35	m	w	IREL	San Francisco	1-Wd San Francisco	79	135
Wm H H	30	m	w	KY	Monterey	Castroville Twp	74	327
GRANADA								
Pancho	50	m	w	MEXI	Monterey	San Antonio Twp	74	318
GRANADO								
Emanuel	38	m	w	MEXI	Fresno	Millerton P O	72	154
GRANADOS								
Valentine	40	m	w	MEXI	Calaveras	San Andreas P O	70	154
GRANBY								
John	33	m	w	HCAS	Santa Clara	Santa Clara Twp	88	144
GRANCLOSE								
Mary	15	f	w	FRAN	Santa Clara	Fremont Twp	88	51
GRANCOURT								
John B	47	m	w	FRAN	San Francisco	2-Wd San Francisco	79	138
GRAND								
Ellen G	22	f	w	MA	Santa Clara	Santa Clara Twp	88	137
Fredk	28	m	w	ITAL	San Francisco	San Francisco P O	85	851
Louis	51	m	w	FRAN	El Dorado	White Oak Twp	72	138
Samuel	30	m	w	PRUS	Los Angeles	Santa Ana Twp	73	612
Winnie	18	f	w	NY	San Francisco	8-Wd San Francisco	82	388
GRANDBOES								
Lewis	40	m	w	CANA	Sierra	Sears Twp	89	557
GRANDE								
John	36	m	w	SWIT	Marin	San Rafael Twp	74	32
John	26	m	w	SWIT	Marin	Tomales Twp	74	76
John	25	m	w	SWIT	Marin	Nicasio Twp	74	15
John	25	m	w	SWIT	Marin	San Antonio Twp	74	61
Louis	20	m	w	SWIT	Marin	Nicasio Twp	74	15
GRANDESON								
C	55	m	w	MEXI	Yuba	Marysville	93	617
GRANDHILL								
John	5	m	i	CA	Colusa	Colusa	71	288
GRANDHOLM								
Victor	28	m	w	FINL	Placer	Bath P O	76	457
GRANDIE								
Antone	20	m	w	SWIT	Marin	Tomales Twp	74	79
John	23	m	w	SWIT	Marin	Tomales Twp	74	79
GRANDIZ								
Sebastian	20	m	w	WURT	San Francisco	San Francisco P O	80	461
GRANDMAN								
Christopher	30	m	w	ENGL	Santa Cruz	Santa Cruz Twp	89	395
GRANDOLER								
Ellen	50	f	w	ENGL	San Francisco	8-Wd San Francisco	82	320
GRANDOS								
Francisco	47	m	w	MEXI	Santa Cruz	Pajaro Twp	89	360
GRANDOVER								
George	31	m	w	ENGL	San Francisco	5-Wd San Francisco	81	33
GRANDPREE								
Henry	35	m	w	CANA	Sierra	Sears Twp	89	557
GRANDSHAFF								
Jacob	44	m	w	IN	San Luis Obispo	Morro Twp	87	284
GRANDUNA								
August	30	m	w	ITAL	San Francisco	2-Wd San Francisco	79	233
GRANDY								
Henry	40	m	w	NY	El Dorado	Mud Springs Twp	72	83
James	53	m	w	ENGL	El Dorado	Mud Springs Twp	72	91
James	49	m	w	ENGL	Sacramento	Sutter Twp	77	384
John	44	m	w	ENGL	Sacramento	Sutter Twp	77	384
GRANE								
Samuel S	44	m	w	NY	Yuba	Long Bar Twp	93	564
GRANEDINO								
Manl	53	m	w	PERU	Tuolumne	Sonora P O	93	331
GRANEL								
Arron	25	m	w	FRAN	Los Angeles	Los Angeles	73	521
GRANER								
Andrew	43	m	w	IREL	Mendocino	Point Arena Twp	74	206
O N	38	m	w	VA	San Francisco	San Francisco P O	83	137
GRANES								
Bernard	29	m	w	HAMB	San Francisco	San Francisco P O	80	352
GRANEY								
Bridget	40	f	w	IREL	Nevada	Grass Valley Twp	75	198
Catherine	55	f	w	IREL	San Francisco	11-Wd San Francisc	84	502
Geo P	40	m	w	IREL	San Francisco	San Francisco P O	83	369
Margaret	26	f	w	IREL	San Francisco	11-Wd San Francisc	84	462
Michael	30	m	w	IREL	San Francisco	San Francisco P O	83	7
GRANFALL								
John	33	m	w	ENGL	Nevada	Grass Valley Twp	75	181
Richard	19	m	w	ENGL	Nevada	Grass Valley Twp	75	181
William	35	m	w	ENGL	Nevada	Grass Valley Twp	75	198
GRANFELL								
William P	37	m	w	ENGL	Stanislaus	Branch Twp	92	7
GRANGAN								
E E	45	m	w	MD	Humboldt	Pacific Twp	72	299
GRANGE								
Hiram	28	m	w	IA	Stanislaus	Buena Vista Twp	92	11
Nevene	29	m	w	FRAN	San Francisco	San Francisco P O	83	367
GRANGENE								
Laura	14	f	w	CA	Stanislaus	Empire Twp	92	59
GRANGER								
Chas	38	m	w	MA	San Joaquin	Elkhorn Twp	86	55
Farley B	42	m	w	NY	Alameda	Washington Twp	68	268
Frank	22	m	w	VT	Sutter	Yuba Twp	92	148
Fredk	32	m	w	ENGL	Fresno	Millerton P O	72	155
John	28	m	w	KY	San Mateo	Half Moon Bay P O	87	403
Julius	48	m	w	ENGL	San Francisco	5-Wd San Francisco	81	12
Lewis C	51	m	w	OH	Butte	Ophir Twp	70	114
Loui	50	m	w	CANA	Alameda	Brooklyn	68	38
Marrion	25	m	w	TN	San Joaquin	Dent Twp	86	18
Nattie W	24	f	w	LA	San Francisco	5-Wd San Francisco	81	5
Oel	31	m	w	MI	San Francisco	8-Wd San Francisco	82	365
Pane	19	m	w	KY	San Mateo	Half Moon Bay P O	87	394
Saml	22	m	w	CANA	Alameda	Brooklyn Twp	68	51
Samuel	36	m	w	NY	Marin	San Antonio Twp	74	64
Samuel	34	m	w	ME	Nevada	Grass Valley Twp	75	145
Silas	21	m	w	KY	San Mateo	Half Moon Bay P O	87	403
W	19	m	w	NJ	Sacramento	3-Wd Sacramento	77	293
W M	29	m	w	VT	Sutter	Yuba Twp	92	148
W N	38	m	w	NY	Yuba	Marysville	93	583
Wm C	19	m	w	NJ	Sacramento	4-Wd Sacramento	77	321
GRANGO								
S K	42	m	w	GA	San Joaquin	Dent Twp	86	23
GRANGRE								
Nazaire	45	m	w	CANA	Nevada	Grass Valley Twp	75	154
GRANIA								
Antone	38	m	w	SPAI	Amador	Jackson P O	69	342
GRANIDAS								
Joan	39	m	w	MEXI	Fresno	Millerton P O	72	153
GRANIER								
Ammie	48	m	w	FRAN	Calaveras	San Andreas P O	70	198
Julius	27	m	w	ALGE	San Francisco	1-Wd San Francisco	79	42
GRANIS								
Alden G	45	m	w	MA	Placer	Auburn P O	76	360
Concepcion	45	f	w	MEXI	San Diego	Coronado	78	466

© 2001 by Heritage Quest. All rights reserved.

California 1870 Census

Name	Age	S	R	B-PL	County	Locale	Series M593 Roll	Pg
GRANISON								
George	31	m	w	PRUS	Fresno	Millerton P O	72	192
GRANJE								
Moses	49	m	w	CANA	San Francisco	8-Wd San Francisco	82	431
GRANJON								
Charles	50	m	w	FRAN	Nevada	Grass Valley Twp	75	219
Chas	57	m	w	FRAN	Yuba	Marysville	93	615
GRANLIN								
Clara	27	f	w	VT	San Francisco	San Francisco P O	80	477
GRANNELL								
Wm H	43	m	w	CANA	Sonoma	Petaluma Twp	91	325
GRANNER								
August	24	m	w	FRAN	Butte	Chico Twp	70	58
GRANNIER								
Zoe	57	f	w	FRAN	San Francisco	6-Wd San Francisco	81	86
GRANNIS								
Charles A	38	m	w	NY	Los Angeles	Los Angeles Twp	73	483
M S	25	m	w	NY	Klamath	Trinidad Twp	73	392
Olan	25	m	w	MI	Los Angeles	Los Angeles	73	567
GRANNISS								
D W	45	m	w	CT	San Francisco	1-Wd San Francisco	79	18
George W	45	m	w	CT	San Francisco	San Francisco P O	83	261
GRANNON								
Isaac	9	m	w	CA	San Francisco	San Francisco P O	83	373
GRANNUGH								
Geo	41	m	w	FRAN	San Francisco	11-Wd San Francisc	84	424
GRANODOS								
Fredrick	15	m	w	CA	Calaveras	San Andreas P O	70	156
GRANPREE								
Lewis	30	m	w	CANA	Sierra	Sears Twp	89	556
GRANS								
Henry S	46	m	w	CT	Calaveras	San Andreas P O	70	158
GRANSON								
Cyrus	42	m	w	MO	Mendocino	Point Arena Twp	74	214
Rosa	10	f	b	VA	Inyo	Bishop Crk Twp	73	316
GRANT								
---	38	m	w	IREL	Sacramento	4-Wd Sacramento	77	370
Abner	44	m	w	NY	Siskiyou	Yreka Twp	89	666
Abraham	28	m	w	NY	San Joaquin	Castoria Twp	86	6
Ada	47	f	w	GA	Sacramento	3-Wd Sacramento	77	287
Adam	42	m	w	PRUS	San Francisco	5-Wd San Francisco	81	31
Alex	35	m	w	CANA	Sierra	Sears Twp	89	561
Alexander	25	m	w	ME	San Mateo	San Mateo P O	87	355
Alfred	44	m	w	RI	San Diego	San Diego	78	488
Alfred M	35	m	w	ME	San Mateo	Schoolhouse Statio	87	333
Algebra	45	m	w	ME	San Francisco	7-Wd San Francisco	81	230
Alte	40	m	w	NJ	San Francisco	11-Wd San Francisc	84	531
Andrew	37	m	w	IREL	Placer	Rocklin P O	76	462
Andrew J	33	m	w	ME	San Bernardino	Chino Twp	78	410
Angles	30	m	w	CANA	El Dorado	Coloma Twp	72	7
Annie	1	f	w	CA	San Francisco	11-Wd San Francisc	84	572
B P	45	m	w	NY	Del Norte	Crescent	71	466
Barbara	43	f	w	SCOT	San Francisco	2-Wd San Francisco	79	160
Benjamin	40	m	w	NY	San Francisco	1-Wd San Francisco	79	71
C	50	m	w	NY	San Joaquin	Tulare Twp	86	252
Catherine	29	f	w	IREL	San Francisco	7-Wd San Francisco	81	204
Charles	28	m	w	MA	San Francisco	11-Wd San Francisc	84	571
Chas	29	m	w	BADE	Butte	Chico Twp	70	43
Chas B	46	m	w	IREL	San Francisco	7-Wd San Francisco	81	280
Cyrus	40	m	w	NY	Butte	Hamilton Twp	70	66
Daniel	48	m	w	ME	Placer	Rocklin Twp	76	466
Daniel M	39	m	w	PA	San Francisco	2-Wd San Francisco	79	258
Donald	30	m	w	SCOT	San Francisco	7-Wd San Francisco	81	253
E A	49	m	w	CT	Sacramento	Sutter Twp	77	389
Ed	42	m	w	MA	Sierra	Table Rock Twp	89	579
Elija	45	m	w	KY	Amador	Volcano P O	69	372
Elijah	34	m	w	NY	Solano	Rio Vista Twp	90	70
Elisha	57	m	w	ME	Calaveras	San Andreas P O	70	212
Elizur	41	m	w	CT	El Dorado	Placerville Twp	72	92
Ellen	20	f	w	MA	San Francisco	11-Wd San Francisc	84	511
Ellen A	23	f	w	NY	San Francisco	San Francisco P O	83	113
Erastus	27	m	w	CANA	Sonoma	Petaluma Twp	91	360
Everett	21	m	w	MA	Contra Costa	Martinez P O	71	377
Falia	24	f	w	NY	Alameda	Washington Twp	68	292
Fannie	14	f	w	CA	Alameda	Oakland	68	242
Fergus	63	m	w	SCOT	Mendocino	Navarro & Big Rvr	74	176
Franklin	51	m	w	ME	San Mateo	Half Moon Bay P O	87	406
Geo	33	m	w	NY	Butte	Chico Twp	70	18
Geo	27	m	w	IA	Yuba	Marysville	93	610
Geo	25	m	w	SCOT	Yuba	Marysville	93	603
Geo W	37	m	w	ENGL	San Francisco	San Francisco P O	83	119
George	47	m	w	IN	Nevada	Rough & Ready Twp	75	323
George	45	m	w	NH	Alameda	Brooklyn	68	24
George	43	m	w	MA	Santa Clara	Fremont Twp	88	62
George	34	m	w	NY	Santa Clara	1-Wd San Jose	88	278
George	28	m	w	IREL	San Mateo	San Mateo P O	87	360
George A	32	m	w	CANA	San Francisco	11-Wd San Francisc	84	704
George R	50	m	w	NY	Placer	Roseville P O	76	349
George W	38	m	w	NH	San Mateo	Half Moon Bay P O	87	398
Good	39	m	w	ME	Santa Cruz	Santa Cruz Twp	89	395
Hattie	8	f	w	CA	Monterey	Alisal Twp	74	304
Henrietta	17	f	w	NY	San Francisco	11-Wd San Francisc	84	598
Henry	45	m	w	FRAN	San Francisco	3-Wd San Francisco	79	320
Henry	32	m	w	ENGL	Nevada	Grass Valley Twp	75	207
Henry	30	m	w	NY	Nevada	Eureka Twp	75	138
Hiland	50	m	w	CANA	Sonoma	Analy Twp	91	222
Hugh	24	m	w	CANA	Humboldt	Arcata Twp	72	226
J D	30	m	w	IREL	San Francisco	San Francisco P O	83	274
James	45	m	w	NY	San Francisco	11-Wd San Francisc	84	704
James	40	m	w	AR	Kern	Linns Valley P O	73	349
James	36	m	w	SCOT	Tuolumne	Columbia P O	93	344
James	36	m	w	SCOT	Nevada	Meadow Lake Twp	75	260
James	30	m	w	NC	San Francisco	3-Wd San Francisco	79	308
James	30	m	w	VA	San Francisco	2-Wd San Francisco	79	214
James A	30	m	w	CANA	Placer	Bath P O	76	436
James M	40	m	w	ME	San Francisco	San Francisco P O	83	200
James W	30	m	w	CANA	Sutter	Yuba Twp	92	142
Jane	39	m	w	SCOT	Solano	Benicia	90	11
Jas	50	m	w	CANA	San Joaquin	Elkhorn Twp	86	54
Jenny	23	f	w	CANA	San Francisco	5-Wd San Francisco	81	8
Jenny	17	f	w	ENGL	San Francisco	6-Wd San Francisco	81	93
Jesse R	44	m	w	NJ	Sonoma	Russian Rvr	91	375
Jno	28	m	w	IREL	San Francisco	5-Wd San Francisco	81	35
Jno D	43	m	w	NJ	Sonoma	Russian Rvr	91	374
Job	55	m	w	ME	San Francisco	11-Wd San Francisc	84	584
John	55	m	w	IREL	San Francisco	San Francisco P O	83	92
John	55	m	w	CT	Monterey	Monterey Twp	74	347
John	40	m	w	IREL	Sacramento	4-Wd Sacramento	77	369
John	40	m	w	ENGL	Butte	Ophir Twp	70	92
John	39	m	w	SCOT	San Francisco	San Francisco P O	83	129
John	37	m	w	IREL	San Francisco	2-Wd San Francisco	79	215
John	36	m	w	SCOT	San Francisco	1-Wd San Francisco	79	98
John	35	m	w	CANA	Klamath	Sawyers Bar	73	377
John	33	m	w	IREL	Contra Costa	Martinez P O	71	416
John	32	m	w	CANA	Plumas	Plumas Twp	77	32
John	32	m	w	SCOT	Kern	Bakersfield P O	73	363
John	31	m	w	SCOT	Santa Clara	Fremont Twp	88	50
John	25	m	w	IREL	Santa Clara	2-Wd San Jose	88	330
John	15	m	w	CA	Santa Clara	Santa Clara Twp	88	177
John B	34	m	w	KY	Alameda	Washington Twp	68	300
John H	41	m	w	MA	El Dorado	Salmon Falls Twp	72	129
John L	34	m	w	MT	El Dorado	Mud Springs Twp	72	74
Jos	20	m	w	MA	San Francisco	San Francisco P O	83	117
Joseph	30	m	w	SWIT	Kern	Bakersfield P O	73	365
Joseph	30	m	b	VA	Napa	Napa	75	11
Joseph	30	m	b	MD	Napa	Napa	75	57
Joseph	27	m	w	PORT	Shasta	American Ranch P O	89	496
Joseph	27	m	w	NY	Solano	Silveyville Twp	90	78
Kenneth	24	m	w	CANA	Santa Barbara	San Buenaventura P	87	437
L	33	m	w	ME	Sierra	Gibson Twp	89	540
Laughlin	27	m	w	CANA	Sonoma	Petaluma Twp	91	359
Laughlin	27	m	w	CANA	Marin	Tomales Twp	74	77
Libbie	27	f	b	VA	Los Angeles	Los Angeles	73	547
Louis	40	m	w	NY	San Francisco	7-Wd San Francisco	81	197
Manuel	35	m	w	PORT	Trinity	Douglas	92	236
Mary	74	f	w	ME	Alameda	Brooklyn	68	22
Mary	38	f	w	IREL	Tuolumne	Chinese Camp P O	93	366
Mary	28	f	w	IREL	San Francisco	San Francisco P O	83	49
Michl	37	m	w	IREL	Marin	San Rafael Twp	74	38
Mike	28	m	w	IREL	Sonoma	Salt Point	91	380
Mitchell	40	m	w	CANA	Calaveras	San Andreas P O	70	201
Murdo	30	m	w	SCOT	Mendocino	Gualala Twp	74	225
O P	39	m	w	ME	Trinity	Canyon City Pct	92	201
Orland	47	m	w	SCOT	Stanislaus	Empire Twp	92	27
P	45	m	w	IREL	Sierra	Downieville Twp	89	517
Pat	50	m	w	IREL	Alameda	Oakland	68	154
Pat	39	m	w	IREL	San Joaquin	3-Wd Stockton	86	244
Pat	35	m	w	IREL	San Francisco	7-Wd San Francisco	81	242
Patrick	42	m	w	IREL	San Mateo	Schoolhouse Statio	87	337
Patrick	28	m	w	IREL	San Francisco	7-Wd San Francisco	81	169
Peter	24	m	w	OH	San Francisco	7-Wd San Francisco	81	238
Philip B	59	m	w	NJ	Monterey	Monterey	74	357
R P	44	m	w	MA	Alameda	Oakland	68	208
Richard	47	m	w	ME	Calaveras	San Andreas P O	70	211
Richd	19	m	b	MI	Sacramento	1-Wd Sacramento	77	204
Robert	45	m	w	IL	Kern	Tehachapi P O	73	352
Robert	36	m	w	MA	San Francisco	11-Wd San Francisc	84	602
Robert	18	m	w	NY	San Francisco	11-Wd San Francisc	84	509
Robert M	45	m	w	IL	Yolo	Grafton Twp	93	489
Robt	3	m	w	CA	San Francisco	San Francisco P O	85	828
Ruhaney	48	f	w	KY	Monterey	Alisal Twp	74	304
Saml	22	m	w	CANA	Butte	Kimshew Tpw	70	78
Samuel	32	m	w	PA	San Diego	Julian Dist	78	470
Sophie	15	f	w	MA	Santa Clara	2-Wd San Jose	88	337
Stillman	37	m	w	ME	Yuba	Marysville Twp	93	571
Sylvester	27	m	w	IREL	San Mateo	San Mateo P O	87	348
Theodore	42	m	w	MA	Santa Clara	Fremont Twp	88	62
Thomas	42	m	w	IN	Los Angeles	Los Angeles	73	571
Thomas	30	m	w	MA	San Francisco	11-Wd San Francisc	84	572
Thomas R	31	m	w	CANA	Colusa	Colusa	71	288
Thos	24	m	w	IREL	Solano	Vallejo	90	215
Thos W	30	m	w	IN	Shasta	Stillwater P O	89	479
Tom	22	m	i	CA	Fresno	Millerton P O	72	183
Willburn	41	m	w	IN	Shasta	Stillwater P O	89	479
William	50	m	w	MA	San Francisco	San Francisco P O	83	273
William	48	m	w	ME	Kern	Havilah P O	73	340
William	46	m	w	SCOT	Santa Clara	1-Wd San Jose	88	252
William	37	m	w	SCOT	Contra Costa	Martinez P O	71	367
William	31	m	w	MO	Inyo	Cerro Gordo Twp	73	321
William	24	m	w	MA	Contra Costa	Martinez P O	71	436
Wm	47	m	w	SCOT	Tuolumne	Sonora P O	93	318
Wm	41	m	w	NY	San Francisco	2-Wd San Francisco	79	213
Wm	31	m	w	NY	Monterey	Alisal Twp	74	298
Wm	30	m	w	ENGL	Sonoma	Analy Twp	91	222

© 2001 by Heritage Quest. All rights reserved.

Name	Age	S	R	B-PL	County	Locale	Roll	Pg
						Series M593		
Wm B	40	m	w	MA	San Francisco	1-Wd San Francisco	79	95
GRANTHEM								
Alonzo	42	m	b	VA	Tuolumne	Sonora P O	93	321
GRANTLY								
Julia	30	f	w	NY	San Francisco	8-Wd San Francisco	82	305
GRANTMAN								
John	32	m	w	PRUS	San Francisco	San Francisco P O	80	474
GRANTWELL								
Thos	40	m	w	ENGL	Nevada	Nevada Twp	75	287
GRANTZ								
Adolph	22	m	w	SHOL	San Francisco	1-Wd San Francisco	79	110
GRANVILL								
Conrod	25	m	w	NY	San Francisco	7-Wd San Francisco	81	164
GRANVILLE								
Catherine	33	f	w	IREL	Sonoma	Salt Point	91	392
Geo	29	m	w	CT	San Francisco	8-Wd San Francisco	82	370
George	30	m	w	ENGL	Stanislaus	Empire Twp	92	60
George E	26	m	w	WI	Stanislaus	Empire Twp	92	66
H J	30	m	w	ENGL	El Dorado	Mud Springs Twp	72	81
Henderson	25	m	b	LA	San Joaquin	3-Wd Stockton	86	218
Hugh	20	m	w	ENGL	Nevada	Grass Valley Twp	75	168
James	34	m	w	IREL	San Francisco	1-Wd San Francisco	79	44
James H	33	m	w	ENGL	Stanislaus	Branch Twp	92	6
GRANY								
Patrick	33	m	w	IREL	San Mateo	Half Moon Bay P O	87	390
Stephen	21	m	w	IREL	Solano	Vallejo	90	163
GRANYA								
J	55	m	w	CANA	Amador	Lancha Plana P O	69	368
GRANZ								
H	29	m	w	SAXO	San Francisco	San Francisco P O	85	813
GRAOLA								
Baden	15	m	w	CA	Stanislaus	Empire Twp	92	43
GRAPE								
Antone	44	m	w	PORT	Trinity	Indian Crk	92	199
GRAPH								
Henry	54	m	w	FRAN	Alameda	Alameda	68	7
GRAPO								
Charles	52	m	w	FRAN	Amador	Jackson P O	69	325
GRARD								
Girard	26	m	w	FRAN	Santa Barbara	Santa Barbara P O	87	493
GRARE								
Jaro	47	m	w	MEXI	San Joaquin	Elliott Twp	86	70
GRARY								
Eleanor	13	f	w	CA	Santa Clara	2-Wd San Jose	88	337
John	30	m	w	MA	San Francisco	11-Wd San Francisc	84	514
GRAS								
Edward	43	m	w	FRAN	Santa Clara	Fremont Twp	88	60
Fredk	40	m	w	PRUS	San Francisco	5-Wd San Francisco	81	18
GRASCH								
John	45	m	w	ITAL	San Luis Obispo	San Luis Obispo Tw	87	297
GRASCONS								
Antoni	25	m	w	PORT	Yuba	Bullards Bar P O	93	550
GRASENI								
John	38	m	w	SWIT	Tuolumne	Columbia P O	93	341
GRASER								
Henry	45	m	w	PRUS	San Francisco	5-Wd San Francisco	81	3
Josephine	24	f	w	FRAN	San Francisco	6-Wd San Francisco	81	65
Mary	38	f	w	MEXI	Tuolumne	Sonora P O	93	306
GRASETTI								
Wm	24	m	w	SWIT	Sonoma	Bodega Twp	91	260
GRASHMYER								
Fred	42	m	w	BADE	San Joaquin	3-Wd Stockton	86	230
GRASON								
John	26	m	b	VA	Calaveras	Copperopolis P O	70	261
Nathaniel	32	m	w	KY	Yolo	Putah Twp	93	521
Sarah A	68	f	w	KY	Yolo	Putah Twp	93	521
GRASS								
Andrew	33	m	w	HDAR	Yuba	Marysville	93	592
Andrew	33	m	w	HDAR	Yuba	Marysville	93	596
Henry	50	m	w	CANA	Nevada	Little York Twp	75	238
Joseph	58	m	w	HESS	Alameda	Oakland	68	149
Joseph	16	m	b	CAME	San Francisco	8-Wd San Francisco	82	370
William	24	m	w	NY	San Francisco	8-Wd San Francisco	82	363
GRASSBURGER								
Joe	45	m	w	BADE	San Joaquin	2-Wd Stockton	86	190
GRASSETTE								
William	29	m	w	SWIT	Sonoma	Vallejo Twp	91	461
GRASSLE								
John	40	m	w	HANO	San Francisco	7-Wd San Francisco	81	262
GRASSMAN								
Heny	36	m	w	PRUS	San Francisco	2-Wd San Francisco	79	214
Thomas	42	m	w	SWIT	Tuolumne	Sonora P O	93	325
GRASSO								
Charles	50	m	w	FRAN	Amador	Volcano P O	69	388
GRATE								
C	48	m	w	GERM	San Francisco	San Francisco P O	85	785
GRATEHOUSE								
Phil D	34	m	w	IL	Sonoma	Mendocino Twp	91	297
GRATER								
Edwin E	53	m	w	LA	San Luis Obispo	Santa Rosa Twp	87	317
Jno F	34	m	w	WURT	Sonoma	Healdsburg & Mendo	91	283
GRATH								
Daniel	33	m	w	NY	San Francisco	3-Wd San Francisco	79	327
GRATHEN								
C	45	m	w	IREL	San Joaquin	2-Wd Stockton	86	192
John	48	m	w	PRUS	San Francisco	8-Wd San Francisco	82	386
GRATHEY								
Fredrick	33	m	w	PRUS	Inyo	Lone Pine Twp	73	331
GRATIAS								
George	36	m	w	MEXI	Tuolumne	Chinese Camp P O	93	369
GRATIOT								
Henry	42	m	w	MO	Yuba	Rose Bar Twp	93	658
GRATSRANT								
J	49	m	w	NY	Santa Clara	Burnett Twp	88	39
GRATTAN								
Anna	17	f	w	NY	Solano	Vallejo	90	195
John	45	m	w	IREL	San Joaquin	Oneal Twp	86	103
Wm	35	m	w	MA	San Francisco	7-Wd San Francisco	81	263
Wm H	40	m	w	NY	San Francisco	San Francisco P O	85	861
GRATTE								
Joseph M	22	m	w	CANA	Sonoma	Salt Point	91	392
GRATTEN								
Baly	1	f	w	CA	San Joaquin	Oneal Twp	86	102
Richard	38	m	w	CANA	Santa Clara	2-Wd San Jose	88	305
GRATTIN								
John	39	m	w	IREL	Shasta	American Ranch P O	89	496
GRATTO								
Matthew	25	m	w	CANA	San Joaquin	Tulare Twp	86	255
Peter	21	m	w	ITAL	Amador	Jackson P O	69	327
Richard	38	m	w	CANA	Santa Clara	Milpitas Twp	88	112
GRATTON								
Alonzo A	31	m	w	ME	Yuba	North East Twp	93	644
GRAUFANDA								
Joseph	34	m	w	ITAL	San Francisco	2-Wd San Francisco	79	234
GRAUL								
Frank	25	m	w	PRUS	San Francisco	San Francisco P O	85	808
GRAUMAMON								
Sirt	53	m	w	HAMB	Trinity	Canyon City Pct	92	201
GRAUS								
Joel	61	m	w	VA	Amador	Ione City P O	69	356
GRAUT								
Jos O	51	m	w	CT	Solano	Benicia	90	4
GRAVE								
Chas	27	m	w	HAMB	San Francisco	1-Wd San Francisco	79	96
Henry	24	m	w	HANO	San Francisco	11-Wd San Francisc	84	641
GRAVEEL								
Santa Ana	60	m	w	CA	San Luis Obispo	San Luis Obispo Tw	87	308
GRAVELLE								
David	35	m	w	CANA	Nevada	Grass Valley Twp	75	224
GRAVELON								
Adolph	8	m	w	AZ	San Diego	San Pasqual Valley	78	525
GRAVEN								
Joseph	50	m	w	ENGL	El Dorado	Mud Springs Twp	72	78
GRAVENER								
David	38	m	w	WALE	San Francisco	7-Wd San Francisco	81	257
William	55	m	w	ENGL	Santa Clara	2-Wd San Jose	88	327
GRAVER								
C	11	m	w	CA	Solano	Benicia	90	21
Frank	31	m	w	PORT	Alameda	Eden Twp	68	89
Louis	30	m	w	PRUS	San Francisco	San Francisco P O	83	217
Manuel	5	m	w	CA	Santa Cruz	Santa Cruz Twp	89	381
Nicholas	30	m	w	BAVA	Contra Costa	Martinez P O	71	378
GRAVERT								
Carston	45	m	w	SHOL	El Dorado	Diamond Springs Tw	72	35
GRAVES								
Agustus	27	m	w	ME	Mendocino	Gualala Twp	74	225
Alfo	25	m	w	ENGL	Sacramento	3-Wd Sacramento	77	303
Aug	33	m	w	MD	Merced	Snelling P O	74	246
Augustus	37	m	w	NY	San Francisco	2-Wd San Francisco	79	274
B T	35	m	w	PA	Sacramento	1-Wd Sacramento	77	178
Benjamin F	24	m	w	IA	San Luis Obispo	Arroyo Grande Twp	87	274
Charles	55	m	w	ENGL	San Francisco	2-Wd San Francisco	79	205
Charles	37	m	w	KY	San Luis Obispo	Santa Rosa Twp	87	321
Charles W	51	m	w	VT	Placer	Lincoln P O	76	487
Chas	42	m	w	SCOT	Solano	Vallejo	90	165
Converse	37	m	w	MD	San Francisco	2-Wd San Francisco	79	236
Cora	21	f	w	MA	Nevada	Grass Valley Twp	75	177
D H	30	m	w	TN	Nevada	Meadow Lake Twp	75	265
Daniel	52	m	w	ME	Nevada	Grass Valley Twp	75	182
David R	43	m	w	KY	Colusa	Colusa Twp	71	274
Elias Hugh	47	m	w	VA	Mendocino	Point Arena Twp	74	207
Elizabeth	23	f	w	ENGL	San Francisco	11-Wd San Francisc	84	459
Emily	13	f	w	CA	Sonoma	Mendocino Twp	91	288
Emma	13	f	w	CA	Placer	Lincoln P O	76	486
Ernest	16	m	w	CA	Santa Clara	Santa Clara Twp	88	177
Fountain C	42	m	w	KY	Colusa	Monroe Twp	71	317
Frank	18	m	w	MI	Santa Barbara	San Buenaventura P	87	423
Geo	8	m	w	CA	San Francisco	11-Wd San Francisc	84	593
George	8	m	w	CA	San Francisco	6-Wd San Francisco	81	99
George	64	m	w	NY	San Francisco	8-Wd San Francisco	82	384
George	57	m	w	KY	Monterey	Alisal Twp	74	299
George W	37	m	w	VA	Sonoma	Petaluma Twp	91	320
Gusto	50	m	w	GERM	Solano	Vallejo	90	169
H S	42	m	w	CT	Sutter	Butte Twp	92	89
Hanson	30	m	w	ENGL	San Francisco	3-Wd San Francisco	79	312
Heny	60	m	w	VA	San Joaquin	Castoria Twp	86	4
Hilton	35	m	w	MA	Nevada	Grass Valley Twp	75	179
Hiram T	43	m	w	NY	San Francisco	2-Wd San Francisco	79	247
Hugh	15	m	w	CA	Santa Clara	Santa Clara Twp	88	177
Isabella	45	f	w	IREL	Nevada	Nevada Twp	75	287
Isadore R	35	f	w	MA	Sacramento	4-Wd Sacramento	77	327
J	34	m	m	VA	Amador	Ione City P O	69	370
J E	39	m	w	KY	Monterey	Alisal Twp	74	290

© 2001 by Heritage Quest. All rights reserved.

California 1870 Census

Name	Age	S	R	B-PL	County	Locale	Series M593 Roll	Pg
J M	38	m	w	NC	San Joaquin	Douglas Twp	86	46
Jacob	41	m	w	TN	Santa Clara	Redwood Twp	88	118
James	44	m	w	CT	San Francisco	11-Wd San Francisc	84	699
James T	32	m	w	TN	Tulare	Tule Rvr Twp	92	263
Jesse	20	m	w	ME	Monterey	Alisal Twp	74	303
Joel A	65	m	w	VA	Amador	Jackson P O	69	345
John	34	m	w	NY	Solano	Vallejo	90	210
John	28	m	w	MO	San Joaquin	Castoria Twp	86	4
John B	50	m	w	KY	San Mateo	Schoolhouse Statio	87	339
John L	45	m	w	PORT	Alameda	San Leandro	68	96
John M	39	m	w	CT	Tulare	Visalia Twp	92	287
John T	40	m	w	ENGL	Nevada	Grass Valley Twp	75	144
Joseph	43	m	w	ME	San Francisco	San Francisco P O	83	133
Joseph	13	m	w	CA	San Francisco	8-Wd San Francisco	82	356
Martin	56	m	w	NY	Contra Costa	Martinez P O	71	408
Nathan	60	m	w	NY	Calaveras	Copperopolis P O	70	253
Neffie	22	m	w	ENGL	Colusa	Colusa Twp	71	287
Ormand F	40	m	w	ME	Yolo	Grafton Twp	93	481
Perley	63	m	w	ME	Sacramento	4-Wd Sacramento	77	329
Polly	72	f	w	NY	San Francisco	2-Wd San Francisco	79	247
Roswel	33	m	w	PA	Contra Costa	Martinez P O	71	405
S F	29	m	w	MA	Sierra	Table Rock Twp	89	572
S H	34	m	w	NY	San Francisco	8-Wd San Francisco	82	370
Saml	36	m	w	NY	Butte	Chico Twp	70	47
Samuel	76	m	w	NY	San Francisco	2-Wd San Francisco	79	247
Samuel	40	m	w	AR	Siskiyou	Butte Twp	89	584
Simeon	17	m	w	CA	Santa Clara	Santa Clara Twp	88	177
Sylvester	30	m	w	TN	Santa Clara	Redwood Twp	88	117
Thomas	32	m	w	KY	Monterey	Alisal Twp	74	299
Thomas	30	m	w	TX	San Diego	Milquaty Dist	78	477
Wallace	25	m	w	OH	Sutter	Yuba Twp	92	149
Wm	38	m	w	MA	San Joaquin	3-Wd Stockton	86	220
Wm	23	m	w	KY	Sutter	Butte Twp	92	96
Wm	16	m	w	AUST	Butte	Bidwell Twp	70	3
Wm B	40	m	w	KY	Monterey	Castroville Twp	74	338
Wm J	40	m	w	VA	San Luis Obispo	San Luis Obispo Tw	87	309
Wm L	32	m	w	SC	Fresno	Kings Rvr P O	72	211
GRAVIA								
Alfred	38	f	w	FRAN	San Francisco	3-Wd San Francisco	79	319
GRAVID								
I	30	m	w	CA	Alameda	Murray Twp	68	125
GRAVIER								
Edward	28	m	w	FRAN	Marin	Sausalito Twp	74	74
GRAVIES								
Lorenso	25	m	i	MEXI	Inyo	Cerro Gordo Twp	73	319
GRAVIN								
John	30	m	w	ENGL	San Francisco	7-Wd San Francisco	81	187
GRAVINS								
Peter	38	m	w	HDAR	San Diego	Julian Dist	78	468
GRAVISOTA								
Antonio	45	m	w	ITAL	Santa Barbara	Santa Barbara P O	87	492
GRAW								
Edward A	45	m	w	CT	San Bernardino	San Bernardino Twp	78	450
James	27	m	w	MI	San Joaquin	Castoria Twp	86	14
Martha	22	f	w	MA	San Francisco	6-Wd San Francisco	81	72
GRAY								
---	22	m	w	OH	Santa Clara	Gilroy Twp	88	97
A	24	m	w	KY	El Dorado	Mud Springs Twp	72	75
A H	42	m	w	KY	Tehama	Battle Crk Twp	92	157
A R	42	m	w	ME	Sierra	Table Rock Twp	89	572
Alex	35	m	w	SCOT	Santa Barbara	San Buenaventura P	87	444
Alex	25	m	w	SCOT	Santa Clara	Gilroy Twp	88	99
Alexander	41	m	w	FL	San Francisco	2-Wd San Francisco	79	152
Alexander	40	m	w	SCOT	El Dorado	Placerville Twp	72	92
Alexander	30	m	w	SCOT	San Francisco	6-Wd San Francisco	81	80
Alexander	24	m	w	IL	Sutter	Yuba Twp	92	145
Algernon	25	m	w	MO	Sonoma	Analy Twp	91	231
Alice	12	f	w	AUSL	Alameda	Washington Twp	68	277
Allen T	55	m	w	KY	El Dorado	White Oak Twp	72	136
Alonzo	40	m	w	VT	San Francisco	8-Wd San Francisco	82	471
Andrew	34	m	w	IREL	San Francisco	San Francisco P O	80	471
Andrew	34	m	w	MA	Mendocino	Round Valley India	74	180
Ann	24	f	w	IREL	Merced	Snelling P O	74	255
Annie	13	f	w	RI	San Francisco	San Francisco P O	85	858
Ansel	28	m	w	IREL	Solano	Silveyville Twp	90	87
Asaph	55	m	w	MA	Alameda	Oakland	68	200
Benjamin	49	m	w	OH	Butte	Wyandotte Twp	70	143
Benjamin	39	m	w	NC	Napa	Yountville Twp	75	82
Benjamin F	40	m	w	MO	Placer	Auburn P O	76	363
C A	34	m	w	MA	Napa	Yountville Twp	75	80
C F	21	m	w	MO	Mendocino	Calpella Twp	74	183
Catharine	34	f	w	IREL	San Francisco	San Francisco P O	85	849
Celia	33	f	w	IREL	San Francisco	San Francisco P O	83	159
Charles	45	m	w	NY	Yuba	Slate Range Bar Tw	93	675
Charles	36	m	w	SCOT	San Francisco	San Francisco P O	83	100
Charles	35	m	w	ENGL	San Francisco	8-Wd San Francisco	82	357
Charles	32	m	w	VA	Yolo	Cottonwood Twp	93	474
Charles	28	m	w	ME	Mendocino	Navarro & Big Rvr	74	176
Charles H	41	m	w	RI	Yolo	Cache Crk Twp	93	428
Charles H	39	m	w	ME	San Mateo	Woodside P O	87	381
Charles S	15	m	w	MA	Yolo	Cache Crk Twp	93	428
Chas	27	m	w	ENGL	Sacramento	1-Wd Sacramento	77	174
Chas	25	m	w	VA	Yuba	East Bear Rvr Twp	93	542
Chas	24	m	w	MA	Santa Clara	Gilroy Twp	88	104
Clarence	26	m	w	PA	Santa Barbara	Santa Barbara P O	87	455
Col Elmer F	41	m	w	VA	San Diego	San Diego	78	495
D B	34	m	w	OH	Alameda	Oakland	68	218

Name	Age	S	R	B-PL	County	Locale	Series M593 Roll	Pg
D B	29	m	w	ME	Santa Clara	Gilroy Twp	88	80
D C	42	m	w	TN	Sutter	Butte Twp	92	97
D F	44	m	w	ME	Napa	Napa	75	6
D L	26	m	w	WI	Tehama	Tehama Twp	92	193
Dan	35	m	w	IREL	San Joaquin	Tulare Twp	86	255
Danl	35	m	w	SCOT	Solano	Vallejo	90	147
Danl	26	m	w	NY	Butte	Kimshew Tpw	70	79
David	36	m	w	TN	Trinity	North Fork Twp	92	219
David C	32	m	w	TX	Butte	Chico Twp	70	13
Dudley	20	m	w	IL	Nevada	Meadow Lake Twp	75	248
E P	47	m	w	MA	Solano	Benicia	90	14
E T	39	m	w	IN	Sutter	Butte Twp	92	99
Ed	39	m	w	ME	San Joaquin	Elkhorn Twp	86	61
Edward	28	m	w	MI	Sacramento	2-Wd Sacramento	77	238
Edward	27	m	w	IL	Placer	Bath P O	76	457
Edward P	28	m	w	NY	San Francisco	6-Wd San Francisco	81	84
Edwin	29	m	w	ENGL	San Francisco	San Francisco P O	83	366
Ellen	20	f	w	GA	San Francisco	7-Wd San Francisco	81	208
Ellen	18	f	w	NY	San Francisco	11-Wd San Francisc	84	688
Ellen N	66	f	w	MA	Napa	Yountville Twp	75	87
Emila	14	f	w	ENGL	Alameda	Washington Twp	68	277
Emma	16	f	w	CA	Calaveras	San Andreas P O	70	189
Fanny	28	f	w	MO	Yolo	Cache Crk Twp	93	448
Frances	35	m	w	IREL	Placer	Summit P O	76	495
Frances E	32	f	w	CANA	San Francisco	8-Wd San Francisco	82	386
Frank	27	m	w	MO	Solano	Vacaville Twp	90	125
Frank	18	m	w	IL	Placer	Lincoln P O	76	487
Fred	24	m	w	TN	San Joaquin	2-Wd Stockton	86	208
G	14	m	w	CA	Solano	Benicia	90	21
G W	22	m	w	CT	Yuba	Marysville	93	610
G W	18	m	w	IL	Sutter	Yuba Twp	92	145
Galusha	37	m	w	VT	Placer	Lincoln P O	76	485
Garrett	34	m	w	KY	Sonoma	Santa Rosa	91	396
Geo	41	m	w	NY	Solano	Vallejo	90	179
Geo	40	m	w	IN	Butte	Chico Twp	70	59
Geo A	17	m	w	CA	Nevada	Nevada Twp	75	271
Geo F	35	m	w	IL	Nevada	Nevada Twp	75	285
Geo H	34	m	w	IN	Humboldt	Eel Rvr Twp	72	246
Geo W	31	m	w	OH	Butte	Chico Twp	70	19
Geo W	30	m	w	MD	San Francisco	San Francisco P O	83	90
George	43	m	w	OH	Sacramento	Dry Crk Twp	77	103
George	37	m	w	KY	Sonoma	Cloverdale Twp	91	266
George W	38	m	w	KY	Yolo	Cache Crk Twp	93	424
George W	29	m	w	IL	Yolo	Grafton Twp	93	495
George W	24	m	w	LA	Inyo	Bishop Crk Twp	73	316
George W	19	m	w	IL	San Francisco	8-Wd San Francisco	82	462
Giles H	35	m	w	MA	San Francisco	6-Wd San Francisco	81	110
Henry	70	m	w	NY	Mariposa	Maxwell Crk P O	74	145
Henry	48	m	w	NY	Nevada	Little York Twp	75	234
Henry	34	m	w	DENM	Yolo	Cottonwood Twp	93	465
Henry	29	m	w	MO	Solano	Silveyville Twp	90	90
Henry P	38	m	w	IL	Colusa	Monroe Twp	71	320
Heny A	47	m	w	MA	San Francisco	3-Wd San Francisco	79	312
Howard	50	m	w	IREL	San Francisco	San Francisco P O	83	242
Isaac	28	m	w	IN	Sonoma	Mendocino Twp	91	292
J	28	m	w	MA	Alameda	Oakland	68	221
J N	27	m	w	NY	San Francisco	San Francisco P O	83	296
J Thomas C	37	m	w	ENGL	San Diego	San Diego	78	491
J W	31	m	w	CT	Santa Clara	Gilroy Twp	88	83
Jacob	63	m	w	MD	Los Angeles	Los Angeles Twp	73	493
Jacob	60	m	w	TN	Sonoma	Mendocino Twp	91	299
James	53	m	w	ME	Merced	Snelling P O	74	265
James	53	m	w	VA	Los Angeles	Los Angeles	73	572
James	47	m	w	KY	Yuba	Slate Range Bar Tw	93	670
James	39	m	w	SCOT	Merced	Snelling P O	74	265
James	37	m	w	OH	Merced	Snelling P O	74	252
James	36	m	w	MO	Solano	Vacaville Twp	90	133
James	31	m	w	IN	Plumas	Plumas Twp	77	32
James	28	m	w	TN	Merced	Snelling P O	74	278
James	27	m	w	NH	San Francisco	3-Wd San Francisco	79	300
James	19	m	w	MO	San Joaquin	Tulare Twp	86	262
James	17	m	w	NY	San Mateo	Schoolhouse Statio	87	338
James B	48	m	w	PA	Nevada	Nevada Twp	75	275
James C	36	m	w	ME	Butte	Ophir Twp	70	100
James C	28	m	w	IL	Sutter	Yuba Twp	92	145
James H	46	m	w	GA	Los Angeles	El Monte Twp	73	456
James M	51	m	w	CT	Contra Costa	Martinez P O	71	387
James P	40	m	w	MD	Butte	Chico Twp	70	29
Jane	17	f	w	----	El Dorado	Coloma Twp	72	1
Jas	37	m	w	MI	San Joaquin	Elliott Twp	86	81
Jas	23	m	w	AUST	San Joaquin	Dent Twp	86	16
Jas B	34	m	w	IL	Butte	Chico Twp	70	47
Jas P	29	m	w	PA	Fresno	Kingston P O	72	217
Jas W	44	m	w	VA	Sonoma	Santa Rosa	91	402
Jennie	5	f	w	CA	San Francisco	San Francisco P O	85	799
Jennie	24	f	w	IL	El Dorado	Mud Springs Twp	72	81
Jno	35	m	w	IL	Butte	Chico Twp	70	33
Jno C	32	m	w	ME	Butte	Ophir Twp	70	106
Joel	53	m	w	NH	San Francisco	8-Wd San Francisco	82	338
John	49	m	w	SCOT	Alpine	Woodfords P O	69	316
John	43	m	w	NC	Amador	Fiddletown P O	69	431
John	41	m	w	ENGL	Placer	Dutch Flat P O	76	415
John	40	m	w	MA	San Francisco	San Francisco P O	83	91
John	40	m	w	NY	San Francisco	San Francisco P O	83	258
John	40	m	w	US	Santa Cruz	Santa Cruz Twp	89	401
John	39	m	w	IL	Monterey	Monterey Twp	74	344
John	36	m	w	WI	El Dorado	Cosumnes Twp	72	16

© 2001 by Heritage Quest. All rights reserved.

Name	Age	S	R	B-PL	County	Locale	Roll	Pg
						Series M593		
John	35	m	w	ENGL	San Francisco	8-Wd San Francisco	82	460
John	34	m	w	IREL	Solano	Silveyville Twp	90	78
John	33	m	w	ENGL	Placer	Dutch Flat P O	76	403
John	31	m	w	MA	Yolo	Putah Twp	93	515
John	28	m	w	IREL	Solano	Silveyville Twp	90	75
John	28	m	w	IREL	San Francisco	7-Wd San Francisco	81	238
John	26	m	w	NY	Solano	Maine Prairie Twp	90	51
John	26	m	w	NY	Alameda	Oakland	68	264
John	23	m	w	IREL	Placer	Summit P O	76	495
John	18	m	w	ME	Humboldt	Bucksport Twp	72	244
John F	34	m	w	PA	Sacramento	2-Wd Sacramento	77	213
John F	33	m	w	CT	Sutter	Yuba Twp	92	145
John H	43	m	w	IL	Nevada	Nevada Twp	75	285
John H	18	m	w	MA	Sonoma	Vallejo Twp	91	450
John J	36	m	w	ENGL	Sacramento	4-Wd Sacramento	77	338
John T	37	m	w	GA	Amador	Fiddletown P O	69	432
Jonathan	46	m	w	ME	Stanislaus	Buena Vista Twp	92	11
Joseph	55	m	w	IL	Nevada	Nevada Twp	75	318
Joseph	46	m	w	ENGL	Nevada	Meadow Lake Twp	75	252
Joseph	42	m	w	PA	Sonoma	Sonoma Twp	91	432
Joseph	40	m	w	ENGL	San Francisco	San Francisco P O	83	279
Joseph	36	m	w	NY	San Francisco	11-Wd San Francisc	84	511
Joseph C	35	m	w	ENGL	Nevada	Grass Valley Twp	75	154
Joster S	24	m	w	ME	Mendocino	Little Rvr Twp	74	165
Julia	26	f	w	KY	Los Angeles	Los Angeles	73	504
Julia	25	f	w	MA	San Francisco	8-Wd San Francisco	82	385
Lee	18	m	c	CHIN	Monterey	San Juan Twp	74	394
Leonard L	63	m	w	ME	Mendocino	Big Rvr Twp	74	162
Lottie L	4M	f	w	CA	Sonoma	Santa Rosa	91	397
Louisa	22	f	w	NJ	San Francisco	8-Wd San Francisco	82	435
Luke	40	m	w	IREL	San Francisco	11-Wd San Francisc	84	522
M	25	m	w	SCOT	Nevada	Meadow Lake Twp	75	246
M	14	f	w	CA	Lassen	Janesville Twp	73	433
M Mrs	31	f	w	MO	Lake	Kelsey Crk	73	402
M T	32	m	w	PA	Solano	Vallejo	90	200
Mack	40	m	w	TN	Colusa	Colusa Twp	71	277
Malon	38	m	w	IN	Butte	Chico Twp	70	37
Manuel	37	m	w	ENGL	Stanislaus	Washington Twp	92	84
Margaret	40	f	w	IREL	San Francisco	8-Wd San Francisco	82	421
Maria	16	f	w	IREL	San Francisco	San Francisco P O	83	324
Martin L	31	m	w	ME	Contra Costa	Martinez P O	71	373
Mary	38	f	w	ENGL	San Francisco	6-Wd San Francisco	81	123
Mary	35	f	w	IREL	Sonoma	Petaluma Twp	91	345
Mary	16	f	w	CA	Los Angeles	Los Angeles	73	543
Mary	16	f	w	CA	San Francisco	San Francisco P O	83	234
Mary	10	f	w	CA	Calaveras	San Andreas P O	70	192
Matilda N	6	f	w	CA	Placer	Auburn P O	76	363
Michael	43	m	w	TN	Santa Clara	Gilroy Twp	88	84
Michael	35	m	w	IREL	San Francisco	San Francisco P O	83	374
Nancy	23	f	w	TX	Santa Clara	Gilroy Twp	88	84
Nason	54	m	w	ME	Monterey	Salinas Twp	74	310
Nathaniel	64	m	w	MA	San Francisco	6-Wd San Francisco	81	112
Nellie	1	f	w	CA	Sacramento	4-Wd Sacramento	77	378
Nichls R	47	m	w	ENGL	Fresno	Millerton P O	72	167
Orin	42	m	w	NY	Alpine	Monitor P O	69	314
Pat F	32	m	w	IREL	San Francisco	7-Wd San Francisco	81	248
Patrick	30	m	w	IREL	San Francisco	1-Wd San Francisco	79	135
Peter	27	m	w	IREL	Solano	Suisun Twp	90	115
Poris	37	m	w	ME	Mendocino	Big Rvr Twp	74	161
R	48	m	w	PORT	Lassen	Janesville Twp	73	433
R N	41	m	w	ENGL	Santa Clara	Almaden Twp	88	4
Reubin	33	m	w	ME	Butte	Chico Twp	70	19
Richard	50	m	w	NY	San Francisco	5-Wd San Francisco	81	23
Richard	37	m	w	CANA	Santa Cruz	Santa Cruz Twp	89	393
Riley	37	m	w	KY	Monterey	Alisal Twp	74	296
Robert	70	m	w	NY	Solano	Vacaville Twp	90	133
Robert B	43	m	w	NH	San Francisco	8-Wd San Francisco	82	378
Robert J	32	m	w	CT	Sutter	Yuba Twp	92	145
Rose	27	f	w	NY	Alameda	Oakland	68	192
S C	53	m	w	MA	Solano	Benicia	90	4
Salina	26	f	w	VA	Sonoma	Santa Rosa	91	400
Sam	39	m	w	GA	Butte	Chico Twp	70	39
Sam	37	m	w	OH	San Joaquin	Elkhorn Twp	86	65
Samuel	56	m	w	PA	Los Angeles	Los Angeles	73	537
Samuel	55	m	w	NC	Calaveras	San Andreas P O	70	216
Sarah	73	f	w	IREL	San Francisco	San Francisco P O	83	245
Sarah	59	f	w	IREL	Santa Barbara	San Buenaventura P	87	444
Sheldon	51	m	w	ME	Butte	Kimshew Tpw	70	85
Simon	38	m	w	PRUS	San Francisco	San Francisco P O	80	349
Susan	30	f	w	LA	Sonoma	Petaluma Twp	91	366
Susan	18	f	w	US	Yuba	Marysville	93	609
Sydney	28	m	w	MO	Sonoma	Petaluma Twp	91	341
T	14	m	w	CA	Solano	Benicia	90	21
Thomas	69	m	w	MA	Tuolumne	Sonora P O	93	308
Thomas	60	m	w	IREL	San Francisco	San Francisco P O	80	541
Thomas	47	m	w	PA	Los Angeles	Los Angeles Twp	73	482
Thomas	45	m	w	IN	Shasta	American Ranch P O	89	498
Thomas	29	m	w	MA	San Francisco	San Francisco P O	83	247
Thomas	24	m	w	ENGL	El Dorado	Placerville	72	127
Thomas	24	m	w	ENGL	Nevada	Grass Valley Twp	75	144
Thos	23	m	w	VT	Alameda	Oakland	68	247
Thos C	56	m	w	TN	Sonoma	Vallejo Twp	91	450
Thos Cal	50	m	w	IREL	Sacramento	1-Wd Sacramento	77	172
W S	41	m	w	KY	Sacramento	3-Wd Sacramento	77	300
Walter	32	m	w	NY	San Francisco	5-Wd San Francisco	81	33
Walter	10	m	w	AUST	San Francisco	San Francisco P O	85	800
William	70	m	w	IREL	San Francisco	11-Wd San Francisc	84	463
William	40	m	w	NY	San Francisco	8-Wd San Francisco	82	481
William	37	m	w	IREL	San Francisco	San Francisco P O	80	396
William	35	m	w	SCOT	Contra Costa	Martinez P O	71	415
William	32	m	w	MA	Stanislaus	Empire Twp	92	51
William	30	m	w	MD	Solano	Vacaville Twp	90	126
William	30	m	w	ENGL	Placer	Dutch Flat P O	76	403
William	29	m	w	VT	San Francisco	3-Wd San Francisco	79	298
William	28	m	w	SCOT	Merced	Snelling P O	74	252
William	27	m	w	MA	Solano	Vacaville Twp	90	126
William	24	m	w	MO	Solano	Maine Prairie Twp	90	46
William	13	m	w	CA	Calaveras	San Andreas P O	70	191
William A	45	m	w	NC	Calaveras	San Andreas P O	70	216
William H	61	m	w	VA	Los Angeles	Los Angeles	73	504
William H	49	m	w	KY	El Dorado	White Oak Twp	72	140
William J	27	m	w	IL	Sutter	Yuba Twp	92	145
Willis L	29	m	w	KY	Santa Cruz	Santa Cruz Twp	89	386
Wm	40	m	w	VA	San Joaquin	Douglas Twp	86	49
Wm	38	m	w	AR	Yuba	W Bear Rvr Twp	93	680
Wm	37	m	w	PA	San Joaquin	Elliott Twp	86	81
Wm	35	m	w	SCOT	San Francisco	11-Wd San Francisc	84	616
Wm	35	m	w	ENGL	San Francisco	San Francisco P O	85	849
Wm	28	m	w	SHOL	San Francisco	11-Wd San Francisc	84	677
Wm	25	m	w	NY	Sonoma	Salt Point	91	388
Wm C	26	m	w	ME	Placer	Clipper Gap P O	76	392
Wm Henry	35	m	w	MA	San Francisco	1-Wd San Francisco	79	44
Wm O	48	m	w	SCOT	San Francisco	San Francisco P O	85	782
Young	52	m	w	KY	El Dorado	White Oak Twp	72	137
Zebeniah	41	m	w	MA	Plumas	Quartz Twp	77	41
GRAYDON								
John	38	m	w	IREL	Placer	Bath P O	76	445
John	21	m	w	NY	San Francisco	San Francisco P O	85	722
GRAYER								
Lewis	20	m	w	NY	Monterey	Alisal Twp	74	304
GRAYHAM								
Eliza	50	f	w	IREL	Alameda	Brooklyn Twp	68	49
Mary	26	f	w	NY	Alameda	Eden Twp	68	93
GRAYSON								
Charles	35	m	w	MO	Yolo	Cottonwood Twp	93	465
Charles	26	m	b	MO	Yolo	Grafton Twp	93	481
Daniel	37	m	w	AL	Stanislaus	Buena Vista Twp	92	15
Frederick	40	m	w	ENGL	Stanislaus	Emory Twp	92	26
Harvery	40	m	w	TX	Stanislaus	Branch Twp	92	10
GRAYSTONE								
Robert	41	m	w	ENGL	Stanislaus	Empire Twp	92	59
GRAZIA								
Bertrand	59	m	w	FRAN	Santa Cruz	Santa Cruz	89	411
Francisco	40	m	w	MEXI	Santa Cruz	Soquel Twp	89	439
GRAZY								
Joseph	33	m	w	PORT	Alameda	Washington Twp	68	281
GRE								
Ah	28	m	c	CHIN	Sacramento	Franklin Twp	77	108
Ah	20	m	c	CHIN	Sacramento	1-Wd Sacramento	77	194
GREADY								
Robert	18	m	w	ENGL	Contra Costa	Martinez P O	71	385
GREALEY								
Walter	2	m	w	CA	Nevada	Nevada Twp	75	307
GREAME								
A L	30	m	w	ENGL	Santa Clara	Gilroy Twp	88	82
GREANEY								
J J	25	m	w	IREL	Solano	Vallejo	90	140
John	24	m	w	IREL	Solano	Vallejo	90	164
Wm	28	m	w	PRUS	Alameda	Oakland	68	182
GREAONY								
Thomas	35	m	w	IREL	Nevada	Grass Valley Twp	75	212
GREAR								
George A	28	m	w	MO	Colusa	Spring Valley Twp	71	338
John	24	m	w	OH	Solano	Rio Vista Twp	90	57
Robert	61	m	w	IREL	San Francisco	11-Wd San Francisc	84	555
William	31	m	w	MO	Colusa	Spring Valley Twp	71	338
GREASIE								
Alta	1	f	w	CA	Fresno	Millerton P O	72	164
GREAT								
John	48	m	w	ME	San Francisco	11-Wd San Francisc	84	677
GREATMAN								
Charles	45	m	w	BADE	Placer	Lincoln P O	76	490
GREATREX								
Thos	61	m	w	ENGL	Santa Clara	Almaden Twp	88	5
GREAVES								
Benja	50	m	w	IREL	San Francisco	8-Wd San Francisco	82	317
Chas	37	m	w	MA	San Joaquin	Elkhorn Twp	86	61
James P	63	m	w	NY	Los Angeles	Los Angeles	73	538
John	37	m	w	VA	Santa Clara	Gilroy Twp	88	71
R L	38	m	w	OH	San Joaquin	Union Twp	86	265
Robert	21	m	w	CANA	Mendocino	Casper & Big Rvr	74	164
William	55	m	w	ENGL	San Francisco	8-Wd San Francisco	82	434
GREBLE								
Benjamin	57	m	w	OH	San Luis Obispo	San Luis Obispo Tw	87	312
GRECELLIN								
Charles	25	m	w	MO	San Francisco	6-Wd San Francisco	81	89
GREDE								
Pal	27	m	w	IREL	San Joaquin	Dent Twp	86	18
GREDER								
John	36	m	w	IL	Calaveras	Copperopolis P O	70	238
John	27	m	w	ITAL	San Francisco	2-Wd San Francisco	79	284
Tobias S	63	m	w	TN	Los Angeles	Los Angeles Twp	73	494
GREDY								
Emma	8	f	w	CA	Mariposa	Maxwell Crk P O	74	143

© 2001 by Heritage Quest. All rights reserved.

California 1870 Census

Name	Age	S	R	B-PL	County	Locale	Roll	Pg
W S	27	m	w	ME	Mariposa	Maxwell Crk P O	74	143
GREEG								
Ellen	28	f	w	IREL	Solano	Vallejo	90	165
John	40	m	w	ENGL	Sutter	Sutter Twp	92	123
GREEGANS								
P W	36	m	w	IREL	San Francisco	7-Wd San Francisco	81	254
GREEHAM								
Jas	20	m	w	IREL	Solano	Vallejo	90	203
GREEHN								
W	35	m	w	PRUS	Lassen	Susanville Twp	73	441
GREELEAF								
William C	44	m	w	ME	Santa Cruz	Santa Cruz	89	412
GREELEY								
Caroline	5	f	w	CA	Nevada	Nevada Twp	75	309
Edmund	48	m	w	IREL	Solano	Benicia	90	5
Frank	40	m	w	FRAN	Alameda	Oakland	68	143
James	35	m	w	IREL	San Francisco	San Francisco P O	83	202
John	42	m	w	IREL	Solano	Vallejo	90	191
John F	38	m	w	VT	Nevada	Meadow Lake Twp	75	247
Joseph	12	m	w	MD	Marin	San Rafael Twp	74	29
Joseph	12	m	w	CA	San Francisco	11-Wd San Francisc	84	593
Justin	40	m	w	ME	Yuba	Marysville	93	587
Mary	18	f	w	CA	Solano	Vallejo	90	166
Maurice	35	m	w	IREL	Santa Clara	1-Wd San Jose	88	225
Sarah	64	f	w	MA	San Francisco	7-Wd San Francisco	81	282
William	49	m	w	IREL	Placer	Auburn P O	76	374
GREELY								
Ada M	10	f	w	ME	Tuolumne	Sonora P O	93	318
Ella	7	f	w	CA	Nevada	Nevada Twp	75	309
Frank	34	m	w	ME	Siskiyou	Scott Valley Twp	89	611
G W	48	m	w	NY	Sacramento	3-Wd Sacramento	77	267
George G	52	m	w	ME	Los Angeles	Santa Ana Twp	73	603
Henry H	32	m	w	VT	Nevada	Meadow Lake Twp	75	246
James	28	m	w	IREL	San Francisco	5-Wd San Francisco	81	35
John	40	m	w	IREL	Placer	Bath P O	76	432
John	15	m	w	NY	San Francisco	11-Wd San Francisc	84	593
Nancy	29	f	w	CANA	Santa Clara	Redwood Twp	88	129
Saml	27	m	w	NY	San Francisco	5-Wd San Francisco	81	31
William	45	m	w	ME	Nevada	Nevada Twp	75	295
GREEMAN								
A	37	m	w	NY	Lake	Morgan Valley	73	425
GREEN								
A	50	m	w	OH	Alameda	Alameda	68	3
A	45	f	w	NY	Solano	Vallejo	90	210
A B	41	m	w	NH	Amador	Amador City P O	69	391
A D	29	m	w	MO	Lake	Big Valley	73	396
A W	21	m	w	IL	Napa	Napa	75	17
Abbie L	30	f	w	NY	Santa Barbara	Santa Barbara P O	87	462
Abednag	45	m	w	OH	Stanislaus	Washington Twp	92	84
Abigail	78	f	w	CANA	San Francisco	11-Wd San Francisc	84	577
Abraham	37	m	w	MA	Santa Cruz	Santa Cruz Twp	89	397
Adam T	36	m	w	PRUS	San Francisco	San Francisco P O	83	112
Alex	30	m	w	SCOT	Alameda	Oakland	68	136
Alexr M	47	m	w	TN	Sonoma	Mendocino Twp	91	296
Alford	42	m	w	MO	Colusa	Colusa	71	297
Alfred	41	m	w	CANA	San Francisco	11-Wd San Francisc	84	615
Alfred F	39	m	w	VT	San Mateo	San Mateo P O	87	358
Alice	14	f	w	HI	San Francisco	8-Wd San Francisco	82	335
Allen	45	m	w	NY	Sacramento	Brighton Twp	77	72
Allen D G	7	m	w	CA	Los Angeles	Los Angeles Twp	73	472
Ann	50	f	b	PA	San Francisco	San Francisco P O	80	485
Ann	45	f	w	ENGL	Yolo	Cache Crk Twp	93	451
Asa	40	m	b	MO	San Joaquin	Douglas Twp	86	40
Augustus	45	m	w	ENGL	Santa Barbara	Santa Maria P O	87	513
Austin	32	m	w	NY	Humboldt	Eureka Twp	72	276
B	62	m	w	CANA	Lake	Upper Lake	73	409
B D	23	m	w	MO	Lake	Scotts Crk	73	426
B P	40	m	w	VA	San Joaquin	2-Wd Stockton	86	188
Barrett	32	m	w	MO	Sutter	Sutter Twp	92	126
Barry	38	m	w	IREL	San Francisco	San Francisco P O	83	36
Barton	23	m	w	OH	San Joaquin	Elliott Twp	86	78
Basley	40	m	w	IREL	Siskiyou	Callahan P O	89	628
Belinde Mrs	38	f	w	ME	Napa	Napa	75	48
Benj	61	m	w	KY	El Dorado	Placerville Twp	72	95
Benjamin F	34	m	w	WI	El Dorado	Placerville	72	121
Benjamin S	38	m	w	CANA	San Mateo	Schoolhouse Statio	87	334
Boardman A	41	m	w	OH	Amador	Sutter Crk P O	69	414
C A	26	m	w	OH	Nevada	Meadow Lake Twp	75	259
Carolin	40	f	w	OH	Yuba	Slate Range Bar Tw	93	670
Catherine	50	f	w	IREL	Alameda	Oakland	68	141
Charles	68	m	w	IREL	Solano	Rio Vista Twp	90	59
Charles	40	m	w	ME	Amador	Drytown P O	69	423
Charles	35	m	w	VT	San Mateo	San Mateo P O	87	349
Charles	33	m	w	MECK	Sonoma	Analy Twp	91	233
Charles	32	m	w	NY	San Francisco	2-Wd San Francisco	79	273
Charles	10	m	w	HI	San Francisco	8-Wd San Francisco	82	335
Charles E	45	m	w	VT	Yolo	Putah Twp	93	524
Chas	38	m	w	MD	Marin	San Rafael Twp	74	42
Christopher	39	m	w	IREL	Sacramento	2-Wd Sacramento	77	226
Cistro	19	m	w	FRAN	San Mateo	San Mateo P O	87	349
Clara	17	f	w	CA	Sonoma	Cloverdale Twp	91	267
Corydon B	40	m	w	VT	San Francisco	San Francisco P O	83	125
D R	27	m	w	IL	Santa Clara	Gilroy Twp	88	83
Daniel	57	m	w	CANA	San Francisco	11-Wd San Francisc	84	577
Daniel	36	m	w	IREL	San Francisco	San Francisco P O	83	13
David	58	m	w	OH	San Francisco	San Francisco P O	83	182
David	28	m	w	BAVA	Sacramento	2-Wd Sacramento	77	216
Dennis D	47	m	w	NY	Stanislaus	Emory Twp	92	20
E	42	m	w	CT	Sacramento	1-Wd Sacramento	77	200
E L	45	m	w	TN	Lake	Upper Lake	73	409
Edmond	45	m	w	PA	San Francisco	8-Wd San Francisco	82	316
Edmonia	65	f	b	NC	Nevada	Nevada Twp	75	296
Edward	47	m	w	IREL	Yolo	Grafton Twp	93	481
Edward	32	m	w	IREL	Santa Barbara	San Buenaventura P	87	431
Edward	25	m	w	NY	San Francisco	6-Wd San Francisco	81	88
Edward	22	m	w	PRUS	Los Angeles	Soledad Twp	73	631
Edward E	50	m	w	NY	Plumas	Indian Twp	77	11
Edward L	34	m	w	IREL	Calaveras	Copperopolis P O	70	247
Edwd	36	m	w	ENGL	San Francisco	San Francisco P O	83	72
Eliza	43	f	w	BELG	Santa Cruz	Santa Cruz	89	404
Ellen	34	f	w	NY	San Francisco	2-Wd San Francisco	79	216
Ellis	26	m	w	MI	Alameda	Alameda	68	13
Ellis	18	m	w	WI	Kern	Bakersfield P O	73	360
Ephraim	61	m	w	CT	Siskiyou	Yreka	89	659
Evaline	38	f	w	MA	Sonoma	Petaluma Twp	91	337
F M	26	m	w	AL	San Joaquin	Liberty Twp	86	88
Francis	55	m	b	MO	Sacramento	Cosumnes Twp	77	92
Francis	25	m	w	NY	Santa Cruz	Santa Cruz Twp	89	400
Francis B	42	m	w	MA	Sonoma	Vallejo Twp	91	459
Frank	52	m	w	PA	Butte	Ophir Twp	70	113
Frank	35	m	w	FRAN	Humboldt	Eureka Twp	72	267
Frank	27	m	w	IN	Klamath	Trinidad Twp	73	390
Frank W	38	m	w	PA	Mendocino	Navarro & Big Rvr	74	176
Fredk	10	m	w	CA	San Francisco	San Francisco P O	85	828
G L	21	m	w	RI	San Joaquin	2-Wd Stockton	86	171
G M	32	m	w	AL	San Joaquin	Liberty Twp	86	88
G P	37	m	w	NY	Amador	Jackson P O	69	319
Geo	51	m	w	ENGL	Fresno	Millerton P O	72	162
Geo	43	m	w	OH	Yuba	Marysville	93	577
Geo	40	m	w	IREL	San Francisco	11-Wd San Francisc	84	691
Geo	30	m	w	NJ	San Joaquin	Douglas Twp	86	40
Geo	25	m	w	IREL	San Francisco	1-Wd San Francisco	79	130
Georg	21	m	w	WI	Calaveras	San Andreas P O	70	152
George	51	m	w	ENGL	San Francisco	2-Wd San Francisco	79	152
George	46	m	w	NY	Kern	Bakersfield P O	73	360
George	42	m	w	NC	Fresno	Millerton P O	72	149
George	39	m	w	ENGL	San Francisco	San Francisco P O	83	95
George	36	m	w	CT	San Francisco	San Francisco P O	80	365
George	35	m	w	MA	San Francisco	San Francisco P O	83	255
George	30	m	w	BADE	Del Norte	Smith Rvr Twp	71	483
George	28	m	w	PA	Santa Clara	Santa Clara Twp	88	147
George	25	m	w	CT	San Francisco	11-Wd San Francisc	84	473
George	25	m	w	SAXO	San Francisco	1-Wd San Francisco	79	63
George	24	m	w	NY	San Francisco	8-Wd San Francisco	82	334
George	23	m	w	NY	San Francisco	3-Wd San Francisco	79	314
George	21	m	w	OH	Sonoma	Petaluma Twp	91	336
George	13	m	w	CA	Colusa	Colusa	71	298
George B	38	m	w	MA	Santa Clara	2-Wd San Jose	88	321
George D	44	m	w	PA	Sonoma	Vallejo Twp	91	450
George S	38	m	w	WI	Amador	Jackson P O	69	346
George W	52	m	w	MO	Siskiyou	Yreka	89	654
George W	44	m	w	NY	San Francisco	6-Wd San Francisco	81	153
George W	44	m	w	MA	Solano	Suisun Twp	90	98
George W	39	m	w	OH	Yolo	Cache Crk Twp	93	432
George W	32	m	w	ME	San Mateo	Belmont P O	87	372
George W	28	m	w	MD	Sacramento	2-Wd Sacramento	77	224
Granvill	36	m	w	MO	Colusa	Monroe Twp	71	321
H P	20	m	w	ME	Sacramento	1-Wd Sacramento	77	174
Hannah	64	f	w	CANA	Solano	Vallejo	90	142
Hannah J	27	f	w	IREL	Alpine	Markleeville P O	69	311
Hanora	26	f	w	IREL	San Mateo	Schoolhouse Statio	87	334
Harris	40	m	w	PRUS	San Francisco	1-Wd San Francisco	79	97
Harris V	40	m	w	POLA	San Francisco	8-Wd San Francisco	82	288
Harry	24	m	w	ENGL	Yuba	Rose Bar Twp	93	662
Henn	7	m	w	CA	San Luis Obispo	Santa Rosa Twp	87	328
Henry	46	m	w	RUSS	Tulare	Visalia	92	295
Henry	44	m	w	PA	San Francisco	San Francisco P O	83	332
Henry	35	m	w	IREL	Napa	Napa Twp	75	31
Henry	28	m	w	MA	San Francisco	San Francisco P O	83	369
Henry	26	m	w	NJ	Los Angeles	Los Angeles Twp	73	491
Henry	26	m	w	NY	San Francisco	2-Wd San Francisco	79	213
Henry	23	m	w	ENGL	Los Angeles	Los Angeles	73	541
Henry D	24	m	w	CANA	San Francisco	San Francisco P O	85	723
Henry H	25	m	w	IA	San Mateo	Pescadero P O	87	411
Henry V	36	m	w	NY	Sacramento	Brighton Twp	77	70
Herrman B	27	m	w	NY	Siskiyou	Yreka	89	651
Hiram	32	m	w	AR	Colusa	Colusa Twp	71	280
Horace	38	m	w	NY	Yolo	Cache Crk Twp	93	454
Horace	38	m	w	NY	Yolo	Cache Crk Twp	93	438
Isaac	32	m	w	IREL	San Francisco	San Francisco P O	83	198
Isaac	32	m	w	MO	Fresno	Kingston P O	72	219
Ishmael	17	m	w	ENGL	Napa	Yountville Twp	75	85
J C	41	m	w	US	San Joaquin	3-Wd Stockton	86	218
J C	35	m	w	VT	San Francisco	San Francisco P O	85	815
J J	25	m	w	IREL	Alameda	Oakland	68	240
J L	35	m	w	WI	Sacramento	1-Wd Sacramento	77	174
J M	34	m	w	AL	San Joaquin	Liberty Twp	86	89
J W B	27	m	w	OH	San Joaquin	3-Wd Stockton	86	218
Jacob	45	m	w	NY	Placer	Auburn P O	76	366
James	50	m	w	ME	San Mateo	Pescadero P O	87	415
James	48	m	w	IREL	Yolo	Grafton Twp	93	482
James	45	m	w	SCOT	Los Angeles	Wilmington Twp	73	640
James	44	m	w	NY	San Francisco	San Francisco P O	80	353
James	41	m	w	IREL	Amador	Volcano P O	69	375

Series M593

© 2001 by Heritage Quest. All rights reserved.

California 1870 Census

Name	Age	S	R	B-PL	County	Locale	Roll	Pg
James	40	m	w	OH	Los Angeles	Los Angeles Twp	73	476
James	40	m	w	OH	Butte	Ophir Twp	70	92
James	38	m	w	OH	Los Angeles	Los Angeles Twp	73	478
James	36	m	w	HOLL	San Francisco	3-Wd San Francisco	79	290
James	35	m	w	ENGL	San Francisco	San Francisco P O	80	333
James	35	m	w	IL	San Mateo	San Mateo P O	87	349
James	30	m	w	IREL	Santa Clara	Santa Clara Twp	88	163
James	30	m	w	IREL	San Francisco	San Francisco P O	83	353
James	26	m	w	NZEA	Mendocino	Casper & Big Rvr	74	164
James	20	m	w	IREL	San Francisco	11-Wd San Francisc	84	489
James B	25	m	w	CANA	Nevada	Grass Valley Twp	75	217
James J	37	m	w	IREL	Marin	San Rafael	74	57
Janie	22	f	w	IREL	San Francisco	San Francisco P O	80	475
Jas	44	m	w	IREL	Sierra	Gibson Twp	89	542
Jas	25	m	w	IREL	Solano	Benicia	90	19
Jas C	5	m	w	CA	Sonoma	Mendocino Twp	91	294
Jas H	42	m	w	ME	Solano	Vallejo	90	151
Jasper N	32	m	w	IN	Santa Cruz	Santa Cruz	89	428
Jay	50	m	w	OH	Yolo	Grafton Twp	93	490
Jefferson	41	m	w	NY	Santa Cruz	Santa Cruz	89	409
Jennie	17	f	w	CA	Alameda	Oakland	68	237
Jesse	60	m	w	TN	San Joaquin	Liberty Twp	86	89
Jesus	22	m	w	CA	Monterey	San Antonio Twp	74	316
Jno L	8	m	w	CA	Sonoma	Santa Rosa	91	418
Jno S	39	m	w	IREL	Sacramento	1-Wd Sacramento	77	179
Joe	52	m	w	ENGL	Alameda	Oakland	68	190
John	60	m	w	CANA	Amador	Ione City P O	69	366
John	53	m	w	IREL	San Francisco	11-Wd San Francisc	84	525
John	50	m	w	IREL	San Francisco	1-Wd San Francisco	79	38
John	50	m	w	IL	Yolo	Grafton Twp	93	488
John	45	m	w	ENGL	Sacramento	4-Wd Sacramento	77	373
John	45	m	w	POLA	San Francisco	San Francisco P O	80	533
John	44	m	w	SWED	Placer	Auburn P O	76	372
John	42	m	w	ENGL	San Francisco	San Francisco P O	83	345
John	41	m	w	ENGL	Mariposa	Mariposa P O	74	113
John	40	m	w	IREL	Alameda	Murray Twp	68	100
John	39	m	w	PRUS	Solano	Silveyville Twp	90	87
John	37	m	w	PA	Sacramento	2-Wd Sacramento	77	214
John	36	m	w	ENGL	Alameda	Alameda	68	20
John	35	m	w	IREL	Amador	Volcano P O	69	373
John	35	m	w	IREL	Sacramento	Center Twp	77	85
John	35	m	w	AUST	Santa Clara	2-Wd San Jose	88	301
John	35	m	w	ENGL	San Francisco	7-Wd San Francisco	81	204
John	34	m	w	IREL	Alameda	Murray Twp	68	121
John	30	m	w	IREL	Mendocino	Gualala Twp	74	225
John	30	m	w	IREL	Santa Barbara	Santa Barbara P O	87	459
John	30	m	w	IREL	San Mateo	Redwood Twp	87	361
John	28	m	w	OH	Sacramento	Dry Crk Twp	77	103
John	27	m	w	CANA	Contra Costa	Martinez P O	71	438
John	25	m	w	AUSL	Alameda	Brooklyn	68	26
John	24	m	w	MD	Marin	Sausalito Twp	74	74
John	24	m	w	IREL	Solano	Vallejo	90	204
John	23	m	w	CANA	Lake	Upper Lake	73	411
John	23	m	w	PA	Marin	San Rafael Twp	74	45
John A	24	m	w	ME	Sutter	Butte Twp	92	97
John B	52	m	w	PA	Mariposa	Mariposa P O	74	136
John C	25	m	w	LA	Sacramento	2-Wd Sacramento	77	244
John H	39	m	w	CT	Yolo	Cottonwood Twp	93	463
John K	71	m	w	RI	Mariposa	Maxwell Crk P O	74	144
John L	56	m	w	CANA	San Francisco	3-Wd San Francisco	79	298
John L	42	m	w	NY	San Francisco	3-Wd San Francisco	79	312
John R	38	m	w	OH	San Mateo	Pescadero P O	87	415
John S	24	m	w	WI	San Francisco	San Francisco P O	83	342
John W	64	m	w	NY	Amador	Drytown P O	69	421
John W	30	m	w	MO	San Luis Obispo	Salinas Twp	87	290
Jones	21	m	w	MO	El Dorado	Mud Springs Twp	72	90
Jones	20	m	w	MO	El Dorado	Mud Springs Twp	72	81
Jos	53	m	w	ENGL	Alameda	Oakland	68	246
Joseph	60	m	w	VA	Solano	Suisun Twp	90	112
Joseph	6	m	w	CA	San Francisco	San Francisco P O	83	279
Joseph	50	m	w	NY	San Francisco	8-Wd San Francisco	82	419
Joseph	47	m	w	PRUS	Sacramento	Franklin Twp	77	114
Joseph	47	m	w	ENGL	San Joaquin	Oneal Twp	86	98
Joseph	28	m	b	MD	San Francisco	1-Wd San Francisco	79	96
Joseph	27	m	w	IREL	Alameda	Oakland	68	147
Joseph R	59	m	w	MA	Mariposa	Mariposa P O	74	123
Joseph R	33	m	w	RI	Mariposa	Mariposa P O	74	118
Joshua	34	m	w	OH	San Joaquin	2-Wd Stockton	86	199
Josiah S	48	m	w	PA	Santa Cruz	Santa Cruz	89	422
Kate	33	f	w	NY	San Joaquin	2-Wd Stockton	86	204
Kate	28	f	w	IREL	San Francisco	San Francisco P O	83	102
Kate	25	f	w	IREL	San Francisco	San Francisco P O	85	779
L	30	m	w	NY	Alameda	Alameda	68	12
L A	25	m	w	OH	Tuolumne	Columbia P O	93	362
L B	50	m	w	OH	San Joaquin	Elliott Twp	86	78
L S P	40	m	w	NY	San Joaquin	Elkhorn Twp	86	64
Larry	38	m	w	NORW	San Francisco	San Francisco P O	85	810
Laura	11	f	w	USSR	Alameda	Oakland	68	171
Levi	35	m	w	CT	Alameda	Brooklyn Twp	68	49
Lewis	35	m	w	PRUS	San Francisco	San Francisco P O	83	150
Lewis	20	m	w	MI	Monterey	Monterey Twp	74	348
Lewis G	42	m	b	NC	Los Angeles	Los Angeles	73	503
Liddy	56	f	w	KY	Monterey	Pajaro Twp	74	377
Lizzie	7	f	w	HI	San Francisco	8-Wd San Francisco	82	335
Louis	42	m	w	NY	San Francisco	San Francisco P O	83	332
Louisa	40	f	w	WURT	Santa Clara	2-Wd San Jose	88	312
Lucretia	18	f	w	HI	San Francisco	8-Wd San Francisco	82	335

Name	Age	S	R	B-PL	County	Locale	Roll	Pg
Lucy	20	f	i	CA	Del Norte	Smith Rvr Twp	71	483
Luther	45	m	w	AL	Kern	Tehachapi P O	73	352
Madison	22	m	b	TX	Santa Clara	2-Wd San Jose	88	333
Manuel	34	m	w	SCOT	Alameda	Brooklyn	68	30
Maria	50	f	m	VA	San Francisco	6-Wd San Francisco	81	71
Marrion	28	m	w	AL	Sutter	Sutter Twp	92	127
Mary	7	f	w	CA	Los Angeles	El Monte Twp	73	452
Mary	56	f	w	IREL	San Francisco	11-Wd San Francisc	84	511
Mary	45	f	w	CT	San Francisco	8-Wd San Francisco	82	335
Mary	40	f	b	LA	San Francisco	8-Wd San Francisco	82	312
Mary	39	f	w	IREL	Santa Clara	2-Wd San Jose	88	327
Mary	21	f	w	IREL	Santa Clara	San Jose Twp	88	187
Mary	16	f	w	CT	San Francisco	8-Wd San Francisco	82	335
Mary	15	f	w	CA	Solano	Benicia	90	17
Mary	14	f	w	CA	San Francisco	11-Wd San Francisc	84	485
Mary Ja	52	f	w	PA	Mariposa	Mariposa P O	74	116
Mary L	16	f	w	CA	San Francisco	8-Wd San Francisco	82	482
Matthew D	33	m	w	TN	Santa Clara	San Jose Twp	88	210
Mattie	47	f	w	IREL	Solano	Vacaville Twp	90	124
Michael	35	m	w	NY	Del Norte	Crescent	71	467
Michael	28	m	w	IREL	San Francisco	San Francisco P O	83	335
Michl J	43	m	w	IREL	San Francisco	San Francisco P O	83	100
Morris	35	m	w	NY	Los Angeles	Los Angeles Twp	73	491
Morris	25	m	b	DC	Alameda	Oakland	68	145
Morris M	38	m	w	NH	Nevada	Nevada Twp	75	317
Myron D	23	m	w	MA	Santa Cruz	Santa Cruz Twp	89	400
Nancy	70	f	w	ME	San Francisco	7-Wd San Francisco	81	249
Nathan	46	m	w	SWED	Tuolumne	Chinese Camp P O	93	363
Nathan	37	m	w	MO	Santa Clara	Gilroy Twp	88	106
Nelson	43	m	w	MS	Colusa	Grand Island Twp	71	308
Nelson	40	m	w	SWED	San Francisco	7-Wd San Francisco	81	274
Noble P	19	m	w	MI	Yolo	Cottonwood Twp	93	467
O B	30	m	w	MO	Sutter	Vernon Twp	92	134
Orson	38	m	w	NY	Siskiyou	Callahan P O	89	632
Patrick	42	m	w	IREL	Santa Clara	2-Wd San Jose	88	307
Patrick	40	m	w	IREL	Colusa	Colusa	71	289
Patrick	34	m	w	IREL	San Francisco	San Francisco P O	80	388
Patrick	27	m	w	IREL	San Francisco	7-Wd San Francisco	81	203
Paul	30	m	w	BAVA	Amador	Volcano P O	69	381
Pauline	25	f	w	IREL	San Francisco	6-Wd San Francisco	81	113
Peter	50	m	w	FRAN	Los Angeles	Los Angeles	73	519
Peter	46	m	w	IREL	Sonoma	Bodega Twp	91	265
Peter	46	m	w	DENM	San Francisco	1-Wd San Francisco	79	122
Peter	45	m	w	IREL	San Francisco	San Francisco P O	83	185
Peter	44	m	w	NY	Kern	Tehachapi P O	73	353
Peter	34	m	w	IREL	San Joaquin	2-Wd Stockton	86	213
Phillip	38	m	w	BADE	Butte	Bidwell Twp	70	1
Possie	9	f	w	CA	Alameda	Oakland	68	246
Puss A	9	f	w	CA	Colusa	Colusa	71	293
R B	12	m	w	CA	Alameda	Oakland	68	243
R H	54	m	w	TN	Merced	Snelling P O	74	258
R J	28	m	w	IL	Alameda	San Leandro	68	98
R S	47	m	w	PA	Siskiyou	Scott Valley Twp	89	608
Reuben P	44	m	w	IL	Colusa	Spring Valley Twp	71	342
Richard	50	m	w	ENGL	Calaveras	San Andreas P O	70	189
Richard	45	m	w	MO	Colusa	Grand Island Twp	71	305
Richard	24	m	w	CANA	San Francisco	11-Wd San Francisc	84	577
Robert	44	m	w	SAXO	Sacramento	2-Wd Sacramento	77	248
Robert	40	m	w	IREL	Marin	San Rafael	74	55
Robert	35	m	w	NY	San Francisco	San Francisco P O	83	158
Robt F	38	m	w	VA	Fresno	Kings Rvr P O	72	211
Robt W	50	m	w	VA	El Dorado	Mountain Twp	72	68
Rosa H	40	f	w	IREL	San Francisco	8-Wd San Francisco	82	416
Rose	26	f	w	IREL	San Francisco	11-Wd San Francisc	84	480
S S	22	m	w	OH	San Francisco	San Francisco P O	83	276
Saml	60	m	w	NJ	San Francisco	5-Wd San Francisco	81	27
Samuel	35	m	w	IREL	San Francisco	San Francisco P O	83	385
Samuel	22	m	w	IREL	San Francisco	San Francisco P O	85	817
Sarah	40	f	b	PA	San Francisco	San Francisco P O	80	486
Sarah	31	f	w	IREL	San Francisco	San Francisco P O	80	477
Seth	40	m	w	NY	Alameda	Oakland	68	262
Sidney A	25	m	w	RI	San Francisco	7-Wd San Francisco	81	250
Silas	34	m	w	ME	Sacramento	1-Wd Sacramento	77	189
Stephen	40	m	w	US	San Mateo	Schoolhouse Statio	87	338
T J	43	m	w	VA	Lake	Big Valley	73	395
T W	30	m	w	NY	San Francisco	3-Wd San Francisco	79	312
Thomas	51	m	w	OH	Nevada	Eureka Twp	75	139
Thomas	40	m	w	IREL	Siskiyou	Big Valley Twp	89	582
Thomas	40	m	w	PA	Yolo	Putah Twp	93	524
Thomas	40	m	w	IREL	San Francisco	7-Wd San Francisco	81	168
Thomas	37	m	w	IREL	San Francisco	11-Wd San Francisc	84	447
Thomas	34	m	w	IREL	Alameda	Oakland	68	180
Thomas	30	m	w	IREL	Yolo	Cache Crk Twp	93	422
Thomas	30	m	w	ENGL	San Francisco	7-Wd San Francisco	81	221
Thomas	29	m	w	IREL	San Francisco	San Francisco P O	83	137
Thomas	25	m	w	TX	Los Angeles	Los Nietos Twp	73	586
W	45	m	w	ENGL	Nevada	Nevada Twp	75	286
W B	55	m	w	NY	Lake	Lower Lake	73	422
W E	33	m	w	ME	San Joaquin	2-Wd Stockton	86	202
W H	23	m	w	MI	Santa Clara	Gilroy Twp	88	97
W O	67	m	w	NY	Amador	Jackson P O	69	345
W O	21	m	w	NY	Amador	Jackson P O	69	345
Wallace	26	m	w	PA	Marin	San Rafael Twp	74	40
Warren	8	m	w	CA	San Francisco	San Francisco P O	85	828
Warren	27	m	w	OH	Yuba	Marysville	93	583
Watson H	12	m	w	WI	San Francisco	6-Wd San Francisco	81	136
Will S	36	m	w	KY	Colusa	Colusa	71	295

© 2001 by Heritage Quest. All rights reserved.

California 1870 Census

Series M593

Name	Age	S	R	B-PL	County	Locale	Roll	Pg
William	53	m	w	SWED	Placer	Bath P O	76	435
William	48	m	w	BADE	San Francisco	7-Wd San Francisco	81	214
William	47	m	w	ENGL	Santa Clara	2-Wd San Jose	88	286
William	45	m	w	VT	San Francisco	3-Wd San Francisco	79	293
William	45	m	w	PRUS	San Francisco	8-Wd San Francisco	82	449
William	40	m	w	ENGL	San Francisco	8-Wd San Francisco	82	482
William	39	m	b	NY	San Francisco	San Francisco P O	80	417
William	36	m	w	SWIT	Siskiyou	Butte Twp	89	587
William	35	m	w	NY	San Francisco	San Francisco P O	83	368
William	34	m	w	MA	Solano	Vacaville Twp	90	131
William	30	m	w	DENM	Humboldt	Eureka Twp	72	276
William	30	m	w	CT	Stanislaus	Empire Twp	92	33
William	26	m	w	IREL	San Mateo	Belmont P O	87	388
William A	50	m	w	KY	El Dorado	Lake Valley Twp	72	63
William A	34	m	w	MO	Yolo	Grafton Twp	93	480
William G	30	m	w	MI	Placer	Auburn P O	76	383
William H	23	m	w	ENGL	Los Angeles	Los Angeles	73	547
William M	50	m	w	NY	Yolo	Washington Twp	93	536
Willis	74	m	w	KY	Lake	Big Valley	73	398
Wm	62	m	w	SWED	Sacramento	Georgianna Twp	77	125
Wm H	49	m	w	PRUS	Mariposa	Mariposa P O	74	104
Wm H	32	m	w	IREL	San Francisco	8-Wd San Francisco	82	348
Wm S	39	m	w	MA	Butte	Kimshew Tpw	70	86
Woods W	43	m	w	MO	Colusa	Colusa	71	295
GREENALSH								
William	31	m	w	ENGL	San Francisco	8-Wd San Francisco	82	415
GREENAN								
Patrick	26	m	w	IREL	Santa Clara	Fremont Twp	88	52
GREENAWAY								
Geo	25	m	w	ENGL	San Francisco	1-Wd San Francisco	79	70
GREENBACK								
John	18	m	w	PRUS	Solano	Suisun Twp	90	110
GREENBAUM								
Alfrano	42	m	w	POLA	Los Angeles	Los Angeles	73	530
J	28	m	w	OH	San Francisco	5-Wd San Francisco	81	14
J	26	m	w	PRUS	San Francisco	8-Wd San Francisco	82	375
Sigmond	28	m	w	BAVA	San Francisco	6-Wd San Francisco	81	130
William	38	m	w	POLA	Santa Cruz	Watsonville	89	366
GREENBECK								
Charles	44	m	w	SWED	Santa Clara	1-Wd San Jose	88	236
GREENBERG								
Charles	55	m	w	PRUS	San Francisco	8-Wd San Francisco	82	462
Henry	51	m	w	BAVA	San Francisco	11-Wd San Francisc	84	423
Mak	29	m	w	PRUS	San Francisco	11-Wd San Francisc	84	551
Morris	46	m	w	POLA	San Francisco	San Francisco P O	83	108
GREENBOUGH								
Asher	40	m	w	POLA	San Luis Obispo	San Luis Obispo Tw	87	309
GREENBOWER								
Henry G	11	m	w	CA	Placer	Bath P O	76	452
John	40	m	w	BAVA	Placer	Bath P O	76	437
GREENBURG								
Louis	54	m	w	PRUS	San Francisco	5-Wd San Francisco	81	1
Thomas	30	m	w	MA	San Francisco	7-Wd San Francisco	81	221
GREENE								
Alex	45	m	w	TN	San Francisco	2-Wd San Francisco	79	223
Benjn J	50	m	w	RI	San Francisco	San Francisco P O	85	716
Charles	32	m	w	CT	Contra Costa	San Pablo Twp	71	360
Chas H	40	m	w	DE	Shasta	Millville P O	89	483
Danl	32	m	w	IREL	Shasta	Shasta P O	89	452
Edward B	40	m	w	IREL	San Francisco	San Francisco P O	83	190
Eloise P	19	f	w	MA	Sonoma	Sonoma Twp	91	445
Frank	28	m	w	IREL	Amador	Volcano P O	69	375
Fredk	44	m	w	ENGL	San Francisco	San Francisco P O	83	286
Geo	46	m	w	VA	Lassen	Long Valley Twp	73	437
Harriet L	65	f	w	NY	Shasta	Shasta P O	89	460
Henry	53	m	w	NY	San Diego	San Diego	78	489
Henry P	56	m	w	NY	San Francisco	1-Wd San Francisco	79	111
Horace W	35	m	w	NY	Shasta	Shasta P O	89	456
James	46	m	w	RI	Santa Cruz	Santa Cruz	89	419
James	31	m	w	IN	Yuba	New York Twp	93	638
John	40	m	w	IREL	San Francisco	2-Wd San Francisco	79	225
Kate Alisia F	20	f	w	NY	San Francisco	1-Wd San Francisco	79	97
Myron S	32	m	w	VT	Sacramento	4-Wd Sacramento	77	336
Shadrick	46	m	w	VA	Mendocino	Ukiah Twp	74	237
Thomas	38	m	w	MO	Shasta	Shasta P O	89	458
Uriah	50	m	w	PA	Calaveras	Copperopolis P O	70	232
William	58	m	w	IREL	San Francisco	11-Wd San Francisc	84	528
William	49	m	w	NY	Sonoma	Sonoma Twp	91	443
GREENEBAUM								
Jacob	58	m	w	BAVA	San Francisco	8-Wd San Francisco	82	497
Louis	36	m	w	PRUS	San Francisco	8-Wd San Francisco	82	468
GREENEMANN								
Adolph	20	m	w	DENM	Placer	Newcastle Twp	76	474
GREENER								
Frank	51	m	w	BADE	San Francisco	San Francisco P O	80	331
James	38	m	w	TN	Siskiyou	Cottonwood Twp	89	592
Richard	58	m	b	MD	Butte	Wyandotte Twp	70	143
Thomas	47	m	w	ENGL	Siskiyou	Yreka	89	653
GREENEY								
Bridget	27	f	w	IREL	San Francisco	San Francisco P O	83	226
GREENFIELD								
Chas P	31	m	w	LA	Butte	Ophir Twp	70	117
Daniel	20	m	w	IREL	Santa Clara	San Jose Twp	88	219
John	45	m	w	CANA	Butte	Ophir Twp	70	96
Lewis	35	m	w	AUST	Sonoma	Petaluma Twp	91	320
Thos J	40	m	w	CANA	Alameda	Washington Twp	68	277
Truman	32	m	w	NY	Yolo	Cache Crk Twp	93	439
GREENHALGH								
Daniel	30	m	w	ENGL	Placer	Bath P O	76	447
John	27	m	w	NY	San Francisco	San Francisco P O	83	144
Thomas	43	m	w	NH	Amador	Jackson P O	69	319
GREENHAM								
Fred	43	m	w	IREL	San Francisco	San Francisco P O	83	394
Robert	42	m	w	OH	Colusa	Colusa	71	288
GREENHOFF								
S	49	m	w	PRUS	Sierra	Forest Twp	89	529
GREENHOOD								
Maurice	54	m	w	AUST	San Francisco	San Francisco P O	83	236
Otto	30	m	w	MA	San Francisco	5-Wd San Francisco	81	35
GREENHOOLT								
Dan	36	m	w	OH	San Joaquin	2-Wd Stockton	86	164
GREENHOUSE								
Isaac	35	m	w	ENGL	Solano	Vacaville Twp	90	125
Wm	50	m	w	AUST	San Francisco	2-Wd San Francisco	79	209
GREENIA								
Joseph	43	m	w	CANA	San Mateo	Belmont P O	87	374
GREENING								
John	44	m	w	CANA	Sonoma	Petaluma Twp	91	354
Robt	39	m	w	KY	Sonoma	Russian Rvr	91	367
Wm	37	m	w	MO	Sonoma	Petaluma Twp	91	341
GREENINGER								
Adolph	27	m	w	PRUS	Santa Clara	1-Wd San Jose	88	259
Jacob	40	m	w	WURT	Alameda	Alvarado	68	303
GREENLAND								
Charles	26	m	w	DENM	Plumas	Quartz Twp	77	40
William	18	m	w	CA	San Francisco	8-Wd San Francisco	82	462
GREENLAW								
A S	37	m	w	ME	Sacramento	3-Wd Sacramento	77	311
Chas E	28	m	w	ME	Sacramento	4-Wd Sacramento	77	366
G H	33	m	w	SCOT	Sacramento	3-Wd Sacramento	77	272
J W	34	m	w	ME	Sacramento	3-Wd Sacramento	77	276
Jno H	34	m	w	ME	Sacramento	3-Wd Sacramento	77	311
John	40	m	w	SCOT	San Francisco	7-Wd San Francisco	81	279
GREENLEAF								
Anna	20	f	w	MO	Fresno	Millerton P O	72	145
Bradford	33	m	w	ME	Solano	Suisun Twp	90	107
Chas	24	m	w	NY	Mendocino	Round Valley Twp	74	220
D M	25	m	w	NY	Nevada	Eureka Twp	75	136
Edwd F	27	m	w	MS	Fresno	Millerton P O	72	167
George	39	m	w	MA	Trinity	Douglas	92	235
Miles	40	m	b	NC	Merced	Snelling P O	74	276
Rhoda S	18	f	w	MO	San Luis Obispo	San Luis Obispo Tw	87	312
Samuel	70	m	b	NC	Tuolumne	Chinese Camp P O	93	380
Samuel	33	m	w	ME	Stanislaus	Empire Twp	92	55
Thomas	20	m	w	NY	Nevada	Eureka Twp	75	136
William	45	m	w	ME	Solano	Montezuma Twp	90	69
Wm	36	m	w	ME	San Francisco	11-Wd San Francisc	84	604
Wm B	30	m	w	ME	Santa Cruz	Santa Cruz Twp	89	396
GREENLEE								
Louis	35	m	w	TN	Napa	Napa	75	15
GREENLEIF								
Wm	46	m	w	NY	Butte	Ophir Twp	70	109
GREENLER								
P M	37	m	w	MO	Napa	Napa	75	14
GREENLEY								
John G	39	m	w	CT	Tuolumne	Sonora P O	93	331
William A	45	m	w	CT	Inyo	Bishop Crk Twp	73	317
Wm	27	m	b	NC	Tuolumne	Sonora P O	93	307
GREENLIEF								
Harriet	15	f	i	CA	Trinity	Hayfork Valley	92	238
GREENLOW								
Isaac	30	m	w	ME	Humboldt	Eureka Twp	72	267
Isaac	26	m	w	CANA	Humboldt	Eureka Twp	72	268
Jesse	36	m	w	CANA	Humboldt	Bucksport Twp	72	244
GREENMAN								
George	34	m	w	NY	Santa Clara	2-Wd San Jose	88	318
H	45	m	w	NY	Lake	Morgan Valley	73	425
John	36	m	w	ENGL	Nevada	Rough & Ready Twp	75	337
John H	45	m	w	MA	San Francisco	6-Wd San Francisco	81	92
W P	25	m	w	WI	Santa Clara	Gilroy Twp	88	95
GREENMIRE								
Peter	38	m	w	IREL	San Joaquin	Tulare Twp	86	252
GREENNADE								
Civility	30	f	w	MO	Los Angeles	San Gabriel Twp	73	597
GREENOUGH								
Charles	41	m	w	NH	Yolo	Washington Twp	93	530
Chas	40	m	w	MA	Calaveras	Copperopolis P O	70	241
Edward	43	m	w	ENGL	Nevada	Grass Valley Twp	75	162
John	23	m	w	ME	San Francisco	8-Wd San Francisco	82	339
GREENOVER								
W B	38	m	w	PA	Tuolumne	Chinese Camp P O	93	387
GREENOW								
Charles	43	m	w	ENGL	Nevada	Eureka Twp	75	138
GREENOWER								
John	29	m	w	ENGL	Stanislaus	Empire Twp	92	45
GREENTREE								
John	45	m	w	MD	San Francisco	San Francisco P O	80	406
Louis	36	m	w	ENGL	Humboldt	South Fork Twp	72	302
GREENWALD								
A	32	m	w	PA	Santa Clara	Almaden Twp	88	18
David	46	m	w	PA	Santa Clara	San Jose Twp	88	199
Julius	45	m	w	GERM	Nevada	Nevada Twp	75	275
W F	30	m	w	HCAS	San Francisco	San Francisco P O	83	269

© 2001 by Heritage Quest. All rights reserved.

Name	Age	S	R	B-PL	County	Locale	Series M593 Roll	Pg
GREENWAY								
Ellen	25	f	w	IREL	San Francisco	San Francisco P O	85	727
Pricilla F	37	f	w	IL	Placer	Bath P O	76	459
GREENWELL								
Benj	47	m	w	ENGL	Butte	Wyandotte Twp	70	148
John	28	m	w	ENGL	Calaveras	Copperopolis P O	70	235
Lemuel	31	m	w	NY	San Francisco	5-Wd San Francisco	81	27
Robert	49	m	w	ENGL	Calaveras	Copperopolis P O	70	245
Stephen T	50	m	w	MO	Nevada	Grass Valley Twp	75	218
Wm E	43	m	w	MD	Santa Barbara	Santa Barbara P O	87	487
GREENWOD								
J T	30	m	w	PA	San Joaquin	2-Wd Stockton	86	203
GREENWOLD								
Bertha	50	f	w	FRAN	San Francisco	2-Wd San Francisco	79	220
Frank	55	m	w	PRUS	San Francisco	2-Wd San Francisco	79	245
Jacob	43	m	w	HDAR	San Francisco	2-Wd San Francisco	79	241
Saml	38	m	w	NY	San Francisco	5-Wd San Francisco	81	33
GREENWOOD								
Britan	43	m	w	MO	Mendocino	Anderson Twp	74	157
C	73	f	w	CANA	Solano	Vallejo	90	212
C	70	f	w	CANA	Solano	Vallejo	90	189
D	55	m	w	MO	Nevada	Meadow Lake Twp	75	265
Dud	28	m	w	MO	Napa	Napa Twp	75	61
F D	64	m	w	KY	Napa	Yountville Twp	75	87
G H	38	m	w	ME	Solano	Vallejo	90	212
H A	36	f	w	IREL	Tuolumne	Sonora P O	93	333
Hannah	45	f	w	IREL	Sonoma	Mendocino Twp	91	297
Henery	36	m	w	ENGL	San Francisco	7-Wd San Francisco	81	197
Henry H	41	m	w	PA	Siskiyou	Yreka	89	662
Herry	40	m	w	HANO	Sonoma	Petaluma Twp	91	333
Hiram	34	m	w	NY	Colusa	Monroe Twp	71	315
Hugh	26	m	w	ENGL	San Joaquin	1-Wd Stockton	86	129
J	40	m	w	BREM	Alameda	Alameda	68	15
Jack	23	m	i	CA	Colusa	Monroe Twp	71	315
James	27	m	w	MO	Mendocino	Cuffeys Cove Twp	74	169
James	17	m	w	ENGL	San Joaquin	1-Wd Stockton	86	135
Jas	43	m	w	ENGL	San Joaquin	Douglas Twp	86	34
John	54	m	w	ENGL	Santa Cruz	Santa Cruz	89	415
John	48	m	w	ENGL	San Francisco	8-Wd San Francisco	82	446
John	43	m	w	ME	Sonoma	Analy Twp	91	237
John	39	m	w	ME	San Francisco	7-Wd San Francisco	81	230
John	36	m	w	KY	Santa Clara	Fremont Twp	88	45
Lawrence	30	m	w	ENGL	Santa Barbara	San Buenaventura P	87	437
M	33	m	w	CANA	Mendocino	Ukiah Twp	74	237
M	19	m	w	BOHE	Alameda	Oakland	68	184
Marcus	37	m	w	NH	San Francisco	6-Wd San Francisco	81	112
Mary	18	f	w	CA	Sonoma	Sonoma Twp	91	445
S S	48	m	w	CANA	Sacramento	3-Wd Sacramento	77	312
Samuel S	51	m	w	CT	Placer	Auburn P O	76	378
Susan	21	f	w	IL	San Francisco	11-Wd San Francisc	84	681
Thomas	37	m	w	ENGL	Siskiyou	Yreka Twp	89	673
Thos	29	m	w	OH	Yuba	Marysville	93	583
W J	25	m	w	BADE	San Joaquin	Oneal Twp	86	112
William	53	m	w	ENGL	Placer	Bath P O	76	436
William	42	m	w	IL	San Diego	Julian Dist	78	473
William	32	m	w	MO	Mendocino	Cuffeys Cove Twp	74	169
William	30	m	w	RUSS	Calaveras	San Andreas P O	70	170
Wm M	50	m	w	NY	San Francisco	3-Wd San Francisco	79	327
GREENY								
Ellen	24	f	w	IREL	Alameda	Oakland	68	137
GREER								
Andy	39	m	w	IREL	Sacramento	Franklin Twp	77	106
Charles	50	m	w	AZOR	El Dorado	Georgetown Twp	72	40
Columbus	15	m	w	MO	Santa Clara	Gilroy Twp	88	98
Craissa	40	f	w	NY	Santa Clara	Santa Clara Twp	88	145
George	54	m	w	IREL	San Mateo	Woodside P O	87	386
George	14	m	w	IL	Santa Clara	Santa Clara Twp	88	145
Henery	60	m	w	PA	San Francisco	7-Wd San Francisco	81	167
Henry H	40	m	w	ME	Santa Barbara	Santa Barbara P O	87	470
James	37	m	w	IREL	San Francisco	8-Wd San Francisco	82	304
James	37	m	w	KY	Kern	Bakersfield P O	73	357
Jerome	56	m	w	VA	Alameda	Oakland	68	133
John	61	m	w	IREL	Santa Clara	Fremont Twp	88	56
John	40	m	w	IREL	Napa	Napa	75	5
John	30	m	w	OH	San Joaquin	Elkhorn Twp	86	54
John J	57	m	w	VA	Yolo	Cache Crk Twp	93	452
Julia A	32	f	w	IL	San Francisco	6-Wd San Francisco	81	87
Lendrum	43	m	w	IREL	Sacramento	Franklin Twp	77	105
Margaret	19	f	w	PA	San Francisco	2-Wd San Francisco	79	273
Mary	40	f	w	IREL	San Francisco	11-Wd San Francisc	84	602
Nathan	58	m	w	VA	El Dorado	Cosumnes Twp	72	16
Newton	33	m	w	MO	Kern	Havilah P O	73	338
Saml	31	m	w	IREL	San Francisco	8-Wd San Francisco	82	304
Thomas	36	m	w	IREL	Napa	Napa	75	3
W H	38	m	w	MA	Monterey	San Juan Twp	74	414
GREES								
Henry	31	m	w	HAMB	San Francisco	1-Wd San Francisco	79	51
GREESON								
Wm	40	m	w	IREL	San Francisco	1-Wd San Francisco	79	43
GREETHOUSEN								
Henry	33	m	w	PRUS	San Francisco	San Francisco P O	83	379
GREETMANN								
L	16	f	w	CA	Yuba	Marysville	93	609
GREEVE								
David	21	m	w	SCOT	San Francisco	7-Wd San Francisco	81	262
GREEVES								
T	41	f	w	SCOT	Alameda	Oakland	68	245

Name	Age	S	R	B-PL	County	Locale	Series M593 Roll	Pg
GREEVINS								
Geo	45	m	w	WURT	Tehama	Tehama Twp	92	187
GREFALVA								
Trinederiol	25	m	w	MEXI	Napa	Napa	75	46
GREFERNIA								
Baptist	30	m	w	ITAL	Stanislaus	Branch Twp	92	7
GREFFOZ								
Julian	53	m	w	FRAN	San Francisco	6-Wd San Francisco	81	103
GREGAN								
Thomas	37	m	w	ENGL	San Francisco	San Francisco P O	83	8
Thos	35	m	w	IREL	San Francisco	San Francisco P O	83	21
GREGEOR								
Otto	36	m	w	PRUS	San Mateo	Belmont P O	87	371
GREGG								
G W	55	m	w	VA	Yuba	Marysville	93	585
Geo T	38	m	w	OH	Sonoma	Santa Rosa	91	425
George	31	m	w	VA	Sacramento	2-Wd Sacramento	77	249
George T	40	m	w	MA	Santa Cruz	Santa Cruz	89	422
Henry	30	m	w	MI	Plumas	Indian Twp	77	16
Isaac	40	m	w	OH	San Francisco	San Francisco P O	83	321
Isaac	36	m	w	OH	Sonoma	Santa Rosa	91	425
J T	23	m	w	IN	Napa	Napa Twp	75	72
James	72	m	w	VA	Alameda	Alvarado	68	304
James	42	m	w	NH	Fresno	Millerton P O	72	184
James	38	m	w	SCOT	San Francisco	2-Wd San Francisco	79	212
James C	26	m	w	NH	Klamath	Trinidad Twp	73	390
James T	43	m	w	NY	Amador	Fiddletown P O	69	431
Jerry	11	m	w	CA	Marin	San Rafael Twp	74	27
John	44	m	w	ENGL	San Francisco	San Francisco P O	85	754
John	43	m	w	KY	Placer	Bath P O	76	424
John	28	m	w	IREL	Stanislaus	Washington Twp	92	86
John W	30	m	w	MO	Sonoma	Russian Rvr	91	378
Joseph	26	m	w	NJ	Calaveras	San Andreas P O	70	195
Joseph	19	m	w	ENGL	San Francisco	1-Wd San Francisco	79	74
Joseph M	42	m	w	OH	Monterey	Monterey	74	362
Joseph W	44	m	w	OH	San Francisco	San Francisco P O	85	735
Levi W	49	m	w	IL	Tulare	Visalia Twp	92	285
Livingston	24	m	w	MO	Stanislaus	San Joaquin Twp	92	78
M G	25	m	w	ENGL	San Francisco	3-Wd San Francisco	79	315
Michael	34	m	w	IREL	Santa Clara	1-Wd San Jose	88	275
Minnie	24	f	w	NH	San Francisco	5-Wd San Francisco	81	13
Morris	36	m	w	VA	Colusa	Colusa	71	291
T	52	m	w	AR	Lake	Lower Lake	73	420
W	75	m	w	NH	Sierra	Forest	89	537
W Lewis	50	m	w	PA	San Diego	San Diego	78	491
William	41	m	w	MO	Solano	Silveyville Twp	90	74
William	11	m	w	CA	Marin	San Rafael Twp	74	27
Wm	35	m	w	NJ	Marin	San Rafael Twp	74	39
Worthington	19	m	w	IN	Tehama	Red Bluff	92	182
GREGGORY								
John J	44	m	w	KY	Nevada	Grass Valley Twp	75	227
Richard	60	m	w	IREL	Nevada	Grass Valley Twp	75	224
William	16	m	w	MO	Nevada	Grass Valley Twp	75	150
GREGGS								
Riley	56	m	w	IL	Stanislaus	San Joaquin Twp	92	78
Walter S	15	m	w	CA	Amador	Fiddletown P O	69	432
GREGIORIO								
Louis	45	m	w	FRAN	San Francisco	San Francisco P O	80	535
GREGIRY								
Julia	40	f	w	IREL	San Francisco	2-Wd San Francisco	79	171
GREGIT								
Leopold	47	m	w	FRAN	San Francisco	San Francisco P O	85	752
GREGO								
Joseph	36	m	w	AUST	San Francisco	1-Wd San Francisco	79	111
GREGOIRE								
Camillo	29	m	w	CANA	Marin	Novato Twp	74	10
James	46	m	w	FRAN	Calaveras	San Andreas P O	70	214
Joseph	27	m	w	BELG	San Francisco	San Francisco P O	83	135
Lewis	32	m	w	FRAN	San Francisco	8-Wd San Francisco	82	306
GREGOR								
Anthony	36	m	w	PRUS	San Francisco	San Francisco P O	83	212
Eilse	27	m	w	CANA	Humboldt	Eureka Twp	72	269
James	31	m	w	CANA	Mendocino	Casper & Big Rvr	74	162
Joseph A	40	m	w	PORT	Nevada	Rough & Ready Twp	75	328
GREGORE								
Gustavo	28	m	w	ITAL	Nevada	Nevada Twp	75	316
John H	50	m	w	ENGL	Siskiyou	Yreka Twp	89	672
GREGORIA								
Farala	44	f	w	MEXI	Nevada	Nevada Twp	75	292
GREGORICH								
Nicholas	39	m	w	AUSL	San Francisco	2-Wd San Francisco	79	154
GREGORIE								
Guitirres	48	m	w	CHIL	Calaveras	San Andreas P O	70	196
GREGORIO								
Antonio	22	m	w	MEXI	Marin	San Rafael Twp	74	43
GREGORRE								
Francis	37	m	w	FRAN	Calaveras	San Andreas P O	70	212
Henry	34	m	w	FRAN	Calaveras	San Andreas P O	70	212
GREGORY								
A B	50	m	w	KY	Nevada	Nevada Twp	75	297
Alfred	38	m	w	MA	Butte	Mountain Spring Tw	70	88
Catherin	50	f	w	IREL	San Francisco	8-Wd San Francisco	82	336
Celina	11	f	w	IA	Solano	Vallejo	90	185
Charles B	38	m	w	CT	Alpine	Woodfords P O	69	315
Clinton	25	m	w	MI	Sacramento	Sutter Twp	77	388
Colbert	64	m	w	CANA	Santa Cruz	Santa Cruz Twp	89	400
D S	45	m	w	VA	Monterey	Monterey	74	354

© 2001 by Heritage Quest. All rights reserved.

California 1870 Census

Name	Age	S	R	B-PL	County	Locale	Series M593 Roll	Pg
Danl	35	m	w	VT	Santa Cruz	Santa Cruz Twp	89	400
David	76	m	w	CT	Contra Costa	Martinez P O	71	447
Depay	27	m	w	CANA	Contra Costa	Martinez P O	71	367
E J	17	m	w	CA	Alameda	Oakland	68	159
Edward	52	m	w	CT	San Diego	San Diego	78	497
Elizabeth	55	f	w	ENGL	San Francisco	San Francisco P O	85	836
Frank	23	m	w	FRAN	San Francisco	8-Wd San Francisco	82	388
Franklin P	35	m	w	PA	San Francisco	San Francisco P O	83	118
Frederich	28	m	w	ME	Calaveras	Copperopolis P O	70	261
George	27	m	w	ENGL	San Diego	Julian Dist	78	469
George	20	m	w	NY	San Francisco	San Francisco P O	85	776
Gilbert	30	m	w	OH	Contra Costa	Martinez P O	71	387
Gillman	35	m	w	OH	Contra Costa	Martinez Twp	71	352
Henry	38	m	w	TN	Colusa	Spring Valley Twp	71	340
Henry	34	m	w	ENGL	Sonoma	Vallejo Twp	91	453
Henry C	30	m	w	NY	Alameda	Washington Twp	68	278
Herman	22	m	w	SHOL	Marin	San Antonio Twp	74	60
I B	51	m	w	TN	Amador	Ione City P O	69	351
J	44	m	w	FRAN	Sacramento	1-Wd Sacramento	77	173
J F	30	m	w	NY	Alameda	Oakland	68	222
J M	26	m	w	CANA	Solano	Vallejo	90	167
J W	27	m	w	NY	Solano	Vallejo	90	204
James	58	m	w	IREL	Placer	Newcastle Twp	76	478
James	36	m	w	MO	Sacramento	Lee Twp	77	157
James	35	m	w	KY	Sacramento	Brighton Twp	77	72
James	35	m	w	IA	Santa Clara	Burnett Twp	88	38
James	22	m	w	CT	Yuba	Marysville	93	605
James F	27	m	w	NY	San Francisco	1-Wd San Francisco	79	69
Jason	65	m	w	NY	El Dorado	Placerville	72	127
Jno C	43	m	w	CT	San Francisco	5-Wd San Francisco	81	11
John	50	m	w	ENGL	San Bernardino	Chino Twp	78	411
John	50	m	w	MO	Yolo	Cache Crk Twp	93	443
John	47	m	w	ENGL	Sonoma	Vallejo Twp	91	453
John H	42	m	w	MD	Los Angeles	Los Angeles	73	568
John S	25	m	w	MO	San Francisco	San Francisco P O	83	138
Joseph	25	m	w	CANA	Santa Cruz	Santa Cruz Twp	89	400
L E	14	f	w	IA	Solano	Vallejo	90	184
Leroy	37	m	w	NY	Shasta	Stillwater P O	89	478
M B	40	m	w	CT	Del Norte	Smith Rvr Twp	71	478
M J	22	f	w	CANA	Mendocino	Round Valley Twp	74	220
Martin	25	m	w	TN	San Francisco	5-Wd San Francisco	81	6
Michael	27	m	w	ITAL	Sacramento	Dry Crk Twp	77	99
Micheal	63	m	w	AUST	Sacramento	Franklin Twp	77	106
Munson	42	m	w	OH	Contra Costa	Martinez P O	71	447
N	31	m	w	OH	Santa Clara	Almaden Twp	88	20
Nancy	58	f	w	KY	Nevada	Nevada Twp	75	280
Paul	33	m	w	SHOL	Marin	San Antonio Twp	74	60
Perosso	23	m	w	ITAL	San Francisco	San Francisco P O	85	842
Samuel	35	m	w	TN	Colusa	Colusa Twp	71	286
Simon	30	m	w	VT	San Francisco	San Francisco P O	83	223
Simon	24	m	w	PRUS	Sacramento	2-Wd Sacramento	77	241
Thomas	26	m	w	CANA	San Francisco	8-Wd San Francisco	82	434
Thomas	16	m	w	CA	Sonoma	Petaluma Twp	91	356
Thomas M	45	m	w	VA	Yolo	Putah Twp	93	509
Thos	29	m	w	IREL	San Francisco	1-Wd San Francisco	79	63
Thos	27	m	w	ENGL	Yuba	Rose Bar Twp	93	657
Thos	27	m	w	ENGL	Yuba	Rose Bar Twp	93	657
Thos	22	m	w	ENGL	Sacramento	1-Wd Sacramento	77	203
William	38	m	w	MO	El Dorado	Diamond Springs Tw	72	34
William	35	m	w	TN	San Bernardino	San Bernardino Twp	78	445
William	30	m	w	IREL	San Francisco	San Francisco P O	83	140
William	30	m	w	ME	San Francisco	11-Wd San Francisc	84	637
Willie A	2	m	w	CA	Amador	Ione City P O	69	353
Wm	52	m	w	SCOT	Butte	Oregon Twp	70	124
GREGSON								
John	17	m	w	CA	Sonoma	Analy Twp	91	233
Jones	47	m	w	ENGL	Sonoma	Analy Twp	91	243
Ole	40	m	w	NORW	Colusa	Spring Valley Twp	71	336
GREGULVA								
Anderson	43	m	w	MEXI	San Diego	Warners Rancho Dis	78	529
Aug	22	m	w	MEXI	San Diego	Warners Rancho Dis	78	529
GREGY								
Andrew	40	m	w	SCOT	Siskiyou	Butte Twp	89	588
GREHALDA								
I	24	f	w	MEXI	Napa	Napa	75	55
GREHALVA								
Juana	55	f	w	MEXI	Los Angeles	Los Angeles	73	519
GREHARE								
Francisco	35	m	w	MEXI	Fresno	Millerton P O	72	158
GREHELVA								
Miguel	38	m	w	MEXI	Los Angeles	Los Angeles	73	519
GREHLER								
Christian	39	m	w	WURT	Sacramento	4-Wd Sacramento	77	377
Elias	45	m	w	WURT	Sacramento	4-Wd Sacramento	77	377
GREILLARD								
Joseph	21	m	w	BELG	San Francisco	2-Wd San Francisco	79	146
GREIMS								
George	41	m	w	BAVA	Amador	Drytown P O	69	415
GREINER								
Fredk	42	m	w	BAVA	San Francisco	San Francisco P O	83	329
Fredrick	36	m	w	AUST	San Francisco	San Francisco P O	80	469
Magt	46	f	w	SWIT	San Francisco	San Francisco P O	83	335
GREIPNER								
Geo	40	m	w	PRUS	San Francisco	San Francisco P O	85	872
GREIS								
Leopold	30	m	w	PRUS	San Francisco	San Francisco P O	83	189
GREISER								
Frederick	23	m	w	BADE	San Francisco	San Francisco P O	85	724
GREISS								
Henry	35	m	b	LA	San Joaquin	2-Wd Stockton	86	166
GREIVE								
August	27	m	w	HANO	Santa Cruz	Santa Cruz	89	404
GREIVES								
Robert	57	m	w	SCOT	Solano	Tremont Twp	90	33
GREJALBA								
Antonio	35	m	w	MEXI	San Luis Obispo	Salinas Twp	87	295
GREJALVA								
Jesus	30	m	w	MEXI	Los Angeles	Los Angeles Twp	73	468
Jose	35	m	w	MEXI	Los Angeles	Los Angeles Twp	73	480
GRELAN								
John	38	m	w	IREL	Sacramento	2-Wd Sacramento	77	240
GRELL								
Henry	21	m	w	PRUS	Sacramento	2-Wd Sacramento	77	232
John	50	m	w	WURT	San Francisco	San Francisco P O	85	877
GRELLET								
August	51	m	w	FRAN	San Francisco	San Francisco P O	83	349
GRELSOFF								
S F	49	m	w	ASEA	Sierra	Lincoln Twp	89	547
GREMENGE								
Michael	31	m	w	MO	San Francisco	11-Wd San Francisc	84	446
GREMERSHAW								
Thomas	26	m	w	ENGL	Nevada	Grass Valley Twp	75	145
GREMFEL								
Thomas	24	m	w	ENGL	Placer	Bath P O	76	428
GREMMINGER								
Chas	18	m	w	MD	San Francisco	11-Wd San Francisc	84	426
Louis	30	m	w	PRUS	San Francisco	11-Wd San Francisc	84	685
GREN								
Ay	30	m	c	CHIN	Marin	San Rafael Twp	74	34
Wm	29	m	w	IREL	San Francisco	San Francisco P O	85	758
GRENAWAY								
Thos	25	m	w	IREL	San Francisco	1-Wd San Francisco	79	129
GRENCIO								
L	30	m	w	PORT	Nevada	Eureka Twp	75	139
GRENELL								
Benj J	42	m	w	NY	San Diego	San Diego	78	500
John	33	m	w	IL	Stanislaus	Washington Twp	92	87
William H	44	m	w	NY	Placer	Bath P O	76	435
GRENEWALD								
J F	48	m	w	HESS	Sutter	Nicolaus Twp	92	112
GRENFELL								
Resco	35	m	w	ENGL	Stanislaus	Empire Twp	92	35
GRENIGER								
Phillip	32	m	w	GERM	Yolo	Putah Twp	93	515
GRENION								
Geo	47	m	w	PRUS	Sacramento	3-Wd Sacramento	77	301
GRENKE								
Henry	40	m	w	HANO	San Francisco	11-Wd San Francisc	84	690
GRENLEAF								
E	55	m	w	TN	Sacramento	Georgianna Twp	77	128
GRENN								
John	39	m	w	IREL	San Francisco	1-Wd San Francisco	79	6
GRENNAN								
Dennis	35	m	w	IREL	San Francisco	San Francisco P O	80	371
Ellen	30	f	w	IREL	San Francisco	8-Wd San Francisco	82	429
John	30	m	w	IREL	San Francisco	San Francisco P O	83	163
Thos	42	m	w	IREL	Solano	Vallejo	90	161
GRENNEL								
Dick	37	m	w	PRUS	Butte	Concow Twp	70	7
GRENNELL								
William	40	m	w	NY	Sonoma	Petaluma Twp	91	353
GRENNON								
John	39	m	w	IREL	Placer	Clipper Gap P O	76	376
GRENSHAW								
Chestopher	23	m	w	ENGL	Los Angeles	Los Angeles Twp	73	466
GRENSO								
Gemento	23	m	i	MEXI	Inyo	Lone Pine Twp	73	335
GRENVILLE								
Jno	35	m	w	ENGL	Santa Clara	Almaden Twp	88	9
Jno H	36	m	w	ENGL	Santa Clara	Almaden Twp	88	9
GRENWALT								
Alonzo	35	m	w	ME	San Francisco	11-Wd San Francisc	84	662
GREOR								
Robert	35	m	w	IREL	Nevada	Nevada Twp	75	308
GREORY								
Mary Ann	4	f	w	CA	Monterey	Salinas Twp	74	310
GREP								
S	26	m	w	KY	San Joaquin	2-Wd Stockton	86	193
GRESAS								
James	21	m	m	NY	San Francisco	San Francisco P O	80	364
GRESCHEL								
Abraham	18	m	w	BAVA	San Francisco	8-Wd San Francisco	82	403
GRESEL								
Christoph	45	m	w	HANO	Alameda	Washington Twp	68	300
GRESHAM								
Urick	26	m	w	KY	Yolo	Buckeye Twp	93	409
GRESHOT								
John	47	m	b	SWIT	San Joaquin	1-Wd Stockton	86	150
GRESKY								
Edward	25	m	w	PRUS	Sacramento	Alabama Twp	77	59
GRESS								
Jno M	26	m	w	PA	Sacramento	1-Wd Sacramento	77	178
William	32	m	w	PRUS	San Francisco	8-Wd San Francisco	82	434

© 2001 by Heritage Quest. All rights reserved.

Name	Age	S	R	B-PL	County	Locale	Roll	Pg
GRESSNER						Series M593		
John M	49	m	w	BAVA	Yuba	Slate Range Bar Tw	93	673
GRESSOT								
Augustus	53	m	w	FRAN	Marin	Novato Twp	74	10
GREST								
Harry	50	m	w	SHOL	Mariposa	Mariposa P O	74	98
GRESTEN								
Elecio	22	m	w	UT	Los Angeles	Los Angeles Twp	73	470
GRETCH								
John	37	m	w	CA	Mono	Bridgeport P O	74	282
GRETH								
Antone	40	m	w	PRUS	Butte	Kimshew Tpw	70	82
GRETHAN								
Geo	55	m	w	OH	San Francisco	7-Wd San Francisco	81	276
GRETTEN								
C W	26	m	w	PA	San Joaquin	Oneal Twp	86	110
Mary	72	f	w	IREL	San Joaquin	Oneal Twp	86	110
GRETZ								
Joseph	40	m	w	FRAN	San Francisco	San Francisco P O	80	461
Wm	28	m	w	PRUS	San Francisco	5-Wd San Francisco	81	15
GREUBER								
Charles	30	m	w	HAMB	San Francisco	6-Wd San Francisco	81	83
GREVE								
Frederick	49	m	w	HANO	Calaveras	San Andreas P O	70	209
GREW								
Ah	30	m	c	CHIN	Trinity	Douglas	92	234
Josiah B	51	m	w	NH	Yolo	Merritt Twp	93	503
GREWARD								
Mary	40	f	w	VA	San Francisco	San Francisco P O	85	734
GREWELL								
John W	23	m	w	IA	Santa Clara	2-Wd San Jose	88	318
L H	54	m	w	IN	Lake	Kelsey Crk	73	403
GREY								
Ah	40	m	c	CHIN	Marin	San Rafael Twp	74	38
Alexander	51	m	w	ENGL	San Francisco	2-Wd San Francisco	79	264
Alfred	38	m	w	ENGL	San Joaquin	2-Wd Stockton	86	165
Benj	26	m	w	IL	Sacramento	San Joaquin Twp	77	404
Chas G	41	m	w	SCOT	Colusa	Spring Valley Twp	71	340
Cyril V	51	m	w	ENGL	San Francisco	8-Wd San Francisco	82	486
Eliza	55	f	w	IREL	San Joaquin	2-Wd Stockton	86	172
Eliza	36	f	w	US	San Joaquin	2-Wd Stockton	86	166
Ellen	27	f	w	ENGL	San Francisco	San Francisco P O	85	783
G H	47	m	w	ME	San Joaquin	2-Wd Stockton	86	179
Geo W	32	m	w	IL	Siskiyou	Scott Valley Twp	89	611
George	15	m	w	CA	Los Angeles	Los Angeles Twp	73	487
George C	49	m	w	OH	Tuolumne	Sonora P O	93	324
Georgiana	18	f	w	IL	Tulare	Tule Rvr Twp	92	263
Gustavus	36	m	w	NY	San Francisco	5-Wd San Francisco	81	27
Henry	39	m	b	KY	Santa Clara	Santa Clara Twp	88	172
Henry	31	m	w	CANA	Santa Clara	Fremont Twp	88	42
Henry M	34	m	w	VT	San Francisco	San Francisco P O	83	181
J	33	m	w	OH	San Joaquin	2-Wd Stockton	86	162
J A	42	m	w	NJ	Tuolumne	Big Oak Flat P O	93	401
James	46	m	w	AR	Tulare	Farmersville Twp	92	244
James T H	31	m	w	AR	Tulare	Tule Rvr Twp	92	268
Jenny	23	f	w	SPAI	San Francisco	5-Wd San Francisco	81	1
John	45	m	w	IREL	San Francisco	2-Wd San Francisco	79	153
John	42	m	w	RI	San Joaquin	3-Wd Stockton	86	235
Jos	40	m	w	IL	San Joaquin	Elliott Twp	86	71
Lydia	53	f	w	MA	San Francisco	11-Wd San Francisc	84	504
Maria	16	f	b	LA	San Francisco	San Francisco P O	83	245
Mary	25	f	w	IREL	San Francisco	11-Wd San Francisc	84	540
Nicholas	29	m	w	MS	San Luis Obispo	San Luis Obispo Tw	87	297
Oskar M	35	m	w	NY	Trinity	Weaverville Pct	92	222
R D	30	m	w	ME	San Joaquin	3-Wd Stockton	86	235
Sylvis	20	m	w	TN	San Joaquin	Elliott Twp	86	71
Thomas	65	m	w	IREL	San Francisco	2-Wd San Francisco	79	231
Thomas	24	m	w	ENGL	Nevada	Nevada Twp	75	322
Thomas	24	m	w	ENGL	Nevada	Grass Valley Twp	75	145
Thos	14	m	w	NY	San Francisco	11-Wd San Francisc	84	588
W	5	m	w	NV	San Joaquin	Oneal Twp	86	108
W H	50	m	b	MA	Alameda	Oakland	68	184
William	25	m	m	CANA	San Francisco	San Francisco P O	80	384
Wm	47	m	w	ENGL	Santa Clara	Almaden Twp	88	4
Wm	37	m	w	TN	San Joaquin	2-Wd Stockton	86	208
GREYBACK								
Joaquin	30	m	w	CA	Santa Clara	Gilroy Twp	88	91
GREYLIN								
David	66	m	w	PA	Humboldt	Pacific Twp	72	296
GREYS								
Ed	53	m	w	NY	San Joaquin	2-Wd Stockton	86	212
GREYSEGA								
A	27	m	w	SWIT	Santa Clara	Gilroy Twp	88	93
Jas	20	m	w	SWIT	Santa Clara	Gilroy Twp	88	93
Manuel	18	m	w	SWIT	Santa Clara	Gilroy Twp	88	93
GREYSON								
Wm	19	m	w	CA	Sonoma	Analy Twp	91	234
GREZALVE								
Modesta	9	f	w	CA	Monterey	San Antonio Twp	74	318
GREZALVO								
Meterio	40	m	w	MEXI	Monterey	San Antonio Twp	74	316
GREZEL								
Adolf	25	m	w	TN	Contra Costa	San Pablo Twp	71	362
GRHUN								
John	45	m	w	IREL	Alameda	Oakland	68	244
GRIAS								
John Adam	33	m	w	BAVA	Plumas	Seneca Twp	77	51

Name	Age	S	R	B-PL	County	Locale	Roll	Pg
GRIBBEN						Series M593		
James	35	m	w	IREL	San Joaquin	Castoria Twp	86	7
Marck	26	m	w	IREL	San Francisco	1-Wd San Francisco	79	63
Robert	26	m	w	IREL	San Luis Obispo	Arroyo Grande Twp	87	279
GRIBBIN								
Wm	34	m	w	IREL	San Francisco	2-Wd San Francisco	79	205
Wm	31	m	w	IREL	Alameda	Brooklyn Twp	68	47
GRIBBLE								
H	40	m	w	PA	Sacramento	1-Wd Sacramento	77	189
James	34	m	w	ENGL	El Dorado	Mud Springs Twp	72	75
James	33	m	w	ENGL	Nevada	Grass Valley Twp	75	163
John	45	m	w	ENGL	Nevada	Grass Valley Twp	75	194
John	30	m	w	ENGL	Nevada	Grass Valley Twp	75	184
John	26	m	w	ENGL	Placer	Dutch Flat P O	76	414
John A	25	m	w	ENGL	Nevada	Grass Valley Twp	75	192
John C	26	m	w	SCOT	San Francisco	1-Wd San Francisco	79	112
Josiah	35	m	w	ENGL	Nevada	Grass Valley Twp	75	188
Mary E	7	f	w	CA	Tulare	Tule Rvr Twp	92	262
Peter A	24	m	w	OH	Los Angeles	Los Angeles	73	546
Richard	50	m	w	ENGL	Trinity	Junction City Pct	92	207
GRIBBON								
Thomas	49	m	w	IREL	Sonoma	Bodega Twp	91	254
GRIBNER								
George	13	m	w	CA	Santa Barbara	Santa Barbara P O	87	492
GRIBNEY								
Anne	30	f	w	IREL	San Francisco	11-Wd San Francisc	84	644
GRIBREL								
A	38	m	w	HCAS	San Joaquin	Tulare Twp	86	264
GRICA								
Edwin	16	m	w	MEXI	Alameda	Oakland	68	159
GRICIOLI								
Charles	28	m	w	SWIT	Yolo	Putah Twp	93	517
GRIDER								
H C	36	m	w	IN	Lake	Kelsey Crk	73	402
John	32	m	w	TN	Solano	Vallejo	90	140
L B	50	m	w	AL	Del Norte	Happy Camp Twp	71	472
W T	25	m	w	MS	Del Norte	Happy Camp Twp	71	471
GRIDI								
Domingo	29	m	w	AUST	Santa Clara	2-Wd San Jose	88	315
GRIDINE								
Joseph	65	m	w	ITAL	Yuba	Marysville	93	616
GRIDLEY								
Alex	44	m	w	NY	Napa	Napa Twp	75	64
Charles	53	m	w	OH	Los Angeles	El Monte Twp	73	448
Charles	45	m	w	NY	Marin	Tomales Twp	74	86
Daniel	45	m	w	NY	Napa	Napa	75	35
Geo	48	m	w	NY	Butte	Hamilton Twp	70	63
George	27	m	w	IL	Tehama	Paskenta Twp	92	164
Rural C	42	m	w	MO	Stanislaus	Empire Twp	92	51
GRIEBNOW								
Frederick	41	m	w	PRUS	Alameda	Hayward	68	77
GRIEF								
E A	43	m	w	HANO	Sierra	Lincoln Twp	89	548
GRIEN								
A	27	m	w	BADE	San Joaquin	Elliott Twp	86	77
Sigmond	40	m	w	WEST	San Francisco	11-Wd San Francisc	84	690
GRIER								
David	36	m	w	SCOT	San Francisco	11-Wd San Francisc	84	707
Herman	32	m	w	DE	Sacramento	2-Wd Sacramento	77	243
Jno	35	m	w	SWED	Sacramento	1-Wd Sacramento	77	184
John	40	m	w	IL	Sacramento	2-Wd Sacramento	77	229
Mark C	37	m	w	VA	San Luis Obispo	Morro Twp	87	282
Mathew	35	m	w	IL	Sacramento	2-Wd Sacramento	77	226
GRIERSON								
Peter	35	m	w	IREL	Sacramento	1-Wd Sacramento	77	178
GRIES								
Adam	44	m	w	PA	Butte	Ophir Twp	70	111
Jacob K	39	m	w	PA	Santa Barbara	San Buenaventura P	87	422
Joseph	40	m	w	OH	Butte	Ophir Twp	70	111
William	38	m	w	DENM	Colusa	Monroe Twp	71	313
GRIESBACK								
Jacob	5	m	w	CA	Amador	Jackson P O	69	323
Jacob	39	m	w	PRUS	Amador	Volcano P O	69	376
Peter	34	m	w	PRUS	Amador	Volcano P O	69	375
GRIESSEN								
Neils	22	m	w	DENM	Butte	Chico Twp	70	42
GRIEST								
Peter	48	m	w	PA	Sonoma	Healdsburg & Mendo	91	285
GRIEVES								
William	49	m	w	KY	Sonoma	Santa Rosa	91	426
GRIEZ								
Henry	23	m	w	SHOL	San Francisco	1-Wd San Francisco	79	104
GRIFF								
John	51	m	w	PRUS	San Francisco	1-Wd San Francisco	79	23
Josephine	49	f	w	FRAN	San Francisco	2-Wd San Francisco	79	184
GRIFFATH								
Alfred	40	m	w	OH	Sonoma	Analy Twp	91	238
GRIFFEM								
Michael	37	m	w	IREL	San Francisco	7-Wd San Francisco	81	167
GRIFFEN								
Danl	37	m	w	IREL	San Francisco	1-Wd San Francisco	79	107
Ellen	70	f	w	IREL	San Francisco	2-Wd San Francisco	79	259
Geo W	49	m	w	PA	Butte	Oregon Twp	70	136
John	28	m	w	IREL	San Francisco	1-Wd San Francisco	79	67
Michael B	37	m	w	IREL	San Francisco	San Francisco P O	83	404
Nathaniel	37	m	w	OH	Placer	Bath P O	76	440

© 2001 by Heritage Quest. All rights reserved.

California 1870 Census

Name	Age	S	R	B-PL	County	Locale	Roll	Pg
GRIFFES								
James W	34	m	w	NY	San Mateo	Belmont P O	87	388
GRIFFETH								
Arthur	39	m	w	MD	Alameda	Brooklyn Twp	68	45
Jacob H	31	m	w	AL	Mendocino	Anderson Twp	74	157
Sam	43	m	w	TN	Trinity	Minersville Pct	92	215
GRIFFIEN								
Robt	20	m	w	IREL	San Joaquin	Castoria Twp	86	11
GRIFFIN								
A	33	m	w	IREL	Alameda	Oakland	68	132
A	32	m	w	ME	Alameda	Oakland	68	262
A	30	m	w	IREL	Alameda	Oakland	68	172
Anne	60	f	w	IREL	San Francisco	San Francisco P O	83	85
Annie	31	f	w	AUSL	Yolo	Merritt Twp	93	506
Barthol	38	m	w	IREL	Marin	Nicasio Twp	74	17
Bartholemew	30	m	w	IREL	Yolo	Putah Twp	93	526
Benjamin	17	m	w	CA	Santa Clara	Santa Clara Twp	88	177
Bridget	40	f	w	IREL	Tuolumne	Big Oak Flat P O	93	406
Bridget	35	f	w	IREL	San Francisco	11-Wd San Francisc	84	701
Burrell	20	m	w	MO	Los Angeles	Los Angeles Twp	73	485
Charles	28	m	w	NY	Calaveras	San Andreas P O	70	151
D R	42	m	w	DE	Del Norte	Crescent Twp	71	457
Daniel	29	m	w	IREL	Alameda	Brooklyn	68	33
Daniel	22	m	w	IREL	San Francisco	11-Wd San Francisc	84	465
Dehlia	34	f	w	ENGL	San Francisco	5-Wd San Francisco	81	10
Dwight	24	m	w	OH	Yolo	Cache Crk Twp	93	430
Edith	21	f	w	IL	San Francisco	8-Wd San Francisco	82	429
Edward	48	m	w	NY	Sonoma	Bodega Twp	91	255
Edward	42	m	w	MA	San Francisco	San Francisco P O	85	864
Elizabeth	23	f	w	IREL	Marin	San Rafael Twp	74	26
Elizth	38	f	w	IREL	San Francisco	San Francisco P O	83	114
Ellen	30	m	w	FRAN	San Francisco	San Francisco P O	85	873
Ellen	25	f	w	IREL	San Francisco	San Francisco P O	83	275
Frank	37	m	w	NY	Napa	Yountville Twp	75	76
Frank	29	m	w	ME	Siskiyou	Butte Twp	89	585
Frederick	32	m	w	NY	Marin	Point Reyes Twp	74	21
G	44	m	w	IREL	Alameda	Oakland	68	184
Geo	62	m	w	PA	Solano	Vallejo	90	169
Geo	53	m	w	VA	Sacramento	3-Wd Sacramento	77	273
George	53	m	w	VA	Placer	Summit P O	76	495
George	23	m	w	PA	Klamath	Trinidad Twp	73	389
George	20	m	w	ME	Mendocino	Little Rvr Twp	74	171
George B	33	m	w	NY	Monterey	Castroville Twp	74	325
George L	42	m	w	OH	Shasta	Shasta P O	89	452
Grace	63	f	w	ENGL	Siskiyou	Callahan P O	89	626
Henry	37	m	w	CANA	San Francisco	2-Wd San Francisco	79	215
Henry	26	m	w	IREL	Los Angeles	Los Angeles	73	547
Henry	26	m	w	ENGL	Santa Clara	San Jose Twp	88	209
Hiram	42	m	w	KY	Nevada	Grass Valley Twp	75	142
James	59	m	w	NY	Placer	Auburn P O	76	369
James	58	m	w	NY	Stanislaus	Empire Twp	92	47
James	57	m	w	IREL	Nevada	Bloomfield Twp	75	92
James	47	m	w	IN	Mendocino	Round Valley Twp	74	220
James	45	m	w	NY	Santa Clara	Gilroy Twp	88	95
James	31	m	w	IREL	San Francisco	2-Wd San Francisco	79	207
James	30	m	w	IREL	San Francisco	7-Wd San Francisco	81	226
James	27	m	w	IREL	San Francisco	7-Wd San Francisco	81	178
James	24	m	w	IREL	San Francisco	7-Wd San Francisco	81	182
James	23	m	w	LA	San Francisco	7-Wd San Francisco	81	180
James A	38	m	w	NY	Nevada	Bridgeport Twp	75	104
James H	41	m	w	IN	Mendocino	Round Valley Twp	74	219
James M	48	m	w	AL	San Diego	San Luis Rey	78	513
James R	43	m	w	OH	El Dorado	Mountain Twp	72	68
Jane	54	f	w	ENGL	Sacramento	4-Wd Sacramento	77	378
Jasper	22	m	w	WI	Solano	Suisun Twp	90	109
Jeremiah	43	m	w	IREL	Nevada	Grass Valley Twp	75	160
Joel W	58	m	w	NC	Stanislaus	Empire Twp	92	33
John	51	m	w	CT	Alameda	Oakland	68	182
John	51	m	w	IREL	San Francisco	San Francisco P O	83	137
John	50	m	w	IREL	San Francisco	6-Wd San Francisco	81	118
John	47	m	w	IREL	Contra Costa	Martinez P O	71	395
John	45	m	w	IREL	Santa Clara	2-Wd San Jose	88	289
John	44	m	w	IREL	Siskiyou	Callahan P O	89	633
John	41	m	w	IREL	Tuolumne	Columbia P O	93	341
John	40	m	w	IREL	San Joaquin	Douglas Twp	86	30
John	40	m	w	IREL	Marin	Tomales Twp	74	84
John	35	m	w	OH	San Joaquin	Douglas Twp	86	37
John	35	m	w	NY	Alameda	Murray Twp	68	108
John	35	m	w	IREL	San Francisco	San Francisco P O	85	776
John	34	m	w	IREL	San Francisco	San Francisco P O	85	832
John	30	m	w	IREL	Los Angeles	Los Angeles	73	527
John	26	m	w	IREL	Santa Clara	2-Wd San Jose	88	322
John	25	m	w	NY	San Francisco	3-Wd San Francisco	79	293
John	19	m	w	MS	San Joaquin	Oneal Twp	86	110
John	15	m	w	CA	San Francisco	11-Wd San Francisc	84	593
John F	39	m	w	KY	Yuba	North East Twp	93	644
John M	22	m	w	MO	Los Angeles	Los Angeles Twp	73	486
John S	54	m	w	VA	Los Angeles	Los Angeles	73	532
Jonas	24	m	w	MO	Stanislaus	Empire Twp	92	38
Joseph	52	m	w	VA	Yolo	Buckeye Twp	93	414
Joseph	50	m	w	IREL	San Francisco	San Francisco P O	83	82
Kate	28	f	w	IREL	Merced	Snelling P O	74	261
Lawrence	32	m	w	IREL	El Dorado	Mud Springs Twp	72	77
Lydia S	62	f	w	ME	San Francisco	6-Wd San Francisco	81	134
M	45	m	w	IREL	Sierra	Lincoln Twp	89	551
M	32	m	w	IREL	Lake	Knoxville Mines	73	404
M	32	m	w	IREL	San Mateo	San Mateo P O	87	359

Name	Age	S	R	B-PL	County	Locale	Roll	Pg
Margaret	40	f	w	IREL	Santa Clara	1-Wd San Jose	88	229
Margaret	30	f	w	IREL	Santa Clara	1-Wd San Jose	88	254
Margaret	28	f	w	MA	San Francisco	11-Wd San Francisc	84	509
Margaret	24	f	w	IREL	San Francisco	San Francisco P O	85	825
Margaret	13	f	w	MA	San Francisco	San Francisco P O	85	818
Maria	7	f	w	CA	Nevada	Grass Valley Twp	75	229
Martin	41	m	w	IREL	Sacramento	3-Wd Sacramento	77	302
Martin	35	m	w	IREL	Monterey	San Benito Twp	74	380
Mary	71	f	w	NJ	Monterey	San Juan Twp	74	407
Mary	45	f	w	IREL	San Francisco	7-Wd San Francisco	81	175
Mary	40	f	w	IREL	San Joaquin	2-Wd Stockton	86	170
Mary	39	f	w	IREL	San Francisco	11-Wd San Francisc	84	701
Mary	32	f	w	IREL	San Francisco	San Francisco P O	85	814
Mary	16	f	w	NY	Santa Clara	2-Wd San Jose	88	337
Mary Ann	37	f	w	IREL	San Francisco	San Francisco P O	83	71
Mary J	20	f	w	MO	Yolo	Buckeye Twp	93	414
Melinda C	40	f	w	VT	Nevada	Grass Valley Twp	75	186
Michael	47	m	w	IREL	Alameda	Brooklyn Twp	68	44
Michael	34	m	w	IREL	Yolo	Putah Twp	93	526
Michael	30	m	w	IREL	San Francisco	11-Wd San Francisc	84	558
Michael	28	m	w	IREL	San Francisco	San Francisco P O	85	769
Michael	15	m	w	CA	Santa Clara	Santa Clara Twp	88	177
Michael	15	m	w	NY	San Joaquin	Douglas Twp	86	30
Mitchell	49	m	w	GA	Stanislaus	Emory Twp	92	16
Morris	45	m	w	CANA	Trinity	Weaverville Pct	92	224
Morris	21	m	w	IREL	Mendocino	Point Arena Twp	74	210
Nellie	14	f	w	NY	Santa Clara	2-Wd San Jose	88	337
Oliver	38	m	w	MA	Placer	Gold Run Twp	76	395
Owen	48	m	w	ENGL	Contra Costa	San Pablo Twp	71	361
P J	72	m	w	IREL	Monterey	San Juan Twp	74	407
Pat	30	m	w	IREL	Merced	Snelling P O	74	261
Pat	28	m	w	IREL	San Francisco	San Francisco P O	83	85
Patrick	35	m	w	IREL	Contra Costa	Martinez P O	71	396
Patrick	30	m	w	IREL	Contra Costa	San Pablo Twp	71	357
Patrick	24	m	w	IREL	San Francisco	7-Wd San Francisco	81	185
Perry L	19	m	w	NY	Napa	Napa	75	50
Peter	50	m	w	IREL	San Francisco	San Francisco P O	83	38
Robert	47	m	w	WALE	Santa Clara	1-Wd San Jose	88	230
Robert M	43	m	w	IN	Santa Cruz	Watsonville	89	367
Thomas	50	m	w	IREL	Santa Clara	2-Wd San Jose	88	304
Thomas	45	m	w	IREL	Contra Costa	Martinez P O	71	367
Thomas	40	m	w	IREL	Marin	San Rafael Twp	74	25
Thomas	16	m	w	CA	Santa Clara	Santa Clara Twp	88	153
Thos	26	m	w	NY	San Francisco	2-Wd San Francisco	79	218
Timothy	36	m	w	IREL	Alameda	Alvarado	68	304
Truman	40	m	w	KY	Placer	Bath P O	76	460
Warren	23	m	w	CT	Yolo	Cache Crk Twp	93	430
William	43	m	w	IN	Los Angeles	Los Angeles	73	520
William	40	m	w	SC	San Diego	Milquaty Dist	78	476
William	18	m	w	MA	Inyo	Bishop Crk Twp	73	311
William A	27	m	w	GA	Stanislaus	Emory Twp	92	17
William R	54	m	w	VA	Yuba	Slate Range Bar Tw	93	669
William R	43	m	w	MA	Mendocino	Albion & Big Rvr T	74	166
Willis	27	m	w	IN	San Joaquin	Castoria Twp	86	7
Wm	52	m	w	IREL	Sacramento	1-Wd Sacramento	77	184
Wm	43	m	w	GA	Fresno	Millerton P O	72	157
Wm	40	m	w	MO	Yuba	East Bear Rvr Twp	93	544
Wm	33	m	w	MA	San Francisco	11-Wd San Francisc	84	573
GRIFFING								
Andrew	40	m	w	NY	San Francisco	5-Wd San Francisco	81	33
F G	60	m	w	CT	Tuolumne	Chinese Camp P O	93	366
Fred	50	m	w	NY	San Francisco	5-Wd San Francisco	81	31
Geo J	30	m	w	NY	San Francisco	San Francisco P O	85	722
GRIFFINGS								
Mary A	34	f	w	ME	San Francisco	8-Wd San Francisco	82	323
GRIFFINS								
James	24	m	w	CANA	Mendocino	Casper & Big Rvr	74	163
GRIFFINSON								
James	33	m	w	WALE	Santa Cruz	Santa Cruz	89	410
GRIFFIS								
J Q	34	m	w	ENGL	Solano	Vallejo	90	184
GRIFFIT								
L	31	m	w	IA	Lake	Morgan Valley	73	424
GRIFFITH								
A	28	f	w	NY	Sacramento	3-Wd Sacramento	77	281
Abram	47	m	w	ENGL	Yolo	Cache Crk Twp	93	453
Alex	33	m	w	IREL	San Francisco	San Francisco P O	85	790
Ann	21	f	w	ENGL	Alameda	Oakland	68	206
Anthoney	40	m	w	MD	San Francisco	2-Wd San Francisco	79	183
Antonia	48	f	w	KY	Sonoma	Sonoma Twp	91	448
Bertran	34	m	w	VT	Tuolumne	Sonora P O	93	317
Bradford	37	m	w	OH	Sacramento	4-Wd Sacramento	77	358
Catharine	25	f	w	PA	Sacramento	2-Wd Sacramento	77	219
Charles	52	m	w	NY	Solano	Maine Prairie Twp	90	46
Charles D	31	m	w	WALE	Yolo	Putah Twp	93	526
Chas	43	m	w	MO	San Joaquin	Tulare Twp	86	264
David	39	m	w	WALE	San Francisco	1-Wd San Francisco	79	61
Ed	5	m	w	US	San Joaquin	3-Wd Stockton	86	218
Edward	62	m	w	MA	Solano	Suisun Twp	90	113
Edward	30	m	w	NY	Tulare	Visalia	92	296
Edward	29	m	w	IREL	Sacramento	4-Wd Sacramento	77	340
Even	49	m	w	WALE	Sutter	Butte Twp	92	101
Frank	24	m	w	MA	San Francisco	San Francisco P O	80	413
Frank	18	m	w	CA	Merced	Snelling P O	74	252
Frederich	23	m	w	NY	San Diego	Julian Dist	78	471
Frederick	19	m	w	ENGL	Sacramento	2-Wd Sacramento	77	241
Geo	30	m	w	IREL	San Francisco	San Francisco P O	83	11

Series M593

© 2001 by Heritage Quest. All rights reserved.

Series M593

Name	Age	S	R	B-PL	County	Locale	Roll	Pg
Geo W	25	m	w	OH	Humboldt	Arcata Twp	72	231
George	30	m	w	MI	Solano	Montezuma Twp	90	69
George W	48	m	w	NJ	Yolo	Washington Twp	93	535
Ger	29	m	w	WALE	Sierra	Sears Twp	89	557
Griffith	46	m	w	WALE	Placer	Newcastle Twp	76	476
Hattie	18	f	w	NY	San Francisco	San Francisco P O	83	413
Henry	12	m	w	CA	Butte	Ophir Twp	70	93
J B	50	m	w	IREL	Tehama	Red Bluff	92	183
J W	27	m	w	PA	San Joaquin	Castoria Twp	86	10
James	38	m	w	WALE	Placer	Dutch Flat P O	76	405
James	34	m	w	MA	San Francisco	11-Wd San Francisc	84	462
James	26	m	w	MA	San Joaquin	Oneal Twp	86	111
James M	40	m	w	MD	Los Angeles	Los Angeles	73	529
Jas M	30	m	w	IL	Shasta	Millville P O	89	483
John	58	m	w	VA	Nevada	Grass Valley Twp	75	217
John	46	m	w	MI	Butte	Ophir Twp	70	113
John	44	m	w	IREL	Tuolumne	Chinese Camp P O	93	371
John	38	m	w	WALE	Monterey	Castroville Twp	74	326
John	36	m	w	KY	Klamath	Trinidad Twp	73	392
John	36	m	w	NY	Butte	Chico Twp	70	33
John	27	m	w	OH	Sutter	Yuba Twp	92	148
John E	43	m	w	VA	Santa Clara	Fremont Twp	88	43
John W	54	m	w	NJ	Monterey	San Juan Twp	74	396
Joshua	70	m	w	PA	Merced	Snelling P O	74	251
Julia	46	f	w	NJ	San Francisco	5-Wd San Francisco	81	11
Mary D	3	f	w	CA	San Francisco	1-Wd San Francisco	79	61
Maurice L	40	m	w	PA	El Dorado	Placerville	72	127
Michael	42	m	w	IREL	Trinity	Canyon City Pct	92	202
Miller	42	m	w	NY	San Francisco	San Francisco P O	83	111
Milton	29	m	w	NY	Los Angeles	Los Angeles	73	507
Morris	45	m	w	WALE	Kern	Bakersfield P O	73	358
Morris	40	m	w	ME	Napa	Napa	75	26
Owen	27	m	w	WALE	Placer	Bath P O	76	454
Price	35	m	w	WALE	Sierra	Gibson Twp	89	538
R L	14	f	w	IA	Sacramento	3-Wd Sacramento	77	271
Robert	60	m	w	PA	Amador	Volcano P O	69	386
Robert	33	m	w	WALE	Contra Costa	Martinez P O	71	425
Saml	19	m	w	WALE	Alameda	Oakland	68	240
Silas	40	m	w	IL	Placer	Bath P O	76	457
Silas W	35	m	w	MD	Alpine	Markleeville P O	69	311
Thomas F	63	m	w	WALE	Santa Cruz	Santa Cruz	89	411
Thos	37	m	w	WALE	Merced	Snelling P O	74	281
Thos E	25	m	w	IL	San Francisco	1-Wd San Francisco	79	65
William	50	m	w	WALE	Nevada	Eureka Twp	75	137
William	45	m	w	WALE	Nevada	Bloomfield Twp	75	92
William	42	m	w	OH	San Francisco	2-Wd San Francisco	79	281
William E C	53	m	w	TN	El Dorado	Diamond Springs Tw	72	32
William P	43	m	w	WALE	Tulare	Visalia	92	298
Wm	35	m	w	IREL	San Francisco	San Francisco P O	83	11
Wm F	39	m	w	OH	Butte	Chico Twp	70	55
Wm H	39	m	w	OH	San Mateo	Half Moon Bay P O	87	398
GRIFFITHS								
Benj I	40	m	w	WALE	Nevada	Little York Twp	75	241
David	40	m	w	WALE	Contra Costa	Martinez P O	71	425
Emma	47	f	w	NY	San Francisco	San Francisco P O	80	388
G	43	m	w	WALE	Sierra	Sears Twp	89	561
G	35	m	w	ENGL	San Francisco	3-Wd San Francisco	79	312
Griffith	35	m	w	WALE	Contra Costa	Martinez P O	71	428
I Y	38	m	w	MO	Mendocino	Calpella Twp	74	185
Isabella	35	f	w	ENGL	San Francisco	6-Wd San Francisco	81	70
Isabella	29	f	w	MO	San Francisco	6-Wd San Francisco	81	45
J H	24	m	w	MA	San Francisco	San Francisco P O	83	23
J T	38	m	w	NY	Solano	Vallejo	90	201
John	35	m	w	WALE	Solano	Vallejo	90	158
John	18	m	w	ME	San Francisco	San Francisco P O	80	473
Jonathan	31	m	w	NY	Siskiyou	Surprise Valley Tw	89	640
Joseph	44	m	w	WALE	Nevada	Grass Valley Twp	75	216
Marion	21	m	w	NY	Solano	Vallejo	90	201
Thomas	57	m	w	WALE	Nevada	Grass Valley Twp	75	172
Thomas	39	m	w	ENGL	San Francisco	San Francisco P O	85	746
W J	38	m	w	ENGL	San Francisco	3-Wd San Francisco	79	293
William	46	m	w	PA	San Francisco	8-Wd San Francisco	82	430
William	35	m	w	WALE	Contra Costa	Martinez P O	71	426
GRIFFITS								
J T	32	m	w	NJ	Sacramento	3-Wd Sacramento	77	262
S J	40	m	w	PA	Sacramento	1-Wd Sacramento	77	178
William	22	m	w	WALE	San Francisco	2-Wd San Francisco	79	261
GRIFFITT								
J A	30	m	w	NY	Sacramento	3-Wd Sacramento	77	311
Robt	60	m	w	OH	El Dorado	Cosumnes Twp	72	13
GRIFFORD								
Benjamin	28	m	w	KY	Colusa	Colusa Twp	71	284
GRIFIN								
Morris	35	m	w	IREL	San Francisco	11-Wd San Francisc	84	678
GRIFITH								
H	48	m	w	PA	Alameda	Oakland	68	253
Thos	35	m	w	ENGL	San Francisco	11-Wd San Francisc	84	687
GRIFTH								
D J	40	m	w	WALE	Sierra	Forest	89	536
GRIG								
Thomas	23	m	w	CANA	Humboldt	Eel Rvr Twp	72	252
GRIGAR								
Paul	50	m	w	AUST	San Francisco	6-Wd San Francisco	81	38
GRIGATTA								
Creandin	28	f	w	MEXI	Santa Clara	Almaden Twp	88	6
GRIGG								
J A	32	m	w	NY	Alameda	Murray Twp	68	106

Series M593

Name	Age	S	R	B-PL	County	Locale	Roll	Pg
John	48	m	w	PA	Alameda	Brooklyn	68	36
Leonard	46	m	w	OH	El Dorado	White Oak Twp	72	142
N	28	m	w	NY	Alameda	Murray Twp	68	106
W J	16	m	w	IN	Alameda	Oakland	68	240
GRIGGINS								
Phillip	36	m	w	IREL	San Francisco	San Francisco P O	83	252
GRIGGS								
Anderson	55	m	w	KY	Yolo	Cache Crk Twp	93	438
Antone	21	m	w	PORT	Alameda	Washington Twp	68	273
Catherine	16	f	w	CA	San Mateo	San Mateo P O	87	352
E	44	m	w	ME	Lake	Lakeport	73	406
Ensign	49	m	w	NY	Humboldt	Eel Rvr Twp	72	248
George	45	m	w	MA	San Francisco	8-Wd San Francisco	82	350
George M	36	m	w	NY	Yolo	Merritt Twp	93	503
Isaac	37	m	w	KY	Klamath	Klamath Twp	73	371
John D	45	m	w	CANA	San Joaquin	Tulare Twp	86	253
John G	40	m	w	IL	Yolo	Cache Crk Twp	93	445
Jos B	50	m	w	VA	Sonoma	Santa Rosa	91	429
M C	43	m	w	MO	Mendocino	Ukiah Twp	74	235
Samuel F	28	m	w	PA	Stanislaus	Empire Twp	92	52
Sarah A	27	f	w	IA	El Dorado	Placerville Twp	72	101
William	21	m	w	MO	Yolo	Cache Crk Twp	93	449
GRIGORNE								
Lewis	24	m	w	FRAN	San Joaquin	2-Wd Stockton	86	172
GRIGS								
Alvin B	32	m	w	IL	Placer	Bath P O	76	441
GRIGSBY								
Acholis	46	m	w	MO	Napa	Yountville Twp	75	76
Alexander	34	m	w	TN	Sonoma	Washington Twp	91	470
Alphonzo	26	m	w	MO	Napa	Yountville Twp	75	83
E D	29	m	w	MO	Napa	Yountville Twp	75	90
Elva	16	f	w	CA	Napa	Yountville Twp	75	78
F T	41	m	w	TN	Napa	Yountville Twp	75	82
Granvill W	41	m	w	TN	Napa	Napa Twp	75	62
Henry	41	m	w	KY	Alameda	San Leandro	68	97
Hiram	43	m	b	TN	Napa	Yountville Twp	75	78
Jesse	51	m	w	TN	Napa	Napa Twp	75	65
John T	25	m	w	MT	Napa	Napa Twp	75	65
John W	23	m	w	MO	San Luis Obispo	Morro Twp	87	284
Lucy	70	f	w	VA	Napa	Yountville Twp	75	76
M	38	m	w	TN	Lake	Lower Lake	73	420
Melissa	27	f	w	GA	San Diego	Julian Dist	78	468
Richd D	31	m	w	MO	Napa	Yountville Twp	75	91
Rot T	31	m	w	MO	Napa	Yountville Twp	75	83
Saml H	76	m	w	VA	Napa	Yountville Twp	75	76
Samuel	35	m	w	OH	Colusa	Colusa	71	289
Samuel	21	m	w	TN	Napa	Yountville Twp	75	76
Tirrell R	52	m	w	TN	Napa	Yountville Twp	75	83
William	26	m	w	MO	Napa	Napa Twp	75	29
GRIGSLEY								
Lafayett	23	m	w	IL	Tehama	Tehama Twp	92	194
GRIJABA								
Francisco	21	m	w	MEXI	Los Angeles	Los Angeles Twp	73	468
GRIJALVA								
Dionisio	51	m	w	MEXI	San Luis Obispo	San Luis Obispo Tw	87	304
Jesus	29	m	w	MEXI	San Luis Obispo	San Luis Obispo Tw	87	305
Lucas	13	m	i	CA	Los Angeles	Los Angeles Twp	73	499
Ramon	23	m	w	MEXI	Santa Barbara	Santa Barbara P O	87	497
Ramona	60	f	w	MEXI	Los Angeles	Los Angeles	73	551
Salvador	34	m	w	MEXI	Los Angeles	Los Angeles Twp	73	492
GRILL								
David	50	m	w	BAVA	Plumas	Plumas Twp	77	33
GRILLARD								
Henry	43	m	w	NY	Mendocino	Sanel Twp	74	228
GRILLET								
Julius	40	m	w	FRAN	San Francisco	San Francisco P O	80	477
GRILLIN								
Frank	44	m	w	FRAN	Sutter	Nicolaus Twp	92	106
GRILLIST								
A	34	m	w	IREL	Alameda	Oakland	68	133
GRILLO								
Andrew	35	m	w	MEXI	Tuolumne	Sonora P O	93	311
James	32	m	w	ITAL	Amador	Volcano P O	69	376
Joseph	40	m	w	ITAL	Calaveras	San Andreas P O	70	157
GRILLOS								
Anton	40	m	w	MEXI	Tuolumne	Sonora P O	93	311
GRILLS								
August	56	m	w	BELG	Calaveras	San Andreas P O	70	210
GRILSER								
William	35	m	w	NY	Stanislaus	Buena Vista Twp	92	13
GRIM								
Abraham	37	m	w	OH	San Francisco	11-Wd San Francisc	84	501
Fredrick	50	m	w	SAXO	Calaveras	San Andreas P O	70	193
George	25	m	w	WURT	Sonoma	Bodega Twp	91	256
Hugh	39	m	w	OH	Yuba	New York Twp	93	641
Otho S	38	m	w	OH	Placer	Auburn P O	76	372
William	24	m	w	CANA	Santa Clara	Santa Clara Twp	88	165
GRIMAEYAR								
Henry J	6	m	w	CA	El Dorado	Placerville Twp	72	101
GRIMANCHI								
Joseph	36	m	w	ITAL	Santa Clara	2-Wd San Jose	88	316
GRIMAND								
Julius	28	m	w	FRAN	Butte	Bidwell Twp	70	3
GRIMAS								
Alex	35	m	w	CANA	San Joaquin	Douglas Twp	86	41
GRIMBALL								
A	30	m	w	NY	San Francisco	7-Wd San Francisco	81	226

© 2001 by Heritage Quest. All rights reserved.

California 1870 Census

Name	Age	S	R	B-PL	County	Locale	Series M593 Roll	Pg
GRIMBERG								
Abraham	27	m	w	RUSS	San Francisco	San Francisco P O	80	460
GRIMENGEN								
Geo	54	m	w	PRUS	Fresno	Millerton P O	72	164
GRIMES								
Albert	50	m	w	NY	San Francisco	2-Wd San Francisco	79	153
Andrew J	38	m	w	TN	Yuba	Slate Range Bar Tw	93	674
Brice	40	m	w	MO	Santa Barbara	San Buenaventura P	87	438
Clayton	45	m	w	KY	Colusa	Grand Island Twp	71	308
Eleanor	21	f	m	CT	Sacramento	2-Wd Sacramento	77	236
Eli	35	m	w	OH	Merced	Snelling P O	74	257
Elizath	36	f	w	IREL	San Francisco	San Francisco P O	83	409
F C	40	m	w	MO	Solano	Vallejo	90	166
G C	19	m	w	MS	Sacramento	1-Wd Sacramento	77	181
Geo R	24	m	w	SC	Solano	Vallejo	90	203
George	36	m	w	MA	San Francisco	San Francisco P O	80	412
George	35	m	w	MA	Yolo	Buckeye Twp	93	416
George A	30	m	w	MA	Los Angeles	Los Angeles	73	542
George C	34	m	w	MA	Yolo	Buckeye Twp	93	415
George E	33	m	m	CT	San Francisco	11-Wd San Francisc	84	707
Henry	30	m	w	IREL	San Francisco	7-Wd San Francisco	81	208
Isaac C	41	m	w	OH	San Bernardino	San Bernardino Twp	78	435
James	45	m	w	PRUS	San Francisco	1-Wd San Francisco	79	52
James	39	m	w	IREL	Fresno	Millerton P O	72	167
James	33	m	w	ENGL	Placer	Cisco P O	76	494
James	22	m	w	NY	Santa Barbara	San Buenaventura P	87	440
Jane	35	f	w	IREL	San Francisco	San Francisco P O	85	860
John	46	m	w	IREL	Nevada	Nevada Twp	75	300
John	45	m	w	OH	Stanislaus	Branch Twp	92	2
John	35	m	w	ENGL	Solano	Vallejo	90	168
John L	22	m	w	OH	Placer	Bath P O	76	444
Lawrence	54	m	w	OH	Sacramento	4-Wd Sacramento	77	357
Lyman	34	m	w	NH	San Francisco	6-Wd San Francisco	81	155
M V	25	m	w	IA	Sacramento	3-Wd Sacramento	77	314
Mary	58	f	w	MA	Contra Costa	Martinez P O	71	375
Mary	45	f	w	IREL	Sonoma	Vallejo Twp	91	455
Michael	45	m	w	IREL	San Francisco	2-Wd San Francisco	79	179
Michael	36	m	w	IREL	Alameda	Brooklyn Twp	68	52
Michael	29	m	w	OH	Solano	Silveyville Twp	90	87
N E	31	m	w	MA	San Francisco	San Francisco P O	85	792
P	54	m	w	KY	Sacramento	3-Wd Sacramento	77	314
P D	44	m	w	PA	Solano	Vallejo	90	141
P G	29	m	w	IREL	Solano	Vallejo	90	166
Patrick	30	m	w	IREL	Yolo	Cache Crk Twp	93	421
Sol	33	m	w	IA	Sacramento	3-Wd Sacramento	77	314
Susan	69	f	w	PA	Colusa	Grand Island Twp	71	308
Wallace	24	m	w	MO	Stanislaus	Empire Twp	92	64
William	34	m	w	IREL	Santa Cruz	Santa Cruz Twp	89	400
William	30	m	w	IN	Inyo	Bishop Crk Twp	73	317
GRIMLEY								
John	24	m	w	IREL	San Francisco	11-Wd San Francisc	84	432
Pat	44	m	w	IREL	Solano	Benicia	90	10
GRIMLY								
Patrick	24	m	w	IREL	Klamath	Camp Gaston	73	373
GRIMM								
Adam	30	m	w	BAVA	San Francisco	8-Wd San Francisco	82	497
Alexander	53	m	w	WURT	San Francisco	San Francisco P O	83	172
Charles	52	m	w	PRUS	San Francisco	San Francisco P O	80	372
Charles	47	m	w	SAXO	San Francisco	2-Wd San Francisco	79	167
Charles	34	m	w	SAXO	Calaveras	San Andreas P O	70	190
Emil	35	m	w	HANO	San Francisco	6-Wd San Francisco	81	82
F K	46	m	w	HAMB	Tuolumne	Big Oak Flat P O	93	404
Mary	40	f	w	ENGL	San Francisco	11-Wd San Francisc	84	538
GRIMS								
Lylo	21	m	w	ITAL	San Joaquin	Elliott Twp	86	70
GRIMSHAW								
Henry	55	m	w	ENGL	Nevada	Grass Valley Twp	75	221
W B	44	m	w	NY	Sacramento	Lee Twp	77	161
GRIMSTY								
John	30	m	w	RUSS	Calaveras	Copperopolis P O	70	262
GRIMWALD								
Hall	32	m	w	BADE	San Francisco	7-Wd San Francisco	81	226
GRIMWOOD								
Adolph	34	m	w	ENGL	San Francisco	San Francisco P O	80	404
John D	35	m	w	NY	Santa Cruz	Soquel Twp	89	436
GRIN								
Manley	20	m	w	NY	San Joaquin	Tulare Twp	86	258
GRINDELCOPEN								
John	39	m	w	PRUS	Amador	Sutter Crk P O	69	411
GRINDELL								
Joseph	43	m	w	ENGL	Alameda	Hayward	68	75
GRINDETT								
August	46	m	w	FRAN	San Francisco	San Francisco P O	80	337
GRINDLEY								
James	30	m	w	SCOT	Sonoma	Bodega Twp	91	262
John H	22	m	w	NY	San Francisco	3-Wd San Francisco	79	297
Thomas K	34	m	w	SCOT	San Bernardino	San Bernardino Twp	78	417
GRINDY								
William	30	m	w	ENGL	Amador	Amador City P O	69	394
GRINELL								
M	22	f	w	CANA	Alameda	Oakland	68	146
GRINENSTINE								
Henry	28	m	w	BREM	San Mateo	Searsville P O	87	382
GRINES								
George	33	m	w	OH	Santa Clara	2-Wd San Jose	88	302
J M	39	m	w	MA	Sierra	Sierra Twp	89	562
GRING								
John	36	m	w	SWED	Contra Costa	Martinez P O	71	394
GRINLY								
Sarah	27	f	w	IREL	San Francisco	8-Wd San Francisco	82	318
GRINN								
David	30	m	w	IL	Yolo	Cottonwood Twp	93	474
GRINNAGE								
Fredk	42	m	b	MD	Placer	Bath P O	76	459
Sarah	65	f	b	GA	San Francisco	8-Wd San Francisco	82	357
GRINNAM								
Richard	54	m	w	ENGL	Santa Clara	Milpitas Twp	88	110
GRINNEL								
Margaret	40	f	w	CANA	Sacramento	4-Wd Sacramento	77	321
GRINNELL								
Alvin	51	m	w	RI	Humboldt	Eel Rvr Twp	72	247
Joshua	36	m	w	MA	Santa Cruz	Santa Cruz Twp	89	398
Philander	38	m	w	RI	Colusa	Spring Valley Twp	71	341
GRINNEN								
Michael	33	m	w	IREL	Contra Costa	Martinez P O	71	396
GRINNEY								
William H	12	m	w	MA	Marin	San Rafael Twp	74	29
GRINS								
Charles	31	m	w	PRUS	San Francisco	11-Wd San Francisc	84	502
Ernest	22	m	w	FRAN	San Francisco	San Francisco P O	80	350
GRINSELL								
Wm P	28	m	w	CANA	Sonoma	Salt Point	91	390
GRINTER								
George W	40	m	w	KY	Marin	Bolinas Twp	74	7
GRINTORE								
George	35	m	w	SCOT	Santa Clara	San Jose Twp	88	219
GRINZES								
Henry	25	m	w	PA	Los Angeles	Los Nietos Twp	73	590
GRIPENBURG								
A	25	m	w	FINL	San Francisco	3-Wd San Francisco	79	291
GRIPP								
Fritz	21	m	w	PRUS	San Francisco	San Francisco P O	80	344
Gottleib	70	m	w	PRUS	San Francisco	San Francisco P O	83	51
GRIPPIN								
E M	39	m	w	NY	Sierra	Downieville Twp	89	515
GRIPPLY								
Aug	42	m	w	SHOL	Sierra	Gibson Twp	89	539
GRISAR								
Adolph	23	m	w	BADE	San Francisco	San Francisco P O	80	406
GRISBACK								
Jacob	63	m	w	PRUS	Amador	Volcano P O	69	386
GRISCH								
Christian	54	m	w	SWIT	San Francisco	6-Wd San Francisco	81	59
GRISER								
Emile	49	m	w	BELG	San Francisco	2-Wd San Francisco	79	246
GRISET								
Ferdinand	39	m	w	FRAN	Siskiyou	Table Rock Twp	89	645
James	33	m	w	OH	Siskiyou	Table Rock Twp	89	647
GRISKEY								
Margaret	21	f	w	IREL	San Francisco	11-Wd San Francisc	84	497
GRISNOLD								
Edwin	54	m	w	VT	Kern	Havilah P O	73	336
GRISON								
Andy	24	m	w	IA	Sonoma	Vallejo Twp	91	456
GRISOS								
John	63	m	w	PORT	Shasta	French Gulch P O	89	470
GRISSIM								
H	55	m	w	NY	San Joaquin	2-Wd Stockton	86	185
Wilson T	43	m	w	TN	Santa Clara	2-Wd San Jose	88	293
GRISSISON								
Wm	59	m	w	TN	Sonoma	Mendocino Twp	91	291
GRISSIZ								
Joseph	38	m	w	AUST	San Francisco	3-Wd San Francisco	79	299
Louis	50	m	w	AUST	San Francisco	3-Wd San Francisco	79	299
GRISSON								
Celia	20	f	w	PRUS	San Francisco	San Francisco P O	83	155
GRISSWOLD								
D C	60	m	w	NY	Amador	Jackson P O	69	340
GRIST								
George	23	m	w	PA	Mendocino	Round Valley Twp	74	220
Isaac	50	m	w	PA	Mendocino	Round Valley Twp	74	219
GRISTER								
Jerry	28	m	w	IREL	Santa Clara	San Jose Twp	88	214
GRISTIEN								
Cornelius	30	m	w	IREL	Alameda	Washington Twp	68	291
GRISWALD								
Andrew	38	m	w	NY	Santa Clara	Redwood Twp	88	131
Augustus	42	m	w	OH	Santa Clara	Santa Clara Twp	88	150
GRISWELL								
Andrew	29	m	w	ME	San Francisco	1-Wd San Francisco	79	85
Wm	27	m	w	ME	San Francisco	1-Wd San Francisco	79	85
GRISWOLD								
Alfred	40	m	w	NY	Solano	Vallejo	90	150
Andrew	42	m	w	OH	Mono	Bridgeport P O	74	283
Benjamin	34	m	w	OH	Calaveras	Copperopolis P O	70	262
Chas	33	m	w	VT	Napa	Napa Twp	75	58
Danl	43	m	w	MO	Butte	Chico Twp	70	33
Elisha	25	m	w	MA	Solano	Suisun Twp	90	102
Geo W	54	m	w	VT	Butte	Ophir Twp	70	116
H	45	m	w	ITAL	Alameda	Alameda	68	1
H M	31	m	w	NY	Alameda	Oakland	68	157
Jacob W	62	m	w	NY	Calaveras	Copperopolis P O	70	229
James	37	m	w	NY	Santa Clara	2-Wd San Jose	88	330

© 2001 by Heritage Quest. All rights reserved.

Name	Age	S	R	B-PL	County	Locale	Roll	Pg
						Series M593		
James	34	m	w	OH	Placer	Roseville P O	76	355
Jane	37	f	w	NY	San Francisco	8-Wd San Francisco	82	420
Jane	26	f	w	NJ	San Francisco	6-Wd San Francisco	81	144
John	42	m	w	GA	San Francisco	San Francisco P O	80	405
John M	33	m	w	WI	Placer	Roseville P O	76	355
Josiah	56	m	w	PA	San Francisco	11-Wd San Francisc	84	466
Mary	60	f	w	NY	Santa Clara	2-Wd San Jose	88	284
P D	29	m	w	IL	Sonoma	Santa Rosa	91	395
Peter	29	m	w	NY	San Francisco	1-Wd San Francisco	79	127
Talmon I	53	m	w	NY	Butte	Chico Twp	70	33
W	23	m	w	NY	Monterey	Alisal Twp	74	303
W N	36	m	w	NY	San Francisco	5-Wd San Francisco	81	3
William	23	m	w	NY	Santa Clara	Fremont Twp	88	49
GRISWOULD								
Martha	13	f	w	CA	Sacramento	Granite Twp	77	136
GRITCHEN								
Joseph	35	m	w	NY	San Francisco	5-Wd San Francisco	81	14
GRITTE								
Jacob	32	m	w	PRUS	San Francisco	6-Wd San Francisco	81	90
GRITZEL								
Edward	28	m	w	BREM	San Francisco	7-Wd San Francisco	81	224
GRIZALBA								
Isaac	30	m	w	MEXI	Los Angeles	Wilmington Twp	73	639
GRIZALVE								
Clama	7	f	w	CA	Monterey	San Antonio Twp	74	317
GRIZZLE								
Conrad	43	m	w	HCAS	Nevada	Washington Twp	75	343
John	35	m	w	PA	Nevada	Washington Twp	75	344
GRO								
Ah	40	m	c	CHIN	Solano	Silveyville Twp	90	92
GROA								
Mum	61	m	c	CHIN	Solano	Vallejo	90	208
GROAD								
Ann	30	f	w	IREL	San Francisco	2-Wd San Francisco	79	200
GROAT								
Elias	39	m	w	NY	Napa	Napa	75	38
James	28	m	w	AR	Stanislaus	Empire Twp	92	33
William	36	m	w	NY	Napa	Napa	75	47
GROB								
Jacob	30	m	w	GERM	Contra Costa	San Pablo Twp	71	359
GROBE								
Ambrose	25	m	w	IL	Fresno	Millerton P O	72	181
GROBER								
Charles	36	m	w	HAMB	San Francisco	2-Wd San Francisco	79	207
GROBMAN								
William	29	m	w	PRUS	Stanislaus	Empire Twp	92	35
GROCH								
Otto	29	m	w	GERM	Sacramento	1-Wd Sacramento	77	178
GROCHY								
John	34	m	w	IREL	Solano	Suisun Twp	90	115
GROCUR								
G	40	f	w	CA	Alameda	Oakland	68	229
GRODEGATE								
Henry	32	m	w	PRUS	Napa	Napa	75	25
GRODHOUSE								
F	30	m	w	HANO	Sonoma	Sonoma Twp	91	447
GROEGOR								
Charles	42	m	w	PRUS	Mariposa	Mariposa P O	74	97
GROENING								
Frances	18	f	w	PRUS	San Francisco	San Francisco P O	83	297
GROESBACK								
Fredrick	24	m	w	GERM	Yolo	Grafton Twp	93	488
GROESBECK								
J R	25	m	w	NY	Napa	Napa Twp	75	72
GROFEL								
Lena	27	f	w	HAMB	San Francisco	6-Wd San Francisco	81	88
GROFF								
Daniel	45	m	w	PA	Placer	Lincoln P O	76	488
George	40	m	w	BAVA	Amador	Volcano P O	69	376
John	45	m	w	FRAN	Sonoma	Sonoma Twp	91	444
Joseph	70	m	w	SAXO	Monterey	San Benito Twp	74	382
Josiah Z	41	m	w	NJ	Yolo	Putah Twp	93	521
Lillie	25	f	w	GA	San Francisco	7-Wd San Francisco	81	207
Wm	38	m	w	PRUS	Tehama	Red Bluff	92	177
GROGAN								
Alexr B	55	m	w	IREL	San Francisco	1-Wd San Francisco	79	111
Alice	28	f	w	IREL	San Francisco	San Francisco P O	80	392
Ann	50	f	w	IREL	San Francisco	San Francisco P O	83	91
Emily	40	f	w	IREL	San Mateo	Menlo Park P O	87	377
J R	32	m	w	ENGL	Tuolumne	Chinese Camp P O	93	367
Jas	32	m	w	IREL	Solano	Benicia	90	18
Linda	28	f	w	IREL	San Francisco	San Francisco P O	80	405
Michael	44	m	w	IREL	San Francisco	8-Wd San Francisco	82	488
Michael	39	m	w	IREL	Amador	Ione City P O	69	362
Patk	31	m	w	IREL	San Francisco	1-Wd San Francisco	79	77
Peter	30	m	w	IREL	San Francisco	San Francisco P O	83	335
Sarah	21	f	w	NY	El Dorado	Coloma Twp	72	2
GROGEN								
Peter	22	m	w	NY	San Bernardino	San Bernardino Twp	78	418
GROGER								
Jacob	30	m	w	SHOL	San Mateo	Half Moon Bay P O	87	403
GROGIN								
William N	35	m	w	ME	San Francisco	6-Wd San Francisco	81	106
GROH								
George	24	m	w	HDAR	San Francisco	San Francisco P O	80	467
GROIN								
Josiah	40	m	w	TN	Klamath	South Fork Twp	73	385

Name	Age	S	R	B-PL	County	Locale	Roll	Pg
						Series M593		
GROINNIA								
Adam	33	m	w	ITAL	San Francisco	7-Wd San Francisco	81	178
GROISBECH								
John	68	m	w	NY	San Diego	San Diego	78	493
GROLICH								
John	35	m	w	PRUS	San Francisco	San Francisco P O	80	531
GROLLIET								
Henry	39	m	w	PRUS	San Francisco	6-Wd San Francisco	81	110
GROMDANA								
D	35	m	w	ITAL	Alameda	Oakland	68	221
GROME								
Geo E	28	m	w	OH	Sonoma	Mendocino Twp	91	303
GROMER								
Andrew	48	m	w	KY	El Dorado	Placerville	72	123
GRON								
Ah	20	m	c	CHIN	Placer	Auburn P O	76	378
C A	28	m	w	VT	Sacramento	3-Wd Sacramento	77	313
John	30	m	w	SPAI	San Joaquin	Douglas Twp	86	49
GRONARD								
Thomas J	35	m	w	MO	Tulare	Visalia	92	296
GRONDONE								
Joseph	51	m	w	ITAL	Sacramento	Sutter Twp	77	385
GRONDONO								
Donquia	46	m	w	ITAL	Santa Barbara	Santa Barbara P O	87	475
GRONEAS								
Greora	30	m	i	MEXI	Inyo	Lone Pine Twp	73	335
GRONER								
Ferdinand	26	m	w	WURT	El Dorado	Diamond Springs Tw	72	29
GRONES								
Frances W	52	m	w	VT	Sonoma	Vallejo Twp	91	450
Jabes S	36	m	w	KY	Sacramento	Dry Crk Twp	77	104
GRONEVELD								
M T	29	m	w	HOLL	Sacramento	3-Wd Sacramento	77	289
GRONSKY								
Henry	27	m	w	POLA	Santa Barbara	Santa Barbara P O	87	455
GRONT								
J S	30	m	w	OH	Sacramento	Sutter Twp	77	387
GROOCH								
Katy	25	f	w	HAMB	Mendocino	Little Lake Twp	74	198
GROOM								
A J	36	m	w	MO	Humboldt	Mattole Twp	72	284
Edward	38	m	w	KY	Placer	Emigrant Gap P O	76	416
Frank	42	m	w	KY	Siskiyou	Scott Valley Twp	89	619
Henry	66	m	w	ENGL	San Francisco	6-Wd San Francisco	81	89
Job	15	m	w	IA	Del Norte	Smith Rvr Twp	71	478
John C	33	m	w	NY	San Francisco	1-Wd San Francisco	79	127
Morrison	26	m	w	OH	Del Norte	Smith Rvr Twp	71	478
Ormsby	39	m	w	KY	Calaveras	San Andreas P O	70	216
Roger	34	m	w	IREL	San Francisco	San Francisco P O	83	303
Theodore	35	m	w	NY	San Francisco	1-Wd San Francisco	79	88
William	32	m	w	IREL	San Francisco	11-Wd San Francisc	84	595
GROOMES								
James	35	m	w	MS	Contra Costa	Martinez P O	71	366
GROOMS								
William	48	m	w	ENGL	Yolo	Washington Twp	93	530
GROOT								
John	30	m	w	CANA	Yolo	Grafton Twp	93	499
GROOTH								
Carston	38	m	w	PRUS	San Francisco	8-Wd San Francisco	82	412
GROOTHER								
M	40	m	w	HANO	El Dorado	Coloma Twp	72	2
GROOVER								
John	34	m	w	PRUS	El Dorado	Coloma Twp	72	9
Rudolph	35	m	w	SHOL	San Mateo	Half Moon Bay P O	87	403
GROPE								
Charles	41	m	w	HANO	San Joaquin	Douglas Twp	86	31
John C	46	m	w	WURT	San Joaquin	Douglas Twp	86	31
GROPENGIEPER								
A	34	m	w	GERM	Solano	Benicia	90	13
GROS								
Alfred	33	m	w	FRAN	San Francisco	San Francisco P O	80	360
Joseph	36	m	w	FRAN	San Francisco	2-Wd San Francisco	79	169
Michael	55	m	w	FRAN	El Dorado	Salmon Falls Twp	72	131
GROSANTIO								
Bennaro	42	f	w	MEXI	San Francisco	San Francisco P O	80	332
GROSARIA								
Veltran	48	f	w	CA	Sacramento	2-Wd Sacramento	77	221
GROSBAUER								
John	30	m	w	PRUS	San Francisco	1-Wd San Francisco	79	92
John F	43	m	w	HANO	San Francisco	1-Wd San Francisco	79	127
John F	42	m	w	HANO	San Francisco	1-Wd San Francisco	79	95
John F	10	m	w	NY	San Francisco	1-Wd San Francisco	79	95
Sophia	41	f	w	HANO	San Francisco	1-Wd San Francisco	79	95
GROSCHINSKY								
August	45	m	w	PRUS	San Joaquin	2-Wd Stockton	86	170
GROSCUP								
John	43	m	w	BAVA	Mendocino	Little Lake Twp	74	196
GROSEDA								
Grosarvera	25	m	w	FRAN	Los Angeles	Los Angeles Twp	73	476
GROSETTE								
John	52	m	w	AUST	San Francisco	2-Wd San Francisco	79	191
Michael	40	m	w	FRAN	San Francisco	2-Wd San Francisco	79	278
GROSEY								
J	22	m	w	PARA	Sierra	Butte Twp	89	511
GROSGROVE								
Thos	40	m	w	OH	Butte	Chico Twp	70	60

© 2001 by Heritage Quest. All rights reserved.

Name	Age	S	R	B-PL	County	Locale	Series M593 Roll	Pg
GROSH								
John	35	m	w	HDAR	San Francisco	8-Wd San Francisco	82	361
Samuel	44	m	w	PA	San Francisco	11-Wd San Francisc	84	423
GROSHENG								
S	19	f	w	CA	Sonoma	Santa Rosa	91	398
GROSHONG								
Henry L	21	m	w	WI	Mendocino	Gualala Twp	74	225
Uriah R	51	m	w	MO	Mendocino	Gualala Twp	74	225
GROSLICHT								
Chas	34	m	w	CZEC	San Francisco	San Francisco P O	83	287
GROSNNER								
Lena	21	f	w	PRUS	San Francisco	6-Wd San Francisco	81	72
GROSS								
A	60	m	b	MD	Alameda	Oakland	68	213
A A	61	m	w	PRUS	Tuolumne	Chinese Camp P O	93	386
A P	52	m	w	MA	Solano	Vallejo	90	205
Augustus	25	m	i	MEXI	Inyo	Lone Pine Twp	73	334
Catharine	44	f	w	PRUS	San Francisco	San Francisco P O	85	817
Charles	45	m	w	MECK	Monterey	San Juan Twp	74	404
Daniel	41	m	w	ENGL	Amador	Sutter Crk P O	69	402
Elean	38	m	w	POLA	San Francisco	1-Wd San Francisco	79	58
Emile	9	m	w	CA	San Francisco	San Francisco P O	83	90
F	50	m	w	PRUS	Yuba	Marysville	93	605
Frank	44	m	w	PA	San Luis Obispo	Santa Rosa Twp	87	322
Frank	39	m	w	SAXO	Los Angeles	Wilmington Twp	73	641
Frank	36	m	w	PORT	San Francisco	1-Wd San Francisco	79	119
Frank X	33	m	w	FRAN	San Francisco	8-Wd San Francisco	82	416
Fred	44	m	w	SWIT	Yuba	Linda Twp	93	558
Fred	40	m	w	BADE	Placer	Dutch Flat P O	76	404
George	31	m	w	IN	Tuolumne	Chinese Camp P O	93	386
George	26	m	w	OH	Shasta	Fort Crook P O	89	476
J L	28	m	w	ME	Trinity	Junction City Pct	92	209
Jacob	30	m	w	SWIT	San Francisco	San Francisco P O	85	754
Jacob L	28	m	w	PA	San Francisco	1-Wd San Francisco	79	61
James	45	m	w	BAVA	Solano	Vacaville Twp	90	131
John	58	m	w	PRUS	San Francisco	San Francisco P O	83	132
John F	42	m	w	NY	San Francisco	San Francisco P O	83	365
John L	31	m	w	HCAS	San Francisco	San Francisco P O	85	788
Joseph	29	m	w	BAVA	San Francisco	1-Wd San Francisco	79	14
Leopold	20	m	w	PRUS	San Joaquin	1-Wd Stockton	86	135
Manuel	15	m	i	CHIL	Inyo	Lone Pine Twp	73	333
Maria	27	f	w	ME	Sonoma	Salt Point	91	387
Mary	22	f	w	PRUS	San Francisco	6-Wd San Francisco	81	135
Mary	14	f	w	CA	Solano	Benicia	90	17
Noah	38	m	w	PA	Plumas	Indian Twp	77	15
Peter	33	m	w	HDAR	El Dorado	Placerville Twp	72	104
Rasher	53	m	w	MA	San Francisco	San Francisco P O	83	372
Robert	49	m	b	SWED	Calaveras	San Andreas P O	70	181
Stephen	41	m	w	DC	Tuolumne	Columbia P O	93	353
William	40	m	w	PRUS	San Francisco	6-Wd San Francisco	81	124
William	23	m	w	NY	Sacramento	2-Wd Sacramento	77	244
Wm	30	m	w	ME	Sonoma	Salt Point	91	386
GROSSEN								
Joseph	40	m	w	BELG	San Francisco	1-Wd San Francisco	79	54
GROSSETT								
J	52	m	w	FRAN	Amador	Jackson P O	69	347
GROSSFIELD								
Edward	22	m	w	PRUS	San Francisco	San Francisco P O	83	198
GROSSMAN								
Charles	47	m	w	HDAR	San Francisco	San Francisco P O	83	181
Geo	45	m	w	FRAN	San Francisco	San Francisco P O	83	322
Marks	40	m	w	POLA	San Francisco	2-Wd San Francisco	79	157
GROSSO								
Constantine	48	m	w	ITAL	San Francisco	1-Wd San Francisco	79	111
GROTE								
Chas E	46	m	w	HANO	San Francisco	1-Wd San Francisco	79	52
Fred H	35	m	w	HANO	San Francisco	San Francisco P O	85	868
Frederick	45	m	w	HANO	Placer	Newcastle Twp	76	474
Wm P	30	m	w	MO	San Francisco	San Francisco P O	83	87
GROTEFANT								
Alice	11	f	w	CA	Santa Cruz	Watsonville	89	364
GROTEFEND								
Augustus	46	m	w	HANO	Shasta	Shasta P O	89	459
Chas	44	m	w	MO	Shasta	Shasta P O	89	457
GROTEGER								
L	37	f	w	PRUS	San Joaquin	2-Wd Stockton	86	174
GROTER								
Fredk	38	m	w	PRUS	San Francisco	1-Wd San Francisco	79	46
Henery	26	m	w	BREM	San Francisco	7-Wd San Francisco	81	224
Henry	39	m	w	HANO	San Mateo	Half Moon Bay P O	87	390
GROTEVANT								
Hiram	8	m	w	CA	Santa Cruz	Pajaro Twp	89	351
GROTFORD								
Preston	30	m	w	IA	Monterey	San Antonio Twp	74	318
GROTH								
Henry	40	m	w	PRUS	San Francisco	6-Wd San Francisco	81	136
John	35	m	w	PRUS	Yuba	W Bear Rvr Twp	93	680
GROTON								
Nat	32	m	w	ME	Yuba	Marysville	93	605
GROTTEGUT								
Caroline	1	f	w	OR	San Francisco	11-Wd San Francisc	84	711
GROTTO								
Frederick	22	m	w	CANA	Santa Clara	Milpitas Twp	88	108
GROU								
Peter	45	m	w	PA	Placer	Colfax P O	76	389
GROUCH								
Fred	23	m	w	GERM	Solano	Vallejo	90	204

Name	Age	S	R	B-PL	County	Locale	Series M593 Roll	Pg
GROUL								
Ferdinand S	39	m	w	CANA	Santa Barbara	San Buenaventura P	87	430
GROUND								
Robt	29	m	w	IL	Napa	Napa Twp	75	67
GROUNLOCK								
R	50	m	w	SCOT	Lassen	Susanville Twp	73	440
GROUPP								
John	44	m	w	WURT	San Francisco	2-Wd San Francisco	79	145
GROUS								
Joseph	40	m	w	VA	San Joaquin	Douglas Twp	86	43
William H	40	m	w	OH	Yuba	Slate Range Bar Tw	93	675
GROUSA								
Frederick	45	m	w	PRUS	San Francisco	San Francisco P O	83	400
GROUSEBACK								
Theodore	46	m	w	NY	Sacramento	Granite Twp	77	142
GROUT								
Isaac	45	m	w	CANA	Solano	Vallejo	90	161
Jas	45	m	w	IREL	Solano	Vallejo	90	164
John	31	m	w	IREL	Solano	Vacaville Twp	90	135
GROVALES								
John	23	m	w	BELG	Solano	Vallejo	90	201
GROVAN								
William	40	m	w	NY	Contra Costa	Martinez P O	71	398
GROVE								
Catherine M	46	f	w	MD	Yolo	Cache Crk Twp	93	450
Charles	42	m	w	MA	Yolo	Cottonwood Twp	93	474
Chas	50	m	w	ENGL	Solano	Vallejo	90	171
Chas	22	m	b	MEXI	Marin	San Rafael Twp	74	39
David	56	m	w	VA	Sonoma	Russian Rvr	91	373
David	38	m	w	PA	Santa Barbara	San Buenaventura P	87	438
Elbridge	21	m	w	OH	Yolo	Cache Crk Twp	93	450
Henry	62	m	w	TN	El Dorado	Placerville	72	123
John M	40	m	w	TN	Yolo	Grafton Twp	93	499
Joseph	20	m	w	CANA	Nevada	Grass Valley Twp	75	149
Leah M	24	f	w	IN	San Francisco	San Francisco P O	83	160
Lucy	30	f	w	VA	San Joaquin	2-Wd Stockton	86	179
Susan H	49	f	w	NC	Stanislaus	Empire Twp	92	31
William G	22	m	w	VA	Mariposa	Mariposa P O	74	131
William H	45	m	w	VA	Nevada	Bloomfield Twp	75	97
Wm H	26	m	w	OH	Sonoma	Russian Rvr	91	374
GROVELLA								
G	36	m	w	ITAL	Amador	Sutter Crk P O	69	411
GROVER								
Alexander	36	m	w	IL	Los Angeles	Los Nietos Twp	73	579
Alwin M	26	m	w	ME	Alpine	Markleeville P O	69	311
Annie	20	f	w	NY	Sacramento	4-Wd Sacramento	77	329
Barbary	27	f	w	KY	Butte	Ophir Twp	70	112
Benj P	32	m	w	ME	Sonoma	Petaluma Twp	91	313
Carlton D	28	m	w	MI	Sonoma	Vallejo Twp	91	450
Charles H	28	m	w	ME	El Dorado	White Oak Twp	72	139
Christian	30	m	w	PRUS	Inyo	Cerro Gordo Twp	73	323
David	46	m	w	NY	Butte	Concow Twp	70	6
David	31	m	w	PA	Tehama	Tehama Twp	92	192
E W	41	m	w	ME	Alameda	Oakland	68	130
Edward	32	m	w	NY	Los Angeles	Wilmington Twp	73	636
Eliphlet	50	m	w	MA	Alameda	Brooklyn	68	27
Erner	31	m	w	PRUS	San Francisco	11-Wd San Francisc	84	541
George R	40	m	w	ME	Stanislaus	Branch Twp	92	5
Henderson L	40	m	w	OH	Yolo	Cache Crk Twp	93	437
Henery	38	m	w	BADE	San Francisco	7-Wd San Francisco	81	170
Henry	36	m	w	OH	Nevada	Nevada Twp	75	308
Henry	36	m	w	OH	Nevada	Nevada Twp	75	320
Henry E	40	m	w	MA	Yolo	Merritt Twp	93	504
Ira E	52	m	w	OH	Contra Costa	Martinez P O	71	374
James R	50	m	w	ME	Santa Cruz	Santa Cruz	89	428
John	50	m	w	NY	Yuba	Marysville Twp	93	567
John	43	m	w	WI	Butte	Ophir Twp	70	110
L P	43	m	w	ME	Mendocino	Calpella Twp	74	187
Mansfield	44	m	w	ME	Tulare	Tule Rvr Twp	92	259
Mary	50	f	w	MA	San Francisco	8-Wd San Francisco	82	433
Mary	25	f	w	NY	San Mateo	Pescadero P O	87	412
Nancy B	35	m	w	ME	El Dorado	Kelsey Twp	72	60
Reuben	15	m	w	IREL	Contra Costa	Martinez P O	71	406
Saml	36	m	w	NY	San Francisco	5-Wd San Francisco	81	33
Samuel B	41	m	w	PA	San Francisco	8-Wd San Francisco	82	451
Stephen L	40	m	w	ME	Santa Cruz	Soquel Twp	89	448
William	58	m	w	ENGL	Butte	Oregon Twp	70	126
William	42	m	w	NY	Contra Costa	Martinez P O	71	407
Wm	45	m	w	NY	San Joaquin	2-Wd Stockton	86	174
Wm A	51	m	w	CT	San Francisco	San Francisco P O	83	333
GROVES								
A W	37	m	w	IN	Monterey	Monterey Twp	74	348
Chas	25	m	w	ME	San Francisco	7-Wd San Francisco	81	233
Columbia	28	f	w	TN	Nevada	Little York Twp	75	240
Edward	38	m	w	SCOT	San Francisco	11-Wd San Francisc	84	600
F	28	m	w	ME	Yuba	Marysville	93	595
G H	38	m	w	IREL	Monterey	San Juan Twp	74	400
J Samuel	40	m	w	IL	Yolo	Merritt Twp	93	506
Jacob	61	m	w	WURT	San Francisco	2-Wd San Francisco	79	160
Jerome	35	m	w	NY	Solano	Silveyville Twp	90	86
John	35	m	w	PRUS	San Mateo	Schoolhouse Statio	87	333
Johnson	32	m	w	ME	Sonoma	Petaluma Twp	91	323
Joseph	45	m	w	OH	Yuba	Slate Range Bar Tw	93	672
Lewis D	35	m	w	OH	Placer	Emigrant Gap P O	76	416
Perry	32	m	w	CANA	Shasta	Millville P O	89	488
Philip	65	m	w	RI	San Joaquin	3-Wd Stockton	86	220
William	27	m	w	IREL	Colusa	Spring Valley Twp	71	341

© 2001 by Heritage Quest. All rights reserved.

Series M593

Name	Age	S	R	B-PL	County	Locale	Roll	Pg
William	22	m	w	POLA	San Mateo	Schoolhouse Statio	87	340
Wm B	43	m	w	ME	Butte	Chico Twp	70	39
Wm C	37	m	w	OH	Nevada	Nevada Twp	75	271
GROVET								
George	25	m	w	ENGL	Butte	Ophir Twp	70	92
GROVETT								
Wm	54	m	w	VA	San Joaquin	1-Wd Stockton	86	139
GROVIER								
T J	34	m	w	KY	Mendocino	Sanel Twp	74	229
GROW								
Jacob	51	m	w	FRAN	Calaveras	San Andreas P O	70	194
James	40	m	w	FRAN	El Dorado	Diamond Springs Tw	72	34
Joseph	52	m	w	FRAN	Amador	Jackson P O	69	329
Mary	26	f	w	FRAN	Sacramento	2-Wd Sacramento	77	239
S L	45	m	w	VT	Del Norte	Smith Rvr Twp	71	478
Sarah	38	f	w	IL	San Francisco	San Francisco P O	83	158
Thos	40	m	w	ENGL	Solano	Vallejo	90	170
Timothy	42	m	w	VT	Santa Cruz	Watsonville	89	371
Valentine	34	m	w	US	Yuba	Marysville	93	632
William	22	m	w	IREL	Solano	Rio Vista Twp	90	64
GROWDER								
George	24	m	w	IL	Yolo	Grafton Twp	93	487
Phillip	89	m	w	VA	Yolo	Grafton Twp	93	487
GROWE								
J E	41	m	w	NC	San Joaquin	Douglas Twp	86	47
GROWELL								
James	33	m	w	MA	Solano	Rio Vista Twp	90	60
GROWLEY								
John	40	m	w	BADE	Contra Costa	San Pablo Twp	71	353
GROWNE								
Thomas	38	m	w	MA	San Francisco	7-Wd San Francisco	81	156
GROWNEY								
Own	30	m	w	IREL	San Francisco	7-Wd San Francisco	81	254
GROZELIER								
Simon	36	m	w	FRAN	Santa Clara	1-Wd San Jose	88	267
GROZIER								
Josephine	28	f	w	ME	San Francisco	6-Wd San Francisco	81	106
GROZINGER								
George	46	m	w	WURT	San Francisco	6-Wd San Francisco	81	114
GROZINSKI								
Max	28	m	w	PRUS	San Francisco	8-Wd San Francisco	82	433
GROZIOLO								
Feliciano	30	m	w	CA	Monterey	Monterey Twp	74	347
GROZZELLY								
Eugene	46	m	w	FRAN	San Francisco	San Francisco P O	80	354
GRRILL								
Eliza	60	f	w	VA	Butte	Chico Twp	70	41
John	41	m	w	VA	Butte	Chico Twp	70	41
GRU								
Wo	42	m	c	CHIN	San Joaquin	Oneal Twp	86	116
GRUB								
John	24	m	w	HAMB	Santa Barbara	San Buenaventura P	87	424
GRUBB								
Albert	39	m	m	KY	Sacramento	2-Wd Sacramento	77	217
Caswell W	33	m	w	TN	Yolo	Grafton Twp	93	485
David	60	m	w	OH	Napa	Napa Twp	75	61
G N	36	m	w	IN	Mendocino	Little Lake Twp	74	194
Mary E	8	f	w	CA	Tulare	Venice Twp	92	274
Robert W	38	m	w	TN	Santa Clara	San Jose Twp	88	210
Saml	33	m	w	MD	San Francisco	2-Wd San Francisco	79	224
Thompson	38	m	w	IN	Mendocino	Little Lake Twp	74	194
GRUBBS								
E P	43	m	w	VA	Lassen	Susanville Twp	73	441
Jas	23	m	w	PA	Butte	Chico Twp	70	46
Richard C	39	m	w	GA	Butte	Ophir Twp	70	94
Wm J	45	m	w	GA	Butte	Bidwell Twp	70	4
GRUBE								
Martin	24	m	w	PRUS	San Diego	San Diego	78	486
Wm	39	m	w	PRUS	San Francisco	San Francisco P O	85	871
GRUBENSHUK								
Willm	25	m	w	BADE	San Francisco	6-Wd San Francisco	81	139
GRUBER								
Charles	36	m	w	BAVA	San Francisco	8-Wd San Francisco	82	390
James	29	m	w	MA	San Francisco	8-Wd San Francisco	82	295
John H	40	m	w	PRUS	San Francisco	San Francisco P O	83	346
Joseph	40	m	w	AUST	San Francisco	San Francisco P O	80	430
Lawrence	42	m	w	FRAN	San Francisco	San Francisco P O	83	141
Rupert	29	m	w	PRUS	San Francisco	6-Wd San Francisco	81	93
Samuel	26	m	w	MO	Inyo	Bishop Crk Twp	73	315
GRUBS								
Eli H	53	m	w	VA	Yolo	Cache Crk Twp	93	433
William	36	m	w	MO	Nevada	Rough & Ready Twp	75	325
GRUBY								
M	43	f	w	IREL	Sierra	Forest Twp	89	531
GRUCELLI								
Baptist	18	m	w	ITAL	San Francisco	San Francisco P O	80	469
GRUCH								
Antoine	30	m	w	AUST	Santa Clara	2-Wd San Jose	88	324
John	39	m	w	WURT	San Francisco	11-Wd San Francisc	84	644
GRUCHER								
Frank	34	m	w	ENGL	Tuolumne	Columbia P O	93	360
GRUE								
George	35	m	w	ENGL	Santa Clara	Santa Clara Twp	88	148
GRUEL								
James	20	m	w	IL	San Luis Obispo	Santa Rosa Twp	87	317
GRUELL								
Elizabeth	49	f	w	OH	San Luis Obispo	Santa Rosa Twp	87	320
Jacob	63	m	w	IN	Solano	Vacaville Twp	90	136
Laban H	31	m	w	IL	Colusa	Stony Crk Twp	71	334
Melvin	43	m	w	IN	Santa Clara	Redwood Twp	88	117
Samuel	44	m	w	IN	San Luis Obispo	Santa Rosa Twp	87	320
GRUELLE								
Wm C	29	m	w	MO	Siskiyou	Surprise Valley Tw	89	636
GRUELLER								
Henry	26	m	w	HAMB	San Francisco	6-Wd San Francisco	81	92
GRUENHEGEN								
Caroline	55	f	w	PRUS	San Francisco	San Francisco P O	80	378
GRUETT								
John	23	m	w	MD	San Francisco	San Francisco P O	83	292
P W	39	m	w	ME	Tuolumne	Big Oak Flat P O	93	405
GRUEY								
John	15	m	w	CA	Alameda	Oakland	68	138
GRUGAN								
Ann	45	f	w	IREL	San Francisco	San Francisco P O	83	180
Annie	50	f	w	IREL	San Francisco	San Francisco P O	83	180
GRUGES								
Framsua	40	m	w	FRAN	Los Angeles	Los Angeles	73	566
GRUHLER								
William	32	m	w	SAXO	Los Angeles	Santa Ana Twp	73	610
GRUILLETTE								
Treffle	26	m	w	FRAN	Calaveras	San Andreas P O	70	158
GRUIN								
John	38	m	w	WURT	Humboldt	Eureka Twp	72	278
Maria S	56	f	w	CA	Los Angeles	San Gabriel Twp	73	593
GRUISTMAN								
Jacob H	35	m	w	IN	El Dorado	Cosumnes Twp	72	17
GRUMBLES								
Samuel	28	m	w	TX	San Diego	Milquaty Dist	78	477
GRUMELL								
Henry	23	m	w	MA	San Francisco	San Francisco P O	85	725
GRUMLEY								
Peter	26	m	w	IREL	Santa Clara	Fremont Twp	88	60
GRUMLICH								
Jno Y	40	m	w	OH	Sonoma	Healdsburg & Mendo	91	276
GRUMMERSOL								
James	18	m	w	CANA	Stanislaus	Empire Twp	92	66
GRUMMETT								
Albt	47	m	w	PRUS	Butte	Oregon Twp	70	123
GRUMMOCK								
Merina	48	f	w	SCOT	San Francisco	11-Wd San Francisc	84	688
GRUMMOND								
Jas	9	m	w	IA	Shasta	Horsetown P O	89	506
GRUMP								
Chas	30	m	w	IL	San Joaquin	Oneal Twp	86	105
GRUNBAUM								
Joseph	29	m	w	BAVA	Humboldt	Arcata Twp	72	230
GRUNBOCK								
J W	35	m	w	ASEA	Sierra	Forest Twp	89	529
GRUND								
B	40	m	w	HAMB	San Francisco	San Francisco P O	83	134
GRUNDAL								
Emma	43	f	w	SAXO	Alameda	Hayward	68	77
GRUNDI								
Fredrick	29	m	w	BADE	Calaveras	San Andreas P O	70	205
GRUNDIKE								
J	40	m	w	PA	San Joaquin	Dent Twp	86	27
GRUNDY								
James	30	m	w	VA	Stanislaus	Branch Twp	92	6
Josiah	40	m	w	ENGL	Amador	Amador City P O	69	392
Thos E	41	m	w	ENGL	Sonoma	Healdsburg	91	275
GRUNELL								
S	27	m	w	IL	Lake	Big Valley	73	397
GRUNEN								
Henry	32	m	w	BAVA	Inyo	Cerro Gordo Twp	73	323
GRUNER								
Emil	36	m	w	SWIT	San Francisco	San Francisco P O	80	480
Ferd	35	m	w	SAXO	San Francisco	San Francisco P O	85	794
Ferdinand	55	m	w	BADE	El Dorado	Diamond Springs Tw	72	26
John	37	m	w	WURT	Santa Cruz	Watsonville	89	365
GRUNES								
Alice	26	f	w	IREL	Santa Clara	1-Wd San Jose	88	262
Peter	13	m	w	CANA	Stanislaus	Washington Twp	92	84
GRUNG								
Low	29	m	c	CHIN	Amador	Volcano P O	69	384
GRUNIG								
Henry	37	m	w	HDAR	Santa Barbara	Santa Barbara P O	87	453
GRUNLES								
Danl	40	m	w	SCOT	Humboldt	Bucksport Twp	72	244
GRUNN								
Agoston	20	m	w	CA	Los Angeles	El Monte Twp	73	454
John	33	m	w	IREL	San Francisco	San Francisco P O	83	140
GRUNSELL								
Andrew	50	m	w	ENGL	Butte	Ophir Twp	70	95
GRUNSKY								
Chas	45	m	w	PRUS	San Joaquin	3-Wd Stockton	86	233
GRUNTMAN								
Carole	70	f	w	IREL	San Francisco	11-Wd San Francisc	84	431
GRUNWALD								
Mathias	51	m	w	FRAN	San Francisco	San Francisco P O	80	429
Richd	28	m	w	POLA	San Francisco	3-Wd San Francisco	79	297
GRUNWOLD								
Alexander	55	m	w	PRUS	San Francisco	8-Wd San Francisco	82	438
GRUP								
Ah	44	m	c	CHIN	San Joaquin	1-Wd Stockton	86	145

© 2001 by Heritage Quest. All rights reserved.

California 1870 Census

Series M593

Name	Age	S	R	B-PL	County	Locale	Roll	Pg
GRUPHY								
Kate	34	f	w	IREL	Monterey	Alisal Twp	74	291
GRUSH								
Charles	22	m	w	MA	San Francisco	8-Wd San Francisco	82	458
David	36	m	w	PA	San Francisco	San Francisco P O	83	160
Henry	44	m	w	MA	San Francisco	San Francisco P O	85	726
GRUSS								
Moses	29	m	w	TX	Santa Clara	Santa Clara Twp	88	166
GRUTH								
Jos H	35	m	w	PRUS	Sacramento	3-Wd Sacramento	77	258
GRUTHER								
Adrian M	35	m	w	MD	Placer	Gold Run Twp	76	395
Robert	38	m	w	SAXO	Humboldt	Eureka Twp	72	279
GRUTSCH								
Henry	57	m	w	HDAR	Shasta	Shasta P O	89	453
GRUTTNER								
Oswold	26	m	w	BOHE	Tehama	Red Bluff	92	177
GRUTZ								
F	25	m	w	WURT	San Joaquin	1-Wd Stockton	86	138
GRUTZE								
Chas	49	m	w	SAXO	Siskiyou	Scott Valley Twp	89	621
GRUVE								
Peter	35	m	w	BAVA	San Francisco	3-Wd San Francisco	79	317
GRUWELL								
Asa	68	m	w	OH	Santa Clara	Santa Clara Twp	88	159
James	25	m	w	IA	Santa Clara	Redwood Twp	88	126
Robert	63	m	w	OH	Santa Clara	Santa Clara Twp	88	164
William	33	m	w	IL	Santa Clara	Redwood Twp	88	126
GRY								
Ah	30	m	c	CHIN	Sacramento	Georgianna Twp	77	125
Ah	19	m	c	CHIN	Plumas	Plumas Twp	77	30
GRYAHARAGAN								
Garret	36	m	w	IREL	San Francisco	San Francisco P O	83	161
GRYDER								
C C	36	m	w	MO	Siskiyou	Surprise Valley Tw	89	641
GRYFF								
Jno A	44	m	w	HOLL	Sonoma	Washington Twp	91	469
GSCHWIND								
John	41	m	w	SWIT	Mendocino	Anderson Twp	74	151
Joseph	37	m	w	SWIT	Mendocino	Anderson Twp	74	155
GU								
Ah	29	m	c	CHIN	Mendocino	Gualala Twp	74	223
Ah	20	m	c	CHIN	Sacramento	Franklin Twp	77	116
Ah	19	m	c	CHIN	Placer	Colfax P O	76	391
Kee	23	f	c	CHIN	Siskiyou	Yreka	89	652
GUA								
Um	18	m	c	CHIN	Santa Clara	Santa Clara Twp	88	164
GUADA								
Lupi	30	f	w	MEXI	San Francisco	11-Wd San Francisc	84	615
GUADALAJARA								
Juan	43	m	w	MEXI	Los Angeles	Los Angeles Twp	73	489
GUADALOUPE								
Jose	40	m	w	MEXI	Stanislaus	Emory Twp	92	26
GUADALUPE								
James	26	m	w	ITAL	Santa Clara	Fremont Twp	88	48
Jose	23	m	w	CA	Santa Cruz	Santa Cruz Twp	89	385
Juan	35	m	w	MEXI	Marin	Point Reyes Twp	74	23
GUADER								
Michal	24	m	w	IN	Butte	Chico Twp	70	56
GUADRO								
M	26	m	w	CHIL	Alameda	Alameda	68	3
GUALED								
Miguel	29	m	w	ITAL	Contra Costa	San Pablo Twp	71	356
GUALT								
Andrew D	28	m	w	CANA	Mendocino	Navarro & Big Rvr	74	177
GUALZESTA								
C	38	m	w	SWIT	San Francisco	San Francisco P O	85	785
GUAMEZ								
Felipa D	70	f	w	MEXI	Monterey	Monterey	74	355
GUAMOS								
Joseph	32	m	w	AZOR	Monterey	Castroville Twp	74	336
GUAN								
Ah	29	m	c	CHIN	Stanislaus	Buena Vista Twp	92	13
Maria	20	f	w	CA	San Diego	San Luis Rey	78	515
Nin	22	m	c	CHIN	Placer	Bath P O	76	443
GUANEL								
James	32	m	w	CANA	Alameda	Oakland	68	172
GUANOICH								
Juan	45	m	w	FRAN	Los Angeles	San Juan Twp	73	628
GUANORNA								
Joano	19	m	w	SWIT	Marin	Nicasio Twp	74	20
GUARD								
Charles	46	m	w	MO	Merced	Snelling P O	74	274
George	30	m	w	OH	Los Angeles	Los Angeles	73	529
Isaac W	17	m	w	CA	Sonoma	Healdsburg	91	275
Lizzie	24	f	w	IN	Sacramento	2-Wd Sacramento	77	208
Lotta	18	f	w	PRUS	Yuba	Marysville	93	601
Malissa A	32	f	w	DC	Mariposa	Mariposa P O	74	116
GUARDERTH								
Jacob	28	m	w	SWIT	Santa Clara	2-Wd San Jose	88	320
GUARDIS								
Mary	23	f	w	HANO	San Francisco	San Francisco P O	85	778
GUAREZ								
Carlos	30	m	w	MEXI	San Francisco	San Francisco P O	80	472
GUARO								
Trinidad	45	m	w	MEXI	Fresno	Millerton P O	72	164
GUARRA								
Dominick	52	m	w	ITAL	Calaveras	San Andreas P O	70	209
GUARREZ								
Dolores	36	f	w	MEXI	San Francisco	San Francisco P O	80	457
GUATAMALA								
Pheba	17	f	w	MEXI	San Diego	Coronado	78	465
GUAY								
Ah	30	m	c	CHIN	Sonoma	Sonoma Twp	91	434
GUB								
Ah	28	m	c	CHIN	Placer	Lincoln P O	76	483
GUBAR								
John	22	m	w	FRAN	Alameda	Murray Twp	68	128
GUBBAY								
Frank	29	m	w	ENGL	Placer	Auburn P O	76	367
GUBBINS								
John	40	m	w	IREL	Amador	Jackson P O	69	318
GUBENHEIM								
Frederick	45	m	w	HDAR	El Dorado	Placerville	72	109
GUBENNER								
Henry	34	m	w	HANO	San Francisco	2-Wd San Francisco	79	284
GUBER								
Louis	64	m	w	NY	Stanislaus	Empire Twp	92	61
GUBERT								
Wm	33	m	w	BAVA	Butte	Mountain Spring Tw	70	87
GUBIOTTI								
Carmel	57	m	w	ITAL	Santa Clara	1-Wd San Jose	88	258
GUBLER								
John	43	m	w	SWIT	San Francisco	1-Wd San Francisco	79	49
GUBRASO								
Frado	34	m	w	MEXI	San Joaquin	1-Wd Stockton	86	154
GUBSER								
Frank	31	m	w	SWIT	Santa Clara	2-Wd San Jose	88	324
GUCER								
Manuel	18	m	w	PORT	Sacramento	Georgianna Twp	77	127
GUCKER								
Peter	52	m	w	FRAN	Solano	Benicia	90	17
GUD								
Ahu	15	m	c	CHIN	San Francisco	San Francisco P O	83	175
GUDDE								
Christian	44	m	w	HOLL	San Francisco	1-Wd San Francisco	79	110
GUDDY								
Collus	46	m	w	KY	Lassen	Susanville Twp	73	441
GUDECI								
Jesusa	23	f	w	CA	Santa Clara	2-Wd San Jose	88	300
GUDEHUS								
Christina	33	m	w	HANO	San Francisco	3-Wd San Francisco	79	290
GUDELLA								
Andrew	50	m	w	ITAL	Butte	Ophir Twp	70	108
GUDGEL								
George	46	m	w	KY	Colusa	Stony Crk Twp	71	332
GUDIN								
William	42	m	w	ENGL	Inyo	Independence Twp	73	327
GUDOPP								
Henrietta	32	f	w	HAMB	San Francisco	San Francisco P O	85	736
GUDSKINSKI								
Carl	35	m	w	PRUS	San Francisco	San Francisco P O	85	844
GUE								
Ah	40	m	c	CHIN	Alameda	Alameda	68	17
Ah	40	m	c	CHIN	Alameda	Alameda	68	6
Ah	38	m	c	CHIN	Alameda	Alameda	68	17
Ah	35	m	c	CHIN	Alameda	Oakland	68	260
Ah	30	m	c	CHIN	Alameda	Alameda	68	16
Ah	30	m	c	CHIN	Alameda	Alameda	68	17
Ah	30	m	c	CHIN	Alameda	Alameda	68	6
Ah	30	m	c	CHIN	Alameda	Alameda	68	9
Ah	29	m	c	CHIN	Alameda	Alameda	68	16
Ah	28	m	c	CHIN	Alameda	Oakland	68	210
Ah	27	m	c	CHIN	Sacramento	1-Wd Sacramento	77	198
Ah	26	m	c	CHIN	Butte	Ophir Twp	70	109
Ah	25	m	c	CHIN	Sonoma	Sonoma Twp	91	447
Ah	23	m	c	CHIN	Alameda	Oakland	68	210
Ah	18	m	c	CHIN	Sacramento	1-Wd Sacramento	77	199
Ah	17	m	c	CHIN	Sonoma	Russian Rvr	91	370
Ah	15	m	c	CHIN	Stanislaus	Emory Twp	92	16
Fang	27	m	c	CHIN	San Mateo	Schoolhouse Statio	87	336
Hoy	21	m	c	CHIN	Marin	Novato Twp	74	12
Shin	32	m	c	CHIN	Klamath	Dillon Twp	73	369
Ung	32	m	c	CHIN	Solano	Suisun Twp	90	105
Ung	24	m	c	CHIN	Solano	Suisun Twp	90	105
GUEARNASION								
F	32	f	w	CA	Napa	Napa	75	54
GUEHNE								
Fredk	34	m	w	PRUS	San Francisco	San Francisco P O	85	720
GUEI								
Ni	40	m	c	CHIN	Nevada	Nevada Twp	75	298
GUEL								
Ah	28	m	c	CHIN	Mendocino	Point Arena Twp	74	208
GUELENETARTE								
F	30	m	w	ITAL	Siskiyou	Callahan P O	89	628
GUELEY								
Rochwell	30	m	w	ME	Merced	Snelling P O	74	278
GUELHEMPBY								
G	46	m	w	FRAN	El Dorado	Greenwood Twp	72	53
GUEMNIE								
Piere	45	m	w	ITAL	Sonoma	Sonoma Twp	91	438
GUEN								
Ah	15	m	c	CHIN	San Francisco	San Francisco P O	83	259

© 2001 by Heritage Quest. All rights reserved.

Name	Age	S	R	B-PL	County	Locale	Series M593 Roll	Pg
Gee	32	m	c	CHIN	Solano	Suisun Twp	90	106
GUENIEZ								
Felipe	38	m	w	CA	Monterey	Monterey	74	355
GUENIN								
Ernest	9	m	w	CA	Marin	San Rafael Twp	74	28
Leoni	38	m	w	FRAN	San Francisco	2-Wd San Francisco	79	180
Thaddeus	39	m	w	IREL	San Francisco	6-Wd San Francisco	81	105
GUENN								
Louis	40	m	w	FRAN	San Francisco	6-Wd San Francisco	81	73
GUENO								
Dominick	28	m	w	ITAL	Alpine	Woodfords P O	69	310
GUENSLEY								
Joseph	55	m	w	FRAN	Santa Clara	1-Wd San Jose	88	228
GUERADO								
Ana	83	f	w	MEXI	Los Angeles	Los Angeles	73	525
GUERALD								
L	34	m	w	SPAI	San Joaquin	1-Wd Stockton	86	132
GUERARD								
Joseph	50	m	w	FRAN	San Francisco	8-Wd San Francisco	82	395
GUEREAS								
Simona	15	m	w	CA	Monterey	Monterey Twp	74	352
GUERERO								
Porfereo	18	m	w	CA	Monterey	Alisal Twp	74	304
GUERIN								
Alice	17	f	w	CANA	San Francisco	San Francisco P O	85	775
Caroline	19	f	w	CANA	San Francisco	San Francisco P O	80	414
Ferdinand	14	m	w	FRAN	Solano	Benicia	90	16
Jane	37	f	w	IREL	San Francisco	1-Wd San Francisco	79	101
John	32	m	w	IREL	San Francisco	11-Wd San Francisc	84	643
John	21	m	w	IREL	San Francisco	San Francisco P O	83	34
Oscar	23	m	w	IA	San Francisco	San Francisco P O	83	144
Pat	30	m	w	IREL	San Francisco	11-Wd San Francisc	84	643
Richard	44	m	w	FRAN	San Francisco	San Francisco P O	80	348
Richard	44	m	w	FRAN	San Francisco	San Francisco P O	80	347
GUERMAN								
Christian	62	m	w	BREM	San Francisco	2-Wd San Francisco	79	240
GUERNE								
Agustus	30	m	w	SWIT	Sonoma	Mendocino Twp	91	303
GUERNES								
Satan	30	m	i	MEXI	Inyo	Independence Twp	73	325
GUERNEY								
Eugene	29	m	w	ENGL	San Francisco	5-Wd San Francisco	81	35
GUERNI								
Michl	52	m	w	IREL	San Francisco	San Francisco P O	83	107
GUERNIE								
Peter	50	m	w	FRAN	San Francisco	8-Wd San Francisco	82	311
GUERNSEY								
W H	37	m	w	NY	Tehama	Antelope Twp	92	155
GUERRA								
Cleotilda	39	f	w	CA	Santa Barbara	Santa Barbara P O	87	463
Dolores	30	f	w	MEXI	San Francisco	San Francisco P O	80	464
Felipa	27	m	w	MEXI	San Francisco	San Francisco P O	80	470
Neverta	36	m	w	CHIL	Butte	Kimshew Tpw	70	82
GUERRARO								
Juan	45	m	w	CHIL	Santa Clara	Alviso Twp	88	24
GUERRAZ								
John	65	m	w	SWIT	Santa Clara	Santa Clara Twp	88	172
GUERRERO								
Augustine	27	m	w	CA	San Mateo	Half Moon Bay P O	87	391
John B	22	m	w	CA	San Francisco	2-Wd San Francisco	79	163
Jose	50	f	w	MEXI	Napa	Napa	75	54
Joseph	22	m	w	CA	San Francisco	2-Wd San Francisco	79	137
Victorine	20	m	w	CA	San Mateo	Half Moon Bay P O	87	389
GUERRERRO								
Juana	50	f	w	MEXI	Los Angeles	Wilmington Twp	73	640
GUERREZ								
Henry	15	m	w	CA	Santa Clara	Santa Clara Twp	88	177
GUERRIN								
Felix	14	m	w	CA	Marin	San Rafael Twp	74	25
GUERRO								
Antonia	45	f	w	MEXI	San Francisco	San Francisco P O	80	422
John	20	m	w	CA	Santa Cruz	Pajaro Twp	89	355
Jose de L	27	m	w	MEXI	Santa Barbara	Santa Barbara P O	87	452
Rosso	50	m	w	CA	San Francisco	6-Wd San Francisco	81	91
Sylvester	16	m	w	MEXI	San Francisco	2-Wd San Francisco	79	147
GUERRY								
John	39	m	w	NY	San Francisco	7-Wd San Francisco	81	284
GUERWICK								
Ada	4	f	i	CA	Yolo	Cottonwood Twp	93	471
Charles	30	m	w	FRAN	Yolo	Cottonwood Twp	93	471
GUESE								
Stephen	30	m	w	SWIT	El Dorado	Placerville Twp	72	93
GUESI								
Nora	21	f	w	CANA	San Francisco	San Francisco P O	85	789
GUESPAS								
Ramon	37	m	w	MEXI	Fresno	Millerton P O	72	164
GUESS								
Henry	50	m	m	MD	San Francisco	San Francisco P O	80	365
James	30	m	w	ME	San Francisco	1-Wd San Francisco	79	92
Roger	45	m	w	MI	Alameda	Washington Twp	68	291
Solomen	43	m	w	AL	Santa Clara	Redwood Twp	88	118
GUEST								
James	36	m	w	ENGL	Monterey	San Antonio Twp	74	322
John W	16	m	w	OH	Mariposa	Mariposa P O	74	112
GUESTINE								
Jno	38	m	w	OH	San Francisco	5-Wd San Francisco	81	21

Name	Age	S	R	B-PL	County	Locale	Series M593 Roll	Pg
GUETERREZ								
Benigno	40	m	w	CHIL	Santa Barbara	Santa Barbara P O	87	450
GUEVARA								
Jose	34	m	w	CA	Santa Barbara	Santa Barbara P O	87	471
GUEY								
Ah	25	m	c	CHIN	Yuba	Marysville	93	620
Ah	18	m	c	CHIN	San Francisco	8-Wd San Francisco	82	385
Gee	44	m	c	CHIN	Plumas	Mineral Twp	77	24
Yon	42	m	c	CHIN	Yuba	Marysville	93	624
GUFFICK								
Ann	40	f	w	IREL	San Francisco	2-Wd San Francisco	79	216
GUFFIE								
Wm M	42	m	w	OH	San Luis Obispo	Salinas Twp	87	292
GUFFIN								
A	30	f	w	ME	Alameda	Alameda	68	3
Cathrine	70	f	w	IREL	San Francisco	11-Wd San Francisc	84	492
Chas	9	m	w	CA	San Francisco	San Francisco P O	85	800
Jas	39	m	w	IREL	San Joaquin	2-Wd Stockton	86	211
Mary	26	f	w	IREL	San Francisco	11-Wd San Francisc	84	428
Thomas	71	m	w	IREL	San Francisco	11-Wd San Francisc	84	492
William	30	m	w	IREL	San Francisco	11-Wd San Francisc	84	457
GUFFY								
Alex	44	m	w	PA	Solano	Vallejo	90	143
Wm P	24	m	w	IREL	San Francisco	3-Wd San Francisco	79	300
GUGEGO								
Asencion	13	m	w	CA	San Luis Obispo	San Luis Obispo Tw	87	315
GUGGEIS								
Louis	25	m	w	BADE	San Francisco	San Francisco P O	83	177
GUGGENHEIM								
Leon	21	m	w	GERM	San Francisco	8-Wd San Francisco	82	291
GUGGINHAM								
C	20	f	w	PRUS	Yuba	Marysville	93	582
GUGGS								
Nelson	55	m	w	CANA	Amador	Ione City P O	69	349
GUH								
Lip	28	m	c	CHIN	San Joaquin	Oneal Twp	86	116
GUHALBA								
Miguel	60	m	w	MEXI	Santa Barbara	Las Cruces P O	87	515
GUHL								
Johanna	42	f	w	BADE	Yuba	Marysville	93	590
GUHN								
Max H	40	m	w	SHOL	Napa	Napa Twp	75	68
GUHRIE								
Samuel	38	m	w	OH	Sutter	Yuba Twp	92	147
GUI								
---	28	m	c	CHIN	Siskiyou	Yreka	89	661
Ah	30	m	c	CHIN	Fresno	Millerton P O	72	200
Ah	28	m	c	CHIN	Placer	Lincoln P O	76	483
GUIADO								
Rafael	69	m	w	MEXI	Los Angeles	Los Angeles	73	560
GUIAGA								
Jesus	34	m	w	MEXI	Los Angeles	Los Angeles Twp	73	477
GUIAGO								
Jose	36	m	w	MEXI	Los Angeles	Los Angeles	73	504
GUIANPANCISCHI								
Ferdinand	41	m	w	ITAL	Santa Clara	Santa Clara Twp	88	176
GUIBARD								
Frank	33	m	w	FRAN	Nevada	Nevada Twp	75	305
GUIBERSON								
Saml	36	m	w	OH	Santa Barbara	San Buenaventura P	87	429
Simon	30	m	w	OH	Alameda	Washington Twp	68	283
GUICARO								
Jesus	40	m	w	MEXI	Siskiyou	Scott Valley Twp	89	612
GUICETTI								
Battiste	37	m	w	SWIT	Nevada	Nevada Twp	75	313
GUICHETTO								
Frank	35	m	w	FRAN	San Francisco	San Francisco P O	80	350
GUIDER								
James	38	m	w	IREL	Calaveras	San Andreas P O	70	181
GUIDICI								
Frank	50	m	w	SWIT	El Dorado	Diamond Springs Tw	72	29
GUIDIE								
Pedro	36	m	w	SWIT	San Francisco	San Francisco P O	80	478
GUIDOLA								
Jaques	26	m	w	AUST	Calaveras	San Andreas P O	70	205
GUIDOTTI								
Andrea	14	m	w	SWIT	San Francisco	2-Wd San Francisco	79	146
GUIDRY								
Timothy	48	m	w	IREL	Sutter	Butte Twp	92	102
GUIE								
Ah	51	m	c	CHIN	Nevada	Eureka Twp	75	127
Ah	22	m	c	CHIN	Nevada	Meadow Lake Twp	75	266
Lee	43	m	c	CHIN	Nevada	Eureka Twp	75	141
Ong	26	m	c	CHIN	Nevada	Nevada Twp	75	316
Ong	25	m	c	CHIN	Nevada	Eureka Twp	75	129
GUIEGUA								
Laurezane	50	m	w	MEXI	Santa Barbara	Santa Barbara P O	87	477
GUIETT								
Mary	30	f	w	NY	San Francisco	San Francisco P O	80	535
GUIETTELLO								
John	26	m	w	ITAL	San Francisco	2-Wd San Francisco	79	147
GUIFRA								
Pasquelin	52	f	w	ITAL	San Francisco	2-Wd San Francisco	79	284
GUIGER								
Jake	40	m	w	OH	Yolo	Putah Twp	93	512
GUIGNON								
John	40	m	w	SWIT	San Francisco	6-Wd San Francisco	81	110

© 2001 by Heritage Quest. All rights reserved.

California 1870 Census

Name	Age	S	R	B-PL	County	Locale	Roll	Pg
GUIJABBA								
Jesus	30	m	w	MEXI	Los Angeles	Los Angeles Twp	73	468
GUIJADO								
Juan	50	m	w	MEXI	Los Angeles	Los Angeles Twp	73	467
GUIKAS								
Mary	28	f	w	MEXI	San Francisco	2-Wd San Francisco	79	149
GUILALMERA								
Antonio	24	m	w	SWIT	Santa Cruz	Santa Cruz Twp	89	399
GUILAP								
A H	21	m	w	MO	San Francisco	3-Wd San Francisco	79	315
GUILBARD								
August	56	m	w	SWIT	El Dorado	Coloma Twp	72	3
GUILBERT								
Buenaventura	48	m	w	FRAN	Siskiyou	Yreka	89	654
George	28	m	w	PA	Siskiyou	Table Rock Twp	89	647
GUILD								
Frank G	46	m	w	NY	Nevada	Nevada Twp	75	278
John	40	m	w	FRAN	Solano	Tremont Twp	90	34
Jonathan H	56	m	w	NY	Santa Cruz	Santa Cruz	89	404
Joseph	28	m	w	OH	Sonoma	Petaluma Twp	91	320
Lemuel	48	m	w	VA	San Francisco	8-Wd San Francisco	82	335
GUILDERSLEER								
J W	28	m	w	NY	San Francisco	8-Wd San Francisco	82	339
GUILDERSTEIN								
Wm	50	m	w	CT	San Bernardino	Chino Twp	78	410
GUILDFRY								
Thomas	40	m	w	NY	San Francisco	San Francisco P O	80	370
GUILE								
Ah	31	m	c	CHIN	Nevada	Bridgeport Twp	75	122
James	28	m	w	OR	Humboldt	Eureka Twp	72	275
Silas S	49	m	w	NY	Yolo	Putah Twp	93	524
GUILERMO								
John	40	m	w	ITAL	San Francisco	San Francisco P O	80	471
GUILETT								
Peter	40	m	w	CANA	Alameda	Oakland	68	249
GUILFILE								
Bridget	40	f	w	IREL	Sonoma	Petaluma Twp	91	342
GUILFOILE								
John	29	m	w	IREL	San Francisco	11-Wd San Francisc	84	430
GUILFORD								
Mary	40	f	w	IREL	San Francisco	11-Wd San Francisc	84	514
William M	28	m	w	PA	Solano	Silveyville Twp	90	83
GUILFOY								
Kate	26	f	w	IREL	San Francisco	San Francisco P O	83	165
GUILL								
Stephen	31	m	w	KY	Shasta	Millville P O	89	494
GUILLAMO								
Juan	49	m	w	MEXI	Santa Clara	Almaden Twp	88	15
GUILLARD								
Jean	42	m	w	FRAN	San Francisco	San Francisco P O	80	533
GUILLEMIN								
Claude	43	m	w	FRAN	San Luis Obispo	San Luis Obispo Tw	87	312
Frank	53	m	w	FRAN	San Luis Obispo	San Luis Obispo Tw	87	312
GUILLEN								
Isidora	20	f	w	CA	Santa Cruz	Pajaro Twp	89	360
Petra	25	m	w	SWIT	Marin	San Antonio Twp	74	63
GUILLER								
L	25	m	w	FRAN	Alameda	Alameda	68	9
GUILLET								
Jules	30	m	w	FRAN	San Francisco	7-Wd San Francisco	81	234
Vaine	43	f	w	FRAN	San Francisco	8-Wd San Francisco	82	306
GUILLIAME								
Eugene	28	m	w	FRAN	Santa Clara	2-Wd San Jose	88	313
GUILLIERMO								
Teodo	39	m	w	PORT	San Francisco	1-Wd San Francisco	79	68
GUILLISON								
Henry	47	m	w	NORW	San Francisco	San Francisco P O	83	141
GUILLOME								
Premo	60	m	w	FRAN	Santa Clara	Fremont Twp	88	49
GUILLON								
Victor	46	m	w	FRAN	San Francisco	San Francisco P O	80	483
GUILLOT								
Jacob	63	m	w	FRAN	San Francisco	2-Wd San Francisco	79	144
GUILLY								
Leopold	25	m	w	FRAN	San Francisco	San Francisco P O	80	350
GUIM								
Thomas	44	m	w	PRUS	San Francisco	San Francisco P O	83	371
GUIN								
Ah	35	f	c	CHIN	Santa Barbara	Santa Barbara P O	87	487
Ah	25	m	c	CHIN	Nevada	Grass Valley Twp	75	209
Ah	20	m	c	CHIN	San Francisco	San Francisco P O	83	263
GUINAND								
L A	43	m	w	KY	Amador	Fiddletown P O	69	427
GUINDE								
Stephen	53	m	w	FRAN	San Francisco	2-Wd San Francisco	79	159
GUINDON								
Francis	51	m	w	VT	Tuolumne	Sonora P O	93	315
GUINE								
V	29	m	w	PORT	Alameda	Alameda	68	15
GUINES								
Denis	25	m	w	IA	Calaveras	San Andreas P O	70	186
S R	43	m	w	TN	Merced	Snelling P O	74	279
GUING								
Ah	16	m	c	CHIN	San Francisco	3-Wd San Francisco	79	309
GUINN								
Charles F	25	m	w	PA	Yolo	Grafton Twp	93	487
Thos	34	m	w	VA	Yuba	Marysville Twp	93	567
William	22	m	b	VA	Sacramento	2-Wd Sacramento	77	216
GUINNAN								
Louis	23	m	w	MO	Yolo	Cache Crk Twp	93	439
GUINNANE								
James	24	m	w	IREL	San Francisco	1-Wd San Francisco	79	70
GUINNEA								
S	40	m	w	SCOT	Alameda	Oakland	68	175
GUINNESS								
Joseph	65	m	w	ITAL	San Francisco	2-Wd San Francisco	79	161
Mary	24	f	w	NY	San Francisco	6-Wd San Francisco	81	108
Thomas	23	m	w	ITAL	San Francisco	2-Wd San Francisco	79	161
GUIO								
Ah	34	m	c	CHIN	Placer	Bath P O	76	445
GUIOD								
Alexis	64	m	w	FRAN	San Francisco	11-Wd San Francisc	84	642
GUION								
Ah	26	m	c	CHIN	Placer	Bath P O	76	445
Ah	22	m	c	CHIN	Placer	Bath P O	76	445
Ann Eliza	42	f	w	CANA	Santa Clara	Fremont Twp	88	56
Catholix	42	m	w	FRAN	Calaveras	San Andreas P O	70	214
Geo W	60	m	w	NY	San Francisco	5-Wd San Francisco	81	5
Leonard	38	m	w	NY	San Francisco	San Francisco P O	80	537
Milton	37	m	w	NY	Santa Clara	Santa Clara Twp	88	155
Oscar	26	m	w	NY	San Francisco	3-Wd San Francisco	79	322
GUIPE								
Victor	21	m	w	FRAN	Monterey	Alisal Twp	74	298
GUIR								
John	40	m	c	CHIN	Yolo	Putah Twp	93	514
GUIRADO								
Bernadino	24	m	w	CA	Los Angeles	Los Nietos Twp	73	585
Rafael	75	m	w	MEXI	Los Angeles	Wilmington Twp	73	639
Seccondino	33	f	w	CA	Los Angeles	Los Angeles	73	528
GUIRE								
Bern	46	m	w	OH	Shasta	Horsetown P O	89	506
Joseph M	32	m	w	IREL	Fresno	Millerton P O	72	155
Wm	28	m	w	US	Sacramento	1-Wd Sacramento	77	188
GUIROOS								
Snyavano	35	m	w	MEXI	Los Angeles	Soledad Twp	73	631
GUIS								
Reuben	32	m	w	PA	Plumas	Indian Twp	77	16
GUISALDA								
Felipe	9	m	w	CA	Los Angeles	Los Angeles	73	566
GUISLER								
John	36	m	w	PA	Alameda	Oakland	68	165
GUISSE								
Geo F	36	m	w	PA	Butte	Concow Twp	70	6
GUIT								
Ong	28	m	c	CHIN	Nevada	Washington Twp	75	342
GUITANO								
Ignatio	29	m	w	ITAL	Calaveras	San Andreas P O	70	184
GUITEREZ								
Diego	28	m	w	MEXI	San Francisco	San Francisco P O	80	335
Jose	25	m	w	CA	Santa Cruz	Pajaro Twp	89	362
GUITERREZ								
Antonie M	42	m	w	CA	Santa Barbara	Santa Barbara P O	87	463
Antonio	37	m	w	MEXI	Santa Barbara	Santa Barbara P O	87	479
Celadona	62	f	w	CA	Santa Barbara	Santa Barbara P O	87	457
Francisco	64	m	w	MEXI	Santa Barbara	Santa Barbara P O	87	475
Joseph	42	m	w	PORT	San Francisco	1-Wd San Francisco	79	102
Miguel	47	m	w	MEXI	Santa Barbara	Las Cruces P O	87	506
GUITIERREZ								
Anastacio	50	m	w	MEXI	Santa Barbara	Santa Barbara P O	87	472
GUIZOT								
Paul	50	m	w	ITAL	San Francisco	San Francisco P O	80	350
GUK								
Chi	31	m	c	CHIN	Solano	Green Valley Twp	90	42
GUKE								
Ah	29	m	c	CHIN	Nevada	Meadow Lake Twp	75	266
GUL								
Ah	37	m	c	CHIN	Sacramento	1-Wd Sacramento	77	200
GULARTE								
John	20	m	w	PORT	Alameda	Eden Twp	68	61
GULCH								
Alferdo	70	m	w	AUST	San Diego	Temecula Dist	78	527
GULDAGER								
Hans	37	m	w	DENM	Marin	Tomales Twp	74	79
Louis	37	m	w	DENM	Marin	Tomales Twp	74	88
Otho	44	m	w	SHOL	Sonoma	Petaluma Twp	91	327
GULENE								
N C	24	m	w	FRAN	Monterey	San Juan Twp	74	407
GULER								
Christian	50	m	w	SWIT	Placer	Bath P O	76	453
GULICHHUMN								
Antone	50	m	w	ITAL	Calaveras	San Andreas P O	70	168
GULICK								
Jas H	30	m	w	NJ	Humboldt	Table Bluff Twp	72	306
Samuel	50	m	w	NJ	Tuolumne	Chinese Camp P O	93	375
GULIG								
John	45	m	w	PRUS	San Francisco	5-Wd San Francisco	81	30
GULING								
Ah	30	m	c	CHIN	Santa Clara	Gilroy Twp	88	75
GULKINSON								
Saul	37	m	w	ENGL	San Francisco	5-Wd San Francisco	81	33
GULLAN								
Jose M	51	m	w	MEXI	Santa Cruz	Santa Cruz Twp	89	381
GULLEFER								
Elizabeth	40	f	w	ME	Alameda	Oakland	68	203

© 2001 by Heritage Quest. All rights reserved.

Series M593

Name	Age	S	R	B-PL	County	Locale	Roll	Pg
GULLEST								
Joseph	24	m	w	AZOR	Nevada	Washington Twp	75	346
GULLETT								
Charles	33	m	w	SWIT	San Francisco	San Francisco P O	83	222
GULLEVER								
Joseph	17	m	w	PORT	Solano	Suisun Twp	90	110
GULLEY								
Ashley	56	m	w	KY	Mendocino	Sanel Twp	74	228
S G	27	m	w	IN	Lake	Upper Lake	73	409
GULLIARD								
Joseph	18	m	w	FRAN	Marin	San Antonio Twp	74	64
GULLICKSON								
Louis	30	m	w	NORW	Alpine	Silver Mtn P O	69	307
GULLILAND								
A	33	m	w	SCOT	Sacramento	3-Wd Sacramento	77	272
GULLITT								
John	54	m	w	ENGL	Sacramento	Granite Twp	77	148
GULLIVER								
George W	25	m	w	NJ	Santa Cruz	Soquel Twp	89	447
Harriet	45	f	w	ENGL	San Francisco	San Francisco P O	85	762
GULLOYA								
M	16	f	w	CA	Alameda	Oakland	68	242
GULLY								
Bryant	20	m	w	TN	Santa Clara	San Jose Twp	88	209
James	50	m	w	PRUS	San Francisco	8-Wd San Francisco	82	356
Michael	34	m	w	IREL	San Francisco	San Francisco P O	83	92
William	24	m	w	IREL	Solano	Silveyville Twp	90	84
GULMON								
G C	27	m	w	GA	Alameda	Oakland	68	235
GULNAC								
Charles	39	m	w	CA	Santa Clara	San Jose Twp	88	213
Eugene	22	m	w	CA	Santa Clara	1-Wd San Jose	88	226
Jesusa	28	f	w	CA	Santa Clara	Milpitas Twp	88	112
GULSER								
George L	33	m	w	IN	Yolo	Putah Twp	93	522
GULSTINE								
Geo	40	m	w	DALM	Butte	Ophir Twp	70	93
GULSTON								
David	28	m	w	PRUS	Solano	Vallejo	90	139
GULTHOFF								
Henry	53	m	w	PRUS	El Dorado	Mud Springs Twp	72	77
GULU								
H	52	m	w	FRAN	Alameda	Alameda	68	9
GUM								
Ah	42	m	c	CHIN	Calaveras	San Andreas P O	70	174
Ah	40	m	c	CHIN	Amador	Volcano P O	69	387
Ah	34	m	c	CHIN	Tuolumne	Big Oak Flat P O	93	397
Ah	33	m	c	CHIN	Merced	Snelling P O	74	257
Ah	31	m	c	CHIN	Placer	Bath P O	76	443
Ah	27	m	c	CHIN	Alameda	Washington Twp	68	297
Ah	27	f	c	CHIN	Amador	Drytown P O	69	421
Ah	27	m	c	CHIN	Solano	Suisun Twp	90	105
Ah	27	m	c	CHIN	Placer	Clipper Gap P O	76	376
Ah	25	f	c	CHIN	Nevada	Meadow Lake Twp	75	255
Ah	24	m	c	CHIN	Placer	Auburn P O	76	358
Ah	24	m	c	CHIN	San Francisco	8-Wd San Francisco	82	318
Ah	24	m	c	CHIN	Placer	Auburn P O	76	375
Ah	23	m	c	CHIN	Solano	Suisun Twp	90	107
Ah	22	m	c	CHIN	Placer	Lincoln P O	76	484
Ah	18	f	c	CHIN	Tuolumne	Sonora P O	93	312
Ah	17	m	c	CHIN	Marin	Point Reyes Twp	74	21
Gee	32	m	c	CHIN	El Dorado	Coloma Twp	72	3
James	28	m	w	NY	Solano	Tremont Twp	90	28
John	55	m	w	SCOT	Alameda	Alameda	68	17
Luig	36	m	c	CHIN	San Francisco	11-Wd San Francisc	84	560
Pharo	19	m	w	CANA	Butte	Ophir Twp	70	118
Tuck	40	m	c	CHIN	Tuolumne	Chinese Camp P O	93	385
Wha	25	m	c	CHIN	Solano	Rio Vista Twp	90	64
Yon	18	f	c	CHIN	Placer	Auburn P O	76	371
GUMAS								
Anna	24	f	w	PORT	Placer	Auburn P O	76	381
Salstine	40	m	m	PORT	Placer	Auburn P O	76	381
GUMBA								
M	45	m	w	ITAL	Alameda	Oakland	68	239
GUMBEY								
A	25	m	w	PRUS	Alameda	Oakland	68	184
GUMBINES								
Anna	18	f	w	PRUS	San Francisco	2-Wd San Francisco	79	173
GUMBO								
Ah	25	f	c	CHIN	Solano	Vallejo	90	174
Avelina	15	f	w	MEXI	San Francisco	San Francisco P O	80	411
M	28	m	w	ENGL	Alameda	Oakland	68	246
GUMM								
Isaac	34	m	w	IN	Sonoma	Healdsburg & Mendo	91	284
GUMMER								
Fredk	25	m	w	ENGL	San Francisco	8-Wd San Francisco	82	344
Jacob	26	m	w	SWIT	San Francisco	11-Wd San Francisc	84	649
Samuel	40	m	w	ME	Santa Clara	Santa Clara Twp	88	154
GUMMO								
Richard Jr	23	m	w	ENGL	Nevada	Grass Valley Twp	75	189
GUMMOW								
Wm	41	m	w	ENGL	Yuba	Marysville	93	607
GUMP								
Gustav	31	m	w	BADE	San Francisco	8-Wd San Francisco	82	477
Solomon	37	m	w	BADE	San Francisco	8-Wd San Francisco	82	477
GUMPAR								
John	35	m	w	WURT	Santa Cruz	Watsonville	89	365

Series M593

Name	Age	S	R	B-PL	County	Locale	Roll	Pg
GUMPE								
Chas	40	m	w	PRUS	San Joaquin	Elliott Twp	86	71
GUMPERT								
E	43	m	w	PRUS	San Joaquin	1-Wd Stockton	86	134
GUMY								
Patrick	40	m	w	IREL	Alameda	Oakland	68	260
GUN								
---	22	m	c	CHIN	Siskiyou	Yreka Twp	89	667
Ah	50	m	c	CHIN	Santa Clara	1-Wd San Jose	88	273
Ah	50	m	c	CHIN	Tuolumne	Chinese Camp P O	93	370
Ah	50	m	c	CHIN	Sacramento	San Joaquin Twp	77	398
Ah	45	m	c	CHIN	Tuolumne	Big Oak Flat P O	93	394
Ah	44	m	c	CHIN	Tuolumne	Chinese Camp P O	93	364
Ah	42	m	c	CHIN	Amador	Ione City P O	69	349
Ah	42	m	c	CHIN	Sacramento	Georgianna Twp	77	132
Ah	40	m	c	CHIN	Tuolumne	Chinese Camp P O	93	364
Ah	40	m	c	CHIN	Fresno	Kings Rvr P O	72	206
Ah	40	m	c	CHIN	San Francisco	2-Wd San Francisco	79	285
Ah	40	m	c	CHIN	Nevada	Nevada Twp	75	320
Ah	39	m	c	CHIN	Alameda	Oakland	68	250
Ah	37	f	c	CHIN	Amador	Jackson P O	69	344
Ah	35	m	c	CHIN	Nevada	Little York Twp	75	245
Ah	34	m	c	CHIN	Stanislaus	Emory Twp	92	17
Ah	33	m	c	CHIN	Merced	Snelling P O	74	251
Ah	32	m	c	CHIN	Mariposa	Mariposa P O	74	132
Ah	31	f	c	CHIN	Placer	Auburn P O	76	370
Ah	30	f	c	CHIN	Tuolumne	Sonora P O	93	331
Ah	28	m	c	CHIN	Sierra	Gibson Twp	89	540
Ah	28	f	c	CHIN	Calaveras	San Andreas P O	70	169
Ah	28	m	c	CHIN	Mariposa	Maxwell Crk P O	74	141
Ah	28	m	c	CHIN	Sacramento	Cosumnes Twp	77	92
Ah	28	m	c	CHIN	Plumas	Plumas Twp	77	32
Ah	28	m	c	CHIN	Sacramento	Georgianna Twp	77	133
Ah	28	m	c	CHIN	Sacramento	1-Wd Sacramento	77	196
Ah	28	m	c	CHIN	Solano	Suisun Twp	90	107
Ah	28	m	c	CHIN	Tuolumne	Chinese Camp P O	93	377
Ah	28	m	c	CHIN	Calaveras	San Andreas P O	70	204
Ah	27	m	c	CHIN	Del Norte	Happy Camp Twp	71	469
Ah	26	m	c	CHIN	Sacramento	1-Wd Sacramento	77	200
Ah	25	m	c	CHIN	Sonoma	Bodega Twp	91	264
Ah	25	m	c	CHIN	Sacramento	1-Wd Sacramento	77	202
Ah	22	m	c	CHIN	Napa	Napa	75	56
Ah	21	m	c	CHIN	Trinity	North Fork Twp	92	217
Ah	20	m	c	CHIN	Napa	Napa	75	57
Ah	19	m	c	CHIN	Santa Clara	1-Wd San Jose	88	269
Ah	19	m	c	CHIN	Tuolumne	Chinese Camp P O	93	369
Ah	17	m	c	CHIN	Sacramento	1-Wd Sacramento	77	200
Ah	16	m	c	CHIN	Santa Clara	Fremont Twp	88	47
Ah	16	m	c	CHIN	Alameda	Oakland	68	172
Ah	15	m	c	CHIN	San Francisco	7-Wd San Francisco	81	190
An	18	m	c	CHIN	San Francisco	8-Wd San Francisco	82	437
Charles A	40	m	w	NY	Mendocino	Little Lake Twp	74	198
Fat	26	m	c	CHIN	San Francisco	5-Wd San Francisco	81	16
Gee	28	m	c	CHIN	Yolo	Washington Twp	93	537
Gin	30	m	c	CHIN	Yuba	Marysville	93	626
Ham	27	m	c	CHIN	Del Norte	Happy Camp Twp	71	470
Ho	28	m	c	CHIN	San Joaquin	1-Wd Stockton	86	142
Ho	20	f	c	CHIN	Yuba	Marysville	93	601
Kee	37	m	c	CHIN	Yuba	Marysville	93	623
Kee	36	m	c	CHIN	El Dorado	Georgetown Twp	72	44
Kim	30	m	c	CHIN	San Francisco	San Francisco P O	83	277
Lee	36	m	c	CHIN	Yuba	Marysville	93	631
Long	23	m	c	CHIN	Solano	Rio Vista Twp	90	64
Lung	55	m	c	CHIN	Siskiyou	Yreka Twp	89	667
Sam	48	m	c	CHIN	Placer	Blue Canyon P O	76	418
Tim	31	m	c	CHIN	Yuba	Marysville	93	630
Ting	12	f	c	CHIN	San Francisco	3-Wd San Francisco	79	308
Wau	35	m	c	CHIN	Del Norte	Happy Camp Twp	71	468
Wee	36	m	c	CHIN	Yuba	Marysville	93	620
Wo	25	m	c	CHIN	San Francisco	8-Wd San Francisco	82	359
Yee	34	m	c	CHIN	San Francisco	6-Wd San Francisco	81	50
Yong	34	m	c	CHIN	San Francisco	8-Wd San Francisco	82	472
GUNANNI								
Antonio	27	m	w	ITAL	Amador	Jackson P O	69	327
GUNARD								
B	48	m	w	SWIT	Alameda	Oakland	68	191
GUNCKEL								
William	50	m	w	OH	Santa Clara	San Jose Twp	88	185
GUNDER								
Delia	25	f	w	PRUS	San Francisco	San Francisco P O	83	98
GUNDERSEN								
Christian	40	m	w	NORW	San Francisco	7-Wd San Francisco	81	283
GUNDERSON								
Herman	36	m	w	NORW	San Francisco	San Francisco P O	83	215
Thos	62	m	w	NORW	Solano	Vallejo	90	156
GUNDLACH								
Fred	26	m	w	BREM	San Francisco	2-Wd San Francisco	79	149
Jacob	50	m	w	BAVA	San Francisco	2-Wd San Francisco	79	144
Jacob	42	m	w	BAVA	San Francisco	San Francisco P O	80	355
Julia	19	f	w	HCAS	Santa Clara	1-Wd San Jose	88	232
William	30	m	w	PRUS	San Francisco	8-Wd San Francisco	82	436
GUNDLACK								
Henry	63	m	w	PRUS	Santa Clara	Santa Clara Twp	88	155
GUNDLEFAYN								
J	30	m	w	PRUS	Alameda	Oakland	68	247
GUNDLEFIELD								
Louis	20	m	w	WURT	San Francisco	7-Wd San Francisco	81	206

© 2001 by Heritage Quest. All rights reserved.

California 1870 Census

Name	Age	S	R	B-PL	County	Locale	Series M593 Roll	Pg
GUNDLEFINGER								
C D	32	m	w	PRUS	Alameda	Oakland	68	222
D	30	m	w	PRUS	Alameda	Oakland	68	262
GUNDLICH								
John	29	m	w	HANO	San Francisco	11-Wd San Francisc	84	624
GUNDREY								
Richard	24	m	w	ENGL	El Dorado	Mud Springs Twp	72	81
GUNDRY								
George	30	m	w	ENGL	Nevada	Grass Valley Twp	75	228
GUNDY								
Conry	16	f	w	CA	Nevada	Eureka Twp	75	133
Henry	56	m	w	ENGL	Tuolumne	Big Oak Flat P O	93	401
Henry	37	m	w	WURT	Butte	Concow Twp	70	7
Van H	40	m	w	OH	Santa Clara	Gilroy Twp	88	93
GUNE								
Ah	19	m	c	CHIN	Placer	Auburn P O	76	377
Ah	19	m	c	CHIN	Nevada	Rough & Ready Twp	75	331
Ah	17	m	c	CHIN	Monterey	Monterey Twp	74	347
Ah	16	m	c	CHIN	San Francisco	San Francisco P O	83	131
Jung	18	m	c	CHIN	Sonoma	Salt Point	91	387
GUNEAU								
Thos	34	m	w	CANA	Sacramento	1-Wd Sacramento	77	173
GUNESS								
Anna	22	f	w	IREL	Alameda	Oakland	68	145
GUNFLO								
William	52	m	w	FRAN	Los Angeles	Santa Ana Twp	73	610
GUNG								
Ah	51	m	c	CHIN	Calaveras	Copperopolis P O	70	222
Ah	42	m	c	CHIN	Amador	Drytown P O	69	420
Ah	41	m	c	CHIN	Tuolumne	Chinese Camp P O	93	374
Ah	40	m	c	CHIN	Tuolumne	Sonora P O	93	311
Ah	38	m	c	CHIN	San Francisco	San Francisco P O	80	448
Ah	38	m	c	CHIN	Placer	Dutch Flat P O	76	408
Ah	31	m	c	CHIN	San Francisco	San Francisco P O	80	503
Ah	30	m	c	CHIN	Trinity	Douglas	92	235
Ah	30	m	c	CHIN	San Diego	San Diego	78	498
Ah	27	m	c	CHIN	Sierra	Eureka Twp	89	525
Ah	25	m	c	CHIN	Santa Clara	Alviso Twp	88	25
Ah	24	m	c	CHIN	San Francisco	San Francisco P O	80	503
Ah	23	m	c	CHIN	Placer	Clipper Gap P O	76	392
Ah	20	m	c	CHIN	San Francisco	8-Wd San Francisco	82	385
Ah	20	m	c	CHIN	Amador	Jackson P O	69	330
Ah	19	m	c	CHIN	Alameda	Oakland	68	225
Ah	18	f	c	CHIN	San Francisco	San Francisco P O	80	453
Ah	15	m	c	CHIN	El Dorado	Mud Springs Twp	72	78
Ti	29	m	c	CHIN	Solano	Green Valley Twp	90	42
We	20	m	c	CHIN	Nevada	Bridgeport Twp	75	111
Woon	25	m	c	CHIN	San Francisco	8-Wd San Francisco	82	350
GUNIS								
Jose	49	m	w	SCOT	San Luis Obispo	Santa Rosa Twp	87	323
GUNK								
Mic	31	m	c	CHIN	San Joaquin	Liberty Twp	86	97
GUNKEL								
Richard	27	m	w	SAXO	Santa Clara	Fremont Twp	88	55
Sophia	62	f	w	PRUS	San Francisco	San Francisco P O	85	824
GUNN								
Ah	50	m	c	CHIN	El Dorado	Mud Springs Twp	72	75
Ah	40	m	c	CHIN	Placer	Auburn P O	76	373
Ah	30	m	c	CHIN	El Dorado	Coloma Twp	72	3
Ah	30	m	c	CHIN	San Joaquin	Castoria Twp	86	13
Ah	24	m	c	CHIN	San Francisco	6-Wd San Francisco	81	43
Ah	21	m	c	CHIN	Calaveras	San Andreas P O	70	173
Ah	19	m	c	CHIN	Tehama	Tehama Twp	92	189
Alex	23	m	w	SCOT	San Francisco	7-Wd San Francisco	81	242
Anna	22	f	w	CANA	San Mateo	Schoolhouse Statio	87	340
Charles	39	m	w	ENGL	Calaveras	San Andreas P O	70	153
Charles	20	m	w	ENGL	San Francisco	San Francisco P O	83	31
Douglas	29	m	w	OH	San Diego	San Diego	78	490
E	41	m	w	NJ	Sacramento	1-Wd Sacramento	77	200
Enos	27	m	w	OH	Butte	Chico Twp	70	44
Enos	21	m	w	OH	Butte	Chico Twp	70	56
Francis	26	m	w	IREL	San Francisco	San Francisco P O	80	399
Fredrick	60	m	w	IREL	San Francisco	7-Wd San Francisco	81	177
G	50	m	w	BADE	San Joaquin	Tulare Twp	86	264
George	38	m	w	US	Sonoma	Analy Twp	91	233
George	36	m	w	MI	Butte	Bidwell Twp	70	4
H T	36	m	w	IL	Sutter	Butte Twp	92	104
Hannah	67	f	w	IREL	Solano	Benicia	90	11
Henry	32	m	w	IL	Butte	Chico Twp	70	58
Isaac	25	m	w	CANA	Contra Costa	Martinez P O	71	423
James	62	m	w	KY	Sutter	Butte Twp	92	104
James	28	m	w	IREL	San Mateo	Schoolhouse Statio	87	334
Jane	60	f	w	KY	San Joaquin	Elkhorn Twp	86	59
John	60	m	w	SCOT	Alameda	Oakland	68	230
John	60	m	w	MA	Mendocino	Big Rvr Twp	74	160
John	36	m	w	VT	San Francisco	5-Wd San Francisco	81	22
John	32	m	w	CANA	Mono	Bridgeport P O	74	285
John	28	m	w	IREL	San Francisco	11-Wd San Francisc	84	515
John	21	m	w	IREL	Solano	Tremont Twp	90	29
Joseph	54	m	w	CT	San Francisco	11-Wd San Francisc	84	427
Lewis C	56	m	w	NY	San Francisco	San Francisco P O	85	724
Maria	20	f	b	TN	San Joaquin	1-Wd Stockton	86	127
Mary A	44	f	w	CANA	San Francisco	8-Wd San Francisco	82	294
May	22	f	w	ME	San Joaquin	Dent Twp	86	24
Miles G	38	m	w	TN	Yuba	Bullards Bar P O	93	553
Nicholas	63	m	w	TN	Santa Cruz	Santa Cruz Twp	89	388
Patrick	50	m	w	IREL	El Dorado	Mud Springs Twp	72	87
Patrick	40	m	w	IREL	San Francisco	San Francisco P O	83	171
Philip	45	m	w	IREL	Sacramento	2-Wd Sacramento	77	243
Smith R	41	m	w	IN	Santa Clara	Santa Clara Twp	88	152
Space	34	m	w	IL	San Joaquin	Elkhorn Twp	86	59
Susan	48	f	w	IREL	San Francisco	San Francisco P O	83	45
Thomas F	7	m	w	CA	Santa Barbara	San Buenaventura P	87	425
William	50	m	w	SCOT	San Francisco	8-Wd San Francisco	82	491
William	29	m	w	CANA	San Francisco	8-Wd San Francisco	82	327
William A	24	m	w	CT	Santa Barbara	Santa Barbara P O	87	473
Z	40	m	w	OH	Siskiyou	Scott Valley Twp	89	613
GUNNELL								
Jno C	45	m	w	VA	Butte	Hamilton Twp	70	69
GUNNELSON								
George	40	m	w	NORW	Placer	Dutch Flat P O	76	406
GUNNER								
Eugene	40	m	w	IREL	San Francisco	San Francisco P O	83	359
GUNNGAN								
Hannah	19	f	w	IREL	San Francisco	San Francisco P O	83	365
GUNNING								
A H	45	m	w	ENGL	Solano	Vallejo	90	192
James	38	m	w	IREL	San Francisco	8-Wd San Francisco	82	434
James	31	m	w	IREL	San Mateo	Redwood Twp	87	365
Mary	35	f	w	IREL	Alameda	Murray Twp	68	126
Sam	36	m	w	IREL	Yuba	Rose Bar Twp	93	654
Wm	40	m	w	WALE	Alameda	Murray Twp	68	122
Wm	30	m	w	SCOT	Alameda	Oakland	68	234
GUNNIP								
Philip	33	m	w	IREL	Nevada	Little York Twp	75	237
GUNNIS								
J M	33	m	w	PA	Alameda	Oakland	68	262
GUNNISON								
Albert	39	m	w	NH	San Francisco	San Francisco P O	83	341
Andrew	47	m	w	NH	San Francisco	8-Wd San Francisco	82	425
Clarissa	60	f	w	ME	San Francisco	San Francisco P O	83	70
David D	47	m	w	VT	Inyo	Independence Twp	73	325
Geo	28	m	w	NORW	Humboldt	Eureka Twp	72	282
Nathann	51	m	w	NH	Sonoma	Analy Twp	91	235
Robt	40	m	w	NORW	San Francisco	San Francisco P O	83	36
GUNNOND								
C J	29	m	w	IREL	Napa	Napa	75	47
GUNOE								
Ah	20	m	c	CHIN	Napa	Napa Twp	75	32
GUNOZ								
Francisco	34	m	w	MEXI	Fresno	Millerton P O	72	167
GUNPORT								
E	43	m	w	PRUS	San Joaquin	2-Wd Stockton	86	194
GUNS								
Ah	39	m	c	CHIN	Amador	Ione City P O	69	349
GUNSLER								
Jacob	48	m	w	SWIT	Calaveras	San Andreas P O	70	178
GUNSON								
H	42	m	w	DENM	San Joaquin	2-Wd Stockton	86	203
Robert	36	m	w	NORW	Nevada	Nevada Twp	75	318
GUNT								
Con	30	m	c	CHIN	Sacramento	1-Wd Sacramento	77	201
GUNTER								
August	30	m	w	PRUS	San Francisco	11-Wd San Francisc	84	530
Eliza	60	f	w	CANA	San Francisco	2-Wd San Francisco	79	157
Elonzo	21	m	w	IA	Sacramento	Sutter Twp	77	388
George	42	m	w	PRUS	Inyo	Independence Twp	73	326
Henry	19	m	w	IA	Mono	Bridgeport P O	74	284
Jacob	55	m	w	PA	Inyo	Bishop Crk Twp	73	314
GUNTHER								
Augusta	10	f	w	CA	Yuba	Marysville	93	579
Ernest	41	m	w	PRUS	San Francisco	San Francisco P O	80	459
Fanny	28	f	w	SWIT	San Francisco	San Francisco P O	80	338
Henry	33	m	w	SAXO	Nevada	Nevada Twp	75	279
Jacob	81	m	w	PRUS	San Francisco	8-Wd San Francisco	82	407
Jacob	38	m	w	FRNK	Yuba	Marysville	93	578
John	28	m	w	BADE	San Francisco	2-Wd San Francisco	79	218
Jos	29	m	w	NY	Sacramento	1-Wd Sacramento	77	190
Lawrence	48	m	w	BADE	Los Angeles	Santa Ana Twp	73	613
Louis	17	m	w	WURT	Santa Clara	2-Wd San Jose	88	318
William	46	m	w	BREM	San Francisco	San Francisco P O	80	403
GUNTIS								
Alfred	26	m	w	IL	Sacramento	San Joaquin Twp	77	394
GUNTO								
John	60	m	w	FRAN	Alameda	Murray Twp	68	124
GUNTZ								
Abram	52	m	w	PRUS	San Francisco	8-Wd San Francisco	82	346
Augusta	19	f	w	PRUS	San Francisco	San Francisco P O	85	809
GUNY								
Aot	19	m	c	CHIN	Napa	Napa Twp	75	58
Ho	45	m	c	CHIN	Sacramento	1-Wd Sacramento	77	187
GUNZ								
Albert E	30	m	w	ME	Santa Cruz	Soquel Twp	89	445
John	40	m	w	SWIT	San Francisco	3-Wd San Francisco	79	324
GUNZENDORFER								
F	32	m	w	BAVA	Santa Clara	Gilroy Twp	88	74
GUO								
Ah	20	m	c	CHIN	San Francisco	San Francisco P O	80	513
GUON								
Gee	29	m	c	CHIN	Butte	Hamilton Twp	70	71
Ling	39	m	c	CHIN	Butte	Hamilton Twp	70	72
GUP								
Ah	39	m	c	CHIN	Marin	San Rafael Twp	74	39
Ah	37	m	c	CHIN	San Joaquin	1-Wd Stockton	86	145

© 2001 by Heritage Quest. All rights reserved.

Name	Age	S	R	B-PL	County	Locale	Series M593 Roll	Pg
Ah	37	m	c	CHIN	Sacramento	1-Wd Sacramento	77	201
Ah	28	m	c	CHIN	San Joaquin	1-Wd Stockton	86	145
Ho	40	m	c	CHIN	San Joaquin	1-Wd Stockton	86	144
Lee	24	m	c	CHIN	San Joaquin	1-Wd Stockton	86	145
GUPAM								
Mave Addie	28	f	w	MEXI	Los Angeles	Los Angeles	73	519
GUPPY								
A R	33	m	w	NH	Alameda	Oakland	68	212
Edward	33	m	w	ENGL	Santa Clara	1-Wd San Jose	88	247
GUPSER								
Frank	31	m	w	SWIT	Santa Clara	1-Wd San Jose	88	266
GUPTEL								
A N	50	m	w	ME	Humboldt	Eureka Twp	72	274
E H	54	m	w	ME	Humboldt	Pacific Twp	72	299
GUPTELL								
James	29	m	w	ME	Sacramento	Georgianna Twp	77	133
Lucius	28	m	w	IL	Solano	Vacaville Twp	90	130
GUPTIL								
Albert	24	m	w	ME	Humboldt	Bucksport Twp	72	242
E W	32	m	w	ME	Humboldt	Bucksport Twp	72	242
Melville	17	m	w	ME	Humboldt	Pacific Twp	72	296
GUPTILL								
B S	40	m	w	ME	Trinity	Junction City Pct	92	205
Wm N	56	m	w	ME	Shasta	Millville P O	89	491
GUPTON								
James	26	m	w	MO	Colusa	Monroe Twp	71	314
John	34	m	w	SHOL	Tehama	Red Bluff	92	183
Kindred	28	m	w	IA	Colusa	Monroe Twp	71	314
GUR								
Knyhkaussen	33	m	w	OH	Humboldt	Pacific Twp	72	297
Ralf	12	m	w	OR	Humboldt	Eureka Twp	72	276
GURADO								
Leandro	26	m	w	CA	Los Angeles	Los Nietos Twp	73	586
GURAIN								
Antonio	40	m	w	ITAL	San Francisco	San Francisco P O	80	346
Antonio	40	m	w	ITAL	San Francisco	San Francisco P O	80	346
GURANI								
Pedro	20	m	w	ITAL	Nevada	Meadow Lake Twp	75	267
GURBER								
John	35	m	w	LA	Alameda	Oakland	68	209
GURBO								
G	30	m	w	CANA	Alameda	Oakland	68	267
GURCIA								
Gartrudes	54	f	w	MEXI	Mariposa	Mariposa P O	74	95
GURD								
Mike	17	m	w	CA	Sacramento	Alabama Twp	77	59
GURDIKA								
Louis	30	m	w	DENM	San Francisco	2-Wd San Francisco	79	173
GURDLEY								
John P	48	m	w	NY	Santa Clara	San Jose Twp	88	208
GURGEON								
N	36	m	w	PRUS	San Francisco	San Francisco P O	85	847
GURGER								
Nichols	33	m	w	IREL	San Francisco	7-Wd San Francisco	81	173
GURIN								
John	35	m	w	IREL	Santa Clara	Fremont Twp	88	57
GURLACH								
Adam	36	m	w	IL	Yolo	Cache Crk Twp	93	426
GURLEY								
Frank	34	m	w	NY	Trinity	Douglas	92	235
Henry	33	m	w	IREL	Yuba	Rose Bar Twp	93	667
Henry	28	m	w	CANA	Sacramento	Granite Twp	77	140
James	38	m	w	MO	Tehama	Paskenta Twp	92	165
Jas	39	m	w	IREL	Solano	Vallejo	90	178
GURLLA								
George	20	m	w	GERM	Sonoma	Sonoma Twp	91	449
GURMAN								
Owen	29	m	w	SCOT	San Francisco	5-Wd San Francisco	81	32
GURMAR								
Joseph	22	m	w	SWIT	San Francisco	8-Wd San Francisco	82	398
GURN								
Elizabeth	27	f	w	GA	San Francisco	8-Wd San Francisco	82	447
K R	64	m	w	SWIT	Sonoma	Sonoma Twp	91	434
GURNAINE								
James	22	m	w	IREL	San Francisco	11-Wd San Francisc	84	540
GURNDY								
M J	25	m	w	IREL	Amador	Jackson P O	69	335
GURNE								
Gionani	26	m	w	SWIT	San Francisco	3-Wd San Francisco	79	319
GURNECK								
A	50	m	w	FRAN	San Francisco	San Francisco P O	83	285
GURNELL								
E	23	m	w	NY	Alameda	Oakland	68	210
GURNER								
James	24	m	w	PRUS	San Francisco	San Francisco P O	80	473
Jno	47	m	w	SWIT	Sacramento	3-Wd Sacramento	77	304
GURNET								
Alphonso	51	m	w	FRAN	San Francisco	San Francisco P O	80	477
Chas	36	m	w	PRUS	Sacramento	4-Wd Sacramento	77	354
GURNETT								
Albert	25	m	w	NY	Santa Clara	1-Wd San Jose	88	236
John	34	m	w	SCOT	Alameda	Murray Twp	68	109
GURNEY								
Benjamin	29	m	w	MA	Yuba	Marysville	93	575
Case John	25	m	w	SCOT	Alameda	Oakland	68	205
Charles	38	m	w	NH	Sacramento	2-Wd Sacramento	77	214
David	40	m	w	ME	El Dorado	Placerville Twp	72	100
Dennis	20	m	w	CANA	San Joaquin	Oneal Twp	86	111
E B	34	m	w	ME	Tuolumne	Big Oak Flat P O	93	405
Elisha	29	m	w	ME	Tuolumne	Sonora P O	93	318
George	36	m	w	MS	Santa Clara	Redwood Twp	88	131
John	36	m	w	IREL	Alameda	Oakland	68	205
S B	34	m	w	MA	Solano	Benicia	90	3
S H	45	m	w	NY	Sutter	Yuba Twp	92	141
GURNSEY								
A A	63	m	w	NH	San Joaquin	Oneal Twp	86	108
James	37	m	w	MO	Santa Clara	Santa Clara Twp	88	151
GURNT								
Chas	32	m	w	NY	Sacramento	1-Wd Sacramento	77	190
GURPONVITCH								
A	41	m	w	AUST	Amador	Sutter Crk P O	69	406
GURRCHVICH								
Stephen	34	m	w	AUST	Plumas	Quartz Twp	77	35
GURRERA								
Flora	26	f	w	MEXI	San Francisco	San Francisco P O	80	476
GURRIN								
Peter	55	m	w	HOLL	Sonoma	Bodega Twp	91	257
GURRINGTON								
Leondas	23	m	w	IA	Sacramento	Georgianna Twp	77	131
GURRY								
Henry	22	m	w	NY	San Francisco	San Francisco P O	80	391
John	31	m	w	MA	San Francisco	11-Wd San Francisc	84	676
GURS								
John	43	m	w	PRUS	San Joaquin	3-Wd Stockton	86	230
GURT								
John	20	m	w	SWIT	Sacramento	Sutter Twp	77	389
GURTH								
Margt	57	f	w	OH	Fresno	Kings Rvr P O	72	214
GURTY								
William	26	m	w	CANA	Santa Clara	Redwood Twp	88	119
GURVAL								
Louisa	18	f	w	FRAN	San Francisco	2-Wd San Francisco	79	176
GURVIS								
Archibald	35	m	w	SCOT	Sonoma	Vallejo Twp	91	452
GUS								
Mow	29	m	c	CHIN	San Bernardino	San Bernardino Twp	78	452
GUSALES								
Joseph	38	m	w	PERU	San Mateo	Half Moon Bay P O	87	393
GUSANO								
Charles	40	m	w	FRAN	Los Angeles	Los Angeles	73	528
GUSBO								
J	20	m	w	FRAN	Alameda	Oakland	68	240
GUSCASTTO								
Jacoman	34	m	w	SWIT	Amador	Jackson P O	69	336
GUSEE								
Jacob	44	m	w	CA	Sacramento	3-Wd Sacramento	77	309
GUSETTI								
Peter	35	m	w	SWIT	Plumas	Seneca Twp	77	47
GUSHARD								
Charles	40	m	w	LA	Los Angeles	Soledad Twp	73	630
GUSHAW								
George F	54	m	w	PA	Yolo	Grafton Twp	93	491
J F	52	m	w	PA	Humboldt	Eel Rvr Twp	72	255
GUSHEE								
Fredk A	57	m	w	MA	Santa Cruz	Santa Cruz	89	407
George C	23	m	w	ME	Marin	Point Reyes Twp	74	23
Horace	55	m	w	MA	Santa Cruz	Santa Cruz	89	404
GUSHIE								
Elisebeth	81	f	w	BREM	Sonoma	Petaluma Twp	91	316
GUSHLEA								
Geo	37	m	w	ENGL	Sacramento	4-Wd Sacramento	77	353
GUSINA								
Marco	45	m	w	DALM	San Francisco	11-Wd San Francisc	84	489
GUSKE								
Henry	24	m	w	HANO	San Francisco	San Francisco P O	83	120
GUSMAN								
Domingo	30	m	w	MEXI	Santa Clara	1-Wd San Jose	88	251
Pedro	44	m	w	CHIL	Santa Clara	Gilroy Twp	88	79
GUSMANO								
Pedro	45	m	w	MEXI	San Mateo	Half Moon Bay P O	87	393
GUSS								
Ah	23	m	c	CHIN	Tuolumne	Big Oak Flat P O	93	406
GUSSEN								
H	36	m	w	CA	Alameda	Murray Twp	68	112
GUSSER								
Phillip	47	m	w	AUSL	Mariposa	Mariposa P O	74	99
GUSSHEN								
John	39	m	w	HANO	Alameda	Oakland	68	176
GUSSISAMANI								
Liner	35	m	w	ITAL	San Francisco	1-Wd San Francisco	79	83
GUSSMANDEZ								
I	12	m	w	CA	San Francisco	San Francisco P O	85	827
GUSSMENDEZ								
Eloise	16	f	w	CA	San Francisco	San Francisco P O	85	826
GUSSRIDGE								
Annie	26	f	w	IREL	San Francisco	11-Wd San Francisc	84	505
GUST								
Charles	24	m	w	SWED	San Francisco	3-Wd San Francisco	79	292
GUSTAF								
Huff	35	m	w	SWED	Humboldt	Bald Hills	72	238
Johnston	40	m	w	SWED	Humboldt	Bald Hills	72	238
GUSTARA								
Mary	10M	f	w	CA	Alameda	Oakland	68	168

© 2001 by Heritage Quest. All rights reserved.

California 1870 Census

Series M593

Name	Age	S	R	B-PL	County	Locale	Roll	Pg
GUSTASON								
A	48	m	w	SWED	San Francisco	7-Wd San Francisco	81	167
GUSTAV								
John	40	m	w	PRUS	Los Angeles	Los Angeles	73	546
GUSTAVESON								
Aug	28	m	w	SWED	Sierra	Table Rock Twp	89	573
GUSTAVISON								
Alex	45	m	w	SWEE	Humboldt	Eureka Twp	72	276
GUSTAVUS								
Rev	40	m	w	IREL	Alameda	Oakland	68	137
GUSTE								
Joseph	28	m	w	ITAL	San Francisco	6-Wd San Francisco	81	93
GUSTELLA								
J	56	f	w	LA	San Francisco	San Francisco P O	85	798
GUSTELO								
A	36	m	w	FRAN	Alameda	Oakland	68	166
GUSTENSON								
G	40	m	w	SWED	Alameda	Oakland	68	238
GUSTIN								
Christine	25	f	w	DENM	San Joaquin	1-Wd Stockton	86	136
Columbus	42	m	w	PA	Sonoma	Petaluma Twp	91	309
Peter	35	m	w	GERM	Santa Clara	Gilroy Twp	88	103
Piere	31	m	w	ITAL	San Francisco	11-Wd San Francisc	84	709
William	28	m	w	ENGL	Alameda	Oakland	68	172
GUSTNER								
Samuel	30	m	w	SWIT	Alameda	Eden Twp	68	86
GUSTO								
Alex	29	m	w	FRAN	San Francisco	2-Wd San Francisco	79	169
Arad	29	m	w	ITAL	San Francisco	11-Wd San Francisc	84	710
GUSTON								
Gillis	25	m	w	ITAL	San Francisco	11-Wd San Francisc	84	709
GUSUSE								
J	50	f	w	MEXI	Alameda	Alameda	68	10
GUT								
Ah	50	m	c	CHIN	Mariposa	Mariposa P O	74	125
Ah	50	m	c	CHIN	Stanislaus	Emory Twp	92	22
Ah	44	m	c	CHIN	Placer	Dutch Flat P O	76	408
Ah	42	m	c	CHIN	Trinity	Lewiston Pct	92	212
Ah	30	m	c	CHIN	Tuolumne	Chinese Camp P O	93	369
Ah	26	m	c	CHIN	Nevada	Meadow Lake Twp	75	257
Ah	23	m	c	CHIN	Sacramento	1-Wd Sacramento	77	201
John	28	m	w	SWIT	Santa Clara	Santa Clara Twp	88	164
GUTBALET								
Joseph	29	m	w	PRUS	San Francisco	1-Wd San Francisco	79	45
GUTBRIE								
And	22	m	w	SCOT	Merced	Snelling P O	74	260
GUTCHER								
Wm	32	m	w	NY	San Francisco	San Francisco P O	85	824
GUTCHIN								
Adolph	25	m	w	BREM	San Francisco	San Francisco P O	83	160
GUTCHOW								
Charles	42	m	w	PRUS	Calaveras	Copperopolis P O	70	246
GUTE								
Ah	20	m	c	CHIN	Trinity	Lewiston Pct	92	215
GUTH								
Geo	36	m	w	FRAN	Sacramento	3-Wd Sacramento	77	258
Helen	25	f	w	BAVA	Placer	Auburn P O	76	383
John	28	m	w	FRAN	San Joaquin	3-Wd Stockton	86	229
GUTHER								
A	30	m	w	PRUS	Yuba	Marysville	93	586
GUTHERIE								
Celestia	60	f	w	IREL	San Francisco	11-Wd San Francisc	84	650
John	23	m	w	IL	San Joaquin	2-Wd Stockton	86	189
Patrick	43	m	w	IREL	Contra Costa	Martinez P O	71	402
GUTHIRE								
L P	54	m	w	VA	Sierra	Sierra Twp	89	566
GUTHRE								
Anna	30	f	w	SCOT	Sonoma	Petaluma Twp	91	323
GUTHRIDGE								
Thos	26	m	w	MO	Monterey	Alisal Twp	74	300
GUTHRIE								
A B	41	m	w	MO	Sacramento	4-Wd Sacramento	77	372
A P	44	m	w	IL	Humboldt	South Fork Twp	72	302
Alexander	24	m	w	SCOT	Alameda	Brooklyn	68	24
Alexander	20	m	w	CANA	Colusa	Grand Island Twp	71	305
Bartholemew	41	m	w	VA	Solano	Tremont Twp	90	31
Daniel	32	m	w	ENGL	Yuba	Long Bar Twp	93	566
Flavel	24	m	w	ENGL	Santa Clara	2-Wd San Jose	88	281
Florence	18	f	w	OH	Solano	Benicia	90	17
Francis	32	m	w	MO	Mendocino	Round Valley Twp	74	221
G B	26	m	w	CANA	Amador	Amador City P O	69	391
Henry W	33	m	w	MO	Tulare	Venice Twp	92	275
J	30	m	w	ME	Alameda	Oakland	68	237
James	35	m	w	IL	San Francisco	6-Wd San Francisco	81	92
James	33	m	w	TN	Tulare	Farmersville Twp	92	246
James	32	m	w	IREL	Marin	Bolinas Twp	74	1
John J	50	m	w	MO	Sacramento	Sutter Twp	77	390
Joseph	39	m	w	OH	Monterey	Monterey	74	356
Julia	23	f	w	MA	San Francisco	1-Wd San Francisco	79	107
L B	60	m	w	VA	Nevada	Bridgeport Twp	75	116
N L	27	m	w	OH	Alameda	Oakland	68	242
Nathan	30	m	w	OH	Santa Clara	2-Wd San Jose	88	297
Nellie	22	f	w	PA	Santa Clara	2-Wd San Jose	88	297
Robt M	40	m	w	MO	Santa Barbara	San Buenaventura P	87	425
Thomas	58	m	w	ENGL	San Francisco	7-Wd San Francisco	81	182
Thomas W	41	m	w	VA	Yolo	Buckeye Twp	93	409
Wash	39	m	w	KY	Sonoma	Santa Rosa	91	404
William	27	m	w	MO	San Diego	Milquaty Dist	78	476
Wm	36	m	w	SCOT	San Francisco	1-Wd San Francisco	79	68
GUTHRISS								
Frank	36	m	w	IREL	Humboldt	Mattole Twp	72	288
GUTHRY								
Henry	17	m	w	MI	Sacramento	4-Wd Sacramento	77	340
GUTHWASSER								
Charles	26	m	w	FRAN	Santa Cruz	Santa Cruz Twp	89	397
GUTIERES								
Candido	48	m	w	MEXI	San Francisco	2-Wd San Francisco	79	189
GUTIEREZ								
Clemente	61	m	w	MEXI	Monterey	San Benito Twp	74	380
Jesus	53	m	w	MEXI	Santa Cruz	Pajaro Twp	89	361
Nicolasa	12	f	w	MEXI	Santa Clara	2-Wd San Jose	88	337
GUTIERREZ								
Abram	10	m	w	CA	Monterey	San Benito Twp	74	380
Ignacio	18	m	w	MEXI	San Francisco	11-Wd San Francisc	84	593
Jose	50	m	w	MEXI	Santa Barbara	Santa Barbara P O	87	487
Jose	39	m	w	CA	Santa Barbara	Santa Barbara P O	87	496
Juan	75	m	w	MEXI	Los Angeles	San Jose Twp	73	622
Louis	37	m	w	CA	Marin	Bolinas Twp	74	1
M	46	m	w	MEXI	Sierra	Butte Twp	89	512
Marcello	16	m	w	MEXI	San Francisco	11-Wd San Francisc	84	593
Maria	12	f	w	CA	Los Angeles	San Juan Twp	73	627
Maria E	38	f	w	CA	Los Angeles	San Juan Twp	73	626
Modesto	35	m	w	MEXI	Monterey	San Juan Twp	74	407
Nicholasa	15	f	w	CA	Santa Clara	1-Wd San Jose	88	263
Rosa	44	f	w	MEXI	San Francisco	2-Wd San Francisco	79	252
GUTIREZ								
Jose M	38	m	w	MEXI	Santa Cruz	Pajaro Twp	89	357
GUTMANN								
Adolph	45	m	w	HANO	Shasta	Shasta P O	89	458
GUTNER								
Lewis S	23	m	w	OH	Yolo	Grafton Twp	93	497
GUTREA								
Joseph	25	m	w	PORT	Alameda	Washington Twp	68	273
GUTRIDGE								
William	39	m	w	IREL	San Francisco	8-Wd San Francisco	82	430
GUTRUTO								
John	42	m	w	ITAL	San Joaquin	3-Wd Stockton	86	238
GUTSTEIN								
Samuel	44	m	w	RUSS	San Francisco	San Francisco P O	83	389
GUTT								
James	30	m	w	CHIL	Alameda	Murray Twp	68	112
Lip	26	m	c	CHIN	San Joaquin	1-Wd Stockton	86	144
Oscar	34	m	w	FRAN	Napa	Napa	75	11
GUTTEL								
Bernard	30	m	w	PRUS	San Francisco	8-Wd San Francisco	82	403
GUTTELEWIST								
John	30	m	w	GERM	San Diego	Julian Dist	78	469
GUTTENBERGER								
Wm	41	m	w	PRUS	Sacramento	4-Wd Sacramento	77	349
GUTTER								
John B	51	m	w	ENGL	San Francisco	6-Wd San Francisco	81	102
GUTTERMAN								
August	47	m	w	HANO	El Dorado	Georgetown Twp	72	37
GUTTINGDE								
John	37	m	w	WV	El Dorado	Georgetown Twp	72	41
GUTTMAN								
Saml	45	m	w	PRUS	San Francisco	1-Wd San Francisco	79	49
GUTTO								
Gawby	62	m	w	SWIT	El Dorado	Diamond Springs Tw	72	30
GUTZ								
Augustus	32	m	w	FRAN	Monterey	San Antonio Twp	74	321
GUTZET								
Henry	30	m	w	PRUS	San Francisco	San Francisco P O	83	415
GUTZKOW								
Frederick	38	m	w	PRUS	San Francisco	San Francisco P O	83	410
GUVANDITCH								
Mark	37	m	w	AUST	Santa Clara	2-Wd San Jose	88	300
GUY								
Ah	47	m	c	CHIN	Alameda	Oakland	68	254
Ah	35	m	c	CHIN	Trinity	Indian Crk	92	199
Ah	35	m	c	CHIN	Solano	Vallejo	90	174
Ah	28	m	c	CHIN	Placer	Alta P O	76	413
Ah	26	m	c	CHIN	Nevada	Eureka Twp	75	141
Ah	24	m	c	CHIN	Yolo	Putah Twp	93	513
Ah	19	m	c	CHIN	San Francisco	San Francisco P O	83	85
Ah	17	m	c	CHIN	San Francisco	8-Wd San Francisco	82	401
Chas A	36	m	w	CT	Siskiyou	Scott Valley Twp	89	611
Eng	27	m	c	CHIN	Alpine	Monitor P O	69	313
George	25	m	w	FRAN	Los Angeles	Santa Ana Twp	73	610
Go	29	m	c	CHIN	San Joaquin	Oneal Twp	86	116
Henry	23	m	w	ENGL	Calaveras	San Andreas P O	70	152
Hong	32	m	c	CHIN	Nevada	Nevada Twp	75	289
John	26	m	w	CANA	Marin	Tomales Twp	74	78
Loo	27	m	c	CHIN	San Mateo	Schoolhouse Statio	87	344
Michael	30	m	w	IREL	Alameda	Brooklyn	68	24
Sang	19	m	c	CHIN	Solano	Suisun Twp	90	105
Victor A	51	m	w	FRAN	Plumas	Mineral Twp	77	21
Wm	47	m	w	ENGL	Sacramento	Granite Twp	77	141
GUYDEN								
Vincent	30	m	w	FRAN	Placer	Lincoln P O	76	482
GUYDER								
F P	25	m	w	IREL	San Francisco	3-Wd San Francisco	79	315
GUYER								
Louisa	34	f	b	NJ	Yolo	Washington Twp	93	533

© 2001 by Heritage Quest. All rights reserved.

Series M593

Name	Age	S	R	B-PL	County	Locale	Roll	Pg
GUYLBRIDE								
T	34	m	w	IREL	Sacramento	3-Wd Sacramento	77	317
GUYLER								
John	50	m	w	IREL	Yolo	Putah Twp	93	523
GUYNN								
Charles	27	m	w	ENGL	Contra Costa	Martinez P O	71	426
GUYOT								
Volney	42	m	w	FRAN	Solano	Denverton Twp	90	27
GUYTHER								
George	50	m	w	ENGL	San Francisco	2-Wd San Francisco	79	250
GUZMAN								
Domingo	25	m	w	MEXI	Santa Clara	1-Wd San Jose	88	231
M	34	m	w	CHIL	Alameda	Oakland	68	170
Mateo	27	m	i	CHIL	Inyo	Cerro Gordo Twp	73	318
GWAY								
Ben	40	m	w	FRAN	Butte	Ophir Twp	70	101
GWELL								
Francois	52	m	w	FRAN	Amador	Volcano P O	69	386
GWIM								
P N	33	m	w	MO	Butte	Chico Twp	70	55
GWIN								
Abby S	40	f	w	WI	Butte	Ophir Twp	70	95
Ah	20	m	c	CHIN	San Francisco	6-Wd San Francisco	81	87
Catherine	25	f	w	PA	San Francisco	2-Wd San Francisco	79	196
Enos M	62	m	w	PA	Napa	Napa Twp	75	33
Franklin S	36	m	w	MO	Yolo	Grafton Twp	93	482
Frederick P	32	m	w	CANA	Santa Clara	Alviso Twp	88	22
George	31	m	w	MO	Sonoma	Vallejo Twp	91	461
Horatio J	61	m	w	PA	Santa Barbara	San Buenaventura P	87	420
James H	31	m	w	OH	Los Angeles	Santa Ana Twp	73	600
Olney	30	m	w	MO	Yolo	Grafton Twp	93	483
S W	37	f	w	LA	Alameda	Oakland	68	177
Thomas	26	m	w	IREL	Santa Clara	2-Wd San Jose	88	291
Washington	38	m	w	WI	Napa	Napa	75	19
William	36	m	w	KY	Trinity	North Fork Twp	92	218
William	35	m	w	IREL	San Francisco	7-Wd San Francisco	81	165
William M	64	m	w	TN	Calaveras	San Andreas P O	70	203
GWINN								
A A	27	m	w	OH	Solano	Vallejo	90	162
Belden R	38	m	w	MO	Yolo	Grafton Twp	93	484
Cyral	27	m	w	OH	Butte	Chico Twp	70	44
Harrison	61	m	w	TN	Yolo	Grafton Twp	93	484
John	53	m	w	OH	Butte	Chico Twp	70	45
John	25	m	w	IREL	Humboldt	Arcata Twp	72	226
John E	36	m	w	MA	Sonoma	Petaluma Twp	91	323
John M	33	m	w	MO	Yolo	Grafton Twp	93	484
Landie	14	f	w	CA	Butte	Chico Twp	70	47
GWO								
Ah	35	m	c	CHIN	Sacramento	Georgianna Twp	77	123
GWON								
Ah	30	m	c	CHIN	Nevada	Nevada Twp	75	297
On	27	m	c	CHIN	Butte	Hamilton Twp	70	72
GWYNE								
Abraham T	42	m	w	TN	Nevada	Nevada Twp	75	302
William	8	m	w	CA	Sacramento	4-Wd Sacramento	77	319
GWYNN								
Ed	36	m	w	CANA	Sierra	Gibson Twp	89	542
John R	72	m	w	MD	Placer	Auburn P O	76	368
William	42	m	w	CANA	San Francisco	8-Wd San Francisco	82	456
GWYNNE								
Thos	40	m	w	IREL	San Francisco	1-Wd San Francisco	79	62
William	47	m	w	MD	Sacramento	4-Wd Sacramento	77	319
GWYTHER								
George	49	m	w	ENGL	San Bernardino	San Bernardino Twp	78	452
GY								
Ah	38	m	c	CHIN	Nevada	Little York Twp	75	234
GYE								
Ah	39	m	c	CHIN	Sacramento	Georgianna Twp	77	125
Ah	26	m	c	CHIN	Plumas	Washington Twp	77	53
GYLE								
Herman	24	m	w	RUSS	Tehama	Tehama Twp	92	191
Lewis A	34	m	w	RUSS	Tehama	Tehama Twp	92	190
Saml A	37	m	w	RUSS	Tehama	Tehama Twp	92	190
GYN								
Ah	40	m	c	CHIN	Sacramento	Georgianna Twp	77	131
GYNOR								
Wm	30	m	w	IREL	San Francisco	San Francisco P O	83	39
GYNT								
John	37	m	w	IREL	San Francisco	11-Wd San Francisc	84	572
GYSER								
Daniel	50	m	w	LA	Nevada	Meadow Lake Twp	75	246
GYTE								
Joseph	40	m	w	ENGL	Napa	Yountville Twp	75	83
H								
Ah	24	m	c	CHIN	Sacramento	Georgianna Twp	77	123
HA								
Ah	45	m	c	CHIN	Mono	Bridgeport P O	74	284
Ah	42	m	c	CHIN	Sacramento	1-Wd Sacramento	77	193
Ah	21	f	c	CHIN	San Francisco	San Francisco P O	80	492
Ah	20	f	c	CHIN	Los Angeles	Los Angeles	73	565
Ah	20	m	c	CHIN	Sutter	Sutter Twp	92	127
Good	39	m	c	CHIN	San Joaquin	1-Wd Stockton	86	151
Hee	27	f	c	CHIN	San Francisco	6-Wd San Francisco	81	59
I	22	f	c	CHIN	Stanislaus	Emory Twp	92	22
Joe	20	m	c	CHIN	San Joaquin	3-Wd Stockton	86	246
Kung	43	m	c	CHIN	San Mateo	Half Moon Bay P O	87	396
Lee	35	m	c	CHIN	Yuba	Marysville	93	628
Ma Fo	20	m	c	CHIN	Amador	Ione City P O	69	367
Ma Iuc	21	m	c	CHIN	Amador	Ione City P O	69	367
Mah Nou	36	m	c	CHIN	Amador	Ione City P O	69	367
Matt Um	18	m	c	CHIN	Amador	Ione City P O	69	367
Poo	40	m	c	CHIN	San Francisco	6-Wd San Francisco	81	40
We Tor	30	m	c	CHIN	San Francisco	6-Wd San Francisco	81	58
HAACKE								
Charles	31	m	w	HANO	San Francisco	San Francisco P O	83	182
HAAF								
Jacob	35	m	w	PRUS	San Francisco	San Francisco P O	85	780
Louis	40	m	w	HDAR	Solano	Vallejo	90	172
HAAG								
Adam	42	m	w	BAVA	Tuolumne	Sonora P O	93	310
Ah	25	m	c	CHIN	Fresno	Millerton P O	72	200
Lot	20	m	w	CHIN	San Joaquin	2-Wd Stockton	86	166
HAAGEN								
L A	45	m	w	PRUS	Tuolumne	Sonora P O	93	310
HAAK								
Robt	30	m	w	PRUS	San Francisco	8-Wd San Francisco	82	375
HAAKE								
John	45	m	w	BREM	Napa	Napa Twp	75	65
John	37	m	w	OLDE	San Francisco	11-Wd San Francisc	84	574
Joseph	19	m	w	HANO	Santa Clara	2-Wd San Jose	88	329
Mary	27	f	w	PRUS	San Francisco	8-Wd San Francisco	82	430
HAAR								
Martin	45	m	w	FRAN	Sonoma	Petaluma Twp	91	333
Thomas	35	m	w	IREL	Santa Clara	2-Wd San Jose	88	286
HAARER								
Gustavus	40	m	w	GERM	Yolo	Cottonwood Twp	93	470
HAAS								
Abraham	28	m	w	BAVA	Calaveras	Copperopolis P O	70	246
Augt	45	m	w	PRUS	San Francisco	8-Wd San Francisco	82	360
Benj	55	m	w	VA	Tehama	Red Bluff	92	179
Chas	42	m	w	BADE	San Joaquin	1-Wd Stockton	86	139
Christ	47	m	w	BADE	Santa Barbara	San Buenaventura P	87	437
David L	27	m	w	HESS	Napa	Napa	75	43
Francis	73	f	w	BADE	San Francisco	2-Wd San Francisco	79	142
Fred G	32	m	w	WURT	Trinity	Junction City Pct	92	209
Fredk	43	m	w	HANO	San Francisco	San Francisco P O	83	120
Hannah	50	f	w	HDAR	San Francisco	8-Wd San Francisco	82	356
Henry	32	m	w	PRUS	San Francisco	5-Wd San Francisco	81	10
Henry	22	m	w	BAVA	San Francisco	8-Wd San Francisco	82	386
Herman	34	m	w	PRUS	San Francisco	6-Wd San Francisco	81	93
Herman	34	m	w	HDAR	Sacramento	2-Wd Sacramento	77	221
Jacob	40	m	w	PRUS	San Francisco	San Francisco P O	83	57
Kalman	29	m	w	BAVA	San Francisco	8-Wd San Francisco	82	362
L	44	f	w	PA	San Joaquin	2-Wd Stockton	86	203
Martin L	36	m	w	HDAR	San Francisco	8-Wd San Francisco	82	346
Mary	46	f	w	SCOT	Alameda	Brooklyn Twp	68	45
Mathew	49	m	w	PRUS	Solano	Maine Prairie Twp	90	54
Robert	30	m	w	HDAR	San Francisco	8-Wd San Francisco	82	362
S L	28	m	w	HDAR	Solano	Vallejo	90	147
Samuel	45	m	w	PRUS	San Francisco	8-Wd San Francisco	82	412
Samuel	44	m	w	BADE	San Francisco	8-Wd San Francisco	82	368
Samuel	29	m	w	PRUS	San Francisco	San Francisco P O	83	137
Shar	19	m	w	BADE	San Joaquin	Elliott Twp	86	71
Solomon	52	m	w	BAVA	San Francisco	8-Wd San Francisco	82	425
Valentino	31	m	w	BAVA	Monterey	Castroville Twp	74	333
William	23	m	w	BAVA	San Francisco	San Francisco P O	83	195
HAASE								
Maks	27	m	w	PRUS	San Francisco	2-Wd San Francisco	79	238
Peter	40	m	w	HANO	Sacramento	Granite Twp	77	155
HAASI								
Minnie	20	f	w	PRUS	San Francisco	San Francisco P O	83	96
HABAL								
Eliza K	38	f	w	ENGL	Sacramento	2-Wd Sacramento	77	224
HABARLIN								
James	39	m	w	IREL	San Francisco	2-Wd San Francisco	79	152
HABASCUS								
Vincent	5	m	w	CA	Santa Clara	Santa Clara Twp	88	157
HABBY								
William	62	m	w	OH	Yolo	Cache Crk Twp	93	457
HABENICHT								
Henry	30	m	w	PRUS	San Francisco	San Francisco P O	83	27
HABER								
John	40	m	w	BADE	Colusa	Spring Valley Twp	71	343
Stephen	24	m	w	CANA	Santa Cruz	Santa Cruz Twp	89	399
HABERACKER								
Leonard	21	m	w	BADE	San Bernardino	San Bernardino Twp	78	414
HABERLAND								
Isaac	35	m	w	PRUS	Colusa	Stony Crk Twp	71	331
HABERLEY								
Chas	40	m	w	IREL	San Diego	San Diego	78	508
HABERLIN								
James	29	m	w	IREL	San Francisco	San Francisco P O	85	762
John	28	m	w	IREL	San Francisco	1-Wd San Francisco	79	68
HABERMACHER								
Ferdinand	25	m	w	SWIT	San Francisco	8-Wd San Francisco	82	417
HABERMEHL								
Henry	40	m	w	BAVA	San Francisco	11-Wd San Francisc	84	512
HABERSTICK								
John	27	m	w	PA	Kern	Tehachapi P O	73	353
HABERT								
Charles	47	m	w	ENGL	Inyo	Cerro Gordo Twp	73	318
Rosamond	72	f	w	IA	San Mateo	Half Moon Bay P O	87	400
HABICH								
Henry	43	m	w	HANO	Shasta	Shasta P O	89	460

© 2001 by Heritage Quest. All rights reserved.

Name	Age	S	R	B-PL	County	Locale	Roll	Pg
Theodore	39	m	w	HANO	Shasta	Shasta P O	89	459
HABICK								
August	32	m	w	HCAS	Santa Clara	Santa Clara Twp	88	155
HABIS								
B	39	m	w	HAMB	Sierra	Forest Twp	89	532
HABISHAN								
I	20	m	w	ENGL	Napa	Napa	75	24
HABISHAW								
Isaac	46	m	w	ENGL	Sonoma	Washington Twp	91	468
HABISHEEN								
T	24	m	w	ENGL	Napa	Napa	75	24
HABLE								
John	40	m	w	POLA	Yuba	Marysville	93	583
HABNER								
Conrad	14	m	w	CA	San Francisco	11-Wd San Francisc	84	577
HACE								
Ah	15	m	c	CHIN	San Francisco	1-Wd San Francisco	79	87
Edward J	32	m	w	PA	Sonoma	Petaluma Twp	91	311
HACH								
Hirem	34	m	w	MA	Humboldt	Mattole Twp	72	285
HACHAEL								
John	26	m	w	NY	San Mateo	Half Moon Bay P O	87	402
HACHEL								
Conrad	53	m	w	HANO	Los Angeles	Santa Ana Twp	73	614
HACHERLEN								
Lewis A	37	m	w	PA	San Francisco	San Francisco P O	83	34
HACHET								
David	38	m	w	IREL	Solano	Vallejo	90	173
HACHETT								
Lucy	17	f	w	MA	San Joaquin	1-Wd Stockton	86	121
William	35	m	w	IREL	San Mateo	San Mateo P O	87	357
HACHMAN								
Jacob	33	m	w	SHOL	Colusa	Grand Island Twp	71	303
HACHSPIL								
Oscar	30	m	w	PRUS	San Francisco	8-Wd San Francisco	82	443
HACK								
Ah	52	m	c	CHIN	Mariposa	Mariposa P O	74	103
Ah	50	m	c	CHIN	Sacramento	Granite Twp	77	141
Geo W	24	m	w	NY	Sacramento	Franklin Twp	77	113
George	51	m	w	ENGL	Sacramento	Franklin Twp	77	107
Henry	34	m	w	HDAR	San Francisco	11-Wd San Francisc	84	516
Henry L	27	m	w	NY	Sacramento	2-Wd Sacramento	77	239
John	25	m	w	IN	Solano	Vallejo	90	197
Julius F	34	m	w	GERM	Yolo	Washington Twp	93	528
Kee	34	m	c	CHIN	San Francisco	6-Wd San Francisco	81	53
Low	23	m	c	CHIN	Solano	Green Valley Twp	90	42
Mary	12	f	w	CA	Contra Costa	Martinez P O	71	390
Nicholas	34	m	w	PRUS	Placer	Lincoln P O	76	491
Toon	25	m	c	CHIN	Siskiyou	Yreka Twp	89	668
HACKABOUT								
Benj	37	m	w	NJ	Contra Costa	Martinez P O	71	413
HACKE								
Christopher	40	m	w	HANO	San Francisco	6-Wd San Francisco	81	78
HACKELHITE								
Mat	50	m	w	PRUS	San Joaquin	Tulare Twp	86	252
HACKEN								
John C	58	m	w	TN	Stanislaus	Emory Twp	92	19
Wm	33	m	w	PA	San Joaquin	Tulare Twp	86	263
HACKENHEIMER								
Louiza	22	f	w	PRUS	San Francisco	2-Wd San Francisco	79	187
HACKER								
C	16	f	w	NY	San Francisco	San Francisco P O	85	809
Chas	32	m	w	PRUS	San Francisco	7-Wd San Francisco	81	287
Edward	35	m	w	ME	Stanislaus	San Joaquin Twp	92	81
Eli	60	m	w	TN	Yuba	East Bear Rvr Twp	93	540
John	63	m	w	PRUS	San Francisco	7-Wd San Francisco	81	287
John	39	m	w	BADE	Trinity	Junction City Pct	92	210
Jonathan	79	m	w	VA	Humboldt	South Fork Twp	72	300
Joseph	25	m	w	MO	Stanislaus	Buena Vista Twp	92	13
Martin	27	m	w	IREL	San Francisco	7-Wd San Francisco	81	270
HACKERMAN								
Geo	28	m	w	NY	Santa Clara	Gilroy Twp	88	95
HACKET								
Denis J	35	m	w	NY	San Francisco	1-Wd San Francisco	79	62
James	55	m	w	IREL	San Francisco	7-Wd San Francisco	81	234
Jas	30	m	w	NY	San Francisco	1-Wd San Francisco	79	91
Joseph	13	m	w	CA	San Francisco	San Francisco P O	85	873
Mart	22	m	w	IREL	Sonoma	Bodega Twp	91	260
Patrick	30	m	w	IREL	Sacramento	Dry Crk Twp	77	101
William	42	m	w	IREL	Yolo	Grafton Twp	93	496
HACKETT								
Adaline	24	f	w	WI	Siskiyou	Yreka	89	657
Alva	34	m	w	MA	San Francisco	8-Wd San Francisco	82	445
Charles	21	m	w	MI	Placer	Gold Run Twp	76	394
Charles W	23	m	w	MI	Placer	Gold Run Twp	76	396
Chester	62	m	w	NY	Placer	Bath P O	76	450
Cornilus	49	m	w	HOLL	San Francisco	San Francisco P O	80	532
Elen	14	f	w	MA	Alameda	Oakland	68	132
F M	42	m	w	VT	Napa	Napa Twp	75	73
Fred	19	m	w	CA	San Francisco	San Francisco P O	83	87
G W	32	m	w	MA	Yuba	Marysville	93	591
George	53	m	w	NY	Santa Cruz	Santa Cruz Twp	89	386
H E	30	m	w	ME	Solano	Benicia	90	12
J J	39	m	w	IREL	Sonoma	Bodega Twp	91	250
J M	55	m	w	ME	San Francisco	San Francisco P O	83	288
Jacob P	43	m	w	DE	San Francisco	San Francisco P O	83	145
Jane	70	f	w	IREL	San Francisco	San Francisco P O	83	44
Jeremiah	45	m	w	IREL	San Francisco	11-Wd San Francisc	84	450
Jesse	30	m	w	OH	Stanislaus	Empire Twp	92	37
Mary Ann	23	f	w	IREL	San Francisco	San Francisco P O	83	344
Nathan	45	m	w	ME	Stanislaus	Branch Twp	92	4
Oliver	24	m	w	IREL	San Joaquin	2-Wd Stockton	86	165
Pat	44	m	w	IREL	Alameda	Oakland	68	145
Saml W	30	m	w	NY	Santa Cruz	Santa Cruz Twp	89	386
Samuel	39	m	w	MA	San Diego	San Diego	78	484
Thomas	48	m	w	IREL	Nevada	Grass Valley Twp	75	193
Thos	29	m	w	IREL	Solano	Vallejo	90	195
William	45	m	w	IREL	Nevada	Rough & Ready Twp	75	335
William	14	m	w	NY	Yolo	Grafton Twp	93	496
Wm	38	m	w	MA	San Francisco	11-Wd San Francisc	84	429
HACKIN								
Dennis	27	m	w	IREL	Solano	Suisun Twp	90	100
HACKINGS								
Chas	50	m	w	VT	San Francisco	5-Wd San Francisco	81	9
HACKLER								
John	40	m	w	TN	Contra Costa	Martinez P O	71	406
HACKLEY								
De Witt C	44	m	w	IN	Mendocino	Point Arena Twp	74	211
Francis S	71	m	w	KY	Mendocino	Point Arena Twp	74	211
George W	63	m	w	KY	Placer	Auburn P O	76	363
S	36	m	w	NY	Alameda	Oakland	68	151
HACKMAN								
Alexr	34	m	w	PRUS	San Francisco	5-Wd San Francisco	81	29
John	24	m	w	PRUS	Placer	Bath P O	76	421
John	23	m	w	OH	San Francisco	3-Wd San Francisco	79	297
Richd	44	m	w	NY	Calaveras	Copperopolis P O	70	236
Wm	52	m	w	ENGL	Siskiyou	Callahan P O	89	633
HACKNEY								
Elmira	41	f	w	PA	Sacramento	4-Wd Sacramento	77	329
H W	37	m	w	TN	Napa	Napa	75	21
John	30	m	w	MA	San Luis Obispo	Santa Rosa Twp	87	326
M	50	m	w	MA	Amador	Jackson P O	69	338
Mary	23	f	w	TX	Tulare	Venice Twp	92	273
Mathew	52	m	w	NY	Amador	Volcano P O	69	377
Robt H	22	m	w	LA	San Francisco	San Francisco P O	83	330
William	28	m	w	OH	Yolo	Cache Crk Twp	93	446
HACKS								
Joseph	35	m	w	IREL	San Francisco	San Francisco P O	85	848
HACKSHAW								
Brodis	21	f	w	IL	Calaveras	Copperopolis P O	70	241
HADA								
Pedro	44	m	w	CHIL	Santa Clara	2-Wd San Jose	88	312
HADALER								
John	51	m	w	HANO	San Francisco	2-Wd San Francisco	79	241
HADAN								
William	35	m	w	KY	Humboldt	South Fork Twp	72	300
HADAR								
Robt	43	m	w	AL	Napa	Napa	75	53
HADCOCK								
John	49	m	w	NY	Nevada	Eureka Twp	75	132
John	39	m	w	SCOT	Amador	Amador City P O	69	391
HADDAN								
James	33	m	w	IA	Yolo	Cottonwood Twp	93	462
HADDEN								
John M	42	m	w	VA	Santa Barbara	Santa Barbara P O	87	491
Thos	54	m	w	TN	Fresno	Millerton P O	72	192
Wm J	65	m	w	MD	Tuolumne	Chinese Camp P O	93	377
HADDER								
Thomas	31	m	w	ME	Nevada	Meadow Lake Twp	75	268
HADDICAN								
John	38	m	w	IREL	Yolo	Cottonwood Twp	93	461
HADDICK								
Joseph	43	m	w	TN	Colusa	Stony Crk Twp	71	328
HADDING								
William	30	m	w	NY	San Francisco	5-Wd San Francisco	81	21
HADDLER								
H A	47	m	w	HANO	San Francisco	San Francisco P O	85	783
L F	18	m	w	IN	San Francisco	San Francisco P O	85	783
HADDOCH								
Jessee	30	m	w	KY	El Dorado	Georgetown Twp	72	46
HADDOCK								
Chas	32	m	w	MI	San Joaquin	Elliott Twp	86	70
Geo	40	m	w	ENGL	San Joaquin	Oneal Twp	86	109
Katie	3	f	w	CA	Colusa	Stony Crk Twp	71	328
Michael	38	m	w	IREL	Nevada	Eureka Twp	75	135
Robert W	32	m	w	CANA	Inyo	Bishop Crk Twp	73	313
Wm	42	m	w	ENGL	Santa Clara	Almaden Twp	88	14
HADDON								
Mary	37	f	w	BAVA	San Francisco	San Francisco P O	80	349
HADDOX								
William	32	m	w	OH	Los Angeles	El Monte Twp	73	449
HADEN								
Anna	59	f	w	NY	Santa Clara	Santa Clara Twp	88	148
Henry	25	m	w	HANO	San Francisco	7-Wd San Francisco	81	218
Jos	35	m	w	KY	San Francisco	8-Wd San Francisco	82	376
Pat	31	m	w	IREL	Sierra	Eureka Twp	89	523
William	33	m	w	IREL	San Francisco	San Francisco P O	83	249
HADINGTON								
Peter	31	m	w	MA	San Francisco	11-Wd San Francisc	84	676
HADLER								
George	35	m	w	SHOL	Calaveras	San Andreas P O	70	206
Jacob	41	m	w	PRUS	San Francisco	San Francisco P O	80	394
John	24	m	w	HAMB	San Francisco	San Francisco P O	85	815
W	46	f	w	PRUS	San Joaquin	2-Wd Stockton	86	171

© 2001 by Heritage Quest. All rights reserved.

Name	Age	S	R	B-PL	County	Locale	Series M593 Roll	Pg
HADLESON								
Charles M	40	m	w	OH	Yolo	Cache Crk Twp	93	447
HADLEY								
Anson	60	m	w	NY	Tulare	Tule Rvr Twp	92	260
Charles W	33	m	w	IL	Yolo	Cache Crk Twp	93	453
Chas	42	m	w	BAVA	Tuolumne	Big Oak Flat P O	93	394
D L	43	m	w	NY	San Francisco	San Francisco P O	85	862
Daniel	40	m	w	NY	Santa Clara	1-Wd San Jose	88	269
David	26	m	w	NJ	Colusa	Spring Valley Twp	71	343
Edward W	46	m	w	NH	Los Angeles	Santa Ana Twp	73	599
George	36	m	w	VT	Amador	Fiddletown P O	69	427
Halsey	51	m	w	OH	Colusa	Colusa	71	297
Harvey	53	m	w	NY	Yolo	Cache Crk Twp	93	453
Henry	23	m	w	ENGL	Alameda	Oakland	68	133
Hiram	35	m	w	MA	San Francisco	5-Wd San Francisco	81	26
James	35	m	w	NY	Solano	Denverton Twp	90	27
James	26	m	w	NY	Trinity	Douglas	92	236
James T	45	m	w	NY	Solano	Rio Vista Twp	90	58
James T	34	m	w	OH	Yolo	Grafton Twp	93	488
Jas	45	m	w	ENGL	San Francisco	7-Wd San Francisco	81	252
John	35	m	w	MA	Solano	Vallejo	90	200
John	31	m	w	NH	Placer	Bath P O	76	435
Moses	45	m	w	MA	San Francisco	San Francisco P O	80	374
Phebe	16	f	w	MO	Solano	Benicia	90	17
Samuel	44	m	w	NY	Solano	Rio Vista Twp	90	58
William	20	m	w	ME	Colusa	Spring Valley Twp	71	341
HADLICK								
Louis	47	m	w	MECK	Mariposa	Mariposa P O	74	97
HADLOCK								
Hubard	66	m	w	MA	Santa Clara	2-Wd San Jose	88	291
Josiah B	46	m	w	MA	Calaveras	San Andreas P O	70	199
Samuel	40	m	w	NH	San Mateo	Redwood City P O	87	375
HADNER								
Frank	41	m	w	IREL	Santa Clara	Redwood Twp	88	118
HADRICH								
Jacob	47	m	w	IREL	El Dorado	White Oak Twp	72	135
HADRICK								
Fred	31	m	w	PRUS	Colusa	Monroe Twp	71	320
H	21	m	w	PA	Amador	Sutter Crk P O	69	411
Hermann	25	m	w	PA	San Francisco	8-Wd San Francisco	82	351
Joseph	33	m	w	KY	Butte	Ophir Twp	70	114
HADRICKS								
Joseph	28	m	w	NY	San Bernardino	San Bernardino Twp	78	445
HADROCK								
John	25	m	w	ME	San Francisco	8-Wd San Francisco	82	307
HADSALL								
Chas	40	m	w	MA	Alameda	Murray Twp	68	106
HADSELL								
Chas A	49	m	w	SWED	San Francisco	1-Wd San Francisco	79	3
Edmund	44	m	w	MI	Marin	San Rafael Twp	74	41
J R	60	m	w	CT	Monterey	Monterey Twp	74	349
HADSKIN								
John	36	m	w	US	San Joaquin	2-Wd Stockton	86	164
HADSON								
Geo A	43	m	w	NY	Monterey	San Antonio Twp	74	315
Jno	25	m	w	MO	San Joaquin	Elliott Twp	86	73
HADWACK								
Edward	29	m	w	ENGL	Sonoma	Salt Point	91	387
HADWICK								
William	40	m	w	IREL	Sacramento	2-Wd Sacramento	77	224
HAE								
Ah	58	m	c	CHIN	Sacramento	Sutter Twp	77	382
Ah	42	m	c	CHIN	Sacramento	San Joaquin Twp	77	405
Ah	34	m	c	CHIN	Sacramento	Granite Twp	77	139
HAECKER								
John G	70	m	w	SAXO	Santa Clara	1-Wd San Jose	88	267
HAECKL								
Louis	38	m	w	FRAN	Napa	Napa	75	46
HAEFES								
Charles	23	m	w	PRUS	Sonoma	Sonoma Twp	91	438
HAEHL								
Louis	25	m	w	WURT	Mariposa	Mariposa P O	74	116
HAEHNLEN								
Albert K	26	m	w	PA	Santa Clara	2-Wd San Jose	88	329
HAELER								
Frank	35	m	w	SWIT	Yolo	Grafton Twp	93	482
HAELY								
James	68	m	w	VT	Lassen	Susanville Twp	73	439
HAEN								
Mon Hap	28	m	c	CHIN	Calaveras	Copperopolis P O	70	260
HAENNY								
Jane	8	f	w	NY	San Joaquin	Oneal Twp	86	98
HAERDER								
John	33	m	w	HOLL	El Dorado	Lake Valley Twp	72	65
HAEY								
Leon	36	m	c	CHIN	Yuba	Slate Range Bar Tw	93	674
HAFEE								
William C	30	m	w	ME	San Francisco	7-Wd San Francisco	81	176
HAFENRICHTER								
Ferdd	35	m	w	BOHE	San Francisco	San Francisco P O	83	113
HAFER								
Augustus	41	m	w	PA	Mariposa	Mariposa P O	74	136
George	53	m	w	PA	Mariposa	Mariposa P O	74	136
HAFERKORN								
Antoine	34	m	w	SAXO	San Francisco	San Francisco P O	83	265
HAFFEL								
Robt	27	m	w	ENGL	Sonoma	Russian Rvr	91	369
HAFFEN								
James	40	m	w	PA	San Francisco	11-Wd San Francisc	84	596
HAFFEND								
H B	40	m	w	NY	Sierra	Gibson Twp	89	542
HAFFER								
Wilhelm	30	m	w	WURT	San Francisco	6-Wd San Francisco	81	70
HAFFERTY								
Bridget	38	f	w	IREL	San Francisco	1-Wd San Francisco	79	94
Bridgt	33	f	w	IREL	Sacramento	3-Wd Sacramento	77	302
Michael	20	m	w	MA	San Francisco	8-Wd San Francisco	82	314
Patrick	32	m	w	IREL	San Francisco	7-Wd San Francisco	81	179
HAFFEY								
James	27	m	w	IREL	Contra Costa	Martinez P O	71	422
William	39	m	w	IREL	Contra Costa	Martinez P O	71	422
HAFFLECK								
Jacob	22	m	w	VA	Stanislaus	Emory Twp	92	21
HAFFMAN								
Wyatt	40	m	w	OH	Nevada	Nevada Twp	75	295
HAFFNER								
Joseph	30	m	w	WURT	Solano	Silveyville Twp	90	88
Lewis	42	m	w	WURT	Solano	Tremont Twp	90	36
Wm	45	m	w	SAXO	San Joaquin	Oneal Twp	86	102
Wm	42	m	w	SAXO	San Joaquin	2-Wd Stockton	86	191
HAFFORD								
Josephine	17	f	w	IA	Butte	Ophir Twp	70	113
Myra	34	f	w	MA	San Francisco	8-Wd San Francisco	82	448
Solomon	32	m	w	IN	Butte	Chico Twp	70	16
HAFFOTER								
Nicholas	66	m	w	SWIT	Placer	Newcastle Twp	76	477
HAFFRON								
N	43	m	w	IREL	Humboldt	Arcata Twp	72	228
HAFFRY								
John	29	m	w	NY	Sierra	Table Rock Twp	89	571
HAFFY								
Edward	25	m	w	IREL	Contra Costa	Martinez P O	71	420
Patrick	27	m	w	IREL	Contra Costa	Martinez P O	71	423
HAFKA								
L	35	m	w	AUST	San Francisco	San Francisco P O	85	842
HAFKY								
Isaac	43	m	w	PRUS	Yolo	Cache Crk Twp	93	427
HAFLER								
Joseph	27	m	w	BAVA	San Francisco	8-Wd San Francisco	82	434
HAFLICH								
Jacob	48	m	w	PA	San Joaquin	3-Wd Stockton	86	229
HAFNAGLE								
Charles	47	m	w	PRUS	El Dorado	Cosumnes Twp	72	17
HAFNER								
Chas	42	m	w	HCAS	San Francisco	11-Wd San Francisc	84	605
HAFT								
E E	35	m	w	PA	San Francisco	8-Wd San Francisco	82	333
HAG								
Ah	37	m	c	CHIN	Nevada	Meadow Lake Twp	75	257
John	56	m	w	SWED	Marin	San Rafael	74	50
HAGADORN								
A H	38	m	w	NY	Nevada	Nevada Twp	75	278
David F	28	m	w	OH	Sacramento	2-Wd Sacramento	77	237
William	48	m	w	NY	Contra Costa	Martinez P O	71	416
HAGAN								
---	28	m	w	CANA	Humboldt	Eureka Twp	72	273
Albert	28	m	w	MO	Santa Cruz	Santa Cruz	89	426
Anastasia	21	f	w	NY	San Francisco	San Francisco P O	80	359
C C	24	m	w	ME	Solano	Vallejo	90	160
Chris	61	m	w	DENM	Contra Costa	Martinez Twp	71	352
Eliza	10	f	w	MA	Santa Clara	1-Wd San Jose	88	247
George	23	m	w	ME	San Mateo	Half Moon Bay P O	87	408
Henry	55	m	w	IREL	Sonoma	Santa Rosa	91	423
Henry	31	m	w	NY	Tehama	Tehama Twp	92	191
Hugh	40	m	w	IREL	Yolo	Buckeye Twp	93	409
Isabella	32	f	w	IREL	San Francisco	11-Wd San Francisc	84	491
James	43	m	w	IREL	Santa Clara	Fremont Twp	88	49
James	40	m	w	IREL	Santa Clara	1-Wd San Jose	88	237
James	27	m	w	IREL	Los Angeles	Santa Ana Twp	73	601
James	25	m	w	ENGL	Alameda	Hayward	68	76
John	49	m	w	NY	San Francisco	San Francisco P O	85	867
John	31	m	w	DENM	Yuba	Marysville Twp	93	570
John	30	m	w	IREL	San Francisco	7-Wd San Francisco	81	251
John	26	m	w	IREL	Tehama	Red Bluff	92	183
John	25	m	w	ENGL	Humboldt	Eureka Twp	72	273
John	21	m	w	MO	Napa	Napa Twp	75	71
John E	22	m	w	ME	Santa Cruz	Santa Cruz Twp	89	394
L	46	f	w	SAXO	Sacramento	3-Wd Sacramento	77	262
Margaret	35	f	w	IREL	Santa Clara	1-Wd San Jose	88	227
Michael	38	m	w	IREL	San Francisco	3-Wd San Francisco	79	327
Patrick	39	m	w	IREL	San Francisco	San Francisco P O	83	69
Patrick	20	m	w	IREL	Solano	Denverton Twp	90	27
Peter	42	m	w	IREL	San Francisco	7-Wd San Francisco	81	241
Peter	29	m	w	NORW	San Francisco	1-Wd San Francisco	79	74
Peter	23	m	w	IREL	Marin	Sausalito Twp	74	68
Robert	26	m	w	NY	Nevada	Meadow Lake Twp	75	252
Robt	53	m	w	PRUS	San Francisco	2-Wd San Francisco	79	224
Rose	57	f	w	IREL	San Joaquin	2-Wd Stockton	86	170
Thomas	24	m	w	SCOT	Yolo	Putah Twp	93	519
W	35	m	w	PRUS	Sacramento	4-Wd Sacramento	77	324
HAGANKAMP								
Adolf	44	m	w	PRUS	San Francisco	San Francisco P O	83	407
HAGANS								
Edward	28	m	w	ENGL	Santa Clara	2-Wd San Jose	88	327

© 2001 by Heritage Quest. All rights reserved.

California 1870 Census

Name	Age	S	R	B-PL	County	Locale	Roll	Pg
						Series M593		
Jno S	68	m	w	KY	Sonoma	Santa Rosa	91	426
W A	37	m	w	IL	Mendocino	Sanel Twp	74	227
W H	62	m	w	KY	Mendocino	Ukiah Twp	74	236
Wm E	4	m	w	CA	Mendocino	Sanel Twp	74	227
HAGAR								
E P	27	m	w	ME	Yuba	Rose Bar Twp	93	654
Edward	40	m	w	PA	San Francisco	San Francisco P O	80	533
H	28	m	w	BADE	Alameda	Oakland	68	164
Henry	30	m	w	OH	Yolo	Putah Twp	93	524
Jno S	55	m	w	PRUS	San Francisco	5-Wd San Francisco	81	19
John	34	m	w	BADE	Yolo	Putah Twp	93	526
Thos S	29	m	w	NY	San Francisco	San Francisco P O	83	124
HAGARD								
Gardner	59	m	w	RI	San Francisco	San Francisco P O	83	52
HAGARMAN								
M	22	f	w	PRUS	Alameda	Murray Twp	68	100
HAGARTY								
James	40	m	w	IREL	Calaveras	San Andreas P O	70	186
Patrick	24	m	w	IREL	Yolo	Cache Crk Twp	93	453
Timothy	14	m	w	NY	San Francisco	11-Wd San Francisc	84	588
HAGE								
John T	22	m	w	NORW	San Francisco	3-Wd San Francisco	79	297
Tobias	29	m	w	NORW	San Francisco	3-Wd San Francisco	79	297
HAGEDEN								
Eber A	33	m	w	WI	El Dorado	Placerville Twp	72	100
HAGEDON								
Charles	31	m	w	WI	Sonoma	Analy Twp	91	218
William	37	m	w	HANO	Sonoma	Petaluma Twp	91	350
HAGEDORN								
William	48	m	w	BREM	San Francisco	San Francisco P O	83	189
HAGEL								
John	28	m	w	PA	Solano	Benicia	90	19
Nicholas	45	m	w	BADE	Solano	Vallejo	90	207
HAGEMAN								
Eliza	55	f	w	BADE	Solano	Silveyville Twp	90	86
George	16	m	w	CA	Solano	Silveyville Twp	90	86
HAGEMANN								
Ernest	26	m	w	HANO	Sacramento	4-Wd Sacramento	77	367
Fred	46	m	w	HANO	San Francisco	San Francisco P O	83	176
HAGEMEYER								
Englebert	27	m	w	PRUS	San Francisco	San Francisco P O	83	138
HAGEN								
C C [Dr]	51	m	w	CANA	Monterey	Salinas Twp	74	309
Chas	26	m	w	SWED	San Francisco	1-Wd San Francisco	79	75
E D	24	m	w	NY	Solano	Benicia	90	12
Henry	59	m	w	HANO	Monterey	San Juan Twp	74	395
Henry	34	m	w	BADE	San Francisco	2-Wd San Francisco	79	171
Jacob	20	m	w	NH	San Francisco	San Francisco P O	83	107
James	25	m	w	IREL	San Bernardino	San Bernardino Twp	78	418
Lizzy E	38	f	w	IREL	San Francisco	6-Wd San Francisco	81	118
Maggie	43	f	w	IREL	San Francisco	San Francisco P O	83	173
Mary E	12	f	w	MA	San Francisco	6-Wd San Francisco	81	119
Peter	29	m	w	NY	San Francisco	3-Wd San Francisco	79	320
Sarah	25	f	w	IREL	San Francisco	8-Wd San Francisco	82	407
HAGENAH								
Ferdind	32	m	w	HANO	San Francisco	1-Wd San Francisco	79	96
William	24	m	w	PRUS	San Francisco	San Francisco P O	80	352
HAGENMEYER								
Gebhord	38	m	w	WURT	Mendocino	Big Rvr Twp	74	162
Joseph	41	m	w	WURT	Mendocino	Little Rvr Twp	74	171
HAGENS								
Edwin B	27	m	w	IL	Yuba	New York Twp	93	637
HAGER								
Geo B	42	m	w	MA	San Francisco	San Francisco P O	83	381
George	48	m	w	NY	Placer	Cisco P O	76	494
George	23	m	w	WI	Fresno	Millerton P O	72	189
Henry	25	m	w	PRUS	Solano	Rio Vista Twp	90	70
Jacob	37	m	w	SWIT	Siskiyou	Yreka	89	653
Jacob	33	m	w	BAVA	Trinity	Junction City Pct	92	209
James H	33	m	w	MO	Sonoma	Analy Twp	91	228
John	55	m	w	GERM	Los Angeles	Los Angeles	73	516
John	48	m	w	IREL	Sonoma	Vallejo Twp	91	462
HAGERLY								
Robert	30	m	w	IREL	San Francisco	11-Wd San Francisc	84	541
HAGERMAN								
Chas	38	m	w	HANO	Sierra	Gibson Twp	89	538
Geo	20	m	w	IL	San Joaquin	Liberty Twp	86	86
Henry	50	m	w	HANO	Amador	Jackson P O	69	343
J	40	m	w	PRUS	Sutter	Butte Twp	92	93
Jacob	39	m	w	NY	Butte	Mountain Spring Tw	70	87
John	53	m	w	HANO	Amador	Jackson P O	69	343
Jos	40	m	w	PRUS	Sutter	Butte Twp	92	102
Louisa	5	f	w	NY	Los Angeles	Los Angeles	73	538
Peter	20	m	w	NY	Sacramento	Franklin Twp	77	109
HAGERMANN								
Henry	51	m	w	HANO	San Francisco	3-Wd San Francisco	79	287
HAGERMON								
Fredk	35	m	w	PRUS	Sonoma	Sonoma Twp	91	443
HAGERS								
Mary	31	f	w	IREL	San Francisco	1-Wd San Francisco	79	113
HAGERSTON								
Charles	33	m	w	SWED	San Francisco	7-Wd San Francisco	81	201
HAGERTY								
Catharine	47	f	w	IREL	San Francisco	11-Wd San Francisc	84	568
Catherine	24	f	w	IREL	San Francisco	San Francisco P O	83	260
Daniel	34	m	w	NY	San Francisco	11-Wd San Francisc	84	704
David	42	m	w	IREL	San Francisco	7-Wd San Francisco	81	187
Dennis	32	m	w	IREL	San Joaquin	Elkhorn Twp	86	59
Ellen	25	f	w	IREL	San Francisco	San Francisco P O	83	288
James	37	m	w	IREL	San Francisco	8-Wd San Francisco	82	312
James	28	m	w	NY	San Francisco	San Francisco P O	83	251
John	40	m	w	NY	San Francisco	San Francisco P O	83	288
John	38	m	w	IREL	San Francisco	1-Wd San Francisco	79	100
John	38	m	w	IREL	Sacramento	Cosumnes Twp	77	91
Julia	23	f	w	IREL	San Francisco	San Francisco P O	83	322
Kate	22	f	w	IREL	San Francisco	San Francisco P O	85	774
Kate	16	f	w	IREL	Yolo	Cache Crk Twp	93	453
Margt	32	f	w	IREL	San Francisco	San Francisco P O	83	111
Mary	45	f	w	IREL	San Francisco	7-Wd San Francisco	81	198
Mich	27	m	w	IREL	San Francisco	1-Wd San Francisco	79	59
Michael	40	m	w	IREL	San Francisco	6-Wd San Francisco	81	88
Michl	30	m	w	IREL	San Francisco	1-Wd San Francisco	79	92
P R	25	m	w	PA	Sierra	Butte Twp	89	508
Patrick	50	m	w	IREL	San Francisco	11-Wd San Francisc	84	592
Patrick	35	m	w	IREL	San Francisco	San Francisco P O	83	211
Peter	40	m	w	IREL	San Francisco	San Francisco P O	83	299
Thomas	47	m	w	IREL	San Mateo	Schoolhouse Statio	87	337
Timothy	37	m	w	IREL	Marin	San Rafael	74	52
HAGES								
Thos	14	m	w	CA	Yuba	W Bear Rvr Twp	93	684
HAGESSON								
Jacob	47	m	w	PRUS	Tuolumne	Sonora P O	93	328
HAGESTEN								
Ludwick	28	m	w	SWED	Santa Clara	Redwood Twp	88	125
HAGETHE								
Hiram E	23	m	w	WI	Santa Clara	Santa Clara Twp	88	150
HAGG								
Andrew	32	m	w	SWED	Stanislaus	Emory Twp	92	26
HAGGAN								
Peter	60	m	w	IREL	El Dorado	Placerville Twp	72	92
HAGGARD								
Thomas L	39	m	w	TN	Plumas	Rich Bar Twp	77	8
HAGGART								
Denis	27	m	w	IREL	San Francisco	11-Wd San Francisc	84	670
HAGGARTY								
Dennis	24	m	w	IREL	Santa Cruz	Watsonville	89	366
Dora	19	f	w	IREL	Solano	Vallejo	90	214
Edgar	24	m	w	CANA	Santa Cruz	Pajaro Twp	89	351
James	48	m	w	IREL	Yuba	Marysville	93	588
Jerry	24	m	w	IREL	Solano	Benicia	90	1
M	38	m	w	IREL	Merced	Snelling P O	74	255
Morris	47	m	w	IREL	Yuba	Rose Bar Twp	93	658
Patk	74	m	w	IREL	Solano	Vallejo	90	149
Patk	45	m	w	IREL	Solano	Vallejo	90	144
Thomas	25	m	w	IREL	San Mateo	Woodside P O	87	380
William	58	m	w	IREL	Nevada	Grass Valley Twp	75	210
William	30	m	w	NY	San Francisco	San Francisco P O	83	186
HAGGEDOM								
Alex	23	m	w	BREM	San Francisco	2-Wd San Francisco	79	222
HAGGER								
Jos	36	m	w	PA	Tehama	Antelope Twp	92	158
HAGGERTY								
Corneil	35	m	w	IREL	San Francisco	7-Wd San Francisco	81	263
Dennis	25	m	w	IREL	San Francisco	11-Wd San Francisc	84	595
Edward	31	m	w	VT	Marin	Point Reyes Twp	74	21
George	60	m	w	IREL	San Francisco	San Francisco P O	83	130
James	28	m	w	IREL	San Francisco	1-Wd San Francisco	79	101
John	40	m	w	IREL	San Francisco	San Francisco P O	83	383
Jos	41	m	w	NJ	San Diego	Warners Rancho Dis	78	529
Martin	52	m	w	IREL	Marin	Point Reyes Twp	74	21
Michl	36	m	w	IREL	Marin	Tomales Twp	74	87
Michl	30	m	w	NY	San Francisco	1-Wd San Francisco	79	58
Norah	26	f	w	IREL	San Francisco	San Francisco P O	83	102
Patrick	72	m	w	IREL	Santa Clara	San Jose Twp	88	195
Saml	55	m	w	KY	Tuolumne	Columbia P O	93	336
Thos	25	m	w	IREL	San Francisco	San Francisco P O	83	133
HAGGET								
Nathaniel	18	m	w	OR	Monterey	Alisal Twp	74	294
HAGGIN								
James	45	m	w	KY	San Francisco	San Francisco P O	80	405
Patrick	28	m	w	IREL	El Dorado	Placerville Twp	72	92
HAGGUM								
James	48	m	w	ENGL	Mendocino	Point Arena Twp	74	208
HAGHAN								
Jas	35	m	w	IREL	San Francisco	San Francisco P O	83	2
HAGHMEISTER								
Julius	28	m	w	PRUS	Los Angeles	Los Angeles	73	557
HAGIN								
John	34	m	w	TN	San Francisco	1-Wd San Francisco	79	65
John	27	m	w	IREL	Sacramento	American Twp	77	64
HAGINS								
Thos	28	m	w	IREL	Solano	Vallejo	90	197
HAGIR								
Henry	49	m	w	BAVA	San Francisco	2-Wd San Francisco	79	244
HAGLE								
Alex	30	m	w	POLA	San Francisco	3-Wd San Francisco	79	315
Dora	8	f	i	CA	Colusa	Grand Island Twp	71	308
HAGLEMAN								
John	38	m	w	BAVA	Trinity	Weaverville Pct	92	223
HAGLER								
John	43	m	w	BADE	Sacramento	4-Wd Sacramento	77	331
Paul	40	m	w	NC	Sonoma	Mendocino Twp	91	307
HAGLEY								
Josephine	10	f	i	CA	Shasta	Millville P O	89	495

© 2001 by Heritage Quest. All rights reserved.

Name	Age	S	R	B-PL	County	Locale	Roll	Pg
HAGMAN								
Robt	37	m	w	RUSS	San Francisco	8-Wd San Francisco	82	357
HAGMAYRE								
Govelove	22	m	w	WURT	Sonoma	Cloverdale Twp	91	268
HAGNEA								
Pierre	27	m	w	FRAN	San Francisco	San Francisco P O	80	458
HAGNER								
John	33	m	w	WURT	Santa Cruz	Santa Cruz Twp	89	386
HAGUE								
A	36	m	w	SCOT	Sacramento	3-Wd Sacramento	77	311
Lewis L	47	m	w	PA	Yuba	Long Bar Twp	93	563
M W	45	m	w	TN	Butte	Chico Twp	70	56
Robert	36	m	w	MO	Fresno	Millerton P O	72	160
Wm	58	m	w	OH	Butte	Oroville Twp	70	138
HAGUS								
John	45	m	w	FRAN	San Francisco	11-Wd San Francisc	84	695
HAGY								
Adam	39	m	w	PA	Contra Costa	Martinez P O	71	438
Anne	21	f	w	IREL	San Francisco	11-Wd San Francisc	84	538
HAH								
Ah	35	m	c	CHIN	Plumas	Plumas Twp	77	31
Ah	25	m	c	CHIN	San Francisco	San Francisco P O	80	445
Ah	24	m	c	CHIN	Colusa	Butte Twp	71	269
Ah	22	m	c	CHIN	Merced	Snelling P O	74	279
Ah	20	m	c	CHIN	San Mateo	Half Moon Bay P O	87	396
Ah	20	m	c	CHIN	San Francisco	1-Wd San Francisco	79	21
Berry	32	m	c	CHIN	San Joaquin	Castoria Twp	86	7
He	29	f	c	CHIN	San Francisco	6-Wd San Francisco	81	51
Hen	34	m	c	CHIN	Tuolumne	Columbia P O	93	357
Hop	50	m	c	CHIN	Colusa	Butte Twp	71	269
Lack	39	m	c	CHIN	Yuba	Marysville	93	631
Len	35	m	c	CHIN	San Joaquin	3-Wd Stockton	86	231
Quoi	20	f	c	CHIN	San Francisco	6-Wd San Francisco	81	44
Wang	26	m	c	CHIN	Solano	Rio Vista Twp	90	64
We	60	m	c	CHIN	Yolo	Washington Twp	93	536
HAHAN								
P	36	m	w	PA	Sacramento	1-Wd Sacramento	77	191
HAHN								
Albert V	42	m	w	SAXO	Yuba	New York Twp	93	638
Alfred	32	m	w	SAXO	San Francisco	San Francisco P O	80	348
August	42	m	w	PRUS	San Francisco	San Francisco P O	85	841
August	34	m	w	HCAS	San Francisco	San Francisco P O	85	844
Barbara	36	f	w	PRUS	San Francisco	8-Wd San Francisco	82	309
Charles	19	m	w	PRUS	San Francisco	2-Wd San Francisco	79	255
Chas	41	m	w	PRUS	Fresno	Millerton P O	72	184
Chas	40	m	w	BAVA	San Francisco	11-Wd San Francisc	84	424
Daniel D	30	m	w	IL	Siskiyou	Yreka Twp	89	664
Geo H	30	m	w	HANO	San Francisco	San Francisco P O	83	135
Godlibt	42	m	w	WURT	Contra Costa	Martinez Twp	71	352
Henry	45	m	w	MECK	San Francisco	2-Wd San Francisco	79	244
Henry	44	m	w	PRUS	San Francisco	6-Wd San Francisco	81	129
Jacob	38	m	w	PRUS	Nevada	Nevada Twp	75	278
John	32	m	w	HANO	Nevada	Nevada Twp	75	277
John	28	m	w	IREL	San Francisco	San Francisco P O	85	773
Joseph	39	m	w	FRAN	San Francisco	2-Wd San Francisco	79	224
Jost	25	m	w	BADE	Colusa	Spring Valley Twp	71	343
Mary	19	f	w	BAVA	San Francisco	San Francisco P O	83	416
Nicholas	35	m	w	PRUS	Yolo	Cache Crk Twp	93	428
Peter	50	m	w	IREL	San Francisco	1-Wd San Francisco	79	92
Seligman	44	m	w	BAVA	San Francisco	8-Wd San Francisco	82	432
William	40	m	w	HCAS	San Francisco	San Francisco P O	85	716
William	28	m	w	PRUS	San Francisco	6-Wd San Francisco	81	129
HAHNEMAN								
Chas	28	m	w	OH	San Francisco	1-Wd San Francisco	79	104
HAHOE								
John	35	m	w	ENGL	San Francisco	San Francisco P O	83	340
HAI								
Chi	38	m	c	CHIN	Tuolumne	Columbia P O	93	346
Chi	36	m	c	CHIN	Tuolumne	Columbia P O	93	356
HAID								
Ah	25	m	c	CHIN	Trinity	Lewiston Pct	92	211
HAIG								
Anna	40	f	w	SWED	San Francisco	San Francisco P O	85	853
D C	28	m	m	OR	Humboldt	Eureka Twp	72	278
D C	26	m	w	NY	Sacramento	San Joaquin Twp	77	399
Wm S	38	m	w	NY	Sierra	Sears Twp	89	555
HAIGH								
G B	38	m	w	ENGL	Mariposa	Maxwell Crk P O	74	141
Geo W	26	m	w	MO	Sonoma	Healdsburg & Mendo	91	284
Jno B	55	m	w	ENGL	Sonoma	Mendocino Twp	91	291
Patrick	40	m	w	IREL	San Francisco	11-Wd San Francisc	84	649
HAIGHT								
Abraham	40	m	w	OH	Yolo	Putah Twp	93	523
Alen J	40	m	w	NY	San Francisco	5-Wd San Francisco	81	2
Amos	37	m	w	LA	San Francisco	7-Wd San Francisco	81	274
Charles	32	m	w	MI	Siskiyou	Table Rock Twp	89	647
Charles B	8	m	w	CA	Placer	Bath P O	76	441
Charlie	5	m	i	CA	Del Norte	Smith Rvr Twp	71	477
Daniel	41	m	w	OH	Del Norte	Smith Rvr Twp	71	476
Emmor J	27	m	w	NY	Yolo	Putah Twp	93	515
Fanny	18	f	i	CA	Del Norte	Smith Rvr Twp	71	477
Geo	26	m	w	CANA	Solano	Vallejo	90	139
George S	64	m	w	NY	Siskiyou	Table Rock Twp	89	648
Harrison	43	m	w	NY	San Francisco	8-Wd San Francisco	82	410
Henry	45	m	w	NY	Alameda	Alameda	68	11
J A	27	m	w	IA	Del Norte	Crescent	71	466
J H	28	m	w	WI	Sacramento	4-Wd Sacramento	77	351
J M	38	m	w	NY	Sacramento	3-Wd Sacramento	77	271
James	17	m	w	IA	Del Norte	Smith Rvr Twp	71	477
James H	55	m	w	NY	San Francisco	1-Wd San Francisco	79	55
Job	52	m	w	OH	Del Norte	Smith Rvr Twp	71	477
John	28	m	w	NY	San Mateo	Redwood Twp	87	366
John E	33	m	w	NY	Santa Clara	Santa Clara Twp	88	152
Joseph	40	m	w	ME	Colusa	Monroe Twp	71	312
Louis	35	m	w	FRAN	Marin	Bolinas Twp	74	3
Malone H	41	m	w	CANA	Mendocino	Point Arena Twp	74	210
Weltha	45	f	w	NY	San Francisco	8-Wd San Francisco	82	313
William K	46	m	w	NY	Santa Clara	2-Wd San Jose	88	283
HAIKE								
Andrew	22	m	w	HAMB	San Francisco	11-Wd San Francisc	84	497
HAIL								
August	24	m	w	PRUS	Napa	Napa	75	41
Frank	25	m	w	GA	Los Angeles	Los Angeles	73	541
Lee	53	m	w	KY	Colusa	Spring Valley Twp	71	335
Louis	36	m	w	PA	Tuolumne	Chinese Camp P O	93	373
Wm	28	m	w	IL	Sacramento	3-Wd Sacramento	77	290
HAILDE								
Francis	48	m	w	PRUS	Placer	Auburn P O	76	380
HAILE								
C S	24	m	w	NY	Alameda	Alameda	68	2
Charles H	38	m	w	VT	Alameda	Alameda	68	3
Richard C	54	m	w	TN	Solano	Suisun Twp	90	101
HAILEY								
Pat	40	m	w	IREL	Alameda	Oakland	68	258
HAILLE								
Joseph	43	m	w	FRAN	San Francisco	2-Wd San Francisco	79	148
HAILMAN								
Peter	66	m	w	PA	Sonoma	Santa Rosa	91	409
HAILS								
Mary	70	f	w	HOLL	Contra Costa	Martinez P O	71	397
HAILSTONE								
William	35	m	w	ENGL	Contra Costa	Martinez P O	71	418
HAILY								
Robbert	28	m	w	IREL	Alameda	Oakland	68	267
HAIN								
Ah	15	m	c	CHIN	Santa Barbara	San Buenaventura P	87	446
Carl	45	m	w	AUST	San Francisco	6-Wd San Francisco	81	86
H R	38	m	w	NY	Alameda	Murray Twp	68	117
Henry	39	m	w	OH	Los Angeles	Soledad Twp	73	630
James H	40	m	w	NH	San Francisco	San Francisco P O	85	778
Jno	20	m	w	PA	Sierra	Gibson Twp	89	541
John C C	49	f	w	HANO	San Francisco	San Francisco P O	85	783
Quoy	34	f	c	CHIN	San Francisco	6-Wd San Francisco	81	65
HAINE								
Carl	25	m	w	SHOL	San Francisco	2-Wd San Francisco	79	217
Carlos	45	m	w	PRUS	San Francisco	7-Wd San Francisco	81	197
Joseph	60	m	w	BELG	San Francisco	8-Wd San Francisco	82	305
HAINES								
Abner	46	m	w	ME	Santa Barbara	San Buenaventura P	87	431
Abram	33	m	w	PRUS	Yolo	Cottonwood Twp	93	463
D M	64	m	w	RI	Alameda	Oakland	68	220
Ephraim	69	m	w	IA	Fresno	Millerton P O	72	157
Frank	22	m	w	MA	Alameda	Oakland	68	256
G J	54	m	w	PRUS	Sacramento	3-Wd Sacramento	77	282
George	42	m	w	NY	Calaveras	San Andreas P O	70	215
George	32	m	w	CANA	Solano	Maine Prairie Twp	90	48
Heny	56	m	w	PA	San Joaquin	Castoria Twp	86	2
Israel	38	m	w	PA	Alameda	Washington Twp	68	299
J	41	m	w	VA	Siskiyou	Scott Rvr Twp	89	604
J W	39	m	w	NY	Sierra	Downieville Twp	89	516
John	44	m	w	MD	El Dorado	Greenwood Twp	72	55
John	40	m	w	MA	Stanislaus	North Twp	92	67
John	23	m	w	PA	Colusa	Spring Valley Twp	71	344
John C	70	m	w	NH	Colusa	Butte Twp	71	271
Margaret	25	f	w	ME	San Francisco	11-Wd San Francisc	84	537
Maria	22	f	w	IREL	Alameda	Oakland	68	191
Minor B	34	m	w	MS	Fresno	Millerton P O	72	160
Prince	60	m	w	NY	Santa Clara	Almaden Twp	88	17
R	44	m	w	NY	Sierra	Downieville Twp	89	516
Robert	35	m	w	IREL	Kern	Bakersfield P O	73	357
Rufus B	44	m	w	ME	Placer	Auburn P O	76	367
Samuel	40	m	w	PRUS	Yolo	Cottonwood Twp	93	463
Samuel	35	m	w	GERM	Yolo	Cache Crk Twp	93	447
Thomas	21	m	w	IN	Amador	Volcano P O	69	379
Thos	46	m	w	CHIL	Shasta	Horsetown P O	89	501
Titus G B	50	m	w	IL	Los Angeles	Los Nietos Twp	73	578
Wm	46	m	w	NY	Alameda	Oakland	68	182
Wm R	25	m	w	PA	San Luis Obispo	San Luis Obispo Tw	87	316
HAINS								
Benjamin	36	m	w	MO	Los Angeles	Los Nietos Twp	73	590
David	50	m	w	KY	Tehama	Paskenta Twp	92	165
David	45	m	w	MO	Tehama	Paskenta Twp	92	165
Geo	59	m	w	KY	Tehama	Paskenta Twp	92	165
Geo	50	m	w	ME	Amador	Drytown P O	69	421
George	30	m	w	IL	Solano	Silveyville Twp	90	90
George	21	m	w	IREL	Nevada	Meadow Lake Twp	75	268
James	36	m	w	DENM	Placer	Auburn P O	76	383
James	30	m	w	ENGL	Nevada	Grass Valley Twp	75	231
Jno	44	m	w	IN	San Joaquin	Douglas Twp	86	37
Joshua	38	m	w	NY	Calaveras	San Andreas P O	70	209
Martin	23	m	w	NY	San Francisco	7-Wd San Francisco	81	287
Wm	30	m	w	PA	San Joaquin	2-Wd Stockton	86	163
HAINY								
Jas	20	m	w	NC	San Joaquin	Dent Twp	86	25

© 2001 by Heritage Quest. All rights reserved.

Name	Age	S	R	B-PL	County	Locale	Series M593 Roll	Pg
HAIR								
Emma	12	f	w	CA	Alameda	Oakland	68	259
HAIRFIELD								
Wm	15	m	w	NY	San Francisco	7-Wd San Francisco	81	262
HAIRLOCKER								
L	22	m	w	OH	Sonoma	Mendocino Twp	91	301
HAIS								
Joseph	32	m	w	PRUS	San Francisco	San Francisco P O	83	358
HAISE								
Samuel	43	m	w	IREL	Santa Cruz	Santa Cruz Twp	89	395
HAISER								
Joseph	31	m	w	MI	Marin	San Rafael	74	56
HAISH								
George	42	m	w	OH	Placer	Auburn P O	76	359
HAISLEP								
Alex	83	m	w	VA	Del Norte	Crescent	71	463
Benj F	29	m	w	VA	Stanislaus	Empire Twp	92	33
HAISLIP								
Alexander	81	m	w	VA	Humboldt	Eureka Twp	72	256
HAIT								
James	56	m	w	IREL	Colusa	Colusa	71	294
James	50	m	w	IREL	Alameda	Oakland	68	236
HAITCH								
Samuel	25	m	w	NY	San Francisco	6-Wd San Francisco	81	122
HAITER								
James	49	m	w	NY	San Joaquin	3-Wd Stockton	86	234
HAITON								
Otho W	14	m	w	HI	Santa Cruz	Santa Cruz	89	422
HAITT								
Jno F	43	m	w	MA	Sacramento	3-Wd Sacramento	77	273
HAJEMANN								
Bartha	62	f	w	DENM	Los Angeles	Los Angeles Twp	73	476
HAK								
Ah	32	m	c	CHIN	Nevada	Grass Valley Twp	75	208
Ah	28	m	c	CHIN	San Francisco	6-Wd San Francisco	81	47
Sue	30	f	c	CHIN	Sacramento	1-Wd Sacramento	77	193
Sui	18	f	c	CHIN	Sacramento	1-Wd Sacramento	77	193
HAKE								
Harmon	40	m	w	PRUS	Amador	Volcano P O	69	373
Joseph	30	m	w	IREL	Sacramento	Georgianna Twp	77	124
HAKEMAN								
Henry	37	m	w	PRUS	Tulare	Tule Rvr Twp	92	263
HAKERMAN								
Henry	22	m	w	PRUS	Colusa	Colusa Twp	71	273
HAKES								
Dorr	31	m	w	NY	Sonoma	Bodega Twp	91	252
Emery	44	m	w	OH	Sonoma	Bodega Twp	91	248
Harry	67	m	w	NY	Butte	Bidwell Twp	70	2
HAKI								
Ah	45	m	c	CHIN	Nevada	Little York Twp	75	242
HAKKS								
J T	40	m	w	CT	Sierra	Butte Twp	89	509
HAKMAN								
Chas	45	m	w	HAMB	Napa	Napa	75	17
Henry	41	m	w	PRUS	Solano	Tremont Twp	90	33
HAKOLISKIO								
David	84	m	w	SAXO	El Dorado	Placerville	72	125
HAKOMOLLER								
Henry	40	m	w	HANO	El Dorado	Kelsey Twp	72	60
HAL								
Ah	38	m	c	CHIN	Fresno	Millerton P O	72	201
HALADAY								
Margaret	45	f	w	IREL	San Joaquin	2-Wd Stockton	86	170
HALAI								
Manuel	42	m	w	CHIL	Tuolumne	Chinese Camp P O	93	380
HALAN								
Timothy	39	m	w	IREL	Santa Clara	2-Wd San Jose	88	289
HALAND								
J C	46	m	w	TN	Alameda	Oakland	68	142
Patrick	24	m	w	IREL	San Francisco	7-Wd San Francisco	81	181
HALARD								
Peter	48	m	w	FRAN	Calaveras	Copperopolis P O	70	251
HALBERD								
O	38	m	w	ME	Alameda	Murray Twp	68	124
Samuel	40	m	w	ME	Stanislaus	Emory Twp	92	25
HALBERSON								
Hugh	28	m	w	NORW	Stanislaus	Empire Twp	92	53
HALBERSTADT								
Luis	37	m	w	AUST	Los Angeles	Santa Ana Twp	73	599
HALBERT								
George	50	m	w	KY	Kern	Linns Valley P O	73	345
H	55	m	w	SCOT	Alameda	Oakland	68	184
Jasper G	48	m	w	NY	Plumas	Quartz Twp	77	40
John	41	m	w	IREL	San Francisco	San Francisco P O	80	367
M E	34	m	w	OH	Tuolumne	Big Oak Flat P O	93	401
HALBOT								
Henry	24	m	w	MO	Solano	Silveyville Twp	90	80
HALBURT								
Hughes	40	m	w	SCOT	Alameda	Oakland	68	207
HALCOMB								
Antonette C	57	f	w	NJ	Yuba	Parks Bar Twp	93	649
C S	24	m	w	CT	Tuolumne	Big Oak Flat P O	93	391
Jonas	31	m	w	AR	Shasta	Fort Crook P O	89	477
HALD								
Nellie	23	f	w	ME	Sonoma	Petaluma Twp	91	324
HALDEN								
Thomas	26	m	w	AL	Inyo	Lone Pine Twp	73	335
HALDINES								
Jacob	42	m	w	SWIT	Siskiyou	Cottonwood Twp	89	595
HALE								
Abednago	52	m	w	TN	Yuba	Rose Bar Twp	93	665
Alfred W	55	m	w	NY	San Francisco	6-Wd San Francisco	81	117
C E	54	f	w	VT	Tuolumne	Big Oak Flat P O	93	395
Ceylon L	39	m	w	OH	Butte	Ophir Twp	70	111
David	31	m	w	MO	Solano	Denverton Twp	90	24
David	30	m	w	IN	Solano	Montezuma Twp	90	65
Eli	12	m	i	CA	Lake	Lower Lake	73	420
Elizabeth	11	f	w	CA	Los Angeles	El Monte Twp	73	449
Fred	18	m	w	OH	Butte	Chico Twp	70	33
G E	55	m	w	ME	Sierra	Sierra Twp	89	567
G W	38	m	w	ME	Tuolumne	Big Oak Flat P O	93	406
Geo	25	m	w	NY	Butte	Chico Twp	70	46
George	40	m	w	HDAR	San Francisco	San Francisco P O	83	257
Hannah	32	f	w	DC	San Francisco	San Francisco P O	83	144
Henry	42	m	w	CT	San Francisco	6-Wd San Francisco	81	121
Henry	37	m	w	OH	Contra Costa	Martinez P O	71	432
Henry C	22	m	w	MA	San Francisco	1-Wd San Francisco	79	65
Henry M	45	m	w	MA	San Francisco	8-Wd San Francisco	82	422
Horace	46	m	w	NH	Nevada	Nevada Twp	75	317
Horace P	45	m	w	NH	Contra Costa	Martinez P O	71	372
Hubbard	38	m	w	MA	San Francisco	San Francisco P O	83	420
J R	37	m	w	TN	Lake	Lower Lake	73	422
J W	36	m	w	OH	Nevada	Nevada Twp	75	307
James	40	m	w	IREL	San Francisco	7-Wd San Francisco	81	205
James C	37	m	w	TN	Merced	Snelling P O	74	254
James H	35	m	w	MD	San Francisco	6-Wd San Francisco	81	86
Jane F	49	f	w	MA	San Francisco	San Francisco P O	83	178
Jessee S	31	m	w	MO	Merced	Snelling P O	74	263
Jno B	30	m	w	ENGL	Sacramento	3-Wd Sacramento	77	303
John	43	m	w	AL	Tehama	Red Bluff	92	184
John	33	m	w	TN	Mariposa	Mariposa P O	74	124
John	23	m	w	OH	Kern	Linns Valley P O	73	349
John	20	m	w	MO	Solano	Denverton Twp	90	27
John B	57	m	w	TN	San Diego	San Diego	78	490
John B	35	m	w	ENGL	Sacramento	2-Wd Sacramento	77	246
John C	40	m	w	TN	Merced	Snelling P O	74	254
Joseph	37	m	w	ME	San Joaquin	2-Wd Stockton	86	203
Joseph	31	m	w	TN	Solano	Denverton Twp	90	26
Joseph P	36	m	w	IREL	San Francisco	8-Wd San Francisco	82	464
L	40	m	w	NH	Lake	Morgan Valley	73	424
Laura	25	f	w	OH	Solano	Montezuma Twp	90	65
Lester P	22	m	w	NY	Santa Barbara	San Buenaventura P	87	418
Lucinda	10	f	w	CA	Mendocino	Ukiah Twp	74	234
M A	32	m	w	LA	San Joaquin	Union Twp	86	265
Marion	40	m	w	TN	Napa	Yountville Twp	75	77
Mary B	33	f	w	IREL	Solano	Benicia	90	16
Mathew	43	m	w	CT	Sonoma	Healdsburg	91	275
Owen	32	m	w	MA	Nevada	Washington Twp	75	341
Reubin	67	m	w	TN	Merced	Snelling P O	74	254
Robert	35	m	w	NY	Los Angeles	Wilmington Twp	73	642
Rosanna	7	f	w	CA	Tulare	Tule Rvr Twp	92	266
Rose	7	f	w	CA	Santa Cruz	Santa Cruz	89	417
Samuel	40	m	w	ME	San Francisco	San Francisco P O	80	364
Samuel	40	m	w	NY	Amador	Volcano P O	69	377
Simeon	36	m	w	BAVA	Humboldt	Eureka Twp	72	281
Taylor	36	m	w	PA	Santa Clara	1-Wd San Jose	88	232
Thomas	48	m	w	NY	San Francisco	6-Wd San Francisco	81	80
Thomas	43	m	w	MA	Santa Cruz	Santa Cruz	89	407
Thomas	28	m	w	IREL	Sonoma	Analy Twp	91	226
Titus	36	m	w	MO	Santa Cruz	Soquel Twp	89	437
W	27	m	w	MA	Alameda	Oakland	68	263
W F	32	m	w	ME	San Francisco	San Francisco P O	83	312
W W	59	m	w	TN	Lake	Lower Lake	73	420
William	60	m	w	NY	San Francisco	San Francisco P O	80	419
William	39	m	w	OH	Contra Costa	Martinez P O	71	432
William	25	m	w	MA	San Francisco	1-Wd San Francisco	79	39
William J	38	m	w	PA	Mariposa	Mariposa P O	74	118
Wm	41	m	w	KY	El Dorado	Kelsey Twp	72	58
Wm J	34	m	w	MA	San Francisco	8-Wd San Francisco	82	365
HALEM								
William	43	m	w	AR	Shasta	Millville P O	89	484
HALEN								
Maria	7	f	w	CT	Sacramento	4-Wd Sacramento	77	348
HALER								
George	45	m	w	HAMB	Placer	Gold Run Twp	76	395
Lon	22	m	w	ME	San Joaquin	2-Wd Stockton	86	203
William	20	m	w	MO	San Francisco	San Francisco P O	83	159
HALEROW								
John	29	m	w	SCOT	Santa Cruz	Soquel Twp	89	437
HALES								
Bedford	36	m	w	KY	Monterey	Salinas Twp	74	311
Duncan	36	m	w	ENGL	Mendocino	Navarro & Big Rvr	74	176
HALEY								
Ann	36	f	w	IREL	San Francisco	7-Wd San Francisco	81	202
Ann	17	f	w	IREL	Solano	Vallejo	90	172
Anne	50	f	w	IREL	Monterey	San Juan Twp	74	398
Annie	18	f	w	MA	San Francisco	8-Wd San Francisco	82	387
Bridget	70	f	w	IREL	San Francisco	San Francisco P O	83	300
Bridget	26	f	w	IREL	Solano	Vallejo	90	204
Caleb S	37	m	w	CANA	Alameda	Washington Twp	68	273
Caroline	67	f	w	MD	Santa Clara	Milpitas Twp	88	115
Catherine	30	f	w	IREL	Sonoma	Sonoma Twp	91	439
Catherine	25	f	w	IREL	San Francisco	6-Wd San Francisco	81	132
Charles	4	m	w	CA	San Francisco	San Francisco P O	85	800

© 2001 by Heritage Quest. All rights reserved.

Name	Age	S	R	B-PL	County	Locale	Series M593 Roll	Pg
Charles	32	m	w	VT	San Francisco	11-Wd San Francisc	84	501
Charles	30	m	w	LA	Marin	San Rafael Twp	74	46
Charles	24	m	w	IREL	San Francisco	San Francisco P O	80	335
Charles	19	m	w	ME	Butte	Oroville Twp	70	138
Chas M	40	m	w	NY	San Francisco	5-Wd San Francisco	81	27
Chas M	30	m	w	NY	San Francisco	5-Wd San Francisco	81	27
Chas M	28	m	w	NY	San Francisco	5-Wd San Francisco	81	22
Chas M Mrs	25	f	w	NY	San Francisco	5-Wd San Francisco	81	27
Cornelius	22	m	w	IREL	Marin	San Rafael Twp	74	36
Daniel	24	m	w	NY	Contra Costa	San Pablo Twp	71	355
Daniel	13	m	w	CA	Santa Clara	San Jose Twp	88	194
Delp	64	m	w	FRAN	Trinity	Lewiston Pct	92	212
Dennis	40	m	w	IREL	San Francisco	San Francisco P O	80	379
Dennis	27	m	w	IREL	Marin	San Rafael	74	50
Dominick	21	f	w	IREL	Merced	Snelling P O	74	259
Dora	21	f	w	IREL	Solano	Maine Prairie Twp	90	52
Ebenezer	70	m	w	CANA	Alameda	Washington Twp	68	273
Ed	43	m	w	US	Humboldt	Eureka Twp	72	273
Edward	40	m	w	IREL	Santa Clara	San Jose Twp	88	192
Edward	30	m	w	IREL	Santa Clara	1-Wd San Jose	88	239
Edward	27	m	w	IREL	Napa	Napa	75	6
Elisha	27	m	w	CT	Humboldt	Pacific Twp	72	289
Eliza	25	f	w	NY	San Francisco	8-Wd San Francisco	82	345
Eliza	25	f	w	NY	San Francisco	8-Wd San Francisco	82	335
Elizabeth	16	f	w	NY	San Francisco	San Francisco P O	83	163
Elizabeth	13	f	w	IL	San Francisco	8-Wd San Francisco	82	462
Ellen	63	f	w	IREL	Santa Clara	2-Wd San Jose	88	303
F H	31	m	w	CT	Alameda	Murray Twp	68	113
Garner	39	m	w	VA	Placer	Auburn P O	76	380
George H	50	m	w	MI	Santa Clara	Santa Clara Twp	88	143
H W	42	m	w	MA	Lassen	Janesville Twp	73	433
Hanry	58	m	b	VA	Del Norte	Happy Camp Twp	71	472
Isaac M	39	m	w	ME	Yolo	Putah Twp	93	510
J M	67	m	w	ME	San Francisco	San Francisco P O	85	854
James	50	m	w	IREL	Sierra	Eureka Twp	89	523
James	50	m	w	IREL	Nevada	Eureka Twp	75	137
James	32	m	w	CANA	San Francisco	7-Wd San Francisco	81	267
James	25	m	w	ME	Sonoma	Salt Point	91	386
James	25	m	w	MA	San Francisco	7-Wd San Francisco	81	190
James	24	m	w	IREL	Sonoma	Santa Rosa	91	398
James F	30	m	w	CANA	San Francisco	San Francisco P O	83	221
James P	38	m	w	IREL	San Francisco	8-Wd San Francisco	82	405
Jas	36	m	w	IREL	Sacramento	1-Wd Sacramento	77	187
Jas	27	m	w	NY	Solano	Vallejo	90	160
Jas	26	m	w	IREL	Solano	Vallejo	90	200
Jeremiah	55	m	w	IREL	Nevada	Grass Valley Twp	75	175
Jeremiah	36	m	w	IREL	San Francisco	1-Wd San Francisco	79	36
Jeremiah	30	m	w	IREL	San Francisco	San Francisco P O	85	764
Jno J	55	m	w	NY	San Francisco	5-Wd San Francisco	81	25
John	8	m	w	NY	Alameda	Eden Twp	68	85
John	6	m	w	NY	San Francisco	5-Wd San Francisco	81	27
John	58	m	w	MD	Santa Clara	Milpitas Twp	88	113
John	57	m	w	IREL	Placer	Bath P O	76	446
John	48	m	w	IREL	Santa Clara	Alviso Twp	88	29
John	45	m	w	KY	Santa Clara	Santa Clara Twp	88	142
John	40	m	w	IREL	Nevada	Washington Twp	75	340
John	40	m	w	IREL	San Francisco	8-Wd San Francisco	82	419
John	40	m	w	IREL	San Francisco	San Francisco P O	83	69
John	35	m	w	IREL	Yolo	Cache Crk Twp	93	438
John	34	m	w	IREL	San Francisco	8-Wd San Francisco	82	319
John	28	m	w	IREL	San Francisco	11-Wd San Francisc	84	586
John	23	m	w	IREL	San Francisco	7-Wd San Francisco	81	199
John E	32	m	w	IA	Santa Clara	Milpitas Twp	88	113
Kate	30	f	w	IREL	San Francisco	7-Wd San Francisco	81	277
Lawrence	26	m	w	IREL	El Dorado	Georgetown Twp	72	40
Lucy	45	f	w	NY	San Francisco	5-Wd San Francisco	81	25
Margaret	20	f	w	IREL	San Francisco	8-Wd San Francisco	82	469
Margaret	18	f	w	ENGL	San Francisco	8-Wd San Francisco	82	471
Mark	25	m	w	IREL	San Francisco	San Francisco P O	83	70
Martin	43	m	w	IREL	Santa Clara	1-Wd San Jose	88	249
Martin	25	m	w	IREL	Santa Clara	Redwood Twp	88	127
Mary	80	f	w	IREL	San Francisco	7-Wd San Francisco	81	255
Mary	8	f	w	IREL	San Francisco	San Francisco P O	85	799
Mary	49	f	w	IREL	San Francisco	11-Wd San Francisc	84	574
Mary	30	f	w	IREL	San Francisco	San Francisco P O	83	148
Mary	30	f	w	ENGL	San Francisco	5-Wd San Francisco	81	33
Mary	30	f	w	ENGL	San Francisco	1-Wd San Francisco	79	97
Mary	25	f	w	IREL	San Francisco	7-Wd San Francisco	81	212
Mary	25	f	w	IREL	San Francisco	San Francisco P O	83	144
Mary	23	f	w	IREL	San Francisco	11-Wd San Francisc	84	445
Mary	22	f	w	IREL	Solano	Vallejo	90	188
Mary	19	f	w	IREL	San Francisco	11-Wd San Francisc	84	494
Mary	15	f	w	NY	San Francisco	5-Wd San Francisco	81	27
Mary	15	f	w	CT	San Francisco	8-Wd San Francisco	82	413
Maurice	29	m	w	IREL	San Francisco	San Francisco P O	83	239
Michael	60	m	w	IREL	San Francisco	San Francisco P O	83	193
Michael	40	m	w	IREL	Yolo	Putah Twp	93	517
Michael	34	m	w	IREL	San Francisco	San Francisco P O	83	299
Michl	28	m	w	IREL	San Francisco	1-Wd San Francisco	79	48
Morgan	40	m	w	IREL	San Francisco	San Francisco P O	83	146
Morris	37	m	w	IREL	Sacramento	3-Wd Sacramento	77	255
Nellie	18	f	w	IA	San Francisco	8-Wd San Francisco	82	352
Nicholas	35	m	w	IREL	Solano	Rio Vista Twp	90	60
Pat	40	m	w	IREL	Placer	Auburn P O	76	359
Pat	37	m	w	IREL	San Francisco	San Francisco P O	83	125
Pat	35	m	w	IREL	Alameda	Oakland	68	213
Pat	35	m	w	IREL	Alameda	Oakland	68	186
Pat	23	m	w	IREL	San Joaquin	3-Wd Stockton	86	217
Patrick	45	m	w	IREL	San Francisco	San Francisco P O	85	765
Patrick	40	m	w	IREL	Napa	Napa	75	18
Patrick	39	m	w	IREL	San Francisco	San Francisco P O	85	840
Patrick	37	m	w	IREL	Nevada	Grass Valley Twp	75	166
Patrick	36	m	w	IREL	Santa Clara	2-Wd San Jose	88	331
Patrick	35	m	w	IREL	Santa Clara	Milpitas Twp	88	111
Patrick	30	m	w	CANA	San Francisco	7-Wd San Francisco	81	177
Patrick	20	m	w	IREL	San Francisco	3-Wd San Francisco	79	315
Paul	10	m	m	CA	San Francisco	2-Wd San Francisco	79	249
Peter	23	m	w	IREL	San Francisco	5-Wd San Francisco	81	28
Richd	26	m	w	IREL	Santa Clara	Almaden Twp	88	9
Robbert	46	m	w	CANA	Alameda	Alameda	68	16
Robert	52	m	w	ME	San Francisco	2-Wd San Francisco	79	170
Salsbury	48	m	w	NH	Los Angeles	Los Angeles	73	523
Samuel	30	m	w	LA	San Francisco	San Francisco P O	80	458
Sarah	11	f	w	IL	San Francisco	San Francisco P O	85	827
Thomas	57	m	w	CANA	San Francisco	San Francisco P O	85	859
Thomas	44	m	w	IREL	Calaveras	San Andreas P O	70	163
Thomas	39	m	w	IREL	San Francisco	San Francisco P O	83	269
Thomas	33	m	w	IREL	San Francisco	San Francisco P O	85	773
Thomas	28	m	w	IREL	San Francisco	1-Wd San Francisco	79	65
Thomas	27	m	w	IREL	San Francisco	11-Wd San Francisc	84	433
Thomas	22	m	w	IREL	San Francisco	San Francisco P O	83	174
Thos H	19	m	w	NY	San Francisco	8-Wd San Francisco	82	365
Timothy	40	m	w	CANA	Klamath	Salmon Twp	73	388
W F	32	m	w	KY	Santa Clara	Gilroy Twp	88	70
W J	33	m	w	NH	Solano	Vallejo	90	162
William	50	m	w	MI	Santa Clara	Santa Clara Twp	88	170
William	42	m	w	IREL	Santa Clara	San Jose Twp	88	214
William	38	m	w	KY	San Luis Obispo	San Luis Obispo Tw	87	307
William	28	m	w	IREL	San Francisco	1-Wd San Francisco	79	44
Wm	44	m	w	IREL	San Francisco	San Francisco P O	85	762
Wm	42	m	w	IREL	San Francisco	San Francisco P O	85	764
Wm	36	m	w	IREL	San Francisco	1-Wd San Francisco	79	100
HALF								
Charles	38	m	w	FRAN	Tuolumne	Sonora P O	93	310
John	54	m	w	ENGL	Tuolumne	Sonora P O	93	313
HALFTERMYER								
Amand	58	m	w	FRAN	El Dorado	Placerville	72	118
HALI								
Wm J	47	m	w	TN	Calaveras	Copperopolis P O	70	235
HALIBURTON								
Swain	24	m	w	DENM	San Mateo	Half Moon Bay P O	87	407
HALILTON								
William	44	m	w	PA	Sonoma	Petaluma Twp	91	357
HALIN								
Hartly L	40	m	w	IREL	San Joaquin	2-Wd Stockton	86	196
HALING								
F	40	m	w	HANO	Nevada	Eureka Twp	75	135
William	21	m	w	IN	Nevada	Grass Valley Twp	75	185
HALION								
Thomas	36	m	w	IREL	Marin	Nicasio Twp	74	15
HALIY								
William	15	m	w	MD	San Francisco	11-Wd San Francisc	84	628
HALK								
Charles	36	m	w	PRUS	Tuolumne	Chinese Camp P O	93	383
Joseph	35	m	w	BADE	Calaveras	San Andreas P O	70	193
HALKUM								
Andrew	24	m	w	SWIT	Yolo	Fremont Twp	93	476
HALL								
---	22	m	w	NY	Sacramento	1-Wd Sacramento	77	182
A	45	m	w	NH	Siskiyou	Surprise Valley Tw	89	641
A	11	f	w	CA	Sacramento	3-Wd Sacramento	77	317
A B	13	f	w	CA	Alameda	Oakland	68	258
A J	38	m	w	MA	Yuba	Marysville Twp	93	568
A S	46	m	w	IL	Solano	Vallejo	90	143
Abraham	44	m	w	MA	San Francisco	San Francisco P O	85	722
Ada	32	f	w	ENGL	San Francisco	San Francisco P O	80	475
Adelia	24	f	w	KY	Alameda	Washington Twp	68	276
Adeline	44	f	w	OH	Butte	Ophir Twp	70	112
Agnes	61	f	w	VA	Del Norte	Crescent	71	462
Albert	38	m	w	IL	Monterey	Castroville Twp	74	338
Albert S	29	m	w	ME	Sonoma	Petaluma Twp	91	348
Albion P	33	m	w	ME	El Dorado	Placerville	72	110
Alexander	45	m	w	SCOT	Marin	Novato Twp	74	13
Alexander	40	m	w	SCOT	San Mateo	Belmont P O	87	374
Alma	9	f	w	MO	Tulare	Visalia Twp	92	285
Alvarado	24	m	w	ME	Sacramento	1-Wd Sacramento	77	178
Alvarado	22	m	w	ME	Sacramento	2-Wd Sacramento	77	236
Amelia	24	f	w	NY	San Francisco	San Francisco P O	83	212
Amelia	23	f	w	HCAS	San Francisco	San Francisco P O	83	275
Amelia	12	f	w	CA	Solano	Silveyville Twp	90	73
Amelia	11	f	w	CA	Solano	Silveyville Twp	90	88
Amos	31	m	w	OH	Mendocino	Point Arena Twp	74	209
Andrew	45	m	w	KY	Colusa	Butte Twp	71	268
Andrew	27	m	m	WIND	San Francisco	San Francisco P O	80	368
Andrew J	48	m	w	ME	Mendocino	Point Arena Twp	74	207
Andrew J	32	m	w	KY	Yolo	Cache Crk Twp	93	454
Angene	22	m	w	WI	San Francisco	San Francisco P O	85	738
Ann	25	f	w	SCOT	San Francisco	8-Wd San Francisco	82	317
Ann Mrs	53	f	w	US	Nevada	Grass Valley Twp	75	147
Arden E	37	m	w	MA	Santa Cruz	Santa Cruz	89	420
Atwell	35	m	w	ME	Alameda	Hayward	68	77
Barney	50	m	w	MA	Sonoma	Sonoma Twp	91	436
Benjamin	50	m	w	RI	San Francisco	San Francisco P O	83	176
C J	34	m	w	VT	Del Norte	Crescent	71	464

© 2001 by Heritage Quest. All rights reserved.

California 1870 Census

Name	Age	S	R	B-PL	County	Locale	Roll	Pg
						Series M593		
C S	25	m	w	KY	Napa	Napa Twp	75	61
Catharine	42	f	w	NY	Calaveras	Copperopolis P O	70	236
Catherine	57	f	w	IREL	San Francisco	8-Wd San Francisco	82	438
Catherine	45	f	w	NY	San Francisco	2-Wd San Francisco	79	204
Charles	53	m	w	MD	Marin	Bolinas Twp	74	1
Charles	43	m	w	KY	San Francisco	San Francisco P O	85	858
Charles	34	m	w	MO	Solano	Vacaville Twp	90	135
Charles	29	m	w	MD	San Francisco	San Francisco P O	80	538
Charles	13	m	w	CA	Santa Barbara	Santa Barbara P O	87	456
Charles F	25	m	w	MI	Placer	Rocklin Twp	76	465
Charles G	18	m	w	ME	San Francisco	3-Wd San Francisco	79	303
Charles H	46	m	w	MA	Santa Cruz	Soquel Twp	89	442
Charles H	26	m	w	MO	Sonoma	Petaluma Twp	91	334
Charles T	26	m	w	RI	Sonoma	Analy Twp	91	224
Charlotte	43	f	w	ENGL	San Francisco	2-Wd San Francisco	79	168
Chas	45	m	w	TN	Sonoma	Santa Rosa	91	402
Chas	22	m	w	OR	Sacramento	3-Wd Sacramento	77	300
Chas C	50	m	w	NY	Solano	Vallejo	90	147
Chas E	38	m	w	VA	San Francisco	San Francisco P O	83	131
Chas F	36	m	w	NH	San Francisco	San Francisco P O	83	339
Chase	10	m	m	CA	San Joaquin	1-Wd Stockton	86	136
Christiana	33	f	b	PA	San Francisco	San Francisco P O	80	393
Daniel	40	m	w	ME	San Francisco	11-Wd San Francisc	84	543
Daniel R	36	m	w	NY	Sonoma	Analy Twp	91	231
Daniel T	45	m	w	NY	El Dorado	Mud Springs Twp	72	84
David	48	m	w	MO	Trinity	Trinity Center Pct	92	205
David	40	m	w	MA	San Francisco	8-Wd San Francisco	82	297
David	36	m	w	OH	Solano	Vacaville Twp	90	124
David	34	m	w	PA	Amador	Sutter Crk P O	69	398
David C	48	m	w	VT	San Francisco	San Francisco P O	85	764
David F	42	m	w	RI	Los Angeles	San Gabriel Twp	73	593
David W	53	m	w	NY	Sonoma	Cloverdale Twp	91	270
Davis Clark	33	m	w	ME	Plumas	Washington Twp	77	56
Dean	22	m	w	IL	San Mateo	Schoolhouse Statio	87	339
Debora	40	f	w	PA	San Joaquin	Oneal Twp	86	99
Demon J	26	m	w	ENGL	Sierra	Sears Twp	89	554
E	32	m	w	WALE	Sierra	Lincoln Twp	89	551
E H	42	m	w	ME	Siskiyou	Callahan P O	89	628
E M	43	m	w	PA	Alameda	Oakland	68	157
E O	34	m	w	ME	Tuolumne	Columbia P O	93	344
E S	61	m	w	CT	Amador	Jackson P O	69	339
E S	23	m	w	NY	San Joaquin	3-Wd Stockton	86	229
Ed G	44	m	w	OH	Fresno	Millerton P O	72	191
Edmond	25	m	w	NJ	San Francisco	5-Wd San Francisco	81	27
Edward	45	m	w	KY	Kern	Tehachapi P O	73	355
Edward	41	m	w	MA	San Joaquin	Oneal Twp	86	119
Edward	38	m	w	NY	Klamath	Trinidad Twp	73	389
Edward	34	m	w	CT	Alameda	Brooklyn	68	31
Edward	33	m	w	NJ	Stanislaus	Branch Twp	92	2
Edward	28	m	w	ME	San Francisco	8-Wd San Francisco	82	463
Edward	26	m	w	AUSL	San Francisco	7-Wd San Francisco	81	166
Edward B	35	m	w	MA	San Francisco	San Francisco P O	85	729
Edward Dickenson	33	m	w	PA	Plumas	Indian Twp	77	16
Edward E	53	m	w	ENGL	San Francisco	11-Wd San Francisc	84	712
Edward F	31	m	w	MA	San Mateo	San Mateo P O	87	350
Edward G	38	m	w	KY	Yolo	Cache Crk Twp	93	432
Edwin	32	m	w	IREL	San Francisco	7-Wd San Francisco	81	205
Eldridge	29	m	w	NY	San Francisco	San Francisco P O	80	539
Eliza	67	f	w	MA	San Francisco	San Francisco P O	85	714
Eliza	52	f	w	VA	Del Norte	Crescent	71	464
Eliza Jane	45	f	w	NY	Los Angeles	Los Angeles Twp	73	488
Elizabeth	54	f	w	ENGL	San Francisco	11-Wd San Francisc	84	707
Elizabeth M	26	f	w	AUSL	Colusa	Grand Island Twp	71	302
Ellman G	34	m	w	MD	San Francisco	8-Wd San Francisco	82	384
Elmore G	34	m	w	MD	Inyo	Independence Twp	73	325
Emily	59	f	m	KY	Shasta	Shasta P O	89	461
Emma	8	f	w	CA	Mendocino	Ukiah Twp	74	234
Emma	25	f	w	ENGL	Alameda	Oakland	68	246
En	2	f	w	CA	Sacramento	3-Wd Sacramento	77	313
Enma	13	f	w	CA	San Francisco	11-Wd San Francisc	84	664
Ennis	37	m	w	NY	Contra Costa	Martinez P O	71	367
Ethota	55	f	m	NC	San Francisco	San Francisco P O	80	364
Ezra	46	m	w	PA	Butte	Chico Twp	70	15
F A	22	m	w	MA	Solano	Vallejo	90	164
F B	34	m	w	ME	San Joaquin	Dent Twp	86	21
F C	66	m	w	CT	Amador	Ione City P O	69	351
F D	41	m	w	VT	Monterey	Castroville Twp	74	330
F E	21	m	w	IA	El Dorado	Greenwood Twp	72	55
F J	46	m	w	VT	Merced	Snelling P O	74	263
Fletcher	50	m	w	IL	Mendocino	Calpella Twp	74	184
Francis	60	f	w	IREL	San Francisco	7-Wd San Francisco	81	185
Francis	24	m	w	ENGL	Yuba	Rose Bar Twp	93	663
Frank	32	m	w	ME	Alameda	Oakland	68	189
Frank	29	m	w	OH	Solano	Tremont Twp	90	29
Frank	16	m	w	NY	San Francisco	San Francisco P O	83	197
Frank	15	m	w	CA	Alameda	Oakland	68	257
Frank	14	m	w	CA	Sonoma	Santa Rosa	91	402
Franklin	30	m	w	NY	Solano	Tremont Twp	90	28
Franklin	28	m	w	LA	Yolo	Buckeye Twp	93	412
Franklin B	39	m	w	NY	San Mateo	Half Moon Bay P O	87	403
Fred	50	m	w	IREL	San Francisco	11-Wd San Francisc	84	642
Fred	30	m	w	PA	San Mateo	Belmont P O	87	372
Fred G	46	m	w	ME	Tulare	Visalia	92	293
Fred S	20	m	w	ME	Napa	Napa Twp	75	73
Frederick	39	m	w	VT	Santa Clara	2-Wd San Jose	88	330
Fredrick	28	m	w	ME	San Francisco	7-Wd San Francisco	81	208
G	50	m	w	PA	Lake	Knoxville Mines	73	404
G C	37	m	w	OH	Sacramento	4-Wd Sacramento	77	350
Geo	20	m	w	IA	Sacramento	Sutter Twp	77	392
Geo A	42	m	w	NY	Santa Barbara	San Buenaventura P	87	430
Geo E	40	m	w	ME	San Francisco	San Francisco P O	83	276
Georg H	19	m	w	MO	Tulare	Visalia Twp	92	281
George	65	m	w	IREL	Solano	Suisun Twp	90	115
George	52	m	w	VA	Calaveras	San Andreas P O	70	206
George	44	m	w	IREL	Placer	Bath P O	76	430
George	42	m	w	OH	Fresno	Kingston P O	72	220
George	40	m	w	NC	Tulare	Visalia Twp	92	285
George	40	m	w	ME	San Francisco	San Francisco P O	83	386
George	36	m	w	IL	Yolo	Merritt Twp	93	503
George	33	m	w	MI	Santa Clara	2-Wd San Jose	88	298
George	32	m	w	ENGL	Sacramento	Georgianna Twp	77	128
George	32	m	w	NY	San Francisco	2-Wd San Francisco	79	204
George	32	m	w	AUSL	Colusa	Grand Island Twp	71	302
George	28	m	w	CANA	Tulare	Tule Rvr Twp	92	270
George	25	m	w	OH	Los Angeles	Wilmington Twp	73	642
George	25	m	w	CANA	Klamath	Trinidad Twp	73	392
George	21	m	w	VT	Colusa	Colusa	71	298
George L	39	m	w	ENGL	Yuba	North East Twp	93	646
George S	32	m	w	WI	San Francisco	6-Wd San Francisco	81	80
George W	49	m	w	OH	Colusa	Grand Island Twp	71	303
George W	41	m	w	MA	Solano	Green Valley Twp	90	44
George W	39	m	w	OH	Solano	Montezuma Twp	90	68
George W	30	m	w	IREL	Colusa	Colusa Twp	71	279
George W	28	m	w	TN	Santa Clara	Fremont Twp	88	61
H C	35	m	w	MA	Solano	Vallejo	90	176
H E	44	m	w	NY	San Joaquin	2-Wd Stockton	86	197
H F	37	m	w	CA	Amador	Ione City P O	69	351
H J	45	m	w	CT	Amador	Sutter Crk P O	69	410
Hannah	55	f	b	MA	Alameda	Oakland	68	180
Harris	35	m	w	OH	Solano	Tremont Twp	90	29
Harry	34	m	w	NY	Nevada	Meadow Lake Twp	75	263
Harry	27	m	w	NH	Sacramento	4-Wd Sacramento	77	375
Harvey	40	m	w	ME	San Francisco	11-Wd San Francisc	84	623
Helen	27	f	w	ME	San Francisco	6-Wd San Francisco	81	148
Henry	60	m	m	KY	Placer	Colfax P O	76	384
Henry	57	m	w	RI	Sonoma	Analy Twp	91	224
Henry	45	m	w	CT	Sonoma	Petaluma Twp	91	321
Henry	45	m	w	IREL	San Francisco	San Francisco P O	83	106
Henry	37	m	w	SCOT	Solano	Vallejo	90	201
Henry	37	m	m	TX	Mariposa	Mariposa P O	74	110
Henry	35	m	w	IREL	El Dorado	Mud Springs Twp	72	81
Henry	28	m	w	SC	San Francisco	8-Wd San Francisco	82	388
Henry	21	m	w	TX	Butte	Chico Twp	70	14
Henry	21	m	w	NY	Yolo	Cache Crk Twp	93	450
Henry	20	m	w	MO	Santa Clara	San Jose Twp	88	211
Henry	17	m	w	LA	San Francisco	San Francisco P O	83	417
Henry F	35	m	w	NH	Placer	Gold Run Twp	76	397
Horace B	32	m	w	ME	San Francisco	San Francisco P O	83	345
Horace R	59	m	w	NY	Santa Clara	San Jose Twp	88	182
Hurbert E	25	m	w	NY	San Joaquin	3-Wd Stockton	86	229
Ira	24	m	w	VT	Marin	San Rafael Twp	74	38
Isaac	50	m	w	MA	Solano	Vallejo	90	180
Isaac	45	m	w	ENGL	El Dorado	Georgetown Twp	72	38
Isaac	44	m	w	PA	Sacramento	4-Wd Sacramento	77	349
Isaac	40	m	w	ME	Sacramento	2-Wd Sacramento	77	226
Isaac	40	m	w	NY	Plumas	Indian Twp	77	10
Isaac M	60	m	w	VT	San Francisco	8-Wd San Francisco	82	468
Isaac R	35	m	w	NY	Solano	Maine Prairie Twp	90	53
Iver X	38	m	w	SWED	Colusa	Butte Twp	71	267
J	26	m	w	TN	Lake	Lower Lake	73	429
J A	38	m	w	NY	Solano	Vallejo	90	140
J A	32	m	w	VT	Alameda	Oakland	68	221
J B	50	m	w	MD	San Joaquin	2-Wd Stockton	86	184
J C	37	m	w	BAVA	Solano	Vallejo	90	179
J D	47	m	w	NY	Tehama	Paskenta Twp	92	165
J D	32	m	w	TN	Amador	Jackson P O	69	340
J J	38	m	w	MO	Del Norte	Smith Rvr Twp	71	479
J K	55	m	w	ME	Napa	Napa	75	10
J P	34	m	w	WI	San Joaquin	Douglas Twp	86	40
J Q	38	m	w	NC	Solano	Vallejo	90	189
J W	68	m	w	ENGL	Solano	Vallejo	90	193
J W	28	m	w	KY	Sonoma	Santa Rosa	91	397
J W	25	m	w	NY	Alameda	Oakland	68	264
Jabez C	43	m	w	KY	Amador	Drytown P O	69	418
Jacob	39	m	w	BAVA	Mendocino	Little Lake Twp	74	202
Jacob	33	m	w	PRUS	San Francisco	5-Wd San Francisco	81	9
James	48	m	w	CT	Sacramento	2-Wd Sacramento	77	243
James	46	m	w	ENGL	Placer	Rocklin Twp	76	468
James	44	m	w	CANA	Shasta	Shasta P O	89	457
James	43	m	w	PA	Amador	Volcano P O	69	374
James	40	m	w	IREL	San Francisco	San Francisco P O	85	767
James	37	m	w	ENGL	Yolo	Washington Twp	93	528
James	36	m	w	PA	San Mateo	Half Moon Bay P O	87	394
James	35	m	w	VA	Mendocino	Cuffeys Cove Twp	74	169
James	34	m	w	IREL	San Francisco	11-Wd San Francisc	84	615
James	30	m	w	MO	Siskiyou	Big Valley Twp	89	580
James	27	m	w	VA	San Francisco	11-Wd San Francisc	84	612
James	27	m	w	IREL	San Francisco	7-Wd San Francisco	81	157
James	22	m	w	TX	Kern	Tehachapi P O	73	355
James	13	m	w	CA	San Francisco	11-Wd San Francisc	84	593
James B	27	m	w	VA	Tulare	Farmersville Twp	92	245
James D	28	m	w	IN	Tulare	Visalia	92	292
James H	61	m	w	DE	Sonoma	Petaluma Twp	91	343
James H	40	m	w	IL	Del Norte	Smith Rvr Twp	71	478

© 2001 by Heritage Quest. All rights reserved.

Series M593

Name	Age	S	R	B-PL	County	Locale	Roll	Pg
James H	26	m	w	NY	San Francisco	San Francisco P O	85	737
James L	41	m	w	NJ	Yuba	Long Bar Twp	93	563
James Neal	54	m	w	ME	Plumas	Goodwin Twp	77	2
Jane	40	f	w	PA	Placer	Colfax P O	76	389
Jane A	46	f	w	NC	San Francisco	8-Wd San Francisco	82	459
Jane R	34	f	w	ME	Sacramento	3-Wd Sacramento	77	281
Jas	35	m	w	IREL	Solano	Vallejo	90	152
Jefferson	32	m	w	ENGL	Monterey	San Antonio Twp	74	321
Jno	68	m	w	OH	Butte	Oregon Twp	70	134
Jno S	63	m	w	ENGL	Santa Clara	Gilroy Twp	88	68
Jobe	21	m	w	MO	Alameda	Washington Twp	68	289
John	65	m	w	KY	Butte	Ophir Twp	70	120
John	55	m	w	ENGL	San Francisco	San Francisco P O	83	274
John	54	m	w	VA	Sacramento	Cosumnes Twp	77	90
John	48	m	w	OH	Alameda	Washington Twp	68	268
John	45	m	w	MA	Humboldt	Eureka Twp	72	273
John	44	m	w	ENGL	Sacramento	4-Wd Sacramento	77	355
John	43	m	w	SCOT	Placer	Bath P O	76	452
John	42	m	w	ENGL	Tuolumne	Sonora P O	93	320
John	40	m	w	IREL	Humboldt	Eureka Twp	72	279
John	40	m	w	LA	Tuolumne	Sonora P O	93	305
John	38	m	w	IREL	Marin	San Rafael Twp	74	25
John	38	m	w	ME	Plumas	Quartz Twp	77	42
John	35	m	w	NY	San Francisco	6-Wd San Francisco	81	79
John	33	m	w	AR	Colusa	Butte Twp	71	271
John	31	m	w	MO	Napa	Napa	75	25
John	31	m	w	ENGL	Santa Clara	Burnett Twp	88	32
John	30	m	w	CANA	Contra Costa	Martinez P O	71	369
John	30	m	b	MO	Los Angeles	Los Angeles	73	543
John	30	m	w	ENGL	San Francisco	San Francisco P O	83	335
John	28	m	w	IL	San Joaquin	Douglas Twp	86	46
John	28	m	w	CANA	San Francisco	San Francisco P O	83	188
John	27	m	b	NY	San Francisco	San Francisco P O	80	485
John	26	m	w	NY	San Francisco	7-Wd San Francisco	81	179
John	24	m	w	IREL	San Francisco	6-Wd San Francisco	81	86
John	23	m	w	NY	Trinity	Weaverville Pct	92	223
John	16	m	w	IN	Del Norte	Smith Rvr Twp	71	479
John D	33	m	w	TN	Amador	Volcano P O	69	387
John E C	39	m	w	IN	Nevada	Nevada Twp	75	307
John F	45	m	w	MO	El Dorado	Placerville	72	118
John F	32	m	w	CANA	Plumas	Plumas Twp	77	27
John L	27	m	w	MA	San Francisco	San Francisco P O	83	176
John P	18	m	m	FL	Trinity	Weaverville Pct	92	225
John T	60	m	w	NH	Yolo	Fremont Twp	93	476
John W	16	m	w	CA	Nevada	Nevada Twp	75	306
Jon	16	m	w	CA	Yuba	Rose Bar Twp	93	664
Jonathan	46	m	w	NH	Calaveras	San Andreas P O	70	164
Jos W	56	m	w	NY	Butte	Concow Twp	70	6
Joseph	63	m	w	SC	Contra Costa	Martinez P O	71	443
Joseph	58	m	w	ME	San Francisco	San Francisco P O	83	86
Joseph	21	m	w	OH	Siskiyou	Butte Twp	89	585
Joseph	13	m	w	IN	Del Norte	Crescent Twp	71	456
Joseph F	57	m	w	MA	San Francisco	6-Wd San Francisco	81	152
Joseph H	63	m	w	NY	Yolo	Cache Crk Twp	93	437
Joseph W	48	m	w	NY	Sacramento	Dry Crk Twp	77	99
Joseph W	40	m	w	ENGL	Solano	Rio Vista Twp	90	56
Joshua A	50	m	w	VA	San Mateo	Belmont P O	87	372
Joshua R	42	m	w	IL	Santa Clara	2-Wd San Jose	88	279
Josiah	54	m	w	ENGL	Tuolumne	Sonora P O	93	309
Kate	5M	f	w	CA	San Francisco	7-Wd San Francisco	81	255
Kate	22	f	w	IREL	San Francisco	San Francisco P O	83	99
Kate	22	f	w	NY	San Francisco	San Francisco P O	83	157
L B	49	m	w	KY	Sonoma	Santa Rosa	91	397
L M	58	m	w	MA	Mendocino	Little Lake Twp	74	200
L P	49	m	w	KY	Sacramento	1-Wd Sacramento	77	183
Lester E	26	m	w	OH	Placer	Alta P O	76	412
Levy	53	m	w	PA	Butte	Chico Twp	70	15
Lewis	44	m	w	TN	Mendocino	Calpella Twp	74	186
Libby	26	f	w	NY	San Francisco	8-Wd San Francisco	82	391
Lienallen J	44	m	w	MO	Sonoma	Washington Twp	91	467
Louis	23	m	w	NH	San Francisco	San Francisco P O	85	815
Louisa	28	f	w	MA	San Francisco	6-Wd San Francisco	81	129
Lucinda	20	f	w	LA	Santa Barbara	San Buenaventura P	87	426
Lucy A	25	f	m	MO	Del Norte	Smith Rvr Twp	71	479
Luther	34	m	w	PA	Contra Costa	Martinez P O	71	433
M H	51	m	w	VA	Merced	Snelling P O	74	265
M J	37	m	w	ME	San Joaquin	Oneal Twp	86	99
Maggie	18	f	w	IREL	San Francisco	San Francisco P O	83	363
Marcos	22	m	w	MA	San Francisco	6-Wd San Francisco	81	95
Margaret	45	f	w	NY	San Francisco	2-Wd San Francisco	79	267
Martha E	15	f	w	UT	El Dorado	Placerville	72	118
Martin	50	m	w	NH	San Francisco	San Francisco P O	83	339
Martin	28	m	w	NY	Solano	Tremont Twp	90	28
Martin V	34	m	w	NY	Sonoma	Cloverdale Twp	91	268
Mary	25	f	w	IREL	San Francisco	8-Wd San Francisco	82	442
Mary	24	f	w	MA	San Francisco	6-Wd San Francisco	81	79
Mary	14	f	w	CA	Solano	Benicia	90	17
Mary F	28	f	w	NY	Marin	San Rafael	74	48
Matie	25	f	w	OH	Sacramento	4-Wd Sacramento	77	350
Maud M	11	f	w	IL	Yolo	Grafton Twp	93	485
Micheal	30	m	w	IREL	San Francisco	7-Wd San Francisco	81	186
Milton	62	m	w	RI	Mariposa	Maxwell Crk P O	74	141
Minnie	3	f	w	CA	San Francisco	5-Wd San Francisco	81	4
Miriam W	41	m	w	TN	Calaveras	Copperopolis P O	70	245
Morman H	24	m	w	NY	San Francisco	San Francisco P O	83	49
Moses	35	m	w	OH	Kern	Tehachapi P O	73	353
Moses Andrew	37	m	w	KY	Plumas	Washington Twp	77	52
Myron W	39	m	w	PA	Contra Costa	Martinez P O	71	377
N	45	m	w	VA	Sutter	Vernon Twp	92	131
Nathan	41	m	w	NY	Santa Clara	Fremont Twp	88	64
Nellie D	32	f	w	VT	Contra Costa	Martinez P O	71	377
Newell	50	m	w	VT	Butte	Chico Twp	70	21
Nicholas C	38	m	w	GERM	Nevada	Grass Valley Twp	75	174
Oretas K	38	m	w	OH	Butte	Chico Twp	70	13
Patrick	38	m	w	IREL	Nevada	Grass Valley Twp	75	192
Peter	16	m	w	CA	Tehama	Antelope Twp	92	160
Pierne	64	m	w	NY	Butte	Chico Twp	70	40
R	42	m	w	VA	El Dorado	Greenwood Twp	72	55
R B	49	m	w	SCOT	Alameda	Oakland	68	157
R B	45	m	w	IN	Sacramento	Franklin Twp	77	112
R M	36	m	w	TN	Sonoma	Santa Rosa	91	419
R R	62	m	w	ENGL	Santa Clara	Gilroy Twp	88	79
Reuben B	42	m	w	VA	Stanislaus	Empire Twp	92	59
Rich M	47	m	w	NH	Tehama	Red Bluff	92	183
Richard	53	m	w	IREL	Solano	Silveyville Twp	90	73
Richard	46	m	w	VA	Monterey	Pajaro Twp	74	371
Richard	45	m	w	IREL	Santa Clara	Fremont Twp	88	58
Richard	34	m	w	KY	Contra Costa	Martinez P O	71	399
Richard	32	m	w	RI	Contra Costa	Martinez P O	71	416
Richard	30	m	w	IREL	Amador	Jackson P O	69	328
Richard B	61	m	w	NY	Alameda	Washington Twp	68	276
Richard B	50	m	w	NY	Santa Clara	1-Wd San Jose	88	246
Richard H	46	m	w	MA	Santa Cruz	Santa Cruz Twp	89	397
Robert	52	m	w	SCOT	San Francisco	San Francisco P O	83	188
Robert	44	m	w	ENGL	Alameda	Brooklyn	68	25
Robert	37	m	w	ME	San Francisco	San Francisco P O	83	354
Robert	35	m	w	NY	San Francisco	11-Wd San Francisc	84	529
Robert	32	m	b	DE	San Francisco	1-Wd San Francisco	79	96
Robert	30	m	w	FRAN	Santa Clara	Fremont Twp	88	44
Robert	29	m	w	ENGL	Santa Clara	1-Wd San Jose	88	236
Robt	31	m	w	NY	Sierra	Sears Twp	89	555
Robt	21	m	w	ENGL	Solano	Vallejo	90	201
Roderick	63	m	w	CT	Placer	Bath P O	76	433
Rosa	85	f	w	CT	San Francisco	8-Wd San Francisco	82	444
Rowland	64	m	w	NY	Napa	Napa	75	12
Rufus	48	m	w	VA	Sutter	Vernon Twp	92	131
Rufus L	35	m	w	TN	Sonoma	Santa Rosa	91	426
S H	27	m	w	ENGL	San Francisco	San Francisco P O	85	805
S J	40	f	w	OH	Sacramento	3-Wd Sacramento	77	257
Salina	19	f	w	IREL	San Francisco	San Francisco P O	83	217
Saml	22	m	b	MD	San Francisco	1-Wd San Francisco	79	96
Saml A	54	m	w	MA	Santa Cruz	Soquel Twp	89	440
Saml M	40	m	w	MD	San Francisco	San Francisco P O	85	729
Samuel	62	m	w	TN	Santa Clara	Fremont Twp	88	46
Samuel	57	m	w	ENGL	Sonoma	Petaluma Twp	91	332
Samuel	47	m	w	PA	Inyo	Bishop Crk Twp	73	316
Samuel	45	m	w	PA	Tehama	Tehama Twp	92	196
Samuel	45	m	w	PA	Inyo	Bishop Crk Twp	73	313
Samuel	40	m	w	OH	Sacramento	Natomas Twp	77	165
Samuel	37	m	w	MO	San Mateo	Searsville P O	87	382
Samuel	19	m	w	IN	Del Norte	Smith Rvr Twp	71	477
Samuel B	45	m	w	VA	Mendocino	Albion & Big Rvr T	74	167
Sarah	70	f	w	ENGL	Solano	Vallejo	90	193
Sarah	58	f	w	NY	Sacramento	Dry Crk Twp	77	101
Sarah	47	f	w	LA	San Diego	Milquaty Dist	78	478
Sarah L	37	f	m	NY	San Francisco	6-Wd San Francisco	81	135
Solomon	43	m	w	ME	Klamath	Trinidad Twp	73	389
Stephen	36	m	w	WALE	Contra Costa	Martinez P O	71	427
T H	35	m	w	VT	San Francisco	8-Wd San Francisco	82	358
T W	33	m	w	ENGL	Solano	Vallejo	90	193
Taylor	36	m	w	PA	Placer	Auburn P O	76	370
Thomas	64	m	w	MD	Los Angeles	Los Angeles Twp	73	493
Thomas	55	m	w	ENGL	San Francisco	11-Wd San Francisc	84	633
Thomas	47	m	w	ENGL	San Francisco	San Francisco P O	83	394
Thomas	41	m	w	NY	Yolo	Cottonwood Twp	93	468
Thomas	37	m	w	IREL	San Luis Obispo	Morro Twp	87	287
Thomas	30	m	w	ENGL	San Francisco	San Francisco P O	83	172
Thomas	24	m	w	CANA	San Francisco	San Francisco P O	83	318
Thomas	18	m	w	GA	Marin	San Rafael Twp	74	45
Thos	27	m	w	IREL	San Francisco	7-Wd San Francisco	81	247
Thos	24	m	w	IL	Sacramento	3-Wd Sacramento	77	316
Thos J	51	m	w	KY	Sonoma	Mendocino Twp	91	288
Thos J	38	m	w	IN	Fresno	Millerton P O	72	193
Timothy	35	m	w	ME	Shasta	Shasta P O	89	456
W A	14	m	w	CA	Alameda	Oakland	68	243
W G	39	m	w	MO	Tehama	Battle Crk Twp	92	157
W H	27	m	w	ME	Lassen	Janesville Twp	73	435
W P	35	m	w	ME	Lassen	Janesville Twp	73	434
W R	37	m	w	WI	San Joaquin	Dent Twp	86	27
Warren	13	m	w	CA	Colusa	Butte Twp	71	268
Wesley	52	m	w	TN	Plumas	Plumas Twp	77	27
Wilhelmina	35	f	w	SWED	San Francisco	8-Wd San Francisco	82	494
Willerd L	37	m	w	ME	Yuba	North East Twp	93	644
William	75	m	w	IREL	Tulare	Venice Twp	92	279
William	70	m	w	KY	Sonoma	Washington Twp	91	468
William	60	m	w	NY	Solano	Suisun Twp	90	103
William	55	m	w	NY	Sonoma	Mendocino Twp	91	304
William	48	m	w	IREL	San Francisco	11-Wd San Francisc	84	576
William	43	m	w	NY	Colusa	Grand Island Twp	71	303
William	40	m	w	IREL	Contra Costa	San Pablo Twp	71	354
William	39	m	w	MO	Trinity	Trinity Center Pct	92	204
William	38	m	w	NY	Santa Cruz	Soquel Twp	89	446
William	37	m	w	TN	Alameda	Eden Twp	68	66
William	36	m	w	MD	San Francisco	San Francisco P O	80	484

© 2001 by Heritage Quest. All rights reserved.

California 1870 Census

Series M593

Name	Age	S	R	B-PL	County	Locale	Roll	Pg
William	36	m	w	MO	Kern	Tehachapi P O	73	356
William	35	m	w	IREL	San Luis Obispo	Morro Twp	87	287
William	26	m	w	NY	San Francisco	5-Wd San Francisco	81	33
William	25	m	w	CANA	San Francisco	San Francisco P O	83	188
William	23	m	b	TN	San Francisco	8-Wd San Francisco	82	355
William	21	m	w	IN	Calaveras	San Andreas P O	70	200
William A	23	m	w	MO	Tulare	Visalia Twp	92	284
William G	59	m	w	NC	Santa Clara	1-Wd San Jose	88	264
William G	34	m	w	VA	San Mateo	San Mateo P O	87	354
William H	50	m	w	NY	Los Angeles	Wilmington Twp	73	643
William H	50	m	w	NY	Los Angeles	Los Angeles	73	571
William H	47	m	w	NY	Santa Clara	2-Wd San Jose	88	300
William H	47	m	b	DC	San Francisco	6-Wd San Francisco	81	135
William J	27	m	w	IL	El Dorado	White Oak Twp	72	142
William S	55	m	w	ME	Santa Clara	Redwood Twp	88	130
William W	46	m	w	NY	San Mateo	Belmont P O	87	371
Wilson	27	m	w	NH	San Francisco	San Francisco P O	80	456
Winslow	47	m	w	NY	Mendocino	Anderson Twp	74	157
Winslow	45	m	w	NY	San Francisco	8-Wd San Francisco	82	311
Wm	66	m	w	GA	San Joaquin	Douglas Twp	86	46
Wm	45	m	w	NY	San Francisco	11-Wd San Francisc	84	692
Wm	43	m	w	OH	El Dorado	Georgetown Twp	72	41
Wm	41	m	w	SC	San Joaquin	2-Wd Stockton	86	197
Wm	36	m	w	IREL	San Francisco	11-Wd San Francisc	84	615
Wm	35	m	w	MA	Alameda	Oakland	68	169
Wm	29	m	w	IL	Sacramento	3-Wd Sacramento	77	316
Wm	28	m	w	CA	Fresno	Millerton P O	72	158
Wm	24	m	w	SCOT	San Francisco	7-Wd San Francisco	81	236
Wm	18	m	w	IREL	San Joaquin	Tulare Twp	86	255
Wm H	24	m	w	NY	San Francisco	8-Wd San Francisco	82	371
Wm Henry	37	m	w	NY	Napa	Napa	75	57
Wm Henry	21	m	w	MO	Sonoma	Washington Twp	91	468
Wm P	31	m	w	CT	Sonoma	Analy Twp	91	225
Wm S	28	m	w	IL	Sonoma	Bodega Twp	91	256
Wm W	26	m	w	NY	San Francisco	8-Wd San Francisco	82	359
HALLADAY								
Frank	22	m	w	SPAI	San Francisco	3-Wd San Francisco	79	317
Levi	36	m	w	CANA	San Bernardino	San Bernardino Twp	78	430
HALLAGAN								
Mary C	36	f	w	NY	Placer	Bath P O	76	439
HALLAHAN								
Florence	34	m	w	IREL	Santa Cruz	Santa Cruz	89	407
O	45	m	w	IREL	Alameda	Oakland	68	260
Pat	31	m	w	IREL	Sacramento	1-Wd Sacramento	77	204
Rosa	25	f	w	IREL	Sacramento	1-Wd Sacramento	77	204
Thomas	37	m	w	IREL	San Francisco	San Francisco P O	83	378
HALLAM								
Labeaux	50	m	w	WIND	Calaveras	San Andreas P O	70	190
Mary	35	f	w	IREL	San Francisco	San Francisco P O	83	146
Wm	38	m	w	NORW	San Francisco	1-Wd San Francisco	79	74
HALLAND								
Richd	35	m	w	ENGL	Santa Clara	Burnett Twp	88	36
HALLARAN								
Danl	40	m	w	IREL	Humboldt	Eureka Twp	72	277
Danl	38	m	w	IREL	Humboldt	Eureka Twp	72	277
Danl	31	m	w	IREL	Humboldt	Eureka Twp	72	271
Dennis	33	m	w	IREL	Humboldt	Eureka Twp	72	271
HALLBECK								
Theo	38	m	w	SWED	San Francisco	11-Wd San Francisc	84	472
HALLECK								
C L	20	m	w	MI	Tehama	Tehama Twp	92	156
Chas	38	m	w	GERM	Tuolumne	Sonora P O	93	308
Henry	35	m	w	MO	Nevada	Grass Valley Twp	75	229
Joseph	29	m	w	PRUS	Nevada	Grass Valley Twp	75	144
HALLEGAN								
Hugh	34	m	w	IA	Nevada	Washington Twp	75	346
HALLEGH								
Mary A	39	f	w	OH	San Joaquin	Elkhorn Twp	86	62
HALLEM								
John Jackson	45	m	w	PA	Plumas	Seneca Twp	77	49
HALLEN								
---	31	m	c	CHIN	Amador	Ione City P O	69	349
Frederick	29	m	w	SWED	Mendocino	Point Arena Twp	74	208
Geo	32	m	w	NY	Yuba	Marysville	93	604
John	24	m	w	IREL	Amador	Sutter Crk P O	69	399
Peter	35	m	w	IREL	San Francisco	1-Wd San Francisco	79	88
HALLENHOFF								
August	25	m	w	HANO	Sacramento	1-Wd Sacramento	77	172
HALLER								
Elam	63	m	w	TN	Sonoma	Healdsburg & Mendo	91	285
Iredell	30	m	w	IN	Sonoma	Healdsburg & Mendo	91	285
John	32	m	w	WURT	San Francisco	San Francisco P O	85	747
Lucus	40	m	w	FRAN	San Francisco	8-Wd San Francisco	82	464
Michel	52	m	w	FRAN	Napa	Napa	75	45
William	38	m	w	PA	Nevada	Meadow Lake Twp	75	262
HALLERAN								
Edward	45	m	w	IREL	Sonoma	Sonoma Twp	91	431
HALLET								
Andrew	56	m	w	MA	Butte	Chico Twp	70	21
Edwd	41	m	w	MS	Butte	Chico Twp	70	55
George	44	m	w	MA	Napa	Napa	75	56
Heny	48	m	w	MA	Butte	Chico Twp	70	22
Roland	41	m	w	ENGL	Yuba	Rose Bar Twp	93	666
HALLETE								
Mary	30	f	w	CANA	Sacramento	3-Wd Sacramento	77	295
HALLETT								
Albert H	24	m	w	ME	Yuba	Slate Range Bar Tw	93	674

Series M593

Name	Age	S	R	B-PL	County	Locale	Roll	Pg
Francis	45	m	w	ME	San Francisco	San Francisco P O	83	313
George H	38	m	w	MA	San Francisco	8-Wd San Francisco	82	390
J R	45	m	w	MA	Alameda	Oakland	68	182
James	60	m	w	NY	Contra Costa	San Pablo Twp	71	355
Jas	23	m	w	IREL	San Joaquin	Dent Twp	86	29
Joseph	45	m	w	MA	San Francisco	11-Wd San Francisc	84	513
Oliver	32	m	w	MA	San Francisco	8-Wd San Francisco	82	461
Otis L	52	m	w	MA	Humboldt	Bald Hills	72	237
Winslow	25	m	w	MA	San Francisco	8-Wd San Francisco	82	461
HALLEY								
A A	40	m	w	OH	Humboldt	Mattole Twp	72	286
Frank	23	m	w	NY	Alameda	Alameda	68	7
George W	57	m	w	VA	Colusa	Monroe Twp	71	318
Henry	18	m	w	BADE	Butte	Concow Twp	70	7
John	29	m	w	IREL	Humboldt	Pacific Twp	72	293
Margaret	28	f	w	CANA	Santa Barbara	Santa Barbara P O	87	502
Morton	33	m	w	IREL	Plumas	Quartz Twp	77	34
HALLEYMOUTH								
W	38	m	w	GERM	Yuba	Marysville	93	614
HALLIBURTON								
Andres	30	m	w	ME	San Mateo	Woodside P O	87	381
HALLICK								
Edward	21	m	w	AUSL	San Francisco	11-Wd San Francisc	84	708
HALLIDAY								
A	40	m	w	IREL	Solano	Vallejo	90	174
Geo	28	m	w	CANA	Humboldt	Table Bluff Twp	72	307
HALLIDIE								
Andrew	32	m	w	SCOT	San Francisco	San Francisco P O	80	410
HALLIDIN								
Dennis	28	m	w	IREL	San Francisco	8-Wd San Francisco	82	318
HALLIGAN								
Alice	65	f	w	IREL	Nevada	Nevada Twp	75	290
Hannah	16	f	w	ME	San Francisco	San Francisco P O	85	735
John	73	m	w	IREL	San Francisco	8-Wd San Francisco	82	290
Vincentia	28	f	w	PA	Santa Cruz	Santa Cruz	89	417
HALLIHAN								
Eugene	44	m	w	IREL	San Francisco	11-Wd San Francisc	84	459
John	40	m	w	IREL	Alameda	Oakland	68	166
HALLIMAN								
Jas	25	m	w	KY	Calaveras	Copperopolis P O	70	238
Jas	20	m	w	IREL	Sonoma	Santa Rosa	91	423
John	37	m	w	ENGL	Napa	Napa Twp	75	31
Nathaniel	42	m	w	IREL	San Francisco	11-Wd San Francisc	84	698
HALLIMON								
Michel	25	m	w	IREL	Napa	Napa Twp	75	32
HALLIN								
Fred	36	m	w	DENM	Mendocino	Big Rvr Twp	74	171
HALLINA								
Kate	24	f	w	IREL	San Francisco	7-Wd San Francisco	81	285
HALLINAN								
John	37	m	w	IREL	Mariposa	Maxwell Crk P O	74	141
HALLINEN								
Thos	39	m	w	IREL	San Francisco	San Francisco P O	83	12
HALLING								
Charles	24	m	w	OLDE	Sonoma	Vallejo Twp	91	451
HALLINGS								
A F	18	m	w	CA	Alameda	Oakland	68	242
HALLMAN								
Geo	16	m	w	PA	Solano	Vallejo	90	212
M	73	f	w	PA	Solano	Vallejo	90	182
Robt S	14	m	w	PA	Nevada	Grass Valley Twp	75	150
HALLOCK								
E B	19	m	w	ME	Alameda	Oakland	68	260
Frank	29	m	w	PRUS	Nevada	Grass Valley Twp	75	230
James V	45	m	w	PA	San Francisco	5-Wd San Francisco	81	29
R F M	35	m	w	AL	Tuolumne	Sonora P O	93	317
Thomas	23	m	w	TX	Yolo	Grafton Twp	93	496
HALLON								
Ambrose	33	m	w	NY	Butte	Chico Twp	70	36
HALLORAN								
Benjamin	27	m	w	IREL	Solano	Montezuma Twp	90	66
Bridget	40	f	w	IREL	San Francisco	San Francisco P O	83	239
James	34	m	w	IREL	San Bernardino	San Bernardino Twp	78	452
Jas	38	m	w	IREL	Sonoma	Santa Rosa	91	423
Thos E	25	m	w	IREL	Sacramento	4-Wd Sacramento	77	319
Timothy	36	m	w	IREL	San Francisco	11-Wd San Francisc	84	628
William	44	m	w	IREL	San Francisco	6-Wd San Francisco	81	143
HALLOREN								
Michael	45	m	w	IREL	Sacramento	2-Wd Sacramento	77	208
HALLOWAY								
James	42	m	w	IREL	Yuba	Marysville Twp	93	568
Jo	49	m	w	ENGL	San Francisco	5-Wd San Francisco	81	12
Mary	52	f	w	KY	Sonoma	Russian Rvr	91	378
Sarah	30	f	w	IL	Sonoma	Petaluma Twp	91	329
HALLOWELL								
Bessie H	22	f	w	PA	San Francisco	San Francisco P O	83	340
HALLOWER								
P	40	m	w	PRUS	Sacramento	3-Wd Sacramento	77	310
HALLSTEAD								
John	32	m	w	CANA	San Francisco	2-Wd San Francisco	79	216
Lausing A	33	m	w	OH	Plumas	Rich Bar Twp	77	46
Peter L	36	m	w	OH	Plumas	Plumas Twp	77	26
HALLSTROM								
M Wm	33	m	w	DENM	San Francisco	San Francisco P O	83	136
HALLUP								
Robert	36	m	w	AR	San Joaquin	Castoria Twp	86	8

© 2001 by Heritage Quest. All rights reserved.

Name	Age	S	R	B-PL	County	Locale	Series M593 Roll	Pg
HALLUVIER								
Louisa	50	f	w	FRAN	San Francisco	San Francisco P O	80	539
HALLY								
Frances	2	f	w	CA	Sacramento	Franklin Twp	77	110
Henry	29	m	w	MO	San Joaquin	Union Twp	86	267
John	34	m	w	IREL	Calaveras	San Andreas P O	70	170
HALLYAN								
Cecelia	23	f	w	LA	San Francisco	11-Wd San Francisc	84	711
HALM								
Ah	14	m	c	CHIN	Sonoma	Russian Rvr	91	373
Conradine	30	f	w	WURT	San Francisco	1-Wd San Francisco	79	57
Louis	34	m	w	WURT	San Francisco	1-Wd San Francisco	79	57
HALMAR								
N	33	m	w	TX	Sonoma	Petaluma Twp	91	362
HALMER								
R J	37	m	w	NY	Trinity	North Fork Twp	92	217
HALNER								
J T	25	m	w	MA	Alameda	Oakland	68	163
HALNNAN								
F G	47	m	w	SAXO	Sonoma	Santa Rosa	91	403
HALO								
Gill	47	m	c	CHIN	San Joaquin	Liberty Twp	86	97
HALON								
Martha	40	f	b	VA	San Joaquin	2-Wd Stockton	86	167
HALPE								
George	30	m	w	PRUS	San Francisco	San Francisco P O	83	225
HALPHEN								
Eli	70	m	w	FRAN	Nevada	Grass Valley Twp	75	200
HALPHIN								
Alexander	62	m	w	FRAN	San Francisco	8-Wd San Francisco	82	459
HALPIN								
David	36	m	w	IREL	Santa Cruz	Santa Cruz Twp	89	399
Edward	20	m	w	IREL	Santa Clara	Santa Clara Twp	88	147
Hannah	40	f	w	IREL	San Francisco	1-Wd San Francisco	79	27
James	37	m	w	MA	San Francisco	1-Wd San Francisco	79	30
James	32	m	w	IREL	San Francisco	1-Wd San Francisco	79	9
John	34	m	w	IREL	San Francisco	San Francisco P O	83	68
Miguel	45	m	w	NY	Los Angeles	Los Angeles Twp	73	483
Thomas	30	m	w	PORT	San Mateo	Half Moon Bay P O	87	400
Thos	42	m	w	IREL	Sacramento	4-Wd Sacramento	77	362
Wm	40	m	w	CANA	San Francisco	San Francisco P O	85	765
Wm	30	m	w	MA	Fresno	Kings Rvr P O	72	213
HALPINE								
Edwd S	21	m	w	IREL	San Francisco	San Francisco P O	85	746
HALS								
Julia	38	f	w	IREL	Plumas	Mineral Twp	77	20
HALSAL								
Thomas	38	m	w	ENGL	Nevada	Grass Valley Twp	75	172
HALSBY								
Robert	40	m	w	CANA	Kern	Linns Valley P O	73	349
HALSE								
A W	44	m	w	NY	Merced	Snelling P O	74	266
James	41	m	w	PA	San Mateo	Schoolhouse Statio	87	336
HALSELL								
Wilson F	38	m	w	TN	Santa Barbara	Santa Barbara P O	87	502
HALSER								
Alvina	20	f	w	IREL	San Joaquin	1-Wd Stockton	86	121
HALSEY								
Abraham	40	m	w	NJ	Stanislaus	Buena Vista Twp	92	11
Benj B	35	m	w	NJ	Amador	Volcano P O	69	387
Benjamin	34	m	w	NY	San Mateo	Half Moon Bay P O	87	408
Brogan B	21	m	w	NY	Placer	Clipper Gap P O	76	376
Charles	58	m	w	NY	San Francisco	2-Wd San Francisco	79	261
David	48	m	w	NY	Napa	Napa Twp	75	61
E A	78	f	w	ENGL	Sonoma	Bodega Twp	91	252
Edward	26	m	w	MI	Santa Clara	2-Wd San Jose	88	290
Eli	24	m	w	MO	Colusa	Butte Twp	71	265
Emma	15	f	w	CA	Calaveras	San Andreas P O	70	198
Hiram H	31	m	w	NY	Placer	Dutch Flat P O	76	407
Julie	57	f	w	NY	Sonoma	Petaluma Twp	91	341
Nancy A	79	f	w	ENGL	Shasta	Fort Crook P O	89	477
Samuel J	54	m	w	NJ	Placer	Dutch Flat P O	76	415
Sanford H	46	m	w	NY	San Francisco	San Francisco P O	83	203
Sarah	17	f	w	CA	Santa Clara	Redwood Twp	88	134
William	51	m	w	NY	San Francisco	San Francisco P O	83	259
Wm H	42	m	w	NY	Sacramento	4-Wd Sacramento	77	321
Wm M	38	m	w	NY	San Francisco	1-Wd San Francisco	79	7
HALSIG								
Henry	20	m	w	PRUS	Placer	Pino Twp	76	470
HALSMAN								
C	38	m	w	PRUS	Sacramento	3-Wd Sacramento	77	262
Henry	21	m	w	HAMB	Sonoma	Petaluma Twp	91	316
HALSON								
W A	63	m	w	DENM	Tuolumne	Columbia P O	93	354
HALST								
Charles	36	m	w	DENM	Los Angeles	Los Angeles Twp	73	476
HALSTAB								
Jacob	38	m	w	SWIT	Nevada	Nevada Twp	75	281
HALSTEAD								
Allen	41	m	w	OH	Butte	Ophir Twp	70	114
Benj	52	m	w	VA	Santa Barbara	San Buenaventura P	87	436
Chas D	39	m	w	IL	Del Norte	Happy Camp Twp	71	470
David	68	m	w	ENGL	Contra Costa	Martinez P O	71	404
Frank	23	m	w	MI	Merced	Snelling P O	74	247
G W Jr	29	m	w	MI	Merced	Snelling P O	74	248
G W Sr	62	m	w	NY	Merced	Snelling P O	74	253
James	17	m	w	IL	Merced	Snelling P O	74	253
M	27	m	w	NY	San Francisco	8-Wd San Francisco	82	363
Nellie	22	f	w	NY	San Francisco	8-Wd San Francisco	82	353
HALSTED								
Cornelius	30	m	w	OH	Fresno	Millerton P O	72	186
Henry	36	m	w	NJ	San Francisco	San Francisco P O	83	111
Humphrey	36	m	w	IN	Tulare	Packwood Twp	92	257
James	29	m	w	IN	Tulare	Packwood Twp	92	257
James L	39	m	w	NY	Santa Cruz	Watsonville	89	371
Jas	31	m	w	ENGL	San Joaquin	Tulare Twp	86	249
Jasper W	34	m	w	IN	Tulare	Packwood Twp	92	257
Marget	30	f	w	NY	San Francisco	7-Wd San Francisco	81	235
Melvin	49	m	w	NY	Solano	Vallejo	90	197
Richd	26	m	w	MO	San Joaquin	2-Wd Stockton	86	174
Timothy	38	m	w	OH	Tulare	Packwood Twp	92	257
HALSTEIN								
George	38	m	w	IL	Amador	Volcano P O	69	379
HALSTON								
I T	42	m	w	NY	Amador	Amador City P O	69	391
HALSY								
T H	53	m	w	NY	Alameda	Oakland	68	208
HALT								
George W	38	m	w	MO	Siskiyou	Cottonwood Twp	89	592
HALTDIENER								
Peter	30	m	w	PRUS	San Francisco	8-Wd San Francisco	82	373
HALTER								
F	63	m	w	KY	San Joaquin	Elkhorn Twp	86	62
HALTERMAN								
Joseph	46	m	w	OH	Napa	Napa	75	23
L	17	f	w	OH	Napa	Yountville Twp	75	80
HALTERMON								
Rinehart	28	f	w	TN	Santa Clara	Fremont Twp	88	46
HALTEZHEISER								
Peter	27	m	w	PRUS	San Francisco	11-Wd San Francisc	84	503
HALTIN								
A H	33	m	w	SWED	San Francisco	3-Wd San Francisco	79	291
HALTON								
Edward	35	m	b	DC	Solano	Silveyville Twp	90	92
Edward	35	m	w	NY	Sonoma	Sonoma Twp	91	442
Francis	30	m	w	VT	San Francisco	5-Wd San Francisco	81	18
Harry	30	m	w	NORW	Del Norte	Crescent Twp	71	455
James	29	m	w	IN	Butte	Chico Twp	70	24
HALTZ								
Ernst	29	m	w	SWED	San Joaquin	2-Wd Stockton	86	213
Peter	58	m	w	BAVA	Amador	Jackson P O	69	332
Peter	37	m	w	SHOL	Amador	Jackson P O	69	346
HALVERSON								
A	36	m	w	NORW	Klamath	Dillon Twp	73	369
Andrew	50	m	w	NORW	Nevada	Bridgeport Twp	75	100
Carl	27	m	w	NORW	Sacramento	Brighton Twp	77	74
Christian	46	m	w	NORW	Alpine	Bullion P O	69	314
Isaac	43	m	w	DENM	El Dorado	Salmon Falls Twp	72	129
Joseph	39	m	w	NORW	Nevada	Washington Twp	75	345
HALVESTOTT								
Henry W	36	m	w	OH	Yolo	Cottonwood Twp	93	465
Jacob	40	m	w	OH	Yolo	Cottonwood Twp	93	468
HALVORSON								
Peter	47	m	w	NJ	Alameda	Eden Twp	68	89
HALY								
Charles	38	m	w	ME	San Francisco	San Francisco P O	83	407
Cornelius	27	m	w	IREL	Sacramento	Franklin Twp	77	108
Ellen	38	f	w	IREL	San Joaquin	Douglas Twp	86	40
Jeremiah	32	m	w	IREL	San Francisco	San Francisco P O	83	209
John	40	m	w	IREL	Placer	Gold Run Twp	76	399
Martin	27	m	w	IREL	Santa Cruz	Soquel Twp	89	446
Mary	25	f	w	IREL	San Francisco	San Francisco P O	85	775
Miche	26	m	w	IREL	Alameda	Oakland	68	267
Nelly	21	f	w	IREL	San Francisco	7-Wd San Francisco	81	228
Pat	40	m	w	IREL	Alameda	Oakland	68	137
Patrick	35	m	w	IREL	Sacramento	Granite Twp	77	139
William	30	m	w	IREL	San Francisco	San Francisco P O	83	173
HAM								
Ah	65	m	c	CHIN	El Dorado	White Oak Twp	72	136
Ah	49	m	c	CHIN	Tuolumne	Chinese Camp P O	93	377
Ah	48	m	c	CHIN	San Mateo	San Mateo P O	87	350
Ah	47	m	c	CHIN	San Francisco	San Francisco P O	80	527
Ah	47	m	c	CHIN	Alameda	Eden Twp	68	62
Ah	46	m	c	CHIN	San Francisco	San Francisco P O	80	443
Ah	40	m	c	CHIN	San Francisco	6-Wd San Francisco	81	48
Ah	40	m	c	CHIN	Alameda	Alvarado	68	305
Ah	40	m	c	CHIN	Placer	Auburn P O	76	361
Ah	40	m	c	CHIN	Alameda	Oakland	68	253
Ah	38	m	c	CHIN	Tuolumne	Chinese Camp P O	93	367
Ah	37	m	c	CHIN	El Dorado	Mud Springs Twp	72	76
Ah	37	m	c	CHIN	San Francisco	6-Wd San Francisco	81	61
Ah	36	m	c	CHIN	Tuolumne	Big Oak Flat P O	93	395
Ah	34	m	c	CHIN	Fresno	Millerton P O	72	202
Ah	33	m	c	CHIN	San Francisco	San Francisco P O	80	499
Ah	32	m	c	CHIN	Tehama	Tehama Twp	92	188
Ah	32	m	c	CHIN	Sacramento	Granite Twp	77	155
Ah	32	m	c	CHIN	Fresno	Millerton P O	72	201
Ah	31	m	c	CHIN	San Francisco	San Francisco P O	80	529
Ah	31	m	c	CHIN	San Francisco	San Francisco P O	80	510
Ah	31	m	c	CHIN	Nevada	Nevada Twp	75	286
Ah	30	m	c	CHIN	Sierra	Gibson Twp	89	538
Ah	30	m	c	CHIN	Tuolumne	Columbia P O	93	346
Ah	28	m	c	CHIN	San Francisco	San Francisco P O	80	440
Ah	27	m	c	CHIN	San Francisco	San Francisco P O	80	515

© 2001 by Heritage Quest. All rights reserved.

Series M593

Name	Age	S	R	B-PL	County	Locale	Roll	Pg
Ah	22	m	c	CHIN	Placer	Summit P O	76	496
Ah	22	m	c	CHIN	Nevada	Meadow Lake Twp	75	251
Ah	20	m	c	CHIN	San Francisco	2-Wd San Francisco	79	246
Ah	20	m	c	CHIN	Tehama	Red Bluff	92	184
Ah	20	m	c	CHIN	Tehama	Red Bluff	92	175
Ah	20	m	c	CHIN	San Francisco	6-Wd San Francisco	81	85
Ah	19	m	c	CHIN	Yuba	Marysville Twp	93	569
Ah	18	m	c	CHIN	San Francisco	8-Wd San Francisco	82	337
Ah	17	m	c	CHIN	San Luis Obispo	Arroyo Grande Twp	87	279
Ah	17	m	c	CHIN	San Francisco	8-Wd San Francisco	82	357
Ah	17	m	c	CHIN	Napa	Napa Twp	75	58
Ah	15	m	c	CHIN	San Francisco	11-Wd San Francisc	84	607
Ah	15	m	c	CHIN	Contra Costa	San Pablo Twp	71	358
Ah	14	m	c	CHIN	San Francisco	8-Wd San Francisco	82	317
Ah	13	m	c	CHIN	San Mateo	Half Moon Bay P O	87	403
Amelia	25	f	i	OR	San Francisco	11-Wd San Francisc	84	601
Ann	40	f	w	IREL	Sacramento	4-Wd Sacramento	77	323
Charles	26	m	w	ME	San Francisco	8-Wd San Francisco	82	443
Chas W	50	m	w	NH	Nevada	Grass Valley Twp	75	207
Chung	24	m	c	CHIN	San Francisco	6-Wd San Francisco	81	83
Elen A	32	f	w	MA	Sacramento	4-Wd Sacramento	77	332
Fan	28	m	c	CHIN	Los Angeles	Los Angeles	73	509
Gee	42	m	c	CHIN	Yuba	Marysville	93	625
Geo F	55	m	w	NH	El Dorado	Georgetown Twp	72	47
Heny	25	m	w	GERM	Humboldt	Eureka Twp	72	273
James T	47	m	w	CANA	San Francisco	6-Wd San Francisco	81	105
John	28	m	w	ENGL	Yuba	Rose Bar Twp	93	657
John C	60	m	w	ME	Amador	Volcano P O	69	379
John T	23	m	w	MO	Sonoma	Analy Twp	91	237
Joseph	38	m	w	NH	Trinity	Douglas	92	237
Ki	19	m	c	CHIN	Tehama	Deer Crk Twp	92	171
Lee	38	m	w	IL	Calaveras	San Andreas P O	70	209
Lo	28	m	c	CHIN	Tehama	Red Bluff	92	182
Lo	18	m	c	CHIN	Tuolumne	Sonora P O	93	312
Luing	22	m	c	CHIN	Tehama	Deer Crk Twp	92	170
Margaret	60	f	w	IREL	Sacramento	4-Wd Sacramento	77	331
May	20	f	c	CHIN	Tehama	Red Bluff	92	184
Merritt	33	m	w	ME	Tuolumne	Columbia P O	93	335
Patrick	24	m	w	IREL	San Francisco	11-Wd San Francisc	84	459
Quoi	13	m	c	CHIN	San Francisco	6-Wd San Francisco	81	45
Randall	30	m	w	ME	Tuolumne	Columbia P O	93	348
Richard K	48	m	w	NH	Santa Clara	Santa Clara Twp	88	175
Richd	26	m	w	ENGL	Sierra	Table Rock Twp	89	572
Sam	22	m	c	CHIN	Tehama	Tehama Twp	92	189
Sarah	12	f	w	CA	San Mateo	Schoolhouse Statio	87	339
Sing	42	m	c	CHIN	Tuolumne	Big Oak Flat P O	93	400
So	23	m	c	CHIN	Tehama	Tehama Twp	92	192
Sung	38	m	c	CHIN	San Francisco	11-Wd San Francisc	84	477
Thos J	54	m	w	VA	Sonoma	Mendocino Twp	91	301
William	28	m	w	IL	San Diego	Julian Dist	78	470
Wm	30	m	w	ENGL	Fresno	Millerton P O	72	165
HAMACK								
H B	35	m	w	OH	Siskiyou	Scott Valley Twp	89	614
HAMAH								
Robt	40	m	w	IREL	San Francisco	San Francisco P O	83	138
HAMAHAN								
Dennis	37	m	w	IREL	Napa	Napa Twp	75	72
HAMAN								
J C	22	m	w	DE	Nevada	Meadow Lake Twp	75	255
James	45	m	w	BREM	San Francisco	8-Wd San Francisco	82	357
Jesus	40	m	w	MEXI	San Francisco	San Francisco P O	80	466
HAMANN								
Jacob	45	m	w	SHOL	San Francisco	1-Wd San Francisco	79	36
HAMARD								
Wm	25	m	w	IREL	Solano	Benicia	90	8
HAMB								
John	52	m	w	BADE	Yuba	New York Twp	93	638
HAMBEE								
George	28	m	w	OH	Tulare	Visalia	92	296
HAMBERG								
John F	32	m	w	HCAS	Mendocino	Little Lake Twp	74	192
Mary	43	f	w	SWIT	Sacramento	4-Wd Sacramento	77	340
HAMBERGER								
Chas	38	m	w	BADE	San Francisco	11-Wd San Francisc	84	568
HAMBERLY								
Phillip	30	m	w	ENGL	Amador	Drytown P O	69	425
HAMBERTON								
John	19	m	w	ENGL	San Francisco	11-Wd San Francisc	84	642
HAMBIDGE								
E	34	m	w	CANA	Mariposa	Maxwell Crk P O	74	146
HAMBIER								
Chas	16	m	w	PRUS	San Francisco	8-Wd San Francisco	82	344
HAMBLAY								
Nicholas	36	m	w	ENGL	Nevada	Grass Valley Twp	75	182
HAMBLEN								
D E	39	m	w	VA	Sutter	Yuba Twp	92	140
Gong	16	m	c	CHIN	Sutter	Yuba Twp	92	140
HAMBLET								
George	27	m	w	ME	Colusa	Monroe Twp	71	312
HAMBLETON								
Albert	16	m	w	CA	Yolo	Cache Crk Twp	93	445
Jacob	39	m	w	NY	San Francisco	5-Wd San Francisco	81	23
James	21	m	w	CANA	San Mateo	Pescadero P O	87	416
John	53	m	w	KY	Mariposa	Mariposa P O	74	125
Joseph	30	m	w	TN	San Francisco	5-Wd San Francisco	81	28
HAMBLEY								
David W	48	m	w	ENGL	Plumas	Plumas Twp	77	30

Series M593

Name	Age	S	R	B-PL	County	Locale	Roll	Pg
HAMBLIN								
Alamagon G	32	m	w	CT	Santa Cruz	Pajaro Twp	89	363
Alpers	54	m	w	MA	San Francisco	San Francisco P O	83	83
Charles	39	m	w	ME	San Francisco	6-Wd San Francisco	81	126
Sylvanus F	45	m	w	MA	Siskiyou	Yreka	89	656
Thomas	37	m	w	ME	Stanislaus	Washington Twp	92	85
HAMBLY								
Anne	26	f	w	PA	Yuba	Rose Bar Twp	93	666
William D	24	m	w	WI	Santa Clara	2-Wd San Jose	88	284
HAMBORG								
Conrad	49	m	w	HANO	San Francisco	2-Wd San Francisco	79	191
HAMBRECHT								
Louisa	52	f	w	BADE	San Francisco	11-Wd San Francisc	84	621
HAMBRET								
Doras	35	f	w	PRUS	San Francisco	6-Wd San Francisco	81	142
HAMBRICK								
Benj A	32	m	w	PRUS	San Mateo	Schoolhouse Statio	87	341
Peter	45	m	w	PRUS	Napa	Napa	75	57
HAMBRIGHT								
Benj	68	m	w	SC	Tulare	Farmersville Twp	92	242
James	29	m	w	TN	El Dorado	Mountain Twp	72	69
James M	40	m	w	KY	Tulare	Farmersville Twp	92	242
HAMBURG								
Adam	28	m	w	PRUS	Santa Clara	1-Wd San Jose	88	268
Frank	52	m	w	PRUS	Napa	Napa	75	22
John	42	m	w	GERM	Yolo	Merritt Twp	93	508
Valentine	36	m	w	PRUS	Santa Clara	1-Wd San Jose	88	232
HAMBURGER								
Becky	23	f	w	PRUS	San Francisco	San Francisco P O	83	311
Gustave	36	m	w	PRUS	San Francisco	San Francisco P O	83	199
Max	47	m	w	BAVA	Siskiyou	Yreka	89	653
HAMBURGH								
Chas	41	m	w	PRUS	Alameda	Alameda	68	19
HAMBURGHER								
Adam	49	m	w	BAVA	Sacramento	2-Wd Sacramento	77	217
HAMBURY								
Thos	40	m	w	IREL	Sonoma	Analy Twp	91	221
HAMBY								
W J	23	m	w	MO	Sierra	Sierra Twp	89	569
HAMDORFF								
Chas	21	m	w	PRUS	San Luis Obispo	Salinas Twp	87	293
HAME								
Ah	22	m	c	CHIN	Shasta	French Gulch P O	89	470
James B	40	m	w	NY	El Dorado	Placerville	72	112
HAMEAU								
Bartler	30	m	w	IREL	San Francisco	11-Wd San Francisc	84	679
HAMEL								
Mary	23	f	w	GERM	Yolo	Grafton Twp	93	485
Mary	14	f	w	CA	Monterey	Monterey	74	358
Robt	22	m	w	CA	Monterey	Monterey	74	366
Wm	49	m	w	HESS	Monterey	Monterey	74	354
HAMELDENBERG								
C	25	m	w	GERM	Alameda	Oakland	68	161
F	20	m	w	GERM	Alameda	Oakland	68	162
HAMELIN								
Arthur	30	m	w	FRAN	Santa Clara	Fremont Twp	88	49
Joseph	30	m	w	ME	San Francisco	San Francisco P O	83	353
HAMELL								
Henry	36	m	w	PRUS	Solano	Tremont Twp	90	29
HAMELSBERG								
W	49	m	w	PRUS	Alameda	Oakland	68	130
HAMEN								
Charles	24	m	w	DENM	Alameda	Brooklyn Twp	68	43
Chas	20	m	w	IL	Sonoma	Santa Rosa	91	429
Timothy	39	m	w	IREL	Sacramento	Granite Twp	77	147
HAMENWAY								
V B	40	m	w	ME	Sacramento	4-Wd Sacramento	77	329
HAMER								
Andrew	21	m	w	PRUS	San Francisco	1-Wd San Francisco	79	60
Emaline	43	f	w	IN	Alameda	Hayward	68	75
George	42	m	b	MD	San Francisco	San Francisco P O	80	353
Herbert	28	m	w	MD	San Francisco	1-Wd San Francisco	79	15
John	28	m	w	HOLL	San Francisco	3-Wd San Francisco	79	292
Joseph C	46	m	w	MA	Santa Barbara	Santa Barbara P O	87	475
L	50	m	w	NY	Nevada	Bloomfield Twp	75	94
Solomon	50	m	w	IN	Contra Costa	Martinez P O	71	370
Wm	40	m	w	GERM	San Francisco	8-Wd San Francisco	82	311
HAMERGAS								
Fred	37	m	w	BADE	Alameda	Oakland	68	149
HAMERLON								
Peter	45	m	w	SWED	Butte	Oroville Twp	70	137
HAMERSLY								
Andrew	41	m	w	IN	Siskiyou	Surprise Valley Tw	89	637
Catherine	70	f	w	TN	Siskiyou	Surprise Valley Tw	89	642
Jacob	36	m	w	IN	Siskiyou	Surprise Valley Tw	89	642
Wm	42	m	w	IN	Siskiyou	Surprise Valley Tw	89	636
HAMERTON								
Henry W	37	m	w	ENGL	Los Angeles	Los Nietos Twp	73	573
HAMES								
Adolphus	40	m	w	HANO	San Francisco	11-Wd San Francisc	84	444
Benjamin	23	m	w	CA	Monterey	San Antonio Twp	74	321
Charles	30	m	w	IL	Sacramento	American Twp	77	69
George T	29	m	w	ENGL	San Francisco	3-Wd San Francisco	79	298
Jefferson	32	m	w	AR	Tulare	Kings Rvr Twp	92	252
John	58	m	w	NY	Santa Cruz	Soquel Twp	89	443
John	37	m	w	LA	Sacramento	American Twp	77	65
Mary	41	f	w	CHIL	Santa Cruz	Pajaro Twp	89	355

© 2001 by Heritage Quest. All rights reserved.

Series M593

Name	Age	S	R	B-PL	County	Locale	Roll	Pg
Thos	33	m	w	SC	Lake	Coyote Valley	73	400
HAMEY								
James	29	m	w	IREL	Nevada	Meadow Lake Twp	75	267
John	43	m	w	IREL	Tuolumne	Chinese Camp P O	93	368
Samuel	29	m	w	IREL	Tuolumne	Chinese Camp P O	93	368
HAMGSBERGER								
Solomon	47	m	w	BAVA	Alameda	Eden Twp	68	83
HAMIER								
Vctor	28	m	w	CA	Los Angeles	Los Angeles Twp	73	479
HAMIESON								
Clauk	40	m	m	OH	Colusa	Stony Crk Twp	71	327
HAMIL								
Chas	37	m	w	FRAN	Monterey	Alisal Twp	74	296
John	45	m	w	IREL	San Francisco	San Francisco P O	85	777
HAMILL								
Arthur	24	m	w	RI	San Diego	San Diego	78	487
B	24	m	w	IREL	Sonoma	Bodega Twp	91	249
John	38	m	w	IREL	San Francisco	11-Wd San Francisc	84	498
HAMILTON								
--- Mrs	45	f	w	MD	Alameda	Oakland	68	144
A	15	f	w	CA	San Joaquin	Elliott Twp	86	73
A J	28	m	w	TN	Siskiyou	Callahan P O	89	627
A S	25	m	w	OH	San Joaquin	Tulare Twp	86	250
Absolom	57	m	w	IN	Sacramento	San Joaquin Twp	77	402
Albert	45	m	w	NC	Placer	Lincoln P O	76	487
Alex	27	m	w	CANA	San Francisco	San Francisco P O	85	877
Alexander	29	m	w	SCOT	Inyo	Independence Twp	73	324
Alexander	27	m	w	MO	Stanislaus	Empire Twp	92	47
Alexdr	27	m	w	MO	Stanislaus	Branch Twp	92	2
Alonzo	40	m	w	NY	San Francisco	5-Wd San Francisco	81	6
Alonzo B	40	m	w	MI	Santa Clara	1-Wd San Jose	88	246
Alx	55	m	b	CT	El Dorado	Coloma Twp	72	9
Amer	50	m	w	KY	Sonoma	Washington Twp	91	469
Andrew	40	m	w	IREL	San Francisco	8-Wd San Francisco	82	419
Andrew	28	m	w	IREL	San Francisco	1-Wd San Francisco	79	62
Ann	35	f	w	MD	San Francisco	8-Wd San Francisco	82	363
Anne	34	f	w	IREL	San Francisco	1-Wd San Francisco	79	31
Annie	50	f	w	ENGL	Sacramento	2-Wd Sacramento	77	221
Annie	20	f	w	NY	San Bernardino	San Bernardino Twp	78	438
Anson	22	m	w	CANA	Santa Cruz	Soquel Twp	89	445
B F	29	m	b	MD	Alameda	Oakland	68	185
Baset W	25	m	w	CANA	Mendocino	Navarro & Big Rvr	74	174
Bell	15	f	w	CA	Yuba	Marysville	93	609
Byron J	34	m	w	IREL	Nevada	Rough & Ready Twp	75	326
C	47	m	w	OH	Nevada	Meadow Lake Twp	75	246
C	24	m	w	KY	Sutter	Sutter Twp	92	127
C H	36	m	w	VA	San Joaquin	Tulare Twp	86	263
C J	35	m	w	IL	Nevada	Meadow Lake Twp	75	247
C L	19	f	w	NY	Santa Clara	Burnett Twp	88	31
C Simon	28	m	w	PA	San Diego	San Diego	78	495
Caleb	35	m	w	NY	Santa Clara	1-Wd San Jose	88	225
Carrie	9	f	w	KS	San Joaquin	1-Wd Stockton	86	133
Catherin	44	f	w	ENGL	Sacramento	Granite Twp	77	149
Charles	82	m	w	IREL	Tulare	Farmersville Twp	92	247
Charles	45	m	w	ENGL	San Francisco	San Francisco P O	83	253
Charles	41	m	w	VA	Santa Clara	Redwood Twp	88	120
Charles	38	m	w	OH	Sacramento	2-Wd Sacramento	77	226
Charles	34	m	w	NY	San Francisco	San Francisco P O	83	206
Charles W	55	m	w	MA	Los Angeles	El Monte Twp	73	454
Chas	22	m	b	JAMA	San Joaquin	1-Wd Stockton	86	129
Chas	22	m	w	OH	San Diego	San Diego	78	496
Chas F	45	m	w	IREL	San Francisco	San Francisco P O	83	360
Christopher	58	m	m	PA	San Francisco	San Francisco P O	80	333
D D	53	m	w	TN	Tehama	Paskenta Twp	92	164
Daniel	53	m	w	SWED	Yolo	Cache Crk Twp	93	440
David	44	m	w	IL	Yolo	Grafton Twp	93	484
David	30	m	w	KY	Sonoma	Salt Point	91	389
David	28	m	w	NY	San Francisco	7-Wd San Francisco	81	159
E	48	m	w	MA	Yuba	Marysville	93	590
E	25	f	w	CANA	San Francisco	San Francisco P O	85	791
E R	39	m	w	PA	Sacramento	3-Wd Sacramento	77	301
Ed G	37	m	w	IL	San Francisco	6-Wd San Francisco	81	93
Edward	40	m	w	CANA	Santa Cruz	Soquel Twp	89	441
Edward	40	m	w	NY	Nevada	Meadow Lake Twp	75	264
Edward G	28	m	w	MS	San Francisco	8-Wd San Francisco	82	341
Edwd	31	m	w	IREL	San Francisco	1-Wd San Francisco	79	93
Edwin	35	m	w	NY	Placer	Rocklin Twp	76	465
Elizabeth	40	f	w	IREL	El Dorado	Georgetown Twp	72	45
Enna	12	f	w	CA	Butte	Concow Twp	70	9
F P	31	m	w	MI	Napa	Napa Twp	75	74
Francis	30	m	w	NH	San Francisco	San Francisco P O	83	104
Frank	36	m	w	LA	Alameda	Oakland	68	260
Frank	18	m	w	ENGL	Marin	San Rafael Twp	74	43
Gallagher	48	m	w	IREL	San Francisco	San Francisco P O	83	138
Garwin	51	m	w	ME	Nevada	Grass Valley Twp	75	160
Geo	40	m	w	IREL	Merced	Snelling P O	74	252
Geo	23	m	w	MO	Sonoma	Santa Rosa	91	420
Geo	20	m	w	CA	Sacramento	1-Wd Sacramento	77	177
Geo W	36	m	w	OH	Sonoma	Analy Twp	91	230
George	63	m	w	TN	Santa Clara	San Jose Twp	88	208
Gilbert S	37	m	w	PA	Santa Cruz	Watsonville	89	368
H	29	m	w	ENGL	Solano	Vallejo	90	175
H J	47	m	w	OH	Butte	Wyandotte Twp	70	149
Henry	40	m	w	IREL	Los Angeles	Los Angeles	73	542
Henry	40	m	w	NY	San Francisco	2-Wd San Francisco	79	257
Henry	28	m	w	MI	Stanislaus	San Joaquin Twp	92	71
Henry M	39	m	w	TN	Stanislaus	Emory Twp	92	25

Series M593

Name	Age	S	R	B-PL	County	Locale	Roll	Pg
Heny	40	m	w	NY	San Francisco	8-Wd San Francisco	82	374
Hill	24	m	w	IOFM	Sacramento	4-Wd Sacramento	77	373
Hugh	47	m	w	VA	Tulare	Farmersville Twp	92	247
Isaac	41	m	w	OH	Siskiyou	Scott Valley Twp	89	610
Isabell	10	f	w	CA	San Francisco	8-Wd San Francisco	82	363
Isaiah	44	m	w	NY	Santa Clara	Milpitas Twp	88	114
J	49	m	w	PA	Lake	Coyote Valley	73	400
J	25	m	w	ME	Sierra	Sierra Twp	89	565
J A	25	m	w	NY	Monterey	Alisal Twp	74	290
J B	55	m	w	TN	Humboldt	Pacific Twp	72	291
J D	48	m	w	OH	San Joaquin	2-Wd Stockton	86	177
J D	28	m	w	PA	Monterey	San Juan Twp	74	399
Jacob	43	m	w	MO	Yuba	W Bear Rvr Twp	93	682
Jaennette	22	f	w	IL	San Diego	San Diego	78	501
James	50	m	w	KY	Stanislaus	Empire Twp	92	56
James	49	m	b	VA	San Diego	Temecula Dist	78	526
James	40	m	w	NJ	Solano	Tremont Twp	90	34
James	40	m	w	SWED	Stanislaus	Buena Vista Twp	92	14
James	39	m	w	KY	Sacramento	Cosumnes Twp	77	89
James	38	m	w	ENGL	Nevada	Grass Valley Twp	75	199
James	37	m	w	IREL	Yolo	Grafton Twp	93	478
James	36	m	w	IREL	San Diego	San Diego	78	492
James	36	m	w	ME	San Francisco	11-Wd San Francisc	84	676
James	32	m	w	CANA	Solano	Suisun Twp	90	116
James	31	m	w	MA	Marin	San Rafael Twp	74	43
James	31	m	w	NY	Mariposa	Mariposa P O	74	135
James	30	m	w	SCOT	Contra Costa	Martinez P O	71	422
James	28	m	w	IREL	Stanislaus	Emory Twp	92	26
James	25	m	w	CANA	Solano	Rio Vista Twp	90	56
James	23	m	w	NY	San Francisco	11-Wd San Francisc	84	586
James	22	m	w	DE	Napa	Napa	75	26
James E	68	m	w	IREL	San Francisco	San Francisco P O	83	108
James H	38	m	w	IREL	Santa Clara	Fremont Twp	88	52
James P	45	m	w	ENGL	Sonoma	Petaluma Twp	91	361
James P	42	m	w	SCOT	Sonoma	Sonoma Twp	91	435
James W	42	m	w	TN	Yolo	Cottonwood Twp	93	460
Jas	45	f	w	NY	San Joaquin	2-Wd Stockton	86	192
Jas	40	m	w	IREL	Solano	Vallejo	90	160
Jas	35	m	w	IL	Sutter	Vernon Twp	92	134
Jas	14	m	w	OR	Siskiyou	Big Valley Twp	89	580
Jas A	31	m	w	IL	Humboldt	Pacific Twp	72	298
Jas G	25	m	w	IL	San Francisco	1-Wd San Francisco	79	103
Jesse	40	m	m	TN	San Joaquin	1-Wd Stockton	86	125
Jo	45	m	w	MD	Sacramento	4-Wd Sacramento	77	353
Jo	40	m	w	IREL	San Joaquin	2-Wd Stockton	86	174
Jo	38	m	w	KY	Placer	Auburn P O	76	381
John	60	m	b	VA	Nevada	Nevada Twp	75	274
John	45	m	w	VA	Plumas	Seneca Twp	77	51
John	42	m	w	IREL	San Francisco	8-Wd San Francisco	82	405
John	40	m	w	IREL	San Francisco	7-Wd San Francisco	81	225
John	38	m	w	TN	Placer	Lincoln P O	76	486
John	37	m	w	PA	Nevada	Nevada Twp	75	295
John	34	m	w	ENGL	Solano	Vallejo	90	170
John	32	m	w	OH	Tehama	Tehama Twp	92	193
John	31	m	w	MO	Yuba	East Bear Rvr Twp	93	543
John	30	m	w	OH	Mariposa	Mariposa P O	74	135
John	30	m	w	IREL	Solano	Benicia	90	20
John	28	m	w	ME	Kern	Tehachapi P O	73	352
John	28	m	w	IREL	San Francisco	11-Wd San Francisc	84	452
John	25	m	w	CA	Placer	Rocklin Twp	76	466
John	25	m	w	MS	San Francisco	San Francisco P O	80	540
John	22	m	w	IN	Merced	Snelling P O	74	276
John A	43	m	w	NH	Mendocino	Point Arena Twp	74	209
John B	42	m	w	OH	Contra Costa	Martinez P O	71	378
John C	49	m	w	NY	Mariposa	Mariposa P O	74	116
John C	33	m	w	MS	Colusa	Monroe Twp	71	317
John F	52	m	w	CT	Nevada	Grass Valley Twp	75	146
John F	39	m	w	CT	San Francisco	San Francisco P O	83	302
John K	30	m	w	SCOT	San Francisco	San Francisco P O	83	65
John Newton	36	m	w	TN	Plumas	Indian Twp	77	19
John P	40	m	w	NY	Placer	Cisco P O	76	494
Jos	52	m	w	IREL	San Francisco	San Francisco P O	83	108
Joseph	50	m	w	TN	Colusa	Spring Valley Twp	71	337
Joseph	25	m	w	VA	San Diego	Warners Rancho Dis	78	530
L	43	m	w	NY	Alameda	Oakland	68	160
L	19	f	w	NY	Alameda	Oakland	68	237
Lewis E	32	m	w	OH	Colusa	Colusa	71	288
Luther	38	m	w	NY	Butte	Ophir Twp	70	96
Lydia	35	f	w	ME	Placer	Auburn P O	76	357
M	27	f	w	IREL	Solano	Benicia	90	14
M B	34	f	w	IREL	Solano	Vallejo	90	189
M M	42	f	w	GA	Tehama	Mill Crk Twp	92	168
Maggie	20	f	w	IA	San Francisco	7-Wd San Francisco	81	281
Marena F	30	m	w	MEXI	Alameda	Murray Twp	68	107
Margaret R	33	f	w	LA	Butte	Ophir Twp	70	96
Martin	29	m	w	IL	Butte	Oregon Twp	70	129
Mary	47	f	w	IN	Alameda	Eden Twp	68	71
Mary	25	f	w	SCOT	San Francisco	8-Wd San Francisco	82	386
Mary	18	f	w	IL	Sonoma	Petaluma Twp	91	335
Matilda	34	f	w	IREL	San Francisco	11-Wd San Francisc	84	538
Moses	37	m	w	ME	Butte	Chico Twp	70	38
Moses	30	m	b	TN	San Joaquin	1-Wd Stockton	86	136
Nancy	40	f	w	MO	Stanislaus	Empire Twp	92	43
Nathl	36	m	w	NY	San Francisco	San Francisco P O	83	105
Noah	31	m	w	IL	Sonoma	Vallejo Twp	91	460
Noble	46	m	w	IN	Alameda	San Leandro	68	94
Oliver	35	m	w	FINL	Mendocino	Navarro & Big Rvr	74	177

© 2001 by Heritage Quest. All rights reserved.

Name	Age	S	R	B-PL	County	Locale	Roll	Pg
Penelope Mrs	58	f	w	MO	Monterey	Monterey Twp	74	348
Peter	33	m	w	SCOT	Mendocino	Albion & Big Rvr T	74	166
Phillip	21	m	w	NY	Plumas	Indian Twp	77	11
R	38	m	w	SCOT	Sacramento	3-Wd Sacramento	77	314
R	38	m	w	ME	Alameda	Oakland	68	157
Rich	27	m	w	CANA	Butte	Chico Twp	70	34
Robert	46	m	w	TN	Tulare	Venice Twp	92	273
Robert	40	m	w	SCOT	San Francisco	6-Wd San Francisco	81	93
Robert	40	m	w	IREL	Santa Clara	1-Wd San Jose	88	278
Robert	25	m	w	IREL	San Francisco	7-Wd San Francisco	81	218
Robt	42	m	w	SCOT	Alameda	Murray Twp	68	107
Robt	40	m	w	IREL	San Francisco	San Francisco P O	83	293
Robt	37	m	w	MO	Tehama	Paskenta Twp	92	166
Robt	35	m	w	MO	San Francisco	5-Wd San Francisco	81	28
Robt	31	m	w	NY	Butte	Chico Twp	70	30
Robt	30	m	w	CANA	San Francisco	1-Wd San Francisco	79	59
Roger	66	m	b	TN	San Joaquin	1-Wd Stockton	86	129
S	35	m	w	IA	Merced	Snelling P O	74	255
S	24	m	w	MD	Solano	Vallejo	90	166
S W	49	m	w	OH	Amador	Sutter Crk P O	69	397
Saml	22	m	w	NJ	San Francisco	8-Wd San Francisco	82	317
Saml	21	m	w	NY	San Francisco	1-Wd San Francisco	79	135
Samuel	39	m	w	IREL	Monterey	Salinas Twp	74	308
Samuel	22	m	w	MO	Stanislaus	San Joaquin Twp	92	80
Sarah	64	f	w	IREL	Sonoma	Salt Point	91	385
Sarah	60	f	b	NC	San Francisco	6-Wd San Francisco	81	92
Sarah	25	f	m	LA	San Francisco	San Francisco P O	80	402
Sarah E	27	f	w	PA	Humboldt	Bucksport Twp	72	244
Sarah E	26	f	w	TN	Sacramento	Franklin Twp	77	110
Siras	25	m	w	ME	San Francisco	11-Wd San Francisc	84	694
Susan	18	f	w	CA	San Francisco	San Francisco P O	83	231
Sylvester	32	m	w	OH	Stanislaus	San Joaquin Twp	92	70
Thomas	40	m	w	IREL	Santa Clara	San Jose Twp	88	210
Thomas	39	m	w	KY	Solano	Silveyville Twp	90	90
Thomas	33	m	w	OH	Colusa	Spring Valley Twp	71	343
Thomas	29	m	w	ENGL	San Francisco	6-Wd San Francisco	81	98
Thomas	25	m	w	NY	Placer	Blue Canyon P O	76	418
Thomas	24	m	w	NY	Inyo	Independence Twp	73	324
Thos	38	m	w	KY	San Joaquin	3-Wd Stockton	86	230
Thos	24	m	w	OISL	San Francisco	5-Wd San Francisco	81	7
Tim	21	m	w	MA	San Francisco	11-Wd San Francisc	84	684
W	33	m	w	IL	Sierra	Sierra Twp	89	563
W	24	m	w	IREL	Solano	Vallejo	90	181
W	17	m	w	CA	San Joaquin	Douglas Twp	86	34
W A	48	m	w	KY	Del Norte	Crescent	71	466
W D	30	m	w	CANA	Calaveras	Copperopolis P O	70	257
W D	28	m	w	PA	Amador	Jackson P O	69	333
W H	48	m	w	MA	San Joaquin	1-Wd Stockton	86	153
W S	44	m	w	IL	Lassen	Janesville Twp	73	430
William	50	m	w	IN	Stanislaus	San Joaquin Twp	92	83
William	46	m	w	PA	Santa Barbara	Santa Barbara P O	87	489
William	42	m	w	OH	Alameda	Brooklyn	68	37
William	40	m	w	IL	Nevada	Grass Valley Twp	75	171
William	40	m	w	GA	Stanislaus	Empire Twp	92	37
William	40	m	w	IREL	Placer	Auburn P O	76	358
William	38	m	w	TX	Colusa	Colusa Twp	71	286
William	38	m	w	CT	Yolo	Merritt Twp	93	506
William	36	m	w	IL	Santa Clara	San Jose Twp	88	197
William	29	m	w	MO	Stanislaus	Empire Twp	92	36
William	26	m	w	SCOT	El Dorado	White Oak Twp	72	135
William	19	m	w	DENM	Colusa	Monroe Twp	71	314
William	14	m	w	AUST	Santa Clara	Milpitas Twp	88	114
William B	37	m	w	VA	San Diego	San Diego	78	493
William D	49	m	w	TN	Placer	Bath P O	76	460
Wm	57	m	w	OH	Marin	Tomales Twp	74	83
Wm	55	m	w	IREL	San Francisco	7-Wd San Francisco	81	281
Wm	40	m	w	MD	Santa Barbara	San Buenaventura P	87	449
Wm B	10	m	w	MO	San Joaquin	Douglas Twp	86	34
Wm R	32	m	w	NY	San Diego	San Diego	78	501
Zack	37	m	w	TN	Butte	Chico Twp	70	36
Zeri	59	m	w	NY	Santa Clara	San Jose Twp	88	188
HAMIN								
Henry	27	m	w	ME	San Mateo	Menlo Park P O	87	378
Wm	35	m	w	NY	Sonoma	Analy Twp	91	222
HAMING								
Pat	25	m	w	IREL	Alameda	Oakland	68	266
HAMIS								
Thomas H	39	m	w	OH	Yuba	Slate Range Bar Tw	93	676
HAMISA								
P J	40	m	w	MEXI	Tuolumne	Chinese Camp P O	93	386
HAMISH								
B F	28	m	w	PA	Solano	Vallejo	90	203
HAMIWELL								
Freeman	35	m	w	ME	Solano	Vacaville Twp	90	130
HAMK								
---	25	m	c	CHIN	Siskiyou	Cottonwood Twp	89	592
HAMLER								
Frederick	38	m	w	BADE	San Francisco	San Francisco P O	83	355
HAMLET								
Charles	41	m	w	BAVA	Tuolumne	Chinese Camp P O	93	365
E J	50	m	w	KY	San Joaquin	3-Wd Stockton	86	241
John	37	m	w	TN	Marin	Tomales Twp	74	77
Jonas	59	m	w	MA	Nevada	Bloomfield Twp	75	92
HAMLEY								
Edward W	41	m	w	VT	Los Angeles	El Monte Twp	73	460
HAMLIN								
Benjamin	36	m	w	SWED	San Francisco	San Francisco P O	80	475
Charles	23	m	w	ME	Plumas	Washington Twp	77	52
Doc	35	m	w	MO	Siskiyou	Scott Valley Twp	89	619
E H	35	m	w	ME	Sierra	Sierra Twp	89	563
Elias	31	m	w	OH	Napa	Napa Twp	75	73
Francis	52	m	w	ME	Sutter	Butte Twp	92	97
Fred	32	m	w	WI	Butte	Chico Twp	70	59
Geo	26	m	w	IL	San Francisco	11-Wd San Francisc	84	602
Geo L	47	m	w	NY	Butte	Chico Twp	70	29
George C	44	m	w	NY	San Francisco	San Francisco P O	85	752
H	63	m	w	MA	Sonoma	Santa Rosa	91	429
H H	33	m	w	IREL	Sacramento	3-Wd Sacramento	77	313
Henry K	38	m	w	ME	El Dorado	Salmon Falls Twp	72	132
Hiram	36	m	w	PA	San Bernardino	San Bernardino Twp	78	439
Hugh P	40	m	w	MI	Yolo	Grafton Twp	93	483
James	34	m	w	NY	Yolo	Putah Twp	93	524
John	58	m	w	IREL	Monterey	Alisal Twp	74	292
John	26	m	w	IREL	Mono	Bridgeport P O	74	284
John C	34	m	w	ME	Yuba	North East Twp	93	643
Louis	58	m	w	FRAN	Contra Costa	Martinez P O	71	421
Mark J	52	m	w	CT	San Francisco	11-Wd San Francisc	84	703
N S	35	m	w	PA	Sutter	Yuba Twp	92	141
Orin	33	m	w	ME	Yuba	North East Twp	93	643
Ralph	27	m	w	IL	Alameda	Brooklyn Twp	68	45
Ross	30	m	w	ME	Plumas	Quartz Twp	77	39
Simeon	84	m	w	MA	Sacramento	Cosumnes Twp	77	93
Sumner	38	m	w	ME	San Francisco	11-Wd San Francisc	84	515
William	47	m	w	PA	Colusa	Monroe Twp	71	316
William	35	m	w	MO	Colusa	Spring Valley Twp	71	344
HAMLING								
---	18	m	c	CHIN	Sutter	Sutter Twp	92	117
HAMLON								
James	28	m	w	IREL	Sonoma	Washington Twp	91	471
Wm	24	m	w	ME	Sierra	Lincoln Twp	89	547
HAMLY								
Umbery	34	m	w	TN	Sonoma	Salt Point Twp	91	383
HAMM								
Jeremiah	47	m	w	NY	Santa Cruz	Watsonville	89	370
Michael	25	m	w	IREL	Los Angeles	Los Nietos Twp	73	576
Pat	44	m	w	IREL	San Francisco	11-Wd San Francisc	84	673
Stephen	42	m	w	NY	Sacramento	4-Wd Sacramento	77	377
HAMMA								
T W	34	m	w	ENGL	Klamath	Klamath Twp	73	370
HAMMACK								
C	37	m	w	TN	Amador	Amador City P O	69	393
HAMMARS								
Davie	62	m	w	BREM	Alameda	Brooklyn	68	32
HAMMATT								
Robert W	50	m	w	MA	Mariposa	Mariposa P O	74	109
HAMMEAL								
J H	40	m	w	NY	Amador	Sutter Crk P O	69	401
HAMMEL								
B	45	m	w	WURT	El Dorado	Greenwood Twp	72	55
George	38	m	w	WURT	Klamath	Salmon Twp	73	387
Henry	34	m	w	OH	Sonoma	Petaluma Twp	91	354
James	50	m	w	IREL	Solano	Rio Vista Twp	90	63
Pete	37	m	w	PRUS	San Joaquin	1-Wd Stockton	86	155
Thos	41	m	w	IREL	Tuolumne	Big Oak Flat P O	93	401
William	48	m	w	VA	San Diego	Julian Dist	78	471
HAMMELL								
Bradford	45	m	w	NY	El Dorado	Mud Springs Twp	72	77
Chas W	31	m	w	OH	Humboldt	Pacific Twp	72	291
James	42	m	w	OH	Santa Barbara	Santa Barbara P O	87	473
John	46	m	w	IREL	Shasta	Millville P O	89	494
Julian	54	m	w	CANA	Solano	Vallejo	90	192
Thos	6	m	w	CA	Marin	San Rafael Twp	74	28
HAMMER								
Fredk	29	m	w	PRUS	San Francisco	San Francisco P O	85	729
Gutlip	54	m	w	WURT	San Francisco	11-Wd San Francisc	84	523
H	44	m	w	PRUS	San Joaquin	2-Wd Stockton	86	206
Henry C	44	m	w	MA	Calaveras	San Andreas P O	70	198
L H	42	m	w	MD	Sacramento	3-Wd Sacramento	77	258
Martin B	53	m	w	PA	San Diego	San Diego	78	494
Me	32	m	w	MA	Sacramento	3-Wd Sacramento	77	318
Samuel	34	m	w	VA	Santa Cruz	Pajaro Twp	89	350
Saws	41	m	w	SWED	San Francisco	2-Wd San Francisco	79	284
Smith C	27	m	w	NY	San Francisco	6-Wd San Francisco	81	93
HAMMERLY								
Fred	34	m	w	GERM	El Dorado	Diamond Springs Tw	72	27
HAMMEROUIST								
Martin	50	m	w	HANO	San Francisco	2-Wd San Francisco	79	137
HAMMERS								
Enos F	39	m	w	MO	Tuolumne	Sonora P O	93	327
HAMMERSLAGG								
Abram	26	m	w	PRUS	San Francisco	3-Wd San Francisco	79	326
HAMMERSLAY								
Marten	26	m	w	AUST	San Luis Obispo	San Luis Obispo Tw	87	316
HAMMERSMITH								
Cornelius	43	m	w	PRUS	Calaveras	Copperopolis P O	70	241
S	59	m	w	SWIT	San Francisco	8-Wd San Francisco	82	370
HAMMERSTRAND								
Harris W	41	m	w	SWED	Inyo	Cerro Gordo Twp	73	318
HAMMERTHSMITT								
John	39	m	w	PRUS	San Francisco	San Francisco P O	85	809
HAMMETT								
Austin W	46	m	w	OH	Contra Costa	Martinez P O	71	379
Elwood	39	m	w	OH	Humboldt	Table Bluff Twp	72	307
George	48	m	w	KY	Contra Costa	Martinez P O	71	377

Series M593

© 2001 by Heritage Quest. All rights reserved.

Name	Age	S	R	B-PL	County	Locale	Series M593 Roll	Pg
J B	38	m	w	MA	Napa	Napa Twp	75	28
Johnson	52	m	w	OH	Humboldt	Eel Rvr Twp	72	247
HAMMEY								
George	36	m	w	SWIT	Sonoma	Salt Point	91	380
HAMMICK								
W C	44	m	w	NC	Tuolumne	Chinese Camp P O	93	377
HAMMIL								
Jesse	54	m	w	PA	Tuolumne	Sonora P O	93	308
Uriah H	55	m	w	VT	Los Angeles	Santa Ana Twp	73	611
HAMMILL								
Amelia	37	f	w	NY	San Francisco	San Francisco P O	83	312
Henry	42	m	w	SC	San Diego	San Jacinto Dist	78	517
Henry	36	m	w	GERM	Los Angeles	Los Angeles	73	547
J	45	m	w	LA	Solano	Vallejo	90	163
John	29	m	w	ENGL	Nevada	Grass Valley Twp	75	142
John	11	m	w	CA	Marin	San Rafael Twp	74	27
Wernar	22	m	w	IREL	San Francisco	San Francisco P O	83	203
William	44	m	w	PRUS	Los Angeles	Los Angeles	73	529
William	22	m	w	ENGL	Nevada	Grass Valley Twp	75	199
HAMMILTON								
Martha	30	f	w	IREL	Los Angeles	Los Angeles	73	502
Wm	18	m	w	OH	Sacramento	1-Wd Sacramento	77	176
HAMMINE								
John	35	m	w	IREL	San Francisco	7-Wd San Francisco	81	261
HAMMING								
Luke	42	m	w	IREL	Marin	Tomales Twp	74	84
HAMMOCK								
L A Mrs	38	f	w	MO	Lake	Big Valley	73	398
M	78	m	w	NC	Lake	Big Valley	73	398
HAMMON								
Andrew	27	m	w	BADE	San Joaquin	Tulare Twp	86	254
James	39	m	w	RI	Yolo	Washington Twp	93	530
James	22	f	w	IREL	San Joaquin	1-Wd Stockton	86	135
Mary	8	f	w	CA	San Francisco	11-Wd San Francisc	84	711
HAMMOND								
A	33	m	w	ME	San Joaquin	Tulare Twp	86	252
A J	25	m	w	IA	Tehama	Red Bluff	92	181
Albert N	51	m	w	ME	San Mateo	Woodside P O	87	387
Alen	38	m	w	RI	San Joaquin	Oneal Twp	86	112
Andrew	27	m	w	IA	Tehama	Paynes Crk Twp	92	160
Andw	45	m	w	IREL	San Francisco	1-Wd San Francisco	79	11
B	54	m	w	TN	Sutter	Nicolaus Twp	92	112
B C	28	m	w	MO	Mendocino	Little Lake Twp	74	195
C	42	m	w	PRUS	San Joaquin	3-Wd Stockton	86	235
C F	88	m	w	IL	Trinity	Trinity Center Pct	92	204
Chas F	38	m	w	ENGL	Siskiyou	Scott Valley Twp	89	614
Chas Y	43	m	w	NY	Yolo	Cache Crk Twp	93	419
Clara	48	f	w	FRAN	San Francisco	8-Wd San Francisco	82	364
E	39	m	w	NCOD	Yuba	W Bear Rvr Twp	93	680
E A	34	m	w	KY	Napa	Napa	75	24
Ed H	45	m	w	MD	San Francisco	San Francisco P O	83	104
Edward	23	m	w	NY	San Francisco	8-Wd San Francisco	82	389
Edwin	30	m	w	MA	Sacramento	Sutter Twp	77	390
Elizabeth	38	f	w	ENGL	San Francisco	8-Wd San Francisco	82	490
Emory	48	m	w	NY	Stanislaus	Emory Twp	92	23
Fred	38	m	w	SAXO	Sierra	Gibson Twp	89	540
G W	23	m	w	IA	Tehama	Paynes Crk Twp	92	160
Geo	59	m	w	GA	San Joaquin	Douglas Twp	86	43
H A	22	m	w	MA	San Joaquin	Elliott Twp	86	72
Henry	52	m	w	VA	Shasta	Millville P O	89	484
Henry	29	m	w	OH	Santa Clara	San Jose Twp	88	191
J H	36	m	w	ENGL	Yuba	W Bear Rvr Twp	93	682
J R	35	m	w	PA	Mendocino	Little Lake Twp	74	199
J S	26	m	w	MA	San Joaquin	3-Wd Stockton	86	228
J S	25	m	w	MA	San Joaquin	3-Wd Stockton	86	230
J W	60	m	w	MA	San Joaquin	1-Wd Stockton	86	139
J W	21	m	w	IA	Mariposa	Maxwell Crk P O	74	142
James	35	m	w	NY	San Francisco	11-Wd San Francisc	84	703
Jas	29	m	w	ME	San Francisco	11-Wd San Francisc	84	622
John	68	m	w	RI	San Francisco	3-Wd San Francisco	79	308
John	53	m	b	MD	Nevada	Grass Valley Twp	75	201
John	42	m	w	IREL	San Francisco	11-Wd San Francisc	84	441
John	41	m	w	PRUS	San Joaquin	3-Wd Stockton	86	237
John	40	m	w	ME	Alameda	Alameda	68	3
John	36	m	w	MA	Placer	Rocklin Twp	76	465
John	30	m	w	IREL	San Francisco	San Francisco P O	83	133
John	25	m	w	NY	Solano	Suisun Twp	90	97
John	19	m	w	MO	Napa	Yountville Twp	75	90
John T	24	m	w	MA	Solano	Suisun Twp	90	99
Joseph	60	m	w	ME	Santa Clara	1-Wd San Jose	88	254
Joseph	40	m	w	CANA	San Francisco	11-Wd San Francisc	84	506
Julia	12	f	i	CA	Del Norte	Mountain Twp	71	475
L A	45	f	w	CT	Sacramento	1-Wd Sacramento	77	202
M	60	f	w	IREL	Solano	Vallejo	90	141
Moses	70	m	w	MA	San Joaquin	Oneal Twp	86	112
Nathaniel	50	m	w	KY	Tulare	Farmersville Twp	92	241
Richard P	50	m	w	MD	San Francisco	8-Wd San Francisco	82	479
Robert	45	m	w	NJ	Yolo	Grafton Twp	93	489
Robt	48	m	w	IREL	Butte	Chico Twp	70	56
S	38	m	w	OH	El Dorado	Coloma Twp	72	1
S A	63	m	w	ME	San Joaquin	Douglas Twp	86	34
S K	64	m	w	ENGL	Sierra	Forest	89	536
Samuel	71	m	w	NY	Yolo	Cache Crk Twp	93	419
Samuel	40	m	w	OH	Humboldt	Pacific Twp	72	295
Seth	30	m	w	VT	Santa Barbara	San Buenaventura P	87	444
T	25	m	w	ENGL	Yuba	W Bear Rvr Twp	93	681
T C	46	m	w	MA	Sutter	Vernon Twp	92	136

Name	Age	S	R	B-PL	County	Locale	Series M593 Roll	Pg
T J	44	m	w	MD	Del Norte	Mountain Twp	71	475
Teaching	53	m	w	BREM	Alameda	Washington Twp	68	268
Thomas	40	m	w	IREL	San Francisco	11-Wd San Francisc	84	554
Thos	60	m	w	MA	San Joaquin	Douglas Twp	86	37
Thos	41	m	w	PA	Sonoma	Salt Point	91	385
Thos	41	m	w	NY	San Joaquin	2-Wd Stockton	86	175
Thos	39	m	w	MO	San Joaquin	2-Wd Stockton	86	198
Thos	23	m	w	MO	Napa	Yountville Twp	75	90
W	49	m	w	OH	Amador	Drytown P O	69	418
W	47	m	w	NY	San Francisco	San Francisco P O	83	274
W D	30	m	w	ME	Sacramento	3-Wd Sacramento	77	316
William	35	m	w	IREL	Contra Costa	Martinez P O	71	428
William	34	m	w	IN	Kern	Havilah P O	73	340
William	32	m	w	TN	Stanislaus	Branch Twp	92	9
William	28	m	w	NY	Santa Barbara	Santa Barbara P O	87	455
William C	46	m	w	KY	Stanislaus	San Joaquin Twp	92	71
Wm	37	m	w	SWED	San Francisco	1-Wd San Francisco	79	121
Wm B	24	m	w	TN	San Francisco	1-Wd San Francisco	79	118
Wm P	58	m	w	CT	Napa	Napa	75	49
Worthington	46	m	w	MD	Tulare	Tule Rvr Twp	92	267
HAMMUS								
Philip	67	m	w	SILE	Los Angeles	Santa Ana Twp	73	609
HAMNER								
Thomas	39	m	w	IN	Santa Cruz	Pajaro Twp	89	353
HAMNETT								
Levy	33	m	w	OH	Butte	Chico Twp	70	14
HAMNIL								
John	61	m	w	IREL	San Francisco	3-Wd San Francisco	79	308
HAMON								
Jno	45	m	m	HI	Butte	Concow Twp	70	6
Thomas	29	m	w	PRUS	Marin	San Rafael	74	56
HAMOND								
Geo	55	m	w	MA	San Joaquin	Elliott Twp	86	73
John	46	m	w	TN	San Joaquin	1-Wd Stockton	86	136
John	23	m	w	MI	San Joaquin	2-Wd Stockton	86	179
Joseph	38	m	w	GA	Los Angeles	Los Angeles	73	502
W H	12	m	w	CA	Alameda	Oakland	68	257
Wm	35	m	w	MA	San Joaquin	Castoria Twp	86	15
HAMONSTEIN								
Jacob	45	m	w	SWIT	Calaveras	Copperopolis P O	70	262
HAMPE								
Charles	38	m	w	BADE	San Francisco	San Francisco P O	80	474
HAMPEL								
Conrad	46	m	w	PRUS	Alameda	Brooklyn	68	34
John	43	m	w	PRUS	Alameda	Brooklyn Twp	68	51
HAMPELL								
Henry	38	m	w	PRUS	Alameda	Brooklyn	68	35
HAMPSHIRE								
J	28	m	w	PA	Yuba	Marysville	93	581
William	52	m	w	SWED	San Francisco	7-Wd San Francisco	81	213
HAMPSON								
Henry A	30	m	w	OH	Sonoma	Cloverdale Twp	91	267
Henry C	50	m	w	OH	Plumas	Washington Twp	77	53
Ira	37	m	w	CHIN	Klamath	Trinidad Twp	73	392
Wm	20	m	w	ENGL	San Francisco	1-Wd San Francisco	79	116
HAMPSTEAD								
Mary	25	f	w	IREL	San Mateo	Belmont P O	87	372
HAMPTON								
---	27	m	w	ENGL	Sierra	Butte Twp	89	508
Adaline	50	f	w	TN	Sonoma	Petaluma Twp	91	344
Ann E	28	f	w	MO	San Joaquin	2-Wd Stockton	86	161
E M	47	m	w	PA	Tuolumne	Sonora P O	93	307
E P	55	m	w	NY	Trinity	Lewiston Pct	92	213
Ed	30	m	w	VA	San Joaquin	3-Wd Stockton	86	218
Geo	38	m	w	SCOT	San Joaquin	Oneal Twp	86	111
Geo	34	m	w	VA	Napa	Napa	75	21
Henry	56	m	w	VA	Santa Barbara	San Buenaventura P	87	445
Henry	33	m	w	VA	San Francisco	8-Wd San Francisco	82	474
Henry C	40	m	w	CT	San Francisco	6-Wd San Francisco	81	88
J M	35	m	w	PA	Tuolumne	Sonora P O	93	307
James	45	m	w	KY	Santa Cruz	Pajaro Twp	89	347
James	42	m	w	OH	Siskiyou	Hamburg Twp	89	596
James	42	m	w	IREL	San Mateo	San Mateo P O	87	351
James M	35	m	w	NC	Sonoma	Analy Twp	91	237
Joel H	23	m	w	IA	Shasta	Fort Crook P O	89	475
John	33	m	w	IREL	San Mateo	San Mateo P O	87	351
John	22	m	w	SCOT	San Joaquin	1-Wd Stockton	86	129
Lina	16	f	w	KY	Santa Barbara	San Buenaventura P	87	445
Mary	60	f	w	SCOT	San Joaquin	3-Wd Stockton	86	225
Mary	38	f	w	NY	Alameda	Oakland	68	153
Rich	23	m	w	IL	Butte	Chico Twp	70	40
Robert	46	m	w	IREL	San Francisco	8-Wd San Francisco	82	421
Wade	58	m	w	VA	Santa Barbara	San Buenaventura P	87	446
William	41	m	w	NY	Santa Barbara	Las Cruces P O	87	516
William	22	m	w	MS	Los Angeles	Los Nietos Twp	73	580
William H	39	m	w	PA	Yolo	Putah Twp	93	509
William H	39	m	w	PA	Yolo	Putah Twp	93	514
William H	38	m	w	AL	Mendocino	Navarro & Big Rvr	74	177
William H	25	m	w	ENGL	Nevada	Grass Valley Twp	75	145
Wm	41	m	w	NY	Santa Barbara	Santa Barbara P O	87	478
Wm R	44	m	w	NY	Fresno	Millerton P O	72	150
HAMRA								
E	32	m	w	DENM	Sierra	Butte Twp	89	513
HAMRICH								
Peter	40	m	w	PRUS	Sacramento	2-Wd Sacramento	77	253
HAMRICK								
G R	30	m	w	KY	Amador	Ione City P O	69	361

© 2001 by Heritage Quest. All rights reserved.

Series M593

Name	Age	S	R	B-PL	County	Locale	Roll	Pg
J E	22	m	w	MO	Amador	Ione City P O	69	352
James	22	m	w	MO	Amador	Ione City P O	69	363
Jesse C	47	m	w	KY	Amador	Ione City P O	69	352
HAMS								
Daniel	35	m	w	KY	Kern	Bakersfield P O	73	357
H H	44	m	w	NY	Alameda	Oakland	68	190
HAMSEL								
John H	31	m	w	OH	Santa Clara	Santa Clara Twp	88	147
HAMSON								
J B	46	m	w	ENGL	San Francisco	San Francisco P O	85	849
HAMSTREET								
Adam	37	m	w	NY	Colusa	Monroe Twp	71	325
HAMWOOD								
H S	14	m	w	CA	Alameda	Oakland	68	159
J H	16	m	w	CA	Alameda	Oakland	68	159
HAN								
---	28	m	c	CHIN	Siskiyou	Yreka	89	661
---	15	m	c	CHIN	Siskiyou	Cottonwood Twp	89	593
A	21	m	c	CHIN	Santa Cruz	Soquel Twp	89	448
Ah	8	m	c	CHIN	San Francisco	San Francisco P O	80	441
Ah	53	m	c	CHIN	El Dorado	Mud Springs Twp	72	79
Ah	50	m	c	CHIN	Sacramento	Natomas Twp	77	167
Ah	46	m	c	CHIN	Calaveras	San Andreas P O	70	174
Ah	42	m	c	CHIN	El Dorado	Placerville	72	115
Ah	40	m	c	CHIN	San Francisco	11-Wd San Francisc	84	515
Ah	40	m	c	CHIN	Sierra	Eureka Twp	89	525
Ah	40	m	c	CHIN	Alameda	Murray Twp	68	114
Ah	40	m	c	CHIN	Sacramento	Franklin Twp	77	108
Ah	38	m	c	CHIN	Tuolumne	Chinese Camp P O	93	370
Ah	37	m	c	CHIN	San Francisco	San Francisco P O	80	521
Ah	36	m	c	CHIN	San Francisco	San Francisco P O	80	527
Ah	35	m	c	CHIN	Sierra	Table Rock Twp	89	579
Ah	34	m	c	CHIN	Shasta	French Gulch P O	89	469
Ah	33	m	c	CHIN	Calaveras	Copperopolis P O	70	248
Ah	31	m	c	CHIN	Tuolumne	Big Oak Flat P O	93	392
Ah	31	m	c	CHIN	Fresno	Millerton P O	72	200
Ah	31	m	c	CHIN	San Francisco	3-Wd San Francisco	79	306
Ah	31	m	c	CHIN	Sutter	Yuba Twp	92	144
Ah	31	m	c	CHIN	San Francisco	San Francisco P O	80	519
Ah	30	m	c	CHIN	San Francisco	San Francisco P O	80	479
Ah	30	m	c	CHIN	Sacramento	1-Wd Sacramento	77	197
Ah	29	m	c	CHIN	San Francisco	6-Wd San Francisco	81	58
Ah	29	m	c	CHIN	San Francisco	San Francisco P O	80	511
Ah	29	m	c	CHIN	Sacramento	Granite Twp	77	151
Ah	26	m	c	CHIN	San Francisco	San Francisco P O	80	524
Ah	25	f	c	CHIN	Solano	Vallejo	90	179
Ah	25	m	c	CHIN	San Francisco	11-Wd San Francisc	84	560
Ah	25	m	c	CHIN	Calaveras	San Andreas P O	70	204
Ah	22	m	c	CHIN	Placer	Dutch Flat P O	76	410
Ah	21	m	c	CHIN	Solano	Vallejo	90	175
Ah	21	m	c	CHIN	San Francisco	6-Wd San Francisco	81	48
Ah	20	m	c	CHIN	Plumas	Seneca Twp	77	47
Ah	20	m	c	CHIN	Sacramento	1-Wd Sacramento	77	194
Ah	19	m	c	CHIN	Solano	Silveyville Twp	90	91
Ah	18	m	c	CHIN	San Francisco	6-Wd San Francisco	81	49
Ah	17	m	c	CHIN	Sonoma	Sonoma Twp	91	449
Ah	17	m	c	CHIN	Santa Clara	Santa Clara Twp	88	165
Ah	14	m	c	CHIN	Mariposa	Maxwell Crk P O	74	142
Ah	14	m	c	CHIN	Contra Costa	San Pablo Twp	71	356
Be	20	m	c	CHIN	Yuba	Marysville	93	628
Chuc	20	m	c	CHIN	Santa Clara	Santa Clara Twp	88	163
Coon	30	m	c	CHIN	Trinity	North Fork Twp	92	216
Dan	18	m	c	CHIN	San Francisco	San Francisco P O	83	352
Flat	45	m	c	CHIN	Siskiyou	Yreka Twp	89	666
Gee	51	m	c	CHIN	Plumas	Rich Bar Twp	77	46
James	40	m	w	IREL	Amador	Sutter Crk P O	69	405
James H	59	m	w	KY	Plumas	Plumas Twp	77	28
Kee	27	m	c	CHIN	Amador	Drytown P O	69	422
Koo	30	m	c	CHIN	San Francisco	6-Wd San Francisco	81	63
Lee	40	m	c	CHIN	Siskiyou	Yreka Twp	89	665
Lee	40	m	c	CHIN	Shasta	American Ranch P O	89	496
Lee	38	m	c	CHIN	Fresno	Millerton P O	72	201
Lon	41	m	c	CHIN	Calaveras	Copperopolis P O	70	264
Mary A	22	f	w	MO	San Francisco	8-Wd San Francisco	82	313
Michael	50	m	w	SCOT	San Francisco	San Francisco P O	80	372
Sing	17	f	c	CHIN	Butte	Kimshew Tpw	70	85
Sut	21	m	c	CHIN	Sutter	Nicolaus Twp	92	106
Wood	45	m	w	PA	Nevada	Rough & Ready Twp	75	329
Yee	27	m	c	CHIN	Placer	Auburn P O	76	367
HANA								
Hamilton	37	m	w	PA	Stanislaus	Branch Twp	92	3
HANABERY								
Patrick	29	m	w	IREL	Alameda	Eden Twp	68	65
HANAEN								
John	40	m	w	HANO	Sacramento	4-Wd Sacramento	77	339
HANAFER								
Alice	11	f	w	CA	Alameda	Oakland	68	206
HANAFORD								
A M	39	m	w	NY	Sacramento	1-Wd Sacramento	77	189
E T	35	m	w	ME	San Francisco	7-Wd San Francisco	81	235
J G	40	m	w	ME	Alameda	Oakland	68	141
HANAGAN								
David	37	m	w	IREL	San Francisco	11-Wd San Francisc	84	473
HANAHAN								
John	38	m	w	IREL	Fresno	Millerton P O	72	168
Pat	30	m	w	IREL	Santa Clara	Gilroy Twp	88	78
HANAHEN								
Wm	30	m	w	IREL	San Francisco	11-Wd San Francisc	84	603
HANAJ								
Michael	40	m	w	SAXO	Amador	Ione City P O	69	350
HANAN								
Bridgit	68	f	w	IREL	Alameda	Oakland	68	205
Edward	36	m	w	IREL	Inyo	Independence Twp	73	328
Mary	50	f	w	IREL	San Francisco	7-Wd San Francisco	81	170
HANAR								
F L	14	m	w	CA	Alameda	Oakland	68	243
Simon S	22	f	w	PA	Santa Cruz	Santa Cruz	89	434
HANAVAN								
Bridget	68	f	w	IREL	San Francisco	San Francisco P O	83	167
HANBURY								
James T	31	m	w	ENGL	San Francisco	1-Wd San Francisco	79	97
Peter	36	m	w	IREL	San Francisco	11-Wd San Francisc	84	589
HANBY								
Saml	41	m	w	AR	San Joaquin	Dent Twp	86	25
HANCE								
Samuel	42	m	w	NY	Siskiyou	Scott Valley Twp	89	617
William	68	m	w	ME	San Mateo	Half Moon Bay P O	87	405
HANCH								
Michael	24	m	w	CANA	Humboldt	Bucksport Twp	72	241
HANCHETT								
Cath	30	f	w	IREL	San Francisco	2-Wd San Francisco	79	217
HANCHIN								
Wm	26	m	w	VA	Butte	Kimshew Tpw	70	78
HANCHON								
Hercher	50	f	w	SHOL	San Francisco	3-Wd San Francisco	79	326
HANCK								
Felix	46	m	w	OH	Merced	Snelling P O	74	266
Lizzie	21	f	w	IN	Sacramento	4-Wd Sacramento	77	327
Margaret	17	f	w	IN	Sacramento	4-Wd Sacramento	77	346
Morten	10	m	w	CA	Sacramento	4-Wd Sacramento	77	327
Peter	39	m	w	BAVA	Humboldt	Eel Rvr Twp	72	251
HANCKMAN								
Thomas	51	m	w	MO	Yolo	Grafton Twp	93	488
HANCLIFF								
Hyman	28	m	w	NY	San Francisco	5-Wd San Francisco	81	30
HANCOCK								
Bessie	20	f	w	IA	San Francisco	San Francisco P O	80	394
Edward	51	m	w	ENGL	San Mateo	Redwood Twp	87	367
Frank	26	m	w	MA	Solano	Vallejo	90	146
G W	34	m	w	MA	Sutter	Vernon Twp	92	132
Geo	2M	m	w	VT	Butte	Ophir Twp	70	108
George	40	m	w	ENGL	Contra Costa	Martinez P O	71	425
Henry	48	m	w	NH	Los Angeles	Los Angeles	73	572
J P	36	m	w	MO	San Joaquin	2-Wd Stockton	86	172
James	37	m	w	TN	El Dorado	Placerville Twp	72	96
Jane	25	f	w	IREL	Monterey	San Juan Twp	74	395
Jno C	35	m	w	MA	San Diego	San Diego	78	484
John	70	m	w	IREL	San Francisco	San Francisco P O	83	284
John	47	m	w	TN	Stanislaus	Empire Twp	92	32
John	44	m	w	PA	San Francisco	San Francisco P O	80	367
John	37	m	w	OH	Nevada	Washington Twp	75	343
Joseph	48	m	w	OH	San Bernardino	San Bernardino Twp	78	420
Richd	50	m	w	IREL	San Francisco	1-Wd San Francisco	79	129
S	52	f	w	CT	Yuba	Marysville	93	596
S	42	m	w	IREL	San Francisco	San Francisco P O	85	777
Santiago	50	m	w	KY	Santa Clara	1-Wd San Jose	88	258
T	40	m	w	IN	San Joaquin	Oneal Twp	86	101
Thomas	21	m	w	ME	Nevada	Washington Twp	75	344
HANCY								
Ah	35	m	c	CHIN	Monterey	Salinas Twp	74	313
HAND								
Ah	45	m	c	CHIN	Trinity	Indian Crk	92	199
Ah	26	m	c	CHIN	San Francisco	3-Wd San Francisco	79	303
Andrew	40	m	w	CANA	Stanislaus	Emory Twp	92	22
Anna	25	f	w	IREL	San Francisco	8-Wd San Francisco	82	420
Anna M	49	f	w	VA	Tehama	Tehama Twp	92	195
David	40	m	w	IREL	San Francisco	8-Wd San Francisco	82	351
Geo W	36	m	w	PA	San Francisco	8-Wd San Francisco	82	314
George	38	m	w	NY	Yolo	Putah Twp	93	523
J	32	m	w	PA	Alameda	Oakland	68	256
James	27	m	w	IL	Sonoma	Russian Rvr	91	372
Jas	30	m	w	NY	Siskiyou	Callahan P O	89	633
Jno	38	m	w	IREL	Santa Clara	Gilroy Twp	88	86
Jno	30	m	w	IA	San Joaquin	Douglas Twp	86	50
John	27	m	w	IREL	San Francisco	7-Wd San Francisco	81	225
John E	22	m	w	NY	Sonoma	Salt Point	91	385
John S	28	m	w	NY	San Francisco	6-Wd San Francisco	81	84
Joseph	71	m	w	GA	Los Angeles	Los Angeles	73	521
Joseph	37	m	w	IN	El Dorado	Lake Valley Twp	72	63
Joseph	25	m	w	NY	San Francisco	7-Wd San Francisco	81	228
Mary E	50	f	w	NY	San Francisco	8-Wd San Francisco	82	378
Oscar	25	m	w	PRUS	San Francisco	San Francisco P O	83	190
Patrick	32	m	w	IREL	Santa Clara	2-Wd San Jose	88	319
Samuel	50	m	w	AL	San Diego	Poway Dist	78	481
Sarah	72	f	w	PA	Sonoma	Analy Twp	91	234
Stephen	37	m	w	NY	San Francisco	2-Wd San Francisco	79	189
Thomas	36	m	w	IREL	Siskiyou	Scott Valley Twp	89	619
William	45	m	w	IREL	El Dorado	Salmon Falls Twp	72	130
William	28	m	w	MA	San Francisco	San Francisco P O	85	725
William	23	m	w	WI	Solano	Tremont Twp	90	31
William	23	m	w	MO	Plumas	Quartz Twp	77	39
Wm Dawson	40	m	w	OH	Nevada	Grass Valley Twp	75	193

© 2001 by Heritage Quest. All rights reserved.

Series M593

Name	Age	S	R	B-PL	County	Locale	Roll	Pg
HANDBURY								
Thos	30	m	w	KY	San Francisco	1-Wd San Francisco	79	54
HANDEL								
Phillipine	18	f	w	BAVA	Santa Clara	2-Wd San Jose	88	285
HANDERHAN								
Edward	38	m	w	IREL	San Francisco	San Francisco P O	83	393
Lot	40	m	w	IREL	Tuolumne	Columbia P O	93	348
HANDEST								
J E	24	m	w	IL	San Joaquin	Castoria Twp	86	6
HANDLEN								
Charles	35	m	w	MA	San Francisco	7-Wd San Francisco	81	217
HANDLEY								
Henry	25	m	w	NY	San Francisco	San Francisco P O	83	173
James	48	m	w	MA	San Francisco	6-Wd San Francisco	81	106
John	60	m	w	IREL	Santa Cruz	Santa Cruz	89	415
John	42	m	w	ME	Calaveras	Copperopolis P O	70	262
Peter	44	m	w	IREL	San Francisco	7-Wd San Francisco	81	200
Thomas	55	m	w	IREL	Santa Cruz	Santa Cruz	89	431
Thomas	28	m	w	IREL	Santa Cruz	Santa Cruz Twp	89	383
Walter	50	m	w	SCOT	Santa Cruz	Santa Cruz Twp	89	383
Wm M	42	m	w	IREL	Alameda	Murray Twp	68	106
HANDLIN								
Andrew	35	m	w	IREL	Sacramento	Franklin Twp	77	109
Jos	25	m	w	MD	Solano	Vallejo	90	167
HANDLY								
M A	40	f	w	MA	Sierra	Forest	89	536
HANDON								
J B	47	m	w	KY	Alameda	Oakland	68	207
HANDORFF								
William	27	m	w	PRUS	San Diego	Fort Yuma Dist	78	463
HANDS								
Constantine	45	m	w	NY	Santa Clara	Alviso Twp	88	23
George L	36	m	w	IREL	Los Angeles	Wilmington Twp	73	634
Thomas	25	m	w	ENGL	San Francisco	7-Wd San Francisco	81	218
HANDSCHUH								
B	40	f	w	PRUS	San Francisco	San Francisco P O	85	832
HANDY								
A E	46	f	w	MA	San Francisco	7-Wd San Francisco	81	168
A G	45	m	w	IL	Humboldt	Arcata Twp	72	227
Anna	24	f	w	IREL	San Francisco	7-Wd San Francisco	81	163
Edward	30	m	b	MA	San Francisco	2-Wd San Francisco	79	230
Elizabeth	25	f	m	MD	San Francisco	2-Wd San Francisco	79	230
Geo	37	m	w	OH	El Dorado	Georgetown Twp	72	48
Henry	16	m	b	CA	San Francisco	8-Wd San Francisco	82	466
John	36	m	w	NY	Calaveras	Copperopolis P O	70	221
Jos K	30	m	w	IREL	San Francisco	8-Wd San Francisco	82	332
Lucien	40	m	w	MA	San Francisco	San Francisco P O	80	485
Martin	25	m	w	CANA	Solano	Silveyville Twp	90	86
Mary	23	f	w	IL	Butte	Chico Twp	70	36
N A	41	m	w	RI	San Francisco	8-Wd San Francisco	82	364
Philo	28	m	w	OH	Mendocino	Round Valley Twp	74	220
Raymond B	47	m	w	MA	Santa Cruz	Santa Cruz	89	418
Rhodelphus D	32	m	w	MA	Santa Barbara	Santa Barbara P O	87	468
Samuel W	70	m	w	IREL	Nevada	Grass Valley Twp	75	208
Thos	25	m	w	IREL	San Francisco	11-Wd San Francisc	84	475
William	8	m	w	CA	Colusa	Butte Twp	71	271
William L	45	m	w	WURT	San Francisco	8-Wd San Francisco	82	480
HANE								
Ah	30	m	c	CHIN	Tulare	Tule Rvr Twp	92	261
Ah	25	m	c	CHIN	Trinity	Junction City Pct	92	207
Joseph	56	m	w	IREL	Sonoma	Sonoma Twp	91	449
Pat	28	m	w	IREL	Alameda	Oakland	68	202
HANEAU								
Julia	18	f	w	PRUS	San Francisco	2-Wd San Francisco	79	231
HANEGAN								
Dennis	33	m	w	IREL	San Mateo	Half Moon Bay P O	87	405
Hiram	48	m	w	IREL	Sutter	Vernon Twp	92	131
Jos	50	m	w	IREL	Solano	Vallejo	90	184
N	5	f	w	CA	San Francisco	San Francisco P O	85	827
Rose	7	f	w	CA	San Francisco	San Francisco P O	85	827
HANEHAN								
Thomas	35	m	w	IREL	Santa Cruz	Santa Cruz	89	430
HANEKE								
Charles	64	m	w	PRUS	San Francisco	San Francisco P O	85	731
Sophie	75	f	w	HANO	San Francisco	San Francisco P O	85	731
HANER								
N B	25	m	w	US	Sacramento	1-Wd Sacramento	77	184
HANERTY								
James	35	m	w	IREL	San Francisco	7-Wd San Francisco	81	241
HANES								
E A	40	m	w	OH	Alameda	Oakland	68	150
Jacob	42	m	w	OH	San Francisco	3-Wd San Francisco	79	299
John	39	m	w	OH	Napa	Napa Twp	75	68
Joseph I	27	m	w	ME	San Mateo	Pescadero P O	87	409
Oliver	28	m	w	MA	San Francisco	San Francisco P O	83	203
Samuel	20	m	b	TN	Inyo	Bishop Crk Twp	73	312
Z	39	m	w	IL	Del Norte	Smith Rvr Twp	71	477
HANEVELT								
Elisa	35	f	w	IREL	San Joaquin	1-Wd Stockton	86	126
HANEY								
Anna	10	f	w	CA	San Joaquin	Liberty Twp	86	91
Christ	34	m	w	SWIT	Placer	Lincoln P O	76	481
Dan	37	m	w	IREL	Placer	Colfax P O	76	390
E C	40	m	w	NY	Tehama	Paskenta Twp	92	164
Edward	46	m	w	IREL	San Francisco	7-Wd San Francisco	81	253
Edward	27	m	w	PRUS	San Francisco	San Francisco P O	80	467
Elizabeth	23	f	w	MA	San Francisco	8-Wd San Francisco	82	426

Series M593

Name	Age	S	R	B-PL	County	Locale	Roll	Pg
Hannah	27	f	w	CANA	San Francisco	2-Wd San Francisco	79	201
Hugh	28	m	w	IREL	San Francisco	11-Wd San Francisc	84	673
John	35	m	w	IREL	San Francisco	1-Wd San Francisco	79	28
John	24	m	w	IREL	San Francisco	1-Wd San Francisco	79	88
John	24	m	w	IREL	San Diego	Julian Dist	78	472
L O	36	m	w	OH	San Francisco	San Francisco P O	83	274
Richd	39	m	w	IREL	San Joaquin	3-Wd Stockton	86	244
Squire	42	m	w	CT	San Joaquin	Elliott Twp	86	72
William	61	m	w	VA	Contra Costa	Martinez P O	71	412
William	35	m	w	ENGL	San Francisco	San Francisco P O	80	362
William W	45	m	w	MD	San Francisco	8-Wd San Francisco	82	403
Wm	35	m	w	ENGL	San Francisco	1-Wd San Francisco	79	6
HANFIELD								
John	50	m	w	HANO	Calaveras	San Andreas P O	70	190
HANFIN								
Nellie	18	f	w	MA	San Francisco	8-Wd San Francisco	82	292
HANFORD								
Benj T	45	m	w	NY	San Francisco	San Francisco P O	85	718
George	23	m	w	ENGL	Nevada	Washington Twp	75	343
Harvy	41	m	w	NY	Amador	Volcano P O	69	374
Isaac	43	m	w	NY	Siskiyou	Yreka	89	656
James M	40	m	w	NY	Sacramento	4-Wd Sacramento	77	334
James W	38	m	w	ENGL	Sacramento	Granite Twp	77	146
Jessee	41	m	w	NY	Santa Barbara	Santa Barbara P O	87	480
Jno	39	m	w	IREL	Sacramento	1-Wd Sacramento	77	179
John	52	m	w	ENGL	Nevada	Little York Twp	75	244
John	42	m	w	ENGL	Solano	Vallejo	90	181
Joseph	48	m	w	NY	San Francisco	11-Wd San Francisc	84	614
Saml	38	m	w	NY	Amador	Volcano P O	69	374
Samuel	29	m	w	ENGL	Santa Clara	Redwood Twp	88	132
HANG								
---	35	m	c	CHIN	Siskiyou	Yreka	89	650
---	20	m	c	CHIN	San Francisco	6-Wd San Francisco	81	51
---	20	m	c	CHIN	Shasta	American Ranch P O	89	496
Ah	60	m	c	CHIN	Trinity	Weaverville Pct	92	229
Ah	60	m	c	CHIN	Tuolumne	Chinese Camp P O	93	375
Ah	6	m	c	CHIN	San Francisco	San Francisco P O	80	528
Ah	50	m	c	CHIN	Tuolumne	Big Oak Flat P O	93	401
Ah	50	m	c	CHIN	San Francisco	6-Wd San Francisco	81	44
Ah	50	m	c	CHIN	Placer	Auburn P O	76	377
Ah	47	m	c	CHIN	Butte	Wyandotte Twp	70	143
Ah	45	m	c	CHIN	San Francisco	San Francisco P O	80	439
Ah	43	m	c	CHIN	San Francisco	San Francisco P O	80	442
Ah	42	m	c	CHIN	Marin	Tomales Twp	74	85
Ah	42	m	c	CHIN	San Francisco	San Francisco P O	80	521
Ah	42	m	c	CHIN	Butte	Wyandotte Twp	70	146
Ah	41	m	c	CHIN	San Francisco	San Francisco P O	80	442
Ah	41	m	c	CHIN	Nevada	Grass Valley Twp	75	183
Ah	40	m	c	CHIN	San Francisco	6-Wd San Francisco	81	58
Ah	40	m	c	CHIN	Placer	Emigrant Gap P O	76	416
Ah	40	m	c	CHIN	San Francisco	San Francisco P O	80	526
Ah	40	m	c	CHIN	Santa Clara	1-Wd San Jose	88	272
Ah	40	m	c	CHIN	Siskiyou	Yreka	89	661
Ah	4	f	c	CHIN	San Francisco	San Francisco P O	80	440
Ah	39	m	c	CHIN	Placer	Auburn P O	76	371
Ah	39	m	c	CHIN	San Francisco	1-Wd San Francisco	79	92
Ah	39	m	c	CHIN	San Francisco	San Francisco P O	80	447
Ah	39	m	c	CHIN	San Francisco	San Francisco P O	80	446
Ah	39	m	c	CHIN	San Francisco	San Francisco P O	80	521
Ah	38	m	c	CHIN	San Francisco	6-Wd San Francisco	81	57
Ah	38	m	c	CHIN	Nevada	Grass Valley Twp	75	206
Ah	37	m	c	CHIN	San Francisco	San Francisco P O	80	450
Ah	37	m	c	CHIN	San Francisco	San Francisco P O	80	443
Ah	37	m	c	CHIN	San Francisco	San Francisco P O	80	452
Ah	37	m	c	CHIN	San Francisco	San Francisco P O	80	522
Ah	36	m	c	CHIN	San Francisco	San Francisco P O	80	439
Ah	36	m	c	CHIN	San Francisco	San Francisco P O	80	442
Ah	36	m	c	CHIN	San Francisco	San Francisco P O	80	452
Ah	36	m	c	CHIN	San Francisco	San Francisco P O	80	530
Ah	35	m	c	CHIN	San Francisco	San Francisco P O	80	445
Ah	35	m	c	CHIN	San Mateo	Pescadero P O	87	416
Ah	35	m	c	CHIN	Butte	Wyandotte Twp	70	141
Ah	35	m	c	CHIN	Placer	Lincoln P O	76	484
Ah	34	m	c	CHIN	San Francisco	San Francisco P O	80	499
Ah	34	m	c	CHIN	Placer	Rocklin Twp	76	464
Ah	34	m	c	CHIN	San Francisco	San Francisco P O	80	436
Ah	34	m	c	CHIN	San Francisco	San Francisco P O	80	451
Ah	34	m	c	CHIN	San Francisco	San Francisco P O	80	524
Ah	34	m	c	CHIN	San Francisco	San Francisco P O	80	513
Ah	34	m	c	CHIN	Mariposa	Mariposa P O	74	98
Ah	34	m	c	CHIN	Sacramento	1-Wd Sacramento	77	196
Ah	33	f	c	CHIN	San Francisco	San Francisco P O	80	523
Ah	32	m	c	CHIN	San Francisco	6-Wd San Francisco	81	54
Ah	32	m	c	CHIN	San Francisco	San Francisco P O	80	516
Ah	31	m	c	CHIN	Sierra	Sears Twp	89	553
Ah	31	m	c	CHIN	Butte	Bidwell Twp	70	5
Ah	31	m	c	CHIN	Placer	Auburn P O	76	363
Ah	30	m	c	CHIN	Shasta	Shasta P O	89	456
Ah	30	m	c	CHIN	Placer	Auburn P O	76	371
Ah	30	m	c	CHIN	Alameda	Oakland	68	237
Ah	30	m	c	CHIN	San Francisco	San Francisco P O	80	517
Ah	30	m	c	CHIN	Mariposa	Maxwell Crk P O	74	147
Ah	29	m	c	CHIN	Calaveras	Copperopolis P O	70	240
Ah	29	m	c	CHIN	Calaveras	San Andreas P O	70	205
Ah	28	m	c	CHIN	San Francisco	6-Wd San Francisco	81	39
Ah	28	m	c	CHIN	Fresno	Millerton P O	72	199
Ah	28	m	c	CHIN	Alameda	Oakland	68	267

© 2001 by Heritage Quest. All rights reserved.

Name	Age	S	R	B-PL	County	Locale	Roll	Pg
						Series M593		
Ah	27	m	c	CHIN	Stanislaus	Branch Twp	92	6
Ah	27	m	c	CHIN	Santa Clara	San Jose Twp	88	191
Ah	27	m	c	CHIN	San Francisco	San Francisco P O	80	441
Ah	26	m	c	CHIN	San Francisco	San Francisco P O	80	451
Ah	25	m	c	CHIN	Santa Clara	Alviso Twp	88	25
Ah	25	m	c	CHIN	Tuolumne	Chinese Camp P O	93	364
Ah	25	m	c	CHIN	San Francisco	6-Wd San Francisco	81	42
Ah	25	m	c	CHIN	San Francisco	San Francisco P O	80	453
Ah	25	m	c	CHIN	Nevada	Nevada Twp	75	314
Ah	24	m	c	CHIN	Solano	Vallejo	90	162
Ah	24	m	c	CHIN	San Francisco	6-Wd San Francisco	81	56
Ah	24	m	c	CHIN	San Francisco	San Francisco P O	80	496
Ah	24	m	c	CHIN	Placer	Auburn P O	76	373
Ah	24	f	c	CHIN	San Francisco	San Francisco P O	80	449
Ah	24	m	c	CHIN	Colusa	Colusa	71	299
Ah	23	m	c	CHIN	Tuolumne	Big Oak Flat P O	93	397
Ah	23	m	c	CHIN	San Francisco	6-Wd San Francisco	81	60
Ah	23	m	c	CHIN	Amador	Jackson P O	69	332
Ah	22	m	c	CHIN	San Francisco	San Francisco P O	80	443
Ah	22	m	c	CHIN	Nevada	Grass Valley Twp	75	145
Ah	22	m	c	CHIN	Placer	Lincoln P O	76	483
Ah	21	m	c	CHIN	San Joaquin	1-Wd Stockton	86	145
Ah	21	m	c	CHIN	San Francisco	1-Wd San Francisco	79	87
Ah	21	m	c	CHIN	Shasta	American Ranch P O	89	499
Ah	20	m	c	CHIN	San Francisco	6-Wd San Francisco	81	85
Ah	20	m	c	CHIN	San Francisco	6-Wd San Francisco	81	67
Ah	20	m	c	CHIN	San Francisco	6-Wd San Francisco	81	46
Ah	20	m	c	CHIN	Butte	Chico Twp	70	28
Ah	20	m	c	CHIN	San Francisco	6-Wd San Francisco	81	55
Ah	20	m	c	CHIN	San Francisco	6-Wd San Francisco	81	53
Ah	20	m	c	CHIN	Colusa	Colusa	71	300
Ah	20	m	c	CHIN	Placer	Bath P O	76	456
Ah	19	m	c	CHIN	Santa Cruz	Santa Cruz	89	408
Ah	19	m	c	CHIN	San Francisco	6-Wd San Francisco	81	54
Ah	19	m	c	CHIN	Sonoma	Healdsburg & Mendo	91	280
Ah	18	m	c	CHIN	San Francisco	6-Wd San Francisco	81	68
Ah	18	m	c	CHIN	San Francisco	6-Wd San Francisco	81	60
Ah	18	m	c	CHIN	Santa Clara	1-Wd San Jose	88	272
Ah	18	m	c	CHIN	Alameda	Oakland	68	161
Ah	16	m	c	CHIN	San Francisco	6-Wd San Francisco	81	46
Ah	16	m	c	CHIN	San Francisco	6-Wd San Francisco	81	75
Ah	15	m	c	CHIN	San Francisco	San Francisco P O	83	311
Ah	14	m	c	CHIN	San Francisco	6-Wd San Francisco	81	49
Am	40	m	c	CHIN	Tuolumne	Sonora P O	93	303
Ar	50	m	c	CHIN	Sonoma	Petaluma Twp	91	363
Chang	22	m	c	CHIN	San Francisco	3-Wd San Francisco	79	325
Charles	34	m	w	PRUS	Tuolumne	Chinese Camp P O	93	378
Christian	30	m	w	WURT	Santa Cruz	Santa Cruz	89	408
Chung	36	m	c	CHIN	Amador	Jackson P O	69	331
Con	25	m	c	CHIN	Klamath	Salmon Twp	73	388
Fwa	30	m	c	CHIN	Plumas	Goodwin Twp	77	4
Get	19	m	c	CHIN	San Francisco	3-Wd San Francisco	79	301
Ham	35	m	c	CHIN	Yuba	Marysville	93	629
He	19	m	c	CHIN	Tehama	Bell Mills Twp	92	159
High	20	m	c	CHIN	San Francisco	6-Wd San Francisco	81	128
Hoh	28	m	c	CHIN	San Francisco	San Francisco P O	83	277
Jim	20	m	c	CHIN	Sacramento	3-Wd Sacramento	77	283
Joe	26	m	c	CHIN	San Bernardino	San Bernardino Twp	78	433
Joo	32	m	c	CHIN	San Joaquin	Elkhorn Twp	86	66
Kee	25	m	c	CHIN	Santa Clara	San Jose Twp	88	189
Kee	21	m	c	CHIN	Santa Clara	2-Wd San Jose	88	325
Kin	38	m	c	CHIN	Shasta	American Ranch P O	89	497
King	16	m	c	CHIN	San Francisco	2-Wd San Francisco	79	207
Kong	25	m	c	CHIN	Yuba	Marysville	93	625
Le	34	m	c	CHIN	Sacramento	1-Wd Sacramento	77	199
Lee	39	m	c	CHIN	Plumas	Indian Twp	77	9
Leen	15	f	c	CHIN	San Francisco	6-Wd San Francisco	81	67
Lo	26	m	c	CHIN	Tuolumne	Chinese Camp P O	93	388
Long	25	m	c	CHIN	San Francisco	2-Wd San Francisco	79	256
Luck	21	m	c	CHIN	Yuba	Marysville	93	628
Nim	30	m	c	CHIN	Sacramento	Franklin Twp	77	116
Sam	35	m	c	CHIN	San Joaquin	2-Wd Stockton	86	169
See Up	27	m	c	CHIN	Santa Clara	San Jose Twp	88	190
Sing	36	m	c	CHIN	San Francisco	6-Wd San Francisco	81	75
Sing	21	m	c	CHIN	San Francisco	1-Wd San Francisco	79	43
Sing	15	m	c	CHIN	San Francisco	6-Wd San Francisco	81	44
Soon	22	m	c	CHIN	Nevada	Bridgeport Twp	75	111
Tay	36	m	c	CHIN	Yuba	Marysville	93	625
Tom	31	m	c	CHIN	Butte	Chico Twp	70	28
Tong	34	m	c	CHIN	Fresno	Millerton P O	72	152
Wa	27	m	c	CHIN	San Francisco	San Francisco P O	80	481
Wah	27	m	c	CHIN	Butte	Wyandotte Twp	70	142
We	31	m	c	CHIN	Santa Clara	San Jose Twp	88	193
Wo	30	m	c	CHIN	Tuolumne	Chinese Camp P O	93	388
Wong	32	m	c	CHIN	Mariposa	Mariposa P O	74	103
Yeh	42	m	c	CHIN	Alameda	Hayward	68	77
Yep	20	m	c	CHIN	San Francisco	8-Wd San Francisco	82	301
HANGER								
Anton	60	m	w	PRUS	San Francisco	1-Wd San Francisco	79	104
Frederick	39	m	w	FRAN	El Dorado	Placerville	72	109
J	40	m	w	WURT	Yuba	Marysville	93	616
James	30	m	w	IN	Inyo	Lone Pine Twp	73	331
HANGLON								
Jerry	52	m	w	IREL	Placer	Newcastle Twp	76	476
HANGREY								
Annie	35	f	w	PA	San Francisco	San Francisco P O	83	207

Name	Age	S	R	B-PL	County	Locale	Roll	Pg
						Series M593		
HANH								
Yong	23	m	c	CHIN	San Francisco	2-Wd San Francisco	79	166
HANHAGAN								
Henry	32	m	w	HANO	San Francisco	7-Wd San Francisco	81	224
HANHAGEN								
John	35	m	w	HANO	San Francisco	San Francisco P O	83	190
HANHANARH								
Patrick	29	m	w	IREL	San Francisco	7-Wd San Francisco	81	172
HANHY								
Wm	29	m	w	US	San Joaquin	3-Wd Stockton	86	231
HANI								
Jno A	32	m	w	PA	Santa Clara	Gilroy Twp	88	81
HANIBAL								
H	42	m	w	IREL	Solano	Benicia	90	19
HANIES								
Chr	20	m	w	OH	Sacramento	1-Wd Sacramento	77	190
HANIFAN								
John	36	m	w	IREL	San Francisco	San Francisco P O	83	242
HANIFEL								
John	40	m	w	IREL	San Francisco	8-Wd San Francisco	82	360
HANIFORD								
Thos	40	m	w	IREL	San Francisco	8-Wd San Francisco	82	356
HANIGAN								
Barney	39	m	w	IREL	San Francisco	11-Wd San Francisc	84	450
Edward	25	m	w	IREL	Alameda	Washington Twp	68	298
John	13	m	w	NV	San Francisco	7-Wd San Francisco	81	184
Mich	30	m	w	IREL	Tehama	Tehama Twp	92	187
HANIGAR								
J	46	m	w	IREL	Sacramento	3-Wd Sacramento	77	311
HANIHAN								
Jake	30	m	w	IREL	Solano	Vallejo	90	215
HANIKE								
Peter	25	m	w	PRUS	San Francisco	San Francisco P O	83	393
HANIKEN								
John	31	m	w	IREL	Mariposa	Mariposa P O	74	130
HANINIO								
Doleres	17	m	i	MEXI	Sonoma	Analy Twp	91	231
HANISCH								
Gottlieb	49	m	w	AUST	Placer	Roseville P O	76	349
HANISON								
John	42	m	w	ENGL	San Francisco	2-Wd San Francisco	79	198
HANK								
Ah	25	m	c	CHIN	Sacramento	1-Wd Sacramento	77	204
Elizabeth	14	f	w	CA	San Francisco	11-Wd San Francisc	84	710
Jacob	22	m	w	HDAR	Santa Clara	2-Wd San Jose	88	330
Sam	35	m	w	PRUS	San Francisco	San Francisco P O	83	379
HANKE								
Harmon	45	m	w	PRUS	Solano	Tremont Twp	90	28
James	24	m	w	ENGL	Amador	Amador City P O	69	392
Richard	39	m	w	ENGL	El Dorado	Mud Springs Twp	72	81
HANKER								
John	38	m	w	HANO	Calaveras	San Andreas P O	70	200
HANKES								
John	38	m	w	IREL	San Francisco	San Francisco P O	83	141
HANKET								
A W	44	m	w	NY	Alameda	Oakland	68	153
HANKEY								
D L	21	m	w	IL	Sutter	Sutter Twp	92	124
Edward	40	m	w	PRUS	San Francisco	6-Wd San Francisco	81	94
John	35	m	w	ME	San Francisco	7-Wd San Francisco	81	216
HANKIE								
Julius	30	m	w	DENM	San Francisco	1-Wd San Francisco	79	71
HANKIN								
John	34	m	w	HANO	Calaveras	San Andreas P O	70	210
HANKINS								
B P	37	m	w	TN	Mendocino	Little Lake Twp	74	196
Benjamin	34	m	w	ME	Placer	Bath P O	76	420
Chas H	39	m	w	NJ	Nevada	Little York Twp	75	237
Geo	20	m	w	IA	Lassen	Milford Twp	73	438
J Sm	28	m	w	IL	Sutter	Sutter Twp	92	117
Jennie	7	f	w	CA	Sacramento	Center Twp	77	83
Jessee	40	m	w	TN	Placer	Roseville P O	76	352
John	39	m	w	ENGL	Fresno	Millerton P O	72	165
Mary	53	f	w	IREL	Placer	Colfax P O	76	387
Mary	23	f	w	PA	San Francisco	11-Wd San Francisc	84	498
HANKS								
Charles	42	m	w	IREL	San Francisco	7-Wd San Francisco	81	221
E	24	m	w	CT	Sierra	Butte Twp	89	509
Henry	43	m	w	OH	San Francisco	11-Wd San Francisc	84	563
Henry	29	m	w	OH	Nevada	Meadow Lake Twp	75	267
Isabel	46	f	w	MEXI	Santa Clara	1-Wd San Jose	88	276
Jno	24	m	w	MI	San Joaquin	2-Wd Stockton	86	193
John	59	m	w	VT	Solano	Vallejo	90	172
Marshall	24	m	w	MI	San Francisco	7-Wd San Francisco	81	166
R V	36	m	w	ME	San Joaquin	2-Wd Stockton	86	187
Saml	26	m	w	CA	Santa Clara	Burnett Twp	88	33
Samuel	27	m	w	MEXI	Santa Clara	1-Wd San Jose	88	242
Thomas	32	m	w	OH	San Francisco	7-Wd San Francisco	81	170
W W	26	m	w	NH	Santa Clara	Gilroy Twp	88	82
W Wm	34	m	w	OH	Santa Clara	Gilroy Twp	88	92
William T	26	m	w	NY	San Francisco	6-Wd San Francisco	81	96
HANLAN								
Catherine	76	f	w	IREL	Calaveras	San Andreas P O	70	188
John	50	m	w	IREL	Calaveras	San Andreas P O	70	188
John	43	m	w	IREL	San Francisco	11-Wd San Francisc	84	451
Michael	35	m	w	IREL	San Francisco	San Francisco P O	83	165
Timothy	30	m	w	IREL	Santa Clara	1-Wd San Jose	88	276

© 2001 by Heritage Quest. All rights reserved.

Series M593

Name	Age	S	R	B-PL	County	Locale	Roll	Pg
HANLEN								
John	55	m	w	PA	Santa Clara	San Jose Twp	88	211
Martin	30	m	w	IREL	San Francisco	5-Wd San Francisco	81	32
Rodger	44	m	w	IREL	Humboldt	Eureka Twp	72	280
Tim	38	m	w	IREL	Placer	Blue Canyon P O	76	419
HANLEY								
Albert	39	m	w	PRUS	Yolo	Buckeye Twp	93	414
Alfred	32	m	w	ME	Mendocino	Little Rvr Twp	74	171
Andrew	35	m	w	WURT	El Dorado	Mud Springs Twp	72	73
Anna	47	f	w	IREL	Alameda	Oakland	68	163
Benjamin F	43	m	w	NY	Yolo	Cache Crk Twp	93	446
Bridget	30	f	w	IREL	San Francisco	8-Wd San Francisco	82	451
Charles	42	m	w	NH	San Francisco	11-Wd San Francisc	84	652
Danial	35	m	w	IREL	San Francisco	7-Wd San Francisco	81	172
E J	18	m	w	CA	Alameda	Oakland	68	258
Edwd	36	m	w	IREL	San Francisco	1-Wd San Francisco	79	101
F	8	m	w	CA	San Francisco	San Francisco P O	85	799
Hannah	18	f	w	CANA	San Francisco	San Francisco P O	83	307
Hugh	12	m	w	CA	Santa Cruz	Pajaro Twp	89	343
James	42	m	w	IREL	Santa Cruz	Watsonville	89	367
James	32	m	w	IREL	Marin	Point Reyes Twp	74	22
James	23	m	w	IREL	Placer	Rocklin Twp	76	465
John	52	m	w	IREL	Nevada	Nevada Twp	75	314
John	45	m	w	IREL	Yolo	Washington Twp	93	528
John	35	m	w	IREL	San Francisco	1-Wd San Francisco	79	60
John	31	m	w	IREL	San Francisco	San Francisco P O	85	745
John	28	m	w	IREL	San Francisco	San Francisco P O	85	773
John	23	m	w	NY	Santa Cruz	Santa Cruz Twp	89	388
M	11	m	w	CA	San Francisco	San Francisco P O	85	799
Margaret	45	f	w	IREL	Yuba	Rose Bar Twp	93	653
Mary	44	f	w	IREL	San Francisco	11-Wd San Francisc	84	487
Mary	30	f	w	IREL	San Francisco	7-Wd San Francisco	81	183
Mary	11	f	w	MD	San Francisco	8-Wd San Francisco	82	331
Michael	37	m	w	IREL	Nevada	Nevada Twp	75	319
Michael	30	m	w	IREL	Colusa	Stony Crk Twp	71	326
Michael	30	m	w	IREL	Marin	Sausalito Twp	74	73
Michael	29	m	w	IREL	Nevada	Meadow Lake Twp	75	249
Michael W	26	m	w	IREL	Santa Cruz	Santa Cruz Twp	89	393
Nellie	28	f	w	IREL	Sacramento	4-Wd Sacramento	77	373
P	44	m	w	IREL	Sierra	Table Rock Twp	89	572
Patk	37	m	w	IREL	San Francisco	1-Wd San Francisco	79	8
Patrick	63	m	w	IREL	San Francisco	11-Wd San Francisc	84	500
Patrick	37	m	w	IREL	San Francisco	San Francisco P O	83	250
Philip	42	m	w	IREL	Placer	Bath P O	76	421
Richard	40	m	w	IREL	El Dorado	Kelsey Twp	72	58
Sarah	13	f	w	CA	Nevada	Nevada Twp	75	291
Victoria	12	f	w	CA	Nevada	Nevada Twp	75	276
W M	42	m	w	CT	Alameda	Oakland	68	256
William	36	m	w	IREL	Alameda	Brooklyn	68	33
HANLIN								
Ann	24	f	w	PRUS	Alameda	Oakland	68	208
John	30	m	w	PA	Sierra	Table Rock Twp	89	577
Mathew	30	m	w	PRUS	Butte	Ophir Twp	70	119
Peter	42	m	w	IREL	Shasta	Stillwater P O	89	480
HANLON								
Con	25	m	w	IREL	Contra Costa	Martinez P O	71	427
Danl	35	m	w	IREL	San Francisco	1-Wd San Francisco	79	108
David	59	m	w	PA	Sacramento	Brighton Twp	77	75
David	41	m	w	IREL	San Francisco	11-Wd San Francisc	84	627
Eliza	35	f	w	IREL	Butte	Kimshew Tpw	70	81
George	77	m	w	OH	Sacramento	Brighton Twp	77	75
James	24	m	w	IREL	San Francisco	11-Wd San Francisc	84	548
Jas	49	m	w	IREL	Sacramento	1-Wd Sacramento	77	176
John	39	m	w	IL	Sacramento	Lee Twp	77	161
John	39	m	w	IREL	Solano	Vallejo	90	201
John	33	m	w	IREL	Trinity	Weaverville Pct	92	222
John	31	m	w	IREL	San Francisco	2-Wd San Francisco	79	216
Joseph F	45	m	w	IREL	San Francisco	San Francisco P O	83	355
Julia	18	f	w	IN	Sacramento	2-Wd Sacramento	77	235
Mary	65	f	w	IREL	San Francisco	11-Wd San Francisc	84	627
Michael	52	m	w	IREL	Nevada	Grass Valley Twp	75	175
Michael	36	m	w	IREL	El Dorado	Mountain Twp	72	70
Michael	30	m	w	IREL	Nevada	Grass Valley Twp	75	215
Richard	29	m	w	IREL	San Francisco	7-Wd San Francisco	81	259
Robt	49	m	w	OH	Shasta	Buckeye P O	89	482
Rose	34	f	w	IREL	San Francisco	San Francisco P O	83	246
Stephen	31	m	w	IREL	San Francisco	San Francisco P O	83	72
Valentine	44	m	w	IREL	San Francisco	1-Wd San Francisco	79	5
Wm	61	m	w	OH	Shasta	American Ranch P O	89	498
HANLY								
Charles L	33	m	w	ME	Mendocino	Little Rvr Twp	74	171
Danl	38	m	w	IREL	San Francisco	1-Wd San Francisco	79	74
Hugh	11	m	w	CA	Placer	Dutch Flat P O	76	410
John	47	m	w	IREL	San Mateo	San Mateo P O	87	350
John	43	m	w	IREL	Butte	Wyandotte Twp	70	142
John	34	m	w	IREL	San Francisco	San Francisco P O	83	390
Joseph	35	m	w	IREL	Sacramento	Franklin Twp	77	118
Kate	9	f	w	CA	Nevada	Grass Valley Twp	75	230
Mary	15	f	w	IREL	Alameda	Oakland	68	166
Mary	10	f	w	CA	Yolo	Buckeye Twp	93	414
Mary A	7	f	w	CA	Nevada	Grass Valley Twp	75	230
Thomas	37	m	w	IREL	Nevada	Little York Twp	75	235
HANMER								
Ed	39	m	w	VA	Humboldt	Pacific Twp	72	291
HANN								
Adam	18	m	w	NY	Siskiyou	Scott Valley Twp	89	608
Ah	21	m	c	CHIN	San Francisco	7-Wd San Francisco	81	245
David	67	m	w	NY	Sutter	Vernon Twp	92	131
Geo	43	m	w	BADE	Butte	Ophir Twp	70	108
Israel	46	m	w	NH	San Francisco	11-Wd San Francisc	84	607
Jane	70	f	w	KY	Santa Clara	Santa Clara Twp	88	152
John	45	m	w	NY	San Francisco	San Francisco P O	83	308
John	23	m	w	HAMB	San Joaquin	1-Wd Stockton	86	131
Kate M	42	f	w	KY	San Francisco	San Francisco P O	83	195
L E	40	m	w	IL	Santa Clara	Burnett Twp	88	31
Lizzie	22	f	w	IREL	San Francisco	San Francisco P O	83	138
Lovina	46	f	w	IN	Santa Clara	Redwood Twp	88	120
M E	38	f	w	NY	Santa Clara	Gilroy Twp	88	77
Peter	77	m	w	OH	Santa Clara	Santa Clara Twp	88	152
Thomas	13	m	w	CA	Santa Clara	San Jose Twp	88	194
Wm	22	m	w	MO	Monterey	Alisal Twp	74	298
Z	48	m	w	MO	Santa Clara	Gilroy Twp	88	99
HANNA								
A W	35	m	w	PA	San Francisco	8-Wd San Francisco	82	333
Davis	39	m	w	DE	El Dorado	Mountain Twp	72	67
Edward	21	m	w	MI	Sacramento	Center Twp	77	85
Eli	32	m	w	MO	Marin	San Rafael Twp	74	40
Francis	39	m	w	IREL	Marin	San Rafael Twp	74	59
Frank	45	m	w	VA	El Dorado	Mud Springs Twp	72	82
Frank	21	m	w	PORT	San Mateo	Half Moon Bay P O	87	390
Fredrick	32	m	w	PRUS	San Francisco	San Francisco P O	80	482
George	38	m	w	IREL	Tuolumne	Chinese Camp P O	93	381
George G	35	m	w	ME	San Diego	San Diego	78	490
J	29	m	w	IL	Alameda	Oakland	68	262
James	64	m	w	PA	Humboldt	Eureka Twp	72	272
James	38	m	w	IN	Santa Clara	Gilroy Twp	88	93
James G	40	m	w	MO	Sonoma	Petaluma Twp	91	361
John	65	m	w	IREL	Solano	Vallejo	90	161
John	58	m	w	MD	San Francisco	2-Wd San Francisco	79	284
John	42	m	w	TN	Napa	Napa	75	26
John	41	m	w	VA	Colusa	Colusa	71	289
John	39	m	w	OH	Los Angeles	Santa Ana Twp	73	601
John	35	m	w	PA	San Francisco	8-Wd San Francisco	82	476
John	30	m	c	IREL	Calaveras	San Andreas P O	70	184
John A	37	m	w	CANA	Humboldt	Arcata Twp	72	227
Levi	35	m	w	ME	Santa Cruz	Santa Cruz	89	424
Lydia	27	f	w	NY	San Joaquin	1-Wd Stockton	86	121
Michael	32	m	w	IREL	Placer	Newcastle Twp	76	476
Robert	44	m	w	IN	San Joaquin	2-Wd Stockton	86	165
Robert	35	m	w	SCOT	San Francisco	11-Wd San Francisc	84	668
Robt	45	m	w	IREL	San Francisco	San Francisco P O	85	777
William	38	m	w	MO	Kern	Havilah P O	73	336
Wm	56	m	w	IN	Santa Clara	Gilroy Twp	88	74
Wm	51	m	w	KY	Santa Clara	Gilroy Twp	88	82
Wm H	35	m	w	CANA	Sonoma	Petaluma Twp	91	318
HANNAFIN								
I I	36	m	w	MA	Alameda	Oakland	68	184
HANNAFORD								
John	37	m	w	ENGL	San Francisco	San Francisco P O	83	249
Sarah	22	f	w	ME	San Joaquin	1-Wd Stockton	86	126
HANNAGON								
Thos	26	m	w	NJ	Alameda	Murray Twp	68	113
HANNAH								
Charles	47	m	w	IREL	Trinity	Weaverville Pct	92	230
Elbridge	27	m	w	ME	Sacramento	4-Wd Sacramento	77	348
Eliza	23	f	w	NY	Nevada	Grass Valley Twp	75	172
Hariett	50	f	w	ENGL	San Francisco	San Francisco P O	83	255
J W	27	m	w	KY	Lake	Lower Lake	73	416
James	31	m	w	ENGL	Humboldt	Pacific Twp	72	298
James	18	m	w	NY	San Francisco	San Francisco P O	83	142
Jas K P	24	m	w	MO	Sonoma	Cloverdale Twp	91	272
Joe	25	m	w	BAVA	Alameda	Oakland	68	192
John	43	m	w	FRAN	Colusa	Spring Valley Twp	71	345
Margaret	32	f	w	FRAN	Sacramento	2-Wd Sacramento	77	243
Micheal	44	m	w	IREL	San Francisco	7-Wd San Francisco	81	193
Robt T	37	m	w	CANA	Monterey	Monterey	74	361
W A	26	m	w	CANA	Nevada	Meadow Lake Twp	75	246
William	32	m	w	CANA	Yolo	Grafton Twp	93	501
Wm	38	m	w	IL	Santa Clara	Gilroy Twp	88	97
HANNAHAN								
John	38	m	w	IREL	Klamath	Klamath Twp	73	370
HANNAM								
Moses	50	m	w	BADE	Marin	San Rafael	74	54
HANNAN								
Charles	22	m	w	NY	San Francisco	San Francisco P O	83	361
Hugh	35	m	w	IREL	Nevada	Grass Valley Twp	75	210
Jas	22	m	w	NY	San Francisco	7-Wd San Francisco	81	250
Michl	28	m	w	IREL	San Francisco	1-Wd San Francisco	79	87
Patrick	40	m	w	IREL	Santa Clara	San Jose Twp	88	193
Patrick	30	m	w	IREL	Sonoma	Petaluma Twp	91	337
Rbt	42	m	w	VA	Sutter	Nicolaus Twp	92	106
Wm	65	m	w	IREL	Sierra	Gibson Twp	89	542
HANNASACKER								
Nichs	44	m	w	IL	San Diego	San Diego	78	490
HANNATH								
Chas G	58	m	w	ENGL	San Francisco	7-Wd San Francisco	81	248
J C	61	m	w	ENGL	Sonoma	Santa Rosa	91	418
HANNAY								
Andrew	28	m	w	SWIT	El Dorado	Georgetown Twp	72	42
HANNEFAN								
Timothy	29	m	w	NY	Nevada	Meadow Lake Twp	75	264
HANNEFEN								
Timothy	24	m	w	IREL	Nevada	Meadow Lake Twp	75	252

© 2001 by Heritage Quest. All rights reserved.

California 1870 Census

Name	Age	S	R	B-PL	County	Locale	Roll	Pg
						Series M593		
HANNEGAN								
James	35	m	w	IREL	Placer	Alta P O	76	412
John	35	m	w	IREL	San Francisco	1-Wd San Francisco	79	48
Wm	46	m	w	IREL	San Francisco	1-Wd San Francisco	79	19
HANNEKEN								
Hes	40	m	w	SHOL	Marin	San Antonio Twp	74	61
HANNEN								
Anna	32	f	w	IREL	San Francisco	7-Wd San Francisco	81	171
Margaret	33	f	w	IREL	Sacramento	Granite Twp	77	146
HANNENS								
Elisha	45	m	w	MA	Mariposa	Maxwell Crk P O	74	144
HANNER								
John	48	m	w	IREL	Sonoma	Vallejo Twp	91	452
John	27	m	w	NY	Solano	Vallejo	90	160
Wm	35	m	w	ENGL	San Francisco	San Francisco P O	83	89
Wm	22	m	w	ENGL	Sonoma	Salt Point	91	386
HANNEY								
Andrew	25	m	w	TX	Butte	Chico Twp	70	29
Chas H	41	m	w	CANA	Humboldt	Eureka Twp	72	271
Christan	60	m	w	WURT	Placer	Bath P O	76	447
Jas	34	m	w	MI	San Joaquin	Dent Twp	86	28
HANNIBAL								
Russell	21	m	w	CANA	San Luis Obispo	San Luis Obispo Tw	87	316
William	60	m	w	ENGL	Santa Clara	Santa Clara Twp	88	164
HANNIGAN								
Bridget	35	f	w	IREL	San Francisco	7-Wd San Francisco	81	284
David	13	m	w	IREL	Marin	San Rafael Twp	74	30
James	40	m	w	IREL	San Francisco	11-Wd San Francisc	84	494
John	12	m	w	IREL	Placer	Cisco P O	76	494
Mally	23	f	w	ENGL	San Francisco	San Francisco P O	85	721
Patrick	68	m	w	IREL	San Francisco	San Francisco P O	85	715
Samuel	40	m	w	IREL	Placer	Cisco P O	76	494
HANNIN								
Cathine	65	f	w	IREL	San Francisco	San Francisco P O	85	834
HANNING								
Fredrick	22	m	w	PRUS	San Francisco	San Francisco P O	80	349
George	50	m	w	IREL	San Francisco	San Francisco P O	83	221
Jacob	35	m	w	MI	Tehama	Tehama Twp	92	194
Paul	46	m	w	HAMB	Placer	Bath P O	76	430
William	40	m	w	IREL	Santa Clara	Redwood Twp	88	123
HANNIS								
Thos J	32	m	w	SC	Fresno	Kingston P O	72	222
HANNON								
Amanda	17	f	w	OR	San Diego	San Diego	78	490
Anna Maria	70	f	c	CHIN	San Francisco	2-Wd San Francisco	79	202
David	23	m	w	ENGL	San Francisco	3-Wd San Francisco	79	314
David G	44	m	w	NC	Mono	Bridgeport P O	74	282
Fritz	30	m	w	GERM	Yolo	Cache Crk Twp	93	452
J S	40	m	w	KY	San Joaquin	Liberty Twp	86	90
James C	40	m	w	ENGL	Los Angeles	El Monte Twp	73	450
Jennie	24	f	w	SC	San Francisco	8-Wd San Francisco	82	359
John	46	m	w	IREL	San Francisco	San Francisco P O	85	876
John	35	m	w	IREL	San Francisco	3-Wd San Francisco	79	315
John	33	m	w	IREL	San Francisco	San Francisco P O	85	742
John	27	m	w	WURT	San Francisco	San Francisco P O	83	304
Mary	19	f	w	MA	San Mateo	Redwood Twp	87	365
Michael	40	m	w	IREL	San Francisco	San Francisco P O	85	733
Michael	35	m	w	IREL	Nevada	Grass Valley Twp	75	169
Miles	44	m	w	NY	Sonoma	Petaluma Twp	91	344
Nora	25	f	w	IREL	San Francisco	2-Wd San Francisco	79	202
Owen	49	m	w	IREL	Sacramento	1-Wd Sacramento	77	180
Patrick	33	m	w	IREL	San Francisco	2-Wd San Francisco	79	191
Thomas	40	m	w	IREL	Nevada	Eureka Twp	75	130
Thos	55	m	w	IREL	Sacramento	4-Wd Sacramento	77	324
Tom	22	m	w	IREL	San Francisco	8-Wd San Francisco	82	359
HANNOR								
James	45	m	w	IREL	Yolo	Grafton Twp	93	500
HANNOVER								
M S	28	m	w	OH	Sacramento	1-Wd Sacramento	77	176
HANNOWY								
John	30	m	w	IREL	San Francisco	3-Wd San Francisco	79	316
HANNSBERRY								
Patrick	25	m	w	IREL	San Mateo	San Mateo P O	87	360
HANNSON								
Christian	32	m	w	DENM	Yolo	Cottonwood Twp	93	471
HANNUM								
Warren W	42	m	w	TN	Yolo	Cache Crk Twp	93	452
HANNUN								
Alice	30	f	w	PA	San Francisco	San Francisco P O	83	267
HANNY								
P	25	m	w	NY	Alameda	Oakland	68	184
Phillip	40	m	w	IREL	Sacramento	4-Wd Sacramento	77	341
W E	29	m	w	VT	Alameda	Oakland	68	239
HANOCK								
H	29	m	w	PRUS	Alameda	Oakland	68	164
Jacob	26	m	w	BOHE	San Francisco	8-Wd San Francisco	82	414
HANOLD								
George	27	m	w	NY	San Francisco	5-Wd San Francisco	81	12
James	52	m	w	NY	San Francisco	2-Wd San Francisco	79	202
HANON								
Henry	39	m	w	CANA	Solano	Rio Vista Twp	90	64
James	26	m	w	MO	Solano	Rio Vista Twp	90	61
Thomas	37	m	w	CANA	San Diego	San Diego	78	487
HANOVAN								
Cathrine	62	f	w	IREL	San Francisco	San Francisco P O	83	382
John	35	m	w	IREL	San Francisco	San Francisco P O	83	96
HANOVEN								
John	26	m	w	NY	San Francisco	San Francisco P O	83	378
HANOVER								
William	40	m	w	IREL	San Francisco	6-Wd San Francisco	81	136
HANOWE								
Juan	4	m	w	CA	San Francisco	San Francisco P O	80	478
HANOWER								
Wm	28	m	w	SCOT	Sonoma	Mendocino Twp	91	298
HANOY								
Mary	33	f	w	IREL	Alameda	Brooklyn	68	22
HANPER								
James	29	m	w	SWIT	San Francisco	San Francisco P O	80	533
HANPT								
Casper	47	m	w	PRUS	Sacramento	4-Wd Sacramento	77	342
HANQUINEL								
Peter	32	m	w	BELG	San Francisco	8-Wd San Francisco	82	358
HANRAHAN								
Edward	75	m	w	IREL	Santa Clara	Redwood Twp	88	123
Statia	18	f	w	IREL	San Francisco	San Francisco P O	85	800
HANRATHY								
Thos	21	m	w	ENGL	Solano	Vallejo	90	201
HANRATTY								
Patrick	42	m	w	IREL	Sonoma	Analy Twp	91	219
HANRETTY								
Patk	46	m	w	IREL	San Francisco	1-Wd San Francisco	79	59
Wm	26	m	w	IREL	Lake	Knoxville Mines	73	404
HANS								
Elizabeth	35	f	w	HDAR	San Francisco	2-Wd San Francisco	79	187
Hanson	32	m	w	BADE	Solano	Suisun Twp	90	104
John	60	m	w	BADE	San Francisco	San Francisco P O	85	865
Nicholas	22	m	w	DENM	San Francisco	2-Wd San Francisco	79	284
Wm D	37	m	w	TN	Tuolumne	Sonora P O	93	329
HANSALT								
John	39	m	w	BAVA	Calaveras	Copperopolis P O	70	256
HANSARD								
Calvin	55	m	w	TN	Yuba	Linda Twp	93	557
Elinda	77	f	w	NC	Yuba	Linda Twp	93	557
J	76	m	w	VA	Yuba	Linda Twp	93	557
John	27	m	w	TN	Mendocino	Calpella Twp	74	183
HANSBERRY								
P	31	m	w	IREL	San Francisco	San Francisco P O	83	310
HANSBROUGH								
Eliab	61	m	w	KY	Santa Clara	Milpitas Twp	88	114
HANSBROW								
G	13	m	w	CA	Solano	Benicia	90	20
L	30	f	w	KY	Sacramento	3-Wd Sacramento	77	302
HANSCELMAN								
Jacob	50	m	w	OH	Stanislaus	Emory Twp	92	21
HANSCH								
Henry	42	m	w	PRUS	Sacramento	2-Wd Sacramento	77	230
HANSCHILD								
Thos	22	m	w	PRUS	San Francisco	5-Wd San Francisco	81	20
HANSCOM								
J W	48	m	w	ME	San Joaquin	Dent Twp	86	21
Meldon	28	m	w	ME	San Francisco	11-Wd San Francisc	84	647
HANSCOMB								
Heny	35	m	w	CANA	Butte	Chico Twp	70	39
HANSCUM								
E L	43	m	w	GERM	Sacramento	1-Wd Sacramento	77	188
HANSE								
Emma	14	f	w	CA	San Joaquin	Elkhorn Twp	86	61
HANSEL								
Christian	49	m	w	BADE	Shasta	Fort Crook P O	89	474
Danl	39	m	w	PRUS	Tuolumne	Big Oak Flat P O	93	404
Henry	15	m	w	CA	Humboldt	Eel Rvr Twp	72	251
Michael	60	m	w	PA	Shasta	Shasta P O	89	457
HANSELL								
Amos	44	m	w	PA	Humboldt	South Fork Twp	72	301
Joe	35	m	w	NY	San Joaquin	2-Wd Stockton	86	212
Louis	40	m	w	NY	San Joaquin	2-Wd Stockton	86	207
W	28	m	w	IL	San Joaquin	Liberty Twp	86	86
HANSELMAN								
Andrew	40	m	w	SWIT	Sacramento	American Twp	77	66
HANSELTON								
Ruben	35	m	w	VT	Placer	Bath P O	76	425
HANSEMAN								
S	45	m	w	SWIT	Alameda	Oakland	68	250
HANSEN								
Albert	34	m	w	DENM	San Francisco	San Francisco P O	83	403
Andreas	33	m	w	DENM	Santa Cruz	Pajaro Twp	89	356
Andrew	51	m	w	NORW	Nevada	Bridgeport Twp	75	122
Andrew	44	m	w	PA	San Francisco	San Francisco P O	80	538
Andrew	37	m	w	DENM	Alameda	Eden Twp	68	85
Anton	22	m	w	DENM	San Francisco	1-Wd San Francisco	79	85
Artemus	31	m	w	PRUS	San Francisco	8-Wd San Francisco	82	428
Asmus	36	m	w	SHOL	San Francisco	11-Wd San Francisc	84	424
Asmus	32	m	w	SHOL	San Francisco	11-Wd San Francisc	84	469
Charles E	36	m	w	PRUS	San Francisco	8-Wd San Francisco	82	474
Chas	27	m	w	DENM	San Francisco	1-Wd San Francisco	79	122
Christ	47	m	w	PRUS	Butte	Chico Twp	70	16
Christian	40	m	w	DENM	San Francisco	3-Wd San Francisco	79	324
Danil	59	m	w	SHOL	San Francisco	1-Wd San Francisco	79	70
Elisabeth	80	f	w	DENM	Alameda	Eden Twp	68	57
Etsphe	46	m	w	PRUS	San Francisco	11-Wd San Francisc	84	685
Frank	27	m	w	HANO	San Francisco	1-Wd San Francisco	79	122
Frederick	60	m	w	NORW	Nevada	Bridgeport Twp	75	122
Fritz	26	m	w	PRUS	San Francisco	1-Wd San Francisco	79	112

© 2001 by Heritage Quest. All rights reserved.

Name	Age	S	R	B-PL	County	Locale	Roll	Pg
H C	43	m	w	DENM	San Joaquin	2-Wd Stockton	86	164
Hans	30	m	w	DENM	San Francisco	1-Wd San Francisco	79	70
Hanse	24	m	w	DENM	Monterey	Alisal Twp	74	293
Henry	44	m	w	NORW	San Francisco	1-Wd San Francisco	79	122
Henry	34	m	w	SWED	Marin	Tomales Twp	74	79
Henry	27	m	w	NORW	San Francisco	8-Wd San Francisco	82	386
James	42	m	w	DENM	Sierra	Downieville Twp	89	514
James	27	m	w	DENM	Alameda	Eden Twp	68	59
John	45	m	w	BREM	Marin	Sausalito Twp	74	71
John	44	m	w	DENM	Alameda	Eden Twp	68	57
John	42	m	w	NY	San Francisco	1-Wd San Francisco	79	124
John	35	m	w	DENM	Monterey	Castroville Twp	74	336
John	29	m	w	DENM	Alameda	Eden Twp	68	86
John	28	m	w	SHOL	Sutter	Sutter Twp	92	119
John	26	m	w	DENM	Santa Cruz	Pajaro Twp	89	346
Lauria	12	f	w	CA	Alameda	San Leandro	68	94
Loranz	35	m	w	DENM	Santa Cruz	Pajaro Twp	89	356
Louis	42	m	w	SHOL	San Francisco	2-Wd San Francisco	79	170
Louis	27	m	w	DENM	San Francisco	1-Wd San Francisco	79	121
M	26	f	w	IREL	San Joaquin	2-Wd Stockton	86	173
Madeline	52	f	w	DENM	Placer	Lincoln P O	76	487
Martin	30	m	w	DENM	Alameda	Eden Twp	68	71
N	22	m	w	VT	Alameda	Oakland	68	261
Nellie	25	f	i	CA	Nevada	Grass Valley Twp	75	222
Peter	46	m	w	DENM	San Francisco	11-Wd San Francisc	84	601
Peter	41	m	w	PRUS	San Francisco	San Francisco P O	80	533
Peter	38	m	w	DENM	Butte	Chico Twp	70	38
Peter	36	m	w	DENM	San Francisco	San Francisco P O	80	467
Peter	32	m	w	DENM	Alameda	Brooklyn Twp	68	46
Peter	31	m	w	DENM	San Francisco	11-Wd San Francisc	84	519
Peter	30	m	w	SHOL	Sonoma	Salt Point	91	389
Peter	25	m	w	PRUS	Alameda	Hayward	68	78
Peter	22	m	w	NORW	San Francisco	1-Wd San Francisco	79	122
Peter A	28	m	w	DENM	San Francisco	1-Wd San Francisco	79	119
Peter N	38	m	w	NORW	Nevada	Grass Valley Twp	75	222
R	36	m	w	DENM	Alameda	Murray Twp	68	118
Stello	47	m	w	NORW	San Francisco	San Francisco P O	83	65
Thomas	33	m	w	DENM	San Francisco	San Francisco P O	80	467
Tolof	44	m	w	NORW	Santa Cruz	Pajaro Twp	89	348
Victor	35	m	w	MI	Santa Clara	Fremont Twp	88	43
William	21	m	w	PRUS	San Francisco	San Francisco P O	80	478
Wm	36	m	w	NORW	Sonoma	Santa Rosa	91	405
HANSERA								
Benito	50	m	w	CHIL	Santa Clara	Alviso Twp	88	28
HANSESSY								
Lawrence	27	m	w	DENM	Monterey	San Juan Twp	74	389
HANSEY								
Anna	74	f	m	MD	San Joaquin	3-Wd Stockton	86	226
HANSHUE								
Amelia	16	f	w	NY	San Francisco	8-Wd San Francisco	82	322
HANSICK								
Margrett	42	f	w	HANO	San Francisco	1-Wd San Francisco	79	5
HANSIN								
Fredk	33	m	w	DENM	San Francisco	1-Wd San Francisco	79	125
HANSMAN								
Wm	50	m	w	SAXO	San Joaquin	2-Wd Stockton	86	195
HANSOM								
A J	44	m	w	ME	El Dorado	Greenwood Twp	72	54
Jane	17	f	w	IREL	San Francisco	11-Wd San Francisc	84	504
Oliver	31	m	w	NORW	San Francisco	7-Wd San Francisco	81	274
Peter	41	m	w	DENM	Placer	Auburn P O	76	357
Saml K	52	m	w	OH	Tuolumne	Sonora P O	93	322
HANSON								
A	40	m	w	PRUS	San Joaquin	3-Wd Stockton	86	223
A B	35	m	w	ME	Sutter	Sutter Twp	92	124
A B	27	m	w	ME	Sutter	Sutter Twp	92	122
A H	41	m	w	CANA	Nevada	Nevada Twp	75	276
A P	38	m	w	DENM	Sutter	Nicolaus Twp	92	108
Albert	30	m	w	SHOL	San Francisco	1-Wd San Francisco	79	127
Albert C	34	m	w	VT	Inyo	Independence Twp	73	325
Ames	36	m	w	ME	Mendocino	Anderson Twp	74	156
Andrew	55	m	w	NORW	Stanislaus	Branch Twp	92	6
Andrew	45	m	w	DENM	Monterey	Monterey	74	355
Andrew	35	m	w	SWED	San Francisco	7-Wd San Francisco	81	218
Andrew	32	m	w	DENM	San Francisco	3-Wd San Francisco	79	294
Andrew	28	m	w	PA	San Francisco	1-Wd San Francisco	79	18
Andrew	27	m	w	DENM	San Francisco	1-Wd San Francisco	79	26
Andrew	26	m	w	DENM	Alameda	Eden Twp	68	62
Andrew	19	m	w	IA	Santa Clara	Santa Clara Twp	88	151
Anthon W	36	m	w	NORW	Sonoma	Cloverdale Twp	91	268
Asa	34	m	w	ME	Mendocino	Ukiah Twp	74	244
Asmus J	31	m	w	SHOL	San Francisco	1-Wd San Francisco	79	116
B H	21	m	w	SWED	San Francisco	7-Wd San Francisco	81	223
Berry	30	m	w	IREL	San Joaquin	Tulare Twp	86	255
C M	43	m	w	HOLL	Klamath	Salmon Twp	73	387
C R	25	m	w	DENM	Solano	Vallejo	90	201
C S	50	m	w	DENM	Del Norte	Crescent	71	465
Carl	54	m	w	DENM	Nevada	Grass Valley Twp	75	168
Charles	42	m	w	PA	Plumas	Mineral Twp	77	20
Charles	38	m	w	BADE	San Francisco	San Francisco P O	83	158
Charles	37	m	w	DENM	San Mateo	Redwood Twp	87	369
Charles	37	m	w	ENGL	Placer	Colfax P O	76	387
Charles	35	m	w	DENM	Mendocino	Navarro & Big Rvr	74	177
Charles	30	m	w	DENM	Sonoma	Bodega Twp	91	260
Charles	30	m	w	NORW	Plumas	Quartz Twp	77	35
Charles	28	m	w	DENM	San Francisco	San Francisco P O	83	218
Charles	26	m	w	NORW	Mendocino	Navarro & Big Rvr	74	177
Charles	24	m	w	SWED	San Mateo	Schoolhouse Statio	87	335
Charles	22	m	w	NORW	Sonoma	Bodega Twp	91	260
Charles F	24	m	w	ME	Klamath	Camp Gaston	73	372
Charles G	40	m	w	PA	Inyo	Cerro Gordo Twp	73	318
Charles O	33	m	w	SWED	Yolo	Washington Twp	93	530
Chas	42	m	w	PA	Butte	Ophir Twp	70	98
Chas	40	m	w	DENM	San Francisco	1-Wd San Francisco	79	26
Chas	37	m	w	NY	San Francisco	1-Wd San Francisco	79	90
Chas	31	m	w	NORW	Humboldt	Bucksport Twp	72	242
Chas	29	m	w	ME	Humboldt	Bucksport Twp	72	242
Chas	24	m	w	HAMB	San Francisco	San Francisco P O	83	95
Chas E	36	m	w	NY	San Francisco	1-Wd San Francisco	79	111
Christ	24	m	w	DENM	Alameda	Eden Twp	68	62
Christian	28	m	w	HAMB	San Francisco	6-Wd San Francisco	81	81
Christian	28	m	w	DENM	Sonoma	Salt Point	91	387
Christian	24	m	w	SHOL	Sonoma	Vallejo Twp	91	457
Christn	53	m	w	DENM	Alameda	Eden Twp	68	57
Chrristian	24	m	w	DENM	Nevada	Eureka Twp	75	130
Con	37	m	w	GERM	San Joaquin	2-Wd Stockton	86	167
Conrad	42	m	w	DENM	Tuolumne	Chinese Camp P O	93	390
D A	31	m	w	IL	Sutter	Yuba Twp	92	152
Daniel	61	m	w	ME	Butte	Ophir Twp	70	94
Daniel	34	m	w	DENM	San Francisco	San Francisco P O	80	538
David	32	m	w	NORW	San Francisco	3-Wd San Francisco	79	294
Detliff	35	m	w	SHOL	Trinity	Weaverville Pct	92	223
Dun	33	m	w	IL	Lake	Lower Lake	73	419
Ede	45	f	w	ME	San Joaquin	2-Wd Stockton	86	175
Edwd	41	m	w	NY	Solano	Vallejo	90	152
Eliza	16	f	w	CA	San Francisco	2-Wd San Francisco	79	224
Emile	27	m	w	DENM	San Diego	San Diego	78	492
F E	28	m	w	MO	Tuolumne	Big Oak Flat P O	93	405
Felix	28	m	w	PRUS	San Francisco	6-Wd San Francisco	81	118
Ferdinand	33	m	w	PRUS	San Francisco	2-Wd San Francisco	79	187
Francisco	46	m	w	NH	Alameda	Washington Twp	68	296
Frank	42	m	w	PRUS	Trinity	Junction City Pct	92	210
Frank	37	m	w	IL	Lake	Scotts Crk	73	428
Frank	25	m	w	NY	Sonoma	Sonoma Twp	91	442
Fred	25	m	w	SHOL	San Francisco	11-Wd San Francisc	84	641
Fred	25	m	w	DENM	Fresno	Kings Rvr P O	72	212
Frederick	40	m	w	PRUS	Kern	Linns Valley P O	73	343
Frederick	28	m	w	FINL	Placer	Bath P O	76	457
Fredk	31	m	w	DENM	San Francisco	1-Wd San Francisco	79	79
Fredrick	29	m	w	DENM	Mendocino	Little Rvr Twp	74	171
G	38	m	w	PRUS	San Francisco	San Francisco P O	83	62
Geo M	71	m	w	VA	Santa Clara	Gilroy Twp	88	74
George	46	m	w	AUST	Los Angeles	Los Angeles	73	565
George	34	m	w	DENM	San Francisco	11-Wd San Francisc	84	519
H C	32	m	w	DENM	Humboldt	Bald Hills	72	237
Han	28	m	w	SWED	San Francisco	3-Wd San Francisco	79	308
Hance	39	m	w	DENM	Alameda	Eden Twp	68	65
Hans	59	m	w	PRUS	Yolo	Merritt Twp	93	503
Hans	35	m	w	GERM	Yolo	Putah Twp	93	517
Hans	32	m	w	DENM	Solano	Suisun Twp	90	97
Hans	30	m	w	NORW	Siskiyou	Callahan P O	89	632
Hans	28	m	w	DENM	Mendocino	Navarro & Big Rvr	74	177
Hans C	39	m	w	DENM	San Francisco	1-Wd San Francisco	79	79
Henry	42	m	w	DENM	Los Angeles	Los Angeles	73	545
Henry	36	m	w	DENM	San Francisco	3-Wd San Francisco	79	300
Henry	34	m	w	ENGL	Los Angeles	Wilmington Twp	73	642
Henry	33	m	w	DENM	San Francisco	7-Wd San Francisco	81	223
Henry	32	m	w	PRUS	Yolo	Merritt Twp	93	503
Henry	25	m	w	ENGL	San Francisco	7-Wd San Francisco	81	223
Herman	46	m	w	GERM	Tuolumne	Columbia P O	93	336
Herman	28	m	w	DENM	San Francisco	San Francisco P O	83	213
Holtz	30	m	w	NY	Sutter	Yuba Twp	92	145
Isaac N	40	m	w	OH	San Mateo	Redwood Twp	87	363
J	28	m	w	SWED	Sonoma	Petaluma Twp	91	357
Jacob	40	m	w	NORW	Siskiyou	Yreka	89	658
Jacob	34	m	w	DENM	San Francisco	7-Wd San Francisco	81	262
Jacob	33	m	w	FINL	Mendocino	Casper & Big Rvr	74	164
Jacob	31	m	w	DENM	Alameda	Eden Twp	68	64
James	57	m	w	ME	San Francisco	11-Wd San Francisc	84	489
James	52	m	w	MA	San Francisco	San Francisco P O	83	200
James	43	m	w	DENM	San Francisco	2-Wd San Francisco	79	153
James H	46	m	w	MD	Yuba	New York Twp	93	636
Jane	60	f	w	NY	Sutter	Yuba Twp	92	152
Jane	105	f	w	SCOT	San Francisco	11-Wd San Francisc	84	611
Jas J	38	m	w	DENM	San Francisco	1-Wd San Francisco	79	35
Jeff	30	m	w	DENM	Solano	Vallejo	90	213
Jessee G	28	m	w	ME	Santa Barbara	Las Cruces P O	87	515
John	59	m	w	NY	El Dorado	White Oak Twp	72	142
John	55	m	w	ME	San Francisco	11-Wd San Francisc	84	443
John	54	m	w	HANO	Plumas	Washington Twp	77	25
John	44	m	w	NORW	San Francisco	2-Wd San Francisco	79	166
John	42	m	w	NORW	Yuba	Slate Range Bar Tw	93	673
John	40	m	w	DENM	San Francisco	San Francisco P O	83	42
John	40	m	w	OH	Contra Costa	Martinez P O	71	412
John	38	m	w	DENM	San Francisco	1-Wd San Francisco	79	129
John	32	m	w	DENM	Humboldt	Eureka Twp	72	256
John	30	m	w	DENM	Mendocino	Big Rvr Twp	74	171
John	27	m	w	FINL	San Francisco	1-Wd San Francisco	79	128
John	27	m	w	DENM	Butte	Chico Twp	70	42
John	23	m	w	NORW	Contra Costa	Martinez P O	71	383
John	22	m	w	SWED	Santa Clara	Milpitas Twp	88	109
John A	56	m	w	NY	Santa Clara	2-Wd San Jose	88	281
John B	23	m	w	DENM	Mendocino	Casper & Big Rvr	74	164
Johns	28	m	w	NORW	Humboldt	Mattole Twp	72	285

© 2001 by Heritage Quest. All rights reserved.

California 1870 Census

Name	Age	S	R	B-PL	County	Locale	Series M593 Roll	Pg
Laurena	35	m	w	DENM	Solano	Rio Vista Twp	90	59
Lawrence	38	m	w	DENM	San Francisco	3-Wd San Francisco	79	302
Lewis	19	m	w	SHOL	Alameda	Eden Twp	68	63
Louis	27	m	w	PRUS	San Francisco	7-Wd San Francisco	81	213
Lucy [Squaw]	30	f	i	CA	Lake	Scotts Crk	73	428
M	35	m	w	PRUS	Alameda	Oakland	68	253
M	26	m	w	IREL	Lake	Morgan Valley	73	425
Maggie	12	f	w	IA	San Francisco	San Francisco P O	83	196
March P	21	m	w	SHOL	Contra Costa	Martinez P O	71	392
Marion	41	m	w	DENM	Sacramento	2-Wd Sacramento	77	221
Markham	21	m	w	SWED	El Dorado	Diamond Springs Tw	72	26
Martin	27	m	w	PRUS	Solano	Tremont Twp	90	31
Martin	27	m	w	DENM	El Dorado	Lake Valley Twp	72	64
Mary	36	f	w	NORW	Los Angeles	Wilmington Twp	73	635
Mary	34	f	w	IREL	Alpine	Monitor P O	69	313
Mary	32	f	w	MA	Santa Clara	2-Wd San Jose	88	299
Mary	30	f	i	CA	Mariposa	Mariposa P O	74	98
Max	33	m	w	SILE	San Francisco	2-Wd San Francisco	79	255
Merriam	16	m	w	CA	San Francisco	San Francisco P O	83	15
N	34	m	w	KY	San Francisco	8-Wd San Francisco	82	359
Nathan	44	m	w	DENM	Calaveras	San Andreas P O	70	179
Nels	28	m	w	DENM	Mendocino	Casper & Big Rvr	74	163
Nels	27	m	w	DENM	Mendocino	Casper & Big Rvr	74	164
Nelson	30	m	w	NORW	Nevada	Eureka Twp	75	133
Nicholas	42	m	w	DENM	Calaveras	San Andreas P O	70	194
Nichols	44	m	w	NORW	Tuolumne	Sonora P O	93	326
Niels	24	m	w	DENM	Solano	Vallejo	90	183
O F	30	m	w	ME	Santa Clara	Gilroy Twp	88	73
O W	25	m	w	NORW	Humboldt	Eureka Twp	72	272
Ole	59	m	w	DENM	San Francisco	San Francisco P O	83	235
Otte	35	m	w	NORW	Sacramento	2-Wd Sacramento	77	237
P	39	m	w	HOLL	San Joaquin	Tulare Twp	86	264
P	32	m	w	NORW	Lake	Morgan Valley	73	425
Peter	53	m	w	DENM	Contra Costa	Martinez P O	71	446
Peter	45	m	w	NORW	Del Norte	Happy Camp Twp	71	471
Peter	42	m	w	NORW	Mendocino	Big Rvr Twp	74	159
Peter	40	m	w	MA	San Francisco	7-Wd San Francisco	81	221
Peter	38	m	w	DENM	Marin	Novato Twp	74	9
Peter	38	m	w	DENM	Alameda	San Leandro	68	97
Peter	36	m	w	DENM	Trinity	Weaverville Pct	92	222
Peter	35	m	w	SWED	Contra Costa	Martinez P O	71	371
Peter	34	m	w	PRUS	Calaveras	Copperopolis P O	70	242
Peter	34	f	w	CHIL	Mendocino	Point Arena Twp	74	211
Peter	32	m	w	PRUS	San Francisco	11-Wd San Francisc	84	703
Peter	32	m	w	DENM	Nevada	Grass Valley Twp	75	180
Peter	32	m	w	SWED	Sacramento	Georgianna Twp	77	126
Peter	30	m	w	DENM	San Francisco	1-Wd San Francisco	79	70
Peter	30	m	w	IREL	San Francisco	7-Wd San Francisco	81	212
Peter	28	m	w	SWED	San Francisco	1-Wd San Francisco	79	57
Peter	28	m	w	DENM	Alameda	Eden Twp	68	64
Peter	27	m	w	DENM	San Francisco	3-Wd San Francisco	79	297
Peter	26	m	w	DENM	Marin	San Rafael Twp	74	25
Peter	25	m	w	DENM	San Mateo	Half Moon Bay P O	87	408
Peter	22	m	w	DENM	Alameda	Eden Twp	68	59
R	21	m	w	SHOL	Sonoma	Bodega Twp	91	249
Rufus S	26	m	w	IA	Napa	Napa	75	14
Samuel	24	m	w	MD	San Francisco	San Francisco P O	85	758
Samuel H	31	m	w	SWED	San Mateo	Woodside P O	87	385
Sanford	44	m	w	OH	El Dorado	Georgetown Twp	72	43
Sarah	41	f	w	IREL	San Francisco	2-Wd San Francisco	79	179
Sarah E	39	f	w	CANA	San Francisco	San Francisco P O	83	189
Stephen	33	m	w	NY	San Francisco	11-Wd San Francisc	84	511
Stephen	33	m	w	PA	San Francisco	11-Wd San Francisc	84	502
T C	30	m	w	ME	Alameda	Oakland	68	156
Theodore	24	m	w	HAMB	Napa	Napa	75	4
Thomas	28	m	w	NY	San Francisco	11-Wd San Francisc	84	464
Thomas H	46	m	w	VA	Marin	San Rafael	74	55
Thos	44	m	w	NORW	San Francisco	7-Wd San Francisco	81	262
Thos	43	m	w	DENM	San Francisco	1-Wd San Francisco	79	6
Thos	31	m	w	NORW	San Francisco	7-Wd San Francisco	81	262
W H	44	m	w	SWED	Tuolumne	Columbia P O	93	346
W H	23	m	w	IL	Tuolumne	Chinese Camp P O	93	381
W J	47	m	w	SHOL	Amador	Fiddletown P O	69	426
W T	45	m	w	KY	Amador	Fiddletown P O	69	438
William	6	m	w	CA	Marin	San Rafael Twp	74	28
William	45	m	w	DENM	San Francisco	San Francisco P O	83	221
William	45	m	w	SWED	Mendocino	Casper & Big Rvr	74	164
William	43	m	w	ME	San Francisco	San Francisco P O	83	334
William	40	m	w	ENGL	Mariposa	Mariposa P O	74	98
William	29	m	w	ENGL	Placer	Alta P O	76	412
William	25	m	w	PRUS	Yolo	Merritt Twp	93	503
William D	23	m	w	CANA	Solano	Montezuma Twp	90	66
Wm	23	m	w	CANA	Sacramento	Georgianna Twp	77	130
Wm P	44	m	w	KY	Sutter	Nicolaus Twp	92	110
Wm T	45	m	w	KY	El Dorado	Cosumnes Twp	72	15
HANSPRICH								
Louis	41	m	w	PRUS	San Francisco	San Francisco P O	80	426
HANSTRIM								
Wm	56	m	w	NY	Alameda	Brooklyn	68	24
HANSY								
Thomas	40	m	w	IREL	San Mateo	Redwood City P O	87	375
HANT								
Wm	25	m	w	NJ	Butte	Concow Twp	70	9
HANTON								
C D	45	m	w	NY	Trinity	Douglas	92	237
HANTS								
C E	42	m	w	PRUS	Tuolumne	Chinese Camp P O	93	389
Geo	34	m	w	HCAS	San Francisco	11-Wd San Francisc	84	617
HANURNY								
Jas	28	m	w	SCOT	Solano	Vallejo	90	198
HANUS								
Herman	37	m	w	HANO	San Francisco	San Francisco P O	83	69
HANVER								
Harvey	28	m	w	NY	San Diego	Julian Dist	78	469
HANVILLE								
Thomas C	34	m	w	ENGL	El Dorado	Placerville	72	107
HANWAY								
Daniel	19	m	w	IN	Santa Clara	1-Wd San Jose	88	226
HANWOOD								
Jas	32	m	w	ENGL	Santa Clara	Almaden Twp	88	9
HANY								
Christiani	36	m	w	GERM	Marin	San Rafael Twp	74	37
Leonora	26	f	i	CA	Los Angeles	Los Angeles Twp	73	498
Mark	44	m	w	IREL	Placer	Bath P O	76	438
Nicholas	45	m	w	PRUS	Sutter	Butte Twp	92	97
HANYMAN								
Hans	54	m	w	GERM	San Mateo	Schoolhouse Statio	87	338
HANZO								
Aug	43	m	w	FRAN	Alameda	Oakland	68	214
HAON								
Ah	28	m	c	CHIN	Nevada	Meadow Lake Twp	75	251
HAP								
Ah	45	m	c	CHIN	Sacramento	Georgianna Twp	77	126
Ah	35	m	c	CHIN	Shasta	American Ranch P O	89	499
Ah	35	m	c	CHIN	Trinity	Canyon City Pct	92	201
Ah	34	m	c	CHIN	Fresno	Millerton P O	72	200
Ah	33	m	c	CHIN	Sacramento	Natomas Twp	77	167
Ah	32	m	c	CHIN	Butte	Chico Twp	70	27
Ah	30	m	c	CHIN	Sacramento	Cosumnes Twp	77	94
Ah	27	m	c	CHIN	San Francisco	6-Wd San Francisco	81	65
Ah	26	m	c	CHIN	Butte	Concow Twp	70	10
Ah	25	m	c	CHIN	San Francisco	1-Wd San Francisco	79	98
Ah	24	m	c	CHIN	Sacramento	Georgianna Twp	77	134
Ah	24	m	c	CHIN	San Mateo	San Mateo P O	87	356
Ah	20	m	w	CHIN	Sacramento	1-Wd Sacramento	77	191
Ah	18	m	c	CHIN	Butte	Bidwell Twp	70	4
Gayeg	43	m	w	CHIN	Plumas	Mineral Twp	77	24
Kee	21	m	c	CHIN	Santa Clara	2-Wd San Jose	88	314
Lee	38	m	c	CHIN	Trinity	Weaverville Pct	92	228
Loe	16	m	c	CHIN	Santa Clara	San Jose Twp	88	194
See	19	m	c	CHIN	Santa Clara	1-Wd San Jose	88	269
Sing	23	m	c	CHIN	Santa Clara	1-Wd San Jose	88	269
Sing	23	m	c	CHIN	San Francisco	6-Wd San Francisco	81	50
You	32	m	c	CHIN	Sacramento	1-Wd Sacramento	77	191
HAPE								
Ah	63	m	c	CHIN	Trinity	Weaverville Pct	92	226
HAPEN								
William	30	m	w	SALT	San Francisco	San Francisco P O	85	729
HAPER								
James	33	m	w	RI	San Francisco	1-Wd San Francisco	79	123
HAPGOOD								
Joseph	47	m	w	MA	Plumas	Quartz Twp	77	37
Nathan Harry	21	m	w	NH	Plumas	Plumas Twp	77	26
Thos	22	m	w	AUSL	San Francisco	1-Wd San Francisco	79	81
HAPHART								
Charles	28	m	w	PRUS	San Francisco	6-Wd San Francisco	81	81
HAPIGON								
S J	44	m	w	DE	Alameda	Oakland	68	158
HAPMAN								
John	42	m	w	PRUS	San Francisco	8-Wd San Francisco	82	386
HAPNER								
Jennie	20	f	w	PRUS	San Francisco	San Francisco P O	83	52
HAPP								
Anna	19	f	w	NY	Los Angeles	Los Angeles	73	520
Kate	12	f	w	NY	Los Angeles	Los Angeles	73	525
HAPPE								
John	41	m	w	PRUS	Solano	Rio Vista Twp	90	60
HAPPELER								
Conrad	51	m	w	SWIT	San Francisco	2-Wd San Francisco	79	143
HAPPER								
M M	41	f	w	OH	San Joaquin	Castoria Twp	86	1
Maggie A	24	f	w	IL	San Joaquin	2-Wd Stockton	86	160
Zack	59	m	w	NC	Sonoma	Cloverdale Twp	91	267
HAPPIE								
Henry	49	m	w	PRUS	Trinity	North Fork Twp	92	217
HAPPINGER								
Joseph	45	m	w	VA	San Francisco	11-Wd San Francisc	84	532
HAPPUTATT								
Thos	36	m	w	PRUS	Sacramento	Brighton Twp	77	76
HAPPY								
Jack	40	m	w	IREL	Tulare	Visalia	92	297
John H	71	m	w	NY	Sonoma	Bodega Twp	91	259
Max	6	m	w	CA	Butte	Ophir Twp	70	111
HAR								
Ah	3	f	c	CA	San Francisco	San Francisco P O	80	521
Ah	23	m	c	CHIN	San Francisco	6-Wd San Francisco	81	60
Ah	22	m	c	CHIN	San Francisco	6-Wd San Francisco	81	49
Tuey	18	m	c	CHIN	Yuba	Marysville	93	628
HARA								
Ann	40	f	w	IREL	San Francisco	2-Wd San Francisco	79	209
Bridget	32	f	w	IREL	San Francisco	San Francisco P O	83	176
Enacio	4	f	w	CA	San Mateo	Half Moon Bay P O	87	394
Horace F	43	m	w	OH	Santa Cruz	Pajaro Twp	89	349
James	42	m	w	IREL	San Francisco	11-Wd San Francisc	84	671

© 2001 by Heritage Quest. All rights reserved.

Name	Age	S	R	B-PL	County	Locale	Roll	Pg
						Series M593		
John	40	m	w	IREL	San Francisco	11-Wd San Francisc	84	664
Lorenzo	12	m	w	CA	San Mateo	Half Moon Bay P O	87	397
Sebastion	20	m	w	MEXI	San Mateo	Pescadero P O	87	412
HARAGE								
Jurgen	33	m	w	HANO	Yuba	Slate Range Bar Tw	93	677
HARAHAN								
Ellen	23	f	w	IREL	San Francisco	7-Wd San Francisco	81	280
Wm	24	m	w	IREL	Sutter	Sutter Twp	92	129
HARALAND								
James F	45	m	w	OH	Colusa	Butte Twp	71	272
HARALSON								
Wm	41	m	w	AL	Alameda	Brooklyn	68	35
HARAN								
John	25	m	w	IREL	Placer	Roseville P O	76	351
HARASTHY								
A F	35	m	w	HUNG	Sonoma	Sonoma Twp	91	447
Francis	69	m	w	MA	Sonoma	Sonoma Twp	91	435
HARASZTHY								
Arpad	29	m	w	HUNG	San Francisco	8-Wd San Francisco	82	380
Otillo	19	f	w	WI	Los Angeles	Los Angeles	73	572
HARATHY								
B	24	m	w	WI	San Francisco	8-Wd San Francisco	82	363
HARAZTHY								
Bela	27	m	w	MD	Los Angeles	San Gabriel Twp	73	595
HARB								
Loring	30	m	w	MA	Yuba	Parks Bar Twp	93	650
HARBACK								
Daniel L	43	m	w	NY	Sonoma	Salt Point	91	387
HARBAL								
Eliza	23	f	w	TN	Sutter	Nicolaus Twp	92	109
HARBE								
Cora	36	f	w	PRUS	San Francisco	5-Wd San Francisco	81	10
HARBEAU								
Christian	35	m	w	DENM	Marin	Nicasio Twp	74	18
HARBECK								
Adele	21	f	w	PRUS	San Francisco	San Francisco P O	83	134
HARBEN								
G L	27	m	w	CA	Yuba	Marysville	93	632
HARBERT								
John	24	m	w	MO	Santa Barbara	San Buenaventura P	87	445
Mathew	66	m	w	KY	Mendocino	Ukiah Twp	74	242
W F	31	m	w	IL	Mendocino	Calpella Twp	74	183
HARBIN								
A H	44	m	w	TN	Lake	Lower Lake	73	414
J C	52	m	w	AL	Lake	Coyote Valley	73	417
Mat	48	m	w	TN	Lake	Lower Lake	73	423
Sarah	78	f	w	TN	Yolo	Cache Crk Twp	93	437
Wm B	33	m	w	IN	Humboldt	Pacific Twp	72	294
HARBINE								
Leander	50	m	w	PA	Sonoma	Analy Twp	91	240
HARBISON								
Fredk	36	m	w	NJ	Stanislaus	Empire Twp	92	53
Hugh	34	m	w	MI	Sacramento	2-Wd Sacramento	77	252
James	33	m	w	IL	Stanislaus	Empire Twp	92	29
John	52	m	w	OH	Colusa	Monroe Twp	71	311
John	42	m	w	GA	Stanislaus	Empire Twp	92	64
John H	37	m	w	PA	Sacramento	Sutter Twp	77	386
HARBOLT								
Zeritha	46	f	w	KY	Los Angeles	Los Nietos Twp	73	590
HARBON								
W	26	m	w	ENGL	Sierra	Butte Twp	89	510
HARBOO								
Clementina	27	f	w	MD	Alameda	Eden Twp	68	86
HARBOR								
Ben	42	m	w	PRUS	Butte	Kimshew Tpw	70	85
Thomas	33	m	w	IREL	San Francisco	San Francisco P O	80	537
HARBORT								
Eiza	57	f	w	NY	Butte	Chico Twp	70	40
HARBOULE								
Victor	26	m	w	PA	San Francisco	7-Wd San Francisco	81	164
HARBOUR								
Benj F	37	m	w	TN	Mariposa	Mariposa P O	74	131
Hiram	51	m	w	VA	Sutter	Butte Twp	92	98
HARBOURN								
Henry	50	m	w	IREL	San Francisco	San Francisco P O	83	222
HARBRAY								
Mary	28	f	w	IREL	San Francisco	7-Wd San Francisco	81	207
HARBUR								
Antoine	28	m	w	PRUS	San Francisco	11-Wd San Francisc	84	643
HARBURTON								
Mary A	54	f	w	ENGL	San Francisco	San Francisco P O	85	765
HARBUS								
Louis	23	m	w	PRUS	Mendocino	Sanel Twp	74	228
HARBY								
Rosalie	43	f	w	LA	San Francisco	San Francisco P O	83	397
HARCHAN								
Henry	38	m	w	IREL	Sacramento	4-Wd Sacramento	77	339
HARCHER								
Baron	30	m	w	NY	Colusa	Stony Crk Twp	71	332
HARCUAS								
Denis	39	m	w	FRAN	San Joaquin	2-Wd Stockton	86	168
HARD								
A E	11	f	w	CA	Alameda	Oakland	68	258
Ah	35	m	c	CHIN	Placer	Bath P O	76	433
Joseph	19	m	w	NY	Sonoma	Analy Twp	91	222
Lorenzo	37	m	w	CHIL	San Mateo	Half Moon Bay P O	87	395
M S	51	m	w	NY	Alameda	Oakland	68	209

Name	Age	S	R	B-PL	County	Locale	Roll	Pg
						Series M593		
Peter	35	m	w	SHOL	Sutter	Nicolaus Twp	92	114
Roswell	42	m	w	VT	Contra Costa	Martinez P O	71	371
Sarah	40	f	w	NY	Napa	Napa	75	7
William H	41	m	w	MD	Nevada	Meadow Lake Twp	75	248
Willis	32	m	w	GA	San Joaquin	Douglas Twp	86	47
HARDCASTLE								
J W	42	m	w	KY	Sonoma	Sonoma Twp	91	445
HARDEE								
James	30	m	w	IN	Stanislaus	Empire Twp	92	44
HARDELL								
August	37	m	w	FRAN	Sacramento	Granite Twp	77	141
HARDELO								
Nicholas	55	m	w	AUST	San Francisco	2-Wd San Francisco	79	181
HARDEMAN								
Anne	35	f	w	IREL	San Francisco	San Francisco P O	83	82
HARDEN								
A B	50	m	w	KY	Siskiyou	Big Valley Twp	89	581
A M	30	m	w	TN	Monterey	San Juan Twp	74	391
Abraham W	54	m	w	OH	Shasta	Millville P O	89	488
Claus	32	m	w	PRUS	San Francisco	5-Wd San Francisco	81	16
Ed	30	m	w	ENGL	San Joaquin	Elliott Twp	86	71
Elizabeth	40	f	w	KY	Humboldt	South Fork Twp	72	300
G E	31	m	w	IL	Alameda	Oakland	68	263
George	26	m	w	MO	Stanislaus	Washington Twp	92	85
H	25	m	w	GERM	San Joaquin	2-Wd Stockton	86	174
J H	31	m	w	OH	Alameda	Alameda	68	13
James	52	m	w	KY	Stanislaus	Washington Twp	92	85
James	45	m	w	PRUS	Stanislaus	Branch Twp	92	8
James H	19	m	w	OH	Yolo	Grafton Twp	93	478
John	45	m	w	ENGL	Tuolumne	Big Oak Flat P O	93	394
John	45	m	w	SHOL	Sonoma	Vallejo Twp	91	457
John	44	m	w	PA	Nevada	Grass Valley Twp	75	162
John	28	m	w	AR	Merced	Snelling P O	74	263
L	40	m	w	ENGL	San Joaquin	2-Wd Stockton	86	176
Riley	12	m	w	CA	Siskiyou	Butte Twp	89	588
Willm L	40	m	w	ENGL	Siskiyou	Yreka	89	662
HARDENBECH								
David	35	m	w	NY	San Francisco	2-Wd San Francisco	79	219
HARDENBURG								
Charles	30	m	w	NJ	San Francisco	San Francisco P O	83	341
J R	56	m	w	NJ	Amador	Jackson P O	69	348
John H	55	m	w	NJ	San Francisco	6-Wd San Francisco	81	132
W	32	m	w	NY	Alameda	Alameda	68	1
HARDENBURGH								
--- [Rev]	31	m	w	NY	San Francisco	5-Wd San Francisco	81	28
HARDENSTEIN								
Frederick	53	m	w	SWIT	San Francisco	San Francisco P O	83	164
HARDENT								
E	20	f	w	GA	Alameda	Oakland	68	163
HARDER								
Alonzo	24	m	w	PRUS	San Francisco	5-Wd San Francisco	81	15
Conrad	38	m	w	SWIT	San Francisco	1-Wd San Francisco	79	128
Jacob	22	m	w	SHOL	Alameda	Eden Twp	68	63
James	36	m	w	SWIT	Yuba	Marysville	93	592
John	40	m	w	CHIL	El Dorado	White Oak Twp	72	139
Lewis	35	m	w	SHOL	San Francisco	3-Wd San Francisco	79	287
Theodore	25	m	w	NORW	San Francisco	1-Wd San Francisco	79	125
Theodore	24	m	w	PRUS	Solano	Tremont Twp	90	34
HARDERS								
Fredrick	40	m	w	PRUS	San Francisco	San Francisco P O	83	248
HARDESS								
Fred	10	m	w	CA	San Francisco	11-Wd San Francisc	84	588
Geo	13	m	w	CA	San Francisco	11-Wd San Francisc	84	588
HARDESTY								
A P	43	m	w	KY	Monterey	Alisal Twp	74	304
Benjamin	44	m	w	KY	Colusa	Colusa Twp	71	286
H C	25	m	w	KY	Sonoma	Santa Rosa	91	425
Henry	42	m	w	LA	San Francisco	2-Wd San Francisco	79	152
Jacob	32	m	w	KY	Sonoma	Santa Rosa	91	408
Jos	25	m	w	OH	Solano	Vallejo	90	200
K	35	m	w	KY	Sonoma	Santa Rosa	91	421
S W	33	m	w	KY	Sonoma	Santa Rosa	91	394
T J	30	m	w	KY	Yuba	Marysville	93	608
T P	31	m	w	IN	Placer	Newcastle Twp	76	475
Thos D	39	m	w	MO	Napa	Napa	75	57
HARDEY								
John	30	m	w	IREL	Humboldt	Bald Hills	72	239
Kimbol	42	m	w	MA	Los Angeles	Los Angeles Twp	73	482
Versey M	30	m	w	ENGL	Los Angeles	Los Angeles Twp	73	483
HARDGRAM								
John B	59	m	w	KY	Mendocino	Anderson Twp	74	150
HARDGRAVE								
Charles	26	m	w	IN	Mendocino	Big Rvr Twp	74	159
John	52	m	w	CANA	Plumas	Indian Twp	77	10
Sipio	63	m	w	OH	Mendocino	Point Arena Twp	74	215
HARDGRAVES								
Frederick	50	m	w	TN	Plumas	Quartz Twp	77	36
HARDIE								
Angus M	30	m	w	SCOT	San Luis Obispo	Morro Twp	87	280
Dudrich	46	m	w	HANO	San Francisco	11-Wd San Francisc	84	509
James	33	m	w	IREL	San Francisco	San Francisco P O	85	876
Porter	33	m	w	IA	Mendocino	Point Arena Twp	74	224
Thomas	77	m	w	SCOT	San Luis Obispo	Morro Twp	87	280
HARDIGAN								
David	20	m	w	PA	Sutter	Sutter Twp	92	122
John	40	m	w	IREL	Sacramento	4-Wd Sacramento	77	357

© 2001 by Heritage Quest. All rights reserved.

California 1870 Census

Name	Age	S	R	B-PL	County	Locale	Roll	Pg
HARDIMAN								
John	30	m	w	IREL	San Francisco	San Francisco P O	83	76
Mary	15	f	w	NY	San Francisco	2-Wd San Francisco	79	248
HARDIN								
Agnes	47	f	w	KY	Sonoma	Vallejo Twp	91	451
Andrew	38	m	w	MO	Sonoma	Vallejo Twp	91	458
D	48	m	w	MO	Lassen	Susanville Twp	73	443
David	42	m	w	OH	Trinity	Weaverville Pct	92	226
Geo	41	m	w	LA	San Joaquin	Liberty Twp	86	95
Henry	34	m	w	ENGL	Nevada	Eureka Twp	75	130
Isaac	40	m	w	IL	Monterey	San Juan Twp	74	412
James	19	m	w	OH	Yolo	Fremont Twp	93	477
James T	25	m	w	MO	Sonoma	Santa Rosa	91	413
Jno R	36	m	w	IN	Santa Clara	Gilroy Twp	88	82
John	50	m	w	IREL	Nevada	Nevada Twp	75	303
John	45	m	w	ME	Mendocino	Calpella Twp	74	183
John	30	m	w	KY	San Mateo	Woodside P O	87	387
John H	68	m	w	KY	Santa Clara	Milpitas Twp	88	112
John W	22	m	w	KY	Yolo	Grafton Twp	93	479
L A	47	m	w	CANA	Tuolumne	Big Oak Flat P O	93	393
Maria	30	f	w	CA	Mariposa	Mariposa P O	74	93
R S	47	m	w	KY	Napa	Napa	75	25
Simeon	38	m	w	MO	Siskiyou	Yreka Twp	89	673
W H	48	m	w	GA	Tuolumne	Chinese Camp P O	93	383
William	56	m	w	VA	Colusa	Grand Island Twp	71	309
William	35	m	w	OH	Los Angeles	Los Angeles Twp	73	493
William A	41	m	w	VA	Los Angeles	Santa Ana Twp	73	612
William H	27	m	w	MO	Sonoma	Vallejo Twp	91	460
William J	49	m	w	KY	Sonoma	Vallejo Twp	91	460
Wm	34	m	w	KY	San Joaquin	Castoria Twp	86	11
HARDINAN								
Patrick	30	m	w	IREL	San Francisco	11-Wd San Francisc	84	541
HARDING								
A	56	m	w	PRUS	Alameda	Oakland	68	153
Alex	48	m	w	NY	Amador	Volcano P O	69	380
August	22	m	w	PRUS	Plumas	Goodwin Twp	77	7
Bartha	52	m	w	ENGL	Fresno	Millerton P O	72	167
Charles	37	m	w	ENGL	Plumas	Mineral Twp	77	22
Charles	32	m	w	ENGL	Plumas	Indian Twp	77	15
Chas	45	m	w	KY	Yuba	W Bear Rvr Twp	93	683
Dinah	20	f	w	PRUS	San Francisco	8-Wd San Francisco	82	307
Edward A	42	m	w	MA	Yuba	Slate Range Bar Tw	93	673
Edward B	40	m	w	MA	San Francisco	San Francisco P O	85	727
Elizabeth	45	f	w	OH	Sutter	Yuba Twp	92	145
F	35	m	w	MA	Alameda	Oakland	68	200
Frank	28	m	w	HAMB	San Francisco	1-Wd San Francisco	79	56
George	29	m	w	ENGL	San Francisco	2-Wd San Francisco	79	253
George	25	m	w	PRUS	San Francisco	5-Wd San Francisco	81	15
George W	25	m	w	MA	Yolo	Putah Twp	93	516
Isaac	45	m	w	MA	Sonoma	Sonoma Twp	91	437
J	61	m	w	MA	Sacramento	3-Wd Sacramento	77	274
James G	45	m	w	MA	San Francisco	6-Wd San Francisco	81	95
James R	30	m	w	MA	Los Angeles	El Monte Twp	73	450
Jane	44	f	w	ME	San Francisco	8-Wd San Francisco	82	382
Jane	42	f	w	ME	San Francisco	8-Wd San Francisco	82	458
Jane	11	f	w	CA	Solano	Benicia	90	8
Jno	34	m	w	VA	Butte	Chico Twp	70	18
Jno	27	m	w	MA	Butte	Chico Twp	70	25
John	54	m	w	CANA	Yolo	Merritt Twp	93	505
John	43	m	w	CANA	Plumas	Plumas Twp	77	29
John H	32	m	w	MA	San Francisco	San Francisco P O	83	112
Joseph	28	m	w	ME	Marin	San Rafael	74	56
Joseph D	55	m	w	KY	San Mateo	Woodside P O	87	386
Lockwood	40	m	b	IL	Shasta	French Gulch P O	89	468
Lowell	26	m	w	ME	San Francisco	6-Wd San Francisco	81	99
Mary E	26	f	w	OH	Plumas	Goodwin Twp	77	2
Mathew	40	m	w	CANA	Klamath	Sawyers Bar	73	377
Melvin L	29	m	w	OH	Shasta	Millville P O	89	488
R L	21	m	w	ME	Sacramento	3-Wd Sacramento	77	272
Robert	27	m	w	TN	Stanislaus	Empire Twp	92	28
Robert	25	m	w	MO	Stanislaus	Branch Twp	92	1
Rosco	23	m	w	ME	San Joaquin	Elkhorn Twp	86	65
Saml	30	m	w	IL	Yuba	W Bear Rvr Twp	93	682
Samuel	44	m	w	RI	San Francisco	San Francisco P O	80	391
Spencer	33	m	w	MI	Solano	Silveyville Twp	90	76
Thomas	26	m	w	CANA	Kern	Linns Valley P O	73	349
Timothy	48	m	w	MA	Calaveras	San Andreas P O	70	178
William	41	m	w	NY	San Mateo	San Mateo P O	87	371
William	31	m	w	KY	Los Angeles	Los Angeles	73	504
Wm	47	m	w	KY	Yuba	East Bear Rvr Twp	93	539
Wm	42	m	w	OH	Sutter	Vernon Twp	92	133
Wm	32	m	w	ME	Nevada	Meadow Lake Twp	75	265
Wm	28	m	w	SC	Butte	Chico Twp	70	42
HARDINGE								
Robert	39	m	w	ENGL	San Francisco	1-Wd San Francisco	79	125
HARDISLY								
Sarah	16	f	w	CA	Santa Clara	2-Wd San Jose	88	337
HARDISON								
Walace L	19	m	w	ME	Humboldt	Eureka Twp	72	266
HARDLEY								
Thomas	40	m	w	ENGL	Yolo	Grafton Twp	93	494
HARDMAN								
James	50	m	w	DC	San Francisco	11-Wd San Francisc	84	468
Joshua	55	m	w	OH	Napa	Napa	75	23
Sophia	30	f	w	OH	Marin	Bolinas Twp	74	2
William F	23	m	w	IA	Colusa	Stony Crk Twp	71	332
HARDMEY								
William	31	m	w	SWIT	San Francisco	2-Wd San Francisco	79	161
HARDMEYER								
William	32	m	w	SWIT	San Francisco	11-Wd San Francisc	84	499
HARDNER								
Caroline	21	f	w	BAVA	San Francisco	11-Wd San Francisc	84	551
HARDNET								
Hannah	32	f	w	IREL	San Francisco	8-Wd San Francisco	82	476
HARDNUT								
Delia	24	f	w	IREL	San Francisco	8-Wd San Francisco	82	404
HARDOC								
Charles	33	m	w	PRUS	Los Angeles	Wilmington Twp	73	642
HARDON								
Thomas	35	m	w	IREL	San Francisco	San Francisco P O	83	267
HARDRICKS								
J	57	m	w	KY	San Joaquin	Douglas Twp	86	42
HARDRIX								
James A	39	m	w	KY	Sonoma	Petaluma Twp	91	314
HARDRUM								
James	45	m	w	NY	Alameda	Oakland	68	192
HARDSCRABBLE								
Benj	30	m	b	MO	Yolo	Grafton Twp	93	500
HARDWICH								
C	26	m	w	MO	Monterey	Alisal Twp	74	290
HARDWICK								
Geo M	58	m	w	GA	Mariposa	Mariposa P O	74	99
George	24	m	w	MA	Mendocino	Bourns Landing Twp	74	223
H J	17	f	w	AR	Mariposa	Maxwell Crk P O	74	142
J	34	m	w	AL	Merced	Snelling P O	74	276
John	30	m	w	OH	Sacramento	Brighton Twp	77	72
John	26	m	w	ENGL	Sacramento	Brighton Twp	77	80
John W	59	m	w	KY	Santa Clara	2-Wd San Jose	88	282
Joseph	53	m	w	ENGL	Siskiyou	Butte Twp	89	586
R F	40	m	w	MA	Sonoma	Salt Point	91	387
Richard	21	m	w	MA	Sonoma	Salt Point	91	390
T J	61	m	w	GA	Merced	Snelling P O	74	276
Thomas	50	m	w	KY	Mendocino	Little Lake Twp	74	199
Thos	65	m	w	MA	Alameda	Oakland	68	249
William	35	m	w	MA	San Francisco	7-Wd San Francisco	81	206
Wm	23	m	w	IL	Santa Clara	Gilroy Twp	88	95
HARDWIDGE								
Mary	30	f	w	IREL	San Francisco	8-Wd San Francisco	82	290
HARDWOOD								
Thos	50	m	w	ENGL	San Francisco	2-Wd San Francisco	79	199
HARDY								
Aaron	29	m	w	OH	Yuba	Marysville	93	611
Alford	28	m	w	PA	San Francisco	7-Wd San Francisco	81	179
Alfred	32	m	w	IREL	San Francisco	11-Wd San Francisc	84	708
Allen	25	m	w	NORW	Stanislaus	Emory Twp	92	16
Aun	55	m	w	ENGL	San Joaquin	2-Wd Stockton	86	168
B	30	m	w	ME	Lake	Knoxville Mines	73	405
B F	61	m	w	ME	San Francisco	San Francisco P O	83	277
Bridget	25	f	w	IREL	Sacramento	4-Wd Sacramento	77	374
Caroline	37	f	w	VT	San Francisco	8-Wd San Francisco	82	422
E J	27	f	w	MA	Alameda	Oakland	68	192
Edwin H	24	m	w	ME	San Francisco	San Francisco P O	83	329
Eliza	47	f	w	OH	Solano	Vallejo	90	193
Ezra T	44	m	w	ME	Nevada	Eureka Twp	75	129
Geo	29	m	w	BAVA	San Francisco	1-Wd San Francisco	79	69
George	60	m	w	ENGL	Calaveras	Copperopolis P O	70	226
George	41	m	w	NY	Placer	Lincoln P O	76	485
George	40	m	w	ENGL	Nevada	Eureka Twp	75	131
Henry	30	m	w	ENGL	Monterey	San Juan Twp	74	417
Henry	30	m	w	PRUS	Santa Clara	San Jose Twp	88	210
Hiram	44	m	w	NH	Contra Costa	Martinez P O	71	369
Horatio	67	m	w	ME	San Francisco	8-Wd San Francisco	82	476
Isaac	36	m	w	MA	Contra Costa	Martinez P O	71	399
Jacob	43	m	w	MA	Alameda	Oakland	68	195
James	40	m	w	MO	Sonoma	Russian Rvr	91	375
James	29	m	w	ENGL	Contra Costa	Martinez P O	71	378
James	24	m	w	NY	Solano	Maine Prairie Twp	90	46
James H	38	m	w	IL	San Francisco	San Francisco P O	83	101
Jane	21	f	w	IREL	San Francisco	San Francisco P O	80	457
Jno	34	m	b	NC	San Joaquin	1-Wd Stockton	86	122
Joanna	42	f	w	VT	Santa Clara	1-Wd San Jose	88	227
John	45	m	w	ENGL	San Luis Obispo	Santa Rosa Twp	87	324
John	35	m	w	PRUS	San Francisco	6-Wd San Francisco	81	133
John	33	m	w	ENGL	Sierra	Eureka Twp	89	524
John	31	m	w	MO	Solano	Vacaville Twp	90	118
Joseph	73	m	w	VA	Mendocino	Anderson Twp	74	155
Joseph	45	m	w	OH	Sutter	Yuba Twp	92	147
L	53	m	w	MA	Alameda	Oakland	68	207
Lewis	19	m	w	IL	Lake	Lower Lake	73	419
Margaret	17	f	w	IL	El Dorado	Placerville Twp	72	95
Marion	30	m	w	IA	Humboldt	Pacific Twp	72	296
Mary	80	f	w	MA	Santa Clara	1-Wd San Jose	88	238
Oscar	30	m	w	PRUS	Sacramento	3-Wd Sacramento	77	273
Oswell	37	m	w	SCOT	El Dorado	Placerville Twp	72	105
Otis	59	m	w	VT	Santa Clara	2-Wd San Jose	88	299
Patrick	24	m	w	IREL	Yolo	Cottonwood Twp	93	468
R	51	f	w	KY	Sacramento	3-Wd Sacramento	77	265
R	29	m	w	ME	Lake	Lower Lake	73	418
Robin A	27	m	w	MO	Mendocino	Anderson Twp	74	155
Robt	40	m	w	IREL	Nevada	Meadow Lake Twp	75	250
Sabina	24	f	w	IREL	San Francisco	San Francisco P O	80	396
Thomas	53	m	w	MA	San Francisco	San Francisco P O	85	770
Thomas	44	m	w	ENGL	Yolo	Grafton Twp	93	498

Series M593

© 2001 by Heritage Quest. All rights reserved.

Name	Age	S	R	B-PL	County	Locale	Roll	Pg
Thomas	35	m	w	IREL	San Francisco	7-Wd San Francisco	81	209
W B	43	m	w	IL	Alameda	Oakland	68	145
W J	22	m	w	IL	San Francisco	7-Wd San Francisco	81	168
William	26	m	w	NY	San Francisco	3-Wd San Francisco	79	317
William B	30	m	w	VA	Santa Clara	2-Wd San Jose	88	305
William C	54	m	w	NY	El Dorado	Placerville Twp	72	101
William P	26	m	w	MI	Stanislaus	Empire Twp	92	42
HARDYMAN								
Julia	75	f	w	IREL	San Francisco	11-Wd San Francisc	84	475
HARE								
Ah	30	m	c	CHIN	Sacramento	2-Wd Sacramento	77	250
Alexander	53	m	w	PA	Los Angeles	Los Angeles	73	552
Alexander	45	m	w	PA	San Francisco	8-Wd San Francisco	82	313
C A	42	m	w	BAVA	Tuolumne	Big Oak Flat P O	93	395
Charles	49	m	w	ENGL	San Francisco	San Francisco P O	83	113
Daniel	40	m	w	FRAN	Tehama	Cottonwood Twp	92	161
David	32	m	w	IN	Tulare	Farmersville Twp	92	247
Ed Q	22	m	w	MA	Santa Barbara	Santa Barbara P O	87	456
Edward	35	m	w	OH	Sonoma	Bodega Twp	91	248
Edward	35	m	w	IREL	San Francisco	8-Wd San Francisco	82	324
Elias C	34	m	w	OH	San Francisco	11-Wd San Francisc	84	698
Ellen	38	f	w	IREL	San Francisco	11-Wd San Francisc	84	492
George H	30	m	w	MA	Santa Clara	2-Wd San Jose	88	293
Henrietta	51	f	w	MA	Santa Clara	2-Wd San Jose	88	293
Hugh	45	m	w	IREL	Santa Clara	Fremont Twp	88	41
James	14	m	w	CA	San Francisco	11-Wd San Francisc	84	593
John S	29	m	w	OH	San Francisco	11-Wd San Francisc	84	698
Kate	50	f	w	PRUS	San Francisco	6-Wd San Francisco	81	154
Levi H	58	m	w	MA	Santa Clara	2-Wd San Jose	88	293
Maggie	20	f	w	IREL	San Francisco	11-Wd San Francisc	84	504
Margaret	30	f	w	IREL	San Francisco	San Francisco P O	83	270
Mary	19	f	w	CA	Contra Costa	Martinez Twp	71	346
Pat	28	m	w	IREL	San Francisco	5-Wd San Francisco	81	28
Sebastian	37	m	w	CHIL	San Mateo	Half Moon Bay P O	87	390
HARELD								
H C	38	m	w	OH	San Joaquin	Oneal Twp	86	105
HARELSON								
D O	30	m	w	MS	San Joaquin	Oneal Twp	86	113
Elijah	69	m	w	NC	San Joaquin	Dent Twp	86	21
HAREN								
Margrett	28	f	w	IREL	San Francisco	1-Wd San Francisco	79	5
HARENBURG								
Edward	31	m	w	PRUS	Solano	Silveyville Twp	90	79
HARENS								
Anna	56	f	w	NY	San Joaquin	2-Wd Stockton	86	179
HARES								
Emma	13	f	w	CA	Santa Clara	2-Wd San Jose	88	337
Marcus	40	m	w	PRUS	San Francisco	11-Wd San Francisc	84	483
HARET								
Mathew D	39	m	w	KY	Los Angeles	Los Angeles	73	559
HARFELDT								
Herman	39	m	w	HDAR	San Francisco	San Francisco P O	80	478
HARFF								
Charles	43	m	w	PRUS	Sacramento	Granite Twp	77	141
HARFORD								
E C	61	m	w	ME	Solano	Vallejo	90	146
Ed E	30	m	w	MA	San Francisco	7-Wd San Francisco	81	250
Fred	36	m	w	NY	Placer	Lincoln P O	76	485
John	42	m	w	NY	San Luis Obispo	San Luis Obispo Tw	87	298
John	32	m	w	IL	Sacramento	2-Wd Sacramento	77	236
Thos	36	m	w	IREL	San Francisco	1-Wd San Francisco	79	112
W G W	43	m	w	NY	Sonoma	Petaluma Twp	91	343
William	45	m	w	MI	San Francisco	San Francisco P O	80	540
HARGAN								
John	30	m	w	IREL	Santa Clara	Alviso Twp	88	26
Urich	26	m	w	FL	Sutter	Vernon Twp	92	138
HARGARTY								
John	35	m	w	IREL	San Francisco	7-Wd San Francisco	81	173
HARGDEN								
Patrick	55	m	w	IREL	San Francisco	8-Wd San Francisco	82	388
HARGEN								
George	46	m	w	KY	Santa Barbara	Santa Barbara P O	87	499
HARGIS								
L D	34	m	w	KY	Sacramento	Dry Crk Twp	77	98
Wm	40	m	w	NJ	San Joaquin	Dent Twp	86	22
HARGMAN								
John	30	m	w	SWED	San Francisco	San Francisco P O	80	427
HARGOOD								
August	35	m	w	WURT	San Francisco	San Francisco P O	83	257
HARGOTTE								
John	65	m	w	FRAN	El Dorado	White Oak Twp	72	136
HARGRAVE								
Alf	54	m	w	MO	Butte	Chico Twp	70	17
Caroline	52	f	m	NC	Sacramento	2-Wd Sacramento	77	227
Edward	40	m	w	IL	Mariposa	Mariposa P O	74	110
John M	34	m	w	LA	Los Angeles	Los Nietos Twp	73	589
Pitman	23	m	w	TX	Mendocino	Anderson Twp	74	155
Robert	38	m	w	IREL	El Dorado	Diamond Springs Tw	72	34
HARGRAVES								
Hannibal	50	m	w	OH	Sonoma	Bodega Twp	91	253
Leroy B	32	m	w	TN	Sonoma	Salt Point	91	390
Leroy B	30	m	w	IL	Sonoma	Bodega Twp	91	253
Thos	40	m	w	IL	San Joaquin	Douglas Twp	86	31
Wm	52	m	w	MO	Napa	Napa	75	42
Zip	70	m	w	OH	Sonoma	Salt Point	91	390
HARGREAVES								
S	54	m	w	ENGL	Del Norte	Crescent Twp	71	455
HARGRO								
Ah	18	m	c	CHIN	San Joaquin	Tulare Twp	86	251
HARGROVE								
Henry	31	m	w	ENGL	San Francisco	11-Wd San Francisc	84	457
James	41	m	b	MD	San Francisco	6-Wd San Francisco	81	110
John	48	m	w	IL	Mendocino	Ukiah Twp	74	233
Solomon	70	m	w	GA	Tulare	Farmersville Twp	92	245
HARGUE								
Noel	51	m	w	FRAN	Siskiyou	Callahan P O	89	627
HARGUES								
Simeon	42	m	w	NH	Santa Clara	Redwood Twp	88	119
HARGUS								
Susan E	32	f	w	NY	Santa Clara	Redwood Twp	88	117
Walter	45	m	w	TN	Santa Clara	Santa Clara Twp	88	173
HARGUTA								
N	21	f	w	IREL	Alameda	Oakland	68	143
HARI								
Andrew	32	m	w	NJ	Placer	Cisco P O	76	494
HARIGUEZ								
Jesus	39	f	w	MEXI	San Francisco	San Francisco P O	80	342
HARINGER								
Jno	36	m	w	PA	Butte	Ophir Twp	70	116
HARINGTON								
Charles	35	m	w	IREL	San Francisco	7-Wd San Francisco	81	213
Jas	35	m	w	IREL	Butte	Chico Twp	70	42
W	26	m	w	IREL	San Francisco	7-Wd San Francisco	81	168
HARIOT								
Corinne	15	f	w	WA	Los Angeles	Los Nietos Twp	73	574
HARIS								
Chs	35	m	w	PRUS	San Francisco	2-Wd San Francisco	79	215
Hezakiah	36	m	w	NY	Mendocino	Point Arena Twp	74	206
John	35	m	w	ENGL	Sacramento	4-Wd Sacramento	77	340
William	24	m	w	BAVA	San Francisco	2-Wd San Francisco	79	283
HARISON								
Liddia	53	f	w	IL	Sacramento	2-Wd Sacramento	77	210
Nelson	24	m	w	DENM	Mendocino	Little Rvr Twp	74	171
HARJES								
Lina	35	f	w	BREM	San Francisco	2-Wd San Francisco	79	220
Richard	34	m	w	BREM	Santa Clara	Fremont Twp	88	44
HARK								
Adam	50	m	w	PA	San Francisco	8-Wd San Francisco	82	447
Ah	32	m	c	CHIN	San Francisco	6-Wd San Francisco	81	53
Jno	30	m	w	MO	Monterey	San Juan Twp	74	405
HARKEE								
Christena	42	f	w	PRUS	Sutter	Butte Twp	92	102
Joseph	17	m	w	LA	Sutter	Butte Twp	92	102
HARKEN								
Mary	29	f	w	IREL	San Francisco	San Francisco P O	83	343
Patrick	25	m	w	IREL	San Francisco	San Francisco P O	83	376
HARKER								
Andrew	32	m	w	BADE	San Francisco	6-Wd San Francisco	81	84
Annie	17	f	w	SAXO	San Francisco	San Francisco P O	85	803
Charles H	32	m	w	NY	Santa Clara	Alviso Twp	88	23
Chas W	26	m	w	IL	Nevada	Meadow Lake Twp	75	266
Christopher	30	m	w	IL	Nevada	Bloomfield Twp	75	93
George	31	m	w	ME	Nevada	Meadow Lake Twp	75	267
Henry	21	m	w	TN	Nevada	Meadow Lake Twp	75	267
James	36	m	w	IREL	San Francisco	San Francisco P O	85	746
John	54	m	w	BAVA	Amador	Volcano P O	69	384
Mifflin	71	m	w	PA	Contra Costa	Martinez P O	71	445
HARKEY								
James	42	m	w	NC	Santa Barbara	San Buenaventura P	87	424
James	35	m	w	ENGL	San Francisco	1-Wd San Francisco	79	78
W P	42	m	w	NY	Sutter	Sutter Twp	92	128
HARKIN								
B C	22	m	w	ENGL	Tuolumne	Big Oak Flat P O	93	402
C	20	m	w	ENGL	Tuolumne	Big Oak Flat P O	93	402
Catherine	48	f	w	IREL	Santa Clara	1-Wd San Jose	88	233
Edwd	35	m	w	IREL	San Francisco	1-Wd San Francisco	79	132
Edwd	21	m	w	IREL	San Francisco	1-Wd San Francisco	79	132
John	40	m	w	MA	San Mateo	Half Moon Bay P O	87	406
John	30	m	w	ENGL	Tuolumne	Big Oak Flat P O	93	402
Michel	24	m	w	IREL	Napa	Napa	75	38
Patrick	28	m	w	IREL	Sacramento	2-Wd Sacramento	77	240
Robt	25	m	w	ENGL	San Francisco	1-Wd San Francisco	79	59
HARKINS								
C A	38	m	w	NY	Solano	Vallejo	90	205
Charles	51	m	w	IREL	Yuba	Slate Range Bar Tw	93	673
Charles	47	m	w	IREL	Calaveras	San Andreas P O	70	182
Chas	55	m	w	IREL	San Francisco	7-Wd San Francisco	81	255
Daniel	34	m	w	IREL	Calaveras	San Andreas P O	70	182
Daniel	25	m	w	MA	Alameda	Brooklyn	68	26
Denis	22	m	w	IREL	San Francisco	1-Wd San Francisco	79	82
Eliza	54	f	w	IL	Sacramento	Lee Twp	77	158
Hugh V	33	m	w	OH	Contra Costa	Martinez P O	71	392
James	42	m	w	IREL	Sacramento	4-Wd Sacramento	77	375
James	33	m	w	IREL	Calaveras	San Andreas P O	70	182
Jas	37	m	w	IREL	San Francisco	1-Wd San Francisco	79	49
John	23	m	w	IREL	Yuba	Rose Bar Twp	93	662
John P	34	m	w	IREL	Sacramento	2-Wd Sacramento	77	247
Lucy	74	f	w	NH	Sonoma	Petaluma Twp	91	330
Margaret	27	f	w	IREL	San Francisco	San Francisco P O	85	798
Mary	24	f	w	IREL	San Francisco	San Francisco P O	85	798
Michel	36	m	w	IREL	Sacramento	4-Wd Sacramento	77	319
Owen	33	m	w	CANA	San Francisco	11-Wd San Francisc	84	691
Patrick	35	m	w	IREL	Plumas	Goodwin Twp	77	58
Patrick	26	m	w	IREL	Plumas	Goodwin Twp	77	6

© 2001 by Heritage Quest. All rights reserved.

Name	Age	S	R	B-PL	County	Locale	Roll	Pg
Robt	70	m	w	MD	San Francisco	San Francisco P O	83	85
Susan	55	f	w	UNKN	San Joaquin	2-Wd Stockton	86	166
Thomas	34	m	w	IREL	Trinity	Weaverville Pct	92	223
HARKINSON								
John	25	m	w	SCOT	San Francisco	San Francisco P O	83	188
HARKISHAAH								
Vilcola	33	m	w	GERM	Los Angeles	Los Angeles	73	517
HARKISON								
Chas	44	m	w	NY	Solano	Vallejo	90	179
HARKLESS								
Mary	30	f	w	ME	San Francisco	8-Wd San Francisco	82	460
HARKMAN								
Chas	35	m	w	HDAR	Solano	Rio Vista Twp	90	70
F	42	m	w	WURT	Yuba	Marysville	93	612
H	47	m	w	PRUS	San Joaquin	2-Wd Stockton	86	163
Philip	19	m	w	CANA	Santa Cruz	Soquel Twp	89	445
HARKNESS								
Edson	26	m	w	OH	Yolo	Grafton Twp	93	478
Edward	30	m	w	IREL	San Francisco	11-Wd San Francisc	84	700
John	58	m	w	CT	San Francisco	7-Wd San Francisco	81	287
M E	27	f	w	IL	Alameda	Oakland	68	196
Mat	31	m	b	GA	Butte	Ophir Twp	70	105
Osmer	53	m	w	OH	Placer	Gold Run Twp	76	394
Rod D	45	m	w	OH	El Dorado	Georgetown Twp	72	42
Samuel	40	m	m	WIND	San Francisco	6-Wd San Francisco	81	99
Thomas	34	m	w	SCOT	Contra Costa	Martinez P O	71	373
Timothy	30	m	w	IREL	Santa Clara	Santa Clara Twp	88	155
Walter	45	m	w	NY	Plumas	Washington Twp	77	25
HARKNETT								
Morris	30	m	w	IREL	San Mateo	Menlo Park P O	87	377
HARKNEY								
John	37	m	w	VA	San Francisco	6-Wd San Francisco	81	79
HARKRADER								
Joseph	55	m	w	VA	Napa	Yountville Twp	75	87
HARKSON								
T C	32	m	w	NORW	Alameda	Oakland	68	153
HARKUM								
Geo	27	m	w	KY	San Joaquin	Douglas Twp	86	48
HARLAN								
Benjamin	41	m	w	KY	Kern	Bakersfield P O	73	365
Chas	23	m	w	OH	San Francisco	8-Wd San Francisco	82	331
Edward	32	m	w	PA	Monterey	San Juan Twp	74	390
Frank	40	m	w	DENM	Tuolumne	Chinese Camp P O	93	384
George	47	m	w	IN	Alameda	Brooklyn Twp	68	45
George W	40	m	w	VA	Stanislaus	Branch Twp	92	4
J C	18	m	w	CA	Alameda	Oakland	68	257
Jacob	41	m	w	IN	Alameda	Eden Twp	68	91
Joel	42	m	w	IN	Contra Costa	Martinez P O	71	392
Micajah O	25	m	w	KY	Yolo	Buckeye Twp	93	415
HARLAND								
Edward	32	m	w	CANA	Nevada	Grass Valley Twp	75	172
Geo	38	m	w	IL	Alameda	Murray Twp	68	105
Grace	10	f	w	MO	Colusa	Spring Valley Twp	71	335
Jacob	44	m	w	CANA	San Francisco	San Francisco P O	83	266
Nellie	29	f	w	IREL	Santa Clara	Redwood Twp	88	129
Thomas	44	m	w	ENGL	Nevada	Grass Valley Twp	75	183
William	49	m	w	IREL	Tulare	Visalia	92	296
HARLDIN								
Samuel S	24	m	w	TN	Yolo	Buckeye Twp	93	415
HARLDSON								
James B	43	m	w	TN	Stanislaus	Branch Twp	92	4
HARLE								
John	42	m	w	IREL	San Francisco	San Francisco P O	83	155
Neal	45	m	w	IREL	Stanislaus	Buena Vista Twp	92	12
HARLEHAY								
Wm	40	m	w	IREL	San Joaquin	Liberty Twp	86	93
HARLEM								
John	22	m	w	NY	San Francisco	San Francisco P O	80	338
William	60	m	w	IREL	Contra Costa	Martinez P O	71	423
HARLES								
A	23	m	w	IA	San Joaquin	Elliott Twp	86	77
Miles W	41	m	w	KY	Stanislaus	North Twp	92	67
HARLETT								
Ebenezer B	34	m	w	PA	San Diego	San Diego	78	493
HARLEY								
Aaron	45	m	w	PA	Yolo	Grafton Twp	93	488
Charles	34	m	w	SCOT	San Francisco	11-Wd San Francisc	84	467
Chas	24	m	w	IREL	San Francisco	San Francisco P O	85	794
Danl	40	m	w	IREL	San Francisco	11-Wd San Francisc	84	614
Danl	26	m	w	IREL	San Francisco	1-Wd San Francisco	79	36
David	26	m	w	MA	San Francisco	San Francisco P O	83	41
Elias	55	m	w	PA	Yolo	Grafton Twp	93	488
Hannah	25	f	w	IREL	Contra Costa	Martinez Twp	71	351
I H	39	m	w	CANA	Sacramento	3-Wd Sacramento	77	318
J N	38	m	w	ENGL	Alameda	Murray Twp	68	118
J R	42	m	w	KY	Solano	Benicia	90	9
James	41	m	w	NY	San Francisco	3-Wd San Francisco	79	316
James	30	m	w	MO	Sutter	Nicolaus Twp	92	110
Jeanette	65	f	w	SCOT	San Francisco	11-Wd San Francisc	84	625
John	35	m	w	VT	Sacramento	4-Wd Sacramento	77	327
John	30	m	w	IREL	San Francisco	San Francisco P O	85	846
Jos W	24	m	w	ENGL	San Francisco	8-Wd San Francisco	82	344
Joseph	24	m	w	IL	San Diego	Julian Dist	78	473
Julia	22	f	w	CHIL	San Francisco	San Francisco P O	80	465
M N	28	m	w	URUG	Monterey	Salinas Twp	74	314
Michael F	40	m	w	IREL	Santa Clara	1-Wd San Jose	88	266
Micheal	26	m	w	IREL	San Francisco	7-Wd San Francisco	81	180
Pat	30	m	w	IREL	San Joaquin	Oneal Twp	86	103
Thos	39	m	w	ENGL	Monterey	Alisal Twp	74	290
W	36	m	w	TX	Monterey	San Antonio Twp	74	316
Wm	25	m	w	IREL	Butte	Chico Twp	70	56
HARLIN								
Benjamin	33	m	w	MO	Yolo	Cache Crk Twp	93	450
Joanna	6	f	w	CA	Yolo	Cache Crk Twp	93	451
John	35	m	w	FRAN	San Francisco	11-Wd San Francisc	84	614
Josph	46	m	w	MO	Yolo	Cache Crk Twp	93	451
Michael	62	m	w	IREL	Alameda	Washington Twp	68	275
Thomas J	32	m	w	TN	Yolo	Cache Crk Twp	93	442
HARLINE								
William	30	m	w	IREL	San Francisco	7-Wd San Francisco	81	178
HARLING								
Charles	34	m	w	PRUS	Santa Cruz	Santa Cruz Twp	89	388
HARLINGER								
Von John	46	m	w	OH	Tuolumne	Sonora P O	93	305
HARLIS								
Harrison	34	m	w	VA	Napa	Napa	75	53
James	48	m	w	ENGL	Tuolumne	Columbia P O	93	357
S A	18	f	w	ENGL	Tuolumne	Columbia P O	93	339
HARLOCK								
Harvey	30	m	w	ENGL	San Francisco	5-Wd San Francisco	81	28
Henry	22	m	w	AUSL	San Francisco	11-Wd San Francisc	84	674
Robt	27	m	w	AUSL	San Francisco	11-Wd San Francisc	84	477
HARLOE								
Marcus	37	m	w	IREL	Santa Barbara	Santa Barbara P O	87	501
R G	31	m	w	NY	San Francisco	San Francisco P O	83	25
HARLOW								
Antonio	25	m	w	IL	Santa Clara	Santa Clara Twp	88	137
Dora M	26	m	w	IL	Tulare	Farmersville Twp	92	250
E A	44	m	w	MA	Tuolumne	Chinese Camp P O	93	378
Emma	18	f	w	OH	Santa Clara	Santa Clara Twp	88	137
Fayette S	29	m	w	NY	San Francisco	1-Wd San Francisco	79	61
G W	42	m	w	IL	Sacramento	Brighton Twp	77	73
Geo	30	m	w	ME	San Francisco	1-Wd San Francisco	79	71
Ichabod	46	m	w	MA	Sonoma	Salt Point Twp	91	383
Jacob	28	m	w	SHOL	San Mateo	Half Moon Bay P O	87	403
James	40	m	w	MA	Sonoma	Analy Twp	91	220
James	32	m	w	NY	Sacramento	4-Wd Sacramento	77	343
John	45	m	w	IA	Yolo	Cottonwood Twp	93	474
John M	28	m	w	OH	Alameda	Oakland	68	136
Joseph	37	m	w	ME	Yolo	Grafton Twp	93	500
Peter	27	m	w	IREL	Solano	Tremont Twp	90	31
Robert B	28	m	w	NY	San Francisco	1-Wd San Francisco	79	69
Robt C	35	m	w	IN	Fresno	Millerton P O	72	168
Urial	57	m	w	ME	Tulare	Farmersville Twp	92	249
HARLSON								
John H	54	m	w	GA	Marin	Nicasio Twp	74	16
HARLUNG								
Gustave	31	m	w	HANO	San Francisco	2-Wd San Francisco	79	190
HARLY								
Mary	35	f	w	IREL	San Joaquin	2-Wd Stockton	86	169
HARM								
James	35	m	w	IL	Alameda	Oakland	68	263
John	33	m	w	MECK	Tuolumne	Sonora P O	93	325
HARMACK								
Jesus	40	m	i	MEXI	San Luis Obispo	San Luis Obispo Tw	87	307
HARMAN								
A M	35	m	w	IL	Nevada	Eureka Twp	75	135
Andrew	38	m	w	KY	San Francisco	5-Wd San Francisco	81	12
Daniel	23	m	w	NY	Inyo	Independence Twp	73	328
Eliza	17	f	w	US	Yuba	Marysville	93	609
Fred	28	m	w	PRUS	Contra Costa	Martinez P O	71	398
George	34	m	w	MD	San Francisco	San Francisco P O	80	485
George S	39	m	w	ME	Santa Clara	Fremont Twp	88	49
Henry	22	m	w	HAMB	San Joaquin	Oneal Twp	86	110
John	29	m	w	NY	San Francisco	San Francisco P O	80	540
John	27	m	w	IREL	San Francisco	11-Wd San Francisc	84	455
John	26	m	w	US	San Joaquin	3-Wd Stockton	86	231
John L	31	m	w	NY	Placer	Dutch Flat P O	76	415
M	39	m	w	IL	San Joaquin	Tulare Twp	86	264
Mary	49	m	w	CANA	San Francisco	1-Wd San Francisco	79	123
Nancy	73	f	w	KY	San Joaquin	Douglas Twp	86	34
Sam	42	m	w	ME	San Francisco	7-Wd San Francisco	81	285
William	27	m	w	ENGL	Inyo	Bishop Crk Twp	73	313
Winifred	29	f	w	IREL	San Francisco	San Francisco P O	83	124
Wm	35	m	w	PA	Sonoma	Vallejo Twp	91	458
HARMANN								
L	58	m	w	LA	San Francisco	San Francisco P O	85	783
HARMEN								
Henry B	45	m	w	ENGL	San Francisco	1-Wd San Francisco	79	133
Jose	49	m	w	IREL	San Joaquin	3-Wd Stockton	86	226
HARMENSING								
Edward	48	m	w	DENM	Stanislaus	San Joaquin Twp	92	72
HARMER								
Amanda	7	f	w	PA	San Francisco	6-Wd San Francisco	81	98
Geo	29	m	w	ENGL	San Francisco	7-Wd San Francisco	81	235
Nelson	38	m	w	NY	Trinity	Weaverville Pct	92	225
Sol	40	m	w	IN	Alameda	Alameda	68	7
William	38	m	w	CANA	Santa Clara	2-Wd San Jose	88	308
HARMES								
Charles	31	m	w	HANO	Inyo	Cerro Gordo Twp	73	319
HARMESS								
Jacob	51	m	w	PRUS	San Francisco	5-Wd San Francisco	81	16
HARMINN								
Frederick	40	m	w	NY	San Diego	Julian Dist	78	468

Series M593

© 2001 by Heritage Quest. All rights reserved.

California 1870 Census

Series M593

Name	Age	S	R	B-PL	County	Locale	Roll	Pg
HARMIOT								
Tohal	38	m	w	ITAL	San Francisco	San Francisco P O	80	469
HARMMOND								
J	40	m	w	IL	Amador	Sutter Crk P O	69	410
HARMON								
---	35	m	w	PA	Sonoma	Bodega Twp	91	257
A	58	m	w	PRUS	Sierra	Butte Twp	89	511
A B	50	m	w	NC	Amador	Jackson P O	69	330
A K P	50	m	w	ME	San Francisco	San Francisco P O	83	115
Alexander	51	m	w	KY	Santa Cruz	Pajaro Twp	89	351
Arthur	40	m	w	NH	Solano	Suisun Twp	90	114
Austin	22	m	w	ME	Santa Cruz	Santa Cruz Twp	89	396
C A	45	f	w	NY	San Francisco	San Francisco P O	85	798
C T	33	m	w	ME	Humboldt	Eureka Twp	72	264
Charles	23	m	w	OH	Santa Barbara	San Buenaventura P	87	448
Chas	24	m	w	MO	Nevada	Bloomfield Twp	75	95
Daniel	63	m	w	ME	Placer	Lincoln P O	76	492
Dewitt	47	m	w	IL	Calaveras	Copperopolis P O	70	258
E D	39	m	w	OH	Alameda	Oakland	68	250
Frank	25	m	w	MO	Tulare	Farmersville Twp	92	245
George D	37	m	w	GERM	Tulare	Visalia	92	297
George K	31	m	w	MO	Tulare	Visalia Twp	92	288
George W	20	m	w	MO	Tulare	Venice Twp	92	275
Hen J	26	m	w	IN	Butte	Oregon Twp	70	130
Henry	41	m	w	NY	Santa Barbara	Santa Barbara P O	87	476
J	28	m	w	MO	Nevada	Meadow Lake Twp	75	269
J B	47	m	w	OH	Alameda	Oakland	68	161
James	50	m	w	GA	Amador	Fiddletown P O	69	433
James	48	m	w	TN	Amador	Fiddletown P O	69	430
James H	42	m	w	TN	Tulare	Farmersville Twp	92	248
John	36	m	w	IL	Nevada	Little York Twp	75	242
John	32	m	w	CT	Sonoma	Analy Twp	91	224
John	18	m	w	MO	Amador	Sutter Crk P O	69	413
John R	49	m	w	PA	Nevada	Bridgeport Twp	75	125
John R	45	m	w	GERM	Los Angeles	Los Angeles	73	535
Johnthas	28	m	w	NY	Sonoma	Petaluma Twp	91	345
Leonard S	38	m	w	ME	Santa Cruz	Santa Cruz	89	418
Logan	20	m	w	CANA	Mendocino	Point Arena Twp	74	224
Luther N	59	m	w	CANA	Sonoma	Petaluma Twp	91	345
Martin	38	m	w	IREL	San Francisco	11-Wd San Francisc	84	561
Myron	40	m	w	NY	Kern	Linns Valley P O	73	348
Oscar R	22	m	w	ME	Santa Cruz	Santa Cruz Twp	89	396
Pulaski	22	m	w	OH	Mendocino	Navarro & Big Rvr	74	174
R	35	m	w	PRUS	San Joaquin	2-Wd Stockton	86	163
R A	40	m	w	NY	Alameda	Murray Twp	68	126
Rachael	17	m	w	OR	Butte	Chico Twp	70	42
Robert	29	m	w	NY	San Francisco	5-Wd San Francisco	81	35
Rufus B	29	m	w	ME	Sacramento	2-Wd Sacramento	77	245
Sherlock	24	m	w	ME	Santa Cruz	Santa Cruz Twp	89	389
Silas S	51	m	w	NY	Santa Barbara	Santa Barbara P O	87	467
Soln	27	m	w	MO	Siskiyou	Surprise Valley Tw	89	636
T O	38	m	w	VA	Sutter	Vernon Twp	92	130
William	33	m	w	ENGL	San Francisco	San Francisco P O	83	412
William	26	m	w	ME	Nevada	Nevada Twp	75	321
Wm	51	m	w	VA	Sutter	Vernon Twp	92	130
Wm	25	m	w	NY	San Francisco	7-Wd San Francisco	81	231
Wm H	55	m	w	VT	Amador	Volcano P O	69	372
HARMONY								
Isabella	31	f	w	IREL	San Francisco	San Francisco P O	80	474
Katrina	36	f	w	BAVA	Siskiyou	Yreka	89	656
HARMS								
Christian	40	m	w	HANO	El Dorado	Diamond Springs Tw	72	25
Hy	35	m	w	HANO	San Francisco	11-Wd San Francisc	84	623
John	43	m	w	SHOL	San Francisco	San Francisco P O	83	269
John	41	m	w	HANO	San Francisco	2-Wd San Francisco	79	155
Mathew	29	m	w	PRUS	San Francisco	San Francisco P O	83	321
Peter	27	m	w	PRUS	San Francisco	San Francisco P O	83	318
Riley	30	m	w	NY	Sonoma	Petaluma Twp	91	351
HARMSTEAD								
Joseph	55	m	w	MA	San Francisco	11-Wd San Francisc	84	603
HARN								
Ah	20	m	c	CHIN	San Francisco	6-Wd San Francisco	81	49
Ah	19	m	c	CHIN	San Francisco	6-Wd San Francisco	81	138
Charles F R	44	m	w	SAXO	Inyo	Cerro Gordo Twp	73	321
George	36	m	w	ME	Inyo	Independence Twp	73	328
Lut	15	m	c	CHIN	San Francisco	San Francisco P O	83	99
Theron	13	m	w	IL	Nevada	Rough & Ready Twp	75	334
HARNDON								
Asbury P	39	m	w	AL	San Luis Obispo	San Luis Obispo Tw	87	312
HARNED								
Alex	36	m	w	LA	San Francisco	7-Wd San Francisco	81	284
Jacob A M	40	m	w	NJ	Los Angeles	Los Angeles	73	540
Katie	19	f	w	IREL	Los Angeles	Los Angeles	73	548
Stephen K	40	m	w	NY	Placer	Auburn P O	76	374
HARNELL								
John	28	m	w	IREL	Nevada	Nevada Twp	75	282
HARNEN								
Michael	39	m	w	IREL	San Francisco	2-Wd San Francisco	79	257
HARNER								
Edward	31	m	w	NJ	Alameda	Washington Twp	68	276
Thos	29	m	w	ENGL	Sacramento	3-Wd Sacramento	77	273
HARNESS								
Charles	30	m	w	IL	Inyo	Bishop Crk Twp	73	316
Jedediah F	53	m	w	VT	Los Angeles	Los Angeles	73	505
John	32	m	w	VA	Colusa	Colusa	71	296
HARNET								
Danl	28	m	w	IREL	San Francisco	7-Wd San Francisco	81	242
HARNETT								
Edwd	25	m	w	IREL	San Francisco	1-Wd San Francisco	79	41
Ellen	26	f	w	IREL	San Francisco	San Francisco P O	80	386
James	31	m	w	VA	Sutter	Yuba Twp	92	143
John	23	m	w	IREL	San Francisco	1-Wd San Francisco	79	41
Maurice	30	m	w	IREL	Santa Clara	Fremont Twp	88	57
HARNEY								
Catherine	35	f	w	IREL	Santa Clara	2-Wd San Jose	88	328
Charles	40	m	w	CANA	El Dorado	Coloma Twp	72	10
D H	36	m	w	NY	Yuba	Marysville	93	612
Daniel	40	m	w	IREL	San Francisco	8-Wd San Francisco	82	290
Edmond	21	m	w	IREL	Tuolumne	Big Oak Flat P O	93	404
Hugh	26	m	w	IREL	Mariposa	Mariposa P O	74	111
I S	28	m	w	SWIT	San Joaquin	2-Wd Stockton	86	200
James	50	m	w	ENGL	Placer	Alta P O	76	412
James	37	m	w	ENGL	San Francisco	San Francisco P O	83	171
James	29	m	w	SCOT	Santa Clara	San Jose Twp	88	221
John	45	m	w	IREL	Tuolumne	Big Oak Flat P O	93	404
John	45	m	w	IREL	Humboldt	Pacific Twp	72	297
John	36	m	w	SCOT	Santa Clara	San Jose Twp	88	221
John	17	m	w	IL	San Francisco	8-Wd San Francisco	82	359
Joseph	42	m	w	MO	Mono	Bridgeport P O	74	286
Joseph	40	m	w	TN	El Dorado	Greenwood Twp	72	50
Joseph	38	m	w	ENGL	San Francisco	11-Wd San Francisc	84	580
Martin	43	m	w	IREL	Sacramento	4-Wd Sacramento	77	346
Martin	40	m	w	IREL	Solano	Vallejo	90	155
Mary	38	f	w	IREL	Yolo	Washington Twp	93	533
Mary A	15	f	w	MA	San Francisco	San Francisco P O	83	181
Michael	58	m	w	IREL	San Francisco	San Francisco P O	83	242
Mike	71	m	w	IREL	San Francisco	11-Wd San Francisc	84	613
Mike	24	m	w	NY	San Francisco	11-Wd San Francisc	84	694
P M	34	m	w	IREL	Tuolumne	Big Oak Flat P O	93	400
Patrick	40	m	w	IREL	Tuolumne	Big Oak Flat P O	93	404
Patrick	35	m	w	IREL	San Francisco	2-Wd San Francisco	79	252
Rosa	52	f	w	IREL	San Francisco	11-Wd San Francisc	84	505
Sten D	54	m	w	NH	Butte	Ophir Twp	70	118
Stewart	46	m	w	NH	Butte	Ophir Twp	70	101
Thomas	30	m	w	IREL	San Francisco	7-Wd San Francisco	81	194
Thos	30	m	w	ENGL	San Francisco	11-Wd San Francisc	84	674
William	50	m	w	IREL	Sutter	Nicolaus Twp	92	115
William	31	m	w	NY	San Francisco	6-Wd San Francisco	81	146
Wm	63	m	w	IREL	San Francisco	11-Wd San Francisc	84	573
HARNION								
William	39	m	w	IREL	San Francisco	San Francisco P O	83	361
HARNIS								
Fred	20	m	w	NY	Napa	Napa Twp	75	75
HARNISTER								
Noah	35	m	w	KY	San Francisco	6-Wd San Francisco	81	88
HARNOIS								
Octa	26	m	w	CANA	Mendocino	Round Valley Twp	74	217
HARNS								
A	40	m	w	PRUS	Alameda	Murray Twp	68	102
Fritz	46	m	w	HANO	Yolo	Washington Twp	93	537
George	21	m	w	ENGL	Nevada	Nevada Twp	75	301
Henry	50	m	w	HANO	Yolo	Washington Twp	93	537
Solomon	31	m	w	PRUS	San Francisco	8-Wd San Francisco	82	291
HARNSE								
A	27	f	w	MEXI	Sierra	Downieville Twp	89	520
HARNSTON								
Robt	26	m	w	NY	San Francisco	1-Wd San Francisco	79	103
HAROEY								
Thos	69	m	w	MD	San Francisco	11-Wd San Francisc	84	613
HAROHER								
Patrick	45	m	w	IREL	San Francisco	8-Wd San Francisco	82	402
HAROLD								
Barney	42	m	w	IREL	Calaveras	Copperopolis P O	70	241
Charles	45	m	w	ENGL	San Francisco	6-Wd San Francisco	81	89
Eli	42	m	w	TN	El Dorado	Placerville Twp	72	95
Henry	60	m	w	GA	Tulare	Visalia Twp	92	282
James	60	m	w	IREL	Calaveras	Copperopolis P O	70	241
John	36	m	w	MO	Tulare	Kings Rvr Twp	92	253
John	34	m	w	IREL	San Francisco	1-Wd San Francisco	79	93
Martin	25	m	w	PRUS	Sacramento	American Twp	77	66
Mary	22	f	w	AR	Tulare	Visalia	92	290
Philip	44	m	w	HCAS	San Francisco	11-Wd San Francisc	84	648
Simon	22	m	w	TX	Tulare	Visalia Twp	92	283
W H	29	m	w	PA	Solano	Vallejo	90	203
HAROLDSON								
Margret	44	f	w	TN	San Joaquin	Oneal Twp	86	113
HAROUN								
J D	37	m	w	NY	Nevada	Washington Twp	75	340
HAROW								
Mary	17	f	w	IREL	Sonoma	Cloverdale Twp	91	267
HAROY								
David	45	m	w	ENGL	Alameda	Washington Twp	68	283
HARP								
Adam M	35	m	w	AR	Stanislaus	Empire Twp	92	52
Ah	27	m	c	CHIN	San Francisco	San Francisco P O	83	131
Campbell S	33	m	w	TN	Tulare	Visalia Twp	92	287
James A	55	m	w	TN	Tulare	Visalia Twp	92	287
James D	24	m	w	AR	Stanislaus	Empire Twp	92	56
Lemuel	22	m	w	AR	Stanislaus	Empire Twp	92	53
Lucinda	52	f	w	KY	Calaveras	Copperopolis P O	70	245
Samuel	33	m	w	AR	Tulare	Visalia Twp	92	288
Samuel	33	m	w	AR	Tulare	Visalia	92	295
Sarah A	39	f	w	IL	Stanislaus	Empire Twp	92	52
Simon	27	m	w	NY	San Francisco	5-Wd San Francisco	81	31

© 2001 by Heritage Quest. All rights reserved.

Name	Age	S	R	B-PL	County	Locale	Roll	Pg
Swan	38	m	w	MO	Stanislaus	Empire Twp	92	61
T D	43	m	w	TN	San Joaquin	Castoria Twp	86	10
Thomas	45	m	w	TN	Stanislaus	Empire Twp	92	56
William	45	m	w	SWIT	San Joaquin	2-Wd Stockton	86	167
William	32	m	w	AR	Tulare	Venice Twp	92	273
William	32	m	w	GA	Stanislaus	Emory Twp	92	25
William S	52	m	w	TN	Stanislaus	Empire Twp	92	59
HARPE								
J A	33	m	w	NY	Humboldt	South Fork Twp	72	301
HARPEN								
Benjamin	45	m	w	KY	San Francisco	7-Wd San Francisco	81	182
HARPENDING								
Asburg	30	m	w	KY	San Francisco	7-Wd San Francisco	81	278
HARPER								
A B	53	m	w	VA	Sonoma	Bodega Twp	91	256
Aaron	24	m	w	MS	Solano	Vacaville Twp	90	123
Albert	39	m	w	IREL	Santa Clara	Santa Clara Twp	88	178
Alfred	18	m	w	CA	Sutter	Butte Twp	92	90
Amos	35	m	w	MO	Sonoma	Russian Rvr	91	369
Andrew J	54	m	w	TN	Stanislaus	North Twp	92	67
Arnold	35	m	w	OH	Contra Costa	Martinez P O	71	376
Arthur	50	m	w	ENGL	San Francisco	6-Wd San Francisco	81	104
Caroline	38	f	w	PA	San Francisco	11-Wd San Francisc	84	634
Charles	19	m	w	OH	Placer	Lincoln P O	76	487
Charles A	44	m	w	PA	San Francisco	3-Wd San Francisco	79	315
Charles F	38	m	w	NC	Los Angeles	Los Angeles Twp	73	489
Chas	40	m	w	NY	Sacramento	3-Wd Sacramento	77	291
Chas W	38	m	w	IN	Sonoma	Mendocino Twp	91	296
David	40	m	w	MI	Solano	Denverton Twp	90	25
David	37	m	w	NY	Solano	Suisun Twp	90	99
E	14	m	w	CA	San Joaquin	Oneal Twp	86	112
Edward	34	m	w	ENGL	San Francisco	7-Wd San Francisco	81	199
Edward	22	m	b	MA	San Francisco	San Francisco P O	80	417
Eli A	45	m	w	VA	San Diego	Julian Dist	78	473
Eliott	29	m	w	SCOT	Santa Clara	Gilroy Twp	88	69
Elizabeth	40	f	w	OH	Placer	Lincoln P O	76	491
Gustavus	18	m	w	CA	San Francisco	San Francisco P O	85	754
Harper W H	28	m	w	OH	Sacramento	3-Wd Sacramento	77	261
Henry	46	m	w	PA	Alameda	Brooklyn Twp	68	51
Henry	42	m	w	MO	Placer	Auburn P O	76	358
Henry	29	m	w	GERM	Los Angeles	Los Angeles	73	529
Henry	28	m	w	ENGL	Nevada	Nevada Twp	75	301
Henry	28	m	w	TN	Inyo	Independence Twp	73	325
Henry T	37	m	w	ME	Calaveras	San Andreas P O	70	156
J	36	m	w	SCOT	San Joaquin	1-Wd Stockton	86	153
James	33	m	w	ENGL	San Francisco	San Francisco P O	85	830
James	27	m	w	ENGL	San Francisco	1-Wd San Francisco	79	112
Jane	26	f	m	CANA	San Francisco	San Francisco P O	80	475
Jerome W	41	m	w	ENGL	Placer	Bath P O	76	454
Jessie	40	m	w	OH	San Bernardino	San Bernardino Twp	78	453
Jno	19	m	w	ENGL	Santa Clara	Almaden Twp	88	9
John	52	m	w	IREL	San Francisco	1-Wd San Francisco	79	24
John	52	m	w	IN	Calaveras	San Andreas P O	70	215
John	40	m	w	MO	San Joaquin	Liberty Twp	86	86
John	38	m	w	IREL	San Francisco	San Francisco P O	85	868
John	30	m	w	ENGL	San Francisco	11-Wd San Francisc	84	434
John	19	m	w	PA	San Francisco	San Francisco P O	83	336
John F	42	m	w	SWED	Stanislaus	Emory Twp	92	24
John H	35	m	w	NY	Santa Cruz	Santa Cruz Twp	89	395
Josephine	23	f	w	IREL	Sacramento	4-Wd Sacramento	77	364
L Mrs	47	f	w	VA	Napa	Napa Twp	75	63
Laurence	28	m	w	SCOT	Monterey	Monterey Twp	74	351
Margaret	72	f	w	SC	Stanislaus	North Twp	92	67
Margaret	20	f	w	AUSL	Yuba	Long Bar Twp	93	561
Martha	46	f	b	SC	El Dorado	Placerville	72	114
Milton	11	m	w	OR	San Francisco	11-Wd San Francisc	84	588
Moses H	45	m	w	TN	Stanislaus	North Twp	92	68
O S	44	m	w	PA	Tuolumne	Big Oak Flat P O	93	400
O T	56	m	w	GA	Tuolumne	Big Oak Flat P O	93	396
Richard	49	m	w	ENGL	San Francisco	11-Wd San Francisc	84	446
Richard	37	m	w	IREL	San Francisco	San Francisco P O	80	336
Richard	27	m	w	ENGL	Nevada	Grass Valley Twp	75	199
Rienzi	20	m	w	PA	San Mateo	Pescadero P O	87	412
Robt	21	m	w	MO	Siskiyou	Big Valley Twp	89	581
S	35	m	w	MA	Alameda	Oakland	68	226
Samuel	37	m	w	IREL	Los Angeles	Soledad Twp	73	631
Samuel	28	m	b	VA	Sacramento	2-Wd Sacramento	77	242
Samuel N	54	m	w	IN	Calaveras	San Andreas P O	70	215
Sterling G	30	m	w	AL	Yolo	Cache Crk Twp	93	429
Thoaph	47	m	w	PA	Sonoma	Healdsburg & Mendo	91	280
Thomas B	38	m	w	VA	Placer	Lincoln P O	76	484
Thomas N	33	m	w	MO	Placer	Dutch Flat P O	76	415
Thos	32	m	w	ENGL	Sacramento	1-Wd Sacramento	77	186
Troyman W	40	m	w	VA	Tulare	Tule Rvr Twp	92	264
W H	27	m	w	IL	Merced	Snelling P O	74	270
William	60	m	w	ME	Placer	Emigrant Gap P O	76	417
William	54	m	w	ME	San Francisco	6-Wd San Francisco	81	133
William	36	m	w	MD	San Francisco	San Francisco P O	80	473
William	36	m	w	PA	San Francisco	San Francisco P O	80	374
William	35	m	w	IA	Stanislaus	Empire Twp	92	55
William	35	m	w	NY	San Francisco	2-Wd San Francisco	79	246
William	33	m	w	OH	Los Angeles	Los Angeles Twp	73	494
William	32	m	w	PA	San Francisco	8-Wd San Francisco	82	462
William	23	m	b	MA	San Francisco	San Francisco P O	80	475
William A	24	m	w	MO	Yolo	Grafton Twp	93	495
William C	52	m	w	TN	Stanislaus	North Twp	92	67
William C	50	m	w	TN	Alpine	Woodfords P O	69	310

Name	Age	S	R	B-PL	County	Locale	Roll	Pg
William H	54	m	b	MD	Sacramento	2-Wd Sacramento	77	236
Wm	40	m	w	VA	San Joaquin	Douglas Twp	86	38
Wm	30	m	w	ENGL	Solano	Vallejo	90	212
Wm K	60	f	w	PA	Santa Clara	Gilroy Twp	88	95
HARPIN								
Louis	36	m	w	FRAN	Los Angeles	Los Angeles	73	524
HARPMAN								
Wm	26	m	w	SWED	Sonoma	Bodega Twp	91	256
HARPOOL								
J	22	m	w	MO	Lake	Lower Lake	73	420
HARPS								
A	23	m	w	PRUS	Alameda	Oakland	68	175
George	41	m	w	PA	Humboldt	Bald Hills	72	239
Joseph	18	m	w	POLA	San Francisco	8-Wd San Francisco	82	374
HARPST								
John	32	m	w	OH	Humboldt	Arcata Twp	72	235
HARPSTER								
Chas	64	m	w	PA	Yuba	Marysville	93	589
HARR								
J W	32	m	w	MA	El Dorado	Greenwood Twp	72	56
HARRA								
Domingo	35	m	w	MEXI	Los Angeles	Los Angeles Twp	73	466
John	25	m	w	FRAN	San Francisco	San Francisco P O	85	772
Jose	46	m	w	CHIL	Amador	Jackson P O	69	337
Nathan	60	m	w	MO	Santa Clara	Gilroy Twp	88	89
HARRAGAN								
Ellen	27	f	w	IREL	San Francisco	8-Wd San Francisco	82	404
HARRAH								
Asa	33	m	w	MO	Tulare	Kings Rvr Twp	92	252
Nancy	63	f	w	GA	Tulare	Visalia	92	289
HARRAHAN								
John	30	m	w	NY	Inyo	Lone Pine Twp	73	330
M	40	f	w	IREL	Alameda	Oakland	68	237
HARRANT								
Eloise	25	f	w	FRAN	San Francisco	San Francisco P O	80	460
HARRARD								
Allen S	34	m	w	RI	San Luis Obispo	Santa Rosa Twp	87	325
HARRAS								
George	51	m	w	RUSS	Inyo	Lone Pine Twp	73	331
Joseph	28	m	w	PRUS	Inyo	Independence Twp	73	325
HARRAWAY								
William	30	m	w	SCOT	Contra Costa	Martinez P O	71	412
HARRCHAUSON								
Fredrick	30	m	w	HDAR	Calaveras	San Andreas P O	70	206
HARRELL								
Eden	19	m	w	ME	Marin	Tomales Twp	74	79
Edward	69	m	w	GA	Tuolumne	Chinese Camp P O	93	378
John	39	m	w	GA	San Francisco	11-Wd San Francisc	84	693
HARRER								
David H	40	m	w	AR	Santa Barbara	San Buenaventura P	87	424
Evan	80	m	w	VA	Santa Barbara	San Buenaventura P	87	424
Nathl G	28	m	w	AR	Santa Barbara	San Buenaventura P	87	424
Obediena	75	f	w	GA	Santa Barbara	San Buenaventura P	87	424
Redmond	33	m	w	AR	Santa Barbara	San Buenaventura P	87	424
Wilson	49	m	w	AR	Santa Barbara	San Buenaventura P	87	420
HARRES								
Alford	47	m	w	IN	Humboldt	Mattole Twp	72	286
Ellene	18	f	i	CA	Humboldt	Mattole Twp	72	286
Henry	19	m	w	PRUS	Contra Costa	Martinez P O	71	431
HARREY								
Henry	43	m	w	ENGL	Yuba	North East Twp	93	643
Thos	45	m	w	TN	San Joaquin	Oneal Twp	86	113
HARRIATT								
William	40	m	w	IREL	San Francisco	8-Wd San Francisco	82	422
HARRICK								
Henry	29	m	w	PRUS	San Francisco	1-Wd San Francisco	79	103
Patrick	31	m	w	IREL	San Francisco	San Francisco P O	83	311
HARRIDEN								
James	35	m	w	MA	Klamath	Camp Gaston	73	373
HARRIDGE								
John	70	m	w	SAXO	San Francisco	San Francisco P O	83	194
HARRIE								
John	52	m	w	IREL	San Francisco	7-Wd San Francisco	81	214
John	30	m	w	GERM	Sonoma	Mendocino Twp	91	291
HARRIER								
D W	35	m	w	PA	Solano	Vallejo	90	188
HARRIES								
Jas	53	m	w	SCOT	Sacramento	1-Wd Sacramento	77	188
John	40	m	w	PA	Mendocino	Round Valley Twp	74	218
John W	47	m	w	IL	Los Angeles	El Monte Twp	73	460
HARRIET								
Christian	40	m	w	NY	Tulare	Visalia	92	290
HARRIETT								
Frank	40	m	w	MA	San Diego	San Diego	78	502
HARRIETY								
James	41	m	w	IREL	San Francisco	7-Wd San Francisco	81	188
Mary	35	f	w	IREL	San Francisco	7-Wd San Francisco	81	188
HARRIGAN								
Albert	10	m	w	CA	Marin	San Rafael Twp	74	29
Andrew	60	m	w	IREL	San Francisco	2-Wd San Francisco	79	245
Auguste	40	m	w	PRUS	San Francisco	San Francisco P O	83	167
Corneilus	43	m	w	IREL	San Francisco	San Francisco P O	80	381
Daniel	22	m	w	IREL	San Francisco	11-Wd San Francisc	84	475
Daniel	18	m	w	NY	San Francisco	San Francisco P O	83	383
Danl	58	m	w	IREL	Shasta	French Gulch P O	89	467
Danl	36	m	w	IREL	San Francisco	7-Wd San Francisco	81	270
Denis	46	m	w	IREL	San Francisco	1-Wd San Francisco	79	63

© 2001 by Heritage Quest. All rights reserved.

Series M593

Name	Age	S	R	B-PL	County	Locale	Roll	Pg
Dennis	32	m	w	IREL	San Francisco	San Francisco P O	80	398
Edwd	31	m	w	IREL	San Francisco	1-Wd San Francisco	79	72
Edwd	27	m	w	NY	San Francisco	1-Wd San Francisco	79	42
Ellen	16	f	w	CA	San Francisco	11-Wd San Francisc	84	437
Hanna	32	f	w	IREL	Placer	Bath P O	76	423
James	8	m	w	CA	Marin	San Rafael Twp	74	29
James	67	m	w	IREL	Santa Barbara	Las Cruces P O	87	515
James	38	m	w	IREL	Sacramento	4-Wd Sacramento	77	335
James	33	m	w	IREL	Nevada	Grass Valley Twp	75	160
Jeffrey	7	m	w	CA	Marin	San Rafael Twp	74	28
Jeremiah	21	m	w	IREL	San Francisco	7-Wd San Francisco	81	280
John	45	m	w	IREL	San Francisco	11-Wd San Francisc	84	487
John	44	m	w	IREL	San Francisco	11-Wd San Francisc	84	536
John	42	m	w	IREL	San Joaquin	3-Wd Stockton	86	232
John	41	m	w	IREL	Santa Clara	Redwood Twp	88	125
John	38	m	w	IREL	San Francisco	San Francisco P O	83	72
John	36	m	w	IREL	Santa Clara	2-Wd San Jose	88	303
John	35	m	w	IREL	Yolo	Putah Twp	93	509
John	30	m	w	IREL	Santa Clara	Alviso Twp	88	26
John	29	m	w	NJ	San Francisco	San Francisco P O	80	336
Josephine	32	f	w	IREL	San Francisco	1-Wd San Francisco	79	66
Kate	25	f	w	IREL	Sacramento	4-Wd Sacramento	77	344
Margaret	48	f	w	IREL	Santa Cruz	Santa Cruz Twp	89	388
Margaret	34	f	w	IREL	Shasta	French Gulch P O	89	468
Margerett	54	f	w	NY	Sacramento	Sutter Twp	77	389
Mary	19	f	w	IREL	San Francisco	8-Wd San Francisco	82	329
Mathew	35	m	w	IREL	San Francisco	San Francisco P O	83	146
May	30	f	w	IREL	San Francisco	8-Wd San Francisco	82	374
Michael	40	m	w	IREL	San Francisco	7-Wd San Francisco	81	241
Michael	22	m	w	IREL	Yolo	Putah Twp	93	514
Mike	44	m	w	IREL	San Francisco	11-Wd San Francisc	84	595
Patrick	35	m	w	IREL	San Francisco	11-Wd San Francisc	84	497
Patrick	32	m	w	IREL	San Francisco	11-Wd San Francisc	84	442
Sarah	26	f	w	IREL	Sacramento	2-Wd Sacramento	77	253
Sarah A	44	f	w	NJ	Nevada	Nevada Twp	75	306
Timothy	36	m	w	IREL	San Francisco	7-Wd San Francisco	81	251
William W	30	m	w	NY	Yolo	Washington Twp	93	531
HARRIGTON								
Levi A	44	m	w	MA	Colusa	Stony Crk Twp	71	332
HARRIHILL								
J L	25	m	w	IREL	San Francisco	8-Wd San Francisco	82	361
HARRILL								
Drury D	61	m	w	NC	Shasta	Shasta P O	89	457
HARRIMAN								
Chas	33	m	w	ENGL	San Francisco	San Francisco P O	85	763
Christopher I	36	m	w	MO	Nevada	Rough & Ready Twp	75	334
Elizabeth	36	f	w	ME	San Francisco	8-Wd San Francisco	82	467
Henry	25	m	w	PRUS	San Luis Obispo	Arroyo Grande Twp	87	279
John	62	m	w	NH	Tuolumne	Chinese Camp P O	93	367
John H	32	m	w	TN	Solano	Silveyville Twp	90	83
M B	49	m	w	ME	Tuolumne	Columbia P O	93	357
Rufus	37	m	w	ME	Santa Cruz	Santa Cruz Twp	89	394
Samuel Q	41	m	w	VT	Placer	Dutch Flat P O	76	401
Shadrock	56	m	w	VA	Yolo	Buckeye Twp	93	416
Stephen	36	m	w	ME	Yuba	Parks Bar Twp	93	648
William	70	m	w	SC	Solano	Silveyville Twp	90	83
HARRIMON								
George W	29	m	w	ME	San Francisco	San Francisco P O	83	237
HARRINA								
Wm S	38	m	w	ME	San Luis Obispo	San Luis Obispo Tw	87	297
HARRING								
Eugene	27	m	w	IREL	Yuba	Rose Bar Twp	93	662
John V	48	m	w	NY	Placer	Bath P O	76	452
HARRINGS								
Wm	53	m	w	BOHE	San Francisco	11-Wd San Francisc	84	584
HARRINGTON								
And J	40	m	w	NY	Santa Barbara	San Buenaventura P	87	435
Andrew	41	m	w	MA	Alameda	Hayward	68	73
Ann	30	f	w	IREL	San Francisco	San Francisco P O	85	806
Ann	14	f	w	MA	San Francisco	8-Wd San Francisco	82	341
Benj	46	m	w	NY	San Francisco	3-Wd San Francisco	79	301
Benj	40	m	w	ME	Marin	Tomales Twp	74	84
Benjamin W	51	m	w	VT	San Francisco	8-Wd San Francisco	82	474
Bryan	56	m	w	IREL	San Francisco	1-Wd San Francisco	79	62
C	25	m	w	WI	Sierra	Sierra Twp	89	564
C C	52	m	w	RI	Yuba	Marysville	93	596
C M	20	f	w	IREL	San Francisco	San Francisco P O	85	810
Chester	49	m	w	NY	Tehama	Tehama Twp	92	186
Cobb C	56	m	w	RI	Nevada	Grass Valley Twp	75	167
Cornelius	34	m	w	IREL	San Francisco	7-Wd San Francisco	81	258
Cornelius	30	m	w	IREL	San Francisco	11-Wd San Francisc	84	598
Cornelius	28	m	w	IREL	San Francisco	1-Wd San Francisco	79	62
Cunningham	27	m	w	IA	Shasta	Millville P O	89	483
D	35	m	w	KY	Lake	Lower Lake	73	414
D	35	m	w	IL	Alameda	Murray Twp	68	110
D	27	m	w	IREL	Solano	Vallejo	90	169
D	26	m	w	MO	Marin	San Rafael Twp	74	43
D	25	m	w	NY	Solano	Vallejo	90	152
Dan	4	m	w	CA	San Francisco	San Francisco P O	83	14
Daniel	40	m	w	CANA	Marin	San Rafael	74	53
Daniel	33	m	w	IREL	Calaveras	Copperopolis P O	70	252
Daniel	22	m	w	IREL	Colusa	Grand Island Twp	71	306
Danl	38	m	w	IREL	San Francisco	San Francisco P O	83	312
Danl	35	m	w	IREL	San Francisco	11-Wd San Francisc	84	555
Demas	38	m	w	IREL	San Luis Obispo	Arroyo Grande Twp	87	279
Denis	34	m	w	IREL	San Francisco	San Francisco P O	80	369
Dennis	36	m	w	IREL	Nevada	Grass Valley Twp	75	196
Dennis W	48	m	w	IN	Santa Clara	Santa Clara Twp	88	152
E	35	m	w	VT	Yuba	Marysville	93	590
Edward	43	m	w	IL	Stanislaus	Branch Twp	92	1
Eliza	32	f	w	IREL	San Francisco	11-Wd San Francisc	84	477
Ellen	26	f	w	IREL	San Francisco	San Francisco P O	83	23
Ellen	24	f	w	MA	San Francisco	8-Wd San Francisco	82	444
Emily	47	f	w	MO	Monterey	San Juan Twp	74	385
Emma M	26	f	w	MA	Placer	Colfax P O	76	384
Eugene	30	m	w	IREL	San Francisco	San Francisco P O	83	417
F	56	m	w	IREL	Amador	Ione City P O	69	365
F H	30	m	w	PRUS	Alameda	Oakland	68	219
Frederick	22	m	w	MA	Calaveras	San Andreas P O	70	190
Geor	36	m	w	CANA	Sonoma	Petaluma Twp	91	342
George	50	m	w	IA	Calaveras	San Andreas P O	70	162
George	45	m	w	VT	Santa Cruz	Santa Cruz Twp	89	400
George	35	m	w	ENGL	Sonoma	Petaluma Twp	91	319
George W	25	m	w	IA	Yolo	Cache Crk Twp	93	419
H S	41	m	w	ME	San Joaquin	3-Wd Stockton	86	236
Henry	45	m	w	KY	Solano	Rio Vista Twp	90	62
Henry	45	m	w	VA	Solano	Rio Vista Twp	90	63
Hiram	65	m	w	NY	El Dorado	Placerville	72	118
Isaac	28	m	w	NY	San Francisco	San Francisco P O	83	346
J	40	f	w	IREL	San Francisco	San Francisco P O	85	789
J W	39	m	w	MA	Amador	Drytown P O	69	415
James	56	m	w	OH	Sonoma	Analy Twp	91	241
James	35	m	w	IL	Yolo	Cache Crk Twp	93	446
James	30	m	w	IREL	Napa	Napa	75	37
Jane	50	f	w	IREL	San Francisco	8-Wd San Francisco	82	455
Jeffery	58	m	w	IREL	San Francisco	11-Wd San Francisc	84	613
Jeremiah	37	m	w	IREL	San Francisco	8-Wd San Francisco	82	497
Jerry	60	m	w	IREL	Yolo	Cache Crk Twp	93	421
Jerry	30	m	w	IREL	Nevada	Bridgeport Twp	75	105
Jno	44	m	w	IREL	San Francisco	San Francisco P O	83	308
Joel	24	m	w	VA	San Francisco	6-Wd San Francisco	81	113
Johanna	87	f	w	IREL	San Francisco	11-Wd San Francisc	84	478
John	60	m	w	GA	Merced	Snelling P O	74	252
John	54	m	w	IREL	Placer	Newcastle Twp	76	475
John	52	m	w	IREL	Santa Clara	Santa Clara Twp	88	152
John	47	m	w	CANA	San Francisco	San Francisco P O	85	843
John	40	m	w	MA	Sacramento	Natomas Twp	77	166
John	40	m	w	IREL	San Francisco	11-Wd San Francisc	84	448
John	40	m	w	IREL	Solano	Vallejo	90	148
John	39	m	w	IREL	San Francisco	San Francisco P O	85	806
John	38	m	w	ME	San Francisco	11-Wd San Francisc	84	609
John	30	m	w	IREL	San Diego	San Diego	78	496
John	23	m	w	CANA	Mendocino	Bourns Landing Twp	74	223
John	22	m	w	ENGL	Monterey	Castroville Twp	74	338
John	21	m	w	IA	Sonoma	Analy Twp	91	244
John	12	m	w	NY	San Francisco	5-Wd San Francisco	81	7
John	12	m	w	NY	San Francisco	5-Wd San Francisco	81	7
John	12	m	w	CA	Santa Clara	Santa Clara Twp	88	177
John A	33	m	w	OH	Nevada	Bridgeport Twp	75	101
John A	30	m	w	CANA	Santa Clara	Santa Clara Twp	88	169
John S	25	m	w	MO	Placer	Colfax P O	76	389
Jubal`	67	m	w	MA	Tuolumne	Columbia P O	93	339
Julia	67	f	w	IREL	San Francisco	San Francisco P O	85	735
Julia	30	f	w	IREL	San Francisco	11-Wd San Francisc	84	478
Kate	55	f	w	IREL	San Francisco	11-Wd San Francisc	84	674
Kate	27	f	w	IREL	San Francisco	8-Wd San Francisco	82	322
Kate	27	f	w	IREL	Solano	Benicia	90	6
Kate	25	f	w	IREL	San Francisco	1-Wd San Francisco	79	67
L A	40	m	w	MA	Tehama	Tehama Twp	92	187
L G	35	m	w	MO	Amador	Sutter Crk P O	69	411
Louis	21	m	w	MA	Calaveras	San Andreas P O	70	152
M	35	m	w	VA	Solano	Vallejo	90	186
M	21	f	w	IREL	Alameda	Oakland	68	219
Martin B	44	m	w	NY	San Francisco	San Francisco P O	83	168
Mary	57	f	w	IREL	Contra Costa	Martinez P O	71	425
Mary	40	f	w	NY	San Francisco	1-Wd San Francisco	79	24
Mary	35	f	w	IREL	San Francisco	7-Wd San Francisco	81	181
Mary	18	f	w	IREL	Contra Costa	Martinez Twp	71	349
Michael	27	m	w	IREL	San Francisco	San Francisco P O	80	336
Michael	26	m	w	IREL	San Francisco	San Francisco P O	83	241
Micheal	29	m	w	IREL	San Francisco	11-Wd San Francisc	84	440
Mike	27	m	w	IREL	Sacramento	4-Wd Sacramento	77	369
N	60	m	w	NC	Amador	Drytown P O	69	420
Nero	49	m	w	OH	Shasta	Millville P O	89	483
Owen	43	m	w	IREL	San Francisco	11-Wd San Francisc	84	433
P	20	m	w	IREL	Solano	Vallejo	90	188
Pat	40	m	w	CANA	Humboldt	Eureka Twp	72	278
Pat	35	m	w	SCOT	San Joaquin	1-Wd Stockton	86	137
Pat	30	m	w	IREL	Alameda	Murray Twp	68	128
Pat	27	m	w	IREL	Sierra	Gibson Twp	89	542
Patrick	58	m	w	IREL	San Francisco	San Francisco P O	83	399
Paul	37	m	w	IREL	Tuolumne	Columbia P O	93	357
Phineas	56	m	w	MA	Contra Costa	Martinez P O	71	375
T S	26	m	w	IL	Merced	Snelling P O	74	270
Thomas	28	m	w	NY	Sacramento	2-Wd Sacramento	77	246
Thos	38	m	w	CANA	Alameda	Oakland	68	221
Thos	36	m	w	IREL	Contra Costa	Martinez P O	71	369
Thos	30	m	w	IREL	San Francisco	1-Wd San Francisco	79	94
Timothy	35	m	w	IREL	San Francisco	San Francisco P O	83	76
Timothy	34	m	w	IREL	Mendocino	Point Arena Twp	74	224
W	44	m	w	NY	Santa Clara	2-Wd San Jose	88	320
W	14	m	w	CA	Alameda	Oakland	68	182
W B	49	m	w	VT	Placer	Newcastle Twp	76	476
Warren	39	m	w	OH	Nevada	Bridgeport Twp	75	100

© 2001 by Heritage Quest. All rights reserved.

California 1870 Census

Series M593

Name	Age	S	R	B-PL	County	Locale	Roll	Pg
William	40	m	w	TN	Tulare	Farmersville Twp	92	248
William	37	m	w	AR	Tulare	Visalia Twp	92	282
William P	44	m	w	ME	Colusa	Colusa	71	297
Winnie	38	f	w	IREL	San Francisco	7-Wd San Francisco	81	286
Wm	44	m	w	VT	Yuba	Marysville	93	586
Wm	35	m	w	MA	San Francisco	2-Wd San Francisco	79	253
Wm	30	m	w	NY	Fresno	Kingston P O	72	217
Wm	26	m	w	TN	Marin	San Rafael Twp	74	47
Wm	24	m	w	IA	Sonoma	Russian Rvr	91	376
Wm P	32	m	w	OH	San Francisco	8-Wd San Francisco	82	336
HARRINTON								
Michael	29	m	w	ME	San Diego	Julian Dist	78	468
HARRIS								
A P	38	m	w	PA	Sierra	Forest Twp	89	530
A S	40	m	w	NY	San Francisco	1-Wd San Francisco	79	54
Aaron	36	m	w	PRUS	Tuolumne	Sonora P O	93	313
Aaron	28	m	w	PRUS	Nevada	Bridgeport Twp	75	100
Aaron	24	m	w	RUSS	Plumas	Goodwin Twp	77	6
Abraham	25	m	w	PRUS	Los Angeles	Los Angeles	73	525
Abram	30	m	b	VA	San Francisco	San Francisco P O	80	402
Abram	29	m	w	POLA	San Francisco	San Francisco P O	80	361
Ada	19	f	m	MO	Sacramento	2-Wd Sacramento	77	233
Adolph	31	m	w	PRUS	Los Angeles	Los Angeles	73	549
Al	62	m	w	PRUS	San Francisco	San Francisco P O	83	368
Albert	50	m	w	MO	Mendocino	Point Arena Twp	74	211
Albert	42	m	w	NC	Merced	Snelling P O	74	272
Albert	40	m	w	PA	San Francisco	5-Wd San Francisco	81	29
Albert	40	m	w	IREL	Contra Costa	Martinez P O	71	403
Albert S	53	m	w	NC	Los Angeles	El Monte Twp	73	455
Alexander	55	m	w	POLA	San Francisco	7-Wd San Francisco	81	186
Alexander	40	m	w	ENGL	Calaveras	San Andreas P O	70	170
Alfred	37	m	b	KY	Alameda	Alameda	68	6
Alich	40	m	b	OH	Tulare	Tule Rvr Twp	92	271
Allen	45	m	w	NY	Calaveras	San Andreas P O	70	209
Alva	60	m	w	OH	El Dorado	Diamond Springs Tw	72	30
Alvin	37	m	w	ME	Santa Clara	San Jose Twp	88	195
Amasa H	26	m	w	MI	Nevada	Grass Valley Twp	75	185
Amelia	37	f	w	POLA	San Francisco	San Francisco P O	83	208
Amelia	20	f	w	ENGL	Monterey	San Juan Twp	74	409
Andrew J	15	m	w	CA	San Luis Obispo	Arroyo Grande Twp	87	278
Ann E	48	f	w	NJ	Tuolumne	Sonora P O	93	319
Anna L	6M	f	w	CA	Santa Cruz	Santa Cruz	89	428
Anson	40	m	w	ME	San Francisco	San Francisco P O	85	851
Ant	22	m	w	TX	Merced	Snelling P O	74	263
Augusta	39	f	w	ME	San Francisco	8-Wd San Francisco	82	458
Avery	59	m	w	MA	San Francisco	7-Wd San Francisco	81	282
B	37	m	w	IN	Sutter	Vernon Twp	92	135
B C	45	m	w	VA	San Joaquin	Elkhorn Twp	86	64
Barney	36	m	w	ENGL	San Francisco	7-Wd San Francisco	81	186
Benj	39	m	w	VA	San Bernardino	San Bernardino Twp	78	432
Benj	25	m	w	IL	Marin	San Rafael Twp	74	40
Benj R	44	m	w	ENGL	Sonoma	Santa Rosa	91	404
Benjamin	44	m	w	BRAN	Santa Barbara	Santa Barbara P O	87	465
Benjamin	35	m	w	NY	San Francisco	7-Wd San Francisco	81	221
Benjamin F	42	m	w	PA	Nevada	Grass Valley Twp	75	148
Benjm	30	m	w	NY	San Francisco	8-Wd San Francisco	82	362
Bradford	12	m	w	IL	Sacramento	Natomas Twp	77	166
C B	30	m	w	IN	Sutter	Nicolaus Twp	92	106
C C	52	m	w	ENGL	Tuolumne	Columbia P O	93	359
C H	46	m	b	GA	Sacramento	4-Wd Sacramento	77	323
Carl	24	m	w	AR	San Joaquin	Castoria Twp	86	6
Caroline	27	f	w	ENGL	Nevada	Grass Valley Twp	75	151
Celia	39	f	w	PRUS	San Francisco	San Francisco P O	83	219
Charles	45	m	w	ENGL	Santa Barbara	Santa Barbara P O	87	459
Charles	43	m	w	MO	Siskiyou	Table Rock Twp	89	647
Charles	30	m	w	MA	Sonoma	Analy Twp	91	229
Charles	30	m	w	POLA	San Francisco	San Francisco P O	80	429
Charles	25	m	w	PA	Siskiyou	Butte Twp	89	586
Charles	24	m	w	ENGL	Plumas	Quartz Twp	77	34
Charles	19	m	w	IL	Mariposa	Mariposa P O	74	123
Charles T	43	m	w	NY	Calaveras	San Andreas P O	70	210
Chas	35	m	w	IL	San Francisco	1-Wd San Francisco	79	90
Chas	30	m	w	RUSS	San Francisco	1-Wd San Francisco	79	52
Chas	28	m	w	PA	San Francisco	5-Wd San Francisco	81	28
Chas	27	m	w	ENGL	San Francisco	1-Wd San Francisco	79	121
Chs P	25	m	w	NY	Merced	Snelling P O	74	274
Clara	6	m	w	CA	Santa Clara	Almaden Twp	88	4
Daniel	38	m	w	ENGL	Monterey	San Juan Twp	74	408
Daniel	33	m	w	PRUS	San Francisco	11-Wd San Francisc	84	540
Danl H	30	m	w	NY	Sonoma	Mendocino Twp	91	291
David	47	m	w	WALE	Sierra	Sears Twp	89	559
David	47	m	w	NH	Butte	Chico Twp	70	13
David	46	m	w	WALE	San Francisco	San Francisco P O	85	776
David	38	m	w	ENGL	Sacramento	3-Wd Sacramento	77	283
David	32	m	w	MD	Placer	Rocklin Twp	76	465
David	24	m	w	FL	Placer	Rocklin Twp	76	468
Dayton J	45	m	w	IN	Yolo	Grafton Twp	93	497
Doctor	35	m	w	MO	Mariposa	Mariposa P O	74	124
Dwight C	23	m	w	NY	Calaveras	San Andreas P O	70	210
E B	46	m	w	NY	Nevada	Bridgeport Twp	75	106
E F	37	m	w	NC	Monterey	Alisal Twp	74	299
Edward	38	m	m	MO	Colusa	Butte Twp	71	269
Edward	33	m	w	ME	Santa Cruz	Santa Cruz Twp	89	395
Edward	30	m	w	IN	Tulare	Kings Rvr Twp	92	253
Edward	28	m	w	TX	Kern	Bakersfield P O	73	360
Edward	28	m	w	MO	San Bernardino	San Bernardino Twp	78	417
Edward	24	m	w	ENGL	San Francisco	6-Wd San Francisco	81	98
Edward	23	m	w	IL	San Luis Obispo	Salinas Twp	87	296
Edwd	38	m	w	RI	San Francisco	1-Wd San Francisco	79	98
Edwin	39	m	w	RI	Alameda	Oakland	68	144
Einhour	37	m	w	NY	San Francisco	1-Wd San Francisco	79	42
Eli W	39	m	w	IN	Santa Cruz	Watsonville	89	373
Elijah	45	m	w	AR	San Diego	Milquaty Dist	78	475
Elisha A	42	m	w	NY	Colusa	Grand Island Twp	71	306
Emiel	27	m	w	PRUS	Los Angeles	Los Angeles	73	532
Emily	32	f	w	WI	Mariposa	Mariposa P O	74	121
Ephrain	10	m	w	CA	Sonoma	Analy Twp	91	229
Estrella	40	m	w	ENGL	Nevada	Grass Valley Twp	75	220
Ethelbert S	50	m	w	MO	San Luis Obispo	Santa Rosa Twp	87	322
Evan	24	m	w	WALE	Amador	Sutter Crk P O	69	408
Few W	26	m	w	IL	Siskiyou	Big Valley Twp	89	581
Francis	12	f	w	CA	Yolo	Cache Crk Twp	93	419
Frank	24	m	i	NV	Sacramento	Franklin Twp	77	111
Frank	22	m	w	OH	Solano	Vacaville Twp	90	125
G	63	m	w	KY	Sierra	Downieville Twp	89	516
G B	56	m	w	NY	Amador	Drytown P O	69	423
G F	24	m	w	KY	Del Norte	Smith Rvr Twp	71	479
Geo	30	m	w	PRUS	San Francisco	11-Wd San Francisc	84	422
Geo	25	m	w	ENGL	San Joaquin	Douglas Twp	86	47
Geo	25	m	w	NY	Alameda	Oakland	68	253
Geo	24	m	w	MD	San Francisco	11-Wd San Francisc	84	687
Geo	24	m	w	NY	San Francisco	1-Wd San Francisco	79	86
Geo A	19	m	w	CANA	Sonoma	Bodega Twp	91	264
Geo L	35	m	w	NY	San Francisco	5-Wd San Francisco	81	30
George	58	m	w	VT	Sonoma	Petaluma Twp	91	310
George	50	m	w	MA	Yolo	Cache Crk Twp	93	448
George	46	m	w	NY	San Francisco	8-Wd San Francisco	82	378
George	40	m	w	MD	San Francisco	San Francisco P O	80	538
George	40	m	w	MA	Tuolumne	Big Oak Flat P O	93	405
George	39	m	w	ENGL	Nevada	Rough & Ready Twp	75	331
George	39	m	w	MA	Yolo	Cache Crk Twp	93	452
George	38	m	w	PA	San Bernardino	San Bernardino Twp	78	448
George	35	m	w	AR	Klamath	Klamath Twp	73	371
George	35	m	w	IL	Yolo	Merritt Twp	93	506
George	33	m	w	SCOT	Colusa	Spring Valley Twp	71	344
George	33	m	m	KY	Tulare	Visalia Twp	92	286
George	32	m	w	MA	San Francisco	San Francisco P O	83	207
George	32	m	w	NY	San Francisco	8-Wd San Francisco	82	388
George	31	m	w	PRUS	San Francisco	1-Wd San Francisco	79	118
George	26	m	w	ENGL	Nevada	Nevada Twp	75	301
George A	39	m	w	PA	Placer	Auburn P O	76	380
George C	45	m	w	NY	Monterey	Monterey	74	366
George W	35	m	w	MA	San Francisco	San Francisco P O	85	717
Granville	11	m	w	CA	Sonoma	Sonoma Twp	91	437
H	54	m	w	PRUS	Amador	Jackson P O	69	320
H	29	m	w	PRUS	Amador	Sutter Crk P O	69	398
H B	28	m	w	TN	Santa Clara	Gilroy Twp	88	72
H F	24	m	w	KY	Mendocino	Round Valley Twp	74	219
H H	32	m	w	MO	Napa	Yountville Twp	75	90
H M	41	m	w	MA	Yuba	Marysville	93	578
H R	18	m	w	CA	Napa	Yountville Twp	75	90
H W	62	m	w	NY	Humboldt	Eureka Twp	72	272
Hannah	26	f	w	MO	Santa Cruz	Santa Cruz	89	432
Henery	22	m	w	ENGL	San Francisco	7-Wd San Francisco	81	156
Henery	18	m	w	PA	San Francisco	7-Wd San Francisco	81	164
Henry	83	m	w	VA	Yuba	Marysville	93	613
Henry	51	m	w	ENGL	Santa Clara	Santa Clara Twp	88	160
Henry	45	m	w	RI	Alameda	Oakland	68	204
Henry	40	m	w	NORW	Santa Barbara	Santa Maria P O	87	512
Henry	36	m	w	ENGL	Nevada	Grass Valley Twp	75	148
Henry	35	m	w	HAMB	San Francisco	6-Wd San Francisco	81	111
Henry	34	m	w	ENGL	Santa Barbara	San Buenaventura P	87	427
Henry	34	m	w	IREL	Siskiyou	Scott Valley Twp	89	613
Henry	30	m	w	PRUS	San Francisco	1-Wd San Francisco	79	98
Henry	22	m	w	ENGL	Contra Costa	Martinez P O	71	423
Henry T	37	m	w	KY	Santa Barbara	San Buenaventura P	87	426
Henry W	38	m	w	NY	Contra Costa	Martinez P O	71	382
Herman	40	m	w	POLA	San Francisco	San Francisco P O	83	363
Hiram	47	m	w	VA	San Francisco	3-Wd San Francisco	79	323
Hiram	36	m	w	IL	Yolo	Putah Twp	93	514
I H	60	m	w	NC	Santa Clara	Gilroy Twp	88	85
Isaac	62	m	w	KY	Santa Barbara	San Buenaventura P	87	425
Isaac	57	m	w	KY	Calaveras	San Andreas P O	70	164
Isaac	50	m	w	AUST	San Francisco	7-Wd San Francisco	81	212
Isaac	40	m	w	POLA	San Francisco	1-Wd San Francisco	79	41
Isaac	38	m	w	PRUS	Inyo	Independence Twp	73	324
Isaac	37	m	w	BAVA	Nevada	Meadow Lake Twp	75	268
Isaac	19	m	w	PRUS	San Francisco	1-Wd San Francisco	79	93
Isaac W	44	m	w	NJ	Mariposa	Mariposa P O	74	119
Isadore	16	m	w	POLA	San Francisco	San Francisco P O	83	21
J	50	m	w	ENGL	San Joaquin	Elliott Twp	86	77
J	35	m	w	CANA	Merced	Snelling P O	74	261
J A	44	m	w	AR	Humboldt	Pacific Twp	72	294
J B	44	m	w	IN	Sutter	Nicolaus Twp	92	106
J J	45	m	w	NY	Sacramento	Sutter Twp	77	389
J T	41	m	w	IN	Yuba	Marysville Twp	93	571
J W	30	m	w	MO	San Joaquin	Douglas Twp	86	41
J W	26	m	w	IN	San Joaquin	3-Wd Stockton	86	219
J [Capt]	40	m	w	MS	San Francisco	8-Wd San Francisco	82	309
Jabez	35	m	w	ENGL	Fresno	Millerton P O	72	165
Jacob	44	m	w	PRUS	San Francisco	5-Wd San Francisco	81	1
Jacob	36	m	w	PRUS	San Francisco	San Francisco P O	80	425
Jacob	27	m	w	NY	San Francisco	San Francisco P O	83	117
Jacob	25	m	m	MA	San Francisco	2-Wd San Francisco	79	153

© 2001 by Heritage Quest. All rights reserved.

Series M593

Name	Age	S	R	B-PL	County	Locale	Roll	Pg
James	73	m	w	IREL	Calaveras	San Andreas P O	70	164
James	60	m	w	OR	San Joaquin	Tulare Twp	86	253
James	42	m	w	MO	Colusa	Monroe Twp	71	315
James	34	m	w	CANA	Sacramento	Natomas Twp	77	166
James	33	m	w	OH	Contra Costa	Martinez P O	71	387
James	30	m	w	PA	Lake	Lower Lake	73	420
James	30	m	w	MO	Amador	Volcano P O	69	388
James	30	m	w	ENGL	Nevada	Grass Valley Twp	75	161
James	27	m	b	DC	Sacramento	2-Wd Sacramento	77	233
James	26	m	w	CT	Tuolumne	Chinese Camp P O	93	366
James	18	m	b	PA	San Francisco	1-Wd San Francisco	79	96
James B	22	m	w	IN	Santa Cruz	Santa Cruz	89	410
James H	43	m	w	MD	San Francisco	San Francisco P O	83	191
James H	23	m	w	MA	Calaveras	San Andreas P O	70	170
James M	39	m	w	OH	Monterey	San Antonio Twp	74	324
James R	30	m	w	IREL	Napa	Napa Twp	75	63
Jane	77	f	w	MD	Monterey	Monterey	74	359
Jane	46	f	w	IL	San Luis Obispo	Santa Rosa Twp	87	322
Jas	54	m	w	OH	San Joaquin	Dent Twp	86	27
Jas	30	m	w	IREL	Sacramento	1-Wd Sacramento	77	188
Jas B	24	m	w	LA	Butte	Chico Twp	70	56
Jas H	54	m	w	TN	Santa Barbara	Santa Maria P O	87	510
Jas T	42	m	w	NY	San Francisco	1-Wd San Francisco	79	112
Jefferson	40	m	w	TX	Kern	Bakersfield P O	73	365
Jennie	24	f	w	NY	San Francisco	San Francisco P O	80	484
Jessee	40	m	w	TX	Merced	Snelling P O	74	263
Jno H	23	m	w	ENGL	Butte	Ophir Twp	70	117
Joe	40	m	w	PRUS	Alameda	Murray Twp	68	125
Joh H	20	m	w	NJ	Inyo	Bishop Crk Twp	73	313
John	57	m	w	KY	El Dorado	Mud Springs Twp	72	85
John	57	m	w	ENGL	Calaveras	San Andreas P O	70	174
John	47	m	w	IREL	Sacramento	Granite Twp	77	148
John	46	m	w	ENGL	Solano	Vallejo	90	153
John	45	m	w	ENGL	Mendocino	Round Valley Twp	74	221
John	45	m	w	PA	Solano	Vallejo	90	140
John	45	m	w	KY	Colusa	Spring Valley Twp	71	336
John	43	m	w	TN	San Bernardino	San Bernardino Twp	78	448
John	40	m	w	NJ	Mendocino	Round Valley Twp	74	221
John	40	m	w	PRUS	Contra Costa	Martinez P O	71	436
John	38	m	w	ENGL	Marin	San Rafael Twp	74	43
John	38	m	w	ENGL	Santa Clara	Almaden Twp	88	5
John	38	m	m	MD	San Francisco	6-Wd San Francisco	81	128
John	36	m	w	ENGL	Nevada	Grass Valley Twp	75	223
John	36	m	w	WALE	Solano	Vallejo	90	202
John	36	m	w	ENGL	Tuolumne	Chinese Camp P O	93	365
John	35	m	w	SCOT	Monterey	San Juan Twp	74	387
John	34	m	w	WALE	Solano	Vallejo	90	198
John	34	m	w	CANA	San Joaquin	1-Wd Stockton	86	141
John	31	m	w	ENGL	Nevada	Grass Valley Twp	75	194
John	30	m	w	NY	San Francisco	San Francisco P O	80	471
John	29	m	w	MO	Solano	Silveyville Twp	90	74
John	28	m	w	NY	San Francisco	1-Wd San Francisco	79	95
John	28	m	w	ENGL	Mariposa	Mariposa P O	74	98
John	27	m	w	NY	San Joaquin	Elliott Twp	86	70
John	27	m	w	ENGL	Stanislaus	San Joaquin Twp	92	78
John	25	m	b	WIND	Solano	Vallejo	90	203
John	25	m	w	OH	Yuba	Marysville Twp	93	571
John	20	m	w	MD	Colusa	Monroe Twp	71	315
John F	38	m	w	ENGL	San Francisco	San Francisco P O	83	387
John F	28	m	w	WI	Mariposa	Mariposa P O	74	123
John H	26	m	w	ENGL	Nevada	Grass Valley Twp	75	224
John H	10	m	w	TX	Los Angeles	Los Nietos Twp	73	591
John J	41	m	w	ENGL	Mendocino	Point Arena Twp	74	204
John J	40	m	w	IREL	San Francisco	San Francisco P O	83	232
John M	20	m	w	MO	Contra Costa	Martinez P O	71	384
Jonas	35	m	w	KY	San Bernardino	San Bernardino Twp	78	440
Jones	35	m	w	CA	San Bernardino	San Bernardino Twp	78	450
Joseph	61	m	w	PRUS	Sacramento	2-Wd Sacramento	77	242
Joseph	54	m	w	ENGL	Contra Costa	Martinez P O	71	413
Joseph	40	m	w	PRUS	San Francisco	San Francisco P O	80	534
Joseph	35	m	w	IREL	San Francisco	1-Wd San Francisco	79	86
Joseph	35	m	w	PRUS	San Francisco	San Francisco P O	83	368
Joseph	34	m	w	PRUS	San Francisco	San Francisco P O	83	213
Joseph	30	m	w	ENGL	Nevada	Grass Valley Twp	75	193
Joseph	29	m	b	MD	El Dorado	Mud Springs Twp	72	84
Joseph	28	m	w	CANA	San Joaquin	2-Wd Stockton	86	186
Joseph	23	m	w	WALE	Contra Costa	Martinez P O	71	428
Joseph	22	m	w	PRUS	San Francisco	San Francisco P O	83	138
Joseph	21	m	w	IL	Colusa	Spring Valley Twp	71	338
Joseph	19	m	w	CANA	San Joaquin	Douglas Twp	86	39
Julius	56	m	w	POLA	San Francisco	San Francisco P O	83	229
Julius	48	m	w	PRUS	Plumas	Indian Twp	77	9
L	26	m	w	CANA	Sierra	Table Rock Twp	89	578
L B	51	m	w	NY	Sacramento	3-Wd Sacramento	77	306
L C	50	m	w	MO	Calaveras	Copperopolis P O	70	251
L E	38	m	w	NY	Tuolumne	Chinese Camp P O	93	366
L W	55	m	w	MA	Siskiyou	Surprise Valley Tw	89	639
Leonard	41	m	w	NY	Marin	San Rafael Twp	74	35
Leopold	34	m	w	PRUS	Los Angeles	Los Angeles	73	539
Lewel	32	m	w	ME	Sutter	Sutter Twp	92	125
Louis	36	m	w	PRUS	San Francisco	1-Wd San Francisco	79	124
Louis	28	m	w	NY	Los Angeles	Los Angeles	73	561
Luther	37	m	w	OH	Amador	Jackson P O	69	319
M	47	f	w	NY	Sacramento	3-Wd Sacramento	77	264
M B	31	m	w	KY	Merced	Snelling P O	74	268
M J	39	f	w	IN	Lassen	Janesville Twp	73	434
Marcus	35	m	w	IREL	Contra Costa	Martinez P O	71	403
Margaret	22	f	w	CANA	Yolo	Cache Crk Twp	93	432
Marion K	24	m	w	MO	Santa Barbara	San Buenaventura P	87	425
Mark	43	m	w	ENGL	San Francisco	6-Wd San Francisco	81	78
Marks	45	m	w	AUST	San Francisco	8-Wd San Francisco	82	355
Marks	38	m	w	POLA	San Francisco	1-Wd San Francisco	79	79
Marshall	35	m	w	MO	Mariposa	Mariposa P O	74	137
Mary	55	f	w	ME	Calaveras	San Andreas P O	70	190
Mary	40	f	w	MA	Nevada	Grass Valley Twp	75	177
Mary	31	f	w	IREL	San Francisco	San Francisco P O	80	426
Mary	29	f	w	PRUS	San Francisco	6-Wd San Francisco	81	88
Mary	25	f	w	ENGL	San Francisco	6-Wd San Francisco	81	72
Mary	17	f	w	NY	San Francisco	11-Wd San Francisc	84	509
Mathew	30	m	w	SCOT	San Francisco	San Francisco P O	85	823
Mathew	28	m	w	IL	San Francisco	San Francisco P O	83	10
Mich	38	m	w	IREL	Alameda	Oakland	68	240
Michael	59	m	w	PRUS	San Francisco	1-Wd San Francisco	79	72
Michael	50	m	w	ENGL	Nevada	Grass Valley Twp	75	188
Michael	45	m	w	ENGL	Nevada	Grass Valley Twp	75	147
Minnie	17	f	w	RUSS	San Francisco	San Francisco P O	85	803
Mitchell	38	m	w	PRUS	San Francisco	San Francisco P O	83	382
Morgan	35	m	w	IL	Monterey	Castroville Twp	74	333
Morris	48	m	w	PRUS	Nevada	Grass Valley Twp	75	170
Moses	52	m	w	PRUS	San Francisco	7-Wd San Francisco	81	197
Nathan	67	m	w	NC	Placer	Bath P O	76	425
Nathan A	42	m	w	NH	Butte	Oregon Twp	70	124
Nathan H	47	m	w	CANA	Sonoma	Petaluma Twp	91	325
Nathan T	48	m	w	CANA	Sonoma	Petaluma Twp	91	363
Nathaniel	44	m	w	ENGL	Santa Clara	2-Wd San Jose	88	290
Nicholas R	36	m	w	MA	Santa Clara	2-Wd San Jose	88	327
O C	42	m	w	NY	Butte	Oroville Twp	70	137
Pat	44	m	w	IREL	San Francisco	1-Wd San Francisco	79	125
Patrick	40	m	w	IREL	San Francisco	7-Wd San Francisco	81	209
Patrick	25	m	w	IREL	Santa Clara	Fremont Twp	88	60
Paul W	62	m	w	VT	Sutter	Nicolaus Twp	92	106
Pemelia	70	f	w	VT	Yuba	Marysville	93	578
Peter	36	m	w	IREL	Solano	Silveyville Twp	90	78
Peter Y	69	m	w	NY	Yuba	Parks Bar Twp	93	648
Phil	32	m	w	PA	Butte	Chico Twp	70	50
Phoebe	74	f	w	KY	Sonoma	Santa Rosa	91	425
Pinkus	40	m	w	PRUS	San Francisco	6-Wd San Francisco	81	154
Pleasant	44	m	w	TN	Sonoma	Vallejo Twp	91	455
Presly F	64	m	w	KY	Napa	Yountville Twp	75	79
R B	32	m	w	AR	Mendocino	Round Valley Twp	74	220
R H	30	m	w	NY	Solano	Vallejo	90	153
Rachel	21	f	w	RUSS	San Francisco	San Francisco P O	83	359
Raney B	62	m	w	NC	Fresno	Millerton P O	72	194
Richard	50	m	w	IREL	Sonoma	Petaluma Twp	91	348
Richard	46	m	w	WALE	Placer	Colfax P O	76	392
Richard	44	m	b	MD	Alameda	Washington Twp	68	272
Richard	39	m	w	IREL	San Francisco	San Francisco P O	85	752
Richard	19	m	w	ENGL	Nevada	Grass Valley Twp	75	186
Richard M	51	m	w	KY	Plumas	Indian Twp	77	13
Robbey D	25	m	w	OH	Placer	Bath P O	76	427
Robert	64	m	w	KY	Colusa	Colusa Twp	71	277
Robert	50	m	b	NJ	San Francisco	6-Wd San Francisco	81	79
Robert	41	m	w	TN	Tulare	Tule Rvr Twp	92	260
Robert	38	m	w	MO	San Luis Obispo	San Luis Obispo Tw	87	314
Robert	31	m	w	NY	San Francisco	San Francisco P O	80	348
Robert L	36	m	w	NH	San Francisco	San Francisco P O	85	723
Robt R	37	m	w	MO	San Luis Obispo	Arroyo Grande Twp	87	276
Ruben C	44	m	w	VA	Mariposa	Mariposa P O	74	124
S	8	f	w	MEXI	San Francisco	San Francisco P O	85	827
S	44	m	w	RI	Yuba	Marysville	93	591
S B	56	m	w	PA	Tuolumne	Chinese Camp P O	93	386
S E	35	f	w	KY	San Francisco	San Francisco P O	85	876
Sabine	49	m	w	NY	Alameda	Oakland	68	155
Saml	36	m	w	POLA	San Francisco	7-Wd San Francisco	81	261
Saml	23	m	w	PRUS	San Francisco	5-Wd San Francisco	81	5
Samuel	54	m	w	NY	San Francisco	San Francisco P O	80	531
Samuel	38	m	w	ENGL	Monterey	San Juan Twp	74	409
Samuel	35	m	w	NY	Mendocino	Point Arena Twp	74	214
Samuel	27	m	w	PRUS	San Francisco	San Francisco P O	83	395
Samuel	22	m	w	ME	San Francisco	6-Wd San Francisco	81	88
Samuel T	60	m	w	MA	Sacramento	2-Wd Sacramento	77	247
Sarah	49	f	w	CANA	Sonoma	Sonoma Twp	91	437
Sary	60	f	w	GERM	San Francisco	8-Wd San Francisco	82	371
Simon	43	m	w	POLA	San Francisco	San Francisco P O	80	430
Simon	41	m	w	FRAN	San Francisco	San Francisco P O	80	470
Simon	39	m	w	PRUS	San Francisco	San Francisco P O	83	382
Soloman	23	m	w	POLA	San Francisco	7-Wd San Francisco	81	166
Sophia	41	f	w	PA	Santa Cruz	Santa Cruz	89	410
Stephen M	41	m	w	DE	Nevada	Grass Valley Twp	75	168
Stephen R	69	m	w	NY	San Francisco	3-Wd San Francisco	79	321
Stewart	52	m	w	KY	Colusa	Colusa	71	298
Susan	23	f	w	MA	San Francisco	1-Wd San Francisco	79	58
Susan	21	f	w	SC	San Francisco	7-Wd San Francisco	81	186
T	28	m	w	OH	Sierra	Butte Twp	89	509
T B	45	m	w	OH	San Joaquin	Elliott Twp	86	70
T C	44	m	w	PA	Solano	Vallejo	90	202
T Spencer	36	m	w	NY	Sacramento	2-Wd Sacramento	77	248
Thomas	50	m	w	NY	San Francisco	San Francisco P O	85	875
Thomas	50	m	w	NY	San Francisco	8-Wd San Francisco	82	440
Thomas	45	m	w	ENGL	San Mateo	Half Moon Bay P O	87	407
Thomas	42	m	w	ENGL	El Dorado	Diamond Springs Tw	72	23
Thomas	38	m	w	IA	Los Angeles	Los Angeles Twp	73	490
Thomas	36	m	w	WALE	Nevada	Bridgeport Twp	75	104
Thomas	35	m	w	ENGL	Nevada	Nevada Twp	75	315

© 2001 by Heritage Quest. All rights reserved.

California 1870 Census

Series M593

Name	Age	S	R	B-PL	County	Locale	Roll	Pg
Thomas	35	m	w	IREL	San Francisco	8-Wd San Francisco	82	402
Thomas	35	m	w	ENGL	San Francisco	11-Wd San Francisc	84	447
Thomas	27	m	w	ENGL	Nevada	Grass Valley Twp	75	164
Thomas	26	m	w	WI	Mariposa	Mariposa P O	74	123
Thomas	22	m	w	ENGL	San Francisco	5-Wd San Francisco	81	32
Thomas	21	m	w	AL	Calaveras	San Andreas P O	70	163
Thomas B	40	m	w	ENGL	Santa Clara	1-Wd San Jose	88	258
Thomas L	30	m	w	MI	Los Angeles	Los Angeles	73	505
Thos	40	m	w	NORW	San Francisco	1-Wd San Francisco	79	134
Thos	28	m	w	MO	Lassen	Janesville Twp	73	432
Timothy	43	m	w	CANA	San Francisco	11-Wd San Francisc	84	509
Valentine H	21	m	w	NZEA	Santa Clara	San Jose Twp	88	212
W	37	m	w	IN	Lake	Big Valley	73	396
W	35	m	w	IREL	Alameda	Oakland	68	229
W	22	m	w	PA	Sacramento	1-Wd Sacramento	77	190
W B	35	m	w	OH	Lake	Lakeport	73	407
W H	28	m	w	IREL	San Francisco	San Francisco P O	83	287
W H	28	m	w	MI	Klamath	Trinidad Twp	73	390
W J	25	m	w	IN	Sutter	Butte Twp	92	92
Wash G	37	m	w	PA	Siskiyou	Yreka	89	662
Westly	58	m	w	NY	Contra Costa	Martinez P O	71	404
Wilber F	31	m	w	VA	Sonoma	Washington Twp	91	469
William	60	m	w	VA	Colusa	Colusa Twp	71	281
William	50	m	w	IN	Sutter	Butte Twp	92	97
William	48	m	w	ENGL	Nevada	Grass Valley Twp	75	164
William	43	m	w	IREL	Stanislaus	San Joaquin Twp	92	72
William	40	m	w	IREL	Tuolumne	Chinese Camp P O	93	374
William	39	m	w	MO	Los Angeles	Los Nietos Twp	73	580
William	38	m	w	WALE	Nevada	Bloomfield Twp	75	92
William	36	m	w	ME	Sutter	Butte Twp	92	91
William	36	m	w	MO	Contra Costa	Martinez P O	71	403
William	36	m	w	SWED	San Francisco	7-Wd San Francisco	81	218
William	35	m	w	PRUS	Sacramento	2-Wd Sacramento	77	248
William	32	m	w	KY	Kern	Havilah P O	73	351
William	30	m	m	CANA	San Francisco	6-Wd San Francisco	81	99
William	28	m	w	ENGL	Nevada	Grass Valley Twp	75	224
William	13	m	w	CA	San Francisco	San Francisco P O	83	361
William C	51	m	w	NY	Placer	Gold Run Twp	76	396
William H	38	m	w	NY	San Mateo	Half Moon Bay P O	87	402
William M	34	m	w	ENGL	Nevada	Grass Valley Twp	75	168
William N	39	m	w	MA	Placer	Gold Run Twp	76	395
Wilson	36	m	w	GA	Stanislaus	Branch Twp	92	5
Wm	54	m	w	PA	El Dorado	Greenwood Twp	72	52
Wm	50	m	w	KY	Monterey	San Antonio Twp	74	324
Wm	42	m	w	GA	Fresno	Millerton P O	72	194
Wm	38	m	w	IREL	San Francisco	5-Wd San Francisco	81	35
Wm	33	m	b	IREL	Sacramento	1-Wd Sacramento	77	190
Wm	32	m	w	PRUS	San Francisco	1-Wd San Francisco	79	127
Wm	30	m	m	EIND	San Francisco	1-Wd San Francisco	79	95
Wm	30	m	w	HANO	San Francisco	11-Wd San Francisc	84	479
Wm	27	m	w	PRUS	Nevada	Meadow Lake Twp	75	261
Wm	26	m	w	MA	Fresno	Kings Rvr P O	72	214
Wm B	50	m	w	GA	Fresno	Millerton P O	72	183
Wm H	27	m	w	IL	Merced	Snelling P O	74	275
Wm Henry	30	m	w	ENGL	Nevada	Grass Valley Twp	75	181
Y	26	m	w	MI	Sierra	Butte Twp	89	508
HARRISMAN								
John	30	m	w	BREM	San Francisco	7-Wd San Francisco	81	224
HARRISON								
Aaron	32	m	w	ENGL	San Bernardino	San Bernardino Twp	78	420
Adam	36	m	w	OH	Placer	Rocklin Twp	76	467
And	46	m	w	NY	San Francisco	8-Wd San Francisco	82	378
Andrew	33	m	w	SWED	Placer	Gold Run Twp	76	394
Anna	16	m	w	UT	Lake	Lower Lake	73	414
Anthony	44	m	w	CANA	San Francisco	San Francisco P O	83	91
Arthur	38	m	w	MI	San Mateo	Belmont P O	87	374
Benj J	38	m	w	MO	Sonoma	Bodega Twp	91	259
Benjamin	15	m	w	TX	Tulare	Farmersville Twp	92	242
Bridget	51	f	w	IREL	San Francisco	3-Wd San Francisco	79	290
Bridget	25	f	w	IREL	San Francisco	San Francisco P O	83	77
Burk	34	m	w	KY	Shasta	French Gulch P O	89	464
C	30	m	w	VA	San Joaquin	2-Wd Stockton	86	194
Carrie	27	f	w	RI	San Francisco	8-Wd San Francisco	82	357
Charles	58	m	w	PA	San Francisco	San Francisco P O	83	343
Charles	25	m	w	FINL	Mendocino	Casper & Big Rvr	74	163
Chas	32	m	w	DENM	Nevada	Meadow Lake Twp	75	260
Chas A	43	m	w	NJ	Humboldt	Table Bluff Twp	72	307
Clinton	22	m	w	NY	Sacramento	Brighton Twp	77	71
Cornelius G	41	m	w	IL	Santa Clara	2-Wd San Jose	88	279
D	43	m	w	VA	San Joaquin	Oneal Twp	86	101
Dennis	38	m	w	TN	Kern	Linns Valley P O	73	347
E	46	m	w	OH	Lake	Lower Lake	73	414
E B	33	m	w	VA	Sacramento	Brighton Twp	77	76
Edmund	37	m	w	VA	Santa Clara	Fremont Twp	88	63
Edward	36	m	w	VA	San Francisco	11-Wd San Francisc	84	430
Eli W	38	m	w	MA	Santa Clara	2-Wd San Jose	88	279
Elisabeth	46	f	w	TN	Butte	Oroville Twp	70	139
Ferris	45	m	w	NY	Santa Barbara	San Buenaventura P	87	441
Francis P	57	m	w	TN	Placer	Rocklin Twp	76	468
Frank	36	m	w	IREL	San Francisco	San Francisco P O	83	65
G W	38	m	w	KY	Solano	Vallejo	90	162
Geo	38	m	w	ENGL	Sonoma	Santa Rosa	91	401
Geo	38	m	w	ENGL	San Francisco	7-Wd San Francisco	81	264
Geo	31	m	w	MO	San Joaquin	Castoria Twp	86	15
Geo	19	m	w	NY	San Francisco	San Francisco P O	83	263
Geor W	41	m	w	NY	Nevada	Meadow Lake Twp	75	246
George	48	m	w	GA	Marin	San Rafael Twp	74	46
George	40	m	w	SWED	Calaveras	San Andreas P O	70	215
Ham C	40	m	w	VA	Sacramento	2-Wd Sacramento	77	235
Henry	52	m	w	WIND	San Francisco	11-Wd San Francisc	84	603
Henry	45	m	w	ENGL	San Francisco	2-Wd San Francisco	79	209
Henry	43	m	w	NORW	Mendocino	Casper & Big Rvr	74	163
Henry	32	m	w	MA	San Diego	San Diego	78	485
Henry	26	m	w	MO	Tehama	Paskenta Twp	92	164
Henry S	38	m	w	MO	Nevada	Eureka Twp	75	131
I R	57	m	w	NY	Nevada	Nevada Twp	75	288
J E	46	m	w	TN	Santa Clara	Gilroy Twp	88	72
J F	48	m	w	VA	San Joaquin	2-Wd Stockton	86	179
J F	35	m	w	CANA	Sacramento	3-Wd Sacramento	77	283
J H	31	m	w	PA	San Francisco	8-Wd San Francisco	82	368
Jackson	38	m	m	PA	Nevada	Grass Valley Twp	75	148
James S	46	m	w	ENGL	San Francisco	8-Wd San Francisco	82	491
James V	43	m	w	OH	San Francisco	San Francisco P O	85	764
Jas	41	m	w	TN	Santa Clara	Gilroy Twp	88	98
Jas E	22	m	b	TN	San Francisco	11-Wd San Francisc	84	708
Jno W	38	m	w	NC	Shasta	French Gulch P O	89	469
John	61	m	w	OH	Trinity	North Fork Twp	92	219
John	55	m	w	ENGL	Santa Clara	Gilroy Twp	88	87
John	40	m	w	OH	Tehama	Cottonwood Twp	92	162
John	40	m	w	IREL	Santa Cruz	Santa Cruz Twp	89	402
John	39	m	w	IREL	Yolo	Cache Crk Twp	93	426
John	36	m	w	MD	San Francisco	1-Wd San Francisco	79	116
John	31	m	w	NY	Placer	Colfax P O	76	391
John	29	m	w	VA	Sutter	Nicolaus Twp	92	107
John	29	m	w	ENGL	Amador	Fiddletown P O	69	430
John	27	m	w	IREL	San Francisco	San Francisco P O	85	754
John	24	m	w	NY	San Francisco	8-Wd San Francisco	82	425
John	19	m	w	MD	Sacramento	2-Wd Sacramento	77	252
John C	46	m	w	SWED	San Francisco	San Francisco P O	83	103
John H	42	m	w	NY	Nevada	Nevada Twp	75	306
John W	9	m	w	NY	Placer	Pino Twp	76	470
John W	49	m	w	ENGL	Sonoma	Sonoma Twp	91	443
Jos	31	m	w	MA	Sacramento	1-Wd Sacramento	77	172
Joseph	32	m	m	SC	Sacramento	2-Wd Sacramento	77	243
Joseph R	58	m	w	PA	Santa Clara	2-Wd San Jose	88	322
Julia	15	f	w	CA	Butte	Oroville Twp	70	138
Kate E	20	f	w	IL	Butte	Oregon Twp	70	125
M M	33	m	w	PA	Nevada	Nevada Twp	75	310
M M	32	m	w	PA	Placer	Alta P O	76	413
Maria	29	f	w	IREL	Santa Clara	1-Wd San Jose	88	245
Martin	32	m	w	IREL	Sacramento	Center Twp	77	85
Mary	80	f	w	VT	San Francisco	San Francisco P O	83	107
Mary	37	f	w	MO	Yuba	Linda Twp	93	554
Michael E	37	m	w	DE	Nevada	Grass Valley Twp	75	228
N	41	m	w	MI	Alameda	Oakland	68	262
Nathaniel	38	m	w	VA	Colusa	Colusa Twp	71	280
Orville F	57	m	w	PA	Nevada	Grass Valley Twp	75	185
P H	25	m	w	NJ	Alameda	Oakland	68	158
Pat	50	m	w	IREL	Santa Clara	Almaden Twp	88	3
Patrick	48	m	w	MA	Calaveras	San Andreas P O	70	185
Patrick	47	m	w	IREL	Sacramento	Center Twp	77	85
Pierce T	4	m	w	MO	Placer	Bath P O	76	458
R	11	m	w	ENGL	Solano	Benicia	90	21
R J	30	m	w	KY	San Joaquin	Oneal Twp	86	109
R J	25	m	w	ENGL	San Francisco	San Francisco P O	85	800
Ralf C	38	m	w	CT	San Francisco	8-Wd San Francisco	82	329
Rebecca	38	f	w	PA	San Francisco	11-Wd San Francisc	84	657
Richd	42	m	w	VA	Sonoma	Cloverdale Twp	91	268
S N	30	m	w	IN	Lassen	Susanville Twp	73	441
Samul	66	m	w	KY	El Dorado	Cosumnes Twp	72	13
Thomas	48	m	w	IREL	Santa Clara	Milpitas Twp	88	113
Thomas	30	m	w	IL	Yolo	Washington Twp	93	532
Thomas	26	m	w	ENGL	San Francisco	San Francisco P O	85	758
Thos	37	m	w	VA	Mendocino	Ukiah Twp	74	236
Thos	36	m	w	ENGL	Sonoma	Bodega Twp	91	252
Thos J	44	m	w	TN	Shasta	Buckeye P O	89	482
Thos W	33	m	w	IN	Mendocino	Little Lake Twp	74	201
W	33	m	w	OH	Sierra	Forest Twp	89	530
W	30	m	w	NY	San Francisco	8-Wd San Francisco	82	373
W B	38	m	w	MO	San Joaquin	Dent Twp	86	29
W H	5	m	w	CA	San Francisco	San Francisco P O	83	323
W H	26	m	w	VA	San Joaquin	Douglas Twp	86	39
William	70	m	w	KY	Sonoma	Santa Rosa	91	406
William	48	m	w	CANA	San Francisco	6-Wd San Francisco	81	93
William	38	m	w	CANA	Stanislaus	San Joaquin Twp	92	71
William	35	m	w	MA	Sonoma	Sonoma Twp	91	436
William	28	m	w	OH	Siskiyou	Yreka	89	661
William	26	m	w	AUSL	San Francisco	7-Wd San Francisco	81	172
William	24	m	w	NY	San Francisco	8-Wd San Francisco	82	430
William B	30	m	b	WIND	San Francisco	6-Wd San Francisco	81	109
Wm	79	m	w	ENGL	Sonoma	Santa Rosa	91	405
Wm	36	m	w	KY	Alameda	Murray Twp	68	126
Wm	35	m	w	IREL	San Francisco	San Francisco P O	83	88
Wm	32	m	w	KY	San Joaquin	3-Wd Stockton	86	216
Wm	29	m	w	MO	Sonoma	Santa Rosa	91	413
Wm	26	m	w	PA	Sacramento	1-Wd Sacramento	77	189
Wm C	25	m	w	NY	San Francisco	1-Wd San Francisco	79	125
Wm J	43	m	w	MO	Sonoma	Cloverdale Twp	91	269
Wm P	34	m	w	MA	San Francisco	San Francisco P O	83	96
HARRISS								
John W	35	m	w	ME	Sonoma	Petaluma Twp	91	322
W M	39	m	w	KY	Lassen	Long Valley Twp	73	437
HARRISSON								
Joe	45	m	w	ENGL	Humboldt	Eureka Twp	72	279

© 2001 by Heritage Quest. All rights reserved.

Name	Age	S	R	B-PL	County	Locale	Series M593 Roll	Pg
William	26	m	w	NY	San Mateo	Schoolhouse Statio	87	338
HARRITY								
John	13	m	w	MA	San Francisco	2-Wd San Francisco	79	215
HARRIVAN								
J N	30	f	w	CANA	Mendocino	Ukiah Twp	74	244
HARROD								
William H	31	m	w	MD	San Bernardino	San Bernardino Twp	78	448
HARROL								
Columbus	18	m	w	IA	Tehama	Tehama Twp	92	193
HARROLD								
Alf	44	m	w	KY	Merced	Snelling P O	74	258
C B	53	m	w	ENGL	San Joaquin	Douglas Twp	86	34
Catherine	40	f	w	IREL	Sacramento	4-Wd Sacramento	77	368
Charles	66	m	w	NH	El Dorado	White Oak Twp	72	142
Christopher	53	m	w	ENGL	Alpine	Woodfords P O	69	310
E W	29	m	w	IN	Sutter	Yuba Twp	92	149
Elizabeth	70	f	w	IREL	San Francisco	2-Wd San Francisco	79	218
Elizabeth	45	f	w	TN	Plumas	Indian Twp	77	14
Frank	43	m	w	PRUS	San Joaquin	2-Wd Stockton	86	188
Joel	41	m	w	IL	Merced	Snelling P O	74	254
Joel	30	m	w	IN	Shasta	Millville P O	89	486
John	40	m	w	NY	San Francisco	2-Wd San Francisco	79	218
John	35	m	w	SWED	San Joaquin	Oneal Twp	86	104
John W	34	m	w	IREL	San Francisco	San Francisco P O	83	339
Mike	41	m	w	IREL	Sonoma	Santa Rosa	91	396
N S	37	m	w	PA	San Joaquin	Douglas Twp	86	46
Richard	34	m	w	NY	San Francisco	San Francisco P O	83	141
Rudolph	16	m	w	CA	San Francisco	San Francisco P O	83	360
Sarah	39	f	w	PA	Napa	Napa	75	13
HARROLDSON								
N	39	m	w	KY	San Joaquin	Oneal Twp	86	109
HARROLSON								
Harry	24	m	w	LA	Sacramento	American Twp	77	65
Zechial	45	m	w	KY	San Joaquin	Oneal Twp	86	100
HARROP								
John	49	m	w	ENGL	San Francisco	San Francisco P O	85	753
Joseph	50	m	w	ENGL	Sutter	Butte Twp	92	92
HARROW								
Annie	13	f	w	IA	Napa	Napa	75	17
H M	60	m	w	MA	Sacramento	3-Wd Sacramento	77	302
Isaac	56	m	w	VA	Mariposa	Mariposa P O	74	106
J W	20	m	w	IN	Humboldt	Mattole Twp	72	284
Jane	13	f	w	IL	Solano	Benicia	90	14
R	40	m	w	IREL	Lake	Kelsey Crk	73	402
HARROWITZ								
Adolph	23	m	w	AUST	San Bernardino	San Bernardino Twp	78	418
HARRY								
Alexander	25	m	w	ENGL	Nevada	Grass Valley Twp	75	174
Edward	20	m	w	ENGL	Nevada	Grass Valley Twp	75	221
Henry	38	m	w	NY	Sacramento	4-Wd Sacramento	77	369
Henry	21	m	w	IL	San Joaquin	Douglas Twp	86	43
Henry	10	m	w	ME	Butte	Chico Twp	70	49
James	38	m	w	IREL	Trinity	Minersville Pct	92	203
James	36	m	w	ENGL	Nevada	Grass Valley Twp	75	198
John	55	m	w	IREL	San Mateo	Belmont P O	87	374
John	35	m	w	FRAN	Placer	Auburn P O	76	361
John	27	m	w	ENGL	San Joaquin	Liberty Twp	86	97
John	23	m	w	VA	San Francisco	San Francisco P O	83	130
John	16	m	c	CHIN	Tehama	Antelope Twp	92	155
John C	23	m	w	ENGL	Sacramento	Georgianna Twp	77	127
Joseph	29	m	w	ENGL	Nevada	Grass Valley Twp	75	191
Joseph	25	m	w	ENGL	Nevada	Nevada Twp	75	314
Mary	14	f	w	CA	San Francisco	7-Wd San Francisco	81	166
Michael	45	m	w	IREL	Sacramento	Lee Twp	77	157
Ohio	40	m	w	MI	San Joaquin	Dent Twp	86	24
Pete	35	m	w	IREL	San Francisco	5-Wd San Francisco	81	27
Thomas	48	m	w	ENGL	El Dorado	Placerville Twp	72	93
William	26	m	w	IREL	Kern	Havilah P O	73	339
HARRYHASSEN								
Fredrick	35	m	w	PRUS	Calaveras	San Andreas P O	70	211
HARRYHAUSSEN								
Christian	27	m	w	PRUS	Calaveras	San Andreas P O	70	211
Henry	31	m	w	PRUS	Calaveras	San Andreas P O	70	211
HARSACK								
Rodrick	42	m	w	SCOT	Sacramento	Lee Twp	77	160
HARSAID								
John	42	m	w	IREL	San Mateo	San Mateo P O	87	360
HARSBURG								
Patrick	25	m	w	IREL	San Francisco	San Francisco P O	83	156
HARSCHAL								
Gerson	34	m	w	PRUS	San Francisco	San Francisco P O	83	231
HARSH								
Lewis	44	m	w	WURT	Santa Cruz	Soquel Twp	89	444
HARSHA								
John B	40	m	w	OH	San Mateo	Half Moon Bay P O	87	408
HARSHFIELD								
Lemuel	43	m	w	AR	Fresno	Millerton P O	72	149
HARSHMAN								
Isabel	28	f	w	MO	Yolo	Grafton Twp	93	500
HARSO								
John	38	m	w	PRUS	San Mateo	Half Moon Bay P O	87	404
HARSON								
Jas	50	m	w	IREL	San Joaquin	1-Wd Stockton	86	136
HARSTED								
Alanson	66	m	w	NY	San Francisco	2-Wd San Francisco	79	214
HARSTLEY								
A	40	m	w	PRUS	San Joaquin	1-Wd Stockton	86	157
HARSWELL								
Fred	60	m	w	ENGL	Contra Costa	Martinez P O	71	444
HARSY								
Frank	9	m	w	NY	San Francisco	5-Wd San Francisco	81	31
HART								
A	35	m	w	OH	Siskiyou	Scott Valley Twp	89	611
Abner	42	m	w	OH	Siskiyou	Hamburg Twp	89	596
Abram	23	m	w	PA	Solano	Vallejo	90	201
Agust	44	m	w	NY	San Francisco	7-Wd San Francisco	81	156
Albert	40	m	w	WIND	Alameda	Brooklyn	68	27
Albert	18	m	w	IL	El Dorado	Diamond Springs Tw	72	29
Albert	15	m	w	CA	Monterey	Pajaro Twp	74	368
Albert L	33	m	w	OH	Sacramento	2-Wd Sacramento	77	251
Alison	42	m	w	MO	Mendocino	Big Rvr Twp	74	171
Andrew	18	m	w	CA	Humboldt	Arcata Twp	72	235
Andrew	16	m	w	IL	Humboldt	Table Bluff Twp	72	305
Andrew J	38	m	w	ME	Stanislaus	Empire Twp	92	51
Ann	42	f	w	IREL	San Francisco	San Francisco P O	83	354
Anthony	37	m	w	IREL	Sierra	Gibson Twp	89	543
Bartlett	54	m	w	CANA	Stanislaus	San Joaquin Twp	92	83
Bernard	60	m	w	IREL	San Francisco	San Francisco P O	83	133
Bridget	45	f	w	IREL	San Francisco	San Francisco P O	83	18
Bridget	42	f	w	IREL	Solano	Rio Vista Twp	90	59
C B	28	m	w	VT	Humboldt	Pacific Twp	72	290
Catharine	62	f	w	IREL	San Francisco	San Francisco P O	85	816
Charles	64	m	w	CT	El Dorado	Mud Springs Twp	72	88
Charles	42	m	w	OH	Kern	Bakersfield P O	73	358
Charles	38	m	w	MO	Santa Cruz	Soquel Twp	89	447
Charles B	32	m	w	OH	San Francisco	8-Wd San Francisco	82	488
Charles D	44	m	w	CT	Tulare	Farmersville Twp	92	241
Chas	27	m	w	NY	San Luis Obispo	Santa Rosa Twp	87	326
Chas J	34	m	w	NY	Merced	Snelling P O	74	268
Conrad	46	m	w	PA	Santa Clara	San Jose Twp	88	205
Daniel	60	m	w	IREL	San Francisco	San Francisco P O	85	765
Daniel	32	m	w	IREL	San Francisco	San Francisco P O	83	383
Daniel	27	m	w	MA	San Francisco	11-Wd San Francisc	84	434
Daniel B	37	m	w	WV	Calaveras	Copperopolis P O	70	258
David	46	m	w	TN	Mariposa	Mariposa P O	74	121
David	40	m	w	ENGL	Santa Cruz	Santa Cruz	89	406
David	40	m	w	PA	Humboldt	Arcata Twp	72	235
E C	50	m	w	IREL	Humboldt	Pacific Twp	72	296
E Jane	37	f	w	MO	Placer	Auburn P O	76	361
E S	38	m	w	NY	Sacramento	Brighton Twp	77	70
Eben	25	m	w	MA	San Francisco	San Francisco P O	85	746
Edward P	48	m	w	NY	Tulare	Visalia	92	294
Elerson	54	m	b	GA	Merced	Snelling P O	74	249
Elias	46	m	w	KY	Lassen	Janesville Twp	73	432
Eliza	35	f	w	IREL	San Francisco	San Francisco P O	80	389
Etha L	11	f	w	CA	El Dorado	Mud Springs Twp	72	86
F	41	m	w	NY	Alameda	Murray Twp	68	128
F J	47	f	w	ME	San Joaquin	2-Wd Stockton	86	203
Frances	60	f	w	NY	San Francisco	San Francisco P O	80	427
Francis	30	m	w	IREL	San Francisco	11-Wd San Francisc	84	536
Frank	30	m	w	IREL	Merced	Snelling P O	74	259
Fred	34	m	w	SAXO	San Francisco	11-Wd San Francisc	84	599
Fred W	30	m	w	PRUS	San Francisco	7-Wd San Francisco	81	246
G P	30	m	w	OH	San Francisco	San Francisco P O	85	776
G W	34	m	w	ME	Humboldt	Eureka Twp	72	271
Geo A	40	m	w	ENGL	San Francisco	2-Wd San Francisco	79	236
Geo C	30	m	w	ME	Humboldt	Eureka Twp	72	277
George	35	m	w	PA	San Francisco	5-Wd San Francisco	81	31
George	30	m	w	OH	San Diego	Julian Dist	78	468
Gram Tonn	40	m	w	AR	San Joaquin	Douglas Twp	86	43
Hagot T	43	m	w	HOLL	El Dorado	Salmon Falls Twp	72	130
Henry	73	m	w	VA	Solano	Rio Vista Twp	90	61
Henry	36	m	w	IREL	San Francisco	San Francisco P O	85	715
Henry	34	m	w	ENGL	Nevada	Washington Twp	75	344
Henry	26	m	w	PA	Inyo	Cerro Gordo Twp	73	320
Henry H	40	m	w	IREL	San Francisco	8-Wd San Francisco	82	419
Henry H	39	m	w	IREL	San Francisco	1-Wd San Francisco	79	45
Henry H	24	m	w	NY	San Francisco	1-Wd San Francisco	79	31
Henry H	17	m	w	ENGL	San Francisco	1-Wd San Francisco	79	91
Hiram	43	m	w	MO	San Joaquin	Elliott Twp	86	78
Hiram M	47	m	w	VA	Inyo	Bishop Crk Twp	73	317
Horace G	46	m	w	ME	Santa Clara	San Jose Twp	88	189
Hugh	41	m	w	IREL	Santa Clara	Almaden Twp	88	3
Isaac	34	m	w	PRUS	Kern	Tehachapi P O	73	352
J	41	m	w	IL	Lassen	Janesville Twp	73	432
J H	46	m	w	IREL	Humboldt	Pacific Twp	72	292
Jackson	35	m	w	MO	Colusa	Colusa	71	298
Jacob	24	m	w	IN	San Diego	Fort Yuma Dist	78	463
James	60	m	w	IREL	San Luis Obispo	Santa Rosa Twp	87	325
James	56	m	w	NY	San Luis Obispo	Salinas Twp	87	295
James	53	m	w	ENGL	Santa Clara	1-Wd San Jose	88	234
James	39	m	w	IL	El Dorado	Mud Springs Twp	72	86
James	39	m	w	IREL	San Bernardino	San Bernardino Twp	78	419
James	35	m	w	IREL	Santa Barbara	Santa Barbara P O	87	498
James	31	m	w	NY	San Francisco	7-Wd San Francisco	81	190
James	30	m	w	IREL	Santa Clara	2-Wd San Jose	88	325
James	28	m	w	IREL	San Francisco	6-Wd San Francisco	81	119
James	28	m	w	CANA	Colusa	Monroe Twp	71	325
James	23	m	w	MO	Santa Clara	Gilroy Twp	88	79
James	20	m	w	IA	Placer	Lincoln P O	76	485
James A	43	m	w	ENGL	Santa Cruz	Santa Cruz Twp	89	395
James H	42	m	w	ENGL	Santa Cruz	Santa Cruz	89	427
Jas	26	m	w	MI	Tehama	Antelope Twp	92	153
Jerome	18	m	w	CA	San Francisco	San Francisco P O	83	48

© 2001 by Heritage Quest. All rights reserved.

Name	Age	S	R	B-PL	County	Locale	Series M593 Roll	Pg
Jno	43	m	w	SCOT	San Joaquin	Douglas Twp	86	36
Jno E	37	m	w	OH	Butte	Ophir Twp	70	120
Joe	52	m	w	PRUS	San Joaquin	2-Wd Stockton	86	197
John	49	m	w	IREL	San Francisco	San Francisco P O	83	151
John	48	m	w	IREL	San Francisco	7-Wd San Francisco	81	192
John	43	m	w	IREL	San Francisco	11-Wd San Francisc	84	479
John	43	m	w	GERM	Los Angeles	Santa Ana Twp	73	599
John	42	m	w	IREL	Nevada	Eureka Twp	75	137
John	37	m	w	MA	San Joaquin	2-Wd Stockton	86	208
John	36	m	w	IREL	San Francisco	1-Wd San Francisco	79	91
John	34	m	w	IREL	San Francisco	11-Wd San Francisc	84	636
John	28	m	w	MD	Los Angeles	Los Angeles	73	544
John	28	m	w	IREL	San Francisco	1-Wd San Francisco	79	41
John	23	m	w	IREL	San Mateo	Pescadero P O	87	411
John W	31	m	w	VA	Nevada	Nevada Twp	75	296
John W	17	m	w	IA	Placer	Auburn P O	76	365
Joseph	76	m	w	KY	Kern	Tehachapi P O	73	355
Joseph	32	m	w	BREM	Los Angeles	Santa Ana Twp	73	615
Joseph	26	m	w	TX	Kern	Tehachapi P O	73	352
Josephine	50	f	w	ENGL	San Francisco	San Francisco P O	83	211
Leopold	39	m	w	FRAN	Santa Clara	Santa Clara Twp	88	142
Lewis	13	m	w	CA	San Francisco	11-Wd San Francisc	84	588
Louis	64	m	w	HDAR	San Francisco	2-Wd San Francisco	79	173
Louisa	34	f	w	OH	Siskiyou	Table Rock Twp	89	648
Malachi	35	m	w	CANA	Contra Costa	Martinez P O	71	415
Marcus	28	m	w	PRUS	San Francisco	8-Wd San Francisco	82	408
Margaret	57	f	w	CANA	San Joaquin	3-Wd Stockton	86	231
Margaret	25	f	w	NH	Sacramento	4-Wd Sacramento	77	320
Marian	40	f	w	ENGL	San Francisco	1-Wd San Francisco	79	91
Martha	24	f	w	IREL	San Francisco	11-Wd San Francisc	84	489
Mary	63	f	w	IREL	San Francisco	San Francisco P O	83	244
Mary	50	f	w	ENGL	San Francisco	7-Wd San Francisco	81	286
Mary	40	f	w	ENGL	San Francisco	San Francisco P O	80	390
Mary	28	f	w	MA	San Francisco	1-Wd San Francisco	79	90
Mary	26	f	w	IREL	San Francisco	1-Wd San Francisco	79	31
Mary	25	f	w	IREL	San Francisco	San Francisco P O	83	377
Mary	25	f	w	NY	San Francisco	7-Wd San Francisco	81	165
Mary	24	f	w	AR	San Francisco	8-Wd San Francisco	82	310
Mary	24	f	w	IREL	San Francisco	San Francisco P O	80	418
Mary	24	f	w	OH	San Francisco	6-Wd San Francisco	81	132
Mary	11	f	w	CA	Placer	Auburn P O	76	382
Mary A	47	f	w	IREL	San Francisco	San Francisco P O	83	248
Mary A	21	f	w	IREL	San Francisco	8-Wd San Francisco	82	426
Michael	35	m	w	IREL	San Francisco	San Francisco P O	83	299
Michael	35	m	w	MO	Tulare	Venice Twp	92	276
Michael	30	m	w	IREL	Mendocino	Casper & Big Rvr	74	164
Micheal	40	m	w	IREL	San Francisco	7-Wd San Francisco	81	168
Morris	50	m	w	IREL	San Francisco	1-Wd San Francisco	79	20
Moses	36	m	w	AR	Kern	Tehachapi P O	73	355
Myredith	25	m	w	TX	Kern	Tehachapi P O	73	352
Nathan	39	m	w	NY	Santa Cruz	Soquel Twp	89	447
Oliver	42	m	w	PA	Calaveras	San Andreas P O	70	180
Oliver B	42	m	w	TN	El Dorado	Mud Springs Twp	72	81
Otto	37	m	w	HANO	San Francisco	San Francisco P O	83	75
P F	36	m	w	VT	Humboldt	Pacific Twp	72	299
Patrick	47	m	w	IREL	Sacramento	Natomas Twp	77	168
Patrick	40	m	w	IREL	Inyo	Lone Pine Twp	73	334
Patrick	35	m	w	IREL	Kern	Kernville P O	73	368
Patrick	32	m	w	IREL	San Francisco	San Francisco P O	83	316
Peter	45	m	w	PRUS	Alameda	Murray Twp	68	101
Powell	45	m	w	HOLL	El Dorado	Salmon Falls Twp	72	130
Rena	70	f	b	GA	Merced	Snelling P O	74	249
Richard	43	m	w	BELG	San Diego	San Diego	78	495
Rogers	35	m	w	IREL	San Francisco	8-Wd San Francisco	82	337
Ruth	12	f	w	CA	San Mateo	Pescadero P O	87	411
Sally	20	f	w	OH	San Francisco	San Francisco P O	83	96
Sampson	85	m	w	TN	Stanislaus	Empire Twp	92	56
Samuel	33	m	w	PRUS	San Francisco	8-Wd San Francisco	82	420
Sewell	55	m	w	VT	El Dorado	Mud Springs Twp	72	85
Stephen	50	m	w	RI	El Dorado	Mud Springs Twp	72	79
Susan	36	f	w	ME	San Francisco	San Francisco P O	83	313
Thomas	46	m	w	ENGL	Humboldt	Eel Rvr Twp	72	249
Thomas	45	m	w	IREL	El Dorado	Mud Springs Twp	72	83
Thomas	40	m	w	OH	Sutter	Vernon Twp	92	138
Thomas	38	m	w	PA	Yuba	Long Bar Twp	93	565
Thomas	32	m	w	IREL	San Francisco	San Francisco P O	83	224
Thomas	28	m	w	IN	Colusa	Colusa	71	294
Thomas	27	m	w	ENGL	Monterey	Castroville Twp	74	330
Thomas	25	m	w	IREL	San Bernardino	San Bernardino Twp	78	427
Thomas	25	m	w	IREL	San Francisco	1-Wd San Francisco	79	41
Thomas	24	m	w	IREL	San Francisco	San Francisco P O	83	290
Thomas R	27	m	w	OH	San Francisco	3-Wd San Francisco	79	326
Thos	38	m	w	ENGL	Fresno	Millerton P O	72	167
Thos	36	m	w	IREL	San Joaquin	2-Wd Stockton	86	163
Thos	28	m	w	IREL	San Francisco	1-Wd San Francisco	79	90
Thos P	39	m	w	KY	Tehama	Red Bluff	92	177
W S	44	m	w	TN	San Joaquin	Douglas Twp	86	46
Warren	43	m	w	ME	Santa Clara	1-Wd San Jose	88	247
William	45	m	w	ENGL	San Francisco	San Francisco P O	83	250
William	45	m	w	IREL	San Francisco	6-Wd San Francisco	81	119
William	32	m	w	MO	Colusa	Colusa	71	298
William A	26	m	w	NY	Tulare	Visalia Twp	92	284
Willie	14	m	w	CA	San Francisco	San Francisco P O	83	125
Wm	55	m	w	KY	El Dorado	Georgetown Twp	72	40
Wm	30	m	w	SHOL	Sonoma	Salt Point	91	385
Wm	15	m	w	CA	Sacramento	Granite Twp	77	136
Wm J	59	m	w	CT	Merced	Snelling P O	74	247

Name	Age	S	R	B-PL	County	Locale	Series M593 Roll	Pg
HARTAL								
Fred	28	m	w	BAVA	Sierra	Sears Twp	89	553
HARTCORN								
Chas	34	m	w	WURT	San Francisco	1-Wd San Francisco	79	41
HARTE								
J H	24	m	w	NY	Mendocino	Ukiah Twp	74	237
John	37	m	w	TN	Humboldt	South Fork Twp	72	301
Mary	56	f	w	IREL	Santa Clara	1-Wd San Jose	88	254
HARTEL								
Charles	46	m	w	GERM	Contra Costa	Martinez P O	71	406
HARTER								
Bloomfield	32	m	w	NY	Sonoma	Petaluma Twp	91	324
Chris	27	m	w	IN	San Joaquin	Dent Twp	86	23
Daniel	41	m	w	PA	Amador	Jackson P O	69	319
Eli	20	m	w	IN	Sutter	Yuba Twp	92	150
Elizabeth	30	f	w	NY	San Francisco	8-Wd San Francisco	82	421
George	37	m	w	OH	Sutter	Yuba Twp	92	149
Isaac W	35	m	w	OH	Tulare	Visalia Twp	92	282
John	35	m	w	PRUS	Sonoma	Analy Twp	91	225
Pedro	40	m	w	FRAN	Calaveras	Copperopolis P O	70	221
S	45	m	w	OH	Mendocino	Calpella Twp	74	183
HARTERY								
Bridget	21	f	w	IREL	Plumas	Goodwin Twp	77	4
Thomas	44	m	w	IREL	Plumas	Quartz Twp	77	43
HARTEY								
Dan	38	m	w	IREL	Merced	Snelling P O	74	261
Wm	25	m	w	NY	San Joaquin	2-Wd Stockton	86	169
HARTFIELD								
Charles	40	m	w	FRAN	San Mateo	Half Moon Bay P O	87	393
HARTFORD								
Joanna	32	f	w	IL	Tulare	Kings Rvr Twp	92	252
John	47	m	w	IREL	San Francisco	1-Wd San Francisco	79	15
HARTHAN								
L	42	m	w	NH	Sacramento	Granite Twp	77	144
L E	40	m	w	NH	Trinity	Junction City Pct	92	208
Siles	30	m	w	ME	Sierra	Sears Twp	89	555
HARTHORN								
Henry	40	m	w	ENGL	San Francisco	San Francisco P O	85	771
HARTICK								
Absolon	46	m	w	PA	Amador	Fiddletown P O	69	437
HARTIE								
John	29	m	w	TX	San Joaquin	Tulare Twp	86	260
HARTIGAN								
Kate	40	f	w	IREL	San Francisco	San Francisco P O	80	364
M	40	m	w	IREL	Amador	Ione City P O	69	360
M	35	m	w	IREL	Amador	Sutter Crk P O	69	397
Richard	38	m	w	IREL	Calaveras	San Andreas P O	70	214
Timothy	31	m	w	IREL	San Francisco	6-Wd San Francisco	81	88
HARTIN								
Lary	40	m	w	MS	San Joaquin	2-Wd Stockton	86	194
HARTING								
Jacob	38	m	w	BADE	San Francisco	San Francisco P O	80	472
Wm	35	m	w	PA	San Francisco	1-Wd San Francisco	79	122
HARTINGAN								
James	35	m	w	IREL	San Francisco	7-Wd San Francisco	81	159
HARTINGS								
D N	48	m	w	MA	Solano	Benicia	90	1
HARTLE								
Benjamin	36	m	w	ME	Mendocino	Point Arena Twp	74	206
HARTLEB								
Fred	5	m	w	GERM	Sonoma	Petaluma Twp	91	346
HARTLEBARN								
Otto	29	m	w	PRUS	San Francisco	San Francisco P O	85	746
HARTLEY								
A J	35	m	w	CANA	Tuolumne	Columbia P O	93	343
Benjiman F	28	m	w	MO	Los Angeles	Los Angeles Twp	73	467
David	30	m	w	AR	Santa Cruz	Santa Cruz Twp	89	393
Geo	39	m	w	NY	Santa Barbara	Santa Barbara P O	87	461
H H	33	f	w	MO	Sacramento	3-Wd Sacramento	77	265
Henry	36	m	w	IL	Tulare	Visalia	92	299
Henry G	33	m	w	ENGL	Yolo	Putah Twp	93	526
Henry J	41	m	w	ENGL	El Dorado	Placerville Twp	72	98
Jane	35	f	w	SCOT	Alameda	Alameda	68	18
Jeremiah	44	m	w	IREL	Plumas	Plumas Twp	77	33
John	9	m	w	SCOT	Alameda	Alameda	68	7
John	55	m	w	ENGL	Alameda	Hayward	68	74
John	39	m	w	ENGL	Sacramento	4-Wd Sacramento	77	349
Margaret	50	f	w	CANA	San Francisco	San Francisco P O	80	480
Marquis De	34	m	w	IL	Tulare	Farmersville Twp	92	249
Michael	30	m	w	IREL	Solano	Benicia	90	9
Sarah	14	f	w	CA	Amador	Ione City P O	69	355
Stephen	35	m	w	MA	Calaveras	Copperopolis P O	70	264
William	54	m	w	ENGL	Nevada	Rough & Ready Twp	75	331
William	23	m	w	IREL	San Francisco	San Francisco P O	83	209
Wm	26	m	w	ENGL	Solano	Vallejo	90	202
HARTLIFF								
Jacob	44	m	w	PRUS	Calaveras	Copperopolis P O	70	241
HARTLING								
V	38	m	w	HDAR	Sierra	Downieville Twp	89	516
HARTLY								
Charles	27	m	w	IA	Los Angeles	Los Nietos Twp	73	590
H H	35	m	w	PA	Sierra	Sierra Twp	89	563
Henry	36	m	w	IREL	San Francisco	1-Wd San Francisco	79	72
Rathmus	23	m	w	OH	Calaveras	San Andreas P O	70	159
HARTMAN								
---	50	m	w	MA	Alameda	Oakland	68	261
Adam	22	m	w	BADE	San Francisco	San Francisco P O	80	459

© 2001 by Heritage Quest. All rights reserved.

Series M593

Name	Age	S	R	B-PL	County	Locale	Roll	Pg
Albert	24	m	w	MO	Colusa	Colusa	71	290
Amelia	12	f	w	CA	San Francisco	8-Wd San Francisco	82	440
Anna	68	f	w	PRUS	Alameda	Eden Twp	68	59
Annie	20	f	w	BAVA	San Francisco	San Francisco P O	83	211
Antone	51	m	w	PRUS	Calaveras	San Andreas P O	70	218
B F	43	m	w	PA	Nevada	Nevada Twp	75	295
C	35	m	w	PRUS	San Francisco	San Francisco P O	85	847
C	30	m	w	PRUS	Yuba	Marysville	93	587
Casper	70	m	w	PRUS	San Francisco	San Francisco P O	85	752
Catherine	23	f	w	BAVA	El Dorado	Georgetown Twp	72	46
Charles	45	m	w	RUSS	Santa Clara	2-Wd San Jose	88	322
Charles	31	m	w	FRAN	Trinity	Weaverville Pct	92	223
Charles	28	m	w	HOLL	Santa Clara	San Jose Twp	88	209
Charles	28	m	w	OH	Colusa	Colusa Twp	71	278
Chas W	28	m	w	OH	Butte	Chico Twp	70	41
Chris	30	m	w	PRUS	Solano	Rio Vista Twp	90	58
Christin	25	m	w	HDAR	San Francisco	San Francisco P O	80	353
Christine	12	f	w	IA	El Dorado	Placerville	72	117
Christopher	33	m	w	PRUS	San Francisco	San Francisco P O	83	63
Claus	38	m	w	PRUS	San Francisco	8-Wd San Francisco	82	386
David	40	m	w	LA	Stanislaus	Branch Twp	92	5
Edward C	44	m	w	OH	Yolo	Putah Twp	93	523
Elizabeth A	35	f	w	NY	El Dorado	Placerville	72	118
Ernst	29	m	w	PRUS	San Francisco	11-Wd San Francisc	84	422
F	28	m	w	WURT	Sierra	Table Rock Twp	89	575
Felix	25	m	w	MO	Santa Clara	2-Wd San Jose	88	319
Francis	13	m	w	CA	Nevada	Rough & Ready Twp	75	325
Fred	68	m	w	PA	Alameda	Alameda	68	18
Fred	50	m	w	FRAN	Alameda	Murray Twp	68	128
Fred	40	m	w	PRUS	Alameda	Murray Twp	68	117
Frederick	35	m	w	BADE	San Francisco	8-Wd San Francisco	82	474
Geo	30	m	w	ENGL	Humboldt	Arcata Twp	72	235
George	49	m	w	FRAN	Amador	Volcano P O	69	380
George E	48	m	w	FRAN	Amador	Jackson P O	69	338
George W	48	m	w	PRUS	San Francisco	San Francisco P O	85	752
Gotlip	31	m	w	NCOD	Nevada	Grass Valley Twp	75	144
Henry	58	m	w	FRAN	San Francisco	2-Wd San Francisco	79	224
Henry	40	m	w	HDAR	San Francisco	6-Wd San Francisco	81	89
Heny	42	m	w	PRUS	Alameda	Murray Twp	68	117
Isaac	46	m	w	NJ	San Francisco	8-Wd San Francisco	82	364
Isaac	40	m	w	NY	San Francisco	3-Wd San Francisco	79	318
Israel	33	m	w	PRUS	San Francisco	8-Wd San Francisco	82	432
J	43	m	w	FRAN	Alameda	Murray Twp	68	112
J W	40	m	w	FRNK	Sonoma	Santa Rosa	91	394
Jacob	63	m	w	VA	Santa Clara	Redwood Twp	88	120
Jacob	50	m	w	PA	San Francisco	5-Wd San Francisco	81	8
Jacob	42	m	w	PA	San Francisco	11-Wd San Francisc	84	424
Jacob	28	m	w	PRUS	San Francisco	San Francisco P O	85	831
James S	55	m	w	PA	El Dorado	Cosumnes Twp	72	18
John	60	m	w	BAVA	El Dorado	Placerville	72	117
John	45	m	w	MO	Amador	Jackson P O	69	326
John	45	m	w	NY	San Francisco	5-Wd San Francisco	81	19
John	44	m	w	BREM	Del Norte	Happy Camp Twp	71	471
John	43	m	w	BAVA	Amador	Ione City P O	69	354
John	43	m	w	NY	El Dorado	Placerville	72	107
John	22	m	w	CA	Sonoma	Petaluma Twp	91	336
John H	22	m	w	MO	Santa Clara	2-Wd San Jose	88	302
John W	35	m	w	NY	San Francisco	San Francisco P O	83	238
Joseph	59	m	w	HDAR	Santa Clara	1-Wd San Jose	88	256
Julus	28	m	w	FRAN	San Francisco	2-Wd San Francisco	79	224
Kicholas	52	m	w	FRAN	El Dorado	Cosumnes Twp	72	17
Lewis	35	m	w	FRAN	Yuba	Marysville	93	590
Max	39	m	w	PRUS	Calaveras	San Andreas P O	70	189
Morris	20	m	w	PRUS	San Francisco	San Francisco P O	80	537
Nicholas	40	m	w	PRUS	San Francisco	San Francisco P O	83	20
Philip	42	m	w	HDAR	Sacramento	2-Wd Sacramento	77	247
Philip	19	m	w	MO	Nevada	Nevada Twp	75	279
Philip	19	m	w	MO	Sacramento	2-Wd Sacramento	77	218
S S	48	m	w	PA	Amador	Jackson P O	69	337
Solomon	15	m	w	MO	Yolo	Merritt Twp	93	508
Stephen	16	m	w	PRUS	Tulare	Tule Rvr Twp	92	261
W	38	m	w	WURT	Nevada	Eureka Twp	75	134
William	49	m	w	HDAR	San Francisco	San Francisco P O	83	139
William	29	m	w	AUST	Santa Clara	2-Wd San Jose	88	335
William	26	m	w	SWED	San Mateo	San Mateo P O	87	359
William D	47	m	w	VA	Yolo	Cache Crk Twp	93	438
Wm	40	m	w	MA	Alameda	Alameda	68	18
Wm D	47	m	w	VA	Yolo	Cache Crk Twp	93	429
HARTMANN								
Adolf	30	m	w	OLDE	San Francisco	3-Wd San Francisco	79	287
Adolph	26	m	w	SAXO	San Francisco	San Francisco P O	85	724
Chas J W	55	m	w	SWIT	Shasta	Stillwater P O	89	481
Ernest	34	m	w	ITAL	El Dorado	Mud Springs Twp	72	80
Hyman	26	m	w	GERM	San Bernardino	San Bernardino Twp	78	452
Margaret	14	f	w	CA	El Dorado	Placerville	72	108
Wm P	28	m	w	FRAN	Shasta	Shasta P O	89	458
HARTMEYER								
George	25	m	w	PRUS	Napa	Napa	75	16
Louis	28	m	w	MI	San Francisco	2-Wd San Francisco	79	195
HARTNAGLE								
Theodore	22	m	w	PRUS	San Francisco	6-Wd San Francisco	81	91
HARTNEL								
Jas	43	m	w	IN	San Joaquin	Dent Twp	86	22
Pallo	29	m	w	CA	Monterey	Castroville Twp	74	331
HARTNELL								
Alberto	39	m	w	CA	Santa Barbara	Santa Maria P O	87	514
Ellen	25	f	w	IREL	Los Angeles	Los Angeles	73	537
H F	46	m	w	VT	San Joaquin	Oneal Twp	86	109
Jose G	36	m	w	CA	Monterey	Alisal Twp	74	295
Juan	38	m	w	CA	Santa Barbara	Santa Barbara P O	87	467
Mary	35	f	w	IREL	Los Angeles	Los Angeles	73	531
William	44	m	w	CA	Santa Barbara	Santa Maria P O	87	513
HARTNER								
Emil	30	m	w	PRUS	San Francisco	8-Wd San Francisco	82	428
HARTNESS								
Kate	32	f	w	IREL	San Francisco	8-Wd San Francisco	82	322
HARTNET								
Edward	45	m	w	IREL	San Francisco	11-Wd San Francisc	84	700
Ellen	20	f	w	IREL	San Francisco	8-Wd San Francisco	82	473
William	25	m	w	IREL	San Francisco	7-Wd San Francisco	81	183
HARTNETT								
Danl	37	m	w	IREL	San Francisco	1-Wd San Francisco	79	67
Harvey	21	m	w	NY	San Francisco	1-Wd San Francisco	79	89
Jeremia S	50	m	w	IREL	San Francisco	San Francisco P O	85	755
Maurice	54	m	w	IREL	Plumas	Washington Twp	77	53
Michael	42	m	w	IREL	San Francisco	San Francisco P O	83	284
Patk	35	m	w	IREL	San Francisco	1-Wd San Francisco	79	125
Thomas	30	m	w	IREL	San Francisco	San Francisco P O	83	243
HARTNEY								
Edwd H	30	m	w	MA	San Francisco	1-Wd San Francisco	79	97
Gustave	32	m	w	HANO	San Francisco	11-Wd San Francisc	84	541
James	30	m	w	IREL	San Francisco	San Francisco P O	83	372
Jane	65	f	w	ENGL	San Francisco	San Francisco P O	83	156
Johana	16	f	w	IREL	Los Angeles	Los Angeles	73	518
John	37	m	w	NJ	Santa Cruz	Soquel Twp	89	440
Julia	21	f	w	NJ	San Francisco	San Francisco P O	85	729
Mary	25	f	w	IREL	San Francisco	San Francisco P O	85	734
Polley	36	f	w	NY	Sonoma	Healdsburg & Mendo	91	284
Stephen	18	m	w	NY	Solano	Vallejo	90	201
HARTOF								
H	37	m	w	PRUS	San Joaquin	Tulare Twp	86	263
HARTOG								
Edward	43	m	w	BELG	San Francisco	3-Wd San Francisco	79	326
James	23	m	w	FRAN	San Francisco	San Francisco P O	80	456
HARTON								
Joe	31	m	w	CANA	Alameda	Murray Twp	68	124
John	25	m	w	HAMB	Placer	Newcastle Twp	76	478
John	25	m	w	CT	San Mateo	Woodside P O	87	380
William T	26	m	w	TX	Los Angeles	El Monte Twp	73	460
HARTONG								
Theodore	35	m	w	HANO	San Francisco	San Francisco P O	83	61
HARTRE								
John	39	m	w	NJ	Plumas	Indian Twp	77	12
HARTRICH								
Henrietta	40	f	w	PRUS	San Francisco	San Francisco P O	83	371
J	43	m	w	NY	San Joaquin	Tulare Twp	86	253
HARTS								
John	43	m	w	IREL	Alameda	Murray Twp	68	127
HARTSALL								
Jacob L	34	m	w	NC	Calaveras	Copperopolis P O	70	241
HARTSEFF								
John	39	m	w	CANA	Contra Costa	Martinez P O	71	444
HARTSEY								
Hans	59	m	w	DENM	Tuolumne	Sonora P O	93	308
HARTSHORM								
B M	44	m	w	NJ	San Francisco	1-Wd San Francisco	79	103
HARTSHORN								
A K	40	m	w	NY	Sutter	Sutter Twp	92	116
E D	40	m	w	OH	Amador	Drytown P O	69	423
Frank	46	m	w	MA	Santa Barbara	Santa Barbara P O	87	482
J	23	m	w	NH	Lake	Morgan Valley	73	425
Saml	37	m	w	NY	San Francisco	8-Wd San Francisco	82	300
Wm	56	m	w	ENGL	Santa Clara	Gilroy Twp	88	99
HARTSHORNE								
Ben	43	m	w	NH	Mono	Bridgeport P O	74	286
Benjamin	43	m	w	NJ	San Francisco	8-Wd San Francisco	82	497
Eldridge	52	m	w	MA	San Francisco	11-Wd San Francisc	84	553
Wm	40	m	w	VT	Sacramento	Franklin Twp	77	113
HARTSIG								
William	23	m	w	LA	Tuolumne	Sonora P O	93	304
HARTSOCK								
Adolph	36	m	w	IN	Sonoma	Cloverdale Twp	91	271
Florena	3	f	w	CA	Sonoma	Cloverdale Twp	91	273
HARTSON								
Chanoher	44	m	w	NY	Napa	Napa	75	51
Charles	28	m	w	RUSS	San Francisco	San Francisco P O	80	467
Henry	36	m	w	ENGL	San Francisco	1-Wd San Francisco	79	59
Nettie	15	f	w	CA	Plumas	Plumas Twp	77	33
HARTSOUGH								
David B	65	m	w	MI	Sacramento	2-Wd Sacramento	77	224
HARTT								
Edwd	45	m	w	NH	Solano	Vallejo	90	199
HARTUNG								
Adolphe	74	m	w	PRUS	Nevada	Rough & Ready Twp	75	329
Frederick	70	m	w	HANO	Los Angeles	Santa Ana Twp	73	610
Henry	1	m	w	CA	Nevada	Rough & Ready Twp	75	329
HARTVIG								
Henny	42	m	w	HAMB	San Francisco	6-Wd San Francisco	81	155
HARTWELL								
---	51	m	w	US	Sacramento	1-Wd Sacramento	77	183
Charles N	44	m	w	MA	Sacramento	2-Wd Sacramento	77	220
Chas	28	m	w	BADE	San Joaquin	Oneal Twp	86	103
Clarence H	33	m	w	VT	Alpine	Markleeville P O	69	311
Derias	31	m	w	CT	Sutter	Butte Twp	92	99

© 2001 by Heritage Quest. All rights reserved.

California 1870 Census

Name	Age	S	R	B-PL	County	Locale	Roll	Pg
Edwd	28	m	w	NJ	Sacramento	1-Wd Sacramento	77	172
Ella	26	f	w	IREL	San Francisco	6-Wd San Francisco	81	132
Geo	46	m	w	VT	San Francisco	11-Wd San Francisc	84	643
Geo	45	m	w	VT	San Francisco	11-Wd San Francisc	84	564
Geo	26	m	w	IREL	San Francisco	5-Wd San Francisco	81	27
George	56	m	w	MA	Yolo	Grafton Twp	93	493
George	24	m	w	MA	San Francisco	San Francisco P O	85	874
J F	43	m	w	LA	San Francisco	San Francisco P O	85	774
John F	44	m	w	ME	Plumas	Plumas Twp	77	29
Julia	30	f	w	IREL	San Francisco	2-Wd San Francisco	79	282
Mary	52	f	w	IREL	Sacramento	3-Wd Sacramento	77	264
Mat	24	m	w	IL	Yuba	Marysville	93	591
Mathew	34	m	w	PA	Sutter	Butte Twp	92	96
S E	28	m	w	MA	Solano	Vallejo	90	178
W H	55	m	w	ME	Yuba	Marysville	93	578
HARTWICK								
Charles	42	m	w	BADE	San Francisco	San Francisco P O	83	227
Christian	58	m	w	NY	Santa Clara	Santa Clara Twp	88	160
The	42	m	w	HAMB	Alameda	Oakland	68	145
HARTY								
Annie	25	f	w	IREL	Sacramento	4-Wd Sacramento	77	350
Johanna	37	f	w	IREL	San Francisco	San Francisco P O	85	796
John	34	m	w	MA	San Francisco	1-Wd San Francisco	79	115
John	32	m	w	IREL	San Joaquin	2-Wd Stockton	86	206
John	30	m	w	IREL	Contra Costa	Martinez P O	71	380
Larry	45	m	w	IREL	San Joaquin	2-Wd Stockton	86	186
Margaret	11	f	w	CA	Nevada	Grass Valley Twp	75	229
Patrick	32	m	w	IREL	San Francisco	San Francisco P O	83	354
Robert	39	m	w	IREL	Nevada	Meadow Lake Twp	75	258
Thomas	26	m	w	IREL	Alameda	Murray Twp	68	125
Thos	30	m	w	IREL	San Francisco	7-Wd San Francisco	81	260
W	54	m	w	ENGL	Sierra	Sierra Twp	89	568
HARTZ								
Antony	40	m	w	FRAN	Klamath	Sawyers Bar	73	377
Edward	21	m	w	PRUS	San Francisco	6-Wd San Francisco	81	104
John	34	m	w	GERM	San Mateo	Schoolhouse Statio	87	342
Matilda	30	f	w	BAVA	San Francisco	San Francisco P O	83	214
HARTZBERG								
M	40	m	w	HANO	San Francisco	San Francisco P O	85	842
HARTZELL								
Christian	32	m	w	NORW	San Francisco	7-Wd San Francisco	81	224
HARVEAN								
Febian	34	m	w	CANA	Siskiyou	Hamburg Twp	89	598
HARVERE								
Francisco	35	m	w	CA	Alameda	Washington Twp	68	287
HARVERY								
Thos	37	m	w	IREL	Napa	Napa Twp	75	74
HARVESON								
Charles	40	m	w	MA	San Bernardino	San Bernardino Twp	78	453
HARVEY								
A B	33	m	w	IN	Monterey	Salinas Twp	74	307
A L	37	f	w	NY	San Francisco	San Francisco P O	85	774
Abraham	27	m	w	ENGL	Napa	Napa Twp	75	70
Abraham	26	m	w	ENGL	Napa	Napa Twp	75	69
Alfred	42	m	w	ENGL	San Francisco	San Francisco P O	80	359
Andrew	39	m	w	SCOT	San Francisco	2-Wd San Francisco	79	206
Andrew	26	m	w	CANA	Kern	Linns Valley P O	73	345
Andrew J	28	m	w	NY	San Francisco	1-Wd San Francisco	79	115
Andrew W	41	m	w	VA	El Dorado	Mud Springs Twp	72	76
Anna	24	f	w	CANA	San Mateo	Half Moon Bay P O	87	404
August	35	m	w	IREL	Solano	Silveyville Twp	90	78
B P	40	m	w	MS	Tehama	Red Bluff	92	179
Benj P	48	m	w	NH	San Francisco	1-Wd San Francisco	79	40
Bernard	46	m	w	IREL	San Francisco	San Francisco P O	80	473
Bernard	36	m	w	IREL	San Francisco	San Francisco P O	80	536
Betsy	66	f	w	OH	Sacramento	4-Wd Sacramento	77	358
C W	45	m	w	NY	El Dorado	Lake Valley Twp	72	63
Charles	20	m	w	ENGL	Trinity	Weaverville Pct	92	229
Charles H	37	m	w	MA	San Francisco	6-Wd San Francisco	81	94
Chas	38	m	w	IREL	Tehama	Tehama Twp	92	195
Chs Sr	35	m	w	ME	San Francisco	2-Wd San Francisco	79	263
David B	45	m	w	NY	San Francisco	5-Wd San Francisco	81	19
Delia	17	f	w	IREL	Santa Barbara	Santa Barbara P O	87	487
Eden	45	m	w	VA	Placer	Blue Canyon P O	76	419
Edward	45	m	w	VA	Nevada	Nevada Twp	75	308
Edward	38	m	w	NH	San Francisco	San Francisco P O	83	208
Eliza	53	f	w	ENGL	San Francisco	San Francisco P O	83	68
Eliza	39	f	w	IREL	San Francisco	11-Wd San Francisc	84	688
Eliza	18	f	w	IREL	San Joaquin	2-Wd Stockton	86	160
Elizabeth	32	f	w	LA	San Francisco	11-Wd San Francisc	84	698
Eugene	27	m	w	IL	Nevada	Nevada Twp	75	286
Francis S	43	m	w	NH	San Francisco	1-Wd San Francisco	79	131
G H	33	m	w	ME	Sacramento	3-Wd Sacramento	77	263
George	42	m	w	KY	Nevada	Meadow Lake Twp	75	267
George	32	m	w	KY	Placer	Dutch Flat P O	76	403
George	32	m	w	OH	Santa Cruz	Watsonville	89	368
George	22	m	w	MA	Los Angeles	Los Angeles Twp	73	487
Harry	32	m	w	MI	Del Norte	Mountain Twp	71	475
Henry	34	m	w	ENGL	Yuba	Rose Bar Twp	93	661
Henry	33	m	w	VA	El Dorado	Mud Springs Twp	72	76
Henry	32	m	w	ENGL	Trinity	Weaverville Pct	92	229
Hezekiah	44	m	w	PA	Plumas	Seneca Twp	77	47
Hugh	36	m	w	IREL	Butte	Oregon Twp	70	127
J A	32	m	w	NY	Solano	Vallejo	90	178
James	52	m	w	IREL	San Francisco	7-Wd San Francisco	81	227
James	41	m	w	ENGL	Sonoma	Petaluma Twp	91	332
James	40	m	w	IREL	San Francisco	7-Wd San Francisco	81	199
James	38	m	w	ME	Marin	San Rafael	74	50
James	34	m	w	ENGL	Trinity	Weaverville Pct	92	229
James	23	m	w	OH	San Francisco	1-Wd San Francisco	79	106
James	20	m	w	NY	San Francisco	2-Wd San Francisco	79	165
James C	52	m	w	MA	San Francisco	6-Wd San Francisco	81	131
Jeremiah	25	m	w	ENGL	Nevada	Grass Valley Twp	75	203
Jno C	34	m	w	ME	Sonoma	Santa Rosa	91	399
Joel	69	m	w	VT	Marin	Tomales Twp	74	76
John	45	m	w	WALE	El Dorado	Mud Springs Twp	72	76
John	43	m	w	IREL	Calaveras	San Andreas P O	70	209
John	40	m	w	NJ	Merced	Snelling P O	74	272
John	40	m	w	SCOT	Solano	Vallejo	90	189
John	38	m	w	NY	Alameda	Eden Twp	68	68
John	35	m	w	MA	San Francisco	7-Wd San Francisco	81	207
John	35	m	w	IREL	Siskiyou	Surprise Valley Tw	89	638
John	29	m	w	FRAN	Calaveras	San Andreas P O	70	200
John	28	m	w	OH	San Bernardino	San Bernardino Twp	78	453
John	14	m	w	CA	Colusa	Grand Island Twp	71	310
John F	49	m	w	ME	Yolo	Washington Twp	93	534
John F	49	m	w	ME	Yolo	Cache Crk Twp	93	431
John W	16	m	w	IL	Yolo	Grafton Twp	93	486
Joseph	54	m	w	RI	San Francisco	San Francisco P O	83	228
Joseph	18	m	w	US	San Joaquin	3-Wd Stockton	86	218
Joseph W	38	m	w	KY	Alpine	Woodfords P O	69	315
Joshua	25	m	w	ENGL	Nevada	Grass Valley Twp	75	232
Kate	30	f	w	IREL	San Francisco	San Francisco P O	83	61
Lewellyn	29	m	w	IL	Marin	Tomales Twp	74	76
Louisa	35	f	w	SC	San Francisco	8-Wd San Francisco	82	335
Lydia	71	f	w	MA	Sonoma	Sonoma Twp	91	437
M	40	m	w	PRUS	Alameda	Alameda	68	9
M C	47	f	w	ME	Sacramento	3-Wd Sacramento	77	276
Martin	26	m	w	IREL	San Francisco	1-Wd San Francisco	79	41
Mary A	36	f	w	ME	Trinity	Douglas	92	233
Michael	35	m	c	CHIN	Del Norte	Mountain Twp	71	475
Michael	30	m	w	IREL	Yolo	Cache Crk Twp	93	422
N	6	m	w	CA	San Francisco	San Francisco P O	85	799
O B	35	m	w	OH	San Joaquin	Elliott Twp	86	73
Obed	43	m	w	NY	Sacramento	Dry Crk Twp	77	100
Oscar	32	m	w	IN	Solano	Tremont Twp	90	30
Patk	35	m	w	IREL	San Francisco	1-Wd San Francisco	79	9
Peter	22	m	w	ENGL	Klamath	Liberty Twp	73	374
R	28	m	w	ENGL	Sacramento	1-Wd Sacramento	77	189
R B	31	m	w	IL	Lassen	Susanville Twp	73	444
Ransom A	44	m	w	NH	Sonoma	Sonoma Twp	91	436
Richard	51	m	w	WALE	El Dorado	Mud Springs Twp	72	79
Robert	60	m	w	IREL	Siskiyou	Hamburg Twp	89	596
Robert G	37	m	w	VT	Placer	Blue Canyon P O	76	418
Robt	70	m	w	NH	Tehama	Battle Crk Meadows	92	168
S	66	m	w	MD	Sonoma	Santa Rosa	91	428
Stoddard G	40	m	w	NY	Los Angeles	Los Angeles	73	545
Sylvester P	37	m	w	NH	Alameda	Washington Twp	68	268
Thomas	42	m	w	ENGL	Plumas	Indian Twp	77	15
Thomas J	22	m	w	MA	San Francisco	6-Wd San Francisco	81	135
Thomas J	16	m	w	CA	Los Angeles	Los Angeles	73	536
Thos	45	m	w	SCOT	Solano	Vallejo	90	181
Thos C	50	m	w	SCOT	Calaveras	Copperopolis P O	70	250
W C	40	m	w	ENGL	Amador	Amador City P O	69	393
Walter W	27	m	w	MO	Alpine	Woodfords P O	69	315
Warren	23	m	w	NH	Alameda	Washington Twp	68	298
William	51	m	w	CT	El Dorado	Placerville	72	125
William	43	m	w	ENGL	Nevada	Grass Valley Twp	75	176
William	42	m	w	TN	Monterey	Pajaro Twp	74	370
William	36	m	w	NC	Napa	Napa	75	25
William	35	m	w	ENGL	San Francisco	11-Wd San Francisc	84	434
William	28	m	w	OH	Solano	Montezuma Twp	90	69
William	22	m	w	ENGL	Nevada	Grass Valley Twp	75	143
William	22	m	w	CANA	San Francisco	3-Wd San Francisco	79	294
Wm	8	m	w	CA	San Francisco	San Francisco P O	85	799
Wm	45	m	w	NY	Solano	Vallejo	90	143
Wm	35	m	w	ENGL	Yuba	Marysville	93	584
Wm	34	m	w	ENGL	San Joaquin	1-Wd Stockton	86	152
Wm Jr	22	m	w	ENGL	Nevada	Grass Valley Twp	75	190
HARVILLE								
John	44	m	w	NH	San Francisco	11-Wd San Francisc	84	553
Willis	59	m	w	NY	Tehama	Deer Crk Twp	92	172
HARVY								
Alvery	24	m	w	AR	Inyo	Lone Pine Twp	73	332
Anna	37	f	w	IREL	Alameda	Alameda	68	3
Asa L	38	m	w	CANA	Solano	Benicia	90	15
Catherine	28	f	w	SCOT	Placer	Cisco P O	76	495
Charles	35	m	w	PORT	Alameda	Eden Twp	68	82
David	21	m	w	DE	Solano	Montezuma Twp	90	65
Eliza	25	f	w	IREL	San Francisco	11-Wd San Francisc	84	437
Henry	59	m	w	FRAN	Inyo	Cerro Gordo Twp	73	318
Henry	21	m	w	ENGL	Amador	Jackson P O	69	321
James	61	m	w	NY	San Joaquin	1-Wd Stockton	86	131
James	47	m	w	KY	Solano	Rio Vista Twp	90	58
John	32	m	w	IREL	Inyo	Independence Twp	73	328
John	27	m	w	PORT	Alameda	Eden Twp	68	85
Pheobe	40	f	w	CANA	San Francisco	8-Wd San Francisco	82	323
Robt	21	m	w	NY	Alameda	Oakland	68	234
Wm	37	m	w	ME	San Joaquin	1-Wd Stockton	86	126
HARWELL								
Fred B	33	m	w	OH	Alameda	Brooklyn	68	25
HARWICK								
Felix F	42	m	w	NY	Stanislaus	Empire Twp	92	66

© 2001 by Heritage Quest. All rights reserved.

Name	Age	S	R	B-PL	County	Locale	Series M593 Roll	Pg
HARWOOD								
Benj	55	m	w	MD	Calaveras	Copperopolis P O	70	249
Charles	38	m	w	SC	San Francisco	San Francisco P O	83	373
D M	39	m	w	NY	Santa Clara	Almaden Twp	88	17
David	31	m	w	NY	Santa Clara	Fremont Twp	88	41
Henry	38	m	w	CANA	Contra Costa	Martinez P O	71	376
James	40	m	w	ME	Amador	Jackson P O	69	325
Thos	49	m	w	GA	San Francisco	1-Wd San Francisco	79	63
Thos J	32	m	w	ME	San Francisco	3-Wd San Francisco	79	320
W	56	m	w	NY	Alameda	Oakland	68	138
William	29	m	w	ENGL	Contra Costa	Martinez P O	71	431
William	24	m	w	NJ	Santa Clara	2-Wd San Jose	88	295
Wm	38	m	w	MA	Alameda	Oakland	68	256
HARWORTH								
Jas	52	m	w	ENGL	Solano	Benicia	90	15
HARY								
Ah	40	m	c	CHIN	Sacramento	Granite Twp	77	141
Frank	25	m	w	IREL	Placer	Summit P O	76	496
Jno	40	m	w	PRUS	Butte	Chico Twp	70	26
Wm	45	m	w	IREL	San Francisco	11-Wd San Francisc	84	667
HASALTME								
Charles	39	m	w	ME	San Francisco	San Francisco P O	83	207
HASAR								
Jno	40	m	w	IN	Butte	Oregon Twp	70	135
HASBACH								
Henry	33	m	w	PRUS	San Francisco	San Francisco P O	83	293
HASBROCK								
Geo	39	m	w	PRUS	Butte	Ophir Twp	70	97
HASBROOK								
John	35	m	w	NY	Sonoma	Petaluma Twp	91	354
Joseph	30	m	w	NY	San Francisco	San Francisco P O	85	826
Josiah	41	m	w	NY	Sonoma	Mendocino Twp	91	287
HASBROUGH								
Christopher	32	m	w	IL	San Mateo	Redwood Twp	87	361
HASBROUK								
Augustus	35	m	w	NY	San Francisco	8-Wd San Francisco	82	399
Hiram B	40	m	w	NY	Sonoma	Petaluma Twp	91	325
HASCALL								
Melvin	20	m	w	ME	Sacramento	Brighton Twp	77	80
HASE								
Ah	18	m	c	CHIN	Solano	Suisun Twp	90	109
HASELBERG								
T	59	m	w	BAVA	Sacramento	3-Wd Sacramento	77	315
HASELBUSH								
Wm	20	m	w	PRUS	Butte	Chico Twp	70	35
HASELTINE								
Frank	37	m	w	VT	Calaveras	Copperopolis P O	70	231
George W	28	m	w	OH	Los Angeles	El Monte Twp	73	458
HASELTON								
James	44	m	w	OH	Nevada	Grass Valley Twp	75	231
HASELWOOD								
Jas	18	m	w	NY	Tehama	Antelope Twp	92	153
HASEMAN								
Jno	18	m	w	HANO	Sacramento	3-Wd Sacramento	77	291
HASEN								
James	34	m	w	NY	Nevada	Meadow Lake Twp	75	267
Jerom B	34	m	w	OH	San Luis Obispo	Morro Twp	87	280
HASENBERG								
M	37	m	w	SHOL	Sacramento	1-Wd Sacramento	77	176
HASENFELDT								
G	37	m	w	HESS	Amador	Jackson P O	69	318
HASENFLUTH								
Caroline	21	f	w	WURT	San Francisco	8-Wd San Francisco	82	380
HASERICK								
Anton	61	m	w	SALT	Siskiyou	Cottonwood Twp	89	592
HASEY								
Ellen	30	f	w	IREL	Alameda	Oakland	68	197
Henry C	53	m	b	NY	El Dorado	Coloma Twp	72	10
John	32	m	w	IREL	San Mateo	San Mateo P O	87	351
John	23	m	w	WURT	San Francisco	1-Wd San Francisco	79	39
John J	29	m	w	MI	Tulare	Visalia	92	294
HASFORD								
Wm	53	m	w	NY	San Francisco	San Francisco P O	85	859
HASH								
John	28	m	w	PA	San Francisco	11-Wd San Francisc	84	690
Rosina	65	f	w	WURT	San Francisco	7-Wd San Francisco	81	277
HASHAGAN								
C	25	f	w	HANO	Sacramento	3-Wd Sacramento	77	295
HASHANA								
Muller	25	m	w	PRUS	San Francisco	5-Wd San Francisco	81	20
HASHBRING								
Abe	28	m	w	POLA	San Francisco	2-Wd San Francisco	79	163
HASHELL								
Joseph	40	m	w	OH	San Joaquin	Dent Twp	86	24
Thos	32	m	w	KY	San Joaquin	Castoria Twp	86	11
HASHHAGEN								
Chris	19	m	w	PRUS	San Francisco	San Francisco P O	83	310
HASHIE								
Joshua	64	m	w	ME	Los Angeles	Los Angeles	73	548
HASKALL								
Danl H	56	m	w	MA	San Francisco	3-Wd San Francisco	79	329
J C	29	m	w	ME	Tuolumne	Columbia P O	93	356
L S	56	m	w	ME	Tuolumne	Columbia P O	93	356
HASKE								
Henry H	61	m	w	IREL	Placer	Gold Run Twp	76	394
HASKEL								
Alford	44	m	w	OH	Placer	Bath P O	76	447

Name	Age	S	R	B-PL	County	Locale	Series M593 Roll	Pg
Augt	10	m	w	CA	Merced	Snelling P O	74	281
Benjm	27	m	w	ME	Tuolumne	Sonora P O	93	318
Chas L	29	m	w	ME	San Francisco	8-Wd San Francisco	82	308
James	50	m	w	MA	San Francisco	5-Wd San Francisco	81	23
Josiah	17	m	w	ME	Merced	Snelling P O	74	277
W B	27	m	w	NY	Sonoma	Petaluma Twp	91	335
Walter	9	m	w	CA	Yuba	Rose Bar Twp	93	663
Walter	24	m	w	ENGL	Yuba	Rose Bar Twp	93	662
HASKELL								
A B	33	m	w	IREL	Tehama	Red Bluff	92	184
Charles	25	m	w	ME	Colusa	Grand Island Twp	71	307
D H	43	m	w	MO	Sacramento	4-Wd Sacramento	77	337
Ed W	50	m	w	VT	San Francisco	San Francisco P O	83	110
Frank	18	m	w	ME	San Francisco	11-Wd San Francisc	84	628
Frank	12	m	w	CA	San Francisco	San Francisco P O	80	413
Fred	26	m	w	ME	Humboldt	Eel Rvr Twp	72	249
G H	52	m	w	MA	San Francisco	3-Wd San Francisco	79	316
Geo	50	m	w	MA	San Francisco	7-Wd San Francisco	81	286
Geo	33	m	w	ME	Butte	Kimshew Tpw	70	80
Geo S	47	m	w	MA	San Francisco	San Francisco P O	83	137
Geo W	30	m	w	ME	San Francisco	San Francisco P O	83	121
Geor E	34	m	w	MA	San Francisco	San Francisco P O	83	195
George E	34	m	w	MA	San Francisco	San Francisco P O	83	170
Gilbert	40	m	w	ME	San Francisco	11-Wd San Francisc	84	571
H	45	m	w	MA	Yuba	Marysville	93	614
Harry	24	m	w	ME	Yuba	Marysville	93	610
Henry J	41	m	w	DC	Santa Clara	1-Wd San Jose	88	251
J	35	m	w	ME	Alameda	Murray Twp	68	122
Jacob W	49	m	w	ME	Santa Clara	2-Wd San Jose	88	298
James	39	m	w	OH	Los Angeles	Los Angeles	73	524
James T	42	m	w	ME	Placer	Dutch Flat P O	76	407
John	35	m	w	NY	San Bernardino	San Bernardino Twp	78	451
John	28	m	w	IREL	San Francisco	San Francisco P O	83	415
John	25	m	w	ME	Klamath	Trinidad Twp	73	392
John F	9	m	w	CA	El Dorado	White Oak Twp	72	143
John M	40	m	w	ME	San Francisco	5-Wd San Francisco	81	35
John W	44	m	w	ME	Santa Barbara	Santa Barbara P O	87	467
Joseph	60	m	w	PRUS	San Francisco	San Francisco P O	83	255
Joseph	28	m	w	IL	San Francisco	San Francisco P O	83	313
Louisa	29	f	w	ME	Marin	Tomales Twp	74	78
Lyman	55	m	w	ME	Merced	Snelling P O	74	264
M	32	m	w	MA	Sutter	Nicolaus Twp	92	111
Mary	72	f	w	VT	Solano	Vallejo	90	206
Mary M	20	f	w	MA	Marin	Bolinas Twp	74	2
R	38	m	w	ME	Solano	Vallejo	90	160
Saml	37	m	w	NC	Mendocino	Ukiah Twp	74	235
Simon	29	m	w	MA	San Francisco	5-Wd San Francisco	81	35
Thomas	29	m	w	DENM	Alameda	Oakland	68	264
Violina	16	f	w	CA	Santa Clara	2-Wd San Jose	88	337
W H	58	m	w	MA	San Francisco	San Francisco P O	83	321
William	15	m	w	CA	Calaveras	Copperopolis P O	70	223
Wm	42	m	w	MA	Sierra	Sears Twp	89	561
Wm	25	m	w	MA	San Luis Obispo	Morro Twp	87	285
Wm A	29	m	w	ME	Sonoma	Bodega Twp	91	251
HASKER								
Johannah	25	f	w	HAMB	San Francisco	San Francisco P O	83	179
Wm	36	m	w	ENGL	Humboldt	Eureka Twp	72	272
HASKIE								
Louis	60	m	w	KY	Tuolumne	Sonora P O	93	327
HASKILL								
Barnelos	54	m	w	CT	Sonoma	Petaluma Twp	91	333
Chas	39	m	w	OH	Nevada	Eureka Twp	75	138
George	28	m	w	MA	Alameda	Alameda	68	6
HASKIN								
David H	29	m	w	IL	Siskiyou	Yreka	89	657
Ellen A	21	m	w	IA	San Luis Obispo	Santa Rosa Twp	87	321
Henry C	33	m	w	OH	Santa Barbara	San Buenaventura P	87	429
R	29	m	w	ENGL	Sierra	Butte Twp	89	509
Wm A	58	m	w	NY	Napa	Napa	75	5
HASKING								
J	46	m	w	ENGL	Calaveras	Copperopolis P O	70	232
W	35	m	w	PA	Alameda	Oakland	68	164
Y	25	m	w	ENGL	Sierra	Butte Twp	89	508
HASKINS								
Aaron	46	m	w	NY	San Mateo	Half Moon Bay P O	87	407
Albert P	33	m	w	NY	Trinity	Trinity Center Pct	92	204
Charles	29	m	w	IN	Mendocino	Noyo & Big Rvr Twp	74	173
Charles W	43	m	w	MA	El Dorado	Placerville Twp	72	102
Chas	37	m	w	IN	Nevada	Bloomfield Twp	75	94
Clayton	22	m	w	WI	Sacramento	Lee Twp	77	159
D C	45	m	w	OH	Solano	Vallejo	90	209
D H	25	m	w	IREL	Alameda	Oakland	68	260
Daniel	30	m	w	RI	San Francisco	2-Wd San Francisco	79	236
E W	19	m	w	NY	Solano	Vallejo	90	209
Erastus M	63	m	w	NY	El Dorado	Diamond Springs Tw	72	24
Freeman	37	m	w	NY	San Joaquin	Elkhorn Twp	86	57
H B	64	m	w	VT	Napa	Yountville Twp	75	84
H H	28	m	w	NY	Nevada	Nevada Twp	75	273
Henry R	50	m	w	NY	San Francisco	6-Wd San Francisco	81	147
Hiram	39	m	w	VT	Humboldt	Eureka Twp	72	259
Honora	40	f	w	IREL	Sacramento	4-Wd Sacramento	77	361
J W	45	m	w	OH	Solano	Vallejo	90	210
John	35	m	w	IREL	San Francisco	11-Wd San Francisc	84	679
John A	16	m	w	CA	Placer	Bath P O	76	424
Joseph	28	m	w	NY	Napa	Napa	75	5
R A	38	m	w	NY	Solano	Vallejo	90	206
Samuel	64	m	w	ENGL	Inyo	Cerro Gordo Twp	73	323

© 2001 by Heritage Quest. All rights reserved.

California 1870 Census

Series M593

Name	Age	S	R	B-PL	County	Locale	Roll	Pg
Samuel	30	m	w	ENGL	San Diego	Poway Dist	78	481
Thomas	51	m	w	OH	Calaveras	San Andreas P O	70	151
Thomas	41	m	w	KY	Mariposa	Mariposa P O	74	129
Thomas	33	m	w	ENGL	Solano	Vacaville Twp	90	123
W	44	m	w	ENGL	Sierra	Forest	89	536
William	35	m	w	NY	San Francisco	7-Wd San Francisco	81	184
William	16	m	w	CA	Yolo	Grafton Twp	93	482
Wilson	21	m	b	CA	San Bernardino	San Bernardino Twp	78	419
Wm	32	m	w	IA	Fresno	Kings Rvr P O	72	213
Wm A	24	m	w	IL	Napa	Napa	75	5
HASLACHER								
Jacob	27	m	w	NY	Stanislaus	Emory Twp	92	21
HASLAM								
C S	35	m	w	ME	Tuolumne	Sonora P O	93	318
David J	44	m	w	PA	Santa Cruz	Santa Cruz	89	404
Henry A	37	m	w	ENGL	San Francisco	San Francisco P O	85	720
James	32	m	w	ME	Kern	Havilah P O	73	350
Sarah E	17	f	w	MA	San Luis Obispo	Santa Rosa Twp	87	328
Wm A	56	m	w	MD	San Luis Obispo	San Luis Obispo Tw	87	308
HASLAND								
Wm	36	m	w	NY	Alameda	Oakland	68	142
HASLEHURST								
George	71	m	w	ENGL	Alameda	San Leandro	68	98
Wm	37	m	w	ENGL	Alameda	San Leandro	68	98
HASLEM								
Henry	30	m	w	ENGL	Placer	Bath P O	76	460
HASLEP								
Jno	40	m	w	PA	Butte	Kimshew Tpw	70	77
HASLER								
David	60	m	w	HUNG	San Francisco	San Francisco P O	85	815
Eunice	53	f	w	PA	Santa Clara	San Jose Twp	88	210
John	49	m	w	PRUS	Santa Clara	San Jose Twp	88	212
HASLET								
Elizabeth	19	f	w	IL	Santa Clara	2-Wd San Jose	88	303
Henrietta	10	f	w	CA	Santa Clara	1-Wd San Jose	88	228
Matthew	43	m	w	IREL	Placer	Bath P O	76	444
Newell	22	f	w	MI	Colusa	Monroe Twp	71	324
HASLETT								
Charles	47	m	w	ME	San Francisco	San Francisco P O	83	42
Henry John	4	m	w	CA	Sacramento	4-Wd Sacramento	77	378
John	43	m	w	GA	Fresno	Millerton P O	72	189
HASLEY								
Joseph	35	m	w	NY	Butte	Kimshew Tpw	70	79
Russell D	48	m	w	VT	Butte	Ophir Twp	70	101
HASLICK								
Wm	14	m	w	CA	Alameda	Eden Twp	68	71
HASLIN								
Patrick	35	m	w	IREL	Calaveras	Copperopolis P O	70	227
HASLINGS								
Asbury	38	m	w	MO	Santa Barbara	San Buenaventura P	87	420
HASLOCK								
Thos	30	m	w	AUST	San Francisco	11-Wd San Francisc	84	681
Wm	40	m	w	NH	San Francisco	San Francisco P O	85	779
HASLOP								
Fred	35	m	w	HANO	San Francisco	11-Wd San Francisc	84	672
HASLUM								
Solon	38	m	w	ME	Tuolumne	Columbia P O	93	354
HASLUP								
Geo	40	m	w	BADE	Butte	Ophir Twp	70	120
HASMER								
C C	46	m	w	MA	Tuolumne	Chinese Camp P O	93	382
HASNER								
Charles	29	m	w	MA	Calaveras	San Andreas P O	70	194
HASNETT								
Jas	24	m	w	NC	San Joaquin	Liberty Twp	86	91
HASO								
Francisco	30	m	w	FRAN	Los Angeles	Soledad Twp	73	632
HASOK								
Saul	41	m	w	NY	San Francisco	5-Wd San Francisco	81	21
HASOPHA								
M	58	m	w	MEXI	Sierra	Butte Twp	89	509
HASP								
Daniel	30	m	w	NY	Solano	Vacaville Twp	90	118
HASPER								
Thos	47	m	w	IREL	San Francisco	San Francisco P O	83	118
HASPIR								
Deborah	43	f	b	NC	Los Angeles	Los Angeles Twp	73	489
HASS								
Agnes	35	f	w	IREL	San Francisco	8-Wd San Francisco	82	464
Bernard	45	m	w	BAVA	San Francisco	San Francisco P O	83	227
Charles N	40	m	w	GERM	Los Angeles	Los Angeles	73	505
Fritz	43	m	w	SWIT	Sutter	Yuba Twp	92	145
George	30	m	w	PRUS	San Francisco	San Francisco P O	85	776
H R	30	m	w	PRUS	Alameda	Hayward	68	79
J	30	m	w	PA	Alameda	Oakland	68	261
J	15	m	w	CA	Solano	Benicia	90	21
Jacob	37	m	w	FRAN	Plumas	Goodwin Twp	77	8
Jacob	35	m	w	WURT	San Francisco	8-Wd San Francisco	82	388
John B	34	m	w	MO	Amador	Volcano P O	69	386
Joseph	55	m	w	BADE	San Joaquin	Oneal Twp	86	118
M D	48	m	w	IREL	Sierra	Lincoln Twp	89	545
Mary	27	f	w	GERM	San Joaquin	2-Wd Stockton	86	167
HASSA								
N B	50	m	w	FRAN	Tuolumne	Chinese Camp P O	93	376
HASSAN								
James	40	m	w	IREL	San Francisco	San Francisco P O	83	98

Series M593

Name	Age	S	R	B-PL	County	Locale	Roll	Pg
HASSAR								
Esteven	33	m	w	AUST	San Luis Obispo	San Luis Obispo Tw	87	314
HASSARD								
Richard	24	m	w	CANA	San Mateo	Menlo Park P O	87	377
HASSATH								
Malica	30	m	w	IREL	San Francisco	San Francisco P O	83	348
HASSE								
Fred	42	m	w	OLDE	Sacramento	Alabama Twp	77	60
John	44	m	w	HAMB	Klamath	Trinidad Twp	73	392
HASSEL								
C	16	f	m	OH	Sacramento	1-Wd Sacramento	77	187
Thomas	35	m	w	PA	Santa Clara	Gilroy Twp	88	89
HASSELBACK								
Geo	33	m	w	HDAR	San Francisco	7-Wd San Francisco	81	261
HASSELBACKER								
C	19	m	w	GERM	Solano	Vallejo	90	202
HASSELL								
Fredk W	43	m	w	PRUS	Tuolumne	Sonora P O	93	318
Harris	27	m	w	NY	San Francisco	San Francisco P O	83	48
J C	38	m	b	AL	Nevada	Nevada Twp	75	279
HASSEN								
Henry	50	m	w	NY	San Francisco	8-Wd San Francisco	82	368
Henry	40	m	w	CANA	Solano	Rio Vista Twp	90	59
Jno	30	m	w	BADE	San Joaquin	2-Wd Stockton	86	186
Joseph	21	m	w	NY	San Joaquin	Liberty Twp	86	83
Moses	61	m	w	ENGL	San Francisco	1-Wd San Francisco	79	99
HASSENGER								
A J	35	m	w	PA	Butte	Chico Twp	70	46
HASSET								
James H	32	m	w	IREL	Sonoma	Bodega Twp	91	257
Mike	32	m	w	GERM	San Joaquin	2-Wd Stockton	86	172
HASSETT								
Aron	33	m	w	OH	Sonoma	Healdsburg & Mendo	91	280
Bridget	45	f	w	IREL	Santa Clara	2-Wd San Jose	88	295
Chas	28	m	w	OH	Sonoma	Healdsburg & Mendo	91	281
John	43	m	w	IREL	Santa Clara	San Jose Twp	88	194
John	28	m	w	IREL	San Francisco	7-Wd San Francisco	81	182
John D	38	m	w	OH	Sonoma	Healdsburg & Mendo	91	281
Mary	70	f	w	IREL	San Francisco	11-Wd San Francisc	84	487
Mary	20	f	w	IREL	San Francisco	San Francisco P O	83	110
Pat	30	m	w	IREL	Solano	Vallejo	90	166
Patrick	69	m	w	IREL	San Francisco	11-Wd San Francisc	84	487
Stephen	30	m	w	IREL	San Francisco	7-Wd San Francisco	81	185
HASSEY								
Catherine	39	f	w	IREL	Santa Cruz	Watsonville	89	378
Edgar	39	m	w	ME	San Francisco	5-Wd San Francisco	81	25
Elbridge M	58	m	w	ME	Santa Cruz	Pajaro Twp	89	358
Frank	45	m	w	PA	San Francisco	5-Wd San Francisco	81	29
George	30	m	w	OH	Alameda	Oakland	68	265
James	32	m	w	OH	Alameda	Oakland	68	265
Thos	40	m	w	NY	San Francisco	5-Wd San Francisco	81	11
HASSIG								
Adolphus E	31	m	w	NY	Plumas	Washington Twp	77	52
HASSILUGER								
John	32	m	w	PRUS	San Francisco	San Francisco P O	80	413
HASSLER								
Jacob	26	m	w	SWIT	San Francisco	11-Wd San Francisc	84	646
HASSNER								
Valentine	40	m	w	HDAR	San Francisco	San Francisco P O	83	53
HASSON								
Mary	15	f	w	CA	San Francisco	8-Wd San Francisco	82	477
HASSOW								
Louis	40	m	w	PRUS	San Francisco	1-Wd San Francisco	79	110
HAST								
L	46	m	w	FRAN	Trinity	North Fork Twp	92	217
Sarah J	16	f	w	CA	Santa Cruz	Santa Cruz	89	429
HASTE								
Edward S	35	m	w	ENGL	Tuolumne	Sonora P O	93	324
J H	55	m	w	DENM	Alameda	Oakland	68	225
Julia	17	f	w	CA	San Francisco	8-Wd San Francisco	82	322
HASTIE								
Robert	38	m	w	SCOT	Napa	Napa	75	4
HASTING								
Flora	13	f	w	CA	Santa Clara	2-Wd San Jose	88	337
G	36	m	w	TN	Lake	Lower Lake	73	419
Harry	33	m	w	MA	Santa Clara	Milpitas Twp	88	111
Joseph	23	m	w	NY	San Francisco	1-Wd San Francisco	79	133
Norman L	37	m	w	OH	Alameda	Alvarado	68	302
S A	66	m	w	NY	Alameda	Alameda	68	7
S W	24	m	w	NY	Alameda	Alameda	68	6
William	40	m	w	MA	San Francisco	6-Wd San Francisco	81	133
HASTINGS								
A S	29	m	w	PA	Sacramento	1-Wd Sacramento	77	188
Alonzo P	32	m	w	ME	San Francisco	San Francisco P O	83	23
Alx	42	m	w	PA	Tuolumne	Sonora P O	93	332
Astley	58	m	w	MA	San Francisco	3-Wd San Francisco	79	300
Augusta	27	f	w	WI	Santa Cruz	Santa Cruz	89	427
Benjamin	27	m	w	OH	Yolo	Cache Crk Twp	93	435
Cathrin	38	f	w	IREL	Sacramento	Sutter Twp	77	383
Clara	27	f	w	IREL	San Francisco	6-Wd San Francisco	81	72
D J	18	m	w	CA	Napa	Yountville Twp	75	90
Delay	30	m	w	TN	Sonoma	Santa Rosa	91	430
E F	40	m	w	PA	Nevada	Meadow Lake Twp	75	247
Elizabeth	12	f	w	CA	San Francisco	San Francisco P O	80	373
Ella	11	f	w	CA	Santa Clara	2-Wd San Jose	88	338
Fanny	20	f	w	VA	San Francisco	8-Wd San Francisco	82	354
Frank	45	m	w	NY	San Francisco	San Francisco P O	83	228

© 2001 by Heritage Quest. All rights reserved.

Series M593

Name	Age	S	R	B-PL	County	Locale	Roll	Pg
Frank	30	m	w	AR	Sonoma	Petaluma Twp	91	340
Frank	21	f	w	MI	Santa Clara	1-Wd San Jose	88	252
George	40	m	w	NH	San Francisco	San Francisco P O	83	376
George H	46	m	w	MA	Calaveras	San Andreas P O	70	181
George S	35	m	w	ENGL	San Francisco	8-Wd San Francisco	82	381
George W	35	m	w	OH	Colusa	Colusa Twp	71	273
H F	30	m	w	PA	Sacramento	3-Wd Sacramento	77	262
Henry	34	m	w	MA	Alameda	San Leandro	68	94
Henry	11	m	w	CA	Contra Costa	Martinez Twp	71	346
Honora	38	f	w	IREL	Yuba	Linda Twp	93	556
Horace G	29	m	w	ME	Placer	Dutch Flat P O	76	414
I F	40	m	w	NC	San Joaquin	Tulare Twp	86	257
J C	57	m	w	TN	Sonoma	Santa Rosa	91	423
J F	35	m	w	MA	San Joaquin	1-Wd Stockton	86	135
J O	39	m	w	NY	Napa	Napa	75	18
James	30	m	w	IN	Yolo	Putah Twp	93	524
Jno	45	m	w	MA	San Francisco	5-Wd San Francisco	81	8
John	50	m	w	NY	San Francisco	7-Wd San Francisco	81	286
John	40	m	w	MA	San Francisco	8-Wd San Francisco	82	309
John	40	m	w	PA	San Francisco	6-Wd San Francisco	81	86
John	38	m	w	IREL	Nevada	Grass Valley Twp	75	176
John	34	m	w	IREL	San Mateo	Redwood Twp	87	366
John	30	m	w	NY	Sonoma	Analy Twp	91	224
Jos	33	m	w	PA	Sacramento	1-Wd Sacramento	77	188
Libius	33	m	w	NY	San Francisco	San Francisco P O	83	165
Luther L Y	69	m	w	MA	Shasta	Fort Crook P O	89	477
Lyman H	41	m	w	OH	Contra Costa	Martinez P O	71	373
Marshal	28	m	w	IA	Contra Costa	Martinez P O	71	441
Mary	51	f	w	OH	Contra Costa	Martinez Twp	71	349
Mary	30	f	w	NY	Yolo	Cottonwood Twp	93	474
Mary	25	f	w	NZEA	San Francisco	7-Wd San Francisco	81	174
May	28	f	w	NZEA	San Francisco	San Francisco P O	83	195
Michael	30	m	w	IREL	San Joaquin	1-Wd Stockton	86	129
Nathl	56	m	w	MA	San Francisco	San Francisco P O	85	731
Saml C	55	m	w	NY	San Francisco	6-Wd San Francisco	81	132
William	38	m	w	OH	Stanislaus	San Joaquin Twp	92	76
William W	21	m	w	CA	Contra Costa	Martinez P O	71	383
Wm	58	m	w	ENGL	Fresno	Millerton P O	72	163
HASTLER								
Josephine	24	f	b	MA	San Francisco	6-Wd San Francisco	81	121
HASTON								
Edward T	24	m	w	MO	Colusa	Colusa	71	298
John	33	m	w	ENGL	Sacramento	2-Wd Sacramento	77	246
Robt	45	m	w	CANA	Alameda	Oakland	68	244
HASTS								
Herman	33	m	w	PRUS	Napa	Napa Twp	75	73
HASTY								
Charles	8	m	w	CA	Humboldt	Eureka Twp	72	278
James	39	m	w	NY	Butte	Ophir Twp	70	117
James C	42	m	w	ME	Butte	Kimshew Tpw	70	77
Robert	42	m	w	SCOT	Contra Costa	Martinez P O	71	445
Wm H	42	m	w	ME	Butte	Kimshew Tpw	70	77
HASUS								
Mattie	35	m	w	MEXI	Yuba	Marysville	93	600
HASWELL								
C E	30	m	w	RI	Tuolumne	Big Oak Flat P O	93	398
Chas S	55	m	w	VT	Sacramento	3-Wd Sacramento	77	289
George C	55	m	w	NY	Sacramento	2-Wd Sacramento	77	210
John C	58	m	w	VT	San Francisco	2-Wd San Francisco	79	195
Wm	25	m	w	OH	Sutter	Nicolaus Twp	92	107
HAT								
Ah	21	m	c	CHIN	Placer	Emigrant Gap P O	76	416
Lip	42	m	c	CHIN	San Joaquin	Liberty Twp	86	97
HATABOUGH								
Wm	27	m	w	IN	San Francisco	11-Wd San Francisc	84	586
HATAWAY								
John	45	m	w	MA	Stanislaus	North Twp	92	67
HATCH								
Abner	27	m	w	ME	San Joaquin	Elkhorn Twp	86	66
Alonzo	16	m	w	MO	Yolo	Grafton Twp	93	498
Angeline	24	f	w	WI	Sacramento	San Joaquin Twp	77	406
Anne	24	f	w	IREL	San Francisco	7-Wd San Francisco	81	231
Annie	74	f	w	TN	Yolo	Grafton Twp	93	487
Arthur	43	m	w	MA	Santa Clara	1-Wd San Jose	88	238
Asa D	56	m	w	ME	San Francisco	8-Wd San Francisco	82	297
C L	27	m	w	NY	San Francisco	3-Wd San Francisco	79	312
Charles M	33	m	w	ME	Calaveras	San Andreas P O	70	213
Charles S	44	m	w	MA	Mariposa	Mariposa P O	74	128
Chas	48	m	w	NY	San Francisco	San Francisco P O	85	838
Chester	10	m	w	CA	Sacramento	4-Wd Sacramento	77	344
Chester P	56	m	w	CT	Sonoma	Petaluma Twp	91	330
Cutter	61	m	w	MA	Humboldt	Pacific Twp	72	289
Dennis	21	m	w	NH	Merced	Snelling P O	74	252
E M	30	m	w	VT	Amador	Sutter Crk P O	69	397
Edward S	26	m	w	NY	Santa Clara	2-Wd San Jose	88	291
Ephraim	38	m	w	VT	Stanislaus	Empire Twp	92	58
F L	47	m	w	AL	Santa Clara	Gilroy Twp	88	68
F W	45	m	w	VA	Sacramento	3-Wd Sacramento	77	306
F W	21	m	w	TX	San Joaquin	2-Wd Stockton	86	172
Frank S	38	m	w	ME	Calaveras	Copperopolis P O	70	256
Ger W	20	m	w	WI	Monterey	Salinas Twp	74	306
H C	37	m	w	ME	San Francisco	7-Wd San Francisco	81	222
Henry L	57	m	w	VT	Nevada	Rough & Ready Twp	75	334
Hiram	39	m	w	NY	Mendocino	Little Lake Twp	74	198
Hiram F	52	m	w	ME	Calaveras	San Andreas P O	70	215
Isaac H	45	m	w	VT	Santa Clara	2-Wd San Jose	88	280
Isaih	52	m	w	MA	Santa Clara	Gilroy Twp	88	100
Jabez	44	m	w	MA	Solano	Benicia	90	18
James	70	m	w	VT	Yolo	Grafton Twp	93	487
James	43	m	w	CANA	San Mateo	Half Moon Bay P O	87	399
James	30	m	w	ME	San Francisco	11-Wd San Francisc	84	519
James D	39	m	w	NY	Placer	Cisco P O	76	494
James H	42	m	w	ME	Mariposa	Mariposa P O	74	134
Jas G	33	m	w	ME	San Francisco	San Francisco P O	83	91
Jennie	14	f	w	CA	Santa Clara	1-Wd San Jose	88	226
John	67	m	w	NH	Sacramento	2-Wd Sacramento	77	236
John	49	m	w	ME	Solano	Vallejo	90	197
Jonathan	30	m	w	OH	Contra Costa	Martinez P O	71	386
Joseph	8	m	w	CA	Santa Clara	San Jose Twp	88	182
Joseph	65	m	w	VT	Santa Cruz	Watsonville	89	373
L L	46	m	w	PA	Napa	Napa	75	2
L S	40	m	w	IL	Alameda	Oakland	68	259
L S	36	m	w	MA	Alameda	Oakland	68	247
Laura	48	f	w	VT	Marin	San Rafael Twp	74	33
Martin P	28	m	w	VT	Nevada	Rough & Ready Twp	75	334
Mary	45	f	w	IREL	San Francisco	7-Wd San Francisco	81	231
Morris W	45	m	w	OH	Mono	Bridgeport P O	74	286
Moses	30	m	w	NY	Yuba	Marysville	93	583
R T	30	m	w	ME	Nevada	Meadow Lake Twp	75	255
Rufus H	39	m	w	NY	San Mateo	Half Moon Bay P O	87	402
S B	43	m	w	NY	Mendocino	Little Lake Twp	74	198
S T	38	m	w	NY	Alameda	Oakland	68	261
Stephen	35	m	w	OH	Monterey	Castroville Twp	74	325
Theo H	36	m	w	ME	San Francisco	8-Wd San Francisco	82	313
W G	44	m	w	VA	Tehama	Red Bluff	92	184
Wallace	32	m	w	NH	San Joaquin	3-Wd Stockton	86	217
Wallace	24	m	w	NY	San Francisco	7-Wd San Francisco	81	175
Wilbur M	18	m	w	ME	El Dorado	Mud Springs Twp	72	83
William	36	m	w	PORT	Marin	San Rafael Twp	74	25
William	25	m	w	MA	San Francisco	7-Wd San Francisco	81	208
William	12	m	w	MO	Yolo	Grafton Twp	93	485
Williard	25	m	w	ME	San Francisco	2-Wd San Francisco	79	161
Wilson	26	m	w	CANA	Sacramento	2-Wd Sacramento	77	247
Wm H	35	m	w	NH	San Francisco	8-Wd San Francisco	82	369
Wm H H	34	m	w	MA	Sacramento	4-Wd Sacramento	77	326
HATCHER								
George	30	m	w	ME	San Francisco	7-Wd San Francisco	81	199
Joseph	37	m	w	ENGL	Nevada	Bloomfield Twp	75	99
Robt	8	m	w	CA	San Francisco	11-Wd San Francisc	84	494
HATE								
John R	38	m	w	VA	Mariposa	Mariposa P O	74	130
HATEN								
Thos	47	m	w	KY	San Joaquin	Oneal Twp	86	119
HATFIELD								
Anna	35	f	w	IREL	San Francisco	San Francisco P O	83	181
Edward L	37	m	w	NY	Los Angeles	Los Angeles	73	568
Hanry	31	m	b	NY	San Francisco	San Francisco P O	80	481
Isaac	32	m	w	ENGL	Santa Cruz	Santa Cruz Twp	89	393
Jno	41	m	w	MO	Sonoma	Mendocino Twp	91	295
Robert	55	m	w	IA	Calaveras	San Andreas P O	70	208
S	27	m	w	NY	San Joaquin	Tulare Twp	86	249
William	38	m	w	NY	Los Angeles	San Juan Twp	73	629
Wm	44	m	w	IN	El Dorado	Coloma Twp	72	3
Wm H	65	m	w	NY	Nevada	Bridgeport Twp	75	103
HATGER								
Godlip	54	m	w	SAXO	Placer	Auburn P O	76	357
HATH								
John C	25	m	w	NY	Yolo	Washington Twp	93	538
John H	42	m	w	PA	Placer	Bath P O	76	422
R Thomas	30	m	w	ME	Placer	Summit P O	76	496
HATHAWAY								
A	28	m	w	MI	Alameda	Oakland	68	146
A H	35	m	w	MA	San Francisco	San Francisco P O	85	784
Alden	31	m	w	MA	Marin	Bolinas Twp	74	1
Andrew	50	m	w	DENM	Sacramento	4-Wd Sacramento	77	361
Ben H	37	m	w	NY	San Francisco	1-Wd San Francisco	79	107
Charles	54	m	w	MA	Solano	Montezuma Twp	90	66
Charles	52	m	w	NORW	Mendocino	Little Rvr Twp	74	170
Charles D	35	m	w	ME	Los Angeles	Los Angeles	73	538
Chas	49	m	w	MA	Alameda	Eden Twp	68	82
Danl F	53	m	w	OH	Santa Barbara	Santa Barbara P O	87	482
E E	34	m	w	MA	Napa	Yountville Twp	75	89
E V	40	m	w	MA	San Francisco	San Francisco P O	83	96
Embira	16	f	w	CA	Tulare	Tule Rvr Twp	92	258
F M	32	m	w	PA	Nevada	Washington Twp	75	341
Fielding	62	m	w	VA	Tulare	Visalia	92	290
Fred	36	m	w	MA	San Francisco	11-Wd San Francisc	84	601
G	30	m	w	PA	Solano	Vallejo	90	194
Geo B	67	m	w	RI	Sonoma	Bodega Twp	91	256
Geo W	60	m	w	MA	Sonoma	Analy Twp	91	236
Hale	43	m	w	KY	San Bernardino	Chino Twp	78	409
Hiram J	37	m	w	NY	Plumas	Indian Twp	77	13
Isaac H	36	m	w	MA	Sacramento	4-Wd Sacramento	77	326
James	41	m	w	TX	San Bernardino	Chino Twp	78	410
James B	30	m	w	NY	Sonoma	Bodega Twp	91	261
Jno	37	m	w	IL	San Joaquin	2-Wd Stockton	86	191
Jno C	58	m	w	MA	Sonoma	Analy Twp	91	235
Job J	23	m	w	MA	San Francisco	San Francisco P O	83	161
John	60	m	w	MA	Sonoma	Bodega Twp	91	259
Joseph B	41	m	w	VT	Plumas	Quartz Twp	77	37
Lysander	54	m	w	MA	Shasta	Shasta P O	89	462
M	35	m	w	MO	San Bernardino	Chino Twp	78	410
Mary C	53	f	w	RI	Mendocino	Point Arena Twp	74	210
Nathan	50	m	w	ME	San Francisco	11-Wd San Francisc	84	603

© 2001 by Heritage Quest. All rights reserved.

Name	Age	S	R	B-PL	County	Locale	Series M593 Roll	Pg
Oromon W	43	m	w	NY	Nevada	Grass Valley Twp	75	147
R B	36	m	w	NH	Sacramento	1-Wd Sacramento	77	178
Russell	44	m	w	NY	Contra Costa	Martinez P O	71	434
S	65	m	w	MA	Solano	Vallejo	90	173
S A	30	m	w	OH	San Joaquin	1-Wd Stockton	86	127
Samuel	39	m	w	IL	Amador	Fiddletown P O	69	438
Sarah	22	f	w	ME	Marin	Tomales Twp	74	76
Stphn K	45	m	w	RI	Sonoma	Petaluma Twp	91	346
Susan	24	f	w	ME	Los Angeles	Wilmington Twp	73	634
Valentine	45	m	w	MA	Napa	Napa Twp	75	29
Welcome	42	m	w	MA	Placer	Auburn P O	76	357
HATHERLAND								
Danl	30	m	w	NY	San Francisco	7-Wd San Francisco	81	234
HATHEWAY								
B R	40	m	w	MA	Sacramento	Natomas Twp	77	170
Charles	40	m	w	MA	San Francisco	San Francisco P O	80	380
Jno W	18	m	w	IN	Shasta	Millville P O	89	492
R W	41	m	w	MA	Tuolumne	Columbia P O	93	336
HATHORNE								
Jacob S	47	m	w	ME	Los Angeles	Los Angeles Twp	73	496
HATHWAY								
Francis	38	m	w	PA	San Francisco	San Francisco P O	83	240
James	64	m	w	RI	Merced	Snelling P O	74	249
HATHWEN								
M	28	m	w	IREL	San Francisco	San Francisco P O	85	786
HATIEBRING								
Henry	35	m	w	PRUS	Alameda	Brooklyn Twp	68	44
HATLAN								
Rebecca	6	f	m	NE	Sacramento	3-Wd Sacramento	77	262
HATLER								
Chas H	25	m	w	MO	Sacramento	4-Wd Sacramento	77	337
HATLEY								
Walter	28	m	w	NY	Sacramento	2-Wd Sacramento	77	210
HATMAN								
Henry	42	m	w	HESS	Calaveras	San Andreas P O	70	160
HATT								
Ah	24	m	c	CHIN	Amador	Jackson P O	69	331
Saml S	22	m	w	NY	San Francisco	5-Wd San Francisco	81	10
HATTABOUGH								
Isaac J	48	m	w	DE	Santa Clara	Santa Clara Twp	88	173
William	26	m	w	IN	San Francisco	11-Wd San Francisc	84	658
HATTEN								
Amanda	52	f	w	SCOT	Placer	Gold Run Twp	76	398
C B	73	m	w	KY	San Joaquin	Elkhorn Twp	86	65
Charles	17	m	w	MO	Sonoma	Analy Twp	91	240
Chas	27	m	w	NY	San Joaquin	2-Wd Stockton	86	212
G R	21	m	w	MO	San Joaquin	Liberty Twp	86	82
John	35	m	w	IREL	Amador	Jackson P O	69	329
Josephine	22	f	w	IA	Butte	Chico Twp	70	21
Sarah	27	f	w	IREL	Tulare	Visalia	92	297
Wm	52	m	w	ENGL	Sonoma	Analy Twp	91	218
HATTER								
Alexander	59	m	w	KY	Santa Cruz	Santa Cruz Twp	89	390
HATTERSLEY								
John	21	m	w	IN	Amador	Amador City P O	69	392
HATTESLEY								
Martha	40	f	w	CANA	San Joaquin	Tulare Twp	86	249
HATTIGAN								
Ellen	5	f	w	ME	Napa	Napa Twp	75	64
HATTIN								
Catherine	27	f	w	IREL	Alameda	Brooklyn	68	28
HATTING								
Elizabeth	40	f	w	PRUS	San Francisco	San Francisco P O	83	327
HATTLE								
Peter G	27	m	w	OH	Napa	Yountville Twp	75	91
HATTON								
David	40	m	w	ENGL	Butte	Chico Twp	70	39
Ellen	24	f	w	MO	Sonoma	Mendocino Twp	91	293
Fanny	12	f	w	CA	Sonoma	Russian Rvr	91	373
James	22	m	w	IREL	Amador	Jackson P O	69	329
Jas	60	m	b	SC	Solano	Vallejo	90	157
John	30	m	w	ME	Butte	Hamilton Twp	70	71
John	30	m	w	IREL	Calaveras	San Andreas P O	70	205
Joseph S	33	m	b	MA	Napa	Napa	75	50
Laura	14	f	w	CA	San Francisco	2-Wd San Francisco	79	280
M	33	m	w	IREL	Amador	Jackson P O	69	330
William	33	m	w	CANA	Santa Clara	1-Wd San Jose	88	257
Wm M	50	m	w	MO	Sonoma	Russian Rvr	91	373
HATZEL								
Charles	43	m	w	WURT	Santa Clara	1-Wd San Jose	88	255
HAUB								
George	30	m	w	HDAR	San Francisco	San Francisco P O	83	415
HAUBERT								
C	53	m	w	PRUS	Napa	Napa Twp	75	28
Jacob	38	m	w	BAVA	Sonoma	Sonoma Twp	91	446
HAUBRICH								
F Wm	36	m	w	PRUS	San Francisco	San Francisco P O	83	91
HAUCH								
Charles	50	m	w	PRUS	San Francisco	San Francisco P O	83	355
HAUCK								
Chris	51	m	w	FRAN	San Francisco	11-Wd San Francisc	84	662
Louis	50	m	w	PRUS	San Francisco	San Francisco P O	80	424
Stephen	48	m	w	PRUS	San Francisco	San Francisco P O	83	168
HAUFF								
Chas A	29	m	w	GERM	San Francisco	8-Wd San Francisco	82	368
HAUFMAN								
Charles	33	m	w	GERM	Santa Clara	1-Wd San Jose	88	229
John	45	m	w	BADE	Santa Clara	1-Wd San Jose	88	230
HAUFMANN								
Leopold	38	m	w	BADE	San Francisco	2-Wd San Francisco	79	240
HAUFORT								
George	40	m	w	BAVA	Sonoma	Petaluma Twp	91	350
HAUFT								
Casper	28	m	w	PRUS	Nevada	Washington Twp	75	340
HAUG								
Ah	52	m	c	CHIN	Placer	Lincoln P O	76	483
Koy	40	m	c	CHIN	Placer	Auburn P O	76	370
HAUGH								
J	30	m	w	ITAL	Sierra	Butte Twp	89	512
Jno A	45	m	w	NY	San Francisco	5-Wd San Francisco	81	36
John	42	m	w	IREL	Yuba	Rose Bar Twp	93	665
HAUGHAN								
James	34	m	w	CANA	Sacramento	American Twp	77	66
HAUGHBY								
Augusta	35	f	w	PRUS	San Francisco	6-Wd San Francisco	81	89
HAUGHLAND								
Errick	48	m	w	SWED	San Francisco	1-Wd San Francisco	79	20
HAUGHT								
Enos	31	m	w	NY	San Diego	San Diego	78	488
Fred	19	m	w	PRUS	Alameda	Oakland	68	195
HAUGHTON								
James	20	m	w	AUSL	San Francisco	1-Wd San Francisco	79	113
W	28	m	w	MO	San Joaquin	2-Wd Stockton	86	205
Watson	47	m	w	CANA	Butte	Kimshew Tpw	70	78
HAUGLIN								
James B	29	m	w	NY	San Francisco	San Francisco P O	83	358
HAUGSE								
Lewis	35	m	w	NORW	Napa	Napa	75	16
HAUHN								
Sarah A	42	f	w	BAVA	El Dorado	Coloma Twp	72	10
HAUKINS								
Vardiman	59	m	w	KY	Solano	Vacaville Twp	90	117
HAUKS								
Harriet	40	f	w	NY	San Francisco	San Francisco P O	83	201
John H	30	m	w	IN	San Francisco	San Francisco P O	83	353
HAULK								
Talk	44	m	c	CHIN	Placer	Bath P O	76	443
HAULY								
Timothy	36	m	w	IREL	Amador	Volcano P O	69	375
HAUM								
---	35	m	c	CHIN	Siskiyou	Yreka Twp	89	668
Ah	54	m	c	CHIN	Calaveras	Copperopolis P O	70	238
Louis	29	m	w	NJ	Sierra	Gibson Twp	89	539
HAUN								
E	33	m	w	CANA	Sierra	Sierra Twp	89	563
J	27	m	w	GERM	Sacramento	1-Wd Sacramento	77	182
M J	12	f	w	CA	Santa Clara	Burnett Twp	88	33
HAUP								
Ah	41	m	c	CHIN	Plumas	Rich Bar Twp	77	8
John	26	m	w	HDAR	San Francisco	1-Wd San Francisco	79	60
John	25	m	w	HDAR	San Francisco	San Francisco P O	80	456
Rudolph	29	m	w	SWIT	San Francisco	8-Wd San Francisco	82	368
Wo	17	m	c	CHIN	San Francisco	1-Wd San Francisco	79	43
HAUPLER								
John	38	m	w	WURT	Alameda	Washington Twp	68	290
HAUPT								
Andreas	46	m	w	WURT	Plumas	Quartz Twp	77	40
Charles	39	m	w	SAXO	Sonoma	Salt Point	91	381
Fredk	35	m	w	PRUS	San Francisco	1-Wd San Francisco	79	120
Gustavus	49	m	w	PRUS	Calaveras	San Andreas P O	70	187
Herman	30	m	w	PRUS	Los Angeles	Los Angeles Twp	73	470
HAUPTMAN								
Fredericka	24	f	w	PRUS	San Francisco	8-Wd San Francisco	82	410
HAUR								
George	19	m	w	PRUS	Solano	Silveyville Twp	90	88
HAURI								
Tomas	24	m	w	ITAL	San Francisco	San Francisco P O	80	472
HAUS								
Benjamin	39	m	w	KY	Calaveras	San Andreas P O	70	160
James O	20	m	w	MA	Los Angeles	Los Angeles	73	543
Keller I	31	m	w	SAXO	Napa	Napa	75	18
Lewis	14	m	w	CA	Sutter	Nicolaus Twp	92	113
Maggie	9	f	i	CA	San Francisco	San Francisco P O	83	342
HAUSBURGH								
John	24	m	w	PRUS	Sacramento	2-Wd Sacramento	77	246
HAUSCH								
Criss	38	m	w	PRUS	Sonoma	Mendocino Twp	91	295
HAUSCHELDT								
Finn	40	m	w	SHOL	Alameda	Eden Twp	68	65
HAUSCHILDS								
John	40	m	w	SHOL	Plumas	Quartz Twp	77	34
HAUSCOM								
William	30	m	w	ME	San Francisco	8-Wd San Francisco	82	410
HAUSE								
Alfred	35	m	w	IREL	Stanislaus	San Joaquin Twp	92	82
Augt	31	m	w	NY	San Francisco	8-Wd San Francisco	82	376
Henry	40	m	w	RI	Los Angeles	Los Angeles	73	513
John L	40	m	w	SWIT	Sacramento	Granite Twp	77	147
HAUSEN								
John O	33	m	w	ME	San Francisco	8-Wd San Francisco	82	444
HAUSER								
Conrad	28	m	w	HDAR	San Francisco	San Francisco P O	80	356
Danl	43	m	w	PA	San Joaquin	Castoria Twp	86	2
David	41	m	w	GERM	Santa Clara	1-Wd San Jose	88	225

© 2001 by Heritage Quest. All rights reserved.

Series M593

Name	Age	S	R	B-PL	County	Locale	Roll	Pg
George	45	m	w	BADE	San Francisco	San Francisco P O	80	427
George	37	m	w	PRUS	Placer	Roseville P O	76	351
George	34	m	w	WURT	Santa Clara	1-Wd San Jose	88	260
George	34	m	w	WURT	Santa Clara	2-Wd San Jose	88	317
J	35	m	w	SWIT	Amador	Jackson P O	69	346
John	73	m	w	PRUS	Placer	Roseville P O	76	354
John	45	m	w	HDAR	San Francisco	San Francisco P O	80	461
Joseph	48	m	w	NY	Placer	Dutch Flat P O	76	406
Julius	23	m	w	BADE	Yolo	Washington Twp	93	530
Mina	23	f	w	WURT	San Francisco	11-Wd San Francisc	84	510
Rudolph	31	m	w	SWIT	San Francisco	8-Wd San Francisco	82	430
Solomon	30	m	w	SWIT	Yolo	Cache Crk Twp	93	424
William	12	m	w	CA	Santa Cruz	Pajaro Twp	89	343
HAUSHILD								
Edward	30	m	w	HANO	San Francisco	7-Wd San Francisco	81	226
HAUSKINS								
John	68	m	w	CANA	Mariposa	Maxwell Crk P O	74	141
HAUSLER								
Fred	29	m	w	WURT	San Francisco	1-Wd San Francisco	79	55
John	32	m	w	SWIT	San Francisco	7-Wd San Francisco	81	248
HAUSMAN								
Charles	40	m	w	SWED	Plumas	Washington Twp	77	54
HAUSS								
Freeman	17	m	w	SHOL	Inyo	Lone Pine Twp	73	330
HAUSSIN								
Christian	35	m	w	MA	Butte	Ophir Twp	70	120
HAUSSLER								
Leonardt	47	m	w	WURT	San Francisco	1-Wd San Francisco	79	104
HAUSSMANN								
Adolph	62	m	w	FRAN	San Francisco	2-Wd San Francisco	79	156
HAUTHY								
Frank	35	m	w	IREL	San Francisco	7-Wd San Francisco	81	172
HAUTIER								
Peter	40	m	w	GERM	Santa Clara	2-Wd San Jose	88	323
HAUTMANN								
Ed	55	m	w	FRAN	San Francisco	2-Wd San Francisco	79	233
HAUX								
Chris The	41	m	w	WURT	Sacramento	4-Wd Sacramento	77	365
HAUXHURST								
Geo	42	m	w	NY	Contra Costa	Martinez P O	71	420
HAVARD								
Eugene	44	m	w	FRAN	Siskiyou	Yreka Twp	89	668
Phineas	43	m	w	MA	San Francisco	11-Wd San Francisc	84	642
Thos D	39	m	w	WALE	Sierra	Sears Twp	89	557
HAVE								
Ah	30	f	c	CHIN	Mariposa	Mariposa P O	74	132
John	22	m	w	ENGL	Fresno	Millerton P O	72	167
Lyman	39	m	w	CT	Sacramento	San Joaquin Twp	77	407
HAVEMOND								
Rebecca	28	f	w	MD	San Francisco	San Francisco P O	83	360
HAVEN								
A L	53	m	w	NH	Alameda	Oakland	68	201
Albert	21	m	w	MA	San Francisco	6-Wd San Francisco	81	96
C B	38	m	w	OH	San Joaquin	Elkhorn Twp	86	53
Conrad	45	m	w	SWIT	Los Angeles	Los Angeles	73	510
E D	30	m	w	IL	San Francisco	3-Wd San Francisco	79	310
Elijah	26	m	w	MI	Nevada	Bloomfield Twp	75	98
Elisha	27	m	w	MI	Nevada	Nevada Twp	75	310
Eugene	30	m	w	IL	San Francisco	11-Wd San Francisc	84	595
George	33	m	w	ME	Marin	Novato Twp	74	11
George D	40	m	w	MO	Tulare	Visalia	92	300
Henry	37	m	w	NH	Sonoma	Santa Rosa	91	412
James	41	m	w	NY	San Francisco	11-Wd San Francisc	84	599
John G	62	m	w	ME	Marin	Novato Twp	74	12
Joktan G	80	m	w	MA	Nevada	Grass Valley Twp	75	204
Lisander	28	m	w	PORT	San Joaquin	2-Wd Stockton	86	172
Mary	30	f	w	IREL	Marin	San Rafael Twp	74	31
P A	52	m	w	NY	Sierra	Butte Twp	89	511
Patrick	31	m	w	IREL	Marin	San Rafael Twp	74	31
Roderick	34	m	w	SC	Tuolumne	Columbia P O	93	353
Wm S	43	m	w	MA	San Francisco	5-Wd San Francisco	81	23
HAVENER								
James	35	m	w	ME	San Francisco	7-Wd San Francisco	81	194
HAVENEY								
Patk	28	m	w	IREL	Solano	Vallejo	90	216
HAVENS								
Henry T	51	m	w	NY	San Francisco	7-Wd San Francisco	81	236
Howard	50	m	w	NY	San Francisco	8-Wd San Francisco	82	299
J F	58	m	w	NY	Alameda	Oakland	68	157
John	47	m	w	CANA	San Diego	San Diego	78	488
John H	36	m	w	NJ	Los Angeles	Los Angeles Twp	73	488
Sam	25	m	w	IN	San Joaquin	2-Wd Stockton	86	179
William	40	m	w	NY	Sacramento	4-Wd Sacramento	77	370
HAVER								
C D	33	m	w	NY	Alameda	Oakland	68	208
Daniel	51	m	w	NY	San Mateo	San Mateo P O	87	355
William H	29	m	w	OH	Santa Cruz	Pajaro Twp	89	340
HAVERCOST								
John	17	m	w	HI	Butte	Oregon Twp	70	126
HAVERGY								
M J	20	m	w	MA	San Francisco	San Francisco P O	85	869
HAVERIN								
Mary C	25	f	w	NY	San Francisco	San Francisco P O	83	50
HAVERLIN								
Mark	25	m	w	IREL	Santa Barbara	Santa Barbara P O	87	492
HAVERSON								
John	31	m	w	HANO	San Francisco	1-Wd San Francisco	79	124
HAVERTICK								
George	42	m	w	PA	Amador	Volcano P O	69	373
HAVERTON								
Edwd	39	m	w	ENGL	San Francisco	1-Wd San Francisco	79	98
HAVERTY								
Ann	27	f	w	IREL	San Francisco	San Francisco P O	83	115
John	30	m	w	IREL	Santa Clara	Fremont Twp	88	45
Thomas	22	m	w	MA	Amador	Amador City P O	69	390
HAVEY								
Bernard	28	m	w	IREL	San Francisco	San Francisco P O	83	137
Christopher	50	m	w	IREL	Inyo	Cerro Gordo Twp	73	320
Elizabeth	16	f	w	CT	San Francisco	8-Wd San Francisco	82	418
Isrod J	53	m	w	IN	Monterey	Salinas Twp	74	307
James	44	m	w	IREL	Contra Costa	San Pablo Twp	71	354
James	18	m	w	IREL	Contra Costa	Martinez Twp	71	346
John	21	m	w	NJ	Yuba	Rose Bar Twp	93	661
Patrick	56	m	w	IREL	Yuba	Rose Bar Twp	93	658
Rosa	23	f	w	IREL	Yuba	Rose Bar Twp	93	659
William	40	m	w	IREL	San Mateo	Redwood Twp	87	362
HAVIAL								
Romero	56	m	w	CA	Marin	Bolinas Twp	74	2
HAVIEL								
Francisco	30	m	w	SCOT	San Luis Obispo	San Luis Obispo Tw	87	297
HAVIL								
Joseph F	22	m	w	PORT	Inyo	Cerro Gordo Twp	73	321
HAVILAND								
James T	51	m	w	NY	San Francisco	6-Wd San Francisco	81	87
HAVILLO								
Jesus	46	m	w	OH	Marin	San Rafael Twp	74	37
HAVILO								
Bernardo	34	m	w	MEXI	San Francisco	San Francisco P O	80	466
HAVING								
Agnus	32	f	w	IL	San Joaquin	2-Wd Stockton	86	163
HAVINS								
G W	54	m	w	NY	San Joaquin	1-Wd Stockton	86	121
HAVLEY								
Wm	20	m	w	ME	Sacramento	3-Wd Sacramento	77	286
HAVLIN								
Thomas	44	m	w	BAVA	San Francisco	2-Wd San Francisco	79	140
HAVNER								
---	20	m	w	CT	San Francisco	7-Wd San Francisco	81	250
HAVON								
George A	30	m	w	MO	Tulare	Visalia Twp	92	284
HAVRE								
---	32	m	w	FRAN	San Francisco	11-Wd San Francisc	84	592
HAW								
Ah	43	m	c	CHIN	Amador	Volcano P O	69	387
Ah	42	m	c	CHIN	San Francisco	San Francisco P O	80	499
Ah	37	m	c	CHIN	San Francisco	6-Wd San Francisco	81	63
Ah	33	m	c	CHIN	Placer	Bath P O	76	442
Ah	32	m	c	CHIN	Yuba	W Bear Rvr Twp	93	682
Ah	30	m	c	CHIN	San Francisco	3-Wd San Francisco	79	302
Ah	30	m	c	CHIN	San Francisco	1-Wd San Francisco	79	85
Ah	28	m	c	CHIN	San Francisco	11-Wd San Francisc	84	527
Ah	27	m	c	CHIN	San Francisco	San Francisco P O	83	285
Ah	26	m	c	CHIN	Santa Clara	Gilroy Twp	88	81
Ah	26	m	c	CHIN	Shasta	French Gulch P O	89	470
Ah	25	m	c	CHIN	Santa Clara	Gilroy Twp	88	81
Ah	24	m	c	CHIN	Shasta	French Gulch P O	89	467
Ah	22	m	c	CHIN	San Francisco	6-Wd San Francisco	81	54
Ah	22	m	c	CHIN	San Francisco	6-Wd San Francisco	81	39
Ah	22	m	c	CHIN	San Francisco	6-Wd San Francisco	81	45
Ah	21	m	c	CHIN	San Francisco	6-Wd San Francisco	81	67
Ah	19	f	c	CHIN	San Francisco	San Francisco P O	80	438
Ah	17	m	c	CHIN	Santa Clara	Santa Clara Twp	88	158
Ah	11	m	c	CHIN	San Francisco	San Francisco P O	83	367
Gee	30	m	c	CHIN	Plumas	Mineral Twp	77	23
Ha	22	m	c	CHIN	San Francisco	6-Wd San Francisco	81	46
Ha	18	m	c	CHIN	San Francisco	San Francisco P O	83	113
Lee	28	f	c	CHIN	San Francisco	6-Wd San Francisco	81	52
Muck	35	m	c	CHIN	Yuba	Marysville	93	601
Richard	21	m	w	ENGL	San Francisco	San Francisco P O	83	370
Robt A	40	m	w	IREL	Humboldt	Bucksport Twp	72	245
Tem	35	m	c	CHIN	Yuba	Marysville	93	623
William	27	m	w	ENGL	Contra Costa	Martinez P O	71	403
Ye	20	f	c	CHIN	Yuba	Rose Bar Twp	93	655
HAWA								
Saml A	34	m	w	NY	Placer	Gold Run Twp	76	395
HAWARD								
Stephen	37	m	w	NY	Tuolumne	Sonora P O	93	329
HAWBER								
John	27	m	w	IREL	San Joaquin	2-Wd Stockton	86	172
HAWBERRY								
John	45	m	w	IREL	San Francisco	San Francisco P O	83	213
HAWE								
Thomas	25	m	w	IREL	Sonoma	Bodega Twp	91	262
HAWEL								
Wm	45	m	w	IL	San Joaquin	Liberty Twp	86	86
HAWELKE								
Edwin	33	m	w	PRUS	San Francisco	San Francisco P O	83	349
HAWES								
Alexr	30	m	w	NY	San Francisco	5-Wd San Francisco	81	26
Alfred	36	m	w	NY	Mariposa	Mariposa P O	74	117
Daniel M	52	m	w	PA	Yolo	Washington Twp	93	533
Eben	50	m	w	MA	San Francisco	2-Wd San Francisco	79	178
Elijah	43	m	w	ME	San Francisco	San Francisco P O	83	84
Eunice	13	f	w	CA	Placer	Roseville P O	76	356

© 2001 by Heritage Quest. All rights reserved.

California 1870 Census

Name	Age	S	R	B-PL	County	Locale	Roll	Pg
Francis	40	m	w	IL	San Bernardino	San Bernardino Twp	78	434
Francis	40	m	w	NY	San Bernardino	San Bernardino Twp	78	434
Geo H	20	m	w	MA	Alameda	Oakland	68	179
J E	39	m	w	CANA	Alameda	Oakland	68	137
James E	60	m	w	KY	Siskiyou	Yreka Twp	89	668
Madison	61	m	w	ME	Alameda	Brooklyn Twp	68	49
Mary E	10	f	w	CA	Los Angeles	Los Nietos Twp	73	578
Pierce	18	m	w	PA	Tulare	Kings Rvr Twp	92	252
R S	48	m	w	NY	Nevada	Eureka Twp	75	139
Valentine C	37	m	w	ME	Nevada	Rough & Ready Twp	75	333
Wm	45	m	w	NH	San Francisco	San Francisco P O	85	866
Wm	34	m	w	NY	Shasta	Millville P O	89	483
HAWETH								
Henry	15	m	w	CA	Mariposa	Maxwell Crk P O	74	142
HAWEY								
Chas	44	m	w	ENGL	San Francisco	11-Wd San Francisc	84	607
Lizzie	22	f	w	NY	San Francisco	5-Wd San Francisco	81	33
Lona	45	m	w	ENGL	Sacramento	3-Wd Sacramento	77	309
HAWITT								
Frank	28	m	w	RI	Contra Costa	Martinez P O	71	384
HAWK								
Ah	46	m	c	CHIN	Nevada	Nevada Twp	75	292
Ah	32	m	c	CHIN	Placer	Bath P O	76	440
Foan	50	m	c	CHIN	Klamath	Orleans Twp	73	380
Geo	60	m	w	ENGL	Monterey	Alisal Twp	74	299
James	55	m	b	VA	Sacramento	Cosumnes Twp	77	88
John	50	m	w	BADE	Yolo	Merritt Twp	93	507
John	19	m	w	ENGL	Plumas	Quartz Twp	77	34
John N	33	m	w	IN	Plumas	Quartz Twp	77	41
Nathan	46	m	w	IN	Yolo	Washington Twp	93	536
Peter	39	m	w	NY	Napa	Napa	75	43
William H	20	m	w	NH	Yolo	Merritt Twp	93	505
HAWKE								
C W	24	f	w	MA	Sacramento	3-Wd Sacramento	77	305
John	50	m	w	ENGL	Nevada	Nevada Twp	75	308
HAWKEN								
John	42	m	w	ENGL	Tuolumne	Sonora P O	93	327
HAWKER								
William	23	m	w	PRUS	San Mateo	Half Moon Bay P O	87	406
HAWKES								
Edward	39	m	w	VT	Alameda	Oakland	68	153
Eugene	34	m	w	ME	Yuba	Rose Bar Twp	93	653
F F	36	m	w	ME	Yuba	Rose Bar Twp	93	653
HAWKIN								
Joseph	23	m	w	ENGL	Nevada	Grass Valley Twp	75	217
HAWKINGS								
Jos P	40	m	w	CANA	San Francisco	8-Wd San Francisco	82	298
M S H	45	m	w	ENGL	San Francisco	San Francisco P O	83	151
HAWKINS								
A B	65	m	w	KY	Sacramento	American Twp	77	69
Abraham	22	m	w	MO	Colusa	Colusa Twp	71	280
Alice	25	f	w	IREL	Placer	Bath P O	76	427
Arculus	62	m	w	KY	Solano	Vacaville Twp	90	126
Augustine	43	m	w	OH	Siskiyou	Yreka	89	656
Azanox	40	m	w	NY	Tehama	Tehama Twp	92	196
B B	55	m	w	OH	Sonoma	Bodega Twp	91	252
B F	42	m	w	MO	Marin	San Rafael Twp	74	42
Bart	50	m	w	ENGL	Fresno	Millerton P O	72	166
Benj B	55	m	w	OH	Shasta	Fort Crook P O	89	476
C G	50	m	w	DC	Amador	Sutter Crk P O	69	401
Chas	23	m	w	MEXI	Napa	Napa	75	17
Cory	39	m	w	RI	Marin	San Rafael	74	55
Creth	25	m	w	KY	Solano	Vacaville Twp	90	126
Daniel R	25	m	w	OH	Alpine	Markleeville P O	69	312
Devine	25	m	w	TN	Santa Clara	Fremont Twp	88	61
Duff G	32	m	w	MO	Sonoma	Healdsburg & Mendo	91	279
E	30	f	w	PA	Yuba	Marysville	93	584
Elizabeth	26	f	w	PA	San Francisco	2-Wd San Francisco	79	234
Frank	30	m	w	CA	Merced	Snelling P O	74	277
Frank	28	m	w	MA	Solano	Vallejo	90	139
Fredrick	32	m	w	IREL	San Francisco	7-Wd San Francisco	81	221
Geo	45	m	w	IL	Santa Clara	Burnett Twp	88	33
Geo	29	m	w	MO	San Joaquin	2-Wd Stockton	86	176
George	57	m	w	SPAI	Placer	Bath P O	76	455
George	48	m	b	NY	Napa	Napa	75	34
George	38	m	w	DC	Alameda	Alameda	68	12
George	35	m	w	MO	Solano	Vacaville Twp	90	123
George	28	m	w	IREL	Plumas	Quartz Twp	77	44
George C	25	m	w	RI	San Mateo	Woodside P O	87	384
H	30	m	w	NY	Monterey	Alisal Twp	74	304
H	25	m	w	MI	Alameda	Alameda	68	13
H	22	m	w	MO	Lake	Morgan Valley	73	425
H B	22	m	w	MO	Solano	Vallejo	90	205
Henry	26	m	w	HANO	San Francisco	7-Wd San Francisco	81	218
Henry	26	m	w	NY	Marin	Novato Twp	74	9
Henry A	45	m	w	RI	Los Angeles	Los Angeles Twp	73	465
Henry P	37	m	w	VA	Santa Cruz	Santa Cruz Twp	89	380
Hugh J	25	m	w	NY	Santa Cruz	Santa Cruz	89	408
Isaac	46	m	w	CANA	Marin	San Rafael Twp	74	38
J	24	m	w	MO	Lake	Morgan Valley	73	425
J N	31	m	w	IN	Sierra	Eureka Twp	89	524
J W	40	m	w	MA	San Joaquin	1-Wd Stockton	86	153
Jacob	38	m	w	KY	San Joaquin	1-Wd Stockton	86	127
James	69	m	w	IREL	San Francisco	8-Wd San Francisco	82	469
James	45	m	w	ENGL	Trinity	Weaverville Pct	92	231
James	37	m	w	KY	Nevada	Washington Twp	75	344
James	29	m	w	ENGL	Placer	Dutch Flat P O	76	402
James	26	m	w	IREL	San Francisco	1-Wd San Francisco	79	94
James E	35	m	w	MO	Humboldt	Pacific Twp	72	293
James O	28	m	w	IA	Santa Clara	2-Wd San Jose	88	279
John	45	m	w	OH	Solano	Vacaville Twp	90	130
John	40	m	w	IREL	El Dorado	Salmon Falls Twp	72	132
John	39	m	w	KY	Amador	Volcano P O	69	382
John	35	m	w	VA	San Francisco	7-Wd San Francisco	81	179
John	30	m	w	MO	Monterey	San Juan Twp	74	404
John	29	m	w	ENGL	Nevada	Nevada Twp	75	309
John	24	m	w	ENGL	San Francisco	1-Wd San Francisco	79	119
John L	39	m	w	OH	Marin	San Rafael Twp	74	37
John P	50	m	w	NY	San Francisco	8-Wd San Francisco	82	319
Jos P	40	m	w	CANA	San Francisco	8-Wd San Francisco	82	298
Joseph	67	m	w	VA	Sonoma	Mendocino Twp	91	294
Joseph	39	m	w	CANA	San Francisco	San Francisco P O	80	385
Julia	22	f	w	ENGL	San Francisco	5-Wd San Francisco	81	25
Levy	34	m	w	ENGL	San Francisco	7-Wd San Francisco	81	228
Lizzie	26	f	w	IREL	San Francisco	1-Wd San Francisco	79	94
M	27	m	w	NY	Sierra	Sierra Twp	89	566
Marion	39	m	w	NY	Inyo	Lone Pine Twp	73	332
Mary	73	f	w	OH	Santa Clara	2-Wd San Jose	88	279
Mary	45	f	w	IREL	Alpine	Woodfords P O	69	315
Mary	35	f	w	KY	San Joaquin	2-Wd Stockton	86	163
Mary	30	f	w	IL	Sonoma	Santa Rosa	91	427
Mary	20	f	w	MA	San Francisco	11-Wd San Francisc	84	514
May	30	f	b	MO	Amador	Sutter Crk P O	69	397
Mudgett	40	f	w	CANA	Humboldt	Eureka Twp	72	258
Nathan	30	m	w	PRUS	San Francisco	5-Wd San Francisco	81	31
Nettie	2	f	w	CA	Napa	Napa Twp	75	67
Nich	58	m	w	KY	Santa Clara	Gilroy Twp	88	101
Olva	19	f	w	CA	Monterey	Pajaro Twp	74	373
Pat	41	m	w	IREL	San Francisco	2-Wd San Francisco	79	221
Patrick	26	m	w	IREL	Nevada	Grass Valley Twp	75	213
Ralph	38	m	w	TN	San Francisco	11-Wd San Francisc	84	520
Richd	46	m	w	ENGL	Fresno	Millerton P O	72	166
Rose	51	f	w	IREL	San Joaquin	1-Wd Stockton	86	152
Rufus	27	m	w	MO	Tulare	Farmersville Twp	92	245
S	60	m	w	KY	Sacramento	3-Wd Sacramento	77	315
Samuel A	36	m	w	NY	Alpine	Monitor P O	69	313
Sarah	16	f	w	CA	Alameda	San Leandro	68	93
Susan	43	f	w	HDAR	San Francisco	11-Wd San Francisc	84	628
Telford	22	m	w	MO	Sonoma	Analy Twp	91	240
Thomas	34	m	w	MO	Tulare	Tule Rvr Twp	92	269
Thomas	29	m	w	ME	Monterey	Pajaro Twp	74	377
Thomas H	2	m	w	CA	Tulare	Tule Rvr Twp	92	265
Thos	33	m	w	KY	Monterey	San Juan Twp	74	406
Thos	30	m	w	IREL	Alameda	Murray Twp	68	113
Walter	76	m	w	NY	San Francisco	11-Wd San Francisc	84	630
William	38	m	w	SCOT	San Francisco	San Francisco P O	83	293
William	30	m	w	CANA	Sacramento	2-Wd Sacramento	77	207
William J	45	m	w	NY	Yolo	Grafton Twp	93	495
Wm	55	m	w	RI	San Francisco	San Francisco P O	83	88
Wm	38	m	w	KY	Santa Barbara	San Buenaventura P	87	420
Wm	37	m	w	IL	San Joaquin	3-Wd Stockton	86	216
Wm	21	m	w	ME	San Francisco	7-Wd San Francisco	81	234
Wm H	9	m	w	CA	El Dorado	Placerville Twp	72	96
HAWKINSON								
James	58	m	w	NJ	Merced	Snelling P O	74	257
HAWKS								
A A	48	m	w	CA	Humboldt	Table Bluff Twp	72	307
Carrie M	19	f	w	NY	Trinity	Lewiston Pct	92	213
Catherine	28	f	w	IREL	Alameda	Brooklyn Twp	68	53
Harry D	12	m	w	CA	San Francisco	San Francisco P O	83	200
James	50	m	w	NY	Sacramento	Sutter Twp	77	383
Louisa	56	f	w	NY	Santa Clara	San Jose Twp	88	183
Miner	52	m	w	OH	Alameda	Eden Twp	68	66
Robt	27	m	w	IREL	San Francisco	San Francisco P O	83	271
HAWLAND								
Eli	38	m	w	OH	Del Norte	Crescent Twp	71	456
HAWLETT								
Wm	30	m	w	ENGL	Alameda	Oakland	68	133
HAWLEY								
Abe	22	m	w	IL	Butte	Chico Twp	70	34
Agustus S	42	m	w	CT	Placer	Rocklin Twp	76	468
Albert T	38	m	w	KY	Santa Cruz	Santa Cruz	89	405
Alexander	47	m	w	KY	Solano	Rio Vista Twp	90	59
Anna	15	f	w	CA	Humboldt	Eureka Twp	72	271
Anne	75	f	w	IREL	San Francisco	11-Wd San Francisc	84	497
Asa H	57	m	w	VT	El Dorado	Lake Valley Twp	72	63
Ashbel D	47	m	w	VT	Yolo	Cache Crk Twp	93	446
B F	39	m	w	KY	Nevada	Meadow Lake Twp	75	261
C B	38	m	w	CANA	Nevada	Bloomfield Twp	75	99
Chas	34	m	w	CT	San Francisco	7-Wd San Francisco	81	235
Chas J	41	m	w	CANA	San Francisco	San Francisco P O	83	160
D N	46	m	w	CT	San Francisco	San Francisco P O	83	274
David	33	m	w	CANA	Humboldt	Eel Rvr Twp	72	249
E R	53	m	w	OH	San Francisco	San Francisco P O	83	82
Elijah H	28	m	w	CT	Santa Clara	2-Wd San Jose	88	325
Eliza	17	f	w	LA	Humboldt	Table Bluff Twp	72	309
Ernest	11	m	w	NV	Sonoma	Sonoma Twp	91	442
Frank	31	m	w	IA	San Francisco	5-Wd San Francisco	81	23
Geo T	30	m	w	MA	San Francisco	San Francisco P O	83	99
Hattie	7	f	w	CA	Sonoma	Russian Rvr	91	378
Horace H	49	m	w	CT	Marin	Point Reyes Twp	74	23
Isaac	34	m	w	MO	San Bernardino	San Bernardino Twp	78	424
J Frank	26	m	w	SC	San Diego	San Diego	78	511
Jacob	49	m	w	VT	San Francisco	San Francisco P O	85	842

Series M593

© 2001 by Heritage Quest. All rights reserved.

Name	Age	S	R	B-PL	County	Locale (Series M593)	Roll	Pg
James	48	m	w	IREL	San Francisco	11-Wd San Francisc	84	497
James	48	m	w	ENGL	Alameda	Alvarado	68	304
James	42	m	w	OH	Nevada	Washington Twp	75	344
James	25	m	w	CANA	Stanislaus	San Joaquin Twp	92	79
Jas	39	m	w	IL	San Joaquin	3-Wd Stockton	86	217
Joel F	37	m	w	NC	Stanislaus	Empire Twp	92	55
John	28	m	w	IN	Tehama	Tehama Twp	92	193
John M	51	m	w	NY	Los Angeles	San Gabriel Twp	73	595
L H	36	m	w	CT	Santa Clara	Gilroy Twp	88	74
Marks	21	m	w	SHOL	Yolo	Putah Twp	93	524
Mary	13	f	w	NY	San Mateo	San Mateo P O	87	371
Nathan	45	m	w	NY	San Francisco	11-Wd San Francisc	84	628
Niram	62	m	w	VT	Siskiyou	Yreka	89	659
Oscar T	39	m	w	CANA	Placer	Colfax P O	76	384
W N	40	m	w	CT	San Francisco	San Francisco P O	83	289
William	28	m	w	OH	Solano	Silveyville Twp	90	72
Wm	18	m	w	MO	Nevada	Nevada Twp	75	271
HAWLY								
Patrick	42	m	w	IREL	San Francisco	San Francisco P O	83	45
Wm	51	m	w	VT	Yuba	Marysville	93	576
HAWN								
Henry C	28	m	w	IL	Inyo	Bishop Crk Twp	73	312
HAWORTH								
Abraham	35	m	w	ENGL	Yuba	Parks Bar Twp	93	648
James	50	m	w	ENGL	Yolo	Washington Twp	93	537
James	47	m	w	ENGL	Yuba	Marysville	93	605
Richard	40	m	w	ENGL	Santa Barbara	San Buenaventura P	87	435
Thomas	62	m	w	ENGL	Yuba	Parks Bar Twp	93	648
HAWPE								
John	50	m	w	VA	Tulare	Visalia Twp	92	280
HAWRITE								
H	41	m	w	ITAL	San Joaquin	3-Wd Stockton	86	231
HAWS								
Ah	17	m	c	CHIN	San Francisco	6-Wd San Francisco	81	66
Artemus	71	m	w	OH	Mariposa	Maxwell Crk P O	74	147
Betsey	48	f	w	NH	Santa Clara	Santa Clara Twp	88	136
Fred R	40	m	w	ME	El Dorado	Georgetown Twp	72	47
Oliver	30	m	w	MA	Alameda	Oakland	68	163
HAWSER								
George	40	m	w	WURT	Inyo	Lone Pine Twp	73	332
HAWTEN								
N H	30	m	w	ENGL	Sierra	Butte Twp	89	511
HAWTHORN								
Augustus	50	f	w	ME	Los Angeles	Los Angeles Twp	73	470
B A	34	m	w	ME	Klamath	Trinidad Twp	73	389
Chas	22	m	w	LA	San Francisco	7-Wd San Francisco	81	228
M	34	f	w	IREL	Yuba	Marysville	93	593
HAWTHORNE								
Danel M	28	m	w	NY	San Francisco	8-Wd San Francisco	82	382
Henry	37	m	w	ME	San Francisco	San Francisco P O	83	64
Hix	40	m	w	NY	San Francisco	5-Wd San Francisco	81	14
HAWTON								
Ann	37	f	w	NY	San Francisco	5-Wd San Francisco	81	11
David	26	m	w	IREL	Nevada	Meadow Lake Twp	75	252
HAWVER								
C	8	f	w	CA	Los Angeles	Los Angeles	73	570
Dewitt	60	m	w	OH	Colusa	Grand Island Twp	71	304
M J	12	f	w	CA	Los Angeles	Los Angeles	73	570
Micholas	40	m	w	BELG	El Dorado	Diamond Springs Tw	72	34
HAWWORTH								
Henry	34	m	w	PA	Calaveras	San Andreas P O	70	199
HAXE								
George I	37	m	w	PRUS	San Francisco	8-Wd San Francisco	82	427
HAXHALL								
Henry	50	m	w	PA	Kern	Tehachapi P O	73	355
HAXON								
W M	43	m	w	ENGL	Alameda	Alameda	68	5
HAXTON								
Minnie	18	f	w	NY	San Francisco	7-Wd San Francisco	81	285
HAY								
---	26	m	c	CHIN	Siskiyou	Yreka Twp	89	666
---	15	m	c	CHIN	Siskiyou	Yreka Twp	89	669
Ah	68	m	c	CHIN	Calaveras	Copperopolis P O	70	255
Ah	57	m	c	CHIN	Sacramento	Granite Twp	77	139
Ah	53	m	c	CHIN	Trinity	Lewiston Pct	92	213
Ah	44	m	c	CHIN	Sacramento	Granite Twp	77	137
Ah	42	m	c	CHIN	San Francisco	6-Wd San Francisco	81	57
Ah	41	m	c	CHIN	Santa Cruz	Pajaro Twp	89	344
Ah	40	m	c	CHIN	Yolo	Cache Crk Twp	93	437
Ah	40	m	c	CHIN	Placer	Rocklin Twp	76	464
Ah	40	m	c	CHIN	Sacramento	Natomas Twp	77	171
Ah	40	m	c	CHIN	Sierra	Table Rock Twp	89	571
Ah	40	m	c	CHIN	Mendocino	Point Arena Twp	74	208
Ah	40	m	c	CHIN	Sacramento	Granite Twp	77	138
Ah	40	m	c	CHIN	Plumas	Goodwin Twp	77	2
Ah	38	m	c	CHIN	Solano	Vallejo	90	139
Ah	38	m	c	CHIN	Sacramento	Granite Twp	77	138
Ah	35	m	c	CHIN	Stanislaus	North Twp	92	68
Ah	35	m	c	CHIN	Placer	Bath P O	76	444
Ah	34	m	c	CHIN	San Joaquin	Oneal Twp	86	116
Ah	32	m	c	CHIN	San Francisco	6-Wd San Francisco	81	39
Ah	31	m	c	CHIN	Nevada	Meadow Lake Twp	75	251
Ah	31	m	c	CHIN	Sacramento	Dry Crk Twp	77	104
Ah	30	m	c	CHIN	Trinity	Douglas	92	237
Ah	30	m	c	CHIN	Tuolumne	Chinese Camp P O	93	380
Ah	30	m	c	CHIN	Los Angeles	Los Angeles	73	564
Ah	29	m	c	CHIN	Butte	Hamilton Twp	70	68
Ah	29	m	c	CHIN	Butte	Mountain Spring Tw	70	89
Ah	28	m	c	CHIN	Sacramento	Cosumnes Twp	77	89
Ah	27	m	c	CHIN	Sonoma	Salt Point	91	380
Ah	27	m	c	CHIN	Trinity	Junction City Pct	92	206
Ah	27	m	c	CHIN	Amador	Jackson P O	69	332
Ah	26	m	c	CHIN	Yuba	Marysville Twp	93	569
Ah	25	m	c	CHIN	Yolo	Putah Twp	93	515
Ah	25	m	c	CHIN	Yolo	Grafton Twp	93	479
Ah	25	m	c	CHIN	Mendocino	Point Arena Twp	74	205
Ah	25	m	c	CHIN	Yuba	Marysville	93	605
Ah	24	m	c	CHIN	Amador	Jackson P O	69	338
Ah	22	m	c	CHIN	Los Angeles	Los Angeles	73	527
Ah	21	m	c	CHIN	Merced	Snelling P O	74	256
Ah	20	m	c	CHIN	El Dorado	Diamond Springs Tw	72	35
Ah	20	f	c	CHIN	Sacramento	Granite Twp	77	152
Ah	19	m	c	CHIN	Marin	San Rafael Twp	74	45
Ah	19	m	c	CHIN	Nevada	Bloomfield Twp	75	98
Ah	18	m	c	CHIN	San Mateo	San Mateo P O	87	355
Ah	16	f	c	CHIN	San Francisco	San Francisco P O	80	440
Ah	16	m	c	CHIN	Santa Cruz	Santa Cruz Twp	89	388
Ah	14	f	c	CHIN	Solano	Vallejo	90	176
Alex	35	m	w	CANA	San Francisco	7-Wd San Francisco	81	246
Alexander	30	m	w	SCOT	San Francisco	11-Wd San Francisc	84	632
Alfred	47	m	w	KY	San Francisco	2-Wd San Francisco	79	203
Allen	38	m	w	ENGL	Santa Clara	Redwood Twp	88	130
August	60	m	w	FRAN	San Francisco	San Francisco P O	80	483
Ban	36	m	c	CHIN	San Francisco	11-Wd San Francisc	84	574
Catherine	32	f	w	IREL	San Diego	San Diego	78	510
David C	30	m	w	SCOT	Mariposa	Maxwell Crk P O	74	144
H P	30	m	w	AR	San Joaquin	3-Wd Stockton	86	240
Henry	52	m	w	FRAN	El Dorado	Placerville	72	117
Henry	31	m	w	PA	Nevada	Bridgeport Twp	75	120
James	44	m	w	SCOT	Yolo	Washington Twp	93	528
James	39	m	w	ENGL	Nevada	Nevada Twp	75	301
James	38	m	w	SCOT	Marin	San Rafael	74	48
James	36	m	w	ENGL	San Joaquin	Tulare Twp	86	252
James	13	m	w	MO	Sonoma	Mendocino Twp	91	291
Jno	35	m	w	NY	San Francisco	5-Wd San Francisco	81	19
John	40	m	w	IREL	Sonoma	Vallejo Twp	91	461
John	40	m	w	MA	Solano	Denverton Twp	90	23
John	37	m	w	ENGL	San Joaquin	Tulare Twp	86	252
John	34	m	w	SCOT	Contra Costa	Martinez P O	71	419
John	30	m	w	ENGL	Solano	Vallejo	90	174
John	27	m	w	ME	San Francisco	7-Wd San Francisco	81	243
John	24	m	w	OH	Solano	Vacaville Twp	90	122
John	24	m	w	IREL	Solano	Silveyville Twp	90	90
Josephine	23	f	w	IN	Yuba	Marysville	93	588
Kate	45	f	w	IREL	San Francisco	1-Wd San Francisco	79	3
Lee	30	m	c	CHIN	Sacramento	1-Wd Sacramento	77	198
Lee	25	m	c	CHIN	Alameda	Washington Twp	68	288
Leng	38	m	c	CHIN	San Francisco	11-Wd San Francisc	84	574
Lewis	28	m	w	PA	San Francisco	3-Wd San Francisco	79	297
Long	26	m	c	CHIN	Solano	Green Valley Twp	90	43
M A	35	m	w	IREL	Tuolumne	Columbia P O	93	355
Song	48	m	c	CHIN	Nevada	Nevada Twp	75	313
Thomas	36	m	w	CANA	Alpine	Silver Mtn P O	69	307
William	34	m	w	IREL	Solano	Vacaville Twp	90	123
William	28	m	w	IREL	Solano	Silveyville Twp	90	81
William	23	m	w	IREL	San Francisco	3-Wd San Francisco	79	308
William G	40	m	w	GA	Santa Cruz	Santa Cruz	89	414
Wm	48	m	w	MO	Santa Clara	Almaden Twp	88	19
Won	29	f	c	CHIN	Yuba	Marysville	93	627
Won	24	f	c	CHIN	Klamath	Sawyers Bar	73	378
HAYARD								
A	63	m	w	NY	San Joaquin	Dent Twp	86	25
J D	30	m	w	OH	Alameda	Oakland	68	135
HAYAS								
Henry	46	m	w	ENGL	Tuolumne	Chinese Camp P O	93	374
HAYBURG								
John J	43	m	w	SCOT	Mendocino	Cuffeys Cove Twp	74	169
HAYBURN								
Jas C	47	m	w	PA	San Francisco	San Francisco P O	83	20
Sophie	20	f	w	BAVA	San Francisco	8-Wd San Francisco	82	480
HAYCOCK								
James F	42	m	w	ENGL	San Francisco	6-Wd San Francisco	81	152
Jennette	43	f	w	NY	Santa Clara	Redwood Twp	88	133
Job	30	m	w	WALE	Contra Costa	Martinez P O	71	428
Thomas	44	m	w	CANA	Plumas	Mineral Twp	77	23
HAYCROFF								
Elser	35	m	w	GERM	Yolo	Grafton Twp	93	492
HAYCROFT								
J W	21	m	w	RI	San Francisco	7-Wd San Francisco	81	223
HAYDE								
Martina	39	f	w	CA	Monterey	Monterey	74	359
HAYDEN								
A	25	f	w	IREL	San Joaquin	2-Wd Stockton	86	162
Amaziah	55	m	w	ME	Marin	Novato Twp	74	11
Andrew	42	m	w	PRUS	San Joaquin	3-Wd Stockton	86	246
Benj F	34	m	w	MA	San Francisco	San Francisco P O	85	874
C	45	m	w	CT	San Joaquin	Douglas Twp	86	41
C C	53	m	w	MA	Sacramento	1-Wd Sacramento	77	174
Catherine	59	f	w	KY	Santa Cruz	Santa Cruz	89	426
Charles	23	m	w	MO	San Mateo	Half Moon Bay P O	87	399
Charles M	36	m	w	IREL	Los Angeles	Los Angeles	73	521
Chas H	41	m	w	ME	Siskiyou	Callahan P O	89	625
Danl	40	m	w	IREL	San Francisco	1-Wd San Francisco	79	135
E G	57	m	w	CT	Tehama	Red Bluff	92	174

© 2001 by Heritage Quest. All rights reserved.

California 1870 Census

Name	Age	S	R	B-PL	County	Locale	Series M593 Roll	Pg
E Willis	22	m	w	WI	Nevada	Nevada Twp	75	275
Edgar	35	m	w	LA	San Francisco	5-Wd San Francisco	81	26
Edwin	45	m	w	MA	Fresno	Millerton P O	72	148
Edwin	41	m	w	ME	Fresno	Millerton P O	72	168
Enoch	35	m	w	ME	Marin	Novato Twp	74	11
Frank	28	m	w	IREL	San Francisco	8-Wd San Francisco	82	460
George	50	m	w	VT	Tulare	Tule Rvr Twp	92	263
Grenville	50	m	w	MA	San Francisco	San Francisco P O	83	203
H H	38	m	w	KY	Amador	Sutter Crk P O	69	397
Henry	43	m	w	PRUS	San Francisco	San Francisco P O	80	533
Iva	43	f	w	VA	San Francisco	2-Wd San Francisco	79	218
J H	47	m	w	KY	Amador	Amador City P O	69	395
J H	15	m	w	OR	Santa Clara	Gilroy Twp	88	97
James	39	m	w	IREL	San Francisco	7-Wd San Francisco	81	161
James	30	m	w	SCOT	San Francisco	San Francisco P O	83	139
James	30	m	w	IREL	San Francisco	San Francisco P O	83	420
James	23	m	w	KY	Amador	Sutter Crk P O	69	396
Jane L	50	f	w	KY	San Francisco	San Francisco P O	83	322
Jas	39	m	w	MS	San Francisco	8-Wd San Francisco	82	368
Jas B	36	m	w	ME	Siskiyou	Callahan P O	89	625
John	44	m	w	MA	San Francisco	11-Wd San Francisc	84	627
John	43	m	w	MECK	San Francisco	11-Wd San Francisc	84	596
John	27	m	w	IREL	San Francisco	San Francisco P O	83	370
John S	19	m	w	CA	Sonoma	Salt Point Twp	91	382
Lawrence	35	m	w	IREL	San Francisco	11-Wd San Francisc	84	479
Louisa A	51	f	w	CT	Mendocino	Big Rvr Twp	74	160
M	35	m	w	IN	Alameda	Oakland	68	181
Marion	32	m	w	MO	San Diego	Milquaty Dist	78	475
Michl	34	m	w	IREL	San Francisco	1-Wd San Francisco	79	70
Nancy	56	f	w	OH	Amador	Drytown P O	69	425
Nelly	31	f	w	CT	San Francisco	6-Wd San Francisco	81	88
R C	50	m	w	MA	Lassen	Janesville Twp	73	432
Richard	28	m	w	CT	Nevada	Meadow Lake Twp	75	251
S C	41	m	w	PA	Monterey	San Juan Twp	74	401
Sam	14	m	w	CA	Santa Clara	Gilroy Twp	88	102
Thomas	52	m	w	IL	Santa Clara	2-Wd San Jose	88	295
Thomas	32	m	w	PA	Nevada	Meadow Lake Twp	75	255
Thomas	28	m	w	IREL	San Francisco	7-Wd San Francisco	81	210
W W	48	m	w	CT	San Joaquin	3-Wd Stockton	86	236
William	45	m	w	MA	San Francisco	8-Wd San Francisco	82	428
William	45	m	w	ENGL	Placer	Gold Run Twp	76	397
William	40	m	w	IL	Butte	Chico Twp	70	25
Wm	37	m	w	MO	Santa Clara	Burnett Twp	88	38
Wm	32	m	w	ENGL	Solano	Vallejo	90	207
Wm G	52	m	w	IREL	Tuolumne	Chinese Camp P O	93	382
Wm J	54	m	w	KY	Mendocino	Calpella Twp	74	189
Zedekiah	54	m	w	PA	San Diego	San Diego	78	509
HAYDN								
Peter	30	m	w	IREL	San Francisco	San Francisco P O	83	2
HAYDON								
John	26	m	w	IREL	San Francisco	San Francisco P O	83	388
Valney	6	m	w	NV	Butte	Chico Twp	70	50
HAYE								
Ah	25	m	c	CHIN	Placer	Dutch Flat P O	76	408
HAYEMAN								
William	28	m	w	PRUS	Los Angeles	Los Angeles	73	546
HAYEN								
James	38	m	w	MO	Nevada	Nevada Twp	75	314
HAYENOR								
J P	43	m	w	PRUS	Sierra	Downieville Twp	89	521
HAYES								
A N	44	m	w	NH	San Francisco	San Francisco P O	83	307
Anna	35	f	w	IREL	San Francisco	8-Wd San Francisco	82	388
Anna	18	f	w	MO	San Francisco	San Francisco P O	83	359
Anna	18	f	w	WI	San Francisco	San Francisco P O	83	395
B	40	m	w	IREL	San Francisco	San Francisco P O	85	779
Benj	55	m	w	MD	San Diego	San Diego	78	483
Benj W	31	m	w	MA	San Francisco	San Francisco P O	85	846
Bridget	74	f	w	IREL	San Francisco	San Francisco P O	83	146
Bridget	44	f	w	IREL	San Francisco	11-Wd San Francisc	84	505
C D	34	m	w	MA	Alameda	Oakland	68	201
Cath	35	f	w	ASEA	San Francisco	San Francisco P O	85	793
Cathrain	48	f	w	IREL	San Francisco	San Francisco P O	80	340
Charles	45	m	w	ME	San Francisco	San Francisco P O	83	236
Chas	30	m	w	IREL	San Francisco	1-Wd San Francisco	79	78
Cornelius	45	m	w	IREL	Tuolumne	Sonora P O	93	328
Cornelius	22	m	w	MA	San Francisco	8-Wd San Francisco	82	408
D H	47	m	w	IREL	Solano	Vallejo	90	139
Daniel	45	m	w	IREL	San Francisco	8-Wd San Francisco	82	417
Daniel	32	m	w	ME	San Francisco	11-Wd San Francisc	84	624
Daniel	17	m	w	MA	San Francisco	11-Wd San Francisc	84	631
Danl	24	m	w	NY	Sierra	Table Rock Twp	89	575
David	39	m	w	KY	Yolo	Cache Crk Twp	93	442
David	35	m	w	NY	San Francisco	11-Wd San Francisc	84	485
David	35	m	w	OH	Sacramento	Mississippi Twp	77	162
Dennis	42	m	w	IREL	Yuba	Marysville	93	607
Dennis	40	m	w	IREL	San Francisco	San Francisco P O	85	848
Dennis	40	m	w	IREL	Santa Clara	Santa Clara Twp	88	169
Dennis	36	m	w	IREL	San Francisco	San Francisco P O	85	851
Donphon	21	m	w	MO	Trinity	Lewiston Pct	92	214
E D	45	m	w	KY	Siskiyou	Scott Valley Twp	89	617
Ed B	19	m	w	IREL	Alameda	Oakland	68	182
Edward	43	m	w	CT	Sutter	Yuba Twp	92	143
Edward	36	m	w	IREL	San Francisco	11-Wd San Francisc	84	570
Edward	27	m	w	CANA	Yolo	Buckeye Twp	93	416
Edward	24	m	w	IREL	San Francisco	11-Wd San Francisc	84	450
Eli	34	m	w	KY	Yolo	Putah Twp	93	525
Elihu R	45	m	w	NY	San Francisco	8-Wd San Francisco	82	424
Eliza	31	f	w	CANA	San Francisco	San Francisco P O	83	17
Ellen	19	f	w	CT	San Francisco	1-Wd San Francisco	79	96
Eugene	38	m	w	IREL	San Francisco	San Francisco P O	85	817
Frederick	35	m	w	IREL	San Francisco	6-Wd San Francisco	81	80
G R B	26	m	w	IREL	San Francisco	San Francisco P O	83	160
Geo A	49	m	w	ME	Mariposa	Mariposa P O	74	123
Geo W	39	m	w	OH	Siskiyou	Scott Valley Twp	89	618
George	40	m	w	NY	San Francisco	San Francisco P O	80	361
Green	69	m	w	KY	San Francisco	11-Wd San Francisc	84	459
H	22	m	w	CA	Alameda	Oakland	68	159
H C	35	m	w	ME	San Francisco	San Francisco P O	83	87
H M	34	m	w	IN	Monterey	San Juan Twp	74	405
Hannah	45	f	w	IREL	San Francisco	San Francisco P O	85	820
Hannah	30	f	w	IREL	Sacramento	4-Wd Sacramento	77	326
Henry	28	m	w	MO	Napa	Napa Twp	75	66
Hiram B	24	m	w	MO	Trinity	Lewiston Pct	92	213
Honora	31	f	w	IREL	San Francisco	1-Wd San Francisco	79	97
Irvin W	27	m	w	MO	Nevada	Grass Valley Twp	75	154
Isaac N	44	m	w	VA	Nevada	Rough & Ready Twp	75	335
Isaac N	34	m	w	MI	Santa Cruz	Santa Cruz Twp	89	394
Jacob	62	m	w	TN	Yolo	Putah Twp	93	525
James	50	m	w	IREL	Santa Clara	2-Wd San Jose	88	297
James	42	m	w	IREL	Klamath	South Fork Twp	73	384
James	37	m	w	IREL	San Francisco	San Francisco P O	83	17
James	37	m	w	TX	San Francisco	5-Wd San Francisco	81	33
James	35	m	w	IREL	Amador	Sutter Crk P O	69	396
James	23	m	w	NY	San Francisco	1-Wd San Francisco	79	69
James	22	m	w	KY	Napa	Yountville Twp	75	85
James S	28	m	w	CANA	Yolo	Buckeye Twp	93	416
Jas	41	m	w	NY	Sierra	Table Rock Twp	89	579
Jas	37	m	w	NY	San Francisco	7-Wd San Francisco	81	259
Jeremiah	32	m	w	IREL	Santa Clara	2-Wd San Jose	88	297
Jno	20	m	w	IREL	Butte	Oregon Twp	70	130
Johanna	35	f	w	IREL	San Francisco	8-Wd San Francisco	82	399
Johanna	24	f	w	IREL	San Francisco	San Francisco P O	85	778
John	55	m	w	IREL	San Francisco	2-Wd San Francisco	79	214
John	51	m	w	VA	San Francisco	San Francisco P O	85	809
John	50	m	w	IREL	San Francisco	8-Wd San Francisco	82	417
John	50	m	w	IREL	Sacramento	Alabama Twp	77	60
John	46	m	w	PRUS	Solano	Silveyville Twp	90	87
John	46	m	w	IREL	Fresno	Millerton P O	72	167
John	40	m	w	IREL	San Francisco	San Francisco P O	85	836
John	39	m	w	IREL	San Francisco	11-Wd San Francisc	84	471
John	38	m	w	IREL	Alameda	Oakland	68	244
John	30	m	w	IREL	San Francisco	6-Wd San Francisco	81	153
John	26	m	w	MO	Yolo	Putah Twp	93	521
John	26	m	w	CANA	Humboldt	Bucksport Twp	72	244
John	25	m	w	IREL	Monterey	Pajaro Twp	74	374
John	24	m	w	MA	San Francisco	1-Wd San Francisco	79	96
John	23	m	w	IREL	San Francisco	1-Wd San Francisco	79	135
John	22	m	w	PA	Solano	Vacaville Twp	90	123
John	19	m	w	VT	San Francisco	San Francisco P O	83	308
John	11	m	w	CA	San Francisco	11-Wd San Francisc	84	593
John C	30	m	w	TN	Mendocino	Point Arena Twp	74	211
John C	29	m	w	IREL	Marin	San Rafael Twp	74	39
John C	17	m	w	CA	Santa Clara	Santa Clara Twp	88	177
John H	38	m	w	PA	Stanislaus	Empire Twp	92	33
John J	39	m	w	NY	Marin	San Rafael Twp	74	45
John T	33	m	w	OH	San Francisco	1-Wd San Francisco	79	107
Katy	23	f	w	NY	Santa Clara	1-Wd San Jose	88	243
L W	52	m	w	DE	Tulare	Tule Rvr Twp	92	272
Louise R	27	f	w	NY	San Francisco	2-Wd San Francisco	79	218
Luther	47	m	w	TN	Mendocino	Calpella Twp	74	183
M	37	m	w	IREL	Napa	Napa Twp	75	31
M	34	m	w	OH	Yuba	Marysville	93	586
Mack	27	m	w	NY	Santa Clara	1-Wd San Jose	88	258
Margaret	32	f	w	IREL	San Francisco	San Francisco P O	85	859
Margaret	30	f	w	IREL	San Francisco	San Francisco P O	80	406
Margaret	24	f	w	IREL	San Francisco	11-Wd San Francisc	84	571
Margaret	23	f	w	IREL	San Francisco	8-Wd San Francisco	82	387
Margaret	20	f	w	IREL	Yolo	Cache Crk Twp	93	421
Mary	70	f	w	IREL	San Francisco	8-Wd San Francisco	82	431
Mary	42	f	w	IREL	San Francisco	San Francisco P O	80	340
Mary	38	f	w	SCOT	San Francisco	8-Wd San Francisco	82	451
Mary	37	f	w	IREL	San Francisco	San Francisco P O	80	383
Mary	26	f	w	IREL	San Francisco	San Francisco P O	83	143
Mary A	33	f	w	IREL	Santa Clara	2-Wd San Jose	88	291
Michael	50	m	w	IREL	San Francisco	San Francisco P O	80	406
Michael	39	m	w	NY	San Francisco	San Francisco P O	85	804
Michael	33	m	w	IREL	San Francisco	1-Wd San Francisco	79	6
Michl	32	m	w	IREL	San Francisco	1-Wd San Francisco	79	44
Morris	27	m	w	IREL	San Francisco	11-Wd San Francisc	84	653
Moses	42	m	w	IREL	Kern	Kernville P O	73	367
P	28	m	w	IREL	Lake	Knoxville Mines	73	405
Pat	25	m	w	VA	San Francisco	San Francisco P O	83	130
Patrick	50	m	w	IREL	Alameda	Oakland	68	136
Patrick	28	m	w	IREL	Colusa	Spring Valley Twp	71	337
Patrick	21	m	w	NY	Butte	Oregon Twp	70	128
Patrick	16	m	w	NY	San Francisco	7-Wd San Francisco	81	257
Philip	40	m	w	IREL	San Francisco	2-Wd San Francisco	79	264
Putman	56	m	w	KY	Contra Costa	Martinez P O	71	451
Robert I	31	m	w	PA	Nevada	Rough & Ready Twp	75	335
Robt R	40	m	w	KY	Sonoma	Santa Rosa	91	404
S L	21	m	w	TN	Yuba	Marysville	93	604
Sarah	33	f	w	ENGL	Contra Costa	Martinez P O	71	425
Talbot	40	m	w	IN	Yolo	Cache Crk Twp	93	447

© 2001 by Heritage Quest. All rights reserved.

Name	Age	S	R	B-PL	County	Locale	Series M593 Roll	Pg
Talbot	39	m	w	KY	Yolo	Putah Twp	93	520
Tan S	31	m	w	IREL	San Francisco	8-Wd San Francisco	82	368
Thomas	43	m	w	IL	Trinity	Indian Crk	92	200
Thomas	42	m	w	IREL	Tuolumne	Columbia P O	93	337
Thomas	40	m	w	IREL	Santa Clara	Fremont Twp	88	62
Thomas	40	m	w	NY	Alameda	Brooklyn Twp	68	54
Thomas	37	m	w	CANA	Yolo	Grafton Twp	93	480
Thomas	35	m	w	IREL	San Francisco	San Francisco P O	85	762
Thomas	28	m	w	PA	Siskiyou	Callahan P O	89	624
Thomas	25	m	w	ENGL	Yolo	Cottonwood Twp	93	473
Thomas	24	m	w	NY	San Francisco	1-Wd San Francisco	79	90
Thomas B	42	m	w	IREL	Los Angeles	Wilmington Twp	73	643
Thomas R	24	m	w	ME	San Francisco	8-Wd San Francisco	82	470
Thos	40	m	w	IREL	San Joaquin	Douglas Twp	86	33
Thos	33	m	w	IREL	Sierra	Sears Twp	89	560
Thos	30	m	w	IREL	San Francisco	1-Wd San Francisco	79	123
Victoria A	31	f	w	CANA	San Francisco	6-Wd San Francisco	81	140
W B	40	m	w	PA	Yuba	Marysville	93	591
William	57	m	w	IREL	San Francisco	San Francisco P O	83	360
William	54	m	w	NH	Alameda	Eden Twp	68	57
William	40	m	w	TN	Los Angeles	Los Nietos Twp	73	578
William	40	m	w	IREL	Sonoma	Sonoma Twp	91	437
William	33	m	w	KY	Yolo	Cottonwood Twp	93	463
William	20	m	w	OH	San Francisco	3-Wd San Francisco	79	316
William O	51	m	w	NY	Yolo	Putah Twp	93	520
Wm	40	m	w	NH	Marin	San Rafael Twp	74	42
Wm	20	m	w	IREL	Alameda	Oakland	68	182
Wm E	42	m	w	VA	Sonoma	Petaluma Twp	91	311
HAYETT								
John	30	m	w	CANA	Shasta	Shasta P O	89	459
HAYFIELD								
John	27	m	w	TX	Inyo	Bishop Crk Twp	73	315
HAYFORD								
Captain	30	m	w	NH	Sacramento	Natomas Twp	77	166
Columbus	58	m	w	ME	El Dorado	White Oak Twp	72	142
Edward	44	m	w	NH	Santa Clara	2-Wd San Jose	88	297
William B	33	m	w	ME	Placer	Colfax P O	76	386
HAYHALL								
Horace	40	m	w	IL	Tehama	Tehama Twp	92	186
HAYIN								
Alice	16	f	w	OH	San Joaquin	2-Wd Stockton	86	174
HAYLAND								
Henry	52	m	w	IREL	Alameda	Brooklyn Twp	68	51
HAYLE								
Jas M	36	m	w	TN	Butte	Chico Twp	70	22
HAYLETT								
William	30	m	w	MA	Placer	Cisco P O	76	494
HAYLEY								
John	32	m	w	NY	Contra Costa	Martinez P O	71	409
John	27	m	w	IREL	Contra Costa	San Pablo Twp	71	364
HAYLOCK								
Isaac	53	m	w	ENGL	Mendocino	Point Arena Twp	74	209
Isaac	30	m	w	ENGL	Trinity	Minersville Pct	92	203
HAYMAKER								
Ed	29	m	w	OH	Alameda	Murray Twp	68	116
John	59	m	w	PA	San Joaquin	3-Wd Stockton	86	242
HAYMAN								
Benjamin	26	m	w	ENGL	San Francisco	San Francisco P O	80	358
Luther T	26	m	w	IN	Colusa	Spring Valley Twp	71	339
HAYMER								
Martha J	24	f	w	MO	Yolo	Grafton Twp	93	489
HAYMON								
Jon	52	m	w	MA	Solano	Vallejo	90	168
HAYMOND								
Leonard	27	m	w	TX	Tulare	Tule Rvr Twp	92	263
HAYMOR								
Chas	40	m	b	MD	Sacramento	3-Wd Sacramento	77	256
HAYNARD								
Clemente	29	m	w	GERM	Los Angeles	Los Angeles	73	567
HAYNE								
Arthur	48	m	w	SC	San Francisco	6-Wd San Francisco	81	37
Arthur	47	m	w	SC	San Francisco	San Francisco P O	80	479
Doretta	30	f	w	PRUS	San Francisco	San Francisco P O	83	349
Edd	26	m	w	MD	San Francisco	5-Wd San Francisco	81	22
G	30	m	w	NORW	San Francisco	San Francisco P O	85	820
George	30	m	w	MD	San Francisco	5-Wd San Francisco	81	22
Jane	62	f	w	NY	Alameda	Alameda	68	9
Joseph	60	m	w	IREL	San Francisco	San Francisco P O	83	354
Robt	16	m	w	CA	San Francisco	San Francisco P O	85	789
Willm A	49	m	w	SC	Santa Barbara	Santa Barbara P O	87	490
HAYNER								
Rachel	65	f	w	PRUS	San Francisco	San Francisco P O	83	344
HAYNES								
Ann	11	f	w	CA	Klamath	Dillon Twp	73	369
Bridget	70	f	w	IREL	San Francisco	San Francisco P O	83	402
Chas	20	m	w	CT	San Francisco	11-Wd San Francisc	84	687
Daniel	43	m	w	IREL	Tuolumne	Columbia P O	93	340
Dennis	35	m	w	IREL	San Francisco	8-Wd San Francisco	82	475
F	13	m	w	CA	Solano	Benicia	90	21
Geo W	45	m	w	NY	Napa	Yountville Twp	75	85
George	30	m	w	ENGL	Sonoma	Sonoma Twp	91	436
George W	42	m	w	OH	Solano	Suisun Twp	90	103
H E	26	m	w	OH	Lake	Morgan Valley	73	425
Isadore	44	f	b	AFRI	Stanislaus	Empire Twp	92	48
J H	21	m	w	ME	Lake	Lower Lake	73	419
James	29	m	w	IREL	San Francisco	San Francisco P O	83	402
John	45	m	w	VA	San Francisco	11-Wd San Francisc	84	631
John	43	m	w	IREL	Yolo	Putah Twp	93	520
John	42	m	w	IREL	San Francisco	San Francisco P O	83	164
John	37	m	w	ME	Sonoma	Salt Point	91	387
John P	43	m	w	KY	Humboldt	Eureka Twp	72	259
Joseph	40	m	w	VA	San Francisco	8-Wd San Francisco	82	371
Joseph	36	m	w	ENGL	Santa Barbara	San Buenaventura P	87	430
Justin C	31	m	w	ME	Plumas	Quartz Twp	77	39
Kate	38	f	w	IREL	San Francisco	5-Wd San Francisco	81	33
Kecca	45	m	w	IREL	San Francisco	11-Wd San Francisc	84	670
Louisa	15	f	w	CA	San Francisco	San Francisco P O	85	798
Louisa	13	f	w	IL	San Francisco	San Francisco P O	85	725
Lucretia	41	f	w	MEXI	Santa Clara	1-Wd San Jose	88	257
Mary	29	f	w	IREL	San Francisco	8-Wd San Francisco	82	350
Nahum	62	m	w	ME	San Francisco	2-Wd San Francisco	79	193
P L [Rev]	41	m	w	US	Santa Cruz	Santa Cruz	89	406
Patrick	37	m	w	IREL	Tuolumne	Columbia P O	93	339
Peter	38	m	w	IREL	San Francisco	11-Wd San Francisc	84	669
Peter	25	m	w	ME	Humboldt	Eureka Twp	72	275
Santa	50	m	w	NY	Butte	Chico Twp	70	57
Sarah	54	f	w	VA	Napa	Napa	75	52
Theodore P	21	m	w	IREL	Sonoma	Salt Point Twp	91	384
Thomas	45	m	w	NY	San Francisco	5-Wd San Francisco	81	34
Wash	22	m	w	MI	San Joaquin	Tulare Twp	86	258
Washington	41	m	w	OH	Contra Costa	Martinez P O	71	379
William	41	m	w	IREL	Tuolumne	Columbia P O	93	340
William	21	m	w	MO	Los Angeles	Santa Ana Twp	73	611
Wm	52	m	w	PA	Butte	Chico Twp	70	32
Wm W	40	m	w	NY	Santa Barbara	Santa Barbara P O	87	493
HAYNESS								
John	33	m	w	FRAN	San Francisco	7-Wd San Francisco	81	218
HAYNIE								
Wm M	43	m	w	MD	Sacramento	Sutter Twp	77	393
HAYNS								
Benja	44	m	w	MA	San Francisco	8-Wd San Francisco	82	300
HAYONG								
---	32	m	c	CHIN	Shasta	Horsetown P O	89	504
HAYRE								
Henry	22	m	w	MA	San Joaquin	2-Wd Stockton	86	192
John	29	m	w	IREL	Monterey	Salinas Twp	74	308
HAYS								
Andrew E	26	m	w	IL	Sonoma	Washington Twp	91	469
Annie	22	f	w	ME	Solano	Silveyville Twp	90	89
Catherine	27	f	w	IREL	San Francisco	7-Wd San Francisco	81	184
David	39	m	w	CT	Mono	Bridgeport P O	74	282
Dennis	36	m	w	IREL	Nevada	Grass Valley Twp	75	179
Dennis	32	m	w	IREL	Santa Clara	Gilroy Twp	88	84
Dora L	10	f	w	CA	Yuba	Long Bar Twp	93	566
Florence	28	f	w	MO	San Luis Obispo	San Luis Obispo Tw	87	310
Frank	35	m	w	NY	San Francisco	3-Wd San Francisco	79	318
Frank	23	m	w	NY	San Francisco	3-Wd San Francisco	79	323
George	44	m	w	ENGL	Butte	Oregon Twp	70	134
George	16	m	w	CA	Tuolumne	Chinese Camp P O	93	386
George T	14	m	w	CA	Yuba	Bullards Bar P O	93	550
Henery	25	m	w	VA	San Francisco	7-Wd San Francisco	81	179
Henery	25	m	w	SCOT	San Francisco	7-Wd San Francisco	81	165
Henry	40	m	w	MA	Solano	Denverton Twp	90	25
Henry A	67	m	w	VT	Tehama	Tehama Twp	92	192
Jacob	36	m	w	IN	Stanislaus	Empire Twp	92	43
James	55	m	w	KY	Siskiyou	Surprise Valley Tw	89	641
James	51	m	w	PRUS	Tuolumne	Chinese Camp P O	93	383
James	40	m	w	TN	Siskiyou	Big Valley Twp	89	582
James	34	m	w	MI	Placer	Cisco P O	76	494
James	22	m	w	RI	Inyo	Bishop Crk Twp	73	314
Jerry	29	m	w	IREL	Solano	Benicia	90	19
Jno C	50	m	w	TN	Alameda	Oakland	68	257
John	45	m	w	IREL	San Francisco	7-Wd San Francisco	81	197
John	45	m	w	IREL	San Mateo	Redwood City P O	87	376
John	37	m	w	IREL	Solano	Silveyville Twp	90	78
John	36	m	w	ENGL	Plumas	Seneca Twp	77	48
John	35	m	w	IREL	San Francisco	11-Wd San Francisc	84	422
John	28	m	w	ME	San Francisco	7-Wd San Francisco	81	179
John	24	m	w	OH	Solano	Maine Prairie Twp	90	45
John	24	m	w	TN	Calaveras	Copperopolis P O	70	221
John	24	m	w	MA	San Francisco	3-Wd San Francisco	79	299
John	23	m	w	IREL	Marin	San Rafael Twp	74	40
Joseph	25	m	w	IREL	Yolo	Cache Crk Twp	93	446
Julia	26	f	w	IREL	Alameda	Eden Twp	68	81
Kate	24	f	w	IREL	Sonoma	Petaluma Twp	91	350
Lillie	7	f	w	CA	Alpine	Monitor P O	69	313
Luke C	36	m	w	KY	Solano	Suisun Twp	90	111
Maggie	27	f	w	IREL	San Francisco	7-Wd San Francisco	81	246
Margaret	70	f	w	IREL	San Mateo	Redwood City P O	87	376
Margaret	18	f	w	IREL	San Mateo	Redwood Twp	87	365
Mary	30	f	w	IREL	San Mateo	Schoolhouse Statio	87	341
Mary C	15	f	w	CA	Santa Cruz	Santa Cruz	89	417
Mary J	24	f	w	SC	San Francisco	8-Wd San Francisco	82	368
Mathew	37	m	w	TN	Sonoma	Washington Twp	91	464
Matthew	50	m	w	IREL	Santa Clara	2-Wd San Jose	88	316
Michael	22	m	w	IREL	Placer	Cisco P O	76	494
P M	55	m	w	MO	Siskiyou	Surprise Valley Tw	89	639
Patrick	50	m	w	IREL	Nevada	Eureka Twp	75	132
Patrick	43	m	w	IREL	Marin	San Rafael Twp	74	33
Patrick	30	m	w	IREL	San Francisco	7-Wd San Francisco	81	223
Permelia	14	f	w	IA	Yolo	Cache Crk Twp	93	447
Peter	26	m	w	MO	Solano	Montezuma Twp	90	68
Robert	51	m	w	PA	Alameda	Hayward	68	73
Robert	45	m	w	IREL	San Francisco	2-Wd San Francisco	79	157

© 2001 by Heritage Quest. All rights reserved.

California 1870 Census

Series M593

Name	Age	S	R	B-PL	County	Locale	Roll	Pg
Robert T	45	m	w	OH	Los Angeles	Los Angeles	73	533
Saml M	54	m	w	VA	Sonoma	Healdsburg & Mendo	91	280
Samuel	30	m	w	MO	Mono	Bridgeport P O	74	287
Shadrock L	28	m	w	KY	Yolo	Buckeye Twp	93	417
Susan	44	f	w	IREL	San Francisco	7-Wd San Francisco	81	161
Sylvester	61	m	w	MO	Sonoma	Mendocino Twp	91	307
T K	43	m	w	IN	Tehama	Antelope Twp	92	154
Thomas	29	m	w	VA	Los Angeles	Los Angeles Twp	73	494
Thomas	28	m	w	IREL	Solano	Vacaville Twp	90	120
Thomas K	49	m	w	PA	Marin	San Rafael Twp	74	46
Thos	37	m	w	CANA	Solano	Vallejo	90	210
Thos C	38	m	w	LA	San Luis Obispo	Santa Rosa Twp	87	326
Timothy	50	m	w	IREL	San Mateo	Redwood City P O	87	376
W P	28	m	w	IREL	Nevada	Eureka Twp	75	139
Wade	42	m	w	MO	Siskiyou	Surprise Valley Tw	89	643
Wade	42	m	w	MO	Contra Costa	Martinez P O	71	393
William	38	m	w	IREL	El Dorado	Mud Springs Twp	72	85
William	33	m	w	IREL	San Francisco	San Francisco P O	83	140
William	23	m	w	PA	Solano	Silveyville Twp	90	78
Wm	50	m	w	IREL	Solano	Benicia	90	18
Wm M	32	m	w	MD	San Luis Obispo	San Luis Obispo Tw	87	310
HAYSDEN								
James	20	m	w	ENGL	San Francisco	7-Wd San Francisco	81	165
HAYSE								
Fredrick	37	m	w	BADE	Amador	Ione City P O	69	356
John W	28	m	w	IREL	Nevada	Grass Valley Twp	75	221
Patrick	60	m	w	IREL	Nevada	Grass Valley Twp	75	217
HAYT								
James	25	m	w	NH	San Diego	Milquaty Dist	78	478
Martha C	40	f	w	ME	San Francisco	San Francisco P O	83	140
HAYTEN								
Chas	50	m	w	NJ	San Francisco	5-Wd San Francisco	81	25
HAYTHROP								
Edward	63	m	w	MD	San Francisco	8-Wd San Francisco	82	327
HAYTON								
G M	44	m	w	ENGL	Sacramento	1-Wd Sacramento	77	177
Jessie	37	m	w	ENGL	Sacramento	2-Wd Sacramento	77	211
HAYUM								
H	36	m	w	WURT	Sacramento	4-Wd Sacramento	77	340
HAYWARD								
Alvira	48	m	w	VT	San Mateo	San Mateo P O	87	357
Bazell	40	m	w	MA	San Mateo	Pescadero P O	87	411
Claudeus	31	m	w	OH	Santa Clara	Redwood Twp	88	129
D L	39	m	w	NY	Sonoma	Santa Rosa	91	411
D L	39	m	w	NY	Sonoma	Santa Rosa	91	400
George	38	m	w	NY	San Francisco	San Francisco P O	85	768
J R	45	m	w	IL	Mendocino	Little Lake Twp	74	198
James	45	m	w	MA	San Francisco	5-Wd San Francisco	81	22
James A	24	m	w	WI	San Mateo	San Mateo P O	87	357
Louisa	40	f	w	MD	San Francisco	8-Wd San Francisco	82	384
Luther	55	m	w	MA	San Francisco	11-Wd San Francisc	84	497
Sarah L	30	f	w	MA	Yolo	Cache Crk Twp	93	456
Silas	38	m	w	MA	San Francisco	8-Wd San Francisco	82	468
Thomas	23	m	w	CANA	San Francisco	11-Wd San Francisc	84	505
William	54	m	w	MA	Alameda	Eden Twp	68	81
Wm B	40	m	w	ME	San Francisco	San Francisco P O	85	722
HAYWOOD								
Abel	43	m	w	ME	Alpine	Silver Mtn P O	69	306
Anna	35	f	w	MEXI	San Francisco	2-Wd San Francisco	79	174
Chas F	35	m	w	VT	San Francisco	5-Wd San Francisco	81	18
Hannah	40	f	w	ENGL	San Francisco	8-Wd San Francisco	82	447
Johnn A	74	m	w	ENGL	Nevada	Grass Valley Twp	75	178
Martha	28	f	b	JAMA	San Francisco	8-Wd San Francisco	82	386
Robert	10	m	m	JAMA	San Francisco	8-Wd San Francisco	82	386
Saml	64	m	w	ME	Tuolumne	Columbia P O	93	338
Saml	37	m	w	ME	Alameda	Oakland	68	250
Thomas	40	m	w	ENGL	Sonoma	Petaluma Twp	91	315
W A	30	m	b	NC	Tuolumne	Chinese Camp P O	93	387
William	47	m	b	DE	San Francisco	6-Wd San Francisco	81	107
HAYWORTH								
---	35	m	w	WURT	Colusa	Spring Valley Twp	71	343
Frank	18	m	w	IA	Colusa	California Twp	71	279
J S	65	m	w	NC	Siskiyou	Surprise Valley Tw	89	637
HAZ								
Ah	23	m	c	CHIN	Tuolumne	Big Oak Flat P O	93	401
Conrad	34	m	w	HCAS	Mariposa	Mariposa P O	74	105
HAZARD								
Andrew	35	m	w	IREL	San Francisco	8-Wd San Francisco	82	409
Augustus C	45	m	w	MI	Santa Clara	Santa Clara Twp	88	135
Betsy	76	f	w	VT	Butte	Oregon Twp	70	122
Charles	37	m	w	CANA	Los Angeles	Los Angeles	73	534
Edward	30	m	w	IREL	San Francisco	11-Wd San Francisc	84	654
Ellenor	54	f	w	SCOT	Los Angeles	Los Angeles	73	535
Margt	40	f	w	IREL	San Francisco	6-Wd San Francisco	81	120
Peggy	86	f	b	CT	Santa Clara	San Jose Twp	88	202
Robert	45	m	w	IREL	San Francisco	San Francisco P O	83	331
Sarah	35	f	w	ENGL	San Francisco	San Francisco P O	83	214
Stewart	68	m	w	NY	Butte	Oregon Twp	70	122
William	23	m	w	ENGL	San Francisco	San Francisco P O	83	219
HAZE								
Daniel	40	m	w	IREL	Alameda	Washington Twp	68	284
John	23	m	w	IREL	Alameda	San Leandro	68	96
S W	39	m	w	IL	Merced	Snelling P O	74	268
Stephen D	22	m	w	IL	Merced	Snelling P O	74	268
HAZEL								
---	50	m	w	ENGL	Yuba	Rose Bar Twp	93	663
Cyrus	21	m	w	IL	San Mateo	San Mateo P O	87	359

Series M593

Name	Age	S	R	B-PL	County	Locale	Roll	Pg
Eli	24	m	w	OH	Alameda	Washington Twp	68	280
Elia	22	m	w	OH	Alameda	Washington Twp	68	278
James	30	m	w	NY	Santa Clara	2-Wd San Jose	88	335
John	23	m	w	NY	Santa Clara	2-Wd San Jose	88	335
Samuel	23	m	w	IL	San Francisco	San Francisco P O	85	874
HAZELL								
Henson	45	m	w	KY	Mendocino	Ukiah Twp	74	239
John	25	m	w	NY	San Francisco	San Francisco P O	80	538
Wm	28	m	w	IL	San Francisco	San Francisco P O	85	876
HAZELQUIST								
Albert	31	m	w	SWED	San Francisco	San Francisco P O	80	427
Louis	40	m	w	SWED	San Francisco	San Francisco P O	80	427
HAZELTINE								
Ana	50	f	w	IREL	Sacramento	4-Wd Sacramento	77	343
Benj	47	m	w	KY	Butte	Chico Twp	70	58
Charles	28	m	w	CANA	San Mateo	Pescadero P O	87	411
F P	43	m	w	OH	Del Norte	Smith Rvr Twp	71	479
John	51	m	w	ME	Contra Costa	Martinez P O	71	449
Justin	34	m	w	CANA	San Mateo	Pescadero P O	87	410
Lucy	40	f	w	IL	San Francisco	7-Wd San Francisco	81	232
Thos	45	m	w	ENGL	Yuba	W Bear Rvr Twp	93	681
HAZELTON								
Francis M	24	m	w	MO	Shasta	Millville P O	89	487
Frank	26	m	w	MA	Sacramento	1-Wd Sacramento	77	186
Royal	21	m	w	TX	Shasta	Millville P O	89	487
Saml	54	m	w	VT	Humboldt	Pacific Twp	72	296
Saml N	47	m	w	IN	Shasta	Millville P O	89	487
Thomas	40	m	w	IREL	San Francisco	3-Wd San Francisco	79	313
Timothy	44	m	w	ME	Mariposa	Mariposa P O	74	135
Walter S	28	m	w	VT	Yolo	Cache Crk Twp	93	454
Wm	45	m	w	NY	Fresno	Kings Rvr P O	72	204
HAZEN								
Edmond	57	m	w	VT	Contra Costa	Martinez P O	71	367
Edward	49	m	w	NY	Santa Clara	Santa Clara Twp	88	160
Hiram C	41	m	w	CT	Monterey	San Juan Twp	74	403
Sears	42	m	w	PA	Shasta	Fort Crook P O	89	474
W	70	m	w	KS	San Francisco	8-Wd San Francisco	82	365
W B	32	m	w	NY	Tehama	Battle Crk Twp	92	172
Willard	53	m	w	VT	Sacramento	Franklin Twp	77	113
HAZER								
M	28	m	w	PA	Mendocino	Sanel Twp	74	230
HAZETT								
Elijah	39	m	w	KY	Mendocino	Anderson Twp	74	154
HAZLE								
Thomas	25	m	w	ENGL	Yolo	Cache Crk Twp	93	448
HAZLEBUSH								
Fredk	26	m	w	HANO	Butte	Hamilton Twp	70	70
Heny	37	m	w	PRUS	Butte	Ophir Twp	70	99
HAZLEP								
John B	53	m	w	MD	Siskiyou	Callahan P O	89	625
HAZLERIGG								
Charles	39	m	w	IN	Santa Cruz	Watsonville	89	366
HAZLETON								
Aaron C	47	m	w	NY	El Dorado	Mud Springs Twp	72	71
James	42	m	w	NH	Placer	Auburn P O	76	360
Jos	37	m	w	MI	San Francisco	8-Wd San Francisco	82	353
HAZLETT								
Chas F	38	m	w	IL	Shasta	Fort Crook P O	89	476
Flora	14	f	w	IA	Nevada	Bridgeport Twp	75	123
Henry	14	m	w	CA	Siskiyou	Cottonwood Twp	89	591
Robert	20	m	w	IREL	San Francisco	11-Wd San Francisc	84	697
William	35	m	w	TX	Calaveras	San Andreas P O	70	159
HAZLETTE								
John	28	m	w	TX	Calaveras	San Andreas P O	70	152
HAZOROWSKI								
Frank	44	m	w	POLA	Mariposa	Mariposa P O	74	108
HAZZ								
A	45	m	w	MEXI	Sierra	Downieville Twp	89	519
HAZZARD								
Elizabeth	30	f	w	GERM	San Luis Obispo	Morro Twp	87	280
George	26	m	w	IREL	San Diego	San Diego	78	494
Jerry R	44	m	w	RI	San Luis Obispo	Morro Twp	87	280
Robert	25	m	w	ENGL	San Francisco	3-Wd San Francisco	79	313
Wm H	40	m	w	RI	El Dorado	Mountain Twp	72	68
HAZZELTON								
Martin	38	m	w	ME	Mendocino	Big Rvr Twp	74	161
HE								
Aad	40	m	c	CHIN	Sacramento	3-Wd Sacramento	77	316
Ah	42	m	c	CHIN	Butte	Concow Twp	70	10
Ah	42	m	c	CHIN	Monterey	Monterey Twp	74	352
Ah	41	m	c	CHIN	Nevada	Washington Twp	75	343
Ah	41	m	c	CHIN	Shasta	French Gulch P O	89	469
Ah	40	m	c	CHIN	Sacramento	Georgianna Twp	77	123
Ah	40	m	c	CHIN	Butte	Chico Twp	70	28
Ah	40	m	c	CHIN	Calaveras	San Andreas P O	70	190
Ah	40	m	c	CHIN	San Francisco	San Francisco P O	80	518
Ah	39	m	c	CHIN	San Francisco	6-Wd San Francisco	81	60
Ah	36	m	c	CHIN	Tuolumne	Chinese Camp P O	93	371
Ah	36	m	c	CHIN	Placer	Roseville P O	76	348
Ah	36	m	c	CHIN	Sacramento	American Twp	77	68
Ah	35	m	c	CHIN	San Francisco	San Francisco P O	83	193
Ah	35	m	c	CHIN	Sacramento	Georgianna Twp	77	124
Ah	35	m	c	CHIN	Sonoma	Petaluma Twp	91	357
Ah	34	m	c	CHIN	Calaveras	San Andreas P O	70	199
Ah	33	f	c	CHIN	Calaveras	Copperopolis P O	70	242
Ah	32	m	c	CHIN	Fresno	Millerton P O	72	199
Ah	31	m	c	CHIN	Nevada	Meadow Lake Twp	75	255

© 2001 by Heritage Quest. All rights reserved.

Series M593

Name	Age	S	R	B-PL	County	Locale	Roll	Pg
Ah	30	m	c	CHIN	Sacramento	Natomas Twp	77	168
Ah	30	m	c	CHIN	Nevada	Nevada Twp	75	297
Ah	30	m	c	CHIN	Tuolumne	Chinese Camp P O	93	381
Ah	30	m	c	CHIN	Yuba	East Bear Rvr Twp	93	546
Ah	30	f	c	CHIN	San Francisco	6-Wd San Francisco	81	60
Ah	27	m	c	CHIN	Sacramento	American Twp	77	68
Ah	27	m	c	CHIN	Sacramento	American Twp	77	68
Ah	27	m	c	CHIN	Sacramento	Georgianna Twp	77	134
Ah	26	m	c	CHIN	Shasta	French Gulch P O	89	466
Ah	25	m	c	CHIN	Sacramento	Mississippi Twp	77	163
Ah	25	m	c	CHIN	Calaveras	San Andreas P O	70	161
Ah	25	m	c	CHIN	Shasta	American Ranch P O	89	500
Ah	25	m	c	CHIN	Solano	Vallejo	90	209
Ah	24	m	c	CHIN	Nevada	Meadow Lake Twp	75	259
Ah	24	m	c	CHIN	San Francisco	8-Wd San Francisco	82	361
Ah	24	m	c	CHIN	Tuolumne	Chinese Camp P O	93	381
Ah	24	f	c	CHIN	Santa Clara	1-Wd San Jose	88	270
Ah	23	m	c	CHIN	Calaveras	San Andreas P O	70	176
Ah	23	m	c	CHIN	Sacramento	Georgianna Twp	77	131
Ah	22	m	c	CHIN	El Dorado	Diamond Springs Tw	72	27
Ah	22	m	c	CHIN	Tehama	Tehama Twp	92	189
Ah	22	m	c	CHIN	San Francisco	San Francisco P O	85	806
Ah	21	m	c	CHIN	Sacramento	Georgianna Twp	77	134
Ah	20	m	c	CHIN	Sacramento	2-Wd Sacramento	77	243
Ah	20	m	c	CHIN	San Francisco	8-Wd San Francisco	82	430
Ah	20	f	c	CHIN	San Francisco	6-Wd San Francisco	81	74
Ah	18	m	c	CHIN	San Francisco	6-Wd San Francisco	81	66
Ah	17	m	c	CHIN	San Francisco	6-Wd San Francisco	81	44
Ah	16	m	c	CHIN	Yuba	Marysville	93	582
Ah	16	m	c	CHIN	Sacramento	1-Wd Sacramento	77	198
Ah	16	f	c	CHIN	Sacramento	Granite Twp	77	153
Ah	15	m	c	CHIN	San Francisco	San Francisco P O	85	830
Ar	16	m	c	CHIN	Sonoma	Vallejo Twp	91	452
Chat	44	m	c	CHIN	Shasta	French Gulch P O	89	466
Chi	50	m	c	CHIN	Butte	Concow Twp	70	10
Chong	31	m	c	CHIN	Calaveras	San Andreas P O	70	205
Chong	29	m	c	CHIN	Butte	Chico Twp	70	49
Chun	45	m	c	CHIN	Butte	Concow Twp	70	10
Con	38	m	c	CHIN	Butte	Chico Twp	70	51
Con	38	m	c	CHIN	Butte	Chico Twp	70	52
Cow	40	m	c	CHIN	Butte	Hamilton Twp	70	75
Cow	19	m	c	CHIN	Butte	Hamilton Twp	70	71
Foy	28	f	c	CHIN	Los Angeles	Santa Ana Twp	73	613
Hang Toy	28	m	c	CHIN	San Francisco	6-Wd San Francisco	81	52
Kim	22	m	c	CHIN	Tehama	Tehama Twp	92	188
Lam	27	m	c	CHIN	Calaveras	San Andreas P O	70	205
Lany	29	m	c	CHIN	Butte	Concow Twp	70	12
Lap	20	m	c	CHIN	Tehama	Tehama Twp	92	188
Les	28	m	c	CHIN	Nevada	Eureka Twp	75	140
Long	40	m	c	CHIN	Placer	Blue Canyon P O	76	417
Long	24	f	c	CHIN	Calaveras	Copperopolis P O	70	260
Low Tow	16	f	c	CHIN	Nevada	Meadow Lake Twp	75	254
Quon	39	m	c	CHIN	Butte	Hamilton Twp	70	74
Sam	26	m	c	CHIN	Tehama	Tehama Twp	92	189
Sap	20	m	c	CHIN	Tehama	Tehama Twp	92	191
See	38	m	c	CHIN	El Dorado	Cosumnes Twp	72	20
See	35	m	c	CHIN	Butte	Hamilton Twp	70	71
Sow	10	f	c	CHIN	San Francisco	6-Wd San Francisco	81	39
Soy	55	m	c	CHIN	Calaveras	Copperopolis P O	70	242
Sue	28	f	c	CHIN	Mariposa	Mariposa P O	74	103
Sung	23	m	c	CHIN	Solano	Suisun Twp	90	106
Tek	23	m	c	CHIN	Solano	Green Valley Twp	90	42
Tin	34	m	c	CHIN	Butte	Concow Twp	70	11
Tin	19	m	c	CHIN	Nevada	Nevada Twp	75	311
War	24	m	c	CHIN	San Francisco	6-Wd San Francisco	81	52
Wee	27	f	c	CHIN	San Francisco	6-Wd San Francisco	81	53
Wong Loon	22	m	c	CHIN	San Francisco	6-Wd San Francisco	81	52
Wot	27	m	c	CHIN	San Joaquin	1-Wd Stockton	86	151
You	23	m	c	CHIN	Tehama	Stony Crk	92	166
Yuen	38	m	c	CHIN	Calaveras	San Andreas P O	70	205
HEA								
Ah	40	m	c	CHIN	Plumas	Washington Twp	77	57
Ah	20	f	c	CHIN	Mariposa	Maxwell Crk P O	74	138
HEABER								
Edward	25	m	w	KY	Los Angeles	Los Angeles	73	549
HEACH								
Harry	37	m	w	IN	Tehama	Tehama Twp	92	186
HEACOCK								
Daniel	67	m	w	MA	Marin	San Rafael Twp	74	26
Edwin H	39	m	w	NY	Santa Cruz	Santa Cruz	89	414
Henry	32	m	w	OH	San Francisco	11-Wd San Francisc	84	555
J	48	m	w	PA	Amador	Ione City P O	69	350
Judson	26	m	w	MA	Solano	Vallejo	90	160
Lewis	37	m	w	OH	Sacramento	2-Wd Sacramento	77	227
Thos	30	m	w	WI	San Diego	San Diego	78	507
HEACOCKS								
Frank	26	m	w	DE	San Francisco	San Francisco P O	83	230
HEAD								
Albert	24	m	w	CANA	Colusa	Colusa	71	288
Alfred	37	m	w	ME	Mendocino	Point Arena Twp	74	204
Clara	17	f	w	CA	Sacramento	3-Wd Sacramento	77	317
E F	51	m	w	MA	Alameda	Oakland	68	146
E R	30	m	w	NY	San Francisco	San Francisco P O	83	50
George	32	m	w	NY	Napa	Napa	75	45
James R	48	m	w	MA	Amador	Fiddletown P O	69	430
Robt	49	m	w	NY	San Joaquin	Tulare Twp	86	262
Samuel	50	m	w	PA	San Francisco	3-Wd San Francisco	79	316
William	7	m	w	PA	San Francisco	San Francisco P O	80	331
HEADDEN								
Nancy	56	f	w	IL	San Diego	San Pasqual	78	522
HEADEN								
Geo T	28	m	w	IN	Santa Clara	Gilroy Twp	88	80
Nellie	16	f	w	CA	Santa Clara	Gilroy Twp	88	84
HEADING								
Jo	30	m	w	MI	San Joaquin	Elliott Twp	86	70
HEADLEN								
Joseph	30	m	w	WURT	Placer	Bath P O	76	455
HEADLEY								
Arnold E	46	m	w	VT	Plumas	Indian Twp	77	9
Charles	34	m	w	HANO	San Francisco	11-Wd San Francisc	84	534
Saml	42	m	w	PA	Alameda	Brooklyn Twp	68	51
HEADMAN								
Mathias	42	m	w	FINL	Placer	Bath P O	76	441
HEADMANS								
P	47	m	w	WALE	Sierra	Forest	89	536
HEADON								
Benjamin F	55	m	w	VA	Santa Clara	Santa Clara Twp	88	161
HEADRICK								
Fred	31	m	w	BADE	Butte	Kimshew Tpw	70	80
HEAFFER								
John	40	m	w	PRUS	Del Norte	Happy Camp Twp	71	471
HEAGLE								
Catherine	88	f	w	FRAN	San Francisco	7-Wd San Francisco	81	185
Christian	80	m	w	FRAN	San Francisco	7-Wd San Francisco	81	185
HEAGY								
David W	22	m	w	PA	Yolo	Cache Crk Twp	93	453
HEAL								
Annie M	42	f	w	BREM	San Francisco	8-Wd San Francisco	82	387
David	24	m	w	CANA	Santa Clara	2-Wd San Jose	88	317
John	37	m	w	ME	Nevada	Bloomfield Twp	75	99
Joseph	38	m	w	VA	San Francisco	7-Wd San Francisco	81	211
HEALAND								
Alice	65	f	w	IREL	Solano	Benicia	90	2
HEALD								
Allen	48	m	w	ME	Alameda	Brooklyn	68	28
Danl G	40	m	w	ME	Sonoma	Petaluma Twp	91	346
Edward	40	m	w	NY	Alameda	Washington Twp	68	292
Fred	13	m	w	ENGL	Solano	Maine Prairie Twp	90	47
Geo W	15	m	w	CA	Sonoma	Russian Rvr	91	372
George L	34	m	w	ME	San Diego	San Diego	78	497
Harietta	7	f	w	CA	Sonoma	Sonoma Twp	91	434
J	27	m	w	IREL	Lake	Morgan Valley	73	425
J L	35	m	w	ME	Solano	Vallejo	90	193
Jacob G	42	m	w	OH	Sonoma	Cloverdale Twp	91	272
John	50	m	w	ME	San Francisco	San Francisco P O	85	727
John	29	m	w	ME	Solano	Tremont Twp	90	33
Lasen	43	m	w	MA	Contra Costa	Martinez P O	71	446
Moses	54	m	w	MA	Placer	Dutch Flat P O	76	410
Samuel	50	m	w	OH	San Francisco	San Francisco P O	83	293
Thos S	44	m	w	OH	Sonoma	Mendocino Twp	91	306
William	42	m	w	NY	San Mateo	Belmont P O	87	372
HEALER								
H C	35	m	w	NY	Merced	Snelling P O	74	263
HEALEY								
Allen	78	m	w	VT	Tehama	Cottonwood Twp	92	162
Daniel D	36	m	w	ENGL	Alameda	Brooklyn	68	38
Dennis	27	m	w	IREL	San Francisco	San Francisco P O	83	336
E	35	m	w	IREL	Yuba	Marysville	93	614
Elinor	9	f	w	NY	Solano	Benicia	90	17
Eliza S	71	f	w	ME	Tehama	Cottonwood Twp	92	162
Frank	37	m	w	IREL	San Francisco	2-Wd San Francisco	79	170
Geo H	38	m	w	NY	San Francisco	San Francisco P O	85	737
George	25	m	w	MA	Nevada	Eureka Twp	75	133
John	43	m	w	OH	Nevada	Washington Twp	75	346
John	32	m	w	MO	Kern	Linns Valley P O	73	349
John	32	m	w	IREL	Marin	San Rafael	74	53
Lucia B	41	m	w	VT	Tehama	Cottonwood Twp	92	162
Mary A	26	f	w	CANA	San Francisco	San Francisco P O	85	845
Mary A	15	f	w	MD	Mariposa	Mariposa P O	74	121
Patrick	50	m	w	IREL	San Francisco	2-Wd San Francisco	79	267
Peter	46	m	w	IREL	San Francisco	11-Wd San Francisc	84	654
Richd	28	m	w	IREL	Solano	Vallejo	90	156
Terrence	32	m	w	IREL	San Francisco	San Francisco P O	83	230
Thomas	35	m	w	IREL	San Francisco	San Francisco P O	83	410
Thomas	28	m	w	IREL	Alameda	Murray Twp	68	124
HEALING								
James	22	m	w	ENGL	San Francisco	3-Wd San Francisco	79	303
HEALLY								
Geo	44	m	w	NY	San Francisco	11-Wd San Francisc	84	663
Mike	20	m	w	ME	San Francisco	11-Wd San Francisc	84	678
HEALY								
Bartholomw	35	m	w	IREL	San Francisco	11-Wd San Francisc	84	655
Charles	28	m	w	CANA	San Francisco	11-Wd San Francisc	84	586
Daniel	38	m	w	IREL	San Francisco	8-Wd San Francisco	82	319
Daniel	20	m	w	IA	Inyo	Cerro Gordo Twp	73	323
Dom	17	m	w	IREL	Yuba	Marysville	93	599
Edward	6	m	w	CA	San Francisco	11-Wd San Francisc	84	593
Edward	45	m	w	ENGL	Sacramento	San Joaquin Twp	77	404
Edward	34	m	w	IREL	Yuba	Marysville	93	593
Edward	25	m	w	HAMB	Sacramento	Sutter Twp	77	382
Horace	21	m	w	NJ	San Francisco	6-Wd San Francisco	81	98
J M	35	m	w	ENGL	Alameda	Oakland	68	265
James	34	m	w	IREL	Alameda	Washington Twp	68	294
James	33	m	w	NY	San Francisco	8-Wd San Francisco	82	351

© 2001 by Heritage Quest. All rights reserved.

Name	Age	S	R	B-PL	County	Locale	Roll	Pg
						Series M593		
Jesse	58	m	w	NY	Alameda	Oakland	68	131
John	42	m	w	IREL	San Francisco	San Francisco P O	83	133
John	40	m	w	IREL	San Francisco	San Francisco P O	83	133
John	35	m	w	IREL	San Francisco	San Francisco P O	83	350
John	29	m	w	IREL	San Francisco	1-Wd San Francisco	79	94
John	25	m	w	MA	San Francisco	11-Wd San Francisc	84	535
Joseph	67	m	w	VT	San Francisco	San Francisco P O	83	254
Kate	22	f	w	CANA	Alameda	Oakland	68	199
M	33	m	w	IREL	Alameda	Murray Twp	68	128
Mary	42	f	w	IREL	Santa Clara	Gilroy Twp	88	95
Mary	30	f	w	IREL	Alameda	Oakland	68	153
Mary A	30	f	w	ME	San Francisco	San Francisco P O	83	175
Morris	30	m	w	IREL	Contra Costa	Martinez P O	71	394
Pat	40	m	w	IREL	Alameda	Murray Twp	68	102
Peter	8	m	w	MEXI	San Francisco	11-Wd San Francisc	84	593
Thomas	5	m	w	CA	San Francisco	San Francisco P O	83	198
Thomas	33	m	w	IREL	San Francisco	San Francisco P O	83	234
William	35	m	w	ENGL	San Mateo	Menlo Park P O	87	377
William	30	m	w	IREL	San Francisco	San Francisco P O	83	363
Willm	35	m	w	IREL	Alameda	Murray Twp	68	112
Wm	35	m	w	IREL	San Francisco	1-Wd San Francisco	79	100
HEAMS								
Mayer	31	m	w	NY	Placer	Auburn P O	76	363
Thomas	22	m	w	MA	Calaveras	Copperopolis P O	70	246
HEAN								
Ah	19	m	c	CHIN	Shasta	French Gulch P O	89	469
HEANEY								
James	34	m	w	IREL	San Francisco	San Francisco P O	83	122
John	29	m	w	CANA	San Francisco	San Francisco P O	83	81
Mary A	39	f	w	PA	San Francisco	San Francisco P O	83	152
Thomas	40	m	w	IREL	San Francisco	San Francisco P O	85	869
William	50	m	w	NY	San Francisco	8-Wd San Francisco	82	461
HEANG								
Ah	40	m	c	CHIN	Mono	Bridgeport P O	74	282
Ah	22	m	c	CHIN	Shasta	French Gulch P O	89	469
HEANY								
C	35	f	w	IREL	Alameda	Oakland	68	139
HEAP								
Ah	38	m	c	CHIN	Placer	Rocklin P O	76	462
HEAPS								
G P	41	m	w	NY	Lassen	Susanville Twp	73	441
HEARCH								
John	48	m	w	PRUS	Yuba	Marysville	93	603
HEARD								
Edwd	58	m	w	IREL	Butte	Kimshew Tpw	70	83
Elijah H	46	m	w	KY	Siskiyou	Yreka	89	663
Francis	36	f	w	ENGL	San Francisco	1-Wd San Francisco	79	77
Freeman	64	m	w	MA	San Francisco	7-Wd San Francisco	81	184
Geo W	38	m	w	KY	Siskiyou	Scott Valley Twp	89	608
Jno	52	m	w	KY	Sacramento	3-Wd Sacramento	77	275
John	40	m	w	PA	Tehama	Antelope Twp	92	154
Joseph	25	m	w	NY	San Francisco	2-Wd San Francisco	79	193
HEARDING								
John C	33	m	w	SWIT	San Francisco	8-Wd San Francisco	82	355
HEARLEY								
Hannah	26	f	w	IREL	Solano	Vallejo	90	186
John	35	m	w	MO	Santa Barbara	Santa Maria P O	87	513
HEARN								
Annie	22	f	w	IREL	San Francisco	San Francisco P O	80	421
Fleming G	44	m	w	KY	Siskiyou	Yreka	89	653
Geo W	38	m	w	MD	Nevada	Bridgeport Twp	75	114
James	55	m	w	KY	Colusa	Grand Island Twp	71	303
James	24	m	w	IREL	San Francisco	San Francisco P O	83	218
Jeremiah	35	m	w	IREL	San Francisco	San Francisco P O	83	391
John	39	m	w	IREL	San Francisco	11-Wd San Francisc	84	632
John	29	m	w	IREL	San Francisco	San Francisco P O	85	745
HEARNE								
David	23	m	w	IREL	San Francisco	7-Wd San Francisco	81	180
Endorgues	39	f	w	CA	Santa Barbara	Santa Barbara P O	87	457
James	41	m	w	IREL	San Francisco	San Francisco P O	85	874
James	21	m	w	IREL	San Francisco	San Francisco P O	83	26
Peter	25	m	w	IREL	Nevada	Grass Valley Twp	75	220
William	24	m	w	ENGL	Nevada	Eureka Twp	75	139
Wm	27	m	w	ME	Nevada	Eureka Twp	75	126
HEARNS								
Christian	51	m	w	HANO	San Francisco	6-Wd San Francisco	81	40
HEARSCH								
John B	23	m	w	CANA	Nevada	Grass Valley Twp	75	151
HEARST								
George	45	m	w	MO	Santa Clara	Santa Clara Twp	88	167
John P	40	m	w	BADE	Siskiyou	Scott Rvr Twp	89	603
W B	40	m	w	MD	Tehama	Red Bluff	92	182
HEART								
Bates	44	m	w	CANA	Merced	Snelling P O	74	274
John	49	m	w	CANA	Merced	Snelling P O	74	274
William	31	m	w	ENGL	Amador	Amador City P O	69	393
HEARTH								
Hermen	40	m	w	PRUS	San Francisco	San Francisco P O	83	264
HEARTON								
Frank	40	m	w	ENGL	Nevada	Eureka Twp	75	131
HEARTSHAND								
P A	49	m	w	SWED	Siskiyou	Callahan P O	89	624
HEARTY								
James	45	m	w	IREL	San Francisco	1-Wd San Francisco	79	32
Mary	16	f	w	OH	Sacramento	3-Wd Sacramento	77	291
Stephen	28	m	w	IREL	San Francisco	1-Wd San Francisco	79	82

Name	Age	S	R	B-PL	County	Locale	Roll	Pg
						Series M593		
HEARY								
John	45	m	w	IREL	San Francisco	8-Wd San Francisco	82	461
Michael	40	m	w	IREL	Yuba	Rose Bar Twp	93	659
HEASE								
Albert	31	m	w	NORW	San Francisco	1-Wd San Francisco	79	124
HEASTON								
Richard	35	m	w	TX	Tulare	Tule Rvr Twp	92	267
HEATH								
A	31	m	w	US	San Joaquin	2-Wd Stockton	86	171
Albert	44	m	w	NY	Santa Cruz	Santa Cruz	89	403
Alexander	38	m	w	CANA	San Joaquin	2-Wd Stockton	86	166
Alfred	53	m	w	ENGL	Santa Cruz	Santa Cruz	89	403
Alfred	50	m	w	VA	Sacramento	Dry Crk Twp	77	100
Alfred	48	m	w	VT	Placer	Newcastle Twp	76	477
Alphonso	50	m	w	CANA	Fresno	Millerton P O	72	150
Anna	30	f	w	ME	Sonoma	Petaluma Twp	91	314
Aron	50	m	w	OH	Sutter	Yuba Twp	92	144
Charles	48	m	w	GERM	Tuolumne	Columbia P O	93	336
Elander	40	m	w	NY	San Francisco	San Francisco P O	85	796
Elisha A	42	m	w	NH	Plumas	Plumas Twp	77	26
Era	16	f	w	MA	Santa Cruz	Santa Cruz	89	419
Fannie	7	f	w	AUST	San Francisco	San Francisco P O	85	827
G G	52	m	w	NY	Monterey	Monterey	74	361
G W	53	m	w	OH	Sacramento	Cosumnes Twp	77	93
Geo J	39	m	w	NY	Shasta	Stillwater P O	89	478
George	40	m	w	NY	Colusa	Spring Valley Twp	71	335
George	25	m	w	BADE	Inyo	Independence Twp	73	328
H C	35	m	w	ME	San Francisco	3-Wd San Francisco	79	311
Higer Hamon	27	m	w	IL	Plumas	Seneca Twp	77	47
Hiland	16	m	w	WI	Plumas	Seneca Twp	77	47
Issac	36	m	w	OH	Siskiyou	Surprise Valley Tw	89	638
J R	36	m	w	OH	Sacramento	3-Wd Sacramento	77	259
J W	55	m	w	MA	Solano	Vallejo	90	169
James	30	m	w	ME	Santa Clara	1-Wd San Jose	88	277
Jemima	41	f	w	ENGL	San Francisco	2-Wd San Francisco	79	185
Jemmima	50	f	w	ENGL	Plumas	Goodwin Twp	77	8
Jno	72	m	w	WALE	Butte	Oregon Twp	70	136
John	43	m	w	ENGL	Fresno	Millerton P O	72	147
John	41	m	w	CA	Merced	Snelling P O	74	248
John	33	m	w	MO	Butte	Hamilton Twp	70	62
John	12	m	w	AUST	San Francisco	San Francisco P O	85	827
John W	23	m	w	IN	Sacramento	Cosumnes Twp	77	93
Jos W	34	m	w	AL	San Francisco	8-Wd San Francisco	82	368
Josiah R	35	m	w	OH	Sacramento	3-Wd Sacramento	77	287
L J	42	m	w	IN	Sierra	Sierra Twp	89	568
Levi	10	m	w	AUST	San Francisco	San Francisco P O	85	827
Loren	50	m	w	ME	Placer	Auburn P O	76	381
Lucien	51	m	w	NY	Santa Cruz	Santa Cruz	89	406
Marion	18	m	b	CA	Los Angeles	Los Angeles	73	530
Maris J Mrs	32	f	w	IREL	Monterey	Monterey Twp	74	343
Mary	23	f	w	SWIT	Amador	Sutter Crk P O	69	401
Mary H	35	f	w	NC	Santa Clara	1-Wd San Jose	88	264
Michael	28	m	w	IREL	Sonoma	Salt Point	91	391
Pat	30	m	w	IREL	San Joaquin	Douglas Twp	86	43
Richd	48	m	w	NY	San Francisco	5-Wd San Francisco	81	33
Richd W	28	m	w	VA	San Francisco	San Francisco P O	83	47
Rudolph	36	m	w	SWIT	San Francisco	2-Wd San Francisco	79	148
Russel	44	m	w	NY	Santa Barbara	Santa Barbara P O	87	485
S W	30	m	w	VT	Merced	Snelling P O	74	261
Samuel	55	m	w	MA	San Francisco	San Francisco P O	80	419
Samuel M	54	m	w	MS	Los Angeles	Los Angeles Twp	73	495
Serena	14	f	w	MA	Santa Cruz	Santa Cruz	89	417
Stephen R	29	m	w	VT	Nevada	Bridgeport Twp	75	114
T P	23	m	w	NH	San Joaquin	Douglas Twp	86	44
Thomas	48	m	w	NH	San Francisco	San Francisco P O	85	747
Thos J	61	m	w	NH	Shasta	Stillwater P O	89	481
Webster	39	m	w	VA	Kern	Bakersfield P O	73	358
William	66	m	w	ENGL	Marin	San Antonio Twp	74	60
William	65	m	w	ENGL	Sonoma	Petaluma Twp	91	366
William	33	m	w	NY	Stanislaus	Buena Vista Twp	92	11
William	24	m	w	ENGL	Santa Clara	Milpitas Twp	88	112
Wm	42	m	w	RI	San Joaquin	2-Wd Stockton	86	206
Wm	31	m	w	IN	Tehama	Merrill	92	198
HEATHCOTE								
Edward	43	m	w	ENGL	Colusa	Butte Twp	71	266
Theode	54	m	w	ENGL	San Francisco	1-Wd San Francisco	79	64
HEATHERLY								
John	23	m	w	ENGL	Santa Barbara	Santa Maria P O	87	513
HEATHLY								
Edward	48	m	w	ENGL	San Francisco	2-Wd San Francisco	79	203
HEATING								
Nellie	22	f	w	IREL	Solano	Vallejo	90	139
Wm	24	m	w	NY	Marin	San Rafael Twp	74	39
HEATON								
Charles A	23	m	w	OH	Colusa	Colusa	71	300
Damiel	28	m	w	PA	Mariposa	Mariposa P O	74	124
John	43	m	w	OH	Colusa	Stony Crk Twp	71	334
Richard	27	m	w	IREL	Marin	Nicasio Twp	74	16
Robbert	31	m	w	NY	Alameda	Oakland	68	265
Viota	20	f	w	ENGL	Napa	Napa	75	52
W	46	m	w	OH	Sacramento	3-Wd Sacramento	77	311
W R	35	m	w	IN	Sacramento	4-Wd Sacramento	77	375
Warren	47	m	w	OH	Placer	Lincoln P O	76	488
William	42	m	w	MA	Placer	Bath P O	76	436
HEATOR								
Humphrey B	35	m	w	OH	Placer	Bath P O	76	456

© 2001 by Heritage Quest. All rights reserved.

Name	Age	S	R	B-PL	County	Locale	Series M593 Roll	Pg
HEATY								
Michael	42	m	w	NY	Yuba	Marysville	93	583
HEAVENS								
T H	58	m	w	NY	Alameda	Oakland	68	165
HEAVER								
George	25	m	w	US	Santa Cruz	Pajaro Twp	89	349
HEAVEY								
John	30	m	w	IREL	Tehama	Paskenta Twp	92	165
John	22	m	w	IREL	San Francisco	1-Wd San Francisco	79	127
Martin	36	m	w	SC	Alameda	Brooklyn	68	35
Patrick	35	m	w	IREL	San Francisco	1-Wd San Francisco	79	69
HEBB								
Henry	35	m	w	ENGL	Santa Clara	San Jose Twp	88	220
HEBBARD								
C	16	m	w	NV	Solano	Benicia	90	21
James	42	m	w	CANA	Nevada	Nevada Twp	75	293
HEBEN								
Fredrika L	39	f	w	BREM	Sacramento	4-Wd Sacramento	77	321
HEBER								
Augustus	38	m	w	HAMB	San Francisco	6-Wd San Francisco	81	104
Lewis	24	m	w	FRAN	Solano	Denverton Twp	90	22
Mary	61	f	w	BAVA	San Francisco	2-Wd San Francisco	79	159
William	40	m	w	MO	Solano	Denverton Twp	90	27
Wm	36	m	w	AUST	San Francisco	2-Wd San Francisco	79	233
HEBERS								
Franz	40	m	w	PRUS	San Francisco	1-Wd San Francisco	79	57
HEBERT								
L D	30	m	w	NY	Trinity	Junction City Pct	92	210
Margaret	26	f	w	CANA	San Mateo	Half Moon Bay P O	87	400
HEBNER								
Charles	36	m	w	PRUS	Marin	Sausalito Twp	74	67
HEBOLD								
Tobock	42	m	w	FRAN	Butte	Oregon Twp	70	132
HEBORN								
Ann	72	f	w	ENGL	Sonoma	Mendocino Twp	91	296
George	53	m	w	ENGL	Yolo	Cache Crk Twp	93	445
Henry	46	m	w	ENGL	Sonoma	Mendocino Twp	91	296
HEBRAND								
Theodore	61	m	w	FRAN	San Mateo	Woodside P O	87	384
HEBREW								
James	40	m	w	IREL	Monterey	San Benito Twp	74	382
HEBRON								
William	23	m	w	CANA	Alpine	Markleeville P O	69	312
William Mc	45	m	w	NY	Santa Cruz	Santa Cruz	89	423
HECAL								
Bernard	33	m	w	AUST	San Luis Obispo	San Luis Obispo Tw	87	310
HECHL								
David	29	m	w	BAVA	Butte	Ophir Twp	70	91
Isaac	37	m	w	BAVA	San Francisco	8-Wd San Francisco	82	428
HECHT								
Edward	40	m	w	FRAN	San Francisco	2-Wd San Francisco	79	165
John M	34	m	w	SAXO	San Francisco	2-Wd San Francisco	79	153
Louisa	49	f	w	HDAR	San Francisco	2-Wd San Francisco	79	193
HECK								
Ah	48	m	c	CHIN	Calaveras	San Andreas P O	70	165
Ah	24	m	c	CHIN	Los Angeles	Los Angeles	73	507
Anna	30	f	w	SWED	Sonoma	Sonoma Twp	91	447
Emilias	30	m	w	PRUS	Alameda	Murray Twp	68	123
HECKE								
Cristopher	40	m	w	PRUS	San Francisco	8-Wd San Francisco	82	473
HECKEL								
John	31	m	w	NY	Inyo	Independence Twp	73	324
HECKELS								
Wm	28	m	w	NY	Sierra	Table Rock Twp	89	578
HECKENDORN								
John	56	m	w	PA	Calaveras	Copperopolis P O	70	262
HECKER								
Caroline	20	f	w	SAXO	San Francisco	2-Wd San Francisco	79	219
Fred	27	m	w	PRUS	Butte	Ophir Twp	70	91
Jno	51	m	w	NH	Sacramento	1-Wd Sacramento	77	185
Samuel	34	m	w	PA	Nevada	Nevada Twp	75	319
HECKERTHORN								
David	35	m	w	OH	Sonoma	Mendocino Twp	91	291
HECKET								
L F	45	m	w	OH	San Joaquin	Castoria Twp	86	8
HECKHAUSEN								
John P	44	m	w	PRUS	Los Angeles	Los Angeles	73	528
HECKLE								
Charles	36	m	w	PRUS	Inyo	Bishop Crk Twp	73	317
Francis	38	m	w	PRUS	Plumas	Seneca Twp	77	49
James Alexander	32	m	w	LA	Plumas	Indian Twp	77	9
HECKLER								
Charles	35	m	w	PRUS	Tulare	Tule Rvr Twp	92	259
HECKMAN								
Henry	41	m	w	GERM	Tuolumne	Columbia P O	93	358
J A	32	m	w	AL	Napa	Napa Twp	75	61
John	9	m	w	WI	San Francisco	San Francisco P O	85	800
Martin	30	m	w	SHOL	San Francisco	1-Wd San Francisco	79	119
Mary	14	f	w	UT	Siskiyou	Yreka	89	659
Thomas	44	m	w	BAVA	San Francisco	San Francisco P O	83	315
HECKOX								
George	46	m	w	IL	Napa	Napa Twp	75	64
HECLOTFISHER								
Sam	25	m	w	BAVA	San Francisco	11-Wd San Francisc	84	662
HECOX								
Adna A	64	m	w	MI	Santa Cruz	Santa Cruz	89	434
Oscar T	30	m	w	IL	Santa Cruz	Santa Cruz	89	427

Name	Age	S	R	B-PL	County	Locale	Series M593 Roll	Pg
HECTON								
Newton	28	m	w	MO	Nevada	Eureka Twp	75	131
HECTOR								
A B	38	m	w	SWED	Tuolumne	Chinese Camp P O	93	363
Chas	28	m	w	KY	San Joaquin	Liberty Twp	86	96
Christopher	26	m	w	MA	San Francisco	3-Wd San Francisco	79	325
George W	35	m	w	OH	Tulare	Venice Twp	92	274
Harrison	30	m	w	IL	Santa Barbara	San Buenaventura P	87	444
John	48	m	w	PRUS	Sacramento	4-Wd Sacramento	77	334
John	40	m	w	AR	San Joaquin	Elliott Twp	86	80
John J	38	m	w	OH	Santa Barbara	San Buenaventura P	87	431
John Jr	65	m	w	NJ	Santa Barbara	San Buenaventura P	87	431
Oschwald	19	m	w	PRUS	Sacramento	2-Wd Sacramento	77	245
William B	49	m	w	OH	Tulare	Venice Twp	92	274
Wm	34	m	w	AR	San Joaquin	Tulare Twp	86	259
Wm	27	m	w	CA	San Joaquin	Castoria Twp	86	1
Wm	21	m	w	ME	San Joaquin	Tulare Twp	86	253
HEDDEN								
Byron	28	m	w	NJ	Siskiyou	Table Rock Twp	89	647
Joel	26	m	w	IL	Sutter	Nicolaus Twp	92	106
Sanford	24	m	w	IN	Marin	San Rafael Twp	74	37
HEDDING								
Albert	30	m	w	HANO	San Francisco	1-Wd San Francisco	79	53
J	22	f	w	WI	Sutter	Yuba Twp	92	151
HEDDY								
Ed	44	m	w	IREL	Alameda	Oakland	68	208
HEDENBERG								
J	66	m	w	ME	Sacramento	3-Wd Sacramento	77	302
HEDERINGTON								
Lizzi	19	f	w	IREL	San Luis Obispo	Salinas Twp	87	295
HEDGE								
Albert	35	m	w	OH	Yuba	Rose Bar Twp	93	653
Galvin M	33	m	w	OH	Yuba	New York Twp	93	635
Geo	51	m	w	OH	Butte	Ophir Twp	70	115
Joseph	54	m	w	OH	Yuba	New York Twp	93	635
Leonard	35	m	w	OH	Butte	Ophir Twp	70	111
Mareus	41	m	w	NY	Tuolumne	Sonora P O	93	313
Martha	20	f	w	OH	Butte	Ophir Twp	70	116
Martha	10	m	w	MO	Butte	Ophir Twp	70	94
Mathew	30	m	w	IREL	San Mateo	Redwood Twp	87	369
Nathan M	48	m	w	NY	Sonoma	Petaluma Twp	91	328
P	32	m	w	IREL	Amador	Sutter Crk P O	69	398
HEDGEPETH								
Joel	29	m	w	MO	Monterey	Pajaro Twp	74	371
HEDGES								
Augustes	38	m	w	NY	Trinity	North Fork Twp	92	218
Ben	31	m	w	PA	San Francisco	7-Wd San Francisco	81	262
C W	24	m	w	MI	Trinity	Hayfork Valley	92	238
Charles	27	m	w	MA	Sonoma	Bodega Twp	91	254
Chas H	48	m	w	NY	Yuba	Linda Twp	93	558
E R	40	m	w	NJ	San Joaquin	3-Wd Stockton	86	244
Geo	30	m	w	NY	San Francisco	11-Wd San Francisc	84	432
Jabe	37	m	w	NY	Trinity	North Fork Twp	92	220
Jares J	22	m	w	ENGL	Sacramento	Franklin Twp	77	117
John H	34	m	w	VA	Tulare	Tule Rvr Twp	92	270
Joseph	31	m	w	OH	Butte	Ophir Twp	70	96
Josiah B	36	m	w	NY	Inyo	Bishop Crk Twp	73	313
L D	46	m	w	OH	Sutter	Nicolaus Twp	92	109
Lewis	27	m	w	IREL	Butte	Ophir Twp	70	120
M A	76	f	w	NY	Tuolumne	Sonora P O	93	308
William H	56	m	w	NY	Sonoma	Petaluma Twp	91	313
HEDGPATH								
Joel	60	m	w	KY	Tulare	Farmersville Twp	92	249
HEDLER								
John	45	m	w	HANO	San Francisco	San Francisco P O	83	75
HEDLEY								
Peter D	41	m	w	NY	San Francisco	8-Wd San Francisco	82	380
HEDLY								
Edwd	36	m	w	ENGL	Butte	Kimshew Tpw	70	79
Robert	30	m	w	CANA	Solano	Green Valley Twp	90	41
HEDMAN								
Charles	28	m	w	HAMB	San Francisco	8-Wd San Francisco	82	432
William	28	m	w	PRUS	San Francisco	3-Wd San Francisco	79	318
HEDNERSON								
Hugh	38	m	w	IREL	San Diego	Coronado	78	467
HEDRICK								
Charles	30	m	w	AR	San Bernardino	San Bernardino Twp	78	451
Duskin	30	m	w	IA	Plumas	Indian Twp	77	16
Geo P	56	m	w	VA	Santa Barbara	Santa Barbara P O	87	496
Hamden	37	m	w	OH	Shasta	Stillwater P O	89	480
Henry	46	m	w	IN	Calaveras	San Andreas P O	70	170
Jacob	46	m	w	MD	Siskiyou	Butte Twp	89	586
Joseph	23	m	w	OH	Nevada	Rough & Ready Twp	75	324
HEDRICKS								
Harvey	46	m	w	IL	Calaveras	San Andreas P O	70	176
Jos	40	m	w	KY	Sonoma	Santa Rosa	91	404
Robt	52	m	w	PA	Santa Barbara	Santa Barbara P O	87	495
HEDWICK								
---	25	f	w	BADE	Yuba	W Bear Rvr Twp	93	682
HEE								
A	35	m	c	CHIN	Placer	Bath P O	76	444
Ah	65	m	c	CHIN	Sacramento	Granite Twp	77	141
Ah	60	m	c	CHIN	Sacramento	Dry Crk Twp	77	101
Ah	60	m	c	CHIN	Sacramento	Granite Twp	77	155
Ah	59	m	c	CHIN	Nevada	Grass Valley Twp	75	206
Ah	50	m	c	CHIN	Trinity	Trinity Center Pct	92	240
Ah	46	m	c	CHIN	Trinity	Junction City Pct	92	208

© 2001 by Heritage Quest. All rights reserved.

California 1870 Census

Name	Age	S	R	B-PL	County	Locale	Series M593 Roll	Pg
Ah	45	m	c	CHIN	Sacramento	Center Twp	77	85
Ah	45	m	c	CHIN	Calaveras	Copperopolis P O	70	242
Ah	44	m	c	CHIN	Placer	Bath P O	76	445
Ah	44	m	c	CHIN	Trinity	Lewiston Pct	92	212
Ah	44	m	c	CHIN	San Francisco	2-Wd San Francisco	79	285
Ah	43	m	c	CHIN	Calaveras	Copperopolis P O	70	233
Ah	42	m	c	CHIN	Calaveras	Copperopolis P O	70	232
Ah	42	m	c	CHIN	Mariposa	Mariposa P O	74	137
Ah	41	m	c	CHIN	Nevada	Rough & Ready Twp	75	337
Ah	41	m	c	CHIN	San Francisco	6-Wd San Francisco	81	58
Ah	41	m	c	CHIN	San Francisco	6-Wd San Francisco	81	69
Ah	40	m	c	CHIN	Santa Clara	Santa Clara Twp	88	148
Ah	40	m	c	CHIN	San Joaquin	2-Wd Stockton	86	173
Ah	40	m	c	CHIN	Trinity	Weaverville Pct	92	232
Ah	37	m	c	CHIN	Nevada	Little York Twp	75	242
Ah	36	m	c	CHIN	Butte	Mountain Spring Tw	70	89
Ah	36	m	c	CHIN	Santa Clara	1-Wd San Jose	88	277
Ah	35	m	c	CHIN	San Joaquin	Elkhorn Twp	86	53
Ah	35	m	c	CHIN	San Joaquin	2-Wd Stockton	86	171
Ah	35	f	c	CHIN	San Francisco	6-Wd San Francisco	81	37
Ah	35	f	c	CHIN	Amador	Fiddletown P O	69	428
Ah	32	m	c	CHIN	Sacramento	Granite Twp	77	139
Ah	32	m	c	CHIN	San Francisco	6-Wd San Francisco	81	39
Ah	32	f	c	CHIN	San Francisco	6-Wd San Francisco	81	58
Ah	32	m	c	CHIN	Trinity	Trinity Center Pct	92	240
Ah	31	m	c	CHIN	Amador	Volcano P O	69	384
Ah	31	m	c	CHIN	Solano	Silveyville Twp	90	87
Ah	30	m	c	CHIN	Sacramento	Granite Twp	77	139
Ah	30	m	c	CHIN	Siskiyou	Yreka	89	650
Ah	30	f	c	CHIN	Trinity	Weaverville Pct	92	228
Ah	30	m	c	CHIN	San Francisco	6-Wd San Francisco	81	65
Ah	29	m	c	CHIN	Sacramento	Granite Twp	77	155
Ah	29	f	c	CHIN	San Francisco	6-Wd San Francisco	81	75
Ah	29	m	c	CHIN	Siskiyou	Hamburg Twp	89	597
Ah	29	m	c	CHIN	San Francisco	2-Wd San Francisco	79	285
Ah	28	m	c	CHIN	Sacramento	Granite Twp	77	141
Ah	28	m	c	CHIN	Sacramento	Granite Twp	77	152
Ah	28	m	c	CHIN	Tehama	Tehama Twp	92	189
Ah	28	m	c	CHIN	Shasta	Horsetown P O	89	503
Ah	28	f	c	CHIN	San Francisco	6-Wd San Francisco	81	76
Ah	28	f	c	CHIN	San Francisco	6-Wd San Francisco	81	77
Ah	28	m	c	CHIN	Yuba	Rose Bar Twp	93	655
Ah	28	m	c	CHIN	San Francisco	6-Wd San Francisco	81	60
Ah	28	m	c	CHIN	Sacramento	Franklin Twp	77	119
Ah	27	m	c	CHIN	Placer	Auburn P O	76	363
Ah	26	m	c	CHIN	Kern	Bakersfield P O	73	361
Ah	26	m	c	CHIN	San Francisco	6-Wd San Francisco	81	63
Ah	25	m	c	CHIN	Sacramento	Cosumnes Twp	77	93
Ah	25	f	c	CHIN	Calaveras	Copperopolis P O	70	234
Ah	25	m	c	CHIN	Alameda	Alameda	68	6
Ah	25	m	c	CHIN	Mariposa	Mariposa P O	74	126
Ah	24	f	c	CHIN	Amador	Ione City P O	69	354
Ah	24	m	c	CHIN	Sonoma	Bodega Twp	91	251
Ah	24	f	c	CHIN	Santa Cruz	Watsonville	89	377
Ah	24	m	c	CHIN	Santa Barbara	Santa Barbara P O	87	458
Ah	24	m	c	CHIN	Santa Clara	San Jose Twp	88	219
Ah	24	m	c	CHIN	San Francisco	3-Wd San Francisco	79	307
Ah	23	f	c	CHIN	San Francisco	6-Wd San Francisco	81	51
Ah	23	f	c	CHIN	San Francisco	6-Wd San Francisco	81	77
Ah	23	m	c	CHIN	San Francisco	7-Wd San Francisco	81	182
Ah	23	m	c	CHIN	San Francisco	2-Wd San Francisco	79	282
Ah	22	f	c	CHIN	Amador	Fiddletown P O	69	428
Ah	22	m	c	CHIN	Alameda	Eden Twp	68	72
Ah	22	m	c	CHIN	Solano	Suisun Twp	90	106
Ah	22	m	c	CHIN	Nevada	Rough & Ready Twp	75	324
Ah	22	m	c	CHIN	Butte	Mountain Spring Tw	70	90
Ah	21	f	c	CHIN	Nevada	Grass Valley Twp	75	205
Ah	21	m	c	CHIN	Sacramento	Natomas Twp	77	167
Ah	20	m	c	CHIN	Sacramento	Granite Twp	77	137
Ah	20	m	c	CHIN	San Francisco	6-Wd San Francisco	81	62
Ah	20	m	c	CHIN	San Francisco	6-Wd San Francisco	81	55
Ah	20	m	c	CHIN	Yuba	Marysville	93	619
Ah	20	m	c	CHIN	San Francisco	6-Wd San Francisco	81	85
Ah	20	m	c	CHIN	San Francisco	3-Wd San Francisco	79	324
Ah	19	m	c	CHIN	Trinity	Lewiston Pct	92	214
Ah	19	m	c	CHIN	Santa Clara	Gilroy Twp	88	75
Ah	19	f	c	CHIN	San Francisco	6-Wd San Francisco	81	76
Ah	19	m	c	CHIN	San Francisco	6-Wd San Francisco	81	57
Ah	19	m	c	CHIN	San Francisco	6-Wd San Francisco	81	129
Ah	19	m	c	CHIN	Marin	San Rafael Twp	74	39
Ah	18	m	c	CHIN	San Francisco	11-Wd San Francisc	84	444
Ah	18	f	c	CHIN	San Francisco	6-Wd San Francisco	81	74
Ah	18	m	c	CHIN	San Francisco	6-Wd San Francisco	81	85
Ah	18	m	c	CHIN	Placer	Auburn P O	76	371
Ah	17	f	c	CHIN	San Francisco	6-Wd San Francisco	81	75
Ah	17	f	c	CHIN	San Francisco	6-Wd San Francisco	81	74
Ah	17	m	c	CHIN	Placer	Auburn P O	76	371
Ah	17	m	c	CHIN	San Francisco	2-Wd San Francisco	79	139
Ah	17	m	c	CHIN	Alameda	Oakland	68	185
Ah	16	m	c	CHIN	Placer	Clipper Gap P O	76	393
Ah	15	m	c	CHIN	San Francisco	3-Wd San Francisco	79	307
Ah	14	m	c	CHIN	San Francisco	6-Wd San Francisco	81	47
Ah	14	m	c	CHIN	San Francisco	7-Wd San Francisco	81	208
Ah	13	m	c	CHIN	San Francisco	7-Wd San Francisco	81	212
Choy	32	f	c	CHIN	Nevada	Grass Valley Twp	75	205
Cong	24	m	c	CHIN	Calaveras	San Andreas P O	70	220
Fook	34	m	c	CHIN	Calaveras	San Andreas P O	70	218

Name	Age	S	R	B-PL	County	Locale	Series M593 Roll	Pg
Gee	27	m	c	CHIN	Yuba	Marysville	93	631
Hah	42	m	c	CHIN	San Francisco	6-Wd San Francisco	81	61
Hi	24	f	c	CHIN	San Francisco	6-Wd San Francisco	81	53
Hing	16	f	c	CHIN	San Francisco	6-Wd San Francisco	81	76
Hop	25	m	c	CHIN	Nevada	Nevada Twp	75	279
Ling	38	m	c	CHIN	Mariposa	Mariposa P O	74	104
Lis	7	m	c	CHIN	Sacramento	1-Wd Sacramento	77	193
Si	38	m	c	CHIN	Nevada	Nevada Twp	75	311
Sin	28	f	c	CHIN	Mariposa	Mariposa P O	74	103
Sin	28	f	c	CHIN	Mariposa	Mariposa P O	74	104
Sing	19	m	c	CHIN	San Francisco	2-Wd San Francisco	79	158
Sung	21	m	c	CHIN	Sonoma	Petaluma Twp	91	342
Ti	19	m	c	CHIN	San Francisco	1-Wd San Francisco	79	80
Tom	24	m	c	CHIN	Tehama	Tehama Twp	92	189
Tong	25	m	c	CHIN	San Francisco	11-Wd San Francisc	84	661
Tong	21	f	c	CHIN	Placer	Dutch Flat P O	76	409
Tye	29	m	c	CHIN	Solano	Suisun Twp	90	107
Wing	48	m	c	CHIN	San Francisco	11-Wd San Francisc	84	546
Wy	24	m	c	CHIN	Solano	Suisun Twp	90	107
Yee	36	m	c	CHIN	San Francisco	2-Wd San Francisco	79	286
Yon	29	m	c	CHIN	San Joaquin	Union Twp	86	266
HEEBE								
Phillip	45	m	w	GERM	Sonoma	Washington Twp	91	471
HEED								
W Y	48	m	w	KY	Alameda	Oakland	68	213
HEEGAARD								
Chas	20	m	w	DENM	Shasta	Millville P O	89	486
HEEGAN								
James	38	m	w	NORW	San Francisco	7-Wd San Francisco	81	274
HEEK								
Ah	16	f	c	CHIN	San Francisco	6-Wd San Francisco	81	74
HEELD								
M	40	m	w	CA	Alameda	Murray Twp	68	116
HEELY								
Hugh	40	m	w	IREL	San Francisco	7-Wd San Francisco	81	162
HEEM								
Ah	34	m	c	CHIN	Butte	Mountain Spring Tw	70	90
Ah	17	m	c	CHIN	San Francisco	6-Wd San Francisco	81	45
HEEMAY								
Chas	28	m	w	NH	Alameda	Oakland	68	213
HEEN								
Ah	49	m	c	CHIN	Merced	Snelling P O	74	278
Ah	31	m	c	CHIN	San Francisco	6-Wd San Francisco	81	85
Ah	27	f	c	CHIN	San Francisco	6-Wd San Francisco	81	53
Ah	24	f	c	CHIN	San Francisco	6-Wd San Francisco	81	75
Ah	20	m	c	CHIN	San Francisco	San Francisco P O	80	487
Ah	20	m	c	CHIN	San Francisco	6-Wd San Francisco	81	90
Ah	19	m	c	CHIN	San Francisco	6-Wd San Francisco	81	46
Ah	18	f	c	CHIN	San Francisco	6-Wd San Francisco	81	74
Ah	16	f	c	CHIN	San Francisco	6-Wd San Francisco	81	75
Ah	13	f	c	CHIN	San Francisco	6-Wd San Francisco	81	61
Fong	20	m	c	CHIN	San Francisco	6-Wd San Francisco	81	47
HEENAN								
Charles O	22	m	w	SCOT	Santa Cruz	Santa Cruz	89	427
Dennis	31	m	w	IREL	San Francisco	San Francisco P O	80	400
J	50	m	w	IREL	Alameda	Murray Twp	68	123
James	37	m	w	IREL	Placer	Auburn P O	76	377
James P	33	m	w	IREL	San Francisco	1-Wd San Francisco	79	132
Mich	30	m	w	IREL	San Francisco	1-Wd San Francisco	79	44
Michl	32	m	w	IREL	Alameda	Murray Twp	68	106
Nora	30	f	w	IREL	Alameda	Oakland	68	163
Pat	35	m	w	IREL	Alameda	Murray Twp	68	106
Pat	30	m	w	IREL	San Francisco	7-Wd San Francisco	81	274
Patrick	33	m	w	IREL	Yuba	Linda Twp	93	554
HEENEY								
Anne	40	f	w	IREL	Alameda	Oakland	68	196
James	30	m	w	IREL	Santa Barbara	San Buenaventura P	87	430
James	20	m	w	IREL	Merced	Snelling P O	74	269
John	33	m	w	MA	Alameda	Oakland	68	181
Mary	35	f	w	IREL	San Francisco	San Francisco P O	83	256
Patrick	40	m	w	IREL	Stanislaus	Empire Twp	92	48
HEENG								
Ah	28	f	c	CHIN	San Francisco	6-Wd San Francisco	81	74
HEENY								
Sarah	40	f	w	IREL	Alameda	Oakland	68	162
HEEP								
Ah	25	m	c	CHIN	San Francisco	6-Wd San Francisco	81	61
Ah	15	m	c	CHIN	San Francisco	6-Wd San Francisco	81	68
Low	32	m	c	CHIN	San Francisco	6-Wd San Francisco	81	39
Phillip	37	m	w	PRUS	San Francisco	6-Wd San Francisco	81	108
HEEPS								
Joseph	22	m	w	UT	San Bernardino	San Bernardino Twp	78	432
HEER								
Ah	27	m	c	CHIN	San Francisco	6-Wd San Francisco	81	56
Ah	24	m	c	CHIN	San Francisco	6-Wd San Francisco	81	61
Ah	16	f	c	CHIN	San Francisco	6-Wd San Francisco	81	75
HEERE								
Henry	25	m	w	BREM	San Francisco	3-Wd San Francisco	79	321
HEERING								
John H	55	m	w	PRUS	Santa Clara	2-Wd San Jose	88	324
HEES								
Charles	48	m	w	PRUS	San Francisco	6-Wd San Francisco	81	79
HEESCH								
John	37	m	w	SHOL	San Francisco	3-Wd San Francisco	79	287
HEESER								
William	47	m	w	PRUS	Mendocino	Big Rvr Twp	74	170

© 2001 by Heritage Quest. All rights reserved.

Name	Age	S	R	B-PL	County	Locale	Series M593 Roll	Pg
HEET								
Ah	54	m	c	CHIN	San Francisco	6-Wd San Francisco	81	56
Ah	51	m	c	CHIN	San Francisco	6-Wd San Francisco	81	57
Ha	20	m	c	CHIN	San Francisco	6-Wd San Francisco	81	49
HEETH								
Joseph	31	m	w	PA	Inyo	Independence Twp	73	326
HEETS								
Charles	61	m	w	PA	Sacramento	Alabama Twp	77	60
HEFELFINGER								
William	13	m	w	LA	Shasta	Shasta P O	89	457
HEFENAN								
Jno	34	m	w	US	San Joaquin	2-Wd Stockton	86	166
HEFER								
John A	35	m	w	WURT	San Francisco	8-Wd San Francisco	82	307
HEFERMAN								
Charles	53	m	w	PRUS	Sacramento	San Joaquin Twp	77	405
HEFERON								
Sarah	29	f	w	NY	San Francisco	San Francisco P O	83	271
HEFFELFINGER								
S	27	m	w	OH	Sierra	Butte Twp	89	508
HEFFEMAN								
Charles	12	m	w	CA	Marin	San Rafael Twp	74	27
HEFFER								
Henery	38	m	w	IREL	San Francisco	7-Wd San Francisco	81	195
HEFFERMAN								
Charles	13	m	w	CA	Sonoma	Sonoma Twp	91	449
Edward	19	m	w	NY	Stanislaus	Emory Twp	92	24
Lawrence	24	m	w	OH	Sonoma	Petaluma Twp	91	326
Patk	35	m	w	IREL	San Francisco	1-Wd San Francisco	79	7
HEFFERN								
James	43	m	w	IREL	San Francisco	San Francisco P O	83	249
HEFFERNAN								
Henry	43	m	w	HOLL	Calaveras	San Andreas P O	70	201
P	53	m	w	IREL	San Joaquin	Oneal Twp	86	101
Thos	36	m	w	IREL	San Joaquin	Oneal Twp	86	111
Thos	35	m	w	IREL	San Joaquin	Oneal Twp	86	100
Wm	22	m	w	CT	San Francisco	1-Wd San Francisco	79	70
HEFFERNAND								
John	12	m	w	CA	Contra Costa	Martinez P O	71	372
HEFFERNON								
John	35	m	w	IREL	San Francisco	San Francisco P O	83	114
HEFFERON								
James J	40	m	w	NY	Inyo	Independence Twp	73	324
Martin	30	m	w	IREL	San Francisco	San Francisco P O	83	312
Michael	25	m	w	IREL	San Francisco	8-Wd San Francisco	82	465
HEFFILBERG								
John	19	m	w	OH	Sutter	Yuba Twp	92	147
HEFFIN								
Michael	36	m	w	IREL	San Bernardino	San Bernardino Twp	78	417
HEFFLIFINGER								
Wm	24	m	w	PA	Sonoma	Salt Point	91	389
HEFFNER								
Adam	24	m	w	WURT	San Francisco	11-Wd San Francisc	84	424
Fred	43	m	w	BADE	Butte	Chico Twp	70	23
Henry	28	m	w	GERM	Tulare	Packwood Twp	92	255
Philip	46	m	w	OH	Butte	Ophir Twp	70	116
HEFFRAN								
Patrick	39	m	w	IREL	San Francisco	11-Wd San Francisc	84	467
HEFFREN								
William	9	m	w	CA	San Francisco	11-Wd San Francisc	84	652
Wm	34	m	w	IREL	Solano	Vallejo	90	170
HEFFRON								
Albert	28	m	w	MA	Sonoma	Bodega Twp	91	251
John	38	m	w	IREL	Alameda	Eden Twp	68	72
M H	39	m	w	IREL	Amador	Ione City P O	69	351
Mary	13	f	w	CA	Yuba	Rose Bar Twp	93	666
Patrick	25	m	w	IREL	Marin	San Rafael Twp	74	31
Thomas	35	m	w	IREL	Marin	Tomales Twp	74	77
HEFFUR								
Thomas	49	m	w	MO	Sonoma	Vallejo Twp	91	458
HEFLE								
William	45	m	w	PA	San Francisco	8-Wd San Francisco	82	288
HEFLICE								
Henry	10	m	w	CA	Stanislaus	North Twp	92	68
HEFLIN								
H M	30	m	w	VT	Sonoma	Mendocino Twp	91	298
Joseph	36	m	w	PA	Sacramento	Sutter Twp	77	389
HEFNER								
John	33	m	w	AR	Siskiyou	Butte Twp	89	587
William	46	m	w	PRUS	San Francisco	8-Wd San Francisco	82	428
HEFRENAN								
Margaret	20	f	w	IREL	Santa Clara	2-Wd San Jose	88	297
HEFRON								
John	23	m	w	CANA	Sacramento	Franklin Twp	77	117
Margaret	29	f	w	IREL	Siskiyou	Scott Valley Twp	89	610
Mary	16	f	w	NJ	Sacramento	4-Wd Sacramento	77	361
HEFT								
Henry	27	m	w	SWIT	Los Angeles	Los Angeles	73	565
Jacob	40	m	w	GERM	Santa Clara	1-Wd San Jose	88	224
HEFTE								
Fredeline	28	m	w	BAVA	Inyo	Independence Twp	73	324
HEGAERA								
Alveno	48	m	w	CA	Alameda	Washington Twp	68	287
HEGAN								
James	25	m	w	IREL	San Francisco	11-Wd San Francisc	84	678
John	45	m	w	IREL	Solano	Vallejo	90	180
W	38	m	w	HANO	Alameda	Oakland	68	164
HEGARTY								
Anna	30	f	w	IREL	Nevada	Eureka Twp	75	126
Chas	36	m	w	IREL	Nevada	Eureka Twp	75	126
Michael	50	m	w	IREL	San Mateo	Schoolhouse Statio	87	343
HEGECOTH								
Jas	38	m	w	TN	Shasta	Stillwater P O	89	479
Pleasant	51	m	w	TN	Shasta	Stillwater P O	89	481
HEGEILSTEIN								
Gus	14	m	w	CA	Sacramento	3-Wd Sacramento	77	273
HEGELAN								
John	25	m	w	GERM	Yolo	Grafton Twp	93	493
HEGELER								
Gerhardt	11	m	w	CA	Sonoma	Analy Twp	91	237
Henry	51	m	w	OLDE	Sonoma	Bodega Twp	91	252
John	48	m	w	ENGL	San Francisco	5-Wd San Francisco	81	11
HEGEMAN								
Samuel J	47	m	w	NY	San Francisco	8-Wd San Francisco	82	427
Victor	32	m	w	FRAN	San Francisco	8-Wd San Francisco	82	458
HEGER								
Jacob	35	m	w	WURT	Napa	Napa Twp	75	70
HEGERHORST								
Chris	30	m	w	HANO	San Francisco	11-Wd San Francisc	84	446
HEGG								
Ann	40	f	w	SWED	San Francisco	3-Wd San Francisco	79	300
HEGGINS								
T A	29	m	w	NY	San Francisco	7-Wd San Francisco	81	226
Thomas	10	m	w	CA	Marin	San Rafael Twp	74	26
HEGIRA								
Joseph	30	m	w	CA	Napa	Napa Twp	75	31
HEGLAND								
Chas J	40	m	w	SWED	San Diego	San Diego	78	497
Henry	36	m	w	NORW	Marin	San Rafael	74	57
Silas	48	m	w	OH	Humboldt	South Fork Twp	72	302
HEGMANN								
George	34	m	w	PRUS	San Francisco	San Francisco P O	83	219
HEGOBY								
Rose	20	f	w	IREL	San Francisco	7-Wd San Francisco	81	229
HEGS								
W D	28	m	w	NY	Sutter	Butte Twp	92	98
HEGUENA								
Pedro	45	m	w	CA	Contra Costa	Martinez P O	71	369
HEH								
Hot	25	m	c	CHIN	Sacramento	1-Wd Sacramento	77	198
HEI								
Ah	30	f	c	CHIN	Amador	Jackson P O	69	344
HEIBLIN								
James	48	m	w	SAXO	San Francisco	San Francisco P O	80	531
HEICHTIS								
O P	26	m	w	GERM	San Joaquin	2-Wd Stockton	86	170
HEICK								
Chas	40	m	w	OLDE	San Francisco	San Francisco P O	83	43
HEICKA								
Heurn	26	m	w	BRUN	Napa	Napa Twp	75	70
HEICKLEY								
George	27	m	w	NY	Fresno	Millerton P O	72	158
HEIDAECK								
Mark	24	m	w	BADE	San Francisco	San Francisco P O	83	352
HEIDECKER								
Wm	58	m	w	PRUS	Fresno	Millerton P O	72	147
HEIDEN								
Christian	38	m	w	NORW	Calaveras	San Andreas P O	70	204
HEIDENFELD								
Solomon	25	m	w	AL	San Francisco	8-Wd San Francisco	82	438
HEIDENFELT								
Geo	33	m	w	GERM	San Francisco	8-Wd San Francisco	82	375
HEIDENHEIMER								
J	45	m	w	PRUS	San Francisco	8-Wd San Francisco	82	375
J	42	m	w	GERM	San Francisco	8-Wd San Francisco	82	375
HEIDER								
Chris	22	m	w	BADE	San Francisco	San Francisco P O	83	273
Christian	33	m	w	PRUS	Tehama	Tehama Twp	92	195
HEIDHOFF								
Albert	30	m	w	PRUS	San Francisco	San Francisco P O	83	207
HEIDINGER								
Chas	30	m	w	FRAN	San Francisco	San Francisco P O	83	58
HEIDMAN								
Matilda	26	f	w	PRUS	San Francisco	8-Wd San Francisco	82	390
HEIDORN								
Clark	43	m	w	GERM	Alameda	Washington Twp	68	293
HEIDRICH								
H	20	m	w	PA	Amador	Sutter Crk P O	69	396
HEIDRICK								
Fredk	37	m	w	HCAS	San Francisco	1-Wd San Francisco	79	51
HEIDRIDK								
D E	31	m	w	IL	Yuba	Marysville Twp	93	569
HEIFFRAN								
Oscar	46	m	w	NY	Yuba	Linda Twp	93	554
HEIGAL								
Johana	44	f	w	GERM	Sacramento	1-Wd Sacramento	77	177
HEIGGINS								
Elisha W	48	m	w	TN	San Luis Obispo	Santa Rosa Twp	87	319
HEIGH								
Chang	40	m	c	CHIN	Nevada	Meadow Lake Twp	75	254
HEIGHT								
John	47	m	m	NJ	Solano	Vallejo	90	161
HEIGHTMAN								
H	48	m	w	PRUS	Sonoma	Santa Rosa	91	422

© 2001 by Heritage Quest. All rights reserved.

Series M593

Name	Age	S	R	B-PL	County	Locale	Roll	Pg
HEIGLEHER								
Godfrey	24	m	w	WURT	San Francisco	8-Wd San Francisco	82	305
HEIGLER								
Jos	26	m	w	PRUS	San Francisco	8-Wd San Francisco	82	335
HEIGUENEY								
Alex	51	m	w	BELG	San Francisco	2-Wd San Francisco	79	148
HEIKINS								
Henry	46	m	w	HANO	Sutter	Sutter Twp	92	124
HEIL								
Christina	22	f	w	HDAR	Sacramento	4-Wd Sacramento	77	338
Constantine	40	m	w	PRUS	San Francisco	8-Wd San Francisco	82	386
Fred	26	m	w	GERM	Sacramento	1-Wd Sacramento	77	173
HEILBROM								
August	35	m	w	PRUS	Sacramento	2-Wd Sacramento	77	219
Augustus	37	m	w	PRUS	Sacramento	2-Wd Sacramento	77	219
HEILBRON								
F	29	m	w	HANO	Sacramento	3-Wd Sacramento	77	298
Frederick	51	m	w	HANO	Santa Cruz	Watsonville	89	368
Rose	24	f	w	ENGL	San Francisco	6-Wd San Francisco	81	100
HEILBRUN								
Caroline	18	f	w	AFRI	San Francisco	8-Wd San Francisco	82	459
HEILDERBRAND								
Chs	45	m	w	PRUS	San Francisco	2-Wd San Francisco	79	154
HEILER								
Henry	33	m	w	GERM	Marin	San Rafael Twp	74	46
Jno	23	m	w	PA	Santa Clara	Almaden Twp	88	12
HEILL								
Warrel	21	m	w	GA	Fresno	Millerton P O	72	186
HEILMAN								
Frederick	28	m	w	AUST	San Francisco	8-Wd San Francisco	82	434
HEILONDOFER								
Ernst	35	m	w	PRUS	Alpine	Monitor P O	69	314
HEILRATH								
Christian	36	m	w	SWED	San Francisco	San Francisco P O	80	463
HEILTON								
Charles A	26	m	w	ME	Placer	Dutch Flat P O	76	415
HEILUNNYER								
Peter	38	m	w	CANA	Calaveras	San Andreas P O	70	158
HEIM								
Ah	27	m	c	CHIN	Tehama	Red Bluff	92	182
Herman	29	m	w	PRUS	San Francisco	8-Wd San Francisco	82	310
Jacob	37	m	w	GERM	Sacramento	1-Wd Sacramento	77	174
HEIMBURG								
E S	40	f	w	PRUS	San Francisco	San Francisco P O	85	833
Emil	25	m	w	WURT	San Francisco	1-Wd San Francisco	79	124
Louis	24	m	w	PRUS	San Francisco	2-Wd San Francisco	79	219
HEIMEL								
Simon	39	m	w	WURT	San Francisco	1-Wd San Francisco	79	134
HEIMERLE								
Fred	38	m	w	HDAR	San Francisco	11-Wd San Francisc	84	535
HEIN								
Ah	45	m	c	CHIN	Nevada	Nevada Twp	75	317
Ah	40	m	c	CHIN	Nevada	Nevada Twp	75	312
Ah	37	m	c	CHIN	Nevada	Eureka Twp	75	140
Ah	32	m	c	CHIN	Nevada	Nevada Twp	75	311
Ah	32	m	c	CHIN	Napa	Napa	75	19
Ah	30	m	c	CHIN	Nevada	Eureka Twp	75	126
Ah	25	m	c	CHIN	Nevada	Eureka Twp	75	126
Ah	22	m	c	CHIN	Sierra	Sears Twp	89	553
Ah	19	m	c	CHIN	Santa Clara	Alviso Twp	88	25
Anak	36	m	c	CHIN	Plumas	Plumas Twp	77	29
Catherine	55	f	w	WURT	Santa Cruz	Santa Cruz	89	426
Henry	28	m	w	PRUS	Kern	Kernville P O	73	368
Henry	24	m	w	PRUS	San Francisco	8-Wd San Francisco	82	435
Henry A	27	m	w	MD	Santa Cruz	Santa Cruz	89	415
John	39	m	w	PRUS	Napa	Napa	75	38
John	30	m	w	WURT	San Francisco	11-Wd San Francisc	84	584
Marcus	23	m	w	SHOL	San Francisco	1-Wd San Francisco	79	116
Nicholas	27	m	w	NY	Napa	Napa	75	38
Sing	25	m	c	CHIN	San Francisco	11-Wd San Francisc	84	574
Tam	45	m	c	CHIN	San Francisco	11-Wd San Francisc	84	478
HEINBAUGH								
E	42	m	w	PA	Sonoma	Santa Rosa	91	397
HEINBERG								
Abraham	53	m	w	PRUS	San Francisco	San Francisco P O	83	337
HEINBRIN								
Wm	25	m	w	HANO	Alameda	Eden Twp	68	86
HEINCH								
Herman	36	m	w	PRUS	Los Angeles	Los Angeles	73	525
HEINCKEN								
A C	45	m	w	BREM	Sierra	Sierra Twp	89	562
HEINDEN								
William	21	m	w	HANO	Alameda	Eden Twp	68	86
HEINE								
Ato	29	m	w	PRUS	San Francisco	3-Wd San Francisco	79	305
Chas	25	m	w	GERM	San Francisco	7-Wd San Francisco	81	240
HEINECK								
Julius	31	m	w	PRUS	Sacramento	3-Wd Sacramento	77	284
HEINECKE								
Thomas	42	m	w	FRAN	San Francisco	San Francisco P O	80	354
HEINED								
Henry	27	m	w	PRUS	Kern	Havilah P O	73	350
HEINEMAN								
Henry	24	m	w	PRUS	San Francisco	8-Wd San Francisco	82	349
HEINER								
Isaac	19	m	m	MD	San Francisco	San Francisco P O	80	419
HEINES								
Charles	26	m	w	HANO	Santa Barbara	Santa Barbara P O	87	473
HEING								
Ah	45	m	c	CHIN	Nevada	Bridgeport Twp	75	110
Ah	33	m	c	CHIN	Nevada	Bridgeport Twp	75	110
Ah	30	m	c	CHIN	Nevada	Nevada Twp	75	320
Ah	30	m	c	CHIN	Sacramento	3-Wd Sacramento	77	309
Ah	30	m	c	CHIN	Nevada	Meadow Lake Twp	75	254
Ah	26	m	c	CHIN	Nevada	Meadow Lake Twp	75	259
Ah	14	m	c	CHIN	San Francisco	7-Wd San Francisco	81	206
Conrad	58	m	w	HDAR	El Dorado	Mud Springs Twp	72	84
HEINHAM								
Fred	41	m	w	SHOL	San Francisco	1-Wd San Francisco	79	86
HEINHFELA								
Peter	29	m	w	PRUS	San Francisco	San Francisco P O	83	412
HEINICK								
Charles	40	m	w	PRUS	Sacramento	2-Wd Sacramento	77	246
Morris	35	m	w	PRUS	Sacramento	2-Wd Sacramento	77	246
HEINLEN								
John	51	m	w	PA	Santa Clara	2-Wd San Jose	88	296
HEINOMAN								
Charles	29	m	w	GERM	Los Angeles	Los Angeles	73	539
HEINRICH								
Carl	20	m	w	HAMB	San Francisco	6-Wd San Francisco	81	81
Christina	2	f	w	CA	Santa Cruz	Santa Cruz	89	434
Gustave	21	m	w	PRUS	San Francisco	1-Wd San Francisco	79	64
Henry	28	m	w	BREM	San Francisco	2-Wd San Francisco	79	192
Louis	38	m	w	FRAN	San Diego	San Diego	78	498
HEINRICHS								
John E	37	m	w	PRUS	Santa Cruz	Santa Cruz	89	410
HEINRICK								
Charles	46	m	w	HANO	Sacramento	2-Wd Sacramento	77	244
Fredk	35	m	w	WURT	San Francisco	1-Wd San Francisco	79	85
R	16	m	w	CA	Alameda	Oakland	68	159
HEINRICKS								
Aug	24	m	w	HAMB	San Francisco	1-Wd San Francisco	79	96
Nichl	34	m	w	HAMB	San Francisco	1-Wd San Francisco	79	96
HEINS								
Herman	35	m	w	HANO	San Francisco	1-Wd San Francisco	79	29
Jacob	38	m	w	GERM	San Francisco	San Francisco P O	83	145
Richard	18	m	w	HANO	San Francisco	San Francisco P O	85	795
Robert	33	m	w	PRUS	San Francisco	7-Wd San Francisco	81	227
HEINSBERG								
Benjamin	48	m	w	PRUS	San Francisco	11-Wd San Francisc	84	558
HEINSDORF								
John	46	m	w	PRUS	Calaveras	Copperopolis P O	70	255
HEINSEN								
Henry	37	m	w	HANO	Nevada	Washington Twp	75	341
HEINSON								
H P	24	m	w	DENM	Monterey	Salinas Twp	74	307
John	50	m	w	SHOL	Nevada	Little York Twp	75	237
HEINTON								
Saml	29	m	w	BAVA	Butte	Hamilton Twp	70	65
HEINTZ								
Fred R	36	m	w	BADE	Napa	Napa Twp	75	70
Jacob	31	m	w	NY	Sacramento	2-Wd Sacramento	77	233
Thebaud	34	m	w	FRAN	Butte	Ophir Twp	70	94
HEINTZEN								
C	44	m	w	PA	Sierra	Forest	89	536
HEINZ								
A M	52	f	w	FRAN	Solano	Vallejo	90	162
Jacob	24	m	w	ENGL	Plumas	Washington Twp	77	55
Louis C F	29	m	w	KY	Sacramento	4-Wd Sacramento	77	320
Phillip	40	m	w	PRUS	San Francisco	San Francisco P O	83	304
HEINZE								
Joe	39	m	w	PRUS	San Joaquin	2-Wd Stockton	86	201
Joseph	39	m	w	PRUS	San Joaquin	2-Wd Stockton	86	160
Louis	35	m	w	SWED	San Francisco	1-Wd San Francisco	79	71
Moses	26	m	w	PRUS	Solano	Vallejo	90	206
HEINZENBERGER								
Julius	63	m	w	HAMB	San Francisco	2-Wd San Francisco	79	240
HEIPMER								
Francis	41	m	w	PRUS	San Francisco	San Francisco P O	83	217
HEIR								
Henry	29	m	w	HCAS	San Diego	Julian Dist	78	470
HEIRSHALD								
Henry	24	m	w	PRUS	Placer	Newcastle Twp	76	474
HEISCH								
Augustus	48	m	w	HDAR	Sacramento	2-Wd Sacramento	77	226
Geo C	32	m	w	HDAR	Sacramento	3-Wd Sacramento	77	307
Mark	32	m	w	PRUS	Sacramento	2-Wd Sacramento	77	225
Phil	27	m	w	HDAR	Sacramento	3-Wd Sacramento	77	307
HEISE								
Chas Edwd	28	m	w	BREM	San Francisco	San Francisco P O	83	64
HEISEL								
Hans P	16	m	w	DENM	Santa Cruz	Pajaro Twp	89	356
Paul	40	m	w	PRUS	Sonoma	Santa Rosa	91	402
HEISELL								
William	38	m	w	OH	San Francisco	San Francisco P O	83	254
HEISER								
Conrad	35	m	w	HDAR	Calaveras	Copperopolis P O	70	263
Jacob	36	m	w	HDAR	San Francisco	8-Wd San Francisco	82	310
Koenig	35	m	w	BAVA	San Francisco	1-Wd San Francisco	79	30
HEISKELL								
Tyler D	46	m	w	VA	Stanislaus	Buena Vista Twp	92	12
HEISLER								
Conrad	28	m	w	PRUS	San Francisco	San Francisco P O	80	411

© 2001 by Heritage Quest. All rights reserved.

Name	Age	S	R	B-PL	County	Locale	Roll (Series M593)	Pg
HEISMAN								
M	21	m	w	PRUS	San Francisco	7-Wd San Francisco	81	226
HEISONER								
A	39	m	w	FRAN	Sierra	Downieville Twp	89	518
HEISS								
Charles	35	m	w	INDI	Sutter	Sutter Twp	92	117
Joseph	24	m	w	BAVA	Marin	Sausalito Twp	74	73
HEISTAND								
H	50	m	w	IA	Nevada	Meadow Lake Twp	75	265
HEISTER								
Amos	34	m	w	OH	San Francisco	San Francisco P O	80	400
HEISZ								
John	46	m	w	IL	Amador	Volcano P O	69	388
HEIT								
John	42	m	w	FRAN	Los Angeles	Los Angeles	73	504
HEITMAN								
Henry	43	m	w	HANO	Santa Cruz	Santa Cruz	89	410
Henry	28	m	w	PRUS	San Francisco	San Francisco P O	83	59
John H	22	m	w	HANO	Santa Cruz	Santa Cruz	89	404
N	46	m	w	PRUS	San Francisco	San Francisco P O	85	815
HEITMULLER								
Herman	30	m	w	HANO	San Francisco	San Francisco P O	83	70
HEITSHAN								
Samuel	30	m	w	PA	San Francisco	San Francisco P O	80	407
HEITZ								
Arthur	42	m	w	HDAR	San Francisco	3-Wd San Francisco	79	324
Herman	40	m	w	PRUS	San Francisco	San Francisco P O	83	317
Johanna	43	f	w	PRUS	Santa Cruz	Watsonville	89	365
Joseph	45	m	w	BADE	Napa	Napa	75	17
Peter	35	m	w	GERM	Alameda	Oakland	68	131
HEITZBERG								
Paul	38	m	w	FRAN	San Francisco	8-Wd San Francisco	82	493
HEITZIG								
Melville	10	m	w	MO	Butte	Wyandotte Twp	70	149
HEIVENER								
Peter	40	m	w	PA	Tehama	Red Bluff	92	174
HEIZENBURG								
Chs	33	m	w	PRUS	San Francisco	8-Wd San Francisco	82	356
HEIZER								
Herman	25	m	w	BADE	San Francisco	8-Wd San Francisco	82	362
Robert	60	m	w	VA	Sonoma	Washington Twp	91	464
HEIZMAN								
John	40	m	w	BADE	San Francisco	8-Wd San Francisco	82	339
HEIZNER								
Henry	33	m	w	PRUS	Sonoma	Analy Twp	91	235
HEK								
Ah	36	m	c	CHIN	San Francisco	6-Wd San Francisco	81	56
HEKER								
Adolph	18	m	w	BAVA	San Francisco	8-Wd San Francisco	82	375
HEL								
Ah	38	m	c	CHIN	Fresno	Millerton P O	72	201
Lop	22	m	c	CHIN	San Joaquin	3-Wd Stockton	86	246
HELARY								
Jacques	46	m	w	FRAN	Plumas	Rich Bar Twp	77	45
HELBACH								
Andr	27	m	w	PRUS	Sierra	Gibson Twp	89	542
HELBERT								
John	30	m	w	ENGL	San Francisco	7-Wd San Francisco	81	194
HELBLECK								
Charles	49	m	w	SWIT	Placer	Auburn P O	76	357
HELBRICH								
Conrad E	40	m	w	HCAS	Nevada	Grass Valley Twp	75	155
HELBURG								
Henry	58	m	w	PRUS	Solano	Tremont Twp	90	32
HELBUSCH								
Frank	13	m	w	PRUS	San Francisco	8-Wd San Francisco	82	486
HELCHA								
Andrew	39	m	w	PRUS	San Francisco	San Francisco P O	83	225
HELCHER								
Margarita	6	f	w	CA	Sacramento	4-Wd Sacramento	77	351
HELD								
Bernard	34	m	w	BADE	San Francisco	8-Wd San Francisco	82	470
Ernest	31	m	w	HDAR	San Francisco	11-Wd San Francisc	84	493
George	35	m	w	HDAR	San Francisco	11-Wd San Francisc	84	509
John	28	m	w	PRUS	San Joaquin	2-Wd Stockton	86	161
Wm	25	m	w	WURT	San Francisco	2-Wd San Francisco	79	233
HELDA								
Maria	35	f	w	MEXI	Santa Clara	1-Wd San Jose	88	251
HELDIE								
J	31	m	w	OH	Lake	Morgan Valley	73	425
HELDSTAB								
Christine	72	f	w	SWIT	El Dorado	Diamond Springs Tw	72	30
John	74	m	w	SWIT	El Dorado	Diamond Springs Tw	72	30
HELDT								
Fredrick	38	m	w	FRAN	Mendocino	Casper & Big Rvr	74	164
HELEBRENZ								
Carstin	37	m	w	PRUS	San Francisco	San Francisco P O	85	766
HELEM								
C	40	m	w	HANO	San Joaquin	Tulare Twp	86	256
HELEN								
Augustus	22	m	w	SWED	Sacramento	Georgianna Twp	77	125
J	39	m	w	DENM	Monterey	Alisal Twp	74	293
J Harvey	44	m	w	NY	Nevada	Nevada Twp	75	284
Thos	37	m	w	CANA	Fresno	Millerton P O	72	155
HELENA								
Antonio	60	m	w	CA	Los Angeles	Wilmington Twp	73	637
HELEP								
Carrie	18	f	w	PA	Alameda	Oakland	68	228
HELEY								
Ellen	21	f	w	IREL	Merced	Snelling P O	74	259
John	45	m	w	IREL	San Francisco	San Francisco P O	85	717
HELF								
John C	36	m	w	DENM	San Francisco	San Francisco P O	83	134
HELFERICK								
Elizabeth	16	f	w	NY	Calaveras	Copperopolis P O	70	262
HELFORDS								
Thoroughgood	44	m	w	OH	Santa Clara	San Jose Twp	88	185
HELFRICH								
John	32	m	w	HESS	Colusa	Colusa Twp	71	273
HELFSE								
Anne	28	f	w	HANO	Placer	Rocklin Twp	76	467
HELGE								
Charlotte	32	f	w	ENGL	San Joaquin	3-Wd Stockton	86	242
HELGER								
W G	31	m	w	MA	Alameda	Oakland	68	263
HELGERSON								
Peter	41	m	w	NORW	Nevada	Rough & Ready Twp	75	330
Peter	37	m	w	NORW	Nevada	Grass Valley Twp	75	230
HELGESON								
Peter	41	m	w	NORW	Nevada	Bridgeport Twp	75	101
HELGOTH								
A	39	m	w	BAVA	San Francisco	San Francisco P O	83	273
HELHAM								
--- Mr	52	m	w	NY	Alameda	Alameda	68	7
HELIGEST								
Geo	45	m	w	NY	San Francisco	1-Wd San Francisco	79	134
HELILY								
J	36	m	w	PRUS	Alameda	Oakland	68	238
HELISSY								
Helen	23	f	w	MA	Alameda	Oakland	68	153
HELKE								
Charles	48	m	w	SAXO	San Francisco	11-Wd San Francisc	84	698
HELL								
Melvin	26	m	w	IN	Santa Barbara	San Buenaventura P	87	419
Wm R	55	m	w	NY	Santa Barbara	San Buenaventura P	87	419
HELLBECK								
Charles	42	m	w	PRUS	San Francisco	San Francisco P O	83	185
HELLBING								
Mary	22	f	w	PRUS	San Francisco	8-Wd San Francisco	82	307
HELLBUSH								
Hy L	48	m	w	PRUS	San Francisco	San Francisco P O	83	90
HELLEBRAND								
H	45	m	w	BADE	Alameda	Oakland	68	139
HELLEGASS								
Jennie	13	f	w	CA	Alameda	Oakland	68	259
Mary	10	f	w	CA	Alameda	Oakland	68	259
HELLEN								
Julia	28	f	w	IREL	Solano	Benicia	90	12
HELLER								
Albert	44	m	w	GERM	Los Angeles	Los Angeles	73	540
Charles L	48	m	w	MECK	San Francisco	2-Wd San Francisco	79	189
Chas	39	m	w	PRUS	San Francisco	11-Wd San Francisc	84	662
Emanuel	23	m	w	NY	San Francisco	8-Wd San Francisco	82	406
Ester	70	f	w	HAMB	San Francisco	7-Wd San Francisco	81	166
George	43	m	w	NY	San Mateo	Redwood Twp	87	364
Jacob	76	m	w	HAMB	Santa Cruz	Santa Cruz	89	433
Jacob	29	m	w	MEXI	Calaveras	San Andreas P O	70	174
Jno	53	m	w	WURT	Sacramento	1-Wd Sacramento	77	174
K	72	m	w	HAMB	San Francisco	7-Wd San Francisco	81	166
Louis	30	m	w	HDAR	Siskiyou	Yreka	89	652
Martin	48	m	w	BAVA	San Francisco	8-Wd San Francisco	82	460
Morris	52	m	w	BAVA	San Francisco	8-Wd San Francisco	82	440
Peter	27	m	w	DENM	San Francisco	3-Wd San Francisco	79	293
Wm	47	m	w	NY	San Francisco	5-Wd San Francisco	81	24
HELLERBRICK								
Fredrick	28	m	w	HANO	Yolo	Washington Twp	93	538
HELLERICH								
Henry	40	m	w	PRUS	San Francisco	8-Wd San Francisco	82	337
HELLERIUS								
Gustave	36	m	w	FINL	Contra Costa	Martinez P O	71	406
HELLERMAN								
Christian	49	m	w	HANO	San Francisco	8-Wd San Francisco	82	383
R	50	m	w	ENGL	Alameda	Oakland	68	199
HELLETT								
Eliza	40	f	w	IREL	San Francisco	San Francisco P O	83	268
J	55	m	w	ME	Lassen	Janesville Twp	73	433
HELLEY								
David	30	m	w	CT	San Francisco	San Francisco P O	83	170
HELLGER								
Franz	20	m	w	PRUS	San Francisco	San Francisco P O	83	375
HELLIGER								
Oscar	30	m	w	IREL	Solano	Vacaville Twp	90	122
HELLIKIN								
John	32	m	w	ENGL	Sutter	Nicolaus Twp	92	115
HELLING								
August	45	m	w	BAVA	San Francisco	San Francisco P O	80	397
Frederick	36	m	w	PRUS	San Francisco	8-Wd San Francisco	82	381
Henry	30	m	w	IL	San Francisco	San Francisco P O	83	6
J	40	m	w	NY	San Joaquin	Tulare Twp	86	252
Louis	23	m	w	PRUS	San Francisco	5-Wd San Francisco	81	8
W F	36	m	w	CANA	San Francisco	San Francisco P O	85	791
HELLMAN								
Henry	46	m	w	FRAN	San Francisco	San Francisco P O	83	420

© 2001 by Heritage Quest. All rights reserved.

California 1870 Census

Series M593

Name	Age	S	R	B-PL	County	Locale	Roll	Pg
Isah M	39	m	w	BAVA	Los Angeles	Los Angeles	73	530
John	40	m	w	PRUS	San Francisco	San Francisco P O	80	465
Joseph	28	m	w	PORT	Los Angeles	Wilmington Twp	73	639
Samuel	31	m	w	BAVA	Los Angeles	Los Angeles	73	543
William	46	m	w	BAVA	San Francisco	8-Wd San Francisco	82	387
HELLMUCH								
Frederick	29	m	w	BAVA	Siskiyou	Callahan P O	89	628
HELLOR								
Alexr	21	m	w	NY	San Francisco	5-Wd San Francisco	81	19
HELLREHL								
John	30	m	w	GERM	Yolo	Grafton Twp	93	489
HELLSTEN								
Charles	30	m	w	FINL	Sonoma	Salt Point	91	392
HELLWIG								
Chas F	55	m	w	PRUS	Nevada	Nevada Twp	75	308
Henry	60	m	w	HDAR	San Francisco	11-Wd San Francisc	84	656
Philip	40	m	w	PRUS	Alameda	Alvarado	68	302
HELLYER								
Daniel	45	m	w	OH	Santa Clara	San Jose Twp	88	210
George W	48	m	w	OH	Santa Clara	San Jose Twp	88	206
HELM								
Alfred	33	m	w	IA	San Mateo	Half Moon Bay P O	87	408
Catherine	46	f	w	OH	Nevada	Nevada Twp	75	296
Ed	31	m	w	IL	Mendocino	Little Lake Twp	74	195
Henry	61	m	w	TN	Nevada	Bridgeport Twp	75	116
I	42	m	w	VA	Lake	Upper Lake	73	410
James	31	m	w	CANA	Fresno	Millerton P O	72	156
John	61	m	w	IREL	San Francisco	11-Wd San Francisc	84	612
L S	53	m	w	VA	Sonoma	Santa Rosa	91	421
S W	41	m	w	MO	Lake	Upper Lake	73	410
Solomon F	33	m	w	IA	San Mateo	Half Moon Bay P O	87	408
W H	38	m	w	IN	Sierra	Sears Twp	89	555
Wm	35	m	w	CANA	Fresno	Millerton P O	72	155
HELMAN								
Charles	49	m	w	SWED	El Dorado	Lake Valley Twp	72	63
HELMAR								
John	37	m	w	PRUS	Sierra	Table Rock Twp	89	573
HELME								
Turner	33	m	w	GA	San Diego	Warners Rancho Dis	78	528
Wm	35	m	w	GA	San Diego	Warners Rancho Dis	78	528
HELMER								
Andrew	32	m	w	CANA	San Francisco	8-Wd San Francisco	82	288
C J	43	m	w	NY	Butte	Wyandotte Twp	70	149
Charles	50	m	w	BADE	San Francisco	7-Wd San Francisco	81	209
James	28	m	w	NY	Sutter	Butte Twp	92	103
Jno	47	m	w	PRUS	San Joaquin	Elliott Twp	86	71
Julius	47	m	w	DENM	San Francisco	8-Wd San Francisco	82	313
Lawrence	35	m	w	PRUS	Solano	Rio Vista Twp	90	62
Peter	27	m	w	DENM	Santa Cruz	Watsonville	89	367
William	28	m	w	CANA	San Francisco	3-Wd San Francisco	79	328
HELMERING								
C A	40	m	w	PRUS	San Francisco	8-Wd San Francisco	82	294
HELMERS								
Nelson S	35	m	w	SWED	San Francisco	San Francisco P O	83	96
HELMES								
Martin	24	m	w	NY	San Francisco	5-Wd San Francisco	81	15
HELMESLEY								
Charles	40	m	w	SCOT	San Francisco	2-Wd San Francisco	79	259
HELMF								
William	31	m	w	HANO	Alameda	Eden Twp	68	62
HELMKE								
Frederick	39	m	w	HANO	Sonoma	Salt Point	91	388
John	20	m	w	HANO	San Francisco	2-Wd San Francisco	79	217
William	29	m	w	HANO	San Francisco	San Francisco P O	83	190
HELMKEN								
John T	40	m	w	BREM	San Francisco	6-Wd San Francisco	81	135
HELMOT								
J	37	m	w	SWED	Sierra	Lincoln Twp	89	547
HELMOTH								
George	45	m	w	BAVA	Shasta	Horsetown P O	89	503
HELMREICH								
Edward	18	m	w	BAVA	Butte	Mountain Spring Tw	70	88
HELMS								
Allen	30	m	w	MO	Merced	Snelling P O	74	258
Benton	39	m	w	MO	Merced	Snelling P O	74	264
C T	21	m	w	MO	Merced	Snelling P O	74	258
H W	31	m	w	PRUS	San Francisco	San Francisco P O	83	321
Houston	46	m	w	IN	Butte	Ophir Twp	70	100
J W	28	m	w	MO	Merced	Snelling P O	74	258
John	30	m	w	HANO	San Francisco	11-Wd San Francisc	84	423
Napoleon	22	m	w	MO	San Diego	Julian Dist	78	473
Olive	9	f	w	CA	Merced	Snelling P O	74	255
HELMSEN								
E	29	m	w	HANO	Yuba	Marysville	93	604
HELMSLEY								
Robt J	37	m	w	ENGL	Sacramento	2-Wd Sacramento	77	209
HELNEY								
Cong	34	m	c	CHIN	Trinity	Weaverville Pct	92	228
HELON								
Allen	68	m	w	NC	Merced	Snelling P O	74	264
HELPER								
John	31	m	w	OH	San Joaquin	1-Wd Stockton	86	150
Pat	33	m	w	IREL	Santa Clara	Almaden Twp	88	5
HELPHENSTINE								
Lowis H	57	m	w	KY	Colusa	Monroe Twp	71	311
HELPHINSTINE								
Benj	47	m	w	KY	Colusa	Monroe Twp	71	316

Series M593

Name	Age	S	R	B-PL	County	Locale	Roll	Pg
HELPIN								
John	21	m	w	NJ	San Francisco	7-Wd San Francisco	81	178
HELRETA								
Roma	37	f	w	ITAL	San Joaquin	3-Wd Stockton	86	220
HELSKY								
John B	48	m	w	HDAR	San Francisco	2-Wd San Francisco	79	274
HELSON								
Richard	35	m	w	MA	San Francisco	7-Wd San Francisco	81	216
HELSTOUP								
Edwd	30	m	w	DENM	San Francisco	San Francisco P O	83	53
HELT								
Catharine	27	f	w	HDAR	San Francisco	11-Wd San Francisc	84	611
James	47	m	w	IN	San Joaquin	1-Wd Stockton	86	135
HELTON								
William	45	m	w	VA	Colusa	Grand Island Twp	71	302
HELTOR								
Stephen	30	m	w	IL	Yolo	Cottonwood Twp	93	460
HELTS								
Miles A	31	m	w	NY	Stanislaus	Emory Twp	92	21
HELVEY								
Theodore	22	m	w	CANA	San Francisco	1-Wd San Francisco	79	69
HELVING								
Dora	19	f	w	PRUS	San Francisco	San Francisco P O	85	824
HELVIS								
Juan	37	m	w	CHIL	San Luis Obispo	Morro Twp	87	284
HELVY								
Matilda	35	f	w	SWIT	Sacramento	1-Wd Sacramento	77	200
HELWIG								
Charles	43	m	w	PRUS	Placer	Auburn P O	76	370
HELY								
George	40	m	w	WI	Fresno	Millerton P O	72	152
John	36	m	w	MI	San Francisco	San Francisco P O	83	342
Robt	21	m	w	NY	Alameda	Oakland	68	255
Susan	23	f	w	IREL	San Francisco	8-Wd San Francisco	82	471
HEM								
Ah	35	m	c	CHIN	San Francisco	6-Wd San Francisco	81	52
Ah	27	m	c	CHIN	Yuba	Marysville	93	620
Ah	26	m	c	CHIN	San Francisco	3-Wd San Francisco	79	310
Ah	24	m	c	CHIN	Alameda	Eden Twp	68	62
Ah	23	m	c	CHIN	San Francisco	3-Wd San Francisco	79	304
Ah	19	m	c	CHIN	Sonoma	Santa Rosa	91	424
Ah	15	m	c	CHIN	Sierra	Eureka Twp	89	525
Ah	15	m	c	CHIN	San Francisco	11-Wd San Francisc	84	561
Con	46	m	c	CHIN	Inyo	Cerro Gordo Twp	73	319
Gee	28	m	c	CHIN	Alameda	Alvarado	68	303
Gee	25	m	c	CHIN	Yuba	Marysville	93	628
Hong	16	m	c	CHIN	San Francisco	3-Wd San Francisco	79	307
Peter	40	m	w	MO	Fresno	Millerton P O	72	193
You	44	m	c	CHIN	Yuba	North East Twp	93	646
HEMAL								
Anatole	52	m	w	FRAN	San Francisco	8-Wd San Francisco	82	413
HEMAN								
Cerea	16	m	w	CA	Merced	Snelling P O	74	267
Michael	59	m	w	IREL	Solano	Benicia	90	14
Robt	45	m	w	GERM	Solano	Vallejo	90	180
Rosa	18	f	w	PRUS	El Dorado	Georgetown Twp	72	45
HEMANS								
James	40	m	w	SPAI	San Francisco	5-Wd San Francisco	81	7
HEMASY								
Elisabeth	25	f	w	IREL	Alameda	Washington Twp	68	282
HEMBEART								
Morones	63	m	w	FRAN	Sacramento	2-Wd Sacramento	77	249
HEMBECKER								
N	45	m	w	PRUS	Amador	Jackson P O	69	345
Nicholas	21	m	w	PRUS	Amador	Jackson P O	69	345
HEMBOLDT								
Charles	22	m	w	PRUS	Los Angeles	Los Angeles	73	567
HEMBOLT								
J F	32	m	w	PRUS	Alameda	Oakland	68	226
HEMBRA								
Ellen	38	f	w	IREL	Yuba	East Bear Rvr Twp	93	540
HEMBREE								
Mary	57	f	w	TN	Sonoma	Analy Twp	91	238
HEMBRY								
La Fayette	39	m	w	TN	Stanislaus	Empire Twp	92	52
HEMD								
Nancy	32	f	w	IL	Sonoma	Santa Rosa	91	429
HEMDON								
George W	37	m	w	KY	Colusa	Stony Crk Twp	71	333
HEMENA								
Refugia	23	f	w	MEXI	Santa Clara	1-Wd San Jose	88	258
HEMENWAY								
A	31	m	w	NY	San Francisco	8-Wd San Francisco	82	362
M D	23	m	w	ME	Amador	Volcano P O	69	382
M J	44	m	w	VT	Del Norte	Crescent	71	462
HEMEY								
H	51	m	w	FRAN	Alameda	Oakland	68	177
HEMING								
David	50	m	w	OH	Amador	Jackson P O	69	340
M	48	m	w	HOLL	San Joaquin	2-Wd Stockton	86	174
HEMINGWAY								
---	25	m	w	NY	Yuba	Marysville	93	617
F	46	m	w	NY	Napa	Napa	75	24
HEMINWAY								
Nathan	43	m	w	OH	Napa	Napa	75	43
HEMIS								
George W	49	m	w	IN	Santa Cruz	Soquel Twp	89	447

© 2001 by Heritage Quest. All rights reserved.

Name	Age	S	R	B-PL	County	Locale	Roll	Pg
						Series M593		
HEMIZKE								
William	27	m	w	PRUS	Inyo	Cerro Gordo Twp	73	319
HEMLIKER								
Gertrude	21	f	w	MO	Solano	Silveyville Twp	90	72
HEMLY								
Samuel	40	m	w	ENGL	Mariposa	Maxwell Crk P O	74	144
HEMME								
August	36	m	w	HANO	San Francisco	San Francisco P O	85	729
HEMMEGER								
Henry	25	m	w	BADE	Los Angeles	Los Angeles	73	528
HEMMENWAY								
George	43	m	w	ME	Sacramento	2-Wd Sacramento	77	226
Heny	26	m	w	MO	San Francisco	2-Wd San Francisco	79	277
Oliver	22	m	w	MO	Santa Barbara	San Buenaventura P	87	418
Sylvester	53	m	w	MA	San Francisco	2-Wd San Francisco	79	277
W P	41	m	w	MA	San Francisco	San Francisco P O	85	839
HEMMER								
Albert	23	m	w	PRUS	San Francisco	San Francisco P O	85	819
Henry	34	m	w	BAVA	San Francisco	3-Wd San Francisco	79	328
Mary J	12	f	w	MO	Los Angeles	Los Angeles	73	506
Thomas	10	m	w	IL	Marin	Tomales Twp	74	78
William	22	m	w	GERM	Los Angeles	Los Angeles	73	565
HEMMIGHOFEN								
Henry	37	m	w	PRUS	Calaveras	San Andreas P O	70	195
HEMMING								
Augustus	30	m	w	PRUS	San Diego	San Diego	78	489
Thomas	34	m	w	IREL	Santa Barbara	San Buenaventura P	87	432
HEMMINGWAY								
Daid B	39	m	w	NY	Sonoma	Petaluma Twp	91	324
W H	61	m	w	MA	Tuolumne	Chinese Camp P O	93	369
HEMMOND								
Henry	39	m	w	ENGL	Plumas	Indian Twp	77	14
HEMMY								
Peter	32	m	w	SWIT	San Luis Obispo	Arroyo Grande Twp	87	274
HEMP								
Ah	26	m	c	CHIN	Tehama	Red Bluff	92	184
HEMPEL								
A H	32	m	w	PRUS	San Francisco	San Francisco P O	85	762
Gustavus	37	m	w	HANO	Sacramento	Granite Twp	77	142
Hermann	36	m	w	PRUS	San Francisco	8-Wd San Francisco	82	305
W C	41	m	w	PRUS	Tuolumne	Chinese Camp P O	93	387
HEMPELL								
A G	17	m	w	UT	Alameda	Oakland	68	159
HEMPFIELD								
Frink	35	m	w	OH	Humboldt	Arcata Twp	72	235
H	26	m	w	IREL	San Joaquin	2-Wd Stockton	86	206
J	43	m	w	OH	Humboldt	Arcata Twp	72	235
HEMPHILL								
Anderson	42	m	w	IREL	Placer	Alta P O	76	412
Charlote	75	f	w	OH	Alameda	Oakland	68	170
Henry	15	m	w	IREL	San Francisco	2-Wd San Francisco	79	207
I	40	m	w	NY	Alameda	Oakland	68	170
James H	28	m	w	LA	Yolo	Putah Twp	93	516
John	43	m	w	OH	San Joaquin	Elkhorn Twp	86	55
HEMPHREYS								
Alexander	60	m	w	MO	Los Angeles	San Jose Twp	73	623
HEMPHRY								
William	35	m	w	ENGL	Yuba	Parks Bar Twp	93	648
HEMPLE								
Henry G	28	m	w	PRUS	San Francisco	5-Wd San Francisco	81	9
HEMPLEY								
Michl	23	m	w	IREL	San Francisco	5-Wd San Francisco	81	19
HEMPSTEAD								
Billings	50	m	w	CT	San Francisco	11-Wd San Francisc	84	444
HEMPSTREET								
Charles	60	m	w	NY	Santa Cruz	Santa Cruz Twp	89	393
HEMROD								
---	25	m	w	NY	Sacramento	4-Wd Sacramento	77	372
HEMS								
David	20	m	w	IREL	San Francisco	7-Wd San Francisco	81	180
HEMSALTH								
Barnard	20	m	w	HANO	Sierra	Gibson Twp	89	542
HEMSETH								
Eliza	29	f	w	OR	Solano	Suisun Twp	90	113
HEMSON								
John	29	m	w	LDET	Sacramento	4-Wd Sacramento	77	376
Peter	26	m	w	DENM	San Diego	Julian Dist	78	470
HEMSOTH								
Christian	25	m	w	BAVA	Monterey	Alisal Twp	74	294
HEMSTE								
John	44	m	w	BADE	Calaveras	San Andreas P O	70	197
HEMSTED								
Chas	37	m	w	PRUS	San Joaquin	Elliott Twp	86	70
Henry	34	m	w	PRUS	Tulare	Kings Rvr Twp	92	254
Peter	29	m	w	NY	Butte	Kimshew Tpw	70	82
HEMSTREET								
Oliver	31	m	w	NY	Alameda	Brooklyn	68	25
HEMSY								
Chas	38	m	w	PRUS	Tehama	Paskenta Twp	92	164
HEN								
---	32	m	c	CHIN	Siskiyou	Cottonwood Twp	89	594
---	30	m	c	CHIN	Siskiyou	Cottonwood Twp	89	594
Ah	60	m	c	CHIN	Tuolumne	Big Oak Flat P O	93	397
Ah	46	m	c	CHIN	Trinity	Lewiston Pct	92	214
Ah	45	m	c	CHIN	Calaveras	San Andreas P O	70	176
Ah	40	m	c	CHIN	Calaveras	Copperopolis P O	70	243
Ah	38	m	c	CHIN	Nevada	Nevada Twp	75	280
Ah	36	m	c	CHIN	Placer	Dutch Flat P O	76	410
Ah	36	m	c	CHIN	San Francisco	San Francisco P O	80	489
Ah	35	m	c	CHIN	Nevada	Eureka Twp	75	136
Ah	32	m	c	CHIN	San Mateo	Schoolhouse Statio	87	334
Ah	32	m	c	CHIN	Placer	Auburn P O	76	362
Ah	32	m	c	CHIN	Nevada	Nevada Twp	75	311
Ah	30	m	c	CHIN	Calaveras	San Andreas P O	70	169
Ah	30	m	c	CHIN	San Francisco	2-Wd San Francisco	79	184
Ah	30	m	c	CHIN	San Francisco	11-Wd San Francisc	84	522
Ah	28	m	c	CHIN	Tuolumne	Chinese Camp P O	93	383
Ah	28	m	c	CHIN	Calaveras	Copperopolis P O	70	234
Ah	28	m	c	CHIN	Nevada	Washington Twp	75	343
Ah	28	m	c	CHIN	Trinity	Canyon City Pct	92	202
Ah	27	m	c	CHIN	Nevada	Meadow Lake Twp	75	255
Ah	27	m	c	CHIN	Placer	Auburn P O	76	378
Ah	25	m	c	CHIN	Monterey	San Juan Twp	74	407
Ah	25	m	c	CHIN	Sacramento	Granite Twp	77	151
Ah	24	m	c	CHIN	Plumas	Seneca Twp	77	48
Ah	20	m	c	CHIN	Placer	Auburn P O	76	359
Ah	20	m	c	CHIN	Placer	Auburn P O	76	380
Ah	19	f	c	CHIN	Santa Clara	1-Wd San Jose	88	274
Ah	16	m	c	CHIN	El Dorado	Placerville	72	113
Ah	15	m	c	CHIN	Tehama	Tehama Twp	92	188
Chen	43	m	c	CHIN	Shasta	Horsetown P O	89	507
Chi	40	m	c	CHIN	Butte	Wyandotte Twp	70	143
Chow	54	m	c	CHIN	Klamath	South Fork Twp	73	382
Fuch	32	m	c	CHIN	Klamath	Liberty Twp	73	375
Fwe	60	m	c	CHIN	Plumas	Washington Twp	77	57
Gee	19	m	c	CHIN	Klamath	South Fork Twp	73	384
Hawk	50	m	c	CHIN	Klamath	Sawyers Bar	73	378
Hen	25	m	c	CHIN	Marin	Novato Twp	74	12
La	28	m	c	CHIN	San Joaquin	1-Wd Stockton	86	143
Lee	27	m	c	CHIN	Nevada	Eureka Twp	75	141
Maw	25	m	c	CHIN	San Francisco	San Francisco P O	83	227
Paugh	24	m	c	CHIN	Nevada	Nevada Twp	75	314
Too	15	m	c	CHIN	Nevada	Bridgeport Twp	75	110
Wah	18	m	c	CHIN	San Francisco	San Francisco P O	83	279
Wo	20	m	c	CHIN	San Francisco	8-Wd San Francisco	82	389
Won	26	m	c	CHIN	Butte	Hamilton Twp	70	74
Ye	59	m	c	CHIN	Nevada	Meadow Lake Twp	75	255
HENAIS								
Pedro	22	m	w	CA	Tuolumne	Sonora P O	93	314
HENAN								
John	40	m	w	IREL	Colusa	Spring Valley Twp	71	335
HENANE								
D V B	46	m	w	NJ	San Francisco	6-Wd San Francisco	81	116
HENAR								
A Q	18	m	w	PRUS	Sierra	Downieville Twp	89	518
Isaiah	19	m	w	MD	San Francisco	1-Wd San Francisco	79	133
HENAS								
James	35	m	w	IREL	Inyo	Bishop Crk Twp	73	313
HENBLIN								
Lorenz	43	m	w	SAXO	Sacramento	Granite Twp	77	142
HENCEL								
Adolphus	35	m	w	HANO	Stanislaus	Emory Twp	92	22
HENCH								
Erastus	34	m	w	PA	Solano	Rio Vista Twp	90	55
HENCHE								
A A	28	m	w	SWIT	Tuolumne	Sonora P O	93	308
John B	43	m	w	CT	San Joaquin	1-Wd Stockton	86	130
HENCHEN								
Claus	34	m	w	HANO	San Francisco	2-Wd San Francisco	79	139
Louis	33	m	w	HANO	San Francisco	11-Wd San Francisc	84	462
HENCHFELD								
Herman	27	m	w	PRUS	Kern	Havilah P O	73	336
HENCHINS								
Rich	27	m	w	MI	San Francisco	2-Wd San Francisco	79	213
HENCHMAN								
Frank	60	m	w	PRUS	San Francisco	2-Wd San Francisco	79	171
HENCHY								
Laurence	40	m	w	IREL	San Francisco	1-Wd San Francisco	79	87
HENCK								
Edward	41	m	w	BAVA	San Diego	San Diego	78	486
Hannah H	50	f	w	AUST	San Francisco	San Francisco P O	83	348
HENCKE								
August	17	m	w	HANO	San Francisco	11-Wd San Francisc	84	627
HENCKEL								
Geo K	50	m	w	PA	Butte	Ophir Twp	70	94
HENCKEN								
Wm	50	m	w	HANO	San Francisco	San Francisco P O	83	107
HENCKLEMAN								
Wm	40	m	w	GERM	Tuolumne	Columbia P O	93	348
HENDAY								
Jalius G	27	m	w	WI	Santa Clara	Redwood Twp	88	129
HENDEE								
E S L	35	m	w	NY	Solano	Vallejo	90	188
Edwin P	46	m	w	VT	San Francisco	San Francisco P O	83	172
Geo	30	m	w	MA	Solano	Vallejo	90	202
Mary H	60	f	w	NH	San Francisco	San Francisco P O	85	739
HENDELL								
S	30	m	w	ENGL	San Joaquin	Liberty Twp	86	86
HENDEN								
Philip	36	m	w	HESS	Monterey	San Juan Twp	74	396
HENDER								
C H	40	m	w	VT	Humboldt	Eel Rvr Twp	72	250
S I	30	m	w	ENGL	Tuolumne	Sonora P O	93	317

© 2001 by Heritage Quest. All rights reserved.

Name	Age	S	R	B-PL	County	Locale	Roll	Pg
						Series M593		
HENDERHAN								
James	30	m	w	IREL	San Francisco	1-Wd San Francisco	79	82
HENDERHOLS								
John	30	m	w	PRUS	Colusa	Colusa	71	297
HENDERHOLY								
Matthew	32	m	w	PRUS	Colusa	Grand Island Twp	71	302
HENDERICKS								
Louis	36	m	w	HANO	San Francisco	6-Wd San Francisco	81	141
HENDERKEN								
Wm	40	m	w	IREL	San Francisco	7-Wd San Francisco	81	260
HENDERN								
Ellen	16	f	w	OR	Sacramento	3-Wd Sacramento	77	297
HENDERSHOT								
William D	40	m	w	NY	Placer	Bath P O	76	458
HENDERSON								
A	45	m	w	PA	San Joaquin	2-Wd Stockton	86	189
Abel	35	m	m	MD	San Francisco	1-Wd San Francisco	79	95
Ada	23	f	w	LA	Solano	Vallejo	90	163
Alex	37	m	w	NY	Merced	Snelling P O	74	248
Alexander	50	m	w	ENGL	San Francisco	8-Wd San Francisco	82	457
Alexander	43	m	w	SCOT	Nevada	Grass Valley Twp	75	172
Alexander	23	m	w	SCOT	Stanislaus	Empire Twp	92	28
Alexdr	55	m	w	NY	Stanislaus	Branch Twp	92	5
Alexr	24	m	w	CANA	Santa Clara	Milpitas Twp	88	110
Andrew J	42	m	w	VA	Los Angeles	Los Angeles	73	546
B R	54	m	w	NC	San Joaquin	Liberty Twp	86	88
B T	37	m	w	GA	Sutter	Sutter Twp	92	116
Balder	30	m	w	TN	Yolo	Cottonwood Twp	93	464
Beatrice	11	f	w	ENGL	Santa Clara	Fremont Twp	88	47
Benj	38	m	w	SCOT	Mendocino	Ukiah Twp	74	233
Benj	34	m	w	NORW	San Francisco	5-Wd San Francisco	81	1
Brit	35	m	w	PA	Yuba	Rose Bar Twp	93	658
C H	31	m	w	NJ	Amador	Ione City P O	69	370
Charles	50	m	w	TN	Trinity	Trinity Center Pct	92	204
Charles	43	m	w	SAXO	Inyo	Lone Pine Twp	73	332
Charles	25	m	w	PA	Santa Clara	Redwood Twp	88	133
Chas	30	m	w	IREL	Santa Clara	Gilroy Twp	88	78
Christ	28	m	w	DENM	Mendocino	Little Rvr Twp	74	171
Cyrus	30	m	w	IL	Santa Clara	Fremont Twp	88	64
D	24	m	w	NY	Yuba	Marysville	93	604
Dancan	42	m	w	CANA	San Francisco	11-Wd San Francisc	84	608
David	40	m	w	SCOT	San Bernardino	San Bernardino Twp	78	442
David	40	m	w	ME	San Francisco	San Francisco P O	83	284
David	35	m	w	IREL	Tuolumne	Sonora P O	93	322
David	28	m	w	SCOT	San Bernardino	San Bernardino Twp	78	447
David	27	m	w	PA	Los Angeles	Los Nietos Twp	73	577
Don	38	m	w	SCOT	Alameda	Oakland	68	166
Duncan	48	m	w	GA	Sonoma	Mendocino Twp	91	288
Duncan	42	m	w	CANA	San Francisco	11-Wd San Francisc	84	553
E	40	f	w	IREL	San Francisco	San Francisco P O	83	314
Ebenezer	76	m	w	SC	Solano	Suisun Twp	90	103
Ed	20	f	w	MO	Alameda	Oakland	68	235
Edward	38	m	w	ME	San Francisco	San Francisco P O	83	308
Edward	26	m	w	ENGL	San Francisco	San Francisco P O	85	874
Emma J	22	f	w	MO	San Joaquin	Elkhorn Twp	86	56
F B	31	m	w	OH	Amador	Drytown P O	69	415
Florance	30	f	w	LA	San Francisco	6-Wd San Francisco	81	79
Frank	49	m	w	IREL	San Francisco	8-Wd San Francisco	82	377
Fredk	40	m	w	SCOT	San Francisco	1-Wd San Francisco	79	86
G	16	m	w	MO	Sierra	Sierra Twp	89	569
G H	34	m	w	MO	Sutter	Nicolaus Twp	92	109
G W	39	m	w	OH	Alameda	Oakland	68	247
George	48	m	w	IN	Contra Costa	Martinez P O	71	404
George	40	m	w	NORW	San Francisco	San Francisco P O	83	73
George C	41	m	w	NY	Stanislaus	Empire Twp	92	53
Gilbert	77	m	w	IREL	Alameda	Eden Twp	68	85
H	52	m	w	VA	Amador	Jackson P O	69	341
H	40	m	w	IREL	Merced	Snelling P O	74	264
Hannah	48	f	w	IREL	Yolo	Merritt Twp	93	503
Henry	54	m	w	MD	Siskiyou	Surprise Valley Tw	89	637
Henry	36	m	m	DC	San Francisco	2-Wd San Francisco	79	179
Henry C	33	m	w	IN	Solano	Suisun Twp	90	100
Horace	25	m	w	AR	Stanislaus	Empire Twp	92	52
Ira	32	m	w	MO	Stanislaus	Washington Twp	92	87
Isaac	44	m	w	ENGL	Calaveras	San Andreas P O	70	201
J	31	m	w	SCOT	Sierra	Butte Twp	89	508
J	26	m	w	CT	Sacramento	4-Wd Sacramento	77	373
J C	39	m	w	KY	Siskiyou	Surprise Valley Tw	89	643
J F	29	m	w	ENGL	San Francisco	5-Wd San Francisco	81	36
J H	29	m	w	NY	Sonoma	Santa Rosa	91	409
J L	45	f	w	SCOT	San Francisco	San Francisco P O	83	294
J M	10	f	w	CA	Amador	Drytown P O	69	416
J R	36	m	w	KY	Lake	Upper Lake	73	411
Jacob	40	m	w	NY	San Francisco	5-Wd San Francisco	81	30
James	68	m	w	GA	Stanislaus	Empire Twp	92	41
James	42	m	w	SCOT	San Francisco	11-Wd San Francisc	84	575
James	40	m	w	CANA	Stanislaus	Empire Twp	92	29
James	36	m	w	NY	Colusa	Butte Twp	71	270
James	30	m	w	SCOT	Yolo	Washington Twp	93	532
James	27	m	w	CANA	Santa Clara	Redwood Twp	88	131
James	27	m	w	PA	Yolo	Putah Twp	93	521
James	25	m	w	CANA	Tulare	Visalia Twp	92	285
James	24	m	w	SCOT	San Francisco	11-Wd San Francisc	84	518
James T	57	m	w	SC	El Dorado	Cosumnes Twp	72	14
James W	67	m	w	GA	Stanislaus	Washington Twp	92	87
Jane	30	f	w	IREL	San Francisco	5-Wd San Francisco	81	7
Jas	30	m	w	ENGL	San Francisco	San Francisco P O	85	874
Jas W	42	m	w	NY	Humboldt	Eureka Twp	72	273
Jerry	27	m	b	MO	San Francisco	San Francisco P O	83	302
Jno A	30	m	w	ME	Butte	Ophir Twp	70	114
Johanna	3	m	w	CA	Calaveras	San Andreas P O	70	216
John	65	m	w	SCOT	San Francisco	11-Wd San Francisc	84	536
John	64	m	w	SCOT	San Francisco	San Francisco P O	80	469
John	58	m	w	KY	Los Angeles	Los Angeles Twp	73	493
John	54	m	w	SCOT	San Joaquin	2-Wd Stockton	86	208
John	34	m	w	NORW	Yolo	Cache Crk Twp	93	432
John	32	m	w	IREL	San Francisco	San Francisco P O	83	150
John	24	m	w	PA	San Francisco	7-Wd San Francisco	81	164
John	22	m	w	IREL	San Francisco	San Francisco P O	83	60
John H	50	m	w	IREL	Nevada	Grass Valley Twp	75	146
John P	45	m	w	IL	Stanislaus	Empire Twp	92	42
John R	51	m	w	KY	Klamath	Klamath Twp	73	371
Joseph	40	m	w	OH	Colusa	Monroe Twp	71	314
Joseph P	48	m	w	TN	Los Angeles	Los Nietos Twp	73	584
Joshua M	40	m	w	GA	Stanislaus	Empire Twp	92	27
Julia	12	f	w	CA	Stanislaus	Emory Twp	92	20
Justus	36	m	w	SWED	San Francisco	7-Wd San Francisco	81	253
Louisa	26	f	m	ME	San Joaquin	Douglas Twp	86	37
M H	28	f	w	MO	Sacramento	1-Wd Sacramento	77	184
Maggie	19	f	w	MA	San Francisco	San Francisco P O	83	289
Margaret	41	f	w	MO	Los Angeles	Los Nietos Twp	73	591
Margaret	40	f	w	ENGL	Sacramento	4-Wd Sacramento	77	352
Martha	37	f	w	MO	Stanislaus	Empire Twp	92	41
Mary	65	f	w	IREL	Tehama	Tehama Twp	92	195
Mary	58	f	w	OH	Del Norte	Crescent Twp	71	456
Mary	30	f	w	NY	San Francisco	San Francisco P O	83	262
Mary	30	f	w	ENGL	San Francisco	7-Wd San Francisco	81	204
Mary	29	f	w	NORW	Calaveras	San Andreas P O	70	152
Mary	24	f	w	PRUS	San Francisco	San Francisco P O	83	354
Mary	21	f	w	NY	San Francisco	7-Wd San Francisco	81	208
Mary	20	f	w	AUSL	Marin	San Antonio Twp	74	64
Mary	15	f	w	CA	Nevada	Nevada Twp	75	289
Mary	15	f	w	US	Nevada	Grass Valley Twp	75	229
Melvin	36	m	w	MO	San Joaquin	2-Wd Stockton	86	189
Michael	37	m	w	SCOT	San Luis Obispo	San Luis Obispo Tw	87	309
Michael	28	m	w	IREL	Colusa	Colusa	71	298
Milton M	55	m	w	KY	Santa Barbara	San Buenaventura P	87	438
Mitton C	37	m	w	IL	Santa Barbara	Santa Barbara P O	87	502
Nancy	72	f	w	IN	Santa Clara	Santa Clara Twp	88	140
Nettie	33	f	w	VT	Marin	Point Reyes Twp	74	22
Niel	37	m	w	ENGL	San Francisco	San Francisco P O	83	245
O	35	m	w	ME	Solano	Vallejo	90	176
Oliver W	37	m	w	GA	Placer	Bath P O	76	424
Peter	36	m	m	MD	Calaveras	San Andreas P O	70	202
Phillis M	29	f	w	ENGL	San Francisco	5-Wd San Francisco	81	36
Pleasant	48	m	w	TN	Stanislaus	Empire Twp	92	46
R	46	m	w	KY	Lake	Big Valley	73	395
Richard	25	m	w	NY	San Francisco	7-Wd San Francisco	81	208
Robe	24	m	w	CANA	Colusa	Spring Valley Twp	71	337
Robert	39	m	w	AL	Tulare	Venice Twp	92	278
Robert	38	m	w	TX	Yolo	Buckeye Twp	93	409
Robert	32	m	w	CANA	Yolo	Putah Twp	93	521
Robert	28	m	w	SCOT	San Francisco	San Francisco P O	83	259
Robert	25	m	w	SCOT	San Francisco	7-Wd San Francisco	81	277
Rush	24	m	w	NY	Contra Costa	San Pablo Twp	71	364
S	24	m	w	IREL	Napa	Napa Twp	75	66
S S	42	m	w	MO	Del Norte	Smith Rvr Twp	71	476
Sally	35	f	i	CA	Klamath	Klamath Twp	73	371
Sam	42	m	w	IN	San Joaquin	2-Wd Stockton	86	165
Saml C	43	m	w	OH	El Dorado	Placerville Twp	72	99
Samuel	75	m	w	KY	Santa Clara	Santa Clara Twp	88	140
Samuel	68	m	w	ENGL	Santa Clara	Alviso Twp	88	25
Samuel	24	m	w	IN	Napa	Yountville Twp	75	90
Thomas	36	m	w	IN	Solano	Suisun Twp	90	101
Thomas	28	m	w	SCOT	Stanislaus	Empire Twp	92	66
Thos	66	m	w	PA	San Joaquin	Elkhorn Twp	86	56
Thos	36	m	w	SCOT	San Francisco	1-Wd San Francisco	79	113
Thos	30	m	w	NY	San Joaquin	Tulare Twp	86	256
Thos	19	m	w	MA	San Francisco	3-Wd San Francisco	79	323
Thos D	32	m	w	SCOT	San Francisco	1-Wd San Francisco	79	78
Vincent	39	m	w	IN	Yuba	W Bear Rvr Twp	93	680
W	65	m	w	IREL	Sierra	Sierra Twp	89	569
W	51	m	w	SCOT	Merced	Snelling P O	74	265
W	35	m	w	CANA	Sierra	Sierra Twp	89	569
W	35	m	w	LA	Sacramento	1-Wd Sacramento	77	190
Walter	30	m	w	SCOT	Santa Clara	Fremont Twp	88	54
Warren	31	m	w	IL	Plumas	Quartz Twp	77	35
William	60	m	w	SCOT	Stanislaus	Empire Twp	92	30
William	49	m	w	MO	Calaveras	San Andreas P O	70	219
William	41	m	w	MD	Calaveras	San Andreas P O	70	157
William	35	m	w	IREL	San Francisco	San Francisco P O	80	485
William	28	m	w	MO	Santa Clara	2-Wd San Jose	88	326
William	24	m	w	SCOT	Stanislaus	Empire Twp	92	29
William	20	m	w	CANA	Santa Cruz	Santa Cruz	89	426
William F	59	m	w	MA	El Dorado	Placerville	72	113
William K	28	m	w	OH	Contra Costa	Martinez P O	71	386
William T	23	m	w	NY	Mendocino	Navarro & Big Rvr	74	177
Wm	60	m	w	NY	Humboldt	Pacific Twp	72	298
Wm	57	m	w	SCOT	Butte	Chico Twp	70	21
Wm	41	m	w	PA	Sonoma	Russian Rvr	91	377
Wm	38	m	w	SC	Marin	San Rafael Twp	74	47
Wm	34	m	w	IREL	San Diego	San Diego	78	489
Wm	28	m	w	NY	San Francisco	1-Wd San Francisco	79	21
Wm I	42	m	w	PA	Mariposa	Mariposa P O	74	135

© 2001 by Heritage Quest. All rights reserved.

Name	Age	S	R	B-PL	County	Locale	Roll	Pg
						Series M593		
HENDESON								
Jno	39	m	w	SCOT	San Joaquin	2-Wd Stockton	86	187
HENDGE								
Heny	70	m	w	VT	Nevada	Nevada Twp	75	283
HENDLE								
Chas W	38	m	w	SAXO	Sierra	Sears Twp	89	561
M	40	f	w	MO	Sacramento	1-Wd Sacramento	77	184
HENDLEY								
Barclay	28	m	w	IN	Sonoma	Santa Rosa	91	414
Charles	42	m	w	ENGL	Stanislaus	Empire Twp	92	44
James	50	m	w	ENGL	San Francisco	7-Wd San Francisco	81	176
John	49	m	w	KY	Sonoma	Santa Rosa	91	405
Patrick	29	m	w	IREL	Sonoma	Vallejo Twp	91	453
Sarah	12	f	w	PA	San Francisco	2-Wd San Francisco	79	202
William	42	m	w	VA	Mendocino	Albion & Big Rvr T	74	166
HENDLY								
Pat O	48	m	w	VA	Butte	Ophir Twp	70	108
HENDRE								
John	55	m	w	ENGL	Nevada	Nevada Twp	75	309
HENDRIC								
James	50	m	w	AR	Santa Cruz	Santa Cruz Twp	89	389
Wm C	45	m	w	PA	Butte	Oregon Twp	70	123
HENDRICK								
Antone	44	m	w	SWED	Del Norte	Happy Camp Twp	71	468
Charles	28	m	w	IREL	San Francisco	San Francisco P O	83	192
Edward	31	m	w	IL	San Francisco	11-Wd San Francisc	84	510
H	50	f	w	VA	Napa	Napa	75	21
H	20	m	w	OH	Amador	Sutter Crk P O	69	410
Jno A	41	m	w	TN	Shasta	Stillwater P O	89	481
John	31	m	w	MO	Nevada	Bloomfield Twp	75	98
Richard	45	m	w	PA	Calaveras	San Andreas P O	70	202
S P	34	m	w	MO	San Francisco	San Francisco P O	85	853
William L	39	m	w	IN	Colusa	Colusa	71	293
HENDRICKS								
Abram	66	m	w	NY	Santa Cruz	Santa Cruz Twp	89	386
Alice	33	f	w	IL	Santa Clara	San Jose Twp	88	201
Anks J	30	m	w	IA	Santa Clara	1-Wd San Jose	88	244
Anna	11	f	w	SHOL	Sutter	Vernon Twp	92	136
August	25	m	w	PRUS	Contra Costa	Martinez P O	71	400
Charles	50	m	w	ENGL	San Francisco	San Francisco P O	80	532
Chas J	50	m	w	CT	Santa Cruz	Santa Cruz Twp	89	379
Elizabeh	41	f	w	ENGL	San Francisco	11-Wd San Francisc	84	500
Frank	37	m	w	IA	Nevada	Washington Twp	75	339
G B	42	m	w	TN	Lake	Lakeport	73	406
George	37	m	w	SHOL	Napa	Napa Twp	75	29
H	36	m	w	DENM	El Dorado	Salmon Falls Twp	72	132
Harret	23	f	w	NY	San Francisco	8-Wd San Francisco	82	459
Harrison	47	m	w	TN	Santa Clara	Santa Clara Twp	88	158
J D	37	m	w	NY	San Francisco	3-Wd San Francisco	79	312
J J	54	m	w	MA	San Francisco	8-Wd San Francisco	82	370
J J	50	m	w	KY	Lake	Lakeport	73	406
J M	44	m	w	NY	Mariposa	Maxwell Crk P O	74	139
J W	46	m	w	OH	Sutter	Butte Twp	92	91
John	41	m	w	NORW	Contra Costa	Martinez P O	71	435
John	40	m	w	OH	Siskiyou	Yreka	89	652
John	40	m	w	SHOL	Napa	Napa Twp	75	67
John	40	m	w	IL	Yuba	Parks Bar Twp	93	648
John	32	m	w	FINL	Mendocino	Big Rvr Twp	74	171
M B	35	m	w	WI	San Joaquin	Oneal Twp	86	115
Moses	49	m	w	KY	Solano	Green Valley Twp	90	42
Nathan H	39	m	w	IL	Stanislaus	Empire Twp	92	62
Peter	39	m	w	SHOL	Napa	Napa Twp	75	29
Thos P	29	m	w	PA	Butte	Ophir Twp	70	113
W	39	m	w	BREM	San Francisco	8-Wd San Francisco	82	356
William	47	m	w	RI	Contra Costa	Martinez P O	71	435
William	37	m	w	IL	Stanislaus	Empire Twp	92	62
Wm	30	m	w	MO	San Joaquin	Elliott Twp	86	81
HENDRICKSEN								
August	22	m	w	NORW	San Francisco	1-Wd San Francisco	79	128
HENDRICKSON								
Chas	50	m	w	NJ	San Francisco	11-Wd San Francisc	84	437
H	52	m	w	SWED	Sacramento	4-Wd Sacramento	77	377
Hen W	36	m	w	NY	San Francisco	San Francisco P O	83	108
I	32	m	w	PA	Del Norte	Happy Camp Twp	71	472
J J	48	m	w	NY	Monterey	Alisal Twp	74	297
Jn	30	m	w	NY	Napa	Napa Twp	75	64
John	30	m	w	PRUS	Kern	Tehachapi P O	73	353
Jonathan	24	m	w	PA	Nevada	Eureka Twp	75	137
Mary	49	f	w	PRUS	San Francisco	5-Wd San Francisco	81	1
Tona	27	m	w	IREL	Napa	Napa	75	57
HENDRICS								
A H	26	m	w	IL	Sutter	Yuba Twp	92	144
HENDRICSON								
Gordon	61	m	w	OH	San Luis Obispo	Arroyo Grande Twp	87	278
HENDRIKS								
Charles	37	m	w	HAMB	San Francisco	6-Wd San Francisco	81	120
HENDRIX								
Ebin W	41	m	w	OH	Sonoma	Healdsburg & Mendo	91	280
Franklin	33	m	w	KY	San Mateo	Half Moon Bay P O	87	394
Joseph	28	m	w	MO	Sonoma	Mendocino Twp	91	307
Lewis	55	m	w	OH	Sonoma	Santa Rosa	91	429
William	51	m	w	OH	El Dorado	Placerville Twp	72	97
HENDRIXSON								
W A	34	m	w	KY	Monterey	Monterey Twp	74	351
HENDROM								
Thomas M	49	m	w	IL	Mendocino	Albion & Big Rvr T	74	166

Name	Age	S	R	B-PL	County	Locale	Roll	Pg
						Series M593		
HENDRY								
Chas J	26	m	w	MA	San Francisco	San Francisco P O	83	175
Emma S	35	f	w	MA	San Francisco	San Francisco P O	83	104
Frank	43	m	w	NH	Marin	San Rafael Twp	74	45
James	28	m	w	IREL	Marin	San Rafael Twp	74	45
John	50	m	w	SCOT	Calaveras	San Andreas P O	70	203
Wm M	45	m	w	SCOT	San Francisco	San Francisco P O	83	94
HENDSCH								
Charles	45	m	w	PRUS	Calaveras	Copperopolis P O	70	227
HENDY								
E M	22	f	m	MD	Sacramento	3-Wd Sacramento	77	262
J B	45	m	b	MD	Sacramento	3-Wd Sacramento	77	262
James	50	m	w	ENGL	San Francisco	2-Wd San Francisco	79	190
Jas	25	m	w	IREL	Butte	Chico Twp	70	43
John H	28	m	w	MA	San Francisco	San Francisco P O	85	813
Robt	45	m	w	SCOT	Alameda	Oakland	68	140
HENE								
Ah	35	m	c	CHIN	Monterey	San Antonio Twp	74	318
Ah	31	m	c	CHIN	Nevada	Grass Valley Twp	75	206
HENEBERRY								
James	13	m	w	CA	Alpine	Markleeville P O	69	312
HENEFORD								
Anna	18	f	w	MA	Solano	Silveyville Twp	90	92
HENEGAN								
Patk	34	m	w	IREL	Fresno	Millerton P O	72	164
HENELY								
Mary	50	f	w	IREL	San Francisco	San Francisco P O	83	362
HENEMAN								
Eliza Mrs	35	f	w	ME	Calaveras	San Andreas P O	70	212
HENEN								
Jas	35	m	w	IREL	San Joaquin	2-Wd Stockton	86	199
John	40	m	w	IREL	Sutter	Butte Twp	92	104
HENER								
William	30	m	w	PRUS	San Diego	Fort Yuma Dist	78	464
HENEREY								
Michael	34	m	w	IREL	San Francisco	7-Wd San Francisco	81	272
HENERICKSON								
E	26	m	w	DENM	San Francisco	7-Wd San Francisco	81	192
H	21	m	w	NY	San Francisco	7-Wd San Francisco	81	192
HENERTY								
Thomas	36	m	w	IREL	Santa Clara	2-Wd San Jose	88	313
HENERY								
Alice	35	f	w	HI	San Francisco	7-Wd San Francisco	81	206
John	52	m	w	SHOL	San Joaquin	Oneal Twp	86	111
HENESEY								
P O M	40	m	w	IREL	Trinity	North Fork Twp	92	219
Peter	40	m	w	IREL	San Francisco	San Francisco P O	85	869
HENESLY								
Wm	38	m	w	MO	San Francisco	2-Wd San Francisco	79	201
HENESSEY								
David	45	m	w	IREL	San Francisco	11-Wd San Francisc	84	429
HENESY								
David	48	m	w	IREL	Trinity	Weaverville Pct	92	230
HENETH								
Frank	31	m	w	FRAN	San Francisco	San Francisco P O	80	456
HENEY								
Ah	50	m	c	CHIN	Mendocino	Point Arena Twp	74	208
Anne	78	f	w	IREL	San Francisco	San Francisco P O	83	320
Chas	52	m	w	IREL	Contra Costa	San Pablo Twp	71	363
James	35	m	w	IREL	San Francisco	7-Wd San Francisco	81	218
Jas	27	m	w	KY	San Joaquin	1-Wd Stockton	86	153
John	28	m	w	HANO	San Francisco	7-Wd San Francisco	81	224
Richard	48	m	w	IREL	San Francisco	San Francisco P O	83	297
William	27	m	w	NY	San Francisco	8-Wd San Francisco	82	476
HENFFNER								
Gottleib	31	m	w	WURT	San Francisco	San Francisco P O	80	421
HENFIELD								
J	48	m	w	KY	Lake	Big Valley	73	396
Joseph	39	m	w	MA	Marin	Novato Twp	74	12
Stillman	12	m	w	CA	Marin	Novato Twp	74	13
HENFRY								
Anna	28	f	w	MO	Mendocino	Round Valley Twp	74	218
John	38	m	w	ENGL	Mendocino	Round Valley Twp	74	217
HENG								
Ah	9	m	c	CHIN	San Francisco	6-Wd San Francisco	81	50
Ah	50	m	c	CHIN	Calaveras	San Andreas P O	70	184
Ah	35	m	c	CHIN	Nevada	Nevada Twp	75	317
Ah	32	m	c	CHIN	Nevada	Eureka Twp	75	127
Ah	28	m	c	CHIN	Marin	San Rafael Twp	74	38
Ah	25	m	c	CHIN	Los Angeles	Los Angeles	73	527
Ah	20	m	c	CHIN	San Francisco	6-Wd San Francisco	81	56
Ah	20	m	c	CHIN	Sonoma	Washington Twp	91	471
Ah	17	m	c	CHIN	El Dorado	Diamond Springs Tw	72	24
Ah	12	m	c	CHIN	Plumas	Indian Twp	77	9
Chong	24	m	c	CHIN	Nevada	Meadow Lake Twp	75	256
Eh	35	m	c	CHIN	San Mateo	San Mateo P O	87	351
Fung	18	m	c	CHIN	Monterey	Castroville Twp	74	327
Gim	16	m	c	CHIN	San Francisco	San Francisco P O	85	792
Gum	20	m	c	CHIN	Yuba	Marysville	93	623
Hy	20	m	c	CHIN	Contra Costa	Martinez P O	71	430
James	48	m	w	CT	Amador	Volcano P O	69	380
Sing	32	m	c	CHIN	San Francisco	6-Wd San Francisco	81	40
Vop	20	m	c	CHIN	Sonoma	Sonoma Twp	91	437
HENGARA								
Santiago	28	m	w	MEXI	Los Angeles	Los Angeles Twp	73	477
HENGER								
Nicholas	27	m	w	PRUS	San Francisco	6-Wd San Francisco	81	100

© 2001 by Heritage Quest. All rights reserved.

Name	Age	S	R	B-PL	County	Locale	Roll	Pg
						Series M593		
HENGY								
Henry	23	m	w	US	San Joaquin	3-Wd Stockton	86	218
William B	25	m	w	WI	Stanislaus	Emory Twp	92	26
HENI								
Ah	45	m	c	CHIN	Nevada	Nevada Twp	75	307
Ah	16	m	c	CHIN	Nevada	Bridgeport Twp	75	122
HENIELY								
John	40	m	w	IREL	San Francisco	11-Wd San Francisc	84	603
HENIGAN								
Michael	25	m	w	IREL	Alameda	Brooklyn Twp	68	55
Thomas	47	m	w	IREL	Sutter	Yuba Twp	92	143
HENIGER								
Gottfred	29	m	w	BADE	San Francisco	San Francisco P O	85	718
HENIKE								
Adam	40	m	w	PRUS	San Francisco	5-Wd San Francisco	81	4
HENIKEN								
A	22	m	w	MO	Solano	Vallejo	90	185
HENINGER								
Charles	35	m	w	BADE	Yuba	Bullards Bar P O	93	547
William K	52	m	w	VA	Los Angeles	San Gabriel Twp	73	598
HENINGTON								
D G	49	m	w	KY	Lake	Kelsey Crk	73	402
HENION								
Daniel	46	m	w	NY	Alameda	Washington Twp	68	289
I	28	m	w	NY	Alameda	Murray Twp	68	125
John K	80	m	w	NJ	Alameda	Washington Twp	68	289
HENIS								
Vincent	50	m	w	HI	Yolo	Merritt Twp	93	505
HENISEY								
Timothy	35	m	w	IREL	Trinity	Indian Crk	92	200
HENKE								
C Thom	29	m	w	SAXO	San Diego	San Diego	78	500
Daniel	41	m	w	PRUS	San Francisco	San Francisco P O	80	462
John W	42	m	w	PRUS	Calaveras	San Andreas P O	70	158
Joseph	34	m	w	PRUS	San Francisco	San Francisco P O	80	461
William	39	m	w	PRUS	El Dorado	Diamond Springs Tw	72	21
William	35	m	w	HAMB	San Francisco	San Francisco P O	83	352
HENKEL								
W	36	m	w	PRUS	San Francisco	San Francisco P O	85	831
HENKELMAN								
E G	44	m	w	GERM	Tuolumne	Columbia P O	93	340
HENKEN								
John	34	m	w	HESS	Stanislaus	Empire Twp	92	32
Martin	38	m	w	HANO	San Francisco	11-Wd San Francisc	84	438
P	32	m	w	HANO	Mariposa	Mariposa P O	74	131
HENKEY								
Fred	31	m	w	HANO	Alameda	Brooklyn	68	35
HENKLE								
Joseph	47	m	w	SWEE	Calaveras	San Andreas P O	70	202
HENKS								
William	28	m	w	HAMB	San Francisco	San Francisco P O	80	358
HENLAND								
George	35	m	w	NY	San Luis Obispo	Morro Twp	87	287
HENLEY								
Amazien	15	f	w	AUSL	San Francisco	1-Wd San Francisco	79	73
Anna	15	f	w	CA	Sonoma	Petaluma Twp	91	357
Archibald	52	m	w	VA	Sacramento	4-Wd Sacramento	77	338
Charles	21	m	w	NC	Sonoma	Russian Rvr	91	376
Charles	21	m	w	NY	San Francisco	6-Wd San Francisco	81	83
Chas	45	m	w	SWIT	Sacramento	3-Wd Sacramento	77	259
D	23	m	w	IREL	Sierra	Sierra Twp	89	566
E S	21	m	w	TN	Amador	Ione City P O	69	360
Frank	22	m	w	MO	Sacramento	3-Wd Sacramento	77	312
Geo W	36	m	w	IN	Mendocino	Round Valley Twp	74	218
J S	48	m	w	TN	Amador	Ione City P O	69	361
James	21	m	w	IREL	Nevada	Meadow Lake Twp	75	252
John F	40	m	w	ENGL	San Francisco	San Francisco P O	83	209
Nellie	22	f	w	ME	Del Norte	Mountain Twp	71	475
Simon	39	m	w	IREL	Placer	Roseville P O	76	355
Thomas	55	m	w	ENGL	Del Norte	Mountain Twp	71	475
Thomas	39	m	w	IREL	Santa Barbara	Santa Maria P O	87	510
Thomas	35	m	w	IREL	Inyo	Lone Pine Twp	73	331
William	49	m	w	PA	Amador	Sutter Crk P O	69	396
HENLY								
Ann	45	f	w	IREL	Humboldt	Eureka Twp	72	261
Ann	45	f	w	IREL	Humboldt	Eureka Twp	72	262
Henry	40	m	w	CANA	Humboldt	Bucksport Twp	72	243
Hetty	38	f	w	IREL	Solano	Vallejo	90	199
J D	35	m	w	IREL	Nevada	Eureka Twp	75	134
J H	39	m	w	WURT	Sacramento	Sutter Twp	77	383
James	39	m	w	VA	Butte	Ophir Twp	70	120
John	45	m	w	IREL	Sacramento	4-Wd Sacramento	77	369
John	31	m	w	NY	Solano	Maine Prairie Twp	90	50
John C	34	m	w	TN	Humboldt	Pacific Twp	72	297
Jonathan	50	m	w	IN	Plumas	Washington Twp	77	54
Joseph	38	m	w	IREL	Solano	Silveyville Twp	90	81
Joseph	35	m	w	VA	Butte	Ophir Twp	70	120
Pat	65	m	w	IREL	Alameda	Oakland	68	231
Patrick	51	m	w	IREL	Amador	Jackson P O	69	341
Patrick	35	m	w	IREL	San Mateo	San Mateo P O	87	357
Robert	29	m	w	ENGL	Calaveras	San Andreas P O	70	199
Thomas	35	m	w	MA	Solano	Suisun Twp	90	114
Tim	35	m	w	IREL	Alameda	Oakland	68	239
W N	37	m	w	IN	Tehama	Paskenta Twp	92	164
William	17	m	w	CA	Solano	Silveyville Twp	90	74
HENMAN								
A	30	m	w	NY	Alameda	Oakland	68	255

Name	Age	S	R	B-PL	County	Locale	Roll	Pg
						Series M593		
Daniel	45	m	w	ENGL	Placer	Lincoln P O	76	482
HENN								
John	34	m	w	IREL	Contra Costa	Martinez P O	71	412
Patrick	40	m	w	IREL	Contra Costa	Martinez P O	71	412
Richard J	23	m	w	IREL	San Luis Obispo	Arroyo Grande Twp	87	278
HENNABERRY								
Thos	48	m	w	IREL	Sierra	Gibson Twp	89	538
HENNAN								
Francis	58	m	w	BELG	Colusa	Monroe Twp	71	312
Jacob	37	m	w	HOLL	Contra Costa	Martinez P O	71	411
HENNE								
John	56	m	b	NY	Stanislaus	Branch Twp	92	5
HENNEBERRY								
Michael	42	m	w	IREL	San Francisco	8-Wd San Francisco	82	456
HENNEBURY								
Patrick	40	m	w	IREL	Humboldt	Eureka Twp	72	264
Patrick	35	m	w	IREL	San Francisco	1-Wd San Francisco	79	114
HENNECKE								
Jno	25	m	w	GERM	Marin	San Rafael Twp	74	38
HENNEFAUTH								
Peter	60	m	w	BAVA	Nevada	Nevada Twp	75	321
HENNEGAN								
Johanna	22	f	w	IREL	San Francisco	8-Wd San Francisco	82	394
HENNEKE								
William	26	f	w	GERM	Yolo	Buckeye Twp	93	411
HENNELL								
Abbie	55	f	w	MA	San Francisco	7-Wd San Francisco	81	240
HENNEMAN								
Antoine	45	m	w	BOHE	Nevada	Nevada Twp	75	272
HENNENFIELD								
Peter	23	m	w	HUNG	San Francisco	3-Wd San Francisco	79	320
HENNEQUER								
Anne	47	f	w	FRAN	Santa Clara	2-Wd San Jose	88	284
HENNER								
Ah	22	m	c	CHIN	Placer	Cisco P O	76	494
Micheal	26	m	w	IREL	San Francisco	7-Wd San Francisco	81	212
HENNESAY								
Edward	28	m	w	IREL	San Francisco	7-Wd San Francisco	81	185
Henery	30	m	w	IREL	San Francisco	7-Wd San Francisco	81	177
Micheal	40	m	w	IREL	San Francisco	7-Wd San Francisco	81	178
HENNESEE								
David	30	m	w	IREL	San Francisco	7-Wd San Francisco	81	202
HENNESEY								
Andrew	35	m	w	IREL	San Francisco	8-Wd San Francisco	82	450
Daniel	32	m	w	IREL	San Francisco	San Francisco P O	80	458
Jane	26	f	w	IREL	San Francisco	8-Wd San Francisco	82	490
John	54	m	w	ME	Del Norte	Crescent	71	467
Margaret	25	f	w	CT	Nevada	Grass Valley Twp	75	144
HENNESSE								
Catherin	40	f	w	IREL	San Francisco	7-Wd San Francisco	81	194
HENNESSEL								
Thos	26	m	w	KY	San Joaquin	Oneal Twp	86	112
HENNESSEY								
Bridget	24	f	w	IREL	San Francisco	San Francisco P O	83	206
Dennis	21	m	w	IREL	San Francisco	San Francisco P O	83	280
James	30	m	w	IREL	Nevada	Grass Valley Twp	75	231
James	28	m	w	IREL	San Francisco	San Francisco P O	83	235
James	27	m	w	IREL	Nevada	Washington Twp	75	344
John	36	m	w	IREL	Nevada	Grass Valley Twp	75	180
John	28	m	w	IREL	Placer	Roseville P O	76	351
John	28	m	w	IREL	San Francisco	San Francisco P O	83	298
John	25	m	w	IREL	Nevada	Grass Valley Twp	75	214
Margaret	65	f	w	IREL	San Francisco	San Francisco P O	83	242
Michael	46	m	w	IREL	Tuolumne	Sonora P O	93	328
Michael	42	m	w	IREL	San Francisco	San Francisco P O	83	197
Owen	39	m	w	IREL	San Francisco	San Francisco P O	83	312
Patrick	60	m	w	IREL	San Francisco	11-Wd San Francisc	84	456
Patrick	39	m	w	IREL	Nevada	Grass Valley Twp	75	211
Patrick	36	m	w	IREL	San Francisco	11-Wd San Francisc	84	513
Thomas	22	m	w	IREL	Nevada	Grass Valley Twp	75	230
William	30	m	w	PA	San Francisco	San Francisco P O	83	216
HENNESSY								
Ann	50	f	w	IREL	Solano	Vacaville Twp	90	127
Dennis	24	m	w	IREL	Tuolumne	Sonora P O	93	329
Helen	32	f	w	IREL	San Francisco	11-Wd San Francisc	84	514
James	7	m	w	CA	Marin	San Rafael Twp	74	27
James	55	m	w	IREL	Solano	Vacaville Twp	90	127
James	40	m	w	ENGL	San Francisco	5-Wd San Francisco	81	2
James	30	m	w	IREL	San Francisco	2-Wd San Francisco	79	250
James	20	m	w	CANA	San Francisco	8-Wd San Francisco	82	346
Jas	42	m	w	IREL	Solano	Vallejo	90	191
John	35	m	w	IREL	San Francisco	8-Wd San Francisco	82	417
Lawrence	6	m	w	CA	Marin	San Rafael Twp	74	27
M	34	m	w	IREL	Alameda	Oakland	68	216
Margt	40	f	w	IREL	Tuolumne	Sonora P O	93	328
Michael	37	m	w	IREL	Marin	San Rafael	74	56
Michael	33	m	w	IREL	Sacramento	4-Wd Sacramento	77	319
Michael	31	m	w	IREL	Marin	San Rafael	74	56
Michael	30	m	w	IREL	Marin	Point Reyes Twp	74	23
Michael	28	m	w	IREL	Santa Cruz	Santa Cruz	89	429
Micheal	30	m	w	IREL	San Francisco	11-Wd San Francisc	84	440
Michl	30	m	w	IREL	San Francisco	1-Wd San Francisco	79	94
Robt	30	m	w	IREL	San Francisco	San Francisco P O	83	75
Thomas	29	m	w	IREL	Solano	Green Valley Twp	90	39
Thos	39	m	w	NY	San Joaquin	Tulare Twp	86	256
Thos	27	m	w	IREL	San Francisco	11-Wd San Francisc	84	604
William	63	m	w	IREL	Solano	Vacaville Twp	90	127

© 2001 by Heritage Quest. All rights reserved.

Name	Age	S	R	B-PL	County	Locale	Roll	Pg
William	28	m	w	IREL	San Francisco	11-Wd San Francisc	84	540
HENNESY								
James	38	m	w	MA	Mariposa	Mariposa P O	74	131
James	12	m	w	CA	Sonoma	Sonoma Twp	91	443
John	41	m	w	IREL	Sacramento	4-Wd Sacramento	77	366
M	34	m	w	IREL	Sacramento	3-Wd Sacramento	77	274
T I	29	m	w	IREL	Sacramento	4-Wd Sacramento	77	364
Thomas	23	m	w	IREL	Nevada	Grass Valley Twp	75	178
Wm	40	m	w	IREL	Sutter	Vernon Twp	92	133
HENNEUSE								
John F	47	m	w	BELG	Santa Cruz	Santa Cruz	89	432
HENNEY								
Ah	35	m	c	CHIN	Nevada	Nevada Twp	75	311
Chas	26	m	w	CANA	Humboldt	Eureka Twp	72	267
James	26	m	w	IREL	San Francisco	2-Wd San Francisco	79	257
HENNEYSEE								
Pat	43	m	w	IREL	El Dorado	Coloma Twp	72	8
HENNHOD								
Henry	23	m	w	PRUS	San Francisco	8-Wd San Francisco	82	338
HENNI								
Christian	44	m	w	WURT	Los Angeles	Los Angeles	73	543
HENNICK								
Max	28	m	w	PRUS	Solano	Vallejo	90	139
HENNICKE								
William	35	m	w	PRUS	San Francisco	San Francisco P O	83	371
HENNIG								
Augt	43	m	w	PRUS	San Francisco	8-Wd San Francisco	82	309
HENNIGEN								
P W	58	m	w	LA	Sierra	Gibson Twp	89	542
HENNIGER								
Geo	5	m	w	NV	Sacramento	San Joaquin Twp	77	396
HENNING								
Abraham	23	m	w	MO	Kern	Havilah P O	73	339
Addine	36	m	w	MO	Kern	Bakersfield P O	73	358
Alpha	58	m	w	VA	Santa Clara	1-Wd San Jose	88	224
Ewing P	29	m	w	MO	Santa Clara	San Jose Twp	88	209
John	59	m	w	VA	Plumas	Indian Twp	77	14
John	40	m	w	OH	Santa Clara	Santa Clara Twp	88	138
John	34	m	w	PRUS	Napa	Napa	75	7
John S	40	m	w	KY	Yolo	Grafton Twp	93	479
Max	36	m	w	PRUS	Solano	Tremont Twp	90	32
Otte	37	m	w	PRUS	San Francisco	2-Wd San Francisco	79	225
Thomas	40	m	w	IREL	Los Angeles	Soledad Twp	73	630
W	30	m	w	IREL	Tehama	Antelope Twp	92	155
William	35	m	w	HANO	San Mateo	Pescadero P O	87	410
HENNINGS								
John	40	m	w	BADE	Solano	Vallejo	90	165
Joseph	48	m	w	ENGL	Calaveras	Copperopolis P O	70	258
HENNINGSEN								
George	42	m	w	SHOL	Plumas	Washington Twp	77	54
HENNINGSON								
Henry	31	m	w	PRUS	San Francisco	11-Wd San Francisc	84	703
HENNISEY								
Wm	52	m	w	IREL	Santa Barbara	San Buenaventura P	87	422
HENNISON								
Milton	30	m	w	IN	Santa Barbara	San Buenaventura P	87	420
HENNISSY								
Daniel	32	m	w	NH	Tuolumne	Columbia P O	93	344
HENNY								
Ah	30	m	c	CHIN	Butte	Wyandotte Twp	70	146
F	37	m	w	ME	Alameda	Oakland	68	263
Geo	38	m	w	PRUS	Tehama	Paskenta Twp	92	165
John	35	m	w	IREL	San Joaquin	Elliott Twp	86	79
Robert	30	m	w	NY	Marin	Sausalito Twp	74	73
Saml H	35	m	w	ENGL	San Francisco	2-Wd San Francisco	79	187
HENNYBRESSER								
William	40	m	w	PA	Santa Clara	2-Wd San Jose	88	330
HENO								
Henry	24	m	w	NY	Solano	Denverton Twp	90	24
HENON								
C B	37	m	w	GERM	San Joaquin	Elkhorn Twp	86	68
Wm G	38	m	w	OLDE	Sonoma	Washington Twp	91	465
HENRI								
Juliette	45	f	w	FRAN	San Francisco	11-Wd San Francisc	84	643
HENRICE								
Caspar	34	m	w	PRUS	San Francisco	8-Wd San Francisco	82	475
HENRICH								
Charles	22	m	w	PRUS	San Francisco	San Francisco P O	80	343
George	48	m	w	GERM	Yolo	Cottonwood Twp	93	466
John	28	m	w	PRUS	San Francisco	San Francisco P O	85	757
HENRICHS								
Edward	17	m	w	DENM	Santa Cruz	Santa Cruz	89	415
Manuel	18	m	w	AZOR	Monterey	Alisal Twp	74	304
HENRICHSON								
Clonus	40	m	w	HAMB	Los Angeles	Los Angeles Twp	73	475
Peter	43	m	w	DENM	Sonoma	Petaluma Twp	91	316
HENRICI								
Mary	35	f	w	IREL	Solano	Vallejo	90	216
HENRICK								
J M	51	m	w	PRUS	Monterey	Castroville Twp	74	334
Louis	26	m	w	PRUS	San Francisco	5-Wd San Francisco	81	5
HENRICKE								
Hannah	70	f	w	POLA	San Francisco	San Francisco P O	83	184
Herman	35	m	w	BREM	San Francisco	7-Wd San Francisco	81	223
HENRICKS								
Christian	30	m	w	NORW	San Francisco	1-Wd San Francisco	79	120
Henry	30	m	w	PRUS	San Francisco	San Francisco P O	83	21
HENRICKSON								
Frank	28	m	w	FINL	San Francisco	3-Wd San Francisco	79	291
Henry	35	m	w	BAVA	San Francisco	7-Wd San Francisco	81	218
Henry	28	m	w	ME	San Francisco	3-Wd San Francisco	79	293
HENRICO								
Frank	30	m	w	GERM	Solano	Vallejo	90	216
HENRIES								
Henry	23	m	w	NY	Sacramento	Center Twp	77	83
HENRIETTA								
John	45	m	w	IREL	Monterey	San Juan Twp	74	404
HENRIGUES								
Catherine	19	f	w	PRUS	San Francisco	2-Wd San Francisco	79	172
Joseph	32	m	b	BRAZ	San Francisco	2-Wd San Francisco	79	145
HENRIHAN								
William S	30	m	w	VA	Tulare	Tule Rvr Twp	92	270
HENRIOT								
Jules	42	m	w	FRAN	San Francisco	11-Wd San Francisc	84	643
HENRIQUES								
Jean	23	m	w	FRAN	San Francisco	San Francisco P O	80	484
Tomaso	31	m	w	ITAL	San Francisco	San Francisco P O	80	426
HENRIQUEZ								
D	49	m	w	WIND	San Francisco	8-Wd San Francisco	82	371
Hendacula	30	m	w	MEXI	Los Angeles	Los Angeles	73	557
Manuel	35	m	w	PERU	Los Angeles	Los Angeles	73	524
HENRITTY								
Patrick	34	m	w	IREL	Santa Clara	2-Wd San Jose	88	309
HENRITZ								
E	34	f	w	NY	Alameda	Oakland	68	201
Henry	17	m	w	PRUS	San Francisco	3-Wd San Francisco	79	318
HENRY								
A	30	m	w	PORT	Sierra	Butte Twp	89	509
A C	41	m	w	OH	Alameda	Oakland	68	161
A C	35	m	w	OH	Lake	Kelsey Crk	73	402
A H	29	m	w	MO	Trinity	Weaverville Pct	92	223
A M	28	m	w	SC	Solano	Vallejo	90	161
Agness	55	f	w	IREL	Alameda	Eden Twp	68	70
Ah	41	m	c	CHIN	Monterey	Salinas Twp	74	308
Ah	38	m	c	CHIN	Sacramento	1-Wd Sacramento	77	198
Ah	35	m	c	CHIN	Siskiyou	Cottonwood Twp	89	592
Ah	32	m	c	CHIN	Los Angeles	Los Angeles	73	544
Ah	29	m	c	CHIN	Nevada	Washington Twp	75	343
Ah	18	m	c	CHIN	Tehama	Tehama Twp	92	188
Ah	17	m	c	CHIN	Nevada	Nevada Twp	75	298
Alexander	30	m	w	SCOT	Los Angeles	Santa Ana Twp	73	603
Alfred	31	m	w	NY	Los Angeles	Los Angeles	73	524
Allen	32	m	w	VA	Butte	Chico Twp	70	26
Allen	26	m	w	IL	Los Angeles	Soledad Twp	73	630
Annie	24	f	w	CANA	San Francisco	San Francisco P O	85	809
Augustus	31	m	w	FRAN	San Francisco	San Francisco P O	80	538
Ausust	41	m	w	IL	Mendocino	Anderson Twp	74	153
Butler	70	m	w	DC	Sacramento	1-Wd Sacramento	77	180
C M	72	m	w	CT	San Joaquin	Oneal Twp	86	114
Charles	50	m	w	SAXO	Colusa	Grand Island Twp	71	302
Charles	35	m	w	NORW	Monterey	San Antonio Twp	74	318
Charles	31	m	w	MO	Merced	Snelling P O	74	267
Charles	30	m	w	MO	Alameda	Alameda	68	12
Charles	18	m	w	NY	San Francisco	San Francisco P O	85	745
Charles D	38	m	w	VT	San Francisco	6-Wd San Francisco	81	116
Chas	37	m	w	IN	Sacramento	Alabama Twp	77	61
Chas	22	m	w	IL	Sacramento	Dry Crk Twp	77	102
Chow	20	m	c	CHIN	San Francisco	6-Wd San Francisco	81	91
Daniel	45	m	w	SCOT	San Luis Obispo	San Luis Obispo Tw	87	316
Edward	25	m	w	IREL	San Mateo	Schoolhouse Statio	87	341
Edward	10	m	w	CA	Santa Clara	Redwood Twp	88	125
Edward A	23	m	w	PA	Tulare	Kings Rvr Twp	92	252
Edward S	18	m	w	PA	Sacramento	2-Wd Sacramento	77	237
Edwin	31	m	w	NY	Kern	Havilah P O	73	339
Elizabeth	49	f	w	NY	San Francisco	San Francisco P O	85	873
Francis	37	m	w	PA	Nevada	Eureka Twp	75	126
Frank	36	m	w	MO	Colusa	Colusa Twp	71	287
Fred	25	m	w	PA	San Francisco	San Francisco P O	83	416
Geo	42	m	w	ME	San Francisco	1-Wd San Francisco	79	116
Geo	30	m	w	SCOT	Siskiyou	Scott Valley Twp	89	611
Geo	28	m	w	ENGL	San Joaquin	2-Wd Stockton	86	187
George	69	m	w	IREL	El Dorado	Diamond Springs Tw	72	31
George	55	m	w	NY	Inyo	Lone Pine Twp	73	333
George	39	m	w	MA	Sonoma	Vallejo Twp	91	451
George	32	m	w	NY	Tuolumne	Sonora P O	93	326
George	30	m	w	IL	Mariposa	Mariposa P O	74	137
H	28	m	w	MI	San Joaquin	2-Wd Stockton	86	193
Harbester	64	m	w	KY	San Joaquin	Castoria Twp	86	1
Harm K	26	m	w	SWIT	Sacramento	1-Wd Sacramento	77	173
Henri	35	m	w	PRUS	San Francisco	5-Wd San Francisco	81	27
Henry	42	m	w	IREL	San Francisco	San Francisco P O	83	313
Henry	36	m	w	IREL	San Mateo	Schoolhouse Statio	87	331
Henry A	64	m	w	ENGL	San Francisco	2-Wd San Francisco	79	239
Hinman	50	m	w	CT	Sacramento	2-Wd Sacramento	77	226
J	36	m	w	IREL	Sierra	Sierra Twp	89	565
J B	34	m	w	US	Sacramento	1-Wd Sacramento	77	179
J Davis	14	m	w	IL	San Mateo	Pescadero P O	87	417
J R	28	m	w	PA	Nevada	Bloomfield Twp	75	95
Jacob	32	m	w	MO	Los Angeles	Wilmington Twp	73	639
James	52	m	w	SCOT	Monterey	Monterey Twp	74	348
James	40	m	w	AL	Butte	Hamilton Twp	70	66
James	40	m	w	IREL	Santa Clara	Santa Clara Twp	88	176
James	35	m	w	IREL	Sonoma	Salt Point	91	384
James	33	m	w	IREL	San Francisco	San Francisco P O	85	745

© 2001 by Heritage Quest. All rights reserved.

California 1870 Census

Name	Age	S	R	B-PL	County	Locale	Roll	Pg
James	30	m	w	PA	Sonoma	Analy Twp	91	232
James	25	m	w	MO	Sonoma	Salt Point	91	385
James	21	m	w	CANA	Stanislaus	San Joaquin Twp	92	76
James Jr	43	m	w	VT	San Francisco	5-Wd San Francisco	81	11
James R	46	m	w	TN	San Joaquin	Douglas Twp	86	47
Jas	51	m	w	CANA	Solano	Benicia	90	9
Jean B	43	m	w	FRAN	Santa Cruz	Watsonville	89	374
Jeanna	28	f	w	IREL	Santa Clara	Redwood Twp	88	120
Jemima	13	f	w	CA	El Dorado	Cosumnes Twp	72	16
Johanna	12	f	w	NY	Yolo	Cottonwood Twp	93	465
John	50	m	w	IREL	San Francisco	San Francisco P O	85	848
John	47	m	w	PA	Sacramento	Franklin Twp	77	106
John	40	m	w	OH	Solano	Suisun Twp	90	98
John	40	m	w	FRAN	Placer	Bath P O	76	448
John	39	m	c	CHIN	Inyo	Cerro Gordo Twp	73	318
John	39	m	w	IREL	San Francisco	2-Wd San Francisco	79	169
John	38	m	w	PRUS	San Francisco	San Francisco P O	80	423
John	38	m	w	SCOT	Lake	Lower Lake	73	422
John	37	m	w	NY	Humboldt	Eel Rvr Twp	72	252
John	36	m	w	MO	Tulare	Visalia Twp	92	283
John	35	m	w	IREL	Solano	Vallejo	90	198
John	35	m	w	IREL	San Francisco	San Francisco P O	85	850
John	35	m	w	WURT	Humboldt	Eel Rvr Twp	72	254
John	34	m	w	TN	Santa Clara	Fremont Twp	88	54
John	33	m	w	IN	Sonoma	Mendocino Twp	91	306
John	33	m	w	ENGL	San Francisco	San Francisco P O	83	80
John	31	m	w	IREL	San Francisco	1-Wd San Francisco	79	63
John	29	m	w	IREL	Solano	Vallejo	90	200
John	29	m	w	IREL	Solano	Vallejo	90	215
John	28	m	w	NY	Santa Clara	Redwood Twp	88	119
John	28	m	w	PA	San Francisco	San Francisco P O	80	533
John	24	m	w	IREL	Marin	San Rafael Twp	74	40
John	24	m	w	NY	Tehama	Tehama Twp	92	191
John	22	m	w	NY	San Mateo	Redwood Twp	87	369
John	22	m	w	IREL	Alameda	Brooklyn	68	22
John	21	m	w	CANA	Nevada	Meadow Lake Twp	75	259
John	20	m	w	CA	Marin	San Rafael Twp	74	37
John	14	m	w	CA	Nevada	Grass Valley Twp	75	223
John	13	m	w	CA	Santa Clara	Redwood Twp	88	125
John A	42	m	w	FRAN	Mariposa	Mariposa P O	74	114
John F	27	m	w	AR	Calaveras	San Andreas P O	70	207
John H	40	m	w	HANO	San Francisco	2-Wd San Francisco	79	234
John R	33	m	w	IL	Mendocino	Sanel Twp	74	227
Joseph	41	m	w	OH	Napa	Napa Twp	75	68
Joseph	40	m	w	TN	El Dorado	Greenwood Twp	72	51
Joseph	30	m	w	OH	Humboldt	Table Bluff Twp	72	306
Laura	26	f	w	FRAN	San Francisco	6-Wd San Francisco	81	78
Levy J	39	m	w	NY	San Francisco	6-Wd San Francisco	81	41
Long	45	m	w	GERM	Santa Clara	Fremont Twp	88	58
Louis	33	m	w	MO	San Francisco	San Francisco P O	80	345
Louis	31	m	w	BAVA	Tuolumne	Big Oak Flat P O	93	398
Louis	21	m	w	HANO	San Francisco	11-Wd San Francisc	84	428
Low	25	m	w	IREL	Sacramento	1-Wd Sacramento	77	179
Lucinda	36	f	w	IL	San Francisco	San Francisco P O	80	343
Maggie	21	f	w	IA	Humboldt	Arcata Twp	72	233
Margaret	20	f	w	IREL	San Francisco	8-Wd San Francisco	82	389
Margaret	11	f	w	IREL	San Francisco	San Francisco P O	85	814
Martin	45	m	w	IREL	Yuba	Rose Bar Twp	93	660
Mary	40	f	w	MD	Nevada	Rough & Ready Twp	75	332
Mary	4	f	w	CA	San Joaquin	Douglas Twp	86	47
Mary	22	f	w	IREL	San Mateo	Schoolhouse Statio	87	341
Mary	15	f	w	IREL	Nevada	Meadow Lake Twp	75	251
Mathew	40	m	w	IREL	San Joaquin	Douglas Twp	86	41
Michael	45	m	w	IREL	San Joaquin	Douglas Twp	86	32
Oscar	28	m	w	IN	Colusa	Colusa	71	294
Oser	6	m	i	CA	Del Norte	Smith Rvr Twp	71	483
Patrick	64	m	w	IREL	Nevada	Nevada Twp	75	277
Patrick	45	m	w	IREL	San Francisco	San Francisco P O	83	379
Patrick	28	m	w	IREL	Solano	Silveyville Twp	90	75
Patrick	18	m	w	CANA	Nevada	Meadow Lake Twp	75	259
Peter	45	m	w	IREL	Calaveras	San Andreas P O	70	195
Purdy	41	m	w	KY	Mendocino	Ukiah Twp	74	236
Robert	50	m	w	MO	Nevada	Bloomfield Twp	75	99
Robert	48	m	w	NY	San Francisco	San Francisco P O	83	349
Robert	35	m	w	IREL	Calaveras	San Andreas P O	70	187
Robert M	38	m	w	NY	Yolo	Putah Twp	93	515
Sam T W	43	m	w	PA	Nevada	Eureka Twp	75	126
Saml	38	m	w	POLA	San Francisco	2-Wd San Francisco	79	173
Samuel	39	m	w	POLA	San Francisco	San Francisco P O	83	368
Sarah E	32	f	w	VA	San Francisco	5-Wd San Francisco	81	1
Simon	47	m	w	NY	San Francisco	2-Wd San Francisco	79	171
Simon	40	m	w	OH	Butte	Chico Twp	70	50
Simon W	27	m	w	IREL	Fresno	Millerton P O	72	194
Sing	22	m	c	CHIN	Sacramento	4-Wd Sacramento	77	330
Stephen	32	m	w	OH	Napa	Napa Twp	75	68
Sylvanus H	60	m	w	NY	San Francisco	8-Wd San Francisco	82	467
Thomas	41	m	w	IREL	Shasta	French Gulch P O	89	464
Thomas	35	m	w	IREL	San Francisco	San Francisco P O	85	822
Thomas	30	m	w	ENGL	Nevada	Eureka Twp	75	133
Thomas	28	m	w	NY	San Francisco	6-Wd San Francisco	81	87
Turner	1	m	w	CA	Merced	Snelling P O	74	246
W F	23	m	w	SC	Merced	Snelling P O	74	255
William	73	m	w	IL	San Bernardino	San Bernardino Twp	78	447
William	64	m	w	VA	Colusa	Spring Valley Twp	71	337
William	62	m	w	KY	Mendocino	Little Lake Twp	74	203
William	59	m	w	KY	Mendocino	Ukiah Twp	74	242
William	56	m	w	PA	Calaveras	San Andreas P O	70	209

Name	Age	S	R	B-PL	County	Locale	Roll	Pg
William	45	m	w	SHOL	Trinity	Douglas	92	234
William	40	m	w	MD	San Francisco	San Francisco P O	80	463
William	38	m	w	NY	Nevada	Meadow Lake Twp	75	267
William	35	m	w	SCOT	Siskiyou	Scott Valley Twp	89	613
William	35	m	w	AL	Colusa	Colusa Twp	71	287
William	33	m	w	IREL	Calaveras	San Andreas P O	70	187
William	30	m	w	PA	Alpine	Bullion P O	69	314
William	27	m	w	NY	Inyo	Cerro Gordo Twp	73	321
William	26	m	w	IREL	San Francisco	1-Wd San Francisco	79	99
William	17	m	b	MD	San Francisco	5-Wd San Francisco	81	2
William C	33	m	w	CANA	Colusa	Spring Valley Twp	71	341
Wilson A	37	m	w	KY	Yolo	Cache Crk Twp	93	430
Wm	52	m	w	PA	Sacramento	Franklin Twp	77	106
Wm	45	m	w	CANA	San Francisco	11-Wd San Francisc	84	615
Wm	38	m	w	PA	San Francisco	San Francisco P O	83	46
Wm	28	m	w	IREL	San Mateo	San Mateo P O	87	359
Wm	25	m	w	IREL	San Francisco	San Francisco P O	83	81
Wm	23	m	w	IA	Humboldt	Arcata Twp	72	228
Wm	22	m	w	NJ	San Joaquin	Elkhorn Twp	86	54
Wm B	27	m	w	ENGL	Nevada	Nevada Twp	75	315
Wm F	45	m	w	OH	San Joaquin	Elkhorn Twp	86	62
Wm J	41	m	w	ENGL	Nevada	Meadow Lake Twp	75	247
Wm Sr	63	m	w	KY	Merced	Snelling P O	74	267
Zelikah	14	f	w	MA	San Joaquin	Oneal Twp	86	114
HENRYS								
Edwin	52	m	w	IL	Calaveras	Copperopolis P O	70	257
HENSCHER								
John	31	m	w	HANO	San Francisco	7-Wd San Francisco	81	222
HENSEL								
August	28	m	w	PRUS	San Francisco	7-Wd San Francisco	81	287
George	40	m	w	MO	Santa Clara	San Jose Twp	88	211
Harry	46	m	w	PRUS	Calaveras	Copperopolis P O	70	241
Isabel	45	f	w	VA	Santa Clara	San Jose Twp	88	215
John	55	m	w	PRUS	El Dorado	White Oak Twp	72	135
Max	25	m	w	PRUS	San Francisco	1-Wd San Francisco	79	69
HENSELL								
C C	36	f	w	MO	Tuolumne	Chinese Camp P O	93	373
G H	18	m	w	MO	Tuolumne	Chinese Camp P O	93	373
HENSELY								
Abram	22	m	w	MO	Fresno	Millerton P O	72	194
Geo W	14	m	w	CA	Fresno	Millerton P O	72	194
John	20	m	w	MO	Fresno	Millerton P O	72	194
Pinkny J	16	m	w	CA	Fresno	Millerton P O	72	194
Saml P	24	m	w	MO	Fresno	Millerton P O	72	194
Thos J	26	m	w	MO	Fresno	Millerton P O	72	194
Wm C	18	m	w	MO	Fresno	Millerton P O	72	194
HENSEN								
Chas	27	m	w	DENM	San Joaquin	2-Wd Stockton	86	172
Christopher	29	m	w	DENM	Calaveras	San Andreas P O	70	205
HENSER								
J	45	m	w	ENGL	Sierra	Sierra Twp	89	569
HENSEY								
Samuel	40	m	w	PA	Placer	Rocklin Twp	76	467
HENSHAW								
Alexander	26	m	w	KY	Stanislaus	Washington Twp	92	85
C	37	m	w	NY	San Joaquin	Douglas Twp	86	40
Edward T	20	m	w	IL	Placer	Bath P O	76	441
H	50	m	w	IREL	San Joaquin	Douglas Twp	86	40
Harvey	25	m	w	NY	Santa Barbara	San Buenaventura P	87	431
Jonathan	30	m	w	NC	Santa Clara	Fremont Twp	88	44
Wast	62	m	w	VA	Butte	Chico Twp	70	40
William	28	m	w	KY	Stanislaus	Washington Twp	92	85
HENSHILWOOD								
T R	33	m	w	SCOT	San Francisco	San Francisco P O	85	859
HENSHON								
Park	25	m	w	MO	Butte	Chico Twp	70	17
HENSLER								
John	36	m	w	GERM	Yolo	Grafton Twp	93	492
John D	48	m	w	WURT	El Dorado	Coloma Twp	72	8
HENSLEY								
Amti	16	f	w	MO	San Joaquin	1-Wd Stockton	86	139
Anita	25	f	w	MO	San Francisco	San Francisco P O	83	199
Frederick	21	m	w	LA	San Francisco	San Francisco P O	83	185
H L	44	m	w	MO	Mendocino	Ukiah Twp	74	240
John	43	m	w	ENGL	San Francisco	San Francisco P O	83	303
John	35	m	w	MO	Sonoma	Analy Twp	91	247
John	35	m	w	MO	Yolo	Putah Twp	93	523
John J	53	m	w	MO	Fresno	Millerton P O	72	148
Lucinda	49	f	w	MA	Sacramento	4-Wd Sacramento	77	366
Mary H	35	f	w	NY	Santa Clara	2-Wd San Jose	88	294
Michael	33	m	w	CA	Fresno	Millerton P O	72	160
Preston	35	m	w	MO	Solano	Rio Vista Twp	90	57
Rebecca	42	f	w	MO	Colusa	Colusa Twp	71	275
Robt Geo	37	m	w	ENGL	Sacramento	4-Wd Sacramento	77	343
Thos L	57	m	w	TN	Shasta	American Ranch P O	89	497
Timothy	27	m	w	NY	San Francisco	1-Wd San Francisco	79	100
William	37	m	w	MO	Santa Cruz	Santa Cruz	89	433
William	14	m	w	IA	Los Angeles	Los Angeles	73	570
Wm S	34	m	w	MO	Shasta	American Ranch P O	89	497
HENSLY								
Frank	60	m	w	CANA	Los Angeles	Wilmington Twp	73	640
Tobias A	42	m	w	OH	Butte	Chico Twp	70	38
HENSON								
E	22	m	w	HAMB	San Francisco	San Francisco P O	83	95
Henry	23	m	w	IN	Tehama	Tehama Twp	92	193
Hibbard	13	m	w	CANA	San Francisco	San Francisco P O	83	189
James	30	m	w	TN	Colusa	Spring Valley Twp	71	340

© 2001 by Heritage Quest. All rights reserved.

Series M593

Name	Age	S	R	B-PL	County	Locale	Roll	Pg
James A H	17	m	b	NY	Yolo	Cache Crk Twp	93	433
John	29	m	w	DENM	Sacramento	Center Twp	77	82
John	16	m	w	CA	San Francisco	San Francisco P O	83	152
Tousa W	23	m	w	PRUS	Alpine	Markleeville P O	69	312
HENSOR								
Antone	24	m	w	HDAR	Yuba	Slate Range Bar Tw	93	669
HENSPIN								
Nelson	36	m	m	MS	San Francisco	San Francisco P O	83	51
HENSTEON								
Ella	9	f	w	CA	Yolo	Cache Crk Twp	93	435
HENSTON								
H	28	m	w	MO	Lake	Big Valley	73	399
J M	66	m	w	KY	Lake	Big Valley	73	399
James	43	m	w	NY	Monterey	Alisal Twp	74	298
James E	55	m	w	OH	Contra Costa	Martinez P O	71	376
Joseph W	39	m	w	ME	Sacramento	Natomas Twp	77	169
Lewis	32	m	w	TX	Fresno	Millerton P O	72	192
Robert	22	m	w	IN	Sonoma	Petaluma Twp	91	337
W	8	m	w	HI	San Francisco	San Francisco P O	85	800
HENT								
L Eva	11	f	w	CA	Amador	Volcano P O	69	379
Robert W	36	m	w	IL	San Francisco	6-Wd San Francisco	81	124
HENTADO								
Agostin	40	m	w	PERU	Los Angeles	Santa Ana Twp	73	616
HENTAGE								
Joseph	47	m	w	NJ	Monterey	San Juan Twp	74	410
HENTCHISON								
J	40	m	w	SCOT	Sierra	Butte Twp	89	513
HENTER								
William	40	m	w	IA	Los Angeles	Los Angeles Twp	73	481
HENTH								
Francis	34	m	w	HANO	Nevada	Little York Twp	75	238
HENTIN								
William	30	m	w	CANA	Alameda	Washington Twp	68	296
HENTZ								
August	28	m	w	SHOL	San Francisco	San Francisco P O	83	74
Augustus	34	m	w	PRUS	San Francisco	San Francisco P O	83	176
Frank	26	m	w	PRUS	San Francisco	San Francisco P O	80	477
H F	28	m	w	NY	Nevada	Nevada Twp	75	294
HENTZELL								
Frank	21	m	w	BREM	San Francisco	8-Wd San Francisco	82	368
HENWOOD								
Joseph	36	m	w	ENGL	Placer	Newcastle Twp	76	474
HENY								
Gee Gin	38	m	c	CHIN	Calaveras	San Andreas P O	70	155
Mary	35	f	w	CANA	Marin	San Rafael	74	52
Yon	35	m	c	CHIN	San Joaquin	1-Wd Stockton	86	149
HENYON								
John	31	m	w	KY	Los Angeles	San Juan Twp	73	628
HENZLEY								
Thomas	35	m	w	MO	Siskiyou	Butte Twp	89	585
HEOFS								
John	44	m	w	BELG	Monterey	Monterey	74	355
HEON								
---	55	m	c	CHIN	Sierra	Eureka Twp	89	526
W	28	m	w	ENGL	Sacramento	3-Wd Sacramento	77	295
HEONG								
Ah	32	m	c	CHIN	Nevada	Eureka Twp	75	136
Ah	26	m	c	CHIN	Placer	Lincoln P O	76	483
HEOP								
Yo	23	m	c	CHIN	Fresno	Millerton P O	72	181
HEORTSAY								
S	40	m	w	BADE	Sierra	Butte Twp	89	508
HEOW								
Ah	36	m	c	CHIN	Amador	Jackson P O	69	331
HEP								
Ah	38	m	c	CHIN	Sacramento	American Twp	77	68
Ah	37	m	c	CHIN	Sacramento	Georgianna Twp	77	134
Ah	30	m	c	CHIN	Sacramento	Georgianna Twp	77	133
Ah	28	m	c	CHIN	Sacramento	Georgianna Twp	77	133
Ah	28	m	c	CHIN	Sacramento	Georgianna Twp	77	135
Lah	30	m	c	CHIN	San Joaquin	1-Wd Stockton	86	142
Son	65	m	c	CHIN	Sacramento	1-Wd Sacramento	77	197
HEPBERSON								
T R	41	m	w	ENGL	Monterey	Alisal Twp	74	298
HEPBURN								
Emma	37	f	w	PA	Marin	San Rafael	74	51
I W	30	m	w	PA	Sacramento	3-Wd Sacramento	77	302
James	71	m	w	PA	Calaveras	San Andreas P O	70	198
Louisa	24	f	w	IL	Butte	Ophir Twp	70	104
HEPHTULY								
Wm	17	m	w	BOHE	Sacramento	1-Wd Sacramento	77	172
HEPION								
Wm	40	m	w	IREL	Solano	Benicia	90	12
HEPLE								
Conrad	50	m	w	SWIT	Santa Clara	2-Wd San Jose	88	333
HEPLER								
John	43	m	w	IREL	San Francisco	San Francisco P O	80	534
Susan	24	f	w	MS	Sacramento	2-Wd Sacramento	77	243
HEPP								
Henrietta	30	f	w	AL	Yolo	Cottonwood Twp	93	472
HEPPE								
Charles	35	m	w	OLDE	Santa Clara	1-Wd San Jose	88	262
HEPPENETTE								
E O	31	m	w	PRUS	Alameda	Oakland	68	263
HEPPLER								
Charles	43	m	w	PRUS	Monterey	San Juan Twp	74	400
HEPPORD								
George W	40	m	w	PA	Placer	Gold Run Twp	76	397
HEPSBARGER								
Eliza	32	f	w	PRUS	San Francisco	5-Wd San Francisco	81	8
HEPSTEINE								
Jno P	58	m	w	KY	Butte	Chico Twp	70	58
HEPT								
George	24	m	w	PRUS	San Francisco	8-Wd San Francisco	82	431
HEPWORTH								
Susan	36	f	w	IREL	San Francisco	San Francisco P O	80	401
HEQUILLY								
Francis	65	m	w	FRAN	Nevada	Grass Valley Twp	75	146
HER								
Ah	40	m	c	CHIN	Amador	Volcano P O	69	386
Ah	24	f	c	CHIN	Placer	Dutch Flat P O	76	409
HERALD								
Frank	32	m	w	IREL	Placer	Lincoln P O	76	486
James	35	m	w	AL	Los Angeles	Los Angeles Twp	73	493
Jasper	39	m	w	GA	Tulare	Visalia	92	290
Jos	30	m	w	NY	Sacramento	1-Wd Sacramento	77	172
Robert T	30	m	w	KY	Tulare	White Rvr Twp	92	301
Thomas	25	m	w	ENGL	Nevada	Grass Valley Twp	75	203
William	45	m	w	ENGL	Nevada	Bridgeport Twp	75	122
HERAN								
John H	35	m	w	KY	Stanislaus	San Joaquin Twp	92	77
HERANGAR								
John	51	m	w	HOLL	Yolo	Merritt Twp	93	504
HERANS								
Bonifacio	36	m	w	CA	Fresno	Millerton P O	72	151
HERANZ								
Nevais	38	m	w	TX	Los Angeles	Los Angeles	73	511
HERAT								
George	32	m	w	FRAN	Mendocino	Casper & Big Rvr	74	163
HERBACK								
Arnold	35	m	w	SWED	Solano	Vallejo	90	188
HERBAN								
Simon	40	m	w	MEXI	Fresno	Millerton P O	72	155
HERBEC								
Frank	39	m	w	AUST	Mariposa	Maxwell Crk P O	74	146
HERBER								
John	21	m	w	PRUS	San Francisco	6-Wd San Francisco	81	100
HERBERGER								
Carl	42	m	w	HANO	Yuba	Marysville	93	575
HERBERSON								
Adam	53	m	w	SCOT	Placer	Newcastle Twp	76	478
HERBERT								
Afred	25	m	w	ENGL	San Francisco	1-Wd San Francisco	79	17
Alfred W	48	m	w	ENGL	Calaveras	San Andreas P O	70	210
Allen	42	m	w	IA	San Francisco	5-Wd San Francisco	81	14
Amy	40	f	w	WALE	San Francisco	1-Wd San Francisco	79	62
Annie E	13	f	w	NJ	Santa Cruz	Santa Cruz	89	425
Annie H	13	f	w	NJ	Santa Barbara	Santa Barbara P O	87	473
Arthur	26	m	w	NY	San Francisco	11-Wd San Francisc	84	527
Catharine	22	f	w	MA	San Francisco	San Francisco P O	83	292
Franklin	18	m	w	PA	Santa Barbara	Santa Barbara P O	87	499
G W	45	m	w	KY	San Joaquin	Dent Twp	86	26
George	56	m	w	ME	Santa Barbara	San Buenaventura P	87	437
George	29	m	w	WALE	San Francisco	1-Wd San Francisco	79	118
Henrietta	39	f	w	GA	Santa Cruz	Santa Cruz	89	431
Henry	38	m	w	NY	San Francisco	11-Wd San Francisc	84	557
J E	31	m	w	PA	Solano	Vallejo	90	200
J T	30	m	w	MO	Yuba	Marysville	93	604
James	43	m	w	NY	San Francisco	11-Wd San Francisc	84	573
Jas	29	m	w	IREL	San Francisco	1-Wd San Francisco	79	94
Jessey	28	f	w	PA	Amador	Sutter Crk P O	69	409
John	36	m	w	IREL	San Francisco	San Francisco P O	83	199
John	30	m	w	IREL	Yuba	Marysville	93	612
John	19	m	w	SCOT	San Joaquin	Douglas Twp	86	51
Joseph	26	m	w	IREL	San Francisco	1-Wd San Francisco	79	96
Lewis	47	m	w	FRAN	Stanislaus	Empire Twp	92	52
Lewis	28	m	w	ENGL	Sacramento	Dry Crk Twp	77	97
Mary	14	f	w	WALE	San Francisco	1-Wd San Francisco	79	62
Matthew	41	m	w	IL	Stanislaus	Branch Twp	92	1
Maurice	45	m	w	IREL	Sonoma	Petaluma Twp	91	360
Richard	35	m	w	NJ	San Francisco	San Francisco P O	83	367
Samuel	22	m	w	CANA	Yolo	Cache Crk Twp	93	456
Sarah	24	f	w	IREL	Butte	Oregon Twp	70	124
Thomas	32	m	w	AUST	Monterey	San Antonio Twp	74	324
Thomas	30	m	w	IREL	Santa Cruz	Santa Cruz Twp	89	391
William	16	m	w	WALE	San Francisco	1-Wd San Francisco	79	62
William B	51	m	w	MD	Solano	Tremont Twp	90	31
Wm	42	m	w	WALE	Butte	Oregon Twp	70	125
Wm	41	m	w	WALE	San Francisco	1-Wd San Francisco	79	61
Z	43	m	w	LA	Monterey	Alisal Twp	74	298
HERBESON								
Mathew	70	m	w	IREL	Sonoma	Analy Twp	91	223
HERBET								
Danl S	63	m	w	VA	Plumas	Plumas Twp	77	28
HERBISON								
William	24	m	w	CANA	Solano	Green Valley Twp	90	39
HERBST								
Adolph	34	m	w	FRNK	San Francisco	2-Wd San Francisco	79	229
HERBTS								
Charles	40	m	w	PRUS	Mendocino	Gualala Twp	74	226
HERCE								
Henry	24	m	w	NY	Tulare	Visalia	92	290

© 2001 by Heritage Quest. All rights reserved.

Name	Age	S	R	B-PL	County	Locale	Roll	Pg
						Series M593		
HERCHELL								
Rudolph	39	m	w	PRUS	San Francisco	San Francisco P O	83	253
HERCHFELD								
William	44	m	w	BAVA	San Francisco	San Francisco P O	83	255
HERCOG								
Gustavus	39	m	w	BAVA	San Francisco	2-Wd San Francisco	79	189
HERD								
Anne	49	f	w	ENGL	San Francisco	7-Wd San Francisco	81	273
Barton	31	m	w	ME	San Joaquin	Oneal Twp	86	113
James	35	m	w	SCOT	San Bernardino	San Bernardino Twp	78	453
Jane	28	f	w	IREL	San Francisco	7-Wd San Francisco	81	169
Julia	38	f	w	PRUS	San Francisco	San Francisco P O	85	820
William	52	m	w	NJ	Santa Clara	Redwood Twp	88	126
HERDICH								
Jos	25	m	w	HOLL	Alameda	Oakland	68	222
HERDINK								
John	41	m	w	HOLL	San Francisco	11-Wd San Francisc	84	466
HERDON								
Otis H	67	m	w	MA	El Dorado	Placerville Twp	72	94
HERDY								
Thomas	43	m	w	SCOT	El Dorado	Placerville Twp	72	94
HERED								
Robert	38	m	b	NY	Los Angeles	Los Angeles	73	528
HEREFORD								
Ann C	36	f	w	OH	Los Angeles	Los Angeles	73	518
B	46	m	w	MO	Mendocino	Ukiah Twp	74	234
Daniel	56	m	w	TN	Placer	Auburn P O	76	361
Edmond H	25	m	w	MO	Los Angeles	San Gabriel Twp	73	596
Esther	68	f	w	VA	Los Angeles	San Gabriel Twp	73	596
Pierce	35	m	w	OH	Los Angeles	Los Nietos Twp	73	587
Thos	28	m	w	MO	San Joaquin	Elkhorn Twp	86	63
HEREL								
Daniel	50	m	w	IREL	Santa Clara	1-Wd San Jose	88	262
HERENA								
Phillip	40	m	w	SPAI	San Francisco	6-Wd San Francisco	81	82
HERFIELD								
Henry	47	m	w	PRUS	Marin	Sausalito Twp	74	72
HERGASON								
John	60	m	w	IREL	Amador	Jackson P O	69	335
HERGERT								
John	40	m	w	FRAN	Placer	Colfax P O	76	389
HERGES								
William	34	m	w	PRUS	San Francisco	2-Wd San Francisco	79	153
HERGET								
J B	43	m	w	GERM	Sacramento	1-Wd Sacramento	77	201
Mar	65	f	w	HESS	Sacramento	3-Wd Sacramento	77	290
HERGETT								
John	27	m	w	FRAN	Sacramento	4-Wd Sacramento	77	373
HERGITT								
Godfrey	47	m	w	ENGL	San Francisco	8-Wd San Francisco	82	428
HERGOT								
Geo	43	m	w	PRUS	Sacramento	American Twp	77	67
Henry	14	m	w	CA	San Francisco	11-Wd San Francisc	84	588
HERGOTT								
Alex P	37	m	w	FRAN	San Francisco	6-Wd San Francisco	81	122
HERGUSHAMER								
J	8	m	w	IA	Mendocino	Calpella Twp	74	190
HERHEIM								
Conrad	34	m	w	GERM	Marin	San Rafael Twp	74	26
HERI								
George	40	m	w	BREM	Monterey	Alisal Twp	74	301
HERIENSE								
G	28	m	w	NY	San Francisco	San Francisco P O	85	790
HERIFORD								
John	63	m	w	TN	El Dorado	Diamond Springs Tw	72	27
William	39	m	w	KY	El Dorado	Diamond Springs Tw	72	26
HERIGAULT								
Emiel	35	m	w	FRAN	Sacramento	2-Wd Sacramento	77	246
HERIN								
Mary	12	f	w	CA	El Dorado	Mud Springs Twp	72	84
HERING								
Corydon D	44	m	w	IL	San Francisco	San Francisco P O	83	230
HERINGER								
Henry	23	m	w	PA	San Francisco	San Francisco P O	83	362
HERIONA								
Jose	50	m	w	MEXI	Stanislaus	Empire Twp	92	41
HERIOT								
William	45	m	w	SCOT	El Dorado	White Oak Twp	72	137
HERIST								
John	53	m	w	GERM	Tuolumne	Columbia P O	93	346
HERITTON								
A	21	m	w	ME	Sierra	Sierra Twp	89	564
HERKES								
Peter	30	m	w	SCOT	Solano	Rio Vista Twp	90	62
HERKIMER								
James B	33	m	w	CANA	San Diego	Julian Dist	78	472
Thomas	37	m	w	CANA	San Diego	San Diego	78	487
HERKNESS								
G S	44	m	w	NY	San Joaquin	2-Wd Stockton	86	187
HERKULIS								
Fredrick	29	m	w	HANO	San Francisco	7-Wd San Francisco	81	213
HERLEIGH								
William	40	m	w	IREL	San Francisco	7-Wd San Francisco	81	216
HERLEMAN								
J F	40	m	w	BADE	Amador	Drytown P O	69	419
HERLEY								
Jerry	32	m	w	IREL	San Francisco	7-Wd San Francisco	81	212
Jerry	29	m	w	IREL	Placer	Bath P O	76	459
HERLIAHY								
Rich	33	m	w	IREL	San Francisco	2-Wd San Francisco	79	265
HERLIHY								
Edmond	33	m	w	IREL	San Francisco	1-Wd San Francisco	79	68
Morris	46	m	w	IREL	San Francisco	11-Wd San Francisc	84	482
HERLIN								
John	26	m	w	SWED	San Francisco	7-Wd San Francisco	81	259
HERLOCK								
Maria	68	f	w	MD	Yolo	Washington Twp	93	538
HERLVILLE								
Lewis	40	m	w	BADE	Placer	Auburn P O	76	380
HERM								
Pat	32	m	w	NY	Sacramento	1-Wd Sacramento	77	191
See	25	f	c	CHIN	Sacramento	1-Wd Sacramento	77	198
HERMAIS								
N A	23	m	w	MEXI	Tuolumne	Sonora P O	93	306
HERMAL								
George	19	m	w	PRUS	Solano	Tremont Twp	90	28
HERMAN								
Adam	36	m	w	HDAR	Los Angeles	Santa Ana Twp	73	615
Antone	23	m	w	CA	Contra Costa	Martinez P O	71	441
August	23	m	w	BADE	Alameda	Washington Twp	68	290
Benjamin	29	m	w	PRUS	San Francisco	8-Wd San Francisco	82	407
Bernard	26	m	w	MD	Santa Clara	2-Wd San Jose	88	320
C	25	m	w	BAVA	Amador	Ione City P O	69	369
Carl	20	m	w	PRUS	El Dorado	Placerville Twp	72	93
Carlos	25	m	w	PRUS	San Francisco	6-Wd San Francisco	81	96
Charles	27	m	w	PRUS	San Francisco	7-Wd San Francisco	81	195
Charles	26	m	w	HANO	Santa Clara	2-Wd San Jose	88	331
Charles	16	m	w	BADE	San Francisco	San Francisco P O	83	255
Chas	37	m	w	GERM	San Francisco	8-Wd San Francisco	82	368
Chas	36	m	w	SAXO	San Francisco	San Francisco P O	83	323
Christopher	22	m	w	BADE	San Francisco	San Francisco P O	80	461
Conrad	23	m	w	GERM	Sacramento	Sutter Twp	77	390
Conrad	19	m	w	BAVA	San Francisco	3-Wd San Francisco	79	324
Domina	86	f	w	CA	Monterey	Monterey Twp	74	349
Edward	40	m	w	DENM	San Francisco	11-Wd San Francisc	84	655
Edward	23	m	w	IREL	San Diego	Julian Dist	78	472
Elias S	34	m	w	POLA	San Francisco	San Francisco P O	83	51
Frank	13	m	w	CA	Amador	Jackson P O	69	342
Franklin	41	m	w	PA	Amador	Sutter Crk P O	69	408
George	33	m	w	PRUS	San Francisco	6-Wd San Francisco	81	113
George	25	m	w	GERM	Yolo	Grafton Twp	93	499
Gregory	50	m	w	FRAN	San Francisco	6-Wd San Francisco	81	89
Hance	25	m	w	SHOL	Alameda	Hayward	68	75
Henrietta	22	f	w	NY	San Francisco	8-Wd San Francisco	82	453
Henry	40	m	w	PRUS	San Francisco	San Francisco P O	83	318
Isaac	52	m	w	PRUS	San Francisco	8-Wd San Francisco	82	298
Jas A	37	m	w	CA	San Francisco	San Francisco P O	85	781
John	29	m	w	OH	Fresno	Millerton P O	72	183
John	24	m	w	KY	Siskiyou	Butte Twp	89	585
John	22	m	w	NY	San Francisco	2-Wd San Francisco	79	213
Juan	27	m	w	MEXI	Santa Barbara	San Buenaventura P	87	427
Levi	32	m	w	POLA	San Francisco	San Francisco P O	83	141
M D	22	m	w	PRUS	San Francisco	7-Wd San Francisco	81	226
Margaret	24	f	w	PRUS	San Francisco	San Francisco P O	80	421
Peter	36	m	w	SHOL	San Francisco	1-Wd San Francisco	79	130
Peter	35	m	w	HDAR	San Francisco	11-Wd San Francisc	84	632
Richd	42	m	w	HANO	Solano	Vallejo	90	165
Robert	43	m	w	DENM	San Francisco	7-Wd San Francisco	81	218
Robert	22	m	w	AUST	Los Angeles	Santa Ana Twp	73	611
Rudolph	39	m	w	PRUS	San Francisco	San Francisco P O	85	757
Samuel	60	m	w	LA	San Francisco	8-Wd San Francisco	82	464
T H	35	m	w	NY	Solano	Vallejo	90	142
Ursula	22	f	w	SWIT	San Francisco	8-Wd San Francisco	82	471
William	37	m	w	BAVA	Inyo	Lone Pine Twp	73	335
William	30	m	w	ENGL	San Francisco	San Francisco P O	80	427
William	25	m	w	BAVA	San Francisco	8-Wd San Francisco	82	391
William Z	24	m	w	ENGL	San Francisco	6-Wd San Francisco	81	82
HERMANCE								
F	15	f	w	CA	Sacramento	3-Wd Sacramento	77	313
Fred	44	m	w	SWED	Sacramento	Brighton Twp	77	74
Hannah	23	f	w	NH	Solano	Tremont Twp	90	30
John	49	m	w	NY	San Joaquin	Elkhorn Twp	86	58
Lemuel S	34	m	w	NY	Sacramento	2-Wd Sacramento	77	240
Peter	43	m	w	NY	Humboldt	Eureka Twp	72	256
HERMAND								
Adolph	38	m	w	FRAN	San Francisco	San Francisco P O	85	752
HERMANDEZ								
Benito	28	m	w	CA	Santa Clara	1-Wd San Jose	88	262
Juan	31	m	w	MEXI	Santa Clara	2-Wd San Jose	88	335
Juan	30	m	w	MEXI	Santa Clara	Burnett Twp	88	35
Tomasa	71	f	w	CA	Santa Clara	Santa Clara Twp	88	158
HERMANDO								
Jose	26	m	w	CA	Santa Cruz	Santa Cruz	89	431
Juan	18	m	w	MEXI	Fresno	Millerton P O	72	166
HERMANDS								
D	16	f	w	CA	Alameda	Oakland	68	237
HERMANN								
Adam	34	m	w	WURT	Los Angeles	Santa Ana Twp	73	605
Chis	45	m	w	PRUS	San Francisco	2-Wd San Francisco	79	261
Christian	29	m	w	NY	Alameda	Hayward	68	77
Francis	38	m	w	PRUS	San Francisco	11-Wd San Francisc	84	624
Lyman	45	m	w	PRUS	San Francisco	8-Wd San Francisco	82	307
Otto	36	m	w	FRNK	San Francisco	11-Wd San Francisc	84	690

© 2001 by Heritage Quest. All rights reserved.

Series M593

Name	Age	S	R	B-PL	County	Locale	Roll	Pg
HERMANNY								
Austin	28	m	w	SAXO	Sonoma	Salt Point	91	386
HERMER								
Ann	25	f	w	PRUS	San Francisco	6-Wd San Francisco	81	104
Henry	30	m	w	PRUS	San Francisco	6-Wd San Francisco	81	92
HERMEY								
Martin	40	m	w	PRUS	Nevada	Nevada Twp	75	305
HERMIDA								
Aug	33	m	w	ECUA	San Francisco	1-Wd San Francisco	79	117
HERMILLIA								
Amelia	50	f	w	NJ	San Francisco	2-Wd San Francisco	79	265
HERMIN								
Augustus	52	m	w	SAXO	Sutter	Butte Twp	92	90
HERMINAN								
Maria	15	f	w	MEXI	San Francisco	San Francisco P O	80	346
HERMINGER								
T J	45	m	w	IA	Sacramento	4-Wd Sacramento	77	373
HERMINGHAM								
Gustave	45	m	w	MO	Fresno	Millerton P O	72	157
HERMIS								
Mary	60	f	w	FRAN	San Francisco	2-Wd San Francisco	79	151
HERMON								
Phillip	46	m	w	PRUS	Contra Costa	San Pablo Twp	71	360
R E	35	m	w	PA	Alameda	Oakland	68	180
HERMOSILLA								
Rosa	60	f	w	CHIL	Sacramento	2-Wd Sacramento	77	207
HERN								
Ack	22	m	c	CHIN	Contra Costa	Martinez P O	71	430
Ezra	27	m	w	MO	Solano	Vacaville Twp	90	133
James	23	m	w	TN	Fresno	Kings Rvr P O	72	213
Joshua	29	m	w	MO	Fresno	Millerton P O	72	155
Levi	44	m	w	MO	Fresno	Millerton P O	72	146
Patrick A	36	m	w	IREL	San Francisco	San Francisco P O	83	5
R	35	m	w	MO	Santa Clara	Burnett Twp	88	36
U N	24	m	w	IREL	Yuba	Marysville	93	604
William	45	m	w	KY	Inyo	Independence Twp	73	326
William	26	m	w	IREL	Placer	Newcastle Twp	76	477
William	20	m	w	CANA	Sacramento	Franklin Twp	77	112
HERNANDES								
Carlos	40	m	w	CHIL	Plumas	Goodwin Twp	77	1
Domingo	45	m	w	MEXI	Los Angeles	Los Angeles	73	515
H	34	m	w	PORT	San Joaquin	Douglas Twp	86	43
Jesus	58	m	w	MEXI	Los Angeles	Los Angeles Twp	73	474
Juan	33	m	w	CA	San Luis Obispo	Morro Twp	87	286
Olean	45	m	i	CHIL	Inyo	Lone Pine Twp	73	333
Silver	50	m	w	CA	San Luis Obispo	Santa Rosa Twp	87	330
Torivio	40	m	w	MEXI	San Luis Obispo	San Luis Obispo Tw	87	306
HERNANDEZ								
Andy	50	m	w	CHIL	Butte	Kimshew Tpw	70	82
Antonio	38	m	w	CA	San Mateo	Half Moon Bay P O	87	394
Augustino	55	m	w	CA	Fresno	Millerton P O	72	161
E	44	m	w	MEXI	Monterey	San Juan Twp	74	401
F J	50	m	w	CHIL	Tuolumne	Sonora P O	93	306
Francisco	21	m	w	CA	San Francisco	11-Wd San Francisc	84	573
Gregorio	32	m	w	MEXI	Santa Clara	Almaden Twp	88	1
J	37	m	w	MEXI	Santa Clara	Almaden Twp	88	10
Jamila	26	f	w	MEXI	Sacramento	2-Wd Sacramento	77	221
Johnan	24	f	w	MEXI	San Bernardino	San Salvador Twp	78	456
Jose	63	m	w	CA	Contra Costa	Martinez P O	71	441
Jose	41	m	w	MEXI	Fresno	Millerton P O	72	193
Jose	35	m	w	MEXI	San Diego	San Diego	78	504
Joaquin	30	m	w	CA	Contra Costa	Martinez P O	71	438
Julian	27	m	w	MEXI	Los Angeles	Los Angeles	73	559
Manuela	25	f	w	MEXI	Los Angeles	Los Angeles	73	552
Mariano	23	m	w	CA	Santa Clara	2-Wd San Jose	88	302
Nicholas	50	m	w	MEXI	Plumas	Quartz Twp	77	35
Pedro	60	m	w	CA	Santa Clara	Santa Clara Twp	88	158
Rafael	50	m	w	MEXI	Monterey	San Juan Twp	74	412
Raphael S	44	m	w	FL	El Dorado	Placerville	72	108
Stanislais	33	m	w	MEXI	Marin	San Rafael	74	56
Teofilo	60	m	w	MEXI	Monterey	San Benito Twp	74	381
Victor	18	m	w	CA	Los Angeles	Los Angeles	73	525
HERNANDO								
Anton	54	m	w	MEXI	Tuolumne	Columbia P O	93	355
Anton	30	m	w	MEXI	Tuolumne	Chinese Camp P O	93	335
J A	49	m	w	MEXI	Tuolumne	Columbia P O	93	355
J H	51	m	w	MEXI	Tuolumne	Columbia P O	93	335
HERNANDOZ								
Lean	2	m	w	CA	San Francisco	San Francisco P O	80	331
HERNDEN								
N	61	m	w	TN	Lake	Lower Lake	73	421
Wm L	47	m	w	VA	Sacramento	4-Wd Sacramento	77	345
HERNDON								
A M	40	f	w	KY	Sacramento	1-Wd Sacramento	77	184
David	50	m	w	KY	Kern	Tehachapi P O	73	356
F M	36	m	w	KY	Lake	Lower Lake	73	418
George	24	m	w	MO	Lake	Lower Lake	73	418
John	46	m	w	VA	Santa Clara	San Jose Twp	88	213
Wm	30	m	w	MO	Lake	Lower Lake	73	420
HERNE								
Jeremiah	32	m	w	IREL	San Francisco	San Francisco P O	83	182
Jeremiah	30	m	w	IREL	Santa Clara	2-Wd San Jose	88	307
Thos	43	m	w	IREL	Butte	Ophir Twp	70	102
HERNEDY								
Abel	29	m	w	NY	San Francisco	5-Wd San Francisco	81	12
Abel Mrs	24	m	w	NY	San Francisco	5-Wd San Francisco	81	12
HERNEN								
Peter	24	m	w	NY	Alameda	Eden Twp	68	81
HERNEY								
Chas	28	m	w	IREL	San Francisco	San Francisco P O	85	851
Michael	25	m	w	IREL	San Francisco	San Francisco P O	83	236
Patrick	18	m	w	IREL	San Francisco	San Francisco P O	83	236
HERNIGER								
J C	29	m	w	PA	San Francisco	San Francisco P O	85	839
HERNMAN								
Herman	31	m	w	BAVA	San Francisco	6-Wd San Francisco	81	70
HERNOLD								
Daniel	38	m	w	OH	El Dorado	Georgetown Twp	72	37
HERNSHIMER								
---	25	m	w	BADE	Yuba	Marysville	93	616
HERNSTAY								
William	28	m	w	PRUS	Stanislaus	Emory Twp	92	25
HERNSTER								
Geo	44	m	w	BAVA	Santa Barbara	Santa Barbara P O	87	452
HERNTER								
Jas	48	m	w	BELG	Solano	Vallejo	90	201
HERNUBST								
Wm	41	m	w	GERM	Yuba	Marysville	93	592
HERO								
Ah	20	m	c	CHIN	Mendocino	Point Arena Twp	74	213
HEROD								
Reuben	40	m	w	ENGL	Nevada	Rough & Ready Twp	75	333
HEROLD								
Conrad	39	m	w	PRUS	San Francisco	San Francisco P O	83	73
Nicholas	40	m	w	PRUS	San Bernardino	San Bernardino Twp	78	415
Peter N	23	m	w	OH	Santa Clara	2-Wd San Jose	88	324
HERON								
David	42	m	w	SCOT	Yolo	Buckeye Twp	93	407
James	42	m	w	VA	San Francisco	11-Wd San Francisc	84	609
Joseph	50	m	w	CHIL	El Dorado	Diamond Springs Tw	72	34
Matthew E	38	m	w	MA	San Francisco	1-Wd San Francisco	79	93
Peter	32	m	w	IREL	Monterey	Alisal Twp	74	299
William	35	m	w	TN	Mendocino	Point Arena Twp	74	214
William	29	m	w	CANA	Marin	Point Reyes Twp	74	21
HERONIMUS								
George	35	m	w	FRAN	Plumas	Seneca Twp	77	47
HERPE								
W N	41	m	w	PRUS	Sacramento	3-Wd Sacramento	77	268
HERPST								
Andrew	35	m	w	PRUS	San Francisco	6-Wd San Francisco	81	133
HERR								
Abraham	63	m	w	PA	El Dorado	Cosumnes Twp	72	17
Con	26	m	w	IREL	Sutter	Sutter Twp	92	121
Cornelius	28	m	w	IREL	Sutter	Sutter Twp	92	129
Francis	42	m	w	BADE	Siskiyou	Yreka Twp	89	665
G W	27	m	w	CA	Del Norte	Crescent Twp	71	455
James J	34	m	w	OH	San Francisco	8-Wd San Francisco	82	475
John	42	m	w	WURT	Yuba	New York Twp	93	640
Mary	54	f	w	BADE	Siskiyou	Yreka	89	658
Max	39	m	w	BAVA	San Francisco	2-Wd San Francisco	79	138
HERRALDSON								
Jno	51	m	w	KY	San Joaquin	Douglas Twp	86	40
HERRANDA								
Dario	40	m	w	MEXI	Mariposa	Mariposa P O	74	110
HERRANDES								
Victorio	8	f	w	MEXI	Mariposa	Mariposa P O	74	94
HERRARA								
Isabel	49	f	b	WIND	San Francisco	San Francisco P O	80	421
Tranfila	46	f	w	MEXI	San Francisco	San Francisco P O	80	481
HERRARAS								
Nicholas	53	f	w	MEXI	Mariposa	Mariposa P O	74	92
Pedro M	29	m	w	MEXI	Mariposa	Mariposa P O	74	93
HERRE								
L	27	m	w	BAVA	Alameda	Oakland	68	222
HERREICH								
Augustus	54	m	w	HAMB	San Mateo	San Mateo P O	87	358
HERREN								
Anna M	46	f	w	IREL	Placer	Roseville P O	76	348
Elizabeth	16	f	w	CA	San Francisco	11-Wd San Francisc	84	656
James	41	m	w	OH	Humboldt	Pacific Twp	72	289
HERRENHOFFER								
John	23	m	w	IN	San Francisco	San Francisco P O	85	862
HERRERA								
Antonio	40	m	w	SAME	Monterey	San Juan Twp	74	385
Antonio	34	m	w	NM	San Luis Obispo	San Luis Obispo Tw	87	312
Delmorus	38	m	w	MEXI	San Luis Obispo	Salinas Twp	87	288
Domingo	25	m	w	PORT	Marin	Nicasio Twp	74	20
Francisco	39	m	w	CHIL	San Francisco	7-Wd San Francisco	81	157
Frank	37	m	w	MEXI	Monterey	San Juan Twp	74	410
Thos	21	m	w	CA	San Luis Obispo	Salinas Twp	87	289
Tomas	70	m	w	NM	San Luis Obispo	San Luis Obispo Tw	87	312
Visalia	24	m	w	CA	San Luis Obispo	Salinas Twp	87	288
HERRES								
Daniel	49	m	w	MA	San Francisco	San Francisco P O	83	203
HERRET								
David	18	m	w	SCOT	Plumas	Washington Twp	77	53
HERRETT								
Geo	30	m	w	VA	Santa Barbara	San Buenaventura P	87	431
Joseph	50	m	m	MD	Sacramento	2-Wd Sacramento	77	219
HERREY								
J B	50	m	w	IN	Alameda	Oakland	68	260
Richd	26	m	w	ENGL	Santa Clara	Almaden Twp	88	11

© 2001 by Heritage Quest. All rights reserved.

Name	Age	S	R	B-PL	County	Locale	Series M593 Roll	Pg
HERRGUTH								
Samuel	40	m	w	PRUS	San Francisco	8-Wd San Francisco	82	485
HERRIA								
Guadalupe	16	f	w	CA	Santa Barbara	Santa Barbara P O	87	501
HERRIC								
Patric	39	m	w	IREL	Trinity	Junction City Pct	92	206
HERRICK								
Alfred	30	m	w	ME	San Francisco	8-Wd San Francisco	82	446
Amos P	38	m	w	VT	Butte	Ophir Twp	70	118
Benjamin	46	m	w	ME	Sonoma	Analy Twp	91	219
Coit	40	m	w	MA	Tehama	Antelope Twp	92	155
Curtiss	25	m	w	MA	Shasta	Fort Crook P O	89	474
E	22	m	w	IA	Lassen	Susanville Twp	73	443
Edward	32	m	w	IREL	Humboldt	Table Bluff Twp	72	308
Ellen A	28	f	w	MI	Colusa	Colusa	71	298
Geo E	35	m	w	VT	San Francisco	3-Wd San Francisco	79	327
H H	37	m	w	KY	Lake	Lower Lake	73	421
H L	38	m	w	MA	Tehama	Mill Crk Twp	92	167
Hazard	49	m	w	VT	San Francisco	7-Wd San Francisco	81	246
Isera A	26	m	w	NY	Santa Barbara	Santa Barbara P O	87	499
J B	32	m	w	ME	Humboldt	Eureka Twp	72	277
Jack	32	m	w	ME	Sonoma	Analy Twp	91	247
James E	42	m	w	MA	Placer	Bath P O	76	437
John	50	m	w	NY	San Francisco	San Francisco P O	83	188
Lorenzo	30	m	i	MEXI	Inyo	Cerro Gordo Twp	73	320
Loring	44	m	w	NY	El Dorado	Kelsey Twp	72	60
Mary	30	f	w	MA	San Francisco	San Francisco P O	80	472
Nelson	50	m	w	PA	San Francisco	San Francisco P O	85	765
R F	40	m	w	OH	Humboldt	Pacific Twp	72	292
Saml W	36	m	w	NY	Solano	Vallejo	90	148
Sanford E	37	m	w	NY	San Francisco	8-Wd San Francisco	82	497
Walter B	32	m	w	IA	Stanislaus	Branch Twp	92	3
Wm	43	m	w	NH	San Francisco	11-Wd San Francisc	84	580
HERRIG								
Henry	37	m	w	OLDE	Nevada	Bloomfield Twp	75	94
HERRIGAN								
James	40	m	w	IREL	San Diego	San Diego	78	501
John	60	m	w	IREL	San Francisco	11-Wd San Francisc	84	465
HERRIMAN								
Martha	27	f	w	OH	Santa Clara	2-Wd San Jose	88	328
Moralas	50	m	w	MEXI	Inyo	Bishop Crk Twp	73	310
HERRIN								
Dan	26	m	w	IREL	Alameda	Oakland	68	143
John	23	m	w	CANA	San Francisco	San Francisco P O	83	89
Lewis	40	m	w	FRAN	Yuba	Long Bar Twp	93	560
HERRING								
A W	36	m	w	NC	Nevada	Nevada Twp	75	276
Ann	30	f	w	PA	Yolo	Cache Crk Twp	93	432
Bernard	44	m	w	PRUS	San Francisco	San Francisco P O	83	259
Charity	52	f	w	NC	San Bernardino	San Bernardino Twp	78	422
Charles	39	m	w	PRUS	Stanislaus	Empire Twp	92	35
Chas	31	m	w	IN	Sonoma	Bodega Twp	91	258
Chas	31	m	w	TN	Sonoma	Santa Rosa	91	401
Daniel	73	m	w	ME	Butte	Mountain Spring Tw	70	88
Fred K	47	m	w	ME	Butte	Oroville Twp	70	137
G W	36	m	w	IN	Sutter	Yuba Twp	92	152
Geo	49	m	w	BAVA	El Dorado	Coloma Twp	72	7
George Henry	36	m	w	TN	Plumas	Indian Twp	77	11
James	27	m	b	DE	San Francisco	1-Wd San Francisco	79	95
John	62	m	w	NY	Solano	Vallejo	90	146
John	28	m	w	IREL	Placer	Rocklin Twp	76	468
Joseph	27	m	w	MI	Napa	Napa Twp	75	64
Michel	40	m	w	IREL	Butte	Mountain Spring Tw	70	89
Morris	38	m	w	ENGL	San Francisco	San Francisco P O	83	16
Morris	35	m	w	IREL	San Francisco	1-Wd San Francisco	79	59
Rosa	27	f	w	ENGL	Butte	Oroville Twp	70	138
Thomas	23	m	w	PA	San Francisco	7-Wd San Francisco	81	184
Tillman	21	m	w	PA	San Francisco	7-Wd San Francisco	81	239
W J	46	m	w	NY	Monterey	Alisal Twp	74	296
Wm	56	m	w	PA	Butte	Chico Twp	70	24
Wm	45	m	w	PRUS	Alameda	Murray Twp	68	113
Wm	44	m	w	ME	Butte	Oroville Twp	70	137
HERRINGER								
Charles	60	m	w	PRUS	Santa Clara	2-Wd San Jose	88	280
Joseph	50	m	w	VA	Monterey	Alisal Twp	74	297
HERRINGTON								
Edward B	28	m	w	ENGL	Monterey	Alisal Twp	74	302
James	32	m	w	IREL	San Francisco	San Francisco P O	83	144
John	45	m	w	IREL	Sonoma	Petaluma Twp	91	340
O F	37	m	w	MA	Alameda	Oakland	68	189
Peter	30	m	w	IREL	Alameda	Murray Twp	68	113
William	64	m	w	IREL	Placer	Dutch Flat P O	76	409
William	44	m	w	MO	Tulare	Farmersville Twp	92	247
Wm H	30	m	w	NY	Tuolumne	Sonora P O	93	323
HERRION								
Thomas	40	m	w	MS	Los Angeles	Los Angeles Twp	73	478
HERRIS								
John	57	m	w	NY	San Joaquin	Elliott Twp	86	79
HERRITAGE								
John	42	m	w	NC	San Francisco	San Francisco P O	85	795
HERRITT								
S	30	m	w	CA	San Joaquin	Douglas Twp	86	48
HERRLEY								
James	30	m	w	IREL	Sacramento	4-Wd Sacramento	77	373
HERRMAN								
Daniel E	38	m	w	GERM	San Diego	San Diego	78	496
James	50	m	w	IREL	San Francisco	11-Wd San Francisc	84	540
John F	19	m	w	NY	Placer	Gold Run Twp	76	395
HERRMANN								
Adolph	31	m	w	HANO	Santa Clara	San Jose Twp	88	181
Michael	49	m	w	NY	El Dorado	Cosumnes Twp	72	14
Seigmund	53	m	w	GERM	San Francisco	8-Wd San Francisco	82	364
HERROD								
Andrew H	23	m	w	KY	Colusa	Colusa	71	288
HERRON								
Charles W	35	m	w	IREL	Mendocino	Casper & Big Rvr	74	164
Cornelius	37	m	w	IREL	San Francisco	San Francisco P O	83	364
Edward	50	m	w	IREL	Marin	Point Reyes Twp	74	23
James	42	m	w	NY	Fresno	Millerton P O	72	183
Jas	27	m	w	ENGL	Sacramento	1-Wd Sacramento	77	182
John	44	m	w	TN	Fresno	Millerton P O	72	150
John	31	m	w	AR	Fresno	Millerton P O	72	183
John	22	m	w	MO	Stanislaus	Empire Twp	92	58
John A	48	m	w	IREL	Sacramento	2-Wd Sacramento	77	209
Jos	30	m	w	CT	San Francisco	8-Wd San Francisco	82	364
S G	18	f	w	MO	Solano	Vallejo	90	161
Samuel P	37	m	w	TN	Mariposa	Mariposa P O	74	131
Susan	69	f	w	PA	San Francisco	6-Wd San Francisco	81	121
Thomas	45	m	w	IREL	Butte	Oroville Twp	70	140
William	45	m	b	JAMA	San Francisco	2-Wd San Francisco	79	262
HERRONA								
Jenute	48	m	w	MEXI	Stanislaus	Empire Twp	92	27
HERRONS								
R Q	40	m	w	NY	Yuba	Marysville	93	608
HERROT								
John	50	m	w	SCOT	Nevada	Bridgeport Twp	75	108
HERRYMAN								
Jacob	40	m	w	MO	Colusa	Stony Crk Twp	71	332
HERSANT								
Louisa	52	f	w	FRAN	Nevada	Nevada Twp	75	295
HERSCH								
Charles	26	m	w	SAXO	San Francisco	8-Wd San Francisco	82	364
Jacob	25	m	w	BADE	San Bernardino	San Bernardino Twp	78	417
James	32	m	w	SCOT	Marin	Sausalito Twp	74	73
Phillip	27	m	w	HDAR	Sacramento	3-Wd Sacramento	77	259
HERSE								
Eugene	35	m	w	FRAN	San Francisco	6-Wd San Francisco	81	131
HERSEM								
Aud	33	m	w	ME	Sierra	Sears Twp	89	555
HERSER								
Sarah	24	f	w	IL	Placer	Dutch Flat P O	76	404
HERSEY								
Amos	56	m	w	ME	Alameda	Oakland	68	171
Charles A	51	m	w	MA	Plumas	Plumas Twp	77	26
E A	25	m	w	MA	Solano	Vallejo	90	140
George	10	m	w	CA	Placer	Auburn P O	76	363
Joseph	45	m	w	NY	San Francisco	3-Wd San Francisco	79	299
Price	26	m	w	MA	Yolo	Cache Crk Twp	93	449
Thomas F	49	m	w	MA	Plumas	Plumas Twp	77	26
Wm	36	m	w	ENGL	San Joaquin	3-Wd Stockton	86	219
HERSHAW								
Eliza	29	f	w	ENGL	Santa Clara	Redwood Twp	88	129
HERSHBERGER								
Frank	15	m	i	CA	Colusa	Spring Valley Twp	71	342
HERSHIAN								
Michael	40	m	w	IREL	Stanislaus	Empire Twp	92	48
HERSIC								
John	46	m	w	ENGL	San Francisco	11-Wd San Francisc	84	677
HERSINGER								
John	45	m	w	GERM	Nevada	Nevada Twp	75	287
HERSLAND								
David	26	m	w	NY	San Francisco	1-Wd San Francisco	79	135
HERSLER								
Hail	40	m	w	SWIT	Sacramento	San Joaquin Twp	77	403
HERSOM								
Nathaniel	30	m	w	ME	Plumas	Goodwin Twp	77	7
HERSPTS								
August	25	m	w	PRUS	Colusa	Spring Valley Twp	71	344
HERT								
Courg	27	m	w	WALD	San Francisco	11-Wd San Francisc	84	684
George	34	m	w	WURT	Sonoma	Analy Twp	91	232
John	34	m	w	ENGL	Tuolumne	Sonora P O	93	325
Lewis	37	m	w	ENGL	San Francisco	2-Wd San Francisco	79	144
HERTEL								
Charles	40	m	w	BAVA	Santa Clara	2-Wd San Jose	88	322
Ottilie	15	f	w	BAVA	Santa Clara	Redwood Twp	88	134
Rudolph	44	m	w	PRUS	Sonoma	Healdsburg & Mendo	91	285
Sophia	33	f	w	PRUS	San Francisco	San Francisco P O	83	2
HERTEMAN								
Edward	40	m	w	FRAN	San Francisco	San Francisco P O	80	535
HERTHIRCK								
William	25	m	w	WURT	San Francisco	11-Wd San Francisc	84	446
HERTICK								
Anna	22	f	w	STUT	San Diego	San Diego	78	485
HERTIG								
Gottlieb	38	m	w	SWIT	El Dorado	Mud Springs Twp	72	74
HERTLE								
William	40	m	w	BADE	Santa Cruz	Santa Cruz	89	411
HERTLING								
Joseph	41	m	w	BADE	San Mateo	Half Moon Bay P O	87	389
HERTMAN								
Charles	34	m	w	SHOL	Solano	Suisun Twp	90	114
Fredrick	54	m	w	DENM	Calaveras	San Andreas P O	70	154
John	20	m	w	SHOL	Santa Cruz	Santa Cruz	89	410

© 2001 by Heritage Quest. All rights reserved.

Name	Age	S	R	B-PL	County	Locale	Series M593 Roll	Pg
HERTMULLER								
Fred	44	m	w	HANO	San Francisco	1-Wd San Francisco	79	127
HERTNETZ								
William	30	m	w	PRUS	San Francisco	San Francisco P O	80	533
HERTOLIE								
Picard	42	m	w	FRAN	San Francisco	San Francisco P O	80	342
HERTON								
Richard	29	m	w	CANA	Placer	Gold Run Twp	76	394
HERTREL								
L	45	m	w	GERM	Contra Costa	San Pablo Twp	71	363
HERTS								
John	38	m	w	ENGL	San Francisco	8-Wd San Francisco	82	394
HERTWECK								
Joseph	38	m	w	BADE	Nevada	Eureka Twp	75	134
HERTZ								
Albert	35	m	w	SWIT	San Francisco	8-Wd San Francisco	82	434
Carle	49	m	w	WURT	Calaveras	San Andreas P O	70	194
Henry	37	m	w	HANO	San Francisco	1-Wd San Francisco	79	64
Lazarus	37	m	w	AUST	San Francisco	1-Wd San Francisco	79	53
Leon	21	m	w	HANO	San Francisco	7-Wd San Francisco	81	200
HERTZER								
John	37	m	w	OH	Calaveras	San Andreas P O	70	212
HERTZLEWICH								
Mather	27	m	w	LUXE	San Joaquin	Oneal Twp	86	112
HERUPEL								
E	29	m	w	PRUS	Alameda	Oakland	68	185
HERVE								
Julia	60	f	w	FRAN	San Francisco	6-Wd San Francisco	81	132
HERVEGEULT								
Mary	57	f	w	FRAN	San Francisco	8-Wd San Francisco	82	390
HERVEY								
Herman	52	m	w	NY	Santa Clara	San Jose Twp	88	180
Mi	35	m	c	CHIN	Placer	Bath P O	76	425
Michael	45	m	w	IREL	Contra Costa	San Pablo Twp	71	361
Nelson	47	m	w	NH	Sonoma	Santa Rosa	91	396
William W	37	m	w	MO	Placer	Gold Run Twp	76	400
HERVILLE								
Lizzie	30	f	w	ENGL	Sacramento	4-Wd Sacramento	77	350
HERVISON								
Charles	29	m	w	HANO	Los Angeles	Wilmington Twp	73	640
HERWIG								
Henry	33	m	w	GERM	Los Angeles	Los Angeles	73	505
James T	32	m	w	NJ	Nevada	Meadow Lake Twp	75	267
HERYFORD								
Clemens R	49	m	w	MO	Shasta	Millville P O	89	492
M A	17	f	w	LA	Alameda	Oakland	68	258
HERZER								
Hugo	24	m	w	BAVA	San Francisco	8-Wd San Francisco	82	442
HERZO								
Ann	70	f	w	AUST	San Francisco	San Francisco P O	80	361
John	42	m	w	AUST	San Francisco	San Francisco P O	80	361
HERZOG								
C T	50	m	w	PRUS	San Francisco	3-Wd San Francisco	79	319
Charles	40	m	w	PRUS	Siskiyou	Yreka	89	660
Christian	52	m	w	PRUS	San Francisco	San Francisco P O	80	423
Henry	25	m	w	SAXO	San Francisco	8-Wd San Francisco	82	433
Joseph	40	m	w	AUST	San Francisco	8-Wd San Francisco	82	472
Josephine	33	f	w	SWIT	Santa Clara	2-Wd San Jose	88	302
Philip	35	m	w	OH	Sacramento	2-Wd Sacramento	77	214
HERZSBURG								
Julius	55	m	w	PRUS	San Francisco	2-Wd San Francisco	79	280
HESANBERG								
F	45	m	w	HAMB	San Francisco	7-Wd San Francisco	81	166
HESAULT								
Jean	35	m	w	FRAN	San Francisco	San Francisco P O	80	535
HESER								
Andrew	21	m	w	SWED	Sonoma	Vallejo Twp	91	454
HESFELDT								
Maurice	19	m	w	PRUS	Los Angeles	Wilmington Twp	73	643
HESKELL								
Ellen	35	f	w	ME	San Francisco	11-Wd San Francisc	84	580
HESKETH								
Geo	35	m	w	ENGL	San Francisco	11-Wd San Francisc	84	692
Wm	51	m	w	NY	San Francisco	7-Wd San Francisco	81	243
HESKINS								
Robert	47	m	w	ENGL	Sonoma	Petaluma Twp	91	333
HESLEM								
Joseph	42	m	w	CANA	Tuolumne	Sonora P O	93	319
HESLEP								
Augustus	65	m	w	VA	San Francisco	San Francisco P O	80	368
B F	48	m	w	PA	Tuolumne	Chinese Camp P O	93	366
E W	59	f	w	OH	Alameda	Oakland	68	179
O	14	m	w	CANA	Alameda	Oakland	68	228
P C	30	m	w	VA	Alameda	Eden Twp	68	81
HESLER								
Adam	35	m	w	PRUS	Santa Clara	San Jose Twp	88	212
Charles	34	m	w	PRUS	San Francisco	San Francisco P O	83	246
John	37	m	w	NORW	Mariposa	Mariposa P O	74	119
Martin	26	m	w	BAVA	Marin	Nicasio Twp	74	16
HESLINGTON								
Jas	65	m	w	ENGL	Sierra	Eureka Twp	89	524
HESLIP								
Joseph	19	m	w	IL	San Francisco	7-Wd San Francisco	81	165
HESLOP								
Adam	25	m	w	SCOT	San Francisco	San Francisco P O	83	57
HESMOND								
Chas	40	m	w	ITAL	San Francisco	1-Wd San Francisco	79	44
HESNER								
Joseph	35	m	w	HAMB	Sacramento	Sutter Twp	77	382
HESON								
John	32	m	w	WURT	San Francisco	1-Wd San Francisco	79	48
HESPELT								
Wm	26	m	w	PRUS	San Francisco	San Francisco P O	85	745
HESPERIOSA								
Jose	80	m	w	MEXI	San Joaquin	Douglas Twp	86	39
HESS								
Adam	59	m	w	HDAR	El Dorado	White Oak Twp	72	143
Adolph	34	m	w	BADE	San Francisco	8-Wd San Francisco	82	370
Alexander	64	m	w	SAXO	Napa	Napa	75	11
Alexander	46	m	w	IN	Santa Clara	Santa Clara Twp	88	165
Andrew	40	m	w	MD	San Francisco	San Francisco P O	80	333
August	10	m	w	HDAR	El Dorado	Lake Valley Twp	72	66
Conrad	43	m	w	HDAR	San Francisco	2-Wd San Francisco	79	147
D F	30	m	w	PRUS	Alameda	Oakland	68	265
E	38	m	w	FRAN	Alameda	Oakland	68	147
Edwin L	38	m	w	NY	Siskiyou	Yreka	89	660
Eliza	42	f	w	PA	Sacramento	3-Wd Sacramento	77	315
F G	44	m	w	PRUS	Alameda	Oakland	68	186
Fred	36	m	w	TN	Yuba	Linda Twp	93	557
Fred	31	m	w	PRUS	Alameda	Alameda	68	17
Fredrick	48	m	w	BAVA	Sonoma	Petaluma Twp	91	315
George B	39	m	w	MD	San Francisco	6-Wd San Francisco	81	37
H	27	m	w	HDAR	Yuba	Marysville Twp	93	569
Henry	37	m	w	BAVA	Solano	Benicia	90	12
Hermann	40	m	w	POLA	San Francisco	8-Wd San Francisco	82	310
Ingia	37	f	w	SHOL	Alameda	Eden Twp	68	65
J	32	m	w	HANO	Sierra	Butte Twp	89	509
James B	45	m	w	IN	Santa Clara	Santa Clara Twp	88	165
James W	25	m	w	OH	Humboldt	Bald Hills	72	239
John	44	m	w	BAVA	Sacramento	3-Wd Sacramento	77	286
John	41	m	w	FRNK	San Joaquin	Liberty Twp	86	82
John	40	m	w	IL	Siskiyou	Scott Valley Twp	89	620
John	39	m	w	FRAN	Sacramento	Lee Twp	77	161
John	33	m	w	KY	San Joaquin	Union Twp	86	267
John	29	m	w	PRUS	Solano	Tremont Twp	90	32
John	23	m	w	NY	San Joaquin	Dent Twp	86	22
John B	23	m	w	IL	Humboldt	Bald Hills	72	239
Jos	42	m	w	GERM	Sacramento	1-Wd Sacramento	77	174
Joseph	60	m	w	AR	Siskiyou	Big Valley Twp	89	582
Joseph	44	m	w	MD	San Francisco	San Francisco P O	80	393
Julius	24	m	w	PRUS	San Francisco	7-Wd San Francisco	81	218
Levi	57	m	w	HDAR	San Francisco	8-Wd San Francisco	82	308
Louis	26	m	w	HDAR	Santa Clara	1-Wd San Jose	88	231
Malinda	21	f	w	LA	San Francisco	8-Wd San Francisco	82	294
Maria	25	f	w	BAVA	San Francisco	San Francisco P O	80	532
Solomon H	50	m	w	NY	Shasta	Fort Crook P O	89	477
Thomas C	33	m	w	AR	Siskiyou	Big Valley Twp	89	582
William	53	m	w	PA	Nevada	Bridgeport Twp	75	122
HESSAN								
Wm	36	m	w	PRUS	San Francisco	11-Wd San Francisc	84	571
HESSE								
Catherine	22	f	w	PRUS	San Francisco	2-Wd San Francisco	79	172
Charles	20	m	w	PRUS	San Francisco	San Francisco P O	83	374
Frances	62	f	w	ENGL	San Francisco	San Francisco P O	83	335
Frederick	35	m	w	PRUS	San Francisco	6-Wd San Francisco	81	97
Frederick	30	m	w	WURT	Marin	Bolinas Twp	74	1
Henry	44	m	w	PRUS	San Francisco	6-Wd San Francisco	81	134
Madalina	22	f	w	WURT	Marin	Bolinas Twp	74	1
Manuel	30	m	w	PERU	Sacramento	2-Wd Sacramento	77	243
Mathew	26	m	w	PRUS	San Francisco	7-Wd San Francisco	81	226
Philomena	17	f	w	OH	Sacramento	4-Wd Sacramento	77	359
William	61	m	w	PRUS	San Francisco	San Francisco P O	83	335
HESSEL								
Geo	34	m	w	GERM	San Joaquin	2-Wd Stockton	86	213
HESSELL								
John	22	m	w	HESS	Colusa	Grand Island Twp	71	307
W F	43	m	w	GERM	Tuolumne	Columbia P O	93	348
HESSELWOOD								
M F	53	f	w	ENGL	Tehama	Mill Crk Twp	92	167
HESSEM								
Milton F	35	m	w	ME	Stanislaus	Empire Twp	92	51
HESSEN								
F H	40	m	w	ME	Sacramento	3-Wd Sacramento	77	267
HESSENGER								
John A	38	m	w	GERM	Los Angeles	Los Angeles	73	565
HESSENICH								
Henry	46	m	w	PRUS	Sonoma	Petaluma Twp	91	317
HESSER								
Geo W	35	m	w	OH	Nevada	Rough & Ready Twp	75	323
Lafayette	30	m	w	MA	San Francisco	San Francisco P O	83	36
S C	37	m	w	VA	Sacramento	3-Wd Sacramento	77	270
HESSI								
Victoria	36	f	w	PRUS	San Francisco	San Francisco P O	80	419
HESSIAN								
Michael	35	m	w	IREL	San Francisco	San Francisco P O	80	370
HESSIC								
Ben	43	m	w	PA	Trinity	Weaverville Pct	92	229
Louis	27	m	w	IL	Humboldt	Bald Hills	72	238
HESSIER								
Richard	42	m	w	IREL	Inyo	Bishop Crk Twp	73	311
HESSIG								
Jacob	38	m	w	BAVA	Butte	Mountain Spring Tw	70	87
HESSING								
John	40	m	w	HANO	San Francisco	11-Wd San Francisc	84	607

© 2001 by Heritage Quest. All rights reserved.

Name	Age	S	R	B-PL	County	Locale	Series M593 Roll	Pg
HESSION								
Thomas	35	m	w	IREL	Tuolumne	Sonora P O	93	325
HESSLER								
Mary	48	f	w	BADE	El Dorado	Diamond Springs Tw	72	27
William	45	m	w	BAVA	San Francisco	San Francisco P O	80	535
HESSMAN								
James	29	m	w	PRUS	Alameda	Oakland	68	157
HESSNAUER								
John	39	m	w	BADE	Siskiyou	Yreka	89	651
HESSON								
H	28	m	w	PRUS	Alameda	Murray Twp	68	119
HESTALL								
Anna	17	f	w	ENGL	San Francisco	San Francisco P O	83	145
HESTEL								
Chas	40	m	w	PRUS	San Francisco	5-Wd San Francisco	81	6
HESTER								
Craven P	73	m	w	KY	Santa Clara	Santa Clara Twp	88	136
George	28	m	w	ME	San Francisco	7-Wd San Francisco	81	225
James	25	m	w	IREL	Los Angeles	Los Angeles	73	566
Jerry	26	m	w	HAMB	Sonoma	Petaluma Twp	91	316
John H	47	m	w	IN	Sonoma	Petaluma Twp	91	351
Lena	14	f	w	CA	San Francisco	11-Wd San Francisc	84	559
Martha T	70	f	w	PA	Santa Clara	Santa Clara Twp	88	136
Martin	45	m	w	IREL	San Francisco	2-Wd San Francisco	79	192
Robert	40	m	w	TN	Los Angeles	Los Angeles	73	560
Robert F	36	m	w	AR	Yolo	Merritt Twp	93	503
Wm H	26	m	w	ENGL	Napa	Napa	75	51
HESTERS								
Frank	25	m	w	PRUS	San Francisco	6-Wd San Francisco	81	125
HESTMAN								
Lemuel	37	m	w	ENGL	San Francisco	5-Wd San Francisco	81	33
HESTON								
Mary L	32	f	w	WI	Tulare	Visalia	92	294
HESTRAHA								
G	23	m	w	SWIT	San Joaquin	2-Wd Stockton	86	172
HESTRUP								
Geo	40	m	w	ENGL	Humboldt	Eureka Twp	72	265
HET								
Charles	41	m	w	HCAS	San Francisco	2-Wd San Francisco	79	144
HETCHEL								
J	12	m	w	AZ	Alameda	Oakland	68	150
HETCHERICH								
John	33	m	w	PRUS	Sacramento	4-Wd Sacramento	77	351
HETCHT								
John	30	m	w	PRUS	San Francisco	8-Wd San Francisco	82	292
HETHER								
Henry	26	m	w	ENGL	Nevada	Grass Valley Twp	75	220
HETHEREN								
Bat	29	m	w	IREL	San Francisco	San Francisco P O	85	866
HETHERINGTON								
Henry	41	m	w	ENGL	San Francisco	San Francisco P O	83	345
HETHERSA								
Frederick	16	m	w	IN	Plumas	Quartz Twp	77	43
HETHINGTON								
Smith	30	m	w	NY	Nevada	Little York Twp	75	235
HETHRINGTON								
Chris	25	m	w	CANA	Sacramento	Sutter Twp	77	381
HETIAN								
James	31	m	w	IREL	San Mateo	Redwood Twp	87	366
HETKIN								
John	37	m	w	HOLL	San Joaquin	Tulare Twp	86	261
HETMAN								
Henry	19	m	w	PRUS	Sacramento	2-Wd Sacramento	77	241
HETON								
Saml O	39	m	w	KY	Sonoma	Mendocino Twp	91	290
HETRICK								
Jacob	35	m	w	OH	San Francisco	7-Wd San Francisco	81	250
Jacob	32	m	w	OH	Plumas	Washington Twp	77	55
HETTEL								
Jacob	26	m	w	PA	San Francisco	8-Wd San Francisco	82	482
HETTEN								
John	26	m	w	IREL	Amador	Drytown P O	69	416
HETTENHAUSEN								
L	28	m	w	PRUS	Alameda	Alameda	68	5
HETTICH								
Wm	35	m	w	PRUS	San Francisco	San Francisco P O	83	12
HETTICK								
A	49	m	w	BADE	Calaveras	Copperopolis P O	70	226
Andrew	21	m	w	CA	Sacramento	Cosumnes Twp	77	96
George	23	m	w	OH	Yolo	Grafton Twp	93	480
HETTY								
Asbury	30	m	w	CA	Fresno	Millerton P O	72	160
John	48	m	w	BADE	Santa Clara	Santa Clara Twp	88	156
HETZEL								
David	24	m	w	WI	San Francisco	1-Wd San Francisco	79	69
Geo	42	m	w	OH	Sacramento	3-Wd Sacramento	77	310
HETZER								
Jonas B	39	m	w	BAVA	Placer	Colfax P O	76	391
HETZLER								
Alfred	26	m	w	BAVA	Santa Cruz	Pajaro Twp	89	352
Conrad	35	m	w	BADE	Shasta	French Gulch P O	89	469
HEUBER								
Jacob	49	m	w	PA	El Dorado	Georgetown Twp	72	48
HEUBNER								
Hugo	28	m	w	PRUS	Santa Clara	2-Wd San Jose	88	322
HEUER								
Earnest	28	m	w	HANO	San Francisco	San Francisco P O	85	814

Name	Age	S	R	B-PL	County	Locale	Series M593 Roll	Pg
HEUGHES								
Larson W	18	m	w	IA	Los Angeles	Los Angeles	73	541
HEULINGS								
George	28	m	w	WALE	San Francisco	San Francisco P O	83	200
HEUMSKIN								
Hy	17	m	w	BREM	San Francisco	11-Wd San Francisc	84	588
HEUNG								
Ah	30	m	c	CHIN	Shasta	French Gulch P O	89	470
Ah	30	m	c	CHIN	Placer	Lincoln P O	76	493
HEUP								
Ah	60	m	c	CHIN	Shasta	French Gulch P O	89	470
Ah	20	m	c	CHIN	Tehama	Red Bluff	92	184
HEUPHHER								
John	42	m	w	IREL	Tehama	Red Bluff	92	183
HEURING								
Jos	31	m	w	IN	Sacramento	1-Wd Sacramento	77	178
HEUSCH								
Charles	34	m	w	FRAN	San Francisco	11-Wd San Francisc	84	556
HEUSILER								
Geo	34	m	w	SWIT	Sacramento	1-Wd Sacramento	77	173
HEUSNER								
Conrad	37	m	w	HESS	El Dorado	Mud Springs Twp	72	86
HEUSTACE								
Chas	36	m	w	HANO	San Francisco	San Francisco P O	83	269
HEUSTDEN								
J	27	m	w	IREL	Yuba	Marysville	93	604
HEUSTER								
David	28	m	w	NORW	Contra Costa	Martinez P O	71	415
HEUSTISS								
John	26	m	w	ENGL	Nevada	Grass Valley Twp	75	185
HEUSTON								
Calvin	37	m	w	ME	Yolo	Cache Crk Twp	93	422
D	10	f	w	HI	Alameda	Oakland	68	217
George N	24	m	w	KY	Contra Costa	Martinez P O	71	375
John	45	m	w	PA	San Francisco	8-Wd San Francisco	82	328
William L	34	m	w	OH	Contra Costa	Martinez P O	71	376
HEVEL								
Christopher	25	m	w	IL	Yolo	Cache Crk Twp	93	447
Jacob	42	m	w	PA	Yolo	Cache Crk Twp	93	437
John	45	m	w	OH	Yolo	Cache Crk Twp	93	447
HEVEN								
Matilda	25	f	w	SWED	San Francisco	2-Wd San Francisco	79	278
HEVENER								
W H	38	m	w	NJ	Sacramento	3-Wd Sacramento	77	276
HEVENS								
Mary	32	f	w	MA	Siskiyou	Scott Valley Twp	89	615
HEVERIN								
Michael	44	m	w	ENGL	San Francisco	2-Wd San Francisco	79	193
Michael	40	m	w	IREL	San Francisco	San Francisco P O	80	366
HEVIN								
Louis	54	m	w	FRAN	San Francisco	San Francisco P O	83	135
HEW								
Ah	40	m	c	CHIN	Sierra	Lincoln Twp	89	546
Ah	38	m	c	CHIN	Fresno	Millerton P O	72	201
Ah	34	m	c	CHIN	San Joaquin	1-Wd Stockton	86	144
Ah	30	m	c	CHIN	San Francisco	11-Wd San Francisc	84	708
Ah	26	m	c	CHIN	San Francisco	11-Wd San Francisc	84	499
Ah	17	m	c	CHIN	Nevada	Nevada Twp	75	298
Noo	41	m	c	CHIN	Tuolumne	Big Oak Flat P O	93	400
Quong	24	m	c	CHIN	Solano	Rio Vista Twp	90	70
HEWEL								
Mare	36	f	w	NY	San Francisco	5-Wd San Francisco	81	33
Mose	42	m	w	NY	San Francisco	5-Wd San Francisco	81	33
HEWELKE								
Wm	33	m	w	PRUS	San Francisco	5-Wd San Francisco	81	20
HEWELL								
James C	21	m	w	MO	Nevada	Rough & Ready Twp	75	323
Jno	34	m	w	NY	Butte	Chico Twp	70	36
HEWER								
Geo C W	32	m	w	PRUS	San Francisco	San Francisco P O	83	364
Philip	37	m	w	HANO	San Francisco	2-Wd San Francisco	79	229
HEWES								
G	11	f	w	MA	Alameda	Oakland	68	236
James F	40	m	w	IREL	Nevada	Grass Valley Twp	75	232
John C	44	m	w	TN	Calaveras	Copperopolis P O	70	254
R C W	50	m	w	MA	Alameda	Oakland	68	237
Samuel	61	m	w	NJ	San Francisco	7-Wd San Francisco	81	223
Thos	37	m	w	ENGL	Sacramento	1-Wd Sacramento	77	186
HEWESTON								
Nelson	38	m	w	VA	Colusa	Colusa Twp	71	280
HEWET								
Joseph	53	m	w	FRAN	Trinity	Lewiston Pct	92	212
HEWETT								
A J	40	m	w	IN	Yuba	Marysville	93	589
Abijah	60	m	w	NY	Plumas	Rich Bar Twp	77	8
Ambrose R	25	m	w	VA	El Dorado	Placerville Twp	72	105
Charles H	47	m	w	ENGL	San Francisco	San Francisco P O	85	772
Geo F	38	m	w	ENGL	Sacramento	1-Wd Sacramento	77	187
Henry	38	m	w	IREL	Sierra	Sears Twp	89	558
James	40	m	w	AR	Nevada	Rough & Ready Twp	75	333
James	37	m	w	ENGL	Alameda	Eden Twp	68	81
James	22	m	w	AR	Nevada	Rough & Ready Twp	75	328
John	35	m	w	MA	San Francisco	7-Wd San Francisco	81	205
Mary	30	f	w	MA	San Francisco	7-Wd San Francisco	81	205
Rosswell	52	m	w	NY	Santa Barbara	San Buenaventura P	87	420
Thomas	35	m	w	VA	Calaveras	Copperopolis P O	70	262
William	18	m	w	CA	Placer	Gold Run Twp	76	396

© 2001 by Heritage Quest. All rights reserved.

Name	Age	S	R	B-PL	County	Locale	Roll	Pg
						Series M593		
HEWEY								
Ernest	6	m	w	CA	San Francisco	San Francisco P O	83	54
Samuel	50	m	w	NJ	San Francisco	San Francisco P O	83	54
Thos	12	m	w	CA	San Joaquin	Elkhorn Twp	86	59
HEWINS								
Richard	59	m	w	ENGL	Sacramento	Lee Twp	77	161
HEWIT								
C	25	m	w	TN	Sutter	Sutter Twp	92	117
George	44	m	w	IN	Alameda	Brooklyn	68	34
John B	18	m	w	IREL	Yolo	Grafton Twp	93	497
Joshua	26	m	w	IREL	Los Angeles	Los Angeles	73	567
Martin	33	m	w	ME	Alameda	Oakland	68	187
William	58	m	w	OH	Colusa	Monroe Twp	71	313
HEWITT								
Absalom	26	m	w	VA	Marin	San Rafael Twp	74	36
Agnes	60	f	w	NY	San Francisco	San Francisco P O	83	390
Amos L	36	m	w	CT	San Francisco	6-Wd San Francisco	81	122
Andrew	32	m	w	ENGL	Merced	Snelling P O	74	277
Andrew J	40	m	w	MO	Nevada	Bridgeport Twp	75	116
Edwin E	42	m	w	NY	Los Angeles	Wilmington Twp	73	638
Geo T	34	m	w	IREL	Nevada	Nevada Twp	75	296
Henry	63	m	w	TX	Kern	Tehachapi P O	73	356
Henry T	38	m	w	CT	Sonoma	Santa Rosa	91	411
James	34	m	w	SCOT	Sonoma	Santa Rosa	91	419
Jason	27	m	w	ME	San Francisco	2-Wd San Francisco	79	215
John C	42	m	w	GA	Fresno	Millerton P O	72	155
Joseph	63	m	w	NY	Solano	Suisun Twp	90	100
Joseph	37	m	w	OH	Solano	Vacaville Twp	90	132
Joseph	20	m	w	OH	San Francisco	7-Wd San Francisco	81	278
Mary	20	f	w	NJ	San Francisco	7-Wd San Francisco	81	174
Moses	36	m	w	ME	Alameda	Oakland	68	185
Orson P	22	m	w	ENGL	Los Angeles	Los Nietos Twp	73	578
Roscoe	30	m	w	IL	Solano	Silveyville Twp	90	91
S	40	m	w	IA	San Joaquin	Douglas Twp	86	50
Sam	18	m	w	IL	San Joaquin	Liberty Twp	86	86
W	14	m	w	MD	Napa	Yountville Twp	75	82
HEWLAN								
Isaac	20	m	w	KY	Los Angeles	Los Angeles	73	509
HEWLAND								
Geo W	37	m	w	MO	Solano	Vacaville Twp	90	117
HEWLET								
Alexd	21	m	b	TN	Sonoma	Russian Rvr	91	373
F	9	m	w	CA	Solano	Benicia	90	21
Jerry	21	m	w	MO	Yolo	Cottonwood Twp	93	469
Jno B	50	m	w	NY	Butte	Ophir Twp	70	102
P B	50	m	w	NY	Sonoma	Russian Rvr	91	373
HEWLETT								
Alonzo	35	m	w	NY	Sonoma	Analy Twp	91	237
Eva	21	f	w	VT	Sonoma	Bodega Twp	91	250
H H	38	m	w	NY	San Joaquin	2-Wd Stockton	86	178
James	44	m	w	IREL	San Francisco	San Francisco P O	83	280
James	22	m	w	MO	Yolo	Buckeye Twp	93	413
John	46	m	w	KY	San Joaquin	Liberty Twp	86	84
Sam	38	m	w	NY	San Joaquin	2-Wd Stockton	86	177
HEWMAN								
John	38	m	w	NY	San Francisco	San Francisco P O	83	258
HEWS								
G W	22	m	w	MO	Lassen	Janesville Twp	73	433
Owen	29	m	w	IREL	Merced	Snelling P O	74	272
HEWSLEY								
Isaac L	36	m	w	IL	San Francisco	San Francisco P O	83	32
HEWSON								
James	35	m	w	IREL	Fresno	Millerton P O	72	164
John B	45	m	w	NJ	Santa Clara	2-Wd San Jose	88	336
Palheur	26	m	w	NY	Santa Clara	2-Wd San Jose	88	287
HEWSTON								
George	43	m	w	PA	San Francisco	San Francisco P O	83	226
James	25	m	w	CANA	Sonoma	Salt Point Twp	91	382
Josephine	14	f	m	MA	Placer	Bath P O	76	428
Saml	44	m	w	NY	Butte	Ophir Twp	70	108
William	50	m	w	IREL	El Dorado	Placerville Twp	72	99
HEWY								
Edward F	44	m	w	NY	Siskiyou	Scott Valley Twp	89	608
Elias W	39	m	w	VT	Amador	Volcano P O	69	377
HEXA								
E W	38	m	w	MA	San Joaquin	Tulare Twp	86	250
HEXLEY								
George J	52	m	w	ENGL	Santa Cruz	Pajaro Twp	89	353
HEXT								
Thomas	42	m	w	ENGL	Yolo	Putah Twp	93	526
HEXTER								
Kaufman	44	m	w	HDAR	Calaveras	San Andreas P O	70	193
HEY								
Ah	45	m	c	CHIN	Sacramento	American Twp	77	68
Ah	38	m	c	CHIN	Butte	Ophir Twp	70	109
Ah	28	m	c	CHIN	Calaveras	San Andreas P O	70	173
Ah	26	m	c	CHIN	Sacramento	Georgianna Twp	77	133
Ah	20	f	c	CHIN	Sacramento	Granite Twp	77	152
Chung	29	m	c	CHIN	Butte	Concow Twp	70	12
Come	32	m	c	CHIN	Trinity	Junction City Pct	92	206
Elizabeth	49	f	w	SCOT	Alameda	Oakland	68	218
John J	27	m	w	PRUS	San Francisco	San Francisco P O	83	231
Michael	40	m	w	IREL	Sacramento	2-Wd Sacramento	77	252
Wm	63	m	w	VA	San Joaquin	Tulare Twp	86	249
Wm J	22	m	w	HANO	San Francisco	San Francisco P O	83	94
HEYDEMANN								
Henry	47	m	w	MECK	Merced	Snelling P O	74	273

Name	Age	S	R	B-PL	County	Locale	Roll	Pg
						Series M593		
HEYDENFELDT								
Chs	27	m	w	SHOL	San Francisco	2-Wd San Francisco	79	174
Elken	45	m	w	GA	San Francisco	2-Wd San Francisco	79	203
Solomon	51	m	w	MD	San Francisco	San Francisco P O	80	487
HEYDENFELT								
Annie	43	f	w	LA	San Francisco	San Francisco P O	80	428
HEYDENREICH								
Fredk	43	m	w	PRUS	Marin	Sausalito Twp	74	74
HEYDER								
William	50	m	w	PRUS	Nevada	Grass Valley Twp	75	216
HEYDLAUFF								
Frederick	33	m	w	MI	Nevada	Little York Twp	75	239
HEYEMAN								
James S F	50	m	w	BRUN	Los Angeles	Santa Ana Twp	73	613
HEYER								
Albert	40	m	w	HANO	San Francisco	San Francisco P O	83	61
Julius	34	m	w	HANO	Alameda	Hayward	68	76
HEYES								
E E	55	m	w	NH	Del Norte	Crescent Twp	71	456
J F	37	m	w	IREL	Sacramento	3-Wd Sacramento	77	276
HEYFRON								
Joseph	34	m	w	IREL	San Francisco	San Francisco P O	83	405
HEYHER								
S J	40	m	w	CANA	Alameda	Oakland	68	262
HEYL								
Charles N	45	m	w	PA	Plumas	Goodwin Twp	77	6
HEYMAN								
Arnold	44	m	w	PRUS	Sacramento	3-Wd Sacramento	77	290
H	26	m	w	PRUS	San Francisco	8-Wd San Francisco	82	310
Hannah	42	f	w	PRUS	Alameda	Oakland	68	170
Hegenberg L	82	m	w	PRUS	Alameda	Oakland	68	170
Henry	26	m	w	PRUS	San Francisco	6-Wd San Francisco	81	37
Jacob	32	m	w	PRUS	Nevada	Grass Valley Twp	75	157
Jno	38	m	w	IREL	San Francisco	San Francisco P O	83	32
Julius	24	m	w	POLA	Placer	Rocklin Twp	76	466
L H	47	m	w	POLA	Sonoma	Santa Rosa	91	401
Moses	54	m	w	PRUS	Placer	Roseville P O	76	356
S	54	m	w	BADE	Nevada	Meadow Lake Twp	75	253
Simon	24	m	w	BAVA	San Francisco	7-Wd San Francisco	81	281
Wolfe	39	m	w	PRUS	San Francisco	San Francisco P O	83	310
HEYMANN								
Chris	28	m	w	HANO	San Francisco	11-Wd San Francisc	84	433
E	25	m	w	PRUS	Napa	Napa	75	3
HEYMON								
B	23	m	w	MI	Sierra	Alleghany & Forest	89	534
HEYNE								
Earnest	59	m	w	PERS	Monterey	Alisal Twp	74	294
John	22	m	w	PA	Yolo	Putah Twp	93	514
HEYNEMAN								
Hermann	37	m	w	HAMB	San Francisco	2-Wd San Francisco	79	204
HEYS								
William	53	m	w	IREL	Sonoma	Petaluma Twp	91	315
HEYSANT								
Wm	29	m	w	BAVA	Nevada	Meadow Lake Twp	75	253
HEYSEL								
William	56	m	w	OH	Santa Cruz	Pajaro Twp	89	363
HEYVAN								
Ceprian	10	m	w	CA	Fresno	Millerton P O	72	157
HEYWARD								
Ada	18	f	w	ENGL	San Francisco	11-Wd San Francisc	84	620
HEYWOOD								
C W	37	m	w	ME	Alameda	Oakland	68	253
Erastus W	45	m	w	ME	Nevada	Grass Valley Twp	75	146
J J	46	m	w	SC	Tuolumne	Chinese Camp P O	93	368
James	33	m	w	OH	Napa	Yountville Twp	75	90
John	40	m	b	GA	Calaveras	Copperopolis P O	70	241
Thos	42	m	w	ENGL	Sonoma	Salt Point	91	393
Zimeriah	67	m	w	ME	San Francisco	San Francisco P O	85	728
HEZELRIDD								
Arthur	47	m	w	IN	Santa Cruz	Santa Cruz	89	430
HEZERA								
Jose	28	m	w	CA	Fresno	Millerton P O	72	159
HEZLEP								
James	56	m	w	OH	Alameda	Brooklyn	68	27
HEZOG								
Fritz	32	m	w	SWIT	Inyo	Bishop Crk Twp	73	310
HEZUEMO								
Leandro	32	m	w	CA	Fresno	Millerton P O	72	160
HEZZOG								
Michael	29	m	w	PRUS	San Francisco	San Francisco P O	83	23
HI								
---	30	m	c	CHIN	Siskiyou	Cottonwood Twp	89	592
---	19	m	c	CHIN	San Francisco	6-Wd San Francisco	81	51
Ah	65	m	c	CHIN	Tuolumne	Big Oak Flat P O	93	392
Ah	45	m	c	CHIN	El Dorado	Mud Springs Twp	72	79
Ah	42	m	c	CHIN	Nevada	Grass Valley Twp	75	218
Ah	40	m	c	CHIN	Plumas	Plumas Twp	77	31
Ah	40	m	c	CHIN	San Francisco	6-Wd San Francisco	81	44
Ah	40	m	c	CHIN	San Francisco	6-Wd San Francisco	81	62
Ah	37	m	c	CHIN	San Joaquin	Liberty Twp	86	97
Ah	34	m	c	CHIN	Sacramento	1-Wd Sacramento	77	205
Ah	34	m	c	CHIN	San Joaquin	Union Twp	86	265
Ah	32	m	c	CHIN	Nevada	Little York Twp	75	245
Ah	31	m	c	CHIN	Yolo	Putah Twp	93	524
Ah	31	m	c	CHIN	Los Angeles	El Monte Twp	73	460
Ah	30	m	c	CHIN	Sacramento	Georgianna Twp	77	123
Ah	30	m	c	CHIN	Sierra	Downieville Twp	89	520

© 2001 by Heritage Quest. All rights reserved.

Name	Age	S	R	B-PL	County	Locale	Series M593 Roll	Pg
Ah	30	m	c	CHIN	Colusa	Grand Island Twp	71	304
Ah	30	m	c	CHIN	Sacramento	Granite Twp	77	153
Ah	29	m	c	CHIN	Tuolumne	Chinese Camp P O	93	388
Ah	27	m	c	CHIN	San Francisco	San Francisco P O	80	502
Ah	26	m	c	CHIN	San Francisco	San Francisco P O	80	514
Ah	26	m	c	CHIN	Tuolumne	Columbia P O	93	348
Ah	26	m	c	CHIN	Marin	San Rafael Twp	74	59
Ah	25	m	c	CHIN	San Francisco	1-Wd San Francisco	79	106
Ah	21	m	c	CHIN	Sacramento	Georgianna Twp	77	133
Ah	20	f	c	CHIN	San Francisco	San Francisco P O	80	501
Ah	20	m	c	CHIN	San Francisco	1-Wd San Francisco	79	106
Ah	19	f	c	CHIN	San Francisco	San Francisco P O	80	508
Ah	18	f	c	CHIN	Los Angeles	Los Angeles	73	565
Ah	12	m	c	CHIN	Napa	Napa	75	56
Cal	30	m	c	CHIN	Sacramento	1-Wd Sacramento	77	192
Chine	32	m	c	CHIN	Trinity	North Fork Twp	92	217
Chuck	21	m	c	CHIN	San Joaquin	1-Wd Stockton	86	151
Comb	30	m	c	CHIN	Yuba	Marysville	93	625
Coo	29	m	c	CHIN	Yuba	Marysville	93	623
Dee	30	m	c	CHIN	San Mateo	Half Moon Bay P O	87	396
Eh	13	m	c	CHIN	San Francisco	8-Wd San Francisco	82	463
Fai	28	m	c	CHIN	San Francisco	11-Wd San Francisc	84	477
Foo	32	m	c	CHIN	Fresno	Millerton P O	72	202
Go	28	m	c	CHIN	Sacramento	1-Wd Sacramento	77	196
Hing	32	m	c	CHIN	Sacramento	1-Wd Sacramento	77	205
Ho	19	m	c	CHIN	Tehama	Tehama Twp	92	188
Hung	40	m	c	CHIN	Sacramento	1-Wd Sacramento	77	197
Jeo	38	m	c	CHIN	Sacramento	1-Wd Sacramento	77	193
Juhe	26	m	c	CHIN	Yolo	Washington Twp	93	537
Kam	30	m	c	CHIN	Fresno	Millerton P O	72	202
Kee	39	m	c	CHIN	San Francisco	6-Wd San Francisco	81	61
Ki	40	m	c	CHIN	Yolo	Putah Twp	93	525
Kim	35	f	c	CHIN	Yuba	Marysville	93	627
Kum	18	m	c	CHIN	Tehama	Deer Crk Twp	92	172
Lay	41	m	c	CHIN	Alameda	Washington Twp	68	272
Lee	30	f	c	CHIN	Yuba	Marysville	93	627
Lee	26	m	c	CHIN	San Joaquin	2-Wd Stockton	86	163
Lee	18	m	c	CHIN	San Joaquin	1-Wd Stockton	86	147
Lee	13	m	c	CHIN	San Francisco	1-Wd San Francisco	79	106
Lin	25	m	c	CHIN	Yuba	Marysville	93	630
Ling	20	m	c	CHIN	Tehama	Tehama Twp	92	188
Ling	19	m	c	CHIN	Yuba	Marysville	93	595
Lo	20	m	c	CHIN	San Joaquin	1-Wd Stockton	86	151
Long	27	m	c	CHIN	Solano	Rio Vista Twp	90	64
Long	26	m	c	CHIN	Tehama	Tehama Twp	92	188
Loo	18	m	c	CHIN	San Francisco	1-Wd San Francisco	79	60
Low	43	m	c	CHIN	San Francisco	11-Wd San Francisc	84	631
Low	32	m	c	CHIN	San Joaquin	3-Wd Stockton	86	246
Lue	30	m	c	CHIN	Yuba	Marysville	93	630
Lun	48	m	c	CHIN	Fresno	Millerton P O	72	201
Lung	22	m	c	CHIN	Tehama	Tehama Twp	92	188
Mi Sham	19	m	c	CHIN	Amador	Ione City P O	69	367
Ming	34	m	c	CHIN	Fresno	Millerton P O	72	191
Pi	23	m	c	CHIN	Yuba	Marysville	93	631
Pon	30	m	c	CHIN	Sacramento	1-Wd Sacramento	77	192
Qo	35	m	c	CHIN	Alameda	Eden Twp	68	58
Qua Ah	20	m	c	CHIN	San Francisco	6-Wd San Francisco	81	48
Quon	30	m	c	CHIN	Sacramento	1-Wd Sacramento	77	199
Sam	23	m	c	CHIN	Tehama	Merrill	92	197
Shi	24	m	c	CHIN	San Francisco	1-Wd San Francisco	79	109
Shi	21	m	c	CHIN	San Francisco	1-Wd San Francisco	79	120
Sing	26	m	c	CHIN	Yuba	Marysville	93	630
Sky	17	m	c	CHIN	San Francisco	1-Wd San Francisco	79	106
Soo	42	m	c	CHIN	San Joaquin	3-Wd Stockton	86	246
Sung	30	m	c	CHIN	Sacramento	1-Wd Sacramento	77	197
Sung	28	m	c	CHIN	Fresno	Millerton P O	72	191
Suni	18	f	c	CHIN	Sacramento	1-Wd Sacramento	77	192
Tai	28	m	c	CHIN	San Francisco	11-Wd San Francisc	84	481
Tee	20	m	c	CHIN	Sacramento	1-Wd Sacramento	77	202
Tip	19	m	c	CHIN	San Joaquin	1-Wd Stockton	86	156
Wak	21	m	c	CHIN	Sacramento	1-Wd Sacramento	77	205
War	22	m	c	CHIN	San Francisco	6-Wd San Francisco	81	52
We	30	m	c	CHIN	Yolo	Washington Twp	93	537
Win	42	m	c	CHIN	San Joaquin	1-Wd Stockton	86	142
Wot	16	m	c	CHIN	San Joaquin	2-Wd Stockton	86	203
Yack	21	m	c	CHIN	Fresno	Millerton P O	72	191
Young	20	m	c	CHIN	Sacramento	1-Wd Sacramento	77	196
Yup	40	m	c	CHIN	San Joaquin	1-Wd Stockton	86	151
Yup	36	m	c	CHIN	San Joaquin	1-Wd Stockton	86	142
Yup	23	m	c	CHIN	Fresno	Millerton P O	72	184
HIA								
Mon	22	m	c	CHIN	San Mateo	Schoolhouse Statio	87	336
HIALY								
Augusta	24	f	w	MA	San Francisco	San Francisco P O	83	141
HIAM								
Tar	21	m	c	CHIN	San Francisco	6-Wd San Francisco	81	56
HIANG								
Yi	30	m	c	CHIN	Solano	Vacaville Twp	90	130
HIATT								
Lee	27	m	w	VA	Sacramento	Franklin Twp	77	108
Wm T	33	m	w	KY	Shasta	Buckeye P O	89	482
HIB								
Sang	40	m	c	CHIN	Tuolumne	Big Oak Flat P O	93	397
Woo	18	m	c	CHIN	Tuolumne	Columbia P O	93	350
HIBAGERT								
John	42	m	w	GERM	Marin	San Rafael Twp	74	25
HIBBARD								
A	41	f	w	ME	Alameda	Oakland	68	232
A A	22	m	w	NY	Tehama	Red Bluff	92	176
Allert A	22	m	w	NY	Tehama	Red Bluff	92	183
Chas	42	m	w	PRUS	Solano	Vallejo	90	182
Chas W	31	m	w	ME	Santa Cruz	Santa Cruz Twp	89	394
David	32	m	w	CANA	Alameda	Washington Twp	68	284
Eugene	22	m	w	MO	Yuba	Marysville Twp	93	571
James	39	m	w	NY	Amador	Volcano P O	69	382
James	38	m	w	NY	Amador	Sutter Crk P O	69	409
Joel	38	m	w	KY	Nevada	Nevada Twp	75	310
John G	62	m	w	CT	San Francisco	San Francisco P O	83	128
Lewis	49	m	w	NY	Santa Clara	Redwood Twp	88	132
Thomas J	28	m	w	ME	Yuba	Long Bar Twp	93	563
Thos	36	m	w	CANA	Yuba	Marysville Twp	93	571
HIBBERT								
John	44	m	w	IREL	Tehama	Tehama Twp	92	187
John	34	m	w	PA	Nevada	Eureka Twp	75	137
P S	33	m	w	ME	San Francisco	8-Wd San Francisco	82	363
HIBBETS								
Henderson	51	m	w	OH	Plumas	Seneca Twp	77	48
HIBBS								
John	45	m	w	LA	Siskiyou	Butte Twp	89	588
Robert	33	m	w	VA	Sacramento	Alabama Twp	77	61
Roswell	37	m	w	VA	Sacramento	Alabama Twp	77	61
HIBERT								
Augustus	23	m	w	ME	Sacramento	Georgianna Twp	77	130
HIC								
Ah	29	m	c	CHIN	Butte	Hamilton Twp	70	68
Ah	25	m	c	CHIN	Sacramento	1-Wd Sacramento	77	201
HICHBORN								
A	26	m	w	MA	Solano	Vallejo	90	140
John E	39	m	w	ME	Humboldt	Eureka Twp	72	277
HICHCOCK								
Chord	35	m	w	NY	Sonoma	Vallejo Twp	91	463
HICHINGS								
Rebecca	22	f	w	CANA	Humboldt	Eureka Twp	72	266
HICINBOTHEN								
David	56	m	w	IREL	San Francisco	3-Wd San Francisco	79	310
HICK								
Ah	48	m	c	CHIN	Plumas	Indian Twp	77	19
Ah	37	m	c	CHIN	Plumas	Washington Twp	77	58
Ah	30	m	c	CHIN	San Mateo	Schoolhouse Statio	87	332
Ah	18	m	c	CHIN	San Francisco	1-Wd San Francisco	79	84
Frederick	25	m	w	GERM	Contra Costa	San Pablo Twp	71	364
G L	44	m	w	ME	Sacramento	Mississippi Twp	77	163
James	45	m	w	ME	Kern	Bakersfield P O	73	360
Victor	27	m	w	NY	San Joaquin	2-Wd Stockton	86	212
William	33	m	w	ENGL	San Francisco	8-Wd San Francisco	82	492
HICKAY								
John	55	m	w	IREL	San Francisco	San Francisco P O	83	100
HICKCOCK								
Joel B	50	m	w	MD	San Francisco	5-Wd San Francisco	81	18
Sylus	33	m	w	PA	San Joaquin	Elkhorn Twp	86	54
HICKEL								
M	30	m	w	IREL	Solano	Vallejo	90	202
HICKEMAN								
Alick	30	m	w	VA	Tulare	Visalia	92	291
HICKEN								
John B	34	m	w	PRUS	Placer	Roseville P O	76	354
HICKENBERY								
Fredrica	27	f	w	BAVA	San Francisco	2-Wd San Francisco	79	245
HICKENBOTHAM								
F	23	m	w	AL	Stanislaus	Empire Twp	92	32
HICKENS								
Richard	38	m	w	ENGL	Nevada	Nevada Twp	75	301
HICKER								
Adam	57	m	w	PA	Butte	Oregon Twp	70	133
Henry	38	m	w	ENGL	San Francisco	San Francisco P O	83	408
HICKERSON								
Andrew J	58	m	w	TN	Plumas	Indian Twp	77	13
C	32	m	w	TN	Lake	Lower Lake	73	419
Fines W	30	m	w	IL	Plumas	Indian Twp	77	13
George	46	m	w	NY	Solano	Green Valley Twp	90	40
Isaac	36	m	w	MO	Solano	Green Valley Twp	90	39
Michael	28	m	w	ME	San Francisco	San Francisco P O	83	209
HICKES								
G	28	m	w	SCOT	Alameda	Oakland	68	263
HICKESON								
M	44	m	w	IREL	Yuba	Linda Twp	93	556
HICKET								
M M	42	m	w	PRUS	Tuolumne	Chinese Camp P O	93	383
HICKEY								
Bautiste	35	m	w	CANA	Santa Clara	Fremont Twp	88	58
Bridget	60	f	w	IREL	Santa Cruz	Santa Cruz	89	429
Cornelias	35	m	w	NY	Trinity	Lewiston Pct	92	211
Daniel	10	m	w	CA	Trinity	Minersville Pct	92	203
Dennis	28	m	w	IREL	Sacramento	4-Wd Sacramento	77	357
E A	42	m	w	PA	Yuba	East Bear Rvr Twp	93	540
Edward	43	m	w	IREL	Solano	Suisun Twp	90	100
Edward	19	m	w	CA	Sacramento	Brighton Twp	77	73
Ellen	37	f	w	IREL	Sacramento	4-Wd Sacramento	77	323
Henry	30	m	w	AUSL	San Francisco	1-Wd San Francisco	79	73
Isaac	51	m	w	TN	San Diego	Julian Dist	78	471
J H	50	m	w	OH	Sierra	Sierra Twp	89	570
James	47	m	w	IREL	San Francisco	11-Wd San Francisc	84	651
James	45	m	w	IREL	San Francisco	San Francisco P O	80	430

© 2001 by Heritage Quest. All rights reserved.

Name	Age	S	R	B-PL	County	Locale	Series M593 Roll	Pg
James	40	m	w	IREL	Monterey	Salinas Twp	74	313
James	38	m	w	IREL	Mendocino	Navarro & Big Rvr	74	167
James	35	m	w	IREL	San Francisco	1-Wd San Francisco	79	80
James	31	m	w	IREL	Humboldt	Arcata Twp	72	226
James	30	m	w	IREL	San Francisco	San Francisco P O	83	310
James	23	m	w	IREL	San Francisco	1-Wd San Francisco	79	135
James E	27	m	w	IL	San Francisco	6-Wd San Francisco	81	104
Jno W	23	m	w	RUSS	Sacramento	3-Wd Sacramento	77	283
John	50	m	w	IREL	San Joaquin	Elliott Twp	86	71
John	45	m	w	IREL	San Francisco	San Francisco P O	83	126
John	40	m	w	IREL	Yolo	Putah Twp	93	510
John	40	m	w	IREL	Santa Clara	Redwood Twp	88	122
John	37	m	w	IREL	Marin	San Rafael Twp	74	42
John	35	m	w	IREL	San Francisco	7-Wd San Francisco	81	268
John	31	m	w	NY	San Francisco	San Francisco P O	83	219
John	30	m	w	IREL	Alameda	Oakland	68	206
John	29	m	w	IREL	San Mateo	Schoolhouse Statio	87	333
John	28	m	w	NY	Solano	Vallejo	90	202
John	27	m	w	IREL	Contra Costa	San Pablo Twp	71	362
John	25	m	w	IREL	San Francisco	San Francisco P O	85	745
John	22	m	w	MA	San Francisco	2-Wd San Francisco	79	250
John	11	m	w	CA	Santa Cruz	Pajaro Twp	89	343
John M	34	m	w	NY	Nevada	Eureka Twp	75	130
Julia	35	f	w	IREL	San Francisco	8-Wd San Francisco	82	411
Lawrence	54	m	w	IREL	Placer	Lincoln P O	76	486
Maggie	26	f	w	IREL	San Francisco	San Francisco P O	83	337
Margaret	21	f	w	IREL	San Francisco	8-Wd San Francisco	82	411
Margrate	26	f	w	MA	San Francisco	7-Wd San Francisco	81	165
Martin	54	m	w	IREL	Solano	Benicia	90	16
Mary	40	f	w	IREL	San Francisco	6-Wd San Francisco	81	95
Mary	27	f	w	IREL	Santa Clara	Redwood Twp	88	123
Mary	18	f	w	IREL	San Francisco	San Francisco P O	83	146
Matthew	33	m	w	IREL	Placer	Lincoln P O	76	485
Michael	50	m	w	IREL	Placer	Rocklin Twp	76	466
Michael	38	m	w	RI	Santa Cruz	Santa Cruz Twp	89	401
Michael	28	m	w	IREL	El Dorado	Mud Springs Twp	72	80
Michael B	48	m	w	IREL	Shasta	Shasta P O	89	454
Morris	25	m	w	ME	Sonoma	Petaluma Twp	91	311
Pat	27	m	w	IREL	Alameda	Oakland	68	208
Patt	26	m	w	IREL	Solano	Vallejo	90	200
Richd	45	m	w	ENGL	Fresno	Millerton P O	72	167
Thomas	65	m	w	IREL	San Francisco	San Francisco P O	83	247
Thomas	37	m	w	IREL	Klamath	Liberty Twp	73	375
Thomas	35	m	w	IREL	San Francisco	1-Wd San Francisco	79	87
Thomas	24	m	w	IREL	Alameda	Brooklyn	68	37
W W	30	m	w	ME	Solano	Vallejo	90	176
William	40	m	w	IREL	Placer	Pino Twp	76	472
William	40	m	w	IREL	San Francisco	7-Wd San Francisco	81	203
William	24	m	w	TX	San Diego	Temecula Dist	78	527
William	24	m	w	IREL	Marin	San Rafael Twp	74	26
William	21	m	w	IREL	San Francisco	San Francisco P O	83	243
William F	34	m	w	IREL	Placer	Newcastle Twp	76	476
Wm	35	m	w	IREL	San Francisco	1-Wd San Francisco	79	99
Wm	29	m	w	IREL	San Francisco	1-Wd San Francisco	79	94
Wm F	32	m	w	IREL	San Francisco	San Francisco P O	83	11
HICKINS								
Ambrose	52	m	w	ENGL	Placer	Bath P O	76	422
HICKISH								
Charles	31	m	w	PRUS	Kern	Havilah P O	73	350
HICKLAN								
Tolman	20	m	w	MO	Sonoma	Washington Twp	91	468
HICKLAND								
Louis	15	m	w	CA	Solano	Denverton Twp	90	24
Mar	18	f	w	MO	Sonoma	Russian Rvr	91	367
Thomas	48	m	w	MO	Solano	Montezuma Twp	90	69
William	40	m	w	MO	Solano	Denverton Twp	90	24
HICKLE								
James	40	m	w	IL	Sonoma	Mendocino Twp	91	297
HICKLES								
Wm	52	m	w	MA	San Francisco	11-Wd San Francisc	84	665
HICKLEY								
Cornelius	42	m	w	IREL	Monterey	San Juan Twp	74	394
Isaiah	22	m	w	MA	San Francisco	8-Wd San Francisco	82	468
Robert	20	m	w	CA	Sacramento	2-Wd Sacramento	77	239
HICKLIN								
Agnes	21	f	w	IN	Marin	San Rafael Twp	74	31
E F	31	m	w	MO	Mendocino	Ukiah Twp	74	237
Edwd	40	m	w	MO	Sonoma	Mendocino Twp	91	308
Thomas	23	m	w	IN	San Francisco	San Francisco P O	83	54
HICKMAN								
A	28	m	w	MO	Sacramento	3-Wd Sacramento	77	285
Al	35	m	w	TX	Napa	Napa Twp	75	66
Claybourn	30	m	w	TN	Nevada	Bloomfield Twp	75	93
Elija	43	m	w	MO	Tehama	Antelope Twp	92	153
Ellenor	56	f	w	VA	Sonoma	Analy Twp	91	220
Frank	27	m	w	HDAR	San Francisco	1-Wd San Francisco	79	30
Harry	14	m	w	CA	El Dorado	Placerville	72	113
Henry	28	m	w	FL	Kern	Kernville P O	73	368
Iasih	52	m	w	TN	Yolo	Grafton Twp	93	490
Isaac	47	m	w	ENGL	Santa Clara	Gilroy Twp	88	70
Isaac	47	m	w	ENGL	Santa Clara	Gilroy Twp	88	79
James	23	m	w	MO	Sonoma	Salt Point	91	381
Jeff	28	m	w	MO	Tehama	Mill Crk Twp	92	168
Jno	39	m	w	TN	Butte	Oregon Twp	70	122
John	21	m	w	GA	Marin	Point Reyes Twp	74	21
John B	22	m	w	ENGL	Sacramento	Granite Twp	77	142
John H	45	m	w	PA	Los Angeles	Wilmington Twp	73	635

Name	Age	S	R	B-PL	County	Locale	Series M593 Roll	Pg
Joseph C	46	m	w	KY	Plumas	Seneca Twp	77	47
L M	39	m	w	DC	San Joaquin	2-Wd Stockton	86	176
L Peter	42	m	w	PA	Sacramento	4-Wd Sacramento	77	331
Louisa	41	f	w	TN	Nevada	Grass Valley Twp	75	220
Mary A	67	f	w	KY	Sonoma	Analy Twp	91	223
P J	52	m	b	DE	Sacramento	3-Wd Sacramento	77	301
R	50	m	w	MA	San Joaquin	Liberty Twp	86	97
Susan	25	f	w	TN	Sacramento	3-Wd Sacramento	77	294
Thom	40	m	w	US	Yuba	Marysville	93	576
Thos	56	m	w	KY	Tehama	Paynes Crk Twp	92	167
Thos J	21	m	w	IN	Calaveras	Copperopolis P O	70	257
W J	24	m	w	TN	Napa	Napa	75	17
William	47	m	w	ENGL	Nevada	Rough & Ready Twp	75	336
William	31	m	w	MO	Placer	Lincoln P O	76	482
HICKOCK								
J	45	m	w	PA	San Joaquin	2-Wd Stockton	86	187
Noah	63	m	w	NY	San Joaquin	Elkhorn Twp	86	64
HICKOK								
Elizabeth	53	f	w	PA	Santa Cruz	Watsonville	89	372
Frank	50	m	w	VT	Butte	Chico Twp	70	43
Geo	28	m	w	LA	Yuba	Marysville	93	591
H D	38	m	w	NY	Sacramento	3-Wd Sacramento	77	291
Henry	30	m	w	NY	Del Norte	Crescent Twp	71	455
Seth	24	m	w	WI	Inyo	Independence Twp	73	328
HICKON								
Albert	19	m	w	NY	San Francisco	11-Wd San Francisc	84	603
Wesley	22	m	w	NY	San Francisco	11-Wd San Francisc	84	603
HICKOX								
Alfred	46	m	w	IL	Los Angeles	Los Nietos Twp	73	587
Geo C	38	m	w	MA	San Francisco	San Francisco P O	85	733
Sophia M	61	f	w	NY	San Francisco	San Francisco P O	85	732
W S	44	m	w	MI	Klamath	Orleans Twp	73	380
HICKRICH								
Frank	46	m	w	BADE	Sacramento	3-Wd Sacramento	77	289
HICKS								
Amos	30	m	w	MO	Merced	Snelling P O	74	279
Augustus	30	m	w	MO	Plumas	Seneca Twp	77	47
Augustus C	43	m	w	GA	Monterey	Castroville Twp	74	325
Barney	21	m	w	NY	Alameda	Brooklyn Twp	68	49
Bedford	22	m	w	CANA	Santa Clara	Santa Clara Twp	88	144
Benjamin	35	m	w	ENGL	Santa Clara	Almaden Twp	88	14
Benjamin	33	m	w	CANA	Tulare	Venice Twp	92	278
Beverly	44	m	w	VA	Santa Barbara	Santa Barbara P O	87	498
Bridget	65	f	w	IREL	San Francisco	San Francisco P O	80	360
Charles	31	m	w	OH	Kern	Bakersfield P O	73	360
Charles	22	m	w	IL	Sacramento	2-Wd Sacramento	77	220
Chas W	38	m	w	CANA	Nevada	Meadow Lake Twp	75	258
Chas W	38	m	w	OH	Nevada	Meadow Lake Twp	75	261
Christian	82	m	w	PA	Shasta	Millville P O	89	489
Chs	50	m	w	GA	Merced	Snelling P O	74	262
Daniel	18	m	w	MO	Butte	Chico Twp	70	57
Dave C	45	m	w	TN	Butte	Chico Twp	70	14
Dave F	18	m	w	MO	Butte	Chico Twp	70	21
Desire	55	f	w	NY	Santa Clara	San Jose Twp	88	214
E	40	m	w	ENGL	Alameda	Oakland	68	221
Edward	40	m	w	ENGL	Santa Clara	Gilroy Twp	88	67
Emma	15	f	w	OH	Shasta	Fort Crook P O	89	477
G A	40	m	w	TN	Siskiyou	Scott Rvr Twp	89	603
George	31	m	w	US	Santa Clara	Santa Clara Twp	88	162
George D	47	m	w	ME	Mariposa	Mariposa P O	74	114
Gilbert	28	m	w	WI	El Dorado	Diamond Springs Tw	72	35
H B	27	f	w	NY	Sacramento	3-Wd Sacramento	77	269
Henry	40	m	w	MO	El Dorado	Salmon Falls Twp	72	132
Hyland	78	m	w	VA	Butte	Chico Twp	70	57
J C	36	m	w	GA	Tuolumne	Chinese Camp P O	93	377
J E	46	m	w	MO	Merced	Snelling P O	74	247
J M	39	m	w	KY	Sutter	Nicolaus Twp	92	111
J M	28	m	w	MO	Merced	Snelling P O	74	259
Jacob	36	m	w	MO	Calaveras	San Andreas P O	70	218
James	56	m	w	VT	Placer	Auburn P O	76	363
James	48	m	w	NJ	San Joaquin	3-Wd Stockton	86	231
James	48	m	w	AL	Tuolumne	Big Oak Flat P O	93	394
James	30	m	w	MO	San Joaquin	3-Wd Stockton	86	231
James L	40	m	w	IREL	San Francisco	San Francisco P O	83	164
James S	20	m	b	CT	Sacramento	2-Wd Sacramento	77	236
James W	24	m	w	OH	Nevada	Meadow Lake Twp	75	267
Jno W	50	m	w	IL	Butte	Chico Twp	70	57
John	57	m	w	ENGL	Merced	Snelling P O	74	267
John	42	m	w	ENGL	Nevada	Nevada Twp	75	300
John	41	m	w	CANA	Sonoma	Healdsburg & Mendo	91	281
John	40	m	w	ENGL	Nevada	Nevada Twp	75	302
John	35	m	w	ENGL	Nevada	Grass Valley Twp	75	183
John	28	m	w	ME	San Francisco	7-Wd San Francisco	81	204
John	23	m	w	TX	Inyo	Lone Pine Twp	73	334
John	23	m	w	TX	Inyo	Lone Pine Twp	73	334
John D	42	m	w	MA	Los Angeles	Los Angeles	73	545
John J	32	m	w	IREL	San Francisco	2-Wd San Francisco	79	272
John R	40	m	w	ME	San Francisco	San Francisco P O	83	107
John T	26	m	w	ENGL	Nevada	Nevada Twp	75	309
Jos	43	m	w	TN	San Joaquin	Liberty Twp	86	83
Joseph	52	m	w	CANA	Fresno	Millerton P O	72	163
Joseph	52	m	w	CANA	Fresno	Millerton P O	72	193
Kate	1	f	w	CA	Merced	Snelling P O	74	247
L	31	m	w	NY	Lassen	Janesville Twp	73	433
L S	32	m	w	VT	Humboldt	Table Bluff Twp	72	307
Louis J	50	m	w	NC	Los Angeles	El Monte Twp	73	456
M	60	f	w	IREL	San Francisco	San Francisco P O	83	133

© 2001 by Heritage Quest. All rights reserved.

California 1870 Census

Name	Age	S	R	B-PL	County	Locale	Series M593 Roll	Pg
M	15	f	w	OH	Sonoma	Bodega Twp	91	252
Mahilda	44	f	w	TN	Los Angeles	El Monte Twp	73	448
Margaret H	13	f	w	MI	El Dorado	Cosumnes Twp	72	16
Mary	35	f	w	IREL	San Francisco	San Francisco P O	83	234
Marye	15	f	w	CA	Santa Clara	2-Wd San Jose	88	337
Michl	30	m	w	ENGL	Sierra	Table Rock Twp	89	573
Napoleon B	31	m	w	GA	Santa Cruz	Santa Cruz Twp	89	392
Nathaniel	67	m	w	GA	Santa Clara	San Jose Twp	88	188
Nathaniel	1	m	w	CA	Monterey	Castroville Twp	74	326
Oliver	52	m	b	DE	El Dorado	Georgetown Twp	72	45
Patrick	31	m	w	IREL	San Francisco	2-Wd San Francisco	79	217
Peter	42	m	w	IREL	Napa	Napa	75	49
Radolphis	30	m	w	IL	Inyo	Cerro Gordo Twp	73	320
Richard	45	m	w	IREL	San Francisco	7-Wd San Francisco	81	157
Richard	33	m	w	TN	Napa	Yountville Twp	75	79
Rubenn	21	m	w	ME	San Francisco	7-Wd San Francisco	81	157
Saml P	51	m	w	NY	Tehama	Red Bluff	92	178
Samuel H	70	m	m	CANA	Mariposa	Mariposa P O	74	131
Sarah	54	f	w	ENGL	El Dorado	Placerville Twp	72	99
Seraphine	29	f	w	NY	Tulare	Tule Rvr Twp	92	261
Thomas	43	m	w	ENGL	Santa Clara	Almaden Twp	88	14
Thos	40	m	w	IREL	Yuba	Rose Bar Twp	93	663
Thos	35	m	w	ENGL	Yuba	Rose Bar Twp	93	663
Thos	26	m	w	CUBA	Tehama	Red Bluff	92	182
Thos	16	m	w	CA	Nevada	Nevada Twp	75	304
W H	53	m	w	NY	Humboldt	Pacific Twp	72	291
William	45	m	w	NY	San Bernardino	San Bernardino Twp	78	445
William	40	m	w	MO	Stanislaus	Empire Twp	92	47
William	28	m	w	ENGL	Nevada	Grass Valley Twp	75	172
Willis	53	m	w	KY	Merced	Snelling P O	74	277
Wm	49	m	w	TN	Sacramento	Dry Crk Twp	77	104
Wm H	24	m	w	ENGL	Nevada	Grass Valley Twp	75	183
HICKSON								
Thomas	42	m	w	IREL	San Francisco	7-Wd San Francisco	81	192
HICKY								
David	25	m	w	TX	San Bernardino	Chino Twp	78	409
Jane	31	f	w	CA	San Bernardino	Chino Twp	78	410
John	32	m	w	TX	San Bernardino	Chino Twp	78	409
M C	58	m	w	NY	San Francisco	8-Wd San Francisco	82	367
Patrick	41	m	w	IREL	El Dorado	Diamond Springs Tw	72	21
Thomas	40	m	w	IREL	San Francisco	8-Wd San Francisco	82	320
Walter	26	m	w	TX	San Bernardino	Chino Twp	78	409
HICOCK								
Jos	28	m	w	PA	Solano	Vallejo	90	150
HICOK								
John J	56	m	w	PA	Colusa	Grand Island Twp	71	305
HICOMBA								
Labella	50	f	w	MEXI	San Francisco	San Francisco P O	80	332
HICON								
Wm	24	m	w	PA	Butte	Hamilton Twp	70	62
HICSLETTER								
Charles	25	m	w	AUST	San Francisco	6-Wd San Francisco	81	90
HID								
Mon	28	m	c	CHIN	San Mateo	Schoolhouse Statio	87	335
HIDALGO								
Felix	40	m	w	CHIL	Calaveras	San Andreas P O	70	154
Florence	3	f	w	CA	San Francisco	11-Wd San Francisc	84	711
Guadalupa	2	f	w	CA	San Francisco	11-Wd San Francisc	84	711
Jacinto	45	m	w	CHIL	San Mateo	Half Moon Bay P O	87	405
Maria	4	f	w	CA	San Francisco	11-Wd San Francisc	84	711
HIDDEN								
Charles	67	m	w	VT	Sacramento	Sutter Twp	77	385
Nancy	54	f	w	IL	San Diego	San Diego	78	503
HIDE								
E J	24	m	w	ENGL	Tuolumne	Big Oak Flat P O	93	396
Frank R	30	m	w	NY	San Francisco	7-Wd San Francisco	81	188
George	41	m	w	NY	Alameda	Eden Twp	68	84
Hanna	28	f	w	IREL	San Joaquin	2-Wd Stockton	86	165
Michael	32	m	w	IREL	Inyo	Independence Twp	73	328
HIDEMAN								
Christian	28	m	w	PRUS	San Francisco	San Francisco P O	80	474
HIDEN								
Chas	38	m	w	SWED	Klamath	Liberty Twp	73	374
HIDER								
Chas	48	m	w	PA	Solano	Vallejo	90	160
HIDLEY								
N P	20	m	w	NY	Mariposa	Maxwell Crk P O	74	146
HIE								
Ah	55	m	c	CHIN	Sacramento	Natomas Twp	77	167
Ah	50	m	c	CHIN	Sacramento	Cosumnes Twp	77	90
Ah	45	m	c	CHIN	Sacramento	San Joaquin Twp	77	398
Ah	43	m	c	CHIN	San Francisco	San Francisco P O	80	506
Ah	43	m	c	CHIN	San Joaquin	1-Wd Stockton	86	149
Ah	40	m	c	CHIN	Sacramento	Granite Twp	77	153
Ah	40	m	c	CHIN	Sacramento	Granite Twp	77	153
Ah	40	m	c	CHIN	Trinity	Lewiston Pct	92	212
Ah	36	m	c	CHIN	Fresno	Millerton P O	72	200
Ah	35	m	c	CHIN	Sacramento	Cosumnes Twp	77	94
Ah	34	m	c	CHIN	San Joaquin	1-Wd Stockton	86	144
Ah	32	m	c	CHIN	Sacramento	Cosumnes Twp	77	95
Ah	31	m	c	CHIN	Sacramento	Granite Twp	77	152
Ah	30	m	c	CHIN	Sacramento	Cosumnes Twp	77	92
Ah	28	m	c	CHIN	Fresno	Millerton P O	72	199
Ah	28	m	c	CHIN	Sacramento	Brighton Twp	77	70
Ah	28	m	c	CHIN	Sacramento	Granite Twp	77	155
Ah	27	m	c	CHIN	Butte	Hamilton Twp	70	72
Ah	25	m	c	CHIN	Plumas	Goodwin Twp	77	3
Ah	25	m	c	CHIN	San Francisco	3-Wd San Francisco	79	328
Ah	20	m	c	CHIN	Sacramento	Brighton Twp	77	79
Ah	19	m	c	CHIN	San Francisco	1-Wd San Francisco	79	110
Ale	22	m	c	CHIN	San Joaquin	1-Wd Stockton	86	144
Gee	13	f	c	CHIN	Sacramento	1-Wd Sacramento	77	192
Koot	14	m	c	CHIN	Sacramento	1-Wd Sacramento	77	197
Lon	39	m	c	CHIN	San Joaquin	3-Wd Stockton	86	246
Loo	28	m	c	CHIN	Solano	Vacaville Twp	90	129
Tong	30	m	c	CHIN	Solano	Vacaville Twp	90	132
Wa	22	m	c	CHIN	Solano	Rio Vista Twp	90	56
Yang	24	m	c	CHIN	Solano	Vacaville Twp	90	131
Yo	35	m	c	CHIN	Alameda	Washington Twp	68	297
HIEBUER								
Wm	52	m	w	PRUS	Solano	Vallejo	90	170
HIEDER								
William	23	m	w	PRUS	Mendocino	Point Arena Twp	74	213
HIEGEL								
Nicholas	45	m	w	FRAN	San Francisco	11-Wd San Francisc	84	575
HIEGHAL								
Alice	50	f	w	IREL	San Francisco	7-Wd San Francisco	81	185
Charles	15	m	w	NJ	San Francisco	7-Wd San Francisco	81	185
HIEGUERRA								
Ygnatio	96	m	w	CA	Santa Barbara	Santa Barbara P O	87	465
HIEM								
George	43	m	w	FRAN	Tuolumne	Columbia P O	93	353
HIEN								
Ah	28	m	c	CHIN	Solano	Suisun Twp	90	106
John	33	m	w	HANO	San Francisco	San Francisco P O	85	762
HIENDS								
John H	39	m	w	HAMB	San Francisco	7-Wd San Francisco	81	262
HIENK								
B	26	m	w	CANA	Sierra	Sierra Twp	89	565
HIENREAUS								
David	36	m	w	WURT	Calaveras	San Andreas P O	70	206
HIENREUS								
Daniel	66	m	w	WURT	Calaveras	San Andreas P O	70	206
HIER								
August	45	m	w	HANO	Alameda	Alvarado	68	303
Julius	33	m	w	HAMB	Alameda	Hayward	68	78
HIERLIHY								
P	34	m	w	IREL	Sacramento	1-Wd Sacramento	77	188
HIERMAN								
Fredrick	36	m	w	PRUS	San Francisco	San Francisco P O	80	461
HIESER								
George	31	m	w	OH	Mariposa	Maxwell Crk P O	74	139
HIETAL								
Juan	60	m	w	ENGL	Butte	Kimshew Tpw	70	82
HIETMAN								
Henry	23	m	w	HANO	San Francisco	11-Wd San Francisc	84	469
HIETT								
George	53	m	w	VA	Sonoma	Salt Point	91	385
Thomas L	25	m	w	OH	Mendocino	Point Arena Twp	74	212
HIG								
Ah	20	m	c	CHIN	San Francisco	San Francisco P O	80	492
Win	36	m	c	CHIN	Tuolumne	Chinese Camp P O	93	385
HIGARA								
Manwell	60	m	w	MEXI	Santa Clara	San Jose Twp	88	220
HIGBEE								
Henry C	36	m	w	VT	Tulare	Visalia Twp	92	280
John H	30	m	w	NY	San Francisco	San Francisco P O	83	202
L P	46	m	w	NY	San Francisco	San Francisco P O	83	281
HIGBEY								
Geo	46	m	w	NY	Sacramento	Sutter Twp	77	381
HIGBY								
Albert	54	m	w	NY	Los Angeles	Wilmington Twp	73	634
Charles	27	m	w	NY	Calaveras	San Andreas P O	70	198
Charles C	13	m	w	IN	Placer	Colfax P O	76	390
Christopher C	40	m	w	NY	Los Angeles	Los Angeles	73	541
Geo	21	m	w	PRUS	San Francisco	2-Wd San Francisco	79	166
James O	60	m	w	VT	Placer	Dutch Flat P O	76	403
Levi	56	m	w	NY	Alameda	Oakland	68	209
Walter E	33	m	w	CT	Shasta	Horsetown P O	89	505
HIGDON								
J W	38	m	w	KY	Nevada	Eureka Twp	75	130
HIGELSON								
Jacob	30	m	w	BAVA	San Francisco	San Francisco P O	80	482
HIGERA								
Antonio	23	m	w	CA	Santa Clara	1-Wd San Jose	88	276
Pitre	50	f	w	CA	Santa Clara	2-Wd San Jose	88	280
Ramon	8	m	w	CA	Santa Clara	Fremont Twp	88	61
Ramon	44	m	w	CA	Santa Clara	Fremont Twp	88	56
HIGGARTY								
Michael	30	m	w	IREL	Monterey	Castroville Twp	74	329
HIGGENBOTHAN								
Ed	39	m	w	ME	San Joaquin	3-Wd Stockton	86	244
HIGGENS								
Frank	25	m	w	IREL	Mariposa	Mariposa P O	74	111
Jno	27	m	w	IREL	Butte	Chico Twp	70	47
John	40	m	w	IREL	Santa Clara	2-Wd San Jose	88	294
Thos W	37	m	w	ME	Nevada	Nevada Twp	75	315
William S	42	m	w	ME	Butte	Ophir Twp	70	95
Wm	50	m	w	PA	Siskiyou	Callahan P O	89	632
HIGGIN								
Arthur	30	m	w	IREL	Santa Clara	Gilroy Twp	88	97
Dennis	30	m	w	SCOT	Alameda	Oakland	68	258
James	40	m	w	IREL	Sonoma	Salt Point Twp	91	383
James	18	m	w	ENGL	San Francisco	San Francisco P O	83	298

© 2001 by Heritage Quest. All rights reserved.

Name	Age	S	R	B-PL	County	Locale	Roll	Pg
Joseph	37	m	w	KY	San Francisco	8-Wd San Francisco	82	346
R	30	m	w	IREL	Alameda	Oakland	68	213
HIGGINBOTHAM								
Elizabeth	63	f	w	ENGL	Santa Clara	2-Wd San Jose	88	283
Geo B	40	m	w	IREL	San Francisco	3-Wd San Francisco	79	330
HIGGINBOTTOM								
J B	50	m	w	NY	Tehama	Red Bluff	92	183
Jno	40	m	w	CT	San Joaquin	3-Wd Stockton	86	215
John W	52	m	w	VA	Tulare	Visalia	92	300
HIGGINBOTTON								
Jo	40	m	w	NY	San Francisco	5-Wd San Francisco	81	13
HIGGINE								
John W	29	m	w	NY	Monterey	Castroville Twp	74	340
HIGGINGS								
H L	30	m	w	MA	Lassen	Susanville Twp	73	446
James	29	m	w	SCOT	Calaveras	San Andreas P O	70	154
HIGGINS								
A B	33	m	w	ME	Humboldt	Arcata Twp	72	227
Abraham	20	m	w	IREL	Napa	Napa Twp	75	31
Alexr	40	m	w	IREL	Sonoma	Salt Point Twp	91	383
Alf	19	m	w	IL	Mendocino	Sanel Twp	74	231
Alfred	62	m	w	KY	Mendocino	Sanel Twp	74	227
Alice	24	f	w	MA	San Francisco	7-Wd San Francisco	81	230
Andr	64	m	w	PA	Sacramento	4-Wd Sacramento	77	376
Andrew	61	m	w	AUSL	Solano	Suisun Twp	90	116
Andrew	39	m	w	IREL	Santa Clara	2-Wd San Jose	88	309
Ann	32	f	w	IREL	Santa Cruz	Watsonville	89	378
Ann	30	f	w	IREL	Alameda	Oakland	68	210
Anne	24	f	w	IREL	San Francisco	1-Wd San Francisco	79	62
Asa	39	m	w	MA	Sonoma	Vallejo Twp	91	452
B	37	m	w	IREL	Alameda	Oakland	68	203
Benjamin	43	m	w	MA	Placer	Auburn P O	76	373
Bridget	60	f	w	IREL	San Francisco	San Francisco P O	85	751
Bridget	39	f	w	IREL	San Francisco	6-Wd San Francisco	81	116
Celia	15	f	w	UT	Alameda	Eden Twp	68	57
Charles	45	m	w	AL	Santa Cruz	Santa Cruz Twp	89	387
Charles	41	m	w	IREL	Placer	Auburn P O	76	369
Charles	34	m	w	IREL	San Mateo	Woodside P O	87	384
Charles	33	m	w	IREL	Monterey	San Juan Twp	74	399
Charles C	30	m	w	PA	Placer	Blue Canyon P O	76	418
Cornelius	40	m	w	MA	Santa Clara	Santa Clara Twp	88	163
Dallas	23	m	w	OR	San Diego	San Pasqual	78	523
Dan	32	m	w	IREL	Alameda	Oakland	68	205
Daniel	49	m	w	CT	San Francisco	San Francisco P O	85	809
Daniel	26	m	w	IREL	Siskiyou	Surprise Valley Tw	89	638
Dennis	39	m	w	IREL	El Dorado	Mud Springs Twp	72	78
Eben	47	m	w	ME	Nevada	Nevada Twp	75	315
Ed	29	m	w	IL	Mendocino	Sanel Twp	74	231
Edward	33	m	w	IREL	San Francisco	11-Wd San Francisc	84	704
Elijah B	46	m	w	NY	Santa Barbara	Santa Barbara P O	87	467
Elisha	50	m	w	MA	San Francisco	2-Wd San Francisco	79	189
Elizabeth	63	f	w	ME	San Francisco	8-Wd San Francisco	82	413
Elizabeth	21	f	w	AUSL	Solano	Suisun Twp	90	94
Ellen	37	f	w	IREL	San Francisco	San Francisco P O	80	418
Ellen	26	f	w	IREL	San Joaquin	2-Wd Stockton	86	171
Flora	27	f	w	IREL	San Francisco	San Francisco P O	80	457
Francis	72	m	w	IREL	Santa Clara	San Jose Twp	88	196
Frank	48	m	w	CT	San Joaquin	2-Wd Stockton	86	185
Frank	25	m	w	IREL	Mariposa	Maxwell Crk P O	74	142
G B	42	m	w	OH	Tuolumne	Columbia P O	93	340
G W	33	m	w	IL	Mendocino	Sanel Twp	74	227
Henry	58	m	w	MO	Los Angeles	Wilmington Twp	73	645
Henry	25	m	w	MA	Sacramento	Franklin Twp	77	116
Henry W	36	m	w	ME	Sacramento	2-Wd Sacramento	77	220
Honora	67	f	w	IREL	San Francisco	San Francisco P O	85	769
Hugh	40	m	w	IREL	Yolo	Cottonwood Twp	93	461
Hugh	25	m	w	IREL	San Joaquin	2-Wd Stockton	86	172
Isaac N	36	m	w	IL	San Francisco	8-Wd San Francisco	82	330
J H	38	m	w	ME	Solano	Vallejo	90	160
Jackson	20	m	w	GA	Kern	Tehachapi P O	73	352
Jacob	56	m	w	ENGL	Fresno	Millerton P O	72	163
James	57	m	w	IREL	Siskiyou	Yreka Twp	89	667
James	56	m	w	IREL	San Francisco	1-Wd San Francisco	79	117
James	43	m	w	IL	San Francisco	5-Wd San Francisco	81	24
James	40	m	w	ENGL	San Joaquin	2-Wd Stockton	86	166
James	40	m	w	IREL	San Francisco	2-Wd San Francisco	79	158
James	39	m	w	IL	San Diego	Julian Dist	78	469
James	32	m	w	IREL	Marin	San Rafael	74	56
James	32	m	w	IREL	Monterey	Pajaro Twp	74	375
James	30	m	w	MA	Marin	Sausalito Twp	74	73
James	25	m	w	IREL	Santa Clara	San Jose Twp	88	220
James	25	m	w	IREL	San Francisco	1-Wd San Francisco	79	100
James	25	m	w	OR	San Diego	San Pasqual	78	523
James B	39	m	w	IL	Butte	Bidwell Twp	70	2
James S	53	m	w	MA	San Francisco	2-Wd San Francisco	79	195
Jas	36	m	b	MO	Tehama	Red Bluff	92	182
Jefferson	18	m	w	NV	Alameda	Washington Twp	68	296
Jenny	25	f	w	CA	San Bernardino	Chino Twp	78	410
Jeramiah	35	m	w	ME	Napa	Napa	75	16
Jno	29	m	w	NY	Monterey	San Juan Twp	74	418
John	9	m	w	CA	San Francisco	11-Wd San Francisc	84	707
John	60	m	w	MA	Sonoma	Analy Twp	91	227
John	58	m	w	ENGL	San Francisco	1-Wd San Francisco	79	58
John	50	m	w	IREL	Humboldt	Bucksport Twp	72	243
John	47	m	w	ME	Sonoma	Healdsburg & Mendo	91	280
John	40	m	w	IREL	San Mateo	Half Moon Bay P O	87	401
John	40	m	w	IREL	San Francisco	San Francisco P O	83	4

Name	Age	S	R	B-PL	County	Locale	Roll	Pg
John	39	m	w	IREL	San Francisco	7-Wd San Francisco	81	198
John	39	m	w	TN	Mendocino	Sanel Twp	74	231
John	38	m	w	IREL	San Francisco	1-Wd San Francisco	79	62
John	34	m	w	PRUS	San Francisco	2-Wd San Francisco	79	281
John	32	m	w	IREL	San Francisco	San Francisco P O	83	268
John	30	m	w	IREL	San Francisco	San Francisco P O	80	536
John	30	m	w	NY	Monterey	Castroville Twp	74	335
John	30	m	w	IREL	San Francisco	San Francisco P O	83	346
John	17	m	w	ENGL	Stanislaus	Empire Twp	92	63
John	17	m	w	AUSL	San Francisco	11-Wd San Francisc	84	588
John C	35	m	w	IREL	Marin	Sausalito Twp	74	74
John F	33	m	w	IREL	San Francisco	7-Wd San Francisco	81	242
John P	4	m	w	CA	San Francisco	1-Wd San Francisco	79	62
Jos	36	m	w	KY	San Joaquin	Oneal Twp	86	100
Kate	18	f	w	MO	Mendocino	Sanel Twp	74	229
Kate	17	f	w	MA	San Francisco	11-Wd San Francisc	84	541
L	27	m	w	NY	Yuba	Marysville	93	605
L B	37	m	w	OH	Sacramento	American Twp	77	64
Lester	37	m	w	AR	Santa Barbara	Santa Barbara P O	87	493
Lucy	25	f	w	IREL	Alameda	Oakland	68	241
Margret	1	f	w	CA	San Francisco	1-Wd San Francisco	79	62
Mark	26	m	w	IREL	San Francisco	San Francisco P O	83	395
Mark W	34	m	w	IREL	San Francisco	San Francisco P O	83	350
Martin	42	m	w	IREL	Santa Cruz	Watsonville	89	364
Mary	45	f	w	IREL	San Francisco	6-Wd San Francisco	81	124
Mary	39	f	b	MA	Nevada	Rough & Ready Twp	75	329
Mary	30	f	w	IREL	San Francisco	8-Wd San Francisco	82	444
Mary	25	f	w	AUSL	San Francisco	2-Wd San Francisco	79	234
Mary	23	f	w	IREL	San Francisco	8-Wd San Francisco	82	359
Mary	23	f	w	IREL	Sonoma	Vallejo Twp	91	453
Mary A	6	f	w	CA	San Francisco	1-Wd San Francisco	79	62
Mich	45	m	w	IREL	Alameda	Oakland	68	249
Michael	40	m	w	IREL	Nevada	Little York Twp	75	239
Michael	35	m	w	IREL	Placer	Summit P O	76	496
Michael	33	m	w	IREL	San Francisco	7-Wd San Francisco	81	262
Michael	31	m	w	MA	San Francisco	San Francisco P O	80	337
Michael	30	m	w	IREL	San Francisco	San Francisco P O	80	366
Micheal	37	m	w	IREL	Monterey	Alisal Twp	74	289
Monica	23	f	w	AUSL	Santa Cruz	Santa Cruz	89	417
Morton	24	m	w	IREL	Mendocino	Point Arena Twp	74	224
Nicke	15	m	w	CA	San Joaquin	Douglas Twp	86	35
O P	51	m	w	IL	Alameda	Murray Twp	68	105
O P	24	m	w	IA	Shasta	Shasta P O	89	453
P	27	m	w	IREL	San Joaquin	2-Wd Stockton	86	171
Patk	36	m	w	IREL	Marin	Nicasio Twp	74	14
Patrick	57	m	w	IREL	San Joaquin	3-Wd Stockton	86	222
Patrick	47	m	w	IREL	San Francisco	San Francisco P O	83	213
Patrick	45	m	w	IREL	Sutter	Sutter Twp	92	128
Patrick	36	m	w	IREL	San Francisco	11-Wd San Francisc	84	434
Patrick	33	m	w	IREL	Yuba	Marysville	93	579
Patrick	29	m	w	IREL	Colusa	Grand Island Twp	71	307
Patrick	24	m	w	IREL	Marin	San Rafael Twp	74	38
Peter	30	m	w	IREL	San Francisco	San Francisco P O	83	133
Robert	36	m	w	AL	San Mateo	San Mateo P O	87	357
Robert	33	m	w	AL	San Francisco	San Francisco P O	83	366
Robert	28	m	w	MA	San Francisco	6-Wd San Francisco	81	88
S M	58	f	w	MA	Humboldt	Arcata Twp	72	235
Sam	45	m	w	OH	Placer	Gold Run Twp	76	396
Samuel	36	m	w	IREL	Tuolumne	Chinese Camp P O	93	373
Samuel C	21	m	w	MA	San Francisco	San Francisco P O	83	350
Sarah	29	f	w	ENGL	San Francisco	8-Wd San Francisco	82	439
Sarah	27	f	w	ENGL	San Francisco	San Francisco P O	83	240
Sarah	22	f	w	IREL	San Francisco	San Francisco P O	85	871
Solomon	50	m	w	MA	San Francisco	San Francisco P O	83	342
Thomas	66	m	w	CANA	Yuba	Parks Bar Twp	93	648
Thomas	42	m	w	IREL	Placer	Auburn P O	76	493
Thomas	28	m	w	IREL	Alameda	Oakland	68	182
Thom B	42	m	w	CANA	San Diego	San Diego	78	495
Thos	48	m	w	IREL	San Francisco	1-Wd San Francisco	79	22
Thos P	29	m	w	IREL	Santa Barbara	Las Cruces P O	87	515
Uriah	70	m	w	VT	San Francisco	5-Wd San Francisco	81	13
Walter	30	m	w	MA	San Francisco	11-Wd San Francisc	84	494
Warren	22	m	w	MA	San Francisco	8-Wd San Francisco	82	339
William	54	m	w	CT	Tehama	Antelope Twp	92	156
William	51	m	w	IREL	San Francisco	San Francisco P O	80	397
William	50	m	w	MO	Kern	Linns Valley P O	73	344
William	45	m	w	IREL	Solano	Green Valley Twp	90	37
William	45	m	w	IREL	Napa	Napa Twp	75	30
William	40	m	w	VA	San Francisco	11-Wd San Francisc	84	538
William	40	m	w	NY	Contra Costa	Martinez Twp	71	348
William	38	m	w	MS	Nevada	Rough & Ready Twp	75	329
William	34	m	w	PA	Nevada	Grass Valley Twp	75	207
William	29	m	w	IREL	Nevada	Washington Twp	75	344
William	26	m	w	ENGL	Nevada	Nevada Twp	75	310
William M	44	m	w	NJ	Los Angeles	Santa Ana Twp	73	611
Wm	40	m	w	MA	San Francisco	5-Wd San Francisco	81	6
Wm	36	m	w	IL	Mendocino	Sanel Twp	74	231
Wm	36	m	w	NY	San Francisco	San Francisco P O	85	769
Wm	21	m	w	IREL	San Francisco	1-Wd San Francisco	79	62
HIGGINSON								
S P	8	m	w	CA	Santa Clara	Gilroy Twp	88	79
HIGGOLD								
Arnold	31	m	w	PRUS	Sacramento	2-Wd Sacramento	77	239
HIGGS								
Elizabeth	44	f	w	ENGL	San Francisco	San Francisco P O	80	414
HIGH								
Ah	40	m	c	CHIN	Mariposa	Mariposa P O	74	105

© 2001 by Heritage Quest. All rights reserved.

California 1870 Census

Name	Age	S	R	B-PL	County	Locale	Roll	Pg
Ah	35	m	c	CHIN	Placer	Bath P O	76	445
Ah	29	m	c	CHIN	Yuba	Marysville	93	601
Ah	29	m	c	CHIN	Yuba	Marysville	93	619
Ah	25	m	c	CHIN	Yolo	Grafton Twp	93	479
Ah	24	m	c	CHIN	Tehama	Tehama Twp	92	192
Ah	24	m	c	CHIN	Yuba	Marysville	93	619
Ah	19	m	c	CHIN	San Francisco	1-Wd San Francisco	79	60
Alfred	20	m	w	IL	Yolo	Cottonwood Twp	93	473
Charles	24	m	w	IL	Yolo	Cottonwood Twp	93	473
Deston	26	m	w	IL	Yolo	Cottonwood Twp	93	473
Elizabeth	43	f	w	OH	Yolo	Cache Crk Twp	93	450
George	13	m	w	CA	Sonoma	Analy Twp	91	238
Govan	47	m	w	VA	Yolo	Cottonwood Twp	93	473
Hung	30	m	c	CHIN	Butte	Chico Twp	70	52
John E	36	m	w	PA	San Diego	San Diego	78	496
Kim	24	f	c	CHIN	Yuba	Marysville	93	627
Lee	40	f	c	CHIN	Butte	Chico Twp	70	27
Rufus	40	m	w	TN	Mariposa	Mariposa P O	74	126
Solomon	26	m	w	WALE	Contra Costa	Martinez P O	71	425
William	49	m	w	NY	Los Angeles	Wilmington Twp	73	635
Wo	21	m	c	CHIN	Butte	Chico Twp	70	51
Won	40	m	c	CHIN	Yuba	Marysville	93	624
HIGHDOTZ								
George	46	m	w	HANO	Sutter	Butte Twp	92	100
HIGHER								
Henry	27	m	w	HANO	San Francisco	7-Wd San Francisco	81	224
HIGHES								
Wm	40	m	w	PA	San Francisco	8-Wd San Francisco	82	368
HIGHION								
Edward	58	m	w	ENGL	San Francisco	11-Wd San Francisc	84	571
HIGHLAND								
Daniel	20	m	w	IREL	San Francisco	8-Wd San Francisco	82	375
David	37	m	w	IREL	San Francisco	5-Wd San Francisco	81	7
H J	23	m	w	NY	San Joaquin	Dent Twp	86	29
Michael	40	m	w	IREL	San Francisco	11-Wd San Francisc	84	450
Michel	30	m	w	IREL	San Joaquin	1-Wd Stockton	86	136
Moses	12	m	w	CA	El Dorado	White Oak Twp	72	142
HIGHLEY								
Wm	44	m	w	PA	Sonoma	Salt Point	91	385
HIGHMAN								
Chas	26	m	w	PRUS	San Francisco	8-Wd San Francisco	82	320
HIGHT								
Alfred	61	m	w	MO	Kern	Linns Valley P O	73	347
Charles	32	m	w	MO	Kern	Linns Valley P O	73	343
H A	20	m	w	PA	Siskiyou	Scott Valley Twp	89	610
James	25	m	w	PA	Del Norte	Crescent Twp	71	456
Wm	28	m	w	PA	Butte	Chico Twp	70	17
HIGHTINGER								
Leopold	45	m	w	WURT	San Francisco	San Francisco P O	83	343
HIGHTMAN								
E J	39	f	w	VA	San Joaquin	Douglas Twp	86	39
Lena	20	f	w	PRUS	San Francisco	San Francisco P O	80	362
HIGHTON								
Ed	30	m	w	ENGL	Alameda	Oakland	68	206
HIGHTOWER								
Allen	64	m	w	VA	Sonoma	Analy Twp	91	228
Geo W	41	m	w	KY	Mono	Bridgeport P O	74	284
J D	41	m	w	NC	Tehama	Paskenta Twp	92	166
T J	29	m	w	AR	San Joaquin	Oneal Twp	86	109
HIGHY								
Pat	25	m	w	IREL	Solano	Vallejo	90	215
HIGINBOTHAM								
Green H	44	m	w	TN	Shasta	American Ranch P O	89	499
HIGINGS								
William	24	m	w	ENGL	Trinity	Weaverville Pct	92	230
HIGINS								
Bridget	45	m	w	IREL	San Joaquin	2-Wd Stockton	86	168
Ger	87	m	w	MS	San Joaquin	Oneal Twp	86	105
HIGINSEINMON								
---	33	m	w	POLA	Yuba	Marysville	93	616
HIGLEY								
Henry T	41	m	w	NY	Sacramento	2-Wd Sacramento	77	236
Truman	53	m	w	NY	Los Angeles	Los Angeles Twp	73	483
HIGMAN								
Henry	60	m	w	SWED	Calaveras	San Andreas P O	70	182
John	45	m	w	ENGL	Mariposa	Mariposa P O	74	117
Wm	24	m	m	NC	San Joaquin	1-Wd Stockton	86	124
HIGMETT								
Thos J	50	m	w	DE	Sacramento	Franklin Twp	77	113
HIGNER								
Frank	34	m	w	CUBA	Humboldt	Arcata Twp	72	235
HIGNIGHT								
S B	95	m	w	MO	Lake	Kelsey Crk	73	402
HIGSON								
Alexr	34	m	w	ME	Sonoma	Mendocino Twp	91	302
HIGUARA								
Jesus	26	m	w	CA	Santa Clara	San Jose Twp	88	222
HIGUERA								
Francisco	36	m	w	CA	Santa Clara	San Jose Twp	88	184
Francisco	25	m	w	CA	Monterey	San Juan Twp	74	385
Jose	58	m	w	CA	Santa Clara	San Jose Twp	88	184
Juan	34	m	w	CA	Monterey	San Juan Twp	74	385
Juan A	40	m	w	CA	Monterey	San Juan Twp	74	385
Madalina	22	f	w	MEXI	Los Angeles	Wilmington Twp	73	635
Valentine	60	m	w	CA	Santa Clara	Milpitas Twp	88	109
HIGUERIA								
Thos	20	m	w	CA	San Luis Obispo	Santa Rosa Twp	87	330

Name	Age	S	R	B-PL	County	Locale	Roll	Pg
HIGUERRA								
Manuel	70	f	w	CA	Santa Barbara	Santa Barbara P O	87	464
HIHN								
Frederick A	40	m	w	BRUN	Santa Cruz	Santa Cruz	89	421
Lewis E	31	m	w	BRUN	Santa Cruz	Santa Cruz	89	419
HII								
Ah	46	m	c	CHIN	San Francisco	San Francisco P O	80	508
Ah	17	f	c	CHIN	San Francisco	San Francisco P O	80	439
HIIGGINS								
Lank S	27	m	w	MO	Napa	Napa	75	44
HIIM								
Ah	25	m	c	CHIN	San Francisco	6-Wd San Francisco	81	98
HIK								
Ah	40	m	c	CHIN	San Francisco	6-Wd San Francisco	81	116
Ah	29	m	c	CHIN	San Francisco	6-Wd San Francisco	81	61
Saney	29	m	c	CHIN	Solano	Vacaville Twp	90	129
HIKE								
John W	40	m	w	NY	San Francisco	1-Wd San Francisco	79	3
HILAIRE								
Remillart	35	m	w	CANA	San Francisco	11-Wd San Francisc	84	560
HILAND								
Ellen	45	f	w	IREL	Nevada	Nevada Twp	75	281
John	38	m	w	IREL	El Dorado	Placerville	72	125
John	23	m	w	NJ	San Francisco	San Francisco P O	83	282
Michael	65	m	w	IREL	Monterey	Pajaro Twp	74	374
HILANDS								
J W	48	m	w	PA	Sierra	Sears Twp	89	555
HILARD								
William	37	m	w	IREL	Solano	Tremont Twp	90	32
HILBERO								
Philip	33	m	w	BADE	San Francisco	San Francisco P O	85	821
HILBERT								
Baren S	24	m	w	ME	Sonoma	Salt Point	91	392
Charles	43	m	w	BADE	El Dorado	Placerville	72	119
Jacob	33	m	w	PA	Colusa	Colusa	71	298
Jo	34	m	w	NY	San Joaquin	2-Wd Stockton	86	212
Mike	38	m	w	NY	Sacramento	3-Wd Sacramento	77	272
HILBIE								
Charles	40	m	w	PRUS	San Francisco	8-Wd San Francisco	82	347
HILBING								
Wm	45	m	w	BAVA	San Francisco	8-Wd San Francisco	82	346
HILBORN								
S G	36	m	w	ME	Solano	Vallejo	90	165
Stener	26	m	w	MO	Inyo	Bishop Crk Twp	73	312
HILBRETH								
Frank	36	m	w	PRUS	San Francisco	San Francisco P O	85	758
HILBRON								
Alfred	26	m	w	PRUS	San Francisco	8-Wd San Francisco	82	357
HILBROOK								
Margaret	65	f	w	SAXO	San Joaquin	Douglas Twp	86	33
HILBURN								
Edward	39	m	w	ME	Solano	Suisun Twp	90	95
Robert E	14	m	w	CA	Los Angeles	Los Angeles Twp	73	473
HILBY								
John	49	m	w	SWIT	Napa	Napa Twp	75	70
HILCHER								
Edward	45	m	w	PRUS	Placer	Bath P O	76	443
HILDBERGH								
Henry	34	m	w	PA	San Francisco	5-Wd San Francisco	81	26
HILDBRAND								
Alexander	44	m	w	PRUS	San Francisco	11-Wd San Francisc	84	486
HILDBURG								
Louis	28	m	w	NY	Sonoma	Petaluma Twp	91	320
HILDEBRAND								
Chas	34	m	w	PRUS	San Francisco	1-Wd San Francisco	79	103
Conrad	26	m	w	PRUS	San Francisco	San Francisco P O	80	470
Conrad	22	m	w	HDAR	San Francisco	2-Wd San Francisco	79	181
Geo	36	m	w	HDAR	Yuba	Marysville	93	605
Henry M	42	m	w	NY	Santa Cruz	Watsonville	89	366
Jacob	33	m	w	HDAR	San Francisco	San Francisco P O	80	346
Jacob	25	m	w	HDAR	San Francisco	San Francisco P O	80	460
James	60	m	w	PA	San Luis Obispo	Santa Rosa Twp	87	324
John	42	m	w	BAVA	San Francisco	1-Wd San Francisco	79	54
John	35	m	w	IN	Yolo	Cottonwood Twp	93	462
John	35	m	w	OH	Yuba	Marysville Twp	93	567
John	27	m	w	HANO	San Francisco	1-Wd San Francisco	79	47
Levi	41	m	w	PA	Tuolumne	Sonora P O	93	317
Michael	50	m	w	FRAN	San Francisco	11-Wd San Francisc	84	538
HILDEBRANDE								
Martin	45	m	w	PRUS	Santa Clara	1-Wd San Jose	88	249
HILDEBRANDT								
Fritz	28	m	w	HANO	Los Angeles	Santa Ana Twp	73	613
Geo W	41	m	w	PRUS	San Francisco	San Francisco P O	83	193
Wm	24	m	w	HANO	San Francisco	11-Wd San Francisc	84	626
HILDEBRANT								
Henry	27	m	w	ENGL	Los Angeles	Wilmington Twp	73	638
HILDEGOOD								
Gustave	20	f	w	SWED	San Francisco	2-Wd San Francisco	79	274
HILDEN								
John	22	m	w	SWED	Sonoma	Russian Rvr	91	370
Reno	38	m	w	FRAN	Marin	Nicasio Twp	74	18
HILDERBRAND								
---	30	m	w	GERM	Contra Costa	Martinez P O	71	438
A W	59	m	w	PA	Santa Clara	Gilroy Twp	88	78
Charlotte	22	f	w	PRUS	San Francisco	8-Wd San Francisco	82	412
Elias	46	m	w	TN	Colusa	Colusa Twp	71	280
Frank	58	m	w	HANO	San Francisco	11-Wd San Francisc	84	672

© 2001 by Heritage Quest. All rights reserved.

Name	Age	S	R	B-PL	County	Locale	Roll	Pg
						Series M593		
Geo	46	m	w	PRUS	San Francisco	6-Wd San Francisco	81	103
Henry	27	m	w	PRUS	Contra Costa	San Pablo Twp	71	358
R	24	m	w	BADE	Tehama	Deer Crk Twp	92	170
S D	26	m	w	IN	Santa Clara	Gilroy Twp	88	89
HILDERBRANDT								
Henry	34	m	w	BREM	San Francisco	8-Wd San Francisco	82	348
James	35	m	w	IA	Monterey	San Juan Twp	74	398
HILDERBRANT								
Wm	25	m	w	PRUS	San Francisco	8-Wd San Francisco	82	355
HILDERS								
Wm	30	m	w	PRUS	Butte	Ophir Twp	70	97
HILDETH								
I	25	m	w	NY	San Joaquin	Dent Twp	86	28
HILDRETH								
Alfred	37	m	w	NY	Shasta	Stillwater P O	89	481
Chatherine	26	f	w	NY	San Francisco	7-Wd San Francisco	81	204
Columbus	36	m	w	IL	Monterey	Castroville Twp	74	327
D W	45	m	w	ME	Solano	Vallejo	90	167
E S	35	m	w	ME	Nevada	Nevada Twp	75	321
Emph J	44	m	w	MO	Fresno	Millerton P O	72	146
Frank	24	m	w	NH	Sonoma	Petaluma Twp	91	324
G W	25	m	w	NY	Alameda	Oakland	68	214
Geo	32	m	w	MO	Sonoma	Analy Twp	91	224
George	35	m	w	KY	San Francisco	7-Wd San Francisco	81	204
H	30	m	w	NY	Lake	Lower Lake	73	419
James	44	m	w	NY	San Francisco	11-Wd San Francisc	84	613
James	28	m	w	DENM	San Francisco	7-Wd San Francisco	81	221
Jno	25	m	w	PRUS	San Francisco	5-Wd San Francisco	81	5
Joseph	39	m	w	MO	Santa Cruz	Pajaro Twp	89	342
Lewis	28	m	w	MA	Solano	Vallejo	90	139
Mary	68	f	w	MD	Santa Clara	1-Wd San Jose	88	276
Richard	18	m	i	CA	Sonoma	Bodega Twp	91	250
Richd	50	m	w	MA	San Francisco	San Francisco P O	83	24
Thomas	53	m	w	KY	Santa Clara	1-Wd San Jose	88	276
Torry	11	m	w	CA	San Francisco	11-Wd San Francisc	84	593
Wm H	55	m	w	VT	Placer	Roseville P O	76	355
HILDRITH								
Geo	32	m	w	OH	Humboldt	Pacific Twp	72	290
J H	38	m	w	KY	Mendocino	Ukiah Twp	74	243
Lowis A	62	m	w	MA	Butte	Chico Twp	70	19
Robt	32	m	w	MO	Mendocino	Ukiah Twp	74	234
William	43	m	w	KY	Monterey	San Juan Twp	74	387
Wm	35	m	w	MO	Mendocino	Ukiah Twp	74	241
HILDROTH								
John	43	m	w	NY	Alameda	Eden Twp	68	58
HILDS								
James	27	m	w	IREL	Sacramento	Georgianna Twp	77	129
HILE								
John	40	m	w	NY	Tehama	Tehama Twp	92	192
HILEMAN								
Chs	30	m	w	BREM	Yuba	Marysville	93	581
John	24	m	w	WURT	Contra Costa	Martinez P O	71	380
Wm	40	m	w	BADE	Butte	Ophir Twp	70	105
HILEMON								
Archi	48	m	w	TN	Butte	Oregon Twp	70	130
HILENER								
August	32	m	w	HANO	Alameda	Brooklyn	68	33
HILEPROM								
Doris	27	f	w	HANO	Placer	Bath P O	76	426
HILER								
John	32	m	w	NJ	Contra Costa	Martinez P O	71	423
HILES								
Catherine	45	f	w	IL	Los Angeles	San Juan Twp	73	628
Davis	39	m	w	OH	Sonoma	Cloverdale Twp	91	269
HILGEMANN								
H	36	m	w	HANO	Sierra	Forest	89	537
HILGROVE								
Harvey	36	m	w	HDAR	San Francisco	San Francisco P O	83	213
HILKER								
N C	39	m	w	PRUS	San Joaquin	3-Wd Stockton	86	218
HILL								
---	37	m	w	CANA	Humboldt	Arcata Twp	72	225
A	14	f	w	CA	Alameda	Oakland	68	242
A B	31	m	w	CT	San Francisco	San Francisco P O	85	863
A B	30	m	w	NY	Napa	Napa	75	20
A D	65	m	w	IREL	San Francisco	San Francisco P O	85	856
A E	37	m	w	IREL	Sacramento	Granite Twp	77	145
A H	42	m	w	ME	Tuolumne	Chinese Camp P O	93	386
Adelia	43	f	w	IREL	Placer	Bath P O	76	455
Agapito	56	m	w	CA	Santa Barbara	Santa Barbara P O	87	496
Ah	30	m	c	CHIN	San Francisco	San Francisco P O	80	500
Ah	24	m	c	CHIN	San Joaquin	1-Wd Stockton	86	145
Alex	36	m	w	SCOT	Sacramento	3-Wd Sacramento	77	263
Alex C	41	m	w	NC	Shasta	Fort Crook P O	89	473
Alexander B	7	m	w	CA	Sonoma	Petaluma Twp	91	319
Alfred	51	m	w	NY	Sacramento	Granite Twp	77	136
Alice	14	f	w	CA	Nevada	Bridgeport Twp	75	109
Allison	70	m	b	VA	El Dorado	Kelsey Twp	72	60
Alonzo	45	m	w	NY	Contra Costa	San Pablo Twp	71	359
Amos	50	m	w	OH	Sonoma	Mendocino Twp	91	302
Andrew	35	m	w	NY	San Francisco	8-Wd San Francisco	82	445
Andrew J	41	m	w	OH	Napa	Napa Twp	75	62
Andrew P	16	m	w	CA	Santa Clara	Santa Clara Twp	88	177
Andrew P	16	m	w	LA	San Mateo	Menlo Park P O	87	378
Ashlel	27	m	w	PA	San Francisco	11-Wd San Francisc	84	575
Ben P	27	m	w	MO	San Diego	San Diego	78	506
Benjamin	51	m	w	MA	San Francisco	8-Wd San Francisco	82	429
C S	40	m	w	NY	Mariposa	Maxwell Crk P O	74	140
Calantha	23	f	w	NY	Sonoma	Petaluma Twp	91	325
Caleb	48	m	w	IN	San Francisco	5-Wd San Francisco	81	29
Catherine	35	f	w	IREL	San Joaquin	2-Wd Stockton	86	169
Cesar	32	m	w	CT	San Francisco	5-Wd San Francisco	81	12
Charles	31	m	m	VA	San Francisco	San Francisco P O	80	423
Charles	26	m	w	OH	Shasta	Millville P O	89	486
Charles	14	m	w	CA	Sonoma	Santa Rosa	91	411
Charles G	60	m	w	NH	San Diego	Milquaty Dist	78	476
Chas	33	m	w	ENGL	San Francisco	11-Wd San Francisc	84	600
Chas	20	m	w	PA	San Francisco	11-Wd San Francisc	84	643
Chas	11	m	w	CA	San Francisco	11-Wd San Francisc	84	593
Chas H	37	m	w	CT	Napa	Napa	75	56
Chas W	33	m	w	CANA	Humboldt	Eureka Twp	72	264
Christopher S	43	m	w	ENGL	San Francisco	5-Wd San Francisco	81	12
Cornelia	39	f	w	VT	Santa Clara	San Jose Twp	88	199
Cyrus F	28	m	w	ME	Sonoma	Bodega Twp	91	264
Cyrus R	41	m	w	NY	Nevada	Grass Valley Twp	75	183
Daniel	52	m	w	MD	Santa Cruz	Pajaro Twp	89	350
Daniel	40	m	w	ENGL	San Francisco	San Francisco P O	85	875
Daniel	33	m	w	CANA	Humboldt	Bald Hills	72	238
David	33	m	w	ME	San Francisco	3-Wd San Francisco	79	319
David	30	m	w	ENGL	San Francisco	11-Wd San Francisc	84	662
David L	40	m	w	ENGL	Nevada	Little York Twp	75	243
Deming D	33	m	w	OH	Napa	Yountville Twp	75	84
Doctor	47	m	w	OH	Butte	Ophir Twp	70	120
Dudley B	37	m	w	ME	Santa Clara	2-Wd San Jose	88	287
E B	10	m	w	CA	Alameda	Oakland	68	257
E G	40	m	w	MA	Merced	Snelling P O	74	265
E M	40	m	w	VT	Alameda	Oakland	68	227
E P	40	m	w	ME	San Francisco	San Francisco P O	85	778
Edward	48	m	w	IREL	San Francisco	11-Wd San Francisc	84	457
Edward	36	m	w	MA	San Francisco	San Francisco P O	83	149
Elizabeth	73	f	w	NC	Solano	Vacaville Twp	90	133
Elizabeth	37	f	w	IREL	San Francisco	San Francisco P O	83	220
Ellen A	40	f	w	TN	Calaveras	San Andreas P O	70	158
Enoch	24	m	w	CANA	Yuba	Marysville	93	611
Ephraim	40	m	w	NY	San Francisco	6-Wd San Francisco	81	92
Erastus B	43	m	w	VT	Santa Cruz	Santa Cruz	89	409
F A	31	m	w	OH	Yuba	Marysville	93	599
F C	26	m	w	POLA	San Francisco	7-Wd San Francisco	81	226
Francis	35	m	w	PA	Plumas	Mineral Twp	77	21
Francis	32	m	w	FRAN	Amador	Ione City P O	69	355
Frank	40	m	w	NY	Sacramento	4-Wd Sacramento	77	329
Frank	28	m	w	MO	Sonoma	Russian Rvr	91	376
Frank	26	m	w	ENGL	San Francisco	3-Wd San Francisco	79	324
Frank K	4	m	w	ME	Stanislaus	Empire Twp	92	45
Fredrick	30	m	w	PA	San Francisco	San Francisco P O	80	532
Fulton F	22	m	w	MO	Los Angeles	Santa Ana Twp	73	616
G P	55	m	w	VT	Napa	Napa	75	25
G W	21	m	w	IN	Sutter	Butte Twp	92	90
Geo	45	m	w	SCOT	San Francisco	7-Wd San Francisco	81	229
Geo H	23	m	w	CANA	Sacramento	1-Wd Sacramento	77	203
Geo S	38	m	w	CANA	Sacramento	Center Twp	77	82
George	6	m	w	CA	San Francisco	11-Wd San Francisc	84	494
George	47	m	w	IREL	El Dorado	Greenwood Twp	72	55
George	45	m	w	OH	Humboldt	Pacific Twp	72	292
George	40	m	w	ME	Yolo	Grafton Twp	93	481
George	30	m	w	PRUS	Placer	Roseville P O	76	354
George	21	m	w	IN	Sutter	Butte Twp	92	92
George A	46	m	w	RI	San Francisco	6-Wd San Francisco	81	137
George H	9	m	w	CA	San Francisco	San Francisco P O	85	721
George W	42	m	w	NY	Nevada	Grass Valley Twp	75	155
Gilbert	33	m	w	WI	Calaveras	San Andreas P O	70	201
H B	51	m	w	ME	Alameda	Oakland	68	222
Harmon	24	m	w	PRUS	Nevada	Little York Twp	75	240
Harry	32	m	w	TN	Solano	Vacaville Twp	90	133
Helen L	11	f	w	MO	Los Angeles	Santa Ana Twp	73	617
Henery	17	m	w	CT	San Francisco	7-Wd San Francisco	81	156
Henry	51	m	w	ENGL	Nevada	Nevada Twp	75	294
Henry	35	m	w	IREL	Yolo	Putah Twp	93	510
Henry	33	m	w	NY	San Francisco	2-Wd San Francisco	79	155
Henry	30	m	b	KY	Nevada	Meadow Lake Twp	75	265
Henry	29	m	w	HAMB	San Francisco	San Francisco P O	83	54
Henry P	24	m	w	KY	San Francisco	8-Wd San Francisco	82	365
Hiram	69	m	w	NY	Sonoma	Santa Rosa	91	404
Hiram	48	m	w	ME	Yolo	Cottonwood Twp	93	465
Hiram	30	m	w	IA	Sonoma	Santa Rosa	91	404
Hiram H	37	m	w	NY	Santa Barbara	Santa Barbara P O	87	499
Horace	32	m	w	PA	San Francisco	San Francisco P O	80	532
Howard	23	m	w	ENGL	Napa	Napa	75	18
Hugh	25	m	w	PRUS	Solano	Vallejo	90	165
Iley	62	f	w	OH	Santa Clara	San Jose Twp	88	190
Isaac L	35	m	w	ENGL	Nevada	Grass Valley Twp	75	223
J B	31	m	w	CANA	Sutter	Butte Twp	92	97
J B	22	m	w	OH	Monterey	San Juan Twp	74	393
J Bryant	48	m	w	VT	Humboldt	Pacific Twp	72	296
J Ellis	42	m	w	PA	San Francisco	8-Wd San Francisco	82	360
J H	44	m	w	MD	San Joaquin	Oneal Twp	86	100
J J	15	m	w	CA	Solano	Vallejo	90	162
J K	20	m	w	IREL	Alameda	Oakland	68	265
J S	42	m	w	VA	Mariposa	Maxwell Crk P O	74	144
Jacob	32	m	w	TN	Monterey	San Antonio Twp	74	321
James	39	m	w	OH	Monterey	San Antonio Twp	74	321
James	37	m	w	IREL	Placer	Bath P O	76	441
James	25	m	w	SCOT	Plumas	Indian Twp	77	17
James A	39	m	w	MO	Sonoma	Analy Twp	91	228

© 2001 by Heritage Quest. All rights reserved.

California 1870 Census

Name	Age	S	R	B-PL	County	Locale	Series M593 Roll	Pg
James A	25	m	w	MD	Siskiyou	Surprise Valley Tw	89	638
James C	57	m	w	KY	Los Angeles	Santa Ana Twp	73	616
James Fred	33	m	w	SCOT	San Francisco	San Francisco P O	83	46
James M	50	m	w	MO	Santa Cruz	Santa Cruz Twp	89	393
James M	25	m	w	NY	Monterey	Castroville Twp	74	336
James S	38	m	w	ENGL	San Francisco	2-Wd San Francisco	79	270
James T	28	m	w	MO	Sutter	Butte Twp	92	100
Jas M	60	m	w	KY	Sonoma	Mendocino Twp	91	300
Jas P	40	m	w	MA	San Francisco	8-Wd San Francisco	82	379
Jasper C	29	m	w	MO	Los Angeles	Santa Ana Twp	73	616
Jerome H	32	m	w	VT	Santa Clara	San Jose Twp	88	203
Jesse	50	m	w	VA	Santa Clara	2-Wd San Jose	88	292
Jessee	45	m	w	VA	Santa Barbara	Santa Barbara P O	87	458
Jno	34	m	w	NY	San Francisco	8-Wd San Francisco	82	372
Jno M	38	m	w	IL	Butte	Chico Twp	70	17
Joel F	46	m	w	ME	San Diego	San Diego	78	501
John	9	m	w	CA	San Francisco	5-Wd San Francisco	81	29
John	67	m	w	WV	Sonoma	Santa Rosa	91	411
John	59	m	w	IREL	Placer	Bath P O	76	442
John	50	m	w	KY	Kern	Bakersfield P O	73	357
John	50	m	w	NY	Nevada	Bridgeport Twp	75	103
John	49	m	w	MO	Solano	Vacaville Twp	90	125
John	48	m	b	ENGL	Los Angeles	Los Nietos Twp	73	586
John	43	m	w	IREL	Solano	Denverton Twp	90	23
John	41	m	w	ME	Solano	Vallejo	90	162
John	40	m	w	IREL	San Francisco	San Francisco P O	83	276
John	39	m	w	KY	Calaveras	San Andreas P O	70	177
John	39	m	w	PRUS	San Francisco	San Francisco P O	85	809
John	36	m	w	CANA	Humboldt	Arcata Twp	72	225
John	35	m	w	SCOT	Alameda	Murray Twp	68	106
John	28	m	w	CANA	Humboldt	Eureka Twp	72	281
John	28	m	w	NY	Stanislaus	Empire Twp	92	66
John	27	m	w	PA	San Francisco	San Francisco P O	80	352
John	26	m	w	CANA	Humboldt	Eureka Twp	72	281
John	26	m	w	IREL	San Francisco	1-Wd San Francisco	79	82
John	26	m	w	IREL	Yolo	Grafton Twp	93	494
John	25	m	w	SCOT	San Francisco	7-Wd San Francisco	81	239
John	24	m	w	IREL	San Francisco	1-Wd San Francisco	79	70
John	23	m	w	NY	Colusa	Colusa Twp	71	286
John	19	m	w	NY	San Francisco	San Francisco P O	80	333
John C	20	m	w	MO	Placer	Clipper Gap P O	76	376
John E	40	m	w	NY	Yolo	Cache Crk Twp	93	434
John G	25	m	w	MO	Santa Barbara	San Buenaventura P	87	422
John H	78	m	w	NJ	Sonoma	Sonoma Twp	91	432
John M	44	m	w	VA	Nevada	Nevada Twp	75	278
John O	33	m	w	ENGL	Placer	Rocklin P O	76	462
John P	45	m	w	ENGL	San Diego	San Diego	78	491
John P	28	m	w	PA	Los Angeles	Santa Ana Twp	73	600
John Peabody	48	m	w	ME	Plumas	Quartz Twp	77	35
John R	40	m	w	ENGL	San Diego	San Diego	78	500
John W	33	m	w	OH	Colusa	Grand Island Twp	71	308
John W	32	m	m	VA	El Dorado	Placerville	72	110
John W	19	m	w	CA	Yuba	Long Bar Twp	93	566
Johnathan	35	m	w	MO	Nevada	Grass Valley Twp	75	209
Jos	50	m	w	IREL	Sacramento	1-Wd Sacramento	77	179
Jos	40	m	w	CANA	Sacramento	3-Wd Sacramento	77	256
Jos Reo	41	m	w	NJ	Sacramento	3-Wd Sacramento	77	259
Jose M	35	m	w	CA	Santa Barbara	Santa Barbara P O	87	496
Joseph	41	m	w	CANA	Yolo	Buckeye Twp	93	417
Joseph	19	m	w	MEXI	Fresno	Millerton P O	72	156
Joseph C	38	m	w	MA	San Francisco	8-Wd San Francisco	82	301
Joseph J	42	m	w	IREL	San Mateo	Schoolhouse Statio	87	331
Josephine C	38	f	w	OH	Sacramento	Lee Twp	77	159
Katy	23	f	w	NY	San Francisco	5-Wd San Francisco	81	2
L	40	m	w	AL	Sierra	Forest Twp	89	530
Laura	11	f	w	CA	Santa Cruz	Santa Cruz	89	410
Laura	1	f	w	MEXI	San Francisco	San Francisco P O	80	337
Lelia	14	f	w	CA	Santa Clara	2-Wd San Jose	88	338
Levi	33	m	w	CANA	Yolo	Buckeye Twp	93	417
Lizzie	21	f	w	CANA	Solano	Silveyville Twp	90	75
Louisa	6	f	w	CA	San Francisco	5-Wd San Francisco	81	29
Louisa	24	f	w	ME	Placer	Bath P O	76	435
Lydia	62	f	w	NY	Shasta	Stillwater P O	89	478
M G	11	m	w	CA	Alameda	Oakland	68	257
M J	22	m	w	IL	Tehama	Tehama Twp	92	187
Maggie	34	f	w	ENGL	San Francisco	San Francisco P O	80	457
Margaret	64	f	w	IREL	San Francisco	San Francisco P O	83	212
Maria	46	f	w	SC	Merced	Snelling P O	74	258
Maria A	33	f	w	CA	Santa Barbara	Santa Barbara P O	87	459
Maria A	33	f	w	MD	Nevada	Nevada Twp	75	287
Marian	44	f	w	CT	San Francisco	8-Wd San Francisco	82	410
Martha A	13	f	w	CA	Shasta	Millville P O	89	493
Martha F	14	f	w	CA	Placer	Rocklin P O	76	462
Mary	49	f	w	NY	San Francisco	2-Wd San Francisco	79	193
Mary A	35	f	w	TN	Nevada	Bridgeport Twp	75	102
Mary H	48	f	w	NY	Santa Cruz	Watsonville	89	375
Mary J	27	f	w	OH	Mariposa	Mariposa P O	74	124
Mary M	76	f	w	MA	Amador	Jackson P O	69	325
Mathew	50	m	w	KY	Sonoma	Santa Rosa	91	420
Matilda	49	f	w	PA	Santa Clara	Santa Clara Twp	88	136
Max	36	m	w	PRUS	Solano	Silveyville Twp	90	73
Maxwell G	34	m	w	OH	Plumas	Goodwin Twp	77	7
Michl	24	m	w	IREL	San Francisco	1-Wd San Francisco	79	62
Moses	61	m	w	NH	Amador	Ione City P O	69	360
Moses	59	m	w	NH	Amador	Volcano P O	69	388
Moses	55	m	w	MA	Amador	Volcano P O	69	381
Nancy Mrs	53	f	w	KY	Napa	Napa Twp	75	32
Niel	40	m	w	IREL	Humboldt	Arcata Twp	72	233
Oscar	35	m	w	NY	Alameda	Eden Twp	68	82
Oscar W	19	m	w	IN	Shasta	Millville P O	89	484
Otis	43	m	w	NY	Alameda	Eden Twp	68	82
P M	44	m	w	IN	Siskiyou	Big Valley Twp	89	582
Pat	41	m	w	IREL	Sacramento	3-Wd Sacramento	77	266
Patrick	26	m	w	IREL	Merced	Snelling P O	74	272
Peter	57	m	w	LA	Yuba	Slate Range Bar Tw	93	670
Pleasant	38	m	w	VA	Kern	Linns Valley P O	73	349
R	34	m	w	NY	Sierra	Sierra Twp	89	569
Rafaela	56	f	w	CA	Santa Barbara	Santa Barbara P O	87	496
Ralph F	37	m	w	CT	San Francisco	3-Wd San Francisco	79	328
Ramon J	36	m	w	CA	Santa Barbara	Santa Barbara P O	87	498
Refigas	33	f	w	CA	San Luis Obispo	San Luis Obispo Tw	87	314
Richmond	44	m	w	ENGL	San Francisco	San Francisco P O	80	345
Robert	49	m	w	ENGL	Shasta	Stillwater P O	89	479
Robert	28	m	w	SCOT	San Francisco	11-Wd San Francisc	84	672
Robert B	44	m	w	KY	Los Angeles	Los Angeles Twp	73	496
Robert L	36	m	w	CANA	Santa Barbara	Santa Maria P O	87	514
Robt	21	m	w	CANA	Humboldt	Arcata Twp	72	231
Robt	14	m	w	CA	San Francisco	11-Wd San Francisc	84	649
Robt R	38	m	w	IREL	San Luis Obispo	Arroyo Grande Twp	87	278
S D	49	m	w	NH	Sierra	Downieville Twp	89	522
S P	21	m	w	MA	San Francisco	8-Wd San Francisco	82	373
Sam	25	m	w	NY	San Joaquin	Oneal Twp	86	105
Saml	40	m	w	IREL	San Francisco	8-Wd San Francisco	82	354
Samuel	54	m	w	IREL	San Francisco	6-Wd San Francisco	81	121
Samuel	54	m	w	ENGL	Amador	Ione City P O	69	355
Samuel	53	m	w	IREL	Los Angeles	Santa Ana Twp	73	603
Samuel	51	m	w	MA	Tuolumne	Sonora P O	93	303
Samuel	50	m	w	ENGL	Nevada	Grass Valley Twp	75	190
Samuel	47	m	w	OH	El Dorado	Mud Springs Twp	72	81
Samuel	41	m	w	CA	Marin	San Rafael Twp	74	42
Samuel H	64	m	w	KY	Sonoma	Analy Twp	91	228
Sarah	56	f	w	TN	Sonoma	Mendocino Twp	91	301
Sarah E	31	f	w	ME	Stanislaus	Empire Twp	92	51
Sarah G	38	f	w	MA	San Diego	San Diego	78	501
Stephen	57	m	w	KY	Yolo	Buckeye Twp	93	410
Stephen	57	m	w	KY	Solano	Vacaville Twp	90	119
Stephen	38	m	w	CANA	Humboldt	Eureka Twp	72	281
Stephen S	57	m	w	VT	Stanislaus	Emory Twp	92	24
Steven	57	m	w	KY	Inyo	Bishop Crk Twp	73	317
Sumner	26	m	w	MA	San Francisco	7-Wd San Francisco	81	277
Susan	40	f	w	ENGL	Nevada	Meadow Lake Twp	75	270
Sylvester	39	m	w	NY	Placer	Bath P O	76	441
T J	32	m	w	IL	Sacramento	Granite Twp	77	145
Taylor	48	m	w	ENGL	Yuba	W Bear Rvr Twp	93	682
Theodore	20	m	w	OH	Monterey	San Juan Twp	74	393
Thomas	52	m	w	KY	El Dorado	Cosumnes Twp	72	13
Thomas	48	m	w	MADE	Alameda	Brooklyn	68	38
Thomas	47	m	w	NY	San Francisco	San Francisco P O	85	763
Thomas	38	m	w	KY	Santa Clara	Santa Clara Twp	88	170
Thomas	36	m	w	IREL	Yolo	Grafton Twp	93	479
Thomas	32	m	w	CA	Santa Barbara	Santa Maria P O	87	510
Thomas W	41	m	w	RI	Inyo	Independence Twp	73	324
Thos	60	m	w	IREL	San Francisco	1-Wd San Francisco	79	83
Thos	50	m	w	ENGL	Fresno	Millerton P O	72	162
Thos	45	m	w	NY	San Francisco	1-Wd San Francisco	79	104
Trimira	14	m	w	CA	Santa Clara	Santa Clara Twp	88	158
Uriah	39	m	w	NY	San Diego	San Diego	78	505
V W	50	m	w	MI	Alameda	Oakland	68	195
Vicente	42	m	w	CA	Santa Barbara	Santa Barbara P O	87	497
W H	40	m	w	LA	San Francisco	7-Wd San Francisco	81	165
W P	54	m	w	ME	San Francisco	3-Wd San Francisco	79	313
Whitman H	36	m	w	GA	El Dorado	Placerville	72	110
William	7	m	w	CA	Solano	Suisun Twp	90	109
William	58	m	w	OH	Nevada	Grass Valley Twp	75	167
William	53	m	w	ENGL	Nevada	Grass Valley Twp	75	190
William	40	m	w	LA	San Bernardino	San Bernardino Twp	78	453
William	40	m	w	IREL	Tuolumne	Sonora P O	93	328
William	40	m	w	ENGL	San Francisco	8-Wd San Francisco	82	495
William	35	m	w	CANA	Yolo	Putah Twp	93	516
William	34	m	w	OH	Tulare	Visalia	92	289
William	34	m	w	CANA	Humboldt	Eureka Twp	72	281
William	32	m	w	IREL	Placer	Bath P O	76	461
William	29	m	w	IL	El Dorado	Georgetown Twp	72	46
William	28	m	w	MO	Solano	Vacaville Twp	90	135
William	25	m	w	ENGL	Alameda	Oakland	68	182
William	24	m	w	MO	Solano	Silveyville Twp	90	74
William	24	m	w	ENGL	Solano	Silveyville Twp	90	75
William	23	m	w	NY	Colusa	Monroe Twp	71	322
William	22	m	w	IREL	Los Angeles	Santa Ana Twp	73	600
William A	32	m	w	IN	Siskiyou	Surprise Valley Tw	89	643
William B	47	m	w	MA	San Francisco	3-Wd San Francisco	79	312
William H	42	m	w	NY	San Francisco	7-Wd San Francisco	81	174
William H	33	m	w	ENGL	El Dorado	Placerville Twp	72	105
William J	35	m	w	IREL	Nevada	Little York Twp	75	241
William W	47	m	w	MO	Solano	Maine Prairie Twp	90	53
Wm	40	m	w	NY	Sonoma	Petaluma Twp	91	319
Wm	35	m	w	ENGL	Solano	Vallejo	90	200
Wm	33	m	w	PRUS	San Francisco	San Francisco P O	83	67
Wm G	30	m	w	MO	San Diego	San Diego	78	506
Wm H	54	m	w	CT	Sacramento	3-Wd Sacramento	77	290
Wm H	39	m	w	MO	Nevada	Meadow Lake Twp	75	262
Wm H	30	m	w	PA	San Francisco	8-Wd San Francisco	82	302
Wm R	55	m	w	TN	Napa	Napa Twp	75	71
Wm R	37	m	w	AR	Fresno	Millerton P O	72	149

© 2001 by Heritage Quest. All rights reserved.

Name	Age	S	R	B-PL	County	Locale	Series M593 Roll	Pg
Wm W	41	m	w	TN	Fresno	Millerton P O	72	145
HILLAR								
Thomas	46	m	w	MD	Alameda	Eden Twp	68	65
HILLARD								
Benjamin	42	m	w	VA	San Francisco	11-Wd San Francisc	84	636
Frederick	48	m	w	CT	San Luis Obispo	San Luis Obispo Tw	87	298
Mary	28	f	w	IREL	Contra Costa	Martinez P O	71	388
HILLBERRY								
Andrew	30	m	w	IREL	San Francisco	2-Wd San Francisco	79	232
HILLBRANDT								
Henry	34	m	w	PRUS	San Francisco	San Francisco P O	83	63
HILLBRANT								
Jno Q A	14	m	w	MO	Shasta	Stillwater P O	89	479
HILLDEBRAND								
David	50	m	w	BAVA	Calaveras	San Andreas P O	70	209
John	37	m	w	HDAR	San Francisco	San Francisco P O	80	358
HILLDEBRANT								
Ernest	37	m	w	PRUS	San Francisco	San Francisco P O	80	467
HILLDO								
M	40	m	w	CA	Alameda	Murray Twp	68	115
HILLEBRADT								
John	38	m	w	HANO	San Francisco	11-Wd San Francisc	84	560
HILLEBRAND								
August	33	m	w	HANO	Sacramento	4-Wd Sacramento	77	339
Henry	26	m	w	PRUS	San Francisco	San Francisco P O	83	72
HILLEGAS								
Wm	42	m	w	PA	Alameda	Oakland	68	244
HILLEGENDORFER								
J	40	m	w	GERM	San Francisco	8-Wd San Francisco	82	373
HILLEN								
Barney	36	m	w	IREL	Mariposa	Mariposa P O	74	124
Diedrich	28	m	w	HANO	San Francisco	San Francisco P O	85	718
Frederick	20	m	w	FRAN	San Francisco	7-Wd San Francisco	81	188
HILLENBRAND								
Henry	53	m	w	BAVA	Butte	Wyandotte Twp	70	148
HILLEPP								
C A	18	f	w	CA	Alameda	Oakland	68	237
HILLER								
Bertha	15	f	w	CA	Los Angeles	El Monte Twp	73	459
Chas	35	m	w	BADE	Butte	Kimshew Tpw	70	80
Edward	42	m	w	MA	Contra Costa	Martinez Twp	71	348
Fred	40	m	w	HANO	San Francisco	2-Wd San Francisco	79	280
Fred	28	m	w	FRAN	Humboldt	Bucksport Twp	72	241
Geo	36	m	w	CA	Humboldt	Eel Rvr Twp	72	246
Geo	31	m	w	ME	Alameda	Oakland	68	183
Henry	42	m	w	BAVA	Nevada	Meadow Lake Twp	75	261
James	39	m	w	CANA	San Francisco	San Francisco P O	83	188
John A	49	m	w	NY	Yolo	Putah Twp	93	510
John R	43	m	w	PA	Yolo	Cache Crk Twp	93	429
Peter	60	m	w	FRAN	San Francisco	San Francisco P O	85	765
Philip	29	m	w	FRAN	Shasta	American Ranch P O	89	496
HILLERS								
Diedrich	22	m	w	BREM	San Francisco	1-Wd San Francisco	79	54
HILLERY								
I H	33	m	w	TN	Alameda	Murray Twp	68	107
Wm H	27	m	m	VA	San Francisco	San Francisco P O	85	743
HILLES								
John	70	m	w	KY	El Dorado	Mountain Twp	72	70
HILLEY								
Jas	38	m	w	IREL	Sonoma	Cloverdale Twp	91	267
Michael	34	m	w	IREL	El Dorado	Georgetown Twp	72	39
HILLGASS								
G	35	m	w	IN	Merced	Snelling P O	74	262
HILLGEN								
Henry	25	m	w	HANO	San Francisco	11-Wd San Francisc	84	428
HILLGER								
John	27	m	w	BAVA	San Joaquin	Tulare Twp	86	258
HILLHOUSE								
John	21	m	w	WI	Amador	Volcano P O	69	386
John	21	m	w	WI	Amador	Sutter Crk P O	69	411
William	43	m	w	KY	Placer	Dutch Flat P O	76	406
HILLIARD								
Chester	50	m	w	NH	Amador	Jackson P O	69	333
Henry	46	m	w	FRAN	San Francisco	San Francisco P O	80	535
Jacob	38	m	w	PA	Trinity	Hayfork Valley	92	238
John	39	m	w	PA	San Francisco	11-Wd San Francisc	84	586
M	38	m	w	CANA	Mariposa	Maxwell Crk P O	74	143
Martin	51	m	w	SWED	Placer	Bath P O	76	421
Mary E	52	f	w	PA	Stanislaus	Empire Twp	92	62
Moses	64	m	w	VA	Stanislaus	Empire Twp	92	62
Reuben	40	m	w	PA	Colusa	Monroe Twp	71	325
Thomas	45	m	w	IL	Stanislaus	Empire Twp	92	62
HILLICK								
Geo	26	m	w	PRUS	Sonoma	Salt Point	91	393
HILLING								
B	46	m	w	HANO	Calaveras	Copperopolis P O	70	224
HILLINGER								
Jacob	24	m	w	HDAR	Sacramento	4-Wd Sacramento	77	347
HILLINTELL								
Barnard	46	m	w	BAVA	San Francisco	San Francisco P O	83	212
HILLIS								
Bolivar	33	m	w	OH	El Dorado	Mud Springs Twp	72	82
James	26	m	w	CANA	Humboldt	Eureka Twp	72	267
Thomas	44	m	w	IREL	San Mateo	Pescadero P O	87	413
W H	43	m	w	MI	Tuolumne	Columbia P O	93	352
HILLMAN								
Henry	49	m	w	BRUN	San Francisco	11-Wd San Francisc	84	556
Isais W	27	m	w	BAVA	Los Angeles	Los Angeles	73	511
John	48	m	w	ENGL	Plumas	Goodwin Twp	77	1
John	35	m	w	RUSS	San Francisco	1-Wd San Francisco	79	50
Jonathan	39	m	w	MA	Marin	Point Reyes Twp	74	21
Levi C	45	m	w	NY	Santa Clara	Redwood Twp	88	123
R	40	m	w	ME	Lassen	Susanville Twp	73	443
S	49	m	w	MA	Del Norte	Crescent	71	464
Theodore	9	m	w	CA	Humboldt	Bucksport Twp	72	243
Wm	23	m	w	MO	San Joaquin	Dent Twp	86	19
HILLMANN								
Isaac	73	m	w	VT	San Francisco	San Francisco P O	83	400
HILLMANTLE								
Bernard	46	m	w	PRUS	San Francisco	San Francisco P O	83	386
HILLOCK								
Thomas	25	m	w	ENGL	San Francisco	3-Wd San Francisco	79	297
HILLPERT								
Leonard	30	m	w	BAVA	San Francisco	8-Wd San Francisco	82	381
HILLS								
Austin	45	m	w	ME	San Francisco	7-Wd San Francisco	81	247
Austin	30	m	w	CT	Marin	Bolinas Twp	74	1
F M	31	m	w	IL	Trinity	Hayfork Valley	92	238
Frank W	46	m	w	VT	Sacramento	Dry Crk Twp	77	98
Geo	32	m	w	IREL	San Francisco	5-Wd San Francisco	81	28
Harvey E	37	m	w	MA	Santa Clara	2-Wd San Jose	88	299
Illoc	71	m	w	NH	Humboldt	Eel Rvr Twp	72	252
James A	40	m	w	ENGL	Tulare	Visalia Twp	92	284
John	55	m	w	MA	San Mateo	San Mateo P O	87	355
John	36	m	w	NH	Sonoma	Vallejo Twp	91	456
Joseph M	26	m	w	ENGL	Nevada	Grass Valley Twp	75	193
Josiah	49	m	w	ENGL	San Francisco	2-Wd San Francisco	79	179
Mary A	55	f	w	IN	Colusa	Colusa	71	296
Miles	50	m	w	CT	Santa Clara	San Jose Twp	88	196
Mt T	25	m	w	CANA	Humboldt	Eureka Twp	72	274
Samuel M	38	m	w	ME	San Francisco	6-Wd San Francisco	81	89
Spencer W	40	m	w	ME	Mendocino	Big Rvr Twp	74	161
Thomas S	24	m	w	ENGL	Merced	Snelling P O	74	258
HILLSBURY								
Adam	34	m	w	PA	Humboldt	Eel Rvr Twp	72	250
HILLSON								
Gus	28	m	w	GERM	Solano	Vallejo	90	170
John	30	m	w	ENGL	Kern	Havilah P O	73	350
HILLTON								
L	50	m	w	SCOT	Alameda	Murray Twp	68	120
HILLUKER								
Enoch	25	m	w	CANA	Solano	Silveyville Twp	90	86
HILLY								
James	22	m	w	CANA	Sacramento	Franklin Twp	77	109
HILLYARD								
Abraham	51	m	w	PA	Tulare	Venice Twp	92	274
Philip	41	m	w	PA	Tulare	Venice Twp	92	274
HILLYER								
C T	38	m	w	MA	Nevada	Eureka Twp	75	133
David	35	m	w	OH	Santa Cruz	Santa Cruz Twp	89	389
E C	13	m	w	CA	Alameda	Oakland	68	243
Francis	28	f	w	NY	Alameda	Brooklyn Twp	68	40
Hiram	34	m	w	MO	San Joaquin	2-Wd Stockton	86	189
Horace	56	m	w	OH	Alameda	Eden Twp	68	72
James	51	m	w	VA	Amador	Sutter Crk P O	69	398
Samuel	54	m	w	PRUS	Yolo	Cache Crk Twp	93	436
HILLYSMER								
Joseph	42	m	w	DENM	San Francisco	3-Wd San Francisco	79	320
HILMAN								
Henry	36	m	w	HOLL	Nevada	Meadow Lake Twp	75	265
HILMER								
Charles	32	m	w	CANA	Merced	Snelling P O	74	257
Louis	23	m	w	PRUS	Sacramento	4-Wd Sacramento	77	326
HILO								
Laura	38	f	w	MEXI	San Francisco	San Francisco P O	80	466
HILONE								
Cong	40	m	c	CHIN	Trinity	Weaverville Pct	92	228
HILPERT								
John	52	m	w	PRUS	San Francisco	7-Wd San Francisco	81	271
HILSTROM								
Louis J	46	m	w	SWED	San Diego	San Diego	78	497
HILT								
C W	40	m	w	OH	Solano	Vallejo	90	159
Chas W	35	m	w	IL	Siskiyou	Cottonwood Twp	89	590
John	45	m	w	IL	Siskiyou	Cottonwood Twp	89	591
William	80	m	w	OH	Siskiyou	Cottonwood Twp	89	590
HILTMAN								
Frederick	50	m	w	HAMB	El Dorado	Mud Springs Twp	72	79
HILTON								
C C	18	m	w	CA	Alameda	Oakland	68	159
Caddie	28	f	w	ME	Santa Clara	Gilroy Twp	88	83
Charles	21	m	w	ME	Alameda	Oakland	68	193
Chas	37	m	w	OH	Santa Clara	Gilroy Twp	88	78
Danl	37	m	w	ME	Butte	Ophir Twp	70	105
Deborah	35	f	w	TN	Sonoma	Petaluma Twp	91	343
Dilia	33	f	w	IREL	San Francisco	San Francisco P O	83	186
Eben	43	m	w	ME	Napa	Napa	75	11
Edwd	37	m	w	CANA	San Francisco	1-Wd San Francisco	79	98
Edwin	32	m	w	ME	Solano	Vallejo	90	148
Elma	14	f	w	CA	Sonoma	Petaluma Twp	91	343
Emma	18	f	w	NY	Contra Costa	Martinez P O	71	379
Frank	13	m	w	CA	Sacramento	3-Wd Sacramento	77	290
Frederick	52	m	w	CANA	Alameda	Washington Twp	68	277
Geo K	38	m	w	NH	San Francisco	8-Wd San Francisco	82	340

© 2001 by Heritage Quest. All rights reserved.

California 1870 Census

Name	Age	S	R	B-PL	County	Locale	Roll	Pg
						Series M593		
George	35	m	w	ME	Nevada	Meadow Lake Twp	75	248
George	20	m	w	CANA	Marin	San Rafael	74	48
Henry	39	m	w	NY	Napa	Yountville Twp	75	81
J D	38	m	w	ME	Nevada	Meadow Lake Twp	75	253
J H	39	m	w	FRAN	Sacramento	4-Wd Sacramento	77	377
J R	52	m	w	OH	Tehama	Tehama Twp	92	194
J W	61	m	w	IL	Alameda	Murray Twp	68	108
James	45	m	w	ENGL	San Mateo	Redwood Twp	87	365
James	30	m	w	IREL	San Francisco	San Francisco P O	83	133
James B	56	m	w	ENGL	Yolo	Washington Twp	93	535
John	46	m	w	ME	Yuba	North East Twp	93	644
John	43	m	w	NY	Tulare	White Rvr Twp	92	302
John	41	m	w	ENGL	Alameda	Oakland	68	245
John	30	m	w	ENGL	Marin	San Rafael	74	55
John M	49	m	w	ENGL	Sacramento	Cosumnes Twp	77	88
John W	38	m	w	ME	San Francisco	San Francisco P O	83	218
Joseph	35	m	w	NY	San Francisco	5-Wd San Francisco	81	35
Joseph	22	m	w	MI	Inyo	Independence Twp	73	327
Joshua	50	m	w	ME	Marin	Sausalito Twp	74	70
L	39	m	w	IL	Alameda	Murray Twp	68	108
Lydia	30	f	w	ME	Santa Clara	Gilroy Twp	88	83
Margaret	21	f	w	IL	Butte	Ophir Twp	70	105
Mary	44	f	w	CANA	Alameda	Washington Twp	68	277
Osgood	42	m	w	ME	Solano	Vallejo	90	180
Philip	40	m	w	CANA	Nevada	Bridgeport Twp	75	101
Primas	30	m	w	ME	Sonoma	Sonoma Twp	91	446
Richard	43	m	w	NY	Inyo	Bishop Crk Twp	73	314
Samuel	28	m	w	ME	San Francisco	11-Wd San Francisc	84	500
Sarah	43	f	w	ME	Solano	Vallejo	90	172
Sarah	38	f	w	WIND	San Francisco	San Francisco P O	80	486
Stanford	41	m	w	ME	San Francisco	11-Wd San Francisc	84	619
Stephen	37	m	w	ME	Alameda	Brooklyn	68	27
Thomas	39	m	w	IL	San Francisco	5-Wd San Francisco	81	21
William	37	m	w	NY	Colusa	Monroe Twp	71	321
William	22	m	w	ENGL	Placer	Cisco P O	76	494
Wm	37	m	m	NY	San Joaquin	1-Wd Stockton	86	134
Wm H	37	m	w	NY	Tuolumne	Columbia P O	93	347
HIM								
Ah	55	m	c	CHIN	Plumas	Mineral Twp	77	25
Ah	51	m	c	CHIN	Butte	Wyandotte Twp	70	147
Ah	51	m	c	CHIN	Trinity	North Fork Twp	92	218
Ah	46	m	c	CHIN	Nevada	Nevada Twp	75	312
Ah	41	m	c	CHIN	San Francisco	San Francisco P O	80	528
Ah	40	m	c	CHIN	Trinity	Douglas	92	236
Ah	40	m	c	CHIN	Placer	Colfax P O	76	387
Ah	40	m	c	CHIN	San Francisco	San Francisco P O	80	454
Ah	40	m	c	CHIN	San Mateo	Schoolhouse Statio	87	335
Ah	4	f	c	CA	San Francisco	San Francisco P O	80	528
Ah	39	m	c	CHIN	Amador	Volcano P O	69	383
Ah	37	m	c	CHIN	San Francisco	San Francisco P O	80	529
Ah	36	m	c	CHIN	Nevada	Nevada Twp	75	277
Ah	35	m	c	CHIN	Placer	Colfax P O	76	387
Ah	34	m	c	CHIN	San Francisco	San Francisco P O	80	436
Ah	34	m	c	CHIN	San Francisco	San Francisco P O	80	526
Ah	32	m	c	CHIN	Tuolumne	Big Oak Flat P O	93	402
Ah	32	m	c	CHIN	Placer	Colfax P O	76	384
Ah	32	m	c	CHIN	Trinity	Junction City Pct	92	206
Ah	30	m	c	CHIN	San Francisco	3-Wd San Francisco	79	304
Ah	3	m	c	CA	San Francisco	San Francisco P O	80	527
Ah	29	m	c	CHIN	San Joaquin	Oneal Twp	86	117
Ah	29	m	c	CHIN	Marin	San Rafael Twp	74	59
Ah	29	m	c	CHIN	Sacramento	1-Wd Sacramento	77	190
Ah	28	m	c	CHIN	Napa	Napa	75	56
Ah	28	m	c	CHIN	Plumas	Plumas Twp	77	33
Ah	28	m	c	CHIN	San Francisco	6-Wd San Francisco	81	50
Ah	28	m	c	CHIN	San Francisco	San Francisco P O	80	516
Ah	28	m	c	CHIN	Tehama	Tehama Twp	92	189
Ah	27	m	c	CHIN	San Francisco	San Francisco P O	85	748
Ah	27	m	c	CHIN	Placer	Colfax P O	76	386
Ah	27	f	c	CHIN	San Francisco	San Francisco P O	80	433
Ah	27	m	c	CHIN	San Francisco	San Francisco P O	80	525
Ah	27	m	c	CHIN	Santa Clara	Santa Clara Twp	88	166
Ah	26	m	c	CHIN	Marin	San Rafael Twp	74	42
Ah	26	m	c	CHIN	Plumas	Indian Twp	77	16
Ah	26	m	c	CHIN	Butte	Concow Twp	70	11
Ah	26	m	c	CHIN	San Francisco	6-Wd San Francisco	81	49
Ah	26	m	c	CHIN	Santa Clara	Santa Clara Twp	88	147
Ah	25	m	c	CHIN	Trinity	Douglas	92	235
Ah	25	m	c	CHIN	San Mateo	Schoolhouse Statio	87	335
Ah	25	m	c	CHIN	Trinity	Lewiston Pct	92	214
Ah	24	m	c	CHIN	Shasta	American Ranch P O	89	499
Ah	24	m	c	CHIN	Nevada	Nevada Twp	75	320
Ah	24	m	c	CHIN	Plumas	Quartz Twp	77	43
Ah	24	m	c	CHIN	Placer	Newcastle Twp	76	477
Ah	24	m	c	CHIN	Plumas	Goodwin Twp	77	5
Ah	24	m	c	CHIN	San Francisco	San Francisco P O	80	511
Ah	23	m	c	CHIN	San Francisco	6-Wd San Francisco	81	39
Ah	23	m	c	CHIN	San Francisco	San Francisco P O	80	489
Ah	22	m	c	CHIN	San Francisco	6-Wd San Francisco	81	66
Ah	22	m	c	CHIN	Placer	Auburn P O	76	364
Ah	22	m	c	CHIN	Placer	Roseville P O	76	350
Ah	21	m	c	CHIN	Shasta	French Gulch P O	89	470
Ah	21	f	c	CHIN	San Francisco	6-Wd San Francisco	81	67
Ah	21	m	c	CHIN	Placer	Bath P O	76	444
Ah	21	f	c	CHIN	San Francisco	San Francisco P O	80	434
Ah	20	m	c	CHIN	San Mateo	San Mateo P O	87	357
Ah	20	m	c	CHIN	Marin	San Rafael Twp	74	38
						Series M593		
Ah	19	m	c	CHIN	Placer	Clipper Gap P O	76	393
Ah	19	m	c	CHIN	San Francisco	8-Wd San Francisco	82	310
Ah	19	m	c	CHIN	Trinity	Junction City Pct	92	208
Ah	19	m	c	CHIN	Trinity	Douglas	92	234
Ah	18	m	c	CHIN	Shasta	French Gulch P O	89	465
Ah	18	m	c	CHIN	San Francisco	6-Wd San Francisco	81	42
Ah	18	m	c	CHIN	Amador	Jackson P O	69	331
Ah	18	m	c	CHIN	El Dorado	Salmon Falls Twp	72	130
Ah	17	m	c	CHIN	San Francisco	1-Wd San Francisco	79	55
Ah	17	m	c	CHIN	San Francisco	1-Wd San Francisco	79	60
Ah	17	m	c	CHIN	San Francisco	3-Wd San Francisco	79	329
Ah	17	m	c	CHIN	Calaveras	San Andreas P O	70	155
Ah	16	m	c	CHIN	Sacramento	2-Wd Sacramento	77	234
Ah	15	m	c	CHIN	Trinity	Douglas	92	235
Ah	14	m	c	CHIN	Nevada	Nevada Twp	75	292
Ah	14	m	c	CHIN	Placer	Auburn P O	76	382
Ah	12	m	c	CHIN	San Francisco	2-Wd San Francisco	79	262
Ah	12	m	c	CHIN	San Francisco	2-Wd San Francisco	79	218
Chew	20	m	c	CHIN	Shasta	American Ranch P O	89	500
Choy	22	m	c	CHIN	Sierra	Eureka Twp	89	527
Chu	25	m	c	CHIN	Placer	Newcastle Twp	76	477
King	50	m	c	CHIN	Del Norte	Happy Camp Twp	71	468
Kou	28	m	c	CHIN	Sierra	Eureka Twp	89	527
Kun	26	m	c	CHIN	Tehama	Tehama Twp	92	188
Sing	17	m	c	CHIN	San Mateo	Schoolhouse Statio	87	335
Yan	21	m	c	CHIN	Plumas	Goodwin Twp	77	4
You	35	m	c	CHIN	Tehama	Tehama Twp	92	188
You	25	m	c	CHIN	Placer	Newcastle Twp	76	477
Yow	21	m	c	CHIN	San Francisco	6-Wd San Francisco	81	57
HIMBER								
Chs	45	m	w	VT	Merced	Snelling P O	74	254
HIMBLE								
Christian	41	m	w	DENM	Contra Costa	Martinez P O	71	424
HIME								
Ah	50	m	c	CHIN	Trinity	Lewiston Pct	92	211
Ah	39	m	c	CHIN	Nevada	Meadow Lake Twp	75	257
Ah	39	m	c	CHIN	Butte	Mountain Spring Tw	70	90
Ah	30	m	c	CHIN	Sonoma	Sonoma Twp	91	443
Ah	20	m	c	CHIN	Trinity	North Fork Twp	92	219
Ah	17	m	c	CHIN	Merced	Snelling P O	74	278
HIMENO								
Juan	30	m	w	CHIL	Los Angeles	San Jose Twp	73	618
HIMES								
James	43	m	w	MA	Santa Barbara	Santa Barbara P O	87	455
James	18	m	w	IA	Santa Cruz	Soquel Twp	89	445
John	38	m	w	OH	Nevada	Rough & Ready Twp	75	335
Ruth	13	f	w	MO	Santa Cruz	Soquel Twp	89	439
Wm H	28	m	w	IL	Napa	Yountville Twp	75	82
HIMETONBURG								
Micheal	21	m	w	WURT	San Francisco	7-Wd San Francisco	81	176
HIMMELMAN								
Daniel	30	m	w	PRUS	San Francisco	San Francisco P O	85	768
HIMMELMANN								
Jacob	63	m	w	PRUS	San Francisco	San Francisco P O	83	20
HIMMINGER								
Benj K	42	m	w	PA	Yolo	Buckeye Twp	93	407
HIMMURLY								
Ellen	39	f	w	IREL	Sutter	Butte Twp	92	102
HIMP								
Jacob	33	m	w	PRUS	Tehama	Tehama Twp	92	186
HIN								
---	40	m	c	CHIN	Siskiyou	Yreka Twp	89	668
---	25	m	c	CHIN	Shasta	Shasta P O	89	454
Ah	65	m	c	CHIN	Placer	Auburn P O	76	362
Ah	61	m	c	CHIN	Amador	Drytown P O	69	420
Ah	60	m	c	CHIN	Placer	Roseville P O	76	348
Ah	50	m	c	CHIN	Nevada	Nevada Twp	75	313
Ah	50	m	c	CHIN	Amador	Ione City P O	69	361
Ah	50	m	c	CHIN	Amador	Fiddletown P O	69	428
Ah	49	m	c	CHIN	Tuolumne	Chinese Camp P O	93	377
Ah	49	m	c	CHIN	Tuolumne	Chinese Camp P O	93	377
Ah	49	m	c	CHIN	San Francisco	San Francisco P O	80	522
Ah	47	m	c	CHIN	Placer	Auburn P O	76	371
Ah	47	m	c	CHIN	Amador	Fiddletown P O	69	427
Ah	46	m	c	CHIN	Calaveras	Copperopolis P O	70	259
Ah	46	m	c	CHIN	San Francisco	San Francisco P O	80	514
Ah	45	m	c	CHIN	San Francisco	San Francisco P O	80	517
Ah	44	m	c	CHIN	Tuolumne	Chinese Camp P O	93	364
Ah	43	m	c	CHIN	Amador	Jackson P O	69	328
Ah	41	m	c	CHIN	San Francisco	San Francisco P O	80	509
Ah	40	m	c	CHIN	Sierra	Sears Twp	89	553
Ah	40	m	c	CHIN	Mariposa	Mariposa P O	74	99
Ah	40	m	c	CHIN	Placer	Blue Canyon P O	76	419
Ah	40	m	c	CHIN	San Francisco	San Francisco P O	80	450
Ah	40	m	c	CHIN	San Francisco	San Francisco P O	80	454
Ah	40	m	c	CHIN	San Francisco	San Francisco P O	80	523
Ah	4	m	c	CA	San Francisco	San Francisco P O	80	453
Ah	39	m	c	CHIN	San Francisco	San Francisco P O	80	442
Ah	38	m	c	CHIN	San Francisco	San Francisco P O	80	435
Ah	38	m	c	CHIN	Calaveras	San Andreas P O	70	204
Ah	38	m	c	CHIN	Solano	Suisun Twp	90	105
Ah	38	m	c	CHIN	Amador	Drytown P O	69	423
Ah	37	m	c	CHIN	San Joaquin	1-Wd Stockton	86	144
Ah	37	m	c	CHIN	Nevada	Grass Valley Twp	75	217
Ah	36	m	c	CHIN	Stanislaus	Branch Twp	92	9
Ah	36	m	c	CHIN	San Francisco	San Francisco P O	80	449
Ah	36	m	c	CHIN	San Francisco	San Francisco P O	80	513

© 2001 by Heritage Quest. All rights reserved.

Name	Age	S	R	B-PL	County	Locale	Roll	Pg
Ah	36	m	c	CHIN	San Francisco	San Francisco P O	80	463
Ah	35	m	c	CHIN	Placer	Colfax P O	76	388
Ah	35	m	c	CHIN	Amador	Fiddletown P O	69	428
Ah	35	m	c	CHIN	San Francisco	6-Wd San Francisco	81	54
Ah	35	m	c	CHIN	San Francisco	San Francisco P O	80	499
Ah	35	m	c	CHIN	Sacramento	Georgianna Twp	77	126
Ah	35	m	c	CHIN	Amador	Ione City P O	69	355
Ah	35	m	c	CHIN	Amador	Drytown P O	69	420
Ah	35	m	c	CHIN	Amador	Drytown P O	69	422
Ah	34	m	c	CHIN	San Francisco	1-Wd San Francisco	79	87
Ah	34	m	c	CHIN	Placer	Dutch Flat P O	76	410
Ah	34	m	c	CHIN	El Dorado	Cosumnes Twp	72	18
Ah	33	m	c	CHIN	San Francisco	1-Wd San Francisco	79	87
Ah	33	m	c	CHIN	Amador	Sutter Crk P O	69	413
Ah	32	m	c	CHIN	Sacramento	Georgianna Twp	77	125
Ah	32	m	c	CHIN	Sacramento	1-Wd Sacramento	77	198
Ah	31	m	c	CHIN	Plumas	Rich Bar Twp	77	45
Ah	31	m	c	CHIN	Solano	Suisun Twp	90	107
Ah	31	m	c	CHIN	San Mateo	Schoolhouse Statio	87	332
Ah	31	m	c	CHIN	San Francisco	San Francisco P O	80	499
Ah	31	m	c	CHIN	Amador	Sutter Crk P O	69	401
Ah	30	m	c	CHIN	Sonoma	Salt Point	91	393
Ah	30	m	c	CHIN	San Francisco	6-Wd San Francisco	81	40
Ah	30	m	c	CHIN	Placer	Lincoln P O	76	483
Ah	30	m	c	CHIN	Placer	Gold Run Twp	76	398
Ah	30	m	c	CHIN	Placer	Emigrant Gap P O	76	416
Ah	30	m	c	CHIN	Placer	Dutch Flat P O	76	408
Ah	30	m	c	CHIN	Sacramento	Sutter Twp	77	382
Ah	29	m	c	CHIN	Solano	Vallejo	90	208
Ah	29	m	c	CHIN	San Francisco	San Francisco P O	80	496
Ah	29	f	c	CHIN	San Francisco	San Francisco P O	80	450
Ah	29	m	c	CHIN	Butte	Hamilton Twp	70	67
Ah	29	m	c	CHIN	Calaveras	San Andreas P O	70	169
Ah	29	m	c	CHIN	Amador	Jackson P O	69	336
Ah	29	m	c	CHIN	Amador	Amador City P O	69	395
Ah	28	m	c	CHIN	Placer	Clipper Gap P O	76	393
Ah	27	m	c	CHIN	Plumas	Indian Twp	77	16
Ah	27	m	c	CHIN	Mariposa	Maxwell Crk P O	74	142
Ah	27	m	c	CHIN	Solano	Suisun Twp	90	104
Ah	27	m	c	CHIN	San Mateo	Half Moon Bay P O	87	395
Ah	27	m	c	CHIN	Amador	Ione City P O	69	363
Ah	27	m	c	CHIN	Amador	Sutter Crk P O	69	413
Ah	26	m	c	CHIN	Tuolumne	Chinese Camp P O	93	377
Ah	26	m	c	CHIN	San Joaquin	1-Wd Stockton	86	145
Ah	26	f	c	CHIN	San Francisco	San Francisco P O	80	444
Ah	26	f	c	CHIN	San Francisco	San Francisco P O	80	431
Ah	26	m	c	CHIN	San Mateo	Schoolhouse Statio	87	334
Ah	26	m	c	CHIN	El Dorado	Diamond Springs Tw	72	35
Ah	25	m	c	CHIN	Tuolumne	Chinese Camp P O	93	363
Ah	25	f	c	CHIN	Tuolumne	Columbia P O	93	341
Ah	25	m	c	CHIN	Placer	Clipper Gap P O	76	392
Ah	25	m	c	CHIN	Napa	Napa Twp	75	71
Ah	25	m	c	CHIN	Plumas	Washington Twp	77	58
Ah	23	m	c	CHIN	San Joaquin	1-Wd Stockton	86	149
Ah	23	m	c	CHIN	Butte	Hamilton Twp	70	73
Ah	22	m	c	CHIN	San Francisco	San Francisco P O	80	510
Ah	21	m	c	CHIN	Placer	Colfax P O	76	388
Ah	21	m	c	CHIN	San Francisco	San Francisco P O	80	510
Ah	20	m	c	CHIN	Sierra	Eureka Twp	89	526
Ah	20	m	c	CHIN	San Francisco	6-Wd San Francisco	81	63
Ah	20	m	c	CHIN	Placer	Clipper Gap P O	76	393
Ah	20	m	c	CHIN	San Francisco	3-Wd San Francisco	79	304
Ah	20	f	c	CHIN	San Francisco	San Francisco P O	80	450
Ah	20	m	c	CHIN	San Francisco	6-Wd San Francisco	81	50
Ah	20	m	c	CHIN	Sacramento	Georgianna Twp	77	125
Ah	19	f	c	CHIN	San Francisco	San Francisco P O	80	490
Ah	19	m	c	CHIN	San Francisco	San Francisco P O	80	491
Ah	19	f	c	CHIN	San Francisco	San Francisco P O	80	449
Ah	19	m	c	CHIN	Monterey	Castroville Twp	74	338
Ah	19	m	c	CHIN	Alameda	Washington Twp	68	299
Ah	18	m	c	CHIN	San Francisco	San Francisco P O	85	791
Ah	16	m	c	CHIN	Tuolumne	Columbia P O	93	349
Ah	16	m	c	CHIN	San Francisco	San Francisco P O	80	412
Ah	14	m	c	CHIN	San Francisco	8-Wd San Francisco	82	371
Ah	13	m	c	CHIN	San Francisco	San Francisco P O	80	444
Ah	12	m	c	CHIN	San Francisco	6-Wd San Francisco	81	50
Ah	11	m	c	CHIN	Plumas	Seneca Twp	77	51
Ah	10	m	c	CHIN	San Francisco	6-Wd San Francisco	81	60
Aqh	21	f	c	CHIN	San Francisco	San Francisco P O	80	439
Bin	19	m	c	CHIN	San Mateo	Schoolhouse Statio	87	336
Fin	27	m	c	CHIN	San Mateo	Schoolhouse Statio	87	339
Fung	19	m	c	CHIN	San Francisco	3-Wd San Francisco	79	329
Gick	60	m	c	CHIN	Calaveras	San Andreas P O	70	171
Gin	18	m	c	CHIN	San Francisco	San Francisco P O	85	805
Gu	27	m	c	CHIN	San Joaquin	Liberty Twp	86	97
Leet	40	m	c	CHIN	San Francisco	6-Wd San Francisco	81	67
Lu	50	m	c	CHIN	El Dorado	Mud Springs Twp	72	76
Lum	38	m	c	CHIN	Marin	San Rafael Twp	74	38
Lung	30	m	c	CHIN	Calaveras	San Andreas P O	70	211
Pan	53	f	c	CHIN	Calaveras	San Andreas P O	70	161
Sai	29	m	c	CHIN	Tuolumne	Columbia P O	93	356
See	20	m	c	CHIN	San Francisco	3-Wd San Francisco	79	306
Shing	41	m	c	CHIN	Amador	Jackson P O	69	332
Shon	35	m	c	CHIN	Calaveras	San Andreas P O	70	205
Sing	45	m	c	CHIN	San Francisco	11-Wd San Francisc	84	477
Sing	18	m	c	CHIN	San Francisco	2-Wd San Francisco	79	158
Tin	63	m	c	CHIN	Calaveras	San Andreas P O	70	161

Name	Age	S	R	B-PL	County	Locale	Roll	Pg
Too	15	m	c	CHIN	Nevada	Bridgeport Twp	75	111
Toy	27	f	c	CHIN	Yuba	Marysville	93	626
Yan	28	m	c	CHIN	Plumas	Plumas Twp	77	33
Yip	55	m	c	CHIN	Shasta	American Ranch P O	89	499
Yo	28	f	c	CHIN	Mariposa	Mariposa P O	74	103
HINA								
Ah	30	m	c	CHIN	San Mateo	Schoolhouse Statio	87	335
HINCH								
Charles	50	m	w	PRUS	Stanislaus	Empire Twp	92	35
John H	31	m	w	HANO	San Francisco	2-Wd San Francisco	79	169
John W	22	m	w	MA	Sacramento	2-Wd Sacramento	77	224
Joseph	45	m	w	CANA	Humboldt	Bucksport Twp	72	243
Thomas	32	m	w	CANA	Humboldt	Bucksport Twp	72	243
William	28	m	w	HAMB	San Francisco	6-Wd San Francisco	81	70
HINCHCLIFFE								
William	39	m	w	ENGL	San Francisco	6-Wd San Francisco	81	126
HINCHERS								
Kate	15	f	w	MA	San Francisco	San Francisco P O	83	405
HINCHEY								
James	29	m	w	IREL	San Francisco	San Francisco P O	85	758
Joseph	21	m	w	ENGL	San Francisco	2-Wd San Francisco	79	283
HINCHIN								
Herman	22	m	w	BAVA	Sacramento	1-Wd Sacramento	77	174
HINCHMAN								
Aug	46	m	w	NY	San Francisco	8-Wd San Francisco	82	334
August	50	m	w	PRUS	Amador	Ione City P O	69	355
C H	54	m	w	NY	San Francisco	6-Wd San Francisco	81	139
Chas	31	m	w	ENGL	San Francisco	8-Wd San Francisco	82	292
Chas	16	m	w	PA	Alameda	Brooklyn	68	23
Henri	30	f	w	NJ	Alameda	Brooklyn	68	24
HINCK								
Henry	28	m	w	HANO	San Francisco	San Francisco P O	83	119
HINCKEL								
Wm	18	m	w	CA	San Francisco	San Francisco P O	83	49
HINCKEY								
George	45	m	w	OH	Solano	Vacaville Twp	90	132
HINCKLEY								
Alice	23	f	w	IA	Napa	Napa	75	49
Anne	8	f	w	ME	Siskiyou	Callahan P O	89	630
Chas	30	m	w	DENM	Butte	Ophir Twp	70	120
Edward	40	m	w	NY	San Francisco	San Francisco P O	83	258
George	27	m	w	TN	Tulare	Visalia Twp	92	282
George W	46	m	w	OH	Mendocino	Cuffeys Cove Twp	74	168
George W	45	m	w	OH	Yolo	Buckeye Twp	93	411
Henry	24	m	w	CA	San Francisco	San Francisco P O	83	314
James P	47	m	w	ME	Mendocino	Point Arena Twp	74	206
Lilian G	12	f	w	ME	San Francisco	8-Wd San Francisco	82	449
Luther	35	m	w	MA	Alameda	Washington Twp	68	297
Margaret	33	f	w	IREL	Solano	Suisun Twp	90	112
Mark	58	m	w	ME	San Francisco	11-Wd San Francisc	84	648
Nehemiah	33	m	w	MA	San Francisco	San Francisco P O	83	19
Oliver	40	m	w	ME	San Francisco	San Francisco P O	83	117
Oscar	31	m	w	MA	Monterey	San Juan Twp	74	389
Roger G	65	m	w	NY	Santa Cruz	Soquel Twp	89	442
Sallie	31	f	w	MA	San Francisco	3-Wd San Francisco	79	318
Saml	35	m	w	OH	Stanislaus	Empire Twp	92	27
Stephen	36	m	w	ME	San Francisco	San Francisco P O	83	210
Thos	40	m	w	NY	San Francisco	San Francisco P O	83	282
Timothy	49	m	w	MA	Amador	Jackson P O	69	328
HINCKLY								
Akors	32	m	w	NY	San Francisco	6-Wd San Francisco	81	96
Frank	34	m	w	NY	San Francisco	San Francisco P O	80	414
Lydia	29	f	w	IN	Butte	Chico Twp	70	13
Walter	36	m	w	MA	San Francisco	San Francisco P O	80	388
HINCLY								
William	40	m	w	IREL	San Francisco	11-Wd San Francisc	84	639
HINCOCK								
Benj	39	m	w	AR	Fresno	Millerton P O	72	181
HIND								
James	31	m	w	IL	Los Angeles	San Gabriel Twp	73	596
Mina	6	f	w	CA	Stanislaus	Branch Twp	92	5
HINDE								
Chas	35	m	w	IREL	San Francisco	1-Wd San Francisco	79	3
Henry	26	m	w	NY	San Francisco	7-Wd San Francisco	81	207
HINDERS								
Henry	33	m	w	BAVA	San Francisco	8-Wd San Francisco	82	439
HINDLEY								
H	48	m	w	ENGL	Humboldt	Eel Rvr Twp	72	249
HINDLY								
George	24	m	w	CANA	Trinity	Weaverville Pct	92	230
HINDMAN								
Chs	28	m	w	VT	San Francisco	2-Wd San Francisco	79	212
Eliphlett	45	m	w	WI	Stanislaus	Branch Twp	92	4
Robt	60	m	w	IREL	Sonoma	Santa Rosa	91	409
HINDRBODE								
Patrick	35	m	w	IREL	San Francisco	11-Wd San Francisc	84	490
HINDS								
Alfred	23	m	w	NY	San Joaquin	Tulare Twp	86	254
Alfred J	25	m	w	ENGL	Santa Cruz	Santa Cruz	89	420
Ambrose	42	m	w	MA	San Francisco	San Francisco P O	80	387
Archibald	32	m	w	AR	Tulare	Farmersville Twp	92	243
David	56	m	w	NY	Santa Cruz	Santa Cruz	89	418
Edward	24	m	w	NJ	Santa Clara	2-Wd San Jose	88	324
Eliza	30	f	w	IREL	San Francisco	San Francisco P O	85	790
F S	21	m	w	KY	San Joaquin	1-Wd Stockton	86	135
H B	38	m	w	TN	Sonoma	Bodega Twp	91	258
H M	56	m	w	KY	Nevada	Nevada Twp	75	272

© 2001 by Heritage Quest. All rights reserved.

California 1870 Census

Name	Age	S	R	B-PL	County	Locale	Series M593 Roll	Pg
James	39	m	w	ASEA	Colusa	Monroe Twp	71	318
James	28	m	w	TN	San Diego	San Diego	78	483
John	45	m	w	ME	San Francisco	11-Wd San Francisc	84	509
John J	35	m	w	KY	Los Angeles	El Monte Twp	73	457
John W	31	m	w	TN	Nevada	Nevada Twp	75	308
Joseph	34	m	w	NY	San Joaquin	Tulare Twp	86	254
Joseph	27	m	w	IN	San Joaquin	Liberty Twp	86	86
Maggie	22	f	w	TN	Nevada	Nevada Twp	75	276
Maria	64	f	w	CT	Solano	Vallejo	90	194
Marietta	51	f	w	NY	Santa Cruz	Santa Cruz	89	433
Patrick	45	m	w	IREL	San Francisco	1-Wd San Francisco	79	38
Sumner	40	m	w	ME	San Francisco	2-Wd San Francisco	79	140
Thomas	40	m	w	WALE	San Mateo	Belmont P O	87	373
Thomas W	52	m	w	ENGL	Santa Cruz	Santa Cruz	89	419
Wiley	40	m	w	MO	Tulare	Farmersville Twp	92	250
William	39	m	w	VT	Amador	Drytown P O	69	422
William	28	m	w	NC	Trinity	North Fork Twp	92	217
William	28	m	w	IREL	San Francisco	7-Wd San Francisco	81	213
William J	21	m	w	IA	Santa Cruz	Santa Cruz	89	420
HINDY								
Mary	90	f	w	IREL	San Francisco	8-Wd San Francisco	82	366
HINE								
Ah	38	m	c	CHIN	Yolo	Putah Twp	93	510
Ah	36	m	c	CHIN	Nevada	Bridgeport Twp	75	110
Ah	31	m	c	CHIN	San Francisco	3-Wd San Francisco	79	298
Ah	30	m	c	CHIN	Nevada	Meadow Lake Twp	75	257
Ah	30	m	c	CHIN	Nevada	Meadow Lake Twp	75	255
Ah	28	m	c	CHIN	Santa Clara	1-Wd San Jose	88	270
Ah	25	m	c	CHIN	Placer	Rocklin Twp	76	464
Ah	18	m	c	CHIN	San Francisco	11-Wd San Francisc	84	448
Ah	15	m	c	CHIN	San Francisco	11-Wd San Francisc	84	435
Benjamin	31	m	w	NY	Napa	Yountville Twp	75	82
Bertha	20	f	w	SHOL	Mendocino	Ukiah Twp	74	242
Frank E	21	m	w	ME	San Diego	Milquaty Dist	78	478
Henry	26	m	w	PA	San Francisco	2-Wd San Francisco	79	191
Jacob	40	m	w	PRUS	San Francisco	San Francisco P O	83	153
John	30	m	w	MO	Yolo	Cache Crk Twp	93	438
John	25	m	w	BAVA	Sutter	Butte Twp	92	101
John	23	m	w	NY	San Francisco	San Francisco P O	83	293
Nelson	52	m	w	NY	San Francisco	San Francisco P O	83	362
William	16	m	w	CA	San Francisco	3-Wd San Francisco	79	312
HINEBAUGH								
Henry	42	m	w	PA	Sonoma	Vallejo Twp	91	457
HINEBOLT								
Joseph	44	m	w	NY	Sacramento	Cosumnes Twp	77	90
HINES								
Anne	24	f	w	IREL	San Francisco	San Francisco P O	83	277
Bertha	38	f	w	PRUS	San Francisco	2-Wd San Francisco	79	175
Danl L	35	m	w	MD	Napa	Napa Twp	75	64
Debusa	41	m	i	MEXI	Inyo	Cerro Gordo Twp	73	323
Edward	39	m	w	AR	Tulare	Venice Twp	92	273
Ellen	44	f	w	IREL	San Francisco	San Francisco P O	83	273
Frank	22	m	w	VT	San Francisco	1-Wd San Francisco	79	69
Fred	34	m	w	MI	Lassen	Susanville Twp	73	439
George	50	m	w	MD	San Francisco	6-Wd San Francisco	81	70
George	36	m	w	IN	Tehama	Merrill	92	197
H	25	m	w	ENGL	Alameda	Oakland	68	191
Henry	7	m	w	CA	Marin	San Rafael Twp	74	29
Henry	38	m	w	CANA	Sutter	Sutter Twp	92	116
Henry	24	m	w	PRUS	San Francisco	6-Wd San Francisco	81	70
Herman	40	m	w	BAVA	San Francisco	San Francisco P O	83	225
Jacob	39	m	w	HESS	San Francisco	2-Wd San Francisco	79	155
James	37	m	w	IREL	Sacramento	Natomas Twp	77	168
James	22	m	w	WI	San Francisco	San Francisco P O	85	812
James	11	m	w	CA	Marin	San Rafael Twp	74	29
John	37	m	w	IREL	San Francisco	11-Wd San Francisc	84	542
John	34	m	w	IREL	Solano	Vacaville Twp	90	125
John	25	m	w	NY	San Francisco	San Francisco P O	83	360
John	23	m	w	AR	Plumas	Quartz Twp	77	42
John	12	m	w	MA	Marin	San Rafael Twp	74	29
Joseph	9	m	w	CA	Marin	San Rafael Twp	74	29
Joseph W	43	m	w	NY	Santa Clara	Santa Clara Twp	88	136
Josephine	18	f	w	NY	Alameda	Washington Twp	68	294
Lawrence	42	m	w	WURT	Yolo	Putah Twp	93	525
M E	42	m	w	NY	Alameda	Oakland	68	255
M J	38	m	w	IREL	Solano	Benicia	90	6
Mary	55	f	w	IREL	San Joaquin	2-Wd Stockton	86	169
Mike	30	m	w	IREL	Solano	Vallejo	90	215
Nellie	15	f	w	MA	San Francisco	11-Wd San Francisc	84	487
P J	28	m	w	IREL	Solano	Benicia	90	1
Patrick	27	m	w	IREL	Placer	Auburn P O	76	366
Patrick	25	m	w	IREL	San Francisco	7-Wd San Francisco	81	194
Patrick	24	m	w	IREL	Solano	Vacaville Twp	90	125
Peter	33	m	w	FRAN	Sutter	Sutter Twp	92	117
Rachael	20	f	w	PRUS	San Francisco	San Francisco P O	83	390
Robert	30	m	w	MO	Yolo	Cache Crk Twp	93	454
Sylvester B	30	m	w	AR	Plumas	Quartz Twp	77	42
Theodore	4	m	w	CA	Yolo	Putah Twp	93	525
Thomas	33	m	w	IN	Monterey	Alisal Twp	74	292
Thomas	21	m	w	IREL	Santa Clara	Gilroy Twp	88	83
Thomas	21	m	w	NY	Marin	Sausalito Twp	74	72
Timothy	25	m	w	IREL	Solano	Vallejo	90	215
William	42	m	w	NY	Calaveras	San Andreas P O	70	191
William	38	m	w	PRUS	San Francisco	2-Wd San Francisco	79	263
William	28	m	w	IA	Solano	Silveyville Twp	90	79
HING								
---	21	m	c	CHIN	San Francisco	6-Wd San Francisco	81	51
Ah	60	m	c	CHIN	Mariposa	Mariposa P O	74	106
Ah	6	m	c	CA	San Francisco	San Francisco P O	80	452
Ah	56	m	c	CHIN	San Francisco	San Francisco P O	80	433
Ah	54	m	c	CHIN	Tuolumne	Chinese Camp P O	93	369
Ah	51	m	c	CHIN	Calaveras	San Andreas P O	70	169
Ah	50	f	c	CHIN	San Francisco	San Francisco P O	80	431
Ah	50	f	c	CHIN	San Francisco	San Francisco P O	80	441
Ah	50	m	c	CHIN	Mariposa	Mariposa P O	74	93
Ah	50	m	c	CHIN	Mariposa	Mariposa P O	74	126
Ah	50	m	c	CHIN	Tuolumne	Chinese Camp P O	93	363
Ah	49	m	c	CHIN	Nevada	Nevada Twp	75	298
Ah	48	m	c	CHIN	San Francisco	San Francisco P O	80	437
Ah	48	m	c	CHIN	Mariposa	Mariposa P O	74	106
Ah	46	m	c	CHIN	El Dorado	Mud Springs Twp	72	76
Ah	45	m	c	CHIN	San Francisco	6-Wd San Francisco	81	54
Ah	45	m	c	CHIN	El Dorado	Mud Springs Twp	72	89
Ah	45	m	c	CHIN	El Dorado	Mud Springs Twp	72	74
Ah	45	m	c	CHIN	Mariposa	Mariposa P O	74	92
Ah	45	m	c	CHIN	Butte	Chico Twp	70	28
Ah	44	m	c	CHIN	Plumas	Rich Bar Twp	77	45
Ah	44	m	c	CHIN	Mariposa	Mariposa P O	74	106
Ah	42	m	c	CHIN	San Francisco	San Francisco P O	80	525
Ah	42	m	c	CHIN	Humboldt	Eureka Twp	72	280
Ah	42	m	c	CHIN	San Francisco	San Francisco P O	80	440
Ah	42	m	c	CHIN	San Francisco	San Francisco P O	80	447
Ah	42	m	c	CHIN	San Francisco	San Francisco P O	80	445
Ah	41	m	c	CHIN	San Francisco	San Francisco P O	80	527
Ah	41	m	c	CHIN	Amador	Ione City P O	69	361
Ah	41	m	c	CHIN	Mariposa	Mariposa P O	74	133
Ah	41	m	c	CHIN	Mariposa	Mariposa P O	74	107
Ah	41	m	c	CHIN	El Dorado	Placerville	72	114
Ah	40	m	c	CHIN	San Francisco	San Francisco P O	80	525
Ah	40	m	c	CHIN	San Francisco	San Francisco P O	80	529
Ah	40	m	c	CHIN	Amador	Jackson P O	69	331
Ah	40	m	c	CHIN	Nevada	Eureka Twp	75	140
Ah	40	m	c	CHIN	Nevada	Nevada Twp	75	299
Ah	40	m	c	CHIN	Nevada	Grass Valley Twp	75	205
Ah	40	m	c	CHIN	Sacramento	Georgianna Twp	77	132
Ah	40	m	c	CHIN	San Francisco	San Francisco P O	80	443
Ah	40	f	c	CHIN	San Francisco	San Francisco P O	80	440
Ah	40	m	c	CHIN	San Francisco	San Francisco P O	80	448
Ah	40	m	c	CHIN	San Francisco	San Francisco P O	80	444
Ah	40	m	c	CHIN	San Francisco	San Francisco P O	80	447
Ah	40	m	c	CHIN	El Dorado	Placerville Twp	72	98
Ah	40	m	c	CHIN	Tuolumne	Columbia P O	93	353
Ah	4	m	c	CA	San Francisco	San Francisco P O	80	448
Ah	4	f	c	CA	San Francisco	San Francisco P O	80	450
Ah	39	m	c	CHIN	San Francisco	6-Wd San Francisco	81	70
Ah	39	m	c	CHIN	San Francisco	San Francisco P O	80	453
Ah	39	m	c	CHIN	San Francisco	San Francisco P O	80	510
Ah	39	m	c	CHIN	Sierra	Downieville Twp	89	521
Ah	39	m	c	CHIN	El Dorado	Mud Springs Twp	72	74
Ah	39	m	c	CHIN	San Francisco	San Francisco P O	80	447
Ah	39	m	c	CHIN	Tuolumne	Sonora P O	93	311
Ah	38	m	c	CHIN	San Francisco	San Francisco P O	80	452
Ah	38	m	c	CHIN	Amador	Lancha Plana P O	69	369
Ah	38	m	c	CHIN	Mariposa	Mariposa P O	74	130
Ah	38	m	c	CHIN	Tuolumne	Chinese Camp P O	93	390
Ah	38	m	c	CHIN	San Francisco	San Francisco P O	80	503
Ah	37	f	c	CHIN	San Francisco	San Francisco P O	80	521
Ah	37	m	c	CHIN	El Dorado	White Oak Twp	72	136
Ah	37	m	c	CHIN	San Francisco	San Francisco P O	80	444
Ah	37	m	c	CHIN	San Francisco	San Francisco P O	80	447
Ah	37	m	c	CHIN	Nevada	Meadow Lake Twp	75	257
Ah	37	m	c	CHIN	Merced	Snelling P O	74	278
Ah	37	m	c	CHIN	Mariposa	Mariposa P O	74	106
Ah	37	m	c	CHIN	Mariposa	Mariposa P O	74	127
Ah	37	m	c	CHIN	San Joaquin	Castoria Twp	86	12
Ah	36	m	c	CHIN	San Francisco	San Francisco P O	80	503
Ah	36	m	c	CHIN	San Francisco	San Francisco P O	80	522
Ah	36	m	c	CHIN	San Francisco	San Francisco P O	80	435
Ah	36	m	c	CHIN	San Francisco	San Francisco P O	80	444
Ah	36	m	c	CHIN	San Francisco	San Francisco P O	80	436
Ah	36	m	c	CHIN	San Francisco	San Francisco P O	80	449
Ah	36	m	c	CHIN	San Francisco	San Francisco P O	80	451
Ah	36	m	c	CHIN	San Francisco	San Francisco P O	80	445
Ah	36	m	c	CHIN	San Francisco	San Francisco P O	80	446
Ah	36	m	c	CHIN	Santa Cruz	Santa Cruz	89	434
Ah	36	m	c	CHIN	Tuolumne	Sonora P O	93	312
Ah	36	m	c	CHIN	San Francisco	San Francisco P O	80	501
Ah	35	m	c	CHIN	San Francisco	San Francisco P O	80	512
Ah	35	m	c	CHIN	San Francisco	San Francisco P O	80	431
Ah	35	m	c	CHIN	San Francisco	San Francisco P O	80	452
Ah	35	m	c	CHIN	Sacramento	3-Wd Sacramento	77	316
Ah	35	m	c	CHIN	Placer	Alta P O	76	411
Ah	35	m	c	CHIN	Placer	Auburn P O	76	373
Ah	35	m	c	CHIN	Trinity	Weaverville Pct	92	231
Ah	35	m	c	CHIN	San Francisco	6-Wd San Francisco	81	38
Ah	34	m	c	CHIN	San Francisco	San Francisco P O	80	518
Ah	34	m	c	CHIN	Amador	Drytown P O	69	419
Ah	34	m	c	CHIN	Nevada	Nevada Twp	75	312
Ah	34	m	c	CHIN	San Francisco	San Francisco P O	80	436
Ah	34	m	c	CHIN	San Francisco	San Francisco P O	80	454
Ah	34	m	c	CHIN	San Francisco	San Francisco P O	80	443
Ah	34	m	c	CHIN	Tuolumne	Columbia P O	93	341
Ah	33	m	c	CHIN	San Francisco	San Francisco P O	80	509
Ah	33	m	c	CHIN	Plumas	Goodwin Twp	77	2

© 2001 by Heritage Quest. All rights reserved.

Name	Age	S	R	B-PL	County	Locale	Series M593 Roll	Pg
Ah	33	m	c	CHIN	Nevada	Nevada Twp	75	298
Ah	32	m	c	CHIN	Placer	Dutch Flat P O	76	414
Ah	32	m	c	CHIN	San Francisco	San Francisco P O	80	350
Ah	32	m	c	CHIN	San Francisco	San Francisco P O	80	439
Ah	32	m	c	CHIN	San Francisco	San Francisco P O	80	453
Ah	32	m	c	CHIN	Napa	Napa Twp	75	58
Ah	32	m	c	CHIN	Calaveras	San Andreas P O	70	172
Ah	32	m	c	CHIN	El Dorado	Cosumnes Twp	72	20
Ah	32	m	c	CHIN	Tuolumne	Columbia P O	93	341
Ah	32	m	c	CHIN	San Joaquin	1-Wd Stockton	86	144
Ah	32	m	c	CHIN	San Francisco	San Francisco P O	80	492
Ah	32	m	c	CHIN	San Francisco	San Francisco P O	80	509
Ah	31	m	c	CHIN	San Francisco	San Francisco P O	80	521
Ah	31	m	c	CHIN	San Francisco	San Francisco P O	80	523
Ah	31	m	c	CHIN	Amador	Ione City P O	69	362
Ah	31	m	c	CHIN	El Dorado	Greenwood Twp	72	50
Ah	31	m	c	CHIN	Yuba	Marysville	93	618
Ah	31	m	c	CHIN	Placer	Auburn P O	76	364
Ah	31	m	c	CHIN	Tuolumne	Columbia P O	93	352
Ah	31	m	c	CHIN	San Francisco	6-Wd San Francisco	81	37
Ah	30	m	c	CHIN	San Francisco	6-Wd San Francisco	81	119
Ah	30	m	c	CHIN	San Joaquin	Douglas Twp	86	45
Ah	30	m	c	CHIN	Amador	Fiddletown P O	69	428
Ah	30	m	c	CHIN	Amador	Drytown P O	69	419
Ah	30	m	c	CHIN	Yuba	Rose Bar Twp	93	656
Ah	30	f	c	CHIN	San Francisco	San Francisco P O	80	448
Ah	30	m	c	CHIN	Sacramento	Franklin Twp	77	114
Ah	30	m	c	CHIN	Placer	Blue Canyon P O	76	419
Ah	30	m	c	CHIN	Placer	Auburn P O	76	369
Ah	30	m	c	CHIN	Nevada	Meadow Lake Twp	75	254
Ah	30	m	c	CHIN	Merced	Snelling P O	74	279
Ah	30	m	c	CHIN	Butte	Chico Twp	70	18
Ah	30	m	c	CHIN	Calaveras	San Andreas P O	70	174
Ah	30	m	c	CHIN	Calaveras	San Andreas P O	70	199
Ah	30	m	c	CHIN	Trinity	Douglas	92	237
Ah	30	m	c	CHIN	San Francisco	San Francisco P O	85	748
Ah	3	m	c	CA	San Francisco	San Francisco P O	80	527
Ah	3	f	c	CA	San Francisco	San Francisco P O	80	530
Ah	3	f	c	CA	San Francisco	San Francisco P O	80	449
Ah	3	f	c	CA	San Francisco	San Francisco P O	80	448
Ah	29	f	c	CHIN	San Francisco	San Francisco P O	80	526
Ah	29	m	c	CHIN	San Francisco	San Francisco P O	80	514
Ah	29	m	c	CHIN	Placer	Blue Canyon P O	76	417
Ah	29	m	c	CHIN	Plumas	Indian Twp	77	19
Ah	29	m	c	CHIN	Nevada	Meadow Lake Twp	75	257
Ah	28	m	c	CHIN	Nevada	Nevada Twp	75	311
Ah	28	m	c	CHIN	Nevada	Washington Twp	75	342
Ah	28	m	c	CHIN	Trinity	Douglas	92	232
Ah	28	m	c	CHIN	Sacramento	3-Wd Sacramento	77	317
Ah	28	m	c	CHIN	Sacramento	Granite Twp	77	155
Ah	28	m	w	CHIN	Plumas	Indian Twp	77	19
Ah	28	m	c	CHIN	Placer	Auburn P O	76	381
Ah	28	m	c	CHIN	Sonoma	Sonoma Twp	91	449
Ah	28	m	c	CHIN	San Joaquin	1-Wd Stockton	86	145
Ah	28	m	c	CHIN	San Francisco	San Francisco P O	85	748
Ah	27	m	c	CHIN	San Francisco	San Francisco P O	80	455
Ah	27	m	c	CHIN	Butte	Chico Twp	70	53
Ah	27	m	c	CHIN	Butte	Chico Twp	70	52
Ah	27	m	c	CHIN	San Francisco	San Francisco P O	80	445
Ah	27	m	c	CHIN	Mariposa	Mariposa P O	74	121
Ah	27	m	c	CHIN	Calaveras	San Andreas P O	70	211
Ah	27	m	c	CHIN	San Joaquin	1-Wd Stockton	86	144
Ah	26	f	c	CHIN	San Francisco	San Francisco P O	80	530
Ah	26	m	c	CHIN	San Francisco	San Francisco P O	80	522
Ah	26	f	c	CHIN	San Francisco	San Francisco P O	80	433
Ah	26	f	c	CHIN	San Francisco	San Francisco P O	80	441
Ah	26	m	c	CHIN	San Francisco	San Francisco P O	80	445
Ah	26	f	c	CHIN	San Francisco	San Francisco P O	80	444
Ah	26	m	c	CHIN	Sacramento	4-Wd Sacramento	77	371
Ah	26	m	c	CHIN	Placer	Colfax P O	76	387
Ah	25	m	c	CHIN	San Francisco	11-Wd San Francisc	84	528
Ah	25	m	c	CHIN	Amador	Fiddletown P O	69	428
Ah	25	m	c	CHIN	Sacramento	3-Wd Sacramento	77	310
Ah	25	m	c	CHIN	Sacramento	3-Wd Sacramento	77	310
Ah	25	m	c	CHIN	San Diego	San Diego	78	500
Ah	25	m	c	CHIN	Yuba	Marysville	93	618
Ah	25	f	c	CHIN	San Francisco	San Francisco P O	80	448
Ah	25	m	c	CHIN	Trinity	Douglas	92	236
Ah	25	m	c	CHIN	San Joaquin	Castoria Twp	86	10
Ah	25	m	c	CHIN	San Francisco	11-Wd San Francisc	84	571
Ah	25	m	c	CHIN	San Francisco	6-Wd San Francisco	81	60
Ah	25	m	c	CHIN	San Francisco	San Francisco P O	83	71
Ah	24	m	c	CHIN	San Francisco	7-Wd San Francisco	81	234
Ah	24	f	c	CHIN	San Francisco	San Francisco P O	80	507
Ah	24	f	c	CHIN	San Francisco	San Francisco P O	80	508
Ah	24	m	c	CHIN	San Francisco	San Francisco P O	80	515
Ah	24	m	c	CHIN	San Francisco	San Francisco P O	80	527
Ah	24	m	c	CHIN	Sierra	Eureka Twp	89	525
Ah	24	m	c	CHIN	Butte	Chico Twp	70	51
Ah	24	m	c	CHIN	Butte	Chico Twp	70	53
Ah	24	f	c	CHIN	San Francisco	San Francisco P O	80	435
Ah	24	m	c	CHIN	Monterey	Castroville Twp	74	338
Ah	24	m	c	CHIN	Calaveras	San Andreas P O	70	172
Ah	24	m	c	CHIN	Tuolumne	Columbia P O	93	341
Ah	23	m	c	CHIN	El Dorado	Coloma Twp	72	8
Ah	23	m	c	CHIN	San Francisco	San Francisco P O	80	452
Ah	23	m	c	CHIN	Solano	Suisun Twp	90	105
Ah	22	m	c	CHIN	San Francisco	6-Wd San Francisco	81	49
Ah	22	m	c	CHIN	San Francisco	San Francisco P O	80	489
Ah	22	m	c	CHIN	Tehama	Red Bluff	92	184
Ah	22	m	c	CHIN	Butte	Kimshew Tpw	70	84
Ah	22	m	c	CHIN	Monterey	Castroville Twp	74	341
Ah	22	m	c	CHIN	San Francisco	2-Wd San Francisco	79	282
Ah	22	m	c	CHIN	Placer	Clipper Gap P O	76	393
Ah	22	m	c	CHIN	Placer	Colfax P O	76	386
Ah	22	m	c	CHIN	Mariposa	Maxwell Crk P O	74	147
Ah	22	m	c	CHIN	San Francisco	San Francisco P O	80	496
Ah	21	f	c	CHIN	San Francisco	6-Wd San Francisco	81	76
Ah	21	f	c	CHIN	San Francisco	San Francisco P O	80	527
Ah	21	f	c	CHIN	San Francisco	San Francisco P O	80	508
Ah	21	m	c	CHIN	Plumas	Goodwin Twp	77	3
Ah	21	f	c	CHIN	San Francisco	San Francisco P O	80	438
Ah	21	f	c	CHIN	San Francisco	San Francisco P O	80	451
Ah	21	m	c	CHIN	San Francisco	6-Wd San Francisco	81	63
Ah	21	m	c	CHIN	San Francisco	San Francisco P O	83	48
Ah	21	m	c	CHIN	San Francisco	San Francisco P O	83	62
Ah	20	m	c	CHIN	San Francisco	6-Wd San Francisco	81	57
Ah	20	m	c	CHIN	San Francisco	San Francisco P O	80	503
Ah	20	f	c	CHIN	San Francisco	San Francisco P O	80	526
Ah	20	m	c	CHIN	San Francisco	San Francisco P O	80	524
Ah	20	m	c	CHIN	El Dorado	Georgetown Twp	72	46
Ah	20	m	c	CHIN	Placer	Bath P O	76	446
Ah	20	m	c	CHIN	Sacramento	3-Wd Sacramento	77	296
Ah	20	m	c	CHIN	Sacramento	3-Wd Sacramento	77	302
Ah	20	m	c	CHIN	Sacramento	3-Wd Sacramento	77	291
Ah	20	f	c	CHIN	San Francisco	San Francisco P O	80	438
Ah	20	m	c	CHIN	San Francisco	San Francisco P O	80	435
Ah	20	f	c	CHIN	San Francisco	San Francisco P O	80	442
Ah	20	m	c	CHIN	Sacramento	3-Wd Sacramento	77	311
Ah	20	m	c	CHIN	El Dorado	Placerville	72	115
Ah	20	m	c	CHIN	El Dorado	Cosumnes Twp	72	20
Ah	20	m	c	CHIN	Tuolumne	Chinese Camp P O	93	370
Ah	20	m	c	CHIN	San Francisco	San Francisco P O	80	501
Ah	20	m	c	CHIN	San Francisco	8-Wd San Francisco	82	401
Ah	2	f	c	CA	San Francisco	San Francisco P O	80	525
Ah	19	m	c	CHIN	San Francisco	2-Wd San Francisco	79	139
Ah	19	f	c	CHIN	San Francisco	San Francisco P O	80	453
Ah	19	f	c	CHIN	San Francisco	San Francisco P O	80	454
Ah	19	m	c	CHIN	Nevada	Nevada Twp	75	278
Ah	19	m	c	CHIN	Trinity	Douglas	92	237
Ah	19	m	c	CHIN	San Joaquin	Castoria Twp	86	12
Ah	19	m	c	CHIN	San Joaquin	Castoria Twp	86	13
Ah	18	m	c	CHIN	San Francisco	6-Wd San Francisco	81	47
Ah	18	m	c	CHIN	San Francisco	6-Wd San Francisco	81	49
Ah	18	m	c	CHIN	San Francisco	San Francisco P O	83	176
Ah	18	f	c	CHIN	San Francisco	San Francisco P O	80	434
Ah	18	m	c	CHIN	Sacramento	2-Wd Sacramento	77	223
Ah	18	m	c	CHIN	Mariposa	Mariposa P O	74	120
Ah	18	m	c	CHIN	Trinity	Douglas	92	234
Ah	18	m	c	CHIN	San Francisco	5-Wd San Francisco	81	5
Ah	18	m	c	CHIN	San Francisco	6-Wd San Francisco	81	46
Ah	17	m	c	CHIN	San Francisco	San Francisco P O	80	441
Ah	17	f	c	CHIN	San Francisco	San Francisco P O	80	439
Ah	17	m	c	CHIN	Placer	Clipper Gap P O	76	393
Ah	16	m	c	CHIN	Sacramento	3-Wd Sacramento	77	283
Ah	16	m	c	CHIN	Sacramento	3-Wd Sacramento	77	302
Ah	16	m	c	CHIN	San Francisco	2-Wd San Francisco	79	264
Ah	15	m	c	CHIN	San Francisco	1-Wd San Francisco	79	41
Ah	15	m	c	CHIN	San Francisco	San Francisco P O	80	375
Ah	15	m	c	CHIN	Shasta	French Gulch P O	89	469
Ah	15	m	c	CHIN	San Francisco	6-Wd San Francisco	81	85
Ah	14	m	c	CHIN	Santa Clara	1-Wd San Jose	88	269
Ah	14	m	c	CHIN	Sacramento	3-Wd Sacramento	77	315
Ah	14	m	c	CHIN	Sacramento	3-Wd Sacramento	77	314
Ah	12	m	c	CHIN	Los Angeles	Los Angeles	73	531
Ah	12	m	c	CHIN	Sacramento	3-Wd Sacramento	77	306
Ah	12	f	c	CHIN	San Francisco	San Francisco P O	80	437
Ah	11	m	c	CHIN	Sacramento	3-Wd Sacramento	77	295
Ah	10	m	c	CHIN	San Francisco	San Francisco P O	80	451
Ah	1	m	c	CA	San Francisco	San Francisco P O	80	434
Chang	14	m	c	CHIN	San Francisco	2-Wd San Francisco	79	264
Chas	24	m	c	CHIN	Sacramento	3-Wd Sacramento	77	307
Chas	15	m	c	CHIN	Sacramento	3-Wd Sacramento	77	306
Ching	46	m	c	CHIN	Sierra	Butte Twp	89	513
Chong	28	m	c	CHIN	Tuolumne	Chinese Camp P O	93	385
Chung	19	m	c	CHIN	San Francisco	2-Wd San Francisco	79	264
Co	45	m	c	CHIN	Sierra	Downieville Twp	89	520
Day	34	f	c	CHIN	Placer	Dutch Flat P O	76	408
Fan	31	m	c	CHIN	Sierra	Downieville Twp	89	520
Fok	41	f	c	CHIN	San Francisco	San Francisco P O	80	490
Fong	25	m	c	CHIN	Plumas	Rich Bar Twp	77	46
Fong	25	m	c	CHIN	Plumas	Seneca Twp	77	51
Fong	24	m	c	CHIN	Plumas	Indian Twp	77	16
Frank	40	m	c	CHIN	San Joaquin	1-Wd Stockton	86	144
Fun	18	m	c	CHIN	Solano	Green Valley Twp	90	42
Gee	43	m	c	CHIN	Plumas	Mineral Twp	77	24
Gee	32	m	c	CHIN	Plumas	Mineral Twp	77	23
Gee	2	m	c	CHIN	Butte	Hamilton Twp	70	74
Gee	18	m	c	CHIN	Placer	Dutch Flat P O	76	407
Gine	32	m	c	CHIN	Nevada	Washington Twp	75	342
Gong	29	m	c	CHIN	Butte	Wyandotte Twp	70	143
Hi	71	m	c	CHIN	San Joaquin	1-Wd Stockton	86	146
Hi	29	m	c	CHIN	Yolo	Merritt Twp	93	504
Hin	15	m	c	CHIN	Alameda	Alvarado	68	305

© 2001 by Heritage Quest. All rights reserved.

California 1870 Census

Name	Age	S	R	B-PL	County	Locale	Series M593 Roll	Pg
Hing	37	m	c	CHIN	Amador	Drytown P O	69	422
Hong	20	m	c	CHIN	Sacramento	3-Wd Sacramento	77	276
Hop	42	m	c	CHIN	Placer	Lincoln P O	76	483
How	29	m	c	CHIN	Yuba	Marysville	93	625
Hoy	30	m	c	CHIN	Yuba	Marysville	93	621
Hung	15	m	c	CHIN	San Francisco	1-Wd San Francisco	79	80
Jim	14	m	c	CHIN	Sacramento	3-Wd Sacramento	77	316
Jno	60	m	c	CHIN	Sacramento	3-Wd Sacramento	77	310
Jo	14	m	c	CHIN	Sacramento	3-Wd Sacramento	77	315
Jos	20	m	w	ENGL	San Joaquin	2-Wd Stockton	86	187
Kai	44	m	c	CHIN	Tuolumne	Sonora P O	93	313
Ki	17	m	c	CHIN	San Francisco	8-Wd San Francisco	82	486
Ko	30	m	c	CHIN	Calaveras	San Andreas P O	70	199
Lee	38	m	c	CHIN	Mariposa	Mariposa P O	74	102
Lee	37	m	c	CHIN	Placer	Lincoln P O	76	491
Lee	33	f	c	CHIN	Mariposa	Mariposa P O	74	103
Lee	30	m	c	CHIN	San Francisco	6-Wd San Francisco	81	39
Lee	28	m	c	CHIN	San Francisco	7-Wd San Francisco	81	208
Lee	27	m	c	CHIN	San Francisco	7-Wd San Francisco	81	234
Lee	26	m	c	CHIN	Mariposa	Mariposa P O	74	128
Lee	21	m	c	CHIN	San Joaquin	1-Wd Stockton	86	146
Lee	20	m	c	CHIN	San Francisco	2-Wd San Francisco	79	256
Lee	20	m	c	CHIN	San Francisco	6-Wd San Francisco	81	48
Lee	20	m	c	CHIN	Santa Clara	2-Wd San Jose	88	323
Lo	22	m	c	CHIN	San Francisco	7-Wd San Francisco	81	234
Loo	23	m	c	CHIN	Tuolumne	Chinese Camp P O	93	390
Loo	20	m	c	CHIN	San Joaquin	Elliott Twp	86	71
Lot	29	m	c	CHIN	San Joaquin	1-Wd Stockton	86	144
M	32	m	c	CHIN	Yuba	Marysville	93	625
Mang	36	m	c	CHIN	Yuba	Marysville	93	629
Me	25	f	c	CHIN	San Francisco	6-Wd San Francisco	81	53
On	31	m	c	CHIN	Sierra	Table Rock Twp	89	574
Pae	22	m	c	CHIN	Tuolumne	Columbia P O	93	361
Pee	25	m	c	CHIN	San Francisco	6-Wd San Francisco	81	42
Pi	46	m	c	CHIN	Tuolumne	Chinese Camp P O	93	383
Pong	28	m	c	CHIN	Tuolumne	Chinese Camp P O	93	390
Pow	25	m	c	CHIN	Plumas	Rich Bar Twp	77	46
Sam	63	m	c	CHIN	San Joaquin	1-Wd Stockton	86	147
Sam	36	m	c	CHIN	Kern	Kernville P O	73	367
Sam	28	m	c	CHIN	Tuolumne	Columbia P O	93	346
Sam	19	m	c	CHIN	Tehama	Deer Crk Twp	92	172
Sam	15	m	c	CHIN	San Mateo	Pescadero P O	87	414
Sea	19	m	c	CHIN	El Dorado	Cosumnes Twp	72	19
Seda	36	m	c	CHIN	Mariposa	Mariposa P O	74	133
See	19	m	c	CHIN	San Francisco	San Francisco P O	85	866
Sing	30	m	c	CHIN	Solano	Green Valley Twp	90	44
Sing	28	m	c	CHIN	Tuolumne	Columbia P O	93	342
Sing	28	m	c	CHIN	Tuolumne	Columbia P O	93	357
Sing	28	m	c	CHIN	Stanislaus	Emory Twp	92	23
Sing	26	m	c	CHIN	Tuolumne	Big Oak Flat P O	93	398
Sing	23	m	c	CHIN	Tuolumne	Big Oak Flat P O	93	400
Sip	39	m	c	CHIN	Tuolumne	Sonora P O	93	332
Son	51	m	c	CHIN	Tuolumne	Columbia P O	93	361
Su	41	m	c	CHIN	San Francisco	San Francisco P O	80	492
Ta	20	m	c	CHIN	San Francisco	8-Wd San Francisco	82	387
Tee	31	m	c	CHIN	San Francisco	6-Wd San Francisco	81	61
Tie	35	m	c	CHIN	Monterey	Castroville Twp	74	327
Tung	16	m	c	CHIN	San Francisco	2-Wd San Francisco	79	256
Wa	40	m	c	CHIN	Nevada	Bridgeport Twp	75	111
Wa	24	m	c	CHIN	Solano	Rio Vista Twp	90	64
Wau	32	m	c	CHIN	Sutter	Butte Twp	92	89
Weig	20	m	c	CHIN	San Francisco	3-Wd San Francisco	79	325
Wing	34	m	c	CHIN	San Francisco	San Francisco P O	83	170
Wo	25	m	c	CHIN	Napa	Napa	75	19
Wong	30	m	c	CHIN	San Joaquin	1-Wd Stockton	86	130
Wong Koy	39	m	c	CHIN	Placer	Lincoln P O	76	491
Ye	20	m	c	CHIN	San Francisco	2-Wd San Francisco	79	139
Yen	30	m	c	CHIN	San Francisco	2-Wd San Francisco	79	149
Yo	40	m	c	CHIN	Mariposa	Mariposa P O	74	122
Yo	22	f	c	CHIN	Mariposa	Mariposa P O	74	103
Yong	26	m	c	CHIN	San Francisco	2-Wd San Francisco	79	242
Yong	25	m	c	CHIN	San Francisco	2-Wd San Francisco	79	285
Yung	19	m	c	CHIN	Sacramento	3-Wd Sacramento	77	311
Zoo	34	m	c	CHIN	San Mateo	Schoolhouse Statio	87	336
HINGBERGAN								
H	23	m	w	PRUS	Yuba	Marysville	93	606
HINGOCHOA								
Antonio	32	m	w	MEXI	Los Angeles	San Juan Twp	73	627
Narciso	61	m	w	MEXI	Los Angeles	San Juan Twp	73	627
HINGON								
Chong	26	m	c	CHIN	Monterey	Pajaro Twp	74	372
HINGSLEY								
Ida	15	f	w	CA	Contra Costa	Martinez P O	71	386
HINK								
Chas	26	m	w	BAVA	Sacramento	4-Wd Sacramento	77	340
Federika	18	f	w	BREM	San Francisco	11-Wd San Francisc	84	561
Kie	23	m	c	CHIN	San Francisco	San Francisco P O	83	253
Louis	36	m	w	BAVA	Amador	Fiddletown P O	69	436
Patrick	30	m	w	SHOL	San Francisco	11-Wd San Francisc	84	428
HINKEL								
Charles	53	m	w	PRUS	San Francisco	San Francisco P O	83	52
HINKELBEIN								
Adam	40	m	w	GERM	Santa Clara	2-Wd San Jose	88	301
HINKEY								
Charles	25	m	w	IREL	Solano	Vacaville Twp	90	125
HINKFELD								
Sallie	80	f	w	PRUS	San Francisco	San Francisco P O	83	413
HINKLE								
George B	40	m	w	MD	Plumas	Indian Twp	77	10
J B	44	m	w	VA	Sonoma	Petaluma Twp	91	343
Jesse	40	m	w	CA	Monterey	Monterey	74	356
Solomon	52	m	w	SC	El Dorado	Placerville	72	125
Wm	60	m	w	PRUS	Sacramento	American Twp	77	65
HINKLEMAN								
Fredrick	17	m	w	MD	Inyo	Bishop Crk Twp	73	313
HINKLEY								
Acasia	4	f	w	CA	Sacramento	San Joaquin Twp	77	399
Adkins	64	m	w	ME	Siskiyou	Scott Valley Twp	89	610
Daniel	42	m	w	MA	Alameda	Brooklyn Twp	68	55
Elizabeth	58	f	w	ME	Siskiyou	Scott Valley Twp	89	613
George	26	m	w	MA	San Francisco	7-Wd San Francisco	81	175
I B	30	m	w	ME	San Francisco	7-Wd San Francisco	81	218
James	27	m	w	NY	San Francisco	7-Wd San Francisco	81	183
John Z	33	m	w	MO	Mendocino	Little Lake Twp	74	194
Joseph	35	m	w	ME	Calaveras	San Andreas P O	70	156
P R	55	m	w	IN	Yuba	Marysville	93	608
Rose	32	f	w	ME	Alameda	Washington Twp	68	281
HINKLY								
Wm	60	m	w	MA	San Francisco	8-Wd San Francisco	82	330
HINKS								
Christophe	29	m	w	TX	Contra Costa	Martinez P O	71	443
HINKSON								
A H	64	m	w	MO	Amador	Drytown P O	69	415
Aldney	51	m	w	ME	Yuba	W Bear Rvr Twp	93	684
J M	33	m	w	MO	Amador	Drytown P O	69	415
John F	57	m	w	ME	Alpine	Monitor P O	69	317
Laura	20	f	w	MO	Yolo	Washington Twp	93	536
M A	54	m	w	MO	Amador	Drytown P O	69	418
N C	30	m	w	MO	Amador	Drytown P O	69	416
R S	31	m	w	MO	Amador	Drytown P O	69	420
Sarah	65	f	w	ME	Sonoma	Petaluma Twp	91	330
W R	26	m	w	MO	Amador	Jackson P O	69	324
HINKSTON								
Harlon	70	m	w	NY	Sonoma	Vallejo Twp	91	458
Joseph R	32	m	w	MO	Sonoma	Vallejo Twp	91	451
Nancy	50	f	w	AL	Sonoma	Vallejo Twp	91	456
HINLEY								
Margaret	40	f	w	IREL	San Francisco	11-Wd San Francisc	84	498
HINMAN								
A G	40	m	w	NY	Santa Clara	Gilroy Twp	88	85
Ephraim	49	m	w	NY	Monterey	Pajaro Twp	74	375
Hattie	18	f	w	OH	Amador	Ione City P O	69	352
James M	23	m	w	NY	Alpine	Woodfords P O	69	309
L	23	m	w	PRUS	Sacramento	1-Wd Sacramento	77	184
Louis A	39	m	w	VA	Marin	San Rafael	74	52
M	35	f	w	OH	Amador	Ione City P O	69	353
Marcus D	53	m	w	NY	El Dorado	Mud Springs Twp	72	78
Nelson	52	m	w	NY	Alameda	Oakland	68	131
Walter	45	m	w	NY	Solano	Silveyville Twp	90	73
William	20	m	w	IL	Santa Cruz	Pajaro Twp	89	340
HINN								
---	62	m	c	CHIN	Siskiyou	Hamburg Twp	89	596
Ah	36	m	c	CHIN	Placer	Auburn P O	76	379
Ah	32	m	c	CHIN	Nevada	Nevada Twp	75	277
Ah	22	m	c	CHIN	Sonoma	Sonoma Twp	91	447
HINO								
Lee	32	m	c	CHIN	Sierra	Gibson Twp	89	542
HINS								
Bak	23	m	c	CHIN	San Francisco	1-Wd San Francisco	79	101
HINSDALE								
Seymore	29	m	w	VT	Yolo	Merritt Twp	93	502
HINSDY								
J B	38	m	w	OH	Humboldt	Pacific Twp	72	291
HINSELMANN								
Deitrick	25	m	w	HANO	Yuba	Slate Range Bar Tw	93	672
HINSEY								
Elias	70	m	w	PA	Contra Costa	Martinez P O	71	379
HINSHAW								
Edward	40	m	w	NC	Sonoma	Analy Twp	91	224
Hugh	36	m	w	NC	Marin	Tomales Twp	74	85
John	22	m	w	NC	Marin	Tomales Twp	74	85
Thos	44	m	w	TN	San Joaquin	Liberty Twp	86	90
Wm P	49	m	w	NC	Sonoma	Analy Twp	91	224
HINSLER								
Arnold	28	m	w	SWIT	San Francisco	8-Wd San Francisco	82	366
Jacob	24	m	w	SWIT	San Francisco	8-Wd San Francisco	82	366
HINSLEY								
George	37	m	w	AL	Tulare	Venice Twp	92	275
HINSMAN								
Edith	23	f	w	BELG	San Francisco	8-Wd San Francisco	82	335
HINSONG								
Antoine	37	m	w	FRAN	Shasta	French Gulch P O	89	465
HINSTER								
W P	28	m	w	PA	Humboldt	Eureka Twp	72	272
HINT								
C N	20	m	w	MD	Yuba	Marysville	93	605
William	29	m	w	MO	Santa Cruz	Soquel Twp	89	447
HINTERLANG								
Barnibas	39	m	w	FRAN	Shasta	Stillwater P O	89	481
HINTON								
Frederick	11	m	w	PA	El Dorado	Diamond Springs Tw	72	26
G	30	m	w	MO	Lake	Lower Lake	73	422
John	34	m	w	OH	San Diego	San Diego	78	483
Lewis	54	m	w	NY	Santa Cruz	Santa Cruz Twp	89	379

© 2001 by Heritage Quest. All rights reserved.

Series M593

Name	Age	S	R	B-PL	County	Locale	Roll	Pg
Oscar F	45	m	w	OH	Sonoma	Petaluma Twp	91	335
Rebecca	63	f	w	PA	Sonoma	Petaluma Twp	91	336
William	35	m	w	ENGL	San Francisco	6-Wd San Francisco	81	114
HINTZ								
Jacob	30	m	w	PRUS	San Francisco	8-Wd San Francisco	82	391
HINTZE								
Isaac R	42	m	w	PRUS	San Francisco	San Francisco P O	85	841
HINTZLEY								
John	51	m	w	VA	Contra Costa	Martinez P O	71	442
HINUCK								
Louis	36	m	w	PRUS	Amador	Fiddletown P O	69	440
HINUS								
William	39	m	w	RI	Placer	Colfax P O	76	387
HINY								
Ah	28	m	c	CHIN	Sacramento	1-Wd Sacramento	77	181
Lee	38	m	c	CHIN	San Joaquin	1-Wd Stockton	86	145
Lee	28	m	c	CHIN	San Joaquin	1-Wd Stockton	86	145
My	48	m	c	CHIN	Nevada	Meadow Lake Twp	75	250
HINZ								
Adolph	29	m	w	HAMB	San Francisco	8-Wd San Francisco	82	344
Bertha	19	f	w	PRUS	San Francisco	San Francisco P O	83	169
Chas	44	m	w	GERM	San Francisco	8-Wd San Francisco	82	311
Henry	30	m	w	PRUS	San Francisco	8-Wd San Francisco	82	369
Karl	23	m	w	PRUS	San Francisco	San Francisco P O	83	281
Louis	40	m	w	PRUS	San Francisco	San Francisco P O	80	420
HIO								
---	26	m	c	CHIN	Siskiyou	Cottonwood Twp	89	592
HION								
Ah	28	m	c	CHIN	San Joaquin	1-Wd Stockton	86	144
Victor	50	m	w	FRAN	San Francisco	San Francisco P O	83	78
HIONG								
Ah	47	m	c	CHIN	Mariposa	Mariposa P O	74	132
HIP								
Ah	50	m	c	CHIN	Placer	Auburn P O	76	362
Ah	40	m	c	CHIN	San Joaquin	Oneal Twp	86	117
Ah	40	m	c	CHIN	Amador	Jackson P O	69	332
Ah	37	m	c	CHIN	Mariposa	Mariposa P O	74	102
Ah	36	m	c	CHIN	San Joaquin	1-Wd Stockton	86	147
Ah	36	m	c	CHIN	Tuolumne	Big Oak Flat P O	93	401
Ah	32	m	c	CHIN	Amador	Fiddletown P O	69	427
Ah	31	m	c	CHIN	San Francisco	San Francisco P O	80	492
Ah	30	m	c	CHIN	San Francisco	San Francisco P O	80	507
Ah	30	m	c	CHIN	Sacramento	Georgianna Twp	77	133
Ah	27	m	c	CHIN	San Francisco	San Francisco P O	83	82
Ah	27	m	c	CHIN	Sacramento	Georgianna Twp	77	124
Ah	25	m	c	CHIN	Trinity	Junction City Pct	92	210
Ah	24	m	c	CHIN	San Francisco	6-Wd San Francisco	81	60
Ah	22	m	c	CHIN	San Francisco	6-Wd San Francisco	81	61
Ah	20	m	c	CHIN	San Joaquin	1-Wd Stockton	86	144
Ah	20	f	c	CHIN	San Francisco	San Francisco P O	80	508
Ah	20	f	c	CHIN	Sacramento	Granite Twp	77	151
Ah	20	m	c	CHIN	Sacramento	1-Wd Sacramento	77	199
Ah	19	f	c	CHIN	San Francisco	San Francisco P O	80	507
Ah	14	m	c	CHIN	San Francisco	6-Wd San Francisco	81	68
Foo	21	m	c	CHIN	Tehama	Deer Crk Twp	92	171
Gee	28	m	c	CHIN	Sacramento	1-Wd Sacramento	77	178
How	41	m	c	CHIN	San Francisco	6-Wd San Francisco	81	54
Hup	23	m	c	CHIN	Tehama	Deer Crk Twp	92	172
Kee	28	m	c	CHIN	Tuolumne	Chinese Camp P O	93	363
Lee	62	m	c	CHIN	Tuolumne	Big Oak Flat P O	93	400
Lee	40	m	c	CHIN	El Dorado	Coloma Twp	72	10
Lih	37	m	c	CHIN	San Joaquin	1-Wd Stockton	86	143
Lin	36	m	c	CHIN	San Joaquin	1-Wd Stockton	86	151
Lit	26	m	c	CHIN	San Joaquin	1-Wd Stockton	86	144
Lo	36	m	c	CHIN	San Joaquin	1-Wd Stockton	86	147
Lo	34	m	c	CHIN	San Joaquin	1-Wd Stockton	86	148
Lo	16	m	c	CHIN	Tehama	Tehama Twp	92	188
Lue	22	m	c	CHIN	Sacramento	1-Wd Sacramento	77	199
Sam	47	m	c	CHIN	Tuolumne	Big Oak Flat P O	93	400
Sam	30	m	c	CHIN	Mariposa	Mariposa P O	74	121
Sing	32	m	c	CHIN	Klamath	Orleans Twp	73	380
Up	26	m	c	CHIN	Tehama	Toomes & Grant	92	169
Wo	39	m	c	CHIN	Butte	Chico Twp	70	30
Wo	18	m	c	CHIN	San Francisco	8-Wd San Francisco	82	359
Woo	52	m	c	CHIN	San Francisco	2-Wd San Francisco	79	285
Yah	28	m	c	CHIN	San Francisco	6-Wd San Francisco	81	60
Yung	20	m	c	CHIN	San Francisco	11-Wd San Francisc	84	517
HIPE								
Ah	22	m	c	CHIN	Tehama	Tehama Twp	92	189
HIPMAN								
Julius	34	m	w	PRUS	San Francisco	San Francisco P O	80	479
HIPO								
Ah	23	m	c	CHIN	San Francisco	San Francisco P O	80	491
HIPPING								
William	43	m	w	PRUS	Tuolumne	Sonora P O	93	319
HIPPOLITE								
Augustus	60	m	w	FRAN	Marin	San Rafael Twp	74	40
Riviere	31	m	w	FRAN	Siskiyou	Callahan P O	89	628
HIPPS								
D C	43	m	w	PA	Humboldt	Bucksport Twp	72	241
Fanny	16	f	w	NY	San Francisco	San Francisco P O	83	305
Herman	80	m	w	PRUS	San Francisco	San Francisco P O	83	305
HIPSHER								
Harvey	43	m	w	OH	Shasta	Stillwater P O	89	480
HIPSON								
H	48	m	w	DENM	Nevada	Bridgeport Twp	75	101
John	32	m	w	SCOT	San Francisco	7-Wd San Francisco	81	231

Series M593

Name	Age	S	R	B-PL	County	Locale	Roll	Pg
HIPWELL								
George W	52	m	w	IREL	Los Angeles	San Juan Twp	73	629
HIRAK								
N H	31	m	w	CANA	Sierra	Sierra Twp	89	566
HIRAM								
Johanna	25	f	w	IREL	San Joaquin	1-Wd Stockton	86	130
John	30	m	w	IL	Sutter	Sutter Twp	92	123
Raymond	56	m	w	VT	Klamath	Hoopa Valley India	73	386
HIRANDA								
Augustus	25	m	w	CA	Marin	San Rafael	74	48
HIRCHFELD								
Hermar	41	m	w	BAVA	San Francisco	San Francisco P O	83	295
Julius	60	m	w	PRUS	San Francisco	San Francisco P O	80	349
HIRCHPERGER								
Emily	29	f	w	MS	Sacramento	3-Wd Sacramento	77	299
HIRD								
John	42	m	w	ENGL	San Francisco	San Francisco P O	83	308
HIRDH								
Goodlow	21	m	w	WURT	Sonoma	Petaluma Twp	91	317
HIRE								
Ah	19	m	c	CHIN	Nevada	Eureka Twp	75	141
Benette	32	f	w	NY	San Diego	San Diego	78	506
Henry	44	m	w	BAVA	Calaveras	San Andreas P O	70	211
John	35	m	w	MO	San Diego	San Diego	78	506
HIRECH								
S	23	m	w	PRUS	Nevada	Nevada Twp	75	274
HIRK								
Catherine	16	f	w	OH	Sacramento	4-Wd Sacramento	77	326
HIRKLE								
Gabriel	28	m	w	CA	Monterey	Pajaro Twp	74	376
HIRLEMAN								
Phillip	36	m	w	PRUS	San Francisco	6-Wd San Francisco	81	148
HIRONAMUS								
Jesse	37	m	w	KY	Sacramento	Franklin Twp	77	117
HIRP								
Boniface	30	m	w	PA	San Francisco	8-Wd San Francisco	82	455
HIRRIGOYEN								
Michael	30	m	w	FRAN	San Francisco	San Francisco P O	83	207
HIRS								
Christian	34	m	w	PRUS	San Francisco	San Francisco P O	83	372
HIRSCH								
Benoat S	33	m	w	FRAN	El Dorado	Mud Springs Twp	72	78
Chas	19	m	w	BADE	San Francisco	8-Wd San Francisco	82	375
Emile	23	m	w	PRUS	San Francisco	3-Wd San Francisco	79	327
John	43	m	w	HDAR	San Francisco	San Francisco P O	83	137
Joseph	42	m	w	HDAR	San Francisco	San Francisco P O	83	321
Joseph	38	m	w	BADE	Alameda	Washington Twp	68	283
Julius	30	m	w	FRAN	San Francisco	San Francisco P O	80	349
Solomon	50	m	w	PRUS	San Francisco	San Francisco P O	80	409
HIRSCHEY								
Horace B	41	m	w	AL	San Diego	San Diego	78	491
HIRSCHFELD								
Benj	32	m	w	PRUS	San Francisco	San Francisco P O	83	295
Joseph	34	m	w	BAVA	San Francisco	2-Wd San Francisco	79	225
Mark	26	m	w	BAVA	San Francisco	8-Wd San Francisco	82	404
Minna	48	f	w	PRUS	San Francisco	8-Wd San Francisco	82	442
Simon	33	m	w	PRUS	Sacramento	3-Wd Sacramento	77	284
HIRSCHFELDER								
Henrietta	40	f	w	BAVA	San Francisco	8-Wd San Francisco	82	453
HIRSCHFIELD								
Joseph	39	m	w	HDAR	Nevada	Grass Valley Twp	75	151
HIRSFALL								
John	30	m	w	ENGL	San Diego	San Diego	78	508
HIRSH								
Prospere	24	m	w	FRAN	San Francisco	6-Wd San Francisco	81	112
HIRSHBERGER								
Jno M	23	m	w	IN	Sonoma	Santa Rosa	91	398
HIRSHEMANN								
Jerome	41	m	w	FRAN	Napa	Napa	75	46
HIRSHMAN								
L	46	m	w	BAVA	Nevada	Nevada Twp	75	280
HIRSTEL								
Henry	29	m	w	PRUS	San Francisco	6-Wd San Francisco	81	96
HIRTH								
Christian	22	m	w	WURT	Santa Clara	2-Wd San Jose	88	319
Julius	50	m	w	FRAN	San Francisco	San Francisco P O	80	349
Rose	23	f	w	SWIT	San Francisco	San Francisco P O	83	131
HIRTSFELDT								
Peter	30	m	w	PRUS	San Francisco	San Francisco P O	83	403
HIRTZ								
John	27	m	w	PRUS	San Francisco	2-Wd San Francisco	79	172
HIRZ								
Christian	43	m	w	PRUS	Shasta	Dog Crk P O	89	471
HISCOCK								
H O	24	m	w	CT	Nevada	Bridgeport Twp	75	113
Samuel	45	m	w	ME	Calaveras	Copperopolis P O	70	251
HISCOX								
Alfred	55	m	w	RI	Santa Cruz	Pajaro Twp	89	340
H	35	m	w	NY	San Joaquin	Tulare Twp	86	261
Irvin	10	m	w	CA	Nevada	Bridgeport Twp	75	113
Merrill	51	m	w	CT	Nevada	Bridgeport Twp	75	113
HISELY								
William	27	m	w	ME	San Mateo	Pescadero P O	87	412
HISEMAN								
Henry	23	m	w	WURT	Marin	Sausalito Twp	74	72
HISEN								
John	36	m	w	IA	Tehama	Tehama Twp	92	187

© 2001 by Heritage Quest. All rights reserved.

California 1870 Census

Series M593

Name	Age	S	R	B-PL	County	Locale	Roll	Pg
HISER								
Aluse	50	m	w	SWIT	Sonoma	Sonoma Twp	91	449
HISHEN								
Mary	28	f	w	IREL	San Francisco	2-Wd San Francisco	79	207
HISLER								
John	45	m	w	PRUS	Sutter	Butte Twp	92	101
HISOM								
John	29	m	w	VA	San Joaquin	2-Wd Stockton	86	191
HISS								
Chah	38	m	c	CHIN	Marin	San Rafael Twp	74	59
Elisebeth	50	f	w	PA	Sonoma	Petaluma Twp	91	351
HIST								
Mores	44	m	w	VA	Plumas	Quartz Twp	77	35
HITARS								
E L	28	m	w	ME	Humboldt	Eureka Twp	72	282
HITCH								
Hiram	45	m	w	ENGL	Stanislaus	San Joaquin Twp	92	83
HITCHAISER								
Wm	29	m	w	MO	San Joaquin	Tulare Twp	86	253
HITCHBORN								
Ella	16	f	w	CA	San Francisco	5-Wd San Francisco	81	4
HITCHBURN								
Albert	32	m	w	ME	San Francisco	11-Wd San Francisc	84	537
HITCHCOCK								
A J	12	m	w	CA	Humboldt	Eureka Twp	72	275
Abner	27	m	w	MO	San Joaquin	Douglas Twp	86	34
Benj	34	m	w	CANA	Monterey	Alisal Twp	74	291
Carlos	30	m	w	NY	Tulare	Tule Rvr Twp	92	261
Charles M	57	m	w	MD	San Francisco	San Francisco P O	83	147
Clara	14	f	w	CA	Sacramento	4-Wd Sacramento	77	350
Cortland	33	m	w	NY	Tulare	Visalia	92	296
David	54	m	w	NY	San Francisco	2-Wd San Francisco	79	216
E B	42	m	w	NY	Santa Clara	Gilroy Twp	88	73
Edward	63	m	w	CANA	Nevada	Nevada Twp	75	296
Elizabeth	50	f	w	MA	Santa Clara	Fremont Twp	88	46
Elmore	31	m	w	OH	El Dorado	White Oak Twp	72	141
Fanny C	11	f	w	CA	Stanislaus	Empire Twp	92	28
Geo N	27	m	w	MA	San Diego	San Diego	78	498
Green	35	m	w	MO	Inyo	Lone Pine Twp	73	330
H E	40	m	w	NY	Alameda	Oakland	68	153
Hollis	42	m	w	VT	Sonoma	Bodega Twp	91	252
Isaac	64	m	w	KY	Inyo	Independence Twp	73	327
Isaac	52	m	w	NY	Monterey	Monterey Twp	74	347
Isaac	36	m	w	OH	Colusa	Colusa Twp	71	277
Isaac N	36	m	w	MO	Mendocino	Point Arena Twp	74	210
Isaac P	48	m	w	PA	Calaveras	Copperopolis P O	70	249
J F	44	m	w	MO	Santa Barbara	Santa Barbara P O	87	498
J N W	44	m	w	VA	San Joaquin	Castoria Twp	86	4
James	37	m	w	MO	Santa Barbara	Santa Barbara P O	87	478
John	40	m	w	ME	San Joaquin	Oneal Twp	86	113
John B	46	m	w	NY	San Francisco	6-Wd San Francisco	81	102
Jos B	28	m	w	IA	Nevada	Nevada Twp	75	320
Joseph	14	m	w	CA	Monterey	Monterey Twp	74	345
Kate L	17	f	w	NY	Santa Cruz	Santa Cruz	89	405
Oliver	39	m	w	MO	Inyo	Independence Twp	73	326
Robert	53	m	w	OH	Calaveras	San Andreas P O	70	158
Russell	35	m	w	OH	Alpine	Silver Mtn P O	69	306
S B	48	m	w	NY	Placer	Dutch Flat P O	76	405
Sarah	35	f	w	ME	Alameda	Brooklyn	68	22
Silas	22	m	w	CA	San Mateo	Redwood Twp	87	361
Stephen	29	m	w	OH	San Francisco	San Francisco P O	83	311
Thomas	59	m	w	OH	El Dorado	Mud Springs Twp	72	83
William	40	m	w	ENGL	Nevada	Bloomfield Twp	75	92
William	37	m	w	CANA	San Francisco	San Francisco P O	80	389
William	30	m	w	MO	Los Angeles	El Monte Twp	73	450
Wm	44	m	w	NY	Butte	Kimshew Tpw	70	83
Wm B	36	m	w	VT	Nevada	Nevada Twp	75	320
HITCHCOOK								
Elizabeth	25	f	w	OH	Yuba	Long Bar Twp	93	560
HITCHENS								
Edwin	26	m	w	ENGL	Nevada	Grass Valley Twp	75	188
James	40	m	w	PA	San Francisco	8-Wd San Francisco	82	321
John	29	m	w	ENGL	Nevada	Nevada Twp	75	315
Wm D	21	m	w	MI	San Joaquin	Elliott Twp	86	78
HITCHINGS								
Edward	26	m	w	ENGL	Nevada	Grass Valley Twp	75	148
John	55	m	w	ENGL	El Dorado	Georgetown Twp	72	43
Josiah	27	m	w	ME	Humboldt	Eureka Twp	72	266
William	38	m	w	WALE	Calaveras	Copperopolis P O	70	248
Wm	24	m	w	WALE	Contra Costa	Martinez P O	71	428
HITCHINS								
Andrew	37	m	w	CANA	Humboldt	Eureka Twp	72	267
Edward	45	m	w	MA	San Francisco	6-Wd San Francisco	81	105
Edward W	27	m	w	MA	San Francisco	6-Wd San Francisco	81	105
Kate	14	f	w	CA	Placer	Colfax P O	76	390
Kitty	9	f	w	CA	Santa Barbara	San Buenaventura P	87	422
Mary L	15	f	w	CA	Placer	Colfax P O	76	390
S E	43	m	w	NH	Solano	Vallejo	90	177
HITE								
Ah	32	m	c	CHIN	Tehama	Tehama Twp	92	188
Ah	24	m	c	CHIN	Tehama	Tehama Twp	92	188
Alexander	64	m	w	VA	Sacramento	Franklin Twp	77	105
Allen	39	m	w	VA	Mariposa	Mariposa P O	74	131
David	28	m	w	IL	Yuba	East Bear Rvr Twp	93	545
Edward	50	m	w	VA	Nevada	Nevada Twp	75	275
Isaac	28	m	w	MO	Sutter	Nicolaus Twp	92	115
John P	27	m	w	NY	San Bernardino	San Bernardino Twp	78	453
Philip B	49	m	w	VA	Humboldt	South Fork Twp	72	300
HITEMAN								
H	49	m	w	PRUS	Yuba	Marysville	93	579
HITEN								
Dannel	49	m	w	VA	Napa	Napa Twp	75	29
HITHERTING								
Jacob	22	m	w	PA	Colusa	Colusa	71	288
HITHOWER								
Margaret	11	f	w	CA	Shasta	Horsetown P O	89	505
HITMAN								
John	31	m	w	GERM	Contra Costa	Martinez P O	71	369
HITNER								
F	45	m	w	BAVA	Amador	Ione City P O	69	357
HITO								
Ah	24	m	c	CHIN	Sutter	Butte Twp	92	104
HITOWN								
James	28	m	w	CANA	San Joaquin	Castoria Twp	86	14
HITSMAN								
Marshal	40	m	w	NY	Sierra	Table Rock Twp	89	571
HITT								
Henry F	44	m	w	MA	Los Angeles	El Monte Twp	73	460
HITTEL								
John	44	m	w	PA	San Francisco	11-Wd San Francisc	84	500
HITTELL								
Theodore	40	m	w	PA	San Francisco	San Francisco P O	83	210
HITTER								
Charlotte	32	f	w	GERM	Humboldt	Eel Rvr Twp	72	246
HITZ								
F	43	m	w	BADE	Monterey	Salinas Twp	74	312
HITZELBERGER								
Anthony	45	m	w	MD	Santa Cruz	Santa Cruz	89	403
William	11	m	w	CA	San Francisco	8-Wd San Francisco	82	406
HITZLEMAN								
Chas	24	m	w	FRAN	Santa Cruz	Santa Cruz	89	428
HIVESKER								
Henry	32	m	w	PRUS	Sacramento	2-Wd Sacramento	77	226
HIX								
Thos	30	m	w	IREL	San Francisco	11-Wd San Francisc	84	614
HIXON								
Almira K	49	f	w	NY	Santa Clara	2-Wd San Jose	88	326
Andrew	37	m	w	MO	Sonoma	Santa Rosa	91	416
J H	44	m	w	KY	San Francisco	San Francisco P O	85	802
J M	50	m	w	AL	Tuolumne	Big Oak Flat P O	93	404
John	35	m	w	KY	Colusa	Monroe Twp	71	311
Joseph H	22	m	w	KY	Monterey	San Antonio Twp	74	319
Omin	40	m	w	CANA	San Francisco	8-Wd San Francisco	82	378
Thomas	60	m	w	VA	El Dorado	Placerville	72	114
William	17	m	w	CA	Sonoma	Cloverdale Twp	91	268
HIXSON								
F B	28	m	w	CANA	Solano	Vallejo	90	198
Jno H	11	m	w	CA	Sonoma	Washington Twp	91	464
Jno Mc	40	m	w	TN	Sonoma	Washington Twp	91	464
Josiah	22	m	w	TN	Sonoma	Washington Twp	91	465
HIYEE								
Ah	34	m	c	CHIN	San Francisco	3-Wd San Francisco	79	301
HIZER								
Anna	21	f	w	AR	Sonoma	Mendocino Twp	91	291
HIZERMAN								
John	21	m	w	VA	Monterey	Alisal Twp	74	304
HNSON								
Peter	36	m	w	DENM	Plumas	Mineral Twp	77	22
HO								
Ac	30	m	c	CHIN	Sacramento	Georgianna Twp	77	124
Ah	60	m	c	CHIN	Sacramento	Granite Twp	77	154
Ah	60	m	c	CHIN	Tuolumne	Chinese Camp P O	93	382
Ah	6	m	c	CHIN	Sacramento	Cosumnes Twp	77	94
Ah	55	m	c	CHIN	Sacramento	Center Twp	77	86
Ah	55	m	c	CHIN	Sacramento	Granite Twp	77	152
Ah	55	m	c	CHIN	Sacramento	Granite Twp	77	154
Ah	55	m	c	CHIN	Sacramento	Center Twp	77	86
Ah	51	m	c	CHIN	Sacramento	Granite Twp	77	153
Ah	48	m	c	CHIN	Sacramento	Dry Crk Twp	77	101
Ah	48	m	c	CHIN	Sacramento	Georgianna Twp	77	133
Ah	48	m	c	CHIN	Sacramento	Georgianna Twp	77	133
Ah	47	m	c	CHIN	Amador	Drytown P O	69	424
Ah	46	m	c	CHIN	Sacramento	Natomas Twp	77	167
Ah	45	f	c	CHIN	Amador	Drytown P O	69	424
Ah	45	m	c	CHIN	Sacramento	Georgianna Twp	77	130
Ah	45	m	c	CHIN	Sacramento	Georgianna Twp	77	134
Ah	45	m	c	CHIN	Sacramento	Cosumnes Twp	77	90
Ah	44	m	c	CHIN	Sacramento	Cosumnes Twp	77	95
Ah	44	m	c	CHIN	Calaveras	San Andreas P O	70	174
Ah	44	m	c	CHIN	Sacramento	Granite Twp	77	155
Ah	44	m	c	CHIN	Sacramento	Center Twp	77	87
Ah	44	m	c	CHIN	Sacramento	Center Twp	77	86
Ah	44	m	c	CHIN	Sacramento	Center Twp	77	86
Ah	42	m	c	CHIN	Sacramento	Granite Twp	77	153
Ah	42	m	c	CHIN	Fresno	Millerton P O	72	199
Ah	42	m	c	CHIN	San Francisco	San Francisco P O	85	747
Ah	42	m	c	CHIN	Sacramento	Granite Twp	77	152
Ah	42	m	c	CHIN	Sacramento	Georgianna Twp	77	135
Ah	42	m	c	CHIN	Sacramento	Georgianna Twp	77	134
Ah	41	m	c	CHIN	Sacramento	Center Twp	77	86
Ah	41	m	c	CHIN	Nevada	Grass Valley Twp	75	228
Ah	40	m	c	CHIN	Sacramento	Natomas Twp	77	171
Ah	40	m	c	CHIN	El Dorado	Diamond Springs Tw	72	24
Ah	40	m	c	CHIN	Fresno	Millerton P O	72	200

© 2001 by Heritage Quest. All rights reserved.

Name	Age	S	R	B-PL	County	Locale	Roll	Pg
Ah	40	m	c	CHIN	Amador	Fiddletown P O	69	434
Ah	40	m	c	CHIN	San Joaquin	1-Wd Stockton	86	144
Ah	40	m	c	CHIN	Sacramento	Granite Twp	77	153
Ah	40	m	c	CHIN	Sacramento	Georgianna Twp	77	126
Ah	40	m	c	CHIN	Sacramento	Georgianna Twp	77	129
Ah	40	m	c	CHIN	Sacramento	Georgianna Twp	77	129
Ah	40	m	c	CHIN	Sacramento	Georgianna Twp	77	125
Ah	40	m	c	CHIN	Sacramento	Granite Twp	77	140
Ah	40	m	c	CHIN	Sacramento	Granite Twp	77	141
Ah	40	m	c	CHIN	Sacramento	Cosumnes Twp	77	94
Ah	40	m	c	CHIN	Sacramento	Center Twp	77	86
Ah	40	m	c	CHIN	Sacramento	Cosumnes Twp	77	94
Ah	39	m	c	CHIN	Placer	Pino Twp	76	470
Ah	39	m	c	CHIN	Sacramento	Granite Twp	77	154
Ah	38	m	c	CHIN	Kern	Linns Valley P O	73	343
Ah	38	f	c	CHIN	Tuolumne	Chinese Camp P O	93	375
Ah	38	m	c	CHIN	San Francisco	San Francisco P O	80	499
Ah	38	m	c	CHIN	Sacramento	Georgianna Twp	77	129
Ah	38	m	c	CHIN	Sacramento	Center Twp	77	87
Ah	37	m	c	CHIN	Sacramento	Georgianna Twp	77	124
Ah	37	m	c	CHIN	Sacramento	Georgianna Twp	77	128
Ah	37	m	c	CHIN	Sacramento	Georgianna Twp	77	128
Ah	37	m	c	CHIN	Sacramento	Granite Twp	77	139
Ah	37	m	c	CHIN	Sacramento	Center Twp	77	87
Ah	37	m	c	CHIN	Nevada	Washington Twp	75	347
Ah	37	m	c	CHIN	San Francisco	San Francisco P O	80	511
Ah	36	m	c	CHIN	Sacramento	Natomas Twp	77	171
Ah	36	m	c	CHIN	Sacramento	Center Twp	77	87
Ah	36	m	c	CHIN	Sacramento	Center Twp	77	86
Ah	36	m	c	CHIN	Sacramento	Georgianna Twp	77	125
Ah	36	m	c	CHIN	El Dorado	Mud Springs Twp	72	87
Ah	35	m	c	CHIN	Sacramento	Georgianna Twp	77	125
Ah	35	m	c	CHIN	Sacramento	Center Twp	77	85
Ah	35	m	c	CHIN	Mono	Bridgeport P O	74	282
Ah	35	f	c	CHIN	Tuolumne	Columbia P O	93	342
Ah	35	m	c	CHIN	Sacramento	Georgianna Twp	77	132
Ah	35	m	c	CHIN	Sacramento	Georgianna Twp	77	125
Ah	35	m	c	CHIN	Sacramento	Georgianna Twp	77	132
Ah	35	m	c	CHIN	Sacramento	Cosumnes Twp	77	95
Ah	35	m	c	CHIN	Sacramento	Center Twp	77	86
Ah	34	m	c	CHIN	Los Angeles	Santa Ana Twp	73	613
Ah	34	m	c	CHIN	Tuolumne	Chinese Camp P O	93	389
Ah	34	m	c	CHIN	Sacramento	Georgianna Twp	77	126
Ah	34	m	c	CHIN	Sacramento	Cosumnes Twp	77	93
Ah	34	m	c	CHIN	Sacramento	Center Twp	77	87
Ah	34	f	c	CHIN	Amador	Sutter Crk P O	69	403
Ah	33	f	c	CHIN	Tuolumne	Sonora P O	93	324
Ah	32	m	c	CHIN	Sacramento	Granite Twp	77	153
Ah	32	m	c	CHIN	Sacramento	Georgianna Twp	77	134
Ah	32	m	c	CHIN	Sacramento	Georgianna Twp	77	134
Ah	32	m	c	CHIN	Sacramento	Granite Twp	77	138
Ah	32	m	c	CHIN	Sacramento	Cosumnes Twp	77	94
Ah	32	m	c	CHIN	Calaveras	San Andreas P O	70	161
Ah	32	m	c	CHIN	San Francisco	San Francisco P O	80	523
Ah	31	m	c	CHIN	San Joaquin	1-Wd Stockton	86	149
Ah	31	m	c	CHIN	Sacramento	Georgianna Twp	77	132
Ah	31	f	c	CHIN	Nevada	Grass Valley Twp	75	205
Ah	31	f	c	CHIN	Nevada	Grass Valley Twp	75	205
Ah	30	m	c	CHIN	Sacramento	Georgianna Twp	77	124
Ah	30	m	c	CHIN	Sacramento	Natomas Twp	77	168
Ah	30	m	c	CHIN	Sacramento	Mississippi Twp	77	162
Ah	30	m	c	CHIN	Sacramento	American Twp	77	68
Ah	30	f	c	CHIN	El Dorado	Mud Springs Twp	72	79
Ah	30	m	c	CHIN	Calaveras	Copperopolis P O	70	241
Ah	30	m	c	CHIN	Sacramento	Georgianna Twp	77	133
Ah	30	m	c	CHIN	Sacramento	Georgianna Twp	77	131
Ah	30	m	c	CHIN	Sacramento	Georgianna Twp	77	125
Ah	30	m	c	CHIN	Sacramento	Georgianna Twp	77	129
Ah	30	m	c	CHIN	Sacramento	Georgianna Twp	77	126
Ah	30	m	c	CHIN	Sacramento	Georgianna Twp	77	133
Ah	30	m	c	CHIN	Sacramento	Cosumnes Twp	77	94
Ah	30	m	c	CHIN	Sacramento	Center Twp	77	87
Ah	3	m	c	CA	Sacramento	Granite Twp	77	152
Ah	29	m	c	CHIN	Sacramento	Georgianna Twp	77	129
Ah	29	m	c	CHIN	Sacramento	Granite Twp	77	155
Ah	29	m	c	CHIN	Calaveras	San Andreas P O	70	169
Ah	29	m	c	CHIN	Sacramento	Granite Twp	77	153
Ah	29	m	c	CHIN	Sacramento	Granite Twp	77	151
Ah	29	m	c	CHIN	Sacramento	Georgianna Twp	77	132
Ah	29	m	c	CHIN	Sacramento	Georgianna Twp	77	133
Ah	28	m	c	CHIN	Sacramento	Georgianna Twp	77	124
Ah	28	m	c	CHIN	Sacramento	Granite Twp	77	153
Ah	28	m	c	CHIN	Sacramento	Granite Twp	77	155
Ah	28	m	c	CHIN	San Francisco	San Francisco P O	83	131
Ah	28	m	c	CHIN	Sacramento	Natomas Twp	77	168
Ah	28	m	c	CHIN	Sacramento	Dry Crk Twp	77	101
Ah	28	m	c	CHIN	Sacramento	Georgianna Twp	77	122
Ah	28	m	c	CHIN	Sacramento	Georgianna Twp	77	131
Ah	28	m	c	CHIN	Sacramento	Granite Twp	77	149
Ah	28	m	c	CHIN	Sacramento	Granite Twp	77	153
Ah	28	m	c	CHIN	Sacramento	Center Twp	77	85
Ah	28	m	c	CHIN	Alameda	Eden Twp	68	61
Ah	28	m	c	CHIN	Fresno	Millerton P O	72	199
Ah	28	f	c	CHIN	San Francisco	San Francisco P O	80	490
Ah	27	m	c	CHIN	Sacramento	Natomas Twp	77	171
Ah	27	m	c	CHIN	Sacramento	Natomas Twp	77	168
Ah	27	m	c	CHIN	Sacramento	Georgianna Twp	77	135

Name	Age	S	R	B-PL	County	Locale	Roll	Pg
Ah	27	m	c	CHIN	Sacramento	Georgianna Twp	77	135
Ah	27	m	c	CHIN	Sacramento	Georgianna Twp	77	133
Ah	27	m	c	CHIN	Sacramento	Georgianna Twp	77	131
Ah	27	m	c	CHIN	Sacramento	Georgianna Twp	77	133
Ah	27	m	c	CHIN	Sacramento	Georgianna Twp	77	134
Ah	27	m	c	CHIN	Sacramento	Cosumnes Twp	77	94
Ah	27	m	c	CHIN	Sacramento	Cosumnes Twp	77	94
Ah	26	m	c	CHIN	Sacramento	Georgianna Twp	77	125
Ah	26	m	c	CHIN	Sacramento	Natomas Twp	77	171
Ah	26	m	c	CHIN	Santa Cruz	Santa Cruz	89	434
Ah	26	m	c	CHIN	Sacramento	Center Twp	77	85
Ah	25	f	c	CHIN	Sacramento	Granite Twp	77	152
Ah	25	m	c	CHIN	Sacramento	American Twp	77	67
Ah	25	m	c	CHIN	Placer	Colfax P O	76	385
Ah	25	m	c	CHIN	Sacramento	Granite Twp	77	138
Ah	25	m	c	CHIN	Sacramento	Georgianna Twp	77	131
Ah	25	m	c	CHIN	Sacramento	Georgianna Twp	77	127
Ah	25	m	c	CHIN	Sacramento	Granite Twp	77	137
Ah	25	m	c	CHIN	Calaveras	San Andreas P O	70	155
Ah	25	f	c	CHIN	El Dorado	Placerville	72	115
Ah	24	m	c	CHIN	Sacramento	Georgianna Twp	77	132
Ah	23	f	c	CHIN	San Francisco	San Francisco P O	80	433
Ah	23	m	c	CHIN	Sacramento	Granite Twp	77	155
Ah	23	f	c	CHIN	San Francisco	6-Wd San Francisco	81	74
Ah	22	m	c	CHIN	Placer	Auburn P O	76	364
Ah	22	m	c	CHIN	Sacramento	Granite Twp	77	152
Ah	22	m	c	CHIN	Sacramento	Georgianna Twp	77	127
Ah	22	m	c	CHIN	Sacramento	Center Twp	77	86
Ah	22	m	c	CHIN	Alameda	Oakland	68	220
Ah	22	f	c	CHIN	El Dorado	Placerville	72	116
Ah	22	m	c	CHIN	Los Angeles	Los Angeles	73	547
Ah	21	m	c	CHIN	Sacramento	Granite Twp	77	155
Ah	21	f	c	CHIN	San Francisco	San Francisco P O	80	434
Ah	21	f	c	CHIN	San Francisco	San Francisco P O	80	440
Ah	21	f	c	CHIN	El Dorado	Placerville	72	116
Ah	20	m	c	CHIN	Sacramento	Center Twp	77	85
Ah	20	m	c	CHIN	Sacramento	Center Twp	77	86
Ah	20	m	c	CHIN	San Francisco	3-Wd San Francisco	79	324
Ah	20	m	c	CHIN	Sutter	Sutter Twp	92	126
Ah	20	f	c	CHIN	San Diego	San Diego	78	494
Ah	20	m	c	CHIN	El Dorado	Mud Springs Twp	72	85
Ah	19	f	c	CHIN	Nevada	Grass Valley Twp	75	205
Ah	18	f	c	CHIN	Sacramento	Granite Twp	77	153
Ah	18	m	c	CHIN	Sacramento	Granite Twp	77	152
Ah	18	m	c	CHIN	Solano	Benicia	90	14
Ah	18	m	c	CHIN	Sierra	Gibson Twp	89	544
Ah	17	m	c	CHIN	Sonoma	Russian Rvr	91	371
Ah	17	f	c	CHIN	Amador	Fiddletown P O	69	427
Ah	17	m	c	CHIN	Sonoma	Santa Rosa	91	424
Ah	16	m	c	CHIN	San Francisco	8-Wd San Francisco	82	359
Ah	16	m	c	CHIN	Sacramento	Georgianna Twp	77	132
Ah	14	m	c	CHIN	San Francisco	7-Wd San Francisco	81	286
Chin	30	m	c	CHIN	Butte	Chico Twp	70	51
Con	23	m	c	CHIN	Butte	Hamilton Twp	70	72
Cum	31	f	c	CHIN	Fresno	Millerton P O	72	200
Fok	28	m	c	CHIN	San Francisco	6-Wd San Francisco	81	44
Foo	45	m	c	CHIN	Butte	Chico Twp	70	51
Foo	30	m	c	CHIN	Fresno	Millerton P O	72	202
Gee	38	m	c	CHIN	Sacramento	1-Wd Sacramento	77	202
Gee	29	m	c	CHIN	Sacramento	1-Wd Sacramento	77	194
Goo	40	m	c	CHIN	San Joaquin	2-Wd Stockton	86	181
Har	31	m	c	CHIN	San Joaquin	1-Wd Stockton	86	155
Him	40	m	c	CHIN	Solano	Green Valley Twp	90	42
Hoy	28	m	c	CHIN	Sacramento	1-Wd Sacramento	77	202
Hung	30	m	c	CHIN	San Francisco	6-Wd San Francisco	81	44
Hunt	54	m	w	OH	San Joaquin	Liberty Twp	86	89
Jim	29	f	c	CHIN	Kern	Havilah P O	73	338
Kee	42	m	c	CHIN	Sacramento	2-Wd Sacramento	77	217
Kee	37	m	c	CHIN	Sacramento	2-Wd Sacramento	77	217
Kee	36	m	c	CHIN	San Francisco	6-Wd San Francisco	81	61
Kee	24	m	c	CHIN	Solano	Suisun Twp	90	106
King	40	m	c	CHIN	San Francisco	11-Wd San Francisc	84	546
Kong	43	m	c	CHIN	Trinity	Weaverville Pct	92	231
Lee	47	m	c	CHIN	Calaveras	San Andreas P O	70	219
Lin	39	m	c	CHIN	Butte	Wyandotte Twp	70	143
Lin	20	f	c	CHIN	El Dorado	Placerville	72	115
Ling	32	m	c	CHIN	Yuba	Marysville	93	621
Lom	38	m	c	CHIN	San Joaquin	1-Wd Stockton	86	156
Lon	22	m	c	CHIN	Butte	Hamilton Twp	70	72
Lop	16	m	c	CHIN	San Joaquin	1-Wd Stockton	86	151
Man	31	m	c	CHIN	Calaveras	San Andreas P O	70	203
Me	17	f	c	CHIN	San Francisco	6-Wd San Francisco	81	60
Oh	25	f	c	CHIN	Nevada	Nevada Twp	75	299
Own	28	m	c	CHIN	Calaveras	San Andreas P O	70	211
Quon	45	m	c	CHIN	Calaveras	San Andreas P O	70	161
Quong	45	m	c	CHIN	Calaveras	San Andreas P O	70	211
Sam	43	m	c	CHIN	Santa Clara	Santa Clara Twp	88	168
Sam	19	m	c	CHIN	Tehama	Antelope Twp	92	155
Sin	18	m	c	CHIN	Sacramento	1-Wd Sacramento	77	182
Sing	23	f	c	CHIN	San Francisco	6-Wd San Francisco	81	67
Sing	18	m	c	CHIN	Tehama	Deer Crk Twp	92	171
Sing	18	m	c	CHIN	Yuba	Marysville	93	621
Sung	28	m	c	CHIN	San Francisco	6-Wd San Francisco	81	43
Wa	28	m	c	CHIN	Fresno	Millerton P O	72	202
Wang	24	m	c	CHIN	San Francisco	8-Wd San Francisco	82	358
Wenn	16	m	c	CHIN	San Joaquin	1-Wd Stockton	86	151
Wun	30	m	c	CHIN	Sacramento	1-Wd Sacramento	77	202

© 2001 by Heritage Quest. All rights reserved.

Name	Age	S	R	B-PL	County	Locale	Roll (Series M593)	Pg
Yack	16	m	c	CHIN	Trinity	Junction City Pct	92	206
Yan	33	m	c	CHIN	Calaveras	San Andreas P O	70	204
Yo	26	f	c	CHIN	El Dorado	Mud Springs Twp	72	87
Yong	55	m	c	CHIN	Calaveras	San Andreas P O	70	204
Yop	28	m	c	CHIN	Sacramento	1-Wd Sacramento	77	202
Yot	17	m	c	CHIN	San Luis Obispo	Arroyo Grande Twp	87	278
Yoy Too	22	m	c	CHIN	Amador	Ione City P O	69	366
Yum	40	m	c	CHIN	Fresno	Millerton P O	72	184
HOA								
Ah	51	m	c	CHIN	Humboldt	Arcata Twp	72	233
Ah	40	m	c	CHIN	Sonoma	Salt Point	91	387
Ah	35	m	c	CHIN	Sacramento	Franklin Twp	77	118
Ah	25	m	c	CHIN	Sonoma	Salt Point	91	387
HOACHENSCHILD								
H	21	m	w	LA	San Francisco	San Francisco P O	83	297
HOAD								
John H	68	m	w	ENGL	Butte	Bidwell Twp	70	4
Lewis	38	m	w	OH	Butte	Chico Twp	70	32
HOADLEY								
Catharine	52	f	w	IREL	San Francisco	San Francisco P O	83	44
Elias A	37	m	w	VT	Klamath	Dillon Twp	73	369
James	38	m	w	NY	Trinity	Lewiston Pct	92	213
James H	38	m	w	CT	San Francisco	2-Wd San Francisco	79	254
Milo	60	m	w	CT	San Francisco	San Francisco P O	85	770
HOADY								
John	35	m	w	IREL	San Francisco	7-Wd San Francisco	81	193
HOAFT								
John	16	m	w	HANO	San Francisco	San Francisco P O	85	756
HOAG								
---	23	m	c	CHIN	Shasta	Horsetown P O	89	503
Abraham	28	m	w	NY	San Bernardino	San Salvador Twp	78	457
Benjamin H	37	m	w	NY	Yolo	Washington Twp	93	532
Caroline	30	f	w	CT	Marin	San Rafael	74	57
Charles	18	m	w	NY	Marin	Tomales Twp	74	83
Charles P	27	m	w	MA	San Francisco	8-Wd San Francisco	82	462
David	24	m	w	NY	Sonoma	Analy Twp	91	219
Delavan	47	m	w	NY	Santa Clara	Fremont Twp	88	57
Elizabeth	42	f	w	IL	Alameda	Oakland	68	174
George	50	m	w	NY	San Francisco	7-Wd San Francisco	81	171
George H	27	m	w	MA	San Francisco	8-Wd San Francisco	82	302
George W	45	m	w	NY	Colusa	Monroe Twp	71	313
George W	30	m	w	PA	San Mateo	Belmont P O	87	374
Horace	52	m	w	NY	San Francisco	11-Wd San Francisc	84	623
Isaac N	47	m	w	NY	Yolo	Washington Twp	93	531
J V	52	m	w	NY	Nevada	Meadow Lake Twp	75	258
Jared C	36	m	w	NY	Sonoma	Analy Twp	91	221
John	35	m	w	WURT	San Francisco	2-Wd San Francisco	79	168
John	22	m	w	MA	Solano	Tremont Twp	90	30
Jonathan	56	m	w	NH	Contra Costa	Martinez P O	71	394
Mary	22	f	i	CA	Colusa	Monroe Twp	71	313
Newman B	54	m	w	NY	Sonoma	Analy Twp	91	221
Obediah H	31	m	w	NY	Sonoma	Analy Twp	91	221
Soloman	42	m	w	NY	Sonoma	Analy Twp	91	247
Walter	32	m	w	ENGL	San Francisco	8-Wd San Francisco	82	362
William	31	m	w	IREL	Solano	Rio Vista Twp	90	59
William H	61	m	w	NY	Sacramento	2-Wd Sacramento	77	207
HOAGE								
Oscar S	38	m	w	NH	Santa Clara	1-Wd San Jose	88	252
Wm	26	m	w	MA	San Francisco	11-Wd San Francisc	84	667
HOAGLAN								
John E	48	m	w	PA	Yolo	Washington Twp	93	529
HOAGLAND								
John	37	m	w	NY	San Joaquin	Tulare Twp	86	261
John	26	m	w	SWED	Nevada	Grass Valley Twp	75	162
Lucas	43	m	w	MI	San Bernardino	San Bernardino Twp	78	441
Rose	28	f	w	CT	San Francisco	San Francisco P O	83	288
HOAGLY								
Henry	30	m	w	NY	San Mateo	Menlo Park P O	87	378
HOAH								
Toy	41	m	c	CHIN	San Joaquin	Oneal Twp	86	115
HOAK								
George	18	m	w	CA	Alpine	Woodfords P O	69	309
HOAM								
Manuell	23	m	w	PORT	San Mateo	Pescadero P O	87	415
HOAN								
Ah	38	m	c	CHIN	Shasta	French Gulch P O	89	469
Michl	29	m	w	IREL	San Francisco	1-Wd San Francisco	79	69
HOANG								
Ah	23	m	c	CHIN	Santa Clara	San Jose Twp	88	193
HOAR								
Benj F	30	m	w	US	Nevada	Grass Valley Twp	75	225
Charles A	31	m	w	ME	Alpine	Woodfords P O	69	316
Charles A	28	m	w	US	Nevada	Grass Valley Twp	75	225
Chas W	24	m	w	ENGL	San Francisco	8-Wd San Francisco	82	343
James	40	m	w	MA	San Francisco	5-Wd San Francisco	81	6
John	19	m	w	ENGL	Nevada	Grass Valley Twp	75	191
Wesley N	19	m	w	ME	Alpine	Woodfords P O	69	316
William	61	m	w	ME	Alpine	Woodfords P O	69	316
William	30	m	w	ENGL	Amador	Amador City P O	69	393
HOARAY								
John	36	m	w	IREL	San Francisco	San Francisco P O	83	370
HOARD								
H G	45	m	w	TN	Amador	Fiddletown P O	69	430
Ramslar	59	m	w	NY	Santa Clara	Santa Clara Twp	88	171
HOARE								
Mikel	30	m	w	IREL	San Francisco	San Francisco P O	83	6

Name	Age	S	R	B-PL	County	Locale	Roll (Series M593)	Pg
HOARTH								
Emil	40	m	w	DENM	Los Angeles	Los Angeles	73	565
HOARY								
John	40	m	w	IREL	San Francisco	8-Wd San Francisco	82	398
HOAS								
---	68	m	c	CHIN	Siskiyou	Yreka Twp	89	669
HOASA								
Ann	26	f	w	IREL	Alameda	Alameda	68	10
HOAY								
Geo S	28	m	w	MA	San Francisco	8-Wd San Francisco	82	337
HOB								
Ah	33	m	c	CHIN	Nevada	Grass Valley Twp	75	190
Ah	20	m	c	CHIN	San Francisco	8-Wd San Francisco	82	410
Sing	28	m	c	CHIN	Solano	Green Valley Twp	90	42
HOBAR								
F	25	f	w	PRUS	Alameda	Alameda	68	11
HOBART								
Allen P	55	m	w	VT	Butte	Chico Twp	70	50
Bell	25	f	w	IREL	San Francisco	5-Wd San Francisco	81	27
Benjamin Jr	45	m	w	MA	San Francisco	San Francisco P O	85	776
Edward	39	m	w	NJ	El Dorado	Mud Springs Twp	72	71
Edward	30	m	w	WALE	San Francisco	7-Wd San Francisco	81	276
Harvey	35	m	w	TX	Nevada	Bloomfield Twp	75	94
J A	62	m	w	MA	Alameda	Oakland	68	227
James P	50	m	w	MA	Nevada	Nevada Twp	75	302
John	22	m	w	NY	San Francisco	1-Wd San Francisco	79	130
Lewis	2	m	w	CA	San Francisco	6-Wd San Francisco	81	105
Paul	35	m	w	FRAN	San Francisco	San Francisco P O	85	841
Sarah E	70	f	w	US	Santa Cruz	Santa Cruz	89	411
HOBBE								
Louis	26	m	w	AUST	San Joaquin	Tulare Twp	86	250
HOBBIE								
Joseph E	23	m	w	MA	Sacramento	3-Wd Sacramento	77	284
HOBBLER								
Albert	28	m	w	AUSL	Alameda	Murray Twp	68	122
HOBBS								
Abraham	48	m	w	IREL	Solano	Silveyville Twp	90	78
Alexander	42	m	w	NC	San Bernardino	Chino Twp	78	410
C H	27	m	w	PA	San Joaquin	2-Wd Stockton	86	161
Caleb	60	m	w	NH	San Francisco	7-Wd San Francisco	81	157
Dickrey	50	m	w	ENGL	Sacramento	San Joaquin Twp	77	406
Emory	35	m	w	LA	Tuolumne	Sonora P O	93	318
Ezekial	34	m	w	OH	Solano	Vacaville Twp	90	127
Fredrick	34	m	w	ME	San Francisco	San Francisco P O	83	226
Gashom	35	m	w	PA	Sonoma	Analy Twp	91	227
George B	33	m	w	ME	Placer	Dutch Flat P O	76	409
H P	39	m	w	ME	Santa Clara	Gilroy Twp	88	74
Hiram H	37	m	w	ME	Santa Cruz	Santa Cruz	89	405
J W	32	m	w	KY	Sutter	Sutter Twp	92	117
James	50	m	w	MO	Tulare	White Rvr Twp	92	302
L M	31	m	w	MA	Alameda	Oakland	68	163
Moses F	39	m	w	MA	Marin	Bolinas Twp	74	1
P K	41	m	w	ME	Solano	Vallejo	90	197
Saml	45	m	w	VT	San Diego	San Diego	78	492
Samuel	39	m	w	IN	Santa Barbara	Arroyo Burro P O	87	509
Selden X	37	m	w	TN	Santa Clara	1-Wd San Jose	88	255
William H	34	m	w	ME	Santa Cruz	Soquel Twp	89	443
Wm H	35	m	m	LA	Butte	Ophir Twp	70	104
HOBBY								
D A	43	m	w	CT	Sierra	Lincoln Twp	89	547
Elizabeth	45	f	w	KY	Nevada	Grass Valley Twp	75	143
James	28	m	w	KY	Placer	Cisco P O	76	494
John	40	m	w	NY	San Francisco	5-Wd San Francisco	81	30
Spencer	29	m	w	KY	Nevada	Meadow Lake Twp	75	255
W H	40	m	w	CT	Sacramento	3-Wd Sacramento	77	263
William	57	m	w	KY	Nevada	Grass Valley Twp	75	142
HOBE								
Adolphus	41	m	w	HAMB	San Francisco	11-Wd San Francisc	84	557
George J	45	m	w	HAMB	San Francisco	2-Wd San Francisco	79	247
HOBEN								
Harry	28	m	w	NY	San Francisco	1-Wd San Francisco	79	125
John	27	m	w	MI	Nevada	Grass Valley Twp	75	217
HOBENIGH								
Richard	30	m	w	HANO	San Francisco	7-Wd San Francisco	81	224
HOBER								
Adolph	40	m	w	GERM	San Francisco	8-Wd San Francisco	82	370
HOBERSON								
Louisa	5	f	w	CA	Stanislaus	Empire Twp	92	53
HOBERT								
Ada	13	f	w	CA	Sacramento	San Joaquin Twp	77	394
J B	54	m	w	MA	Calaveras	Copperopolis P O	70	224
John	31	m	w	PRUS	San Francisco	5-Wd San Francisco	81	13
HOBERTI								
Thomas	19	m	w	ITAL	San Francisco	San Francisco P O	80	413
HOBERY								
Wm	49	m	w	MD	San Francisco	11-Wd San Francisc	84	422
HOBEY								
George	29	m	w	SWED	San Francisco	3-Wd San Francisco	79	300
HOBIN								
Henry	35	m	w	ENGL	San Francisco	11-Wd San Francisc	84	519
John	33	m	w	IREL	Stanislaus	Empire Twp	92	66
HOBINE								
Augusta	19	f	w	MO	San Francisco	San Francisco P O	80	423
HOBKINS								
Micheal	34	m	w	IREL	San Francisco	7-Wd San Francisco	81	210
HOBLER								
George	70	m	w	ENGL	Alameda	Alameda	68	2

© 2001 by Heritage Quest. All rights reserved.

Series M593

Name	Age	S	R	B-PL	County	Locale	Roll	Pg
HOBLEY								
Spencer	26	m	w	MO	Nevada	Meadow Lake Twp	75	266
HOBLITZEL								
H S	41	m	w	MD	Yuba	Marysville	93	605
HOBSON								
A M	41	m	w	NY	Klamath	Sawyers Bar	73	378
Abraham	77	m	w	ENGL	San Francisco	6-Wd San Francisco	81	106
Alf D	44	m	w	NC	Sonoma	Mendocino Twp	91	300
An	22	m	w	PA	Sierra	Eureka Twp	89	525
Caroline	36	f	w	NY	Napa	Napa	75	26
Catherine	39	f	w	IREL	Shasta	Shasta P O	89	454
Charles	26	m	w	NC	Santa Clara	2-Wd San Jose	88	281
David	48	m	w	NC	Santa Clara	San Jose Twp	88	203
David J	42	m	w	NC	Santa Clara	San Jose Twp	88	203
Eliza	45	f	w	ENGL	San Francisco	6-Wd San Francisco	81	79
Eliza D	64	f	w	IL	Santa Barbara	San Buenaventura P	87	440
G W	42	m	w	ME	Mariposa	Maxwell Crk P O	74	143
George	47	m	w	NC	Santa Clara	2-Wd San Jose	88	296
George	13	m	w	CA	San Francisco	8-Wd San Francisco	82	487
Henry	25	m	w	ENGL	San Francisco	11-Wd San Francisc	84	709
Henry C	12	m	w	KS	Santa Clara	San Jose Twp	88	214
Isaac	52	m	w	IN	Sutter	Yuba Twp	92	143
J E	40	m	w	ENGL	Yuba	Marysville	93	590
J M	38	m	w	IA	Tehama	Stony Crk	92	166
Jacob	29	m	w	NC	Santa Clara	Burnett Twp	88	38
Jacob	29	m	w	NC	Santa Clara	Gilroy Twp	88	102
James R	45	m	w	IN	Colusa	Colusa Twp	71	283
Jesse	53	m	w	NC	Santa Clara	2-Wd San Jose	88	285
John	55	m	w	ENGL	San Joaquin	2-Wd Stockton	86	174
John B	27	m	w	NY	Sacramento	4-Wd Sacramento	77	334
Stephen	41	m	w	NC	Santa Clara	San Jose Twp	88	203
Thaddeus	20	m	w	CA	Santa Clara	2-Wd San Jose	88	319
Thomas	45	m	w	IREL	San Francisco	San Francisco P O	80	387
William	42	m	w	OH	Sacramento	2-Wd Sacramento	77	210
Winton	32	m	w	IL	Napa	Yountville Twp	75	79
Wm	32	m	w	SCOT	San Francisco	2-Wd San Francisco	79	209
Wm D	41	m	w	IL	Santa Barbara	San Buenaventura P	87	436
HOBURN								
John	30	m	w	IREL	San Francisco	11-Wd San Francisc	84	516
HOC								
Ah	53	m	c	CHIN	Placer	Newcastle Twp	76	479
Ah	41	m	c	CHIN	Butte	Kimshew Tpw	70	86
Ah	38	m	c	CHIN	Calaveras	San Andreas P O	70	176
Cho	42	m	c	CHIN	Butte	Concow Twp	70	10
Cho	40	m	c	CHIN	Butte	Concow Twp	70	11
Chon	32	m	c	CHIN	Butte	Concow Twp	70	10
Choy	33	m	c	CHIN	Butte	Concow Twp	70	10
Mary	29	f	w	FL	Butte	Oregon Twp	70	131
Ton	45	m	c	CHIN	Butte	Concow Twp	70	10
Woh	42	m	c	CHIN	Butte	Concow Twp	70	11
Yan	36	m	c	CHIN	Butte	Concow Twp	70	10
Yon	22	m	c	CHIN	Butte	Hamilton Twp	70	73
HOCH								
Frantz	29	m	w	HAMB	San Francisco	San Francisco P O	80	352
Fredk	40	m	w	WURT	San Francisco	1-Wd San Francisco	79	60
Isach	32	m	w	POLA	Los Angeles	Los Angeles	73	549
John C	28	m	w	HAMB	San Francisco	2-Wd San Francisco	79	238
Loin	50	m	c	CHIN	San Francisco	6-Wd San Francisco	81	47
William	25	m	w	HAMB	San Francisco	2-Wd San Francisco	79	238
HOCHHEIMER								
Letri	20	f	w	BADE	Solano	Silveyville Twp	90	85
HOCHHOLZER								
Huge	42	m	w	HUNG	San Francisco	San Francisco P O	80	359
HOCHING								
C B	30	m	w	MI	San Joaquin	Oneal Twp	86	107
HOCHKLER								
R	43	m	w	ITAL	Alameda	Oakland	68	161
HOCHSTADTER								
S	26	m	w	PRUS	Yuba	Marysville	93	591
HOCK								
Ah	50	m	c	CHIN	Placer	Auburn P O	76	362
Ah	47	m	c	CHIN	Amador	Fiddletown P O	69	428
Ah	45	m	c	CHIN	Placer	Auburn P O	76	362
Ah	42	m	c	CHIN	Plumas	Goodwin Twp	77	5
Ah	35	m	c	CHIN	Placer	Dutch Flat P O	76	409
Ah	30	m	c	CHIN	Sacramento	Cosumnes Twp	77	90
Ah	26	m	c	CHIN	Amador	Volcano P O	69	378
Ah	24	f	c	CHIN	Tuolumne	Chinese Camp P O	93	375
Ah	22	m	c	CHIN	Sonoma	Sonoma Twp	91	447
Ah	18	m	c	CHIN	Placer	Clipper Gap P O	76	393
Ah	17	m	c	CHIN	Alameda	Oakland	68	237
Foy	25	m	c	CHIN	Yuba	Marysville	93	628
Frank	38	m	w	NC	Sacramento	San Joaquin Twp	77	405
Gim	20	m	c	CHIN	San Francisco	San Francisco P O	85	806
Hong	19	m	c	CHIN	Yuba	Marysville	93	631
John	34	m	w	OH	Trinity	North Fork Twp	92	217
John	26	m	w	MA	Alameda	Oakland	68	261
Kin	60	m	c	CHIN	Plumas	Washington Twp	77	57
Know	40	m	c	CHIN	Calaveras	San Andreas P O	70	162
Lich	33	m	c	CHIN	Sonoma	Petaluma Twp	91	343
Mena	27	f	w	PRUS	San Joaquin	2-Wd Stockton	86	199
Nicholas	45	m	w	AUST	Placer	Clipper Gap P O	76	392
Ny	24	m	c	CHIN	Butte	Chico Twp	70	52
Ong	41	m	c	CHIN	Yuba	Marysville	93	631
Poo	31	f	c	CHIN	Yuba	Marysville	93	627
Sue	34	m	c	CHIN	Yuba	Marysville	93	630
Sum	33	m	c	CHIN	Klamath	Liberty Twp	73	374
Suon	30	m	c	CHIN	Calaveras	San Andreas P O	70	162
Tongue	48	m	c	CHIN	Plumas	Washington Twp	77	57
Wa	19	m	c	CHIN	Nevada	Bridgeport Twp	75	111
Wm	37	m	w	OH	Sacramento	3-Wd Sacramento	77	279
Woey	35	m	c	CHIN	Yuba	Marysville	93	624
HOCKBEE								
Thos	32	m	w	MO	San Joaquin	2-Wd Stockton	86	171
HOCKENSMITH								
J T	39	m	w	KY	Amador	Jackson P O	69	342
HOCKER								
Catherine	57	f	w	BADE	San Francisco	11-Wd San Francisc	84	440
George A	33	m	w	NY	Sonoma	Petaluma Twp	91	313
Henry	46	m	w	HANO	Trinity	Weaverville Pct	92	223
HOCKETT								
John B	42	m	w	IL	Tulare	Tule Rvr Twp	92	270
HOCKETY								
John W	36	m	w	VA	Mendocino	Point Arena Twp	74	213
HOCKEY								
William	33	m	w	ENGL	Nevada	Grass Valley Twp	75	166
HOCKHOUSE								
Joannah	50	f	w	PRUS	San Francisco	6-Wd San Francisco	81	134
HOCKIN								
Charles	32	m	w	ENGL	Nevada	Grass Valley Twp	75	188
HOCKING								
Edmund	38	m	w	ENGL	Nevada	Grass Valley Twp	75	159
Edward	36	m	w	ENGL	Nevada	Grass Valley Twp	75	193
Jno	44	m	w	ENGL	Santa Clara	Almaden Twp	88	9
John	22	m	w	ENGL	Nevada	Grass Valley Twp	75	224
Joseph	28	m	w	ENGL	Nevada	Grass Valley Twp	75	224
Samuel	26	m	w	ENGL	Nevada	Grass Valley Twp	75	144
Stephen	35	m	w	ENGL	Nevada	Grass Valley Twp	75	203
Thomas	35	m	w	ENGL	Nevada	Grass Valley Twp	75	193
William	44	m	w	ENGL	Nevada	Grass Valley Twp	75	164
William	29	m	w	ENGL	San Francisco	6-Wd San Francisco	81	144
HOCKINGS								
---	26	m	w	PA	Sacramento	3-Wd Sacramento	77	280
HOCKISS								
G C	40	m	w	CT	Tuolumne	Chinese Camp P O	93	368
HOCKLING								
William	42	m	w	ENGL	Nevada	Nevada Twp	75	315
HOCKMAN								
H	26	m	w	PRUS	Yuba	Marysville	93	605
Jacob	46	m	w	VA	Sonoma	Washington Twp	91	467
Mary	19	f	w	HANO	San Francisco	San Francisco P O	83	26
HOCKMEYER								
Adam	26	m	w	BADE	San Francisco	2-Wd San Francisco	79	165
HOCKMUTH								
B	30	m	w	SAXO	Sutter	Yuba Twp	92	143
HOCKSTRAT								
Antone	36	m	w	PRUS	Colusa	Butte Twp	71	272
HOCKURCE								
Peter	56	m	w	ENGL	Sacramento	2-Wd Sacramento	77	206
HOCTOR								
John	25	m	w	IREL	San Francisco	11-Wd San Francisc	84	642
Patrick	30	m	w	IREL	San Francisco	San Francisco P O	80	540
HOCY								
John	36	m	w	IREL	Sacramento	3-Wd Sacramento	77	311
HODAPP								
Sebastin	45	m	w	HDAR	Solano	Rio Vista Twp	90	62
HODDEN								
James	34	m	w	NY	Alameda	Oakland	68	130
HODDY								
Diedrich	40	m	w	PRUS	San Francisco	2-Wd San Francisco	79	261
O P	30	m	w	OH	Mendocino	Ukiah Twp	74	238
HODECKER								
Philip	63	m	w	HANO	Calaveras	San Andreas P O	70	172
HODEN								
Edmund	34	m	w	IREL	San Francisco	11-Wd San Francisc	84	533
Henry	32	m	w	MA	San Joaquin	2-Wd Stockton	86	165
John	25	m	w	IREL	San Francisco	San Francisco P O	83	41
HODES								
Gustina	58	f	w	HANO	San Francisco	8-Wd San Francisco	82	357
Lebareous	42	m	w	HANO	Calaveras	San Andreas P O	70	182
HODESTY								
John	39	m	w	OH	San Joaquin	1-Wd Stockton	86	132
HODGDEN								
Phebe	29	f	w	ME	Calaveras	San Andreas P O	70	188
HODGDON								
Ambrose	42	m	w	ME	San Francisco	11-Wd San Francisc	84	524
Charles	66	m	w	NH	Santa Clara	San Jose Twp	88	180
Elizabeth	35	f	w	MA	San Francisco	8-Wd San Francisco	82	487
J R	33	m	w	ME	Monterey	San Juan Twp	74	410
John P	32	m	w	NH	Placer	Colfax P O	76	386
Wadsworth	55	m	w	ME	Yolo	Washington Twp	93	534
HODGE								
Alexander	45	m	w	SCOT	San Francisco	San Francisco P O	83	235
Alexander	39	m	w	NH	Marin	Tomales Twp	74	81
Ben O	44	m	w	NY	San Francisco	8-Wd San Francisco	82	354
Charlotte	60	f	b	VA	Sacramento	Cosumnes Twp	77	92
Chas	24	m	w	IL	Alameda	Oakland	68	146
David C	29	m	w	NH	Sacramento	Franklin Twp	77	110
George	32	m	w	ENGL	Napa	Napa	75	24
George M	21	m	w	IN	Alpine	Markleeville P O	69	311
Henry	38	m	w	ENGL	Del Norte	Crescent Twp	71	457
Hugh W	40	m	w	GA	El Dorado	Placerville	72	124
James	30	m	w	NY	Contra Costa	San Pablo Twp	71	360
Jno	38	m	w	MA	San Joaquin	1-Wd Stockton	86	130

© 2001 by Heritage Quest. All rights reserved.

California 1870 Census

Name	Age	S	R	B-PL	County	Locale	Series M593 Roll	Pg
John	29	m	w	ENGL	Nevada	Nevada Twp	75	300
John F	36	m	w	IL	Yolo	Buckeye Twp	93	410
Joseph	30	m	w	KS	San Joaquin	Elkhorn Twp	86	67
Kenny	40	m	w	VA	San Joaquin	3-Wd Stockton	86	233
L C	42	m	w	NY	Sutter	Yuba Twp	92	149
Mary J	33	f	w	ENGL	Nevada	Grass Valley Twp	75	198
Matthea	49	m	w	IREL	Sacramento	4-Wd Sacramento	77	354
Michael	38	m	w	IREL	San Francisco	1-Wd San Francisco	79	3
Richard	27	m	w	ENGL	Tuolumne	Sonora P O	93	324
Samuel	55	m	w	ENGL	Nevada	Grass Valley Twp	75	192
Thomas	45	m	w	AL	San Diego	Milquaty Dist	78	478
Thomas	37	m	w	NY	Tuolumne	Sonora P O	93	317
Thomas	32	m	w	ENGL	Nevada	Grass Valley Twp	75	192
Thomas	26	m	w	ENGL	Yuba	North East Twp	93	646
Thomas	21	m	w	NC	Marin	San Rafael Twp	74	45
W C	39	m	w	IL	Sutter	Vernon Twp	92	137
William	22	m	w	WI	Stanislaus	Emory Twp	92	17
Wm	36	m	w	HANO	San Francisco	11-Wd San Francisc	84	426
Wm	28	m	w	ENGL	Tuolumne	Sonora P O	93	326
HODGEKINS								
Otis	60	m	w	ME	Los Angeles	Los Angeles Twp	73	495
HODGEN								
I R	44	m	w	KY	Tehama	Antelope Twp	92	158
John	40	m	w	CT	San Francisco	San Francisco P O	83	329
Saml J	32	m	w	ME	San Francisco	1-Wd San Francisco	79	34
HODGERS								
A D	23	m	w	NY	San Francisco	5-Wd San Francisco	81	36
John	50	m	w	ENGL	El Dorado	Georgetown Twp	72	38
Richard	20	m	w	MO	Solano	Suisun Twp	90	115
HODGES								
Albert	24	m	w	MA	San Francisco	7-Wd San Francisco	81	278
Anna A	16	f	w	CA	San Mateo	Redwood City P O	87	376
Benjamin	43	m	w	IL	Contra Costa	Martinez P O	71	387
Charles	30	m	w	VA	Tulare	Visalia Twp	92	285
Daniel	42	m	w	MO	Santa Cruz	Santa Cruz Twp	89	386
Geo	27	m	w	VA	San Joaquin	Tulare Twp	86	263
Geo Z	54	m	w	NH	Calaveras	Copperopolis P O	70	228
H	29	m	w	NY	San Francisco	8-Wd San Francisco	82	373
Henry	27	m	w	WI	Tulare	Tule Rvr Twp	92	266
Isac	36	m	w	ENGL	Merced	Snelling P O	74	247
James	50	m	w	ENGL	San Francisco	8-Wd San Francisco	82	368
James	39	m	w	CT	Placer	Bath P O	76	425
James C	39	m	w	TN	Monterey	San Juan Twp	74	399
John	34	m	w	TX	Los Angeles	Los Angeles Twp	73	483
John	24	m	w	AR	Los Angeles	Los Angeles Twp	73	493
John B	50	m	w	TN	El Dorado	Mountain Twp	72	69
Jos H	24	m	w	RI	San Francisco	San Francisco P O	83	36
Joseph	37	m	w	WI	Tulare	Packwood Twp	92	255
Martin	36	m	w	VA	Monterey	San Antonio Twp	74	319
Mary	59	f	w	IREL	San Francisco	7-Wd San Francisco	81	280
P C	45	m	w	NC	Santa Clara	Gilroy Twp	88	98
Preston	37	m	w	NC	Santa Clara	Milpitas Twp	88	114
Sahra	24	f	w	NY	San Francisco	7-Wd San Francisco	81	278
Samuel	40	m	w	IL	Contra Costa	Martinez P O	71	373
Sephas	30	m	w	IL	Contra Costa	Martinez P O	71	376
Thomas	40	m	w	NJ	Calaveras	San Andreas P O	70	202
William	45	m	w	CANA	Marin	San Rafael	74	48
William	22	m	w	WI	Tuolumne	Chinese Camp P O	93	365
HODGESON								
Richd	43	m	w	ENGL	Sonoma	Santa Rosa	91	407
HODGETTS								
Joseph	47	m	w	ENGL	Santa Clara	1-Wd San Jose	88	244
HODGIN								
Thomas	60	m	w	ENGL	Nevada	Grass Valley Twp	75	162
HODGINS								
John	39	m	w	VA	Amador	Fiddletown P O	69	437
HODGKIN								
John W	47	m	w	NY	San Francisco	11-Wd San Francisc	84	698
Mary	29	f	w	SAME	Sacramento	2-Wd Sacramento	77	242
HODGKINS								
C H	41	m	w	MA	Solano	Vallejo	90	188
E A	50	m	w	MA	Solano	Vallejo	90	177
Edward	55	m	w	MO	Los Angeles	Wilmington Twp	73	634
George	37	m	w	ME	San Bernardino	San Bernardino Twp	78	448
George W	43	m	w	NH	Plumas	Indian Twp	77	9
Henry	38	m	w	ENGL	San Francisco	11-Wd San Francisc	84	705
James Wm	50	m	w	NH	Plumas	Indian Twp	77	9
Leonard	34	m	w	NY	San Francisco	11-Wd San Francisc	84	587
Peter	45	m	w	ME	San Francisco	7-Wd San Francisco	81	163
Wm	51	m	w	VT	Del Norte	Crescent	71	464
HODGKINSON								
Robt	28	m	w	IL	Solano	Vallejo	90	150
HODGKIS								
Theo	44	m	w	NY	San Francisco	San Francisco P O	85	808
HODGSON								
George	40	m	w	ENGL	San Francisco	1-Wd San Francisco	79	118
George	28	m	w	ENGL	San Francisco	5-Wd San Francisco	81	5
Thomas	53	m	w	ENGL	Mariposa	Mariposa P O	74	126
Wm	28	m	w	ENGL	Merced	Snelling P O	74	267
HODINS								
Kate	30	f	w	IREL	San Joaquin	2-Wd Stockton	86	173
HODKESKIN								
Edwin	36	m	w	VT	San Francisco	San Francisco P O	83	240
HODKIN								
George H	6	m	w	CA	Nevada	Grass Valley Twp	75	176
HODKINS								
John	45	m	w	VT	Tuolumne	Big Oak Flat P O	93	397
M W	44	m	w	NY	Sacramento	1-Wd Sacramento	77	183
William	35	m	w	ENGL	San Francisco	San Francisco P O	83	220
HODLEY								
Fred	19	m	w	ME	San Francisco	8-Wd San Francisco	82	316
HODMET								
Florida	30	f	w	CA	Los Angeles	Los Angeles	73	553
HODNETT								
Alfred	39	m	w	ENGL	Yuba	East Bear Rvr Twp	93	543
Jeremiah	32	m	w	IREL	San Francisco	11-Wd San Francisc	84	551
Michael	35	m	w	IREL	San Francisco	11-Wd San Francisc	84	620
Thomas	36	m	w	IREL	Amador	Drytown P O	69	417
Wm	63	m	w	ENGL	San Francisco	11-Wd San Francisc	84	613
HODOY								
Hosa	50	m	w	CHIL	Amador	Drytown P O	69	415
HODSKIFF								
W	50	m	w	VT	El Dorado	Georgetown Twp	72	46
HODSON								
George	49	m	w	ENGL	Marin	Bolinas Twp	74	6
George	27	m	w	ENGL	Sacramento	2-Wd Sacramento	77	246
Wm Henry	20	m	w	CANA	Sacramento	Sutter Twp	77	381
HODUP								
Edwin	40	m	w	BADE	Butte	Concow Twp	70	7
HOE								
---	50	m	c	CHIN	Shasta	Shasta P O	89	454
---	26	f	c	CHIN	Siskiyou	Yreka	89	650
Ah	63	m	c	CHIN	Mariposa	Mariposa P O	74	132
Ah	58	m	c	CHIN	Santa Clara	1-Wd San Jose	88	276
Ah	58	m	c	CHIN	Sacramento	Granite Twp	77	150
Ah	58	m	c	CHIN	Los Angeles	Los Angeles	73	565
Ah	48	m	c	CHIN	Amador	Ione City P O	69	351
Ah	48	m	c	CHIN	Fresno	Millerton P O	72	200
Ah	48	m	c	CHIN	Mariposa	Mariposa P O	74	113
Ah	48	m	c	CHIN	Mariposa	Mariposa P O	74	105
Ah	44	m	c	CHIN	Sacramento	Granite Twp	77	150
Ah	44	m	c	CHIN	Sacramento	Granite Twp	77	138
Ah	44	m	c	CHIN	Calaveras	Copperopolis P O	70	259
Ah	42	m	c	CHIN	Sacramento	Granite Twp	77	139
Ah	41	m	c	CHIN	Sacramento	Cosumnes Twp	77	90
Ah	41	m	c	CHIN	Sacramento	Granite Twp	77	138
Ah	40	m	c	CHIN	Trinity	Lewiston Pct	92	211
Ah	40	m	c	CHIN	Sacramento	Granite Twp	77	150
Ah	40	m	c	CHIN	Sacramento	Natomas Twp	77	167
Ah	38	f	c	CHIN	Mariposa	Maxwell Crk P O	74	138
Ah	37	f	c	CHIN	San Francisco	6-Wd San Francisco	81	76
Ah	37	m	c	CHIN	Sacramento	Georgianna Twp	77	124
Ah	36	m	c	CHIN	Sacramento	Center Twp	77	86
Ah	36	m	c	CHIN	Sacramento	Granite Twp	77	140
Ah	36	m	c	CHIN	San Francisco	6-Wd San Francisco	81	48
Ah	33	m	c	CHIN	Amador	Fiddletown P O	69	441
Ah	32	m	c	CHIN	Solano	Suisun Twp	90	104
Ah	32	m	c	CHIN	Mariposa	Mariposa P O	74	103
Ah	31	m	c	CHIN	Nevada	Grass Valley Twp	75	202
Ah	31	m	c	CHIN	Tuolumne	Sonora P O	93	311
Ah	31	m	c	CHIN	Mariposa	Mariposa P O	74	115
Ah	30	m	c	CHIN	Shasta	American Ranch P O	89	497
Ah	30	f	c	CHIN	San Francisco	6-Wd San Francisco	81	75
Ah	30	m	c	CHIN	Sacramento	Georgianna Twp	77	123
Ah	30	m	c	CHIN	Yuba	Marysville	93	618
Ah	30	m	c	CHIN	San Joaquin	Oneal Twp	86	118
Ah	30	f	c	CHIN	Merced	Snelling P O	74	279
Ah	30	m	c	CHIN	Sacramento	Granite Twp	77	151
Ah	28	m	c	CHIN	Sacramento	Georgianna Twp	77	134
Ah	28	m	c	CHIN	Sacramento	Georgianna Twp	77	125
Ah	28	m	c	CHIN	Fresno	Kings Rvr P O	72	211
Ah	28	m	c	CHIN	Sacramento	Franklin Twp	77	108
Ah	28	m	c	CHIN	Sacramento	Natomas Twp	77	167
Ah	26	f	c	CHIN	Merced	Snelling P O	74	279
Ah	25	m	c	CHIN	Sacramento	Granite Twp	77	150
Ah	25	m	c	CHIN	Alameda	Eden Twp	68	92
Ah	25	m	c	CHIN	San Francisco	6-Wd San Francisco	81	44
Ah	25	m	c	CHIN	Butte	Bidwell Twp	70	1
Ah	23	m	c	CHIN	Alameda	Eden Twp	68	62
Ah	21	f	c	CHIN	Santa Clara	2-Wd San Jose	88	303
Ah	21	f	c	CHIN	Merced	Snelling P O	74	279
Ah	20	f	c	CHIN	Santa Clara	1-Wd San Jose	88	270
Ah	20	f	c	CHIN	Santa Clara	1-Wd San Jose	88	274
Ah	20	m	c	CHIN	San Francisco	6-Wd San Francisco	81	64
Ah	20	f	c	CHIN	Butte	Concow Twp	70	8
Ah	19	m	c	CHIN	San Francisco	8-Wd San Francisco	82	412
Ah	18	m	c	CHIN	San Francisco	6-Wd San Francisco	81	85
Ah	17	f	c	CHIN	Placer	Bath P O	76	429
Ah	16	f	c	CHIN	Santa Clara	Gilroy Twp	88	75
Ah	16	m	c	CHIN	San Francisco	San Francisco P O	83	263
Ah	14	m	c	CHIN	San Francisco	6-Wd San Francisco	81	42
Ah	10	m	c	CHIN	San Francisco	8-Wd San Francisco	82	350
George	31	m	w	CANA	Mendocino	Casper & Big Rvr	74	164
Jane	37	f	w	IREL	San Francisco	11-Wd San Francisc	84	534
Jen	3	m	c	CHIN	Butte	Chico Twp	70	52
Kie	20	m	c	CHIN	Calaveras	San Andreas P O	70	151
Lee	26	m	c	CHIN	San Francisco	San Francisco P O	83	380
Syne	17	f	c	CHIN	Sacramento	1-Wd Sacramento	77	191
Tai	35	m	c	CHIN	Butte	Concow Twp	70	8
Teon	30	m	c	CHIN	Siskiyou	Yreka Twp	89	667
Ye	34	f	c	CHIN	Mariposa	Mariposa P O	74	102
Yon	28	m	c	CHIN	Butte	Chico Twp	70	52
Young	28	f	c	CHIN	Placer	Dutch Flat P O	76	407

© 2001 by Heritage Quest. All rights reserved.

Name	Age	S	R	B-PL	County	Locale	Roll	Pg
						Series M593		
HOEBERLEIN								
Hugo	22	m	w	PRUS	San Francisco	San Francisco P O	85	758
HOEELL								
William	37	m	w	ENGL	Nevada	Rough & Ready Twp	75	323
HOEFFER								
Heny	42	m	w	SAXO	San Francisco	6-Wd San Francisco	81	100
HOEFIELD								
W	39	m	w	NY	Alameda	Murray Twp	68	104
HOEG								
Jane	47	f	w	MA	San Francisco	San Francisco P O	83	359
HOEL								
M	55	f	w	NY	Nevada	Nevada Twp	75	273
HOELACHER								
Ernest	40	m	w	PRUS	San Francisco	8-Wd San Francisco	82	469
HOELLE								
George	29	m	w	BADE	San Francisco	San Francisco P O	85	785
HOELMAN								
Herman	26	m	w	PRUS	San Francisco	6-Wd San Francisco	81	109
HOELSCHER								
Joseph	19	m	w	PRUS	San Francisco	3-Wd San Francisco	79	321
HOELSHAUN								
J	23	m	w	GERM	Solano	Vallejo	90	186
HOEMER								
J J	36	m	w	OH	San Joaquin	1-Wd Stockton	86	141
HOEN								
Ah	40	m	c	CHIN	Calaveras	San Andreas P O	70	162
Ah	38	m	c	CHIN	Fresno	Millerton P O	72	201
Ah	30	m	c	CHIN	Calaveras	San Andreas P O	70	161
Ah	30	m	c	CHIN	Sacramento	1-Wd Sacramento	77	197
Berthold	47	m	w	PRUS	Sonoma	Santa Rosa	91	422
HOENCHIELD								
Geo	29	m	w	PRUS	San Francisco	2-Wd San Francisco	79	278
HOENSHELL								
A	19	m	w	PA	San Joaquin	Oneal Twp	86	105
HOERCHNER								
Adolph H	46	m	w	SAXO	Calaveras	San Andreas P O	70	197
Carle	52	m	w	SAXO	Calaveras	San Andreas P O	70	192
Sophia	42	f	w	HANO	San Francisco	2-Wd San Francisco	79	148
HOERDT								
Conrad	23	m	w	BADE	San Francisco	8-Wd San Francisco	82	434
HOERL								
John	17	m	w	NY	San Francisco	San Francisco P O	83	377
HOERLIUN								
Charles	35	m	w	GERM	Yolo	Grafton Twp	93	499
HOERNLEIN								
Emiel	34	m	w	GERM	Yolo	Cache Crk Twp	93	432
HOERNLEINA								
Emil	34	m	w	PRUS	Yolo	Cache Crk Twp	93	437
HOERSHMER								
Andrew	31	m	w	OH	San Joaquin	Elkhorn Twp	86	55
HOES								
Geo H	26	m	w	MD	Siskiyou	Big Valley Twp	89	582
HOESH								
Josephine	40	f	w	PRUS	Yuba	Marysville	93	596
HOESSEL								
George	29	m	w	PRUS	San Francisco	San Francisco P O	80	469
HOET								
George	31	m	w	MA	Tuolumne	Sonora P O	93	307
Gules	50	m	w	FRAN	Mariposa	Mariposa P O	74	130
HOEY								
Ah	42	m	c	CHIN	Sacramento	Granite Twp	77	139
Ah	41	m	c	CHIN	Shasta	French Gulch P O	89	465
Ah	33	m	c	CHIN	Shasta	French Gulch P O	89	466
Ah	24	m	c	CHIN	Amador	Jackson P O	69	332
Ah	15	m	c	CHIN	Shasta	American Ranch P O	89	497
David	23	m	w	CANA	San Francisco	11-Wd San Francisc	84	477
Hong	11	m	c	CHIN	San Francisco	3-Wd San Francisco	79	320
Jane	60	f	w	IREL	San Francisco	8-Wd San Francisco	82	484
John	40	m	w	IREL	Sacramento	Brighton Twp	77	77
John	40	m	w	IREL	Shasta	Shasta P O	89	453
John	25	m	w	IREL	San Francisco	San Francisco P O	83	285
John L	30	m	w	IL	Calaveras	San Andreas P O	70	192
Katie	14	f	w	CA	Sacramento	4-Wd Sacramento	77	327
King	41	m	c	CHIN	Solano	Vacaville Twp	90	132
P F	34	m	w	IL	Santa Clara	Gilroy Twp	88	68
Patrick	40	m	w	IREL	Sacramento	Brighton Twp	77	70
Peter	29	m	w	IREL	Sacramento	Brighton Twp	77	77
Robert	29	m	w	NY	San Francisco	1-Wd San Francisco	79	37
Thomas	43	m	w	IREL	San Francisco	San Francisco P O	83	17
Thomas	19	m	w	NY	San Francisco	3-Wd San Francisco	79	316
HOF								
Ah	22	m	c	CHIN	Sacramento	Georgianna Twp	77	123
John	38	m	w	FRAN	Los Angeles	El Monte Twp	73	458
HOFER								
Rudolph	53	m	w	SWIT	Amador	Jackson P O	69	321
Valentine	41	m	w	PA	Sonoma	Sonoma Twp	91	438
HOFF								
Albert	30	m	w	OH	San Francisco	6-Wd San Francisco	81	83
Alex H	47	m	w	PA	Marin	Sausalito Twp	74	72
Bion D	23	m	w	ME	Mendocino	Little Rvr Twp	74	171
Charles	37	m	w	PRUS	Plumas	Washington Twp	77	56
Charles	30	m	w	ME	Mendocino	Little Rvr Twp	74	170
Charles R	32	m	w	NY	Santa Cruz	Santa Cruz	89	420
Francis M	30	m	w	SWIT	San Francisco	San Francisco P O	85	754
Geo T	35	m	w	NY	Monterey	Monterey	74	358
J W	50	m	w	PRUS	San Francisco	San Francisco P O	85	853
John	72	m	w	ME	Tuolumne	Sonora P O	93	322
Man A	40	m	w	PRUS	Sacramento	1-Wd Sacramento	77	189
Peter	36	m	w	PRUS	Shasta	Shasta P O	89	457
Peter	23	m	w	SHOL	Plumas	Washington Twp	77	54
Richard W	30	m	w	US	Santa Cruz	Santa Cruz Twp	89	387
Rose	30	f	w	PRUS	Santa Clara	2-Wd San Jose	88	299
Victor	39	m	w	PRUS	Santa Clara	2-Wd San Jose	88	290
William	64	m	w	NY	San Francisco	11-Wd San Francisc	84	560
HOFFAMN								
Joseph	24	m	w	HANO	San Francisco	6-Wd San Francisco	81	112
HOFFEL								
Peter	48	m	w	PRUS	Sacramento	2-Wd Sacramento	77	252
HOFFEN								
Gustave	22	m	w	LA	Solano	Vallejo	90	173
HOFFER								
Clarence	36	m	w	FRAN	San Francisco	8-Wd San Francisco	82	342
HOFFERD								
Walter	16	m	w	IA	Santa Clara	2-Wd San Jose	88	284
HOFFERKAMP								
---	38	m	w	HANO	San Francisco	2-Wd San Francisco	79	210
HOFFGUARD								
Carl	46	m	w	NORW	Sonoma	Healdsburg & Mendo	91	277
HOFFLEGER								
Clara	19	f	w	PA	San Francisco	7-Wd San Francisco	81	238
HOFFLING								
Frederick	46	m	w	HOLL	San Francisco	San Francisco P O	83	166
HOFFMAN								
A	53	m	w	PRUS	Nevada	Nevada Twp	75	295
A	36	m	w	IN	San Joaquin	Elliott Twp	86	71
A	22	m	w	GERM	San Francisco	8-Wd San Francisco	82	375
Abe	30	m	w	PRUS	San Francisco	San Francisco P O	83	182
Abraham	55	m	m	VA	San Francisco	2-Wd San Francisco	79	241
Adam	40	m	w	PRUS	Plumas	Seneca Twp	77	47
Adam J	42	m	w	SAXO	Sonoma	Petaluma Twp	91	321
Adele	34	f	w	FRAN	San Francisco	8-Wd San Francisco	82	385
Andrew	26	m	w	CANA	Butte	Chico Twp	70	34
Andrew	25	m	w	NY	San Diego	San Diego	78	487
Anna	19	f	w	LA	Nevada	Nevada Twp	75	274
Annie	47	f	w	PRUS	San Francisco	San Francisco P O	83	416
Barbette	23	f	w	BAVA	San Francisco	8-Wd San Francisco	82	401
Bertha	26	f	w	BREM	San Francisco	8-Wd San Francisco	82	448
Birdsall	68	m	w	HDAR	San Francisco	2-Wd San Francisco	79	211
C	27	m	w	AUST	Mendocino	Ukiah Twp	74	236
C A	37	m	w	MO	Klamath	Camp Gaston	73	373
C H	55	m	w	PRUS	San Francisco	San Francisco P O	83	286
Carey	47	m	w	IL	Santa Clara	Milpitas Twp	88	111
Catharine	70	f	w	HDAR	Santa Clara	1-Wd San Jose	88	258
Chancy B	40	m	w	NY	El Dorado	Salmon Falls Twp	72	129
Charles	50	m	w	PRUS	San Francisco	San Francisco P O	80	476
Charles S	30	m	w	FRAN	San Francisco	8-Wd San Francisco	82	392
Charlotte	50	f	w	NY	San Francisco	San Francisco P O	83	88
Chas	35	m	w	NY	San Francisco	11-Wd San Francisc	84	676
Chas	34	m	w	PRUS	San Francisco	1-Wd San Francisco	79	124
Chas E	30	m	w	NY	San Francisco	5-Wd San Francisco	81	19
Christian	46	m	w	SAXO	San Francisco	San Francisco P O	83	181
Christian	34	m	w	HDAR	Santa Cruz	Santa Cruz	89	416
Chs	38	m	w	PRUS	Tuolumne	Big Oak Flat P O	93	401
Clara	52	f	w	FRAN	San Francisco	San Francisco P O	83	222
Conrad	43	m	w	HDAR	San Francisco	San Francisco P O	80	476
Cyrus	19	m	w	MO	Solano	Silveyville Twp	90	74
Daniel	26	m	w	PA	Solano	Denverton Twp	90	27
Daniel C	32	m	w	OH	Yolo	Grafton Twp	93	495
David	40	m	w	NY	San Diego	San Diego	78	483
Edward	29	m	w	PRUS	San Francisco	2-Wd San Francisco	79	142
Edward	26	m	w	PRUS	Santa Clara	1-Wd San Jose	88	236
Emanuel	32	m	w	OH	Yolo	Grafton Twp	93	485
F	26	m	w	PRUS	Alameda	Murray Twp	68	113
Fannie	28	f	w	IREL	San Francisco	San Francisco P O	85	759
Ferd	42	m	w	PRUS	Contra Costa	Martinez P O	71	406
Ferdinand	35	m	w	PRUS	San Francisco	San Francisco P O	80	532
Frank	47	m	w	PA	Tuolumne	Sonora P O	93	327
Frank	43	m	w	SCOG	Amador	Jackson P O	69	323
Frank	36	m	w	BAVA	Napa	Napa	75	3
Franklin	38	m	w	HOLL	Placer	Bath P O	76	443
Fred	32	m	w	GERM	Nevada	Bridgeport Twp	75	115
Fred	28	m	w	BREM	San Francisco	2-Wd San Francisco	79	222
Fred W	29	m	w	PRUS	Sonoma	Analy Twp	91	223
Frederick	41	m	w	FRAN	Placer	Bath P O	76	431
Frederick	39	m	w	PRUS	Kern	Havilah P O	73	338
Frederick	34	m	w	HCAS	Santa Clara	2-Wd San Jose	88	327
Frederick W	34	m	w	BAVA	Santa Clara	2-Wd San Jose	88	331
Geo	32	m	w	HDAR	Sacramento	3-Wd Sacramento	77	295
George	59	m	w	PA	Calaveras	San Andreas P O	70	153
George	43	m	w	BREM	Santa Clara	1-Wd San Jose	88	248
George	39	m	w	FRAN	San Francisco	2-Wd San Francisco	79	158
George	26	m	w	FRAN	Los Angeles	Santa Ana Twp	73	611
George L	40	m	w	NY	Fresno	Millerton P O	72	156
George W	40	m	w	PA	Yolo	Grafton Twp	93	485
Gilbert W	31	m	w	OH	Placer	Bath P O	76	435
Gotlieb	44	m	w	PRUS	San Francisco	2-Wd San Francisco	79	139
Gustav	20	m	w	NY	San Francisco	8-Wd San Francisco	82	477
H	39	m	w	HANO	El Dorado	Greenwood Twp	72	55
Henry	53	m	w	NY	Butte	Ophir Twp	70	118
Henry	46	m	w	MA	San Francisco	11-Wd San Francisc	84	428
Henry	41	m	w	BAVA	San Francisco	San Francisco P O	80	470
Henry	38	m	w	HAMB	San Francisco	6-Wd San Francisco	81	88
Henry	37	m	w	FRAN	San Francisco	2-Wd San Francisco	79	248
Henry	31	m	w	HCAS	San Francisco	1-Wd San Francisco	79	51

© 2001 by Heritage Quest. All rights reserved.

California 1870 Census

Series M593

Name	Age	S	R	B-PL	County	Locale	Roll	Pg
Henry	28	m	w	WURT	San Francisco	San Francisco P O	83	218
Henry	17	m	w	PRUS	Tulare	Visalia	92	298
Henry C	46	m	w	PA	Yolo	Grafton Twp	93	479
Henry I	38	m	w	IN	Nevada	Rough & Ready Twp	75	332
Herman	42	m	w	MO	Santa Clara	1-Wd San Jose	88	256
J W	30	m	w	PRUS	San Francisco	7-Wd San Francisco	81	226
Jacob	40	m	w	PA	Yolo	Grafton Twp	93	496
James	52	m	w	PRUS	San Francisco	11-Wd San Francisc	84	445
James	31	m	w	PRUS	Nevada	Nevada Twp	75	295
Jno	22	m	w	DENM	San Francisco	5-Wd San Francisco	81	9
John	57	m	w	DENM	San Francisco	2-Wd San Francisco	79	252
John	45	m	w	HDAR	Solano	Vacaville Twp	90	117
John	40	m	w	SAXO	San Francisco	1-Wd San Francisco	79	89
John	40	m	w	MO	Solano	Vacaville Twp	90	126
John	38	m	w	MI	Solano	Benicia	90	9
John	35	m	w	BAVA	San Francisco	2-Wd San Francisco	79	181
John	34	m	w	NY	Colusa	Colusa Twp	71	283
John	34	m	w	NY	Sacramento	2-Wd Sacramento	77	207
John	30	m	w	MA	San Diego	San Pasqual	78	523
John	24	m	w	BAVA	San Francisco	8-Wd San Francisco	82	419
John	13	m	w	PA	San Francisco	11-Wd San Francisc	84	613
John A	31	m	w	GERM	Santa Cruz	Santa Cruz Twp	89	396
John P	44	m	w	PA	Mendocino	Ukiah Twp	74	243
Joseph	31	m	w	PA	San Francisco	7-Wd San Francisco	81	156
Joseph	28	m	w	BAVA	San Francisco	8-Wd San Francisco	82	293
Julien	37	m	w	PRUS	Solano	Benicia	90	12
Kate	44	f	w	HDAR	San Francisco	1-Wd San Francisco	79	23
L	21	m	w	SWIT	Sacramento	1-Wd Sacramento	77	190
Leonhard	27	m	w	GERM	Klamath	Camp Gaston	73	372
Lewis	56	m	w	PRUS	Yuba	Bullards Bar P O	93	550
Lottie E	18	f	w	PA	Sacramento	4-Wd Sacramento	77	327
Louis	29	m	w	PRUS	Sacramento	3-Wd Sacramento	77	283
Louis	25	m	w	BADE	San Francisco	3-Wd San Francisco	79	325
M P	25	m	w	PA	Solano	Vallejo	90	161
Martin	45	m	w	PRUS	San Francisco	San Francisco P O	80	460
Martin	41	m	w	BAVA	San Francisco	8-Wd San Francisco	82	383
Mary	77	f	w	PA	Yolo	Grafton Twp	93	485
Mary	71	f	w	PA	Yolo	Grafton Twp	93	485
Mary	30	f	w	IREL	San Francisco	2-Wd San Francisco	79	216
Mary	11	f	w	PA	San Francisco	San Francisco P O	85	826
Michael	52	m	w	LUXE	Placer	Auburn P O	76	366
O H	35	m	w	PRUS	Sacramento	4-Wd Sacramento	77	344
Ogden	48	m	w	NY	San Francisco	3-Wd San Francisco	79	327
Olympia	52	f	w	HUNG	San Francisco	San Francisco P O	83	24
Paul	37	m	w	HESS	San Francisco	San Francisco P O	83	73
Ruben	45	m	w	PRUS	San Francisco	8-Wd San Francisco	82	340
S	35	m	w	NJ	Lassen	Janesville Twp	73	433
S S	32	m	w	NJ	Calaveras	Copperopolis P O	70	236
Saml	22	m	w	NJ	San Francisco	11-Wd San Francisc	84	484
Samuel	45	m	w	OH	Calaveras	San Andreas P O	70	201
Seymour	47	m	w	POLA	San Francisco	11-Wd San Francisc	84	654
Simon	41	m	w	PRUS	San Francisco	San Francisco P O	83	220
Simon	40	m	w	BAVA	Calaveras	San Andreas P O	70	216
Solan	23	m	w	PA	Marin	Novato Twp	74	12
Sullivan	30	m	w	PA	Sacramento	2-Wd Sacramento	77	239
Thomas	36	m	w	PRUS	San Francisco	7-Wd San Francisco	81	226
Victor	39	m	w	PRUS	Santa Clara	2-Wd San Jose	88	288
W	40	m	w	KY	Nevada	Nevada Twp	75	283
W H	39	m	w	NY	Mendocino	Round Valley Twp	74	216
Walter	43	m	w	NY	San Francisco	8-Wd San Francisco	82	496
William	49	m	w	PRUS	Contra Costa	Martinez Twp	71	349
William	42	m	w	SCOG	Placer	Dutch Flat P O	76	401
William	40	m	w	PRUS	San Francisco	San Francisco P O	80	460
William	39	m	w	NY	San Francisco	8-Wd San Francisco	82	492
William	32	m	w	WI	Kern	Havilah P O	73	350
William	30	m	w	PRUS	San Francisco	6-Wd San Francisco	81	147
Wm	43	m	w	PRUS	San Francisco	San Francisco P O	85	824
Wm	42	m	w	PRUS	San Francisco	San Francisco P O	85	757
Wm	41	m	w	PA	El Dorado	Kelsey Twp	72	60
Wm	23	m	w	NY	San Joaquin	Liberty Twp	86	96
Wm P	39	m	w	NY	San Francisco	San Francisco P O	83	89
HOFFMANN								
August	40	m	w	GERM	Yolo	Cottonwood Twp	93	463
John D	40	m	w	FRAN	San Francisco	San Francisco P O	83	99
Rudolph	52	m	w	BRUN	San Bernardino	San Bernardino Twp	78	414
HOFFMASTER								
Charles	29	m	w	HANO	San Francisco	7-Wd San Francisco	81	164
E	74	m	w	IL	Yuba	W Bear Rvr Twp	93	680
G	48	m	w	GERM	Yuba	Rose Bar Twp	93	657
Henry	38	m	w	PRUS	Kern	Havilah P O	73	350
Wm C	31	m	w	MA	San Francisco	1-Wd San Francisco	79	111
HOFFMEISTER								
Willis	40	f	w	VA	San Francisco	6-Wd San Francisco	81	41
HOFFNER								
Christiane	55	f	w	GERM	Sonoma	Sonoma Twp	91	439
Fredrk	36	m	w	OH	Placer	Bath P O	76	427
P	35	m	w	WEST	Yuba	Marysville	93	586
Wm	37	m	w	PRUS	San Joaquin	Castoria Twp	86	15
Wm	26	m	w	PRUS	Butte	Ophir Twp	70	116
HOFFRAN								
M	26	f	w	NY	San Francisco	San Francisco P O	85	793
Mathew	65	m	w	IREL	San Francisco	San Francisco P O	83	106
HOFFSCHMIDT								
Frederick	33	m	w	HUNG	San Francisco	8-Wd San Francisco	82	455
John	24	m	w	HANO	San Francisco	6-Wd San Francisco	81	79
HOFFSCHNEIDER								
William	32	m	w	PRUS	San Francisco	8-Wd San Francisco	82	413
HOFFSES								
Melyer	25	m	w	ME	Nevada	Eureka Twp	75	138
Nabzar J	25	m	w	ME	Nevada	Eureka Twp	75	135
HOFFSTATTER								
L	26	f	w	IREL	Yuba	Marysville	93	602
HOFFSTETER								
Christina	16	f	w	HI	Sonoma	Petaluma Twp	91	314
HOFFSTETTER								
Gregoire	35	m	w	FRAN	Marin	San Rafael	74	54
Henry	13	m	w	CA	Colusa	Spring Valley Twp	71	336
J G	52	m	w	NJ	Calaveras	Copperopolis P O	70	230
J N	30	m	w	SWIT	Yuba	Marysville	93	587
HOFFTETTER								
Henry	37	m	w	IL	Los Angeles	El Monte Twp	73	463
HOFMAN								
Chas	50	m	w	PRUS	Sonoma	Santa Rosa	91	406
HOFMEISTER								
Frederick	41	m	w	BAVA	El Dorado	Placerville	72	107
HOFRAKER								
Joseph	38	m	w	BAVA	Sacramento	Sutter Twp	77	380
HOFSOMER								
John	48	m	w	PRUS	Sacramento	American Twp	77	68
HOFSTEAD								
Fredrick	43	m	w	WURT	Yolo	Washington Twp	93	528
HOFSTETTER								
Louis	44	m	w	BADE	Klamath	Salmon Twp	73	387
HOG								
Ah	50	m	c	CHIN	Tuolumne	Chinese Camp P O	93	377
Ah	36	m	c	CHIN	Mariposa	Mariposa P O	74	107
Ah	34	m	c	CHIN	Nevada	Meadow Lake Twp	75	259
Ah	31	m	c	CHIN	Mariposa	Mariposa P O	74	120
Ah	29	m	c	CHIN	Santa Clara	1-Wd San Jose	88	273
Ah	28	m	c	CHIN	El Dorado	Cosumnes Twp	72	15
Ah	26	m	c	CHIN	Mariposa	Mariposa P O	74	118
Ah	18	m	c	CHIN	Tuolumne	Chinese Camp P O	93	370
Gen	45	m	c	CHIN	Klamath	Orleans Twp	73	381
HOGA								
Ah	12	m	c	CHIN	San Francisco	San Francisco P O	83	91
HOGABOOM								
James H	54	m	w	VT	Sacramento	Franklin Twp	77	117
HOGADOINE								
Mary E	22	f	w	AUSL	Sacramento	Georgianna Twp	77	129
HOGALOON								
Lawrence	31	m	w	CANA	Yolo	Grafton Twp	93	482
HOGAN								
Annie	42	f	w	IREL	San Francisco	11-Wd San Francisc	84	506
Catherine	27	f	w	IREL	San Francisco	8-Wd San Francisco	82	424
Charles	32	m	w	IREL	Los Angeles	Los Angeles Twp	73	482
Charles	27	m	w	IA	El Dorado	Diamond Springs Tw	72	24
Charles	23	m	w	NY	Los Angeles	El Monte Twp	73	451
Charlotte M	48	f	w	IREL	San Francisco	San Francisco P O	83	26
Dahl	55	m	w	GA	Stanislaus	Empire Twp	92	32
Daniel	45	m	w	IREL	San Francisco	11-Wd San Francisc	84	471
Daniel	13	m	w	NY	San Francisco	San Francisco P O	80	378
David	30	m	w	CA	Sonoma	Santa Rosa	91	413
Dennis	46	m	w	IREL	San Francisco	11-Wd San Francisc	84	461
Dennis	24	m	w	IREL	Alameda	Oakland	68	154
Derius	27	m	w	IREL	San Francisco	San Francisco P O	83	348
Edmund T	42	m	w	NY	Plumas	Plumas Twp	77	26
Edw	70	m	w	IREL	Alameda	Oakland	68	219
Edward	35	m	w	IREL	San Francisco	11-Wd San Francisc	84	630
Ellen	70	f	w	IREL	Napa	Napa	75	52
Ellen	35	f	w	IREL	San Francisco	San Francisco P O	83	279
Ellen	32	f	w	ENGL	San Francisco	7-Wd San Francisco	81	174
Ellen	30	f	w	IREL	San Francisco	8-Wd San Francisco	82	343
Ellen	22	f	w	IREL	San Francisco	8-Wd San Francisco	82	318
Ellen R	42	f	w	NY	San Francisco	San Francisco P O	83	24
Eugene	37	m	w	IREL	San Francisco	San Francisco P O	83	385
Geo	33	m	w	NY	San Joaquin	Elkhorn Twp	86	60
George	45	m	w	IREL	San Francisco	8-Wd San Francisco	82	301
Henry	52	m	w	ME	San Francisco	7-Wd San Francisco	81	277
Henry	37	m	w	IREL	Santa Clara	2-Wd San Jose	88	307
Honora	41	f	w	IREL	San Francisco	San Francisco P O	80	372
Ida	13	f	w	CA	San Francisco	San Francisco P O	85	798
Isabel	14	f	w	MO	Santa Clara	Fremont Twp	88	46
J M	37	m	w	OH	San Joaquin	2-Wd Stockton	86	204
J S	33	m	w	IREL	Napa	Napa	75	52
James	40	m	w	IREL	San Francisco	1-Wd San Francisco	79	36
James	39	m	w	IL	Tehama	Tehama Twp	92	186
James	37	m	w	IREL	San Francisco	2-Wd San Francisco	79	280
James	33	m	w	IREL	Alameda	Oakland	68	219
James	30	m	w	IREL	Yolo	Cache Crk Twp	93	449
Jeramiah	33	m	w	IREL	Alameda	Eden Twp	68	61
Jerry	22	m	w	IREL	Yuba	Rose Bar Twp	93	663
Johanah	40	f	w	IREL	Yolo	Washington Twp	93	533
John	47	m	w	IREL	San Francisco	11-Wd San Francisc	84	540
John	46	m	w	IREL	San Francisco	San Francisco P O	83	335
John	44	m	w	IREL	San Diego	Julian Dist	78	473
John	40	m	w	IREL	San Francisco	San Francisco P O	85	773
John	40	m	w	NY	San Francisco	7-Wd San Francisco	81	178
John	39	m	w	IREL	San Francisco	11-Wd San Francisc	84	641
John	38	m	w	IREL	San Francisco	11-Wd San Francisc	84	506
John	37	m	w	IREL	San Joaquin	Oneal Twp	86	98
John	35	m	w	ME	Nevada	Bridgeport Twp	75	101
John	35	m	w	IREL	San Francisco	11-Wd San Francisc	84	675
John	33	m	w	NY	Sacramento	2-Wd Sacramento	77	243
John	31	m	w	IREL	Alameda	Murray Twp	68	109

© 2001 by Heritage Quest. All rights reserved.

Series M593

Name	Age	S	R	B-PL	County	Locale	Roll	Pg
John	31	m	w	IREL	Nevada	Eureka Twp	75	134
John	31	m	w	IREL	Solano	Vallejo	90	187
John	28	m	w	IREL	Stanislaus	Empire Twp	92	47
John	28	m	w	IREL	San Francisco	11-Wd San Francisc	84	496
John	28	m	w	IREL	San Francisco	11-Wd San Francisc	84	535
John	27	m	w	IREL	Stanislaus	Emory Twp	92	16
John	27	m	w	IREL	Monterey	San Antonio Twp	74	320
John	26	m	w	IREL	San Francisco	San Francisco P O	83	158
John	25	m	w	IREL	San Francisco	San Francisco P O	83	170
John	16	m	w	DC	Sacramento	4-Wd Sacramento	77	344
John E	38	m	w	IREL	San Francisco	San Francisco P O	85	765
John P	33	m	w	IREL	Stanislaus	Emory Twp	92	26
Kate	35	f	w	IREL	San Francisco	7-Wd San Francisco	81	246
Lizzie	22	f	w	NY	San Francisco	5-Wd San Francisco	81	33
M A	27	m	w	IREL	San Francisco	San Francisco P O	85	863
M C	32	m	w	ME	Yuba	Marysville	93	583
M G	26	m	w	IREL	San Francisco	7-Wd San Francisco	81	226
Margaret	24	f	w	IREL	San Francisco	8-Wd San Francisco	82	442
Margaret	18	f	w	IREL	Sacramento	Granite Twp	77	143
Maria	23	f	w	IREL	San Francisco	8-Wd San Francisco	82	495
Maria	23	f	w	IREL	San Francisco	8-Wd San Francisco	82	328
Martin	32	m	w	NY	San Francisco	2-Wd San Francisco	79	214
Martin	28	m	w	IREL	San Francisco	11-Wd San Francisc	84	581
Martin	15	m	w	CA	Santa Clara	Burnett Twp	88	31
Mary	32	f	w	IREL	San Francisco	5-Wd San Francisco	81	29
Mary	25	f	w	IREL	Santa Clara	1-Wd San Jose	88	278
Mary	18	f	w	IREL	Sonoma	Cloverdale Twp	91	270
Matthew	40	m	w	IREL	San Francisco	San Francisco P O	80	366
Matthew	39	m	w	IREL	San Francisco	1-Wd San Francisco	79	62
Michael	50	m	w	IREL	San Francisco	2-Wd San Francisco	79	161
Michael	45	m	w	IREL	San Francisco	San Francisco P O	83	92
Michael	40	m	w	IREL	San Francisco	San Francisco P O	80	366
Michael	40	m	w	IREL	San Francisco	San Francisco P O	80	363
Michael	39	m	w	IREL	Nevada	Grass Valley Twp	75	158
Michael	36	m	w	IREL	San Francisco	San Francisco P O	83	93
Michael	35	m	w	IREL	San Francisco	11-Wd San Francisc	84	524
Michael	34	m	w	CUBA	San Mateo	Belmont P O	87	374
Michael	31	m	w	IREL	San Francisco	San Francisco P O	83	335
Michael	28	m	w	IREL	San Francisco	San Francisco P O	83	156
Michael	25	m	w	IREL	Sonoma	Vallejo Twp	91	453
Michael	22	m	w	IREL	Stanislaus	Empire Twp	92	37
Mike	34	m	w	IREL	San Francisco	11-Wd San Francisc	84	694
Ned	25	m	w	IREL	San Francisco	San Francisco P O	83	335
Nellie	17	f	w	MA	San Francisco	San Francisco P O	80	385
Nichola	26	f	i	CA	Mariposa	Mariposa P O	74	137
Owen	20	m	w	VA	San Francisco	6-Wd San Francisco	81	121
Pat	40	m	w	IREL	El Dorado	Lake Valley Twp	72	65
Pat	37	m	w	IREL	San Joaquin	3-Wd Stockton	86	224
Patrick	45	m	w	IREL	San Francisco	1-Wd San Francisco	79	82
Patrick	40	m	w	IREL	San Francisco	7-Wd San Francisco	81	203
Patrick	35	m	w	IREL	Santa Clara	Fremont Twp	88	52
Patrick	34	m	w	IREL	Napa	Napa	75	41
Patrick	32	m	w	IREL	San Francisco	1-Wd San Francisco	79	132
Patrick	30	m	w	IREL	San Francisco	San Francisco P O	83	156
Patrick	30	m	w	IREL	San Francisco	San Francisco P O	83	179
Patrick	30	m	w	IREL	San Francisco	San Francisco P O	83	302
Patrick	30	m	w	IREL	San Francisco	San Francisco P O	80	367
Patrick	30	m	w	IREL	San Francisco	San Francisco P O	80	409
Patrick	27	m	w	IREL	Napa	Yountville Twp	75	76
Patrick	25	m	w	IREL	Nevada	Grass Valley Twp	75	148
Patrick	23	m	w	IREL	San Francisco	11-Wd San Francisc	84	573
Patrick S	28	m	w	IREL	Mendocino	Big Rvr Twp	74	159
Peter	43	m	w	IREL	San Francisco	San Francisco P O	83	312
Peter	38	m	w	IREL	Solano	Vallejo	90	153
Peter	27	m	w	IREL	Sonoma	Salt Point	91	392
Peter	24	m	w	IREL	Napa	Napa	75	52
Philip B	55	m	w	IN	El Dorado	Diamond Springs Tw	72	24
Phillip	45	m	w	IREL	San Francisco	7-Wd San Francisco	81	184
Reuben	38	m	w	IREL	San Joaquin	1-Wd Stockton	86	125
Richard	45	m	w	IREL	San Francisco	7-Wd San Francisco	81	186
Roger	35	m	w	IREL	Monterey	San Juan Twp	74	387
Samuel L	35	m	w	MO	Mariposa	Mariposa P O	74	137
Thomas	39	m	w	IREL	Sutter	Nicolaus Twp	92	107
Thomas	38	m	w	IREL	San Francisco	San Francisco P O	85	863
Thomas	36	m	w	IREL	San Francisco	1-Wd San Francisco	79	136
Thomas	35	m	w	IREL	San Francisco	San Francisco P O	83	209
Thomas	25	m	w	IREL	San Francisco	8-Wd San Francisco	82	423
Thomas	22	m	w	NY	Colusa	Grand Island Twp	71	304
Thos	45	m	w	IREL	Solano	Benicia	90	12
Thos	34	m	w	IREL	San Joaquin	1-Wd Stockton	86	141
Thos C	40	m	w	IREL	San Francisco	7-Wd San Francisco	81	266
Timothy	25	m	w	IREL	San Francisco	San Francisco P O	83	209
William	55	m	w	IREL	San Francisco	3-Wd San Francisco	79	310
William	41	m	w	IREL	Nevada	Eureka Twp	75	131
William	34	m	w	ME	Colusa	Stony Crk Twp	71	331
William	30	m	w	IREL	San Francisco	6-Wd San Francisco	81	143
William	28	m	w	CANA	Mendocino	Anderson Twp	74	157
William	12	m	w	IREL	Santa Clara	Santa Clara Twp	88	176
Wm	37	m	w	WURT	San Francisco	8-Wd San Francisco	82	359
Wm	27	m	w	IREL	San Francisco	2-Wd San Francisco	79	212
Wm J	35	m	w	CANA	San Francisco	8-Wd San Francisco	82	367
Wm W	41	m	w	OH	Fresno	Millerton P O	72	158
HOGAND								
Alex	26	m	w	NJ	Sacramento	1-Wd Sacramento	77	183
HOGANI								
Peter	22	m	w	SWED	San Francisco	1-Wd San Francisco	79	126
HOGANS								
John	30	m	w	IREL	San Francisco	7-Wd San Francisco	81	160
Richard	25	m	b	KY	Santa Clara	1-Wd San Jose	88	236
Wm	38	m	w	KY	Siskiyou	Surprise Valley Tw	89	638
HOGARTH								
George	26	m	w	SCOT	San Francisco	11-Wd San Francisc	84	520
Henry	39	m	w	SCOT	Yuba	Rose Bar Twp	93	652
Mary J	22	f	w	IREL	San Francisco	San Francisco P O	83	184
HOGARTY								
Daniel	26	m	w	IREL	San Francisco	11-Wd San Francisc	84	698
John	29	m	w	IREL	San Francisco	1-Wd San Francisco	79	85
Jos B	30	m	w	OH	Alameda	Brooklyn Twp	68	50
Wm	39	m	w	IREL	San Francisco	1-Wd San Francisco	79	76
HOGATE								
Samuel	34	m	w	NJ	Plumas	Washington Twp	77	53
HOGBERG								
Augusta	36	f	w	SWED	San Francisco	6-Wd San Francisco	81	150
HOGBREN								
Thos	35	m	w	PRUS	Sacramento	4-Wd Sacramento	77	359
HOGDON								
Charles	50	m	w	NH	Santa Cruz	Santa Cruz	89	423
Samuel	32	m	w	ME	San Francisco	San Francisco P O	80	429
HOGE								
Charles	11	m	w	CA	Santa Clara	Santa Clara Twp	88	177
Ellis	29	m	w	MI	Tehama	Tehama Twp	92	193
George	38	m	w	DE	San Francisco	San Francisco P O	80	348
George	35	m	w	SCOT	Tehama	Merrill	92	198
James P	59	m	w	OH	San Francisco	San Francisco P O	83	338
Lucas	62	m	w	WURT	San Francisco	San Francisco P O	80	349
HOGEBOOM								
Frank R	35	m	w	NY	Siskiyou	Yreka	89	657
Louis	40	m	w	NY	San Francisco	San Francisco P O	83	371
HOGENANT								
N	32	m	w	SWED	San Francisco	8-Wd San Francisco	82	358
HOGER								
Ernest	43	m	w	PRUS	San Francisco	8-Wd San Francisco	82	315
HOGERBAUM								
Jos	46	m	w	NY	Sutter	Butte Twp	92	95
HOGERS								
Mary	24	f	w	ENGL	Nevada	Nevada Twp	75	304
HOGERTEIN								
Louis	29	m	w	AUST	San Francisco	San Francisco P O	80	363
HOGES								
Silas	68	m	w	CT	El Dorado	Greenwood Twp	72	50
HOGG								
Fredrick	25	m	w	ENGL	Sonoma	Petaluma Twp	91	320
J B	52	m	w	TN	El Dorado	Greenwood Twp	72	51
Lawrence	28	m	w	IREL	San Francisco	11-Wd San Francisc	84	519
Thomas E	35	m	w	PRUS	San Francisco	5-Wd San Francisco	81	19
HOGGENMASTER								
John	30	m	w	PRUS	San Francisco	2-Wd San Francisco	79	206
HOGGLAND								
Wm C	55	m	w	NJ	Alameda	Brooklyn	68	23
HOGH								
John P	36	m	w	ME	Tuolumne	Columbia P O	93	350
HOGHAN								
N	40	m	w	PRUS	Alameda	Oakland	68	146
HOGIN								
Barney	63	m	w	IREL	San Francisco	San Francisco P O	85	765
HOGINS								
Daniel	41	m	w	NY	Placer	Newcastle Twp	76	475
HOGLAN								
Fred	37	m	w	IL	San Joaquin	Oneal Twp	86	106
HOGLAND								
Christian	35	m	w	DENM	Nevada	Bloomfield Twp	75	92
H W	38	m	w	OH	Merced	Snelling P O	74	261
Jane	64	f	w	NY	Mendocino	Sanel Twp	74	230
HOGLE								
James G	50	m	w	VT	Santa Clara	Santa Clara Twp	88	135
Jane	55	f	w	KY	Napa	Napa	75	49
Martin	31	m	w	HANO	San Francisco	11-Wd San Francisc	84	478
Nelson	28	m	w	CANA	San Francisco	8-Wd San Francisco	82	485
Silas	50	m	w	NY	San Mateo	Half Moon Bay P O	87	403
William	38	m	w	NY	Yuba	Long Bar Twp	93	563
HOGLEY								
Mary	42	f	w	NY	San Francisco	7-Wd San Francisco	81	162
HOGOBOOM								
Hiram	40	m	w	NY	Humboldt	Eel Rvr Twp	72	252
HOGONA								
R	21	m	w	HANO	Klamath	Trinidad Twp	73	392
HOGQUIST								
Charles	38	m	w	SWED	Santa Cruz	Santa Cruz	89	415
HOGTENMILLER								
Bennett	27	m	w	BAVA	Marin	San Antonio Twp	74	64
HOGUE								
Caleb	26	m	w	IL	Colusa	Colusa Twp	71	279
Catherine	32	f	w	IREL	Solano	Vallejo	90	157
James M	57	m	w	TN	Placer	Newcastle Twp	76	475
HOGUN								
Milton	48	m	w	GA	Sacramento	4-Wd Sacramento	77	325
HOGY								
Caroline	20	f	w	ENGL	San Francisco	San Francisco P O	83	201
James R	23	m	w	SCOT	Sonoma	Petaluma Twp	91	349
HOH								
Ah	39	m	c	CHIN	San Francisco	6-Wd San Francisco	81	116
Ah	32	m	c	CHIN	San Francisco	6-Wd San Francisco	81	131
Ah	25	f	c	CHIN	San Francisco	6-Wd San Francisco	81	39

© 2001 by Heritage Quest. All rights reserved.

Name	Age	S	R	B-PL	County	Locale	Roll	Pg
						Series M593		
Qui	17	m	c	CHIN	San Francisco	6-Wd San Francisco	81	43
Why	40	m	c	CHIN	San Joaquin	1-Wd Stockton	86	151
HOHER								
Henry	36	m	w	PRUS	San Francisco	8-Wd San Francisco	82	312
HOHING								
Ming	42	m	c	CHIN	San Francisco	San Francisco P O	80	522
HOHLMAN								
D	20	m	w	CT	Sacramento	1-Wd Sacramento	77	182
HOHLNEY								
Frank	20	m	w	BAVA	San Francisco	3-Wd San Francisco	79	311
HOHM								
Bertha	18	f	w	SWED	San Francisco	8-Wd San Francisco	82	330
HOHMAN								
M	32	m	w	PRUS	El Dorado	Greenwood Twp	72	52
HOHN								
Ah	22	m	c	CHIN	Calaveras	San Andreas P O	70	165
Ah	22	m	c	CHIN	Calaveras	San Andreas P O	70	166
Geo	34	m	w	BADE	San Francisco	8-Wd San Francisco	82	368
Geo	30	m	w	WURT	Sacramento	1-Wd Sacramento	77	173
Henry	33	m	w	PRUS	San Francisco	8-Wd San Francisco	82	319
Peeterson	47	m	w	DENM	Alameda	Eden Twp	68	57
V A	60	m	w	PA	Tuolumne	Columbia P O	93	351
William	18	m	w	PRUS	Sacramento	2-Wd Sacramento	77	244
HOHNER								
Thos J	45	m	w	KY	San Joaquin	Elkhorn Twp	86	62
HOHNISTIN								
J	22	f	w	HANO	Sacramento	3-Wd Sacramento	77	308
HOHSTADT								
John	41	m	w	VT	San Luis Obispo	San Luis Obispo Tw	87	302
HOI								
Ah	50	m	c	CHIN	Nevada	Grass Valley Twp	75	205
Ah	40	m	c	CHIN	San Francisco	San Francisco P O	80	492
Ah	38	m	c	CHIN	Nevada	Grass Valley Twp	75	205
Ah	36	m	c	CHIN	San Francisco	San Francisco P O	80	496
Ah	34	m	c	CHIN	Mariposa	Maxwell Crk P O	74	145
Ah	31	m	c	CHIN	Fresno	Millerton P O	72	202
Ah	30	m	c	CHIN	Nevada	Grass Valley Twp	75	209
Ah	29	m	c	CHIN	Sacramento	1-Wd Sacramento	77	197
Ah	27	m	c	CHIN	San Francisco	11-Wd San Francisc	84	666
Ah	27	m	c	CHIN	Nevada	Grass Valley Twp	75	208
Ah	23	m	c	CHIN	Nevada	Nevada Twp	75	321
Ah	19	f	c	CHIN	San Francisco	San Francisco P O	80	492
Ah	10	m	c	CA	San Francisco	6-Wd San Francisco	81	44
Hung	28	m	c	CHIN	Solano	Vacaville Twp	90	130
Lo	44	m	c	CHIN	Solano	Vacaville Twp	90	130
Lung	47	m	c	CHIN	Solano	Vacaville Twp	90	132
Tak	23	m	c	CHIN	Nevada	Grass Valley Twp	75	184
HOIGG								
Jas	39	m	w	CANA	San Francisco	7-Wd San Francisco	81	287
HOIGN								
Waign	25	m	c	CHIN	San Francisco	8-Wd San Francisco	82	434
HOILT								
Frank	37	m	w	ME	San Francisco	7-Wd San Francisco	81	199
HOIN								
M E	18	f	w	KY	San Francisco	San Francisco P O	85	781
P P	55	m	w	FRAN	San Francisco	San Francisco P O	85	781
HOING								
Ah	29	m	c	CHIN	Placer	Lincoln P O	76	483
HOISE								
S D	30	m	w	NY	Monterey	San Juan Twp	74	400
HOIT								
Ann	40	f	b	NC	Sacramento	Dry Crk Twp	77	97
Charles W	53	m	w	NH	Sacramento	Sutter Twp	77	384
Isaac	30	m	w	MI	Santa Clara	San Jose Twp	88	219
John S	42	m	w	NY	Trinity	Hayfork Valley	92	239
M B	40	m	w	NY	Alameda	Oakland	68	222
Mary	29	f	w	KY	Sacramento	2-Wd Sacramento	77	253
Peter	21	m	w	NY	San Francisco	San Francisco P O	83	255
HOITT								
Ira G	36	m	w	NY	San Francisco	8-Wd San Francisco	82	329
HOK								
Ah	41	m	c	CHIN	Nevada	Meadow Lake Twp	75	259
Ah	26	m	c	CHIN	Sierra	Sierra Twp	89	562
Ah	24	m	c	CHIN	Nevada	Rough & Ready Twp	75	338
Ah	20	m	c	CHIN	Sacramento	1-Wd Sacramento	77	200
Ah	20	m	c	CHIN	San Francisco	6-Wd San Francisco	81	52
Ah	16	m	c	CHIN	San Francisco	6-Wd San Francisco	81	68
Kee	18	m	c	CHIN	Tehama	Tehama Twp	92	188
Wong	20	m	c	CHIN	San Francisco	6-Wd San Francisco	81	39
HOKE								
Ah	41	m	c	CHIN	Amador	Drytown P O	69	423
Ah	37	m	c	CHIN	Sierra	Downieville Twp	89	520
Ah	37	m	c	CHIN	Amador	Ione City P O	69	370
George	18	m	w	CA	Sacramento	Natomas Twp	77	165
Jacob	33	m	w	OH	San Diego	San Diego	78	490
HOKEY								
Ernest	47	m	w	HAMB	San Joaquin	Elkhorn Twp	86	61
Frederick	55	m	w	PRUS	Sutter	Butte Twp	92	99
HOKINS								
M	35	m	w	IREL	Alameda	Oakland	68	166
HOL								
Lun	18	m	c	CHIN	San Joaquin	1-Wd Stockton	86	151
HOLABIRD								
Mary	30	f	w	VT	Yuba	East Bear Rvr Twp	93	539
HOLADAY								
Thomas	35	m	w	TN	San Bernardino	San Bernardino Twp	78	444
HOLAM								
Robinson	48	m	w	NY	Stanislaus	Buena Vista Twp	92	13
HOLAN								
Charles	35	m	w	IREL	San Francisco	San Francisco P O	85	714
John	28	m	w	NY	Santa Cruz	Santa Cruz Twp	89	390
HOLAND								
John	40	m	w	IREL	San Francisco	7-Wd San Francisco	81	226
Johnana	25	f	w	IREL	San Francisco	7-Wd San Francisco	81	211
Saml	28	m	w	MI	Butte	Oregon Twp	70	134
HOLAWAY								
J C	32	m	w	KY	Monterey	Salinas Twp	74	309
HOLBECK								
Alexander	45	m	w	AUST	San Francisco	San Francisco P O	80	338
HOLBERT								
Henry T	27	m	w	ENGL	San Francisco	San Francisco P O	83	255
John K	37	m	w	ME	San Francisco	San Francisco P O	83	254
Louisa	22	f	w	ENGL	San Francisco	5-Wd San Francisco	81	1
HOLBORN								
John	36	m	w	ENGL	San Francisco	11-Wd San Francisc	84	470
HOLBRESON								
Newton	28	m	w	NORW	Stanislaus	Empire Twp	92	61
HOLBROCK								
Augustus	30	m	w	MA	San Francisco	San Francisco P O	85	834
HOLBROOK								
Andrew W	40	m	w	MA	Calaveras	San Andreas P O	70	186
Benjm F	35	m	w	NY	San Francisco	8-Wd San Francisco	82	316
C E	29	m	w	MA	Solano	Benicia	90	6
Charles	59	m	w	CT	San Francisco	San Francisco P O	83	413
Charles A	35	m	w	VT	San Francisco	6-Wd San Francisco	81	86
Charles D	45	m	w	NY	Santa Cruz	Santa Cruz	89	407
Charles E	39	m	w	CT	Alpine	Woodfords P O	69	316
Chas	39	m	w	NH	San Francisco	8-Wd San Francisco	82	322
Chas H	24	m	w	ME	Butte	Chico Twp	70	26
Danl P	48	m	w	MA	Nevada	Grass Valley Twp	75	146
Flora	15	f	w	CA	Nevada	Nevada Twp	75	288
Frederick	24	m	w	PA	Santa Clara	2-Wd San Jose	88	317
Henry	28	m	w	MA	Marin	San Rafael Twp	74	35
J S	43	m	w	WI	Nevada	Washington Twp	75	340
John	24	m	w	MA	Nevada	Nevada Twp	75	271
Josepha	22	f	w	IL	Butte	Chico Twp	70	26
Laura	40	f	w	VA	San Francisco	8-Wd San Francisco	82	447
Lucius D	38	m	w	NY	Santa Cruz	Watsonville	89	369
O S	55	m	w	ME	Nevada	Nevada Twp	75	291
Wm	30	m	w	PRUS	San Francisco	1-Wd San Francisco	79	50
HOLBURT								
Henry	54	m	w	PA	Sonoma	Analy Twp	91	246
HOLBY								
Robert	23	m	w	CANA	Kern	Bakersfield P O	73	365
HOLCES								
Andrew	35	m	w	ITAL	Stanislaus	Branch Twp	92	8
HOLCHAR								
Peter	38	m	w	HDAR	San Francisco	8-Wd San Francisco	82	361
HOLCHAUSER								
Fredk	44	m	w	SCHW	Siskiyou	Callahan P O	89	631
HOLCHER								
August	35	m	w	PRUS	Solano	Suisun Twp	90	113
HOLCHSTER								
Paul	40	m	w	PRUS	San Francisco	San Francisco P O	83	416
HOLCOMB								
Benijah	23	m	w	CT	San Diego	San Pasqual	78	522
C W	32	m	w	NY	Trinity	Minersville Pct	92	203
C W	30	m	w	NY	Placer	Colfax P O	76	385
Frank	65	m	w	NY	San Francisco	1-Wd San Francisco	79	18
Frank	32	m	w	MA	Placer	Gold Run Twp	76	395
George W	34	m	w	MO	El Dorado	Diamond Springs Tw	72	35
Gus	30	m	w	SWED	Butte	Chico Twp	70	55
Isaac	42	m	w	MO	Santa Cruz	Soquel Twp	89	443
J P	35	m	w	OH	Nevada	Nevada Twp	75	293
James	42	m	w	NY	San Francisco	San Francisco P O	83	301
James A	41	m	w	MO	Monterey	San Juan Twp	74	399
M T	60	m	w	VT	Alameda	Oakland	68	167
Saml E	39	m	w	NJ	San Francisco	8-Wd San Francisco	82	331
Sarah	62	f	w	MO	Monterey	San Juan Twp	74	399
Sarah	34	f	w	IN	Butte	Chico Twp	70	21
W H	36	m	w	VT	San Francisco	6-Wd San Francisco	81	125
Weslley	38	m	w	VT	San Francisco	11-Wd San Francisc	84	542
William	40	m	w	IN	San Bernardino	San Bernardino Twp	78	442
William	38	m	w	IA	Amador	Volcano P O	69	379
HOLCOMBE								
Albert	41	m	w	NY	Siskiyou	Surprise Valley Tw	89	642
HOLCON								
J	36	m	w	SWIT	Alameda	Oakland	68	153
HOLCROFT								
G M	23	m	w	IN	Lake	Lower Lake	73	421
HOLD								
Let	50	m	c	CHIN	Yuba	Marysville	93	623
HOLDCROFT								
David	32	m	w	ENGL	Shasta	Fort Crook P O	89	474
HOLDEN								
---	13	m	w	CA	San Francisco	11-Wd San Francisc	84	593
Abraham	53	m	w	ENGL	El Dorado	White Oak Twp	72	138
Albert	25	m	w	CT	San Francisco	San Francisco P O	83	325
Alex C	36	m	w	TN	Fresno	Millerton P O	72	189
E S	60	m	w	ME	San Joaquin	2-Wd Stockton	86	160
E S	54	m	w	MA	San Joaquin	2-Wd Stockton	86	196
Ed	25	m	w	AUSL	Alameda	Murray Twp	68	121
Edward	25	m	w	IREL	San Francisco	2-Wd San Francisco	79	162

© 2001 by Heritage Quest. All rights reserved.

Series M593

Name	Age	S	R	B-PL	County	Locale	Roll	Pg
Edwin	9	m	w	CA	San Francisco	11-Wd San Francisc	84	593
F P	60	m	w	MA	San Joaquin	2-Wd Stockton	86	201
Frances	13	f	w	CA	San Francisco	8-Wd San Francisco	82	405
Francis	60	m	w	MA	San Joaquin	3-Wd Stockton	86	242
Fredrick	54	m	w	ENGL	Butte	Ophir Twp	70	95
Geo	18	m	w	IL	Yuba	Marysville Twp	93	571
Giles	42	m	w	CANA	Fresno	Millerton P O	72	162
Gilman	49	m	w	NY	San Francisco	8-Wd San Francisco	82	350
Henry C	41	m	w	IN	Butte	Chico Twp	70	39
Ira	26	m	w	ME	Sutter	Yuba Twp	92	151
J A	35	m	w	ENGL	Alameda	Oakland	68	263
James	63	m	w	ENGL	San Francisco	11-Wd San Francisc	84	602
James	46	m	w	IREL	San Francisco	San Francisco P O	83	361
James	45	m	w	IREL	San Francisco	1-Wd San Francisco	79	87
James	38	m	w	IREL	Los Angeles	Los Angeles Twp	73	478
James	32	m	w	NY	San Francisco	11-Wd San Francisc	84	455
James	30	m	w	NY	Contra Costa	San Pablo Twp	71	363
James B	38	m	w	NY	San Francisco	San Francisco P O	83	176
Jarvis	34	m	w	NY	Stanislaus	Emory Twp	92	25
John	43	m	w	SWED	El Dorado	Mud Springs Twp	72	83
John	41	m	w	ENGL	Placer	Bath P O	76	438
John	22	m	w	ENGL	San Francisco	7-Wd San Francisco	81	213
John A	38	m	w	SWED	El Dorado	Mud Springs Twp	72	72
John G	33	m	w	MI	Nevada	Bridgeport Twp	75	116
John M	45	m	w	VT	Sacramento	Dry Crk Twp	77	100
Justin E	41	m	w	MA	Nevada	Grass Valley Twp	75	146
Lucinda	49	f	w	CT	Placer	Pino Twp	76	471
Martin	51	m	w	IREL	San Francisco	2-Wd San Francisco	79	250
Michael	50	m	w	IREL	Placer	Gold Run Twp	76	395
Nicholas	25	m	w	ENGL	Santa Clara	1-Wd San Jose	88	228
S	36	m	w	MO	Sacramento	3-Wd Sacramento	77	267
Saml P	29	m	w	ENGL	San Francisco	2-Wd San Francisco	79	277
T A	25	m	w	OH	Alameda	Oakland	68	263
T J	32	m	w	RI	Sacramento	1-Wd Sacramento	77	186
Teresa	37	f	w	OH	San Francisco	6-Wd San Francisco	81	78
Thos	45	m	w	CT	Sacramento	3-Wd Sacramento	77	257
William	48	m	w	KY	Marin	San Rafael Twp	74	36
HOLDER								
Daniel J	34	m	w	CANA	Sonoma	Salt Point	91	393
John	45	m	w	NC	Placer	Newcastle Twp	76	473
HOLDERNESS								
James	38	m	w	LA	San Francisco	San Francisco P O	80	539
HOLDERSBERG								
John	35	m	w	BAVA	San Francisco	1-Wd San Francisco	79	23
HOLDGATE								
Schofield	26	m	w	ENGL	Los Angeles	Los Nietos Twp	73	591
HOLDING								
J A	15	m	w	ME	Alameda	Oakland	68	257
HOLDIREUS								
Fritz	20	m	w	BADE	San Francisco	2-Wd San Francisco	79	227
HOLDMAN								
J H	39	m	w	IN	Amador	Drytown P O	69	417
J W	52	m	w	TN	Amador	Drytown P O	69	424
HOLDREDGE								
Edwin D	37	m	w	NY	Placer	Auburn P O	76	378
HOLDRICH								
Ambrose	30	m	w	CT	Solano	Tremont Twp	90	31
HOLDRIDGE								
D H	28	m	w	IL	El Dorado	Lake Valley Twp	72	64
Fred	30	m	w	OH	Sonoma	Bodega Twp	91	264
H A	38	m	w	NY	San Francisco	San Francisco P O	85	801
Jacob	23	m	w	OH	Solano	Silveyville Twp	90	88
Lewis	58	m	w	NY	El Dorado	White Oak Twp	72	141
T R	25	m	w	NY	San Francisco	5-Wd San Francisco	81	36
Wm	60	m	w	NY	Butte	Wyandotte Twp	70	141
HOLDRIEF								
William	65	m	w	IREL	Santa Clara	San Jose Twp	88	208
HOLDRITH								
Wm	31	m	w	ENGL	San Joaquin	Union Twp	86	267
HOLDRON								
Harriett	39	f	w	IREL	San Francisco	8-Wd San Francisco	82	345
HOLDSWORTH								
Geo	28	m	w	ENGL	San Joaquin	2-Wd Stockton	86	158
HOLDT								
Chas	30	m	w	OH	Tehama	Merrill	92	197
Lemuel	60	m	w	CT	Tehama	Tehama Twp	92	192
HOLE								
Mary E	22	f	w	NY	Monterey	San Juan Twp	74	414
R M C	47	m	w	VA	Merced	Snelling P O	74	271
HOLEHAN								
Timothy	36	m	w	IREL	Inyo	Cerro Gordo Twp	73	318
HOLEMAN								
Junius	33	m	w	VA	Siskiyou	Surprise Valley Tw	89	636
HOLENBACK								
Julia	14	f	w	CA	Inyo	Bishop Crk Twp	73	316
Sarah	43	f	w	PA	Inyo	Independence Twp	73	324
HOLENBECK								
Benjamin	50	m	w	NY	Santa Clara	Redwood Twp	88	122
Wm	25	m	w	NY	San Joaquin	Liberty Twp	86	89
HOLENBERG								
Maguns	42	m	w	SWED	Placer	Gold Run Twp	76	400
HOLERREN								
John	36	m	w	IREL	Plumas	Quartz Twp	77	34
HOLEY								
Benjiman	53	m	w	VA	Monterey	Alisal Twp	74	294
John	32	m	w	IREL	Monterey	San Juan Twp	74	398
John	25	m	w	NY	Solano	Vallejo	90	161
Wm	37	m	w	IREL	San Francisco	11-Wd San Francisc	84	695
HOLFFMAN								
J	43	m	w	PRUS	Sierra	Forest Twp	89	529
HOLFMONN								
E	38	m	w	PA	Sierra	Forest Twp	89	531
HOLGERSON								
Harris	45	m	w	DENM	Contra Costa	San Pablo Twp	71	359
HOLGIN								
Mersey	46	m	w	CHIL	Sacramento	2-Wd Sacramento	77	221
HOLGREEN								
John	27	m	w	DENM	Plumas	Quartz Twp	77	34
HOLIAN								
Mary	24	f	w	IREL	Nevada	Grass Valley Twp	75	143
HOLIBIRD								
Frederick	35	m	w	VT	Santa Clara	San Jose Twp	88	180
HOLIDAY								
James	35	m	w	MO	Tulare	Kings Rvr Twp	92	253
John	39	m	w	NY	Alameda	Brooklyn	68	23
Juelliett P	10	f	w	IN	Yolo	Cache Crk Twp	93	437
Trotten	40	m	w	IREL	Sutter	Butte Twp	92	102
Wm F	38	m	w	VA	Mendocino	Sanel Twp	74	231
HOLIGER								
Fred	40	m	w	PRUS	Sacramento	San Joaquin Twp	77	401
HOLIN								
Mary	30	f	w	NY	San Francisco	5-Wd San Francisco	81	19
HOLINGER								
Henery	23	m	w	SWED	San Francisco	7-Wd San Francisco	81	221
HOLINS								
John	50	m	w	BREM	Alameda	Eden Twp	68	59
HOLISTER								
Dwight	46	m	w	OH	Sacramento	Franklin Twp	77	114
Hiram	41	m	w	NY	Humboldt	South Fork Twp	72	301
HOLJE								
John	47	m	w	PRUS	San Francisco	San Francisco P O	80	332
HOLJES								
John H	28	m	w	BREM	San Francisco	1-Wd San Francisco	79	73
HOLKIN								
Hansen	31	m	w	PRUS	San Francisco	San Francisco P O	83	174
HOLKINS								
Wm	50	m	w	MA	Alameda	Oakland	68	172
HOLL								
Frederick W	38	m	w	ENGL	Mariposa	Mariposa P O	74	124
S S	37	m	w	PA	Sacramento	3-Wd Sacramento	77	264
HOLLADAY								
Ben J	24	m	w	MO	San Francisco	3-Wd San Francisco	79	327
F	30	m	w	MO	Yuba	Rose Bar Twp	93	662
Isaac	34	m	w	PA	San Francisco	San Francisco P O	83	288
Jesse	42	m	w	ME	San Francisco	8-Wd San Francisco	82	425
HOLLAHAN								
Eliza	24	f	w	IREL	San Francisco	San Francisco P O	83	97
HOLLAN								
Alfred	27	m	w	ME	San Joaquin	Douglas Twp	86	51
Benj P	32	m	w	MO	Marin	San Antonio Twp	74	61
HOLLAND								
A H	43	m	w	TN	Sutter	Butte Twp	92	91
Andrew	35	m	w	IREL	San Francisco	7-Wd San Francisco	81	241
Andrew W	41	m	w	GA	Sacramento	Center Twp	77	82
Ann	40	f	w	IREL	Plumas	Indian Twp	77	16
Augustus	37	m	w	ME	Butte	Oroville Twp	70	137
Bridget	25	f	w	HOLL	Marin	San Rafael	74	55
Catharine	26	f	w	IREL	San Francisco	San Francisco P O	83	111
Charles	27	m	w	IREL	San Diego	Julian Dist	78	471
Charles H	30	m	w	IN	Solano	Green Valley Twp	90	40
Chas	6	m	w	CA	San Francisco	San Francisco P O	85	800
Chris	31	m	w	IREL	Klamath	Trinidad Twp	73	390
Clara	27	f	w	VT	San Francisco	San Francisco P O	83	221
Corneils	40	m	w	NY	San Francisco	1-Wd San Francisco	79	134
Crawford	40	m	w	PA	Yuba	East Bear Rvr Twp	93	542
Curly	38	m	w	NY	San Francisco	San Francisco P O	80	464
Daniel	45	m	w	IREL	Nevada	Bridgeport Twp	75	112
David L	50	m	w	ENGL	Inyo	Cerro Gordo Twp	73	318
Dennis	23	m	w	IREL	Solano	Vallejo	90	145
Edith	14	f	w	IN	Colusa	Colusa Twp	71	277
Edmund	4	m	w	CA	Marin	San Rafael Twp	74	29
Edward	42	m	w	IREL	Alameda	Eden Twp	68	86
Elisab	60	f	w	ENGL	Alameda	Oakland	68	191
Ellen	24	f	w	CANA	San Francisco	7-Wd San Francisco	81	244
Geo	28	m	w	IREL	San Francisco	7-Wd San Francisco	81	258
Geo M	39	m	w	NY	Nevada	Washington Twp	75	342
George	32	m	w	ENGL	Monterey	San Antonio Twp	74	319
George	22	m	w	PA	Sacramento	2-Wd Sacramento	77	228
Gustave	48	m	w	WURT	San Francisco	8-Wd San Francisco	82	360
Henry	51	m	w	PRUS	San Francisco	2-Wd San Francisco	79	176
Henry	42	m	w	IREL	Alameda	Washington Twp	68	292
Henry	16	m	b	CA	Tehama	Battle Crk Twp	92	158
Henry	15	m	b	CA	Tehama	Tehama Twp	92	190
Hugh	74	m	w	IREL	San Joaquin	1-Wd Stockton	86	137
Isaac	38	m	w	TN	Tuolumne	Sonora P O	93	305
J	48	m	w	MA	Sierra	Lincoln Twp	89	550
J L	32	m	w	MO	Nevada	Eureka Twp	75	137
J R	50	m	m	MO	Nevada	Meadow Lake Twp	75	265
Jacob	24	m	w	MO	Nevada	Washington Twp	75	345
James	50	m	w	IREL	Alameda	Oakland	68	179
James	45	m	w	IREL	San Francisco	11-Wd San Francisc	84	667
James	43	m	w	CANA	San Francisco	11-Wd San Francisc	84	691
James	36	m	w	IREL	San Francisco	11-Wd San Francisc	84	532
James	35	m	w	IREL	San Francisco	San Francisco P O	83	225

© 2001 by Heritage Quest. All rights reserved.

Name	Age	S	R	B-PL	County	Locale	Series M593 Roll	Pg
James	30	m	w	IREL	San Francisco	7-Wd San Francisco	81	272
James	28	m	w	IREL	San Francisco	1-Wd San Francisco	79	74
James C	35	m	w	ENGL	San Diego	San Diego	78	502
Jane	26	f	w	IREL	San Francisco	11-Wd San Francisc	84	489
Jno	60	m	w	PA	Sacramento	3-Wd Sacramento	77	307
Jno	48	m	w	NORW	Butte	Chico Twp	70	58
Jno	28	m	w	SCOT	Alameda	Oakland	68	258
Jno V	44	m	w	IL	Butte	Chico Twp	70	33
Joh	17	m	b	CA	Tehama	Tehama Twp	92	193
John	71	m	w	MA	Marin	Tomales Twp	74	86
John	50	m	w	ENGL	Solano	Vallejo	90	199
John	45	m	w	OH	San Joaquin	2-Wd Stockton	86	168
John	34	m	w	IREL	Solano	Vallejo	90	186
John	30	m	w	IL	Alameda	Oakland	68	172
John	30	m	w	IREL	Colusa	Monroe Twp	71	314
John	30	m	w	ENGL	San Francisco	11-Wd San Francisc	84	558
John	25	m	w	MD	Fresno	Millerton P O	72	151
John	24	m	w	HANO	Sacramento	2-Wd Sacramento	77	225
John	21	m	w	IREL	San Francisco	1-Wd San Francisco	79	91
Joseph	48	m	w	IREL	Fresno	Millerton P O	72	187
Joseph	33	m	w	ENGL	Santa Clara	San Jose Twp	88	214
Julia	19	f	w	IREL	San Francisco	San Francisco P O	83	111
Kate	22	f	w	IREL	Alameda	Oakland	68	152
Kate	15	f	w	CANA	Alameda	Brooklyn	68	27
Louis	32	m	w	HANO	San Francisco	1-Wd San Francisco	79	135
Louis W	33	m	w	MA	Marin	Tomales Twp	74	86
Louisa	2	f	w	CA	Santa Clara	Burnett Twp	88	36
M	19	f	w	MEXI	Sierra	Butte Twp	89	509
M P	77	f	w	IREL	Alameda	Oakland	68	251
Maggie	22	f	w	MA	Contra Costa	San Pablo Twp	71	353
Margaret	38	f	w	IREL	Santa Clara	1-Wd San Jose	88	233
Margt	23	f	w	IREL	San Francisco	8-Wd San Francisco	82	309
Martin	52	m	w	IREL	Plumas	Plumas Twp	77	32
Mary	73	f	w	MA	Marin	Tomales Twp	74	86
Mary	25	f	w	IREL	San Francisco	8-Wd San Francisco	82	449
Michael	63	m	w	IREL	San Francisco	2-Wd San Francisco	79	237
Michael	50	m	w	IREL	San Francisco	San Francisco P O	85	751
Michl	42	m	w	IREL	Alameda	Oakland	68	175
Michl	27	m	w	IREL	Marin	Bolinas Twp	74	2
N	24	m	w	IREL	Sacramento	3-Wd Sacramento	77	318
Nathaniel	55	m	w	PA	San Francisco	San Francisco P O	80	403
Nicholas	48	m	w	IREL	San Francisco	San Francisco P O	83	251
Owen	28	m	w	IREL	Solano	Vallejo	90	171
P	32	m	w	IREL	Sierra	Butte Twp	89	508
Pat	50	m	w	IREL	Alameda	Oakland	68	154
Pat	49	m	w	IREL	Alameda	Oakland	68	147
Patrick	50	m	w	IREL	San Francisco	11-Wd San Francisc	84	650
Patrick	30	m	w	IREL	Marin	Sausalito Twp	74	72
Patrick	23	m	w	IREL	Nevada	Bridgeport Twp	75	120
Patrick O	23	m	w	IREL	Yolo	Putah Twp	93	523
Perry	40	m	w	KY	Mariposa	Mariposa P O	74	130
Peter	31	m	w	MS	San Joaquin	Tulare Twp	86	257
Rose	28	f	w	IREL	San Francisco	San Francisco P O	85	753
Simeon	41	m	w	ENGL	Santa Clara	San Jose Twp	88	214
Thomas	42	m	w	IREL	Inyo	Independence Twp	73	327
Thomas	26	m	w	ENGL	Santa Clara	San Jose Twp	88	200
Thos	50	m	w	IREL	San Francisco	11-Wd San Francisc	84	611
Timy	27	m	w	IREL	Yuba	Rose Bar Twp	93	662
W	31	m	w	PA	Klamath	Trinidad Twp	73	392
Washington	30	m	w	MO	Nevada	Washington Twp	75	345
William	50	m	w	PRUS	Calaveras	San Andreas P O	70	184
William	38	m	w	IREL	San Francisco	San Francisco P O	83	145
William	36	m	w	IREL	San Francisco	11-Wd San Francisc	84	647
William	19	m	w	CA	Napa	Yountville Twp	75	80
Wm	32	m	w	MS	San Joaquin	Tulare Twp	86	258
Wm D	30	m	w	ENGL	San Francisco	8-Wd San Francisco	82	312
Wm R	33	m	w	IL	Butte	Chico Twp	70	33
HOLLANDER								
Fred	37	m	w	HAMB	Placer	Gold Run Twp	76	399
Theo	30	m	w	HUNG	San Francisco	San Francisco P O	83	330
HOLLANDS								
Alfred	42	m	w	ENGL	Santa Clara	Fremont Twp	88	47
James	25	m	w	IREL	San Francisco	1-Wd San Francisco	79	68
HOLLANO								
Dan	25	m	w	IN	Merced	Snelling P O	74	254
HOLLAWAY								
Charles	26	m	w	NY	Placer	Bath P O	76	460
Henry C	38	m	w	ME	Sonoma	Petaluma Twp	91	354
James	48	m	w	MA	Calaveras	Copperopolis P O	70	262
HOLLDRENER								
John	32	m	w	PRUS	San Francisco	8-Wd San Francisco	82	374
HOLLEHAN								
John	38	m	w	IREL	Sacramento	4-Wd Sacramento	77	333
HOLLEN								
Green S P	34	m	w	SWED	Sonoma	Mendocino Twp	91	305
HOLLENBACK								
John	48	m	w	PRUS	Solano	Rio Vista Twp	90	71
John	35	m	w	NY	San Joaquin	Oneal Twp	86	98
Lucy	50	f	w	MA	San Francisco	2-Wd San Francisco	79	173
HOLLENBEAK								
Asa	28	m	w	MO	Shasta	Fort Crook P O	89	475
Benj Q	57	m	w	KY	Shasta	Fort Crook P O	89	475
Stephen B	23	m	w	IA	Shasta	Fort Crook P O	89	475
Wm H	30	m	w	IL	Shasta	Fort Crook P O	89	475
HOLLENBECK								
---	36	m	w	NY	Tehama	Antelope Twp	92	156
Barton	23	m	w	TN	Santa Clara	Fremont Twp	88	64

Name	Age	S	R	B-PL	County	Locale	Series M593 Roll	Pg
James	38	m	w	IL	Santa Clara	Fremont Twp	88	64
James C	40	m	w	TN	San Francisco	2-Wd San Francisco	79	225
John	38	m	w	NY	San Luis Obispo	Santa Rosa Twp	87	323
Lawrence	36	m	w	IL	Santa Clara	Milpitas Twp	88	115
Orrin	38	m	w	MA	Placer	Auburn P O	76	366
Walter	25	m	w	NY	Santa Clara	2-Wd San Jose	88	324
William	63	m	w	NY	Santa Clara	Fremont Twp	88	64
HOLLENBURGH								
Geo	48	m	w	PRUS	San Francisco	1-Wd San Francisco	79	14
HOLLENMILLER								
Henry	41	m	w	PRUS	Nevada	Grass Valley Twp	75	144
Mary	1	f	w	CA	Nevada	Grass Valley Twp	75	144
HOLLENSTEIN								
Herman	38	m	w	PRUS	San Francisco	San Francisco P O	80	536
HOLLER								
Andrew	41	m	w	SWIT	Placer	Auburn P O	76	366
Antoine	27	m	w	BADE	San Francisco	1-Wd San Francisco	79	52
Caroline T	22	f	w	IA	Plumas	Indian Twp	77	9
Edward	14	m	w	IA	Plumas	Plumas Twp	77	28
Jane	54	f	w	VA	Plumas	Plumas Twp	77	27
HOLLERAN								
Mark	35	m	w	IREL	San Francisco	San Francisco P O	83	248
HOLLES								
Barton	40	m	w	ME	Amador	Sutter Crk P O	69	410
HOLLEY								
Adelia	9	f	w	MO	Sacramento	Franklin Twp	77	116
Bird	31	m	w	MO	Placer	Auburn P O	76	377
Edward F	41	m	w	SAXO	Placer	Auburn P O	76	370
Francis	38	m	w	KY	Colusa	Spring Valley Twp	71	341
Fredrick	24	m	w	FRAN	San Francisco	7-Wd San Francisco	81	218
John	30	m	w	MO	Placer	Auburn P O	76	365
Richard	24	m	w	TX	Kern	Tehachapi P O	73	352
William	36	m	w	MO	Placer	Auburn P O	76	359
HOLLFELDER								
P	45	m	w	BAVA	Sacramento	3-Wd Sacramento	77	296
HOLLIDAY								
Benjn	23	m	w	MO	San Francisco	5-Wd San Francisco	81	14
Beverly	45	m	w	KY	Contra Costa	Martinez P O	71	453
Burt	34	m	w	MO	Yuba	Rose Bar Twp	93	654
Geo	30	m	w	NY	Solano	Vallejo	90	165
George M	52	m	w	IN	Los Angeles	San Jose Twp	73	621
Jessy	52	m	w	NY	San Francisco	5-Wd San Francisco	81	33
John	55	m	w	NY	Shasta	Horsetown P O	89	504
M	39	f	w	IREL	Sonoma	Santa Rosa	91	414
Maria	45	f	w	IREL	Sonoma	Santa Rosa	91	425
Thomas	68	m	w	IREL	Yuba	Long Bar Twp	93	560
Thomas	28	m	w	ENGL	Nevada	Grass Valley Twp	75	231
Wm H	45	m	w	MA	Napa	Napa	75	49
HOLLIEB								
Adolphus	49	m	w	BOHE	San Francisco	San Francisco P O	85	834
HOLLIHAN								
Dennis W	32	m	w	IREL	Contra Costa	Martinez P O	71	379
HOLLING								
Antone	26	m	w	MO	El Dorado	Greenwood Twp	72	54
Charles H	38	m	w	PRUS	San Francisco	8-Wd San Francisco	82	474
H	32	m	w	PRUS	Sierra	Forest	89	537
Rebecca	25	f	w	HANO	San Francisco	San Francisco P O	85	753
HOLLINGS								
Bard	26	m	w	PRUS	San Francisco	San Francisco P O	85	737
HOLLINGSHEAD								
A	43	m	w	CANA	Yuba	W Bear Rvr Twp	93	681
Daniel	55	m	w	OH	Los Angeles	Los Angeles	73	527
Daniel	52	m	w	OH	Los Angeles	Los Angeles Twp	73	497
J	30	m	w	CANA	Yuba	W Bear Rvr Twp	93	681
Kate	20	f	w	OH	Nevada	Eureka Twp	75	136
Thos	75	m	w	CANA	Yuba	W Bear Rvr Twp	93	681
Wm D	22	m	w	PA	Nevada	Grass Valley Twp	75	180
HOLLINGSWORTH								
Amos	33	m	w	IL	Plumas	Mineral Twp	77	22
B S	68	m	w	VA	San Francisco	San Francisco P O	83	303
H	42	m	w	IL	Napa	Yountville Twp	75	81
J	60	m	w	KY	Los Angeles	Los Angeles Twp	73	469
Mallisa	37	f	w	MO	El Dorado	Georgetown Twp	72	48
Miles	60	m	w	IN	Monterey	Pajaro Twp	74	375
HOLLINGWOOD								
Frank	38	m	w	IREL	Contra Costa	Martinez P O	71	420
HOLLINGWORTH								
John	52	m	w	KY	Yolo	Cache Crk Twp	93	435
HOLLINS								
Henry	40	m	w	PRUS	San Francisco	8-Wd San Francisco	82	420
Susan	24	f	w	IREL	San Francisco	8-Wd San Francisco	82	472
HOLLINSHEAD								
Jeremiah B	63	m	w	NJ	San Mateo	Pescadero P O	87	415
Joseph B	37	m	w	KY	San Mateo	Pescadero P O	87	411
HOLLINSWORTH								
D P	61	m	w	CA	Merced	Snelling P O	74	272
D P	57	m	w	GA	Merced	Snelling P O	74	272
J L	35	m	w	IN	Mendocino	Calpella Twp	74	184
Rosa	26	f	w	ITAL	San Francisco	San Francisco P O	80	339
W D	22	m	w	CA	Mendocino	Calpella Twp	74	181
HOLLIS								
Charles	29	m	w	ENGL	Sacramento	Franklin Twp	77	111
Chas	14	m	w	CA	Santa Clara	Burnett Twp	88	30
Henry	33	m	w	ENGL	San Francisco	1-Wd San Francisco	79	83
James	40	m	w	ME	Nevada	Meadow Lake Twp	75	252
Joseph	31	m	w	ITAL	San Francisco	2-Wd San Francisco	79	166
Larry	32	m	w	IREL	San Joaquin	3-Wd Stockton	86	231

© 2001 by Heritage Quest. All rights reserved.

Series M593

Name	Age	S	R	B-PL	County	Locale	Roll	Pg
Reuben	46	m	w	VT	Sutter	Yuba Twp	92	143
Thomas	57	m	w	ENGL	Amador	Ione City P O	69	365
Thomas Q	35	m	w	MA	Placer	Auburn P O	76	369
William	48	m	w	KY	Santa Clara	1-Wd San Jose	88	241
William	29	m	w	IA	San Francisco	San Francisco P O	83	291
HOLLIST								
Fred	45	m	w	PRUS	San Francisco	San Francisco P O	83	103
HOLLISTER								
Corydon	54	m	w	NY	Solano	Suisun Twp	90	103
Daniel	36	m	w	NY	San Francisco	San Francisco P O	80	458
Henry M	38	m	w	NY	Nevada	Meadow Lake Twp	75	264
J	38	m	w	MA	Yuba	W Bear Rvr Twp	93	680
Jane	50	f	w	NY	San Francisco	San Francisco P O	83	97
Joseph H	50	m	w	OH	San Luis Obispo	San Luis Obispo Tw	87	303
Oscar	37	m	w	NY	San Diego	Julian Dist	78	474
Page	40	m	w	VT	Santa Clara	1-Wd San Jose	88	239
Peter	24	m	w	PA	Solano	Vacaville Twp	90	123
Saml	55	m	w	NY	San Francisco	11-Wd San Francisc	84	576
Wm W	51	m	w	OH	Santa Barbara	Santa Barbara P O	87	499
HOLLISWORTH								
Hiram	14	m	w	TX	Stanislaus	Emory Twp	92	16
HOLLIWAY								
Charles	37	m	w	HANO	Plumas	Indian Twp	77	18
James P	35	m	w	CT	Sonoma	Analy Twp	91	220
HOLLMAN								
David	27	m	w	FRAN	San Francisco	San Francisco P O	80	420
E W	45	m	w	MS	Yuba	Linda Twp	93	558
Francis	48	m	w	MA	Marin	San Rafael	74	51
H	64	m	w	BAVA	San Francisco	San Francisco P O	83	301
John	30	m	w	BREM	Santa Clara	Santa Clara Twp	88	178
HOLLMANN								
Chas G	34	m	w	HANO	San Francisco	San Francisco P O	83	94
HOLLMAR								
Patrick	20	m	w	SHOL	San Francisco	11-Wd San Francisc	84	428
HOLLNAD								
Byron	20	m	w	IREL	San Francisco	San Francisco P O	83	417
HOLLO								
Herman	42	m	w	HANO	San Francisco	7-Wd San Francisco	81	156
HOLLODAY								
H H	47	m	w	NY	San Francisco	San Francisco P O	85	772
Jane	30	f	w	IREL	San Francisco	7-Wd San Francisco	81	280
HOLLOHAN								
Mark	32	m	w	IREL	Marin	San Rafael Twp	74	31
Thomas	22	m	w	IREL	Marin	San Rafael Twp	74	31
HOLLOMAN								
---	26	m	w	MO	Sutter	Yuba Twp	92	142
Jos	50	m	w	TN	Sutter	Butte Twp	92	89
HOLLON								
Richard	31	m	w	ENGL	San Luis Obispo	San Luis Obispo Tw	87	309
William	60	m	w	ENGL	San Francisco	San Francisco P O	80	337
HOLLORAN								
Tom	30	m	w	IREL	San Francisco	1-Wd San Francisco	79	46
HOLLORY								
Patrick	35	m	w	IREL	San Mateo	San Mateo P O	87	357
HOLLOW								
Thomas	28	m	w	ENGL	Nevada	Bridgeport Twp	75	119
HOLLOWAY								
Adam	45	m	w	BAVA	Santa Clara	2-Wd San Jose	88	324
Andrew	6	m	w	CA	Santa Clara	Milpitas Twp	88	110
Barnes	57	m	w	TN	Contra Costa	Martinez P O	71	372
Benj	43	m	w	TN	Sonoma	Mendocino Twp	91	306
Chas	45	m	w	NY	San Diego	San Diego	78	508
Cyrus	49	m	w	MA	Santa Barbara	Santa Barbara P O	87	451
D W	29	m	w	IL	Santa Clara	Gilroy Twp	88	83
Edward	8	m	w	CA	San Francisco	San Francisco P O	80	537
Geo	23	m	w	IL	Santa Clara	Gilroy Twp	88	82
H C	26	m	w	IL	Santa Clara	Gilroy Twp	88	83
Henry S	31	m	w	RI	Sacramento	Franklin Twp	77	109
Horace	35	m	w	ME	Contra Costa	Martinez P O	71	414
J	42	m	w	MO	Lake	Lower Lake	73	421
J B	41	m	w	TN	Lake	Kelsey Crk	73	402
J G	30	m	w	MO	Sutter	Vernon Twp	92	135
John	40	m	c	CHIN	Sutter	Vernon Twp	92	135
John	31	m	w	KY	Sonoma	Russian Rvr	91	368
John	22	m	w	IL	Monterey	San Benito Twp	74	380
John F	56	m	w	VA	Santa Clara	San Jose Twp	88	214
John J	35	m	w	MO	Santa Barbara	Santa Maria P O	87	513
Laban	37	m	w	MD	Santa Clara	Gilroy Twp	88	82
Leonidas	29	m	w	KY	Santa Clara	2-Wd San Jose	88	334
Thomas	28	m	w	MO	Santa Barbara	Santa Maria P O	87	513
William H	25	m	w	MO	Santa Barbara	Santa Maria P O	87	513
Wm	28	m	w	IREL	Solano	Benicia	90	16
HOLLOWELL								
Benjamin	46	m	w	PA	Monterey	San Benito Twp	74	383
Charles	23	m	w	MA	San Francisco	7-Wd San Francisco	81	156
HOLLOWWAY								
Lipscomb	45	m	w	TN	San Luis Obispo	Arroyo Grande Twp	87	279
HOLLUM								
Mathias	28	m	w	PRUS	Solano	Suisun Twp	90	110
HOLLY								
Amos	34	m	w	IL	Solano	Silveyville Twp	90	82
Daniel	47	m	w	NY	Sonoma	Petaluma Twp	91	327
Henry	34	m	w	MA	Mendocino	Little Lake Twp	74	193
James	44	m	w	IREL	Butte	Ophir Twp	70	117
James	41	m	w	IREL	Butte	Ophir Twp	70	99
James	24	m	w	IA	San Bernardino	San Bernardino Twp	78	415
John	30	m	w	PA	Klamath	Trinidad Twp	73	392

Series M593

Name	Age	S	R	B-PL	County	Locale	Roll	Pg
John C	39	m	w	AL	Fresno	Millerton P O	72	147
Stephen	57	m	w	NH	Butte	Chico Twp	70	59
Venia	25	f	w	PA	Klamath	Trinidad Twp	73	392
Walter	28	m	w	NY	San Francisco	5-Wd San Francisco	81	26
HOLLYFIELD								
Benjiman	46	m	w	AL	Los Angeles	Los Angeles Twp	73	494
Newton	35	m	w	MO	Los Angeles	Los Angeles Twp	73	494
HOLLYMAN								
Charles	25	m	w	VA	Colusa	Monroe Twp	71	313
HOLLYWOOD								
J Sr	65	m	w	IREL	Alameda	Oakland	68	218
Rose	25	f	w	IREL	Marin	San Rafael	74	51
HOLM								
Ah	47	m	c	CHIN	Calaveras	San Andreas P O	70	155
Charles	27	m	w	DENM	San Francisco	San Francisco P O	83	157
Clous	35	m	w	PRUS	Humboldt	Eureka Twp	72	277
Hance P	28	m	w	DENM	Alameda	Washington Twp	68	300
Harris	22	m	w	PRUS	San Francisco	7-Wd San Francisco	81	174
Henry	60	m	w	NY	San Francisco	3-Wd San Francisco	79	297
Jacob	32	m	w	DENM	Butte	Kimshew Tpw	70	83
John	44	m	w	WURT	Sacramento	3-Wd Sacramento	77	288
Meta	26	f	w	SHOL	San Francisco	1-Wd San Francisco	79	28
Michael	24	m	w	FINL	Placer	Bath P O	76	457
Nista	36	m	w	DENM	Alameda	Eden Twp	68	59
Peter	30	m	w	DENM	Merced	Snelling P O	74	265
Peter	15	m	w	CA	San Francisco	11-Wd San Francisc	84	593
Thos	45	m	w	DENM	San Francisco	8-Wd San Francisco	82	306
Thos	37	m	w	ENGL	Lassen	Susanville Twp	73	446
Victor	32	m	w	FINL	Yuba	Marysville Twp	93	567
HOLMAN								
D B	59	m	w	KY	Mendocino	Little Lake Twp	74	196
David	47	m	w	PA	Siskiyou	Surprise Valley Tw	89	643
E	45	f	w	IREL	Alameda	Oakland	68	181
Ellen	12	f	w	CA	San Francisco	11-Wd San Francisc	84	489
Geo	45	m	w	ENGL	Mariposa	Mariposa P O	74	105
Geo	35	m	w	IREL	San Francisco	7-Wd San Francisco	81	286
Geo S	47	m	b	VA	Mariposa	Mariposa P O	74	137
H	48	m	w	KY	Mendocino	Ukiah Twp	74	244
Henry	30	m	w	HANO	San Francisco	2-Wd San Francisco	79	187
Ira	46	m	w	MO	Calaveras	San Andreas P O	70	158
J H	54	m	w	TN	Sonoma	Santa Rosa	91	407
James	40	m	w	IL	Sacramento	Granite Twp	77	136
James	19	m	b	MO	Napa	Napa Twp	75	29
Jane	20	f	w	WI	Nevada	Grass Valley Twp	75	189
Jno B	39	m	w	MA	Butte	Oregon Twp	70	130
John	24	m	w	SAME	Sacramento	Franklin Twp	77	117
Julia	18	f	w	PA	Yolo	Cache Crk Twp	93	435
Nickolas	46	m	w	ENGL	Trinity	Weaverville Pct	92	229
R	29	m	w	IREL	Alameda	Oakland	68	247
Saml	34	m	w	MO	Mendocino	Little Lake Twp	74	193
Saml	22	m	w	ENGL	Fresno	Millerton P O	72	165
Symotee	30	f	i	CA	Siskiyou	Surprise Valley Tw	89	643
W J	52	m	w	IN	Tehama	Red Bluff	92	182
Wm	19	m	w	ENGL	Fresno	Millerton P O	72	165
HOLME								
Marcus	27	m	w	MA	Butte	Chico Twp	70	41
William	50	m	w	ENGL	Contra Costa	Martinez P O	71	413
HOLMER								
Cal H	44	m	w	TN	Sonoma	Mendocino Twp	91	287
Elmena	38	f	w	IN	Los Angeles	Los Angeles	73	518
Hans	33	m	w	DENM	San Francisco	3-Wd San Francisco	79	297
Henderson	45	m	w	TX	Kern	Havilah P O	73	341
Jno	58	m	w	BADE	Sacramento	3-Wd Sacramento	77	313
HOLMES								
A C	37	m	w	CT	Solano	Vallejo	90	202
Aaron	56	m	w	MA	San Francisco	8-Wd San Francisco	82	425
Albert	26	m	w	MO	Sonoma	Petaluma Twp	91	321
Albert	11	m	w	CA	Merced	Snelling P O	74	275
Alfred C	37	m	w	CANA	Solano	Vallejo	90	198
Anna	18	f	w	NY	Santa Clara	2-Wd San Jose	88	296
Anne M	37	f	w	MA	San Francisco	San Francisco P O	83	278
Arthur C	37	m	w	ME	Los Angeles	Los Angeles	73	537
Aug P	26	m	w	ME	Tuolumne	Sonora P O	93	318
Carrie	22	f	w	CT	Santa Clara	1-Wd San Jose	88	275
Carrie	10	f	w	CA	San Francisco	San Francisco P O	83	143
Charles	37	m	w	SC	San Francisco	11-Wd San Francisc	84	520
Charles B	43	m	w	OH	El Dorado	Diamond Springs Tw	72	21
Charles H	30	m	w	ENGL	Colusa	Spring Valley Twp	71	343
Charles J	28	m	w	CT	San Francisco	2-Wd San Francisco	79	254
Chas	37	m	w	SWED	Alameda	Murray Twp	68	99
Chas	36	m	w	ME	San Francisco	11-Wd San Francisc	84	622
Chas	35	m	w	ME	San Francisco	11-Wd San Francisc	84	657
Cornelius	48	m	w	MA	San Francisco	6-Wd San Francisco	81	154
D	9	f	w	IA	Lassen	Milford Twp	73	438
Daniel	51	m	w	ENGL	Nevada	Nevada Twp	75	292
David	24	m	w	OH	Solano	Vacaville Twp	90	127
E B	35	m	w	GA	San Francisco	San Francisco P O	85	856
E K	43	m	w	ME	San Francisco	7-Wd San Francisco	81	235
E S	40	m	w	MA	Tuolumne	Chinese Camp P O	93	367
Edmund B	34	m	w	NY	San Francisco	8-Wd San Francisco	82	381
Edward	40	m	w	NY	San Francisco	6-Wd San Francisco	81	79
Edward H	45	m	w	MA	San Francisco	6-Wd San Francisco	81	107
Edwd	60	m	b	NY	Butte	Chico Twp	70	18
Elisha	74	m	w	NY	El Dorado	Georgetown Twp	72	43
Elizabeth	53	f	w	KY	Plumas	Seneca Twp	77	51
Ella	29	f	w	VT	Colusa	Colusa Twp	71	287
Ella	15	f	w	NJ	San Francisco	San Francisco P O	85	798

© 2001 by Heritage Quest. All rights reserved.

Name	Age	S	R	B-PL	County	Locale	Series M593 Roll	Pg
Ellen	13	f	w	CA	Placer	Gold Run Twp	76	400
Elliott H	40	m	w	NY	Plumas	Quartz Twp	77	43
Emma	8	f	w	CA	Santa Clara	San Jose Twp	88	182
Frank	22	m	w	PORT	San Francisco	11-Wd San Francisc	84	615
G C	41	m	w	PA	Tuolumne	Chinese Camp P O	93	372
George	72	m	w	MA	Santa Clara	1-Wd San Jose	88	247
George	37	m	w	ENGL	San Francisco	San Francisco P O	85	741
George	34	m	w	KY	Marin	San Rafael Twp	74	40
George	31	m	w	ENGL	San Francisco	2-Wd San Francisco	79	153
George	29	m	w	DENM	San Francisco	7-Wd San Francisco	81	223
George A	51	m	w	NY	San Francisco	6-Wd San Francisco	81	151
George S	31	m	w	MA	Napa	Napa Twp	75	28
Gersham	28	m	w	NY	Sacramento	4-Wd Sacramento	77	347
Gordon V	45	m	w	SC	El Dorado	Mountain Twp	72	69
Grace O	34	f	w	OH	San Francisco	3-Wd San Francisco	79	330
H	21	m	w	CT	Alameda	Oakland	68	222
H P	49	m	w	TN	Sonoma	Santa Rosa	91	419
H P	40	m	w	KY	San Joaquin	Tulare Twp	86	261
Harrietta	26	f	w	IREL	Sacramento	2-Wd Sacramento	77	243
Henry	44	m	w	MA	San Francisco	11-Wd San Francisc	84	606
Henry	28	m	w	LA	Sonoma	Healdsburg & Mendo	91	283
Henry B	38	m	w	MA	Calaveras	San Andreas P O	70	195
Henry E	39	m	w	MA	Santa Cruz	Pajaro Twp	89	355
Henry P	38	m	w	MO	Butte	Chico Twp	70	36
Henry T	41	m	w	NY	San Francisco	8-Wd San Francisco	82	293
Horace	29	m	w	NY	Butte	Chico Twp	70	46
Horace	29	m	w	ME	Nevada	Little York Twp	75	244
Huldy	40	f	w	OH	Lassen	Milford Twp	73	438
I I	53	m	w	PA	Napa	Napa Twp	75	71
Ira	42	m	w	MA	San Francisco	8-Wd San Francisco	82	393
J K	59	m	w	PRUS	Sierra	Alleghany & Forest	89	534
Jacob P	43	m	w	OH	Yolo	Cache Crk Twp	93	438
James	42	m	w	IREL	Tuolumne	Sonora P O	93	329
James	41	m	w	ME	Placer	Gold Run Twp	76	400
James	39	m	w	ENGL	Los Angeles	Wilmington Twp	73	638
James R	35	m	w	MA	Los Angeles	Los Angeles Twp	73	489
Jas	33	m	w	IREL	Solano	Vallejo	90	215
Jasper	27	m	w	MO	Plumas	Seneca Twp	77	50
John	44	m	w	MA	Sonoma	Salt Point	91	393
John	44	m	w	HANO	Nevada	Rough & Ready Twp	75	330
John	41	m	w	ME	Placer	Emigrant Gap P O	76	417
John	40	m	w	IREL	San Francisco	San Francisco P O	83	63
John	36	m	w	KY	Placer	Auburn P O	76	360
John	35	m	w	ME	San Francisco	7-Wd San Francisco	81	249
John	34	m	i	AR	Yolo	Grafton Twp	93	499
John	33	m	w	ME	San Mateo	Half Moon Bay P O	87	402
John	29	m	w	ENGL	Tuolumne	Chinese Camp P O	93	378
John	27	m	w	NY	San Francisco	11-Wd San Francisc	84	518
John	25	m	w	NY	San Francisco	11-Wd San Francisc	84	564
John	22	m	w	IREL	San Francisco	1-Wd San Francisco	79	81
John	22	m	w	OH	Butte	Ophir Twp	70	96
John C	33	m	w	NC	Monterey	Alisal Twp	74	305
Joseph	52	m	w	SCOT	San Francisco	11-Wd San Francisc	84	610
K H	15	f	w	CA	Alameda	Oakland	68	237
L	7	f	w	CA	San Francisco	San Francisco P O	85	798
Lewis	30	m	w	ME	San Francisco	7-Wd San Francisco	81	231
Loren	49	m	w	PA	Sacramento	4-Wd Sacramento	77	376
Lucindy A	50	f	w	NY	El Dorado	Salmon Falls Twp	72	133
Lucretia F	62	f	w	NY	Los Angeles	Los Angeles	73	539
Lucy T	58	f	w	MA	Sonoma	Petaluma Twp	91	339
M A	47	f	w	NH	Tuolumne	Columbia P O	93	340
Marcus D	19	m	w	MI	Mariposa	Mariposa P O	74	123
Margaret	45	f	w	IREL	San Francisco	San Francisco P O	85	862
Margaret	18	f	w	ENGL	San Francisco	11-Wd San Francisc	84	481
Maria	45	f	w	ENGL	San Bernardino	San Bernardino Twp	78	449
Mary	45	f	w	IN	Sacramento	3-Wd Sacramento	77	266
Mary	26	f	w	OR	San Francisco	San Francisco P O	80	465
Mary	18	f	w	MA	San Francisco	8-Wd San Francisco	82	345
Mary J	38	f	w	NJ	Alameda	Washington Twp	68	293
Milo P	37	m	w	NY	San Francisco	8-Wd San Francisco	82	349
Moses	23	m	w	NC	Monterey	Alisal Twp	74	304
Nat R	13	m	w	NJ	Sonoma	Cloverdale Twp	91	268
Nathaniel B	42	m	w	NH	Calaveras	Copperopolis P O	70	256
Oliver	35	m	w	NY	Alameda	Washington Twp	68	295
Owen	11	m	w	MS	Fresno	Millerton P O	72	152
Parker B	43	m	w	NY	Santa Clara	Santa Clara Twp	88	146
Peter	28	m	w	IREL	San Francisco	8-Wd San Francisco	82	430
R	42	m	w	NY	San Joaquin	3-Wd Stockton	86	242
Ralph	40	m	w	IREL	San Francisco	7-Wd San Francisco	81	173
Robert	50	m	w	SCOT	Plumas	Indian Twp	77	19
Rosa	15	f	w	WI	Stanislaus	Empire Twp	92	38
Russell R R	27	m	w	MO	El Dorado	Diamond Springs Tw	72	32
S	42	m	w	MO	El Dorado	Greenwood Twp	72	51
S F	29	f	w	IL	Sacramento	3-Wd Sacramento	77	281
Sam A	21	m	w	ME	Placer	Gold Run Twp	76	398
Saml A	39	m	w	NC	Fresno	Millerton P O	72	152
Samuel G	22	m	w	ME	Placer	Gold Run Twp	76	394
Sarah	26	f	w	VA	Santa Clara	1-Wd San Jose	88	245
Seth	40	m	w	MA	Tuolumne	Sonora P O	93	318
Stephen	37	m	w	MA	Stanislaus	Empire Twp	92	49
T B	33	m	w	ME	Yuba	Rose Bar Twp	93	652
Thomas	47	m	w	IREL	San Francisco	San Francisco P O	85	870
Thomas W	37	m	w	CANA	Santa Barbara	Santa Maria P O	87	512
Thos	40	m	w	ENGL	Butte	Chico Twp	70	57
Thos K	36	m	w	ME	Nevada	Nevada Twp	75	310
W C	67	m	w	MA	Merced	Snelling P O	74	266
William	45	m	w	NY	San Francisco	San Francisco P O	83	178

Name	Age	S	R	B-PL	County	Locale	Series M593 Roll	Pg
William	24	m	w	ENGL	San Francisco	San Francisco P O	83	284
William H	37	m	w	IREL	Calaveras	San Andreas P O	70	216
Wm	39	m	w	ENGL	Nevada	Nevada Twp	75	271
Wm	35	m	w	PRUS	San Francisco	1-Wd San Francisco	79	124
Wm	30	m	w	IREL	San Francisco	1-Wd San Francisco	79	96
Wm	15	m	w	IN	Santa Clara	Almaden Twp	88	15
Wm M	40	m	w	TN	Sonoma	Santa Rosa	91	419
HOLMEYER								
Kate	24	f	w	PRUS	San Francisco	2-Wd San Francisco	79	141
Mary	18	f	w	AUST	San Francisco	6-Wd San Francisco	81	72
HOLMN								
Edwd	41	m	w	ENGL	San Francisco	1-Wd San Francisco	79	37
HOLMON								
F S	37	m	w	ENGL	Alameda	Oakland	68	132
HOLMS								
Burch	40	m	w	MO	San Joaquin	Elliott Twp	86	80
G	28	m	w	IN	Alameda	Oakland	68	264
George	36	m	w	ENGL	San Francisco	San Francisco P O	83	135
Henry	24	m	w	PRUS	San Francisco	7-Wd San Francisco	81	224
J H	40	m	w	ENGL	Sutter	Nicolaus Twp	92	106
Oscar	39	m	w	OH	San Francisco	7-Wd San Francisco	81	226
HOLOHAN								
Margaret	25	f	w	IREL	San Francisco	San Francisco P O	80	487
Richard	63	m	w	IREL	San Francisco	2-Wd San Francisco	79	157
Richard	34	m	w	IREL	Santa Cruz	Pajaro Twp	89	346
HOLOISON								
W	16	m	w	NORW	Sierra	Butte Twp	89	509
HOLOLAN								
S	18	f	w	CA	Alameda	Oakland	68	239
HOLOWAY								
Parker	34	m	w	OH	San Luis Obispo	Santa Rosa Twp	87	320
HOLRAN								
Thos	30	m	w	IREL	Solano	Vallejo	90	162
HOLROYLD								
Wm	25	m	w	ENGL	Contra Costa	Martinez P O	71	428
HOLSCHER								
John	42	m	w	HOLL	San Francisco	San Francisco P O	83	122
HOLSCLAW								
M T	44	m	w	MO	Santa Clara	Gilroy Twp	88	69
William	40	m	w	KY	Nevada	Bloomfield Twp	75	92
HOLSENBEGGAR								
Chas	48	m	w	PRUS	Nevada	Nevada Twp	75	316
HOLSER								
John	34	m	w	PA	Santa Barbara	Santa Barbara P O	87	497
Sarah	49	f	w	FRAN	Santa Cruz	Santa Cruz	89	418
HOLSEUR								
Joseph	29	m	w	PRUS	Tulare	Tule Rvr Twp	92	263
HOLSEY								
George	48	m	w	NY	Alameda	Washington Twp	68	278
George M	26	m	w	NY	Placer	Dutch Flat P O	76	404
HOLSINGER								
Fred	48	m	w	WURT	Sacramento	Granite Twp	77	143
HOLSON								
Betsy	19	f	w	NORW	Sacramento	2-Wd Sacramento	77	214
Charlie	14	m	c	CHIN	Sacramento	1-Wd Sacramento	77	183
Jno	35	m	w	IREL	Sacramento	1-Wd Sacramento	77	183
William	20	m	w	LA	San Francisco	11-Wd San Francisc	84	709
HOLSTEAN								
Andrew	50	m	w	SWED	Siskiyou	Scott Valley Twp	89	617
HOLSTED								
Frank	23	m	w	MI	Mariposa	Maxwell Crk P O	74	146
HOLSTEIN								
John	40	m	w	HANO	Stanislaus	Empire Twp	92	44
HOLSTER								
F G	43	m	w	NY	Monterey	Castroville Twp	74	338
HOLSTINE								
Nelson	34	m	w	PRUS	Sutter	Sutter Twp	92	121
HOLSTMAN								
Joseph	50	m	w	BAVA	San Francisco	San Francisco P O	80	338
HOLSWORTH								
Thomas	27	m	w	MA	Humboldt	Bucksport Twp	72	244
HOLT								
A H	33	m	w	ME	Nevada	Meadow Lake Twp	75	247
Adeline F	31	f	w	MS	Nevada	Rough & Ready Twp	75	337
Andrew	40	m	b	MO	El Dorado	Mud Springs Twp	72	85
Andrew J	36	m	w	ME	Nevada	Nevada Twp	75	310
C H	26	m	w	ME	Humboldt	Eureka Twp	72	282
Charles	24	m	w	NH	San Francisco	San Francisco P O	83	87
Charles	23	m	w	NY	Los Angeles	El Monte Twp	73	451
Chas	27	m	w	MA	San Francisco	San Francisco P O	83	319
Chas	25	m	w	ME	Humboldt	Eureka Twp	72	273
E G	57	m	w	MA	Solano	Benicia	90	2
Edward	44	m	w	ENGL	El Dorado	Diamond Springs Tw	72	30
Elizabeth	37	f	w	NY	San Francisco	San Francisco P O	83	258
F P	34	m	w	NY	Solano	Vallejo	90	192
Frank	32	m	w	PORT	Alameda	Eden Twp	68	85
George	27	m	w	CT	Humboldt	Eureka Twp	72	277
Gustavus	45	m	w	NY	San Francisco	5-Wd San Francisco	81	31
J W	46	m	w	ME	Humboldt	Table Bluff Twp	72	307
J W	43	m	w	CANA	Monterey	San Juan Twp	74	389
Jessie	15	f	w	CANA	Santa Clara	Milpitas Twp	88	115
John	78	m	w	VA	Los Angeles	San Gabriel Twp	73	596
John E	41	m	w	LA	San Francisco	1-Wd San Francisco	79	95
John O	24	m	w	AL	Yolo	Putah Twp	93	509
L M	30	m	w	MI	Sacramento	3-Wd Sacramento	77	271
Levi	33	m	w	NH	San Joaquin	Tulare Twp	86	250
Lucy	20	f	w	NY	San Francisco	5-Wd San Francisco	81	1

© 2001 by Heritage Quest. All rights reserved.

Name	Age	S	R	B-PL	County	Locale	Roll	Pg
Michael	29	m	w	FINL	Placer	Bath P O	76	457
Noah	49	m	w	CANA	Humboldt	Bucksport Twp	72	243
O J	55	m	w	DENM	Butte	Mountain Spring Tw	70	89
Pierre	25	m	w	SWED	San Francisco	11-Wd San Francisc	84	662
R M	46	m	w	NY	Alameda	Alameda	68	10
Saml S	22	m	w	NC	San Francisco	5-Wd San Francisco	81	1
Samuel	64	m	w	ENGL	Placer	Roseville P O	76	349
Samuel	39	m	w	CANA	Monterey	San Juan Twp	74	389
Sarah	56	f	w	NH	San Francisco	7-Wd San Francisco	81	247
Sylvanus	50	m	w	ME	San Francisco	San Francisco P O	83	313
Thomas	55	m	w	ENGL	San Francisco	San Francisco P O	83	348
Thomas	40	m	w	ENGL	San Francisco	7-Wd San Francisco	81	171
Thomas H	55	m	w	KY	San Francisco	2-Wd San Francisco	79	194
W C	46	m	w	VA	San Francisco	San Francisco P O	83	16
Warren	60	m	w	MA	San Francisco	San Francisco P O	80	393
Warren	55	m	w	MA	San Francisco	6-Wd San Francisco	81	84
William	41	m	w	HAMB	Alameda	Alameda	68	15
William	28	m	w	MA	San Francisco	2-Wd San Francisco	79	214
Wm	46	m	w	ASEA	Napa	Napa	75	36
Wm F	20	m	w	MD	San Francisco	1-Wd San Francisco	79	100
HOLTEN								
Chester	23	m	w	MA	Sonoma	Vallejo Twp	91	460
HOLTFORTH								
Frederick	41	m	w	PRUS	Solano	Tremont Twp	90	30
HOLTHAUS								
Henry	42	m	w	HANO	Plumas	Indian Twp	77	11
HOLTMAN								
Henry	40	m	w	NORW	San Francisco	San Francisco P O	83	232
John	32	m	w	SWED	San Francisco	San Francisco P O	83	225
HOLTMIER								
Henry	37	m	w	PRUS	San Francisco	2-Wd San Francisco	79	254
HOLTOG								
J J	41	m	w	DENM	Solano	Vallejo	90	212
HOLTON								
Chas	22	m	w	MA	San Joaquin	2-Wd Stockton	86	174
David	34	m	w	PA	Siskiyou	Surprise Valley Tw	89	639
Edward R	33	m	w	MO	Yolo	Cottonwood Twp	93	460
Eliza	36	f	w	MA	San Francisco	8-Wd San Francisco	82	441
Henry I	40	m	w	MA	Sonoma	Petaluma Twp	91	315
Horace	57	m	w	NH	Sacramento	4-Wd Sacramento	77	337
Lewis	47	m	w	FRAN	San Francisco	11-Wd San Francisc	84	485
Michel	28	m	w	NY	Humboldt	Mattole Twp	72	284
Moses	35	m	b	FRAN	San Joaquin	3-Wd Stockton	86	232
Ora S	32	m	w	NY	Shasta	Shasta P O	89	462
Wm	36	m	w	ENGL	Sacramento	Georgianna Twp	77	122
HOLTS								
Anna	34	f	w	SWED	Monterey	Monterey	74	361
Chas	35	m	w	GERM	Yuba	Marysville	93	607
HOLTZ								
Gerhard	26	m	w	DENM	Santa Cruz	Pajaro Twp	89	356
Gustave	45	m	w	BADE	San Francisco	San Francisco P O	83	250
Henry	37	m	w	BAVA	Calaveras	San Andreas P O	70	205
John	39	m	w	WURT	El Dorado	Placerville	72	127
John	28	m	w	PRUS	San Francisco	7-Wd San Francisco	81	218
Lewis	34	m	w	HDAR	Sutter	Sutter Twp	92	122
Louis F	34	m	w	BREM	San Francisco	San Francisco P O	85	719
Madaline	25	f	w	PA	San Francisco	San Francisco P O	83	54
Wm	45	m	w	GERM	Sacramento	1-Wd Sacramento	77	184
HOLTZEL								
Daniel	47	m	w	FRAN	Mariposa	Maxwell Crk P O	74	142
HOLTZER								
Sebastian	50	m	w	FRAN	El Dorado	Placerville	72	126
HOLTZMAN								
Fred	37	m	w	GERM	Yolo	Cache Crk Twp	93	437
HOLUBAR								
Peter	30	m	w	BOHE	Sacramento	Georgianna Twp	77	132
HOLVERSTADT								
Charles	33	m	w	PRUS	San Francisco	San Francisco P O	80	422
HOLVERSTOTTS								
John	54	m	w	PRUS	Solano	Silveyville Twp	90	77
HOLVEY								
August	41	m	w	PRUS	San Francisco	7-Wd San Francisco	81	274
HOLWAY								
Saml P	37	m	w	RI	San Francisco	8-Wd San Francisco	82	335
Thos F	63	m	w	ME	Sierra	Gibson Twp	89	539
HOLWORTH								
B	36	m	w	ENGL	Alameda	Oakland	68	227
HOLY								
Ann	62	f	w	IREL	San Francisco	6-Wd San Francisco	81	118
Jane Mrs	35	f	w	IREL	San Francisco	5-Wd San Francisco	81	19
HOLYON								
Jane	26	f	w	IREL	San Joaquin	2-Wd Stockton	86	192
HOLYROOD								
John	28	m	w	PRUS	San Francisco	5-Wd San Francisco	81	16
HOLYWOOD								
Andrew	25	m	w	IREL	San Francisco	San Francisco P O	83	218
Ann	50	f	w	IREL	San Joaquin	2-Wd Stockton	86	164
HOLZ								
Caspar	72	m	w	WURT	Siskiyou	Yreka Twp	89	666
James	35	m	w	PRUS	Amador	Amador City P O	69	393
John J	40	m	w	SHOL	Amador	Jackson P O	69	328
Lewis	35	m	w	BADE	San Francisco	8-Wd San Francisco	82	308
HOLZHAWER								
Hermann	35	m	w	PRUS	San Francisco	2-Wd San Francisco	79	173
HOM								
Ah	39	m	c	CHIN	San Francisco	6-Wd San Francisco	81	57
Ah	30	m	c	CHIN	Fresno	Millerton P O	72	201

Name	Age	S	R	B-PL	County	Locale	Roll	Pg
Ah	29	m	c	CHIN	San Francisco	6-Wd San Francisco	81	60
Ah	18	m	c	CHIN	Napa	Napa	75	9
Ah	17	m	c	CHIN	San Francisco	8-Wd San Francisco	82	310
Ah	16	m	c	CHIN	Tehama	Tehama Twp	92	189
Andrew J	41	m	w	VA	Los Angeles	El Monte Twp	73	448
Au	18	f	c	CHIN	Tulare	Visalia	92	299
Ho	25	m	c	CHIN	Yuba	Marysville	93	621
Hun	35	m	c	CHIN	Yuba	Marysville	93	621
John	32	m	w	VA	San Francisco	6-Wd San Francisco	81	130
Leo	19	f	c	CHIN	Tulare	Visalia	92	299
Peter	39	m	w	NORW	Contra Costa	Martinez P O	71	415
HOMA								
Peter	28	m	w	PRUS	El Dorado	Greenwood Twp	72	52
Theodore	54	m	w	PRUS	Sierra	Table Rock Twp	89	577
HOMAGE								
Wm	32	m	w	PRUS	San Francisco	San Francisco P O	85	848
HOMAN								
Edd	25	m	w	FRAN	San Francisco	5-Wd San Francisco	81	9
John	44	m	w	SHOL	Sacramento	4-Wd Sacramento	77	338
Peter	39	m	w	NORW	San Francisco	1-Wd San Francisco	79	83
Richard H	42	m	w	VA	Mariposa	Mariposa P O	74	124
Thomas	55	m	w	ENGL	Mariposa	Mariposa P O	74	117
Valentine	45	m	w	PRUS	San Francisco	5-Wd San Francisco	81	3
Wm	35	m	w	NY	San Francisco	5-Wd San Francisco	81	10
HOMANS								
John	28	m	w	NY	Sonoma	Analy Twp	91	233
Peter	38	m	w	NORW	San Francisco	1-Wd San Francisco	79	125
William	48	m	w	MA	Calaveras	San Andreas P O	70	160
HOMARTER								
Lizetta	19	f	w	CAME	San Joaquin	1-Wd Stockton	86	121
HOMB								
Jos	40	m	w	IREL	San Joaquin	Elliott Twp	86	77
HOMBECK								
W P	22	m	w	NY	Sacramento	3-Wd Sacramento	77	300
HOMBERG								
Laurence	45	m	w	HCAS	Contra Costa	Martinez P O	71	381
Martin	44	m	w	PRUS	Contra Costa	Martinez P O	71	371
HOMBOLDT								
Henry	39	m	w	SAXO	Sonoma	Sonoma Twp	91	448
HOMBROOK								
Geo	26	m	w	IREL	Nevada	Meadow Lake Twp	75	246
Jas M	40	m	w	OH	Butte	Chico Twp	70	15
HOMBY								
James	56	m	w	ENGL	Placer	Bath P O	76	457
HOME								
Ah	42	m	c	CHIN	Butte	Mountain Spring Tw	70	89
Ah	31	m	c	CHIN	Tuolumne	Chinese Camp P O	93	364
Ah	29	m	c	CHIN	Sacramento	Lee Twp	77	160
George	32	m	w	SCOT	Humboldt	Eureka Twp	72	256
John	34	m	w	ME	Santa Cruz	Santa Cruz	89	419
Sing	27	m	c	CHIN	Nevada	Nevada Twp	75	314
HOMEN								
Manual	40	m	w	PORT	Yuba	Parks Bar Twp	93	649
HOMENY								
Jacob	42	m	w	PRUS	Siskiyou	Callahan P O	89	631
HOMER								
Clayton	11	m	w	TN	Yolo	Cache Crk Twp	93	444
David H	28	m	w	MD	Yolo	Grafton Twp	93	496
Emma	24	f	w	NY	San Francisco	San Francisco P O	83	387
Fredk	30	m	w	NY	San Francisco	8-Wd San Francisco	82	302
Fredrick	32	m	w	NY	Calaveras	San Andreas P O	70	220
H	27	m	w	MD	Sierra	Butte Twp	89	512
Henry	48	m	w	NY	Placer	Summit P O	76	496
Henry	35	m	w	NY	San Francisco	San Francisco P O	83	390
Herand	45	m	w	PA	Merced	Snelling P O	74	253
J R C H	22	m	w	PRUS	Sacramento	1-Wd Sacramento	77	174
Jno	31	m	w	IREL	Sacramento	3-Wd Sacramento	77	267
John	40	m	w	WURT	San Francisco	San Francisco P O	83	374
John	39	m	w	WURT	San Francisco	8-Wd San Francisco	82	338
Joshua	33	m	w	LA	Tulare	Farmersville Twp	92	249
Marie	54	f	w	NY	San Francisco	San Francisco P O	80	361
Mary	32	f	w	HDAR	San Francisco	2-Wd San Francisco	79	267
Peter	41	m	w	DENM	San Francisco	2-Wd San Francisco	79	268
Valentine	26	m	w	IL	Yolo	Washington Twp	93	537
William	18	m	w	MO	Stanislaus	Empire Twp	92	46
William	13	m	w	CA	Santa Clara	1-Wd San Jose	88	243
HOMERAN								
James	36	m	w	DENM	Alameda	Oakland	68	264
HOMGBERGER								
H	43	m	w	BAVA	San Francisco	7-Wd San Francisco	81	179
HOMICK								
Francis	53	m	w	BAVA	Solano	Benicia	90	9
HOMICKS								
Henry	35	m	w	PRUS	San Francisco	6-Wd San Francisco	81	120
HOMIER								
Max	55	m	w	BAVA	San Francisco	2-Wd San Francisco	79	197
HOMMEL								
Sebastian	44	m	w	BADE	Shasta	Shasta P O	89	455
HOMMRICK								
Christopher	46	m	w	PRUS	San Francisco	2-Wd San Francisco	79	155
HOMOGEN								
Henry	35	m	b	VA	San Francisco	6-Wd San Francisco	81	110
HOMPH								
Wm	38	m	w	BADE	Sacramento	3-Wd Sacramento	77	287
HOMY								
Ah	38	m	c	CHIN	Los Angeles	Los Angeles	73	507
William	38	m	w	HANO	Los Angeles	Santa Ana Twp	73	613

© 2001 by Heritage Quest. All rights reserved.

Name	Age	S	R	B-PL	County	Locale	Roll	Pg
HON								
Ah	65	m	c	CHIN	Butte	Ophir Twp	70	98
Ah	60	m	c	CHIN	Calaveras	San Andreas P O	70	191
Ah	53	m	c	CHIN	Placer	Auburn P O	76	363
Ah	52	m	c	CHIN	Shasta	Horsetown P O	89	506
Ah	49	m	c	CHIN	Tuolumne	Sonora P O	93	325
Ah	48	m	c	CHIN	Nevada	Grass Valley Twp	75	205
Ah	46	m	c	CHIN	Calaveras	San Andreas P O	70	156
Ah	45	m	c	CHIN	Amador	Volcano P O	69	387
Ah	42	m	c	CHIN	Yuba	Marysville	93	577
Ah	41	m	c	CHIN	Tuolumne	Chinese Camp P O	93	377
Ah	40	m	c	CHIN	Mariposa	Mariposa P O	74	128
Ah	40	m	c	CHIN	Tuolumne	Chinese Camp P O	93	363
Ah	40	m	c	CHIN	Tuolumne	Chinese Camp P O	93	377
Ah	40	m	c	CHIN	Sacramento	Granite Twp	77	151
Ah	40	m	c	CHIN	San Francisco	San Francisco P O	80	505
Ah	40	m	c	CHIN	Santa Clara	1-Wd San Jose	88	273
Ah	38	m	c	CHIN	Sacramento	Sutter Twp	77	382
Ah	36	m	c	CHIN	El Dorado	Placerville Twp	72	98
Ah	35	m	c	CHIN	San Francisco	1-Wd San Francisco	79	110
Ah	35	m	c	CHIN	Sierra	Eureka Twp	89	525
Ah	34	m	c	CHIN	Mariposa	Mariposa P O	74	135
Ah	34	m	w	CHIN	Alameda	Murray Twp	68	114
Ah	34	m	c	CHIN	Calaveras	San Andreas P O	70	191
Ah	32	m	c	CHIN	San Francisco	San Francisco P O	85	749
Ah	31	m	c	CHIN	Mariposa	Mariposa P O	74	132
Ah	31	m	c	CHIN	Amador	Ione City P O	69	356
Ah	30	m	c	CHIN	Mariposa	Mariposa P O	74	131
Ah	30	m	c	CHIN	Placer	Auburn P O	76	373
Ah	30	m	c	CHIN	Sierra	Gibson Twp	89	544
Ah	30	m	c	CHIN	Sacramento	3-Wd Sacramento	77	315
Ah	30	m	c	CHIN	Calaveras	San Andreas P O	70	169
Ah	30	m	c	CHIN	Amador	Fiddletown P O	69	427
Ah	29	m	c	CHIN	San Francisco	San Francisco P O	80	447
Ah	28	m	c	CHIN	Sierra	Sears Twp	89	561
Ah	28	m	c	CHIN	Sacramento	Granite Twp	77	138
Ah	26	m	c	CHIN	Sacramento	1-Wd Sacramento	77	192
Ah	26	f	c	CHIN	San Francisco	San Francisco P O	80	526
Ah	24	m	c	CHIN	Sacramento	Georgianna Twp	77	131
Ah	24	m	c	CHIN	Contra Costa	Martinez P O	71	452
Ah	22	f	c	CHIN	Butte	Ophir Twp	70	103
Ah	22	m	c	CHIN	Trinity	Canyon City Pct	92	201
Ah	21	m	c	CHIN	Tuolumne	Big Oak Flat P O	93	393
Ah	21	m	c	CHIN	San Francisco	6-Wd San Francisco	81	46
Ah	20	m	c	CHIN	Sacramento	Georgianna Twp	77	132
Ah	20	m	c	CHIN	San Francisco	San Francisco P O	80	506
Ah	20	m	c	CHIN	Santa Clara	Gilroy Twp	88	80
Ah	19	f	c	CHIN	Calaveras	San Andreas P O	70	167
Ah	19	m	c	CHIN	San Francisco	3-Wd San Francisco	79	329
Ah	18	m	c	CHIN	San Francisco	6-Wd San Francisco	81	44
Ah	18	m	c	CHIN	Nevada	Grass Valley Twp	75	206
Ah	18	m	c	CHIN	San Francisco	San Francisco P O	83	169
Chin	28	f	c	CHIN	Mariposa	Mariposa P O	74	102
Chung	40	m	c	CHIN	Klamath	Liberty Twp	73	376
Drue	18	m	c	CHIN	Marin	Tomales Twp	74	77
Frederick	61	m	w	MO	Tulare	Tule Rvr Twp	92	262
Gacy	35	m	c	CHIN	Trinity	North Fork Twp	92	221
Gee	44	m	c	CHIN	Butte	Kimshew Tpw	70	86
Go	51	m	c	CHIN	Trinity	North Fork Twp	92	221
Hoa	40	m	c	CHIN	San Francisco	6-Wd San Francisco	81	37
I	24	f	c	CHIN	Stanislaus	Emory Twp	92	20
Kee	26	m	c	CHIN	Sierra	Lincoln Twp	89	547
Kim	26	f	c	CHIN	Yuba	Marysville	93	627
Lip	40	m	c	CHIN	San Joaquin	1-Wd Stockton	86	144
Lung	38	m	c	CHIN	Yuba	Marysville	93	625
Lut	29	m	c	CHIN	Yuba	Marysville	93	601
Mow	25	m	c	CHIN	San Francisco	6-Wd San Francisco	81	98
On	19	m	c	CHIN	Butte	Kimshew Tpw	70	84
See	46	m	c	CHIN	Butte	Concow Twp	70	11
Sing	40	m	c	CHIN	San Francisco	7-Wd San Francisco	81	245
Sun	19	m	c	CHIN	Yuba	Marysville	93	631
Tia	23	m	c	CHIN	San Mateo	Schoolhouse Statio	87	337
Tim	50	m	c	CHIN	Mariposa	Mariposa P O	74	102
Wah	45	m	c	CHIN	Placer	Newcastle Twp	76	479
Wi	35	m	c	CHIN	Sacramento	1-Wd Sacramento	77	202
Wing	26	m	c	CHIN	Butte	Concow Twp	70	11
Wo	27	m	c	CHIN	San Joaquin	1-Wd Stockton	86	142
Yup	40	m	c	CHIN	Trinity	Weaverville Pct	92	229
HONAN								
Henry	45	m	w	ENGL	Fresno	Millerton P O	72	165
Jno	40	m	w	PRUS	San Francisco	5-Wd San Francisco	81	15
HONARSON								
Annie	23	f	w	NY	Sacramento	1-Wd Sacramento	77	173
HONCE								
John	20	m	w	PORT	San Francisco	San Francisco P O	85	756
HONCHARENKO								
Agapius	39	m	w	PRUS	San Francisco	2-Wd San Francisco	79	284
HONDA								
Pedro	31	m	w	PORT	San Francisco	1-Wd San Francisco	79	118
HONE								
Ah	42	m	c	CHIN	Amador	Jackson P O	69	343
Ah	38	m	c	CHIN	Amador	Drytown P O	69	419
Ah	36	m	c	CHIN	Amador	Jackson P O	69	330
Ah	35	m	c	CHIN	Trinity	Douglas	92	235
Ah	30	m	c	CHIN	Butte	Mountain Spring Tw	70	90
Ah	25	m	c	CHIN	Contra Costa	Martinez P O	71	440
Elisha W	42	m	w	RI	San Luis Obispo	Morro Twp	87	283
George C	22	m	w	MA	San Francisco	San Francisco P O	83	188
John	35	m	w	IREL	San Francisco	7-Wd San Francisco	81	251
HONEBRIN								
John	59	m	w	OLDE	Sonoma	Analy Twp	91	237
HONEL								
Isaac	72	m	w	NY	San Luis Obispo	Arroyo Grande Twp	87	275
HONEMAN								
J S	19	m	w	NY	Solano	Benicia	90	21
HONENSHELL								
A	48	m	w	PA	San Joaquin	Oneal Twp	86	105
HONEREURE								
Henry	65	m	w	BAVA	San Francisco	2-Wd San Francisco	79	145
HONESS								
Frank	45	m	w	NORW	Contra Costa	Martinez P O	71	415
HONETTE								
Constant	35	m	w	FRAN	San Francisco	San Francisco P O	83	374
HONEUR								
Felix	41	m	w	FRAN	San Francisco	San Francisco P O	80	348
Felix	41	m	w	FRAN	San Francisco	San Francisco P O	80	347
HONEY								
Calvin	55	m	w	NY	Calaveras	Copperopolis P O	70	226
Cong	32	m	c	CHIN	Butte	Hamilton Twp	70	72
John	19	m	w	MA	Stanislaus	Empire Twp	92	66
Richd	30	m	w	ENGL	Yuba	Rose Bar Twp	93	658
Wm	22	m	w	WALE	Butte	Oregon Twp	70	125
HONEYCHURCH								
John	45	m	w	ENGL	Amador	Amador City P O	69	390
HONEYCUTT								
William	37	m	w	IL	Monterey	Alisal Twp	74	295
HONEYJANGER								
Wm	30	m	w	SHOL	San Francisco	1-Wd San Francisco	79	104
HONEYMAN								
M	36	m	w	DENM	Yuba	Marysville	93	611
HONEYWELL								
Henry	51	m	w	MA	Alameda	Brooklyn Twp	68	42
HONG								
---	45	m	c	CHIN	Shasta	Shasta P O	89	461
---	30	m	c	CHIN	Shasta	Shasta P O	89	454
---	26	m	c	CHIN	Siskiyou	Cottonwood Twp	89	594
---	20	m	c	CHIN	Siskiyou	Cottonwood Twp	89	592
Ah	52	m	c	CHIN	Trinity	Junction City Pct	92	209
Ah	52	m	c	CHIN	Sierra	Gibson Twp	89	540
Ah	50	m	c	CHIN	Mariposa	Mariposa P O	74	102
Ah	50	m	c	CHIN	Sacramento	3-Wd Sacramento	77	316
Ah	50	m	c	CHIN	San Francisco	San Francisco P O	80	523
Ah	50	m	c	CHIN	San Francisco	San Francisco P O	80	523
Ah	49	m	c	CHIN	Santa Clara	San Jose Twp	88	192
Ah	48	m	c	CHIN	Trinity	North Fork Twp	92	220
Ah	46	m	c	CHIN	San Francisco	11-Wd San Francisc	84	694
Ah	46	m	c	CHIN	Mariposa	Mariposa P O	74	126
Ah	46	m	c	CHIN	San Francisco	San Francisco P O	80	438
Ah	45	m	c	CHIN	Trinity	Weaverville Pct	92	228
Ah	45	m	c	CHIN	San Francisco	San Francisco P O	80	438
Ah	45	m	c	CHIN	Mariposa	Maxwell Crk P O	74	142
Ah	45	m	c	CHIN	Nevada	Eureka Twp	75	127
Ah	45	m	c	CHIN	Trinity	North Fork Twp	92	221
Ah	44	m	c	CHIN	Calaveras	San Andreas P O	70	172
Ah	43	m	c	CHIN	San Francisco	11-Wd San Francisc	84	694
Ah	43	m	c	CHIN	San Francisco	San Francisco P O	80	527
Ah	42	m	c	CHIN	Placer	Lincoln P O	76	482
Ah	41	m	c	CHIN	Yolo	Grafton Twp	93	479
Ah	41	m	c	CHIN	San Francisco	San Francisco P O	80	514
Ah	40	m	c	CHIN	Sierra	Eureka Twp	89	525
Ah	40	m	c	CHIN	Amador	Drytown P O	69	423
Ah	40	m	c	CHIN	Mariposa	Mariposa P O	74	127
Ah	40	m	c	CHIN	Plumas	Goodwin Twp	77	4
Ah	40	m	c	CHIN	Yuba	Marysville	93	601
Ah	40	m	c	CHIN	Amador	Volcano P O	69	388
Ah	40	m	c	CHIN	Nevada	Eureka Twp	75	127
Ah	40	m	c	CHIN	San Francisco	San Francisco P O	80	520
Ah	40	m	c	CHIN	Trinity	Weaverville Pct	92	228
Ah	39	m	c	CHIN	Nevada	Bridgeport Twp	75	110
Ah	39	m	c	CHIN	San Francisco	6-Wd San Francisco	81	56
Ah	39	m	c	CHIN	Trinity	Weaverville Pct	92	227
Ah	38	m	c	CHIN	Mariposa	Mariposa P O	74	131
Ah	38	m	c	CHIN	Alameda	Washington Twp	68	299
Ah	38	m	c	CHIN	San Francisco	San Francisco P O	80	502
Ah	38	m	c	CHIN	San Francisco	San Francisco P O	80	517
Ah	37	m	c	CHIN	Calaveras	San Andreas P O	70	203
Ah	37	f	c	CHIN	Butte	Chico Twp	70	28
Ah	37	m	c	CHIN	Alameda	Murray Twp	68	114
Ah	37	m	c	CHIN	Mariposa	Mariposa P O	74	106
Ah	37	m	c	CHIN	San Francisco	San Francisco P O	80	443
Ah	37	m	c	CHIN	Plumas	Rich Bar Twp	77	45
Ah	36	m	c	CHIN	San Francisco	11-Wd San Francisc	84	696
Ah	36	m	c	CHIN	San Francisco	San Francisco P O	80	437
Ah	36	f	c	CHIN	San Francisco	San Francisco P O	80	446
Ah	36	m	c	CHIN	San Francisco	San Francisco P O	80	435
Ah	36	m	c	CHIN	Nevada	Nevada Twp	75	311
Ah	36	m	c	CHIN	Sierra	Table Rock Twp	89	573
Ah	35	m	c	CHIN	Plumas	Goodwin Twp	77	5
Ah	35	m	c	CHIN	Stanislaus	Emory Twp	92	23
Ah	34	m	c	CHIN	Yolo	Cache Crk Twp	93	451
Ah	34	m	c	CHIN	Nevada	Meadow Lake Twp	75	261
Ah	34	m	c	CHIN	Alameda	Eden Twp	68	62
Ah	34	m	c	CHIN	San Francisco	San Francisco P O	80	517
Ah	34	m	c	CHIN	San Francisco	San Francisco P O	80	520

© 2001 by Heritage Quest. All rights reserved.

Name	Age	S	R	B-PL	County	Locale	Series M593 Roll	Pg
Ah	33	m	c	CHIN	Amador	Volcano P O	69	387
Ah	33	m	c	CHIN	Trinity	Junction City Pct	92	208
Ah	32	m	c	CHIN	San Francisco	San Francisco P O	80	436
Ah	32	m	c	CHIN	Nevada	Nevada Twp	75	312
Ah	32	m	c	CHIN	San Francisco	San Francisco P O	80	515
Ah	32	m	c	CHIN	Trinity	Douglas	92	234
Ah	30	m	c	CHIN	San Mateo	San Mateo P O	87	350
Ah	30	m	c	CHIN	Calaveras	Copperopolis P O	70	242
Ah	30	m	c	CHIN	Los Angeles	Los Nietos Twp	73	581
Ah	30	f	c	CHIN	San Francisco	San Francisco P O	80	448
Ah	30	m	c	CHIN	Nevada	Nevada Twp	75	307
Ah	30	m	c	CHIN	San Francisco	San Francisco P O	80	519
Ah	30	m	c	CHIN	San Francisco	San Francisco P O	80	516
Ah	30	m	c	CHIN	Trinity	Junction City Pct	92	210
Ah	30	m	c	CHIN	Trinity	Lewiston Pct	92	214
Ah	29	m	c	CHIN	Siskiyou	Cottonwood Twp	89	593
Ah	29	m	c	CHIN	Solano	Suisun Twp	90	105
Ah	29	m	c	CHIN	Yuba	Marysville	93	631
Ah	28	m	c	CHIN	Tuolumne	Big Oak Flat P O	93	392
Ah	28	m	c	CHIN	San Francisco	San Francisco P O	80	498
Ah	28	m	c	CHIN	Mariposa	Mariposa P O	74	132
Ah	28	m	c	CHIN	Placer	Lincoln P O	76	484
Ah	28	m	c	CHIN	Placer	Auburn P O	76	371
Ah	28	m	c	CHIN	Nevada	Meadow Lake Twp	75	255
Ah	28	m	c	CHIN	Alameda	Eden Twp	68	59
Ah	28	m	c	CHIN	Sacramento	Georgianna Twp	77	132
Ah	28	m	c	CHIN	Nevada	Grass Valley Twp	75	208
Ah	28	m	c	CHIN	San Francisco	6-Wd San Francisco	81	44
Ah	27	m	c	CHIN	Tulare	Visalia	92	299
Ah	27	m	c	CHIN	San Francisco	San Francisco P O	80	499
Ah	27	m	c	CHIN	San Francisco	San Francisco P O	80	450
Ah	27	m	c	CHIN	San Bernardino	San Bernardino Twp	78	433
Ah	27	m	c	CHIN	Sacramento	1-Wd Sacramento	77	195
Ah	27	m	c	CHIN	Sacramento	Sutter Twp	77	388
Ah	27	m	c	CHIN	Nevada	Eureka Twp	75	136
Ah	26	m	c	CHIN	San Francisco	San Francisco P O	85	748
Ah	26	m	c	CHIN	San Francisco	6-Wd San Francisco	81	42
Ah	26	f	c	CHIN	San Francisco	San Francisco P O	80	449
Ah	26	m	c	CHIN	El Dorado	Mountain Twp	72	70
Ah	26	m	c	CHIN	Santa Clara	1-Wd San Jose	88	272
Ah	25	f	c	CHIN	San Francisco	San Francisco P O	80	434
Ah	25	m	c	CHIN	Placer	Auburn P O	76	363
Ah	25	m	c	CHIN	Contra Costa	Martinez P O	71	398
Ah	25	m	c	CHIN	Fresno	Millerton P O	72	145
Ah	25	m	c	CHIN	Sacramento	Center Twp	77	86
Ah	25	m	c	CHIN	Nevada	Eureka Twp	75	136
Ah	25	m	c	CHIN	Sonoma	Sonoma Twp	91	447
Ah	24	m	c	CHIN	San Joaquin	Union Twp	86	266
Ah	24	f	c	CHIN	San Francisco	San Francisco P O	80	493
Ah	24	m	c	CHIN	San Francisco	San Francisco P O	80	441
Ah	24	m	c	CHIN	San Francisco	3-Wd San Francisco	79	309
Ah	24	m	c	CHIN	Placer	Newcastle Twp	76	475
Ah	24	m	c	CHIN	Amador	Ione City P O	69	351
Ah	24	m	c	CHIN	Placer	Lincoln P O	76	484
Ah	24	m	c	CHIN	Placer	Bath P O	76	442
Ah	24	m	c	CHIN	Santa Clara	Fremont Twp	88	47
Ah	24	m	c	CHIN	Trinity	Junction City Pct	92	207
Ah	24	m	c	CHIN	Solano	Suisun Twp	90	105
Ah	23	m	c	CHIN	Solano	Suisun Twp	90	107
Ah	23	m	c	CHIN	Yolo	Washington Twp	93	534
Ah	23	m	c	CHIN	San Joaquin	Dent Twp	86	16
Ah	23	m	c	CHIN	San Francisco	6-Wd San Francisco	81	43
Ah	23	f	c	CHIN	San Francisco	San Francisco P O	80	437
Ah	23	m	c	CHIN	Sacramento	Georgianna Twp	77	122
Ah	23	m	c	CHIN	Plumas	Washington Twp	77	58
Ah	23	m	c	CHIN	Napa	Napa	75	1
Ah	23	m	c	CHIN	Alameda	Murray Twp	68	114
Ah	23	m	c	CHIN	Napa	Napa Twp	75	31
Ah	23	m	c	CHIN	Sierra	Eureka Twp	89	525
Ah	22	m	c	CHIN	Yolo	Cottonwood Twp	93	469
Ah	22	f	c	CHIN	Plumas	Goodwin Twp	77	4
Ah	22	m	c	CHIN	Nevada	Nevada Twp	75	311
Ah	22	m	c	CHIN	Nevada	Nevada Twp	75	311
Ah	21	m	c	CHIN	Placer	Newcastle Twp	76	477
Ah	20	m	c	CHIN	Siskiyou	Yreka	89	650
Ah	20	m	c	CHIN	Santa Clara	San Jose Twp	88	192
Ah	20	m	c	CHIN	San Francisco	6-Wd San Francisco	81	46
Ah	20	m	c	CHIN	San Francisco	6-Wd San Francisco	81	60
Ah	20	m	c	CHIN	Calaveras	Copperopolis P O	70	260
Ah	20	m	c	CHIN	Calaveras	Copperopolis P O	70	260
Ah	20	m	c	CHIN	Alameda	Murray Twp	68	120
Ah	20	f	c	CHIN	San Francisco	San Francisco P O	80	444
Ah	20	m	c	CHIN	Placer	Auburn P O	76	381
Ah	20	m	c	CHIN	San Francisco	6-Wd San Francisco	81	50
Ah	20	m	c	CHIN	San Francisco	6-Wd San Francisco	81	46
Ah	20	m	c	CHIN	Sonoma	Healdsburg & Mendo	91	280
Ah	20	m	c	CHIN	Trinity	Lewiston Pct	92	214
Ah	20	m	c	CHIN	Trinity	North Fork Twp	92	216
Ah	19	m	c	CHIN	San Francisco	6-Wd San Francisco	81	45
Ah	19	m	c	CHIN	San Francisco	San Francisco P O	83	131
Ah	19	m	c	CHIN	Placer	Auburn P O	76	370
Ah	19	m	c	CHIN	San Francisco	San Francisco P O	83	132
Ah	18	m	c	CHIN	Los Angeles	Los Angeles	73	510
Ah	18	m	c	CHIN	San Francisco	San Francisco P O	80	510
Ah	18	m	c	CHIN	Santa Clara	Fremont Twp	88	47
Ah	17	m	c	CHIN	San Francisco	3-Wd San Francisco	79	329
Ah	17	m	c	CHIN	Sacramento	1-Wd Sacramento	77	187
Ah	17	m	c	CHIN	Alameda	Oakland	68	133
Ah	17	m	c	CHIN	Alameda	Oakland	68	188
Ah	17	m	c	CHIN	Butte	Kimshew Tpw	70	84
Ah	17	m	c	CHIN	Siskiyou	Yreka Twp	89	664
Ah	16	m	c	CHIN	San Joaquin	Tulare Twp	86	262
Ah	16	f	c	CHIN	San Francisco	San Francisco P O	80	491
Ah	16	m	c	CHIN	Placer	Lincoln P O	76	484
Ah	15	m	c	CHIN	San Francisco	San Francisco P O	80	500
Ah	15	m	c	CHIN	Placer	Clipper Gap P O	76	393
Ah	15	m	c	CHIN	San Francisco	San Francisco P O	85	731
Ah	14	m	c	CHIN	Yolo	Cache Crk Twp	93	424
Ah	14	m	c	CHIN	Merced	Snelling P O	74	279
Ah	14	m	c	CHIN	Sacramento	3-Wd Sacramento	77	312
Ah	13	m	c	CHIN	Solano	Benicia	90	3
Ah	12	m	c	CHIN	Sonoma	Russian Rvr	91	370
Ah	10	m	c	CHIN	Yolo	Grafton Twp	93	481
Bee	34	m	c	CHIN	Yuba	Marysville	93	626
Bing	30	m	c	CHIN	Yuba	Marysville	93	622
Bug	11	m	c	CHIN	San Francisco	San Francisco P O	85	867
Chee	27	m	c	CHIN	San Mateo	Schoolhouse Statio	87	338
Chi	17	m	c	CHIN	San Joaquin	1-Wd Stockton	86	149
Chong	40	m	c	CHIN	Trinity	Weaverville Pct	92	228
Chong	33	m	c	CHIN	Plumas	Rich Bar Twp	77	46
Chong	26	m	c	CHIN	Placer	Pino Twp	76	470
Chong	24	m	c	CHIN	San Francisco	2-Wd San Francisco	79	229
Chong	19	m	c	CHIN	Yuba	Marysville	93	631
Chong	15	m	c	CHIN	San Francisco	2-Wd San Francisco	79	229
Chou	24	m	c	CHIN	Yuba	Marysville	93	620
Choug	18	f	c	CHIN	Lassen	Susanville Twp	73	441
Chow	31	m	c	CHIN	Solano	Green Valley Twp	90	43
Choy	27	m	c	CHIN	Butte	Ophir Twp	70	106
Chung	53	m	c	CHIN	Placer	Auburn P O	76	363
Cow	30	m	c	CHIN	Yuba	Marysville	93	620
Dock	30	m	w	CHIN	Plumas	Mineral Twp	77	24
Eu Po	43	m	c	CHIN	Siskiyou	Cottonwood Twp	89	594
Fa	21	f	c	CHIN	Nevada	Grass Valley Twp	75	204
Foo	35	m	c	CHIN	Butte	Chico Twp	70	49
Foo	34	m	c	CHIN	Butte	Hamilton Twp	70	67
Foo	31	m	c	CHIN	Solano	Vacaville Twp	90	132
Foo	25	m	c	CHIN	Butte	Ophir Twp	70	106
Fook	40	m	c	CHIN	Siskiyou	Yreka	89	650
Fung	34	m	c	CHIN	Yuba	Marysville	93	624
Gar	34	m	c	CHIN	Yuba	Marysville	93	624
Gee	52	m	c	CHIN	San Francisco	11-Wd San Francisc	84	574
Gee	38	m	w	CHIN	Plumas	Mineral Twp	77	24
Gee	30	m	c	CHIN	Marin	Point Reyes Twp	74	22
Gee	27	m	c	CHIN	Yuba	Marysville	93	622
Gee	22	m	c	CHIN	Solano	Vallejo	90	139
Gee Hong	54	m	c	CHIN	Plumas	Rich Bar Twp	77	46
Gee Hong	54	m	c	CHIN	Plumas	Washington Twp	77	58
Ging	18	m	c	CHIN	San Francisco	3-Wd San Francisco	79	317
Go	40	m	c	CHIN	San Joaquin	1-Wd Stockton	86	153
Go	26	m	c	CHIN	San Joaquin	Liberty Twp	86	97
Haw	28	m	c	CHIN	Plumas	Rich Bar Twp	77	46
Hi	36	m	c	CHIN	Nevada	Eureka Twp	75	140
Hi	30	m	c	CHIN	Nevada	Nevada Twp	75	276
Hin	17	m	c	CHIN	San Francisco	3-Wd San Francisco	79	306
Hing	19	m	c	CHIN	San Francisco	2-Wd San Francisco	79	242
Hing	15	m	c	CHIN	San Francisco	8-Wd San Francisco	82	313
Ho	19	m	c	CHIN	Santa Clara	2-Wd San Jose	88	325
Hock	38	m	c	CHIN	Nevada	Nevada Twp	75	277
Hoo	24	m	c	CHIN	Sierra	Forest Twp	89	529
How	42	m	c	CHIN	Nevada	Washington Twp	75	339
Hoy	27	m	c	CHIN	Santa Clara	San Jose Twp	88	192
Huck	30	m	c	CHIN	Yuba	Marysville	93	632
James	45	m	w	OH	Placer	Bath P O	76	424
John	26	m	w	ITAL	San Mateo	Schoolhouse Statio	87	345
Kee	44	m	c	CHIN	Santa Clara	San Jose Twp	88	190
Kee	37	m	c	CHIN	San Joaquin	Oneal Twp	86	115
Kee	36	m	c	CHIN	Sacramento	1-Wd Sacramento	77	194
Kee	29	m	c	CHIN	San Francisco	6-Wd San Francisco	81	40
Kee	24	m	c	CHIN	San Francisco	6-Wd San Francisco	81	60
Kee	18	m	c	CHIN	San Francisco	2-Wd San Francisco	79	234
Keong	41	m	c	CHIN	Nevada	Nevada Twp	75	314
Kong	30	m	c	CHIN	Alameda	Oakland	68	267
La	19	m	c	CHIN	Solano	Vacaville Twp	90	122
Lee	48	m	c	CHIN	Sierra	Lincoln Twp	89	548
Lee	45	m	c	CHIN	Butte	Chico Twp	70	28
Lee	44	m	c	CHIN	Butte	Hamilton Twp	70	74
Lee	44	m	c	CHIN	San Mateo	Half Moon Bay P O	87	395
Lee	42	m	c	CHIN	Butte	Hamilton Twp	70	67
Lee	38	m	c	CHIN	Tulare	Venice Twp	92	274
Lee	35	m	c	CHIN	Solano	Tremont Twp	90	34
Lee	35	m	c	CHIN	Placer	Bath P O	76	460
Lee	35	m	c	CHIN	Yuba	Marysville	93	629
Lee	27	m	c	CHIN	Plumas	Goodwin Twp	77	2
Lee	24	m	c	CHIN	Butte	Ophir Twp	70	103
Lee	19	m	c	CHIN	Santa Clara	San Jose Twp	88	190
Lee	14	f	c	CHIN	Butte	Hamilton Twp	70	73
Lew	34	m	c	CHIN	Yuba	Marysville	93	624
Lewy	18	m	c	CHIN	Yuba	Marysville	93	631
Lo	42	m	c	CHIN	San Joaquin	3-Wd Stockton	86	237
Lo	30	m	c	CHIN	San Joaquin	1-Wd Stockton	86	130
Lon	26	f	c	CHIN	Yuba	Marysville	93	627
Lon	19	m	c	CHIN	Sacramento	2-Wd Sacramento	77	250
Long	30	m	c	CHIN	Napa	Napa	75	2
Loo	38	m	c	CHIN	San Mateo	Schoolhouse Statio	87	332

© 2001 by Heritage Quest. All rights reserved.

California 1870 Census

Series M593

Name	Age	S	R	B-PL	County	Locale	Roll	Pg
Loo	13	m	c	CHIN	San Francisco	11-Wd San Francisc	84	573
Lu	18	m	c	CHIN	San Francisco	8-Wd San Francisco	82	412
Me	38	m	c	CHIN	San Joaquin	1-Wd Stockton	86	156
Ming	36	m	c	CHIN	Yuba	Marysville	93	621
Mow	37	m	c	CHIN	Butte	Hamilton Twp	70	74
Pan	41	m	c	CHIN	San Luis Obispo	Arroyo Grande Twp	87	279
Pay	20	m	c	CHIN	Sacramento	1-Wd Sacramento	77	194
Qua	20	m	c	CHIN	Placer	Bath P O	76	443
Que	25	m	c	CHIN	Fresno	Millerton P O	72	156
Quen	62	m	c	CHIN	Butte	Ophir Twp	70	106
Ray	27	m	c	CHIN	Yuba	Marysville	93	629
Roo	28	m	c	CHIN	San Mateo	Schoolhouse Statio	87	336
Sang	22	m	c	CHIN	Shasta	Horsetown P O	89	503
See	14	m	c	CHIN	Sierra	Forest Twp	89	530
Shong	61	m	c	CHIN	Trinity	Weaverville Pct	92	228
Sing	42	m	c	CHIN	Butte	Chico Twp	70	27
Sing	41	m	c	CHIN	Yuba	Slate Range Bar Tw	93	676
Sing	35	m	c	CHIN	San Francisco	6-Wd San Francisco	81	103
Sing	28	m	c	CHIN	Nevada	Meadow Lake Twp	75	254
Sing	27	m	c	CHIN	Butte	Chico Twp	70	42
Sing	25	m	c	CHIN	San Francisco	5-Wd San Francisco	81	36
Sing	23	m	c	CHIN	San Francisco	8-Wd San Francisco	82	425
Sing	22	m	c	CHIN	Klamath	South Fork Twp	73	382
Song	44	m	c	CHIN	Siskiyou	Hamburg Twp	89	597
Song	35	m	c	CHIN	Yuba	Marysville	93	620
Soon	20	m	c	CHIN	San Francisco	San Francisco P O	83	346
Soon	19	m	c	CHIN	San Francisco	San Francisco P O	83	374
Sue	19	m	c	CHIN	Yuba	Marysville	93	630
Suen	46	m	c	CHIN	Yuba	Marysville	93	623
Sun	40	m	c	CHIN	Fresno	Millerton P O	72	202
Sun	32	m	c	CHIN	Yuba	Marysville	93	629
Tacy	17	m	c	CHIN	San Joaquin	Liberty Twp	86	97
Te Ock	33	m	c	CHIN	Plumas	Rich Bar Twp	77	46
Tek	59	m	c	CHIN	San Francisco	San Francisco P O	80	435
Ti	27	m	c	CHIN	Solano	Vacaville Twp	90	133
Tie	37	m	c	CHIN	San Joaquin	Oneal Twp	86	116
Tie	35	m	c	CHIN	Butte	Chico Twp	70	51
Tim	38	m	c	CHIN	Nevada	Nevada Twp	75	312
Ton	40	m	c	CHIN	Del Norte	Mountain Twp	71	474
Ton	30	m	c	CHIN	San Francisco	2-Wd San Francisco	79	177
Toy	45	m	c	CHIN	Butte	Chico Twp	70	28
Toy	29	m	c	CHIN	Yolo	Grafton Twp	93	484
Wa	15	m	c	CHIN	Fresno	Millerton P O	72	201
Wan	20	m	c	CHIN	San Francisco	San Francisco P O	83	162
Wang	45	m	c	CHIN	Yuba	Slate Range Bar Tw	93	668
We	25	m	c	CHIN	San Francisco	8-Wd San Francisco	82	428
Wi	36	m	c	CHIN	Sacramento	2-Wd Sacramento	77	250
Wing	47	m	c	CHIN	Plumas	Rich Bar Twp	77	46
Wing	24	m	c	CHIN	San Francisco	8-Wd San Francisco	82	412
Wo	29	m	c	CHIN	San Francisco	3-Wd San Francisco	79	328
Wo	22	m	c	CHIN	Santa Clara	San Jose Twp	88	190
Wo Yeek	18	m	c	CHIN	San Francisco	6-Wd San Francisco	81	69
Wong	20	m	c	CHIN	San Francisco	3-Wd San Francisco	79	307
Woo	33	m	c	CHIN	Solano	Silveyville Twp	90	84
Woo	31	m	c	CHIN	Solano	Rio Vista Twp	90	64
Woo	26	m	c	CHIN	Yuba	Marysville	93	626
Woo	16	m	c	CHIN	San Joaquin	1-Wd Stockton	86	151
Ye	65	m	c	CHIN	Klamath	Sawyers Bar	73	378
Ye	32	m	c	CHIN	San Joaquin	1-Wd Stockton	86	149
Yee	40	m	c	CHIN	Yuba	Marysville	93	629
Yek	6	m	c	CHIN	Butte	Kimshew Tpw	70	77
Yek	36	m	c	CHIN	Butte	Ophir Twp	70	121
Yick	15	m	c	CHIN	Plumas	Rich Bar Twp	77	46
Yin	49	m	c	CHIN	San Francisco	6-Wd San Francisco	81	47
Yo	18	m	c	CHIN	San Francisco	San Francisco P O	85	802
Yon	35	m	c	CHIN	Butte	Concow Twp	70	10
Yon J	21	m	c	CHIN	El Dorado	Georgetown Twp	72	36
You	49	m	c	CHIN	Placer	Bath P O	76	454
Yun	25	m	c	CHIN	Butte	Ophir Twp	70	97
Zon	29	m	c	CHIN	Butte	Chico Twp	70	52
HONGBERG								
Lawrence	32	m	w	SWED	Mendocino	Point Arena Twp	74	215
HONGS								
Lah	30	m	c	CHIN	San Joaquin	Liberty Twp	86	97
HONICK								
Andrew L	35	m	w	NY	Santa Clara	2-Wd San Jose	88	280
HONICO								
Jabal	40	m	w	ITAL	San Mateo	Schoolhouse Statio	87	334
HONIG								
Morris	30	m	w	PRUS	Sacramento	Granite Twp	77	143
HONIS								
J	38	m	w	WALE	Calaveras	Copperopolis P O	70	235
HONK								
Ah	22	m	c	CHIN	San Francisco	6-Wd San Francisco	81	106
Chow	28	m	c	CHIN	Placer	Newcastle Twp	76	475
HONN								
George W	56	m	w	MD	Placer	Clipper Gap P O	76	376
HONNER								
Chas Mrs	50	f	w	NY	San Francisco	5-Wd San Francisco	81	30
HONNESSEE								
Thos	26	m	w	ME	Sonoma	Salt Point	91	386
HONO								
Hor	23	m	c	CHIN	San Francisco	6-Wd San Francisco	81	98
HONOE								
Pedro	36	m	w	MEXI	Plumas	Mineral Twp	77	22
HONOFT								
Wm	4	m	w	CA	Nevada	Nevada Twp	75	288
HONOLD								
Herman	35	m	w	WURT	Sierra	Table Rock Twp	89	573
HONON								
Henry	30	m	w	MA	Calaveras	San Andreas P O	70	193
HONOR								
James	20	m	w	ENGL	Sacramento	Franklin Twp	77	115
HONREA								
Tabee	35	m	w	MEXI	Tulare	Tule Rvr Twp	92	266
HONS								
Fredk	40	m	w	PRUS	Butte	Hamilton Twp	70	69
Geo	20	m	w	BADE	Butte	Chico Twp	70	33
Nelson	27	m	w	DENM	Butte	Oregon Twp	70	135
HONSBY								
Christina	36	f	w	SWED	San Francisco	3-Wd San Francisco	79	300
HONSELL								
May J	45	f	w	NY	Nevada	Nevada Twp	75	290
HONSLEY								
Louisa	50	f	b	DE	San Francisco	8-Wd San Francisco	82	449
HONSON								
Peter	22	m	w	DENM	Sonoma	Petaluma Twp	91	349
HONSOR								
William	20	m	w	TX	Los Angeles	Los Nietos Twp	73	585
HONTER								
Joseph	52	m	w	BADE	Trinity	North Fork Twp	92	216
HONTURAS								
D	55	m	w	CHIL	Amador	Jackson P O	69	343
HONY								
Ah	50	m	c	CHIN	Amador	Volcano P O	69	378
Gee	38	m	c	CHIN	Butte	Chico Twp	70	53
Lee	34	m	w	CHIN	Butte	Chico Twp	70	17
HOO								
Ah	64	m	c	CHIN	Tuolumne	Sonora P O	93	311
Ah	59	m	c	CHIN	Calaveras	San Andreas P O	70	176
Ah	58	m	c	CHIN	Placer	Lincoln P O	76	484
Ah	58	m	c	CHIN	Nevada	Grass Valley Twp	75	171
Ah	56	m	c	CHIN	San Francisco	6-Wd San Francisco	81	55
Ah	51	m	c	CHIN	Nevada	Rough & Ready Twp	75	324
Ah	46	m	c	CHIN	Sierra	Lincoln Twp	89	546
Ah	45	m	c	CHIN	Placer	Newcastle Twp	76	477
Ah	42	m	c	CHIN	Tuolumne	Big Oak Flat P O	93	395
Ah	42	m	c	CHIN	Amador	Jackson P O	69	343
Ah	41	m	c	CHIN	Tuolumne	Chinese Camp P O	93	370
Ah	41	m	c	CHIN	Santa Clara	1-Wd San Jose	88	276
Ah	40	m	c	CHIN	San Joaquin	1-Wd Stockton	86	143
Ah	40	m	c	CHIN	San Joaquin	Oneal Twp	86	107
Ah	40	m	c	CHIN	Tuolumne	Columbia P O	93	349
Ah	40	m	c	CHIN	Tuolumne	Chinese Camp P O	93	382
Ah	40	m	c	CHIN	Tuolumne	Big Oak Flat P O	93	401
Ah	39	m	c	CHIN	San Joaquin	Oneal Twp	86	117
Ah	39	m	c	CHIN	Tuolumne	Chinese Camp P O	93	388
Ah	39	m	c	CHIN	San Francisco	11-Wd San Francisc	84	522
Ah	38	m	c	CHIN	San Francisco	San Francisco P O	80	439
Ah	37	m	c	CHIN	Sacramento	2-Wd Sacramento	77	208
Ah	36	m	c	CHIN	San Francisco	San Francisco P O	80	446
Ah	36	m	c	CHIN	San Joaquin	Oneal Twp	86	117
Ah	36	m	c	CHIN	Sierra	Forest Twp	89	529
Ah	36	m	c	CHIN	San Francisco	San Francisco P O	80	509
Ah	35	m	c	CHIN	San Francisco	San Francisco P O	80	437
Ah	34	f	c	CHIN	San Francisco	6-Wd San Francisco	81	63
Ah	34	m	c	CHIN	San Francisco	San Francisco P O	80	491
Ah	32	m	c	CHIN	Fresno	Millerton P O	72	162
Ah	32	f	c	CHIN	Monterey	Monterey Twp	74	352
Ah	31	m	c	CHIN	San Francisco	11-Wd San Francisc	84	695
Ah	30	m	c	CHIN	Sacramento	Franklin Twp	77	118
Ah	30	m	c	CHIN	San Francisco	San Francisco P O	80	507
Ah	29	f	c	CHIN	San Francisco	San Francisco P O	80	449
Ah	29	m	c	CHIN	Tuolumne	Columbia P O	93	349
Ah	28	f	c	CHIN	El Dorado	Coloma Twp	72	1
Ah	28	m	c	CHIN	Sacramento	Franklin Twp	77	118
Ah	28	m	c	CHIN	San Francisco	San Francisco P O	80	447
Ah	28	m	c	CHIN	Nevada	Grass Valley Twp	75	202
Ah	27	m	c	CHIN	San Joaquin	Elliott Twp	86	71
Ah	27	m	c	CHIN	San Joaquin	Elliott Twp	86	77
Ah	27	m	c	CHIN	Solano	Suisun Twp	90	106
Ah	26	m	c	CHIN	San Joaquin	2-Wd Stockton	86	169
Ah	25	m	c	CHIN	San Francisco	3-Wd San Francisco	79	304
Ah	25	m	c	CHIN	San Francisco	San Francisco P O	80	512
Ah	24	m	c	CHIN	Placer	Auburn P O	76	364
Ah	24	m	c	CHIN	Yolo	Cache Crk Twp	93	424
Ah	24	m	c	CHIN	Placer	Auburn P O	76	362
Ah	24	m	c	CHIN	San Francisco	6-Wd San Francisco	81	62
Ah	22	m	c	CHIN	San Francisco	San Francisco P O	80	443
Ah	22	m	c	CHIN	San Francisco	6-Wd San Francisco	81	85
Ah	22	m	c	CHIN	San Joaquin	1-Wd Stockton	86	144
Ah	22	f	c	CHIN	Amador	Fiddletown P O	69	427
Ah	22	m	c	CHIN	San Joaquin	Elkhorn Twp	86	52
Ah	21	m	c	CHIN	San Francisco	11-Wd San Francisc	84	556
Ah	21	m	c	CHIN	Solano	Suisun Twp	90	105
Ah	21	m	c	CHIN	Sierra	Downieville Twp	89	520
Ah	21	m	c	CHIN	Santa Cruz	Pajaro Twp	89	341
Ah	21	m	c	CHIN	San Francisco	2-Wd San Francisco	79	229
Ah	20	m	c	CHIN	Calaveras	Copperopolis P O	70	242
Ah	20	m	c	CHIN	Tuolumne	Chinese Camp P O	93	380
Ah	20	f	c	CHIN	Butte	Ophir Twp	70	103
Ah	20	m	c	CHIN	San Joaquin	Elliott Twp	86	71
Ah	19	m	c	CHIN	San Joaquin	1-Wd Stockton	86	149
Ah	19	f	c	CHIN	San Francisco	San Francisco P O	80	508

© 2001 by Heritage Quest. All rights reserved.

Name	Age	S	R	B-PL	County	Locale	Series M593 Roll	Pg
Ah	16	m	c	CHIN	San Francisco	3-Wd San Francisco	79	307
Ah	16	m	c	CHIN	San Joaquin	1-Wd Stockton	86	146
Chee	37	m	c	CHIN	Tuolumne	Big Oak Flat P O	93	400
Choo	21	m	c	CHIN	Tuolumne	Big Oak Flat P O	93	398
Chow	30	m	c	CHIN	San Joaquin	Elliott Twp	86	71
Chum	29	m	c	CHIN	Nevada	Grass Valley Twp	75	208
Cunn	18	m	c	CHIN	Mendocino	Big Rvr Twp	74	170
Hame	30	m	c	CHIN	Shasta	American Ranch P O	89	500
Ing	20	m	c	CHIN	Santa Cruz	Pajaro Twp	89	341
Kee	42	m	c	CHIN	Santa Clara	1-Wd San Jose	88	270
Mai	26	f	c	CHIN	Tuolumne	Big Oak Flat P O	93	404
Owe	41	m	c	CHIN	Sierra	Lincoln Twp	89	546
She	36	m	c	CHIN	San Joaquin	Oneal Twp	86	117
Shee	40	m	c	CHIN	Klamath	South Fork Twp	73	382
Shum	12	m	c	CHIN	San Francisco	3-Wd San Francisco	79	304
Soon	33	m	c	CHIN	Shasta	Shasta P O	89	453
Sun	28	m	c	CHIN	Sacramento	1-Wd Sacramento	77	198
Toy	24	f	c	CHIN	Amador	Fiddletown P O	69	429
Tye	23	m	c	CHIN	Solano	Suisun Twp	90	107
Wah	28	m	c	CHIN	San Francisco	San Francisco P O	83	137
Yon	24	m	c	CHIN	Yuba	Marysville	93	629
Yr	43	f	c	CHIN	Sierra	Lincoln Twp	89	546
HOOBER								
Fredrick	28	m	w	BADE	San Francisco	7-Wd San Francisco	81	226
W W	21	m	w	IA	Alameda	Oakland	68	177
HOOBS								
Isaac	48	m	w	ME	Solano	Vallejo	90	147
HOOD								
Aaron	41	m	w	NY	Inyo	Bishop Crk Twp	73	310
Aaron	31	m	w	MO	Solano	Denverton Twp	90	25
Albert H	43	m	w	RI	Stanislaus	Emory Twp	92	18
Benjamin	25	m	w	PA	Inyo	Lone Pine Twp	73	334
Charles	62	m	w	MECK	San Francisco	San Francisco P O	80	347
Charles	60	m	w	SCOT	San Francisco	San Francisco P O	80	427
Christopher	30	m	w	ENGL	Nevada	Meadow Lake Twp	75	270
Christopher	27	m	w	ENGL	Plumas	Indian Twp	77	19
D B	70	m	w	OH	Calaveras	Copperopolis P O	70	223
David	30	m	w	ENGL	Plumas	Quartz Twp	77	40
E E	30	m	w	NY	San Joaquin	2-Wd Stockton	86	176
Edward	26	m	w	NH	Inyo	Independence Twp	73	328
Frank	22	m	w	VA	Santa Clara	Redwood Twp	88	131
George	47	m	w	SCOT	Sonoma	Santa Rosa	91	400
George	35	m	w	FRAN	Plumas	Seneca Twp	77	51
Heny	28	m	w	PRUS	San Francisco	2-Wd San Francisco	79	284
James	60	m	w	TN	Yolo	Putah Twp	93	518
Jennie	58	f	w	ME	Siskiyou	Yreka	89	657
John	50	m	w	IREL	San Francisco	11-Wd San Francisc	84	439
Lafayette	15	m	w	IA	Solano	Tremont Twp	90	28
Mary	37	f	w	NY	Sacramento	Brighton Twp	77	73
Mingo W	36	m	w	NY	Yolo	Putah Twp	93	514
Oscar	35	m	w	VT	Yolo	Grafton Twp	93	497
Samuell	60	m	w	NC	Humboldt	Bald Hills	72	238
Smith F	37	m	w	NC	Sonoma	Bodega Twp	91	264
Thomas	48	m	w	ENGL	Nevada	Grass Valley Twp	75	187
Thos B	41	m	w	SC	Sonoma	Santa Rosa	91	414
W	46	m	w	SCOT	Lassen	Long Valley Twp	73	436
William	51	m	w	SCOT	Sonoma	Santa Rosa	91	424
William	36	m	w	IL	Colusa	Monroe Twp	71	316
William	28	m	w	VT	Solano	Silveyville Twp	90	89
HOODEN								
Nancy	26	f	w	MO	Sacramento	4-Wd Sacramento	77	327
HOODLEY								
James H	39	m	w	CT	Nevada	Meadow Lake Twp	75	250
HOODS								
William	37	m	w	MA	San Francisco	San Francisco P O	83	397
HOOF								
M J	31	m	w	PRUS	Alameda	Murray Twp	68	109
HOOFMAN								
Wm	28	m	w	NY	Fresno	Millerton P O	72	192
HOOGE								
Ann	40	f	w	CANA	San Francisco	8-Wd San Francisco	82	444
HOOGSTAD								
Abram	55	m	w	HOLL	San Francisco	3-Wd San Francisco	79	295
James	45	m	w	HOLL	San Francisco	2-Wd San Francisco	79	154
HOOK								
Ah	62	m	c	CHIN	El Dorado	Mud Springs Twp	72	88
Ah	50	m	c	CHIN	Calaveras	San Andreas P O	70	190
Ah	42	m	c	CHIN	Contra Costa	Martinez P O	71	436
Ah	38	m	c	CHIN	Mariposa	Mariposa P O	74	122
Ah	34	m	c	CHIN	Calaveras	San Andreas P O	70	178
Ah	28	m	c	CHIN	Placer	Auburn P O	76	364
Ah	28	m	c	CHIN	Calaveras	San Andreas P O	70	172
Ah	28	m	c	CHIN	San Joaquin	Oneal Twp	86	118
Ah	26	m	c	CHIN	Yolo	Grafton Twp	93	479
Ah	22	m	c	CHIN	Yolo	Cache Crk Twp	93	424
Ah	17	f	c	CHIN	San Francisco	6-Wd San Francisco	81	74
Charles	27	m	w	HCAS	San Francisco	2-Wd San Francisco	79	275
Dick	40	m	w	AL	San Joaquin	Tulare Twp	86	259
Edmond	38	m	w	NY	San Francisco	5-Wd San Francisco	81	26
Elijah	32	m	w	MO	Contra Costa	Martinez P O	71	433
Frank	37	m	w	AL	San Joaquin	Tulare Twp	86	259
Freman	52	m	w	GERM	El Dorado	Placerville	72	109
George	21	m	w	OH	Contra Costa	Martinez P O	71	427
George Y	41	m	w	NY	Nevada	Meadow Lake Twp	75	268
Henry	24	m	w	AUSL	San Francisco	2-Wd San Francisco	79	205
Henry	22	m	w	IREL	San Francisco	San Francisco P O	83	112
J H	47	m	w	ENGL	Humboldt	Arcata Twp	72	235

Name	Age	S	R	B-PL	County	Locale	Series M593 Roll	Pg
James	45	m	w	ME	San Diego	Milquaty Dist	78	475
James H	23	m	w	MO	El Dorado	Lake Valley Twp	72	64
John	37	m	w	HOLL	San Francisco	1-Wd San Francisco	79	110
John	25	m	w	HAMB	San Francisco	2-Wd San Francisco	79	251
John	20	m	w	OH	El Dorado	Placerville	72	109
John F	39	m	w	GERM	Nevada	Nevada Twp	75	279
Joseph	58	m	w	ME	Alameda	Brooklyn	68	26
Lin	35	m	c	CHIN	Solano	Vacaville Twp	90	132
Peter	32	m	w	SHOL	San Francisco	11-Wd San Francisc	84	469
Sing	25	m	c	CHIN	Monterey	Monterey	74	367
Solomon	45	m	w	MO	Solano	Vacaville Twp	90	133
Solomon	39	m	w	IL	Solano	Vacaville Twp	90	137
Thos K	53	m	w	PA	San Joaquin	3-Wd Stockton	86	242
Tobias	34	m	w	AUST	San Francisco	8-Wd San Francisco	82	306
Tong	50	m	c	CHIN	Trinity	North Fork Twp	92	221
William	63	m	w	VA	Contra Costa	Martinez P O	71	448
Wm	56	m	w	HANO	Butte	Wyandotte Twp	70	144
Wm	31	m	w	NH	Humboldt	Arcata Twp	72	226
HOOKE								
Josiah S	49	m	w	ME	Napa	Napa	75	40
Thomas	19	m	w	CANA	Mendocino	Casper & Big Rvr	74	164
Wm H	46	m	w	ME	San Francisco	7-Wd San Francisco	81	282
HOOKER								
Alonzo	22	m	w	VT	San Francisco	11-Wd San Francisc	84	645
C J	31	m	w	PRUS	Tuolumne	Chinese Camp P O	93	386
Chas G	47	m	w	NH	San Francisco	8-Wd San Francisco	82	348
Chester H	54	m	w	CT	Nevada	Grass Valley Twp	75	223
Geo H	15	m	w	CA	Sacramento	Sutter Twp	77	381
Henry C D	38	m	w	NH	El Dorado	Placerville	72	118
J H	36	m	w	NY	Sacramento	3-Wd Sacramento	77	278
Jerry	44	m	w	NY	Shasta	Horsetown P O	89	502
John D	32	m	w	NH	San Francisco	6-Wd San Francisco	81	141
Jos B	30	m	w	NY	San Diego	San Diego	78	509
Joshua	30	m	w	NY	San Diego	San Diego	78	495
M R	24	f	w	NH	Sacramento	3-Wd Sacramento	77	270
S W	47	m	w	IN	Tehama	Antelope Twp	92	155
Van B	36	m	w	VA	El Dorado	Placerville	72	124
William	60	m	w	ENGL	Santa Clara	Redwood Twp	88	131
Wm D	40	m	w	MA	San Francisco	San Francisco P O	83	86
York	46	m	w	BADE	San Francisco	3-Wd San Francisco	79	319
HOOKEY								
Robert	56	m	w	ENGL	Alameda	Eden Twp	68	58
HOOKLEY								
Captain	35	m	i	CA	Colusa	Monroe Twp	71	322
HOOKS								
Chas A	27	m	w	AL	Sonoma	Santa Rosa	91	410
Frank	30	m	w	SCOT	San Francisco	7-Wd San Francisco	81	181
William	30	m	w	WALE	Contra Costa	Martinez P O	71	425
HOOKWAY								
William	28	m	w	HANO	Placer	Bath P O	76	428
HOOL								
Ah	35	m	c	CHIN	Calaveras	Copperopolis P O	70	234
HOOLE								
David P	30	m	w	MA	San Francisco	5-Wd San Francisco	81	11
John	27	m	w	ENGL	San Francisco	3-Wd San Francisco	79	312
HOOLEY								
Patrick	42	m	w	IREL	Butte	Oregon Twp	70	126
Rhody	27	m	w	IREL	Nevada	Bridgeport Twp	75	112
HOOLY								
C	20	m	w	MA	Alameda	Oakland	68	177
HOOMER								
William	28	m	w	MA	Solano	Maine Prairie Twp	90	53
HOON								
Ah	46	m	c	CHIN	San Joaquin	1-Wd Stockton	86	151
Ah	42	m	c	CHIN	Santa Cruz	Santa Cruz	89	418
Ah	36	m	c	CHIN	Sacramento	Georgianna Twp	77	124
Ah	31	m	c	CHIN	Sierra	Lincoln Twp	89	546
Ah	30	m	c	CHIN	Sacramento	3-Wd Sacramento	77	292
Ah	30	m	c	CHIN	Sonoma	Sonoma Twp	91	435
Ah	27	m	c	CHIN	Tuolumne	Columbia P O	93	352
Ah	24	m	c	CHIN	San Francisco	San Francisco P O	85	748
Ah	23	m	c	CHIN	San Francisco	6-Wd San Francisco	81	61
Ah	22	m	c	CHIN	Sacramento	3-Wd Sacramento	77	309
Ah	20	m	c	CHIN	Sacramento	Franklin Twp	77	107
Ah	18	m	c	CHIN	San Francisco	6-Wd San Francisco	81	57
Ah	18	f	c	CHIN	El Dorado	Placerville	72	116
Ah	16	m	c	CHIN	San Francisco	6-Wd San Francisco	81	58
Chas A	46	m	w	NJ	Sierra	Sears Twp	89	559
Jay	38	m	c	CHIN	San Francisco	6-Wd San Francisco	81	37
John	40	m	w	MO	Butte	Hamilton Twp	70	69
Li	36	m	c	CHIN	San Francisco	11-Wd San Francisc	84	661
HOONEY								
Ah	41	m	c	CHIN	Nevada	Bloomfield Twp	75	94
HOONG								
Ah	30	m	c	CHIN	Shasta	French Gulch P O	89	465
Ah	19	m	c	CHIN	San Francisco	8-Wd San Francisco	82	310
Fon	30	m	c	CHIN	San Francisco	11-Wd San Francisc	84	574
HOOP								
Ah	40	m	c	CHIN	San Joaquin	Elkhorn Twp	86	59
Ah	38	m	c	CHIN	San Francisco	6-Wd San Francisco	81	57
Ah	33	m	c	CHIN	San Joaquin	1-Wd Stockton	86	147
Ah	30	m	c	CHIN	Alameda	Oakland	68	224
Ah	27	m	c	CHIN	San Joaquin	1-Wd Stockton	86	148
Ah	27	m	c	CHIN	San Joaquin	3-Wd Stockton	86	230
Ah	26	m	c	CHIN	San Joaquin	1-Wd Stockton	86	149
Ah	21	m	c	CHIN	Sacramento	Cosumnes Twp	77	90
Henry	42	m	w	BAVA	Alameda	Eden Twp	68	58

© 2001 by Heritage Quest. All rights reserved.

California 1870 Census

Name	Age	S	R	B-PL	County	Locale	Roll	Pg
Henry	31	m	w	HDAR	Solano	Silveyville Twp	90	89
Ida	8	f	w	CA	Santa Clara	Gilroy Twp	88	99
Kee	45	m	c	CHIN	San Francisco	6-Wd San Francisco	81	61
Lee	14	m	c	CHIN	San Francisco	San Francisco P O	83	346
Loo	22	m	c	CHIN	Yolo	Merritt Twp	93	506
Soo	26	m	c	CHIN	Yolo	Grafton Twp	93	484
HOOPER								
Aaron	31	m	w	NY	Nevada	Grass Valley Twp	75	149
Benj	37	m	w	NC	Butte	Ophir Twp	70	106
Chas	28	m	w	MA	Sacramento	3-Wd Sacramento	77	270
David	47	m	w	NC	Butte	Chico Twp	70	21
E	38	m	w	ENGL	Sierra	Butte Twp	89	509
E	30	m	w	ENGL	Sierra	Butte Twp	89	513
E F	45	m	w	PA	San Francisco	San Francisco P O	85	851
Edward	57	m	w	MD	Yuba	Marysville	93	586
Edward J	70	m	w	ENGL	San Francisco	8-Wd San Francisco	82	322
Emery	31	m	w	ENGL	Contra Costa	Martinez P O	71	453
F M	52	m	w	NY	Siskiyou	Scott Valley Twp	89	613
Geo	24	m	w	ME	San Francisco	7-Wd San Francisco	81	249
Geo F	43	m	w	VA	San Francisco	San Francisco P O	83	111
George W	44	m	w	NY	Stanislaus	Empire Twp	92	65
Henry	35	m	w	ENGL	Nevada	Grass Valley Twp	75	232
Henry	31	m	w	ENGL	Nevada	Grass Valley Twp	75	187
Henry O	46	m	w	MA	El Dorado	Diamond Springs Tw	72	32
J	29	m	w	ENGL	Alameda	Oakland	68	241
J K	30	m	w	ME	Alameda	Oakland	68	138
J M	47	m	w	GA	Mendocino	Ukiah Twp	74	234
James	28	m	w	ENGL	Nevada	Grass Valley Twp	75	215
John	50	m	w	TN	San Joaquin	Tulare Twp	86	252
John	46	m	w	IA	Amador	Jackson P O	69	341
John	41	m	w	MA	Solano	Vacaville Twp	90	126
John	40	m	w	NY	San Francisco	San Francisco P O	83	374
John	37	m	w	ENGL	Shasta	French Gulch P O	89	465
John	30	m	w	ENGL	Nevada	Nevada Twp	75	301
John A	30	m	w	ME	San Francisco	San Francisco P O	83	113
John B	36	m	w	ENGL	San Francisco	1-Wd San Francisco	79	16
John M	45	m	w	MA	San Francisco	8-Wd San Francisco	82	315
John W	50	m	w	ENGL	Tulare	Packwood Twp	92	255
Jos	33	m	w	ENGL	Sacramento	3-Wd Sacramento	77	256
Julia	11	f	w	CA	Butte	Chico Twp	70	40
O C	73	m	w	GA	Yuba	East Bear Rvr Twp	93	540
Peter	36	m	w	ENGL	Nevada	Grass Valley Twp	75	191
Richard	25	m	w	ENGL	Nevada	Grass Valley Twp	75	188
Samuel	35	m	w	ENGL	Nevada	Grass Valley Twp	75	175
Sylvester	35	m	w	NY	Plumas	Indian Twp	77	15
Thomas	51	m	w	PA	Alameda	Oakland	68	173
Thomas	29	m	w	ENGL	Nevada	Grass Valley Twp	75	215
Thomas	28	m	w	ENGL	Nevada	Grass Valley Twp	75	186
Thomas P	58	m	w	MA	Solano	Montezuma Twp	90	65
Thomas P Jr	30	m	w	MA	Solano	Montezuma Twp	90	67
Thomas W	32	m	w	RI	Yolo	Grafton Twp	93	494
V C W	38	m	w	GA	Yuba	East Bear Rvr Twp	93	541
W	36	m	w	ENGL	Sierra	Forest Twp	89	532
W T	55	m	w	NC	Merced	Snelling P O	74	272
William	60	m	w	MA	San Francisco	San Francisco P O	80	405
William	40	m	w	MA	Contra Costa	Martinez Twp	71	347
William	30	m	w	TX	Colusa	Stony Crk Twp	71	333
William	29	m	w	MA	Solano	Denverton Twp	90	26
Wm	50	m	w	MD	Solano	Vallejo	90	143
Wm	38	m	w	AR	Fresno	Kings Rvr P O	72	214
Wm	35	m	w	OH	El Dorado	Coloma Twp	72	9
Wm	33	m	w	MA	Butte	Kimshew Tpw	70	83
Wm B	34	m	w	VA	San Francisco	2-Wd San Francisco	79	276
Wm Bailey	52	m	w	OH	Plumas	Washington Twp	77	53
Wm H	40	m	w	ENGL	San Francisco	San Francisco P O	83	193
Wm H	35	m	w	ME	Amador	Drytown P O	69	418
HOOPES								
Abram	52	m	w	PA	Santa Cruz	Santa Cruz Twp	89	399
Lavinia	46	f	w	PA	San Francisco	11-Wd San Francisc	84	561
HOOPS								
Fred	23	m	w	PRUS	San Francisco	11-Wd San Francisc	84	533
Fredk	30	m	w	HAMB	San Francisco	1-Wd San Francisco	79	124
Hans T	51	m	w	HAMB	Nevada	Washington Twp	75	341
Louis W	31	m	w	PRUS	Butte	Ophir Twp	70	96
Mike	39	m	w	BADE	Butte	Ophir Twp	70	118
HOOPT								
Chapt	2	m	i	CA	Sonoma	Salt Point Twp	91	382
HOORLE								
Henry	38	m	w	HDAR	San Francisco	San Francisco P O	83	134
HOORN								
Ah	50	m	c	CHIN	Sierra	Downieville Twp	89	520
HOORT								
Amandus	24	m	w	PRUS	Contra Costa	Martinez P O	71	371
HOOS								
Fredrick C	40	m	w	BAVA	Placer	Dutch Flat P O	76	402
John F	43	m	w	PRUS	Placer	Dutch Flat P O	76	405
Stephen	44	m	w	PRUS	Placer	Dutch Flat P O	76	403
HOOSE								
Charles	48	m	w	PRUS	Stanislaus	Buena Vista Twp	92	12
Jane Mrs	44	f	w	ENGL	San Diego	San Diego	78	502
HOOT								
Ah	28	m	c	CHIN	San Francisco	6-Wd San Francisco	81	61
Ah	28	m	c	CHIN	San Francisco	6-Wd San Francisco	81	61
Ah	14	m	c	CHIN	San Francisco	6-Wd San Francisco	81	60
Kee	28	m	c	CHIN	San Francisco	6-Wd San Francisco	81	66
War	50	m	c	CHIN	San Francisco	6-Wd San Francisco	81	57
HOOTER								
Manuel	47	m	w	VA	Kern	Kernville P O	73	368
HOOTMAN								
Lyman	80	m	w	VT	Solano	Maine Prairie Twp	90	54
HOOTON								
Jas	24	m	w	MO	Sonoma	Mendocino Twp	91	293
Mars V	31	m	w	MO	Sonoma	Mendocino Twp	91	294
Patrick	23	m	w	IREL	San Francisco	8-Wd San Francisco	82	339
S	31	m	w	NY	San Joaquin	Dent Twp	86	28
Saml B	46	m	w	MA	Shasta	Shasta P O	89	454
HOOVEL								
Philip	47	m	w	PRUS	Sacramento	Sutter Twp	77	384
HOOVER								
Alexander	25	m	w	SCOT	Sonoma	Vallejo Twp	91	459
Amelia H	14	f	w	CA	Humboldt	Eel Rvr Twp	72	247
Conrad	45	m	w	OH	Santa Clara	Gilroy Twp	88	84
Daniel	36	m	w	OH	Colusa	Grand Island Twp	71	303
Ephram	32	m	w	NC	Mendocino	Point Arena Twp	74	215
George	44	m	w	TN	Napa	Napa	75	13
George	20	m	w	WI	Inyo	Independence Twp	73	327
Henry	30	m	w	IL	Monterey	Alisal Twp	74	299
Henry	29	m	w	IL	Monterey	San Antonio Twp	74	315
Irwin	23	m	w	IN	San Bernardino	San Bernardino Twp	78	445
J Frank	36	m	w	OH	Siskiyou	Yreka Twp	89	664
Jacob	69	m	w	PA	Napa	Napa	75	13
James	54	m	w	MO	Santa Clara	Gilroy Twp	88	105
Jenny	23	f	i	CA	Siskiyou	Yreka Twp	89	668
John	33	m	w	IL	Napa	Napa	75	15
John A	30	m	w	OH	El Dorado	Salmon Falls Twp	72	132
Saml B	38	m	w	OH	Butte	Chico Twp	70	24
Samuel	42	m	w	PA	Sacramento	San Joaquin Twp	77	405
Vincent A	44	m	w	PA	Los Angeles	Los Angeles	73	516
Wesley	46	m	w	TN	Santa Clara	San Jose Twp	88	191
Wm	28	m	w	IN	El Dorado	Georgetown Twp	72	45
Wm H	27	m	w	IA	Santa Clara	Gilroy Twp	88	86
HOOW								
Ah	25	f	c	CHIN	Santa Cruz	Pajaro Twp	89	345
HOP								
Ac	40	m	c	CHIN	Sacramento	Georgianna Twp	77	124
Ah	64	m	c	CHIN	Sacramento	Granite Twp	77	155
Ah	60	m	c	CHIN	Sacramento	Cosumnes Twp	77	92
Ah	60	m	c	CHIN	Tuolumne	Big Oak Flat P O	93	406
Ah	55	m	c	CHIN	Sacramento	Granite Twp	77	153
Ah	55	m	c	CHIN	Sacramento	Cosumnes Twp	77	95
Ah	55	m	c	CHIN	Sacramento	Granite Twp	77	151
Ah	54	m	c	CHIN	Sacramento	Mississippi Twp	77	163
Ah	51	m	c	CHIN	Sacramento	Granite Twp	77	155
Ah	50	m	c	CHIN	Sacramento	Dry Crk Twp	77	101
Ah	50	m	c	CHIN	Sacramento	Center Twp	77	86
Ah	50	m	c	CHIN	Sacramento	Granite Twp	77	153
Ah	50	m	c	CHIN	Sacramento	Natomas Twp	77	171
Ah	47	m	c	CHIN	Sacramento	Dry Crk Twp	77	101
Ah	46	m	c	CHIN	Sacramento	Georgianna Twp	77	132
Ah	46	m	c	CHIN	Butte	Hamilton Twp	70	72
Ah	44	m	c	CHIN	Sacramento	Granite Twp	77	139
Ah	44	m	c	CHIN	Butte	Chico Twp	70	53
Ah	44	m	c	CHIN	Sacramento	American Twp	77	68
Ah	44	m	c	CHIN	Sacramento	Mississippi Twp	77	162
Ah	43	m	c	CHIN	Sacramento	Georgianna Twp	77	135
Ah	43	m	c	CHIN	Sacramento	Georgianna Twp	77	131
Ah	42	m	c	CHIN	Sacramento	Cosumnes Twp	77	92
Ah	42	m	c	CHIN	Stanislaus	Branch Twp	92	9
Ah	42	m	c	CHIN	San Joaquin	1-Wd Stockton	86	148
Ah	42	m	c	CHIN	Sacramento	Natomas Twp	77	171
Ah	42	m	c	CHIN	Placer	Blue Canyon P O	76	418
Ah	40	m	c	CHIN	Sacramento	Georgianna Twp	77	125
Ah	40	m	c	CHIN	Sacramento	Georgianna Twp	77	125
Ah	40	m	c	CHIN	Sacramento	Georgianna Twp	77	133
Ah	40	m	c	CHIN	Sacramento	Granite Twp	77	150
Ah	40	m	c	CHIN	Sacramento	Granite Twp	77	153
Ah	40	m	c	CHIN	Sacramento	Granite Twp	77	152
Ah	40	m	c	CHIN	Sacramento	Center Twp	77	86
Ah	40	m	c	CHIN	Sacramento	Cosumnes Twp	77	94
Ah	40	m	c	CHIN	Butte	Hamilton Twp	70	71
Ah	40	m	c	CHIN	Santa Clara	2-Wd San Jose	88	314
Ah	40	m	c	CHIN	Stanislaus	Emory Twp	92	20
Ah	40	m	c	CHIN	Monterey	Castroville Twp	74	338
Ah	40	m	c	CHIN	Butte	Hamilton Twp	70	68
Ah	40	m	c	CHIN	Sacramento	Center Twp	77	87
Ah	40	m	c	CHIN	Sacramento	Georgianna Twp	77	127
Ah	40	m	c	CHIN	Sacramento	Granite Twp	77	153
Ah	40	m	c	CHIN	Sacramento	Georgianna Twp	77	124
Ah	40	m	c	CHIN	Sacramento	Granite Twp	77	151
Ah	40	m	c	CHIN	Sacramento	Natomas Twp	77	167
Ah	40	m	c	CHIN	Placer	Auburn P O	76	371
Ah	4	f	c	CHIN	Butte	Chico Twp	70	30
Ah	39	m	c	CHIN	Sacramento	Cosumnes Twp	77	95
Ah	39	m	c	CHIN	Nevada	Eureka Twp	75	136
Ah	39	m	c	CHIN	Butte	Chico Twp	70	52
Ah	39	m	c	CHIN	Stanislaus	Emory Twp	92	26
Ah	39	m	c	CHIN	Butte	Hamilton Twp	70	74
Ah	38	m	c	CHIN	Sacramento	Georgianna Twp	77	128
Ah	38	m	c	CHIN	Sacramento	Cosumnes Twp	77	95
Ah	38	m	c	CHIN	Fresno	Millerton P O	72	200
Ah	38	m	c	CHIN	Tuolumne	Sonora P O	93	312
Ah	38	m	c	CHIN	Tuolumne	Sonora P O	93	312
Ah	38	m	c	CHIN	Sacramento	Cosumnes Twp	77	94

Series M593

© 2001 by Heritage Quest. All rights reserved.

Name	Age	S	R	B-PL	County	Locale	Roll	Pg
						Series M593		
Ah	38	m	c	CHIN	Sacramento	Cosumnes Twp	77	94
Ah	37	m	c	CHIN	Sacramento	Georgianna Twp	77	125
Ah	37	m	c	CHIN	Sacramento	Georgianna Twp	77	134
Ah	37	m	c	CHIN	Sacramento	Georgianna Twp	77	134
Ah	37	m	c	CHIN	Sacramento	Dry Crk Twp	77	101
Ah	37	m	c	CHIN	Sacramento	Center Twp	77	86
Ah	37	m	c	CHIN	Sacramento	Cosumnes Twp	77	92
Ah	37	m	c	CHIN	Stanislaus	Emory Twp	92	24
Ah	37	m	c	CHIN	Butte	Kimshew Tpw	70	77
Ah	36	m	c	CHIN	Sacramento	Georgianna Twp	77	131
Ah	36	m	c	CHIN	Sacramento	Georgianna Twp	77	134
Ah	36	m	c	CHIN	Sacramento	1-Wd Sacramento	77	204
Ah	35	m	c	CHIN	Sacramento	Georgianna Twp	77	134
Ah	35	m	c	CHIN	Sacramento	Georgianna Twp	77	135
Ah	35	m	c	CHIN	Sacramento	Georgianna Twp	77	127
Ah	35	m	c	CHIN	Sacramento	Granite Twp	77	151
Ah	35	m	c	CHIN	Sacramento	Granite Twp	77	152
Ah	35	m	c	CHIN	Sacramento	Cosumnes Twp	77	94
Ah	35	m	c	CHIN	Sacramento	Center Twp	77	87
Ah	35	m	c	CHIN	Sacramento	Cosumnes Twp	77	94
Ah	35	m	c	CHIN	Calaveras	San Andreas P O	70	199
Ah	35	m	c	CHIN	Sacramento	American Twp	77	68
Ah	34	m	c	CHIN	Sacramento	Georgianna Twp	77	126
Ah	34	m	c	CHIN	Sacramento	Georgianna Twp	77	132
Ah	34	m	c	CHIN	Sacramento	Center Twp	77	87
Ah	34	m	c	CHIN	San Joaquin	1-Wd Stockton	86	143
Ah	34	m	c	CHIN	Calaveras	San Andreas P O	70	216
Ah	34	m	c	CHIN	Sacramento	Natomas Twp	77	171
Ah	34	m	c	CHIN	Placer	Auburn P O	76	374
Ah	33	m	c	CHIN	Sacramento	Georgianna Twp	77	131
Ah	33	m	c	CHIN	Butte	Hamilton Twp	70	72
Ah	33	m	c	CHIN	Monterey	Castroville Twp	74	338
Ah	32	m	c	CHIN	Sacramento	Georgianna Twp	77	132
Ah	32	m	c	CHIN	Sacramento	Georgianna Twp	77	128
Ah	32	m	c	CHIN	Sacramento	Georgianna Twp	77	133
Ah	32	m	c	CHIN	Plumas	Rich Bar Twp	77	45
Ah	32	m	c	CHIN	Calaveras	San Andreas P O	70	213
Ah	32	m	c	CHIN	Sacramento	Natomas Twp	77	168
Ah	32	m	c	CHIN	Sacramento	Natomas Twp	77	168
Ah	32	m	c	CHIN	Yuba	Marysville	93	601
Ah	31	m	c	CHIN	Amador	Sutter Crk P O	69	399
Ah	31	m	c	CHIN	San Joaquin	1-Wd Stockton	86	147
Ah	30	m	c	CHIN	Sacramento	Georgianna Twp	77	125
Ah	30	m	c	CHIN	Sacramento	Georgianna Twp	77	132
Ah	30	m	c	CHIN	Sacramento	Georgianna Twp	77	134
Ah	30	m	c	CHIN	Sacramento	Granite Twp	77	152
Ah	30	m	c	CHIN	Sacramento	Granite Twp	77	152
Ah	30	m	c	CHIN	Sacramento	Center Twp	77	86
Ah	30	m	c	CHIN	Sacramento	Center Twp	77	87
Ah	30	m	c	CHIN	Sacramento	Center Twp	77	86
Ah	30	m	c	CHIN	Sacramento	Cosumnes Twp	77	93
Ah	30	m	c	CHIN	Sacramento	Cosumnes Twp	77	92
Ah	30	m	c	CHIN	Yolo	Merritt Twp	93	503
Ah	30	m	c	CHIN	Tuolumne	Columbia P O	93	361
Ah	30	m	c	CHIN	Sacramento	American Twp	77	68
Ah	30	m	c	CHIN	Sacramento	American Twp	77	67
Ah	30	m	c	CHIN	Sacramento	Georgianna Twp	77	127
Ah	30	m	c	CHIN	Sacramento	Mississippi Twp	77	162
Ah	30	m	c	CHIN	Sacramento	Granite Twp	77	155
Ah	30	m	c	CHIN	Sacramento	Granite Twp	77	153
Ah	29	m	c	CHIN	Sacramento	1-Wd Sacramento	77	201
Ah	29	m	c	CHIN	Sacramento	Granite Twp	77	150
Ah	29	m	c	CHIN	San Joaquin	1-Wd Stockton	86	154
Ah	29	m	c	CHIN	Los Angeles	Wilmington Twp	73	634
Ah	28	m	c	CHIN	Sacramento	Georgianna Twp	77	125
Ah	28	m	c	CHIN	Sacramento	Granite Twp	77	138
Ah	28	m	c	CHIN	Sacramento	Georgianna Twp	77	134
Ah	28	m	c	CHIN	Sacramento	Georgianna Twp	77	128
Ah	28	m	c	CHIN	Sacramento	Granite Twp	77	141
Ah	28	m	c	CHIN	Sacramento	Cosumnes Twp	77	93
Ah	28	m	c	CHIN	Sacramento	Center Twp	77	85
Ah	28	m	c	CHIN	Sacramento	Cosumnes Twp	77	94
Ah	28	m	c	CHIN	Sacramento	Center Twp	77	85
Ah	28	m	c	CHIN	Sacramento	Georgianna Twp	77	130
Ah	28	m	c	CHIN	Sacramento	Natomas Twp	77	171
Ah	28	m	c	CHIN	Sacramento	Natomas Twp	77	168
Ah	28	m	c	CHIN	Sacramento	Mississippi Twp	77	162
Ah	28	m	c	CHIN	Sacramento	Natomas Twp	77	167
Ah	28	m	c	CHIN	San Francisco	1-Wd San Francisco	79	52
Ah	27	m	c	CHIN	Sacramento	Granite Twp	77	138
Ah	27	m	c	CHIN	Sacramento	Georgianna Twp	77	132
Ah	27	m	c	CHIN	Sacramento	Georgianna Twp	77	134
Ah	27	m	c	CHIN	Sacramento	Georgianna Twp	77	129
Ah	27	m	c	CHIN	Sacramento	Granite Twp	77	153
Ah	27	m	c	CHIN	Sacramento	Cosumnes Twp	77	90
Ah	27	m	c	CHIN	Sacramento	Center Twp	77	86
Ah	27	m	c	CHIN	Butte	Hamilton Twp	70	67
Ah	27	m	c	CHIN	Santa Clara	1-Wd San Jose	88	271
Ah	27	m	c	CHIN	Sierra	Butte Twp	89	513
Ah	27	m	c	CHIN	Butte	Hamilton Twp	70	73
Ah	27	m	c	CHIN	Sacramento	Natomas Twp	77	171
Ah	27	m	c	CHIN	Sacramento	Natomas Twp	77	166
Ah	27	m	c	CHIN	Sacramento	Natomas Twp	77	171
Ah	27	m	c	CHIN	Nevada	Nevada Twp	75	300
Ah	26	m	c	CHIN	Sacramento	Georgianna Twp	77	133
Ah	26	m	c	CHIN	Sacramento	Georgianna Twp	77	129
Ah	26	m	c	CHIN	Sacramento	Georgianna Twp	77	132
Ah	26	m	c	CHIN	Sacramento	Georgianna Twp	77	132
Ah	26	m	c	CHIN	Sacramento	Georgianna Twp	77	131
Ah	26	m	c	CHIN	Sacramento	Granite Twp	77	153
Ah	26	m	c	CHIN	Santa Clara	San Jose Twp	88	190
Ah	26	m	c	CHIN	Sacramento	American Twp	77	68
Ah	26	m	c	CHIN	Sacramento	Dry Crk Twp	77	101
Ah	26	m	c	CHIN	Sacramento	Georgianna Twp	77	123
Ah	26	m	c	CHIN	Nevada	Nevada Twp	75	300
Ah	25	m	c	CHIN	Sacramento	Georgianna Twp	77	126
Ah	25	m	c	CHIN	Sacramento	Georgianna Twp	77	125
Ah	25	m	c	CHIN	Sacramento	Georgianna Twp	77	131
Ah	25	m	c	CHIN	Sacramento	Georgianna Twp	77	129
Ah	25	m	c	CHIN	Sacramento	Cosumnes Twp	77	94
Ah	25	m	c	CHIN	Plumas	Washington Twp	77	58
Ah	24	m	c	CHIN	Sacramento	Georgianna Twp	77	123
Ah	24	m	c	CHIN	Sacramento	Georgianna Twp	77	131
Ah	24	m	c	CHIN	Sacramento	Georgianna Twp	77	131
Ah	24	m	c	CHIN	Sacramento	1-Wd Sacramento	77	198
Ah	24	m	c	CHIN	Sacramento	Granite Twp	77	154
Ah	24	m	c	CHIN	Sacramento	Granite Twp	77	141
Ah	24	m	c	CHIN	Santa Clara	1-Wd San Jose	88	274
Ah	24	m	c	CHIN	Tehama	Tehama Twp	92	193
Ah	24	m	c	CHIN	Butte	Oregon Twp	70	133
Ah	24	m	c	CHIN	Sacramento	Granite Twp	77	155
Ah	23	m	c	CHIN	Sacramento	Granite Twp	77	155
Ah	23	m	c	CHIN	San Francisco	6-Wd San Francisco	81	49
Ah	23	m	c	CHIN	Tuolumne	Chinese Camp P O	93	367
Ah	22	m	c	CHIN	Sacramento	Georgianna Twp	77	132
Ah	22	m	c	CHIN	Sacramento	Georgianna Twp	77	126
Ah	22	m	c	CHIN	Sacramento	Georgianna Twp	77	129
Ah	22	m	c	CHIN	Sacramento	Georgianna Twp	77	134
Ah	22	m	c	CHIN	Sacramento	Cosumnes Twp	77	93
Ah	22	m	c	CHIN	Solano	Vallejo	90	208
Ah	22	m	c	CHIN	San Francisco	6-Wd San Francisco	81	97
Ah	22	m	c	CHIN	Sacramento	Natomas Twp	77	167
Ah	22	m	c	CHIN	Sacramento	Natomas Twp	77	171
Ah	21	m	c	CHIN	Sacramento	Georgianna Twp	77	131
Ah	21	m	c	CHIN	Sacramento	Georgianna Twp	77	134
Ah	21	m	c	CHIN	Sacramento	Granite Twp	77	154
Ah	20	m	c	CHIN	Sacramento	Georgianna Twp	77	129
Ah	20	m	c	CHIN	Sacramento	Georgianna Twp	77	134
Ah	20	m	c	CHIN	Sacramento	Georgianna Twp	77	131
Ah	20	m	c	CHIN	Tehama	Red Bluff	92	184
Ah	20	m	c	CHIN	San Francisco	6-Wd San Francisco	81	52
Ah	20	m	c	CHIN	Siskiyou	Yreka Twp	89	668
Ah	20	m	c	CHIN	San Francisco	San Francisco P O	83	86
Ah	19	m	c	CHIN	Solano	Suisun Twp	90	106
Ah	19	m	c	CHIN	Yuba	Marysville	93	619
Ah	19	m	c	CHIN	San Francisco	6-Wd San Francisco	81	59
Ah	18	m	c	CHIN	Yolo	Buckeye Twp	93	412
Ah	18	m	c	CHIN	San Mateo	San Mateo P O	87	351
Ah	17	m	c	CHIN	San Francisco	6-Wd San Francisco	81	68
Ah	16	m	c	CHIN	Sacramento	Granite Twp	77	153
Ah	16	m	c	CHIN	Tehama	Tehama Twp	92	189
Ah	16	m	c	CHIN	Santa Clara	1-Wd San Jose	88	225
Ah	16	m	c	CHIN	Yolo	Grafton Twp	93	498
Ah	16	f	c	CHIN	Sacramento	Granite Twp	77	153
Ah	14	m	c	CHIN	Napa	Yountville Twp	75	80
Ah Jo	17	m	c	CHIN	Monterey	Castroville Twp	74	338
Ah Lee	20	m	c	CHIN	Monterey	Castroville Twp	74	338
Charlie	25	m	c	CHIN	Sacramento	4-Wd Sacramento	77	373
Chong	30	m	c	CHIN	Santa Clara	2-Wd San Jose	88	301
Choy	36	f	c	CHIN	Santa Clara	1-Wd San Jose	88	269
Cow	23	m	c	CHIN	Solano	Rio Vista Twp	90	59
Dan	32	m	c	CHIN	Tehama	Tehama Twp	92	188
Eh	40	m	c	CHIN	Sonoma	Petaluma Twp	91	342
Eu	23	m	c	CHIN	Sonoma	Petaluma Twp	91	366
Fow	24	m	c	CHIN	Santa Clara	San Jose Twp	88	192
Gee	38	m	c	CHIN	Sacramento	1-Wd Sacramento	77	198
Gee	21	m	c	CHIN	San Francisco	San Francisco P O	83	308
Gee	19	m	c	CHIN	Plumas	Mineral Twp	77	24
Gin	27	m	c	CHIN	Solano	Rio Vista Twp	90	64
Gol	30	m	c	CHIN	Sacramento	1-Wd Sacramento	77	202
Gon	20	m	c	CHIN	San Joaquin	3-Wd Stockton	86	246
Gu	41	m	c	CHIN	Amador	Jackson P O	69	332
Gun	20	m	c	CHIN	San Francisco	7-Wd San Francisco	81	190
Hang	50	m	c	CHIN	Placer	Auburn P O	76	379
Hay	27	m	c	CHIN	Santa Clara	1-Wd San Jose	88	271
Hee	20	m	c	CHIN	Santa Clara	San Jose Twp	88	191
Hi	36	m	c	CHIN	San Joaquin	1-Wd Stockton	86	148
Hi	29	m	c	CHIN	Tehama	Tehama Twp	92	189
Ho	26	m	c	CHIN	San Joaquin	1-Wd Stockton	86	156
Hog	19	m	c	CHIN	Santa Clara	2-Wd San Jose	88	322
Hoy	31	m	c	CHIN	Santa Clara	1-Wd San Jose	88	274
Hoy	19	m	c	CHIN	Santa Clara	Alviso Twp	88	29
Hoy	18	m	c	CHIN	Santa Clara	1-Wd San Jose	88	225
Hoy	15	m	c	CHIN	Santa Clara	1-Wd San Jose	88	272
Hung	50	m	c	CHIN	Yolo	Merritt Twp	93	504
Jack	22	m	c	CHIN	San Francisco	8-Wd San Francisco	82	301
Jim	32	m	c	CHIN	San Joaquin	1-Wd Stockton	86	143
Jim	30	m	c	CHIN	Santa Clara	1-Wd San Jose	88	272
John	30	m	c	CHIN	San Joaquin	1-Wd Stockton	86	143
Kee	38	m	c	CHIN	Plumas	Indian Twp	77	10
Kee	37	m	c	CHIN	San Francisco	11-Wd San Francisc	84	477
Kee	35	m	c	CHIN	San Mateo	Half Moon Bay P O	87	395
Kee	30	m	c	CHIN	Tehama	Red Bluff	92	184
Kee	29	m	c	CHIN	Solano	Green Valley Twp	90	43

© 2001 by Heritage Quest. All rights reserved.

California 1870 Census

Name	Age	S	R	B-PL	County	Locale	Roll	Pg
Kee	27	m	c	CHIN	Yuba	Marysville	93	632
Kee	26	m	c	CHIN	Tehama	Tehama Twp	92	188
Kee	25	m	c	CHIN	San Mateo	Half Moon Bay P O	87	396
Kee	25	m	c	CHIN	San Francisco	8-Wd San Francisco	82	312
Kee	25	m	c	CHIN	Solano	Rio Vista Twp	90	64
Kee	24	m	c	CHIN	Solano	Vacaville Twp	90	132
Kee	24	m	c	CHIN	San Mateo	Schoolhouse Statio	87	344
Kee	20	m	c	CHIN	Tehama	Deer Crk Twp	92	171
Kee	20	m	c	CHIN	Tehama	Antelope Twp	92	155
Kee	18	m	c	CHIN	Tuolumne	Chinese Camp P O	93	388
Ki	40	m	c	CHIN	San Francisco	6-Wd San Francisco	81	62
Ki	24	m	c	CHIN	Tehama	Tehama Twp	92	188
Kim	28	m	c	CHIN	Tehama	Tehama Twp	92	189
King	22	m	c	CHIN	Tehama	Tehama Twp	92	195
Kum	22	m	c	CHIN	Tehama	Merrill	92	197
Lah	34	m	c	CHIN	Marin	Tomales Twp	74	83
Le	28	m	c	CHIN	Sonoma	Petaluma Twp	91	342
Lee	64	m	c	CHIN	Butte	Chico Twp	70	27
Lee	54	m	c	CHIN	San Francisco	2-Wd San Francisco	79	285
Lee	50	m	c	CHIN	Alameda	Eden Twp	68	58
Lee	49	m	c	CHIN	San Francisco	2-Wd San Francisco	79	286
Lee	49	m	c	CHIN	San Francisco	2-Wd San Francisco	79	285
Lee	42	m	c	CHIN	Butte	Chico Twp	70	49
Lee	42	m	c	CHIN	Fresno	Millerton P O	72	201
Lee	42	m	c	CHIN	San Joaquin	1-Wd Stockton	86	151
Lee	41	m	c	CHIN	Nevada	Nevada Twp	75	318
Lee	39	m	c	CHIN	San Francisco	11-Wd San Francisc	84	661
Lee	37	m	c	CHIN	Placer	Bath P O	76	441
Lee	35	m	c	CHIN	Yolo	Buckeye Twp	93	411
Lee	31	m	c	CHIN	Mendocino	Ukiah Twp	74	239
Lee	31	m	c	CHIN	San Joaquin	Douglas Twp	86	36
Lee	30	m	c	CHIN	Trinity	Canyon City Pct	92	202
Lee	30	m	c	CHIN	Sacramento	1-Wd Sacramento	77	197
Lee	30	m	c	CHIN	Nevada	Eureka Twp	75	140
Lee	30	m	c	CHIN	Butte	Ophir Twp	70	104
Lee	30	m	c	CHIN	San Mateo	Pescadero P O	87	412
Lee	30	m	c	CHIN	Yolo	Grafton Twp	93	495
Lee	28	m	c	CHIN	Alameda	Washington Twp	68	297
Lee	28	m	c	CHIN	Fresno	Millerton P O	72	188
Lee	28	m	c	CHIN	Colusa	Monroe Twp	71	324
Lee	28	m	c	CHIN	San Mateo	Schoolhouse Statio	87	337
Lee	28	m	c	CHIN	San Joaquin	1-Wd Stockton	86	148
Lee	26	m	c	CHIN	Sacramento	3-Wd Sacramento	77	255
Lee	23	m	c	CHIN	Butte	Ophir Twp	70	106
Lee	22	m	c	CHIN	Alameda	Washington Twp	68	273
Lee	21	m	c	CHIN	San Francisco	San Francisco P O	83	374
Lee	20	m	c	CHIN	Santa Clara	1-Wd San Jose	88	233
Lee	19	m	c	CHIN	San Francisco	San Francisco P O	83	270
Lee	18	m	c	CHIN	Sacramento	2-Wd Sacramento	77	242
Lie	27	m	c	CHIN	Fresno	Millerton P O	72	191
Lim	20	m	c	CHIN	San Francisco	San Francisco P O	83	298
Lin	35	m	c	CHIN	Butte	Concow Twp	70	9
Lin	30	m	c	CHIN	Butte	Concow Twp	70	8
Ling	32	m	c	CHIN	El Dorado	Georgetown Twp	72	44
Ling	19	m	c	CHIN	San Joaquin	Liberty Twp	86	97
Long	34	m	c	CHIN	Sonoma	Sonoma Twp	91	447
Loo	30	m	c	CHIN	Solano	Rio Vista Twp	90	64
Loo	16	m	c	CHIN	Tehama	Tehama Twp	92	189
Low	32	m	c	CHIN	Butte	Concow Twp	70	8
Low	32	m	c	CHIN	Fresno	Millerton P O	72	202
Loy	17	m	c	CHIN	Santa Clara	1-Wd San Jose	88	272
Lun	37	m	c	CHIN	Butte	Ophir Twp	70	121
Lun	25	m	c	CHIN	Tehama	Antelope Twp	92	153
Lung	34	m	c	CHIN	Yuba	Marysville	93	626
Mang	35	m	c	CHIN	Plumas	Washington Twp	77	57
Mi	34	m	c	CHIN	Fresno	Millerton P O	72	202
Moon	32	m	c	CHIN	San Francisco	11-Wd San Francisc	84	558
Mow	40	m	c	CHIN	Butte	Chico Twp	70	27
Mow	22	m	c	CHIN	San Francisco	6-Wd San Francisco	81	57
Mung	42	m	c	CHIN	Yuba	Marysville	93	622
Nue	23	f	c	CHIN	Sacramento	1-Wd Sacramento	77	197
Poy	51	m	c	CHIN	Santa Clara	San Jose Twp	88	190
Poy	42	m	c	CHIN	Butte	Chico Twp	70	27
Qua	28	m	c	CHIN	Fresno	Millerton P O	72	202
Sam	44	m	c	CHIN	Stanislaus	Emory Twp	92	26
Sam	22	m	c	CHIN	Tehama	Antelope Twp	92	155
Sam	18	m	c	CHIN	Santa Clara	2-Wd San Jose	88	324
San	61	m	c	CHIN	Mariposa	Mariposa P O	74	125
See	40	m	c	CHIN	Nevada	Nevada Twp	75	311
See	30	m	c	CHIN	Fresno	Millerton P O	72	191
See	28	m	c	CHIN	San Francisco	6-Wd San Francisco	81	104
See	26	m	c	CHIN	Nevada	Eureka Twp	75	140
Shi	35	m	c	CHIN	San Francisco	6-Wd San Francisco	81	53
Sho	32	m	c	CHIN	Fresno	Millerton P O	72	188
Si	38	m	c	CHIN	Stanislaus	Emory Twp	92	19
Si	28	f	c	CHIN	Stanislaus	Branch Twp	92	9
Sick	63	m	c	CHIN	El Dorado	Georgetown Twp	72	44
Sim	30	m	c	CHIN	Alameda	Washington Twp	68	270
Sincy	30	m	c	CHIN	Sutter	Yuba Twp	92	145
Sing	57	m	c	CHIN	Nevada	Washington Twp	75	342
Sing	43	m	c	CHIN	Plumas	Rich Bar Twp	77	45
Sing	40	m	c	CHIN	Humboldt	Eureka Twp	72	266
Sing	40	m	c	CHIN	Stanislaus	Emory Twp	92	22
Sing	40	m	c	CHIN	Tehama	Antelope Twp	92	153
Sing	40	m	c	CHIN	Butte	Chico Twp	70	27
Sing	37	m	c	CHIN	Butte	Chico Twp	70	27
Sing	36	m	c	CHIN	Sutter	Yuba Twp	92	147
Sing	36	m	c	CHIN	Amador	Sutter Crk P O	69	403
Sing	36	m	c	CHIN	Sutter	Butte Twp	92	91
Sing	31	m	c	CHIN	San Francisco	5-Wd San Francisco	81	17
Sing	27	m	c	CHIN	San Joaquin	3-Wd Stockton	86	246
Sing	27	m	c	CHIN	San Joaquin	3-Wd Stockton	86	230
Sing	24	m	c	CHIN	Sutter	Butte Twp	92	94
Sing	24	m	c	CHIN	San Joaquin	1-Wd Stockton	86	142
Sing	22	m	c	CHIN	Sutter	Vernon Twp	92	131
Sing	22	m	c	CHIN	Sutter	Yuba Twp	92	150
Sing	21	m	c	CHIN	Sutter	Butte Twp	92	95
Sing	20	m	c	CHIN	Sutter	Sutter Twp	92	125
Sing	20	m	c	CHIN	Santa Clara	2-Wd San Jose	88	325
Sing	20	m	c	CHIN	Sutter	Sutter Twp	92	122
Sing	19	f	c	CHIN	Sutter	Vernon Twp	92	134
Sing	19	m	c	CHIN	Alameda	Oakland	68	144
Sing	18	m	c	CHIN	Sutter	Yuba Twp	92	149
Sing	18	m	c	CHIN	Sutter	Butte Twp	92	93
Sing	17	m	c	CHIN	San Francisco	5-Wd San Francisco	81	17
Sing	15	m	c	CHIN	Sutter	Butte Twp	92	98
So	16	m	c	CHIN	San Francisco	6-Wd San Francisco	81	64
Song	40	m	c	CHIN	Placer	Lincoln P O	76	484
Soo	46	m	c	CHIN	Tuolumne	Big Oak Flat P O	93	402
Soon	24	m	c	CHIN	Plumas	Washington Twp	77	57
Sow	33	m	c	CHIN	Fresno	Millerton P O	72	202
Sum	32	m	c	CHIN	Tehama	Red Bluff	92	182
Sun	26	m	c	CHIN	Solano	Vacaville Twp	90	129
Tai	27	m	c	CHIN	Butte	Ophir Twp	70	117
Tee	27	m	c	CHIN	San Francisco	6-Wd San Francisco	81	65
Ti	54	m	c	CHIN	San Francisco	6-Wd San Francisco	81	61
Ti	22	m	c	CHIN	Santa Clara	1-Wd San Jose	88	271
Tie	14	m	c	CHIN	Santa Clara	2-Wd San Jose	88	325
Tok	31	m	c	CHIN	San Francisco	6-Wd San Francisco	81	67
Toy	23	m	c	CHIN	Santa Clara	2-Wd San Jose	88	325
Toy	19	m	c	CHIN	Santa Clara	San Jose Twp	88	192
Toy	14	m	c	CHIN	Santa Clara	1-Wd San Jose	88	274
Ve	16	m	c	CHIN	Alameda	Oakland	68	152
Vee	31	m	c	CHIN	Alameda	Washington Twp	68	276
W E	35	m	c	CHIN	Tehama	Tehama Twp	92	188
Wa	35	m	c	CHIN	Fresno	Millerton P O	72	201
Wah	32	m	c	CHIN	San Francisco	San Francisco P O	83	308
Wang	47	m	c	CHIN	Plumas	Washington Twp	77	57
We	18	m	c	CHIN	Yolo	Merritt Twp	93	503
Wee	32	m	c	CHIN	San Francisco	11-Wd San Francisc	84	703
Wo	36	m	c	CHIN	Butte	Kimshew Tpw	70	77
Wo	20	m	c	CHIN	Solano	Suisun Twp	90	95
Woh	24	m	c	CHIN	Fresno	Millerton P O	72	181
Wong	18	m	c	CHIN	Santa Clara	1-Wd San Jose	88	233
Woo	21	m	c	CHIN	Solano	Vacaville Twp	90	132
Ye	25	m	c	CHIN	Sacramento	1-Wd Sacramento	77	201
Ye	22	m	c	CHIN	Alameda	Washington Twp	68	300
Yee	30	m	c	CHIN	Alameda	Alvarado	68	303
Yep	30	m	c	CHIN	San Francisco	7-Wd San Francisco	81	190
Yet	35	m	c	CHIN	Butte	Concow Twp	70	8
Yick	24	m	c	CHIN	San Francisco	8-Wd San Francisco	82	359
Yock	36	m	c	CHIN	Sierra	Eureka Twp	89	526
Yoke	42	m	c	CHIN	San Joaquin	Elkhorn Twp	86	62
Yon	63	m	c	CHIN	San Mateo	Schoolhouse Statio	87	334
Yon	38	m	c	CHIN	Placer	Bath P O	76	442
Yon	25	m	c	CHIN	San Mateo	Schoolhouse Statio	87	335
Yon	21	m	c	CHIN	Sacramento	1-Wd Sacramento	77	183
You	22	m	c	CHIN	Solano	Silveyville Twp	90	92
Yow	45	m	c	CHIN	Trinity	Weaverville Pct	92	232
Yuen	48	m	c	CHIN	Yuba	Marysville	93	620
Yum	22	m	c	CHIN	Solano	Rio Vista Twp	90	70
HOPE								
Ah	28	m	c	CHIN	San Francisco	6-Wd San Francisco	81	64
Ah	25	m	c	CHIN	Humboldt	Eureka Twp	72	266
Ah	24	m	c	CHIN	Butte	Mountain Spring Tw	70	90
Ah	22	m	c	CHIN	Tehama	Red Bluff	92	184
Alexander	37	m	w	SCOT	San Francisco	6-Wd San Francisco	81	81
Aquila M	65	m	w	MD	Calaveras	San Andreas P O	70	207
Edgar	30	m	w	MO	Calaveras	San Andreas P O	70	209
Edward	33	m	w	NY	San Bernardino	San Bernardino Twp	78	426
Flora	32	f	w	PA	San Francisco	11-Wd San Francisc	84	566
Henry Harlan	35	m	w	KY	Plumas	Seneca Twp	77	48
John	9	m	w	CA	Santa Barbara	Santa Barbara P O	87	492
John	34	m	w	NY	San Francisco	San Francisco P O	80	473
Joseph	45	m	w	IN	Colusa	Monroe Twp	71	325
Michael	42	m	w	OH	San Francisco	5-Wd San Francisco	81	29
Philip	42	m	w	ENGL	Mariposa	Maxwell Crk P O	74	143
Rose	10	f	w	CA	Santa Cruz	Santa Cruz	89	417
Thomas	49	m	w	IREL	Santa Barbara	Santa Barbara P O	87	494
William	18	m	w	ME	Stanislaus	North Twp	92	67
Wm	26	m	w	KY	Sacramento	Georgianna Twp	77	131
HOPEE								
Joseph	36	m	w	RI	Marin	San Rafael	74	52
HOPEMAN								
Albert	36	m	w	NY	Sacramento	4-Wd Sacramento	77	352
HOPES								
Edward	36	m	w	CANA	Sonoma	Petaluma Twp	91	329
James	27	m	w	MO	Stanislaus	San Joaquin Twp	92	77
HOPFE								
Fred	48	m	w	PRUS	Sacramento	4-Wd Sacramento	77	340
Henry	25	m	w	PRUS	Sacramento	4-Wd Sacramento	77	342
HOPFELT								
Gustavus	31	m	w	SAXO	El Dorado	Cosumnes Twp	72	16

Series M593

© 2001 by Heritage Quest. All rights reserved.

Name	Age	S	R	B-PL	County	Locale (Series M593)	Roll	Pg
HOPKING								
Robert D	47	m	w	MD	Napa	Napa Twp	75	46
HOPKINS								
A	20	m	w	NY	Nevada	Eureka Twp	75	136
A S	33	m	w	VT	Sacramento	4-Wd Sacramento	77	323
Albert	28	m	w	PRUS	San Francisco	San Francisco P O	83	217
Albridge	29	m	w	ME	Sonoma	Petaluma Twp	91	311
Ambrose D	46	m	w	NY	Yolo	Fremont Twp	93	476
Andrew	25	m	w	WI	Colusa	Grand Island Twp	71	309
Anna	36	f	w	IREL	San Francisco	11-Wd San Francisc	84	442
Aron	50	m	w	KY	Siskiyou	Surprise Valley Tw	89	638
C C	40	m	w	IN	Yuba	Marysville	93	595
Casper	44	m	w	PA	Alameda	Brooklyn Twp	68	53
Charles	22	m	w	IL	Colusa	Colusa	71	292
Charles B	60	m	w	VT	Calaveras	San Andreas P O	70	172
Chas	44	m	w	NY	Solano	Vallejo	90	140
Chas	40	m	w	OH	San Joaquin	2-Wd Stockton	86	179
D	57	m	w	NC	San Joaquin	3-Wd Stockton	86	239
Daniel	29	m	w	ENGL	Butte	Oregon Twp	70	126
Dwight	24	m	w	OH	Yolo	Grafton Twp	93	497
E C	20	m	w	VT	Sacramento	1-Wd Sacramento	77	177
Edward	40	m	w	PA	Monterey	Pajaro Twp	74	376
Edward	40	m	w	IREL	San Francisco	San Francisco P O	83	180
Edward	33	m	w	WALE	Plumas	Washington Twp	77	54
Edwd	40	m	w	IREL	San Francisco	San Francisco P O	83	2
Eliza	31	f	w	PA	Solano	Vacaville Twp	90	124
Elizabeth	39	f	w	MO	Santa Clara	1-Wd San Jose	88	242
Ellen	50	f	w	ENGL	San Francisco	2-Wd San Francisco	79	226
Ellen	28	f	w	NY	San Francisco	8-Wd San Francisco	82	426
Frank	29	m	w	IREL	San Mateo	San Mateo P O	87	360
G B	34	m	w	IN	Yuba	Marysville	93	595
George	45	m	w	MD	San Francisco	San Francisco P O	80	402
Griffith	40	m	w	ENGL	El Dorado	Placerville Twp	72	98
H H	38	m	w	ME	Klamath	Klamath Twp	73	370
Henry	19	m	w	LA	Santa Cruz	Watsonville	89	374
Hopkins	42	m	w	WALE	Inyo	Cerro Gordo Twp	73	319
Ira	38	m	w	NY	Santa Clara	Santa Clara Twp	88	172
Isiah	43	m	w	PA	Butte	Chico Twp	70	14
Isiah	37	m	w	MD	Tulare	Visalia	92	290
J J	40	m	w	ME	Klamath	Klamath Twp	73	370
Jack	29	m	w	MA	San Francisco	San Francisco P O	83	355
James	47	m	w	ENGL	Santa Cruz	Watsonville	89	374
James	39	m	w	IREL	San Francisco	San Francisco P O	83	263
James	38	m	w	IREL	Mariposa	Mariposa P O	74	113
James	23	m	w	IREL	Klamath	Camp Gaston	73	372
James S	28	m	w	ME	Alpine	Markleeville P O	69	316
Jane	50	f	m	LA	San Francisco	San Francisco P O	80	430
Jas	37	m	w	OH	Mendocino	Calpella Twp	74	181
Jas	30	m	m	ENGL	Humboldt	Eureka Twp	72	279
Jas P	29	m	w	ENGL	Humboldt	Eureka Twp	72	265
John	45	m	w	IREL	San Francisco	San Francisco P O	83	161
John	38	m	w	KY	Tehama	Paskenta Twp	92	163
John	38	m	w	KY	Tehama	Paskenta Twp	92	164
John	30	m	w	ENGL	Amador	Amador City P O	69	392
John	25	m	w	IREL	Kern	Bakersfield P O	73	366
John	23	m	w	IL	Yuba	Marysville	93	585
John	21	m	w	IREL	San Francisco	3-Wd San Francisco	79	313
John H	35	m	w	IREL	San Francisco	1-Wd San Francisco	79	123
John L	40	m	w	ENGL	San Francisco	1-Wd San Francisco	79	106
Jos	48	m	w	MO	Tehama	Paskenta Twp	92	165
Joseph	26	m	w	ENGL	San Francisco	San Francisco P O	83	237
Kate	30	f	w	IREL	Los Angeles	Wilmington Twp	73	643
Kate	17	f	w	IREL	San Francisco	San Francisco P O	85	775
L	51	m	w	NY	Los Angeles	Soledad Twp	73	631
L	38	m	w	PRUS	Alameda	Alameda	68	15
L B	46	f	w	IL	San Francisco	San Francisco P O	83	280
L C	40	m	w	PA	Merced	Snelling P O	74	259
Laura	30	f	w	NY	San Francisco	San Francisco P O	83	394
Lawrence W	49	m	w	OH	San Diego	San Diego	78	490
Levi	45	m	w	ME	Solano	Vallejo	90	160
M	55	f	w	ENGL	San Joaquin	2-Wd Stockton	86	165
M S	44	m	w	PA	Monterey	San Juan Twp	74	389
Mark	54	m	w	NY	Sacramento	4-Wd Sacramento	77	320
Mary A	29	f	w	KY	Yolo	Cache Crk Twp	93	430
Mat	32	m	b	NC	Butte	Chico Twp	70	18
Mike	50	m	w	NY	San Francisco	11-Wd San Francisc	84	680
More	48	m	w	MO	Sutter	Nicolaus Twp	92	107
Mortimer D	31	m	w	MA	San Mateo	Pescadero P O	87	409
Morton	34	m	w	MI	Napa	Napa Twp	75	29
Nathan P	57	m	w	RI	San Francisco	San Francisco P O	83	172
Peter	39	m	w	NY	San Francisco	San Francisco P O	83	110
Peter	35	m	w	CANA	Placer	Pino Twp	76	472
Peter	33	m	w	NY	San Francisco	San Francisco P O	83	45
R	16	f	w	US	Yuba	Marysville	93	609
R L	35	m	w	VA	Amador	Jackson P O	69	337
R N	60	m	w	MA	Yuba	Marysville	93	634
Raymond	3	m	w	CA	Sacramento	2-Wd Sacramento	77	211
Rebecca	72	f	w	ENGL	Alameda	Alameda	68	8
Rienzo	29	m	w	IL	Calaveras	San Andreas P O	70	181
Rufus	53	m	w	VA	San Francisco	11-Wd San Francisc	84	508
S F	60	m	w	VT	Sacramento	4-Wd Sacramento	77	323
S H	27	m	w	IL	Napa	Napa	75	15
Saml J	27	m	w	NY	Sonoma	Petaluma Twp	91	337
Samuel	41	m	w	CANA	San Francisco	7-Wd San Francisco	81	223
Simeon W	63	m	w	VT	Yolo	Cache Crk Twp	93	433
Stephen	52	m	w	PA	Amador	Sutter Crk P O	69	413
Theron	51	m	w	NY	San Francisco	1-Wd San Francisco	79	29
Thomas	71	m	w	ENGL	Alameda	Alameda	68	8
Thomas	43	m	w	IN	Santa Clara	Gilroy Twp	88	100
Thomas	35	m	w	IREL	San Francisco	San Francisco P O	80	400
Thos	62	m	w	ENGL	Del Norte	Crescent	71	467
Thos	36	m	w	NJ	Merced	Snelling P O	74	272
Thos	30	m	w	IREL	San Francisco	11-Wd San Francisc	84	677
Thos	30	m	w	IREL	Alameda	Oakland	68	172
Thos	26	m	w	CANA	Santa Cruz	Santa Cruz Twp	89	394
W H	54	m	w	KY	Napa	Napa	75	21
Walter	26	m	w	ME	Amador	Sutter Crk P O	69	403
Walter L	27	m	w	IL	Calaveras	San Andreas P O	70	164
William	57	m	w	AL	Stanislaus	San Joaquin Twp	92	74
William	40	m	w	NJ	Alameda	Washington Twp	68	288
William	39	m	w	NY	San Diego	Coronado	78	467
William	35	m	w	PA	Los Angeles	Los Angeles Twp	73	468
William	29	m	w	AL	Stanislaus	San Joaquin Twp	92	74
William	27	m	w	IREL	Calaveras	San Andreas P O	70	205
William L	42	m	w	NY	San Francisco	8-Wd San Francisco	82	387
William W	35	m	w	RI	San Francisco	8-Wd San Francisco	82	444
Wirt	36	m	w	NY	San Francisco	San Francisco P O	85	732
Wm	79	m	w	ME	Klamath	Klamath Twp	73	370
Wm	54	m	w	OH	Santa Clara	Gilroy Twp	88	100
Wm	45	m	w	IL	San Francisco	2-Wd San Francisco	79	214
Wm	12	m	w	CA	San Francisco	11-Wd San Francisc	84	588
HOPKINSON								
Samuel B	38	m	w	NY	Nevada	Grass Valley Twp	75	162
HOPLEY								
J	44	m	w	CANA	Sacramento	1-Wd Sacramento	77	182
HOPMAN								
Otto	24	m	w	BAVA	Sonoma	Sonoma Twp	91	446
HOPNER								
Chas	35	m	w	ENGL	Alameda	Oakland	68	152
HOPO								
Ah	30	m	c	CHIN	Sacramento	Cosumnes Twp	77	94
HOPP								
Ah	35	m	c	CHIN	Amador	Ione City P O	69	354
Ah	30	m	c	CHIN	Amador	Volcano P O	69	384
Ah	26	m	c	CHIN	Amador	Ione City P O	69	354
Uriah	32	m	w	OH	Butte	Oregon Twp	70	130
HOPPA								
G B	27	m	w	MO	Mendocino	Ukiah Twp	74	237
HOPPE								
Conrad	30	m	w	PRUS	San Francisco	San Francisco P O	80	427
Fernandi	49	m	w	HAMB	San Francisco	11-Wd San Francisc	84	467
H	16	m	w	HANO	Sacramento	3-Wd Sacramento	77	295
Henry	43	m	w	PRUS	Marin	Sausalito Twp	74	71
Monroe C	23	m	w	CA	San Bernardino	San Bernardino Twp	78	453
HOPPEL								
Rosania	35	f	w	GERM	San Joaquin	2-Wd Stockton	86	166
HOPPER								
A J	36	m	w	NJ	Siskiyou	Scott Valley Twp	89	608
Benjamin	28	m	w	ENGL	Sacramento	Lee Twp	77	159
Charles	61	m	w	NC	Mendocino	Calpella Twp	74	182
Charles	23	m	w	MO	Mendocino	Calpella Twp	74	182
Charles	13	m	w	CA	Napa	Napa	75	15
Charles H	29	m	w	MO	Mendocino	Point Arena Twp	74	210
Chas	70	m	w	NC	Napa	Yountville Twp	75	77
D C	46	m	w	SC	Sutter	Nicolaus Twp	92	110
David	44	m	w	TN	Sonoma	Mendocino Twp	91	307
Eli	46	m	w	MO	Santa Barbara	San Buenaventura P	87	430
Eliza	48	f	w	----	San Joaquin	2-Wd Stockton	86	169
Ellen E	30	f	w	ME	San Francisco	6-Wd San Francisco	81	94
G D	37	m	w	NY	Sacramento	3-Wd Sacramento	77	257
Garrett	46	m	w	NY	San Francisco	1-Wd San Francisco	79	56
Garrett H	44	m	w	NY	San Francisco	1-Wd San Francisco	79	127
George L	22	m	w	CA	Mendocino	Calpella Twp	74	189
Jacob	34	m	w	OH	Calaveras	San Andreas P O	70	212
James	40	m	w	VA	Alpine	Markleeville P O	69	316
James	21	m	w	MO	Mendocino	Anderson Twp	74	157
John	53	m	w	SC	Los Angeles	El Monte Twp	73	457
John	47	m	w	MO	Mendocino	Calpella Twp	74	187
John	38	m	w	CANA	San Francisco	11-Wd San Francisc	84	693
Josephine	41	f	w	IREL	Yolo	Cache Crk Twp	93	456
Levi	37	m	w	NY	Santa Clara	Gilroy Twp	88	82
Martha	3	f	w	CA	San Luis Obispo	Salinas Twp	87	296
Mary	40	f	w	SCOT	San Joaquin	3-Wd Stockton	86	220
Mollie	21	f	w	IL	San Joaquin	1-Wd Stockton	86	133
Thos B	31	m	w	MO	Napa	Yountville Twp	75	84
William	63	m	w	KY	Monterey	San Juan Twp	74	401
William	45	m	w	MO	Mendocino	Little Lake Twp	74	203
William	40	m	w	ENGL	Sacramento	2-Wd Sacramento	77	225
William	26	m	w	OH	Solano	Silveyville Twp	90	74
William	22	m	w	CANA	Sacramento	2-Wd Sacramento	77	252
Wm	63	m	w	NC	Sonoma	Cloverdale Twp	91	271
HOPPERS								
David C	35	m	w	MO	San Luis Obispo	Salinas Twp	87	294
HOPPERSTEAD								
O	25	m	w	NORW	San Joaquin	2-Wd Stockton	86	206
HOPPERT								
Christopher H	38	m	w	SAXO	Placer	Bath P O	76	455
HOPPICH								
John H	52	m	w	NJ	Placer	Colfax P O	76	385
HOPPIN								
Charles R	40	m	w	NY	Yolo	Cache Crk Twp	93	451
John	30	m	w	MI	Yolo	Cache Crk Twp	93	451
John E	30	m	w	MI	Yolo	Cache Crk Twp	93	451
Nathan S	56	m	w	MA	Yolo	Cache Crk Twp	93	451

© 2001 by Heritage Quest. All rights reserved.

California 1870 Census

Name	Age	S	R	B-PL	County	Locale	Roll	Pg
						Series M593		
Thadeus C	45	m	w	MA	Yolo	Cache Crk Twp	93	451
HOPPING								
Harriet	33	f	w	NJ	Shasta	Shasta P O	89	463
W C	53	m	w	NY	Sacramento	3-Wd Sacramento	77	314
W C	47	m	w	NY	Sacramento	3-Wd Sacramento	77	278
Wm E	40	m	w	NJ	Shasta	Shasta P O	89	463
HOPPINS								
John	32	m	w	ENGL	Solano	Vallejo	90	203
HOPPMAN								
Chas	26	m	w	SAXO	San Francisco	1-Wd San Francisco	79	89
HOPPS								
Charles	63	m	w	ENGL	San Francisco	8-Wd San Francisco	82	394
Charles	35	m	w	MA	San Francisco	8-Wd San Francisco	82	417
Frank W	26	m	w	MA	San Francisco	8-Wd San Francisco	82	413
James H	19	m	w	MA	San Francisco	8-Wd San Francisco	82	395
Joseph	45	m	w	CANA	Solano	Maine Prairie Twp	90	45
Peter J	40	m	w	NJ	Sacramento	Granite Twp	77	142
HOPPY								
Ellen	17	f	w	CA	Napa	Napa Twp	75	63
HOPSE								
Kim	42	m	c	CHIN	San Joaquin	Liberty Twp	86	97
HOPWOOD								
Franklin M	36	m	w	VA	El Dorado	White Oak Twp	72	137
Madame	65	f	w	ENGL	Santa Barbara	Santa Barbara P O	87	475
HOPZARD								
F	18	m	w	ME	Sierra	Sierra Twp	89	567
HOR								
Ah	50	m	c	CHIN	El Dorado	Georgetown Twp	72	41
Jow	25	m	c	CHIN	Sonoma	Salt Point	91	386
Morris	39	m	w	IREL	Alameda	Oakland	68	151
HORA								
William H	44	m	w	ME	Santa Cruz	Santa Cruz	89	430
HORABIN								
Thomas	50	m	w	ENGL	San Francisco	6-Wd San Francisco	81	101
HORACE								
Austin	34	m	w	MA	Butte	Ophir Twp	70	91
J	47	m	w	HANO	Sierra	Forest Twp	89	531
HORAM								
Bridget	26	f	w	IREL	San Francisco	San Francisco P O	83	110
HORAN								
Edward	72	m	w	IREL	Contra Costa	Martinez P O	71	390
Frank	44	m	w	IREL	Solano	Suisun Twp	90	108
Gabriella	30	f	w	IREL	Sonoma	Petaluma Twp	91	339
James	44	m	w	IREL	Nevada	Grass Valley Twp	75	151
James	30	m	w	CANA	Contra Costa	Martinez P O	71	390
John	55	m	w	IREL	San Francisco	1-Wd San Francisco	79	93
John	46	m	w	IREL	Calaveras	San Andreas P O	70	216
John	39	m	w	IREL	Santa Clara	2-Wd San Jose	88	328
John	20	m	w	IREL	San Francisco	5-Wd San Francisco	81	20
John J	19	m	w	NY	San Francisco	8-Wd San Francisco	82	353
Maggie	27	f	w	IREL	San Francisco	San Francisco P O	83	129
Mary	47	f	w	IREL	Sacramento	4-Wd Sacramento	77	344
Mary	18	f	w	NY	San Francisco	San Francisco P O	80	352
Mary	18	f	w	NY	San Francisco	8-Wd San Francisco	82	422
Michael	40	m	w	IREL	Nevada	Grass Valley Twp	75	231
Patrick	56	m	w	IREL	San Francisco	1-Wd San Francisco	79	100
Patrick	35	m	w	CANA	Contra Costa	Martinez P O	71	390
Patrick	35	m	w	MA	Siskiyou	Surprise Valley Tw	89	637
Rosana	27	f	w	IREL	San Francisco	2-Wd San Francisco	79	276
Thomas	30	m	w	IREL	San Francisco	11-Wd San Francisc	84	441
Thomas	29	m	w	TN	Nevada	Meadow Lake Twp	75	268
HORAND								
Michael	41	m	w	MA	Colusa	California Twp	71	279
HORARO								
Jesus	36	m	w	MEXI	Alameda	Eden Twp	68	65
HORATA								
Paine	47	m	w	CA	San Joaquin	3-Wd Stockton	86	220
HORBACK								
Isaac	41	m	w	PRUS	San Francisco	San Francisco P O	80	456
HORCE								
Michael	30	m	w	IREL	Nevada	Grass Valley Twp	75	197
HORCH								
Fredrick	35	m	w	PRUS	San Francisco	7-Wd San Francisco	81	223
Joseph	33	m	w	AUST	San Francisco	San Francisco P O	80	461
HORCHE								
Catharine	7	f	w	NV	Yuba	Long Bar Twp	93	560
HORD								
Bell	20	f	w	KY	San Francisco	San Francisco P O	83	340
John R	72	m	w	KY	Alameda	Brooklyn	68	23
W	28	m	w	ENGL	Sierra	Alleghany & Forest	89	534
HORDES								
Richard	25	m	w	ENGL	San Diego	Julian Dist	78	472
HORDING								
Valentine A	22	m	w	CANA	San Mateo	Searsville P O	87	382
HORDON								
M	51	m	w	NJ	Sierra	Sierra Twp	89	564
HORDY								
Cyrus	40	m	w	MD	Mendocino	Casper & Big Rvr	74	162
Phelix	41	m	w	IREL	Mendocino	Big Rvr Twp	74	162
HORE								
James	38	m	w	IREL	San Francisco	San Francisco P O	85	829
HORECK								
Alfred	24	m	w	ENGL	Yuba	Marysville	93	594
HOREIS								
William	36	m	w	HANO	Placer	Newcastle Twp	76	474
HORENDER								
Frank	25	m	w	IREL	San Francisco	11-Wd San Francisc	84	649

Name	Age	S	R	B-PL	County	Locale	Roll	Pg
						Series M593		
HORENLE								
Michel	44	m	w	WURT	Napa	Napa	75	45
HORG								
Jos	20	f	c	CHIN	San Joaquin	1-Wd Stockton	86	153
HORGAN								
Andrew	30	m	w	IREL	Yolo	Grafton Twp	93	490
Cornelius	38	m	w	IREL	Yolo	Grafton Twp	93	489
Cornelius	32	m	w	IREL	San Francisco	San Francisco P O	85	839
Daniel	23	m	w	IREL	San Francisco	San Francisco P O	85	877
Edward	26	m	w	MA	San Francisco	San Francisco P O	83	258
Eliza	18	f	w	IREL	Nevada	Grass Valley Twp	75	151
Hannah	37	f	w	IREL	San Francisco	8-Wd San Francisco	82	380
John	30	m	w	IREL	Yolo	Cache Crk Twp	93	421
Michael	35	m	w	IREL	Yolo	Grafton Twp	93	496
Pat	27	m	w	IREL	Yuba	Marysville	93	613
Patrick	37	m	w	IREL	San Diego	San Luis Rey	78	515
Timothy	23	m	w	IREL	San Francisco	1-Wd San Francisco	79	69
HORGELOH								
Chas	24	m	w	HANO	San Francisco	11-Wd San Francisc	84	446
HORGENS								
Dor	32	m	w	SHOL	Monterey	Alisal Twp	74	294
HORGON								
John	56	m	w	IREL	Solano	Rio Vista Twp	90	57
HORINE								
Henry	39	m	w	KY	Placer	Auburn P O	76	374
HORING								
James	30	m	w	IREL	Yolo	Fremont Twp	93	476
HORINO								
James L	38	m	w	VA	El Dorado	Cosumnes Twp	72	14
HORISH								
Beng	42	m	w	OH	Butte	Chico Twp	70	48
HORKINS								
Samuel	35	m	w	ENGL	El Dorado	Cosumnes Twp	72	15
HORLEY								
John	42	m	w	GA	Merced	Snelling P O	74	269
HORLIN								
Wm C	41	m	w	BAVA	Tuolumne	Chinese Camp P O	93	384
HORM								
Christian	29	m	w	PRUS	San Francisco	7-Wd San Francisco	81	171
Jacob	15	m	w	CA	San Joaquin	Elkhorn Twp	86	65
William	42	m	w	IREL	Calaveras	San Andreas P O	70	159
HORN								
Ah	56	m	c	CHIN	El Dorado	Diamond Springs Tw	72	24
Ah	32	m	c	CHIN	Placer	Bath P O	76	452
Ah	30	m	c	CHIN	Placer	Auburn P O	76	379
Ah	21	m	c	CHIN	San Joaquin	Oneal Twp	86	118
Alex	55	m	w	NY	Stanislaus	Empire Twp	92	58
Alex	42	m	w	NY	Solano	Vallejo	90	202
Alfred	42	m	w	IL	Sutter	Vernon Twp	92	130
Amos A	43	m	w	MO	Napa	Napa Twp	75	59
Andrew	35	m	w	NY	Santa Barbara	Santa Barbara P O	87	473
Charles	20	m	w	HANO	Del Norte	Smith Rvr Twp	71	479
Christian	19	m	w	HANO	San Francisco	1-Wd San Francisco	79	53
Daniel	35	m	w	OH	Los Angeles	El Monte Twp	73	457
David	27	m	w	OH	Siskiyou	Scott Valley Twp	89	608
Dora M	33	f	w	SHOL	San Mateo	Woodside P O	87	384
Genevie	59	f	w	BAVA	Solano	Vallejo	90	170
George	64	m	w	PA	San Joaquin	Oneal Twp	86	114
George	39	m	w	PRUS	Calaveras	Copperopolis P O	70	251
Greenberry M	38	m	w	NC	Santa Cruz	Pajaro Twp	89	350
Gy	55	m	c	CHIN	Placer	Bath P O	76	442
Ida	21	f	w	OH	San Francisco	San Francisco P O	80	396
Isaiah	47	m	w	NC	Stanislaus	Empire Twp	92	56
J R	30	m	w	ME	Sierra	Sears Twp	89	556
Jacob E	36	m	w	NH	Klamath	South Fork Twp	73	385
James	45	m	w	IREL	Sonoma	Vallejo Twp	91	456
James	35	m	w	IREL	Santa Clara	2-Wd San Jose	88	316
James	30	m	w	SCOT	Contra Costa	Martinez P O	71	427
James B	32	m	w	IL	Alameda	Washington Twp	68	288
James F	32	m	w	AL	San Mateo	Woodside P O	87	384
James M	50	m	w	NC	Santa Cruz	Soquel Twp	89	436
Jerome	33	m	w	HDAR	San Francisco	8-Wd San Francisco	82	381
Jos P	36	m	w	MA	San Francisco	San Francisco P O	83	112
Joseph	42	m	w	PRUS	San Francisco	San Francisco P O	83	133
Levi	48	m	w	MO	Stanislaus	Branch Twp	92	5
Margerita	22	f	w	PRUS	San Francisco	San Francisco P O	83	23
Martin	40	m	w	SWED	Solano	Vallejo	90	145
Phillip	53	m	w	PA	San Francisco	7-Wd San Francisco	81	232
Piere H	29	m	w	IL	San Francisco	8-Wd San Francisco	82	332
R	26	m	w	HANO	San Francisco	San Francisco P O	85	806
Richard	24	m	w	NY	San Francisco	5-Wd San Francisco	81	19
Sarah	29	f	w	NY	Sacramento	2-Wd Sacramento	77	220
Sim	30	m	w	IN	Humboldt	South Fork Twp	72	301
Sylvester	25	m	w	ME	Yuba	New York Twp	93	639
Thomas	40	m	w	IREL	San Francisco	7-Wd San Francisco	81	166
Thomas	39	m	w	CT	San Francisco	2-Wd San Francisco	79	194
William	40	m	w	NORW	San Francisco	11-Wd San Francisc	84	519
William	35	m	w	ENGL	San Francisco	7-Wd San Francisco	81	221
William	22	m	w	PRUS	San Francisco	6-Wd San Francisco	81	97
William S	50	m	w	CT	Yolo	Cache Crk Twp	93	437
Wm	45	m	w	PRUS	Sierra	Sears Twp	89	561
HORNAGE								
James	40	m	w	OH	Calaveras	San Andreas P O	70	154
HORNAY								
Julius	24	m	w	PRUS	Sutter	Sutter Twp	92	122
HORNBACK								
Jas	43	m	w	WI	Butte	Chico Twp	70	50

© 2001 by Heritage Quest. All rights reserved.

Name	Age	S	R	B-PL	County	Locale	Series M593 Roll	Pg
Jus	31	m	w	MO	Butte	Chico Twp	70	25
Samuel	50	m	w	ENGL	San Francisco	7-Wd San Francisco	81	183
HORNBECK								
James	68	m	w	KY	Contra Costa	Martinez P O	71	401
Jas H	35	m	w	MO	Santa Barbara	San Buenaventura P	87	440
HORNBERGER								
John H	32	m	w	PA	Santa Clara	Fremont Twp	88	46
HORNBLOWER								
F A	42	m	w	ENGL	Sacramento	1-Wd Sacramento	77	172
HORNBROOK								
S	48	m	w	KY	Mendocino	Round Valley Twp	74	217
HORNBUCK								
William	22	m	w	MO	Colusa	Monroe Twp	71	315
HORNDOLPH								
Henry	40	m	w	PRUS	San Francisco	6-Wd San Francisco	81	122
HORNE								
Ah	36	m	c	CHIN	Amador	Jackson P O	69	331
Ann Mrs	35	f	w	IREL	Santa Clara	Burnett Twp	88	31
Barney	36	m	w	NY	San Francisco	11-Wd San Francisc	84	666
Charles D	40	m	w	VT	Amador	Jackson P O	69	325
Frank	37	m	w	BADE	Siskiyou	Callahan P O	89	624
George	37	m	w	ME	Calaveras	San Andreas P O	70	203
James	58	m	w	ENGL	Amador	Jackson P O	69	328
James	55	m	w	ENGL	San Francisco	San Francisco P O	83	205
John	45	m	w	IREL	San Francisco	11-Wd San Francisc	84	512
John	18	m	w	NY	Santa Clara	1-Wd San Jose	88	235
Marcus P	52	m	w	ME	San Francisco	San Francisco P O	83	157
Pat	30	m	w	IREL	San Francisco	San Francisco P O	83	115
Patrick	33	m	w	IREL	Siskiyou	Callahan P O	89	627
Thomas	38	m	w	IREL	San Francisco	8-Wd San Francisco	82	383
HORNER								
C W	31	m	w	ENGL	San Francisco	San Francisco P O	85	774
Charles	26	m	w	BADE	San Francisco	San Francisco P O	83	180
David H	25	m	w	MD	Yolo	Grafton Twp	93	490
Eunice M	34	f	w	CANA	Sacramento	Brighton Twp	77	79
Horatio G	29	m	w	ENGL	San Francisco	San Francisco P O	85	717
Isaac	49	m	w	NJ	Alameda	Washington Twp	68	277
J C	40	m	w	IREL	Alameda	Oakland	68	153
John	60	m	w	MO	San Joaquin	Liberty Twp	86	94
John M	49	m	w	NJ	Alameda	Washington Twp	68	288
Leonard	20	m	w	MO	Sacramento	4-Wd Sacramento	77	366
Margaret	17	f	w	CANA	Santa Clara	1-Wd San Jose	88	237
Rulof J	40	m	w	NJ	Alameda	Washington Twp	68	284
Sarah	75	f	w	NJ	Alameda	Washington Twp	68	288
William	57	m	w	ENGL	San Francisco	11-Wd San Francisc	84	525
William	42	m	w	NJ	Alameda	Washington Twp	68	288
HORNERES								
Henry	36	m	w	FRAN	San Francisco	San Francisco P O	80	408
HORNESS								
James	40	m	w	OH	Santa Cruz	Santa Cruz	89	427
HORNET								
Jno	50	m	w	IREL	Butte	Kimshew Tpw	70	80
Patrick	28	m	w	IREL	San Francisco	San Francisco P O	85	755
HORNETT								
Daniel	45	m	w	IREL	Klamath	Sawyers Bar	73	377
J	24	m	w	IN	Alameda	Oakland	68	172
HORNEY								
G	44	m	w	SWED	Sierra	Butte Twp	89	512
HORNING								
D G	32	m	w	SC	Sacramento	3-Wd Sacramento	77	268
Frank C	37	m	w	HCAS	San Francisco	San Francisco P O	83	80
Jacob	38	m	w	NY	Yolo	Putah Twp	93	509
Odolph	35	m	w	GERM	Yolo	Cottonwood Twp	93	472
Richard	30	m	w	GERM	Yolo	Cottonwood Twp	93	472
HORNISH								
George B	38	m	w	VA	Colusa	Colusa	71	297
HORNMAN								
Herman	51	m	w	HANO	Placer	Bath P O	76	447
HORNSBERG								
Louis	54	m	w	BAVA	San Francisco	8-Wd San Francisco	82	456
HORNSTEIN								
Anne	20	f	w	PRUS	San Francisco	6-Wd San Francisco	81	62
Jacob	45	m	w	HUNG	San Francisco	San Francisco P O	80	419
HORNSUCKER								
George	30	m	w	MO	Yolo	Cache Crk Twp	93	451
HORNUNCE								
Jacob	47	m	w	PRUS	Humboldt	Eureka Twp	72	258
HORNUNG								
---	45	m	w	GERM	Yuba	Marysville	93	614
G	48	m	w	HCAS	Yuba	Marysville	93	582
HORR								
Almon	24	m	w	HANO	Marin	Sausalito Twp	74	66
Bennett	24	m	w	MA	San Francisco	San Francisco P O	80	401
Josephine	30	f	w	NY	Stanislaus	Empire Twp	92	34
Milton	21	m	w	ME	Nevada	Grass Valley Twp	75	167
Wm H	22	m	w	NY	San Francisco	8-Wd San Francisco	82	374
HORRA								
Ah	23	m	c	CHIN	San Francisco	1-Wd San Francisco	79	60
HORRAGAN								
Patrick	35	m	w	IREL	Nevada	Eureka Twp	75	129
HORRALD								
Sarah	49	f	w	IN	Napa	Napa	75	38
HORRAN								
John	34	m	w	ENGL	Marin	Nicasio Twp	74	14
HORRAS								
Thomas	25	m	w	NY	San Francisco	11-Wd San Francisc	84	712

Name	Age	S	R	B-PL	County	Locale	Series M593 Roll	Pg
HORRELL								
Alex B	45	m	w	KY	Amador	Fiddletown P O	69	441
Alxa J	45	m	w	MO	El Dorado	Cosumnes Twp	72	18
Jackson	42	m	w	PA	Contra Costa	San Pablo Twp	71	364
John	43	m	w	VA	Amador	Fiddletown P O	69	435
John B	62	m	w	PA	Napa	Napa	75	52
T M	53	m	w	DC	Amador	Jackson P O	69	321
Thomas	34	m	w	PA	Napa	Napa	75	52
HORRICKS								
George	32	m	w	LA	San Francisco	San Francisco P O	83	210
HORRIDGE								
John	31	m	w	ENGL	San Francisco	San Francisco P O	83	151
HORRIGAN								
Cornelius	45	m	w	IREL	San Francisco	San Francisco P O	83	7
Eliz	60	f	w	IREL	San Francisco	San Francisco P O	83	134
Ellen	23	f	w	IREL	San Francisco	San Francisco P O	83	134
John	9	m	w	CA	Marin	San Rafael Twp	74	28
John	22	m	w	IREL	San Francisco	San Francisco P O	83	132
Mary	25	f	w	IREL	San Francisco	San Francisco P O	83	134
Michael	26	m	w	IREL	San Francisco	7-Wd San Francisco	81	230
Patk	39	m	w	IREL	San Francisco	San Francisco P O	83	311
Timothy	38	m	w	IREL	San Francisco	San Francisco P O	83	334
HORRINGTON								
J	30	m	w	IREL	Napa	Napa Twp	75	69
HORSCHE								
John	43	m	w	BAVA	San Francisco	11-Wd San Francisc	84	439
HORSELEY								
John A	42	m	w	OH	Sonoma	Analy Twp	91	220
HORSELY								
Cathr S	75	f	w	PA	Sonoma	Healdsburg & Mendo	91	282
James C	21	m	w	IN	Stanislaus	Buena Vista Twp	92	14
Joseph	43	m	w	OH	Stanislaus	Buena Vista Twp	92	14
HORSLEY								
Chas	20	m	w	KY	Sacramento	1-Wd Sacramento	77	174
John	45	m	w	ENGL	Amador	Volcano P O	69	381
HORSMAN								
Henry	67	m	w	ENGL	Butte	Oregon Twp	70	125
Henry	38	m	w	HANO	Los Angeles	Santa Ana Twp	73	614
Mary	8	f	w	CA	Los Angeles	Santa Ana Twp	73	609
HORSNER								
Charles	40	m	w	BAVA	San Francisco	8-Wd San Francisco	82	389
HORST								
Henry	45	m	w	SWED	San Francisco	1-Wd San Francisco	79	27
Hugo	32	m	w	PRUS	San Francisco	8-Wd San Francisco	82	484
Hugo	32	m	w	GERM	San Luis Obispo	San Luis Obispo Tw	87	311
Thos	38	m	w	IREL	San Joaquin	2-Wd Stockton	86	172
William	38	m	w	HANO	Alameda	Alameda	68	11
HORSTINGER								
F W	44	m	w	PRUS	Sacramento	3-Wd Sacramento	77	290
HORSTMAN								
C	34	m	w	PRUS	Sacramento	3-Wd Sacramento	77	295
Clemens	40	m	w	PRUS	San Francisco	8-Wd San Francisco	82	486
Elizabeth	76	f	w	PRUS	San Francisco	8-Wd San Francisco	82	486
Henry	44	m	w	PRUS	San Francisco	8-Wd San Francisco	82	290
Herman	30	m	w	PRUS	San Francisco	8-Wd San Francisco	82	486
Jos	36	m	w	PRUS	San Francisco	8-Wd San Francisco	82	337
HORSTMANN								
Christopher	29	m	w	PRUS	San Francisco	11-Wd San Francisc	84	708
HORSTMIRE								
Henry	48	m	w	PRUS	Trinity	Canyon City Pct	92	202
HORSTMYER								
Fredk W	41	m	w	PRUS	Sacramento	4-Wd Sacramento	77	348
H C	21	m	w	IN	Napa	Napa	75	41
HORSY								
James	70	m	w	MA	Santa Clara	Redwood Twp	88	121
HORT								
Charles	42	m	w	BAVA	Calaveras	San Andreas P O	70	220
Gottlieb	36	m	w	HOLL	Calaveras	San Andreas P O	70	202
Samuel	54	m	w	ENGL	San Francisco	11-Wd San Francisc	84	660
HORTEL								
George	43	m	w	HAMB	San Francisco	8-Wd San Francisco	82	304
HORTER								
Henry	42	m	w	NY	San Francisco	San Francisco P O	83	393
HORTEX								
G	35	m	w	PRUS	Alameda	Oakland	68	265
HORTH								
Charles	27	m	w	PA	San Francisco	5-Wd San Francisco	81	19
HORTON								
Alex	26	m	w	IL	Tehama	Antelope Twp	92	160
Alonzo	45	m	w	CT	San Diego	San Diego	78	483
Bernard	33	m	w	FRAN	San Francisco	San Francisco P O	83	89
Charles	38	m	w	NY	Los Angeles	Soledad Twp	73	630
Charles	30	m	w	CANA	Yolo	Grafton Twp	93	481
Charles A	46	m	w	MA	San Francisco	8-Wd San Francisco	82	437
Chs H	48	m	w	NY	San Francisco	2-Wd San Francisco	79	282
Daniel	40	m	w	ENGL	San Francisco	5-Wd San Francisco	81	19
Daniel	25	m	w	NY	Los Angeles	Wilmington Twp	73	642
Frank	35	m	w	NY	Siskiyou	Callahan P O	89	630
Geo C	52	m	w	OH	Butte	Ophir Twp	70	120
George	39	m	w	NY	San Francisco	1-Wd San Francisco	79	19
George	19	m	w	MA	San Francisco	7-Wd San Francisco	81	157
Gerard	32	m	w	NY	Alameda	Eden Twp	68	66
Gilbert	23	m	w	NY	Napa	Yountville Twp	75	80
Griffith	30	m	w	CT	Sacramento	Dry Crk Twp	77	104
Homer	46	m	w	NY	Santa Clara	1-Wd San Jose	88	255
Horton	27	m	w	CT	Yuba	East Bear Rvr Twp	93	542
James	35	m	w	NY	Santa Barbara	San Buenaventura P	87	428

© 2001 by Heritage Quest. All rights reserved.

California 1870 Census

Name	Age	S	R	B-PL	County	Locale	Series M593 Roll	Pg
John	40	m	w	IREL	Alameda	Washington Twp	68	287
John	35	m	w	IL	Amador	Ione City P O	69	361
John	34	m	w	TN	Los Angeles	El Monte Twp	73	462
John	28	m	w	VT	San Francisco	8-Wd San Francisco	82	382
Joseph	26	m	w	MA	Butte	Chico Twp	70	29
Levi	29	m	w	NY	Marin	Bolinas Twp	74	7
Lewis	42	m	w	NY	Nevada	Rough & Ready Twp	75	332
Lover E	37	m	w	NY	Placer	Colfax P O	76	389
M L	36	m	w	TN	Tehama	Antelope Twp	92	156
Martha S	49	f	w	MO	Santa Clara	Santa Clara Twp	88	141
Nathaniel	20	m	w	VA	Napa	Napa Twp	75	32
Neamiah	34	m	w	VT	Stanislaus	North Twp	92	67
Nickolos	32	m	w	ME	Sonoma	Salt Point	91	386
Orrin	30	m	w	TN	Los Angeles	Los Nietos Twp	73	580
Pemberton	26	m	w	NJ	San Francisco	San Francisco P O	80	407
S T	44	m	w	NY	Napa	Napa	75	47
Stephen	47	m	w	GA	El Dorado	Georgetown Twp	72	40
Thomas	35	m	w	IREL	San Francisco	7-Wd San Francisco	81	191
Thomas R	48	m	w	MA	San Francisco	6-Wd San Francisco	81	141
Wallac J	23	m	w	IL	Yolo	Putah Twp	93	521
Wallace J	23	m	w	IL	Yolo	Cache Crk Twp	93	447
William	59	m	w	NY	Inyo	Bishop Crk Twp	73	313
William	35	m	w	PRUS	San Francisco	8-Wd San Francisco	82	389
William	35	m	w	TN	Los Angeles	Los Nietos Twp	73	578
William	15	m	w	CA	Amador	Ione City P O	69	363
William	15	m	w	CA	Amador	Ione City P O	69	360
William H	63	m	w	NC	Los Angeles	Los Nietos Twp	73	573
William L	61	m	w	NY	Los Angeles	Los Nietos Twp	73	589
Wm	44	m	w	KY	Butte	Bidwell Twp	70	3
Wm	35	m	w	KY	Tehama	Tehama Twp	92	193
Wm	28	m	w	NY	San Francisco	San Francisco P O	83	102
Wm	26	m	w	NY	San Joaquin	1-Wd Stockton	86	130
Wm T	46	m	w	NY	Plumas	Quartz Twp	77	39
HORTONS								
Cyrus	28	m	w	NY	Sacramento	San Joaquin Twp	77	406
HORTOYA								
Ellis	32	m	w	CA	Fresno	Millerton P O	72	151
HORTUN								
Gourd	40	m	w	OH	Sacramento	Alabama Twp	77	60
HORUM								
Mike	38	m	w	IREL	Sacramento	1-Wd Sacramento	77	188
HORWEGO								
Henry	11	m	w	CA	San Francisco	7-Wd San Francisco	81	264
HORWOOD								
Charles	35	m	w	ENGL	Yolo	Putah Twp	93	523
Esther	26	f	w	ENGL	Sacramento	2-Wd Sacramento	77	214
HORY								
Ah	30	m	c	CHIN	Kern	Kernville P O	73	368
Elizabeth	10	f	w	CA	Colusa	Grand Island Twp	71	307
Gan	30	m	c	CHIN	San Francisco	11-Wd San Francisc	84	574
HOSA								
S	64	m	w	MEXI	Amador	Drytown P O	69	418
HOSACK								
John	56	m	w	PA	Kern	Tehachapi P O	73	355
HOSADA								
Frances	30	f	w	MEXI	Yuba	Marysville	93	614
HOSAFER								
M	28	f	w	CA	Alameda	Alameda	68	3
HOSANI								
Henry	41	m	w	ITAL	San Francisco	San Francisco P O	80	460
HOSBIER								
Henry	39	m	w	BADE	San Francisco	11-Wd San Francisc	84	459
HOSCH								
William	17	m	w	CA	Santa Barbara	Santa Barbara P O	87	492
HOSEA								
A	37	m	w	MEXI	Mariposa	Mariposa P O	74	106
Alfred	31	m	w	MEXI	Mariposa	Mariposa P O	74	135
Jesus	69	m	w	MEXI	Tuolumne	Columbia P O	93	354
Juan	40	m	w	MEXI	Colusa	Monroe Twp	71	325
Manual	44	m	w	CHIL	El Dorado	Coloma Twp	72	5
Mary	25	f	w	SCOT	Alameda	Brooklyn Twp	68	45
Robert	22	m	w	MA	San Francisco	San Francisco P O	85	758
HOSEFETA								
Martin	38	m	w	PA	Sacramento	2-Wd Sacramento	77	218
HOSEFUS								
J	40	f	w	MEXI	Alameda	Murray Twp	68	106
HOSELKUS								
Edwin Douglass	41	m	w	NY	Plumas	Indian Twp	77	10
Nicholas	70	m	w	NY	Plumas	Indian Twp	77	10
HOSEN								
Joseph	40	m	w	CHIL	El Dorado	Placerville	72	125
HOSENDORF								
Gustav	35	m	w	PRUS	San Francisco	6-Wd San Francisco	81	132
HOSENMEIR								
Fred	37	m	w	WURT	San Francisco	2-Wd San Francisco	79	222
HOSER								
Lopoldt	32	m	w	BADE	Sonoma	Vallejo Twp	91	455
HOSEY								
John	33	m	w	IREL	San Francisco	5-Wd San Francisco	81	35
Patrick	65	m	w	IREL	Santa Clara	Redwood Twp	88	124
HOSFORD								
Lizzie	21	f	w	NY	San Francisco	7-Wd San Francisco	81	243
HOSIA								
Antonia	29	f	w	GERM	San Francisco	8-Wd San Francisco	82	366
Joseph	26	m	m	WIND	San Francisco	8-Wd San Francisco	82	366
HOSIER								
Jacob	29	m	w	VA	Yuba	Marysville	93	600

Name	Age	S	R	B-PL	County	Locale	Series M593 Roll	Pg
HOSKEN								
Wm	20	m	w	ENGL	Yuba	Rose Bar Twp	93	661
HOSKENS								
Chas T	59	m	w	ENGL	Mariposa	Mariposa P O	74	126
Emanuel	32	m	w	ENGL	Yuba	Rose Bar Twp	93	657
HOSKIM								
Richard	43	m	w	ENGL	Plumas	Indian Twp	77	17
HOSKIN								
John	35	m	w	ENGL	San Mateo	Woodside P O	87	386
John	20	m	w	ENGL	Nevada	Grass Valley Twp	75	191
John H	35	m	w	ENGL	Placer	Gold Run Twp	76	397
John H	18	m	w	ENGL	Nevada	Grass Valley Twp	75	203
Joseph	44	m	w	ENGL	Nevada	Grass Valley Twp	75	191
Joseph	27	m	w	ENGL	Yuba	Rose Bar Twp	93	656
HOSKING								
James	27	m	w	ENGL	Nevada	Grass Valley Twp	75	230
James	26	m	w	ENGL	Nevada	Grass Valley Twp	75	187
John	39	m	w	ENGL	Santa Cruz	Santa Cruz Twp	89	399
John	19	m	w	ENGL	Nevada	Grass Valley Twp	75	230
Richard	41	m	w	ENGL	Butte	Wyandotte Twp	70	146
Thomas	36	m	w	ENGL	Nevada	Grass Valley Twp	75	176
William	36	m	w	ENGL	Nevada	Grass Valley Twp	75	170
HOSKINGS								
Jas	19	m	w	ENGL	Santa Clara	Almaden Twp	88	9
HOSKINS								
Edwd	45	m	w	PA	Alameda	Oakland	68	173
H	51	m	w	NY	Sacramento	3-Wd Sacramento	77	318
James	49	m	w	ENGL	San Francisco	2-Wd San Francisco	79	281
James	23	m	w	ENGL	Mariposa	Mariposa P O	74	111
John G	51	m	w	KY	Fresno	Millerton P O	72	148
M	50	m	w	VT	San Francisco	San Francisco P O	85	820
Richard	46	m	w	ENGL	Nevada	Nevada Twp	75	304
Richard	46	m	w	ENGL	Nevada	Nevada Twp	75	292
Samuel	41	m	w	NY	Calaveras	San Andreas P O	70	208
Solomon	25	m	w	ENGL	El Dorado	Mountain Twp	72	69
Thos	44	m	w	ENGL	Nevada	Nevada Twp	75	301
Walker	40	m	m	KY	Nevada	Grass Valley Twp	75	188
Wm	58	m	w	PA	Alameda	Oakland	68	183
Wm	29	m	w	IL	Merced	Snelling P O	74	269
Wm	15	m	w	CA	Nevada	Nevada Twp	75	292
HOSLER								
Jas W	50	m	w	PA	Butte	Chico Twp	70	49
HOSLET								
John	33	m	w	OH	Yolo	Cache Crk Twp	93	434
HOSLINGER								
V	34	m	w	GERM	Santa Clara	Gilroy Twp	88	69
HOSMAN								
John F	45	m	w	DENM	Yolo	Merritt Twp	93	507
HOSMER								
Anita	15	f	w	CA	Los Angeles	Los Angeles	73	538
Chas	52	m	w	NY	San Francisco	5-Wd San Francisco	81	29
Daniel M	37	m	w	ME	San Francisco	San Francisco P O	83	107
Horace	51	m	w	VT	San Francisco	11-Wd San Francisc	84	512
Rich N	34	m	w	NY	Santa Barbara	Santa Barbara P O	87	478
Robert	19	m	w	NY	Sacramento	2-Wd Sacramento	77	253
Stephen	44	m	w	MA	Santa Clara	Fremont Twp	88	65
Theodore	29	m	w	OH	San Francisco	San Francisco P O	83	202
Thomas	36	m	w	ME	San Francisco	11-Wd San Francisc	84	500
Thomas N	47	m	w	ME	Placer	Bath P O	76	446
Winslow	24	m	w	MA	Colusa	Stony Crk Twp	71	327
HOSS								
Ah	30	m	c	CHIN	Amador	Ione City P O	69	358
Ah	26	m	c	CHIN	Amador	Lancha Plana P O	69	369
Ah	15	m	c	CHIN	Monterey	Alisal Twp	74	297
Archibald B	43	m	w	TN	Fresno	Millerton P O	72	148
Ching	27	m	c	CHIN	San Luis Obispo	Salinas Twp	87	296
George	50	m	w	WURT	Shasta	Shasta P O	89	456
John	35	m	w	WURT	San Francisco	1-Wd San Francisco	79	42
See	39	m	c	CHIN	San Luis Obispo	Salinas Twp	87	296
Valentine	34	m	w	SHOL	San Francisco	San Francisco P O	83	21
William C	34	m	w	MO	Amador	Volcano P O	69	387
Yoa	34	m	c	CHIN	San Mateo	Schoolhouse Statio	87	337
HOSSACK								
Chas	25	m	w	DENM	Napa	Napa	75	18
David	43	m	w	SCOT	Santa Cruz	Santa Cruz Twp	89	395
HOSSELKUSS								
W	34	m	w	NY	Lassen	Susanville Twp	73	440
HOSSLER								
George	52	m	w	OH	Calaveras	San Andreas P O	70	186
HOSSMAN								
Henry	41	m	w	HANO	San Francisco	2-Wd San Francisco	79	177
HOSSTEN								
George	20	m	w	PRUS	San Francisco	San Francisco P O	80	477
HOST								
Geo	40	m	w	OH	Alameda	Murray Twp	68	128
Herman	33	m	w	PRUS	San Francisco	6-Wd San Francisco	81	96
William	36	m	w	BAVA	Mendocino	Big Rvr Twp	74	160
HOSTA								
Ellen	40	f	w	MEXI	San Francisco	2-Wd San Francisco	79	237
HOSTELL								
James	43	m	w	MD	San Francisco	2-Wd San Francisco	79	262
HOSTER								
L	38	m	w	CANA	Alameda	Alameda	68	3
HOSTES								
William	50	m	w	HANO	Mariposa	Mariposa P O	74	135
HOSTETER								
Mary	17	f	w	CA	Sutter	Butte Twp	92	102

© 2001 by Heritage Quest. All rights reserved.

Name	Age	S	R	B-PL	County	Locale	Series M593 Roll	Pg
S	26	f	w	OH	Alameda	Oakland	68	232
HOSTETLER								
Jacob	40	m	w	NC	Tulare	Tule Rvr Twp	92	264
HOSTETTER								
Augustus	35	m	w	OH	San Francisco	San Francisco P O	83	398
E	20	m	w	IA	Lassen	Milford Twp	73	438
F	39	m	w	MO	Lassen	Janesville Twp	73	431
George	13	m	w	CA	San Francisco	11-Wd San Francisc	84	647
J E	22	m	w	IA	Lassen	Janesville Twp	73	431
Joseph	35	m	w	MO	Santa Clara	San Jose Twp	88	212
Margaret	30	f	w	IL	Santa Clara	Gilroy Twp	88	100
Phebe	29	f	w	NY	San Francisco	8-Wd San Francisco	82	292
Willard D	30	m	w	NY	Tulare	Tule Rvr Twp	92	261
HOSTETTERS								
Frank	39	m	w	IN	Alameda	Brooklyn	68	35
HOSTICKER								
Jno	35	m	w	OH	Santa Clara	Gilroy Twp	88	107
HOSY								
Ah	26	m	c	CHIN	Sierra	Lincoln Twp	89	551
HOT								
Ah	33	m	c	CHIN	San Francisco	6-Wd San Francisco	81	58
Ah	27	m	c	CHIN	Nevada	Eureka Twp	75	140
Ah	18	m	c	CHIN	San Francisco	San Francisco P O	85	748
Lot	30	m	c	CHIN	Colusa	Monroe Twp	71	318
Pung	13	m	c	CHIN	San Francisco	8-Wd San Francisco	82	358
HOTALING								
Anson	42	m	w	NY	San Francisco	11-Wd San Francisc	84	511
Conrad	46	m	w	NY	Kern	Havilah P O	73	337
Conrad	45	m	w	NY	Nevada	Grass Valley Twp	75	158
HOTALLEY								
Thos J	55	m	w	NY	Tehama	Tehama Twp	92	192
HOTARB								
August	37	m	w	HANO	San Francisco	2-Wd San Francisco	79	224
HOTCH								
Jo	38	m	w	MO	San Joaquin	2-Wd Stockton	86	172
HOTCHESTER								
P	30	m	w	ENGL	Alameda	Oakland	68	264
HOTCHKISS								
Blanch	10	f	w	NY	Placer	Bath P O	76	455
Burr M	38	m	w	CT	Yolo	Cache Crk Twp	93	446
Chauncy L	44	m	w	VT	Placer	Lincoln P O	76	485
F S	46	m	w	CT	Sacramento	2-Wd Sacramento	77	208
Jayson Hall	34	m	w	CT	Plumas	Indian Twp	77	11
Robert	25	m	w	NY	San Francisco	11-Wd San Francisc	84	518
HOTE								
Augustus	32	m	w	SHOL	Sacramento	American Twp	77	64
Charles	34	m	w	AR	Placer	Roseville P O	76	349
HOTEL								
James S	11	m	w	CA	Sonoma	Analy Twp	91	228
Mariam D	20	f	w	WI	Sonoma	Petaluma Twp	91	329
HOTELL								
Lucinda	14	f	w	CA	Sonoma	Petaluma Twp	91	360
HOTH								
George	36	m	w	PRUS	Placer	Newcastle Twp	76	474
HOTHAM								
David	38	m	w	ME	Yuba	Rose Bar Twp	93	663
Wm	33	m	w	MI	Sierra	Eureka Twp	89	523
HOTHERSALL								
Elijah	41	m	w	ENGL	Nevada	Nevada Twp	75	296
HOTINGER								
D	25	m	w	PRUS	Alameda	Oakland	68	162
HOTMAN								
John	23	m	w	TN	Napa	Yountville Twp	75	79
HOTOATER								
Peter	40	m	w	FRAN	Nevada	Bloomfield Twp	75	94
HOTOP								
Charles	32	m	w	HANO	San Francisco	3-Wd San Francisco	79	297
HOTSANER								
Wm	26	m	w	PRUS	San Francisco	8-Wd San Francisco	82	351
HOTTE								
Wm	31	m	w	HCAS	San Francisco	11-Wd San Francisc	84	616
HOTTENEGER								
Rosalie	30	f	w	MEXI	San Francisco	6-Wd San Francisco	81	123
HOTTER								
Mattheas	31	m	w	PRUS	San Francisco	1-Wd San Francisco	79	86
HOTTGSCHEITER								
Fred	74	m	w	BADE	Mariposa	Mariposa P O	74	117
HOTTINGER								
Bernhard	30	m	w	BADE	Nevada	Little York Twp	75	234
HOTTMAN								
Thos	45	m	w	BAVA	Shasta	Horsetown P O	89	504
HOTTON								
James	24	m	w	CANA	San Francisco	7-Wd San Francisco	81	275
HOTZ								
Jno M	28	m	w	PA	Sacramento	3-Wd Sacramento	77	285
Katie	30	f	w	BAVA	San Francisco	11-Wd San Francisc	84	659
HOU								
Ah	18	m	c	CHIN	Nevada	Eureka Twp	75	141
HOUBER								
R J	39	m	w	ASEA	Sierra	Alleghany & Forest	89	535
HOUCADE								
Adolph	50	m	w	FRAN	San Francisco	San Francisco P O	80	350
HOUCHE								
Chas H	35	m	w	CT	San Francisco	7-Wd San Francisco	81	267
James P	32	m	w	CT	Plumas	Plumas Twp	77	28
HOUCHO								
Sam	37	m	w	PRUS	San Joaquin	Castoria Twp	86	15
HOUCK								
Anthony	29	m	w	OH	Napa	Napa Twp	75	32
Frederick	43	m	w	PRUS	Santa Clara	1-Wd San Jose	88	261
John A	37	m	w	VA	Calaveras	Copperopolis P O	70	246
Louis	29	m	w	VA	Calaveras	Copperopolis P O	70	247
HOUD								
A	19	m	w	WURT	Alameda	Oakland	68	148
HOUE								
Samuel I	34	m	w	OH	San Luis Obispo	Arroyo Grande Twp	87	271
HOUENDUM								
Chas	40	m	w	ENGL	Siskiyou	Callahan P O	89	633
HOUG								
Ah	30	m	c	CHIN	Amador	Volcano P O	69	378
Ah	30	m	c	CHIN	Placer	Emigrant Gap P O	76	416
Chas H	29	m	w	NY	Santa Cruz	Santa Cruz	89	419
Fut	28	m	c	CHIN	San Francisco	San Francisco P O	83	71
HOUGAN								
John	42	m	w	IREL	Monterey	Pajaro Twp	74	377
HOUGEIT								
John	37	m	w	FRAN	San Francisco	1-Wd San Francisco	79	131
HOUGH								
Ah	40	m	c	CHIN	Plumas	Goodwin Twp	77	3
Ah	29	m	c	CHIN	Plumas	Indian Twp	77	19
Assul	48	m	w	NY	Los Angeles	Los Angeles	73	536
Clark A	44	m	w	NY	Sonoma	Petaluma Twp	91	335
Edward	46	m	w	NY	Contra Costa	Martinez Twp	71	348
Fredk	22	m	w	NY	Fresno	Millerton P O	72	151
Howard M	32	m	w	ME	San Francisco	San Francisco P O	85	728
James	55	m	w	NY	Nevada	Grass Valley Twp	75	213
James F	42	m	w	NY	San Francisco	San Francisco P O	85	767
Jeremiah	34	m	w	IL	Plumas	Indian Twp	77	12
John	35	m	w	ME	Contra Costa	Martinez P O	71	398
Milo J	48	m	w	NY	Contra Costa	Martinez P O	71	378
Noah	41	m	w	PA	Placer	Bath P O	76	440
Oliver S	61	f	w	NY	San Mateo	Menlo Park P O	87	377
Orlando	32	m	w	NY	Contra Costa	Martinez P O	71	373
Rollin	38	m	w	NY	Plumas	Indian Twp	77	13
S R	43	m	w	MI	Tuolumne	Big Oak Flat P O	93	396
Sylvanus	62	m	w	VT	Contra Costa	Martinez P O	71	374
William	40	m	w	TN	Mendocino	Ukiah Twp	74	238
Wm B	51	m	w	ME	Humboldt	Eureka Twp	72	273
HOUGHAN								
Michiel	30	m	w	IREL	Sonoma	Vallejo Twp	91	459
HOUGHLEGGER								
Clara	20	f	w	PRUS	San Francisco	San Francisco P O	83	199
HOUGHMAN								
H D	35	m	w	ENGL	Alameda	Oakland	68	175
HOUGHSON								
H	42	m	w	US	San Joaquin	Castoria Twp	86	9
HOUGHTALING								
Abram	40	m	w	NY	San Francisco	1-Wd San Francisco	79	29
Edward	39	m	w	NY	Yuba	Slate Range Bar Tw	93	671
HOUGHTLAM								
D K	40	m	w	NY	San Francisco	1-Wd San Francisco	79	71
HOUGHTON								
A R	39	m	w	VT	Sacramento	3-Wd Sacramento	77	264
C B	47	m	w	MA	Solano	Benicia	90	2
Charles	46	m	w	CT	Stanislaus	Empire Twp	92	64
Charles	31	m	w	ME	San Francisco	11-Wd San Francisc	84	565
Edward	41	m	w	IREL	Amador	Volcano P O	69	386
F G	45	m	w	MA	Alameda	Oakland	68	171
Frank	32	m	w	MO	Tehama	Stony Crk	92	198
Geo	62	m	w	MA	Alameda	Brooklyn	68	29
George	18	m	w	CA	Napa	Yountville Twp	75	89
George Wm	42	m	w	CANA	Plumas	Mineral Twp	77	20
H A	27	m	w	IA	Santa Clara	Gilroy Twp	88	75
J F	40	m	w	MA	Sacramento	3-Wd Sacramento	77	305
J N	30	m	w	MI	Solano	Benicia	90	4
John	42	m	w	ME	Tuolumne	Chinese Camp P O	93	390
John	28	m	w	ENGL	Colusa	Stony Crk Twp	71	326
Joseph	39	m	w	ME	San Francisco	11-Wd San Francisc	84	559
Luther	58	m	w	MA	Klamath	Klamath Twp	73	371
Miles	38	m	w	ENGL	San Francisco	7-Wd San Francisco	81	196
R J	16	f	w	MO	San Joaquin	2-Wd Stockton	86	184
Robert	43	m	w	MI	Nevada	Rough & Ready Twp	75	332
Robert	43	m	w	PA	Nevada	Grass Valley Twp	75	217
Roscoe	30	m	w	ME	San Francisco	8-Wd San Francisco	82	404
Saml	44	m	w	VA	San Francisco	San Francisco P O	85	872
Sherman O	42	m	w	NY	Santa Clara	2-Wd San Jose	88	292
Thos	33	m	w	TX	Merced	Snelling P O	74	277
Warren	36	m	w	ME	San Francisco	San Francisco P O	85	763
William	35	m	w	ENGL	Sacramento	2-Wd Sacramento	77	235
William	20	m	w	NY	Solano	Maine Prairie Twp	90	54
HOUGLAND								
John A	32	m	w	OH	Placer	Emigrant Gap P O	76	416
HOUI								
Thos	35	m	w	OR	San Francisco	11-Wd San Francisc	84	694
HOUK								
Ah	23	m	c	CHIN	Marin	San Rafael Twp	74	37
Andrew	43	m	w	BADE	Placer	Bath P O	76	458
D	38	m	w	NC	Lassen	Janesville Twp	73	434
Martin L	32	m	w	KY	Monterey	Alisal Twp	74	299
HOUKINS								
Ann	40	f	w	NH	Merced	Snelling P O	74	266
HOULAHAN								
James	40	m	w	IREL	San Joaquin	1-Wd Stockton	86	131

© 2001 by Heritage Quest. All rights reserved.

California 1870 Census

Name	Age	S	R	B-PL	County	Locale	Series M593 Roll	Pg
HOULAND								
Ridge	13	m	w	CA	Santa Cruz	Pajaro Twp	89	360
Rufus	60	m	w	MA	San Francisco	11-Wd San Francisc	84	686
HOULD								
L G	49	m	w	CANA	San Francisco	San Francisco P O	85	776
HOULE								
Jas	29	m	w	CANA	Sierra	Sears Twp	89	557
HOULIHAN								
Sine	35	m	w	IREL	Solano	Benicia	90	11
HOULK								
Peter	28	m	w	BAVA	San Francisco	San Francisco P O	85	756
HOULSTON								
John	40	m	w	NORW	San Francisco	7-Wd San Francisco	81	216
HOULT								
J C	40	m	w	IA	San Joaquin	Douglas Twp	86	50
Margaret	32	f	w	CANA	San Francisco	2-Wd San Francisco	79	139
HOUNG								
Ah	22	m	c	CHIN	Placer	Auburn P O	76	363
HOUNIHAN								
Michael	30	m	w	IREL	Alameda	Washington Twp	68	290
HOUPTZ								
--- [Father]	30	m	w	PRUS	Del Norte	Crescent	71	463
HOUR								
Charles	47	m	w	NY	San Francisco	San Francisco P O	83	414
HOURANGA								
Manuel	50	m	w	SPAI	Marin	Bolinas Twp	74	2
HOURCK								
John	30	m	w	FRAN	Nevada	Grass Valley Twp	75	154
HOURS								
Horace	57	m	w	NY	San Mateo	Menlo Park P O	87	379
HOUS								
H N	36	m	w	IN	San Joaquin	2-Wd Stockton	86	182
HOUSE								
Alfred S	38	m	w	ENGL	Yolo	Cache Crk Twp	93	425
Andrew C	35	m	w	TN	Mariposa	Mariposa P O	74	97
Daniel H	29	m	w	ENGL	Mariposa	Mariposa P O	74	124
Dolores B	42	m	w	CHIL	San Mateo	San Mateo P O	87	354
Elish	41	m	w	IL	San Francisco	7-Wd San Francisco	81	275
Ezekiel	35	m	w	MO	Santa Clara	Gilroy Twp	88	103
Francis M	47	m	w	OH	Placer	Bath P O	76	428
Frank	25	m	w	MA	Nevada	Meadow Lake Twp	75	252
Frank R	22	m	w	CT	Placer	Rocklin Twp	76	463
George W	30	m	w	NY	Santa Cruz	Santa Cruz	89	426
Iza	70	f	w	IREL	San Francisco	2-Wd San Francisco	79	216
J	35	m	w	IL	Alameda	Murray Twp	68	110
J C	34	m	w	NY	Sierra	Gibson Twp	89	539
J T	31	m	w	MO	Santa Clara	Gilroy Twp	88	94
Jno	56	m	w	NY	Santa Clara	Almaden Twp	88	17
John C	38	m	w	NY	Butte	Bidwell Twp	70	3
Joseph	48	m	w	MO	Santa Clara	Gilroy Twp	88	103
Kitty	66	f	w	TN	Santa Clara	Gilroy Twp	88	94
William B	41	m	w	NY	El Dorado	Placerville	72	122
Wm H	34	m	w	CT	Tuolumne	Chinese Camp P O	93	375
HOUSEDON								
Annie	41	f	w	IREL	San Francisco	11-Wd San Francisc	84	447
HOUSELDT								
Conrad	37	m	w	SAME	Calaveras	Copperopolis P O	70	254
HOUSELL								
David	39	m	w	OH	Nevada	Nevada Twp	75	297
HOUSEMAN								
Andrw	21	m	w	LA	San Francisco	2-Wd San Francisco	79	245
Barnet	61	m	w	NY	El Dorado	Salmon Falls Twp	72	131
Fred	37	m	w	HANO	San Francisco	2-Wd San Francisco	79	181
Henry	36	m	w	HANO	Sacramento	2-Wd Sacramento	77	251
James	49	m	w	PA	San Francisco	7-Wd San Francisco	81	243
Jno	53	m	w	NY	San Joaquin	2-Wd Stockton	86	177
HOUSEN								
Nicholus	30	m	w	OH	San Mateo	Searsville P O	87	382
HOUSER								
A W	33	m	w	MO	Yuba	Linda Twp	93	555
Alfred	43	m	w	KY	Yuba	Linda Twp	93	557
Antone	54	m	w	PRUS	Amador	Volcano P O	69	376
Frank	34	m	w	BAVA	Santa Clara	Santa Clara Twp	88	155
Frank	31	m	w	FRAN	Santa Clara	Santa Clara Twp	88	149
Fred	26	m	w	PRUS	San Joaquin	1-Wd Stockton	86	135
George	44	m	w	OH	Butte	Wyandotte Twp	70	146
John	51	m	w	SWIT	Santa Clara	1-Wd San Jose	88	226
John	30	m	w	MO	Butte	Ophir Twp	70	120
Louis	32	m	w	PRUS	Placer	Auburn P O	76	369
Louis	27	m	w	HDAR	San Francisco	2-Wd San Francisco	79	181
R H	46	m	w	KY	Yuba	East Bear Rvr Twp	93	546
Reuben	38	m	w	PA	Sacramento	American Twp	77	67
Sarah	70	f	w	KY	Yuba	Linda Twp	93	557
Victor	27	m	w	POLA	San Francisco	San Francisco P O	83	301
HOUSEWORTH								
Benj	43	m	w	VA	Placer	Newcastle Twp	76	479
Thos	42	m	w	NY	San Francisco	San Francisco P O	85	727
HOUSH								
A W	28	m	w	IN	Sutter	Yuba Twp	92	147
Joseph	22	m	w	IL	Colusa	Spring Valley Twp	71	344
HOUSHARD								
Taylor	18	m	w	CA	Solano	Rio Vista Twp	90	61
HOUSHELD								
H	23	m	w	PRUS	Alameda	Oakland	68	164
HOUSHOLD								
James	39	m	w	OH	Yolo	Grafton Twp	93	484

Name	Age	S	R	B-PL	County	Locale	Series M593 Roll	Pg
HOUSING								
Otto	53	m	w	HDAR	San Francisco	San Francisco P O	83	26
HOUSINGER								
Aaron	45	m	w	NY	San Mateo	Pescadero P O	87	414
HOUSKIN								
Geo	32	m	w	NORW	San Joaquin	Elkhorn Twp	86	53
HOUSLEY								
Ed	42	m	w	ENGL	San Francisco	11-Wd San Francisc	84	657
George	29	m	w	ENGL	Sutter	Vernon Twp	92	130
J W	38	m	w	MA	Solano	Vallejo	90	142
John	40	m	w	MA	Solano	Vallejo	90	174
John	37	m	w	ENGL	Solano	Benicia	90	7
HOUSMAN								
George	40	m	w	GERM	Yolo	Cache Crk Twp	93	451
Joshua	45	m	w	WURT	Sacramento	4-Wd Sacramento	77	376
L	38	m	w	PA	Nevada	Nevada Twp	75	303
HOUSSEL								
Geo	35	m	w	PRUS	San Francisco	2-Wd San Francisco	79	218
HOUSSTON								
Charles	38	m	w	ENGL	Los Angeles	Los Angeles Twp	73	466
HOUSTED								
H	35	m	w	PRUS	Alameda	Murray Twp	68	102
HOUSTEN								
Erastus	42	m	w	IL	Calaveras	San Andreas P O	70	212
Jas	26	m	w	IREL	San Francisco	8-Wd San Francisco	82	309
Robert	56	m	w	PRUS	Monterey	Monterey	74	364
Robt	45	m	w	IREL	Solano	Vallejo	90	155
HOUSTER								
Fretz	37	m	w	NORW	Mendocino	Casper & Big Rvr	74	163
HOUSTIN								
John	36	m	w	IREL	Trinity	Weaverville Pct	92	223
John	34	m	w	SCOT	Placer	Auburn P O	76	382
Robt	37	m	w	OH	Contra Costa	Martinez P O	71	404
HOUSTING								
R T	63	m	b	SC	San Francisco	8-Wd San Francisco	82	357
HOUSTIS								
Solomon	27	m	w	IL	Santa Cruz	Soquel Twp	89	448
HOUSTON								
August	18	m	w	BADE	San Joaquin	Oneal Twp	86	104
Benjamin F	30	m	w	IL	Contra Costa	Martinez P O	71	389
C W	43	m	w	MA	El Dorado	Georgetown Twp	72	46
Charles	33	m	w	TN	Kern	Bakersfield P O	73	357
David	38	m	w	OH	Nevada	Grass Valley Twp	75	147
Edward	30	m	w	IREL	San Joaquin	Tulare Twp	86	256
Elie	35	m	w	OH	Alameda	Washington Twp	68	299
Emma	40	f	w	SCOT	San Francisco	11-Wd San Francisc	84	469
Ezra	19	m	w	IREL	San Diego	San Diego	78	494
Fredrick	33	m	w	PA	San Francisco	San Francisco P O	83	258
Geo W	45	m	w	ME	Santa Barbara	San Buenaventura P	87	441
George	41	m	w	ENGL	San Francisco	San Francisco P O	80	540
H	31	m	w	NY	San Joaquin	Dent Twp	86	17
Henry F	38	m	w	PRUS	San Francisco	1-Wd San Francisco	79	133
Henry F	36	m	w	NY	San Francisco	1-Wd San Francisco	79	19
Henry G	37	m	w	ENGL	San Francisco	1-Wd San Francisco	79	111
James	59	m	w	TN	Tulare	Venice Twp	92	278
James	46	m	w	SCOT	Placer	Auburn P O	76	380
James	21	m	w	NY	Nevada	Bloomfield Twp	75	96
Jane	44	f	w	IREL	San Francisco	1-Wd San Francisco	79	48
John	58	m	w	NY	San Francisco	3-Wd San Francisco	79	315
John	30	m	w	NY	San Francisco	San Francisco P O	80	381
John A	39	m	w	SCOT	San Diego	San Diego	78	494
Jos	23	m	w	MA	San Francisco	8-Wd San Francisco	82	365
Mary	58	f	w	VA	Tulare	Kings Rvr Twp	92	253
Ned	45	m	w	IREL	San Joaquin	Tulare Twp	86	252
Robert	42	m	w	AR	Los Angeles	El Monte Twp	73	450
Robert	41	m	w	SCOT	Nevada	Nevada Twp	75	306
Thos R	49	m	w	MA	San Francisco	7-Wd San Francisco	81	241
William	40	m	w	MO	Tulare	Kings Rvr Twp	92	253
William	34	m	w	MS	Los Angeles	Los Nietos Twp	73	579
William J	30	m	w	NY	Stanislaus	Empire Twp	92	63
Wm	44	m	w	MD	Shasta	Stillwater P O	89	479
Wm	30	m	w	NY	San Francisco	11-Wd San Francisc	84	687
HOUSTOR								
Robert	28	m	w	NY	Yolo	Grafton Twp	93	480
HOUT								
Frank	38	m	w	FRAN	Alameda	Washington Twp	68	300
HOUTALING								
Thos G	55	m	w	NY	Shasta	Shasta P O	89	463
HOUTNER								
Henry	35	m	w	GERM	San Francisco	8-Wd San Francisco	82	311
HOUTON								
J	36	m	w	SCOT	Alameda	Oakland	68	261
HOUTT								
D C	20	m	w	OH	Sutter	Sutter Twp	92	116
HOUX								
Benjamin	25	m	w	MO	Sonoma	Sonoma Twp	91	448
F A [Widow]	41	f	w	KY	Lake	Big Valley	73	397
Frederick W	38	m	w	MO	Yolo	Cache Crk Twp	93	445
John	63	m	w	KY	Mendocino	Sanel Twp	74	229
John M	46	m	w	MO	Sonoma	Analy Twp	91	224
Leonard	63	m	w	KY	Yolo	Grafton Twp	93	490
Mahala	39	f	w	MO	Mendocino	Sanel Twp	74	229
HOUY								
Jee	36	m	c	CHIN	San Joaquin	2-Wd Stockton	86	163
Up	25	m	c	CHIN	San Joaquin	1-Wd Stockton	86	146
HOVART								
Jno	41	m	w	ITAL	San Joaquin	3-Wd Stockton	86	231

© 2001 by Heritage Quest. All rights reserved.

Name	Age	S	R	B-PL	County	Locale	Roll	Pg
HOVEL								
Hiram M	40	m	w	VA	Yolo	Cache Crk Twp	93	440
HOVELAND								
Thomas	43	m	w	IREL	Placer	Rocklin Twp	76	467
HOVER								
David	39	m	w	PA	Tulare	Farmersville Twp	92	246
E	42	m	w	FRAN	Monterey	Alisal Twp	74	298
Israel	35	m	w	PA	San Joaquin	Elkhorn Twp	86	52
HOVERA								
Antone	41	m	w	CHIL	El Dorado	Greenwood Twp	72	54
HOVERHOUSE								
Thomas	24	m	w	IREL	Monterey	Castroville Twp	74	337
HOVERY								
W P	34	m	w	VT	Sierra	Downieville Twp	89	522
HOVET								
Albert A	38	m	w	HANO	Sacramento	2-Wd Sacramento	77	244
HOVEY								
Asa E	39	m	w	VT	San Francisco	San Francisco P O	83	75
David	17	m	w	NY	Sacramento	Sutter Twp	77	392
David M	17	m	w	CA	Santa Clara	Santa Clara Twp	88	177
Elizabeth	40	f	w	MO	Sacramento	4-Wd Sacramento	77	327
Geo A	22	m	w	CANA	San Francisco	1-Wd San Francisco	79	134
George	26	m	w	NY	San Francisco	San Francisco P O	83	243
James J	29	m	w	NH	Placer	Rocklin Twp	76	466
John	47	m	w	NY	Shasta	Dog Crk P O	89	471
John B	48	m	w	NY	Shasta	Stillwater P O	89	479
Michael	39	m	w	IREL	San Francisco	1-Wd San Francisco	79	17
Peletiah	42	m	w	AL	Tulare	Visalia	92	298
Perkins D	32	m	w	NH	Placer	Roseville P O	76	349
Richard	53	m	w	NH	Shasta	Stillwater P O	89	479
Su	25	m	c	CHIN	Nevada	Nevada Twp	75	311
W	42	m	w	NY	Sierra	Sears Twp	89	561
William A	49	m	w	VT	Siskiyou	Yreka	89	655
William T	29	m	w	ME	San Francisco	San Francisco P O	83	143
HOVIONS								
James H	33	m	w	KY	San Mateo	Half Moon Bay P O	87	403
Silas	65	m	w	KY	San Mateo	Half Moon Bay P O	87	403
HOW								
---	43	m	c	CHIN	San Francisco	11-Wd San Francisc	84	695
Ah	60	m	c	CHIN	Trinity	Weaverville Pct	92	228
Ah	60	m	c	CHIN	El Dorado	Mud Springs Twp	72	74
Ah	60	m	c	CHIN	Amador	Fiddletown P O	69	440
Ah	6	f	c	CHIN	San Francisco	6-Wd San Francisco	81	78
Ah	56	m	c	CHIN	Amador	Fiddletown P O	69	440
Ah	52	m	c	CHIN	El Dorado	Diamond Springs Tw	72	25
Ah	50	m	c	CHIN	San Joaquin	Oneal Twp	86	118
Ah	50	m	c	CHIN	Santa Barbara	Santa Barbara P O	87	499
Ah	50	m	c	CHIN	Trinity	North Fork Twp	92	221
Ah	50	f	c	CHIN	San Francisco	San Francisco P O	80	432
Ah	50	m	c	CHIN	San Francisco	San Francisco P O	80	443
Ah	48	m	c	CHIN	Butte	Hamilton Twp	70	73
Ah	47	m	c	CHIN	Shasta	French Gulch P O	89	465
Ah	46	m	c	CHIN	San Francisco	San Francisco P O	80	519
Ah	45	m	c	CHIN	San Joaquin	Oneal Twp	86	115
Ah	45	m	c	CHIN	Placer	Auburn P O	76	373
Ah	45	m	c	CHIN	Trinity	Junction City Pct	92	207
Ah	45	m	c	CHIN	Trinity	Indian Crk	92	199
Ah	44	m	c	CHIN	Butte	Ophir Twp	70	103
Ah	44	m	c	CHIN	San Francisco	San Francisco P O	80	515
Ah	41	m	c	CHIN	Shasta	Horsetown P O	89	507
Ah	40	m	c	CHIN	San Francisco	6-Wd San Francisco	81	66
Ah	40	m	c	CHIN	Placer	Auburn P O	76	375
Ah	40	m	c	CHIN	San Francisco	San Francisco P O	80	514
Ah	40	m	c	CHIN	San Francisco	San Francisco P O	80	512
Ah	40	m	c	CHIN	Trinity	North Fork Twp	92	217
Ah	40	m	c	CHIN	Alameda	Oakland	68	260
Ah	40	m	c	CHIN	Amador	Ione City P O	69	369
Ah	39	m	c	CHIN	San Francisco	San Francisco P O	80	450
Ah	38	m	c	CHIN	Mariposa	Mariposa P O	74	105
Ah	38	m	c	CHIN	Trinity	Lewiston Pct	92	214
Ah	37	m	c	CHIN	San Joaquin	2-Wd Stockton	86	212
Ah	37	m	c	CHIN	Butte	Concow Twp	70	11
Ah	36	m	c	CHIN	Nevada	Nevada Twp	75	314
Ah	36	m	c	CHIN	San Francisco	San Francisco P O	80	435
Ah	36	m	c	CHIN	San Francisco	San Francisco P O	80	466
Ah	36	m	c	CHIN	San Francisco	San Francisco P O	80	524
Ah	36	m	c	CHIN	San Francisco	San Francisco P O	80	515
Ah	35	m	c	CHIN	Calaveras	Copperopolis P O	70	252
Ah	35	m	c	CHIN	Alameda	Alameda	68	16
Ah	35	m	c	CHIN	Sonoma	Salt Point	91	380
Ah	34	m	c	CHIN	Plumas	Plumas Twp	77	33
Ah	34	m	c	CHIN	San Francisco	San Francisco P O	80	440
Ah	34	m	c	CHIN	San Francisco	San Francisco P O	80	514
Ah	34	m	c	CHIN	Amador	Ione City P O	69	370
Ah	34	m	c	CHIN	Yuba	Marysville	93	620
Ah	33	m	c	CHIN	San Joaquin	Castoria Twp	86	13
Ah	33	m	c	CHIN	San Francisco	6-Wd San Francisco	81	57
Ah	33	m	c	CHIN	Calaveras	Copperopolis P O	70	235
Ah	32	m	c	CHIN	San Francisco	San Francisco P O	80	520
Ah	32	m	c	CHIN	Fresno	Millerton P O	72	200
Ah	31	m	c	CHIN	Fresno	Millerton P O	72	199
Ah	31	m	c	CHIN	Calaveras	Copperopolis P O	70	233
Ah	31	m	c	CHIN	Yuba	Marysville	93	601
Ah	31	f	c	CHIN	Santa Clara	1-Wd San Jose	88	274
Ah	31	m	w	CHIN	Plumas	Indian Twp	77	19
Ah	30	m	c	CHIN	Stanislaus	Emory Twp	92	23
Ah	30	m	c	CHIN	Stanislaus	Washington Twp	92	85
Ah	30	m	c	CHIN	Placer	Colfax P O	76	387
Ah	30	f	c	CHIN	Nevada	Bridgeport Twp	75	110
Ah	30	m	c	CHIN	Nevada	Meadow Lake Twp	75	255
Ah	30	f	c	CHIN	San Francisco	San Francisco P O	80	432
Ah	30	f	c	CHIN	San Francisco	San Francisco P O	80	453
Ah	30	m	c	CHIN	Merced	Snelling P O	74	274
Ah	30	f	c	CHIN	Mariposa	Mariposa P O	74	126
Ah	30	m	c	CHIN	El Dorado	Diamond Springs Tw	72	23
Ah	30	m	c	CHIN	Calaveras	Copperopolis P O	70	258
Ah	30	m	c	CHIN	San Francisco	6-Wd San Francisco	81	103
Ah	30	m	c	CHIN	Trinity	Lewiston Pct	92	214
Ah	30	m	c	CHIN	Santa Clara	Fremont Twp	88	47
Ah	30	m	c	CHIN	Butte	Kimshew Tpw	70	85
Ah	29	m	c	CHIN	San Francisco	San Francisco P O	85	748
Ah	29	m	c	CHIN	Placer	Auburn P O	76	370
Ah	29	m	c	CHIN	Butte	Mountain Spring Tw	70	90
Ah	29	m	c	CHIN	Yuba	Marysville	93	619
Ah	28	m	c	CHIN	San Joaquin	1-Wd Stockton	86	148
Ah	28	m	c	CHIN	San Francisco	6-Wd San Francisco	81	65
Ah	28	m	c	CHIN	Nevada	Nevada Twp	75	313
Ah	28	m	c	CHIN	Plumas	Goodwin Twp	77	4
Ah	28	f	c	CHIN	San Francisco	6-Wd San Francisco	81	75
Ah	28	m	c	CHIN	San Francisco	San Francisco P O	80	530
Ah	28	m	c	CHIN	San Francisco	San Francisco P O	80	509
Ah	28	m	c	CHIN	San Francisco	San Francisco P O	80	512
Ah	28	m	c	CHIN	Merced	Snelling P O	74	257
Ah	28	m	c	CHIN	Amador	Ione City P O	69	351
Ah	27	m	c	CHIN	Nevada	Meadow Lake Twp	75	255
Ah	27	m	c	CHIN	San Francisco	San Francisco P O	80	450
Ah	27	m	c	CHIN	Butte	Bidwell Twp	70	1
Ah	27	m	c	CHIN	San Francisco	San Francisco P O	80	512
Ah	27	f	c	CHIN	Nevada	Eureka Twp	75	127
Ah	27	m	c	CHIN	Sacramento	Georgianna Twp	77	132
Ah	26	m	c	CHIN	Santa Barbara	Santa Barbara P O	87	484
Ah	26	m	c	CHIN	San Francisco	San Francisco P O	80	501
Ah	26	m	c	CHIN	Placer	Newcastle Twp	76	477
Ah	26	m	c	CHIN	San Francisco	San Francisco P O	80	529
Ah	26	m	c	CHIN	Sacramento	Granite Twp	77	138
Ah	26	m	c	CHIN	Alameda	Oakland	68	135
Ah	25	m	c	CHIN	Plumas	Mineral Twp	77	25
Ah	25	m	c	CHIN	Merced	Snelling P O	74	278
Ah	25	f	c	CHIN	Mariposa	Mariposa P O	74	127
Ah	25	m	c	CHIN	Nevada	Grass Valley Twp	75	214
Ah	25	m	c	CHIN	Klamath	Liberty Twp	73	375
Ah	25	m	c	CHIN	Yuba	Rose Bar Twp	93	660
Ah	24	m	c	CHIN	San Joaquin	Castoria Twp	86	15
Ah	24	m	c	CHIN	Santa Clara	San Jose Twp	88	194
Ah	24	m	c	CHIN	Santa Clara	San Jose Twp	88	189
Ah	24	m	c	CHIN	San Francisco	6-Wd San Francisco	81	61
Ah	24	m	c	CHIN	San Francisco	San Francisco P O	80	498
Ah	24	m	c	CHIN	Sacramento	2-Wd Sacramento	77	250
Ah	24	f	c	CHIN	Butte	Hamilton Twp	70	73
Ah	24	m	c	CHIN	San Francisco	San Francisco P O	80	513
Ah	24	m	c	CHIN	San Francisco	San Francisco P O	80	524
Ah	24	m	c	CHIN	Placer	Auburn P O	76	362
Ah	24	m	c	CHIN	Plumas	Washington Twp	77	53
Ah	24	m	c	CHIN	Amador	Ione City P O	69	367
Ah	24	m	c	CHIN	Yuba	Marysville	93	619
Ah	22	m	c	CHIN	San Francisco	San Francisco P O	85	748
Ah	22	m	c	CHIN	San Francisco	6-Wd San Francisco	81	75
Ah	22	m	c	CHIN	San Francisco	6-Wd San Francisco	81	62
Ah	22	f	c	CHIN	San Francisco	San Francisco P O	80	440
Ah	22	f	c	CHIN	San Francisco	San Francisco P O	80	447
Ah	22	f	c	CHIN	San Francisco	San Francisco P O	80	449
Ah	22	m	c	CHIN	Plumas	Goodwin Twp	77	3
Ah	21	m	c	CHIN	San Francisco	6-Wd San Francisco	81	84
Ah	21	f	c	CHIN	San Francisco	San Francisco P O	80	501
Ah	21	f	c	CHIN	San Francisco	San Francisco P O	80	440
Ah	21	f	c	CHIN	San Francisco	San Francisco P O	80	439
Ah	21	m	c	CHIN	Yuba	Marysville	93	590
Ah	21	m	c	CHIN	San Francisco	San Francisco P O	80	505
Ah	21	f	c	CHIN	San Francisco	San Francisco P O	80	529
Ah	21	m	c	CHIN	Contra Costa	Martinez P O	71	397
Ah	21	f	c	CHIN	Amador	Ione City P O	69	354
Ah	20	f	c	CHIN	San Francisco	6-Wd San Francisco	81	75
Ah	20	m	c	CHIN	San Francisco	6-Wd San Francisco	81	69
Ah	20	m	c	CHIN	Shasta	French Gulch P O	89	465
Ah	20	m	c	CHIN	Placer	Colfax P O	76	389
Ah	20	f	c	CHIN	Mariposa	Mariposa P O	74	113
Ah	20	m	c	CHIN	San Francisco	6-Wd San Francisco	81	131
Ah	20	m	c	CHIN	Sierra	Gibson Twp	89	538
Ah	20	m	c	CHIN	Santa Clara	Fremont Twp	88	47
Ah	20	f	c	CHIN	Nevada	Eureka Twp	75	136
Ah	20	m	c	CHIN	Nevada	Eureka Twp	75	136
Ah	20	m	c	CHIN	Plumas	Washington Twp	77	57
Ah	19	m	c	CHIN	San Francisco	6-Wd San Francisco	81	43
Ah	19	m	c	CHIN	San Francisco	6-Wd San Francisco	81	43
Ah	19	m	c	CHIN	Santa Cruz	Santa Cruz	89	405
Ah	19	m	c	CHIN	San Francisco	3-Wd San Francisco	79	309
Ah	19	f	c	CHIN	San Francisco	San Francisco P O	80	444
Ah	19	f	c	CHIN	San Francisco	6-Wd San Francisco	81	74
Ah	19	m	c	CHIN	Santa Clara	Santa Clara Twp	88	165
Ah	19	m	c	CHIN	Monterey	Monterey	74	354
Ah	19	f	c	CHIN	Amador	Ione City P O	69	354
Ah	18	m	c	CHIN	San Francisco	San Francisco P O	83	138
Ah	18	m	c	CHIN	San Francisco	6-Wd San Francisco	81	68
Ah	18	m	c	CHIN	Napa	Napa Twp	75	67

Series M593

© 2001 by Heritage Quest. All rights reserved.

California 1870 Census

Name	Age	S	R	B-PL	County	Locale	Roll	Pg
Ah	18	m	c	CHIN	Nevada	Nevada Twp	75	297
Ah	18	f	c	CHIN	Nevada	Meadow Lake Twp	75	254
Ah	18	m	c	CHIN	Mendocino	Gualala Twp	74	225
Ah	18	m	c	CHIN	San Francisco	6-Wd San Francisco	81	85
Ah	17	m	c	CHIN	San Francisco	1-Wd San Francisco	79	61
Ah	17	m	c	CHIN	Mendocino	Point Arena Twp	74	208
Ah	17	m	c	CHIN	Plumas	Goodwin Twp	77	2
Ah	16	m	c	CHIN	San Francisco	6-Wd San Francisco	81	68
Ah	16	m	c	CHIN	San Francisco	6-Wd San Francisco	81	46
Ah	16	m	c	CHIN	Sacramento	4-Wd Sacramento	77	336
Ah	16	m	c	CHIN	San Francisco	3-Wd San Francisco	79	317
Ah	16	m	c	CHIN	San Francisco	6-Wd San Francisco	81	49
Ah	16	m	c	CHIN	Plumas	Goodwin Twp	77	3
Ah	15	f	c	CHIN	Mariposa	Mariposa P O	74	114
Ah	14	m	c	CHIN	Plumas	Goodwin Twp	77	3
Bock	27	m	c	CHIN	Sierra	Lincoln Twp	89	546
Bridget	39	f	w	IREL	Amador	Sutter Crk P O	69	399
Chee	49	f	c	CHIN	Yuba	Marysville	93	627
Chin	35	m	c	CHIN	Alameda	Washington Twp	68	297
Choo	41	m	c	CHIN	Marin	Tomales Twp	74	77
Chop	26	m	c	CHIN	San Joaquin	3-Wd Stockton	86	230
Chung	19	m	c	CHIN	San Francisco	3-Wd San Francisco	79	306
Coon	37	m	c	CHIN	Yuba	Marysville	93	623
Dow	59	m	c	CHIN	Calaveras	Copperopolis P O	70	226
Fy	21	f	c	CHIN	Placer	Dutch Flat P O	76	410
Gee	42	m	c	CHIN	Plumas	Mineral Twp	77	23
Gee	35	m	c	CHIN	Butte	Chico Twp	70	53
Gee	30	f	c	CHIN	Yuba	Marysville	93	626
Gow	42	m	c	CHIN	Yuba	Marysville	93	625
Gue	37	f	c	CHIN	Yuba	Marysville	93	627
Ham	35	m	c	CHIN	Yuba	Marysville	93	629
Harriett A	40	f	m	NY	San Francisco	6-Wd San Francisco	81	100
Harry	20	m	w	US	Sacramento	1-Wd Sacramento	77	173
Hung	46	m	c	CHIN	Solano	Vallejo	90	208
Io	21	f	c	CHIN	Contra Costa	Martinez P O	71	398
Jime	11	m	c	CHIN	Contra Costa	Martinez Twp	71	350
John	31	m	w	NC	Mendocino	Anderson Twp	74	156
John C	46	m	w	NY	Trinity	Lewiston Pct	92	212
Kee	20	f	c	CHIN	Los Angeles	Los Angeles	73	564
Kim	28	f	c	CHIN	Yuba	Marysville	93	626
Kin Sim	16	m	c	CHIN	Amador	Ione City P O	69	367
King	23	m	c	CHIN	Sierra	Lincoln Twp	89	546
Kow	40	m	c	CHIN	San Francisco	11-Wd San Francisc	84	631
Koy	20	m	c	CHIN	San Francisco	6-Wd San Francisco	81	65
Lee	34	m	c	CHIN	Yuba	Marysville	93	629
Lee	29	m	c	CHIN	San Francisco	6-Wd San Francisco	81	56
Lee	29	m	c	CHIN	Alameda	Washington Twp	68	270
Limb	24	m	c	CHIN	Yuba	Marysville	93	630
Ling	48	m	c	CHIN	El Dorado	Salmon Falls Twp	72	133
Ling	27	m	c	CHIN	Yuba	Marysville	93	624
Linn	18	m	c	CHIN	San Francisco	San Francisco P O	83	261
Long	25	m	c	CHIN	Yuba	Marysville	93	632
Mathew	20	m	w	IREL	Klamath	Trinidad Twp	73	392
Mut	37	m	c	CHIN	Yuba	Marysville	93	625
O M	15	f	w	WI	Sierra	Forest Twp	89	530
Peep	28	m	c	CHIN	Nevada	Bridgeport Twp	75	111
Saml	45	m	w	NY	San Francisco	5-Wd San Francisco	81	23
Saml	24	m	c	CHIN	El Dorado	Cosumnes Twp	72	14
Sin	22	f	c	CHIN	Mariposa	Mariposa P O	74	102
Sin	17	f	c	CHIN	Solano	Vallejo	90	208
Sloon	34	m	c	CHIN	Trinity	Junction City Pct	92	206
Tie	46	f	c	CHIN	Placer	Auburn P O	76	374
Timothy	42	m	w	IREL	Amador	Sutter Crk P O	69	399
Tin	40	m	c	CHIN	Nevada	Nevada Twp	75	313
Ting	52	m	c	CHIN	Trinity	Trinity Center Pct	92	240
Top	40	m	c	CHIN	San Francisco	11-Wd San Francisc	84	661
Wa	16	m	c	CHIN	Solano	Vallejo	90	212
William	61	m	w	ENGL	Contra Costa	Martinez P O	71	443
Wing	47	m	c	CHIN	Mariposa	Mariposa P O	74	125
Wm	41	m	w	IREL	San Francisco	San Francisco P O	85	852
Won	42	m	c	CHIN	Yuba	Marysville	93	623
Ye	28	m	c	CHIN	Yuba	East Bear Rvr Twp	93	546
Ye	20	f	c	CHIN	Yuba	Marysville	93	601
Yee	22	f	c	CHIN	Yuba	Marysville	93	627
Yet	26	m	c	CHIN	Yuba	Marysville	93	628
Young	19	m	c	CHIN	Yuba	Marysville	93	628
HOWALLEN								
James	40	m	w	MEXI	Fresno	Kings Rvr P O	72	213
HOWARD								
A	27	m	w	RI	San Joaquin	2-Wd Stockton	86	193
Abraham	24	m	w	OH	Calaveras	San Andreas P O	70	219
Abram	43	m	b	MO	Yolo	Cottonwood Twp	93	460
Ada	19	f	w	CA	San Joaquin	Douglas Twp	86	32
Adison	38	m	w	TN	Yolo	Washington Twp	93	537
Alba	24	m	w	ME	Mendocino	Round Valley Twp	74	217
Albert	30	m	w	MA	San Francisco	5-Wd San Francisco	81	7
Albert	19	m	w	OH	El Dorado	Lake Valley Twp	72	64
Allen	31	m	w	MO	Solano	Vacaville Twp	90	135
Allen	24	m	w	TN	Solano	Vacaville Twp	90	137
Allen F	30	m	w	IL	Napa	Napa	75	11
Amos	37	m	w	ME	Nevada	Grass Valley Twp	75	153
Andrew	62	m	w	IREL	Marin	San Rafael	74	54
Andrew	36	m	w	NY	San Francisco	San Francisco P O	80	474
Ann	35	f	w	IREL	Santa Clara	2-Wd San Jose	88	294
Ann	32	f	w	IREL	Santa Clara	2-Wd San Jose	88	332
Asa	54	m	w	MA	Siskiyou	Scott Valley Twp	89	619
Austin	21	m	w	VT	San Joaquin	1-Wd Stockton	86	130
Azbury A	46	m	w	KY	El Dorado	White Oak Twp	72	140
B	45	m	w	MO	Lake	Upper Lake	73	413
B F	49	m	w	MA	Sacramento	Franklin Twp	77	114
Benj	30	f	w	PA	San Francisco	7-Wd San Francisco	81	283
Benj F	31	m	w	MO	Sonoma	Analy Twp	91	247
Benjamin C	57	m	w	GA	Colusa	Colusa	71	297
Bertha	43	f	w	NY	San Francisco	8-Wd San Francisco	82	385
Briant	35	m	w	NY	San Diego	San Diego	78	489
Burrell	38	m	b	KY	Siskiyou	Yreka	89	651
C	34	m	w	NY	Lake	Morgan Valley	73	425
C B	53	m	w	MD	Merced	Snelling P O	74	261
C G	44	m	w	ENGL	Alameda	Oakland	68	177
C W	39	m	w	VT	Alameda	Oakland	68	161
Calvin	33	m	w	TN	Solano	Vacaville Twp	90	137
Calvin	29	m	w	MO	Solano	Vacaville Twp	90	135
Calvin P	35	m	w	VT	Santa Clara	1-Wd San Jose	88	275
Caroline	34	f	w	PA	Yolo	Cache Crk Twp	93	438
Carrie	33	f	w	IL	San Francisco	San Francisco P O	83	288
Celina	23	f	w	MA	San Francisco	San Francisco P O	80	540
Charles	34	m	w	PA	Santa Clara	2-Wd San Jose	88	322
Charles	33	m	w	NY	Contra Costa	Martinez P O	71	367
Charles	32	m	w	NY	Mariposa	Mariposa P O	74	134
Charles	30	m	w	ME	Marin	Bolinas Twp	74	2
Charles	18	m	w	IL	Sacramento	Alabama Twp	77	59
Charles E	40	m	w	MA	Contra Costa	Martinez P O	71	382
Chas	34	m	w	NY	San Francisco	1-Wd San Francisco	79	56
Chas	25	m	w	IN	San Joaquin	Liberty Twp	86	92
Chas W	29	m	w	ENGL	Solano	Rio Vista Twp	90	60
Clark	25	m	w	MO	Yuba	Marysville Twp	93	569
D	39	m	w	MA	San Joaquin	Elliott Twp	86	77
Dan	54	m	w	MA	Placer	Gold Run Twp	76	397
David	43	m	w	NY	Tehama	Bell Mills Twp	92	159
E B	46	m	w	NY	Sacramento	Natomas Twp	77	169
E H	53	m	w	NY	Humboldt	Bucksport Twp	72	244
E J	42	m	w	MO	Sutter	Butte Twp	92	100
E M	40	m	w	IL	Mendocino	Ukiah Twp	74	239
Edward R	45	m	w	MO	Yolo	Cottonwood Twp	93	460
Edwd	40	m	w	MA	Butte	Hamilton Twp	70	63
Eli	45	m	w	NY	Alameda	Oakland	68	218
Elias B	56	m	w	NY	Siskiyou	Yreka Twp	89	668
Elisha	50	m	w	CT	Sacramento	Center Twp	77	85
Elizabeth	13	f	w	CA	Alameda	Oakland	68	149
Ella	10	f	w	MA	San Francisco	7-Wd San Francisco	81	247
Ellen	62	f	w	IREL	Marin	San Rafael	74	52
Emma	30	f	w	ENGL	San Francisco	San Francisco P O	80	462
Etty W	25	f	w	ME	San Francisco	6-Wd San Francisco	81	104
F A	37	m	w	MA	Amador	Amador City P O	69	395
Fannie	36	f	w	IREL	San Francisco	8-Wd San Francisco	82	411
Fimas	44	m	w	US	San Mateo	Schoolhouse Statio	87	338
Frances	28	f	w	IREL	San Francisco	8-Wd San Francisco	82	450
Francis	34	m	w	NY	Colusa	Spring Valley Twp	71	340
Francis M	24	m	w	MO	Santa Cruz	Soquel Twp	89	447
Frank	40	m	w	NY	Santa Cruz	Santa Cruz Twp	89	390
Frank	30	m	w	ME	Solano	Rio Vista Twp	90	62
Frank C	35	m	w	KY	Butte	Hamilton Twp	70	65
G	30	m	w	NY	Alameda	Oakland	68	262
G M	36	m	w	NY	Amador	Jackson P O	69	342
G T	42	m	w	ENGL	Alameda	Murray Twp	68	116
G W	29	m	w	IN	Lassen	Janesville Twp	73	434
Garrett	28	m	w	IREL	San Francisco	1-Wd San Francisco	79	94
Geo	47	m	w	PA	San Joaquin	Elkhorn Twp	86	54
Geo	32	m	w	CANA	Sonoma	Mendocino Twp	91	287
Geo	29	m	w	ENGL	San Francisco	San Francisco P O	83	83
Geo M	40	m	w	US	Nevada	Rough & Ready Twp	75	336
Geo M	39	m	w	NY	Nevada	Rough & Ready Twp	75	323
George	34	m	w	MA	San Francisco	7-Wd San Francisco	81	262
George H	43	m	w	MA	San Mateo	San Mateo P O	87	359
Gilliam	45	m	w	CANA	Colusa	Butte Twp	71	272
H	31	m	w	NY	Alameda	Oakland	68	262
H A	61	m	w	MA	Tuolumne	Chinese Camp P O	93	366
Harry	32	m	w	ENGL	Sacramento	4-Wd Sacramento	77	326
Harry	25	m	w	ENGL	Sacramento	1-Wd Sacramento	77	178
Harry	22	m	w	NY	San Francisco	1-Wd San Francisco	79	127
Harry	19	m	w	NY	Sacramento	San Joaquin Twp	77	399
Harry	10	m	w	CA	Marin	San Rafael Twp	74	29
Henry	40	m	w	NY	Fresno	Kings Rvr P O	72	214
Henry	31	m	w	ENGL	Sacramento	1-Wd Sacramento	77	179
Henry C	48	m	w	MI	San Francisco	6-Wd San Francisco	81	79
Henry G	34	m	w	NY	Yuba	Parks Bar Twp	93	649
Henry O	33	m	w	MA	San Francisco	3-Wd San Francisco	79	323
Hiram	20	m	w	SCOT	Inyo	Cerro Gordo Twp	73	318
Hobert E	43	m	w	WI	Fresno	Kings Rvr P O	72	214
Hollis	31	m	w	OH	Monterey	Alisal Twp	74	293
Homer	23	m	w	IA	Alameda	Eden Twp	68	70
Horace Z	35	m	w	CT	San Francisco	San Francisco P O	83	60
Irving	44	m	w	ENGL	San Francisco	San Francisco P O	85	803
Isaac	36	m	w	GA	Tuolumne	Sonora P O	93	314
J	35	m	w	NY	Calaveras	Copperopolis P O	70	236
J	29	m	w	MI	Sierra	Butte Twp	89	508
J B	33	m	w	MO	Humboldt	Bald Hills	72	237
J J	42	m	w	VA	Tehama	Red Bluff	92	182
J M	37	m	w	IL	Mendocino	Calpella Twp	74	184
James	79	m	w	IREL	Butte	Oroville Twp	70	138
James	57	m	w	NY	San Francisco	San Francisco P O	80	462
James	55	m	w	TN	Solano	Vacaville Twp	90	135
James	49	m	w	NY	San Joaquin	Elliott Twp	86	70
James	38	m	w	MA	Sacramento	Lee Twp	77	158

Series M593

© 2001 by Heritage Quest. All rights reserved.

Series M593

Name	Age	S	R	B-PL	County	Locale	Roll	Pg
James	35	m	w	IREL	Santa Clara	2-Wd San Jose	88	332
James	27	m	w	DE	Nevada	Eureka Twp	75	139
James	27	m	w	IL	Napa	Napa	75	21
James	25	m	w	IREL	San Francisco	6-Wd San Francisco	81	109
James	23	m	w	PA	Sonoma	Salt Point	91	390
James	20	m	w	ENGL	San Francisco	1-Wd San Francisco	79	91
James G	40	m	w	NY	Los Angeles	Los Angeles	73	531
James L	43	m	w	NY	Colusa	Spring Valley Twp	71	345
Jane	40	f	w	IREL	Santa Clara	Almaden Twp	88	14
Jas	36	m	w	ME	Solano	Vallejo	90	211
Jas E	30	m	w	WI	Fresno	Millerton P O	72	187
Jas L	32	m	w	TN	Tehama	Cottonwood Twp	92	161
Jefferson	50	m	w	MO	Santa Clara	San Jose Twp	88	222
Jeremiah	46	m	w	NC	Stanislaus	Empire Twp	92	49
Jeremiah	26	m	w	CANA	San Francisco	1-Wd San Francisco	79	86
Jerry	39	m	w	NY	Amador	Sutter Crk P O	69	397
Jessie	13	m	w	CA	Monterey	Alisal Twp	74	298
Jno	13	m	w	IA	Sacramento	3-Wd Sacramento	77	257
Johana	47	f	w	IREL	San Francisco	San Francisco P O	80	482
John	44	m	w	AL	Contra Costa	Martinez P O	71	400
John	40	m	w	IREL	San Francisco	1-Wd San Francisco	79	80
John	37	m	w	IREL	San Francisco	11-Wd San Francisc	84	649
John	35	m	w	IREL	San Francisco	5-Wd San Francisco	81	20
John	35	m	w	ENGL	Alameda	Oakland	68	180
John	35	m	w	MO	Stanislaus	North Twp	92	67
John	33	m	w	NY	San Francisco	11-Wd San Francisc	84	432
John	30	m	w	IREL	Kern	Bakersfield P O	73	357
John	29	m	w	IREL	Alameda	Washington Twp	68	300
John	26	m	w	NY	San Francisco	1-Wd San Francisco	79	93
John Charles	24	m	w	IL	Plumas	Indian Twp	77	19
John F	41	m	w	VT	Sonoma	Petaluma Twp	91	336
John W	26	m	w	MI	Calaveras	Copperopolis P O	70	223
Jos S	47	m	w	NY	Sonoma	Cloverdale Twp	91	271
Joseph	43	m	w	IREL	Plumas	Quartz Twp	77	39
Joseph	40	m	w	PA	Siskiyou	Surprise Valley Tw	89	637
Joseph	35	m	w	HAMB	Colusa	Grand Island Twp	71	304
Joseph	27	m	w	MA	Solano	Vacaville Twp	90	129
Joseph F	40	m	w	IL	Calaveras	San Andreas P O	70	160
Julia	13	f	w	CA	Plumas	Indian Twp	77	14
L	44	m	w	NY	San Joaquin	3-Wd Stockton	86	230
L	40	m	w	MA	Alameda	Oakland	68	259
L	28	m	w	VT	Alameda	Oakland	68	247
L	28	m	w	ME	Alameda	Oakland	68	212
L	26	m	w	MI	San Joaquin	2-Wd Stockton	86	193
L D	47	m	w	NY	Amador	Sutter Crk P O	69	396
Larry	40	m	w	IREL	Santa Barbara	San Buenaventura P	87	427
Larry	40	m	w	NJ	San Francisco	5-Wd San Francisco	81	13
Lizzie	32	f	w	IREL	San Francisco	San Francisco P O	80	457
Louis	30	m	w	NH	Inyo	Bishop Crk Twp	73	313
Loyd	61	m	m	MD	El Dorado	Placerville	72	110
Lucas R	34	m	w	OH	Colusa	Colusa	71	296
M	37	m	w	ENGL	San Francisco	8-Wd San Francisco	82	375
M	26	m	w	IL	San Joaquin	Dent Twp	86	28
M B	22	m	w	MA	San Francisco	San Francisco P O	85	829
M V	28	m	w	TN	Tehama	Cottonwood Twp	92	161
M W	52	m	w	NC	Mendocino	Ukiah Twp	74	243
Maggie	22	f	w	NY	San Francisco	8-Wd San Francisco	82	328
Mark	25	m	w	IL	Sacramento	Dry Crk Twp	77	102
Mark	25	m	w	IL	El Dorado	Lake Valley Twp	72	65
Martha	12	f	w	CA	Santa Clara	1-Wd San Jose	88	266
Mary	47	f	w	IREL	San Francisco	6-Wd San Francisco	81	148
Mary	47	f	w	ENGL	San Francisco	8-Wd San Francisco	82	301
Mary	45	f	w	IREL	San Mateo	Schoolhouse Statio	87	333
Mary	30	f	w	CT	San Francisco	8-Wd San Francisco	82	425
Mary	27	f	w	ENGL	San Joaquin	2-Wd Stockton	86	169
Mary H	72	f	w	KY	Tehama	Cottonwood Twp	92	161
Matthew	39	m	w	ENGL	El Dorado	White Oak Twp	72	138
Matthew	32	m	w	IREL	Santa Clara	2-Wd San Jose	88	332
Mattie	29	f	w	IN	San Francisco	8-Wd San Francisco	82	384
Michael	48	m	b	SC	San Francisco	San Francisco P O	80	383
Nathan	18	m	m	MI	San Francisco	1-Wd San Francisco	79	132
Nathaniel S	51	m	w	MA	Contra Costa	Martinez P O	71	382
Nicholas	45	m	b	VA	Sacramento	2-Wd Sacramento	77	234
O H	32	m	w	OH	Nevada	Eureka Twp	75	132
Pat	35	m	w	IREL	Sacramento	1-Wd Sacramento	77	204
Patrick	32	m	w	IREL	Solano	Maine Prairie Twp	90	53
Patrick	28	m	w	IREL	Solano	Maine Prairie Twp	90	47
Patrick	25	m	w	IREL	Santa Clara	2-Wd San Jose	88	332
Paul	56	m	w	FRAN	Inyo	Bishop Crk Twp	73	317
Paul	27	m	w	FRAN	Inyo	Bishop Crk Twp	73	310
Peter	54	m	w	FRAN	Los Angeles	Los Angeles	73	551
Peter	33	m	w	NY	Plumas	Plumas Twp	77	33
R W	38	m	w	NY	Napa	Yountville Twp	75	87
Richard	45	m	w	CT	Sonoma	Analy Twp	91	225
Richard	30	m	w	ENGL	San Francisco	2-Wd San Francisco	79	138
Robert	51	m	w	ENGL	Sacramento	Dry Crk Twp	77	100
Robert	39	m	w	MA	San Joaquin	3-Wd Stockton	86	221
Robt	38	m	w	SCOT	San Joaquin	2-Wd Stockton	86	163
Rose	23	f	w	VA	San Francisco	6-Wd San Francisco	81	95
S C	35	m	w	PA	Del Norte	Happy Camp Twp	71	471
Sam	42	m	w	NY	San Joaquin	Liberty Twp	86	91
Samuel	42	m	w	IREL	Inyo	Cerro Gordo Twp	73	319
Shadrack	53	m	b	MA	San Francisco	3-Wd San Francisco	79	310
Silas L	30	m	w	KY	Colusa	Colusa	71	288
Sophia M	47	f	w	VT	Nevada	Little York Twp	75	241
Stephen	38	m	w	MO	Yolo	Buckeye Twp	93	416
T B	30	m	w	NY	San Francisco	San Francisco P O	83	110

Series M593

Name	Age	S	R	B-PL	County	Locale	Roll	Pg
T J	38	m	w	OH	Mendocino	Round Valley Twp	74	216
Terry	34	m	w	KY	Plumas	Indian Twp	77	12
Tho	37	m	w	KY	El Dorado	Greenwood Twp	72	50
Thomas	21	m	w	ENGL	Santa Clara	2-Wd San Jose	88	317
Thos	45	m	w	PA	San Francisco	San Francisco P O	83	55
Thos	40	m	w	ENGL	Yuba	Marysville	93	594
Thos	38	m	w	RI	San Francisco	1-Wd San Francisco	79	70
Thos	23	m	w	IREL	San Francisco	8-Wd San Francisco	82	311
Timothy	31	m	w	IREL	Alameda	Washington Twp	68	295
Volney	30	m	w	MA	Santa Clara	Gilroy Twp	88	80
Volney E	60	m	w	ME	Los Angeles	San Gabriel Twp	73	598
W	36	m	w	NY	Alameda	Oakland	68	264
W F	51	m	w	NH	Tehama	Red Bluff	92	179
W H	46	m	w	TN	Tehama	Cottonwood Twp	92	161
W H	38	m	w	SC	Marin	San Rafael Twp	74	38
Wash	24	m	w	IA	Yolo	Putah Twp	93	521
Willes L	35	m	w	NY	Butte	Oregon Twp	70	122
William	46	m	w	DENM	Sonoma	Bodega Twp	91	259
William	45	m	w	MA	Los Angeles	Santa Ana Twp	73	600
William	42	m	w	VA	Stanislaus	Buena Vista Twp	92	12
William	40	m	w	CANA	Nevada	Eureka Twp	75	129
William	39	m	w	IN	Yolo	Cache Crk Twp	93	454
William	37	m	w	OH	Nevada	Eureka Twp	75	138
William	35	m	w	IREL	Santa Clara	1-Wd San Jose	88	225
William	30	m	w	IREL	San Bernardino	Belleville Twp	78	408
William G	38	m	w	MA	San Francisco	San Francisco P O	83	369
William L	38	m	w	IN	Yolo	Cache Crk Twp	93	454
Wm	45	m	w	IREL	Butte	Wyandotte Twp	70	141
Wm	38	m	w	CANA	San Francisco	2-Wd San Francisco	79	270
Wm	37	m	w	MO	Tuolumne	Sonora P O	93	308
Wm	28	m	w	AR	Mendocino	Little Lake Twp	74	201
Wm A	36	m	w	NY	Santa Cruz	Soquel Twp	89	448
Wshington	23	m	w	IL	Yolo	Cache Crk Twp	93	448
Zader	16	f	w	MA	Humboldt	Eureka Twp	72	271
HOWARDS								
Chatherine	32	f	w	IREL	Santa Clara	1-Wd San Jose	88	278
HOWARDSON								
Lee	23	m	w	MA	Sacramento	1-Wd Sacramento	77	182
HOWATH								
William	29	m	w	MA	San Francisco	11-Wd San Francisc	84	555
HOWATT								
Georgiana	26	f	w	NY	San Francisco	8-Wd San Francisco	82	449
HOWD								
W L	38	m	w	NY	Solano	Vallejo	90	210
HOWE								
A J	52	m	w	NY	Sierra	Table Rock Twp	89	573
Ah	22	m	c	CHIN	San Francisco	7-Wd San Francisco	81	227
Alphonso	36	m	w	VT	El Dorado	Mud Springs Twp	72	84
Andrew J	31	m	w	OH	San Francisco	11-Wd San Francisc	84	698
Annie	29	f	w	IREL	San Francisco	San Francisco P O	80	460
Anthony	40	m	w	NY	Napa	Napa	75	8
Arrilla C	49	f	w	MA	Sacramento	4-Wd Sacramento	77	324
B	36	m	w	MA	Alameda	Alameda	68	14
B F	29	m	w	MA	Solano	Vallejo	90	208
C S	30	m	w	MA	San Joaquin	2-Wd Stockton	86	174
Catherine	49	f	w	OH	Santa Clara	Fremont Twp	88	65
Chas	65	m	w	CT	San Francisco	5-Wd San Francisco	81	13
Chas	44	m	w	MA	Monterey	Salinas Twp	74	306
Clara	40	f	w	ENGL	San Francisco	2-Wd San Francisco	79	254
David	19	m	w	IL	Butte	Chico Twp	70	34
Delos J	30	m	w	NY	San Francisco	San Francisco P O	83	46
E A	37	m	w	NY	Sonoma	Santa Rosa	91	414
E R	25	m	w	NY	San Francisco	5-Wd San Francisco	81	36
Edgar	36	m	w	IL	San Francisco	San Francisco P O	85	871
Edward A	53	m	w	ENGL	Calaveras	San Andreas P O	70	162
Edwd	27	m	w	CT	Solano	Vallejo	90	201
Elizabeth	40	f	w	PA	Napa	Napa	75	45
Elizabeth Mrs	57	f	w	VA	San Diego	San Diego	78	501
Ella	13	f	w	CA	Yuba	Marysville	93	609
Ellen	48	f	b	MD	Napa	Napa Twp	75	75
Ellen	48	f	b	MD	Napa	Napa	75	27
Emma	33	f	w	NY	San Francisco	6-Wd San Francisco	81	71
Fenelon W	41	m	w	MA	Placer	Rocklin Twp	76	468
Frank	16	m	w	CA	Marin	San Antonio Twp	74	63
George	35	m	w	NY	San Francisco	2-Wd San Francisco	79	152
George	22	m	w	ME	San Francisco	8-Wd San Francisco	82	399
George S	31	m	w	MI	Nevada	Grass Valley Twp	75	156
George W	36	m	w	NY	San Francisco	San Francisco P O	85	722
Gottleib	49	m	w	HDAR	Shasta	Horsetown P O	89	503
Hannah	47	f	w	NY	Alpine	Monitor P O	69	313
Henry	50	m	w	ME	Santa Clara	San Jose Twp	88	199
Henry	17	m	w	CA	Marin	Novato Twp	74	12
Henry W	50	m	w	ME	San Mateo	Woodside P O	87	384
Ira	43	m	w	NY	Santa Cruz	Santa Cruz	89	419
J B	40	m	w	IN	Del Norte	Mountain Twp	71	474
J W M	51	m	w	OH	Lassen	Susanville Twp	73	441
James	40	m	w	NY	Shasta	Horsetown P O	89	505
James	33	m	w	OH	San Francisco	7-Wd San Francisco	81	276
James	20	m	w	IREL	San Joaquin	2-Wd Stockton	86	162
James	15	m	w	CA	Contra Costa	Martinez Twp	71	349
James S	49	m	w	ME	Santa Cruz	Santa Cruz Twp	89	389
Joannah	31	f	w	BAVA	San Francisco	6-Wd San Francisco	81	72
Joel	46	m	w	VT	Nevada	Nevada Twp	75	306
John	44	m	w	ENGL	Colusa	Monroe Twp	71	314
John	33	m	w	IREL	San Francisco	11-Wd San Francisc	84	494
John	29	m	w	IL	Napa	Napa Twp	75	63
John F	40	m	w	OH	Sacramento	Granite Twp	77	142

© 2001 by Heritage Quest. All rights reserved.

Name	Age	S	R	B-PL	County	Locale	Series M593 Roll	Pg
John M	68	m	w	VT	Alameda	Eden Twp	68	91
Jos H	46	m	w	NY	San Francisco	8-Wd San Francisco	82	346
Joseph	38	m	w	ENGL	Tulare	Visalia Twp	92	281
Joseph H	6	m	w	CA	San Luis Obispo	Morro Twp	87	283
Laura	13	f	w	WI	Alameda	Murray Twp	68	128
Leland	43	m	w	VT	Sacramento	4-Wd Sacramento	77	340
Louise	13	f	w	CA	Contra Costa	Martinez P O	71	407
Lucilia	36	f	w	OH	Sacramento	Granite Twp	77	142
Lucy	25	f	w	MS	San Francisco	8-Wd San Francisco	82	388
M	42	m	w	NH	Alameda	Oakland	68	239
M M	41	m	w	NY	Alameda	Oakland	68	185
Mary	40	f	w	IREL	Sacramento	4-Wd Sacramento	77	331
Mary	38	f	w	CA	Marin	San Antonio Twp	74	64
Mary W	14	f	w	CA	Santa Cruz	Santa Cruz	89	406
Maurice	40	m	w	NH	San Francisco	San Francisco P O	83	245
Michael	42	m	w	IREL	Sonoma	Salt Point	91	384
Norman A W	49	m	w	CT	Santa Clara	Santa Clara Twp	88	145
Philip	51	m	w	NH	Solano	Silveyville Twp	90	87
Philip	51	m	w	NH	Solano	Suisun Twp	90	112
Robert	38	m	w	NY	San Francisco	11-Wd San Francisc	84	607
Robert	26	m	w	SCOT	Sonoma	Salt Point	91	385
Robt	25	m	w	IREL	San Francisco	San Francisco P O	83	53
Samuel	50	m	w	NH	Tulare	White Rvr Twp	92	301
Susan	39	f	w	FRAN	San Francisco	8-Wd San Francisco	82	295
Thaddeus C	37	m	w	NY	Shasta	American Ranch P O	89	498
Thomas	40	m	w	IREL	San Francisco	2-Wd San Francisco	79	170
William	59	m	w	MA	San Francisco	8-Wd San Francisco	82	329
William	38	m	w	FRAN	Plumas	Goodwin Twp	77	7
William	38	m	w	ENGL	Napa	Napa Twp	75	64
William	36	m	w	ENGL	Los Angeles	Wilmington Twp	73	643
William	22	m	w	MA	San Francisco	7-Wd San Francisco	81	208
Wm	40	m	w	NY	San Joaquin	Douglas Twp	86	46
HOWEL								
Birds	20	m	w	CANA	Solano	Vallejo	90	216
Carroll	39	m	w	KY	Monterey	San Juan Twp	74	386
S A	46	m	w	OH	Sacramento	Lee Twp	77	159
Sarora Bet	11	f	w	IA	Monterey	Salinas Twp	74	307
HOWELL								
A J	38	m	w	AR	Del Norte	Crescent	71	462
Abial B	25	m	w	ME	Santa Cruz	Santa Cruz Twp	89	394
Alfred	41	m	w	ENGL	Amador	Sutter Crk P O	69	408
Alfred	17	m	w	ENGL	San Francisco	8-Wd San Francisco	82	392
Anna	18	f	w	ENGL	Amador	Jackson P O	69	334
Anna	13	f	m	CA	Sonoma	Healdsburg & Mendo	91	282
B F	50	m	w	TN	Sonoma	Sonoma Twp	91	445
Charles	75	m	m	VA	Sonoma	Mendocino Twp	91	307
Christ	50	m	w	NY	San Joaquin	Tulare Twp	86	259
Daniel Wm	53	m	w	WALE	Plumas	Quartz Twp	77	35
David	41	m	w	NY	Napa	Napa	75	8
Delina	44	f	w	OH	Santa Clara	Gilroy Twp	88	82
E P	66	m	w	VA	Solano	Benicia	90	20
Eddy	21	m	w	WI	San Joaquin	Liberty Twp	86	93
Edward	37	m	w	IREL	San Francisco	San Francisco P O	83	145
Elizabeth	40	f	w	MA	San Francisco	7-Wd San Francisco	81	158
Flint	23	m	w	MO	Santa Cruz	Santa Cruz Twp	89	390
Francis	38	m	w	MO	Sonoma	Santa Rosa	91	427
Frank	30	m	w	WI	San Joaquin	Liberty Twp	86	93
Frederick	42	m	w	WALE	Contra Costa	Martinez P O	71	429
Geo	23	m	w	WI	San Joaquin	Liberty Twp	86	93
George	42	m	w	NY	Colusa	Grand Island Twp	71	305
Henry	27	m	w	ME	Santa Cruz	Santa Cruz	89	429
Isaac	65	m	w	NY	Colusa	Grand Island Twp	71	308
J A	55	m	w	TN	Calaveras	Copperopolis P O	70	221
J B	65	m	w	TN	Del Norte	Smith Rvr Twp	71	477
J H	27	m	w	MO	San Joaquin	Castoria Twp	86	4
Jabez	41	m	w	MA	San Francisco	6-Wd San Francisco	81	70
James	52	m	w	KY	Santa Clara	Redwood Twp	88	130
Jas M	27	m	w	MO	Tehama	Paskenta Twp	92	164
Jesse H	4	f	w	CA	San Joaquin	Liberty Twp	86	93
Jno	30	m	w	IREL	Butte	Chico Twp	70	56
Jno G	33	m	w	OH	Sonoma	Healdsburg	91	274
John	50	m	w	BAVA	Santa Cruz	Soquel Twp	89	440
John	45	m	w	NY	Napa	Napa	75	21
John	33	m	w	CANA	Santa Clara	1-Wd San Jose	88	253
John	25	m	w	VA	Yolo	Grafton Twp	93	495
Joseph	55	m	w	ENGL	Amador	Volcano P O	69	381
Joseph	45	m	w	NY	Napa	Napa	75	37
Joseph A	31	m	w	PA	Napa	Napa	75	25
Joseph H	45	m	w	NY	San Francisco	6-Wd San Francisco	81	149
Josiah	40	m	w	ENGL	Sacramento	3-Wd Sacramento	77	291
Lewis H	40	m	w	NJ	Sonoma	Analy Twp	91	242
Lorain P	42	m	w	NY	Los Angeles	Los Angeles	73	535
Louisa	13	f	w	CA	Colusa	Grand Island Twp	71	310
Marcus W	42	m	w	PA	Yolo	Cache Crk Twp	93	441
Mark	28	m	w	MO	Merced	Snelling P O	74	253
Martin	40	m	w	NY	San Francisco	5-Wd San Francisco	81	33
Minerva	50	f	w	VA	Stanislaus	Washington Twp	92	87
Moses	50	m	w	NY	San Francisco	1-Wd San Francisco	79	33
N F	16	m	w	MO	San Joaquin	Castoria Twp	86	4
Newton	30	m	w	MO	Tehama	Paskenta Twp	92	164
Orin	30	m	w	NY	Mendocino	Sanel Twp	74	230
Philip	37	m	w	NY	Mendocino	Ukiah Twp	74	241
Robert	21	m	w	PA	San Diego	Julian Dist	78	469
Saml P	25	m	w	NJ	Mono	Bridgeport P O	74	286
Seth	20	m	w	PA	San Francisco	San Francisco P O	80	335
Stephen F	36	m	w	TN	Sonoma	Petaluma Twp	91	344
Sylv Sr	28	m	w	OH	Sonoma	Healdsburg	91	274

Name	Age	S	R	B-PL	County	Locale	Series M593 Roll	Pg
Thomas	39	m	w	ENGL	San Francisco	8-Wd San Francisco	82	392
Thomas	35	m	w	ENGL	Santa Cruz	Soquel Twp	89	448
Thomas W	28	m	w	ENGL	Colusa	Colusa Twp	71	285
Thos	24	m	w	VA	Fresno	Kings Rvr P O	72	203
Thos B	40	m	w	WALE	Siskiyou	Scott Valley Twp	89	614
Thos M	30	m	w	MO	Tehama	Tehama Twp	92	186
Watkins F	44	m	w	KY	Santa Clara	Redwood Twp	88	130
William	40	m	w	PA	Calaveras	San Andreas P O	70	198
William	37	m	w	ENGL	San Francisco	San Francisco P O	80	379
William H	56	m	w	NY	Tulare	Farmersville Twp	92	245
Wm	42	m	w	WALE	Sierra	Sears Twp	89	555
Wm M	63	m	w	NY	Sonoma	Cloverdale Twp	91	272
HOWELLS								
Morgan	45	m	w	WALE	Placer	Bath P O	76	446
HOWELS								
Thomas	37	m	w	PA	Nevada	Bridgeport Twp	75	124
HOWERD								
Emma	22	f	w	IN	Yuba	North East Twp	93	644
HOWERTON								
Andrew	25	m	w	IL	Amador	Amador City P O	69	391
Andrew D	39	m	w	MO	Los Angeles	El Monte Twp	73	460
Henry	40	m	w	KY	Sonoma	Salt Point	91	388
HOWES								
David	28	m	w	CANA	Santa Cruz	Santa Cruz Twp	89	393
E	39	m	w	MA	Los Angeles	Los Angeles	73	544
Edward	21	m	w	ENGL	San Francisco	6-Wd San Francisco	81	137
Eliza D	7	f	w	CA	San Francisco	San Francisco P O	85	867
J H	42	m	b	MD	Sierra	Downieville Twp	89	521
John	50	m	w	MA	San Francisco	3-Wd San Francisco	79	305
John	40	m	w	IREL	San Francisco	7-Wd San Francisco	81	223
Samuel B	36	m	w	MA	Santa Clara	2-Wd San Jose	88	329
Samuel P	37	m	w	MA	San Francisco	San Francisco P O	85	774
HOWETH								
Charles	11	m	w	CA	Mariposa	Maxwell Crk P O	74	142
Frank	5	m	w	CA	Mariposa	Maxwell Crk P O	74	144
James	44	m	w	SCOT	Placer	Bath P O	76	429
James	38	m	w	ENGL	Placer	Bath P O	76	454
James T	41	m	w	ENGL	Placer	Bath P O	76	453
Jeff	8	m	w	CA	Mariposa	Maxwell Crk P O	74	146
Jeff	38	m	w	TN	Mariposa	Maxwell Crk P O	74	144
Nelson	47	m	w	AL	Santa Cruz	Pajaro Twp	89	352
Wm	17	m	w	CA	Mariposa	Maxwell Crk P O	74	141
Wm S	16	m	w	MEXI	Mariposa	Maxwell Crk P O	74	142
HOWETT								
E B	18	m	w	SCOT	Alameda	Oakland	68	221
George	18	m	w	CANA	Mendocino	Navarro & Big Rvr	74	167
Henry B	37	m	w	NY	San Francisco	8-Wd San Francisco	82	415
HOWEY								
James	36	m	w	PA	Yolo	Cache Crk Twp	93	424
HOWGATE								
Geo	50	m	w	ENGL	San Francisco	7-Wd San Francisco	81	268
HOWHARD								
John	28	m	w	CANA	Solano	Vallejo	90	144
HOWISON								
James	33	m	w	MO	Tulare	Visalia Twp	92	285
Richard	59	m	w	VA	Tulare	Visalia Twp	92	286
HOWITT								
Arther	25	m	w	ENGL	Monterey	Alisal Twp	74	303
S	37	m	w	MA	San Joaquin	Douglas Twp	86	50
Thomas	32	m	w	ENGL	Monterey	Alisal Twp	74	303
HOWITZ								
Selina	18	f	w	PRUS	San Francisco	San Francisco P O	85	727
HOWITZEN								
A	30	m	w	NORW	San Francisco	7-Wd San Francisco	81	224
HOWK								
Ah	52	m	c	CHIN	San Francisco	6-Wd San Francisco	81	55
Ah	26	m	c	CHIN	San Francisco	San Francisco P O	85	749
Andrew	36	m	w	BADE	El Dorado	Cosumnes Twp	72	17
Corel	41	m	w	OH	Plumas	Quartz Twp	77	39
James Henry	36	m	w	NY	Plumas	Plumas Twp	77	28
Jno	55	m	w	GERM	Sacramento	1-Wd Sacramento	77	177
HOWKE								
J A	28	m	w	PA	Solano	Vallejo	90	202
HOWL								
William	30	m	w	PA	Sonoma	Washington Twp	91	468
HOWLAN								
I Seth	45	m	w	NY	Butte	Oregon Twp	70	133
HOWLAND								
Ada	10	f	w	CA	San Francisco	San Francisco P O	85	798
Albert	37	m	w	NY	Yuba	Long Bar Twp	93	563
Benj P	52	m	w	VT	Nevada	Grass Valley Twp	75	142
Benjamin	41	m	w	MA	San Francisco	11-Wd San Francisc	84	569
C	50	m	w	NY	Mariposa	Maxwell Crk P O	74	141
C F	30	m	w	OH	San Joaquin	Castoria Twp	86	7
Carie	16	f	w	CA	Alameda	Oakland	68	259
Chas M	40	m	w	NY	Sonoma	Mendocino Twp	91	302
Daniel	70	m	w	ME	Trinity	Weaverville Pct	92	225
David	48	m	w	NY	El Dorado	Lake Valley Twp	72	64
Edwd D	56	m	w	MA	San Francisco	San Francisco P O	83	27
Frank	25	m	w	OH	Los Angeles	Soledad Twp	73	631
Geo	31	m	w	NY	San Joaquin	Douglas Twp	86	40
H S	43	m	w	MA	San Joaquin	Castoria Twp	86	11
Harriet	30	f	w	IN	El Dorado	Placerville Twp	72	102
Henry	80	m	w	NY	San Joaquin	Douglas Twp	86	44
J	13	m	w	CA	Solano	Benicia	90	21
J H	41	m	w	MA	Napa	Napa	75	51
James	22	m	w	IREL	Solano	Tremont Twp	90	29

© 2001 by Heritage Quest. All rights reserved.

Name	Age	S	R	B-PL	County	Locale	Roll	Pg
						Series M593		
Jasper	36	m	w	IREL	Sonoma	Sonoma Twp	91	435
Jno	40	m	w	NY	San Joaquin	Elliott Twp	86	80
Joel	45	m	w	ME	Stanislaus	San Joaquin Twp	92	80
John	30	m	w	SWIT	Monterey	Alisal Twp	74	304
Joseph	36	m	w	IREL	Sonoma	Sonoma Twp	91	443
Joseph	32	m	w	PORT	Santa Clara	Gilroy Twp	88	89
Koit	19	m	w	PORT	Santa Clara	Gilroy Twp	88	89
Levi	42	m	w	MA	San Diego	Julian Dist	78	471
Levi L	42	m	w	MA	Stanislaus	Empire Twp	92	38
Lydia	65	f	w	MA	San Francisco	11-Wd San Francisc	84	569
Maria	47	f	w	NY	San Joaquin	Douglas Twp	86	44
Mary	17	f	w	NY	Alameda	Oakland	68	163
Max	30	m	w	CA	San Francisco	5-Wd San Francisco	81	14
Nathaniel	38	m	w	MA	Yolo	Grafton Twp	93	483
Sabin	47	m	w	NH	Santa Cruz	Soquel Twp	89	442
Thos	25	m	w	ME	San Francisco	11-Wd San Francisc	84	566
William	48	m	w	PORT	Los Angeles	Wilmington Twp	73	640
Wm	35	m	w	PORT	Santa Clara	Gilroy Twp	88	89
Wm	30	m	w	NY	San Joaquin	Douglas Twp	86	48
HOWLARD								
L	37	m	w	ME	San Joaquin	2-Wd Stockton	86	181
HOWLER								
Jacob	28	m	w	GERM	Yolo	Cache Crk Twp	93	451
HOWLET								
Harritt	30	f	w	KY	Yolo	Cache Crk Twp	93	423
Mary	45	f	w	CANA	San Francisco	7-Wd San Francisco	81	271
HOWLETT								
Charles	45	m	w	ENGL	Alameda	Eden Twp	68	80
George W	40	m	w	CT	El Dorado	Placerville	72	108
J W	30	m	w	IA	Sutter	Yuba Twp	92	147
James	38	m	w	IREL	Nevada	Bloomfield Twp	75	95
John	42	m	w	ENGL	Kern	Bakersfield P O	73	361
Wallace J	9	m	w	CA	Sutter	Yuba Twp	92	147
HOWLEY								
Charles	34	m	w	ENGL	San Francisco	7-Wd San Francisco	81	159
John	57	m	w	OH	Sacramento	Natomas Twp	77	166
Patk	38	m	w	IREL	Solano	Vallejo	90	183
Patrick	23	m	w	IREL	San Francisco	San Francisco P O	83	33
HOWLITE								
Jacob	50	m	w	PRUS	San Francisco	2-Wd San Francisco	79	155
HOWLLER								
Sebastin	48	m	w	FRAN	Trinity	Lewiston Pct	92	212
HOWN								
Ah	26	m	c	CHIN	Mendocino	Point Arena Twp	74	205
Levi	35	m	w	CANA	Monterey	Alisal Twp	74	293
HOWORTH								
John	35	m	w	NJ	San Francisco	San Francisco P O	80	373
HOWRARD								
Austin	49	m	w	VA	Alameda	Eden Twp	68	69
HOWS								
Ah	32	m	c	CHIN	Mariposa	Maxwell Crk P O	74	142
HOWSEN								
Andrew	30	m	w	MO	Sonoma	Sonoma Twp	91	433
HOWSENNA								
A	25	m	w	BADE	Alameda	Oakland	68	175
HOWSER								
Fredk	31	m	w	CT	Yuba	Rose Bar Twp	93	662
HOWSON								
Andrew	28	m	w	PRUS	Sonoma	Petaluma Twp	91	318
Frank	40	m	w	NY	San Francisco	1-Wd San Francisco	79	134
Leroy	24	m	w	NY	Alameda	Brooklyn Twp	68	42
HOWTON								
Lewis	40	m	w	OH	Mendocino	Point Arena Twp	74	215
HOWY								
Jas	34	m	w	FRAN	Alameda	Oakland	68	248
HOXETT								
Thos	43	m	w	IREL	Santa Clara	Gilroy Twp	88	69
HOXHALL								
Ernest	45	m	w	GERM	Yolo	Cache Crk Twp	93	451
HOXIE								
Benjamin	30	m	w	MA	Solano	Suisun Twp	90	98
Former	43	m	w	NY	El Dorado	Georgetown Twp	72	48
Ira C	33	m	w	OH	Mendocino	Round Valley Twp	74	218
Ira C	24	m	w	CT	Solano	Vallejo	90	161
John	21	m	w	MA	Fresno	Millerton P O	72	194
Peleg B	52	m	w	RI	El Dorado	Placerville	72	122
Ruth P	60	f	w	NY	Santa Cruz	Santa Cruz	89	406
HOXTON								
P H	22	m	w	VA	Monterey	San Juan Twp	74	394
HOY								
A	21	m	c	CHIN	Klamath	South Fork Twp	73	383
Ah	62	m	c	CHIN	Amador	Drytown P O	69	423
Ah	60	m	c	CHIN	Tuolumne	Chinese Camp P O	93	381
Ah	6	f	c	CA	San Francisco	San Francisco P O	80	454
Ah	55	m	c	CHIN	Amador	Volcano P O	69	387
Ah	54	m	c	CHIN	San Francisco	San Francisco P O	80	436
Ah	54	m	c	CHIN	Tuolumne	Big Oak Flat P O	93	397
Ah	53	m	c	CHIN	Yolo	Merritt Twp	93	504
Ah	51	m	c	CHIN	Placer	Newcastle Twp	76	479
Ah	50	m	c	CHIN	Calaveras	San Andreas P O	70	199
Ah	50	m	c	CHIN	Amador	Drytown P O	69	420
Ah	50	m	c	CHIN	Nevada	Nevada Twp	75	312
Ah	48	m	c	CHIN	Nevada	Rough & Ready Twp	75	324
Ah	47	m	c	CHIN	Amador	Volcano P O	69	378
Ah	47	m	c	CHIN	Sacramento	Georgianna Twp	77	126
Ah	46	m	c	CHIN	Sierra	Table Rock Twp	89	579
Ah	45	m	c	CHIN	Stanislaus	Emory Twp	92	22

Name	Age	S	R	B-PL	County	Locale	Roll	Pg
						Series M593		
Ah	45	m	c	CHIN	Nevada	Nevada Twp	75	299
Ah	43	m	c	CHIN	Butte	Chico Twp	70	51
Ah	43	m	c	CHIN	San Francisco	San Francisco P O	80	494
Ah	42	m	c	CHIN	Merced	Snelling P O	74	264
Ah	42	m	c	CHIN	Mariposa	Mariposa P O	74	102
Ah	42	m	c	CHIN	Calaveras	Copperopolis P O	70	234
Ah	41	m	c	CHIN	Amador	Fiddletown P O	69	427
Ah	41	m	c	CHIN	Nevada	Meadow Lake Twp	75	251
Ah	41	m	c	CHIN	San Francisco	San Francisco P O	80	518
Ah	41	m	c	CHIN	Mariposa	Mariposa P O	74	103
Ah	41	m	c	CHIN	Tuolumne	Big Oak Flat P O	93	394
Ah	40	m	c	CHIN	El Dorado	Placerville Twp	72	98
Ah	40	m	c	CHIN	Butte	Concow Twp	70	8
Ah	40	m	c	CHIN	Placer	Bath P O	76	445
Ah	40	m	c	CHIN	San Francisco	San Francisco P O	80	518
Ah	40	m	c	CHIN	San Francisco	San Francisco P O	80	503
Ah	40	m	c	CHIN	Mariposa	Mariposa P O	74	126
Ah	40	m	c	CHIN	Mariposa	Mariposa P O	74	126
Ah	40	m	c	CHIN	Sacramento	Natomas Twp	77	166
Ah	40	m	c	CHIN	Placer	Auburn P O	76	363
Ah	40	m	c	CHIN	Trinity	Douglas	92	235
Ah	40	m	c	CHIN	San Francisco	San Francisco P O	80	491
Ah	39	m	c	CHIN	Alameda	Hayward	68	77
Ah	39	m	c	CHIN	Amador	Ione City P O	69	349
Ah	39	m	c	CHIN	Santa Clara	1-Wd San Jose	88	273
Ah	38	m	c	CHIN	San Francisco	6-Wd San Francisco	81	51
Ah	38	m	c	CHIN	Mariposa	Mariposa P O	74	129
Ah	38	m	c	CHIN	Fresno	Millerton P O	72	202
Ah	37	m	c	CHIN	Mariposa	Mariposa P O	74	133
Ah	37	m	c	CHIN	Calaveras	San Andreas P O	70	211
Ah	37	m	c	CHIN	San Francisco	San Francisco P O	80	436
Ah	36	m	c	CHIN	Trinity	North Fork Twp	92	220
Ah	36	m	c	CHIN	Santa Clara	1-Wd San Jose	88	274
Ah	36	m	c	CHIN	Mariposa	Mariposa P O	74	106
Ah	36	f	c	CHIN	Butte	Hamilton Twp	70	74
Ah	35	m	c	CHIN	Amador	Ione City P O	69	361
Ah	35	m	c	CHIN	Placer	Lincoln P O	76	483
Ah	35	m	c	CHIN	Merced	Snelling P O	74	279
Ah	35	m	c	CHIN	San Joaquin	Liberty Twp	86	88
Ah	35	m	c	CHIN	San Francisco	San Francisco P O	85	747
Ah	34	m	c	CHIN	San Francisco	San Francisco P O	80	498
Ah	32	m	c	CHIN	Amador	Ione City P O	69	359
Ah	32	m	c	CHIN	Calaveras	San Andreas P O	70	169
Ah	32	m	c	CHIN	Sierra	Table Rock Twp	89	574
Ah	32	m	c	CHIN	Placer	Newcastle Twp	76	478
Ah	32	m	c	CHIN	Placer	Colfax P O	76	392
Ah	31	m	c	CHIN	Tuolumne	Sonora P O	93	321
Ah	30	m	c	CHIN	Plumas	Plumas Twp	77	29
Ah	30	m	c	CHIN	Sacramento	Dry Crk Twp	77	101
Ah	30	m	c	CHIN	Kern	Tehachapi P O	73	353
Ah	30	m	c	CHIN	San Francisco	3-Wd San Francisco	79	307
Ah	30	m	c	CHIN	Placer	Summit P O	76	497
Ah	30	m	c	CHIN	Sacramento	3-Wd Sacramento	77	312
Ah	30	m	c	CHIN	Solano	Suisun Twp	90	106
Ah	30	m	c	CHIN	Yolo	Cache Crk Twp	93	431
Ah	30	m	c	CHIN	Yolo	Grafton Twp	93	486
Ah	30	m	c	CHIN	Yolo	Cottonwood Twp	93	470
Ah	30	m	c	CHIN	Yuba	East Bear Rvr Twp	93	545
Ah	29	m	c	CHIN	Butte	Kimshew Tpw	70	85
Ah	29	m	c	CHIN	Calaveras	San Andreas P O	70	179
Ah	29	m	c	CHIN	Sacramento	Georgianna Twp	77	134
Ah	29	m	c	CHIN	Sacramento	Dry Crk Twp	77	101
Ah	29	m	c	CHIN	Santa Clara	1-Wd San Jose	88	277
Ah	29	m	c	CHIN	San Francisco	6-Wd San Francisco	81	58
Ah	29	m	c	CHIN	San Francisco	6-Wd San Francisco	81	61
Ah	28	m	c	CHIN	Plumas	Mineral Twp	77	23
Ah	28	m	c	CHIN	Plumas	Mineral Twp	77	25
Ah	28	m	c	CHIN	Placer	Auburn P O	76	379
Ah	27	m	c	CHIN	Butte	Ophir Twp	70	103
Ah	27	m	c	CHIN	San Francisco	3-Wd San Francisco	79	302
Ah	26	m	c	CHIN	Alameda	Eden Twp	68	61
Ah	26	m	c	CHIN	San Francisco	San Francisco P O	80	501
Ah	26	m	c	CHIN	Nevada	Nevada Twp	75	300
Ah	26	m	c	CHIN	San Francisco	San Francisco P O	80	490
Ah	26	m	c	CHIN	Santa Clara	San Jose Twp	88	190
Ah	26	m	c	CHIN	Santa Clara	San Jose Twp	88	192
Ah	26	m	c	CHIN	Santa Clara	San Jose Twp	88	194
Ah	25	f	c	CHIN	Amador	Fiddletown P O	69	428
Ah	25	m	c	CHIN	Sierra	Sears Twp	89	553
Ah	25	m	c	CHIN	Yolo	Grafton Twp	93	496
Ah	25	m	c	CHIN	San Francisco	6-Wd San Francisco	81	60
Ah	24	m	c	CHIN	Amador	Ione City P O	69	364
Ah	24	m	c	CHIN	Santa Clara	2-Wd San Jose	88	325
Ah	24	m	c	CHIN	Santa Clara	1-Wd San Jose	88	271
Ah	24	m	c	CHIN	Santa Clara	1-Wd San Jose	88	272
Ah	24	m	c	CHIN	Yuba	Marysville	93	595
Ah	23	m	c	CHIN	Plumas	Plumas Twp	77	31
Ah	23	m	c	CHIN	San Francisco	6-Wd San Francisco	81	55
Ah	23	f	c	CHIN	San Francisco	San Francisco P O	80	431
Ah	23	m	c	CHIN	San Francisco	6-Wd San Francisco	81	62
Ah	23	m	c	CHIN	San Francisco	6-Wd San Francisco	81	66
Ah	22	m	c	CHIN	Plumas	Plumas Twp	77	31
Ah	22	m	c	CHIN	Plumas	Goodwin Twp	77	3
Ah	22	m	c	CHIN	Yolo	Buckeye Twp	93	411
Ah	22	m	c	CHIN	San Francisco	6-Wd San Francisco	81	75
Ah	22	m	c	CHIN	San Francisco	6-Wd San Francisco	81	58
Ah	21	m	c	CHIN	Butte	Concow Twp	70	12

© 2001 by Heritage Quest. All rights reserved.

Name	Age	S	R	B-PL	County	Series M593 Locale	Roll	Pg
Ah	21	f	c	CHIN	San Francisco	San Francisco P O	80	435
Ah	21	f	c	CHIN	Napa	Napa	75	56
Ah	21	m	c	CHIN	San Francisco	6-Wd San Francisco	81	46
Ah	20	m	c	CHIN	Sierra	Table Rock Twp	89	571
Ah	20	m	c	CHIN	San Francisco	6-Wd San Francisco	81	50
Ah	20	f	c	CHIN	San Francisco	San Francisco P O	80	438
Ah	20	f	c	CHIN	San Francisco	San Francisco P O	80	437
Ah	20	m	c	CHIN	San Francisco	6-Wd San Francisco	81	66
Ah	19	f	c	CHIN	Butte	Hamilton Twp	70	74
Ah	19	m	c	CHIN	Santa Clara	1-Wd San Jose	88	274
Ah	19	m	c	CHIN	Santa Clara	1-Wd San Jose	88	272
Ah	19	m	c	CHIN	San Francisco	6-Wd San Francisco	81	49
Ah	19	m	c	CHIN	Mariposa	Maxwell Crk P O	74	142
Ah	19	m	c	CHIN	Yolo	Putah Twp	93	515
Ah	19	f	c	CHIN	San Francisco	San Francisco P O	80	495
Ah	18	m	c	CHIN	Sacramento	3-Wd Sacramento	77	288
Ah	18	m	c	CHIN	Santa Clara	San Jose Twp	88	190
Ah	18	m	c	CHIN	San Francisco	11-Wd San Francisc	84	560
Ah	18	f	c	CHIN	Yuba	Marysville	93	627
Ah	18	m	c	CHIN	Yolo	Cottonwood Twp	93	467
Ah	16	m	c	CHIN	Santa Clara	1-Wd San Jose	88	272
Ah	16	m	c	CHIN	San Francisco	6-Wd San Francisco	81	123
Ah	16	m	c	CHIN	Mariposa	Mariposa P O	74	103
Ah	16	m	c	CHIN	Plumas	Washington Twp	77	58
Ah	15	m	c	CHIN	Placer	Colfax P O	76	388
Ah	14	m	c	CHIN	Santa Clara	1-Wd San Jose	88	277
Ah	14	m	c	CHIN	Nevada	Nevada Twp	75	282
Ah	13	m	c	CHIN	Placer	Clipper Gap P O	76	393
Ah	12	f	c	CHIN	San Francisco	San Francisco P O	80	528
Ah	12	m	c	CHIN	San Francisco	San Francisco P O	80	388
Ah Lee	32	m	c	CHIN	Calaveras	Copperopolis P O	70	259
Ah Su	32	m	c	CHIN	Calaveras	San Andreas P O	70	174
Alexander	52	m	w	NJ	San Francisco	6-Wd San Francisco	81	142
Band	28	f	c	CHIN	Yuba	Marysville	93	627
Catherine	46	f	w	BAVA	Colusa	Grand Island Twp	71	309
Charles A	20	m	w	MD	Placer	Blue Canyon P O	76	419
Charley	30	m	c	CHIN	Monterey	San Juan Twp	74	394
Chas A	32	m	w	ME	Nevada	Meadow Lake Twp	75	252
Chee	18	f	c	CHIN	Placer	Auburn P O	76	371
Fat	19	m	c	CHIN	Napa	Napa Twp	75	58
Gin	20	f	c	CHIN	Mariposa	Mariposa P O	74	103
Hang	30	m	c	CHIN	Placer	Auburn P O	76	370
Isaac	40	m	b	VA	San Francisco	San Francisco P O	80	383
J W	41	m	w	OH	Nevada	Meadow Lake Twp	75	263
James	45	m	w	IREL	Placer	Auburn P O	76	360
John	37	m	w	OH	Nevada	Meadow Lake Twp	75	268
John	25	m	c	CHIN	Placer	Colfax P O	76	388
John M C	40	m	w	SCOT	San Francisco	6-Wd San Francisco	81	91
Joseph	20	m	w	NY	San Francisco	6-Wd San Francisco	81	89
Le Ung	38	m	c	CHIN	Siskiyou	Yreka	89	657
Lee	28	m	c	CHIN	Placer	Auburn P O	76	377
Lee	16	m	c	CHIN	Solano	Vallejo	90	217
Len	30	f	c	CHIN	Placer	Auburn P O	76	371
Len Tin	20	m	c	CHIN	Amador	Ione City P O	69	366
Lo Noy	22	m	c	CHIN	Amador	Ione City P O	69	366
Mary	23	f	w	IREL	Merced	Snelling P O	74	273
Richard	20	m	w	ENGL	Colusa	Monroe Twp	71	313
Sam	45	m	c	CHIN	Yuba	Bullards Bar P O	93	552
Senne	37	m	c	CHIN	Nevada	Nevada Twp	75	311
Sim	17	f	c	CHIN	Placer	Bath P O	76	439
Sing	25	m	c	CHIN	Tulare	Tule Rvr Twp	92	259
Thomas	40	m	w	IREL	San Francisco	San Francisco P O	83	142
To	17	m	c	CHIN	San Francisco	8-Wd San Francisco	82	441
Ton Loy	17	m	c	CHIN	Amador	Ione City P O	69	366
Tong	38	f	c	CHIN	San Francisco	11-Wd San Francisc	84	611
Too	30	m	c	CHIN	Siskiyou	Hamburg Twp	89	597
Wah	27	m	c	CHIN	Solano	Tremont Twp	90	31
Way	51	m	c	CHIN	Calaveras	San Andreas P O	70	162
Yen	35	m	c	CHIN	Butte	Chico Twp	70	52
Yen How	34	m	c	CHIN	Amador	Ione City P O	69	366
Yon	40	f	c	CHIN	Calaveras	San Andreas P O	70	214
Yun	49	m	c	CHIN	Placer	Bath P O	76	439
HOYD								
Susan E	39	f	w	NY	Placer	Emigrant Gap P O	76	416
HOYE								
Ah	27	m	c	CHIN	Amador	Drytown P O	69	423
Micheal	45	m	w	IREL	San Francisco	7-Wd San Francisco	81	201
HOYER								
Wm	36	m	w	HAMB	San Francisco	2-Wd San Francisco	79	206
HOYES								
A M	42	f	w	CT	San Francisco	7-Wd San Francisco	81	206
HOYL								
Manus	24	m	w	PRUS	Solano	Silveyville Twp	90	75
HOYLE								
Alfred	31	m	w	STHO	San Francisco	7-Wd San Francisco	81	281
Edwds	48	m	w	NY	Butte	Chico Twp	70	21
Elizabeth	5	f	w	CA	Butte	Chico Twp	70	20
Frank W	46	m	w	KY	Butte	Chico Twp	70	58
Grace M	9	f	w	MA	Nevada	Grass Valley Twp	75	225
Henry	39	m	w	IREL	Solano	Montezuma Twp	90	67
John	49	m	w	ENGL	Nevada	Grass Valley Twp	75	171
Louis	38	m	w	ENGL	Stanislaus	Emory Twp	92	24
Mary	38	f	w	ENGL	Marin	Bolinas Twp	74	6
Thos	29	m	w	IREL	Butte	Chico Twp	70	55
William	52	m	w	PA	Placer	Dutch Flat P O	76	401
HOYLEN								
Patrick	26	m	w	IREL	San Francisco	San Francisco P O	83	382

Name	Age	S	R	B-PL	County	Series M593 Locale	Roll	Pg
HOYMAN								
Alexander	17	m	w	OH	Placer	Roseville P O	76	350
HOYNE								
Julia R	1	f	w	CA	Nevada	Grass Valley Twp	75	158
Michael	32	m	w	IREL	Nevada	Grass Valley Twp	75	158
HOYT								
A A	43	m	w	CANA	Monterey	San Juan Twp	74	388
Abby	25	f	w	IREL	Solano	Suisun Twp	90	103
Abel	30	m	w	IREL	Solano	Denverton Twp	90	23
Ah	22	m	c	CHIN	San Francisco	San Francisco P O	83	126
Amherst	26	m	w	RI	Santa Clara	Fremont Twp	88	46
Calvin	50	m	w	ME	San Francisco	San Francisco P O	83	117
Charles	24	m	w	PA	Solano	Silveyville Twp	90	84
Chas	39	m	w	NY	Solano	Vallejo	90	149
Chas T	40	m	w	NY	Napa	Napa	75	49
David	62	m	w	NH	San Francisco	8-Wd San Francisco	82	291
David	27	m	w	MA	Solano	Vacaville Twp	90	127
Dexter B	56	m	w	CANA	El Dorado	Mountain Twp	72	69
Dudley	31	m	w	NY	Nevada	Grass Valley Twp	75	208
Elijah	54	m	w	NY	Sonoma	Santa Rosa	91	407
Emily	38	f	w	NY	San Francisco	6-Wd San Francisco	81	153
Geo A	23	m	w	CANA	El Dorado	Placerville Twp	72	103
Hazen	37	m	w	CANA	Solano	Vacaville Twp	90	135
Henry	43	m	w	NY	El Dorado	Placerville Twp	72	105
Henry	24	m	w	NY	San Francisco	2-Wd San Francisco	79	169
Henry M	42	m	w	VT	Yolo	Grafton Twp	93	480
Hiram	34	m	w	OH	Tulare	Tule Rvr Twp	92	268
Hiram	24	m	w	OH	Sonoma	Santa Rosa	91	407
Hoffman	27	m	w	NY	San Francisco	San Francisco P O	85	874
Homa	27	m	w	MA	San Mateo	Schoolhouse Statio	87	333
James	48	m	w	CT	San Francisco	8-Wd San Francisco	82	370
James	40	m	w	NY	San Francisco	11-Wd San Francisc	84	578
Jas	42	m	w	IREL	San Francisco	7-Wd San Francisco	81	238
John	50	m	w	NY	Santa Cruz	Santa Cruz Twp	89	395
John	38	m	w	NY	Solano	Vacaville Twp	90	123
John	29	m	w	KY	Solano	Montezuma Twp	90	68
John A	25	m	w	MO	San Luis Obispo	San Luis Obispo Tw	87	302
John M	39	m	w	BADE	Amador	Drytown P O	69	417
John M	27	m	w	IL	San Francisco	8-Wd San Francisco	82	484
Jos	39	m	w	NH	Solano	Benicia	90	1
Joseph	37	m	w	MO	Solano	Silveyville Twp	90	90
Joseph	23	m	w	OH	Fresno	Kings Rvr P O	72	203
Julian	43	m	w	VT	Solano	Suisun Twp	90	112
Leonard	58	m	w	NY	Sacramento	Sutter Twp	77	384
M C	43	m	w	ME	Amador	Sutter Crk P O	69	398
Marcellus G	58	m	w	NH	Amador	Volcano P O	69	372
Mary E	35	f	w	NY	Los Angeles	Los Angeles	73	540
Merritt	27	m	w	OH	Colusa	Colusa	71	294
Moses	37	m	w	ME	Sacramento	2-Wd Sacramento	77	250
Moses	34	m	w	OH	Santa Cruz	Santa Cruz Twp	89	400
Nathaniel	51	m	w	NH	Calaveras	Copperopolis P O	70	256
Perry	40	m	w	OH	Siskiyou	Table Rock Twp	89	646
Peter	25	m	w	BADE	Solano	Montezuma Twp	90	65
Philo F	51	m	w	NY	Placer	Auburn P O	76	379
Porter	30	m	w	NH	Mendocino	Navarro & Big Rvr	74	167
Robert	24	m	w	PA	Amador	Jackson P O	69	341
Samuel	38	m	w	ME	Alameda	Oakland	68	187
Stephen T	49	m	w	CANA	Solano	Vacaville Twp	90	117
Sterling E	25	m	w	CT	San Francisco	8-Wd San Francisco	82	347
Sylvanious S	57	m	w	VT	Mendocino	Point Arena Twp	74	206
Terrence	40	m	w	IREL	San Francisco	San Francisco P O	83	168
Thos	28	m	w	WI	Tehama	Tehama Twp	92	192
W H	55	m	w	NY	Sacramento	3-Wd Sacramento	77	299
Walter	24	m	w	MA	Sacramento	3-Wd Sacramento	77	316
William	22	m	w	MO	Solano	Vacaville Twp	90	133
William	19	m	w	DE	Solano	Montezuma Twp	90	65
William K	40	m	w	ME	Solano	Suisun Twp	90	93
William W	27	m	w	CANA	El Dorado	Diamond Springs Tw	72	25
HOYTE								
Isaac	57	m	w	NY	Amador	Ione City P O	69	357
T S	43	m	w	NH	Amador	Jackson P O	69	321
HOZEN								
Ada M	21	f	w	ME	San Francisco	San Francisco P O	83	303
HRAY								
Philander	39	m	w	NY	El Dorado	Mud Springs Twp	72	90
HU								
Ah	60	m	c	CHIN	Amador	Fiddletown P O	69	429
Ah	35	m	c	CHIN	Sierra	Downieville Twp	89	521
Ah	31	m	c	CHIN	Solano	Suisun Twp	90	106
Ah	28	m	c	CHIN	Placer	Dutch Flat P O	76	408
Ah	22	m	c	CHIN	Sacramento	Georgianna Twp	77	133
Ah	17	m	c	CHIN	Sutter	Sutter Twp	92	125
Ah	14	m	c	CHIN	San Francisco	8-Wd San Francisco	82	293
Howk	45	m	c	CHIN	Plumas	Washington Twp	77	57
HUALA								
J	42	m	w	BADE	El Dorado	Greenwood Twp	72	52
HUAND								
Paul	40	m	w	FRAN	San Francisco	2-Wd San Francisco	79	241
HUANT								
Michael	41	m	w	FRAN	San Francisco	San Francisco P O	80	533
Paul	28	m	w	FRAN	San Francisco	San Francisco P O	80	468
HUARD								
Louis	62	m	w	FRAN	San Francisco	San Francisco P O	80	481
HUBART								
D A	38	m	w	NY	Trinity	Weaverville Pct	92	222
HUBASH								
Jas	35	m	w	GERM	San Francisco	8-Wd San Francisco	82	357

© 2001 by Heritage Quest. All rights reserved.

Name	Age	S	R	B-PL	County	Locale	Roll	Pg
						Series M593		
HUBBAD								
Geo	20	m	w	CANA	San Francisco	11-Wd San Francisc	84	684
HUBBARD								
A W	35	m	w	VA	Santa Clara	Gilroy Twp	88	76
Adam	50	m	w	MI	Santa Clara	San Jose Twp	88	206
Albert	55	m	w	FRAN	Nevada	Grass Valley Twp	75	228
Albert	37	m	w	ME	Plumas	Quartz Twp	77	37
Albert	25	m	w	ENGL	San Francisco	San Francisco P O	83	225
Arthur	20	m	w	MO	Yolo	Cache Crk Twp	93	445
Arthur	19	m	w	MO	Yolo	Cache Crk Twp	93	435
B S	24	m	w	OH	Butte	Bidwell Twp	70	3
Bessie	38	f	w	ME	San Francisco	7-Wd San Francisco	81	229
C H	25	m	w	MA	Sacramento	4-Wd Sacramento	77	324
C V D	30	m	w	OH	Alameda	Alameda	68	4
Catherine	50	f	w	IREL	San Francisco	11-Wd San Francisc	84	700
Charles	23	m	m	KY	Sacramento	2-Wd Sacramento	77	212
Chauncy	53	m	w	OH	Yolo	Washington Twp	93	535
Daniel	50	m	w	MO	San Francisco	5-Wd San Francisco	81	9
David C	63	m	w	KY	Yolo	Cache Crk Twp	93	435
Early	27	m	w	GA	Los Angeles	El Monte Twp	73	456
Edward	23	m	w	CT	San Francisco	11-Wd San Francisc	84	519
Edward R	33	m	w	IL	Los Angeles	Santa Ana Twp	73	604
Edwin	26	m	w	ME	San Francisco	7-Wd San Francisco	81	233
Eliza	23	f	w	OH	Yolo	Grafton Twp	93	489
Emma	24	f	w	WI	Yolo	Washington Twp	93	535
Enos P	43	m	w	NY	Nevada	Little York Twp	75	244
Eveline	11	f	w	CA	Yolo	Cache Crk Twp	93	419
F G	28	m	w	MI	Alameda	Murray Twp	68	116
Frank	20	m	w	CA	Santa Clara	Santa Clara Twp	88	177
Geo	50	m	w	NY	San Francisco	5-Wd San Francisco	81	15
Geo	23	m	w	CT	Santa Clara	Gilroy Twp	88	90
Geo W	17	m	w	MO	Santa Cruz	Santa Cruz Twp	89	394
George	40	m	w	NY	San Diego	San Luis Rey	78	515
George	20	m	w	ITAL	Santa Barbara	Las Cruces P O	87	506
George	19	m	w	MD	Colusa	Spring Valley Twp	71	340
H	47	m	w	NH	San Joaquin	2-Wd Stockton	86	197
H W	58	m	w	VT	San Francisco	8-Wd San Francisco	82	312
Hanford	29	m	w	OH	Yolo	Washington Twp	93	535
Henry	45	m	w	MA	Solano	Suisun Twp	90	93
Henry	30	m	w	CT	San Francisco	2-Wd San Francisco	79	262
Henry	25	m	w	VT	Santa Cruz	Soquel Twp	89	440
Henry S	29	m	w	VT	San Francisco	San Francisco P O	85	754
I	40	m	w	VA	Lake	Lower Lake	73	428
J E	27	m	w	CHIL	Solano	Vallejo	90	161
J H	56	m	w	CT	Sacramento	3-Wd Sacramento	77	265
Jacob	38	m	w	PRUS	San Francisco	San Francisco P O	83	384
James	35	m	w	GA	Los Angeles	Santa Ana Twp	73	599
James	32	m	m	MD	Nevada	Grass Valley Twp	75	167
James	26	m	w	WI	Sacramento	2-Wd Sacramento	77	242
Jane	30	f	w	ME	San Francisco	San Francisco P O	80	425
Jas H	52	m	w	NY	San Francisco	8-Wd San Francisco	82	328
Jno H	49	m	w	VA	Sierra	Sears Twp	89	555
John	65	m	w	PRUS	Stanislaus	San Joaquin Twp	92	82
John	55	m	w	NY	San Francisco	5-Wd San Francisco	81	28
John	45	m	w	MA	Solano	Vacaville Twp	90	134
John C	53	m	w	VA	San Francisco	7-Wd San Francisco	81	253
Joseph	42	m	w	GA	San Diego	Julian Dist	78	473
Joseph	36	m	w	NH	Monterey	San Juan Twp	74	415
Lavin	51	m	w	MD	Marin	Novato Twp	74	10
Lorenza	59	m	w	NY	San Francisco	1-Wd San Francisco	79	63
Lozien	29	m	w	ME	Plumas	Quartz Twp	77	36
Margaret	56	f	w	TN	Los Angeles	El Monte Twp	73	448
Marshall	54	m	w	MA	San Francisco	11-Wd San Francisc	84	500
Mary	35	f	m	OH	Nevada	Grass Valley Twp	75	191
Michael	24	m	w	IREL	San Francisco	San Francisco P O	83	237
Mike	25	m	w	IREL	Solano	Vallejo	90	199
Moses	40	m	w	ME	San Francisco	San Francisco P O	83	24
Nathan	60	m	w	TN	San Diego	Julian Dist	78	473
Parker M	27	m	w	ME	Santa Cruz	Santa Cruz Twp	89	393
Samuel	39	m	w	MA	San Mateo	San Mateo P O	87	350
Stephen R	54	m	w	OH	Shasta	Shasta P O	89	455
Sylvester	21	m	w	TX	Fresno	Millerton P O	72	158
T J	37	m	w	NY	Trinity	Trinity Center Pct	92	240
Thomas	44	m	w	CT	Colusa	Monroe Twp	71	311
Thos W	30	m	w	NY	San Francisco	5-Wd San Francisco	81	28
Uri	27	m	w	IL	Los Angeles	Santa Ana Twp	73	604
W	30	m	w	TN	Tehama	Red Bluff	92	183
W G	49	m	w	CT	Monterey	San Juan Twp	74	413
Warren	42	m	w	NY	San Francisco	6-Wd San Francisco	81	147
William	54	m	w	NY	El Dorado	Diamond Springs Tw	72	23
William	39	m	w	MO	Santa Cruz	Santa Cruz Twp	89	392
William	20	m	w	OH	Yolo	Washington Twp	93	535
William H	25	m	w	RI	Placer	Auburn P O	76	368
Wm	39	m	w	MO	Santa Cruz	Santa Cruz Twp	89	394
Wm W	39	m	w	TN	Monterey	Castroville Twp	74	331
HUBBEL								
Carrie	20	f	w	MA	San Joaquin	1-Wd Stockton	86	133
Chas	37	m	w	NY	San Francisco	5-Wd San Francisco	81	25
Thomas J	33	m	w	PA	San Mateo	Pescadero P O	87	412
Wm	26	m	w	NY	Sonoma	Santa Rosa	91	414
HUBBELL								
C J	33	m	w	NY	Nevada	Eureka Twp	75	135
Edgar	26	m	w	OH	Contra Costa	San Pablo Twp	71	359
Edward	21	m	w	NY	Nevada	Eureka Twp	75	138
Ezra S	45	m	w	CANA	Plumas	Washington Twp	77	54
George	46	m	w	NY	San Bernardino	San Bernardino Twp	78	424
John S	42	m	w	MO	Santa Cruz	Santa Cruz Twp	89	397
Orton	37	m	w	NY	Marin	Tomales Twp	74	81
Steven C	29	m	w	NY	San Bernardino	San Bernardino Twp	78	417
Taithanica	31	f	w	WI	Siskiyou	Scott Valley Twp	89	609
HUBBERD								
Henry	38	m	w	NY	Inyo	Bishop Crk Twp	73	310
HUBBERT								
L	60	m	w	ME	Sierra	Downieville Twp	89	520
HUBBERTY								
George	75	m	w	HANO	Calaveras	San Andreas P O	70	184
John	41	m	w	HANO	Calaveras	San Andreas P O	70	184
HUBBLE								
De Wit	33	m	w	NY	Monterey	Monterey	74	359
J	40	m	w	AR	Yuba	Marysville	93	618
Marshal	56	m	w	AR	Sonoma	Mendocino Twp	91	291
Samuel	30	m	w	NY	Trinity	Trinity Center Pct	92	240
Thos	15	m	w	HI	San Francisco	11-Wd San Francisc	84	588
W B	53	m	w	OH	Amador	Sutter Crk P O	69	396
HUBBORD								
C H	47	m	w	CT	San Joaquin	2-Wd Stockton	86	168
HUBBS								
Adam	40	m	w	CANA	Yuba	Linda Twp	93	555
Bun A	26	m	w	ENGL	Butte	Chico Twp	70	13
James	45	m	w	IL	Tulare	Tule Rvr Twp	92	267
Paul R	61	m	w	NJ	Solano	Vallejo	90	165
Walter	50	m	w	GA	Stanislaus	Washington Twp	92	85
William	26	m	w	OH	Solano	Tremont Twp	90	28
HUBBUCK								
Ed	23	m	w	ENGL	Alameda	Oakland	68	256
HUBBURD								
Jakin	40	m	w	VA	Trinity	North Fork Twp	92	217
HUBELL								
Jno	50	m	w	FRAN	Butte	Oregon Twp	70	132
HUBER								
Apolina	56	f	w	BADE	Los Angeles	Los Angeles	73	503
Catherine	64	f	w	PRUS	San Francisco	San Francisco P O	83	227
Charles	25	m	w	WURT	San Francisco	8-Wd San Francisco	82	432
David	68	m	w	PA	Santa Clara	Gilroy Twp	88	71
Elizabeth	51	f	w	PA	Yolo	Grafton Twp	93	492
Elizabeth	29	f	w	IREL	Napa	Napa Twp	75	58
Geo J	30	m	w	BADE	San Francisco	2-Wd San Francisco	79	180
George	53	m	w	SWIT	San Francisco	7-Wd San Francisco	81	211
Gotlieb	45	f	w	BADE	San Mateo	Redwood Twp	87	363
John	49	m	w	CANA	Placer	Colfax P O	76	389
John	28	m	w	BADE	San Francisco	1-Wd San Francisco	79	21
John	19	m	w	OH	San Francisco	7-Wd San Francisco	81	277
Joseph	38	m	w	NY	San Francisco	7-Wd San Francisco	81	253
Joseph	35	m	w	KY	Los Angeles	Los Angeles	73	533
Joseph	32	m	w	BAVA	San Francisco	2-Wd San Francisco	79	160
Joseph	25	m	w	BADE	El Dorado	Georgetown Twp	72	47
Louis	26	m	w	HAMB	San Francisco	1-Wd San Francisco	79	124
Rosa	25	f	w	BAVA	San Francisco	2-Wd San Francisco	79	187
Susan	32	f	w	MA	San Francisco	San Francisco P O	83	159
HUBERT								
Agnes	11	f	w	ENGL	Solano	Benicia	90	5
Charles	40	m	w	PRUS	San Francisco	8-Wd San Francisco	82	441
Deco	43	m	w	FRAN	Plumas	Plumas Twp	77	32
Eva	53	f	w	HUNG	Nevada	Nevada Twp	75	305
Frank	40	m	w	FRAN	San Francisco	San Francisco P O	80	350
Fred	45	m	w	SWIT	Tehama	Merrill	92	197
J W	51	m	w	PA	Sutter	Yuba Twp	92	144
Joab	70	m	w	ITAL	Calaveras	San Andreas P O	70	174
John	46	m	w	FRAN	Calaveras	Copperopolis P O	70	263
Nellie	20	f	w	SCOT	Contra Costa	Martinez P O	71	419
Numa	50	m	w	LA	San Francisco	3-Wd San Francisco	79	318
Peter	37	m	w	FRAN	Nevada	Eureka Twp	75	138
HUBIE								
Philip	22	m	w	ENGL	Nevada	Rough & Ready Twp	75	332
HUBLER								
James N	39	m	w	PA	Monterey	San Juan Twp	74	398
HUBLEY								
George	38	m	w	ENGL	San Francisco	6-Wd San Francisco	81	79
HUBLY								
Homer	36	m	w	NY	San Diego	Fort Yuma Dist	78	463
HUBNER								
C G	39	m	w	SAXO	San Joaquin	2-Wd Stockton	86	181
Fritz	40	m	w	SAXO	Los Angeles	Wilmington Twp	73	641
Harry	28	m	w	PRUS	San Francisco	5-Wd San Francisco	81	16
J C	27	m	w	MI	San Francisco	3-Wd San Francisco	79	311
HUBRAND								
L	30	m	w	SWED	San Francisco	7-Wd San Francisco	81	221
HUBRICH								
Leonard	33	m	w	PRUS	Sonoma	Petaluma Twp	91	321
HUBSON								
C	36	m	w	ENGL	Sierra	Lincoln Twp	89	545
HUBY								
Eli	65	m	w	FRAN	San Francisco	11-Wd San Francisc	84	613
HUCH								
F	36	m	w	HCAS	San Joaquin	Tulare Twp	86	259
HUCHABAY								
B	51	m	w	NC	Lake	Upper Lake	73	413
HUCHARD								
Francis	53	m	w	FRAN	Placer	Auburn P O	76	361
HUCHELGON								
Hanora	21	f	w	BAVA	San Francisco	San Francisco P O	83	233
HUCHICON								
James	27	m	w	OH	Humboldt	Mattole Twp	72	286

© 2001 by Heritage Quest. All rights reserved.

California 1870 Census

Name	Age	S	R	B-PL	County	Locale	Series M593 Roll	Pg
HUCHIER								
George	35	m	w	PRUS	Sacramento	San Joaquin Twp	77	403
HUCHINGS								
Luther	25	m	w	MI	Sacramento	Sutter Twp	77	388
HUCHINS								
John	39	m	w	IL	Humboldt	Bald Hills	72	237
HUCHINSON								
J H	41	m	w	OH	Klamath	Sawyers Bar	73	377
HUCHISON								
Elick	50	m	w	OH	Sacramento	Cosumnes Twp	77	89
HUCK								
Andrew	30	m	w	IREL	Marin	San Rafael Twp	74	26
Anthony	27	m	w	NY	Marin	Novato Twp	74	9
John	42	m	w	SHOL	San Francisco	2-Wd San Francisco	79	185
Valentine	35	m	w	BAVA	San Francisco	San Francisco P O	83	414
HUCKALY								
David	40	m	w	KY	Fresno	Kings Rvr P O	72	213
HUCKER								
John	33	m	w	TN	Trinity	Trinity Center Pct	92	205
HUCKINS								
John A	41	m	w	NH	San Mateo	Redwood Twp	87	365
Louis	28	m	w	CANA	Solano	Vacaville Twp	90	131
Robert	38	m	w	ME	Nevada	Bridgeport Twp	75	103
Samuel	47	m	w	NH	San Francisco	8-Wd San Francisco	82	421
HUCKLEMAN								
John	48	m	w	IN	Trinity	North Fork Twp	92	218
HUCKS								
James	60	m	w	ENGL	San Francisco	2-Wd San Francisco	79	223
John J	65	m	w	ENGL	San Francisco	2-Wd San Francisco	79	223
HUDD								
Patrick	40	m	w	IREL	Butte	Chico Twp	70	42
HUDDART								
Rd Townsend	61	m	w	IREL	San Francisco	San Francisco P O	83	136
HUDDER								
Chas	38	m	w	HANO	Tuolumne	Big Oak Flat P O	93	400
HUDDLESON								
James	44	m	w	KY	Stanislaus	Empire Twp	92	65
James	35	m	w	NY	San Francisco	2-Wd San Francisco	79	166
Mary	75	f	w	SCOT	San Francisco	2-Wd San Francisco	79	166
William	34	m	w	MO	Stanislaus	Empire Twp	92	45
HUDDLESTON								
Wm	27	m	w	ENGL	Alameda	Eden Twp	68	81
HUDDLESTONE								
G	27	m	w	KY	Stanislaus	Empire Twp	92	42
HUDDLETON								
Lewis B	24	m	w	TN	Santa Cruz	Santa Cruz Twp	89	395
HUDDY								
Wm	32	m	w	CA	San Francisco	San Francisco P O	83	264
HUDEMAN								
H	49	m	w	PRUS	Napa	Napa Twp	75	68
HUDEPHAL								
R	47	m	w	PRUS	Placer	Dutch Flat P O	76	404
HUDEPOHL								
Charles	21	m	w	HANO	Placer	Dutch Flat P O	76	404
H	38	m	w	PRUS	Placer	Dutch Flat P O	76	404
HUDERSON								
Harry	38	m	w	MA	Sonoma	Petaluma Twp	91	335
HUDEWRICH								
John	42	m	w	PRUS	Sacramento	Mississippi Twp	77	163
HUDLER								
Henery	38	m	w	HAMB	San Francisco	7-Wd San Francisco	81	223
HUDNALL								
Preston M	28	m	w	MO	Yolo	Grafton Twp	93	495
HUDNER								
James	42	m	w	IREL	Monterey	San Juan Twp	74	396
HUDNOT								
Alexr	16	m	w	CA	Monterey	Monterey Twp	74	350
HUDNUT								
Joseph	37	m	w	NY	Kern	Linns Valley P O	73	343
Respers	33	f	w	CA	Monterey	Monterey	74	354
Richard	42	m	w	NJ	Kern	Bakersfield P O	73	360
HUDON								
Eliza	50	f	b	VA	San Francisco	2-Wd San Francisco	79	281
HUDSICK								
Alfd W	40	m	w	MO	Butte	Chico Twp	70	46
HUDSON								
Andrew J	37	m	w	MO	Santa Barbara	San Buenaventura P	87	429
Andrew J	33	m	w	MI	San Luis Obispo	Morro Twp	87	281
Andy	45	m	w	IL	Yolo	Putah Twp	93	524
Charles M	18	m	w	VA	San Francisco	3-Wd San Francisco	79	320
Chas	30	m	w	DE	Solano	Vallejo	90	171
D	37	m	w	MI	San Joaquin	Elliott Twp	86	71
David	52	m	w	ENGL	San Francisco	11-Wd San Francisc	84	710
David	49	m	w	MO	Napa	Napa	75	11
Ed	25	m	w	ME	Yuba	Marysville	93	587
Frank	30	m	w	ME	Colusa	Colusa	71	298
Frank	20	m	w	NC	Marin	San Rafael Twp	74	39
Geo	30	m	w	MA	San Francisco	San Francisco P O	83	284
George	35	m	w	CANA	Monterey	San Juan Twp	74	409
George	30	m	w	PA	Los Angeles	Los Angeles	73	505
H S	42	m	w	ENGL	Alameda	Oakland	68	196
Harry	40	m	w	CANA	Monterey	San Juan Twp	74	408
Hattie	34	f	w	MA	Sacramento	2-Wd Sacramento	77	253
Henery	50	m	w	ENGL	San Francisco	7-Wd San Francisco	81	187
Henry	52	m	w	NJ	San Francisco	2-Wd San Francisco	79	210
Henry	38	m	w	NY	San Francisco	6-Wd San Francisco	81	137
Henry	30	m	w	IA	Tehama	Tehama Twp	92	192
Issac	40	m	w	MD	Placer	Dutch Flat P O	76	401
J K	26	m	w	NY	Los Angeles	Los Angeles	73	571
J L	26	m	w	MA	Sonoma	Sonoma Twp	91	439
Jacob	41	m	w	AUST	San Francisco	5-Wd San Francisco	81	26
Jacob	39	m	w	NY	Shasta	Shasta P O	89	456
James	37	m	b	MO	San Joaquin	2-Wd Stockton	86	163
James	34	m	w	IL	Placer	Auburn P O	76	375
James G	36	m	w	DENM	San Bernardino	San Bernardino Twp	78	452
James L	36	m	w	NY	San Mateo	Redwood Twp	87	366
Jas	45	m	w	NY	Solano	Vallejo	90	181
Jas	36	m	w	ENGL	San Francisco	San Francisco P O	83	36
Jennie	16	f	w	NY	San Francisco	7-Wd San Francisco	81	285
Joel	42	m	w	MA	Tuolumne	Columbia P O	93	346
John	48	m	w	PA	Tuolumne	Big Oak Flat P O	93	391
John	48	m	w	RI	Solano	Vallejo	90	162
John	40	m	w	ENGL	San Luis Obispo	Arroyo Grande Twp	87	274
John	39	m	w	ENGL	San Francisco	2-Wd San Francisco	79	158
John	36	m	w	SC	San Bernardino	San Bernardino Twp	78	422
John	25	m	w	RI	San Francisco	11-Wd San Francisc	84	559
John	24	m	w	ENGL	Solano	Vacaville Twp	90	128
John F	22	m	w	CA	Napa	Napa	75	6
John Hamilton	44	m	w	DE	Plumas	Plumas Twp	77	31
John W	42	m	w	IREL	San Francisco	San Francisco P O	83	156
Joseph	40	m	w	MD	San Francisco	6-Wd San Francisco	81	79
Joshua A	43	m	w	MI	Santa Clara	1-Wd San Jose	88	242
Ln P	35	m	w	NY	Sacramento	Franklin Twp	77	112
Mark	25	m	w	IA	Monterey	Pajaro Twp	74	368
Martha	63	f	w	KY	Napa	Napa	75	7
Martin	63	m	w	TN	Sonoma	Santa Rosa	91	424
Martin C	41	m	w	TN	Yolo	Cottonwood Twp	93	463
Molton	52	m	w	DE	Santa Clara	Redwood Twp	88	120
Moses	30	m	w	NY	Yolo	Cottonwood Twp	93	467
Nelson	34	m	w	NY	San Francisco	San Francisco P O	80	393
P	15	m	w	CA	Sierra	Sierra Twp	89	564
Phineas	67	m	w	NY	Alameda	Eden Twp	68	91
Phineas	33	m	w	NY	San Francisco	3-Wd San Francisco	79	315
Pliny E	31	m	w	NY	San Francisco	San Francisco P O	85	753
R T	30	m	w	IL	Amador	Fiddletown P O	69	429
Robert	35	m	w	IL	Amador	Fiddletown P O	69	436
Robt	37	m	w	NY	Solano	Vallejo	90	143
Rosa	3	f	w	CA	San Francisco	6-Wd San Francisco	81	38
Saml	22	m	w	KY	Lake	Lakeport	73	407
Saml N	36	m	w	TN	Sonoma	Bodega Twp	91	248
Samuel	77	m	w	CANA	Sonoma	Sonoma Twp	91	439
Samuel	46	m	w	CANA	Sacramento	American Twp	77	64
Susan	82	f	w	PA	San Joaquin	Castoria Twp	86	3
Thomas	28	m	w	TX	Tulare	Venice Twp	92	273
Thos	65	m	w	NY	San Francisco	San Francisco P O	83	129
Thos J	41	m	w	IREL	Santa Clara	Gilroy Twp	88	86
Thos W	41	m	w	VA	Sonoma	Healdsburg & Mendo	91	285
W K	45	m	w	OH	Sutter	Butte Twp	92	91
W K	42	m	w	ME	Yuba	Marysville	93	596
William	47	m	w	VA	Kern	Tehachapi P O	73	355
William	47	m	w	KY	Santa Clara	Santa Clara Twp	88	151
William	45	m	w	MD	Placer	Dutch Flat P O	76	401
William	31	m	w	MI	Monterey	Pajaro Twp	74	368
William	21	m	w	IN	San Bernardino	San Bernardino Twp	78	448
Wm	41	m	w	IN	Sacramento	San Joaquin Twp	77	405
Wm	40	m	w	IL	Sacramento	Alabama Twp	77	59
Wm	40	m	w	NY	San Francisco	San Francisco P O	83	132
Wm G	37	m	w	MA	Nevada	Grass Valley Twp	75	142
Wm J	30	m	w	MO	San Luis Obispo	Morro Twp	87	281
Wm T	22	m	w	MO	Sonoma	Russian Rvr	91	377
HUDSPETH								
James	57	m	w	AL	Sonoma	Analy Twp	91	234
William	60	m	w	ENGL	Trinity	Weaverville Pct	92	223
HUDSPETT								
Wm	26	m	w	MO	Siskiyou	Surprise Valley Tw	89	639
HUDSPETTE								
Jas	70	m	w	TN	Sonoma	Santa Rosa	91	429
Nancy A	70	f	w	TN	Sonoma	Santa Rosa	91	429
HUE								
Ah	38	m	c	CHIN	Trinity	Weaverville Pct	92	227
Ah	38	m	c	CHIN	San Joaquin	Oneal Twp	86	117
Ah	31	m	c	CHIN	Sierra	Forest	89	537
Ah	30	m	c	CHIN	San Joaquin	Castoria Twp	86	12
Ah	28	m	c	CHIN	Sacramento	Georgianna Twp	77	124
Ah	28	m	c	CHIN	San Francisco	San Francisco P O	80	487
Ah	27	m	c	CHIN	San Joaquin	Castoria Twp	86	12
Ah	24	m	c	CHIN	Sacramento	Natomas Twp	77	171
Ah	22	m	c	CHIN	El Dorado	Coloma Twp	72	3
Ah	21	m	c	CHIN	San Joaquin	Tulare Twp	86	262
Ah	19	m	c	CHIN	San Joaquin	Dent Twp	86	22
Ah	17	m	c	CHIN	San Francisco	San Francisco P O	80	349
Ah	16	m	c	CHIN	San Francisco	1-Wd San Francisco	79	85
Ah	14	m	c	CHIN	San Francisco	6-Wd San Francisco	81	154
Chow	40	m	c	CHIN	Butte	Chico Twp	70	28
Edward	8	m	w	CA	Sacramento	4-Wd Sacramento	77	343
Hi	26	m	c	CHIN	San Joaquin	1-Wd Stockton	86	156
Wa	26	m	c	CHIN	Solano	Vacaville Twp	90	132
HUECKINS								
Harris	29	m	w	MI	Placer	Emigrant Gap P O	76	416
HUEFNER								
Otto	23	m	w	PRUS	San Francisco	6-Wd San Francisco	81	95
HUEN								
Ah	21	m	c	CHIN	San Francisco	San Francisco P O	80	336
Jane	24	f	w	HANO	San Francisco	11-Wd San Francisc	84	658

© 2001 by Heritage Quest. All rights reserved.

Series M593

Name	Age	S	R	B-PL	County	Locale	Roll	Pg
HUENART								
Fred A	46	m	w	WEST	San Francisco	6-Wd San Francisco	81	37
HUENT								
William B	33	m	w	NJ	Los Angeles	Los Angeles Twp	73	471
HUENTE								
Rossa	56	m	w	CHIL	Calaveras	Copperopolis P O	70	247
HUER								
Walter H	28	m	w	MO	San Francisco	6-Wd San Francisco	81	79
HUERNE								
Etienne	49	m	w	FRAN	San Francisco	11-Wd San Francisc	84	575
Jaspar	31	m	w	FRAN	San Francisco	San Francisco P O	80	470
HUERTA								
Juan Joseph	42	m	w	MEXI	Plumas	Quartz Twp	77	34
HUES								
Robbert	41	m	w	CANA	Trinity	Douglas	92	233
Wm A	16	m	w	NY	Butte	Oroville Twp	70	138
HUESMAN								
Charles	22	m	w	PRUS	Sacramento	Center Twp	77	84
Jacob	34	m	w	BADE	San Francisco	7-Wd San Francisco	81	194
HUESTER								
Wm	28	m	w	NY	Tehama	Tehama Twp	92	193
HUESTIS								
John E	23	m	w	IA	Humboldt	Table Bluff Twp	72	306
W F	34	m	w	VA	Humboldt	Bucksport Twp	72	244
Washington	31	m	w	NJ	Humboldt	Bucksport Twp	72	242
HUESTON								
James	38	m	w	OH	Tehama	Toomes & Grant	92	169
Michael	35	m	w	IREL	Contra Costa	Martinez P O	71	431
William	50	m	w	IL	Calaveras	Copperopolis P O	70	249
HUET								
Alex	38	m	w	FRAN	Sierra	Sears Twp	89	556
HUETT								
Henery	30	m	w	FRAN	San Francisco	7-Wd San Francisco	81	180
HUEY								
Ah	30	m	c	CHIN	El Dorado	Salmon Falls Twp	72	131
Ah	25	m	c	CHIN	Plumas	Goodwin Twp	77	4
Ah	23	m	c	CHIN	San Francisco	6-Wd San Francisco	81	60
Charles	39	m	w	MD	Placer	Bath P O	76	459
Chung	44	m	c	CHIN	Placer	Auburn P O	76	372
Het Sue	24	m	c	CHIN	Yuba	Marysville	93	620
James	55	m	w	PA	Humboldt	Table Bluff Twp	72	307
James	35	m	w	IREL	San Francisco	1-Wd San Francisco	79	123
Lo	47	m	c	CHIN	San Joaquin	Oneal Twp	86	116
Sam	24	m	c	CHIN	Yuba	North East Twp	93	647
William R	36	m	w	IN	El Dorado	Mountain Twp	72	68
HUFF								
Abram	39	m	w	NY	Marin	Point Reyes Twp	74	21
Ah	32	m	c	CHIN	Plumas	Goodwin Twp	77	3
Amberson	35	m	w	PA	Napa	Napa	75	57
Angeline	28	f	w	MO	Santa Clara	2-Wd San Jose	88	327
Annie	11	f	w	CA	Nevada	Nevada Twp	75	283
Chas	56	m	b	TN	Yuba	Marysville Twp	93	568
Daniel	30	m	w	NY	Solano	Silveyville Twp	90	86
Daniel E	60	m	w	MA	Yolo	Buckeye Twp	93	412
Edward	36	m	w	MI	Alameda	Alvarado	68	304
Elizabeth	76	f	w	PRUS	San Bernardino	San Bernardino Twp	78	445
Frederick	26	m	w	WURT	Los Angeles	Los Angeles	73	545
Geo	15	m	w	MS	San Joaquin	Liberty Twp	86	91
Hampton	24	m	w	MI	Santa Clara	Fremont Twp	88	42
J J	61	m	w	NY	Solano	Vallejo	90	161
James	40	m	w	FRAN	Sacramento	2-Wd Sacramento	77	248
James E	37	m	w	OH	Santa Clara	Fremont Twp	88	43
Leonard C	57	m	w	TN	Santa Barbara	San Buenaventura P	87	430
Levi	36	m	w	ME	Santa Clara	Fremont Twp	88	65
Lucien	41	m	w	MI	Alameda	Brooklyn	68	27
Mary	30	f	i	MEXI	Inyo	Independence Twp	73	324
Oliver B	45	m	w	ME	San Francisco	8-Wd San Francisco	82	331
Saml D	35	m	w	NY	Butte	Chico Twp	70	26
Socrates	43	m	w	OH	Alameda	San Leandro	68	98
Valentine	46	m	w	VA	Monterey	Castroville Twp	74	335
William	40	m	m	GA	Inyo	Independence Twp	73	324
William D	58	m	w	PA	Santa Cruz	Santa Cruz	89	410
Wm	52	m	b	TN	Yuba	Marysville Twp	93	568
Wm	17	m	w	CA	San Francisco	11-Wd San Francisc	84	593
HUFFAKER								
C C	27	m	w	KY	Sutter	Sutter Twp	92	119
Chris	28	m	w	KY	Sutter	Nicolaus Twp	92	110
Columbus	50	m	w	KY	San Mateo	Belmont P O	87	373
Frances	30	f	w	KY	San Luis Obispo	Morro Twp	87	285
George	33	m	w	TN	Tulare	Venice Twp	92	277
J M	45	m	w	KY	Sutter	Sutter Twp	92	119
Samuel M	46	m	w	IN	Placer	Bath P O	76	438
HUFFARD								
J H	32	m	b	MD	Yuba	Marysville	93	606
Newman	28	m	w	NY	Contra Costa	Martinez P O	71	415
HUFFEKER								
Robert	39	m	w	KY	San Francisco	11-Wd San Francisc	84	637
HUFFERD								
David	42	m	w	KY	Contra Costa	Martinez P O	71	444
HUFFERT								
Barny	42	m	w	LUXE	Sutter	Sutter Twp	92	116
HUFFINE								
Wm	22	m	w	PRUS	San Francisco	San Francisco P O	83	127
HUFFMAN								
C	55	m	w	PA	Monterey	Salinas Twp	74	312
David	56	m	w	VA	Sacramento	Alabama Twp	77	61
Ellis	29	m	w	TN	San Joaquin	Union Twp	86	265

Series M593

Name	Age	S	R	B-PL	County	Locale	Roll	Pg
Frederick	33	m	w	BAVA	Stanislaus	Emory Twp	92	23
Henry	40	m	w	BADE	Stanislaus	San Joaquin Twp	92	78
Henry C	39	m	w	LA	Stanislaus	Empire Twp	92	49
J W	56	m	w	PA	San Joaquin	Elkhorn Twp	86	57
Jeus	35	f	w	LA	San Joaquin	Elkhorn Twp	86	68
L	24	m	w	IA	Napa	Napa Twp	75	68
Robert	50	m	w	PA	Los Angeles	El Monte Twp	73	455
Wm	35	m	w	RI	San Francisco	5-Wd San Francisco	81	18
HUFFMASTER								
Joseph	38	m	w	MA	Kern	Havilah P O	73	350
HUFFORD								
Jacob	70	m	w	MO	Contra Costa	Martinez P O	71	435
John	74	m	w	KY	Shasta	Millville P O	89	492
Solomon	38	m	w	IN	Shasta	Millville P O	89	490
HUFFSCHMIDT								
Louis	28	m	w	PRUS	San Francisco	San Francisco P O	80	394
HUFFT								
Philip W	51	m	w	KY	El Dorado	Diamond Springs Tw	72	22
HUFFUM								
J	29	m	w	PRUS	San Joaquin	Dent Twp	86	25
HUFLEY								
Richard	38	m	w	NC	Humboldt	Table Bluff Twp	72	308
HUFMASTER								
J W	33	m	w	TN	Merced	Snelling P O	74	252
HUG								
Ah	45	m	c	CHIN	Sierra	Table Rock Twp	89	544
Ah	26	m	c	CHIN	Tuolumne	Chinese Camp P O	93	382
Ah	25	m	c	CHIN	Placer	Blue Canyon P O	76	419
Ah	19	m	c	CHIN	Santa Clara	Alviso Twp	88	25
Ah	13	m	c	CHIN	Yuba	Marysville	93	602
Casper	30	m	w	SWIT	San Francisco	San Francisco P O	80	469
Charles	40	m	w	BADE	San Francisco	11-Wd San Francisc	84	528
Fat	22	m	c	CHIN	Solano	Rio Vista Twp	90	64
Fredrick	20	m	w	BADE	Napa	Yountville Twp	75	77
Hoo	27	m	c	CHIN	Sierra	Lincoln Twp	89	548
John	24	m	w	SWIT	San Francisco	San Francisco P O	80	469
Joseph	46	m	w	BADE	San Francisco	San Francisco P O	83	175
HUGABON								
Cornelius	33	m	w	NY	Yolo	Merritt Twp	93	503
HUGAN								
George	50	m	w	MA	Colusa	Colusa	71	300
John	40	m	w	IREL	Napa	Yountville Twp	75	91
John	40	m	w	IREL	Santa Clara	2-Wd San Jose	88	304
John	40	m	w	IREL	San Joaquin	Dent Twp	86	25
HUGAR								
Adelia	28	f	w	IREL	San Joaquin	2-Wd Stockton	86	165
Henry	39	m	w	PRUS	El Dorado	Placerville Twp	72	102
HUGART								
Adam	40	m	w	SAXO	San Francisco	8-Wd San Francisco	82	383
HUGCK								
Johnson	46	m	w	OH	Placer	Cisco P O	76	494
HUGEL								
Joseph	50	m	w	FRAN	San Francisco	San Francisco P O	80	350
HUGENO								
James	25	m	w	CANA	San Joaquin	Liberty Twp	86	92
HUGER								
Lynch P	24	m	w	SC	Santa Barbara	Santa Barbara P O	87	454
HUGERRA								
Nicholas	60	m	w	MEXI	Contra Costa	Martinez P O	71	401
HUGES								
David	40	m	w	MO	Santa Clara	Redwood Twp	88	118
Hugh	55	m	w	NY	Stanislaus	Emory Twp	92	18
Michael	27	m	w	IREL	San Francisco	11-Wd San Francisc	84	541
Patrick G	29	m	w	IREL	Mono	Bridgeport P O	74	282
HUGG								
Benjamin P	43	m	w	DE	Yuba	Slate Range Bar Tw	93	676
Henry	46	m	w	DE	San Francisco	San Francisco P O	83	25
S W	57	m	w	NY	Sacramento	3-Wd Sacramento	77	289
HUGGEN								
Maggie	25	f	w	IREL	San Francisco	San Francisco P O	83	269
HUGGINS								
Clara	9	f	w	CA	San Francisco	San Francisco P O	85	827
E R	30	m	w	NY	Klamath	Liberty Twp	73	374
Emma	10	f	w	CA	San Francisco	San Francisco P O	85	827
L	37	m	w	AR	Sonoma	Santa Rosa	91	395
Wm	30	m	w	NORW	Sacramento	Georgianna Twp	77	130
HUGH								
Ah	31	m	c	CHIN	Nevada	Meadow Lake Twp	75	254
Ah	22	m	c	CHIN	San Joaquin	Elliott Twp	86	71
Charles	30	m	w	CANA	Mendocino	Cuffeys Cove Twp	74	169
Felix Peter	15	m	w	CA	Humboldt	Arcata Twp	72	235
H	41	m	w	WALE	Alameda	Murray Twp	68	99
James	23	m	w	FRAN	San Francisco	San Francisco P O	83	163
John	28	m	w	ENGL	San Francisco	11-Wd San Francisc	84	674
John W	45	m	w	PA	Humboldt	Bald Hills	72	239
L May	40	m	w	PA	Sonoma	Petaluma Twp	91	345
Thomas	44	m	w	ENGL	San Francisco	7-Wd San Francisco	81	217
Thos	37	m	w	PA	San Joaquin	Dent Twp	86	18
Wm	24	m	w	GUAT	Santa Clara	Gilroy Twp	88	104
HUGHELL								
Joseph	87	m	w	PA	Plumas	Quartz Twp	77	42
Phebe	85	f	w	SC	Plumas	Quartz Twp	77	42
HUGHES								
Abe	40	m	w	WALE	San Francisco	2-Wd San Francisco	79	160
Abraham	57	m	w	OH	Tuolumne	Sonora P O	93	329
Alfred	42	m	w	OH	Santa Cruz	Pajaro Twp	89	349
Alfred	40	m	w	IL	San Francisco	5-Wd San Francisco	81	15

© 2001 by Heritage Quest. All rights reserved.

California 1870 Census

Series M593

Name	Age	S	R	B-PL	County	Locale	Roll	Pg
Amelia	64	f	w	MO	Santa Clara	Santa Clara Twp	88	167
Andrew	62	m	w	MO	Shasta	Stillwater P O	89	479
Andrew	36	m	w	CANA	Solano	Vallejo	90	169
Andrew C	8	m	w	CA	Stanislaus	Empire Twp	92	28
Ann	70	f	w	IREL	San Francisco	San Francisco P O	83	173
Ann	30	f	w	IREL	San Francisco	8-Wd San Francisco	82	448
Ann	26	f	w	IREL	San Francisco	8-Wd San Francisco	82	468
Anna M	49	f	w	ENGL	Siskiyou	Scott Valley Twp	89	609
Annie	8	f	w	RI	San Francisco	11-Wd San Francisc	84	639
Benj	49	m	w	PA	Tehama	Red Bluff	92	179
Benjamin	29	m	w	WALE	San Francisco	2-Wd San Francisco	79	261
Brice	28	m	w	IREL	San Luis Obispo	Salinas Twp	87	291
Byron	29	m	w	MS	Del Norte	Happy Camp Twp	71	472
C B	44	m	w	OH	Lake	Lower Lake	73	429
Calvin	28	m	w	OH	Kern	Tehachapi P O	73	353
Charles	42	m	w	IN	Stanislaus	Empire Twp	92	44
Charles	26	m	w	MO	Yolo	Buckeye Twp	93	407
Charles	20	m	w	PA	Sacramento	2-Wd Sacramento	77	237
Charles G	41	m	w	ME	San Francisco	8-Wd San Francisco	82	402
Chas	41	m	w	IREL	Contra Costa	Martinez P O	71	448
Christian	47	m	w	IL	Calaveras	San Andreas P O	70	214
D J	42	m	w	WALE	Tuolumne	Columbia P O	93	351
Daniel	70	m	w	IREL	Calaveras	Copperopolis P O	70	222
Daniel	35	m	w	MO	Mendocino	Calpella Twp	74	187
Daniel	30	m	w	NJ	Kern	Bakersfield P O	73	365
Daniel	25	m	w	NY	Marin	Bolinas Twp	74	5
David	55	m	w	WALE	Marin	San Rafael Twp	74	42
David	55	m	w	WALE	San Francisco	2-Wd San Francisco	79	261
David	47	m	w	NJ	San Francisco	11-Wd San Francisc	84	510
David	28	m	w	NY	San Francisco	8-Wd San Francisco	82	401
David P	22	m	w	WALE	Santa Cruz	Santa Cruz	89	410
Ebbert R	38	m	w	AR	Nevada	Grass Valley Twp	75	219
Ed F	40	m	w	WALE	Sierra	Sears Twp	89	554
Edward	44	m	w	WALE	San Francisco	San Francisco P O	83	258
Edward	33	m	w	ENGL	San Francisco	11-Wd San Francisc	84	466
Edward	30	m	w	IREL	San Francisco	San Francisco P O	83	38
Edward	27	m	w	MO	San Francisco	San Francisco P O	80	428
Edward	27	m	w	IREL	San Francisco	San Francisco P O	83	250
Edward	22	m	w	NY	San Francisco	San Francisco P O	83	224
Edwd	26	m	w	IREL	Marin	San Rafael Twp	74	38
Eliza	48	f	w	IREL	San Francisco	8-Wd San Francisco	82	312
Elizabeth	36	f	w	IREL	San Francisco	San Francisco P O	85	798
Ellen	8	f	w	NY	San Francisco	San Francisco P O	83	42
Ellen	40	f	w	IREL	Nevada	Grass Valley Twp	75	164
Ellen	35	f	w	IREL	San Francisco	San Francisco P O	83	303
Ellis	48	m	w	WALE	San Francisco	San Francisco P O	85	873
Francis	34	m	w	IREL	San Francisco	11-Wd San Francisc	84	464
Frank	44	m	w	IREL	Colusa	Spring Valley Twp	71	340
Frank	33	m	w	GERM	Contra Costa	Martinez P O	71	401
G M	41	m	w	WALE	Nevada	Nevada Twp	75	286
Geo H	42	m	w	NY	San Francisco	1-Wd San Francisco	79	59
George	49	m	w	ENGL	Alameda	Alameda	68	14
George	28	m	w	VT	Solano	Silveyville Twp	90	87
George	24	m	w	PA	Stanislaus	Empire Twp	92	45
George F	24	m	w	PA	Stanislaus	San Joaquin Twp	92	74
H	30	m	w	WALE	Lake	Lower Lake	73	415
Helen	29	f	w	IREL	San Francisco	San Francisco P O	80	390
Henry	43	m	w	ENGL	San Francisco	San Francisco P O	83	124
Henry	41	m	w	PA	Santa Clara	Santa Clara Twp	88	147
Henry	39	m	w	NY	San Diego	San Diego	78	486
Henry	36	m	w	PA	Santa Clara	2-Wd San Jose	88	329
Henry	30	m	w	CANA	San Mateo	Woodside P O	87	386
Henry	25	m	w	ENGL	San Francisco	8-Wd San Francisco	82	364
Henry V	12	m	w	CA	Sacramento	4-Wd Sacramento	77	348
Hiram	61	m	w	KY	Stanislaus	Emory Twp	92	26
Horace M	39	m	w	NY	Colusa	Colusa	71	296
Hugh	40	m	w	WALE	San Francisco	1-Wd San Francisco	79	45
Hugh	38	m	w	WALE	Sierra	Table Rock Twp	89	572
Hugh	32	m	w	ENGL	San Francisco	San Francisco P O	80	373
J	32	m	w	IREL	Sierra	Downieville Twp	89	520
J G	27	m	w	KY	Tuolumne	Sonora P O	93	316
J J	20	m	w	NY	San Francisco	San Francisco P O	85	856
J W	51	m	w	WALE	San Francisco	San Francisco P O	83	12
James	65	m	w	IREL	San Francisco	5-Wd San Francisco	81	32
James	64	m	w	PA	San Francisco	3-Wd San Francisco	79	319
James	53	m	w	ENGL	Del Norte	Crescent	71	465
James	44	m	w	IREL	San Francisco	San Francisco P O	83	154
James	43	m	w	KY	Mendocino	Calpella Twp	74	188
James	40	m	w	NY	San Joaquin	Douglas Twp	86	32
James	39	m	w	IREL	Tuolumne	Big Oak Flat P O	93	402
James	35	m	w	IREL	San Francisco	11-Wd San Francisc	84	435
James	35	m	w	IREL	San Francisco	11-Wd San Francisc	84	632
James	35	m	w	IREL	San Francisco	11-Wd San Francisc	84	428
James	31	m	w	WALE	San Francisco	1-Wd San Francisco	79	78
James	30	m	w	ENGL	San Francisco	11-Wd San Francisc	84	636
James	24	m	w	NY	San Francisco	8-Wd San Francisco	82	366
James	22	m	w	IREL	Inyo	Independence Twp	73	326
James	20	m	w	OH	Santa Barbara	San Buenaventura P	87	446
James	18	m	w	CA	El Dorado	Placerville	72	124
Jane	61	f	w	KY	Mendocino	Calpella Twp	74	187
Jane	55	f	w	IREL	San Francisco	San Francisco P O	83	167
Jas	40	m	w	IREL	Solano	Vallejo	90	149
Jas	37	m	w	IREL	Sierra	Gibson Twp	89	538
Jas	28	m	w	MI	San Francisco	8-Wd San Francisco	82	379
Jas H	55	m	w	KY	Mendocino	Ukiah Twp	74	233
Jas R	34	m	w	LA	Klamath	Liberty Twp	73	374
Jeremiah	35	m	w	IREL	Nevada	Little York Twp	75	241

Series M593

Name	Age	S	R	B-PL	County	Locale	Roll	Pg
Jesse	50	m	b	VA	San Francisco	6-Wd San Francisco	81	109
Jesse	41	m	w	WALE	Sierra	Sears Twp	89	527
Jessee	30	m	w	VA	Stanislaus	Empire Twp	92	48
Joah J	40	m	w	OH	Los Angeles	Los Angeles Twp	73	478
John	50	m	w	IREL	Nevada	Eureka Twp	75	134
John	49	m	w	AR	Fresno	Kings Rvr P O	72	203
John	47	m	w	IREL	Nevada	Eureka Twp	75	136
John	45	m	w	WALE	Nevada	Bridgeport Twp	75	102
John	41	m	w	KY	Sonoma	Santa Rosa	91	423
John	40	m	w	IREL	San Francisco	11-Wd San Francisc	84	535
John	40	m	w	IREL	San Mateo	Redwood Twp	87	361
John	38	m	w	WALE	Contra Costa	Martinez P O	71	426
John	38	m	w	IREL	San Francisco	San Francisco P O	83	92
John	33	m	w	IREL	San Francisco	1-Wd San Francisco	79	7
John	32	m	w	ENGL	San Francisco	6-Wd San Francisco	81	103
John	32	m	w	OH	Mariposa	Mariposa P O	74	113
John	31	m	w	WALE	Contra Costa	Martinez Twp	71	348
John	31	m	w	NY	San Francisco	11-Wd San Francisc	84	585
John	30	m	w	OH	Lake	Big Valley	73	396
John	30	m	w	NY	Inyo	Independence Twp	73	325
John	29	m	w	NY	Mendocino	Round Valley Twp	74	217
John	29	m	w	IREL	San Francisco	San Francisco P O	80	335
John	28	m	w	IREL	San Francisco	San Francisco P O	80	473
John	28	m	w	IREL	Santa Clara	Redwood Twp	88	123
John	28	m	w	CANA	El Dorado	Placerville Twp	72	105
John	27	m	w	IREL	San Francisco	San Francisco P O	83	183
John	25	m	w	IREL	Yolo	Putah Twp	93	516
John	23	m	w	MO	San Joaquin	Dent Twp	86	24
John	23	m	w	AL	San Bernardino	San Bernardino Twp	78	448
John	17	m	w	NY	Placer	Cisco P O	76	494
John E	30	m	w	AR	Stanislaus	North Twp	92	69
John R	46	m	w	NY	Inyo	Independence Twp	73	327
John S	40	m	w	NY	Klamath	Sawyers Bar	73	377
John W	38	m	w	VA	Siskiyou	Yreka	89	656
Johnathan	25	m	w	CANA	Yuba	Marysville	93	577
Joseph	35	m	w	OH	Napa	Napa Twp	75	68
Joseph	33	m	w	IREL	San Francisco	1-Wd San Francisco	79	35
Joseph	32	m	w	VT	Marin	San Rafael Twp	74	40
Joseph	28	m	w	ENGL	San Francisco	San Francisco P O	83	133
Julius	28	m	w	BADE	Sacramento	3-Wd Sacramento	77	304
Kate	35	f	w	IREL	San Francisco	San Francisco P O	80	358
Kate	27	f	w	IREL	San Francisco	6-Wd San Francisco	81	118
Kate	20	f	w	NY	San Francisco	San Francisco P O	85	720
Kimber	45	m	w	KY	Santa Cruz	Soquel Twp	89	437
Lawrence	49	m	w	IREL	Shasta	French Gulch P O	89	467
Leander	34	m	w	KY	Siskiyou	Surprise Valley Tw	89	640
Leonora	6	f	w	CA	Siskiyou	Scott Valley Twp	89	612
Lewis	21	m	w	IA	Tulare	Venice Twp	92	277
Lizzy	8	f	w	CA	Siskiyou	Scott Valley Twp	89	611
Louis	37	m	w	OH	Siskiyou	Callahan P O	89	631
Louisa	27	f	w	MO	Napa	Napa Twp	75	68
M E	44	m	w	IREL	Tuolumne	Sonora P O	93	308
M E	39	m	w	IREL	San Francisco	San Francisco P O	85	812
Margaret	9	f	w	IREL	San Francisco	San Francisco P O	85	776
Margaret	35	f	w	IREL	San Francisco	8-Wd San Francisco	82	390
Martin	45	m	w	IREL	Sacramento	4-Wd Sacramento	77	340
Martin	40	m	w	IREL	Yolo	Putah Twp	93	523
Martin	32	m	w	NY	Solano	Vallejo	90	197
Mary	40	f	w	IL	Yolo	Grafton Twp	93	487
Mary	40	f	w	IL	Yolo	Grafton Twp	93	487
Mary	35	f	w	IREL	San Francisco	1-Wd San Francisco	79	81
Mary	35	f	w	IREL	Alameda	Brooklyn	68	29
Mary	34	f	w	IREL	San Francisco	San Francisco P O	83	221
Mary	33	f	w	IREL	San Francisco	8-Wd San Francisco	82	472
Mary	30	f	w	IREL	San Francisco	San Francisco P O	83	52
Mathew	34	m	w	WI	Placer	Gold Run Twp	76	400
Matthew	49	m	w	IREL	San Francisco	1-Wd San Francisco	79	76
Michael	58	m	w	IREL	Santa Clara	Alviso Twp	88	28
Michael	34	m	w	IREL	Yuba	Rose Bar Twp	93	654
Michael	26	m	w	MO	Santa Clara	Milpitas Twp	88	112
Michael	26	m	w	IREL	Santa Clara	2-Wd San Jose	88	329
Mike	40	m	w	IREL	San Francisco	11-Wd San Francisc	84	657
Mike	35	m	w	IREL	San Francisco	San Francisco P O	85	785
Napoleon	32	m	w	MO	Stanislaus	Emory Twp	92	26
Nicholas	20	m	w	MO	Yolo	Cottonwood Twp	93	460
O C	33	m	w	IREL	San Francisco	San Francisco P O	83	312
Owen	50	m	w	IREL	San Francisco	11-Wd San Francisc	84	612
Owen	35	m	w	IREL	San Francisco	11-Wd San Francisc	84	530
Owen	29	m	w	IREL	Merced	Snelling P O	74	272
Owen	21	m	w	WALE	Colusa	Monroe Twp	71	321
P	22	f	w	IREL	San Francisco	San Francisco P O	83	132
Pat	33	m	w	IREL	San Francisco	San Francisco P O	83	82
Patk	30	m	w	IREL	Sacramento	4-Wd Sacramento	77	341
Patrick	46	m	w	IREL	San Francisco	11-Wd San Francisc	84	651
Patrick	40	m	w	IREL	San Francisco	1-Wd San Francisco	79	81
Patrick	38	m	w	IREL	Shasta	French Gulch P O	89	468
Patrick	38	m	w	IREL	Santa Clara	2-Wd San Jose	88	310
Patrick	37	m	w	IREL	Santa Clara	Santa Clara Twp	88	176
Patrick	33	m	w	IREL	San Francisco	San Francisco P O	83	333
Patrick	33	m	w	IREL	San Francisco	5-Wd San Francisco	81	7
Patrick	30	m	w	IREL	Santa Cruz	Santa Cruz Twp	89	387
Patrick	27	m	w	IREL	San Francisco	7-Wd San Francisco	81	186
Peter	43	m	w	ENGL	Sacramento	4-Wd Sacramento	77	367
Peter P	53	m	w	OH	El Dorado	Cosumnes Twp	72	19
Peter P	19	m	w	WI	El Dorado	Cosumnes Twp	72	19
Richard	55	m	w	WALE	Tuolumne	Columbia P O	93	351
Richd	32	m	w	IREL	Sacramento	4-Wd Sacramento	77	325

© 2001 by Heritage Quest. All rights reserved.

Series M593

Name	Age	S	R	B-PL	County	Locale	Roll	Pg
Robert	50	m	w	ENGL	Inyo	Lone Pine Twp	73	331
Robert	29	m	w	ME	San Joaquin	Tulare Twp	86	262
Robert	19	m	w	ENGL	Los Angeles	Los Angeles	73	536
Robert J	41	m	w	WALE	Nevada	Bridgeport Twp	75	108
Robt	30	m	w	VA	San Joaquin	1-Wd Stockton	86	131
Robt J H	43	m	w	ENGL	San Francisco	1-Wd San Francisco	79	92
Rowland	41	m	w	MO	Sonoma	Analy Twp	91	231
Ryan	33	m	w	NY	San Francisco	8-Wd San Francisco	82	457
Samuel	27	m	w	MO	Amador	Volcano P O	69	385
Samuel	10	m	w	CA	Napa	Yountville Twp	75	84
Sarah A	25	f	w	ENGL	San Francisco	8-Wd San Francisco	82	290
Terence	36	m	w	IREL	Solano	Vallejo	90	153
Tho M	40	f	w	ENGL	San Francisco	8-Wd San Francisco	82	329
Thomas	8	m	w	CA	Yolo	Cache Crk Twp	93	420
Thomas	73	m	w	ENGL	Stanislaus	North Twp	92	69
Thomas	40	m	w	WALE	Plumas	Mineral Twp	77	21
Thomas	32	m	w	WALE	Yolo	Cache Crk Twp	93	429
Thomas	29	m	w	IREL	San Francisco	San Francisco P O	83	251
Thomas	28	m	w	IREL	San Francisco	7-Wd San Francisco	81	221
Thomas	26	m	w	WALE	Contra Costa	Martinez P O	71	428
Thomas	25	m	w	NY	Inyo	Independence Twp	73	325
Thomas E	40	m	w	NC	Stanislaus	North Twp	92	69
Thomas L	47	m	w	NH	Nevada	Nevada Twp	75	310
Thos	41	m	w	WALE	Sierra	Sears Twp	89	559
Thos	30	m	w	IREL	Nevada	Nevada Twp	75	282
Thos F	37	m	w	PA	Colusa	Spring Valley Twp	71	339
W	44	m	w	ITAL	Sierra	Butte Twp	89	512
W	41	m	w	NY	Sierra	Downieville Twp	89	518
W J	15	m	w	MA	San Francisco	San Francisco P O	83	202
W W	14	m	w	CA	El Dorado	Greenwood Twp	72	52
Washington	52	m	w	MO	Amador	Volcano P O	69	383
Watson	34	m	w	MO	Alameda	Eden Twp	68	71
Wesley	35	m	w	IN	Siskiyou	Yreka	89	652
William	59	m	w	NY	Nevada	Bloomfield Twp	75	99
William	52	m	w	ENGL	Kern	Bakersfield P O	73	364
William	52	m	w	MO	San Francisco	San Francisco P O	80	382
William	48	m	w	ENGL	San Francisco	San Francisco P O	80	336
William	47	m	w	OH	Mariposa	Mariposa P O	74	118
William	40	m	w	NY	San Francisco	11-Wd San Francisc	84	511
William	39	m	w	MO	Mendocino	Calpella Twp	74	187
William	38	m	w	IREL	San Francisco	San Francisco P O	80	373
William	36	m	w	ME	San Mateo	Searsville P O	87	382
William	35	m	w	ENGL	Santa Clara	Fremont Twp	88	49
William	35	m	w	ENGL	Santa Clara	1-Wd San Jose	88	233
William	32	m	w	WALE	Contra Costa	Martinez P O	71	430
William	30	m	w	VA	San Francisco	San Francisco P O	80	486
William	29	m	w	ENGL	San Francisco	San Francisco P O	83	161
William	24	m	w	IREL	San Francisco	San Francisco P O	80	333
William	19	m	w	WALE	Contra Costa	Martinez P O	71	428
William	17	m	w	IA	Los Angeles	Los Angeles Twp	73	491
William	15	m	w	MA	San Francisco	7-Wd San Francisco	81	205
William C	42	m	w	NC	Stanislaus	Empire Twp	92	37
William H	18	m	w	ME	Stanislaus	Empire Twp	92	37
Wm	49	m	w	PA	San Joaquin	Castoria Twp	86	3
Wm	42	m	w	LA	San Joaquin	2-Wd Stockton	86	182
Wm	40	m	w	ENGL	San Francisco	San Francisco P O	83	48
Wm	34	m	w	IL	Marin	San Rafael Twp	74	38
Wm	32	m	w	PA	Santa Barbara	San Buenaventura P	87	418
Wm B	30	m	w	CANA	Solano	Vallejo	90	181
Wm S	56	m	w	PA	Marin	San Rafael	74	56
Wm W	30	m	w	SWED	San Francisco	1-Wd San Francisco	79	71
HUGHEY								
George	24	m	w	OH	Yolo	Cache Crk Twp	93	426
HUGHLETT								
John	31	m	w	TN	Shasta	Fort Crook P O	89	476
HUGHS								
Agness	28	f	w	IREL	San Francisco	7-Wd San Francisco	81	156
Andrew	38	m	w	IL	San Luis Obispo	Morro Twp	87	285
Arto	42	m	w	IREL	San Francisco	11-Wd San Francisc	84	675
Cathren	35	f	w	IREL	San Joaquin	2-Wd Stockton	86	168
Charles	34	m	w	FRAN	Sonoma	Sonoma Twp	91	440
Clara	6	f	w	NV	San Luis Obispo	Arroyo Grande Twp	87	270
Ellen	22	f	w	MO	San Joaquin	Liberty Twp	86	88
Frank	28	m	w	MO	Sonoma	Cloverdale Twp	91	271
Franklin	22	m	w	MO	Alameda	Eden Twp	68	71
G W	38	m	w	IN	Sierra	Downieville Twp	89	519
G Wm	32	m	w	VA	San Joaquin	2-Wd Stockton	86	174
George W	26	m	w	OH	San Luis Obispo	San Luis Obispo Tw	87	316
Henry	36	m	w	OH	Sacramento	Cosumnes Twp	77	91
Henry	36	m	w	IREL	Amador	Fiddletown P O	69	440
Henry	35	m	w	IL	Sutter	Butte Twp	92	103
Hugh	30	m	w	WALE	Sonoma	Salt Point	91	384
James H	48	m	w	ME	San Mateo	Belmont P O	87	373
John	63	m	b	TN	San Joaquin	1-Wd Stockton	86	129
John	61	m	w	IREL	Mariposa	Maxwell Crk P O	74	142
John	46	m	w	MD	Mariposa	Maxwell Crk P O	74	145
John	42	m	w	PA	Sutter	Butte Twp	92	96
John	28	m	w	IREL	San Joaquin	Oneal Twp	86	112
John	26	m	w	ENGL	Contra Costa	Martinez P O	71	423
John	24	m	w	IL	Sutter	Butte Twp	92	103
Josiah	46	m	w	NJ	Calaveras	San Andreas P O	70	189
Maria	70	f	w	ENGL	San Mateo	Belmont P O	87	372
Mary	70	f	w	SC	Calaveras	San Andreas P O	70	152
Mary	55	f	w	WALE	Calaveras	San Andreas P O	70	188
Mary	40	f	w	IL	Yolo	Cache Crk Twp	93	453
Mary	26	f	w	IREL	San Francisco	7-Wd San Francisco	81	192
Michael	34	m	w	IREL	Monterey	Salinas Twp	74	306

Series M593

Name	Age	S	R	B-PL	County	Locale	Roll	Pg
Patrick	46	m	w	IREL	San Francisco	San Francisco P O	85	807
Patrick	37	m	w	IREL	Sacramento	American Twp	77	66
Patrick	30	m	w	IREL	San Mateo	San Mateo P O	87	360
Patrick	24	m	w	IREL	Sonoma	Vallejo Twp	91	459
Peter	35	m	w	IREL	Sacramento	Granite Twp	77	140
Richard R	31	m	w	NY	Placer	Bath P O	76	453
Robert	35	m	w	IREL	Alameda	Washington Twp	68	285
Samuel	40	m	w	TN	Calaveras	San Andreas P O	70	165
Thomas	41	m	w	WALE	Alameda	Brooklyn	68	24
Thomas	33	m	w	NY	San Joaquin	Oneal Twp	86	98
Thomas	31	m	w	IREL	San Francisco	7-Wd San Francisco	81	221
Thomas	24	m	w	IREL	Sonoma	Vallejo Twp	91	454
W J	24	m	w	WALE	Lake	Lower Lake	73	416
William	51	m	w	IREL	San Mateo	Belmont P O	87	372
William	48	m	w	ENGL	San Francisco	7-Wd San Francisco	81	182
Wm	45	m	w	SCOT	San Joaquin	2-Wd Stockton	86	174
Wm	39	m	w	IREL	Sierra	Table Rock Twp	89	571
Wm C	42	m	w	NC	San Joaquin	Castoria Twp	86	5
HUGHSON								
Elias	66	m	w	NY	San Francisco	San Francisco P O	80	402
Henry	31	m	w	ENGL	San Francisco	1-Wd San Francisco	79	89
M	12	f	w	HI	Alameda	Oakland	68	215
HUGHSTON								
Dora	10	f	w	PA	San Francisco	San Francisco P O	85	789
Geo	31	m	w	NY	San Francisco	11-Wd San Francisc	84	522
William	56	m	w	PA	Santa Clara	Milpitas Twp	88	116
HUGO								
L	27	m	w	PRUS	Sacramento	4-Wd Sacramento	77	335
Victor	46	m	w	FRAN	San Francisco	San Francisco P O	80	345
Victor	16	m	w	SWIT	San Francisco	8-Wd San Francisco	82	318
HUGS								
Julia	19	f	w	IREL	San Francisco	San Francisco P O	85	776
HUGUES								
B	68	m	w	FRAN	Sonoma	Petaluma Twp	91	333
HUGUNIN								
Edward	57	m	w	NY	Napa	Napa	75	36
William	38	m	w	NY	Nevada	Grass Valley Twp	75	176
HUI								
Ah	31	m	c	CHIN	San Francisco	San Francisco P O	80	490
HUIE								
George	46	m	w	KY	San Francisco	11-Wd San Francisc	84	499
John	50	m	w	KY	San Francisco	11-Wd San Francisc	84	483
Philip	32	m	w	OH	Nevada	Meadow Lake Twp	75	253
HUIET								
Wm J	33	m	w	MO	Sonoma	Analy Twp	91	231
HUIETT								
John	16	m	w	CA	San Francisco	San Francisco P O	80	482
HUIM								
Marie	40	f	w	FRAN	San Francisco	San Francisco P O	80	464
HUING								
Ah	28	m	c	CHIN	Santa Cruz	Watsonville	89	369
HUISTER								
Louis	17	m	w	PRUS	Shasta	Millville P O	89	486
HUL								
Leonard P	52	m	w	NY	Sacramento	Franklin Twp	77	111
Thos	30	m	w	MS	San Joaquin	Dent Twp	86	17
HULA								
P	22	m	w	PRUS	San Joaquin	2-Wd Stockton	86	165
HULAN								
Saml	60	m	w	NJ	Humboldt	Eel Rvr Twp	72	255
HULBART								
J H	27	m	w	OH	Nevada	Meadow Lake Twp	75	252
HULBERD								
Martha	26	f	w	OH	Santa Clara	1-Wd San Jose	88	252
HULBERT								
A	33	m	w	CANA	Monterey	Salinas Twp	74	309
Ephraim	29	m	w	ENGL	San Francisco	San Francisco P O	85	867
H	26	m	w	WI	Sutter	Yuba Twp	92	151
Hiram	45	m	w	WI	Yolo	Grafton Twp	93	492
James	33	m	w	IREL	Sonoma	Salt Point Twp	91	383
John W	27	m	w	PA	Placer	Blue Canyon P O	76	419
S O	25	m	w	NY	Sacramento	Franklin Twp	77	121
Wm	53	m	w	NY	San Francisco	San Francisco P O	85	769
HULBRESON								
Henry	8	m	w	CA	Stanislaus	Empire Twp	92	61
Ole	32	m	w	NORW	Stanislaus	Empire Twp	92	61
HULBURT								
B G	50	m	w	CT	Sutter	Sutter Twp	92	126
Hiland S	52	m	w	VT	El Dorado	Placerville	72	124
Hiram	20	m	w	WI	Sutter	Butte Twp	92	97
Josiah	61	m	w	CANA	Sutter	Yuba Twp	92	150
HULDORT								
A	40	m	w	BAVA	San Joaquin	Tulare Twp	86	259
HULE								
Chas	38	m	w	NJ	San Joaquin	Union Twp	86	268
Cyrill	51	m	w	CANA	Inyo	Cerro Gordo Twp	73	319
HULEN								
David	40	m	w	OH	Butte	Chico Twp	70	37
HULESTOCK								
Alx	45	m	b	MD	San Joaquin	2-Wd Stockton	86	175
HULETT								
Nathan	70	m	w	CT	Santa Barbara	Santa Barbara P O	87	494
HULEY								
James	42	m	w	IREL	Siskiyou	Butte Twp	89	588
Robert	38	m	w	IREL	San Francisco	11-Wd San Francisc	84	486
HULFORD								
E W	34	m	w	ENGL	El Dorado	Greenwood Twp	72	53

© 2001 by Heritage Quest. All rights reserved.

Name	Age	S	R	B-PL	County	Locale	Series M593 Roll	Pg
HULIHAN								
John	52	m	w	IREL	San Francisco	7-Wd San Francisco	81	197
HULING								
Chas	23	m	w	IN	Yuba	Rose Bar Twp	93	665
HULIT								
S J	48	m	w	LA	Butte	Mountain Spring Tw	70	88
HULL								
Benjamin J	40	m	w	CT	San Francisco	6-Wd San Francisco	81	96
Charles	35	m	w	CT	San Francisco	San Francisco P O	83	174
Chas A	40	m	w	VT	Sacramento	Franklin Twp	77	109
Chas J	33	m	w	PA	Sierra	Table Rock Twp	89	574
Clarence	28	m	w	OH	Placer	Roseville P O	76	355
Clarrence	27	m	w	OH	Sutter	Vernon Twp	92	130
Clemiclas	26	m	w	IL	Colusa	Stony Crk Twp	71	333
Cyrus V	54	m	w	NY	Colusa	Stony Crk Twp	71	333
David	4	m	w	CA	San Francisco	11-Wd San Francisc	84	635
Dellezell	30	m	w	VA	Yolo	Grafton Twp	93	494
E A	30	m	w	MO	San Joaquin	Liberty Twp	86	82
Edwin	24	m	w	ENGL	Sacramento	1-Wd Sacramento	77	204
Frank	16	m	w	NV	Sacramento	Lee Twp	77	160
G L	39	m	w	RI	San Francisco	San Francisco P O	85	839
George S	40	m	w	NY	San Francisco	6-Wd San Francisco	81	154
John M	40	m	w	NC	Sonoma	Salt Point Twp	91	383
Joseph	57	m	w	OH	Sacramento	Sutter Twp	77	389
Joseph	40	m	w	IREL	Napa	Napa Twp	75	69
Philip	61	m	w	OH	Sacramento	Dry Crk Twp	77	103
Richard	50	m	w	IREL	Santa Clara	1-Wd San Jose	88	225
Saml	29	m	w	MA	Sacramento	1-Wd Sacramento	77	186
Saml H	69	m	w	CT	Shasta	Stillwater P O	89	480
Sylvester	39	m	w	OH	Shasta	Stillwater P O	89	480
T	30	m	w	IL	San Joaquin	Liberty Twp	86	86
T B	36	m	w	NY	Sutter	Sutter Twp	92	121
Thos B	40	m	w	OH	Sacramento	American Twp	77	66
W P	41	m	w	OH	Trinity	Trinity Center Pct	92	204
William	76	m	w	HANO	San Francisco	3-Wd San Francisco	79	299
William	33	m	w	AL	Calaveras	San Andreas P O	70	218
Wm	40	m	w	PA	San Francisco	8-Wd San Francisco	82	367
Z T	23	m	w	IL	San Joaquin	Elliott Twp	86	74
HULLAN								
George	52	m	w	ENGL	San Francisco	7-Wd San Francisco	81	210
HULLENBECK								
Henry	39	m	w	NY	Contra Costa	Martinez P O	71	368
HULLERY								
Annie	22	f	w	MO	Mariposa	Mariposa P O	74	118
HULLEY								
Albert	20	m	w	NY	San Francisco	San Francisco P O	83	244
Martha	52	f	w	ENGL	Lassen	Long Valley Twp	73	436
HULLMAN								
Louisa	24	f	w	PRUS	Sacramento	2-Wd Sacramento	77	226
HULMAN								
John	26	m	w	PRUS	San Francisco	7-Wd San Francisco	81	224
Saml R	57	m	w	DE	Santa Cruz	Santa Cruz	89	408
HULME								
James	31	m	w	NJ	San Francisco	11-Wd San Francisc	84	526
Wm	22	m	w	ENGL	San Francisco	7-Wd San Francisco	81	241
HULON								
George	48	m	w	FRAN	Tehama	Merrill	92	197
HULS								
Joseph	55	m	w	KY	Yolo	Cottonwood Twp	93	469
HULSE								
Albert P	42	m	w	OH	Santa Clara	2-Wd San Jose	88	305
Danl A	24	m	w	NY	San Francisco	5-Wd San Francisco	81	16
HULSEMAN								
C	16	m	w	BADE	Sacramento	3-Wd Sacramento	77	311
Peter H	18	m	w	HANO	San Francisco	8-Wd San Francisco	82	381
HULSEY								
Chas	47	m	w	GA	Shasta	American Ranch P O	89	496
Robt	22	m	w	GA	Sacramento	American Twp	77	67
HULSH								
Fulgarth	39	m	w	HOLL	San Francisco	7-Wd San Francisco	81	269
HULSMAN								
J	31	m	w	PRUS	Lassen	Susanville Twp	73	439
HULT								
John	30	m	w	SWED	San Francisco	San Francisco P O	80	334
HULTON								
Henry	30	m	w	NY	San Francisco	7-Wd San Francisco	81	270
Hugh	42	m	w	ENGL	San Francisco	2-Wd San Francisco	79	257
James	29	m	w	NY	Kern	Tehachapi P O	73	356
John	43	m	w	ME	San Francisco	11-Wd San Francisc	84	498
John	27	m	w	MO	San Joaquin	2-Wd Stockton	86	206
Wm	32	m	w	SCOT	San Francisco	7-Wd San Francisco	81	259
HULTZ								
Claus	40	m	w	PRUS	Amador	Sutter Crk P O	69	409
Conrad F	39	m	w	BAVA	San Francisco	1-Wd San Francisco	79	111
S D	50	m	w	NY	Yuba	Marysville Twp	93	568
HULY								
Henry	30	m	w	VA	Sacramento	4-Wd Sacramento	77	324
HUM								
Ah	51	m	c	CHIN	Nevada	Meadow Lake Twp	75	255
Ah	45	m	c	CHIN	El Dorado	Cosumnes Twp	72	13
Ah	41	m	c	CHIN	Marin	San Rafael Twp	74	39
Ah	33	m	c	CHIN	Fresno	Millerton P O	72	202
Ah	32	m	c	CHIN	San Francisco	San Francisco P O	80	521
Ah	32	m	c	CHIN	San Francisco	San Francisco P O	80	512
Ah	30	m	c	CHIN	Sacramento	Sutter Twp	77	385
Ah	26	m	c	CHIN	Tehama	Tehama Twp	92	188
Ah	20	m	c	CHIN	San Francisco	6-Wd San Francisco	81	42
Ah	18	m	c	CHIN	San Francisco	6-Wd San Francisco	81	48
Ah	17	m	c	CHIN	San Francisco	6-Wd San Francisco	81	49
Bouy	28	m	c	CHIN	Humboldt	Arcata Twp	72	233
Bow	24	m	c	CHIN	San Mateo	Half Moon Bay P O	87	395
Cha	38	m	c	CHIN	Yuba	Marysville	93	623
Cook	46	m	c	CHIN	Yuba	Marysville	93	623
Cook	36	m	c	CHIN	Yuba	Marysville	93	621
Fee	48	m	c	CHIN	Yuba	Marysville	93	623
Ho	40	m	c	CHIN	San Joaquin	Liberty Twp	86	97
Ho	40	m	c	CHIN	San Joaquin	1-Wd Stockton	86	156
Lee	29	m	c	CHIN	Yuba	Marysville	93	623
Lop	38	m	c	CHIN	Sacramento	1-Wd Sacramento	77	198
Si	45	m	c	CHIN	Yuba	Marysville	93	623
Soo	35	m	c	CHIN	Yuba	Marysville	93	623
HUMASTON								
Eliza	44	f	w	NY	San Francisco	San Francisco P O	85	826
HUMBART								
Albert	60	m	w	PRUS	San Francisco	6-Wd San Francisco	81	81
HUMBERHAND								
Charles	27	m	w	ME	Mendocino	Navarro & Big Rvr	74	174
HUMBERT								
Charles E	34	m	w	PRUS	Santa Clara	2-Wd San Jose	88	323
I	42	m	w	NY	Alameda	Oakland	68	136
Joseph	48	m	w	FRAN	Los Angeles	Los Angeles	73	567
Louisa	22	f	w	OH	Santa Clara	2-Wd San Jose	88	314
HUMBLE								
Helen	35	f	w	BADE	San Francisco	11-Wd San Francisc	84	611
HUMBOLD								
Danl M	36	m	w	PA	Sonoma	Cloverdale Twp	91	268
HUMBOLT								
M	30	m	w	GERM	San Francisco	8-Wd San Francisco	82	375
HUMBRUT								
Auguste	36	m	w	HCAS	San Francisco	11-Wd San Francisc	84	513
HUMDEN								
W H	33	m	w	MA	Alameda	Alameda	68	7
HUME								
Ah	44	m	c	CHIN	Trinity	Lewiston Pct	92	212
Andrew	34	m	w	IREL	Calaveras	San Andreas P O	70	177
David N	23	m	w	MO	Santa Cruz	Santa Cruz Twp	89	392
George	9	m	i	OR	Sonoma	Analy Twp	91	230
Jas	33	m	w	IREL	San Joaquin	3-Wd Stockton	86	225
John	26	m	w	MO	Tehama	Tehama Twp	92	187
Mary J	22	f	w	CANA	San Francisco	San Francisco P O	83	94
Reuben	28	m	w	ENGL	Santa Clara	San Jose Twp	88	195
Robt	40	m	w	IREL	El Dorado	Coloma Twp	72	2
William	40	m	w	GERM	Sutter	Nicolaus Twp	92	106
Wilson T	10	m	w	CA	Santa Cruz	Watsonville	89	368
HUMES								
D M	22	m	w	MO	Monterey	Monterey Twp	74	346
Thompson	65	m	w	CANA	Nevada	Nevada Twp	75	294
HUMISTON								
Elood E	22	m	w	NY	El Dorado	Mud Springs Twp	72	72
Frank	46	m	w	OH	Kern	Kernville P O	73	367
HUMIWELL								
Nelson B	41	m	w	ME	Mono	Bridgeport P O	74	282
HUMMEL								
George	31	m	w	PRUS	San Francisco	San Francisco P O	80	392
James F	50	m	w	WURT	Sacramento	2-Wd Sacramento	77	237
John	45	m	w	BADE	San Francisco	2-Wd San Francisco	79	164
William	20	m	w	BAVA	Yolo	Cache Crk Twp	93	420
HUMMELL								
Augustus	31	m	w	BAVA	San Francisco	San Francisco P O	83	34
HUMMELMAN								
Andrew	44	m	w	PRUS	San Francisco	8-Wd San Francisco	82	421
HUMPHREY								
Annie	5	f	w	CA	Nevada	Grass Valley Twp	75	230
Augustus	48	m	w	MA	San Mateo	Half Moon Bay P O	87	398
Burt	41	m	w	KY	Stanislaus	Empire Twp	92	60
C D	40	m	w	NY	Sacramento	3-Wd Sacramento	77	278
Catherine	3	f	w	CA	Nevada	Grass Valley Twp	75	229
Charles	32	m	w	OH	Yolo	Cache Crk Twp	93	426
D T	39	m	w	WALE	Siskiyou	Scott Valley Twp	89	612
E A	38	m	w	VA	Napa	Yountville Twp	75	86
Eliza	70	f	w	PA	San Bernardino	San Bernardino Twp	78	443
G W	50	m	w	VA	El Dorado	Cosumnes Twp	72	16
H	37	m	w	VT	Lake	Lower Lake	73	419
Henry	26	m	w	NY	San Francisco	San Francisco P O	83	254
Hugh	30	m	w	ENGL	San Francisco	6-Wd San Francisco	81	90
Humphrey	39	m	w	WALE	Yuba	Slate Range Bar Tw	93	675
Irvin	34	m	w	OH	San Francisco	San Francisco P O	85	824
J H	40	m	w	IL	Sacramento	3-Wd Sacramento	77	270
J W	43	m	w	VA	Sutter	Sutter Twp	92	121
James	45	m	w	KY	Nevada	Meadow Lake Twp	75	251
James	40	m	w	IREL	San Francisco	8-Wd San Francisco	82	397
James	37	m	w	MA	Stanislaus	San Joaquin Twp	92	73
James	24	m	w	IREL	San Francisco	San Francisco P O	83	190
Jn	36	m	w	MA	San Francisco	5-Wd San Francisco	81	22
John	38	m	w	ENGL	San Francisco	8-Wd San Francisco	82	305
John	36	m	w	MA	San Francisco	5-Wd San Francisco	81	23
John	26	m	w	PRUS	San Francisco	7-Wd San Francisco	81	218
Julia	28	f	w	MA	San Francisco	6-Wd San Francisco	81	103
Julius	62	m	w	CT	San Francisco	8-Wd San Francisco	82	316
Lawren E	42	m	w	CT	Placer	Bath P O	76	423
Mary S	8	f	w	CA	Los Angeles	Los Angeles	73	549
Milton	39	m	w	OH	Santa Clara	1-Wd San Jose	88	241
Patrick H	34	m	w	VA	San Francisco	8-Wd San Francisco	82	383
Robt	30	m	w	NY	Solano	Vallejo	90	184

© 2001 by Heritage Quest. All rights reserved.

Series M593

Name	Age	S	R	B-PL	County	Locale	Roll	Pg
Saml	22	m	w	RI	Tuolumne	Chinese Camp P O	93	386
Smith	65	m	w	RI	San Bernardino	San Bernardino Twp	78	443
Thos	57	m	w	CT	San Joaquin	2-Wd Stockton	86	200
William	56	m	w	NJ	Stanislaus	Empire Twp	92	63
William	53	m	w	IL	Los Angeles	El Monte Twp	73	462
William	50	m	w	NY	Stanislaus	Empire Twp	92	62
Wm	35	m	w	OH	Butte	Mountain Spring Tw	70	88
HUMPHREYS								
Anna	27	f	w	TN	San Francisco	8-Wd San Francisco	82	458
Anne	21	f	w	NH	San Francisco	8-Wd San Francisco	82	444
C	8	m	w	CA	San Francisco	San Francisco P O	85	799
Chas	59	m	w	ENGL	Marin	Nicasio Twp	74	15
Chas W	43	m	w	OH	Placer	Pino Twp	76	471
Davis	39	m	w	WALE	Yuba	Marysville	93	605
G	11	m	w	CA	San Francisco	San Francisco P O	85	799
J C	35	m	w	MO	Merced	Snelling P O	74	257
John	30	m	w	IREL	San Francisco	7-Wd San Francisco	81	172
Saml	23	m	w	ENGL	San Francisco	1-Wd San Francisco	79	130
Wm	45	m	w	RI	San Francisco	San Francisco P O	85	727
Wm	13	m	w	GA	San Francisco	11-Wd San Francisc	84	588
HUMPHRIES								
Alice	18	f	w	ENGL	San Francisco	San Francisco P O	80	532
Chs	19	m	w	NY	San Francisco	San Francisco P O	83	264
Georgie	21	f	w	VT	Nevada	Nevada Twp	75	287
M A	21	f	w	MA	Monterey	Castroville Twp	74	326
Sarah	42	m	w	IL	Nevada	Bloomfield Twp	75	94
Stella	4	f	w	NY	San Francisco	San Francisco P O	83	32
Thos	35	m	w	ENGL	Shasta	American Ranch P O	89	499
HUMPHRY								
Ann	20	f	i	CA	Del Norte	Happy Camp Twp	71	472
James	40	m	w	NY	Sacramento	Granite Twp	77	143
John J	44	m	w	CT	Yuba	New York Twp	93	637
John N	40	m	w	AL	Fresno	Millerton P O	72	183
Mary	26	f	w	MA	San Francisco	San Francisco P O	83	160
R	42	m	w	WALE	Del Norte	Happy Camp Twp	71	472
Robert	35	m	w	WALE	Yuba	Slate Range Bar Tw	93	672
HUMPREY								
Holley	24	m	w	NY	Placer	Lincoln P O	76	482
Very	42	m	w	NY	Santa Cruz	Soquel Twp	89	449
HUMPRIES								
Chas	47	m	w	VA	Sonoma	Petaluma Twp	91	361
HUMSEY								
Patrick	31	m	w	IREL	San Francisco	San Francisco P O	83	193
HUMSTED								
William	15	m	w	CA	Solano	Silveyville Twp	90	88
HUN								
---	37	m	c	CHIN	Siskiyou	Scott Valley Twp	89	611
---	19	m	c	CHIN	San Francisco	6-Wd San Francisco	81	51
Ah	60	m	c	CHIN	Sacramento	Center Twp	77	86
Ah	50	m	c	CHIN	Sacramento	Center Twp	77	86
Ah	50	m	c	CHIN	Sacramento	Cosumnes Twp	77	92
Ah	45	m	c	CHIN	Sacramento	Center Twp	77	86
Ah	44	m	c	CHIN	Sacramento	Center Twp	77	86
Ah	44	m	c	CHIN	Amador	Ione City P O	69	365
Ah	44	m	c	CHIN	Sacramento	Center Twp	77	86
Ah	44	m	c	CHIN	Sacramento	Center Twp	77	85
Ah	44	m	c	CHIN	Sacramento	Center Twp	77	85
Ah	43	m	c	CHIN	Sacramento	Center Twp	77	85
Ah	40	m	c	CHIN	Sacramento	Dry Crk Twp	77	101
Ah	40	m	c	CHIN	Calaveras	San Andreas P O	70	179
Ah	40	m	c	CHIN	Sacramento	1-Wd Sacramento	77	196
Ah	40	m	c	CHIN	Nevada	Little York Twp	75	242
Ah	38	m	c	CHIN	Mariposa	Mariposa P O	74	126
Ah	38	m	c	CHIN	Sacramento	Cosumnes Twp	77	90
Ah	37	m	c	CHIN	San Francisco	San Francisco P O	80	516
Ah	37	m	c	CHIN	Sacramento	Granite Twp	77	151
Ah	37	m	c	CHIN	Sacramento	Center Twp	77	86
Ah	36	m	c	CHIN	Sierra	Lincoln Twp	89	546
Ah	36	m	c	CHIN	Sacramento	Center Twp	77	86
Ah	35	m	c	CHIN	Mariposa	Mariposa P O	74	126
Ah	35	m	c	CHIN	Sacramento	Cosumnes Twp	77	94
Ah	34	m	c	CHIN	San Francisco	5-Wd San Francisco	81	14
Ah	33	m	c	CHIN	San Francisco	6-Wd San Francisco	81	66
Ah	32	m	c	CHIN	Sacramento	Granite Twp	77	152
Ah	32	m	c	CHIN	El Dorado	Placerville	72	108
Ah	32	m	c	CHIN	El Dorado	Mud Springs Twp	72	79
Ah	32	m	c	CHIN	Alameda	Eden Twp	68	59
Ah	30	m	c	CHIN	Yuba	Marysville	93	584
Ah	30	m	c	CHIN	Sacramento	American Twp	77	68
Ah	30	m	c	CHIN	Fresno	Millerton P O	72	202
Ah	30	m	c	CHIN	El Dorado	Mud Springs Twp	72	88
Ah	30	m	c	CHIN	Placer	Alta P O	76	412
Ah	29	m	c	CHIN	Sacramento	Franklin Twp	77	119
Ah	28	m	c	CHIN	Contra Costa	Martinez P O	71	436
Ah	28	m	c	CHIN	Fresno	Millerton P O	72	200
Ah	28	m	c	CHIN	El Dorado	Mud Springs Twp	72	79
Ah	28	m	c	CHIN	Amador	Fiddletown P O	69	428
Ah	27	m	c	CHIN	Sacramento	Dry Crk Twp	77	101
Ah	27	m	c	CHIN	Sacramento	Georgianna Twp	77	131
Ah	27	m	c	CHIN	Sacramento	Granite Twp	77	150
Ah	27	m	c	CHIN	Sacramento	Georgianna Twp	77	131
Ah	26	m	c	CHIN	Sacramento	Center Twp	77	86
Ah	25	m	c	CHIN	San Francisco	6-Wd San Francisco	81	44
Ah	25	m	c	CHIN	San Francisco	San Francisco P O	80	515
Ah	25	m	c	CHIN	Sacramento	Georgianna Twp	77	125
Ah	24	m	c	CHIN	Calaveras	San Andreas P O	70	191
Ah	22	m	c	CHIN	Butte	Kimshew Tpw	70	84

Series M593

Name	Age	S	R	B-PL	County	Locale	Roll	Pg
Ah	20	f	c	CHIN	San Francisco	San Francisco P O	80	529
Ah	20	m	c	CHIN	Sacramento	1-Wd Sacramento	77	199
Chun	25	m	c	CHIN	San Francisco	7-Wd San Francisco	81	260
Fod	28	m	c	CHIN	Solano	Vacaville Twp	90	130
Him	21	m	c	CHIN	San Mateo	Half Moon Bay P O	87	395
Lee	41	m	c	CHIN	San Francisco	6-Wd San Francisco	81	56
Sang	40	m	c	CHIN	Tuolumne	Big Oak Flat P O	93	392
Sing	25	m	c	CHIN	Yuba	Marysville	93	622
Sun	25	m	c	CHIN	Yuba	Marysville	93	630
HUNAN								
Patreick	38	m	w	IREL	San Francisco	11-Wd San Francisc	84	654
HUNCE								
Andrew	23	m	w	OH	Santa Clara	Santa Clara Twp	88	171
HUNCK								
John	25	m	w	PRUS	San Francisco	San Francisco P O	80	351
HUND								
Catharine	45	f	w	NY	San Francisco	San Francisco P O	83	51
HUNDEMAN								
Henry	25	m	w	BADE	San Diego	Coronado	78	465
HUNDERSON								
Chas	48	m	w	PRUS	San Francisco	7-Wd San Francisco	81	250
HUNDLEY								
Mary	50	f	w	IREL	San Francisco	3-Wd San Francisco	79	288
HUNDMAN								
Andw	35	m	w	SAXO	San Francisco	1-Wd San Francisco	79	3
HUNE								
Ah	30	m	c	CHIN	Santa Clara	Santa Clara Twp	88	148
Ah	30	m	c	CHIN	Merced	Snelling P O	74	265
Ah	24	m	c	CHIN	San Francisco	3-Wd San Francisco	79	310
Antone	39	m	w	PRUS	Siskiyou	Scott Valley Twp	89	611
HUNEY								
Susan	31	f	w	MA	San Francisco	San Francisco P O	83	199
HUNFREVILLE								
White	36	m	w	OH	San Luis Obispo	San Luis Obispo Tw	87	309
HUNG								
---	42	m	c	CHIN	Siskiyou	Cottonwood Twp	89	593
Ah	68	m	c	CHIN	Tuolumne	Chinese Camp P O	93	363
Ah	57	m	c	CHIN	Sacramento	American Twp	77	68
Ah	55	m	c	CHIN	El Dorado	Placerville	72	126
Ah	53	m	c	CHIN	San Francisco	6-Wd San Francisco	81	61
Ah	52	m	c	CHIN	Calaveras	Copperopolis P O	70	234
Ah	51	m	c	CHIN	San Francisco	San Francisco P O	80	446
Ah	51	m	c	CHIN	Mariposa	Mariposa P O	74	125
Ah	47	m	c	CHIN	Butte	Ophir Twp	70	106
Ah	46	m	c	CHIN	Calaveras	Copperopolis P O	70	242
Ah	45	m	c	CHIN	Mariposa	Mariposa P O	74	103
Ah	45	m	c	CHIN	Mono	Bridgeport P O	74	282
Ah	45	m	c	CHIN	Calaveras	San Andreas P O	70	171
Ah	44	m	c	CHIN	Sierra	Gibson Twp	89	538
Ah	44	m	c	CHIN	Placer	Auburn P O	76	364
Ah	42	m	c	CHIN	Mono	Bridgeport P O	74	282
Ah	42	m	c	CHIN	Butte	Chico Twp	70	51
Ah	41	m	c	CHIN	San Francisco	San Francisco P O	80	454
Ah	40	m	c	CHIN	San Francisco	San Francisco P O	80	450
Ah	40	m	c	CHIN	San Francisco	San Francisco P O	80	453
Ah	40	m	c	CHIN	Placer	Auburn P O	76	362
Ah	40	m	c	CHIN	Placer	Auburn P O	76	378
Ah	40	m	c	CHIN	Placer	Auburn P O	76	372
Ah	40	m	c	CHIN	Calaveras	Copperopolis P O	70	249
Ah	40	m	c	CHIN	Trinity	Lewiston Pct	92	214
Ah	40	m	c	CHIN	San Francisco	6-Wd San Francisco	81	58
Ah	40	m	c	CHIN	Sacramento	Granite Twp	77	151
Ah	40	m	c	CHIN	Placer	Dutch Flat P O	76	409
Ah	39	m	c	CHIN	Butte	Hamilton Twp	70	73
Ah	39	m	c	CHIN	San Francisco	6-Wd San Francisco	81	57
Ah	38	m	c	CHIN	San Francisco	San Francisco P O	80	435
Ah	38	m	c	CHIN	San Francisco	San Francisco P O	80	447
Ah	38	m	c	CHIN	Yuba	Marysville	93	619
Ah	37	m	c	CHIN	Yuba	Marysville	93	583
Ah	37	m	c	CHIN	Placer	Auburn P O	76	362
Ah	37	m	c	CHIN	Nevada	Grass Valley Twp	75	218
Ah	37	m	c	CHIN	Amador	Fiddletown P O	69	429
Ah	36	m	c	CHIN	San Francisco	San Francisco P O	80	496
Ah	36	m	c	CHIN	San Francisco	San Francisco P O	80	447
Ah	36	m	c	CHIN	San Francisco	San Francisco P O	80	450
Ah	36	m	c	CHIN	San Francisco	San Francisco P O	80	497
Ah	36	m	c	CHIN	Calaveras	Copperopolis P O	70	233
Ah	35	m	c	CHIN	San Francisco	6-Wd San Francisco	81	42
Ah	35	m	c	CHIN	Plumas	Plumas Twp	77	32
Ah	35	m	c	CHIN	Mariposa	Mariposa P O	74	107
Ah	35	m	c	CHIN	Mariposa	Mariposa P O	74	106
Ah	35	m	c	CHIN	Mariposa	Mariposa P O	74	103
Ah	35	m	c	CHIN	Calaveras	Copperopolis P O	70	254
Ah	35	m	c	CHIN	Butte	Concow Twp	70	10
Ah	35	m	c	CHIN	Tehama	Tehama Twp	92	189
Ah	34	m	c	CHIN	Tuolumne	Chinese Camp P O	93	375
Ah	34	m	c	CHIN	Nevada	Rough & Ready Twp	75	329
Ah	34	m	c	CHIN	Calaveras	Copperopolis P O	70	248
Ah	34	m	c	CHIN	Trinity	Junction City Pct	92	208
Ah	34	m	c	CHIN	Fresno	Millerton P O	72	202
Ah	33	m	c	CHIN	Trinity	Douglas	92	236
Ah	33	m	c	CHIN	El Dorado	Mud Springs Twp	72	89
Ah	32	m	c	CHIN	San Francisco	San Francisco P O	80	452
Ah	32	m	c	CHIN	Mariposa	Mariposa P O	74	103
Ah	32	m	c	CHIN	Butte	Concow Twp	70	10
Ah	32	m	c	CHIN	Calaveras	San Andreas P O	70	167
Ah	31	m	c	CHIN	Fresno	Millerton P O	72	202

© 2001 by Heritage Quest. All rights reserved.

Name	Age	S	R	B-PL	County	Locale	Roll	Pg
						Series M593		
Ah	31	m	c	CHIN	Kern	Kernville P O	73	368
Ah	30	m	c	CHIN	Yolo	Grafton Twp	93	482
Ah	30	m	c	CHIN	Plumas	Washington Twp	77	57
Ah	30	m	c	CHIN	Nevada	Nevada Twp	75	277
Ah	30	m	c	CHIN	Calaveras	San Andreas P O	70	169
Ah	30	m	c	CHIN	Calaveras	San Andreas P O	70	176
Ah	30	m	c	CHIN	Tehama	Tehama Twp	92	189
Ah	30	m	c	CHIN	Plumas	Seneca Twp	77	48
Ah	30	m	c	CHIN	Amador	Drytown P O	69	424
Ah	30	m	c	CHIN	Amador	Volcano P O	69	388
Ah	30	m	c	CHIN	El Dorado	Salmon Falls Twp	72	129
Ah	30	m	c	CHIN	Stanislaus	Emory Twp	92	23
Ah	30	m	c	CHIN	Yuba	Marysville	93	619
Ah	30	m	c	CHIN	Yuba	Marysville	93	604
Ah	29	m	c	CHIN	San Joaquin	1-Wd Stockton	86	145
Ah	29	m	c	CHIN	San Francisco	San Francisco P O	80	445
Ah	29	m	c	CHIN	Placer	Auburn P O	76	370
Ah	29	m	c	CHIN	Marin	Tomales Twp	74	86
Ah	29	m	c	CHIN	Calaveras	San Andreas P O	70	205
Ah	28	m	c	CHIN	Yolo	Washington Twp	93	530
Ah	28	m	c	CHIN	San Francisco	3-Wd San Francisco	79	306
Ah	28	m	c	CHIN	Sacramento	American Twp	77	68
Ah	28	m	c	CHIN	El Dorado	Placerville Twp	72	92
Ah	28	m	c	CHIN	Fresno	Millerton P O	72	181
Ah	28	m	c	CHIN	Trinity	Junction City Pct	92	206
Ah	28	m	c	CHIN	San Francisco	6-Wd San Francisco	81	58
Ah	28	m	c	CHIN	Mariposa	Maxwell Crk P O	74	147
Ah	28	m	c	CHIN	El Dorado	Salmon Falls Twp	72	130
Ah	28	m	c	CHIN	Contra Costa	Martinez P O	71	441
Ah	27	m	c	CHIN	San Francisco	San Francisco P O	80	444
Ah	27	m	c	CHIN	Placer	Bath P O	76	428
Ah	27	m	c	CHIN	Placer	Dutch Flat P O	76	410
Ah	27	m	c	CHIN	San Francisco	San Francisco P O	80	481
Ah	25	m	c	CHIN	Sierra	Table Rock Twp	89	574
Ah	25	m	c	CHIN	Yolo	Grafton Twp	93	486
Ah	25	m	c	CHIN	San Francisco	San Francisco P O	83	276
Ah	25	m	c	CHIN	San Francisco	6-Wd San Francisco	81	43
Ah	25	f	c	CHIN	Mariposa	Mariposa P O	74	125
Ah	25	m	c	CHIN	San Francisco	6-Wd San Francisco	81	58
Ah	25	m	c	CHIN	El Dorado	Placerville	72	122
Ah	24	m	c	CHIN	San Francisco	6-Wd San Francisco	81	49
Ah	24	m	c	CHIN	San Francisco	6-Wd San Francisco	81	48
Ah	24	f	c	CHIN	San Francisco	San Francisco P O	80	444
Ah	23	m	c	CHIN	Solano	Suisun Twp	90	107
Ah	22	m	c	CHIN	Tehama	Red Bluff	92	184
Ah	22	m	c	CHIN	San Francisco	6-Wd San Francisco	81	54
Ah	22	m	c	CHIN	Yuba	Rose Bar Twp	93	664
Ah	21	m	c	CHIN	Solano	Vallejo	90	208
Ah	21	m	c	CHIN	San Francisco	3-Wd San Francisco	79	304
Ah	21	m	c	CHIN	San Francisco	San Francisco P O	80	452
Ah	21	m	c	CHIN	Trinity	Canyon City Pct	92	201
Ah	21	m	c	CHIN	Plumas	Goodwin Twp	77	3
Ah	20	m	c	CHIN	San Francisco	6-Wd San Francisco	81	49
Ah	20	m	c	CHIN	San Francisco	6-Wd San Francisco	81	57
Ah	18	m	c	CHIN	San Francisco	6-Wd San Francisco	81	55
Ah	18	m	c	CHIN	San Francisco	6-Wd San Francisco	81	47
Ah	18	m	c	CHIN	Napa	Napa Twp	75	30
Ah	18	m	c	CHIN	Nevada	Little York Twp	75	234
Ah	17	m	c	CHIN	Tehama	Tehama Twp	92	188
Ah	17	m	c	CHIN	Amador	Jackson P O	69	331
Ah	16	m	c	CHIN	San Francisco	6-Wd San Francisco	81	84
Ah	16	m	c	CHIN	San Francisco	8-Wd San Francisco	82	497
Ah	13	m	c	CHIN	San Francisco	San Francisco P O	83	162
Ah	12	m	c	CHIN	San Francisco	7-Wd San Francisco	81	238
Am	38	m	c	CHIN	Yuba	Marysville	93	601
An	54	m	c	CHIN	Calaveras	San Andreas P O	70	174
Ban	22	m	c	CHIN	Yuba	Marysville	93	580
Bit	34	m	c	CHIN	Yuba	Marysville	93	623
Chang	31	m	c	CHIN	Plumas	Mineral Twp	77	25
Chee	19	m	c	CHIN	Yolo	Washington Twp	93	536
Chin	35	m	c	CHIN	Yuba	Marysville	93	621
Chun	26	m	c	CHIN	Solano	Rio Vista Twp	90	64
Chung	29	m	c	CHIN	Tehama	Tehama Twp	92	189
Cow	26	m	c	CHIN	Santa Clara	1-Wd San Jose	88	271
Dot	55	m	c	CHIN	San Francisco	6-Wd San Francisco	81	40
Far	30	m	c	CHIN	Yuba	Marysville	93	623
Foo	36	m	c	CHIN	Yuba	Marysville	93	623
Foo	30	m	c	CHIN	Butte	Kimshew Tpw	70	84
Foo	26	m	c	CHIN	Yolo	Cache Crk Twp	93	424
Foy	28	m	c	CHIN	Sierra	Eureka Twp	89	527
Fung	30	m	c	CHIN	Santa Clara	1-Wd San Jose	88	271
Furt	24	m	c	CHIN	San Francisco	San Francisco P O	83	404
Gee	40	m	c	CHIN	Plumas	Goodwin Twp	77	5
Gee	36	m	c	CHIN	Placer	Newcastle Twp	76	479
Ha	20	m	c	CHIN	Yuba	Marysville	93	624
Hang	31	m	c	CHIN	Yuba	Marysville	93	623
Hin	30	m	c	CHIN	Calaveras	San Andreas P O	70	220
Kee	48	m	c	CHIN	Yuba	Marysville	93	624
Kee	40	m	c	CHIN	Yuba	Marysville	93	623
Kee	18	m	c	CHIN	San Francisco	7-Wd San Francisco	81	174
Kim	29	f	c	CHIN	Yuba	Marysville	93	626
La	21	m	c	CHIN	Solano	Vacaville Twp	90	124
Lee	40	m	c	CHIN	San Francisco	6-Wd San Francisco	81	49
Lee	26	m	c	CHIN	Solano	Vacaville Twp	90	131
Lee	24	m	c	CHIN	Solano	Rio Vista Twp	90	64
Lee	19	m	c	CHIN	Yuba	Marysville	93	594
Lewy	31	m	c	CHIN	Yuba	Marysville	93	623

Name	Age	S	R	B-PL	County	Locale	Roll	Pg
						Series M593		
Li	22	m	c	CHIN	Tehama	Deer Crk Twp	92	172
Ling	23	m	c	CHIN	Yuba	Marysville	93	620
Lo	34	m	c	CHIN	Yuba	Marysville	93	631
Lo	34	m	c	CHIN	San Joaquin	1-Wd Stockton	86	142
Long	24	m	c	CHIN	Calaveras	San Andreas P O	70	205
Lue	25	m	c	CHIN	Yuba	Marysville	93	629
Lung	40	m	c	CHIN	Solano	Montezuma Twp	90	68
May	22	f	c	CHIN	Tehama	Red Bluff	92	184
Ming	32	m	c	CHIN	Calaveras	Copperopolis P O	70	263
Moy	26	m	c	CHIN	Santa Clara	1-Wd San Jose	88	271
Mung	27	m	c	CHIN	Santa Clara	1-Wd San Jose	88	271
Nun	41	m	c	CHIN	Yuba	Marysville	93	623
Que	42	m	c	CHIN	Sacramento	1-Wd Sacramento	77	193
Que	34	m	c	CHIN	Yuba	Marysville	93	629
Quon	37	m	c	CHIN	Butte	Concow Twp	70	11
Shing	31	m	c	CHIN	Plumas	Goodwin Twp	77	5
Sing	42	m	c	CHIN	Plumas	Goodwin Twp	77	4
Sing	28	m	c	CHIN	Yolo	Buckeye Twp	93	411
Sing	26	m	c	CHIN	Yuba	Marysville	93	580
Sing	25	m	c	CHIN	San Francisco	8-Wd San Francisco	82	430
Sing	19	m	c	CHIN	San Francisco	San Francisco P O	83	346
Son	31	m	c	CHIN	Solano	Rio Vista Twp	90	70
Sue	20	m	c	CHIN	Yuba	Marysville	93	625
Sun	36	m	c	CHIN	Nevada	Rough & Ready Twp	75	327
Sun	19	m	c	CHIN	Yuba	Marysville	93	628
Sung	36	m	c	CHIN	Yuba	Marysville	93	624
Tho	66	m	w	TN	El Dorado	Mountain Twp	72	67
Tie	35	m	c	CHIN	Placer	Bath P O	76	456
Ty	22	f	c	CHIN	Placer	Dutch Flat P O	76	409
Waah	40	m	c	CHIN	Humboldt	Eureka Twp	72	277
Wah	40	m	c	CHIN	Sacramento	1-Wd Sacramento	77	193
Wan	35	m	c	CHIN	Yuba	Marysville	93	623
Wee	32	m	c	CHIN	Santa Clara	1-Wd San Jose	88	271
Wee	29	m	c	CHIN	Placer	Bath P O	76	430
Wo	36	m	c	CHIN	Yuba	Marysville	93	624
Won	35	m	c	CHIN	Yuba	Marysville	93	624
Woo	40	m	c	CHIN	Sacramento	1-Wd Sacramento	77	205
Y	30	m	c	CHIN	Yuba	Marysville	93	623
Yah	30	m	c	CHIN	Fresno	Millerton P O	72	191
Yee	45	m	c	CHIN	Nevada	Little York Twp	75	242
Yo	32	m	c	CHIN	Yuba	Marysville	93	624
Yo	25	m	c	CHIN	San Joaquin	1-Wd Stockton	86	142
You	53	m	c	CHIN	Amador	Volcano P O	69	378
You	16	m	c	CHIN	Yolo	Cache Crk Twp	93	437
HUNGATE								
Harrison H	34	m	w	IL	Yolo	Cottonwood Twp	93	469
J D P	39	m	w	IN	Monterey	San Juan Twp	74	400
HUNGER								
Augustus	35	m	w	FRAN	El Dorado	Placerville	72	127
L	32	m	w	SWIT	Lake	Big Valley	73	395
Mathew	48	m	w	SWIT	San Francisco	8-Wd San Francisco	82	321
HUNGERFORD								
Ada	11	f	w	PA	Santa Clara	2-Wd San Jose	88	338
Byron	25	m	w	MI	San Francisco	7-Wd San Francisco	81	240
Chas B	44	m	w	NY	Placer	Gold Run Twp	76	398
Eveline	45	f	w	NY	San Francisco	San Francisco P O	83	147
G W	31	m	w	MI	Trinity	Trinity Center Pct	92	204
K	9	f	w	GA	Alameda	Oakland	68	176
Luana	52	f	w	CT	San Francisco	7-Wd San Francisco	81	240
M C	40	m	w	OH	Sutter	Butte Twp	92	93
HUNGERFORTH								
John	60	m	w	BAVA	San Francisco	San Francisco P O	83	216
HUNGUNG								
Ho Ah	40	m	c	CHIN	San Francisco	San Francisco P O	85	749
HUNIGE								
Manuel	40	m	i	CAME	Sacramento	4-Wd Sacramento	77	377
HUNKEN								
John	36	m	w	HANO	Nevada	Washington Twp	75	346
HUNKIN								
Nicholas	32	m	w	WURT	Nevada	Washington Twp	75	344
HUNN								
Ah	49	m	c	CHIN	Amador	Fiddletown P O	69	427
HUNNAM								
J F	44	m	w	IN	Lassen	Janesville Twp	73	431
HUNNEMAN								
John	25	m	w	WURT	Yolo	Cache Crk Twp	93	420
HUNNETT								
Form	55	m	w	FRAN	Yuba	Rose Bar Twp	93	652
HUNNEWELL								
Chas	37	m	w	NY	Sacramento	4-Wd Sacramento	77	370
Eliza E	35	f	w	PA	Napa	Napa	75	51
HUNNICRETT								
Wm J	33	m	w	IL	Placer	Colfax P O	76	389
HUNOGA								
Margaret	20	f	w	SWIT	San Francisco	8-Wd San Francisco	82	390
HUNPTON								
Joseph	32	m	w	NY	Trinity	Lewiston Pct	92	212
HUNSACKER								
A W	44	m	w	NC	San Joaquin	Dent Twp	86	17
Eliza	60	f	w	VA	Solano	Maine Prairie Twp	90	52
Harrison	32	m	w	MO	Contra Costa	Martinez Twp	71	347
John	45	m	w	MO	Solano	Vacaville Twp	90	127
HUNSAKER								
Allen	38	m	w	KY	Tulare	Tule Rvr Twp	92	267
Budd	25	m	w	MO	Tulare	Tule Rvr Twp	92	269
Daniel	66	m	w	KY	Tulare	Tule Rvr Twp	92	266
Geo W	33	m	w	MO	Tulare	Tule Rvr Twp	92	265

© 2001 by Heritage Quest. All rights reserved.

Series M593

Name	Age	S	R	B-PL	County	Locale	Roll	Pg
George	23	m	w	MO	Tulare	Tule Rvr Twp	92	267
Henry	35	m	w	IL	Tulare	Tule Rvr Twp	92	265
Isaac	63	m	w	KY	Contra Costa	Martinez P O	71	373
Jeptha	30	m	w	IL	Tulare	Tule Rvr Twp	92	267
Joseph	40	m	w	IL	Tulare	Tule Rvr Twp	92	266
William	30	m	w	IA	Tulare	Tule Rvr Twp	92	265
HUNSCHEL								
Wm	30	m	w	GERM	San Francisco	8-Wd San Francisco	82	362
HUNSINGER								
Benj F	42	m	w	IL	Plumas	Indian Twp	77	10
S A	37	f	w	ENGL	Napa	Napa	75	51
HUNT								
A	57	m	w	MO	San Joaquin	Liberty Twp	86	83
Abbie	29	f	w	MA	San Francisco	11-Wd San Francisc	84	538
Ah	40	m	c	CHIN	Stanislaus	Emory Twp	92	23
Albert	25	m	w	MS	Santa Clara	Gilroy Twp	88	97
Albert H	42	m	w	NY	Los Angeles	El Monte Twp	73	456
Albert N	11	m	w	ME	Yuba	Slate Range Bar Tw	93	673
Alex	63	m	w	NY	Nevada	Nevada Twp	75	279
Alexander	28	m	w	ME	Yolo	Grafton Twp	93	481
Allen W	33	m	w	NY	Yolo	Buckeye Twp	93	412
Allen W	32	m	w	NY	Yolo	Putah Twp	93	515
Ambrose	42	m	w	ENGL	San Bernardino	San Bernardino Twp	78	439
Andrew	52	m	w	OH	Sonoma	Santa Rosa	91	417
Anna	30	f	w	IREL	San Francisco	7-Wd San Francisco	81	205
Arthur L	31	m	w	ME	El Dorado	Mud Springs Twp	72	91
Asa	51	m	w	IN	San Diego	San Diego	78	501
B Henry	30	m	w	CANA	Santa Clara	Gilroy Twp	88	98
Benj W	47	m	w	PA	Sonoma	Analy Twp	91	229
Benjamin T	38	m	w	KY	El Dorado	Placerville	72	110
Byron	28	m	w	IL	Napa	Napa	75	3
C A	48	m	w	MA	San Francisco	San Francisco P O	85	860
C J	46	m	w	NY	Humboldt	Eureka Twp	72	265
Caleb	19	m	w	VA	Santa Clara	Milpitas Twp	88	109
Catherine	20	f	w	IREL	San Francisco	San Francisco P O	83	208
Charles	43	m	w	MO	Colusa	Butte Twp	71	265
Charles	40	m	w	BADE	Placer	Gold Run Twp	76	399
Charles	39	m	w	ME	Santa Clara	1-Wd San Jose	88	226
Charles	25	m	w	CANA	San Francisco	7-Wd San Francisco	81	178
Charles	24	m	w	NY	San Francisco	San Francisco P O	83	264
Charles E	28	m	w	MA	San Francisco	3-Wd San Francisco	79	330
Charles M	30	m	w	ME	Yolo	Washington Twp	93	529
Charles R	35	m	w	NY	Yolo	Putah Twp	93	513
Charles S	34	m	w	ME	Klamath	Orleans Twp	73	379
Chas	50	m	w	NY	Sonoma	Petaluma Twp	91	323
Curtis N	35	m	w	NH	Stanislaus	San Joaquin Twp	92	73
D O	39	m	w	MA	Napa	Napa	75	10
D R	50	m	w	VT	Sacramento	Franklin Twp	77	107
Daniel	45	m	w	NH	Stanislaus	North Twp	92	68
Daniel Augustus	36	m	w	MA	Plumas	Mineral Twp	77	22
Danl G	37	m	w	MO	Shasta	Millville P O	89	489
David	63	m	w	MA	San Francisco	11-Wd San Francisc	84	494
David	27	m	w	NY	San Francisco	San Francisco P O	83	210
David	20	m	w	CA	San Joaquin	Oneal Twp	86	105
Dennis	24	m	w	IREL	Santa Clara	Fremont Twp	88	42
E S	30	m	w	ME	Sacramento	4-Wd Sacramento	77	373
E W	42	m	w	NY	Monterey	San Juan Twp	74	396
Ed	36	m	w	ME	Alameda	Oakland	68	198
Ed R	38	m	w	SC	San Francisco	2-Wd San Francisco	79	212
Edwin	24	m	w	ENGL	San Mateo	San Mateo P O	87	371
Elbridge	47	m	w	ENGL	Mariposa	Mariposa P O	74	112
Eli	27	m	w	ENGL	Nevada	Grass Valley Twp	75	221
Elizabeth	84	f	w	PA	San Bernardino	San Bernardino Twp	78	417
Elizabeth	12	f	w	CA	Tulare	Farmersville Twp	92	249
Enoch	44	m	w	NC	Napa	Napa Twp	75	72
Ephraim	35	m	w	ME	Santa Clara	Redwood Twp	88	125
Frank C	28	m	w	ME	Tulare	Visalia	92	296
Franklin M	28	m	w	MO	Yolo	Buckeye Twp	93	415
Fredk	27	m	w	PRUS	San Francisco	San Francisco P O	83	305
Fredrick	33	m	w	MA	San Francisco	7-Wd San Francisco	81	226
G H	38	m	w	IN	Alameda	Oakland	68	260
George	45	m	w	MO	San Francisco	2-Wd San Francisco	79	277
George	26	m	w	MA	Sacramento	2-Wd Sacramento	77	219
George E P	29	m	w	MA	San Francisco	San Francisco P O	83	409
George S	41	m	w	ENGL	Sacramento	2-Wd Sacramento	77	207
Georgia	18	f	w	ME	San Francisco	7-Wd San Francisco	81	236
Giles	35	m	w	MO	Klamath	Klamath Twp	73	370
Gustave	48	m	w	DENM	Mendocino	Anderson Twp	74	156
H C	26	m	w	NC	Sacramento	Dry Crk Twp	77	98
H M	26	m	w	IREL	San Joaquin	Oneal Twp	86	113
H W	69	m	w	NC	San Joaquin	2-Wd Stockton	86	196
Hammond	63	m	w	ME	San Francisco	San Francisco P O	83	258
Henery	30	m	w	IREL	San Francisco	7-Wd San Francisco	81	185
Henry	29	m	w	ME	Sacramento	2-Wd Sacramento	77	237
Henry	28	m	w	MO	Yuba	Long Bar Twp	93	564
Henry	28	m	w	OH	Solano	Denverton Twp	90	25
Ho	50	m	c	CHIN	San Joaquin	1-Wd Stockton	86	144
Isaac W	23	m	w	KY	Inyo	Lone Pine Twp	73	331
J	67	m	w	VT	Alameda	Oakland	68	239
J	35	m	w	VT	Sierra	Forest Twp	89	529
J A	60	m	w	NC	Tuolumne	Big Oak Flat P O	93	396
J B	39	m	w	ENGL	Tehama	Merrill	92	198
J E	24	m	w	NY	Solano	Vallejo	90	191
J K	62	m	w	VT	Tuolumne	Big Oak Flat P O	93	395
Jacob	42	m	w	BADE	San Joaquin	Oneal Twp	86	105
James	30	m	w	IREL	Yolo	Cache Crk Twp	93	421
Jas	30	m	w	RI	Sacramento	1-Wd Sacramento	77	188
Jas J	29	m	w	VA	Monterey	San Juan Twp	74	405
Jno	52	m	w	OH	Santa Clara	Gilroy Twp	88	96
Jno	24	m	w	PA	San Francisco	8-Wd San Francisco	82	371
Jno Edwd	36	m	w	NY	San Francisco	San Francisco P O	83	75
John	60	m	w	OH	San Francisco	San Francisco P O	80	391
John	56	m	w	NY	Santa Clara	2-Wd San Jose	88	296
John	40	m	w	ME	San Francisco	San Francisco P O	83	176
John	40	m	b	KY	Siskiyou	Yreka	89	651
John	40	m	w	ENGL	Alameda	Hayward	68	75
John	39	m	w	ENGL	Los Angeles	Los Angeles	73	536
John	34	m	w	IREL	Yolo	Putah Twp	93	524
John	22	m	w	CANA	San Francisco	San Francisco P O	83	53
John A	47	m	w	MA	Sacramento	2-Wd Sacramento	77	208
John B	40	m	w	MO	Shasta	Millville P O	89	489
John D	62	m	w	MA	San Francisco	San Francisco P O	83	18
John H	40	m	w	AL	San Bernardino	San Bernardino Twp	78	452
John H	33	m	w	MA	San Francisco	7-Wd San Francisco	81	243
John J	44	m	w	KY	Tulare	Visalia Twp	92	281
Jos	32	m	w	ENGL	Alameda	Oakland	68	240
Jos R	14	m	w	CA	Shasta	Millville P O	89	489
Joseph S	38	m	w	MO	Tuolumne	Sonora P O	93	325
Kate	26	f	w	IREL	Alameda	Oakland	68	208
Kate	25	f	w	IREL	San Francisco	San Francisco P O	80	408
L L	58	f	w	VT	Tuolumne	Big Oak Flat P O	93	395
Levi	49	m	w	NJ	Plumas	Indian Twp	77	13
Levi	28	m	w	MO	Santa Cruz	Soquel Twp	89	437
Lewis	43	m	w	MA	Placer	Auburn P O	76	379
Lewis E	26	m	w	MO	Yolo	Buckeye Twp	93	415
Lizzie	16	f	w	KY	Yuba	Marysville	93	598
Lizzie C	32	f	w	MA	San Francisco	7-Wd San Francisco	81	245
Lucius	9	m	w	CA	Santa Clara	Gilroy Twp	88	97
Lyman	19	m	w	MI	Humboldt	Eel Rvr Twp	72	248
Manson	50	m	w	CANA	Sonoma	Petaluma Twp	91	348
Margaret	50	f	w	NJ	San Francisco	San Francisco P O	83	48
Mark	47	m	w	IREL	San Francisco	11-Wd San Francisc	84	430
Martin	26	m	w	WI	Yolo	Putah Twp	93	510
Mary	8	f	w	CA	Tulare	Farmersville Twp	92	241
Mary	63	f	w	MD	San Francisco	11-Wd San Francisc	84	699
Mary	36	f	w	NY	San Francisco	San Francisco P O	83	205
Mary	15	f	w	DC	San Francisco	11-Wd San Francisc	84	665
Mary A	50	f	w	IREL	San Francisco	8-Wd San Francisco	82	443
Merrick	68	m	w	KY	Sacramento	2-Wd Sacramento	77	251
Michael	50	m	w	IREL	San Francisco	San Francisco P O	85	841
Michael	30	m	w	ENGL	San Francisco	7-Wd San Francisco	81	159
Orlando	29	m	w	OH	Santa Clara	2-Wd San Jose	88	321
P C	45	m	w	PRUS	Yuba	Marysville	93	603
P C	15	m	w	CA	Alameda	Oakland	68	243
Phebe P	63	f	w	ME	Santa Clara	Redwood Twp	88	125
Philander	49	m	w	RI	Napa	Napa	75	25
R M	42	m	w	NY	Nevada	Nevada Twp	75	280
Robert	22	m	w	ENGL	Sacramento	Sutter Twp	77	390
Rosa	24	f	i	CA	Siskiyou	Yreka	89	651
Rosanna	33	f	w	IREL	Santa Clara	Gilroy Twp	88	77
S A	32	m	w	NY	Tuolumne	Columbia P O	93	336
Samuel L	60	m	w	ME	Yolo	Washington Twp	93	533
Samul	60	m	w	NC	Humboldt	Arcata Twp	72	233
Seth B	20	m	w	ME	Santa Clara	2-Wd San Jose	88	295
Stephen H	43	m	w	IL	Santa Cruz	Santa Cruz Twp	89	379
Susan	24	f	i	CA	Klamath	Orleans Twp	73	379
T C	45	m	w	WALD	Yuba	Marysville	93	586
T P	50	m	w	ENGL	Yuba	Marysville	93	603
Thomas	66	m	w	NC	El Dorado	Georgetown Twp	72	40
Thomas	33	m	w	AL	Tulare	Visalia	92	295
Thomas	11	m	w	CA	Santa Clara	Gilroy Twp	88	97
Thos B	38	m	w	MO	Butte	Mountain Spring Tw	70	87
Thos H	40	m	w	MO	Sacramento	Franklin Twp	77	110
Thos J	29	m	w	MD	Klamath	Trinidad Twp	73	391
Truman L	43	m	w	NY	Los Angeles	Los Angeles Twp	73	494
W	60	m	w	CT	San Joaquin	Liberty Twp	86	82
W B	50	m	w	PRUS	San Joaquin	2-Wd Stockton	86	168
W G	40	m	w	IN	Alameda	Oakland	68	189
Walter R	25	m	w	CANA	Nevada	Grass Valley Twp	75	227
Warren W	33	m	w	NH	Santa Barbara	Santa Maria P O	87	511
William	64	m	w	IREL	El Dorado	White Oak Twp	72	143
William	56	m	w	OH	Santa Clara	San Jose Twp	88	195
William	45	m	w	ENGL	Nevada	Grass Valley Twp	75	181
William	43	m	w	IREL	San Francisco	San Francisco P O	83	59
William	35	m	w	KY	Yolo	Cache Crk Twp	93	435
William	30	m	w	TN	Placer	Roseville P O	76	355
William B	45	m	w	MA	Sacramento	2-Wd Sacramento	77	248
William G	38	m	w	MD	Yolo	Cache Crk Twp	93	449
William H	30	m	w	VA	Placer	Gold Run Twp	76	396
William T	36	m	w	KY	Yolo	Cache Crk Twp	93	430
Wilson	32	m	w	OH	Placer	Bath P O	76	438
Wm	48	m	w	IREL	San Francisco	San Francisco P O	85	852
Wm	37	m	w	ME	San Joaquin	2-Wd Stockton	86	168
Wm H	40	m	w	MD	San Francisco	San Francisco P O	83	1
Wm S	39	m	w	PA	Sacramento	1-Wd Sacramento	77	184
HUNTEE								
H	38	m	w	WURT	Alameda	Oakland	68	214
P H	49	m	w	NY	Napa	Napa	75	8
HUNTER								
A	50	m	w	IREL	San Joaquin	Douglas Twp	86	42
A A	28	m	w	OH	Mendocino	Round Valley Twp	74	218
A K	43	m	w	OH	Butte	Oroville Twp	70	139
Alex	40	m	w	IL	Butte	Hamilton Twp	70	66
Alexander	47	m	w	PA	Stanislaus	Empire Twp	92	51

© 2001 by Heritage Quest. All rights reserved.

Name	Age	S	R	B-PL	County	Locale (Series M593)	Roll	Pg
Alexander	42	m	w	NY	Inyo	Independence Twp	73	327
Alexander	32	m	w	MO	Colusa	Spring Valley Twp	71	340
Andrew	34	m	w	SCOT	San Mateo	Half Moon Bay P O	87	406
Annie	23	f	w	MA	San Francisco	San Francisco P O	83	149
Asa	37	m	w	IL	Los Angeles	Soledad Twp	73	632
Augustus	41	m	w	VA	Santa Clara	Santa Clara Twp	88	166
Benj A	69	m	w	TN	Los Angeles	El Monte Twp	73	462
Charles	35	m	w	ENGL	San Francisco	8-Wd San Francisco	82	435
Charles	33	m	w	HANO	San Francisco	6-Wd San Francisco	81	155
Chas	36	m	w	ME	San Francisco	1-Wd San Francisco	79	49
Chas	30	m	w	CANA	Solano	Vallejo	90	210
Chas	21	m	w	NY	Solano	Vallejo	90	203
Christopher	40	m	w	ENGL	San Francisco	San Francisco P O	83	236
D R	65	m	w	TN	Nevada	Nevada Twp	75	296
Daniel D	64	m	w	VT	Yolo	Cache Crk Twp	93	429
David	47	m	w	SCOT	San Francisco	San Francisco P O	85	800
David	42	m	w	SCOT	San Francisco	1-Wd San Francisco	79	53
David	38	m	w	CANA	San Francisco	11-Wd San Francisc	84	491
David	34	m	w	NJ	Amador	Sutter Crk P O	69	408
David	29	m	w	SCOT	San Francisco	1-Wd San Francisco	79	88
David	25	m	w	MI	Shasta	French Gulch P O	89	466
David E	41	m	w	NY	Inyo	Independence Twp	73	325
E	48	m	w	MA	Solano	Vallejo	90	173
E	11	f	w	CA	San Francisco	San Francisco P O	85	826
Edmond	52	m	w	AR	Los Angeles	San Jose Twp	73	621
Eliza	59	f	w	HAMB	San Francisco	8-Wd San Francisco	82	331
Enos C	49	m	w	OH	Colusa	Monroe Twp	71	311
F	22	m	w	OH	Sierra	Downieville Twp	89	521
F B	36	m	w	VA	Monterey	Alisal Twp	74	301
Fred G	35	m	w	MA	San Francisco	6-Wd San Francisco	81	115
G W	41	m	w	IN	El Dorado	Greenwood Twp	72	55
Geo	45	m	w	IREL	Monterey	Alisal Twp	74	288
George	38	m	w	IN	Los Angeles	Los Nietos Twp	73	578
George	32	m	w	SCOT	Amador	Sutter Crk P O	69	401
George H	40	m	w	CANA	Calaveras	Copperopolis P O	70	257
Giles	40	m	w	NY	Monterey	Pajaro Twp	74	372
J K	41	m	w	IN	Tuolumne	Columbia P O	93	345
James	57	m	w	TN	Kern	Linns Valley P O	73	343
James	41	m	w	IREL	Marin	San Rafael	74	57
James	38	m	w	IREL	San Francisco	8-Wd San Francisco	82	313
James	38	m	w	SCOT	San Luis Obispo	Salinas Twp	87	295
James	35	m	w	SCOT	San Francisco	11-Wd San Francisc	84	551
James	30	m	w	SCOT	Contra Costa	Martinez P O	71	420
James	26	m	w	NC	Stanislaus	Branch Twp	92	2
James	21	m	w	IREL	Merced	Snelling P O	74	246
James	20	m	w	SCOT	San Francisco	3-Wd San Francisco	79	323
James T	38	m	w	CT	Mendocino	Anderson Twp	74	150
Jas	48	m	w	IREL	Solano	Vallejo	90	214
Jas	39	m	w	IREL	Shasta	Portugese Flat P O	89	471
Jeno	40	m	w	CANA	Stanislaus	San Joaquin Twp	92	80
Jessee	28	m	w	IA	Los Angeles	Los Angeles Twp	73	481
Jessee D	33	m	w	CA	Los Angeles	Los Angeles Twp	73	481
Jessie D	64	m	w	KY	Los Angeles	Los Angeles	73	543
Jno	40	m	w	MO	Butte	Kimshew Tpw	70	80
Jno	32	m	w	CA	San Joaquin	1-Wd Stockton	86	153
Jno	27	m	w	IREL	Butte	Hamilton Twp	70	71
John	60	m	w	ME	San Francisco	11-Wd San Francisc	84	637
John	48	m	w	NY	San Francisco	11-Wd San Francisc	84	701
John	45	m	w	IREL	Marin	San Rafael Twp	74	25
John	40	m	w	CANA	San Joaquin	2-Wd Stockton	86	175
John	39	m	w	SCOT	San Francisco	San Francisco P O	83	413
John	37	m	w	PA	Mendocino	Anderson Twp	74	157
John	36	m	w	MI	Shasta	French Gulch P O	89	467
John	36	m	w	IREL	Humboldt	Eureka Twp	72	282
John	35	m	w	ME	San Francisco	7-Wd San Francisco	81	249
John	33	m	w	BADE	Santa Clara	Gilroy Twp	88	79
John	26	m	w	NH	Colusa	Colusa	71	294
John	25	m	w	NY	San Francisco	6-Wd San Francisco	81	94
John	24	m	w	IREL	Sonoma	Bodega Twp	91	252
John	15	m	b	MO	Marin	San Rafael Twp	74	36
John B	39	m	w	NY	Nevada	Bridgeport Twp	75	103
John H	41	m	w	MO	Humboldt	Mattole Twp	72	284
Julia	36	f	w	NY	San Francisco	8-Wd San Francisco	82	369
Julia	22	f	w	MA	San Francisco	11-Wd San Francisc	84	611
Laura	19	f	w	NY	San Francisco	5-Wd San Francisco	81	22
Laura	12	f	w	CA	San Francisco	San Francisco P O	85	826
Levi	29	m	w	IN	Santa Clara	Burnett Twp	88	31
Louis C	33	m	w	NY	San Francisco	6-Wd San Francisco	81	152
M	36	f	w	TN	Calaveras	Copperopolis P O	70	230
M E	29	m	w	MA	Santa Clara	Gilroy Twp	88	81
Mason	39	m	w	SCOT	Sacramento	4-Wd Sacramento	77	376
Merritt A	50	m	w	NY	El Dorado	Mud Springs Twp	72	73
Nathan	32	m	w	CT	San Francisco	6-Wd San Francisco	81	78
Peter	60	m	w	SCOT	San Francisco	San Francisco P O	83	143
Peter	35	m	w	PRUS	San Francisco	7-Wd San Francisco	81	274
Philander	41	m	w	NY	San Diego	Poway Dist	78	481
Philipi	20	m	w	NY	San Francisco	11-Wd San Francisc	84	694
R C	48	m	w	ENGL	Sutter	Yuba Twp	92	140
Robert	52	m	w	SCOT	Sutter	Vernon Twp	92	130
Robert E	52	m	w	NY	San Francisco	11-Wd San Francisc	84	712
Robt	34	m	w	CANA	Klamath	Trinidad Twp	73	389
Robt	21	m	w	CA	Calaveras	Copperopolis P O	70	229
Robt A	46	m	w	SCOT	San Francisco	San Francisco P O	85	736
S A	50	m	w	TN	Nevada	Nevada Twp	75	297
S J	41	m	w	MO	Sutter	Yuba Twp	92	141
S S	36	m	w	MO	Humboldt	Mattole Twp	72	284
Saml	43	m	w	NY	Mariposa	Maxwell Crk P O	74	145
Samuel	47	m	w	NY	Mariposa	Maxwell Crk P O	74	139
Samuel	25	m	w	IL	Los Angeles	Soledad Twp	73	633
Samuel C	34	m	w	CT	Mendocino	Point Arena Twp	74	204
Sank A	23	m	w	MI	Shasta	French Gulch P O	89	467
Theo	38	m	w	MA	San Francisco	8-Wd San Francisco	82	339
Thomas	38	m	w	MO	Humboldt	Mattole Twp	72	283
Thomas	33	m	w	ENGL	Contra Costa	Martinez P O	71	419
Thomas	32	m	w	NY	San Francisco	1-Wd San Francisco	79	65
Thomas G	43	m	w	NY	Los Angeles	Los Angeles	73	527
Thomas J	29	m	w	CANA	Napa	Napa	75	16
Thorn	25	m	w	LA	San Diego	San Diego	78	508
Thos	22	m	w	SCOT	San Francisco	San Francisco P O	83	73
Victor	53	m	w	FRAN	Stanislaus	Branch Twp	92	2
Walker	39	m	w	MO	Humboldt	Mattole Twp	72	283
William	59	m	w	VA	Marin	San Rafael Twp	74	36
William	54	m	w	ENGL	Butte	Oregon Twp	70	122
William	44	m	w	MA	San Francisco	3-Wd San Francisco	79	308
William	42	m	w	OH	Plumas	Mineral Twp	77	20
William	40	m	w	NY	San Diego	San Diego	78	486
William	38	m	w	IL	Los Angeles	Los Angeles Twp	73	496
William	37	m	w	PA	San Mateo	Woodside P O	87	385
William	36	m	w	IREL	Colusa	Monroe Twp	71	325
William	35	m	w	ENGL	Contra Costa	Martinez P O	71	419
William	35	m	w	MI	San Mateo	Redwood Twp	87	361
William	28	m	w	SCOT	Colusa	Monroe Twp	71	312
William	27	m	w	VA	Inyo	Cerro Gordo Twp	73	321
William	27	m	w	AUSL	San Bernardino	San Bernardino Twp	78	425
William	25	m	w	SCOT	San Francisco	3-Wd San Francisco	79	297
William E	28	m	w	AR	Los Angeles	San Jose Twp	73	623
William L	29	m	w	VA	Inyo	Lone Pine Twp	73	331
William T	40	m	w	NY	Santa Cruz	Santa Cruz	89	412
Wm	40	m	w	IREL	Nevada	Nevada Twp	75	321
Wm	32	m	w	AR	Fresno	Millerton P O	72	192
Wm	27	m	w	CANA	Napa	Napa	75	52
Wm W	36	m	w	PA	Mariposa	Mariposa P O	74	114
Yough	20	m	c	CHIN	San Francisco	11-Wd San Francisc	84	712
HUNTERMANN								
August	38	m	w	PRUS	San Francisco	2-Wd San Francisco	79	269
HUNTHOON								
F J	43	m	w	PRUS	Sierra	Downieville Twp	89	522
HUNTING								
B F	41	m	w	VT	San Joaquin	Castoria Twp	86	13
C W	54	m	w	VT	San Joaquin	Liberty Twp	86	84
Chas	20	m	w	SAME	San Joaquin	Dent Twp	86	17
Thos	28	m	w	DE	San Joaquin	Dent Twp	86	23
HUNTINGBERG								
August	46	m	w	HAMB	San Francisco	San Francisco P O	83	7
HUNTINGDON								
Harry	45	m	w	ME	San Francisco	7-Wd San Francisco	81	281
Henry	50	m	w	NH	Plumas	Indian Twp	77	12
Jacob	42	m	w	OH	Siskiyou	Callahan P O	89	626
HUNTINGTON								
Carlin	22	m	w	NY	San Bernardino	San Bernardino Twp	78	452
Clark	38	m	w	NY	San Joaquin	1-Wd Stockton	86	122
E B	26	m	w	CT	Alameda	Alameda	68	18
Frank	35	m	w	NY	San Francisco	5-Wd San Francisco	81	19
Geo H	35	m	w	NY	Nevada	Grass Valley Twp	75	192
Hariett	9	f	w	CA	San Bernardino	San Bernardino Twp	78	417
Heber	28	m	w	IL	San Bernardino	San Bernardino Twp	78	425
Henry	45	m	w	ME	Butte	Wyandotte Twp	70	145
John	39	m	w	OH	Santa Cruz	Santa Cruz	89	432
John	39	m	w	OH	Santa Cruz	Santa Cruz	89	406
John A	45	m	w	OH	Placer	Bath P O	76	459
Joshua	27	m	w	CANA	Sonoma	Vallejo Twp	91	462
Josiah L	50	m	w	ME	Contra Costa	Martinez P O	71	378
Sallie	24	f	w	OH	Yuba	Marysville	93	596
Saml	47	m	w	MA	Tulare	Farmersville Twp	92	246
Uriel	54	m	w	ME	Contra Costa	Martinez P O	71	377
W C	28	m	w	MA	Monterey	Alisal Twp	74	303
Wilbur	32	m	w	MI	Santa Cruz	Santa Cruz	89	405
HUNTINTON								
Johann C	65	m	w	VT	Santa Cruz	Santa Cruz Twp	89	384
HUNTLEY								
Albert	41	m	w	ME	Monterey	Salinas Twp	74	309
Antonette M	25	f	w	ME	Alpine	Woodfords P O	69	316
Ashael	32	m	w	NY	Placer	Bath P O	76	431
B F	40	m	w	PA	Sacramento	1-Wd Sacramento	77	180
Carles C	32	m	w	NY	Plumas	Quartz Twp	77	40
Eli	36	m	w	CT	Nevada	Bloomfield Twp	75	92
Geo W	31	m	w	NY	Sonoma	Bodega Twp	91	248
Geo W C	39	m	w	ME	Sonoma	Bodega Twp	91	263
Giles W	39	m	w	NJ	San Francisco	5-Wd San Francisco	81	12
Harriet	56	f	w	NY	Santa Clara	Gilroy Twp	88	78
Jas S	50	m	w	NY	San Diego	San Diego	78	509
John J	62	m	w	ENGL	Nevada	Bridgeport Twp	75	107
John M	35	m	w	NY	Tulare	Visalia	92	290
Joseph	49	m	w	ME	Marin	Tomales Twp	74	82
P C	52	m	w	NY	San Francisco	San Francisco P O	83	23
Phoebe	39	f	w	CANA	Marin	Tomales Twp	74	84
Russell	26	m	w	NY	Mendocino	Point Arena Twp	74	215
S N	45	m	w	PA	San Joaquin	Dent Twp	86	19
Stephen	27	m	w	ENGL	Nevada	Bridgeport Twp	75	107
Trestiom B	31	m	w	IL	Yolo	Cache Crk Twp	93	421
Tristmon	32	m	w	IL	Yolo	Cache Crk Twp	93	438
Willard	66	m	w	NH	Yolo	Cache Crk Twp	93	438
William	23	m	w	ME	Marin	Tomales Twp	74	84

© 2001 by Heritage Quest. All rights reserved.

Series M593

Name	Age	S	R	B-PL	County	Locale	Roll	Pg
HUNTLY								
Augustas	23	m	w	ME	Sonoma	Petaluma Twp	91	352
Elijah	32	m	w	CANA	Nevada	Nevada Twp	75	322
HUNTON								
John L	50	m	w	SCOT	San Bernardino	San Bernardino Twp	78	453
John W	24	m	w	AR	Mendocino	Anderson Twp	74	157
W D	28	m	w	ME	San Joaquin	Elkhorn Twp	86	65
HUNTOON								
D R	30	m	w	VT	Sacramento	3-Wd Sacramento	77	274
Edward	39	m	w	NY	Sacramento	Dry Crk Twp	77	100
J L	48	m	w	VT	Sacramento	4-Wd Sacramento	77	338
Jane	65	f	w	IREL	Sacramento	Brighton Twp	77	71
Lydia	13	f	w	CA	Tehama	Cottonwood Twp	92	162
Mary	55	f	w	OH	San Francisco	7-Wd San Francisco	81	231
Moses	25	m	w	CANA	Mono	Bridgeport P O	74	282
R	20	m	w	MI	Lake	Knoxville Mines	73	404
Sidney	39	m	w	CANA	Mono	Bridgeport P O	74	287
Thos	19	m	w	SWED	Sacramento	Franklin Twp	77	119
HUNTRESS								
Jas S	36	m	w	ME	Nevada	Rough & Ready Twp	75	328
HUNTS								
Harry	12	m	w	CA	Mariposa	Mariposa P O	74	93
HUNTSINGER								
E	33	m	w	IN	Sacramento	3-Wd Sacramento	77	318
HUNTSMAN								
Danl	35	m	w	MO	Monterey	San Juan Twp	74	393
David	40	m	w	OH	Shasta	Shasta P O	89	456
Geo H	39	m	w	ENGL	San Francisco	8-Wd San Francisco	82	318
Thomas Jefferson	45	m	w	KY	Plumas	Mineral Twp	77	20
William	38	m	w	OH	Santa Cruz	Pajaro Twp	89	352
HUNTSMEN								
Jacob	35	m	w	OH	San Bernardino	San Salvador Twp	78	460
HUNTSON								
Anna	3	f	w	ENGL	Sacramento	Sutter Twp	77	383
H P	30	m	w	NORW	Sierra	Butte Twp	89	508
HUNTZ								
Henry F	49	m	w	PRUS	Butte	Kimshew Tpw	70	83
HUNY								
Hig	34	m	c	CHIN	San Joaquin	1-Wd Stockton	86	147
HUNZ								
Fred	34	m	w	PRUS	San Francisco	1-Wd San Francisco	79	92
HUONG								
Ah	34	m	c	CHIN	Sacramento	3-Wd Sacramento	77	316
Ah	14	m	c	CHIN	San Francisco	11-Wd San Francisc	84	595
HUP								
Ah	40	m	c	CHIN	San Joaquin	1-Wd Stockton	86	149
Ah	33	m	c	CHIN	Sierra	Sears Twp	89	553
Ah	24	f	c	CHIN	San Francisco	San Francisco P O	80	507
Ah	21	f	c	CHIN	San Francisco	San Francisco P O	80	489
Ah	18	m	c	CHIN	San Francisco	San Francisco P O	80	492
Bo	25	m	c	CHIN	Nevada	Grass Valley Twp	75	205
George	53	m	w	HDAR	San Francisco	San Francisco P O	80	355
Lee	43	m	c	CHIN	San Joaquin	1-Wd Stockton	86	149
HUPE								
Ah	26	m	c	CHIN	Tehama	Red Bluff	92	184
Ed	45	m	w	FRAN	Butte	Ophir Twp	70	101
HUPERS								
M	39	m	w	PRUS	Alameda	Murray Twp	68	125
HUPP								
John	39	m	w	OH	Butte	Kimshew Tpw	70	78
W P	34	m	w	OH	Trinity	Weaverville Pct	92	222
HUPPENS								
John	28	m	w	OLDE	Sonoma	Bodega Twp	91	262
HUPPER								
J B	35	m	w	MO	Monterey	San Antonio Twp	74	320
HURBERT								
Amon	45	m	w	FRAN	El Dorado	Cosumnes Twp	72	18
HURCH								
John	25	m	w	NH	San Francisco	11-Wd San Francisc	84	545
HURCHISON								
---	25	m	w	IN	San Joaquin	Tulare Twp	86	252
HURD								
Ann	52	f	w	ENGL	San Joaquin	Oneal Twp	86	111
Ann	40	f	w	ENGL	San Francisco	San Francisco P O	83	115
C E	26	m	w	ME	San Joaquin	Oneal Twp	86	112
Casse	8	f	w	CA	Colusa	California Twp	71	279
Chas	27	m	w	ME	San Joaquin	Oneal Twp	86	118
Chas H	25	m	w	IREL	Sonoma	Russian Rvr	91	375
Ezra D	36	m	w	ME	Placer	Bath P O	76	439
Henry H	42	m	w	NY	Sonoma	Healdsburg & Mendo	91	277
Hugh	30	m	w	WI	San Joaquin	Douglas Twp	86	32
J	24	m	w	MA	Sacramento	1-Wd Sacramento	77	182
J H	40	m	w	MA	San Joaquin	3-Wd Stockton	86	219
James M	29	m	w	NY	San Francisco	1-Wd San Francisco	79	107
Jas	32	m	w	OH	Solano	Vallejo	90	190
Jno	30	m	w	NY	Sacramento	1-Wd Sacramento	77	182
Justus	33	m	w	NY	Mariposa	Mariposa P O	74	134
Robert S	36	m	w	NY	Placer	Dutch Flat P O	76	415
Robrt	8	m	w	ENGL	Placer	Lincoln P O	76	489
T B	63	m	w	VT	San Francisco	3-Wd San Francisco	79	310
Washington	52	m	w	MA	Sonoma	Petaluma Twp	91	346
William	35	m	w	KY	Colusa	Butte Twp	71	270
William	32	m	w	KY	Nevada	Meadow Lake Twp	75	246
Wm C	39	m	w	ME	San Luis Obispo	San Luis Obispo Tw	87	303
HURDES								
John A	45	m	w	PA	San Luis Obispo	Morro Twp	87	283
HURDLE								
Thomas	21	m	w	OH	San Francisco	San Francisco P O	80	335
HURDS								
James	40	m	w	IA	San Joaquin	Liberty Twp	86	87
HURDY								
Albert W	35	m	w	IREL	San Francisco	8-Wd San Francisco	82	343
Alice	13	f	w	CA	San Francisco	5-Wd San Francisco	81	24
James	40	m	w	IREL	San Francisco	San Francisco P O	83	38
Jane	24	f	w	IREL	Alameda	Oakland	68	210
Jno Mrs	33	f	w	NY	San Francisco	5-Wd San Francisco	81	24
HURE								
John J	39	m	w	ME	Placer	Dutch Flat P O	76	401
HURGUET								
John	49	m	w	SAXO	San Francisco	1-Wd San Francisco	79	32
HURIANGE								
Hugo	29	m	w	MEXI	San Francisco	8-Wd San Francisco	82	388
HURICHO								
Marry	37	f	w	IREL	Santa Clara	Almaden Twp	88	12
HURINS								
Lyman	18	f	w	PRUS	San Francisco	5-Wd San Francisco	81	15
HURLAHY								
John	42	m	w	IREL	San Francisco	San Francisco P O	85	743
HURLBERT								
Bell D	22	f	w	NY	Sacramento	4-Wd Sacramento	77	372
Clara	56	f	w	NY	Sacramento	Franklin Twp	77	110
Daniel B	58	m	w	NY	Yolo	Cottonwood Twp	93	465
E	22	m	w	NY	Solano	Vallejo	90	141
Thomas B	47	m	w	VT	Yolo	Buckeye Twp	93	417
HURLBURT								
D	40	m	w	IL	Lassen	Susanville Twp	73	444
George C	40	m	w	SC	San Francisco	2-Wd San Francisco	79	252
I M	39	m	w	KY	Tehama	Hunters Twp	92	187
John W	48	m	w	OH	Los Angeles	Los Angeles	73	527
William	31	m	w	NH	Marin	Nicasio Twp	74	17
HURLBUT								
D	49	m	w	NY	Nevada	Nevada Twp	75	278
James M	41	m	w	NJ	San Francisco	San Francisco P O	85	783
O	65	m	w	NY	Sacramento	3-Wd Sacramento	77	286
William	40	m	w	NY	Tehama	Tehama Twp	92	196
HURLBUTT								
Louis	23	m	w	NH	Humboldt	Pacific Twp	72	292
Nathaniel	28	m	w	NH	Humboldt	Pacific Twp	72	296
HURLD								
Henery	38	m	w	ENGL	San Francisco	7-Wd San Francisco	81	180
HURLES								
Smith	43	m	w	IREL	Butte	Wyandotte Twp	70	149
HURLEY								
Alfred	38	m	w	AL	Monterey	Alisal Twp	74	290
Charles	37	m	w	IREL	San Francisco	11-Wd San Francisc	84	505
Daniel	58	m	w	IREL	Napa	Napa	75	57
Daniel	30	m	w	IREL	Mendocino	Point Arena Twp	74	213
Danl	38	m	w	IREL	San Francisco	11-Wd San Francisc	84	642
Isaac	45	m	w	MO	Plumas	Quartz Twp	77	43
J W	45	m	w	MD	Tehama	Red Bluff	92	183
J W	28	m	w	CANA	Monterey	Alisal Twp	74	290
James	28	m	w	IREL	San Francisco	San Francisco P O	83	8
James G	36	m	w	IL	Sacramento	Cosumnes Twp	77	91
Jane	32	f	w	IREL	San Francisco	11-Wd San Francisc	84	660
Jeremiah	34	m	w	IREL	Nevada	Grass Valley Twp	75	190
Jeremiah	32	m	w	IREL	Santa Clara	1-Wd San Jose	88	266
Jeremiah	31	m	w	IREL	San Luis Obispo	San Luis Obispo Tw	87	316
Johanna	30	f	w	IREL	San Francisco	2-Wd San Francisco	79	234
John	60	m	w	IREL	San Francisco	San Francisco P O	83	382
John	55	m	w	IREL	Solano	Vallejo	90	186
John	49	m	w	IREL	Amador	Sutter Crk P O	69	396
John	45	m	w	IREL	Nevada	Nevada Twp	75	295
John	40	m	w	IL	Sacramento	Cosumnes Twp	77	91
John	40	m	w	IREL	San Francisco	San Francisco P O	80	378
John	38	m	w	IREL	Sacramento	2-Wd Sacramento	77	240
John	37	m	w	IREL	Tehama	Battle Crk Twp	92	157
John	33	m	w	IREL	San Francisco	11-Wd San Francisc	84	433
John	28	m	w	MA	San Francisco	San Francisco P O	83	361
John	26	m	w	IREL	San Francisco	7-Wd San Francisco	81	157
John	22	m	w	PA	Solano	Vallejo	90	203
John H	22	m	w	AR	Plumas	Quartz Twp	77	43
Julia	17	f	w	IREL	San Francisco	7-Wd San Francisco	81	185
Margaret	45	f	w	IREL	Solano	Suisun Twp	90	102
Margaret	30	f	w	IREL	San Francisco	8-Wd San Francisco	82	456
Margarett	50	f	w	IREL	Solano	Vallejo	90	140
Margt E	35	f	w	IREL	Sacramento	3-Wd Sacramento	77	287
Mary	24	f	w	IREL	Alameda	Alameda	68	18
Mary A	33	f	w	CANA	San Francisco	San Francisco P O	83	279
Maurice	11	m	w	CA	Marin	San Rafael Twp	74	29
Mercy G	61	f	w	MA	San Francisco	San Francisco P O	85	727
Michael	50	m	w	IREL	San Francisco	San Francisco P O	83	374
Michael	31	m	w	IREL	San Francisco	San Francisco P O	83	396
Micheal	50	m	w	IREL	San Francisco	7-Wd San Francisco	81	203
Morris	35	m	w	IREL	El Dorado	Cosumnes Twp	72	16
Morris	21	m	w	IREL	San Francisco	8-Wd San Francisco	82	470
Morris	10	m	w	CA	Marin	San Rafael Twp	74	27
Pat	39	m	w	IREL	Alameda	Oakland	68	261
Pat	30	m	w	IREL	Solano	Vallejo	90	215
Patrick	53	m	w	IREL	San Francisco	San Francisco P O	85	715
Patrick	45	m	w	IREL	San Francisco	San Francisco P O	83	239
Patrick	32	m	w	IREL	Nevada	Grass Valley Twp	75	211
Patrick	32	m	w	IREL	San Francisco	1-Wd San Francisco	79	127
Patrick	30	m	w	IREL	San Francisco	San Francisco P O	83	142

© 2001 by Heritage Quest. All rights reserved.

Name	Age	S	R	B-PL	County	Locale	Series M593 Roll	Pg
Patrick	25	m	w	IREL	San Francisco	San Francisco P O	83	194
Timothy	50	m	w	IREL	San Francisco	7-Wd San Francisco	81	186
Tom	33	m	w	IREL	Alameda	Oakland	68	186
William	9	m	w	CA	Marin	San Rafael Twp	74	29
William	37	m	w	NY	Sacramento	2-Wd Sacramento	77	240
William	27	m	w	CANA	Marin	San Rafael	74	52
William S	40	m	w	VA	Stanislaus	Empire Twp	92	41
HURLIMAN								
John	45	m	w	SWIT	Placer	Bath P O	76	425
HURLLEY								
Thomas	40	m	w	IREL	San Francisco	7-Wd San Francisco	81	164
HURLY								
Anna	7	f	w	CA	San Francisco	11-Wd San Francisc	84	711
D J	33	m	w	IREL	San Joaquin	1-Wd Stockton	86	122
Daniel	27	m	w	IREL	Sonoma	Vallejo Twp	91	456
Fanny	19	f	w	CA	San Francisco	San Francisco P O	80	473
John	34	m	w	IREL	San Francisco	8-Wd San Francisco	82	312
John	30	m	w	IREL	San Francisco	San Francisco P O	80	458
Kate	20	f	w	NY	San Francisco	7-Wd San Francisco	81	240
Mary	8	f	w	CA	San Francisco	11-Wd San Francisc	84	711
Patrick	54	m	w	IREL	Butte	Wyandotte Twp	70	142
Thomas	30	m	w	IREL	Alameda	Oakland	68	145
Thos	30	m	w	IREL	San Joaquin	1-Wd Stockton	86	133
Timothy	25	m	w	IREL	El Dorado	White Oak Twp	72	135
William	25	m	w	IREL	Yolo	Grafton Twp	93	480
HURM								
Ah	23	m	c	CHIN	Nevada	Little York Twp	75	234
John	40	m	w	WURT	Monterey	Monterey Twp	74	352
John	37	m	w	GERM	Monterey	Monterey Twp	74	352
HURMAN								
Jason	40	m	w	NY	Butte	Chico Twp	70	17
Justus	57	m	w	NY	Sacramento	San Joaquin Twp	77	395
HURMS								
Chas	30	m	w	PRUS	San Francisco	5-Wd San Francisco	81	20
HURN								
John	13	m	w	MO	Monterey	Pajaro Twp	74	368
HURNANDEZ								
Frank	25	m	w	SAME	San Joaquin	1-Wd Stockton	86	135
HURNE								
James	31	m	w	ENGL	San Francisco	1-Wd San Francisco	79	135
HURNEY								
Jno W	16	m	w	IL	Butte	Oregon Twp	70	134
Mary	17	f	w	MS	San Francisco	11-Wd San Francisc	84	688
HURREY								
George	26	m	w	ME	Marin	Point Reyes Twp	74	22
John	28	m	w	ME	Marin	Point Reyes Twp	74	22
HURRI								
William	17	m	w	MO	Santa Cruz	Watsonville	89	375
HURSEY								
Valentine	43	m	w	IREL	San Mateo	Menlo Park P O	87	379
HURSHEY								
David	50	m	w	MD	Yolo	Grafton Twp	93	490
HURSON								
Edward	23	m	w	IREL	San Francisco	8-Wd San Francisco	82	401
HURST								
Anderson	35	m	w	VA	Placer	Auburn P O	76	378
Anna	46	f	w	HAMB	Sacramento	2-Wd Sacramento	77	214
Charles	17	m	w	NY	San Mateo	Schoolhouse Statio	87	342
Francis	27	m	w	BADE	Yolo	Cache Crk Twp	93	422
Frank	34	m	w	IN	Tehama	Paynes Crk Twp	92	160
George	37	m	w	IN	Placer	Auburn P O	76	359
Henry	47	m	w	IREL	Yuba	Rose Bar Twp	93	666
Henry	40	m	w	NY	Butte	Bidwell Twp	70	4
Henry	32	m	w	NY	Nevada	Nevada Twp	75	300
Henry C	37	m	w	VA	Contra Costa	Martinez P O	71	383
J H	30	m	w	ENGL	Mendocino	Round Valley Twp	74	217
James	22	m	w	VA	San Diego	Julian Dist	78	469
John	45	m	w	GERM	Nevada	Nevada Twp	75	274
John	31	m	w	CANA	Merced	Snelling P O	74	249
Rolandus P	40	m	w	OH	Siskiyou	Butte Twp	89	585
W	14	m	w	KS	San Joaquin	Elkhorn Twp	86	64
William H	13	m	w	CA	El Dorado	Mud Springs Twp	72	83
Wm J	41	m	w	ENGL	Tuolumne	Chinese Camp P O	93	377
HURSTER								
A J	64	m	w	NH	Humboldt	Bucksport Twp	72	245
HURSTON								
Matilda	25	f	w	ME	Humboldt	Eureka Twp	72	259
HURT								
Hiram	27	m	w	KY	San Bernardino	Chino Twp	78	409
J	32	m	w	IN	Alameda	Oakland	68	261
James	35	m	w	MO	Lake	Scotts Crk	73	426
John	50	m	w	IN	San Joaquin	Liberty Twp	86	92
William J	33	m	w	ME	Santa Cruz	Soquel Twp	89	445
Wm	42	m	w	TN	Lake	Scotts Crk	73	427
HURTADO								
Francisco	42	m	w	MEXI	Marin	Bolinas Twp	74	3
Pedro P	44	m	w	PERU	Sacramento	2-Wd Sacramento	77	242
HURTEADO								
Julepe	21	m	w	MEXI	Merced	Snelling P O	74	259
HURTELS								
C	22	f	w	NGRA	San Francisco	San Francisco P O	83	318
HURTER								
Mary E	40	f	w	NY	Monterey	San Juan Twp	74	416
HURTHNABANK								
Jas	35	m	w	ENGL	Humboldt	Eel Rvr Twp	72	250
HURTROCK								
Joseph	51	m	w	SWIT	Sutter	Butte Twp	92	100

Name	Age	S	R	B-PL	County	Locale	Series M593 Roll	Pg
HURTT								
Harvey	64	m	w	VA	Humboldt	Eel Rvr Twp	72	253
Wm	47	m	w	MD	San Francisco	11-Wd San Francisc	84	610
HURTZ								
Ah	28	m	c	CHIN	Sierra	Sears Twp	89	553
Charles	32	m	w	BADE	San Francisco	7-Wd San Francisco	81	213
Joseph	37	m	w	PRUS	San Francisco	5-Wd San Francisco	81	14
HURTZIG								
Nathaiel	43	m	w	PRUS	Placer	Bath P O	76	432
HURY								
Ah	28	m	c	CHIN	Sacramento	Granite Twp	77	139
Andrew	45	m	w	MA	Sonoma	Petaluma Twp	91	322
William	35	m	w	VA	Los Angeles	Wilmington Twp	73	634
HUSBAND								
David	38	m	w	PA	Stanislaus	Empire Twp	92	35
Edgar	36	m	w	MO	Calaveras	San Andreas P O	70	220
Hamilton	38	m	w	MA	Placer	Rocklin Twp	76	464
William	41	m	w	WALE	Santa Clara	Santa Clara Twp	88	162
HUSBANDS								
W H	26	m	w	DE	Napa	Napa	75	6
HUSBY								
George	42	m	w	CANA	Sacramento	Georgianna Twp	77	124
HUSCROFT								
John J	38	m	w	OH	Yuba	North East Twp	93	645
HUSE								
Alice	10	f	w	CA	Santa Barbara	Santa Barbara P O	87	462
Chas E	45	m	w	MA	Santa Barbara	Santa Barbara P O	87	460
Colm	40	m	w	PA	Butte	Kimshew Tpw	70	80
E F	42	m	w	VT	Amador	Sutter Crk P O	69	396
John	20	m	w	IN	Amador	Fiddletown P O	69	440
Margaret	15	f	w	CA	Amador	Jackson P O	69	341
Samuel E	49	m	w	VT	Amador	Fiddletown P O	69	438
Stephen	33	m	w	MA	Amador	Jackson P O	69	330
Washington	53	m	w	KY	Amador	Sutter Crk P O	69	409
Wm	42	m	w	VT	Butte	Ophir Twp	70	115
HUSELY								
Kate	47	f	w	ME	Butte	Kimshew Tpw	70	80
HUSEMAN								
Louis	38	m	w	HANO	Siskiyou	Yreka	89	655
HUSER								
Geo	40	m	w	HCAS	El Dorado	Georgetown Twp	72	45
HUSHBACK								
Lewis	45	m	w	MD	Santa Cruz	Pajaro Twp	89	344
HUSHBURGHER								
J	30	m	w	PRUS	Humboldt	Eureka Twp	72	275
HUSHER								
Emanuel	51	m	w	BAVA	Alameda	San Leandro	68	97
HUSHFELTER								
E	44	m	w	WURT	Sierra	Downieville Twp	89	521
HUSHING								
Joseph	27	m	w	IREL	San Mateo	Schoolhouse Statio	87	331
HUSHNER								
C	36	f	w	HAMB	San Joaquin	Oneal Twp	86	110
HUSHON								
Patrick	40	m	w	IREL	Humboldt	Pacific Twp	72	292
HUSICK								
M	19	f	w	NY	Alameda	Alameda	68	3
HUSING								
Henry	39	m	w	HANO	San Mateo	San Mateo P O	87	355
Henry	24	m	w	PRUS	San Francisco	8-Wd San Francisco	82	434
Heny	30	m	w	PRUS	San Francisco	8-Wd San Francisco	82	352
John	35	m	w	PRUS	San Francisco	8-Wd San Francisco	82	307
Richd	24	m	w	PRUS	San Francisco	San Francisco P O	85	747
HUSKEY								
George	26	m	w	OH	San Francisco	San Francisco P O	83	370
HUSLER								
Fred	36	m	w	PRUS	San Francisco	2-Wd San Francisco	79	226
HUSLEY								
Daniel	40	m	w	IREL	San Francisco	San Francisco P O	83	167
HUSMAN								
Nathan H	65	f	w	HANO	Los Angeles	Santa Ana Twp	73	613
HUSMONN								
O	40	m	w	HANO	Sierra	Butte Twp	89	509
HUSNER								
Henry	36	m	w	PRUS	Sonoma	Analy Twp	91	243
HUSNETTER								
John	48	m	w	GERM	Yolo	Cottonwood Twp	93	461
HUSOM								
Andrew	38	m	w	NORW	Nevada	Grass Valley Twp	75	229
HUSON								
Cornelius	38	m	w	NY	Nevada	Bridgeport Twp	75	114
Thos R	18	m	w	GA	Tehama	Tehama Twp	92	194
HUSS								
Bador	47	m	w	BADE	Sacramento	Sutter Twp	77	389
Benj	18	m	w	OH	Yuba	Marysville	93	597
Frank	46	m	w	PRUS	Nevada	Grass Valley Twp	75	142
HUSSCROFT								
George L	32	m	w	OH	Colusa	Monroe Twp	71	322
HUSSEY								
Albine	40	m	w	MA	San Francisco	San Francisco P O	83	371
Bartholemew	29	m	w	IREL	Solano	Vallejo	90	217
C	47	f	w	WI	San Joaquin	2-Wd Stockton	86	180
Charles S	50	m	w	MA	Santa Cruz	Soquel Twp	89	442
Chas	23	m	w	LA	San Francisco	San Francisco P O	83	62
Danl	36	m	w	NH	Solano	Vallejo	90	173
Edwd	40	m	w	IREL	Solano	Vallejo	90	214
G S	40	m	w	ME	Tuolumne	Columbia P O	93	357

© 2001 by Heritage Quest. All rights reserved.

Name	Age	S	R	B-PL	County	Locale	Roll	Pg
Geo V	46	m	w	NH	Butte	Hamilton Twp	70	64
Harriet	5	f	w	CA	San Joaquin	Douglas Twp	86	47
Henry J	35	m	w	IREL	San Francisco	San Francisco P O	83	44
Homer	21	m	w	IL	Stanislaus	Emory Twp	92	24
J H	50	m	w	ME	Sacramento	3-Wd Sacramento	77	269
John	41	m	w	IREL	Nevada	Little York Twp	75	239
John	40	m	w	NY	San Joaquin	Union Twp	86	267
Joseph	60	m	w	IREL	San Francisco	1-Wd San Francisco	79	26
Lawrence	45	m	w	IREL	San Francisco	San Francisco P O	83	40
Lewis	40	m	w	BAVA	El Dorado	Greenwood Twp	72	57
Margret	19	f	w	NY	San Francisco	1-Wd San Francisco	79	107
Mathew	45	m	w	AZOR	Plumas	Indian Twp	77	12
Michael	33	m	w	IREL	Nevada	Nevada Twp	75	319
Michael	32	m	w	IREL	Nevada	Grass Valley Twp	75	230
Michael	21	m	w	NY	San Francisco	3-Wd San Francisco	79	325
Patrick	42	m	w	IREL	San Francisco	San Francisco P O	83	321
Patrick	27	m	w	NY	San Francisco	3-Wd San Francisco	79	325
S S	54	m	w	ME	Nevada	Bridgeport Twp	75	101
Sarah	42	f	w	IREL	San Francisco	1-Wd San Francisco	79	31
Sarah	35	f	w	ENGL	San Francisco	7-Wd San Francisco	81	269
Simon	56	m	w	IREL	San Francisco	1-Wd San Francisco	79	26
Stephen	53	m	w	ME	Butte	Concow Twp	70	7
Ulric J	29	m	w	ME	San Francisco	8-Wd San Francisco	82	494
Wm M	41	m	w	ME	San Francisco	8-Wd San Francisco	82	289
HUSSING								
Everetto	21	m	w	HANO	San Mateo	San Mateo P O	87	354
Rathye	29	m	w	HANO	San Francisco	11-Wd San Francisc	84	597
Richard	37	m	w	HANO	San Mateo	Schoolhouse Statio	87	331
HUSSON								
Frank	43	m	w	FRAN	Santa Cruz	Watsonville	89	365
John	40	m	w	FRAN	San Francisco	San Francisco P O	80	539
HUSSY								
Frank S	43	m	w	MA	Calaveras	San Andreas P O	70	156
Harvey	34	m	w	MA	Calaveras	San Andreas P O	70	204
Mathew	26	m	w	BAVA	Calaveras	San Andreas P O	70	184
Morris	23	m	w	CANA	San Mateo	Woodside P O	87	385
Simon	35	m	w	OH	San Joaquin	Liberty Twp	86	95
William	23	m	w	ME	Marin	San Rafael Twp	74	36
HUST								
John	39	m	w	BADE	Trinity	Douglas	92	236
HUSTED								
Mary	57	f	w	VT	Sonoma	Analy Twp	91	229
William	40	m	w	ME	San Francisco	8-Wd San Francisco	82	487
HUSTEDT								
Herman	22	m	w	CANA	Contra Costa	Martinez P O	71	386
HUSTEL								
Henry	31	m	w	PA	San Francisco	6-Wd San Francisco	81	103
HUSTEN								
Elie	34	m	w	OH	Alameda	Alvarado	68	302
HUSTER								
Louis	20	m	w	DENM	San Francisco	7-Wd San Francisco	81	224
HUSTES								
John	37	m	w	ENGL	Nevada	Bridgeport Twp	75	108
HUSTIN								
N	40	m	w	ME	El Dorado	Greenwood Twp	72	51
HUSTIS								
Joseph	30	m	w	WI	Nevada	Bridgeport Twp	75	117
HUSTLER								
A B	42	m	w	MD	Sacramento	Franklin Twp	77	113
HUSTON								
Charles	24	m	w	TX	Kern	Tehachapi P O	73	352
Daniel T	45	m	w	OH	San Bernardino	San Bernardino Twp	78	419
E	13	f	w	CA	Los Angeles	Los Angeles	73	569
Frank H	4	m	w	OR	Humboldt	Eureka Twp	72	259
John	31	m	w	CANA	Santa Clara	Fremont Twp	88	62
John	30	m	w	IREL	San Francisco	San Francisco P O	83	188
John	28	m	w	SCOT	Santa Barbara	Santa Maria P O	87	511
Joseph	35	m	w	VA	Yolo	Buckeye Twp	93	411
Lewis H	28	m	w	OH	Colusa	Butte Twp	71	268
Martha	70	f	w	NH	San Francisco	San Francisco P O	83	104
Nich	40	m	w	BADE	San Joaquin	Oneal Twp	86	104
Samuel B	33	m	w	PA	Mariposa	Mariposa P O	74	137
Samuel B	32	m	w	PA	Mariposa	Mariposa P O	74	130
W S	37	m	w	ME	Nevada	Nevada Twp	75	283
Walter S	40	m	w	MO	Yolo	Grafton Twp	93	481
HUSUDER								
John	39	m	w	PRUS	Yolo	Cache Crk Twp	93	427
HUT								
Ah	39	m	c	CHIN	San Joaquin	1-Wd Stockton	86	156
Ah	35	m	c	CHIN	Amador	Drytown P O	69	421
Ah	15	m	c	CHIN	San Francisco	6-Wd San Francisco	81	68
I	22	f	c	CHIN	Stanislaus	Emory Twp	92	22
HUTAFF								
Henry	37	m	w	PRUS	San Francisco	8-Wd San Francisco	82	477
HUTCH								
V	46	m	w	PA	Sacramento	3-Wd Sacramento	77	304
Wesley W	32	m	w	ME	Santa Cruz	Pajaro Twp	89	350
HUTCHENSON								
David	35	m	w	OH	Placer	Newcastle Twp	76	476
HUTCHER								
William	42	m	w	TN	Yolo	Grafton Twp	93	488
HUTCHERSON								
William	38	m	w	IREL	San Francisco	6-Wd San Francisco	81	109
HUTCHESON								
Sylvester	58	m	w	ME	Sonoma	Petaluma Twp	91	323
HUTCHESS								
Morris	26	m	w	IL	Sonoma	Analy Twp	91	223
HUTCHIN								
J	42	m	w	PA	San Joaquin	Tulare Twp	86	256
Jas	43	m	w	NY	San Joaquin	Tulare Twp	86	255
John	36	m	w	CANA	San Joaquin	Elkhorn Twp	86	58
Thomas	40	m	w	ENGL	Santa Clara	1-Wd San Jose	88	232
HUTCHING								
John W	42	m	w	ME	Placer	Bath P O	76	460
Joseph S	45	m	w	OH	Los Angeles	Los Angeles Twp	73	495
HUTCHINGS								
B F	39	m	w	ME	Tuolumne	Chinese Camp P O	93	368
Chas	45	m	w	ME	San Francisco	11-Wd San Francisc	84	610
Chas V	27	m	w	MA	Placer	Gold Run Twp	76	397
Cyrus	45	m	w	CANA	Butte	Oregon Twp	70	131
F W	49	m	w	IREL	Butte	Ophir Twp	70	118
Galvin	30	m	w	CANA	Butte	Ophir Twp	70	115
George	30	m	w	IREL	Plumas	Plumas Twp	77	30
George	26	m	w	ENGL	Mendocino	Navarro & Big Rvr	74	167
Gid	47	m	w	NC	Sutter	Nicolaus Twp	92	114
H N	60	m	w	VA	Monterey	San Juan Twp	74	396
Henry	56	m	w	ENGL	Plumas	Plumas Twp	77	29
Henry	38	m	w	PA	Trinity	Trinity Center Pct	92	205
Isaac	54	m	w	NC	Sonoma	Analy Twp	91	224
J B R	38	m	w	MO	Monterey	San Juan Twp	74	399
J L	52	m	w	ME	Tuolumne	Columbia P O	93	339
J M	47	m	w	ENGL	Mariposa	Mariposa P O	74	135
James	31	m	w	NY	Placer	Cisco P O	76	494
Jno L	42	m	w	NH	Nevada	Little York Twp	75	244
John	42	m	w	ME	San Francisco	2-Wd San Francisco	79	224
John	21	m	w	IL	Sacramento	4-Wd Sacramento	77	338
Jus	45	m	w	CANA	Butte	Oregon Twp	70	135
Lemuel	36	m	w	ME	San Francisco	11-Wd San Francisc	84	589
Liman	41	m	w	OH	Monterey	Pajaro Twp	74	372
M	15	f	w	CA	Yuba	Marysville	93	598
P L	37	m	w	MO	Yuba	East Bear Rvr Twp	93	539
Phin R	57	m	w	CANA	Butte	Ophir Twp	70	115
S	64	m	w	KY	Yuba	Linda Twp	93	554
Saml	23	m	w	ME	Humboldt	Eureka Twp	72	281
Samuel C	35	m	w	MO	Yuba	Long Bar Twp	93	562
T C	24	m	w	LA	Monterey	San Juan Twp	74	413
Thos	35	m	w	ENGL	Marin	Nicasio Twp	74	15
HUTCHINGSON								
Fannie	32	f	w	NY	San Francisco	San Francisco P O	83	413
Henry L	40	m	w	NY	Plumas	Quartz Twp	77	40
Hiram	41	m	w	CT	Yuba	W Bear Rvr Twp	93	684
J	46	m	w	SCOT	Alameda	Oakland	68	231
James	25	m	w	AR	Colusa	Colusa	71	294
L	45	m	w	ENGL	Lake	Morgan Valley	73	425
Mary	42	f	w	CANA	San Francisco	San Francisco P O	85	779
P	35	m	w	IREL	San Francisco	7-Wd San Francisco	81	176
R	30	m	w	ME	Lake	Morgan Valley	73	425
Richd	45	m	w	IREL	Sonoma	Petaluma Twp	91	321
Robert	44	m	w	SCOT	Colusa	Spring Valley Twp	71	345
Wm	50	m	w	SCOT	Monterey	Pajaro Twp	74	370
HUTCHINS								
Charles H	44	m	w	PA	Sonoma	Petaluma Twp	91	334
Chas	41	m	w	VA	San Francisco	San Francisco P O	83	107
Cherine	55	f	w	IA	San Joaquin	Elkhorn Twp	86	58
Edwd P	54	m	w	VT	San Francisco	6-Wd San Francisco	81	73
Elizabeth	35	f	w	IREL	San Francisco	8-Wd San Francisco	82	463
George	38	m	w	AL	Los Angeles	Los Nietos Twp	73	576
Horace	50	m	m	MO	Sonoma	Healdsburg & Mendo	91	285
James	40	m	w	NC	El Dorado	Lake Valley Twp	72	63
Luther	25	m	w	MI	Sacramento	Franklin Twp	77	110
M W	39	m	w	AL	Los Angeles	Los Nietos Twp	73	576
Martha	43	f	w	NY	San Francisco	8-Wd San Francisco	82	341
Martin	28	m	w	MO	Yolo	Merritt Twp	93	507
Pierce	48	m	w	NY	San Francisco	6-Wd San Francisco	81	95
Reuben	21	m	w	VT	Sonoma	Vallejo Twp	91	454
Robt	48	m	w	CANA	Nevada	Nevada Twp	75	292
Robt H	23	m	w	MD	Humboldt	Pacific Twp	72	293
T E	29	m	w	CANA	San Joaquin	Elkhorn Twp	86	62
William	22	m	w	MO	Inyo	Independence Twp	73	325
Wm	25	m	w	CANA	Sonoma	Salt Point	91	392
HUTCHINSON								
---	25	m	w	ENGL	Humboldt	Eureka Twp	72	277
Abel	40	m	w	MA	San Francisco	5-Wd San Francisco	81	14
Alex	18	m	w	NY	San Francisco	San Francisco P O	83	353
Alexander	30	m	w	NY	Santa Clara	Redwood Twp	88	123
Alonzo	40	m	w	NY	Butte	Ophir Twp	70	100
Anne	20	f	m	MA	San Francisco	6-Wd San Francisco	81	109
Avil	51	m	w	NY	Sonoma	Petaluma Twp	91	310
Benjamin	28	m	w	TN	Inyo	Cerro Gordo Twp	73	319
Bjm	13	m	w	CA	San Francisco	11-Wd San Francisc	84	593
C	40	m	w	AL	Mendocino	Ukiah Twp	74	242
Champion	54	m	w	CT	San Francisco	8-Wd San Francisco	82	424
Charles J	49	m	w	NH	Los Angeles	San Gabriel Twp	73	594
Chas	29	m	w	OH	Colusa	Grand Island Twp	71	309
D	48	m	w	OH	San Francisco	San Francisco P O	83	275
Daniel	35	m	w	CT	San Mateo	Schoolhouse Statio	87	339
David	30	m	w	PA	Nevada	Nevada Twp	75	286
David	30	m	w	NY	San Francisco	3-Wd San Francisco	79	327
Del	19	m	w	NY	San Joaquin	Tulare Twp	86	249
E A	28	m	w	MA	San Joaquin	Tulare Twp	86	251
E I	40	m	w	ME	Nevada	Bloomfield Twp	75	98
Ed	50	m	w	MA	San Joaquin	Tulare Twp	86	252
Eliza G	23	f	w	ENGL	San Francisco	8-Wd San Francisco	82	304
Enma	25	f	w	PA	San Francisco	8-Wd San Francisco	82	444

© 2001 by Heritage Quest. All rights reserved.

California 1870 Census

Name	Age	S	R	B-PL	County	Locale	Roll	Pg
Ezra	30	m	w	VT	San Francisco	8-Wd San Francisco	82	381
Friz	25	m	w	ME	San Joaquin	Elliott Twp	86	74
Geo O	55	m	w	MA	San Francisco	San Francisco P O	83	54
J C	32	m	w	MA	San Joaquin	Tulare Twp	86	251
Jame	42	m	w	CANA	El Dorado	Salmon Falls Twp	72	132
James	53	m	w	PA	Contra Costa	Martinez P O	71	413
James	44	m	w	PA	San Francisco	11-Wd San Francisc	84	510
James	23	m	w	ME	Placer	Emigrant Gap P O	76	416
James	21	m	w	PA	Yolo	Buckeye Twp	93	408
James E	36	m	w	ME	Mariposa	Mariposa P O	74	131
Jane	30	f	w	ENGL	San Francisco	San Francisco P O	83	241
Jas	34	m	w	IREL	Sutter	Sutter Twp	92	123
Jno	49	m	w	OH	Santa Clara	Burnett Twp	88	33
John	53	m	b	NJ	Tehama	Red Bluff	92	173
John	49	m	w	ENGL	San Francisco	11-Wd San Francisc	84	635
John	48	m	w	GA	Santa Clara	Redwood Twp	88	121
John	47	m	w	ME	San Francisco	San Francisco P O	83	235
John	44	m	w	DC	San Francisco	San Francisco P O	83	192
John	41	m	w	SCOT	Nevada	Nevada Twp	75	290
John	35	m	w	IREL	San Francisco	2-Wd San Francisco	79	275
John	33	m	w	PA	Yolo	Grafton Twp	93	496
John	30	m	w	KY	Placer	Auburn P O	76	369
John J	44	m	w	ENGL	San Francisco	8-Wd San Francisco	82	296
Joseph	32	m	w	MA	San Francisco	11-Wd San Francisc	84	514
Joseph	32	m	w	ME	Solano	Suisun Twp	90	96
Louis	29	m	w	NY	San Francisco	3-Wd San Francisco	79	324
M	40	f	w	CANA	Alameda	Oakland	68	141
Marian	33	f	w	IREL	Santa Cruz	Santa Cruz	89	406
Mathias	46	m	w	CT	Solano	Suisun Twp	90	96
Pat	30	m	w	IREL	Contra Costa	Martinez P O	71	421
Prince	38	m	b	WIND	San Francisco	San Francisco P O	80	458
R	50	m	w	MO	Sutter	Vernon Twp	92	134
Rich	60	m	w	NH	Butte	Oregon Twp	70	125
Robert	58	m	w	ME	Santa Clara	Alviso Twp	88	23
Robert	32	m	w	SCOT	San Francisco	San Francisco P O	85	758
Robert M	51	m	w	OH	Santa Clara	1-Wd San Jose	88	275
Saml	48	m	w	VA	Solano	Vacaville Twp	90	121
Sanl	42	m	w	IREL	Sutter	Sutter Twp	92	123
Sarah	37	f	w	IREL	San Francisco	11-Wd San Francisc	84	611
Seaborn	45	m	w	GA	Santa Clara	Redwood Twp	88	121
Thomas J	34	m	w	MO	Yolo	Cache Crk Twp	93	437
Thos A	32	m	w	IREL	Santa Cruz	Santa Cruz Twp	89	385
W S	40	m	w	PA	Tuolumne	Columbia P O	93	336
William	53	m	w	IREL	Calaveras	San Andreas P O	70	197
William	40	m	w	ENGL	San Francisco	6-Wd San Francisco	81	90
William H	31	m	w	NC	Yolo	Putah Twp	93	510
Wm	51	m	w	OH	Siskiyou	Yreka Twp	89	672
Wm	51	m	w	ME	Humboldt	Eureka Twp	72	276
Wm	43	m	w	ENGL	San Francisco	San Francisco P O	83	177
Wm	36	m	w	ME	San Francisco	11-Wd San Francisc	84	668
Wm	36	m	w	TN	Fresno	Kings Rvr P O	72	211
HUTCHISON								
Abram	59	m	w	VA	Amador	Volcano P O	69	388
Frank	38	m	w	IL	Inyo	Bishop Crk Twp	73	312
Franklin	58	m	w	VA	Fresno	Kings Rvr P O	72	206
G N	52	m	w	SCOT	Solano	Vallejo	90	147
Harvey F	25	m	w	KY	Fresno	Kings Rvr P O	72	206
John B	38	m	w	GA	Placer	Cisco P O	76	494
Malinda	54	f	w	KY	Placer	Newcastle Twp	76	473
Richard	37	m	w	CANA	Mendocino	Gualala Twp	74	225
Robert	27	m	w	OH	Placer	Alta P O	76	412
Tho	72	m	w	KY	San Joaquin	3-Wd Stockton	86	224
Thomas	37	m	w	IL	Inyo	Bishop Crk Twp	73	312
Wm	31	m	w	RI	Solano	Benicia	90	4
HUTCHMAN								
S	45	m	w	PA	San Francisco	8-Wd San Francisco	82	375
T O	27	m	w	GA	Alameda	Oakland	68	227
HUTCHTRIMOR								
James S	22	m	w	PA	Yolo	Cottonwood Twp	93	466
HUTEN								
F N	37	m	w	FRAN	San Francisco	San Francisco P O	85	851
HUTFIELD								
Bill	40	m	w	MO	San Joaquin	Liberty Twp	86	86
M	33	m	w	WURT	San Joaquin	Dent Twp	86	17
HUTH								
Charles	48	m	w	BRUN	San Francisco	2-Wd San Francisco	79	237
John C	20	m	w	NY	San Francisco	2-Wd San Francisco	79	238
HUTLON								
Hester	40	f	w	IREL	San Francisco	1-Wd San Francisco	79	10
HUTNER								
C E A	48	m	w	PRUS	Sierra	Forest Twp	89	531
HUTOP								
Katrine	71	f	w	BADE	San Francisco	San Francisco P O	80	352
HUTSLEY								
Martin	45	m	w	WURT	El Dorado	Diamond Springs Tw	72	24
HUTSON								
Andw J	24	m	w	MO	Shasta	Fort Crook P O	89	477
Danl	40	m	w	NC	Tuolumne	Big Oak Flat P O	93	404
HUTT								
Albert	27	m	w	PRUS	Napa	Napa	75	35
John	50	m	w	NY	Humboldt	Bald Hills	72	237
HUTTER								
Esabella	26	f	w	NY	Sonoma	Petaluma Twp	91	312
HUTTLESON								
Geo	48	m	w	NY	Yuba	Marysville	93	610
HUTTON								
Alexander	36	m	w	NJ	Stanislaus	San Joaquin Twp	92	74

Name	Age	S	R	B-PL	County	Locale	Roll	Pg
Alice	24	f	w	IREL	San Francisco	San Francisco P O	83	340
Arvilios W	23	m	w	AL	Los Angeles	Los Angeles	73	546
Chas E	34	m	w	MD	Sonoma	Healdsburg & Mendo	91	282
Daniel D	42	m	w	MO	Mendocino	Point Arena Twp	74	211
Frederick	40	m	w	OH	Solano	Vacaville Twp	90	126
Henry	57	m	w	NY	Santa Clara	Redwood Twp	88	127
Isaac H	38	m	w	OH	Yolo	Cache Crk Twp	93	449
James	39	m	w	ME	San Francisco	San Francisco P O	80	365
James	35	m	w	MO	Mendocino	Point Arena Twp	74	207
James	33	m	w	GA	Butte	Oregon Twp	70	135
James A	53	m	w	KY	Yolo	Cache Crk Twp	93	455
John	45	m	w	ENGL	San Francisco	San Francisco P O	83	73
Joseph	44	m	w	MO	Del Norte	Happy Camp Twp	71	471
Richd	29	m	w	NY	San Francisco	1-Wd San Francisco	79	74
Robt F	40	m	w	SCOT	Solano	Vallejo	90	172
Stephen O	32	m	w	IN	Los Angeles	El Monte Twp	73	461
William	25	m	w	NY	Santa Clara	2-Wd San Jose	88	313
HUTZ								
Edward	39	m	w	RUSS	Nevada	Nevada Twp	75	317
HUTZELL								
George	31	m	w	OH	Plumas	Quartz Twp	77	36
HUTZLER								
Fredrick	48	m	w	GERM	Humboldt	Bald Hills	72	237
HUVER								
W	19	m	w	GERM	San Joaquin	2-Wd Stockton	86	162
HUY								
Ah	50	m	c	CHIN	Sacramento	Georgianna Twp	77	133
Ah	27	m	c	CHIN	Sacramento	Granite Twp	77	150
Ah	20	m	c	CHIN	Yolo	Buckeye Twp	93	413
Ah	20	m	c	CHIN	Sacramento	1-Wd Sacramento	77	179
Ah	17	m	c	CHIN	Yolo	Cottonwood Twp	93	465
Lui	38	m	c	CHIN	Fresno	Millerton P O	72	201
HUYLAND								
Francis	60	m	w	IREL	Sutter	Vernon Twp	92	136
HUYSINK								
Benjamin	43	m	w	HOLL	Placer	Dutch Flat P O	76	404
HWELL								
Ellen	18	f	w	MO	Amador	Fiddletown P O	69	426
HY								
Ah	40	m	c	CHIN	Sacramento	Natomas Twp	77	165
Ah	30	m	c	CHIN	Sacramento	Cosumnes Twp	77	95
Ah	28	m	c	CHIN	Mariposa	Mariposa P O	74	107
Ah	26	m	c	CHIN	Sacramento	Georgianna Twp	77	133
Ah	26	m	c	CHIN	Sacramento	Georgianna Twp	77	133
Ah	22	m	c	CHIN	Sacramento	Georgianna Twp	77	125
Ah	22	m	c	CHIN	Sacramento	Georgianna Twp	77	133
Ah	18	m	c	CHIN	Napa	Napa Twp	75	30
Chn	29	m	c	CHIN	Butte	Hamilton Twp	70	75
Chong	30	m	c	CHIN	Butte	Chico Twp	70	54
Sing	35	m	c	CHIN	Butte	Chico Twp	70	19
Yin	42	m	c	CHIN	Butte	Concow Twp	70	11
Yon	48	m	c	CHIN	Placer	Bath P O	76	442
HYAM								
Frank	32	m	w	HDAR	San Francisco	8-Wd San Francisco	82	383
HYAMS								
Ann	24	f	w	PRUS	San Francisco	6-Wd San Francisco	81	139
D S	41	m	w	SC	Yuba	Marysville	93	607
Geo J S	40	m	w	ENGL	San Francisco	8-Wd San Francisco	82	333
HYASEN								
Henery	22	m	w	PRUS	San Francisco	7-Wd San Francisco	81	205
HYAT								
John	28	m	w	MO	Sutter	Sutter Twp	92	125
HYATT								
Alex	39	m	w	NY	San Francisco	2-Wd San Francisco	79	220
B S J	41	m	w	KY	Sutter	Vernon Twp	92	138
Campbell D	60	m	w	SCOT	Contra Costa	Martinez P O	71	382
Ellitt	39	m	w	OH	Santa Clara	Gilroy Twp	88	98
Geo H	40	m	w	NY	Tehama	Tehama Twp	92	195
Isaac M	34	m	w	CANA	Shasta	Stillwater P O	89	478
J C	36	m	w	CANA	San Joaquin	3-Wd Stockton	86	236
Jacob	64	m	w	CANA	Nevada	Rough & Ready Twp	75	332
James	42	m	w	NY	Nevada	Little York Twp	75	242
James	32	m	w	NY	San Francisco	8-Wd San Francisco	82	441
Lionel B	37	m	w	MO	Placer	Pino Twp	76	471
Mary A	10	f	w	CA	Sutter	Vernon Twp	92	139
O A	34	m	w	CANA	Sierra	Sierra Twp	89	568
Thomas H	61	m	w	NY	San Francisco	San Francisco P O	85	725
W H	30	m	w	MO	Sutter	Sutter Twp	92	125
Washington	42	m	w	MO	Sutter	Sutter Twp	92	125
William	53	m	w	NY	Humboldt	Mattole Twp	72	287
HYBROOK								
Henry	30	m	w	PRUS	Siskiyou	Yreka Twp	89	670
HYDA								
Jehn	42	m	w	OH	Butte	Bidwell Twp	70	1
HYDE								
A F	35	m	w	PA	San Joaquin	Tulare Twp	86	254
Aaron	44	m	w	NH	Tuolumne	Sonora P O	93	322
C L	38	m	w	ME	Solano	Vallejo	90	185
Charles	14	m	w	AR	Tulare	Venice Twp	92	273
Charles Wm	41	m	w	ENGL	Plumas	Rich Bar Twp	77	46
Chas J	39	m	w	IREL	San Francisco	1-Wd San Francisco	79	93
Elizabeth J	36	f	w	OH	Fresno	Millerton P O	72	183
Frederick	23	m	w	NY	San Francisco	8-Wd San Francisco	82	415
Geo	31	m	w	NH	Solano	Vallejo	90	211
Geo	14	m	w	CA	Solano	Benicia	90	1
H F	44	m	w	MA	Yuba	Marysville	93	610
Henry	40	m	w	PA	San Joaquin	2-Wd Stockton	86	158

© 2001 by Heritage Quest. All rights reserved.

Name	Age	S	R	B-PL	County	Locale	Series M593 Roll	Pg
Henry	40	m	w	MI	Butte	Oregon Twp	70	134
Henry	34	m	w	NY	San Francisco	7-Wd San Francisco	81	286
Issaac	42	m	w	CT	Alameda	Oakland	68	188
Jerry E	40	m	w	NY	Tulare	Visalia	92	291
John	30	m	w	IREL	San Francisco	8-Wd San Francisco	82	338
Julia	16	f	w	IREL	San Francisco	11-Wd San Francisc	84	527
Kate	25	f	w	IREL	Alameda	Oakland	68	179
Kate	14	f	w	MA	Butte	Oregon Twp	70	127
Louisa	51	f	w	FRAN	San Francisco	2-Wd San Francisco	79	251
M	12	f	w	CA	Alameda	Oakland	68	242
Martin	42	m	w	IREL	Solano	Benicia	90	10
Mike	50	m	w	IREL	San Francisco	11-Wd San Francisc	84	656
Morris	39	m	w	IREL	Trinity	Weaverville Pct	92	222
Nellie	10	f	w	CA	Alameda	Oakland	68	242
Olivier	54	m	w	MA	Alameda	Oakland	68	143
Patrick	33	m	w	IREL	San Mateo	San Mateo P O	87	353
Richard E	38	m	w	NY	Tulare	Visalia	92	291
Samuel	28	m	w	NY	San Francisco	8-Wd San Francisco	82	329
Septa F	50	m	w	VT	Solano	Tremont Twp	90	30
Thomas R	36	m	w	MD	San Francisco	3-Wd San Francisco	79	318
W H	47	m	w	ME	Nevada	Eureka Twp	75	133
William	49	m	w	NY	San Francisco	11-Wd San Francisc	84	544
Wm	40	m	w	KY	Butte	Chico Twp	70	22
Wm	37	m	w	IREL	Solano	Benicia	90	7
Wm B	29	m	w	MD	Alameda	Oakland	68	134
Wm C	31	m	w	VT	San Francisco	San Francisco P O	83	72
HYDELIFF								
Martin	40	m	w	NY	San Francisco	San Francisco P O	85	733
HYDER								
Henry	33	m	w	FRAN	San Francisco	1-Wd San Francisco	79	71
HYDO								
David H	39	m	w	NY	Siskiyou	Callahan P O	89	624
HYE								
Ah	30	m	c	CHIN	Sacramento	Natomas Twp	77	168
Emil	30	m	w	PRUS	San Francisco	San Francisco P O	80	427
Joseph	27	m	w	IN	San Joaquin	1-Wd Stockton	86	150
Ye	25	m	c	CHIN	Sonoma	Petaluma Twp	91	359
HYER								
Adeline	21	f	i	CA	Siskiyou	Scott Valley Twp	89	618
Charles	32	m	w	WEST	Alameda	Oakland	68	188
Fred	45	m	w	RUSS	Santa Clara	Santa Clara Twp	88	148
Henry	45	m	w	SHOL	Alameda	Eden Twp	68	65
Henry P	37	m	b	NY	Siskiyou	Scott Valley Twp	89	618
Richard	35	m	w	MD	Alameda	Alvarado	68	302
Wm	32	m	w	RUSS	Butte	Chico Twp	70	56
Wm	32	m	b	NY	San Joaquin	1-Wd Stockton	86	141
HYES								
Michael	45	m	w	IREL	Yuba	Rose Bar Twp	93	666
HYKES								
Oscar	26	m	w	NY	Yuba	Marysville	93	594
HYLAND								
Anne	40	f	w	IREL	San Francisco	San Francisco P O	83	108
Bernard	36	m	w	IREL	San Francisco	San Francisco P O	83	381
Catharine	60	f	w	IREL	Butte	Wyandotte Twp	70	144
Dennis	39	m	w	IREL	Placer	Bath P O	76	426
Edwd	39	m	w	IREL	San Francisco	1-Wd San Francisco	79	89
H	15	m	w	IL	Amador	Sutter Crk P O	69	414
H P	23	m	w	MA	Sierra	Gibson Twp	89	541
John J	40	m	w	NY	Placer	Bath P O	76	457
Patrick	22	m	w	IREL	San Francisco	San Francisco P O	83	203
R M	14	m	w	CA	Amador	Jackson P O	69	323
William	26	m	w	NY	San Francisco	San Francisco P O	83	418
HYLLIER								
John	38	m	w	ME	Calaveras	San Andreas P O	70	207
HYLOR								
Thomas	43	m	w	KY	Sutter	Nicolaus Twp	92	109
HYLOW								
Peter	24	m	w	OH	Solano	Silveyville Twp	90	80
HYLPING								
Kate	24	f	w	IREL	San Francisco	7-Wd San Francisco	81	283
HYLTON								
T de M	43	m	w	ENGL	San Francisco	8-Wd San Francisco	82	358
HYMAN								
A	45	m	w	POLA	Sacramento	1-Wd Sacramento	77	173
A C	60	m	w	POLA	Sacramento	4-Wd Sacramento	77	322
Deborah	22	f	w	NY	San Francisco	8-Wd San Francisco	82	289
Edward	31	m	w	MO	Solano	Tremont Twp	90	29
Ernestina	22	f	w	PRUS	San Francisco	8-Wd San Francisco	82	290
Felix	41	m	w	BAVA	San Francisco	6-Wd San Francisco	81	104
Ferdinand	32	m	w	PRUS	San Francisco	San Francisco P O	80	479
Henry	48	m	w	HAMB	San Francisco	San Francisco P O	83	7
Herman	27	m	w	PRUS	San Francisco	6-Wd San Francisco	81	113
Isaac	36	m	w	PRUS	San Francisco	1-Wd San Francisco	79	124
Jacob	40	m	w	POLA	Sacramento	Granite Twp	77	143
Jacob	32	m	w	POLA	Sacramento	3-Wd Sacramento	77	283
Jan	13	m	w	CA	Sacramento	4-Wd Sacramento	77	323
Johanna	40	f	w	ME	San Francisco	11-Wd San Francisc	84	632
Maria	6	f	w	CA	Los Angeles	Los Angeles	73	552
Marks	23	m	w	POLA	Placer	Bath P O	76	438
Morris	39	m	w	POLA	San Francisco	San Francisco P O	80	344
Morris	38	m	w	PRUS	Yolo	Cache Crk Twp	93	420
Moses	29	m	w	BAVA	San Francisco	8-Wd San Francisco	82	491
Peter	21	m	w	WURT	San Francisco	San Francisco P O	80	468
Samuel	29	m	m	WIND	San Francisco	San Francisco P O	80	386
Sarah	44	f	w	FRNK	San Francisco	San Francisco P O	80	342
Selig	43	m	w	PRUS	Yolo	Cache Crk Twp	93	434
HYMANS								
Joseph	41	m	w	MO	Solano	Denverton Twp	90	25
HYMELL								
Jacob	34	m	w	PRUS	Yuba	Marysville	93	614
HYMER								
Charles	29	m	w	MEXI	Amador	Jackson P O	69	322
Howard	35	m	w	BAVA	Inyo	Cerro Gordo Twp	73	320
Israel	44	m	w	PRUS	San Francisco	2-Wd San Francisco	79	163
HYMES								
Agnes	25	f	w	IREL	Solano	Vallejo	90	197
HYNDMAN								
William	37	m	w	IREL	Alpine	Markleeville P O	69	311
HYNE								
William H	30	m	w	OH	Sonoma	Petaluma Twp	91	344
HYNER								
Bernard	28	m	w	IREL	Sonoma	Russian Rvr	91	374
Patk	42	m	w	IREL	San Francisco	San Francisco P O	83	70
HYNES								
Andrews	50	m	w	KY	San Francisco	8-Wd San Francisco	82	333
B F	30	m	w	ME	Lake	Lower Lake	73	419
Bridget	36	f	w	IREL	San Francisco	5-Wd San Francisco	81	3
Charles	36	m	w	SWED	San Francisco	3-Wd San Francisco	79	313
Chas	16	m	w	PA	Yuba	Marysville Twp	93	569
George	42	m	w	KY	Stanislaus	Branch Twp	92	2
James	50	m	w	IREL	Santa Clara	San Jose Twp	88	210
James	37	m	w	IREL	Sonoma	Petaluma Twp	91	346
Kate	21	f	w	IREL	San Francisco	6-Wd San Francisco	81	154
Martin	29	m	w	IREL	Sacramento	2-Wd Sacramento	77	245
William H	42	m	w	MA	San Francisco	11-Wd San Francisc	84	705
HYNG								
Up	29	m	c	CHIN	San Joaquin	1-Wd Stockton	86	149
HYNN								
Bertha	73	f	w	NH	San Francisco	San Francisco P O	83	256
John H	13	m	w	CA	Tehama	Tehama Twp	92	192
HYNOK								
John	54	m	w	IREL	Monterey	San Juan Twp	74	408
HYNSON								
John H	35	m	w	DE	San Francisco	1-Wd San Francisco	79	69
John R	23	m	w	AR	Sonoma	Analy Twp	91	239
HYORTHE								
Edward	27	m	w	DENM	San Francisco	7-Wd San Francisco	81	241
HYPATYT								
Gillaron	52	m	w	FRAN	Inyo	Lone Pine Twp	73	332
HYPOLYTE								
Ellen	28	m	w	NY	San Francisco	San Francisco P O	85	835
HYRE								
Herman	18	m	w	BAVA	Inyo	Lone Pine Twp	73	330
John	33	m	w	PRUS	Inyo	Lone Pine Twp	73	330
HYRER								
Henry	52	m	w	PRUS	Sacramento	Sutter Twp	77	386
HYRS								
Anna M	15	f	m	NY	Sacramento	4-Wd Sacramento	77	320
Samuel B	40	m	b	NY	Sacramento	4-Wd Sacramento	77	320
HYSELL								
W S	29	m	w	OH	Monterey	San Juan Twp	74	411
HYSLIP								
John	28	m	w	MA	San Francisco	7-Wd San Francisco	81	157
Robert	36	m	w	BAVA	Nevada	Meadow Lake Twp	75	250
HYSLOP								
John	30	m	w	CANA	Humboldt	Eureka Twp	72	278
Wm	41	m	w	SCOT	Napa	Napa Twp	75	69
HYST								
Ellet	38	m	w	WI	Stanislaus	San Joaquin Twp	92	77
HYSTRES								
Emile	55	f	w	FRAN	San Francisco	11-Wd San Francisc	84	544
I								
Hiram	50	m	w	NY	Merced	Snelling P O	74	266
Yen	41	m	c	CHIN	Calaveras	San Andreas P O	70	201
IACHUM								
E C	34	f	w	GERM	Tuolumne	Sonora P O	93	313
IAGO								
Katie H	35	f	w	CA	Santa Cruz	Santa Cruz	89	428
IAK								
Ah	25	m	c	CHIN	Nevada	Bloomfield Twp	75	96
IAM								
Ah	31	m	c	CHIN	Yuba	Marysville	93	622
IANEZ								
Remji	40	m	w	MEXI	Los Angeles	Los Angeles Twp	73	465
IAPELLO								
Jacob	67	m	w	ITAL	Sacramento	Georgianna Twp	77	129
IASSCS								
Albert	38	m	w	POLA	San Francisco	2-Wd San Francisco	79	158
IASTONS								
Fanny	30	f	w	PRUS	Solano	Tremont Twp	90	33
IAY								
William	30	m	w	IA	Solano	Denverton Twp	90	27
IAZLYN								
A P	38	m	w	NY	Lake	Scotts Crk	73	428
IBANA								
Cayetano	34	m	w	CA	Los Angeles	San Jose Twp	73	618
Jesus	30	m	w	CA	Los Angeles	San Jose Twp	73	618
Lewis	36	m	w	CA	Los Angeles	San Jose Twp	73	618
Maria G	29	f	w	CA	Los Angeles	Wilmington Twp	73	637
IBARIA								
Lewis	55	m	w	MEXI	Los Angeles	Santa Ana Twp	73	615
IBASLA								
John	37	m	w	CHIL	Inyo	Lone Pine Twp	73	332

© 2001 by Heritage Quest. All rights reserved.

California 1870 Census

Series M593

Name	Age	S	R	B-PL	County	Locale	Roll	Pg
IBEN								
Julius	45	m	w	PRUS	Butte	Kimshew Tpw	70	77
IBENSINO								
Joseph	36	m	w	ITAL	San Francisco	1-Wd San Francisco	79	105
IBY								
Jos	47	m	w	PRUS	San Joaquin	Tulare Twp	86	259
ICHAVA								
Antonio	55	m	w	CA	Santa Cruz	Soquel Twp	89	450
ICHBORN								
Edward	39	m	w	FRAN	Santa Clara	San Jose Twp	88	200
ICHE								
Pierre	59	m	w	FRAN	San Francisco	11-Wd San Francisc	84	648
ICHEY								
Henry	35	m	w	BAVA	San Joaquin	Tulare Twp	86	258
ICHLER								
George	41	m	w	PRUS	Inyo	Cerro Gordo Twp	73	323
ICHTASH								
Michael	37	m	w	FRAN	Solano	Tremont Twp	90	34
ICK								
Ah	28	m	c	CHIN	Nevada	Little York Twp	75	242
ICKE								
Catharine	15	f	w	CA	Alameda	Brooklyn	68	34
Jacob	49	m	w	PRUS	San Francisco	San Francisco P O	80	481
ICKEL								
Adolph	43	m	w	PRUS	San Francisco	8-Wd San Francisco	82	356
ICKLEHEIMER								
Herman	46	m	w	BAVA	San Francisco	San Francisco P O	85	866
ICKO								
Joseph	21	m	w	PORT	San Mateo	Pescadero P O	87	413
ICKS								
Charles	35	m	w	HANO	San Mateo	Half Moon Bay P O	87	404
Jacob	39	m	w	HANO	San Mateo	Half Moon Bay P O	87	404
IDALGO								
--- Mrs	47	f	w	PORT	San Joaquin	2-Wd Stockton	86	174
IDDE								
James	24	m	w	NY	San Francisco	San Francisco P O	83	374
IDE								
D W	35	m	w	OH	Tehama	Tehama Twp	92	190
Hubert	34	m	w	PA	Calaveras	San Andreas P O	70	174
Isrial	26	m	w	IL	Colusa	Monroe Twp	71	316
James	25	m	w	NH	San Francisco	2-Wd San Francisco	79	247
L H C	33	m	w	OH	Tehama	Cottonwood Twp	92	162
L H C	12	m	w	CA	Alameda	Oakland	68	257
W C	44	m	w	CT	Tehama	Tehama Twp	92	196
IDES								
Nelson	39	m	w	TURK	Alpine	Silver Mtn P O	69	307
IDEUS								
Joseph	50	m	w	ENGL	Amador	Jackson P O	69	328
IDIE								
Jennie	41	f	w	ENGL	San Francisco	San Francisco P O	83	216
IDLE								
Martin	50	m	w	BAVA	Butte	Wyandotte Twp	70	142
William	20	m	w	ENGL	Sutter	Vernon Twp	92	132
IE								
Yow	25	f	c	CHIN	Sacramento	1-Wd Sacramento	77	202
IEDALE								
Thomas	26	m	w	CANA	San Francisco	7-Wd San Francisco	81	178
IEKON								
Edward	30	m	w	HANO	San Francisco	2-Wd San Francisco	79	138
IENG								
Yeng	19	m	c	CHIN	San Francisco	11-Wd San Francisc	84	505
IFFERT								
Leonard	35	m	w	HESS	Santa Clara	Fremont Twp	88	53
IGARO								
Thomas	53	m	w	CA	San Luis Obispo	San Luis Obispo Tw	87	307
IGELL								
Augusta	18	f	w	PRUS	Solano	Vallejo	90	165
IGERA								
Francisco	48	m	w	CA	Los Angeles	Los Angeles Twp	73	489
Majin	24	m	w	CA	Los Angeles	Los Angeles Twp	73	487
Ramijo	23	m	w	CA	Los Angeles	Los Angeles	73	521
IGLANER								
Sigmond	18	m	w	GERM	San Diego	San Diego	78	497
IGNACIO								
Jose	35	m	i	CA	Yolo	Cottonwood Twp	93	474
Manuel	25	m	w	PORT	San Francisco	3-Wd San Francisco	79	294
IGNACO								
Paula	29	m	w	ITAL	Amador	Volcano P O	69	385
IGNALLO								
Mary	55	f	w	MEXI	San Francisco	2-Wd San Francisco	79	150
IGNIO								
Gilech	44	m	w	ITAL	Nevada	Little York Twp	75	238
IGNITIO								
E	50	m	w	MEXI	San Joaquin	Douglas Twp	86	36
IGNOLI								
Rudolphe	37	m	w	BELG	Sacramento	4-Wd Sacramento	77	370
IGNOTO								
Juan	5	m	w	CA	Santa Cruz	Pajaro Twp	89	343
IGO								
Ah	20	m	c	CHIN	Fresno	Millerton P O	72	156
James	39	m	w	IREL	Yolo	Putah Twp	93	520
James	38	m	w	IREL	Yolo	Putah Twp	93	513
John	17	m	w	CT	Santa Cruz	Santa Cruz Twp	89	402
Orrin	39	m	w	IREL	San Mateo	Schoolhouse Statio	87	342
Patrick	50	m	w	IREL	Butte	Chico Twp	70	41
IGORA								
Emilia	30	f	w	MEXI	Los Angeles	San Jose Twp	73	623

Series M593

Name	Age	S	R	B-PL	County	Locale	Roll	Pg
IH								
Inn	40	m	c	CHIN	Calaveras	San Andreas P O	70	167
Un	28	m	c	CHIN	Calaveras	San Andreas P O	70	172
Yon	20	f	c	CHIN	Calaveras	San Andreas P O	70	167
IHREE								
Theodore	48	m	w	PRUS	Plumas	Rich Bar Twp	77	46
IJAMS								
John	24	m	w	NY	San Francisco	San Francisco P O	80	427
IKART								
John	65	m	w	PA	Napa	Napa	75	52
IKE								
Ah	27	m	c	CHIN	Nevada	Grass Valley Twp	75	208
IKENBERRY								
William	38	m	w	OH	Stanislaus	Empire Twp	92	29
IKENBERY								
Samuel	35	m	w	AR	Stanislaus	Empire Twp	92	52
IKMILLER								
Charles	43	m	w	SWIT	Alameda	Hayward	68	76
ILDEFENCE								
Cuenin	21	m	w	FRAN	San Francisco	3-Wd San Francisco	79	311
ILDNER								
William	34	m	w	PRUS	Solano	Silveyville Twp	90	73
ILEGAN								
John	70	m	i	MEXI	Inyo	Cerro Gordo Twp	73	323
ILER								
Benjamin	35	m	w	IL	Santa Cruz	Santa Cruz Twp	89	396
George	20	m	w	IL	Sutter	Sutter Twp	92	116
John H	31	m	w	VA	San Diego	San Diego	78	505
Joseph	40	m	w	IL	Sutter	Sutter Twp	92	123
Richard	30	m	w	IL	Santa Cruz	Santa Cruz Twp	89	396
Seth W	59	m	w	OH	Los Angeles	San Juan Twp	73	625
ILES								
Elizabeth	37	f	w	GA	Monterey	San Juan Twp	74	398
Francis	23	m	w	IREL	San Francisco	1-Wd San Francisco	79	63
John W	28	m	w	KY	Los Angeles	El Monte Twp	73	457
ILEY								
Charles	30	m	w	PRUS	San Bernardino	Chino Twp	78	411
ILINGTON								
Hugh	30	m	w	SCOT	San Francisco	7-Wd San Francisco	81	184
ILL								
Ah	24	m	c	CHIN	San Francisco	San Francisco P O	80	489
ILLARDO								
Joseph	34	m	w	ITAL	Solano	Montezuma Twp	90	67
ILLEMORE								
Robt	50	m	w	ME	Mono	Bridgeport P O	74	284
ILLICH								
Jerome	24	m	w	AUST	San Francisco	San Francisco P O	80	354
ILLICK								
Jas B	53	m	w	PA	Calaveras	Copperopolis P O	70	240
ILLIES								
Eimer	23	m	w	BREM	Nevada	Little York Twp	75	244
ILLIFF								
Edward	59	m	w	TN	San Diego	Julian Dist	78	472
ILLINGSWORTH								
J	33	m	w	ENGL	Sonoma	Santa Rosa	91	416
ILLMAN								
Edwd	38	m	w	PRUS	San Francisco	1-Wd San Francisco	79	2
ILLUNIO								
Francisco	53	m	w	SPAI	Marin	San Rafael Twp	74	41
ILS								
Elizabeth	7	f	w	MA	Santa Cruz	Santa Cruz	89	417
John G	47	m	w	BAVA	San Francisco	1-Wd San Francisco	79	109
ILSOHN								
John F D	38	m	w	HAMB	El Dorado	Diamond Springs Tw	72	22
ILTERS								
Domingo	36	m	i	MEXI	Inyo	Cerro Gordo Twp	73	322
IM								
Ah	44	m	c	CHIN	San Luis Obispo	San Luis Obispo Tw	87	297
Fu	22	f	c	CHIN	Sacramento	1-Wd Sacramento	77	195
IMAS								
Hiram A	66	m	w	NY	Santa Cruz	Santa Cruz	89	416
IMBER								
A C	47	m	w	FRAN	Tuolumne	Sonora P O	93	308
IMBERT								
Ferdinand	27	m	w	FRAN	Santa Barbara	Santa Barbara P O	87	450
IMBONIG								
Chas	40	m	w	LA	San Francisco	5-Wd San Francisco	81	1
IMBRIE								
Augustus C	38	m	w	PA	San Francisco	8-Wd San Francisco	82	381
IMER								
Peter	50	m	w	WALE	Butte	Kimshew Tpw	70	82
Peter	42	m	w	BADE	Butte	Kimshew Tpw	70	76
IMHAUS								
Louis	49	m	w	PRUS	San Francisco	2-Wd San Francisco	79	224
IMHOFF								
Caroline	36	f	w	PRUS	Sacramento	Granite Twp	77	147
S G	32	m	w	PA	Alameda	Oakland	68	213
IMLAY								
William F	41	m	w	NJ	Alameda	Washington Twp	68	272
IMMON								
Glover	21	m	w	TN	Tulare	Visalia Twp	92	283
IMODA								
Henry	38	m	w	ITAL	Santa Clara	Santa Clara Twp	88	175
IMP								
Ah	20	m	c	CHIN	San Francisco	San Francisco P O	80	499
IMPELLO								
Antonio	25	m	w	MEXI	San Diego	Fort Yuma Dist	78	463

© 2001 by Heritage Quest. All rights reserved.

Name	Age	S	R	B-PL	County	Locale	Series M593 Roll	Pg
Francisco	32	m	w	MEXI	San Diego	Warners Rancho Dis	78	529
IN								
Ah	60	m	c	CHIN	Placer	Roseville P O	76	348
Ah	45	m	c	CHIN	Sacramento	Georgianna Twp	77	123
Ah	43	m	c	CHIN	El Dorado	Mud Springs Twp	72	87
Ah	34	m	c	CHIN	San Joaquin	Oneal Twp	86	116
Ah	20	m	c	CHIN	El Dorado	Mud Springs Twp	72	76
Ih	52	m	c	CHIN	El Dorado	Salmon Falls Twp	72	129
Ih	24	m	c	CHIN	El Dorado	Placerville Twp	72	92
Un	54	m	c	CHIN	El Dorado	Salmon Falls Twp	72	129
INBORN								
Charles P	50	m	w	DENM	Santa Clara	2-Wd San Jose	88	301
INBURG								
Mary	31	f	w	IREL	San Francisco	3-Wd San Francisco	79	296
INCE								
John	38	m	w	MO	Del Norte	Happy Camp Twp	71	471
M N	41	m	w	ENGL	San Francisco	San Francisco P O	85	783
INCH								
Richard	49	m	w	ENGL	El Dorado	Placerville	72	124
William	22	m	w	ENGL	Amador	Jackson P O	69	342
INCHAN								
Tim	15	m	i	CA	Humboldt	Eel Rvr Twp	72	248
INCHES								
Robert	49	m	w	SCOT	San Francisco	San Francisco P O	85	804
Robert	24	m	w	AUSL	San Francisco	7-Wd San Francisco	81	163
INCO								
Jose	38	m	w	MEXI	Los Angeles	Los Angeles	73	512
INCOM								
Anton	39	m	w	CHIL	Tuolumne	Chinese Camp P O	93	383
IND								
Charley	18	m	w	CA	Humboldt	Eureka Twp	72	257
Vane	24	m	c	CHIN	Sacramento	1-Wd Sacramento	77	204
INDAGINS								
Flores	20	m	w	MEXI	San Francisco	San Francisco P O	83	98
INDART								
Thomas	18	m	w	CA	Los Angeles	Los Angeles	73	570
INDEL								
Christ	27	m	w	PRUS	Sutter	Sutter Twp	92	124
INDER								
J S	31	m	w	ENGL	Nevada	Bridgeport Twp	75	120
John	35	m	w	FRAN	San Francisco	8-Wd San Francisco	82	446
Robert	22	m	j	CA	Humboldt	Eureka Twp	72	281
INDERTON								
Saml	31	m	w	SWED	San Francisco	1-Wd San Francisco	79	75
INDIAN								
--- [Bill's Mother]	50	f	i	CA	Del Norte	Crescent Twp	71	454
--- [Bill's Sister]	44	f	i	CA	Del Norte	Crescent Twp	71	454
--- [Charlie's Father]	60	m	i	CA	Del Norte	Happy Camp Twp	71	473
--- [Dick's Father]	50	m	i	CA	Del Norte	Happy Camp Twp	71	472
--- [Frank's Father]	50	m	i	CA	Del Norte	Happy Camp Twp	71	473
--- [Noonan's Mother]	50	f	i	CA	Del Norte	Crescent Twp	71	454
--- [Wantsy's Father]	60	m	i	CA	Del Norte	Smith Rvr Twp	71	482
Abe	38	m	i	CA	Fresno	Kings Rvr P O	72	209
Abe	12	m	i	CA	Napa	Napa	75	19
Adelaida	42	f	i	CA	Los Angeles	Los Angeles	73	500
Adella	12	f	i	----	Marin	San Rafael	74	89
Adofo	3	m	i	CA	Los Angeles	Los Angeles	73	500
Aheman	45	m	i	CA	Fresno	Millerton P O	72	176
Alak	31	m	i	CA	Colusa	Spring Valley Twp	71	338
Alapore	40	m	i	CA	Fresno	Millerton P O	72	171
Alberto	18	m	i	CA	Los Angeles	Los Angeles	73	500
Alegracia	18	f	i	CA	Los Angeles	Los Angeles	73	501
Alex	16	m	i	CA	Colusa	Stony Crk Twp	71	333
Alex	15	m	i	CA	Napa	Napa	75	18
Alic	20	m	i	CA	Lake	Lower Lake	73	421
Alicano	47	m	i	CA	San Luis Obispo	San Luis Obispo Tw	87	308
Alick	30	m	i	CA	Colusa	Grand Island Twp	71	310
Alie	15	f	i	CA	Del Norte	Crescent Twp	71	457
Alix	30	m	i	CA	Del Norte	Crescent Twp	71	458
Allchatonah	40	m	i	CA	Fresno	Millerton P O	72	174
Almite	12	f	i	MEXI	Alameda	Murray Twp	68	103
Alpa	45	m	i	CA	Fresno	Millerton P O	72	171
Amadeo	45	m	i	CA	Monterey	San Benito Twp	74	381
Amapni	30	m	i	CA	Fresno	Millerton P O	72	175
Ambrocia	8	f	i	CA	Alameda	Murray Twp	68	106
Amfosil	25	m	i	CA	Fresno	Millerton P O	72	172
Anastasio	9	m	i	----	Marin	Nicasio Twp	74	89
Anastasio	30	m	i	CA	San Diego	San Luis Rey	78	512
Anatotis	40	m	i	CA	Monterey	San Juan Twp	74	412
Anats	10	f	i	CA	Del Norte	Smith Rvr Twp	71	482
Andrea	40	f	i	CA	Monterey	San Juan Twp	74	385
Andrew	60	m	i	CA	Los Angeles	Los Angeles	73	500
Andrew	32	m	i	CA	Fresno	Kings Rvr P O	72	206
Andria	7	f	i	----	Marin	Nicasio Twp	74	89
Andria	16	f	i	----	Marin	Nicasio Twp	74	89
Aniceto	56	m	i	CA	Santa Barbara	Santa Maria P O	87	514
Anna	5	f	i	CA	Yolo	Grafton Twp	93	484
Annie	23	f	j	CA	Humboldt	Eureka Twp	72	277
Annie	20	f	i	CA	Del Norte	Happy Camp Twp	71	472
Annie	20	f	i	CA	Del Norte	Happy Camp Twp	71	472
Annie	20	f	i	CA	Del Norte	Crescent Twp	71	459
Annie	20	f	i	CA	Del Norte	Crescent Twp	71	455
Annie	20	f	i	CA	Del Norte	Happy Camp Twp	71	473
Annie	16	f	i	CA	Del Norte	Crescent Twp	71	455
Ansunta	20	m	i	MEXI	Alameda	Murray Twp	68	103
Antenia	35	f	i	----	Marin	Nicasio Twp	74	89
Antenio	29	m	i	----	Marin	Nicasio Twp	74	89
Antolina	42	f	i	----	Marin	Nicasio Twp	74	89
Antone	70	f	i	CA	Alameda	Murray Twp	68	106
Antone	64	m	i	CA	Fresno	Kings Rvr P O	72	208
Antone	40	m	i	CA	Fresno	Millerton P O	72	189
Antone	32	f	i	MEXI	Alameda	Murray Twp	68	103
Antone	25	m	i	MEXI	Alameda	Murray Twp	68	103
Antone	24	m	i	CA	Fresno	Kingston P O	72	217
Antone	20	m	i	CA	Lake	Zim Zim	73	417
Antoni	35	m	i	CA	Yolo	Grafton Twp	93	484
Antonia	20	f	i	CA	Alameda	Murray Twp	68	106
Antonio	18	m	i	CA	Sonoma	Bodega Twp	91	265
Antonio	14	m	i	CA	Los Angeles	Los Angeles	73	501
Antuck	50	m	i	CA	Fresno	Millerton P O	72	173
Aria	23	f	i	CA	Los Angeles	Los Angeles Twp	73	498
Arick	25	m	i	CA	Del Norte	Smith Rvr Twp	71	482
Arson	30	m	i	CA	Del Norte	Crescent Twp	71	458
Artose	34	m	i	CA	Fresno	Millerton P O	72	184
Ary Melia	30	f	i	CA	Del Norte	Crescent Twp	71	454
Asentie	48	f	i	MEXI	Alameda	Murray Twp	68	103
Asesciona	14	f	i	CA	Los Angeles	Los Angeles Twp	73	499
Asito	40	f	i	CA	Alameda	Murray Twp	68	106
Astasia	30	f	i	----	Marin	Sausalito Twp	74	89
Athrusen	55	f	i	CA	Del Norte	Crescent Twp	71	454
Attma	18	f	i	CA	Del Norte	Smith Rvr Twp	71	482
Augustin	38	m	i	CA	Napa	Napa Twp	75	74
Augustina	56	f	i	----	Marin	Novato Twp	74	89
Augustina	25	f	i	----	Marin	Nicasio Twp	74	89
Augustina	24	f	i	----	Marin	Tomales Twp	74	89
Augustina	10	f	i	CA	Napa	Napa Twp	75	73
Aunteo	25	f	i	MEXI	Alameda	Murray Twp	68	103
Ausento	2	f	i	MEXI	Alameda	Murray Twp	68	103
Auvessten	40	f	i	CA	Los Angeles	Los Angeles	73	500
Awacoopee	26	m	i	CA	Fresno	Millerton P O	72	180
Babtiste	40	m	i	CA	Fresno	Millerton P O	72	171
Badger	26	m	i	CA	Fresno	Kings Rvr P O	72	209
Balscea	28	m	i	MEXI	Alameda	Murray Twp	68	103
Baltizar	22	m	i	CA	San Diego	San Luis Rey	78	512
Bartcoh	50	m	i	MEXI	Alameda	Murray Twp	68	103
Beach	37	m	i	CA	Colusa	Stony Crk Twp	71	334
Beattice	19	m	i	OR	Del Norte	Smith Rvr Twp	71	481
Becintd	28	m	i	CA	Colusa	Butte Twp	71	270
Behinia	9	f	i	----	Marin	Bolinas Twp	74	89
Bell	38	f	i	CA	Fresno	Millerton P O	72	197
Bellon	10	m	i	----	Marin	Point Reyes Twp	74	89
Ben	35	m	i	CA	Colusa	Monroe Twp	71	322
Ben	24	m	i	CA	Fresno	Kings Rvr P O	72	206
Ben	24	m	i	CA	Fresno	Millerton P O	72	188
Ben	18	m	i	CA	Del Norte	Happy Camp Twp	71	472
Benito	49	m	i	CA	Fresno	Millerton P O	72	155
Benito	30	m	i	CA	Fresno	Millerton P O	72	179
Bernabel	30	m	i	CA	Los Angeles	Los Angeles	73	501
Betsey	18	f	i	CA	Del Norte	Smith Rvr Twp	71	482
Bettie	13	f	i	AZ	Napa	Napa Twp	75	67
Big Bob	35	m	i	CA	Del Norte	Smith Rvr Twp	71	480
Big Dick	35	m	i	CA	Del Norte	Smith Rvr Twp	71	480
Big George	35	m	i	CA	Del Norte	Crescent Twp	71	459
Big Jack	46	m	i	CA	Fresno	Kings Rvr P O	72	205
Big Jim	30	m	i	CA	Colusa	Stony Crk Twp	71	328
Bigbob	25	m	i	CA	Del Norte	Smith Rvr Twp	71	480
Bigfeet	40	m	i	CA	Del Norte	Crescent Twp	71	458
Bil	34	m	i	CA	Fresno	Millerton P O	72	183
Bill	48	m	i	CA	Fresno	Millerton P O	72	181
Bill	38	m	i	CA	Colusa	Butte Twp	71	270
Bill	38	m	i	CA	Fresno	Millerton P O	72	195
Bill	38	m	i	CA	Fresno	Kings Rvr P O	72	203
Bill	36	m	i	CA	Colusa	Monroe Twp	71	322
Bill	35	m	i	CA	Del Norte	Happy Camp Twp	71	472
Bill	30	m	i	CA	Del Norte	Crescent	71	466
Bill	30	m	i	CA	Fresno	Kingston P O	72	224
Bill	30	m	i	CA	Yolo	Grafton Twp	93	484
Bill	28	m	i	CA	Fresno	Kingston P O	72	222
Bill	28	m	i	CA	Fresno	Kings Rvr P O	72	215
Bill	25	m	i	CA	Del Norte	Crescent Twp	71	454
Bill	25	m	i	CA	Del Norte	Crescent Twp	71	454
Bill	24	m	i	CA	Fresno	Kings Rvr P O	72	207
Bill	24	m	i	CA	Fresno	Kings Rvr P O	72	208
Bill	24	m	i	CA	Fresno	Millerton P O	72	189
Bill	23	m	i	CA	Fresno	Kings Rvr P O	72	206
Bill	21	m	i	CA	Fresno	Millerton P O	72	185
Bill	21	m	i	CA	Fresno	Kings Rvr P O	72	208
Bill	20	m	i	CA	Yolo	Grafton Twp	93	478
Billy	30	m	i	CA	Del Norte	Crescent Twp	71	458
Billy	30	m	i	CA	Del Norte	Crescent Twp	71	458
Billy	25	f	i	CA	Del Norte	Happy Camp Twp	71	473
Billy	24	m	i	CA	Del Norte	Smith Rvr Twp	71	481
Billy	21	m	i	OR	Sacramento	1-Wd Sacramento	77	204
Billy	20	m	i	CA	Del Norte	Crescent Twp	71	457
Billy	20	m	i	CA	Del Norte	Crescent Twp	71	459
Billy	20	m	i	CA	Del Norte	Crescent Twp	71	457
Billy Crook	30	m	i	CA	Del Norte	Smith Rvr Twp	71	480
Billy Kieffer	25	m	i	CA	Del Norte	Crescent Twp	71	460
Black Jim	40	m	i	CA	Del Norte	Smith Rvr Twp	71	480
Black Jim	25	m	i	CA	Del Norte	Happy Camp Twp	71	472
Black Tom	50	m	i	CA	Colusa	Grand Island	71	310
Boatwright	38	m	i	CA	Fresno	Millerton P O	72	182
Bob	50	m	i	CA	Fresno	Millerton P O	72	188
Bob	40	m	i	CA	Fresno	Kingston P O	72	221

© 2001 by Heritage Quest. All rights reserved.

Name	Age	S	R	B-PL	County	Locale	Roll	Pg
Bob	33	m	i	CA	Fresno	Kings Rvr P O	72	213
Bob	32	m	i	CA	Fresno	Millerton P O	72	187
Bob	30	m	i	CA	Del Norte	Crescent Twp	71	458
Bob	28	m	i	CA	Fresno	Kingston P O	72	224
Bob	26	m	i	CA	Fresno	Millerton P O	72	192
Bob	25	m	i	CA	Del Norte	Crescent	71	467
Bob	24	m	i	CA	Fresno	Kings Rvr P O	72	215
Bob	20	m	i	CA	Del Norte	Crescent Twp	71	459
Boneteo	33	m	i	CA	Colusa	Stony Crk Twp	71	326
Bonjee	70	f	i	CA	Del Norte	Smith Rvr Twp	71	482
Borrow	35	m	i	CA	Fresno	Millerton P O	72	176
Boston	20	m	i	CA	Del Norte	Smith Rvr Twp	71	482
Branford	22	m	i	CA	Fresno	Millerton P O	72	190
Branson	27	m	i	CA	Fresno	Kings Rvr P O	72	205
Bries	50	m	i	CA	Colusa	Monroe Twp	71	317
Brisco	30	m	i	CA	Colusa	Stony Crk Twp	71	331
Bruno	55	m	i	CA	Los Angeles	Los Angeles Twp	73	499
Buck Smith	18	m	i	CA	Humboldt	Pacific Twp	72	297
Buckskin	50	m	i	CA	Fresno	Kings Rvr P O	72	204
Buckskin	50	m	i	CA	Fresno	Kings Rvr P O	72	215
Bucksnort	25	m	i	CA	Fresno	Kings Rvr P O	72	216
Buffalo Bill	31	m	i	CA	Fresno	Kings Rvr P O	72	216
Bull Frog	3	m	i	CA	Fresno	Kings Rvr P O	72	213
Bully	16	m	i	CA	Del Norte	Smith Rvr Twp	71	481
Bush	25	m	i	CA	Colusa	Colusa Twp	71	285
Calastra	80	f	i	----	Marin	Nicasio Twp	74	89
Calda	40	m	i	CA	Colusa	Monroe Twp	71	322
Calistoo	25	m	i	CA	Fresno	Millerton P O	72	171
Calistra	17	f	i	CA	Napa	Napa Twp	75	74
Calostico	66	m	i	----	Marin	Point Reyes Twp	74	89
Camlick	46	m	i	CA	Colusa	Spring Valley Twp	71	338
Candido	30	m	i	CA	Napa	Napa Twp	75	74
Capt Charly	44	m	i	CA	Fresno	Kingston P O	72	221
Capt Eagle	42	m	i	CA	Fresno	Kings Rvr P O	72	209
Capt George	54	m	i	CA	Fresno	Kings Rvr P O	72	207
Capt Joe	38	m	i	CA	Fresno	Kingston P O	72	217
Capt Jose	42	m	i	CA	Fresno	Millerton P O	72	189
Capt Mike	45	m	i	CA	Del Norte	Crescent Twp	71	459
Capt Tom	52	m	i	CA	Fresno	Millerton P O	72	185
Capt Tom	48	m	i	CA	Fresno	Millerton P O	72	187
Carlos	60	m	i	CA	Los Angeles	Los Angeles Twp	73	498
Carlos	35	m	i	----	Marin	Nicasio Twp	74	89
Carlos	35	m	i	----	Marin	Nicasio Twp	74	89
Carmel	30	f	i	CA	Napa	Napa Twp	75	74
Carver	20	f	i	CA	Del Norte	Crescent Twp	71	457
Casen	30	m	i	CA	Los Angeles	Los Angeles	73	500
Casmer	45	m	i	CA	Fresno	Kings Rvr P O	72	216
Catarina	54	f	i	CA	Monterey	Monterey Twp	74	348
Catchup	30	m	i	CA	Del Norte	Crescent Twp	71	457
Cawan	40	f	i	CA	Del Norte	Crescent Twp	71	458
Celso	75	m	i	----	Marin	Novato Twp	74	89
Chacaltjee	40	m	i	CA	Fresno	Millerton P O	72	176
Chack	25	m	i	CA	Del Norte	Crescent Twp	71	458
Chackratt	30	f	i	CA	Fresno	Millerton P O	72	174
Chajackee	28	m	i	CA	Fresno	Millerton P O	72	172
Chajaii	20	m	i	CA	Fresno	Millerton P O	72	175
Chakesa	40	f	i	CA	Fresno	Millerton P O	72	195
Chamaij	20	m	i	CA	Fresno	Millerton P O	72	177
Chamchem	40	m	i	CA	Fresno	Millerton P O	72	180
Chamesan	40	m	i	CA	Fresno	Millerton P O	72	170
Chamewah	30	f	i	CA	Fresno	Millerton P O	72	178
Chapo	60	m	i	CA	Colusa	Stony Crk Twp	71	334
Chapo	17	m	i	CA	Los Angeles	Los Angeles	73	500
Chappe	40	m	i	CA	Colusa	Stony Crk Twp	71	328
Chappe	40	m	i	CA	Colusa	Colusa Twp	71	285
Chappoc	16	m	i	CA	Colusa	Butte Twp	71	265
Charaway	55	m	i	CA	Colusa	Spring Valley Twp	71	338
Charles	30	m	i	CA	Colusa	Spring Valley Twp	71	337
Charles	30	m	i	CA	Sacramento	American Twp	77	67
Charles	25	m	i	CA	Colusa	Monroe Twp	71	317
Charley	50	m	i	CA	Colusa	Stony Crk Twp	71	329
Charley	40	m	i	CA	Fresno	Kingston P O	72	217
Charley	38	m	i	CA	Fresno	Millerton P O	72	192
Charley	34	m	i	CA	Fresno	Kings Rvr P O	72	207
Charley	33	m	i	CA	Fresno	Millerton P O	72	198
Charley	32	m	i	CA	Fresno	Millerton P O	72	196
Charley	32	m	i	CA	Fresno	Millerton P O	72	196
Charley	32	m	i	CA	Fresno	Kingston P O	72	223
Charley	28	m	i	CA	Fresno	Millerton P O	72	189
Charley	26	m	i	CA	Fresno	Millerton P O	72	181
Charley	25	m	i	CA	Fresno	Millerton P O	72	196
Charley	25	m	i	CA	Sonoma	Salt Point	91	390
Charley	24	m	i	CA	Fresno	Kings Rvr P O	72	215
Charley	24	m	i	CA	Fresno	Kings Rvr P O	72	210
Charley	23	m	i	CA	Fresno	Millerton P O	72	198
Charley	21	m	i	CA	Fresno	Kings Rvr P O	72	216
Charley	16	m	i	CA	Colusa	Stony Crk Twp	71	331
Charley	15	m	i	CA	Colusa	Monroe Twp	71	317
Charley	15	m	i	CA	Colusa	Butte Twp	71	270
Charley	10	m	i	CA	Monterey	San Benito Twp	74	380
Charlie	9	m	i	CA	Yolo	Cottonwood Twp	93	468
Charlie	30	m	i	CA	Del Norte	Happy Camp Twp	71	473
Charlie	30	m	i	CA	Del Norte	Crescent	71	466
Charlie	30	m	i	CA	Del Norte	Smith Rvr Twp	71	482
Charlie	30	m	i	CA	Del Norte	Smith Rvr Twp	71	481
Charlie	25	m	i	CA	Del Norte	Crescent Twp	71	459
Charlie	25	m	i	CA	Del Norte	Happy Camp Twp	71	472
Charlie	22	m	i	CA	Yolo	Cottonwood Twp	93	470
Charlie	18	m	i	CA	Del Norte	Crescent Twp	71	459
Charlie	18	m	i	CA	Del Norte	Crescent Twp	71	454
Charlie	18	m	i	CA	Del Norte	Crescent Twp	71	458
Charlie Stateter	25	m	i	CA	Del Norte	Crescent Twp	71	460
Charlot	60	f	i	CA	Yolo	Buckeye Twp	93	412
Chartos	25	m	i	CA	Del Norte	Crescent Twp	71	459
Chatal	50	m	i	CA	Fresno	Millerton P O	72	172
Chavackles	40	m	i	CA	Fresno	Millerton P O	72	171
Cheata	35	m	i	CA	Del Norte	Smith Rvr Twp	71	480
Checoo	35	m	i	CA	Fresno	Millerton P O	72	172
Cheenortho	40	m	i	CA	Fresno	Millerton P O	72	175
Cheepak	25	m	i	CA	Fresno	Millerton P O	72	175
Chehue	36	m	i	CA	Napa	Napa Twp	75	74
Chemavatt	30	f	i	CA	Fresno	Millerton P O	72	176
Chemotick	32	m	i	CA	Fresno	Kings Rvr P O	72	215
Chenkeller	35	f	i	CA	Fresno	Millerton P O	72	174
Cher	25	m	i	CA	Del Norte	Crescent Twp	71	457
Cheropee	40	m	i	CA	Colusa	Stony Crk Twp	71	334
Cherpettnault	25	f	i	CA	Del Norte	Crescent Twp	71	457
Chewaha	48	m	i	CA	Fresno	Millerton P O	72	195
Chewaha	34	m	i	CA	Fresno	Millerton P O	72	195
Chico	16	m	i	CA	Los Angeles	Los Angeles	73	500
Chicoro	17	m	i	MEXI	Alameda	Murray Twp	68	103
Chimisa	45	m	i	CA	Los Angeles	Los Angeles Twp	73	498
China John	35	m	i	CA	Del Norte	Smith Rvr Twp	71	480
Chintima	30	f	i	CA	Del Norte	Smith Rvr Twp	71	481
Chockjah	45	m	i	CA	Fresno	Millerton P O	72	179
Chocomah	40	m	i	CA	Fresno	Millerton P O	72	172
Chocowah	80	m	i	CA	Fresno	Millerton P O	72	178
Choechoe	40	m	i	CA	Fresno	Millerton P O	72	171
Chokitte	45	m	i	CA	Fresno	Millerton P O	72	174
Chokowah	45	m	i	CA	Fresno	Millerton P O	72	173
Cholacke	27	m	i	CA	Fresno	Millerton P O	72	186
Cholikee	38	m	i	CA	Fresno	Kings Rvr P O	72	215
Chomat	64	m	i	CA	Fresno	Kings Rvr P O	72	215
Chomut	40	f	i	CA	Fresno	Millerton P O	72	170
Choppo	71	m	i	CA	Fresno	Millerton P O	72	197
Choppo	21	m	i	CA	Fresno	Millerton P O	72	184
Chrispo	14	m	i	CA	Los Angeles	Los Angeles	73	500
Chrochta	20	f	i	CA	Del Norte	Crescent Twp	71	454
Chuca	65	f	i	----	Marin	Tomales Twp	74	89
Chungosey	50	m	i	CA	Del Norte	Smith Rvr Twp	71	480
Chunnaih	35	m	i	CA	Fresno	Millerton P O	72	178
Chupechak	25	f	i	CA	Fresno	Millerton P O	72	177
Chutuly	30	f	i	CA	Fresno	Millerton P O	72	176
Clapobla	30	f	i	CA	Del Norte	Crescent Twp	71	459
Clara	40	f	i	CA	Los Angeles	Los Angeles	73	501
Clawcoer	10	m	i	CA	Del Norte	Crescent Twp	71	458
Clemento	6	m	i	CA	San Diego	San Luis Rey	78	512
Clubshins	23	f	i	CA	Fresno	Kings Rvr P O	72	213
Clumps	35	m	i	CA	Del Norte	Crescent Twp	71	454
Cluton	50	m	i	CA	Del Norte	Smith Rvr Twp	71	481
Cluttebar	22	m	i	CA	Colusa	Spring Valley Twp	71	338
Cocheo	24	m	i	CA	Fresno	Kings Rvr P O	72	205
Cocsoučock	36	m	i	CA	Colusa	Spring Valley Twp	71	338
Cohil	40	m	i	CA	Fresno	Millerton P O	72	181
Col	24	m	i	CA	Fresno	Kings Rvr P O	72	209
Colomosoner	35	m	i	CA	Fresno	Millerton P O	72	169
Colonel	50	m	i	CA	Del Norte	Smith Rvr Twp	71	479
Colonokee	61	m	i	CA	Fresno	Millerton P O	72	198
Comach	38	m	i	CA	Fresno	Millerton P O	72	197
Comaheva	32	m	i	CA	Fresno	Millerton P O	72	190
Come Took	45	f	i	CA	Colusa	Spring Valley Twp	71	343
Comipehah	54	m	i	CA	Fresno	Millerton P O	72	196
Commahoe	64	m	i	CA	Fresno	Kingston P O	72	223
Como	23	m	i	CA	Contra Costa	Martinez P O	71	441
Concepciona	32	f	i	CA	Los Angeles	Los Angeles	73	500
Concicion	60	f	i	CA	Napa	Napa Twp	75	74
Connecticutt	30	m	i	CA	Del Norte	Crescent Twp	71	460
Conock	48	m	i	CA	Fresno	Millerton P O	72	188
Cononda	50	f	i	CA	Los Angeles	Los Angeles Twp	73	498
Coper	50	f	i	CA	Fresno	Millerton P O	72	173
Cora	15	f	i	CA	Humboldt	Arcata Twp	72	234
Coree	40	m	i	CA	Colusa	Spring Valley Twp	71	338
Cortoope	25	m	i	CA	Fresno	Millerton P O	72	179
Cotapee	50	m	i	CA	Fresno	Millerton P O	72	169
Couite	32	m	i	CA	Fresno	Millerton P O	72	184
Cowan	35	f	i	CA	Del Norte	Crescent Twp	71	458
Cowshipe	30	m	i	CA	Fresno	Kings Rvr P O	72	216
Coyogette	30	m	i	CA	Fresno	Millerton P O	72	189
Craw Mouth	55	m	i	CA	Del Norte	Crescent Twp	71	459
Crazy Jake	30	m	i	CA	Del Norte	Smith Rvr Twp	71	480
Crecencia	20	f	i	CA	Los Angeles	Los Angeles	73	501
Crisanto	20	m	i	CA	Alameda	Murray Twp	68	106
Crisato	2	m	i	CA	Alameda	Murray Twp	68	106
Crisosta	40	f	i	MEXI	Los Angeles	Los Angeles Twp	73	498
Crisparo	26	m	i	----	Marin	Nicasio Twp	74	89
Criste	8	f	i	MEXI	Alameda	Murray Twp	68	103
Cristoval	50	m	i	CA	Los Angeles	Los Angeles Twp	73	498
Crow	37	m	i	CA	Colusa	Monroe Twp	71	322
Cuchner	30	f	i	CA	Del Norte	Crescent Twp	71	458
Cusivis	50	m	i	CA	Monterey	San Antonio Twp	74	317
Damas	66	f	i	CA	Napa	Napa Twp	75	74
Damas	32	m	i	CA	San Luis Obispo	Salinas Twp	87	295
Damte	45	f	i	CA	Colusa	Spring Valley Twp	71	343
Dane	15	m	i	CA	Humboldt	Eureka Twp	72	281

Series M593

© 2001 by Heritage Quest. All rights reserved.

Name	Age	S	R	B-PL	County	Locale	Roll	Pg
						Series M593		
Daniel	18	m	i	CA	San Diego	San Luis Rey	78	512
Datuch	20	m	i	CA	Fresno	Millerton P O	72	170
Dave	15	m	i	CA	Sacramento	4-Wd Sacramento	77	327
Deck	24	m	i	CA	Fresno	Millerton P O	72	190
Deck	13	m	i	CA	Colusa	Monroe Twp	71	318
Deetor	36	m	i	CA	Fresno	Millerton P O	72	197
Delgardo	60	f	i	CA	Los Angeles	Los Angeles Twp	73	498
Delida	12	f	i	----	Marin	Bolinas Twp	74	89
Demas	58	m	i	CA	Monterey	Alisal Twp	74	295
Demas	18	m	i	CA	Yolo	Cottonwood Twp	93	474
Deonicio	18	m	i	CA	Monterey	San Antonio Twp	74	321
Devorcio	42	m	i	MEXI	San Luis Obispo	San Luis Obispo Tw	87	298
Dick	38	m	i	CA	Fresno	Millerton P O	72	198
Dick	36	m	i	CA	Fresno	Kings Rvr P O	72	206
Dick	35	m	i	CA	Del Norte	Crescent Twp	71	454
Dick	35	m	i	CA	Fresno	Kingston P O	72	223
Dick	32	m	i	CA	Fresno	Millerton P O	72	187
Dick	31	m	i	CA	Colusa	Stony Crk Twp	71	326
Dick	30	m	i	CA	Fresno	Kingston P O	72	223
Dick	30	m	i	CA	Del Norte	Crescent Twp	71	459
Dick	26	m	i	CA	Fresno	Kingston P O	72	223
Dick	25	m	i	CA	Del Norte	Happy Camp Twp	71	472
Dick	24	m	i	----	Marin	No Twp Listed	74	89
Dick	22	m	i	----	Marin	No Twp Listed	74	89
Dick	22	m	i	CA	Del Norte	Smith Rvr Twp	71	481
Dick	21	m	i	CA	Fresno	Millerton P O	72	191
Dick	18	m	i	CA	Del Norte	Crescent Twp	71	460
Dick	16	m	i	CA	San Luis Obispo	San Luis Obispo Tw	87	307
Dick	16	m	i	CA	Del Norte	Smith Rvr Twp	71	480
Dick	12	m	i	CA	Colusa	Colusa Twp	71	274
Dinah	13	f	i	CA	Yolo	Cottonwood Twp	93	470
Dixie	30	m	i	CA	Del Norte	Crescent Twp	71	459
Docelo	37	m	i	MEXI	Alameda	Murray Twp	68	103
Doctor	48	m	i	CA	Fresno	Kingston P O	72	221
Doctor	46	m	i	CA	Fresno	Kings Rvr P O	72	208
Dogood	25	m	i	CA	Fresno	Millerton P O	72	192
Dolores	40	f	i	CA	Yolo	Grafton Twp	93	484
Dolores	38	f	i	CA	Napa	Napa Twp	75	74
Dolores	30	f	i	CA	Yolo	Grafton Twp	93	484
Domingo	48	m	i	----	Marin	Point Reyes Twp	74	89
Domingo	26	m	i	CA	Los Angeles	Los Angeles Twp	73	498
Domingo	25	m	i	CA	Fresno	Millerton P O	72	175
Domingo	24	m	i	----	Marin	Bolinas Twp	74	89
Dominguez	50	m	i	CA	Los Angeles	Los Angeles	73	500
Doolittle	23	m	i	CA	Fresno	Millerton P O	72	198
Dorotia	88	f	i	CA	Monterey	Monterey Twp	74	344
Dowing	40	m	i	CA	Alameda	Murray Twp	68	106
Downing	28	m	i	CA	Colusa	Stony Crk Twp	71	328
Doxie	18	f	i	CA	Del Norte	Crescent Twp	71	460
Dulce	14	f	i	CA	Los Angeles	Los Angeles Twp	73	498
Eduardo	54	m	i	CA	Los Angeles	Los Angeles Twp	73	498
Edward	24	m	i	CA	Fresno	Kings Rvr P O	72	209
Eleck	30	m	i	CA	Colusa	Monroe Twp	71	317
Elejo	40	m	i	CA	Los Angeles	Los Angeles Twp	73	498
Elizabeth	35	f	i	CA	Colusa	Stony Crk Twp	71	326
Ellick	20	m	i	CA	Lake	Lower Lake	73	428
Emanuel	24	m	i	CA	Fresno	Kings Rvr P O	72	207
Emilio	45	m	i	CA	Fresno	Millerton P O	72	172
Enanuel	12	m	i	CA	Yolo	Grafton Twp	93	484
Encarnacion	20	f	i	CA	Los Angeles	Los Angeles	73	501
Ennassio	12	m	i	CA	Alameda	Murray Twp	68	106
Epatech	50	m	i	CA	Fresno	Millerton P O	72	174
Esedore	45	m	i	CA	Alameda	Murray Twp	68	106
Esinelle	62	f	i	CA	Fresno	Millerton P O	72	182
Espiridiona	8	m	i	CA	San Luis Obispo	San Luis Obispo Tw	87	310
Euckoto	30	m	i	CA	Fresno	Kingston P O	72	223
Euconomah	43	m	i	CA	Fresno	Millerton P O	72	197
Eumoca	58	f	i	CA	Fresno	Kings Rvr P O	72	209
Eva	55	m	i	CA	Colusa	Spring Valley Twp	71	338
Fahconndra	70	m	i	----	Marin	San Rafael	74	89
Fanney	18	f	i	CA	Del Norte	Crescent Twp	71	460
Fanni	14	f	i	CA	Colusa	Butte Twp	71	268
Fannie	15	f	i	CA	Del Norte	Crescent Twp	71	459
Fanny	18	f	i	CA	Del Norte	Happy Camp Twp	71	473
Fasten	17	m	i	CA	Los Angeles	Los Angeles Twp	73	498
Feliciano	35	m	i	CA	Monterey	San Benito Twp	74	380
Felicida	33	f	i	----	Marin	Bolinas Twp	74	89
Felicita	24	f	i	CA	Los Angeles	Los Angeles Twp	73	498
Felipe	40	m	i	MEXI	Los Angeles	Los Angeles Twp	73	498
Femanda	60	f	i	CA	Alameda	Murray Twp	68	106
Fernando	99	m	i	CA	Contra Costa	Martinez P O	71	442
Fernando	17	m	i	CA	Los Angeles	Los Angeles Twp	73	498
Floho	27	m	i	----	Marin	Nicasio Twp	74	89
Forty	20	f	i	CA	Del Norte	Smith Rvr Twp	71	482
Francasu	40	m	i	CA	Napa	Napa Twp	75	74
Francisca	21	f	i	----	Marin	Nicasio Twp	74	89
Francisco	8	f	i	CA	San Diego	San Luis Rey	78	512
Francisco	50	m	i	MEXI	Los Angeles	Los Angeles Twp	73	498
Francisco	42	m	i	CA	Fresno	Kings Rvr P O	72	216
Francisco	40	m	i	----	Marin	Bolinas Twp	74	89
Francisco	40	m	i	CA	Los Angeles	Los Angeles	73	500
Francisco	35	m	i	CA	Los Angeles	Los Angeles	73	500
Francisco	24	m	i	CA	Santa Barbara	San Buenaventura P	87	441
Francisco	20	m	i	CA	San Diego	San Luis Rey	78	512
Francisco	18	m	i	CA	Los Angeles	Los Angeles	73	500
Francisco	18	m	i	CA	Los Angeles	Los Angeles Twp	73	499
Francisco	12	m	i	CA	Santa Barbara	Las Cruces P O	87	505

Name	Age	S	R	B-PL	County	Locale	Roll	Pg
						Series M593		
Frank	9	m	i	CA	Sacramento	Dry Crk Twp	77	104
Frank	42	m	i	CA	Fresno	Kingston P O	72	217
Frank	35	m	i	CA	Fresno	Kings Rvr P O	72	206
Frank	3	m	i	CA	Del Norte	Happy Camp Twp	71	473
Frank	20	f	i	CA	Del Norte	Happy Camp Twp	71	473
Frank	19	m	i	CA	Colusa	Colusa Twp	71	273
Franky	17	f	i	CA	Colusa	Stony Crk Twp	71	326
Fred	35	m	i	CA	Del Norte	Smith Rvr Twp	71	481
Frederica	24	f	i	MEXI	Los Angeles	Los Angeles Twp	73	498
Frederico	3	m	i	CA	Los Angeles	Los Angeles Twp	73	499
Freeball	33	m	i	CA	Fresno	Kingston P O	72	222
Gabreal	20	m	i	CA	San Luis Obispo	Salinas Twp	87	295
Gabriel	50	m	i	MEXI	Los Angeles	Los Angeles Twp	73	499
Garcia	40	m	i	CA	Sonoma	Bodega Twp	91	261
Gaspar	28	m	i	CA	Los Angeles	Los Angeles	73	501
Gensalda	10	f	i	CA	Los Angeles	Los Angeles Twp	73	498
George	8	m	i	CA	Del Norte	Smith Rvr Twp	71	482
George	35	m	i	CA	Del Norte	Smith Rvr Twp	71	480
George	30	m	i	CA	Fresno	Kings Rvr P O	72	216
George	30	m	i	CA	Colusa	Stony Crk Twp	71	331
George	28	m	i	CA	Fresno	Kingston P O	72	217
George	25	m	i	CA	Fresno	Kingston P O	72	217
George	25	m	i	CA	Del Norte	Crescent Twp	71	454
George	25	m	i	CA	Del Norte	Happy Camp Twp	71	472
George	25	m	i	CA	Colusa	Grand Island	71	310
George	23	m	i	CA	Del Norte	Crescent Twp	71	458
George	22	m	i	CA	Fresno	Kings Rvr P O	72	216
George	21	m	i	CA	Fresno	Millerton P O	72	182
George	15	m	i	CA	Alameda	Murray Twp	68	106
George	15	m	i	CA	Yolo	Buckeye Twp	93	412
George	13	m	i	CA	Yolo	Putah Twp	93	514
George Mrs	14	f	i	CA	Del Norte	Crescent Twp	71	458
Gertrudes	35	f	i	CA	Los Angeles	Los Angeles	73	500
Gertrudes	30	f	i	CA	Los Angeles	Los Angeles Twp	73	498
Gilmore	50	m	i	CA	Colusa	Stony Crk Twp	71	334
Giullemo	20	m	i	CA	San Diego	San Luis Rey	78	512
Gomeset	40	f	i	CA	Colusa	Spring Valley Twp	71	343
Goodege	34	m	i	CA	Fresno	Kings Rvr P O	72	207
Governor Briggs	25	m	i	CA	Del Norte	Crescent Twp	71	460
Granis	43	m	i	MEXI	Los Angeles	Los Angeles Twp	73	498
Grant	24	m	i	CA	Fresno	Kingston P O	72	221
Greaser	30	m	i	CA	Del Norte	Happy Camp Twp	71	472
Gregorio	1	m	i	CA	San Diego	San Luis Rey	78	512
Grujah	40	m	i	CA	Fresno	Millerton P O	72	176
Guillermo	38	m	i	CA	Los Angeles	Los Angeles Twp	73	498
Gussi	16	f	i	CA	Yolo	Cottonwood Twp	93	474
Hacoh	45	m	i	CA	Fresno	Millerton P O	72	174
Hacoh	35	m	i	CA	Fresno	Millerton P O	72	174
Hager	34	f	i	CA	Colusa	Spring Valley Twp	71	343
Hagetts	36	m	i	CA	Fresno	Millerton P O	72	171
Hagotch	35	m	i	CA	Del Norte	Crescent Twp	71	458
Hainchanah	45	m	i	CA	Fresno	Millerton P O	72	171
Hairlip	30	m	i	CA	Del Norte	Smith Rvr Twp	71	482
Halletto	31	m	i	CA	Fresno	Millerton P O	72	195
Hallith	36	m	i	CA	Fresno	Millerton P O	72	180
Hallock	40	m	i	CA	Colusa	Spring Valley Twp	71	338
Hamanahow	48	m	i	CA	Fresno	Kings Rvr P O	72	210
Hamella	42	f	i	CA	Colusa	Spring Valley Twp	71	343
Hammertop	61	m	i	CA	Fresno	Millerton P O	72	182
Hamtulle	27	f	i	CA	Colusa	Spring Valley Twp	71	343
Haner	25	m	i	CA	Del Norte	Crescent Twp	71	458
Hannah	25	f	i	CA	Yolo	Cottonwood Twp	93	474
Hanovirat	35	f	i	CA	Fresno	Millerton P O	72	169
Hanun	43	m	i	CA	Fresno	Millerton P O	72	182
Hapense	50	m	i	CA	Fresno	Millerton P O	72	148
Happy Camp Bill	25	m	i	CA	Del Norte	Happy Camp Twp	71	472
Harna	63	m	i	CA	Fresno	Kingston P O	72	224
Harry	9	m	i	CA	Yolo	Grafton Twp	93	484
Harry	16	m	i	CA	Colusa	Monroe Twp	71	311
Hasachee	30	m	i	CA	Fresno	Millerton P O	72	176
Hasanoch	50	f	i	CA	Fresno	Millerton P O	72	170
Hasuck	29	m	i	CA	Fresno	Millerton P O	72	181
Hatcha	42	m	i	CA	Fresno	Millerton P O	72	195
Hatchee	36	m	i	CA	Fresno	Millerton P O	72	196
Hatee	35	m	i	CA	Fresno	Millerton P O	72	171
Hathee	40	f	i	CA	Fresno	Millerton P O	72	179
Hatsea	28	m	i	CA	Fresno	Millerton P O	72	171
Hawanotte	34	m	i	CA	Fresno	Millerton P O	72	190
Hawitch	30	m	i	CA	Del Norte	Crescent Twp	71	457
Heldfa	35	m	i	CA	Colusa	Stony Crk Twp	71	334
Hem Tan	56	m	i	CA	Colusa	Stony Crk Twp	71	334
Hemah	47	m	i	CA	Fresno	Kings Rvr P O	72	209
Henriquez	45	m	i	CA	Los Angeles	Los Angeles	73	500
Henriquez	22	m	i	CA	Los Angeles	Los Angeles	73	500
Henry	32	m	i	CA	Colusa	Stony Crk Twp	71	331
Henry	31	m	i	CA	Butte	Wyandotte Twp	70	143
Henry	30	m	i	CA	Colusa	Monroe Twp	71	317
Henry	25	m	i	CA	Del Norte	Smith Rvr Twp	71	482
Henry	13	m	i	CA	Del Norte	Smith Rvr Twp	71	482
Henry	10	m	i	CA	Colusa	Butte Twp	71	270
Henry	1	m	i	CA	Sacramento	Dry Crk Twp	77	98
Heoah	22	m	i	CA	Colusa	Spring Valley Twp	71	338
Herman	28	m	i	CA	Fresno	Kings Rvr P O	72	207
Hevayooh	44	f	i	CA	Colusa	Spring Valley Twp	71	343
Hewaijun	60	f	i	CA	Fresno	Millerton P O	72	178
Higatte	50	m	i	CA	Fresno	Millerton P O	72	172
Hill	40	m	i	CA	Colusa	Stony Crk Twp	71	334

© 2001 by Heritage Quest. All rights reserved.

California 1870 Census

Name	Age	S	R	B-PL	County	Locale	Roll (Series M593)	Pg
Hillihah	34	m	i	CA	Fresno	Millerton P O	72	195
Hinpah	40	m	i	CA	Fresno	Kings Rvr P O	72	207
Hocaitah	25	f	i	CA	Fresno	Millerton P O	72	180
Hochack	30	m	i	CA	Fresno	Millerton P O	72	179
Hochochansu	36	m	i	CA	Fresno	Millerton P O	72	198
Hogannet	18	f	i	CA	Fresno	Millerton P O	72	173
Hoganrich	40	m	i	CA	Fresno	Millerton P O	72	173
Hoikee	26	m	i	CA	Fresno	Millerton P O	72	169
Hoioppa	33	m	i	CA	Fresno	Millerton P O	72	196
Holloopa	27	m	i	CA	Colusa	Stony Crk Twp	71	331
Holyan	30	m	i	CA	Colusa	Stony Crk Twp	71	328
Homegh	45	m	i	CA	Fresno	Kings Rvr P O	72	207
Homosa	30	m	i	CA	Fresno	Millerton P O	72	195
Honapo	22	f	i	CA	Colusa	Spring Valley Twp	71	343
Honemah	62	m	i	CA	Fresno	Millerton P O	72	197
Hoocatcher	60	f	i	CA	Fresno	Millerton P O	72	169
Hookah	40	m	i	CA	Fresno	Millerton P O	72	176
Hooker B	22	m	i	CA	Fresno	Kings Rvr P O	72	209
Hookley Captain	35	m	i	CA	Colusa	Monroe Twp	71	322
Hoonas	25	m	i	CA	Del Norte	Crescent Twp	71	457
Hoosach	70	m	i	CA	Fresno	Kings Rvr P O	72	208
Hooto	30	m	i	CA	Yolo	Grafton Twp	93	484
Hopansmar	25	m	i	CA	Fresno	Millerton P O	72	172
Hopchuenah	80	f	i	CA	Fresno	Millerton P O	72	177
Horn Buff	15	m	i	CA	Napa	Napa Twp	75	59
Hortoci	50	m	i	CA	Fresno	Millerton P O	72	177
Hortoie	30	m	i	CA	Fresno	Millerton P O	72	175
Hortoloo	25	f	i	CA	Fresno	Millerton P O	72	174
Hosa	35	m	i	CA	Colusa	Stony Crk Twp	71	331
Hose	28	m	i	CA	Fresno	Millerton P O	72	187
Hose	24	m	i	CA	Fresno	Kings Rvr P O	72	208
Hose	21	m	i	CA	Fresno	Millerton P O	72	185
Hoso	20	m	i	CA	Alameda	Murray Twp	68	106
Hoso	2	m	i	CA	Alameda	Murray Twp	68	106
Hotspur	50	m	i	CA	Del Norte	Crescent Twp	71	459
Houchca	30	m	i	CA	Fresno	Millerton P O	72	171
Howich	62	m	i	CA	Fresno	Millerton P O	72	186
Hownow	48	m	i	CA	Fresno	Kingston P O	72	222
Hududa	26	f	i	MEXI	Santa Barbara	San Buenaventura P	87	428
Humphry	60	m	i	CA	Colusa	Colusa Twp	71	285
Hunena	27	m	i	CA	Fresno	Millerton P O	72	182
Hunter	50	m	i	CA	Del Norte	Smith Rvr Twp	71	482
Hunter	28	m	i	CA	Fresno	Kings Rvr P O	72	207
Hunter	25	m	i	CA	Fresno	Millerton P O	72	190
Hupalla	26	m	i	CA	Fresno	Millerton P O	72	170
Indui	70	m	i	CA	Alameda	Murray Twp	68	106
Inguato	30	f	i	CA	Fresno	Millerton P O	72	196
Iruila	15	f	i	CA	Los Angeles	Los Angeles	73	500
Isabel	30	f	i	CA	Los Angeles	Los Angeles	73	500
Isabela	25	f	i	CA	Los Angeles	Los Angeles	73	500
Isabella	35	f	i	CA	Sacramento	Dry Crk Twp	77	98
Iseeaton	25	m	i	CA	Del Norte	Smith Rvr Twp	71	481
Isolletta	54	f	i	CA	Fresno	Kings Rvr P O	72	208
Jack	58	m	i	CA	Colusa	Stony Crk Twp	71	329
Jack	45	m	i	CA	Del Norte	Happy Camp Twp	71	473
Jack	44	m	i	CA	Colusa	Stony Crk Twp	71	326
Jack	40	m	i	CA	Colusa	Stony Crk Twp	71	331
Jack	30	m	i	CA	Del Norte	Smith Rvr Twp	71	481
Jack	30	m	i	CA	Fresno	Kings Rvr P O	72	210
Jack	30	m	i	CA	Del Norte	Happy Camp Twp	71	472
Jack	26	m	i	CA	Fresno	Kings Rvr P O	72	205
Jack	25	m	i	CA	Yolo	Cottonwood Twp	93	474
Jack	25	m	i	CA	Fresno	Millerton P O	72	175
Jack	25	m	i	CA	Del Norte	Crescent Twp	71	460
Jack	25	m	i	CA	Del Norte	Crescent Twp	71	459
Jack	24	m	i	CA	Colusa	Grand Island Twp	71	309
Jack	20	m	i	CA	Yolo	Cottonwood Twp	93	469
Jack	20	m	i	CA	Fresno	Kings Rvr P O	72	216
Jack	18	m	i	CA	Del Norte	Crescent Twp	71	457
Jack	18	m	i	CA	Colusa	Stony Crk Twp	71	334
Jack	13	m	i	CA	Colusa	Colusa	71	292
Jack Clam	40	m	i	CA	Del Norte	Crescent Twp	71	455
Jack N	28	m	i	CA	Fresno	Kings Rvr P O	72	209
Jackson	45	m	i	CA	Del Norte	Crescent Twp	71	459
Jackson	23	m	i	CA	Fresno	Kingston P O	72	222
James	8	m	i	CA	Sonoma	Mendocino Twp	91	293
James	40	m	i	CA	Del Norte	Crescent Twp	71	457
James	11	m	i	CA	Los Angeles	Los Angeles	73	500
Jane	30	f	i	CA	Colusa	Monroe Twp	71	322
Jane	18	f	i	CA	Del Norte	Crescent Twp	71	459
Jane	15	f	i	AR	Fresno	Kings Rvr P O	72	206
Jane	14	f	i	CA	Yolo	Cottonwood Twp	93	474
Jane	1	f	i	CA	Yolo	Cottonwood Twp	93	470
Janhatch	50	m	i	CA	Fresno	Millerton P O	72	172
Jaranna	70	f	i	----	Marin	Nicasio Twp	74	89
Jasina	40	f	i	CA	Alameda	Murray Twp	68	106
Jasper	31	m	i	CA	Fresno	Kings Rvr P O	72	205
Javil	58	m	i	MEXI	Los Angeles	Los Angeles Twp	73	498
Jebs	18	m	i	CA	Yolo	Buckeye Twp	93	412
Jeff	30	m	i	CA	Fresno	Kingston P O	72	221
Jeff	27	m	i	CA	Fresno	Kings Rvr P O	72	215
Jeff	20	m	i	CA	Fresno	Kings Rvr P O	72	203
Jefferson	28	m	i	CA	Fresno	Millerton P O	72	192
Jelor	30	f	i	CA	Yolo	Cottonwood Twp	93	474
Jene	12	f	i	CA	Humboldt	Pacific Twp	72	298
Jennie	50	f	i	CA	Colusa	Colusa Twp	71	285
Jennie	27	f	i	CA	Del Norte	Crescent Twp	71	454
Jennie	25	f	i	CA	Del Norte	Crescent Twp	71	458
Jennie	25	f	i	CA	Del Norte	Crescent	71	466
Jennie	20	f	i	CA	Del Norte	Smith Rvr Twp	71	482
Jennie	20	f	i	CA	Del Norte	Smith Rvr Twp	71	482
Jennie	16	f	i	CA	Del Norte	Happy Camp Twp	71	472
Jennie	14	f	i	CA	Del Norte	Smith Rvr Twp	71	482
Jennie	14	f	i	CA	Del Norte	Smith Rvr Twp	71	483
Jennie	10	f	i	UNKN	San Francisco	8-Wd San Francisco	82	300
Jerry	30	m	i	CA	Del Norte	Crescent Twp	71	459
Jerry	23	m	i	CA	Fresno	Millerton P O	72	198
Jerry	20	m	i	CA	Fresno	Millerton P O	72	198
Jese	25	m	i	CA	Sonoma	Salt Point	91	390
Jessee	30	m	i	CA	Del Norte	Smith Rvr Twp	71	482
Jestcilla	40	m	i	CA	Fresno	Millerton P O	72	171
Jesus	13	f	i	CA	Los Angeles	Los Angeles Twp	73	498
Jesus	12	m	i	----	Marin	Point Reyes Twp	74	89
Jesus	10	m	i	CA	Los Angeles	Los Angeles	73	500
Jim	50	m	i	CA	Colusa	Colusa Twp	71	285
Jim	45	m	i	CA	Colusa	Stony Crk Twp	71	329
Jim	42	m	i	CA	Colusa	Monroe Twp	71	323
Jim	40	m	i	CA	Sonoma	Salt Point	91	390
Jim	36	m	i	CA	Colusa	Butte Twp	71	270
Jim	35	m	i	CA	Colusa	Grand Island	71	310
Jim	35	m	i	CA	Del Norte	Smith Rvr Twp	71	481
Jim	32	m	i	CA	Fresno	Millerton P O	72	195
Jim	30	m	i	CA	Fresno	Millerton P O	72	191
Jim	30	m	i	CA	Fresno	Millerton P O	72	198
Jim	30	m	i	CA	Colusa	Monroe Twp	71	322
Jim	30	m	i	CA	Yolo	Grafton Twp	93	478
Jim	30	m	i	CA	Yolo	Grafton Twp	93	484
Jim	30	m	i	CA	Fresno	Millerton P O	72	184
Jim	30	m	i	CA	Del Norte	Smith Rvr Twp	71	480
Jim	30	m	i	CA	Del Norte	Smith Rvr Twp	71	479
Jim	30	m	i	CA	Del Norte	Crescent Twp	71	460
Jim	30	m	i	IN	Nevada	Meadow Lake Twp	75	248
Jim	28	m	i	CA	Fresno	Kings Rvr P O	72	210
Jim	28	m	i	CA	Fresno	Kingston P O	72	221
Jim	25	m	i	CA	Del Norte	Happy Camp Twp	71	472
Jim	25	m	i	CA	Del Norte	Crescent Twp	71	459
Jim	25	m	i	CA	Colusa	Stony Crk Twp	71	329
Jim	25	m	i	CA	Del Norte	Crescent Twp	71	459
Jim	25	m	i	CA	Del Norte	Crescent Twp	71	460
Jim	25	m	i	CA	Del Norte	Crescent Twp	71	459
Jim	25	m	i	CA	Del Norte	Smith Rvr Twp	71	480
Jim	25	f	i	CA	Del Norte	Happy Camp Twp	71	472
Jim	22	m	i	CA	Fresno	Millerton P O	72	150
Jim	21	m	i	CA	Fresno	Millerton P O	72	195
Jim	20	m	i	CA	Colusa	Colusa Twp	71	283
Jim	20	m	i	CA	Colusa	Colusa Twp	71	278
Jim	20	m	i	CA	Yolo	Buckeye Twp	93	412
Jim	18	m	i	CA	Del Norte	Smith Rvr Twp	71	482
Jim	18	m	i	CA	Fresno	Kings Rvr P O	72	213
Jim	18	m	i	CA	Yolo	Grafton Twp	93	485
Jim	18	m	i	CA	Yolo	Cottonwood Twp	93	461
Jim	18	m	i	CA	Del Norte	Crescent Twp	71	457
Jim	18	m	i	CA	Del Norte	Crescent Twp	71	460
Jim	17	m	i	CA	Colusa	Spring Valley Twp	71	338
Jim	16	m	i	CA	Colusa	Stony Crk Twp	71	326
Jim	13	m	i	CA	Yolo	Grafton Twp	93	492
Jim	12	m	i	CA	Del Norte	Happy Camp Twp	71	472
Jisalvaro	40	m	i	----	Marin	Nicasio Twp	74	89
Joaquin	45	m	i	CA	Monterey	Alisal Twp	74	297
Joaquin	28	m	i	CA	Los Angeles	Los Angeles	73	500
Joaquin	25	m	i	MEXI	Los Angeles	Los Angeles	73	501
Joe	50	m	i	CA	Yolo	Buckeye Twp	93	412
Joe	40	m	i	CA	Colusa	Monroe Twp	71	323
Joe	38	m	i	CA	Fresno	Millerton P O	72	187
Joe	37	m	i	CA	Colusa	Stony Crk Twp	71	326
Joe	35	m	i	CA	Fresno	Kings Rvr P O	72	203
Joe	35	m	i	CA	Fresno	Millerton P O	72	174
Joe	30	m	i	CA	Fresno	Kingston P O	72	223
Joe	28	m	i	CA	Colusa	Spring Valley Twp	71	336
Joe	28	m	i	CA	Del Norte	Crescent Twp	71	459
Joe	28	m	i	CA	Fresno	Millerton P O	72	190
Joe	25	m	i	CA	Del Norte	Smith Rvr Twp	71	480
Joe	24	m	i	CA	Fresno	Kingston P O	72	218
Joe	22	m	i	CA	Fresno	Millerton P O	72	185
Joe	21	m	i	CA	Fresno	Kingston P O	72	218
Joe	20	m	i	CA	Del Norte	Crescent Twp	71	459
Joe	18	m	i	CA	Colusa	Stony Crk Twp	71	334
Joe	18	m	i	CA	Sacramento	Sutter Twp	77	384
Joe	18	m	i	CA	Del Norte	Crescent Twp	71	457
Joe	17	m	i	CA	Colusa	Monroe Twp	71	318
Joe	14	m	i	CA	Sonoma	Analy Twp	91	239
Joe	13	m	i	UT	Colusa	Spring Valley Twp	71	335
Joe Hostler	30	m	i	CA	Del Norte	Smith Rvr Twp	71	480
Johana	60	f	i	CA	Yolo	Cache Crk Twp	93	428
John	40	m	i	CA	Del Norte	Crescent Twp	71	457
John	40	m	i	CA	Colusa	Stony Crk Twp	71	334
John	40	m	i	CA	Colusa	Stony Crk Twp	71	331
John	39	m	i	----	Marin	No Twp Listed	74	89
John	38	m	i	CA	Yolo	Buckeye Twp	93	412
John	35	m	i	CA	Del Norte	Crescent Twp	71	460
John	35	m	i	CA	Del Norte	Crescent Twp	71	459
John	34	m	i	CA	Colusa	Stony Crk Twp	71	331
John	30	m	i	CA	Del Norte	Smith Rvr Twp	71	482
John	30	m	i	CA	Del Norte	Smith Rvr Twp	71	481

© 2001 by Heritage Quest. All rights reserved.

Series M593

Name	Age	S	R	B-PL	County	Locale	Roll	Pg
John	30	m	i	CA	Del Norte	Smith Rvr Twp	71	483
John	30	m	i	CA	Del Norte	Crescent Twp	71	460
John	30	m	i	CA	Colusa	Monroe Twp	71	317
John	30	m	i	CA	Del Norte	Crescent	71	465
John	30	m	i	CA	Colusa	Monroe Twp	71	317
John	25	m	i	CA	Del Norte	Crescent Twp	71	457
John	25	m	i	ENGL	Mariposa	Maxwell Crk P O	74	142
John	24	m	i	CA	Yolo	Cottonwood Twp	93	474
John	23	m	i	CA	Fresno	Millerton P O	72	182
John	20	m	i	CA	Del Norte	Crescent	71	467
John	20	m	i	CA	Del Norte	Happy Camp Twp	71	472
John	20	m	i	CA	Humboldt	Table Bluff Twp	72	304
John	18	m	i	CA	Yolo	Cottonwood Twp	93	469
John	18	m	i	CA	Del Norte	Crescent Twp	71	459
John	18	m	i	CA	Napa	Yountville Twp	75	78
John	13	m	i	CA	Del Norte	Crescent Twp	71	460
John	11	m	i	CA	Colusa	Spring Valley Twp	71	345
Johnny	20	m	i	CA	Del Norte	Crescent Twp	71	458
Johnny	12	m	i	NV	Yolo	Grafton Twp	93	499
Johnson	36	m	i	CA	Fresno	Kingston P O	72	222
Johnson	30	m	i	CA	Del Norte	Smith Rvr Twp	71	480
Johnson	25	m	i	CA	Fresno	Millerton P O	72	176
Johnson	20	m	i	CA	Del Norte	Crescent Twp	71	460
Johoo	25	m	i	CA	Fresno	Millerton P O	72	170
Jonas	25	m	i	CA	Del Norte	Crescent Twp	71	459
Jonas	21	m	i	CA	Del Norte	Crescent Twp	71	454
Jonas	20	m	i	CA	Del Norte	Crescent Twp	71	460
Jonas	18	m	i	CA	Del Norte	Crescent Twp	71	460
Jones	15	m	i	CA	Del Norte	Smith Rvr Twp	71	482
Jose	5M	m	i	CA	Los Angeles	Los Angeles Twp	73	498
Jose	55	m	i	CA	Los Angeles	Los Angeles	73	500
Jose	54	m	i	CA	Santa Barbara	San Buenaventura P	87	429
Jose	50	m	i	CA	Los Angeles	Los Angeles	73	501
Jose	4M	m	i	CA	Los Angeles	Los Angeles Twp	73	498
Jose	43	m	i	CA	Fresno	Millerton P O	72	184
Jose	35	m	i	----	Marin	Novato Twp	74	89
Jose	34	m	i	CA	San Diego	San Luis Rey	78	512
Jose	31	m	i	----	Marin	No Twp Listed	74	89
Jose	30	m	i	----	Marin	Nicasio Twp	74	89
Jose	30	m	i	----	Marin	Point Reyes Twp	74	89
Jose	30	m	i	CA	Los Angeles	Los Angeles	73	500
Jose	30	m	i	CA	Los Angeles	Los Angeles	73	500
Jose	30	m	i	CA	Los Angeles	Los Angeles	73	500
Jose	30	m	i	CA	Napa	Napa	75	11
Jose	30	m	i	CA	Sonoma	Salt Point Twp	91	382
Jose	25	m	i	CA	Los Angeles	Los Angeles	73	500
Jose	25	m	i	CA	Santa Barbara	San Buenaventura P	87	442
Jose	19	m	i	CA	Monterey	San Antonio Twp	74	321
Jose	17	m	i	----	Marin	Point Reyes Twp	74	89
Jose	15	m	i	CA	Napa	Napa Twp	75	74
Jose	12	m	i	CA	Los Angeles	Los Angeles	73	500
Jose	10	m	i	MEXI	Los Angeles	Los Angeles Twp	73	498
Jose Maria	18	m	i	CA	Los Angeles	Los Angeles	73	500
Josefa	50	f	i	CA	Los Angeles	Los Angeles Twp	73	498
Josefa	25	f	i	CA	Los Angeles	Los Angeles	73	500
Josepha	40	f	i	CA	San Diego	San Luis Rey	78	512
Juan	60	m	i	MEXI	Los Angeles	Los Angeles	73	500
Juan	40	m	i	----	Marin	No Twp Listed	74	89
Juan	35	m	i	CA	Los Angeles	Los Angeles Twp	73	498
Juan	32	m	i	----	Marin	Bolinas Twp	74	89
Juan	32	m	i	CA	Napa	Napa Twp	75	74
Juan	25	m	i	CA	Los Angeles	Los Angeles	73	500
Juan	24	m	i	CA	Los Angeles	Los Angeles	73	500
Juan	24	m	i	CA	Los Angeles	Los Angeles	73	500
Juan	24	m	i	CA	Monterey	Monterey Twp	74	344
Juan	24	m	i	CA	Fresno	Kings Rvr P O	72	215
Juan	23	m	i	CA	Monterey	Monterey Twp	74	344
Juan	22	m	i	CA	Los Angeles	Los Angeles Twp	73	498
Juan	21	m	i	CA	Los Angeles	Los Angeles Twp	73	498
Juan	20	m	i	----	Marin	Novato Twp	74	89
Juan	2	m	i	----	Marin	Nicasio Twp	74	89
Juan	17	m	i	CA	Los Angeles	Los Angeles Twp	73	499
Juana	8	f	i	----	Marin	Nicasio Twp	74	89
Juana	50	f	i	CA	Los Angeles	Los Angeles	73	500
Juana	15	f	i	CA	Los Angeles	Los Angeles Twp	73	498
Juanita	23	f	i	CA	San Francisco	San Francisco P O	83	134
Juchenea	20	f	i	CA	Fresno	Millerton P O	72	180
Julia	30	f	i	CA	Del Norte	Smith Rvr Twp	71	480
Julia	25	f	i	CA	Yolo	Cottonwood Twp	93	474
Julia	18	f	i	CA	Del Norte	Crescent Twp	71	460
Julia	18	f	i	CA	Del Norte	Crescent Twp	71	455
Julia	16	f	i	CA	Del Norte	Happy Camp Twp	71	472
Julia	16	f	i	CA	Del Norte	Happy Camp Twp	71	472
Julian	16	m	i	CA	Napa	Napa Twp	75	74
Julius	20	m	i	CA	Del Norte	Crescent Twp	71	459
Jutchoul	25	m	i	CA	Fresno	Millerton P O	72	172
Ka Tope	48	f	i	CA	Colusa	Stony Crk Twp	71	329
Kachilla	40	m	i	CA	Fresno	Millerton P O	72	175
Kaiipah	25	m	i	CA	Fresno	Millerton P O	72	177
Kaitaino	45	m	i	CA	Fresno	Millerton P O	72	171
Kalpat	25	m	i	CA	Fresno	Millerton P O	72	179
Kamaso	35	m	i	CA	Fresno	Millerton P O	72	170
Kanumber	60	m	i	CA	Del Norte	Crescent Twp	71	458
Kapett	50	m	i	CA	Del Norte	Crescent Twp	71	458
Karihapah	28	m	i	CA	Fresno	Millerton P O	72	171
Kartui	45	m	i	CA	Fresno	Millerton P O	72	173
Kaso	25	f	i	CA	Alameda	Murray Twp	68	106
Katchua	25	f	i	CA	Del Norte	Crescent Twp	71	457
Kate	28	f	i	CA	Fresno	Kings Rvr P O	72	204
Kate	25	f	i	CA	San Francisco	San Francisco P O	83	134
Kate	12	f	i	CA	Colusa	Spring Valley Twp	71	337
Kavor	25	m	i	CA	Fresno	Millerton P O	72	169
Kawne	30	m	i	CA	Fresno	Millerton P O	72	176
Keanosto	24	m	i	CA	Fresno	Millerton P O	72	187
Keel	35	m	i	CA	Colusa	Stony Crk Twp	71	328
Keena	61	m	i	CA	Fresno	Kings Rvr P O	72	205
Keross	46	f	i	CA	Colusa	Spring Valley Twp	71	343
Ketchup	30	m	i	CA	Del Norte	Crescent	71	467
Ketchup	25	m	i	CA	Del Norte	Crescent Twp	71	457
Ketoah	22	m	i	CA	Colusa	Spring Valley Twp	71	338
Kissumque	34	f	i	CA	Fresno	Millerton P O	72	177
Kitara	40	f	i	CA	Alameda	Murray Twp	68	103
Kitty	35	f	i	CA	Del Norte	Crescent Twp	71	458
Klaklie	30	f	i	CA	Del Norte	Crescent	71	467
Klanart	50	f	i	CA	Del Norte	Smith Rvr Twp	71	482
Koennah	54	m	i	CA	Fresno	Millerton P O	72	196
Kohowelett	25	m	i	CA	Fresno	Millerton P O	72	174
Kolcala	28	m	i	CA	Fresno	Millerton P O	72	177
Konokonoh	35	m	i	CA	Fresno	Millerton P O	72	176
Kooker	40	m	i	CA	Fresno	Millerton P O	72	191
Kowat	32	m	i	CA	Fresno	Millerton P O	72	190
Koweah	48	m	i	CA	Fresno	Kingston P O	72	221
Kowem	35	m	i	CA	Fresno	Millerton P O	72	173
Kuchitcha	25	f	i	CA	Fresno	Millerton P O	72	177
Kuska	60	m	i	CA	Del Norte	Smith Rvr Twp	71	481
Lafonso	55	m	i	----	Marin	Nicasio Twp	74	89
Lafonso	35	m	i	----	Marin	Nicasio Twp	74	89
Lahusatt	50	f	i	CA	Fresno	Millerton P O	72	179
Lalhane	60	f	i	CA	Fresno	Millerton P O	72	177
Lamoon	30	m	i	CA	Colusa	Stony Crk Twp	71	326
Lan	16	f	i	CA	San Francisco	San Francisco P O	83	321
Lasing	70	f	i	CA	Del Norte	Crescent	71	467
Laucisco	30	m	i	CA	Colusa	Colusa Twp	71	285
Laures	24	f	i	CA	Los Angeles	Los Angeles	73	501
Layelld	34	m	i	CA	Colusa	Spring Valley Twp	71	338
Lazy Bill	30	m	i	CA	Colusa	Grand Island	71	310
Lazzarus	22	m	i	----	Marin	No Twp Listed	74	89
Lee	21	m	i	CA	Colusa	Spring Valley Twp	71	337
Legan	14	m	i	OR	Sonoma	Salt Point	91	393
Leka	45	f	i	CA	Del Norte	Smith Rvr Twp	71	482
Lem	24	m	i	CA	Fresno	Kingston P O	72	223
Leonardo	40	m	i	CA	Napa	Napa Twp	75	74
Leonora	30	f	i	CA	San Diego	San Luis Rey	78	512
Lew	33	m	i	CA	Fresno	Millerton P O	72	186
Lilla	5	f	i	----	Marin	Point Reyes Twp	74	89
Lino	60	f	i	CA	Los Angeles	Los Angeles Twp	73	498
Lipta	40	f	i	CA	Del Norte	Happy Camp Twp	71	472
Liptmas	35	m	i	CA	Del Norte	Happy Camp Twp	71	472
Little Dick	20	m	i	CA	Del Norte	Smith Rvr Twp	71	481
Lizzettea	24	m	i	CA	Fresno	Millerton P O	72	196
Lizzie	60	m	i	CA	Colusa	Stony Crk Twp	71	334
Lockhock	45	m	i	CA	Fresno	Millerton P O	72	177
Lohotma	40	f	i	CA	Del Norte	Crescent Twp	71	458
Lohures	50	m	i	CA	Alameda	Murray Twp	68	106
Lol	35	m	i	CA	Yolo	Buckeye Twp	93	412
Lom	28	m	i	CA	Fresno	Kings Rvr P O	72	209
Lomio	40	f	i	CA	Yolo	Buckeye Twp	93	412
Lonanah	41	f	i	CA	Fresno	Millerton P O	72	198
Lonely Jack	30	m	i	CA	Del Norte	Crescent Twp	71	461
Loney	30	m	i	CA	Colusa	Stony Crk Twp	71	331
Long Adams	20	m	i	CA	Del Norte	Smith Rvr Twp	71	480
Long Tom	40	m	i	CA	Colusa	Stony Crk Twp	71	331
Lonoha	48	f	i	CA	Fresno	Kings Rvr P O	72	209
Loren	35	m	i	CA	Colusa	Stony Crk Twp	71	326
Lorenz	70	m	i	CA	Alameda	Murray Twp	68	106
Lorenzo	21	m	i	CA	Colusa	Butte Twp	71	270
Lot	80	m	i	CA	Yolo	Buckeye Twp	93	412
Lot Louse	60	m	i	CA	Del Norte	Smith Rvr Twp	71	481
Loue	30	m	i	CA	Colusa	Monroe Twp	71	317
Louis	35	m	i	CA	Del Norte	Smith Rvr Twp	71	482
Louis	30	m	i	CA	Del Norte	Crescent Twp	71	460
Louis	25	m	i	CA	Yolo	Buckeye Twp	93	412
Louisa	24	f	i	CA	Los Angeles	Los Angeles	73	500
Louisa	23	f	i	CA	Los Angeles	Los Angeles	73	501
Louisa	2	f	i	----	Marin	Point Reyes Twp	74	89
Louriance	40	m	i	CA	Monterey	Monterey Twp	74	344
Loutham	35	f	i	CA	Fresno	Millerton P O	72	172
Lucas	14	m	i	CA	Monterey	Alisal Twp	74	289
Luciano	65	m	i	MEXI	Santa Barbara	San Buenaventura P	87	429
Lucus	70	m	i	CA	Alameda	Murray Twp	68	106
Lucy	50	m	i	CA	Del Norte	Crescent Twp	71	460
Lucy	35	f	i	CA	Del Norte	Crescent Twp	71	454
Lucy	26	f	i	CA	Colusa	Stony Crk Twp	71	334
Lucy	19	f	i	CA	Napa	Yountville Twp	75	77
Luis	6	m	i	CA	Los Angeles	Los Angeles Twp	73	498
Luke	13	m	i	CA	Sacramento	Dry Crk Twp	77	103
Lulla	25	f	i	CA	Del Norte	Crescent Twp	71	458
Lurey	23	m	i	CA	Fresno	Kingston P O	72	221
Lusa	65	f	i	CA	Del Norte	Smith Rvr Twp	71	482
Lusema	70	m	i	CA	Del Norte	Smith Rvr Twp	71	482
Luterio	50	m	i	CA	Santa Barbara	Las Cruces P O	87	506
M?ooles	35	m	i	CA	Colusa	Spring Valley Twp	71	338
Macan	25	m	i	CA	Del Norte	Crescent Twp	71	458
Macey	30	m	i	CA	Fresno	Kings Rvr P O	72	208

© 2001 by Heritage Quest. All rights reserved.

Series M593

Name	Age	S	R	B-PL	County	Locale	Roll	Pg
Macks	32	m	i	CA	Fresno	Kingston P O	72	223
Magan	60	m	i	CA	Del Norte	Crescent Twp	71	460
Magell	45	m	i	CA	Colusa	Stony Crk Twp	71	326
Maggie	22	m	i	CA	Colusa	Stony Crk Twp	71	326
Maggie	20	f	i	CA	Yolo	Buckeye Twp	93	412
Magill	24	m	i	CA	Colusa	Colusa Twp	71	285
Magney	34	m	i	----	Marin	No Twp Listed	74	89
Maguaunus	50	m	i	CA	Del Norte	Crescent Twp	71	457
Mahaheetta	20	f	i	CA	Fresno	Kings Rvr P O	72	208
Mahaletta	50	f	i	CA	Fresno	Kings Rvr P O	72	208
Mahalot	43	m	i	CA	Fresno	Kingston P O	72	224
Majincle	18	m	i	CA	Del Norte	Crescent Twp	71	454
Major	30	m	i	CA	Fresno	Kings Rvr P O	72	210
Malutt	20	f	i	CA	Fresno	Millerton P O	72	169
Mamville	25	f	i	CA	Colusa	Stony Crk Twp	71	334
Manewall	35	m	i	CA	Colusa	Stony Crk Twp	71	328
Mangrow	38	m	i	CA	Fresno	Kings Rvr P O	72	206
Manishwa	64	m	i	CA	Fresno	Kingston P O	72	223
Manserace	30	m	i	CA	Los Angeles	Los Angeles Twp	73	498
Manuel	90	m	i	CA	Yolo	Buckeye Twp	93	412
Manuel	60	m	i	CA	Monterey	Monterey Twp	74	344
Manuel	45	m	i	CA	Yolo	Buckeye Twp	93	412
Manuel	35	m	i	CA	Monterey	San Antonio Twp	74	322
Manuel	30	m	i	MEXI	Los Angeles	Los Angeles Twp	73	498
Manuel	22	m	i	----	Marin	No Twp Listed	74	89
Manuel	16	m	i	CA	San Luis Obispo	San Luis Obispo Tw	87	308
Manul	40	m	i	CA	Fresno	Millerton P O	72	177
Manutah	38	m	i	CA	Fresno	Millerton P O	72	190
Mapto	20	m	i	CA	Alameda	Murray Twp	68	106
Marcus	6	m	i	CA	Napa	Napa Twp	75	74
Margarita	30	f	i	----	Marin	Point Reyes Twp	74	89
Maria	90	f	i	----	Marin	Nicasio Twp	74	89
Maria	6M	f	i	----	Marin	Novato Twp	74	89
Maria	6M	f	i	----	Marin	Sausalito Twp	74	89
Maria	5	f	i	CA	Los Angeles	Los Angeles Twp	73	498
Maria	45	f	i	----	Marin	Point Reyes Twp	74	89
Maria	45	f	i	CA	Los Angeles	Los Angeles	73	500
Maria	30	f	i	----	Marin	Bolinas Twp	74	89
Maria	30	f	i	CA	Colusa	Stony Crk Twp	71	334
Maria	30	f	i	CA	Los Angeles	Los Angeles	73	500
Maria	30	f	i	CA	Los Angeles	Los Angeles Twp	73	498
Maria	30	f	i	MEXI	Los Angeles	Los Angeles Twp	73	498
Maria	25	f	i	CA	Los Angeles	Los Angeles	73	500
Maria	25	f	i	CA	Los Angeles	Los Angeles	73	501
Maria	24	f	i	CA	Los Angeles	Los Angeles	73	500
Maria	21	f	i	CA	San Francisco	San Francisco P O	83	134
Maria	20	f	i	CA	Colusa	Colusa Twp	71	285
Maria	18	f	i	CA	San Diego	San Luis Rey	78	512
Maria	1	f	i	CA	Los Angeles	Los Angeles	73	500
Maria Antonia	7	f	i	CA	San Diego	San Luis Rey	78	512
Maria Jose	38	m	i	----	Marin	Nicasio Twp	74	89
Maria Los Angeles	30	f	i	CA	Monterey	Monterey Twp	74	345
Maria Madelana	36	f	i	CA	Monterey	Monterey Twp	74	345
Maria R	47	f	i	CA	Santa Barbara	San Buenaventura P	87	432
Maria Ygnacia	90	f	i	CA	Monterey	Monterey Twp	74	345
Mariano	50	m	i	CA	Monterey	San Antonio Twp	74	318
Marker	42	m	i	CA	Colusa	Stony Crk Twp	71	334
Marmot	45	m	i	CA	Del Norte	Crescent Twp	71	458
Marohana	48	m	i	CA	Fresno	Millerton P O	72	198
Marta	17	f	i	MEXI	Alameda	Murray Twp	68	103
Martha	16	f	i	CA	Colusa	Butte Twp	71	270
Martin	16	m	i	CA	Colusa	Monroe Twp	71	317
Martinez	50	m	i	MEXI	Los Angeles	Los Angeles Twp	73	498
Martino	30	m	i	----	Marin	Tomales Twp	74	89
Martwheep	40	m	i	CA	Fresno	Millerton P O	72	196
Mary	60	f	i	CA	Yolo	Cottonwood Twp	93	474
Mary	40	f	i	CA	Colusa	Stony Crk Twp	71	328
Mary	35	f	i	CA	Del Norte	Crescent Twp	71	460
Mary	32	f	i	CA	Yolo	Cottonwood Twp	93	470
Mary	30	f	i	----	Marin	Nicasio Twp	74	89
Mary	30	f	i	CA	Colusa	Stony Crk Twp	71	329
Mary	25	f	i	CA	Yolo	Grafton Twp	93	484
Mary	25	f	i	CA	Del Norte	Crescent Twp	71	455
Mary	25	f	i	CA	Del Norte	Crescent Twp	71	458
Mary	21	f	i	CA	Colusa	Butte Twp	71	270
Mary	20	f	i	CA	Del Norte	Crescent Twp	71	455
Mary	20	m	i	CA	Colusa	Stony Crk Twp	71	326
Mary	20	f	i	CA	Del Norte	Happy Camp Twp	71	472
Mary	20	f	i	CA	Del Norte	Happy Camp Twp	71	472
Mary	18	f	i	CA	Yolo	Buckeye Twp	93	412
Mary	18	f	i	CA	Humboldt	Table Bluff Twp	72	308
Mary	18	f	i	CA	Del Norte	Happy Camp Twp	71	473
Mary	18	f	i	CA	Del Norte	Happy Camp Twp	71	472
Mary	18	f	i	CA	Del Norte	Crescent Twp	71	460
Mary	16	f	i	CA	Del Norte	Crescent Twp	71	460
Mary	14	f	i	CA	Humboldt	Eureka Twp	72	261
Mary	14	f	i	CA	Humboldt	Eureka Twp	72	262
Mary	14	f	i	CA	Del Norte	Happy Camp Twp	71	473
Mary	14	f	i	CA	Del Norte	Smith Rvr Twp	71	483
Mary	12	f	i	CA	Colusa	Colusa Twp	71	285
Mary	12	f	i	CA	Los Angeles	Los Angeles	73	500
Mary	11	f	i	CA	Humboldt	Eureka Twp	72	261
Mary	11	f	i	CA	Del Norte	Smith Rvr Twp	71	482
Maryanna	20	f	i	CA	Colusa	Stony Crk Twp	71	326
Maryannie	18	f	i	CA	Colusa	Stony Crk Twp	71	326
Masamoha	34	m	i	CA	Fresno	Millerton P O	72	195
Masoo	50	m	i	CA	Fresno	Millerton P O	72	172
Masoo	20	m	i	CA	Fresno	Millerton P O	72	173
Massahat	38	m	i	CA	Fresno	Millerton P O	72	195
Mastoo	70	f	i	CA	Fresno	Millerton P O	72	169
Mastra	5	m	i	CA	Napa	Napa Twp	75	74
Masut	18	f	i	CA	Fresno	Millerton P O	72	169
Mathias	15	m	i	CA	Napa	Napa Twp	75	66
Matias	45	m	i	CA	Los Angeles	Los Angeles	73	500
Matilda	14	f	i	CA	Los Angeles	Los Angeles	73	501
Mawema	65	m	i	CA	Del Norte	Smith Rvr Twp	71	482
Mawemas	70	m	i	CA	Del Norte	Smith Rvr Twp	71	481
Mawemas	50	m	i	CA	Del Norte	Happy Camp Twp	71	472
Mawemas	50	m	i	CA	Del Norte	Crescent Twp	71	457
May	20	f	i	CA	Colusa	Monroe Twp	71	322
May	11	f	i	CA	Humboldt	Eureka Twp	72	262
Meannie	25	f	i	CA	Colusa	Grand Island	71	310
Meguiel	12	m	i	CA	Los Angeles	Los Angeles	73	500
Mejawat	25	f	i	CA	Fresno	Millerton P O	72	172
Meluel	35	m	i	CA	Fresno	Millerton P O	72	172
Mendoza	30	m	i	----	Marin	Bolinas Twp	74	89
Mercalomah	64	m	i	CA	Fresno	Kingston P O	72	217
Merito	40	m	i	MEXI	Alameda	Murray Twp	68	103
Mersed	35	f	i	CA	Monterey	Monterey	74	362
Message	25	m	i	CA	Del Norte	Crescent Twp	71	457
Metser	35	m	i	CA	Del Norte	Crescent Twp	71	459
Mickle	23	m	i	CA	Colusa	Stony Crk Twp	71	331
Micks	30	m	i	CA	Colusa	Grand Island	71	310
Miggie	45	m	i	CA	Del Norte	Crescent	71	467
Miguel	21	m	i	CA	Santa Barbara	San Buenaventura P	87	428
Miguel	20	m	i	CA	Los Angeles	Los Angeles Twp	73	498
Minapich	64	m	i	CA	Fresno	Kings Rvr P O	72	216
Minencee	55	m	i	CA	Colusa	Butte Twp	71	270
Minihaha	18	f	i	CA	San Francisco	6-Wd San Francisco	81	93
Minrod	21	m	i	CA	Fresno	Kings Rvr P O	72	210
Mittama	25	m	i	CA	Del Norte	Smith Rvr Twp	71	482
Mochell	48	m	i	CA	Fresno	Millerton P O	72	190
Mockcha	65	m	i	CA	Fresno	Millerton P O	72	189
Mockehetah	65	m	i	CA	Fresno	Kings Rvr P O	72	205
Mockshaw	56	m	i	CA	Fresno	Kingston P O	72	217
Mocksun	50	m	i	CA	Fresno	Kings Rvr P O	72	208
Mocsai	70	f	i	CA	Fresno	Millerton P O	72	180
Mohajatts	50	m	i	CA	Fresno	Millerton P O	72	179
Mohawk	33	m	i	CA	Fresno	Millerton P O	72	190
Moleta	30	m	i	CA	Colusa	Stony Crk Twp	71	327
Molly	40	f	i	CA	Yolo	Grafton Twp	93	484
Monace	17	f	i	CA	Alameda	Murray Twp	68	103
Monah	30	m	i	CA	Fresno	Millerton P O	72	178
Monarcha	36	f	i	PA	Trinity	Weaverville Pct	92	227
Monetra	40	m	i	CA	Alameda	Murray Twp	68	106
Monkey	30	m	i	CA	Del Norte	Smith Rvr Twp	71	482
Monomah	27	m	i	CA	Fresno	Millerton P O	72	198
Monosonry	40	m	i	CA	San Luis Obispo	Salinas Twp	87	292
Morenita	25	f	i	CA	Los Angeles	Los Angeles Twp	73	498
Morgan	26	m	i	CA	Fresno	Millerton P O	72	187
Morin	18	f	i	MEXI	Alameda	Murray Twp	68	103
Morissa	35	m	i	CA	Colusa	Stony Crk Twp	71	331
Mose	50	m	i	CA	Colusa	Monroe Twp	71	317
Mose	24	m	i	CA	Fresno	Kingston P O	72	223
Mose	20	m	i	CA	Colusa	Monroe Twp	71	317
Motartene	34	m	i	CA	Fresno	Millerton P O	72	178
Mowahwah	25	m	i	CA	Fresno	Millerton P O	72	172
Moziner	40	f	i	CA	Colusa	Stony Crk Twp	71	326
Muckwash	22	m	i	CA	Fresno	Kings Rvr P O	72	215
Muroho	72	m	i	CA	Fresno	Kings Rvr P O	72	210
Murook	50	f	i	CA	Colusa	Spring Valley Twp	71	343
Muscovero	30	m	i	MEXI	Alameda	Murray Twp	68	103
Mustash	50	m	i	CA	Fresno	Kings Rvr P O	72	208
Nahalt	15	m	i	CA	Del Norte	Crescent Twp	71	458
Napamepa	50	m	i	CA	Fresno	Millerton P O	72	171
Napolemo	10	m	i	----	Marin	Nicasio Twp	74	89
Napoleon	34	m	i	CA	Fresno	Millerton P O	72	191
Nash	50	m	i	CA	Del Norte	Smith Rvr Twp	71	481
Nason	25	m	i	CA	Del Norte	Crescent Twp	71	460
Natapa	45	m	i	CA	Fresno	Millerton P O	72	172
Nattie	40	f	i	CA	Del Norte	Crescent Twp	71	458
Naugurade	50	f	i	CA	Del Norte	Crescent Twp	71	454
Neck	30	m	i	CA	Fresno	Millerton P O	72	183
Necosh	65	m	i	CA	Fresno	Kingston P O	72	222
Necosh	23	m	i	CA	Fresno	Millerton P O	72	188
Ned	50	m	i	CA	Colusa	Butte Twp	71	270
Ned	40	m	i	CA	Fresno	Millerton P O	72	197
Ned	40	m	i	CA	Del Norte	Smith Rvr Twp	71	482
Ned	36	m	i	CA	Fresno	Millerton P O	72	197
Ned	31	m	i	CA	Fresno	Millerton P O	72	183
Ned	30	m	i	CA	Fresno	Millerton P O	72	184
Ned	28	m	i	CA	Fresno	Millerton P O	72	192
Ned	23	m	i	CA	Fresno	Millerton P O	72	182
Neeockee	53	m	i	CA	Fresno	Millerton P O	72	184
Nellie	30	f	i	CA	Colusa	Stony Crk Twp	71	331
Nellie	10	f	i	CA	Colusa	Stony Crk Twp	71	332
Nemanchio	61	m	i	CA	Fresno	Kings Rvr P O	72	215
Nenohow	22	f	i	CA	Fresno	Millerton P O	72	178
Neppotas	30	m	i	CA	Fresno	Millerton P O	72	198
Neppy	46	m	i	CA	Fresno	Millerton P O	72	185
Nerweris	12	f	i	CA	Del Norte	Crescent Twp	71	457
Newsul	26	m	i	CA	Colusa	Spring Valley Twp	71	338
Nhotah	60	m	i	CA	Fresno	Millerton P O	72	170
Nic	50	m	i	CA	Yolo	Buckeye Twp	93	412

© 2001 by Heritage Quest. All rights reserved.

Name	Age	S	R	B-PL	County	Locale	Roll	Pg
						Series M593		
Nick	40	m	i	CA	Colusa	Stony Crk Twp	71	326
Nick	30	m	i	CA	Fresno	Kings Rvr P O	72	213
Nick	16	m	i	CA	Colusa	Stony Crk Twp	71	334
Nickowa	22	m	i	CA	Fresno	Kingston P O	72	223
Nicolaus	7	m	i	----	Marin	Bolinas Twp	74	89
Nicolaus	60	m	i	----	Marin	No Twp Listed	74	89
Nimpha	2	f	i	----	Marin	Bolinas Twp	74	89
Nippy	21	m	i	CA	Fresno	Millerton P O	72	198
Niptuck	31	m	i	CA	Fresno	Kings Rvr P O	72	215
Nocklas	50	m	i	CA	Del Norte	Happy Camp Twp	71	472
Nolberto	35	m	i	CA	San Diego	San Luis Rey	78	512
Nomaha	51	m	i	CA	Fresno	Millerton P O	72	186
Nomoho	50	f	i	CA	Fresno	Kings Rvr P O	72	213
Nonan	25	f	i	CA	Del Norte	Crescent Twp	71	454
Nonsemah	60	m	i	CA	Del Norte	Crescent Twp	71	460
Noonan	18	f	i	CA	Del Norte	Crescent Twp	71	454
Nosiech	23	m	i	CA	Fresno	Kings Rvr P O	72	207
Nosikah	68	f	i	CA	Fresno	Kings Rvr P O	72	205
Nullpeco	50	m	i	CA	Colusa	Stony Crk Twp	71	328
Nuwash	36	m	i	CA	Fresno	Kings Rvr P O	72	215
Obrien	30	m	i	CA	Fresno	Kingston P O	72	221
Oceola	45	m	i	CA	Del Norte	Crescent Twp	71	459
Ochumlat	20	f	i	CA	Fresno	Millerton P O	72	178
Ockchawe	51	m	i	CA	Fresno	Millerton P O	72	192
Ocoksee	35	f	i	CA	Fresno	Millerton P O	72	170
Ofracia	36	f	i	----	Marin	Point Reyes Twp	74	89
Ohbin	34	m	i	CA	Fresno	Kings Rvr P O	72	207
Oheman	25	m	i	CA	Fresno	Millerton P O	72	172
Ohmeenah	38	m	i	CA	Fresno	Millerton P O	72	190
Ohnaho	56	f	i	CA	Fresno	Kings Rvr P O	72	208
Old Adams	50	m	i	CA	Del Norte	Smith Rvr Twp	71	480
Old Asick	60	m	i	CA	Del Norte	Smith Rvr Twp	71	482
Old Bela	60	f	i	CA	Del Norte	Smith Rvr Twp	71	482
Old Bill	43	m	i	CA	Fresno	Millerton P O	72	197
Old Bill	43	m	i	CA	Fresno	Kingston P O	72	223
Old Billy	30	m	i	CA	Del Norte	Crescent Twp	71	460
Old Bob	50	m	i	CA	Del Norte	Crescent Twp	71	460
Old Clutchman	70	f	i	CA	Del Norte	Smith Rvr Twp	71	483
Old Doctor	65	m	i	CA	Del Norte	Crescent Twp	71	460
Old Dolly	50	f	i	CA	Del Norte	Smith Rvr Twp	71	482
Old Grimes	65	m	i	CA	Del Norte	Smith Rvr Twp	71	482
Old Jane	50	f	i	CA	Del Norte	Smith Rvr Twp	71	482
Old Jim	60	m	i	CA	Colusa	Monroe Twp	71	323
Old Kentrick	70	m	i	CA	Del Norte	Smith Rvr Twp	71	482
Old Lucy	60	f	i	CA	Del Norte	Crescent Twp	71	454
Old Mike	70	m	i	CA	Del Norte	Smith Rvr Twp	71	479
Old Molly	56	f	i	CA	Fresno	Millerton P O	72	191
Old Peggie	45	f	i	CA	Del Norte	Smith Rvr Twp	71	483
Old Peggy	65	f	i	CA	Del Norte	Crescent Twp	71	458
Old Pennie	50	f	i	CA	Del Norte	Crescent Twp	71	458
Old Phil	60	m	i	CA	Del Norte	Crescent Twp	71	459
Old Phophet	60	m	i	CA	Del Norte	Happy Camp Twp	71	472
Old Sam	46	m	i	CA	Fresno	Millerton P O	72	197
Old Scrub	60	m	i	CA	Fresno	Millerton P O	72	190
Old Slocum	63	m	i	CA	Fresno	Millerton P O	72	195
Old Squaw	70	f	i	CA	Del Norte	Smith Rvr Twp	71	482
Old Squaw	65	f	i	CA	Del Norte	Smith Rvr Twp	71	482
Old Squaw	65	f	i	CA	Del Norte	Smith Rvr Twp	71	482
Old Squaw	60	f	i	CA	Del Norte	Smith Rvr Twp	71	481
Old Squaw	50	f	i	CA	Del Norte	Smith Rvr Twp	71	480
Old Squaw	50	f	i	CA	Del Norte	Happy Camp Twp	71	472
Old Tom	50	m	i	CA	Del Norte	Crescent Twp	71	460
Old Tom	45	m	i	CA	Fresno	Kings Rvr P O	72	207
Oltewitch	50	m	i	CA	Fresno	Millerton P O	72	178
Olympia	90	f	i	----	Marin	Tomales Twp	74	89
Omut	38	m	i	CA	Fresno	Millerton P O	72	169
One Eyed Rily	25	m	i	CA	Del Norte	Crescent	71	466
Oneil	40	m	i	CA	Fresno	Kings Rvr P O	72	216
Onita	15	f	i	CA	San Francisco	7-Wd San Francisco	81	245
Ontahkinoson	75	m	i	CA	Del Norte	Crescent Twp	71	461
Opimia	130	f	i	CA	Monterey	Monterey Twp	74	345
Oput	18	m	i	CA	Fresno	Millerton P O	72	169
Ordon	50	m	i	CA	Los Angeles	Los Angeles Twp	73	498
Osackao	34	m	i	CA	Fresno	Millerton P O	72	185
Osbe	6	m	i	MEXI	Alameda	Murray Twp	68	103
Oscar	20	m	i	CA	Del Norte	Crescent Twp	71	456
Oser	45	m	i	CA	Del Norte	Happy Camp Twp	71	472
Osker	35	m	i	CA	Del Norte	Crescent Twp	71	459
Osker	30	m	i	CA	Del Norte	Crescent Twp	71	458
Oso	30	f	i	MEXI	Alameda	Murray Twp	68	103
Ossomotta	30	m	i	CA	Fresno	Millerton P O	72	198
Ostta	18	m	i	CA	Del Norte	Happy Camp Twp	71	472
Otaga	14	m	i	CA	Los Angeles	Los Angeles Twp	73	498
Otaro	7	f	i	CA	Los Angeles	Los Angeles Twp	73	498
Ottoche	22	m	i	CA	Fresno	Millerton P O	72	177
Ottowat	53	m	i	CA	Fresno	Millerton P O	72	192
Otuejuch	30	f	i	CA	Fresno	Millerton P O	72	179
Overah	40	f	i	CA	Fresno	Millerton P O	72	197
Paakizoh	40	m	i	CA	Fresno	Millerton P O	72	173
Paasoo	50	m	i	CA	Fresno	Millerton P O	72	171
Pablo	35	m	i	CA	Los Angeles	Los Angeles Twp	73	498
Pachtan	25	m	i	CA	Fresno	Millerton P O	72	179
Pachtaw	20	m	i	CA	Fresno	Millerton P O	72	171
Pacifico	26	m	i	----	Marin	No Twp Listed	74	89
Pacifico	20	m	i	CA	Los Angeles	Los Angeles	73	500
Palcopa	35	m	i	CA	Los Angeles	Los Angeles Twp	73	498
Palsah	45	f	i	CA	Fresno	Millerton P O	72	177
Panasker	45	m	i	CA	Fresno	Millerton P O	72	173
Park	20	m	i	CA	Del Norte	Happy Camp Twp	71	472
Parola	36	f	i	CA	Los Angeles	Los Angeles Twp	73	498
Parscher	25	m	i	CA	Fresno	Millerton P O	72	174
Patchew	25	m	i	CA	Fresno	Millerton P O	72	175
Pathuce	25	m	i	CA	Fresno	Millerton P O	72	178
Patricio	35	m	i	CA	San Diego	San Luis Rey	78	512
Patrino	1	m	i	----	Marin	Nicasio Twp	74	89
Pauchan	28	m	i	CA	Fresno	Millerton P O	72	180
Paughnoes	15	f	i	CA	Del Norte	Happy Camp Twp	71	471
Paul	23	m	i	CA	Fresno	Kings Rvr P O	72	208
Paysmel	55	f	i	CA	Del Norte	Crescent Twp	71	458
Peacock Bill	25	m	i	CA	Del Norte	Smith Rvr Twp	71	480
Pedro	42	m	i	CA	Los Angeles	Los Angeles	73	500
Pedro	40	f	i	CA	Alameda	Murray Twp	68	106
Pedro	38	m	i	CA	Los Angeles	Los Angeles	73	500
Pedro	35	m	i	CA	Los Angeles	Los Angeles Twp	73	498
Pedro	26	m	i	CA	San Diego	San Luis Rey	78	512
Pedro	19	m	i	CA	Los Angeles	Los Angeles	73	500
Pedro	18	m	i	CA	Los Angeles	Los Angeles	73	500
Peggy	23	f	i	CA	Klamath	Salmon Twp	73	387
Pelamhat	40	f	i	CA	Fresno	Millerton P O	72	177
Pelenrehal	50	f	i	CA	Fresno	Millerton P O	72	174
Pellean	42	m	i	CA	Fresno	Kings Rvr P O	72	204
Peltopa	19	m	i	CA	Colusa	Spring Valley Twp	71	338
Pemonah	20	m	i	CA	Fresno	Millerton P O	72	175
Perry	65	f	i	CA	Del Norte	Crescent Twp	71	458
Pesatah	30	m	i	CA	Fresno	Millerton P O	72	175
Pete	50	m	i	CA	Yolo	Grafton Twp	93	479
Pete	13	m	i	CA	Yolo	Cottonwood Twp	93	470
Peter	35	m	i	CA	Colusa	Grand Island	71	310
Phil	20	m	i	CA	Del Norte	Happy Camp Twp	71	472
Picaniche	49	m	i	CA	Fresno	Millerton P O	72	182
Pike	16	m	i	CA	Colusa	Monroe Twp	71	323
Pinto	18	m	i	CA	Yolo	Grafton Twp	93	489
Pishwash	34	m	i	CA	Fresno	Millerton P O	72	181
Pitchelow	35	m	i	CA	Fresno	Millerton P O	72	178
Pocoesor	30	m	i	CA	Fresno	Millerton P O	72	174
Pogornches	40	m	i	CA	Fresno	Millerton P O	72	172
Poholin	50	m	i	CA	Fresno	Millerton P O	72	172
Poholowtech	45	m	i	CA	Fresno	Millerton P O	72	177
Pohosick	35	m	i	CA	Fresno	Millerton P O	72	173
Pohosick	20	m	i	CA	Fresno	Millerton P O	72	169
Polimino	46	m	i	----	Marin	No Twp Listed	74	89
Poliss	28	m	i	CA	Fresno	Kingston P O	72	217
Polly	50	f	i	CA	Del Norte	Crescent Twp	71	460
Polly	50	m	i	CA	Del Norte	Crescent Twp	71	460
Polly	5	f	i	CA	Del Norte	Smith Rvr Twp	71	482
Polly	30	f	i	CA	Del Norte	Smith Rvr Twp	71	482
Polly	20	m	i	CA	Del Norte	Happy Camp Twp	71	472
Polly	20	f	i	CA	Del Norte	Happy Camp Twp	71	473
Polly	14	f	i	CA	Del Norte	Crescent Twp	71	455
Pololeno	60	m	i	CA	Fresno	Millerton P O	72	173
Pomico	55	m	i	CA	Yolo	Grafton Twp	93	484
Ponatche	30	m	i	CA	Fresno	Millerton P O	72	175
Poncho	30	m	i	----	Marin	Nicasio Twp	74	89
Poncho	30	m	i	----	Marin	Point Reyes Twp	74	89
Poohee	45	f	i	CA	Fresno	Millerton P O	72	178
Poorama	42	f	i	CA	Colusa	Spring Valley Twp	71	343
Popeai	23	m	i	CA	Fresno	Kings Rvr P O	72	203
Porecel	30	m	i	MEXI	Alameda	Murray Twp	68	103
Porkillo	6	m	i	----	Marin	Nicasio Twp	74	89
Porote	40	m	i	CA	Alameda	Murray Twp	68	103
Posgal	40	m	i	CA	Alameda	Murray Twp	68	103
Potortoo	35	m	i	CA	Fresno	Millerton P O	72	169
Powhemaii	50	f	i	CA	Fresno	Millerton P O	72	175
Procopia	10	m	i	CA	Los Angeles	Los Angeles Twp	73	498
Prudencia	21	f	i	----	Marin	Bolinas Twp	74	89
Pucha	47	m	i	CA	Colusa	Spring Valley Twp	71	338
Punch	22	m	i	CA	Butte	Mountain Spring Tw	70	90
Queanah	28	m	i	CA	Fresno	Millerton P O	72	186
Quin Taw	25	m	i	CA	Del Norte	Smith Rvr Twp	71	481
Rafael	85	m	i	CA	Los Angeles	Los Angeles Twp	73	498
Rafael	35	m	i	CA	Los Angeles	Los Angeles Twp	73	498
Rafella	14	f	i	----	Marin	Nicasio Twp	74	89
Raffell	30	m	i	CA	Colusa	Monroe Twp	71	322
Rainmando	12	m	i	CA	San Diego	San Luis Rey	78	512
Ramon	8	f	i	CA	Napa	Napa Twp	75	74
Ramon	20	m	i	MEXI	Los Angeles	Los Angeles Twp	73	498
Ramon	16	m	i	CA	Los Angeles	Los Angeles Twp	73	498
Ramon	15	m	i	MEXI	Los Angeles	Los Angeles Twp	73	498
Rasoss	40	m	i	CA	Colusa	Stony Crk Twp	71	334
Reacher	40	m	i	CA	Del Norte	Crescent Twp	71	458
Rebecca	20	f	i	CA	Napa	Napa Twp	75	66
Redsaw	30	m	i	CA	Del Norte	Crescent Twp	71	459
Refugia	35	f	i	CA	Los Angeles	Los Angeles Twp	73	498
Refugia	30	f	i	MEXI	Los Angeles	Los Angeles	73	500
Refugio	35	m	i	CA	Los Angeles	Los Angeles	73	500
Refugio	14	m	i	CA	Los Angeles	Los Angeles	73	500
Restaka	40	m	i	CA	Fresno	Kings Rvr P O	72	215
Reuben	38	m	i	CA	Fresno	Millerton P O	72	198
Richd	23	m	i	CA	Fresno	Millerton P O	72	185
Ricorswa	20	f	i	CA	Del Norte	Crescent Twp	71	457
Rigutor	18	f	i	CA	Humboldt	Arcata Twp	72	233
Riley	18	m	i	CA	Colusa	Monroe Twp	71	317
Rinder	22	m	i	CA	Fresno	Kings Rvr P O	72	206
Rita	21	f	i	CA	Los Angeles	Los Angeles	73	500

© 2001 by Heritage Quest. All rights reserved.

California 1870 Census

Name	Age	S	R	B-PL	County	Locale	Roll	Pg
Robert	11	m	i	CA	Lake	Lower Lake	73	422
Rodger	30	m	i	CA	Fresno	Kingston P O	72	223
Rodger	25	m	i	CA	Fresno	Millerton P O	72	190
Rodger	21	m	i	CA	Fresno	Kings Rvr P O	72	209
Roger	28	m	i	CA	Fresno	Kingston P O	72	222
Rogers	35	m	i	CA	Del Norte	Crescent Twp	71	457
Rokario	60	m	i	CA	Los Angeles	Los Angeles Twp	73	498
Roley	28	m	i	CA	Colusa	Monroe Twp	71	317
Romaldo	4	m	i	----	Marin	Point Reyes Twp	74	89
Roman	30	m	i	CA	San Diego	San Luis Rey	78	512
Ronudo	30	m	i	CA	Alameda	Murray Twp	68	106
Rosa	30	f	i	CA	Los Angeles	Los Angeles Twp	73	499
Rosa	30	f	i	CA	Los Angeles	Los Angeles	73	500
Rosa	28	f	i	CA	Santa Barbara	San Buenaventura P	87	428
Rosa	15	f	i	CA	Monterey	Monterey	74	364
Rosalie	30	f	i	CA	Yolo	Grafton Twp	93	484
Rosaria	24	f	i	CA	Los Angeles	Los Angeles	73	500
Rosario	60	f	i	CA	Napa	Napa Twp	75	74
Rosario	28	m	i	CA	Los Angeles	Los Angeles	73	501
Rosario	26	m	i	CA	Santa Barbara	San Buenaventura P	87	429
Rosena	21	f	i	CA	Alameda	Murray Twp	68	106
Rosinda	3	f	i	CA	Los Angeles	Los Angeles Twp	73	498
Roundhead	35	f	i	CA	Del Norte	Smith Rvr Twp	71	482
Roxey	50	m	i	CA	Colusa	Stony Crk Twp	71	329
Rube	34	m	i	CA	Fresno	Kings Rvr P O	72	210
Rube	32	m	i	CA	Fresno	Kingston P O	72	217
Rube	28	m	i	CA	Fresno	Kingston P O	72	222
Rube	23	m	i	CA	Fresno	Kingston P O	72	223
Rube	22	m	i	CA	Fresno	Millerton P O	72	185
Rufujie	18	f	i	CA	Monterey	Monterey	74	367
Rufus	34	m	i	CA	Fresno	Kings Rvr P O	72	210
Rumah	53	m	i	CA	Fresno	Millerton P O	72	196
Rupe	22	m	i	CA	Fresno	Millerton P O	72	190
Sabemah	60	m	i	CA	Fresno	Millerton P O	72	195
Sacar	35	m	i	CA	Colusa	Spring Valley Twp	71	338
Sack	50	m	i	CA	Yolo	Buckeye Twp	93	412
Sadonah	30	f	i	CA	Fresno	Millerton P O	72	175
Sagamah	45	m	i	CA	Del Norte	Crescent Twp	71	460
Sailleo	37	f	i	CA	Colusa	Spring Valley Twp	71	343
Sajanat	25	f	i	CA	Fresno	Millerton P O	72	171
Salale	30	m	i	CA	Fresno	Millerton P O	72	149
Sallie	45	f	i	CA	Colusa	Stony Crk Twp	71	329
Sallie	22	f	i	CA	Colusa	Spring Valley Twp	71	336
Sally	50	f	i	CA	Del Norte	Crescent Twp	71	460
Sally	45	f	i	CA	Del Norte	Crescent Twp	71	460
Sally	45	f	i	CA	Del Norte	Crescent Twp	71	459
Sally	45	f	i	CA	Yolo	Cache Crk Twp	93	428
Sally	40	f	i	CA	Del Norte	Smith Rvr Twp	71	481
Sally	40	f	i	CA	Del Norte	Happy Camp Twp	71	472
Sally	35	f	i	CA	Del Norte	Crescent Twp	71	455
Sally	33	f	i	CA	Fresno	Millerton P O	72	197
Sally	30	f	i	CA	Del Norte	Crescent Twp	71	455
Sally	25	f	i	CA	Del Norte	Crescent Twp	71	459
Sally	25	f	i	CA	Del Norte	Crescent Twp	71	460
Sally	25	f	i	CA	Del Norte	Happy Camp Twp	71	472
Sally	20	f	i	CA	Del Norte	Crescent Twp	71	459
Sally	18	f	i	CA	Del Norte	Crescent Twp	71	460
Sally	18	f	i	CA	Del Norte	Happy Camp Twp	71	473
Salmon Claw	40	m	i	CA	Del Norte	Crescent Twp	71	459
Salmon Mouth	25	m	i	CA	Del Norte	Smith Rvr Twp	71	480
Salvadore	28	m	i	----	Marin	No Twp Listed	74	89
Salvadoro	40	m	i	----	Marin	Tomales Twp	74	89
Salvadoro	40	m	i	----	Marin	Tomales Twp	74	89
Salvinio	45	m	i	----	Marin	Point Reyes Twp	74	89
Sam	55	m	i	CA	Colusa	Monroe Twp	71	322
Sam	44	m	i	CA	Fresno	Millerton P O	72	192
Sam	40	m	i	CA	Colusa	Grand Island	71	310
Sam	40	m	i	CA	Fresno	Millerton P O	72	175
Sam	38	m	i	CA	Fresno	Millerton P O	72	181
Sam	37	m	i	CA	Fresno	Kingston P O	72	221
Sam	35	m	i	CA	Colusa	Monroe Twp	71	322
Sam	35	m	i	CA	Fresno	Kings Rvr P O	72	213
Sam	33	m	i	CA	Fresno	Millerton P O	72	184
Sam	32	m	i	CA	Fresno	Millerton P O	72	189
Sam	32	m	i	CA	Fresno	Kingston P O	72	218
Sam	30	m	i	CA	Fresno	Kings Rvr P O	72	213
Sam	30	m	i	CA	Fresno	Millerton P O	72	196
Sam	30	m	i	CA	Fresno	Millerton P O	72	189
Sam	25	m	i	CA	Sacramento	Dry Crk Twp	77	104
Sam	23	m	i	CA	Sonoma	Salt Point	91	390
Sam	21	m	i	CA	Fresno	Kings Rvr P O	72	208
Sam	20	m	i	CA	Fresno	Millerton P O	72	197
Sam	15	m	i	CA	Colusa	Stony Crk Twp	71	331
Sam	14	m	i	CA	Humboldt	Table Bluff Twp	72	308
Sam	12	m	i	CA	Yolo	Grafton Twp	93	494
Samaco	42	m	i	CA	Fresno	Millerton P O	72	195
Sampler	24	m	i	CA	Fresno	Millerton P O	72	192
Sampson	41	m	i	CA	Fresno	Millerton P O	72	187
Sampson	30	m	i	CA	Fresno	Kings Rvr P O	72	206
Samshoe	56	m	i	CA	Fresno	Millerton P O	72	185
San Shor	18	m	i	CA	Colusa	Monroe Twp	71	315
Santa	45	m	i	CA	Butte	Bidwell Twp	70	2
Santos	47	m	i	MEXI	Santa Barbara	San Buenaventura P	87	442
Santos	16	m	i	----	Marin	Nicasio Twp	74	89
Santrey	25	m	i	CA	Alameda	Murray Twp	68	103
Sapp	45	f	i	CA	Del Norte	Crescent Twp	71	457
Sapua	40	f	i	CA	Del Norte	Crescent Twp	71	457

Name	Age	S	R	B-PL	County	Locale	Roll	Pg
Sarsahoe	35	m	i	CA	Fresno	Kings Rvr P O	72	210
Sarvo	72	m	i	CA	Fresno	Kings Rvr P O	72	206
Sathoie	45	m	i	CA	Fresno	Millerton P O	72	174
Saunders	34	m	i	CA	Fresno	Kingston P O	72	221
Savage	35	m	i	CA	Fresno	Millerton P O	72	174
Savajock	20	f	i	CA	Fresno	Millerton P O	72	170
Sawatyn	20	f	i	CA	Fresno	Millerton P O	72	177
Sawey	11	m	i	CA	Yolo	Putah Twp	93	516
Saxey	70	m	i	CA	Del Norte	Crescent Twp	71	459
Saxey	30	m	i	CA	Del Norte	Crescent Twp	71	459
Saygiva	13	f	i	CA	Del Norte	Crescent Twp	71	457
Scamp	20	m	i	CA	Del Norte	Crescent Twp	71	457
Schaneassca	30	m	i	CA	Fresno	Millerton P O	72	178
Scovalmo	40	m	i	CA	Colusa	Spring Valley Twp	71	338
Sebastian	70	m	i	----	Marin	Tomales Twp	74	89
Sedick	35	m	i	CA	Fresno	Millerton P O	72	177
Seekill	26	m	i	CA	Colusa	Spring Valley Twp	71	338
Seepakee	30	m	i	CA	Fresno	Millerton P O	72	172
Seki	14	m	i	CA	Monterey	Castroville Twp	74	341
Senchajaha	44	m	i	CA	Fresno	Millerton P O	72	196
Sewhejat	35	f	i	CA	Fresno	Millerton P O	72	179
Shack	12	m	i	CA	Yolo	Putah Twp	93	521
Shasta	30	f	i	CA	Del Norte	Smith Rvr Twp	71	480
Sheemuck	22	m	i	CA	Fresno	Kings Rvr P O	72	207
Shitkano	23	m	i	CA	Fresno	Millerton P O	72	189
Shitkill	47	m	i	CA	Fresno	Kings Rvr P O	72	209
Shitkill	30	m	i	CA	Fresno	Millerton P O	72	181
Shoetop	18	m	i	CA	Fresno	Millerton P O	72	182
Short John	35	m	i	CA	Colusa	Stony Crk Twp	71	331
Short Tom	40	m	i	CA	Colusa	Monroe Twp	71	317
Sicool	42	f	i	CA	Colusa	Spring Valley Twp	71	343
Simon	32	m	i	CA	Fresno	Kings Rvr P O	72	206
Sing Song	18	f	i	CA	Fresno	Kings Rvr P O	72	213
Singhee	18	m	i	CA	Fresno	Kings Rvr P O	72	207
Skena Joe	15	m	i	CA	Del Norte	Happy Camp Twp	71	473
Skety	45	f	i	CA	Del Norte	Smith Rvr Twp	71	483
Skow	30	m	i	CA	Del Norte	Crescent Twp	71	457
Skow	25	m	i	CA	Del Norte	Crescent	71	467
Skow	25	m	i	CA	Del Norte	Crescent Twp	71	457
Slickey	23	m	i	CA	Colusa	Grand Island	71	310
Slipa	35	m	i	CA	Colusa	Butte Twp	71	270
Snaton	14	f	i	CA	Del Norte	Smith Rvr Twp	71	482
Socatoh	40	m	i	CA	Fresno	Millerton P O	72	171
Socatoh	40	m	i	CA	Fresno	Millerton P O	72	171
Socheo	50	m	i	CA	Fresno	Millerton P O	72	171
Soitoo	40	m	i	CA	Fresno	Millerton P O	72	169
Sola	18	f	i	CA	Del Norte	Crescent Twp	71	459
Soldad	50	m	i	CA	Fresno	Millerton P O	72	189
Soldado	42	m	i	CA	Fresno	Kings Rvr P O	72	208
Soldado	28	m	i	CA	Fresno	Millerton P O	72	191
Solic	50	m	i	CA	Yolo	Grafton Twp	93	484
Solocomit	50	m	i	CA	Fresno	Millerton P O	72	170
Solome	60	f	i	CA	Monterey	Monterey	74	367
Sonata	14	f	i	----	Marin	Point Reyes Twp	74	89
Sooll	60	f	i	CA	Fresno	Millerton P O	72	173
Sopengreter	49	m	i	CA	Fresno	Millerton P O	72	181
Sopona	37	m	i	CA	Fresno	Millerton P O	72	188
Sosomat	31	m	i	CA	Fresno	Millerton P O	72	197
Soune	25	m	i	CA	Colusa	Spring Valley Twp	71	338
Spome	31	m	i	CA	Colusa	Spring Valley Twp	71	338
Sport	27	m	i	CA	Fresno	Millerton P O	72	190
Spot	30	m	i	CA	Del Norte	Crescent Twp	71	457
Spriggie	25	m	i	CA	Del Norte	Crescent Twp	71	456
Stan Claws	45	m	i	CA	Del Norte	Smith Rvr Twp	71	483
Startow	30	m	i	CA	Fresno	Kings Rvr P O	72	209
Statery	11	f	i	CA	Del Norte	Smith Rvr Twp	71	482
Steve	43	m	i	CA	Fresno	Millerton P O	72	181
Stuco	14	m	i	CA	Monterey	Alisal Twp	74	290
Succosuck	25	m	i	CA	Fresno	Millerton P O	72	170
Suckfock	53	m	i	CA	Fresno	Millerton P O	72	182
Suisul	25	m	i	CA	Fresno	Millerton P O	72	169
Sults	25	m	i	CA	Del Norte	Crescent Twp	71	456
Sumata	20	m	i	CA	Fresno	Millerton P O	72	197
Sumcul	60	m	i	CA	Fresno	Millerton P O	72	169
Sumooah	35	m	i	CA	Fresno	Kings Rvr P O	72	205
Sumuck	36	m	i	CA	Fresno	Kings Rvr P O	72	206
Sundy	15	m	i	CA	Yolo	Cache Crk Twp	93	437
Susa	14	f	i	CA	Los Angeles	Los Angeles	73	500
Susan	25	f	i	CA	Del Norte	Happy Camp Twp	71	473
Susan	25	f	i	CA	Yolo	Cottonwood Twp	93	474
Susan	23	f	i	CA	Fresno	Millerton P O	72	182
Susanna	40	m	i	CA	Colusa	Monroe Twp	71	317
Susanna	25	f	i	CA	Colusa	Stony Crk Twp	71	329
Susie	40	f	i	CA	Yolo	Grafton Twp	93	484
Susie	26	f	i	CA	Colusa	Stony Crk Twp	71	331
Susie	25	f	i	CA	Yolo	Cottonwood Twp	93	470
Susie	20	f	i	CA	Del Norte	Smith Rvr Twp	71	482
Susy	26	f	i	CA	Fresno	Millerton P O	72	195
Suto	65	m	i	CA	Alameda	Murray Twp	68	106
Swissiano	55	m	i	----	Marin	No Twp Listed	74	89
Sylvester	22	m	i	CA	San Diego	San Luis Rey	78	512
Tagire	50	m	i	CA	Del Norte	Crescent Twp	71	457
Tahro Colla	30	m	i	CA	Del Norte	Crescent Twp	71	460
Taimaiger	30	m	i	CA	Fresno	Millerton P O	72	172
Taitum	50	m	i	CA	Fresno	Millerton P O	72	172
Taklar	40	f	i	CA	Alameda	Murray Twp	68	106
Tally Ho	32	m	i	CA	Fresno	Kingston P O	72	224

Series M593

© 2001 by Heritage Quest. All rights reserved.

Series M593

Name	Age	S	R	B-PL	County	Locale	Roll	Pg
Tamahu	47	m	i	CA	Fresno	Millerton P O	72	190
Tamainee	25	m	i	CA	Fresno	Millerton P O	72	171
Tanavee	40	f	i	CA	Fresno	Millerton P O	72	176
Tanhart	28	m	i	CA	Fresno	Millerton P O	72	169
Tania	19	f	i	AK	San Francisco	6-Wd San Francisco	81	141
Tansan	20	m	i	CA	Del Norte	Crescent Twp	71	458
Tantine	50	m	i	CA	Fresno	Millerton P O	72	172
Tarcena	45	m	i	CA	Del Norte	Crescent Twp	71	457
Tarquist	80	m	i	CA	Del Norte	Smith Rvr Twp	71	481
Taska	35	m	i	CA	Del Norte	Crescent Twp	71	460
Taska	30	m	i	CA	Del Norte	Crescent Twp	71	458
Tauchopa	28	m	i	CA	Fresno	Kings Rvr P O	72	205
Tawonee	25	m	i	CA	Fresno	Millerton P O	72	171
Taylor	33	m	i	CA	Colusa	Stony Crk Twp	71	326
Te Lea	52	f	i	CA	Monterey	Monterey	74	360
Techner	45	f	i	CA	Del Norte	Crescent Twp	71	458
Telespard	25	m	i	CA	Los Angeles	Los Angeles Twp	73	498
Tenanton	70	m	i	CA	Del Norte	Smith Rvr Twp	71	482
Tennie	12	f	i	CA	Napa	Napa Twp	75	46
Tentura	19	f	i	----	Marin	Point Reyes Twp	74	89
Teodoro	34	m	i	----	Marin	Bolinas Twp	74	89
Tepeckuha	45	m	i	CA	Fresno	Millerton P O	72	175
Terah	28	m	i	CA	Del Norte	Crescent Twp	71	457
Teremes	95	m	i	----	Marin	Tomales Twp	74	89
Teresa	14	f	i	CA	Los Angeles	Los Angeles Twp	73	498
Texano	38	m	i	CA	Sonoma	Salt Point	91	381
Thaiatemary	26	f	i	CA	Fresno	Millerton P O	72	180
Thaiipaiie	25	f	i	CA	Fresno	Millerton P O	72	177
Thatchers	30	m	i	CA	Fresno	Kings Rvr P O	72	215
Theelaugma	40	f	i	CA	Fresno	Millerton P O	72	177
Theharac	20	m	i	CA	Fresno	Millerton P O	72	174
Thochoie	30	m	i	CA	Fresno	Millerton P O	72	173
Thohertoie	30	m	i	CA	Fresno	Millerton P O	72	179
Thomas	8	m	i	UT	Los Angeles	Los Angeles Twp	73	498
Thomas	20	m	i	CA	Colusa	Butte Twp	71	270
Thomenece	22	m	i	CA	Fresno	Millerton P O	72	180
Thompson	40	m	i	CA	Del Norte	Crescent Twp	71	456
Thompson	30	m	i	CA	Del Norte	Crescent Twp	71	459
Thompson	25	m	i	CA	Del Norte	Crescent Twp	71	458
Thoponock	46	m	i	CA	Fresno	Millerton P O	72	197
Thorleppe	35	m	i	CA	Fresno	Millerton P O	72	179
Thowejacane	40	m	i	CA	Fresno	Millerton P O	72	180
Three Claws	60	m	i	CA	Del Norte	Crescent Twp	71	454
Thursa	20	f	i	CA	Del Norte	Happy Camp Twp	71	472
Ticorbe	7	m	i	CA	Alameda	Murray Twp	68	103
Tiffy John	26	m	i	CA	Colusa	Stony Crk Twp	71	326
Tikos	64	f	i	CA	Fresno	Kings Rvr P O	72	206
Tim	23	m	i	CA	Fresno	Millerton P O	72	184
Tim	23	m	i	CA	Fresno	Kingston P O	72	223
Tim	17	m	i	CA	Colusa	Colusa Twp	71	284
Tim	13	m	i	CA	Del Norte	Smith Rvr Twp	71	483
Timina	36	m	i	----	Marin	No Twp Listed	74	89
Tipsy	40	m	i	CA	Del Norte	Crescent Twp	71	458
Tivasio	65	m	i	----	Marin	Nicasio Twp	74	89
Tivasio	45	m	i	----	Marin	Point Reyes Twp	74	89
To Na	50	f	i	CA	Del Norte	Crescent Twp	71	460
To Na Cul	50	m	i	CA	Del Norte	Crescent Twp	71	460
Toartee	35	m	i	CA	Fresno	Millerton P O	72	178
Tobin	17	m	i	CA	Napa	Yountville Twp	75	80
Toceeenah	20	m	i	CA	Fresno	Millerton P O	72	175
Tockemah	35	m	i	CA	Fresno	Millerton P O	72	176
Tocojoh	75	m	i	CA	Fresno	Millerton P O	72	178
Tocowhee	70	f	i	CA	Fresno	Millerton P O	72	178
Toemkool	45	f	i	CA	Colusa	Spring Valley Twp	71	343
Tokowlarvee	34	f	i	CA	Fresno	Millerton P O	72	178
Toliegum	45	f	i	CA	Fresno	Millerton P O	72	172
Tom	60	m	i	CA	Colusa	Stony Crk Twp	71	329
Tom	60	m	i	CA	Yolo	Cottonwood Twp	93	474
Tom	40	m	i	CA	Fresno	Kings Rvr P O	72	210
Tom	35	m	i	CA	Colusa	Monroe Twp	71	317
Tom	34	m	i	CA	Fresno	Kingston P O	72	218
Tom	34	m	i	CA	Fresno	Kingston P O	72	223
Tom	34	m	i	CA	Fresno	Millerton P O	72	189
Tom	30	m	i	CA	Fresno	Kings Rvr P O	72	213
Tom	30	m	i	CA	Del Norte	Happy Camp Twp	71	472
Tom	26	m	i	CA	Del Norte	Happy Camp Twp	71	473
Tom	26	m	i	CA	Fresno	Millerton P O	72	185
Tom	25	m	i	CA	Del Norte	Smith Rvr Twp	71	480
Tom	25	m	i	CA	Del Norte	Smith Rvr Twp	71	480
Tom	25	m	i	CA	Yolo	Cottonwood Twp	93	460
Tom	25	m	i	CA	Yolo	Grafton Twp	93	478
Tom	25	m	i	CA	Yolo	Grafton Twp	93	495
Tom	24	m	i	CA	Fresno	Kings Rvr P O	72	206
Tom	23	m	i	CA	Fresno	Kingston P O	72	222
Tom	23	m	i	CA	Del Norte	Crescent Twp	71	459
Tom	20	m	i	CA	Fresno	Kings Rvr P O	72	215
Tom	20	m	i	CA	Del Norte	Crescent Twp	71	459
Tom	15	m	i	CA	Colusa	Stony Crk Twp	71	331
Tom	12	m	i	CA	Del Norte	Smith Rvr Twp	71	482
Tomaie	50	m	i	CA	Fresno	Millerton P O	72	179
Tomas	50	m	i	CA	Los Angeles	Los Angeles Twp	73	498
Tomas	18	m	i	CA	Los Angeles	Los Angeles Twp	73	498
Tomasa	65	f	i	CA	San Diego	San Luis Rey	78	512
Tomoha	32	m	i	CA	Fresno	Kings Rvr P O	72	205
Ton	15	m	i	CA	Monterey	Monterey Twp	74	346
Toncheo	31	m	i	CA	Fresno	Millerton P O	72	198
Tonvis	32	f	i	CA	Colusa	Spring Valley Twp	71	343
Toocoyoh	30	m	i	CA	Fresno	Millerton P O	72	178
Tookee	35	m	i	CA	Fresno	Millerton P O	72	178
Topka	20	m	i	CA	Colusa	Stony Crk Twp	71	326
Topoxy	37	f	i	CA	Colusa	Spring Valley Twp	71	343
Toppy	24	m	i	CA	Fresno	Millerton P O	72	183
Topsey	20	f	i	CA	Del Norte	Happy Camp Twp	71	473
Torquo	28	m	i	CA	Fresno	Millerton P O	72	187
Tospedo	28	m	i	CA	Fresno	Kings Rvr P O	72	207
Totcomat	60	f	i	CA	Fresno	Millerton P O	72	170
Totochoo	45	m	i	CA	Fresno	Millerton P O	72	170
Toucher	31	m	i	CA	Fresno	Millerton P O	72	188
Towedare	35	f	i	CA	Colusa	Spring Valley Twp	71	343
Trapper	23	m	i	CA	Fresno	Kings Rvr P O	72	207
Trimmer	30	m	i	CA	Fresno	Millerton P O	72	187
Trinidaz	79	f	i	----	Marin	Point Reyes Twp	74	89
Trocumah	17	m	i	CA	Fresno	Kings Rvr P O	72	209
Troni	30	m	i	CA	Fresno	Millerton P O	72	197
Tully	40	f	i	CA	Del Norte	Crescent Twp	71	460
Tumory	37	m	i	CA	Colusa	Spring Valley Twp	71	338
Tuniva	27	m	i	CA	Fresno	Millerton P O	72	182
Twach	20	m	i	CA	Del Norte	Crescent Twp	71	457
Ucolmey	50	f	i	CA	Colusa	Spring Valley Twp	71	343
Umalla	45	f	i	CA	Colusa	Spring Valley Twp	71	343
Uslat	15	m	i	CA	Del Norte	Happy Camp Twp	71	472
Utah	20	m	i	CA	Colusa	Colusa Twp	71	283
Valentine	41	m	i	CA	San Luis Obispo	Salinas Twp	87	292
Velentie	40	m	i	CA	Alameda	Murray Twp	68	106
Ventura	13	m	i	CA	Los Angeles	Los Angeles Twp	73	499
Venturo	70	m	i	CA	Monterey	Monterey Twp	74	344
Vesitasion	17	f	i	CA	Monterey	San Juan Twp	74	385
Victor	10	m	i	CA	Los Angeles	Los Angeles	73	500
Vicuta	32	f	i	CA	Los Angeles	Los Angeles	73	500
Visaria	5	m	i	CA	Los Angeles	Los Angeles Twp	73	499
Vixtorino	32	m	i	----	Marin	Tomales Twp	74	89
Wacanocho	50	m	i	CA	Fresno	Kings Rvr P O	72	205
Wahoneta	33	m	i	CA	Fresno	Millerton P O	72	198
Wakamechee	45	m	i	CA	Fresno	Millerton P O	72	170
Wakanoche	48	m	i	CA	Fresno	Millerton P O	72	198
Walahai	28	m	i	CA	Fresno	Millerton P O	72	172
Walelten	4	m	i	CA	Fresno	Millerton P O	72	170
Walker	36	m	i	CA	Fresno	Kings Rvr P O	72	208
Wallach	28	m	i	CA	Fresno	Kings Rvr P O	72	209
Walletin	35	m	i	CA	Fresno	Millerton P O	72	173
Walter	25	m	i	CA	Fresno	Kings Rvr P O	72	216
Wam	50	m	i	CA	Alameda	Murray Twp	68	106
Wamahah	26	m	i	CA	Fresno	Millerton P O	72	196
Wannaha	30	m	i	CA	Fresno	Millerton P O	72	195
Wanomette	40	m	i	CA	Fresno	Millerton P O	72	190
Wantsy	24	m	i	CA	Del Norte	Smith Rvr Twp	71	482
Warsan	30	m	i	CA	Del Norte	Crescent Twp	71	458
Wash	9	m	i	CA	Colusa	Stony Crk Twp	71	332
Wassamert	38	m	i	CA	Fresno	Millerton P O	72	190
Watavotch	30	m	i	CA	Fresno	Millerton P O	72	186
Watchill	25	m	i	CA	Colusa	Spring Valley Twp	71	338
Watinas	40	m	i	CA	Del Norte	Smith Rvr Twp	71	481
Watoka	56	m	i	CA	Fresno	Kings Rvr P O	72	215
Watoka	35	m	i	CA	Fresno	Kings Rvr P O	72	213
Wattanape	54	m	i	CA	Fresno	Millerton P O	72	197
Wecamio	40	m	i	CA	Fresno	Kings Rvr P O	72	210
Wehuher	30	m	i	CA	Fresno	Millerton P O	72	170
Wenaseit	45	f	i	CA	Fresno	Millerton P O	72	171
Weptonah	28	m	i	CA	Fresno	Millerton P O	72	182
Wesaset	25	f	i	CA	Fresno	Millerton P O	72	170
Westoca	40	m	i	CA	Fresno	Kingston P O	72	221
Whahaquitch	20	f	i	CA	Fresno	Millerton P O	72	178
Whallece	45	m	i	CA	Fresno	Millerton P O	72	177
Whallis	30	m	i	CA	Fresno	Millerton P O	72	171
Whaloo	40	m	i	CA	Fresno	Millerton P O	72	169
Whatepa	20	f	i	CA	Fresno	Millerton P O	72	177
Whattnis	40	m	i	CA	Del Norte	Crescent	71	467
Whenhuvah	35	m	i	CA	Fresno	Millerton P O	72	171
Whesah	40	m	i	CA	Fresno	Millerton P O	72	173
Whipple	20	m	i	CA	Del Norte	Smith Rvr Twp	71	482
White	17	m	i	CA	Yolo	Buckeye Twp	93	412
Whitehead	30	m	i	CA	Del Norte	Smith Rvr Twp	71	480
Wietowa	56	m	i	CA	Fresno	Kings Rvr P O	72	210
Wilkes	20	m	i	CA	Del Norte	Smith Rvr Twp	71	479
Will	35	m	i	CA	Colusa	Stony Crk Twp	71	334
Will	30	m	i	CA	Yolo	Cottonwood Twp	93	474
William	30	m	i	CA	Fresno	Millerton P O	72	198
William	25	m	i	CA	Colusa	Colusa Twp	71	285
William	12	m	i	CA	Napa	Yountville Twp	75	85
Willie	15	m	i	OR	Napa	Napa Twp	75	28
Willie	10	m	i	CA	Yolo	Cottonwood Twp	93	470
Winesoho	30	m	i	CA	Fresno	Millerton P O	72	198
Witonasah	30	m	i	CA	Fresno	Millerton P O	72	198
Witonomahah	33	m	i	CA	Fresno	Millerton P O	72	198
Wolf	48	m	i	CA	Fresno	Kingston P O	72	218
Wolonier	47	m	i	CA	Colusa	Spring Valley Twp	71	338
Wonatha	38	m	i	CA	Fresno	Millerton P O	72	196
Wononanah	43	m	i	CA	Fresno	Millerton P O	72	197
Woontalah	32	m	i	CA	Colusa	Spring Valley Twp	71	338
Workah	42	m	i	CA	Colusa	Spring Valley Twp	71	338
Workonatch	47	m	i	CA	Fresno	Millerton P O	72	181
Wotac	40	m	i	CA	Fresno	Kings Rvr P O	72	209
Woulapinee	20	f	i	CA	Fresno	Millerton P O	72	177
Yalven	33	m	i	CA	Colusa	Monroe Twp	71	323

© 2001 by Heritage Quest. All rights reserved.

Series M593

Name	Age	S	R	B-PL	County	Locale	Roll	Pg
Yarl	26	f	i	CA	Colusa	Spring Valley Twp	71	343
Yaumah	42	m	i	CA	Fresno	Millerton P O	72	185
Yeboss	33	m	i	CA	Colusa	Spring Valley Twp	71	338
Yehmach	24	m	i	CA	Fresno	Kings Rvr P O	72	207
Yessee Seemer	46	f	i	CA	Colusa	Spring Valley Twp	71	343
Yocartlah	70	m	i	CA	Del Norte	Crescent Twp	71	461
Yockeanai	20	f	i	CA	Fresno	Millerton P O	72	176
Yockollo	26	m	i	CA	Colusa	Grand Island Twp	71	304
Yokawaig	20	m	i	CA	Fresno	Millerton P O	72	178
Yokee	50	m	i	CA	Fresno	Millerton P O	72	171
Yomanas	35	m	i	CA	Fresno	Kingston P O	72	224
Yomum	25	m	i	CA	Colusa	Spring Valley Twp	71	338
Yonapah	25	m	i	CA	Colusa	Spring Valley Twp	71	338
Yones	22	f	i	CA	Colusa	Spring Valley Twp	71	343
Yonker	20	m	i	CA	Del Norte	Smith Rvr Twp	71	482
Yookecum	40	f	i	CA	Fresno	Millerton P O	72	178
Yotohroh	32	m	i	CA	Fresno	Kings Rvr P O	72	207
Yotoxee	37	m	i	CA	Fresno	Millerton P O	72	182
Yuba	26	m	i	CA	Colusa	Monroe Twp	71	323
Yuheta	48	f	i	CA	Fresno	Kings Rvr P O	72	203
Yumappa	30	m	i	CA	Fresno	Millerton P O	72	182
Yuva	25	m	i	CA	Colusa	Colusa Twp	71	281
Zitaro	25	m	i	CA	Del Norte	Crescent Twp	71	458
INDLEKOFER								
Jacob	30	m	w	BADE	Amador	Sutter Crk P O	69	399
INDODA								
Miguel	70	m	w	CA	San Diego	San Pasqual	78	521
Yadar	30	m	w	CA	San Diego	San Pasqual	78	521
INDRAN								
Joe	28	m	w	CA	Humboldt	Eel Rvr Twp	72	254
INE								
Dute	23	m	c	CHIN	Sacramento	Georgianna Twp	77	126
INEL								
Palita	2	f	w	CA	Los Angeles	Los Angeles	73	515
INEMAY								
Louisa	17	f	w	FRAN	San Francisco	San Francisco P O	80	427
INEZ								
Joachim	35	m	w	SCOT	Siskiyou	Callahan P O	89	628
Manuel	25	m	w	PORT	Santa Clara	San Jose Twp	88	195
INFIELD								
G W	27	m	w	OH	Amador	Sutter Crk P O	69	403
ING								
Ah	50	m	c	CHIN	Sacramento	Granite Twp	77	141
Ah	48	m	c	CHIN	Placer	Auburn P O	76	379
Ah	46	m	c	CHIN	Placer	Pino Twp	76	470
Ah	42	m	c	CHIN	San Francisco	2-Wd San Francisco	79	285
Ah	40	m	c	CHIN	Calaveras	Copperopolis P O	70	238
Ah	40	m	c	CHIN	Sonoma	Sonoma Twp	91	449
Ah	38	m	c	CHIN	Nevada	Nevada Twp	75	312
Ah	34	m	c	CHIN	Sierra	Forest Twp	89	528
Ah	31	m	c	CHIN	Sacramento	1-Wd Sacramento	77	193
Ah	31	m	c	CHIN	Sierra	Butte Twp	89	513
Ah	29	m	c	CHIN	Sacramento	1-Wd Sacramento	77	200
Ah	26	m	c	CHIN	San Francisco	2-Wd San Francisco	79	282
Ah	25	m	c	CHIN	Placer	Lincoln P O	76	483
Ah	24	m	c	CHIN	Amador	Jackson P O	69	331
Ah	24	m	c	CHIN	Placer	Bath P O	76	445
Ah	24	m	c	CHIN	Sacramento	2-Wd Sacramento	77	245
Ah	23	m	c	CHIN	Yuba	Marysville	93	593
Ah	22	m	c	CHIN	Contra Costa	Martinez P O	71	435
Ah	22	m	c	CHIN	Sonoma	Sonoma Twp	91	449
Ah	20	m	c	CHIN	Sacramento	1-Wd Sacramento	77	199
Ah	18	m	c	CHIN	Santa Clara	Alviso Twp	88	25
Ah	17	m	c	CHIN	Butte	Ophir Twp	70	103
Ah	11	m	c	CHIN	El Dorado	Placerville	72	118
Hi	20	m	c	CHIN	Calaveras	San Andreas P O	70	190
Jno C	45	m	w	OH	Sacramento	1-Wd Sacramento	77	203
Lee	29	m	c	CHIN	Placer	Bath P O	76	444
Long	20	m	c	CHIN	San Francisco	2-Wd San Francisco	79	243
Lop	34	m	c	CHIN	San Joaquin	Elkhorn Twp	86	52
Wy	36	m	c	CHIN	Sierra	Forest Twp	89	529
Yon	30	m	c	CHIN	Stanislaus	Emory Twp	92	23
INGALES								
F S	20	m	w	IREL	Alameda	Oakland	68	159
INGALLS								
Benjamin	58	m	w	ME	Alameda	Eden Twp	68	57
Frank	19	m	w	IA	Sacramento	1-Wd Sacramento	77	204
Geo	36	m	w	SCOT	Sacramento	3-Wd Sacramento	77	268
Harvey	43	m	w	NY	Plumas	Indian Twp	77	10
J F	34	m	w	OH	Sacramento	3-Wd Sacramento	77	279
James	32	m	w	OH	Napa	Yountville Twp	75	90
Kuyler	30	m	w	NY	San Francisco	5-Wd San Francisco	81	13
Luther	32	m	w	ME	Santa Clara	Fremont Twp	88	55
Lydia	13	f	w	IA	Alameda	Hayward	68	75
Miles	46	m	w	IL	Tehama	Antelope Twp	92	156
N P	45	m	w	NH	Sacramento	3-Wd Sacramento	77	272
R F	40	m	w	ME	Tuolumne	Sonora P O	93	322
Saml E	48	m	w	NY	Tehama	Merrill	92	197
Susan	72	f	w	MA	Solano	Vallejo	90	172
Wesley	29	m	w	OH	Santa Cruz	Watsonville	89	371
INGALOTTI								
Frank	36	m	w	ITAL	Tuolumne	Columbia P O	93	345
INGALS								
Mehetable	28	f	w	ME	San Francisco	6-Wd San Francisco	81	141
INGALSBY								
D	40	m	w	NY	Merced	Snelling P O	74	254

Series M593

Name	Age	S	R	B-PL	County	Locale	Roll	Pg
INGALSHE								
A	43	m	w	CA	Merced	Snelling P O	74	281
INGARD								
Abe	42	m	w	MO	San Joaquin	2-Wd Stockton	86	169
INGARGIOLA								
Augustus	5	m	w	CA	San Francisco	San Francisco P O	83	364
INGARGOLA								
Laurence	42	m	w	ITAL	San Francisco	11-Wd San Francisc	84	531
INGELBOT								
J	44	m	w	PRUS	San Joaquin	2-Wd Stockton	86	195
INGELLS								
Albert	23	m	w	GERM	Marin	San Rafael Twp	74	45
Jonathan	24	m	w	MA	San Francisco	11-Wd San Francisc	84	548
Sarah	29	f	w	CANA	San Francisco	11-Wd San Francisc	84	548
INGELS								
J J	31	m	w	NY	San Joaquin	2-Wd Stockton	86	171
INGERHAM								
Augustus	41	m	w	TN	Inyo	Cerro Gordo Twp	73	318
INGERHAN								
Joseph	50	m	w	ME	San Francisco	7-Wd San Francisco	81	182
INGERMAN								
Albert	39	m	w	PRUS	Marin	Bolinas Twp	74	6
INGERSOL								
John	39	m	w	ENGL	Solano	Rio Vista Twp	90	60
L	20	m	w	LA	San Joaquin	3-Wd Stockton	86	240
INGERSOLL								
Darius	34	m	w	IN	Placer	Bath P O	76	447
Gaylord	21	m	w	MA	San Francisco	San Francisco P O	80	535
George	33	m	w	OH	Sutter	Butte Twp	92	104
Hiram	37	m	w	OH	El Dorado	Diamond Springs Tw	72	22
J J	27	m	w	KY	Lassen	Susanville Twp	73	445
Juliet	34	f	w	MI	Marin	Bolinas Twp	74	7
Julietta	31	f	w	MI	Marin	Bolinas Twp	74	2
Mary	11	f	w	CA	El Dorado	Coloma Twp	72	2
Owen	64	m	w	NY	Sacramento	Natomas Twp	77	165
Thomas	60	m	w	CT	Santa Clara	1-Wd San Jose	88	233
W B	36	m	w	MA	Alameda	Oakland	68	196
Wm E	27	m	w	MA	San Francisco	San Francisco P O	83	201
INGHAM								
Alice	20	f	w	IL	San Diego	San Diego	78	498
And H	29	m	w	MD	Sonoma	Mendocino Twp	91	305
C G	46	m	w	NY	Sacramento	4-Wd Sacramento	77	376
Catherine	49	f	w	NY	San Diego	San Diego	78	498
Geo H	45	m	w	NY	El Dorado	Coloma Twp	72	7
Joseph	43	m	w	ENGL	Santa Clara	1-Wd San Jose	88	231
Richd	35	m	w	RI	San Francisco	San Francisco P O	83	70
S S	44	m	w	IL	Monterey	San Antonio Twp	74	322
INGHAN								
Mary	25	f	w	IN	San Francisco	San Francisco P O	83	413
INGILS								
Jno	26	m	w	NY	San Joaquin	3-Wd Stockton	86	216
INGLASS								
John	37	m	w	ME	San Joaquin	Oneal Twp	86	104
INGLE								
George	29	m	w	HAMB	San Francisco	San Francisco P O	83	31
John	40	m	w	ENGL	Shasta	Portugese Flat P O	89	472
Josiah	42	m	w	PA	Alameda	Hayward	68	75
William	26	m	w	MS	Tulare	Visalia Twp	92	284
INGLEDOW								
John	43	m	w	NY	Humboldt	Eureka Twp	72	258
INGLEHAM								
Charles	15	m	w	CA	Yolo	Cottonwood Twp	93	467
INGLEHART								
John	38	m	w	BAVA	San Diego	Julian Dist	78	472
Saml	25	m	w	MO	Sonoma	Mendocino Twp	91	290
INGLEMAN								
Arthur	31	m	w	CA	San Francisco	2-Wd San Francisco	79	166
INGLEMIRE								
Robt	39	m	w	PA	San Diego	San Diego	78	499
INGLES								
Anna	28	f	w	NY	Sonoma	Petaluma Twp	91	366
Benjamin	28	m	w	MA	San Francisco	San Francisco P O	85	805
Benjamin F	38	m	w	IN	Santa Cruz	Pajaro Twp	89	363
David	52	m	w	SCOT	San Francisco	San Francisco P O	83	322
Edward	39	m	w	NY	Sacramento	Mississippi Twp	77	162
Frank	25	m	w	PRUS	Sacramento	Brighton Twp	77	75
Harrison	36	m	w	IN	Sacramento	2-Wd Sacramento	77	243
Harry	45	m	w	AR	Stanislaus	Empire Twp	92	42
John	29	m	w	CANA	Sonoma	Petaluma Twp	91	316
INGLESBY								
A C	38	m	w	NY	Santa Clara	Gilroy Twp	88	89
Charles	40	m	w	IREL	San Mateo	Belmont P O	87	372
INGLESON								
Charles	47	m	w	MD	Santa Clara	Alviso Twp	88	22
INGLEWOOD								
Hans C	25	m	w	ENGL	San Francisco	1-Wd San Francisco	79	75
INGLEY								
David A	45	m	w	NY	Nevada	Bloomfield Twp	75	99
INGLIBRIDSEN								
Jas	25	m	w	PRUS	Humboldt	Eureka Twp	72	267
INGLIS								
T	41	m	w	SCOT	Sierra	Downieville Twp	89	516
Wm	42	m	w	SCOT	San Joaquin	2-Wd Stockton	86	213
INGMON								
James	64	m	w	PA	Humboldt	Arcata Twp	72	227
INGO								
Mani	40	m	w	SWIT	Sonoma	Russian Rvr	91	377

© 2001 by Heritage Quest. All rights reserved.

Name	Age	S	R	B-PL	County	Locale	Roll	Pg
INGOLD								
Geo	50	m	w	MO	Sonoma	Analy Twp	91	221
Peter	40	m	w	SCOT	Sonoma	Analy Twp	91	234
INGOLDSBY								
James	23	m	w	IREL	Santa Clara	Fremont Twp	88	42
INGOLL								
Peter	47	m	w	HDAR	Yuba	Marysville	93	613
INGOLS								
J E	35	m	w	MA	Alameda	Oakland	68	162
Levi	72	m	w	MA	Alameda	Oakland	68	162
Robert F	42	m	w	ME	Tuolumne	Sonora P O	93	319
T A	42	m	w	NY	Alameda	Oakland	68	148
INGOMAN								
Chas	43	m	w	BAVA	Solano	Benicia	90	19
INGORT								
John	25	m	w	MO	Yolo	Grafton Twp	93	500
INGRAHAM								
Alfred	50	m	w	NY	Contra Costa	Martinez P O	71	368
Duncan	39	m	w	PA	San Francisco	San Francisco P O	83	140
Duncan G	32	m	w	NJ	Santa Cruz	Santa Cruz	89	414
Frank	25	m	w	MA	San Francisco	San Francisco P O	83	140
H Clay	11	m	w	CA	Humboldt	Eel Rvr Twp	72	248
Horace P	34	m	w	NH	San Francisco	8-Wd San Francisco	82	386
James	53	m	w	MA	Marin	San Rafael Twp	74	42
Jasper	60	m	w	KY	San Luis Obispo	Salinas Twp	87	293
John	35	m	w	IL	Tehama	Tehama Twp	92	156
Jos	35	m	w	ME	Solano	Vallejo	90	142
Leroy T	18	m	w	KY	Sonoma	Washington Twp	91	464
Lewis	18	m	w	IN	Placer	Auburn P O	76	366
Newton	40	m	w	IL	Alameda	Murray Twp	68	100
Ossian	23	m	w	ME	San Francisco	11-Wd San Francisc	84	567
Richard B	36	m	w	ME	San Francisco	7-Wd San Francisco	81	250
Robert	30	m	w	IREL	San Francisco	San Francisco P O	83	190
William	51	m	w	SCOT	Santa Clara	1-Wd San Jose	88	257
William	44	m	w	NY	San Diego	San Pasqual	78	520
William	40	m	w	NY	San Diego	San Pasqual Valley	78	525
Wm	45	m	w	MO	Fresno	Kingston P O	72	220
Wm	29	m	w	MO	Napa	Napa	75	57
INGRAHM								
Robert	39	m	w	IREL	Marin	Bolinas Twp	74	7
INGRAIM								
J C M	40	m	w	IL	Lake	Scotts Crk	73	427
Thomas	50	m	w	MEXI	Tuolumne	Sonora P O	93	324
INGRAM								
A B	36	m	w	OH	Mendocino	Ukiah Twp	74	234
Fredk John	40	m	w	ENGL	Santa Cruz	Santa Cruz Twp	89	401
George	19	m	w	OH	Inyo	Bishop Crk Twp	73	316
Horace	50	m	w	CT	Napa	Napa Twp	75	67
Isaac	50	m	w	NY	Sonoma	Vallejo Twp	91	456
Isaac	39	m	w	ME	San Francisco	11-Wd San Francisc	84	689
J	38	m	w	MO	Yuba	Marysville	93	614
J M	35	m	w	KY	Sonoma	Vallejo Twp	91	463
James	32	m	w	ENGL	San Francisco	San Francisco P O	83	340
John	56	m	w	NC	Sonoma	Santa Rosa	91	403
John	24	m	w	NY	Stanislaus	Empire Twp	92	38
Jonas	41	m	w	IL	Lake	Big Valley	73	398
Joseph	33	m	w	SCOT	San Bernardino	San Bernardino Twp	78	429
Nathan B	25	m	w	IA	Mendocino	Anderson Twp	74	156
Nathan V	26	m	w	IL	Mendocino	Anderson Twp	74	150
Rebecca	40	f	w	ME	San Francisco	San Francisco P O	83	27
Rebecca	40	f	w	HI	San Francisco	San Francisco P O	83	130
Riley	40	m	w	GA	Calaveras	Copperopolis P O	70	238
Samuel H	58	m	w	VA	Mendocino	Anderson Twp	74	152
Thos	44	m	w	KY	Sonoma	Santa Rosa	91	394
William	28	m	w	SCOT	Nevada	Eureka Twp	75	137
Wm	60	m	w	SCOT	Sacramento	4-Wd Sacramento	77	361
Wm	42	m	w	IREL	San Francisco	2-Wd San Francisco	79	253
Wm	36	m	w	VA	Yuba	Marysville	93	577
INGRANE								
Silas D	49	m	w	NY	Sonoma	Salt Point	91	381
INGREM								
John	27	m	w	TX	Santa Clara	Redwood Twp	88	118
Traverse	30	m	w	TX	Santa Clara	Redwood Twp	88	120
INGRHAM								
Samuel W	38	m	w	OH	Yolo	Cache Crk Twp	93	442
INGRIM								
Godfrey	43	m	w	PA	Colusa	Spring Valley Twp	71	336
Joseph J	38	m	w	PA	Colusa	Spring Valley Twp	71	336
INGSTEN								
Richd	40	m	w	ENGL	Solano	Vallejo	90	178
INGUS								
Antonio	30	m	w	PORT	Santa Clara	Santa Clara Twp	88	138
INHOFF								
Antoni	26	m	w	RUSS	San Francisco	11-Wd San Francisc	84	648
F G	25	m	w	IREL	Alameda	Oakland	68	260
INK								
Wm P	51	m	w	NY	Sutter	Sutter Twp	92	119
INKLER								
Frederck	21	m	w	WI	San Bernardino	San Bernardino Twp	78	452
INKS								
James	40	m	w	MO	Calaveras	Copperopolis P O	70	253
INLAND								
J C	25	m	w	CANA	Sacramento	3-Wd Sacramento	77	261
John	46	m	w	KY	San Joaquin	Castoria Twp	86	4
INLOW								
Joseph	26	m	w	MO	Yuba	Linda Twp	93	559
S E	33	m	w	MO	Yuba	Linda Twp	93	557

Name	Age	S	R	B-PL	County	Locale	Roll	Pg
INMAN								
Ann E	34	f	w	MO	Napa	Napa	75	49
Eli	28	m	w	OH	Siskiyou	Surprise Valley Tw	89	639
Eliza	35	f	w	ME	San Diego	San Diego	78	503
Frank	18	m	w	ME	Santa Clara	Redwood Twp	88	133
James	46	m	w	ENGL	San Francisco	11-Wd San Francisc	84	543
Mary	34	f	w	ENGL	San Francisco	7-Wd San Francisco	81	241
Nathaniel D	37	m	w	ME	Sonoma	Salt Point	91	387
Saml B	53	m	w	NY	San Luis Obispo	Santa Rosa Twp	87	325
Walter W	38	m	w	ME	Inyo	Lone Pine Twp	73	333
INMANN								
Jerry	36	m	w	ME	Humboldt	Bucksport Twp	72	242
INMANS								
Chas	33	m	w	HAMB	San Francisco	1-Wd San Francisco	79	116
INN								
An	44	m	c	CHIN	Amador	Jackson P O	69	331
INNER								
Joseph	38	m	w	BADE	El Dorado	Coloma Twp	72	2
INNES								
Daniel	35	m	w	IREL	San Francisco	San Francisco P O	85	873
John C	29	m	w	NY	San Francisco	San Francisco P O	85	718
INNIS								
Alex	34	m	w	CANA	Alameda	Alameda	68	16
John	67	m	w	IREL	San Francisco	2-Wd San Francisco	79	216
INNMAN								
Hiram K	60	m	w	KY	Sonoma	Vallejo Twp	91	461
J	29	m	w	ME	Humboldt	Eureka Twp	72	264
INNOCENCIO								
Salinas	28	m	w	CHIL	Sacramento	2-Wd Sacramento	77	221
INO								
Thomas	48	m	w	IREL	Alameda	Eden Twp	68	90
INOCENT								
James	23	m	w	CA	Santa Clara	Santa Clara Twp	88	178
INOCENTI								
Paul	53	m	w	ITAL	Amador	Jackson P O	69	327
INOK								
Ah	29	m	c	CHIN	Nevada	Bridgeport Twp	75	110
INOY								
Ah	20	m	c	CHIN	Placer	Colfax P O	76	384
INRIGHT								
Peter	25	m	w	IREL	San Francisco	11-Wd San Francisc	84	705
INSKEEP								
Elizth	38	f	w	IREL	San Francisco	San Francisco P O	83	83
Florence	23	f	w	MO	Santa Clara	San Jose Twp	88	195
Geo W	38	m	w	MO	Santa Cruz	Santa Cruz	89	408
INSKIP								
Wm	35	m	w	IREL	San Francisco	San Francisco P O	83	131
INSKIPP								
William S	48	m	w	OH	Nevada	Rough & Ready Twp	75	333
INSLEE								
George W	43	m	w	NY	San Francisco	8-Wd San Francisco	82	418
INSUNIA								
Hosee	55	f	i	MEXI	Inyo	Cerro Gordo Twp	73	320
INTEMANN								
H	24	m	w	PRUS	San Francisco	San Francisco P O	83	134
INTOSH								
James	40	m	w	SCOT	San Mateo	Schoolhouse Statio	87	342
INTRIES								
Robert	3	m	w	CA	Sacramento	2-Wd Sacramento	77	242
INTTS								
Leonard	50	m	w	CT	Marin	San Rafael Twp	74	41
INWALD								
John	25	m	w	IN	Sacramento	2-Wd Sacramento	77	218
INWALL								
John H	30	m	w	OH	Sacramento	2-Wd Sacramento	77	235
INWOOD								
George	40	m	w	ENGL	San Francisco	2-Wd San Francisco	79	238
George	35	m	w	ENGL	San Francisco	San Francisco P O	85	737
IONE								
Salvador	34	m	w	MEXI	Butte	Oroville Twp	70	137
IPOLITA								
Dotah	41	m	w	FRAN	Amador	Volcano P O	69	378
IPOLITO								
Ramonia	50	f	w	MEXI	Santa Clara	San Jose Twp	88	211
IPPS								
Robert	24	m	w	SC	Marin	Bolinas Twp	74	4
IPSEN								
Peter	47	m	w	DENM	Contra Costa	Martinez P O	71	393
IRACKS								
Mike	42	m	w	PA	Sierra	Gibson Twp	89	538
IRANN								
G	13	m	b	CA	Sierra	Downieville Twp	89	519
IRANSETAR								
Jose	45	m	w	CA	Fresno	Millerton P O	72	157
IRBA								
Teodosio	22	m	w	CA	Los Angeles	El Monte Twp	73	459
IREBOST								
Annie	11	f	w	MD	San Francisco	San Francisco P O	85	835
IREDALE								
Alfred S	45	m	w	KY	San Francisco	San Francisco P O	83	300
IREDELL								
Joseph B	65	m	w	NJ	San Francisco	2-Wd San Francisco	79	211
IRELAN								
Lambert	52	m	w	OH	Santa Cruz	Watsonville	89	377
Rebecca	14	f	w	CA	Santa Clara	2-Wd San Jose	88	337
William	29	m	w	DE	San Francisco	6-Wd San Francisco	81	148

© 2001 by Heritage Quest. All rights reserved.

California 1870 Census

Name	Age	S	R	B-PL	County	Locale	Roll	Pg
						Series M593		
IRELAND								
E	37	m	w	NJ	San Joaquin	Liberty Twp	86	83
Eberly	24	m	w	IN	Monterey	Pajaro Twp	74	376
James	40	m	w	SCOT	Alameda	Brooklyn Twp	68	54
John	25	m	w	NY	Sacramento	3-Wd Sacramento	77	283
John	20	m	w	CANA	Sacramento	Franklin Twp	77	105
L F	35	m	w	NY	San Francisco	6-Wd San Francisco	81	95
M C	47	m	w	OH	Monterey	Monterey Twp	74	344
N W	31	m	w	NY	Sacramento	4-Wd Sacramento	77	374
Patrick	44	m	w	IREL	Santa Clara	San Jose Twp	88	194
Preston	24	m	w	ME	Alpine	Markleeville P O	69	312
R D	34	m	w	NY	Sacramento	3-Wd Sacramento	77	262
Richd	33	m	w	NY	Sacramento	3-Wd Sacramento	77	283
Saml	32	m	w	MA	Solano	Vallejo	90	141
Sarah	43	f	w	MD	San Francisco	San Francisco P O	83	243
Sidney	28	m	w	IL	Yolo	Cache Crk Twp	93	454
William	43	m	w	NJ	San Francisco	San Francisco P O	83	222
William	43	m	w	ENGL	Contra Costa	Martinez P O	71	434
William	25	m	w	IA	Santa Clara	Santa Clara Twp	88	166
Wm	43	m	w	IREL	Sacramento	Lee Twp	77	158
IREN								
Ah	25	m	c	CHIN	Sacramento	Franklin Twp	77	119
IRER								
Ah	22	m	c	CHIN	Sacramento	Franklin Twp	77	109
IRETT								
John	51	m	w	ENGL	Merced	Snelling P O	74	249
IRETTA								
Sebastian	33	m	w	CA	Santa Clara	Gilroy Twp	88	90
IRIBANNE								
G	45	m	w	FRAN	Calaveras	Copperopolis P O	70	225
IRING								
Ah Bow	25	m	c	CHIN	Sacramento	1-Wd Sacramento	77	182
IRION								
Louis	25	m	w	WURT	San Francisco	8-Wd San Francisco	82	381
IRIS								
E H	42	m	w	NY	San Joaquin	Union Twp	86	268
Eli	37	m	w	MEXI	Yolo	Putah Twp	93	520
IRISE								
G W	44	m	w	ALOR	Sacramento	1-Wd Sacramento	77	178
IRISH								
Albert H	46	m	w	ME	Nevada	Nevada Twp	75	314
Alice	18	f	w	NY	San Francisco	San Francisco P O	83	416
George	28	m	w	CANA	Sonoma	Salt Point Twp	91	384
Henry O	50	m	w	NY	Mendocino	Anderson Twp	74	156
James	50	m	w	IREL	Nevada	Grass Valley Twp	75	165
James	35	m	w	IREL	Santa Clara	Santa Clara Twp	88	162
Joe	28	m	w	IREL	Sacramento	Sutter Twp	77	392
John	45	m	w	IREL	Sacramento	Granite Twp	77	136
Joseph	38	m	w	ME	El Dorado	Kelsey Twp	72	60
Mike	28	m	w	IREL	Sacramento	Cosumnes Twp	77	96
Samuel L	41	m	w	NY	Placer	Alta P O	76	412
Stephen L	42	m	w	NY	Placer	Bath P O	76	447
Thos	38	m	w	IREL	Sacramento	Mississippi Twp	77	163
Will	24	m	w	IREL	Sacramento	Sutter Twp	77	384
William S	42	m	w	CANA	Santa Clara	1-Wd San Jose	88	240
IRLAN								
J	25	m	w	SWIT	Alameda	Oakland	68	168
IRLAND								
Cherly	24	m	w	MO	Monterey	Alisal Twp	74	288
IRMAN								
Thos	32	m	w	NY	Butte	Oregon Twp	70	132
IRMES								
William	53	m	w	NY	Calaveras	San Andreas P O	70	197
IRNIN								
Leonora	28	f	w	ENGL	San Francisco	San Francisco P O	83	187
IROARD								
A	41	m	w	FRAN	Nevada	Nevada Twp	75	276
IROLA								
Baptista	36	m	w	CHIL	Calaveras	San Andreas P O	70	204
Joseph	29	m	w	ITAL	Calaveras	San Andreas P O	70	176
IROLI								
Giouvana	29	m	w	ITAL	Calaveras	San Andreas P O	70	201
IROM								
Edwin	12	m	w	CA	Humboldt	Eel Rvr Twp	72	254
IRONMONGER								
C	44	m	w	VA	Alameda	Oakland	68	131
IRONS								
Amos A	40	m	w	RI	San Francisco	1-Wd San Francisco	79	24
Elijah	50	m	w	VT	El Dorado	Georgetown Twp	72	37
Hiram	23	m	w	ENGL	San Francisco	8-Wd San Francisco	82	376
William	37	m	w	LA	Santa Clara	Redwood Twp	88	121
William	24	m	w	PA	San Francisco	8-Wd San Francisco	82	373
IRONSIDES								
James	28	m	w	SCOT	Alameda	Washington Twp	68	269
IROYZAGAN								
Frank	44	m	w	FRAN	San Francisco	1-Wd San Francisco	79	50
IRVIN								
Ah	25	m	c	CHIN	Sutter	Nicolaus Twp	92	115
Alexander	24	m	w	SCOT	Yolo	Grafton Twp	93	483
B	60	m	b	NC	Amador	Lancha Plana P O	69	368
Brown	66	m	w	PA	San Francisco	San Francisco P O	85	859
Charles	28	m	w	IREL	San Francisco	San Francisco P O	83	237
George	40	m	w	ENGL	San Mateo	Menlo Park P O	87	377
Harry	35	m	w	NY	Alameda	Alameda	68	6
Henry	23	m	w	PA	San Mateo	Half Moon Bay P O	87	405
I H	37	m	w	IN	Tehama	Antelope Twp	92	155
James	51	m	w	PRUS	Solano	Tremont Twp	90	35
Jas	28	m	w	CANA	Solano	Vallejo	90	141
John	36	m	w	IREL	Yuba	Long Bar Twp	93	561
Mary	22	f	w	IREL	Santa Clara	Fremont Twp	88	48
Mary	12	f	w	CA	Sonoma	Petaluma Twp	91	335
Newton	28	m	w	OH	Santa Clara	Almaden Twp	88	9
Sepee	40	m	w	MO	San Joaquin	2-Wd Stockton	86	205
W	39	m	w	MO	Amador	Ione City P O	69	365
William	36	m	w	IREL	Mendocino	Big Rvr Twp	74	158
William	29	m	w	CANA	Marin	San Rafael	74	57
Willie	10	m	w	MS	Monterey	Castroville Twp	74	341
Wm	15	m	w	CA	Sacramento	Sutter Twp	77	390
IRVINE								
Andrew	35	m	w	NY	San Francisco	6-Wd San Francisco	81	94
Chas A	35	m	w	NY	Mendocino	Little Lake Twp	74	192
Geo	55	m	w	IREL	San Francisco	San Francisco P O	83	322
Henry	37	m	w	ME	Nevada	Bridgeport Twp	75	109
James	45	m	w	SCOT	Nevada	Nevada Twp	75	289
John	40	m	w	NY	Santa Clara	San Jose Twp	88	199
John H	30	m	w	VA	Marin	San Rafael Twp	74	36
Joseph	27	m	w	CANA	San Francisco	6-Wd San Francisco	81	133
Mary	30	f	w	IREL	San Francisco	San Francisco P O	83	109
Samuel	39	m	w	IREL	Monterey	Castroville Twp	74	332
William	44	m	w	NY	San Francisco	3-Wd San Francisco	79	328
IRVING								
A V	38	m	w	SCOT	Solano	Vallejo	90	180
Alexander	29	m	w	IREL	Plumas	Quartz Twp	77	44
Anna	60	f	w	IREL	San Francisco	8-Wd San Francisco	82	327
Charles	30	m	w	IREL	Sonoma	Salt Point	91	380
Daniel	38	m	w	NY	Stanislaus	Emory Twp	92	24
David	51	m	w	SCOT	San Francisco	San Francisco P O	83	143
David	26	m	w	IREL	Sacramento	2-Wd Sacramento	77	240
Elizabeth	23	f	w	ENGL	San Francisco	San Francisco P O	85	833
Elizabeth	13	f	w	CA	Nevada	Grass Valley Twp	75	147
Elizabeth	13	f	w	NV	San Francisco	San Francisco P O	85	842
George	43	m	w	ME	San Francisco	8-Wd San Francisco	82	474
George	29	m	w	ENGL	San Francisco	San Francisco P O	83	200
Gerard	28	m	w	CANA	El Dorado	Cosumnes Twp	72	13
Herbert	28	m	w	ME	San Francisco	8-Wd San Francisco	82	298
James	42	m	w	IREL	San Francisco	11-Wd San Francisc	84	505
James	32	m	w	MD	Yuba	W Bear Rvr Twp	93	682
James	30	m	w	IREL	Santa Clara	San Jose Twp	88	197
Jane	35	f	w	NY	Placer	Lincoln P O	76	488
John	33	m	w	SCOT	San Francisco	San Francisco P O	80	396
L Fayette	22	m	w	WI	Santa Clara	2-Wd San Jose	88	329
Lizzie	50	f	w	IREL	Alameda	Oakland	68	250
Mary	45	f	w	IREL	San Francisco	San Francisco P O	83	140
Mary	19	f	w	CANA	San Francisco	8-Wd San Francisco	82	466
Mary L	56	f	w	ME	Santa Clara	Fremont Twp	88	43
Peter	39	m	w	SCOT	Marin	Nicasio Twp	74	17
Peter	31	m	w	KY	Butte	Chico Twp	70	60
Robert	44	m	w	AL	Kern	Havilah P O	73	336
Robert	40	m	w	ENGL	Nevada	Grass Valley Twp	75	152
Robert	34	m	w	IREL	San Francisco	7-Wd San Francisco	81	251
Sally	23	f	w	GA	Yolo	Cache Crk Twp	93	423
Saml	39	m	w	SCOT	San Francisco	8-Wd San Francisco	82	308
Susan	48	f	w	ENGL	Alameda	Alameda	68	5
Thos	25	m	w	IREL	Sacramento	3-Wd Sacramento	77	271
Washington	31	m	w	MD	San Francisco	2-Wd San Francisco	79	238
William	47	m	w	SCOT	Placer	Colfax P O	76	386
William	39	m	w	SCOT	Alameda	Oakland	68	179
William J	21	m	w	IREL	Sacramento	2-Wd Sacramento	77	240
Wm	33	m	w	IREL	San Francisco	San Francisco P O	85	852
Wm	32	m	w	NY	Santa Clara	Burnett Twp	88	33
IRVINS								
Christopher	40	m	w	IREL	San Francisco	1-Wd San Francisco	79	100
IRWIN								
Alexander	20	m	w	CANA	Inyo	Cerro Gordo Twp	73	319
Andrew	34	m	w	IL	Sonoma	Santa Rosa	91	420
Britton	39	m	w	OH	Siskiyou	Yreka	89	652
Charles	37	m	w	NY	Alameda	Washington Twp	68	290
Charles F	42	m	w	NY	El Dorado	Placerville	72	113
Daniel	37	m	w	OH	Placer	Dutch Flat P O	76	414
Daniel	30	m	w	IREL	Nevada	Meadow Lake Twp	75	264
E G	31	m	w	NY	Sacramento	Cosumnes Twp	77	93
Edward	60	m	w	IREL	Solano	Maine Prairie Twp	90	48
Edward	32	m	w	CANA	San Diego	San Luis Rey	78	513
Francis	40	m	w	IREL	San Francisco	1-Wd San Francisco	79	6
George E	37	m	w	OH	Trinity	Minersville Pct	92	215
Henry	36	m	w	WURT	San Francisco	11-Wd San Francisc	84	689
Isabel	20	f	w	IL	Monterey	Salinas Twp	74	306
James	78	m	w	IREL	San Francisco	San Francisco P O	83	90
James	58	m	w	VA	Santa Clara	San Jose Twp	88	196
James	45	m	w	IREL	Sutter	Sutter Twp	92	123
James	40	m	w	ME	El Dorado	Cosumnes Twp	72	13
James	35	m	w	IREL	Contra Costa	Martinez P O	71	419
James	31	m	w	NY	San Francisco	7-Wd San Francisco	81	175
James	20	m	w	IREL	Sierra	Sears Twp	89	559
James W	49	m	w	AL	El Dorado	Mud Springs Twp	72	81
Jas	42	m	w	NY	San Francisco	San Francisco P O	83	90
Jerard	24	m	w	CANA	Inyo	Lone Pine Twp	73	331
John	50	m	w	TN	San Francisco	6-Wd San Francisco	81	90
John	41	m	w	IREL	San Francisco	San Francisco P O	85	850
John	28	m	w	SCOT	Solano	Vallejo	90	139
John	28	m	w	PA	San Bernardino	San Bernardino Twp	78	417
John	27	m	w	IREL	Contra Costa	Martinez P O	71	430
John	21	m	w	CANA	Inyo	Bishop Crk Twp	73	317
Katie	4	f	w	CA	Sacramento	4-Wd Sacramento	77	378

© 2001 by Heritage Quest. All rights reserved.

Series M593

Name	Age	S	R	B-PL	County	Locale	Roll	Pg
Kirby	40	m	w	KY	San Francisco	5-Wd San Francisco	81	15
Lizzie	30	f	w	NY	Plumas	Rich Bar Twp	77	8
M W	60	m	w	PA	Nevada	Eureka Twp	75	137
Mary	24	f	w	IREL	Yolo	Washington Twp	93	530
Mary A	69	f	w	IREL	Sacramento	2-Wd Sacramento	77	253
Nathaniel L	39	m	w	TN	Yolo	Buckeye Twp	93	412
Newton C	49	m	w	TN	Sonoma	Salt Point Twp	91	382
R J	33	m	w	MO	Solano	Vallejo	90	196
Rebecca	38	f	w	IREL	Mariposa	Mariposa P O	74	93
Rebecca	25	f	w	IREL	San Mateo	Menlo Park P O	87	377
Robert	43	m	w	IN	Sonoma	Analy Twp	91	245
Robert	41	m	w	IREL	San Francisco	San Francisco P O	80	412
Robert	34	m	w	CANA	Sonoma	Bodega Twp	91	258
Robert	30	m	w	IREL	San Francisco	San Francisco P O	85	720
Robt	10	m	w	CA	San Francisco	11-Wd San Francisc	84	588
Robt T	45	m	w	IREL	Shasta	Horsetown P O	89	503
S	35	m	w	NY	Alameda	Oakland	68	258
Thomas	30	m	w	OH	Trinity	North Fork Twp	92	218
Thos N	41	m	w	TN	Sonoma	Santa Rosa	91	404
W A	47	m	w	OH	Amador	Drytown P O	69	417
Walter	35	m	w	NY	San Francisco	8-Wd San Francisco	82	420
William	45	m	w	PA	Marin	Bolinas Twp	74	5
William	43	m	w	OH	Siskiyou	Yreka	89	652
William	38	m	w	PA	Placer	Lincoln P O	76	488
William	34	m	w	IREL	San Francisco	7-Wd San Francisco	81	169
Wm	20	m	w	NY	Napa	Napa Twp	75	66
Wm H	42	m	w	IREL	Alameda	Oakland	68	154
IRWINCE								
R	23	m	w	CA	Alameda	Oakland	68	159
IRWINGHAM								
Henry	55	m	w	NY	Solano	Tremont Twp	90	29
ISAAC								
Allice	57	f	w	ENGL	Sacramento	4-Wd Sacramento	77	324
Caleb L	26	m	w	MO	Contra Costa	Martinez P O	71	373
George	30	m	w	NORW	San Francisco	3-Wd San Francisco	79	297
Havens	27	m	w	PRUS	San Joaquin	2-Wd Stockton	86	179
Henry	27	m	w	PRUS	San Joaquin	1-Wd Stockton	86	134
Isaac	41	m	w	SHOL	Mendocino	Ukiah Twp	74	235
Jennie	10	f	w	CA	San Francisco	San Francisco P O	85	798
John	66	m	w	POLA	Siskiyou	Scott Rvr Twp	89	603
John	57	m	w	OH	Sacramento	4-Wd Sacramento	77	324
John	38	m	w	SWIT	Tuolumne	Chinese Camp P O	93	377
Joseph	35	m	w	HAMB	San Francisco	San Francisco P O	83	27
Lizzie	7	f	w	CA	San Francisco	San Francisco P O	85	798
Lotta	20	f	w	PRUS	San Francisco	1-Wd San Francisco	79	99
Michael	30	m	w	PRUS	Amador	Ione City P O	69	353
Ole	28	m	w	NORW	San Francisco	3-Wd San Francisco	79	297
Richard	41	m	w	OH	Monterey	San Juan Twp	74	386
Simon	25	m	w	PRUS	Amador	Sutter Crk P O	69	400
Soloman	37	m	w	PRUS	San Francisco	7-Wd San Francisco	81	169
Wm	43	m	w	TN	Santa Clara	Gilroy Twp	88	78
ISAACKS								
Saml	49	m	w	KY	Shasta	Shasta P O	89	457
ISAACS								
Alfred S	40	m	w	PRUS	San Francisco	8-Wd San Francisco	82	391
Anderson	42	m	w	NC	Sonoma	Mendocino Twp	91	300
Augustus	27	m	w	NGRA	San Francisco	San Francisco P O	83	32
Benjamin	53	m	w	ENGL	San Francisco	11-Wd San Francisc	84	530
Carl	36	m	w	POLA	Napa	Napa	75	44
David	56	m	w	ENGL	Shasta	Shasta P O	89	458
David	18	m	w	CA	San Francisco	6-Wd San Francisco	81	149
Emma	13	f	w	CA	San Francisco	8-Wd San Francisco	82	449
George W	48	m	w	NY	Fresno	Millerton P O	72	149
Henry M	34	m	w	ENGL	Inyo	Independence Twp	73	324
Herman	50	m	w	PRUS	San Francisco	8-Wd San Francisco	82	383
Hyman	39	m	w	PRUS	San Francisco	San Francisco P O	83	359
Jacob	28	m	w	RUSS	San Francisco	San Francisco P O	83	370
Jacob W	29	m	w	NY	San Francisco	6-Wd San Francisco	81	88
Joseph	45	m	w	ENGL	Shasta	Shasta P O	89	459
Joseph	14	m	w	NJ	San Francisco	11-Wd San Francisc	84	563
Joshua	36	m	w	RUSS	San Francisco	San Francisco P O	80	531
Kate	40	f	w	ENGL	San Francisco	3-Wd San Francisco	79	302
Martin	38	m	w	PRUS	San Francisco	San Francisco P O	80	534
Mary	70	f	w	PRUS	San Francisco	San Francisco P O	83	367
Mendel L	30	m	w	PRUS	Santa Clara	2-Wd San Jose	88	317
Michael	45	m	w	PRUS	San Francisco	San Francisco P O	83	284
Morris L	40	m	w	PRUS	Santa Clara	2-Wd San Jose	88	317
Ruben	30	m	w	POLA	San Francisco	San Francisco P O	83	352
S	50	f	w	POLA	San Francisco	San Francisco P O	85	806
Samuel	36	m	w	RUSS	San Francisco	San Francisco P O	83	347
Samuel	31	m	w	PRUS	San Francisco	San Francisco P O	83	373
W B	31	m	w	NY	San Francisco	San Francisco P O	85	842
William	37	m	w	ME	Sutter	Yuba Twp	92	148
William	30	m	w	PA	Placer	Newcastle Twp	76	477
Wm	6	m	w	CA	San Francisco	San Francisco P O	85	800
Wm	39	m	w	RI	San Joaquin	3-Wd Stockton	86	228
ISAACSON								
George	12	m	w	CA	San Francisco	San Francisco P O	83	366
Henry	33	m	w	NORW	San Francisco	1-Wd San Francisco	79	95
ISABEL								
Edward	33	m	w	NY	San Joaquin	Elliott Twp	86	80
James F	21	m	w	MO	Los Angeles	Los Nietos Twp	73	587
Sevilla	35	f	w	MEXI	Calaveras	San Andreas P O	70	196
Thomas	13	m	w	TX	Los Angeles	Los Nietos Twp	73	590
ISABELL								
J H	24	m	w	KY	Napa	Yountville Twp	75	86
Jane	22	f	w	SCOT	San Joaquin	2-Wd Stockton	86	183

Series M593

Name	Age	S	R	B-PL	County	Locale	Roll	Pg
ISABELLA								
Anthony	65	m	w	ITAL	San Francisco	San Francisco P O	83	311
ISABY								
John	35	m	w	FRAN	Calaveras	Copperopolis P O	70	241
ISACS								
Robert	40	m	w	SCOT	Mono	Bridgeport P O	74	287
Ross	24	m	w	NY	Sutter	Vernon Twp	92	133
ISADOR								
Isaac	38	m	w	POLA	San Francisco	1-Wd San Francisco	79	54
ISAIAH								
F H	47	m	w	MO	Lake	Big Valley	73	397
ISAMAN								
John	37	m	w	PA	Sierra	Sears Twp	89	558
Jonathan	37	m	w	PA	Sierra	Sears Twp	89	556
ISAMENGA								
Laura L	10	f	w	MO	Monterey	Alisal Twp	74	302
ISARES								
Mary	30	f	w	POLA	San Francisco	San Francisco P O	80	479
ISBELL								
Henry	40	m	w	MO	Yolo	Cache Crk Twp	93	441
Isaac C	54	m	w	NY	Santa Barbara	San Buenaventura P	87	441
Philo B	45	m	w	CT	El Dorado	Georgetown Twp	72	36
ISCHIE								
Emil	40	m	w	FRAN	San Francisco	8-Wd San Francisco	82	292
ISCHROTH								
Max	26	m	w	BADE	Sacramento	3-Wd Sacramento	77	299
ISEDORE								
Dennis	32	m	w	PRUS	Trinity	Douglas	92	233
ISEFELT								
Theodore	55	m	w	PRUS	El Dorado	Placerville Twp	72	96
ISEMONGA								
Thos	25	m	w	FRAN	Napa	Napa Twp	75	69
ISEN								
Chas	39	m	w	HANO	Sacramento	3-Wd Sacramento	77	291
ISENBURG								
J	38	m	w	GERM	Alameda	Oakland	68	147
ISENDORF								
Fred	39	m	w	GERM	Tuolumne	Columbia P O	93	341
Hernan	23	m	w	GERM	Tuolumne	Columbia P O	93	341
ISER								
August	34	m	w	WURT	Humboldt	Eureka Twp	72	270
Conrad	40	m	w	HDAR	Sacramento	3-Wd Sacramento	77	288
ISERMAN								
Fredrick	48	m	w	PRUS	San Francisco	San Francisco P O	80	422
George	41	m	w	PA	Nevada	Meadow Lake Twp	75	266
Harriet	48	f	w	FRAN	Placer	Bath P O	76	452
Henry	35	m	w	PA	Nevada	Meadow Lake Twp	75	261
ISERMANN								
Charles	52	m	w	WURT	El Dorado	Diamond Springs Tw	72	29
ISERT								
Henry F	47	m	w	PRUS	Los Angeles	Los Angeles	73	539
ISH								
C W	55	m	w	TN	Napa	Yountville Twp	75	87
Columbus	40	m	w	MO	Solano	Montezuma Twp	90	65
ISHAM								
Alfred	25	m	w	VT	San Francisco	11-Wd San Francisc	84	640
Byron	22	m	w	VT	San Francisco	11-Wd San Francisc	84	645
Daniel	34	m	w	MA	Santa Clara	Fremont Twp	88	61
James	23	m	w	AL	Sutter	Sutter Twp	92	120
Susan	40	f	w	IL	Napa	Yountville Twp	75	88
William	25	m	w	AL	Sutter	Sutter Twp	92	120
William	25	m	w	MO	Santa Clara	Milpitas Twp	88	111
ISHAN								
Ben	15	m	w	CA	Alameda	Oakland	68	195
ISHERWOOD								
B F	47	m	w	NY	Solano	Vallejo	90	199
ISHMAEL								
John	31	m	w	IN	Calaveras	Copperopolis P O	70	262
ISINMINGER								
S	35	m	w	OH	Amador	Drytown P O	69	417
ISLAI								
Anton	46	m	w	MEXI	Tuolumne	Columbia P O	93	344
ISLAS								
Leonado	35	m	w	MEXI	Fresno	Millerton P O	72	159
ISLEP								
Geo	14	m	w	CA	San Francisco	11-Wd San Francisc	84	588
ISLI								
John	38	m	w	SWIT	El Dorado	Greenwood Twp	72	54
ISLIP								
Joseph	45	m	w	CANA	Stanislaus	Empire Twp	92	41
ISLISS								
Florentine	35	m	w	SPAI	San Francisco	2-Wd San Francisco	79	198
ISLY								
John	35	m	w	SWIT	El Dorado	Greenwood Twp	72	54
ISMERT								
Peter	46	m	w	FRAN	Nevada	Grass Valley Twp	75	203
ISNER								
D	45	m	w	BOHE	San Joaquin	Tulare Twp	86	256
ISOARD								
August	49	m	w	FRAN	Nevada	Grass Valley Twp	75	146
ISOARDI								
Juan B	44	m	w	ITAL	Santa Barbara	San Buenaventura P	87	433
ISOCHLEMAN								
John	31	m	w	SWIT	San Francisco	San Francisco P O	80	360
ISOLA								
Giovanni	38	m	w	ITAL	San Francisco	11-Wd San Francisc	84	603
Louis	33	m	w	ITAL	San Francisco	2-Wd San Francisco	79	163

© 2001 by Heritage Quest. All rights reserved.

California 1870 Census

Name	Age	S	R	B-PL	County	Locale	Roll	Pg
Louisa	30	m	w	ITAL	Amador	Sutter Crk P O	69	407
ISOM								
Hugh	39	m	w	VA	Sonoma	Analy Twp	91	219
Ira	37	m	w	VA	Santa Cruz	Santa Cruz Twp	89	391
ISON								
Delos E	31	m	w	NY	Stanislaus	Branch Twp	92	2
ISRAAEL								
Abraham	30	m	w	PRUS	San Francisco	San Francisco P O	80	469
Ernest	26	m	w	FRAN	San Francisco	San Francisco P O	80	347
Ernest	26	m	w	FRAN	San Francisco	San Francisco P O	80	348
Myer	24	m	w	PRUS	San Francisco	San Francisco P O	80	423
Samuel	24	m	w	PRUS	San Francisco	San Francisco P O	80	469
ISRAEL								
Archibald	38	m	w	CANA	Stanislaus	Empire Twp	92	38
B	39	m	w	GERM	Santa Clara	Gilroy Twp	88	68
E S	56	f	w	ME	San Francisco	San Francisco P O	83	323
George	32	m	w	IL	Contra Costa	Martinez P O	71	396
Grant	40	m	w	PA	San Francisco	5-Wd San Francisco	81	2
Isaac	45	m	w	NY	San Francisco	5-Wd San Francisco	81	13
Jacob	56	m	w	RUSS	San Francisco	2-Wd San Francisco	79	246
Jas P	36	m	w	IN	Tehama	Tehama Twp	92	191
Julius	30	m	w	PRUS	San Francisco	San Francisco P O	83	234
P G	70	m	w	MD	Placer	Roseville P O	76	356
Simon	30	m	w	PRUS	San Francisco	8-Wd San Francisco	82	356
William	42	m	w	PA	Contra Costa	Martinez P O	71	398
ISRAILSKY								
Julius	33	m	w	PRUS	Napa	Napa	75	50
ISSLEY								
Bernhard	27	m	w	ITAL	Amador	Amador City P O	69	393
ISSON								
Saml	43	m	w	PRUS	San Francisco	1-Wd San Francisco	79	81
ISTEAD								
Ira	39	m	w	CA	Monterey	Monterey	74	357
IT								
Ah	30	m	c	CHIN	El Dorado	Placerville	72	127
ITA								
Carmel	8	f	w	CA	Santa Clara	Burnett Twp	88	37
Pabla	3	f	w	CA	Santa Clara	Burnett Twp	88	37
ITALIAN								
Jacoim	19	m	w	ITAL	Sacramento	Sutter Twp	77	385
Joe	20	m	w	ITAL	Sacramento	Sutter Twp	77	384
ITALIN								
---	30	m	w	ITAL	Sonoma	Sonoma Twp	91	431
ITENHOUSER								
Nicholas	35	m	w	FRAN	Solano	Vallejo	90	154
ITENI								
Louis	29	m	w	ITAL	Santa Clara	2-Wd San Jose	88	281
ITKEN								
Johanna	38	f	w	HANO	San Francisco	1-Wd San Francisco	79	5
ITORIC								
Itty	38	m	w	ITAL	Sacramento	Sutter Twp	77	385
IUSH								
Edwin	41	m	w	NY	Napa	Napa Twp	75	72
IVANS								
Chas H	40	m	w	NJ	San Luis Obispo	Santa Rosa Twp	87	321
IVARA								
Andres	12	m	w	CA	Los Angeles	Los Angeles Twp	73	482
Elario	50	m	w	CA	Los Angeles	Los Angeles	73	551
Jesus	24	f	w	CA	Los Angeles	Los Angeles	73	556
Jose	22	m	w	CA	Los Angeles	Los Angeles	73	553
Maria	38	f	w	CA	Los Angeles	Los Angeles	73	558
Ramon	42	m	w	MEXI	San Luis Obispo	San Luis Obispo Tw	87	300
Timotia	21	f	w	CA	Los Angeles	Los Angeles	73	553
IVARRO								
Miguel	31	m	w	CA	San Francisco	1-Wd San Francisco	79	43
IVARS								
Rafella	35	f	w	CHIL	Contra Costa	Martinez P O	71	367
IVENS								
Henry	24	m	w	IN	Nevada	Grass Valley Twp	75	145
Rich	38	m	w	IREL	Merced	Snelling P O	74	260
IVENSON								
Henry	18	m	w	SHOL	Alameda	Eden Twp	68	67
IVER								
Andrew	40	m	w	OH	Tehama	Tehama Twp	92	193
IVERS								
James	13	m	w	IL	Shasta	American Ranch P O	89	498
John	15	m	w	CA	San Francisco	11-Wd San Francisc	84	588
Richard	42	m	w	IREL	San Francisco	San Francisco P O	83	152
Robt	50	m	w	IREL	Solano	Vallejo	90	154
IVERSEN								
John	30	m	w	DENM	San Francisco	San Francisco P O	83	80
IVERSON								
Christy	26	m	w	DENM	Sonoma	Salt Point	91	388
Hans	35	m	w	BADE	San Francisco	2-Wd San Francisco	79	279
Iver G	28	m	w	NORW	Mendocino	Point Arena Twp	74	210
J B	34	m	w	DENM	Monterey	Salinas Twp	74	307
John	23	m	w	PRUS	Monterey	Alisal Twp	74	299
Michael	32	m	w	DENM	Mendocino	Point Arena Twp	74	209
Niels	40	m	w	DENM	Mendocino	Point Arena Twp	74	209
Petero	23	m	w	DENM	San Francisco	1-Wd San Francisco	79	122
Samuel	33	m	w	DENM	Mendocino	Point Arena Twp	74	207
IVERY								
Chas	38	m	w	NY	San Joaquin	Elkhorn Twp	86	58
IVES								
Bridget	30	f	w	IREL	San Francisco	San Francisco P O	80	534
C	40	m	w	CT	Lake	Lower Lake	73	414
Caroline	17	f	w	CA	Yuba	Marysville	93	582

Name	Age	S	R	B-PL	County	Locale	Roll	Pg
Frank T	15	m	w	CA	Santa Clara	Santa Clara Twp	88	155
L	31	m	w	IREL	Lake	Knoxville Mines	73	405
Mary	49	f	w	MO	Napa	Napa Twp	75	62
Richard	55	m	w	VA	Napa	Napa Twp	75	62
Richard	40	m	w	NY	San Francisco	5-Wd San Francisco	81	26
Richard	24	m	w	MO	Napa	Napa	75	24
Thomas	37	m	w	IN	Butte	Oroville Twp	70	140
William	52	m	w	VT	Amador	Volcano P O	69	373
William	24	m	w	TN	Yolo	Grafton Twp	93	494
Wm S	24	m	w	VA	Sacramento	1-Wd Sacramento	77	174
IVESTON								
Wm	22	m	w	IREL	San Francisco	1-Wd San Francisco	79	69
IVEY								
James	42	m	w	TN	Marin	San Rafael Twp	74	39
John	25	m	w	ENGL	Yuba	Long Bar Twp	93	562
IVIN								
John	28	m	w	IREL	San Francisco	1-Wd San Francisco	79	115
Joseph	36	m	w	IREL	San Francisco	1-Wd San Francisco	79	115
IVIS								
R O	30	m	w	NY	Alameda	Oakland	68	195
IVORA								
Alvin	30	m	w	AZOR	San Francisco	1-Wd San Francisco	79	119
IVORY								
E H	41	m	w	IREL	Solano	Vallejo	90	139
Edward	36	m	w	IREL	Solano	Maine Prairie Twp	90	51
Henry W	32	m	w	NY	Santa Clara	San Jose Twp	88	201
J A	28	m	w	IL	Solano	Vallejo	90	140
John	50	m	w	IREL	Nevada	Grass Valley Twp	75	169
Jonas	65	m	w	MA	San Joaquin	3-Wd Stockton	86	220
Mark B	38	m	w	PA	Contra Costa	Martinez P O	71	377
Peter	30	m	w	IREL	Solano	Maine Prairie Twp	90	47
IVY								
Harrison	30	m	w	MS	Sacramento	Franklin Twp	77	114
John	38	m	w	MS	Yolo	Merritt Twp	93	504
IWANAM								
Benj F	9	m	w	CA	Monterey	Castroville Twp	74	331
IWANSON								
Neal	25	m	w	SWED	San Mateo	Belmont P O	87	372
IWE								
Ah	37	m	c	CHIN	Placer	Bath P O	76	445
IYANZ								
Marco	34	m	w	CHIL	Calaveras	San Andreas P O	70	208
IYO								
John	25	m	w	IREL	Marin	Nicasio Twp	74	16
IZLER								
Antonio	18	m	w	ITAL	San Francisco	2-Wd San Francisco	79	185
IZZULES								
Jacob	49	m	w	NJ	Calaveras	Copperopolis P O	70	243
J								
Wm	46	m	w	IREL	Alameda	Eden Twp	68	82
JAACH								
Martin	38	m	w	HANO	Nevada	Bridgeport Twp	75	120
JAACOBS								
James R	55	m	w	VT	Santa Clara	2-Wd San Jose	88	325
JABEL								
Jno	50	m	w	FRAN	Sacramento	1-Wd Sacramento	77	201
JABENS								
George	39	m	w	PRUS	San Francisco	8-Wd San Francisco	82	468
JABEZ								
Jack	47	m	w	PORT	Alameda	Murray Twp	68	105
JABLE								
August	50	m	w	GERM	San Joaquin	2-Wd Stockton	86	166
JABOR								
F H	20	m	w	NY	San Joaquin	2-Wd Stockton	86	174
JACABY								
John	39	m	w	ENGL	Trinity	Trinity Center Pct	92	204
JACAMAN								
M	50	m	w	FRAN	Amador	Ione City P O	69	355
JACANER								
Louis	21	m	w	ITAL	Tuolumne	Columbia P O	93	342
JACANO								
John	40	m	w	PORT	Tuolumne	Columbia P O	93	345
JACCOMANS								
M	18	m	w	SWIT	Sonoma	Petaluma Twp	91	320
JACEK								
Adam	46	m	w	BADE	San Francisco	1-Wd San Francisco	79	37
JACEN								
Antone	35	m	w	PORT	Alameda	Eden Twp	68	71
Jace	42	m	w	DENM	Alameda	Eden Twp	68	83
Manuel	36	m	w	PORT	Alameda	Eden Twp	68	89
JACENNEZ								
Frank	9	m	w	CA	Yuba	Bullards Bar P O	93	550
Joseph	43	m	w	FRAN	Yuba	Bullards Bar P O	93	550
JACH								
Ah	40	m	c	CHIN	Sacramento	Georgianna Twp	77	124
L S	38	m	w	TN	San Joaquin	Douglas Twp	86	31
M H	14	f	w	IN	Alameda	Oakland	68	237
JACHIN								
Ah	42	m	c	CHIN	San Francisco	11-Wd San Francisc	84	522
JACILLA								
Anton	56	m	w	NM	Humboldt	South Fork Twp	72	301
Anton	36	m	h	NM	Humboldt	South Fork Twp	72	301
JACINTO								
Antonio	34	m	w	PORT	Nevada	Rough & Ready Twp	75	327
John	45	m	w	PORT	Alameda	Washington Twp	68	301
Manuel	26	m	w	PORT	San Francisco	3-Wd San Francisco	79	290
Manuell	49	m	w	PORT	San Mateo	Half Moon Bay P O	87	401

© 2001 by Heritage Quest. All rights reserved.

Name	Age	S	R	B-PL	County	Locale	Series M593 Roll	Pg
JACK								
---	45	m	c	CHIN	Siskiyou	Yreka Twp	89	669
---	40	m	w	IREL	Sonoma	Santa Rosa	91	401
---	35	m	c	CHIN	Siskiyou	Hamburg Twp	89	596
---	33	m	c	CHIN	Siskiyou	Yreka Twp	89	668
---	28	m	c	CHIN	Siskiyou	Cottonwood Twp	89	592
---	24	m	c	CHIN	Siskiyou	Yreka Twp	89	673
Ah	6	m	c	CA	Tuolumne	Chinese Camp P O	93	375
Ah	56	m	c	CHIN	Calaveras	San Andreas P O	70	191
Ah	47	m	c	CHIN	Mariposa	Mariposa P O	74	119
Ah	45	m	c	CHIN	Butte	Ophir Twp	70	104
Ah	45	m	c	CHIN	El Dorado	Mud Springs Twp	72	86
Ah	43	m	c	CHIN	Mariposa	Mariposa P O	74	103
Ah	42	m	c	CHIN	Sacramento	Granite Twp	77	151
Ah	42	m	c	CHIN	Sacramento	Granite Twp	77	137
Ah	40	m	c	CHIN	San Francisco	11-Wd San Francisc	84	695
Ah	40	m	c	CHIN	Placer	Lincoln P O	76	483
Ah	40	m	c	CHIN	Merced	Snelling P O	74	252
Ah	39	m	c	CHIN	Trinity	Minersville Pct	92	203
Ah	39	m	c	CHIN	San Francisco	San Francisco P O	80	496
Ah	37	m	c	CHIN	Merced	Snelling P O	74	274
Ah	37	m	c	CHIN	Sacramento	1-Wd Sacramento	77	196
Ah	36	m	c	CHIN	Fresno	Millerton P O	72	199
Ah	35	m	c	CHIN	Amador	Fiddletown P O	69	436
Ah	35	m	c	CHIN	Amador	Lancha Plana P O	69	369
Ah	34	m	c	CHIN	Placer	Dutch Flat P O	76	408
Ah	34	m	c	CHIN	Mariposa	Mariposa P O	74	109
Ah	33	m	c	CHIN	El Dorado	Mud Springs Twp	72	75
Ah	33	m	c	CHIN	Santa Clara	San Jose Twp	88	194
Ah	33	m	c	CHIN	Nevada	Nevada Twp	75	322
Ah	31	m	c	CHIN	Placer	Dutch Flat P O	76	411
Ah	31	m	c	CHIN	Mariposa	Mariposa P O	74	92
Ah	31	m	c	CHIN	Butte	Hamilton Twp	70	75
Ah	30	m	c	CHIN	Santa Clara	Alviso Twp	88	25
Ah	30	m	c	CHIN	Fresno	Millerton P O	72	150
Ah	30	m	c	CHIN	Nevada	Bloomfield Twp	75	92
Ah	30	m	c	CHIN	San Francisco	11-Wd San Francisc	84	478
Ah	28	m	c	CHIN	Butte	Concow Twp	70	8
Ah	27	m	c	CHIN	Nevada	Meadow Lake Twp	75	257
Ah	27	m	c	CHIN	Mariposa	Mariposa P O	74	100
Ah	25	m	c	CHIN	Sacramento	Franklin Twp	77	114
Ah	25	m	c	CHIN	Alameda	Murray Twp	68	111
Ah	24	m	c	CHIN	Nevada	Meadow Lake Twp	75	266
Ah	22	m	c	CHIN	Amador	Drytown P O	69	420
Ah	16	m	c	CHIN	Yuba	Rose Bar Twp	93	655
Ak	34	m	c	CHIN	Sacramento	Georgianna Twp	77	122
Alex	35	m	w	ENGL	Solano	Benicia	90	12
Ar	20	m	c	CHIN	Sonoma	Petaluma Twp	91	342
China	24	m	c	CHIN	Trinity	North Fork Twp	92	221
D J	40	m	w	ENGL	San Joaquin	1-Wd Stockton	86	154
E W	12	m	w	CA	Alameda	Oakland	68	243
Ed	30	m	w	ENGL	San Joaquin	1-Wd Stockton	86	154
J L	27	m	w	PA	Solano	Vallejo	90	172
James T	28	m	w	MO	San Joaquin	Castoria Twp	86	4
John	40	m	w	SCOT	Nevada	Nevada Twp	75	274
Joseph P	31	m	w	BOHE	Colusa	Colusa Twp	71	275
Kate	26	f	w	PA	San Francisco	San Francisco P O	83	156
Lee	24	m	c	CHIN	Tehama	Tehama Twp	92	195
Lizzie	27	f	w	SCOT	San Francisco	1-Wd San Francisco	79	135
Mary	13	f	w	SCOT	Sonoma	Petaluma Twp	91	324
Nellie	28	f	w	IREL	San Francisco	7-Wd San Francisco	81	283
Peter	50	m	w	SCOT	San Francisco	San Francisco P O	80	346
Robt	27	m	w	IREL	Alameda	Oakland	68	136
Sarah	41	f	w	SCOT	Alameda	Oakland	68	200
Sarah	30	f	w	SCOT	Marin	Point Reyes Twp	74	21
Thomas E	32	m	w	OH	El Dorado	Placerville	72	125
JACKA								
Elias	26	m	w	ENGL	Amador	Sutter Crk P O	69	400
JACKAMO								
Joseph	27	m	w	SWIT	Los Angeles	Los Angeles	73	565
JACKEL								
Dennis	40	m	w	FRAN	Shasta	Shasta P O	89	455
JACKELL								
Willm	38	m	w	PRUS	Siskiyou	Yreka	89	655
JACKEORA								
Louis	27	m	w	ITAL	Santa Clara	San Jose Twp	88	193
JACKER								
Thomas	35	m	w	ENGL	Amador	Amador City P O	69	394
JACKES								
Mark W	42	m	w	ENGL	El Dorado	Mud Springs Twp	72	72
Thomas	25	m	w	ENGL	San Francisco	San Francisco P O	83	224
JACKESBERRY								
B J	24	m	w	NY	Nevada	Meadow Lake Twp	75	249
JACKETS								
Heman S	45	m	w	NY	El Dorado	Diamond Springs Tw	72	34
JACKETT								
Frank	42	m	w	SWIT	Napa	Napa	75	22
JACKEY								
John	55	m	w	PRUS	Sonoma	Santa Rosa	91	414
Rich W	44	m	w	ENGL	Tehama	Red Bluff	92	173
JACKINS								
Daniel	36	m	w	ME	Santa Clara	2-Wd San Jose	88	294
JACKITT								
Allen J	46	m	w	VA	Nevada	Bridgeport Twp	75	103
JACKLIN								
William	36	m	w	ENGL	Santa Clara	Milpitas Twp	88	111

Name	Age	S	R	B-PL	County	Locale	Series M593 Roll	Pg
JACKMAN								
Edwd	25	m	w	ENGL	Marin	Nicasio Twp	74	16
Fred	47	m	w	PRUS	Santa Clara	Santa Clara Twp	88	150
J F	37	m	w	ME	Klamath	Trinidad Twp	73	391
J L	43	m	w	MO	Tehama	Antelope Twp	92	153
Jehiel B	44	m	w	VT	San Francisco	San Francisco P O	85	735
Joseph	21	m	b	WIND	San Francisco	San Francisco P O	80	409
P	27	m	w	MO	Lassen	Susanville Twp	73	446
Warili	24	m	w	ITAL	Santa Clara	2-Wd San Jose	88	315
Wm	37	m	w	NY	Mono	Bridgeport P O	74	286
JACKMIN								
Metreo	21	m	w	SWIT	San Mateo	Woodside P O	87	384
JACKMO								
Cilio	32	m	w	SWIT	Monterey	Monterey Twp	74	344
JACKNEY								
John	37	m	w	CANA	Sacramento	Center Twp	77	84
JACKS								
Ah	25	m	c	CHIN	Tuolumne	Big Oak Flat P O	93	401
Christina	35	f	w	SCOT	San Francisco	6-Wd San Francisco	81	118
Cubb	38	m	w	AR	Fresno	Kings Rvr P O	72	214
David	47	m	w	SCOT	Monterey	Monterey	74	367
Edgar R	26	m	w	ME	San Luis Obispo	Salinas Twp	87	291
Elias B	36	m	w	MO	Plumas	Mineral Twp	77	23
Francois	33	m	w	FRAN	Santa Clara	Almaden Twp	88	2
Fredrick	24	m	w	PRUS	San Francisco	San Francisco P O	80	477
Geo C	31	m	w	IA	Butte	Chico Twp	70	47
J M	40	m	w	KY	Yuba	East Bear Rvr Twp	93	539
Jenny	45	f	w	ENGL	Sierra	Gibson Twp	89	541
John	20	m	w	SCOT	Sutter	Butte Twp	92	94
Lillie	6	f	w	CA	Lake	Lower Lake	73	421
Mary S	55	f	w	NJ	Napa	Napa	75	38
Richard	39	m	w	MO	Plumas	Mineral Twp	77	21
Robert	41	m	w	IREL	Sierra	Gibson Twp	89	540
Samuel W	29	m	w	NY	Napa	Napa	75	4
Squire	41	m	w	KY	Plumas	Mineral Twp	77	21
William S	61	m	w	NY	Napa	Napa	75	36
Wm H	40	m	w	IREL	Sierra	Gibson Twp	89	541
JACKSON								
A	42	m	b	OH	Sierra	Lincoln Twp	89	550
A J	42	m	w	OH	Butte	Chico Twp	70	55
A Jones	41	m	w	NY	Santa Clara	Santa Clara Twp	88	168
A W	33	m	w	ENGL	San Francisco	1-Wd San Francisco	79	17
A W	32	m	w	ME	San Francisco	San Francisco P O	83	89
Abraim	55	m	w	MA	San Francisco	11-Wd San Francisc	84	666
Adam	35	m	w	NY	Calaveras	San Andreas P O	70	173
Alex	34	m	w	MO	Mendocino	Calpella Twp	74	181
Alexand	33	m	w	TN	San Mateo	Woodside P O	87	387
Alexander	30	m	w	CANA	Santa Clara	1-Wd San Jose	88	225
Alexr	30	m	w	IREL	San Francisco	1-Wd San Francisco	79	74
Alexr	25	m	w	MA	San Francisco	5-Wd San Francisco	81	35
Alfred	41	m	w	NY	San Francisco	6-Wd San Francisco	81	79
Alich	30	m	w	MO	Butte	Chico Twp	70	43
Amanda	32	f	w	NY	Santa Clara	Santa Clara Twp	88	171
Amos	34	m	w	IL	Sonoma	Analy Twp	91	232
Andrew	55	m	w	OH	Kern	Bakersfield P O	73	362
Andrew	54	m	w	PA	San Joaquin	Elkhorn Twp	86	53
Andrew	50	m	w	ME	Tuolumne	Sonora P O	93	318
Andrew	48	m	w	NY	San Francisco	1-Wd San Francisco	79	30
Andrew	47	m	w	OH	Sacramento	Franklin Twp	77	108
Andrew	45	m	w	LA	Marin	San Rafael Twp	74	42
Andrew	44	m	w	PA	Siskiyou	Hamburg Twp	89	596
Andrew	40	m	w	KY	Nevada	Bloomfield Twp	75	99
Andrew	40	m	w	NY	Contra Costa	Martinez P O	71	384
Andrew	40	m	w	SC	Calaveras	Copperopolis P O	70	253
Andrew	40	m	w	MI	San Luis Obispo	Salinas Twp	87	288
Andrew	36	m	w	OH	Plumas	Quartz Twp	77	36
Andrew	24	m	w	MI	Santa Barbara	San Buenaventura P	87	422
Andrew P	49	m	w	IN	Solano	Suisun Twp	90	101
Antone	37	m	w	PORT	Trinity	Douglas	92	236
Antone	30	m	w	SWIT	Humboldt	Mattole Twp	72	283
Archibald	45	m	b	MD	San Francisco	2-Wd San Francisco	79	281
Arthur	40	m	w	NY	San Francisco	5-Wd San Francisco	81	30
B B	48	m	w	PA	Solano	Vallejo	90	197
Barney	50	m	b	NY	Butte	Wyandotte Twp	70	143
Bart	32	m	w	PRUS	Stanislaus	Emory Twp	92	19
Bell	13	f	w	MO	Sonoma	Analy Twp	91	233
Benard	22	m	w	SWED	Solano	Vallejo	90	203
Byron	32	m	w	OH	Yolo	Cache Crk Twp	93	446
C A	21	m	w	AUST	San Francisco	8-Wd San Francisco	82	376
Calvin	40	m	w	VA	Yolo	Cache Crk Twp	93	452
Calvin	34	m	w	IA	Butte	Chico Twp	70	34
Caroline	42	f	b	VA	Sacramento	2-Wd Sacramento	77	207
Carter	47	m	b	VA	Sacramento	San Joaquin Twp	77	401
Catherine	55	f	b	KY	Solano	Benicia	90	5
Charles	55	m	w	CANA	Sacramento	San Joaquin Twp	77	401
Charles	53	m	w	NY	San Francisco	6-Wd San Francisco	81	140
Charles	27	m	w	VT	Inyo	Independence Twp	73	328
Charles	21	m	w	CANA	San Francisco	3-Wd San Francisco	79	312
Charles	20	m	m	CT	Placer	Bath P O	76	459
Charles R	30	m	w	NY	San Mateo	Redwood Twp	87	361
Chas	37	m	w	ME	Humboldt	Eureka Twp	72	274
Chas	35	m	w	NY	Sacramento	1-Wd Sacramento	77	202
Chas G	30	m	w	NY	San Francisco	San Francisco P O	83	113
Chas L	38	m	w	PA	Sonoma	Sonoma Twp	91	439
Chesterfield	52	m	m	KY	Sacramento	2-Wd Sacramento	77	207
Chs H	35	m	w	ME	Monterey	San Antonio Twp	74	315
Clouse	29	m	w	PRUS	Stanislaus	Emory Twp	92	19

© 2001 by Heritage Quest. All rights reserved.

California 1870 Census

Name	Age	S	R	B-PL	County	Locale	Roll	Pg
						Series M593		
D S	54	m	w	NY	Sacramento	3-Wd Sacramento	77	267
Daniel A	53	m	w	RI	Contra Costa	Martinez P O	71	394
Daniel A	39	m	w	OH	Yolo	Cache Crk Twp	93	446
Danl	29	m	w	CANA	Sierra	Gibson Twp	89	544
David	42	m	w	NY	San Francisco	2-Wd San Francisco	79	172
David	35	m	w	IREL	Amador	Sutter Crk P O	69	401
David	25	m	w	IA	San Mateo	Pescadero P O	87	411
Dawson	51	m	w	MD	Napa	Napa Twp	75	62
Deitrich	30	m	w	RUSS	San Mateo	Schoolhouse Statio	87	342
E	60	f	w	ENGL	Sierra	Downieville Twp	89	517
Ed	35	m	w	VA	Sonoma	Santa Rosa	91	427
Eda	15	f	w	CA	Solano	Benicia	90	17
Edgar	30	m	w	MA	Kern	Bakersfield P O	73	365
Edward	48	m	w	IREL	Alameda	Eden Twp	68	92
Edward	45	m	b	KY	Stanislaus	Emory Twp	92	22
Edward R	43	m	w	OH	Yolo	Putah Twp	93	525
Edward T	34	m	w	CANA	Yuba	Slate Range Bar Tw	93	677
Edwd	8	m	b	CA	Butte	Chico Twp	70	18
Edwd	36	m	w	IREL	San Francisco	1-Wd San Francisco	79	79
Elias	37	m	w	NY	Nevada	Bridgeport Twp	75	116
Eliza	51	f	w	CANA	San Francisco	San Francisco P O	83	187
Elizabeth	52	f	b	MD	Alameda	Oakland	68	180
Ellen	50	f	w	AL	San Francisco	8-Wd San Francisco	82	436
Enoch	42	m	w	NY	Placer	Bath P O	76	428
Eugene J	40	m	w	NY	Siskiyou	Yreka	89	663
Eunice	48	f	w	NY	Sonoma	Vallejo Twp	91	460
Evans	30	m	w	SCOT	Mendocino	Ten Mile Rvr Twp	74	172
Eziele	23	m	w	ME	Mendocino	Navarro & Big Rvr	74	174
F	56	m	w	VA	San Joaquin	Liberty Twp	86	93
F	35	m	w	VA	Sacramento	3-Wd Sacramento	77	304
F	20	m	w	CA	Yuba	Marysville	93	604
F W	25	m	w	ENGL	San Francisco	San Francisco P O	83	273
Frances	19	f	b	MS	San Francisco	San Francisco P O	80	402
Francis	37	m	w	IREL	Plumas	Rich Bar Twp	77	46
Francis	37	m	w	FRAN	Los Angeles	Los Angeles Twp	73	479
Francis M	31	m	w	IA	Shasta	Fort Crook P O	89	476
Frank	45	m	w	SCOT	Alameda	Brooklyn Twp	68	56
Franklin	43	m	w	IN	Solano	Suisun Twp	90	101
Franklin	26	m	w	OH	Yolo	Cottonwood Twp	93	461
Fred K	55	m	w	WALE	Butte	Kimshew Tpw	70	86
Frederick	3	m	w	CA	Santa Clara	San Jose Twp	88	213
Frederick	27	m	w	SWED	San Francisco	3-Wd San Francisco	79	295
G B	27	m	w	NY	San Francisco	3-Wd San Francisco	79	317
G W	41	m	w	IN	Mendocino	Ukiah Twp	74	237
Geo	50	m	w	HANO	San Joaquin	Douglas Twp	86	31
Geo	25	m	w	TX	El Dorado	Placerville Twp	72	94
Geo C	27	m	w	NH	Butte	Ophir Twp	70	101
Geo H	30	m	w	NY	El Dorado	Georgetown Twp	72	48
Geo L	30	m	w	IREL	El Dorado	Placerville Twp	72	100
Geo W	37	m	w	NY	Shasta	Stillwater P O	89	481
George	35	m	w	MA	San Francisco	7-Wd San Francisco	81	221
George	30	m	w	IREL	Placer	Alta P O	76	412
George	28	m	w	IREL	Inyo	Bishop Crk Twp	73	311
George	27	m	w	FRAN	Sacramento	2-Wd Sacramento	77	227
George	26	m	w	ME	Sacramento	2-Wd Sacramento	77	233
George	25	m	w	MA	San Francisco	San Francisco P O	80	335
George C	42	m	w	NY	Yolo	Merritt Twp	93	505
George E	36	m	w	ENGL	Mendocino	Round Valley Twp	74	217
George H	27	m	w	KY	Yolo	Cache Crk Twp	93	435
George H	27	m	w	DE	San Francisco	6-Wd San Francisco	81	40
Griffin	44	m	w	NY	Santa Clara	Redwood Twp	88	131
H	62	m	w	SC	Amador	Ione City P O	69	350
H E	25	m	w	MO	Alameda	Oakland	68	149
Hannah	36	f	w	OH	El Dorado	Placerville	72	126
Hannah	25	f	w	CANA	Sonoma	Analy Twp	91	218
Harvey I	51	m	w	NY	Sacramento	San Joaquin Twp	77	400
Henry	60	m	w	CUBA	San Francisco	11-Wd San Francisc	84	577
Henry	48	m	w	PA	Yolo	Cache Crk Twp	93	422
Henry	38	m	w	ENGL	Humboldt	Bald Hills	72	238
Henry	16	m	m	CA	Nevada	Grass Valley Twp	75	188
Henry	13	m	b	CA	Sacramento	4-Wd Sacramento	77	366
Homer	51	m	w	NC	Shasta	French Gulch P O	89	469
Horace J	26	m	w	NY	Mariposa	Mariposa P O	74	97
Hugh	50	m	w	SCOT	Sierra	Gibson Twp	89	539
Isaac P	43	m	w	NC	El Dorado	Georgetown Twp	72	46
J	60	m	w	KY	Amador	Ione City P O	69	358
J	41	m	w	ENGL	Santa Clara	Gilroy Twp	88	88
J A	46	m	w	NY	San Joaquin	2-Wd Stockton	86	181
J A	41	m	w	VA	Napa	Napa	75	47
J D	21	m	w	US	Sacramento	1-Wd Sacramento	77	184
J G	53	m	w	VT	San Francisco	8-Wd San Francisco	82	316
J G	34	m	w	NY	Santa Clara	Gilroy Twp	88	95
J M	40	m	w	PA	Solano	Vallejo	90	167
J M	36	m	w	IN	Sacramento	4-Wd Sacramento	77	345
J M	30	m	w	ME	Alameda	Oakland	68	264
J S	28	m	w	KY	San Joaquin	Tulare Twp	86	255
Jacob	30	m	w	POLA	San Francisco	2-Wd San Francisco	79	191
James	48	m	w	MO	Calaveras	San Andreas P O	70	151
James	45	m	w	PRUS	Alameda	Alameda	68	19
James	44	m	w	ENGL	San Francisco	2-Wd San Francisco	79	255
James	43	m	w	ENGL	Inyo	Bishop Crk Twp	73	314
James	40	m	b	TN	Yolo	Putah Twp	93	520
James	40	m	b	TN	Yolo	Putah Twp	93	519
James	37	m	w	KY	Yolo	Putah Twp	93	517
James	34	m	w	ENGL	San Joaquin	Elliott Twp	86	74
James	27	m	w	ME	Sacramento	Sutter Twp	77	388
James	23	m	w	MO	San Joaquin	Castoria Twp	86	11

Name	Age	S	R	B-PL	County	Locale	Roll	Pg
						Series M593		
James	14	m	w	ENGL	Sacramento	San Joaquin Twp	77	398
James	14	m	w	ENGL	Sacramento	2-Wd Sacramento	77	232
James J	26	m	w	ENGL	San Francisco	6-Wd San Francisco	81	41
James M	49	m	w	PA	San Diego	Julian Dist	78	471
James W	38	m	w	KY	Colusa	Stony Crk Twp	71	326
Jane	42	f	b	VA	San Francisco	San Francisco P O	80	486
Jane	40	f	w	IREL	San Francisco	San Francisco P O	83	350
Jas	28	m	w	CANA	San Joaquin	Elkhorn Twp	86	63
Jas	22	m	w	PA	Humboldt	Pacific Twp	72	289
Jeff A	37	m	w	TN	Tehama	Merrill	92	197
Jerry	44	m	w	ME	Sonoma	Petaluma Twp	91	338
Jim	8	m	i	CA	Sacramento	Granite Twp	77	136
Joe	30	m	w	VA	San Joaquin	Elkhorn Twp	86	66
Joel R	45	m	w	OH	Yolo	Cache Crk Twp	93	437
John	60	m	w	VA	San Joaquin	Liberty Twp	86	84
John	59	m	w	ENGL	San Francisco	San Francisco P O	85	738
John	57	m	w	MO	Napa	Napa	75	14
John	55	m	w	ENGL	San Francisco	1-Wd San Francisco	79	70
John	55	m	w	CANA	Mendocino	Point Arena Twp	74	215
John	54	m	w	NY	Solano	Suisun Twp	90	99
John	50	m	w	FINL	San Francisco	2-Wd San Francisco	79	232
John	45	m	w	NY	Kern	Bakersfield P O	73	361
John	44	m	w	IREL	Trinity	Weaverville Pct	92	227
John	37	m	w	NH	San Joaquin	3-Wd Stockton	86	235
John	37	m	w	OH	El Dorado	Georgetown Twp	72	47
John	35	m	w	CANA	Solano	Vallejo	90	147
John	34	m	w	CA	Marin	San Rafael Twp	74	41
John	33	m	w	TN	Tulare	Packwood Twp	92	255
John	33	m	w	NORW	San Joaquin	3-Wd Stockton	86	229
John	32	m	w	NY	San Francisco	1-Wd San Francisco	79	133
John	30	m	w	TX	Santa Barbara	Santa Maria P O	87	513
John	30	m	w	NJ	San Francisco	7-Wd San Francisco	81	188
John	28	m	w	NY	Calaveras	San Andreas P O	70	173
John	25	m	w	PA	San Joaquin	Elkhorn Twp	86	53
John	24	m	w	ME	Sacramento	2-Wd Sacramento	77	239
John	24	m	w	SWED	San Francisco	3-Wd San Francisco	79	292
John	21	m	w	HANO	San Francisco	1-Wd San Francisco	79	101
John A	56	m	w	MD	Mariposa	Mariposa P O	74	122
John A	52	m	w	CT	San Joaquin	1-Wd Stockton	86	141
John A	23	m	w	MD	Mariposa	Mariposa P O	74	118
John D	30	m	w	CANA	San Francisco	6-Wd San Francisco	81	84
John E	31	m	w	IREL	Mendocino	Anderson Twp	74	154
John H	43	m	w	MO	Yolo	Grafton Twp	93	487
John H	28	m	w	NY	Yolo	Buckeye Twp	93	412
John P	40	m	w	KY	San Francisco	8-Wd San Francisco	82	322
John P	30	m	w	NY	Yolo	Putah Twp	93	511
John S	34	m	w	KY	Sonoma	Analy Twp	91	242
John S	30	m	w	ENGL	San Francisco	San Francisco P O	83	93
John T	20	m	w	MO	Colusa	Colusa	71	288
Jonathan	60	m	w	ME	Siskiyou	Surprise Valley Tw	89	637
Joseph	64	m	w	MA	Siskiyou	Scott Rvr Twp	89	602
Joseph	48	m	w	ENGL	Butte	Oroville Twp	70	137
Joseph	40	m	w	TN	Mendocino	Point Arena Twp	74	210
Joseph	29	m	w	CANA	Plumas	Goodwin Twp	77	2
Joseph	27	m	w	CANA	San Francisco	San Francisco P O	80	467
Joseph	25	m	w	MD	Mariposa	Mariposa P O	74	118
Joseph	25	m	w	MD	Mariposa	Mariposa P O	74	122
Josiah	40	m	b	VA	Nevada	Grass Valley Twp	75	188
Josiah	28	m	b	NY	Butte	Chico Twp	70	19
Josiah	20	m	w	ENGL	Santa Clara	San Jose Twp	88	209
Julia	37	f	w	IN	Santa Clara	San Jose Twp	88	186
Julia A	55	f	w	KY	Sonoma	Healdsburg	91	274
Julius D	41	m	w	NY	Nevada	Meadow Lake Twp	75	258
Kate	14	f	w	NY	San Francisco	San Francisco P O	85	782
Lewis F	45	m	w	KY	Mendocino	Ten Mile Rvr Twp	74	172
Lindsey	46	m	w	MO	El Dorado	Mountain Twp	72	67
Louisa	36	f	m	PA	Sacramento	4-Wd Sacramento	77	347
Louise	32	f	w	IL	Sonoma	Santa Rosa	91	395
Lydia	36	f	b	DE	San Francisco	San Francisco P O	83	176
M	28	m	w	GA	Napa	Yountville Twp	75	87
M A	39	m	m	NY	Tuolumne	Sonora P O	93	309
Manuel	48	m	w	PORT	Los Angeles	Wilmington Twp	73	640
Marcus A	30	m	w	LA	San Luis Obispo	Salinas Twp	87	290
Maria	45	f	m	DC	San Joaquin	2-Wd Stockton	86	178
Mary	40	f	m	VA	San Francisco	San Francisco P O	80	417
Mary	37	f	w	IREL	Sacramento	4-Wd Sacramento	77	360
Mary	33	f	b	CT	Sacramento	2-Wd Sacramento	77	236
Mary	26	f	w	IREL	Mendocino	Ten Mile Rvr Twp	74	172
Mary	22	f	w	AR	Butte	Kimshew Tpw	70	78
Mary	20	f	w	NJ	San Francisco	8-Wd San Francisco	82	481
Mary M	33	f	m	LA	Mariposa	Mariposa P O	74	119
Mathew H	24	m	w	AR	Nevada	Rough & Ready Twp	75	332
Matilda	7	f	m	CA	Santa Clara	Fremont Twp	88	61
Monroe P	39	m	w	TN	Fresno	Millerton P O	72	181
Morris Wm	63	m	w	VA	Plumas	Quartz Twp	77	36
Orin H	49	m	w	CT	Yolo	Washington Twp	93	530
Oscar T	23	m	w	NY	Santa Cruz	Watsonville	89	364
Perry	48	m	b	MD	Butte	Chico Twp	70	18
Peter	42	m	w	ME	San Francisco	1-Wd San Francisco	79	124
Peter	34	m	b	NY	Butte	Chico Twp	70	18
Philo	42	m	w	KY	Butte	Ophir Twp	70	118
Poloman	30	m	w	CA	San Bernardino	San Bernardino Twp	78	443
R W	45	m	w	PA	Sacramento	1-Wd Sacramento	77	176
R Y	31	m	w	ENGL	Sierra	Downieville Twp	89	519
Richard	40	m	b	MS	Monterey	Monterey	74	354
Richard	32	m	w	MO	Amador	Sutter Crk P O	69	412
Richard	25	m	w	ENGL	Amador	Sutter Crk P O	69	411

© 2001 by Heritage Quest. All rights reserved.

Name	Age	S	R	B-PL	County	Locale	Series M593 Roll	Pg
Richd	54	m	m	NY	San Francisco	1-Wd San Francisco	79	133
Robert	51	m	w	IREL	Sonoma	Petaluma Twp	91	359
Robert	48	m	w	RUSS	San Francisco	3-Wd San Francisco	79	287
Robert	37	m	b	MO	San Joaquin	1-Wd Stockton	86	152
Robert	35	m	w	OH	Santa Barbara	San Buenaventura P	87	448
Robert	33	m	w	PRUS	San Francisco	1-Wd San Francisco	79	72
Robert	30	m	w	CANA	Marin	Sausalito Twp	74	68
Robert	30	m	w	CANA	San Francisco	1-Wd San Francisco	79	101
Robert	26	m	w	NY	Plumas	Indian Twp	77	19
Robert	25	m	w	IREL	San Francisco	San Francisco P O	83	207
Robert E	50	m	w	OH	Los Angeles	Los Angeles	73	542
Robertia R	28	f	w	ENGL	San Francisco	5-Wd San Francisco	81	2
Roswell	48	m	w	IA	Del Norte	Smith Rvr Twp	71	476
S	30	m	w	IREL	Solano	Vallejo	90	215
S J	40	m	w	NC	Sacramento	4-Wd Sacramento	77	345
Saml	40	m	w	MS	Butte	Chico Twp	70	50
Saml	25	m	b	LA	Tehama	Tehama Twp	92	190
Saml	20	m	w	CANA	Sonoma	Bodega Twp	91	254
Saml H	27	m	w	NY	Sacramento	4-Wd Sacramento	77	331
Saml P	47	m	w	SC	Merced	Snelling P O	74	276
Samuel	43	m	w	VA	Siskiyou	Butte Twp	89	587
Samuel	42	m	w	KY	Sonoma	Analy Twp	91	240
Samuel	34	m	w	LA	Colusa	Monroe Twp	71	324
Samuel	25	m	w	CANA	Sonoma	Salt Point	91	380
Samuel A	40	m	w	VT	Los Angeles	El Monte Twp	73	454
Sarah	60	f	b	MO	San Joaquin	Elliott Twp	86	74
Sarah	50	f	w	IREL	San Francisco	San Francisco P O	85	831
Sarah	35	f	w	SC	San Francisco	8-Wd San Francisco	82	368
Sarah	35	f	w	NY	Sacramento	San Joaquin Twp	77	401
Sarah A	32	f	w	MA	San Francisco	5-Wd San Francisco	81	5
Simon	52	m	w	PRUS	San Bernardino	San Bernardino Twp	78	416
Sol	42	m	w	WI	Butte	Oregon Twp	70	128
Sophronia	13	f	w	MS	Alameda	Hayward	68	76
Spier	37	m	w	NY	Tuolumne	Sonora P O	93	318
St Jno	53	m	w	PA	Butte	Ophir Twp	70	107
Stephen	45	m	w	NH	Sierra	Table Rock Twp	89	578
Ster	9	m	w	AUSL	Alameda	Oakland	68	258
Susan	25	f	w	MS	Merced	Snelling P O	74	255
Susie	24	f	w	RI	San Francisco	1-Wd San Francisco	79	110
T B	23	m	w	ENGL	San Francisco	San Francisco P O	83	302
T P	40	m	w	MO	Sutter	Vernon Twp	92	132
Tertius	45	m	w	ENGL	San Francisco	2-Wd San Francisco	79	187
Thead	36	m	w	VA	Sacramento	4-Wd Sacramento	77	340
Theodore	30	m	w	MA	San Francisco	1-Wd San Francisco	79	110
Thomas	58	m	w	KY	Contra Costa	Martinez Twp	71	347
Thomas	55	m	w	MA	Butte	Ophir Twp	70	91
Thomas	52	m	w	SWED	Placer	Bath P O	76	460
Thomas	48	m	w	ENGL	San Francisco	San Francisco P O	83	331
Thomas	30	m	w	MO	Yolo	Grafton Twp	93	479
Thomas	25	m	w	NJ	Contra Costa	San Pablo Twp	71	364
Thomas B	28	m	w	IREL	Mendocino	Anderson Twp	74	154
Thomas W	29	m	w	NY	San Francisco	San Francisco P O	85	757
Thomas W	17	m	w	ENGL	Nevada	Grass Valley Twp	75	147
Thompson	25	m	w	IREL	San Francisco	San Francisco P O	85	758
Thos	40	m	w	ENGL	Solano	Vallejo	90	160
Thos	36	m	w	OH	Sacramento	Sutter Twp	77	391
Thos	34	m	w	IREL	Marin	San Rafael Twp	74	39
Thos H	48	m	w	PA	Sacramento	4-Wd Sacramento	77	343
Tom	27	m	w	ENGL	San Francisco	San Francisco P O	83	414
W	41	m	w	MA	Alameda	Oakland	68	202
W	27	m	w	IREL	Amador	Jackson P O	69	329
W	24	m	w	NY	Sacramento	1-Wd Sacramento	77	189
W F	52	m	w	NY	Humboldt	Eureka Twp	72	277
W H	34	m	w	NY	Amador	Volcano P O	69	383
W M	39	m	w	SWED	San Francisco	San Francisco P O	83	283
William	42	m	w	DE	Nevada	Meadow Lake Twp	75	253
William	41	m	w	MD	Placer	Colfax P O	76	387
William	35	m	w	IREL	San Francisco	7-Wd San Francisco	81	172
William	35	m	w	CANA	Mendocino	Albion & Big Rvr T	74	167
William	35	m	w	TN	Santa Cruz	Santa Cruz	89	427
William	34	m	w	PA	Shasta	Shasta P O	89	459
William	23	m	m	ME	Sacramento	2-Wd Sacramento	77	229
William	21	m	w	CANA	Sonoma	Petaluma Twp	91	321
William A	30	m	w	ME	Mendocino	Big Rvr Twp	74	170
William B	58	m	w	VA	Placer	Auburn P O	76	381
William D	46	m	w	ENGL	Los Angeles	Wilmington Twp	73	637
William H	46	m	w	CANA	Placer	Bath P O	76	436
William H	41	m	w	PRUS	Santa Cruz	Watsonville	89	373
William L	37	m	w	OH	Yolo	Cache Crk Twp	93	441
William M	39	m	w	OH	Yolo	Cache Crk Twp	93	445
Wm	50	m	w	SWED	San Joaquin	1-Wd Stockton	86	121
Wm	47	m	w	TN	San Luis Obispo	San Luis Obispo Tw	87	311
Wm	42	m	w	OH	Fresno	Kingston P O	72	222
Wm	36	m	w	IN	Lassen	Susanville Twp	73	441
Wm	35	m	w	OH	Yuba	Marysville	93	606
Wm	35	m	w	VA	Marin	San Rafael Twp	74	43
Wm	29	m	w	SWED	San Francisco	San Francisco P O	83	88
Wm	29	m	w	PRUS	Sacramento	Georgianna Twp	77	122
Wm	20	m	w	PA	Humboldt	Pacific Twp	72	289
Wm C	34	m	w	ME	San Francisco	7-Wd San Francisco	81	228
Wm P	27	m	w	MO	San Joaquin	1-Wd Stockton	86	155
Wm S	45	m	w	ME	Plumas	Washington Twp	77	55
JACKTER								
George	28	m	w	PRUS	San Francisco	7-Wd San Francisco	81	218
JACKWAY								
S	37	m	w	MO	Santa Clara	Gilroy Twp	88	105
W	34	m	w	OH	Santa Clara	Gilroy Twp	88	106
JACKY								
Ge	30	m	c	CHIN	Sacramento	Franklin Twp	77	107
JACOB								
A F	30	m	w	PRUS	Tuolumne	Columbia P O	93	343
Atta	41	m	w	GERM	San Joaquin	3-Wd Stockton	86	222
August	43	m	w	FRAN	El Dorado	Salmon Falls Twp	72	131
Charles	38	m	w	BADE	San Francisco	11-Wd San Francisc	84	464
Charles	29	m	w	BAVA	Santa Cruz	Santa Cruz	89	406
David	34	m	w	POLA	San Francisco	3-Wd San Francisco	79	294
Elias	30	m	w	PRUS	Tulare	Visalia	92	296
Erastus	40	m	w	NY	Butte	Chico Twp	70	50
Harris	18	m	w	ENGL	Placer	Dutch Flat P O	76	404
Harry	40	m	w	SWED	Sacramento	Georgianna Twp	77	126
John	23	m	w	MI	San Francisco	San Francisco P O	85	790
Joseph	18	m	w	PRUS	San Francisco	8-Wd San Francisco	82	310
Julius	29	m	w	PRUS	San Francisco	8-Wd San Francisco	82	289
Lewis	24	m	w	OH	Colusa	Monroe Twp	71	322
Marie	22	f	w	FRAN	San Francisco	6-Wd San Francisco	81	78
Morris	38	m	w	RUSS	San Francisco	1-Wd San Francisco	79	55
R N	36	m	w	MI	San Francisco	8-Wd San Francisco	82	369
JACOBI								
Aaron	36	m	w	BAVA	San Francisco	8-Wd San Francisco	82	476
Jacob	40	m	w	POLA	San Francisco	6-Wd San Francisco	81	100
JACOBIN								
Chas	30	m	w	AUST	San Francisco	1-Wd San Francisco	79	126
JACOBINSON								
Hans	40	m	w	DENM	Tuolumne	Columbia P O	93	353
JACOBS								
A B	45	m	w	CANA	El Dorado	Georgetown Twp	72	47
A D	59	m	w	KY	Napa	Napa	75	49
Abner D	30	m	w	OH	Sonoma	Petaluma Twp	91	351
Abraham	36	m	w	PRUS	San Francisco	8-Wd San Francisco	82	475
Abraham	18	m	w	PRUS	Merced	Snelling P O	74	256
Abram	12	m	w	CT	San Francisco	1-Wd San Francisco	79	104
Adam	43	m	w	PRUS	Lassen	Susanville Twp	73	446
Adoph	21	m	w	PRUS	Merced	Snelling P O	74	256
Albert	37	m	w	MA	San Francisco	2-Wd San Francisco	79	198
Albert	30	m	w	IL	Butte	Ophir Twp	70	112
Albrecht	53	m	w	PRUS	Kern	Havilah P O	73	340
Allred	33	m	w	PRUS	Sonoma	Analy Twp	91	233
Andrew	43	m	w	FRAN	Yuba	New York Twp	93	641
Baron	28	m	w	ENGL	Sacramento	3-Wd Sacramento	77	282
Bartle	33	m	w	PRUS	Trinity	Junction City Pct	92	210
Benj	42	m	w	MA	Siskiyou	Scott Rvr Twp	89	602
C S	43	m	w	NY	Solano	Vallejo	90	175
Carl	41	m	w	HAMB	San Francisco	1-Wd San Francisco	79	129
Caroline	52	f	w	PRUS	Santa Clara	1-Wd San Jose	88	236
Catherine A	26	f	w	NY	San Francisco	11-Wd San Francisc	84	699
Charles	18	m	w	NY	Sonoma	Petaluma Twp	91	321
Danl	17	m	w	ENGL	Solano	Vallejo	90	201
David	35	m	w	OH	Marin	San Rafael Twp	74	38
E S	28	m	w	ENGL	Sacramento	1-Wd Sacramento	77	174
Elias	26	m	w	POLA	Sonoma	Healdsburg & Mendo	91	278
Elijah	50	m	w	ENGL	Sacramento	2-Wd Sacramento	77	227
Ely	50	m	w	PA	Sonoma	Santa Rosa	91	403
Enos	31	m	w	PA	Sutter	Sutter Twp	92	116
Ephakim	80	m	w	PRUS	San Francisco	San Francisco P O	83	367
Erastus	43	m	w	NY	Yolo	Grafton Twp	93	490
Eugene	49	m	w	CUBA	Calaveras	San Andreas P O	70	214
Frank	36	m	w	PRUS	San Bernardino	Belleville Twp	78	408
Frank	27	m	w	ENGL	San Joaquin	2-Wd Stockton	86	170
Frank	26	m	w	ME	San Mateo	Pescadero P O	87	413
Geo F	44	m	w	NY	Nevada	Nevada Twp	75	293
Geo H	39	m	w	PA	Sonoma	Washington Twp	91	468
George	40	m	w	FRAN	San Francisco	11-Wd San Francisc	84	463
George	18	m	w	ME	Santa Cruz	Santa Cruz Twp	89	400
Gustav	28	m	w	PRUS	San Francisco	8-Wd San Francisco	82	466
H	19	m	w	GERM	Lake	Lower Lake	73	420
Harry	25	m	w	ENGL	Sacramento	1-Wd Sacramento	77	180
Henry	55	m	w	HCAS	Nevada	Nevada Twp	75	289
Henry	43	m	w	PRUS	San Francisco	1-Wd San Francisco	79	104
Henry	40	m	w	PRUS	Yolo	Cache Crk Twp	93	424
Henry	28	m	w	PRUS	Trinity	Junction City Pct	92	210
Henry	23	m	w	PRUS	Merced	Snelling P O	74	258
Henry	19	m	w	ENGL	San Francisco	1-Wd San Francisco	79	59
Henry	18	m	i	MEXI	Sacramento	Brighton Twp	77	74
Henry T	20	m	w	OH	Sonoma	Petaluma Twp	91	320
Isaac W	49	m	w	VA	Yolo	Grafton Twp	93	492
Isador	40	m	w	PRUS	Nevada	Nevada Twp	75	278
J H	45	m	w	DENM	Alameda	Oakland	68	250
J H	31	m	w	PRUS	Merced	Snelling P O	74	247
Jacob	45	m	w	PRUS	San Francisco	2-Wd San Francisco	79	238
Jacob	40	m	w	BAVA	San Francisco	11-Wd San Francisc	84	500
James	53	m	w	POLA	San Francisco	11-Wd San Francisc	84	423
James	36	m	w	OH	Placer	Bath P O	76	427
James A	43	m	w	KY	Yolo	Cottonwood Twp	93	459
Jas B	45	m	w	PA	Sonoma	Washington Twp	91	468
Jas H	46	m	w	VT	Santa Barbara	Santa Barbara P O	87	499
Jehu	28	m	w	OH	Siskiyou	Cottonwood Twp	89	591
Jeremiah	22	m	w	MO	Yolo	Cache Crk Twp	93	440
John	50	m	w	KY	Amador	Amador City P O	69	393
John	41	m	w	ENGL	Sutter	Vernon Twp	92	136
John	40	m	w	NY	Contra Costa	Martinez P O	71	385
John	26	m	w	FRAN	Santa Cruz	Santa Cruz Twp	89	399
John	24	m	w	NY	San Francisco	5-Wd San Francisco	81	4
John	18	m	w	PRUS	San Joaquin	2-Wd Stockton	86	206
John J	53	m	w	PRUS	Sierra	Table Rock Twp	89	571

© 2001 by Heritage Quest. All rights reserved.

California 1870 Census

Name	Age	S	R	B-PL	County	Locale	Roll	Pg
John J	31	m	w	NY	San Francisco	1-Wd San Francisco	79	88
John N	31	m	w	IN	Siskiyou	Surprise Valley Tw	89	640
Joseph	46	m	w	POLA	San Francisco	1-Wd San Francisco	79	35
Joseph	37	m	w	POLA	Merced	Snelling P O	74	246
Leopold	19	m	w	RUSS	Fresno	Kings Rvr P O	72	211
Lewis	49	m	w	POLA	Sacramento	2-Wd Sacramento	77	246
Lewis	30	m	w	PRUS	Nevada	Nevada Twp	75	276
Louis	41	m	w	PRUS	San Bernardino	San Bernardino Twp	78	425
Louis	34	m	w	PRUS	Tuolumne	Chinese Camp P O	93	335
Lydia	49	f	w	CT	San Francisco	11-Wd San Francisc	84	508
Manheim	44	m	w	PRUS	San Francisco	8-Wd San Francisco	82	427
Mark	40	m	w	RUSS	San Francisco	San Francisco P O	83	229
Mary	29	f	w	PRUS	Sacramento	2-Wd Sacramento	77	243
Matilda	23	f	w	PRUS	Placer	Bath P O	76	451
Morris	35	m	w	PRUS	San Francisco	San Francisco P O	83	53
Morris	26	m	w	RUSS	Contra Costa	Martinez P O	71	397
Nathan	42	m	w	ENGL	Sacramento	4-Wd Sacramento	77	327
Nathaniel	43	m	w	ENGL	San Francisco	San Francisco P O	85	877
Nellie	25	f	w	NY	Santa Clara	1-Wd San Jose	88	236
Ole	48	m	w	DENM	Napa	Yountville Twp	75	79
P	35	m	w	POLA	San Francisco	San Francisco P O	85	818
Perry	33	m	w	MO	Yolo	Cache Crk Twp	93	441
Rachel	40	f	w	PRUS	San Francisco	8-Wd San Francisco	82	414
Rodney	58	m	w	ME	Nevada	Rough & Ready Twp	75	323
Rose	44	f	w	ENGL	San Francisco	8-Wd San Francisco	82	458
S	36	m	w	POLA	San Francisco	San Francisco P O	85	803
Samueel	33	m	w	PRUS	Nevada	Bloomfield Twp	75	93
Samuel	67	m	w	RUSS	San Francisco	San Francisco P O	83	402
Samuel	30	m	w	SCOT	Santa Clara	1-Wd San Jose	88	228
Samuel	27	m	w	PRUS	Yolo	Cache Crk Twp	93	431
Samuel	18	m	w	NY	San Francisco	San Francisco P O	80	480
Sarah	13	f	w	PA	San Francisco	San Francisco P O	83	234
Sible	82	f	w	VT	San Bernardino	San Bernardino Twp	78	443
Soloman	36	m	w	POLA	El Dorado	Georgetown Twp	72	45
Soloman	35	m	w	BAVA	San Francisco	8-Wd San Francisco	82	455
Thomas B	29	m	w	SCOT	Sonoma	Petaluma Twp	91	321
Tobias A	41	m	w	PA	Yolo	Cache Crk Twp	93	420
William	50	m	w	HANO	Contra Costa	San Pablo Twp	71	366
William	42	m	w	NY	San Francisco	San Francisco P O	83	369
William	35	m	w	PRUS	San Francisco	San Francisco P O	85	720
William	24	m	w	OH	Solano	Rio Vista Twp	90	63
Wm	10	m	w	CA	Sacramento	3-Wd Sacramento	77	259
Wm H	38	m	w	NY	San Francisco	San Francisco P O	83	138
Wm W	32	m	w	ENGL	Sacramento	1-Wd Sacramento	77	176
Woolf	42	m	w	RUSS	Plumas	Goodwin Twp	77	58
JACOBSEN								
John	48	m	w	PRUS	San Francisco	San Francisco P O	83	135
John	39	m	w	PRUS	San Francisco	San Francisco P O	80	470
JACOBSON								
Alx	39	m	w	DENM	El Dorado	Coloma Twp	72	3
Benjamin	27	m	w	FINL	Santa Clara	2-Wd San Jose	88	312
Carson	29	m	w	DENM	Marin	San Rafael Twp	74	31
Christian	25	m	w	DENM	Alameda	Eden Twp	68	58
Chs	40	m	w	DENM	San Francisco	2-Wd San Francisco	79	225
David	28	m	w	RUSS	San Francisco	San Francisco P O	83	392
Fred	36	m	w	DENM	San Francisco	3-Wd San Francisco	79	300
Hans	40	m	w	SWED	El Dorado	Placerville Twp	72	101
Hans	28	m	w	DENM	San Francisco	1-Wd San Francisco	79	128
Henry A	20	m	w	CA	Marin	San Rafael Twp	74	59
Jacob	55	m	w	DENM	Butte	Ophir Twp	70	108
Jacob	41	m	w	PRUS	Sacramento	Franklin Twp	77	110
Jacob	41	m	w	SHOL	Sonoma	Analy Twp	91	237
Jno	27	m	w	NC	San Joaquin	2-Wd Stockton	86	188
John	35	m	w	DENM	San Francisco	1-Wd San Francisco	79	119
John	31	m	w	DENM	El Dorado	White Oak Twp	72	138
Julius	45	m	w	PRUS	San Francisco	San Francisco P O	83	198
Louis	38	m	w	RUSS	San Mateo	Half Moon Bay P O	87	396
Nicholas	27	m	w	SWED	San Francisco	San Francisco P O	80	401
Niels	42	m	w	DENM	Amador	Ione City P O	69	353
P	36	m	w	DENM	San Francisco	8-Wd San Francisco	82	366
Peter	45	m	w	SHOL	San Francisco	2-Wd San Francisco	79	224
Peter	27	m	w	SWED	San Francisco	3-Wd San Francisco	79	292
Rudolph	40	m	w	SHOL	El Dorado	Placerville	72	125
Saml	48	m	w	HUNG	San Francisco	San Francisco P O	85	795
Theodore	38	m	w	MA	San Francisco	1-Wd San Francisco	79	124
William	25	m	w	DENM	San Francisco	11-Wd San Francisc	84	519
JACOBSSON								
Jacob	53	m	w	SWED	Inyo	Cerro Gordo Twp	73	320
JACOBUS								
Elizabet S	34	f	w	ME	San Mateo	Searsville P O	87	382
J F	47	m	w	NY	Lake	Big Valley	73	395
James J	46	m	w	NJ	San Mateo	Woodside P O	87	386
Rebecca	36	f	w	SC	Santa Cruz	Santa Cruz	89	431
JACOBY								
Abram	53	m	w	PRUS	San Bernardino	San Bernardino Twp	78	416
Arthur	44	m	w	OH	Tehama	Tehama Twp	92	191
Francis	60	m	w	FRAN	San Francisco	2-Wd San Francisco	79	173
Herman	28	m	w	PRUS	Los Angeles	Wilmington Twp	73	643
Jacob	43	m	w	PRUS	San Francisco	8-Wd San Francisco	82	449
Jacob	19	m	w	CA	San Francisco	2-Wd San Francisco	79	245
John	53	m	w	PA	Fresno	Millerton P O	72	183
Joseph	35	m	w	PRUS	San Francisco	San Francisco P O	85	823
Joseph	32	m	w	BELG	Inyo	Independence Twp	73	328
Louis	48	m	w	PRUS	San Francisco	8-Wd San Francisco	82	404
Morris	23	m	w	PRUS	Kern	Bakersfield P O	73	360
Nathan	31	m	w	PRUS	Los Angeles	Wilmington Twp	73	643
Samuel	48	m	w	PRUS	San Francisco	San Francisco P O	80	534

Name	Age	S	R	B-PL	County	Locale	Roll	Pg
JACOP								
Louis	43	m	w	PRUS	Butte	Ophir Twp	70	95
JACOPE								
Peter	36	m	w	ITAL	Calaveras	Copperopolis P O	70	249
JACOTI								
Julius C	42	m	w	ITAL	San Francisco	1-Wd San Francisco	79	110
JACOTT								
Dan	29	m	w	WI	San Joaquin	Tulare Twp	86	261
JACOX								
Oliver	36	m	w	MI	Alameda	Washington Twp	68	274
JACQUART								
Constantine	36	m	w	FRAN	San Francisco	11-Wd San Francisc	84	699
JACQUEL								
Julian	50	m	w	FRAN	Plumas	Quartz Twp	77	35
JACQUELINE								
Emile	38	m	w	FRAN	San Francisco	San Francisco P O	83	172
JACQUEMOT								
John B	61	m	w	FRAN	Santa Clara	1-Wd San Jose	88	268
JACQUES								
A	37	m	w	CANA	Nevada	Eureka Twp	75	139
Aufranguez	25	m	w	FRAN	Monterey	Monterey Twp	74	346
Bevikill	24	m	w	ENGL	Santa Barbara	Santa Maria P O	87	513
Dennis	41	m	w	CANA	Sacramento	4-Wd Sacramento	77	377
Prine	17	m	w	FRAN	San Francisco	San Francisco P O	83	186
William	16	m	w	CA	Sacramento	Franklin Twp	77	109
JACQUINOT								
Jean	19	f	w	FRAN	San Francisco	San Francisco P O	80	481
Louis	27	m	w	FRAN	San Francisco	San Francisco P O	80	533
JACQUNTO								
Xavier	33	m	w	FRAN	Alameda	Brooklyn Twp	68	39
JACQUOT								
Joseph	43	m	w	FRAN	San Francisco	11-Wd San Francisc	84	704
JACRASS								
T	35	m	w	PA	Lake	Knoxville Mines	73	405
JACUELIN								
Joseph	40	m	w	FRAN	Santa Clara	2-Wd San Jose	88	331
JAEGER								
Chas	29	m	w	PRUS	San Francisco	8-Wd San Francisco	82	374
George	42	m	w	PRUS	San Francisco	San Francisco P O	83	377
Lewis J F	46	m	w	PA	San Diego	Fort Yuma Dist	78	463
JAEGERS								
Augustus J	40	m	w	AUST	San Francisco	8-Wd San Francisco	82	390
JAEGMIN								
C	49	m	w	FRAN	Amador	Drytown P O	69	417
JAENSCH								
William	32	m	w	PRUS	Napa	Napa	75	43
JAESON								
Christ	28	m	w	HAMB	Alameda	Eden Twp	68	83
JAFFA								
Henry	52	m	w	ENGL	San Francisco	11-Wd San Francisc	84	508
JAFFE								
Louis	34	m	w	PRUS	San Francisco	8-Wd San Francisco	82	407
JAFFLIN								
Jim	30	m	w	EIND	Sutter	Yuba Twp	92	149
JAFFREY								
John	32	m	w	SCOT	Santa Clara	Milpitas Twp	88	115
JAFFURT								
M	28	m	w	FRAN	San Joaquin	2-Wd Stockton	86	162
JAFREY								
Gilles	57	m	w	FRAN	San Joaquin	2-Wd Stockton	86	166
JAFUAS								
Ben	60	m	w	IL	Butte	Ophir Twp	70	101
JAGARDS								
Philip	48	m	w	CHIL	Shasta	American Ranch P O	89	496
Toribio	51	m	w	CHIL	Shasta	American Ranch P O	89	496
JAGEMAN								
William	27	m	w	PRUS	San Francisco	San Francisco P O	80	469
JAGEN								
Jno	32	m	w	OH	San Joaquin	3-Wd Stockton	86	230
JAGER								
Charles E	51	m	w	GERM	Santa Clara	1-Wd San Jose	88	264
Frank	38	m	w	NY	Sacramento	Sutter Twp	77	381
Henry	25	m	w	OH	San Joaquin	3-Wd Stockton	86	230
Wm	37	m	w	ENGL	San Francisco	7-Wd San Francisco	81	279
JAGGE								
John	27	m	w	SWIT	San Francisco	8-Wd San Francisco	82	352
JAGGI								
Albert	40	m	w	SWIT	Santa Clara	Fremont Twp	88	58
JAGO								
Ephriam B	39	m	w	KY	Nevada	Grass Valley Twp	75	216
John	36	m	w	SPAI	San Joaquin	Oneal Twp	86	115
Robert H	35	m	w	IREL	San Francisco	San Francisco P O	83	383
JAGOR								
Pastor	35	m	w	OH	Alameda	Eden Twp	68	82
JAH								
Ah	37	m	c	CHIN	Sacramento	3-Wd Sacramento	77	316
Ah	28	m	c	CHIN	Merced	Snelling P O	74	278
Sim	30	m	c	CHIN	Santa Clara	Santa Clara Twp	88	161
JAHANT								
Lewis	37	m	w	FRAN	San Joaquin	1-Wd Stockton	86	136
Otis	36	m	w	MA	San Joaquin	1-Wd Stockton	86	140
Peter	40	m	w	FRAN	San Joaquin	1-Wd Stockton	86	140
Peter	29	m	w	FRAN	San Joaquin	1-Wd Stockton	86	154
JAHEGER								
James	28	m	w	PRUS	San Francisco	San Francisco P O	80	533
JAHENT								
V	38	m	w	OH	San Joaquin	Liberty Twp	86	93

Series M593

© 2001 by Heritage Quest. All rights reserved.

Name	Age	S	R	B-PL	County	Locale	Series M593 Roll	Pg
JAHLE								
Mary	39	f	w	----	San Francisco	3-Wd San Francisco	79	314
JAIKINS								
C	35	m	w	ENGL	Sierra	Butte Twp	89	512
JAIM								
Ah	29	m	c	CHIN	Sacramento	Mississippi Twp	77	162
Ah	26	m	c	CHIN	Sacramento	Brighton Twp	77	72
JAIMESON								
James	40	m	w	NY	Sacramento	Sutter Twp	77	381
Robert	68	m	w	PA	Sacramento	San Joaquin Twp	77	407
JAIN								
Ah	35	m	c	CHIN	Sacramento	Dry Crk Twp	77	101
Ah	32	m	c	CHIN	Yolo	Cache Crk Twp	93	426
JAIRA								
Gerard	40	m	w	FRAN	Santa Clara	Almaden Twp	88	17
JAISON								
Charles	25	m	w	PRUS	San Francisco	6-Wd San Francisco	81	137
Gustave	58	m	w	DENM	San Joaquin	2-Wd Stockton	86	165
JAK								
Ah	22	m	c	CHIN	Sacramento	Franklin Twp	77	109
JAKE								
Ah	60	m	c	CHIN	Trinity	Douglas	92	235
Ah	50	m	c	CHIN	Trinity	Junction City Pct	92	207
Ah	47	m	c	CHIN	Butte	Kimshew Tpw	70	84
Ah	40	m	c	CHIN	Plumas	Plumas Twp	77	31
Ah	38	m	c	CHIN	Sierra	Lincoln Twp	89	546
Ah	37	m	c	CHIN	Sierra	Sears Twp	89	553
Ah	36	m	c	CHIN	Trinity	Weaverville Pct	92	231
Ah	35	m	c	CHIN	El Dorado	White Oak Twp	72	140
Ah	35	m	c	CHIN	Sierra	Sears Twp	89	554
Ah	27	m	c	CHIN	Monterey	Monterey Twp	74	347
Ah	27	m	c	CHIN	El Dorado	Placerville Twp	72	105
Ah	27	m	c	CHIN	Nevada	Washington Twp	75	343
Ah	25	m	c	CHIN	Mendocino	Point Arena Twp	74	215
Ah	25	m	c	CHIN	Stanislaus	Emory Twp	92	17
Ah	25	m	c	CHIN	Sierra	Lincoln Twp	89	551
Ah	23	m	c	CHIN	Placer	Gold Run Twp	76	395
Ah	22	m	c	CHIN	Trinity	Douglas	92	236
Ah	21	m	c	CHIN	Solano	Suisun Twp	90	104
Ah	20	m	c	CHIN	Nevada	Washington Twp	75	342
Ah	18	m	c	CHIN	Mendocino	Point Arena Twp	74	208
Clawhammer	35	m	w	PA	Marin	San Rafael Twp	74	43
Hip	24	m	c	CHIN	San Francisco	1-Wd San Francisco	79	58
King	35	m	c	CHIN	Tehama	Antelope Twp	92	153
Moy	31	m	c	CHIN	Fresno	Millerton P O	72	184
JAKEN								
Berry	23	m	w	ITAL	Santa Clara	Fremont Twp	88	48
JAKNAY								
Alirgal	55	m	w	NY	Solano	Maine Prairie Twp	90	54
JALIA								
Frances	28	f	w	MEXI	Yuba	Marysville	93	614
JALINE								
John	40	m	w	NY	Tehama	Tehama Twp	92	192
JALK								
Ah	31	m	c	CHIN	Santa Clara	Fremont Twp	88	45
JALL								
Wm H	42	m	w	PA	San Francisco	1-Wd San Francisco	79	31
JALUMSTEIN								
John	39	m	w	POLA	Tuolumne	Sonora P O	93	311
JALWITCH								
John	29	m	w	ITAL	Amador	Sutter Crk P O	69	407
JAM								
Ah	52	m	c	CHIN	Sacramento	Granite Twp	77	137
Ah	35	m	c	CHIN	San Mateo	San Mateo P O	87	352
Ah	34	m	c	CHIN	Siskiyou	Hamburg Twp	89	599
Ah	34	m	c	CHIN	San Joaquin	Oneal Twp	86	117
Ah	25	m	c	CHIN	San Francisco	San Francisco P O	83	131
Ah	25	m	c	CHIN	El Dorado	Diamond Springs Tw	72	25
Ah	14	m	c	CHIN	San Francisco	3-Wd San Francisco	79	328
JAMAR								
Eva	19	f	w	ENGL	San Francisco	11-Wd San Francisc	84	688
JAMARD								
Chas	40	m	w	FRAN	San Francisco	8-Wd San Francisco	82	361
JAMATE								
Joseph	37	m	w	ITAL	San Mateo	Schoolhouse Statio	87	334
JAMBER								
Henry	30	m	w	PRUS	San Joaquin	2-Wd Stockton	86	164
JAMBERS								
Peter J M	58	m	w	BELG	Nevada	Nevada Twp	75	317
JAME								
Ah	27	m	c	CHIN	Placer	Emigrant Gap P O	76	416
JAMEISON								
John	59	m	w	SCOT	El Dorado	Placerville	72	109
Samel E	34	m	w	OH	Sonoma	Petaluma Twp	91	329
JAMES								
---	10	m	w	CA	Sacramento	4-Wd Sacramento	77	339
A W	23	m	w	VA	Mendocino	Round Valley Twp	74	217
Aaron	21	m	w	PRUS	San Bernardino	Chino Twp	78	409
Ah	22	m	c	CHIN	Calaveras	Copperopolis P O	70	257
Alford	38	m	w	OH	Los Angeles	Los Angeles Twp	73	466
Alice	10	f	w	CA	Sonoma	Santa Rosa	91	414
Bartholmew	28	m	w	ENGL	San Francisco	San Francisco P O	80	375
Benjn	38	m	w	NY	San Francisco	5-Wd San Francisco	81	23
Bennett	44	m	w	IL	Napa	Napa Twp	75	67
C	22	m	w	PA	Lake	Lower Lake	73	414
Calvin	45	m	w	MO	Sutter	Nicolaus Twp	92	114
Charles	55	m	w	VA	Sonoma	Analy Twp	91	235

Name	Age	S	R	B-PL	County	Locale	Series M593 Roll	Pg
Charles	38	m	w	RI	San Francisco	San Francisco P O	83	340
Charles	36	m	w	NY	Sacramento	4-Wd Sacramento	77	332
Charles	30	m	w	IA	San Mateo	Woodside P O	87	380
Chas	25	m	w	ENGL	Santa Clara	Almaden Twp	88	5
Chas	21	m	w	MD	San Diego	Warners Rancho Dis	78	528
Chas	19	m	w	ENGL	Santa Clara	Almaden Twp	88	9
David	65	m	w	ENGL	San Bernardino	San Bernardino Twp	78	445
David	36	m	w	ENGL	San Francisco	8-Wd San Francisco	82	459
David	32	m	w	MO	Solano	Green Valley Twp	90	38
David	26	m	w	WALE	Santa Clara	San Jose Twp	88	210
David A	71	m	w	VA	Solano	Green Valley Twp	90	39
Duery W	42	m	w	KY	San Luis Obispo	San Luis Obispo Tw	87	305
Edward	65	m	b	KY	Nevada	Rough & Ready Twp	75	332
Edward	44	m	w	ENGL	San Francisco	7-Wd San Francisco	81	264
Edward	39	m	w	NY	San Francisco	7-Wd San Francisco	81	165
Edward	33	m	w	ENGL	Nevada	Grass Valley Twp	75	193
Edward Jr	5M	m	w	CA	Nevada	Grass Valley Twp	75	193
Edwd	33	m	w	ENGL	San Francisco	1-Wd San Francisco	79	59
Edwd	29	m	w	ENGL	San Francisco	1-Wd San Francisco	79	59
Edwd	25	m	w	NY	Yuba	Marysville Twp	93	571
Edwd	22	m	w	CA	San Francisco	1-Wd San Francisco	79	57
Edwin	43	m	w	ENGL	Nevada	Grass Valley Twp	75	180
Elizabeth	39	f	w	PA	San Francisco	San Francisco P O	83	340
Ellen	50	f	w	WALE	Santa Clara	2-Wd San Jose	88	284
F	27	m	w	ENGL	Sierra	Butte Twp	89	508
Francis	47	m	w	MO	Alameda	Brooklyn	68	26
Francis E	32	m	w	AL	Los Angeles	El Monte Twp	73	449
Francis W	44	m	w	MO	Santa Clara	1-Wd San Jose	88	234
Frank	37	m	w	ENGL	Santa Clara	Gilroy Twp	88	76
Frank	22	m	w	IREL	Solano	Tremont Twp	90	29
Frederick	39	m	w	NY	San Francisco	6-Wd San Francisco	81	87
G	12	m	w	CA	Solano	Benicia	90	21
Gabriel	31	m	w	GREE	San Joaquin	1-Wd Stockton	86	152
George C	45	m	w	VT	Santa Clara	Santa Clara Twp	88	163
George F	8	m	w	CA	San Francisco	San Francisco P O	83	340
George W	55	m	w	CT	Stanislaus	Branch Twp	92	5
George W	40	m	w	NY	Sacramento	Georgianna Twp	77	130
H F	66	m	w	VA	Humboldt	Arcata Twp	72	227
H R	30	m	w	IL	Monterey	San Juan Twp	74	394
Henery	45	m	w	ENGL	San Francisco	7-Wd San Francisco	81	171
Henry	58	m	w	MO	Tehama	Stony Crk	92	198
Henry	54	m	w	VT	San Francisco	11-Wd San Francisc	84	601
Henry	41	m	w	KY	El Dorado	Cosumnes Twp	72	15
Henry	30	m	w	NY	San Mateo	Schoolhouse Statio	87	340
Henry	28	m	w	VA	San Francisco	7-Wd San Francisco	81	222
Henry G	39	m	w	ENGL	Stanislaus	Empire Twp	92	34
Horatio	22	m	w	MO	Kern	Havilah P O	73	340
Ireto	35	m	w	GREE	Sacramento	Georgianna Twp	77	130
J B	43	m	w	WALE	Tuolumne	Big Oak Flat P O	93	396
J M	20	m	w	MO	Lake	Big Valley	73	396
James	44	m	w	WALE	Contra Costa	Martinez P O	71	426
James	42	m	w	ENGL	Nevada	Grass Valley Twp	75	190
James	42	m	w	ENGL	Sonoma	Petaluma Twp	91	320
James	35	m	w	ENGL	Kern	Bakersfield P O	73	357
James	35	m	w	ENGL	San Francisco	7-Wd San Francisco	81	164
James C	34	m	w	VA	San Francisco	5-Wd San Francisco	81	13
James G	26	m	w	ENGL	Nevada	Grass Valley Twp	75	184
James W	48	m	w	ENGL	Nevada	Grass Valley Twp	75	152
Jasper M	38	m	w	WI	Humboldt	Arcata Twp	72	227
Jasper N	30	m	w	MO	Mendocino	Point Arena Twp	74	206
Jeremiah	40	m	w	PA	San Mateo	San Mateo P O	87	355
Jeremiah	34	m	w	PRUS	San Francisco	11-Wd San Francisc	84	494
Jesse	26	m	w	KY	Kern	Bakersfield P O	73	360
Jesse	25	m	w	IL	Colusa	Colusa Twp	71	274
Jno P	14	m	w	CA	Sonoma	Mendocino Twp	91	295
Jo	30	m	w	ENGL	Alameda	Alameda	68	12
John	61	m	w	ENGL	Sacramento	Sutter Twp	77	386
John	50	m	w	NC	Monterey	Monterey Twp	74	347
John	45	m	w	KY	El Dorado	Cosumnes Twp	72	19
John	43	m	w	ENGL	El Dorado	Placerville	72	117
John	40	m	w	ENGL	Tehama	Tehama Twp	92	195
John	38	m	w	ENGL	Nevada	Grass Valley Twp	75	148
John	37	m	w	WALE	Nevada	Bridgeport Twp	75	118
John	36	m	w	NY	Marin	Tomales Twp	74	77
John	35	m	w	ENGL	Nevada	Grass Valley Twp	75	183
John	31	m	w	PA	Placer	Roseville P O	76	351
John	30	m	w	NJ	San Francisco	5-Wd San Francisco	81	22
John	29	m	w	ENGL	Nevada	Grass Valley Twp	75	202
John	28	m	w	ENGL	Mariposa	Mariposa P O	74	111
John	26	m	w	IN	Tehama	Tehama Twp	92	187
John	26	m	w	WI	Solano	Tremont Twp	90	31
John	25	m	w	ENGL	Nevada	Grass Valley Twp	75	200
John	24	m	w	ENGL	San Francisco	7-Wd San Francisco	81	171
John	24	m	w	ENGL	Solano	Benicia	90	15
John	23	m	w	ENGL	Nevada	Grass Valley Twp	75	143
John	16	m	w	NY	Contra Costa	Martinez Twp	71	350
John	15	m	w	CA	Sonoma	Healdsburg & Mendo	91	279
John B	61	m	w	MO	Tehama	Stony Crk	92	166
John D	57	m	w	WALE	Sierra	Gibson Twp	89	543
John H	49	m	w	MO	Solano	Green Valley Twp	90	39
John Henry	31	m	w	ENGL	Nevada	Grass Valley Twp	75	201
John M	54	m	w	TN	San Bernardino	San Bernardino Twp	78	448
John M	52	m	w	TN	San Bernardino	San Bernardino Twp	78	428
John W	39	m	w	ENGL	Nevada	Grass Valley Twp	75	165
John W	35	m	w	WALE	Inyo	Lone Pine Twp	73	335
John W	21	m	w	ENGL	Stanislaus	Emory Twp	92	25
Jordan	42	m	w	CT	Amador	Volcano P O	69	386

© 2001 by Heritage Quest. All rights reserved.

California 1870 Census

Name	Age	S	R	B-PL	County	Locale	Roll	Pg
Joseph	34	m	w	MO	Colusa	Stony Crk Twp	71	332
Joseph	28	m	w	ENGL	Nevada	Grass Valley Twp	75	198
Joseph	26	m	w	PRUS	Placer	Rocklin Twp	76	468
Joseph T	21	m	w	MO	Humboldt	Arcata Twp	72	227
Josh	27	m	w	NY	Alameda	Oakland	68	230
Joshua	25	m	b	MA	San Francisco	1-Wd San Francisco	79	55
Josiah P	50	m	w	NY	San Francisco	5-Wd San Francisco	81	12
Juan	35	m	w	NY	Monterey	San Juan Twp	74	418
Julia	75	f	w	VA	Tehama	Stony Crk	92	166
Julius S	39	m	w	NY	San Francisco	5-Wd San Francisco	81	11
Laura C	40	f	w	VA	San Francisco	8-Wd San Francisco	82	299
Leroy	32	m	w	MO	Amador	Volcano P O	69	380
Lewis	32	m	w	LA	Alameda	Oakland	68	141
Lewis	24	m	w	NY	Solano	Montezuma Twp	90	65
Lewis	22	m	w	CA	San Francisco	2-Wd San Francisco	79	259
Louisa	34	f	w	CT	Amador	Volcano P O	69	382
Lucy	32	f	w	CT	San Francisco	8-Wd San Francisco	82	468
M L	28	m	w	GERM	Tuolumne	Chinese Camp P O	93	384
Maria	40	f	w	MEXI	San Joaquin	1-Wd Stockton	86	133
Marris	31	m	w	GA	Kern	Havilah P O	73	350
Mary	64	f	b	NJ	Sacramento	2-Wd Sacramento	77	217
Mary	48	f	w	CANA	San Francisco	11-Wd San Francisc	84	484
Mary A	17	f	w	OH	Sonoma	Petaluma Twp	91	359
Minor	38	m	w	NY	San Francisco	7-Wd San Francisco	81	235
Oliver	49	m	w	MA	Contra Costa	Martinez Twp	71	347
Oliver	29	m	w	MO	Solano	Green Valley Twp	90	39
Oscar	33	m	w	PRUS	San Francisco	San Francisco P O	85	745
Peter	41	m	w	HANO	El Dorado	Cosumnes Twp	72	13
Peter	29	m	w	ENGL	Placer	Bath P O	76	447
Phebe	27	f	w	NY	El Dorado	Coloma Twp	72	8
R S	51	m	w	TN	Butte	Bidwell Twp	70	2
Reece	36	m	w	WALE	Sierra	Sears Twp	89	556
Richard	30	m	w	IREL	San Bernardino	San Bernardino Twp	78	417
Richard	30	m	w	IA	Napa	Napa	75	49
Richard	14	m	w	PA	San Francisco	11-Wd San Francisc	84	588
Robert	38	m	w	ENGL	Merced	Snelling P O	74	269
Robert	30	m	w	WI	Kern	Kernville P O	73	368
Robert	23	m	w	IREL	Santa Clara	San Jose Twp	88	218
Robert E	40	m	w	ENGL	Mariposa	Mariposa P O	74	101
Robert J	52	m	w	VA	Sacramento	Sutter Twp	77	380
Robert R	22	m	w	IA	Amador	Ione City P O	69	353
Saml L	57	m	w	PA	San Francisco	San Francisco P O	83	288
Samuel	60	m	w	ENGL	El Dorado	Mountain Twp	72	67
Samuel	32	m	w	ENGL	El Dorado	Mud Springs Twp	72	74
Samuel	23	m	w	AR	San Bernardino	San Bernardino Twp	78	429
Saul L	58	m	w	ME	Santa Barbara	Santa Barbara P O	87	500
Seth	37	m	w	NY	San Joaquin	Castoria Twp	86	6
Simeon	20	m	w	PA	Butte	Hamilton Twp	70	71
Solomon	24	m	w	ENGL	Fresno	Millerton P O	72	159
Solomon	15	m	w	PRUS	San Francisco	San Francisco P O	83	394
Susan	58	f	w	TN	San Mateo	San Mateo P O	87	359
Theophilus	54	m	w	VA	Santa Cruz	Santa Cruz	89	434
Thomas	57	m	w	ENGL	San Francisco	San Francisco P O	85	783
Thomas	42	m	w	WALE	Yolo	Grafton Twp	93	480
Thomas	34	m	w	IREL	San Francisco	11-Wd San Francisc	84	640
Thomas	33	m	w	WALE	Sierra	Sears Twp	89	556
Thomas	32	m	w	ENGL	Monterey	San Benito Twp	74	378
Thomas	25	m	w	ENGL	Placer	Auburn P O	76	359
Thomas E	30	m	w	ENGL	Nevada	Grass Valley Twp	75	171
Thos	28	m	w	PA	Tehama	Tehama Twp	92	187
Thos E	49	m	w	VA	Sacramento	Sutter Twp	77	380
Thos J	40	m	w	TN	Calaveras	Copperopolis P O	70	229
Unis	70	f	w	MA	San Francisco	11-Wd San Francisc	84	601
W C	20	m	w	MO	Lassen	Susanville Twp	73	445
W H	33	m	w	BADE	San Joaquin	Elkhorn Twp	86	61
W J	36	m	w	OH	Merced	Snelling P O	74	258
W T	43	m	w	ENGL	San Francisco	San Francisco P O	85	804
Walter	38	m	w	ENGL	Inyo	Cerro Gordo Twp	73	323
Walter	31	m	w	OH	Stanislaus	San Joaquin Twp	92	76
Walter B	31	m	w	NY	Los Angeles	Soledad Twp	73	631
Washington	30	m	w	PA	San Luis Obispo	Morro Twp	87	284
Webber R	56	m	w	ME	Sacramento	4-Wd Sacramento	77	364
William	52	m	w	KY	Calaveras	San Andreas P O	70	153
William	52	m	w	IL	Kern	Tehachapi P O	73	352
William	46	m	w	ENGL	Nevada	Grass Valley Twp	75	198
William	41	m	w	IREL	Placer	Bath P O	76	428
William	40	m	w	ENGL	Nevada	Bridgeport Twp	75	115
William	40	m	w	WALE	Butte	Oregon Twp	70	122
William	40	m	w	ENGL	San Francisco	San Francisco P O	80	423
William	40	m	w	MO	Solano	Suisun Twp	90	109
William	39	m	w	WALE	Siskiyou	Hamburg Twp	89	596
William	37	m	w	PRUS	Marin	Sausalito Twp	74	70
William	37	m	w	WALE	Butte	Oregon Twp	70	125
William	35	m	w	GREE	San Francisco	3-Wd San Francisco	79	294
William	33	m	w	NY	San Francisco	8-Wd San Francisco	82	365
William	30	m	w	SCOT	Santa Clara	Santa Clara Twp	88	168
William	28	m	w	ENGL	Nevada	Grass Valley Twp	75	201
William	28	m	w	WALE	Sierra	Sears Twp	89	556
William	27	m	w	CANA	Solano	Rio Vista Twp	90	64
William	26	m	w	DE	Los Angeles	Los Angeles	73	547
William	25	m	w	WI	El Dorado	Cosumnes Twp	72	13
William	25	m	w	WI	Amador	Sutter Crk P O	69	408
William	25	m	w	IA	Amador	Sutter Crk P O	69	411
William R	35	m	w	WALE	Butte	Oregon Twp	70	125
Wm	70	m	w	PA	Yuba	W Bear Rvr Twp	93	681
Wm	43	m	w	ENGL	San Joaquin	Elkhorn Twp	86	60
Wm	36	m	w	WALE	San Francisco	1-Wd San Francisco	79	57

Name	Age	S	R	B-PL	County	Locale	Roll	Pg
Wm	32	m	w	PA	Sierra	Gibson Twp	89	544
Wm	32	m	w	WALE	San Francisco	11-Wd San Francisc	84	623
Wm	20	m	w	ENGL	Santa Clara	Almaden Twp	88	9
Wm C	51	m	w	AR	Mendocino	Little Lake Twp	74	202
Wm F	39	m	w	MO	Merced	Snelling P O	74	247
Wm H	43	m	w	ENGL	Nevada	Little York Twp	75	242
Wm H	23	m	w	ENGL	Nevada	Grass Valley Twp	75	200
Wm H	23	m	w	ENGL	Nevada	Grass Valley Twp	75	175
Wm Henry	19	m	w	ENGL	Nevada	Grass Valley Twp	75	201
Wm J	28	m	w	ENGL	Nevada	Nevada Twp	75	301
Wm Mathew	28	m	w	ENGL	Nevada	Grass Valley Twp	75	169
Wm S	37	m	w	MA	San Francisco	2-Wd San Francisco	79	221
JAMESON								
Charles	10	m	m	NGRA	San Francisco	San Francisco P O	80	368
Edgar	52	m	w	ENGL	San Francisco	5-Wd San Francisco	81	26
Edward	58	m	w	MA	Placer	Rocklin Twp	76	465
Edward	22	m	w	MD	Sacramento	San Joaquin Twp	77	407
Henry A	57	m	w	MO	Stanislaus	Buena Vista Twp	92	13
Horace D	37	m	w	VA	San Francisco	San Francisco P O	85	726
James	64	m	w	SCOT	Placer	Dutch Flat P O	76	405
James J	39	m	w	MO	San Francisco	1-Wd San Francisco	79	135
John	43	m	w	IREL	San Joaquin	2-Wd Stockton	86	174
John	35	m	w	MO	Stanislaus	North Twp	92	68
John M	67	m	w	VA	Amador	Fiddletown P O	69	436
Mary	42	f	w	MS	San Joaquin	2-Wd Stockton	86	162
Robert	30	m	w	IA	Sacramento	San Joaquin Twp	77	407
Saml E	34	m	w	OH	Sonoma	Petaluma Twp	91	323
Thorndike	56	m	w	ME	Marin	San Rafael	74	51
W T	41	m	w	MO	Amador	Fiddletown P O	69	433
William	42	m	w	IREL	San Francisco	2-Wd San Francisco	79	148
William	14	m	w	CA	Sacramento	2-Wd Sacramento	77	239
Wm	41	m	w	IN	Nevada	Meadow Lake Twp	75	253
JAMESTON								
John	30	m	w	MA	San Francisco	6-Wd San Francisco	81	119
JAMESWORTH								
Chs	42	m	w	MD	San Francisco	2-Wd San Francisco	79	256
JAMIE								
Ah	19	m	c	CHIN	Sacramento	1-Wd Sacramento	77	193
JAMIESON								
Edwd	31	m	w	IREL	San Francisco	1-Wd San Francisco	79	95
Euphemia	58	f	w	SCOT	San Mateo	Redwood Twp	87	362
George	42	m	w	ENGL	Monterey	San Juan Twp	74	409
Gertrude	16	f	w	NY	San Francisco	6-Wd San Francisco	81	72
James	56	m	w	PRUS	Calaveras	San Andreas P O	70	214
Jas	5	m	w	CA	Butte	Ophir Twp	70	102
John	36	m	w	IREL	San Francisco	1-Wd San Francisco	79	79
Martha	27	f	w	PA	San Francisco	6-Wd San Francisco	81	92
Richard	32	m	w	IREL	San Francisco	7-Wd San Francisco	81	275
Thomas	34	m	w	SCOT	Monterey	Pajaro Twp	74	376
JAMISON								
Alfred M	42	m	w	MO	Solano	Suisun Twp	90	99
B T	43	m	w	KY	Humboldt	Eel Rvr Twp	72	254
Chas	78	m	w	CANA	Solano	Vallejo	90	191
Da	49	m	w	MO	Merced	Snelling P O	74	246
Edward	25	m	w	AR	Merced	Snelling P O	74	248
Geo W	41	m	w	MO	Amador	Volcano P O	69	386
George	38	m	w	MD	Sacramento	Center Twp	77	85
Isaac	36	m	w	ME	Butte	Ophir Twp	70	96
Isaac S	41	m	w	KY	Yolo	Cache Crk Twp	93	449
J C	31	m	w	CANA	Sutter	Butte Twp	92	91
James	35	m	w	IREL	Sacramento	Dry Crk Twp	77	104
James	35	m	w	KY	Alameda	Hayward	68	76
James	24	m	w	ENGL	San Francisco	7-Wd San Francisco	81	219
James A	39	m	w	AR	Mendocino	Ukiah Twp	74	243
Jesse	40	m	w	KY	El Dorado	Mud Springs Twp	72	81
John	54	m	w	IREL	San Francisco	8-Wd San Francisco	82	443
John	40	m	w	MO	Alameda	Eden Twp	68	71
John	35	m	w	OH	Sutter	Yuba Twp	92	149
John	29	m	w	IREL	San Joaquin	3-Wd Stockton	86	231
John	29	m	w	NY	San Francisco	1-Wd San Francisco	79	117
John	22	m	w	AR	Merced	Snelling P O	74	246
John B	49	m	w	IL	Solano	Maine Prairie Twp	90	51
Marinda	68	f	w	NY	Amador	Jackson P O	69	342
Mary J	15	f	w	CA	Mendocino	Calpella Twp	74	184
Nancy	74	f	w	VA	Yolo	Grafton Twp	93	478
Oscar	31	m	w	NC	San Joaquin	Tulare Twp	86	258
P T	31	m	w	OH	Lassen	Susanville Twp	73	445
Sam	49	m	w	ME	Butte	Ophir Twp	70	97
Saml	40	m	w	CANA	Solano	Vallejo	90	191
Samuel	38	m	w	KY	Santa Clara	Santa Clara Twp	88	153
Sarah	50	f	w	IREL	San Francisco	3-Wd San Francisco	79	289
Stephen	47	m	w	PA	Placer	Auburn P O	76	357
Thomas	56	m	w	PA	Placer	Auburn P O	76	367
V G	28	m	w	DENM	San Francisco	7-Wd San Francisco	81	221
William	14	m	w	TX	Calaveras	Copperopolis P O	70	249
Z T	36	m	w	MO	Merced	Snelling P O	74	273
JAMMETTE								
Jules	42	m	w	FRAN	San Francisco	San Francisco P O	80	429
JAMMISON								
H	36	m	b	MO	El Dorado	Coloma Twp	72	9
JAMSON								
James	26	m	w	CANA	Napa	Napa Twp	75	67
Martin	37	m	w	NORW	Napa	Napa Twp	75	67
JAMY								
Casper	33	m	w	SWIT	Butte	Bidwell Twp	70	4
Emanuel	17	m	w	CANA	Placer	Gold Run Twp	76	394

© 2001 by Heritage Quest. All rights reserved.

Name	Age	S	R	B-PL	County	Locale	Series M593 Roll	Pg
JAN								
Ah	46	f	c	CHIN	San Francisco	San Francisco P O	80	437
Ah	40	m	c	CHIN	Tuolumne	Sonora P O	93	324
Ah	22	m	c	CHIN	San Francisco	6-Wd San Francisco	81	98
Ah	20	m	c	CHIN	San Francisco	6-Wd San Francisco	81	50
Ah	12	m	c	CHIN	San Francisco	11-Wd San Francisc	84	586
Bung	36	m	c	CHIN	Mariposa	Mariposa P O	74	130
Chin	25	m	c	CHIN	San Joaquin	2-Wd Stockton	86	174
Farth	20	m	c	CHIN	San Mateo	Schoolhouse Statio	87	335
Jim	25	m	c	CHIN	El Dorado	Cosumnes Twp	72	15
Kain	24	m	c	CHIN	San Mateo	Schoolhouse Statio	87	339
Tow	18	f	c	CHIN	Butte	Ophir Twp	70	104
JANDER								
Leonard	58	m	w	BAVA	Los Angeles	Santa Ana Twp	73	613
JANDIN								
Mary	28	f	w	NY	San Francisco	San Francisco P O	80	421
JANE								
Ah	40	m	c	CHIN	Mendocino	Point Arena Twp	74	208
Ah	25	m	c	CHIN	Amador	Fiddletown P O	69	439
Ah	24	m	c	CHIN	Trinity	Indian Crk	92	200
Ann	40	f	w	CANA	Klamath	Liberty Twp	73	376
Anthony	45	m	w	NY	Calaveras	San Andreas P O	70	174
William C	38	m	w	TN	Calaveras	Copperopolis P O	70	259
JANEAU								
Daniel	30	m	w	FRAN	San Francisco	San Francisco P O	80	465
JANEFELDER								
John	30	m	w	FRAN	San Francisco	2-Wd San Francisco	79	221
JANES								
Daniel	41	m	w	MI	Santa Clara	San Jose Twp	88	214
Edw P	54	m	w	VA	Tehama	Tehama Twp	92	156
Emma	30	f	w	OH	Santa Clara	Redwood Twp	88	134
Emma	27	f	w	OH	Nevada	Meadow Lake Twp	75	246
James	37	m	w	ENGL	San Joaquin	Douglas Twp	86	45
James	35	m	w	MO	Santa Clara	Milpitas Twp	88	111
Jennett	15	f	w	WI	Tehama	Cottonwood Twp	92	162
John	33	m	w	NY	Yuba	Marysville Twp	93	571
John F	26	m	w	SCOT	San Francisco	3-Wd San Francisco	79	287
Luther	26	m	w	MO	Santa Clara	Milpitas Twp	88	111
R H	50	m	w	VT	Alameda	Oakland	68	221
Thomas	35	m	w	IREL	San Francisco	11-Wd San Francisc	84	554
Thomas	28	m	w	ENGL	San Francisco	San Francisco P O	80	372
Thos Jefferson	40	m	w	MO	Santa Clara	Milpitas Twp	88	111
JANG								
Ah	40	m	c	CHIN	Nevada	Rough & Ready Twp	75	331
Ah	36	m	c	CHIN	San Francisco	San Francisco P O	80	493
Ah	36	m	c	CHIN	Stanislaus	Emory Twp	92	17
Ah	29	m	c	CHIN	Klamath	Orleans Twp	73	380
JANGER								
Frank	40	m	w	CANA	Yolo	Cache Crk Twp	93	448
Phillip	36	m	w	BADE	San Francisco	San Francisco P O	80	457
JANIN								
Georgiana	60	f	w	PA	San Francisco	5-Wd San Francisco	81	29
Henry	33	m	w	NJ	San Francisco	5-Wd San Francisco	81	31
JANINI								
Joseph	29	m	w	SWIT	El Dorado	Diamond Springs Tw	72	33
JANJON								
Eugene	17	m	w	FRAN	Santa Clara	Santa Clara Twp	88	177
Louis	59	m	w	FRAN	San Francisco	2-Wd San Francisco	79	191
JANKE								
Charles A	30	m	w	HAMB	San Mateo	Belmont P O	87	371
JANLUF								
M B	39	f	w	OH	Alameda	Oakland	68	208
JANNARD								
Adrien	27	m	w	FRAN	San Francisco	San Francisco P O	83	135
JANNESSE								
Louis	27	m	w	FRAN	San Francisco	San Francisco P O	83	288
JANNIN								
Cypian	30	m	w	FRAN	San Francisco	8-Wd San Francisco	82	364
JANNINGS								
Pat	35	m	w	IREL	San Francisco	7-Wd San Francisco	81	256
JANNISON								
Henry	40	m	w	VT	San Francisco	7-Wd San Francisco	81	188
Jno	16	m	w	AR	San Joaquin	Douglas Twp	86	44
Jno C	28	m	w	IA	Sonoma	Santa Rosa	91	398
JANNSEN								
Augustine	54	m	w	GERM	Santa Barbara	Santa Barbara P O	87	466
JANONI								
Peter	45	m	w	FRAN	Tuolumne	Columbia P O	93	348
JANOTI								
James	35	m	w	SWIT	Tuolumne	Columbia P O	93	346
JANOTRON								
J	50	m	w	SWIT	Santa Clara	Gilroy Twp	88	93
JANS								
Ches F	26	m	w	WURT	San Francisco	8-Wd San Francisco	82	361
JANSEN								
Anna	19	f	w	DENM	Santa Cruz	Pajaro Twp	89	356
Arent S	39	m	w	NORW	Nevada	Grass Valley Twp	75	181
Charles	51	m	w	SHOL	San Francisco	3-Wd San Francisco	79	287
Chrisr	28	m	w	NY	San Francisco	1-Wd San Francisco	79	124
David	38	m	w	SWED	San Francisco	1-Wd San Francisco	79	121
Ernest	52	m	w	PRUS	San Francisco	San Francisco P O	80	483
Frederick	28	m	w	PRUS	San Francisco	6-Wd San Francisco	81	126
Fredrick	42	m	w	PRUS	San Francisco	San Francisco P O	80	467
Fredrick	38	m	w	SWED	San Francisco	San Francisco P O	80	468
George	42	m	w	HANO	San Francisco	San Francisco P O	83	120
John	41	m	w	DENM	San Francisco	San Francisco P O	80	466
Margaret	64	f	w	PRUS	San Francisco	San Francisco P O	80	456
Morris	40	m	w	PRUS	San Francisco	5-Wd San Francisco	81	34
Nicholas	60	m	w	PRUS	San Francisco	San Francisco P O	83	294
Peter	48	m	w	DENM	San Francisco	2-Wd San Francisco	79	190
Peter	38	m	w	DENM	Alameda	Brooklyn Twp	68	45
Peter	22	m	w	DENM	Alameda	Eden Twp	68	63
Soren	43	m	w	DENM	Butte	Chico Twp	70	42
JANSES								
Cornelius	45	m	w	PRUS	San Bernardino	San Salvador Twp	78	455
JANSOM								
Joseph	33	m	w	BELG	Amador	Sutter Crk P O	69	403
JANSON								
Amos	26	m	w	PRUS	San Francisco	8-Wd San Francisco	82	359
Charles	48	m	w	SWED	San Francisco	11-Wd San Francisc	84	627
Charles	38	m	w	HDAR	Placer	Auburn P O	76	362
D	28	m	w	BADE	Monterey	San Juan Twp	74	405
Hanse	45	m	w	SWED	San Joaquin	2-Wd Stockton	86	175
Henry	48	m	w	PRUS	San Joaquin	1-Wd Stockton	86	122
Henry	40	m	w	SWED	San Francisco	11-Wd San Francisc	84	644
James	12	m	w	CA	San Francisco	5-Wd San Francisco	81	27
John	9	m	w	NY	San Francisco	5-Wd San Francisco	81	34
John	46	m	w	SWED	Nevada	Washington Twp	75	340
Joseph	36	m	w	SWIT	San Francisco	San Francisco P O	80	533
L H	35	m	w	HANO	Humboldt	Arcata Twp	72	230
Matthew	48	m	w	BOHE	Placer	Bath P O	76	458
Peter	41	m	w	DENM	San Francisco	1-Wd San Francisco	79	86
Peter	32	m	w	DENM	Solano	Denverton Twp	90	23
Saml	26	m	w	SWED	San Joaquin	2-Wd Stockton	86	175
Sarah	17	f	w	NY	San Francisco	5-Wd San Francisco	81	34
JANSSEN								
Otto E	54	m	w	DENM	Humboldt	Pacific Twp	72	296
Truels G	40	m	w	PRUS	San Francisco	San Francisco P O	83	62
JANTEE								
Edward	34	m	w	FRAN	San Francisco	6-Wd San Francisco	81	70
Emily	29	f	w	FRAN	San Francisco	6-Wd San Francisco	81	70
JANTOR								
Edward	42	m	w	IREL	San Francisco	San Francisco P O	85	755
JANTROUT								
Pierre	52	m	w	FRAN	Santa Clara	2-Wd San Jose	88	303
JANTZEN								
August	35	m	w	HANO	San Francisco	7-Wd San Francisco	81	262
Charles	26	m	w	HANO	San Francisco	San Francisco P O	85	756
Eliza	40	f	w	FRAN	San Francisco	8-Wd San Francisco	82	431
Jas	34	m	w	DENM	San Francisco	7-Wd San Francisco	81	264
JANUARY								
William	44	m	w	KY	Santa Clara	1-Wd San Jose	88	234
JAP								
Lee	24	m	c	CHIN	Solano	Suisun Twp	90	105
JAPARA								
Franklin	35	m	w	ITAL	San Mateo	Redwood Twp	87	361
John	38	m	w	ITAL	San Mateo	Menlo Park P O	87	378
Louis	40	m	w	ITAL	San Mateo	Schoolhouse Statio	87	335
Louis	24	m	w	ITAL	San Mateo	Schoolhouse Statio	87	345
Louis	20	m	w	ITAL	San Mateo	Menlo Park P O	87	378
JAPARO								
John	40	m	w	ITAL	San Mateo	Schoolhouse Statio	87	345
John	26	m	w	ITAL	San Mateo	Schoolhouse Statio	87	347
JAPARRA								
Henrico	34	m	w	ITAL	San Mateo	Schoolhouse Statio	87	344
JAPHARDT								
Andrew	25	m	w	HANO	Sacramento	2-Wd Sacramento	77	245
JAPON								
John	50	m	w	ENGL	Contra Costa	Martinez P O	71	403
JAPPARAH								
John	34	m	w	ITAL	San Mateo	Schoolhouse Statio	87	344
Louis	17	m	w	ITAL	San Mateo	Schoolhouse Statio	87	344
JAQUAS								
Berry H	33	m	w	VT	Butte	Oregon Twp	70	128
JAQUAYS								
William	60	m	w	RI	Mendocino	Albion & Big Rvr T	74	166
JAQUERS								
John	60	m	b	FRAN	San Francisco	San Francisco P O	80	415
JAQUES								
James	50	m	w	ENGL	Sonoma	Petaluma Twp	91	315
Jesse	54	m	w	NY	Yolo	Cottonwood Twp	93	459
Moran	58	m	w	FRAN	San Mateo	San Mateo P O	87	348
JAQUET								
Michael	31	m	w	FRAN	Santa Clara	2-Wd San Jose	88	311
JAQUIER								
Louis	30	m	w	SWIT	Alameda	Brooklyn	68	34
JAQUILLARD								
Theobald	40	m	w	FRAN	Contra Costa	Martinez P O	71	405
JAQUITH								
Abram	50	m	w	NH	Calaveras	Copperopolis P O	70	255
Henry	50	m	w	VT	Siskiyou	Surprise Valley Tw	89	636
J S	37	m	w	MA	Sierra	Downieville Twp	89	514
Jessie	54	m	w	NY	Yolo	Putah Twp	93	522
JAQUITT								
Thorn	23	m	w	NJ	San Francisco	2-Wd San Francisco	79	214
JAQUNOTTE								
Frances	59	f	w	FRAN	San Francisco	6-Wd San Francisco	81	41
JAQUOT								
Elene	29	f	w	SWIT	San Francisco	San Francisco P O	80	404
JAR								
Ah	44	m	c	CHIN	Calaveras	Copperopolis P O	70	256
JARAMBO								
Louis	15	m	w	ITAL	San Mateo	Schoolhouse Statio	87	346

© 2001 by Heritage Quest. All rights reserved.

Name	Age	S	R	B-PL	County	Locale	Roll	Pg
						Series M593		
JARAMIEN								
Ramon	34	m	w	CA	Los Angeles	Los Angeles Twp	73	479
JARARD								
Anton	25	m	w	CANA	Placer	Auburn P O	76	368
JARBE								
W B	8	m	w	CA	Lake	Lower Lake	73	428
JARBIS								
Mulford	62	m	w	KY	San Diego	Julian Dist	78	472
JARBO								
Benjamin	35	m	w	FRAN	Colusa	Stony Crk Twp	71	330
Henry	51	m	w	KY	Santa Clara	Redwood Twp	88	120
JARBOE								
Jno R	34	m	w	MD	San Francisco	8-Wd San Francisco	82	329
JARBOW								
Martin	26	m	w	DENM	Contra Costa	Martinez P O	71	404
JARES								
Uren	32	m	w	PORT	Stanislaus	Emory Twp	92	19
JARETZKY								
Augusta	8	f	w	CA	San Francisco	San Francisco P O	85	832
JARGAN								
Christian	50	m	w	HOLL	Sacramento	4-Wd Sacramento	77	336
JARGON								
H	42	m	w	ENGL	San Joaquin	3-Wd Stockton	86	240
Joseph	23	m	w	NORW	Stanislaus	Empire Twp	92	61
JARIES								
Henry	43	m	w	PRUS	San Francisco	San Francisco P O	83	306
JARIMILLO								
Pelipe	34	m	w	CA	San Bernardino	San Salvador Twp	78	457
JARMAN								
Hugh	36	m	w	ENGL	Santa Clara	1-Wd San Jose	88	244
Thomas	24	m	w	ENGL	Santa Clara	1-Wd San Jose	88	232
JARNAGIN								
B F	37	m	w	TN	Humboldt	Bald Hills	72	238
JARP								
F F I	43	m	w	GERM	Tuolumne	Columbia P O	93	350
JARRA								
Simon	45	m	w	MEXI	Los Angeles	Los Angeles Twp	73	483
JARRARD								
Thomas N	40	m	w	GA	Stanislaus	Emory Twp	92	18
JARRET								
Saml	36	m	w	IREL	San Francisco	7-Wd San Francisco	81	234
JARRETT								
Abram	21	m	w	AUSL	San Francisco	1-Wd San Francisco	79	115
Thomas	47	m	w	ENGL	Humboldt	Pacific Twp	72	298
Thomas	25	m	w	AUST	Humboldt	Table Bluff Twp	72	307
JARRIMEO								
Jose	80	m	w	MEXI	San Bernardino	San Salvador Twp	78	455
Quan	26	m	w	MEXI	San Bernardino	San Salvador Twp	78	455
JARSON								
Christ	21	m	w	DENM	San Joaquin	Dent Twp	86	21
JART								
Louis	38	m	w	BAVA	Marin	San Antonio Twp	74	64
JARTENSIO								
Jose	33	m	w	CA	San Bernardino	San Salvador Twp	78	456
JARVASE								
Alexander	54	m	w	FRAN	Santa Clara	2-Wd San Jose	88	310
JARVES								
Wm	57	m	w	DC	Sacramento	Natomas Twp	77	169
JARVIE								
Alex	28	m	w	SCOT	San Francisco	San Francisco P O	85	861
JARVIS								
A H	83	f	w	MA	Tuolumne	Columbia P O	93	346
Alfred	37	m	w	WI	Santa Barbara	San Buenaventura P	87	418
Catherine	32	f	w	MA	Marin	San Rafael	74	51
Chas H	24	m	w	NY	San Francisco	1-Wd San Francisco	79	131
Cow	42	m	w	ENGL	San Joaquin	2-Wd Stockton	86	178
Francis	37	m	w	ME	Alameda	Washington Twp	68	273
Frank	33	m	w	ME	Marin	Novato Twp	74	13
George M	42	m	w	GA	Santa Cruz	Santa Cruz Twp	89	402
Henry	30	m	w	ENGL	Yolo	Cache Crk Twp	93	432
Howard S	34	m	w	ME	Stanislaus	San Joaquin Twp	92	73
J	40	m	w	IREL	San Joaquin	2-Wd Stockton	86	193
John W	37	m	w	KY	Santa Cruz	Santa Cruz Twp	89	385
Louis	36	m	w	MO	Yolo	Grafton Twp	93	487
Luther	32	m	w	OH	Plumas	Quartz Twp	77	39
M C	25	f	w	VT	Amador	Ione City P O	69	357
Moses W	24	m	w	NY	Alpine	Markleeville P O	69	311
Napoleon	31	m	w	CANA	Plumas	Washington Twp	77	25
Smith	60	m	w	NY	Amador	Sutter Crk P O	69	398
Thos	40	m	w	ENGL	San Joaquin	Douglas Twp	86	51
Thos	36	m	w	ENGL	San Francisco	7-Wd San Francisco	81	228
William	24	m	w	NY	Sonoma	Petaluma Twp	91	350
JARVISON								
Kell	45	m	w	DENM	Alameda	Eden Twp	68	64
JARY								
William	29	m	w	ENGL	Placer	Bath P O	76	437
JASCEMO								
Joseph	27	m	w	ITAL	Santa Clara	2-Wd San Jose	88	281
JASCO								
John	39	m	w	FRAN	Tuolumne	Columbia P O	93	344
JASE								
Roise	23	m	w	CA	Colusa	Monroe Twp	71	311
JASEN								
Clous	45	m	w	PRUS	Solano	Silveyville Twp	90	79
JASES								
Mary	70	f	w	SCOT	Alameda	Eden Twp	68	91

Name	Age	S	R	B-PL	County	Locale	Roll	Pg
						Series M593		
JASOBROM								
Sigmund	40	m	w	PRUS	Alameda	San Leandro	68	93
JASON								
Antonio	50	m	w	PORT	Los Angeles	Wilmington Twp	73	637
Christopher	35	m	w	PRUS	Alameda	Murray Twp	68	105
Henry H	44	m	w	SILE	Placer	Bath P O	76	457
JASPER								
Aaron	31	m	w	FINL	Marin	San Rafael	74	55
Antonio	33	m	w	PORT	Alameda	Washington Twp	68	275
C H	32	m	w	HANO	Sacramento	San Joaquin Twp	77	401
Edward	3M	m	w	CA	Tuolumne	Sonora P O	93	321
Francis	25	m	w	BADE	Tuolumne	Sonora P O	93	321
George	42	m	w	PRUS	San Francisco	San Francisco P O	83	216
Gerard	39	m	w	MO	San Luis Obispo	San Luis Obispo Tw	87	302
J M C	31	m	w	VA	Yuba	East Bear Rvr Twp	93	543
James A	23	m	w	MO	Tulare	Farmersville Twp	92	243
John	35	m	w	NY	San Francisco	7-Wd San Francisco	81	188
Mansfield	47	m	b	VA	Contra Costa	Martinez P O	71	380
Merrill	45	m	w	KY	Kern	Linns Valley P O	73	347
Richard	40	m	w	ENGL	Solano	Silveyville Twp	90	75
W H	51	m	w	KY	Monterey	San Juan Twp	74	388
William	29	m	w	GERM	Los Angeles	Los Angeles	73	545
William	28	m	w	OH	Solano	Silveyville Twp	90	79
William R	7M	m	w	CA	Monterey	San Juan Twp	74	387
Wm	32	m	w	KY	Yuba	East Bear Rvr Twp	93	543
JASPERSON								
Lars	36	m	w	NORW	El Dorado	Mud Springs Twp	72	73
JASPIN								
Juan	34	m	w	CA	Monterey	Salinas Twp	74	313
JASSEN								
Matts	31	m	w	DENM	Sierra	Table Rock Twp	89	575
JASSMAN								
Bena A	54	f	w	NY	Sacramento	2-Wd Sacramento	77	220
JASSO								
Fannie	61	f	w	AZOR	Monterey	Castroville Twp	74	333
JAST								
Geo H	35	m	w	CANA	Sacramento	4-Wd Sacramento	77	358
JASZINSKY								
Lewis	22	m	w	MA	San Mateo	San Mateo P O	87	352
JASZYUSKY								
Louis	52	m	w	RUSS	San Francisco	8-Wd San Francisco	82	381
JATERON								
Joseph	39	m	w	MO	Sacramento	Dry Crk Twp	77	99
JATTA								
Joseph N	28	m	w	CANA	San Luis Obispo	Arroyo Grande Twp	87	272
JATUM								
James	35	m	w	MO	Nevada	Grass Valley Twp	75	143
JATUNN								
James	40	m	w	MO	Nevada	Grass Valley Twp	75	218
JAUBERT								
Maurice	38	m	w	FRAN	San Francisco	San Francisco P O	83	223
JAUNER								
Julia	25	f	w	OH	San Francisco	5-Wd San Francisco	81	11
JAVANSVICH								
A	19	m	w	AUST	San Francisco	San Francisco P O	85	793
JAVELRY								
Jean	49	m	w	FRAN	Santa Barbara	Santa Barbara P O	87	450
JAVIESON								
Fred	9	m	w	CA	San Francisco	11-Wd San Francisc	84	577
JAVIS								
William	38	m	w	ENGL	San Francisco	7-Wd San Francisco	81	161
JAVITT								
Frank	32	m	w	FRAN	San Francisco	6-Wd San Francisco	81	94
JAVO								
Charles	27	m	m	EIND	Colusa	Colusa	71	296
JAW								
Ah	30	m	c	CHIN	San Joaquin	Oneal Twp	86	117
Jno	32	m	w	ME	San Joaquin	Douglas Twp	86	39
Young	25	m	c	CHIN	Alameda	Oakland	68	135
JAY								
Ah	38	m	c	CHIN	San Francisco	San Francisco P O	80	489
Ah	31	m	c	CHIN	Nevada	Bloomfield Twp	75	96
Ah	30	m	c	CHIN	San Francisco	San Francisco P O	80	495
Ah	24	m	c	CHIN	San Francisco	San Francisco P O	80	498
Ah	21	m	c	CHIN	San Francisco	San Francisco P O	80	381
Ah	20	f	c	CHIN	San Francisco	San Francisco P O	80	497
Ah	19	m	c	CHIN	San Joaquin	1-Wd Stockton	86	143
David	36	m	w	OH	Sonoma	Petaluma Twp	91	329
Giles	30	m	w	IN	Sutter	Nicolaus Twp	92	115
Hartford	55	m	w	ME	San Francisco	1-Wd San Francisco	79	66
Hong Chung	40	m	c	CHIN	San Francisco	6-Wd San Francisco	81	37
Hoo	21	m	c	CHIN	Santa Cruz	Pajaro Twp	89	342
Mary	74	f	w	MA	San Francisco	11-Wd San Francisc	84	459
Peter	38	m	w	CANA	San Francisco	11-Wd San Francisc	84	665
Toy	19	m	c	CHIN	Siskiyou	Yreka Twp	89	665
JAYCOX								
Charles E	28	m	w	OH	El Dorado	Placerville	72	107
JAYNE								
H E	24	f	w	NY	Alameda	Oakland	68	235
John D	45	m	w	NY	Yuba	Slate Range Bar Tw	93	673
John M	41	m	w	NY	Santa Barbara	Santa Barbara P O	87	486
Nathaniel	50	m	w	TN	Solano	Rio Vista Twp	90	62
JAYNES								
Danl	36	m	b	MO	Sonoma	Russian Rvr	91	375
Samuel	44	m	w	PA	Tehama	Antelope Twp	92	156
JAYNOR								
Nellie	19	f	w	IREL	Solano	Vallejo	90	139

© 2001 by Heritage Quest. All rights reserved.

Name	Age	S	R	B-PL	County	Locale	Series M593 Roll	Pg
JAZER								
Geo F	29	m	w	SHOL	El Dorado	Placerville Twp	72	97
Louis	26	m	w	HOLL	Tulare	Tule Rvr Twp	92	262
JE								
Ah	30	m	c	CHIN	Sacramento	Granite Twp	77	138
Ah	26	m	c	CHIN	Sacramento	Georgianna Twp	77	124
JEA								
Ah	20	m	c	CHIN	Nevada	Nevada Twp	75	298
JEACKI								
John	37	m	w	FRAN	San Francisco	San Francisco P O	80	458
JEAGER								
M J	35	m	w	BADE	Amador	Drytown P O	69	420
JEAN								
Ah	14	m	c	CHIN	San Francisco	San Francisco P O	83	359
Pierre	34	m	w	FRAN	San Francisco	8-Wd San Francisco	82	375
JEANES								
W S	36	m	w	MO	Sacramento	3-Wd Sacramento	77	267
JEANETTE								
Simon	25	m	w	FRAN	San Francisco	1-Wd San Francisco	79	49
JEANNIN								
August	41	m	w	FRAN	San Francisco	3-Wd San Francisco	79	317
JEANPERE								
Chas	35	m	w	BELG	Santa Cruz	Watsonville	89	367
JEANS								
James	70	m	w	KY	Solano	Vacaville Twp	90	128
Thomas J	40	m	w	MO	Solano	Vacaville Twp	90	128
William	39	m	w	NY	Solano	Silveyville Twp	90	75
William	37	m	w	OH	Solano	Montezuma Twp	90	68
JEB								
Ah	25	m	c	CHIN	Solano	Suisun Twp	90	107
JECCO								
Francis	61	m	w	ITAL	San Francisco	2-Wd San Francisco	79	142
JECK								
Ah	16	m	c	CHIN	Tuolumne	Chinese Camp P O	93	382
JECKINSKY								
Zack	24	m	w	POLA	San Francisco	5-Wd San Francisco	81	20
JEDDA								
Catharine	33	f	w	FRAN	San Francisco	11-Wd San Francisc	84	610
JEDSON								
John	35	m	w	SCOT	Siskiyou	Yreka Twp	89	665
JEE								
Ah	6	f	c	CA	San Francisco	San Francisco P O	80	521
Ah	41	m	c	CHIN	San Francisco	San Francisco P O	83	380
Ah	40	m	c	CHIN	Mendocino	Point Arena Twp	74	205
Ah	33	m	c	CHIN	San Francisco	San Francisco P O	80	515
Ah	30	f	c	CHIN	San Francisco	San Francisco P O	80	505
Ah	30	m	c	CHIN	Butte	Wyandotte Twp	70	146
Ah	30	m	c	CHIN	Sierra	Lincoln Twp	89	547
Ah	23	m	c	CHIN	Yolo	Grafton Twp	93	479
Ah	18	m	c	CHIN	Shasta	American Ranch P O	89	497
Ah	17	m	c	CHIN	Sonoma	Salt Point	91	387
No	48	m	c	CHIN	Del Norte	Happy Camp Twp	71	469
JEESINK								
B H	30	m	w	HOLL	Nevada	Meadow Lake Twp	75	250
JEFEAR								
John	40	m	w	FRAN	San Francisco	San Francisco P O	80	348
John	40	m	w	FRAN	San Francisco	San Francisco P O	80	347
JEFF								
Davis	19	m	i	CA	Siskiyou	Butte Twp	89	586
Davis	11	m	i	CA	Lake	Lower Lake	73	420
John	46	m	w	ENGL	Butte	Ophir Twp	70	98
JEFFCOTT								
Cornelius	32	m	w	IREL	San Francisco	1-Wd San Francisco	79	81
JEFFERD								
Samuel	48	m	w	CANA	Yuba	Marysville Twp	93	568
JEFFERDS								
Forrest	42	m	w	ME	Tulare	Farmersville Twp	92	250
JEFFERIES								
Anna	35	f	w	ENGL	San Joaquin	Liberty Twp	86	93
Jas	40	m	w	MA	San Joaquin	3-Wd Stockton	86	217
JEFFERO								
Jno	48	m	w	OH	Santa Clara	Gilroy Twp	88	78
JEFFERS								
Adam	27	m	w	CANA	San Francisco	8-Wd San Francisco	82	482
David	35	m	w	NY	San Francisco	8-Wd San Francisco	82	435
Edwd	65	m	w	IREL	San Francisco	1-Wd San Francisco	79	100
George	30	m	w	ENGL	San Francisco	7-Wd San Francisco	81	192
Isaac G	43	m	w	IREL	El Dorado	Placerville Twp	72	102
J M	41	m	w	IN	Calaveras	Copperopolis P O	70	225
James	40	m	w	IREL	Solano	Vacaville Twp	90	129
Lincoln	39	m	w	KY	Amador	Volcano P O	69	388
Mark	55	m	w	IREL	El Dorado	Mud Springs Twp	72	91
Mary C	32	f	w	IREL	San Francisco	7-Wd San Francisco	81	217
Robert	66	m	w	IREL	San Francisco	7-Wd San Francisco	81	259
Robt	55	m	w	MO	El Dorado	Cosumnes Twp	72	18
JEFFERSON								
Alexander	28	m	w	CANA	Mendocino	Casper & Big Rvr	74	162
Charles	60	m	w	SCOT	Solano	Vacaville Twp	90	132
Charles	30	m	w	MEXI	Contra Costa	Martinez P O	71	396
George	58	m	w	SCOT	Sacramento	4-Wd Sacramento	77	319
George H	39	m	w	MA	Santa Clara	2-Wd San Jose	88	289
John	35	m	w	OH	Monterey	Castroville Twp	74	341
Jos	22	m	w	LA	San Francisco	8-Wd San Francisco	82	372
Nancy	22	f	b	UT	Los Angeles	Los Angeles	73	529
Saml	56	m	w	GERM	Tuolumne	Columbia P O	93	354
Sarah	62	f	b	AL	Los Angeles	Los Angeles	73	537
Stephen	31	m	w	ENGL	San Bernardino	San Bernardino Twp	78	416
Thomas	25	m	w	MA	Humboldt	Eureka Twp	72	267
W	64	m	w	ENGL	Placer	Lincoln P O	76	489
W R	47	m	w	MA	San Joaquin	2-Wd Stockton	86	176
Wm	21	m	w	MO	Tehama	Paskenta Twp	92	165
Wm	19	m	w	AL	San Francisco	1-Wd San Francisco	79	89
JEFFERTS								
Plummer	40	m	w	PA	San Francisco	San Francisco P O	83	223
JEFFERY								
D	45	m	w	IREL	San Joaquin	Liberty Twp	86	82
George	34	m	w	ENGL	Mariposa	Maxwell Crk P O	74	140
Gideon	46	m	w	ENGL	El Dorado	Placerville Twp	72	93
Richard	40	m	w	ENGL	Nevada	Nevada Twp	75	302
Robert J	40	m	w	PA	Placer	Gold Run Twp	76	396
Steven	37	m	w	ENGL	Mariposa	Maxwell Crk P O	74	144
Thos	35	m	w	RI	San Joaquin	Elliott Twp	86	73
William	51	m	w	SCOT	San Francisco	8-Wd San Francisco	82	296
William	35	m	w	ENGL	Nevada	Nevada Twp	75	315
Wm	74	m	w	VT	Nevada	Nevada Twp	75	293
Wm	38	m	w	ENGL	Nevada	Nevada Twp	75	306
JEFFERYS								
Geo	33	m	w	ENGL	Alameda	Oakland	68	245
JEFFEY								
Cyrus	26	m	w	ENGL	Contra Costa	Martinez P O	71	426
JEFFIES								
L D	45	f	w	NE	Mariposa	Maxwell Crk P O	74	143
JEFFIRES								
Edward	35	m	w	MA	Kern	Tehachapi P O	73	356
JEFFORDS								
William M	43	m	w	NY	Yuba	Long Bar Twp	93	563
JEFFREE								
John F	49	m	w	ENGL	Nevada	Grass Valley Twp	75	185
JEFFRES								
Robert	32	m	w	IREL	San Francisco	2-Wd San Francisco	79	174
Samuel	32	m	w	RI	Stanislaus	Empire Twp	92	44
JEFFRESS								
G G	48	m	w	VA	San Francisco	San Francisco P O	83	305
G W	45	m	w	VA	Tehama	Red Bluff	92	176
Maria	14	f	b	VA	San Francisco	San Francisco P O	83	305
JEFFREY								
Alexander	51	m	w	PA	Santa Clara	Fremont Twp	88	42
Alfred	36	m	w	ENGL	San Francisco	San Francisco P O	80	392
Edward	36	m	w	ENGL	Nevada	Grass Valley Twp	75	228
George	41	m	w	CANA	Yuba	Rose Bar Twp	93	662
Hugh	45	m	w	CANA	Sacramento	2-Wd Sacramento	77	232
James	37	m	w	ENGL	Nevada	Bridgeport Twp	75	104
John	35	m	w	ENGL	Alameda	Oakland	68	257
John	25	m	w	ENGL	Nevada	Grass Valley Twp	75	164
John H	26	m	w	ENGL	San Francisco	7-Wd San Francisco	81	246
Jos	70	m	w	ENGL	Alameda	Oakland	68	257
Patrick	33	m	w	IREL	Sacramento	2-Wd Sacramento	77	215
Robert	34	m	w	ENGL	Nevada	Grass Valley Twp	75	193
Sarah	45	f	w	NY	San Francisco	San Francisco P O	83	50
William	23	m	w	SCOT	Contra Costa	Martinez P O	71	427
Wm	32	m	w	ENGL	Santa Clara	Almaden Twp	88	9
Wm	26	m	w	NY	San Francisco	11-Wd San Francisc	84	616
JEFFREYS								
David	28	m	w	ENGL	Santa Barbara	Santa Maria P O	87	514
Henry	22	m	w	AUSL	San Francisco	11-Wd San Francisc	84	449
John	45	m	w	ENGL	San Francisco	11-Wd San Francisc	84	495
Walter	25	m	w	ENGL	San Luis Obispo	Salinas Twp	87	291
JEFFRIDO								
Luis	31	m	w	FRAN	Los Angeles	El Monte Twp	73	457
JEFFRIES								
Benjamin	27	m	w	OH	Solano	Green Valley Twp	90	44
Frank	33	m	w	ENGL	Nevada	Little York Twp	75	241
J G W	21	m	w	MS	Alameda	Oakland	68	253
James	38	m	w	MO	Yolo	Cache Crk Twp	93	457
James	37	m	w	ENGL	El Dorado	Placerville	72	118
Jno	56	m	w	ENGL	Santa Clara	Almaden Twp	88	16
Lenn	27	m	w	ENGL	San Joaquin	Tulare Twp	86	252
Mary	30	f	w	NH	San Francisco	7-Wd San Francisco	81	254
Mary J	36	f	w	IA	Nevada	Grass Valley Twp	75	185
Robt A	51	m	w	VA	El Dorado	Cosumnes Twp	72	14
Robt L	28	m	w	ENGL	Humboldt	Arcata Twp	72	231
Thomas	61	m	w	ENGL	Santa Barbara	Santa Barbara P O	87	472
Thomas	54	m	w	WALE	Colusa	Grand Island Twp	71	302
Thos	45	m	w	NY	Butte	Ophir Twp	70	104
William	38	m	w	ENGL	Kern	Kernville P O	73	368
JEFFRIS								
Lincoln	34	m	w	KY	Amador	Drytown P O	69	415
Wm H	39	m	w	SC	Fresno	Millerton P O	72	168
JEFFROY								
Lucien	60	m	w	FRAN	Yuba	Rose Bar Twp	93	652
JEFFRY								
Thomas	27	m	w	ENGL	Mariposa	Mariposa P O	74	108
William	34	m	w	OH	Solano	Rio Vista Twp	90	62
JEFFS								
Isaac	28	m	w	CANA	Yuba	North East Twp	93	644
JEFFYRS								
Milo	35	m	w	NY	San Francisco	8-Wd San Francisco	82	311
JEFREY								
William	38	m	w	SCOT	San Francisco	2-Wd San Francisco	79	263
JEFRY								
J	39	m	w	ENGL	Sierra	Lincoln Twp	89	545
JEFTS								
James M	50	m	w	MA	San Francisco	2-Wd San Francisco	79	257

© 2001 by Heritage Quest. All rights reserved.

Name	Age	S	R	B-PL	County	Locale	Series M593 Roll	Pg
JEGELING								
Charles	39	m	w	HDAR	San Francisco	8-Wd San Francisco	82	419
JEGUINA								
G	40	m	w	SWIT	El Dorado	Kelsey Twp	72	60
JEH								
Ah	34	m	c	CHIN	Santa Clara	Gilroy Twp	88	97
JEHANA								
Pedro	31	m	w	MEXI	Fresno	Millerton P O	72	163
JEHL								
Adolph	37	m	w	FRAN	San Francisco	8-Wd San Francisco	82	373
JEHN								
Nathan	46	m	w	WALE	San Francisco	San Francisco P O	83	183
JEISLER								
Antone	25	m	w	SWIT	Contra Costa	Martinez P O	71	374
JEK								
Ah	30	m	c	CHIN	Solano	Suisun Twp	90	104
JELA								
Jaques	52	m	w	FRAN	San Francisco	1-Wd San Francisco	79	25
JELETICK								
Nicholas	36	m	w	AUST	Amador	Jackson P O	69	321
JELLE								
Jacob	36	m	w	HAMB	Santa Clara	Gilroy Twp	88	81
JELLERSON								
Reuben	41	m	w	ENGL	Monterey	Castroville Twp	74	338
JELLEY								
Andrew	43	m	w	OH	Tehama	Battle Crk Twp	92	157
JELLINGS								
Wm	38	m	w	ENGL	San Francisco	San Francisco P O	85	802
JELLISON								
Julia	46	f	w	MA	Yuba	Marysville	93	617
JELLITT								
Malissa	16	f	w	ITAL	Amador	Amador City P O	69	392
JELLJI								
Conrad	60	m	w	PRUS	San Francisco	1-Wd San Francisco	79	133
JELLOWTZY								
Marco	30	m	w	PA	San Francisco	5-Wd San Francisco	81	10
JELLY								
Saml	42	m	w	MA	Sacramento	3-Wd Sacramento	77	301
Thomas	40	m	w	IREL	Nevada	Eureka Twp	75	132
Toney	25	m	i	CA	Tehama	Cottonwood Twp	92	162
JELMENI								
John	49	m	w	SWIT	Amador	Sutter Crk P O	69	403
JELMINER								
B	35	m	w	SWIT	Amador	Drytown P O	69	420
JELMINI								
Orris	30	m	w	ITAL	San Francisco	8-Wd San Francisco	82	446
JEM								
Ah	32	m	c	CHIN	Santa Barbara	Santa Barbara P O	87	465
Ah	30	m	c	CHIN	Sacramento	Georgianna Twp	77	122
Ah	26	m	c	CHIN	Siskiyou	Cottonwood Twp	89	594
Yee	40	m	c	CHIN	Yuba	Marysville	93	620
JEMIN								
C A	58	m	w	IL	San Joaquin	Dent Twp	86	29
JEMISON								
Alfred	42	m	w	PA	El Dorado	Georgetown Twp	72	40
Henry	35	m	w	LA	San Francisco	7-Wd San Francisco	81	170
Hiram	26	m	w	MO	Inyo	Bishop Crk Twp	73	310
J H	39	m	w	MO	Lake	Lower Lake	73	423
John J	33	m	w	KY	Alpine	Silver Mtn P O	69	306
P H	25	m	w	PA	Alameda	Oakland	68	172
T B	36	m	w	MD	Monterey	Alisal Twp	74	302
JEMMIE								
Chinaman	41	m	c	CHIN	Calaveras	San Andreas P O	70	153
JEMMINGS								
I A	48	m	w	MA	Tuolumne	Columbia P O	93	350
JEMMISON								
Samuel	41	m	w	MD	Santa Clara	Santa Clara Twp	88	165
JEMOIS								
Joseph	33	m	w	ITAL	Santa Clara	Fremont Twp	88	58
JEMSON								
France	38	m	w	PA	Tehama	Paskenta Twp	92	163
JEN								
Ah	36	m	c	CHIN	Sacramento	Mississippi Twp	77	162
Ah	36	m	c	CHIN	Mariposa	Mariposa P O	74	137
Ah	33	m	c	CHIN	Sacramento	1-Wd Sacramento	77	205
Ah	26	m	c	CHIN	Plumas	Indian Twp	77	17
Ah	25	m	c	CHIN	Kern	Bakersfield P O	73	361
Doon	57	m	c	CHIN	Placer	Pino Twp	76	470
Nee	34	f	c	CHIN	Nevada	Nevada Twp	75	298
JENACIE								
Joseph	35	m	w	ITAL	San Francisco	1-Wd San Francisco	79	92
JENAL								
Alex	49	m	w	FRAN	Alameda	San Leandro	68	98
JENARD								
Adrian	37	m	w	FRAN	Nevada	Grass Valley Twp	75	180
JENARDUS								
Ben	22	m	w	SWIT	San Francisco	11-Wd San Francisc	84	680
Stephen	18	m	w	SWIT	San Francisco	11-Wd San Francisc	84	680
JENARI								
Victor	20	m	w	ITAL	San Francisco	San Francisco P O	80	472
JENAUX								
William	44	m	w	CANA	Solano	Green Valley Twp	90	39
JENDES								
Manuel	30	m	w	CHIL	Marin	San Rafael Twp	74	34
JENET								
Henry	24	m	w	MEXI	San Luis Obispo	San Luis Obispo Tw	87	300
Julien	56	m	w	FRAN	Calaveras	Copperopolis P O	70	249
JENG								
Ah	30	m	c	CHIN	Sierra	Eureka Twp	89	525
JENIGAN								
Henry W	40	m	w	AL	Placer	Emigrant Gap P O	76	417
JENING								
E	33	m	w	ENGL	Sierra	Butte Twp	89	509
JENINGS								
M R	60	m	w	IREL	Sierra	Lincoln Twp	89	546
S	24	f	w	ENGL	Sierra	Lincoln Twp	89	548
Williamson	49	m	w	NC	Amador	Drytown P O	69	420
JENISON								
Ephriam	40	m	w	MO	Yolo	Grafton Twp	93	498
JENK								
W	40	m	w	PRUS	Alameda	Murray Twp	68	123
JENKERSON								
Augustus	32	m	w	MO	El Dorado	Cosumnes Twp	72	13
JENKIN								
Jenkins	25	m	w	WALE	Contra Costa	Martinez P O	71	427
John	25	m	w	ENGL	Nevada	Nevada Twp	75	309
JENKINGS								
Wm	40	m	w	ENGL	San Francisco	8-Wd San Francisco	82	312
JENKINS								
Agnes	75	f	w	SCOT	Alameda	Oakland	68	131
Ann	28	f	w	MD	San Francisco	San Francisco P O	83	172
Anna D	50	f	w	AL	Santa Cruz	Santa Cruz	89	427
Annie	58	f	w	IREL	San Francisco	11-Wd San Francisc	84	656
Annie	23	f	w	ENGL	San Francisco	San Francisco P O	80	338
B	41	m	w	IL	Lassen	Susanville Twp	73	446
B A B	44	m	w	IA	Trinity	North Fork Twp	92	218
C	25	m	w	ENGL	Sierra	Butte Twp	89	513
C N	38	m	w	VT	Yuba	Marysville	93	610
Cath	2	f	w	CA	Butte	Oregon Twp	70	130
Cecelia	32	f	w	IREL	Nevada	Nevada Twp	75	287
Charles L	43	m	w	DE	San Francisco	San Francisco P O	83	223
Charles M	31	m	w	OH	Los Angeles	Los Angeles Twp	73	491
David	20	m	w	ENGL	Contra Costa	Martinez P O	71	414
Dorotea	37	f	m	CA	Santa Barbara	Santa Barbara P O	87	455
E	34	m	w	ENGL	Sierra	Butte Twp	89	508
E S	35	m	w	MA	Solano	Vallejo	90	152
Eali	45	f	w	VT	San Francisco	San Francisco P O	83	97
Edmond P	55	m	w	VT	Monterey	San Antonio Twp	74	323
Edward	19	m	w	CANA	Solano	Denverton Twp	90	24
Elisa	49	f	w	OH	Sonoma	Vallejo Twp	91	462
Ella	25	f	w	MA	San Francisco	San Francisco P O	83	170
Emily	30	f	w	MO	Santa Clara	San Jose Twp	88	188
Emma	23	f	w	OH	Sacramento	Lee Twp	77	158
Evan	41	m	w	WALE	Santa Clara	Fremont Twp	88	42
Evan	41	m	w	WALE	Placer	Bath P O	76	437
Evans	38	m	w	WALE	El Dorado	Georgetown Twp	72	47
Frances	23	f	w	ME	San Francisco	8-Wd San Francisco	82	444
Frank	36	m	w	AZOR	San Francisco	1-Wd San Francisco	79	118
Frank	27	m	w	ENGL	San Francisco	San Francisco P O	83	157
G W	33	m	w	OH	Sacramento	3-Wd Sacramento	77	283
Geo F	38	m	w	NY	Sonoma	Healdsburg & Mendo	91	276
Geo H	48	m	w	ENGL	Solano	Rio Vista Twp	90	56
Geo W	25	m	w	IA	Shasta	Millville P O	89	491
George C	47	m	w	NY	Santa Clara	San Jose Twp	88	185
Griffith	40	m	w	WALE	Nevada	Bridgeport Twp	75	102
Henry	50	m	w	IREL	Tuolumne	Sonora P O	93	331
Henry	31	m	w	ENGL	Nevada	Grass Valley Twp	75	222
Henry	31	m	w	ENGL	San Francisco	5-Wd San Francisco	81	35
Henry J	30	m	w	NY	Yuba	Slate Range Bar Tw	93	674
Isabelle	14	f	w	CA	Alameda	Oakland	68	258
J	70	m	w	NC	Lake	Lower Lake	73	416
J E	47	m	w	KY	San Joaquin	2-Wd Stockton	86	177
J L	40	m	w	US	Yuba	Marysville	93	634
James	44	m	w	IL	San Francisco	San Francisco P O	83	263
James	40	m	w	CANA	Kern	Havilah P O	73	350
James	33	m	b	VA	Nevada	Nevada Twp	75	274
James	28	m	w	MO	Tulare	Visalia Twp	92	284
James	24	m	w	ENGL	Nevada	Nevada Twp	75	300
James C	45	m	w	SCOT	Mariposa	Mariposa P O	74	109
James H	49	m	w	MD	San Francisco	2-Wd San Francisco	79	252
Jane	34	f	w	NY	Del Norte	Crescent	71	467
Jas W	45	m	w	NY	Shasta	Shasta P O	89	463
Jenny	16	f	w	WI	Napa	Napa	75	43
Jesse G	28	m	w	MO	Santa Clara	1-Wd San Jose	88	241
Jno	50	m	w	PA	San Diego	San Diego	78	483
Jno	44	m	w	WALE	Butte	Kimshew Tpw	70	82
Jno C	55	m	m	MD	Butte	Ophir Twp	70	93
John	55	m	w	ENGL	Nevada	Grass Valley Twp	75	226
John	55	m	w	MA	San Francisco	6-Wd San Francisco	81	113
John	46	m	w	SCOT	El Dorado	Salmon Falls Twp	72	132
John	41	m	w	NY	Humboldt	Eureka Twp	72	269
John	40	m	w	KY	Solano	Vallejo	90	158
John	40	m	w	ENGL	Los Angeles	Santa Ana Twp	73	610
John	39	m	w	ENGL	Contra Costa	Martinez P O	71	421
John	36	m	w	ENGL	Tuolumne	Chinese Camp P O	93	365
John	33	m	w	ENGL	San Francisco	1-Wd San Francisco	79	102
John	26	m	w	IREL	San Francisco	7-Wd San Francisco	81	185
John	24	m	w	IL	Solano	Silveyville Twp	90	85
John	23	m	w	WALE	Sacramento	San Joaquin Twp	77	407
John D	61	m	w	ENGL	Nevada	Nevada Twp	75	271
John R	40	m	w	ENGL	San Francisco	1-Wd San Francisco	79	107
John T	26	m	w	ENGL	Nevada	Nevada Twp	75	300
John W	52	m	w	NY	Yuba	North East Twp	93	643
Jonas	47	m	w	IL	San Joaquin	Elliott Twp	86	70

© 2001 by Heritage Quest. All rights reserved.

Name	Age	S	R	B-PL	County	Locale	Roll	Pg
Joseph	21	m	w	ENGL	Nevada	Grass Valley Twp	75	148
Joseph J	34	m	w	CANA	Colusa	Butte Twp	71	272
Joseph P	35	m	w	TN	Placer	Auburn P O	76	357
Joseph W	40	m	w	ME	Los Angeles	Los Angeles	73	506
Josiah	54	m	w	ENGL	Los Angeles	Wilmington Twp	73	645
Josiah	35	m	w	ENGL	San Francisco	1-Wd San Francisco	79	119
Josiah	32	m	w	ENGL	Nevada	Grass Valley Twp	75	200
Josiah	32	m	w	ENGL	Santa Clara	Almaden Twp	88	9
Jus	34	m	w	WALE	Butte	Oregon Twp	70	136
Kate	35	f	w	IREL	San Francisco	8-Wd San Francisco	82	424
Lemon	40	m	w	ENGL	Nevada	Grass Valley Twp	75	232
Louis R	32	m	w	OH	Sacramento	San Joaquin Twp	77	399
M	37	m	w	WALE	Alameda	Murray Twp	68	119
Mary	29	f	w	IREL	San Mateo	Redwood Twp	87	368
Mary	23	f	w	ENGL	San Francisco	5-Wd San Francisco	81	24
Mary	11	f	w	PA	Mariposa	Maxwell Crk P O	74	143
Mercedes	35	f	w	CHIL	San Francisco	8-Wd San Francisco	82	441
Mira	30	f	w	ME	San Joaquin	Douglas Twp	86	32
Morris	50	m	w	WALE	Sacramento	San Joaquin Twp	77	407
Nicholas	30	m	w	ENGL	Plumas	Mineral Twp	77	23
P F	45	m	w	NY	Merced	Snelling P O	74	248
P P	37	m	w	VT	San Francisco	San Francisco P O	85	764
Patrick	40	m	w	IREL	Tuolumne	Sonora P O	93	330
R J	65	m	w	IREL	Sacramento	Granite Twp	77	144
Richard	48	m	w	ENGL	Santa Barbara	Santa Barbara P O	87	455
Robert	26	m	w	PA	San Francisco	San Francisco P O	80	458
Robert	26	m	w	IREL	San Francisco	San Francisco P O	80	356
Robert R	43	m	w	PA	Calaveras	Copperopolis P O	70	259
Rockwell S	40	m	w	NY	Yuba	Bullards Bar P O	93	547
Saml	28	m	w	ENGL	San Francisco	2-Wd San Francisco	79	244
Samuel	28	m	w	VA	Colusa	Colusa Twp	71	284
Sarah	30	f	b	SC	San Francisco	8-Wd San Francisco	82	496
Sarah	24	f	w	IREL	San Francisco	San Francisco P O	80	407
Sarah A	25	f	w	ENGL	Yuba	Parks Bar Twp	93	648
Simon	25	m	w	ENGL	Nevada	Grass Valley Twp	75	231
Thomas	45	m	w	MD	San Francisco	San Francisco P O	80	410
Thomas	43	m	w	WALE	Siskiyou	Cottonwood Twp	89	590
Thomas B W	32	m	w	LA	Contra Costa	Martinez P O	71	382
Thomas H	38	m	w	CANA	Colusa	Butte Twp	71	272
Thos	40	m	w	NY	Merced	Snelling P O	74	275
Thos H	13	m	w	ENGL	Sierra	Sears Twp	89	559
Thos J	45	m	w	KY	Butte	Ophir Twp	70	107
W	43	m	w	ENGL	Sierra	Lincoln Twp	89	550
Washn	35	m	w	MA	San Francisco	San Francisco P O	83	84
William	45	m	w	MS	Solano	Silveyville Twp	90	83
William	38	m	w	OH	Los Angeles	Los Angeles Twp	73	493
William	33	m	w	ENGL	Nevada	Grass Valley Twp	75	185
William	32	m	w	ENGL	Nevada	Grass Valley Twp	75	148
William	30	m	w	AR	Tulare	Kings Rvr Twp	92	252
William	29	m	w	IN	Solano	Silveyville Twp	90	92
William	26	m	w	NY	San Francisco	San Francisco P O	80	390
William H	27	m	w	MA	San Francisco	6-Wd San Francisco	81	126
Wilson	36	m	w	IL	Santa Clara	San Jose Twp	88	197
Wm	35	m	w	NY	San Francisco	1-Wd San Francisco	79	15
Wm	23	m	w	WALE	El Dorado	Kelsey Twp	72	62
Wm	13	m	w	CA	San Francisco	11-Wd San Francisc	84	590
Wm E	7	m	w	CA	Fresno	Millerton P O	72	185
Wm H	33	m	w	ENGL	Nevada	Nevada Twp	75	300
Wm P	39	m	w	WALE	San Francisco	1-Wd San Francisco	79	45
JENKINSON								
Ellen	36	f	w	IREL	San Francisco	8-Wd San Francisco	82	495
JENKS								
A B	49	m	w	RI	San Joaquin	3-Wd Stockton	86	244
Agnes	10	f	w	CA	San Joaquin	3-Wd Stockton	86	225
Andrew	29	m	w	MO	Solano	Silveyville Twp	90	75
Angelie	60	f	w	MO	Alameda	Murray Twp	68	117
C C	39	m	w	PA	Sacramento	3-Wd Sacramento	77	300
Georg H	33	m	w	CANA	Sonoma	Petaluma Twp	91	333
J H	34	m	w	RI	San Francisco	San Francisco P O	85	830
John L	34	m	w	IL	San Mateo	Pescadero P O	87	417
Joseph	22	m	w	MO	Solano	Tremont Twp	90	28
Live	62	m	w	MA	Alameda	Alameda	68	1
William	43	m	w	NY	Los Angeles	Los Angeles	73	518
Wm A	28	m	w	HAMB	San Francisco	8-Wd San Francisco	82	325
JENKUS								
S	40	m	w	ENGL	Calaveras	Copperopolis P O	70	232
JENN								
Peter	50	m	w	PRUS	San Francisco	San Francisco P O	83	30
JENNANIE								
Getana	37	m	w	SWIT	San Francisco	San Francisco P O	85	861
JENNE								
Ah	18	f	c	CHIN	Nevada	Nevada Twp	75	298
JENNER								
E P	48	m	w	ENGL	Siskiyou	Callahan P O	89	629
Elijah K	57	m	w	VT	Sonoma	Healdsburg & Mendo	91	284
Sylvester	33	m	w	NY	Sacramento	4-Wd Sacramento	77	332
Wm A	63	m	w	ENGL	San Francisco	7-Wd San Francisco	81	236
JENNERS								
Levi	36	m	w	NH	Plumas	Rich Bar Twp	77	8
JENNETT								
J P	28	m	w	NY	Monterey	San Juan Twp	74	396
JENNEY								
Caspar	45	m	w	SWIT	San Francisco	San Francisco P O	80	479
JENNIE								
Edward S	38	m	w	CT	San Francisco	3-Wd San Francisco	79	312
Jack	30	m	w	SWIT	Sacramento	Sutter Twp	77	389

Name	Age	S	R	B-PL	County	Locale	Roll	Pg
JENNIFER								
John M	34	m	w	IL	Santa Barbara	San Buenaventura P	87	418
M T	39	m	w	IL	Santa Barbara	San Buenaventura P	87	425
JENNING								
Anna	36	f	w	SCOT	San Francisco	8-Wd San Francisco	82	365
G	28	m	w	GERM	Sacramento	1-Wd Sacramento	77	177
Jas	50	m	w	ENGL	Nevada	Nevada Twp	75	282
Saml	50	m	w	ENGL	Yuba	Rose Bar Twp	93	656
JENNINGS								
Albert	18	m	w	NJ	San Francisco	11-Wd San Francisc	84	593
Alfred J	39	m	w	ENGL	Santa Cruz	Watsonville	89	369
Alice P	11	f	w	CA	El Dorado	Placerville Twp	72	94
Augustus	37	m	w	ME	San Francisco	6-Wd San Francisco	81	130
Benjamin	73	m	w	ME	Santa Clara	San Jose Twp	88	210
Benjamin	29	m	w	ENGL	Nevada	Grass Valley Twp	75	231
Bridget	45	f	w	IREL	San Francisco	8-Wd San Francisco	82	409
Byron	33	m	w	CANA	Santa Clara	1-Wd San Jose	88	259
Caesar	31	m	w	SWIT	Yuba	New York Twp	93	640
Charles B	28	m	w	NY	San Francisco	6-Wd San Francisco	81	128
David	50	m	w	NY	San Francisco	6-Wd San Francisco	81	128
Delia	29	f	w	IREL	San Francisco	San Francisco P O	83	283
Edward	48	m	w	WURT	San Francisco	San Francisco P O	80	353
Elijah	38	m	b	MO	Yolo	Grafton Twp	93	482
Ella	18	f	w	ME	San Mateo	San Mateo P O	87	355
F R	22	m	w	GA	San Francisco	3-Wd San Francisco	79	314
Flora	22	f	b	MO	Yolo	Cottonwood Twp	93	460
Frank	23	m	w	CT	Stanislaus	Empire Twp	92	53
Frederick	26	m	w	CT	San Francisco	San Francisco P O	83	339
George	8	m	w	CA	San Francisco	11-Wd San Francisc	84	593
Hanna	22	f	w	IREL	San Joaquin	2-Wd Stockton	86	170
Henry	4	m	b	MO	Yolo	Cottonwood Twp	93	469
Henry	30	m	w	NY	Butte	Chico Twp	70	54
Henry	21	m	w	IL	Napa	Napa	75	14
Hugh	27	m	w	ENGL	Nevada	Grass Valley Twp	75	195
Isaac	32	m	w	ENGL	San Francisco	3-Wd San Francisco	79	320
J	30	m	w	MO	Yuba	Marysville	93	617
J H	28	m	w	NJ	San Francisco	San Francisco P O	85	797
J L	37	m	w	MD	Yuba	Marysville Twp	93	567
J R	30	m	w	NY	Yuba	Marysville	93	608
Jackson	37	m	w	MO	Alpine	Woodfords P O	69	316
James	46	m	w	PA	San Luis Obispo	Santa Rosa Twp	87	324
James	42	m	w	NY	Yuba	Marysville	93	617
James	37	m	w	NY	Stanislaus	Empire Twp	92	46
James	25	m	w	IREL	San Francisco	3-Wd San Francisco	79	315
James	24	m	w	NY	San Francisco	7-Wd San Francisco	81	190
Jane	38	f	w	MA	San Francisco	5-Wd San Francisco	81	27
Jas H	27	m	w	NY	Butte	Chico Twp	70	26
Jennie	35	f	w	NY	Santa Clara	1-Wd San Jose	88	264
John	60	m	w	ME	San Mateo	San Mateo P O	87	355
John	35	m	w	IREL	San Francisco	San Francisco P O	83	16
John	28	m	w	ENGL	Nevada	Nevada Twp	75	309
John	23	m	w	ENGL	Mendocino	Casper & Big Rvr	74	162
Jos Thos	26	m	w	ENGL	San Francisco	San Francisco P O	83	5
Joseph	49	m	w	CT	San Francisco	11-Wd San Francisc	84	595
Joseph	25	m	w	IREL	San Francisco	5-Wd San Francisco	81	32
Josia	33	m	w	CT	San Joaquin	2-Wd Stockton	86	164
Lawrence	40	m	w	NY	Stanislaus	Empire Twp	92	58
M V	36	m	w	MA	Solano	Vallejo	90	140
Martha	9	f	w	CA	Tulare	Farmersville Twp	92	247
Mary	60	f	w	ME	Yolo	Washington Twp	93	531
Mary	20	f	w	IL	Los Angeles	Los Angeles	73	545
Matilda	24	f	w	IL	Amador	Amador City P O	69	395
May M	48	f	w	ENGL	Nevada	Nevada Twp	75	315
Michael	40	m	w	IREL	Nevada	Washington Twp	75	339
Miller	40	m	w	IREL	Colusa	Monroe Twp	71	313
Moses	35	m	w	ME	Los Angeles	Los Angeles	73	512
Nicholas	45	m	w	ENGL	Nevada	Grass Valley Twp	75	194
O	50	m	w	NY	Sierra	Forest Twp	89	530
Pat	35	m	w	IREL	San Francisco	11-Wd San Francisc	84	614
Patrick	45	m	w	IREL	San Francisco	1-Wd San Francisco	79	93
Peter	33	m	w	IREL	San Francisco	11-Wd San Francisc	84	614
Peter	29	m	w	NY	Santa Clara	Fremont Twp	88	50
Robert	36	m	w	IREL	San Mateo	Schoolhouse Statio	87	342
Robt	22	m	w	CANA	Santa Clara	Almaden Twp	88	14
S R	21	m	w	ME	Solano	Vallejo	90	203
Samuel	46	m	w	PA	Tulare	Visalia Twp	92	287
Thomas	43	m	w	ENGL	Inyo	Cerro Gordo Twp	73	323
Thomas	40	m	w	IREL	San Francisco	San Francisco P O	80	394
Thomas	40	m	w	NJ	San Francisco	8-Wd San Francisco	82	448
Thos	38	m	w	PRUS	San Francisco	5-Wd San Francisco	81	9
Tillman	33	m	w	SC	Amador	Ione City P O	69	349
Tillman	30	m	w	NC	Amador	Drytown P O	69	424
W	60	m	w	ME	Alameda	Oakland	68	220
W C	60	m	w	PA	Yuba	East Bear Rvr Twp	93	542
Walter	38	m	w	ENGL	Nevada	Nevada Twp	75	277
William	29	m	w	ENGL	San Francisco	8-Wd San Francisco	82	455
William	24	m	w	NY	San Francisco	6-Wd San Francisco	81	128
William J	22	m	w	ENGL	Nevada	Grass Valley Twp	75	148
Wm	44	m	w	OH	Amador	Drytown P O	69	416
Worthington H	36	m	w	MA	Nevada	Grass Valley Twp	75	204
JENNIS								
Carlotta	2	f	w	CA	Tuolumne	Sonora P O	93	318
Thomas	38	m	w	ENGL	Tuolumne	Sonora P O	93	316
Wm	24	m	w	NY	Tuolumne	Sonora P O	93	321
JENNISON								
M	35	m	w	IREL	Alameda	Murray Twp	68	120
Saml	65	m	w	NY	Tehama	Paskenta Twp	92	164

Series M593

© 2001 by Heritage Quest. All rights reserved.

Name	Age	S	R	B-PL	County	Locale	Roll	Pg
JENNSON								
William	29	m	w	NORW	Colusa	Colusa Twp	71	283
JENNY								
Ah	30	f	c	CHIN	El Dorado	Placerville	72	115
Mary	38	f	w	GERM	San Francisco	8-Wd San Francisco	82	306
JENSEN								
Asen	45	m	w	PRUS	San Francisco	San Francisco P O	83	134
Carl W	27	m	w	DENM	San Francisco	San Francisco P O	83	135
Errick	32	m	w	SHOL	Alameda	Eden Twp	68	67
Francisco	39	m	w	DENM	Fresno	Millerton P O	72	193
Franciso	41	m	w	DENM	Fresno	Millerton P O	72	192
Frederick	36	m	w	SHOL	Siskiyou	Hamburg Twp	89	596
H P	36	m	w	DENM	San Joaquin	1-Wd Stockton	86	136
Henry	30	m	w	PRUS	San Francisco	San Francisco P O	80	381
Jacob	33	m	w	DENM	San Francisco	San Francisco P O	83	120
John C	41	m	w	PRUS	Placer	Bath P O	76	437
John T	32	m	w	NORW	Placer	Gold Run Twp	76	394
Jurgen	33	m	w	DENM	Monterey	Castroville Twp	74	336
Nathaniel	23	m	w	PRUS	Solano	Rio Vista Twp	90	70
Nohman	17	m	w	SHOL	Alameda	Eden Twp	68	67
Peter	27	m	w	DENM	Marin	Tomales Twp	74	88
Robert	27	m	w	PRUS	San Francisco	San Francisco P O	80	479
JENSENT								
Joseph	29	m	w	PORT	Marin	Tomales Twp	74	88
JENSOHN								
Jacob	30	m	w	CANA	Contra Costa	San Pablo Twp	71	356
JENSON								
Andw	40	m	w	NORW	San Francisco	San Francisco P O	83	118
Hans	40	m	w	DENM	Sacramento	Georgianna Twp	77	128
Hans	30	m	w	RI	Marin	Tomales Twp	74	78
Henry	37	m	w	DENM	Nevada	Washington Twp	75	347
Ingerbery	16	f	w	DENM	Sonoma	Petaluma Twp	91	355
Isabel	14	f	w	CA	Los Angeles	Los Angeles	73	526
J	33	m	w	PRUS	Lassen	Susanville Twp	73	440
J	28	m	w	GERM	Lake	Morgan Valley	73	425
Jens C	42	m	w	DENM	Butte	Chico Twp	70	42
W M	30	m	w	DENM	Alameda	Oakland	68	178
JENTIN								
John	68	m	w	ENGL	San Francisco	6-Wd San Francisco	81	113
JENTREY								
James	35	m	w	MO	Humboldt	South Fork Twp	72	300
JENTS								
Augustas	30	m	w	PRUS	Sonoma	Salt Point	91	387
JEOFFREY								
George	24	m	w	FRAN	Amador	Fiddletown P O	69	433
JEONG								
Ah	21	m	c	CHIN	Sonoma	Salt Point	91	386
JEOW								
Ah	46	m	c	CHIN	Sonoma	Bodega Twp	91	251
JEPSON								
Henry	20	m	w	DENM	Alameda	Eden Twp	68	63
Jacob	55	m	w	DENM	Trinity	Douglas	92	233
Jacob	30	m	w	DENM	Alameda	Oakland	68	176
William	44	m	w	KY	Solano	Vacaville Twp	90	126
JERABUCK								
Charles	45	m	w	PA	Santa Barbara	Santa Barbara P O	87	455
JERAMBO								
Louis	19	m	w	ITAL	San Mateo	Schoolhouse Statio	87	334
JERDES								
Henry	36	m	w	BREM	Calaveras	San Andreas P O	70	158
JERE								
Ah	24	m	c	CHIN	Placer	Bath P O	76	445
JEREMIAH								
Price	70	m	w	WALE	Shasta	Shasta P O	89	453
JEREMONIS								
Jose	24	m	w	CA	Santa Cruz	Soquel Twp	89	448
JEREZ								
Jose	34	m	w	MEXI	San Diego	Coronado	78	467
JERGENSON								
Peter	43	m	w	SILE	Placer	Bath P O	76	458
William	29	m	w	PRUS	Stanislaus	North Twp	92	69
JERGUNSON								
C M	31	m	w	DENM	El Dorado	Greenwood Twp	72	55
JERKE								
Amos	25	m	w	AZOR	Marin	Sausalito Twp	74	68
Manuel	20	m	w	AZOR	Marin	Sausalito Twp	74	68
JERKIN								
Diedrich	29	m	w	HANO	San Francisco	1-Wd San Francisco	79	113
JERLEA								
Henry	33	m	w	FRAN	Placer	Bath P O	76	446
JERMAN								
Fredk	40	m	w	PRUS	Sacramento	Lee Twp	77	160
William	16	m	w	ENGL	Santa Clara	San Jose Twp	88	209
JERMANE								
Frank	47	m	w	BELG	San Joaquin	2-Wd Stockton	86	158
JERMEIN								
Fred	28	m	w	CANA	San Joaquin	Oneal Twp	86	100
JERMINA								
Newant	40	m	w	ITAL	San Francisco	11-Wd San Francisc	84	710
JERMIQUET								
Isaac	36	m	w	SWIT	Trinity	Lewiston Pct	92	214
JERN								
John	28	m	w	ENGL	Fresno	Millerton P O	72	146
Tom	25	m	i	CA	Fresno	Millerton P O	72	146
JERNEGAN								
William	35	m	w	IN	Sacramento	2-Wd Sacramento	77	226

Name	Age	S	R	B-PL	County	Locale	Roll	Pg
JERNES								
Jose A	50	m	w	CA	Monterey	Alisal Twp	74	288
JERNIGAN								
Bryant	58	m	w	GA	Nevada	Little York Twp	75	243
JERNSEN								
Herman	49	m	w	SHOL	Siskiyou	Hamburg Twp	89	596
JEROL								
Constant	18	m	w	ITAL	Sacramento	4-Wd Sacramento	77	369
JEROLAKE								
Peter	62	m	w	FRAN	Alameda	Oakland	68	251
JEROLD								
Wm E	21	m	w	IL	Sacramento	San Joaquin Twp	77	404
JEROME								
Albert	28	m	w	PRUS	San Francisco	San Francisco P O	83	102
Alexander	40	m	w	NY	Amador	Volcano P O	69	373
Antone	22	m	w	PORT	Marin	San Rafael Twp	74	59
Catherine	42	f	w	VT	San Francisco	San Francisco P O	83	29
Charly	20	m	i	CA	Colusa	Grand Island Twp	71	310
Fred	50	m	w	ENGL	San Francisco	2-Wd San Francisco	79	206
Judson	25	m	w	CT	Calaveras	Copperopolis P O	70	253
Louis S	40	m	w	FRAN	San Francisco	6-Wd San Francisco	81	37
Michl	40	m	w	NY	San Francisco	5-Wd San Francisco	81	20
Stephen J	51	m	w	NY	Amador	Volcano P O	69	382
Tamar	29	f	w	NY	Mendocino	Sanel Twp	74	229
Thos	36	m	w	VA	Sonoma	Russian Rvr	91	369
Wm	32	m	w	ENGL	San Diego	San Diego	78	510
JERRALD								
Mary	14	f	w	MA	San Joaquin	Elliott Twp	86	70
JERRARD								
Annie	55	f	w	IREL	San Francisco	San Francisco P O	83	178
JERRETT								
Daniel	40	m	w	NY	El Dorado	Georgetown Twp	72	42
Edward	40	m	w	ME	Placer	Summit P O	76	496
William	45	m	w	GA	Stanislaus	Branch Twp	92	2
JERRIL								
Anna	7	f	w	CA	San Joaquin	1-Wd Stockton	86	127
JERRISON								
A B	53	m	w	NH	Lassen	Susanville Twp	73	441
JERRO								
Joseph	19	m	w	SPAI	Alameda	Brooklyn Twp	68	42
JERROLD								
Sarah	22	f	w	MO	Napa	Napa Twp	75	71
JERRON								
Jake	37	m	w	PRUS	San Joaquin	2-Wd Stockton	86	206
JERSEY								
Richard M	35	m	w	ENGL	Nevada	Grass Valley Twp	75	144
JERUD								
John	40	m	w	FRAN	Shasta	Shasta P O	89	455
JERUE								
John	38	m	w	FRAN	Stanislaus	Branch Twp	92	5
JERURDO								
Marcus	46	m	w	CHIL	Calaveras	San Andreas P O	70	180
JERVIS								
J	29	m	w	IN	Nevada	Eureka Twp	75	139
JERZSPERSON								
J I	43	m	w	DENM	Nevada	Bridgeport Twp	75	101
JESABENA								
Margret	37	f	w	SCOT	Alameda	Brooklyn Twp	68	48
JESAU								
Ortego	28	m	w	MEXI	Fresno	Millerton P O	72	159
JESCHKE								
August	22	m	w	PRUS	Yolo	Cache Crk Twp	93	451
JESEN								
Adam	46	m	w	CT	Yolo	Grafton Twp	93	500
JESEY								
Candelario	31	m	w	MEXI	Los Angeles	El Monte Twp	73	452
JESFERSEN								
Christian H	34	m	w	DENM	Santa Cruz	Watsonville	89	370
JESITEL								
Barnard	21	m	w	FRAN	San Francisco	San Francisco P O	80	472
JESPER								
August	26	m	w	SCOT	Alameda	Brooklyn Twp	68	40
John	32	m	w	BAVA	El Dorado	Placerville Twp	72	101
JESS								
W F	37	m	w	MD	Sierra	Forest Twp	89	530
JESSE								
Antonio	40	m	w	PORT	San Mateo	Half Moon Bay P O	87	400
Robert	30	m	w	ENGL	San Francisco	San Francisco P O	83	21
JESSEE								
James E	23	m	w	CA	San Luis Obispo	Arroyo Grande Twp	87	273
John P	45	m	w	VA	San Luis Obispo	Arroyo Grande Twp	87	273
JESSEN								
Carl	42	m	w	GERM	San Joaquin	2-Wd Stockton	86	172
Frederick	28	m	w	HAMB	San Francisco	6-Wd San Francisco	81	84
Jurgen	33	m	w	PRUS	San Francisco	San Francisco P O	80	363
Lawrence	30	m	w	DENM	Sonoma	Santa Rosa	91	395
JESSES								
Frank	55	m	w	FRAN	Calaveras	San Andreas P O	70	156
JESSIE								
Archie C	48	m	w	VA	San Luis Obispo	Salinas Twp	87	294
E Cowan	1	f	w	CA	Klamath	Hoopa Valley India	73	386
Geo R	37	m	w	VA	San Francisco	San Francisco P O	85	825
Jack	15	m	w	SCOT	San Francisco	San Francisco P O	83	418
JESSIN								
Manuel	35	m	w	AZOR	San Francisco	1-Wd San Francisco	79	133
JESSING								
John	28	m	w	AZOR	Shasta	American Ranch P O	89	496

© 2001 by Heritage Quest. All rights reserved.

Series M593

Name	Age	S	R	B-PL	County	Locale	Roll	Pg
JESSUP								
Adam	24	m	w	ENGL	Contra Costa	Martinez P O	71	415
Addison	47	m	w	NY	Stanislaus	Buena Vista Twp	92	14
Alferd	36	m	w	IREL	Trinity	Lewiston Pct	92	213
Andrew	43	m	w	NY	San Francisco	San Francisco P O	80	385
Henry	27	m	w	PA	Contra Costa	Martinez P O	71	416
Isaac	38	m	w	NY	Marin	San Rafael	74	57
J L	36	m	w	NY	Monterey	San Antonio Twp	74	324
Kate	20	f	w	IREL	San Francisco	3-Wd San Francisco	79	324
Levi A	30	m	w	IA	Placer	Bath P O	76	452
Oscar	30	m	w	NY	Contra Costa	Martinez P O	71	396
Stephen	35	m	w	NY	Contra Costa	Martinez P O	71	398
Thomas C	38	m	w	KY	San Francisco	5-Wd San Francisco	81	6
Thos	48	m	w	OH	San Francisco	8-Wd San Francisco	82	368
William	50	m	w	IN	San Francisco	11-Wd San Francisc	84	503
JESSURUM								
Isaac	25	m	w	JAMA	San Francisco	San Francisco P O	83	156
JESSUS								
Jose	46	m	w	MEXI	Napa	Napa Twp	75	63
JESTER								
Anna	3	f	w	IREL	San Francisco	San Francisco P O	83	72
Frank	30	m	w	ITAL	Sacramento	Sutter Twp	77	384
JESTUS								
Daniel	55	m	w	OH	Humboldt	South Fork Twp	72	300
JESUS								
Antonio	53	m	w	MEXI	Calaveras	Copperopolis P O	70	224
Battol	12	m	i	CA	San Diego	San Luis Rey	78	513
Castado	22	m	w	MEXI	Sacramento	2-Wd Sacramento	77	215
Concepcion	56	f	w	CA	Santa Barbara	Las Cruces P O	87	516
Eusebia	35	f	w	CA	Santa Barbara	Las Cruces P O	87	516
Jose	36	m	w	CA	Santa Barbara	Las Cruces P O	87	516
Jose	30	m	w	MEXI	Stanislaus	Empire Twp	92	29
Jose	28	m	w	CA	Santa Cruz	Pajaro Twp	89	340
Lotta	18	f	w	MEXI	San Bernardino	Chino Twp	78	412
M	30	m	w	MEXI	Alameda	Murray Twp	68	111
Maria	40	f	i	CA	San Luis Obispo	San Luis Obispo Tw	87	301
Maria R	26	f	w	CA	Santa Barbara	Las Cruces P O	87	516
Mary	84	f	w	ARGE	San Francisco	2-Wd San Francisco	79	165
Peter	29	m	w	MA	San Joaquin	Elliott Twp	86	81
JETE								
Ah	26	m	c	CHIN	San Joaquin	2-Wd Stockton	86	185
JETER								
Caroline	45	f	w	MD	Tulare	Visalia Twp	92	287
Henry	60	m	w	VA	Sonoma	Healdsburg & Mendo	91	277
Thos H	66	m	w	KY	Sacramento	San Joaquin Twp	77	396
William R	26	m	w	AR	Santa Cruz	Santa Cruz Twp	89	390
Wm H	31	m	w	VA	Sonoma	Cloverdale Twp	91	271
JETZER								
Anna M	52	f	w	SWIT	Nevada	Grass Valley Twp	75	198
JEUM								
Ah	20	m	c	CHIN	Yuba	East Bear Rvr Twp	93	545
JEUN								
Ah	13	m	c	CHIN	San Francisco	7-Wd San Francisco	81	263
JEW								
Ah	40	m	c	CHIN	Shasta	American Ranch P O	89	497
Ah	39	m	c	CHIN	Yuba	Marysville	93	620
Ah	32	m	c	CHIN	Yuba	East Bear Rvr Twp	93	545
Ah	30	m	c	CHIN	Amador	Jackson P O	69	342
Ah	25	m	c	CHIN	Yuba	Rose Bar Twp	93	655
Dan	25	m	c	CHIN	Nevada	Washington Twp	75	342
Gee	41	m	c	CHIN	Yuba	Marysville	93	624
How	38	f	c	CHIN	Yuba	Marysville	93	626
Young	28	f	c	CHIN	Yuba	Marysville	93	626
JEWEL								
James Wm	46	m	w	ENGL	Plumas	Indian Twp	77	17
Louis	41	m	w	MA	Contra Costa	Martinez P O	71	412
M C	32	m	w	MI	Alameda	Oakland	68	132
Raphael	36	m	w	ENGL	El Dorado	Placerville	72	111
JEWELL								
Abe	34	m	w	NY	El Dorado	Lake Valley Twp	72	65
Ambrose	38	m	w	ME	San Francisco	San Francisco P O	83	90
Ann	31	f	w	PA	San Francisco	8-Wd San Francisco	82	371
Annie	10	f	w	ENGL	Nevada	Grass Valley Twp	75	179
C	35	m	w	NY	Humboldt	Eureka Twp	72	269
David	69	m	w	ENGL	San Francisco	8-Wd San Francisco	82	325
Decatur	25	m	w	VT	Sonoma	Salt Point	91	393
Edward	39	m	w	NY	Yuba	Rose Bar Twp	93	663
Ethelred	23	m	w	ENGL	Nevada	Grass Valley Twp	75	143
Fredrick	38	m	w	BADE	Napa	Yountville Twp	75	88
Godfrey	33	m	w	ENGL	San Francisco	San Francisco P O	80	414
Hassel	27	m	w	TX	Merced	Snelling P O	74	277
Henry	44	m	w	KY	Contra Costa	Martinez P O	71	411
Henry M	40	m	w	NY	San Mateo	Half Moon Bay P O	87	401
Isaac R	50	m	w	VT	Sonoma	Petaluma Twp	91	349
James	26	m	w	IL	San Mateo	Pescadero P O	87	413
Jesse	59	m	w	VT	San Mateo	Redwood Twp	87	365
Joe	33	m	w	ENGL	Del Norte	Mountain Twp	71	474
John	38	m	w	ENGL	San Francisco	2-Wd San Francisco	79	212
Joseph	34	m	w	NY	San Francisco	11-Wd San Francisc	84	519
Libby	9	f	w	CA	Sonoma	Healdsburg & Mendo	91	284
Luimee P	36	f	w	NY	Santa Cruz	Santa Cruz	89	414
Omar	49	m	w	NY	Marin	Bolinas Twp	74	1
Peter	35	m	w	ENGL	Nevada	Grass Valley Twp	75	220
Ruben	47	m	w	NY	Solano	Vacaville Twp	90	138
Sallie	89	f	w	NY	Sonoma	Petaluma Twp	91	350
Samuel	26	m	w	ENGL	Nevada	Grass Valley Twp	75	145
Stephen	48	m	w	ME	San Francisco	San Francisco P O	83	255
Stephen	20	m	w	IL	San Francisco	San Francisco P O	85	866
Susan	25	f	w	ENGL	San Francisco	San Francisco P O	80	334
Thomas C	35	m	w	MA	San Francisco	5-Wd San Francisco	81	35
Thos Rodgers	32	m	w	ENGL	Nevada	Grass Valley Twp	75	184
William	47	m	w	DC	Solano	Rio Vista Twp	90	62
William S	27	m	w	MI	El Dorado	Diamond Springs Tw	72	28
JEWET								
Geo W	30	m	w	IA	Sonoma	Santa Rosa	91	414
JEWETT								
Adam P	37	m	w	ME	Sacramento	2-Wd Sacramento	77	232
Andrew	20	m	w	IL	Marin	Tomales Twp	74	83
Danl G	39	m	w	ME	Sonoma	Healdsburg	91	275
E P	45	m	w	MA	Humboldt	South Fork Twp	72	302
Elizabeth	34	f	w	ME	San Francisco	8-Wd San Francisco	82	463
F	19	f	w	VT	Alameda	Oakland	68	237
Fifield H	56	m	w	ME	Placer	Lincoln P O	76	481
Geo	32	m	w	IREL	Yuba	Marysville	93	608
Geo A	25	m	w	MI	Sutter	Yuba Twp	92	147
Geo P	30	m	w	NY	Humboldt	Eel Rvr Twp	72	253
George E	50	m	w	OH	Sonoma	Petaluma Twp	91	360
Henry	46	m	w	OH	Contra Costa	Martinez P O	71	423
Henry E	28	m	w	VT	San Mateo	Redwood Twp	87	367
Ira	39	m	w	MA	Nevada	Nevada Twp	75	273
J H	43	m	w	NY	Yuba	Marysville	93	597
Jarvis	50	m	w	VT	San Francisco	6-Wd San Francisco	81	119
John	28	m	w	OR	Humboldt	Pacific Twp	72	294
Joseph	34	m	w	OH	Yolo	Washington Twp	93	529
La Fayette	40	m	w	OH	Santa Clara	2-Wd San Jose	88	294
Louis	43	m	w	IL	Humboldt	Table Bluff Twp	72	305
M K	50	f	w	VT	Alameda	Oakland	68	129
Rafila	22	f	w	MEXI	San Francisco	San Francisco P O	80	353
Reuben	46	m	w	OH	Sonoma	Petaluma Twp	91	360
Samrel C	29	m	w	ME	Yuba	Slate Range Bar Tw	93	669
Solomon	35	m	w	VT	Kern	Bakersfield P O	73	359
Stephen	50	m	w	ME	San Francisco	San Francisco P O	83	96
Thos	35	m	w	MEXI	San Francisco	2-Wd San Francisco	79	165
JEWIT								
Chauncey	43	m	w	VT	San Mateo	Redwood Twp	87	365
George	61	m	w	VT	Alameda	Oakland	68	164
JHUM								
Yon	41	m	c	CHIN	San Joaquin	1-Wd Stockton	86	146
JIBAU								
Frank	38	m	w	FRAN	Marin	Nicasio Twp	74	19
JIENGARSON								
Nicholas	46	m	w	PRUS	Placer	Bath P O	76	420
JIERNAN								
Juana	30	f	w	CA	Santa Cruz	Pajaro Twp	89	357
JIK								
Ah	24	m	c	CHIN	San Francisco	6-Wd San Francisco	81	67
JILLETT								
Jas W	25	m	w	CANA	San Francisco	8-Wd San Francisco	82	346
JILLSON								
Carlos D	32	m	w	NY	Sierra	Gibson Twp	89	541
George	18	m	w	RI	Siskiyou	Surprise Valley Tw	89	641
JILMOZA								
Francis	40	m	w	CHIL	Calaveras	San Andreas P O	70	208
JIM								
---	30	m	c	CHIN	Siskiyou	Cottonwood Twp	89	594
---	25	m	c	CHIN	Siskiyou	Yreka Twp	89	669
A	21	m	c	CHIN	Sutter	Butte Twp	92	96
Ah	9	m	c	CHIN	Alameda	Oakland	68	168
Ah	9	m	c	CA	San Francisco	San Francisco P O	80	448
Ah	9	m	c	CA	San Francisco	San Francisco P O	80	441
Ah	9	m	c	CHIN	San Francisco	San Francisco P O	80	440
Ah	9	m	c	CHIN	San Francisco	San Francisco P O	80	528
Ah	9	m	c	CHIN	San Francisco	San Francisco P O	80	452
Ah	8	m	c	CA	San Francisco	San Francisco P O	80	451
Ah	8	m	c	CHIN	San Francisco	San Francisco P O	80	442
Ah	8	m	c	CA	San Francisco	San Francisco P O	80	521
Ah	8	f	c	CHIN	San Francisco	San Francisco P O	80	525
Ah	61	m	c	CHIN	Placer	Auburn P O	76	375
Ah	60	m	c	CHIN	Placer	Lincoln P O	76	483
Ah	6	m	c	CA	San Francisco	San Francisco P O	80	452
Ah	6	m	c	CHIN	San Francisco	San Francisco P O	80	439
Ah	6	m	c	CA	San Francisco	San Francisco P O	80	435
Ah	6	m	c	CHIN	San Francisco	San Francisco P O	80	528
Ah	57	m	c	CHIN	Santa Clara	Alviso Twp	88	24
Ah	56	m	c	CHIN	San Francisco	San Francisco P O	80	431
Ah	55	m	c	CHIN	Trinity	Weaverville Pct	92	231
Ah	54	m	c	CHIN	San Francisco	San Francisco P O	80	431
Ah	54	m	c	CHIN	San Francisco	San Francisco P O	80	432
Ah	54	m	c	CHIN	San Francisco	San Francisco P O	80	435
Ah	52	m	c	CHIN	Sierra	Eureka Twp	89	526
Ah	51	m	c	CHIN	San Francisco	San Francisco P O	80	527
Ah	50	m	c	CHIN	Placer	Lincoln P O	76	493
Ah	50	m	c	CHIN	San Francisco	San Francisco P O	80	438
Ah	50	f	c	CHIN	San Francisco	San Francisco P O	80	506
Ah	50	m	c	CHIN	San Francisco	San Francisco P O	80	520
Ah	50	m	c	CHIN	El Dorado	Salmon Falls Twp	72	130
Ah	5	m	c	CA	San Francisco	San Francisco P O	80	437
Ah	49	m	c	CHIN	San Francisco	San Francisco P O	80	437
Ah	49	m	c	CHIN	San Francisco	San Francisco P O	80	508
Ah	48	m	c	CHIN	Shasta	Horsetown P O	89	506
Ah	48	m	c	CHIN	Nevada	Eureka Twp	75	127
Ah	47	m	c	CHIN	Sacramento	Natomas Twp	77	171
Ah	47	m	c	CHIN	El Dorado	White Oak Twp	72	143
Ah	46	m	c	CHIN	Alameda	Oakland	68	205

© 2001 by Heritage Quest. All rights reserved.

California 1870 Census

Name	Age	S	R	B-PL	County	Series M593 Locale	Roll	Pg
Ah	46	m	c	CHIN	San Francisco	San Francisco P O	80	431
Ah	45	m	c	CHIN	El Dorado	Placerville	72	112
Ah	45	m	c	CHIN	El Dorado	Mud Springs Twp	72	75
Ah	45	m	c	CHIN	Mariposa	Mariposa P O	74	114
Ah	45	m	c	CHIN	Sacramento	Mississippi Twp	77	163
Ah	45	m	c	CHIN	San Francisco	San Francisco P O	80	436
Ah	45	m	c	CHIN	San Francisco	San Francisco P O	80	513
Ah	44	m	c	CHIN	Butte	Ophir Twp	70	103
Ah	42	m	c	CHIN	San Francisco	San Francisco P O	80	440
Ah	42	m	c	CHIN	San Francisco	San Francisco P O	80	440
Ah	42	m	c	CHIN	San Francisco	San Francisco P O	80	431
Ah	42	m	c	CHIN	San Francisco	San Francisco P O	80	529
Ah	42	m	c	CHIN	San Francisco	San Francisco P O	80	521
Ah	42	m	c	CHIN	San Francisco	San Francisco P O	80	523
Ah	42	m	c	CHIN	San Francisco	San Francisco P O	80	523
Ah	42	m	c	CHIN	Nevada	Bridgeport Twp	75	119
Ah	42	m	c	CHIN	Nevada	Nevada Twp	75	307
Ah	42	m	c	CHIN	Nevada	Washington Twp	75	347
Ah	42	m	c	CHIN	Placer	Newcastle Twp	76	475
Ah	42	m	c	CHIN	Amador	Jackson P O	69	347
Ah	42	m	c	CHIN	Fresno	Millerton P O	72	146
Ah	41	m	c	CHIN	San Francisco	San Francisco P O	80	444
Ah	41	m	c	CHIN	San Francisco	San Francisco P O	80	447
Ah	41	m	c	CHIN	San Francisco	San Francisco P O	80	436
Ah	41	m	c	CHIN	San Francisco	San Francisco P O	80	446
Ah	41	m	c	CHIN	San Francisco	2-Wd San Francisco	79	285
Ah	41	m	c	CHIN	Sierra	Lincoln Twp	89	548
Ah	41	m	c	CHIN	San Francisco	San Francisco P O	80	515
Ah	41	m	c	CHIN	San Francisco	San Francisco P O	80	517
Ah	41	m	c	CHIN	San Francisco	San Francisco P O	80	518
Ah	41	m	c	CHIN	Nevada	Washington Twp	75	344
Ah	41	m	c	CHIN	El Dorado	Coloma Twp	72	6
Ah	40	m	c	CHIN	San Francisco	6-Wd San Francisco	81	57
Ah	40	m	c	CHIN	San Joaquin	1-Wd Stockton	86	142
Ah	40	m	c	CHIN	San Joaquin	Oneal Twp	86	117
Ah	40	m	c	CHIN	Calaveras	San Andreas P O	70	167
Ah	40	m	c	CHIN	Amador	Fiddletown P O	69	427
Ah	40	m	c	CHIN	Alameda	Oakland	68	238
Ah	40	m	c	CHIN	Butte	Chico Twp	70	28
Ah	40	m	c	CHIN	Placer	Newcastle Twp	76	479
Ah	40	m	c	CHIN	Placer	Auburn P O	76	372
Ah	40	m	c	CHIN	Nevada	Nevada Twp	75	296
Ah	40	m	c	CHIN	Sacramento	Center Twp	77	86
Ah	40	m	c	CHIN	San Francisco	San Francisco P O	80	448
Ah	40	m	c	CHIN	San Francisco	San Francisco P O	80	446
Ah	40	m	c	CHIN	San Francisco	San Francisco P O	80	447
Ah	40	m	c	CHIN	San Francisco	San Francisco P O	80	443
Ah	40	m	c	CHIN	San Francisco	San Francisco P O	80	448
Ah	40	m	c	CHIN	San Francisco	San Francisco P O	80	445
Ah	40	m	c	CHIN	San Francisco	San Francisco P O	80	442
Ah	40	m	c	CHIN	San Mateo	Schoolhouse Statio	87	341
Ah	40	m	c	CHIN	San Francisco	San Francisco P O	80	529
Ah	40	m	c	CHIN	San Francisco	San Francisco P O	80	529
Ah	40	m	c	CHIN	San Francisco	San Francisco P O	80	452
Ah	40	m	c	CHIN	San Francisco	San Francisco P O	80	512
Ah	40	m	c	CHIN	San Francisco	San Francisco P O	80	515
Ah	40	m	c	CHIN	Nevada	Eureka Twp	75	140
Ah	40	m	c	CHIN	Nevada	Grass Valley Twp	75	197
Ah	40	m	c	CHIN	Placer	Auburn P O	76	364
Ah	40	m	c	CHIN	Nevada	Nevada Twp	75	307
Ah	4	m	c	CA	San Francisco	San Francisco P O	80	454
Ah	4	m	c	CA	San Francisco	San Francisco P O	80	454
Ah	4	m	c	CA	San Francisco	San Francisco P O	80	448
Ah	4	m	c	CA	San Francisco	San Francisco P O	80	447
Ah	4	m	c	CA	San Francisco	San Francisco P O	80	448
Ah	4	m	c	CA	San Francisco	San Francisco P O	80	443
Ah	4	m	c	CA	San Francisco	San Francisco P O	80	530
Ah	39	m	c	CHIN	Siskiyou	Cottonwood Twp	89	593
Ah	39	m	c	CHIN	Butte	Bidwell Twp	70	3
Ah	39	m	c	CHIN	Amador	Fiddletown P O	69	429
Ah	39	m	c	CHIN	San Francisco	San Francisco P O	80	444
Ah	39	m	c	CHIN	San Francisco	San Francisco P O	80	465
Ah	39	m	c	CHIN	San Francisco	San Francisco P O	80	511
Ah	39	m	c	CHIN	San Francisco	San Francisco P O	80	514
Ah	39	m	c	CHIN	San Francisco	San Francisco P O	80	511
Ah	38	m	c	CHIN	Santa Clara	Alviso Twp	88	23
Ah	38	m	c	CHIN	Alameda	Oakland	68	220
Ah	38	m	c	CHIN	Nevada	Meadow Lake Twp	75	257
Ah	38	m	c	CHIN	San Francisco	San Francisco P O	80	433
Ah	38	m	c	CHIN	San Francisco	San Francisco P O	80	512
Ah	38	m	c	CHIN	San Francisco	San Francisco P O	80	521
Ah	38	m	c	CHIN	San Francisco	6-Wd San Francisco	81	55
Ah	38	m	c	CHIN	Nevada	Bridgeport Twp	75	114
Ah	38	m	c	CHIN	El Dorado	Mud Springs Twp	72	74
Ah	38	m	c	CHIN	El Dorado	Salmon Falls Twp	72	129
Ah	37	m	c	CHIN	Monterey	Castroville Twp	74	338
Ah	37	m	c	CHIN	Sacramento	Mississippi Twp	77	163
Ah	37	m	c	CHIN	San Francisco	San Francisco P O	80	449
Ah	37	m	c	CHIN	San Francisco	San Francisco P O	80	450
Ah	37	m	c	CHIN	San Francisco	San Francisco P O	80	442
Ah	37	m	c	CHIN	San Francisco	San Francisco P O	80	527
Ah	37	m	c	CHIN	San Francisco	San Francisco P O	80	509
Ah	37	m	c	CHIN	San Francisco	San Francisco P O	80	521
Ah	37	m	c	CHIN	San Francisco	San Francisco P O	80	525
Ah	37	m	c	CHIN	Nevada	Eureka Twp	75	130
Ah	37	m	c	CHIN	Nevada	Bridgeport Twp	75	119
Ah	36	m	c	CHIN	San Francisco	San Francisco P O	80	501

Name	Age	S	R	B-PL	County	Series M593 Locale	Roll	Pg
Ah	36	m	c	CHIN	Santa Clara	San Jose Twp	88	195
Ah	36	m	c	CHIN	Sacramento	2-Wd Sacramento	77	250
Ah	36	m	c	CHIN	San Francisco	San Francisco P O	80	388
Ah	36	m	c	CHIN	San Francisco	San Francisco P O	80	432
Ah	36	m	c	CHIN	San Francisco	San Francisco P O	80	447
Ah	36	m	c	CHIN	San Francisco	San Francisco P O	80	445
Ah	36	m	c	CHIN	San Francisco	San Francisco P O	80	451
Ah	36	m	c	CHIN	San Francisco	San Francisco P O	80	442
Ah	36	m	c	CHIN	San Francisco	San Francisco P O	80	436
Ah	36	m	c	CHIN	San Francisco	San Francisco P O	80	525
Ah	36	m	c	CHIN	San Francisco	San Francisco P O	80	530
Ah	36	m	c	CHIN	San Francisco	San Francisco P O	80	512
Ah	36	m	c	CHIN	San Francisco	San Francisco P O	80	511
Ah	36	m	c	CHIN	San Francisco	San Francisco P O	80	517
Ah	36	m	c	CHIN	San Francisco	San Francisco P O	80	519
Ah	36	m	c	CHIN	San Francisco	San Francisco P O	80	528
Ah	36	m	c	CHIN	San Francisco	San Francisco P O	80	520
Ah	36	m	c	CHIN	San Francisco	San Francisco P O	80	516
Ah	36	m	c	CHIN	Sacramento	Georgianna Twp	77	132
Ah	35	m	c	CHIN	San Mateo	Redwood Twp	87	367
Ah	35	m	c	CHIN	Fresno	Millerton P O	72	200
Ah	35	m	c	CHIN	Placer	Auburn P O	76	371
Ah	35	m	c	CHIN	Sacramento	Georgianna Twp	77	127
Ah	35	m	c	CHIN	San Francisco	San Francisco P O	80	447
Ah	35	m	c	CHIN	San Francisco	San Francisco P O	80	446
Ah	35	m	c	CHIN	San Francisco	San Francisco P O	80	434
Ah	35	m	c	CHIN	San Francisco	San Francisco P O	80	335
Ah	35	m	c	CHIN	San Francisco	2-Wd San Francisco	79	286
Ah	35	m	c	CHIN	Shasta	American Ranch P O	89	497
Ah	35	m	c	CHIN	San Mateo	San Mateo P O	87	351
Ah	35	m	c	CHIN	San Mateo	Schoolhouse Statio	87	338
Ah	35	m	c	CHIN	San Francisco	San Francisco P O	80	513
Ah	35	m	c	CHIN	San Francisco	San Francisco P O	80	511
Ah	35	m	c	CHIN	San Francisco	San Francisco P O	80	517
Ah	35	m	c	CHIN	Sacramento	1-Wd Sacramento	77	199
Ah	35	m	c	CHIN	Placer	Lincoln P O	76	492
Ah	35	m	c	CHIN	Placer	Summit P O	76	495
Ah	35	m	c	CHIN	Alameda	Oakland	68	252
Ah	35	m	c	CHIN	Alameda	Oakland	68	232
Ah	35	m	c	CHIN	Alameda	Eden Twp	68	58
Ah	35	m	c	CHIN	Calaveras	San Andreas P O	70	180
Ah	35	m	c	CHIN	Calaveras	San Andreas P O	70	184
Ah	35	m	c	CHIN	El Dorado	Diamond Springs Tw	72	31
Ah	34	m	c	CHIN	Napa	Napa	75	56
Ah	34	m	c	CHIN	Nevada	Bridgeport Twp	75	107
Ah	34	m	c	CHIN	San Francisco	San Francisco P O	80	447
Ah	34	m	c	CHIN	San Francisco	San Francisco P O	80	446
Ah	34	m	c	CHIN	San Francisco	San Francisco P O	80	441
Ah	34	m	c	CHIN	San Francisco	San Francisco P O	80	438
Ah	34	m	c	CHIN	San Francisco	San Francisco P O	80	438
Ah	34	m	c	CHIN	San Francisco	San Francisco P O	80	439
Ah	34	m	c	CHIN	San Francisco	San Francisco P O	80	512
Ah	34	m	c	CHIN	San Francisco	San Francisco P O	80	519
Ah	34	m	c	CHIN	San Francisco	San Francisco P O	80	518
Ah	34	m	c	CHIN	San Francisco	San Francisco P O	80	520
Ah	34	m	c	CHIN	San Francisco	San Francisco P O	80	522
Ah	34	m	c	CHIN	San Francisco	San Francisco P O	80	522
Ah	34	m	c	CHIN	El Dorado	Placerville	72	127
Ah	33	m	c	CHIN	Trinity	Junction City Pct	92	207
Ah	33	m	c	CHIN	Santa Clara	1-Wd San Jose	88	269
Ah	33	m	c	CHIN	Santa Clara	1-Wd San Jose	88	273
Ah	32	m	c	CHIN	Butte	Hamilton Twp	70	72
Ah	32	m	c	CHIN	Sacramento	Center Twp	77	85
Ah	32	m	c	CHIN	San Francisco	San Francisco P O	80	435
Ah	32	m	c	CHIN	San Francisco	San Francisco P O	80	443
Ah	32	m	c	CHIN	San Francisco	San Francisco P O	80	437
Ah	32	m	c	CHIN	Sierra	Forest Twp	89	529
Ah	32	m	c	CHIN	Santa Clara	1-Wd San Jose	88	273
Ah	32	m	c	CHIN	San Mateo	Pescadero P O	87	412
Ah	32	m	c	CHIN	San Francisco	San Francisco P O	80	507
Ah	32	m	c	CHIN	San Francisco	San Francisco P O	80	507
Ah	32	m	c	CHIN	Amador	Jackson P O	69	344
Ah	32	m	c	CHIN	El Dorado	Mud Springs Twp	72	76
Ah	31	m	c	CHIN	San Joaquin	Elkhorn Twp	86	69
Ah	31	m	c	CHIN	San Mateo	Belmont P O	87	371
Ah	31	m	c	CHIN	Santa Clara	Alviso Twp	88	27
Ah	31	m	c	CHIN	San Francisco	San Francisco P O	80	512
Ah	31	m	c	CHIN	San Francisco	San Francisco P O	80	515
Ah	31	m	c	CHIN	San Francisco	San Francisco P O	80	521
Ah	31	m	c	CHIN	Monterey	Salinas Twp	74	308
Ah	31	m	c	CHIN	Placer	Dutch Flat P O	76	415
Ah	31	m	c	CHIN	Amador	Ione City P O	69	361
Ah	30	m	c	CHIN	Yolo	Washington Twp	93	537
Ah	30	m	c	CHIN	Yuba	East Bear Rvr Twp	93	540
Ah	30	m	c	CHIN	Sierra	Forest Twp	89	529
Ah	30	m	c	CHIN	Santa Cruz	Santa Cruz	89	421
Ah	30	m	c	CHIN	Solano	Vallejo	90	216
Ah	30	m	c	CHIN	Solano	Vallejo	90	173
Ah	30	m	c	CHIN	San Joaquin	1-Wd Stockton	86	151
Ah	30	m	c	CHIN	San Mateo	San Mateo P O	87	356
Ah	30	m	c	CHIN	Santa Clara	San Jose Twp	88	196
Ah	30	m	c	CHIN	San Mateo	San Mateo P O	87	356
Ah	30	m	c	CHIN	Alameda	Alameda	68	15
Ah	30	m	c	CHIN	Placer	Auburn P O	76	371
Ah	30	m	c	CHIN	Placer	Clipper Gap P O	76	393
Ah	30	m	c	CHIN	Placer	Colfax P O	76	387
Ah	30	m	c	CHIN	Placer	Auburn P O	76	378

© 2001 by Heritage Quest. All rights reserved.

Series M593

Name	Age	S	R	B-PL	County	Locale	Roll	Pg
Ah	30	m	c	CHIN	Placer	Colfax P O	76	384
Ah	30	m	c	CHIN	Placer	Auburn P O	76	374
Ah	30	m	c	CHIN	Placer	Colfax P O	76	385
Ah	30	m	c	CHIN	Napa	Napa Twp	75	71
Ah	30	m	c	CHIN	San Francisco	San Francisco P O	80	453
Ah	30	m	c	CHIN	San Francisco	San Francisco P O	80	440
Ah	30	m	c	CHIN	Shasta	American Ranch P O	89	499
Ah	30	m	c	CHIN	Shasta	American Ranch P O	89	500
Ah	30	m	c	CHIN	Siskiyou	Cottonwood Twp	89	594
Ah	30	m	c	CHIN	Sonoma	Sonoma Twp	91	449
Ah	30	m	c	CHIN	Santa Clara	2-Wd San Jose	88	293
Ah	30	m	c	CHIN	San Mateo	Schoolhouse Statio	87	344
Ah	30	m	c	CHIN	San Mateo	Schoolhouse Statio	87	337
Ah	30	m	c	CHIN	San Mateo	Schoolhouse Statio	87	332
Ah	30	m	c	CHIN	San Joaquin	Elkhorn Twp	86	69
Ah	30	m	c	CHIN	San Joaquin	3-Wd Stockton	86	221
Ah	30	m	c	CHIN	San Francisco	San Francisco P O	80	452
Ah	30	m	c	CHIN	San Francisco	San Francisco P O	80	509
Ah	30	m	c	CHIN	San Francisco	San Francisco P O	80	518
Ah	30	f	c	CHIN	San Francisco	San Francisco P O	80	528
Ah	30	m	c	CHIN	Monterey	Alisal Twp	74	302
Ah	30	m	c	CHIN	Nevada	Nevada Twp	75	298
Ah	30	m	c	CHIN	Nevada	Nevada Twp	75	298
Ah	30	m	c	CHIN	Placer	Bath P O	76	445
Ah	30	m	c	CHIN	Placer	Lincoln P O	76	484
Ah	30	m	c	CHIN	Alameda	Oakland	68	254
Ah	30	m	c	CHIN	Amador	Ione City P O	69	354
Ah	30	m	c	CHIN	Amador	Ione City P O	69	367
Ah	30	m	c	CHIN	Calaveras	San Andreas P O	70	169
Ah	30	m	c	CHIN	El Dorado	Greenwood Twp	72	50
Ah	30	m	c	CHIN	El Dorado	Salmon Falls Twp	72	133
Ah	30	m	c	CHIN	Butte	Mountain Spring Tw	70	89
Ah	3	m	c	CA	San Francisco	San Francisco P O	80	450
Ah	3	m	c	CA	San Francisco	San Francisco P O	80	441
Ah	3	m	c	CA	San Francisco	San Francisco P O	80	450
Ah	3	m	c	CA	San Francisco	San Francisco P O	80	434
Ah	3	m	c	CA	San Francisco	San Francisco P O	80	437
Ah	29	m	c	CHIN	Yolo	Cache Crk Twp	93	430
Ah	29	m	c	CHIN	San Joaquin	1-Wd Stockton	86	145
Ah	29	m	c	CHIN	Calaveras	San Andreas P O	70	166
Ah	29	m	c	CHIN	Klamath	South Fork Twp	73	382
Ah	29	m	c	CHIN	San Francisco	San Francisco P O	80	453
Ah	29	m	c	CHIN	San Francisco	San Francisco P O	80	440
Ah	29	m	c	CHIN	San Francisco	San Francisco P O	80	436
Ah	29	m	c	CHIN	San Francisco	San Francisco P O	80	441
Ah	29	m	c	CHIN	San Francisco	San Francisco P O	80	443
Ah	29	m	c	CHIN	San Francisco	San Francisco P O	80	431
Ah	29	m	c	CHIN	San Francisco	San Francisco P O	80	336
Ah	29	m	c	CHIN	San Mateo	Pescadero P O	87	415
Ah	29	m	c	CHIN	San Francisco	San Francisco P O	80	526
Ah	29	m	c	CHIN	San Francisco	San Francisco P O	80	514
Ah	29	m	c	CHIN	San Francisco	San Francisco P O	80	519
Ah	29	m	c	CHIN	San Francisco	San Francisco P O	80	517
Ah	29	m	c	CHIN	Merced	Snelling P O	74	262
Ah	29	m	c	CHIN	Sacramento	2-Wd Sacramento	77	208
Ah	29	m	c	CHIN	Placer	Dutch Flat P O	76	411
Ah	28	m	c	CHIN	Sierra	Lincoln Twp	89	548
Ah	28	m	c	CHIN	Santa Cruz	Pajaro Twp	89	342
Ah	28	m	c	CHIN	San Francisco	San Francisco P O	80	499
Ah	28	m	c	CHIN	San Francisco	San Francisco P O	83	132
Ah	28	m	c	CHIN	San Mateo	Half Moon Bay P O	87	399
Ah	28	m	c	CHIN	San Mateo	Half Moon Bay P O	87	399
Ah	28	m	c	CHIN	San Mateo	Schoolhouse Statio	87	334
Ah	28	m	c	CHIN	Alameda	Oakland	68	241
Ah	28	m	c	CHIN	Placer	Emigrant Gap P O	76	417
Ah	28	m	c	CHIN	Placer	Auburn P O	76	370
Ah	28	m	c	CHIN	Nevada	Meadow Lake Twp	75	266
Ah	28	m	c	CHIN	Yuba	Marysville	93	602
Ah	28	m	c	CHIN	Sonoma	Bodega Twp	91	261
Ah	28	m	c	CHIN	Santa Clara	Santa Clara Twp	88	166
Ah	28	m	c	CHIN	San Mateo	Schoolhouse Statio	87	340
Ah	28	m	c	CHIN	San Francisco	San Francisco P O	80	509
Ah	28	f	c	CHIN	San Francisco	San Francisco P O	80	506
Ah	28	m	c	CHIN	San Francisco	San Francisco P O	80	519
Ah	28	m	c	CHIN	Nevada	Washington Twp	75	342
Ah	28	m	c	CHIN	Placer	Emigrant Gap P O	76	417
Ah	28	m	c	CHIN	Alameda	Oakland	68	250
Ah	28	m	c	CHIN	Alameda	Oakland	68	223
Ah	28	m	c	CHIN	Alameda	Oakland	68	158
Ah	28	m	c	CHIN	Amador	Fiddletown P O	69	427
Ah	27	m	c	CHIN	San Francisco	6-Wd San Francisco	81	87
Ah	27	m	c	CHIN	Santa Clara	San Jose Twp	88	179
Ah	27	m	c	CHIN	Mendocino	Point Arena Twp	74	208
Ah	27	m	c	CHIN	Placer	Rocklin Twp	76	463
Ah	27	m	c	CHIN	Nevada	Meadow Lake Twp	75	255
Ah	27	m	c	CHIN	San Francisco	San Francisco P O	80	445
Ah	27	m	c	CHIN	San Francisco	San Francisco P O	80	441
Ah	27	m	c	CHIN	Siskiyou	Scott Rvr Twp	89	607
Ah	27	m	c	CHIN	Santa Clara	1-Wd San Jose	88	271
Ah	27	m	c	CHIN	Santa Clara	Fremont Twp	88	60
Ah	27	m	c	CHIN	Santa Barbara	Santa Barbara P O	87	501
Ah	27	m	c	CHIN	San Joaquin	3-Wd Stockton	86	221
Ah	27	m	c	CHIN	San Francisco	San Francisco P O	80	505
Ah	27	m	c	CHIN	San Francisco	San Francisco P O	80	519
Ah	27	m	c	CHIN	Monterey	Alisal Twp	74	296
Ah	27	m	c	CHIN	Sacramento	1-Wd Sacramento	77	205
Ah	26	m	c	CHIN	Siskiyou	Hamburg Twp	89	597
Ah	26	m	c	CHIN	Sierra	Butte Twp	89	513
Ah	26	m	c	CHIN	Klamath	Salmon Twp	73	387
Ah	26	m	c	CHIN	Trinity	Junction City Pct	92	206
Ah	26	m	c	CHIN	Santa Clara	San Jose Twp	88	180
Ah	26	m	c	CHIN	San Francisco	San Francisco P O	80	529
Ah	26	m	c	CHIN	San Francisco	San Francisco P O	80	498
Ah	26	m	c	CHIN	San Francisco	San Francisco P O	80	513
Ah	26	m	c	CHIN	San Francisco	San Francisco P O	80	511
Ah	26	m	c	CHIN	San Francisco	San Francisco P O	80	501
Ah	26	m	c	CHIN	San Francisco	San Francisco P O	80	525
Ah	26	m	c	CHIN	San Francisco	San Francisco P O	80	516
Ah	26	m	c	CHIN	San Francisco	San Francisco P O	80	521
Ah	26	m	c	CHIN	Nevada	Nevada Twp	75	311
Ah	26	m	c	CHIN	Placer	Alta P O	76	411
Ah	26	m	c	CHIN	Alameda	Murray Twp	68	126
Ah	25	m	c	CHIN	San Francisco	San Francisco P O	83	58
Ah	25	m	c	CHIN	San Mateo	San Mateo P O	87	357
Ah	25	m	c	CHIN	San Mateo	Redwood City P O	87	375
Ah	25	m	c	CHIN	Santa Clara	San Jose Twp	88	196
Ah	25	m	c	CHIN	San Mateo	San Mateo P O	87	357
Ah	25	m	c	CHIN	Contra Costa	Martinez P O	71	383
Ah	25	m	c	CHIN	El Dorado	Placerville	72	120
Ah	25	m	c	CHIN	Fresno	Millerton P O	72	199
Ah	25	m	c	CHIN	Placer	Colfax P O	76	384
Ah	25	m	c	CHIN	Nevada	Meadow Lake Twp	75	261
Ah	25	m	c	CHIN	Nevada	Meadow Lake Twp	75	254
Ah	25	m	c	CHIN	Sacramento	3-Wd Sacramento	77	312
Ah	25	m	c	CHIN	San Francisco	San Francisco P O	80	435
Ah	25	m	c	CHIN	Sierra	Table Rock Twp	89	571
Ah	25	m	c	CHIN	Tehama	Tehama Twp	92	189
Ah	25	m	c	CHIN	Santa Clara	Alviso Twp	88	29
Ah	25	m	c	CHIN	Santa Clara	Fremont Twp	88	56
Ah	25	m	c	CHIN	San Francisco	San Francisco P O	80	510
Ah	25	m	c	CHIN	San Francisco	San Francisco P O	85	734
Ah	25	m	c	CHIN	Mendocino	Point Arena Twp	74	212
Ah	25	m	c	CHIN	Napa	Napa Twp	75	34
Ah	25	m	c	CHIN	Nevada	Rough & Ready Twp	75	323
Ah	25	m	c	CHIN	Placer	Dutch Flat P O	76	406
Ah	25	m	c	CHIN	Placer	Dutch Flat P O	76	415
Ah	25	m	c	CHIN	Alameda	Oakland	68	224
Ah	25	m	c	CHIN	Yuba	W Bear Rvr Twp	93	683
Ah	24	m	c	CHIN	Solano	Suisun Twp	90	98
Ah	24	m	c	CHIN	Sonoma	Salt Point	91	386
Ah	24	m	c	CHIN	Sutter	Butte Twp	92	104
Ah	24	m	c	CHIN	San Mateo	Schoolhouse Statio	87	335
Ah	24	m	c	CHIN	San Mateo	San Mateo P O	87	348
Ah	24	m	c	CHIN	Placer	Newcastle Twp	76	477
Ah	24	m	c	CHIN	Plumas	Indian Twp	77	17
Ah	24	m	c	CHIN	San Francisco	2-Wd San Francisco	79	282
Ah	24	m	c	CHIN	Sierra	Forest Twp	89	532
Ah	24	m	c	CHIN	Sierra	Forest Twp	89	528
Ah	24	m	c	CHIN	Santa Clara	1-Wd San Jose	88	277
Ah	24	m	c	CHIN	Santa Clara	1-Wd San Jose	88	277
Ah	24	m	c	CHIN	San Francisco	6-Wd San Francisco	81	131
Ah	24	m	c	CHIN	San Francisco	San Francisco P O	80	498
Ah	24	m	c	CHIN	San Francisco	San Francisco P O	80	509
Ah	24	m	c	CHIN	San Francisco	San Francisco P O	80	511
Ah	24	m	c	CHIN	San Francisco	San Francisco P O	80	524
Ah	24	m	c	CHIN	Mendocino	Gualala Twp	74	223
Ah	24	m	c	CHIN	Nevada	Bridgeport Twp	75	119
Ah	24	m	c	CHIN	Marin	San Rafael Twp	74	39
Ah	24	m	c	CHIN	San Diego	Fort Yuma Dist	78	463
Ah	24	m	c	CHIN	Placer	Dutch Flat P O	76	411
Ah	23	m	c	CHIN	Santa Cruz	Santa Cruz	89	418
Ah	23	m	c	CHIN	Placer	Rocklin P O	76	462
Ah	23	m	c	CHIN	Sierra	Sierra Twp	89	569
Ah	23	m	c	CHIN	Tehama	Red Bluff	92	184
Ah	22	m	c	CHIN	Santa Clara	1-Wd San Jose	88	244
Ah	22	m	c	CHIN	Solano	Suisun Twp	90	105
Ah	22	m	c	CHIN	San Francisco	San Francisco P O	80	497
Ah	22	m	c	CHIN	San Mateo	Redwood Twp	87	362
Ah	22	m	c	CHIN	Placer	Auburn P O	76	379
Ah	22	f	c	CHIN	San Francisco	San Francisco P O	80	433
Ah	22	m	c	CHIN	Santa Clara	Fremont Twp	88	45
Ah	22	m	c	CHIN	San Mateo	Half Moon Bay P O	87	389
Ah	22	m	c	CHIN	San Francisco	6-Wd San Francisco	81	139
Ah	22	m	c	CHIN	San Francisco	San Francisco P O	80	510
Ah	22	m	c	CHIN	San Francisco	6-Wd San Francisco	81	50
Ah	22	m	c	CHIN	Nevada	Bridgeport Twp	75	119
Ah	22	m	c	CHIN	Placer	Auburn P O	76	362
Ah	22	m	c	CHIN	Nevada	Nevada Twp	75	298
Ah	22	m	c	CHIN	Sacramento	Cosumnes Twp	77	94
Ah	22	m	c	CHIN	Alameda	Oakland	68	224
Ah	21	m	c	CHIN	Tuolumne	Chinese Camp P O	93	379
Ah	21	m	c	CHIN	San Francisco	6-Wd San Francisco	81	62
Ah	21	m	c	CHIN	San Francisco	San Francisco P O	80	499
Ah	21	m	c	CHIN	San Francisco	San Francisco P O	80	495
Ah	21	m	c	CHIN	San Joaquin	Oneal Twp	86	116
Ah	21	m	c	CHIN	Contra Costa	Martinez P O	71	431
Ah	21	m	c	CHIN	San Francisco	San Francisco P O	80	451
Ah	21	m	c	CHIN	Trinity	North Fork Twp	92	221
Ah	21	m	c	CHIN	San Francisco	San Francisco P O	80	509
Ah	21	m	c	CHIN	Nevada	Meadow Lake Twp	75	253
Ah	21	f	c	CHIN	Nevada	Washington Twp	75	342
Ah	20	m	c	CHIN	Yolo	Grafton Twp	93	479
Ah	20	m	c	CHIN	Shasta	French Gulch P O	89	465
Ah	20	m	c	CHIN	Solano	Vallejo	90	174

© 2001 by Heritage Quest. All rights reserved.

California 1870 Census

Series M593

Name	Age	S	R	B-PL	County	Locale	Roll	Pg
Ah	20	m	c	CHIN	San Francisco	San Francisco P O	83	132
Ah	20	m	c	CHIN	San Mateo	Pescadero P O	87	416
Ah	20	m	c	CHIN	Santa Clara	San Jose Twp	88	186
Ah	20	m	c	CHIN	Alameda	Oakland	68	148
Ah	20	m	c	CHIN	Butte	Hamilton Twp	70	75
Ah	20	m	c	CHIN	Marin	San Rafael Twp	74	46
Ah	20	m	c	CHIN	Placer	Gold Run Twp	76	396
Ah	20	m	c	CHIN	Placer	Colfax P O	76	387
Ah	20	m	c	CHIN	Santa Clara	1-Wd San Jose	88	252
Ah	20	m	c	CHIN	Santa Clara	San Jose Twp	88	179
Ah	20	m	c	CHIN	San Mateo	Schoolhouse Statio	87	343
Ah	20	m	c	CHIN	San Francisco	6-Wd San Francisco	81	101
Ah	20	m	c	CHIN	San Francisco	San Francisco P O	80	484
Ah	20	m	c	CHIN	San Francisco	San Francisco P O	80	499
Ah	20	f	c	CHIN	San Francisco	San Francisco P O	80	526
Ah	20	m	c	CHIN	San Francisco	6-Wd San Francisco	81	93
Ah	20	m	c	CHIN	Nevada	Grass Valley Twp	75	219
Ah	20	m	c	CHIN	San Francisco	2-Wd San Francisco	79	229
Ah	20	m	c	CHIN	Sacramento	1-Wd Sacramento	77	201
Ah	20	m	c	CHIN	Placer	Bath P O	76	459
Ah	20	f	c	CHIN	Placer	Lincoln P O	76	492
Ah	20	m	c	CHIN	Placer	Summit P O	76	496
Ah	20	m	c	CHIN	Alameda	Oakland	68	253
Ah	20	m	c	CHIN	Alameda	Oakland	68	250
Ah	20	m	c	CHIN	Alameda	Murray Twp	68	119
Ah	2	m	c	CA	San Francisco	San Francisco P O	80	453
Ah	2	m	c	CA	San Francisco	San Francisco P O	80	450
Ah	2	m	c	CA	San Francisco	San Francisco P O	80	454
Ah	2	m	c	CA	San Francisco	San Francisco P O	80	450
Ah	2	m	c	CA	San Francisco	San Francisco P O	80	449
Ah	2	m	c	CA	San Francisco	San Francisco P O	80	448
Ah	2	m	c	CA	San Francisco	San Francisco P O	80	449
Ah	2	m	c	CA	San Francisco	San Francisco P O	80	438
Ah	2	m	c	CA	San Francisco	San Francisco P O	80	530
Ah	2	m	c	CA	San Francisco	San Francisco P O	80	454
Ah	19	m	c	CHIN	Yolo	Washington Twp	93	534
Ah	19	m	c	CHIN	Santa Clara	1-Wd San Jose	88	225
Ah	19	m	c	CHIN	San Francisco	6-Wd San Francisco	81	58
Ah	19	m	c	CHIN	San Francisco	San Francisco P O	80	500
Ah	19	m	c	CHIN	Santa Clara	San Jose Twp	88	194
Ah	19	m	c	CHIN	Amador	Fiddletown P O	69	436
Ah	19	m	c	CHIN	Alameda	Oakland	68	253
Ah	19	m	c	CHIN	Monterey	Castroville Twp	74	338
Ah	19	m	c	CHIN	Napa	Napa Twp	75	46
Ah	19	m	c	CHIN	Santa Clara	Alviso Twp	88	25
Ah	19	m	c	CHIN	San Francisco	San Francisco P O	80	530
Ah	19	m	c	CHIN	San Francisco	7-Wd San Francisco	81	156
Ah	19	m	c	CHIN	San Francisco	San Francisco P O	80	498
Ah	19	m	c	CHIN	San Francisco	San Francisco P O	80	506
Ah	19	m	c	CHIN	San Francisco	11-Wd San Francisc	84	645
Ah	19	m	c	CHIN	Mendocino	Point Arena Twp	74	213
Ah	19	m	c	CHIN	Alameda	Oakland	68	181
Ah	19	m	c	CHIN	Yuba	Rose Bar Twp	93	666
Ah	18	m	c	CHIN	Santa Cruz	Santa Cruz	89	408
Ah	18	m	c	CHIN	San Francisco	San Francisco P O	83	23
Ah	18	m	c	CHIN	San Mateo	San Mateo P O	87	354
Ah	18	m	c	CHIN	Alameda	Oakland	68	232
Ah	18	m	c	CHIN	Placer	Gold Run Twp	76	398
Ah	18	m	c	CHIN	Nevada	Nevada Twp	75	321
Ah	18	m	c	CHIN	Nevada	Meadow Lake Twp	75	261
Ah	18	m	c	CHIN	Santa Clara	Gilroy Twp	88	80
Ah	18	m	c	CHIN	San Mateo	Schoolhouse Statio	87	336
Ah	18	f	c	CHIN	San Francisco	San Francisco P O	80	526
Ah	18	m	c	CHIN	San Francisco	San Francisco P O	80	486
Ah	18	f	c	CHIN	San Francisco	San Francisco P O	80	508
Ah	18	m	c	CHIN	San Francisco	San Francisco P O	80	522
Ah	18	m	c	CHIN	Napa	Yountville Twp	75	80
Ah	18	m	c	CHIN	Nevada	Nevada Twp	75	307
Ah	18	m	c	CHIN	Alameda	Oakland	68	235
Ah	18	m	c	CHIN	Alameda	Oakland	68	249
Ah	17	m	c	CHIN	San Mateo	San Mateo P O	87	355
Ah	17	m	c	CHIN	Placer	Auburn P O	76	366
Ah	17	m	c	CHIN	Nevada	Nevada Twp	75	298
Ah	17	m	c	CHIN	San Francisco	San Francisco P O	80	451
Ah	17	m	c	CHIN	Santa Clara	1-Wd San Jose	88	275
Ah	17	m	c	CHIN	Santa Clara	1-Wd San Jose	88	271
Ah	17	m	c	CHIN	San Francisco	San Francisco P O	80	510
Ah	17	m	c	CHIN	San Francisco	San Francisco P O	83	18
Ah	17	m	c	CHIN	Nevada	Bridgeport Twp	75	112
Ah	17	m	c	CHIN	Napa	Napa	75	9
Ah	17	m	c	CHIN	Alameda	Oakland	68	225
Ah	17	m	c	CHIN	Alameda	Oakland	68	133
Ah	16	m	c	CHIN	Trinity	Douglas	92	235
Ah	16	m	c	CHIN	Santa Clara	San Jose Twp	88	205
Ah	16	m	c	CHIN	Santa Clara	1-Wd San Jose	88	254
Ah	16	m	c	CHIN	Solano	Vallejo	90	174
Ah	16	m	c	CHIN	San Francisco	8-Wd San Francisco	82	309
Ah	16	m	c	CHIN	San Joaquin	1-Wd Stockton	86	145
Ah	16	m	c	CHIN	San Francisco	San Francisco P O	80	396
Ah	16	m	c	CHIN	San Francisco	San Francisco P O	80	451
Ah	16	m	c	CHIN	Solano	Vallejo	90	204
Ah	16	m	c	CHIN	San Francisco	6-Wd San Francisco	81	122
Ah	16	m	c	CHIN	Nevada	Nevada Twp	75	306
Ah	16	m	c	CHIN	Yuba	Marysville	93	602
Ah	15	m	c	CHIN	Shasta	French Gulch P O	89	467
Ah	15	m	c	CHIN	Solano	Vallejo	90	193
Ah	15	m	c	CHIN	San Francisco	8-Wd San Francisco	82	330

Series M593

Name	Age	S	R	B-PL	County	Locale	Roll	Pg
Ah	15	m	c	CHIN	Alameda	Oakland	68	168
Ah	15	m	c	CHIN	Alameda	Murray Twp	68	115
Ah	15	m	c	CHIN	Contra Costa	Martinez P O	71	378
Ah	15	m	c	CHIN	Placer	Colfax P O	76	390
Ah	15	m	c	CHIN	San Francisco	San Francisco P O	80	452
Ah	15	m	c	CHIN	Trinity	Junction City Pct	92	208
Ah	15	m	c	CHIN	Santa Clara	2-Wd San Jose	88	294
Ah	15	m	c	CHIN	San Francisco	8-Wd San Francisco	82	302
Ah	15	m	c	CHIN	Napa	Napa	75	19
Ah	15	m	c	CHIN	Napa	Napa	75	35
Ah	15	m	c	CHIN	Napa	Napa	75	39
Ah	14	m	c	CHIN	San Francisco	San Francisco P O	85	838
Ah	14	m	c	CHIN	Napa	Napa	75	4
Ah	14	m	c	CHIN	Napa	Napa	75	56
Ah	14	m	c	CHIN	San Francisco	6-Wd San Francisco	81	125
Ah	14	m	c	CHIN	Nevada	Bridgeport Twp	75	125
Ah	14	m	c	CHIN	Nevada	Eureka Twp	75	137
Ah	14	m	c	CHIN	Nevada	Grass Valley Twp	75	157
Ah	14	m	c	CHIN	Alameda	Oakland	68	233
Ah	14	m	c	CHIN	Alameda	Oakland	68	219
Ah	14	m	c	CHIN	Alameda	Oakland	68	161
Ah	13	m	c	CHIN	Placer	Clipper Gap P O	76	392
Ah	13	m	c	CHIN	San Francisco	San Francisco P O	80	532
Ah	13	m	c	CHIN	San Francisco	San Francisco P O	85	732
Ah	12	m	c	CHIN	San Francisco	8-Wd San Francisco	82	425
Ah	12	m	c	CHIN	San Francisco	2-Wd San Francisco	79	280
Ah	12	m	c	CHIN	Santa Clara	1-Wd San Jose	88	277
Ah	12	m	c	CHIN	Mendocino	Anderson Twp	74	156
Ah	11	m	c	CHIN	San Francisco	San Francisco P O	80	404
Ah	11	m	c	CHIN	San Francisco	San Francisco P O	80	525
Ah	1	m	c	CA	San Francisco	San Francisco P O	80	453
Ah	1	m	c	CA	San Francisco	San Francisco P O	80	434
Ah	1	m	c	CA	San Francisco	San Francisco P O	80	452
Aw	35	m	c	CHIN	Yuba	Marysville	93	622
Ben	17	m	c	CHIN	Marin	San Rafael	74	55
Bill	35	m	c	CHIN	Siskiyou	Yreka Twp	89	672
Bon Lee	21	m	c	CHIN	Marin	San Rafael	74	58
China	35	m	c	CHIN	Yolo	Merritt Twp	93	503
Cuy	25	m	c	CHIN	Yolo	Putah Twp	93	513
Fing	27	m	c	CHIN	Monterey	San Juan Twp	74	397
Foo	30	m	c	CHIN	Klamath	Sawyers Bar	73	378
Foo	15	m	c	CHIN	Plumas	Plumas Twp	77	26
Go	26	m	c	CHIN	San Joaquin	1-Wd Stockton	86	151
Grin	24	m	c	CHIN	San Luis Obispo	Arroyo Grande Twp	87	279
Haly	20	m	i	CA	Del Norte	Smith Rvr Twp	71	482
Hop	22	m	c	CHIN	Tehama	Antelope Twp	92	153
How	45	m	c	CHIN	Yuba	Marysville	93	630
Hoy	24	m	c	CHIN	Santa Cruz	Santa Cruz	89	405
Hug	22	m	c	CHIN	Santa Clara	Gilroy Twp	88	92
Ih	40	m	c	CHIN	Calaveras	San Andreas P O	70	169
Jim	33	m	c	CHIN	Calaveras	San Andreas P O	70	172
Joe	13	m	c	CHIN	San Francisco	San Francisco P O	83	58
Kee	44	m	c	CHIN	El Dorado	Coloma Twp	72	6
Kee	35	m	c	CHIN	Plumas	Plumas Twp	77	29
Kee	17	m	c	CHIN	San Francisco	San Francisco P O	80	353
Kee	14	m	c	CHIN	San Francisco	San Francisco P O	85	807
Lee	40	m	c	CHIN	Placer	Dutch Flat P O	76	408
Lee	35	m	c	CHIN	Yolo	Putah Twp	93	513
Lee	34	m	c	CHIN	Sierra	Table Rock Twp	89	574
Lee	30	m	c	CHIN	San Francisco	San Francisco P O	83	63
Lenny	20	m	c	CHIN	Marin	Bolinas Twp	74	8
Ling	23	m	c	CHIN	Yolo	Putah Twp	93	525
Ling	18	m	c	CHIN	Tehama	Tehama Twp	92	189
Long	28	m	c	CHIN	San Francisco	11-Wd San Francisc	84	710
Low	27	m	c	CHIN	Santa Clara	Alviso Twp	88	28
Lung	29	m	c	CHIN	Yuba	Marysville	93	630
Lung	27	m	c	CHIN	Marin	San Rafael	74	58
Mon	30	m	c	CHIN	Calaveras	San Andreas P O	70	170
Sam	20	m	c	CHIN	Yolo	Putah Twp	93	515
See	43	m	c	CHIN	San Mateo	San Mateo P O	87	354
See	37	m	c	CHIN	Sierra	Lincoln Twp	89	548
Sing	31	m	c	CHIN	San Joaquin	2-Wd Stockton	86	203
Sing	20	m	c	CHIN	Yolo	Putah Twp	93	524
Sing	14	m	c	CHIN	Santa Clara	Gilroy Twp	88	89
Som	31	m	c	CHIN	Tehama	Tehama Twp	92	189
Som	23	m	c	CHIN	Tehama	Red Bluff	92	184
Ti	37	m	c	CHIN	Marin	San Rafael Twp	74	42
Tom	33	m	c	CHIN	Yolo	Putah Twp	93	516
Wah	16	m	c	CHIN	Sacramento	3-Wd Sacramento	77	264
Wow	27	m	c	CHIN	Santa Clara	Alviso Twp	88	27
Yan	40	m	c	CHIN	Plumas	Mineral Twp	77	22
Yee	32	f	c	CHIN	Yuba	Marysville	93	626
You	33	m	c	CHIN	Yolo	Washington Twp	93	538
Yung	34	m	c	CHIN	Yuba	Marysville	93	630
JIMASON								
Saml	36	m	w	IL	Tehama	Red Bluff	92	184
JIMENES								
Domingo	28	m	w	MEXI	Calaveras	San Andreas P O	70	208
Jose	38	m	w	MEXI	Los Angeles	El Monte Twp	73	462
JIMENEZ								
Domingo	48	m	w	PHIL	Santa Barbara	Santa Barbara P O	87	483
Marcilino	35	m	w	CHIL	San Francisco	2-Wd San Francisco	79	286
JIMINEZ								
Arcadia	30	f	w	MEXI	Los Angeles	Santa Ana Twp	73	600
Luis	22	m	w	MEXI	Los Angeles	Santa Ana Twp	73	600
JIMISON								
James	30	m	w	ME	Inyo	Cerro Gordo Twp	73	318

© 2001 by Heritage Quest. All rights reserved.

Name	Age	S	R	B-PL	County	Locale	Series M593 Roll	Pg
William	69	m	w	VA	Los Angeles	Los Angeles Twp	73	494
JIMM								
Ah	30	m	c	CHIN	Mendocino	Albion & Big Rvr T	74	166
JIMMENES								
J	25	m	w	MO	Solano	Vallejo	90	166
JIMS								
Ronn	30	m	w	AR	Alameda	Washington Twp	68	291
JIN								
Ah	9	f	c	CHIN	San Francisco	San Francisco P O	80	438
Ah	32	m	c	CHIN	Alameda	Eden Twp	68	61
Ah	31	m	c	CHIN	Trinity	Indian Crk	92	200
Ah	30	m	c	CHIN	Alameda	Alameda	68	17
Ah	30	m	c	CHIN	Mendocino	Point Arena Twp	74	215
Ah	28	m	c	CHIN	San Joaquin	1-Wd Stockton	86	145
Ah	22	m	c	CHIN	San Joaquin	Oneal Twp	86	117
Ah	22	m	c	CHIN	Napa	Napa	75	52
Ah	20	m	c	CHIN	Alameda	Alameda	68	4
Ah	20	m	c	CHIN	Alameda	Alameda	68	7
Ah	20	m	c	CHIN	Alameda	Alameda	68	19
Ah	20	m	c	CHIN	Alameda	Alameda	68	2
Ah	14	m	c	CHIN	Napa	Napa Twp	75	58
Lim	35	m	c	CHIN	Marin	Tomales Twp	74	84
Lung	18	m	c	CHIN	San Francisco	11-Wd San Francisc	84	435
JINAN								
Louise	21	m	w	DENM	Sonoma	Bodega Twp	91	253
JINE								
Ah	25	m	c	CHIN	San Francisco	11-Wd San Francisc	84	528
Charley	28	m	c	CHIN	Colusa	Monroe Twp	71	324
JING								
Ah	50	m	c	CHIN	Stanislaus	Emory Twp	92	17
Ah	45	m	c	CHIN	El Dorado	Diamond Springs Tw	72	24
Ah	33	m	c	CHIN	Sierra	Forest Twp	89	528
Ah	27	m	c	CHIN	Napa	Napa	75	56
Ah	24	m	c	CHIN	Nevada	Meadow Lake Twp	75	252
Ah	23	m	c	CHIN	San Joaquin	Union Twp	86	266
Ah	15	m	c	CHIN	Nevada	Nevada Twp	75	282
Ah	14	m	c	CHIN	Nevada	Bridgeport Twp	75	110
JINKS								
--- [Capt]	45	m	w	IREL	San Francisco	7-Wd San Francisco	81	260
James L	34	m	w	CANA	Stanislaus	Emory Twp	92	25
JINN								
---	30	m	c	CHIN	Siskiyou	Hamburg Twp	89	597
---	25	m	c	CHIN	Siskiyou	Cottonwood Twp	89	592
Ah	50	m	c	CHIN	Nevada	Nevada Twp	75	277
Ah	40	m	c	CHIN	Sacramento	Mississippi Twp	77	162
Ah	29	m	c	CHIN	San Francisco	7-Wd San Francisco	81	175
Ah	28	m	c	CHIN	Placer	Auburn P O	76	379
Ah	25	m	c	CHIN	Nevada	Nevada Twp	75	277
Ah	21	m	c	CHIN	Santa Clara	San Jose Twp	88	193
Ah	21	m	c	CHIN	Placer	Dutch Flat P O	76	410
JINO								
Ah	30	m	c	CHIN	Colusa	Colusa	71	298
JIO								
Ah	32	m	c	CHIN	Nevada	Eureka Twp	75	136
JIOU								
Ah	20	m	c	CHIN	San Francisco	San Francisco P O	80	389
JIROD								
Philip	22	m	w	FRAN	Santa Clara	2-Wd San Jose	88	302
JIUSTO								
Braco	24	m	w	ITAL	Amador	Jackson P O	69	329
John	26	m	w	ITAL	Amador	Jackson P O	69	329
JN								
Ah	30	m	c	CHIN	Sacramento	Georgianna Twp	77	124
JNASEZ								
Juan	34	m	w	CHIL	Calaveras	San Andreas P O	70	214
JNES								
James	45	m	w	NY	San Mateo	Pescadero P O	87	411
JO								
Ah	55	m	c	CHIN	Sacramento	Cosumnes Twp	77	90
Ah	54	m	c	CHIN	Sacramento	Granite Twp	77	138
Ah	49	m	c	CHIN	Placer	Dutch Flat P O	76	409
Ah	43	m	c	CHIN	San Francisco	San Francisco P O	80	525
Ah	41	m	c	CHIN	Nevada	Nevada Twp	75	298
Ah	41	m	c	CHIN	San Francisco	San Francisco P O	80	520
Ah	40	m	c	CHIN	Sacramento	1-Wd Sacramento	77	193
Ah	39	m	c	CHIN	San Francisco	San Francisco P O	80	448
Ah	39	m	c	CHIN	Nevada	Nevada Twp	75	321
Ah	39	m	c	CHIN	Nevada	Nevada Twp	75	307
Ah	39	m	c	CHIN	Nevada	Nevada Twp	75	300
Ah	38	m	c	CHIN	San Francisco	San Francisco P O	80	508
Ah	35	m	c	CHIN	Nevada	Nevada Twp	75	307
Ah	34	m	c	CHIN	Sacramento	Granite Twp	77	155
Ah	34	m	c	CHIN	San Francisco	San Francisco P O	80	530
Ah	34	m	c	CHIN	San Francisco	San Francisco P O	80	519
Ah	32	m	c	CHIN	San Francisco	San Francisco P O	80	529
Ah	32	m	c	CHIN	San Francisco	San Francisco P O	80	517
Ah	31	m	c	CHIN	San Francisco	San Francisco P O	80	522
Ah	30	m	c	CHIN	El Dorado	Coloma Twp	72	12
Ah	30	f	c	CHIN	San Francisco	San Francisco P O	80	431
Ah	30	m	c	CHIN	Placer	Auburn P O	76	378
Ah	30	m	c	CHIN	Sacramento	Franklin Twp	77	118
Ah	30	m	c	CHIN	Nevada	Grass Valley Twp	75	210
Ah	29	m	c	CHIN	Tuolumne	Big Oak Flat P O	93	396
Ah	28	m	c	CHIN	Amador	Fiddletown P O	69	436
Ah	28	m	c	CHIN	Sacramento	Georgianna Twp	77	134
Ah	28	m	c	CHIN	Sacramento	1-Wd Sacramento	77	202
Ah	27	m	c	CHIN	San Francisco	San Francisco P O	80	499
Ah	27	m	c	CHIN	Butte	Chico Twp	70	28
Ah	27	m	c	CHIN	Nevada	Eureka Twp	75	140
Ah	27	m	c	CHIN	Napa	Napa Twp	75	67
Ah	27	m	c	CHIN	San Francisco	San Francisco P O	80	523
Ah	26	m	c	CHIN	San Francisco	San Francisco P O	80	516
Ah	25	m	c	CHIN	El Dorado	Diamond Springs Tw	72	27
Ah	25	m	c	CHIN	Placer	Auburn P O	76	377
Ah	24	m	c	CHIN	Nevada	Meadow Lake Twp	75	255
Ah	24	m	c	CHIN	Sacramento	3-Wd Sacramento	77	314
Ah	23	m	c	CHIN	San Francisco	San Francisco P O	85	844
Ah	23	m	c	CHIN	San Francisco	San Francisco P O	80	520
Ah	22	f	c	CHIN	San Francisco	San Francisco P O	80	448
Ah	22	m	c	CHIN	El Dorado	Georgetown Twp	72	38
Ah	22	m	c	CHIN	Los Angeles	Los Angeles	73	527
Ah	22	m	c	CHIN	San Mateo	Schoolhouse Statio	87	334
Ah	22	f	c	CHIN	San Francisco	San Francisco P O	80	530
Ah	21	m	c	CHIN	Alameda	Oakland	68	160
Ah	20	m	c	CHIN	San Joaquin	1-Wd Stockton	86	143
Ah	20	f	c	CHIN	San Francisco	San Francisco P O	80	434
Ah	2	m	c	CA	San Francisco	San Francisco P O	80	527
Ah	19	m	c	CHIN	San Francisco	San Francisco P O	80	518
Ah	18	m	c	CHIN	Sacramento	1-Wd Sacramento	77	201
Ah	18	f	c	CHIN	San Francisco	San Francisco P O	80	527
Ah	15	m	c	CHIN	Nevada	Nevada Twp	75	279
Ah	13	m	c	CHIN	Solano	Vallejo	90	207
Cho	42	m	c	CHIN	Butte	Concow Twp	70	10
Ho	36	m	c	CHIN	San Joaquin	Oneal Twp	86	115
I	30	f	c	CHIN	Stanislaus	Emory Twp	92	17
Ke	37	m	c	CHIN	Sacramento	1-Wd Sacramento	77	205
Lond	27	f	c	CHIN	San Joaquin	1-Wd Stockton	86	153
Sung	48	m	c	CHIN	Sacramento	1-Wd Sacramento	77	197
Sway	26	m	c	CHIN	Stanislaus	San Joaquin Twp	92	73
Ton	36	m	c	CHIN	San Joaquin	3-Wd Stockton	86	246
JOACHIM								
Enos	24	m	w	SCOT	Siskiyou	Yreka Twp	89	668
JOAGAM								
Manuel	26	m	w	PORT	Monterey	San Juan Twp	74	396
JOAGUIN								
M	27	m	w	IA	Merced	Snelling P O	74	262
JOAIRD								
Theodore	37	m	w	UNKN	San Joaquin	2-Wd Stockton	86	166
JOAKI								
Frank	18	m	w	PORT	Marin	Nicasio Twp	74	20
JOALDE								
Valentine	55	m	w	SWIT	El Dorado	Placerville Twp	72	92
JOAN								
Ah	34	m	c	CHIN	Trinity	Canyon City Pct	92	201
John	50	m	i	CA	Yolo	Cache Crk Twp	93	427
JOANINI								
Albert	31	m	w	ITAL	Sonoma	Analy Twp	91	236
JOANIS								
Biago	37	m	w	AUST	El Dorado	Salmon Falls Twp	72	131
JOANNAS								
R	42	m	w	FRAN	Santa Clara	Gilroy Twp	88	95
JOANS								
John	30	m	w	WALE	San Francisco	1-Wd San Francisco	79	90
JOAQUIN								
Antoine	16	m	w	FRAN	San Mateo	Half Moon Bay P O	87	390
Antone	50	m	w	PORT	Alameda	Washington Twp	68	273
Antone	35	m	w	PORT	San Mateo	Half Moon Bay P O	87	401
Balle	36	m	w	MEXI	Alameda	Washington Twp	68	297
Emanuel	31	m	w	PORT	Alameda	Washington Twp	68	285
Gowrean	45	m	w	MEXI	Merced	Snelling P O	74	251
John	37	m	i	MEXI	Tehama	Tehama Twp	92	190
John	26	m	w	MEXI	San Francisco	San Francisco P O	80	474
Jose	25	m	w	AFRI	Sacramento	2-Wd Sacramento	77	242
Joseph	40	m	w	PORT	San Mateo	Half Moon Bay P O	87	401
Manuel	31	m	w	PORT	Contra Costa	San Pablo Twp	71	366
Manuel	28	m	w	PORT	Marin	Sausalito Twp	74	69
Manuel	23	m	w	PORT	Marin	Nicasio Twp	74	20
Rosia	60	f	w	SCOT	Alameda	San Leandro	68	93
Sano	37	m	w	CA	Tulare	Visalia	92	299
Santa	35	m	w	MEXI	Tulare	Tule Rvr Twp	92	261
JOB								
Ah	46	m	c	CHIN	San Joaquin	Oneal Twp	86	117
C E	31	m	w	SCOT	Alameda	Oakland	68	265
Charles	36	m	w	FRAN	San Francisco	6-Wd San Francisco	81	101
Chas	24	m	w	ENGL	San Francisco	11-Wd San Francisc	84	677
Chas E	25	m	w	ENGL	Butte	Hamilton Twp	70	64
Henry	28	m	w	MO	Yolo	Cottonwood Twp	93	464
Jno	33	m	w	ENGL	Santa Clara	Almaden Twp	88	9
John	42	m	w	BADE	Butte	Ophir Twp	70	118
Munroe	19	m	w	MO	Kern	Linns Valley P O	73	344
Peter	47	m	w	FRAN	San Francisco	8-Wd San Francisco	82	347
Richard	25	m	w	ENGL	Nevada	Nevada Twp	75	301
William	34	m	w	ENGL	Nevada	Grass Valley Twp	75	160
JOBB								
William	36	m	w	ENGL	Solano	Montezuma Twp	90	67
JOBE								
Richard	30	m	w	ENGL	Nevada	Grass Valley Twp	75	145
JOBENEGE								
Joseph	38	m	w	SICI	San Francisco	3-Wd San Francisco	79	287
JOBES								
John	40	m	w	VA	San Francisco	11-Wd San Francisc	84	432
Samuel	23	m	w	LA	San Mateo	Belmont P O	87	388
JOBIES								
Thos	42	m	w	WALE	Butte	Concow Twp	70	9

© 2001 by Heritage Quest. All rights reserved.

Name	Age	S	R	B-PL	County	Locale	Roll	Pg
JOBINA								
Jas	55	m	w	ITAL	Butte	Ophir Twp	70	100
JOBIT								
Frank	41	m	w	FRAN	San Francisco	San Francisco P O	80	353
JOBSON								
David	54	m	w	PA	San Francisco	1-Wd San Francisco	79	40
Thomas	50	m	w	PRUS	Sonoma	Bodega Twp	91	262
Wm	21	m	w	WI	Sutter	Nicolaus Twp	92	108
JOBY								
William	24	m	w	MO	Solano	Silveyville Twp	90	73
JOCE								
Ah	32	m	c	CHIN	Contra Costa	Martinez P O	71	370
JOCELYN								
Alvah A	50	m	w	MA	San Francisco	5-Wd San Francisco	81	8
JOCHIM								
Jacob	49	m	w	BAVA	San Francisco	7-Wd San Francisco	81	253
William	42	m	w	FRAN	San Francisco	San Francisco P O	80	456
JOCHIMBA								
Petrano	24	m	w	SWIT	San Francisco	San Francisco P O	80	332
JOCIE								
Thomas	26	m	w	NY	San Francisco	1-Wd San Francisco	79	135
JOCKERS								
Ida	19	f	w	OH	San Joaquin	Oneal Twp	86	112
JOCOLULA								
A S	40	m	w	FINL	San Francisco	3-Wd San Francisco	79	291
JOCY								
James	23	m	w	ENGL	Contra Costa	Martinez P O	71	425
JOD								
Julius	47	m	w	SWIT	Butte	Bidwell Twp	70	3
JODSON								
Melvin	19	m	w	WI	Merced	Snelling P O	74	267
JOE								
Ah	54	m	c	CHIN	Sacramento	Granite Twp	77	137
Ah	47	m	c	CHIN	San Joaquin	2-Wd Stockton	86	203
Ah	46	m	c	CHIN	Placer	Colfax P O	76	388
Ah	44	m	c	CHIN	Nevada	Nevada Twp	75	282
Ah	43	m	c	CHIN	Nevada	Eureka Twp	75	127
Ah	43	m	c	CHIN	Amador	Sutter Crk P O	69	408
Ah	42	m	c	CHIN	Monterey	Castroville Twp	74	338
Ah	41	m	c	CHIN	Sacramento	Granite Twp	77	138
Ah	41	m	c	CHIN	Nevada	Meadow Lake Twp	75	256
Ah	40	m	c	CHIN	Nevada	Nevada Twp	75	299
Ah	40	m	c	CHIN	Sacramento	Sutter Twp	77	382
Ah	40	m	c	CHIN	Sacramento	Brighton Twp	77	72
Ah	40	m	c	CHIN	Placer	Blue Canyon P O	76	418
Ah	39	m	c	CHIN	Placer	Auburn P O	76	362
Ah	37	m	c	CHIN	Nevada	Meadow Lake Twp	75	256
Ah	35	m	c	CHIN	Sonoma	Salt Point	91	386
Ah	35	m	c	CHIN	Trinity	Lewiston Pct	92	213
Ah	34	m	c	CHIN	Stanislaus	Buena Vista Twp	92	13
Ah	31	m	c	CHIN	Merced	Snelling P O	74	257
Ah	30	m	c	CHIN	Contra Costa	Martinez Twp	71	351
Ah	30	m	c	CHIN	San Mateo	San Mateo P O	87	348
Ah	29	m	c	CHIN	Nevada	Bridgeport Twp	75	122
Ah	29	m	c	CHIN	Sacramento	Georgianna Twp	77	127
Ah	29	m	c	CHIN	Sacramento	3-Wd Sacramento	77	255
Ah	27	m	c	CHIN	Sacramento	Franklin Twp	77	109
Ah	27	m	c	CHIN	Stanislaus	Empire Twp	92	46
Ah	26	m	c	CHIN	Nevada	Bridgeport Twp	75	119
Ah	25	m	c	CHIN	Sacramento	Franklin Twp	77	118
Ah	25	m	c	CHIN	San Mateo	Schoolhouse Statio	87	336
Ah	25	m	c	CHIN	Placer	Colfax P O	76	388
Ah	24	m	c	CHIN	Nevada	Bridgeport Twp	75	122
Ah	24	m	c	CHIN	Shasta	American Ranch P O	89	497
Ah	23	m	c	CHIN	Sonoma	Bodega Twp	91	251
Ah	23	m	c	CHIN	Santa Clara	Fremont Twp	88	41
Ah	22	m	c	CHIN	Sacramento	1-Wd Sacramento	77	193
Ah	22	m	c	CHIN	San Francisco	San Francisco P O	83	170
Ah	22	m	c	CHIN	Trinity	Junction City Pct	92	209
Ah	21	m	c	CHIN	Nevada	Washington Twp	75	347
Ah	21	m	c	CHIN	Placer	Gold Run Twp	76	398
Ah	20	m	c	CHIN	San Mateo	Schoolhouse Statio	87	335
Ah	20	m	c	CHIN	Santa Clara	Santa Clara Twp	88	147
Ah	20	m	c	CHIN	San Joaquin	2-Wd Stockton	86	193
Ah	19	m	c	CHIN	Santa Clara	Fremont Twp	88	45
Ah	17	m	c	CHIN	Placer	Auburn P O	76	381
Ah	16	m	c	CHIN	Monterey	Monterey	74	356
Ah	16	m	c	CHIN	Nevada	Nevada Twp	75	297
Ah	11	m	c	CHIN	San Francisco	San Francisco P O	83	58
Ah Poh	28	m	c	CHIN	Sonoma	Salt Point	91	387
An	27	m	c	CHIN	Tuolumne	Big Oak Flat P O	93	399
Ang	32	m	c	CHIN	Klamath	South Fork Twp	73	382
Annie	36	f	w	IREL	San Francisco	7-Wd San Francisco	81	269
Cart	40	m	c	CHIN	San Joaquin	3-Wd Stockton	86	246
China	16	m	c	CHIN	Santa Clara	Gilroy Twp	88	102
Chug	15	m	c	CHIN	Yolo	Putah Twp	93	510
Chum	19	m	c	CHIN	Merced	Snelling P O	74	265
Gem	19	f	c	CHIN	Merced	Snelling P O	74	257
Hop	19	m	c	CHIN	San Francisco	1-Wd San Francisco	79	50
Kain	24	m	c	CHIN	San Mateo	Schoolhouse Statio	87	335
Sam	24	m	c	CHIN	Los Angeles	Los Angeles	73	526
Sign	28	m	c	CHIN	Colusa	Monroe Twp	71	324
Wing	30	m	c	CHIN	Klamath	Sawyers Bar	73	378
Yon	32	m	c	CHIN	San Joaquin	3-Wd Stockton	86	246
JOEHEYER								
August	29	m	w	BAVA	Los Angeles	Wilmington Twp	73	641

Name	Age	S	R	B-PL	County	Locale	Roll	Pg
JOEL								
A M	34	m	w	PRUS	San Francisco	San Francisco P O	85	842
JOES								
Sampson	23	m	w	TN	Colusa	Colusa Twp	71	281
JOEST								
Frank	40	m	w	FRAN	San Francisco	2-Wd San Francisco	79	144
Peter	36	m	w	HDAR	San Francisco	2-Wd San Francisco	79	161
JOEY								
Ah	27	m	c	CHIN	San Francisco	San Francisco P O	80	497
JOG								
Ah	26	m	c	CHIN	Stanislaus	Buena Vista Twp	92	14
JOGH								
Henry	44	m	w	GERM	Los Angeles	Los Angeles	73	528
JOGONA								
D	32	m	w	HANO	San Joaquin	2-Wd Stockton	86	198
JOH								
Ah	42	m	c	CHIN	San Mateo	Half Moon Bay P O	87	389
Ah	40	m	c	CHIN	San Mateo	Belmont P O	87	388
Ah	31	m	c	CHIN	Amador	Jackson P O	69	347
Ah	30	m	c	CHIN	Amador	Ione City P O	69	350
Ah	18	m	c	CHIN	Nevada	Nevada Twp	75	281
JOHAM								
Miller	24	m	w	VT	San Francisco	11-Wd San Francisc	84	708
JOHAN								
Henry	47	m	w	SAXO	San Francisco	11-Wd San Francisc	84	646
JOHANASON								
Goriva	48	f	w	NORW	San Francisco	7-Wd San Francisco	81	269
JOHANESMAN								
A P	32	m	w	PERS	Tuolumne	Columbia P O	93	348
JOHANISUE								
Thomas	45	m	w	GERM	Los Angeles	Los Angeles	73	543
JOHANNA								
Wm E	44	m	w	CT	Solano	Rio Vista Twp	90	58
JOHANNAS								
Cathine	40	f	w	HANO	San Francisco	San Francisco P O	85	844
JOHANNES								
Edwd	40	m	w	AZOR	San Francisco	1-Wd San Francisco	79	130
Geo	50	m	w	ITAL	Santa Clara	Burnett Twp	88	38
William	36	m	w	WURT	Calaveras	San Andreas P O	70	154
JOHANNING								
L W	32	m	w	OH	San Francisco	3-Wd San Francisco	79	301
JOHANSEN								
B	50	m	w	PRUS	San Francisco	San Francisco P O	83	134
Henry	40	m	w	PRUS	San Francisco	8-Wd San Francisco	82	392
John	30	m	w	SHOL	Los Angeles	Santa Ana Twp	73	613
John W	40	m	w	LUEB	Santa Cruz	Santa Cruz	89	410
Peter	32	m	w	PRUS	San Francisco	San Francisco P O	83	387
Rasmus	27	m	w	DENM	Santa Cruz	Pajaro Twp	89	348
JOHE								
Ah	31	m	c	CHIN	Sacramento	Franklin Twp	77	108
Ah	27	m	c	CHIN	Sacramento	Georgianna Twp	77	132
JOHES								
C	55	m	w	PA	El Dorado	Greenwood Twp	72	51
G Andrew	42	m	w	AL	San Diego	San Diego	78	490
JOHHSON								
John J	38	m	w	NY	San Francisco	6-Wd San Francisco	81	104
JOHI								
Peachy	21	m	c	CHIN	Siskiyou	Butte Twp	89	586
JOHIN								
James	26	m	w	NY	Alameda	Murray Twp	68	128
JOHINHISEN								
Andrew	20	m	w	SWED	San Francisco	San Francisco P O	80	334
JOHINS								
Felix	34	m	w	ITAL	San Francisco	San Francisco P O	80	471
JOHN								
---	17	m	c	CHIN	Sacramento	1-Wd Sacramento	77	176
---	12	m	c	CHIN	Sacramento	4-Wd Sacramento	77	327
---	12	m	w	CA	Santa Barbara	Santa Barbara P O	87	492
---	10	m	c	CHIN	Sacramento	4-Wd Sacramento	77	321
--- [China Boy]	16	m	c	CHIN	Sacramento	4-Wd Sacramento	77	352
Ah	9	f	c	CHIN	San Francisco	San Francisco P O	80	444
Ah	9	m	c	CHIN	San Francisco	San Francisco P O	80	530
Ah	7	m	c	CHIN	San Francisco	San Francisco P O	80	447
Ah	7	m	c	CA	San Francisco	San Francisco P O	80	441
Ah	60	m	c	CHIN	El Dorado	Coloma Twp	72	6
Ah	6	m	c	CA	San Francisco	San Francisco P O	80	438
Ah	6	m	c	CA	San Francisco	San Francisco P O	80	437
Ah	6	m	c	CHIN	San Francisco	San Francisco P O	80	528
Ah	50	m	c	CHIN	San Francisco	San Francisco P O	80	486
Ah	50	m	c	CHIN	San Francisco	San Francisco P O	80	521
Ah	50	m	c	CHIN	Trinity	Canyon City Pct	92	202
Ah	48	m	c	CHIN	Placer	Newcastle Twp	76	477
Ah	47	m	c	CHIL	San Mateo	Half Moon Bay P O	87	395
Ah	46	m	c	CHIN	San Francisco	San Francisco P O	80	527
Ah	46	m	c	CHIN	San Mateo	Half Moon Bay P O	87	395
Ah	45	m	c	CHIN	El Dorado	Coloma Twp	72	12
Ah	45	m	c	CHIN	El Dorado	Mud Springs Twp	72	79
Ah	45	m	c	CHIN	Solano	Vallejo	90	210
Ah	45	m	c	CHIN	Placer	Alta P O	76	413
Ah	44	m	c	CHIN	Sacramento	Granite Twp	77	155
Ah	42	m	c	CHIN	Sacramento	Georgianna Twp	77	124
Ah	41	m	c	CHIN	San Francisco	San Francisco P O	80	443
Ah	41	m	c	CHIN	San Francisco	San Francisco P O	80	431
Ah	41	m	c	CHIN	San Francisco	San Francisco P O	80	436
Ah	41	m	c	CHIN	San Francisco	San Francisco P O	80	433
Ah	40	m	c	CHIN	Placer	Rocklin Twp	76	466
Ah	40	m	c	CHIN	El Dorado	Coloma Twp	72	11

© 2001 by Heritage Quest. All rights reserved.

Name	Age	S	R	B-PL	County	Locale	Series M593 Roll	Pg
Ah	40	m	c	CHIN	Monterey	Alisal Twp	74	292
Ah	40	m	c	CHIN	San Mateo	Pescadero P O	87	413
Ah	40	m	c	CHIN	San Joaquin	3-Wd Stockton	86	246
Ah	40	m	c	CHIN	San Joaquin	1-Wd Stockton	86	144
Ah	40	m	c	CHIN	San Francisco	San Francisco P O	80	496
Ah	40	m	c	CHIN	Trinity	Weaverville Pct	92	227
Ah	40	m	c	CHIN	San Francisco	San Francisco P O	80	506
Ah	40	m	c	CHIN	Santa Clara	2-Wd San Jose	88	327
Ah	40	m	c	CHIN	San Mateo	San Mateo P O	87	350
Ah	40	m	c	CHIN	Monterey	Salinas Twp	74	308
Ah	40	m	c	CHIN	El Dorado	Placerville	72	125
Ah	40	m	c	CHIN	Amador	Ione City P O	69	359
Ah	40	m	c	CHIN	Amador	Sutter Crk P O	69	410
Ah	4	m	c	CHIN	San Francisco	San Francisco P O	80	528
Ah	39	m	c	CHIN	San Francisco	San Francisco P O	80	452
Ah	39	m	c	CHIN	San Francisco	San Francisco P O	80	451
Ah	39	m	c	CHIN	Amador	Fiddletown P O	69	438
Ah	39	m	c	CHIN	San Francisco	San Francisco P O	80	523
Ah	38	m	c	CHIN	San Joaquin	Oneal Twp	86	116
Ah	38	m	c	CHIN	Trinity	Douglas	92	233
Ah	38	m	c	CHIN	San Francisco	San Francisco P O	80	513
Ah	38	m	c	CHIN	San Francisco	San Francisco P O	80	530
Ah	37	m	c	CHIN	San Francisco	San Francisco P O	80	435
Ah	37	m	c	CHIN	San Francisco	San Francisco P O	80	527
Ah	36	m	c	CHIN	San Francisco	San Francisco P O	80	447
Ah	36	m	c	CHIN	Merced	Snelling P O	74	257
Ah	36	m	c	CHIN	San Francisco	San Francisco P O	80	520
Ah	36	m	c	CHIN	San Francisco	San Francisco P O	80	518
Ah	36	m	c	CHIN	San Francisco	San Francisco P O	80	518
Ah	36	m	c	CHIN	San Francisco	San Francisco P O	80	519
Ah	35	m	c	CHIN	San Mateo	San Mateo P O	87	371
Ah	35	m	c	CHIN	San Francisco	San Francisco P O	80	515
Ah	35	m	c	CHIN	San Francisco	San Francisco P O	80	517
Ah	35	m	c	CHIN	San Francisco	San Francisco P O	80	527
Ah	34	m	c	CHIN	Nevada	Nevada Twp	75	281
Ah	34	m	c	CHIN	San Francisco	San Francisco P O	80	435
Ah	34	m	c	CHIN	San Mateo	Belmont P O	87	373
Ah	34	m	c	CHIN	San Francisco	San Francisco P O	80	510
Ah	34	m	c	CHIN	San Francisco	San Francisco P O	80	500
Ah	32	m	c	CHIN	Tuolumne	Chinese Camp P O	93	390
Ah	32	m	c	CHIN	San Francisco	San Francisco P O	80	528
Ah	31	m	w	CHIN	Monterey	Castroville Twp	74	329
Ah	31	m	c	CHIN	San Francisco	San Francisco P O	80	518
Ah	31	m	c	CHIN	San Mateo	Schoolhouse Statio	87	344
Ah	30	m	c	CHIN	Sacramento	Franklin Twp	77	118
Ah	30	m	c	CHIN	Sacramento	Georgianna Twp	77	123
Ah	30	m	c	CHIN	Nevada	Meadow Lake Twp	75	248
Ah	30	m	c	CHIN	Monterey	Castroville Twp	74	341
Ah	30	m	c	CHIN	San Mateo	Pescadero P O	87	416
Ah	30	m	c	CHIN	Santa Clara	San Jose Twp	88	191
Ah	30	m	c	CHIN	San Mateo	Schoolhouse Statio	87	334
Ah	30	m	c	CHIN	Solano	Suisun Twp	90	106
Ah	30	m	c	CHIN	San Francisco	San Francisco P O	80	501
Ah	30	m	c	CHIN	San Francisco	San Francisco P O	80	530
Ah	30	m	c	CHIN	Santa Clara	1-Wd San Jose	88	275
Ah	30	m	c	CHIN	San Mateo	Half Moon Bay P O	87	399
Ah	30	m	c	CHIN	San Mateo	Redwood City P O	87	375
Ah	30	m	c	CHIN	San Mateo	Half Moon Bay P O	87	399
Ah	30	m	c	CHIN	Sacramento	Georgianna Twp	77	125
Ah	30	m	c	CHIN	Mendocino	Albion & Big Rvr T	74	166
Ah	30	m	c	CHIN	Nevada	Nevada Twp	75	307
Ah	30	f	c	CHIN	Nevada	Nevada Twp	75	299
Ah	30	m	c	CHIN	El Dorado	Greenwood Twp	72	56
Ah	30	m	c	CHIN	Amador	Sutter Crk P O	69	396
Ah	3	m	c	CA	San Francisco	San Francisco P O	80	529
Ah	29	m	c	CHIN	San Joaquin	1-Wd Stockton	86	145
Ah	29	m	c	CHIN	San Francisco	San Francisco P O	80	501
Ah	29	m	c	CHIN	Tuolumne	Chinese Camp P O	93	377
Ah	29	m	c	CHIN	San Francisco	San Francisco P O	80	522
Ah	28	m	c	CHIN	San Francisco	San Francisco P O	80	444
Ah	28	m	c	CHIN	San Francisco	San Francisco P O	85	722
Ah	28	m	c	CHIN	San Mateo	Schoolhouse Statio	87	340
Ah	28	m	c	CHIN	San Mateo	Half Moon Bay P O	87	389
Ah	28	m	c	CHIN	Sacramento	Sutter Twp	77	386
Ah	28	m	c	CHIN	Sacramento	Granite Twp	77	138
Ah	28	m	c	CHIN	Sacramento	Granite Twp	77	150
Ah	28	m	c	CHIN	Monterey	Monterey Twp	74	349
Ah	27	m	c	CHIN	San Mateo	Pescadero P O	87	411
Ah	27	m	c	CHIN	Trinity	North Fork Twp	92	220
Ah	27	m	c	CHIN	Santa Clara	2-Wd San Jose	88	279
Ah	27	m	c	CHIN	San Mateo	San Mateo P O	87	348
Ah	27	m	c	CHIN	San Mateo	Belmont P O	87	373
Ah	27	m	c	CHIN	San Mateo	San Mateo P O	87	354
Ah	26	m	c	CHIN	Sacramento	Natomas Twp	77	168
Ah	26	m	c	CHIN	Nevada	Washington Twp	75	347
Ah	26	m	c	CHIN	San Francisco	San Francisco P O	80	443
Ah	26	m	c	CHIN	San Mateo	Half Moon Bay P O	87	389
Ah	26	m	c	CHIN	San Francisco	San Francisco P O	80	498
Ah	25	m	c	CHIN	Sacramento	Granite Twp	77	152
Ah	25	m	c	CHIN	Calaveras	Copperopolis P O	70	223
Ah	25	m	c	CHIN	San Francisco	8-Wd San Francisco	82	412
Ah	25	m	c	CHIN	Tuolumne	Big Oak Flat P O	93	393
Ah	25	m	c	CHIN	Santa Cruz	Santa Cruz Twp	89	385
Ah	25	m	c	CHIN	Trinity	Canyon City Pct	92	201
Ah	25	m	c	CHIN	Sacramento	Sutter Twp	77	386
Ah	25	m	c	CHIN	Sacramento	Georgianna Twp	77	129
Ah	25	m	c	CHIN	Nevada	Nevada Twp	75	304

Name	Age	S	R	B-PL	County	Locale	Series M593 Roll	Pg
Ah	24	m	c	CHIN	San Francisco	San Francisco P O	80	436
Ah	24	m	c	CHIN	San Francisco	San Francisco P O	80	497
Ah	24	f	c	CHIN	San Francisco	San Francisco P O	80	526
Ah	24	m	c	CHIN	San Francisco	San Francisco P O	80	525
Ah	24	m	c	CHIN	Santa Clara	Santa Clara Twp	88	136
Ah	24	m	c	CHIN	Trinity	North Fork Twp	92	220
Ah	22	m	c	CHIN	Santa Clara	Gilroy Twp	88	97
Ah	22	m	c	CHIN	San Mateo	Half Moon Bay P O	87	390
Ah	22	m	c	CHIN	San Mateo	Menlo Park P O	87	378
Ah	22	m	c	CHIN	San Mateo	Schoolhouse Statio	87	338
Ah	21	m	c	CHIN	Mendocino	Point Arena Twp	74	212
Ah	21	m	c	CHIN	San Francisco	San Francisco P O	80	502
Ah	21	m	c	CHIN	San Mateo	Schoolhouse Statio	87	343
Ah	21	m	c	CHIN	Monterey	Alisal Twp	74	293
Ah	21	m	c	CHIN	Nevada	Eureka Twp	75	127
Ah	20	m	c	CHIN	San Francisco	San Francisco P O	80	451
Ah	20	m	c	CHIN	Calaveras	Copperopolis P O	70	247
Ah	20	m	c	CHIN	San Mateo	Redwood City P O	87	376
Ah	20	m	c	CHIN	San Mateo	Schoolhouse Statio	87	344
Ah	20	m	c	CHIN	Sutter	Butte Twp	92	96
Ah	20	m	c	CHIN	Trinity	Weaverville Pct	92	228
Ah	20	m	c	CHIN	San Francisco	San Francisco P O	80	501
Ah	20	m	c	CHIN	San Francisco	San Francisco P O	80	498
Ah	20	m	c	CHIN	San Francisco	San Francisco P O	80	530
Ah	20	m	c	CHIN	San Francisco	San Francisco P O	80	538
Ah	20	m	c	CHIN	Trinity	Junction City Pct	92	207
Ah	20	m	c	CHIN	San Joaquin	2-Wd Stockton	86	212
Ah	20	m	c	CHIN	El Dorado	Mud Springs Twp	72	87
Ah	19	m	c	CHIN	San Francisco	1-Wd San Francisco	79	45
Ah	19	m	c	CHIN	San Francisco	San Francisco P O	80	540
Ah	19	m	c	CHIN	Sacramento	Franklin Twp	77	108
Ah	19	m	c	CHIN	Contra Costa	Martinez P O	71	432
Ah	18	f	c	CHIN	Nevada	Meadow Lake Twp	75	254
Ah	18	m	c	CHIN	San Francisco	San Francisco P O	80	445
Ah	18	m	c	CHIN	San Mateo	Pescadero P O	87	414
Ah	18	m	c	CHIN	Santa Cruz	Soquel Twp	89	439
Ah	18	m	c	CHIN	San Francisco	6-Wd San Francisco	81	142
Ah	18	m	c	CHIN	San Francisco	6-Wd San Francisco	81	137
Ah	18	m	c	CHIN	San Francisco	San Francisco P O	85	724
Ah	18	m	c	CHIN	San Mateo	Belmont P O	87	373
Ah	18	m	c	CHIN	San Mateo	Half Moon Bay P O	87	399
Ah	18	m	c	CHIN	Yuba	Marysville	93	619
Ah	17	m	c	CHIN	Placer	Dutch Flat P O	76	414
Ah	17	m	c	CHIN	San Francisco	San Francisco P O	80	485
Ah	17	m	c	CHIN	San Francisco	6-Wd San Francisco	81	150
Ah	17	m	c	CHIN	Solano	Benicia	90	14
Ah	17	m	c	CHIN	San Mateo	San Mateo P O	87	355
Ah	16	m	c	CHIN	San Francisco	San Francisco P O	80	510
Ah	16	m	c	CHIN	Alameda	Washington Twp	68	280
Ah	15	m	c	CHIN	San Francisco	8-Wd San Francisco	82	383
Ah	15	m	c	CHIN	San Francisco	San Francisco P O	85	728
Ah	13	m	c	CHIN	San Francisco	6-Wd San Francisco	81	103
Ah	13	m	c	CHIN	San Francisco	San Francisco P O	85	730
Ah	13	m	c	CHIN	San Mateo	Searsville P O	87	383
Ah	13	m	c	CHIN	Nevada	Eureka Twp	75	140
Ah	11	m	c	CHIN	San Francisco	San Francisco P O	80	409
Ah	11	m	c	CHIN	San Francisco	San Francisco P O	80	534
Ah	1	m	c	CA	San Francisco	San Francisco P O	80	448
Alfred	29	m	w	SWED	San Francisco	8-Wd San Francisco	82	435
Annie	14	f	w	NY	San Francisco	San Francisco P O	83	399
Charles	33	m	w	CANA	Santa Clara	1-Wd San Jose	88	225
Charles	33	m	w	ME	Alameda	Murray Twp	68	119
Chin	20	m	c	CHIN	Siskiyou	Yreka	89	662
China	31	m	c	CHIN	Placer	Lincoln P O	76	484
Chung	35	m	c	CHIN	San Mateo	Pescadero P O	87	409
Conn	39	m	w	IL	El Dorado	Mud Springs Twp	72	90
Cow	35	m	c	CHIN	El Dorado	Greenwood Twp	72	56
E K	27	m	w	SWED	San Francisco	San Francisco P O	80	429
Edward	16	m	w	CA	San Francisco	San Francisco P O	83	173
Ellis	39	m	w	MO	Sutter	Nicolaus Twp	92	114
Ferdenand	23	m	w	SAXO	Sonoma	Petaluma Twp	91	319
Godfrey	35	m	w	HESS	Placer	Bath P O	76	440
H	17	m	w	MA	Alameda	Oakland	68	148
Heivenet	41	m	w	PA	Shasta	Shasta P O	89	454
Henry	55	m	w	SHOL	Alameda	Oakland	68	227
Henry	25	m	w	FRAN	San Francisco	5-Wd San Francisco	81	10
Hi	25	m	c	CHIN	Colusa	Grand Island Twp	71	304
Jacinto	18	m	w	FRAN	Monterey	Monterey	74	361
Jacob	27	m	w	PRUS	Alameda	Murray Twp	68	100
James	9M	m	w	CA	Sonoma	Bodega Twp	91	260
James	25	m	w	PA	Sacramento	Georgianna Twp	77	135
John	55	m	w	PA	Sacramento	Georgianna Twp	77	135
John	35	m	w	NY	Sacramento	Lee Twp	77	160
John	16	m	c	CHIN	Yolo	Washington Twp	93	534
Joo	39	m	c	CHIN	San Joaquin	1-Wd Stockton	86	142
Joseph C	25	m	w	IREL	Mendocino	Navarro & Big Rvr	74	176
Ko	28	m	c	CHIN	El Dorado	Coloma Twp	72	11
Kup	20	m	c	CHIN	El Dorado	Coloma Twp	72	11
Lee	30	m	c	CHIN	San Joaquin	1-Wd Stockton	86	151
Ling	25	m	c	CHIN	Napa	Napa	75	18
Long	22	m	c	CHIN	Yolo	Putah Twp	93	524
Loni	20	m	w	CANA	Marin	San Rafael Twp	74	34
Margt	30	f	w	IREL	San Francisco	San Francisco P O	83	134
Maria	30	f	w	PRUS	Santa Clara	2-Wd San Jose	88	331
Mary	35	f	i	CA	Yolo	Cache Crk Twp	93	427
O Craig	38	m	w	TN	Klamath	Hoopa Valley India	73	386
Oh	30	m	c	CHIN	Monterey	San Juan Twp	74	402

© 2001 by Heritage Quest. All rights reserved.

California 1870 Census

Name	Age	S	R	B-PL	County	Locale	Roll	Pg
Oscar J	16	m	w	CA	San Mateo	Woodside P O	87	387
R	12	m	w	CA	Los Angeles	Los Angeles	73	508
Richard	36	m	w	ENGL	Amador	Amador City P O	69	394
Sam	39	m	c	CHIN	San Joaquin	1-Wd Stockton	86	145
Samuel	25	m	w	PA	Sacramento	Georgianna Twp	77	135
Shed S	33	m	w	ENGL	Shasta	Shasta P O	89	454
Shu	22	m	c	CHIN	San Joaquin	1-Wd Stockton	86	151
Sing	33	m	c	CHIN	Sierra	Downieville Twp	89	521
Sing	27	m	c	CHIN	El Dorado	Greenwood Twp	72	56
Thomas	60	m	w	WALE	Contra Costa	Martinez P O	71	428
Toy	32	m	c	CHIN	San Francisco	6-Wd San Francisco	81	60
W	12	m	w	IREL	Lake	Knoxville Mines	73	404
Walter	42	m	w	OH	San Joaquin	3-Wd Stockton	86	231
Wan	28	m	c	CHIN	Sierra	Downieville Twp	89	520
William	28	m	w	HDAR	Santa Clara	Santa Clara Twp	88	171
Woon	32	m	c	CHIN	Yuba	Marysville	93	626
Yack	24	m	c	CHIN	Tulare	White Rvr Twp	92	302
Yee	21	f	c	CHIN	Yuba	Rose Bar Twp	93	655
Yop	14	m	c	CHIN	Sacramento	1-Wd Sacramento	77	192
JOHNEL								
Antonio	24	m	w	ITAL	Tuolumne	Sonora P O	93	324
John	44	m	w	ITAL	Tuolumne	Sonora P O	93	324
Joseph	48	m	w	ITAL	Tuolumne	Sonora P O	93	324
JOHNES								
Chas	35	m	w	MA	San Francisco	1-Wd San Francisco	79	101
Chas	26	m	w	IREL	San Francisco	1-Wd San Francisco	79	83
Julia	40	f	w	NY	Sacramento	San Joaquin Twp	77	394
JOHNESTONE								
W W	49	m	w	NY	Solano	Benicia	90	7
JOHNEY								
P	23	m	w	PRUS	Alameda	Murray Twp	68	102
JOHNMAN								
Robert	45	m	w	NY	Inyo	Bishop Crk Twp	73	316
JOHNPATISTA								
John	38	m	w	ITAL	San Francisco	San Francisco P O	85	865
JOHNS								
Alfred	44	m	w	MO	Sutter	Nicolaus Twp	92	112
Andrew	42	m	w	MO	Colusa	Monroe Twp	71	315
Benjamin F	38	m	w	MO	Plumas	Seneca Twp	77	47
Benjamin F	37	m	w	TN	El Dorado	Mud Springs Twp	72	80
Carl	47	m	w	GERM	Yolo	Merritt Twp	93	506
Charles	33	m	w	ENGL	Santa Cruz	Watsonville	89	366
D H	35	m	w	OH	Yuba	Marysville Twp	93	569
Daniel	38	m	w	IA	Calaveras	San Andreas P O	70	207
David	50	m	w	GERM	Solano	Vallejo	90	162
David D	45	m	w	OH	El Dorado	Placerville	72	111
Della	12	f	w	CA	Nevada	Grass Valley Twp	75	154
Eugene	18	m	w	PRUS	Sacramento	4-Wd Sacramento	77	366
Ezekiel	26	m	w	ENGL	Nevada	Grass Valley Twp	75	181
George	34	m	w	ENGL	Placer	Dutch Flat P O	76	403
George W	55	m	w	MO	Colusa	Spring Valley Twp	71	339
H D	41	m	w	OH	Solano	Benicia	90	12
Hance	61	m	w	PRUS	Sacramento	Natomas Twp	77	166
Henry	37	m	w	PRUS	Sacramento	4-Wd Sacramento	77	351
Henry	24	m	w	IREL	Solano	Silveyville Twp	90	85
Henry L	34	m	w	VT	Marin	Point Reyes Twp	74	23
J Ema	50	f	b	MD	Alameda	Oakland	68	165
James	59	m	w	TN	Colusa	Spring Valley Twp	71	335
James	55	m	w	GERM	Santa Clara	Gilroy Twp	88	95
James	39	m	w	ENGL	Nevada	Nevada Twp	75	301
John	65	m	w	PRUS	Sacramento	American Twp	77	66
John	37	m	w	ENGL	Nevada	Grass Valley Twp	75	177
John	25	m	w	CANA	Tuolumne	Sonora P O	93	321
John	22	m	w	IREL	San Francisco	San Francisco P O	80	355
Joseph F	51	m	b	AFRI	Calaveras	Copperopolis P O	70	240
Josiah	18	m	w	CA	Sonoma	Washington Twp	91	470
Lewis	25	m	w	NY	Butte	Chico Twp	70	49
Miller	36	m	w	MO	Stanislaus	Empire Twp	92	36
Moses	50	m	w	ENGL	San Joaquin	2-Wd Stockton	86	174
Richard	22	m	w	ENGL	Nevada	Grass Valley Twp	75	194
Robert C	49	m	w	SAXO	Amador	Fiddletown P O	69	440
Rose	28	f	w	CHIL	San Francisco	San Francisco P O	83	106
Stephen	30	m	w	ENGL	Nevada	Grass Valley Twp	75	215
Thomas	52	m	w	MA	Stanislaus	Empire Twp	92	42
Thomas	49	m	w	TN	Stanislaus	North Twp	92	68
Thomas	40	m	w	SWED	San Francisco	3-Wd San Francisco	79	295
Thomas	32	m	w	OH	Stanislaus	Empire Twp	92	49
Thomas	28	m	w	NY	San Francisco	San Francisco P O	80	540
Thomas	18	m	w	NY	San Joaquin	Oneal Twp	86	111
Trehemae	32	m	w	ENGL	San Francisco	3-Wd San Francisco	79	325
Vincent	38	m	w	ENGL	Tuolumne	Sonora P O	93	320
William	45	m	w	ENGL	Tuolumne	Sonora P O	93	320
William	45	m	w	MA	Solano	Denverton Twp	90	25
William	36	m	w	ENGL	San Francisco	San Francisco P O	80	426
William	34	m	w	ENGL	Nevada	Grass Valley Twp	75	147
William	26	m	w	OH	Solano	Silveyville Twp	90	83
William	24	m	w	WI	San Francisco	7-Wd San Francisco	81	207
William	24	m	w	HANO	El Dorado	Mud Springs Twp	72	86
William	22	m	w	ENGL	Nevada	Grass Valley Twp	75	164
Wm	35	m	w	ENGL	Sierra	Table Rock Twp	89	577
Wm	35	m	w	CANA	San Joaquin	Douglas Twp	86	36
Wm	22	m	w	ENGL	San Joaquin	1-Wd Stockton	86	157
Zachariah	64	m	w	ENGL	El Dorado	Salmon Falls Twp	72	133
JOHNSA								
John	27	m	w	IREL	San Mateo	San Mateo P O	87	356
JOHNSEN								
Charles	24	m	w	SWED	San Mateo	Menlo Park P O	87	378

Name	Age	S	R	B-PL	County	Locale	Roll	Pg
Jane	45	f	w	IREL	San Francisco	11-Wd San Francisc	84	623
JOHNSING								
John	25	m	w	PORT	Trinity	Indian Crk	92	199
JOHNSON								
---	38	m	w	NY	Santa Barbara	Santa Barbara P O	87	487
A	6	f	w	CA	Los Angeles	Los Angeles	73	569
A	55	m	w	DENM	El Dorado	Coloma Twp	72	2
A	42	m	w	IREL	Sierra	Alleghany & Forest	89	535
A	40	m	w	SWED	Amador	Ione City P O	69	350
A	36	m	w	TN	Lake	Scotts Crk	73	426
A	30	m	w	SWIT	Alameda	Murray Twp	68	123
A	29	m	w	HANO	San Francisco	San Francisco P O	85	806
A	28	m	w	SWED	Klamath	Trinidad Twp	73	392
A A	22	m	w	GERM	Sacramento	1-Wd Sacramento	77	182
A C	32	m	w	NY	San Joaquin	Dent Twp	86	22
A D	40	m	w	IREL	Klamath	Trinidad Twp	73	390
A L	36	m	w	TN	Monterey	Alisal Twp	74	302
A M	35	m	w	GA	San Joaquin	Douglas Twp	86	43
A S	42	m	w	KY	Santa Clara	Gilroy Twp	88	93
A W	39	m	w	PRUS	Calaveras	Copperopolis P O	70	233
Abagail	70	f	w	CT	Humboldt	Eureka Twp	72	274
Abagail	70	f	w	CT	Humboldt	Table Bluff Twp	72	305
Abraham	27	m	w	FINL	Placer	Bath P O	76	441
Abram	32	m	w	RUSS	San Francisco	1-Wd San Francisco	79	50
Addison	37	m	w	NH	San Francisco	11-Wd San Francisc	84	678
Albert	29	m	w	NORW	Trinity	Trinity Center Pct	92	204
Albert	27	m	w	RI	Marin	Sausalito Twp	74	73
Albert	25	m	w	IREL	Colusa	Monroe Twp	71	318
Albert J	28	m	w	MD	Los Angeles	Los Angeles	73	568
Albert S	11	m	w	CA	Sonoma	Mendocino Twp	91	288
Albion	29	m	w	ME	Contra Costa	Martinez P O	71	400
Alden S	36	m	w	NY	Santa Cruz	Pajaro Twp	89	348
Alex	56	m	w	OH	Butte	Chico Twp	70	32
Alex	56	m	w	IA	Butte	Chico Twp	70	50
Alex	45	m	w	PA	Amador	Sutter Crk P O	69	399
Alex	38	m	w	SWED	Sierra	Table Rock Twp	89	576
Alex	30	m	w	SCOT	San Joaquin	1-Wd Stockton	86	124
Alex J	36	m	w	KY	Colusa	Colusa	71	293
Alexander	33	m	w	SWED	Mendocino	Ten Mile Rvr Twp	74	172
Alexander R	36	m	w	IREL	Los Angeles	Los Angeles	73	566
Alfred	24	m	w	ENGL	Contra Costa	Martinez P O	71	419
Alice	19	f	w	MA	San Francisco	2-Wd San Francisco	79	218
Alice	18	f	m	CA	Sacramento	4-Wd Sacramento	77	324
Allen	39	m	w	SWED	Placer	Gold Run Twp	76	400
Allen	30	m	b	DC	Los Angeles	Los Angeles	73	525
Almon	41	m	w	NY	Sonoma	Petaluma Twp	91	328
Alonzo	22	m	w	IN	Monterey	Pajaro Twp	74	369
Alvin	25	m	w	CT	Santa Clara	Santa Clara Twp	88	145
Amariah	47	m	w	IL	Sacramento	4-Wd Sacramento	77	329
Amasa P	32	m	w	NY	San Mateo	Belmont P O	87	371
Ambrose	12	m	w	CA	Solano	Suisun Twp	90	110
Amos	50	m	w	SWED	Butte	Concow Twp	70	7
Amos	29	m	b	WIND	Sacramento	2-Wd Sacramento	77	217
Amos	28	m	b	WIND	Sacramento	4-Wd Sacramento	77	324
Amos	27	m	w	TN	Mendocino	Big Rvr Twp	74	171
Andrew	60	m	w	NORW	Mendocino	Point Arena Twp	74	212
Andrew	57	m	w	PA	Klamath	Orleans Twp	73	379
Andrew	49	m	w	SWED	Siskiyou	Yreka	89	658
Andrew	48	m	w	NY	Placer	Gold Run Twp	76	399
Andrew	45	m	w	MO	Calaveras	San Andreas P O	70	207
Andrew	43	m	w	SWED	Tehama	Battle Crk Twp	92	158
Andrew	42	m	w	NORW	Mendocino	Point Arena Twp	74	204
Andrew	42	m	b	WIND	San Francisco	San Francisco P O	80	457
Andrew	42	m	w	SWED	Stanislaus	Emory Twp	92	17
Andrew	41	m	w	OH	Colusa	Colusa	71	292
Andrew	41	m	w	NORW	Sonoma	Bodega Twp	91	256
Andrew	41	m	w	NORW	San Francisco	7-Wd San Francisco	81	274
Andrew	40	m	w	SWED	Placer	Bath P O	76	458
Andrew	40	m	w	SWED	Klamath	Klamath Twp	73	371
Andrew	34	m	w	SWIT	San Francisco	San Francisco P O	80	467
Andrew	34	m	w	DENM	San Francisco	11-Wd San Francisc	84	573
Andrew	32	m	w	NORW	Mendocino	Noyo & Big Rvr Twp	74	173
Andrew	30	m	w	IREL	Butte	Oregon Twp	70	126
Andrew	30	m	w	IREL	Sonoma	Petaluma Twp	91	340
Andrew	30	m	w	DENM	San Francisco	1-Wd San Francisco	79	132
Andrew	28	m	w	DENM	San Mateo	Half Moon Bay P O	87	407
Andrew	27	m	w	SWED	Sonoma	Salt Point	91	393
Andrew	26	m	w	MO	Sutter	Butte Twp	92	99
Andrew	25	m	w	SWED	Stanislaus	Emory Twp	92	24
Andrew	23	m	w	DENM	Alameda	Eden Twp	68	84
Andrew	23	m	w	SWED	San Francisco	3-Wd San Francisco	79	292
Andrew F	36	m	w	SWED	San Francisco	1-Wd San Francisco	79	110
Andrew J	33	m	w	SWED	Humboldt	Pacific Twp	72	299
Andrew L	52	m	w	SWED	Plumas	Mineral Twp	77	22
Andrw	29	m	w	SWED	San Francisco	2-Wd San Francisco	79	215
Andw	54	m	w	SWED	San Francisco	San Francisco P O	83	88
Andw	45	m	w	DENM	Fresno	Millerton P O	72	149
Anna	45	f	w	MA	San Francisco	San Francisco P O	83	406
Anna	22	f	w	NORW	San Francisco	8-Wd San Francisco	82	374
Annie	23	f	w	VT	Marin	Tomales Twp	74	79
Annie	21	f	w	HAMB	San Francisco	San Francisco P O	83	191
Annie	21	f	w	IREL	Santa Cruz	Watsonville	89	368
Annie	10	f	w	CA	San Francisco	San Francisco P O	83	141
Annie T	40	f	w	IREL	Tulare	Visalia	92	289
Anson	50	m	w	NY	Placer	Bath P O	76	422
Antoine	27	m	w	SWED	San Francisco	3-Wd San Francisco	79	292
Archibald	58	m	w	VA	Santa Clara	Santa Clara Twp	88	172

© 2001 by Heritage Quest. All rights reserved.

Name	Age	S	R	B-PL	County	Locale	Series M593 Roll	Pg
Arthur	47	m	w	NY	Shasta	Stillwater P O	89	479
August	28	m	w	SWED	San Francisco	1-Wd San Francisco	79	119
Augustus	53	m	w	FINL	Alameda	Eden Twp	68	81
Augustus	45	m	w	DENM	Stanislaus	San Joaquin Twp	92	82
Augustus	27	m	w	NORW	Placer	Dutch Flat P O	76	414
Augustus	15	m	w	CA	San Francisco	11-Wd San Francisc	84	593
Austin	23	m	w	MA	Monterey	Monterey	74	358
B	36	m	w	PRUS	Merced	Snelling P O	74	266
B	35	m	w	SWED	Humboldt	Arcata Twp	72	230
B A	22	m	m	DC	Sacramento	3-Wd Sacramento	77	291
B F	54	m	w	NY	Sacramento	1-Wd Sacramento	77	174
B G	37	m	w	SCOT	Marin	San Rafael Twp	74	46
B R	63	m	w	VA	Sonoma	Sonoma Twp	91	448
B T	37	m	w	NY	Sutter	Sutter Twp	92	128
Barbara	40	f	w	BAVA	San Francisco	8-Wd San Francisco	82	386
Bartelle	39	m	w	NORW	Nevada	Grass Valley Twp	75	146
Barthol	63	m	w	ME	Marin	Novato Twp	74	12
Bell	11	f	b	NY	Sacramento	Lee Twp	77	159
Ben T	23	m	w	MO	Santa Cruz	Santa Cruz Twp	89	393
Benj	67	m	w	NY	Siskiyou	Surprise Valley Tw	89	640
Benjamin	45	m	w	SCOT	Tulare	Tule Rvr Twp	92	267
Benjamin	34	m	w	SWED	Solano	Vacaville Twp	90	133
Benjamin	32	m	w	KY	Yolo	Putah Twp	93	513
Benjamin	21	m	w	SC	San Francisco	11-Wd San Francisc	84	702
Brock	29	m	w	MA	San Francisco	San Francisco P O	83	397
Burwell	35	m	w	MO	Plumas	Seneca Twp	77	50
C	45	m	w	PRUS	Alameda	Murray Twp	68	123
C	38	m	w	NORW	Alameda	Oakland	68	134
C	33	f	w	AR	Nevada	Meadow Lake Twp	75	264
C A	21	m	w	SWED	Klamath	Trinidad Twp	73	391
C K	49	m	w	OH	Amador	Amador City P O	69	391
C M	38	m	w	CANA	Sacramento	1-Wd Sacramento	77	176
C P	33	m	w	ME	Santa Clara	Gilroy Twp	88	69
Caleb	28	m	w	ME	Sacramento	4-Wd Sacramento	77	322
Calvin	36	m	w	OH	Santa Cruz	Soquel Twp	89	448
Carlne	10	f	w	CA	Sonoma	Petaluma Twp	91	345
Caroline	44	f	w	AR	Sonoma	Petaluma Twp	91	349
Carrie	55	f	w	MEXI	Los Angeles	Los Angeles	73	527
Carrie	33	f	w	ME	Alameda	Oakland	68	155
Carrie	13	f	w	CA	Solano	Rio Vista Twp	90	59
Carrie A	20	f	w	MA	San Francisco	8-Wd San Francisco	82	382
Catherin	34	f	w	IREL	San Francisco	San Francisco P O	83	254
Charles	52	m	w	SWED	Placer	Bath P O	76	459
Charles	52	m	w	SWED	San Francisco	3-Wd San Francisco	79	296
Charles	48	m	w	SWED	Placer	Auburn P O	76	367
Charles	48	m	w	SWED	San Francisco	San Francisco P O	85	772
Charles	43	m	w	ME	Trinity	Weaverville Pct	92	222
Charles	40	m	w	SWED	El Dorado	Coloma Twp	72	10
Charles	40	m	w	SWED	Yolo	Putah Twp	93	513
Charles	39	m	w	SWIT	Inyo	Lone Pine Twp	73	334
Charles	39	m	w	NY	Contra Costa	San Pablo Twp	71	358
Charles	39	m	w	SWED	Sacramento	2-Wd Sacramento	77	227
Charles	38	m	w	NY	Placer	Gold Run Twp	76	400
Charles	37	m	w	SWED	Mendocino	Little Rvr Twp	74	171
Charles	36	m	w	SWED	Calaveras	Copperopolis P O	70	255
Charles	36	m	w	SWED	Stanislaus	Empire Twp	92	59
Charles	35	m	w	ME	Humboldt	Eureka Twp	72	258
Charles	35	m	w	FINL	San Francisco	3-Wd San Francisco	79	291
Charles	35	m	w	DENM	San Francisco	San Francisco P O	83	53
Charles	33	m	w	NORW	Marin	Tomales Twp	74	78
Charles	33	m	w	SWED	San Francisco	3-Wd San Francisco	79	292
Charles	30	m	w	NY	San Francisco	8-Wd San Francisco	82	440
Charles	27	m	w	SWED	Placer	Clipper Gap P O	76	376
Charles	25	m	w	VT	San Francisco	San Francisco P O	80	401
Charles	21	m	w	CANA	Yolo	Cache Crk Twp	93	449
Charles	18	m	w	CA	Los Angeles	Los Angeles	73	570
Charles G	33	m	w	NY	San Diego	San Diego	78	495
Charles M F C	33	m	w	DENM	Los Angeles	Wilmington Twp	73	640
Charles R	42	m	w	MA	Los Angeles	Los Angeles	73	567
Charles W	34	m	w	MI	Inyo	Lone Pine Twp	73	333
Charlett	78	f	w	NH	Placer	Dutch Flat P O	76	410
Charlie	40	m	w	SWED	Sacramento	4-Wd Sacramento	77	370
Chars	35	m	w	SWIT	Alameda	Murray Twp	68	123
Chas	49	m	w	ENGL	San Joaquin	1-Wd Stockton	86	152
Chas	44	m	w	PA	Sacramento	1-Wd Sacramento	77	178
Chas	43	m	w	SWED	San Francisco	1-Wd San Francisco	79	13
Chas	41	m	w	NORW	Contra Costa	Martinez P O	71	412
Chas	40	m	w	HAMB	Shasta	Shasta P O	89	463
Chas	39	m	w	SWED	San Francisco	1-Wd San Francisco	79	91
Chas	37	m	w	BADE	Butte	Chico Twp	70	17
Chas	37	m	w	GERM	San Joaquin	3-Wd Stockton	86	221
Chas	34	m	w	NORW	San Francisco	7-Wd San Francisco	81	259
Chas	34	m	w	NORW	San Francisco	San Francisco P O	83	118
Chas	31	m	w	DENM	Solano	Vallejo	90	214
Chas	30	m	w	DENM	Alameda	Eden Twp	68	57
Chas	30	m	w	NORW	Alameda	Oakland	68	236
Chas	29	m	w	FINL	San Francisco	1-Wd San Francisco	79	128
Chas	28	m	w	PA	San Joaquin	Oneal Twp	86	107
Chas	27	m	w	DENM	San Francisco	1-Wd San Francisco	79	70
Chas	26	m	w	SHOL	Alameda	Hayward	68	74
Chas	26	m	w	SWED	San Francisco	3-Wd San Francisco	79	308
Chas	25	m	w	NORW	Nevada	Eureka Twp	75	131
Chas D	44	m	w	MD	San Luis Obispo	San Luis Obispo Tw	87	312
Chas E	60	m	w	ENGL	San Francisco	San Francisco P O	83	178
Chas E	35	m	w	NY	San Francisco	1-Wd San Francisco	79	54
Chris	28	m	w	DENM	Santa Cruz	Pajaro Twp	89	349
Chris	22	m	w	DENM	Yolo	Washington Twp	93	535

Name	Age	S	R	B-PL	County	Locale	Series M593 Roll	Pg
Christ	41	m	w	DENM	Placer	Lincoln P O	76	487
Christ J	50	m	w	IREL	Placer	Pino Twp	76	470
Christian	36	m	w	DENM	San Francisco	San Francisco P O	83	170
Christian	32	m	w	SWED	San Francisco	1-Wd San Francisco	79	91
Christian	25	m	w	DENM	Nevada	Bloomfield Twp	75	92
Christian	25	m	w	SWED	San Francisco	San Francisco P O	83	390
Christian	19	m	w	NORW	San Francisco	1-Wd San Francisco	79	126
Christina	39	f	w	SWED	San Francisco	6-Wd San Francisco	81	117
Christopher	45	m	w	SWED	Nevada	Nevada Twp	75	299
Christopher	29	m	w	NORW	San Francisco	1-Wd San Francisco	79	82
Chs H	44	m	w	NY	Monterey	Monterey Twp	74	350
Chs J	48	m	w	SWED	El Dorado	Coloma Twp	72	7
Clacien	40	m	w	DENM	Nevada	Eureka Twp	75	131
Class	20	m	w	HANO	Sonoma	Petaluma Twp	91	316
Clinis	24	m	w	HAMB	Sacramento	Georgianna Twp	77	129
Conner C	38	m	w	NY	San Diego	San Diego	78	493
Corbley	48	m	w	WI	San Luis Obispo	Salinas Twp	87	296
Corbley	44	m	w	OH	Santa Barbara	Arroyo Grande P O	87	508
Cornelius	32	m	w	IREL	Contra Costa	Martinez P O	71	421
Cullen	44	m	w	NY	San Diego	San Diego	78	484
Cyrenius	58	m	w	NY	Contra Costa	Martinez P O	71	384
Cyrus	34	m	w	MO	Santa Clara	Gilroy Twp	88	76
D	43	m	w	PA	Sacramento	1-Wd Sacramento	77	203
D	40	m	w	IREL	Napa	Napa Twp	75	31
D A	38	m	w	CANA	Tuolumne	Columbia P O	93	351
D F	43	m	w	CT	Sacramento	1-Wd Sacramento	77	182
D J	28	m	w	NY	Humboldt	Table Bluff Twp	72	307
Daniel	44	m	w	SWED	Placer	Roseville P O	76	349
Daniel	37	m	w	ME	Colusa	Stony Crk Twp	71	333
Daniel	35	m	w	NORW	Nevada	Washington Twp	75	341
Daniel	31	m	w	SWED	Calaveras	San Andreas P O	70	190
Daniel	31	m	w	SWED	Tehama	Red Bluff	92	175
Daniel M	52	m	w	NY	Mariposa	Mariposa P O	74	90
David	60	m	w	IREL	Merced	Snelling P O	74	257
David	54	m	w	CT	Butte	Bidwell Twp	70	2
David	48	m	w	TX	Tehama	Paynes Crk Twp	92	160
David	41	m	w	KY	Marin	San Rafael Twp	74	37
David	39	m	w	OH	Nevada	Washington Twp	75	344
David	38	m	w	OH	Solano	Silveyville Twp	90	90
David	33	m	w	IN	Colusa	Colusa Twp	71	282
David	25	m	w	IREL	Monterey	San Antonio Twp	74	315
David	18	m	w	MA	Sacramento	2-Wd Sacramento	77	241
David M	36	m	w	MO	Solano	Vacaville Twp	90	136
Delia M	22	f	w	TX	Tehama	Bell Mills Twp	92	159
Delila	56	f	w	AL	Mendocino	Calpella Twp	74	182
Delwin B	7	m	w	IL	El Dorado	Mud Springs Twp	72	85
Dennis	36	m	w	NY	El Dorado	Lake Valley Twp	72	65
Dennis	20	m	w	CANA	Nevada	Meadow Lake Twp	75	255
Derios	31	m	w	MO	Sutter	Butte Twp	92	92
Dewitt C	44	m	w	NY	Shasta	Stillwater P O	89	479
Dolores	35	f	w	CA	San Diego	San Luis Rey	78	512
Donald M	36	m	w	TN	Mendocino	Point Arena Twp	74	206
Dora	10	f	w	CA	Santa Clara	Fremont Twp	88	64
Dudley	22	m	m	DC	Sacramento	4-Wd Sacramento	77	347
Duncan	50	m	w	CANA	San Francisco	San Francisco P O	83	127
E	13	f	w	OR	San Francisco	San Francisco P O	85	798
E D	57	m	w	MD	Sonoma	Santa Rosa	91	417
E H	40	m	w	NORW	San Joaquin	2-Wd Stockton	86	163
E I	20	m	w	VA	Sierra	Table Rock Twp	89	576
E Mrs	40	f	w	IN	Lake	Upper Lake	73	413
E W	48	m	w	NY	San Joaquin	2-Wd Stockton	86	191
Ebenr	26	m	w	SWED	San Francisco	5-Wd San Francisco	81	5
Ed	47	m	w	VT	San Joaquin	Castoria Twp	86	15
Ed	39	m	w	PRUS	Alameda	Oakland	68	185
Edgar	20	m	w	OH	Sonoma	Petaluma Twp	91	355
Edgar	11	m	w	CA	Yolo	Cache Crk Twp	93	457
Edward	60	m	w	IREL	Tuolumne	Columbia P O	93	343
Edward	48	m	w	SWED	Amador	Ione City P O	69	370
Edward	43	m	w	MD	Santa Clara	1-Wd San Jose	88	259
Edward	41	m	m	VA	Shasta	Shasta P O	89	461
Edward	40	m	w	SWED	San Francisco	3-Wd San Francisco	79	295
Edward	39	m	w	IL	Sacramento	Sutter Twp	77	380
Edward	36	m	w	AR	Santa Cruz	Soquel Twp	89	448
Edward	35	m	w	MS	San Diego	Milquaty Dist	78	476
Edward	34	m	w	SCOT	Mendocino	Anderson Twp	74	154
Edward	33	m	w	SWED	San Francisco	11-Wd San Francisc	84	686
Edward	29	m	w	MD	Nevada	Grass Valley Twp	75	147
Edward	26	m	w	IREL	Colusa	Monroe Twp	71	324
Edward	25	m	w	NY	San Mateo	San Mateo P O	87	355
Edward	21	m	w	NJ	Nevada	Grass Valley Twp	75	196
Edward	18	m	w	SCOT	Mendocino	Anderson Twp	74	154
Edward	12	m	w	CA	Santa Clara	San Jose Twp	88	182
Edward D	45	m	w	MA	Sacramento	2-Wd Sacramento	77	251
Edwd	43	m	b	MA	Shasta	Stillwater P O	89	478
Edwd	26	m	w	MA	Sacramento	1-Wd Sacramento	77	189
Edwd	21	m	w	ENGL	San Francisco	1-Wd San Francisco	79	75
Edwin	28	m	w	ME	Mendocino	Anderson Twp	74	156
Edwin	13	m	w	MA	San Francisco	11-Wd San Francisc	84	588
Eli	44	m	w	PA	Lake	Little Borax	73	419
Eli	35	m	w	VA	San Francisco	11-Wd San Francisc	84	451
Eli	34	m	w	DE	Sutter	Butte Twp	92	99
Eli B	59	m	w	KY	Colusa	Colusa Twp	71	281
Elias S	39	m	w	FINL	Mendocino	Ten Mile Rvr Twp	74	172
Elihu S	33	m	w	NY	Sacramento	4-Wd Sacramento	77	334
Eliza	45	f	b	VA	Butte	Ophir Twp	70	101
Eliza	23	f	m	WIND	San Francisco	San Francisco P O	80	475
Eliza	17	f	w	CA	San Francisco	2-Wd San Francisco	79	268

© 2001 by Heritage Quest. All rights reserved.

California 1870 Census

Series M593

Name	Age	S	R	B-PL	County	Locale	Roll	Pg
Eliza J	50	f	w	ME	San Francisco	6-Wd San Francisco	81	141
Elizabeth	60	f	w	IREL	San Francisco	San Francisco P O	80	379
Elizabeth	39	f	b	VA	San Francisco	8-Wd San Francisco	82	469
Ellen	43	f	w	IREL	San Francisco	San Francisco P O	80	410
Ellen	20	f	w	PA	Stanislaus	Emory Twp	92	22
Ellen	19	f	w	MA	San Francisco	8-Wd San Francisco	82	382
Ely	25	m	w	IL	Kern	Tehachapi P O	73	352
Enoch	40	m	w	DE	Sutter	Butte Twp	92	102
Enos	37	m	w	OH	Butte	Ophir Twp	70	120
Ephraim	42	m	w	MO	Kern	Linns Valley P O	73	347
Erasmus	32	m	w	DENM	Alameda	Brooklyn	68	27
Erastus	40	m	w	PA	Los Angeles	Santa Ana Twp	73	600
Eric	46	m	w	SWED	Santa Barbara	Santa Barbara P O	87	501
Erick A	42	m	w	SWED	San Francisco	1-Wd San Francisco	79	119
Eveline	18	f	w	IN	Santa Clara	Santa Clara Twp	88	148
Ewen	60	m	w	VA	Santa Clara	Gilroy Twp	88	72
Ezra	43	m	w	OH	Placer	Roseville P O	76	353
F	64	m	w	VA	Sonoma	Santa Rosa	91	409
F	56	m	w	NY	Del Norte	Crescent	71	464
F S	45	m	w	SWED	Tuolumne	Columbia P O	93	338
Florencia	7	f	w	CA	Monterey	Monterey	74	367
Floyd	37	m	w	NY	San Francisco	San Francisco P O	83	37
Ford J	51	m	w	ME	Santa Cruz	Pajaro Twp	89	350
Francis	40	m	w	NY	Sonoma	Analy Twp	91	222
Francis	15	m	w	PA	Sutter	Butte Twp	92	97
Frank	44	m	w	NORW	Santa Clara	Gilroy Twp	88	92
Frank	40	m	w	NORW	Amador	Sutter Crk P O	69	413
Frank	39	m	w	LA	San Joaquin	Elliott Twp	86	70
Frank	38	m	w	HAMB	Mendocino	Noyo & Big Rvr Twp	74	173
Frank	37	m	w	IA	Santa Clara	Burnett Twp	88	40
Frank	36	m	w	IREL	San Francisco	1-Wd San Francisco	79	51
Frank	32	m	w	MA	Sierra	Sears Twp	89	557
Frank	30	m	w	ENGL	San Francisco	6-Wd San Francisco	81	92
Frank	27	m	w	SWED	San Francisco	1-Wd San Francisco	79	119
Frank	25	m	w	NY	Yolo	Putah Twp	93	520
Frank	16	m	i	CA	Inyo	Lone Pine Twp	73	334
Frank	13	m	w	NE	Humboldt	Pacific Twp	72	297
Frank	10	m	w	CA	Marin	San Rafael Twp	74	28
Franklin	29	m	w	SWIT	Inyo	Cerro Gordo Twp	73	318
Franklin	28	m	w	PRUS	San Mateo	Schoolhouse Statio	87	339
Fred	45	m	w	NORW	Sonoma	Analy Twp	91	222
Fred	36	m	w	DENM	Sonoma	Salt Point	91	391
Fred	31	m	w	DENM	Santa Clara	Gilroy Twp	88	81
Fred	30	m	w	NY	San Francisco	San Francisco P O	83	350
Fred	26	m	w	HANO	Alameda	Brooklyn	68	37
Fred	26	m	w	SWED	Sacramento	Georgianna Twp	77	135
Frederick	41	m	m	MS	Placer	Roseville P O	76	355
Frederick	40	m	w	NORW	San Francisco	San Francisco P O	85	866
Frederick	25	m	w	DENM	Mendocino	Noyo & Big Rvr Twp	74	173
Frederk	46	m	w	PRUS	Placer	Bath P O	76	426
Fredk	35	m	w	HANO	Alameda	San Leandro	68	98
Freeman	40	m	w	IN	Monterey	Castroville Twp	74	335
G	35	m	w	SWED	Sacramento	American Twp	77	66
G M	35	m	w	SWIT	El Dorado	Greenwood Twp	72	53
G W	47	m	w	MA	Sacramento	3-Wd Sacramento	77	313
Gabriel	48	m	w	NORW	Sutter	Nicolaus Twp	92	115
Geo	50	m	w	SCOT	Sacramento	4-Wd Sacramento	77	367
Geo	46	m	w	IREL	San Francisco	2-Wd San Francisco	79	211
Geo	32	m	w	OH	Yuba	Linda Twp	93	554
Geo	30	m	w	IL	Butte	Chico Twp	70	46
Geo	29	m	w	SWED	San Francisco	7-Wd San Francisco	81	274
Geo	27	m	w	IL	Yuba	Marysville	93	605
Geo	25	m	w	MA	Alameda	Oakland	68	175
Geo B	11	m	w	CA	Nevada	Eureka Twp	75	133
Geo C	55	m	w	NORW	San Francisco	San Francisco P O	83	98
Geo M	31	m	w	ME	Santa Clara	Gilroy Twp	88	74
Geo N	41	m	w	ENGL	Alameda	Oakland	68	142
Georg	42	m	w	IN	Calaveras	San Andreas P O	70	211
George	5	m	w	CA	Santa Barbara	San Buenaventura P	87	445
George	49	m	b	MO	Amador	Ione City P O	69	354
George	48	m	w	ENGL	Santa Clara	2-Wd San Jose	88	281
George	47	m	w	US	San Joaquin	2-Wd Stockton	86	166
George	46	m	w	TN	Calaveras	San Andreas P O	70	219
George	40	m	w	PA	San Francisco	3-Wd San Francisco	79	319
George	39	m	w	LA	Nevada	Eureka Twp	75	137
George	38	m	w	GREE	Santa Clara	2-Wd San Jose	88	314
George	34	m	w	DENM	San Francisco	11-Wd San Francisc	84	460
George	32	m	w	NY	Shasta	French Gulch P O	89	470
George	32	m	w	CANA	Sacramento	2-Wd Sacramento	77	247
George	31	m	w	MO	Napa	Napa	75	23
George	31	m	w	PA	Santa Barbara	Santa Barbara P O	87	455
George	30	m	w	RI	Solano	Silveyville Twp	90	88
George	28	m	w	MD	Santa Clara	Fremont Twp	88	61
George	27	m	w	NY	Colusa	Colusa	71	290
George	27	m	w	MD	Santa Clara	Fremont Twp	88	47
George	27	m	w	IN	Solano	Rio Vista Twp	90	61
George	26	m	w	DENM	Placer	Cisco P O	76	494
George	19	m	w	OH	San Francisco	6-Wd San Francisco	81	88
George A	47	m	w	ME	Nevada	Little York Twp	75	244
George A	33	m	w	MA	Nevada	Grass Valley Twp	75	225
George C	42	m	w	NY	Santa Clara	Santa Clara Twp	88	149
George W	68	m	w	MA	El Dorado	White Oak Twp	72	144
George W	39	m	w	NY	San Bernardino	San Bernardino Twp	78	416
George W	26	m	w	MO	Mendocino	Bourns Landing Twp	74	223
George W	21	m	w	IN	Yolo	Washington Twp	93	534
George W	19	m	w	ME	Santa Cruz	Pajaro Twp	89	341
Gilbert	47	m	w	NY	Sonoma	Cloverdale Twp	91	269
Guadalupe	44	f	w	CA	San Diego	Coronado	78	467
Gustav	54	m	w	FINL	Placer	Alta P O	76	411
Gustave	29	m	w	ENGL	San Francisco	7-Wd San Francisco	81	248
H	60	f	b	MD	Alameda	Oakland	68	136
H	32	m	w	LA	Alameda	Oakland	68	160
H	29	f	w	OH	Amador	Ione City P O	69	363
H	28	m	w	HOLL	Solano	Vallejo	90	203
H	24	m	w	SWED	Nevada	Meadow Lake Twp	75	265
H C	28	m	w	IN	Sacramento	1-Wd Sacramento	77	175
H J	28	m	w	DENM	Monterey	Salinas Twp	74	307
H S	50	m	w	VT	Sierra	Forest Twp	89	532
Hance	41	m	w	DENM	Alameda	Eden Twp	68	83
Hannah	64	f	w	ENGL	Placer	Auburn P O	76	365
Hanry	40	m	w	IREL	San Francisco	San Francisco P O	80	362
Hans	42	m	w	HOLL	San Joaquin	2-Wd Stockton	86	166
Hans	35	m	w	DENM	Nevada	Eureka Twp	75	129
Harford	31	m	w	IREL	San Francisco	1-Wd San Francisco	79	72
Hariett	40	f	w	CANA	San Francisco	San Francisco P O	83	235
Harriett M	44	f	w	LA	San Francisco	8-Wd San Francisco	82	406
Harry	50	m	w	HANO	Butte	Kimshew Tpw	70	82
Haschal	40	m	w	MO	Stanislaus	San Joaquin Twp	92	81
Hector	45	m	w	CANA	Sonoma	Analy Twp	91	235
Henry	9	m	w	CA	Santa Clara	San Jose Twp	88	182
Henry	60	m	w	CT	Sacramento	4-Wd Sacramento	77	342
Henry	57	m	w	NY	Sutter	Sutter Twp	92	123
Henry	50	m	w	CA	San Diego	San Diego	78	502
Henry	45	m	w	SCOT	San Francisco	2-Wd San Francisco	79	209
Henry	43	m	w	IREL	Yolo	Washington Twp	93	533
Henry	43	m	w	MI	Humboldt	Eureka Twp	72	273
Henry	42	m	w	DENM	Contra Costa	Martinez P O	71	423
Henry	42	m	w	HAMB	San Francisco	8-Wd San Francisco	82	432
Henry	40	m	w	CANA	Colusa	Butte Twp	71	271
Henry	40	m	w	DE	Sacramento	Granite Twp	77	155
Henry	39	m	w	HUNG	Sacramento	San Joaquin Twp	77	400
Henry	38	m	w	HANO	Santa Cruz	Soquel Twp	89	444
Henry	37	m	w	PA	Shasta	Millville P O	89	491
Henry	37	m	w	HANO	Sutter	Yuba Twp	92	148
Henry	36	m	w	ENGL	San Francisco	1-Wd San Francisco	79	72
Henry	35	m	w	NY	San Francisco	8-Wd San Francisco	82	423
Henry	34	m	w	RUSS	Santa Clara	San Jose Twp	88	217
Henry	32	m	w	SWED	San Francisco	San Francisco P O	80	385
Henry	30	m	w	SWED	San Francisco	1-Wd San Francisco	79	120
Henry	29	m	b	MD	Monterey	Salinas Twp	74	308
Henry	26	m	w	IREL	San Francisco	San Francisco P O	80	473
Henry	25	m	m	AL	San Francisco	San Francisco P O	80	417
Henry	24	m	w	PRUS	Solano	Maine Prairie Twp	90	47
Henry	22	m	w	IL	Tulare	Tule Rvr Twp	92	270
Henry	21	m	w	IL	Sacramento	4-Wd Sacramento	77	320
Henry	19	m	w	ME	Sacramento	4-Wd Sacramento	77	365
Henry B	30	m	w	AL	Yolo	Cottonwood Twp	93	465
Henry F	43	m	w	MA	Tehama	Red Bluff	92	179
Henry F	37	m	w	NY	Yolo	Putah Twp	93	524
Henry L	55	m	w	NJ	Yuba	Long Bar Twp	93	561
Henry L	42	m	w	OH	San Francisco	San Francisco P O	83	94
Heny	26	m	w	IA	Butte	Chico Twp	70	56
Herman	20	m	w	DENM	Stanislaus	Empire Twp	92	61
Hiram W	43	m	w	NY	Sacramento	Franklin Twp	77	111
Homer	30	m	w	OH	Stanislaus	San Joaquin Twp	92	76
Horace E	41	m	w	VT	Contra Costa	Martinez P O	71	387
Horace H	38	m	w	TN	Placer	Roseville P O	76	348
Hugh	30	m	w	AR	Tulare	Farmersville Twp	92	246
Hugo	28	m	w	PRUS	San Francisco	8-Wd San Francisco	82	369
Hutchinson	22	m	w	IREL	Colusa	Monroe Twp	71	321
Ira	36	m	w	ENGL	San Francisco	San Francisco P O	80	456
Irene	28	f	w	WI	San Joaquin	2-Wd Stockton	86	171
Irvin	52	m	w	KY	San Luis Obispo	San Luis Obispo Tw	87	301
Isaac	38	m	w	KY	Solano	Montezuma Twp	90	67
Isaac	32	m	w	NC	Stanislaus	Branch Twp	92	5
Isaac	30	m	b	VA	Sacramento	2-Wd Sacramento	77	234
Isaac	28	m	w	PRUS	Solano	Rio Vista Twp	90	70
Isaac	25	m	b	GA	San Francisco	San Francisco P O	80	342
Isabel	60	f	w	PA	Placer	Colfax P O	76	390
Isabella	20	f	w	CA	San Francisco	6-Wd San Francisco	81	115
Isabelle	8	f	m	CA	San Francisco	San Francisco P O	80	477
Isreal	40	m	b	AL	Kern	Havilah P O	73	337
Isriel	40	m	w	IN	Monterey	Castroville Twp	74	336
J	57	m	w	MA	Sacramento	3-Wd Sacramento	77	258
J	56	m	w	NH	Sacramento	1-Wd Sacramento	77	202
J	50	m	w	DENM	Alameda	Murray Twp	68	122
J	38	m	w	SWED	Alameda	Alameda	68	15
J	35	m	w	ENGL	Lake	Knoxville Mines	73	405
J	35	m	w	IN	Alameda	Oakland	68	264
J	32	m	w	OH	San Joaquin	Tulare Twp	86	264
J	30	m	w	CANA	Alameda	Oakland	68	217
J	30	m	w	DENM	San Francisco	San Francisco P O	83	87
J	28	m	w	KY	Alameda	Murray Twp	68	127
J	28	m	w	ENGL	San Joaquin	2-Wd Stockton	86	206
J	28	m	w	PRUS	Alameda	Murray Twp	68	101
J	27	m	w	SCOT	San Joaquin	1-Wd Stockton	86	123
J	19	m	w	NY	Alameda	Oakland	68	184
J A	63	m	w	SWED	El Dorado	Cosumnes Twp	72	13
J A	45	m	w	ENGL	Sacramento	1-Wd Sacramento	77	180
J A	41	m	w	NY	Alameda	Oakland	68	263
J A	40	m	w	MA	Alameda	Murray Twp	68	120
J A	35	m	w	IN	Alameda	Oakland	68	214
J A	18	m	w	SWED	Solano	Vallejo	90	203
J B	55	m	w	NY	Nevada	Nevada Twp	75	287

© 2001 by Heritage Quest. All rights reserved.

Name	Age	S	R	B-PL	County	Locale	Series M593 Roll	Pg
J B	38	m	w	VA	Alameda	Oakland	68	143
J B	29	m	w	ME	Santa Clara	Gilroy Twp	88	82
J C	25	m	w	CANA	Alameda	Oakland	68	129
J F	30	m	w	TN	Santa Clara	Gilroy Twp	88	82
J F	27	m	w	NY	Nevada	Meadow Lake Twp	75	261
J G	50	m	w	ME	Sonoma	Sonoma Twp	91	444
J G	39	m	w	MA	Solano	Benicia	90	6
J H	50	m	w	ENGL	San Francisco	San Francisco P O	83	273
J K	40	m	w	NC	Del Norte	Crescent	71	467
J L	38	m	w	GA	Sierra	Sierra Twp	89	569
J M	40	m	w	OH	Sierra	Table Rock Twp	89	578
J M F	45	m	w	PA	Amador	Ione City P O	69	369
J O	38	m	w	IL	Alameda	Oakland	68	148
J O	28	m	w	MO	Solano	Vallejo	90	215
J O	28	m	w	VA	Lake	Lakeport	73	408
J P	33	m	w	IN	Los Angeles	Los Angeles	73	571
J P	24	m	w	CANA	San Joaquin	2-Wd Stockton	86	165
J P	14	m	w	DENM	Solano	Vallejo	90	203
J R	35	m	w	NORW	Del Norte	Crescent Twp	71	455
J S	51	m	w	DENM	Tuolumne	Big Oak Flat P O	93	391
J T	35	m	w	ME	Monterey	Salinas Twp	74	307
J T	30	m	w	IREL	Sierra	Table Rock Twp	89	575
J W	55	m	b	VA	Sierra	Downieville Twp	89	517
J W	45	m	w	VA	Alameda	Oakland	68	193
J W	39	m	w	LA	Sierra	Forest Twp	89	531
J W [Rev]	48	m	w	NH	Sonoma	Petaluma Twp	91	324
J Z	44	m	w	VA	Sonoma	Santa Rosa	91	404
J [Dr]	38	m	w	NY	San Francisco	8-Wd San Francisco	82	359
Jacob	35	m	w	AUST	San Francisco	1-Wd San Francisco	79	57
Jacob	32	m	w	MO	Yuba	Rose Bar Twp	93	663
Jacob	29	m	w	NORW	Butte	Concow Twp	70	9
Jacob	24	m	b	NY	San Francisco	8-Wd San Francisco	82	376
Jacob J	48	m	w	KY	Fresno	Kings Rvr P O	72	213
James	59	m	w	KY	Yolo	Cache Crk Twp	93	428
James	59	m	w	IREL	San Francisco	San Francisco P O	83	151
James	57	m	w	NY	El Dorado	Placerville	72	117
James	55	m	w	IREL	Alameda	Alameda	68	11
James	53	m	w	IREL	San Francisco	11-Wd San Francisc	84	683
James	53	m	w	PA	Amador	Ione City P O	69	369
James	52	m	w	OH	Contra Costa	Martinez P O	71	389
James	50	m	w	SCOT	San Francisco	San Francisco P O	83	184
James	50	m	w	CANA	San Francisco	San Francisco P O	83	325
James	50	m	w	CANA	Tuolumne	Columbia P O	93	337
James	48	m	w	KY	San Francisco	11-Wd San Francisc	84	484
James	45	m	w	ENGL	El Dorado	Placerville	72	108
James	45	m	w	ENGL	Monterey	Alisal Twp	74	304
James	45	m	w	SWED	Nevada	Little York Twp	75	244
James	43	m	w	ENGL	Sutter	Yuba Twp	92	147
James	43	m	w	NY	San Francisco	5-Wd San Francisco	81	11
James	42	m	w	NJ	Los Angeles	El Monte Twp	73	450
James	42	m	w	PRUS	San Francisco	San Francisco P O	80	426
James	42	m	w	ME	Sacramento	2-Wd Sacramento	77	228
James	42	m	w	VT	Sacramento	2-Wd Sacramento	77	210
James	42	m	w	CANA	Trinity	Junction City Pct	92	209
James	42	m	w	MADE	San Francisco	San Francisco P O	83	358
James	42	m	w	ME	San Francisco	11-Wd San Francisc	84	662
James	41	m	w	ENGL	Marin	Nicasio Twp	74	16
James	40	m	w	IL	Los Angeles	Soledad Twp	73	633
James	40	m	w	OH	Napa	Napa	75	50
James	40	m	w	IREL	Marin	San Rafael Twp	74	43
James	40	m	w	MA	San Diego	San Diego	78	502
James	39	m	w	CANA	Los Angeles	Los Angeles	73	557
James	39	m	w	SCOT	San Francisco	1-Wd San Francisco	79	59
James	37	m	w	ENGL	San Francisco	11-Wd San Francisc	84	692
James	37	m	w	KY	Santa Clara	Gilroy Twp	88	105
James	37	m	w	KY	Sonoma	Analy Twp	91	244
James	36	m	w	ENGL	Monterey	Monterey Twp	74	348
James	36	m	w	NORW	Sutter	Yuba Twp	92	149
James	36	m	w	OH	Sutter	Vernon Twp	92	135
James	36	m	w	LA	San Francisco	San Francisco P O	80	540
James	35	m	w	IREL	San Francisco	1-Wd San Francisco	79	62
James	35	m	w	PRUS	San Francisco	San Francisco P O	83	49
James	35	m	w	MO	Solano	Vacaville Twp	90	117
James	35	m	w	IREL	Contra Costa	Martinez Twp	71	349
James	34	m	w	IREL	San Francisco	San Francisco P O	83	19
James	34	m	w	MI	San Mateo	Redwood Twp	87	361
James	34	m	w	DENM	Solano	Rio Vista Twp	90	57
James	34	m	w	IN	Solano	Silveyville Twp	90	90
James	33	m	w	MD	Yolo	Cache Crk Twp	93	442
James	33	m	w	IREL	San Francisco	1-Wd San Francisco	79	13
James	31	m	w	ENGL	San Francisco	1-Wd San Francisco	79	72
James	31	m	w	DENM	San Francisco	1-Wd San Francisco	79	77
James	31	m	w	SCOT	San Francisco	1-Wd San Francisco	79	75
James	30	m	w	IREL	Calaveras	San Andreas P O	70	190
James	30	m	b	WIND	Sacramento	Cosumnes Twp	77	92
James	30	m	w	PRUS	Solano	Rio Vista Twp	90	64
James	30	m	w	NY	San Francisco	6-Wd San Francisco	81	73
James	27	m	w	DENM	San Francisco	San Francisco P O	83	81
James	25	m	w	OH	Butte	Chico Twp	70	15
James	25	m	w	DENM	Sonoma	Salt Point	91	387
James	24	m	w	ENGL	San Francisco	1-Wd San Francisco	79	65
James	24	m	w	IN	Sutter	Sutter Twp	92	123
James	21	m	w	DENM	Stanislaus	Empire Twp	92	51
James	17	m	w	CA	San Francisco	San Francisco P O	83	275
James	14	m	w	CA	Santa Clara	San Jose Twp	88	202
James	13	m	w	CA	Santa Clara	San Jose Twp	88	216
James A	39	m	w	PA	Trinity	Indian Crk	92	200
James C	29	m	w	OH	Los Angeles	Los Angeles Twp	73	491
James E	36	m	w	NY	Mendocino	Navarro & Big Rvr	74	176
James E	25	m	w	NJ	San Francisco	1-Wd San Francisco	79	91
James H	35	m	b	VA	Sacramento	2-Wd Sacramento	77	213
James J	36	m	b	VT	Yolo	Cache Crk Twp	93	433
James J	29	m	w	IREL	San Francisco	6-Wd San Francisco	81	102
James M	40	m	w	PA	Tulare	Visalia	92	298
James T	45	m	w	NY	San Francisco	5-Wd San Francisco	81	19
James W	42	m	w	MO	Santa Clara	Santa Clara Twp	88	171
Jane	50	f	w	DENM	San Francisco	San Francisco P O	80	482
Jane	43	f	w	IREL	Solano	Benicia	90	9
Jane	36	f	w	IREL	Alameda	Oakland	68	209
Jane	35	f	w	PA	San Francisco	6-Wd San Francisco	81	79
Jane	32	f	w	ENGL	San Francisco	San Francisco P O	80	458
Jane	30	f	w	IREL	San Francisco	8-Wd San Francisco	82	301
Jane	26	f	w	IREL	San Francisco	San Francisco P O	83	131
Jane	25	f	i	CA	Nevada	Grass Valley Twp	75	225
Jane	24	f	w	IN	San Luis Obispo	Salinas Twp	87	296
Jane	24	f	w	MO	Mariposa	Mariposa P O	74	136
Jane A	14	f	w	MS	Sacramento	Center Twp	77	84
Jarome B	42	m	w	VT	Yuba	Bullards Bar P O	93	552
Jas	40	m	w	MO	Butte	Chico Twp	70	17
Jas	38	m	w	MO	Tehama	Red Bluff	92	184
Jas	30	m	w	NY	San Joaquin	3-Wd Stockton	86	240
Jas	25	m	w	MO	Shasta	Millville P O	89	489
Jas	22	m	w	MS	Santa Clara	Gilroy Twp	88	106
Jas W	37	m	w	KY	Santa Barbara	San Buenaventura P	87	444
Jas W	37	m	w	KY	Santa Barbara	San Buenaventura P	87	448
Jeff	21	m	w	OH	Fresno	Kingston P O	72	218
Jeff	21	m	w	OH	Fresno	Kingston P O	72	217
Jenny	24	f	w	ITAL	San Francisco	5-Wd San Francisco	81	22
Jenny	23	f	w	DENM	San Joaquin	2-Wd Stockton	86	206
Jeremiah	44	m	w	OH	San Luis Obispo	Santa Rosa Twp	87	317
Jeremiah	34	m	w	CANA	Humboldt	Arcata Twp	72	231
Jeremiah J	45	m	w	VA	San Luis Obispo	San Luis Obispo Tw	87	303
Jerome	50	m	b	WIND	San Francisco	San Francisco P O	80	475
Jerome	29	m	w	MI	Marin	San Rafael Twp	74	37
Jerry	34	m	m	VA	Santa Clara	Gilroy Twp	88	79
Jesse E	35	m	w	NY	Yuba	Bullards Bar P O	93	548
Jim	24	m	b	VA	San Joaquin	Oneal Twp	86	102
Jno	69	m	w	ENGL	Butte	Chico Twp	70	59
Jno	42	m	w	FINL	Sierra	Gibson Twp	89	542
Jno	40	m	w	SWED	Sacramento	1-Wd Sacramento	77	187
Jno	35	m	w	MI	Sacramento	3-Wd Sacramento	77	303
Jno	30	m	w	MA	San Francisco	8-Wd San Francisco	82	371
Jno	29	m	m	VA	San Joaquin	Douglas Twp	86	40
Jno	28	m	w	NY	Alameda	Eden Twp	68	63
Jno R	34	m	w	AL	Butte	Ophir Twp	70	117
Johana	26	f	w	SWED	San Francisco	San Francisco P O	80	531
Johanna	48	f	w	DENM	San Francisco	2-Wd San Francisco	79	226
John	90	m	w	SHOL	Sonoma	Petaluma Twp	91	365
John	62	m	w	NORW	Stanislaus	Empire Twp	92	28
John	60	m	w	ENGL	Sutter	Sutter Twp	92	122
John	60	m	w	GERM	Marin	San Rafael Twp	74	25
John	60	m	w	NORW	Mendocino	Sanel Twp	74	230
John	58	m	w	ENGL	Alpine	Woodfords P O	69	309
John	54	m	w	NORW	Trinity	Trinity Center Pct	92	240
John	52	m	b	MD	Marin	San Rafael Twp	74	43
John	52	m	w	IREL	San Francisco	San Francisco P O	80	462
John	51	m	w	NORW	Santa Clara	Gilroy Twp	88	99
John	50	m	w	HANO	Alameda	Eden Twp	68	59
John	50	m	w	IREL	Sacramento	4-Wd Sacramento	77	335
John	50	m	m	VA	Yuba	Marysville	93	615
John	49	m	w	PORT	Sierra	Table Rock Twp	89	579
John	48	m	w	SWED	San Francisco	1-Wd San Francisco	79	92
John	46	m	w	ENGL	Sutter	Butte Twp	92	88
John	46	m	m	VA	Yuba	Marysville	93	614
John	45	m	w	SCOT	San Mateo	San Mateo P O	87	351
John	45	m	w	IREL	Alameda	Oakland	68	206
John	45	m	w	OH	Sutter	Nicolaus Twp	92	106
John	44	m	w	NORW	San Francisco	11-Wd San Francisc	84	691
John	43	m	w	PA	Solano	Rio Vista Twp	90	61
John	43	m	w	NY	San Joaquin	Castoria Twp	86	8
John	42	m	w	DENM	San Francisco	1-Wd San Francisco	79	119
John	42	m	w	SWED	Amador	Volcano P O	69	381
John	42	m	w	SWED	San Francisco	San Francisco P O	80	474
John	42	m	w	SWED	Placer	Bath P O	76	420
John	40	m	w	SWED	San Francisco	1-Wd San Francisco	79	119
John	40	m	w	RUSS	Sacramento	Granite Twp	77	147
John	40	m	w	TN	Napa	Napa	75	22
John	40	m	w	NORW	Kern	Tehachapi P O	73	355
John	40	m	b	AFRI	El Dorado	Diamond Springs Tw	72	28
John	40	m	w	GERM	Sacramento	Sutter Twp	77	389
John	40	m	w	IREL	San Francisco	2-Wd San Francisco	79	215
John	40	m	b	SC	El Dorado	Placerville Twp	72	103
John	40	m	w	BAVA	Los Angeles	El Monte Twp	73	459
John	40	m	w	ENGL	Tuolumne	Chinese Camp P O	93	365
John	40	m	w	CANA	Sutter	Butte Twp	92	94
John	39	m	w	NY	Butte	Ophir Twp	70	118
John	39	m	w	NC	Santa Clara	2-Wd San Jose	88	304
John	39	m	w	SWED	San Francisco	San Francisco P O	80	371
John	39	m	w	NJ	San Francisco	San Francisco P O	80	410
John	38	m	m	MO	El Dorado	Georgetown Twp	72	42
John	38	m	w	OH	Placer	Rocklin Twp	76	466
John	37	m	w	ME	Alameda	Brooklyn	68	32
John	37	m	w	PRUS	Kern	Havilah P O	73	350
John	37	m	w	MO	Yuba	Rose Bar Twp	93	657

© 2001 by Heritage Quest. All rights reserved.

California 1870 Census

Name	Age	S	R	B-PL	County	Locale	Roll	Pg
						Series M593		
John	37	m	w	DENM	Nevada	Bridgeport Twp	75	100
John	36	m	w	NORW	Placer	Auburn P O	76	359
John	36	m	w	GA	San Francisco	San Francisco P O	83	384
John	36	m	b	WIND	San Francisco	San Francisco P O	80	396
John	35	m	w	MO	Plumas	Plumas Twp	77	31
John	35	m	w	SWED	Mariposa	Mariposa P O	74	135
John	35	m	w	KY	Stanislaus	Empire Twp	92	31
John	34	m	w	NY	Sonoma	Analy Twp	91	222
John	33	m	w	NORW	Alpine	Silver Mtn P O	69	308
John	33	m	w	SHOL	Sonoma	Salt Point	91	386
John	33	m	w	IREL	Colusa	Butte Twp	71	266
John	32	m	w	SWED	Plumas	Indian Twp	77	17
John	32	m	w	NY	San Joaquin	1-Wd Stockton	86	124
John	31	m	w	SWED	Sacramento	2-Wd Sacramento	77	208
John	31	m	w	FINL	San Francisco	11-Wd San Francisc	84	520
John	31	m	w	SWED	San Francisco	11-Wd San Francisc	84	691
John	30	m	w	MO	San Mateo	Half Moon Bay P O	87	407
John	30	m	w	SWED	Solano	Vallejo	90	201
John	30	m	w	IREL	San Joaquin	1-Wd Stockton	86	121
John	29	m	w	ASEA	Monterey	San Juan Twp	74	393
John	29	m	w	NORW	Klamath	Camp Gaston	73	373
John	28	m	w	FINL	San Francisco	3-Wd San Francisco	79	293
John	28	m	w	PRUS	Alameda	Murray Twp	68	101
John	28	m	w	NORW	Mendocino	Big Rvr Twp	74	171
John	27	m	w	NORW	Napa	Napa Twp	75	33
John	27	m	w	DENM	El Dorado	Placerville Twp	72	93
John	26	m	b	MD	San Francisco	San Francisco P O	80	457
John	26	m	w	CANA	Colusa	Colusa Twp	71	282
John	25	m	w	DENM	Placer	Blue Canyon P O	76	418
John	25	m	w	WALE	Nevada	Grass Valley Twp	75	207
John	25	m	w	SHOL	Colusa	Spring Valley Twp	71	344
John	25	m	w	DENM	Mendocino	Gualala Twp	74	226
John	24	m	w	IREL	Santa Clara	2-Wd San Jose	88	330
John	23	m	w	SWED	Mendocino	Point Arena Twp	74	205
John	22	m	w	PRUS	Mendocino	Point Arena Twp	74	213
John	22	m	w	MO	Amador	Sutter Crk P O	69	411
John	22	m	w	NY	San Mateo	Half Moon Bay P O	87	401
John	21	m	w	ME	Stanislaus	Empire Twp	92	48
John	20	m	w	SWED	Los Angeles	Santa Ana Twp	73	599
John	20	m	w	ENGL	Solano	Denverton Twp	90	27
John	20	m	w	MS	Tulare	Visalia Twp	92	284
John	16	m	w	CANA	Sonoma	Analy Twp	91	218
John	11	m	w	PA	Yuba	Marysville Twp	93	571
John A	52	m	w	SC	San Bernardino	San Bernardino Twp	78	440
John A	36	m	w	NORW	Alpine	Silver Mtn P O	69	308
John A	36	m	w	MS	Napa	Yountville Twp	75	84
John A	25	m	w	OH	Tulare	Visalia	92	297
John B	51	m	w	ENGL	El Dorado	Placerville Twp	72	98
John C	48	m	w	OH	El Dorado	Placerville Twp	72	99
John C	20	m	w	NY	Santa Clara	Santa Clara Twp	88	177
John E	36	m	w	SWED	Siskiyou	Cottonwood Twp	89	591
John F C	35	m	w	DENM	Los Angeles	Wilmington Twp	73	639
John G	32	m	w	IL	Nevada	Grass Valley Twp	75	145
John H	44	m	w	NY	San Francisco	San Francisco P O	85	772
John H	38	m	w	AL	Placer	Colfax P O	76	389
John H	36	m	w	IL	Sacramento	4-Wd Sacramento	77	379
John J	48	m	w	NC	Santa Barbara	San Buenaventura P	87	441
John J	27	m	w	OH	Siskiyou	Callahan P O	89	628
John L	50	m	w	PA	Nevada	Nevada Twp	75	302
John M	38	m	w	MO	Alpine	Markleeville P O	69	311
John P	46	m	w	SWED	Mendocino	Big Rvr Twp	74	159
John P	28	m	w	DENM	Nevada	Bridgeport Twp	75	101
John R	43	m	w	SWED	San Luis Obispo	San Luis Obispo Tw	87	316
John R	26	m	w	MO	Siskiyou	Yreka	89	655
John R	20	m	w	MA	San Francisco	2-Wd San Francisco	79	211
John T	38	m	w	NY	Butte	Oroville Twp	70	137
John W	49	m	w	IL	Alpine	Silver Mtn P O	69	306
John W	46	m	w	MD	San Francisco	1-Wd San Francisco	79	116
John W	30	m	w	IL	Sonoma	Analy Twp	91	218
John W	28	m	w	IL	Sonoma	Petaluma Twp	91	365
Jonathan	33	m	w	AL	Stanislaus	Empire Twp	92	61
Jos	49	m	w	MO	Sutter	Butte Twp	92	93
Jos	45	m	w	IREL	San Francisco	7-Wd San Francisco	81	260
Joseph	49	m	w	ENGL	San Francisco	1-Wd San Francisco	79	59
Joseph	49	m	w	OH	Yuba	Marysville	93	599
Joseph	42	m	w	SWED	San Francisco	1-Wd San Francisco	79	109
Joseph	41	m	w	MO	Santa Clara	Gilroy Twp	88	91
Joseph	40	m	w	GERM	Yolo	Cache Crk Twp	93	453
Joseph	40	m	w	SWED	Los Angeles	Wilmington Twp	73	637
Joseph	39	m	w	NC	Nevada	Bridgeport Twp	75	121
Joseph	37	m	w	NY	Santa Barbara	San Buenaventura P	87	448
Joseph	36	m	w	SCOT	Siskiyou	Yreka Twp	89	668
Joseph	36	m	w	IREL	San Francisco	1-Wd San Francisco	79	62
Joseph	36	m	w	IREL	San Francisco	1-Wd San Francisco	79	79
Joseph	34	m	w	VA	Stanislaus	Empire Twp	92	63
Joseph	33	m	w	PRUS	Mendocino	Cuffeys Cove Twp	74	168
Joseph	32	m	w	TN	Mendocino	Cuffeys Cove Twp	74	168
Joseph	31	m	w	ME	Tuolumne	Columbia P O	93	336
Joseph	28	m	w	CANA	San Mateo	Schoolhouse Statio	87	340
Joseph	28	m	w	KY	Yolo	Cache Crk Twp	93	446
Joseph	26	m	w	ENGL	San Francisco	3-Wd San Francisco	79	293
Joseph	18	m	w	DE	San Francisco	11-Wd San Francisc	84	593
Joseph	14	m	w	CANA	Sonoma	Analy Twp	91	218
Joseph	11	m	w	CA	Solano	Rio Vista Twp	90	60
Joseph F	28	m	w	KY	San Luis Obispo	Santa Rosa Twp	87	326
Joseph R	41	m	w	NY	Santa Clara	Santa Clara Twp	88	140
Joseph W	51	m	w	NC	Santa Clara	2-Wd San Jose	88	314
Joshua	33	m	w	MS	Stanislaus	Empire Twp	92	48
Joshua	10	m	w	TN	Yolo	Washington Twp	93	536
Josiah	39	m	w	NH	San Francisco	11-Wd San Francisc	84	488
Judson	24	m	w	MI	Yolo	Cache Crk Twp	93	454
Jule	37	m	w	DENM	Placer	Lincoln P O	76	486
Julia	45	f	w	ME	San Francisco	1-Wd San Francisco	79	42
Julia	42	f	w	SWED	San Francisco	San Francisco P O	80	480
Julia	28	f	w	BAVA	Sonoma	Santa Rosa	91	430
Julius	24	m	w	FINL	San Francisco	1-Wd San Francisco	79	128
Julius	20	m	w	DENM	Stanislaus	Empire Twp	92	60
Julus	17	m	w	SHOL	Sonoma	Analy Twp	91	224
Kate	29	f	w	IREL	San Francisco	8-Wd San Francisco	82	435
Kate	26	f	b	MA	San Francisco	San Francisco P O	80	465
Kit C	22	m	w	MO	Inyo	Cerro Gordo Twp	73	319
Kitty	50	f	b	KY	Siskiyou	Yreka	89	651
L	9	f	w	CA	Los Angeles	Los Angeles	73	569
L	41	m	w	KY	Sacramento	Mississippi Twp	77	162
L	34	m	w	DENM	Monterey	Salinas Twp	74	307
Lafayette	25	m	w	AR	Tulare	Farmersville Twp	92	246
Lancaster	32	m	w	MO	Los Angeles	Los Angeles	73	504
Langford	25	m	w	IL	Napa	Yountville Twp	75	86
Larua	37	f	w	NY	San Francisco	5-Wd San Francisco	81	25
Laughlin	40	m	w	CANA	Mendocino	Navarro & Big Rvr	74	174
Lawrence	20	m	w	AUST	San Francisco	San Francisco P O	80	484
Lena	24	f	w	PRUS	San Francisco	8-Wd San Francisco	82	407
Leopold	21	m	w	HDAR	San Francisco	San Francisco P O	80	460
Lester	27	m	w	NY	Yolo	Putah Twp	93	510
Levis	25	m	w	DENM	Sacramento	Franklin Twp	77	116
Lewis	34	m	w	DENM	San Francisco	3-Wd San Francisco	79	317
Lewis	14	m	w	OH	Sutter	Vernon Twp	92	130
Lewis C	14	m	w	CA	Sonoma	Analy Twp	91	222
Lewis J	32	m	w	SWED	Mendocino	Gualala Twp	74	225
Lizzie J	12	f	w	CA	San Francisco	San Francisco P O	85	716
Lonny	30	m	b	HI	Siskiyou	Cottonwood Twp	89	590
Loren	26	m	w	DENM	San Francisco	2-Wd San Francisco	79	219
Lorenzo	50	m	w	SWED	Yolo	Cache Crk Twp	93	455
Lorenzo	46	m	w	ITAL	Placer	Bath P O	76	451
Louis	50	m	w	FRAN	Sacramento	Franklin Twp	77	112
Louis	36	m	w	SWED	San Francisco	San Francisco P O	80	346
Louis	24	m	w	DENM	San Francisco	11-Wd San Francisc	84	586
Louisa	29	f	b	VA	Sacramento	2-Wd Sacramento	77	226
Louisa	21	f	w	PRUS	Sonoma	Analy Twp	91	225
Ludwig	38	m	w	PRUS	Contra Costa	San Pablo Twp	71	364
Luman	51	m	w	NY	San Francisco	3-Wd San Francisco	79	328
M	8	m	m	CA	Yuba	Marysville	93	615
M	41	m	w	KY	Lake	Upper Lake	73	411
M	22	f	w	CANA	Yuba	Marysville	93	603
M E	20	f	w	MO	Sutter	Yuba Twp	92	148
Maggie	6	f	w	CA	Santa Clara	San Jose Twp	88	187
Maggie	2	f	w	CA	Humboldt	Pacific Twp	72	291
Magnus	27	m	w	SWED	Placer	Bath P O	76	421
Mamy	2	f	w	CA	Sacramento	4-Wd Sacramento	77	378
Margaret	70	f	w	IREL	Sacramento	Franklin Twp	77	109
Margaret	38	f	w	IREL	San Francisco	2-Wd San Francisco	79	183
Margaret	22	f	w	CANA	San Francisco	San Francisco P O	85	776
Margart	45	f	b	VA	San Joaquin	1-Wd Stockton	86	129
Maria	58	f	w	NY	Marin	Tomales Twp	74	85
Maria	43	f	w	PRUS	Sierra	Gibson Twp	89	543
Martha	71	f	w	VA	Tehama	Red Bluff	92	173
Martha	28	f	w	PA	Butte	Chico Twp	70	56
Martin	65	m	w	NORW	San Diego	Temecula Dist	78	527
Martin	45	m	w	NORW	Solano	Denverton Twp	90	23
Martin	32	m	w	DENM	San Francisco	2-Wd San Francisco	79	272
Martin	25	m	w	PRUS	Contra Costa	Martinez P O	71	422
Martin	22	m	w	OH	Yolo	Putah Twp	93	526
Martin	21	m	w	OH	Yolo	Buckeye Twp	93	413
Mary	9	f	w	PA	Sacramento	2-Wd Sacramento	77	253
Mary	88	f	w	VA	Sonoma	Analy Twp	91	235
Mary	71	f	w	KY	Plumas	Quartz Twp	77	43
Mary	53	f	w	MS	Sonoma	Sonoma Twp	91	433
Mary	50	f	w	ME	San Francisco	8-Wd San Francisco	82	315
Mary	47	f	w	KY	Marin	Tomales Twp	74	88
Mary	42	f	w	DE	San Francisco	11-Wd San Francisc	84	425
Mary	40	f	w	NC	Sacramento	3-Wd Sacramento	77	297
Mary	38	f	w	NY	Sutter	Sutter Twp	92	123
Mary	34	f	w	IREL	San Francisco	San Francisco P O	80	459
Mary	32	f	w	NY	Tehama	Red Bluff	92	183
Mary	28	f	w	ME	San Francisco	San Francisco P O	80	457
Mary	26	f	w	IREL	San Francisco	San Francisco P O	80	409
Mary	24	f	i	CA	Shasta	Shasta P O	89	461
Mary	24	f	w	ME	San Francisco	8-Wd San Francisco	82	458
Mary	24	f	w	IREL	San Francisco	8-Wd San Francisco	82	334
Mary	22	f	w	NY	San Francisco	1-Wd San Francisco	79	30
Mary	21	f	w	MO	Sacramento	2-Wd Sacramento	77	242
Mary	18	f	w	DENM	Sonoma	Petaluma Twp	91	354
Mary A	30	f	w	IREL	San Francisco	6-Wd San Francisco	81	72
Mary A C	12	f	b	CA	Yolo	Cache Crk Twp	93	433
Mary E	22	f	w	TX	Los Angeles	Los Nietos Twp	73	581
Mary J	50	f	w	KY	Sutter	Butte Twp	92	93
Mary J	27	f	w	MO	Sonoma	Healdsburg & Mendo	91	279
Mary J	25	f	w	ME	San Francisco	8-Wd San Francisco	82	382
Mary M	23	f	w	MO	Napa	Napa	75	21
Mathew	25	m	w	IL	Sacramento	2-Wd Sacramento	77	235
Matthew	39	m	w	SWED	San Francisco	1-Wd San Francisco	79	115
Matthew	11	m	w	TX	Tehama	Paynes Crk Twp	92	167
Matthew R	46	m	w	MO	Tehama	Red Bluff	92	173
Max	28	m	w	DENM	Los Angeles	Los Angeles	73	542

© 2001 by Heritage Quest. All rights reserved.

Name	Age	S	R	B-PL	County	Locale	Series M593 Roll	Pg
May N	46	f	w	MO	Placer	Colfax P O	76	388
Melo	30	m	w	KS	Sonoma	Santa Rosa	91	410
Merrila	50	f	w	SC	Santa Clara	Almaden Twp	88	12
Michael	38	m	w	NY	Sonoma	Analy Twp	91	224
Michiel	48	m	w	MO	Sonoma	Vallejo Twp	91	455
Michl	27	m	w	FINL	San Francisco	1-Wd San Francisco	79	132
Miles	55	m	w	MA	San Diego	San Diego	78	502
Miles	54	m	w	PA	Alameda	Hayward	68	79
Mollie	12	f	i	CA	San Francisco	San Francisco P O	83	94
Morgan	45	m	w	DC	San Francisco	5-Wd San Francisco	81	36
Moriah	32	f	b	GA	Sacramento	2-Wd Sacramento	77	242
Mork	30	m	w	IREL	San Joaquin	1-Wd Stockton	86	141
Moses	62	m	w	KY	Placer	Roseville P O	76	354
Nat	30	m	w	OH	San Joaquin	Elliott Twp	86	80
Nathan A	25	m	w	NY	San Luis Obispo	Santa Rosa Twp	87	324
Nathaniel	41	m	w	MO	Stanislaus	North Twp	92	69
Neil	31	m	w	DENM	San Francisco	11-Wd San Francisc	84	530
Nellie	22	f	w	HUNG	Sacramento	2-Wd Sacramento	77	238
Nellie	13	f	w	CA	Santa Clara	2-Wd San Jose	88	337
Nelson	43	m	w	NORW	Alpine	Monitor P O	69	313
Nelson	30	m	w	NORW	Stanislaus	Empire Twp	92	61
Nelson	27	m	w	NORW	San Francisco	1-Wd San Francisco	79	119
Nelson C	35	m	w	DENM	Los Angeles	Los Angeles Twp	73	479
Nelson P	26	m	w	SWED	San Francisco	8-Wd San Francisco	82	388
Newman	41	m	w	MA	Colusa	Monroe Twp	71	318
Nicholas	55	m	w	SWED	Mariposa	Mariposa P O	74	128
Nicholas	45	m	w	MO	Sonoma	Sonoma Twp	91	434
Noble	74	m	w	CT	Placer	Roseville P O	76	353
Noble	39	m	w	CANA	Marin	Tomales Twp	74	80
Norman	39	m	w	IL	Amador	Lancha Plana P O	69	368
Norvill	64	m	b	NC	San Francisco	San Francisco P O	80	417
O	70	m	w	NY	San Joaquin	2-Wd Stockton	86	158
O H P	47	m	w	OH	Mendocino	Little Lake Twp	74	200
Oakley	40	m	w	NY	Yuba	Marysville	93	584
Oakley	26	m	w	NY	Nevada	Meadow Lake Twp	75	264
Oasman	32	m	w	NORW	Stanislaus	Empire Twp	92	61
Oli	59	m	w	NORW	Tuolumne	Sonora P O	93	316
Olivia B	49	f	w	MA	San Francisco	San Francisco P O	83	359
Onhoff	26	m	w	DENM	Sacramento	San Joaquin Twp	77	398
Orrin	30	m	w	IL	San Francisco	7-Wd San Francisco	81	242
Oscar	24	m	w	SWED	Marin	Sausalito Twp	74	68
Oscar	17	m	w	PRUS	Sacramento	Granite Twp	77	136
Otte	42	m	w	DENM	San Francisco	2-Wd San Francisco	79	224
Otto	22	m	w	SWED	San Francisco	3-Wd San Francisco	79	292
Owen	40	m	w	IREL	Contra Costa	Martinez P O	71	420
P M	41	m	w	NY	Mendocino	Little Lake Twp	74	203
P M	37	m	w	NC	San Joaquin	3-Wd Stockton	86	233
Pamilia	51	f	w	MO	Butte	Chico Twp	70	56
Parks	46	m	w	KY	Sacramento	Center Twp	77	82
Patrick	47	m	w	IREL	Santa Cruz	Santa Cruz	89	410
Patrick	25	m	w	IREL	El Dorado	Kelsey Twp	72	61
Pauline	26	f	w	NY	Nevada	Meadow Lake Twp	75	262
Pearcee R	31	m	w	MEXI	Napa	Napa	75	10
Perry	41	m	w	VT	Alameda	Oakland	68	132
Perry	40	m	w	MO	Siskiyou	Cottonwood Twp	89	592
Perry	37	m	w	OH	Siskiyou	Cottonwood Twp	89	590
Peter	65	m	w	MD	Mariposa	Mariposa P O	74	101
Peter	64	m	b	VA	El Dorado	Placerville	72	114
Peter	64	m	w	SWED	Mendocino	Gualala Twp	74	225
Peter	61	m	w	SWED	Klamath	Trinidad Twp	73	390
Peter	60	m	b	VA	El Dorado	Mud Springs Twp	72	87
Peter	50	m	w	SWED	San Francisco	1-Wd San Francisco	79	70
Peter	50	m	w	SCOT	San Francisco	11-Wd San Francisc	84	519
Peter	49	m	w	DENM	San Francisco	2-Wd San Francisco	79	205
Peter	48	m	w	OH	Contra Costa	Martinez P O	71	407
Peter	47	m	w	DENM	San Francisco	11-Wd San Francisc	84	675
Peter	47	m	w	NY	San Francisco	2-Wd San Francisco	79	230
Peter	43	m	w	NORW	Nevada	Eureka Twp	75	131
Peter	42	m	w	DENM	San Francisco	1-Wd San Francisco	79	36
Peter	42	m	w	SWED	Sacramento	Granite Twp	77	149
Peter	40	m	w	NY	San Francisco	1-Wd San Francisco	79	35
Peter	40	m	w	ITAL	San Francisco	San Francisco P O	80	416
Peter	40	m	w	DENM	Alameda	Eden Twp	68	84
Peter	40	m	w	NORW	Contra Costa	Martinez P O	71	415
Peter	40	m	m	MA	San Francisco	San Francisco P O	83	37
Peter	39	m	w	DENM	Stanislaus	Branch Twp	92	6
Peter	39	m	w	NORW	Trinity	Hayfork Valley	92	239
Peter	39	m	w	PRUS	Mendocino	Gualala Twp	74	226
Peter	39	m	w	PA	Mariposa	Maxwell Crk P O	74	138
Peter	37	m	w	SWED	San Francisco	7-Wd San Francisco	81	260
Peter	36	m	w	IREL	San Francisco	2-Wd San Francisco	79	214
Peter	35	m	w	IREL	San Mateo	San Mateo P O	87	354
Peter	35	m	w	SWED	San Francisco	3-Wd San Francisco	79	292
Peter	35	m	w	ENGL	San Francisco	3-Wd San Francisco	79	330
Peter	34	m	w	FRAN	San Francisco	1-Wd San Francisco	79	41
Peter	34	m	w	DENM	San Francisco	1-Wd San Francisco	79	24
Peter	34	m	w	SWED	San Francisco	San Francisco P O	80	468
Peter	33	m	w	SWED	San Francisco	3-Wd San Francisco	79	292
Peter	33	m	w	DENM	San Francisco	1-Wd San Francisco	79	75
Peter	31	m	w	DENM	San Francisco	1-Wd San Francisco	79	122
Peter	31	m	w	DENM	Sonoma	Salt Point	91	391
Peter	30	m	w	SWED	Stanislaus	Empire Twp	92	64
Peter	30	m	w	SWED	San Francisco	8-Wd San Francisco	82	357
Peter	30	m	w	SWED	Marin	Bolinas Twp	74	8
Peter	28	m	w	SCOT	Contra Costa	Martinez P O	71	423
Peter	28	m	w	DENM	Sierra	Table Rock Twp	89	576
Peter	27	m	w	DENM	Nevada	Eureka Twp	75	130
Peter	26	m	w	NORW	Santa Clara	Fremont Twp	88	57
Peter	26	m	w	PRUS	Sonoma	Mendocino Twp	91	288
Peter	24	m	w	ME	Solano	Vacaville Twp	90	127
Peter	24	m	w	ENGL	San Francisco	San Francisco P O	83	177
Peter	24	m	w	DENM	San Francisco	3-Wd San Francisco	79	313
Peter	24	m	w	DENM	Marin	Bolinas Twp	74	1
Peter	23	m	w	DENM	Yolo	Merritt Twp	93	507
Peter	23	m	w	NORW	San Francisco	1-Wd San Francisco	79	74
Peter	20	m	w	BREM	San Francisco	1-Wd San Francisco	79	126
Peter	20	m	w	DENM	San Francisco	11-Wd San Francisc	84	685
Peter	19	m	w	DENM	San Francisco	3-Wd San Francisco	79	297
Peter A	28	m	w	SWED	Mendocino	Casper & Big Rvr	74	164
Peter S	34	m	w	DENM	Nevada	Grass Valley Twp	75	162
Philip	70	m	b	MO	Nevada	Grass Valley Twp	75	228
Philip	45	m	w	ME	San Francisco	1-Wd San Francisco	79	124
Phillip F	50	m	w	DENM	Los Angeles	Los Angeles	73	568
R	34	m	w	SCOT	San Joaquin	Douglas Twp	86	44
R	32	m	w	KY	Lake	Upper Lake	73	412
R G	34	m	w	ENGL	San Joaquin	2-Wd Stockton	86	209
R M	30	m	w	NY	Sierra	Sears Twp	89	527
R S	55	m	w	VA	Sonoma	Russian Rvr	91	367
R S	27	m	w	ENGL	San Joaquin	2-Wd Stockton	86	179
R S	22	m	w	CANA	Nevada	Nevada Twp	75	291
Ralph	14	m	w	CA	Sacramento	Brighton Twp	77	79
Rebecca	30	f	w	OH	Butte	Chico Twp	70	56
Reuben	44	m	b	KY	Sacramento	4-Wd Sacramento	77	332
Reuben	35	m	b	MD	San Joaquin	Douglas Twp	86	36
Reuben	21	m	w	KS	Placer	Roseville P O	76	354
Richard	60	m	b	MD	Tuolumne	Chinese Camp P O	93	335
Richard	42	m	w	IL	Kern	Havilah P O	73	350
Richard	38	m	w	SWED	Stanislaus	San Joaquin Twp	92	82
Richard	38	m	w	AR	Los Angeles	El Monte Twp	73	462
Richard	31	m	w	CANA	San Francisco	11-Wd San Francisc	84	531
Richard	30	m	w	IN	San Francisco	San Francisco P O	80	425
Richard M	43	m	w	NY	Shasta	Stillwater P O	89	479
Richard M	22	m	w	MO	Stanislaus	Empire Twp	92	65
Richd	37	m	w	PA	San Francisco	5-Wd San Francisco	81	30
Robert	6	m	w	CA	Sacramento	2-Wd Sacramento	77	242
Robert	51	m	b	TN	Santa Cruz	Pajaro Twp	89	344
Robert	41	m	w	BAVA	San Francisco	San Francisco P O	80	455
Robert	41	m	w	SWED	Sonoma	Salt Point	91	393
Robert	41	m	b	VA	San Francisco	San Francisco P O	80	344
Robert	40	m	w	NY	Monterey	Monterey	74	354
Robert	37	m	w	IREL	Sonoma	Analy Twp	91	234
Robert	32	m	w	ENGL	San Francisco	San Francisco P O	80	430
Robert	28	m	w	SCOT	San Francisco	San Francisco P O	83	80
Robert	26	m	w	MA	San Francisco	San Francisco P O	80	477
Robert	26	m	w	KY	Santa Barbara	Santa Maria P O	87	514
Robert	25	m	w	ENGL	San Francisco	7-Wd San Francisco	81	253
Robert M	42	m	w	NY	Yuba	New York Twp	93	636
Roberts	16	m	w	ME	Contra Costa	Martinez P O	71	450
Robt	65	m	w	ENGL	San Joaquin	2-Wd Stockton	86	210
Robt	54	m	w	ENGL	San Francisco	San Francisco P O	83	106
Robt	30	m	w	ENGL	Sonoma	Santa Rosa	91	424
Robt	11	m	w	MEXI	San Francisco	San Francisco P O	85	828
Robt A	50	m	w	IL	Tehama	Red Bluff	92	184
Robt H	31	m	w	SCOT	San Francisco	1-Wd San Francisco	79	109
Roxy	20	f	w	CANA	El Dorado	Mud Springs Twp	72	82
Rufus	33	m	w	NY	Marin	Point Reyes Twp	74	21
Russell	52	m	w	CT	Butte	Bidwell Twp	70	4
S	38	m	w	ME	Alameda	Murray Twp	68	119
S D	41	m	w	OH	Sacramento	Dry Crk Twp	77	98
S G	40	m	w	OH	Siskiyou	Big Valley Twp	89	581
S W	42	m	w	NY	Monterey	Castroville Twp	74	327
Sam	39	m	w	GA	Butte	Oregon Twp	70	135
Sameriah	63	f	w	CT	Sacramento	4-Wd Sacramento	77	330
Saml	40	m	w	ENGL	San Francisco	2-Wd San Francisco	79	227
Saml	35	m	w	DENM	San Francisco	7-Wd San Francisco	81	253
Saml	30	m	w	NY	Butte	Chico Twp	70	46
Saml	21	m	w	OR	Napa	Napa	75	6
Saml C	28	m	w	TN	Sonoma	Washington Twp	91	468
Sampson	42	m	w	VA	Contra Costa	Martinez P O	71	431
Samuel	61	m	w	NORW	Butte	Wyandotte Twp	70	149
Samuel	44	m	w	SC	Calaveras	Copperopolis P O	70	244
Samuel	42	m	w	ENGL	San Mateo	Redwood City P O	87	375
Samuel	39	m	w	IA	Calaveras	San Andreas P O	70	187
Samuel	38	m	w	VA	Contra Costa	Martinez P O	71	432
Samuel	35	m	w	IL	Alpine	Woodfords P O	69	316
Samuel	35	m	w	DENM	San Francisco	11-Wd San Francisc	84	519
Samuel	27	m	w	IA	Contra Costa	Martinez P O	71	446
Samuel	25	m	w	NY	San Mateo	Redwood Twp	87	365
Samuel	25	m	w	SWED	San Mateo	Half Moon Bay P O	87	402
Samuel	24	m	w	ENGL	San Mateo	San Mateo P O	87	353
Samuel	23	m	w	LA	Sacramento	2-Wd Sacramento	77	249
Samuel	15	m	w	CA	Calaveras	San Andreas P O	70	206
Samuel G	38	m	w	MA	San Francisco	8-Wd San Francisco	82	472
Samuel H	58	m	w	TN	Napa	Napa	75	36
Samuel W	40	m	w	ENGL	Santa Clara	Alviso Twp	88	22
Sanborn	43	m	w	ME	Sonoma	Vallejo Twp	91	452
Sarah	9	f	w	CA	El Dorado	Kelsey Twp	72	58
Sarah	67	f	m	MA	Sacramento	2-Wd Sacramento	77	216
Sarah	44	f	m	TN	Santa Cruz	Pajaro Twp	89	344
Sarah	37	f	w	TX	San Bernardino	San Bernardino Twp	78	432
Sarah	30	f	b	VA	Butte	Ophir Twp	70	104
Sarah	23	f	w	MA	San Francisco	San Francisco P O	80	457
Sarah	20	f	w	NY	San Francisco	11-Wd San Francisc	84	603
Sarah	12	f	w	CA	Humboldt	Eureka Twp	72	257

© 2001 by Heritage Quest. All rights reserved.

California 1870 Census

Name	Age	S	R	B-PL	County	Locale	Series M593 Roll	Pg
Sarah D	32	f	w	ME	San Francisco	San Francisco P O	83	10
Saul	35	m	w	IL	San Francisco	5-Wd San Francisco	81	23
Seymour	35	m	w	OH	Sacramento	4-Wd Sacramento	77	338
Simon	29	m	w	CANA	Solano	Rio Vista Twp	90	56
Smith	28	m	w	IL	Amador	Ione City P O	69	358
Stanton E	46	m	b	JAMA	Plumas	Mineral Twp	77	20
Stephen	45	m	w	MA	Tehama	Red Bluff	92	173
Stephen J	23	m	w	MS	Tulare	Visalia	92	289
Steven	37	m	w	MA	Plumas	Indian Twp	77	18
Susan	24	f	b	VA	Sacramento	2-Wd Sacramento	77	229
T B	38	m	w	ME	Tuolumne	Chinese Camp P O	93	365
T F	59	m	w	KY	Sacramento	4-Wd Sacramento	77	377
T M	59	m	w	KY	San Joaquin	3-Wd Stockton	86	217
T R	48	m	w	PA	San Francisco	San Francisco P O	85	794
Taleff	26	m	w	NORW	Sonoma	Salt Point	91	387
Talifero	52	m	w	TN	Santa Clara	2-Wd San Jose	88	325
Taylor	20	m	w	CA	Sutter	Nicolaus Twp	92	112
Thomas	9	m	w	MEXI	San Francisco	San Francisco P O	85	828
Thomas	55	m	w	AUST	San Francisco	3-Wd San Francisco	79	291
Thomas	55	m	w	KY	Colusa	Colusa	71	297
Thomas	52	m	w	IREL	Merced	Snelling P O	74	255
Thomas	50	m	w	ENGL	Plumas	Rich Bar Twp	77	46
Thomas	45	m	b	VA	Sonoma	Petaluma Twp	91	325
Thomas	45	m	w	NY	San Francisco	6-Wd San Francisco	81	115
Thomas	45	m	w	NORW	Alpine	Markleeville P O	69	311
Thomas	42	m	w	HOLL	San Francisco	San Francisco P O	80	375
Thomas	40	m	w	NORW	Placer	Bath P O	76	424
Thomas	40	m	w	ENGL	San Francisco	San Francisco P O	80	484
Thomas	39	m	w	NORW	Alpine	Silver Mtn P O	69	307
Thomas	38	m	w	SWIT	Nevada	Meadow Lake Twp	75	265
Thomas	37	m	w	SWED	Stanislaus	Buena Vista Twp	92	11
Thomas	36	m	w	IL	Marin	Tomales Twp	74	85
Thomas	36	m	w	BADE	Solano	Denverton Twp	90	22
Thomas	36	m	w	DENM	Marin	Bolinas Twp	74	6
Thomas	35	m	w	SCOT	San Francisco	1-Wd San Francisco	79	126
Thomas	34	m	b	WIND	San Francisco	San Francisco P O	80	342
Thomas	34	m	w	ENGL	Mariposa	Mariposa P O	74	98
Thomas	32	m	w	ENGL	Contra Costa	Martinez P O	71	381
Thomas	30	m	w	ENGL	San Francisco	San Francisco P O	83	224
Thomas	30	m	w	SWED	Humboldt	Eureka Twp	72	268
Thomas	28	m	w	CANA	Humboldt	Eureka Twp	72	274
Thomas	27	m	w	DENM	El Dorado	Mud Springs Twp	72	87
Thomas	27	m	w	MI	Monterey	San Juan Twp	74	391
Thomas	25	m	w	CANA	Sonoma	Petaluma Twp	91	364
Thomas	25	m	w	SWED	San Francisco	San Francisco P O	80	418
Thomas	24	m	w	NY	San Francisco	San Francisco P O	80	338
Thomas	24	m	w	NORW	Butte	Ophir Twp	70	93
Thomas	19	m	m	CA	Nevada	Grass Valley Twp	75	151
Thomas M	32	m	w	IN	Mendocino	Gualala Twp	74	225
Thomas M	28	m	w	NY	Nevada	Grass Valley Twp	75	230
Thomas P	36	m	w	OH	Tulare	Tule Rvr Twp	92	270
Thompson	25	m	w	NY	Placer	Auburn P O	76	375
Thos	63	m	w	ENGL	Sonoma	Cloverdale Twp	91	273
Thos	48	m	w	NORW	San Joaquin	Elkhorn Twp	86	55
Thos	41	m	w	SCOT	San Joaquin	2-Wd Stockton	86	172
Thos	39	m	w	NORW	Alameda	Oakland	68	218
Thos	37	m	w	MEXI	San Joaquin	3-Wd Stockton	86	221
Thos	35	m	w	CT	Sacramento	4-Wd Sacramento	77	349
Thos	34	m	w	ENGL	San Francisco	1-Wd San Francisco	79	35
Thos	30	m	w	IREL	San Francisco	San Francisco P O	83	17
Thos	29	m	w	MO	Tehama	Bell Mills Twp	92	159
Thos	16	m	w	CA	San Francisco	11-Wd San Francisc	84	593
Thos J	6	m	w	CA	San Luis Obispo	Morro Twp	87	280
Thos M	30	m	w	OH	Sonoma	Bodega Twp	91	265
Thos V	47	m	w	ENGL	Santa Cruz	Santa Cruz	89	407
Tom	19	m	w	CA	Sacramento	4-Wd Sacramento	77	363
Toney	13	m	w	CA	Contra Costa	Martinez P O	71	396
Valverda A	3M	f	w	CA	El Dorado	Placerville	72	126
W	7	m	w	NY	San Francisco	San Francisco P O	85	800
W	42	m	w	IREL	Tehama	Red Bluff	92	183
W A	46	m	w	PA	Nevada	Bloomfield Twp	75	94
W B	17	m	w	AR	Merced	Snelling P O	74	264
W H	51	m	w	ME	Sierra	Sears Twp	89	527
W H	40	m	w	TN	El Dorado	Georgetown Twp	72	46
W H	33	m	w	IREL	Humboldt	Eureka Twp	72	259
W H	27	m	w	IL	Sacramento	4-Wd Sacramento	77	372
W J	36	m	w	NJ	Sacramento	1-Wd Sacramento	77	178
W J	30	m	w	KY	Sutter	Butte Twp	92	93
W J	26	m	w	IN	Sutter	Sutter Twp	92	127
W K	41	m	w	PA	Amador	Ione City P O	69	369
W M	51	m	w	PA	Mendocino	Little Lake Twp	74	201
W M	34	m	w	IL	Santa Clara	Gilroy Twp	88	72
W N	38	m	w	IN	Sacramento	1-Wd Sacramento	77	174
W V	21	m	w	OH	Alameda	Oakland	68	201
W W	23	m	w	OR	Alameda	Oakland	68	148
Wade	32	m	w	MO	Calaveras	San Andreas P O	70	176
Wallace	35	m	w	CANA	Santa Clara	San Jose Twp	88	216
Walter	66	m	w	IREL	Sacramento	Franklin Twp	77	108
Walter	42	m	w	MN	Fresno	Millerton P O	72	181
Walter	32	m	w	NY	San Francisco	5-Wd San Francisco	81	9
Walter	30	m	w	ENGL	San Francisco	2-Wd San Francisco	79	268
Walter	11	m	w	CA	Santa Cruz	Watsonville	89	377
Washington	31	m	w	PA	Solano	Vacaville Twp	90	131
Wiley	50	m	w	AL	San Diego	Milquaty Dist	78	478
William	69	m	w	MA	San Francisco	San Francisco P O	83	414
William	48	m	w	NY	Colusa	Monroe Twp	71	320
William	47	m	w	SWED	El Dorado	White Oak Twp	72	141
William	45	m	w	ENGL	Alameda	Eden Twp	68	83
William	45	m	w	MD	San Francisco	San Francisco P O	80	423
William	45	m	m	CT	Sacramento	4-Wd Sacramento	77	342
William	44	m	w	DENM	Placer	Auburn P O	76	360
William	42	m	w	ENGL	Alameda	Brooklyn Twp	68	55
William	42	m	w	ENGL	Solano	Maine Prairie Twp	90	46
William	41	m	w	NY	San Francisco	San Francisco P O	80	469
William	41	m	w	MO	Solano	Silveyville Twp	90	90
William	40	m	w	SCOT	San Francisco	San Francisco P O	83	284
William	40	m	w	IREL	San Francisco	San Francisco P O	80	472
William	40	m	w	MD	Sonoma	Vallejo Twp	91	457
William	40	m	w	PRUS	Plumas	Plumas Twp	77	32
William	38	m	w	PA	Sacramento	2-Wd Sacramento	77	209
William	38	m	w	MA	Santa Cruz	Santa Cruz Twp	89	386
William	38	m	w	NY	San Francisco	8-Wd San Francisco	82	370
William	37	m	w	DENM	Marin	Bolinas Twp	74	6
William	36	m	w	VA	Colusa	Spring Valley Twp	71	335
William	36	m	w	DENM	San Francisco	San Francisco P O	80	422
William	36	m	w	NY	Marin	San Rafael Twp	74	37
William	36	m	w	ENGL	Monterey	San Juan Twp	74	391
William	35	m	w	IREL	San Francisco	2-Wd San Francisco	79	239
William	35	m	w	ME	Tuolumne	Sonora P O	93	325
William	35	m	b	VA	Yolo	Grafton Twp	93	481
William	35	m	w	PRUS	San Francisco	San Francisco P O	83	208
William	34	m	w	PA	Stanislaus	Empire Twp	92	63
William	34	m	w	MO	Tulare	Kings Rvr Twp	92	252
William	33	m	w	TN	Tehama	Red Bluff	92	184
William	33	m	w	IL	San Mateo	Half Moon Bay P O	87	404
William	33	m	w	IREL	Stanislaus	San Joaquin Twp	92	80
William	33	m	w	NORW	Contra Costa	Martinez P O	71	433
William	32	m	w	ENGL	San Francisco	8-Wd San Francisco	82	291
William	32	m	w	ENGL	Stanislaus	Empire Twp	92	47
William	32	m	w	IL	Stanislaus	Emory Twp	92	24
William	31	m	w	ENGL	San Mateo	Woodside P O	87	385
William	31	m	w	ENGL	San Francisco	1-Wd San Francisco	79	59
William	30	m	w	NY	San Diego	Fort Yuma Dist	78	464
William	29	m	w	SWIT	San Francisco	San Francisco P O	80	468
William	28	m	w	ENGL	Siskiyou	Callahan P O	89	629
William	27	m	w	MI	Contra Costa	Martinez P O	71	389
William	27	m	w	MO	Santa Clara	Santa Clara Twp	88	172
William	26	m	w	SWED	Yolo	Cottonwood Twp	93	463
William	26	m	w	ENGL	San Francisco	San Francisco P O	80	338
William	25	m	w	NY	Inyo	Lone Pine Twp	73	334
William	25	m	w	PA	Calaveras	San Andreas P O	70	207
William	24	m	w	MO	San Diego	Poway Dist	78	481
William	24	m	w	KY	Los Angeles	Los Angeles Twp	73	492
William	24	m	w	ENGL	San Mateo	Woodside P O	87	380
William	23	m	w	IREL	Marin	Sausalito Twp	74	73
William	23	m	w	PA	San Francisco	San Francisco P O	83	274
William	21	m	w	MO	Solano	Denverton Twp	90	27
William	20	m	w	IA	Sonoma	Petaluma Twp	91	349
William	19	m	w	PRUS	San Francisco	San Francisco P O	80	463
William A	40	m	w	AL	Yolo	Putah Twp	93	516
William A	38	m	w	GA	Alpine	Markleeville P O	69	311
William B	52	m	w	RI	Calaveras	San Andreas P O	70	164
William C	14	m	w	CA	Santa Clara	Santa Clara Twp	88	177
William H	44	m	m	MD	El Dorado	Placerville	72	110
William H	38	m	w	NY	Mendocino	Navarro & Big Rvr	74	176
William H	30	m	w	ENGL	Sacramento	2-Wd Sacramento	77	224
William J	35	m	w	CHIL	Calaveras	San Andreas P O	70	181
William J	28	m	w	CANA	Yolo	Grafton Twp	93	499
William M	56	m	w	RUSS	Placer	Gold Run Twp	76	396
William T	31	m	w	ENGL	Santa Clara	Alviso Twp	88	22
Willis	61	m	b	VA	Yolo	Buckeye Twp	93	415
Wm	69	m	w	PA	San Joaquin	Elkhorn Twp	86	66
Wm	54	m	w	HAMB	Yuba	Marysville	93	589
Wm	53	m	b	VA	Tuolumne	Chinese Camp P O	93	382
Wm	53	m	w	SWED	Amador	Volcano P O	69	388
Wm	48	m	w	WI	Sutter	Butte Twp	92	89
Wm	47	m	w	MO	Merced	Snelling P O	74	264
Wm	46	m	w	ENGL	San Luis Obispo	San Luis Obispo Tw	87	315
Wm	46	m	w	FINL	Sacramento	Georgianna Twp	77	124
Wm	45	m	w	PRUS	San Francisco	8-Wd San Francisco	82	356
Wm	45	m	w	PRUS	Sacramento	4-Wd Sacramento	77	371
Wm	45	m	w	NORW	Mariposa	Maxwell Crk P O	74	144
Wm	44	m	w	SWED	Humboldt	Eureka Twp	72	268
Wm	43	m	w	UNKN	San Joaquin	2-Wd Stockton	86	172
Wm	43	m	b	NY	San Francisco	1-Wd San Francisco	79	133
Wm	42	m	w	BREM	Sacramento	4-Wd Sacramento	77	370
Wm	41	m	w	PA	Sacramento	Franklin Twp	77	109
Wm	41	m	w	TN	Fresno	Millerton P O	72	156
Wm	40	m	w	ITAL	Mariposa	Mariposa P O	74	91
Wm	40	m	w	SCOT	Monterey	Alisal Twp	74	293
Wm	39	m	b	VA	Butte	Ophir Twp	70	104
Wm	38	m	w	MA	Mendocino	Round Valley Twp	74	221
Wm	38	m	w	FINL	Sonoma	Salt Point Twp	91	383
Wm	37	m	w	MO	San Joaquin	2-Wd Stockton	86	190
Wm	36	m	w	MO	Mendocino	Round Valley Twp	74	221
Wm	36	m	w	OH	Yuba	Rose Bar Twp	93	654
Wm	35	m	w	TN	Alameda	Oakland	68	252
Wm	32	m	w	SWED	San Joaquin	Oneal Twp	86	111
Wm	30	m	w	OH	San Joaquin	Douglas Twp	86	50
Wm	30	m	w	OH	Sonoma	Analy Twp	91	233
Wm	28	m	w	NORW	Sonoma	Bodega Twp	91	262
Wm	28	m	w	MA	Yuba	Marysville	93	632
Wm	27	m	w	PA	San Francisco	8-Wd San Francisco	82	335
Wm	27	m	w	ENGL	Marin	San Rafael Twp	74	30

© 2001 by Heritage Quest. All rights reserved.

Name	Age	S	R	B-PL	County	Locale	Series M593 Roll	Pg
Wm	26	m	w	FINL	San Francisco	1-Wd San Francisco	79	7
Wm	25	m	w	SWED	Solano	Vallejo	90	169
Wm	24	m	w	FINL	San Francisco	1-Wd San Francisco	79	128
Wm	24	m	w	OR	San Joaquin	Tulare Twp	86	254
Wm	19	m	w	TX	Tehama	Tehama Twp	92	193
Wm	17	m	i	CA	San Francisco	11-Wd San Francisc	84	588
Wm A	39	m	w	NY	Siskiyou	Scott Valley Twp	89	619
Wm A	35	m	w	TN	Napa	Napa	75	51
Wm B	43	m	b	KY	Butte	Ophir Twp	70	105
Wm B	32	m	w	NY	Butte	Chico Twp	70	25
Wm C	42	m	w	OH	San Diego	San Diego	78	509
Wm C	37	m	w	PA	San Francisco	3-Wd San Francisco	79	330
Wm F	32	m	w	NY	Sacramento	4-Wd Sacramento	77	332
Wm F	31	m	w	KY	Shasta	Millville P O	89	483
Wm H	58	m	w	NY	Santa Barbara	Santa Barbara P O	87	461
Wm H	54	m	w	ENGL	Marin	San Rafael Twp	74	41
Wm H	43	m	w	TN	San Joaquin	Douglas Twp	86	38
Wm H	29	m	w	PA	San Francisco	3-Wd San Francisco	79	326
Wm L	46	m	w	NY	Monterey	Alisal Twp	74	288
Wm O	40	m	w	PRUS	Sacramento	3-Wd Sacramento	77	274
Wm Rodick	52	m	w	ME	Plumas	Seneca Twp	77	47
Wm S	47	m	w	ENGL	Monterey	Monterey	74	362
Wm S	36	m	w	NY	San Francisco	8-Wd San Francisco	82	334
Wm T	50	m	w	NY	San Luis Obispo	Salinas Twp	87	296
Wm W	45	m	w	IREL	San Francisco	1-Wd San Francisco	79	121
Wright	45	m	w	NY	Stanislaus	Empire Twp	92	45
JOHNSTON								
A	50	m	w	PA	Yuba	Marysville	93	591
Albert	37	m	w	VT	San Francisco	7-Wd San Francisco	81	223
Albert	32	m	w	HANO	San Francisco	7-Wd San Francisco	81	224
Alex	42	m	w	PA	Sonoma	Santa Rosa	91	410
Alexander	52	m	w	NY	Santa Clara	Fremont Twp	88	50
Andrew	50	m	w	SWED	San Francisco	11-Wd San Francisc	84	455
Andrew	25	m	w	FRAN	San Francisco	2-Wd San Francisco	79	241
Anna	30	f	w	POLA	San Francisco	San Francisco P O	85	848
August	22	m	w	PRUS	San Francisco	7-Wd San Francisco	81	218
Balinda	15	f	w	CA	Humboldt	Mattole Twp	72	286
Benjamin	8	m	w	NY	San Francisco	7-Wd San Francisco	81	223
C H	30	m	w	SWED	San Francisco	7-Wd San Francisco	81	219
C M	39	m	w	CANA	San Francisco	San Francisco P O	85	860
Charles	60	m	w	SCOT	San Francisco	San Francisco P O	83	351
Charles	56	m	w	OH	Humboldt	Mattole Twp	72	286
Charles	34	m	w	SCOT	San Francisco	San Francisco P O	80	366
Charles	28	m	w	NORW	San Francisco	7-Wd San Francisco	81	221
Charles	25	m	w	NY	San Francisco	7-Wd San Francisco	81	180
Chas	32	m	w	SWED	San Francisco	11-Wd San Francisc	84	477
Chas	25	m	w	ME	Humboldt	Eureka Twp	72	258
D	43	m	w	ENGL	Lassen	Janesville Twp	73	434
D V	43	m	w	IN	Merced	Snelling P O	74	253
Danial	27	m	w	IREL	San Francisco	7-Wd San Francisco	81	221
Eben	41	m	w	NH	San Francisco	San Francisco P O	85	764
Ed	32	m	w	IREL	San Francisco	San Francisco P O	85	796
Edward	37	m	w	VA	San Francisco	San Francisco P O	83	229
Edward	34	m	w	NY	San Francisco	7-Wd San Francisco	81	211
Edward	34	m	w	IREL	San Francisco	7-Wd San Francisco	81	172
Eliza	42	f	w	MA	San Francisco	11-Wd San Francisc	84	443
Elizabeth	13	f	w	CA	Yuba	Linda Twp	93	557
F E	26	m	w	MO	Napa	Napa	75	41
Franck	28	m	w	OH	San Francisco	7-Wd San Francisco	81	226
Frank	25	m	w	OH	San Francisco	7-Wd San Francisco	81	188
Frank	22	m	w	NY	San Francisco	7-Wd San Francisco	81	216
Geo	42	m	w	PA	San Joaquin	Douglas Twp	86	46
Geo R	1	m	w	CA	Nevada	Nevada Twp	75	271
George	38	m	w	SCOT	Nevada	Grass Valley Twp	75	193
Gilbert	28	m	w	SWED	San Francisco	11-Wd San Francisc	84	519
Hancock	25	m	w	TX	Los Angeles	San Gabriel Twp	73	594
Henery	18	m	w	OH	San Francisco	7-Wd San Francisco	81	188
Henry	44	m	w	PRUS	San Francisco	7-Wd San Francisco	81	224
Henry	41	m	w	NH	San Francisco	11-Wd San Francisc	84	488
Henry	40	m	w	NY	San Francisco	7-Wd San Francisco	81	206
Henry	39	m	w	SHOL	San Francisco	11-Wd San Francisc	84	527
Henry	34	m	w	ENGL	San Bernardino	San Bernardino Twp	78	428
Henry	29	m	w	PRUS	San Francisco	San Francisco P O	83	243
Henry	27	m	w	SCOT	Alameda	Murray Twp	68	105
Henry	25	m	w	PRUS	San Francisco	2-Wd San Francisco	79	242
Henry H	36	m	w	VT	San Francisco	San Francisco P O	83	342
Henry P	20	m	w	OH	Tulare	Tule Rvr Twp	92	265
Isabelle	50	f	w	IREL	San Francisco	San Francisco P O	85	838
J E	41	m	w	CANA	Nevada	Nevada Twp	75	271
J F	27	m	w	SWED	San Francisco	7-Wd San Francisco	81	219
Jacob L	37	m	w	SWED	San Mateo	Half Moon Bay P O	87	396
James	60	m	w	SCOT	Contra Costa	Martinez P O	71	386
James	60	m	w	LA	San Francisco	San Francisco P O	83	348
James	57	m	w	SCOT	San Mateo	Pescadero P O	87	409
James	50	m	w	ENGL	San Francisco	7-Wd San Francisco	81	211
James	35	m	w	IREL	Nevada	Meadow Lake Twp	75	246
James S	50	m	w	IREL	San Francisco	6-Wd San Francisco	81	112
James W	49	m	w	PA	Nevada	Grass Valley Twp	75	150
Jasper	26	m	w	IA	Santa Barbara	Santa Barbara P O	87	493
Jeremiah	45	m	w	IREL	San Francisco	San Francisco P O	85	816
John	63	m	w	PA	Santa Clara	San Jose Twp	88	191
John	58	m	w	SCOT	Contra Costa	Martinez P O	71	385
John	52	m	w	IREL	San Mateo	Searsville P O	87	382
John	50	m	w	ENGL	San Francisco	San Francisco P O	85	776
John	43	m	w	PA	San Mateo	Half Moon Bay P O	87	401
John	40	m	w	NY	San Francisco	7-Wd San Francisco	81	219
John	40	m	w	IREL	Nevada	Grass Valley Twp	75	157

Name	Age	S	R	B-PL	County	Locale	Series M593 Roll	Pg
John	40	m	w	SCOT	San Francisco	San Francisco P O	85	874
John	35	m	w	MA	San Mateo	Pescadero P O	87	413
John	34	m	w	HANO	San Francisco	7-Wd San Francisco	81	224
John	25	m	w	SWED	San Francisco	7-Wd San Francisco	81	223
John	23	m	w	MA	San Francisco	6-Wd San Francisco	81	84
John H	28	m	w	MA	San Mateo	Pescadero P O	87	415
John P	44	m	w	PA	San Mateo	Half Moon Bay P O	87	400
Joseph	51	m	w	IREL	San Francisco	11-Wd San Francisc	84	632
Joseph	35	m	w	IREL	San Francisco	7-Wd San Francisco	81	179
Joseph	27	m	w	IREL	Marin	Novato Twp	74	10
Joseph A	37	m	w	IL	Santa Barbara	Santa Barbara P O	87	455
Juga	11	f	w	CA	San Mateo	San Mateo P O	87	357
L H	10	m	w	CA	Alameda	Oakland	68	243
Louis	35	m	w	PA	San Francisco	11-Wd San Francisc	84	443
M B B	25	m	w	LA	San Francisco	San Francisco P O	85	833
Manuel	28	m	w	SWED	San Francisco	7-Wd San Francisco	81	218
Margaret	8	f	w	US	Nevada	Grass Valley Twp	75	229
Margaret	50	f	w	ENGL	San Francisco	San Francisco P O	83	233
Mary	9	f	w	CA	Yuba	Rose Bar Twp	93	658
Mary	40	f	w	IREL	San Francisco	1-Wd San Francisco	79	104
Nellie	29	f	w	IREL	Santa Clara	2-Wd San Jose	88	333
O N	43	m	w	NY	Lassen	Susanville Twp	73	446
Peter	43	m	w	IREL	Nevada	Grass Valley Twp	75	155
Peter	40	m	w	SCOT	Los Angeles	Los Angeles	73	513
Peter	28	m	w	DENM	San Francisco	7-Wd San Francisco	81	176
Peter	25	m	w	SWED	Klamath	Trinidad Twp	73	392
Peter	24	m	w	SWED	San Francisco	7-Wd San Francisco	81	219
Peter	23	m	w	DENM	San Mateo	Half Moon Bay P O	87	407
R	43	m	w	ENGL	Lassen	Janesville Twp	73	434
R	40	m	w	CANA	Alameda	Oakland	68	216
Richard	47	m	w	IREL	Humboldt	Pacific Twp	72	297
Richard	37	m	w	TN	Merced	Snelling P O	74	253
Robert	56	m	w	VA	Nevada	Bridgeport Twp	75	123
Sam S	45	m	w	MA	Butte	Ophir Twp	70	101
Saml	60	m	w	NORW	Plumas	Washington Twp	77	54
Saml	27	m	w	IREL	Lassen	Susanville Twp	73	441
Samuel	40	m	w	SWED	San Francisco	7-Wd San Francisco	81	219
Sarah	40	f	w	IN	San Francisco	7-Wd San Francisco	81	206
Sarah A	44	f	w	AL	Yolo	Cache Crk Twp	93	422
Silas N	35	m	w	KY	Santa Clara	2-Wd San Jose	88	282
Thoma	35	m	w	UNKN	Humboldt	Mattole Twp	72	283
Thomas	35	m	w	ENGL	San Francisco	7-Wd San Francisco	81	224
Thomas	26	m	w	ENGL	San Francisco	7-Wd San Francisco	81	163
Thomas	25	m	w	NORW	San Francisco	7-Wd San Francisco	81	219
Toomas	54	m	w	SCOT	San Mateo	Half Moon Bay P O	87	394
Valencourt	25	m	w	VT	Alameda	Washington Twp	68	277
William	57	m	w	ENGL	San Francisco	San Francisco P O	83	242
William	55	m	w	NY	San Francisco	11-Wd San Francisc	84	661
William	54	m	w	ENGL	San Francisco	San Francisco P O	83	232
William	50	m	w	MD	San Francisco	San Francisco P O	83	261
William	50	m	w	NY	San Bernardino	San Bernardino Twp	78	433
William	35	m	w	MA	San Francisco	7-Wd San Francisco	81	207
William	31	m	w	IA	Humboldt	Mattole Twp	72	286
William	30	m	w	PRUS	San Francisco	7-Wd San Francisco	81	218
William	30	m	w	CANA	Mono	Bridgeport P O	74	282
William	28	m	w	NY	San Francisco	7-Wd San Francisco	81	186
William	20	m	w	CANA	San Francisco	11-Wd San Francisc	84	536
William C	26	m	w	SWED	San Francisco	7-Wd San Francisco	81	176
Wm	49	m	w	IREL	San Francisco	11-Wd San Francisc	84	649
Wm	45	m	w	PA	San Mateo	Half Moon Bay P O	87	400
Wm	44	m	w	IREL	Humboldt	Pacific Twp	72	291
Wm	37	m	w	ME	San Francisco	11-Wd San Francisc	84	468
Wm	26	m	w	IL	Sonoma	Mendocino Twp	91	298
Wm E	55	m	w	IREL	Sacramento	American Twp	77	65
Wm M	52	m	w	OH	Shasta	American Ranch P O	89	499
JOHNSTONE								
A	44	f	w	OH	Solano	Vallejo	90	178
Hosea H	40	m	w	LA	San Luis Obispo	Arroyo Grande Twp	87	270
JOHONES								
Joseph	63	m	w	FRAN	Santa Clara	2-Wd San Jose	88	287
JOHSE								
H	36	m	w	SHOL	Yuba	East Bear Rvr Twp	93	543
JOI								
---	34	m	c	CHIN	Siskiyou	Hamburg Twp	89	597
JOICE								
Benj C	36	m	w	PA	San Francisco	1-Wd San Francisco	79	102
David	30	m	w	IREL	San Francisco	San Francisco P O	85	773
Edward V	59	m	w	NY	San Francisco	6-Wd San Francisco	81	99
Edwd	43	m	w	IREL	San Francisco	1-Wd San Francisco	79	36
Frederik	32	m	w	FRAN	San Francisco	2-Wd San Francisco	79	253
Henry	31	m	w	ME	Nevada	Meadow Lake Twp	75	267
Henry	18	m	w	ENGL	Sacramento	4-Wd Sacramento	77	331
James	32	m	w	IREL	San Francisco	2-Wd San Francisco	79	178
James	24	m	w	IREL	San Luis Obispo	San Luis Obispo Tw	87	308
John	30	m	w	IREL	Alameda	Oakland	68	182
M A	41	m	w	IREL	Tuolumne	Big Oak Flat P O	93	396
Margaret	30	f	w	IREL	Alameda	Washington Twp	68	291
Martin	37	m	w	MEXI	El Dorado	Greenwood Twp	72	55
Mary	40	f	w	IREL	San Francisco	San Francisco P O	85	818
Mary	30	f	w	IREL	San Francisco	San Francisco P O	85	797
Michael	28	m	w	IREL	Sacramento	Granite Twp	77	154
P J	31	m	w	IREL	Solano	Vallejo	90	156
Saml	25	m	w	IA	Tehama	Tehama Twp	92	193
Sarah	38	f	w	CANA	San Francisco	11-Wd San Francisc	84	535
Sarah	29	f	w	IREL	San Francisco	San Francisco P O	85	835
Thomas	53	m	w	IREL	San Francisco	San Francisco P O	85	821
Thomas	22	m	w	IREL	Solano	Suisun Twp	90	100

© 2001 by Heritage Quest. All rights reserved.

Series M593

Name	Age	S	R	B-PL	County	Locale	Roll	Pg
W W	40	m	w	AL	Monterey	Salinas Twp	74	310
William	29	m	w	ME	Solano	Silveyville Twp	90	89
William	22	m	w	IREL	San Luis Obispo	San Luis Obispo Tw	87	308
JOICHIM								
Richard	41	m	w	ITAL	San Francisco	San Francisco P O	80	413
JOINER								
Benj	42	m	w	NC	El Dorado	Mountain Twp	72	69
Benjamin	38	m	b	KY	Calaveras	San Andreas P O	70	195
George L	5	m	w	UT	Marin	San Rafael Twp	74	29
John	34	m	w	ENGL	San Francisco	11-Wd San Francisc	84	701
William	45	m	w	ENGL	San Francisco	San Francisco P O	83	222
William M	33	m	w	AL	Stanislaus	Emory Twp	92	17
JOINES								
Helena	35	f	w	ENGL	Solano	Benicia	90	1
JOINT								
Victor	36	m	w	FRAN	San Francisco	2-Wd San Francisco	79	176
JOISE								
James	28	m	w	IREL	San Francisco	1-Wd San Francisco	79	20
JOISSON								
A H F	21	m	w	PRUS	San Francisco	San Francisco P O	83	271
JOK								
Ah	39	m	c	CHIN	Butte	Ophir Twp	70	121
Ah	38	f	c	CHIN	San Francisco	6-Wd San Francisco	81	45
Lee	30	m	c	CHIN	Monterey	San Juan Twp	74	400
JOKE								
Ah	51	m	c	CHIN	Nevada	Nevada Twp	75	311
Ah	41	m	c	CHIN	Sierra	Forest Twp	89	532
Ah	30	m	c	CHIN	Placer	Auburn P O	76	363
Ah	29	m	c	CHIN	Sierra	Alleghany & Forest	89	535
Ah	27	m	c	CHIN	Sierra	Butte Twp	89	513
Ah	17	m	c	CHIN	San Francisco	8-Wd San Francisco	82	438
JOKERS								
Joseph	40	m	w	PRUS	San Joaquin	2-Wd Stockton	86	187
JOKIN								
Manuel	35	m	w	SCOT	Alameda	Eden Twp	68	91
JOL								
Ah	37	m	c	CHIN	San Joaquin	Oneal Twp	86	117
JOLAND								
John	45	m	w	SWED	San Joaquin	2-Wd Stockton	86	172
JOLAREZ								
Notale	30	m	w	SWIT	San Francisco	San Francisco P O	80	477
JOLE								
Ah	36	m	c	CHIN	San Joaquin	1-Wd Stockton	86	145
JOLEY								
T	25	m	w	IREL	Lake	Knoxville Mines	73	404
JOLL								
Francis	47	m	w	ENGL	Yuba	Rose Bar Twp	93	663
JOLLEY								
Charles H	36	m	w	PA	Sacramento	Granite Twp	77	145
F M	46	m	w	IN	Monterey	Salinas Twp	74	308
H B	48	m	w	IN	Merced	Snelling P O	74	265
John	46	m	w	ENGL	Tuolumne	Columbia P O	93	338
L C	21	m	w	IL	Merced	Snelling P O	74	265
May	40	f	w	IREL	Alameda	Oakland	68	150
Thomas	35	m	w	IL	Plumas	Washington Twp	77	25
William	41	m	w	ENGL	Placer	Bath P O	76	448
William R	45	m	w	NJ	Santa Cruz	Soquel Twp	89	449
JOLLIE								
John	43	m	w	NY	Shasta	Shasta P O	89	455
JOLLIF								
W B	48	m	w	VA	Tuolumne	Columbia P O	93	338
JOLLIFFE								
William	40	m	w	ENGL	San Francisco	11-Wd San Francisc	84	537
JOLLISON								
Benjamin	28	m	w	ME	San Francisco	San Francisco P O	80	534
JOLLY								
Ah	24	m	c	CHIN	Sacramento	1-Wd Sacramento	77	191
Catharine	35	f	w	IREL	Sacramento	2-Wd Sacramento	77	253
Jack	60	m	w	FRAN	El Dorado	White Oak Twp	72	142
Richard	27	m	w	IL	Sacramento	4-Wd Sacramento	77	322
JOLN								
Ah	30	m	c	CHIN	Sacramento	Georgianna Twp	77	123
JOLSALES								
Pedro	22	m	w	MEXI	Colusa	Colusa Twp	71	283
JOLY								
Ernest	56	m	w	FRAN	Santa Clara	2-Wd San Jose	88	289
Joseph	23	m	w	CANA	Yolo	Cache Crk Twp	93	425
Juliet	15	f	w	FRAN	Santa Clara	2-Wd San Jose	88	326
JOM								
Ah	32	m	c	CHIN	Sacramento	Franklin Twp	77	119
Ah	22	m	c	CHIN	San Francisco	1-Wd San Francisco	79	61
JOMES								
Jane	70	f	w	ENGL	Humboldt	Eel Rvr Twp	72	251
Mary	60	f	w	IREL	San Francisco	7-Wd San Francisco	81	197
JOMICA								
Peter	52	m	b	EIND	San Francisco	San Francisco P O	80	430
JON								
Ah	62	m	c	CHIN	Sacramento	Center Twp	77	85
Ah	50	m	c	CHIN	Sacramento	Georgianna Twp	77	131
Ah	45	m	c	CHIN	Sierra	Table Rock Twp	89	571
Ah	42	m	c	CHIN	Sacramento	Georgianna Twp	77	133
Ah	40	m	c	CHIN	San Joaquin	2-Wd Stockton	86	212
Ah	40	m	c	CHIN	Sacramento	Granite Twp	77	137
Ah	39	m	c	CHIN	Butte	Hamilton Twp	70	68
Ah	37	m	c	CHIN	Sacramento	Georgianna Twp	77	134
Ah	31	m	c	CHIN	Nevada	Meadow Lake Twp	75	256
Ah	30	m	c	CHIN	Contra Costa	Martinez P O	71	397
Ah	30	m	c	CHIN	Butte	Hamilton Twp	70	67
Ah	30	m	c	CHIN	Butte	Wyandotte Twp	70	146
Ah	29	m	c	CHIN	Placer	Newcastle Twp	76	479
Ah	28	m	c	CHIN	Amador	Drytown P O	69	420
Ah	25	m	c	CHIN	San Mateo	San Mateo P O	87	357
Ah	25	m	c	CHIN	Sacramento	Granite Twp	77	137
Ah	24	m	c	CHIN	San Francisco	3-Wd San Francisco	79	303
Ah	24	m	c	CHIN	Stanislaus	Emory Twp	92	17
Ah	20	m	c	CHIN	Alameda	Oakland	68	266
Ah	20	m	c	CHIN	Sacramento	3-Wd Sacramento	77	269
Ah	19	m	c	CHIN	Nevada	Meadow Lake Twp	75	256
Ah	16	m	c	CHIN	Sacramento	1-Wd Sacramento	77	198
Chang	34	m	c	CHIN	San Joaquin	1-Wd Stockton	86	146
Lon	36	m	c	CHIN	San Francisco	2-Wd San Francisco	79	158
Yon	40	m	c	CHIN	San Joaquin	1-Wd Stockton	86	143
Yung	12	m	c	CHIN	San Francisco	San Francisco P O	83	58
JONAN								
Wm	21	m	w	IREL	Santa Clara	Gilroy Twp	88	93
JONARD								
Elysees	19	m	w	FRAN	San Francisco	1-Wd San Francisco	79	111
JONAS								
Alfred	21	m	w	ENGL	San Francisco	San Francisco P O	80	396
Antone	27	m	w	PORT	Monterey	San Juan Twp	74	415
Charles	35	m	w	EIND	San Joaquin	2-Wd Stockton	86	173
Isaac A	59	m	w	ENGL	San Francisco	1-Wd San Francisco	79	99
Morris	36	m	w	OH	Sutter	Butte Twp	92	104
Nathaniel	24	m	w	OH	Sutter	Yuba Twp	92	146
Nathaniel	23	m	w	VT	Sutter	Butte Twp	92	101
Peter	41	m	w	PRUS	Amador	Volcano P O	69	374
Robert	40	m	w	FRAN	San Francisco	San Francisco P O	80	350
William	40	m	w	PRUS	San Joaquin	2-Wd Stockton	86	176
William	24	m	w	IL	Sutter	Butte Twp	92	102
Williams	37	m	w	IN	Sutter	Vernon Twp	92	139
JONATAYO								
Jose	35	m	w	NM	Marin	San Rafael Twp	74	34
JONATHAN								
J	23	m	w	ENGL	Lake	Knoxville Mines	73	404
JONAYIN								
Andrew	35	m	w	MEXI	Napa	Napa Twp	75	68
JONCIERES								
Josephine	54	f	w	FRAN	San Francisco	6-Wd San Francisco	81	45
JONDONI								
Pietro	29	m	w	ITAL	San Francisco	1-Wd San Francisco	79	110
JONE								
Ah	17	m	c	CHIN	Plumas	Plumas Twp	77	30
John	16	m	w	UT	San Joaquin	Oneal Twp	86	104
JONEAS								
Jennie	26	f	w	IREL	San Francisco	San Francisco P O	80	459
JONEES								
David A	46	m	w	WALE	Butte	Oregon Twp	70	125
JONELLE								
Aveline	12	f	w	CA	San Francisco	11-Wd San Francisc	84	501
JONES								
A	52	f	w	KY	Alameda	Oakland	68	198
A	45	m	w	OH	San Joaquin	Oneal Twp	86	115
A J	35	m	w	IREL	San Francisco	San Francisco P O	85	781
A J	20	m	w	OH	Sutter	Yuba Twp	92	148
Aaron	25	m	w	NY	San Francisco	5-Wd San Francisco	81	20
Aaron Sr	40	m	w	IN	Santa Clara	San Jose Twp	88	222
Abby	36	f	w	ME	Yolo	Grafton Twp	93	492
Abert S	23	m	w	IL	El Dorado	Placerville Twp	72	105
Abial J	37	m	w	NY	Tulare	Tule Rvr Twp	92	259
Adam	31	m	w	NC	San Joaquin	Dent Twp	86	18
Adam	25	m	w	NY	San Francisco	5-Wd San Francisco	81	14
Addison	40	m	w	OH	Santa Clara	Fremont Twp	88	52
Albert	41	m	w	ME	Santa Cruz	Santa Cruz	89	433
Albert	38	m	w	IN	Sacramento	Mississippi Twp	77	162
Albert	36	m	w	NY	Merced	Snelling P O	74	261
Albert	24	m	w	ENGL	San Joaquin	Oneal Twp	86	105
Alexander	48	m	w	VA	Los Angeles	Los Nietos Twp	73	590
Alexander	43	m	w	MA	Los Angeles	Wilmington Twp	73	636
Alford	23	m	w	ENGL	San Francisco	7-Wd San Francisco	81	171
Alfred	40	m	w	GA	Tehama	Tehama Twp	92	187
Alfred	36	m	w	VT	Santa Clara	Milpitas Twp	88	108
Alfred	36	m	w	GA	Tehama	Tehama Twp	92	196
Alfred	19	m	w	ME	Los Angeles	Wilmington Twp	73	634
Ambrose	47	m	w	VA	Sonoma	Salt Point	91	381
Amelia	65	f	b	MD	San Joaquin	2-Wd Stockton	86	212
Amos	21	m	w	MO	Santa Barbara	San Buenaventura P	87	434
And	22	m	w	NY	San Joaquin	Elkhorn Twp	86	53
Andrew	41	m	w	SWED	Placer	Bath P O	76	457
Andrew	25	m	w	NY	Sonoma	Petaluma Twp	91	324
Andrew	25	m	b	VA	San Francisco	San Francisco P O	80	417
Andrew	23	m	w	NY	San Joaquin	Elkhorn Twp	86	55
Andrew S	36	m	w	VA	Santa Clara	Santa Clara Twp	88	147
Ann	48	f	w	WALE	Sacramento	3-Wd Sacramento	77	277
Ann	20	f	w	MO	Sacramento	3-Wd Sacramento	77	280
Anna	35	f	w	ENGL	Butte	Oregon Twp	70	127
Anne	27	f	w	IREL	San Francisco	San Francisco P O	83	129
Annie	43	f	w	MA	San Francisco	11-Wd San Francisc	84	514
Annie	18	f	w	CA	Tuolumne	Columbia P O	93	361
Annie	16	f	w	MA	San Francisco	San Francisco P O	83	297
Anson	23	m	w	GA	Placer	Bath P O	76	429
Arthur	32	m	w	PA	San Francisco	1-Wd San Francisco	79	124
Asa M	45	m	w	MO	Siskiyou	Cottonwood Twp	89	590
Aug	20	m	w	AR	San Joaquin	Castoria Twp	86	4
Augustus	51	m	w	NC	Merced	Snelling P O	74	252

© 2001 by Heritage Quest. All rights reserved.

Name	Age	S	R	B-PL	County	Locale	Roll	Pg
						Series M593		
Augustus	39	m	w	MO	Kern	Bakersfield P O	73	359
Austin	36	m	w	ENGL	Plumas	Washington Twp	77	54
Barnard	22	m	w	ME	Alameda	Brooklyn	68	32
Benj	35	m	w	WALE	San Francisco	1-Wd San Francisco	79	45
Benj J	17	m	w	PA	Sierra	Table Rock Twp	89	571
Benjamin	70	m	w	KY	Sonoma	Sonoma Twp	91	449
Benjamin	69	m	w	NC	Sonoma	Sonoma Twp	91	444
Benjamin	44	m	w	ENGL	Contra Costa	Martinez P O	71	414
Benjamin	39	m	w	WALE	Contra Costa	Martinez P O	71	429
Benjamin	38	m	w	PA	San Diego	San Luis Rey	78	513
Benjamin	35	m	w	NY	Amador	Ione City P O	69	362
Benjamin	32	m	w	NY	Contra Costa	San Pablo Twp	71	355
Benjamin	31	m	w	WALE	Placer	Bath P O	76	436
Benjamin	29	m	w	IL	Colusa	Stony Crk Twp	71	327
Benjamin H	43	m	w	PA	Yolo	Cottonwood Twp	93	462
Bessie	26	f	w	IREL	San Francisco	8-Wd San Francisco	82	301
Bollmer	44	m	w	OH	Santa Clara	Santa Clara Twp	88	140
Boon	32	m	w	IL	Nevada	Eureka Twp	75	135
Bridget	24	f	w	IREL	San Francisco	1-Wd San Francisco	79	105
Bryan	31	m	w	ME	Stanislaus	Empire Twp	92	45
Byron S	28	m	w	NY	Nevada	Nevada Twp	75	315
C	37	m	w	WALE	Solano	Vallejo	90	160
C	27	m	w	IL	Lake	Lower Lake	73	423
C B	35	m	w	NY	San Francisco	8-Wd San Francisco	82	364
C E	34	m	w	ME	Sutter	Butte Twp	92	92
C E	25	m	w	US	Sacramento	1-Wd Sacramento	77	183
C M	30	m	w	AR	Lake	Scotts Crk	73	427
Calton B	40	m	w	MO	San Luis Obispo	Salinas Twp	87	290
Carolina	16	f	i	CA	Santa Barbara	Santa Barbara P O	87	458
Carrie A	24	f	w	OH	San Francisco	7-Wd San Francisco	81	255
Catharine	60	f	w	IREL	San Francisco	San Francisco P O	83	87
Catharine	34	m	w	ENGL	San Francisco	7-Wd San Francisco	81	247
Catherine	48	f	w	BADE	Santa Clara	2-Wd San Jose	88	325
Charles	49	m	w	ENGL	San Francisco	7-Wd San Francisco	81	172
Charles	45	m	w	DE	Sacramento	Franklin Twp	77	108
Charles	40	m	w	NY	San Francisco	11-Wd San Francisc	84	626
Charles	40	m	w	NY	Inyo	Lone Pine Twp	73	334
Charles	37	m	w	MO	Stanislaus	Empire Twp	92	38
Charles	35	m	w	PORT	Santa Clara	Milpitas Twp	88	110
Charles	34	m	w	NY	Plumas	Plumas Twp	77	26
Charles	32	m	w	CANA	San Francisco	11-Wd San Francisc	84	531
Charles	32	m	w	US	Nevada	Grass Valley Twp	75	230
Charles	32	m	w	IA	Yolo	Cottonwood Twp	93	473
Charles	31	m	w	MD	San Francisco	1-Wd San Francisco	79	106
Charles	30	m	w	KS	Marin	San Rafael Twp	74	42
Charles	27	m	w	ENGL	Stanislaus	Empire Twp	92	38
Charles	25	m	w	NY	San Francisco	5-Wd San Francisco	81	25
Charles	24	m	w	IL	San Diego	Coronado	78	467
Charles	11	m	w	CA	Mariposa	Mariposa P O	74	94
Charles A	30	m	w	CANA	San Francisco	San Francisco P O	83	180
Charles F	48	m	w	NJ	San Francisco	6-Wd San Francisco	81	79
Chas	32	m	w	IA	Tehama	Tehama Twp	92	192
Chas	21	m	w	NY	San Francisco	1-Wd San Francisco	79	64
Chas H	36	m	w	ME	El Dorado	Greenwood Twp	72	50
Chas P	34	m	w	ENGL	Fresno	Millerton P O	72	155
Chas R	37	m	w	VT	San Francisco	1-Wd San Francisco	79	39
Chs	11	m	w	CA	Merced	Snelling P O	74	254
Clarence	35	m	w	IA	San Francisco	5-Wd San Francisco	81	30
Clayton	39	m	b	VA	Napa	Napa	75	49
Clayton	30	m	b	MO	Solano	Suisun Twp	90	113
Clementina	42	f	w	MA	San Francisco	San Francisco P O	83	47
Cyru	49	m	w	ENGL	San Joaquin	Elliott Twp	86	71
Cyrus	45	m	w	MA	San Francisco	11-Wd San Francisc	84	510
Cyrus	36	m	w	TN	Stanislaus	Branch Twp	92	2
Cyrus	28	m	w	ME	San Francisco	11-Wd San Francisc	84	483
D	26	m	w	WALE	Lake	Lower Lake	73	416
D E	41	m	w	IN	Sacramento	4-Wd Sacramento	77	352
D R	50	m	w	WALE	Humboldt	Eureka Twp	72	272
Daniel	52	m	w	CANA	San Francisco	San Francisco P O	83	60
Daniel	46	m	w	WALE	Contra Costa	Martinez P O	71	425
Daniel	40	m	w	ENGL	Amador	Drytown P O	69	425
Daniel E	32	m	w	OH	Mariposa	Mariposa P O	74	91
Daniel M	31	m	w	PA	Nevada	Eureka Twp	75	126
Danl	68	m	w	WALE	Butte	Kimshew Tpw	70	83
Danl	13	m	w	WI	San Francisco	11-Wd San Francisc	84	640
David	46	m	w	ENGL	Sonoma	Sonoma Twp	91	445
David	46	m	w	WALE	San Francisco	San Francisco P O	83	331
David	42	m	w	WALE	Calaveras	Copperopolis P O	70	243
David	40	m	w	WALE	Contra Costa	Martinez P O	71	425
David	35	m	w	IREL	San Francisco	San Francisco P O	83	151
David	35	m	w	WALE	San Francisco	1-Wd San Francisco	79	61
David	35	m	w	VT	Yuba	East Bear Rvr Twp	93	545
David	32	m	w	IREL	San Francisco	San Francisco P O	80	472
David	32	m	w	IN	Sonoma	Sonoma Twp	91	444
David	30	m	w	WALE	Contra Costa	Martinez P O	71	428
David	27	m	w	ENGL	San Francisco	11-Wd San Francisc	84	501
David	26	m	w	WALE	Contra Costa	Martinez P O	71	427
David	25	m	w	WALE	Solano	Vallejo	90	203
David	25	m	w	WALE	Contra Costa	Martinez P O	71	453
David	24	m	w	KY	Contra Costa	Martinez P O	71	427
David	24	m	w	WALE	Butte	Oregon Twp	70	125
David	24	m	w	IREL	Los Angeles	Los Angeles	73	532
David	18	m	w	MO	San Francisco	7-Wd San Francisco	81	184
David A	37	m	w	PA	Nevada	Rough & Ready Twp	75	325
Dinah	36	f	b	VA	Sacramento	2-Wd Sacramento	77	214
Duglass W Ap	40	m	w	MD	Santa Barbara	Santa Barbara P O	87	458
Dunham	43	m	w	CANA	Sonoma	Analy Twp	91	233

Name	Age	S	R	B-PL	County	Locale	Roll	Pg
						Series M593		
E D	40	m	w	NJ	Trinity	Canyon City Pct	92	201
E Floyd	47	m	w	NY	San Joaquin	2-Wd Stockton	86	178
E J	43	m	w	NY	Alameda	Oakland	68	139
E J	37	m	w	ENGL	Solano	Vallejo	90	182
E T	44	m	w	WALE	Sierra	Sears Twp	89	556
Eben E	44	m	w	WALE	San Francisco	1-Wd San Francisco	79	23
Ebenezer	48	m	w	CANA	Sutter	Butte Twp	92	93
Ed	31	m	w	ENGL	Sierra	Forest Twp	89	530
Edmond	50	m	w	PA	Alameda	Brooklyn Twp	68	46
Edmund	43	m	w	ENGL	Santa Cruz	Santa Cruz	89	405
Edmund	42	m	w	ENGL	San Francisco	San Francisco P O	83	120
Edmund M	28	m	w	ENGL	Mono	Bridgeport P O	74	283
Edward	50	m	w	NY	Yuba	W Bear Rvr Twp	93	684
Edward	45	m	w	IREL	Nevada	Grass Valley Twp	75	214
Edward A	33	m	w	MD	Placer	Auburn P O	76	372
Edward W	21	m	w	WI	Colusa	Colusa	71	288
Edwd	31	m	w	ENGL	San Francisco	1-Wd San Francisco	79	130
Edwd	19	m	w	ME	Butte	Chico Twp	70	58
Edwd R	36	m	w	KY	Shasta	Horsetown P O	89	503
Edwin A	42	m	w	VT	El Dorado	Salmon Falls Twp	72	129
Edwin R	38	m	w	CA	El Dorado	Placerville Twp	72	99
Elias	42	m	w	MA	Tehama	Antelope Twp	92	154
Elias	42	m	w	MA	Tehama	Cottonwood Twp	92	161
Elimina	42	m	w	ME	Sacramento	3-Wd Sacramento	77	305
Eliza	60	f	w	NJ	Yuba	W Bear Rvr Twp	93	681
Eliza	30	f	w	NY	San Francisco	1-Wd San Francisco	79	107
Elizabeth	66	f	w	PA	San Francisco	11-Wd San Francisc	84	561
Elizabeth	64	f	w	ENGL	Santa Barbara	Santa Barbara P O	87	476
Elizabeth	21	f	w	DC	San Francisco	San Francisco P O	83	62
Elizabeth	20	f	w	WALE	Contra Costa	Martinez P O	71	371
Ella	44	f	w	ENGL	Contra Costa	Martinez P O	71	417
Ellen	32	f	w	IREL	San Mateo	Redwood Twp	87	364
Ellsworth L	25	m	w	ME	Santa Cruz	Soquel Twp	89	445
Etta	27	f	w	ME	Sacramento	2-Wd Sacramento	77	221
Eugene C	19	m	w	ME	Santa Cruz	Santa Cruz Twp	89	397
Evan	22	m	w	ENGL	Solano	Tremont Twp	90	28
Evan J	41	m	w	WALE	Sierra	Sears Twp	89	561
Evan L	36	m	w	IN	Shasta	Horsetown P O	89	501
Evan L	29	m	w	WALE	Sierra	Sears Twp	89	554
Ezra A	70	m	w	VT	Los Angeles	San Gabriel Twp	73	596
F E	39	m	w	NY	Trinity	Douglas	92	235
Fillmore	14	m	w	IL	San Francisco	11-Wd San Francisc	84	588
Fleming	20	m	w	WI	El Dorado	Lake Valley Twp	72	65
Flora	20	f	w	CA	Solano	Suisun Twp	90	102
Frances	25	f	w	OH	Napa	Napa	75	51
Frances A	40	f	w	TN	San Francisco	6-Wd San Francisco	81	132
Francis	40	m	w	BADE	Butte	Hamilton Twp	70	70
Francis	25	m	w	ENGL	Nevada	Grass Valley Twp	75	195
Francis	25	m	w	IN	Tehama	Red Bank Twp	92	169
Frank	41	m	w	IREL	Alameda	Oakland	68	175
Frank	37	m	w	BADE	Tehama	Merrill	92	197
Frank	36	m	w	AR	Santa Clara	Burnett Twp	88	36
Frank	32	m	w	NY	San Francisco	2-Wd San Francisco	79	159
Frank	31	m	w	PORT	San Francisco	1-Wd San Francisco	79	101
Frank	30	m	m	US	Nevada	Grass Valley Twp	75	188
Frank	27	m	w	IL	Sacramento	Lee Twp	77	160
Frank	16	m	w	CA	Marin	Novato Twp	74	13
Frank A S	42	m	w	OH	Alpine	Silver Mtn P O	69	307
Franklin P	27	m	w	IL	San Luis Obispo	San Luis Obispo Tw	87	297
Franklyn L	53	m	w	DE	San Francisco	5-Wd San Francisco	81	3
Fredenburgh	41	m	w	MD	Placer	Auburn P O	76	359
Frederick	43	m	w	VT	Solano	Green Valley Twp	90	41
Frederick W	44	m	w	MA	Santa Cruz	Watsonville	89	374
Fredk	35	m	b	MD	Santa Barbara	Santa Barbara P O	87	501
Fredrick	36	m	w	NY	Siskiyou	Big Valley Twp	89	581
Fredrick	27	m	w	NY	San Francisco	San Francisco P O	83	211
Fredrick	24	m	w	FRAN	San Francisco	San Francisco P O	80	336
Fremont	14	m	w	IL	San Francisco	11-Wd San Francisc	84	588
G C	25	m	w	NY	San Francisco	3-Wd San Francisco	79	311
G D	40	m	w	MO	Tehama	Deer Crk Twp	92	170
G E	25	m	w	MA	Yuba	Marysville	93	606
G G	47	m	w	CT	Monterey	San Juan Twp	74	397
G M	54	m	w	VA	San Joaquin	3-Wd Stockton	86	240
G W	31	m	w	WALE	Placer	Newcastle Twp	76	477
Geo	72	m	w	MA	Amador	Ione City P O	69	349
Geo	43	m	w	ME	Tehama	Antelope Twp	92	156
Geo	40	m	w	MO	Tehama	Paskenta Twp	92	163
Geo	30	m	w	NH	Solano	Vallejo	90	210
Geo	14	m	w	ENGL	San Francisco	11-Wd San Francisc	84	588
Geo E	18	m	w	ME	Sacramento	3-Wd Sacramento	77	290
Geo F	43	m	w	NH	Butte	Chico Twp	70	20
Geo H	47	m	w	NY	Santa Cruz	Santa Cruz	89	405
Geo H	37	m	w	MI	Sacramento	3-Wd Sacramento	77	257
Geo H	30	m	w	MI	Sacramento	3-Wd Sacramento	77	257
Geo W	45	m	w	KY	Nevada	Nevada Twp	75	319
Geo W	29	m	w	MD	Sonoma	Santa Rosa	91	414
George	70	m	w	ENGL	Sonoma	Washington Twp	91	468
George	53	m	w	WALE	Sierra	Table Rock Twp	89	577
George	49	m	w	ENGL	Kern	Linns Valley P O	73	343
George	48	m	w	WALE	Siskiyou	Hamburg Twp	89	597
George	43	m	w	ENGL	Placer	Bath P O	76	448
George	37	m	w	MO	Napa	Yountville Twp	75	79
George	36	m	w	PA	Napa	Napa	75	50
George	35	m	w	ENGL	Colusa	Butte Twp	71	269
George	32	m	w	LA	San Luis Obispo	Morro Twp	87	287
George	30	m	w	ENGL	San Francisco	5-Wd San Francisco	81	10
George	26	m	w	ENGL	San Francisco	San Francisco P O	80	337

© 2001 by Heritage Quest. All rights reserved.

California 1870 Census

Name	Age	S	R	B-PL	County	Locale	Roll	Pg
George	25	m	w	ENGL	Los Angeles	Santa Ana Twp	73	601
George A	46	m	w	NY	Santa Clara	San Jose Twp	88	188
George A	32	m	w	ME	Santa Clara	1-Wd San Jose	88	242
George H	32	m	w	VA	Sonoma	Salt Point	91	393
Gideon	14	m	w	CA	San Francisco	2-Wd San Francisco	79	276
Gilman	37	m	w	NH	Colusa	Colusa	71	288
Gilmer	25	m	w	OH	Nevada	Bridgeport Twp	75	112
Grandison	45	m	b	VA	Nevada	Meadow Lake Twp	75	265
Griffith	45	m	w	WALE	Nevada	Bridgeport Twp	75	109
Griffith	44	m	w	WALE	San Francisco	1-Wd San Francisco	79	45
Griffith L	52	m	w	WALE	El Dorado	Placerville Twp	72	99
H	40	f	w	NY	Lassen	Susanville Twp	73	439
H	39	m	w	NY	San Joaquin	2-Wd Stockton	86	200
H	30	m	w	ENGL	Alameda	Alameda	68	5
H G	38	m	w	KY	Santa Clara	Gilroy Twp	88	91
H S	30	m	w	OH	Nevada	Meadow Lake Twp	75	249
Haden F	37	m	w	KY	Butte	Chico Twp	70	24
Hamilton	43	m	b	KY	Nevada	Grass Valley Twp	75	228
Hannah	50	f	w	KY	Sacramento	1-Wd Sacramento	77	177
Hannah	29	f	w	ENGL	Alameda	Oakland	68	238
Hanry	20	m	w	NY	San Francisco	San Francisco P O	80	477
Hanson	30	m	w	WALE	Butte	Hamilton Twp	70	69
Hardy	40	m	w	CT	Sonoma	Analy Twp	91	222
Hariet	38	f	w	NY	Sacramento	Granite Twp	77	147
Harrison	57	m	b	VA	Yolo	Buckeye Twp	93	417
Harrison	46	m	w	VA	San Francisco	6-Wd San Francisco	81	144
Harrison	32	m	w	ME	Los Angeles	Los Angeles	73	533
Harrison C	40	m	w	IN	Butte	Wyandotte Twp	70	147
Harry	45	m	w	ENGL	Yuba	Marysville	93	604
Harvey B	40	m	w	NY	San Luis Obispo	Arroyo Grande Twp	87	278
Harvey N	40	m	w	NH	San Diego	San Diego	78	491
Harvy	37	m	w	CANA	Sutter	Butte Twp	92	97
Hattie	22	f	w	NH	Sacramento	2-Wd Sacramento	77	224
Helen	12	f	w	NY	San Francisco	11-Wd San Francisc	84	526
Henry	60	m	w	OH	Shasta	Shasta P O	89	457
Henry	51	m	w	KY	Yuba	W Bear Rvr Twp	93	683
Henry	48	m	w	VT	San Francisco	San Francisco P O	80	380
Henry	45	m	w	ENGL	San Francisco	11-Wd San Francisc	84	596
Henry	39	m	m	MO	Placer	Auburn P O	76	380
Henry	35	m	w	ENGL	Sacramento	2-Wd Sacramento	77	250
Henry	35	m	w	NY	Placer	Auburn P O	76	383
Henry	31	m	w	ME	San Francisco	7-Wd San Francisco	81	221
Henry	31	m	w	ENGL	Sacramento	4-Wd Sacramento	77	374
Henry	30	m	w	ENGL	Yuba	Marysville	93	603
Henry	30	m	w	NY	Yolo	Putah Twp	93	520
Henry	28	m	w	IL	Tehama	Red Bluff	92	183
Henry	23	m	w	IL	Tehama	Tehama Twp	92	193
Henry	22	m	w	NY	Yolo	Cache Crk Twp	93	426
Henry	22	m	w	NY	Sonoma	Petaluma Twp	91	365
Henry	19	m	w	IN	Butte	Chico Twp	70	54
Henry	19	m	w	ENGL	Butte	Oregon Twp	70	126
Henry	17	m	w	CA	El Dorado	Georgetown Twp	72	41
Henry	12	m	i	CA	Nevada	Bridgeport Twp	75	109
Henry C	36	m	w	MI	San Francisco	3-Wd San Francisco	79	312
Henry J	39	m	w	WALE	Nevada	Bloomfield Twp	75	92
Henry R	33	m	w	AR	Butte	Chico Twp	70	41
Henry T	41	m	w	ENGL	Marin	Novato Twp	74	10
Henry W	25	m	w	NJ	San Francisco	1-Wd San Francisco	79	55
Heny M	34	m	w	CANA	Mendocino	Little Rvr Twp	74	165
Herman	28	m	w	AL	San Francisco	5-Wd San Francisco	81	9
Hesekiah	22	m	w	IREL	Solano	Silveyville Twp	90	79
Hew	16	m	w	CT	San Francisco	San Francisco P O	83	342
Hezekiah	23	m	w	IN	Santa Barbara	Santa Barbara P O	87	500
Hezekiah	22	m	w	IN	Yolo	Buckeye Twp	93	412
Hillard M	45	m	w	MO	Sonoma	Mendocino Twp	91	299
Hiram	44	m	w	NY	San Francisco	San Francisco P O	85	754
Hiram	39	m	w	IN	Nevada	Meadow Lake Twp	75	251
Hiram	33	m	w	PA	Merced	Snelling P O	74	246
Hiram	10	m	m	CA	San Francisco	11-Wd San Francisc	84	707
Horace	18	m	w	CA	Marin	Nicasio Twp	74	15
Hugh	38	m	w	WALE	San Francisco	San Francisco P O	83	132
Hugh	28	m	w	OH	Sutter	Yuba Twp	92	148
Humphrey	42	m	w	MO	Stanislaus	Empire Twp	92	60
Ion	41	m	w	PRUS	Solano	Tremont Twp	90	29
Ira B	45	m	w	IL	Mariposa	Mariposa P O	74	99
Isaac C	44	m	w	OH	San Mateo	Pescadero P O	87	415
Isaac S	43	m	w	VT	Sacramento	2-Wd Sacramento	77	214
Isidora	21	f	w	MEXI	San Francisco	San Francisco P O	80	474
J	41	m	w	NY	Sierra	Lincoln Twp	89	550
J	40	m	w	MI	Sierra	Sierra Twp	89	567
J	37	m	w	WALE	Sierra	Forest Twp	89	531
J A	38	m	w	ENGL	Alameda	Oakland	68	238
J B	28	m	w	IN	Alameda	Oakland	68	260
J C	40	m	w	MD	Napa	Napa	75	47
J E	21	m	w	ME	Monterey	San Antonio Twp	74	323
J H	40	m	w	PA	San Francisco	3-Wd San Francisco	79	310
J J	46	m	w	TN	Amador	Fiddletown P O	69	436
J J	39	m	w	WALE	Sierra	Eureka Twp	89	523
J J	29	m	w	ME	San Joaquin	Dent Twp	86	18
J L	45	m	w	PA	Tehama	Tehama Twp	92	194
J L	34	m	w	ENGL	Sierra	Gibson Twp	89	541
J L	27	m	w	WALE	Solano	Vallejo	90	200
J N	38	m	w	OH	Lassen	Susanville Twp	73	439
J P	38	m	w	ENGL	Sacramento	1-Wd Sacramento	77	179
J P	37	m	w	GA	Santa Clara	Gilroy Twp	88	76
J P	26	m	w	WALE	Alameda	Oakland	68	212
J S	41	m	w	PA	Sacramento	4-Wd Sacramento	77	361

Name	Age	S	R	B-PL	County	Locale	Roll	Pg
J T	38	m	w	WALE	Sierra	Sierra Twp	89	564
J W	58	m	w	VT	Siskiyou	Scott Valley Twp	89	619
J W	48	m	w	ME	Solano	Benicia	90	3
J W	34	m	w	MO	Lake	Upper Lake	73	410
J W	28	m	w	MO	Yuba	W Bear Rvr Twp	93	681
Jack	40	m	w	PRUS	Sacramento	Cosumnes Twp	77	92
Jacob	35	m	w	IREL	San Francisco	5-Wd San Francisco	81	19
Jacob Y	44	m	w	VA	Mariposa	Mariposa P O	74	96
James	51	m	w	IREL	San Joaquin	Elkhorn Twp	86	54
James	47	m	w	AL	San Francisco	5-Wd San Francisco	81	26
James	42	m	w	NY	San Francisco	5-Wd San Francisco	81	26
James	42	m	w	KY	Marin	San Rafael Twp	74	35
James	40	m	w	CANA	Sutter	Butte Twp	92	93
James	40	m	w	IREL	San Francisco	6-Wd San Francisco	81	136
James	40	m	w	TN	Nevada	Nevada Twp	75	307
James	37	m	w	WALE	San Francisco	1-Wd San Francisco	79	130
James	35	m	w	CANA	Sacramento	San Joaquin Twp	77	396
James	35	m	w	CT	San Francisco	San Francisco P O	80	407
James	34	m	w	NH	Alameda	Washington Twp	68	300
James	32	m	w	ME	San Francisco	5-Wd San Francisco	81	19
James	32	m	w	KY	Inyo	Bishop Crk Twp	73	316
James	32	m	w	IN	Contra Costa	Martinez Twp	71	347
James	30	m	w	NY	Nevada	Meadow Lake Twp	75	255
James	30	m	w	NY	San Francisco	San Francisco P O	83	421
James	30	m	w	IREL	Butte	Oregon Twp	70	129
James	28	m	w	MA	Marin	San Rafael Twp	74	39
James	27	m	w	MO	Mendocino	Navarro & Big Rvr	74	167
James	20	m	w	VT	Butte	Chico Twp	70	30
James	15	m	w	MD	Sierra	Gibson Twp	89	540
James A	43	m	w	ENGL	Trinity	Weaverville Pct	92	227
James A	37	m	w	MO	San Luis Obispo	Santa Rosa Twp	87	327
James B	39	m	w	DE	Sacramento	4-Wd Sacramento	77	319
James C	48	m	w	KY	El Dorado	Georgetown Twp	72	38
James J	43	m	w	NY	San Francisco	2-Wd San Francisco	79	269
James J	41	m	w	PA	Inyo	Bishop Crk Twp	73	313
James L	32	m	w	PA	San Francisco	San Francisco P O	83	329
James M	29	m	w	TN	Placer	Lincoln P O	76	489
James S	37	m	w	NY	San Francisco	San Francisco P O	83	140
James S	14	m	w	CA	Santa Clara	Santa Clara Twp	88	173
James T	40	m	w	OH	Colusa	Colusa Twp	71	274
Jane	65	f	w	MA	San Francisco	11-Wd San Francisc	84	493
Jane	38	f	w	ENGL	Yuba	Marysville	93	596
Jane	35	f	w	KY	Trinity	Minersville Pct	92	203
Jas H	48	m	w	DE	Solano	Vallejo	90	200
Jas L	35	m	w	IN	Butte	Concow Twp	70	8
Jas M	30	m	w	TN	Santa Barbara	Santa Barbara P O	87	499
Jas R	47	m	w	VA	Fresno	Millerton P O	72	150
Jas R	11	m	w	CA	San Joaquin	Oneal Twp	86	109
Jasper N	38	m	w	TN	Santa Clara	Fremont Twp	88	45
Jay J	40	m	w	WALE	Siskiyou	Yreka Twp	89	664
Jefferson	36	m	w	KY	Placer	Lincoln P O	76	482
Jerome	35	m	w	NY	Butte	Mountain Spring Tw	70	87
Jno	38	m	w	IREL	Sierra	Gibson Twp	89	543
Jno	35	m	w	NY	Sacramento	3-Wd Sacramento	77	305
Jno	23	m	w	NY	Sacramento	3-Wd Sacramento	77	290
Jno P	45	m	w	NY	San Francisco	5-Wd San Francisco	81	28
Jno R	46	m	w	WALE	Butte	Chico Twp	70	22
Jno W	49	m	w	NC	San Joaquin	Dent Twp	86	18
Joel	25	m	w	ENGL	San Francisco	3-Wd San Francisco	79	326
John	68	m	w	GERM	Los Angeles	Los Angeles	73	522
John	60	m	w	IREL	San Francisco	5-Wd San Francisco	81	19
John	56	m	w	WALE	Trinity	Canyon City Pct	92	201
John	55	m	w	PA	El Dorado	Coloma Twp	72	3
John	54	m	w	ENGL	Amador	Sutter Crk P O	69	414
John	52	m	w	KY	Kern	Linns Valley P O	73	349
John	51	m	w	ENGL	San Francisco	San Francisco P O	83	19
John	50	m	w	WALE	Contra Costa	Martinez P O	71	390
John	50	m	w	VT	Marin	San Rafael Twp	74	34
John	50	m	w	NY	San Francisco	San Francisco P O	83	350
John	50	m	w	WALE	Amador	Amador City P O	69	393
John	48	m	w	WALE	San Bernardino	San Bernardino Twp	78	430
John	48	m	w	TN	Yuba	Linda Twp	93	554
John	48	m	w	IREL	Butte	Mountain Spring Tw	70	88
John	48	m	w	ENGL	Fresno	Millerton P O	72	165
John	46	m	w	ENGL	Placer	Auburn P O	76	374
John	46	m	w	ENGL	San Francisco	San Francisco P O	83	227
John	45	m	w	NY	Placer	Bath P O	76	436
John	45	m	w	MA	Siskiyou	Callahan P O	89	625
John	43	m	w	WIND	San Joaquin	1-Wd Stockton	86	125
John	43	m	w	ENGL	Contra Costa	Martinez P O	71	419
John	42	m	w	NY	Napa	Napa Twp	75	29
John	41	m	m	KY	San Francisco	San Francisco P O	80	399
John	40	m	w	TN	Plumas	Seneca Twp	77	47
John	40	m	w	OH	Colusa	Grand Island Twp	71	309
John	40	m	w	MI	Amador	Fiddletown P O	69	438
John	40	m	w	MA	Tuolumne	Big Oak Flat P O	93	402
John	40	m	w	ENGL	San Francisco	San Francisco P O	83	380
John	36	m	m	VA	San Joaquin	3-Wd Stockton	86	221
John	35	m	w	MD	San Joaquin	2-Wd Stockton	86	195
John	35	m	w	ENGL	Nevada	Grass Valley Twp	75	195
John	34	m	w	NY	Marin	San Rafael Twp	74	46
John	32	m	w	ENGL	Contra Costa	Martinez P O	71	414
John	30	m	w	TN	Placer	Gold Run Twp	76	399
John	30	m	w	PRUS	San Francisco	San Francisco P O	83	13
John	30	m	w	NY	San Francisco	5-Wd San Francisco	81	35
John	30	m	w	SWED	Tehama	Red Bluff	92	182
John	29	m	w	WALE	Contra Costa	Martinez P O	71	429

© 2001 by Heritage Quest. All rights reserved.

Series M593

Name	Age	S	R	B-PL	County	Locale	Roll	Pg
John	28	m	w	ENGL	Marin	Novato Twp	74	11
John	27	m	w	NC	San Joaquin	2-Wd Stockton	86	184
John	26	m	w	ENGL	San Francisco	San Francisco P O	80	336
John	25	m	w	NY	Contra Costa	San Pablo Twp	71	357
John	25	m	w	SWED	San Francisco	7-Wd San Francisco	81	160
John	25	m	w	ME	San Francisco	San Francisco P O	83	371
John	25	m	w	ENGL	Solano	Vallejo	90	201
John	24	m	w	NY	Santa Cruz	Santa Cruz	89	429
John	24	m	w	IL	Tehama	Tehama Twp	92	195
John	18	m	w	IREL	San Francisco	5-Wd San Francisco	81	14
John	14	m	w	CA	San Francisco	11-Wd San Francisc	84	588
John	12	m	w	IN	San Francisco	San Francisco P O	85	828
John A	45	m	w	KY	Colusa	Colusa Twp	71	280
John A	29	m	w	WALE	Siskiyou	Scott Valley Twp	89	612
John B	37	m	w	KY	San Mateo	Half Moon Bay P O	87	395
John B	34	m	w	IL	San Bernardino	San Bernardino Twp	78	434
John C	46	m	w	WALE	Placer	Bath P O	76	446
John C	36	m	w	NY	San Francisco	1-Wd San Francisco	79	116
John C	26	m	w	WALE	Placer	Bath P O	76	436
John C	26	m	w	AUSL	San Francisco	San Francisco P O	83	316
John D	35	m	w	WALE	Butte	Oregon Twp	70	126
John E	49	m	w	WALE	Inyo	Bishop Crk Twp	73	313
John E	25	m	w	OH	Siskiyou	Hamburg Twp	89	596
John F	52	m	w	MA	San Francisco	San Francisco P O	83	209
John F	43	m	w	PRUS	Sonoma	Salt Point	91	391
John F	37	m	w	NY	Amador	Fiddletown P O	69	441
John F	18	m	w	PA	Butte	Ophir Twp	70	96
John G	52	m	w	KY	Butte	Bidwell Twp	70	3
John G	35	m	w	ME	Nevada	Grass Valley Twp	75	226
John G	32	m	w	WALE	Mono	Bridgeport P O	74	284
John H	54	m	w	WALE	Sonoma	Analy Twp	91	218
John H	35	m	w	MA	Los Angeles	Los Angeles	73	543
John J	58	m	w	WALE	San Francisco	1-Wd San Francisco	79	51
John J	38	m	w	SHOL	Siskiyou	Hamburg Twp	89	598
John M	76	m	w	NC	Plumas	Quartz Twp	77	38
John M	38	m	w	KY	Solano	Suisun Twp	90	100
John M	35	m	w	MO	Sonoma	Analy Twp	91	232
John M	27	m	w	IN	Nevada	Meadow Lake Twp	75	248
John M C	42	m	w	OH	Siskiyou	Yreka	89	655
John N	46	m	w	WALE	Placer	Bath P O	76	437
John O	37	m	w	WALE	Yuba	Slate Range Bar Tw	93	676
John O	26	m	w	ME	Sierra	Gibson Twp	89	540
John P	45	m	w	WALE	Nevada	Nevada Twp	75	277
John R	35	m	w	PA	Yolo	Cottonwood Twp	93	462
John S	49	m	w	WALE	San Francisco	San Francisco P O	83	92
John T	39	m	w	IN	Sonoma	Sonoma Twp	91	444
John W	48	m	w	KY	Contra Costa	Martinez P O	71	378
John W	40	m	w	PA	San Francisco	San Francisco P O	83	175
John W	40	m	w	PA	San Diego	Coronado	78	467
John W	35	m	w	IA	Colusa	Stony Crk Twp	71	329
John W	14	m	w	CA	Placer	Roseville P O	76	355
John Y	28	m	w	WALE	Alameda	Washington Twp	68	284
Johnathan	31	m	w	MA	San Francisco	11-Wd San Francisc	84	437
Jona	70	m	w	KY	Sonoma	Mendocino Twp	91	296
Jonas	45	m	w	CANA	Sutter	Butte Twp	92	97
Jonathan	33	m	w	MA	San Francisco	11-Wd San Francisc	84	501
Jonathan	33	m	w	MA	San Francisco	11-Wd San Francisc	84	491
Jones	45	m	w	IREL	San Francisco	11-Wd San Francisc	84	646
Jones	42	m	w	MI	San Joaquin	3-Wd Stockton	86	224
Jones	21	m	w	ENGL	San Francisco	6-Wd San Francisco	81	112
Jos A	41	m	w	NY	Monterey	San Juan Twp	74	415
Jose Maria	17	m	w	CA	Los Angeles	Los Angeles	73	559
Joseph	67	m	w	CANA	Sutter	Butte Twp	92	97
Joseph	63	m	w	VA	Santa Clara	1-Wd San Jose	88	227
Joseph	47	m	w	ENGL	San Francisco	11-Wd San Francisc	84	542
Joseph	46	m	w	WALE	San Francisco	2-Wd San Francisco	79	279
Joseph	44	m	w	ENGL	Nevada	Nevada Twp	75	306
Joseph	40	m	w	CT	Sacramento	4-Wd Sacramento	77	322
Joseph	38	m	w	CANA	Colusa	Colusa	71	292
Joseph	37	m	w	WALE	Contra Costa	Martinez P O	71	430
Joseph	35	m	w	WALE	Klamath	Camp Gaston	73	373
Joseph	32	m	w	IL	Sonoma	Washington Twp	91	467
Joseph	30	m	w	NY	San Francisco	6-Wd San Francisco	81	88
Joseph	20	m	i	NV	Calaveras	Copperopolis P O	70	252
Joseph	18	m	w	ME	San Francisco	1-Wd San Francisco	79	68
Joseph P	37	m	w	CANA	Solano	Denverton Twp	90	23
Joseph S	29	m	w	MO	Yolo	Merritt Twp	93	505
Joshua	63	m	w	NC	Santa Clara	Fremont Twp	88	45
Joshua	44	m	w	VA	Colusa	Butte Twp	71	269
Joshua	40	m	w	MO	Calaveras	San Andreas P O	70	162
Joshua	35	m	w	ME	San Francisco	7-Wd San Francisco	81	269
Kate	30	f	w	IREL	Alameda	Oakland	68	182
Katie	18	f	w	NY	San Francisco	San Francisco P O	80	474
Kenedy	42	m	w	NY	San Joaquin	Oneal Twp	86	107
L D	43	m	w	NY	Mendocino	Calpella Twp	74	182
La Fayette	37	m	w	MO	Santa Clara	Milpitas Twp	88	114
Lee	30	m	w	IL	El Dorado	Mountain Twp	72	68
Lemuel H	44	m	w	OH	San Francisco	5-Wd San Francisco	81	2
Leon E	28	m	w	OH	Santa Clara	1-Wd San Jose	88	246
Levi	25	m	w	TN	Stanislaus	Branch Twp	92	5
Lewis	38	m	w	OH	San Joaquin	Tulare Twp	86	254
Lloyd	32	m	w	ENGL	San Francisco	7-Wd San Francisco	81	280
Lorenzo	27	m	w	ME	Santa Cruz	Soquel Twp	89	448
Louis F	49	m	w	NY	Mariposa	Mariposa P O	74	122
Louisa	48	f	w	ENGL	San Francisco	San Francisco P O	83	97
Luis	38	m	w	PRUS	Los Angeles	Wilmington Twp	73	642
Luther	38	m	w	ME	Del Norte	Smith Rvr Twp	71	476
Lydia	17	f	w	IL	San Francisco	San Francisco P O	83	399
M	37	m	w	IA	San Joaquin	Elliott Twp	86	81
M	17	m	w	NY	San Joaquin	Elliott Twp	86	77
M L	44	m	w	TN	Siskiyou	Scott Valley Twp	89	613
M R	40	f	w	DE	Solano	Vallejo	90	200
M V	40	m	w	NY	Del Norte	Crescent	71	462
M W	60	m	w	WALE	Humboldt	Eureka Twp	72	278
M W	30	m	w	WALE	Placer	Newcastle Twp	76	477
Maggie	12	f	w	CA	Lassen	Janesville Twp	73	430
Maggie [Squaw]	22	f	i	CA	Lake	Lower Lake	73	423
Maria	26	f	b	NICA	San Francisco	8-Wd San Francisco	82	438
Marion	14	m	w	CA	Santa Clara	Santa Clara Twp	88	164
Marshal	16	m	w	IN	Sonoma	Analy Twp	91	246
Martha A	40	f	w	MO	Yolo	Buckeye Twp	93	411
Martin	36	m	w	NY	Tuolumne	Big Oak Flat P O	93	402
Mary	78	f	w	NC	San Joaquin	Dent Twp	86	18
Mary	60	f	w	LA	Sonoma	Petaluma Twp	91	363
Mary	56	f	w	ENGL	San Francisco	San Francisco P O	83	198
Mary	45	f	w	KY	Alameda	Oakland	68	230
Mary	40	f	w	IREL	Sacramento	3-Wd Sacramento	77	282
Mary	36	f	w	IREL	San Francisco	11-Wd San Francisc	84	646
Mary	36	f	w	ENGL	Sacramento	3-Wd Sacramento	77	294
Mary	32	f	w	IREL	Siskiyou	Yreka	89	654
Mary	30	f	w	IREL	San Joaquin	2-Wd Stockton	86	180
Mary	30	f	w	ENGL	El Dorado	Greenwood Twp	72	51
Mary	26	f	w	ENGL	San Francisco	San Francisco P O	80	472
Mary	25	f	i	CA	Tehama	Tehama Twp	92	187
Mary	25	f	w	NY	Alameda	Oakland	68	256
Mary	22	f	w	WALE	Alameda	Oakland	68	182
Mary	20	f	w	IREL	Santa Clara	Santa Clara Twp	88	170
Mary	19	f	w	IREL	San Francisco	San Francisco P O	83	409
Mary A	50	f	w	MD	San Francisco	San Francisco P O	83	244
Mary A	50	f	w	CANA	Alameda	Alameda	68	16
Mary A	45	f	w	TN	Contra Costa	Martinez P O	71	388
Mary J	28	f	w	MO	Shasta	Millville P O	89	491
Mary Jane	39	f	b	MD	Placer	Auburn P O	76	380
Maude	10	f	w	CA	Santa Clara	2-Wd San Jose	88	338
Meyer	30	m	w	PRUS	San Francisco	San Francisco P O	83	392
Mggie	14	f	w	NY	Nevada	Bridgeport Twp	75	101
Michael	57	m	w	OH	Sutter	Sutter Twp	92	117
Michael	40	m	w	NY	San Francisco	San Francisco P O	83	256
Michael	36	m	m	NJ	San Francisco	1-Wd San Francisco	79	132
Micheal	35	m	w	OH	San Francisco	7-Wd San Francisco	81	163
Milo	55	m	w	OH	Santa Clara	San Jose Twp	88	209
Minerva	45	f	w	IL	El Dorado	Placerville Twp	72	103
Monroe	27	m	w	IL	Santa Clara	Alviso Twp	88	28
Morgan C	28	m	w	IREL	Marin	Sausalito Twp	74	73
Morris	25	m	w	PRUS	Amador	Ione City P O	69	350
Moses	42	m	w	WALE	San Francisco	1-Wd San Francisco	79	45
Moses	25	m	w	WALE	Placer	Newcastle Twp	76	477
N	31	m	w	WALE	Sierra	Butte Twp	89	510
N H	62	m	w	SC	Mariposa	Maxwell Crk P O	74	145
N W	46	m	w	VA	Nevada	Nevada Twp	75	294
Nathan	60	m	w	MO	San Diego	San Diego	78	506
Nathan	41	m	w	CT	San Francisco	3-Wd San Francisco	79	297
Nathan	24	m	w	ENGL	San Francisco	San Francisco P O	80	418
Nathaniel	50	m	w	TN	Contra Costa	Martinez P O	71	387
Ned	30	m	w	NY	Contra Costa	Martinez P O	71	448
Norah	9	f	m	CA	Contra Costa	Martinez Twp	71	348
O	38	m	w	IL	Monterey	San Juan Twp	74	394
O S	38	m	w	ME	Tuolumne	Chinese Camp P O	93	375
Oliver	53	m	b	DC	San Francisco	San Francisco P O	80	476
Onesewin	37	m	w	CANA	Sierra	Eureka Twp	89	527
Orrin	55	m	w	MA	San Francisco	7-Wd San Francisco	81	158
Osias E	28	m	w	NY	Butte	Wyandotte Twp	70	141
Owen	46	m	w	WALE	Placer	Bath P O	76	453
Owen	40	m	w	WALE	Santa Clara	Fremont Twp	88	61
Owen	36	m	w	WALE	Placer	Gold Run Twp	76	398
Owen O	60	m	w	WALE	Sierra	Sears Twp	89	559
P H	28	m	w	IREL	San Francisco	San Francisco P O	85	862
Patrick	28	m	w	IREL	Yolo	Cache Crk Twp	93	448
Peter	36	m	w	IL	Shasta	Stillwater P O	89	479
Peter	35	m	w	PRUS	Butte	Chico Twp	70	37
Peter	29	m	w	WALE	San Francisco	1-Wd San Francisco	79	61
Peter	27	m	b	OH	Butte	Chico Twp	70	18
Peter	25	m	w	HANO	San Joaquin	Douglas Twp	86	32
Peter	23	m	w	NY	Tehama	Paskenta Twp	92	163
Phebe	75	f	w	NC	Sonoma	Analy Twp	91	239
Pleasant	36	m	w	MO	Mendocino	Round Valley Twp	74	220
Psorianna	40	m	w	ME	Calaveras	San Andreas P O	70	200
R	47	m	w	IL	Sierra	Sierra Twp	89	568
R	42	m	w	WALE	Sierra	Butte Twp	89	513
R H	42	m	w	ME	Alameda	Oakland	68	263
R M	34	m	w	WALE	Sierra	Table Rock Twp	89	574
Ralph	45	m	w	NY	Mariposa	Maxwell Crk P O	74	140
Rebecca	38	f	w	CANA	Nevada	Nevada Twp	75	288
Rebecca E	24	f	w	IN	Sonoma	Russian Rvr	91	373
Rees M	33	m	w	WALE	Sierra	Sears Twp	89	561
Reuben	45	m	w	VA	San Francisco	2-Wd San Francisco	79	215
Reuben B	34	m	w	OH	Santa Clara	San Jose Twp	88	219
Richard	52	m	w	NC	San Joaquin	Dent Twp	86	18
Richard	44	m	w	WALE	Yolo	Putah Twp	93	510
Richard	41	m	w	ENGL	Amador	Sutter Crk P O	69	406
Richard	30	m	w	NY	Sacramento	4-Wd Sacramento	77	340
Richard	29	m	w	ENGL	Nevada	Grass Valley Twp	75	142
Richard	27	m	w	IL	Colusa	Butte Twp	71	265
Richard	24	m	b	VA	Contra Costa	Martinez P O	71	375

© 2001 by Heritage Quest. All rights reserved.

California 1870 Census

Name	Age	S	R	B-PL	County	Locale	Roll	Pg
						Series M593		
Richard D	38	m	w	IL	Amador	Volcano P O	69	383
Richard R	26	m	w	WALE	Nevada	Bloomfield Twp	75	93
Richd	39	m	w	WALE	San Francisco	1-Wd San Francisco	79	30
Richd	37	m	w	CANA	Sacramento	3-Wd Sacramento	77	300
Robert	44	f	w	ME	Placer	Gold Run Twp	76	400
Robert	42	m	w	WALE	San Francisco	San Francisco P O	80	362
Robert	41	m	w	ENGL	Nevada	Grass Valley Twp	75	173
Robert	35	m	w	SCOT	San Francisco	3-Wd San Francisco	79	327
Robert	35	m	w	VA	Plumas	Quartz Twp	77	43
Robert	33	m	w	WALE	Marin	San Rafael Twp	74	41
Robert	27	m	w	IREL	Santa Clara	1-Wd San Jose	88	225
Robert	25	m	w	WALE	Del Norte	Crescent Twp	71	455
Robert M	44	m	w	PA	Mendocino	Point Arena Twp	74	224
Robt V	41	m	w	WALE	Shasta	Shasta P O	89	455
Rudolph	23	m	w	ME	San Francisco	San Francisco P O	83	255
S	46	m	w	US	Sacramento	1-Wd Sacramento	77	189
S	45	m	w	NY	Sierra	Forest Twp	89	530
S V	25	m	w	MA	Yuba	Marysville	93	595
Sally	25	f	w	NY	San Francisco	6-Wd San Francisco	81	88
Saml	59	m	w	NY	Sacramento	1-Wd Sacramento	77	181
Saml	58	m	w	ENGL	Klamath	South Fork Twp	73	385
Saml	42	m	w	IREL	Fresno	Millerton P O	72	159
Saml	41	m	w	ME	San Francisco	5-Wd San Francisco	81	15
Saml	40	m	w	OH	Butte	Chico Twp	70	32
Saml	33	m	w	MI	Merced	Snelling P O	74	255
Saml	33	m	w	OH	San Francisco	San Francisco P O	83	96
Saml	27	m	w	ENGL	San Joaquin	3-Wd Stockton	86	240
Saml	24	m	w	IREL	San Francisco	5-Wd San Francisco	81	10
Saml	23	m	w	PA	San Joaquin	3-Wd Stockton	86	247
Saml B	50	m	w	PRUS	San Francisco	11-Wd San Francisc	84	643
Saml E	42	m	w	MA	San Francisco	6-Wd San Francisco	81	105
Saml S	36	m	w	CT	San Francisco	1-Wd San Francisco	79	111
Saml W	39	m	w	MO	Merced	Snelling P O	74	277
Sampson M	36	m	w	PA	Fresno	Millerton P O	72	148
Samuel	60	m	w	MA	San Francisco	7-Wd San Francisco	81	157
Samuel	44	m	w	ENGL	San Francisco	11-Wd San Francisc	84	707
Samuel	43	m	w	MA	Marin	Bolinas Twp	74	8
Samuel	40	m	w	AL	San Bernardino	San Bernardino Twp	78	428
Samuel	38	m	w	CANA	Colusa	Monroe Twp	71	315
Samuel	38	m	w	IN	San Francisco	11-Wd San Francisc	84	622
Samuel	36	m	b	MD	San Francisco	San Francisco P O	80	470
Samuel	27	m	w	WALE	Alameda	Murray Twp	68	99
Samuel	26	m	w	NY	Alameda	Washington Twp	68	288
Samuel	22	m	b	VA	Los Angeles	Los Angeles	73	549
Samuel E	32	m	w	OH	Monterey	San Antonio Twp	74	319
Samuel S	22	m	b	MO	Yolo	Cache Crk Twp	93	428
Samuel T	36	m	w	KY	Santa Cruz	Soquel Twp	89	447
Sandy	40	m	w	MO	Stanislaus	Emory Twp	92	16
Santiago	3	m	w	CA	Los Angeles	Los Angeles	73	553
Sarah	8	f	w	CA	San Diego	San Diego	78	491
Sarah	45	f	w	AR	Tulare	Visalia Twp	92	281
Sarah	30	f	w	ENGL	San Joaquin	1-Wd Stockton	86	135
Sarah	28	f	i	CA	Contra Costa	Martinez Twp	71	348
Sarah	16	f	w	CA	Santa Clara	San Jose Twp	88	215
Seaborn	33	m	w	KY	Nevada	Grass Valley Twp	75	230
Seamour	20	m	w	IL	San Francisco	San Francisco P O	85	754
Seneca	25	m	w	DE	San Francisco	San Francisco P O	83	386
Seymour	20	m	w	NY	San Francisco	San Francisco P O	83	149
Shadrach	51	m	w	WALE	Contra Costa	Martinez P O	71	444
Sidney	45	m	w	KY	Sierra	Table Rock Twp	89	578
Silas	39	m	w	MA	Kern	Havilah P O	73	339
Siles	80	m	w	MA	San Joaquin	Elkhorn Twp	86	57
Simon D	36	m	w	WI	San Francisco	San Francisco P O	83	8
Simon L	55	m	w	WALE	San Francisco	7-Wd San Francisco	81	285
Solomon	47	m	w	NY	San Francisco	3-Wd San Francisco	79	308
Solomon	34	m	w	ENGL	Contra Costa	Martinez P O	71	423
Stephen	41	m	m	NJ	Butte	Ophir Twp	70	104
Stephen	35	m	w	MO	Napa	Napa Twp	75	63
Steven	31	m	w	MI	Butte	Ophir Twp	70	100
Steven	28	m	w	TN	Yolo	Grafton Twp	93	487
Susan	60	f	w	IREL	San Francisco	San Francisco P O	83	112
Sybella	42	f	w	PA	Placer	Rocklin Twp	76	466
Sylvester	50	m	w	NY	Tulare	Tule Rvr Twp	92	262
Sylvester A	25	m	w	MA	Yolo	Cache Crk Twp	93	419
T W	36	m	w	WALE	Solano	Vallejo	90	146
Thaddeus	20	m	w	WI	Colusa	Butte Twp	71	266
Thaddeus A	37	m	w	GA	Shasta	Horsetown P O	89	501
Theadore	50	m	w	NY	Tehama	Red Bluff	92	174
Thedora	2	f	w	CA	Trinity	Douglas	92	233
Theo	21	m	w	MI	San Francisco	8-Wd San Francisco	82	370
Theodore	39	m	w	BREM	San Francisco	1-Wd San Francisco	79	51
Theodore	37	m	w	HAMB	San Francisco	1-Wd San Francisco	79	51
Theodore	33	m	w	TN	San Francisco	San Francisco P O	83	46
Thom	34	m	w	ENGL	Sacramento	3-Wd Sacramento	77	317
Thomas	70	m	w	MD	El Dorado	Mud Springs Twp	72	83
Thomas	60	m	w	TN	Santa Clara	Redwood Twp	88	121
Thomas	57	m	b	MD	El Dorado	Diamond Springs Tw	72	28
Thomas	54	m	w	WALE	Contra Costa	Martinez P O	71	427
Thomas	53	m	w	WALE	Amador	Jackson P O	69	334
Thomas	53	m	w	ENGL	Sacramento	2-Wd Sacramento	77	211
Thomas	52	m	w	ENGL	Mendocino	Casper & Big Rvr	74	162
Thomas	48	m	w	NORW	San Francisco	San Francisco P O	80	429
Thomas	46	m	w	ENGL	San Francisco	11-Wd San Francisc	84	647
Thomas	45	m	w	KY	San Francisco	8-Wd San Francisco	82	374
Thomas	45	m	w	ENGL	Santa Cruz	Santa Cruz Twp	89	394
Thomas	44	m	w	WALE	Nevada	Bridgeport Twp	75	101
Thomas	44	m	w	WALE	Calaveras	Copperopolis P O	70	248
Thomas	43	m	w	ENGL	San Francisco	6-Wd San Francisco	81	120
Thomas	42	m	w	ME	San Francisco	11-Wd San Francisc	84	707
Thomas	41	m	w	CANA	San Francisco	7-Wd San Francisco	81	166
Thomas	40	m	w	KY	Amador	Fiddletown P O	69	435
Thomas	40	m	w	IREL	San Francisco	8-Wd San Francisco	82	373
Thomas	40	m	w	WALE	San Francisco	6-Wd San Francisco	81	94
Thomas	40	m	w	ENGL	San Francisco	San Francisco P O	80	458
Thomas	40	m	w	ENGL	Contra Costa	Martinez P O	71	422
Thomas	40	m	w	IREL	Monterey	Alisal Twp	74	292
Thomas	40	m	w	WALE	Nevada	Eureka Twp	75	129
Thomas	39	m	w	UNKN	San Joaquin	2-Wd Stockton	86	167
Thomas	39	m	w	WALE	Tuolumne	Chinese Camp P O	93	382
Thomas	39	m	w	IL	Monterey	Monterey Twp	74	350
Thomas	38	m	w	NY	Sacramento	Granite Twp	77	141
Thomas	37	m	w	WALE	Inyo	Cerro Gordo Twp	73	321
Thomas	35	m	w	ME	Mendocino	Little Rvr Twp	74	171
Thomas	35	m	w	IREL	Contra Costa	San Pablo Twp	71	357
Thomas	33	m	w	WALE	Inyo	Bishop Crk Twp	73	314
Thomas	32	m	w	MO	Colusa	Monroe Twp	71	314
Thomas	30	m	w	NY	Los Angeles	Los Angeles	73	524
Thomas	30	m	w	ENGL	Contra Costa	Martinez P O	71	413
Thomas	30	m	w	WALE	Monterey	Monterey Twp	74	351
Thomas	28	m	w	WALE	Contra Costa	Martinez P O	71	426
Thomas	28	m	b	MD	San Francisco	8-Wd San Francisco	82	345
Thomas	28	m	w	MD	San Francisco	San Francisco P O	85	758
Thomas	28	m	w	WALE	Amador	Sutter Crk P O	69	396
Thomas	27	m	w	IREL	San Francisco	San Francisco P O	85	794
Thomas	27	m	w	OH	Butte	Ophir Twp	70	115
Thomas	25	m	w	VT	San Francisco	11-Wd San Francisc	84	527
Thomas	24	m	w	CANA	Nevada	Meadow Lake Twp	75	253
Thomas	22	m	w	OH	Contra Costa	Martinez P O	71	427
Thomas	20	m	w	ENGL	Solano	Vacaville Twp	90	136
Thomas	17	m	w	SC	Siskiyou	Scott Valley Twp	89	611
Thomas	17	m	w	SC	Siskiyou	Yreka	89	659
Thomas A	20	m	w	AUSL	San Francisco	San Francisco P O	83	185
Thomas C	30	m	w	VA	Stanislaus	Empire Twp	92	31
Thomas E	34	m	w	MA	San Francisco	3-Wd San Francisco	79	313
Thomas H	45	m	w	KY	Amador	Drytown P O	69	418
Thomas J	48	m	w	KY	Contra Costa	Martinez P O	71	395
Thomas L	38	m	w	WALE	Nevada	Bridgeport Twp	75	100
Thomas R	16	m	w	CA	Amador	Amador City P O	69	391
Thomas T	29	m	b	NY	Sacramento	2-Wd Sacramento	77	234
Thomas W	40	m	w	ENGL	Yuba	Bullards Bar P O	93	547
Thos	60	m	w	WALE	San Francisco	11-Wd San Francisc	84	582
Thos	60	m	w	WALE	Butte	Kimshew Tpw	70	82
Thos	45	m	w	MA	Solano	Vallejo	90	170
Thos	42	m	w	WALE	Sierra	Sears Twp	89	557
Thos	39	m	w	WA	Fresno	Millerton P O	72	150
Thos	35	m	w	WALE	Butte	Kimshew Tpw	70	77
Thos	26	m	w	IREL	Fresno	Millerton P O	72	188
Thos	22	m	w	IREL	Lake	Knoxville Mines	73	404
Thos A	42	m	w	WALE	Sierra	Sears Twp	89	556
Thos B	33	m	w	VA	Sonoma	Cloverdale Twp	91	268
Thos C	40	m	w	NY	Sacramento	3-Wd Sacramento	77	292
Thos M	42	m	w	OH	Shasta	Stillwater P O	89	481
Thos P	27	m	w	NY	Shasta	Stillwater P O	89	481
Thos R	37	m	w	ENGL	Butte	Ophir Twp	70	101
Tilman	43	m	w	GA	Colusa	Colusa	71	296
Timothy	36	m	w	NY	San Francisco	1-Wd San Francisco	79	107
Timothy	32	m	w	WALE	Napa	Napa Twp	75	32
Timothy	31	m	w	IREL	San Francisco	1-Wd San Francisco	79	112
Timothy	29	m	w	OH	Sonoma	Russian Rvr	91	376
Uriah	33	m	w	KY	Amador	Volcano P O	69	385
Victor	40	m	w	PRUS	Sacramento	Granite Twp	77	143
W A	49	m	b	DE	Tuolumne	Big Oak Flat P O	93	395
W A	19	m	w	OR	Lassen	Susanville Twp	73	446
W B	35	m	w	NC	Lake	Upper Lake	73	412
W D	57	m	w	PA	Solano	Vallejo	90	155
W E	40	m	w	VA	Lassen	Long Valley Twp	73	436
W G	31	m	w	OH	Alameda	Oakland	68	239
W H	50	m	w	NY	Tehama	Red Bluff	92	183
W H	28	m	w	IN	Tehama	Red Bluff	92	182
W L	42	m	w	ME	Monterey	San Juan Twp	74	412
W T	30	m	w	WALE	Amador	Sutter Crk P O	69	398
Walter	40	m	w	NY	San Francisco	5-Wd San Francisco	81	31
Walter	37	m	w	MS	San Joaquin	Oneal Twp	86	113
Walter	28	m	w	IL	Sacramento	Sutter Twp	77	387
Whitton	35	m	w	VA	Fresno	Millerton P O	72	160
Wilbert	23	m	w	ME	San Francisco	7-Wd San Francisco	81	164
Wiley L	56	m	w	TN	Sonoma	Mendocino Twp	91	297
Willard	40	m	w	NY	Tuolumne	Columbia P O	93	338
William	77	m	b	SC	Sacramento	2-Wd Sacramento	77	210
William	60	m	w	NY	Sonoma	Mendocino Twp	91	296
William	57	m	w	MA	Placer	Gold Run Twp	76	400
William	53	m	w	NY	El Dorado	Placerville	72	109
William	53	m	b	NJ	Contra Costa	Martinez Twp	71	348
William	52	m	w	CANA	Placer	Cisco P O	76	494
William	51	m	w	ENGL	Placer	Lincoln P O	76	490
William	50	m	w	MA	San Francisco	8-Wd San Francisco	82	438
William	48	m	w	IREL	San Francisco	1-Wd San Francisco	79	8
William	47	m	w	IREL	Calaveras	Copperopolis P O	70	252
William	46	m	w	OH	Alameda	Washington Twp	68	301
William	45	m	w	IREL	San Francisco	8-Wd San Francisco	82	437
William	45	m	w	ENGL	Contra Costa	Martinez P O	71	413
William	44	m	w	OH	Tuolumne	Columbia P O	93	340
William	44	m	w	NY	San Diego	San Diego	78	511
William	41	m	w	ENGL	Amador	Sutter Crk P O	69	408

© 2001 by Heritage Quest. All rights reserved.

Name	Age	S	R	B-PL	County	Locale	Series M593 Roll	Pg
William	38	m	w	GA	Stanislaus	Empire Twp	92	37
William	38	m	w	MO	Solano	Montezuma Twp	90	69
William	38	m	w	MO	Colusa	Colusa Twp	71	283
William	37	m	w	NY	Nevada	Meadow Lake Twp	75	267
William	35	m	w	WALE	Contra Costa	Martinez P O	71	429
William	35	m	w	NY	San Francisco	6-Wd San Francisco	81	130
William	35	m	w	ENGL	Santa Clara	Fremont Twp	88	58
William	35	m	w	IREL	Alameda	Oakland	68	182
William	35	m	w	WALE	Napa	Napa Twp	75	31
William	34	m	w	MO	Stanislaus	Empire Twp	92	33
William	34	m	w	IA	Sonoma	Petaluma Twp	91	365
William	32	m	w	NY	Sutter	Butte Twp	92	96
William	32	m	w	SC	Tulare	Visalia Twp	92	281
William	32	m	w	IREL	San Luis Obispo	Salinas Twp	87	296
William	32	m	w	OH	Nevada	Bloomfield Twp	75	93
William	31	m	w	WALE	Contra Costa	Martinez P O	71	427
William	30	m	w	CANA	Sutter	Sutter Twp	92	122
William	30	m	w	RUSS	Humboldt	Arcata Twp	72	225
William	30	m	w	AUST	Santa Clara	San Jose Twp	88	192
William	29	m	w	WALE	San Francisco	11-Wd San Francisc	84	649
William	28	m	w	IREL	San Francisco	San Francisco P O	83	185
William	28	m	w	IREL	Marin	San Rafael Twp	74	43
William	27	m	w	NY	Santa Clara	1-Wd San Jose	88	244
William	27	m	w	WALE	Placer	Bath P O	76	437
William	27	m	w	ENGL	Contra Costa	Martinez P O	71	414
William	26	m	w	IREL	Santa Clara	Milpitas Twp	88	108
William	26	m	w	NY	Sacramento	3-Wd Sacramento	77	316
William	25	m	w	WALE	Santa Clara	San Jose Twp	88	193
William	24	m	w	PA	Yolo	Cache Crk Twp	93	425
William	24	m	w	PA	Yolo	Cache Crk Twp	93	448
William	24	m	w	NY	San Francisco	San Francisco P O	83	361
William	22	m	w	NY	Solano	Suisun Twp	90	114
William	20	m	w	ENGL	Marin	San Rafael Twp	74	59
William	18	m	w	MO	Contra Costa	Martinez P O	71	445
William	18	m	w	KY	Shasta	Millville P O	89	492
William	17	m	w	CA	Marin	San Rafael	74	58
William	17	m	w	NY	Contra Costa	Martinez Twp	71	350
William A	31	m	w	WALE	Placer	Bath P O	76	446
William C	35	m	w	MO	Tulare	Visalia Twp	92	287
William G	40	m	w	MI	Santa Clara	Santa Clara Twp	88	171
William H	50	m	w	NY	Sonoma	Petaluma Twp	91	331
William H	38	m	w	TN	San Francisco	7-Wd San Francisco	81	182
William H	23	m	w	MA	Placer	Rocklin Twp	76	463
William H	22	m	w	GA	Yolo	Buckeye Twp	93	410
William J	48	m	w	WALE	Los Angeles	Soledad Twp	73	630
William J	45	m	w	PA	San Francisco	8-Wd San Francisco	82	392
William J	24	m	w	TX	Los Angeles	Los Angeles	73	502
William L	48	m	w	TX	Los Angeles	El Monte Twp	73	457
William R	32	m	w	WALE	Sacramento	2-Wd Sacramento	77	249
William S	44	m	w	TN	Yuba	Long Bar Twp	93	565
William S	42	m	w	MO	Stanislaus	Empire Twp	92	57
William T	40	m	w	WALE	San Francisco	6-Wd San Francisco	81	142
William T	33	m	w	MS	Yolo	Merritt Twp	93	502
Williard D	34	m	w	ME	Yolo	Grafton Twp	93	479
Willis	39	m	w	GA	Placer	Bath P O	76	429
Wirt	21	m	w	OH	Santa Clara	San Jose Twp	88	219
Wm	7	m	w	IN	San Francisco	San Francisco P O	85	828
Wm	57	m	w	WALE	San Francisco	11-Wd San Francisc	84	612
Wm	48	m	w	WALE	Sierra	Eureka Twp	89	523
Wm	45	m	w	NY	Sonoma	Analy Twp	91	218
Wm	44	m	w	DENM	Sierra	Lincoln Twp	89	549
Wm	42	m	w	IN	Yuba	North East Twp	93	643
Wm	38	m	w	SC	San Francisco	San Francisco P O	85	861
Wm	38	m	w	TN	Lake	Lower Lake	73	423
Wm	37	m	w	ENGL	Sacramento	Natomas Twp	77	167
Wm	36	m	w	IN	Napa	Napa Twp	75	69
Wm	35	m	w	WALE	San Francisco	San Francisco P O	83	111
Wm	33	m	w	WALE	Lassen	Long Valley Twp	73	436
Wm	32	m	w	SCOT	Solano	Vallejo	90	181
Wm	31	m	w	ENGL	San Francisco	1-Wd San Francisco	79	125
Wm	30	m	w	IREL	San Joaquin	Douglas Twp	86	32
Wm	30	m	w	ENGL	San Francisco	1-Wd San Francisco	79	68
Wm	30	m	w	ENGL	San Francisco	7-Wd San Francisco	81	257
Wm	30	m	w	WALE	Solano	Vallejo	90	155
Wm	28	m	w	ENGL	San Joaquin	2-Wd Stockton	86	162
Wm	28	m	w	ENGL	Tehama	Battle Crk Twp	92	158
Wm	28	m	w	WALE	Sierra	Gibson Twp	89	541
Wm	26	m	w	NY	San Francisco	11-Wd San Francisc	84	585
Wm	26	m	w	ENGL	Yuba	Rose Bar Twp	93	662
Wm	24	m	w	WALE	San Francisco	7-Wd San Francisco	81	228
Wm Arthur	40	m	w	WALE	San Francisco	San Francisco P O	83	114
Wm H	31	m	w	WALE	San Francisco	1-Wd San Francisco	79	111
Wm H N	33	m	w	NY	Butte	Wyandotte Twp	70	141
Wm Henry	44	m	w	PA	Nevada	Little York Twp	75	235
Wm J	44	m	w	WALE	Tuolumne	Columbia P O	93	362
Wm R	51	m	w	KY	Santa Barbara	San Buenaventura P	87	434
Wm S	34	m	w	NH	San Francisco	San Francisco P O	83	151
Wm S	34	m	w	WALE	Sierra	Lincoln Twp	89	549
Wm T	36	m	w	WALE	Sierra	Sears Twp	89	561
Y	32	m	w	ENGL	Sierra	Lincoln Twp	89	549
Zechariah	63	m	w	TN	Santa Clara	2-Wd San Jose	88	295
Zephaniah	25	m	w	NY	Plumas	Goodwin Twp	77	5
JONESON								
John	35	m	w	ENGL	San Joaquin	Elkhorn Twp	86	58
JONET								
Angel	28	m	w	SWIT	Tuolumne	Columbia P O	93	346
JONEY								
Jim	25	m	c	CHIN	Sonoma	Sonoma Twp	91	447
JONG								
A	30	m	c	CHIN	Butte	Chico Twp	70	51
Ah	48	m	c	CHIN	Calaveras	Copperopolis P O	70	232
Ah	45	m	c	CHIN	Tuolumne	Big Oak Flat P O	93	401
Ah	42	m	c	CHIN	Fresno	Millerton P O	72	199
Ah	40	m	c	CHIN	Santa Clara	1-Wd San Jose	88	269
Ah	35	m	c	CHIN	Stanislaus	Emory Twp	92	17
Ah	26	m	c	CHIN	Merced	Snelling P O	74	278
Ah	19	m	c	CHIN	San Francisco	8-Wd San Francisco	82	412
Ah	17	m	c	CHIN	Nevada	Nevada Twp	75	271
Ah	16	m	c	CHIN	San Francisco	San Francisco P O	80	388
Ah	14	m	c	CHIN	Nevada	Eureka Twp	75	140
Ah	14	m	c	CHIN	San Francisco	San Francisco P O	80	388
Chong	36	m	c	CHIN	Sacramento	Franklin Twp	77	116
Gee	13	m	c	CHIN	Plumas	Mineral Twp	77	24
Ing	42	m	c	CHIN	Klamath	Liberty Twp	73	375
Tou	30	m	c	CHIN	Sonoma	Bodega Twp	91	251
Toy	41	m	c	CHIN	Nevada	Bridgeport Twp	75	111
JONGSTOFF								
Christian H	28	m	w	PRUS	Los Angeles	Wilmington Twp	73	639
JONHS								
Bela W	43	m	w	NH	Klamath	Orleans Twp	73	381
JONICE								
Carlo	19	m	w	ITAL	San Mateo	Schoolhouse Statio	87	334
JONIER								
Emma J	21	f	w	CANA	San Francisco	San Francisco P O	83	107
JONINE								
Casti	20	m	w	ITAL	San Mateo	Schoolhouse Statio	87	346
John	21	m	w	ITAL	San Mateo	Schoolhouse Statio	87	346
JONIS								
T C	28	m	w	NY	Sutter	Nicolaus Twp	92	106
Wm	46	m	w	GERM	San Diego	San Diego	78	497
JONNES								
John	38	m	w	GA	Placer	Bath P O	76	424
JONRAGA								
Antonio	36	m	w	SPAI	Los Angeles	Los Angeles Twp	73	492
JONS								
Jas	30	m	w	NCOD	San Joaquin	Oneal Twp	86	118
JONSE								
James	39	m	w	WALE	Alameda	Brooklyn	68	29
William	40	m	w	NY	Alameda	Washington Twp	68	290
William	30	m	w	OH	Alameda	Brooklyn Twp	68	51
JONSEN								
Chirt	48	m	w	HAMB	San Francisco	2-Wd San Francisco	79	207
JONSING								
Ah	21	m	c	CHIN	Trinity	Junction City Pct	92	208
JONSON								
M	37	m	w	ENGL	Sierra	Forest Twp	89	529
Manuel	32	m	w	SCOT	Siskiyou	Table Rock Twp	89	646
Peter	44	m	w	SWED	San Francisco	San Francisco P O	83	31
JONSTON								
Mike	36	m	w	IREL	Mono	Bridgeport P O	74	284
JONY								
---	67	m	c	CHIN	Siskiyou	Cottonwood Twp	89	592
JOO								
Ah	48	m	c	CHIN	San Joaquin	Oneal Twp	86	117
Ah	40	m	c	CHIN	San Joaquin	1-Wd Stockton	86	142
Ah	40	m	c	CHIN	San Joaquin	Elkhorn Twp	86	66
Ah	32	m	c	CHIN	San Francisco	San Francisco P O	80	513
Ah	31	m	c	CHIN	San Francisco	San Francisco P O	80	513
Ah	30	m	c	CHIN	San Joaquin	Oneal Twp	86	116
Ah	28	m	c	CHIN	San Joaquin	Oneal Twp	86	117
Ah	24	m	c	CHIN	San Joaquin	1-Wd Stockton	86	146
All	29	m	c	CHIN	San Joaquin	1-Wd Stockton	86	142
Joo	42	m	c	CHIN	San Joaquin	1-Wd Stockton	86	142
La	37	m	c	CHIN	San Joaquin	1-Wd Stockton	86	143
Soo	34	m	c	CHIN	San Joaquin	1-Wd Stockton	86	142
Yo	39	m	c	CHIN	San Joaquin	3-Wd Stockton	86	246
JOONGLE								
Daniel	27	m	w	SCOT	Mariposa	Maxwell Crk P O	74	146
JOOQUIN								
Anton	30	m	w	PORT	Tuolumne	Columbia P O	93	356
JOORSH								
Tobian	37	m	w	HANO	San Francisco	11-Wd San Francisc	84	627
JOORY								
J M	23	m	w	MI	Tuolumne	Chinese Camp P O	93	389
JOOST								
Jacob	18	m	w	HANO	San Francisco	2-Wd San Francisco	79	245
Martin	22	m	w	HANO	San Francisco	San Francisco P O	83	19
Martin	22	m	w	HAMB	San Francisco	11-Wd San Francisc	84	497
Martin	18	m	w	PRUS	San Francisco	8-Wd San Francisco	82	323
Peter	22	m	w	PRUS	San Francisco	2-Wd San Francisco	79	209
JOOT								
Yow	28	f	c	CHIN	San Francisco	6-Wd San Francisco	81	62
JOOTES								
Bernard	26	m	w	NCOD	San Francisco	11-Wd San Francisc	84	682
JOP								
Ah	39	m	c	CHIN	Butte	Kimshew Tpw	70	77
Ah	32	m	c	CHIN	San Joaquin	1-Wd Stockton	86	143
JOPLIN								
J	39	m	w	MO	San Joaquin	Tulare Twp	86	259
Lanclot	60	m	w	ENGL	El Dorado	Placerville Twp	72	97
JOPLING								
Joseph	66	m	w	VA	Nevada	Nevada Twp	75	284

© 2001 by Heritage Quest. All rights reserved.

Name	Age	S	R	B-PL	County	Locale	Series M593 Roll	Pg
JOPPINGTON								
Field	22	m	w	ENGL	Contra Costa	Martinez P O	71	396
JOPSON								
C L	29	f	w	IREL	Alameda	Oakland	68	219
JOQUATH								
William	35	m	w	ME	Alameda	Alameda	68	18
JOQUIN								
James	26	m	w	MEXI	San Francisco	2-Wd San Francisco	79	181
JOR								
G K	44	m	w	HOLL	Sierra	Downieville Twp	89	516
JORAN								
Thomas	26	m	w	FRAN	San Francisco	San Francisco P O	80	535
JORAND								
Yves	48	m	w	FRAN	Plumas	Rich Bar Twp	77	8
JORAVICH								
Saml	51	m	w	AUST	San Francisco	1-Wd San Francisco	79	129
JORD								
George	28	m	w	ENGL	Nevada	Grass Valley Twp	75	232
William	25	m	w	ENGL	Nevada	Grass Valley Twp	75	232
JORDAN								
Addison	28	m	w	IN	San Francisco	11-Wd San Francisc	84	600
Adelia	56	f	w	NY	Santa Clara	Fremont Twp	88	53
Adolp	28	m	w	HCAS	Contra Costa	Martinez P O	71	393
Albert H	50	m	w	ENGL	San Mateo	San Mateo P O	87	352
Alfred	26	m	w	TN	Los Angeles	El Monte Twp	73	463
Andrew	45	m	w	ME	Calaveras	Copperopolis P O	70	255
Andrew Z	37	m	w	AUST	Los Angeles	Los Angeles	73	521
Annis J	25	m	w	ENGL	Los Angeles	Los Angeles	73	571
August	47	m	w	SWIT	San Francisco	San Francisco P O	80	537
Benjamin	45	m	w	OH	Calaveras	San Andreas P O	70	206
Bernell	38	m	w	TN	Butte	Ophir Twp	70	98
Bridget	50	f	w	IREL	San Joaquin	Castoria Twp	86	8
Catherine	56	f	w	KY	Yuba	East Bear Rvr Twp	93	540
Charles	52	m	w	MA	Marin	Bolinas Twp	74	4
Charles	24	m	w	MA	San Francisco	San Francisco P O	85	757
Charles C	22	m	w	ME	Santa Cruz	Santa Cruz	89	429
Chas	24	m	w	NY	San Francisco	1-Wd San Francisco	79	65
Conrod	20	m	w	PRUS	San Francisco	7-Wd San Francisco	81	223
Daniel L	21	m	w	NY	San Francisco	San Francisco P O	83	396
David	37	m	w	PA	Nevada	Grass Valley Twp	75	229
Dennis	38	m	w	IREL	San Francisco	8-Wd San Francisco	82	457
Eliza	53	f	w	PA	Tulare	Farmersville Twp	92	247
Eliza	27	f	b	MO	Sacramento	2-Wd Sacramento	77	234
Elmer E	30	m	w	CT	San Diego	Julian Dist	78	471
F M	29	m	w	ENGL	Sacramento	3-Wd Sacramento	77	318
Francis	53	m	w	IL	Tulare	Packwood Twp	92	256
Frank	65	m	w	AR	Monterey	San Juan Twp	74	394
Frank	16	m	w	IN	San Francisco	11-Wd San Francisc	84	597
Geo	23	m	w	ME	San Francisco	1-Wd San Francisco	79	126
George	41	m	w	NY	Calaveras	San Andreas P O	70	186
George	26	m	w	HAMB	San Francisco	8-Wd San Francisco	82	354
George	24	m	w	VA	Marin	San Rafael Twp	74	45
George	20	m	m	TX	San Francisco	6-Wd San Francisco	81	128
Grace	50	f	w	CANA	San Francisco	8-Wd San Francisco	82	422
Helen V	26	f	w	ME	San Francisco	San Francisco P O	83	23
Henry	50	m	w	ME	Santa Cruz	Santa Cruz	89	428
Herman	28	m	w	PRUS	San Francisco	6-Wd San Francisco	81	91
Jackson	57	m	m	LA	Sacramento	2-Wd Sacramento	77	214
James	43	m	w	IREL	San Francisco	8-Wd San Francisco	82	348
James	39	m	w	IL	Sacramento	2-Wd Sacramento	77	227
James	30	m	w	FRAN	San Francisco	6-Wd San Francisco	81	73
James	28	m	w	IREL	San Francisco	7-Wd San Francisco	81	180
James	21	m	w	TX	Inyo	Lone Pine Twp	73	334
Jas B	39	m	w	MO	Fresno	Kingston P O	72	219
Jas S	52	m	w	VA	Placer	Colfax P O	76	385
John	52	m	w	IREL	San Francisco	8-Wd San Francisco	82	426
John	45	m	w	WURT	San Francisco	11-Wd San Francisc	84	660
John	37	m	w	MO	Tulare	Packwood Twp	92	256
John	35	m	w	MA	Yuba	W Bear Rvr Twp	93	681
John	30	m	w	IREL	San Francisco	1-Wd San Francisco	79	123
John	29	m	w	IA	Sutter	Butte Twp	92	103
John	24	m	w	IREL	San Francisco	1-Wd San Francisco	79	136
John	24	m	w	CANA	Sonoma	Salt Point	91	386
John	22	m	w	TX	Tulare	Farmersville Twp	92	247
John J	35	m	w	IREL	San Francisco	San Francisco P O	83	125
John L	40	m	w	PA	Placer	Clipper Gap P O	76	376
Joseph	37	m	w	OH	San Francisco	San Francisco P O	83	398
Joseph	25	m	w	AUSL	San Francisco	San Francisco P O	83	11
Joshua	62	m	w	ME	Sonoma	Washington Twp	91	464
Judith	40	f	w	IREL	San Francisco	2-Wd San Francisco	79	193
Julius	26	m	w	GERM	Santa Clara	2-Wd San Jose	88	300
Katie	23	f	w	IREL	San Francisco	San Francisco P O	83	344
Lavina	15	f	w	CA	Santa Clara	2-Wd San Jose	88	337
Lewis	44	m	w	ITAL	Tuolumne	Chinese Camp P O	93	371
Lewis C	29	m	w	ME	Sacramento	2-Wd Sacramento	77	250
Louie	35	m	w	ENGL	Alameda	Brooklyn Twp	68	41
Louis J	39	m	w	ENGL	San Francisco	8-Wd San Francisco	82	497
Mary	71	f	w	IREL	San Francisco	San Francisco P O	83	396
Mary	40	f	w	FRAN	San Francisco	San Francisco P O	80	351
Mary	38	f	w	MO	Tulare	Visalia	92	299
Mary	24	f	w	ME	San Joaquin	1-Wd Stockton	86	121
Mary E	32	f	w	MA	Santa Cruz	Santa Cruz	89	405
Michael	37	m	w	IREL	San Francisco	1-Wd San Francisco	79	115
Michael	28	m	w	CANA	San Francisco	San Francisco P O	83	343
Moriano	45	m	w	MEXI	Kern	Tehachapi P O	73	356
Nancy C	29	f	w	ME	San Francisco	8-Wd San Francisco	82	292
Oscar	38	m	w	MI	Sacramento	2-Wd Sacramento	77	243
Pat	60	m	w	IREL	Santa Clara	Gilroy Twp	88	103
Pat	50	m	w	IREL	Santa Clara	Burnett Twp	88	38
Patrick	27	m	w	IREL	San Francisco	1-Wd San Francisco	79	123
Peter	40	m	w	KY	Sonoma	Petaluma Twp	91	332
R K	56	m	w	ME	Alameda	Oakland	68	243
Reason	53	m	w	VA	Santa Clara	San Jose Twp	88	201
Robert	13	m	w	CA	Tulare	Packwood Twp	92	256
Rowle	17	m	w	FRAN	San Francisco	San Francisco P O	85	776
Saml	42	m	w	PA	Mariposa	Maxwell Crk P O	74	140
Stephen	42	m	w	SPAI	Marin	Sausalito Twp	74	70
Talbert	29	m	w	MO	Tulare	Farmersville Twp	92	244
Thomas	43	m	w	OH	Sutter	Nicolaus Twp	92	113
W	35	m	w	NC	Merced	Snelling P O	74	268
William	42	m	w	NY	Marin	Tomales Twp	74	83
William F	31	m	w	TX	Tulare	Farmersville Twp	92	245
William M	33	m	w	IL	Contra Costa	Martinez P O	71	390
Wm	38	m	w	IREL	San Francisco	San Francisco P O	83	72
Wm	26	m	w	CT	San Francisco	8-Wd San Francisco	82	364
Wm C	60	m	w	MA	Sonoma	Petaluma Twp	91	321
JORDEN								
Andrew	82	m	w	VA	Amador	Jackson P O	69	326
C H	37	m	w	OH	San Joaquin	1-Wd Stockton	86	141
C M	21	m	w	MO	Sutter	Nicolaus Twp	92	110
Chas	36	m	w	PRUS	Alameda	Murray Twp	68	99
Jas	42	m	w	IREL	San Joaquin	3-Wd Stockton	86	243
W A	46	m	w	MO	Alameda	Murray Twp	68	109
JORDON								
Adam	37	m	w	CANA	Mariposa	Maxwell Crk P O	74	145
Alexander	24	m	w	CANA	Sonoma	Sonoma Twp	91	443
Charles	53	m	w	ME	San Francisco	11-Wd San Francisc	84	518
Charles	39	m	w	MA	San Francisco	11-Wd San Francisc	84	446
Charles	38	m	w	NY	San Francisco	11-Wd San Francisc	84	533
Daniel M	73	m	w	NY	Solano	Suisun Twp	90	103
David	38	m	w	OH	Sacramento	San Joaquin Twp	77	406
Dennis	30	m	w	MA	Butte	Ophir Twp	70	120
Elsie	54	f	w	TN	Del Norte	Smith Rvr Twp	71	476
Erby	30	m	w	TN	Tehama	Paskenta Twp	92	165
Felix	24	m	w	CA	Los Angeles	San Jose Twp	73	619
Fexes	38	m	w	TX	San Joaquin	Liberty Twp	86	86
George	35	m	w	CANA	Siskiyou	Callahan P O	89	633
George M	36	m	w	ME	Placer	Pino Twp	76	471
Harry	20	m	w	MA	San Joaquin	2-Wd Stockton	86	184
Jane	33	f	m	MD	Mariposa	Maxwell Crk P O	74	145
Jane	24	f	w	SCOT	Amador	Jackson P O	69	340
John	38	m	w	NY	Nevada	Eureka Twp	75	137
John	35	m	w	IREL	San Francisco	11-Wd San Francisc	84	474
John	35	m	w	IREL	Sonoma	Vallejo Twp	91	461
John	30	m	w	IREL	San Francisco	11-Wd San Francisc	84	615
John E	38	m	w	ME	Nevada	Little York Twp	75	239
Joseph	50	m	w	ENGL	San Francisco	1-Wd San Francisco	79	106
Joseph F	40	m	w	ENGL	Amador	Jackson P O	69	340
Josiah	38	m	w	ME	Klamath	South Fork Twp	73	383
Juaquene	45	m	w	SCOT	San Luis Obispo	San Luis Obispo Tw	87	297
M C	45	f	w	MA	Alameda	Oakland	68	162
Margaret	30	f	w	NY	San Francisco	11-Wd San Francisc	84	504
Margaret	25	f	w	IREL	San Francisco	San Francisco P O	85	760
Morris	49	m	w	WURT	San Francisco	3-Wd San Francisco	79	321
Moses	33	m	w	SC	El Dorado	Coloma Twp	72	10
Robt H	70	m	w	NC	Tehama	Paskenta Twp	92	164
Simon C	24	m	w	IA	Nevada	Nevada Twp	75	299
Thos	31	m	w	TN	Tehama	Paskenta Twp	92	165
W B	18	m	w	MO	Del Norte	Smith Rvr Twp	71	479
Wm	37	m	w	MA	San Joaquin	3-Wd Stockton	86	220
Wm	23	m	w	ME	Napa	Napa Twp	75	68
Wm A	47	m	w	ME	Siskiyou	Scott Valley Twp	89	610
JORESLIN								
Thos	28	m	w	IREL	San Francisco	8-Wd San Francisco	82	356
JORGEN								
Thos	26	m	w	NJ	San Joaquin	Douglas Twp	86	48
JORGENSEN								
Hans	42	m	w	DENM	Butte	Kimshew Tpw	70	82
Laura	16	f	w	SWED	San Francisco	11-Wd San Francisc	84	609
Peter	51	m	w	PRUS	Placer	Bath P O	76	451
JORGESEN								
Joseph	33	m	w	DENM	Sonoma	Petaluma Twp	91	319
JORI								
Charles	28	m	w	SWIT	Plumas	Seneca Twp	77	49
JORLEY								
Wm	30	m	w	IREL	San Francisco	San Francisco P O	85	834
JORLIS								
Frank G	30	m	w	CANA	Yolo	Cache Crk Twp	93	438
JORNER								
George	38	m	w	NY	Contra Costa	San Pablo Twp	71	353
JORNOD								
Henri Emile	53	m	w	SWIT	San Francisco	San Francisco P O	83	135
JORRADO								
Basilio	70	m	i	CA	Los Angeles	San Juan Twp	73	626
JORRES								
Wm	26	m	w	PRUS	San Francisco	11-Wd San Francisc	84	641
JORY								
James	24	m	w	ENGL	Nevada	Grass Valley Twp	75	192
John	49	m	w	ENGL	San Francisco	11-Wd San Francisc	84	439
John	27	m	w	ENGL	Nevada	Grass Valley Twp	75	220
William	26	m	w	ENGL	San Francisco	11-Wd San Francisc	84	465
JOSA								
Antorne	30	m	w	PORT	San Mateo	Half Moon Bay P O	87	402
Jesus	26	m	w	MEXI	Stanislaus	Emory Twp	92	26

© 2001 by Heritage Quest. All rights reserved.

Series M593

Name	Age	S	R	B-PL	County	Locale	Roll	Pg
John	38	m	w	PORT	San Mateo	Half Moon Bay P O	87	397
JOSCO								
S	41	f	w	MEXI	San Joaquin	1-Wd Stockton	86	139
JOSE								
Ah	38	m	c	CHIN	Santa Clara	Burnett Twp	88	35
Ale	42	m	c	CHIN	San Joaquin	1-Wd Stockton	86	137
Antone	20	m	w	AZOR	Contra Costa	Martinez P O	71	391
Antonio	60	m	w	AZOR	Contra Costa	San Pablo Twp	71	359
Antonio	40	m	w	ITAL	Calaveras	Copperopolis P O	70	247
Antonio	28	m	w	CA	San Diego	San Luis Rey	78	514
Antonio	25	m	i	CA	Santa Barbara	Las Cruces P O	87	505
Antonio	20	m	i	CA	San Diego	San Luis Rey	78	512
Antonio	1	m	w	CA	San Diego	San Luis Rey	78	515
C	40	m	w	ENGL	Lassen	Susanville Twp	73	443
Celia	40	f	w	CA	Napa	Napa	75	26
De Freitas	31	m	w	PORT	San Francisco	8-Wd San Francisco	82	373
Emanuel	40	m	w	CHIL	Butte	Wyandotte Twp	70	149
Henery	17	m	w	PRUS	San Francisco	7-Wd San Francisco	81	222
Luis	26	m	i	MEXI	Los Angeles	Los Angeles Twp	73	498
Manuel	45	m	w	AZOR	Contra Costa	San Pablo Twp	71	359
Manuel	25	m	w	AZOR	Contra Costa	Martinez P O	71	370
Manuel	23	m	w	AZOR	San Francisco	1-Wd San Francisco	79	123
Maria	30	f	i	CA	San Diego	San Diego	78	505
Maria	30	m	i	MEXI	Los Angeles	Los Angeles	73	501
Martinus	39	m	w	MEXI	Humboldt	South Fork Twp	72	301
Mich H	62	m	w	GA	Sonoma	Santa Rosa	91	413
Michael	31	m	w	MEXI	El Dorado	Cosumnes Twp	72	16
Michael W	22	m	w	MO	Sonoma	Analy Twp	91	239
Miguel	25	m	i	CA	Santa Barbara	San Buenaventura P	87	440
Quentain	30	m	w	NM	Mendocino	Round Valley Twp	74	218
Rush	12	m	w	MO	Sonoma	Analy Twp	91	240
S P	31	m	w	CA	Lake	Coyote Valley	73	401
Salanine	54	m	w	SPAI	Merced	Snelling P O	74	273
Thomase	30	m	w	ENGL	Nevada	Nevada Twp	75	301
Triber	24	m	w	CHIL	Sacramento	2-Wd Sacramento	77	215
JOSEA								
Antone	41	m	w	SCOT	Alameda	Brooklyn Twp	68	56
Patrise	40	m	w	PORT	Alameda	Washington Twp	68	287
JOSEF								
Antonio	19	m	w	ITAL	Calaveras	San Andreas P O	70	214
Johan	21	m	w	ITAL	Calaveras	San Andreas P O	70	214
JOSEFA								
Constant	25	m	w	SWIT	Marin	Novato Twp	74	11
Juan	45	m	w	MEXI	Marin	Tomales Twp	74	85
JOSELYN								
H E	28	f	w	ENGL	Sacramento	3-Wd Sacramento	77	285
Joel S	39	m	w	MA	Sacramento	3-Wd Sacramento	77	285
Lucy	47	f	w	NH	San Francisco	San Francisco P O	83	217
Warren	7	m	w	CA	San Francisco	8-Wd San Francisco	82	452
JOSEMAN								
Cacusin	38	m	w	MEXI	San Diego	Fort Yuma Dist	78	463
JOSEN								
Louise	12	f	w	FRAN	Monterey	Alisal Twp	74	298
JOSEPH								
A	40	m	w	PRUS	Yuba	Marysville	93	593
A	21	m	w	PORT	Sierra	Butte Twp	89	509
Abram	29	m	w	BOHE	San Francisco	1-Wd San Francisco	79	51
Albert	37	m	w	OH	Colusa	Monroe Twp	71	321
Ami	56	m	w	FRAN	San Francisco	San Francisco P O	80	460
Anthony	42	m	w	PORT	Alameda	Oakland	68	137
Antoin	35	m	w	HI	Yolo	Merritt Twp	93	502
Antoine	28	m	w	PORT	Plumas	Quartz Twp	77	34
Anton	40	m	w	PORT	Tuolumne	Columbia P O	93	355
Anton	21	m	w	PORT	Marin	Bolinas Twp	74	4
Antone	53	m	w	AZOR	Santa Cruz	Santa Cruz Twp	89	382
Antone	42	m	w	PORT	Alameda	Washington Twp	68	298
Antone	35	m	w	AZOR	Marin	Sausalito Twp	74	70
Antone	33	m	w	PORT	Siskiyou	Cottonwood Twp	89	590
Antone	33	m	w	ITAL	Santa Clara	Almaden Twp	88	19
Antone	29	m	w	PORT	Marin	San Rafael Twp	74	59
Antone	28	m	w	AZOR	Nevada	Washington Twp	75	346
Antone	25	m	w	PORT	Mendocino	Navarro & Big Rvr	74	177
Antone	20	m	w	SCOT	Alameda	Brooklyn Twp	68	46
Antone	20	m	w	PORT	Trinity	North Fork Twp	92	217
Antonio	50	m	w	PORT	Solano	Suisun Twp	90	110
Antonio	47	m	w	PORT	Solano	Rio Vista Twp	90	61
Antonio	44	m	w	AZOR	San Francisco	1-Wd San Francisco	79	102
Antonio	37	m	w	SCOT	Alameda	Brooklyn Twp	68	44
Antonio	35	m	w	PORT	San Mateo	Half Moon Bay P O	87	400
Antonio	30	m	w	AZOR	San Francisco	1-Wd San Francisco	79	134
August	29	m	w	CHIL	Solano	Vallejo	90	202
Bernhard	42	m	w	PRUS	San Francisco	San Francisco P O	85	864
Buff	13	m	w	ENGL	San Francisco	1-Wd San Francisco	79	45
Carmelo	40	m	w	PORT	Alameda	Eden Twp	68	88
Chas	40	m	w	FRAN	San Francisco	1-Wd San Francisco	79	106
Chas	2	m	w	CA	San Francisco	1-Wd San Francisco	79	106
Chas	15	m	w	CA	Shasta	French Gulch P O	89	466
Dora	30	f	w	PRUS	San Francisco	8-Wd San Francisco	82	403
Edwin	40	m	w	OH	Solano	Silveyville Twp	90	91
Enos	56	m	w	PORT	Tuolumne	Columbia P O	93	338
Eugenie	20	f	w	FRAN	San Francisco	1-Wd San Francisco	79	106
Frances	65	f	w	SC	San Francisco	2-Wd San Francisco	79	173
Francis	42	m	w	MA	El Dorado	Placerville	72	124
Francis	34	m	w	PORT	Nevada	Rough & Ready Twp	75	328
Francis	28	m	w	GERM	Yolo	Cache Crk Twp	93	445
Frank	56	m	w	PORT	Alameda	Hayward	68	73
Frank	56	m	w	FRAN	Nevada	Eureka Twp	75	135

Series M593

Name	Age	S	R	B-PL	County	Locale	Roll	Pg
Frank	45	m	w	PORT	Alameda	Eden Twp	68	89
Frank	43	m	w	PORT	Tuolumne	Sonora P O	93	304
Frank	40	m	w	PORT	Alameda	Hayward	68	77
Frank	38	m	w	PORT	Shasta	American Ranch P O	89	498
Frank	37	m	w	PORT	Alameda	Washington Twp	68	275
Frank	32	m	w	PORT	Alameda	Washington Twp	68	269
Frank	30	m	w	PORT	Santa Clara	Redwood Twp	88	123
Frank	30	m	w	AZOR	Monterey	Castroville Twp	74	341
Frank	30	m	w	PORT	San Francisco	11-Wd San Francisc	84	614
Frank	29	m	w	NCOD	Colusa	Colusa	71	297
Frank	28	m	w	AZOR	San Francisco	1-Wd San Francisco	79	123
Frank	28	m	w	PORT	Mendocino	Big Rvr Twp	74	159
Frank	28	m	w	PORT	Santa Clara	Milpitas Twp	88	111
Frank	28	m	w	AZOR	Yuba	Parks Bar Twp	93	649
Frank	26	m	w	PORT	San Francisco	1-Wd San Francisco	79	101
Frank	25	m	w	AZOR	Sonoma	Analy Twp	91	222
Frank	24	m	w	AZOR	San Francisco	1-Wd San Francisco	79	118
Frank	22	m	w	PORT	Yuba	New York Twp	93	640
Frank	20	m	w	PORT	Alameda	Hayward	68	79
Frank	19	m	w	PORT	Alameda	Washington Twp	68	299
Frank	1	m	w	CA	San Mateo	Pescadero P O	87	414
George	36	m	b	IL	Nevada	Nevada Twp	75	320
Harris	45	m	w	RUSS	San Francisco	1-Wd San Francisco	79	44
Henrico	22	m	w	ITAL	San Mateo	Schoolhouse Statio	87	344
Henry	27	m	m	ENGL	Santa Clara	Gilroy Twp	88	77
Hyman	29	m	w	POLA	San Francisco	San Francisco P O	80	380
I J	38	m	w	PA	Sierra	Sierra Twp	89	565
Isaac	45	m	w	PRUS	San Francisco	San Francisco P O	83	39
Isaac	32	m	w	PRUS	San Francisco	8-Wd San Francisco	82	406
Isaac	30	m	w	POLA	San Francisco	1-Wd San Francisco	79	92
Isaac	18	m	w	PRUS	San Francisco	1-Wd San Francisco	79	118
J	30	m	w	PORT	Nevada	Eureka Twp	75	136
J	22	m	w	PORT	Lassen	Janesville Twp	73	434
Jacob	9	m	w	CA	San Francisco	5-Wd San Francisco	81	34
Jacob	45	m	w	NY	San Francisco	5-Wd San Francisco	81	33
Jo	20	m	i	CA	Yolo	Cache Crk Twp	93	427
Joaquin	47	m	w	PORT	Alameda	Washington Twp	68	297
Joaquin	35	m	w	PORT	Alameda	Hayward	68	77
John	50	m	w	RUSS	Calaveras	San Andreas P O	70	160
John	48	m	w	SCOT	Alameda	Brooklyn Twp	68	47
John	42	m	w	PORT	Tuolumne	Columbia P O	93	342
John	36	m	w	ITAL	San Mateo	Schoolhouse Statio	87	344
John	35	m	w	PORT	Trinity	Minersville Pct	92	203
John	34	m	w	AZOR	Marin	Sausalito Twp	74	71
John	25	m	w	SCOT	Siskiyou	Yreka Twp	89	666
John	25	m	w	PORT	Santa Clara	Milpitas Twp	88	109
John	24	m	w	PORT	Alameda	Eden Twp	68	69
John	24	m	w	PORT	Alameda	Washington Twp	68	274
John	23	m	w	PORT	Nevada	Rough & Ready Twp	75	329
Jose	32	m	b	CA	Santa Barbara	Santa Barbara P O	87	460
Joseph	40	m	w	RUSS	San Francisco	11-Wd San Francisc	84	569
Lewis	51	m	w	FRAN	Placer	Gold Run Twp	76	398
Louis	47	m	w	ENGL	San Francisco	San Francisco P O	83	365
Louis	36	m	w	FRAN	San Francisco	San Francisco P O	80	538
Louis	13	m	w	CA	San Joaquin	1-Wd Stockton	86	139
Louisa	32	f	w	NY	San Francisco	5-Wd San Francisco	81	34
Luce	40	m	w	AZOR	Monterey	Monterey	74	363
M	37	m	w	PORT	Santa Clara	Gilroy Twp	88	92
Manel	40	m	w	SCOT	Alameda	Brooklyn Twp	68	48
Manuel	50	m	w	PORT	Alameda	Washington Twp	68	293
Manuel	47	m	w	HI	Klamath	South Fork Twp	73	383
Manuel	44	m	w	AZOR	Marin	Sausalito Twp	74	69
Manuel	40	m	w	PORT	Klamath	Liberty Twp	73	374
Manuel	40	m	w	SCOT	San Luis Obispo	San Luis Obispo Tw	87	297
Manuel	35	m	w	MEXI	San Francisco	5-Wd San Francisco	81	34
Manuel	34	m	w	PORT	Alameda	Eden Twp	68	87
Manuel	34	m	w	PORT	Tuolumne	Columbia P O	93	355
Manuel	33	m	w	AZOR	Monterey	Monterey Twp	74	343
Manuel	32	m	w	SCOT	Alameda	Brooklyn Twp	68	45
Manuel	30	m	w	PORT	Alameda	Washington Twp	68	291
Manuel	30	m	w	PORT	San Francisco	1-Wd San Francisco	79	14
Manuel	28	m	w	PORT	Alameda	Washington Twp	68	291
Manuel	26	m	w	PORT	Marin	San Rafael Twp	74	42
Manuel	25	m	w	HI	Yolo	Merritt Twp	93	508
Manuel	22	m	w	HI	Yolo	Merritt Twp	93	502
Manuel	20	m	w	AZOR	Contra Costa	Martinez P O	71	367
Manuel	15	m	w	AZOR	San Francisco	1-Wd San Francisco	79	51
Marcelino	35	m	w	AZOR	Monterey	Monterey Twp	74	352
Marcus E	22	m	w	NY	Stanislaus	San Joaquin Twp	92	77
Mary	48	f	w	RUSS	San Francisco	8-Wd San Francisco	82	320
Mary	48	f	w	NY	San Francisco	2-Wd San Francisco	79	147
Mary	28	f	w	IREL	San Francisco	San Francisco P O	83	11
Mary	24	f	w	AZOR	Contra Costa	Martinez P O	71	395
Michael	47	m	w	POLA	Sacramento	4-Wd Sacramento	77	341
Michael	35	m	w	PORT	San Mateo	Pescadero P O	87	414
Michael J	37	m	w	ENGL	San Francisco	8-Wd San Francisco	82	418
Michl	87	m	w	RUSS	San Francisco	1-Wd San Francisco	79	45
Morris H	28	m	w	ENGL	Nevada	Grass Valley Twp	75	145
O A	36	m	w	ITAL	Tuolumne	Columbia P O	93	346
Peter	41	m	w	NY	San Francisco	1-Wd San Francisco	79	132
Peter H	49	m	w	NY	San Francisco	2-Wd San Francisco	79	227
Robrt	49	m	w	PRUS	San Francisco	11-Wd San Francisc	84	494
Rolins	30	m	w	SCOT	Alameda	Brooklyn Twp	68	48
Saml	40	m	w	WIND	Santa Barbara	Santa Barbara P O	87	451
Saml	27	m	w	NY	San Francisco	5-Wd San Francisco	81	34
Sander	27	m	w	AR	Colusa	Monroe Twp	71	322
Sarvanina	30	m	w	ITAL	El Dorado	Placerville Twp	72	93

© 2001 by Heritage Quest. All rights reserved.

California 1870 Census

Series M593

Name	Age	S	R	B-PL	County	Locale	Roll	Pg
Simon	37	m	w	AZOR	Nevada	Eureka Twp	75	139
Suze	62	m	w	FRAN	Trinity	Lewiston Pct	92	212
Thomas	25	m	w	PRUS	Yolo	Cottonwood Twp	93	471
Thos	11	m	w	CA	Sacramento	Sutter Twp	77	382
Ulyesses	34	m	w	OH	Yolo	Putah Twp	93	517
W	44	m	w	VA	Sacramento	1-Wd Sacramento	77	189
William	45	m	w	PORT	San Francisco	3-Wd San Francisco	79	290
William W	41	m	w	OH	Yolo	Putah Twp	93	512
Wm	46	m	w	SPAI	Solano	Vallejo	90	184
Zampetia	18	m	w	ITAL	Napa	Napa Twp	75	68
JOSEPHENSON								
Martin	40	m	w	NORW	Butte	Ophir Twp	70	95
JOSEPHERN								
Mark	23	m	w	ENGL	Stanislaus	San Joaquin Twp	92	83
JOSEPHES								
Joshua	30	m	w	CHIL	Sacramento	2-Wd Sacramento	77	215
JOSEPHI								
Augusta R	29	f	w	MA	San Francisco	San Francisco P O	83	104
David	27	m	w	NY	San Francisco	11-Wd San Francisc	84	562
Eveline	56	f	w	ENGL	San Francisco	11-Wd San Francisc	84	562
John	25	m	w	ITAL	San Mateo	Schoolhouse Statio	87	346
Louis	22	m	w	SWIT	San Francisco	6-Wd San Francisco	81	155
JOSEPHINE								
Isaac S	40	m	w	ENGL	San Francisco	San Francisco P O	83	104
JOSEPHS								
C	24	m	w	IREL	Santa Clara	Almaden Twp	88	20
John	27	m	w	NY	San Francisco	1-Wd San Francisco	79	116
Louisa	42	f	w	ENGL	San Francisco	2-Wd San Francisco	79	143
Mary	48	f	w	NY	Solano	Vallejo	90	162
Peter	47	m	w	PRUS	Yolo	Merritt Twp	93	507
JOSEPHUS								
Antone	29	m	w	PORT	Alameda	Eden Twp	68	67
JOSEPHY								
Joseph	30	m	w	SWED	Santa Clara	San Jose Twp	88	208
JOSEPPI								
Alpirri	28	m	w	ITAL	Sonoma	Analy Twp	91	236
JOSES								
B F	39	m	w	PA	Alameda	Oakland	68	226
JOSH								
Ah	26	f	c	CHIN	San Francisco	San Francisco P O	80	495
JOSHER								
Geo	45	m	w	HANO	Sacramento	4-Wd Sacramento	77	324
JOSHLAN								
Gilbert	27	m	w	MI	Santa Clara	Gilroy Twp	88	98
JOSIAH								
Nelson	25	m	w	NY	Santa Barbara	Santa Barbara P O	87	493
JOSIM								
Absalom	27	m	w	IL	San Joaquin	Douglas Twp	86	46
JOSLIN								
Clark M	59	m	w	VT	Inyo	Lone Pine Twp	73	330
Hardy	38	m	w	MI	Monterey	San Antonio Twp	74	324
Silas	39	m	w	CT	Contra Costa	Martinez P O	71	398
JOSLYN								
Abner	22	m	w	IREL	Solano	Silveyville Twp	90	78
Henry	24	m	w	IREL	Solano	Silveyville Twp	90	88
Henry C	34	m	w	MA	Nevada	Grass Valley Twp	75	177
JOSMAN								
Thos	31	m	w	TN	Butte	Oregon Twp	70	133
JOSOLIN								
Joseph	45	m	w	MA	San Joaquin	Elkhorn Twp	86	54
JOSSAND								
John	19	m	w	FRAN	San Francisco	San Francisco P O	85	752
JOSSE								
Madeline	30	f	w	FRAN	San Francisco	San Francisco P O	80	487
JOSSELAN								
Mary S	27	f	w	NY	San Francisco	5-Wd San Francisco	81	12
JOSSELYN								
B F	37	m	w	MA	San Francisco	3-Wd San Francisco	79	326
JOSSELYNE								
J D	32	m	w	OH	Solano	Vallejo	90	162
JOSSET								
Joseph	48	m	w	FRAN	San Francisco	8-Wd San Francisco	82	366
JOST								
Alexander	20	m	w	IL	Sacramento	2-Wd Sacramento	77	247
Bernard	29	m	w	HANO	San Francisco	11-Wd San Francisc	84	504
Charles	36	m	w	BAVA	San Francisco	2-Wd San Francisco	79	187
Edward	45	m	w	BREM	San Francisco	2-Wd San Francisco	79	143
John D	27	m	w	CANA	Sacramento	4-Wd Sacramento	77	375
JOSTA								
Berlia	22	f	w	NY	San Joaquin	2-Wd Stockton	86	173
JOSUS								
C J	17	m	w	AUSL	Alameda	Oakland	68	258
JOSYLIN								
Henry	45	m	w	MA	San Francisco	8-Wd San Francisco	82	445
JOT								
Ah	44	m	c	CHIN	San Joaquin	Oneal Twp	86	117
Ah	36	m	c	CHIN	San Joaquin	Oneal Twp	86	117
JOTIEN								
J	54	m	w	FRAN	San Joaquin	2-Wd Stockton	86	163
JOTTARD								
John	34	m	w	BELG	San Francisco	2-Wd San Francisco	79	148
JOU								
Wo	25	m	c	CHIN	San Francisco	1-Wd San Francisco	79	43
JOUBERT								
Cesinine	42	m	w	FRAN	Yuba	Slate Range Bar Tw	93	670
Jacques	44	m	w	FRAN	Yuba	Slate Range Bar Tw	93	670
Pierre	31	m	w	FRAN	San Francisco	8-Wd San Francisco	82	373

Series M593

Name	Age	S	R	B-PL	County	Locale	Roll	Pg
JOUGHINS								
Andrew	52	m	w	ENGL	Los Angeles	San Juan Twp	73	624
JOUNG								
Hiram	63	m	w	KY	Sonoma	Santa Rosa	91	398
JOURDAIN								
Leon	64	m	w	FRAN	Santa Barbara	Santa Barbara P O	87	451
JOURDAN								
Andrew	47	m	w	MO	Tuolumne	Sonora P O	93	323
J G	24	m	w	FRAN	San Francisco	8-Wd San Francisco	82	346
Jacques	40	m	w	WIND	San Francisco	11-Wd San Francisc	84	643
John	38	m	w	MI	San Joaquin	Tulare Twp	86	257
Philip	35	m	w	FRAN	San Francisco	San Francisco P O	80	348
Philip	35	m	w	FRAN	San Francisco	San Francisco P O	80	347
Phillip	63	m	w	WI	El Dorado	Diamond Springs Tw	72	24
William	59	m	w	ENGL	San Francisco	San Francisco P O	83	384
JOURGANS								
Jasper	46	m	w	ENGL	El Dorado	White Oak Twp	72	138
JOURGER								
Joseph	39	m	w	FRAN	El Dorado	Lake Valley Twp	72	65
William	52	m	w	HANO	El Dorado	Diamond Springs Tw	72	21
JOURNEY								
Alfred	18	m	w	IA	Sacramento	Lee Twp	77	157
Jas	45	m	w	NY	San Joaquin	3-Wd Stockton	86	239
John	22	m	w	IL	San Joaquin	Elkhorn Twp	86	52
John	18	m	w	NY	Solano	Vallejo	90	204
Peter	42	m	w	IL	Sacramento	San Joaquin Twp	77	407
Richard	10	m	w	IA	Sacramento	Brighton Twp	77	71
JOURNY								
Lina	17	f	w	IN	Sacramento	San Joaquin Twp	77	406
JOUSE								
William	22	m	w	PA	Alameda	Washington Twp	68	289
JOUTIN								
Charles	34	m	w	FRAN	El Dorado	Salmon Falls Twp	72	131
JOUVINTAN								
F	58	f	w	FRAN	Sierra	Sears Twp	89	555
JOVANNI								
Angel	24	m	w	ITAL	Marin	Novato Twp	74	10
JOVANOICH								
Lazarus	28	m	w	DALM	San Francisco	1-Wd San Francisco	79	127
JOVARNY								
Antonio	18	m	w	ITAL	San Mateo	Schoolhouse Statio	87	340
JOVENETTI								
A	35	m	w	ITAL	El Dorado	Greenwood Twp	72	54
JOW								
Ah	30	m	c	CHIN	Alameda	Washington Twp	68	284
Ah	26	m	c	CHIN	San Francisco	6-Wd San Francisco	81	130
Ah	22	m	c	CHIN	Calaveras	Copperopolis P O	70	228
Ah	21	m	c	CHIN	Alameda	Eden Twp	68	81
Ka	24	m	c	CHIN	Santa Clara	San Jose Twp	88	191
JOWARDA								
Margarita	13	f	w	MEXI	San Diego	Coronado	78	467
JOWLEY								
James	28	m	w	IREL	San Francisco	1-Wd San Francisco	79	113
JOWN								
Ah	39	m	c	CHIN	Calaveras	Copperopolis P O	70	226
JOY								
A	48	m	w	NY	Amador	Drytown P O	69	423
A C	34	m	w	MA	Sierra	Sierra Twp	89	568
Ah	43	m	c	CHIN	San Francisco	San Francisco P O	80	502
Ah	40	m	c	CHIN	El Dorado	Coloma Twp	72	12
Ah	39	m	c	CHIN	San Francisco	San Francisco P O	80	445
Ah	38	m	c	CHIN	San Francisco	San Francisco P O	80	508
Ah	32	m	c	CHIN	El Dorado	Coloma Twp	72	11
Ah	31	m	c	CHIN	Nevada	Meadow Lake Twp	75	256
Ah	27	m	c	CHIN	Stanislaus	Buena Vista Twp	92	11
Ah	26	m	c	CHIN	Sierra	Lincoln Twp	89	546
Ah	26	m	c	CHIN	Nevada	Washington Twp	75	342
Ah	25	m	c	CHIN	Santa Clara	Santa Clara Twp	88	148
Ah	21	f	c	CHIN	San Francisco	San Francisco P O	80	524
Ah	21	f	c	CHIN	San Francisco	San Francisco P O	80	432
Ah	20	m	c	CHIN	San Francisco	San Francisco P O	80	517
Ah	20	m	c	CHIN	Contra Costa	Martinez P O	71	370
Alfred	36	m	w	ME	Santa Barbara	San Buenaventura P	87	446
Benjamin	49	m	w	ENGL	Sonoma	Bodega Twp	91	263
Charles H	28	m	w	NH	Mendocino	Navarro & Big Rvr	74	167
E A	39	f	w	ME	Sacramento	3-Wd Sacramento	77	271
Edwin F	37	m	w	VT	San Francisco	6-Wd San Francisco	81	124
H C	34	m	w	MA	Amador	Sutter Crk P O	69	398
H L	50	m	w	ENGL	Amador	Jackson P O	69	324
Henry	24	m	w	MO	Solano	Silveyville Twp	90	83
J A	19	m	w	MN	Amador	Drytown P O	69	423
James	22	m	w	ENGL	Nevada	Grass Valley Twp	75	183
Jim	23	m	c	CHIN	Contra Costa	Martinez Twp	71	346
Jno P	45	m	w	VT	Santa Clara	Burnett Twp	88	39
John	34	m	w	IREL	Solano	Rio Vista Twp	90	64
John H	45	m	w	ME	Santa Clara	Alviso Twp	88	24
Mary A	45	f	w	ME	Sacramento	2-Wd Sacramento	77	235
Michael	35	m	w	IREL	Santa Barbara	Santa Barbara P O	87	461
Oliver H	39	m	w	NH	Mendocino	Navarro & Big Rvr	74	176
Peter	35	m	w	IREL	Calaveras	San Andreas P O	70	183
Robert	45	m	w	ENGL	Sierra	Sears Twp	89	559
Rose C	33	f	w	IREL	Santa Cruz	Santa Cruz	89	420
Saml A	35	m	w	ME	Sierra	Table Rock Twp	89	578
Stephen	35	m	w	ME	Marin	San Rafael	74	51
Thomas A	20	m	w	MA	Yolo	Cache Crk Twp	93	444
Thos	20	m	w	IREL	Solano	Vallejo	90	162
William	32	m	w	ENGL	Calaveras	Copperopolis P O	70	244

© 2001 by Heritage Quest. All rights reserved.

Name	Age	S	R	B-PL	County	Locale	Roll	Pg
William	23	m	w	NY	Amador	Jackson P O	69	339
William	21	m	w	IREL	Solano	Silveyville Twp	90	90
Wm	43	m	w	IREL	Nevada	Nevada Twp	75	282
You	21	f	c	CHIN	Yuba	Marysville	93	627
JOYCE								
Abel	41	m	w	IREL	Solano	Silveyville Twp	90	74
Alf	40	m	w	IREL	San Joaquin	2-Wd Stockton	86	200
Andrew	48	m	w	CANA	Nevada	Little York Twp	75	244
Anne	18	f	w	IREL	San Francisco	6-Wd San Francisco	81	155
Annie	25	f	w	IREL	San Francisco	San Francisco P O	80	391
Catherine	40	f	w	IREL	San Francisco	3-Wd San Francisco	79	300
Chas	18	m	w	DE	San Francisco	11-Wd San Francisc	84	593
Conrad	34	m	w	OH	Solano	Silveyville Twp	90	80
Edmund	28	m	w	IREL	San Francisco	11-Wd San Francisc	84	558
Edward	26	m	w	NY	Plumas	Plumas Twp	77	28
Edward	25	m	w	IREL	Contra Costa	Martinez P O	71	427
Elizabeth	40	f	w	IREL	San Francisco	San Francisco P O	83	92
Elizabeth	24	f	w	IREL	San Francisco	San Francisco P O	83	353
Ellen	35	f	w	IREL	San Francisco	11-Wd San Francisc	84	712
George	75	m	w	HANO	San Francisco	11-Wd San Francisc	84	616
George	40	m	w	ENGL	Sonoma	Salt Point	91	391
Hiram	38	m	w	MO	Solano	Silveyville Twp	90	90
James	8	m	w	CA	Alameda	Oakland	68	258
James	15	m	w	CANA	San Francisco	San Francisco P O	83	319
John	48	m	w	MA	Alameda	Washington Twp	68	282
John	45	m	w	IREL	San Francisco	1-Wd San Francisco	79	76
John	27	m	w	CANA	Alameda	Eden Twp	68	57
John	26	m	w	IL	Tehama	Tehama Twp	92	191
John	26	m	w	PORT	Santa Cruz	Santa Cruz	89	414
Julia	90	f	w	IREL	San Francisco	8-Wd San Francisco	82	433
Julia	26	f	w	IREL	San Francisco	San Francisco P O	83	361
Margaret	29	f	w	IREL	San Francisco	8-Wd San Francisco	82	406
Mat	46	m	w	IREL	San Francisco	7-Wd San Francisco	81	264
Michael	45	m	w	IREL	San Joaquin	Castoria Twp	86	2
Michael	32	m	w	IREL	San Francisco	8-Wd San Francisco	82	418
Micheal	23	m	w	NY	San Francisco	7-Wd San Francisco	81	211
Micheal	20	m	w	NY	San Francisco	7-Wd San Francisco	81	171
Milton E	25	m	w	NY	San Mateo	Half Moon Bay P O	87	398
Patrick	41	m	w	IREL	Nevada	Grass Valley Twp	75	213
Patrick	33	m	w	CANA	Nevada	Little York Twp	75	238
Peter	37	m	w	IREL	Marin	San Rafael Twp	74	32
Thomas	54	m	w	IREL	Sonoma	Petaluma Twp	91	344
Thomas F	65	m	w	ENGL	San Mateo	Belmont P O	87	372
William	36	m	w	CT	Nevada	Bridgeport Twp	75	103
William	30	m	w	IREL	Nevada	Washington Twp	75	339
William	28	m	w	NY	Inyo	Lone Pine Twp	73	331
Winford	50	m	w	IREL	San Francisco	San Francisco P O	83	92
Wm	45	m	w	SC	Santa Clara	Gilroy Twp	88	73
JOYE								
Edmond V	23	m	w	SC	Yuba	Bullards Bar P O	93	549
JOYNER								
Wm P	42	m	w	ENGL	Solano	Benicia	90	2
JOYNES								
George F	23	m	w	VA	San Luis Obispo	Santa Rosa Twp	87	319
JOYNT								
G C	20	m	w	NY	San Francisco	San Francisco P O	85	863
Robert	46	m	w	IREL	Sacramento	Mississippi Twp	77	164
JSRICK								
John C	48	m	w	GERM	Los Angeles	Los Angeles Twp	73	481
JU								
Ah	36	m	c	CHIN	El Dorado	Mountain Twp	72	70
La	31	m	c	CHIN	San Francisco	San Francisco P O	85	764
JUA								
Lun	32	m	c	CHIN	Kern	Bakersfield P O	73	365
JUAN								
Antonio	48	m	i	CA	Santa Barbara	Santa Barbara P O	87	472
Antonio	40	m	w	PORT	Contra Costa	Martinez P O	71	408
Don	46	m	w	MEXI	Mariposa	Mariposa P O	74	125
Frank	28	m	w	FRAN	Alameda	Brooklyn Twp	68	43
Hosen	60	m	w	MEXI	Los Angeles	Los Angeles Twp	73	473
John	36	m	w	MEXI	San Francisco	San Francisco P O	80	430
Jose	48	m	i	MEXI	Merced	Snelling P O	74	251
Jose	30	m	w	CA	San Diego	Warners Rancho Dis	78	530
JUANADA								
Teresa	40	f	w	MEXI	San Francisco	2-Wd San Francisco	79	165
JUANNENCO								
---	38	m	w	CA	Napa	Napa	75	57
JUANS								
Patricia	3	f	i	CA	Merced	Snelling P O	74	251
JUANTES								
Vicenti	50	m	w	MEXI	Kern	Bakersfield P O	73	366
JUARA								
Narcisso	35	m	w	CA	Fresno	Millerton P O	72	159
JUARACE								
Juan	25	m	w	MEXI	Los Angeles	Los Angeles Twp	73	480
JUARD								
Manuel	27	m	w	MEXI	San Diego	Fort Yuma Dist	78	463
JUARES								
Reyes	34	m	w	MEXI	Plumas	Mineral Twp	77	22
JUAREZ								
Benjamin	41	m	w	CA	Santa Barbara	Santa Barbara P O	87	480
Cayelemus	60	m	w	CA	Napa	Napa Twp	75	73
Estalo	34	m	w	MEXI	San Francisco	San Francisco P O	80	470
F	62	m	w	CA	Santa Clara	Almaden Twp	88	19
Felicia	25	f	w	MEXI	San Francisco	San Francisco P O	80	344
Isadorra	24	m	w	CA	Santa Clara	Almaden Twp	88	19
Jose	35	m	w	MEXI	Plumas	Mineral Twp	77	23
Juande B	14	m	w	CA	Santa Barbara	Santa Barbara P O	87	479
Manuel	86	m	w	CA	Contra Costa	Martinez P O	71	449
Maria D	56	f	w	CA	Santa Barbara	Santa Barbara P O	87	489
Ramon	50	m	w	MEXI	Fresno	Millerton P O	72	160
Vicente	18	m	w	CA	Santa Barbara	Santa Barbara P O	87	488
JUARIS								
L	60	m	w	CA	Santa Clara	Almaden Twp	88	19
JUBB								
Geo	40	m	w	ENGL	Sacramento	Franklin Twp	77	108
JUBER								
John	33	m	w	NY	Colusa	Grand Island Twp	71	302
JUCELL								
Ada	39	f	w	ENGL	San Francisco	San Francisco P O	83	404
JUCH								
Ah	19	m	c	CHIN	San Joaquin	Dent Twp	86	29
JUCHIN								
Charly	19	m	j	CA	Humboldt	Eureka Twp	72	275
JUCK								
Kee	20	m	c	CHIN	Yuba	Marysville	93	630
Men	23	m	c	CHIN	Solano	Suisun Twp	90	105
JUDA								
Henry	30	m	w	SWIT	Tulare	Venice Twp	92	276
JUDAH								
Henry	19	m	w	OH	San Francisco	7-Wd San Francisco	81	274
Ida	10	f	b	CA	Santa Clara	1-Wd San Jose	88	257
Oceana	26	f	w	MD	San Francisco	San Francisco P O	80	426
Thomas	29	m	w	KY	Yuba	East Bear Rvr Twp	93	540
JUDAMIAH								
John	55	m	w	GERM	Yolo	Putah Twp	93	520
JUDAS								
Joseph	30	m	w	PORT	San Mateo	San Mateo P O	87	359
JUDD								
Annie	17	f	w	CA	Solano	Benicia	90	17
Benj	50	m	w	NY	Mendocino	Calpella Twp	74	182
Charles	32	m	w	CANA	San Diego	San Diego	78	487
Charles H	30	m	w	OH	Santa Clara	San Jose Twp	88	201
D B	40	m	w	ME	Humboldt	Eureka Twp	72	275
Edwin	40	m	w	VT	Sacramento	2-Wd Sacramento	77	230
George A	17	m	w	IL	Santa Cruz	Pajaro Twp	89	362
Harvey	29	m	w	NY	San Francisco	3-Wd San Francisco	79	308
James	27	m	w	IREL	San Francisco	San Francisco P O	83	419
James	25	m	w	NY	Shasta	Portugese Flat P O	89	471
James	14	m	w	CA	Santa Clara	Santa Clara Twp	88	177
John	31	m	w	ENGL	San Francisco	1-Wd San Francisco	79	127
John	18	m	w	CA	San Francisco	8-Wd San Francisco	82	490
Lee	14	m	w	IL	San Francisco	6-Wd San Francisco	81	128
Noah	41	m	w	ENGL	El Dorado	Mud Springs Twp	72	74
Saml M	45	m	w	NY	San Luis Obispo	Santa Rosa Twp	87	326
Walter E	47	m	w	NY	San Francisco	6-Wd San Francisco	81	90
William	37	m	w	ENGL	Placer	Gold Run Twp	76	395
William	21	m	w	IREL	Solano	Silveyville Twp	90	75
JUDE								
James	25	m	w	PA	San Francisco	11-Wd San Francisc	84	712
JUDEN								
George W	40	m	w	MO	Los Angeles	Los Angeles	73	502
Jacob	17	m	i	CA	Humboldt	Eel Rvr Twp	72	247
JUDGE								
Bridget	45	f	w	IREL	San Joaquin	2-Wd Stockton	86	203
Henry	44	m	w	IREL	San Francisco	San Francisco P O	85	768
Irwin	53	m	w	IREL	Sutter	Sutter Twp	92	123
John	38	m	w	IREL	San Francisco	11-Wd San Francisc	84	691
John	34	m	w	IREL	Solano	Vallejo	90	215
John	32	m	w	IREL	Sacramento	American Twp	77	66
John	29	m	w	IREL	San Francisco	11-Wd San Francisc	84	491
John	26	m	w	IREL	Mariposa	Mariposa P O	74	133
Martin	28	m	w	IREL	Santa Clara	Santa Clara Twp	88	163
Mary	28	f	w	IREL	Santa Clara	San Jose Twp	88	186
Michal	17	m	w	IREL	San Francisco	11-Wd San Francisc	84	712
Mikel	45	m	w	IREL	Sacramento	3-Wd Sacramento	77	272
Rosanna	14	f	w	IREL	San Francisco	11-Wd San Francisc	84	711
Thomas	25	m	w	IL	San Bernardino	San Bernardino Twp	78	444
Timothy	38	m	w	IREL	Sierra	Gibson Twp	89	541
Ware	27	m	w	IREL	San Francisco	11-Wd San Francisc	84	572
JUDICE								
Manuel	38	m	w	SWIT	El Dorado	Diamond Springs Tw	72	31
JUDION								
Mary Jane	14	f	w	CA	Humboldt	Arcata Twp	72	227
JUDKINS								
Albt G	34	m	w	ME	Butte	Chico Twp	70	23
Elinz W	48	m	w	ME	Plumas	Indian Twp	77	15
Frank	29	m	w	ME	Butte	Wyandotte Twp	70	146
Lawrence	53	m	w	ME	Sonoma	Vallejo Twp	91	450
Ra	33	m	w	WI	Sonoma	Santa Rosa	91	423
S	37	m	w	ME	Sierra	Gibson Twp	89	539
Sarah	63	f	w	NH	San Joaquin	3-Wd Stockton	86	233
Wm W	36	m	w	VT	Nevada	Grass Valley Twp	75	169
JUDSON								
Alonzo B	17	m	w	IN	Nevada	Grass Valley Twp	75	146
Andrew	50	m	w	NY	San Francisco	5-Wd San Francisco	81	18
Ann	53	f	w	ENGL	San Joaquin	2-Wd Stockton	86	170
Anson	44	m	w	IN	San Francisco	5-Wd San Francisco	81	11
Charlotta	77	f	w	CT	San Francisco	11-Wd San Francisc	84	517
D L	47	m	w	MA	Merced	Snelling P O	74	267
E	26	m	w	SCOT	Alameda	Oakland	68	265
Edwin	30	m	w	NY	San Francisco	7-Wd San Francisco	81	214
Egbert	58	m	w	NY	San Francisco	11-Wd San Francisc	84	517
Fredrick W	40	m	w	CT	Yolo	Grafton Twp	93	494

Series M593 (Roll/Pg)

© 2001 by Heritage Quest. All rights reserved.

Name	Age	S	R	B-PL	County	Locale	Series M593 Roll	Pg
Gilbert	31	m	w	NY	San Francisco	1-Wd San Francisco	79	88
Ithamer	35	m	w	OH	San Bernardino	San Bernardino Twp	78	454
James	27	m	w	ENGL	Klamath	Klamath Twp	73	370
James	13	m	w	CA	Santa Clara	San Jose Twp	88	220
John B	40	m	w	VT	Sonoma	Analy Twp	91	218
Lemon	65	m	w	VT	Sonoma	Analy Twp	91	226
Mary	6	f	w	CA	Yolo	Buckeye Twp	93	407
Thomas	25	m	w	NY	San Francisco	11-Wd San Francisc	84	652
Timoithy	35	m	w	OH	San Bernardino	San Bernardino Twp	78	454
William	24	m	w	PA	San Bernardino	San Bernardino Twp	78	433
Wm	31	m	w	NY	San Francisco	1-Wd San Francisco	79	71
Wm A	38	m	w	MI	San Luis Obispo	Santa Rosa Twp	87	329
JUDY								
Abe C	52	m	w	VA	San Francisco	7-Wd San Francisco	81	248
JUE								
Ah	30	m	c	CHIN	Sacramento	Sutter Twp	77	393
Ah	28	m	c	CHIN	Solano	Suisun Twp	90	104
Ah	26	m	c	CHIN	Placer	Cisco P O	76	495
Ah	23	m	c	CHIN	Alameda	Alameda	68	3
Lee	10	m	c	CHIN	San Francisco	8-Wd San Francisco	82	386
Tung	33	m	c	CHIN	Yuba	Rose Bar Twp	93	656
JUEL								
Napoleon	54	m	w	FRAN	San Francisco	San Francisco P O	80	536
JUEN								
Ah	18	m	c	CHIN	San Francisco	6-Wd San Francisco	81	138
JUEZZE								
Antone	31	m	w	SWIT	Nevada	Nevada Twp	75	319
JUG								
Ah	25	m	c	CHIN	Yolo	Cache Crk Twp	93	429
JUGANEIT								
Chas	34	m	w	PRUS	Sierra	Table Rock Twp	89	577
JUGGARD								
Jam F	34	m	w	NY	Butte	Chico Twp	70	40
JUHAN								
Antonia	16	f	w	CA	San Diego	San Luis Rey	78	515
JUHL								
John J	29	m	w	DENM	Humboldt	Arcata Twp	72	235
Peter	43	m	w	DENM	Yolo	Cache Crk Twp	93	448
JUHLE								
Herman	32	m	w	PRUS	Placer	Lincoln P O	76	487
JUIELTI								
John	22	m	w	ITAL	San Francisco	2-Wd San Francisco	79	164
JUILLIARD								
Charles	45	m	w	FRAN	Alameda	San Leandro	68	97
JUIN								
Ah	46	m	c	CHIN	San Joaquin	1-Wd Stockton	86	142
Ah	40	m	c	CHIN	San Joaquin	1-Wd Stockton	86	143
Ah	37	m	c	CHIN	San Joaquin	1-Wd Stockton	86	143
Ah	30	m	c	CHIN	Sacramento	Franklin Twp	77	116
Ah	30	m	c	CHIN	San Joaquin	1-Wd Stockton	86	143
Lee	50	m	c	CHIN	Siskiyou	Hamburg Twp	89	599
JUITT								
Robt	34	m	w	TN	San Joaquin	Elliott Twp	86	79
JUK								
Ah	40	f	c	CHIN	Sacramento	Granite Twp	77	151
Theron H	39	m	w	NY	Marin	San Antonio Twp	74	62
JUKE								
Ah	45	m	c	CHIN	Trinity	Canyon City Pct	92	202
Ah	30	m	c	CHIN	El Dorado	Mountain Twp	72	68
JULA								
Ah	25	m	c	CHIN	Placer	Dutch Flat P O	76	411
JULE								
Ah	40	m	c	CHIN	Trinity	Indian Crk	92	199
Ah	35	m	c	CHIN	Trinity	Weaverville Pct	92	230
JULEFF								
Francis	29	m	w	ENGL	Nevada	Grass Valley Twp	75	190
JULEIN								
Eugene	31	m	w	FRAN	San Francisco	1-Wd San Francisco	79	49
JULER								
John	44	m	w	BADE	San Joaquin	2-Wd Stockton	86	206
JULI								
Ah	24	m	c	CHIN	Mendocino	Gualala Twp	74	223
JULIA								
John	33	m	w	TN	San Francisco	8-Wd San Francisco	82	288
JULIAN								
---	39	m	w	TN	Colusa	Stony Crk Twp	71	332
A Henry	35	m	w	AL	San Diego	San Diego	78	493
Alfred	36	m	w	GA	San Diego	Julian Dist	78	470
Charles	47	m	w	SWIT	Amador	Volcano P O	69	378
Cuaver	28	m	w	CA	Los Angeles	Los Angeles Twp	73	497
Emil	19	m	w	LA	San Francisco	San Francisco P O	80	410
Francis	42	m	w	FRAN	San Francisco	1-Wd San Francisco	79	97
Fred	41	m	w	PRUS	Butte	Oregon Twp	70	123
Geo	69	m	w	TN	Sonoma	Analy Twp	91	235
Humphrey	54	m	w	ENGL	Nevada	Grass Valley Twp	75	179
Jacob	48	m	b	NC	El Dorado	Georgetown Twp	72	48
Jacob	38	m	b	SC	El Dorado	Coloma Twp	72	9
Jean	62	m	w	FRAN	San Francisco	8-Wd San Francisco	82	490
Jean J	36	m	w	FRAN	San Francisco	1-Wd San Francisco	79	49
John	49	m	w	FRAN	Tuolumne	Sonora P O	93	303
Joseph	64	m	w	FRAN	Tuolumne	Sonora P O	93	303
Joseph	51	m	w	FRAN	Butte	Mountain Spring Tw	70	87
Juan	40	m	i	CA	Santa Barbara	Las Cruces P O	87	505
Julius	30	m	w	FRAN	San Francisco	San Francisco P O	80	475
Louisa L	36	f	w	OH	Sacramento	4-Wd Sacramento	77	347
Marie	24	f	i	CA	Santa Barbara	San Buenaventura P	87	441
Michael	31	m	w	GA	San Diego	Julian Dist	78	470
Roberto	34	m	i	CA	Santa Barbara	San Buenaventura P	87	441
JULIANA								
Carlo	15	m	w	SWIT	Marin	Nicasio Twp	74	14
JULIANS								
Joseph	35	m	w	FRAN	San Francisco	San Francisco P O	80	348
Joseph	35	m	w	FRAN	San Francisco	San Francisco P O	80	347
JULIE								
Jules E	29	m	w	FRAN	San Francisco	1-Wd San Francisco	79	49
JULIEN								
Emil	60	m	w	FRAN	San Francisco	6-Wd San Francisco	81	73
Jacque	32	m	w	FRAN	San Francisco	San Francisco P O	80	413
John S	43	m	w	IN	Sacramento	Franklin Twp	77	107
Jose	16	m	w	MEXI	Fresno	Millerton P O	72	153
Thos	49	m	w	ENGL	Sierra	Eureka Twp	89	524
JULIER								
Chas F	41	m	w	BADE	Sacramento	4-Wd Sacramento	77	362
JULIET								
George	38	m	w	FRAN	San Francisco	San Francisco P O	80	353
John	56	m	w	FRAN	Contra Costa	Martinez Twp	71	352
JULIFF								
Francis	30	m	w	ENGL	Nevada	Grass Valley Twp	75	152
JULIN								
Alexander	45	m	w	SWIT	Amador	Volcano P O	69	386
JULIO								
Jose	37	m	w	MEXI	Kern	Bakersfield P O	73	358
Jose M	22	m	w	CA	Santa Barbara	San Buenaventura P	87	438
JULITZ								
Hermann	53	m	w	PRUS	San Francisco	2-Wd San Francisco	79	142
JULIUS								
Geo	64	m	w	PRUS	San Francisco	San Francisco P O	83	330
Jacob	22	m	w	POLA	San Francisco	6-Wd San Francisco	81	88
John	30	m	b	SDOM	Yuba	Long Bar Twp	93	564
JULL								
Valentine	41	m	w	BAVA	San Francisco	11-Wd San Francisc	84	465
William	54	m	w	ENGL	Monterey	Monterey Twp	74	347
JULNIN								
Louis	35	m	w	OH	Sacramento	Lee Twp	77	161
JULSON								
M	36	m	w	SWED	Sonoma	Sonoma Twp	91	447
JULY								
Ah	30	m	c	CHIN	Santa Clara	1-Wd San Jose	88	269
Mary	24	f	w	IREL	Santa Clara	Gilroy Twp	88	77
JUM								
Ah	45	m	c	CHIN	Trinity	Weaverville Pct	92	231
Ah	36	m	c	CHIN	Sierra	Sears Twp	89	561
Ah	36	m	c	CHIN	Nevada	Grass Valley Twp	75	225
Ah	22	m	c	CHIN	Santa Clara	San Jose Twp	88	180
Ah	22	m	c	CHIN	El Dorado	Placerville Twp	72	92
Ah	12	m	c	CHIN	Nevada	Grass Valley Twp	75	199
JUMEL								
Andrew	50	m	w	FRAN	San Mateo	Woodside P O	87	386
JUMP								
A	43	m	w	OH	Sierra	Downieville Twp	89	515
Ah	34	m	c	CHIN	San Francisco	San Francisco P O	80	495
Ah	18	m	c	CHIN	San Francisco	San Francisco P O	80	463
JUMPER								
Geo B	38	m	w	ME	Trinity	Weaverville Pct	92	229
JUN								
Ah	42	m	c	CHIN	San Joaquin	1-Wd Stockton	86	142
Ah	42	m	c	CHIN	Sacramento	Granite Twp	77	138
Ah	40	m	c	CHIN	Amador	Drytown P O	69	419
Ah	38	m	c	CHIN	Tuolumne	Sonora P O	93	311
Ah	38	m	c	CHIN	Monterey	Castroville Twp	74	338
Ah	38	m	c	CHIN	El Dorado	Cosumnes Twp	72	18
Ah	36	m	c	CHIN	Nevada	Meadow Lake Twp	75	255
Ah	35	m	c	CHIN	Sacramento	Sutter Twp	77	386
Ah	30	m	c	CHIN	Plumas	Goodwin Twp	77	4
Ah	30	m	c	CHIN	Butte	Kimshew Tpw	70	81
Ah	27	m	c	CHIN	Sacramento	Georgianna Twp	77	129
Ah	25	m	c	CHIN	Nevada	Grass Valley Twp	75	219
Ah	24	m	c	CHIN	Santa Clara	San Jose Twp	88	183
Ah	24	m	c	CHIN	Sacramento	Natomas Twp	77	168
Ah	24	m	c	CHIN	Sacramento	Georgianna Twp	77	131
Ah	22	m	c	CHIN	Alameda	Oakland	68	152
Ah	20	m	c	CHIN	San Francisco	8-Wd San Francisco	82	390
Cu	42	m	c	CHIN	El Dorado	Placerville	72	118
Jon	13	m	c	CHIN	Nevada	Bridgeport Twp	75	111
Joy	24	m	c	CHIN	Solano	Rio Vista Twp	90	70
Su	15	m	c	CHIN	San Francisco	San Francisco P O	83	31
JUNCEL								
Augt	35	m	w	ENGL	Alameda	Murray Twp	68	100
JUNCK								
George	19	m	w	PRUS	San Francisco	8-Wd San Francisco	82	414
JUNDA								
Henry	28	m	w	PRUS	San Francisco	1-Wd San Francisco	79	90
JUNE								
Ah	34	m	c	CHIN	Plumas	Goodwin Twp	77	2
Ah	29	m	c	CHIN	Sacramento	3-Wd Sacramento	77	304
Ah	27	m	c	CHIN	San Joaquin	1-Wd Stockton	86	144
Ah	24	m	c	CHIN	Yuba	Rose Bar Twp	93	656
Ah	22	m	c	CHIN	Santa Clara	1-Wd San Jose	88	277
Lin	45	m	c	CHIN	Placer	Lincoln P O	76	484
Peare	27	m	w	FRAN	Placer	Lincoln P O	76	482
JUNES								
Frank	35	m	w	AZOR	San Francisco	1-Wd San Francisco	79	133
JUNEWIN								
Samuel	59	m	w	TN	San Diego	Julian Dist	78	472

© 2001 by Heritage Quest. All rights reserved.

Name	Age	S	R	B-PL	County	Locale	Series M593 Roll	Pg
JUNG								
---	30	m	c	CHIN	San Francisco	San Francisco P O	85	721
---	20	m	c	CHIN	Siskiyou	Cottonwood Twp	89	594
Ah	45	m	c	CHIN	Placer	Auburn P O	76	378
Ah	35	m	c	CHIN	Santa Barbara	Santa Barbara P O	87	459
Ah	35	m	c	CHIN	Merced	Snelling P O	74	279
Ah	32	m	c	CHIN	San Francisco	San Francisco P O	83	137
Ah	32	m	c	CHIN	Butte	Hamilton Twp	70	68
Ah	29	m	c	CHIN	El Dorado	Placerville Twp	72	105
Ah	29	m	c	CHIN	Sierra	Forest Twp	89	530
Ah	28	m	c	CHIN	Calaveras	Copperopolis P O	70	233
Ah	25	m	c	CHIN	San Francisco	San Francisco P O	80	503
Ah	25	m	c	CHIN	Plumas	Washington Twp	77	57
Ah	24	m	c	CHIN	Plumas	Plumas Twp	77	31
Ah	23	m	c	CHIN	San Joaquin	Dent Twp	86	28
Ah	23	m	c	CHIN	Plumas	Plumas Twp	77	31
Ah	20	m	c	CHIN	San Francisco	6-Wd San Francisco	81	40
Ah	20	m	c	CHIN	San Francisco	6-Wd San Francisco	81	43
Ah	19	f	c	CHIN	San Francisco	San Francisco P O	80	505
Ah	19	m	c	CHIN	Santa Clara	Alviso Twp	88	25
Gee	42	m	c	CHIN	Plumas	Mineral Twp	77	23
Hie	42	m	c	CHIN	Mariposa	Maxwell Crk P O	74	147
Lo	24	m	c	CHIN	Sonoma	Santa Rosa	91	420
Pew	51	m	c	CHIN	Santa Clara	1-Wd San Jose	88	270
JUNGAMAN								
Edward	20	m	w	NY	Contra Costa	Martinez P O	71	415
JUNGE								
Adolph	41	m	w	GERM	Los Angeles	Los Angeles	73	546
JUNGER								
Henry	30	m	w	IREL	Sacramento	4-Wd Sacramento	77	344
JUNGERS								
Ernest	29	m	w	PRUS	San Francisco	San Francisco P O	80	334
JUNGO								
Jules	35	m	w	DENM	San Francisco	8-Wd San Francisco	82	376
JUNIAS								
B	35	m	w	FRAN	Santa Clara	Gilroy Twp	88	95
JUNKER								
August	50	m	w	PRUS	San Francisco	2-Wd San Francisco	79	166
JUNKINS								
Carlotta	9	f	w	CA	Santa Cruz	Soquel Twp	89	439
Henry	41	m	w	PRUS	Trinity	Weaverville Pct	92	222
Walter S	37	m	w	ME	Santa Barbara	San Buenaventura P	87	419
JUNMAN								
Joseph	39	m	w	OH	Inyo	Bishop Crk Twp	73	314
JUNN								
Ah	21	m	c	CHIN	Nevada	Meadow Lake Twp	75	256
JUNNERO								
Francisco	36	m	w	MEXI	Stanislaus	San Joaquin Twp	92	70
JUNOT								
F	46	m	w	FRAN	Sierra	Butte Twp	89	513
JUNS								
D P	29	m	w	PA	Sutter	Nicolaus Twp	92	109
JUNYARO								
---	19	m	j	JAPA	El Dorado	Coloma Twp	72	4
JUO								
Ah	34	m	c	CHIN	San Joaquin	Oneal Twp	86	116
Lio	33	m	c	CHIN	San Joaquin	1-Wd Stockton	86	146
JUONG								
Ah	30	m	c	CHIN	Sacramento	3-Wd Sacramento	77	302
JURADO								
Julia	12	f	w	MEXI	San Francisco	San Francisco P O	83	92
JURANO								
Jose Maria	50	m	w	CA	San Diego	San Luis Rey	78	515
JURAS								
Vicente	57	m	w	CA	Santa Clara	1-Wd San Jose	88	259
JURDAN								
James	35	m	w	US	Sacramento	Cosumnes Twp	77	93
JURDO								
Serile	29	m	w	CANA	Sierra	Sears Twp	89	556
JURDON								
Nathan	40	m	w	OH	Sacramento	Brighton Twp	77	81
JURES								
Refugia	33	f	w	MEXI	Santa Clara	2-Wd San Jose	88	300
JURGENS								
Benj	40	m	w	HANO	Marin	Bolinas Twp	74	7
Berend	48	m	w	HANO	El Dorado	Mud Springs Twp	72	74
JURGUS								
C	25	m	w	PRUS	Alameda	Oakland	68	229
JURI								
Adelaide	18	f	w	SWIT	San Francisco	San Francisco P O	83	257
Ah	48	m	c	CHIN	Placer	Auburn P O	76	364
JURIED								
Abe	20	m	w	AUSL	San Francisco	11-Wd San Francisc	84	687
JURODAY								
Joseph	40	m	w	FRAN	Nevada	Washington Twp	75	339
JURRISON								
Franklin	35	m	w	MO	Yolo	Grafton Twp	93	497
JURTELS								
Thos	30	m	w	CANA	San Joaquin	2-Wd Stockton	86	164
JURVIS								
E A	70	f	w	MA	Tuolumne	Columbia P O	93	346
JURY								
Francisco	37	m	w	MEXI	Los Angeles	Los Angeles	73	520
Louis	37	m	w	SWIT	San Francisco	8-Wd San Francisco	82	466
Peter	38	m	w	SWIT	San Francisco	11-Wd San Francisc	84	653
JUS								
A M	45	m	w	ENGL	Alameda	Oakland	68	255
JUSHART								
Emanuel	41	m	w	PA	San Joaquin	2-Wd Stockton	86	162
JUSHKI								
Simon	42	m	w	PRUS	San Francisco	8-Wd San Francisco	82	310
JUST								
John P	37	m	w	SWIT	Placer	Bath P O	76	453
JUSTA								
O Chaa	27	m	i	MEXI	Inyo	Independence Twp	73	325
JUSTE								
Francis	36	m	w	ITAL	San Francisco	San Francisco P O	80	426
JUSTEMANO								
Jose E	37	m	w	CHIL	Amador	Jackson P O	69	326
JUSTER								
Antone	17	m	w	PORT	Alameda	Washington Twp	68	290
JUSTI								
Charles	64	m	w	SAXO	Sonoma	Sonoma Twp	91	434
Chas R H	23	m	w	SC	San Francisco	San Francisco P O	85	802
Dominico	31	m	w	ITAL	Sonoma	Analy Twp	91	236
Louise	38	m	w	ITAL	Sonoma	Analy Twp	91	241
Norence	42	m	w	ITAL	Sonoma	Analy Twp	91	240
Pedro	35	m	w	ITAL	Sonoma	Analy Twp	91	241
JUSTIC								
Emily	18	f	w	MO	Napa	Yountville Twp	75	81
JUSTICE								
J C	47	m	w	KY	Nevada	Nevada Twp	75	273
John D	42	m	w	OH	Monterey	San Benito Twp	74	381
William	27	m	w	PRUS	Los Angeles	Los Angeles Twp	73	488
JUSTIN								
Henery	34	m	w	NORW	San Francisco	7-Wd San Francisco	81	216
Henry	38	m	w	FRAN	San Francisco	San Francisco P O	80	342
Joseph K	39	m	w	PA	Los Angeles	Wilmington Twp	73	642
Julia	40	f	w	FRAN	San Francisco	6-Wd San Francisco	81	40
M E	30	m	w	IL	Sierra	Forest Twp	89	529
William	48	m	w	PA	Nevada	Grass Valley Twp	75	226
JUSTIS								
Chas	34	m	w	PA	Yuba	East Bear Rvr Twp	93	541
Elijah P	31	m	w	TX	Los Angeles	El Monte Twp	73	463
Jesse	58	m	w	PA	Los Angeles	El Monte Twp	73	463
William	27	m	w	ME	Los Angeles	Los Nietos Twp	73	578
JUSTUS								
Chas	54	m	w	PA	Yuba	East Bear Rvr Twp	93	542
Morgan	38	m	w	IN	Yolo	Grafton Twp	93	495
JUSURCHINI								
John	39	m	w	ITAL	San Francisco	San Francisco P O	80	426
JUSUS								
Felipe	29	m	w	CA	Santa Barbara	Las Cruces P O	87	516
JUT								
Sung	21	m	c	CHIN	Solano	Green Valley Twp	90	42
JUVAL								
John	15	m	w	ITAL	San Mateo	Schoolhouse Statio	87	340
JUVAN								
Constetain	28	m	w	AUST	Yolo	Cache Crk Twp	93	427
JUVIGNY								
Clement	43	m	w	FRAN	Santa Cruz	Pajaro Twp	89	350
JUZIX								
Leopold	38	m	w	FRAN	San Francisco	1-Wd San Francisco	79	83
Valery	14	m	w	AUST	San Francisco	11-Wd San Francisc	84	593
JYO								
James	30	m	w	IREL	San Francisco	11-Wd San Francisc	84	651
K								
Ah	42	m	c	CHIN	Sacramento	Cosumnes Twp	77	92
KA								
Ah	43	m	c	CHIN	Nevada	Eureka Twp	75	127
Ah	35	m	c	CHIN	Contra Costa	Martinez P O	71	398
Ah	30	m	c	CHIN	Sacramento	1-Wd Sacramento	77	193
Ah	27	m	c	CHIN	Nevada	Bridgeport Twp	75	107
Ah	27	m	c	CHIN	El Dorado	Mud Springs Twp	72	89
Ah	25	m	c	CHIN	Sacramento	2-Wd Sacramento	77	251
Ah	15	m	c	CHIN	Nevada	Nevada Twp	75	320
Chang	36	m	c	CHIN	Calaveras	Copperopolis P O	70	264
Fong	30	m	c	CHIN	Klamath	Liberty Twp	73	375
Joy	20	f	c	CHIN	Nevada	Nevada Twp	75	299
Ming	30	m	c	CHIN	Sierra	Eureka Twp	89	527
Pag	34	m	c	CHIN	Calaveras	Copperopolis P O	70	264
Sing	13	m	c	CHIN	Contra Costa	Martinez P O	71	378
Too	29	m	c	CHIN	Nevada	Washington Twp	75	342
KAAHRS								
Chas	30	m	w	HANO	San Francisco	1-Wd San Francisco	79	20
KAALER								
James	43	m	w	IREL	San Francisco	San Francisco P O	85	747
KAARS								
Thomas	24	m	w	IREL	San Mateo	Menlo Park P O	87	379
KAAWA								
Bull	60	m	b	HI	Sutter	Vernon Twp	92	133
KABANASKY								
Chas	44	m	w	POLA	Shasta	Horsetown P O	89	504
KABLER								
Sofler	48	m	w	WURT	Los Angeles	Los Angeles Twp	73	487
KABREY								
Wm	30	m	w	IREL	San Francisco	7-Wd San Francisco	81	270
KACE								
Ah	20	m	c	CHIN	Klamath	Liberty Twp	73	375
KACHLER								
Adolph	29	m	w	BAVA	San Francisco	8-Wd San Francisco	82	373
KACZINSKY								
Joseph	29	m	w	PRUS	Trinity	Weaverville Pct	92	223

© 2001 by Heritage Quest. All rights reserved.

Series M593

Name	Age	S	R	B-PL	County	Locale	Roll	Pg
KADEN								
Peter	40	m	w	IREL	San Francisco	3-Wd San Francisco	79	300
KADER								
Frank	35	m	w	PORT	Colusa	Grand Island Twp	71	302
KADI								
Alexander	35	m	w	HUNG	Marin	Sausalito Twp	74	72
KADING								
Bridget	22	f	w	IREL	San Francisco	San Francisco P O	83	321
Cornelius	44	m	w	IREL	San Francisco	2-Wd San Francisco	79	234
Jno	30	m	w	IREL	Sacramento	3-Wd Sacramento	77	317
John	32	m	w	OH	Inyo	Cerro Gordo Twp	73	319
KADLEY								
Henry	54	m	w	NY	Contra Costa	Martinez P O	71	427
KADY								
Caroline	45	f	w	ME	San Francisco	7-Wd San Francisco	81	240
John	24	m	w	IL	Sacramento	4-Wd Sacramento	77	320
KAEBER								
L	19	m	w	HANO	Alameda	Oakland	68	252
KAEL								
John	28	m	w	PA	San Francisco	San Francisco P O	80	410
KAEN								
John	37	m	w	NJ	San Francisco	11-Wd San Francisc	84	432
KAESTER								
Augt	43	m	w	PRUS	Sonoma	Santa Rosa	91	429
KAETZEL								
Philip	28	m	w	OH	San Luis Obispo	Santa Rosa Twp	87	321
KAFFERMIER								
Wm	35	m	w	PRUS	San Francisco	San Francisco P O	83	280
KAFFERTY								
Peter	40	m	w	IREL	Sacramento	San Joaquin Twp	77	399
KAGAN								
James	24	m	w	IREL	Alameda	Oakland	68	240
Timothy	41	m	w	IREL	Sacramento	4-Wd Sacramento	77	357
KAGER								
George	54	m	w	PA	Solano	Suisun Twp	90	111
KAGHAN								
John	24	m	w	IREL	Contra Costa	Martinez P O	71	413
KAGHT								
Catharine L	5	f	w	CA	El Dorado	White Oak Twp	72	143
KAGLE								
William	40	m	w	TN	San Francisco	8-Wd San Francisco	82	376
KAH								
Ah	45	m	c	CHIN	Santa Clara	Santa Clara Twp	88	161
Ah	40	m	c	CHIN	Nevada	Rough & Ready Twp	75	327
Ah	29	m	c	CHIN	Calaveras	San Andreas P O	70	155
Ah	19	m	c	CHIN	Sacramento	3-Wd Sacramento	77	309
Herman J	45	m	w	BADE	Shasta	Fort Crook P O	89	473
Le	42	m	c	CHIN	El Dorado	Cosumnes Twp	72	19
Woo	25	m	c	CHIN	Solano	Vallejo	90	178
KAHALEE								
Manuel	35	m	w	WURT	San Francisco	6-Wd San Francisco	81	72
KAHELER								
Jerry	31	m	w	IREL	Nevada	Meadow Lake Twp	75	252
KAHEN								
Jacob	27	m	w	PRUS	Sonoma	Petaluma Twp	91	321
KAHILL								
James	28	m	w	NY	Nevada	Nevada Twp	75	316
P	40	m	w	IREL	Sacramento	1-Wd Sacramento	77	179
Rodney	34	m	w	IREL	San Francisco	7-Wd San Francisco	81	168
KAHL								
Adam	44	m	w	PA	Merced	Snelling P O	74	264
Henry	29	m	w	SHOL	Santa Clara	Gilroy Twp	88	95
J A C	44	m	w	HCAS	Tuolumne	Columbia P O	93	352
Jacob	40	m	w	PRUS	Napa	Napa	75	42
KAHLAN								
H	45	m	w	PRUS	San Francisco	San Francisco P O	83	282
KAHLE								
Frank	18	m	w	HANO	San Francisco	11-Wd San Francisc	84	704
KAHLER								
James	39	m	w	IREL	Yolo	Putah Twp	93	515
John	40	m	w	IREL	Nevada	Grass Valley Twp	75	231
KAHLMEYER								
Joseph	40	m	w	WURT	Calaveras	San Andreas P O	70	158
KAHN								
Arnold	35	m	w	PRUS	San Francisco	2-Wd San Francisco	79	173
Briget	80	f	w	IREL	San Francisco	7-Wd San Francisco	81	164
Charles	24	m	w	FRAN	Contra Costa	Martinez P O	71	397
Henry	12	m	w	CA	San Francisco	San Francisco P O	85	828
Joseph	42	m	w	PRUS	San Francisco	San Francisco P O	80	531
Joseph	12	m	w	CA	San Francisco	San Francisco P O	80	531
Joseph	11	m	w	CA	San Francisco	San Francisco P O	85	828
Lazzard	20	m	w	FRAN	Santa Barbara	Santa Barbara P O	87	453
Le	39	m	c	CHIN	El Dorado	Cosumnes Twp	72	19
Leopold	53	m	w	FRAN	San Francisco	San Francisco P O	83	275
Moise	26	m	w	FRAN	Santa Barbara	Santa Barbara P O	87	450
Natale	53	m	w	BAVA	San Francisco	San Francisco P O	83	277
KAHNLINOW								
M	13	f	w	HI	Alameda	Oakland	68	197
KAHOA								
Thos	30	m	w	NY	Sacramento	4-Wd Sacramento	77	371
KAHOE								
James	24	m	w	MA	San Francisco	7-Wd San Francisco	81	177
KAHORHULIS								
J	47	m	b	HI	Sutter	Vernon Twp	92	133
J W	35	m	b	HI	Sutter	Vernon Twp	92	133
KAHOUGH								
Mary	30	f	w	IREL	San Francisco	5-Wd San Francisco	81	33
KAHR								
Wm	30	m	w	FRAN	San Joaquin	Tulare Twp	86	262
KAHRS								
G	44	m	w	NORW	Sierra	Gibson Twp	89	541
John H	26	m	w	PRUS	San Francisco	8-Wd San Francisco	82	409
KAHT								
Ah	53	m	c	CHIN	Marin	San Rafael	74	58
KAHTER								
H	29	m	w	PRUS	Alameda	Oakland	68	185
KAI								
Ah	7	m	c	CA	San Francisco	6-Wd San Francisco	81	44
Ah	45	m	c	CHIN	Tuolumne	Columbia P O	93	342
Ah	33	m	c	CHIN	Santa Clara	Gilroy Twp	88	75
Chum	25	m	c	CHIN	San Mateo	Schoolhouse Statio	87	335
Gai	34	f	c	CHIN	San Joaquin	1-Wd Stockton	86	153
John	40	m	b	HI	Tuolumne	Big Oak Flat P O	93	399
Se	28	m	c	CHIN	Tuolumne	Columbia P O	93	341
Young	40	m	c	CHIN	Tuolumne	Sonora P O	93	311
KAIBEL								
Chas	30	m	w	HDAR	Sacramento	3-Wd Sacramento	77	299
KAIDY								
John	34	m	w	IREL	San Francisco	8-Wd San Francisco	82	376
KAIESER								
Jacob	37	m	w	SWIT	San Francisco	San Francisco P O	80	332
KAIHLER								
Fredrick	60	m	w	MECK	San Francisco	11-Wd San Francisc	84	525
KAILES								
M W	25	m	w	NY	Amador	Jackson P O	69	328
KAILLY								
Terence	58	m	w	IREL	San Francisco	11-Wd San Francisc	84	565
KAIN								
Francis	23	m	w	PA	San Francisco	1-Wd San Francisco	79	63
Henry	30	m	w	NY	Yolo	Cache Crk Twp	93	435
J C	41	m	w	OH	Alameda	Oakland	68	195
John	26	m	w	IREL	San Mateo	San Mateo P O	87	355
John	24	m	w	TN	Napa	Yountville Twp	75	78
John	23	m	w	MA	San Francisco	7-Wd San Francisco	81	279
Jos	34	m	w	IREL	Sacramento	1-Wd Sacramento	77	178
Mary	22	f	w	IREL	San Francisco	San Francisco P O	85	816
Patrick	24	m	w	IREL	San Francisco	San Francisco P O	83	401
Richard	34	m	w	PRUS	San Francisco	5-Wd San Francisco	81	9
Thomas	50	m	w	IREL	San Francisco	11-Wd San Francisc	84	471
Thomas	40	m	w	SCOT	San Francisco	11-Wd San Francisc	84	432
KAINDLER								
James	31	m	w	FRAN	San Francisco	San Francisco P O	80	470
KAINE								
Dennis	35	m	w	IREL	San Francisco	8-Wd San Francisco	82	291
Kate	40	f	w	IREL	Sacramento	3-Wd Sacramento	77	257
KAING								
Emile	29	m	w	PRUS	San Francisco	5-Wd San Francisco	81	15
KAINTZ								
Moritz	61	m	w	HUNG	San Francisco	8-Wd San Francisco	82	420
KAIRN								
Lam	50	m	w	PRUS	San Joaquin	2-Wd Stockton	86	205
KAISER								
Andrew	29	m	w	SWIT	Sacramento	4-Wd Sacramento	77	370
Chas	24	m	w	GERM	Sonoma	Washington Twp	91	471
F	29	m	w	PRUS	Sierra	Downieville Twp	89	522
Frank	30	m	w	HAMB	San Francisco	1-Wd San Francisco	79	57
George	42	m	w	BADE	Siskiyou	Yreka	89	659
George	35	m	w	PRUS	San Francisco	2-Wd San Francisco	79	269
George	20	m	w	NY	Napa	Napa	75	3
Henry	19	m	w	HCAS	Santa Clara	2-Wd San Jose	88	333
Jacob	21	m	w	MO	Placer	Auburn P O	76	359
John	38	m	w	IREL	San Francisco	San Francisco P O	83	393
John	28	m	w	PRUS	San Francisco	1-Wd San Francisco	79	55
Joseph	31	m	w	BAVA	San Francisco	8-Wd San Francisco	82	364
Joseph	24	m	w	NY	Napa	Napa	75	4
Lasarus M	23	m	w	AL	San Luis Obispo	San Luis Obispo Tw	87	310
M P	35	m	w	PRUS	San Joaquin	2-Wd Stockton	86	160
Mary	60	f	w	BADE	Sacramento	3-Wd Sacramento	77	296
S	38	m	w	BADE	San Joaquin	2-Wd Stockton	86	159
Theodore	27	m	w	PRUS	San Francisco	6-Wd San Francisco	81	93
Valentine	24	m	w	PRUS	San Francisco	San Francisco P O	80	536
Wm C	36	m	w	CANA	San Luis Obispo	Santa Rosa Twp	87	323
KAISERLA								
John	30	m	w	PRUS	San Francisco	San Francisco P O	80	532
KAISNEL								
C D	32	m	w	PRUS	Santa Cruz	Santa Cruz	89	404
KAIT								
Ah	18	m	c	CHIN	Sacramento	1-Wd Sacramento	77	185
KAITER								
John	30	m	w	WV	Monterey	Alisal Twp	74	291
KAIZER								
Henry	23	m	w	PRUS	Tulare	Visalia	92	298
Robert	38	m	w	PRUS	Tulare	Tule Rvr Twp	92	266
KAK								
Ah	20	m	c	CHIN	Sacramento	1-Wd Sacramento	77	191
KAKEBREAD								
Robt	32	m	w	ENGL	Contra Costa	Martinez P O	71	420
KAKER								
Wm	40	m	w	HAMB	San Francisco	8-Wd San Francisco	82	344
KALAGHER								
Pat	43	m	w	IREL	Nevada	Nevada Twp	75	288
KALAHAN								
Ellen	35	f	w	IREL	San Francisco	San Francisco P O	83	167

© 2001 by Heritage Quest. All rights reserved.

Series M593

Name	Age	S	R	B-PL	County	Locale	Roll	Pg
KALAHER								
Danial	23	m	w	IREL	San Francisco	7-Wd San Francisco	81	172
Hannah	23	f	w	IREL	Nevada	Grass Valley Twp	75	149
KALARAS								
John	34	m	b	HI	Sutter	Butte Twp	92	97
KALB								
Theodore	23	m	w	PRUS	San Francisco	1-Wd San Francisco	79	51
KALBAUGH								
Reuben	55	m	w	IL	Yolo	Cache Crk Twp	93	430
KALBFELL								
George	39	m	w	WURT	San Francisco	3-Wd San Francisco	79	294
KALCHER								
Patrick	30	m	w	IREL	San Francisco	San Francisco P O	83	389
KALCK								
Florence	19	m	w	FRAN	Mariposa	Maxwell Crk P O	74	145
Jacob	17	m	w	FRAN	Mariposa	Maxwell Crk P O	74	144
KALDAN								
Eugene	19	f	w	CA	Sutter	Sutter Twp	92	124
KALE								
Ah	19	m	c	CHIN	Contra Costa	Martinez P O	71	397
C H	66	m	w	HAMB	Tuolumne	Chinese Camp P O	93	364
Edward	45	m	w	IREL	San Francisco	6-Wd San Francisco	81	87
Mary	40	f	w	IREL	San Joaquin	2-Wd Stockton	86	167
S	37	f	w	NY	San Francisco	San Francisco P O	85	826
KALEBOR								
Mary	18	f	w	IREL	San Mateo	Redwood Twp	87	365
KALER								
Austin	40	m	w	ME	Calaveras	Copperopolis P O	70	256
Jas	33	m	w	NY	Solano	Vallejo	90	179
Thomas	37	m	w	DENM	Placer	Bath P O	76	457
Thomas	30	m	w	ME	Calaveras	Copperopolis P O	70	251
KALEY								
Charles	29	m	w	ENGL	San Bernardino	San Bernardino Twp	78	451
Mary	70	f	w	IREL	San Francisco	San Francisco P O	83	389
KALI								
George	21	m	w	IREL	Tuolumne	Chinese Camp P O	93	373
KALICKER								
Julius	46	m	w	PRUS	San Francisco	San Francisco P O	83	364
KALING								
Margareth	19	f	w	ENGL	Humboldt	Eel Rvr Twp	72	250
Patrick	33	m	w	IREL	San Mateo	San Mateo P O	87	360
KALIS								
Francis	44	m	w	WURT	San Francisco	2-Wd San Francisco	79	174
KALISH								
Marx	40	m	w	PRUS	San Francisco	8-Wd San Francisco	82	396
Max	20	m	w	NJ	Santa Clara	2-Wd San Jose	88	324
KALISHER								
D	40	m	w	BRAN	San Joaquin	3-Wd Stockton	86	230
De	23	m	c	CHIN	San Joaquin	3-Wd Stockton	86	230
KALISKY								
Bertha	52	f	w	PRUS	San Francisco	San Francisco P O	83	179
Samuel	25	m	w	POLA	San Francisco	San Francisco P O	83	173
KALKISHAULER								
Wm	23	m	w	HDAR	San Bernardino	San Bernardino Twp	78	415
KALL								
Burnett	21	m	w	WURT	San Francisco	11-Wd San Francisc	84	452
John	42	m	w	SHOL	Nevada	Washington Twp	75	345
Joseph	34	m	w	BADE	San Francisco	2-Wd San Francisco	79	215
KALLAHER								
Hannah	33	f	w	IREL	San Francisco	San Francisco P O	83	281
Martin	45	m	w	IREL	San Francisco	8-Wd San Francisco	82	398
KALLANDER								
David	7	m	w	CA	San Francisco	8-Wd San Francisco	82	401
KALLBACH								
Charles	53	m	w	PRUS	Sutter	Sutter Twp	92	124
KALLENBACH								
Jacob	32	m	w	BAVA	Santa Cruz	Santa Cruz	89	404
KALLENBERG								
Theo	36	m	w	SWIT	San Francisco	San Francisco P O	83	66
KALLENBERGER								
Geo D	60	m	w	BAVA	Nevada	Eureka Twp	75	134
KALLER								
Henry C	37	m	w	OH	Stanislaus	Branch Twp	92	5
KALLEY								
A M	21	f	w	MA	Solano	Vallejo	90	140
A S	44	m	w	PA	Amador	Jackson P O	69	319
KALLITY								
Michael	36	m	w	IREL	San Francisco	8-Wd San Francisco	82	318
KALLOWAY								
James	40	m	w	NC	Nevada	Eureka Twp	75	133
KALLSCHMIDT								
Oscar	33	m	w	PRUS	San Francisco	5-Wd San Francisco	81	1
KALLSTON								
Henry	39	m	w	SWED	San Francisco	7-Wd San Francisco	81	222
KALLY								
James	44	m	w	IREL	San Francisco	San Francisco P O	83	114
James	42	m	w	IREL	San Francisco	1-Wd San Francisco	79	92
Mary Ann	6	f	w	NY	San Francisco	11-Wd San Francisc	84	711
Wm	24	m	w	HI	San Francisco	San Francisco P O	85	829
KALM								
Henrietta	24	f	w	BADE	San Francisco	6-Wd San Francisco	81	70
Jane	29	f	w	BADE	San Francisco	San Francisco P O	80	471
Phillip	27	m	w	HANO	San Francisco	6-Wd San Francisco	81	70
KALMBACK								
August	32	m	w	WURT	San Francisco	2-Wd San Francisco	79	146
KALMUCK								
Moritz	42	m	w	PRUS	San Francisco	San Francisco P O	83	370

Series M593

Name	Age	S	R	B-PL	County	Locale	Roll	Pg
KALMUK								
Augusta	50	f	w	PRUS	San Francisco	8-Wd San Francisco	82	443
KALON								
Jose M	55	m	w	CA	San Luis Obispo	San Luis Obispo Tw	87	315
KALPH								
George	34	m	w	BAVA	Nevada	Bridgeport Twp	75	104
KALSING								
Martin	40	m	w	PRUS	San Francisco	8-Wd San Francisco	82	478
KALTHOFF								
August	44	m	w	PRUS	San Francisco	San Francisco P O	83	242
KALTMEYER								
E	28	m	w	BREM	Napa	Napa	75	6
KALUN								
Abram	34	m	w	PRUS	San Francisco	San Francisco P O	80	362
KALVER								
Ella	15	f	w	CA	Nevada	Meadow Lake Twp	75	246
KALY								
Patrick	31	m	w	IREL	San Francisco	11-Wd San Francisc	84	601
William	40	m	w	IREL	Yolo	Cache Crk Twp	93	422
KALZENSTEIN								
G B	21	m	w	FRAN	Sacramento	3-Wd Sacramento	77	270
KAM								
Ah	40	m	c	CHIN	Sierra	Eureka Twp	89	523
Ah	24	m	c	CHIN	Santa Clara	San Jose Twp	88	194
Ah	20	m	c	CHIN	Contra Costa	Martinez P O	71	398
Ah	14	m	c	CHIN	San Francisco	11-Wd San Francisc	84	576
John	50	m	w	IREL	Calaveras	San Andreas P O	70	172
Patrick	30	m	w	IREL	Tuolumne	Columbia P O	93	360
KAMACKE								
H	29	m	w	PRUS	Alameda	Oakland	68	191
KAMANA								
Henry	33	m	w	BREM	San Francisco	1-Wd San Francisco	79	11
KAMANSKI								
Selma	20	f	w	POLA	San Francisco	6-Wd San Francisco	81	62
KAMATH								
John	25	m	w	SWIT	Marin	Tomales Twp	74	77
KAMBALL								
David	38	m	w	NJ	Shasta	Shasta P O	89	453
KAME								
Thos	34	m	w	IREL	Sierra	Table Rock Twp	89	578
KAMEBURKE								
Henry	46	m	w	GERM	Yolo	Cache Crk Twp	93	454
KAMER								
Chs A	25	m	w	MA	Monterey	Castroville Twp	74	335
KAMINA								
Bernard	45	m	w	SAXO	San Francisco	San Francisco P O	80	335
KAMLADE								
Fred	19	m	w	HANO	San Francisco	San Francisco P O	83	85
KAMMERER								
Fred	33	m	w	BADE	San Francisco	2-Wd San Francisco	79	163
KAMMERSCHMIDT								
Frederick	30	m	w	BADE	San Francisco	8-Wd San Francisco	82	435
KAMMONS								
Henry	36	m	w	HANO	San Francisco	San Francisco P O	85	844
KAMOSITA								
John	27	m	w	ITAL	Amador	Sutter Crk P O	69	407
KAMP								
Albert	24	m	w	IN	San Francisco	2-Wd San Francisco	79	175
Alexander	36	m	w	NY	San Francisco	San Francisco P O	80	350
Aurelias	25	m	w	MO	Santa Clara	Redwood Twp	88	131
Benedict	64	m	w	BAVA	Santa Clara	2-Wd San Jose	88	293
F W	28	m	w	PRUS	San Francisco	San Francisco P O	83	315
Louis	46	m	w	SWED	Contra Costa	Martinez Twp	71	347
Otho	30	m	w	CA	Santa Clara	2-Wd San Jose	88	293
Simon	32	m	w	PRUS	Santa Clara	San Jose Twp	88	191
William	40	m	w	MA	Santa Cruz	Watsonville	89	373
KAMPE								
Chas	31	m	w	PRUS	San Francisco	8-Wd San Francisco	82	376
KAMPEN								
Aug	26	m	w	PRUS	San Francisco	2-Wd San Francisco	79	216
KAMPFER								
John	35	m	w	BAVA	Nevada	Eureka Twp	75	133
KAMPNER								
Jane	55	f	w	ENGL	Monterey	Monterey	74	363
KAMPS								
William	37	m	w	PRUS	San Francisco	San Francisco P O	83	228
KAMSEY								
William	23	m	w	MO	Siskiyou	Table Rock Twp	89	646
KAN								
Ah	42	m	c	CHIN	San Francisco	San Francisco P O	80	524
Ah	40	m	c	CHIN	El Dorado	White Oak Twp	72	140
Ah	37	m	c	CHIN	San Francisco	San Francisco P O	80	446
Ah	34	m	c	CHIN	Butte	Wyandotte Twp	70	143
Ah	34	m	c	CHIN	San Francisco	San Francisco P O	80	439
Ah	34	m	c	CHIN	Placer	Colfax P O	76	387
Ah	32	m	c	CHIN	Butte	Mountain Spring Tw	70	90
Ah	31	m	c	CHIN	Amador	Sutter Crk P O	69	413
Ah	30	m	c	CHIN	San Francisco	6-Wd San Francisco	81	38
Ah	29	m	c	CHIN	San Francisco	San Francisco P O	80	441
Ah	27	m	c	CHIN	San Francisco	San Francisco P O	83	149
Ah	26	m	c	CHIN	Sacramento	1-Wd Sacramento	77	196
Ah	24	m	c	CHIN	Santa Clara	San Jose Twp	88	180
Ah	24	m	c	CHIN	Butte	Wyandotte Twp	70	146
Ah	23	f	c	CHIN	San Francisco	6-Wd San Francisco	81	73
Ah	22	m	c	CHIN	Solano	Vallejo	90	176
Ah	19	m	c	CHIN	Placer	Clipper Gap P O	76	393
Ah	14	m	c	CHIN	San Francisco	San Francisco P O	83	188

© 2001 by Heritage Quest. All rights reserved.

Name	Age	S	R	B-PL	County	Locale	Roll	Pg
C W	42	m	w	ME	Alameda	Oakland	68	245
Chick	34	m	c	CHIN	Amador	Ione City P O	69	364
Gon	18	m	c	CHIN	San Joaquin	Liberty Twp	86	97
John	65	m	w	IREL	San Francisco	11-Wd San Francisc	84	700
Le	25	m	c	CHIN	El Dorado	Diamond Springs Tw	72	30
Lou	20	m	c	CHIN	San Mateo	Schoolhouse Statio	87	336
Martin	27	m	w	PRUS	San Francisco	5-Wd San Francisco	81	13
Wo	37	m	c	CHIN	San Francisco	6-Wd San Francisco	81	53
KANA								
Ah	15	m	c	CHIN	Sierra	Sears Twp	89	561
KANADAY								
M	29	m	w	IREL	Sierra	Table Rock Twp	89	573
KANADY								
Maliche	58	m	w	NC	Sacramento	Franklin Twp	77	115
KANAGA								
Levi	30	m	w	NY	Tuolumne	Sonora P O	93	321
KANAJAH								
John	35	m	w	VA	Sonoma	Mendocino Twp	91	301
KANAKA								
Moses	40	m	b	HI	Calaveras	Copperopolis P O	70	229
Thos	40	m	b	HI	Calaveras	Copperopolis P O	70	231
KANALY								
John	35	m	w	IREL	San Francisco	San Francisco P O	85	836
KANAN								
Jas	35	m	w	IREL	San Francisco	7-Wd San Francisco	81	287
KANAND								
James	50	m	w	MO	Yolo	Cottonwood Twp	93	462
KANANYER								
J J	25	m	w	IN	Merced	Snelling P O	74	275
KANAWHA								
James	40	m	b	HI	Siskiyou	Cottonwood Twp	89	590
KANCALE								
John	42	m	w	ENGL	Nevada	Grass Valley Twp	75	231
KANCE								
Francis	52	m	w	PRUS	San Francisco	6-Wd San Francisco	81	129
KANCHER								
Fredrika	58	f	w	PRUS	San Francisco	11-Wd San Francisc	84	523
KANE								
Agnes	23	f	w	IREL	San Francisco	San Francisco P O	83	15
Ah	48	m	c	CHIN	Trinity	North Fork Twp	92	220
Ah	30	m	c	CHIN	Trinity	Junction City Pct	92	206
Ah	28	m	c	CHIN	Solano	Silveyville Twp	90	92
Ah	28	m	c	CHIN	San Francisco	San Francisco P O	83	82
Ah	28	m	c	CHIN	Sacramento	Franklin Twp	77	114
Ah	23	m	c	CHIN	Sacramento	1-Wd Sacramento	77	189
Ah	22	m	w	CHIN	Solano	Suisun Twp	90	107
Ah	21	m	c	CHIN	Solano	Suisun Twp	90	106
Ah	14	m	c	CHIN	San Francisco	San Francisco P O	85	730
Alexander	43	m	w	IREL	Alameda	Washington Twp	68	293
Andrew	30	m	w	IREL	Solano	Vallejo	90	206
Anna	27	f	w	IREL	San Francisco	8-Wd San Francisco	82	479
Anna	14	f	w	IREL	San Francisco	6-Wd San Francisco	81	126
Annie	30	f	w	IREL	Nevada	Grass Valley Twp	75	145
Annie	18	f	w	MD	San Francisco	San Francisco P O	83	263
Bridget	28	f	w	IREL	Sonoma	Petaluma Twp	91	334
Cachron	24	m	w	IREL	Yuba	North East Twp	93	646
Catharine	22	f	w	IREL	San Francisco	San Francisco P O	83	64
Catherin	33	f	w	IREL	Alameda	Oakland	68	155
Catherine	4	f	w	PA	San Francisco	11-Wd San Francisc	84	711
Catherine	30	f	w	CT	Marin	Novato Twp	74	12
Charles	37	m	w	IREL	San Francisco	San Francisco P O	83	320
Charles E	38	m	w	MA	Santa Cruz	Santa Cruz Twp	89	398
Corneilus	40	m	w	IREL	San Francisco	San Francisco P O	80	429
D	35	m	w	IREL	Alameda	Oakland	68	178
Daniel	35	m	w	IREL	San Francisco	San Francisco P O	80	410
David	20	m	w	IREL	Sonoma	Bodega Twp	91	263
Dennis	35	m	w	IREL	San Francisco	San Francisco P O	83	215
Edward	30	m	w	IREL	San Francisco	San Francisco P O	85	772
Elizabeth	45	f	w	MD	Sonoma	Analy Twp	91	247
Ellen	20	f	w	IREL	Nevada	Grass Valley Twp	75	160
Eunice	21	f	w	NY	San Francisco	San Francisco P O	83	343
Frank	46	m	w	IREL	Plumas	Washington Twp	77	53
Frank	34	m	w	IREL	San Francisco	San Francisco P O	83	315
Frank	27	m	w	IREL	San Francisco	San Francisco P O	83	172
Frank E	26	m	w	PA	Napa	Napa Twp	75	60
Geo	43	m	w	PA	San Francisco	2-Wd San Francisco	79	215
George	43	m	w	IREL	San Francisco	San Francisco P O	80	335
George	43	m	w	MO	Calaveras	San Andreas P O	70	189
George	40	m	w	KY	Solano	Denverton Twp	90	25
Gilbert	42	m	w	NY	Santa Clara	San Jose Twp	88	215
I	42	m	w	IREL	San Mateo	San Mateo P O	87	359
J	28	m	w	IREL	Sierra	Butte Twp	89	512
James	75	m	w	IREL	San Francisco	San Francisco P O	83	271
James	6	m	w	CA	San Francisco	San Francisco P O	83	384
James	49	m	w	MO	Santa Cruz	Santa Cruz	89	410
James	40	m	w	IREL	San Francisco	6-Wd San Francisco	81	152
James	32	m	w	IREL	Sutter	Yuba Twp	92	151
James	31	m	w	IREL	San Francisco	8-Wd San Francisco	82	445
James	30	m	w	IREL	San Diego	Julian Dist	78	472
James	29	m	w	IREL	San Francisco	San Francisco P O	83	138
James	25	m	w	MD	San Francisco	7-Wd San Francisco	81	205
Jane	5	f	w	CA	Yuba	Rose Bar Twp	93	652
Jas	23	m	w	CANA	San Francisco	7-Wd San Francisco	81	237
Jas	23	m	w	PA	Solano	Vallejo	90	141
Joe	30	m	w	IREL	San Francisco	7-Wd San Francisco	81	265
John	60	m	w	IREL	El Dorado	Placerville	72	120
John	60	m	w	IREL	Sacramento	4-Wd Sacramento	77	343
John	52	m	w	IREL	Monterey	Alisal Twp	74	291
John	38	m	w	IREL	San Francisco	11-Wd San Francisc	84	673
John	34	m	w	IREL	Napa	Napa	75	47
John	33	m	w	DENM	Klamath	Klamath Twp	73	371
John	31	m	w	IREL	Solano	Silveyville Twp	90	85
John	27	m	w	IREL	Calaveras	San Andreas P O	70	174
John	22	m	w	NY	Santa Cruz	Santa Cruz	89	410
John O	50	m	w	IREL	Sacramento	Dry Crk Twp	77	98
John W	40	m	w	IN	San Bernardino	San Bernardino Twp	78	419
Jos	50	m	w	IREL	Solano	Vallejo	90	156
Jos	23	m	w	MD	Sacramento	1-Wd Sacramento	77	182
Julia	80	f	w	IREL	Santa Clara	Gilroy Twp	88	86
Kate	55	f	w	IREL	Solano	Vallejo	90	171
Laura	19	f	b	DE	San Francisco	San Francisco P O	80	465
Laurence	30	m	w	IREL	San Francisco	San Francisco P O	83	56
Lawrence	37	m	w	IREL	San Joaquin	2-Wd Stockton	86	167
Lizzie	24	f	w	IREL	San Francisco	San Francisco P O	83	138
Maggie	23	f	w	IREL	Sacramento	3-Wd Sacramento	77	272
Margaret	36	f	w	IREL	San Francisco	San Francisco P O	80	460
Margaret	22	f	w	IREL	San Francisco	San Francisco P O	83	355
Maria	50	f	w	IREL	San Francisco	San Francisco P O	80	464
Mary	5	f	w	PA	San Francisco	11-Wd San Francisc	84	711
Mary	40	f	w	IREL	San Francisco	11-Wd San Francisc	84	611
Mary	36	f	w	IREL	San Francisco	San Francisco P O	80	457
Mary	27	f	w	IREL	San Francisco	San Francisco P O	85	775
Mathew	37	m	w	IREL	Nevada	Grass Valley Twp	75	166
Michael	60	m	w	IREL	San Francisco	San Francisco P O	83	83
Michael	53	m	w	IREL	San Francisco	8-Wd San Francisco	82	483
Michael	44	m	w	IREL	Nevada	Grass Valley Twp	75	207
Michael	35	m	w	IREL	San Francisco	7-Wd San Francisco	81	230
Michael	29	m	w	IREL	San Francisco	7-Wd San Francisco	81	272
Michael	24	m	w	IREL	San Francisco	San Francisco P O	83	60
Michael J	33	m	w	IREL	San Francisco	7-Wd San Francisco	81	230
Michl	24	m	w	IREL	San Francisco	11-Wd San Francisc	84	613
Milton	52	m	w	OH	El Dorado	Placerville	72	117
Morris	35	m	w	IREL	Yuba	Parks Bar Twp	93	649
Newel	67	m	w	NC	Sacramento	Brighton Twp	77	75
Newell	27	m	w	IN	Sacramento	Granite Twp	77	136
Patk	47	m	w	IREL	Solano	Vallejo	90	184
Patk	35	m	w	IREL	San Francisco	5-Wd San Francisco	81	32
Patrick	45	m	w	IREL	El Dorado	Cosumnes Twp	72	19
Patrick	38	m	w	IREL	San Francisco	8-Wd San Francisco	82	394
Patrick	37	m	w	IREL	San Francisco	11-Wd San Francisc	84	582
Patrick	37	m	w	IREL	El Dorado	Coloma Twp	72	7
Patrick	36	m	w	IREL	Contra Costa	San Pablo Twp	71	358
Patrick	34	m	w	IREL	San Francisco	7-Wd San Francisco	81	187
Patrick	32	m	w	IREL	San Francisco	8-Wd San Francisco	82	369
Penetta	20	f	w	NY	San Francisco	San Francisco P O	83	196
Richd	17	m	w	IREL	San Francisco	1-Wd San Francisco	79	28
Robert	21	m	w	IREL	San Francisco	3-Wd San Francisco	79	323
Robert H	29	m	w	TX	San Bernardino	San Bernardino Twp	78	424
Robt	32	m	w	SCOT	Butte	Chico Twp	70	32
Rosa	27	f	w	DC	San Francisco	6-Wd San Francisco	81	71
Rosa	21	m	w	IREL	Contra Costa	Martinez P O	71	431
Susan	73	f	w	IREL	San Francisco	San Francisco P O	83	271
Susan	21	f	w	PA	San Francisco	8-Wd San Francisco	82	473
Theodore	24	m	w	IN	Sacramento	Granite Twp	77	136
Thomas	5	m	w	PA	San Francisco	11-Wd San Francisc	84	711
Thomas	44	m	w	IREL	San Francisco	7-Wd San Francisco	81	196
Thomas	36	m	w	IREL	Marin	Sausalito Twp	74	68
Thomas	31	m	w	IREL	San Francisco	5-Wd San Francisco	81	32
Thomas	28	m	w	IREL	San Francisco	2-Wd San Francisco	79	204
Thomas	27	m	w	IREL	San Francisco	San Francisco P O	83	162
Thomas	23	m	w	IREL	Santa Clara	Gilroy Twp	88	82
Thomas J	22	m	w	ENGL	San Francisco	11-Wd San Francisc	84	709
W E	23	m	w	IA	San Francisco	3-Wd San Francisco	79	314
W H	35	m	w	NY	San Francisco	San Francisco P O	83	282
William	54	m	w	IREL	Sonoma	Petaluma Twp	91	337
William	37	m	w	MA	San Francisco	1-Wd San Francisco	79	63
William	32	m	w	IREL	San Francisco	7-Wd San Francisco	81	172
William	30	m	w	OH	Solano	Vacaville Twp	90	133
William	26	m	w	IREL	San Francisco	8-Wd San Francisco	82	496
William	24	m	w	IREL	San Francisco	11-Wd San Francisc	84	473
Wm	38	m	w	MA	San Francisco	1-Wd San Francisco	79	134
Wm	15	m	w	CT	San Francisco	11-Wd San Francisc	84	588
Wm A	40	m	w	NC	Sacramento	Franklin Twp	77	119
KANELLY								
David	30	m	w	IREL	San Francisco	11-Wd San Francisc	84	705
Patrick	50	m	w	IREL	San Francisco	11-Wd San Francisc	84	480
KANES								
James	33	m	w	IREL	Solano	Rio Vista Twp	90	55
KANEY								
Peter	40	m	w	IREL	San Francisco	San Francisco P O	85	874
KANG								
Ah	56	m	c	CHIN	San Francisco	San Francisco P O	80	436
Ah	45	m	c	CHIN	Klamath	Orleans Twp	73	380
Ah	40	m	c	CHIN	Plumas	Rich Bar Twp	77	8
Ah	32	m	c	CHIN	Plumas	Washington Twp	77	58
Ah	31	m	c	CHIN	Plumas	Goodwin Twp	77	4
Ah	30	m	c	CHIN	Shasta	French Gulch P O	89	465
Ah	29	m	c	CHIN	Yuba	Marysville	93	631
Ah	28	m	c	CHIN	Sacramento	Center Twp	77	86
Ah	24	m	c	CHIN	Santa Clara	1-Wd San Jose	88	271
Ah	21	m	c	CHIN	Santa Clara	1-Wd San Jose	88	270
Ah	21	m	c	CHIN	Santa Clara	San Jose Twp	88	192
Ah	21	m	c	CHIN	Santa Clara	1-Wd San Jose	88	271
Ah	20	m	c	CHIN	Santa Clara	San Jose Twp	88	196

Series M593

© 2001 by Heritage Quest. All rights reserved.

Name	Age	S	R	B-PL	County	Locale	Series M593 Roll	Pg
Ah	20	m	c	CHIN	Santa Clara	Fremont Twp	88	60
Ah	20	m	c	CHIN	Santa Clara	1-Wd San Jose	88	274
Ah	19	m	c	CHIN	Santa Clara	San Jose Twp	88	193
Ah	18	m	c	CHIN	San Francisco	11-Wd San Francisc	84	558
Ah	17	m	c	CHIN	Santa Clara	Fremont Twp	88	64
Fock	30	m	c	CHIN	Yuba	Marysville	93	628
Kow	30	m	c	CHIN	Santa Clara	San Jose Twp	88	190
Ty	24	m	c	CHIN	Solano	Rio Vista Twp	90	70
KANI								
Chie	28	f	c	CHIN	Sacramento	1-Wd Sacramento	77	202
KANKO								
John	40	m	w	HI	Butte	Oregon Twp	70	135
KANN								
Annie	28	f	w	PRUS	San Francisco	San Francisco P O	83	217
KANNA								
Irvin	36	m	w	NJ	San Francisco	San Francisco P O	83	160
Julia	28	f	w	IREL	San Francisco	San Francisco P O	85	775
KANNE								
Walter	35	m	w	IL	San Francisco	5-Wd San Francisco	81	23
KANNEDY								
Annie	5	f	w	CA	San Francisco	San Francisco P O	85	827
Lucy	7	f	w	CA	San Francisco	San Francisco P O	85	827
KANNING								
Isaac	14	m	w	CA	Sonoma	Mendocino Twp	91	305
KANNON								
G B	19	m	w	CA	Alameda	Oakland	68	159
KANNY								
John	36	m	w	IREL	Sierra	Sears Twp	89	558
KANODE								
David W	21	m	w	MD	Yolo	Grafton Twp	93	490
KANOTHA								
Anthony	44	m	w	SWIT	Colusa	Stony Crk Twp	71	332
KANOYA								
Philip	28	m	w	OH	Mendocino	Little Lake Twp	74	192
KANRICK								
Benj F	36	m	w	IA	Sacramento	Granite Twp	77	150
KANSTADLER								
F	51	m	w	FRAN	Alameda	Oakland	68	130
KANSTON								
Henry	40	m	w	SWED	San Francisco	5-Wd San Francisco	81	20
KANT								
James	30	m	w	IREL	Yolo	Cache Crk Twp	93	431
KANTZ								
Chris	36	m	w	BADE	Butte	Chico Twp	70	17
Henry	41	m	w	GERM	Yolo	Grafton Twp	93	496
KANYON								
Lizzie	30	f	w	SCOT	Yuba	Rose Bar Twp	93	661
KANZ								
Julia	21	f	w	BAVA	San Francisco	8-Wd San Francisco	82	492
KAO								
Hen	40	m	c	CHIN	Solano	Vallejo	90	178
KAONG								
Ah	49	m	c	CHIN	Trinity	Junction City Pct	92	206
KAOULA								
Joseph	42	m	w	ITAL	Nevada	Nevada Twp	75	319
KAP								
Ah	17	f	c	CHIN	San Francisco	1-Wd San Francisco	79	109
KAPES								
Lewis	45	m	w	AUST	San Francisco	8-Wd San Francisco	82	364
KAPF								
Wm	49	m	w	WURT	San Joaquin	Tulare Twp	86	249
KAPLAN								
Louis	35	m	w	PRUS	San Francisco	8-Wd San Francisco	82	480
KAPO								
Jesse	29	m	w	MA	Alameda	Murray Twp	68	125
KAPP								
James	38	m	w	MD	Alameda	Murray Twp	68	112
KAPPELL								
W S	40	m	w	OH	Humboldt	Eureka Twp	72	258
KAPPELLER								
John B	36	m	w	SWIT	Placer	Cisco P O	76	494
KAPPERT								
James	41	m	w	AUST	San Francisco	1-Wd San Francisco	79	51
KAPTER								
Charles	65	m	w	PRUS	Inyo	Bishop Crk Twp	73	315
KAPU								
John	50	m	w	HI	Sutter	Vernon Twp	92	133
Manneha	60	f	b	HI	Sutter	Vernon Twp	92	133
KAR								
---	19	m	c	CHIN	San Francisco	6-Wd San Francisco	81	51
Ah	30	m	c	CHIN	El Dorado	Cosumnes Twp	72	19
Sik	19	m	c	CHIN	San Francisco	11-Wd San Francisc	84	480
KARAGAN								
Edward	30	m	w	IREL	Nevada	Eureka Twp	75	128
KARAN								
Simon	30	m	w	PRUS	San Francisco	8-Wd San Francisco	82	318
KARATAN								
Mark	46	m	w	GREE	San Francisco	San Francisco P O	83	302
KARCHER								
Mat	36	m	w	MA	Sacramento	4-Wd Sacramento	77	328
KARCHNER								
Harry	35	m	w	PA	Placer	Lincoln P O	76	482
KARENNY								
James	46	m	w	IREL	Stanislaus	Branch Twp	92	4
KARGROVE								
George	6	m	w	CA	Marin	San Rafael Twp	74	28
James	7	m	w	CA	Marin	San Rafael Twp	74	28
KARHS								
John	31	m	w	PRUS	San Francisco	7-Wd San Francisco	81	170
KARL								
Andrew	25	m	w	PRUS	San Francisco	San Francisco P O	83	358
Jacob	28	m	w	PRUS	San Francisco	1-Wd San Francisco	79	69
Solomon	36	m	w	OH	Trinity	Canyon City Pct	92	201
William	23	m	w	HANO	San Francisco	San Francisco P O	83	357
KARLEA								
Matilda	18	f	w	MA	San Francisco	7-Wd San Francisco	81	158
KARLSTON								
Louisa	10	f	w	CA	San Francisco	5-Wd San Francisco	81	22
KARMAN								
J	27	m	w	PRUS	San Joaquin	2-Wd Stockton	86	193
KARMER								
Lisetta	62	f	w	SWIT	San Francisco	11-Wd San Francisc	84	499
KARN								
Julia	12	f	w	MO	San Francisco	2-Wd San Francisco	79	199
KARNES								
Michael	33	m	w	IREL	Santa Cruz	Santa Cruz	89	429
KARNEY								
F W	48	m	w	IL	San Joaquin	Liberty Twp	86	88
Jas	27	m	w	IREL	San Joaquin	2-Wd Stockton	86	185
Mike	54	m	w	IREL	San Joaquin	1-Wd Stockton	86	150
Roger	26	m	w	IREL	Santa Clara	2-Wd San Jose	88	306
Rudolph	37	m	w	IREL	San Joaquin	2-Wd Stockton	86	195
Steph	43	m	w	IREL	Yuba	Marysville	93	612
William	45	m	w	IREL	San Francisco	3-Wd San Francisco	79	308
Wm	32	m	w	IREL	San Francisco	11-Wd San Francisc	84	665
KARNHOCK								
George	35	m	w	OLDE	Yuba	Slate Range Bar Tw	93	673
KARNS								
Levi	37	m	w	OH	Solano	Vacaville Twp	90	129
KAROLSA								
Jesus	63	f	w	MEXI	San Francisco	2-Wd San Francisco	79	203
KAROT								
John	30	m	w	PRUS	Monterey	San Juan Twp	74	402
KARR								
David	38	m	w	SCOT	San Francisco	San Francisco P O	83	310
Hellen	6	f	w	CA	Placer	Dutch Flat P O	76	404
I F	35	m	w	PA	San Francisco	3-Wd San Francisco	79	323
John	33	m	w	IREL	Santa Clara	Alviso Twp	88	23
William	28	m	w	SCOT	San Francisco	7-Wd San Francisco	81	216
Wm Jas	27	m	w	NY	San Francisco	San Francisco P O	83	188
KARRIGAN								
John	20	m	w	IREL	San Francisco	San Francisco P O	83	155
Mary	38	f	w	IREL	San Francisco	2-Wd San Francisco	79	267
KARRIKER								
Simon	30	m	w	PA	El Dorado	White Oak Twp	72	140
KARSE								
Joseph	12	m	w	CA	El Dorado	Coloma Twp	72	9
KARSKI								
John	29	m	w	PRUS	San Joaquin	2-Wd Stockton	86	172
KARSON								
Paul	27	m	w	PRUS	San Francisco	7-Wd San Francisco	81	219
KARSTADT								
Fred	42	m	w	PRUS	Alameda	Alameda	68	5
KARVIS								
Henry	33	m	w	ENGL	Nevada	Grass Valley Twp	75	179
KARWIN								
John	24	m	w	IREL	Alameda	Brooklyn Twp	68	44
KASALOW								
Louis	42	m	w	LUEB	Calaveras	Copperopolis P O	70	247
KASCHE								
Ferd	42	m	w	BADE	San Francisco	11-Wd San Francisc	84	427
KASEL								
Henry	38	m	w	HANO	Stanislaus	Branch Twp	92	10
KASER								
Herman	42	m	w	PA	Santa Clara	Almaden Twp	88	2
KASEY								
Orvis G	27	m	w	NORW	Butte	Chico Twp	70	26
KASH								
Nicholas	34	m	w	LUXE	Klamath	Liberty Twp	73	374
KASING								
Albert	35	m	w	HANO	San Francisco	11-Wd San Francisc	84	607
KASKEL								
Adolph	45	m	w	PRUS	San Francisco	6-Wd San Francisco	81	139
Isaac	50	m	w	PRUS	San Francisco	6-Wd San Francisco	81	139
KASKIEFF								
Samuel	50	m	w	PA	Napa	Napa	75	18
KASKIL								
Casper	25	m	w	PRUS	Nevada	Nevada Twp	75	273
KASLER								
Martin	39	m	w	FRAN	Sacramento	3-Wd Sacramento	77	296
Wm	25	m	w	NY	San Francisco	5-Wd San Francisco	81	3
KASMER								
Terrice	60	f	w	RUSS	Amador	Drytown P O	69	416
KASPER								
Jacob	33	m	w	NY	Sonoma	Petaluma Twp	91	358
KASS								
George	43	m	w	PRUS	San Francisco	8-Wd San Francisco	82	436
San	27	m	c	CHIN	San Joaquin	Elliott Twp	86	71
KASSABON								
C	34	m	w	PRUS	Mariposa	Maxwell Crk P O	74	144
KASSALAR								
C G	39	m	w	PRUS	Tuolumne	Big Oak Flat P O	93	396
KASSMAN								
C N	36	m	w	BAVA	Tuolumne	Big Oak Flat P O	93	396

© 2001 by Heritage Quest. All rights reserved.

California 1870 Census

Name	Age	S	R	B-PL	County	Locale	Roll	Pg
						Series M593		
KASSON								
Andrew	32	m	w	NY	Monterey	Monterey Twp	74	352
Geo	65	m	w	CANA	San Joaquin	Tulare Twp	86	263
KAST								
Joseph	60	m	w	BADE	San Francisco	San Francisco P O	83	301
M E	21	f	w	PRUS	San Francisco	San Francisco P O	83	132
KASTA								
L	39	m	w	ITAL	Tuolumne	Big Oak Flat P O	93	391
KASTEL								
Minnie	20	f	w	BAVA	San Francisco	8-Wd San Francisco	82	403
KASTNER								
Jaques	39	m	w	ITAL	Calaveras	San Andreas P O	70	205
Louis	25	m	w	BAVA	San Francisco	San Francisco P O	83	217
KAT								
Ah	50	m	c	CHIN	Amador	Drytown P O	69	421
KATAN								
Joseph	35	m	w	PORT	San Francisco	11-Wd San Francisc	84	610
Manuel	30	m	w	PORT	Marin	Nicasio Twp	74	20
KATCH								
Cyrus M	40	m	w	ME	Santa Clara	1-Wd San Jose	88	252
KATE								
Ac	18	m	c	CHIN	Sacramento	Georgianna Twp	77	124
Ah	30	m	c	CHIN	Santa Clara	1-Wd San Jose	88	233
He	30	m	c	CHIN	Colusa	Colusa	71	299
Hubbard	27	m	w	OH	Colusa	Colusa	71	290
John	21	m	w	MO	San Joaquin	2-Wd Stockton	86	173
Manuel	21	m	w	PORT	Mendocino	Navarro & Big Rvr	74	177
KATEN								
Frank	20	m	w	PORT	Trinity	Indian Crk	92	199
John	32	m	w	PORT	Trinity	Indian Crk	92	199
Jose	30	m	w	PORT	Trinity	Indian Crk	92	199
Joseph	40	m	w	PORT	Alameda	Eden Twp	68	69
Manuel	27	m	w	PORT	Alameda	Eden Twp	68	82
KATER								
Antone	32	m	w	PORT	Trinity	Minersville Pct	92	203
Caroline	19	f	w	HDAR	San Francisco	San Francisco P O	85	727
Manuel	44	m	w	PORT	Trinity	Minersville Pct	92	203
KATERINE								
G	30	m	i	CA	Alameda	Murray Twp	68	103
KATES								
Chas	26	m	w	ENGL	Sacramento	3-Wd Sacramento	77	310
Josiah	40	m	w	NJ	Placer	Bath P O	76	425
KATH								
Crist	41	m	w	SHOL	Trinity	Junction City Pct	92	210
KATHAN								
J B	42	f	w	ME	Sacramento	3-Wd Sacramento	77	297
KATHER								
Albert	32	m	w	PRUS	Napa	Napa	75	52
Charles	36	m	w	PRUS	Napa	Napa	75	55
Jane	14	f	i	CA	Napa	Napa	75	55
KATHERN								
Daniel H	19	m	w	MO	Yolo	Cache Crk Twp	93	451
KATIE								
Hanek	24	f	w	IN	Sacramento	4-Wd Sacramento	77	337
KATINTZ								
Peter	23	m	w	BAVA	San Francisco	San Francisco P O	83	187
KATIS								
Sarah	9	f	w	CA	San Joaquin	Oneal Twp	86	109
KATKA								
Paul	35	m	w	POLA	Los Angeles	Los Angeles Twp	73	479
KATO								
Jesus	13	m	w	MEXI	Alameda	Oakland	68	159
Manual	15	m	w	MEXI	Alameda	Oakland	68	159
KATON								
Ellen	40	f	w	IREL	San Francisco	11-Wd San Francisc	84	550
George R	42	m	w	DC	Yolo	Putah Twp	93	516
William	23	m	w	IREL	Placer	Roseville P O	76	352
KATRUE								
C Mrs	56	f	w	FRAN	Amador	Jackson P O	69	322
KATS								
Saml	42	m	w	HANO	San Joaquin	Liberty Twp	86	94
KATTMAN								
George	34	m	w	PRUS	Los Angeles	Wilmington Twp	73	645
KATTRELL								
Lewis	40	m	w	FRAN	Stanislaus	Branch Twp	92	8
KATZ								
Abraham	29	m	w	HCAS	San Francisco	8-Wd San Francisco	82	381
Alex	44	m	w	WURT	San Francisco	San Francisco P O	85	806
Benjiman	38	m	w	PRUS	Los Angeles	Los Angeles	73	538
Daniel	52	m	w	BREM	Marin	Novato Twp	74	12
Frederik	45	m	w	FRAN	San Francisco	2-Wd San Francisco	79	257
Heny	35	m	w	MA	San Joaquin	Liberty Twp	86	97
Marcus	40	m	w	FRAN	San Bernardino	San Bernardino Twp	78	415
KATZE								
G	42	m	w	PA	Sierra	Sierra Twp	89	570
KATZENBACH								
Frederick	35	m	w	HDAR	San Francisco	8-Wd San Francisco	82	464
KATZENSTEIN								
G B	22	m	w	LA	Sacramento	3-Wd Sacramento	77	282
Maria	40	f	w	FRAN	Sacramento	3-Wd Sacramento	77	282
Meyer	20	m	w	NY	San Francisco	San Francisco P O	83	137
KAUB								
Benj	23	m	w	GERM	Yuba	Marysville	93	604
Bernhard	20	m	w	IL	San Francisco	San Francisco P O	83	347
KAUFFING								
Louis	26	m	w	WI	San Francisco	San Francisco P O	80	533

Name	Age	S	R	B-PL	County	Locale	Roll	Pg
						Series M593		
KAUFFMAN								
A A	34	m	w	PA	Tehama	Bell Mills Twp	92	159
A H	61	m	w	PA	Tehama	Antelope Twp	92	160
Adam	38	m	w	PRUS	San Francisco	1-Wd San Francisco	79	110
Chas	31	m	w	OH	Tehama	Red Bluff	92	181
Chris	36	m	w	PA	Tehama	Bell Mills Twp	92	159
F H	45	m	w	PA	Calaveras	San Andreas P O	70	153
Frank	67	m	w	FRAN	Sonoma	Analy Twp	91	222
Mary A	38	f	w	PA	Nevada	Grass Valley Twp	75	154
KAUFMAN								
Andrew	44	m	w	HANO	San Francisco	6-Wd San Francisco	81	127
August	30	m	w	HANO	San Francisco	2-Wd San Francisco	79	143
August	28	m	w	PRUS	Yolo	Putah Twp	93	527
David	17	m	w	TX	Placer	Auburn P O	76	365
Emil	31	m	w	PRUS	Yolo	Putah Twp	93	522
Fred	21	m	w	PRUS	San Francisco	6-Wd San Francisco	81	101
Frederick	33	m	w	PRUS	San Francisco	8-Wd San Francisco	82	448
Gabriel	40	m	w	BAVA	Yolo	Cache Crk Twp	93	427
Gustave	22	m	w	PRUS	Yolo	Putah Twp	93	525
Jacob	29	m	w	PRUS	San Francisco	San Francisco P O	83	308
Jno A	48	m	w	HESS	Shasta	Stillwater P O	89	481
Joseph	37	m	w	AUST	Santa Clara	Fremont Twp	88	55
Margaret	22	f	w	PRUS	San Francisco	8-Wd San Francisco	82	440
Mike	55	m	w	BAVA	Santa Barbara	San Buenaventura P	87	435
Morris	42	m	w	PRUS	Tuolumne	Sonora P O	93	303
Rebecca	19	f	w	BADE	San Francisco	8-Wd San Francisco	82	449
Saul	40	m	w	NY	San Francisco	6-Wd San Francisco	81	87
Sebastian	26	m	w	PRUS	San Francisco	8-Wd San Francisco	82	460
Solomon	18	m	w	BAVA	San Francisco	7-Wd San Francisco	81	156
KAUGHMAN								
Benjamin	56	m	w	PA	Placer	Auburn P O	76	365
KAULBACK								
Charles C	39	m	w	MA	Plumas	Plumas Twp	77	29
KAULBECK								
W	35	m	w	MA	Nevada	Eureka Twp	75	136
KAULEN								
Abraham	39	m	w	BOHE	San Diego	San Diego	78	498
KAUMMETTER								
Jos	41	m	w	PRUS	San Francisco	8-Wd San Francisco	82	318
KAUNG								
Ah	35	m	c	CHIN	Trinity	Douglas	92	234
KAUNZ								
John	29	m	w	IL	Mendocino	Round Valley Twp	74	218
KAUPERMAN								
Palmres	47	m	w	FRAN	Trinity	Lewiston Pct	92	212
KAUPMAN								
Arthur	42	m	w	PRUS	San Francisco	San Francisco P O	80	394
KAUSSEN								
Chas	41	m	w	GERM	Humboldt	Pacific Twp	72	292
Wm	47	m	w	GERM	Humboldt	Pacific Twp	72	296
KAUSTIN								
Saml	34	m	w	SWIT	San Francisco	8-Wd San Francisco	82	358
KAV								
Ah	63	m	c	CHIN	Sacramento	1-Wd Sacramento	77	199
KAVANAGH								
Barney	48	m	w	IREL	Placer	Bath P O	76	458
Edward	67	m	w	IREL	San Francisco	11-Wd San Francisc	84	703
James	30	m	w	IREL	San Francisco	7-Wd San Francisco	81	180
John	26	m	w	IREL	Contra Costa	Martinez P O	71	390
Mary	56	f	w	IREL	San Francisco	2-Wd San Francisco	79	153
Peter	30	m	w	IREL	Placer	Bath P O	76	457
William	60	m	w	KY	Santa Clara	San Jose Twp	88	197
KAVANAH								
Dora	42	f	w	IREL	San Francisco	11-Wd San Francisc	84	489
Patrick	33	m	w	IREL	San Francisco	San Francisco P O	85	717
KAVANAUGH								
John	43	m	w	NY	Contra Costa	San Pablo Twp	71	361
John	40	m	w	IREL	San Francisco	7-Wd San Francisco	81	183
John	40	m	w	IREL	Placer	Bath P O	76	442
Lucy	33	f	w	IREL	Sacramento	4-Wd Sacramento	77	358
Phillip	52	m	w	IREL	Placer	Bath P O	76	450
Thos	13	m	w	CA	San Francisco	11-Wd San Francisc	84	593
KAVANAUH								
Mary	23	f	w	IL	Alameda	Oakland	68	160
KAVANNAUGH								
James	30	m	w	IREL	Nevada	Grass Valley Twp	75	231
KAVE								
D W	24	m	w	IA	Sacramento	4-Wd Sacramento	77	374
KAVENAGH								
Elizabeth	17	f	w	IA	Santa Clara	San Jose Twp	88	197
KAVENAUGH								
John	45	m	w	IREL	San Francisco	1-Wd San Francisco	79	98
John	33	m	w	IREL	San Francisco	1-Wd San Francisco	79	115
Wm S	56	m	w	AL	Mariposa	Mariposa P O	74	120
KAVICK								
Sarah	28	f	w	ME	San Francisco	11-Wd San Francisc	84	574
KAVIN								
James	31	m	w	SCOT	San Francisco	1-Wd San Francisco	79	88
KAVNAUGH								
James	40	m	w	IREL	San Francisco	11-Wd San Francisc	84	705
KAVOON								
John	33	m	w	NORW	Placer	Roseville P O	76	351
KAW								
Ah	30	m	c	CHIN	San Francisco	6-Wd San Francisco	81	42
Ah	27	m	c	CHIN	Santa Clara	San Jose Twp	88	183
Ah	14	m	c	CHIN	San Francisco	3-Wd San Francisco	79	307
Sung	23	m	c	CHIN	Solano	Suisun Twp	90	105

© 2001 by Heritage Quest. All rights reserved.

Name	Age	S	R	B-PL	County	Locale	Series M593 Roll	Pg
KAWEE								
Jim	20	m	c	CHIN	Santa Clara	Redwood Twp	88	131
KAY								
---	30	m	c	CHIN	Siskiyou	Yreka Twp	89	667
Ah	45	m	c	CHIN	Trinity	Indian Crk	92	199
Ah	40	m	c	CHIN	Nevada	Nevada Twp	75	298
Ah	35	m	c	CHIN	Placer	Newcastle Twp	76	473
Ah	34	m	c	CHIN	Butte	Kimshew Tpw	70	84
Ah	32	m	c	CHIN	Trinity	Lewiston Pct	92	212
Ah	31	m	c	CHIN	Santa Clara	1-Wd San Jose	88	271
Ah	31	m	c	CHIN	Yuba	Marysville	93	619
Ah	30	m	c	CHIN	Mendocino	Point Arena Twp	74	208
Ah	30	m	c	CHIN	Amador	Fiddletown P O	69	427
Ah	28	m	c	CHIN	Santa Clara	Fremont Twp	88	57
Ah	27	m	c	CHIN	Amador	Jackson P O	69	332
Ah	27	m	c	CHIN	El Dorado	Diamond Springs Tw	72	27
Ah	26	m	c	CHIN	San Francisco	San Francisco P O	85	748
Ah	25	m	c	CHIN	Sacramento	1-Wd Sacramento	77	202
Ah	25	m	c	CHIN	Humboldt	Eureka Twp	72	266
Ah	24	m	c	CHIN	Monterey	Salinas Twp	74	307
Ah	24	m	c	CHIN	Placer	Newcastle Twp	76	478
Ah	24	m	c	CHIN	Amador	Jackson P O	69	332
Ah	24	m	c	CHIN	Shasta	French Gulch P O	89	466
Ah	23	m	c	CHIN	San Mateo	Half Moon Bay P O	87	395
Ah	23	m	c	CHIN	Shasta	French Gulch P O	89	470
Ah	22	m	c	CHIN	San Francisco	11-Wd San Francisc	84	559
Ah	18	m	c	CHIN	San Francisco	San Francisco P O	83	95
Ah	18	m	c	CHIN	Trinity	Douglas	92	236
Ah	15	m	c	CHIN	Solano	Benicia	90	20
Ah	15	m	c	CHIN	Santa Clara	Alviso Twp	88	27
Ah	14	m	c	CHIN	San Francisco	San Francisco P O	85	721
Chioo	35	m	c	CHIN	San Francisco	11-Wd San Francisc	84	503
Fong	28	m	c	CHIN	Klamath	Sawyers Bar	73	378
Foo	42	m	c	CHIN	Klamath	Sawyers Bar	73	378
Geo S	53	m	w	SCOT	El Dorado	Georgetown Twp	72	47
Guay	35	m	c	CHIN	Yuba	Marysville	93	632
Hi	19	m	c	CHIN	San Joaquin	Castoria Twp	86	13
Hong	20	m	c	CHIN	San Francisco	1-Wd San Francisco	79	131
Jake Yang	24	m	c	CHIN	El Dorado	Placerville	72	108
James R	24	m	w	SCOT	San Francisco	San Francisco P O	83	218
Jo	38	m	w	IL	Alameda	Alameda	68	19
John	24	m	w	NY	San Francisco	7-Wd San Francisco	81	181
John	23	m	w	ENGL	San Francisco	7-Wd San Francisco	81	264
Mun	45	m	c	CHIN	Yuba	Marysville	93	620
Samuel	48	m	w	ENGL	Sacramento	Granite Twp	77	144
Ti	27	m	c	CHIN	Solano	Montezuma Twp	90	68
Ting	37	m	c	CHIN	Humboldt	Eureka Twp	72	266
Wallace	41	m	w	MA	Amador	Jackson P O	69	325
William	54	m	w	ENGL	El Dorado	White Oak Twp	72	136
William R	44	m	w	MA	Amador	Jackson P O	69	325
KAYANDER								
Henry	26	m	w	FINL	Mendocino	Navarro & Big Rvr	74	177
KAYE								
Charles	31	m	w	ENGL	Santa Cruz	Santa Cruz	89	410
KAYLIM								
Margaret	49	f	w	ENGL	El Dorado	Mountain Twp	72	69
KAYON								
Ah	18	m	c	CHIN	Nevada	Nevada Twp	75	314
KAYOTE								
Francois	22	m	w	FRAN	Marin	Bolinas Twp	74	3
KAYS								
John C	59	m	w	IREL	Santa Barbara	Santa Barbara P O	87	457
KAYSER								
Charles	31	m	w	MO	San Francisco	2-Wd San Francisco	79	258
Otto	36	m	w	BADE	San Francisco	San Francisco P O	80	469
KAYTON								
Jacob	50	m	w	TN	El Dorado	Mud Springs Twp	72	77
KAYTSER								
John	40	m	w	PA	Tuolumne	Sonora P O	93	303
KE								
Ah	50	m	c	CHIN	El Dorado	Placerville	72	108
Ah	50	m	c	CHIN	El Dorado	Mud Springs Twp	72	87
Ah	35	m	c	CHIN	Calaveras	San Andreas P O	70	155
Ah	33	m	c	CHIN	El Dorado	Mountain Twp	72	70
Ah	30	m	c	CHIN	Solano	Suisun Twp	90	106
Ah	21	m	c	CHIN	Sacramento	1-Wd Sacramento	77	205
Ah	20	m	c	CHIN	Sacramento	1-Wd Sacramento	77	199
Ah	19	m	c	CHIN	El Dorado	Placerville Twp	72	105
Chun	31	m	c	CHIN	Solano	Vacaville Twp	90	131
Chung	21	m	c	CHIN	Solano	Vacaville Twp	90	136
Han	33	m	c	CHIN	El Dorado	Mud Springs Twp	72	88
Hoy	49	m	c	CHIN	Butte	Concow Twp	70	10
La	41	m	c	CHIN	Solano	Vacaville Twp	90	130
Lee	36	m	c	CHIN	Solano	Vacaville Twp	90	134
Tin	24	m	c	CHIN	Nevada	Bridgeport Twp	75	111
Tong	20	m	c	CHIN	Nevada	Meadow Lake Twp	75	254
Unf	34	m	c	CHIN	Siskiyou	Cottonwood Twp	89	594
KEACH								
Bernard	35	m	w	SWIT	San Francisco	San Francisco P O	80	480
KEADING								
Margaret	16	f	w	CANA	San Francisco	6-Wd San Francisco	81	145
KEADY								
John	37	m	w	IREL	San Francisco	11-Wd San Francisc	84	444
KEAFIELD								
George	43	m	w	NY	Plumas	Quartz Twp	77	39
KEAGAN								
Bridget	54	f	w	IREL	San Francisco	8-Wd San Francisco	82	292
Mary	34	f	w	IREL	Santa Clara	2-Wd San Jose	88	329
Mary	27	f	w	IREL	San Francisco	San Francisco P O	83	97
KEAGER								
Thomas	40	m	w	IREL	San Francisco	11-Wd San Francisc	84	703
KEAGO								
John	39	m	w	PA	San Joaquin	Elkhorn Twp	86	58
KEAHNE								
J A	42	m	w	HDAR	Sierra	Gibson Twp	89	541
KEAHUY								
Francis	57	m	w	IREL	San Francisco	11-Wd San Francisc	84	612
KEALEY								
Michael	60	m	w	IREL	Santa Clara	San Jose Twp	88	215
KEAM								
Bridget	56	f	w	IREL	Calaveras	Copperopolis P O	70	258
Joseph	22	m	w	PORT	Mendocino	Big Rvr Twp	74	159
KEAMER								
Jos C	33	m	w	MA	San Francisco	8-Wd San Francisco	82	340
KEAN								
Andrew C	49	m	w	VA	Yolo	Cache Crk Twp	93	430
Edward	37	m	w	OH	Napa	Napa	75	23
F	27	m	w	PRUS	San Francisco	San Francisco P O	83	134
J	15	m	w	CA	Solano	Benicia	90	20
J B	53	m	w	NJ	Lake	Upper Lake	73	408
Jas	5	m	w	CA	Solano	Vallejo	90	178
John	38	m	w	OH	Napa	Napa	75	57
John	35	m	w	CANA	Solano	Vallejo	90	178
John	30	m	w	IREL	Sacramento	3-Wd Sacramento	77	301
Lemuel	49	m	w	PA	Sacramento	American Twp	77	67
Mary	70	f	w	IREL	Sierra	Table Rock Twp	89	573
Patrick	38	m	w	IREL	San Francisco	7-Wd San Francisco	81	177
Wm	45	m	w	SCOT	Sacramento	Sutter Twp	77	384
Wm	42	m	w	MA	Sierra	Table Rock Twp	89	572
KEANAN								
Patrick	35	m	w	IREL	San Francisco	7-Wd San Francisco	81	211
KEANE								
Elkan	32	m	w	PRUS	San Francisco	8-Wd San Francisco	82	395
Ellen	40	f	w	IREL	San Francisco	8-Wd San Francisco	82	471
Francis	51	m	w	IREL	Santa Clara	2-Wd San Jose	88	303
James	40	m	w	CANA	San Francisco	7-Wd San Francisco	81	186
James	35	m	w	IREL	San Francisco	San Francisco P O	83	161
John	36	m	w	IREL	San Francisco	San Francisco P O	83	68
John	35	m	w	IREL	San Francisco	7-Wd San Francisco	81	184
Malachi	35	m	w	IREL	San Francisco	11-Wd San Francisc	84	528
Margaret	72	f	w	IREL	Santa Clara	2-Wd San Jose	88	306
Thomas	35	m	w	IREL	San Francisco	8-Wd San Francisco	82	405
KEANER								
Andrew	39	m	w	IREL	El Dorado	Coloma Twp	72	2
KEANG								
Ah	40	m	c	CHIN	Placer	Dutch Flat P O	76	411
Ah	25	m	c	CHIN	San Francisco	6-Wd San Francisco	81	38
KEANN								
Edward	31	m	w	ENGL	San Francisco	5-Wd San Francisco	81	16
KEANNY								
Isabella	40	f	w	IREL	San Francisco	San Francisco P O	83	149
KEAR								
Thomas	22	m	w	MO	Kern	Bakersfield P O	73	359
KEARCE								
John	32	m	w	IREL	Solano	Denverton Twp	90	25
KEARLE								
George	42	m	w	SCOT	Humboldt	Eureka Twp	72	272
KEARLY								
Thomas	36	m	w	ENGL	San Francisco	11-Wd San Francisc	84	491
KEARMAN								
Alice	32	f	w	IREL	San Francisco	7-Wd San Francisco	81	176
KEARN								
Lizzie	15	f	w	NY	San Francisco	2-Wd San Francisco	79	199
Mary	40	f	w	IREL	San Francisco	San Francisco P O	83	20
Michael	50	m	w	IREL	San Francisco	2-Wd San Francisco	79	182
Michael	33	m	w	IREL	San Francisco	San Francisco P O	83	183
Robt	30	m	w	OH	Butte	Ophir Twp	70	107
Samuel	43	m	w	MA	San Francisco	2-Wd San Francisco	79	156
KEARNAN								
Peter	30	m	w	IREL	San Francisco	San Francisco P O	83	372
Peter	26	m	w	NY	Yolo	Cache Crk Twp	93	429
KEARNE								
Patick	24	m	w	IREL	San Francisco	San Francisco P O	85	865
KEARNER								
Fredrick	18	m	w	SWIT	Napa	Yountville Twp	75	77
KEARNEY								
Alice	13	f	w	CA	Sacramento	2-Wd Sacramento	77	235
Andrew	53	m	w	IREL	Amador	Volcano P O	69	378
Annie	37	f	w	IREL	San Francisco	San Francisco P O	85	850
Arthur	22	m	w	IREL	Marin	Bolinas Twp	74	1
Catharine	18	f	w	NY	San Francisco	San Francisco P O	85	835
Frank	30	m	w	NY	Nevada	Grass Valley Twp	75	160
George	56	m	w	IREL	San Francisco	San Francisco P O	83	389
Hannah	32	f	w	IREL	San Francisco	8-Wd San Francisco	82	493
Henry	27	m	w	IREL	San Francisco	San Francisco P O	85	877
James	50	m	w	IREL	San Francisco	7-Wd San Francisco	81	157
James	35	m	w	PA	San Luis Obispo	Salinas Twp	87	293
James	31	m	w	NY	San Diego	San Diego	78	491
James	28	m	w	IREL	San Francisco	San Francisco P O	83	264
John	42	m	w	IREL	Placer	Newcastle Twp	76	476
John	30	m	w	IREL	Santa Cruz	Santa Cruz Twp	89	388
John	27	m	w	IREL	San Francisco	1-Wd San Francisco	79	64
John	18	m	w	IREL	San Francisco	7-Wd San Francisco	81	161
John	18	m	w	IREL	San Francisco	5-Wd San Francisco	81	33

© 2001 by Heritage Quest. All rights reserved.

California 1870 Census

Name	Age	S	R	B-PL	County	Locale	Series M593 Roll	Pg
Kearn	27	m	w	IREL	San Francisco	San Francisco P O	83	42
M F	3	f	w	CA	Los Angeles	Los Angeles	73	569
Mary	60	f	w	IREL	Los Angeles	Los Angeles	73	546
Mary	25	f	w	NY	San Francisco	8-Wd San Francisco	82	395
Mathew	33	m	w	IREL	San Francisco	San Francisco P O	85	764
Matthew	48	m	w	IREL	Santa Cruz	Watsonville	89	364
Michael	38	m	w	IREL	San Francisco	San Francisco P O	83	289
Michael	23	m	w	IREL	Santa Cruz	Santa Cruz	89	430
Michael	13	m	w	NY	San Francisco	11-Wd San Francisc	84	588
Pat	32	m	w	IREL	Alameda	Oakland	68	145
Pathrick	40	m	w	IREL	Monterey	Pajaro Twp	74	375
Patk	27	m	w	IREL	Fresno	Millerton P O	72	168
Patrick	47	m	w	IREL	Fresno	Millerton P O	72	158
Patrick	35	m	w	IREL	San Francisco	San Francisco P O	83	391
Richd M	32	m	w	CANA	San Francisco	San Francisco P O	83	51
Samuel	50	m	w	IREL	Stanislaus	Washington Twp	92	85
Samuel	30	m	w	IREL	Los Angeles	Los Angeles	73	528
Thomas	50	m	w	IREL	San Francisco	San Francisco P O	83	373
Thomas	32	m	w	IREL	Santa Clara	Fremont Twp	88	47
Thomas	28	m	w	IREL	Nevada	Little York Twp	75	235
Winfred	35	f	w	IREL	Santa Cruz	Pajaro Twp	89	359
Wm	26	m	w	IREL	San Francisco	5-Wd San Francisco	81	33
KEARNS								
Bernard	35	m	w	IREL	San Francisco	San Francisco P O	85	733
Eliza	22	f	w	IREL	San Francisco	7-Wd San Francisco	81	159
Johana	65	f	w	IREL	San Francisco	7-Wd San Francisco	81	161
John	38	m	w	IREL	Santa Barbara	San Buenaventura P	87	446
John	30	m	w	IREL	San Francisco	1-Wd San Francisco	79	98
John	25	m	w	IREL	San Francisco	San Francisco P O	85	869
Martin	25	m	w	IREL	San Francisco	11-Wd San Francisc	84	592
Michael	38	m	w	IREL	Sutter	Sutter Twp	92	128
Patrick	42	m	w	IREL	Calaveras	Copperopolis P O	70	256
Patrick	31	m	w	IREL	San Francisco	San Francisco P O	83	393
Rosa	56	f	w	IREL	San Francisco	2-Wd San Francisco	79	265
Thomas	39	m	w	NY	San Francisco	San Francisco P O	83	220
KEARNY								
Dennis	28	m	w	IREL	San Francisco	7-Wd San Francisco	81	251
James	36	m	w	IREL	San Francisco	San Francisco P O	83	153
James M	46	m	w	IREL	San Francisco	San Francisco P O	83	157
John	45	m	w	IREL	San Francisco	San Francisco P O	80	365
John	32	m	w	IREL	Solano	Silveyville Twp	90	74
John H	30	m	w	IREL	San Francisco	San Francisco P O	83	178
Joseph	29	m	w	IREL	Siskiyou	Callahan P O	89	627
Julia	20	f	w	ME	San Francisco	7-Wd San Francisco	81	285
Mary	58	f	w	IREL	San Francisco	11-Wd San Francisc	84	460
Patrick	27	m	w	MA	San Francisco	11-Wd San Francisc	84	442
Peter	25	m	w	NY	San Francisco	7-Wd San Francisco	81	278
KEARSING								
G F	62	m	w	ENGL	Amador	Jackson P O	69	342
L A	64	f	w	ENGL	Amador	Jackson P O	69	342
W F	60	m	w	ENGL	Amador	Jackson P O	69	342
KEARSY								
John	46	m	w	IREL	San Joaquin	2-Wd Stockton	86	166
KEARTH								
William	44	m	w	BAVA	Colusa	Spring Valley Twp	71	342
KEARY								
Oswold	51	m	w	SWIT	Mendocino	Anderson Twp	74	152
KEASE								
Henry	60	m	w	RUSS	Monterey	Alisal Twp	74	298
KEAST								
Wm	43	m	w	ENGL	San Joaquin	Dent Twp	86	19
Wm	40	m	w	ENGL	San Joaquin	Castoria Twp	86	3
KEAT								
Ah	38	m	c	CHIN	Colusa	Grand Island Twp	71	308
Frank	37	m	w	PORT	Monterey	Pajaro Twp	74	373
KEATAN								
Daniel	40	m	w	IREL	Placer	Cisco P O	76	495
KEATEN								
Chas	31	m	w	ME	San Joaquin	Dent Twp	86	29
Joseph	28	m	w	SCOT	Alameda	Eden Twp	68	91
KEATH								
Jno	40	m	w	PA	Butte	Chico Twp	70	35
Mary	24	f	w	IREL	San Francisco	7-Wd San Francisco	81	256
KEATHLY								
James	38	m	w	MO	Placer	Lincoln P O	76	482
KEATING								
Chas	30	m	w	NY	Butte	Ophir Twp	70	99
Chas	28	m	w	IREL	San Francisco	2-Wd San Francisco	79	213
D	24	m	w	IREL	Lake	Knoxville Mines	73	404
Danl	32	m	w	IREL	Humboldt	Bucksport Twp	72	241
Denis	47	m	w	GERM	San Francisco	8-Wd San Francisco	82	313
Edward	40	m	w	IREL	San Francisco	11-Wd San Francisc	84	488
Enos	30	m	w	PORT	Butte	Kimshew Tpw	70	77
James	67	m	w	IREL	Sacramento	4-Wd Sacramento	77	356
James	43	m	w	CANA	Tuolumne	Columbia P O	93	340
James	40	m	w	IREL	Butte	Chico Twp	70	18
James	30	m	w	IREL	San Francisco	San Francisco P O	85	743
John	55	m	w	IREL	San Francisco	8-Wd San Francisco	82	489
John	35	m	w	NY	San Francisco	San Francisco P O	83	132
John	30	m	w	IREL	San Francisco	1-Wd San Francisco	79	88
John	30	m	w	IREL	San Francisco	11-Wd San Francisc	84	659
Mary I	21	f	w	MA	San Francisco	5-Wd San Francisco	81	1
Michael	55	m	w	IREL	San Diego	San Diego	78	488
Michael	50	m	w	IREL	Sacramento	2-Wd Sacramento	77	210
Michael	40	m	w	ENGL	San Francisco	11-Wd San Francisc	84	610
Michael	28	m	w	IREL	Mendocino	Cuffeys Cove Twp	74	169
Nicolas	40	m	w	IREL	Los Angeles	Wilmington Twp	73	636
Owen	36	m	w	IREL	San Francisco	11-Wd San Francisc	84	614
Patrick	45	m	w	IREL	San Francisco	San Francisco P O	83	185
Sarah	8	f	w	CA	San Francisco	11-Wd San Francisc	84	710
Sarah	25	f	w	ME	Mono	Bridgeport P O	74	284
Thomas	25	m	w	NY	San Francisco	7-Wd San Francisco	81	213
Thos	36	m	w	IREL	Solano	Vallejo	90	149
Timothy	45	m	w	IREL	Butte	Ophir Twp	70	98
William	8	m	i	CA	Siskiyou	Surprise Valley Tw	89	643
William	36	m	m	LA	Mariposa	Mariposa P O	74	99
William	25	m	w	IREL	Calaveras	San Andreas P O	70	170
Wm	38	m	w	IREL	San Francisco	7-Wd San Francisco	81	266
KEATON								
Anna	60	f	w	IREL	San Francisco	7-Wd San Francisco	81	205
Ellen M	43	f	w	ENGL	Santa Clara	1-Wd San Jose	88	242
James	14	m	w	CA	Amador	Jackson P O	69	345
John	40	m	w	IREL	Yuba	Marysville Twp	93	569
Patrick	26	m	w	NY	San Mateo	San Mateo P O	87	357
KEATS								
Jacob	35	m	w	NY	San Joaquin	Castoria Twp	86	1
KEATTING								
John	28	m	w	NY	San Francisco	7-Wd San Francisco	81	219
KEAY								
Edward	37	m	w	IREL	San Francisco	7-Wd San Francisco	81	191
KEBBY								
James	30	m	w	IL	Sonoma	Bodega Twp	91	265
KEBER								
Christian	36	m	w	AUST	Sacramento	2-Wd Sacramento	77	240
Jacob	35	m	w	PRUS	Sacramento	2-Wd Sacramento	77	231
John	42	m	w	PRUS	Sacramento	4-Wd Sacramento	77	351
KEBO								
Patrick	50	m	w	IREL	San Mateo	Schoolhouse Statio	87	343
KEBOUGH								
Michl	48	m	w	IREL	Santa Clara	Gilroy Twp	88	72
KECH								
G	40	m	w	PRUS	Alameda	Oakland	68	146
KECHER								
Jo	41	m	w	MO	San Joaquin	Liberty Twp	86	86
KECHLER								
Lizzie	17	f	w	CA	San Francisco	2-Wd San Francisco	79	196
KECHMAN								
A R	29	m	w	OH	Nevada	Meadow Lake Twp	75	252
KECIL								
Catherine	25	f	w	IREL	San Francisco	2-Wd San Francisco	79	234
KECK								
Fred	25	m	w	WURT	San Francisco	11-Wd San Francisc	84	662
Jesse	44	m	w	PA	Placer	Colfax P O	76	385
Joel	54	m	w	PA	Sutter	Yuba Twp	92	141
Robert	21	m	w	PA	Sutter	Yuba Twp	92	141
KECKMAN								
Charles	42	m	w	FINL	Placer	Bath P O	76	457
KEDAUR								
Minnie	20	f	w	BADE	Butte	Oregon Twp	70	124
KEDD								
Malinda	35	f	i	CA	Klamath	Klamath Twp	73	371
Moses	53	m	w	IL	El Dorado	Placerville Twp	72	97
Stephen	45	m	w	ENGL	Amador	Ione City P O	69	355
KEDDIE								
Arthur W	28	m	w	SCOT	Plumas	Plumas Twp	77	26
KEDDINGTON								
John	48	m	w	IREL	Yuba	Rose Bar Twp	93	666
KEDER								
Gustave	33	m	w	HANO	Sonoma	Petaluma Twp	91	320
KEDES								
Pera	50	f	w	MEXI	Yuba	Marysville	93	617
KEDING								
Charles	29	m	w	NY	San Francisco	3-Wd San Francisco	79	326
Henry	45	m	w	MECK	El Dorado	Placerville	72	107
KEDO								
H H	25	m	w	PRUS	Monterey	Castroville Twp	74	325
KEDON								
Martin	38	m	w	IREL	San Francisco	San Francisco P O	83	67
Martin	17	m	w	NY	San Francisco	11-Wd San Francisc	84	593
KEE								
---	30	m	c	CHIN	Siskiyou	Cottonwood Twp	89	594
---	25	m	c	CHIN	Siskiyou	Cottonwood Twp	89	592
A	23	m	c	CHIN	San Mateo	San Mateo P O	87	348
Achee	35	m	c	CHIN	Tulare	Tule Rvr Twp	92	271
Ah	70	m	c	CHIN	Tehama	Red Bluff	92	183
Ah	60	m	c	CHIN	Tuolumne	Columbia P O	93	341
Ah	60	m	c	CHIN	Tuolumne	Chinese Camp P O	93	370
Ah	60	m	c	CHIN	San Francisco	2-Wd San Francisco	79	285
Ah	60	m	c	CHIN	Sacramento	Granite Twp	77	151
Ah	5M	m	c	CHIN	San Francisco	6-Wd San Francisco	81	131
Ah	55	m	c	CHIN	Solano	Vallejo	90	173
Ah	55	m	c	CHIN	Amador	Drytown P O	69	420
Ah	53	m	c	CHIN	Placer	Newcastle Twp	76	476
Ah	52	m	c	CHIN	Butte	Ophir Twp	70	106
Ah	51	m	c	CHIN	Mariposa	Mariposa P O	74	103
Ah	50	m	c	CHIN	Nevada	Nevada Twp	75	317
Ah	49	m	c	CHIN	Calaveras	San Andreas P O	70	165
Ah	49	m	c	CHIN	Sacramento	Cosumnes Twp	77	92
Ah	48	m	c	CHIN	Butte	Hamilton Twp	70	67
Ah	48	m	c	CHIN	San Francisco	San Francisco P O	80	436
Ah	48	m	c	CHIN	Placer	Dutch Flat P O	76	410
Ah	47	m	c	CHIN	Sacramento	Georgianna Twp	77	132
Ah	46	m	c	CHIN	Sonoma	Sonoma Twp	91	437
Ah	46	m	c	CHIN	Calaveras	San Andreas P O	70	167

© 2001 by Heritage Quest. All rights reserved.

Name	Age	S	R	B-PL	County	Locale	Series M593 Roll	Pg
Ah	45	m	c	CHIN	Placer	Newcastle Twp	76	478
Ah	45	m	c	CHIN	Sacramento	Granite Twp	77	155
Ah	45	m	c	CHIN	Sacramento	Granite Twp	77	139
Ah	45	m	c	CHIN	Calaveras	San Andreas P O	70	183
Ah	44	m	c	CHIN	Trinity	Douglas	92	233
Ah	44	m	c	CHIN	Sacramento	Granite Twp	77	155
Ah	44	m	c	CHIN	Amador	Fiddletown P O	69	428
Ah	42	m	c	CHIN	Tuolumne	Columbia P O	93	349
Ah	42	m	c	CHIN	Tuolumne	Big Oak Flat P O	93	399
Ah	42	m	c	CHIN	San Francisco	11-Wd San Francisc	84	554
Ah	42	m	c	CHIN	Sacramento	4-Wd Sacramento	77	340
Ah	42	m	c	CHIN	Sacramento	Natomas Twp	77	171
Ah	42	m	c	CHIN	El Dorado	Georgetown Twp	72	44
Ah	41	m	c	CHIN	Tuolumne	Columbia P O	93	342
Ah	41	m	c	CHIN	Alameda	Oakland	68	245
Ah	41	m	c	CHIN	San Francisco	San Francisco P O	80	465
Ah	40	m	c	CHIN	Tulare	Visalia	92	297
Ah	40	m	c	CHIN	Trinity	Douglas	92	235
Ah	40	m	c	CHIN	Tuolumne	Sonora P O	93	311
Ah	40	m	c	CHIN	Sierra	Lincoln Twp	89	546
Ah	40	m	c	CHIN	San Joaquin	Oneal Twp	86	115
Ah	40	m	c	CHIN	San Joaquin	Castoria Twp	86	12
Ah	40	m	c	CHIN	San Francisco	6-Wd San Francisco	81	38
Ah	40	m	c	CHIN	Mariposa	Mariposa P O	74	127
Ah	40	m	c	CHIN	Alameda	Oakland	68	254
Ah	40	m	c	CHIN	Placer	Gold Run Twp	76	399
Ah	40	m	c	CHIN	Santa Clara	1-Wd San Jose	88	273
Ah	40	m	c	CHIN	Sacramento	Granite Twp	77	152
Ah	40	m	c	CHIN	Placer	Blue Canyon P O	76	418
Ah	40	m	c	CHIN	Sacramento	Center Twp	77	85
Ah	40	m	c	CHIN	Sacramento	Center Twp	77	85
Ah	40	m	c	CHIN	Nevada	Eureka Twp	75	141
Ah	40	m	c	CHIN	Nevada	Little York Twp	75	234
Ah	40	m	c	CHIN	Amador	Drytown P O	69	421
Ah	40	m	c	CHIN	Butte	Chico Twp	70	52
Ah	40	m	c	CHIN	Yuba	Marysville	93	619
Ah	39	m	c	CHIN	Yuba	Marysville	93	578
Ah	39	m	c	CHIN	Santa Barbara	Santa Barbara P O	87	458
Ah	39	m	c	CHIN	San Francisco	6-Wd San Francisco	81	56
Ah	39	m	c	CHIN	Butte	Wyandotte Twp	70	148
Ah	39	m	c	CHIN	Amador	Drytown P O	69	425
Ah	38	m	c	CHIN	Alameda	Oakland	68	238
Ah	38	m	c	CHIN	Calaveras	Copperopolis P O	70	258
Ah	38	m	c	CHIN	Siskiyou	Yreka	89	661
Ah	38	m	c	CHIN	Santa Clara	1-Wd San Jose	88	274
Ah	38	m	c	CHIN	Santa Barbara	Santa Barbara P O	87	458
Ah	38	m	c	CHIN	Sacramento	1-Wd Sacramento	77	196
Ah	38	m	c	CHIN	Placer	Pino Twp	76	472
Ah	38	m	c	CHIN	Placer	Bath P O	76	444
Ah	38	m	c	CHIN	Amador	Ione City P O	69	354
Ah	38	m	c	CHIN	Los Angeles	Los Angeles	73	531
Ah	38	m	c	CHIN	El Dorado	Georgetown Twp	72	38
Ah	37	m	c	CHIN	San Joaquin	Castoria Twp	86	12
Ah	37	m	c	CHIN	Butte	Hamilton Twp	70	73
Ah	37	m	c	CHIN	Santa Clara	1-Wd San Jose	88	269
Ah	37	m	c	CHIN	Placer	Bath P O	76	460
Ah	37	m	c	CHIN	Nevada	Washington Twp	75	347
Ah	37	m	c	CHIN	Alameda	Oakland	68	254
Ah	37	m	c	CHIN	Alameda	Oakland	68	254
Ah	37	m	c	CHIN	Butte	Chico Twp	70	51
Ah	36	m	c	CHIN	San Francisco	San Francisco P O	80	495
Ah	36	m	c	CHIN	Merced	Snelling P O	74	280
Ah	36	m	c	CHIN	Mariposa	Mariposa P O	74	106
Ah	36	m	c	CHIN	Placer	Summit P O	76	497
Ah	36	m	c	CHIN	Nevada	Nevada Twp	75	302
Ah	36	m	c	CHIN	Alpine	Woodfords P O	69	315
Ah	35	m	c	CHIN	Solano	Vallejo	90	174
Ah	35	m	c	CHIN	Mariposa	Mariposa P O	74	121
Ah	35	m	c	CHIN	El Dorado	Cosumnes Twp	72	15
Ah	35	m	c	CHIN	Alameda	Oakland	68	238
Ah	35	m	c	CHIN	Sacramento	Natomas Twp	77	171
Ah	35	m	c	CHIN	Trinity	Indian Crk	92	199
Ah	35	m	c	CHIN	San Francisco	San Francisco P O	80	501
Ah	35	m	c	CHIN	Alameda	Oakland	68	223
Ah	35	m	c	CHIN	Los Angeles	Los Angeles Twp	73	473
Ah	35	m	c	CHIN	El Dorado	Placerville	72	123
Ah	35	m	c	CHIN	El Dorado	Salmon Falls Twp	72	132
Ah	34	m	c	CHIN	Yuba	Marysville	93	577
Ah	34	m	c	CHIN	San Francisco	6-Wd San Francisco	81	46
Ah	34	m	c	CHIN	San Francisco	6-Wd San Francisco	81	76
Ah	34	m	c	CHIN	Nevada	Grass Valley Twp	75	203
Ah	34	m	c	CHIN	Alameda	Oakland	68	152
Ah	34	m	c	CHIN	Alameda	Oakland	68	254
Ah	33	m	c	CHIN	Trinity	North Fork Twp	92	219
Ah	33	m	c	CHIN	Sierra	Lincoln Twp	89	548
Ah	33	m	c	CHIN	Sacramento	1-Wd Sacramento	77	204
Ah	33	m	c	CHIN	Sacramento	Granite Twp	77	151
Ah	32	m	c	CHIN	Mariposa	Mariposa P O	74	126
Ah	32	m	c	CHIN	Nevada	Rough & Ready Twp	75	332
Ah	32	m	c	CHIN	San Francisco	6-Wd San Francisco	81	60
Ah	32	m	c	CHIN	Sacramento	2-Wd Sacramento	77	227
Ah	32	m	c	CHIN	Sacramento	Granite Twp	77	152
Ah	32	m	c	CHIN	Plumas	Washington Twp	77	58
Ah	32	m	c	CHIN	Placer	Roseville P O	76	348
Ah	31	m	c	CHIN	San Francisco	San Francisco P O	80	495
Ah	31	m	c	CHIN	San Francisco	6-Wd San Francisco	81	65
Ah	31	m	c	CHIN	Tehama	Tehama Twp	92	188
Ah	31	m	c	CHIN	Sierra	Forest Twp	89	532
Ah	31	m	c	CHIN	Placer	Auburn P O	76	364
Ah	31	m	c	CHIN	Sacramento	Center Twp	77	85
Ah	31	m	c	CHIN	Calaveras	San Andreas P O	70	155
Ah	31	m	c	CHIN	Butte	Chico Twp	70	51
Ah	30	m	c	CHIN	San Joaquin	Castoria Twp	86	10
Ah	30	m	c	CHIN	San Francisco	6-Wd San Francisco	81	62
Ah	30	m	c	CHIN	Mono	Bridgeport P O	74	282
Ah	30	m	c	CHIN	Mariposa	Mariposa P O	74	129
Ah	30	m	c	CHIN	Butte	Ophir Twp	70	99
Ah	30	m	c	CHIN	Nevada	Nevada Twp	75	311
Ah	30	m	c	CHIN	Sacramento	Sutter Twp	77	390
Ah	30	m	c	CHIN	Plumas	Goodwin Twp	77	4
Ah	30	m	c	CHIN	Sacramento	1-Wd Sacramento	77	172
Ah	30	m	c	CHIN	San Francisco	11-Wd San Francisc	84	528
Ah	30	m	c	CHIN	San Francisco	6-Wd San Francisco	81	55
Ah	30	m	c	CHIN	San Francisco	6-Wd San Francisco	81	69
Ah	30	m	c	CHIN	Sacramento	Granite Twp	77	141
Ah	30	m	c	CHIN	Amador	Sutter Crk P O	69	411
Ah	30	m	c	CHIN	Calaveras	San Andreas P O	70	166
Ah	30	m	c	CHIN	Calaveras	San Andreas P O	70	190
Ah	30	m	c	CHIN	Alameda	Oakland	68	232
Ah	30	m	c	CHIN	Alameda	Oakland	68	254
Ah	30	m	c	CHIN	El Dorado	Coloma Twp	72	4
Ah	29	m	c	CHIN	Tehama	Red Bluff	92	182
Ah	29	m	c	CHIN	Siskiyou	Yreka	89	650
Ah	29	m	c	CHIN	Solano	Suisun Twp	90	106
Ah	29	m	c	CHIN	San Francisco	San Francisco P O	80	495
Ah	29	m	c	CHIN	San Francisco	6-Wd San Francisco	81	58
Ah	29	f	c	CHIN	Merced	Snelling P O	74	279
Ah	29	m	c	CHIN	Butte	Hamilton Twp	70	67
Ah	29	m	c	CHIN	Nevada	Nevada Twp	75	321
Ah	29	m	c	CHIN	Solano	Suisun Twp	90	107
Ah	29	m	c	CHIN	San Francisco	6-Wd San Francisco	81	56
Ah	29	m	c	CHIN	San Francisco	6-Wd San Francisco	81	60
Ah	29	m	c	CHIN	Sacramento	Granite Twp	77	152
Ah	28	m	c	CHIN	Shasta	French Gulch P O	89	465
Ah	28	m	c	CHIN	Calaveras	Copperopolis P O	70	234
Ah	28	m	c	CHIN	Sacramento	Granite Twp	77	151
Ah	28	m	c	CHIN	Santa Clara	Fremont Twp	88	55
Ah	28	m	c	CHIN	Santa Clara	2-Wd San Jose	88	325
Ah	28	m	c	CHIN	Santa Clara	1-Wd San Jose	88	277
Ah	28	m	c	CHIN	San Francisco	6-Wd San Francisco	81	56
Ah	28	m	c	CHIN	San Francisco	6-Wd San Francisco	81	58
Ah	28	m	c	CHIN	Sacramento	Granite Twp	77	138
Ah	28	m	c	CHIN	Alameda	Oakland	68	181
Ah	28	m	c	CHIN	Alameda	Oakland	68	250
Ah	28	m	c	CHIN	Alameda	Oakland	68	232
Ah	27	m	c	CHIN	Sierra	Sears Twp	89	553
Ah	27	m	c	CHIN	Solano	Suisun Twp	90	106
Ah	27	m	c	CHIN	San Francisco	6-Wd San Francisco	81	61
Ah	27	m	c	CHIN	Marin	Bolinas Twp	74	8
Ah	27	m	c	CHIN	Kern	Bakersfield P O	73	361
Ah	27	m	c	CHIN	Butte	Hamilton Twp	70	67
Ah	27	m	c	CHIN	Calaveras	San Andreas P O	70	171
Ah	27	m	c	CHIN	Plumas	Mineral Twp	77	23
Ah	27	f	c	CHIN	Santa Clara	1-Wd San Jose	88	269
Ah	27	m	c	CHIN	San Mateo	Schoolhouse Statio	87	344
Ah	27	m	c	CHIN	San Mateo	Schoolhouse Statio	87	332
Ah	27	m	c	CHIN	San Joaquin	Elkhorn Twp	86	62
Ah	27	m	c	CHIN	Nevada	Little York Twp	75	245
Ah	27	m	c	CHIN	Butte	Concow Twp	70	12
Ah	27	m	c	CHIN	El Dorado	Georgetown Twp	72	36
Ah	27	m	c	CHIN	Yuba	Marysville	93	619
Ah	26	m	c	CHIN	Butte	Hamilton Twp	70	66
Ah	26	m	c	CHIN	Placer	Auburn P O	76	371
Ah	26	m	c	ME	Nevada	Washington Twp	75	344
Ah	26	m	c	CHIN	Stanislaus	Buena Vista Twp	92	13
Ah	26	m	c	CHIN	Tehama	Tehama Twp	92	189
Ah	26	m	c	CHIN	Sierra	Butte Twp	89	510
Ah	26	m	c	CHIN	San Mateo	Schoolhouse Statio	87	344
Ah	26	m	c	CHIN	San Mateo	Schoolhouse Statio	87	344
Ah	26	m	c	CHIN	Sacramento	1-Wd Sacramento	77	201
Ah	26	m	c	CHIN	Placer	Bath P O	76	445
Ah	26	m	c	CHIN	Nevada	Little York Twp	75	245
Ah	26	m	c	CHIN	Nevada	Nevada Twp	75	311
Ah	26	m	c	CHIN	Merced	Snelling P O	74	255
Ah	25	m	c	CHIN	Tehama	Antelope Twp	92	153
Ah	25	m	c	CHIN	Siskiyou	Table Rock Twp	89	647
Ah	25	m	c	CHIN	San Joaquin	Dent Twp	86	17
Ah	25	m	c	CHIN	San Francisco	8-Wd San Francisco	82	465
Ah	25	m	c	CHIN	San Francisco	6-Wd San Francisco	81	47
Ah	25	m	c	CHIN	San Francisco	6-Wd San Francisco	81	59
Ah	25	m	c	CHIN	Los Angeles	Los Angeles	73	511
Ah	25	m	c	CHIN	Alameda	Oakland	68	256
Ah	25	m	c	CHIN	Alameda	Oakland	68	233
Ah	25	m	c	CHIN	Placer	Clipper Gap P O	76	392
Ah	25	m	c	CHIN	Placer	Colfax P O	76	387
Ah	25	m	c	CHIN	Sierra	Gibson Twp	89	538
Ah	25	m	c	CHIN	Santa Clara	Fremont Twp	88	57
Ah	25	m	c	CHIN	San Francisco	San Francisco P O	83	253
Ah	25	m	c	CHIN	San Francisco	San Francisco P O	83	298
Ah	25	m	c	CHIN	Napa	Napa	75	19
Ah	24	m	c	CHIN	Sierra	Sears Twp	89	554
Ah	24	m	c	CHIN	Shasta	French Gulch P O	89	464
Ah	24	m	c	CHIN	San Francisco	6-Wd San Francisco	81	62
Ah	24	m	c	CHIN	Butte	Hamilton Twp	70	75

© 2001 by Heritage Quest. All rights reserved.

California 1870 Census

Name	Age	S	R	B-PL	County	Locale	Roll	Pg
						Series M593		
Ah	24	m	c	CHIN	Nevada	Meadow Lake Twp	75	257
Ah	24	m	c	CHIN	San Francisco	6-Wd San Francisco	81	47
Ah	24	m	c	CHIN	San Francisco	6-Wd San Francisco	81	104
Ah	24	m	c	CHIN	San Francisco	San Francisco P O	80	519
Ah	24	m	c	CHIN	Napa	Napa	75	7
Ah	23	m	c	CHIN	Tuolumne	Chinese Camp P O	93	374
Ah	23	m	c	CHIN	Santa Clara	Alviso Twp	88	25
Ah	23	m	c	CHIN	Sacramento	Sutter Twp	77	386
Ah	23	m	c	CHIN	San Mateo	Belmont P O	87	373
Ah	23	m	c	CHIN	Sacramento	3-Wd Sacramento	77	314
Ah	23	m	c	CHIN	Alameda	Washington Twp	68	299
Ah	22	m	c	CHIN	Tehama	Red Bluff	92	182
Ah	22	m	c	CHIN	Sierra	Sears Twp	89	554
Ah	22	m	c	CHIN	San Francisco	6-Wd San Francisco	81	50
Ah	22	m	c	CHIN	San Francisco	6-Wd San Francisco	81	59
Ah	22	m	c	CHIN	Butte	Hamilton Twp	70	67
Ah	22	m	c	CHIN	Placer	Bath P O	76	459
Ah	22	m	c	CHIN	Placer	Colfax P O	76	385
Ah	22	m	c	CHIN	Napa	Napa Twp	75	32
Ah	22	m	c	CHIN	San Francisco	7-Wd San Francisco	81	263
Ah	22	m	c	CHIN	San Francisco	6-Wd San Francisco	81	67
Ah	22	m	c	CHIN	Nevada	Grass Valley Twp	75	203
Ah	22	m	c	CHIN	Marin	San Rafael Twp	74	45
Ah	22	m	c	CHIN	Alameda	Brooklyn	68	34
Ah	22	m	c	CHIN	Alameda	Washington Twp	68	299
Ah	21	m	c	CHIN	Sierra	Butte Twp	89	512
Ah	21	m	c	CHIN	San Francisco	San Francisco P O	85	844
Ah	21	m	c	CHIN	San Francisco	8-Wd San Francisco	82	322
Ah	21	m	c	CHIN	San Francisco	6-Wd San Francisco	81	49
Ah	21	m	c	CHIN	San Francisco	6-Wd San Francisco	81	62
Ah	21	m	c	CHIN	San Francisco	6-Wd San Francisco	81	46
Ah	21	m	c	CHIN	San Francisco	3-Wd San Francisco	79	303
Ah	21	m	c	CHIN	San Francisco	3-Wd San Francisco	79	310
Ah	21	m	c	CHIN	Sacramento	2-Wd Sacramento	77	233
Ah	21	m	c	CHIN	San Francisco	6-Wd San Francisco	81	55
Ah	21	m	c	CHIN	San Francisco	6-Wd San Francisco	81	56
Ah	21	m	c	CHIN	Plumas	Goodwin Twp	77	3
Ah	21	m	c	CHIN	El Dorado	Georgetown Twp	72	44
Ah	20	m	c	CHIN	Siskiyou	Cottonwood Twp	89	593
Ah	20	m	c	CHIN	San Francisco	8-Wd San Francisco	82	486
Ah	20	m	c	CHIN	San Francisco	San Francisco P O	80	489
Ah	20	m	c	CHIN	San Francisco	6-Wd San Francisco	81	47
Ah	20	m	c	CHIN	Butte	Bidwell Twp	70	1
Ah	20	m	c	CHIN	San Francisco	3-Wd San Francisco	79	309
Ah	20	m	c	CHIN	San Francisco	3-Wd San Francisco	79	304
Ah	20	m	c	CHIN	San Francisco	2-Wd San Francisco	79	144
Ah	20	m	c	CHIN	San Francisco	1-Wd San Francisco	79	80
Ah	20	m	c	CHIN	Placer	Auburn P O	76	364
Ah	20	m	c	CHIN	Santa Clara	Fremont Twp	88	62
Ah	20	m	c	CHIN	Santa Clara	Santa Clara Twp	88	165
Ah	20	m	c	CHIN	San Francisco	6-Wd San Francisco	81	47
Ah	20	m	c	CHIN	San Francisco	6-Wd San Francisco	81	48
Ah	20	m	c	CHIN	San Francisco	6-Wd San Francisco	81	50
Ah	20	m	c	CHIN	San Francisco	6-Wd San Francisco	81	55
Ah	20	m	c	CHIN	San Francisco	6-Wd San Francisco	81	52
Ah	20	m	c	CHIN	Placer	Dutch Flat P O	76	411
Ah	20	m	c	CHIN	San Diego	Julian Dist	78	468
Ah	20	m	c	CHIN	Mendocino	Point Arena Twp	74	213
Ah	20	m	c	CHIN	Contra Costa	Martinez P O	71	404
Ah	19	m	c	CHIN	Yuba	Marysville Twp	93	569
Ah	19	m	c	CHIN	Shasta	French Gulch P O	89	464
Ah	19	m	c	CHIN	San Francisco	6-Wd San Francisco	81	44
Ah	19	m	c	CHIN	San Francisco	6-Wd San Francisco	81	59
Ah	19	m	c	CHIN	San Francisco	3-Wd San Francisco	79	329
Ah	19	m	c	CHIN	Nevada	Nevada Twp	75	271
Ah	19	m	c	CHIN	San Mateo	Schoolhouse Statio	87	332
Ah	19	m	c	CHIN	San Francisco	San Francisco P O	85	749
Ah	19	m	c	CHIN	Butte	Hamilton Twp	70	67
Ah	18	m	c	CHIN	Tehama	Red Bluff	92	184
Ah	18	m	c	CHIN	San Joaquin	Castoria Twp	86	13
Ah	18	m	c	CHIN	Shasta	American Ranch P O	89	499
Ah	18	m	c	CHIN	San Francisco	11-Wd San Francisc	84	602
Ah	18	m	c	CHIN	San Francisco	6-Wd San Francisco	81	53
Ah	18	m	c	CHIN	San Francisco	2-Wd San Francisco	79	170
Ah	18	m	c	CHIN	Alameda	Eden Twp	68	82
Ah	18	m	c	CHIN	Alameda	Alvarado	68	303
Ah	18	m	c	CHIN	Alameda	Oakland	68	235
Ah	18	m	c	CHIN	Butte	Chico Twp	70	54
Ah	17	m	c	CHIN	San Francisco	6-Wd San Francisco	81	68
Ah	17	m	c	CHIN	Placer	Lincoln P O	76	483
Ah	17	m	c	CHIN	Placer	Summit P O	76	496
Ah	16	m	c	CHIN	San Francisco	6-Wd San Francisco	81	50
Ah	16	m	c	CHIN	San Francisco	6-Wd San Francisco	81	83
Ah	16	m	c	CHIN	Santa Clara	2-Wd San Jose	88	280
Ah	16	m	c	CHIN	San Francisco	6-Wd San Francisco	81	63
Ah	16	m	c	CHIN	San Francisco	San Francisco P O	80	490
Ah	15	m	c	CHIN	Trinity	Douglas	92	236
Ah	15	m	c	CHIN	San Francisco	3-Wd San Francisco	79	306
Ah	15	m	c	IREL	San Francisco	San Francisco P O	80	372
Ah	15	m	c	CHIN	San Francisco	6-Wd San Francisco	81	66
Ah	15	m	c	CHIN	Sacramento	4-Wd Sacramento	77	321
Ah	15	m	c	CHIN	Contra Costa	Martinez P O	71	445
Ah	14	m	c	CHIN	San Francisco	San Francisco P O	85	788
Ah	14	m	c	CHIN	San Francisco	8-Wd San Francisco	82	306
Ah	13	m	c	CHIN	San Francisco	6-Wd San Francisco	81	50
Ah	13	m	c	CHIN	San Francisco	3-Wd San Francisco	79	321
Ah	13	m	c	CHIN	San Francisco	2-Wd San Francisco	79	179

Name	Age	S	R	B-PL	County	Locale	Roll	Pg
						Series M593		
Ah	12	m	c	CHIN	San Francisco	6-Wd San Francisco	81	124
Ah	12	m	c	CHIN	San Francisco	2-Wd San Francisco	79	173
Ah	11	m	c	CHIN	San Francisco	2-Wd San Francisco	79	165
Ah	10	f	c	CHIN	San Francisco	6-Wd San Francisco	81	39
Ah	10	m	c	CHIN	San Francisco	2-Wd San Francisco	79	150
Ah	10	m	c	CHIN	Placer	Bath P O	76	422
Ah Foo	49	m	c	CHIN	Amador	Fiddletown P O	69	438
Ah Hip	36	m	c	CHIN	Calaveras	San Andreas P O	70	201
Ahk	16	m	c	CHIN	Nevada	Grass Valley Twp	75	173
Ak	29	m	c	CHIN	Tehama	Tehama Twp	92	192
Anna	15	f	w	MA	Alameda	Eden Twp	68	88
Ark	16	m	c	CHIN	San Francisco	San Francisco P O	83	261
Chap	64	m	c	CHIN	San Francisco	2-Wd San Francisco	79	285
Charles	11	m	c	CHIN	Plumas	Plumas Twp	77	29
Chee	21	m	c	CHIN	Solano	Rio Vista Twp	90	59
Cheung	50	m	c	CHIN	Calaveras	San Andreas P O	70	162
Chin	29	m	c	CHIN	Yuba	Marysville	93	623
Chong Ah	38	m	c	CHIN	Santa Clara	1-Wd San Jose	88	270
Chung	32	m	c	CHIN	Mariposa	Mariposa P O	74	126
Con	34	m	c	CHIN	Sierra	Forest Twp	89	528
Fah	20	m	c	CHIN	San Francisco	6-Wd San Francisco	81	43
Fi	41	m	c	CHIN	Nevada	Grass Valley Twp	75	205
Fing	21	m	c	CHIN	Solano	Rio Vista Twp	90	64
Foo	43	m	c	CHIN	Butte	Hamilton Twp	70	73
Foo	37	m	c	CHIN	San Francisco	San Francisco P O	83	302
Fy	17	m	c	CHIN	Yuba	Marysville	93	630
Gee	53	m	c	CHIN	Plumas	Mineral Twp	77	23
Geo	24	m	w	CT	Sacramento	1-Wd Sacramento	77	190
Go	26	m	c	CHIN	Solano	Suisun Twp	90	104
Hang	34	m	c	CHIN	Santa Barbara	Santa Barbara P O	87	452
He	33	m	c	CHIN	Nevada	Nevada Twp	75	298
He	23	m	c	CHIN	Nevada	Meadow Lake Twp	75	257
Hi	45	m	c	CHIN	Yolo	Putah Twp	93	525
Hi	34	m	c	CHIN	Yolo	Merritt Twp	93	503
Hing	50	m	c	CHIN	Nevada	Nevada Twp	75	299
Hing	20	m	c	CHIN	San Bernardino	San Bernardino Twp	78	433
Hip	36	m	c	CHIN	El Dorado	Placerville	72	115
Hong	27	m	c	CHIN	San Francisco	6-Wd San Francisco	81	51
Hop	43	m	c	CHIN	Kern	Havilah P O	73	337
Hop	35	m	c	CHIN	Sonoma	Russian Rvr	91	373
Hop	20	m	c	CHIN	Placer	Gold Run Twp	76	399
How	22	m	c	CHIN	San Francisco	8-Wd San Francisco	82	361
Hoy	42	m	c	CHIN	Butte	Chico Twp	70	51
Hoy	30	m	c	CHIN	Yuba	Marysville	93	630
Hun	24	m	c	CHIN	San Francisco	1-Wd San Francisco	79	80
Jack	32	m	c	CHIN	San Francisco	3-Wd San Francisco	79	306
James	35	m	w	IREL	Sonoma	Bodega Twp	91	257
Jim	38	m	c	CHIN	Santa Clara	1-Wd San Jose	88	271
Jing	25	m	c	CHIN	Alpine	Markleeville P O	69	316
Jo	33	m	c	CHIN	Mendocino	Gualala Twp	74	226
Kee	24	m	c	CHIN	Solano	Rio Vista Twp	90	70
Ko	19	f	c	CHIN	San Joaquin	1-Wd Stockton	86	153
Kom	30	m	c	CHIN	San Francisco	1-Wd San Francisco	79	52
La	25	m	c	CHIN	San Francisco	11-Wd San Francisc	84	688
Lee	9	f	c	CHIN	Santa Clara	1-Wd San Jose	88	273
Lee	31	m	c	CHIN	Placer	Dutch Flat P O	76	408
Lee	30	m	c	CHIN	Placer	Gold Run Twp	76	399
Lee	21	m	c	CHIN	San Francisco	6-Wd San Francisco	81	71
Lim	31	m	c	CHIN	Tulare	Tule Rvr Twp	92	261
Ling	38	m	c	CHIN	Sierra	Butte Twp	89	513
Ling	37	m	c	CHIN	Kern	Bakersfield P O	73	364
Lo	18	m	c	CHIN	San Francisco	San Francisco P O	85	831
Lo	18	m	c	CHIN	Mariposa	Mariposa P O	74	126
Long	41	m	c	CHIN	Yuba	Marysville	93	630
Long	30	m	c	CHIN	Santa Clara	San Jose Twp	88	213
Long	30	m	c	CHIN	Solano	Suisun Twp	90	107
Long	28	m	c	CHIN	Santa Clara	Redwood Twp	88	133
Long	21	m	c	CHIN	San Joaquin	Elkhorn Twp	86	62
Low	17	m	c	CHIN	Napa	Napa	75	9
Lue	26	m	c	CHIN	Yuba	Marysville	93	628
Lung	47	m	c	CHIN	Sierra	Butte Twp	89	512
Lung	27	m	c	CHIN	Solano	Green Valley Twp	90	43
Lung	21	m	c	CHIN	Contra Costa	Martinez P O	71	397
Mah	25	f	c	CHIN	San Francisco	6-Wd San Francisco	81	46
Man	60	f	c	CHIN	Mariposa	Mariposa P O	74	103
May	22	f	c	CHIN	Tehama	Red Bluff	92	184
Ming	43	m	c	CHIN	San Francisco	2-Wd San Francisco	79	285
Mis	18	m	c	CHIN	San Francisco	San Francisco P O	85	759
Now	1	m	c	CA	Nevada	Nevada Twp	75	299
Ok	37	m	c	CHIN	Colusa	Spring Valley Twp	71	336
On	34	m	c	CHIN	Calaveras	San Andreas P O	70	169
Oo	21	m	c	CHIN	San Francisco	11-Wd San Francisc	84	546
Po	28	f	c	CHIN	San Joaquin	1-Wd Stockton	86	153
Sa Tail	13	m	c	CHIN	San Francisco	2-Wd San Francisco	79	154
Sam	40	m	c	CHIN	San Francisco	6-Wd San Francisco	81	37
Sam	40	m	c	CHIN	Yuba	Long Bar Twp	93	560
Sam	37	m	c	CHIN	El Dorado	Georgetown Twp	72	36
Sam	37	m	c	CHIN	Placer	Bath P O	76	449
Sam	30	m	c	CHIN	Sacramento	3-Wd Sacramento	77	300
Sam	28	m	c	CHIN	San Joaquin	Tulare Twp	86	262
Sam	25	m	c	CHIN	Sonoma	Santa Rosa	91	402
Sam	24	m	c	CHIN	Santa Clara	Santa Clara Twp	88	158
Sam	20	m	c	CHIN	Solano	Suisun Twp	90	104
Sam	19	m	c	CHIN	Colusa	Grand Island Twp	71	310
Sani	18	f	c	CHIN	Sacramento	1-Wd Sacramento	77	192
Shu	57	m	c	CHIN	Sacramento	1-Wd Sacramento	77	198
Si	23	f	c	CHIN	Tuolumne	Big Oak Flat P O	93	397

© 2001 by Heritage Quest. All rights reserved.

Name	Age	S	R	B-PL	County	Locale	Roll	Pg
						Series M593		
Sie	28	m	c	CHIN	Tulare	Visalia	92	299
Sing	64	m	c	CHIN	Mariposa	Mariposa P O	74	106
Sing	50	m	c	CHIN	Placer	Gold Run Twp	76	399
Sing	41	m	c	CHIN	Mariposa	Mariposa P O	74	128
Sing	33	m	c	CHIN	El Dorado	Georgetown Twp	72	36
Sing	30	m	c	CHIN	Mariposa	Mariposa P O	74	133
Sing	28	m	c	CHIN	Mariposa	Mariposa P O	74	133
Sing	20	m	c	CHIN	San Francisco	San Francisco P O	83	157
Son	38	m	c	CHIN	Contra Costa	Martinez P O	71	378
Sue	24	m	c	CHIN	Solano	Rio Vista Twp	90	70
Sum	42	m	c	CHIN	Yuba	Marysville	93	622
Tai	21	m	c	CHIN	Solano	Green Valley Twp	90	43
Ting	22	m	c	CHIN	Solano	Suisun Twp	90	107
Tung	29	m	c	CHIN	Solano	Vallejo	90	208
Tung	26	f	c	CHIN	San Francisco	6-Wd San Francisco	81	52
Wa	20	m	c	CHIN	Solano	Vallejo	90	139
Wan	30	m	c	CHIN	San Francisco	8-Wd San Francisco	82	456
William	50	m	w	IREL	Sonoma	Bodega Twp	91	256
Wing	25	m	c	CHIN	Yolo	Washington Twp	93	537
Wing	22	m	c	CHIN	Solano	Vallejo	90	208
Wo	42	m	c	CHIN	Santa Clara	San Jose Twp	88	192
Wo	38	m	c	CHIN	Nevada	Washington Twp	75	344
Wo	20	m	c	CHIN	Nevada	Nevada Twp	75	271
Woo	38	m	c	CHIN	Sierra	Butte Twp	89	512
Woo	24	m	c	CHIN	Solano	Vacaville Twp	90	133
Wy	28	m	c	CHIN	Amador	Amador City P O	69	395
Yan	52	m	c	CHIN	Butte	Ophir Twp	70	103
Yeck	50	m	c	CHIN	Placer	Lincoln P O	76	483
Yek	56	m	c	CHIN	Placer	Lincoln P O	76	483
Yo	34	f	c	CHIN	Mariposa	Mariposa P O	74	103
Yong	40	m	c	CHIN	Mariposa	Mariposa P O	74	126
Yoo	30	m	c	CHIN	San Joaquin	3-Wd Stockton	86	246
Young	32	m	c	CHIN	Placer	Auburn P O	76	371
Young	14	m	c	CHIN	San Joaquin	Elkhorn Twp	86	61
Yung	22	m	c	CHIN	San Francisco	6-Wd San Francisco	81	39
KEEASLEY								
H	40	m	w	CT	Yuba	Marysville	93	587
KEEBER								
Jacob	38	m	w	BAVA	Sacramento	4-Wd Sacramento	77	375
KEEBLER								
Charles	51	m	w	WURT	San Francisco	San Francisco P O	83	369
KEEBONE								
Pierce	31	m	w	ENGL	Nevada	Grass Valley Twp	75	201
KEECH								
Arnold P	29	m	w	RI	San Francisco	San Francisco P O	83	188
KEED								
J J	22	m	w	TX	Sonoma	Vallejo Twp	91	450
KEEF								
James	22	m	w	IREL	Nevada	Nevada Twp	75	310
Jeremiah	25	m	w	IREL	San Francisco	San Francisco P O	85	852
John	36	m	w	IREL	Tuolumne	Columbia P O	93	351
Joseph	42	m	w	IREL	Santa Clara	San Jose Twp	88	220
Mary	25	f	w	IREL	Sonoma	Sonoma Twp	91	439
Michael	45	m	w	IREL	San Mateo	Schoolhouse Statio	87	341
Wm	27	m	w	IREL	Sierra	Table Rock Twp	89	574
KEEFE								
Bridget	29	f	w	MO	San Francisco	San Francisco P O	83	39
Cornelious	34	m	w	IREL	San Francisco	San Francisco P O	83	332
Daniel	36	m	w	IL	San Francisco	San Francisco P O	83	410
Delia	30	f	w	IREL	San Francisco	2-Wd San Francisco	79	216
Edward	28	m	w	ENGL	San Francisco	San Francisco P O	83	174
Ellen	36	f	w	IREL	San Francisco	8-Wd San Francisco	82	403
Eugene	32	m	w	IREL	Nevada	Grass Valley Twp	75	209
Hannah	40	f	w	IREL	San Francisco	San Francisco P O	80	367
Hanora	35	f	w	IREL	Sacramento	4-Wd Sacramento	77	335
Henry	24	m	w	MA	San Francisco	San Francisco P O	83	61
Jane	20	f	w	IREL	San Francisco	San Francisco P O	83	146
John	39	m	w	IREL	San Francisco	2-Wd San Francisco	79	230
John	29	m	w	IREL	Santa Clara	Fremont Twp	88	58
John	28	m	w	IREL	Sonoma	Salt Point	91	392
Joseph	30	m	w	IREL	San Francisco	7-Wd San Francisco	81	186
Kate	30	f	w	IREL	San Francisco	7-Wd San Francisco	81	275
Maggie	26	f	w	LA	San Francisco	San Francisco P O	80	362
Martin	45	m	w	IREL	Nevada	Little York Twp	75	235
Mary	85	f	w	IREL	Sacramento	Granite Twp	77	150
Michael	35	m	w	IREL	San Francisco	8-Wd San Francisco	82	408
N K	30	m	w	IREL	Sonoma	Bodega Twp	91	256
Patk	40	m	w	IREL	Sacramento	4-Wd Sacramento	77	340
Patrick	21	m	w	IREL	Sonoma	Bodega Twp	91	261
Peter	47	m	w	CANA	San Mateo	San Mateo P O	87	356
Richard	16	m	w	IREL	San Francisco	7-Wd San Francisco	81	200
Robt	38	m	w	IREL	Sacramento	Granite Twp	77	150
Sarah H	50	f	w	IREL	San Francisco	San Francisco P O	83	400
Thomas	34	m	w	IREL	San Francisco	San Francisco P O	85	759
Thomas	29	m	w	IREL	Mariposa	Mariposa P O	74	131
Thos	34	m	w	IREL	San Francisco	7-Wd San Francisco	81	265
Timothy	26	m	w	NY	Mariposa	Mariposa P O	74	127
KEEFER								
Amand	17	m	w	FRAN	San Mateo	Woodside P O	87	387
Geo J	36	m	w	PRUS	Sierra	Gibson Twp	89	540
J V	40	m	w	MO	Siskiyou	Scott Rvr Twp	89	604
J W	43	m	w	OH	Amador	Fiddletown P O	69	430
James L	49	m	w	PA	Butte	Chico Twp	70	44
Jno M	28	m	w	PRUS	Sierra	Gibson Twp	89	540
John	30	m	w	FRAN	Mariposa	Mariposa P O	74	134
John W	38	m	w	PA	El Dorado	White Oak Twp	72	140
Joseph	40	m	w	PA	Yolo	Cache Crk Twp	93	431
Thomas	20	m	w	IREL	Sacramento	2-Wd Sacramento	77	240
Valentine	40	m	w	NY	Siskiyou	Hamburg Twp	89	596
Wm M	53	m	w	PA	El Dorado	Georgetown Twp	72	43
KEEFFE								
Daniel	23	m	w	IREL	San Francisco	3-Wd San Francisco	79	312
Patrick	40	m	w	IREL	Placer	Bath P O	76	448
KEEFFLE								
Artnier P	28	m	w	OH	San Luis Obispo	Santa Rosa Twp	87	327
KEEGAN								
Adelaide	37	f	w	IREL	Nevada	Washington Twp	75	339
Bernard	37	m	w	IREL	San Francisco	11-Wd San Francisc	84	429
Edward	64	m	w	NY	Del Norte	Crescent	71	465
Edward	61	m	w	IREL	Placer	Auburn P O	76	382
Edward	54	m	w	ENGL	El Dorado	Placerville	72	114
Edward	40	m	w	IREL	Placer	Rocklin Twp	76	466
Elizabeth	57	f	w	IREL	Sacramento	4-Wd Sacramento	77	338
Gerard	32	m	w	IREL	Tehama	Red Bluff	92	179
Henriett	17	f	w	IL	Tehama	Red Bluff	92	179
James	36	m	w	IREL	Sacramento	2-Wd Sacramento	77	239
James	35	m	w	IREL	Yuba	Rose Bar Twp	93	656
John	32	m	w	IREL	Los Angeles	Los Angeles Twp	73	473
John	28	m	w	IREL	Mariposa	Mariposa P O	74	125
Julia	38	f	w	IREL	San Francisco	11-Wd San Francisc	84	622
Mary	35	f	w	IREL	San Francisco	7-Wd San Francisco	81	246
Mary	15	f	w	IREL	San Francisco	11-Wd San Francisc	84	533
Michael	44	m	w	IREL	San Francisco	San Francisco P O	83	318
Michl	18	m	w	IREL	San Francisco	1-Wd San Francisco	79	127
Patrick	45	m	w	IREL	Calaveras	San Andreas P O	70	208
Patrick	44	m	w	INDI	San Francisco	11-Wd San Francisc	84	502
Patrick	31	m	w	IREL	Nevada	Meadow Lake Twp	75	268
Robert	49	m	w	IREL	Nevada	Eureka Twp	75	130
Rosa	50	f	w	IREL	San Francisco	2-Wd San Francisco	79	165
Thimotty	55	m	w	IREL	Sonoma	Bodega Twp	91	257
Thomas	29	m	w	IREL	Sacramento	2-Wd Sacramento	77	239
Thos	22	m	w	IREL	Sacramento	3-Wd Sacramento	77	269
Torrance	23	m	w	IREL	Sonoma	Analy Twp	91	224
Wm	27	m	w	IREL	San Francisco	San Francisco P O	83	41
KEEHLER								
John	27	m	w	GERM	San Francisco	8-Wd San Francisco	82	373
KEEHNER								
George A	47	m	w	BADE	Placer	Auburn P O	76	370
Rodolph	27	m	w	BADE	Placer	Auburn P O	76	382
KEEHOLD								
Moses	25	m	w	IREL	San Francisco	7-Wd San Francisco	81	254
KEEL								
Thom	51	m	w	IREL	San Diego	Warners Rancho Dis	78	529
KEELAN								
Hugh	59	m	w	IREL	Shasta	American Ranch P O	89	497
KEELE								
George	30	m	w	ME	Klamath	Trinidad Twp	73	390
Isaac T	40	m	w	MO	Yolo	Grafton Twp	93	480
John	22	m	w	MO	Yolo	Grafton Twp	93	483
KEELER								
Aaron	33	m	w	OH	Placer	Auburn P O	76	378
Arthur T	42	m	w	NY	Nevada	Meadow Lake Twp	75	257
Daniel	45	m	w	IREL	Nevada	Rough & Ready Twp	75	331
George	43	m	w	BAVA	Calaveras	San Andreas P O	70	172
George	31	m	w	NY	Alameda	Hayward	68	80
George	28	m	w	NY	Alameda	Hayward	68	79
J	20	m	w	MI	San Joaquin	2-Wd Stockton	86	208
J H	36	m	w	MI	San Joaquin	2-Wd Stockton	86	208
John	44	m	w	IREL	Santa Clara	1-Wd San Jose	88	275
John	27	m	w	BAVA	San Francisco	San Francisco P O	80	483
Martiner	45	m	w	IREL	San Francisco	2-Wd San Francisco	79	251
Mary A	33	f	w	OH	San Francisco	San Francisco P O	83	64
Orange	62	m	w	CT	Placer	Bath P O	76	423
William	44	m	w	IREL	San Francisco	11-Wd San Francisc	84	527
William	26	m	w	OH	Trinity	Weaverville Pct	92	230
Wm H	29	m	w	PA	San Francisco	5-Wd San Francisco	81	26
KEELEY								
Jas	23	m	w	NY	Solano	Vallejo	90	201
John	35	m	w	IREL	Plumas	Washington Twp	77	54
John	33	m	w	NY	Amador	Sutter Crk P O	69	399
John M	37	m	w	MA	Sacramento	4-Wd Sacramento	77	340
Levi	50	m	w	PA	Tuolumne	Columbia P O	93	357
Mary	50	f	w	IREL	San Francisco	7-Wd San Francisco	81	210
Mary	35	f	w	IREL	San Francisco	San Francisco P O	80	386
Thos D	8	m	w	CA	Solano	Vallejo	90	185
W B	25	m	w	DC	Solano	Vallejo	90	203
William	64	m	w	PA	Napa	Napa Twp	75	66
William	25	m	w	PA	Napa	Napa Twp	75	75
KEELIN								
Harry	29	m	w	ME	Santa Clara	2-Wd San Jose	88	329
KEELING								
Conrad	42	m	w	GERM	Tuolumne	Columbia P O	93	352
John	40	m	w	ENGL	San Francisco	San Francisco P O	83	142
KEELLY								
Brian	40	m	w	IREL	San Luis Obispo	Arroyo Grande Twp	87	272
John	40	m	w	IREL	San Francisco	San Francisco P O	83	36
John	29	m	w	IREL	Nevada	Meadow Lake Twp	75	249
KEELY								
Austin	33	m	w	IREL	San Francisco	San Francisco P O	83	160
Conrad	42	m	w	PA	Tuolumne	Columbia P O	93	357
Dahiel	27	m	w	CANA	Merced	Snelling P O	74	272
Edward	34	m	w	IREL	San Francisco	5-Wd San Francisco	81	29
Frank	38	m	w	IREL	San Francisco	5-Wd San Francisco	81	26
Geo	37	m	w	TN	Siskiyou	Callahan P O	89	627

© 2001 by Heritage Quest. All rights reserved.

Name	Age	S	R	B-PL	County	Locale	Series M593 Roll	Pg
James	47	m	w	IREL	Placer	Bath P O	76	437
James	23	m	w	IN	Merced	Snelling P O	74	261
Jerry	28	m	w	IREL	San Francisco	5-Wd San Francisco	81	4
John	57	m	w	IREL	Trinity	North Fork Twp	92	220
John	29	m	w	IREL	San Francisco	5-Wd San Francisco	81	9
John H	26	m	w	MA	Sacramento	4-Wd Sacramento	77	334
Lucy	19	f	w	IREL	Trinity	Weaverville Pct	92	232
Mike	40	m	w	IREL	Sacramento	4-Wd Sacramento	77	369
Saml	36	m	w	IREL	San Joaquin	Elkhorn Twp	86	69
KEEM								
Ah	30	m	c	CHIN	San Francisco	6-Wd San Francisco	81	56
Ah	24	m	c	CHIN	Yolo	Putah Twp	93	516
Manuel	22	m	w	PORT	Marin	San Rafael Twp	74	32
KEEN								
Ah	55	m	c	CHIN	Sierra	Sears Twp	89	554
Ah	51	m	c	CHIN	Yolo	Merritt Twp	93	504
Ah	31	m	c	CHIN	Placer	Newcastle Twp	76	475
Ah	27	m	c	CHIN	Sacramento	Georgianna Twp	77	124
Ah	21	m	c	CHIN	Solano	Suisun Twp	90	107
Ah	20	m	c	CHIN	San Francisco	6-Wd San Francisco	81	46
Ah	20	m	c	CHIN	San Francisco	8-Wd San Francisco	82	310
Ah	20	m	c	CHIN	San Francisco	San Francisco P O	83	131
Ah	19	m	c	CHIN	Placer	Dutch Flat P O	76	410
Ah	19	m	c	CHIN	San Francisco	6-Wd San Francisco	81	60
Ah	16	m	c	CHIN	San Francisco	11-Wd San Francisc	84	528
Ah	15	m	c	CHIN	Alameda	Oakland	68	173
Ah	15	m	c	CHIN	San Francisco	8-Wd San Francisco	82	437
Alexander	33	m	w	SCOT	Plumas	Washington Twp	77	55
Alson	38	m	w	ME	Solano	Vallejo	90	181
Antone	38	m	w	PORT	Alameda	Eden Twp	68	88
Fred	34	m	w	GERM	San Joaquin	2-Wd Stockton	86	172
Gee	43	m	c	CHIN	Plumas	Mineral Twp	77	24
H J	44	m	w	MO	San Joaquin	Liberty Twp	86	91
Kate	35	f	w	IREL	Alameda	Oakland	68	193
S J	38	m	w	ME	Del Norte	Smith Rvr Twp	71	477
Sarah	36	f	w	IREL	San Francisco	San Francisco P O	85	789
KEENAN								
Annie	22	f	w	IREL	San Francisco	8-Wd San Francisco	82	387
Bernard	37	m	w	IREL	San Francisco	San Francisco P O	80	384
Bridget	35	f	w	IREL	San Francisco	6-Wd San Francisco	81	115
Christopher	27	m	w	IREL	Plumas	Quartz Twp	77	34
Dennis	90	m	w	IREL	Sacramento	4-Wd Sacramento	77	377
Ellen	23	f	w	IREL	San Francisco	7-Wd San Francisco	81	284
Ellen L	27	f	w	LA	Santa Cruz	Santa Cruz	89	417
Frank	35	m	w	IREL	San Francisco	San Francisco P O	83	250
George	23	m	w	IA	Sacramento	2-Wd Sacramento	77	226
Hugh	25	m	w	IREL	San Francisco	5-Wd San Francisco	81	27
Hugh	22	m	w	IREL	San Francisco	San Francisco P O	83	192
James	46	m	w	IREL	Sonoma	Vallejo Twp	91	455
James	45	m	w	IREL	San Joaquin	2-Wd Stockton	86	170
James	27	m	w	IREL	Los Angeles	Santa Ana Twp	73	613
John	38	m	w	IREL	Placer	Bath P O	76	433
John	37	m	w	IREL	Plumas	Indian Twp	77	10
John	37	m	w	IREL	Nevada	Nevada Twp	75	303
John	35	m	w	IREL	Santa Clara	San Jose Twp	88	221
John	28	m	w	IREL	Solano	Vallejo	90	148
John	27	m	w	IREL	San Francisco	11-Wd San Francisc	84	432
Maria	27	f	w	IREL	San Francisco	San Francisco P O	83	178
Mary	48	f	w	ENGL	Sacramento	2-Wd Sacramento	77	206
Mary	35	f	w	IREL	Alameda	Oakland	68	166
Mary J	15	f	w	LA	San Francisco	8-Wd San Francisco	82	392
Mary J M	30	f	w	IREL	Sacramento	2-Wd Sacramento	77	229
Michael	35	m	w	IREL	San Francisco	San Francisco P O	83	379
Pat	25	m	w	IREL	Yuba	Marysville	93	579
Patrick	43	m	w	IREL	Santa Clara	Santa Clara Twp	88	176
Patrick	42	m	w	IREL	San Francisco	San Francisco P O	83	161
Patrick	32	m	w	IREL	Nevada	Grass Valley Twp	75	170
Patrick	30	m	w	IREL	San Bernardino	San Bernardino Twp	78	417
Peter	27	m	w	IREL	San Francisco	11-Wd San Francisc	84	551
Peter	26	m	w	IREL	Butte	Chico Twp	70	55
Phillip	35	m	w	ME	San Francisco	7-Wd San Francisco	81	279
Thomas	33	m	w	ENGL	Yuba	Marysville Twp	93	569
KEENE								
C C	37	m	w	HCAS	San Francisco	San Francisco P O	85	846
Daniel	8	m	w	CA	San Francisco	2-Wd San Francisco	79	150
Elizabeth	28	f	w	IREL	Alameda	Oakland	68	192
Ellen	55	f	w	IREL	San Francisco	8-Wd San Francisco	82	394
Frederick	41	m	w	SHOL	El Dorado	Mud Springs Twp	72	82
Helene	60	m	w	CA	San Francisco	7-Wd San Francisco	81	286
Horace G	32	m	w	MA	Mendocino	Casper & Big Rvr	74	164
James	76	m	w	IREL	San Francisco	2-Wd San Francisco	79	141
James	34	m	w	NH	San Francisco	3-Wd San Francisco	79	314
James R	37	m	w	CA	San Francisco	7-Wd San Francisco	81	286
Mary	20	f	w	IREL	San Francisco	2-Wd San Francisco	79	158
Michael	50	m	w	IREL	San Francisco	11-Wd San Francisc	84	579
Reuben	17	m	w	HCAS	San Francisco	San Francisco P O	85	846
KEENEDY								
John	35	m	w	MA	San Francisco	7-Wd San Francisco	81	166
KEENEN								
James	40	m	w	NY	Nevada	Meadow Lake Twp	75	264
KEENER								
Adolph	36	m	w	RUSS	Sacramento	Cosumnes Twp	77	91
George W	32	m	w	PA	Nevada	Grass Valley Twp	75	225
John D	47	m	w	NC	Tulare	Visalia	92	293
Nancey	40	f	w	TN	Los Angeles	Los Nietos Twp	73	587
KEENEY								
Ali	33	m	w	MO	Shasta	Millville P O	89	491

Name	Age	S	R	B-PL	County	Locale	Series M593 Roll	Pg
Ann	18	f	w	MA	San Francisco	11-Wd San Francisc	84	688
Anna	21	f	w	IREL	Sacramento	3-Wd Sacramento	77	305
Bridget	47	f	w	IREL	Alameda	San Leandro	68	95
Chas C	45	m	w	NY	San Francisco	7-Wd San Francisco	81	245
E W P	35	f	w	NY	Nevada	Nevada Twp	75	287
George D	39	m	w	NY	San Francisco	6-Wd San Francisco	81	78
John	40	m	w	IREL	Contra Costa	San Pablo Twp	71	364
John	30	m	w	IREL	Yuba	Rose Bar Twp	93	660
John R	58	m	w	NY	Tulare	Tule Rvr Twp	92	270
Joseph	30	m	w	NY	San Francisco	5-Wd San Francisco	81	24
Loring	40	m	w	PA	Amador	Volcano P O	69	380
Mike	40	m	w	IREL	Alameda	Oakland	68	228
Sam	40	m	w	IREL	San Francisco	11-Wd San Francisc	84	684
Thos	40	m	w	CANA	San Francisco	11-Wd San Francisc	84	686
KEENG								
Ah	25	m	c	CHIN	Shasta	French Gulch P O	89	465
KEENNA								
James	39	m	w	IREL	Placer	Clipper Gap P O	76	376
KEENNEY								
John	50	m	w	IREL	San Francisco	11-Wd San Francisc	84	694
KEENNY								
Tracy	41	f	w	NY	Sacramento	4-Wd Sacramento	77	342
KEENY								
Armenia	25	f	w	KY	Amador	Volcano P O	69	384
Frank	42	m	w	CT	Sacramento	Cosumnes Twp	77	96
James	10	m	w	CA	Solano	Denverton Twp	90	23
John	25	m	w	CT	Santa Cruz	Santa Cruz	89	426
Wilber F	30	m	w	PA	Amador	Volcano P O	69	378
KEEOO								
Ah	17	m	c	CHIN	San Francisco	11-Wd San Francisc	84	443
KEEP								
Albert	40	m	w	MA	Plumas	Rich Bar Twp	77	8
Henry	43	m	w	MA	Plumas	Rich Bar Twp	77	8
John	50	m	w	IREL	San Joaquin	1-Wd Stockton	86	131
John	40	m	w	IREL	Stanislaus	Empire Twp	92	29
W H	33	m	w	MA	San Joaquin	1-Wd Stockton	86	120
William B	41	m	w	MA	Santa Barbara	Santa Barbara P O	87	462
KEEPE								
George	54	m	w	MA	San Francisco	11-Wd San Francisc	84	706
KEEPER								
Francis	39	m	w	FRAN	San Joaquin	2-Wd Stockton	86	166
John	30	m	w	PRUS	Colusa	Colusa Twp	71	284
Peter P	28	m	w	PRUS	Tulare	Visalia	92	297
KEEPERS								
J T	38	m	w	PA	Sacramento	1-Wd Sacramento	77	176
KEEPLENBURG								
Hermann	29	m	w	SHOL	San Francisco	2-Wd San Francisco	79	174
KEEPLER								
August	44	m	w	PRUS	San Francisco	San Francisco P O	83	314
KEEPS								
Danl	30	m	w	IREL	Solano	Vallejo	90	176
Patrick	26	m	w	CANA	Colusa	Monroe Twp	71	314
KEER								
Alexander	54	m	w	SCOT	San Bernardino	San Bernardino Twp	78	429
Alexander	26	m	w	SCOT	San Bernardino	San Bernardino Twp	78	421
Andrew	28	m	w	SCOT	Solano	Vacaville Twp	90	118
Christ	41	m	w	PRUS	Placer	Lincoln P O	76	481
David	25	m	w	CANA	San Mateo	San Mateo P O	87	349
Jane	62	f	w	PA	Amador	Amador City P O	69	390
John J	43	m	w	MO	Contra Costa	Martinez P O	71	393
Miachel	21	m	w	IREL	Tuolumne	Chinese Camp P O	93	363
William	21	m	w	OH	Colusa	Spring Valley Twp	71	337
KEERAN								
John F	39	m	w	TN	Solano	Rio Vista Twp	90	60
KEERIGAN								
Mary	40	f	w	IREL	San Francisco	San Francisco P O	83	194
KEES								
Patrick	35	m	w	IREL	Solano	Benicia	90	10
KEESER								
Aug	29	m	w	GERM	San Joaquin	2-Wd Stockton	86	171
David	21	m	w	LA	San Francisco	San Francisco P O	83	25
Fredk	30	m	w	LA	San Francisco	San Francisco P O	83	25
KEESING								
Barnett	50	m	w	ENGL	San Francisco	8-Wd San Francisco	82	327
KEESPIE								
Joseph	58	m	w	PRUS	El Dorado	Placerville	72	110
KEET								
Ah	40	m	c	CHIN	El Dorado	Mud Springs Twp	72	75
Ah	39	m	c	CHIN	El Dorado	Coloma Twp	72	10
Ah	29	m	c	CHIN	Placer	Rocklin Twp	76	463
Ah	25	m	c	CHIN	San Francisco	3-Wd San Francisco	79	304
Ah	25	m	c	CHIN	San Mateo	Woodside P O	87	381
Ah	25	m	c	CHIN	El Dorado	Georgetown Twp	72	41
Ah	21	m	c	CHIN	San Francisco	11-Wd San Francisc	84	556
Ah	21	m	c	CHIN	San Francisco	6-Wd San Francisco	81	50
Ah	21	m	c	CHIN	San Francisco	6-Wd San Francisco	81	54
Ah	20	m	c	CHIN	San Francisco	6-Wd San Francisco	81	48
Ah	19	m	c	CHIN	San Francisco	6-Wd San Francisco	81	42
Ah	14	m	c	CHIN	San Francisco	3-Wd San Francisco	79	324
Ah	12	m	c	CHIN	San Joaquin	1-Wd Stockton	86	143
KEETH								
John A	56	m	b	GA	Amador	Sutter Crk P O	69	401
KEETING								
---	28	m	w	PORT	Trinity	North Fork Twp	92	217
Joseph A	21	m	w	IA	Sonoma	Petaluma Twp	91	337
KEETON								
Charles	33	m	w	NY	Santa Cruz	Santa Cruz	89	409

© 2001 by Heritage Quest. All rights reserved.

Series M593

Name	Age	S	R	B-PL	County	Locale	Roll	Pg
KEETS								
Joe	37	m	w	PORT	Merced	Snelling P O	74	263
KEETZ								
Jacob	24	m	w	PRUS	San Francisco	7-Wd San Francisco	81	166
KEEVER								
D W	38	m	w	CANA	San Joaquin	Douglas Twp	86	45
KEEVFER								
George F	35	m	w	VA	San Mateo	Pescadero P O	87	409
KEEY								
Ah	22	m	c	CHIN	Alameda	Eden Twp	68	58
KEFFER								
C M	44	m	w	NY	Tuolumne	Sonora P O	93	333
KEFUA								
Charles	54	m	w	ITAL	Santa Clara	Santa Clara Twp	88	175
KEGAN								
B	25	f	w	IREL	Alameda	Murray Twp	68	125
George	6	m	w	CA	Yuba	Rose Bar Twp	93	655
Hugh	42	m	w	WI	Tehama	Tehama Twp	92	193
Jno	53	m	w	NH	Sacramento	3-Wd Sacramento	77	269
John	26	m	w	NY	El Dorado	Lake Valley Twp	72	63
Martin	13	m	w	NY	San Francisco	11-Wd San Francisc	84	588
O	30	m	w	IREL	Alameda	Oakland	68	182
Patrick	37	m	w	IREL	San Francisco	San Francisco P O	83	391
Rosa	35	f	w	IREL	Marin	Tomales Twp	74	80
KEGART								
King	50	m	w	NC	El Dorado	Coloma Twp	72	4
KEGG								
Francis	54	m	w	CANA	San Mateo	Schoolhouse Statio	87	333
John	43	m	w	PA	Siskiyou	Table Rock Twp	89	648
KEGGAN								
John	35	m	w	IREL	San Francisco	San Francisco P O	85	780
KEGGER								
Christopher	41	m	w	DENM	Placer	Gold Run Twp	76	394
KEGLA								
Josefa	40	m	w	SWIT	San Francisco	San Francisco P O	80	477
KEGLEY								
Henry	27	m	w	OH	Sonoma	Petaluma Twp	91	351
KEHAERE								
David	34	m	w	WALE	Placer	Dutch Flat P O	76	405
KEHAL								
Thomas	29	m	w	MA	Inyo	Lone Pine Twp	73	330
KEHALEIN								
Valentin	55	m	w	BAVA	San Francisco	2-Wd San Francisco	79	261
KEHARI								
---	22	m	j	JAPA	San Francisco	11-Wd San Francisc	84	626
KEHDER								
James T	23	m	w	CANA	Humboldt	Eureka Twp	72	273
KEHER								
Mary	21	f	w	IREL	San Francisco	8-Wd San Francisco	82	294
KEHEREN								
Bridget	40	f	w	IREL	San Francisco	6-Wd San Francisco	81	139
KEHN								
Ah	35	m	c	CHIN	Stanislaus	Buena Vista Twp	92	13
KEHNEMANN								
Minnie	41	f	w	PRUS	San Francisco	San Francisco P O	85	741
KEHO								
Daniel	24	m	w	IREL	Kern	Havilah P O	73	339
John	24	m	w	IREL	Mendocino	Navarro & Big Rvr	74	174
KEHOE								
Catherine	28	f	w	IREL	Marin	Tomales Twp	74	88
Dennis	41	m	w	IREL	Stanislaus	Branch Twp	92	9
Edward	23	m	w	IREL	Marin	Point Reyes Twp	74	22
Edward	20	m	w	NY	Humboldt	Eureka Twp	72	258
James	50	m	w	IREL	San Francisco	8-Wd San Francisco	82	363
Jane	42	f	w	IREL	San Francisco	San Francisco P O	83	31
John	43	m	w	IREL	San Francisco	11-Wd San Francisc	84	500
John	35	m	w	IREL	San Francisco	3-Wd San Francisco	79	316
John	30	m	w	NY	San Francisco	7-Wd San Francisco	81	190
Michael	35	m	w	IREL	Stanislaus	Empire Twp	92	47
Michael	30	m	w	IREL	Marin	Tomales Twp	74	81
Peter	31	m	w	IREL	San Francisco	San Francisco P O	83	208
Rosena	8	f	w	CA	San Francisco	San Francisco P O	85	767
Theresa	25	f	w	IREL	San Francisco	8-Wd San Francisco	82	390
Thomas	54	m	w	IREL	Monterey	Salinas Twp	74	312
Thomas	34	m	w	IREL	San Francisco	San Francisco P O	85	740
Thomas	33	m	w	IREL	San Francisco	San Francisco P O	85	767
Thomas	28	m	w	IREL	Santa Clara	San Jose Twp	88	215
Wm	5	m	w	CA	San Francisco	San Francisco P O	85	818
KEHOO								
John	30	m	w	IREL	Napa	Yountville Twp	75	79
KEHRER								
J	46	m	w	BAVA	Sacramento	3-Wd Sacramento	77	313
KEHRNIN								
Edward	26	m	w	GERM	Marin	San Rafael Twp	74	26
KEHT								
John	35	m	w	HCAS	Santa Clara	San Jose Twp	88	197
KEI								
Ah	23	m	c	CHIN	San Francisco	8-Wd San Francisco	82	430
Chong	22	m	c	CHIN	Solano	Vacaville Twp	90	130
Kee	24	m	c	CHIN	Solano	Vacaville Twp	90	131
Su	38	m	c	CHIN	Amador	Ione City P O	69	365
KEIBLE								
Jerry	19	m	w	PRUS	Napa	Napa Twp	75	46
KEIBLER								
Adolph	32	m	w	SAXO	Calaveras	Copperopolis P O	70	254
KEIF								
James	32	m	w	NY	Monterey	Salinas Twp	74	307
KEIFER								
Barbara	43	f	w	BAVA	San Francisco	San Francisco P O	83	208
Gertrude	14	f	w	CANA	Santa Clara	Gilroy Twp	88	97
James	30	m	w	PA	Nevada	Bridgeport Twp	75	122
John	74	m	w	PA	Santa Clara	Fremont Twp	88	61
John	24	m	w	BAVA	Sonoma	Petaluma Twp	91	365
Lucy A	70	f	w	TN	Santa Clara	Fremont Twp	88	61
Shelby W	27	m	w	KY	Santa Clara	Fremont Twp	88	61
KEIFF								
Cornelius	56	m	w	PA	Sonoma	Petaluma Twp	91	356
John	31	m	w	CANA	Stanislaus	Emory Twp	92	25
KEIFFEN								
Haren	48	m	w	BADE	Trinity	North Fork Twp	92	216
KEIFFER								
Angeline	22	f	w	WI	Yuba	Rose Bar Twp	93	662
Jacob	48	m	w	OH	Del Norte	Crescent Twp	71	458
W A	28	m	w	IL	Yuba	Rose Bar Twp	93	663
KEIGAR								
Rosa	17	f	w	PRUS	San Francisco	6-Wd San Francisco	81	62
KEIGER								
Fritz	23	m	w	PRUS	San Francisco	6-Wd San Francisco	81	125
KEIGHTLY								
Mary	42	f	w	IREL	San Francisco	San Francisco P O	80	538
KEIKER								
Adam	37	m	w	PA	Placer	Gold Run Twp	76	399
KEIL								
Ellen	7	f	w	WI	El Dorado	Diamond Springs Tw	72	22
George	31	m	w	OH	San Francisco	San Francisco P O	83	235
John	28	m	w	GREE	San Francisco	San Francisco P O	83	304
M	64	f	w	FRAN	Alameda	Oakland	68	166
KEILEY								
Annie	24	f	w	ENGL	Marin	San Rafael	74	52
KEILLY								
Mary	36	f	w	IREL	San Francisco	San Francisco P O	83	133
KEILSHORN								
John	19	m	w	LA	Marin	San Antonio Twp	74	64
KEILT								
John	40	m	w	IREL	San Joaquin	Douglas Twp	86	42
KEIM								
Ah	21	m	c	CHIN	San Francisco	San Francisco P O	80	350
Alpha	11	f	w	CA	Marin	Tomales Twp	74	86
Benj	65	m	w	PA	Marin	Tomales Twp	74	81
John	14	m	w	IL	Marin	Tomales Twp	74	88
Oliver	31	m	w	PA	Marin	Tomales Twp	74	82
KEIME								
Henry	25	m	w	BADE	Marin	Tomales Twp	74	77
KEIN								
Ah	39	m	c	CHIN	Nevada	Eureka Twp	75	141
Ah	26	m	c	CHIN	Nevada	Bloomfield Twp	75	96
Choi	26	m	c	CHIN	Calaveras	San Andreas P O	70	199
Levi F	38	m	w	PA	Sonoma	Analy Twp	91	229
Manuel	26	m	w	PORT	Marin	Nicasio Twp	74	20
KEINATH								
Henry A	34	m	w	NY	Santa Clara	1-Wd San Jose	88	241
KEINCLAUSS								
Chas	41	m	w	FRAN	San Francisco	11-Wd San Francisc	84	605
KEING								
Ah	45	m	c	CHIN	Nevada	Nevada Twp	75	299
Joseph	50	m	w	NY	San Francisco	11-Wd San Francisc	84	562
KEINIMANN								
Michael	51	m	w	SWIT	San Francisco	11-Wd San Francisc	84	527
KEIO								
Ah	26	m	c	CHIN	Amador	Fiddletown P O	69	428
Ah	18	m	c	CHIN	Amador	Fiddletown P O	69	428
KEIPP								
Frederick	42	m	w	BAVA	Sacramento	2-Wd Sacramento	77	230
KEIRAN								
Patrick	30	m	w	IREL	Santa Cruz	Santa Cruz Twp	89	397
KEIRN								
Thos	32	m	w	IREL	San Francisco	11-Wd San Francisc	84	656
KEIRNS								
J W	27	m	w	NY	Santa Clara	Gilroy Twp	88	77
KEIRNY								
Lawrence	20	f	w	LA	San Francisco	San Francisco P O	80	370
KEIS								
George O	40	m	w	NY	El Dorado	Placerville	72	125
KEISER								
Charles	44	m	w	SWIT	Nevada	Grass Valley Twp	75	159
Charles	34	m	w	PRUS	San Francisco	San Francisco P O	80	461
Henry	18	m	w	FRAN	Santa Clara	2-Wd San Jose	88	323
John	47	m	w	PA	Nevada	Meadow Lake Twp	75	246
Maggie	23	f	w	CA	Sacramento	Granite Twp	77	144
Maria	52	f	w	PRUS	San Francisco	San Francisco P O	80	463
Rinehart	31	m	w	PRUS	Sacramento	Natomas Twp	77	170
Rosa	22	f	w	BAVA	Santa Cruz	Santa Cruz	89	409
KEISLING								
Calvin	37	m	w	IN	Solano	Silveyville Twp	90	77
KEISNER								
John	40	m	w	FRAN	Santa Clara	San Jose Twp	88	194
KEISON								
H	20	m	w	DENM	Alameda	Murray Twp	68	118
KEISOR								
Orrin	26	m	w	NH	San Joaquin	2-Wd Stockton	86	170
KEIST								
Jacob	35	m	w	HUNG	San Francisco	6-Wd San Francisco	81	83
Michael	34	m	w	PRUS	Colusa	Grand Island Twp	71	308

© 2001 by Heritage Quest. All rights reserved.

California 1870 Census

Name	Age	S	R	B-PL	County	Locale	Roll	Pg
KEISTER								
William	38	m	w	PRUS	Solano	Tremont Twp	90	31
KEIT								
Ah	16	m	c	CHIN	Santa Clara	2-Wd San Jose	88	302
Benjamin	20	m	w	OH	Santa Clara	Fremont Twp	88	63
KEITH								
Adam	57	m	w	PA	Yolo	Cottonwood Twp	93	465
B F	21	m	w	VT	Tuolumne	Columbia P O	93	340
Charles	23	m	w	MO	Yolo	Cottonwood Twp	93	475
Dennis	35	m	w	IREL	San Francisco	San Francisco P O	85	727
Eldridge	66	m	w	MA	San Francisco	7-Wd San Francisco	81	277
Elisha	45	m	w	OH	Fresno	Millerton P O	72	158
G N	51	m	w	TN	San Joaquin	Elkhorn Twp	86	60
Gabriel H	50	m	w	KY	Yolo	Cache Crk Twp	93	442
Granville C	38	m	w	MA	Nevada	Nevada Twp	75	318
Henry	35	m	w	NY	San Diego	San Pasqual	78	520
J W	40	m	w	ME	Tuolumne	Big Oak Flat P O	93	395
James	54	m	w	TN	Monterey	Pajaro Twp	74	369
James	42	m	w	NY	Tehama	Red Bluff	92	181
James	18	m	w	OR	Yolo	Fremont Twp	93	477
James S	16	m	w	OR	Yolo	Grafton Twp	93	496
Jas D	45	m	w	MA	Santa Clara	Gilroy Twp	88	84
Jno M	38	m	w	GA	Santa Clara	Gilroy Twp	88	80
Joannah	25	f	w	MA	San Francisco	6-Wd San Francisco	81	102
John	40	m	w	IREL	Alameda	Oakland	68	166
John	29	m	w	NY	Tehama	Tehama Twp	92	195
John	28	m	w	IREL	San Francisco	2-Wd San Francisco	79	222
John W	45	m	w	MA	San Francisco	8-Wd San Francisco	82	477
Joseph S	49	m	w	OH	Napa	Napa	75	11
L C	50	m	w	NY	Nevada	Nevada Twp	75	282
Laura	17	f	w	PA	Alameda	Hayward	68	74
Louis	69	m	w	PA	Santa Clara	Almaden Twp	88	15
Mary	28	f	w	IREL	San Francisco	San Francisco P O	85	746
Mary	24	f	w	PRUS	Alameda	Oakland	68	157
Mary Ann	33	f	w	TN	San Francisco	San Francisco P O	83	10
Michael	50	m	w	IREL	San Mateo	Belmont P O	87	374
Peter G	46	m	w	OH	Santa Clara	Santa Clara Twp	88	174
Richard H	38	m	w	IN	Yolo	Cottonwood Twp	93	465
Samuel	40	m	w	MA	San Francisco	11-Wd San Francisc	84	552
Steven D	26	m	w	MO	Sonoma	Healdsburg & Mendo	91	286
Thomas	33	m	w	CANA	Kern	Linns Valley P O	73	343
Warren C	54	m	w	KY	Yolo	Grafton Twp	93	495
William	35	m	w	VA	San Francisco	8-Wd San Francisco	82	371
William	25	m	w	SCOT	San Francisco	San Francisco P O	83	190
William T	32	m	w	TN	Santa Cruz	Pajaro Twp	89	352
Wm	50	m	w	ME	San Francisco	11-Wd San Francisc	84	579
Wm H	43	m	w	MA	San Francisco	San Francisco P O	83	132
KEITHLEY								
Abram	36	m	w	MO	Sacramento	American Twp	77	69
KEITHLY								
Harrison	33	m	w	MO	Yolo	Cache Crk Twp	93	448
Harrison	32	m	w	MO	Sacramento	Center Twp	77	82
Jacob	64	m	w	KY	Sonoma	Santa Rosa	91	414
Seth	34	m	w	IL	Sonoma	Santa Rosa	91	413
KEITING								
Eliza	25	f	w	IREL	San Francisco	San Francisco P O	83	283
KEITS								
Henry	70	m	w	HDAR	Sacramento	3-Wd Sacramento	77	278
KEITT								
Francis	54	m	w	ENGL	Stanislaus	Empire Twp	92	51
KEIZER								
George	38	m	w	NY	Siskiyou	Callahan P O	89	628
Jacob	36	m	w	SWIT	San Francisco	11-Wd San Francisc	84	700
John	46	m	w	PA	Santa Clara	Santa Clara Twp	88	150
John	26	m	w	HDAR	San Francisco	8-Wd San Francisco	82	369
Peter	25	m	w	FRAN	Santa Clara	2-Wd San Jose	88	322
Sophia	21	f	w	BREM	San Francisco	6-Wd San Francisco	81	45
KEK								
Minn	18	m	c	CHIN	San Francisco	11-Wd San Francisc	84	528
KEKAE								
B M	46	m	b	HI	Sutter	Vernon Twp	92	133
KEL								
Ah	38	m	c	CHIN	Placer	Bath P O	76	442
KELAN								
Sarah	52	f	w	GA	Santa Clara	San Jose Twp	88	199
KELAND								
Lawrance	36	m	w	IREL	Sierra	Table Rock Twp	89	574
KELAS								
John	41	m	w	GERM	Tuolumne	Chinese Camp P O	93	384
KELBERT								
Jacob	33	m	w	PA	Yolo	Merritt Twp	93	504
KELBY								
John	40	m	w	IREL	Alameda	Oakland	68	130
Julia	36	f	w	SCOT	Sacramento	4-Wd Sacramento	77	327
KELCHAM								
Jenney	19	f	w	VT	San Mateo	San Mateo P O	87	357
KELCHEN								
James R	34	m	w	AR	Santa Cruz	Watsonville	89	365
KELCHEY								
Cornelius	30	m	w	IREL	San Francisco	11-Wd San Francisc	84	691
KELDEN								
Jacob	29	m	w	PRUS	Placer	Bath P O	76	428
KELDERWOOD								
Jas	25	m	w	CA	Siskiyou	Surprise Valley Tw	89	638
KELEGHAN								
Hannah	30	f	w	IREL	San Francisco	8-Wd San Francisco	82	399

Name	Age	S	R	B-PL	County	Locale	Roll	Pg
KELEHAR								
John	36	m	w	IREL	San Francisco	San Francisco P O	83	39
KELEHER								
Johanna	26	f	w	IREL	San Francisco	8-Wd San Francisco	82	471
John	52	m	w	CANA	Humboldt	Eureka Twp	72	274
Micheal	35	m	w	IREL	San Francisco	11-Wd San Francisc	84	436
William	32	m	w	CANA	Contra Costa	Martinez P O	71	446
KELEKER								
Michael	37	m	w	IREL	Monterey	Castroville Twp	74	333
KELER								
Edmund	21	m	w	MI	Marin	San Rafael	74	50
John	42	m	w	BADE	San Francisco	San Francisco P O	80	356
KELEY								
John	32	m	w	IREL	Inyo	Independence Twp	73	328
KELFOY								
Edward	25	m	w	IREL	Santa Clara	1-Wd San Jose	88	278
KELHER								
Daniel	40	m	w	IREL	San Francisco	8-Wd San Francisco	82	314
James	26	m	w	IREL	San Francisco	7-Wd San Francisco	81	172
Patrick	27	m	w	IREL	Santa Clara	1-Wd San Jose	88	251
KELIOR								
Jerry	34	m	w	IREL	Placer	Rocklin Twp	76	464
KELK								
William	54	m	w	ENGL	Amador	Fiddletown P O	69	437
KELL								
Ah	40	m	c	CHIN	Tuolumne	Chinese Camp P O	93	388
Ah	27	m	c	CHIN	Placer	Auburn P O	76	365
James	42	m	w	OH	Shasta	Horsetown P O	89	503
John	33	m	w	BAVA	Sonoma	Petaluma Twp	91	317
Martin	30	m	w	CANA	Santa Clara	San Jose Twp	88	198
Mary	30	f	w	IREL	Santa Clara	Santa Clara Twp	88	163
Robert	54	m	w	ENGL	Alameda	Washington Twp	68	287
Robt	15	m	w	CA	San Francisco	11-Wd San Francisc	84	593
Thomas	65	m	w	ENGL	Santa Clara	San Jose Twp	88	207
Thomas B	15	m	w	CA	Santa Clara	Santa Clara Twp	88	177
William	25	m	w	CANA	Santa Clara	San Jose Twp	88	198
Wm A	25	m	w	IL	Sacramento	American Twp	77	66
KELLAHER								
John	27	m	w	IREL	San Francisco	San Francisco P O	80	387
KELLAN								
Jno	50	m	w	OH	Butte	Ophir Twp	70	117
KELLAR								
William	21	m	w	VA	Los Angeles	Los Nietos Twp	73	580
KELLECER								
Anne	28	f	w	IREL	San Francisco	8-Wd San Francisco	82	422
KELLEGHER								
Annie	8	f	w	CA	Nevada	Grass Valley Twp	75	229
Catherine	29	f	w	IREL	San Francisco	6-Wd San Francisco	81	107
KELLEHAN								
J	45	m	w	IREL	Alameda	Oakland	68	141
KELLEHER								
Corns	33	m	w	IREL	San Francisco	1-Wd San Francisco	79	1
Jeremiah	30	m	w	IREL	Monterey	San Juan Twp	74	386
John	40	m	w	IREL	San Francisco	1-Wd San Francisco	79	83
John	35	m	w	IREL	San Francisco	1-Wd San Francisco	79	87
Timothy	38	m	w	IREL	San Francisco	11-Wd San Francisc	84	438
Timothy	31	m	w	IREL	Napa	Napa	75	52
William	40	m	w	IREL	Yolo	Cache Crk Twp	93	421
William	39	m	w	IREL	Nevada	Grass Valley Twp	75	197
KELLEHOR								
Michael	35	m	w	IREL	Santa Clara	San Jose Twp	88	218
Patrick	27	m	w	IREL	Santa Clara	San Jose Twp	88	218
KELLENBAUGH								
Richd	42	m	w	PRUS	Colusa	Spring Valley Twp	71	337
KELLENBERGER								
Francis	58	m	w	DC	Tulare	Visalia	92	293
Frank	18	m	w	IL	Tulare	Visalia	92	297
KELLENGER								
Ann	35	f	w	IREL	San Francisco	San Francisco P O	83	355
KELLER								
Adam	40	m	w	HCAS	Placer	Auburn P O	76	358
Andrew	58	m	w	IREL	Santa Clara	Santa Clara Twp	88	172
August	34	m	w	IL	Sonoma	Analy Twp	91	240
Benjamin	24	m	w	PA	Inyo	Lone Pine Twp	73	332
C	29	m	w	IREL	Sacramento	1-Wd Sacramento	77	190
C F	33	m	w	CANA	Napa	Napa Twp	75	31
Carrie	28	f	w	IREL	San Francisco	San Francisco P O	83	133
Catharine	65	f	w	SWIT	Sacramento	2-Wd Sacramento	77	207
Charles	29	m	w	GERM	Contra Costa	San Pablo Twp	71	366
Chas	26	m	w	NJ	San Francisco	5-Wd San Francisco	81	31
Chas	21	m	w	GERM	San Diego	San Diego	78	492
David C	28	m	w	NY	San Francisco	San Francisco P O	83	44
Delia	30	f	w	IREL	San Francisco	8-Wd San Francisco	82	378
Ellen	47	f	w	NY	San Francisco	San Francisco P O	85	798
Emma	31	f	w	SWIT	Sacramento	3-Wd Sacramento	77	286
Francis	26	m	w	IL	San Bernardino	San Bernardino Twp	78	454
Frederick	43	m	w	BAVA	El Dorado	Diamond Springs Tw	72	29
Frederick	24	m	w	PRUS	San Francisco	6-Wd San Francisco	81	119
Fritz	57	m	w	PRUS	Napa	Napa	75	10
H Junius	32	m	w	VA	Santa Barbara	Santa Maria P O	87	511
Hanry	42	m	w	HANO	Del Norte	Crescent	71	463
Henry	43	m	w	PA	Placer	Bath P O	76	454
Henry	35	m	w	PRUS	San Francisco	8-Wd San Francisco	82	352
Henry	27	m	w	NY	San Francisco	San Francisco P O	80	399
Henry B	31	m	w	IN	Sacramento	Alabama Twp	77	61
J H	38	m	w	IN	San Francisco	San Francisco P O	85	866
Jacob	59	m	w	SWIT	San Francisco	8-Wd San Francisco	82	318

© 2001 by Heritage Quest. All rights reserved.

Series M593

Name	Age	S	R	B-PL	County	Locale	Roll	Pg
Jacob	53	m	w	WURT	Los Angeles	Santa Ana Twp	73	612
Jacob	33	m	w	SWIT	Solano	Benicia	90	13
James	23	m	w	IREL	San Francisco	San Francisco P O	83	40
James M	40	m	w	OH	Sacramento	Franklin Twp	77	111
John	55	m	w	BADE	Placer	Auburn P O	76	368
John	51	m	w	FRAN	Yuba	Marysville	93	593
John	35	m	w	IREL	Marin	San Rafael Twp	74	36
John	26	m	w	IA	San Joaquin	Oneal Twp	86	104
John	26	m	w	IREL	Nevada	Eureka Twp	75	133
John	23	m	w	MA	San Francisco	San Francisco P O	80	473
John F	34	m	w	IREL	San Francisco	San Francisco P O	83	194
John H	28	m	w	MD	Nevada	Eureka Twp	75	134
Joseph	56	m	w	WURT	Nevada	Bloomfield Twp	75	94
Joseph	26	m	w	GERM	Yolo	Cottonwood Twp	93	462
Lewis	35	m	w	PA	Sutter	Sutter Twp	92	127
Lilly	21	f	w	CA	San Francisco	2-Wd San Francisco	79	277
Lizzie	12	f	w	CA	Santa Clara	2-Wd San Jose	88	337
Louisa	13	f	w	CA	Santa Clara	2-Wd San Jose	88	321
Mary H	9	f	w	CA	Tulare	Tule Rvr Twp	92	265
Mathew	60	m	w	IREL	Los Angeles	Los Angeles	73	520
Mathew	41	m	w	SWIT	San Francisco	San Francisco P O	80	480
Michael	35	m	w	IREL	Sutter	Yuba Twp	92	148
Nicholas	42	m	w	GERM	Nevada	Nevada Twp	75	274
P	47	m	w	HANO	Sierra	Forest Twp	89	531
Patrick H	25	m	w	IREL	San Francisco	San Francisco P O	85	735
Peter	58	m	w	SWED	Calaveras	San Andreas P O	70	181
Richard	34	m	w	PA	Sacramento	4-Wd Sacramento	77	320
Rufus	35	m	w	IL	Solano	Benicia	90	6
Sarah	45	f	w	PRUS	San Francisco	San Francisco P O	85	800
Sarah	40	f	w	TN	Kern	Tehachapi P O	73	353
Simon	23	m	w	GERM	San Francisco	8-Wd San Francisco	82	369
Soloman	22	m	w	IL	San Francisco	San Francisco P O	83	171
Thos	26	m	w	IREL	San Francisco	11-Wd San Francisc	84	578
Warren	45	m	w	IA	Sonoma	Bodega Twp	91	263
William	49	m	w	PA	Yolo	Cache Crk Twp	93	435
William	28	m	w	OH	San Bernardino	San Bernardino Twp	78	429
William	28	m	w	PRUS	San Francisco	3-Wd San Francisco	79	323
William	25	m	w	GERM	Yolo	Cottonwood Twp	93	461
Wm	26	m	w	SWIT	San Francisco	8-Wd San Francisco	82	366
KELLET								
John	52	m	w	IREL	Mariposa	Mariposa P O	74	101
KELLETT								
Chas	39	m	w	IREL	San Francisco	11-Wd San Francisc	84	578
Eliza	12	f	w	CA	San Francisco	11-Wd San Francisc	84	578
Samuel	38	m	w	IREL	San Francisco	San Francisco P O	83	327
KELLEWAY								
James	45	m	w	ENGL	Yolo	Grafton Twp	93	494
KELLEY								
A	28	m	w	IREL	Sacramento	1-Wd Sacramento	77	182
Alice	24	f	w	IREL	Santa Clara	1-Wd San Jose	88	246
Alice	20	f	w	IREL	Solano	Vallejo	90	210
Alxender W	44	m	w	SCOT	El Dorado	Placerville Twp	72	104
An	22	m	w	POLA	San Francisco	11-Wd San Francisc	84	673
Andrew	56	m	w	OH	Sacramento	San Joaquin Twp	77	406
Andrew M	36	m	w	CANA	Placer	Dutch Flat P O	76	414
Ann	27	f	w	IREL	Alameda	Eden Twp	68	80
Ann	23	f	w	IREL	Santa Clara	2-Wd San Jose	88	317
Antone	42	m	w	PORT	Alameda	Washington Twp	68	298
Barbara	35	f	w	PRUS	Santa Clara	San Jose Twp	88	209
Barney	34	m	w	IREL	Calaveras	San Andreas P O	70	193
Bernard	44	m	w	IREL	San Francisco	2-Wd San Francisco	79	280
Bernard	32	m	w	IREL	Mendocino	Point Arena Twp	74	208
Bridget	50	f	w	IREL	Santa Clara	2-Wd San Jose	88	307
Briget	35	f	w	IREL	San Francisco	7-Wd San Francisco	81	188
C J	42	m	w	MA	Humboldt	Eureka Twp	72	259
Calas	51	m	w	IREL	San Joaquin	1-Wd Stockton	86	132
Catherine	40	f	w	IREL	Humboldt	Eureka Twp	72	261
Catherine	32	f	w	IREL	San Francisco	San Francisco P O	83	414
Catherine	26	f	w	IREL	Plumas	Goodwin Twp	77	1
Catherine	17	f	w	IREL	San Francisco	2-Wd San Francisco	79	276
Cathrina	40	f	w	IREL	Humboldt	Eureka Twp	72	262
Cawg	45	m	c	CHIN	Humboldt	Eureka Twp	72	266
Charles	21	m	w	WI	Santa Barbara	San Buenaventura P	87	446
Charles E	38	m	w	MO	San Mateo	Half Moon Bay P O	87	399
Charles W	28	m	w	OH	Inyo	Bishop Crk Twp	73	312
Chas	40	m	w	NY	San Francisco	11-Wd San Francisc	84	672
Cornelius	49	m	w	OH	Plumas	Indian Twp	77	13
D	30	m	w	MI	Sierra	Sierra Twp	89	566
Daniel	34	m	w	CANA	Stanislaus	Emory Twp	92	25
David	28	m	w	CANA	Tehama	Red Bluff	92	183
Dennis	53	m	w	IL	Amador	Volcano P O	69	384
Dennis	49	m	w	IREL	Solano	Vallejo	90	144
Douglass	26	m	w	OH	San Francisco	2-Wd San Francisco	79	274
E H	35	m	w	IREL	Nevada	Meadow Lake Twp	75	246
Ed	33	m	w	CANA	San Francisco	11-Wd San Francisc	84	610
Ed H	41	m	w	VT	Butte	Chico Twp	70	50
Ed R	30	m	w	IREL	Santa Barbara	Santa Barbara P O	87	501
Edward	40	m	w	IREL	Alameda	Washington Twp	68	291
Edward	40	m	w	IREL	Stanislaus	Empire Twp	92	60
Edward	21	m	w	CANA	Santa Clara	Milpitas Twp	88	110
Edward G	38	m	w	IREL	Stanislaus	Empire Twp	92	65
Ellen	72	f	w	IREL	San Francisco	2-Wd San Francisco	79	242
Ellen	44	f	w	IREL	San Francisco	San Francisco P O	83	78
Ellen	23	f	w	IREL	San Francisco	San Francisco P O	83	359
Ellen	16	f	w	CA	San Francisco	2-Wd San Francisco	79	196
Eloy	15	f	w	CA	Alameda	Oakland	68	258
Frances	48	m	w	ME	San Francisco	11-Wd San Francisc	84	663
Francis	33	m	w	IREL	San Francisco	San Francisco P O	83	112
Francis	26	m	w	IREL	Sacramento	3-Wd Sacramento	77	287
Frank	32	m	w	IREL	Placer	Newcastle Twp	76	476
G	35	m	w	PRUS	Alameda	Oakland	68	250
G F	45	m	w	VT	Lassen	Janesville Twp	73	434
Greenbery	38	m	w	AL	Tulare	Visalia Twp	92	284
H B	40	m	w	NY	Amador	Sutter Crk P O	69	401
H S	32	m	w	MA	San Francisco	San Francisco P O	83	307
Hannah	26	f	w	IREL	San Francisco	San Francisco P O	83	393
Henry	45	m	w	IREL	San Francisco	San Francisco P O	83	417
Henry	13	m	w	CA	Alameda	Murray Twp	68	118
Henry C	43	m	w	TN	Santa Clara	San Jose Twp	88	195
Hettie	15	f	w	CA	Alameda	Brooklyn	68	33
Honora	50	f	w	IREL	Calaveras	San Andreas P O	70	197
Hugh	48	m	w	IREL	Sacramento	4-Wd Sacramento	77	377
Isac N	39	m	w	PA	Amador	Volcano P O	69	380
J	50	m	w	SC	Alameda	Alameda	68	18
J	32	m	w	CANA	Sierra	Sierra Twp	89	565
J D	44	m	w	IN	Lassen	Janesville Twp	73	430
J J	18	m	w	VA	Solano	Vallejo	90	203
J P J	22	m	w	NY	Solano	Vallejo	90	200
J T	49	m	w	AR	Amador	Jackson P O	69	339
J W	50	m	w	IREL	San Francisco	8-Wd San Francisco	82	372
Jackson T	40	m	w	MO	Yolo	Cottonwood Twp	93	463
Jacob	54	m	w	VA	Santa Clara	2-Wd San Jose	88	283
James	59	m	w	ME	Alameda	Oakland	68	222
James	40	m	w	IREL	Placer	Bath P O	76	443
James	39	m	w	IREL	Santa Clara	San Jose Twp	88	185
James	38	m	w	IREL	Santa Clara	2-Wd San Jose	88	330
James	38	m	w	IREL	Monterey	Salinas Twp	74	308
James	35	m	w	MA	San Francisco	11-Wd San Francisc	84	685
James	34	m	w	IREL	Alameda	Oakland	68	132
James	33	m	w	ME	Monterey	San Antonio Twp	74	319
James	30	m	w	IREL	Yolo	Cache Crk Twp	93	421
James	30	m	w	IREL	Los Angeles	Soledad Twp	73	630
James	25	m	w	IREL	Trinity	Lewiston Pct	92	212
James	24	m	w	NY	Alameda	Oakland	68	230
James	18	m	w	CA	San Francisco	2-Wd San Francisco	79	216
James B	47	m	w	IREL	Yuba	North East Twp	93	643
James H	39	m	w	IREL	Santa Clara	1-Wd San Jose	88	243
James R	48	m	w	IREL	Tulare	Tule Rvr Twp	92	271
Jas	35	m	w	IREL	Solano	Vallejo	90	191
Jas	25	m	w	IREL	Solano	Vallejo	90	157
Jennie	18	f	w	NY	San Francisco	San Francisco P O	83	371
Jere J	34	m	w	NY	San Francisco	8-Wd San Francisco	82	350
John	8	m	w	CA	Solano	Vallejo	90	190
John	52	m	w	IREL	Alameda	Eden Twp	68	71
John	50	m	w	IREL	San Francisco	2-Wd San Francisco	79	259
John	45	m	w	PA	Solano	Vallejo	90	166
John	45	m	w	IREL	Amador	Jackson P O	69	341
John	40	m	w	IREL	Plumas	Quartz Twp	77	34
John	38	m	w	IREL	Tehama	Red Bluff	92	182
John	37	m	w	IREL	Napa	Napa Twp	75	63
John	37	m	w	NY	Alameda	Brooklyn Twp	68	42
John	35	m	w	NY	Solano	Vallejo	90	211
John	34	m	w	IREL	Napa	Yountville Twp	75	86
John	33	m	w	IREL	Mendocino	Cuffeys Cove Twp	74	168
John	33	m	w	MA	San Francisco	San Francisco P O	83	376
John	31	m	w	IREL	San Francisco	11-Wd San Francisc	84	656
John	30	m	w	IREL	San Francisco	7-Wd San Francisco	81	159
John	30	m	w	MO	Alameda	Washington Twp	68	286
John	28	m	w	NY	San Francisco	San Francisco P O	83	263
John	28	m	w	IREL	Solano	Vallejo	90	170
John	28	m	w	NY	Napa	Napa Twp	75	66
John	25	m	w	IREL	Los Angeles	Soledad Twp	73	630
John	22	m	w	PA	Santa Clara	2-Wd San Jose	88	305
John	22	m	w	IREL	Calaveras	San Andreas P O	70	190
John	12	m	w	CA	Santa Barbara	Santa Barbara P O	87	492
John B	45	m	w	IREL	San Francisco	2-Wd San Francisco	79	184
John C	35	m	w	MD	Colusa	Colusa Twp	71	283
John G	37	m	w	IREL	San Francisco	San Francisco P O	83	416
John H	54	m	w	IREL	Calaveras	San Andreas P O	70	196
John L	48	m	w	KY	Humboldt	South Fork Twp	72	301
John M	29	m	w	NY	San Francisco	2-Wd San Francisco	79	216
Jos J	40	m	w	IREL	San Francisco	8-Wd San Francisco	82	375
Joseph	42	m	w	IREL	Plumas	Plumas Twp	77	32
Joseph	38	m	w	IREL	Santa Clara	Milpitas Twp	88	109
Joseph	25	m	w	NY	Santa Clara	Redwood Twp	88	132
Kate	35	f	w	IREL	Tehama	Mill Crk Twp	92	168
Kate	27	f	w	IREL	San Francisco	8-Wd San Francisco	82	326
Kate	19	f	w	IREL	Alameda	Oakland	68	230
L A	37	m	w	NY	Tehama	Red Bluff	92	176
Lizzie	35	f	w	IREL	Plumas	Washington Twp	77	56
Lucretia	14	f	w	MI	Santa Clara	1-Wd San Jose	88	246
Luke	40	m	w	IREL	San Francisco	San Francisco P O	83	305
Luke	36	m	w	MA	San Francisco	San Francisco P O	83	324
M	30	m	w	MO	Humboldt	Pacific Twp	72	294
M	30	m	w	IREL	Lake	Knoxville Mines	73	404
Margaret	35	f	w	IREL	San Francisco	2-Wd San Francisco	79	190
Margaret	30	f	w	IREL	Plumas	Indian Twp	77	18
Margarett	32	f	w	CANA	Sacramento	Dry Crk Twp	77	100
Maria	11	f	w	CA	Amador	Amador City P O	69	392
Martin	42	m	w	IREL	Tuolumne	Big Oak Flat P O	93	399
Martin	40	m	w	NH	Amador	Sutter Crk P O	69	406
Martin	24	m	w	IREL	San Francisco	San Francisco P O	83	323
Martin	23	m	w	IREL	Tehama	Deer Crk Twp	92	170
Mary	66	f	w	IREL	San Francisco	7-Wd San Francisco	81	195

© 2001 by Heritage Quest. All rights reserved.

Name	Age	S	R	B-PL	County	Locale	Roll	Pg
Mary	60	f	w	IREL	San Francisco	San Francisco P O	83	370
Mary	46	f	w	IREL	Santa Clara	1-Wd San Jose	88	237
Mary	35	f	w	IREL	Alameda	Oakland	68	256
Mary	30	f	w	IREL	Santa Clara	1-Wd San Jose	88	234
Mary	18	f	w	IREL	Alameda	Oakland	68	227
Mary Ann	7	f	w	NY	Monterey	San Antonio Twp	74	322
Mary Ann	19	f	w	MA	Santa Clara	1-Wd San Jose	88	265
Mgt	54	f	w	IREL	San Francisco	San Francisco P O	83	294
Mgt	24	f	w	IREL	San Francisco	San Francisco P O	83	278
Michael	58	m	w	IREL	San Francisco	2-Wd San Francisco	79	192
Michael	43	m	w	IREL	Santa Barbara	Santa Barbara P O	87	478
Michael	42	m	w	IREL	San Francisco	San Francisco P O	83	302
Michael	40	m	w	IREL	Amador	Jackson P O	69	318
Michael	40	m	w	IREL	Alameda	Brooklyn Twp	68	55
Michael	30	m	w	CANA	Inyo	Independence Twp	73	325
Michael	30	m	w	IREL	Placer	Newcastle Twp	76	473
Michael	28	m	w	IREL	Placer	Rocklin Twp	76	464
Michael	28	m	w	IREL	San Francisco	2-Wd San Francisco	79	213
Michael	24	m	w	IREL	Klamath	Camp Gaston	73	372
Micheal	33	m	w	IREL	Monterey	Salinas Twp	74	310
Mike	28	m	w	IREL	Sacramento	1-Wd Sacramento	77	187
Moses	35	m	w	KY	Contra Costa	Martinez P O	71	377
Owen	50	m	w	IREL	San Francisco	San Francisco P O	83	307
P	50	m	w	IREL	Sierra	Downieville Twp	89	517
Patk	40	m	w	IREL	Solano	Vallejo	90	169
Patk	35	m	w	IREL	Solano	Vallejo	90	166
Patk	24	m	w	IREL	Solano	Vallejo	90	201
Patk F	29	m	w	IREL	Sacramento	4-Wd Sacramento	77	369
Patrick	53	m	w	ENGL	Alameda	Brooklyn	68	34
Patrick	46	m	w	IREL	El Dorado	Kelsey Twp	72	58
Patrick	46	m	w	IREL	Santa Clara	2-Wd San Jose	88	334
Patrick	45	m	w	IREL	Alameda	Washington Twp	68	296
Patrick	40	m	w	IREL	San Francisco	San Francisco P O	83	316
Patrick	40	m	w	IREL	Placer	Newcastle Twp	76	477
Patrick	39	m	w	IREL	Santa Clara	Fremont Twp	88	47
Patrick	36	m	w	IREL	Santa Clara	2-Wd San Jose	88	289
Patrick	35	m	w	IREL	Alameda	Eden Twp	68	67
Patrick	35	m	w	IREL	San Francisco	2-Wd San Francisco	79	148
Patrick	34	m	w	IREL	Del Norte	Crescent Twp	71	455
Patrick	34	m	w	IREL	Amador	Sutter Crk P O	69	410
Patrick	29	m	w	CANA	Humboldt	Eureka Twp	72	265
Patrick	26	m	w	IREL	Sacramento	San Joaquin Twp	77	404
Patrick	25	m	w	ME	Plumas	Quartz Twp	77	41
Peter	37	m	w	IREL	Butte	Chico Twp	70	31
Peter	36	m	w	IREL	San Francisco	2-Wd San Francisco	79	184
Richard D	31	m	w	IREL	Mendocino	Navarro & Big Rvr	74	174
Ripley	45	m	w	OH	Sacramento	San Joaquin Twp	77	403
S	3	m	w	RI	Sacramento	1-Wd Sacramento	77	185
S	14	f	w	CA	Alameda	Oakland	68	242
Sarah	11	f	w	CA	Santa Clara	1-Wd San Jose	88	245
Stephen	35	m	w	IREL	San Francisco	San Francisco P O	83	336
Stephen	28	m	w	IREL	Plumas	Washington Twp	77	53
Susan	30	f	w	IREL	San Francisco	2-Wd San Francisco	79	137
Symon	53	m	w	IREL	Trinity	Weaverville Pct	92	222
Thomas	46	m	w	IREL	San Francisco	2-Wd San Francisco	79	213
Thomas	40	m	w	IREL	San Francisco	8-Wd San Francisco	82	410
Thomas	36	m	w	IREL	San Francisco	San Francisco P O	83	266
Thomas	32	m	w	IREL	Colusa	Monroe Twp	71	314
Thomas	31	m	w	MA	San Francisco	2-Wd San Francisco	79	276
Thomas	30	m	w	IREL	Alameda	Eden Twp	68	66
Thomas	28	m	w	MS	Inyo	Bishop Crk Twp	73	311
Thomas	12	m	w	NY	Contra Costa	Martinez P O	71	393
Thomas W	36	m	w	IREL	Amador	Jackson P O	69	321
Thompson	53	m	w	NC	Colusa	Grand Island Twp	71	307
Thos	41	m	w	IREL	San Francisco	11-Wd San Francisc	84	599
Thos	38	m	w	IREL	Sacramento	4-Wd Sacramento	77	330
Thos	31	m	w	IREL	Solano	Vallejo	90	201
Tim	32	m	w	IREL	Sonoma	Mendocino Twp	91	287
Timothy	28	m	w	IREL	Santa Clara	San Jose Twp	88	220
Tryon	38	m	w	OH	Plumas	Indian Twp	77	18
Tyron	39	m	w	OH	Plumas	Plumas Twp	77	32
W C	25	m	w	VT	Lassen	Susanville Twp	73	442
W S	36	m	w	IREL	Solano	Vallejo	90	191
William	50	m	w	IREL	Santa Clara	2-Wd San Jose	88	306
William	42	m	w	NY	Napa	Napa	75	8
William	40	m	w	NY	Santa Clara	San Jose Twp	88	215
William	37	m	w	IREL	Alameda	Oakland	68	203
William	35	m	w	MO	Monterey	San Juan Twp	74	406
William	35	m	w	SCOT	Sacramento	2-Wd Sacramento	77	244
William	30	m	w	MA	San Francisco	San Francisco P O	83	283
William	12	m	w	CA	Santa Clara	Gilroy Twp	88	82
William H	48	m	w	CANA	Mendocino	Big Rvr Twp	74	159
Wm	48	m	w	ENGL	Lake	Big Valley	73	399
Wm	45	m	w	CANA	Solano	Vallejo	90	156
Wm	35	m	w	IREL	Alameda	Oakland	68	262
Wm	21	m	w	IREL	Plumas	Quartz Twp	77	34
Wm A	50	m	w	PA	Calaveras	Copperopolis P O	70	234
Wm T	20	m	w	PA	Trinity	Trinity Center Pct	92	240
KELLIAN								
James	2	m	w	CA	San Francisco	11-Wd San Francisc	84	475
KELLING								
Ellen	30	f	w	IREL	San Francisco	San Francisco P O	83	205
Henry	45	m	w	DENM	San Francisco	2-Wd San Francisco	79	160
Thos	42	m	w	VA	Sacramento	Natomas Twp	77	169
KELLINN								
Elum	45	m	w	NC	Merced	Snelling P O	74	259

Name	Age	S	R	B-PL	County	Locale	Roll	Pg
KELLIS								
M	26	m	w	TN	Santa Clara	Gilroy Twp	88	99
KELLISTON								
Nellie	40	f	w	IREL	San Francisco	8-Wd San Francisco	82	353
KELLMEYER								
Louis	38	m	w	HDAR	San Francisco	2-Wd San Francisco	79	185
KELLN								
Robert W	25	m	w	MA	Mendocino	Big Rvr Twp	74	161
KELLNER								
Joseph	59	m	w	PRUS	San Francisco	San Francisco P O	83	138
Julius	32	m	w	WURT	San Francisco	San Francisco P O	83	219
KELLOG								
Albert	60	m	w	CT	San Francisco	San Francisco P O	80	540
Almira	38	f	w	IN	Amador	Jackson P O	69	328
Alvin S	50	m	w	WI	Placer	Auburn P O	76	372
Chas	21	m	w	OH	Solano	Vallejo	90	203
Chas L	59	m	w	CT	San Francisco	7-Wd San Francisco	81	287
Chester	42	m	w	MA	Placer	Auburn P O	76	372
David	32	m	w	VT	Butte	Oregon Twp	70	128
H B	39	m	w	CT	Yuba	Marysville	93	634
James	53	m	w	CT	Alameda	Brooklyn	68	24
James	42	m	w	VT	San Francisco	San Francisco P O	83	208
John	21	m	w	ME	San Francisco	7-Wd San Francisco	81	234
Justor	23	m	w	IL	Yolo	Cottonwood Twp	93	464
L	40	m	w	NY	San Francisco	San Francisco P O	83	275
Louisa P	35	f	w	NY	San Francisco	San Francisco P O	83	266
Nathan	57	m	w	MO	Sacramento	Brighton Twp	77	80
W E	41	m	w	IN	Amador	Jackson P O	69	328
KELLOGE								
Peter	40	m	w	SWED	San Francisco	7-Wd San Francisco	81	221
KELLOGG								
A F	36	m	w	IL	Siskiyou	Callahan P O	89	633
Austin	30	m	w	US	Siskiyou	Butte Twp	89	585
Barker	48	m	w	ENGL	Nevada	Nevada Twp	75	304
Benj W	47	m	w	OH	Monterey	Monterey Twp	74	350
Benjamin	12	m	w	CA	San Francisco	11-Wd San Francisc	84	593
Benjamin F E	48	m	w	IL	Los Angeles	Santa Ana Twp	73	602
C W	31	m	w	PA	Alameda	Oakland	68	203
Calvin	45	m	w	NY	San Francisco	8-Wd San Francisco	82	447
Charles	50	m	w	NY	San Francisco	11-Wd San Francisc	84	466
Charles	32	m	w	NY	Solano	Maine Prairie Twp	90	48
Cow	29	m	w	CT	Sacramento	3-Wd Sacramento	77	286
D M	41	m	w	NY	Santa Clara	Gilroy Twp	88	85
De Los L	43	m	w	MA	Plumas	Indian Twp	77	15
E	50	m	w	VT	San Joaquin	Liberty Twp	86	89
Edward	12	m	w	CA	San Francisco	11-Wd San Francisc	84	593
Ella	13	f	w	CA	Solano	Benicia	90	17
Erastus	65	m	w	NY	Sutter	Yuba Twp	92	141
F E	54	m	w	NY	Napa	Napa	75	11
Fred	15	m	w	CA	San Francisco	11-Wd San Francisc	84	593
G D	43	m	w	NY	Trinity	Hayfork Valley	92	238
George H	47	m	w	MA	San Mateo	Belmont P O	87	374
George H	23	m	w	IL	San Mateo	San Mateo P O	87	352
Giles P	46	m	w	MA	Monterey	Alisal Twp	74	292
Harrison U	75	m	w	IL	Yolo	Grafton Twp	93	481
Henry Waters	46	m	w	CT	Plumas	Mineral Twp	77	21
Hiram	66	m	w	NY	Yolo	Grafton Twp	93	481
J	48	m	w	IL	Amador	Drytown P O	69	423
J H	22	m	w	IL	Sutter	Sutter Twp	92	125
J J	44	m	w	OH	Trinity	Douglas	92	234
James	53	m	w	PA	San Francisco	3-Wd San Francisco	79	326
James	50	m	w	NY	San Francisco	5-Wd San Francisco	81	2
Jay	20	m	w	IL	Humboldt	Eel Rvr Twp	72	252
L J	41	m	w	MA	Trinity	Hayfork Valley	92	238
Leonard	46	m	w	CT	Sacramento	3-Wd Sacramento	77	286
Levi M	40	m	w	PA	San Francisco	8-Wd San Francisco	82	466
M	50	f	w	MA	Alameda	Oakland	68	227
M	41	m	w	CT	Alameda	Oakland	68	199
Marshal	60	m	w	NY	Tulare	Tule Rvr Twp	92	272
Martin V	36	m	w	IN	Tehama	Red Bluff	92	177
Merritt G	38	m	w	MA	Santa Clara	1-Wd San Jose	88	250
Minnie	10	f	w	CA	San Francisco	8-Wd San Francisco	82	466
Ralph	43	m	w	MA	Alameda	Oakland	68	139
Rose	33	f	w	IREL	Tehama	Red Bluff	92	174
Rose	32	f	w	IREL	Tehama	Red Bluff	92	183
Samuel	39	m	w	CT	San Francisco	6-Wd San Francisco	81	113
Warren S	42	m	w	OH	Sonoma	Mendocino Twp	91	289
William	39	m	w	NY	Trinity	Lewiston Pct	92	211
Wm Winnie	82	m	w	MA	Plumas	Indian Twp	77	15
KELLOGGS								
Jonas	50	m	w	VT	San Joaquin	Elliott Twp	86	73
KELLOGS								
Carrie	28	f	w	IL	San Francisco	7-Wd San Francisco	81	163
KELLOM								
Harvey	37	m	w	NH	San Francisco	11-Wd San Francisc	84	623
KELLOUGH								
John	39	m	w	IN	El Dorado	Coloma Twp	72	5
John	28	m	w	IREL	Humboldt	Eureka Twp	72	261
KELLOY								
Samuel	18	m	w	CA	Tuolumne	Chinese Camp P O	93	381
KELLS								
John	45	m	w	OH	San Francisco	2-Wd San Francisco	79	282
Wm	41	m	w	NY	San Francisco	2-Wd San Francisco	79	166
KELLUM								
B F	53	m	w	VT	Butte	Oroville Twp	70	137
Chas	40	m	w	NH	San Francisco	11-Wd San Francisc	84	680
J	40	m	w	ENGL	San Francisco	8-Wd San Francisco	82	373

© 2001 by Heritage Quest. All rights reserved.

Name	Age	S	R	B-PL	County	Locale	Roll	Pg
John	65	m	w	CA	Fresno	Millerton P O	72	160
William	47	m	w	PA	San Francisco	San Francisco P O	80	391
Z W	40	m	w	NJ	San Francisco	3-Wd San Francisco	79	314
KELLUN								
Bridget	30	f	w	IREL	San Francisco	8-Wd San Francisco	82	411
KELLVEY								
Adam	57	m	w	CT	Placer	Cisco P O	76	494
KELLY								
--- Mrs	38	f	w	IREL	San Francisco	7-Wd San Francisco	81	275
A J	37	m	w	IL	Sutter	Butte Twp	92	104
Albert	52	m	w	VT	Sonoma	Petaluma Twp	91	310
Alecia	12	f	w	CA	San Francisco	8-Wd San Francisco	82	436
Alexander	42	m	w	NY	Placer	Bath P O	76	460
Alexander	27	m	w	IREL	Yolo	Putah Twp	93	516
Alfred	52	m	w	VT	Sonoma	Petaluma Twp	91	335
Alfred	17	m	w	CA	Santa Clara	Santa Clara Twp	88	177
Alfred J	28	m	w	CT	San Francisco	San Francisco P O	83	230
Alice	9	f	w	CA	San Francisco	11-Wd San Francisc	84	710
Alice	5	f	w	MA	San Francisco	San Francisco P O	83	309
Allen	47	m	w	AL	Kern	Bakersfield P O	73	365
Ambrose	22	m	w	PORT	Marin	San Rafael Twp	74	59
Andrew J	40	m	w	IREL	Nevada	Rough & Ready Twp	75	331
Andrew J	40	m	w	VA	Los Angeles	El Monte Twp	73	463
Anna	29	f	w	IREL	San Mateo	San Mateo P O	87	355
Anne	40	f	w	IREL	San Francisco	8-Wd San Francisco	82	486
Anne	35	f	w	IREL	San Francisco	8-Wd San Francisco	82	498
Anne	23	f	w	IREL	San Francisco	11-Wd San Francisc	84	451
Anne	22	f	w	IREL	San Francisco	8-Wd San Francisco	82	480
Anne	16	f	w	ENGL	San Francisco	8-Wd San Francisco	82	426
Annie	30	f	w	LA	San Francisco	San Francisco P O	83	219
Annie	29	f	w	IREL	Alpine	Silver Mtn P O	69	308
Annie	14	f	w	IREL	San Francisco	San Francisco P O	83	160
Annie	11	f	w	CA	Stanislaus	Emory Twp	92	24
Arthur	40	m	w	IREL	San Francisco	7-Wd San Francisco	81	280
Arthur	4	m	w	CA	Alameda	Oakland	68	162
B	24	m	w	CANA	Alameda	Murray Twp	68	121
Barnard	57	m	w	IREL	Butte	Oregon Twp	70	127
Barnard	37	m	w	IREL	San Francisco	7-Wd San Francisco	81	205
Barnd	45	m	w	IREL	Sierra	Gibson Twp	89	542
Belle	20	f	w	OH	San Bernardino	San Bernardino Twp	78	418
Benjn	30	m	w	ENGL	San Francisco	San Francisco P O	83	87
Bernard	35	m	w	IREL	San Francisco	11-Wd San Francisc	84	439
Bernard	34	m	w	IREL	San Francisco	11-Wd San Francisc	84	518
Bessie	7	f	w	CA	Nevada	Grass Valley Twp	75	229
Brian	45	m	w	IREL	San Luis Obispo	Arroyo Grande Twp	87	272
Bridget	60	f	w	IREL	San Francisco	11-Wd San Francisc	84	440
Bridget	45	f	w	IREL	San Joaquin	2-Wd Stockton	86	185
Bridget	45	f	w	IREL	San Francisco	San Francisco P O	85	865
Bridget	35	f	w	IREL	San Francisco	1-Wd San Francisco	79	44
Bridget	31	f	w	IREL	San Francisco	8-Wd San Francisco	82	487
Bridget	30	f	w	IREL	San Francisco	San Francisco P O	83	91
Bridget	28	f	w	IREL	San Francisco	San Francisco P O	83	196
Bridget	27	f	w	IREL	San Francisco	8-Wd San Francisco	82	352
Bridget	26	f	w	IREL	San Francisco	San Francisco P O	83	202
Bridget	25	f	w	IREL	San Francisco	6-Wd San Francisco	81	94
Bridget	23	f	w	IREL	Solano	Vallejo	90	145
Bridget	23	f	w	IREL	San Francisco	7-Wd San Francisco	81	280
C J	32	m	w	VT	Alameda	Oakland	68	179
Caleb	15	m	w	CA	Butte	Chico Twp	70	58
Calvin S	30	m	w	NH	San Mateo	Schoolhouse Statio	87	333
Catharine	68	f	w	MD	San Francisco	11-Wd San Francisc	84	584
Catharine	60	f	w	IREL	San Francisco	San Francisco P O	83	89
Catharine	28	f	w	IREL	San Francisco	7-Wd San Francisco	81	244
Catharine	23	f	w	IREL	San Francisco	San Francisco P O	85	786
Catherine	46	f	w	IREL	San Mateo	Schoolhouse Statio	87	337
Catherine	42	f	w	ENGL	Nevada	Grass Valley Twp	75	142
Catherine	38	f	w	IREL	Solano	Benicia	90	3
Catherine	34	f	w	IREL	Marin	San Rafael	74	57
Cathrine	12	f	w	CA	San Francisco	1-Wd San Francisco	79	121
Celia	46	f	w	IREL	San Francisco	San Francisco P O	83	112
Charles	64	m	w	IREL	San Francisco	11-Wd San Francisc	84	505
Charles	36	m	w	PA	Marin	San Rafael Twp	74	35
Charles	35	m	w	NY	San Francisco	San Francisco P O	83	151
Charles	32	m	w	MD	San Francisco	San Francisco P O	85	757
Charles	27	m	w	IN	Colusa	Colusa Twp	71	280
Charles	24	m	w	IREL	Humboldt	Eel Rvr Twp	72	249
Charles	21	m	w	NY	Yolo	Buckeye Twp	93	409
Chas	50	m	w	IREL	San Francisco	1-Wd San Francisco	79	132
Chris	40	m	w	IREL	Sacramento	3-Wd Sacramento	77	298
Christina	54	f	w	IREL	Amador	Fiddletown P O	69	432
Cornelious	42	m	w	NJ	San Francisco	San Francisco P O	83	308
D	24	f	w	IREL	San Francisco	San Francisco P O	83	132
Dan	44	m	w	PA	San Joaquin	1-Wd Stockton	86	121
Daniel	8	m	w	CA	Marin	San Rafael Twp	74	28
Daniel	50	m	w	IREL	San Francisco	San Francisco P O	83	241
Daniel	37	m	w	IREL	San Joaquin	Elkhorn Twp	86	61
Daniel	35	m	w	IREL	Colusa	Colusa Twp	71	275
Daniel C	45	m	w	MA	Siskiyou	Yreka Twp	89	665
Daniel J	38	m	w	IREL	San Francisco	San Francisco P O	83	16
David	40	m	w	NY	San Joaquin	2-Wd Stockton	86	213
David	36	m	w	CANA	San Diego	San Diego	78	502
David	32	m	w	IREL	San Francisco	7-Wd San Francisco	81	226
David	32	m	w	IREL	San Francisco	7-Wd San Francisco	81	214
David	12	m	w	MA	San Francisco	11-Wd San Francisc	84	588
David	12	m	w	MA	San Francisco	San Francisco P O	80	379
Delia	15	f	w	MA	San Francisco	San Francisco P O	83	298
Dennis	85	m	w	IREL	San Francisco	San Francisco P O	83	168
Dennis	84	m	w	IREL	San Francisco	San Francisco P O	85	774
Dennis	36	m	w	NJ	Tuolumne	Columbia P O	93	339
Dennis	30	m	w	IREL	Fresno	Millerton P O	72	150
E	36	m	w	IREL	Sierra	Lincoln Twp	89	545
E L	39	m	w	IREL	Santa Clara	Gilroy Twp	88	83
Ed	50	m	w	IREL	San Joaquin	Elliott Twp	86	74
Ed C	57	m	w	NY	Mono	Bridgeport P O	74	284
Edward	49	m	w	ME	Sacramento	Brighton Twp	77	77
Edward	42	m	w	IREL	San Francisco	San Francisco P O	85	762
Edward	40	m	w	IREL	Mono	Bridgeport P O	74	284
Edward	39	m	w	IREL	Alameda	Washington Twp	68	290
Edward	34	m	w	IREL	Santa Cruz	Pajaro Twp	89	343
Edward	34	m	w	IREL	Santa Cruz	Pajaro Twp	89	345
Edward	30	m	w	IREL	San Francisco	San Francisco P O	83	156
Edward	27	m	w	IREL	San Francisco	San Francisco P O	83	220
Edward	25	m	w	IREL	San Francisco	11-Wd San Francisc	84	541
Eliza	50	f	w	IREL	San Francisco	7-Wd San Francisco	81	166
Eliza	4	f	w	CA	San Mateo	Woodside P O	87	380
Eliza	35	f	w	VA	Solano	Tremont Twp	90	35
Eliza	21	f	w	NY	San Francisco	San Francisco P O	83	332
Elizabeth	75	f	w	CANA	San Francisco	7-Wd San Francisco	81	236
Elizabeth	32	f	w	IREL	San Francisco	1-Wd San Francisco	79	53
Elizabeth	18	f	w	IREL	Alameda	Brooklyn	68	34
Elizabeth S	35	f	w	ME	Alameda	Oakland	68	197
Ellen	49	f	w	IREL	Sacramento	2-Wd Sacramento	77	219
Ellen	26	f	w	IREL	San Francisco	San Francisco P O	80	457
Ellen	26	f	w	ENGL	San Joaquin	1-Wd Stockton	86	123
Ellen	25	f	w	IREL	San Francisco	San Francisco P O	83	206
Ellen	23	f	w	IREL	San Francisco	8-Wd San Francisco	82	435
Ellen	22	f	w	IREL	San Francisco	San Francisco P O	85	825
Ellen	18	f	w	NY	San Francisco	San Francisco P O	85	726
Ephm	15	m	w	KY	Sonoma	Cloverdale Twp	91	271
Estella	27	f	w	IA	San Francisco	5-Wd San Francisco	81	22
Eugene	9	m	w	CA	San Francisco	11-Wd San Francisc	84	588
Eugene	8	m	w	CA	Marin	San Rafael Twp	74	27
Ezekiel H	33	m	w	OH	Santa Cruz	Santa Cruz Twp	89	379
F L	24	m	w	NY	San Francisco	San Francisco P O	83	64
Francis	38	m	w	IREL	Tuolumne	Columbia P O	93	362
Francis	29	m	w	IREL	San Francisco	San Francisco P O	83	371
Francis	27	m	w	IREL	Humboldt	Bucksport Twp	72	243
Francis	25	m	w	IREL	San Francisco	7-Wd San Francisco	81	281
Frank	9	m	w	CA	San Francisco	11-Wd San Francisc	84	593
Frank	39	m	w	OH	San Francisco	1-Wd San Francisco	79	85
Frank	37	m	w	IREL	San Francisco	11-Wd San Francisc	84	438
Frank	28	m	w	IREL	Colusa	Monroe Twp	71	319
Frank	22	m	w	IREL	San Francisco	7-Wd San Francisco	81	180
Frank	16	m	w	NY	San Francisco	San Francisco P O	80	341
Geo	64	m	w	IREL	Sacramento	San Joaquin Twp	77	396
Geo	40	m	w	IREL	San Francisco	San Francisco P O	83	87
Geo	16	m	w	IA	Butte	Chico Twp	70	47
George	56	m	w	IREL	Alameda	Eden Twp	68	67
George	31	m	w	IREL	San Francisco	San Francisco P O	83	172
George	27	m	w	VA	San Bernardino	San Bernardino Twp	78	448
George	23	m	w	NY	San Francisco	San Francisco P O	85	758
George	20	m	w	MO	Yolo	Buckeye Twp	93	414
George	20	m	w	KY	San Mateo	Woodside P O	87	387
George	18	m	w	CA	Sacramento	San Joaquin Twp	77	406
George W	37	m	w	OH	Klamath	Orleans Twp	73	380
George W	36	m	w	NH	San Mateo	Schoolhouse Statio	87	333
Hannibal	36	m	w	ME	Sacramento	Granite Twp	77	137
Henery	32	m	w	IREL	San Francisco	7-Wd San Francisco	81	198
Henry	36	m	w	MA	San Francisco	5-Wd San Francisco	81	33
Henry	35	m	w	IREL	San Francisco	San Francisco P O	85	811
Henry	28	m	w	ME	San Francisco	7-Wd San Francisco	81	245
Henry	28	m	w	NY	San Joaquin	Elkhorn Twp	86	60
Henry	27	m	w	IREL	Marin	San Rafael Twp	74	47
Henry	24	m	w	CT	Alameda	Murray Twp	68	125
Henry	19	m	w	CA	Calaveras	San Andreas P O	70	174
Henry F	19	m	w	NY	San Francisco	5-Wd San Francisco	81	7
Hezakiah	48	m	w	AL	Tulare	Visalia	92	295
Honora	53	f	w	IREL	San Francisco	11-Wd San Francisc	84	496
Honora	42	f	w	IREL	San Francisco	11-Wd San Francisc	84	482
Hugh	50	m	w	IREL	San Francisco	7-Wd San Francisco	81	204
Hugh	44	m	w	IREL	San Francisco	1-Wd San Francisco	79	51
Hugh	40	m	w	IREL	San Mateo	Searsville P O	87	383
Hugh	40	m	w	IREL	Solano	Vallejo	90	195
Hugh	37	m	w	IREL	Sacramento	2-Wd Sacramento	77	234
Hugh	36	m	w	IREL	San Francisco	San Francisco P O	83	159
Hugh	34	m	w	MA	San Francisco	1-Wd San Francisco	79	132
J	29	m	w	ME	Alameda	Oakland	68	264
J	24	m	w	CANA	San Francisco	San Francisco P O	85	785
J B	40	m	w	IREL	Alameda	Oakland	68	182
J B	30	m	w	IREL	San Francisco	San Francisco P O	85	864
J G	30	m	w	NY	Yuba	Marysville	93	583
J T	28	m	w	MO	Tuolumne	Columbia P O	93	355
J W	68	m	w	MD	Tuolumne	Columbia P O	93	355
J W	47	m	w	ENGL	Sierra	Sears Twp	89	527
James	9M	m	w	IREL	San Francisco	1-Wd San Francisco	79	62
James	62	m	w	IREL	Tuolumne	Columbia P O	93	336
James	53	m	w	IREL	San Francisco	11-Wd San Francisc	84	592
James	52	m	w	IREL	Butte	Concow Twp	70	7
James	51	m	w	IREL	Tuolumne	Sonora P O	93	305
James	5	m	w	CA	Marin	San Rafael Twp	74	28
James	45	m	w	IREL	San Francisco	San Francisco P O	83	171
James	44	m	w	IREL	Santa Clara	San Jose Twp	88	209
James	43	m	w	IREL	San Francisco	San Francisco P O	83	276
James	42	m	w	IREL	San Francisco	San Francisco P O	83	136

Series M593

© 2001 by Heritage Quest. All rights reserved.

Name	Age	S	R	B-PL	County	Locale	Series M593 Roll	Pg
James	42	m	w	PA	San Bernardino	San Bernardino Twp	78	432
James	42	m	w	IREL	San Francisco	7-Wd San Francisco	81	169
James	42	m	w	NY	San Francisco	1-Wd San Francisco	79	100
James	40	m	w	IREL	Tuolumne	Chinese Camp P O	93	386
James	40	m	w	IREL	Mariposa	Maxwell Crk P O	74	141
James	40	m	w	IREL	San Francisco	1-Wd San Francisco	79	13
James	40	m	w	IREL	Monterey	San Juan Twp	74	413
James	38	m	w	IREL	San Mateo	San Mateo P O	87	353
James	38	m	w	IREL	San Francisco	11-Wd San Francisc	84	610
James	38	m	w	IREL	Solano	Vacaville Twp	90	117
James	37	m	w	SCOT	Santa Clara	Santa Clara Twp	88	154
James	37	m	w	IREL	San Joaquin	3-Wd Stockton	86	225
James	35	m	w	MI	Butte	Hamilton Twp	70	64
James	35	m	w	IREL	San Francisco	San Francisco P O	85	810
James	35	m	w	IREL	San Francisco	11-Wd San Francisc	84	512
James	35	m	w	IREL	San Francisco	11-Wd San Francisc	84	484
James	35	m	w	CANA	San Mateo	Woodside P O	87	387
James	34	m	w	IREL	San Francisco	11-Wd San Francisc	84	508
James	34	m	w	NY	San Francisco	8-Wd San Francisco	82	371
James	33	m	w	IREL	San Francisco	San Francisco P O	83	1
James	33	m	w	IREL	Contra Costa	Martinez P O	71	367
James	32	m	w	IREL	San Francisco	San Francisco P O	83	74
James	32	m	w	IREL	Sacramento	2-Wd Sacramento	77	221
James	30	m	w	IREL	Santa Clara	San Jose Twp	88	217
James	30	m	w	IREL	San Mateo	Schoolhouse Statio	87	337
James	30	m	w	IREL	Santa Clara	Redwood Twp	88	122
James	30	m	w	IREL	Sacramento	3-Wd Sacramento	77	313
James	29	m	w	IREL	San Francisco	San Francisco P O	85	866
James	29	m	w	IREL	San Francisco	1-Wd San Francisco	79	44
James	28	m	w	IREL	Alpine	Silver Mtn P O	69	306
James	27	m	w	IREL	Solano	Denverton Twp	90	26
James	27	m	w	IREL	San Luis Obispo	Santa Rosa Twp	87	325
James	27	m	w	IREL	Sacramento	Franklin Twp	77	112
James	25	m	w	OH	San Francisco	8-Wd San Francisco	82	489
James	24	m	w	IREL	San Francisco	San Francisco P O	85	877
James	23	m	w	IREL	San Francisco	7-Wd San Francisco	81	170
James	21	m	w	NY	San Francisco	1-Wd San Francisco	79	87
James	10	m	w	CA	San Francisco	11-Wd San Francisc	84	588
James E	21	m	w	NY	San Francisco	1-Wd San Francisco	79	112
James H	43	m	w	NH	Santa Clara	Santa Clara Twp	88	172
James H	39	m	w	IREL	San Francisco	San Francisco P O	83	162
James T	45	m	w	IREL	San Francisco	1-Wd San Francisco	79	87
James V	23	m	w	NY	San Francisco	3-Wd San Francisco	79	326
James W	34	m	w	IREL	Nevada	Grass Valley Twp	75	231
Jane	35	f	w	NY	Mendocino	Round Valley Twp	74	217
Jane	30	f	w	IREL	San Francisco	8-Wd San Francisco	82	449
Jane	30	f	w	IREL	San Francisco	8-Wd San Francisco	82	288
Jane	25	f	w	IREL	San Francisco	1-Wd San Francisco	79	67
Jane	15	f	w	CA	Nevada	Grass Valley Twp	75	185
Jas	29	m	w	IREL	San Joaquin	1-Wd Stockton	86	157
Jas	14	m	w	CA	San Francisco	11-Wd San Francisc	84	593
Jas C	44	m	w	VA	San Joaquin	3-Wd Stockton	86	240
Jas F	45	m	w	IREL	San Francisco	San Francisco P O	83	178
Jas H	45	m	w	IREL	San Francisco	1-Wd San Francisco	79	132
Jeremiah	60	m	w	IREL	San Francisco	11-Wd San Francisc	84	598
Jeremiah	52	m	w	IREL	Santa Cruz	Santa Cruz	89	411
Jeremiah	45	m	w	IREL	Nevada	Grass Valley Twp	75	198
Jeremiah	27	m	w	IREL	San Francisco	San Francisco P O	80	387
Jno	50	m	w	IREL	Sacramento	3-Wd Sacramento	77	298
Jno	45	m	w	IREL	Sierra	Table Rock Twp	89	574
Jno	32	m	w	MO	Santa Clara	Gilroy Twp	88	82
Jno	25	m	w	ENGL	Santa Clara	Almaden Twp	88	9
Jno	24	m	w	IREL	Santa Clara	Gilroy Twp	88	97
Jno H	45	m	w	NY	Shasta	Horsetown P O	89	505
Jno J	31	m	w	IREL	San Francisco	San Francisco P O	83	70
Joel	29	m	w	IL	San Diego	Temecula Dist	78	526
John	53	m	w	IREL	Alpine	Monitor P O	69	314
John	50	m	w	IREL	Solano	Benicia	90	10
John	50	m	w	IREL	Yolo	Cache Crk Twp	93	445
John	50	m	w	KY	Sutter	Butte Twp	92	91
John	49	m	w	IREL	San Francisco	8-Wd San Francisco	82	431
John	48	m	w	OH	Solano	Silveyville Twp	90	82
John	47	m	w	IREL	San Francisco	11-Wd San Francisc	84	432
John	45	m	w	IREL	Contra Costa	San Pablo Twp	71	363
John	45	m	w	IREL	Butte	Concow Twp	70	6
John	45	m	w	IREL	Sonoma	Petaluma Twp	91	333
John	45	m	w	IREL	Sacramento	4-Wd Sacramento	77	346
John	42	m	w	IREL	San Francisco	San Francisco P O	83	46
John	41	m	w	NY	San Francisco	3-Wd San Francisco	79	319
John	40	m	w	IREL	Calaveras	San Andreas P O	70	180
John	38	m	w	IREL	Solano	Denverton Twp	90	25
John	38	m	w	IREL	San Francisco	San Francisco P O	80	379
John	37	m	w	IREL	Mendocino	Casper & Big Rvr	74	163
John	37	m	w	IREL	Yuba	Marysville	93	574
John	36	m	w	IREL	Santa Clara	Burnett Twp	88	31
John	36	m	w	IREL	San Francisco	San Francisco P O	83	308
John	36	m	w	VA	San Bernardino	San Bernardino Twp	78	430
John	36	m	w	IREL	Nevada	Nevada Twp	75	305
John	36	m	w	IREL	Yuba	Marysville	93	583
John	35	m	w	IREL	Marin	San Rafael Twp	74	26
John	35	m	w	NY	Solano	Vallejo	90	142
John	35	m	w	IREL	San Francisco	San Francisco P O	85	842
John	35	m	w	IREL	Sonoma	Salt Point	91	381
John	35	m	w	IREL	Tuolumne	Big Oak Flat P O	93	394
John	35	m	w	MO	Yolo	Cottonwood Twp	93	465
John	35	m	w	IREL	Los Angeles	Soledad Twp	73	631
John	35	m	w	OH	Butte	Chico Twp	70	33

Name	Age	S	R	B-PL	County	Locale	Series M593 Roll	Pg
John	34	m	w	IREL	Sonoma	Petaluma Twp	91	335
John	34	m	w	IREL	Sonoma	Petaluma Twp	91	360
John	34	m	w	IREL	San Francisco	San Francisco P O	80	335
John	32	m	w	IREL	San Francisco	San Francisco P O	85	746
John	32	m	w	IREL	Sacramento	San Joaquin Twp	77	407
John	30	m	w	IREL	San Francisco	1-Wd San Francisco	79	123
John	30	m	w	IREL	Alameda	Oakland	68	186
John	30	m	w	IREL	San Francisco	11-Wd San Francisc	84	639
John	30	m	w	IREL	San Francisco	San Francisco P O	83	35
John	30	m	w	NY	San Francisco	7-Wd San Francisco	81	202
John	30	m	w	IREL	San Francisco	San Francisco P O	83	137
John	29	m	w	IREL	Santa Cruz	Santa Cruz	89	429
John	28	m	w	MI	San Joaquin	Elkhorn Twp	86	52
John	28	m	w	IREL	San Francisco	8-Wd San Francisco	82	482
John	28	m	w	IREL	San Francisco	San Francisco P O	83	211
John	27	m	w	MA	Marin	San Rafael	74	51
John	27	m	w	IREL	San Francisco	San Francisco P O	83	224
John	27	m	w	NY	San Francisco	San Francisco P O	80	338
John	25	m	w	IREL	San Mateo	Half Moon Bay P O	87	389
John	25	m	w	IREL	San Francisco	11-Wd San Francisc	84	712
John	23	m	w	IREL	San Francisco	San Francisco P O	83	188
John	23	m	w	IREL	Los Angeles	Wilmington Twp	73	641
John	22	m	w	IL	Los Angeles	Los Angeles	73	541
John	22	m	w	IREL	San Francisco	San Francisco P O	85	773
John	22	m	w	IREL	San Francisco	San Francisco P O	85	745
John	22	m	w	IREL	San Francisco	3-Wd San Francisco	79	325
John	21	m	w	NY	San Joaquin	1-Wd Stockton	86	157
John	20	m	w	NY	Marin	San Rafael Twp	74	43
John	12	m	w	CA	San Francisco	11-Wd San Francisc	84	593
John F	47	m	w	IREL	San Francisco	San Francisco P O	85	764
John J	5	m	w	CA	Yuba	Slate Range Bar Tw	93	673
John J	40	m	w	IREL	San Francisco	6-Wd San Francisco	81	122
John J	31	m	w	NY	San Francisco	San Francisco P O	83	254
John Jr	45	m	w	IREL	San Francisco	5-Wd San Francisco	81	29
John L	58	m	w	IREL	Nevada	Grass Valley Twp	75	226
John L	54	m	w	MA	San Francisco	3-Wd San Francisco	79	301
John M	45	m	w	MO	Yolo	Cache Crk Twp	93	436
John M	45	m	w	IREL	Stanislaus	Buena Vista Twp	92	14
John P	35	m	w	IREL	San Francisco	San Francisco P O	83	247
John T	30	m	w	IREL	San Francisco	San Francisco P O	83	186
John W	40	m	w	IREL	San Francisco	San Francisco P O	85	771
Jos	33	m	w	IREL	Solano	Benicia	90	12
Jose	42	m	w	IREL	San Francisco	11-Wd San Francisc	84	426
Joseph	65	m	w	ME	Sacramento	Granite Twp	77	137
Joseph	44	m	w	IREL	Placer	Auburn P O	76	360
Joseph	42	m	w	IREL	Nevada	Bridgeport Twp	75	109
Joseph	25	m	w	IREL	Siskiyou	Scott Valley Twp	89	621
Joseph	25	m	w	NY	San Bernardino	San Bernardino Twp	78	439
Josephine	18	f	w	IREL	San Francisco	1-Wd San Francisco	79	62
Julia	43	f	w	IREL	San Francisco	7-Wd San Francisco	81	231
Julia	27	f	w	IREL	San Francisco	7-Wd San Francisco	81	162
Kate	27	f	w	IREL	San Francisco	San Francisco P O	83	345
Kate	20	f	w	IREL	San Francisco	San Francisco P O	83	280
Kate	20	f	w	IREL	San Francisco	San Francisco P O	83	202
Kate	19	f	w	IREL	San Francisco	8-Wd San Francisco	82	378
Katharine	65	f	w	IREL	San Francisco	San Francisco P O	83	151
Keiron	35	m	w	IREL	San Francisco	San Francisco P O	85	874
Kitty F	24	f	w	MA	Butte	Oroville Twp	70	139
Lawrence	40	m	w	IREL	San Mateo	Half Moon Bay P O	87	406
Lawrence	35	m	w	IREL	San Francisco	6-Wd San Francisco	81	143
Lawrence	30	m	w	IREL	San Francisco	San Francisco P O	83	157
Lilly [Md]	45	m	w	MA	San Francisco	San Francisco P O	83	10
Logan	28	m	w	IREL	Stanislaus	San Joaquin Twp	92	80
Louis A	47	m	b	SCRO	Shasta	American Ranch P O	89	497
Louise	16	f	w	MA	Sonoma	Russian Rvr	91	374
Lucy	26	f	w	IREL	San Francisco	1-Wd San Francisco	79	62
Luke	60	m	w	IREL	San Joaquin	1-Wd Stockton	86	136
M	30	m	w	IREL	Sacramento	4-Wd Sacramento	77	369
M	28	m	w	IREL	Yuba	Rose Bar Twp	93	660
M	19	m	w	WI	Sierra	Lincoln Twp	89	547
M C	32	m	w	MO	Yuba	East Bear Rvr Twp	93	539
M H	37	m	w	IREL	San Francisco	San Francisco P O	85	812
M J	31	m	w	IREL	San Francisco	San Francisco P O	85	812
Maggie	30	f	w	IREL	San Francisco	6-Wd San Francisco	81	95
Maggie	29	f	w	IREL	San Diego	San Diego	78	500
Maggie	27	f	w	IREL	San Francisco	5-Wd San Francisco	81	29
Maggie	21	f	w	IREL	San Francisco	San Francisco P O	80	531
Malachi	40	m	w	IREL	San Francisco	1-Wd San Francisco	79	36
Margaret	7	f	w	CA	San Mateo	Half Moon Bay P O	87	395
Margaret	46	f	w	MA	San Francisco	6-Wd San Francisco	81	141
Margaret	35	f	w	IREL	San Francisco	San Francisco P O	83	213
Margaret	30	f	w	IREL	Marin	Tomales Twp	74	88
Margerite	23	f	w	AUSL	Contra Costa	Martinez P O	71	399
Margrat	30	f	w	MA	San Francisco	7-Wd San Francisco	81	166
Margt	66	f	w	IREL	San Francisco	8-Wd San Francisco	82	331
Margt	20	f	w	IREL	Sacramento	3-Wd Sacramento	77	305
Maria	36	f	w	MA	San Francisco	5-Wd San Francisco	81	2
Maria	23	f	w	IREL	San Francisco	8-Wd San Francisco	82	347
Maria	22	f	w	MA	San Francisco	8-Wd San Francisco	82	342
Maria	16	f	w	IREL	San Francisco	6-Wd San Francisco	81	41
Mark	35	m	w	IREL	San Francisco	7-Wd San Francisco	81	257
Mark	35	m	w	IREL	San Francisco	8-Wd San Francisco	82	304
Mark	25	m	w	IREL	San Francisco	San Francisco P O	83	384
Martin	48	m	w	IREL	San Francisco	San Francisco P O	85	808
Martin	45	m	w	IREL	San Francisco	11-Wd San Francisc	84	647
Martin	25	m	w	IREL	Siskiyou	Callahan P O	89	632
Martin P	28	m	w	NY	Sonoma	Bodega Twp	91	255

© 2001 by Heritage Quest. All rights reserved.

Name	Age	S	R	B-PL	County	Locale	Series M593 Roll	Pg
Mary	9	f	w	CA	San Francisco	11-Wd San Francisc	84	611
Mary	8	f	w	CA	Nevada	Grass Valley Twp	75	229
Mary	72	f	w	IREL	San Francisco	6-Wd San Francisco	81	118
Mary	68	f	w	IREL	San Francisco	San Francisco P O	83	329
Mary	62	f	w	IREL	San Francisco	8-Wd San Francisco	82	396
Mary	60	f	w	IREL	San Francisco	1-Wd San Francisco	79	18
Mary	55	f	w	IREL	San Francisco	11-Wd San Francisc	84	628
Mary	50	f	w	IREL	San Francisco	San Francisco P O	83	134
Mary	45	f	w	IREL	San Francisco	8-Wd San Francisco	82	411
Mary	42	f	w	IREL	San Francisco	San Francisco P O	83	89
Mary	42	f	w	IREL	Sacramento	4-Wd Sacramento	77	320
Mary	35	f	w	IREL	San Mateo	San Mateo P O	87	350
Mary	35	f	w	IREL	San Francisco	7-Wd San Francisco	81	235
Mary	35	f	w	IREL	San Francisco	8-Wd San Francisco	82	477
Mary	30	f	w	CA	San Francisco	11-Wd San Francisc	84	710
Mary	30	f	w	IREL	San Francisco	6-Wd San Francisco	81	110
Mary	30	f	w	IREL	San Francisco	11-Wd San Francisc	84	699
Mary	30	f	w	IREL	San Francisco	1-Wd San Francisco	79	44
Mary	3	f	w	NY	San Francisco	1-Wd San Francisco	79	97
Mary	29	f	w	NY	San Francisco	8-Wd San Francisco	82	460
Mary	29	f	w	IREL	San Francisco	11-Wd San Francisc	84	444
Mary	28	f	w	IREL	San Francisco	San Francisco P O	83	177
Mary	28	f	w	IREL	San Francisco	8-Wd San Francisco	82	427
Mary	28	f	w	IREL	San Francisco	1-Wd San Francisco	79	44
Mary	27	f	w	IREL	San Joaquin	Douglas Twp	86	30
Mary	24	f	w	NY	San Francisco	7-Wd San Francisco	81	165
Mary	24	f	w	MA	San Francisco	8-Wd San Francisco	82	470
Mary	23	f	w	IREL	San Francisco	11-Wd San Francisc	84	423
Mary	20	f	w	IREL	San Francisco	6-Wd San Francisco	81	108
Mary	20	f	w	IREL	Sacramento	4-Wd Sacramento	77	346
Mary	13	f	w	WI	Contra Costa	Martinez P O	71	367
Mary	12	f	w	CA	Sacramento	4-Wd Sacramento	77	321
Mary A	22	f	w	MA	San Francisco	San Francisco P O	85	873
Mary A	19	f	w	NY	San Francisco	1-Wd San Francisco	79	18
Mary A	19	f	w	MA	San Francisco	8-Wd San Francisco	82	288
Mary Ann	19	f	w	MA	San Francisco	San Francisco P O	83	345
Mary T	19	f	w	NY	San Francisco	San Francisco P O	83	287
Mathew	50	m	w	IREL	Nevada	Grass Valley Twp	75	182
Mathew	28	m	w	IREL	Amador	Sutter Crk P O	69	411
Matthew	40	m	w	IREL	Santa Cruz	Pajaro Twp	89	362
Matthew	38	m	w	IREL	San Francisco	1-Wd San Francisco	79	89
Matthew	37	m	w	IREL	San Francisco	1-Wd San Francisco	79	112
Matthew	36	m	w	OH	Marin	San Rafael Twp	74	36
Matthew	31	m	w	IREL	San Francisco	1-Wd San Francisco	79	62
Maud	40	f	w	IREL	Contra Costa	Martinez P O	71	370
Merit	35	m	w	IREL	San Francisco	6-Wd San Francisco	81	111
Michael	52	m	w	IREL	Sonoma	Analy Twp	91	228
Michael	48	m	w	IREL	San Francisco	San Francisco P O	83	235
Michael	45	m	w	IREL	Nevada	Grass Valley Twp	75	215
Michael	42	m	w	IREL	Placer	Auburn P O	76	379
Michael	42	m	w	IREL	San Francisco	San Francisco P O	83	392
Michael	38	m	w	IREL	Placer	Colfax P O	76	390
Michael	36	m	w	NJ	San Francisco	San Francisco P O	83	351
Michael	35	m	w	IREL	Santa Cruz	Santa Cruz Twp	89	388
Michael	35	m	w	MA	Tuolumne	Columbia P O	93	339
Michael	34	m	w	IREL	San Francisco	San Francisco P O	85	714
Michael	33	m	w	IREL	San Francisco	1-Wd San Francisco	79	72
Michael	33	m	w	IREL	San Francisco	San Francisco P O	83	216
Michael	32	m	w	IREL	Marin	San Rafael Twp	74	25
Michael	31	m	w	IREL	San Francisco	San Francisco P O	85	761
Michael	31	m	w	IREL	Stanislaus	Emory Twp	92	20
Michael	30	m	w	IREL	San Francisco	San Francisco P O	83	188
Michael	30	m	w	IREL	Sacramento	2-Wd Sacramento	77	251
Michael	28	m	w	IREL	San Francisco	San Francisco P O	83	132
Michael	27	m	w	IREL	San Francisco	San Francisco P O	85	754
Michael	25	m	w	IREL	San Francisco	San Francisco P O	83	158
Michael	25	m	w	IREL	Placer	Cisco P O	76	494
Michael	22	m	w	IREL	San Francisco	San Francisco P O	83	176
Michael B	38	m	w	IREL	Napa	Napa	75	16
Michael G	48	m	w	IREL	San Mateo	Woodside P O	87	380
Michal	35	m	w	IREL	Placer	Newcastle Twp	76	473
Micheal	31	m	w	ME	San Francisco	7-Wd San Francisco	81	182
Micheal	30	m	w	IREL	San Francisco	7-Wd San Francisco	81	180
Michl	45	m	w	IREL	San Francisco	1-Wd San Francisco	79	37
Michl	33	m	w	IREL	San Francisco	1-Wd San Francisco	79	62
Mike	49	m	w	IREL	Placer	Auburn P O	76	374
Morris	21	m	w	CANA	San Francisco	San Francisco P O	85	745
Moses T	54	m	w	OH	Siskiyou	Hamburg Twp	89	596
Nelson	19	m	w	NY	Colusa	Colusa Twp	71	273
Owen	23	m	w	IREL	Napa	Napa Twp	75	61
P	38	m	w	IREL	Lake	Knoxville Mines	73	404
P	21	m	w	IREL	Sierra	Butte Twp	89	508
P J	30	m	w	IREL	Solano	Vallejo	90	143
P T	27	m	w	ME	Sacramento	Brighton Twp	77	73
Pat	40	m	w	IREL	Alameda	Murray Twp	68	128
Pat	37	m	w	IREL	San Joaquin	3-Wd Stockton	86	216
Pat	25	m	w	IREL	San Francisco	7-Wd San Francisco	81	241
Pat	22	m	w	NY	San Francisco	7-Wd San Francisco	81	262
Patk	38	m	w	IREL	Solano	Vallejo	90	215
Patrick	64	m	w	IREL	Santa Clara	Almaden Twp	88	16
Patrick	63	m	w	IREL	Nevada	Bridgeport Twp	75	121
Patrick	60	m	w	IREL	San Francisco	San Francisco P O	83	218
Patrick	45	m	w	IREL	Contra Costa	Martinez P O	71	368
Patrick	44	m	w	IREL	Santa Cruz	Watsonville	89	366
Patrick	38	m	w	IREL	San Francisco	San Francisco P O	83	41
Patrick	37	m	w	IREL	San Francisco	San Francisco P O	85	821
Patrick	35	m	w	IREL	Yolo	Putah Twp	93	520

Name	Age	S	R	B-PL	County	Locale	Series M593 Roll	Pg
Patrick	35	m	w	IREL	San Francisco	11-Wd San Francisc	84	439
Patrick	35	m	w	IREL	Marin	San Rafael Twp	74	34
Patrick	35	m	w	IREL	San Francisco	11-Wd San Francisc	84	648
Patrick	35	m	w	IREL	Santa Clara	Santa Clara Twp	88	175
Patrick	34	m	w	IREL	Santa Clara	Santa Clara Twp	88	178
Patrick	34	m	w	IREL	San Francisco	11-Wd San Francisc	84	491
Patrick	33	m	w	VT	Sonoma	Vallejo Twp	91	460
Patrick	33	m	w	IREL	San Francisco	San Francisco P O	83	356
Patrick	30	m	w	IREL	Fresno	Millerton P O	72	158
Patrick	28	m	w	IREL	San Francisco	1-Wd San Francisco	79	99
Patrick	26	m	w	IREL	Yolo	Buckeye Twp	93	408
Patrick	26	m	w	IREL	San Francisco	11-Wd San Francisc	84	432
Patrick	26	m	w	IREL	Calaveras	San Andreas P O	70	180
Patrick	24	m	w	IREL	Butte	Wyandotte Twp	70	144
Patrick	21	m	w	IREL	Tuolumne	Columbia P O	93	339
Patrick H	47	m	w	IREL	Santa Cruz	Pajaro Twp	89	345
Patrick J	50	m	w	IREL	Santa Cruz	Watsonville	89	369
Paul	31	m	w	IREL	San Francisco	5-Wd San Francisco	81	27
Peter	48	m	w	IREL	Stanislaus	Empire Twp	92	47
Peter	45	m	w	IREL	Yuba	Rose Bar Twp	93	660
Peter	44	m	w	IREL	Santa Clara	Gilroy Twp	88	76
Peter	33	m	w	IREL	San Francisco	San Francisco P O	85	811
Peter	33	m	w	IREL	Yuba	Rose Bar Twp	93	659
Peter	31	m	w	IREL	Nevada	Grass Valley Twp	75	165
Peter	29	m	w	IREL	Monterey	Alisal Twp	74	292
Peter	28	m	w	IREL	Sutter	Sutter Twp	92	129
Peter	26	m	w	IREL	Tuolumne	Columbia P O	93	339
Philip	36	m	w	IREL	Monterey	Alisal Twp	74	296
Pierre M	32	m	w	OH	Butte	Kimshew Tpw	70	82
Potter	31	m	w	VA	Colusa	Colusa Twp	71	282
R H	40	m	w	NY	Solano	Vallejo	90	192
Rate	35	f	w	IREL	Sacramento	3-Wd Sacramento	77	298
Rebecca H	49	f	w	MA	San Francisco	3-Wd San Francisco	79	288
Richard	47	m	w	IREL	Sacramento	3-Wd Sacramento	77	288
Richard	34	m	w	IREL	San Francisco	5-Wd San Francisco	81	9
Richard	22	m	w	IREL	Solano	Vacaville Twp	90	117
Richd	31	m	w	IREL	San Francisco	1-Wd San Francisco	79	135
Robert	33	m	w	IREL	San Francisco	5-Wd San Francisco	81	29
Robert	31	m	w	PA	San Francisco	San Francisco P O	83	356
Robert	29	m	w	NY	San Francisco	San Francisco P O	83	384
Robert	24	m	w	IREL	Sutter	Sutter Twp	92	128
Robert	20	m	w	IL	Calaveras	San Andreas P O	70	153
Robt	35	m	w	NJ	Santa Clara	Gilroy Twp	88	98
Rose	50	f	w	IREL	San Francisco	San Francisco P O	80	333
Rose	50	f	w	IREL	Alameda	Oakland	68	194
Rose	47	f	w	IREL	San Francisco	San Francisco P O	83	139
Rose	27	f	w	IREL	San Francisco	San Francisco P O	83	60
Rose	24	f	w	IREL	San Francisco	8-Wd San Francisco	82	426
Rossie	30	f	w	CT	Yolo	Putah Twp	93	514
Rossie	28	f	w	CT	Yolo	Putah Twp	93	510
Royal T	64	m	w	VT	Placer	Bath P O	76	427
Salina	32	f	w	ME	San Francisco	San Francisco P O	83	247
Sally	24	f	i	CA	Klamath	Orleans Twp	73	380
Saml	35	m	w	PA	Butte	Ophir Twp	70	108
Samuel	55	m	w	IREL	Contra Costa	Martinez P O	71	367
Samuel W	41	m	w	AL	Tulare	Visalia Twp	92	288
Seda	19	f	w	IREL	Sonoma	Petaluma Twp	91	324
Sidney	52	m	w	MA	San Francisco	11-Wd San Francisc	84	468
Simon	45	m	w	NY	San Francisco	8-Wd San Francisco	82	473
Stephen	35	m	w	NY	Sonoma	Petaluma Twp	91	326
Stephen	20	m	w	MA	Alpine	Silver Mtn P O	69	307
Terence B	43	m	w	IREL	San Francisco	1-Wd San Francisco	79	102
Theodore	24	m	w	NJ	Placer	Gold Run Twp	76	394
Thom	36	m	w	IREL	Yuba	Marysville	93	604
Thomas	54	m	w	TN	Solano	Maine Prairie Twp	90	45
Thomas	50	m	w	IREL	San Francisco	1-Wd San Francisco	79	95
Thomas	50	m	w	IREL	Amador	Drytown P O	69	417
Thomas	50	m	w	ME	Sonoma	Salt Point	91	389
Thomas	48	m	w	IREL	Mariposa	Maxwell Crk P O	74	142
Thomas	45	m	w	OH	Humboldt	Table Bluff Twp	72	305
Thomas	41	m	w	IREL	San Francisco	San Francisco P O	83	146
Thomas	40	m	w	PA	San Francisco	8-Wd San Francisco	82	415
Thomas	38	m	w	IREL	San Francisco	San Francisco P O	85	732
Thomas	37	m	w	IREL	San Francisco	3-Wd San Francisco	79	319
Thomas	35	m	w	PA	San Francisco	3-Wd San Francisco	79	323
Thomas	35	m	w	IREL	Alameda	Oakland	68	178
Thomas	35	m	w	IREL	Santa Clara	2-Wd San Jose	88	294
Thomas	32	m	w	IREL	San Francisco	San Francisco P O	83	166
Thomas	30	m	w	IREL	San Francisco	3-Wd San Francisco	79	323
Thomas	30	m	w	IREL	Monterey	San Benito Twp	74	384
Thomas	30	m	w	IREL	Mariposa	Mariposa P O	74	112
Thomas	30	m	w	IREL	Solano	Vacaville Twp	90	134
Thomas	30	m	w	IREL	San Francisco	11-Wd San Francisc	84	712
Thomas	29	m	w	IREL	San Francisco	7-Wd San Francisco	81	174
Thomas	27	m	w	IREL	San Francisco	5-Wd San Francisco	81	20
Thomas	24	m	w	NJ	Placer	Gold Run Twp	76	394
Thomas	17	m	w	RI	Sonoma	Petaluma Twp	91	319
Thomas	17	m	w	IREL	Amador	Sutter Crk P O	69	411
Thomas	10	m	w	MA	San Francisco	San Francisco P O	83	159
Thomas M	42	m	w	PA	Santa Cruz	Santa Cruz Twp	89	395
Thos	7	m	w	CA	San Francisco	11-Wd San Francisc	84	593
Thos	36	m	w	IREL	San Joaquin	3-Wd Stockton	86	227
Thos	35	m	w	IREL	Sacramento	Franklin Twp	77	106
Thos	31	m	w	IREL	Alameda	Oakland	68	171
Thos	26	m	w	OH	Santa Clara	Burnett Twp	88	38
Thos F	31	m	w	NY	San Francisco	1-Wd San Francisco	79	102
Thos H	28	m	w	NH	San Bernardino	San Bernardino Twp	78	422

© 2001 by Heritage Quest. All rights reserved.

California 1870 Census

Series M593

Name	Age	S	R	B-PL	County	Locale	Roll	Pg
Tim	40	m	w	IREL	Solano	Vallejo	90	215
Timothy	41	m	w	IREL	San Francisco	1-Wd San Francisco	79	75
Timothy	31	m	w	IREL	San Francisco	1-Wd San Francisco	79	94
Timothy	30	m	w	IREL	San Francisco	San Francisco P O	83	133
Timothy	25	m	w	IREL	San Mateo	Schoolhouse Statio	87	337
Timothy	11	m	w	CA	San Francisco	1-Wd San Francisco	79	75
Tom	16	m	w	CA	San Francisco	11-Wd San Francisc	84	648
Tymothy	35	m	w	IREL	San Francisco	San Francisco P O	85	834
Victor J	19	m	w	CA	Los Angeles	Los Angeles	73	546
Virginia	13	f	w	CA	San Joaquin	Elkhorn Twp	86	57
W	32	m	w	IREL	Yuba	Marysville	93	586
William	68	m	w	IREL	San Francisco	6-Wd San Francisco	81	131
William	52	m	w	IREL	Amador	Amador City P O	69	393
William	50	m	w	NY	San Francisco	San Francisco P O	80	363
William	50	m	w	IREL	San Francisco	1-Wd San Francisco	79	44
William	38	m	w	PA	Sierra	Gibson Twp	89	542
William	35	m	w	IREL	Siskiyou	Callahan P O	89	632
William	35	m	w	IREL	San Francisco	1-Wd San Francisco	79	44
William	31	m	w	IREL	Marin	San Rafael Twp	74	45
William	30	m	w	IREL	San Francisco	8-Wd San Francisco	82	433
William	30	m	w	NY	San Francisco	7-Wd San Francisco	81	212
William	27	m	w	IREL	Nevada	Grass Valley Twp	75	228
William	26	m	w	IREL	Alameda	Oakland	68	144
William	26	m	w	MO	Sutter	Vernon Twp	92	132
William	24	m	w	NY	San Francisco	6-Wd San Francisco	81	103
William	22	m	w	ENGL	San Francisco	San Francisco P O	83	248
William	17	m	w	WI	Contra Costa	Martinez P O	71	366
William	10	m	w	IREL	Marin	San Rafael Twp	74	27
William H	17	m	w	CA	Santa Clara	Santa Clara Twp	88	177
Winfred	23	f	w	IREL	San Francisco	8-Wd San Francisco	82	461
Wm	56	m	w	ENGL	Tuolumne	Sonora P O	93	334
Wm	50	m	w	IREL	San Francisco	San Francisco P O	85	873
Wm	35	m	w	IREL	Humboldt	Pacific Twp	72	299
Wm	26	m	w	MO	Butte	Chico Twp	70	55
Wm	25	m	w	MA	Sacramento	3-Wd Sacramento	77	315
Wm	24	m	w	MO	Siskiyou	Big Valley Twp	89	582
Wm A	27	m	w	MN	Butte	Chico Twp	70	55
Wm F	28	m	w	IREL	San Francisco	1-Wd San Francisco	79	113
Wm P	25	m	w	NY	San Francisco	1-Wd San Francisco	79	69
Ysabel	12	f	w	CA	Los Angeles	El Monte Twp	73	455
Z	23	m	w	OH	Solano	Benicia	90	21
Z H	24	m	w	NY	Solano	Benicia	90	15
KELLYN								
John	25	m	w	OH	San Joaquin	Elkhorn Twp	86	55
KELM								
William	29	m	w	PRUS	San Francisco	San Francisco P O	80	386
KELN								
E P	40	m	w	OH	Sierra	Lincoln Twp	89	547
KELNER								
Dedrick	44	m	w	HANO	Klamath	Liberty Twp	73	375
KELNORE								
James	27	m	w	IREL	San Francisco	11-Wd San Francisc	84	690
KELRICK								
Abrah	35	m	w	MA	San Francisco	5-Wd San Francisco	81	24
KELRIDGE								
Wm	30	m	w	ME	San Francisco	5-Wd San Francisco	81	14
KELSE								
John	31	m	w	PA	San Mateo	San Mateo P O	87	360
KELSEA								
Moses H	43	m	w	NH	El Dorado	Mud Springs Twp	72	80
KELSER								
Christian	26	m	w	OH	Yuba	Marysville	93	600
KELSEY								
Anderson R	37	m	w	MO	Colusa	Spring Valley Twp	71	336
Asa	20	m	w	OR	San Luis Obispo	Santa Rosa Twp	87	317
B	37	m	w	KY	Lake	Upper Lake	73	411
Benjamin	55	m	w	KY	Inyo	Lone Pine Twp	73	330
Bryant	28	m	w	NJ	Napa	Napa	75	41
Byron	26	m	w	NY	Nevada	Eureka Twp	75	133
Charles	62	m	w	CT	Alameda	Washington Twp	68	280
D B	58	m	w	ME	Humboldt	Eureka Twp	72	278
Darwin	34	m	w	KY	Santa Clara	1-Wd San Jose	88	253
David	40	m	w	MO	San Mateo	Half Moon Bay P O	87	395
Edward	18	m	w	OR	Contra Costa	Martinez P O	71	389
Fred	36	m	w	OH	Yuba	Marysville Twp	93	571
Geo M	37	m	w	US	San Joaquin	2-Wd Stockton	86	168
Hiram C	36	m	w	ME	Placer	Dutch Flat P O	76	405
Isaac	64	m	b	VA	Sacramento	Granite Twp	77	145
Isiah	53	m	w	KY	San Luis Obispo	Morro Twp	87	280
J M	46	m	w	OH	San Joaquin	2-Wd Stockton	86	158
James	43	m	w	KY	Yolo	Grafton Twp	93	483
Jonathan	42	m	w	CT	Plumas	Quartz Twp	77	37
Joseph D	32	m	w	NJ	Santa Barbara	San Buenaventura P	87	446
M	60	m	w	NY	Alameda	Oakland	68	189
Mary	41	f	w	CANA	San Francisco	7-Wd San Francisco	81	282
Nathaniel	45	m	w	KY	Yolo	Cache Crk Twp	93	441
Noah	25	m	w	CT	Alameda	Oakland	68	199
P Mrs	50	f	w	KY	Lake	Kelsey Crk	73	403
Theodore	25	m	w	NJ	Santa Barbara	San Buenaventura P	87	447
Vasteir	41	m	w	NY	Merced	Snelling P O	74	249
W F	41	m	w	NY	Alameda	Oakland	68	238
William	33	m	w	SCOT	Sacramento	4-Wd Sacramento	77	338
William	19	m	w	WI	Contra Costa	Martinez P O	71	394
William F	19	m	w	MO	Yolo	Cache Crk Twp	93	442
KELSHAW								
Joseph	36	m	w	ENGL	Yolo	Washington Twp	93	529
KELSHER								
Timothy	23	m	w	IREL	Yolo	Washington Twp	93	535
KELSO								
Alice L	17	f	w	MO	Sonoma	Washington Twp	91	465
James	35	m	w	NY	Sonoma	Petaluma Twp	91	321
Mary	70	f	w	IREL	San Francisco	2-Wd San Francisco	79	221
Wm	23	m	w	IREL	San Francisco	11-Wd San Francisc	84	689
KELSOE								
Hugh M	49	m	w	MS	Shasta	Stillwater P O	89	481
KELSOR								
Samuel	31	m	w	NY	San Francisco	San Francisco P O	83	155
KELSTRUP								
L G	41	m	w	NORW	Nevada	Eureka Twp	75	128
KELTING								
Hannah	28	f	w	IREL	San Francisco	San Francisco P O	83	112
Simon M	34	m	w	OH	San Bernardino	San Bernardino Twp	78	419
KELTON								
Charles H	38	m	w	NY	Santa Cruz	Watsonville	89	368
David	30	m	w	NY	San Francisco	11-Wd San Francisc	84	672
Edward G	28	m	w	NY	San Francisco	6-Wd San Francisco	81	96
George	41	m	w	NH	Calaveras	San Andreas P O	70	203
Iver H	24	m	w	ME	Mendocino	Point Arena Twp	74	204
Julia A	38	f	w	MA	Trinity	Weaverville Pct	92	223
M A	27	m	w	TX	Mendocino	Ukiah Twp	74	237
Mary A	25	f	w	MD	Los Angeles	Los Nietos Twp	73	573
KELTS								
Allen	38	m	w	NY	Siskiyou	Callahan P O	89	624
KELTY								
George	45	m	w	SWED	Sonoma	Petaluma Twp	91	338
KELVERY								
Morgaul	27	f	w	IREL	Los Angeles	Los Angeles	73	530
KELVIN								
Geo	19	m	m	PA	San Francisco	1-Wd San Francisco	79	132
KELWIS								
Phillip	33	m	w	BELG	Amador	Fiddletown P O	69	432
KELY								
James	20	m	w	IREL	San Mateo	San Mateo P O	87	359
KEM								
Ah	58	m	c	CHIN	Placer	Pino Twp	76	470
Ah	50	m	c	CHIN	Nevada	Little York Twp	75	234
Ah	40	m	c	CHIN	Nevada	Nevada Twp	75	311
Ah	40	m	c	CHIN	Santa Clara	1-Wd San Jose	88	273
Ah	36	m	c	CHIN	Nevada	Meadow Lake Twp	75	256
Ah	34	m	c	CHIN	Siskiyou	Yreka	89	652
Ah	32	m	c	CHIN	Mariposa	Mariposa P O	74	99
Ah	32	m	c	CHIN	Nevada	Washington Twp	75	344
Ah	30	m	c	CHIN	Solano	Benicia	90	14
Ah	22	m	c	CHIN	Sierra	Lincoln Twp	89	550
Ah	22	m	c	CHIN	Plumas	Plumas Twp	77	31
Ah	19	m	c	CHIN	Nevada	Nevada Twp	75	321
Ah	19	m	c	CHIN	Nevada	Rough & Ready Twp	75	338
Jas H	22	m	w	MO	Shasta	Millville P O	89	491
Jerusha	23	f	w	OH	Yuba	Slate Range Bar Tw	93	670
John J	60	m	w	VA	Shasta	Millville P O	89	491
Joseph	46	m	w	VA	San Francisco	6-Wd San Francisco	81	99
Tea	14	m	c	CHIN	Nevada	Bridgeport Twp	75	110
Yo	25	f	c	CHIN	Mariposa	Mariposa P O	74	102
Yon	21	f	c	CHIN	Yuba	Rose Bar Twp	93	656
KEMAN								
John	28	m	w	NY	Sacramento	4-Wd Sacramento	77	320
Mathew	40	m	w	IREL	Sacramento	Brighton Twp	77	72
KEMBEL								
Conrad	40	m	w	PRUS	San Francisco	1-Wd San Francisco	79	78
KEMBERG								
Louisa	33	m	w	HAMB	San Mateo	Searsville P O	87	382
KEMBLE								
Alfred	26	m	w	ENGL	San Francisco	3-Wd San Francisco	79	316
Jane	26	f	w	NY	San Francisco	San Francisco P O	83	223
Thos	15	m	w	MO	Sacramento	Franklin Twp	77	111
KEMBRO								
J N	52	m	w	KY	Sacramento	3-Wd Sacramento	77	276
KEMERAS								
Antonilla	17	f	w	CA	Placer	Bath P O	76	426
KEMKEN								
Minnie	18	f	w	GERM	Yuba	Marysville	93	609
KEMON								
Levey	34	m	w	IREL	Butte	Concow Twp	70	8
KEMP								
Ah	12	m	c	CHIN	San Francisco	8-Wd San Francisco	82	328
Alexander	32	m	w	SCOT	Los Angeles	Los Angeles Twp	73	496
Andrew	24	m	w	NY	San Francisco	San Francisco P O	80	414
Appalone	73	m	w	GERM	Nevada	Grass Valley Twp	75	191
Chas	44	m	w	ENGL	San Francisco	5-Wd San Francisco	81	3
Chas M	34	m	w	OH	San Francisco	San Francisco P O	83	86
Christopher	44	m	b	VA	San Francisco	San Francisco P O	80	359
Domingo	35	m	w	MEXI	Tehama	Red Bluff	92	181
Emanuel	61	m	w	TN	Monterey	San Juan Twp	74	389
F W	35	m	w	PA	Monterey	San Juan Twp	74	410
Frederick	26	m	w	PRUS	San Diego	Fort Yuma Dist	78	463
Henry	36	m	w	NY	San Francisco	San Francisco P O	80	458
Henry	35	m	w	BRAZ	Santa Clara	Gilroy Twp	88	95
Henry	25	m	w	ENGL	Nevada	Washington Twp	75	342
J B	42	m	w	OH	Tuolumne	Columbia P O	93	348
James	49	m	w	PA	Humboldt	Arcata Twp	72	229
James	40	m	w	IREL	San Francisco	11-Wd San Francisc	84	586
James C	41	m	w	MA	San Francisco	San Francisco P O	83	51
Jas W	28	m	w	ENGL	Santa Barbara	San Buenaventura P	87	429

© 2001 by Heritage Quest. All rights reserved.

Name	Age	S	R	B-PL	County	Locale	Series M593 Roll	Pg
John	42	m	w	CA	El Dorado	Placerville Twp	72	99
John	42	m	w	OH	Tuolumne	Columbia P O	93	360
John B	39	m	w	CANA	Shasta	Fort Crook P O	89	475
John K	33	m	w	NY	San Francisco	San Francisco P O	83	293
John W	40	m	w	VT	Humboldt	Pacific Twp	72	289
John W	25	m	w	IREL	San Francisco	San Francisco P O	83	221
Lewis	30	m	w	IL	Solano	Vallejo	90	202
Louisa	24	f	w	HDAR	San Francisco	8-Wd San Francisco	82	412
Michael	56	m	w	LUXE	Mariposa	Mariposa P O	74	92
Robert	29	m	w	IL	Placer	Rocklin Twp	76	468
Thomas	40	m	w	NY	Sonoma	Petaluma Twp	91	340
William	49	m	w	NY	El Dorado	Placerville	72	110
William	46	m	w	ENGL	Nevada	Grass Valley Twp	75	142
William	38	m	w	BADE	San Francisco	7-Wd San Francisco	81	221
Wm H	35	m	w	OH	Butte	Kimshew Tpw	70	79
Wm M	40	m	w	ENGL	Nevada	Grass Valley Twp	75	186
KEMPE								
Lewis	30	m	w	PRUS	San Francisco	8-Wd San Francisco	82	376
KEMPENSKE								
Henry	37	m	w	PRUS	San Francisco	San Francisco P O	83	215
KEMPER								
Charles	38	m	w	MO	Sonoma	Analy Twp	91	238
Chas	28	m	w	IREL	San Francisco	8-Wd San Francisco	82	320
John	29	m	w	PRUS	San Joaquin	2-Wd Stockton	86	206
KEMPF								
Andrew	24	m	w	WURT	Nevada	Nevada Twp	75	282
G W	39	m	w	WURT	San Francisco	San Francisco P O	85	816
John	40	m	w	WURT	Butte	Chico Twp	70	20
KEMPH								
Chas	26	m	w	FINL	San Francisco	1-Wd San Francisco	79	102
KEMPHER								
Andrew	44	m	w	SWIT	Nevada	Rough & Ready Twp	75	335
Rachel	24	f	w	PRUS	San Francisco	6-Wd San Francisco	81	154
KEMPLE								
John	45	m	w	PRUS	Inyo	Cerro Gordo Twp	73	321
KEMPRANE								
John O	54	m	w	HOLL	San Francisco	11-Wd San Francisc	84	699
KEMPRY								
Thos	30	m	w	IREL	San Joaquin	2-Wd Stockton	86	172
KEMPTER								
Theo	13	m	w	CA	Sacramento	4-Wd Sacramento	77	344
KEMPTHORN								
John H	43	m	w	ENGL	El Dorado	Placerville	72	112
KEMPTON								
Hiram	41	m	w	ME	Sutter	Nicolaus Twp	92	111
John	38	m	w	IREL	Tuolumne	Chinese Camp P O	93	386
Philip	40	m	w	PRUS	San Francisco	2-Wd San Francisco	79	149
Samuel	40	m	w	ME	Nevada	Grass Valley Twp	75	184
KEMPUS								
G	38	m	w	MEXI	Alameda	Murray Twp	68	108
J	50	m	w	MEXI	Alameda	Murray Twp	68	111
KEMS								
John	26	m	w	IREL	San Mateo	Schoolhouse Statio	87	338
KEMSEY								
James	40	m	w	IREL	Nevada	Grass Valley Twp	75	222
KEN								
Ah	60	m	c	CHIN	Yuba	Rose Bar Twp	93	656
Ah	45	m	c	CHIN	San Mateo	San Mateo P O	87	351
Ah	42	m	c	CHIN	Mariposa	Maxwell Crk P O	74	147
Ah	41	m	c	CHIN	Placer	Roseville P O	76	348
Ah	40	m	c	CHIN	Nevada	Bridgeport Twp	75	110
Ah	38	m	c	CHIN	Nevada	Bridgeport Twp	75	111
Ah	36	m	c	CHIN	Nevada	Meadow Lake Twp	75	257
Ah	32	m	c	CHIN	Placer	Bath P O	76	444
Ah	29	m	c	CHIN	Placer	Newcastle Twp	76	477
Ah	28	m	c	CHIN	Calaveras	San Andreas P O	70	162
Ah	27	m	c	CHIN	Tuolumne	Big Oak Flat P O	93	393
Ah	26	f	c	CHIN	Sierra	Downieville Twp	89	521
Ah	25	m	c	CHIN	Nevada	Eureka Twp	75	131
Ah	25	m	c	CHIN	Trinity	Junction City Pct	92	206
Ah	21	m	c	CHIN	Nevada	Rough & Ready Twp	75	331
Ah	20	m	c	CHIN	Merced	Snelling P O	74	272
Ah	18	m	c	CHIN	Nevada	Bridgeport Twp	75	122
Ah	17	m	c	CHIN	Nevada	Bridgeport Twp	75	101
Ah	14	m	c	CHIN	Nevada	Eureka Twp	75	140
Ah	14	m	c	CHIN	Solano	Benicia	90	7
Choy	28	m	c	CHIN	Butte	Kimshew Tpw	70	86
Chu	37	m	c	CHIN	Butte	Ophir Twp	70	104
Foo	40	m	c	CHIN	Klamath	Liberty Twp	73	375
I	45	m	c	CHIN	Nevada	Bridgeport Twp	75	107
I	20	f	c	CHIN	Stanislaus	Emory Twp	92	17
John	30	m	w	IREL	San Joaquin	2-Wd Stockton	86	193
Shan	55	m	c	CHIN	Klamath	Liberty Twp	73	374
Thomas	31	m	w	IREL	San Francisco	11-Wd San Francisc	84	508
Took	29	m	c	CHIN	Klamath	Orleans Twp	73	380
Toy	47	m	c	CHIN	Klamath	Liberty Twp	73	376
Yoak	29	m	c	CHIN	Klamath	South Fork Twp	73	382
Yon	19	m	c	CHIN	Plumas	Goodwin Twp	77	3
KENADA								
Sarah	15	f	w	CA	Colusa	Grand Island Twp	71	302
KENADAY								
Thos	30	m	w	TN	Napa	Napa Twp	75	63
KENADEY								
John	27	m	w	SCOT	Mendocino	Casper & Big Rvr	74	164
KENADY								
Elisabeth	35	f	w	IREL	Alameda	Washington Twp	68	291
Margret	35	f	w	IREL	Alameda	Brooklyn	68	37
Robert M	41	m	w	NY	Placer	Auburn P O	76	366
KENAN								
Ann	57	f	w	IREL	Santa Clara	1-Wd San Jose	88	242
KENARD								
Thomas W	40	m	w	MD	San Francisco	6-Wd San Francisco	81	80
KENARY								
Daniel	29	m	w	IREL	Santa Clara	2-Wd San Jose	88	311
KENAY								
John	34	m	w	IREL	San Francisco	11-Wd San Francisc	84	550
KENBER								
Adam	55	m	w	PRUS	Sacramento	Alabama Twp	77	63
KENCH								
E W	33	m	w	ME	Solano	Vallejo	90	162
John	36	m	w	MO	Trinity	North Fork Twp	92	218
KENDAL								
Cyrus	50	m	w	ME	San Francisco	6-Wd San Francisco	81	94
John	30	m	w	ENGL	San Francisco	1-Wd San Francisco	79	89
Stephen	56	m	w	OH	Sacramento	3-Wd Sacramento	77	285
KENDALE								
John	23	m	w	IA	Calaveras	San Andreas P O	70	208
KENDALL								
Anderson	29	m	w	ME	Mendocino	Little Rvr Twp	74	171
Arabella	24	f	w	ME	San Francisco	8-Wd San Francisco	82	467
Benj	40	m	w	MS	Butte	Concow Twp	70	8
Benjn	35	m	w	ENGL	Mariposa	Mariposa P O	74	111
Cyrus	35	m	w	VT	San Francisco	8-Wd San Francisco	82	382
D B	37	m	w	ME	Sierra	Table Rock Twp	89	577
Eliza	45	f	w	NY	Sacramento	4-Wd Sacramento	77	333
Ellen	19	f	w	NY	San Francisco	8-Wd San Francisco	82	393
George	38	m	w	BAVA	San Diego	Julian Dist	78	471
George	14	m	w	OH	Marin	San Rafael	74	58
H G	50	m	w	ME	Butte	Wyandotte Twp	70	146
Harriet	31	f	w	NY	San Francisco	San Francisco P O	80	457
James	38	m	w	ME	Santa Clara	1-Wd San Jose	88	265
Jennie	11	f	w	CA	Nevada	Rough & Ready Twp	75	327
Jeremiah	45	m	w	OH	El Dorado	Cosumnes Twp	72	13
Jerome F	26	m	w	ME	Mendocino	Point Arena Twp	74	207
John	50	m	w	KY	San Francisco	8-Wd San Francisco	82	447
John	49	m	w	NY	Sonoma	Petaluma Twp	91	358
John M	35	m	w	ME	Sierra	Table Rock Twp	89	573
John R	23	m	w	ME	El Dorado	Cosumnes Twp	72	13
Myra	31	f	w	NY	San Francisco	8-Wd San Francisco	82	455
Norris W	43	m	w	NY	Plumas	Indian Twp	77	9
Samuel S	53	m	w	NH	Contra Costa	Martinez P O	71	388
Sophroni	64	f	w	NY	San Francisco	San Francisco P O	80	384
Stephen	51	m	w	NY	Amador	Jackson P O	69	341
Thos	43	m	w	OH	Mariposa	Mariposa P O	74	90
Thos	30	m	w	ENGL	San Francisco	1-Wd San Francisco	79	31
W	40	m	w	VA	Solano	Vallejo	90	217
William	25	m	w	ENGL	San Francisco	San Francisco P O	80	473
Wm	61	m	w	KY	Sacramento	Sutter Twp	77	392
KENDELL								
J F	25	m	w	CANA	Solano	Vallejo	90	194
John	46	m	w	MA	San Francisco	2-Wd San Francisco	79	274
John	24	m	w	ME	Amador	Sutter Crk P O	69	411
Philip	35	m	w	PRUS	Sacramento	2-Wd Sacramento	77	234
S A	22	f	w	IA	San Joaquin	1-Wd Stockton	86	120
William B	46	m	w	KY	Yuba	New York Twp	93	641
KENDIG								
Daniel	34	m	w	PA	Nevada	Grass Valley Twp	75	143
KENDING								
Daniel	35	m	w	PA	San Francisco	San Francisco P O	85	757
Johanna	30	f	w	PA	San Francisco	San Francisco P O	85	759
KENDLE								
B F	9	f	w	MO	Sacramento	1-Wd Sacramento	77	185
J	54	m	w	IA	San Joaquin	Douglas Twp	86	41
Wm	58	m	w	PA	San Joaquin	Oneal Twp	86	113
KENDLER								
Frederick	29	m	w	FRAN	Klamath	Trinidad Twp	73	392
KENDREYSON								
Melan	22	m	w	NY	Monterey	Monterey Twp	74	347
KENDRICK								
Charles	50	m	w	CANA	Mendocino	Round Valley Twp	74	216
Edwd	32	m	w	NY	San Francisco	1-Wd San Francisco	79	89
Henry W	17	m	w	MA	Mendocino	Point Arena Twp	74	210
J M	45	m	w	AL	Tehama	Stony Crk	92	166
James	52	m	w	IREL	Nevada	Nevada Twp	75	313
James W	37	m	w	MS	Yolo	Buckeye Twp	93	413
Jas	25	m	w	OH	Butte	Chico Twp	70	30
Mulford	36	m	w	MA	Colusa	Monroe Twp	71	314
Thomas G	42	m	w	ME	Yolo	Merritt Twp	93	506
Thos	32	m	w	IREL	San Francisco	San Francisco P O	83	41
KENDRICKS								
Colon	45	m	w	IREL	Nevada	Grass Valley Twp	75	204
J H	29	m	w	GA	Merced	Snelling P O	74	247
Wm	42	m	w	MO	San Francisco	1-Wd San Francisco	79	104
KENDRIGAN								
Margt	23	f	w	IREL	San Francisco	1-Wd San Francisco	79	76
KENEALY								
John	30	m	w	IREL	San Francisco	San Francisco P O	83	280
KENEDA								
Elizabeth	17	f	w	IREL	Monterey	Salinas Twp	74	307
KENEDY								
A	50	m	w	IREL	Amador	Jackson P O	69	318
A W	30	m	w	CANA	Alameda	Alameda	68	19
Allen	40	m	w	SCOT	Sacramento	Granite Twp	77	140
Azeride	31	m	w	MO	Trinity	Weaverville Pct	92	231

© 2001 by Heritage Quest. All rights reserved.

California 1870 Census

Series M593

Name	Age	S	R	B-PL	County	Locale	Roll	Pg
Hannah	25	f	w	IREL	San Francisco	San Francisco P O	83	25
James	47	m	w	IREL	Los Angeles	Los Angeles	73	502
James	33	m	w	IREL	Los Angeles	Los Angeles	73	568
Jane	29	f	w	IREL	Solano	Benicia	90	16
John	24	m	w	OH	Los Angeles	Los Angeles	73	538
Mary	30	f	w	IREL	San Joaquin	2-Wd Stockton	86	173
P J	28	m	w	IREL	Solano	Vallejo	90	172
Patrick	37	m	w	IREL	Yolo	Grafton Twp	93	481
Robert	54	m	w	IL	El Dorado	White Oak Twp	72	143
Rose	20	f	w	NY	San Francisco	San Francisco P O	83	28
T	30	m	w	NY	Sacramento	1-Wd Sacramento	77	177
Thos	30	m	w	IREL	Yuba	Linda Twp	93	558
William L	44	m	w	IREL	Inyo	Cerro Gordo Twp	73	323
KENEERY								
John	10	m	w	CA	Monterey	Castroville Twp	74	331
KENEFIC								
Patrick	35	m	w	IREL	San Francisco	11-Wd San Francisc	84	533
KENELLY								
Jerry	26	m	w	IREL	San Francisco	1-Wd San Francisco	79	84
Nora	28	f	w	IREL	San Francisco	8-Wd San Francisco	82	466
William	37	m	w	UNKN	San Joaquin	2-Wd Stockton	86	167
KENELY								
Mattw	18	m	w	MA	Alameda	Oakland	68	182
KENEN								
James	35	m	w	IREL	Alameda	Murray Twp	68	115
KENEPPER								
A B	39	m	w	PA	Butte	Oroville Twp	70	137
KENER								
David	24	m	w	MD	Stanislaus	Empire Twp	92	32
KENEREY								
Jas	33	m	w	IREL	Fresno	Millerton P O	72	186
KENERN								
John	38	m	w	IREL	Sacramento	4-Wd Sacramento	77	366
KENEVAN								
James	58	m	w	IREL	San Francisco	6-Wd San Francisco	81	103
John	30	m	w	IREL	San Francisco	6-Wd San Francisco	81	118
KENEY								
Martin	23	m	w	IREL	Inyo	Independence Twp	73	328
KENFIELD								
D M	40	m	w	NY	Tuolumne	Sonora P O	93	304
Edgar	18	m	w	IL	Santa Barbara	San Buenaventura P	87	435
Sarah	20	f	w	IL	Alameda	Oakland	68	234
KENG								
Ah	45	m	c	CHIN	Plumas	Washington Twp	77	58
Ah	45	m	c	CHIN	Calaveras	San Andreas P O	70	172
Ah	25	m	c	CHIN	Plumas	Goodwin Twp	77	5
Ah	25	m	c	CHIN	Plumas	Goodwin Twp	77	4
Ah	22	m	c	CHIN	Placer	Blue Canyon P O	76	417
Ah	20	m	c	CHIN	Nevada	Eureka Twp	75	127
Ah	17	m	c	CHIN	San Francisco	3-Wd San Francisco	79	309
Howk	32	m	c	CHIN	Plumas	Seneca Twp	77	48
KENGEN								
Lewis	27	m	w	BAVA	Sacramento	2-Wd Sacramento	77	221
KENGON								
Benjamin	45	m	w	OH	Santa Cruz	Soquel Twp	89	437
KENIFECK								
Teresa	40	f	w	IREL	San Bernardino	San Bernardino Twp	78	433
KENIFF								
Andrew	22	m	w	PA	San Francisco	San Francisco P O	80	397
KENIFIT								
Julia	65	f	w	IREL	San Francisco	2-Wd San Francisco	79	153
KENISON								
Robert	51	m	w	LA	San Francisco	11-Wd San Francisc	84	644
KENISTON								
Daniel	39	m	w	MA	San Diego	San Pasqual	78	519
Daniel	30	m	w	NY	Sonoma	Analy Twp	91	223
Joseph F	38	m	w	ME	Sonoma	Bodega Twp	91	255
KENITH								
Peter	21	m	w	NORW	San Francisco	7-Wd San Francisco	81	276
KENITZER								
Karl	36	m	w	PRUS	San Francisco	San Francisco P O	83	281
KENKLER								
Ernest A	62	m	w	SWIT	El Dorado	Placerville	72	112
KENLEY								
Edward	47	m	w	CANA	Tuolumne	Sonora P O	93	331
John	27	m	w	IREL	Siskiyou	Scott Valley Twp	89	611
KENLOCK								
Fredk	14	m	w	NY	San Francisco	6-Wd San Francisco	81	128
George	38	m	w	CANA	Mendocino	Sanel Twp	74	227
KENLY								
Edward	26	m	w	IREL	Calaveras	San Andreas P O	70	204
KENMORE								
John	29	m	w	SCOT	Amador	Sutter Crk P O	69	398
KENNA								
Joseph	25	m	w	ENGL	Placer	Cisco P O	76	494
Margaret	57	f	w	PA	San Francisco	San Francisco P O	83	355
Mc Jno	30	m	w	IREL	Santa Clara	Gilroy Twp	88	95
Patrick	40	m	w	IREL	Sonoma	Salt Point	91	392
KENNADA								
Mary	35	f	w	IREL	Placer	Lincoln P O	76	489
KENNADY								
Hury	58	m	w	IREL	El Dorado	Kelsey Twp	72	61
J	73	m	w	NH	Lake	Lower Lake	73	418
John	40	m	w	IREL	San Joaquin	Douglas Twp	86	37
Mary	21	f	w	FRAN	Alameda	Brooklyn Twp	68	42
Patrick	35	m	w	IREL	Napa	Napa Twp	75	59
R	48	m	w	NY	Lake	Lakeport	73	406

Series M593

Name	Age	S	R	B-PL	County	Locale	Roll	Pg
Wallace	38	m	w	IN	Napa	Napa	75	42
KENNAN								
Patrick	30	m	w	IREL	San Francisco	11-Wd San Francisc	84	442
KENNARD								
D H	42	m	w	MD	Sutter	Yuba Twp	92	149
Geo	48	m	w	ENGL	San Francisco	San Francisco P O	83	332
S E	41	m	w	ND	Sutter	Yuba Twp	92	140
KENNAW								
Chas E	22	m	w	NY	Sacramento	3-Wd Sacramento	77	285
KENNAY								
Martin	41	m	w	IREL	San Francisco	11-Wd San Francisc	84	436
KENNE								
James	30	m	w	NY	San Francisco	3-Wd San Francisco	79	313
Jos	28	m	w	MA	Sacramento	1-Wd Sacramento	77	185
KENNEALLY								
Edward	42	m	w	IREL	San Francisco	2-Wd San Francisco	79	270
Michael	31	m	w	IREL	Alameda	Washington Twp	68	300
Nora	16	f	w	MA	Santa Clara	2-Wd San Jose	88	337
KENNEAR								
James	30	m	w	SCOT	San Mateo	Half Moon Bay P O	87	408
KENNEDAY								
Frank	50	m	w	IREL	San Francisco	7-Wd San Francisco	81	197
Henry	35	m	w	IREL	San Francisco	1-Wd San Francisco	79	74
James	35	m	w	NY	San Francisco	1-Wd San Francisco	79	39
James	33	m	w	ENGL	Contra Costa	Martinez P O	71	450
John	48	m	w	PA	San Francisco	3-Wd San Francisco	79	302
KENNEDEY								
M J	40	m	w	OH	San Francisco	San Francisco P O	83	283
Michl	55	m	w	IREL	San Francisco	1-Wd San Francisco	79	94
KENNEDUT								
Frank	28	m	w	ITAL	Mariposa	Mariposa P O	74	113
KENNEDY								
A	59	m	w	IREL	San Joaquin	Douglas Twp	86	30
A H	27	m	w	TN	Tehama	Cottonwood Twp	92	161
A J	39	m	w	NY	El Dorado	Kelsey Twp	72	62
Albert	30	m	w	CANA	San Francisco	11-Wd San Francisc	84	451
Alex	40	m	w	MD	Fresno	Millerton P O	72	150
Alexander E	43	m	w	SCOT	Calaveras	San Andreas P O	70	213
Alfred	62	m	w	NC	Sacramento	4-Wd Sacramento	77	377
Alfred	24	m	w	IREL	San Francisco	San Francisco P O	85	795
Almy	31	m	w	IN	Yolo	Cache Crk Twp	93	443
Andrew	49	m	w	IREL	Stanislaus	Emory Twp	92	25
Andrew	30	m	w	NY	San Francisco	5-Wd San Francisco	81	14
Andrew F	36	m	w	IREL	Stanislaus	North Twp	92	69
Andrew J	38	m	w	NY	El Dorado	Placerville	72	127
Ann	50	f	w	PA	San Joaquin	Douglas Twp	86	42
Anna	28	f	w	IREL	San Francisco	8-Wd San Francisco	82	391
Annie	26	f	w	IREL	San Francisco	San Francisco P O	83	299
Annie	25	f	w	SCOT	San Francisco	1-Wd San Francisco	79	2
Archd	36	m	w	WIND	Santa Clara	Gilroy Twp	88	83
Armstrong	26	m	w	MO	Yolo	Cottonwood Twp	93	467
Austin	33	m	w	IREL	Santa Cruz	Soquel Twp	89	442
B B	43	m	w	IREL	San Francisco	San Francisco P O	85	778
Banori	43	m	w	KY	Santa Barbara	Santa Maria P O	87	510
Bartholemu	28	m	w	IREL	San Francisco	San Francisco P O	83	189
Bartholomew	44	m	w	IREL	San Francisco	11-Wd San Francisc	84	530
Bernard	56	m	w	IREL	Santa Cruz	Soquel Twp	89	444
Bridget	33	f	w	IREL	San Francisco	8-Wd San Francisco	82	478
C W	30	m	w	NH	Sonoma	Russian Rvr	91	368
Cath	53	f	w	PA	Butte	Chico Twp	70	45
Catharine	40	f	w	IREL	San Francisco	San Francisco P O	83	36
Cathine	20	f	w	IREL	San Francisco	San Francisco P O	85	860
Charles	26	m	w	IREL	San Francisco	San Francisco P O	83	232
Charles D	36	m	w	OH	Solano	Green Valley Twp	90	39
Charles L	25	m	w	CANA	Santa Clara	1-Wd San Jose	88	237
Dan	30	m	w	IREL	Alameda	Alameda	68	12
Daniel	35	m	w	IREL	San Francisco	8-Wd San Francisco	82	447
Danl W	27	m	w	MI	San Francisco	1-Wd San Francisco	79	104
David	35	m	w	IREL	San Francisco	7-Wd San Francisco	81	203
Delia	20	f	w	IREL	San Francisco	8-Wd San Francisco	82	415
Dennis	45	m	w	IREL	San Francisco	8-Wd San Francisco	82	494
Dennis	37	m	w	IREL	San Francisco	7-Wd San Francisco	81	266
E C	45	m	w	IREL	San Francisco	8-Wd San Francisco	82	335
E C	36	m	w	VA	Siskiyou	Scott Rvr Twp	89	604
E P	63	m	w	IREL	Siskiyou	Scott Valley Twp	89	618
E T	20	m	w	AUSL	San Francisco	San Francisco P O	85	777
Ed	32	m	w	IREL	Merced	Snelling P O	74	266
Edi	35	m	w	ENGL	San Francisco	2-Wd San Francisco	79	219
Edward	7	m	w	CA	Marin	San Rafael Twp	74	28
Edward	5	m	w	NV	San Francisco	11-Wd San Francisc	84	678
Edward	43	m	w	NY	San Francisco	11-Wd San Francisc	84	622
Edward	38	m	w	ENGL	San Francisco	5-Wd San Francisco	81	24
Edwd	21	m	w	IREL	San Francisco	San Francisco P O	83	33
Eliza	65	f	w	IREL	San Francisco	6-Wd San Francisco	81	99
F	40	m	w	OH	San Joaquin	Oneal Twp	86	101
Frank	36	m	w	IREL	San Francisco	11-Wd San Francisc	84	484
Frank B	28	m	w	ENGL	San Francisco	6-Wd San Francisco	81	133
Geo H	32	m	w	MA	Sonoma	Russian Rvr	91	368
George	30	m	w	NJ	San Mateo	Half Moon Bay P O	87	405
George R	53	m	w	FINL	Santa Cruz	Santa Cruz	89	410
H	34	m	w	NH	Lake	Lower Lake	73	419
Hannah	25	f	w	IREL	San Francisco	San Francisco P O	83	341
Hanora	26	f	w	IREL	San Francisco	San Francisco P O	83	258
Henry	5	m	w	CA	San Francisco	7-Wd San Francisco	81	253
Henry	37	m	w	ME	San Diego	San Jacinto Dist	78	517
Houston	21	m	w	TN	Santa Cruz	Pajaro Twp	89	350
Hugh	40	m	w	IREL	San Francisco	7-Wd San Francisco	81	202

© 2001 by Heritage Quest. All rights reserved.

Name	Age	S	R	B-PL	County	Locale	Series M593 Roll	Pg
Hugh	36	m	w	IREL	San Francisco	11-Wd San Francisc	84	612
Hugh	35	m	w	IREL	San Francisco	San Francisco P O	83	372
J	35	m	w	IREL	San Joaquin	Elkhorn Twp	86	62
J E	38	m	w	IREL	Solano	Vallejo	90	166
James	71	m	w	PA	Sonoma	Sonoma Twp	91	443
James	65	m	w	SCOT	Santa Clara	Redwood Twp	88	130
James	40	m	w	IREL	San Francisco	San Francisco P O	83	352
James	40	m	w	IREL	San Francisco	8-Wd San Francisco	82	396
James	40	m	w	IREL	Calaveras	San Andreas P O	70	160
James	39	m	w	ENGL	El Dorado	Placerville Twp	72	100
James	38	m	w	MA	San Francisco	11-Wd San Francisc	84	539
James	37	m	w	IREL	San Francisco	San Francisco P O	83	6
James	36	m	w	IREL	Santa Clara	2-Wd San Jose	88	283
James	32	m	w	IREL	Mendocino	Anderson Twp	74	154
James	30	m	w	IREL	San Francisco	San Francisco P O	83	144
James	30	m	w	IREL	Nevada	Meadow Lake Twp	75	267
James	27	m	w	OH	San Bernardino	San Bernardino Twp	78	448
James	16	m	w	MA	San Mateo	Half Moon Bay P O	87	408
James	15	m	w	CA	Santa Clara	Santa Clara Twp	88	177
James F	25	m	w	PA	Santa Clara	Redwood Twp	88	128
James G	27	m	w	IL	Santa Clara	Santa Clara Twp	88	145
Jane	49	f	w	MD	San Francisco	8-Wd San Francisco	82	345
Jane	40	f	w	IREL	Santa Clara	1-Wd San Jose	88	230
Jas	55	m	w	VT	Sonoma	Russian Rvr	91	368
Jennie	35	f	w	IREL	San Francisco	8-Wd San Francisco	82	328
Jno	40	m	w	PA	Butte	Chico Twp	70	26
Jno R	25	m	w	PA	Butte	Chico Twp	70	26
Joanna	30	f	w	IREL	San Francisco	San Francisco P O	85	723
John	84	m	w	ME	San Diego	San Jacinto Dist	78	517
John	82	m	w	CANA	San Bernardino	San Bernardino Twp	78	424
John	80	m	w	KY	Nevada	Grass Valley Twp	75	227
John	51	m	w	IREL	Marin	San Rafael Twp	74	36
John	50	m	w	IREL	San Francisco	6-Wd San Francisco	81	119
John	40	m	w	IREL	San Francisco	San Francisco P O	83	213
John	38	m	w	KY	Plumas	Washington Twp	77	52
John	37	m	w	IREL	Yuba	Rose Bar Twp	93	665
John	36	m	w	ENGL	San Francisco	San Francisco P O	85	807
John	36	m	w	IREL	Santa Clara	Redwood Twp	88	128
John	36	m	w	IREL	San Francisco	San Francisco P O	85	758
John	35	m	w	IREL	Contra Costa	Martinez P O	71	368
John	34	m	w	MD	Siskiyou	Scott Rvr Twp	89	605
John	33	m	w	SCOT	San Francisco	11-Wd San Francisc	84	495
John	30	m	w	IREL	Santa Clara	1-Wd San Jose	88	246
John	30	m	w	CANA	Solano	Vallejo	90	144
John	30	m	w	SCOT	Alameda	Murray Twp	68	128
John	30	m	w	IREL	Sacramento	2-Wd Sacramento	77	251
John	30	m	w	IREL	San Francisco	1-Wd San Francisco	79	67
John	29	m	w	ENGL	San Francisco	San Francisco P O	80	336
John	27	m	w	NY	San Francisco	San Francisco P O	83	129
John	27	m	w	IREL	San Francisco	San Francisco P O	85	758
John	27	m	w	IREL	Solano	Silveyville Twp	90	85
John	25	m	w	OH	Sacramento	4-Wd Sacramento	77	364
John	25	m	w	IREL	San Francisco	San Francisco P O	83	222
John	19	m	w	IREL	San Francisco	11-Wd San Francisc	84	701
John	14	m	w	KY	San Francisco	8-Wd San Francisco	82	400
John	13	m	w	IL	San Francisco	San Francisco P O	83	159
John	12	m	w	CA	San Francisco	11-Wd San Francisc	84	591
John F	29	m	w	KY	Stanislaus	Empire Twp	92	58
John M	45	m	w	CANA	Santa Clara	1-Wd San Jose	88	229
John R	32	m	w	AL	Yuba	Slate Range Bar Tw	93	670
John T	35	m	w	IREL	San Francisco	San Francisco P O	83	184
Jos	23	m	w	IREL	San Francisco	11-Wd San Francisc	84	693
Joseph	53	m	w	CANA	San Diego	San Jacinto Dist	78	517
Joseph	52	m	w	CANA	San Bernardino	San Bernardino Twp	78	424
Joseph	43	m	w	IREL	El Dorado	Placerville	72	125
Joseph	36	m	w	KY	Yolo	Grafton Twp	93	499
Joseph	34	m	w	OH	Yolo	Grafton Twp	93	478
Joseph	22	m	w	NY	Sacramento	3-Wd Sacramento	77	284
Joseph C	28	m	w	PA	Monterey	Monterey	74	362
Josh	51	m	w	IN	San Joaquin	3-Wd Stockton	86	240
Kate	60	f	w	IREL	San Francisco	San Francisco P O	83	41
Kate	50	f	w	IREL	San Francisco	11-Wd San Francisc	84	442
Kate	35	f	w	IREL	San Francisco	6-Wd San Francisco	81	136
Kate	29	f	w	IREL	San Francisco	8-Wd San Francisco	82	481
Kate	26	f	w	IREL	San Francisco	San Francisco P O	83	271
Kate	26	f	w	IREL	San Francisco	San Francisco P O	83	89
Kate	23	f	w	IREL	San Francisco	8-Wd San Francisco	82	466
L W	41	m	w	NY	San Francisco	8-Wd San Francisco	82	330
Lawrence	55	m	w	IREL	San Francisco	7-Wd San Francisco	81	258
Lawrence	26	m	w	IREL	Nevada	Grass Valley Twp	75	160
Louis	56	m	w	DENM	San Francisco	2-Wd San Francisco	79	213
M	40	m	w	IREL	Amador	Ione City P O	69	364
M	22	f	w	IREL	Alameda	Oakland	68	237
Maggie	30	f	w	ENGL	San Francisco	8-Wd San Francisco	82	377
Margret	36	f	w	IREL	San Francisco	11-Wd San Francisc	84	678
Maria	50	f	w	US	San Francisco	San Francisco P O	83	344
Martha	28	f	w	PA	Tulare	Venice Twp	92	273
Martin	57	m	w	IREL	San Francisco	San Francisco P O	83	77
Martin	22	m	w	IREL	San Francisco	1-Wd San Francisco	79	104
Martin	21	m	w	IREL	Marin	Sausalito Twp	74	74
Mary	80	f	w	CANA	San Bernardino	San Bernardino Twp	78	424
Mary	39	f	w	IREL	San Francisco	San Francisco P O	83	367
Mary	35	f	w	IREL	San Francisco	San Francisco P O	83	99
Mary	26	f	w	IREL	San Francisco	San Francisco P O	85	775
Mary	24	f	w	CANA	Santa Cruz	Santa Cruz Twp	89	394
Mary	24	f	w	IREL	San Francisco	San Francisco P O	83	56
Mary	22	f	w	IREL	San Francisco	San Francisco P O	83	15
Maurice	60	m	w	IREL	San Francisco	San Francisco P O	83	233
Mergeret	20	f	w	IREL	Yuba	North East Twp	93	644
Michael	50	m	w	IREL	Yolo	Cottonwood Twp	93	470
Michael	40	m	w	IREL	San Francisco	7-Wd San Francisco	81	239
Michael	37	m	w	IREL	Tehama	Red Bluff	92	174
Michael	35	m	w	IREL	San Francisco	San Francisco P O	83	239
Michael	32	m	w	IREL	Nevada	Bridgeport Twp	75	122
Michael	31	m	w	IREL	San Francisco	San Francisco P O	83	255
Michael	25	m	w	NJ	Alpine	Monitor P O	69	314
Michael	23	m	w	IREL	San Mateo	San Mateo P O	87	360
Michael W	26	m	w	PA	Plumas	Seneca Twp	77	50
Michl	13	m	w	NY	San Francisco	San Francisco P O	83	5
Mitchell	38	m	w	IREL	San Joaquin	Oneal Twp	86	98
Mortin	30	m	w	IREL	Yuba	Slate Range Bar Tw	93	669
Moses	30	m	w	OH	Stanislaus	Empire Twp	92	51
Oscar	21	m	w	CANA	Santa Clara	2-Wd San Jose	88	322
Oscar	19	m	w	CANA	Santa Clara	2-Wd San Jose	88	318
P	30	m	w	IREL	San Joaquin	2-Wd Stockton	86	182
Pamelia	35	f	w	IREL	San Francisco	San Francisco P O	83	172
Pat	40	m	w	IREL	Butte	Ophir Twp	70	102
Patrick	45	m	w	IREL	Calaveras	San Andreas P O	70	156
Patrick	40	m	w	IREL	San Francisco	11-Wd San Francisc	84	474
Patrick	34	m	w	IREL	San Francisco	San Francisco P O	83	345
Patrick	33	m	w	IREL	San Francisco	6-Wd San Francisco	81	88
Patrick	32	m	w	IREL	San Mateo	Redwood City P O	87	375
Patrick	31	m	w	IREL	San Francisco	11-Wd San Francisc	84	512
Patrick	31	m	w	IREL	San Francisco	11-Wd San Francisc	84	545
Patrick	24	m	w	IREL	San Francisco	San Francisco P O	83	60
Pauline	25	f	m	LA	San Francisco	6-Wd San Francisco	81	150
Peter	40	m	w	IREL	San Diego	Julian Dist	78	472
Phillip	36	m	w	IREL	Amador	Ione City P O	69	365
Polk	35	m	w	IREL	San Francisco	San Francisco P O	83	376
R	40	m	w	IREL	Calaveras	Copperopolis P O	70	223
Richard	38	m	w	IREL	Nevada	Grass Valley Twp	75	179
Robert	40	m	w	IREL	Stanislaus	North Twp	92	69
Robert	38	m	w	CANA	Kern	Bakersfield P O	73	366
Robt	36	m	w	IREL	Shasta	Shasta P O	89	463
Sam	50	m	w	IREL	Sacramento	4-Wd Sacramento	77	342
Sam	44	m	w	ME	San Bernardino	San Bernardino Twp	78	443
Samuel	44	m	w	ME	San Diego	San Jacinto Dist	78	517
Samuel	22	m	w	PA	Santa Clara	Redwood Twp	88	130
Samuel	19	m	w	IA	Sacramento	San Joaquin Twp	77	395
Sarah	35	f	w	ENGL	San Francisco	6-Wd San Francisco	81	94
Stephen	42	m	w	IREL	Monterey	San Benito Twp	74	381
T	32	m	w	IREL	Solano	Vallejo	90	169
Thomas	81	m	w	SCOT	San Francisco	San Francisco P O	85	808
Thomas	55	m	w	IREL	San Francisco	6-Wd San Francisco	81	119
Thomas	44	m	w	IREL	San Francisco	San Francisco P O	85	761
Thomas	43	m	w	IREL	Stanislaus	Emory Twp	92	25
Thomas	40	m	w	IREL	San Francisco	2-Wd San Francisco	79	152
Thomas	37	m	w	IREL	Santa Clara	2-Wd San Jose	88	313
Thomas	36	m	w	IREL	Stanislaus	Emory Twp	92	18
Thomas	35	m	w	IREL	San Francisco	San Francisco P O	83	250
Thomas	35	m	w	IREL	Santa Cruz	Watsonville	89	377
Thomas	34	m	w	MO	Solano	Suisun Twp	90	107
Thomas	30	m	w	IREL	San Francisco	San Francisco P O	83	351
Thomas	30	m	w	IREL	Marin	Bolinas Twp	74	7
Thomas	26	m	w	IREL	Solano	Denverton Twp	90	23
Thomas	26	m	w	IREL	Solano	Suisun Twp	90	99
Thomas	23	m	w	IREL	Nevada	Grass Valley Twp	75	180
Thos	55	m	w	IREL	San Francisco	8-Wd San Francisco	82	360
Thos	37	m	w	CANA	San Francisco	7-Wd San Francisco	81	279
Thos	31	m	w	IREL	San Francisco	1-Wd San Francisco	79	71
Thos	26	m	w	IREL	Tehama	Red Bluff	92	180
Timothy	60	m	w	IREL	Santa Clara	Milpitas Twp	88	111
Timothy	30	m	w	IREL	San Francisco	11-Wd San Francisc	84	502
Tymothy	32	m	w	IREL	San Francisco	San Francisco P O	85	754
Van B	22	m	w	KY	Santa Cruz	Pajaro Twp	89	348
Virginia	36	f	w	IL	Nevada	Grass Valley Twp	75	186
Waiter	23	m	w	CANA	Santa Clara	2-Wd San Jose	88	320
William	48	m	w	ME	San Bernardino	San Bernardino Twp	78	443
William	40	m	w	PA	Alameda	Brooklyn Twp	68	39
William	36	m	w	WI	Yolo	Cottonwood Twp	93	465
William	35	m	w	MO	Calaveras	San Andreas P O	70	206
William	30	m	w	NY	San Francisco	5-Wd San Francisco	81	16
William	28	m	w	IREL	Tulare	Tule Rvr Twp	92	271
William	22	m	w	NY	Los Angeles	Santa Ana Twp	73	601
William C	26	m	w	PA	Santa Clara	2-Wd San Jose	88	336
William J	54	m	w	IREL	Yuba	North East Twp	93	644
William P	54	m	w	VA	Solano	Suisun Twp	90	94
Wm	40	m	w	IREL	San Francisco	1-Wd San Francisco	79	91
Wm	38	m	w	IREL	San Francisco	11-Wd San Francisc	84	584
Wm	38	m	w	IN	San Francisco	San Francisco P O	83	133
Wm	24	m	w	IA	Sacramento	San Joaquin Twp	77	402
KENNEFF								
Jeremiah	60	m	w	IREL	Yolo	Putah Twp	93	515
KENNEFIC								
Bartholw	35	m	w	IREL	San Francisco	1-Wd San Francisco	79	132
Michl	35	m	w	IREL	San Francisco	1-Wd San Francisco	79	132
KENNEFIT								
Wm	40	m	w	IREL	San Francisco	8-Wd San Francisco	82	356
KENNEKE								
Charles	46	m	w	PRUS	San Francisco	7-Wd San Francisco	81	226
KENNEL								
Jacob	36	m	w	BAVA	Sacramento	3-Wd Sacramento	77	295
Owen	31	m	w	IREL	San Francisco	11-Wd San Francisc	84	606

© 2001 by Heritage Quest. All rights reserved.

Name	Age	S	R	B-PL	County	Locale	Series M593 Roll	Pg
KENNELEY								
Jacob	32	m	w	WURT	San Francisco	11-Wd San Francisc	84	674
KENNELL								
Owen	34	m	w	IREL	San Francisco	San Francisco P O	83	263
KENNELLY								
M	45	m	w	IREL	Santa Clara	Burnett Twp	88	39
Mat	40	m	w	IREL	Santa Clara	Burnett Twp	88	38
KENNER								
Andrew	50	m	w	ITAL	Calaveras	San Andreas P O	70	210
James	20	m	w	MS	Nevada	Bridgeport Twp	75	121
Josias A	38	m	w	IREL	San Francisco	3-Wd San Francisco	79	322
Richard	29	m	w	KY	San Joaquin	Elkhorn Twp	86	55
KENNESS								
Adam	40	m	w	PRUS	Kern	Kernville P O	73	368
KENNETH								
Thomas	31	m	w	IREL	Tuolumne	Columbia P O	93	346
KENNETT								
William H	32	m	w	IL	Placer	Bath P O	76	447
Wm	60	m	w	ENGL	Butte	Oregon Twp	70	122
KENNEY								
Arthur	59	m	w	IREL	Trinity	Weaverville Pct	92	224
Arthur	19	m	w	MA	San Francisco	San Francisco P O	83	185
Barthol	40	m	w	IREL	San Francisco	San Francisco P O	85	769
Bridget	42	f	w	IREL	San Francisco	San Francisco P O	85	842
Christopher	31	m	w	NH	San Francisco	8-Wd San Francisco	82	494
Cyrus	37	m	w	PA	Santa Barbara	Santa Barbara P O	87	482
Daniel	26	m	w	IREL	Santa Clara	Fremont Twp	88	41
David	22	m	w	IREL	Nevada	Grass Valley Twp	75	215
Delia	30	f	w	IREL	San Francisco	8-Wd San Francisco	82	481
Edward	26	m	w	IREL	San Francisco	San Francisco P O	85	773
Emily	4	f	w	CA	Nevada	Grass Valley Twp	75	230
Emma	8	f	w	CA	Nevada	Grass Valley Twp	75	230
Ephraim L	49	m	w	ME	El Dorado	Placerville	72	121
Felix	29	m	w	IREL	San Francisco	8-Wd San Francisco	82	461
Geo R	44	m	w	CANA	Humboldt	Eureka Twp	72	271
George	26	m	w	IREL	Santa Clara	San Jose Twp	88	183
Henry	40	m	w	KY	Contra Costa	Martinez P O	71	410
Isaac	49	m	w	NH	Alameda	Brooklyn	68	31
James	40	m	w	IREL	San Francisco	8-Wd San Francisco	82	471
James	38	m	w	IREL	Mendocino	Navarro & Big Rvr	74	175
James	25	m	w	IREL	Sonoma	Petaluma Twp	91	326
James F	28	m	w	IREL	San Francisco	6-Wd San Francisco	81	38
John	40	m	w	IREL	San Francisco	San Francisco P O	85	876
John	40	m	w	IREL	San Francisco	2-Wd San Francisco	79	236
John	33	m	w	ENGL	Napa	Yountville Twp	75	82
John	32	m	w	VT	San Francisco	San Francisco P O	85	846
John	25	m	w	AUSL	Solano	Vallejo	90	146
Joseph	40	m	w	PORT	Santa Cruz	Santa Cruz Twp	89	383
Joseph L	40	m	w	NY	San Francisco	8-Wd San Francisco	82	454
Joseph P	36	m	w	IREL	Nevada	Grass Valley Twp	75	177
Kate	6	f	w	CA	Nevada	Grass Valley Twp	75	230
Kern	23	m	w	IREL	Sacramento	2-Wd Sacramento	77	233
Lizzie	28	f	w	IREL	San Francisco	San Francisco P O	83	144
Lydia	51	f	w	MA	Santa Clara	Fremont Twp	88	49
Mary	22	f	w	IREL	San Francisco	San Francisco P O	85	768
Mary	17	f	w	IREL	San Francisco	San Francisco P O	83	323
Mary	15	f	w	CA	El Dorado	Lake Valley Twp	72	64
Michael	48	m	w	IREL	Contra Costa	San Pablo Twp	71	365
Michael	38	m	w	IREL	Santa Clara	1-Wd San Jose	88	252
Michael	34	m	w	IREL	Santa Clara	2-Wd San Jose	88	307
Michael	32	m	w	IREL	San Francisco	San Francisco P O	85	873
Michael	27	m	w	IREL	Placer	Newcastle Twp	76	476
Michl	21	m	w	IREL	San Francisco	1-Wd San Francisco	79	70
Patk	26	m	w	IREL	Solano	Vallejo	90	182
Patrick	40	m	w	IREL	San Francisco	San Francisco P O	83	348
Patrick	37	m	w	IREL	San Francisco	San Francisco P O	83	301
Patrick	35	m	w	IREL	San Francisco	San Francisco P O	85	850
Peter	30	m	w	IREL	San Francisco	11-Wd San Francisc	84	550
S W	28	m	w	PA	Tehama	Red Bluff	92	174
Sebastian	39	m	w	PORT	Santa Cruz	Soquel Twp	89	438
Susan	24	f	w	IREL	Santa Clara	2-Wd San Jose	88	323
Tho	42	m	w	IREL	El Dorado	Georgetown Twp	72	39
Thomas	40	m	w	IREL	San Francisco	San Francisco P O	83	244
Thomas	37	m	w	IREL	San Francisco	7-Wd San Francisco	81	195
Thomas	27	m	w	IREL	Sacramento	2-Wd Sacramento	77	233
Thomas	27	m	w	IREL	Santa Clara	1-Wd San Jose	88	240
W	46	m	w	NY	Sacramento	3-Wd Sacramento	77	261
William	55	m	w	KY	Contra Costa	Martinez P O	71	410
William	29	m	w	NJ	San Francisco	San Francisco P O	83	188
William H	26	m	w	MA	Santa Clara	Fremont Twp	88	49
William J	42	m	w	IREL	San Francisco	8-Wd San Francisco	82	408
Wm	30	m	w	IREL	San Francisco	San Francisco P O	85	805
KENNICKLE								
J G	32	m	w	OH	Nevada	Meadow Lake Twp	75	246
KENNICOTT								
D	38	m	w	ME	Solano	Vallejo	90	165
KENNIDY								
M	37	m	w	IREL	Amador	Jackson P O	69	329
KENNIF								
Rebecca	25	f	w	PA	San Francisco	2-Wd San Francisco	79	234
KENNING								
Annie	40	f	w	IREL	San Francisco	7-Wd San Francisco	81	286
KENNIS								
John	12	m	w	CA	Marin	San Rafael Twp	74	27
Peter	37	m	w	IREL	Monterey	Salinas Twp	74	307
KENNISKY								
Jas	45	m	w	PRUS	Sacramento	3-Wd Sacramento	77	274

Name	Age	S	R	B-PL	County	Locale	Series M593 Roll	Pg
KENNISON								
Grace	31	f	w	IREL	San Francisco	1-Wd San Francisco	79	6
Joe	42	m	w	ME	San Joaquin	3-Wd Stockton	86	242
Sophia	47	f	w	NH	San Francisco	8-Wd San Francisco	82	425
Wm	40	m	w	ME	San Francisco	1-Wd San Francisco	79	6
KENNISTON								
Daniel	39	m	w	MA	San Diego	San Pasqual Valley	78	524
KENNITT								
John	21	m	w	MD	San Francisco	8-Wd San Francisco	82	371
KENNITZER								
Henry	40	m	w	SAXO	San Francisco	San Francisco P O	85	774
KENNON								
Alexr	40	m	w	SCOT	San Francisco	1-Wd San Francisco	79	78
KENNSE								
J	47	m	w	OH	Nevada	Bloomfield Twp	75	99
KENNY								
Ah	14	m	c	CHIN	Yuba	Marysville	93	619
Ah	14	m	c	CHIN	Sacramento	1-Wd Sacramento	77	185
Ann	56	f	w	IREL	San Francisco	6-Wd San Francisco	81	86
Ann	24	f	w	IREL	Alameda	Brooklyn	68	31
Ann	23	f	w	IREL	San Francisco	San Francisco P O	83	99
Anna	7	f	w	CA	San Francisco	8-Wd San Francisco	82	336
Anne	26	f	w	IREL	San Francisco	San Francisco P O	83	99
Annie S D	19	f	w	NY	San Francisco	1-Wd San Francisco	79	15
Arthur	28	m	w	NY	San Francisco	San Francisco P O	80	371
Bernard	24	m	w	IREL	San Francisco	San Francisco P O	83	132
Bridget	22	f	w	IREL	San Francisco	San Francisco P O	80	361
Catherine	60	f	w	IREL	San Francisco	8-Wd San Francisco	82	472
Chester	23	m	w	NY	Los Angeles	Los Angeles	73	538
Dennis	43	m	w	IREL	Sierra	Sears Twp	89	555
Domingo	56	m	w	IREL	Santa Clara	2-Wd San Jose	88	309
Edward	30	m	w	IREL	San Francisco	8-Wd San Francisco	82	313
Edwd T	27	m	w	NY	San Francisco	1-Wd San Francisco	79	103
Frances	35	f	w	IREL	San Francisco	San Francisco P O	83	202
Francis	35	f	w	IREL	San Francisco	San Francisco P O	83	203
Frank G	28	m	w	IREL	San Francisco	8-Wd San Francisco	82	362
George	28	m	w	MA	Solano	Montezuma Twp	90	67
George S	47	m	w	IREL	San Francisco	2-Wd San Francisco	79	248
Henry	25	m	w	IREL	San Francisco	6-Wd San Francisco	81	92
Henry	23	m	w	IA	Sacramento	San Joaquin Twp	77	396
Hiram	34	m	w	MA	Sonoma	Vallejo Twp	91	460
Isaac	25	m	w	NY	San Francisco	5-Wd San Francisco	81	6
James	48	m	w	IREL	San Francisco	11-Wd San Francisc	84	438
James	40	m	w	MA	San Francisco	San Francisco P O	83	133
James	35	m	w	IREL	San Francisco	1-Wd San Francisco	79	74
James	30	m	w	IREL	San Francisco	5-Wd San Francisco	81	17
James	30	m	w	IREL	Monterey	San Juan Twp	74	410
James	28	m	w	IREL	San Francisco	San Francisco P O	83	221
James	16	m	w	RI	Sacramento	Georgianna Twp	77	129
Jas	40	m	w	IREL	Sierra	Gibson Twp	89	538
Jas	28	m	w	IREL	San Francisco	8-Wd San Francisco	82	339
Johin	70	m	w	ME	Sonoma	Petaluma Twp	91	321
John	41	m	w	IREL	San Francisco	San Francisco P O	83	133
John	38	m	w	IREL	San Francisco	1-Wd San Francisco	79	82
John	36	m	w	IREL	Yuba	Marysville	93	595
John	35	m	w	IREL	San Francisco	San Francisco P O	83	155
John	35	m	w	NY	San Francisco	San Francisco P O	83	395
John	35	m	w	IREL	San Francisco	San Francisco P O	83	133
John	30	m	w	IREL	Sacramento	4-Wd Sacramento	77	359
John	29	m	w	IREL	San Francisco	11-Wd San Francisc	84	586
John	23	m	w	CANA	Sonoma	Vallejo Twp	91	454
John	23	m	w	IREL	San Francisco	1-Wd San Francisco	79	113
John B	24	m	w	IREL	Nevada	Meadow Lake Twp	75	268
Joseph	26	m	w	CT	Sacramento	Granite Twp	77	144
Julia	28	f	w	IREL	San Francisco	5-Wd San Francisco	81	33
Kate	25	f	w	NY	Sonoma	Petaluma Twp	91	345
Kate	23	f	w	IREL	San Francisco	8-Wd San Francisco	82	337
Kate	21	f	w	IREL	San Francisco	8-Wd San Francisco	82	374
Kate	20	f	w	IREL	San Francisco	San Francisco P O	85	747
Lizzie	18	f	w	AL	Santa Clara	2-Wd San Jose	88	309
Margaret	18	f	w	IREL	San Francisco	11-Wd San Francisc	84	510
Margt	40	f	w	IREL	San Francisco	8-Wd San Francisco	82	322
Margt	21	f	w	IREL	San Francisco	8-Wd San Francisco	82	289
Martin	35	m	w	IREL	San Francisco	8-Wd San Francisco	82	369
Mary	60	f	w	NC	San Joaquin	3-Wd Stockton	86	233
Mary	30	f	w	IREL	Yuba	Marysville	93	583
Mary	23	f	w	IREL	San Francisco	8-Wd San Francisco	82	316
Mary Henry	38	f	w	IREL	San Francisco	San Francisco P O	83	129
Mary J	30	f	w	IREL	San Francisco	San Francisco P O	83	155
Michael	55	m	w	IREL	Sutter	Sutter Twp	92	124
Michael	51	m	w	IREL	San Francisco	San Francisco P O	80	398
Michael	25	m	w	IREL	Marin	Point Reyes Twp	74	21
Michl	24	m	w	IREL	San Francisco	1-Wd San Francisco	79	132
Pat	24	m	w	IREL	San Joaquin	Elkhorn Twp	86	69
Patrick	40	m	w	IREL	San Francisco	1-Wd San Francisco	79	104
Patrick	38	m	w	IREL	Sonoma	Vallejo Twp	91	462
Patrick	32	m	w	IREL	San Francisco	11-Wd San Francisc	84	487
Sarah	24	f	w	IREL	San Francisco	8-Wd San Francisco	82	350
Sarah	16	f	w	ENGL	San Francisco	1-Wd San Francisco	79	26
T J	37	m	w	ME	Alameda	Oakland	68	170
Theresa	59	f	w	MO	Shasta	Shasta P O	89	461
Theresa	18	f	w	CA	Santa Clara	Redwood Twp	88	122
Thomas	30	m	w	IREL	San Mateo	Schoolhouse Statio	87	343
Thomas	28	m	w	IREL	San Francisco	1-Wd San Francisco	79	77
Thomas	28	m	w	IREL	Alameda	Oakland	68	183
Thomas	21	m	w	CA	Contra Costa	Martinez P O	71	447
Thos	43	m	w	IREL	Solano	Vallejo	90	190

© 2001 by Heritage Quest. All rights reserved.

							Series M593	
Name	Age	S	R	B-PL	County	Locale	Roll	Pg
Thos	36	m	w	IREL	San Francisco	11-Wd San Francisc	84	641
Wm	86	m	w	IREL	San Francisco	11-Wd San Francisc	84	613
KENOILLE								
Joseph	35	m	w	CANA	Santa Cruz	Santa Cruz	89	403
KENON								
Annie	27	f	w	IREL	San Francisco	San Francisco P O	85	791
KENOYER								
David	47	m	w	IN	Humboldt	Mattole Twp	72	285
KENREO								
Ah	1	f	c	CA	Solano	Vallejo	90	174
KENRICK								
Michael	26	m	w	IREL	Butte	Chico Twp	70	35
KENRY								
James	36	m	w	IREL	Nevada	Eureka Twp	75	135
KENSEL								
William	20	m	w	KY	Siskiyou	Surprise Valley Tw	89	638
KENSHE								
Charles	30	m	w	PRUS	Placer	Bath P O	76	441
KENSON								
S	36	f	w	IREL	Alameda	Oakland	68	175
KENSTER								
Lawrance	57	m	w	PRUS	El Dorado	Cosumnes Twp	72	19
KENSTOR								
Michael	43	m	w	IREL	Nevada	Washington Twp	75	342
KENT								
Ah	16	m	c	CHIN	Nevada	Nevada Twp	75	314
Charity	30	f	b	MD	San Francisco	San Francisco P O	80	371
Charles	49	m	w	ENGL	Santa Clara	Gilroy Twp	88	82
Chas	48	m	w	NY	Nevada	Nevada Twp	75	291
Chas C	36	m	w	MO	San Luis Obispo	Santa Rosa Twp	87	325
Cora N	15	f	w	MA	San Francisco	2-Wd San Francisco	79	282
Cyntha	36	f	w	PA	Amador	Ione City P O	69	356
David	27	m	w	CANA	Santa Cruz	Santa Cruz Twp	89	392
E B	39	m	w	IL	Alameda	Oakland	68	263
Edwin A	46	m	w	NH	Amador	Volcano P O	69	379
Elisu E	21	m	w	ME	Mendocino	Casper & Big Rvr	74	164
Ellen	85	f	w	IREL	Humboldt	Pacific Twp	72	294
Fredk W	28	m	w	CANA	Santa Barbara	Santa Barbara P O	87	453
George W	52	m	w	NH	Monterey	San Antonio Twp	74	318
J E	28	m	w	NY	Solano	Vallejo	90	200
J W	21	m	w	SWED	Alameda	Oakland	68	222
James	22	m	w	CANA	Santa Clara	Santa Clara Twp	88	167
James H	56	m	w	OH	Sacramento	San Joaquin Twp	77	404
James O	10	m	w	MO	El Dorado	Placerville Twp	72	104
Jennie	15	f	w	MA	San Francisco	San Francisco P O	85	746
John	33	m	w	IREL	Santa Clara	1-Wd San Jose	88	230
John	26	m	w	CANA	Santa Cruz	Santa Cruz Twp	89	387
John	25	m	w	SCOT	Yuba	Marysville	93	587
John E	36	m	w	AL	Napa	Napa	75	47
Joshua	21	m	w	ENGL	Marin	San Rafael Twp	74	35
Louis A	28	m	w	VA	San Francisco	8-Wd San Francisco	82	448
Mary	45	f	w	IREL	San Francisco	8-Wd San Francisco	82	487
Michael F	37	m	w	IREL	Sacramento	2-Wd Sacramento	77	227
Morris	43	m	w	CANA	Yolo	Cottonwood Twp	93	470
Owen F	50	m	w	VT	San Luis Obispo	Arroyo Grande Twp	87	272
Peter	50	m	w	MA	San Francisco	6-Wd San Francisco	81	92
R T	33	m	w	OH	San Francisco	San Francisco P O	85	780
Richard	50	m	w	ENGL	San Francisco	2-Wd San Francisco	79	261
S	37	m	w	IREL	San Joaquin	2-Wd Stockton	86	167
Samuel	40	m	w	OH	Sacramento	Natomas Twp	77	166
Samuel H	36	m	w	MA	San Francisco	8-Wd San Francisco	82	298
Sherman	40	m	w	NC	El Dorado	Lake Valley Twp	72	63
Sylvester	22	m	w	IA	Solano	Tremont Twp	90	36
T W	45	m	w	NY	Yuba	Marysville	93	616
Terese	71	f	w	SAXO	San Francisco	San Francisco P O	85	772
Thadius	30	m	w	MA	San Francisco	8-Wd San Francisco	82	347
W H	53	m	w	VA	Sutter	Sutter Twp	92	117
William	36	m	w	VA	Placer	Dutch Flat P O	76	415
William	33	m	w	IREL	Santa Clara	1-Wd San Jose	88	260
William	32	m	w	ENGL	Alpine	Silver Mtn P O	69	307
William H	49	m	w	ME	Mendocino	Casper & Big Rvr	74	164
Wm	53	m	w	NY	Nevada	Nevada Twp	75	295
Wm	27	m	w	VT	Nevada	Washington Twp	75	346
Wm T	31	m	w	KY	Nevada	Meadow Lake Twp	75	268
KENTANA								
Thos	38	m	w	NM	Mendocino	Round Valley Twp	74	216
KENTER								
Henry	21	m	w	BREM	San Francisco	11-Wd San Francisc	84	697
KENTERICK								
Thomas	28	m	w	PA	San Francisco	San Francisco P O	83	218
KENTFIELD								
John	48	m	w	NY	San Francisco	7-Wd San Francisco	81	273
KENTILLEN								
Margaret	39	f	w	IREL	San Francisco	San Francisco P O	85	766
KENTNER								
Jacob S	33	m	w	PA	Shasta	Fort Crook P O	89	474
KENTON								
Thomas	38	m	w	KY	Solano	Suisun Twp	90	100
KENTRICK								
John	24	m	w	PA	Mendocino	Round Valley Twp	74	217
KENTRON								
Stephen	40	m	w	PA	Amador	Drytown P O	69	419
KENTZ								
Andrew	38	m	w	ASEA	San Francisco	7-Wd San Francisco	81	166
Charles	21	m	w	IREL	San Francisco	2-Wd San Francisco	79	213
KENTZEL								
James	27	m	w	PA	San Francisco	San Francisco P O	80	384

							Series M593	
Name	Age	S	R	B-PL	County	Locale	Roll	Pg
William	50	m	w	PA	San Francisco	San Francisco P O	80	397
KENY								
Ah	30	m	c	CHIN	Sacramento	1-Wd Sacramento	77	198
KENYON								
Ah	34	m	c	CHIN	Plumas	Plumas Twp	77	31
Chas	46	m	w	NY	Shasta	Millville P O	89	494
Curtis G	24	m	w	NY	Yolo	Cache Crk Twp	93	453
D K	38	m	w	NY	Humboldt	Eureka Twp	72	280
E B	44	m	w	RI	Calaveras	Copperopolis P O	70	226
E B	30	m	w	NY	Sacramento	3-Wd Sacramento	77	284
Francis	51	m	w	NY	Shasta	Millville P O	89	483
Frank	28	m	w	MI	San Francisco	2-Wd San Francisco	79	230
George	28	m	w	IL	San Bernardino	San Bernardino Twp	78	441
James M	53	m	w	OH	Santa Clara	Santa Clara Twp	88	170
Jas R	36	m	w	NY	Siskiyou	Scott Valley Twp	89	621
Kate	44	f	w	NY	Santa Clara	1-Wd San Jose	88	236
Michael	40	m	w	IREL	Santa Clara	San Jose Twp	88	185
Wm	61	m	w	NY	Shasta	Shasta P O	89	461
KENZ								
Wm B	33	m	w	IA	Shasta	Millville P O	89	487
KENZEE								
Robert	38	m	w	PRUS	San Francisco	San Francisco P O	83	337
KENZIE								
David R M	39	m	w	SCOT	Fresno	Millerton P O	72	147
Emmett	41	m	w	IN	Santa Clara	Burnett Twp	88	40
James	27	m	w	PA	Sacramento	San Joaquin Twp	77	394
Mary	29	f	w	PA	San Francisco	6-Wd San Francisco	81	118
KEO								
Ah	37	m	c	CHIN	Sacramento	1-Wd Sacramento	77	193
Ah	30	m	c	CHIN	Butte	Kimshew Tpw	70	84
Ah	30	m	c	CHIN	El Dorado	Coloma Twp	72	6
Ah	30	m	c	CHIN	San Francisco	8-Wd San Francisco	82	341
Ah	20	f	c	CHIN	Amador	Fiddletown P O	69	428
Chuc	28	m	c	CHIN	Sacramento	1-Wd Sacramento	77	193
KEOBER								
Henery	34	m	w	HANO	San Francisco	7-Wd San Francisco	81	209
KEOCH								
John	30	m	c	CHIN	Contra Costa	Martinez Twp	71	349
KEOFENBACH								
Jas	32	m	w	PRUS	Sutter	Nicolaus Twp	92	106
KEOGH								
Bridget	35	f	w	IREL	San Francisco	11-Wd San Francisc	84	499
John	34	m	w	IREL	San Francisco	San Francisco P O	83	60
John	27	m	w	IREL	Solano	Vallejo	90	200
M	40	f	w	IREL	Sonoma	Bodega Twp	91	258
Martin	49	m	w	IREL	San Francisco	1-Wd San Francisco	79	112
Michael	24	m	w	IREL	Marin	Sausalito Twp	74	73
Patrick	38	m	w	IREL	Monterey	Castroville Twp	74	336
Timothy	35	m	w	IREL	San Francisco	San Francisco P O	83	202
KEOHOE								
Anna	42	f	w	IREL	San Francisco	11-Wd San Francisc	84	462
KEON								
Ah	5	m	c	CHIN	San Francisco	2-Wd San Francisco	79	196
Ah	40	m	c	CHIN	Sierra	Table Rock Twp	89	544
Ah	26	m	c	CHIN	Calaveras	San Andreas P O	70	155
Ah	25	m	c	CHIN	Placer	Clipper Gap P O	76	393
Ah	18	m	c	CHIN	San Francisco	San Francisco P O	83	170
Ah	18	m	c	CHIN	San Francisco	2-Wd San Francisco	79	177
Barney	17	m	w	IREL	San Joaquin	1-Wd Stockton	86	134
How	17	m	c	CHIN	Nevada	Bridgeport Twp	75	111
John	9	m	w	CA	Marin	San Rafael Twp	74	28
Kin	43	m	c	CHIN	Calaveras	San Andreas P O	70	161
KEONARSON								
John	28	m	w	DENM	Sonoma	Petaluma Twp	91	326
KEONG								
Ah	50	m	c	CHIN	Placer	Emigrant Gap P O	76	417
Ah	45	m	c	CHIN	Placer	Auburn P O	76	378
Ah	36	m	c	CHIN	Placer	Clipper Gap P O	76	376
Ah	28	m	c	CHIN	Placer	Dutch Flat P O	76	411
Ah	25	m	c	CHIN	Placer	Dutch Flat P O	76	414
Ah	25	m	c	CHIN	Placer	Summit P O	76	496
Ah	23	m	c	CHIN	Placer	Auburn P O	76	363
Ah	15	m	c	CHIN	San Francisco	3-Wd San Francisco	79	304
KEONIG								
Jacob	36	m	w	BADE	Santa Clara	1-Wd San Jose	88	257
KEORN								
Michael	37	m	w	CANA	San Joaquin	2-Wd Stockton	86	169
KEOUGH								
John	35	m	w	IREL	Solano	Benicia	90	10
John	34	m	w	IREL	Mariposa	Mariposa P O	74	137
John	32	m	w	IN	Kern	Havilah P O	73	341
Martin	26	m	w	IREL	Placer	Dutch Flat P O	76	414
Patrick	38	m	w	IREL	San Francisco	2-Wd San Francisco	79	209
Wm	30	m	w	IREL	San Francisco	8-Wd San Francisco	82	320
KEOW								
Ah	30	m	c	CHIN	Santa Cruz	Watsonville	89	377
KEOWN								
Edward	26	m	w	IREL	Santa Clara	Fremont Twp	88	53
James	23	m	w	ENGL	Santa Clara	Fremont Twp	88	41
KEP								
Ah	44	m	c	CHIN	Sacramento	Granite Twp	77	151
Ah	33	m	c	CHIN	Placer	Pino Twp	76	471
Ah	32	m	c	CHIN	El Dorado	Cosumnes Twp	72	20
Ah	29	m	c	CHIN	Nevada	Meadow Lake Twp	75	256
Ah	15	m	c	CHIN	Nevada	Nevada Twp	75	317
Di	30	m	c	CHIN	Nevada	Nevada Twp	75	314
Wm J	56	m	w	NY	San Francisco	San Francisco P O	85	877

© 2001 by Heritage Quest. All rights reserved.

California 1870 Census

Name	Age	S	R	B-PL	County	Locale	Roll	Pg
						Series M593		
KEPHART								
Geo	41	m	w	OH	El Dorado	Kelsey Twp	72	61
KEPLER								
Henry	27	m	w	PA	Marin	Sausalito Twp	74	74
Lewis	32	m	w	PA	San Francisco	San Francisco P O	83	63
Philip	32	m	w	WURT	San Francisco	1-Wd San Francisco	79	64
William	4	m	w	CA	Amador	Jackson P O	69	318
KEPNER								
S K M	49	m	w	PA	San Francisco	3-Wd San Francisco	79	316
KEPP								
Ah	35	m	c	CHIN	Amador	Jackson P O	69	332
KEPPEL								
Jacob	26	m	w	HOLL	Marin	Tomales Twp	74	86
KEPPER								
Chas	40	m	w	IREL	Butte	Chico Twp	70	46
KEPPLE								
Gariot	40	m	w	MI	Butte	Hamilton Twp	70	63
John	44	m	w	BADE	Butte	Ophir Twp	70	111
Mary	1M	f	w	CA	Butte	Hamilton Twp	70	65
William	25	m	w	ME	San Francisco	8-Wd San Francisco	82	382
KEPPLER								
August	53	m	w	PA	Siskiyou	Yreka Twp	89	664
Chas	35	m	w	FRAN	Siskiyou	Callahan P O	89	624
William	62	m	w	WURT	Shasta	Stillwater P O	89	480
KEPPY								
Martin	22	m	w	IL	Butte	Chico Twp	70	37
KEPTER								
Lara	32	f	w	CAME	San Joaquin	1-Wd Stockton	86	121
Lara	32	f	w	CAME	San Joaquin	1-Wd Stockton	86	120
KER								
Ah	52	m	c	CHIN	Amador	Volcano P O	69	387
Ah	20	m	c	CHIN	Sacramento	1-Wd Sacramento	77	205
Chong	40	m	c	CHIN	Trinity	Weaverville Pct	92	231
KERANARZ								
Gostaf	19	m	w	PRUS	Los Angeles	Los Angeles	73	511
KERAND								
John	47	m	w	FRAN	El Dorado	White Oak Twp	72	142
KERBAZIA								
John	56	m	w	ITAL	Nevada	Bloomfield Twp	75	95
KERBLEY								
Michael	29	m	w	BADE	El Dorado	Mud Springs Twp	72	71
KERBY								
Fred	46	m	w	ENGL	Butte	Ophir Twp	70	99
Fred	37	m	w	MO	Butte	Oregon Twp	70	122
James	32	m	w	IREL	San Francisco	1-Wd San Francisco	79	113
John	44	m	w	IREL	San Francisco	11-Wd San Francisc	84	568
K	43	m	w	CANA	Alameda	Oakland	68	249
Mary	28	f	w	IREL	San Francisco	11-Wd San Francisc	84	585
KERCH								
Julius	55	f	w	PRUS	Alameda	Alameda	68	18
KERCHAM								
M E	12	f	w	CA	Yuba	Marysville	93	609
KERCHBAUM								
Enna	28	f	w	ENGL	Colusa	Colusa	71	291
KERCHEBERD								
J K	31	m	w	PRUS	Alameda	Oakland	68	264
KERCHENTHAL								
H A	50	m	w	ENGL	Amador	Fiddletown P O	69	430
KERCHEVAL								
Reuben	49	m	w	OH	Sacramento	Franklin Twp	77	118
KERCHMAN								
M	25	f	w	GERM	Sacramento	1-Wd Sacramento	77	175
KERCHOFF								
Henry	26	m	w	PRUS	San Francisco	San Francisco P O	83	386
KERE								
Ah	23	m	c	CHIN	Santa Clara	Gilroy Twp	88	75
KEREM								
Chah	20	m	c	CHIN	Marin	San Rafael Twp	74	59
KEREN								
John	45	m	w	IREL	Yolo	Putah Twp	93	514
John	21	m	w	NY	Los Angeles	Los Angeles	73	564
Margareta	1M	f	w	CA	Los Angeles	Los Angeles	73	564
Richard	27	m	w	MD	Los Angeles	Los Angeles	73	558
KEREY								
L	31	m	w	PRUS	San Joaquin	Liberty Twp	86	95
KERFOOT								
Ezra	51	m	w	VA	San Bernardino	San Bernardino Twp	78	424
Ezra	27	m	w	MO	San Bernardino	San Bernardino Twp	78	430
John F	23	m	w	MO	San Bernardino	San Bernardino Twp	78	424
Lee	46	m	w	ENGL	Amador	Sutter Crk P O	69	401
KERGAN								
James	35	m	w	TX	Calaveras	San Andreas P O	70	204
KERGEN								
Frederick	33	m	w	HANO	Sacramento	2-Wd Sacramento	77	210
KERICK								
Richard	40	m	w	IREL	San Francisco	11-Wd San Francisc	84	458
KERIGAN								
Jas	28	m	w	IREL	Solano	Vallejo	90	203
KERIN								
James	36	m	w	LA	Marin	Tomales Twp	74	87
KERINA								
Robert	25	m	w	IREL	Santa Clara	Santa Clara Twp	88	175
KERING								
Abram	42	m	w	MA	Calaveras	San Andreas P O	70	210
KERINS								
Michael	42	m	w	IREL	Tulare	Visalia	92	297

Name	Age	S	R	B-PL	County	Locale	Roll	Pg
						Series M593		
KERK								
J W	45	m	w	NH	San Joaquin	Elliott Twp	86	76
KERKEY								
Henery	40	m	w	NY	San Francisco	7-Wd San Francisco	81	206
KERKWOD								
William	48	m	w	SCOT	Contra Costa	Martinez P O	71	453
KERLAN								
Chas	60	m	w	IREL	San Francisco	1-Wd San Francisco	79	123
KERLEY								
Jas H	38	m	w	TN	Butte	Ophir Twp	70	105
Julia	30	f	w	IREL	Alameda	Eden Twp	68	81
Wm T	32	m	w	TN	Shasta	Fort Crook P O	89	476
KERLIN								
Edward	30	m	w	PA	San Francisco	8-Wd San Francisco	82	437
Rebecca	39	f	w	PA	San Francisco	San Francisco P O	83	140
KERLY								
Oren	20	m	w	CANA	Butte	Chico Twp	70	31
KERM								
Benj F	33	m	w	PA	Marin	Tomales Twp	74	76
Thomas	30	m	w	IREL	Colusa	Colusa Twp	71	284
KERMAN								
Barney	26	m	w	IREL	San Francisco	5-Wd San Francisco	81	7
Jas	50	m	w	IREL	San Francisco	San Francisco P O	83	132
John	21	m	w	NY	San Francisco	San Francisco P O	83	106
Mary	28	f	w	IREL	San Francisco	7-Wd San Francisco	81	273
Peter	25	m	w	NY	San Francisco	San Francisco P O	85	843
KERMOCHTON								
John C	35	m	w	NY	Yolo	Putah Twp	93	523
KERN								
Ah	18	m	c	CHIN	Mendocino	Point Arena Twp	74	205
Charles	32	m	w	GERM	Alameda	Washington Twp	68	290
Chas	43	m	w	BAVA	Shasta	Shasta P O	89	455
Gilroy	40	m	w	NY	San Joaquin	2-Wd Stockton	86	164
Hugh	64	m	w	IREL	Sacramento	Franklin Twp	77	105
Jacob	36	m	w	SWIT	Tulare	Kings Rvr Twp	92	252
James	36	m	w	NY	Santa Cruz	Soquel Twp	89	443
James	19	m	w	OH	San Joaquin	Elkhorn Twp	86	56
John	60	m	w	PA	San Francisco	1-Wd San Francisco	79	80
John	50	m	w	BAVA	Santa Clara	2-Wd San Jose	88	323
John	36	m	w	IL	Tulare	Tule Rvr Twp	92	267
John	28	m	w	NY	San Francisco	San Francisco P O	83	209
John	20	m	w	WURT	Santa Clara	2-Wd San Jose	88	281
John N	46	m	w	NY	Tulare	Visalia	92	295
Paul	40	m	w	SWIT	Los Angeles	Los Angeles	73	513
Peter	43	m	w	PA	Butte	Chico Twp	70	45
Victor	40	m	w	FRAN	Shasta	French Gulch P O	89	467
KERNA								
A W	31	m	w	MI	Alameda	Oakland	68	262
KERNAHAN								
Elizabeth	27	f	w	WI	Inyo	Bishop Crk Twp	73	312
Wm	47	m	w	IREL	Marin	San Rafael Twp	74	34
KERNAL								
Jas	25	m	w	IREL	Solano	Vallejo	90	203
KERNAN								
Anne	45	f	w	IREL	San Francisco	San Francisco P O	83	99
Edward	37	m	w	IREL	Stanislaus	Empire Twp	92	28
Eliza	30	f	w	IREL	San Francisco	11-Wd San Francisc	84	555
John	36	m	w	IREL	Placer	Roseville P O	76	351
Mary	13	f	w	CA	San Francisco	11-Wd San Francisc	84	431
Patrick	36	m	w	IREL	San Francisco	San Francisco P O	85	868
Thomas	40	m	w	MD	Yuba	Marysville	93	583
KERNARD								
Paul	8	m	w	NY	San Francisco	11-Wd San Francisc	84	565
KERNAY								
John	40	m	w	IREL	San Francisco	11-Wd San Francisc	84	485
KERNEL								
Mike	42	m	w	NY	San Francisco	11-Wd San Francisc	84	673
KERNER								
Henry	32	m	w	SAXO	El Dorado	Diamond Springs Tw	72	23
Lizzy	17	f	w	PA	San Francisco	6-Wd San Francisco	81	73
Peter	52	m	w	PRUS	San Francisco	5-Wd San Francisco	81	5
KERNES								
James	34	m	w	IREL	Fresno	Kings Rvr P O	72	214
KERNEY								
Arthur	38	m	w	IREL	San Francisco	San Francisco P O	80	382
Catherine	30	f	w	IREL	Alameda	Brooklyn	68	26
Frank	34	m	w	OH	Alameda	Alameda	68	12
Mary	40	f	w	IREL	San Francisco	San Francisco P O	85	776
Michael	34	m	w	IREL	Tuolumne	Sonora P O	93	329
Thomas	40	m	w	IREL	Inyo	Cerro Gordo Twp	73	319
William	32	m	w	IREL	Alameda	Oakland	68	152
KERNIN								
Patrick	28	m	w	IREL	San Francisco	San Francisco P O	83	7
KERNINISH								
Paul	35	m	w	SWIT	Sonoma	Bodega Twp	91	253
KERNN								
Anderson	50	m	w	MA	Tuolumne	Chinese Camp P O	93	363
KERNON								
Bridget	15	f	w	IREL	San Francisco	San Francisco P O	83	151
John	30	m	w	IREL	San Francisco	San Francisco P O	85	876
KERNOW								
Thomas	39	m	w	ENGL	Nevada	Bridgeport Twp	75	119
KERNS								
A H	38	m	w	MA	Tuolumne	Chinese Camp P O	93	368
Catherine	20	f	w	IREL	Santa Cruz	Pajaro Twp	89	346
Ellen	35	f	w	IREL	Alameda	Oakland	68	178
George W	28	m	w	SCOT	San Francisco	San Francisco P O	83	223

© 2001 by Heritage Quest. All rights reserved.

Name	Age	S	R	B-PL	County	Locale	Roll	Pg
Henry	50	m	w	IREL	Yuba	Marysville	93	577
John	45	m	w	ME	San Francisco	1-Wd San Francisco	79	59
John	28	m	w	IREL	San Francisco	11-Wd San Francisc	84	554
John	15	m	w	CA	Sonoma	Sonoma Twp	91	431
Martin	35	m	w	IREL	Nevada	Grass Valley Twp	75	151
Mathew	40	m	w	IREL	San Francisco	8-Wd San Francisco	82	434
Nicholas	38	m	w	MO	Siskiyou	Surprise Valley Tw	89	640
Richd	22	m	w	ME	San Francisco	1-Wd San Francisco	79	59
Robert	44	m	w	SCOT	San Francisco	San Francisco P O	83	260
Thomas	37	m	w	IREL	Santa Cruz	Pajaro Twp	89	343
Thomas J	33	m	w	IL	Los Angeles	Los Nietos Twp	73	592
KERNY								
Edward	17	m	w	CT	Los Angeles	Los Angeles	73	570
John	40	m	w	IREL	Alameda	Oakland	68	138
Margaret	25	f	w	IREL	San Mateo	Half Moon Bay P O	87	401
KEROS								
Jose	40	m	w	MEXI	San Bernardino	San Salvador Twp	78	458
KEROTH								
Ignatio	38	m	w	MEXI	Sacramento	Cosumnes Twp	77	92
KERR								
A W	42	m	w	PA	Amador	Ione City P O	69	365
Alexander	60	m	w	SCOT	Placer	Roseville P O	76	352
Alexander	30	m	w	PA	Monterey	Pajaro Twp	74	375
Alexander	24	m	w	CANA	Solano	Vallejo	90	212
Andrew	42	m	w	IREL	Alameda	Washington Twp	68	271
Andrew	36	m	w	IREL	San Francisco	1-Wd San Francisco	79	17
Andrew	35	m	w	IREL	San Francisco	1-Wd San Francisco	79	6
Charles	39	m	w	IREL	San Francisco	11-Wd San Francisc	84	431
Cyntha A	13	f	w	OR	Butte	Chico Twp	70	25
David	26	m	w	VT	San Mateo	San Mateo P O	87	360
E J	30	m	w	NY	San Joaquin	2-Wd Stockton	86	188
Earl	30	m	w	IREL	San Francisco	6-Wd San Francisco	81	101
Edward	52	m	w	SCOT	San Francisco	San Francisco P O	83	45
Eliza L	8	f	w	CA	Sacramento	2-Wd Sacramento	77	251
Frederick	28	m	w	MA	San Francisco	8-Wd San Francisco	82	445
G C	52	m	w	MA	Sacramento	3-Wd Sacramento	77	287
Geo H	40	m	w	PA	Sacramento	San Joaquin Twp	77	396
Hiram	26	m	w	MO	Stanislaus	Empire Twp	92	36
Honora	53	f	w	IREL	San Francisco	8-Wd San Francisco	82	480
Israel	46	m	w	NY	Solano	Tremont Twp	90	32
J H	46	m	w	PA	Sacramento	San Joaquin Twp	77	399
James	52	m	w	PA	Placer	Bath P O	76	451
James	40	m	w	IREL	San Francisco	San Francisco P O	83	310
James	27	m	w	IREL	Sonoma	Analy Twp	91	226
James	24	m	w	SCOT	Nevada	Grass Valley Twp	75	179
James E	33	m	w	VA	Sacramento	2-Wd Sacramento	77	251
James P	36	m	w	LA	Sacramento	2-Wd Sacramento	77	251
Jane	27	f	w	IREL	Santa Cruz	Watsonville	89	370
John	41	m	w	IREL	San Francisco	11-Wd San Francisc	84	430
John	40	m	w	IREL	San Francisco	5-Wd San Francisco	81	32
John	39	m	w	MO	Stanislaus	Empire Twp	92	31
John	38	m	w	PA	Amador	Drytown P O	69	417
John	38	m	w	SCOT	Yuba	Marysville	93	574
John	33	m	w	IREL	San Francisco	San Francisco P O	83	77
John	31	m	w	ENGL	Santa Clara	2-Wd San Jose	88	287
John	30	m	w	BADE	San Francisco	7-Wd San Francisco	81	221
John B	24	m	w	OH	San Joaquin	1-Wd Stockton	86	131
Jonathan	50	m	w	MA	Mariposa	Mariposa P O	74	130
Kate	22	f	w	MI	San Diego	San Diego	78	500
Martin	22	m	w	IREL	San Francisco	3-Wd San Francisco	79	312
Matthew	26	m	w	IREL	San Francisco	San Francisco P O	83	246
R H	45	m	w	PA	Amador	Drytown P O	69	416
Robert	36	m	w	IREL	Sonoma	Bodega Twp	91	249
Thomas	27	m	w	PA	Amador	Amador City P O	69	391
Thomas C	68	m	w	MO	Stanislaus	Empire Twp	92	31
Thos	45	m	w	IREL	San Francisco	San Francisco P O	83	103
W J	35	m	w	IL	San Francisco	San Francisco P O	85	807
William	67	m	w	PA	Placer	Bath P O	76	425
William	60	m	w	IREL	Santa Clara	2-Wd San Jose	88	283
William	44	m	w	TN	Humboldt	Mattole Twp	72	287
William	32	m	w	TN	Sonoma	Santa Rosa	91	424
William	29	m	w	IREL	San Francisco	11-Wd San Francisc	84	432
Wm	59	m	w	PA	Yuba	East Bear Rvr Twp	93	541
Wm	38	m	w	TN	Sonoma	Santa Rosa	91	401
Wm J	44	m	w	IREL	San Francisco	1-Wd San Francisco	79	22
KERRAN								
Thoro	38	m	w	NY	San Francisco	8-Wd San Francisco	82	342
KERRAY								
Johnathan	35	m	w	MO	Sutter	Nicolaus Twp	92	110
KERRE								
Sanford H	53	m	w	KY	Monterey	Castroville Twp	74	339
KERREELY								
Patrick	35	m	w	IREL	San Francisco	8-Wd San Francisco	82	335
KERREGAN								
Edward	37	m	w	IREL	San Francisco	11-Wd San Francisc	84	442
Mathew	32	m	w	CANA	Humboldt	Eel Rvr Twp	72	247
KERRICAN								
Jno	22	m	w	ITAL	Butte	Ophir Twp	70	107
KERRICH								
L M	42	m	w	KY	San Joaquin	Douglas Twp	86	30
KERRICK								
Harrison	45	m	w	KY	Stanislaus	San Joaquin Twp	92	78
Joseph	45	m	w	KY	Stanislaus	Buena Vista Twp	92	11
Wallack	38	m	w	KY	San Joaquin	Castoria Twp	86	5
KERRIFIC								
Margaret	31	f	w	IREL	San Joaquin	2-Wd Stockton	86	173

Name	Age	S	R	B-PL	County	Locale	Roll	Pg
KERRIGAN								
A	40	m	w	IREL	Yuba	Rose Bar Twp	93	656
Ambrose	33	m	w	IREL	Yuba	Rose Bar Twp	93	658
Cath	23	f	w	IREL	San Francisco	San Francisco P O	85	791
E	38	f	w	IREL	Calaveras	Copperopolis P O	70	221
Frank	30	m	w	IREL	San Francisco	San Francisco P O	83	264
John	60	m	w	IREL	San Francisco	8-Wd San Francisco	82	460
John	26	m	w	AUSL	San Francisco	San Francisco P O	83	192
John	24	m	w	CHIL	Marin	San Rafael Twp	74	40
Mary	39	f	w	IREL	San Francisco	San Francisco P O	83	161
Michael	45	m	w	IREL	Stanislaus	Empire Twp	92	48
Micheal	40	m	w	IREL	San Francisco	11-Wd San Francisc	84	440
Pak	26	m	w	IREL	San Francisco	San Francisco P O	83	65
Pat	28	m	w	IREL	Yuba	Rose Bar Twp	93	656
Thomas	37	m	w	IL	El Dorado	Diamond Springs Tw	72	25
Tim	27	m	w	IREL	San Francisco	5-Wd San Francisco	81	7
Tin	26	m	w	KY	San Francisco	5-Wd San Francisco	81	9
Wm H	42	m	w	IREL	San Francisco	5-Wd San Francisco	81	12
KERRIN								
Thos	22	m	w	CT	San Francisco	1-Wd San Francisco	79	65
KERRINGTON								
Henry	47	m	w	CT	San Francisco	San Francisco P O	83	9
KERRINS								
Christopher	38	m	w	IREL	San Francisco	11-Wd San Francisc	84	478
KERRIS								
George	27	m	w	PA	San Francisco	San Francisco P O	83	207
KERRISON								
George G	45	m	w	ENGL	San Francisco	2-Wd San Francisco	79	241
Wm	22	m	w	LA	San Francisco	11-Wd San Francisc	84	625
KERRON								
Jane	20	f	w	SCOT	Marin	San Rafael Twp	74	33
KERRUISH								
Edward	47	m	w	IOFM	San Francisco	11-Wd San Francisc	84	581
Thomas	32	m	w	IOFM	San Francisco	11-Wd San Francisc	84	581
KERRY								
Catharine	53	f	w	IREL	San Francisco	11-Wd San Francisc	84	483
James	35	m	w	IREL	Placer	Bath P O	76	443
James	35	m	w	IREL	San Francisco	11-Wd San Francisc	84	501
Kate	28	f	w	IREL	Solano	Vallejo	90	185
Wm	41	m	w	IREL	Solano	Vallejo	90	197
KERSBAUM								
Geo	24	m	w	PRUS	San Joaquin	2-Wd Stockton	86	205
KERSE								
A	21	m	w	GERM	Yuba	Marysville	93	604
David	40	m	w	IREL	Los Angeles	Los Angeles	73	568
Wm	10	m	w	CA	El Dorado	Coloma Twp	72	2
KERSEY								
Gennet	19	f	w	SCOT	Sutter	Butte Twp	92	94
John	33	m	w	IREL	San Francisco	11-Wd San Francisc	84	677
John D	29	m	w	MA	Nevada	Meadow Lake Twp	75	258
Phony	21	m	w	IL	Monterey	Monterey Twp	74	347
Richard	33	m	w	IREL	Placer	Rocklin Twp	76	465
Thomas	37	m	w	KY	Sutter	Butte Twp	92	94
KERSHAW								
Henry	40	m	w	ENGL	San Francisco	San Francisco P O	80	364
Israel	54	m	w	OH	Marin	Sausalito Twp	74	67
John	42	m	w	ENGL	Tuolumne	Big Oak Flat P O	93	397
Marsden	36	m	w	NY	San Francisco	11-Wd San Francisc	84	570
KERSKER								
Margaret	54	f	w	WURT	San Francisco	San Francisco P O	83	212
KERSKI								
Charlotte	23	f	w	PRUS	San Francisco	6-Wd San Francisco	81	152
KERSON								
Michl	28	m	w	HAMB	San Francisco	1-Wd San Francisco	79	133
KERSTING								
Carl	20	m	w	HESS	Napa	Napa	75	11
KERSYLOBOHN								
Kate	19	f	w	POLA	San Francisco	San Francisco P O	83	54
KERTING								
Conrad	42	m	w	BAVA	San Francisco	8-Wd San Francisco	82	369
KERTO								
L	45	m	w	FRAN	Alameda	Murray Twp	68	127
KERTZ								
J	35	m	w	PRUS	Alameda	Murray Twp	68	108
KERVER								
Edwd J C	44	m	w	MO	Los Angeles	San Gabriel Twp	73	595
KERVIN								
James	29	m	w	IREL	Nevada	Grass Valley Twp	75	216
KERWAN								
E	24	f	w	IREL	Sacramento	3-Wd Sacramento	77	259
Michael	23	m	w	IREL	Alameda	Brooklyn Twp	68	44
Morris	32	m	w	IREL	San Francisco	San Francisco P O	83	145
KERWIN								
Annie	26	f	w	IREL	San Francisco	San Francisco P O	83	325
Donnell	23	m	w	SCOT	Kern	Tehachapi P O	73	356
Hugh	28	m	w	IREL	San Francisco	San Francisco P O	85	790
Margaret	24	f	w	IREL	San Francisco	11-Wd San Francisc	84	639
Patrick	32	m	w	IREL	Kern	Havilah P O	73	339
R	38	m	w	CANA	San Joaquin	2-Wd Stockton	86	200
Thomas	40	m	w	IREL	Santa Clara	Redwood Twp	88	122
KES								
Ah	35	m	c	CHIN	Amador	Ione City P O	69	354
Mung	30	m	c	CHIN	Solano	Vallejo	90	208
KESALAW								
John	45	m	w	DENM	San Francisco	2-Wd San Francisco	79	191
KESEBERG								
Louis	56	m	w	PRUS	Napa	Napa	75	18

© 2001 by Heritage Quest. All rights reserved.

Name	Age	S	R	B-PL	County	Locale	Roll	Pg
						Series M593		
KESEBURG								
James W	40	m	w	PRUS	Placer	Roseville P O	76	355
KESER								
Lewis	24	m	w	LA	Colusa	Colusa	71	289
Therese	46	f	w	FRAN	Alameda	Oakland	68	170
KESEY								
William	51	m	w	PA	Lake	Lower Lake	73	429
KESHIN								
Joseph	42	m	w	SWIT	Sonoma	Petaluma Twp	91	310
KESHNER								
Barney	44	m	w	RUSS	Sonoma	Petaluma Twp	91	317
KESINER								
John H	40	m	w	SHOL	Sonoma	Petaluma Twp	91	364
KESKETH								
J H	33	m	w	NY	San Francisco	San Francisco P O	85	795
KESLAR								
Charles	27	m	w	MI	Sonoma	Bodega Twp	91	264
KESLER								
Andrew	46	m	w	BAVA	Amador	Jackson P O	69	327
Daniel	39	m	w	OH	Sutter	Butte Twp	92	104
Fred	25	m	w	SWED	San Francisco	1-Wd San Francisco	79	120
Herman	40	m	w	PRUS	San Francisco	San Francisco P O	83	279
J	39	m	w	MO	Lassen	Long Valley Twp	73	437
Peter	43	m	w	PA	Yuba	Slate Range Bar Tw	93	673
Thimothy	41	m	w	FRAN	Napa	Napa Twp	75	71
KESLICK								
John	11	m	w	CA	Marin	San Rafael Twp	74	27
KESLING								
Connard	26	m	w	PRUS	Colusa	Stony Crk Twp	71	326
KESOSE								
Roman	29	m	w	MEXI	Colusa	Colusa Twp	71	283
KESSE								
Ah	52	m	c	CHIN	Placer	Auburn P O	76	365
Biagys	27	m	w	ITAL	Sonoma	Analy Twp	91	236
KESSEL								
John M	45	m	w	PA	Placer	Bath P O	76	436
KESSELRING								
Adam	80	m	w	BADE	El Dorado	Coloma Twp	72	4
Adam J	46	m	w	BADE	El Dorado	Coloma Twp	72	4
Michel	35	m	w	PA	Butte	Bidwell Twp	70	3
KESSING								
Clem	32	m	w	PRUS	Sonoma	Santa Rosa	91	420
J H	29	m	w	IREL	San Francisco	San Francisco P O	83	26
KESSLER								
Jacob	50	m	w	FRAN	Calaveras	San Andreas P O	70	198
Joseph	44	m	w	BAVA	Siskiyou	Yreka	89	652
Thos C	31	m	w	IL	San Francisco	5-Wd San Francisco	81	23
Wm	46	m	w	KY	Shasta	Shasta P O	89	456
KESSUS								
Jesus	28	m	w	MEXI	Calaveras	San Andreas P O	70	170
KESTEL								
Adolf	29	m	w	BAVA	San Francisco	3-Wd San Francisco	79	324
KESTER								
Arnold	32	m	w	CANA	Sonoma	Salt Point Twp	91	382
James L	48	m	w	IN	San Luis Obispo	Morro Twp	87	281
John B	41	m	w	IN	San Luis Obispo	Morro Twp	87	284
John H	41	m	w	NY	Napa	Napa	75	36
Lewis	14	m	w	CA	Mendocino	Round Valley Twp	74	217
Lydia A	15	f	w	IA	San Luis Obispo	Morro Twp	87	284
KESTLY								
Calvin	37	m	w	IA	Nevada	Washington Twp	75	346
KESTON								
L B	42	m	w	NY	Alameda	Oakland	68	215
KET								
Ah	40	m	c	CHIN	Placer	Bath P O	76	443
Ah	35	m	c	CHIN	Butte	Hamilton Twp	70	72
Ah	33	m	c	CHIN	Placer	Bath P O	76	440
Ah	31	m	c	CHIN	Yuba	Marysville	93	600
Ah	29	m	c	CHIN	Placer	Bath P O	76	424
Su	37	m	c	CHIN	Placer	Bath P O	76	454
KETBRIDE								
Patrick	30	m	w	CANA	San Mateo	Pescadero P O	87	413
KETCHEN								
George	33	m	w	MO	Monterey	Monterey Twp	74	351
KETCHERSIDES								
Henry J	46	m	w	TN	Colusa	Colusa Twp	71	280
KETCHUM								
--- Miss	14	f	w	CA	Sacramento	4-Wd Sacramento	77	338
Alvin	37	m	w	NY	Shasta	Fort Crook P O	89	474
Archer	30	m	w	NY	Sonoma	Petaluma Twp	91	338
Eli	38	m	w	NY	Placer	Cisco P O	76	494
Eli	38	m	w	NY	Placer	Cisco P O	76	494
Ernest	26	m	w	CANA	San Luis Obispo	San Luis Obispo Tw	87	316
F B	30	m	w	MI	San Francisco	San Francisco P O	83	296
Frederick	43	m	w	CANA	San Luis Obispo	San Luis Obispo Tw	87	316
George	38	m	w	NY	San Francisco	5-Wd San Francisco	81	28
Isaac R	52	m	w	NY	Butte	Bidwell Twp	70	1
Jas C	52	m	w	MO	Nevada	Little York Twp	75	240
Joseph	31	m	w	NY	Placer	Rocklin Twp	76	465
Josephus	40	m	w	TN	Santa Clara	Santa Clara Twp	88	170
Lawrence	37	m	w	PA	Los Angeles	Los Angeles Twp	73	491
Lewis N	36	m	w	PA	Siskiyou	Yreka	89	657
Lorin B	38	m	w	NY	Tulare	Tule Rvr Twp	92	271
Melville	45	m	w	NY	Santa Clara	1-Wd San Jose	88	248
Mortmer	30	m	w	NY	Sonoma	Analy Twp	91	224
Nelson	34	m	w	IN	Mendocino	Point Arena Twp	74	210
Robt B	34	m	w	MO	Shasta	Shasta P O	89	453
Wm	40	m	w	MO	Sacramento	4-Wd Sacramento	77	350
KETCHUN								
John M	21	m	w	CA	Fresno	Kingston P O	72	217
KETE								
Ah	42	m	c	CHIN	Sacramento	Granite Twp	77	138
KETELSEN								
August	28	m	w	SILE	San Francisco	3-Wd San Francisco	79	287
John	21	m	w	SHOL	Alameda	Eden Twp	68	67
KETES								
John P	21	m	w	SHOL	Alameda	Eden Twp	68	68
KETHER								
Bernard	36	m	w	IREL	San Francisco	11-Wd San Francisc	84	437
KETING								
M T	27	f	w	IREL	San Joaquin	2-Wd Stockton	86	175
Mary	35	f	w	IREL	San Joaquin	2-Wd Stockton	86	175
Patrick	42	m	w	IREL	Amador	Fiddletown P O	69	433
Thomas	33	m	w	IREL	San Francisco	11-Wd San Francisc	84	703
KETLER								
Charles A	29	m	w	PA	Santa Clara	1-Wd San Jose	88	278
Ed	30	m	w	DC	San Joaquin	2-Wd Stockton	86	167
Saml	41	m	w	PRUS	San Francisco	8-Wd San Francisco	82	365
KETNAUER								
Antone	55	m	w	HDAR	Yuba	Marysville Twp	93	569
KETON								
Catherin	33	f	w	IREL	Alameda	Oakland	68	149
KETRIN								
John	30	m	w	GERM	Marin	San Rafael Twp	74	26
KETT								
Ah	43	m	c	CHIN	Placer	Bath P O	76	445
KETTA								
David	36	m	w	ENGL	Placer	Colfax P O	76	392
KETTELL								
Levey	40	f	w	NORW	San Joaquin	2-Wd Stockton	86	173
KETTERIDGE								
Cullen T	20	m	w	MA	Santa Cruz	Santa Cruz	89	417
George	37	m	w	MA	San Francisco	11-Wd San Francisc	84	629
KETTING								
Joseph A	58	m	w	PA	San Bernardino	San Bernardino Twp	78	417
KETTLEHOOD								
Willm	47	m	w	PRUS	Siskiyou	Cottonwood Twp	89	595
KETTLEMAN								
D	38	m	w	BADE	San Joaquin	Elkhorn Twp	86	60
KETTLESON								
Andrew	40	m	w	SWED	Los Angeles	El Monte Twp	73	449
KETTLEWELL								
J R	45	m	w	PA	San Francisco	San Francisco P O	85	855
KETTO								
James	44	m	w	ENGL	Nevada	Grass Valley Twp	75	195
John	42	m	w	ENGL	Nevada	Grass Valley Twp	75	208
Joseph	40	m	w	ENGL	Mariposa	Maxwell Crk P O	74	138
KETTON								
James M	47	m	w	VA	Mariposa	Mariposa P O	74	109
Saml B	47	m	w	MA	San Francisco	San Francisco P O	83	90
KEU								
Ah	52	m	c	CHIN	Shasta	American Ranch P O	89	499
Ah	35	m	c	CHIN	Calaveras	San Andreas P O	70	172
Gok	43	m	c	CHIN	Shasta	American Ranch P O	89	499
KEUBEN								
George	50	m	w	ENGL	San Francisco	San Francisco P O	83	294
KEUK								
---	40	f	c	CHIN	Shasta	Shasta P O	89	461
KEULEN								
Hendreich	41	m	w	HOLL	San Francisco	2-Wd San Francisco	79	236
KEURTH								
Jacot	41	m	w	GERM	Sacramento	1-Wd Sacramento	77	175
KEUW								
---	30	m	c	CHIN	Shasta	American Ranch P O	89	496
KEW								
Ah	58	m	c	CHIN	Nevada	Grass Valley Twp	75	205
Ah	42	m	c	CHIN	Plumas	Mineral Twp	77	25
Ah	41	m	c	CHIN	Mono	Bridgeport P O	74	283
Ah	38	m	c	CHIN	El Dorado	White Oak Twp	72	141
Ah	35	m	c	CHIN	San Francisco	1-Wd San Francisco	79	55
Ah	35	m	c	CHIN	Mariposa	Mariposa P O	74	134
Ah	30	m	c	CHIN	El Dorado	White Oak Twp	72	135
Ah	25	m	c	CHIN	San Francisco	San Francisco P O	80	507
Ah	25	f	c	CHIN	Mariposa	Mariposa P O	74	127
Ah	22	m	c	CHIN	Shasta	American Ranch P O	89	499
Ah	22	m	c	CHIN	Nevada	Nevada Twp	75	297
Ah	21	m	c	CHIN	Nevada	Nevada Twp	75	282
Ah	20	m	c	CHIN	Nevada	Little York Twp	75	234
Ah	15	m	c	CHIN	Butte	Oroville Twp	70	139
Ah	13	m	c	CHIN	Nevada	Grass Valley Twp	75	197
Ah	10	f	c	CHIN	San Francisco	6-Wd San Francisco	81	53
KEWAN								
William	40	m	w	IOFM	San Francisco	11-Wd San Francisc	84	514
KEWITT								
R	40	m	w	PRUS	San Joaquin	Liberty Twp	86	94
KEWLAND								
Jacob	35	m	w	NY	Tuolumne	Sonora P O	93	327
KEWLEY								
J B	21	m	w	IREL	Nevada	Meadow Lake Twp	75	251
John	45	m	w	ENGL	Nevada	Grass Valley Twp	75	223
KEWYER								
John	35	m	w	NY	Plumas	Plumas Twp	77	29
KEY								
Ah	50	m	c	CHIN	Placer	Lincoln P O	76	484

© 2001 by Heritage Quest. All rights reserved.

Name	Age	S	R	B-PL	County	Locale (Series M593)	Roll	Pg
Ah	45	m	c	CHIN	Merced	Snelling P O	74	279
Ah	38	m	c	CHIN	Kern	Bakersfield P O	73	365
Ah	32	m	c	CHIN	Sacramento	1-Wd Sacramento	77	205
Ah	32	m	c	CHIN	Placer	Clipper Gap P O	76	376
Ah	30	m	c	CHIN	Sacramento	Granite Twp	77	141
Ah	30	m	c	CHIN	Mendocino	Big Rvr Twp	74	170
Ah	28	m	c	CHIN	Trinity	Lewiston Pct	92	214
Ah	27	m	c	CHIN	Placer	Auburn P O	76	379
Ah	25	m	c	CHIN	Sacramento	1-Wd Sacramento	77	196
Ah	25	m	c	CHIN	Sierra	Downieville Twp	89	520
Ah	24	m	c	CHIN	Trinity	Weaverville Pct	92	230
Ah	24	m	c	CHIN	Trinity	Weaverville Pct	92	230
Ah	21	m	c	CHIN	Sonoma	Sonoma Twp	91	449
Ah	17	m	c	CHIN	Amador	Volcano P O	69	376
Ah	16	m	c	CHIN	San Francisco	8-Wd San Francisco	82	395
Amung	14	m	c	CHIN	San Francisco	11-Wd San Francisc	84	422
Ce	18	m	c	CHIN	San Francisco	San Francisco P O	83	172
Charles	30	m	c	CHIN	San Mateo	Woodside P O	87	384
Chas	30	m	w	IREL	Sacramento	3-Wd Sacramento	77	291
Elisha	38	m	w	IN	Calaveras	San Andreas P O	70	210
Gun	17	m	c	CHIN	San Francisco	11-Wd San Francisc	84	422
Hay	46	m	c	CHIN	Butte	Chico Twp	70	52
Hoy	40	m	c	CHIN	Butte	Chico Twp	70	51
I	31	m	w	IREL	Lake	Knoxville Mines	73	404
John	34	m	w	ENGL	Los Angeles	El Monte Twp	73	457
John R	29	m	w	NY	San Francisco	6-Wd San Francisco	81	94
John W	40	m	w	SC	Sutter	Yuba Twp	92	145
Joseph	42	m	w	NJ	San Joaquin	1-Wd Stockton	86	124
Julia	3	f	w	CA	San Francisco	5-Wd San Francisco	81	28
L Allen	64	m	w	VA	San Mateo	Half Moon Bay P O	87	404
Margaret	34	f	w	IREL	San Mateo	Schoolhouse Statio	87	340
Ong	35	m	c	CHIN	Placer	Bath P O	76	443
Oscar	35	m	w	OH	San Mateo	Schoolhouse Statio	87	340
Rosella	14	f	w	OR	Calaveras	San Andreas P O	70	192
Sing	48	m	c	CHIN	Yuba	Bullards Bar P O	93	552
Thomas C	41	m	w	TN	Shasta	Millville P O	89	494
Wan	25	m	c	CHIN	San Francisco	11-Wd San Francisc	84	422
William	38	m	w	NY	San Francisco	5-Wd San Francisco	81	28
William	32	m	w	ENGL	Nevada	Grass Valley Twp	75	216
Ye	40	m	c	CHIN	El Dorado	Georgetown Twp	72	36
KEYEER								
Hannah	30	f	w	SWED	Santa Clara	Fremont Twp	88	54
KEYENHAGEN								
G	49	m	w	HANO	Merced	Snelling P O	74	273
KEYES								
Adele	14	f	w	CA	Santa Clara	2-Wd San Jose	88	336
C	53	f	w	PA	Alameda	Oakland	68	174
Carol	17	m	w	CA	San Francisco	11-Wd San Francisc	84	570
D B	40	m	w	VT	Sierra	Sierra Twp	89	566
E D Col	57	m	w	MA	Napa	Napa	75	27
E D Gerd	57	m	w	MA	Napa	Napa Twp	75	75
Elijah B	38	m	w	VT	San Francisco	San Francisco P O	83	58
Ellen	29	f	w	VT	San Francisco	8-Wd San Francisco	82	465
George	40	m	w	NY	Yolo	Cottonwood Twp	93	469
George B	49	m	w	VT	Los Angeles	Wilmington Twp	73	634
J W	39	m	w	ENGL	Sacramento	3-Wd Sacramento	77	271
James	40	m	w	IREL	San Diego	Milquaty Dist	78	478
James	29	m	w	IREL	Napa	Napa Twp	75	60
John A	60	m	w	NJ	Tulare	Visalia	92	294
M C	34	m	w	IREL	Sierra	Alleghany & Forest	89	533
Manly	33	m	b	VA	Sacramento	1-Wd Sacramento	77	202
Marshal M	53	m	w	VT	Sonoma	Mendocino Twp	91	288
Mitten	16	m	w	CA	Stanislaus	Empire Twp	92	66
O H	40	m	w	NH	San Francisco	San Francisco P O	85	792
Richd M	56	m	w	NY	Fresno	Kings Rvr P O	72	203
Richd R	45	m	w	AL	Sonoma	Russian Rvr	91	373
Robert	23	m	w	MO	San Bernardino	San Bernardino Twp	78	428
Thomas	50	m	w	NY	Stanislaus	Empire Twp	92	65
Thomas	37	m	w	OH	Stanislaus	Empire Twp	92	66
Wm	32	m	w	IREL	San Joaquin	2-Wd Stockton	86	211
Wm N	49	m	w	IL	Sacramento	Center Twp	77	82
KEYKNOVAN								
L	60	m	w	BELG	Alameda	Oakland	68	227
KEYLEY								
Roger	39	m	w	IREL	Yuba	Marysville	93	600
KEYM								
Elizabeth	16	f	w	LA	Santa Cruz	Santa Cruz	89	417
KEYMON								
Ah	18	m	c	CHIN	Yuba	Marysville	93	620
KEYN								
Henry	46	m	w	HDAR	Solano	Suisun Twp	90	96
KEYNE								
Henry	19	m	w	LA	Santa Cruz	Santa Cruz	89	433
KEYNHAVEN								
E	40	m	w	BADE	Alameda	Oakland	68	143
KEYON								
Ah	34	m	c	CHIN	Nevada	Meadow Lake Twp	75	256
Ah	30	f	c	CHIN	Nevada	Meadow Lake Twp	75	254
Ah	22	m	c	CHIN	Nevada	Meadow Lake Twp	75	254
KEYS								
Arther	28	m	w	MA	San Francisco	7-Wd San Francisco	81	159
C C	15	f	w	CA	Alameda	Oakland	68	237
Daniel	38	m	w	PA	Calaveras	San Andreas P O	70	213
Eli	36	m	w	VA	Calaveras	San Andreas P O	70	190
Emma	13	f	w	CA	San Joaquin	3-Wd Stockton	86	215
Frank W	24	m	w	CANA	San Francisco	San Francisco P O	85	740
George	52	m	w	IREL	Marin	Tomales Twp	74	88
Harriet	43	f	w	OH	Sacramento	Center Twp	77	82
Isaac	36	m	w	MO	Yolo	Cache Crk Twp	93	445
John	46	m	w	IREL	Marin	Tomales Twp	74	88
John	44	m	w	VA	Merced	Snelling P O	74	257
John	44	m	w	NY	Amador	Amador City P O	69	395
Levi	23	m	w	LA	Inyo	Independence Twp	73	328
Martin	21	m	w	OH	Solano	Suisun Twp	90	95
Neil	20	m	w	ME	Sonoma	Salt Point	91	392
Patrick	35	m	w	IREL	San Francisco	San Francisco P O	83	43
Rand	59	m	b	KY	San Joaquin	3-Wd Stockton	86	238
Thos	47	m	w	OH	San Joaquin	3-Wd Stockton	86	235
W	38	m	w	NY	Calaveras	Copperopolis P O	70	237
Wm	24	m	w	IREL	Sonoma	Salt Point	91	387
Wm S	41	m	w	VA	Merced	Snelling P O	74	257
KEYSBURG								
L C	33	f	w	OH	Alameda	Oakland	68	174
KEYSER								
Andrew	47	m	w	VA	Solano	Maine Prairie Twp	90	54
Augustus	34	m	w	PA	Santa Clara	Fremont Twp	88	55
C	32	m	w	NY	San Joaquin	Castoria Twp	86	14
Constance	45	f	w	FRAN	San Francisco	San Francisco P O	80	480
Elijah T	44	m	w	PA	Siskiyou	Butte Twp	89	585
Fredrick	50	m	w	HANO	Calaveras	San Andreas P O	70	159
H A	43	m	w	VA	Tuolumne	Columbia P O	93	362
Jacob	56	m	w	WURT	El Dorado	Placerville	72	116
James	35	m	w	PA	El Dorado	Placerville	72	117
John	50	m	w	SWIT	Placer	Newcastle Twp	76	478
Kate	20	f	w	WURT	San Francisco	8-Wd San Francisco	82	386
Kohn	20	m	w	OH	Placer	Newcastle Twp	76	478
Louis	48	m	w	SWIT	San Francisco	8-Wd San Francisco	82	459
Louisa	24	f	w	SAXO	San Francisco	San Francisco P O	80	473
P	22	m	w	MO	Sierra	Lincoln Twp	89	545
P G	38	m	w	WALD	Solano	Benicia	90	19
Phil W	46	m	w	MD	Sutter	Yuba Twp	92	149
Richard	28	m	w	PRUS	San Francisco	San Francisco P O	80	344
Rosie	22	f	w	NJ	Monterey	Castroville Twp	74	329
Rufus	53	m	w	PA	San Francisco	8-Wd San Francisco	82	473
S	15	m	w	POLA	Nevada	Bridgeport Twp	75	100
William	41	m	w	PRUS	Solano	Vacaville Twp	90	135
Wm S	38	m	w	PA	San Francisco	2-Wd San Francisco	79	236
KEYSON								
Henry	20	m	w	VA	Colusa	Monroe Twp	71	314
KEYSTONE								
Saml	49	m	w	ENGL	San Francisco	11-Wd San Francisc	84	642
KEYT								
Abner C	41	m	w	OH	San Francisco	8-Wd San Francisco	82	450
KEYZER								
Eliazer	57	m	w	SAXO	Monterey	Monterey	74	358
Jacob	67	m	w	SWIT	Monterey	Alisal Twp	74	298
Michael	25	m	w	PA	Yolo	Putah Twp	93	521
KEYZIE								
A Frank	29	m	w	TN	San Francisco	8-Wd San Francisco	82	350
KEZER								
John W	43	m	w	ME	Santa Barbara	Santa Barbara P O	87	481
KEZO								
John	38	m	w	ENGL	Tuolumne	Chinese Camp P O	93	363
KHADEN								
Henery	30	m	w	PRUS	San Joaquin	Oneal Twp	86	112
KHAN								
George	50	m	w	GERM	Marin	San Rafael Twp	74	41
KHEE								
Chee	27	m	c	CHIN	San Francisco	11-Wd San Francisc	84	708
KHERN								
Geo	21	m	w	GERM	Sacramento	1-Wd Sacramento	77	190
KHOBECKER								
Phil	32	m	w	PRUS	San Joaquin	2-Wd Stockton	86	208
KI								
Ah	60	m	c	CHIN	El Dorado	Mud Springs Twp	72	88
Ah	60	m	c	CHIN	Santa Clara	1-Wd San Jose	88	274
Ah	53	m	c	CHIN	El Dorado	Mud Springs Twp	72	79
Ah	51	m	c	CHIN	Amador	Ione City P O	69	354
Ah	42	m	c	CHIN	Calaveras	Copperopolis P O	70	258
Ah	42	m	c	CHIN	San Francisco	6-Wd San Francisco	81	47
Ah	41	m	c	CHIN	El Dorado	Diamond Springs Tw	72	28
Ah	40	m	c	CHIN	San Joaquin	1-Wd Stockton	86	143
Ah	40	m	c	CHIN	Siskiyou	Yreka Twp	89	670
Ah	40	m	c	CHIN	Placer	Roseville P O	76	348
Ah	39	m	c	CHIN	El Dorado	Salmon Falls Twp	72	130
Ah	37	m	c	CHIN	Placer	Pino Twp	76	470
Ah	36	m	c	CHIN	Santa Barbara	Las Cruces P O	87	505
Ah	35	m	c	CHIN	El Dorado	Mud Springs Twp	72	76
Ah	34	m	c	CHIN	San Francisco	11-Wd San Francisc	84	522
Ah	32	m	c	CHIN	Nevada	Grass Valley Twp	75	205
Ah	32	m	c	CHIN	Calaveras	Copperopolis P O	70	236
Ah	31	m	c	CHIN	Nevada	Nevada Twp	75	316
Ah	30	m	c	CHIN	Fresno	Millerton P O	72	200
Ah	29	m	c	CHIN	San Joaquin	Castoria Twp	86	15
Ah	28	m	c	CHIN	San Francisco	San Francisco P O	85	748
Ah	27	m	c	CHIN	Amador	Drytown P O	69	424
Ah	27	m	c	CHIN	El Dorado	Mountain Twp	72	67
Ah	25	m	c	CHIN	Calaveras	Copperopolis P O	70	234
Ah	25	m	c	CHIN	El Dorado	Mud Springs Twp	72	88
Ah	24	m	c	CHIN	Solano	Vallejo	90	208
Ah	24	m	c	CHIN	El Dorado	Placerville	72	115
Ah	24	m	c	CHIN	San Francisco	6-Wd San Francisco	81	56
Ah	22	m	c	CHIN	San Luis Obispo	San Luis Obispo Tw	87	297
Ah	21	m	c	CHIN	San Joaquin	Castoria Twp	86	13

© 2001 by Heritage Quest. All rights reserved.

California 1870 Census

Name	Age	S	R	B-PL	County	Locale	Series M593 Roll	Pg
Ah	21	m	c	CHIN	El Dorado	White Oak Twp	72	140
Ah	19	m	c	CHIN	Sacramento	3-Wd Sacramento	77	304
Ah	18	m	c	CHIN	Nevada	Nevada Twp	75	298
Ah	16	m	c	CHIN	El Dorado	Mud Springs Twp	72	88
Ah	16	m	c	CHIN	San Francisco	6-Wd San Francisco	81	50
Ah	15	m	c	CHIN	San Francisco	San Francisco P O	83	131
Ah	12	m	c	CHIN	Solano	Vallejo	90	179
China	28	m	c	CHIN	Calaveras	San Andreas P O	70	205
Han	32	m	c	CHIN	Siskiyou	Cottonwood Twp	89	594
Hoh	14	m	c	CHIN	San Francisco	6-Wd San Francisco	81	63
Hung	34	m	c	CHIN	San Mateo	Half Moon Bay P O	87	396
Jiun	17	m	c	CHIN	Sacramento	3-Wd Sacramento	77	305
Kang	41	m	c	CHIN	Siskiyou	Hamburg Twp	89	597
Keang	45	m	c	CHIN	San Francisco	6-Wd San Francisco	81	47
Kong	20	m	c	CHIN	Yuba	Marysville	93	624
Kum	28	m	c	CHIN	Tehama	Tehama Twp	92	189
Kum	20	m	c	CHIN	San Francisco	6-Wd San Francisco	81	54
Le	18	m	c	CHIN	El Dorado	Mountain Twp	72	70
Li Kee	40	m	c	CHIN	San Francisco	6-Wd San Francisco	81	84
Ling	17	m	c	CHIN	San Luis Obispo	Salinas Twp	87	296
Ming	20	m	c	CHIN	San Francisco	2-Wd San Francisco	79	203
Shon	48	m	c	CHIN	Trinity	Douglas	92	233
Wah	18	m	c	CHIN	Sacramento	3-Wd Sacramento	77	258
Win	28	m	c	CHIN	Butte	Wyandotte Twp	70	143
Yi	34	m	c	CHIN	Yuba	Marysville	93	631
KIB								
Ah	32	m	c	CHIN	Nevada	Meadow Lake Twp	75	254
Ah	15	m	c	CHIN	San Francisco	San Francisco P O	83	7
KIBBE								
Henry C	40	m	w	NY	San Francisco	8-Wd San Francisco	82	440
Jerod	66	m	w	NY	Sacramento	Brighton Twp	77	79
Millard	46	m	w	MA	San Francisco	San Francisco P O	80	488
Thomas R	57	m	w	NY	Nevada	Grass Valley Twp	75	186
KIBBEE								
Albertus	30	m	w	KS	Napa	Yountville Twp	75	88
KIBBEY								
Wm R	34	m	w	DC	San Joaquin	2-Wd Stockton	86	168
KIBBIE								
Amiah	39	m	w	NY	Mendocino	Anderson Twp	74	150
C	26	m	w	VT	Sierra	Alleghany & Forest	89	533
H G	42	m	w	MA	Tuolumne	Columbia P O	93	348
KIBBON								
J E	37	m	w	ME	Sierra	Lincoln Twp	89	550
KIBBY								
George	39	m	w	CT	Los Angeles	Los Angeles	73	506
James	46	m	w	NY	Merced	Snelling P O	74	254
Michael	30	m	w	NORW	San Francisco	7-Wd San Francisco	81	276
KIBLAND								
James	16	m	w	CA	Sacramento	Granite Twp	77	144
KICE								
M	23	m	w	IN	Alameda	Murray Twp	68	105
KICHABOCKNE								
F H	18	m	w	MI	Humboldt	Arcata Twp	72	230
KICHLEN								
Michard	42	m	w	PA	Los Angeles	Los Angeles	73	534
KICK								
Adolph	24	m	w	WURT	Santa Clara	Santa Clara Twp	88	148
Ah	40	m	c	CHIN	Trinity	Weaverville Pct	92	230
KICKAN								
Jno	24	m	w	GERM	Santa Clara	Gilroy Twp	88	100
KICKNER								
Charles	19	m	w	BADE	Placer	Auburn P O	76	381
KID								
Joseph	25	m	w	IREL	Napa	Napa	75	1
KIDD								
Abigail	54	f	w	OH	Sonoma	Russian Rvr	91	372
Alexander	48	m	w	IREL	San Francisco	8-Wd San Francisco	82	301
Chas E	35	m	w	ENGL	Placer	Gold Run Twp	76	397
David	34	m	w	SCOT	San Francisco	7-Wd San Francisco	81	244
Eliza	70	f	w	NY	San Francisco	11-Wd San Francisc	84	625
Geo W	49	m	w	KY	San Joaquin	1-Wd Stockton	86	135
Grace	14	f	w	CA	Sacramento	3-Wd Sacramento	77	301
J R	48	m	w	NJ	San Francisco	3-Wd San Francisco	79	313
James	40	m	w	PA	Siskiyou	Butte Twp	89	588
James A	49	m	w	KY	Klamath	Klamath Twp	73	371
John	37	m	w	IREL	San Francisco	1-Wd San Francisco	79	62
John	34	m	w	IREL	San Francisco	1-Wd San Francisco	79	50
Joseph	37	m	w	IREL	Marin	San Rafael	74	48
Leonard	18	m	w	CA	San Francisco	San Francisco P O	80	362
Robt	29	m	w	SCOT	San Francisco	San Francisco P O	83	122
William	38	m	w	IREL	Mendocino	Navarro & Big Rvr	74	175
Wm	38	m	w	KS	Sonoma	Salt Point	91	380
KIDDER								
Broscoe	38	m	w	ME	Santa Clara	Gilroy Twp	88	74
C A	40	m	w	CANA	Solano	Vallejo	90	151
Charles	49	m	w	ME	Sacramento	Lee Twp	77	157
Chas S	46	m	w	ME	Santa Clara	Santa Clara Twp	88	149
Jno	68	m	w	NY	San Joaquin	Oneal Twp	86	109
John S	32	m	w	NY	Santa Cruz	Watsonville	89	372
Luelling L	50	m	w	ME	Santa Clara	San Jose Twp	88	210
Nathaniel A	60	m	w	ME	Sacramento	2-Wd Sacramento	77	251
Saml R	30	m	w	ME	Placer	Dutch Flat P O	76	401
Susan	60	f	w	VT	Alameda	Oakland	68	150
Wm S	35	m	w	ENGL	Shasta	French Gulch P O	89	466
Wm W	65	m	w	NY	Santa Cruz	Watsonville	89	377
KIDDY								
Jas A	50	m	w	ENGL	Santa Clara	Gilroy Twp	88	78

Name	Age	S	R	B-PL	County	Locale	Series M593 Roll	Pg
KIDSON								
Evans J	36	m	w	MD	Colusa	Grand Island Twp	71	303
KIDWELL								
Joseph	30	m	w	NY	San Francisco	5-Wd San Francisco	81	30
Milton	61	m	w	KY	Colusa	Spring Valley Twp	71	337
Rich	34	m	w	KY	San Joaquin	1-Wd Stockton	86	135
KIE								
---	34	m	c	CHIN	Shasta	Shasta P O	89	454
---	18	m	c	CHIN	San Francisco	6-Wd San Francisco	81	51
Ah	80	m	c	CHIN	Sacramento	Center Twp	77	86
Ah	8	m	c	CHIN	Sacramento	1-Wd Sacramento	77	202
Ah	53	m	c	CHIN	Amador	Drytown P O	69	424
Ah	50	m	c	CHIN	Amador	Ione City P O	69	354
Ah	45	m	c	CHIN	Sierra	Downieville Twp	89	520
Ah	45	m	c	CHIN	Mariposa	Mariposa P O	74	132
Ah	41	m	c	CHIN	Sacramento	Granite Twp	77	138
Ah	41	m	c	CHIN	Sacramento	Granite Twp	77	155
Ah	40	m	c	CHIN	San Joaquin	Oneal Twp	86	116
Ah	40	m	c	CHIN	Sacramento	San Joaquin Twp	77	398
Ah	40	m	c	CHIN	Sacramento	Granite Twp	77	151
Ah	40	m	c	CHIN	Sacramento	Granite Twp	77	151
Ah	40	m	c	CHIN	Sacramento	Cosumnes Twp	77	92
Ah	39	m	c	CHIN	Amador	Ione City P O	69	362
Ah	37	m	c	CHIN	Sierra	Downieville Twp	89	521
Ah	36	m	c	CHIN	Trinity	North Fork Twp	92	217
Ah	36	m	c	CHIN	Trinity	Junction City Pct	92	209
Ah	35	m	c	CHIN	Sacramento	Granite Twp	77	140
Ah	34	m	c	CHIN	Mariposa	Mariposa P O	74	132
Ah	34	m	c	CHIN	San Francisco	3-Wd San Francisco	79	301
Ah	34	m	c	CHIN	Sacramento	Granite Twp	77	138
Ah	32	m	c	CHIN	Mariposa	Maxwell Crk P O	74	145
Ah	30	m	c	CHIN	Mariposa	Mariposa P O	74	134
Ah	30	m	c	CHIN	Mariposa	Mariposa P O	74	122
Ah	29	m	c	CHIN	Sierra	Butte Twp	89	513
Ah	28	m	c	CHIN	San Joaquin	1-Wd Stockton	86	145
Ah	28	m	c	CHIN	Amador	Fiddletown P O	69	428
Ah	27	m	c	CHIN	Plumas	Goodwin Twp	77	3
Ah	24	m	c	CHIN	San Joaquin	Elkhorn Twp	86	52
Ah	24	m	c	CHIN	Mendocino	Point Arena Twp	74	212
Ah	20	m	c	CHIN	San Francisco	6-Wd San Francisco	81	55
Ah	18	m	c	CHIN	Santa Cruz	Pajaro Twp	89	342
Ah John	19	m	c	CHIN	Sonoma	Cloverdale Twp	91	270
Cho	8	m	c	CHIN	Monterey	Monterey Twp	74	352
Houy	29	m	c	CHIN	Butte	Chico Twp	70	52
J B	44	m	w	IN	Trinity	Lewiston Pct	92	212
Jim	17	m	c	CHIN	Santa Clara	Redwood Twp	88	128
Lee	39	m	c	CHIN	Amador	Jackson P O	69	346
Sing	62	m	c	CHIN	Mariposa	Mariposa P O	74	126
Sing	31	m	c	CHIN	Sierra	Forest Twp	89	532
Tie	23	m	c	CHIN	Solano	Vacaville Twp	90	134
Won	60	m	c	CHIN	Nevada	Eureka Twp	75	136
Ye	24	m	c	CHIN	Alameda	Washington Twp	68	297
Yee	30	m	c	CHIN	Placer	Bath P O	76	443
Yet	40	m	c	CHIN	San Francisco	3-Wd San Francisco	79	322
KIEF								
Daniel	36	m	w	IREL	Alameda	Eden Twp	68	91
Patrick	30	m	w	IREL	San Francisco	San Francisco P O	85	759
KIEFER								
Edward C	27	m	w	NY	Yolo	Putah Twp	93	520
Frederick	45	m	w	BADE	Yolo	Cache Crk Twp	93	419
Samuel M	41	m	w	MD	Sacramento	4-Wd Sacramento	77	348
KIEFF								
Mat	40	m	w	IREL	San Francisco	11-Wd San Francisc	84	701
KIEFFING								
Charles	38	m	w	PRUS	San Francisco	7-Wd San Francisco	81	219
KIEHL								
Godfred	34	m	w	PRUS	San Francisco	1-Wd San Francisco	79	116
Jacob	52	m	w	BAVA	San Francisco	3-Wd San Francisco	79	311
KIEHN								
Barbara	32	f	w	BAVA	Sacramento	3-Wd Sacramento	77	289
W W	19	m	w	BAVA	San Francisco	8-Wd San Francisco	82	375
KIEL								
Jarvis	66	m	w	NY	Mariposa	Mariposa P O	74	119
KIELBY								
Nicolas	40	m	w	IREL	San Francisco	7-Wd San Francisco	81	258
KIELEY								
Michael	26	m	w	IREL	San Francisco	11-Wd San Francisc	84	508
KIELLER								
John	40	m	w	SCOT	San Diego	San Diego	78	500
KIELLY								
Bridget	15	f	w	CA	Santa Clara	2-Wd San Jose	88	337
KIELY								
Edward	32	m	w	IREL	Placer	Newcastle Twp	76	476
KIEME								
Mary	35	f	w	IREL	San Francisco	8-Wd San Francisco	82	405
KIEN								
Ah	34	m	c	CHIN	San Francisco	3-Wd San Francisco	79	309
Ah	18	m	c	CHIN	San Francisco	3-Wd San Francisco	79	309
KIENE								
Elizabeth	36	f	w	SAXO	El Dorado	Placerville	72	110
KIENG								
Ah	24	m	c	CHIN	Solano	Suisun Twp	90	105
KIENTY								
Christian	54	m	w	BADE	Amador	Ione City P O	69	366
KIEP								
John	23	m	w	NY	Solano	Suisun Twp	90	108

© 2001 by Heritage Quest. All rights reserved.

Series M593

Name	Age	S	R	B-PL	County	Locale	Roll	Pg
KIER								
Carrie	19	f	w	DENM	Humboldt	Eel Rvr Twp	72	248
H	25	m	w	DENM	Humboldt	Bald Hills	72	237
Henry	40	m	w	DENM	Sonoma	Cloverdale Twp	91	269
Lottie	18	f	w	DENM	Humboldt	Eel Rvr Twp	72	250
Taw	37	m	c	CHIN	Marin	San Rafael Twp	74	34
KIERMAN								
Patric	50	m	w	IREL	Trinity	North Fork Twp	92	219
KIERNA								
John	32	m	w	IREL	San Francisco	11-Wd San Francisc	84	533
KIERNAN								
Catherine	44	f	w	IREL	San Francisco	11-Wd San Francisc	84	433
Francis	70	m	w	IREL	San Francisco	San Francisco P O	83	326
Francis	35	m	w	IREL	Solano	Vallejo	90	157
George	44	m	w	IREL	Contra Costa	Martinez P O	71	372
Jno	32	m	w	IREL	San Francisco	5-Wd San Francisco	81	32
John	53	m	w	IREL	Siskiyou	Butte Twp	89	588
John	30	m	w	IREL	San Francisco	1-Wd San Francisco	79	101
Joseph	30	m	w	IREL	Marin	Sausalito Twp	74	72
Kate	28	f	w	IREL	San Francisco	San Francisco P O	83	133
Maria	20	f	w	IREL	San Francisco	8-Wd San Francisco	82	404
Mike	33	m	w	IREL	Sonoma	Bodega Twp	91	257
Owen	24	m	w	IREL	San Francisco	1-Wd San Francisco	79	63
Patrick	46	m	w	IREL	San Francisco	11-Wd San Francisc	84	479
Patrick	45	m	w	IREL	Siskiyou	Butte Twp	89	588
Patrick	43	m	w	IREL	Marin	Sausalito Twp	74	74
Thomas	35	m	w	CANA	San Francisco	8-Wd San Francisco	82	451
Thomas	35	m	w	IREL	San Francisco	San Francisco P O	83	238
Thomas	25	m	w	MA	Sacramento	2-Wd Sacramento	77	236
Thos	36	m	w	IREL	San Francisco	1-Wd San Francisco	79	88
Thos	26	m	w	IREL	Sacramento	2-Wd Sacramento	77	246
KIERNEY								
Mary	26	f	w	IREL	San Francisco	8-Wd San Francisco	82	490
KIERNS								
Alice	23	f	w	IREL	Santa Cruz	Santa Cruz	89	430
KIERSKI								
John	62	m	w	PRUS	San Joaquin	2-Wd Stockton	86	202
Wm	34	m	w	PRUS	San Joaquin	2-Wd Stockton	86	202
KIERSTEAD								
James A	31	m	w	MI	Sonoma	Bodega Twp	91	262
KIERTOLS								
Kesse	29	m	w	ITAL	Sonoma	Analy Twp	91	236
KIES								
Abe	54	m	w	KY	Trinity	Lewiston Pct	92	213
KIET								
Ah	16	m	c	CHIN	San Francisco	3-Wd San Francisco	79	310
KIEZLER								
Henry	46	m	w	HDAR	San Francisco	San Francisco P O	80	428
KIFER								
Diana	16	f	w	CA	Santa Clara	Redwood Twp	88	134
Emeline	40	f	w	KY	Santa Clara	Santa Clara Twp	88	140
John F	17	m	w	CA	Santa Clara	Santa Clara Twp	88	177
KIFFER								
James W	36	m	w	MO	Colusa	Colusa Twp	71	273
KIG								
Ah	24	m	c	CHIN	San Francisco	San Francisco P O	80	498
KIGAR								
Eliza	70	f	w	OH	El Dorado	Coloma Twp	72	5
KIGEEY								
Saml S	45	m	w	VA	Sonoma	Petaluma Twp	91	331
KIGGAN								
Michael	55	m	w	IREL	San Francisco	San Francisco P O	80	398
KIGLER								
Adam	45	m	w	BAVA	San Francisco	8-Wd San Francisco	82	435
KIGUEROA								
Francisco	35	m	w	MEXI	Los Angeles	El Monte Twp	73	453
KIH								
Yah	36	m	c	CHIN	Santa Clara	Santa Clara Twp	88	158
KIHLI								
Geo	24	m	w	BADE	San Francisco	11-Wd San Francisc	84	617
George	26	m	w	BADE	San Francisco	7-Wd San Francisco	81	226
KIHLMYER								
Jacob	26	m	w	WURT	San Francisco	San Francisco P O	80	359
KII								
Ah	54	m	c	CHIN	San Francisco	San Francisco P O	80	443
KIICHMEYSTER								
H W	32	m	w	HANO	San Francisco	1-Wd San Francisco	79	53
KIIHL								
Herman G	49	m	w	SHOL	San Francisco	6-Wd San Francisco	81	114
KIL								
Ah	30	m	c	CHIN	Colusa	Colusa	71	300
KILBERRY								
Jas T	25	m	w	MO	Siskiyou	Big Valley Twp	89	580
KILBORN								
John	47	m	w	ME	San Francisco	11-Wd San Francisc	84	434
KILBOURNE								
Ada C	25	f	w	ME	San Francisco	San Francisco P O	85	759
Chas E	26	m	w	OH	San Francisco	San Francisco P O	85	757
Walter L	38	m	w	CT	Santa Cruz	Soquel Twp	89	445
KILBRETH								
James	39	m	w	NY	Tulare	Tule Rvr Twp	92	259
KILBRIDE								
John	29	m	w	OH	Plumas	Indian Twp	77	17
Tunis	23	m	w	OH	San Luis Obispo	San Luis Obispo Tw	87	316
KILBURN								
Ann	45	f	w	NY	San Francisco	San Francisco P O	83	51
Benjamin	40	m	w	CANA	Colusa	Butte Twp	71	271
Carrol	32	m	w	PA	San Francisco	7-Wd San Francisco	81	166
Edwin	26	m	w	CANA	San Francisco	7-Wd San Francisco	81	208
Eliza	29	f	w	NY	San Francisco	11-Wd San Francisc	84	435
Fred	21	m	w	ME	Santa Cruz	Santa Cruz Twp	89	393
Guy	36	m	w	PA	Stanislaus	San Joaquin Twp	92	83
Guy	34	m	w	PA	Napa	Napa	75	51
Holton	45	m	w	NY	Colusa	Butte Twp	71	272
John	35	m	w	NY	San Francisco	San Francisco P O	83	205
Lewis L	43	m	w	VT	Colusa	Butte Twp	71	271
Ralph S	60	m	w	PA	Napa	Napa	75	13
Wells	64	m	w	PA	Napa	Napa Twp	75	67
KILBURY								
James	39	m	w	TX	Kern	Bakersfield P O	73	357
KILBY								
William	41	m	w	NY	Sacramento	Franklin Twp	77	108
KILCLINE								
Michael	30	m	w	IREL	San Francisco	8-Wd San Francisco	82	396
KILCOUR								
T S	40	m	w	ENGL	Alameda	Oakland	68	255
KILCUP								
Edward	39	m	w	ME	Sierra	Gibson Twp	89	541
KILDARE								
Ed J	21	m	w	MA	San Francisco	3-Wd San Francisco	79	325
KILDAY								
Bridget	34	f	w	IREL	San Francisco	6-Wd San Francisco	81	132
James	37	m	w	IREL	San Francisco	2-Wd San Francisco	79	272
James	27	m	w	IREL	San Francisco	San Francisco P O	83	146
Michael	27	m	w	IREL	San Francisco	San Francisco P O	83	146
Patrick	32	m	w	IREL	Placer	Rocklin Twp	76	465
William	34	m	w	IREL	San Francisco	San Francisco P O	83	146
KILDER								
Martin	32	m	w	NORW	San Francisco	8-Wd San Francisco	82	482
KILDOHL								
Charles	50	m	w	NORW	Solano	Denverton Twp	90	25
KILDUFF								
Bridget	30	f	w	IREL	San Francisco	11-Wd San Francisc	84	514
Marten	32	m	w	IREL	Napa	Napa	75	8
Patrick	38	m	w	IREL	San Francisco	San Francisco P O	80	366
Sarah	21	f	w	IREL	San Francisco	San Francisco P O	83	323
KILE								
Thomas	37	m	w	IL	Placer	Dutch Flat P O	76	415
William	38	m	w	IL	Solano	Silveyville Twp	90	85
William	28	m	w	PRUS	Solano	Silveyville Twp	90	87
KILEN								
James	30	m	w	IREL	Alameda	Oakland	68	165
KILER								
Jeremiah	48	m	w	NY	Del Norte	Crescent Twp	71	457
KILEY								
Amos W	40	m	w	MD	Sonoma	Petaluma Twp	91	314
J W	27	m	w	NY	Sacramento	3-Wd Sacramento	77	318
Pat	47	m	w	IREL	San Joaquin	Dent Twp	86	25
Robbert	22	m	w	IOFM	Trinity	Trinity Center Pct	92	205
Wm	30	m	w	NY	San Francisco	1-Wd San Francisco	79	34
KILFOIL								
James W	23	m	w	NY	San Francisco	San Francisco P O	83	236
KILGARIFF								
Anna	40	f	w	IREL	Sacramento	2-Wd Sacramento	77	211
John	30	m	w	IREL	San Francisco	San Francisco P O	83	70
KILGARY								
Jos	22	m	w	IREL	Sacramento	3-Wd Sacramento	77	265
KILGHE								
Martin	45	m	w	OH	Solano	Suisun Twp	90	103
KILGLASS								
Martin	20	m	w	IREL	San Francisco	11-Wd San Francisc	84	614
KILGO								
William	38	m	w	GA	Placer	Bath P O	76	447
KILGORE								
D C	33	m	w	IN	Sacramento	Brighton Twp	77	76
Go M	45	m	w	OH	Sacramento	Brighton Twp	77	76
J W	4	m	w	WI	Calaveras	Copperopolis P O	70	237
James	40	m	w	IN	Colusa	Colusa	71	298
Logan	39	m	w	MO	Colusa	Butte Twp	71	265
Mathew	69	m	w	OH	Sacramento	Brighton Twp	77	76
Mike	35	m	w	IREL	Solano	Vallejo	90	186
Mote	30	m	w	MO	Santa Barbara	Las Cruces P O	87	515
William	34	m	w	TN	San Diego	Temecula Dist	78	526
KILGORS								
George	54	m	w	SCOT	Nevada	Little York Twp	75	234
KILHEFFER								
Chris	68	m	w	PA	Calaveras	Copperopolis P O	70	258
KILIAN								
Fredk	50	m	w	BAVA	San Francisco	San Francisco P O	83	7
KILKENNY								
Anthony	27	m	w	IREL	Stanislaus	Empire Twp	92	47
James	29	m	w	IREL	Stanislaus	Empire Twp	92	47
KILL								
Ah	27	m	c	CHIN	Yolo	Cache Crk Twp	93	435
James	30	m	w	NY	Solano	Silveyville Twp	90	85
KILLA								
John	25	m	w	IREL	Sacramento	Granite Twp	77	139
KILLADE								
John	49	m	w	IREL	Santa Clara	2-Wd San Jose	88	330
KILLALEA								
Catherine	24	f	w	IREL	Marin	San Rafael	74	52
Patrick	33	m	w	IREL	San Francisco	San Francisco P O	83	298
KILLBURY								
A M	50	m	w	OH	Nevada	Nevada Twp	75	274

© 2001 by Heritage Quest. All rights reserved.

Name	Age	S	R	B-PL	County	Locale	Series M593 Roll	Pg
KILLCORN								
Patrick	35	m	w	IREL	Santa Clara	San Jose Twp	88	195
KILLDAY								
John	27	m	w	IREL	San Francisco	7-Wd San Francisco	81	172
Patrick	65	m	w	IREL	San Francisco	San Francisco P O	83	332
KILLEBREW								
William	45	m	w	MO	Solano	Silveyville Twp	90	91
KILLEEN								
M N	42	m	w	CANA	Merced	Snelling P O	74	272
Malichi	31	m	w	IREL	San Francisco	San Francisco P O	85	757
KILLELEL								
Jno	35	m	w	IREL	Sacramento	3-Wd Sacramento	77	315
KILLEM								
John	28	m	w	IREL	Sacramento	2-Wd Sacramento	77	224
Richard	35	m	w	CANA	Nevada	Little York Twp	75	241
KILLEN								
Edward	28	m	c	IREL	San Francisco	7-Wd San Francisco	81	185
John	58	m	w	MA	Solano	Vallejo	90	202
KILLENER								
C	59	m	w	NY	Amador	Jackson P O	69	323
KILLER								
Anthony	75	m	w	NC	El Dorado	Georgetown Twp	72	41
James	35	m	w	NY	Sacramento	Franklin Twp	77	120
Martin	27	m	w	HANO	San Francisco	11-Wd San Francisc	84	430
Wm	23	m	w	CAPE	San Francisco	8-Wd San Francisco	82	360
KILLET								
Rose A	31	f	w	IREL	Stanislaus	Emory Twp	92	16
KILLEY								
Alvin M	42	m	w	RI	Plumas	Plumas Twp	77	32
Chas H	44	m	w	RI	San Francisco	San Francisco P O	85	738
Dehlia	32	f	w	IREL	Santa Clara	Gilroy Twp	88	79
John	34	m	w	IREL	San Joaquin	Elliott Twp	86	79
Mary	27	f	w	IREL	San Francisco	San Francisco P O	83	413
Robert P	40	m	w	NY	El Dorado	Mud Springs Twp	72	84
Thos W	50	m	w	VT	Santa Clara	Gilroy Twp	88	79
KILLGANN								
Geo	38	m	w	RUSS	San Francisco	8-Wd San Francisco	82	376
KILLGORE								
Al C	52	m	w	OH	Sonoma	Washington Twp	91	465
F G	29	m	w	OH	Trinity	Weaverville Pct	92	227
KILLHAM								
Thos	27	m	w	NJ	Nevada	Nevada Twp	75	309
KILLIAN								
J	26	m	w	PA	Lake	Knoxville Mines	73	404
Thomas	28	m	w	IREL	San Francisco	11-Wd San Francisc	84	634
KILLIE								
Annie	38	f	w	IREL	San Francisco	San Francisco P O	83	139
KILLIGAN								
John	28	m	w	IREL	Humboldt	Eureka Twp	72	278
KILLIKEN								
Abram	50	m	w	SWIT	Yuba	Marysville	93	616
KILLILEA								
Ryan	42	m	w	IREL	San Francisco	8-Wd San Francisco	82	371
KILLIMADE								
John	27	m	w	IREL	San Francisco	11-Wd San Francisc	84	439
KILLIN								
George	35	m	w	IREL	San Francisco	San Francisco P O	83	331
KILLINER								
Henry C	46	m	w	VA	Placer	Colfax P O	76	389
KILLINGER								
John	50	m	w	IN	Shasta	Dog Crk P O	89	471
KILLIP								
Jasper	35	m	w	WI	San Francisco	8-Wd San Francisco	82	344
W C	28	m	w	CANA	Sierra	Forest	89	536
KILLNARRA								
Micheal	38	m	w	IREL	San Francisco	7-Wd San Francisco	81	189
KILLOG								
Philander	28	m	w	IL	Napa	Napa	75	12
KILLOGG								
George	45	m	w	MA	Napa	Napa	75	8
KILLON								
John	58	m	w	NORW	Solano	Vallejo	90	198
KILLOUGH								
John	28	m	w	IREL	Humboldt	Eureka Twp	72	262
Robt	40	m	w	CANA	Humboldt	Eureka Twp	72	263
KILLPACK								
John	40	m	w	ENGL	San Francisco	11-Wd San Francisc	84	583
KILLPATRICK								
D W	47	m	w	OH	El Dorado	Georgetown Twp	72	47
John	42	m	w	IREL	San Francisco	7-Wd San Francisco	81	207
KILLY								
Jane	70	f	w	IREL	San Francisco	11-Wd San Francisc	84	635
Patrick	29	m	w	IREL	Humboldt	Eureka Twp	72	282
KILMAN								
John	30	m	w	GERM	Yolo	Cottonwood Twp	93	462
KILMER								
Catherin	51	f	w	NY	San Francisco	8-Wd San Francisco	82	451
Wm	22	m	w	PA	Sutter	Sutter Twp	92	121
KILMORE								
George	41	m	w	PRUS	Santa Clara	San Jose Twp	88	214
KILPATRCK								
T H	26	m	w	IREL	Napa	Yountville Twp	75	81
KILPATRICK								
Andrew	34	m	w	IREL	San Mateo	San Mateo P O	87	360
David	38	m	w	IREL	Sacramento	4-Wd Sacramento	77	365
David	29	m	w	IREL	Colusa	Colusa	71	298
James	27	m	w	SCOT	San Francisco	San Francisco P O	83	222
Mary	26	f	w	ENGL	San Francisco	7-Wd San Francisco	81	231
KILROY								
Bridget	40	f	w	IREL	San Francisco	San Francisco P O	85	855
Mathew	61	m	w	IREL	Yuba	W Bear Rvr Twp	93	683
Nathan	60	m	w	IREL	Nevada	Bloomfield Twp	75	97
Patrick	30	m	w	IREL	San Francisco	11-Wd San Francisc	84	585
William	39	m	w	NY	Nevada	Bloomfield Twp	75	97
KILSEY								
Wm	78	m	w	TN	Lake	Big Valley	73	394
KILSON								
Alexander	28	m	w	SCOT	Sacramento	2-Wd Sacramento	77	214
George	37	m	w	PA	Stanislaus	Empire Twp	92	55
KILTHMAN								
Frederick	50	m	w	PRUS	Plumas	Rich Bar Twp	77	46
KILTIE								
John	14	m	w	SCOT	Alameda	Washington Twp	68	295
KILTON								
A K	39	m	w	ME	Alameda	Oakland	68	131
John	35	m	w	ENGL	Sacramento	4-Wd Sacramento	77	358
John	24	m	w	NY	Yuba	Marysville	93	586
KILVEIN								
John	32	m	w	IREL	San Joaquin	Castoria Twp	86	2
KILYN								
James	52	m	w	IREL	Sacramento	Cosumnes Twp	77	89
KIM								
---	25	m	c	CHIN	Siskiyou	Scott Valley Twp	89	611
---	15	m	c	CHIN	Siskiyou	Scott Valley Twp	89	611
Ah	75	m	c	CHIN	El Dorado	Cosumnes Twp	72	16
Ah	60	m	c	CHIN	Placer	Auburn P O	76	378
Ah	6	f	c	CA	San Francisco	San Francisco P O	80	450
Ah	55	m	c	CHIN	El Dorado	Diamond Springs Tw	72	26
Ah	53	m	c	CHIN	Mariposa	Mariposa P O	74	106
Ah	52	m	c	CHIN	Fresno	Millerton P O	72	202
Ah	50	m	c	CHIN	Nevada	Bloomfield Twp	75	96
Ah	50	m	c	CHIN	Klamath	South Fork Twp	73	384
Ah	49	m	c	CHIN	San Francisco	San Francisco P O	80	527
Ah	48	m	c	CHIN	Mariposa	Mariposa P O	74	105
Ah	45	m	c	CHIN	El Dorado	White Oak Twp	72	142
Ah	44	m	c	CHIN	Calaveras	Copperopolis P O	70	264
Ah	43	m	c	CHIN	Placer	Roseville P O	76	349
Ah	42	m	c	CHIN	Placer	Lincoln P O	76	484
Ah	41	f	c	CHIN	San Francisco	San Francisco P O	80	453
Ah	41	m	c	CHIN	Mariposa	Maxwell Crk P O	74	146
Ah	40	m	c	CHIN	Placer	Dutch Flat P O	76	407
Ah	40	f	c	CHIN	Placer	Auburn P O	76	370
Ah	40	m	c	CHIN	Amador	Fiddletown P O	69	436
Ah	4	f	c	CA	San Francisco	San Francisco P O	80	452
Ah	39	m	c	CHIN	Nevada	Washington Twp	75	342
Ah	39	m	c	CHIN	Placer	Newcastle Twp	76	475
Ah	39	m	c	CHIN	El Dorado	White Oak Twp	72	143
Ah	39	m	c	CHIN	El Dorado	Coloma Twp	72	12
Ah	39	m	c	CHIN	Mariposa	Mariposa P O	74	132
Ah	38	m	c	CHIN	Mariposa	Mariposa P O	74	102
Ah	38	m	c	CHIN	Mariposa	Mariposa P O	74	106
Ah	37	m	c	CHIN	Nevada	Washington Twp	75	344
Ah	37	m	c	CHIN	Plumas	Rich Bar Twp	77	46
Ah	37	m	c	CHIN	San Francisco	San Francisco P O	80	446
Ah	36	m	c	CHIN	Sierra	Sears Twp	89	560
Ah	36	m	c	CHIN	San Francisco	San Francisco P O	80	503
Ah	36	m	c	CHIN	San Francisco	San Francisco P O	80	441
Ah	36	m	c	CHIN	San Francisco	San Francisco P O	80	450
Ah	35	m	c	CHIN	Nevada	Little York Twp	75	242
Ah	35	m	c	CHIN	Alameda	Oakland	68	238
Ah	35	m	c	CHIN	Butte	Kimshew Tpw	70	84
Ah	35	m	c	CHIN	Mariposa	Maxwell Crk P O	74	138
Ah	35	m	c	CHIN	Sierra	Eureka Twp	89	525
Ah	35	m	c	CHIN	Stanislaus	Buena Vista Twp	92	13
Ah	34	m	c	CHIN	Sacramento	Cosumnes Twp	77	92
Ah	34	m	c	CHIN	Nevada	Grass Valley Twp	75	204
Ah	34	m	c	CHIN	San Francisco	San Francisco P O	80	447
Ah	34	f	c	CHIN	San Francisco	San Francisco P O	80	449
Ah	34	m	c	CHIN	Mariposa	Mariposa P O	74	134
Ah	34	m	c	CHIN	Yolo	Grafton Twp	93	495
Ah	34	m	c	CHIN	San Francisco	San Francisco P O	83	85
Ah	33	m	c	CHIN	Mariposa	Mariposa P O	74	125
Ah	33	m	c	CHIN	Mariposa	Mariposa P O	74	107
Ah	32	m	c	CHIN	Sierra	Sears Twp	89	554
Ah	32	m	c	CHIN	Santa Clara	Santa Clara Twp	88	168
Ah	32	m	c	CHIN	Santa Clara	1-Wd San Jose	88	273
Ah	32	m	c	CHIN	Mariposa	Mariposa P O	74	91
Ah	32	m	c	CHIN	Mariposa	Mariposa P O	74	98
Ah	32	m	c	CHIN	San Francisco	San Francisco P O	80	495
Ah	31	m	c	CHIN	Mendocino	Gualala Twp	74	225
Ah	31	m	c	CHIN	Solano	Silveyville Twp	90	87
Ah	30	m	c	CHIN	Trinity	Junction City Pct	92	207
Ah	30	m	c	CHIN	San Francisco	San Francisco P O	80	505
Ah	30	m	c	CHIN	Placer	Auburn P O	76	379
Ah	30	m	c	CHIN	San Francisco	3-Wd San Francisco	79	329
Ah	30	f	c	CHIN	San Francisco	San Francisco P O	80	449
Ah	30	m	c	CHIN	El Dorado	Coloma Twp	72	11
Ah	30	m	c	CHIN	Butte	Chico Twp	70	30
Ah	30	m	c	CHIN	Calaveras	Copperopolis P O	70	242
Ah	30	m	c	CHIN	Sierra	Lincoln Twp	89	546
Ah	30	m	c	CHIN	San Francisco	San Francisco P O	80	498
Ah	29	m	c	CHIN	Nevada	Bridgeport Twp	75	125
Ah	28	m	c	CHIN	San Francisco	San Francisco P O	80	512
Ah	28	m	c	CHIN	Nevada	Grass Valley Twp	75	205

© 2001 by Heritage Quest. All rights reserved.

Name	Age	S	R	B-PL	County	Locale	Roll	Pg
						Series M593		
Ah	28	m	c	CHIN	Nevada	Bridgeport Twp	75	125
Ah	27	m	c	CHIN	Nevada	Rough & Ready Twp	75	337
Ah	27	m	c	CHIN	Plumas	Goodwin Twp	77	8
Ah	27	m	c	CHIN	Nevada	Nevada Twp	75	299
Ah	27	m	c	CHIN	Nevada	Little York Twp	75	245
Ah	27	m	c	CHIN	San Francisco	1-Wd San Francisco	79	43
Ah	26	m	c	CHIN	Shasta	French Gulch P O	89	467
Ah	26	f	c	CHIN	Santa Clara	1-Wd San Jose	88	272
Ah	26	m	c	CHIN	San Francisco	San Francisco P O	80	488
Ah	26	m	c	CHIN	Nevada	Grass Valley Twp	75	202
Ah	26	m	c	CHIN	San Francisco	San Francisco P O	80	436
Ah	26	f	c	CHIN	San Francisco	San Francisco P O	80	438
Ah	26	m	c	CHIN	San Francisco	San Francisco P O	80	498
Ah	25	m	c	CHIN	San Francisco	San Francisco P O	80	512
Ah	25	m	c	CHIN	Plumas	Goodwin Twp	77	5
Ah	25	f	c	CHIN	Placer	Dutch Flat P O	76	408
Ah	25	m	c	CHIN	Placer	Dutch Flat P O	76	408
Ah	25	m	c	CHIN	Nevada	Nevada Twp	75	298
Ah	25	m	c	CHIN	Amador	Jackson P O	69	329
Ah	25	m	c	CHIN	Trinity	Douglas	92	232
Ah	25	m	c	CHIN	Sacramento	2-Wd Sacramento	77	246
Ah	25	m	c	CHIN	Placer	Auburn P O	76	377
Ah	25	m	c	CHIN	Placer	Auburn P O	76	373
Ah	25	m	c	CHIN	Mariposa	Mariposa P O	74	92
Ah	25	m	c	CHIN	San Francisco	2-Wd San Francisco	79	285
Ah	25	m	c	CHIN	Sierra	Sears Twp	89	561
Ah	24	m	c	CHIN	Trinity	Junction City Pct	92	207
Ah	24	m	c	CHIN	San Francisco	San Francisco P O	83	298
Ah	24	m	c	CHIN	Nevada	Washington Twp	75	347
Ah	24	m	c	CHIN	Placer	Dutch Flat P O	76	410
Ah	24	m	c	CHIN	San Bernardino	San Bernardino Twp	78	433
Ah	24	f	c	CHIN	San Francisco	San Francisco P O	80	432
Ah	24	m	c	CHIN	San Francisco	San Francisco P O	80	446
Ah	24	m	c	CHIN	Tehama	Red Bluff	92	182
Ah	24	m	c	CHIN	Yuba	Marysville	93	576
Ah	24	m	c	CHIN	San Francisco	11-Wd San Francisc	84	503
Ah	23	m	c	CHIN	Mendocino	Gualala Twp	74	223
Ah	23	f	c	CHIN	San Francisco	San Francisco P O	80	433
Ah	22	m	c	CHIN	Tehama	Tehama Twp	92	192
Ah	22	m	c	CHIN	Placer	Summit P O	76	496
Ah	22	m	c	CHIN	Placer	Auburn P O	76	378
Ah	22	m	c	CHIN	Nevada	Nevada Twp	75	277
Ah	22	f	c	CHIN	San Francisco	San Francisco P O	80	444
Ah	22	f	c	CHIN	San Francisco	San Francisco P O	80	445
Ah	22	m	c	CHIN	El Dorado	Mud Springs Twp	72	88
Ah	22	m	c	CHIN	Sierra	Sears Twp	89	554
Ah	22	m	c	CHIN	San Francisco	San Francisco P O	80	490
Ah	21	f	c	CHIN	San Francisco	San Francisco P O	80	507
Ah	21	f	c	CHIN	San Francisco	San Francisco P O	80	526
Ah	21	m	c	CHIN	Nevada	Eureka Twp	75	134
Ah	21	m	c	CHIN	Sierra	Table Rock Twp	89	544
Ah	20	m	c	CHIN	San Francisco	6-Wd San Francisco	81	140
Ah	20	m	c	CHIN	San Francisco	2-Wd San Francisco	79	227
Ah	20	m	c	CHIN	San Francisco	San Francisco P O	83	152
Ah	20	m	c	CHIN	San Francisco	San Francisco P O	80	437
Ah	20	m	c	CHIN	Yuba	Marysville	93	602
Ah	2	m	c	CA	San Francisco	San Francisco P O	80	451
Ah	19	m	c	CHIN	Santa Clara	Fremont Twp	88	60
Ah	19	f	c	CHIN	San Francisco	San Francisco P O	80	432
Ah	18	m	c	CHIN	Sacramento	2-Wd Sacramento	77	221
Ah	18	m	c	CHIN	Nevada	Nevada Twp	75	314
Ah	18	m	c	CHIN	Nevada	Nevada Twp	75	321
Ah	18	m	c	CHIN	San Francisco	2-Wd San Francisco	79	178
Ah	17	m	c	CHIN	Santa Clara	Fremont Twp	88	60
Ah	17	m	c	CHIN	San Francisco	8-Wd San Francisco	82	493
Ah	17	m	c	CHIN	San Francisco	11-Wd San Francisc	84	522
Ah	17	m	c	CHIN	Nevada	Grass Valley Twp	75	198
Ah	16	m	c	CHIN	San Francisco	San Francisco P O	80	457
Ah	16	m	c	CHIN	Contra Costa	Martinez P O	71	397
Ah	16	m	c	CHIN	San Francisco	6-Wd San Francisco	81	40
Ah	14	m	c	CHIN	San Francisco	3-Wd San Francisco	79	309
Ah	14	m	c	CHIN	Solano	Benicia	90	12
Ah	13	f	c	CHIN	San Francisco	San Francisco P O	80	450
Ang	37	m	c	CHIN	Plumas	Seneca Twp	77	48
Ang	32	m	c	CHIN	Plumas	Seneca Twp	77	48
Aug	26	m	c	CHIN	Yuba	Marysville	93	626
Bung	50	m	c	CHIN	Mariposa	Mariposa P O	74	126
Chim	27	m	c	CHIN	Yuba	Marysville	93	621
Chu	22	f	c	CHIN	Sierra	Lincoln Twp	89	550
Emma	30	f	w	NY	San Francisco	San Francisco P O	80	485
Foo	23	f	c	CHIN	Yuba	Marysville	93	627
Fung	37	f	w	CHIN	Plumas	Mineral Twp	77	24
Gin	22	f	c	CHIN	Yuba	Marysville	93	626
Hi	30	m	c	CHIN	Yuba	Marysville	93	624
How	24	f	c	CHIN	Yuba	Marysville	93	626
Hup	27	m	c	CHIN	Yuba	Marysville	93	621
Jake	37	m	c	CHIN	San Joaquin	Oneal Twp	86	108
Jin	30	m	c	CHIN	Yuba	Marysville	93	624
John	28	m	w	SWIT	San Francisco	8-Wd San Francisco	82	366
Ju	28	m	c	CHIN	Yuba	Marysville	93	629
Kam	34	m	c	CHIN	Yuba	Marysville	93	621
Kei	31	m	c	CHIN	Yuba	Marysville	93	632
Koo	29	m	c	CHIN	Yuba	Marysville	93	624
Lee	27	m	c	CHIN	Yuba	Marysville	93	628
Lee	19	m	c	CHIN	San Francisco	6-Wd San Francisco	81	52
Lew	39	f	c	CHIN	Yuba	Marysville	93	626
Lo	28	m	c	CHIN	Siskiyou	Hamburg Twp	89	599
Lock	22	m	c	CHIN	Placer	Bath P O	76	441
Long	28	f	c	CHIN	Yuba	Marysville	93	626
Lun	32	m	c	CHIN	Yuba	Marysville	93	623
Me	32	f	c	CHIN	Yuba	Marysville	93	627
Moi	24	m	c	CHIN	Yuba	Marysville	93	624
Newey	32	m	c	CHIN	Yuba	Marysville	93	628
On	18	m	c	CHIN	San Francisco	San Francisco P O	83	99
Samuel J	52	m	w	NC	Calaveras	San Andreas P O	70	154
See	22	m	c	CHIN	Yuba	Marysville	93	630
Seo	42	m	c	CHIN	Calaveras	Copperopolis P O	70	264
Sing	34	m	c	CHIN	Yuba	Marysville	93	624
Song	4	m	c	CA	Yuba	Marysville	93	627
Toy	22	f	c	CHIN	Placer	Dutch Flat P O	76	407
Woo	20	m	c	CHIN	San Francisco	2-Wd San Francisco	79	177
Yan	23	f	c	CHIN	Placer	Dutch Flat P O	76	410
Ye	36	m	c	CHIN	Yuba	Marysville	93	625
Yeck	30	m	c	CHIN	San Francisco	San Francisco P O	83	72
Yen	35	m	c	CHIN	Yuba	Marysville	93	630
Yock	51	m	c	CHIN	Placer	Bath P O	76	441
Yon	25	m	c	CHIN	Sierra	Downieville Twp	89	521
Young	45	m	c	CHIN	Yuba	Marysville	93	620
Young	26	m	c	CHIN	San Francisco	San Francisco P O	83	72
Yuen	32	f	c	CHIN	Yuba	Marysville	93	627
Yung	28	m	c	CHIN	Yuba	Marysville	93	621
KIMAN								
John	47	m	w	EIND	San Mateo	San Mateo P O	87	350
KIMB								
Chon	30	m	c	CHIN	Yuba	Marysville	93	623
KIMBA								
Franklin	27	m	w	NH	El Dorado	Placerville	72	127
KIMBALL								
A	25	f	w	ME	Alameda	Oakland	68	151
A G	53	m	w	TN	Alameda	Oakland	68	219
Alixander	25	m	w	ENGL	San Francisco	7-Wd San Francisco	81	180
Alonzo	26	m	w	NY	Amador	Volcano P O	69	377
Annie	9	f	w	CA	Yuba	Long Bar Twp	93	565
Archie	36	m	w	SCOT	Colusa	Monroe Twp	71	324
Asa	33	m	w	VT	Solano	Vallejo	90	172
Bartholomew	66	m	w	TN	Colusa	Spring Valley Twp	71	345
C B	43	m	w	ME	Yuba	Marysville	93	583
C F	48	m	w	ME	San Francisco	San Francisco P O	85	831
C H	52	m	w	ME	Sierra	Butte Twp	89	512
C M	23	m	w	IREL	San Francisco	7-Wd San Francisco	81	223
Chas	30	m	w	ENGL	San Francisco	5-Wd San Francisco	81	18
Chs H	40	m	w	ME	Yuba	Marysville	93	595
D C	45	m	w	MA	Nevada	Meadow Lake Twp	75	247
Dilia	55	f	w	NY	Alameda	Oakland	68	156
E C	23	m	w	OH	Sutter	Yuba Twp	92	142
Edward	31	m	w	ME	Napa	Napa	75	57
Edwin	39	m	w	NY	Alameda	Eden Twp	68	80
Edwin	38	m	w	NH	San Francisco	San Francisco P O	85	778
Frank	40	m	w	CT	Marin	Point Reyes Twp	74	22
Fred	10	m	w	CA	Yuba	Marysville	93	579
G P	40	m	w	MA	San Francisco	San Francisco P O	85	778
Geo	45	m	w	NH	San Diego	San Diego	78	510
Geo W	23	m	w	ME	San Francisco	San Francisco P O	83	26
Geo W	18	m	w	OH	El Dorado	Placerville Twp	72	97
George	64	m	w	IL	Contra Costa	Martinez P O	71	400
George	31	m	w	ENGL	San Francisco	7-Wd San Francisco	81	221
George M	44	m	w	ME	Sonoma	Vallejo Twp	91	454
H	67	m	w	NY	Alameda	Oakland	68	235
H	50	m	w	PA	Yuba	W Bear Rvr Twp	93	680
H	28	m	w	PRUS	San Joaquin	2-Wd Stockton	86	205
Hazen	58	m	w	NH	San Francisco	San Francisco P O	80	404
Henry H	36	m	w	NY	Sierra	Eureka Twp	89	525
J Henry	40	m	w	MA	Humboldt	Eureka Twp	72	265
John	54	m	w	MA	Calaveras	Copperopolis P O	70	252
John	39	m	w	ME	Sutter	Sutter Twp	92	124
John	31	m	w	GERM	San Joaquin	2-Wd Stockton	86	172
John	26	m	w	MO	Solano	Suisun Twp	90	100
John R	33	m	w	NJ	Shasta	Shasta P O	89	456
John S	30	m	w	ME	Mendocino	Navarro & Big Rvr	74	176
Joseph	31	m	w	TN	Colusa	Spring Valley Twp	71	345
Josiah	46	m	w	ME	Tuolumne	Sonora P O	93	331
L S	50	m	w	NY	Sonoma	Salt Point	91	381
Lizzie	45	f	w	ME	San Francisco	8-Wd San Francisco	82	315
Louis W	43	m	w	NH	San Diego	San Diego	78	510
Louisa	17	f	w	CA	San Francisco	San Francisco P O	85	798
Maria	25	f	w	NH	San Francisco	6-Wd San Francisco	81	116
Mary	6	f	w	CA	San Francisco	San Francisco P O	80	385
Mary	40	f	w	UT	Yuba	Marysville	93	582
Mary A	28	f	w	ME	San Francisco	8-Wd San Francisco	82	330
Mathew H	38	m	w	VT	San Francisco	San Francisco P O	83	160
Milton	26	m	w	MA	San Francisco	San Francisco P O	83	388
Moses	43	m	w	ME	San Francisco	San Francisco P O	80	383
Penelope	25	f	w	HAMB	San Francisco	2-Wd San Francisco	79	243
S P	39	m	w	MA	Solano	Vallejo	90	197
Solomon	52	m	w	ME	San Francisco	San Francisco P O	83	115
T F	36	m	w	ME	Yuba	Marysville	93	578
T W	21	m	w	IN	San Joaquin	Liberty Twp	86	92
Thos D	38	m	w	ME	San Francisco	San Francisco P O	83	115
Thos L	33	m	w	NY	San Francisco	San Francisco P O	83	174
W B	32	m	w	IL	Sierra	Eureka Twp	89	525
W C	40	m	w	NH	Alameda	Oakland	68	155
William	37	m	w	ME	Yuba	North East Twp	93	644
KIMBELL								
Charles	51	m	w	PA	Colusa	Colusa Twp	71	286

© 2001 by Heritage Quest. All rights reserved.

Name	Age	S	R	B-PL	County	Locale	Roll	Pg
Chas M	43	m	w	MA	San Francisco	3-Wd San Francisco	79	327
Fernando	31	m	w	VT	San Francisco	8-Wd San Francisco	82	461
George	40	m	w	MA	Placer	Dutch Flat P O	76	414
Tim	21	m	w	MI	San Joaquin	Elkhorn Twp	86	56
KIMBER								
Wm	34	m	w	PA	Sacramento	4-Wd Sacramento	77	332
KIMBERLEY								
Nathaniel	47	m	w	CT	Solano	Vacaville Twp	90	132
KIMBERLIN								
James M	42	m	w	VA	Santa Clara	Santa Clara Twp	88	138
KIMBERLY								
Martin M	43	m	w	CT	Santa Barbara	Santa Barbara P O	87	467
Oliver	45	m	w	NY	Stanislaus	Empire Twp	92	44
KIMBLE								
Aaron P	70	m	w	MA	Sacramento	Mississippi Twp	77	164
Amelia	40	f	w	ME	Alameda	Hayward	68	75
Arthur	24	m	w	MO	Los Angeles	San Jose Twp	73	623
Chas	27	m	w	NJ	San Francisco	11-Wd San Francisc	84	622
Geo	38	m	w	OH	San Joaquin	Oneal Twp	86	108
George H	41	m	w	MA	Stanislaus	Emory Twp	92	25
L	44	m	w	NH	San Joaquin	Elkhorn Twp	86	61
Miranda	37	m	w	RI	Alameda	Brooklyn Twp	68	42
Nathan A	28	m	w	MO	Los Angeles	San Jose Twp	73	623
Thos	45	m	w	ME	San Francisco	11-Wd San Francisc	84	674
KIMD								
Ah	42	m	c	CHIN	Nevada	Eureka Twp	75	141
KIME								
D M	41	m	w	OH	Sierra	Downieville Twp	89	520
Jas H	31	m	w	OH	Solano	Vallejo	90	185
KIMERY								
Martin	41	m	w	OH	Sutter	Sutter Twp	92	125
KIMEVER								
Michael	38	m	w	OH	El Dorado	Diamond Springs Tw	72	28
KIMEY								
Elizabeth	25	f	w	MI	Placer	Lincoln P O	76	490
KIMM								
Ah	30	m	c	CHIN	Mendocino	Point Arena Twp	74	208
Ah	28	m	c	CHIN	San Francisco	11-Wd San Francisc	84	620
Ah	28	m	c	CHIN	San Francisco	6-Wd San Francisco	81	42
Ah	19	m	c	CHIN	Mendocino	Albion & Big Rvr T	74	166
Lee	37	m	c	CHIN	San Francisco	6-Wd San Francisco	81	130
KIMMAR								
Karl	24	m	w	IL	Humboldt	Eureka Twp	72	259
KIMMEL								
Fredk	14	m	w	CA	San Francisco	San Francisco P O	85	782
John	50	m	w	GERM	San Francisco	7-Wd San Francisco	81	241
KIMMELLIEB								
Minnie	8M	f	w	CA	San Francisco	7-Wd San Francisco	81	286
KIMMINS								
Jos	38	m	w	NY	Solano	Vallejo	90	160
KIMP								
Ah	42	m	c	CHIN	San Francisco	San Francisco P O	80	493
William	25	m	w	SC	Alameda	Oakland	68	172
KIMPEY								
John	14	m	w	AUST	Santa Clara	San Jose Twp	88	214
KIMPTON								
William	45	m	w	ENGL	San Mateo	Woodside P O	87	381
KIMSON								
J	41	m	w	IREL	Sierra	Lincoln Twp	89	545
KIMSTELL								
Martin	35	m	w	WURT	San Francisco	San Francisco P O	83	212
KIMSTZ								
Ernest	42	m	w	PRUS	Santa Cruz	Santa Cruz	89	419
KIN								
Ah	60	m	c	CHIN	Tuolumne	Big Oak Flat P O	93	397
Ah	56	m	c	CHIN	Mariposa	Mariposa P O	74	102
Ah	50	m	c	CHIN	Mariposa	Mariposa P O	74	92
Ah	49	m	c	CHIN	Calaveras	San Andreas P O	70	161
Ah	45	m	c	CHIN	Mono	Bridgeport P O	74	282
Ah	43	m	c	CHIN	San Francisco	San Francisco P O	80	502
Ah	41	m	c	CHIN	Plumas	Goodwin Twp	77	4
Ah	41	m	c	CHIN	Butte	Hamilton Twp	70	67
Ah	41	m	c	CHIN	Yuba	Marysville	93	630
Ah	40	m	c	CHIN	San Francisco	6-Wd San Francisco	81	65
Ah	40	m	c	CHIN	El Dorado	Coloma Twp	72	6
Ah	40	m	c	CHIN	Nevada	Grass Valley Twp	75	205
Ah	38	m	c	CHIN	Tuolumne	Sonora P O	93	311
Ah	37	m	c	CHIN	Placer	Pino Twp	76	471
Ah	37	m	c	CHIN	Calaveras	San Andreas P O	70	155
Ah	37	m	c	CHIN	San Francisco	San Francisco P O	80	510
Ah	36	m	c	CHIN	San Francisco	San Francisco P O	80	495
Ah	36	m	c	CHIN	Calaveras	San Andreas P O	70	167
Ah	35	m	c	CHIN	Mariposa	Mariposa P O	74	92
Ah	35	m	c	CHIN	Calaveras	Copperopolis P O	70	230
Ah	34	m	c	CHIN	San Francisco	11-Wd San Francisc	84	503
Ah	33	m	c	CHIN	Amador	Jackson P O	69	330
Ah	33	m	c	CHIN	Mariposa	Maxwell Crk P O	74	141
Ah	33	m	c	CHIN	Nevada	Bridgeport Twp	75	114
Ah	32	m	c	CHIN	Solano	Rio Vista Twp	90	59
Ah	32	m	c	CHIN	San Francisco	San Francisco P O	83	126
Ah	32	m	c	CHIN	San Francisco	San Francisco P O	85	748
Ah	32	m	c	CHIN	San Francisco	San Francisco P O	80	519
Ah	31	m	c	CHIN	Sonoma	Sonoma Twp	91	449
Ah	30	m	c	CHIN	Santa Cruz	Pajaro Twp	89	342
Ah	30	m	c	CHIN	Plumas	Goodwin Twp	77	4
Ah	30	m	c	CHIN	El Dorado	Mud Springs Twp	72	79
Ah	30	m	c	CHIN	Santa Clara	Burnett Twp	88	30
Ah	30	m	c	CHIN	Sonoma	Sonoma Twp	91	436
Ah	30	m	c	CHIN	Del Norte	Happy Camp Twp	71	469
Ah	29	m	c	CHIN	Placer	Auburn P O	76	381
Ah	29	m	c	CHIN	Alameda	Eden Twp	68	64
Ah	29	m	c	CHIN	Napa	Napa	75	7
Ah	28	m	c	CHIN	San Francisco	San Francisco P O	80	501
Ah	28	m	c	CHIN	Mariposa	Maxwell Crk P O	74	142
Ah	28	m	c	CHIN	Calaveras	Copperopolis P O	70	234
Ah	28	m	c	CHIN	Nevada	Nevada Twp	75	298
Ah	26	m	c	CHIN	Nevada	Nevada Twp	75	312
Ah	26	m	c	CHIN	Shasta	American Ranch P O	89	499
Ah	26	m	c	CHIN	Nevada	Nevada Twp	75	311
Ah	24	m	c	CHIN	Solano	Silveyville Twp	90	85
Ah	24	f	c	CHIN	Los Angeles	Los Angeles	73	564
Ah	24	m	c	CHIN	Amador	Lancha Plana P O	69	369
Ah	23	m	c	CHIN	San Francisco	6-Wd San Francisco	81	41
Ah	22	m	c	CHIN	Sierra	Lincoln Twp	89	548
Ah	22	m	c	CHIN	San Francisco	8-Wd San Francisco	82	334
Ah	22	m	c	CHIN	Nevada	Nevada Twp	75	297
Ah	22	m	c	CHIN	El Dorado	Diamond Springs Tw	72	27
Ah	22	m	c	CHIN	Los Angeles	Los Angeles	73	565
Ah	21	m	c	CHIN	San Francisco	3-Wd San Francisco	79	306
Ah	21	m	c	CHIN	Santa Clara	Gilroy Twp	88	75
Ah	21	m	c	CHIN	Placer	Dutch Flat P O	76	410
Ah	20	m	c	CHIN	San Francisco	San Francisco P O	80	513
Ah	19	m	c	CHIN	Tuolumne	Big Oak Flat P O	93	398
Ah	19	m	c	CHIN	Alameda	Alameda	68	16
Ah	19	m	c	CHIN	San Francisco	San Francisco P O	85	725
Ah	18	m	c	CHIN	Placer	Clipper Gap P O	76	393
Ah	17	m	c	CHIN	San Joaquin	1-Wd Stockton	86	143
Ah	15	m	c	CHIN	Nevada	Nevada Twp	75	316
Ah	14	m	c	CHIN	San Francisco	3-Wd San Francisco	79	329
Ah	13	m	c	CHIN	San Francisco	11-Wd San Francisc	84	429
Chi	28	f	c	CHIN	Placer	Auburn P O	76	370
Chong	42	m	c	CHIN	Calaveras	San Andreas P O	70	161
Chow	26	m	c	CHIN	Nevada	Bridgeport Twp	75	111
Far	15	f	c	CHIN	San Francisco	6-Wd San Francisco	81	67
Foo	22	f	c	CHIN	San Francisco	11-Wd San Francisc	84	509
Gee	28	m	c	CHIN	Butte	Chico Twp	70	53
Goo	34	m	c	CHIN	El Dorado	Salmon Falls Twp	72	134
Him	23	f	c	CHIN	Tuolumne	Columbia P O	93	341
Hin	43	m	c	CHIN	Yuba	Marysville	93	620
Hop	20	m	c	CHIN	San Francisco	6-Wd San Francisco	81	50
King	34	m	c	CHIN	Solano	Rio Vista Twp	90	70
Kow	17	m	c	CHIN	San Francisco	6-Wd San Francisco	81	85
Long	36	m	c	CHIN	Placer	Bath P O	76	439
Lou	29	m	c	CHIN	Yuba	Marysville	93	625
Lung	38	m	c	CHIN	Nevada	Rough & Ready Twp	75	329
On	49	m	c	CHIN	Placer	Gold Run Twp	76	400
Poi	39	m	c	CHIN	San Francisco	6-Wd San Francisco	81	48
Sang	40	m	c	CHIN	Tuolumne	Chinese Camp P O	93	370
See	40	m	c	CHIN	El Dorado	Georgetown Twp	72	36
Sen	55	m	c	CHIN	Plumas	Seneca Twp	77	48
Si	25	f	c	CHIN	Tuolumne	Sonora P O	93	312
Sin	24	m	c	CHIN	San Mateo	Schoolhouse Statio	87	336
Sin	22	m	c	CHIN	Solano	Rio Vista Twp	90	70
Son	34	m	c	CHIN	Amador	Jackson P O	69	331
Sow	48	m	c	CHIN	Amador	Ione City P O	69	354
Tah	42	m	c	CHIN	Calaveras	San Andreas P O	70	211
Town	17	m	c	CHIN	Sacramento	Brighton Twp	77	73
Toy	27	f	c	CHIN	Yuba	Marysville	93	601
Wa	48	m	c	CHIN	Nevada	Nevada Twp	75	286
Wang	38	m	c	CHIN	Calaveras	San Andreas P O	70	211
Wong	39	m	c	CHIN	El Dorado	Diamond Springs Tw	72	32
Woo	51	m	c	CHIN	Mariposa	Maxwell Crk P O	74	141
Yac	22	f	c	CHIN	Placer	Bath P O	76	429
Yack	39	m	c	CHIN	Placer	Bath P O	76	445
Yan	27	m	c	CHIN	Mariposa	Maxwell Crk P O	74	139
Yan	24	m	c	CHIN	Solano	Vacaville Twp	90	129
Yan	15	f	c	CHIN	Placer	Bath P O	76	429
KINA								
Ah	30	f	c	CHIN	Yuba	Marysville	93	601
KINAN								
John	45	m	w	IREL	Humboldt	Eureka Twp	72	272
KINCADE								
Charles L	36	m	w	VA	Yolo	Putah Twp	93	518
G W	37	m	w	MO	Sacramento	American Twp	77	66
James	27	m	w	ENGL	Solano	Rio Vista Twp	90	63
John	42	m	w	KY	Inyo	Bishop Crk Twp	73	317
John H	32	m	w	IN	Santa Barbara	Santa Maria P O	87	514
Joseph	55	m	w	IREL	Yolo	Putah Twp	93	520
Joseph H	41	m	w	KY	Santa Barbara	Santa Barbara P O	87	468
Peter	43	m	w	MO	Calaveras	San Andreas P O	70	209
Philander	23	m	w	US	Sacramento	Franklin Twp	77	111
William	43	m	w	VA	Trinity	Weaverville Pct	92	231
KINCAID								
A	45	m	w	MO	Tehama	Paskenta Twp	92	166
Alex	40	m	w	SCOT	San Francisco	6-Wd San Francisco	81	96
Amos	40	m	w	KY	Tehama	Paskenta Twp	92	164
Amos	40	m	w	MO	Tulare	Visalia Twp	92	283
Benjamin	56	m	w	VA	Alpine	Monitor P O	69	314
Campbell C	29	m	w	MO	Santa Clara	Santa Clara Twp	88	167
Charles L	66	m	w	KY	Tulare	Visalia Twp	92	283
Elam O	36	m	w	PA	Santa Barbara	Santa Barbara P O	87	455
Ellen D	40	m	w	MD	Tulare	Visalia Twp	92	283
George H	53	m	w	KY	Tulare	Visalia	92	291
H N	27	m	w	MO	Lake	Kelsey Crk	73	403

Series M593

© 2001 by Heritage Quest. All rights reserved.

Name	Age	S	R	B-PL	County	Locale	Roll	Pg
						Series M593		
Hartley	29	m	w	ME	Solano	Suisun Twp	90	97
Harvey	35	m	w	MO	San Mateo	Redwood Twp	87	366
James	66	m	w	KY	Stanislaus	Branch Twp	92	1
James	33	m	w	PA	Tulare	Tule Rvr Twp	92	262
James	30	m	w	MO	Stanislaus	Branch Twp	92	3
James M	49	m	w	TN	Solano	Green Valley Twp	90	44
James W	37	m	w	MO	Santa Clara	Santa Clara Twp	88	162
Jenney	22	f	w	IL	San Joaquin	1-Wd Stockton	86	126
Jno E	39	m	w	PA	San Francisco	San Francisco P O	83	25
Joseph	42	m	w	MO	Stanislaus	Empire Twp	92	64
L C	28	m	w	OH	Solano	Vallejo	90	209
Logan	32	m	w	VA	El Dorado	Cosumnes Twp	72	15
Mary	28	f	w	IREL	San Francisco	San Francisco P O	83	17
Robert	29	m	w	KY	Marin	San Rafael Twp	74	35
Saml A	40	m	w	ME	Nevada	Grass Valley Twp	75	228
William	47	m	w	IREL	Santa Cruz	Santa Cruz	89	410
Wm	36	m	w	SCOT	San Francisco	San Francisco P O	83	8
KINCARD								
Josep	40	m	w	MO	Fresno	Kings Rvr P O	72	216
KINCELLA								
William	40	m	w	CANA	Plumas	Quartz Twp	77	34
KINCH								
Frances	12	f	w	CA	Amador	Ione City P O	69	361
H P	40	m	w	NY	El Dorado	Georgetown Twp	72	37
Mary	9	f	w	CA	Amador	Ione City P O	69	361
William	37	m	w	IREL	San Francisco	San Francisco P O	83	229
KINCHE								
Leo	30	m	w	SWIT	Yolo	Grafton Twp	93	489
KINCHELO								
George C	45	m	w	VA	El Dorado	Placerville	72	117
Patrick	45	m	w	IREL	San Francisco	8-Wd San Francisco	82	397
KINCHLOE								
Bird	35	m	w	KY	Tulare	Kings Rvr Twp	92	252
KINCHLOW								
Phillip	42	m	w	MO	Yolo	Cache Crk Twp	93	444
Zaghirah B	46	m	w	MO	Yolo	Cache Crk Twp	93	443
KINCUC								
David B	45	m	w	GA	Yuba	Long Bar Twp	93	561
KIND								
Ann M	49	f	w	IREL	San Francisco	8-Wd San Francisco	82	303
Henry	26	m	w	BOHE	Placer	Auburn P O	76	372
Henry	23	m	w	ENGL	San Francisco	8-Wd San Francisco	82	463
Richard	39	m	w	SAXO	San Francisco	2-Wd San Francisco	79	194
KINDAY								
Augustus	40	m	w	GERM	Yolo	Buckeye Twp	93	412
KINDBERG								
Jacob	55	m	w	PRUS	San Francisco	San Francisco P O	83	21
KINDER								
Charles	33	m	w	HANO	San Francisco	7-Wd San Francisco	81	213
Mary	65	f	w	NC	Placer	Gold Run Twp	76	397
KINDLE								
Frank	25	m	w	MA	Alameda	Washington Twp	68	279
Mary	16	f	w	WI	San Joaquin	Oneal Twp	86	100
KINDLEBERGER								
David	35	m	w	OH	San Francisco	2-Wd San Francisco	79	147
Jefferson	38	m	w	OH	San Francisco	11-Wd San Francisc	84	705
KINDRED								
George W	43	m	w	PA	Santa Cruz	Santa Cruz Twp	89	391
KINE								
Ah	27	m	c	CHIN	Trinity	Douglas	92	236
Ah	14	m	c	CHIN	San Luis Obispo	Arroyo Grande Twp	87	278
Michael	40	m	w	IREL	San Francisco	11-Wd San Francisc	84	475
S F	23	m	w	MI	Alameda	Oakland	68	242
Stephen	47	m	w	OH	Calaveras	San Andreas P O	70	154
KINEALY								
Jeremiah	45	m	w	IREL	San Francisco	1-Wd San Francisco	79	3
KINEAR								
Kate	26	f	w	IREL	San Francisco	5-Wd San Francisco	81	27
KINEFICK								
John	28	m	w	IREL	Sacramento	Alabama Twp	77	60
KINER								
D	33	m	w	NY	Sierra	Butte Twp	89	509
KINEVANE								
Patrick	37	m	w	IREL	Santa Barbara	Santa Barbara P O	87	478
KINEY								
Jon	37	m	w	IREL	San Joaquin	1-Wd Stockton	86	137
N	37	m	w	IREL	San Joaquin	2-Wd Stockton	86	182
Robert	28	m	w	CANA	San Francisco	11-Wd San Francisc	84	687
KINFIELD								
John	35	m	w	IREL	Contra Costa	San Pablo Twp	71	354
KING								
A	55	m	w	BADE	Humboldt	Eureka Twp	72	268
A	26	m	c	CHIN	San Diego	San Diego	78	499
Abram	47	m	w	NY	Santa Clara	2-Wd San Jose	88	281
Aganah J	24	m	w	MS	Yolo	Merritt Twp	93	504
Agnes	47	f	w	CANA	Santa Clara	Santa Clara Twp	88	154
Ah	68	m	c	CHIN	Santa Clara	1-Wd San Jose	88	273
Ah	55	m	c	CHIN	Shasta	Shasta P O	89	461
Ah	53	m	c	CHIN	Butte	Ophir Twp	70	99
Ah	51	m	c	CHIN	El Dorado	Mountain Twp	72	70
Ah	50	m	c	CHIN	El Dorado	Mud Springs Twp	72	76
Ah	50	m	c	CHIN	Sacramento	Franklin Twp	77	112
Ah	50	m	c	CHIN	San Francisco	1-Wd San Francisco	79	110
Ah	50	m	c	CHIN	El Dorado	Salmon Falls Twp	72	133
Ah	48	m	c	CHIN	Trinity	Lewiston Pct	92	212
Ah	48	m	c	CHIN	Trinity	Weaverville Pct	92	228
Ah	47	m	c	CHIN	Trinity	Lewiston Pct	92	211
Ah	46	m	c	CHIN	Santa Clara	1-Wd San Jose	88	273
Ah	46	m	c	CHIN	Nevada	Washington Twp	75	344
Ah	46	m	c	CHIN	Butte	Chico Twp	70	53
Ah	46	m	c	CHIN	San Francisco	San Francisco P O	80	496
Ah	42	m	c	CHIN	Sacramento	1-Wd Sacramento	77	195
Ah	42	m	c	CHIN	Trinity	Weaverville Pct	92	227
Ah	42	m	c	CHIN	Sierra	Table Rock Twp	89	577
Ah	42	m	c	CHIN	Sacramento	Franklin Twp	77	113
Ah	42	m	c	CHIN	San Francisco	3-Wd San Francisco	79	298
Ah	41	m	c	CHIN	Mariposa	Mariposa P O	74	127
Ah	40	m	c	CHIN	San Francisco	5-Wd San Francisco	81	14
Ah	40	m	c	CHIN	El Dorado	Diamond Springs Tw	72	31
Ah	40	m	c	CHIN	El Dorado	Mud Springs Twp	72	78
Ah	40	m	c	CHIN	El Dorado	Mud Springs Twp	72	85
Ah	40	m	c	CHIN	Colusa	Colusa	71	300
Ah	40	m	c	CHIN	Butte	Concow Twp	70	11
Ah	40	m	c	CHIN	Amador	Drytown P O	69	419
Ah	40	m	c	CHIN	Tuolumne	Chinese Camp P O	93	371
Ah	40	m	c	CHIN	San Francisco	11-Wd San Francisc	84	503
Ah	40	m	c	CHIN	San Francisco	6-Wd San Francisco	81	38
Ah	40	m	c	CHIN	El Dorado	White Oak Twp	72	140
Ah	37	m	c	CHIN	Butte	Hamilton Twp	70	75
Ah	36	m	c	CHIN	Trinity	Weaverville Pct	92	231
Ah	36	m	c	CHIN	Siskiyou	Hamburg Twp	89	598
Ah	35	m	c	CHIN	San Francisco	6-Wd San Francisco	81	54
Ah	35	m	c	CHIN	Placer	Dutch Flat P O	76	407
Ah	35	m	c	CHIN	El Dorado	Coloma Twp	72	7
Ah	35	m	c	CHIN	Calaveras	San Andreas P O	70	191
Ah	35	m	c	CHIN	Sacramento	Sutter Twp	77	391
Ah	35	m	c	CHIN	San Francisco	3-Wd San Francisco	79	301
Ah	34	m	c	CHIN	Nevada	Nevada Twp	75	312
Ah	33	m	c	CHIN	Amador	Drytown P O	69	419
Ah	32	m	c	CHIN	Plumas	Goodwin Twp	77	2
Ah	32	m	c	CHIN	El Dorado	Cosumnes Twp	72	13
Ah	32	m	c	CHIN	Amador	Jackson P O	69	328
Ah	32	m	c	CHIN	Sierra	Sears Twp	89	553
Ah	32	m	c	CHIN	Sierra	Table Rock Twp	89	579
Ah	32	m	c	CHIN	San Francisco	San Francisco P O	83	126
Ah	32	m	c	CHIN	Butte	Hamilton Twp	70	72
Ah	31	m	c	CHIN	Marin	San Rafael Twp	74	37
Ah	31	m	c	CHIN	Butte	Ophir Twp	70	104
Ah	30	m	c	CHIN	San Francisco	2-Wd San Francisco	79	149
Ah	30	m	c	CHIN	Fresno	Millerton P O	72	199
Ah	30	m	c	CHIN	Solano	Suisun Twp	90	104
Ah	30	m	c	CHIN	Sonoma	Sonoma Twp	91	449
Ah	30	m	c	CHIN	San Francisco	6-Wd San Francisco	81	46
Ah	30	m	c	CHIN	Fresno	Millerton P O	72	199
Ah	30	m	c	CHIN	El Dorado	White Oak Twp	72	138
Ah	29	m	c	CHIN	Butte	Hamilton Twp	70	75
Ah	29	m	c	CHIN	Butte	Hamilton Twp	70	74
Ah	29	m	c	CHIN	Alameda	Oakland	68	238
Ah	28	m	c	CHIN	San Francisco	San Francisco P O	80	502
Ah	28	m	c	CHIN	Plumas	Washington Twp	77	57
Ah	28	m	c	CHIN	Sacramento	3-Wd Sacramento	77	316
Ah	27	m	c	CHIN	Santa Clara	1-Wd San Jose	88	271
Ah	27	m	c	CHIN	Colusa	Colusa	71	300
Ah	26	m	c	CHIN	Amador	Jackson P O	69	328
Ah	24	m	c	CHIN	Santa Clara	2-Wd San Jose	88	314
Ah	24	m	c	CHIN	Sacramento	2-Wd Sacramento	77	250
Ah	24	m	c	CHIN	Butte	Hamilton Twp	70	68
Ah	24	m	c	CHIN	Marin	San Rafael Twp	74	59
Ah	23	m	c	CHIN	Santa Clara	San Jose Twp	88	194
Ah	23	m	c	CHIN	Napa	Napa	75	57
Ah	23	m	c	CHIN	Los Angeles	San Gabriel Twp	73	598
Ah	22	m	c	CHIN	Santa Clara	San Jose Twp	88	179
Ah	22	m	c	CHIN	Alameda	Hayward	68	77
Ah	22	m	c	CHIN	Tulare	Visalia	92	294
Ah	22	m	c	CHIN	Santa Clara	San Jose Twp	88	192
Ah	22	m	c	CHIN	San Francisco	6-Wd San Francisco	81	59
Ah	22	m	c	CHIN	Nevada	Bridgeport Twp	75	110
Ah	21	m	c	CHIN	San Francisco	8-Wd San Francisco	82	386
Ah	21	m	c	CHIN	Plumas	Goodwin Twp	77	2
Ah	21	m	c	CHIN	Nevada	Eureka Twp	75	127
Ah	21	m	c	CHIN	Yolo	Buckeye Twp	93	412
Ah	21	m	c	CHIN	Trinity	Douglas	92	237
Ah	20	m	c	CHIN	Sacramento	3-Wd Sacramento	77	288
Ah	20	m	c	CHIN	Solano	Suisun Twp	90	106
Ah	20	m	c	CHIN	San Francisco	3-Wd San Francisco	79	303
Ah	20	m	c	CHIN	Butte	Bidwell Twp	70	4
Ah	19	m	c	CHIN	San Francisco	6-Wd San Francisco	81	59
Ah	19	m	c	CHIN	Solano	Suisun Twp	90	106
Ah	19	m	c	CHIN	Placer	Clipper Gap P O	76	393
Ah	19	m	c	CHIN	San Francisco	2-Wd San Francisco	79	282
Ah	18	m	c	CHIN	Sonoma	Sonoma Twp	91	449
Ah	18	m	c	CHIN	San Francisco	6-Wd San Francisco	81	39
Ah	17	m	c	CHIN	Placer	Clipper Gap P O	76	392
Ah	16	m	c	CHIN	Santa Clara	1-Wd San Jose	88	271
Ah	16	m	c	CHIN	Plumas	Plumas Twp	77	32
Ah	15	m	c	CHIN	San Francisco	3-Wd San Francisco	79	329
Ah	15	m	c	CHIN	San Francisco	3-Wd San Francisco	79	304
Ah	13	m	c	CHIN	San Francisco	6-Wd San Francisco	81	60
Ah	13	m	c	CHIN	San Francisco	7-Wd San Francisco	81	240
Ah	13	m	c	CHIN	Sacramento	2-Wd Sacramento	77	219
Albert	25	m	w	NY	San Francisco	5-Wd San Francisco	81	18
Albin	14	m	w	CA	Santa Clara	Gilroy Twp	88	99
Alex	35	m	w	IREL	San Joaquin	1-Wd Stockton	86	153
Alice	45	f	w	NY	San Francisco	7-Wd San Francisco	81	164

© 2001 by Heritage Quest. All rights reserved.

California 1870 Census

Name	Age	S	R	B-PL	County	Locale	Roll	Pg
Alx	30	m	w	SWIT	El Dorado	Georgetown Twp	72	48
Amelia	50	f	w	RI	San Joaquin	3-Wd Stockton	86	234
Andrew J	34	m	w	GA	Los Angeles	Los Angeles	73	524
Andrew L	58	m	w	KY	Santa Clara	San Jose Twp	88	222
Anna	27	f	w	OH	Solano	Vallejo	90	142
Anne	22	f	w	IREL	San Francisco	8-Wd San Francisco	82	454
Anthony	36	m	w	CANA	Placer	Bath P O	76	437
Antone	23	m	w	PORT	Sacramento	Franklin Twp	77	106
Barry	20	m	w	AL	Stanislaus	Emory Twp	92	22
Basha F	35	f	w	NY	Santa Clara	Redwood Twp	88	130
Bertha	24	f	w	GERM	Sacramento	1-Wd Sacramento	77	177
Bridget	49	f	w	IREL	Placer	Roseville P O	76	355
Burgiss T	46	m	w	RI	Yolo	Merritt Twp	93	503
C H	28	m	w	NY	Klamath	Trinidad Twp	73	391
Charles	48	m	w	PRUS	Sacramento	American Twp	77	68
Charles	43	m	w	IREL	Placer	Roseville P O	76	352
Charles	38	m	w	IN	San Luis Obispo	Salinas Twp	87	295
Charles	35	m	w	NY	San Francisco	San Francisco P O	83	3
Charles	34	m	w	HANO	Sonoma	Petaluma Twp	91	349
Charles	23	m	w	NY	Alpine	Monitor P O	69	313
Charles	22	m	w	ENGL	San Francisco	San Francisco P O	80	336
Charles	22	m	w	NY	San Joaquin	3-Wd Stockton	86	229
Charles	21	m	b	KY	Santa Cruz	Watsonville	89	371
Charles	20	m	w	BADE	San Francisco	San Francisco P O	85	752
Charles H	38	m	w	CANA	Placer	Gold Run Twp	76	397
Charles M	57	m	w	VT	El Dorado	Placerville	72	110
Chas	8	m	w	CA	Santa Clara	Gilroy Twp	88	99
Chas	45	m	w	PRUS	Napa	Napa	75	7
Chas	37	m	w	IREL	San Joaquin	1-Wd Stockton	86	153
Chas	35	m	w	GERM	Sacramento	Franklin Twp	77	105
Chue	28	m	c	CHIN	San Mateo	Schoolhouse Statio	87	336
Chung	31	m	c	CHIN	Amador	Jackson P O	69	330
Clarence	22	m	w	OH	Amador	Sutter Crk P O	69	412
Constantine	42	m	w	HDAR	Sutter	Sutter Twp	92	123
Cora B	18	f	w	IL	San Mateo	Schoolhouse Statio	87	339
Cyrus	33	m	w	ME	Nevada	Eureka Twp	75	132
Cyrus	28	m	w	US	Nevada	Grass Valley Twp	75	228
Daniel	66	m	w	TN	Solano	Tremont Twp	90	35
Daniel	50	m	w	SC	Placer	Lincoln P O	76	484
Daniel	40	m	w	IREL	Alameda	Oakland	68	133
Daniel	35	m	m	VA	Yuba	Marysville	93	616
Daniel	24	m	w	AUSL	Marin	Tomales Twp	74	87
Daniel V	35	m	w	MS	Napa	Yountville Twp	75	84
David	47	m	w	VT	Yuba	Linda Twp	93	558
David	43	m	w	NY	Shasta	Millville P O	89	493
David H	26	m	w	ME	Humboldt	Bald Hills	72	239
Dwight C	43	m	w	MA	San Francisco	San Francisco P O	83	41
E A	12	f	w	CA	Alameda	Oakland	68	258
E S	36	m	w	NY	Solano	Vallejo	90	167
E W	39	m	w	NY	Mendocino	Ukiah Twp	74	242
Edgar	39	m	w	NY	Santa Clara	Gilroy Twp	88	79
Edward	53	m	w	CANA	Yuba	East Bear Rvr Twp	93	540
Edward	48	m	w	TN	Fresno	Millerton P O	72	148
Edwin J	53	m	w	TN	Fresno	Millerton P O	72	188
Edwin T	12	m	w	CA	Amador	Sutter Crk P O	69	397
Eli H	19	m	w	IL	Los Angeles	Los Nietos Twp	73	578
Elijah	42	m	w	IN	San Luis Obispo	Santa Rosa Twp	87	317
Elizabeth	63	f	w	MO	Monterey	Alisal Twp	74	297
Elizabeth	31	f	w	NY	San Francisco	7-Wd San Francisco	81	167
Ella	14	f	w	CANA	San Francisco	11-Wd San Francisc	84	544
Ellen	58	f	w	IREL	San Francisco	11-Wd San Francisc	84	425
Ellen	56	f	w	IREL	Sacramento	4-Wd Sacramento	77	371
Ellen	40	f	w	ENGL	San Francisco	6-Wd San Francisco	81	100
Ellen	40	f	w	IREL	San Francisco	1-Wd San Francisco	79	114
Emanuel	34	m	w	PORT	Alameda	Hayward	68	78
Emanuel	33	m	w	PORT	Sierra	Sears Twp	89	561
Erastus	26	m	w	CT	Sutter	Butte Twp	92	89
Ervin	45	m	w	NY	Santa Clara	Redwood Twp	88	119
Eue	46	m	c	CHIN	Yuba	Marysville	93	626
Ezra	35	m	w	NY	Solano	Vallejo	90	168
F	34	m	w	IREL	Alameda	Murray Twp	68	105
F H	24	m	w	MA	Solano	Vallejo	90	200
Felix	32	m	w	VA	San Francisco	San Francisco P O	85	874
Fielding A	37	m	w	KY	Nevada	Little York Twp	75	237
Fong	37	m	c	CHIN	Yuba	Marysville	93	621
Foo	45	m	c	CHIN	Yuba	Marysville	93	620
Foo	42	m	c	CHIN	Butte	Kimshew Tpw	70	85
France	51	m	w	KY	Colusa	Monroe Twp	71	313
Francis M	24	m	w	MO	Placer	Auburn P O	76	380
Frank	44	m	w	IREL	Yolo	Merritt Twp	93	503
Frank	35	m	w	IA	San Mateo	Woodside P O	87	384
Frank	26	m	w	IREL	San Francisco	1-Wd San Francisco	79	69
Frank	22	m	w	NY	San Francisco	San Francisco P O	80	487
Franklin J	45	m	w	VA	San Francisco	San Francisco P O	85	776
Fred	53	m	w	ENGL	Tehama	Tehama Twp	92	192
Fred	45	m	w	PRUS	Yuba	Marysville	93	574
Fred	45	m	w	GERM	Yuba	Marysville	93	614
Fredk R	8	m	w	CA	San Francisco	San Francisco P O	83	147
Fredrick	29	m	w	BADE	San Francisco	7-Wd San Francisco	81	213
G A	45	m	w	RI	Alameda	Oakland	68	129
G W	40	m	w	IL	Alameda	Oakland	68	263
Gee	26	m	c	CHIN	El Dorado	Mud Springs Twp	72	77
Geo	47	m	w	BAVA	San Joaquin	2-Wd Stockton	86	168
Geo E	21	m	w	ME	Humboldt	Table Bluff Twp	72	309
Geo W	51	m	w	NY	Humboldt	Eel Rvr Twp	72	249
George	53	m	w	NY	Humboldt	South Fork Twp	72	301
George	48	m	w	OH	Nevada	Nevada Twp	75	278
George	39	m	w	IL	Solano	Silveyville Twp	90	85
George	38	m	b	NY	Santa Clara	2-Wd San Jose	88	329
George	38	m	w	ENGL	San Bernardino	San Bernardino Twp	78	422
George	38	m	w	NY	Calaveras	Copperopolis P O	70	259
George	30	m	m	NY	San Francisco	San Francisco P O	80	339
George	27	m	w	OH	Solano	Silveyville Twp	90	82
George	25	m	w	VA	San Diego	Julian Dist	78	471
George	20	m	w	IREL	San Francisco	2-Wd San Francisco	79	150
George C	42	m	w	OH	Nevada	Grass Valley Twp	75	155
George H	37	m	w	NY	Santa Cruz	Santa Cruz	89	418
George W	48	m	w	MS	Solano	Tremont Twp	90	34
George W	43	m	w	ME	Tuolumne	Columbia P O	93	337
George W	43	m	w	NY	El Dorado	Mud Springs Twp	72	88
George W	36	m	w	MS	Yolo	Merritt Twp	93	503
George W	34	m	w	NC	Amador	Sutter Crk P O	69	410
Gernade	36	m	w	TN	Marin	San Rafael Twp	74	59
Godfrey	26	m	w	WURT	Humboldt	Eureka Twp	72	270
Grover	10	m	w	CA	Yuba	Parks Bar Twp	93	648
H	34	m	w	CHIN	Sacramento	1-Wd Sacramento	77	184
H C	39	m	w	NY	Amador	Ione City P O	69	350
H G	44	m	w	CT	Santa Clara	Almaden Twp	88	19
Hannah	8	f	w	CA	Marin	Tomales Twp	74	88
Hee	27	m	c	CHIN	Solano	Vacaville Twp	90	130
Henry	52	m	w	NY	San Francisco	6-Wd San Francisco	81	103
Henry	46	m	w	OH	Alameda	Eden Twp	68	63
Henry	39	m	w	SWIT	Sierra	Sears Twp	89	553
Henry	36	m	w	IREL	Los Angeles	Los Angeles	73	526
Henry	34	m	w	NY	Los Angeles	Los Angeles Twp	73	470
Henry	31	m	w	KY	San Mateo	Redwood Twp	87	367
Henry	30	m	w	ENGL	San Francisco	11-Wd San Francisc	84	482
Henry	29	m	w	NY	Inyo	Cerro Gordo Twp	73	318
Henry	24	m	w	NY	Los Angeles	El Monte Twp	73	458
Henry G	45	m	w	PA	Sonoma	Analy Twp	91	239
Henry L	40	m	w	AR	Shasta	Horsetown P O	89	506
Hermann	30	m	w	PRUS	San Francisco	San Francisco P O	83	21
Hiram	31	m	w	MO	San Joaquin	Union Twp	86	266
Hiram G	30	m	w	NY	San Luis Obispo	Morro Twp	87	280
Ho	37	m	c	CHIN	San Joaquin	1-Wd Stockton	86	144
Hong	56	m	c	CHIN	Solano	Vallejo	90	208
Hop	40	m	c	CHIN	Tuolumne	Big Oak Flat P O	93	398
Hop	21	m	c	CHIN	Tuolumne	Sonora P O	93	332
How	29	m	c	CHIN	Yuba	Marysville	93	631
Hugh	18	m	w	IREL	Sonoma	Petaluma Twp	91	350
J	50	m	w	ENGL	Alameda	Oakland	68	256
J	47	m	w	FRAN	Sierra	Butte Twp	89	512
J	40	m	w	IL	Humboldt	Arcata Twp	72	228
J B	47	m	w	TN	Sierra	Sierra Twp	89	569
J B	45	m	w	NY	Sacramento	4-Wd Sacramento	77	357
J B	30	m	w	NY	Amador	Jackson P O	69	329
J H	29	m	b	GA	Alameda	Oakland	68	184
J M	68	m	w	IREL	Amador	Ione City P O	69	360
J S	34	m	w	TN	Merced	Snelling P O	74	254
J W	46	m	b	MD	Sierra	Downieville Twp	89	519
James	66	m	w	ENGL	San Mateo	Schoolhouse Statio	87	331
James	65	m	w	DC	San Francisco	San Francisco P O	83	57
James	54	m	w	OH	Santa Clara	1-Wd San Jose	88	277
James	48	m	w	MO	Santa Cruz	Santa Cruz	89	419
James	45	m	w	IREL	Alameda	Washington Twp	68	296
James	40	m	w	MO	Alameda	Murray Twp	68	110
James	39	m	w	ENGL	Placer	Dutch Flat P O	76	402
James	36	m	w	NY	Alameda	Hayward	68	74
James	32	m	w	IREL	San Francisco	6-Wd San Francisco	81	82
James	29	m	w	IREL	Placer	Rocklin Twp	76	463
James	26	m	w	IREL	Stanislaus	San Joaquin Twp	92	72
James	24	m	w	MO	Nevada	Washington Twp	75	343
James	24	m	w	CANA	Yolo	Putah Twp	93	527
James	24	m	w	IREL	San Joaquin	2-Wd Stockton	86	168
James	23	m	w	IN	Los Angeles	Los Nietos Twp	73	586
James	17	m	w	MI	Yolo	Cache Crk Twp	93	457
James C	32	m	w	SC	Siskiyou	Callahan P O	89	629
James E	36	m	w	ME	San Francisco	1-Wd San Francisco	79	111
James H	38	m	w	CT	Sutter	Vernon Twp	92	133
James H	35	m	w	NY	San Francisco	San Francisco P O	83	148
Jas L	42	m	w	NY	San Francisco	5-Wd San Francisco	81	31
Jas L Mrs	30	f	w	FRAN	San Francisco	5-Wd San Francisco	81	31
Jas M	35	m	w	TN	Shasta	Millville P O	89	485
Jennie	10	f	w	CA	Butte	Hamilton Twp	70	71
Jeremiah	45	m	w	IREL	Contra Costa	Martinez P O	71	409
Jerome	43	m	w	NY	Contra Costa	Martinez P O	71	452
Jerome B	61	m	w	NY	San Francisco	2-Wd San Francisco	79	178
Jerry	35	m	w	FRAN	Placer	Summit P O	76	496
Jessie	10	f	w	CA	Sonoma	Petaluma Twp	91	329
Jno H	39	m	w	MO	Sonoma	Healdsburg & Mendo	91	276
Joe	23	m	w	PORT	Siskiyou	Table Rock Twp	89	646
Joel C	57	m	w	NC	El Dorado	Georgetown Twp	72	46
John	8	m	w	CA	Yolo	Putah Twp	93	526
John	8	m	w	CA	Yolo	Buckeye Twp	93	413
John	67	m	w	IREL	Amador	Lancha Plana P O	69	368
John	60	m	w	IREL	Alameda	Murray Twp	68	117
John	56	m	w	SWEE	San Francisco	11-Wd San Francisc	84	662
John	44	m	w	MA	Monterey	San Benito Twp	74	384
John	42	m	w	PA	Nevada	Meadow Lake Twp	75	270
John	40	m	w	IREL	Los Angeles	Los Angeles	73	570
John	38	m	w	CANA	Tuolumne	Columbia P O	93	342
John	35	m	w	NY	San Francisco	7-Wd San Francisco	81	167
John	35	m	w	IREL	San Francisco	San Francisco P O	83	339
John	35	m	w	PORT	San Joaquin	2-Wd Stockton	86	173

Series M593

© 2001 by Heritage Quest. All rights reserved.

Name	Age	S	R	B-PL	County	Locale	Series M593 Roll	Pg
John	32	m	w	AZOR	El Dorado	Salmon Falls Twp	72	132
John	30	m	w	PRUS	Placer	Dutch Flat P O	76	402
John	30	m	w	HI	Yolo	Merritt Twp	93	502
John	30	m	w	IREL	San Francisco	San Francisco P O	83	12
John	30	m	w	HAMB	Mendocino	Navarro & Big Rvr	74	175
John	29	m	w	PRUS	San Francisco	8-Wd San Francisco	82	396
John	29	m	w	PORT	Placer	Bath P O	76	424
John	26	m	w	IREL	San Francisco	7-Wd San Francisco	81	219
John	25	m	w	CANA	San Francisco	8-Wd San Francisco	82	469
John	25	m	w	NY	Sacramento	Sutter Twp	77	391
John	24	m	w	AZOR	Monterey	Monterey Twp	74	343
John	24	m	w	ME	San Francisco	11-Wd San Francisc	84	578
John	24	m	w	ENGL	Contra Costa	Martinez P O	71	419
John	24	m	w	MA	San Francisco	1-Wd San Francisco	79	18
John	24	m	w	ENGL	San Francisco	1-Wd San Francisco	79	91
John	21	m	w	PORT	Stanislaus	Empire Twp	92	42
John	21	m	w	IN	Los Angeles	Los Nietos Twp	73	586
John	14	m	w	CA	Alameda	Murray Twp	68	117
John C	56	m	w	PRUS	San Francisco	6-Wd San Francisco	81	154
John D	23	m	w	PA	Los Angeles	Los Angeles	73	538
John E	18	m	w	IL	Sonoma	Petaluma Twp	91	357
John L	44	m	w	DC	Solano	Vallejo	90	182
John M	52	m	w	MD	Placer	Gold Run Twp	76	395
John S	49	m	w	NY	Napa	Napa	75	14
Joseph	43	m	w	PORT	Alameda	Eden Twp	68	72
Joseph	40	m	w	PORT	Alameda	Eden Twp	68	69
Joseph	38	m	b	CANA	San Francisco	1-Wd San Francisco	79	49
Joseph	36	m	w	PORT	Alameda	Washington Twp	68	291
Joseph	36	m	w	SCOT	Siskiyou	Scott Valley Twp	89	612
Joseph	35	m	w	NY	Calaveras	San Andreas P O	70	175
Joseph	31	m	w	PORT	Alameda	Eden Twp	68	88
Joseph	30	m	w	AZOR	Marin	San Rafael Twp	74	32
Joseph	29	m	w	PORT	Nevada	Rough & Ready Twp	75	328
Joseph	28	m	w	PORT	San Francisco	1-Wd San Francisco	79	4
Joseph	27	m	w	CA	Santa Cruz	Pajaro Twp	89	348
Josephine F	18	f	w	CA	San Francisco	San Francisco P O	83	196
Judson	36	m	w	MS	Yolo	Putah Twp	93	518
Katharina	50	f	w	IREL	San Francisco	San Francisco P O	83	198
Kee	24	m	c	CHIN	Solano	Vacaville Twp	90	130
Ki	16	m	c	CHIN	Sonoma	Petaluma Twp	91	359
L P	22	m	w	CANA	San Francisco	San Francisco P O	83	188
Leonidas	28	m	w	CT	San Francisco	3-Wd San Francisco	79	326
Lewis	15	m	w	CUBA	Alameda	Eden Twp	68	85
Lilly	9	f	w	AR	Placer	Auburn P O	76	357
Louis L	15	m	w	CA	Napa	Napa	75	2
Louisa	10	f	w	CA	San Francisco	6-Wd San Francisco	81	104
Luke	40	m	w	IREL	Napa	Yountville Twp	75	86
Lup	28	m	c	CHIN	Solano	Suisun Twp	90	105
Lusina F	41	f	w	NY	El Dorado	Diamond Springs Tw	72	24
Ly	40	m	c	CHIN	Butte	Concow Twp	70	8
Lyman	48	m	w	CT	Yuba	Rose Bar Twp	93	662
M G	40	m	w	NY	Alameda	Oakland	68	227
Malinda	28	f	w	MO	Los Angeles	Los Angeles	73	538
Manuel	55	m	w	PA	Santa Barbara	Santa Barbara P O	87	490
Manuel J	37	m	w	PORT	Sacramento	2-Wd Sacramento	77	220
Margaret	45	f	w	MO	Napa	Yountville Twp	75	89
Margaret	38	f	w	IREL	San Francisco	11-Wd San Francisc	84	618
Margaret	20	f	w	IREL	San Francisco	8-Wd San Francisco	82	381
Margt S	62	f	w	VA	San Francisco	San Francisco P O	83	129
Martin	32	m	w	IREL	Yuba	Rose Bar Twp	93	659
Mary	56	f	w	CT	Alameda	Oakland	68	175
Mary	54	f	w	IREL	Marin	Tomales Twp	74	83
Mary	40	f	w	IREL	San Francisco	8-Wd San Francisco	82	346
Mary	36	f	w	IREL	Nevada	Little York Twp	75	238
Mary	28	f	w	PA	San Francisco	11-Wd San Francisc	84	634
Mary	24	f	w	SCOT	Alameda	Brooklyn Twp	68	45
Mary	22	f	w	IREL	San Francisco	8-Wd San Francisco	82	477
Mary	20	f	w	MO	Colusa	Spring Valley Twp	71	336
Mary	16	f	w	NY	Sacramento	3-Wd Sacramento	77	301
Mary F	23	f	w	MA	San Francisco	San Francisco P O	83	240
Mary J	55	f	w	IREL	Marin	Sausalito Twp	74	69
Mat S	58	m	w	OH	Sacramento	3-Wd Sacramento	77	294
Mat W	55	m	w	SCOT	Sonoma	Cloverdale Twp	91	268
Me	41	m	c	CHIN	Amador	Jackson P O	69	347
Melinda	30	f	w	MO	Los Angeles	Los Nietos Twp	73	591
Michael	43	m	w	NY	Monterey	Castroville Twp	74	335
Michael	40	m	w	IREL	San Francisco	8-Wd San Francisco	82	495
Michael	38	m	w	IREL	San Francisco	7-Wd San Francisco	81	247
Michael	28	m	w	ECUA	Nevada	Nevada Twp	75	279
Michael	25	m	w	NY	Placer	Summit P O	76	495
Michael	23	m	w	PRUS	Amador	Amador City P O	69	394
Michl [Rev]	40	m	w	IREL	Alameda	Oakland	68	187
Miles	10	m	w	CA	Sacramento	San Joaquin Twp	77	403
Milo F	40	m	w	IA	Solano	Vallejo	90	144
Minor	70	m	w	NY	Santa Clara	Santa Clara Twp	88	160
Morris	36	m	w	MA	Sacramento	2-Wd Sacramento	77	228
N J	47	m	w	ME	Santa Clara	Gilroy Twp	88	95
Napoleon	38	m	w	ENGL	Nevada	Nevada Twp	75	292
Nathan	37	m	w	OH	Nevada	Grass Valley Twp	75	231
Nathan	29	m	w	PA	San Luis Obispo	San Luis Obispo Tw	87	297
Nathan	27	m	w	MA	Sacramento	1-Wd Sacramento	77	185
Nathan C	38	m	w	NY	Nevada	Grass Valley Twp	75	172
Nathan H	37	m	w	MO	Monterey	Alisal Twp	74	297
Nicholas	38	m	w	DC	San Francisco	11-Wd San Francisc	84	548
Norman L	24	m	w	DC	Los Angeles	Los Angeles	73	526
Owen	43	m	w	IREL	Placer	Auburn P O	76	382
Owen	30	m	w	IREL	Solano	Vallejo	90	162
Panthea	26	f	w	AR	Los Angeles	El Monte Twp	73	448
Patrick	45	m	w	IREL	Marin	San Rafael Twp	74	47
Patrick	40	m	w	IREL	Tuolumne	Columbia P O	93	344
Patrick	40	m	w	IREL	San Francisco	San Francisco P O	85	815
Patrick	33	m	w	IREL	San Francisco	7-Wd San Francisco	81	215
Patrick	32	m	w	IREL	Marin	San Rafael Twp	74	38
Patrick	32	m	w	IREL	San Francisco	San Francisco P O	83	28
Patrick	32	m	w	IREL	San Francisco	11-Wd San Francisc	84	545
Patrick	25	m	w	IREL	Humboldt	Pacific Twp	72	299
Peter	28	m	w	DENM	Los Angeles	Los Angeles	73	543
Philip	54	m	w	IREL	San Francisco	2-Wd San Francisco	79	214
Philip	36	m	w	IN	El Dorado	Placerville Twp	72	99
Philip	36	m	w	OH	El Dorado	Placerville Twp	72	97
Po	40	m	c	CHIN	San Joaquin	Oneal Twp	86	114
Richard	50	m	w	CANA	San Francisco	8-Wd San Francisco	82	470
Richard	46	m	w	DE	Santa Barbara	San Buenaventura P	87	449
Richard	38	m	w	IREL	San Francisco	7-Wd San Francisco	81	170
Richard	24	m	w	PA	San Bernardino	San Bernardino Twp	78	453
Robert	60	m	w	KY	Placer	Auburn P O	76	380
Robert	58	m	w	TN	Contra Costa	Martinez P O	71	441
Robert	37	m	w	ENGL	San Francisco	11-Wd San Francisc	84	483
Robert	36	m	w	MA	San Francisco	6-Wd San Francisco	81	82
Rose	30	f	w	IREL	Santa Clara	2-Wd San Jose	88	326
Rufus	37	m	b	TN	Butte	Ophir Twp	70	107
Rufus	36	m	w	AR	Fresno	Kings Rvr P O	72	203
S Henston	34	m	w	GA	Los Angeles	San Jose Twp	73	622
S T	42	m	w	MA	Alameda	Oakland	68	161
Sam	36	m	c	CHIN	Alameda	Washington Twp	68	274
Sam	18	m	c	CHIN	San Francisco	1-Wd San Francisco	79	98
Samuel	51	m	w	NJ	San Francisco	San Francisco P O	80	361
Samuel	40	m	w	AR	Nevada	Meadow Lake Twp	75	261
Samuel	36	m	w	AR	Tulare	Tule Rvr Twp	92	265
Samuel	17	m	w	MO	Placer	Auburn P O	76	380
Sarah	58	f	w	PRUS	San Francisco	11-Wd San Francisc	84	493
Sarah	43	f	w	TN	Colusa	Colusa	71	294
Sarah	27	f	w	AUSL	San Francisco	San Francisco P O	83	71
Sebastian	53	m	w	BAVA	San Joaquin	Oneal Twp	86	100
Sing	41	m	c	CHIN	Tuolumne	Columbia P O	93	342
Sing	21	m	c	CHIN	Tuolumne	Sonora P O	93	312
Soloman	30	m	w	ENGL	Plumas	Washington Twp	77	53
Soon	41	m	c	CHIN	Yuba	Marysville	93	623
Stephen	34	m	w	NY	San Francisco	8-Wd San Francisco	82	379
Stephen	26	m	w	OH	San Francisco	8-Wd San Francisco	82	335
Stephen T	36	m	w	NY	San Francisco	8-Wd San Francisco	82	430
Sue	42	m	c	CHIN	Placer	Dutch Flat P O	76	407
Susan	71	f	w	TN	Solano	Tremont Twp	90	35
T C	48	m	w	CANA	Tuolumne	Big Oak Flat P O	93	396
T P	41	m	w	ENGL	Solano	Vallejo	90	181
Thomas	50	m	w	PA	San Francisco	San Francisco P O	80	531
Thomas	45	m	w	IREL	Calaveras	Copperopolis P O	70	254
Thomas	43	m	w	IREL	San Francisco	San Francisco P O	83	158
Thomas	36	m	w	IL	Colusa	Spring Valley Twp	71	341
Thomas	35	m	w	ENGL	San Francisco	2-Wd San Francisco	79	213
Thomas	31	m	w	IREL	Humboldt	Eureka Twp	72	279
Thomas	29	m	w	MA	Butte	Chico Twp	70	19
Thomas	25	m	w	IREL	San Francisco	San Francisco P O	83	163
Thomas	24	m	w	ENGL	San Francisco	San Francisco P O	80	336
Thomas	19	m	w	CANA	Sonoma	Bodega Twp	91	256
Thomas B	55	m	w	MA	San Francisco	6-Wd San Francisco	81	94
Thomas R	23	m	w	ME	Placer	Dutch Flat P O	76	410
Thomas R	23	m	w	ME	Nevada	Little York Twp	75	242
Thos	53	m	w	ENGL	Sonoma	Mendocino Twp	91	296
Thos	42	m	w	IREL	San Francisco	2-Wd San Francisco	79	177
Thos	42	m	w	ENGL	Butte	Chico Twp	70	46
Thos	36	m	w	ENGL	San Joaquin	Elliott Twp	86	80
Thos	35	m	w	IREL	Alameda	Oakland	68	222
Thos	30	m	w	IREL	San Francisco	1-Wd San Francisco	79	92
Thos	27	m	c	CHIN	San Joaquin	2-Wd Stockton	86	172
Thos T	42	m	w	OH	Klamath	Trinidad Twp	73	390
Timothy	28	m	w	OH	San Francisco	11-Wd San Francisc	84	480
Tom	14	m	c	CHIN	San Francisco	8-Wd San Francisco	82	388
Ton	45	m	c	CHIN	Butte	Kimshew Tpw	70	85
Ton	42	m	c	CHIN	Solano	Vacaville Twp	90	132
Ty	20	m	c	CHIN	Marin	Tomales Twp	74	86
W A	42	m	w	TN	Nevada	Meadow Lake Twp	75	260
W B	38	m	w	OH	Alameda	Oakland	68	211
W E	35	m	w	NY	San Francisco	San Francisco P O	83	284
W Z	21	m	w	OH	Alameda	Oakland	68	201
Walter	21	m	w	ME	San Francisco	7-Wd San Francisco	81	168
Walter C	42	m	w	NY	Colusa	Grand Island Twp	71	304
Warren	50	m	w	VT	Marin	San Rafael	74	54
William	62	m	w	ENGL	San Francisco	San Francisco P O	83	191
William	54	m	w	OH	Plumas	Seneca Twp	77	49
William	50	m	w	VA	Kern	Havilah P O	73	340
William	34	m	w	IREL	Stanislaus	Empire Twp	92	40
William	32	m	w	IREL	Alameda	Washington Twp	68	277
William	31	m	w	MO	Humboldt	Bucksport Twp	72	241
William	31	m	w	TN	Yolo	Putah Twp	93	518
William	26	m	w	MI	Marin	Novato Twp	74	12
William	26	m	w	VA	Marin	San Rafael Twp	74	39
William	24	m	w	GERM	Yolo	Cottonwood Twp	93	468
William	22	m	w	NY	Santa Clara	Santa Clara Twp	88	168
William	21	m	w	ENGL	San Francisco	San Francisco P O	85	745
William	16	m	w	ME	San Francisco	7-Wd San Francisco	81	168
William B	41	m	w	AL	Siskiyou	Surprise Valley Tw	89	642
William C	15	m	w	IN	Yuba	Bullards Bar P O	93	549
William F	43	m	w	NY	Santa Clara	Redwood Twp	88	119

© 2001 by Heritage Quest. All rights reserved.

California 1870 Census

Series M593

Name	Age	S	R	B-PL	County	Locale	Roll	Pg
William R	33	m	w	ME	Placer	Dutch Flat P O	76	401
William S	47	m	w	NY	Santa Clara	1-Wd San Jose	88	228
William T	38	m	w	NY	Yolo	Grafton Twp	93	493
William T	32	m	w	MO	Tulare	Venice Twp	92	273
Wilson	32	m	w	NY	Santa Clara	Redwood Twp	88	119
Win	11	m	c	CHIN	San Francisco	San Francisco P O	80	359
Winnie	60	f	m	NC	San Joaquin	3-Wd Stockton	86	221
Wm	6	m	w	AR	Santa Clara	Gilroy Twp	88	69
Wm	40	m	w	ENGL	San Francisco	San Francisco P O	83	74
Wm	38	m	w	ENGL	Tehama	Paskenta Twp	92	165
Wm	35	m	w	BRAZ	Fresno	Millerton P O	72	146
Wm	31	m	w	KY	Butte	Chico Twp	70	25
Wm	2	m	w	CA	San Francisco	7-Wd San Francisco	81	248
Wm O	50	m	w	NY	Sonoma	Petaluma Twp	91	317
Wm P	45	m	w	IREL	San Francisco	8-Wd San Francisco	82	343
Woo	21	m	c	CHIN	Tuolumne	Columbia P O	93	349
Yee	40	m	c	CHIN	Tuolumne	Sonora P O	93	311
Yen	31	m	c	CHIN	Nevada	Bridgeport Twp	75	111
You	35	f	c	CHIN	Placer	Bath P O	76	429
Yung	34	m	c	CHIN	Yuba	Marysville	93	632
KINGALE								
Helen	36	f	w	ME	Butte	Chico Twp	70	14
KINGCAID								
H B	33	m	w	PA	Merced	Snelling P O	74	262
KINGDELYRO								
---	29	m	j	JAPA	El Dorado	Coloma Twp	72	4
KINGDON								
Henry	33	m	w	ENGL	Sierra	Sears Twp	89	554
Saml	40	m	w	ENGL	Sierra	Sears Twp	89	554
Wm	35	m	w	ENGL	Butte	Oroville Twp	70	137
KINGER								
William H	40	m	w	PRUS	Placer	Dutch Flat P O	76	401
KINGERY								
Danl B	35	m	w	PA	Siskiyou	Scott Valley Twp	89	618
Samuel	45	m	w	OH	San Luis Obispo	Morro Twp	87	285
KINGHORNE								
Clementine	26	f	b	CANA	San Francisco	8-Wd San Francisco	82	386
KINGLAND								
John	41	m	w	PRUS	San Francisco	7-Wd San Francisco	81	221
Wm	57	m	w	LA	San Francisco	11-Wd San Francisc	84	683
KINGLE								
Fredk	15	m	w	NY	San Francisco	5-Wd San Francisco	81	27
KINGLEY								
Jacob	30	m	w	SWIT	Placer	Gold Run Twp	76	396
KINGLOCK								
James	30	m	w	SCOT	San Francisco	7-Wd San Francisco	81	219
KINGLSEY								
Anna J	39	f	w	IREL	Klamath	Sawyers Bar	73	378
KINGMAN								
Alden	41	m	w	ME	San Francisco	San Francisco P O	83	229
Chas	48	m	w	MA	San Francisco	1-Wd San Francisco	79	30
Frank	30	m	w	GERM	Santa Clara	2-Wd San Jose	88	330
J F	36	m	w	MA	Alameda	Oakland	68	167
KINGON								
Robert	34	m	w	SCOT	San Francisco	San Francisco P O	83	23
KINGOULD								
Gee	25	m	w	ME	Sacramento	Brighton Twp	77	74
KINGS								
John	22	m	w	NJ	San Francisco	7-Wd San Francisco	81	262
Kingsley	39	m	w	NY	Santa Cruz	Pajaro Twp	89	340
KINGSBERRY								
Jesse	46	m	w	NY	Colusa	Butte Twp	71	271
KINGSBERY								
L	30	m	w	VT	Alameda	Oakland	68	221
KINGSBURRY								
Albert	14	m	w	MA	Sonoma	Petaluma Twp	91	346
Alonzo	27	m	w	GA	Butte	Ophir Twp	70	114
Elisha	40	m	w	CT	San Francisco	5-Wd San Francisco	81	6
W C	43	m	w	OH	Lassen	Susanville Twp	73	439
KINGSBURY								
Alice	26	f	w	LA	San Bernardino	San Bernardino Twp	78	432
Chas N	38	m	w	NY	Shasta	Horsetown P O	89	501
E	54	f	w	VT	Solano	Vallejo	90	146
Eliza	25	f	w	NY	San Francisco	11-Wd San Francisc	84	685
George W	28	m	w	VT	Klamath	Camp Gaston	73	372
Henry	35	m	w	IREL	San Francisco	San Francisco P O	83	411
Hinry	52	m	w	CANA	Trinity	Hayfork Valley	92	239
Ira F	40	m	w	NY	Fresno	Millerton P O	72	161
J C	28	m	w	NY	Sutter	Yuba Twp	92	148
Joseph	30	m	w	CANA	Nevada	Grass Valley Twp	75	202
Lettie	16	f	w	MA	San Francisco	11-Wd San Francisc	84	625
R	40	m	w	SCOT	Alameda	Oakland	68	263
S J	34	f	w	ME	Alameda	Oakland	68	185
Saml	48	m	w	MA	Alameda	Brooklyn	68	28
Samuel	35	m	w	ENGL	Yolo	Washington Twp	93	530
Squire	35	m	w	ME	Sonoma	Bodega Twp	91	261
William	36	m	w	NY	Contra Costa	San Pablo Twp	71	353
Wm	37	m	w	MA	Butte	Oregon Twp	70	135
KINGSFORD								
Amelia	11	f	w	CA	Santa Clara	2-Wd San Jose	88	321
KINGSLAND								
T G	43	m	w	NJ	Del Norte	Crescent	71	462
KINGSLEY								
--- Mrs	38	f	w	NY	Alameda	Oakland	68	200
Andrew	20	m	w	MA	Solano	Benicia	90	4
Aug	30	m	w	NY	San Francisco	San Francisco P O	83	88
Benjamin	55	m	w	RI	Calaveras	Copperopolis P O	70	249
C D	21	m	w	MI	Sacramento	Dry Crk Twp	77	100
Dewitt	38	m	w	PA	Solano	Vacaville Twp	90	120
Edwin	42	m	w	ME	Santa Cruz	Santa Cruz	89	426
Enma	29	f	w	MA	San Francisco	8-Wd San Francisco	82	421
Ezra	47	m	w	PA	Placer	Clipper Gap P O	76	376
F	61	m	w	ME	Lassen	Susanville Twp	73	442
Frank	12	m	w	CA	Stanislaus	San Joaquin Twp	92	75
Geo	54	m	w	NY	Yuba	W Bear Rvr Twp	93	680
Geo S	42	m	w	NY	Tehama	Red Bluff	92	175
George	35	m	w	PA	Santa Barbara	Santa Barbara P O	87	500
Hubbard	23	m	w	MA	Mendocino	Point Arena Twp	74	204
Hubert	35	m	w	RI	Sonoma	Salt Point	91	390
Isabella	17	f	w	CA	Humboldt	Eureka Twp	72	277
James	25	m	w	PA	San Francisco	5-Wd San Francisco	81	7
James B	40	m	w	IL	Tuolumne	Sonora P O	93	327
Joe W	32	m	w	MA	Mono	Bridgeport P O	74	283
John	30	m	w	NY	San Francisco	7-Wd San Francisco	81	262
John C	61	m	w	MA	Inyo	Bishop Crk Twp	73	312
Lima	11	f	w	IL	Contra Costa	Martinez P O	71	394
N L	49	m	w	NY	Tehama	Mill Crk Twp	92	168
Peter	35	m	w	NJ	Sacramento	4-Wd Sacramento	77	357
S A	44	m	w	CA	Sacramento	Dry Crk Twp	77	99
S B	46	m	w	MA	San Joaquin	Dent Twp	86	16
W A	30	m	w	ENGL	Monterey	San Juan Twp	74	408
Walter	14	m	w	KY	Colusa	Monroe Twp	71	311
William	44	m	w	NY	Santa Clara	Santa Clara Twp	88	148
Wm	50	m	w	ENGL	San Francisco	San Francisco P O	83	50
KINGSLY								
Chas	41	m	w	NY	Butte	Oregon Twp	70	128
I F	36	m	w	OH	San Joaquin	Douglas Twp	86	48
KINGSMILL								
Elizabeth	60	f	w	ENGL	Santa Clara	Fremont Twp	88	60
KINGSTON								
Alice	6	f	w	CA	San Francisco	San Francisco P O	85	828
Chrisr	34	m	w	SCOT	Monterey	Pajaro Twp	74	370
Frank	30	m	w	NY	Santa Clara	Santa Clara Twp	88	147
Henry	40	m	w	PA	San Francisco	11-Wd San Francisc	84	572
J	32	m	w	TN	Santa Clara	Gilroy Twp	88	97
James	45	m	w	IREL	Napa	Napa Twp	75	29
John	51	m	w	MA	Tuolumne	Big Oak Flat P O	93	398
John	43	m	w	IREL	San Francisco	San Francisco P O	83	35
Margaret	28	f	w	IREL	San Francisco	8-Wd San Francisco	82	438
Thomas	45	m	w	IREL	Placer	Colfax P O	76	385
KINGTON								
Jas	29	m	w	ENGL	Sierra	Sears Twp	89	554
KINGWALL								
Mary	63	f	w	IREL	San Francisco	San Francisco P O	83	340
KINGWELL								
James	28	m	w	IREL	San Francisco	8-Wd San Francisco	82	454
Vincent	32	m	w	IREL	San Francisco	San Francisco P O	83	414
KININNIWITH								
A	54	m	w	SCOT	El Dorado	Georgetown Twp	72	36
KINIONES								
John	28	m	w	MEXI	Marin	Novato Twp	74	12
KINJORRUS								
Pedro	60	m	w	MEXI	Calaveras	Copperopolis P O	70	260
KINK								
Thomas	60	m	b	VA	Calaveras	San Andreas P O	70	180
KINKAD								
Andrew	58	m	w	MO	Monterey	Castroville Twp	74	327
James E	25	m	w	MO	Monterey	Castroville Twp	74	327
KINKADE								
John T	44	m	w	VA	Placer	Rocklin Twp	76	464
Wm	42	m	w	NY	San Francisco	5-Wd San Francisco	81	16
KINKARD								
Richd	33	m	w	AR	Fresno	Millerton P O	72	181
KINKEAD								
Wm	66	m	w	KY	Alameda	Oakland	68	133
KINKEL								
Auguste	34	m	w	HANO	San Francisco	11-Wd San Francisc	84	561
Philip	40	m	w	IL	San Francisco	1-Wd San Francisco	79	118
KINKER								
John	43	m	w	PRUS	San Joaquin	2-Wd Stockton	86	166
KINKLAND								
Wm	34	m	w	PA	San Francisco	1-Wd San Francisco	79	39
KINKLBERG								
Carl	32	m	w	BAVA	San Francisco	11-Wd San Francisc	84	529
KINKLE								
Adam J	35	m	w	NY	Sacramento	2-Wd Sacramento	77	246
Charles	30	m	w	BREM	Santa Cruz	Santa Cruz	89	412
Malissa	25	m	w	ITAL	Napa	Napa	75	12
Peter	52	m	w	PA	Yolo	Cache Crk Twp	93	450
Pulaski	25	m	w	IN	Napa	Napa	75	12
KINLEY								
Charles	35	m	w	NY	San Francisco	7-Wd San Francisco	81	185
Thomas	30	m	w	IREL	San Francisco	San Francisco P O	83	150
KINLOCH								
Susan	38	f	w	VA	Solano	Suisun Twp	90	98
KINLOCK								
Jennie	25	f	w	NY	San Francisco	11-Wd San Francisc	84	520
John Wm	29	m	w	CA	Monterey	Monterey	74	366
KINLY								
A	27	m	w	ME	San Joaquin	Tulare Twp	86	264
Moses	35	m	w	MA	San Joaquin	Tulare Twp	86	264
KINMAN								
Charles W	36	m	w	NY	Santa Clara	1-Wd San Jose	88	264
Levi	57	m	w	MO	Sierra	Sears Twp	89	527

© 2001 by Heritage Quest. All rights reserved.

Name	Age	S	R	B-PL	County	Locale	Roll	Pg
Nathan	43	m	w	PA	San Bernardino	San Bernardino Twp	78	415
Nathan	19	m	w	NY	Humboldt	Pacific Twp	72	297
R C	18	m	w	IL	Humboldt	Pacific Twp	72	297
Seth	54	m	w	PA	Humboldt	Table Bluff Twp	72	307
KINN								
Ah	50	m	c	CHIN	Santa Clara	Alviso Twp	88	27
Ah	50	m	c	CHIN	Sierra	Downieville Twp	89	520
Ah	33	m	c	CHIN	Sacramento	1-Wd Sacramento	77	205
Ah	32	m	c	CHIN	Sierra	Lincoln Twp	89	550
Ah	30	m	c	CHIN	San Francisco	San Francisco P O	80	335
Ah	28	m	c	CHIN	Marin	San Rafael Twp	74	34
Ah	21	m	c	CHIN	San Francisco	San Francisco P O	80	499
Ah	20	m	c	CHIN	Contra Costa	Martinez P O	71	404
Ah	19	m	c	CHIN	Placer	Bath P O	76	429
KINNAN								
Matthew	44	m	m	NY	San Francisco	1-Wd San Francisco	79	128
KINNAND								
E	35	m	w	FRAN	Alameda	Oakland	68	172
KINNAR								
Sylvester	37	m	w	PA	Yuba	New York Twp	93	641
KINNE								
Ah	32	m	c	CHIN	Trinity	North Fork Twp	92	220
KINNEAR								
John	54	m	w	MA	San Francisco	3-Wd San Francisco	79	301
KINNELL								
Henry	20	m	w	CANA	Nevada	Grass Valley Twp	75	222
KINNENSON								
Geo	30	m	w	RUSS	San Francisco	2-Wd San Francisco	79	168
KINNEY								
Alonzo	28	m	w	NY	San Francisco	5-Wd San Francisco	81	31
Ann	50	f	w	IREL	Placer	Dutch Flat P O	76	404
Bridget	69	f	w	IREL	San Francisco	7-Wd San Francisco	81	253
C M	29	m	w	NY	San Francisco	San Francisco P O	85	852
Cath	40	f	w	IREL	San Francisco	San Francisco P O	85	793
David	29	m	w	IREL	Tuolumne	Columbia P O	93	345
Ed	38	m	w	IREL	Sacramento	3-Wd Sacramento	77	290
Elizabeth	45	f	w	PRUS	Amador	Amador City P O	69	393
Elizabeth	27	f	w	PA	El Dorado	Coloma Twp	72	7
Ellen	47	f	w	IREL	San Francisco	San Francisco P O	83	91
Geo	38	m	w	ME	Humboldt	Bucksport Twp	72	244
Geo	30	m	w	IL	Humboldt	Arcata Twp	72	226
H L	40	m	w	NY	Nevada	Bloomfield Twp	75	98
Henry	35	m	w	TX	Tulare	Farmersville Twp	92	244
J J	42	m	w	MA	Tuolumne	Big Oak Flat P O	93	394
J W	38	m	w	KY	Mendocino	Little Lake Twp	74	196
James	44	m	w	MA	Tuolumne	Big Oak Flat P O	93	392
James	25	m	w	AUSL	San Francisco	3-Wd San Francisco	79	320
James	20	m	w	MA	San Francisco	7-Wd San Francisco	81	276
Jas	27	m	w	MI	San Joaquin	2-Wd Stockton	86	207
Jeremiah	46	m	w	PA	Plumas	Indian Twp	77	11
John	50	m	w	NY	Amador	Ione City P O	69	370
John	48	m	w	NY	San Francisco	5-Wd San Francisco	81	24
Latza	20	f	w	IREL	Contra Costa	Martinez P O	71	433
Maggie	30	f	w	IREL	San Francisco	8-Wd San Francisco	82	369
Maria	26	f	w	IREL	Sacramento	3-Wd Sacramento	77	293
Mary	26	f	w	CA	Solano	Vallejo	90	154
Michael	40	m	w	IREL	Tuolumne	Sonora P O	93	329
Michael	38	m	w	IREL	Tuolumne	Sonora P O	93	313
Michael	35	m	w	IREL	San Francisco	7-Wd San Francisco	81	233
Norman	58	m	w	NY	Sonoma	Santa Rosa	91	419
Saml S	48	m	w	NY	San Luis Obispo	San Luis Obispo Tw	87	308
Thomas	37	m	w	IREL	San Francisco	11-Wd San Francisc	84	701
Thomas	33	m	w	NY	Mendocino	Albion & Big Rvr T	74	166
Thos	31	m	w	PA	San Francisco	11-Wd San Francisc	84	694
KINNICAN								
Michl	26	m	w	IREL	San Francisco	San Francisco P O	85	852
KINNY								
Barny	34	m	w	IREL	San Joaquin	1-Wd Stockton	86	123
Marshall	24	m	w	CANA	San Mateo	Schoolhouse Statio	87	331
Walter	43	m	w	NY	Sacramento	4-Wd Sacramento	77	377
William	28	m	w	IREL	San Francisco	5-Wd San Francisco	81	32
William H	32	m	w	CANA	San Mateo	Schoolhouse Statio	87	331
KINO								
Ah	42	m	c	CHIN	Los Angeles	Los Angeles Twp	73	466
Ah	28	m	c	CHIN	Sacramento	3-Wd Sacramento	77	316
KINON								
John G	24	m	w	PA	Marin	Sausalito Twp	74	73
KINS								
Ah	35	m	c	CHIN	Sacramento	Alabama Twp	77	59
KINSALA								
Mary	45	f	w	IREL	San Francisco	7-Wd San Francisco	81	181
KINSBERGER								
H	40	m	w	HANO	Sierra	Lincoln Twp	89	546
KINSBURY								
Thomas	35	m	w	NY	Tuolumne	Sonora P O	93	318
KINSELL								
John	25	m	w	IREL	Inyo	Bishop Crk Twp	73	312
KINSELLA								
Sarah	19	f	w	IREL	Monterey	Monterey	74	366
KINSELY								
Jacob	40	m	w	OH	El Dorado	Mud Springs Twp	72	90
KINSEY								
Alice	21	f	w	OH	Sacramento	2-Wd Sacramento	77	248
Arther	20	m	w	ENGL	San Francisco	San Francisco P O	85	864
Arthur	40	m	w	NY	San Francisco	5-Wd San Francisco	81	18
Charles	55	m	w	NY	San Mateo	Pescadero P O	87	417
Chas	56	m	w	PA	Humboldt	Eureka Twp	72	272
Chas	19	m	w	CA	Sierra	Table Rock Twp	89	572
H	66	m	w	ENGL	Sierra	Downieville Twp	89	514
Kerst	42	m	w	PA	Sacramento	2-Wd Sacramento	77	227
Maggie	24	f	w	NJ	Nevada	Nevada Twp	75	299
Mark B	32	m	w	OH	Placer	Lincoln P O	76	489
Mixsell	59	m	w	PA	Plumas	Indian Twp	77	9
Solomon	33	m	w	PA	Napa	Yountville Twp	75	81
KINSHI								
John	30	m	w	PRUS	San Joaquin	1-Wd Stockton	86	130
KINSIE								
Henry	39	m	w	PA	El Dorado	Diamond Springs Tw	72	35
KINSILLER								
John	35	m	w	IREL	San Francisco	11-Wd San Francisc	84	452
KINSLEA								
Elizabeth	50	f	w	ENGL	San Francisco	San Francisco P O	85	718
KINSLEY								
Isabell	17	f	w	CA	San Francisco	2-Wd San Francisco	79	216
John	44	m	w	KY	San Diego	Milquaty Dist	78	476
John E	33	m	w	IREL	San Francisco	San Francisco P O	85	718
Josiah	38	m	w	OH	Humboldt	Eel Rvr Twp	72	255
Martin	38	m	w	IREL	Santa Cruz	Soquel Twp	89	444
Mary	19	f	w	PA	San Francisco	8-Wd San Francisco	82	349
Mary A	10	f	w	CA	Santa Cruz	Santa Cruz	89	417
Michl	45	m	w	IREL	San Francisco	1-Wd San Francisco	79	49
KINSLY								
Adolph	40	m	w	SWIT	Tehama	Tehama Twp	92	193
KINSMA								
Joseph A	42	m	w	MA	Fresno	Millerton P O	72	149
KINSMAN								
Afred	24	m	w	ENGL	Nevada	Nevada Twp	75	301
Chas W	39	m	w	ME	San Francisco	7-Wd San Francisco	81	235
Edwin	27	m	w	ENGL	Nevada	Grass Valley Twp	75	183
Frank	62	m	w	ME	San Francisco	San Francisco P O	83	378
Gertrude	7	f	w	CA	San Francisco	San Francisco P O	83	249
J S	41	m	w	PRUS	San Francisco	8-Wd San Francisco	82	350
Jeremiah	21	m	w	IL	Fresno	Millerton P O	72	148
Joel	41	m	w	ENGL	Nevada	Grass Valley Twp	75	159
John	54	m	w	ENGL	Plumas	Indian Twp	77	14
John	40	m	w	ENGL	Colusa	Colusa Twp	71	279
John	27	m	w	ENGL	Nevada	Grass Valley Twp	75	175
Julius A	48	m	w	NH	Yolo	Washington Twp	93	529
Kate E	24	f	w	TX	San Francisco	8-Wd San Francisco	82	354
M G	30	m	w	ENGL	Siskiyou	Scott Rvr Twp	89	604
Miamin	24	m	w	ENGL	Nevada	Grass Valley Twp	75	145
Michael	32	m	w	ENGL	Siskiyou	Scott Rvr Twp	89	604
Oliver A	40	m	w	MA	Fresno	Millerton P O	72	149
KINSMARK								
I	26	m	w	SWED	Alameda	Oakland	68	172
KINSMILL								
Powers	40	m	w	CANA	Solano	Suisun Twp	90	95
KINSON								
Eli B	54	m	w	NH	Butte	Kimshew Tpw	70	77
George	30	m	w	NH	San Francisco	San Francisco P O	83	207
KINSTEY								
Mos	40	m	w	NY	Solano	Benicia	90	7
KINTANA								
Nelly	14	f	w	CA	Los Angeles	Los Angeles	73	570
R	18	f	w	CA	Los Angeles	Los Angeles	73	570
KINTARO								
---	25	m	j	JAPA	El Dorado	Coloma Twp	72	4
Ramon	38	m	w	MEXI	Calaveras	San Andreas P O	70	207
KINTON								
Stephen	38	m	w	PA	Amador	Amador City P O	69	391
KINTONA								
Andrew	33	m	i	MEXI	Inyo	Cerro Gordo Twp	73	323
KINTZ								
John	38	m	w	PA	San Francisco	San Francisco P O	83	27
KINVAIN								
Edwd	28	m	w	IREL	San Francisco	5-Wd San Francisco	81	28
KINVER								
J	27	m	w	AUST	Sierra	Butte Twp	89	509
KINWORTHY								
D	45	m	w	OH	Mariposa	Maxwell Crk P O	74	145
Jacob	32	m	w	IN	Sonoma	Analy Twp	91	238
Wm	35	m	w	IN	Sonoma	Analy Twp	91	238
KINZER								
George	52	m	w	PA	San Francisco	San Francisco P O	80	359
James W	17	m	w	MO	Contra Costa	Martinez P O	71	372
KIO								
Ah	26	m	c	CHIN	Nevada	Meadow Lake Twp	75	256
KION								
Rose	20	f	w	MA	San Francisco	San Francisco P O	83	288
KIOW								
Ah	18	m	c	CHIN	San Francisco	3-Wd San Francisco	79	329
KIP								
Ah	48	m	c	CHIN	Siskiyou	Hamburg Twp	89	599
Ah	45	m	c	CHIN	Mariposa	Mariposa P O	74	127
Ah	42	m	c	CHIN	Fresno	Millerton P O	72	200
Ah	40	m	c	CHIN	Shasta	French Gulch P O	89	465
Ah	40	m	c	CHIN	San Joaquin	Oneal Twp	86	116
Ah	39	m	c	CHIN	El Dorado	Greenwood Twp	72	56
Ah	39	m	c	CHIN	El Dorado	Greenwood Twp	72	56
Ah	38	m	c	CHIN	Sierra	Butte Twp	89	513
Ah	33	m	c	CHIN	El Dorado	Coloma Twp	72	12
Ah	32	m	c	CHIN	Nevada	Washington Twp	75	344
Ah	32	m	c	CHIN	El Dorado	Mountain Twp	72	68
Ah	30	m	c	CHIN	Fresno	Millerton P O	72	200

© 2001 by Heritage Quest. All rights reserved.

California 1870 Census

Series M593

Name	Age	S	R	B-PL	County	Locale	Roll	Pg
Ah	28	m	c	CHIN	Sierra	Downieville Twp	89	521
Ah	27	m	c	CHIN	El Dorado	Georgetown Twp	72	38
Ah	25	m	c	CHIN	El Dorado	Placerville Twp	72	105
Ah	24	m	c	CHIN	Shasta	American Ranch P O	89	500
Ah	19	m	c	CHIN	El Dorado	Salmon Falls Twp	72	134
Chin	32	m	c	CHIN	San Francisco	11-Wd San Francisc	84	521
George	28	m	w	PRUS	San Francisco	5-Wd San Francisco	81	13
John	38	m	w	SCOT	Alameda	Oakland	68	258
Joseph	35	m	w	PRUS	San Francisco	1-Wd San Francisco	79	98
Low	29	m	c	CHIN	San Joaquin	3-Wd Stockton	86	246
See	50	m	c	CHIN	El Dorado	Greenwood Twp	72	56
Sing	32	m	c	CHIN	El Dorado	Kelsey Twp	72	59
Sing	26	m	c	CHIN	Sierra	Butte Twp	89	513
Sip	40	m	c	CHIN	El Dorado	Georgetown Twp	72	38
So	30	m	c	CHIN	El Dorado	Greenwood Twp	72	56
Song	29	m	c	CHIN	Sierra	Butte Twp	89	513
Sow	33	m	c	CHIN	El Dorado	Kelsey Twp	72	59
Yong	20	m	c	CHIN	Los Angeles	El Monte Twp	73	457
KIPHART								
Chas	41	m	w	IN	Lake	Lower Lake	73	421
KIPLIN								
Joseph	31	m	w	SWIT	Inyo	Cerro Gordo Twp	73	320
KIPP								
Henry	37	m	w	OH	Sacramento	1-Wd Sacramento	77	176
Jocob	54	m	m	NY	Alpine	Monitor P O	69	313
John	25	m	w	GERM	Contra Costa	San Pablo Twp	71	366
John B	47	m	w	NY	Los Angeles	Los Angeles	73	535
John L	38	m	w	PRUS	El Dorado	White Oak Twp	72	139
Margaret	22	f	w	NY	San Francisco	8-Wd San Francisco	82	401
Oliver S	29	m	w	NY	Placer	Gold Run Twp	76	394
KIPPEN								
Juan	11	m	w	AZOR	Marin	San Rafael Twp	74	27
KIPPENBERG								
Ernest	29	m	w	RUSS	San Francisco	1-Wd San Francisco	79	78
KIPPER								
Joseph B	42	m	w	SWIT	San Francisco	San Francisco P O	83	173
William	41	m	w	PRUS	Sacramento	4-Wd Sacramento	77	348
KIPPERMAN								
John	55	m	w	HANO	Stanislaus	Buena Vista Twp	92	13
KIPPLE								
Addam	30	m	w	PRUS	Humboldt	Eureka Twp	72	276
KIPPS								
A K	38	m	w	IREL	Alameda	Oakland	68	190
KIRBEY								
John	46	m	w	KY	Solano	Green Valley Twp	90	38
KIRBY								
Abraham	26	m	w	ENGL	Solano	Silveyville Twp	90	91
Alexander	49	m	w	KY	Plumas	Quartz Twp	77	43
Charles W	30	m	w	IL	San Luis Obispo	Morro Twp	87	285
E C	42	m	w	IREL	San Francisco	San Francisco P O	85	791
Eliza	35	f	w	IREL	San Francisco	San Francisco P O	85	742
Emma	20	f	w	PA	El Dorado	Placerville	72	107
Emma	19	f	w	TN	San Joaquin	2-Wd Stockton	86	181
George K	45	m	w	PA	Placer	Roseville P O	76	351
Gersham H	65	m	w	NY	Santa Cruz	Soquel Twp	89	439
Henry	52	m	w	ENGL	Lassen	Janesville Twp	73	431
Henry	32	m	w	IN	El Dorado	Cosumnes Twp	72	19
James	35	m	w	IREL	Fresno	Millerton P O	72	168
James	33	m	w	IREL	Santa Cruz	Santa Cruz Twp	89	394
James	17	m	w	IREL	Shasta	Shasta P O	89	457
Jno	34	m	w	IREL	Santa Clara	Burnett Twp	88	38
John	62	m	w	IREL	Santa Cruz	Santa Cruz Twp	89	398
John	48	m	w	MO	Solano	Denverton Twp	90	24
John	44	m	w	IREL	San Francisco	6-Wd San Francisco	81	86
John	32	m	w	ENGL	San Francisco	8-Wd San Francisco	82	306
Kate	35	f	w	IREL	San Francisco	8-Wd San Francisco	82	427
Lucy R	37	f	w	IREL	San Francisco	8-Wd San Francisco	82	412
M E	9	f	w	CA	Alameda	Oakland	68	258
Martin	53	m	w	ENGL	Mariposa	Mariposa P O	74	131
Mary	13	f	w	CA	Sacramento	San Joaquin Twp	77	403
O I	46	m	w	PA	Sacramento	1-Wd Sacramento	77	182
P J	50	m	w	PA	Alameda	Oakland	68	132
Patrick	15	m	w	IREL	San Francisco	1-Wd San Francisco	79	46
R C	53	m	w	ENGL	Santa Cruz	Santa Cruz	89	403
Robert J	41	m	w	TN	Placer	Alta P O	76	412
S A	52	m	w	PA	Humboldt	South Fork Twp	72	301
Saml W	36	m	w	NY	Santa Cruz	Santa Cruz	89	424
Seth	29	m	w	IL	Tulare	Tule Rvr Twp	92	266
Silas W	25	m	w	IL	Santa Cruz	Soquel Twp	89	448
Susan M	45	f	w	IREL	San Francisco	San Francisco P O	85	732
Thos	28	m	w	IREL	San Francisco	1-Wd San Francisco	79	55
W	40	m	w	VA	Yuba	Marysville	93	591
Wm	34	m	w	NY	Sacramento	1-Wd Sacramento	77	182
Wm H	50	m	w	IREL	San Francisco	2-Wd San Francisco	79	274
KIRCH								
Charles	42	m	w	HANO	San Francisco	San Francisco P O	83	173
Joseph	35	m	w	PRUS	San Francisco	8-Wd San Francisco	82	312
Lavis B	38	m	w	NY	Alameda	Murray Twp	68	116
KIRCHHEN								
Gollert	37	m	w	WURT	Los Angeles	Los Angeles	73	535
KIRCHIVAL								
Albert T	41	m	w	OH	Los Angeles	Los Angeles	73	505
KIRCHMAN								
Hiram	45	m	w	PRUS	Sacramento	2-Wd Sacramento	77	206
KIRCHNER								
Geo	52	m	w	BAVA	El Dorado	Greenwood Twp	72	50
Henry	51	m	w	HAMB	San Francisco	1-Wd San Francisco	79	118
Henry	49	m	w	WURT	Solano	Benicia	90	8
KIRCHOFF								
George	39	m	w	SAXO	San Francisco	11-Wd San Francisc	84	656
Hermann L	42	m	w	PRUS	San Francisco	San Francisco P O	83	78
KIRCHUN								
Jacob	23	m	w	WURT	San Francisco	San Francisco P O	80	536
KIREENS								
Maggie Mrs	40	f	w	IREL	Monterey	Monterey	74	366
KIRENS								
Margaret	21	f	w	NY	San Francisco	11-Wd San Francisc	84	565
KIRGIL								
August	38	m	w	GERM	Yolo	Grafton Twp	93	488
KIRGIN								
Cora	13	f	w	ME	Marin	San Rafael	74	56
KIRK								
Aggie	70	f	b	VA	San Joaquin	Douglas Twp	86	39
Ah	30	m	c	CHIN	Sacramento	3-Wd Sacramento	77	294
Allie	17	f	w	CA	Butte	Chico Twp	70	41
Ann	45	f	w	IREL	San Francisco	San Francisco P O	83	92
Annie	18	f	w	IREL	San Francisco	11-Wd San Francisc	84	495
Annie J	32	f	w	IREL	Nevada	Bridgeport Twp	75	104
Annie J	32	f	w	IREL	Sonoma	Bodega Twp	91	254
B L	22	m	w	PA	San Francisco	San Francisco P O	85	785
Christian	53	m	w	DENM	San Francisco	8-Wd San Francisco	82	322
D	41	m	w	NY	Alameda	Oakland	68	262
Danl	49	m	w	NY	Butte	Hamilton Twp	70	69
Francis	39	m	w	IN	Santa Barbara	Santa Barbara P O	87	453
Frank	36	m	w	IREL	San Francisco	11-Wd San Francisc	84	703
Henry	50	m	b	VA	San Joaquin	Douglas Twp	86	36
Henry	35	m	b	VA	Calaveras	Copperopolis P O	70	261
Henry	30	m	w	ENGL	Sonoma	Mendocino Twp	91	307
Henry C	39	m	w	PA	Sacramento	4-Wd Sacramento	77	351
Hugh	37	m	w	IREL	Santa Clara	Fremont Twp	88	49
Isaac	47	m	w	IN	Butte	Ophir Twp	70	101
Isiah	50	m	w	ENGL	San Francisco	2-Wd San Francisco	79	215
James	34	m	w	SCOT	San Francisco	1-Wd San Francisco	79	94
James	27	m	w	IREL	San Mateo	San Mateo P O	87	353
Jno	27	m	w	IREL	Sacramento	1-Wd Sacramento	77	200
John	55	m	w	PA	El Dorado	Placerville	72	126
John	38	m	w	IREL	Amador	Ione City P O	69	352
John	37	m	w	NY	Plumas	Goodwin Twp	77	7
John	35	m	w	IREL	San Francisco	7-Wd San Francisco	81	273
John	31	m	w	IL	El Dorado	Coloma Twp	72	6
John	24	m	w	MO	Calaveras	Copperopolis P O	70	262
John	21	m	w	CANA	El Dorado	Cosumnes Twp	72	14
John A	40	m	w	VA	Placer	Bath P O	76	433
John T	22	m	w	OR	San Joaquin	Douglas Twp	86	38
John W	48	m	w	VA	San Joaquin	Douglas Twp	86	38
Jos A	53	m	w	VA	Sutter	Sutter Twp	92	123
Joseph	58	m	w	VA	Placer	Auburn P O	76	367
Julia	36	f	w	IREL	Santa Cruz	Watsonville	89	376
Kate	38	f	w	NY	Placer	Auburn P O	76	367
Kate	20	f	w	IN	Placer	Auburn P O	76	366
Leonard	32	m	w	VA	Humboldt	Pacific Twp	72	295
Margaret	28	f	w	CANA	San Francisco	2-Wd San Francisco	79	261
Mary	50	f	w	WURT	San Francisco	San Francisco P O	80	536
Mary	30	f	w	IREL	San Joaquin	2-Wd Stockton	86	162
Mary	27	f	w	IREL	San Joaquin	2-Wd Stockton	86	207
Michl	43	m	w	IREL	Marin	Tomales Twp	74	78
Miles	32	m	w	VA	Shasta	Millville P O	89	486
Nelly	16	f	w	US	Yuba	Marysville	93	609
Owen	30	m	w	IREL	San Francisco	7-Wd San Francisco	81	226
Robbert	50	m	w	MA	Alameda	Alameda	68	8
S B	40	m	w	ME	Solano	Vallejo	90	187
S T	27	m	w	PA	Santa Clara	Gilroy Twp	88	70
Theopolus	38	m	w	OH	Santa Clara	San Jose Twp	88	197
Thomas	46	m	w	VA	Sutter	Vernon Twp	92	138
Thomas D	79	m	w	VA	Sutter	Sutter Twp	92	123
William	35	m	w	IREL	Sonoma	Petaluma Twp	91	351
William	34	m	w	IREL	Del Norte	Crescent	71	463
William	28	m	w	IREL	Napa	Yountville Twp	75	77
William	25	m	w	MO	Stanislaus	Buena Vista Twp	92	11
Wm	42	m	w	IREL	Sacramento	3-Wd Sacramento	77	264
Wm	40	m	b	VA	San Joaquin	Douglas Twp	86	36
Wm	20	m	w	OR	San Joaquin	Douglas Twp	86	38
KIRKALDIE								
W T	41	m	w	ENGL	San Francisco	San Francisco P O	85	797
KIRKALDY								
H	20	m	w	PRUS	San Francisco	San Francisco P O	85	863
KIRKAM								
W G	38	m	w	OH	Klamath	Klamath Twp	73	371
KIRKE								
Henry M	40	m	w	PA	San Diego	San Pasqual Valley	78	524
KIRKENDALL								
J	40	m	w	NY	San Joaquin	3-Wd Stockton	86	241
Jos S	35	m	w	NY	Mono	Bridgeport P O	74	285
Levy	28	m	w	IN	Amador	Fiddletown P O	69	435
Thos	30	m	w	MO	San Luis Obispo	Arroyo Grande Twp	87	273
W	55	m	w	OH	Amador	Ione City P O	69	359
KIRKENDOFF								
Sylvester	30	m	w	OH	Stanislaus	Empire Twp	92	42
KIRKER								
Andrew	27	m	w	IREL	Solano	Vallejo	90	204
KIRKHAM								
David	54	m	w	NY	Plumas	Seneca Twp	77	48
J D	40	m	w	IL	Del Norte	Crescent Twp	71	456
Maria	15	f	w	CA	Yolo	Cache Crk Twp	93	419

© 2001 by Heritage Quest. All rights reserved.

Name	Age	S	R	B-PL	County	Locale	Series M593 Roll	Pg
R W	49	m	w	MA	Alameda	Oakland	68	147
Richard L	44	m	w	IN	Yolo	Cottonwood Twp	93	466
Samuel	40	m	w	OH	Yolo	Cache Crk Twp	93	447
Thos	54	m	w	OH	Nevada	Nevada Twp	75	317
KIRKLAND								
Barry	21	m	w	MO	Stanislaus	Empire Twp	92	38
Chas	43	m	w	WI	Butte	Chico Twp	70	46
Danl	55	m	w	MA	Butte	Kimshew Tpw	70	78
Garin	17	m	w	AUST	Amador	Amador City P O	69	390
James	63	m	w	SCOT	Amador	Jackson P O	69	328
John	46	m	w	MO	Calaveras	Copperopolis P O	70	251
Joshua	47	m	w	TN	Stanislaus	Buena Vista Twp	92	11
Lyman	43	m	w	NY	Stanislaus	Empire Twp	92	49
Mary A	36	f	w	MO	Los Angeles	El Monte Twp	73	451
R M	46	m	w	MO	Santa Clara	Gilroy Twp	88	70
Robert	9	m	w	CANA	Solano	Vacaville Twp	90	121
W W	25	m	w	ENGL	Amador	Amador City P O	69	390
William	57	m	w	SCOT	El Dorado	Mud Springs Twp	72	72
KIRKMAN								
Catherine	50	f	w	KY	Yolo	Cache Crk Twp	93	455
Thomas	38	m	w	IL	Humboldt	Eel Rvr Twp	72	247
KIRKNY								
John	36	m	w	ENGL	San Francisco	San Francisco P O	85	785
KIRKPATRIC								
Thomas	37	m	w	IL	Colusa	Monroe Twp	71	317
KIRKPATRICK								
Andw	40	m	w	SCOT	San Francisco	San Francisco P O	83	118
Benjamin	34	m	w	IN	Colusa	Colusa	71	298
Charles A	47	m	w	MO	San Mateo	Redwood Twp	87	364
Clem	39	m	w	PA	San Bernardino	San Bernardino Twp	78	454
David	40	m	w	AR	Mariposa	Mariposa P O	74	100
Henry	27	m	w	CANA	Alameda	Eden Twp	68	71
Henry	18	m	w	IL	Sonoma	Sonoma Twp	91	442
J	55	m	w	IREL	Amador	Jackson P O	69	341
J	52	m	w	OH	Sacramento	Brighton Twp	77	81
J	50	m	w	IREL	Amador	Jackson P O	69	334
J M	32	m	w	IL	San Joaquin	Douglas Twp	86	41
James	47	m	w	IREL	San Francisco	8-Wd San Francisco	82	415
James	15	m	w	CA	Santa Clara	Santa Clara Twp	88	168
John	70	m	w	IREL	El Dorado	White Oak Twp	72	142
John	50	m	w	IL	Santa Clara	Redwood Twp	88	119
John	35	m	w	MO	Siskiyou	Butte Twp	89	588
John G	15	m	w	CA	Santa Clara	San Jose Twp	88	196
L	11	f	w	CA	Sierra	Downieville Twp	89	516
Robt	40	m	w	TN	Butte	Kimshew Tpw	70	78
S	33	m	w	IL	Sutter	Nicolaus Twp	92	109
Samuel	60	m	w	KY	Placer	Lincoln P O	76	491
Samuel	26	m	w	IL	Placer	Lincoln P O	76	490
Thomas	20	m	w	IL	Santa Clara	Fremont Twp	88	43
Thos	60	m	w	KY	Sutter	Nicolaus Twp	92	110
W	28	m	w	CANA	San Francisco	San Francisco P O	85	785
William	16	m	w	CA	Santa Clara	Santa Clara Twp	88	166
KIRKUM								
John C	20	m	w	ENGL	Colusa	Butte Twp	71	271
KIRKUP								
George	34	m	w	ENGL	Colusa	Colusa Twp	71	284
KIRKUPP								
Elizabeth	75	f	w	ENGL	Amador	Fiddletown P O	69	433
T S	77	m	w	ENGL	Amador	Fiddletown P O	69	433
V S	40	m	w	ENGL	Amador	Fiddletown P O	69	433
KIRKWOOD								
A C	44	m	w	SCOT	Tuolumne	Big Oak Flat P O	93	391
James	38	m	w	SCOT	Mariposa	Mariposa P O	74	112
Nicholas	36	m	w	SCOT	Contra Costa	Martinez P O	71	445
Robert	42	m	w	SCOT	Stanislaus	San Joaquin Twp	92	74
W T	16	m	w	IA	Mendocino	Ukiah Twp	74	243
Wm A J	41	m	w	OH	Amador	Volcano P O	69	388
Z S	38	m	w	OH	Amador	Jackson P O	69	318
KIRLEY								
Charlotte	23	f	w	IREL	San Francisco	San Francisco P O	80	382
Mary	35	f	w	IREL	San Francisco	San Francisco P O	80	416
KIRM								
Frederick	19	m	w	IL	Yolo	Cache Crk Twp	93	430
KIRMACIRE								
Frank	42	m	w	FRAN	Marin	Novato Twp	74	10
KIRN								
Fred	60	m	w	WURT	Sacramento	3-Wd Sacramento	77	275
KIRR								
John W	44	m	w	PA	Siskiyou	Klamath Twp	89	600
KIRSCH								
John P	36	m	w	PRUS	Solano	Silveyville Twp	90	87
Michael	38	m	w	PRUS	Contra Costa	Martinez P O	71	378
KIRSCHBERG								
Meyer	38	m	w	PRUS	San Francisco	San Francisco P O	83	37
KIRSCHON								
Sohene	26	f	w	RUSS	San Francisco	San Francisco P O	83	99
KIRT								
Holt	43	m	w	SCOT	Monterey	San Antonio Twp	74	321
Micheal	40	m	w	IREL	Monterey	San Antonio Twp	74	318
KIRTCHUM								
D K	44	m	w	OH	Sutter	Sutter Twp	92	118
KIRTH								
Fredrik	28	m	w	WURT	Sonoma	Petaluma Twp	91	339
KIRTLAND								
Thos	36	m	w	OH	Sacramento	Franklin Twp	77	106
KIRTLEY								
E B	34	m	w	KY	Monterey	Alisal Twp	74	290

Name	Age	S	R	B-PL	County	Locale	Series M593 Roll	Pg
KIRTS								
Chas W	34	m	w	VA	Klamath	South Fork Twp	73	383
KIRTZ								
C	18	m	w	PRUS	Alameda	Murray Twp	68	110
James	35	m	w	IREL	San Francisco	5-Wd San Francisco	81	35
Lewis W	27	m	w	MD	San Francisco	5-Wd San Francisco	81	11
Wm L	48	m	w	MD	San Francisco	5-Wd San Francisco	81	13
KIRWAN								
James	25	m	w	IREL	Santa Cruz	Santa Cruz	89	409
Matthew	48	m	w	IREL	Santa Cruz	Santa Cruz Twp	89	393
KIRWIN								
James	28	m	w	IREL	San Francisco	2-Wd San Francisco	79	247
John	40	m	w	IREL	Santa Barbara	Santa Barbara P O	87	492
Michael	35	m	w	IREL	San Francisco	11-Wd San Francisc	84	576
KIRZONE								
Philip	32	m	w	FRAN	San Francisco	San Francisco P O	80	539
KIS								
Yen	36	m	c	CHIN	Mariposa	Maxwell Crk P O	74	138
KISCASE								
David	25	m	w	ENGL	Nevada	Eureka Twp	75	128
KISE								
Cooper	58	m	w	MO	Sonoma	Russian Rvr	91	376
Saml O	54	m	w	KY	Sonoma	Russian Rvr	91	368
KISELLI								
Philippo	57	m	w	ITAL	San Francisco	11-Wd San Francisc	84	591
KISEN								
Richard	68	m	w	VA	Kern	Havilah P O	73	339
KISER								
A	54	m	w	PRUS	Sierra	Butte Twp	89	513
George	6	m	w	CA	Stanislaus	Empire Twp	92	27
Howard	54	m	w	ENGL	Plumas	Plumas Twp	77	26
John P	32	m	w	OH	Sonoma	Petaluma Twp	91	357
Mathew	30	m	w	OH	Sonoma	Petaluma Twp	91	357
Philo C	47	m	w	VT	Plumas	Plumas Twp	77	33
Valentine	43	m	w	HESS	Stanislaus	Empire Twp	92	27
KISFY								
C	60	m	w	HUNG	Nevada	Nevada Twp	75	286
Isabelle	16	f	w	LA	San Francisco	2-Wd San Francisco	79	143
KISH								
Albert	36	m	w	HUNG	San Francisco	6-Wd San Francisco	81	73
KISKAN								
Geo	19	m	w	OH	Alameda	Murray Twp	68	121
KISLICH								
Joseph	38	m	w	GERM	Santa Clara	Fremont Twp	88	44
KISLING								
William C	16	m	w	CA	San Mateo	Redwood City P O	87	376
KISPERT								
John	33	m	w	PRUS	Inyo	Lone Pine Twp	73	330
KISSACK								
Andrew	30	m	w	ENGL	Sonoma	Washington Twp	91	464
KISSANE								
Henry	30	m	w	ENGL	San Francisco	San Francisco P O	83	352
KISSEE								
Henry	60	m	w	KY	Los Angeles	El Monte Twp	73	463
KISSIL								
P	30	m	w	BAVA	Sierra	Butte Twp	89	509
KISSLING								
Wm	15	m	w	CA	San Francisco	11-Wd San Francisc	84	648
KISTER								
John S	42	m	w	PA	Napa	Napa	75	10
KISTING								
Jos	45	m	w	HANO	Shasta	French Gulch P O	89	470
KISTLE								
Gildea	51	f	w	PRUS	Nevada	Bridgeport Twp	75	101
James	26	m	w	WI	Nevada	Little York Twp	75	236
John	19	m	w	ENGL	Nevada	Grass Valley Twp	75	162
William	60	m	w	ENGL	Nevada	Nevada Twp	75	320
KISTNER								
John	21	m	w	BADE	Alameda	Eden Twp	68	60
KISTTLE								
John	33	m	w	ENGL	Nevada	Nevada Twp	75	277
KIT								
Ah	67	m	c	CHIN	Tuolumne	Sonora P O	93	322
Ah	50	m	c	CHIN	Placer	Auburn P O	76	378
Ah	44	m	c	CHIN	Mariposa	Mariposa P O	74	125
Ah	43	m	c	CHIN	Mariposa	Mariposa P O	74	137
Ah	42	m	c	CHIN	Placer	Bath P O	76	430
Ah	40	m	c	CHIN	Placer	Auburn P O	76	362
Ah	40	m	c	CHIN	Trinity	Indian Crk	92	199
Ah	35	m	c	CHIN	Butte	Concow Twp	70	11
Ah	35	m	c	CHIN	El Dorado	Placerville Twp	72	101
Ah	32	m	c	CHIN	El Dorado	Cosumnes Twp	72	13
Ah	32	m	c	CHIN	El Dorado	Cosumnes Twp	72	18
Ah	31	m	c	CHIN	Placer	Clipper Gap P O	76	393
Ah	30	m	c	CHIN	Nevada	Nevada Twp	75	297
Ah	30	m	c	CHIN	Placer	Auburn P O	76	381
Ah	30	m	c	CHIN	Sierra	Sears Twp	89	553
Ah	30	m	c	CHIN	Trinity	Weaverville Pct	92	230
Ah	28	m	c	CHIN	San Mateo	San Mateo P O	87	356
Ah	28	m	c	CHIN	El Dorado	Placerville Twp	72	103
Ah	28	m	c	CHIN	Placer	Dutch Flat P O	76	410
Ah	25	m	c	CHIN	El Dorado	Mountain Twp	72	69
Ah	25	m	c	CHIN	El Dorado	Cosumnes Twp	72	19
Ah	22	m	c	CHIN	San Francisco	3-Wd San Francisco	79	306
Ah	22	m	c	CHIN	El Dorado	Mud Springs Twp	72	73
Ah	18	m	c	CHIN	Solano	Silveyville Twp	90	85
Ah	18	m	c	CHIN	San Francisco	San Francisco P O	80	490

© 2001 by Heritage Quest. All rights reserved.

California 1870 Census

Name	Age	S	R	B-PL	County	Locale	Series M593 Roll	Pg
Ah	16	m	c	CHIN	El Dorado	Mud Springs Twp	72	78
Foon	50	m	c	CHIN	Shasta	American Ranch P O	89	497
He	47	f	c	CHIN	Monterey	Monterey Twp	74	351
Kai	30	m	c	CHIN	Tuolumne	Columbia P O	93	348
Leon	40	m	c	CHIN	Sierra	Downieville Twp	89	521
Y	29	m	c	CHIN	Nevada	Bridgeport Twp	75	111
KITCHAM								
Francis D	51	m	w	NY	Humboldt	Eel Rvr Twp	72	248
KITCHEN								
Abraham	40	m	w	MO	Colusa	Monroe Twp	71	323
Andrew	56	m	w	SCOT	Butte	Wyandotte Twp	70	146
Geo W	38	m	w	AR	Sonoma	Cloverdale Twp	91	269
Isaac	48	m	w	ENGL	Butte	Kimshew Tpw	70	81
Jane	12	f	w	CANA	Solano	Vallejo	90	164
Newton J	41	m	w	TN	Santa Cruz	Watsonville	89	378
R G	42	m	w	NY	San Joaquin	Douglas Twp	86	49
KITCHER								
Geo	36	m	w	MO	Monterey	Monterey Twp	74	350
KITCHIE								
John	48	m	w	ENGL	San Francisco	11-Wd San Francisc	84	559
KITCHING								
Augustus	23	m	w	TX	San Diego	San Luis Rey	78	513
KITCHWELL								
Oliver Mrs	23	m	w	NY	San Francisco	5-Wd San Francisco	81	29
KITE								
Ah	22	m	c	CHIN	Tehama	Red Bluff	92	184
Ah	20	m	c	CHIN	Plumas	Plumas Twp	77	31
Ah	19	m	c	CHIN	Amador	Jackson P O	69	331
Benjamin F	45	m	w	OH	Santa Cruz	Santa Cruz Twp	89	393
Gilmore S	35	m	w	VA	San Luis Obispo	Santa Rosa Twp	87	326
Isaac	33	m	w	OH	Santa Cruz	Santa Cruz Twp	89	391
James	30	m	w	CANA	Alameda	Oakland	68	137
Jas	40	m	w	ENGL	Solano	Vallejo	90	162
To	30	m	c	CHIN	Nevada	Meadow Lake Twp	75	254
To	18	m	c	CHIN	Nevada	Meadow Lake Twp	75	256
KITELEY								
John	27	m	w	PA	Alameda	Hayward	68	74
KITMANER								
P	35	m	w	HDAR	Yuba	Marysville	93	633
KITRELL								
Frank M	25	m	w	AR	Stanislaus	Empire Twp	92	52
G	15	f	w	SC	Alameda	Oakland	68	242
M	10	f	w	SC	Alameda	Oakland	68	242
KITRICK								
Lawrnce	43	m	w	IREL	Yuba	North East Twp	93	644
KITRIDGE								
Jame	30	m	w	ME	Amador	Jackson P O	69	345
KITT								
Ah	19	m	c	CHIN	Nevada	Rough & Ready Twp	75	329
Tom	25	m	i	CA	Fresno	Millerton P O	72	179
KITTCHER								
Joseph	63	m	w	ME	Amador	Volcano P O	69	379
KITTEMAN								
James	35	m	w	LA	San Francisco	2-Wd San Francisco	79	267
KITTERICK								
Edwd	16	m	w	IREL	Sacramento	3-Wd Sacramento	77	278
KITTERIDGE								
George	61	m	w	VT	San Diego	San Diego	78	489
Wm	40	m	w	MA	San Francisco	11-Wd San Francisc	84	428
KITTERMAN								
Harry	54	m	w	VA	San Diego	San Diego	78	496
KITTLE								
Henry M	24	m	w	NY	San Francisco	8-Wd San Francisco	82	411
M	50	m	w	NY	San Francisco	8-Wd San Francisco	82	367
Nicholas G	46	m	w	NY	San Francisco	8-Wd San Francisco	82	411
Thomas	30	m	w	IREL	San Francisco	3-Wd San Francisco	79	315
KITTLEND								
Margaret	34	f	w	BADE	San Joaquin	Elkhorn Twp	86	60
KITTLER								
Auguste	30	m	w	SAXO	San Francisco	San Francisco P O	83	169
Eliza	16	f	w	CA	Placer	Lincoln P O	76	493
Elizabeth	46	f	w	HCAS	Placer	Auburn P O	76	358
KITTLEWOOD								
Wm	39	m	w	DE	Siskiyou	Scott Rvr Twp	89	603
KITTO								
John	34	m	w	ENGL	Nevada	Grass Valley Twp	75	212
John	22	m	w	ENGL	Mariposa	Maxwell Crk P O	74	144
Saml	40	m	w	ENGL	Solano	Vallejo	90	152
Thomas	34	m	w	ENGL	Placer	Colfax P O	76	389
KITTREDGE								
Francis M	59	m	w	MA	Santa Cruz	Santa Cruz	89	425
KITTRELL								
Marion	20	m	w	AR	Stanislaus	Empire Twp	92	52
KITTRIDGE								
Harriet	70	f	w	MA	San Francisco	San Francisco P O	83	340
John	40	m	w	IREL	San Joaquin	Oneal Twp	86	100
Jonathan	44	m	w	MA	San Francisco	8-Wd San Francisco	82	444
Joseph	70	m	w	ME	San Francisco	San Francisco P O	83	340
Joseph	40	m	w	MA	San Francisco	San Francisco P O	83	292
Willard	42	m	w	ME	Los Angeles	Wilmington Twp	73	642
KITTS								
Charles	33	m	w	NY	Mariposa	Mariposa P O	74	112
George	39	m	w	KY	Nevada	Nevada Twp	75	295
George F	27	m	w	CANA	Nevada	Meadow Lake Twp	75	268
James	43	m	w	KY	Nevada	Nevada Twp	75	319
Joseph	34	m	w	IN	Nevada	Nevada Twp	75	319
Philander	40	m	w	NY	Mariposa	Mariposa P O	74	112
Samul	48	m	w	ENGL	Nevada	Eureka Twp	75	137
KITZ								
Aaron	31	m	w	SAXO	San Joaquin	Liberty Twp	86	94
John	62	m	w	PRUS	Shasta	Shasta P O	89	455
Rinhold	45	m	w	PRUS	San Francisco	San Francisco P O	85	807
KIVELL								
Edward	30	m	w	ME	San Francisco	3-Wd San Francisco	79	294
KIYNPENRIE								
Peter	37	m	w	FRAN	Solano	Benicia	90	16
KIZER								
Antone	30	m	w	PRUS	Contra Costa	Martinez P O	71	369
Joseph	45	m	w	PA	Kern	Tehachapi P O	73	354
KLABE								
Albert	54	m	w	PRUS	Sacramento	3-Wd Sacramento	77	288
KLABER								
George	45	m	w	AUST	San Francisco	7-Wd San Francisco	81	156
KLAHN								
Henry	33	m	w	IL	Stanislaus	San Joaquin Twp	92	79
KLAHNER								
L	23	m	w	GERM	Sacramento	1-Wd Sacramento	77	181
KLAIN								
Ernest	17	m	w	PRUS	San Francisco	5-Wd San Francisco	81	3
N L	52	m	w	HUNG	San Francisco	San Francisco P O	83	317
KLAM								
John	28	m	w	BAVA	Amador	Jackson P O	69	323
KLAMAN								
Ewald	26	m	w	PRUS	Alameda	Washington Twp	68	300
John	28	m	w	OLDE	San Francisco	8-Wd San Francisco	82	383
KLAMATH								
George	40	m	i	CA	Del Norte	Crescent Twp	71	459
KLANER								
Balthazar	52	m	w	FRNK	El Dorado	Placerville	72	108
KLAPINSTIEN								
Andrew	38	m	w	OH	San Francisco	11-Wd San Francisc	84	631
KLAPP								
Henry	32	m	w	IREL	Solano	Silveyville Twp	90	78
Henry	29	m	w	IA	Solano	Silveyville Twp	90	79
KLASS								
Matthew	28	m	w	SWIT	San Francisco	San Francisco P O	83	222
KLAT								
James	26	m	w	PRUS	San Francisco	San Francisco P O	83	266
KLATT								
Fred	46	m	w	PRUS	Alameda	Alameda	68	13
KLAUS								
Gertrude	66	f	w	PRUS	San Francisco	8-Wd San Francisco	82	496
Jacop	27	m	w	PA	Butte	Ophir Twp	70	93
John	38	m	w	PRUS	San Francisco	1-Wd San Francisco	79	53
Joseph	30	m	w	PRUS	Sacramento	4-Wd Sacramento	77	353
KLAYS								
Fred	21	m	w	LA	Yolo	Putah Twp	93	510
KLEASE								
James	41	m	w	BAVA	Nevada	Eureka Twp	75	129
KLEASON								
Alice	27	f	w	IREL	Contra Costa	Martinez P O	71	397
KLEBAR								
Charles	31	m	w	PRUS	San Francisco	San Francisco P O	85	717
KLEBE								
Adolph	28	m	w	HAMB	San Francisco	7-Wd San Francisco	81	226
KLEBITZ								
Edward	43	m	w	PRUS	Sacramento	2-Wd Sacramento	77	248
KLEBS								
Theodore	20	m	w	NY	Nevada	Grass Valley Twp	75	145
KLECKNER								
A	43	m	w	PA	Sierra	Sears Twp	89	555
A	34	m	w	PA	Sierra	Sears Twp	89	555
KLEE								
Frederick	27	m	w	SHOL	Placer	Auburn P O	76	366
John	38	m	w	HCAS	Santa Clara	San Jose Twp	88	197
KLEEBER								
Geo	34	m	w	BAVA	El Dorado	Coloma Twp	72	9
KLEENSTRAASS								
Heron	25	m	w	PRUS	San Francisco	1-Wd San Francisco	79	126
KLEES								
Jno	38	m	w	PA	Sacramento	3-Wd Sacramento	77	277
KLEET								
Frank	23	m	w	TX	Los Angeles	Soledad Twp	73	630
KLEGAL								
Benjamin	38	m	w	PRUS	San Francisco	6-Wd San Francisco	81	72
KLEI								
Sam	27	m	c	CHIN	Sacramento	1-Wd Sacramento	77	198
KLEIBER								
Henry	26	m	w	PRUS	San Francisco	3-Wd San Francisco	79	300
KLEIN								
Adolph	27	m	w	GERM	San Francisco	8-Wd San Francisco	82	375
Conrad	39	m	w	HESS	Placer	Bath P O	76	456
Ernest	33	m	w	HANO	San Francisco	11-Wd San Francisc	84	619
Frank	56	m	w	PRUS	Calaveras	Copperopolis P O	70	253
Frederick	30	m	w	BAVA	Santa Clara	2-Wd San Jose	88	314
Fredrick	54	m	w	PRUS	Tuolumne	Chinese Camp P O	93	369
Gabriel	70	m	w	AUST	San Francisco	8-Wd San Francisco	82	324
Geo	23	m	w	OH	Yuba	Marysville Twp	93	568
George	34	m	w	WURT	Shasta	French Gulch P O	89	466
Henry	39	m	w	PRUS	San Francisco	San Francisco P O	80	379
J A	20	m	w	NY	Sacramento	3-Wd Sacramento	77	310
Jacob	48	m	w	BAVA	Sierra	Gibson Twp	89	544
Jacob	32	m	w	PRUS	San Francisco	San Francisco P O	83	193
John	46	m	w	PRUS	Tuolumne	Columbia P O	93	358

© 2001 by Heritage Quest. All rights reserved.

Name	Age	S	R	B-PL	County	Locale	Roll	Pg
						Series M593		
Joseph	25	m	w	IA	Santa Barbara	Santa Barbara P O	87	470
Lotta	20	f	w	CA	Tuolumne	Sonora P O	93	308
Moses	32	m	w	BOHE	San Francisco	1-Wd San Francisco	79	35
Norman	39	m	w	MI	Santa Clara	1-Wd San Jose	88	250
Peter	40	m	w	PRUS	Tuolumne	Columbia P O	93	358
Philip	37	m	w	LA	San Francisco	11-Wd San Francisc	84	679
Simon	30	m	w	AUST	San Francisco	8-Wd San Francisco	82	324
Susman	32	m	w	AUST	San Francisco	8-Wd San Francisco	82	324
William	36	m	w	GERM	Tuolumne	Columbia P O	93	355
KLEINCLAUS								
Gustave	24	m	w	FRAN	Santa Clara	Fremont Twp	88	53
Laura	29	f	w	PRUS	Santa Clara	Fremont Twp	88	51
KLEINDIG								
Henry	46	m	w	PRUS	San Francisco	1-Wd San Francisco	79	86
KLEINE								
Fred	60	m	w	BADE	San Francisco	11-Wd San Francisc	84	613
Henry C	30	m	w	PRUS	Stanislaus	Emory Twp	92	20
KLEINHAMMER								
F	42	m	w	PRUS	Sacramento	4-Wd Sacramento	77	370
KLEINHAUHT								
A	31	m	w	PRUS	Napa	Yountville Twp	75	88
KLEINHAUS								
John	37	m	w	NJ	San Francisco	8-Wd San Francisco	82	413
KLEINING								
Christopher	25	m	w	PRUS	Calaveras	San Andreas P O	70	158
KLEINLEIN								
George	35	m	w	BAVA	Mariposa	Mariposa P O	74	92
KLEINSCHMIT								
Amelia	19	f	w	BAVA	San Francisco	8-Wd San Francisco	82	446
KLEINSORG								
Mary	20	f	w	MO	Sacramento	4-Wd Sacramento	77	338
KLEINSORGE								
C	37	m	w	PRUS	Sacramento	3-Wd Sacramento	77	295
Emma	2	f	w	CA	Sacramento	3-Wd Sacramento	77	295
Wm	28	m	w	PRUS	Sacramento	4-Wd Sacramento	77	351
KLEIR								
Aaron	35	m	w	MI	Butte	Chico Twp	70	14
KLEIS								
Barnard P	40	m	w	BADE	Butte	Chico Twp	70	22
KLEISER								
Jas A	51	m	w	KY	Sonoma	Cloverdale Twp	91	269
KLEM								
E A	60	m	w	BADE	Tuolumne	Big Oak Flat P O	93	392
John E	57	m	w	HANO	San Francisco	1-Wd San Francisco	79	116
KLEMMER								
Antone	60	m	w	HDAR	Yuba	Parks Bar Twp	93	648
Jacob P	32	m	w	HDAR	Plumas	Goodwin Twp	77	6
KLEN								
---	30	m	c	CHIN	Siskiyou	Hamburg Twp	89	597
KLENA								
Barnard	40	m	w	SAXO	Placer	Bath P O	76	421
KLENDAIR								
John	26	m	w	BOHE	Tulare	Packwood Twp	92	255
KLENE								
Mark	35	m	w	FRAN	Contra Costa	Martinez P O	71	418
KLENER								
Rudolph	27	m	w	GERM	Los Angeles	Los Angeles	73	568
KLENHAMER								
Haus	23	m	w	PRUS	San Francisco	San Francisco P O	83	134
KLENKEIM								
Abm	30	m	w	PRUS	San Francisco	5-Wd San Francisco	81	20
KLENTZER								
Herman	42	m	w	BREM	San Francisco	7-Wd San Francisco	81	217
KLEOPFER								
Conrad	54	m	w	PRUS	Tuolumne	Chinese Camp P O	93	390
KLEPFER								
Adam	42	m	w	BAVA	San Francisco	8-Wd San Francisco	82	383
KLEPHARDT								
Otto	33	m	w	HAMB	San Francisco	San Francisco P O	85	809
KLEPPEL								
Jacob	42	m	w	HDAR	Sacramento	4-Wd Sacramento	77	351
Louis	32	m	w	PRUS	San Francisco	San Francisco P O	80	462
KLEPPER								
Lucy	22	f	w	PRUS	San Francisco	San Francisco P O	80	397
KLETTICH								
George	48	m	w	BADE	San Bernardino	San Bernardino Twp	78	416
KLEUNG								
Ah	25	m	c	CHIN	Solano	Vallejo	90	139
KLEVESAHL								
Ernst	46	m	w	SHOL	San Francisco	11-Wd San Francisc	84	641
Ernst H	19	m	w	SHOL	San Francisco	11-Wd San Francisc	84	641
William	14	m	w	CA	San Francisco	11-Wd San Francisc	84	641
KLEY								
Herman	31	m	w	PRUS	San Francisco	San Francisco P O	80	469
Werner	35	m	w	PRUS	Yolo	Buckeye Twp	93	412
KLIBLAK								
Chris	43	m	w	PRUS	Nevada	Nevada Twp	75	274
KLICH								
Deitrich	37	m	w	HANO	Siskiyou	Hamburg Twp	89	596
KLICK								
Jno	50	m	w	PRUS	Sierra	Table Rock Twp	89	572
KLIEN								
Albert	13	m	w	CA	San Francisco	San Francisco P O	85	828
Charles	13	m	w	CA	San Francisco	San Francisco P O	85	828
Cornelia	26	f	w	LA	San Francisco	6-Wd San Francisco	81	98
G W	28	m	w	BADE	Tehama	Deer Crk Twp	92	170
Jacob	30	m	w	PRUS	Sonoma	Analy Twp	91	221

Name	Age	S	R	B-PL	County	Locale	Roll	Pg
						Series M593		
Mary	32	f	w	BAVA	Sacramento	2-Wd Sacramento	77	234
KLIENSMITH								
Charls	27	m	w	PRUS	Mendocino	Big Rvr Twp	74	170
KLIES								
Charles	45	m	w	OH	Sacramento	American Twp	77	66
Michael	41	m	w	IA	Butte	Hamilton Twp	70	62
KLIM								
Ah	24	m	c	CHIN	San Francisco	6-Wd San Francisco	81	75
Christian	59	m	w	PA	San Diego	Milquaty Dist	78	475
Harriet	45	f	w	FRAN	San Francisco	San Francisco P O	80	338
KLIMENS								
John	30	m	w	IREL	Sacramento	Franklin Twp	77	108
KLIMNER								
J H	55	m	w	BADE	Sierra	Eureka Twp	89	524
KLIMZENDORF								
H	24	m	w	PRUS	Sierra	Lincoln Twp	89	547
KLIN								
---	30	m	c	CHIN	Siskiyou	Cottonwood Twp	89	594
KLINCH								
John	40	m	w	IREL	San Francisco	2-Wd San Francisco	79	198
KLINCHER								
James	32	m	w	BADE	San Francisco	San Francisco P O	80	338
KLINCK								
Frederick	27	m	w	PRUS	San Francisco	San Francisco P O	85	757
KLINDER								
Waslof	26	m	w	PRUS	San Francisco	San Francisco P O	83	81
KLINE								
A L	44	m	w	PRUS	Sacramento	3-Wd Sacramento	77	306
Addie	15	f	w	CA	San Francisco	1-Wd San Francisco	79	23
Arthur	24	m	w	FRAN	San Francisco	2-Wd San Francisco	79	140
August	54	m	w	BAVA	San Francisco	8-Wd San Francisco	82	390
Augusta	22	f	w	HAMB	San Francisco	6-Wd San Francisco	81	81
Benjamin	53	m	w	FRAN	San Francisco	San Francisco P O	80	481
C M	29	m	w	OH	San Francisco	3-Wd San Francisco	79	313
Charles	40	m	w	HANO	Nevada	Grass Valley Twp	75	188
Charlotta	54	f	w	BAVA	San Francisco	2-Wd San Francisco	79	144
Conrad	34	m	w	PRUS	San Francisco	San Francisco P O	80	362
Elizabeth	21	f	w	WURT	San Francisco	8-Wd San Francisco	82	384
George	60	m	w	HDAR	San Francisco	San Francisco P O	83	261
George	31	m	w	OR	Monterey	San Juan Twp	74	389
Henry	30	m	w	BAVA	Contra Costa	San Pablo Twp	71	355
Henry	30	m	w	BREM	Alameda	Eden Twp	68	59
Henry	25	m	w	BADE	San Francisco	San Francisco P O	80	425
Herman	27	m	w	HANO	San Francisco	7-Wd San Francisco	81	224
Jacob	52	m	w	BADE	San Francisco	San Francisco P O	80	462
John	70	m	w	PRUS	San Francisco	San Francisco P O	80	385
John	50	m	w	PA	Los Angeles	Los Nietos Twp	73	580
John L	50	m	w	PA	Santa Clara	1-Wd San Jose	88	232
Joseph	24	m	w	IL	Solano	Tremont Twp	90	35
Julius	17	m	w	NY	San Francisco	8-Wd San Francisco	82	458
Louis	46	m	w	BAVA	San Francisco	8-Wd San Francisco	82	424
Margaret	23	f	w	PRUS	San Francisco	San Francisco P O	80	387
Maria	66	f	w	NY	Santa Clara	Gilroy Twp	88	71
Martin	35	m	w	PRUS	El Dorado	Placerville Twp	72	101
Mary	55	f	w	AUST	Alameda	Alameda	68	15
Michael	50	m	w	OH	Plumas	Indian Twp	77	10
Micher	38	m	w	SWIT	El Dorado	Kelsey Twp	72	59
Nick	41	m	w	PA	Placer	Alta P O	76	411
Phillip	32	m	w	GERM	Contra Costa	Martinez P O	71	438
Rosa	21	f	w	PRUS	San Francisco	6-Wd San Francisco	81	65
Rosa	18	f	w	NJ	Calaveras	Copperopolis P O	70	252
Samuel	30	m	w	FRAN	San Francisco	San Francisco P O	83	203
Simon	32	m	w	POLA	San Francisco	7-Wd San Francisco	81	260
Thomas	42	m	w	OH	Amador	Volcano P O	69	380
Vivian L	60	m	w	PA	Tuolumne	Sonora P O	93	324
William	37	m	w	BAVA	Yuba	Marysville	93	575
Willie	9	m	w	CA	Marin	Tomales Twp	74	83
KLINER								
Francis	33	m	w	GERM	San Francisco	11-Wd San Francisc	84	426
KLINESMITH								
Wm	32	m	w	PRUS	San Francisco	7-Wd San Francisco	81	262
KLING								
G W	36	m	w	OH	Amador	Amador City P O	69	391
Mary	28	f	w	ENGL	San Joaquin	Liberty Twp	86	83
Saml	21	m	w	OH	San Joaquin	Union Twp	86	265
KLINGE								
August	37	m	w	GERM	Siskiyou	Yreka	89	654
Carl	45	m	w	HANO	Sonoma	Bodega Twp	91	253
William	32	m	w	PRUS	Shasta	Fort Crook P O	89	473
KLINGEL								
Ferdenand	17	m	w	IL	Los Angeles	Los Angeles	73	544
KLINGENDER								
Mary	15	f	w	HANO	Yuba	Bullards Bar P O	93	549
KLINGENDORF								
Henry	48	m	w	HANO	Yuba	Bullards Bar P O	93	550
KLINGENSPORE								
Chas	43	m	w	GERM	Nevada	Nevada Twp	75	306
KLINGER								
John	25	m	w	PRUS	Amador	Ione City P O	69	358
KLINGMAN								
Chas	46	m	w	HAMB	San Francisco	San Francisco P O	83	283
KLINGO								
Geo	45	m	w	BAVA	San Joaquin	Douglas Twp	86	33
KLININY								
Henry	39	m	w	PRUS	Calaveras	San Andreas P O	70	158
KLINK								
Chrestian	47	m	w	WURT	Sacramento	2-Wd Sacramento	77	206

© 2001 by Heritage Quest. All rights reserved.

California 1870 Census

Name	Age	S	R	B-PL	County	Locale	Series M593 Roll	Pg
Fredrick	35	m	w	PRUS	San Francisco	San Francisco P O	80	473
Jacob	45	m	w	GERM	Trinity	Weaverville Pct	92	227
Jacob	40	m	w	WURT	Butte	Chico Twp	70	23
John	25	m	w	HAMB	Sacramento	Sutter Twp	77	381
Mary	20	f	w	WI	Monterey	San Juan Twp	74	404
Mary	16	f	w	NY	Alameda	Oakland	68	258
N B	47	m	w	NY	Solano	Vallejo	90	149
Peter	34	m	w	PRUS	Tehama	Red Bluff	92	182
Stephen R	49	m	w	NY	Sonoma	Russian Rvr	91	374
Wm	26	m	w	NY	Solano	Vallejo	90	166
KLINKERFOST								
Fred	40	m	w	PRUS	Santa Clara	Santa Clara Twp	88	156
KLINKOSSTROM								
Martin	50	m	w	RUSS	San Francisco	San Francisco P O	83	99
KLINN								
Samuel	32	m	w	ENGL	Marin	San Rafael	74	48
KLINSMITH								
Charles	32	m	w	HDAR	Contra Costa	Martinez Twp	71	352
KLINSON								
H	55	m	w	HESS	Sierra	Lincoln Twp	89	546
KLINT								
P	42	m	w	DENM	Sierra	Butte Twp	89	510
KLIPPLER								
Chas	28	m	w	PRUS	San Francisco	8-Wd San Francisco	82	350
KLIPSTINE								
Aaron	42	m	w	VA	Nevada	Little York Twp	75	243
KLIRBY								
Seth	35	m	w	MA	San Francisco	11-Wd San Francisc	84	436
KLOBER								
Theresa	28	f	w	AUST	San Francisco	8-Wd San Francisco	82	477
KLOCHER								
H	57	m	w	DENM	Alameda	Murray Twp	68	107
KLOKINBAUM								
M	39	m	w	HANO	Sierra	Table Rock Twp	89	574
KLONKBERRY								
David	52	m	w	NY	Butte	Concow Twp	70	6
KLOOFINBURG								
G	24	m	w	HANO	San Francisco	7-Wd San Francisco	81	224
KLOOP								
Henry	41	m	w	OH	Solano	Vacaville Twp	90	124
KLOPPENBERG								
Otto	55	m	w	HANO	San Francisco	San Francisco P O	85	803
KLOPPENBERGH								
Henry C	39	m	w	PRUS	San Francisco	San Francisco P O	83	199
KLOPPENBURG								
Henry	39	m	w	HOLL	San Francisco	San Francisco P O	83	195
Henry	19	m	w	PRUS	Santa Clara	Fremont Twp	88	62
Wm	41	m	w	SHOL	Sonoma	Analy Twp	91	246
KLOPPER								
Alexander	26	m	w	HANO	San Francisco	7-Wd San Francisco	81	226
John	29	m	w	BADE	San Francisco	7-Wd San Francisco	81	213
KLOPPINBURG								
John	50	m	w	PRUS	San Francisco	San Francisco P O	80	345
KLOPSTOCK								
Curtis	34	m	w	PRUS	San Francisco	11-Wd San Francisc	84	423
KLORREN								
Wm	32	m	w	PRUS	Shasta	Shasta P O	89	454
KLOS								
Phillip	33	m	w	HDAR	Butte	Mountain Spring Tw	70	88
KLOSE								
Barbara	65	f	w	PRUS	San Francisco	8-Wd San Francisco	82	401
Charles	44	m	w	PRUS	Contra Costa	San Pablo Twp	71	356
J	36	m	w	BADE	Alameda	Oakland	68	194
KLOSER								
Charles	25	m	w	HAMB	San Francisco	6-Wd San Francisco	81	81
KLOSKOPFF								
Geo	47	m	w	BADE	Shasta	Horsetown P O	89	507
KLOSTERMAN								
Augustus	25	m	w	BREM	Marin	San Rafael	74	54
Fred	33	m	w	GA	Humboldt	Bucksport Twp	72	242
KLOTH								
Hy	32	m	w	MECK	San Francisco	11-Wd San Francisc	84	623
KLOTSCH								
Chas	48	m	w	PRUS	San Francisco	San Francisco P O	83	274
KLOTTS								
John	48	m	w	BAVA	San Francisco	3-Wd San Francisco	79	314
KLOTZ								
August	24	m	w	SAXO	Solano	Vallejo	90	185
Frank	27	m	w	BADE	San Francisco	2-Wd San Francisco	79	175
Henry	36	m	w	NJ	Solano	Vacaville Twp	90	126
John	35	m	w	PRUS	Sacramento	Franklin Twp	77	106
John Y	21	m	w	MD	Shasta	Millville P O	89	488
Joseph E	41	m	w	BADE	El Dorado	Mud Springs Twp	72	89
Rudolph	38	m	w	PRUS	Shasta	Millville P O	89	487
KLOWKOW								
Henry	40	m	w	PRUS	Santa Barbara	San Buenaventura P	87	424
KLU								
---	26	m	c	CHIN	Siskiyou	Cottonwood Twp	89	594
KLUBER								
Henry	35	m	w	PRUS	Placer	Auburn P O	76	358
KLUE								
Ah	26	m	c	CHIN	El Dorado	Mud Springs Twp	72	89
KLUEGAL								
F	54	m	w	CANA	Alameda	Oakland	68	210
KLUG								
Charles	31	m	w	PRUS	Santa Clara	Fremont Twp	88	60

Name	Age	S	R	B-PL	County	Locale	Series M593 Roll	Pg
KLUMB								
Jacob	48	m	w	PRUS	Plumas	Washington Twp	77	54
KLUMPKE								
John	45	m	w	HANO	San Francisco	11-Wd San Francisc	84	631
KLUN								
Kate	25	f	w	BADE	Butte	Ophir Twp	70	94
KLUNDER								
John	24	m	w	SHOL	San Francisco	1-Wd San Francisco	79	117
KLUS								
John	38	m	w	PA	Sacramento	4-Wd Sacramento	77	357
KLUSE								
Charles F	54	m	w	PRUS	San Francisco	8-Wd San Francisco	82	485
KLUTE								
Henry	45	m	w	PRUS	Sonoma	Santa Rosa	91	412
KMITH								
Alex	39	m	w	PRUS	Placer	Dutch Flat P O	76	403
KNAAK								
Augt	41	m	w	PRUS	Sonoma	Healdsburg & Mendo	91	276
KNABB								
John	23	m	w	GERM	Nevada	Nevada Twp	75	274
KNABE								
Peter	28	m	w	DENM	San Francisco	2-Wd San Francisco	79	226
KNACK								
Jacob	37	m	w	FRAN	San Francisco	8-Wd San Francisco	82	373
John	40	m	w	BAVA	San Francisco	8-Wd San Francisco	82	373
KNACKSTADT								
T	18	f	w	PRUS	Sonoma	Santa Rosa	91	414
KNACKSTED								
Henry	40	m	c	BRUN	Sonoma	Petaluma Twp	91	365
KNACKSTEDT								
Henry	50	m	w	BRUN	Sonoma	Sonoma Twp	91	444
KNAFF								
William	32	m	w	PRUS	San Mateo	Pescadero P O	87	413
KNAFT								
Gander	38	m	w	PRUS	Contra Costa	Martinez P O	71	433
KNAP								
Charles	38	m	w	PRUS	San Francisco	3-Wd San Francisco	79	306
John P	40	m	w	LUXE	San Francisco	San Francisco P O	85	757
Kinly	40	m	w	ME	San Joaquin	3-Wd Stockton	86	244
KNAPP								
A J	40	m	w	NY	Siskiyou	Scott Valley Twp	89	609
Abner H	46	m	w	NY	Sonoma	Analy Twp	91	220
Albert	35	m	w	NY	San Francisco	11-Wd San Francisc	84	629
Albert	30	m	w	CANA	San Diego	San Diego	78	494
Amos S	58	m	w	NY	Napa	Napa	75	44
Andrew J	35	m	w	MA	Sonoma	Petaluma Twp	91	331
Charles	38	m	w	ME	Santa Cruz	Watsonville	89	377
Charlotte	17	f	w	PRUS	San Francisco	8-Wd San Francisco	82	476
Clark	31	m	w	NY	Santa Clara	Gilroy Twp	88	78
E	43	m	w	NH	Solano	Vallejo	90	197
E	19	f	w	OH	Sierra	Lincoln Twp	89	546
Ezra	44	m	w	NH	Placer	Rocklin Twp	76	468
George	32	m	w	NY	Yolo	Cache Crk Twp	93	452
George A	16	m	w	IL	Placer	Rocklin P O	76	462
Henery	30	m	w	CANA	San Francisco	7-Wd San Francisco	81	171
Henry H	35	m	w	NY	Napa	Napa	75	44
James	26	m	w	MA	San Joaquin	Elkhorn Twp	86	66
Jaspar	34	m	w	PRUS	Sierra	Table Rock Twp	89	576
Jno L	38	m	w	NY	Butte	Chico Twp	70	49
Jno L	37	m	w	OH	Butte	Chico Twp	70	20
Joel	15	m	w	CA	Contra Costa	Martinez P O	71	384
Johey	49	m	w	OH	San Francisco	11-Wd San Francisc	84	467
John	33	m	w	NY	Siskiyou	Yreka	89	658
John B	41	m	w	VT	Santa Cruz	Santa Cruz	89	421
Joseph	45	m	w	MA	San Francisco	8-Wd San Francisco	82	359
Julia	45	f	w	NY	Sacramento	3-Wd Sacramento	77	283
Peter A	30	m	w	DENM	San Francisco	6-Wd San Francisco	81	101
Richd H	34	m	w	ENGL	San Francisco	San Francisco P O	83	4
Robert I	37	m	w	NY	Sonoma	Petaluma Twp	91	330
Samuel	50	m	w	OH	Santa Clara	San Jose Twp	88	217
Sewel	51	m	w	ME	Tuolumne	Columbia P O	93	361
W A	39	m	w	NY	San Francisco	3-Wd San Francisco	79	328
W B	23	m	w	IN	Tehama	Red Bluff	92	182
Wm	54	m	w	NY	San Francisco	8-Wd San Francisco	82	367
Wm	42	m	w	MA	San Diego	San Diego	78	503
KNAPTON								
Thomas	35	m	w	ENGL	San Francisco	7-Wd San Francisco	81	204
KNAQUEL								
Peter	21	m	w	BAVA	San Francisco	2-Wd San Francisco	79	211
KNARSTON								
James	50	m	w	SCOT	San Francisco	San Francisco P O	83	92
KNAUSS								
Henry	36	m	w	OH	Santa Cruz	Santa Cruz Twp	89	397
KNAVER								
Elias	56	m	w	PA	Yolo	Cache Crk Twp	93	440
KNEACH								
Henry	44	m	w	PRUS	Sacramento	3-Wd Sacramento	77	287
KNEADAND								
Francis	46	m	w	MA	San Francisco	11-Wd San Francisc	84	518
KNEAL								
Tom	50	m	w	CA	Sacramento	3-Wd Sacramento	77	286
KNEASS								
Dallas	53	m	w	PA	San Francisco	7-Wd San Francisco	81	184
KNECHT								
N	44	m	w	PRUS	Yuba	Marysville	93	618
KNEDAN								
Seth	49	m	w	KY	Sacramento	1-Wd Sacramento	77	172

© 2001 by Heritage Quest. All rights reserved.

Series M593

Name	Age	S	R	B-PL	County	Locale	Roll	Pg
KNEDDLER								
John	40	m	w	PA	San Francisco	San Francisco P O	85	738
KNEE								
Hans	35	m	w	PRUS	San Francisco	5-Wd San Francisco	81	20
KNEEDLER								
George N	48	m	w	PA	Santa Clara	2-Wd San Jose	88	298
John	22	m	w	MO	Santa Clara	2-Wd San Jose	88	319
KNEEHOUSE								
George J W	49	m	w	HANO	Alpine	Woodfords P O	69	315
KNEELAN								
Alex	35	m	w	AK	Nevada	Nevada Twp	75	281
KNEELAND								
Chas C	32	m	w	ENGL	San Francisco	1-Wd San Francisco	79	16
Edwd	35	m	w	IREL	Solano	Vallejo	90	191
G S	38	m	w	MA	Humboldt	South Fork Twp	72	302
James	30	m	w	IREL	Solano	Green Valley Twp	90	42
Jane	20	f	w	LA	San Francisco	8-Wd San Francisco	82	475
John	44	m	w	ME	Placer	Colfax P O	76	388
John	35	m	w	IREL	San Francisco	11-Wd San Francisc	84	528
Wm	36	m	w	MA	San Francisco	San Francisco P O	83	98
KNEETTE								
Daniel	38	m	w	MA	Nevada	Nevada Twp	75	307
KNEGER								
Frank	32	m	w	PRUS	Plumas	Indian Twp	77	15
KNEIGBUINES								
Matthew	32	m	w	PRUS	Stanislaus	San Joaquin Twp	92	76
KNEIPP								
Allen	62	m	w	BADE	Nevada	Washington Twp	75	345
KNELL								
Catherine	22	f	w	WURT	San Francisco	2-Wd San Francisco	79	241
Jacob	39	m	w	HDAR	San Francisco	8-Wd San Francisco	82	304
Jacob	35	m	w	PRUS	San Francisco	San Francisco P O	80	462
John H	58	m	w	HDAR	San Francisco	8-Wd San Francisco	82	385
Nicholas	61	m	w	HDAR	Siskiyou	Table Rock Twp	89	645
KNELP								
Francis W	40	m	w	HDAR	Los Angeles	Santa Ana Twp	73	613
KNEO								
James	38	m	w	IREL	Amador	Jackson P O	69	327
KNER								
Amalia	19	f	w	WURT	San Francisco	San Francisco P O	83	134
Clara	24	f	w	WURT	San Francisco	8-Wd San Francisco	82	310
KNESS								
Andrew	31	m	w	OH	Yolo	Grafton Twp	93	480
Andrew	30	m	w	OH	Yolo	Grafton Twp	93	484
KNETTLES								
Joseph	43	m	w	NY	Lassen	Milford Twp	73	438
KNEUTH								
Jacob	45	m	w	WALD	Sacramento	3-Wd Sacramento	77	315
KNEY								
Nelson	20	m	w	CA	San Joaquin	Dent Twp	86	24
KNICHT								
Gustaved	28	m	w	SWIT	San Francisco	1-Wd San Francisco	79	63
KNICKERBOCKER								
Eliza	48	f	w	NY	Santa Clara	2-Wd San Jose	88	279
Fred	41	m	w	CT	Santa Cruz	Santa Cruz Twp	89	400
KNIEF								
John F	37	m	w	PRUS	Napa	Napa Twp	75	67
KNIFFEN								
Marcus	38	m	w	NY	San Francisco	5-Wd San Francisco	81	4
KNIGHT								
---	32	m	w	ENGL	Sierra	Butte Twp	89	509
Abram	25	m	w	NJ	Contra Costa	Martinez P O	71	434
Adam	38	m	w	IN	Napa	Napa Twp	75	32
Adam	32	m	w	IN	Solano	Green Valley Twp	90	40
Amelia	18	f	w	AUSL	San Bernardino	San Bernardino Twp	78	430
Andrew J	31	m	w	MO	San Diego	San Diego	78	498
Annie	10	f	w	ENGL	Yolo	Cache Crk Twp	93	454
Annie	10	f	w	ENGL	Yolo	Cache Crk Twp	93	455
Anson	19	m	w	OR	San Joaquin	Liberty Twp	86	96
Augustus	37	m	w	ME	San Bernardino	San Bernardino Twp	78	420
Benjamin	33	m	w	CT	Santa Cruz	Santa Cruz	89	409
C S	40	m	w	GA	Sutter	Vernon Twp	92	138
Chas	34	m	w	MI	San Francisco	11-Wd San Francisc	84	488
Coleman	34	m	w	VT	Sonoma	Mendocino Twp	91	287
D E	45	m	w	NH	Yuba	Marysville	93	602
Daniel	44	m	w	ME	Mariposa	Mariposa P O	74	135
Daniel	32	m	w	VT	San Francisco	8-Wd San Francisco	82	467
Edmund	39	m	w	VT	San Francisco	San Francisco P O	85	738
Edward	42	m	w	ENGL	San Francisco	11-Wd San Francisc	84	586
Edward	32	m	w	ENGL	Yolo	Cache Crk Twp	93	448
Edward	27	m	w	ME	Humboldt	Arcata Twp	72	225
Edwin	28	m	w	ME	San Francisco	San Francisco P O	83	209
Eliza	44	f	w	OH	Solano	Green Valley Twp	90	44
Eliza T	32	f	w	NY	San Francisco	San Francisco P O	83	136
Ellen	22	f	w	ENGL	Yolo	Grafton Twp	93	488
Ellen	21	f	w	ENGL	Yolo	Grafton Twp	93	491
Ether	36	m	w	MO	San Bernardino	San Bernardino Twp	78	431
Frank	24	m	w	MA	San Francisco	7-Wd San Francisco	81	205
Franklin W	35	m	w	ME	San Mateo	Woodside P O	87	380
Fred	26	m	w	KY	San Joaquin	Liberty Twp	86	86
Geo	33	m	w	ME	San Francisco	11-Wd San Francisc	84	678
Geo	21	m	w	VT	San Joaquin	Liberty Twp	86	85
Geo	18	m	w	CANA	Humboldt	Eureka Twp	72	274
George	58	m	w	NY	Placer	Auburn P O	76	493
George	53	m	w	ENGL	San Bernardino	San Bernardino Twp	78	427
George	33	m	w	ENGL	Mariposa	Mariposa P O	74	136
George	25	m	w	MA	San Francisco	8-Wd San Francisco	82	304
George	22	m	w	MO	Solano	Green Valley Twp	90	37
George S	37	m	w	ME	Nevada	Little York Twp	75	242
H K	25	m	w	CT	San Francisco	8-Wd San Francisco	82	373
H L	50	m	w	ENGL	Humboldt	Eureka Twp	72	274
Harriet	42	f	w	NY	San Francisco	11-Wd San Francisc	84	586
Henrietta	31	f	w	BREM	San Francisco	7-Wd San Francisco	81	166
Henry	40	m	w	PRUS	San Francisco	San Francisco P O	83	355
Henry L	20	m	w	MO	Nevada	Grass Valley Twp	75	202
Henry T	42	m	w	VT	Sacramento	Granite Twp	77	148
Hiram A	45	m	w	VT	San Mateo	Schoolhouse Statio	87	341
Horace	58	m	w	VT	Siskiyou	Yreka Twp	89	672
I C	77	m	w	ME	Humboldt	Table Bluff Twp	72	306
Ira L	40	m	w	OH	Tehama	Antelope Twp	92	153
Isabella	72	f	w	ME	Humboldt	Table Bluff Twp	72	306
J	35	m	w	IL	Alameda	Oakland	68	230
J C	41	m	w	OH	Tehama	Antelope Twp	92	153
James	25	m	w	ENGL	Placer	Bath P O	76	437
James	25	m	w	IREL	Alameda	San Leandro	68	96
Jefferson	29	m	w	ME	Humboldt	Table Bluff Twp	72	306
Jerome	46	m	w	NY	San Francisco	11-Wd San Francisc	84	467
John	40	m	w	NY	Amador	Fiddletown P O	69	429
John	40	m	w	ASEA	Mendocino	Sanel Twp	74	227
John	37	m	w	MA	Tuolumne	Big Oak Flat P O	93	395
John	35	m	w	ENGL	Monterey	San Antonio Twp	74	316
John	28	m	w	CANA	San Francisco	7-Wd San Francisco	81	219
John	27	m	w	ENGL	San Francisco	7-Wd San Francisco	81	231
John	22	m	w	OH	San Francisco	8-Wd San Francisco	82	374
John L	57	m	w	VT	Sacramento	Natomas Twp	77	169
John M	23	m	w	VT	Placer	Alta P O	76	412
Johnson	43	m	w	IN	Solano	Green Valley Twp	90	40
Jones D	44	m	w	ME	Placer	Rocklin Twp	76	466
Joseph	55	m	w	NH	Amador	Amador City P O	69	391
Joseph	28	m	w	ENGL	Mariposa	Mariposa P O	74	98
Leonard	35	m	w	ENGL	Yolo	Cache Crk Twp	93	455
Louis	50	m	w	HDAR	San Francisco	11-Wd San Francisc	84	627
Louisa	38	f	w	ENGL	Nevada	Grass Valley Twp	75	165
Luther	44	m	w	ME	San Francisco	6-Wd San Francisco	81	140
M	12	f	w	CA	Sierra	Lincoln Twp	89	545
Margaret	46	f	w	ENGL	San Joaquin	2-Wd Stockton	86	165
Martin	25	m	w	MA	San Francisco	7-Wd San Francisco	81	245
N	74	m	w	NH	San Joaquin	Liberty Twp	86	91
N A	43	m	w	VT	San Joaquin	Liberty Twp	86	91
Peter	37	m	w	IREL	San Francisco	1-Wd San Francisco	79	44
Peter	30	m	w	ENGL	Nevada	Grass Valley Twp	75	162
Quartus P	44	m	w	MA	Nevada	Grass Valley Twp	75	185
Richd H	35	m	w	GA	Santa Barbara	San Buenaventura P	87	423
Richd S	50	m	w	NY	San Francisco	5-Wd San Francisco	81	19
S N	43	m	w	NY	Amador	Sutter Crk P O	69	402
Sam P	38	m	w	VT	Alameda	Oakland	68	177
Simon L	40	m	w	ME	San Mateo	Redwood Twp	87	366
Theodore	27	m	w	IN	San Francisco	1-Wd San Francisco	79	86
Thomas	49	m	w	VT	Sonoma	Mendocino Twp	91	287
Thomas	27	m	w	IREL	Alameda	San Leandro	68	96
Thomas	26	m	w	ME	Klamath	Trinidad Twp	73	390
Thomas	25	m	w	OR	Siskiyou	Yreka Twp	89	672
Thomas	25	m	w	ENGL	Nevada	Grass Valley Twp	75	222
Thomas S	42	m	w	VT	El Dorado	Mud Springs Twp	72	80
Thos	19	m	w	ENGL	Sacramento	Franklin Twp	77	115
W H	44	m	w	CT	Alameda	Oakland	68	206
W H	42	m	w	ENGL	Yuba	Marysville	93	580
W M	26	m	w	ME	San Francisco	San Francisco P O	83	86
Waller	36	m	w	IA	Calaveras	San Andreas P O	70	182
Westbrook	46	m	w	ME	Marin	Tomales Twp	74	79
William	40	m	w	TX	Tuolumne	Chinese Camp P O	93	377
William	25	m	w	OH	Solano	Montezuma Twp	90	69
William C	57	m	w	NH	Placer	Bath P O	76	423
William H	30	m	w	NY	San Francisco	6-Wd San Francisco	81	135
William L	35	m	w	ME	Yolo	Washington Twp	93	531
Wm	41	m	w	ENGL	San Francisco	2-Wd San Francisco	79	195
Wm	39	m	w	ENGL	Sacramento	Granite Twp	77	139
Wm H	42	m	w	RI	Nevada	Little York Twp	75	242
KNIGHTEN								
Wiley	54	m	w	MO	Mendocino	Little Lake Twp	74	192
KNIGHTON								
David	31	m	w	ENGL	El Dorado	Placerville	72	116
John	55	m	w	ENGL	El Dorado	White Oak Twp	72	138
William	26	m	w	NY	San Bernardino	San Bernardino Twp	78	431
KNILAND								
J A	49	m	w	CANA	Humboldt	Arcata Twp	72	229
KNIP								
Fredk	42	m	w	ENGL	Placer	Bath P O	76	452
KNIPE								
Thomas	47	m	w	MA	San Francisco	2-Wd San Francisco	79	280
KNIPP								
Adam	32	m	w	MD	Sonoma	Salt Point Twp	91	384
KNIPPE								
Hermon H	48	m	w	PRUS	Yolo	Putah Twp	93	512
KNIPPER								
Jacob	22	m	w	ENGL	Santa Clara	1-Wd San Jose	88	264
KNISELEY								
Jacob P	41	m	w	PA	Plumas	Plumas Twp	77	29
KNIZEBERGER								
Gregory	40	m	w	PRUS	Sacramento	4-Wd Sacramento	77	376
KNO								
Peter	43	m	w	FRAN	El Dorado	White Oak Twp	72	144
KNOBLACH								
Fredrick	26	m	w	PA	San Francisco	San Francisco P O	80	481

© 2001 by Heritage Quest. All rights reserved.

California 1870 Census

Series M593

Name	Age	S	R	B-PL	County	Locale	Roll	Pg
KNOBLANCH								
Herman	24	m	w	ANHA	Santa Cruz	Santa Cruz	89	404
KNOBLARY								
Jno	32	m	w	GERM	Sacramento	1-Wd Sacramento	77	177
KNOBLAUCH								
Bary	39	m	w	WURT	Sutter	Yuba Twp	92	142
KNOBLE								
Frederick	35	m	w	FRAN	Plumas	Rich Bar Twp	77	8
KNOBLET								
Julius	47	m	w	FRAN	San Francisco	2-Wd San Francisco	79	184
KNOBLEY								
Mary	40	f	w	ITAL	San Francisco	2-Wd San Francisco	79	180
KNOBLOCK								
---	14	m	w	CA	Alameda	Oakland	68	258
Chris	30	m	w	BADE	Yolo	Washington Twp	93	531
KNOCH								
D	45	m	w	RUSS	Lassen	Susanville Twp	73	440
Peter	42	m	w	PRUS	Alameda	Alvarado	68	302
KNOCHA								
Antonio	43	m	w	ITAL	Amador	Volcano P O	69	376
KNOCHE								
Diedrich	28	m	w	HANO	San Francisco	2-Wd San Francisco	79	211
Ferdinde	47	m	w	HANO	Amador	Volcano P O	69	381
Henry	40	m	w	PRUS	San Francisco	San Francisco P O	83	320
John E	51	m	w	HANO	Santa Clara	2-Wd San Jose	88	293
KNOCHEL								
George	32	m	w	PRUS	San Francisco	San Francisco P O	80	483
KNOCK								
John Frederick	26	m	w	PRUS	Plumas	Washington Twp	77	56
KNOCKE								
Geo	53	m	w	HANO	El Dorado	Kelsey Twp	72	58
KNODE								
Daniel H	48	m	w	MD	Calaveras	Copperopolis P O	70	255
KNODERER								
Theo	34	m	w	NY	San Joaquin	1-Wd Stockton	86	134
KNOESEN								
Chl H	40	m	w	HANO	El Dorado	Kelsey Twp	72	58
KNOFF								
Claus	18	m	w	NY	San Mateo	San Mateo P O	87	354
Michael	38	m	w	HDAR	San Mateo	Half Moon Bay P O	87	392
Peter	40	m	w	PRUS	Sierra	Eureka Twp	89	524
KNOK								
Peter	34	m	w	DENM	Santa Cruz	Pajaro Twp	89	346
KNOLKE								
Henry	35	m	w	ARGE	San Francisco	2-Wd San Francisco	79	166
KNOLL								
John	44	m	w	BAVA	San Francisco	8-Wd San Francisco	82	358
Mathias	45	m	w	BAVA	Plumas	Indian Twp	77	18
Theodore	42	m	w	PRUS	San Francisco	San Francisco P O	80	422
KNOLLES								
Chas	36	m	w	PA	Sacramento	4-Wd Sacramento	77	334
KNON								
Ah	25	m	c	CHIN	Sierra	Table Rock Twp	89	578
KNOOP								
Charles	23	m	w	IN	El Dorado	White Oak Twp	72	141
KNOP								
Elbert	32	m	w	HANO	San Francisco	1-Wd San Francisco	79	40
KNOPLELSKY								
Lena	37	f	w	PRUS	San Francisco	11-Wd San Francisc	84	434
KNOPP								
E	55	m	w	NY	Sierra	Forest	89	536
KNOPS								
Henery	40	m	w	HANO	San Francisco	7-Wd San Francisco	81	212
KNORE								
Edwd	42	m	w	AUST	San Francisco	San Francisco P O	83	134
KNORP								
Albert	34	m	w	WURT	San Francisco	8-Wd San Francisco	82	456
John	33	m	w	PRUS	San Francisco	San Francisco P O	80	370
KNORR								
James	55	m	w	PRUS	San Francisco	San Francisco P O	80	531
KNORSA								
Jacob	40	m	w	HESS	Yuba	Marysville	93	603
KNOST								
Henry	26	m	w	HANO	San Francisco	2-Wd San Francisco	79	241
Lillie	6	f	w	NV	San Francisco	2-Wd San Francisco	79	224
KNOTH								
William	43	m	w	HDAR	Santa Clara	San Jose Twp	88	181
KNOTT								
Abell	37	m	w	ENGL	Placer	Bath P O	76	435
Benj	20	m	w	CA	San Francisco	2-Wd San Francisco	79	209
Benjamin	22	m	w	IA	Santa Clara	Fremont Twp	88	64
Elsina	26	f	w	OH	Sacramento	4-Wd Sacramento	77	331
George	24	m	w	IL	San Francisco	11-Wd San Francisc	84	634
John	28	m	w	IL	San Mateo	Woodside P O	87	387
Jonathan	60	m	w	MD	Los Angeles	Los Angeles	73	545
S W	42	m	w	NY	Tehama	Tehama Twp	92	195
Wm	35	m	w	ENGL	Plumas	Quartz Twp	77	43
Wm	21	m	w	AR	San Joaquin	Tulare Twp	86	263
KNOTWELL								
John	38	m	w	ENGL	Nevada	Eureka Twp	75	132
KNOUFT								
Francis	40	m	w	PRUS	Siskiyou	Callahan P O	89	625
KNOUTH								
Phillip	24	m	w	GERM	Yolo	Cottonwood Twp	93	466
KNOW								
Ah	29	m	c	CHIN	Trinity	Junction City Pct	92	210
James	37	m	w	MO	Santa Cruz	Santa Cruz Twp	89	391
Pe	35	f	c	CHIN	Yuba	Marysville	93	627
Wm	30	m	w	MA	San Francisco	11-Wd San Francisc	84	692
KNOWER								
John	41	m	w	NY	San Francisco	San Francisco P O	80	390
KNOWLAND								
Daniel	40	m	w	IREL	Siskiyou	Callahan P O	89	627
F	41	m	w	IREL	Lake	Morgan Valley	73	425
J F	36	m	w	KY	Humboldt	Eel Rvr Twp	72	246
James	65	m	w	IREL	Solano	Denverton Twp	90	26
Jos	36	m	w	NY	Sonoma	Healdsburg & Mendo	91	285
Wm	40	m	w	IREL	Siskiyou	Scott Valley Twp	89	614
KNOWLBERG								
John	42	m	w	OH	San Francisco	11-Wd San Francisc	84	663
KNOWLES								
Astor F	48	m	w	OH	Stanislaus	Empire Twp	92	49
Benjamin	45	m	w	OH	Solano	Silveyville Twp	90	75
Calvin	52	m	w	NH	Alameda	Brooklyn	68	22
Charles	50	m	w	ME	Sonoma	Sonoma Twp	91	437
Cyrenus	34	m	w	NY	Santa Clara	2-Wd San Jose	88	296
David C	40	m	w	ME	Sonoma	Bodega Twp	91	261
Edgar A	43	m	w	VT	Santa Cruz	Pajaro Twp	89	340
Edwd	34	m	w	OH	Fresno	Kingston P O	72	220
Ellen	26	f	w	NY	San Francisco	6-Wd San Francisco	81	72
Ezra	23	m	w	ME	San Francisco	San Francisco P O	83	310
Fred A	34	m	w	MA	San Francisco	3-Wd San Francisco	79	298
George B	52	m	w	RI	San Francisco	6-Wd San Francisco	81	118
Harry	41	m	w	NY	Santa Clara	San Jose Twp	88	194
Henry	37	m	w	IREL	San Francisco	3-Wd San Francisco	79	316
Henry	32	m	w	ME	Marin	San Rafael Twp	74	34
Horace S	26	m	w	NH	Los Angeles	Los Angeles	73	542
Israel G	41	m	w	OH	San Mateo	Schoolhouse Statio	87	340
J B	43	m	w	ME	Sierra	Forest Twp	89	529
J H	48	m	w	RI	San Joaquin	3-Wd Stockton	86	222
James K	40	m	w	ENGL	Sonoma	Petaluma Twp	91	339
Jas	28	m	w	ENGL	Siskiyou	Big Valley Twp	89	581
John	44	m	w	MO	Stanislaus	Empire Twp	92	37
John	37	m	w	ENGL	Santa Clara	Santa Clara Twp	88	160
John P	46	m	w	NY	Butte	Oregon Twp	70	125
Joseph	55	m	w	ME	Sonoma	Bodega Twp	91	261
Joseph	35	m	w	ME	San Francisco	11-Wd San Francisc	84	631
Joshua	41	m	w	NY	Solano	Rio Vista Twp	90	57
Margaret	55	f	w	WALE	Placer	Bath P O	76	436
Mary A	62	f	w	CANA	San Francisco	8-Wd San Francisco	82	386
Moses L	49	m	w	MA	Nevada	Nevada Twp	75	295
Robert	41	m	w	ME	San Mateo	Pescadero P O	87	416
Robert	25	m	w	CANA	Santa Cruz	Santa Cruz Twp	89	387
Rufus B	47	m	w	MA	Santa Cruz	Santa Cruz Twp	89	382
S W	46	m	w	OH	Mendocino	Sanel Twp	74	229
Seth	32	m	w	IL	San Francisco	5-Wd San Francisco	81	15
Stillman	37	m	w	PA	San Francisco	8-Wd San Francisco	82	471
W C	54	m	w	ENGL	El Dorado	Georgetown Twp	72	47
Wm Henry	43	m	w	NY	Plumas	Washington Twp	77	52
KNOWLS								
C M	39	m	w	DC	Humboldt	Eel Rvr Twp	72	249
Frank	35	m	w	MO	Tulare	Tule Rvr Twp	92	262
G	41	m	w	BADE	Sierra	Downieville Twp	89	522
Henry	38	m	w	NY	Trinity	Hayfork Valley	92	238
James	37	m	w	IREL	San Francisco	7-Wd San Francisco	81	163
John	39	m	w	ENGL	Sacramento	Sutter Twp	77	381
Seth	18	m	w	MA	Mendocino	Navarro & Big Rvr	74	174
W A	20	m	w	CA	Alameda	Oakland	68	159
KNOWLTON								
A	37	m	w	ME	Sierra	Forest Twp	89	531
Agnes	50	f	w	NY	Kern	Bakersfield P O	73	360
Charles	23	m	w	NY	San Francisco	San Francisco P O	80	336
Chas	35	m	w	MA	Solano	Vallejo	90	169
Chas	30	m	w	LA	San Luis Obispo	Salinas Twp	87	293
Chas V	20	m	w	OH	Napa	Napa	75	56
David M	33	m	w	ME	San Mateo	Redwood Twp	87	366
Ebenezer	34	m	w	ME	San Francisco	11-Wd San Francisc	84	561
Edwin L	27	m	w	ME	Calaveras	Copperopolis P O	70	227
Egbert B	32	m	w	NY	El Dorado	Placerville Twp	72	103
Emel	38	m	w	MA	Trinity	Canyon City Pct	92	201
Fred	22	m	w	ME	Butte	Chico Twp	70	42
G H	26	m	w	NY	Santa Clara	Gilroy Twp	88	69
Geo W	35	m	w	NY	San Francisco	San Francisco P O	83	68
James	37	m	w	NY	San Francisco	5-Wd San Francisco	81	11
James J	42	m	w	NH	San Francisco	San Francisco P O	85	741
John	47	m	w	CANA	Butte	Concow Twp	70	6
Mary A	10	f	w	CA	Humboldt	Eel Rvr Twp	72	246
N W	49	m	w	NH	Nevada	Nevada Twp	75	272
Peter D	44	m	w	MA	Plumas	Quartz Twp	77	41
Purlin	35	m	w	MA	Shasta	French Gulch P O	89	464
Saen	39	m	w	ME	Butte	Concow Twp	70	6
Thomas	37	m	w	IREL	Santa Clara	Redwood Twp	88	126
Waller	70	m	w	MA	San Francisco	11-Wd San Francisc	84	504
Walter	70	m	w	MA	San Francisco	11-Wd San Francisc	84	538
William	43	m	w	NY	San Francisco	11-Wd San Francisc	84	504
KNOX								
A C	50	m	w	NC	San Francisco	San Francisco P O	83	324
Alexander S	43	m	w	PA	Santa Clara	1-Wd San Jose	88	277
Annie	14	f	w	NY	San Francisco	1-Wd San Francisco	79	88
B F	27	m	w	MO	San Francisco	3-Wd San Francisco	79	312
Barbary	64	m	w	KY	Butte	Oregon Twp	70	134
C C	41	m	w	NY	Sacramento	3-Wd Sacramento	77	306
Caroline	36	f	w	ME	Sonoma	Analy Twp	91	223
Chas	33	m	w	MA	San Francisco	7-Wd San Francisco	81	285

© 2001 by Heritage Quest. All rights reserved.

Name	Age	S	R	B-PL	County	Locale	Roll	Pg
Chas	30	m	w	MO	Mono	Bridgeport P O	74	285
Daniel	28	m	w	ME	San Francisco	San Francisco P O	83	274
Francis	19	m	w	CANA	Sonoma	Healdsburg & Mendo	91	278
Frank	40	m	w	NY	Sonoma	Analy Twp	91	222
Frank	27	m	w	WI	Butte	Ophir Twp	70	120
Frank	15	m	w	CANA	Butte	Ophir Twp	70	121
Franklin	59	m	w	MA	Del Norte	Crescent	71	462
Geo	36	m	w	IL	Butte	Oregon Twp	70	127
Geo R	48	m	w	NY	Shasta	Shasta P O	89	460
Geo W	36	m	w	WI	Butte	Ophir Twp	70	114
George	42	m	w	BARB	San Francisco	11-Wd San Francisc	84	595
George	28	m	w	SCOT	Santa Clara	Fremont Twp	88	42
George	28	m	w	LA	Los Angeles	Santa Ana Twp	73	610
George	25	m	w	IREL	Contra Costa	Martinez P O	71	368
George	22	m	w	MA	Stanislaus	Empire Twp	92	47
Gilbert	40	m	w	CT	El Dorado	Placerville	72	118
Harry	35	m	w	IREL	San Francisco	7-Wd San Francisco	81	181
Henry	38	m	w	MA	San Francisco	5-Wd San Francisco	81	5
Isaiah	43	m	w	MA	Alameda	Oakland	68	238
Ivor G	38	m	w	MA	Placer	Rocklin Twp	76	468
J	25	m	w	CANA	Alameda	Oakland	68	190
Jack	60	m	w	CANA	Placer	Dutch Flat P O	76	401
John	50	m	w	CANA	Tuolumne	Chinese Camp P O	93	367
John	40	m	w	SCOT	Nevada	Little York Twp	75	235
John	29	m	w	ENGL	San Francisco	2-Wd San Francisco	79	264
John F	27	m	w	SCOT	San Francisco	7-Wd San Francisco	81	253
John G	32	m	w	MO	Tulare	Visalia	92	296
John T	59	m	w	TN	Sonoma	Santa Rosa	91	409
Joseph A	38	m	w	NC	Mendocino	Sanel Twp	74	228
Justice	75	m	w	MA	Alameda	Oakland	68	255
Lee W	31	m	w	TN	Colusa	Colusa	71	300
Lewis	68	m	w	KY	Butte	Oregon Twp	70	134
Lewis	40	m	w	OH	Alameda	Eden Twp	68	88
Lizzie	78	f	w	SCOT	San Francisco	San Francisco P O	83	356
Lizzie	30	f	w	IL	Butte	Oregon Twp	70	127
M D	38	m	w	ENGL	Alameda	Oakland	68	265
Martin	51	m	w	CANA	Yuba	New York Twp	93	638
Mary G	58	f	w	NC	Alameda	Eden Twp	68	90
Mary M	57	f	w	NC	Del Norte	Crescent	71	465
Oliver	50	m	w	NY	San Francisco	5-Wd San Francisco	81	28
Robert T	38	m	w	TN	Santa Clara	Redwood Twp	88	118
Robt	38	m	w	IREL	Solano	Vallejo	90	200
Robt	37	m	w	IREL	Solano	Vallejo	90	198
Sarah L	40	f	w	VA	Santa Clara	1-Wd San Jose	88	234
Shannon	56	m	w	PA	El Dorado	Georgetown Twp	72	45
Thos	45	m	w	KY	Butte	Oregon Twp	70	134
Thos	42	m	w	PA	Butte	Ophir Twp	70	97
W C	11	m	w	CA	Alameda	Oakland	68	243
W T	43	m	w	VA	Sacramento	3-Wd Sacramento	77	307
William	40	m	w	IA	Colusa	Butte Twp	71	266
William	25	m	w	HAMB	Yolo	Cache Crk Twp	93	420
William H	19	m	w	IA	El Dorado	Placerville	72	112
Wilson G	44	m	w	VA	Nevada	Little York Twp	75	237
Wm	63	m	w	OH	El Dorado	Mountain Twp	72	67
Wm	15	m	w	CANA	San Francisco	7-Wd San Francisco	81	229
KNUCK								
Gee	37	m	c	CHIN	Plumas	Mineral Twp	77	24
KNUCKLES								
Joseph	28	m	w	VA	Santa Cruz	Santa Cruz Twp	89	389
KNUCKY								
Richard	38	m	w	ENGL	Plumas	Indian Twp	77	17
KNUD								
James	75	m	w	IREL	San Francisco	San Francisco P O	83	186
KNUDSEN								
Adolf	34	m	w	DENM	San Francisco	3-Wd San Francisco	79	300
Peter	26	m	w	DENM	San Francisco	1-Wd San Francisco	79	122
KNUDSON								
Gunder	30	m	w	NORW	Sacramento	Brighton Twp	77	74
L	41	m	w	NORW	Lassen	Susanville Twp	73	446
Peter	23	m	w	DENM	El Dorado	White Oak Twp	72	136
KNUFF								
John	25	m	w	IREL	Sonoma	Analy Twp	91	225
KNUPPER								
Veit	41	m	w	PRUS	San Francisco	San Francisco P O	83	232
KNUR								
Emile	25	f	w	PRUS	San Francisco	San Francisco P O	83	134
KNUT								
R H	42	m	w	KY	Sacramento	Brighton Twp	77	76
KNUTSEN								
Roder	17	m	w	SHOL	Alameda	Eden Twp	68	67
KNUTSON								
Jno	39	m	w	NORW	Santa Clara	Gilroy Twp	88	86
KNUTZE								
Charles	50	m	w	SWIT	Trinity	North Fork Twp	92	218
KNUTZEN								
Jens P	24	m	w	DENM	Santa Cruz	Watsonville	89	369
KO								
Ah	64	m	c	CHIN	Placer	Roseville P O	76	349
Ah	38	m	c	CHIN	Placer	Roseville P O	76	348
Ah	29	m	c	CHIN	Sacramento	1-Wd Sacramento	77	198
Ah	28	m	c	CHIN	Sacramento	1-Wd Sacramento	77	201
Chun	21	f	c	CHIN	San Joaquin	1-Wd Stockton	86	153
Hong	27	m	c	CHIN	San Francisco	San Francisco P O	83	329
Sue	21	f	c	CHIN	San Joaquin	1-Wd Stockton	86	153
KOACH								
Michael	28	m	w	IREL	San Francisco	11-Wd San Francisc	84	426
KOAN								
---	36	m	c	CHIN	Siskiyou	Cottonwood Twp	89	594
KOBALT								
Louis	50	m	w	FRAN	Humboldt	Eureka Twp	72	272
KOBB								
John	29	m	w	PRUS	Solano	Tremont Twp	90	28
KOBBE								
August	23	m	w	SWED	Sonoma	Santa Rosa	91	424
Martin	27	m	w	SWED	Sonoma	Santa Rosa	91	424
KOBBLE								
U	41	m	w	PRUS	San Francisco	San Francisco P O	85	823
KOBER								
Christopher	30	m	w	BREM	San Francisco	3-Wd San Francisco	79	317
Fredk	48	m	w	WURT	Santa Cruz	Santa Cruz	89	407
KOBEREIN								
Anna	25	f	w	SAXO	San Francisco	San Francisco P O	85	729
KOBERG								
Henry	32	m	w	HANO	Santa Clara	1-Wd San Jose	88	237
KOBISON								
J	38	m	w	ME	Alameda	Oakland	68	135
KOBLER								
John Valentine	46	m	w	SWIT	Plumas	Indian Twp	77	18
KOBSON								
Mary	26	f	w	ME	Alameda	Oakland	68	135
KOCH								
Adam	38	m	w	PRUS	San Francisco	San Francisco P O	83	174
Augusta	47	f	w	PRUS	San Francisco	8-Wd San Francisco	82	315
Barthal	42	m	w	BADE	El Dorado	Diamond Springs Tw	72	22
Bertha	22	f	w	PRUS	San Francisco	8-Wd San Francisco	82	406
C I	43	m	w	BAVA	Tuolumne	Big Oak Flat P O	93	396
Charles	41	m	w	PRUS	Tuolumne	Columbia P O	93	336
Charles	36	m	w	BADE	Napa	Napa	75	43
Charles G	42	m	w	WURT	Yuba	Parks Bar Twp	93	650
Chas	25	m	w	HAMB	Solano	Vallejo	90	204
Edward E	29	m	w	AL	San Francisco	San Francisco P O	85	872
Eliza	20	f	w	PRUS	Alameda	Alameda	68	17
Emil	36	m	w	PRUS	San Francisco	San Francisco P O	80	479
Franz	34	m	w	PRUS	San Francisco	1-Wd San Francisco	79	83
Frederick	41	m	w	PRUS	San Mateo	Redwood Twp	87	365
Jacob	44	m	w	BAVA	San Francisco	11-Wd San Francisc	84	486
John	50	m	w	SWIT	San Francisco	8-Wd San Francisco	82	343
John	30	m	w	PA	Sonoma	Vallejo Twp	91	455
Joseph	22	m	w	OH	San Francisco	8-Wd San Francisco	82	291
Julius	42	m	w	PRUS	San Francisco	1-Wd San Francisco	79	96
Mary	32	f	w	MECK	San Mateo	Menlo Park P O	87	378
Nicholas	49	m	w	PA	Sacramento	2-Wd Sacramento	77	223
W H	40	m	w	HANO	San Francisco	San Francisco P O	85	814
William	38	m	w	LUXE	San Francisco	11-Wd San Francisc	84	629
William	25	m	w	PRUS	San Francisco	8-Wd San Francisco	82	398
William D	25	m	w	HANO	San Francisco	2-Wd San Francisco	79	227
KOCHE								
Pierre	24	m	w	FRAN	San Francisco	8-Wd San Francisco	82	373
KOCHEL								
Lewis	45	m	w	LA	San Francisco	8-Wd San Francisco	82	345
KOCHER								
Catharine	33	f	w	SWIT	Mariposa	Mariposa P O	74	95
Jacob	39	m	w	SWIT	Mariposa	Mariposa P O	74	95
Rudolf	30	m	w	SWIT	Santa Clara	1-Wd San Jose	88	230
KOCHLER								
Adam	25	m	w	PRUS	San Francisco	7-Wd San Francisco	81	261
Hans	12	m	w	CA	San Francisco	2-Wd San Francisco	79	180
Louis	32	m	w	IL	San Francisco	2-Wd San Francisco	79	177
KOCHRAN								
Wm	22	m	w	PRUS	Alameda	Oakland	68	201
KOCK								
Ah	19	m	c	CHIN	Plumas	Washington Twp	77	58
Augustine	40	m	w	BADE	Yuba	Parks Bar Twp	93	648
Claus	37	m	w	PRUS	San Francisco	San Francisco P O	80	467
Fritz John	24	m	w	HAMB	San Francisco	1-Wd San Francisco	79	60
John George	44	m	w	WURT	Sacramento	4-Wd Sacramento	77	340
Peter	32	m	w	PRUS	San Francisco	San Francisco P O	80	467
William	38	m	w	PRUS	Tuolumne	Sonora P O	93	324
KOCKENDARFER								
Henry	29	m	w	GERM	Santa Clara	2-Wd San Jose	88	304
KOCKERMAN								
Jacob	40	m	w	PRUS	Sacramento	Brighton Twp	77	75
KOCKLER								
August	57	m	w	PRUS	San Francisco	2-Wd San Francisco	79	141
KODE								
Ah	38	m	c	CHIN	Mariposa	Maxwell Crk P O	74	138
KOE								
Ah	35	m	c	CHIN	Shasta	French Gulch P O	89	469
Ah	30	m	c	CHIN	Shasta	American Ranch P O	89	499
Ah	29	m	c	CHIN	Sacramento	1-Wd Sacramento	77	204
Ah	27	m	c	CHIN	Sacramento	San Joaquin Twp	77	398
Lun	30	m	c	CHIN	Fresno	Millerton P O	72	184
KOEBELIN								
Lawrence	37	m	w	FRAN	Sonoma	Analy Twp	91	224
KOEBLITZ								
F	28	m	w	BADE	Yuba	Marysville	93	611
KOEDITZ								
Earnst F	51	m	w	PRUS	Plumas	Mineral Twp	77	20
KOEFFLER								
Franklin	32	m	w	BAVA	Plumas	Rich Bar Twp	77	46
KOEHLER								
Chs	40	m	w	MECK	San Francisco	2-Wd San Francisco	79	171
Henery	23	m	w	SAXO	San Francisco	7-Wd San Francisco	81	179

© 2001 by Heritage Quest. All rights reserved.

Name	Age	S	R	B-PL	County	Locale	Series M593 Roll	Pg
Theodore	38	m	w	WURT	San Francisco	2-Wd San Francisco	79	225
KOELS								
Adolphus E	47	m	w	PRUS	San Francisco	8-Wd San Francisco	82	465
Albert E	46	m	w	PA	San Francisco	6-Wd San Francisco	81	102
KOELSKI								
Levi	49	m	w	PRUS	San Francisco	San Francisco P O	83	334
KOEN								
Charles	40	m	w	IREL	San Francisco	San Francisco P O	83	356
Michael	53	m	w	IREL	Placer	Bath P O	76	451
KOENECKE								
Conrad	30	m	w	PRUS	San Francisco	San Francisco P O	80	408
KOENIG								
Frank	32	m	w	LUXE	San Francisco	2-Wd San Francisco	79	217
Fred	24	m	w	PRUS	San Francisco	1-Wd San Francisco	79	54
Fredk	36	m	w	HOLL	San Francisco	1-Wd San Francisco	79	51
Gaspar	46	m	w	SWIT	San Francisco	San Francisco P O	80	360
George	34	m	w	PRUS	San Francisco	11-Wd San Francisc	84	503
Jacob	45	m	w	WALE	San Francisco	1-Wd San Francisco	79	57
Lozence	31	m	w	SHOL	Humboldt	Eureka Twp	72	257
Philo	27	m	w	LA	Sacramento	4-Wd Sacramento	77	376
Richard	46	m	w	PRUS	Sacramento	4-Wd Sacramento	77	367
KOENIGSBERGER								
Ferdinand	35	m	w	BAVA	San Francisco	2-Wd San Francisco	79	241
KOENING								
W H L	25	m	w	HANO	San Francisco	7-Wd San Francisco	81	250
KOEPER								
Fred	37	m	w	HANO	San Francisco	2-Wd San Francisco	79	233
KOERNER								
Christian	25	m	w	HDAR	San Francisco	San Francisco P O	80	401
KOESTER								
Frederick	43	m	w	PRUS	Siskiyou	Yreka Twp	89	666
KOEUN								
Jas	47	m	w	IREL	San Francisco	8-Wd San Francisco	82	311
KOFF								
Honora	22	f	w	IREL	San Francisco	8-Wd San Francisco	82	390
KOFFELL								
George	40	m	w	PRUS	Sacramento	2-Wd Sacramento	77	240
KOFFORD								
Peter	32	m	w	DENM	Solano	Vallejo	90	210
KOFOD								
Paul	54	m	w	DENM	San Francisco	7-Wd San Francisco	81	249
KOG								
Ah	28	m	c	CHIN	Sacramento	1-Wd Sacramento	77	200
KOGAN								
James	25	m	w	IREL	Napa	Napa	75	44
KOGEL								
David	10	m	w	CA	San Francisco	11-Wd San Francisc	84	463
Frank	40	m	w	BADE	San Francisco	11-Wd San Francisc	84	463
KOGELSNEY								
Ed	23	m	w	PRUS	Alameda	Oakland	68	184
KOGH								
Christian	40	m	w	HANO	Nevada	Bridgeport Twp	75	101
KOH								
Henry	34	m	w	HANO	San Francisco	11-Wd San Francisc	84	603
Jack	35	m	w	HANO	San Francisco	11-Wd San Francisc	84	629
KOHEN								
Anne	16	f	w	IREL	San Francisco	6-Wd San Francisco	81	91
Geo	27	m	w	BAVA	San Francisco	7-Wd San Francisco	81	276
Jacob	31	m	w	PRUS	San Diego	San Diego	78	496
KOHL								
Andrew	27	m	w	PRUS	San Francisco	San Francisco P O	83	377
Chas	24	m	w	PRUS	San Francisco	5-Wd San Francisco	81	8
George	47	m	w	BAVA	Santa Cruz	Santa Cruz Twp	89	383
Jacob	30	m	w	FRAN	San Francisco	San Francisco P O	80	332
KOHLBERG								
A	50	m	w	PRUS	San Joaquin	2-Wd Stockton	86	184
KOHLE								
August	49	m	w	PRUS	Sonoma	Santa Rosa	91	420
Emma	16	f	w	NY	Yuba	Marysville	93	602
KOHLEN								
Christopher	29	m	w	HANO	Calaveras	San Andreas P O	70	190
KOHLER								
Abel	45	m	w	PRUS	San Francisco	5-Wd San Francisco	81	18
Alfred	27	m	w	PRUS	Sacramento	4-Wd Sacramento	77	355
Andrew R	35	m	w	RUSS	San Francisco	San Francisco P O	83	151
Charles	40	m	w	PRUS	Calaveras	Copperopolis P O	70	246
Chas	30	m	w	BADE	Butte	Chico Twp	70	40
Chas W	40	m	w	PRUS	Sierra	Table Rock Twp	89	575
Christina	75	f	w	WURT	San Francisco	6-Wd San Francisco	81	111
Fred	38	m	w	SHOL	Tehama	Paskenta Twp	92	165
Frederick	32	m	w	WURT	Mendocino	Gualala Twp	74	226
Gottleib	46	m	w	PRUS	San Francisco	San Francisco P O	80	404
Harvey	39	m	w	GERM	Los Angeles	Los Angeles	73	510
Henry	45	m	w	PRUS	Nevada	Washington Twp	75	341
Henry	40	m	w	IREL	San Francisco	2-Wd San Francisco	79	153
Henry	25	m	w	PRUS	Alameda	Oakland	68	182
Herman	46	m	w	BREM	Sacramento	3-Wd Sacramento	77	283
Herman	23	m	w	PRUS	San Francisco	8-Wd San Francisco	82	428
Jacob	54	m	w	GERM	Los Angeles	Santa Ana Twp	73	600
Jacob	25	m	w	BADE	San Francisco	6-Wd San Francisco	81	146
Jas	20	m	w	SAXO	San Francisco	8-Wd San Francisco	82	368
Jerome	45	m	w	BADE	San Francisco	San Francisco P O	85	723
John	40	m	w	PRUS	Marin	Tomales Twp	74	86
John	39	m	w	ENGL	San Francisco	1-Wd San Francisco	79	30
Richd W	50	m	w	ENGL	San Francisco	1-Wd San Francisco	79	18
Stephen	27	m	w	BADE	Butte	Chico Twp	70	42
William	37	m	w	WURT	Mendocino	Gualala Twp	74	226
Wm	40	m	w	GERM	Nevada	Nevada Twp	75	273
KOHLES								
William	35	m	w	PA	Marin	Tomales Twp	74	87
KOHLIN								
Solomon	40	m	w	BAVA	San Francisco	San Francisco P O	83	232
KOHLMAN								
Morris	32	m	w	BADE	Marin	San Rafael	74	50
Samuel	40	m	w	WURT	San Francisco	San Francisco P O	83	258
Solomon	55	m	w	POLA	San Francisco	1-Wd San Francisco	79	43
KOHLMOOS								
Christne	37	m	w	PRUS	San Francisco	San Francisco P O	83	369
Henry	25	m	w	PRUS	San Francisco	San Francisco P O	83	370
KOHLN								
Wm	31	m	w	HANO	San Francisco	San Francisco P O	85	811
KOHLS								
H T	37	m	w	PRUS	Siskiyou	Scott Rvr Twp	89	604
KOHN								
Abraham	59	m	w	BAVA	Solano	Suisun Twp	90	96
Ah	50	m	c	CHIN	El Dorado	Placerville Twp	72	104
Albert	19	m	w	BAVA	San Francisco	8-Wd San Francisco	82	375
Ephraim	27	m	w	RUSS	San Francisco	7-Wd San Francisco	81	262
Frederick	41	m	w	PRUS	San Luis Obispo	Arroyo Grande Twp	87	278
Gustave	15	m	w	WURT	Sacramento	4-Wd Sacramento	77	350
H	45	m	w	BOHE	San Francisco	San Francisco P O	83	278
Henry	35	m	w	BREM	San Francisco	7-Wd San Francisco	81	280
Henry	26	m	w	BOHE	Sacramento	1-Wd Sacramento	77	172
Isaac	46	m	w	BAVA	San Francisco	San Francisco P O	83	226
Jacob	51	m	w	AUST	El Dorado	Placerville	72	125
Jacob	28	m	w	HUNG	Sacramento	3-Wd Sacramento	77	282
Jno B	53	m	w	PRUS	Sacramento	3-Wd Sacramento	77	317
Joseph	40	m	w	BAVA	San Francisco	11-Wd San Francisc	84	494
Kasper	28	m	w	PRUS	Tehama	Red Bluff	92	184
Lissette	50	f	w	PRUS	San Francisco	11-Wd San Francisc	84	516
Louis	25	m	w	SAXO	San Francisco	2-Wd San Francisco	79	137
Pasqual	38	m	w	MEXI	Contra Costa	Martinez P O	71	367
Saml	23	m	w	PRUS	Sonoma	Santa Rosa	91	402
Sarah	20	f	w	FRAN	El Dorado	Placerville	72	112
Theresa	39	f	w	FRAN	San Francisco	8-Wd San Francisco	82	340
KOHNHA								
Jas	48	m	m	HI	Butte	Concow Twp	70	6
KOHR								
Wm Henry	58	m	w	PA	Plumas	Washington Twp	77	25
KOHRIKE								
Mary	20	f	w	PRUS	San Francisco	San Francisco P O	85	829
KOHRUMEL								
Antone	45	m	w	BADE	Shasta	Horsetown P O	89	507
KOI								
---	22	m	c	CHIN	San Francisco	6-Wd San Francisco	81	51
Ah	38	m	c	CHIN	San Francisco	6-Wd San Francisco	81	57
Ah	30	m	c	CHIN	San Francisco	6-Wd San Francisco	81	38
Ah	29	m	c	CHIN	San Francisco	6-Wd San Francisco	81	58
Ah	21	m	c	CHIN	San Francisco	6-Wd San Francisco	81	43
Ah	21	m	c	CHIN	San Francisco	6-Wd San Francisco	81	62
Ah	17	f	c	CHIN	San Francisco	San Francisco P O	80	492
Ah	16	m	c	CHIN	San Francisco	6-Wd San Francisco	81	69
Jai	20	m	c	CHIN	San Mateo	Schoolhouse Statio	87	336
KOIEN								
Wm	30	m	w	DENM	Solano	Vallejo	90	189
KOING								
Ah	30	m	c	CHIN	San Francisco	6-Wd San Francisco	81	68
KOK								
Ah	47	m	c	CHIN	San Francisco	6-Wd San Francisco	81	84
Ah	4	f	c	CHIN	San Francisco	6-Wd San Francisco	81	75
Ah	32	m	c	CHIN	Sacramento	1-Wd Sacramento	77	205
Ah	22	m	c	CHIN	Sacramento	1-Wd Sacramento	77	201
KOKE								
Charles	34	m	w	KY	Los Angeles	Los Angeles	73	524
KOLB								
A	38	m	w	WURT	San Francisco	San Francisco P O	85	797
Frank	40	m	w	GERM	Yolo	Cache Crk Twp	93	452
Isaac	30	m	w	TX	San Diego	Warners Rancho Dis	78	529
Jonathan	40	m	w	GA	San Diego	Warners Rancho Dis	78	529
M	47	f	w	PRUS	Sierra	Downieville Twp	89	520
KOLEKOFF								
Joseph	45	m	w	OLDE	San Francisco	3-Wd San Francisco	79	324
KOLER								
D	33	m	w	GERM	Yuba	Marysville	93	605
KOLETZKE								
August	33	m	w	PRUS	El Dorado	Placerville	72	116
KOLKMAN								
Herman	30	m	w	PRUS	San Francisco	8-Wd San Francisco	82	407
KOLLER								
John	39	m	w	PRUS	San Francisco	San Francisco P O	80	535
KOLLMEYER								
William A	38	m	w	NY	San Francisco	San Francisco P O	83	193
KOLLOCK								
John W	34	m	w	VA	San Francisco	San Francisco P O	83	147
KOLMAN								
Aaron	48	m	w	POLA	San Joaquin	2-Wd Stockton	86	159
KOLMENSE								
Henry	70	m	w	PRUS	San Francisco	8-Wd San Francisco	82	474
KOLOTZ								
Christian	43	m	w	BADE	Santa Clara	2-Wd San Jose	88	334
KOLPINE								
Jasper	24	m	w	SHOL	Colusa	Grand Island Twp	71	303
KOM								
Ah	9	f	c	CHIN	San Francisco	6-Wd San Francisco	81	74

© 2001 by Heritage Quest. All rights reserved.

Name	Age	S	R	B-PL	County	Locale	Series M593 Roll	Pg
Ah	41	m	c	CHIN	Tuolumne	Chinese Camp P O	93	371
Ah	39	m	c	CHIN	San Francisco	6-Wd San Francisco	81	57
Ah	34	m	c	CHIN	San Francisco	6-Wd San Francisco	81	54
Ah	33	m	c	CHIN	Solano	Benicia	90	14
Ah	29	m	c	CHIN	Mendocino	Point Arena Twp	74	205
Ah	29	m	c	CHIN	San Francisco	6-Wd San Francisco	81	63
Ah	27	m	c	CHIN	Sacramento	Georgianna Twp	77	133
Ah	20	m	c	CHIN	San Francisco	6-Wd San Francisco	81	64
Ah	13	m	c	CHIN	Nevada	Bridgeport Twp	75	106
Sing	30	m	c	CHIN	San Francisco	6-Wd San Francisco	81	38
KOMAS								
Mathew	29	m	w	AUSL	San Francisco	San Francisco P O	83	85
KOMG								
Ar	15	m	c	CHIN	Sonoma	Sonoma Twp	91	431
KOMMERN								
Emanuel	40	m	w	WURT	San Francisco	8-Wd San Francisco	82	434
KOMP								
Kossus	30	f	w	MEXI	Tehama	Red Bluff	92	181
KOMPF								
Ferdinand	37	m	w	PRUS	San Francisco	San Francisco P O	80	357
KOMPT								
Louis	41	m	w	WALD	Calaveras	Copperopolis P O	70	231
KOMS								
Alexander	42	m	w	PA	Napa	Napa	75	12
Geo H	32	m	w	BAVA	Humboldt	Eel Rvr Twp	72	255
KON								
Ah	49	m	c	CHIN	Tuolumne	Columbia P O	93	353
Ah	45	m	c	CHIN	Sacramento	1-Wd Sacramento	77	199
Ah	40	m	c	CHIN	Sacramento	1-Wd Sacramento	77	198
Ah	37	m	c	CHIN	Sacramento	Georgianna Twp	77	133
Ah	36	m	c	CHIN	Mariposa	Maxwell Crk P O	74	145
Ah	35	m	c	CHIN	Placer	Lincoln P O	76	484
Ah	34	m	c	CHIN	Mariposa	Maxwell Crk P O	74	146
Ah	30	m	c	CHIN	Sierra	Sears Twp	89	554
Ah	26	m	c	CHIN	Sierra	Sears Twp	89	554
Ah	24	m	c	CHIN	San Francisco	6-Wd San Francisco	81	57
Ah	22	m	c	CHIN	El Dorado	Diamond Springs Tw	72	27
Ah	20	m	c	CHIN	San Francisco	6-Wd San Francisco	81	49
Ah	17	m	c	CHIN	San Francisco	San Francisco P O	85	740
Ah	13	m	c	CHIN	San Francisco	8-Wd San Francisco	82	316
Charles	18	m	c	CHIN	Yuba	New York Twp	93	636
Fin	26	m	c	CHIN	San Mateo	Schoolhouse Statio	87	335
Heny	37	m	w	PA	San Joaquin	Castoria Twp	86	7
Hin	19	m	c	CHIN	El Dorado	Mud Springs Twp	72	76
Lee	25	m	c	CHIN	San Francisco	8-Wd San Francisco	82	442
See	18	m	c	CHIN	San Francisco	8-Wd San Francisco	82	337
KONARES								
Wilhelmina	26	f	w	PRUS	San Francisco	8-Wd San Francisco	82	479
KONE								
Ah	3	m	c	CA	Trinity	Weaverville Pct	92	228
Ah	25	m	c	CHIN	San Francisco	San Francisco P O	83	132
KONEG								
Peter	26	m	w	GERM	Amador	Sutter Crk P O	69	401
KONEGAN								
Andrew	35	m	w	IREL	San Francisco	11-Wd San Francisc	84	472
KONEGIN								
Nicholes	31	m	w	RUSS	San Francisco	2-Wd San Francisco	79	212
KONENG								
Margaret	28	f	w	PRUS	Santa Clara	1-Wd San Jose	88	266
KONER								
Fred W	25	m	w	HANO	San Francisco	1-Wd San Francisco	79	49
Herman J	50	m	w	HOLL	Fresno	Millerton P O	72	150
KONG								
---	37	m	c	CHIN	Santa Clara	San Jose Twp	88	190
---	22	m	c	CHIN	Siskiyou	Cottonwood Twp	89	594
Ah	60	m	c	CHIN	Mariposa	Mariposa P O	74	132
Ah	55	m	c	CHIN	Placer	Auburn P O	76	372
Ah	52	m	c	CHIN	Santa Clara	Alviso Twp	88	29
Ah	50	m	c	CHIN	Placer	Newcastle Twp	76	479
Ah	48	m	c	CHIN	Nevada	Nevada Twp	75	312
Ah	47	m	c	CHIN	Santa Clara	1-Wd San Jose	88	272
Ah	46	m	c	CHIN	Placer	Newcastle Twp	76	477
Ah	45	m	c	CHIN	San Francisco	11-Wd San Francisc	84	528
Ah	43	m	c	CHIN	Santa Clara	1-Wd San Jose	88	271
Ah	42	m	c	CHIN	Solano	Vallejo	90	208
Ah	42	m	c	CHIN	Fresno	Millerton P O	72	200
Ah	41	m	c	CHIN	Mariposa	Maxwell Crk P O	74	145
Ah	41	m	c	CHIN	Santa Clara	San Jose Twp	88	204
Ah	40	m	c	CHIN	Tuolumne	Sonora P O	93	333
Ah	40	m	c	CHIN	San Francisco	6-Wd San Francisco	81	42
Ah	40	m	c	CHIN	Placer	Colfax P O	76	387
Ah	39	m	c	CHIN	Placer	Lincoln P O	76	483
Ah	39	m	c	CHIN	Placer	Auburn P O	76	357
Ah	38	m	c	CHIN	Plumas	Washington Twp	77	57
Ah	35	m	c	CHIN	Santa Clara	1-Wd San Jose	88	269
Ah	35	m	c	CHIN	Calaveras	San Andreas P O	70	169
Ah	33	m	c	CHIN	Stanislaus	Branch Twp	92	9
Ah	32	m	c	CHIN	Sierra	Sears Twp	89	554
Ah	32	m	c	CHIN	Mariposa	Maxwell Crk P O	74	147
Ah	32	m	c	CHIN	San Francisco	6-Wd San Francisco	81	38
Ah	32	m	c	CHIN	Placer	Colfax P O	76	385
Ah	31	m	c	CHIN	Santa Clara	1-Wd San Jose	88	273
Ah	30	m	c	CHIN	Nevada	Washington Twp	75	342
Ah	30	m	c	CHIN	San Francisco	6-Wd San Francisco	81	42
Ah	30	m	c	CHIN	San Francisco	San Francisco P O	85	747
Ah	30	m	c	CHIN	Sacramento	2-Wd Sacramento	77	250
Ah	28	m	c	CHIN	San Francisco	6-Wd San Francisco	81	38

Name	Age	S	R	B-PL	County	Locale	Series M593 Roll	Pg
Ah	28	m	c	CHIN	El Dorado	Mountain Twp	72	69
Ah	28	m	c	CHIN	Yuba	Marysville	93	618
Ah	28	m	c	CHIN	San Francisco	1-Wd San Francisco	79	118
Ah	28	m	c	CHIN	Placer	Colfax P O	76	390
Ah	27	m	c	CHIN	Santa Clara	2-Wd San Jose	88	325
Ah	27	m	c	CHIN	Santa Barbara	Santa Barbara P O	87	458
Ah	25	m	c	CHIN	San Francisco	11-Wd San Francisc	84	556
Ah	25	m	c	CHIN	Placer	Lincoln P O	76	483
Ah	25	m	c	CHIN	San Francisco	6-Wd San Francisco	81	39
Ah	24	m	c	CHIN	San Francisco	6-Wd San Francisco	81	38
Ah	24	m	c	CHIN	Tuolumne	Columbia P O	93	341
Ah	24	m	c	CHIN	San Francisco	6-Wd San Francisco	81	38
Ah	24	m	c	CHIN	Santa Clara	San Jose Twp	88	189
Ah	23	m	c	CHIN	San Francisco	6-Wd San Francisco	81	67
Ah	23	m	c	CHIN	Santa Clara	San Jose Twp	88	189
Ah	23	m	c	CHIN	Santa Clara	San Jose Twp	88	189
Ah	23	m	c	CHIN	San Francisco	San Francisco P O	85	748
Ah	23	m	c	CHIN	San Francisco	3-Wd San Francisco	79	304
Ah	22	m	c	CHIN	Santa Clara	1-Wd San Jose	88	274
Ah	22	m	c	CHIN	Santa Clara	2-Wd San Jose	88	322
Ah	22	m	c	CHIN	San Francisco	6-Wd San Francisco	81	61
Ah	21	m	c	CHIN	Santa Clara	2-Wd San Jose	88	324
Ah	21	m	c	CHIN	San Joaquin	Douglas Twp	86	51
Ah	21	m	c	CHIN	San Francisco	San Francisco P O	83	138
Ah	21	m	c	CHIN	San Francisco	San Francisco P O	80	500
Ah	20	m	c	CHIN	Santa Clara	1-Wd San Jose	88	273
Ah	20	m	c	CHIN	San Francisco	7-Wd San Francisco	81	281
Ah	20	m	c	CHIN	San Francisco	6-Wd San Francisco	81	110
Ah	20	m	c	CHIN	Placer	Clipper Gap P O	76	393
Ah	20	m	c	CHIN	Napa	Napa Twp	75	58
Ah	19	m	c	CHIN	San Francisco	6-Wd San Francisco	81	60
Ah	19	m	c	CHIN	San Francisco	3-Wd San Francisco	79	329
Ah	18	m	c	CHIN	Santa Clara	1-Wd San Jose	88	277
Ah	18	m	c	CHIN	Santa Clara	2-Wd San Jose	88	297
Ah	18	m	c	CHIN	Sonoma	Sonoma Twp	91	431
Ah	18	m	c	CHIN	San Francisco	2-Wd San Francisco	79	184
Ah	18	m	c	CHIN	San Francisco	6-Wd San Francisco	81	42
Ah	18	m	c	CHIN	San Francisco	6-Wd San Francisco	81	42
Ah	18	m	c	CHIN	San Francisco	3-Wd San Francisco	79	310
Ah	17	m	c	CHIN	San Francisco	6-Wd San Francisco	81	51
Ah	17	m	c	CHIN	Butte	Ophir Twp	70	106
Ah	17	m	c	CHIN	Nevada	Nevada Twp	75	292
Ah	16	m	c	CHIN	Marin	San Rafael Twp	74	45
Ah	14	m	c	CHIN	San Francisco	11-Wd San Francisc	84	524
Ah	14	m	c	CHIN	San Francisco	2-Wd San Francisco	79	184
Ah	14	m	c	CHIN	San Francisco	6-Wd San Francisco	81	40
Ah	14	m	c	CHIN	Santa Clara	San Jose Twp	88	194
Ah	14	m	c	CHIN	San Francisco	1-Wd San Francisco	79	58
Ah	12	m	c	CHIN	San Francisco	11-Wd San Francisc	84	445
Ah	12	m	c	CHIN	San Francisco	2-Wd San Francisco	79	240
Ah	11	m	c	CHIN	Shasta	American Ranch P O	89	497
Boo	35	m	c	CHIN	Yolo	Merritt Twp	93	503
Che	53	m	c	CHIN	Placer	Auburn P O	76	362
Chi	14	m	c	CHIN	Colusa	Colusa	71	293
Chin	21	m	c	CHIN	San Francisco	7-Wd San Francisco	81	220
Chon	37	m	c	CHIN	Santa Clara	1-Wd San Jose	88	272
Chong	35	m	c	CHIN	San Francisco	7-Wd San Francisco	81	220
Chung	22	m	c	CHIN	San Francisco	7-Wd San Francisco	81	260
Em	26	m	c	CHIN	Siskiyou	Hamburg Twp	89	597
Fong Wong	40	m	c	CHIN	San Francisco	San Francisco P O	83	126
Game	33	m	c	CHIN	Shasta	French Gulch P O	89	470
Hi	37	m	c	CHIN	San Francisco	11-Wd San Francisc	84	661
Hing	38	m	c	CHIN	Tuolumne	Sonora P O	93	311
Hong	34	m	c	CHIN	San Joaquin	3-Wd Stockton	86	230
Hong	24	m	c	CHIN	Solano	Suisun Twp	90	107
Hung	22	m	c	CHIN	San Francisco	7-Wd San Francisco	81	260
Jim	24	m	c	CHIN	Santa Clara	1-Wd San Jose	88	272
Kow	38	m	c	CHIN	El Dorado	Greenwood Twp	72	54
Le	30	m	c	CHIN	San Joaquin	Douglas Twp	86	46
Le	27	m	c	CHIN	San Joaquin	3-Wd Stockton	86	230
Lee	29	m	c	CHIN	Sonoma	Petaluma Twp	91	343
Lee	27	m	c	CHIN	Santa Clara	1-Wd San Jose	88	272
Lew	18	m	c	CHIN	San Francisco	6-Wd San Francisco	81	46
Ling	36	m	c	CHIN	Nevada	Bridgeport Twp	75	110
Long	46	m	c	CHIN	Yuba	Marysville	93	621
Long	33	m	c	CHIN	Yolo	Putah Twp	93	516
Long	20	m	c	CHIN	San Francisco	7-Wd San Francisco	81	220
Luck	39	m	c	CHIN	Tuolumne	Sonora P O	93	311
Mi	49	m	c	CHIN	Tuolumne	Sonora P O	93	332
S A	50	m	w	PRUS	Alameda	Oakland	68	174
See	41	m	c	CHIN	Santa Clara	1-Wd San Jose	88	271
See	22	m	c	CHIN	Solano	Green Valley Twp	90	43
Sin	21	m	c	CHIN	Sacramento	1-Wd Sacramento	77	189
Ta	25	m	c	CHIN	San Francisco	6-Wd San Francisco	81	41
Tip	45	m	c	CHIN	Shasta	American Ranch P O	89	499
Top	40	m	c	CHIN	Placer	Roseville P O	76	352
Wah	19	m	c	CHIN	San Francisco	1-Wd San Francisco	79	131
We	31	m	c	CHIN	Santa Clara	San Jose Twp	88	191
Wee	47	m	c	CHIN	Santa Clara	1-Wd San Jose	88	271
Wee	24	m	c	CHIN	Santa Clara	1-Wd San Jose	88	269
Who	32	m	c	CHIN	Yuba	Marysville	93	628
Wo	31	m	c	CHIN	Santa Clara	2-Wd San Jose	88	285
Wo	19	m	c	CHIN	Santa Clara	2-Wd San Jose	88	331
Wong	23	m	c	CHIN	Sacramento	1-Wd Sacramento	77	182
Yune	23	m	c	CHIN	Solano	Montezuma Twp	90	66
KONIG								
Ferdinand	36	m	w	PRUS	San Francisco	San Francisco P O	80	470

© 2001 by Heritage Quest. All rights reserved.

California 1870 Census

Name	Age	S	R	B-PL	County	Locale	Series M593 Roll	Pg
Henry	39	m	w	SWIT	Santa Barbara	San Buenaventura P	87	443
William	40	m	w	PRUS	Alpine	Markleeville P O	69	312
KONINBERG								
Herman	30	m	w	PRUS	San Francisco	San Francisco P O	80	480
KONING								
John	22	m	w	IL	San Francisco	7-Wd San Francisco	81	199
Max	40	m	w	PRUS	San Francisco	2-Wd San Francisco	79	174
Max	13	m	w	HUNG	San Francisco	11-Wd San Francisc	84	593
KONKEY								
A	39	m	w	NY	Lassen	Janesville Twp	73	435
S	64	m	w	NY	Lassen	Janesville Twp	73	435
KONKIN								
William	70	m	w	TN	Calaveras	San Andreas P O	70	200
KONN								
Mary	12	f	w	CA	San Joaquin	Oneal Twp	86	115
KONNIFF								
Mary	14	f	w	IREL	Santa Clara	San Jose Twp	88	183
KONREITER								
Alice	65	f	w	BAVA	San Francisco	8-Wd San Francisco	82	417
KONSEGARSO								
J	39	m	w	ITAL	Amador	Jackson P O	69	327
KONSELMYER								
Fred	38	m	w	BREM	San Francisco	San Francisco P O	83	33
KONUTGAN								
G	58	m	w	NORW	Napa	Napa Twp	75	68
KONY								
George	20	m	c	CHIN	Sacramento	4-Wd Sacramento	77	373
KOO								
Ah	52	m	c	CHIN	Kern	Bakersfield P O	73	361
Ah	50	f	c	CHIN	San Francisco	6-Wd San Francisco	81	50
Ah	47	m	c	CHIN	San Joaquin	1-Wd Stockton	86	147
Ah	43	m	c	CHIN	Butte	Mountain Spring Tw	70	90
Ah	40	m	c	CHIN	Sacramento	Granite Twp	77	149
Ah	40	m	c	CHIN	Napa	Napa Twp	75	58
Ah	40	m	c	CHIN	Napa	Napa	75	52
Ah	40	m	c	CHIN	Yolo	Grafton Twp	93	500
Ah	33	m	c	CHIN	Amador	Drytown P O	69	423
Ah	32	m	c	CHIN	Alameda	Murray Twp	68	102
Ah	31	m	c	CHIN	San Francisco	6-Wd San Francisco	81	77
Ah	29	m	c	CHIN	Sierra	Forest Twp	89	528
Ah	28	m	c	CHIN	Sierra	Butte Twp	89	510
Ah	23	m	c	CHIN	San Francisco	6-Wd San Francisco	81	47
Ah	23	m	c	CHIN	Nevada	Nevada Twp	75	311
Ah	22	m	c	CHIN	San Francisco	6-Wd San Francisco	81	60
Ah	20	m	c	CHIN	San Francisco	6-Wd San Francisco	81	46
Ah	16	m	c	CHIN	San Joaquin	Castoria Twp	86	11
Chee	34	m	c	CHIN	Yuba	Marysville	93	620
Choi	25	m	c	CHIN	Yuba	Marysville	93	632
Chook	27	m	c	CHIN	Yuba	Marysville	93	624
Sin	32	m	c	CHIN	Yuba	Marysville	93	622
Te Kar	25	m	c	CHIN	San Francisco	6-Wd San Francisco	81	64
KOOANG								
Ah	30	m	c	CHIN	San Francisco	6-Wd San Francisco	81	38
KOOHL								
Fred	40	m	w	SWIT	San Francisco	8-Wd San Francisco	82	374
KOOI								
---	18	m	c	CHIN	San Francisco	6-Wd San Francisco	81	64
KOOIE								
How	30	m	c	CHIN	San Francisco	6-Wd San Francisco	81	43
KOOK								
Ah	24	m	c	CHIN	San Francisco	3-Wd San Francisco	79	309
Ako	37	m	w	PRUS	San Joaquin	Dent Twp	86	27
KOOKER								
Jacob	38	m	w	PRUS	Alameda	Oakland	68	192
KOOL								
---	19	m	c	CHIN	San Francisco	6-Wd San Francisco	81	64
KOOLS								
James	36	m	w	VA	Trinity	Minersville Pct	92	215
KOOMB								
John	33	m	w	MO	Yolo	Cache Crk Twp	93	442
KOON								
Ah	60	m	c	CHIN	El Dorado	White Oak Twp	72	136
Ah	60	m	c	CHIN	Sacramento	Granite Twp	77	141
Ah	50	m	c	CHIN	Sacramento	Natomas Twp	77	171
Ah	42	m	c	CHIN	Plumas	Washington Twp	77	58
Ah	42	m	c	CHIN	Sacramento	Center Twp	77	86
Ah	38	m	c	CHIN	Sacramento	Georgianna Twp	77	127
Ah	35	m	c	CHIN	El Dorado	Diamond Springs Tw	72	24
Ah	35	m	c	CHIN	Sacramento	Cosumnes Twp	77	94
Ah	33	m	c	CHIN	Plumas	Goodwin Twp	77	4
Ah	31	m	c	CHIN	San Francisco	6-Wd San Francisco	81	54
Ah	30	m	c	CHIN	San Francisco	6-Wd San Francisco	81	56
Ah	30	m	c	CHIN	Plumas	Goodwin Twp	77	3
Ah	29	m	c	CHIN	Sierra	Sears Twp	89	554
Ah	29	m	c	CHIN	Napa	Napa Twp	75	58
Ah	29	m	c	CHIN	Plumas	Washington Twp	77	52
Ah	27	m	c	CHIN	San Francisco	6-Wd San Francisco	81	52
Ah	24	m	c	CHIN	San Francisco	6-Wd San Francisco	81	40
Ah	24	m	c	CHIN	Colusa	Colusa	71	298
Ah	23	m	c	CHIN	San Francisco	3-Wd San Francisco	79	310
Ah	22	m	c	CHIN	San Francisco	6-Wd San Francisco	81	85
Ah	22	m	c	CHIN	Colusa	Colusa	71	300
Ah	21	m	c	CHIN	Plumas	Goodwin Twp	77	2
Ah	20	m	c	CHIN	Santa Clara	Redwood Twp	88	120
Ah	20	m	c	CHIN	Santa Clara	Santa Clara Twp	88	164
Ah	18	m	c	CHIN	San Francisco	6-Wd San Francisco	81	54
Ang	25	m	c	CHIN	Plumas	Seneca Twp	77	48
Chung	38	m	c	CHIN	Yuba	Marysville	93	625
Ephraim B	27	m	w	NY	San Francisco	San Francisco P O	83	199
Henry	48	m	w	WALD	Santa Clara	Santa Clara Twp	88	138
James	30	m	w	BADE	San Francisco	11-Wd San Francisc	84	507
John	44	m	w	PA	Colusa	Colusa	71	288
Joseph M	69	m	w	NY	Stanislaus	San Joaquin Twp	92	72
Mon	25	m	c	CHIN	San Francisco	11-Wd San Francisc	84	528
Seng	18	m	c	CHIN	San Francisco	11-Wd San Francisc	84	556
Sung	44	m	c	CHIN	Calaveras	Copperopolis P O	70	249
Wah	19	m	c	CHIN	Santa Clara	Santa Clara Twp	88	164
Yung	48	m	c	CHIN	Yuba	Marysville	93	624
KOONER								
S A	13	f	w	CA	Alameda	Oakland	68	258
KOONEY								
Ellen	23	f	w	IREL	San Francisco	8-Wd San Francisco	82	468
Hacob	18	m	w	PRUS	Amador	Sutter Crk P O	69	398
KOONG								
Ah	26	m	c	CHIN	San Francisco	6-Wd San Francisco	81	51
Ah	16	m	c	CHIN	Santa Clara	San Jose Twp	88	194
KOONS								
William N	40	m	w	TX	Santa Cruz	Soquel Twp	89	447
KOONTY								
A	26	m	w	KY	Lake	Lower Lake	73	429
KOONTZ								
Susannah	39	f	w	BAVA	Shasta	Shasta P O	89	457
KOOP								
Ah	38	m	c	CHIN	Santa Clara	Fremont Twp	88	62
Ah	26	m	c	CHIN	Santa Clara	San Jose Twp	88	194
Ah	24	m	c	CHIN	Santa Clara	San Jose Twp	88	195
Ah	23	m	c	CHIN	San Joaquin	1-Wd Stockton	86	148
Pu	50	m	c	CHIN	Sierra	Lincoln Twp	89	546
KOOPMAN								
Henry	45	m	w	PRUS	San Francisco	San Francisco P O	85	733
John	37	m	w	PRUS	San Francisco	San Francisco P O	80	469
KOOPMANN								
Henry	34	m	w	FRAN	San Francisco	San Francisco P O	83	123
KOOPMANSEHOP								
C	44	m	w	HOLL	San Francisco	San Francisco P O	83	304
KOOPS								
Peter	43	m	w	PRUS	San Francisco	San Francisco P O	80	470
KOOSER								
Benjamin P	48	m	w	PA	Santa Cruz	Santa Cruz	89	419
KOOT								
Ah	27	m	c	CHIN	San Francisco	6-Wd San Francisco	81	55
KOP								
Ah	33	m	c	CHIN	San Joaquin	1-Wd Stockton	86	148
Ah	21	m	c	CHIN	Sacramento	1-Wd Sacramento	77	194
Ah	19	m	c	CHIN	San Francisco	6-Wd San Francisco	81	68
Jam	30	m	c	CHIN	Sacramento	1-Wd Sacramento	77	201
Lun	17	m	c	CHIN	Sacramento	1-Wd Sacramento	77	200
KOPER								
Thos	40	m	w	IREL	San Joaquin	3-Wd Stockton	86	236
KOPF								
Claus	46	m	w	PRUS	Colusa	Butte Twp	71	265
Henry	35	m	w	HANO	Calaveras	San Andreas P O	70	209
KOPH								
Harry	31	m	w	HDAR	Solano	Silveyville Twp	90	85
KOPMAN								
Frank Jr	28	m	w	BAVA	Monterey	Castroville Twp	74	329
Frank Sr	69	m	w	BAVA	Monterey	Castroville Twp	74	329
KOPP								
Annie	57	f	w	FRAN	San Francisco	San Francisco P O	80	484
F Wm	52	m	w	PRUS	Humboldt	Eureka Twp	72	271
Ferdinand	35	m	w	PRUS	San Francisco	1-Wd San Francisco	79	63
Henry	42	m	w	BAVA	San Francisco	San Francisco P O	85	747
Jacob	47	m	w	WURT	San Francisco	2-Wd San Francisco	79	172
Joseph	40	m	w	WURT	Nevada	Nevada Twp	75	320
Louis	35	m	w	ENGL	San Francisco	San Francisco P O	85	753
Samuel	32	m	w	PRUS	Santa Clara	2-Wd San Jose	88	323
KOPPEL								
Henry	76	m	w	PRUS	San Francisco	San Francisco P O	83	275
KOPPIKUS								
A	60	m	w	PRUS	Sacramento	3-Wd Sacramento	77	297
KOPPITZ								
Geo	38	m	w	PRUS	San Francisco	San Francisco P O	83	314
KOPPLE								
Joseph	37	m	w	BREM	Santa Clara	1-Wd San Jose	88	265
KOPTEN								
Alice	14	f	w	NY	Lake	Coyote Valley	73	401
KORAN								
John	21	m	w	IREL	San Joaquin	Castoria Twp	86	10
KORANIA								
Peter	30	m	w	ITAL	Marin	Novato Twp	74	13
KORB								
Jacob	46	m	w	PRUS	Yuba	Marysville	93	593
John C H	49	m	w	HAMB	San Francisco	San Francisco P O	83	192
KORBEL								
Francis	39	m	w	AUSL	San Francisco	San Francisco P O	83	80
KORDMEYER								
George	37	m	w	GERM	Tuolumne	Columbia P O	93	336
KORELL								
Jacob	35	m	w	GERM	Santa Clara	Burnett Twp	88	33
John	24	m	w	PRUS	San Joaquin	3-Wd Stockton	86	235
KORGAN								
Fredk	30	m	w	PRUS	San Francisco	8-Wd San Francisco	82	321
KORGEL								
Charles	32	m	w	PRUS	San Francisco	11-Wd San Francisc	84	464

© 2001 by Heritage Quest. All rights reserved.

Name	Age	S	R	B-PL	County	Locale	Series M593 Roll	Pg
KORK								
John C	53	m	w	BREM	Sacramento	Franklin Twp	77	111
KORKOWNAN								
Henry	32	m	w	FINL	San Francisco	3-Wd San Francisco	79	291
KORMINSKEY								
Bernard	40	m	w	PRUS	Sacramento	2-Wd Sacramento	77	237
KORN								
Abraham	32	m	w	POLA	San Francisco	San Francisco P O	83	191
Adam	20	m	w	ENGL	San Francisco	11-Wd San Francisc	84	596
Edward	31	m	w	PRUS	Yolo	Cache Crk Twp	93	420
Frederick S	41	m	w	SAXO	Los Angeles	Santa Ana Twp	73	609
Louis	45	m	w	BADE	Yolo	Cache Crk Twp	93	422
Moses	37	m	w	BADE	Santa Clara	Gilroy Twp	88	70
Teresa	55	f	w	NJ	San Francisco	2-Wd San Francisco	79	156
KORNIPER								
Jacob	34	m	w	ITAL	San Francisco	San Francisco P O	80	331
KORNS								
Jacob R	35	m	w	KY	Los Angeles	Los Nietos Twp	73	575
KOROVIN								
Charles	46	m	w	FRAN	Calaveras	San Andreas P O	70	210
KORRIS								
Max	24	m	w	PRUS	San Francisco	San Francisco P O	83	152
KORS								
Clause	25	m	w	HANO	San Francisco	7-Wd San Francisco	81	250
KORSKEY								
M	30	m	w	PRUS	Trinity	Weaverville Pct	92	226
KORSON								
Andrew	26	m	w	PRUS	San Francisco	San Francisco P O	83	389
KORTEN								
Bend	41	m	w	PRUS	San Francisco	San Francisco P O	85	726
KORTES								
John E	32	m	w	PRUS	San Francisco	San Francisco P O	83	233
KORTS								
Henry	32	m	w	BREM	San Francisco	San Francisco P O	83	334
KORTZ								
George	28	m	w	NY	San Francisco	San Francisco P O	80	390
KOSE								
Martin	30	m	w	PRUS	San Francisco	San Francisco P O	85	847
KOSEE								
William	30	m	w	PRUS	San Francisco	5-Wd San Francisco	81	5
KOSER								
Alfred	9	m	w	CA	San Francisco	11-Wd San Francisc	84	495
KOSH								
Margaret	49	f	w	PRUS	San Francisco	San Francisco P O	85	869
KOSHLAND								
Simon	43	m	w	BAVA	San Francisco	8-Wd San Francisco	82	453
KOSK								
John	41	m	w	RUSS	Shasta	Stillwater P O	89	481
KOSKE								
Henry	39	m	w	BREM	San Francisco	San Francisco P O	83	135
KOSLOSSKY								
August	42	m	w	PRUS	Placer	Bath P O	76	443
KOSMINSKY								
James	23	m	w	PRUS	Yolo	Putah Twp	93	520
Solomon	23	m	w	POLA	Santa Clara	2-Wd San Jose	88	330
KOSOUTH								
F	33	m	w	MEXI	Alameda	Murray Twp	68	107
KOSSETTE								
Amelia	50	f	w	HAMB	San Francisco	8-Wd San Francisco	82	394
KOSSUS								
Wan	24	m	w	MEXI	Tehama	Tehama Twp	92	193
KOSSUTH								
Anton	25	m	w	CA	San Joaquin	Dent Twp	86	19
Jessee	23	m	w	CA	Colusa	Monroe Twp	71	311
Joseph	30	m	w	MEXI	Tulare	White Rvr Twp	92	302
Rivers	35	m	w	MEXI	El Dorado	Placerville Twp	72	93
Romeo	60	f	w	MEXI	Sacramento	2-Wd Sacramento	77	243
KOSTA								
Joseph	38	m	w	WEST	San Francisco	1-Wd San Francisco	79	47
KOSTAR								
Fritz	52	m	w	PRUS	San Francisco	6-Wd San Francisco	81	93
KOSTENSON								
Sarah	47	f	w	MO	Solano	Tremont Twp	90	32
KOSTER								
Albert	48	m	w	PRUS	San Francisco	San Francisco P O	83	372
Frederick	40	m	w	PRUS	San Mateo	Redwood Twp	87	362
Henrich	45	m	w	PRUS	San Francisco	San Francisco P O	80	339
Henry	38	m	w	BREM	Napa	Napa	75	20
Herman	36	m	w	HANO	San Francisco	2-Wd San Francisco	79	217
John T	9	m	w	CA	Napa	Napa	75	47
Philip	52	m	w	GERM	San Diego	San Diego	78	496
William	41	m	w	PRUS	Solano	Tremont Twp	90	32
KOSTERT								
R	53	m	w	FRAN	San Francisco	8-Wd San Francisco	82	376
KOSTIR								
Fred	22	m	w	PRUS	Sacramento	4-Wd Sacramento	77	339
KOSTLE								
Bridget	35	f	w	IREL	Sacramento	4-Wd Sacramento	77	341
KOSTOY								
Philip	40	m	w	PRUS	Calaveras	Copperopolis P O	70	262
KOT								
Ah	30	m	c	CHIN	Sacramento	1-Wd Sacramento	77	197
KOTHEIN								
John	30	m	w	BAVA	San Francisco	2-Wd San Francisco	79	213
KOTTALEN								
Adolf	50	m	w	FINL	San Francisco	3-Wd San Francisco	79	291
KOTTINGER								
J W	50	m	w	AUST	Alameda	Murray Twp	68	109
Rosa	13	f	w	CA	Santa Clara	2-Wd San Jose	88	337
KOTTONBA								
Jasper	34	m	w	HDAR	Solano	Silveyville Twp	90	87
KOTZ								
Daniel	41	m	w	PRUS	Sacramento	Sutter Twp	77	393
Geo	16	m	w	OH	Butte	Oregon Twp	70	136
KOUA								
Ah	46	m	c	CHIN	Calaveras	San Andreas P O	70	155
KOUCKMAN								
E G	23	m	w	HANO	San Francisco	San Francisco P O	85	809
KOUE								
David	51	m	w	BADE	Sacramento	3-Wd Sacramento	77	315
KOUG								
Ah	28	m	c	CHIN	Kern	Havilah P O	73	338
KOUGER								
Charles	36	m	w	PRUS	San Francisco	San Francisco P O	80	460
KOUGH								
Dennis	31	m	w	ME	Napa	Napa Twp	75	31
Dennis	31	m	w	IREL	San Francisco	San Francisco P O	83	326
KOUHN								
Frank	25	m	w	BAVA	Los Angeles	Santa Ana Twp	73	613
KOULE								
Myles	8	m	w	CA	Marin	San Rafael Twp	74	29
KOUP								
Ah	40	m	c	CHIN	Santa Clara	San Jose Twp	88	194
KOUR								
Ah	38	m	c	CHIN	Mariposa	Maxwell Crk P O	74	142
KOUSE								
J H	44	m	w	PA	Yuba	Marysville	93	596
KOUSHE								
Michael	29	m	w	PRUS	San Mateo	San Mateo P O	87	348
KOUTZ								
J	41	m	w	PA	Sierra	Alleghany & Forest	89	534
Louis	40	m	w	PRUS	Yuba	New York Twp	93	642
KOVEY								
William K	23	m	w	PA	Colusa	Monroe Twp	71	319
KOW								
---	28	m	c	CHIN	Siskiyou	Cottonwood Twp	89	595
---	26	m	c	CHIN	Siskiyou	Cottonwood Twp	89	594
Ah	7	m	c	CA	Solano	Vallejo	90	174
Ah	6	f	c	CHIN	San Francisco	San Francisco P O	80	447
Ah	58	f	c	CHIN	San Francisco	San Francisco P O	80	439
Ah	56	m	c	CHIN	San Francisco	San Francisco P O	80	446
Ah	54	m	c	CHIN	San Francisco	San Francisco P O	80	519
Ah	50	f	c	CHIN	San Francisco	San Francisco P O	80	450
Ah	48	m	c	CHIN	San Francisco	San Francisco P O	80	522
Ah	44	m	c	CHIN	San Francisco	6-Wd San Francisco	81	57
Ah	42	m	c	CHIN	San Francisco	San Francisco P O	80	443
Ah	42	m	c	CHIN	San Francisco	San Francisco P O	80	453
Ah	42	m	c	CHIN	San Francisco	San Francisco P O	80	446
Ah	42	m	c	CHIN	San Francisco	San Francisco P O	80	529
Ah	41	m	c	CHIN	San Francisco	San Francisco P O	80	521
Ah	41	m	c	CHIN	San Francisco	San Francisco P O	80	520
Ah	40	m	c	CHIN	San Francisco	San Francisco P O	80	488
Ah	40	m	c	CHIN	San Francisco	San Francisco P O	80	509
Ah	40	m	c	CHIN	San Francisco	San Francisco P O	80	524
Ah	40	m	c	CHIN	Butte	Wyandotte Twp	70	148
Ah	4	f	c	CA	San Francisco	San Francisco P O	80	438
Ah	39	m	c	CHIN	San Francisco	6-Wd San Francisco	81	57
Ah	39	m	c	CHIN	San Francisco	San Francisco P O	80	438
Ah	39	m	c	CHIN	San Francisco	San Francisco P O	80	449
Ah	39	m	c	CHIN	Butte	Mountain Spring Tw	70	89
Ah	39	m	c	CHIN	El Dorado	Coloma Twp	72	6
Ah	38	m	c	CHIN	San Francisco	San Francisco P O	80	451
Ah	38	m	c	CHIN	San Francisco	San Francisco P O	80	520
Ah	38	m	c	CHIN	San Francisco	San Francisco P O	80	530
Ah	37	m	c	CHIN	San Francisco	San Francisco P O	80	446
Ah	37	m	c	CHIN	San Francisco	San Francisco P O	80	512
Ah	37	m	c	CHIN	San Francisco	San Francisco P O	80	511
Ah	37	m	c	CHIN	San Francisco	San Francisco P O	80	528
Ah	37	m	c	CHIN	San Francisco	6-Wd San Francisco	81	60
Ah	36	f	c	CHIN	San Francisco	San Francisco P O	80	500
Ah	36	m	c	CHIN	San Francisco	San Francisco P O	80	510
Ah	35	m	c	CHIN	San Francisco	6-Wd San Francisco	81	53
Ah	34	m	c	CHIN	San Francisco	San Francisco P O	80	498
Ah	34	m	c	CHIN	Trinity	Indian Crk	92	199
Ah	34	m	c	CHIN	San Francisco	San Francisco P O	80	513
Ah	34	m	c	CHIN	San Francisco	San Francisco P O	80	523
Ah	32	f	c	CHIN	San Francisco	San Francisco P O	80	452
Ah	31	m	c	CHIN	San Francisco	San Francisco P O	80	442
Ah	31	m	c	CHIN	San Francisco	San Francisco P O	80	511
Ah	30	m	c	CHIN	San Francisco	San Francisco P O	85	747
Ah	30	f	c	CHIN	San Francisco	San Francisco P O	80	447
Ah	30	f	c	CHIN	San Francisco	San Francisco P O	80	451
Ah	30	f	c	CHIN	San Francisco	San Francisco P O	80	449
Ah	30	f	c	CHIN	San Francisco	San Francisco P O	80	450
Ah	30	f	c	CHIN	San Francisco	San Francisco P O	80	451
Ah	30	m	c	CHIN	Placer	Auburn P O	76	377
Ah	30	m	c	CHIN	Trinity	North Fork Twp	92	217
Ah	30	f	c	CHIN	San Francisco	San Francisco P O	80	507
Ah	30	m	c	CHIN	San Francisco	San Francisco P O	80	501
Ah	29	m	c	CHIN	San Francisco	3-Wd San Francisco	79	306
Ah	29	m	c	CHIN	Santa Clara	1-Wd San Jose	88	270
Ah	29	m	c	CHIN	San Francisco	San Francisco P O	80	512
Ah	29	m	c	CHIN	San Francisco	San Francisco P O	80	511

© 2001 by Heritage Quest. All rights reserved.

California 1870 Census

Series M593

Name	Age	S	R	B-PL	County	Locale	Roll	Pg
Ah	29	m	c	CHIN	San Francisco	San Francisco P O	80	525
Ah	29	m	c	CHIN	San Francisco	San Francisco P O	80	524
Ah	28	m	c	CHIN	San Francisco	3-Wd San Francisco	79	329
Ah	28	m	c	CHIN	San Francisco	San Francisco P O	80	450
Ah	28	m	c	CHIN	Alameda	Alvarado	68	303
Ah	28	m	c	CHIN	Monterey	Monterey	74	355
Ah	28	m	c	CHIN	Napa	Napa	75	8
Ah	26	f	c	CHIN	San Francisco	San Francisco P O	80	495
Ah	26	m	c	CHIN	San Francisco	San Francisco P O	80	479
Ah	26	m	c	CHIN	San Francisco	San Francisco P O	80	527
Ah	26	f	c	CHIN	San Francisco	San Francisco P O	80	526
Ah	25	m	c	CHIN	Solano	Vallejo	90	176
Ah	25	m	c	CHIN	Tuolumne	Columbia P O	93	342
Ah	25	m	c	CHIN	Los Angeles	Wilmington Twp	73	635
Ah	25	m	c	CHIN	San Francisco	San Francisco P O	80	436
Ah	25	f	c	CHIN	San Francisco	San Francisco P O	80	439
Ah	25	m	c	CHIN	Marin	Tomales Twp	74	83
Ah	25	m	c	CHIN	Placer	Auburn P O	76	364
Ah	24	m	c	CHIN	Santa Clara	San Jose Twp	88	193
Ah	24	f	c	CHIN	San Francisco	San Francisco P O	80	449
Ah	24	f	c	CHIN	San Francisco	San Francisco P O	80	450
Ah	24	f	c	CHIN	San Francisco	San Francisco P O	80	447
Ah	24	f	c	CHIN	San Francisco	San Francisco P O	80	449
Ah	23	m	c	CHIN	San Francisco	San Francisco P O	80	530
Ah	22	m	c	CHIN	San Francisco	San Francisco P O	85	748
Ah	22	m	c	CHIN	San Francisco	San Francisco P O	83	132
Ah	22	m	c	CHIN	Tehama	Red Bluff	92	183
Ah	22	f	c	CHIN	San Francisco	San Francisco P O	80	454
Ah	22	m	c	CHIN	Nevada	Little York Twp	75	235
Ah	21	m	c	CHIN	Solano	Suisun Twp	90	106
Ah	21	f	c	CHIN	San Francisco	San Francisco P O	80	440
Ah	21	f	c	CHIN	San Francisco	San Francisco P O	80	454
Ah	21	f	c	CHIN	San Francisco	San Francisco P O	80	447
Ah	21	f	c	CHIN	San Francisco	San Francisco P O	80	454
Ah	21	f	c	CHIN	San Francisco	San Francisco P O	80	492
Ah	21	m	c	CHIN	San Francisco	San Francisco P O	80	516
Ah	21	m	c	CHIN	San Francisco	San Francisco P O	80	518
Ah	21	m	c	CHIN	San Francisco	6-Wd San Francisco	81	138
Ah	20	m	c	CHIN	San Francisco	6-Wd San Francisco	81	59
Ah	20	m	c	CHIN	San Francisco	6-Wd San Francisco	81	42
Ah	20	m	c	CHIN	Calaveras	San Andreas P O	70	160
Ah	20	m	c	CHIN	San Francisco	San Francisco P O	80	335
Ah	20	f	c	CHIN	San Francisco	San Francisco P O	80	448
Ah	20	f	c	CHIN	San Francisco	San Francisco P O	80	452
Ah	20	f	c	CHIN	San Francisco	San Francisco P O	80	490
Ah	20	m	c	CHIN	San Francisco	San Francisco P O	80	528
Ah	20	m	c	CHIN	San Francisco	6-Wd San Francisco	81	41
Ah	19	m	c	CHIN	Tehama	Tehama Twp	92	193
Ah	18	m	c	CHIN	San Francisco	6-Wd San Francisco	81	42
Ah	16	m	c	CHIN	San Francisco	3-Wd San Francisco	79	308
Ah	13	f	c	CHIN	San Francisco	San Francisco P O	80	500
Ah	11	m	c	CHIN	San Francisco	San Francisco P O	80	444
Ah	1	f	c	CA	Contra Costa	Martinez P O	71	398
Ah	1	f	c	CA	San Francisco	San Francisco P O	80	449
Choy	36	m	c	CHIN	San Francisco	6-Wd San Francisco	81	66
Hee	19	m	c	CHIN	Butte	Mountain Spring Tw	70	89
Juin	28	m	c	CHIN	Humboldt	Eureka Twp	72	266
Ok	29	m	c	CHIN	Colusa	Colusa	71	300
Sou	19	m	c	CHIN	Sonoma	Analy Twp	91	233
Suen	43	m	c	CHIN	Yuba	Marysville	93	624
Tee	21	m	c	CHIN	Napa	Napa	75	9
W Y R	25	m	c	CHIN	Mariposa	Maxwell Crk P O	74	145
Wah	15	m	c	CHIN	San Francisco	San Francisco P O	83	176
Wan	37	m	c	CHIN	El Dorado	Diamond Springs Tw	72	33
Yu	45	m	c	CHIN	San Francisco	6-Wd San Francisco	81	39
KOWALSKY								
E H	24	m	w	POLA	Sonoma	Bodega Twp	91	251
KOWE								
Ah	45	m	c	CHIN	Trinity	Junction City Pct	92	208
Ah	35	f	c	CHIN	Nevada	Nevada Twp	75	298
Ah	18	f	c	CHIN	San Francisco	6-Wd San Francisco	81	76
KOWER								
Emill	46	m	w	WURT	San Francisco	2-Wd San Francisco	79	198
KOWINSKI								
Morris	26	m	w	PRUS	Sacramento	4-Wd Sacramento	77	322
KOWISKOSKI								
M	25	m	w	RUSS	San Francisco	6-Wd San Francisco	81	86
KOWLEY								
Susie	18	f	w	ENGL	San Francisco	11-Wd San Francisc	84	568
KOWN								
Mc Alek	23	m	w	CANA	Sacramento	3-Wd Sacramento	77	286
KOWOK								
Ah	28	m	c	CHIN	San Francisco	6-Wd San Francisco	81	45
KOX								
M B	50	m	w	ENGL	San Francisco	7-Wd San Francisco	81	286
KOY								
---	26	m	c	CHIN	Siskiyou	Cottonwood Twp	89	594
A	28	m	c	CHIN	Santa Clara	Fremont Twp	88	57
Ah	54	m	c	CHIN	Placer	Gold Run Twp	76	398
Ah	40	m	c	CHIN	San Francisco	6-Wd San Francisco	81	58
Ah	40	m	c	CHIN	San Francisco	6-Wd San Francisco	81	59
Ah	40	m	c	CHIN	San Francisco	6-Wd San Francisco	81	62
Ah	37	m	c	CHIN	San Francisco	6-Wd San Francisco	81	50
Ah	37	m	c	CHIN	San Francisco	6-Wd San Francisco	81	61
Ah	36	m	c	CHIN	San Francisco	6-Wd San Francisco	81	65
Ah	30	m	c	CHIN	El Dorado	Mud Springs Twp	72	89
Ah	27	m	c	CHIN	Santa Clara	2-Wd San Jose	88	322
Ah	27	m	c	CHIN	Santa Clara	San Jose Twp	88	196
Ah	27	m	c	CHIN	Butte	Wyandotte Twp	70	141
Ah	26	m	c	CHIN	San Francisco	6-Wd San Francisco	81	52
Ah	25	m	c	CHIN	San Francisco	6-Wd San Francisco	81	62
Ah	24	m	c	CHIN	San Francisco	6-Wd San Francisco	81	66
Ah	23	m	c	CHIN	San Francisco	6-Wd San Francisco	81	54
Ah	22	m	c	CHIN	San Francisco	6-Wd San Francisco	81	59
Ah	20	f	c	CHIN	Santa Clara	1-Wd San Jose	88	269
Ah	18	m	c	CHIN	San Francisco	6-Wd San Francisco	81	85
Chee	25	m	c	CHIN	San Francisco	6-Wd San Francisco	81	71
Line	25	f	c	CHIN	Sacramento	1-Wd Sacramento	77	192
Pan	26	m	c	CHIN	Solano	Vacaville Twp	90	130
Sade	20	f	c	CHIN	Sacramento	1-Wd Sacramento	77	192
Ze	34	m	c	CHIN	Yuba	Marysville	93	631
KOYLE								
David	41	m	w	IREL	Solano	Vacaville Twp	90	123
Hiram	34	m	w	HDAR	Solano	Silveyville Twp	90	89
John	11	m	w	CA	Marin	San Rafael Twp	74	29
KOZ								
Henry	42	m	w	HAMB	Sonoma	Salt Point	91	385
KOZMINSKY								
Herman	40	m	w	PRUS	San Francisco	8-Wd San Francisco	82	489
S	26	m	w	POLA	Nevada	Bridgeport Twp	75	100
Simon	35	m	w	PRUS	San Francisco	8-Wd San Francisco	82	480
KRABBINHOFTH								
Peter	44	m	w	SHOL	Santa Clara	1-Wd San Jose	88	250
KRACHT								
John	27	m	w	PRUS	Santa Clara	Gilroy Twp	88	80
KRADT								
Mary	36	f	w	HANO	San Francisco	11-Wd San Francisc	84	490
KRAEMER								
Aug	43	m	w	PRUS	San Diego	San Diego	78	495
August	33	m	w	PRUS	San Francisco	1-Wd San Francisco	79	63
George	34	m	w	BAVA	Nevada	Bridgeport Twp	75	100
KRAETZ								
Aug	44	m	w	PRUS	San Francisco	San Francisco P O	83	135
Joseph	55	m	w	BAVA	San Francisco	San Francisco P O	83	158
KRAFER								
Augustus	24	m	w	PRUS	Santa Clara	Santa Clara Twp	88	164
KRAFT								
August	18	m	w	IL	Nevada	Nevada Twp	75	309
Augusta	30	f	w	BAVA	Marin	Sausalito Twp	74	70
Geo	45	m	w	BADE	Butte	Ophir Twp	70	93
Henry	28	m	w	PRUS	Tehama	Red Bluff	92	177
Herbert	39	m	w	HANO	Tehama	Red Bluff	92	177
Jas M	36	m	w	BAVA	Sonoma	Cloverdale Twp	91	268
Louis	40	m	w	BADE	San Francisco	1-Wd San Francisco	79	47
Peter	47	m	w	SWED	Nevada	Eureka Twp	75	133
Samuel	16	m	w	CA	Calaveras	San Andreas P O	70	196
KRAGER								
Fred	41	m	w	ROMA	San Francisco	11-Wd San Francisc	84	644
KRAHANBERG								
Frederick	41	m	w	PRUS	Santa Clara	San Jose Twp	88	182
KRAIG								
Mary	32	f	w	HESS	Sutter	Nicolaus Twp	92	112
KRAITH								
F K	46	m	w	MD	Alameda	Alameda	68	4
KRAKER								
M	26	m	w	VA	Sacramento	3-Wd Sacramento	77	281
KRAM								
Felix	24	m	w	FRAN	San Francisco	2-Wd San Francisco	79	213
KRAMBACH								
Julius	13	m	w	CA	San Francisco	5-Wd San Francisco	81	1
KRAMBS								
Frederick	45	m	w	PRUS	San Francisco	6-Wd San Francisco	81	100
KRAMER								
Aug	21	m	w	PRUS	Sacramento	4-Wd Sacramento	77	354
August	29	m	w	PA	San Francisco	San Francisco P O	80	335
Bernard	47	m	w	SAXO	San Francisco	11-Wd San Francisc	84	444
Cartney	38	m	w	BAVA	San Diego	Fort Yuma Dist	78	464
Catherine	21	f	w	NY	San Francisco	11-Wd San Francisc	84	651
Cathrain	21	f	w	IREL	San Francisco	San Francisco P O	80	427
Chris	35	m	w	PRUS	Sacramento	4-Wd Sacramento	77	376
Delens	50	m	w	BADE	San Diego	Fort Yuma Dist	78	464
Fred	21	m	w	FRNK	Sacramento	4-Wd Sacramento	77	367
Fredrick	42	m	w	PRUS	San Francisco	7-Wd San Francisco	81	165
Henry	29	m	w	OH	Solano	Benicia	90	11
Isaac	35	m	w	PRUS	San Francisco	3-Wd San Francisco	79	326
Jacob	65	m	w	BADE	San Francisco	2-Wd San Francisco	79	185
Jeremia	36	m	w	IREL	San Francisco	San Francisco P O	83	270
John	45	m	w	HDAR	Siskiyou	Scott Valley Twp	89	621
John	35	m	w	GERM	Yolo	Cache Crk Twp	93	452
John	33	m	w	IREL	San Francisco	San Francisco P O	85	741
John	28	m	w	IREL	San Bernardino	San Bernardino Twp	78	452
Louis	30	m	w	GERM	Los Angeles	Los Angeles	73	548
Mary	42	f	w	PRUS	San Francisco	San Francisco P O	83	409
Philip	25	m	w	HANO	San Francisco	San Francisco P O	83	90
Richard	27	m	w	PRUS	Alameda	Washington Twp	68	300
Theodore	32	m	w	PRUS	San Francisco	8-Wd San Francisco	82	434
KRAMP								
Phillip	35	m	w	WALD	El Dorado	Diamond Springs Tw	72	21
KRAN								
Ah	24	m	c	CHIN	Mendocino	Gualala Twp	74	226
Charls	30	m	w	PRUS	Alameda	Oakland	68	163
KRANDICK								
Henry	36	m	w	HANO	Los Angeles	Los Angeles	73	565

© 2001 by Heritage Quest. All rights reserved.

Name	Age	S	R	B-PL	County	Locale	Series M593 Roll	Pg
KRANS								
John	48	m	w	WURT	Santa Clara	San Jose Twp	88	191
KRANSE								
George	40	m	w	PRUS	San Francisco	San Francisco P O	80	359
KRANSI								
Edward	34	m	w	PRUS	San Diego	San Diego	78	500
KRANTH								
F K	22	m	w	NY	Sacramento	3-Wd Sacramento	77	290
KRANTZ								
Laurence	41	m	w	SAXO	San Francisco	2-Wd San Francisco	79	157
Louis	18	m	w	PRUS	Alameda	Oakland	68	257
KRANTZENSTEIN								
Chs	36	m	w	HANO	San Francisco	2-Wd San Francisco	79	235
KRANZ								
Hulda	18	f	w	PRUS	San Francisco	8-Wd San Francisco	82	430
KRASBOURG								
Mary	18	f	w	NY	San Francisco	11-Wd San Francisc	84	688
KRASCHEWSKI								
Miguel	39	m	w	POLA	Los Angeles	San Juan Twp	73	624
KRASER								
Bernard	35	m	w	PRUS	San Francisco	7-Wd San Francisco	81	224
KRASS								
Augustus	48	m	w	HOLL	Tuolumne	Columbia P O	93	350
KRATES								
Fred	50	m	w	HANO	Amador	Drytown P O	69	421
Henry	44	m	w	HANO	Amador	Drytown P O	69	421
Henry	22	m	w	PRUS	Sonoma	Sonoma Twp	91	446
KRATTIGER								
Jacob	32	m	w	SWIT	Siskiyou	Cottonwood Twp	89	595
John	30	m	w	SWIT	Siskiyou	Cottonwood Twp	89	595
KRATZ								
Henry	29	m	w	BAVA	Santa Clara	San Jose Twp	88	202
John	19	m	w	PRUS	San Joaquin	2-Wd Stockton	86	179
KRATZER								
William K	57	m	w	OH	Contra Costa	Martinez P O	71	389
KRAUGHT								
Ernest	42	m	w	PRUS	Alameda	Oakland	68	144
KRAUL								
Mary	22	f	w	IREL	San Francisco	8-Wd San Francisco	82	464
KRAULL								
William	27	m	w	HANO	Santa Cruz	Santa Cruz	89	433
KRAUM								
Wm D	24	m	w	PA	Sacramento	4-Wd Sacramento	77	320
KRAUPT								
John	30	m	w	PRUS	San Bernardino	San Bernardino Twp	78	415
KRAUS								
Edmund	49	m	w	PRUS	Sacramento	3-Wd Sacramento	77	259
Edward	22	m	w	PRUS	Solano	Montezuma Twp	90	67
Frederick	43	m	w	SWIT	San Francisco	8-Wd San Francisco	82	463
Henry	29	m	w	PRUS	Solano	Silveyville Twp	90	80
Nicolaus	43	m	w	PRUS	San Francisco	San Francisco P O	83	136
KRAUSE								
Catherine	27	f	w	IREL	Yolo	Cottonwood Twp	93	470
Charles	46	m	w	PA	San Francisco	2-Wd San Francisco	79	214
Charles	44	m	w	PRUS	San Francisco	2-Wd San Francisco	79	168
Charles	39	m	w	PRUS	San Francisco	3-Wd San Francisco	79	322
John	38	m	w	BAVA	Calaveras	San Andreas P O	70	190
O	62	m	w	PRUS	Sacramento	3-Wd Sacramento	77	307
Wm B	33	m	w	GERM	Tuolumne	Columbia P O	93	349
KRAUSGRILL								
Philip	47	m	w	HDAR	San Francisco	2-Wd San Francisco	79	186
KRAUSKEL								
John	21	m	w	HDAR	San Francisco	San Francisco P O	80	461
KRAUSS								
Adolphus	24	m	w	GERM	Tuolumne	Columbia P O	93	340
Andrew	26	m	w	PRUS	Solano	Tremont Twp	90	31
Daniel	28	m	w	HDAR	San Francisco	8-Wd San Francisco	82	416
Fred H	29	m	w	PRUS	San Francisco	San Francisco P O	85	771
Kate	44	f	w	BAVA	San Francisco	8-Wd San Francisco	82	483
KRAUSSE								
Frederick	34	m	w	HCAS	El Dorado	Mud Springs Twp	72	71
KRAUST								
Peter	48	m	w	PRUS	San Joaquin	Oneal Twp	86	102
KRAWINKLE								
John	51	m	w	PRUS	Sacramento	American Twp	77	66
KRAWSE								
William	38	m	w	HESS	Calaveras	Copperopolis P O	70	262
KREAGENSPAEK								
M	25	m	w	SWIT	San Francisco	8-Wd San Francisco	82	356
KREATE								
Henry	31	m	w	BREM	Los Angeles	Wilmington Twp	73	642
KREBER								
Fredrick	25	m	w	BAVA	San Francisco	7-Wd San Francisco	81	224
KREBS								
Ernest	35	m	w	GERM	San Luis Obispo	San Luis Obispo Tw	87	311
Julius	30	m	w	PRUS	Colusa	Colusa	71	290
KREE								
Barny	36	m	w	PRUS	Sutter	Butte Twp	92	103
Henry	42	m	w	WURT	Sutter	Butte Twp	92	101
KREELES								
Frederick	25	m	w	ENGL	Monterey	San Antonio Twp	74	320
KREEM								
James	24	m	w	MD	San Diego	Poway Dist	78	481
KREETLES								
George	42	m	w	MA	Sutter	Yuba Twp	92	150
KREGER								
George	19	m	w	OLDE	Sonoma	Vallejo Twp	91	454

Name	Age	S	R	B-PL	County	Locale	Series M593 Roll	Pg
Wm	37	m	w	PA	San Francisco	11-Wd San Francisc	84	581
KREGS								
Z W	48	m	w	VT	Sierra	Downieville Twp	89	515
KREIG								
Charles	32	m	w	GERM	Nevada	Nevada Twp	75	321
Ernest	50	m	w	BELG	Nevada	Washington Twp	75	339
Joseph	35	m	w	BADE	San Mateo	Redwood Twp	87	363
KREINER								
William	36	m	w	SWIT	San Francisco	San Francisco P O	80	430
KREISEL								
Ferdinand	28	m	w	SAXO	San Francisco	1-Wd San Francisco	79	52
KREISS								
Henry	39	m	w	BELG	Nevada	Nevada Twp	75	285
Jacob	35	m	w	NY	San Mateo	Woodside P O	87	380
Michael	37	m	w	FRAN	San Mateo	Redwood Twp	87	361
KREKER								
Amanda	19	f	w	ME	Alameda	Brooklyn	68	23
KREL								
Andreas	32	m	w	PRUS	San Francisco	San Francisco P O	83	81
KRELL								
John C	27	m	w	HDAR	San Francisco	8-Wd San Francisco	82	307
KRELLENBERG								
Peter	42	m	w	SHOL	Yolo	Cache Crk Twp	93	436
KREMER								
Daniel	54	m	w	BAVA	Los Angeles	Santa Ana Twp	73	606
Jacob	38	m	w	LUXE	Placer	Bath P O	76	441
Jas	28	m	w	BADE	Santa Clara	Gilroy Twp	88	99
Morris	42	m	w	FRAN	Los Angeles	Los Angeles	73	533
Samuel	29	m	w	PRUS	San Francisco	8-Wd San Francisco	82	408
William	30	m	w	BAVA	San Francisco	8-Wd San Francisco	82	443
KREN								
Henry	48	m	w	PRUS	Nevada	Grass Valley Twp	75	228
KRENAHRESS								
John	19	m	w	HANO	San Francisco	11-Wd San Francisc	84	431
KRENCE								
Osvald	31	m	w	PRUS	San Francisco	San Francisco P O	85	752
KRENGLE								
Jos	40	m	w	OH	Butte	Ophir Twp	70	117
KRENKEL								
B F	46	m	w	BADE	Tuolumne	Chinese Camp P O	93	374
KREOF								
Eugenia	21	f	w	FRAN	San Francisco	6-Wd San Francisco	81	113
Victor	28	m	w	FRAN	San Francisco	6-Wd San Francisco	81	113
KRESING								
Charles	26	m	w	PRUS	San Francisco	San Francisco P O	83	383
KRESS								
George	45	m	w	PRUS	Nevada	Grass Valley Twp	75	228
Henry	29	m	w	PRUS	Sacramento	2-Wd Sacramento	77	241
Simon P	40	m	w	OH	Butte	Chico Twp	70	16
William	46	m	w	OH	San Diego	Coronado	78	465
KRESSEL								
A	28	m	w	PRUS	Sierra	Butte Twp	89	512
KRESTCHMAR								
Caroline	30	f	w	SAXO	San Francisco	2-Wd San Francisco	79	197
KRESTINE								
Charles	39	m	w	PRUS	San Francisco	7-Wd San Francisco	81	168
KRESTSINGER								
Kate	19	f	w	IL	San Francisco	11-Wd San Francisc	84	576
KRETH								
Fredk	46	m	w	BADE	Amador	Drytown P O	69	424
KRETSCHMANN								
J	45	m	w	BADE	San Francisco	8-Wd San Francisco	82	374
KRETZEN								
Rebecca	25	f	w	CA	San Francisco	2-Wd San Francisco	79	216
KRETZER								
Mary A	12	f	w	CA	Sacramento	4-Wd Sacramento	77	349
Noah	40	m	w	OH	San Francisco	1-Wd San Francisco	79	62
KREUSBERGER								
F	48	m	w	WURT	Sacramento	3-Wd Sacramento	77	302
Louis	42	m	w	WURT	Sacramento	2-Wd Sacramento	77	247
KREUSER								
Andrw	46	m	w	PRUS	San Francisco	San Francisco P O	80	479
Constance	48	f	w	FRAN	San Francisco	6-Wd San Francisco	81	37
KREUTER								
Fred W	32	m	w	PRUS	San Bernardino	San Bernardino Twp	78	415
KREUTZ								
Jacob	45	m	w	PRUS	Siskiyou	Butte Twp	89	588
KREUZ								
Frank	30	m	w	PRUS	San Francisco	1-Wd San Francisco	79	100
KREW								
Chris	88	m	w	WURT	San Joaquin	Oneal Twp	86	111
John	53	m	w	FRAN	Sonoma	Petaluma Twp	91	337
KREYER								
Gertrude	20	f	w	PRUS	San Francisco	8-Wd San Francisco	82	386
KRHEN								
Samuel	37	m	w	SWED	San Francisco	7-Wd San Francisco	81	178
KRIBBS								
L W	27	m	w	IL	Solano	Vallejo	90	166
KRIBS								
Lena	18	f	w	CA	Sacramento	4-Wd Sacramento	77	340
KRICHOFF								
Theodore	42	m	w	PRUS	San Francisco	6-Wd San Francisco	81	79
KRICKER								
Jacob	27	m	w	BAVA	Sacramento	4-Wd Sacramento	77	347
KRICKET								
Carl	45	m	w	PRUS	Stanislaus	San Joaquin Twp	92	83

© 2001 by Heritage Quest. All rights reserved.

California 1870 Census

Series M593

Name	Age	S	R	B-PL	County	Locale	Roll	Pg
KRICKEY								
Louisa	14	f	w	PRUS	Stanislaus	San Joaquin Twp	92	79
KRIDER								
John	15	m	w	CA	Yolo	Buckeye Twp	93	409
KRIDLER								
Prudness	54	m	w	PA	Plumas	Plumas Twp	77	27
William H	33	m	w	OH	San Francisco	8-Wd San Francisco	82	494
KRIECHBAUM								
J G	54	m	w	HDAR	Sonoma	Russian Rvr	91	376
KRIEG								
Fred	26	m	w	BADE	San Francisco	8-Wd San Francisco	82	304
KRIET								
Charles	35	m	w	OLDE	Mendocino	Cuffeys Cove Twp	74	169
KRIETE								
George	30	m	w	PRUS	San Francisco	San Francisco P O	80	358
KRIFT								
Charlie	30	m	w	PRUS	Sacramento	4-Wd Sacramento	77	369
Wm	40	m	w	PRUS	Sacramento	4-Wd Sacramento	77	369
KRIGAN								
J	31	m	w	IREL	Lake	Knoxville Mines	73	405
KRIGEN								
J	31	m	w	IREL	Lake	Knoxville Mines	73	404
KRIIGER								
Jos	21	m	w	PRUS	San Francisco	7-Wd San Francisco	81	249
KRIKWOOD								
Wm	30	m	w	SCOT	Sacramento	4-Wd Sacramento	77	357
KRIL								
Andrew	38	m	w	BAVA	San Francisco	San Francisco P O	83	31
KRIN								
Ah	38	m	c	CHIN	Kern	Bakersfield P O	73	365
KRINGLE								
Joseph	42	m	w	PA	Butte	Bidwell Twp	70	4
KRINNOK								
Michael	38	m	w	IREL	San Diego	San Diego	78	494
KRINTZLER								
Peter	28	m	w	PRUS	San Joaquin	Castoria Twp	86	10
KRIS								
George Mrs	45	f	w	PA	San Francisco	5-Wd San Francisco	81	24
KRISS								
John	46	m	w	HESS	Los Angeles	Los Nietos Twp	73	576
Julia	23	f	w	IREL	Solano	Benicia	90	5
KRITCH								
Henry	25	m	w	BAVA	Marin	San Antonio Twp	74	62
KRITH								
Ar	32	m	c	CHIN	Sonoma	Sonoma Twp	91	447
KRITS								
Henry	43	m	w	PRUS	San Francisco	San Francisco P O	83	372
KRITTER								
Henry	40	m	w	BADE	Mariposa	Mariposa P O	74	122
KRITZER								
Geo	34	m	w	MO	San Francisco	7-Wd San Francisco	81	235
KRNELL								
John D	41	m	w	BAVA	Los Angeles	Los Angeles	73	538
KROCKE								
Henry	29	m	w	PRUS	San Francisco	8-Wd San Francisco	82	321
KROCKLE								
Geo	41	m	w	SAXO	San Joaquin	2-Wd Stockton	86	201
KROEGER								
Henry	37	m	w	SHOL	Los Angeles	Santa Ana Twp	73	613
Th Agst	23	m	w	HANO	San Francisco	San Francisco P O	83	62
KROFFT								
Ferdinand	34	m	w	PRUS	Sonoma	Petaluma Twp	91	322
KROFT								
Joseph	52	m	w	FRAN	Calaveras	San Andreas P O	70	156
William	74	m	w	SC	Contra Costa	Martinez P O	71	416
KROGER								
Christian	37	m	w	SHOL	San Francisco	1-Wd San Francisco	79	129
John	25	m	w	HANO	San Francisco	11-Wd San Francisc	84	623
KROGH								
Andrew	52	m	w	DENM	San Francisco	2-Wd San Francisco	79	224
Wal	29	m	w	DENM	Alameda	Oakland	68	219
KROHM								
John	31	m	w	HAMB	San Francisco	San Francisco P O	85	814
KROHN								
August	27	m	w	PRUS	San Francisco	San Francisco P O	85	865
Henry	39	m	w	PRUS	Sierra	Table Rock Twp	89	574
John	29	m	w	SWED	Mendocino	Point Arena Twp	74	204
KROHNER								
William	47	m	w	GERM	El Dorado	Placerville Twp	72	92
KROHS								
Henry	42	m	w	SHOL	Contra Costa	Martinez P O	71	380
KROHUKE								
Herman	30	m	w	SHOL	San Francisco	3-Wd San Francisco	79	287
KROJER								
August	40	m	w	SHOL	San Francisco	11-Wd San Francisc	84	682
KROLIK								
Saml	35	m	w	PRUS	San Luis Obispo	San Luis Obispo Tw	87	314
KROLL								
Edward	30	m	w	ENGL	Nevada	Grass Valley Twp	75	231
M Mrs	50	f	w	PRUS	Amador	Jackson P O	69	323
KROLLMAN								
Julius	39	m	w	PRUS	San Francisco	San Francisco P O	83	287
KROMP								
Mary	16	f	w	CA	San Francisco	San Francisco P O	85	814
KRON								
Jacob F	46	m	w	PRUS	Santa Cruz	Santa Cruz	89	433
Julius	24	m	w	PRUS	San Francisco	San Francisco P O	80	478
KRONBERG								
Adolph	25	m	w	HUNG	San Francisco	6-Wd San Francisco	81	70
KRONE								
Albert	22	m	w	HOLL	San Francisco	San Francisco P O	83	173
John	24	m	w	WURT	Sonoma	Petaluma Twp	91	347
Louis	66	m	w	PRUS	San Francisco	San Francisco P O	83	292
KRONHOLM								
John J	35	m	w	FINL	San Francisco	3-Wd San Francisco	79	291
KRONICUS								
Sarah	35	f	w	ENGL	San Francisco	8-Wd San Francisco	82	439
KRONIN								
Jac	34	m	w	MA	San Francisco	San Francisco P O	83	167
Joseph	25	m	w	SHOL	Santa Clara	2-Wd San Jose	88	318
KRONING								
John	40	m	w	IREL	San Francisco	San Francisco P O	83	149
Michael	34	m	w	PRUS	Solano	Vacaville Twp	90	125
William	45	m	w	BREM	San Francisco	6-Wd San Francisco	81	78
KRONK								
John	20	m	w	CISL	Alameda	Washington Twp	68	275
KRONKOLM								
Edward	28	m	w	SWED	Santa Clara	2-Wd San Jose	88	313
KRONNE								
Ed	26	m	w	CANA	Humboldt	Bucksport Twp	72	243
KRONTHAL								
Henry	40	m	w	BAVA	San Francisco	8-Wd San Francisco	82	475
KRONY								
Ferdinand	30	m	w	DENM	San Francisco	7-Wd San Francisco	81	274
KROOKES								
Morris	34	m	w	PRUS	San Francisco	San Francisco P O	83	315
KROON								
Thos	20	m	w	ENGL	Sacramento	Sutter Twp	77	393
KROPFF								
Wm	45	m	w	WURT	Sacramento	4-Wd Sacramento	77	320
KROPP								
Edward	26	m	w	GERM	Humboldt	Eureka Twp	72	280
Ernest	28	m	w	PRUS	San Francisco	San Francisco P O	83	272
KROSCHIEL								
Anna	16	f	w	HDAR	San Francisco	2-Wd San Francisco	79	186
KROSE								
Louis	60	m	w	HANO	San Francisco	San Francisco P O	85	771
KROSKY								
Wm	42	m	w	PRUS	San Joaquin	2-Wd Stockton	86	206
KROSPFLI								
B	40	m	w	SWED	Sierra	Downieville Twp	89	520
J	45	m	w	SWED	Sierra	Downieville Twp	89	520
KROSS								
Andrew	42	m	w	PRUS	Solano	Silveyville Twp	90	78
David	42	m	w	PRUS	Solano	Vacaville Twp	90	127
John	45	m	w	PRUS	Napa	Napa Twp	75	34
KROTZ								
Chas	45	m	w	BAVA	San Francisco	11-Wd San Francisc	84	670
KROUGHT								
W	40	m	w	PRUS	Alameda	Oakland	68	259
W	35	m	w	SCOT	Alameda	Oakland	68	247
KROUS								
Matildia	8	f	w	CA	Sacramento	3-Wd Sacramento	77	260
KROUSA								
James	40	m	w	PRUS	San Francisco	6-Wd San Francisco	81	97
KROUSE								
George H	45	m	w	PRUS	Stanislaus	Emory Twp	92	24
John C	38	m	w	WURT	Santa Clara	San Jose Twp	88	185
Richd	22	m	w	PRUS	San Francisco	5-Wd San Francisco	81	15
Wm	32	m	w	PRUS	Yuba	Marysville	93	583
KROUSER								
August	36	m	w	BADE	Sacramento	2-Wd Sacramento	77	241
KROUSS								
Frederick	31	m	w	GERM	Yolo	Cache Crk Twp	93	428
KROUTS								
Wm	37	m	w	PRUS	San Joaquin	2-Wd Stockton	86	206
KROW								
O	23	m	w	IL	San Joaquin	2-Wd Stockton	86	195
KROWING								
James	31	m	w	IREL	San Francisco	7-Wd San Francisco	81	185
KRU								
Sung	35	f	c	CHIN	Inyo	Lone Pine Twp	73	332
KRUCE								
Louis	35	m	w	PRUS	Klamath	South Fork Twp	73	383
KRUEGER								
Lewis	26	m	w	PRUS	San Francisco	7-Wd San Francisco	81	247
KRUG								
Charles	25	m	w	PRUS	San Francisco	San Francisco P O	80	464
William	39	m	w	BADE	San Francisco	San Francisco P O	80	424
KRUGER								
Charles	49	m	w	PRUS	San Francisco	San Francisco P O	80	465
Harmon	46	m	w	SAXO	Sonoma	Sonoma Twp	91	439
J H	25	m	w	MO	Amador	Ione City P O	69	353
Joseph	34	m	w	BAVA	San Francisco	San Francisco P O	80	532
Louis	46	m	w	PRUS	San Francisco	8-Wd San Francisco	82	426
Wm	48	m	w	NY	San Joaquin	Dent Twp	86	25
KRUGLER								
John	36	m	w	PA	Tehama	Toomes & Grant	92	169
KRUGRAMAN								
G	32	m	w	PRUS	San Joaquin	Castoria Twp	86	8
KRULE								
B	26	m	w	IOFM	Alameda	Oakland	68	234
KRULL								
Amos A	36	m	w	HOLL	Yolo	Merritt Twp	93	505

© 2001 by Heritage Quest. All rights reserved.

Name	Age	S	R	B-PL	County	Locale	Series M593 Roll	Pg
Isaac	26	m	w	HOLL	Yolo	Merritt Twp	93	505
Phillip	31	m	w	PRUS	San Francisco	San Francisco P O	83	274
KRUM								
Jacob	27	m	w	GERM	Los Angeles	Los Angeles	73	567
Louis	34	m	w	HDAR	Santa Clara	2-Wd San Jose	88	327
Phillip	27	m	w	HDAR	San Francisco	8-Wd San Francisco	82	368
KRUMACHER								
Charles	25	m	w	PRUS	San Francisco	6-Wd San Francisco	81	140
KRUMBEIN								
Justin	22	m	w	HAMB	San Francisco	San Francisco P O	83	95
KRUMBHALT								
Christian S	45	m	w	SAXO	Placer	Bath P O	76	457
KRUMBLER								
F	22	f	w	PRUS	San Francisco	San Francisco P O	83	280
KRUMLAND								
George	33	m	w	OLDE	Shasta	American Ranch P O	89	500
KRUMLEY								
Arabella	15	f	w	KY	Santa Clara	San Jose Twp	88	198
KRUMMEL								
John	57	m	w	PRUS	El Dorado	Diamond Springs Tw	72	21
KRUNZ								
Frank	37	m	w	BAVA	Sacramento	4-Wd Sacramento	77	372
KRUPPENSTAPPEL								
Antone	46	m	w	SHOL	Sonoma	Sonoma Twp	91	446
KRUSA								
Christian	44	m	w	PRUS	Amador	Jackson P O	69	321
KRUSE								
Anna	15	f	w	CA	Calaveras	Copperopolis P O	70	247
E	39	m	w	SWIT	Sierra	Downieville Twp	89	516
Edward	40	m	w	OLDE	San Francisco	San Francisco P O	83	18
Fredreki	24	f	w	LA	Tehama	Red Bluff	92	175
Henry	41	m	w	BREM	Napa	Napa Twp	75	59
Henry	28	m	w	PRUS	San Francisco	11-Wd San Francisc	84	578
Henry	21	m	w	GERM	Monterey	Alisal Twp	74	290
Herman	41	m	w	PRUS	Nevada	Grass Valley Twp	75	203
J	32	m	w	PRUS	Alameda	Murray Twp	68	102
Jacob	25	m	w	PRUS	San Francisco	6-Wd San Francisco	81	101
James	41	m	w	PRUS	Sonoma	Santa Rosa	91	426
Jocum	34	m	w	PRUS	Solano	Tremont Twp	90	35
Louis	47	m	w	CHIL	San Francisco	8-Wd San Francisco	82	489
M	38	m	w	TN	San Joaquin	2-Wd Stockton	86	192
Mathew	36	m	w	IREL	San Francisco	6-Wd San Francisco	81	120
William	30	m	w	PRUS	Plumas	Washington Twp	77	56
William	18	m	w	HANO	Placer	Colfax P O	76	391
KRUSELL								
George	37	m	w	NJ	Alameda	Brooklyn Twp	68	45
KRUSEN								
Horace B	56	m	w	NY	Butte	Hamilton Twp	70	69
KRUSIC								
Jacob	52	m	w	BADE	Butte	Hamilton Twp	70	64
KRUSON								
James	35	m	w	MO	Lassen	Susanville Twp	73	443
KRUSS								
Frederick	69	m	w	PRUS	El Dorado	White Oak Twp	72	138
KRUTTEL								
Christian	48	m	w	FRAN	Alameda	Washington Twp	68	292
KRUTZ								
Chas	50	m	w	PRUS	Sacramento	3-Wd Sacramento	77	260
Chas	26	m	w	WURT	San Francisco	1-Wd San Francisco	79	57
KRUTZER								
Lizzie	5	f	w	CA	San Francisco	San Francisco P O	83	345
Nicholas	67	m	w	BADE	Amador	Fiddletown P O	69	437
KRUTZNETT								
Elisebeth	54	f	w	WURT	Trinity	Weaverville Pct	92	224
KRUZ								
W B	35	m	w	PRUS	Alameda	Oakland	68	264
KRUZEN								
Christopher	36	m	w	BAVA	Mendocino	Little Lake Twp	74	193
KRY								
Ah	42	m	c	CHIN	Sacramento	Cosumnes Twp	77	93
Ah	30	m	c	CHIN	Sacramento	Cosumnes Twp	77	90
Ah	30	m	c	CHIN	Sacramento	Cosumnes Twp	77	94
Ah	29	m	c	CHIN	Sacramento	Cosumnes Twp	77	90
Ah	27	m	c	CHIN	Sacramento	Cosumnes Twp	77	94
KRYGER								
Christian	43	m	w	DENM	San Francisco	San Francisco P O	85	770
KRYSHER								
William	39	m	w	PA	Placer	Bath P O	76	426
KU								
Ah	42	m	c	CHIN	Sierra	Table Rock Twp	89	574
Ah	42	m	c	CHIN	Sierra	Table Rock Twp	89	574
Ah	41	m	c	CHIN	Los Angeles	Los Angeles	73	541
Ah	37	m	c	CHIN	Sierra	Eureka Twp	89	525
Ah	36	m	c	CHIN	Sierra	Downieville Twp	89	520
Ah	30	m	c	CHIN	Fresno	Millerton P O	72	199
Ah	24	m	c	CHIN	Sierra	Table Rock Twp	89	574
Ah	22	m	c	CHIN	Sacramento	Franklin Twp	77	115
Ah	21	m	c	CHIN	Placer	Colfax P O	76	384
Ah	20	f	c	CHIN	Los Angeles	Los Angeles	73	565
Ah	17	m	c	CHIN	El Dorado	White Oak Twp	72	140
Chee	45	m	c	CHIN	Santa Clara	1-Wd San Jose	88	273
Lin	22	f	c	CHIN	El Dorado	Placerville	72	116
Pi	14	f	c	CHIN	El Dorado	Placerville	72	116
Un	25	f	c	CHIN	El Dorado	Placerville	72	115
KUANER								
Lawrence	59	m	w	PRUS	Sacramento	4-Wd Sacramento	77	347
KUATIG								
Thos	31	m	w	ME	Alameda	Oakland	68	190
KUBBEY								
F M	38	m	w	NC	Sierra	Butte Twp	89	513
KUBI								
C H	38	m	w	PRUS	Sacramento	3-Wd Sacramento	77	284
KUBLER								
Jacob	50	m	w	WURT	Shasta	Millville P O	89	487
Rosenca	45	m	w	WURT	San Francisco	San Francisco P O	83	343
KUCHEL								
Chas	13	m	w	CA	San Francisco	San Francisco P O	83	9
KUCHENBEISSER								
Frederick	38	m	w	PRUS	Santa Clara	1-Wd San Jose	88	259
KUCHENBUCH								
F	24	m	w	PRUS	Siskiyou	Callahan P O	89	624
KUCHMEISTER								
Henry	33	m	w	PRUS	San Francisco	San Francisco P O	80	368
KUCK								
Diedrick	33	m	w	HANO	San Mateo	Redwood City P O	87	375
John	32	m	w	HANO	Alameda	Eden Twp	68	60
Martin	38	m	w	HANO	San Mateo	Redwood Twp	87	369
KUCKING								
Jno	23	m	w	HANO	Santa Clara	Gilroy Twp	88	68
KUDER								
J P	44	m	w	PA	Sierra	Lincoln Twp	89	548
KUE								
---	4M	f	c	CA	Siskiyou	Yreka	89	650
---	24	m	c	CHIN	Siskiyou	Cottonwood Twp	89	594
Ah	35	m	c	CHIN	San Francisco	6-Wd San Francisco	81	83
Ah	22	f	c	CHIN	San Francisco	6-Wd San Francisco	81	62
Chue	27	m	c	CHIN	San Mateo	Schoolhouse Statio	87	335
Sam	38	m	c	CHIN	San Joaquin	Tulare Twp	86	262
KUECHLER								
Martin	31	m	w	PRUS	San Francisco	3-Wd San Francisco	79	328
KUEHNEL								
Lucie	29	f	w	SHOL	San Francisco	San Francisco P O	83	109
KUELLIERN								
Philip	56	m	w	FRAN	Inyo	Lone Pine Twp	73	331
KUEN								
Ah	28	m	c	CHIN	San Francisco	3-Wd San Francisco	79	307
William P	34	m	w	MO	Santa Cruz	Santa Cruz Twp	89	394
KUENECKE								
Louis	50	m	w	PRUS	San Francisco	1-Wd San Francisco	79	111
KUENEMAN								
Leopold	57	m	w	PRUS	Sacramento	4-Wd Sacramento	77	365
KUERNSLY								
Henry	64	m	w	SWIT	Placer	Auburn P O	76	380
KUFE								
Patrick	49	m	w	IREL	Amador	Ione City P O	69	365
KUFFELL								
Isaac	41	m	w	OH	Sonoma	Analy Twp	91	222
KUFOR								
Eliza	17	f	w	PRUS	San Francisco	1-Wd San Francisco	79	46
KUFUS								
Herman	25	m	w	PRUS	Colusa	Stony Crk Twp	71	328
KUGAN								
William	40	m	w	NJ	Nevada	Bloomfield Twp	75	97
KUGLER								
August	30	m	w	HANO	San Francisco	11-Wd San Francisc	84	531
John	35	m	w	OH	Tehama	Tehama Twp	92	192
KUH								
Leopold	54	m	w	HUNG	San Francisco	2-Wd San Francisco	79	192
KUHALE								
Fred	34	m	w	WURT	Sonoma	Petaluma Twp	91	348
KUHEN								
John	43	m	w	PRUS	San Francisco	6-Wd San Francisco	81	91
KUHENS								
Henry	37	m	w	OLDE	Marin	Sausalito Twp	74	67
KUHER								
John	36	m	w	SAXO	San Francisco	2-Wd San Francisco	79	177
KUHIRT								
Charles	32	m	w	PRUS	San Francisco	2-Wd San Francisco	79	149
KUHL								
Henry	35	m	w	PRUS	Sacramento	3-Wd Sacramento	77	284
Jacob	30	m	w	FRAN	Sierra	Table Rock Twp	89	573
John	40	m	w	WURT	San Francisco	8-Wd San Francisco	82	398
Martin	38	m	w	SHOL	San Francisco	1-Wd San Francisco	79	128
Peter	52	m	w	PRUS	Solano	Tremont Twp	90	33
Wm	35	m	w	GERM	San Joaquin	Oneal Twp	86	98
KUHLAND								
Wm	32	m	w	HANO	Solano	Benicia	90	1
KUHLITZ								
Charles	43	m	w	HANO	Santa Cruz	Watsonville	89	376
KUHLMAN								
G W	44	m	w	PRUS	Yuba	Linda Twp	93	556
J G	49	m	w	GERM	Solano	Benicia	90	13
Jacob	41	m	w	BADE	San Francisco	1-Wd San Francisco	79	63
John	42	m	w	HANO	Santa Barbara	Santa Barbara P O	87	455
John	42	m	w	MECK	El Dorado	Diamond Springs Tw	72	33
KUHLMEYER								
Henry	42	m	w	PRUS	San Francisco	San Francisco P O	83	229
KUHLS								
Edward	35	m	w	HANO	San Francisco	2-Wd San Francisco	79	242
KUHMMEL								
George	30	m	w	BADE	San Francisco	San Francisco P O	83	34
KUHN								
Ah	27	m	c	CHIN	El Dorado	Diamond Springs Tw	72	34

© 2001 by Heritage Quest. All rights reserved.

Name	Age	S	R	B-PL	County	Locale	Series M593 Roll	Pg
Bertha	21	f	w	PRUS	San Francisco	San Francisco P O	83	110
Frank	41	m	w	PRUS	Calaveras	Copperopolis P O	70	225
Frank	35	m	w	BAVA	San Joaquin	1-Wd Stockton	86	139
Frank W	57	m	w	PRUS	El Dorado	Placerville	72	125
G M	40	m	w	WURT	Plumas	Plumas Twp	77	26
George F	37	m	w	NY	Mendocino	Casper & Big Rvr	74	163
John	40	m	w	DENM	Calaveras	Copperopolis P O	70	263
John	40	m	w	HANO	Calaveras	Copperopolis P O	70	245
Leopold	28	m	w	BAVA	San Francisco	8-Wd San Francisco	82	381
S	24	m	w	BAVA	San Francisco	San Francisco P O	85	793
KUHNERT								
George W	26	m	w	MD	Colusa	Colusa	71	290
KUHUGEN								
Frank	31	m	w	OH	Solano	Rio Vista Twp	90	60
KUI								
Ah	26	f	c	CHIN	Placer	Auburn P O	76	370
KUIKENDALL								
Geo	52	m	w	IN	Sonoma	Santa Rosa	91	426
KUISACK								
---	30	m	w	IREL	Alameda	Oakland	68	143
KUISER								
D	36	m	w	HANO	Alameda	Oakland	68	156
KUJ								
Houp	44	m	c	CHIN	Sacramento	Franklin Twp	77	114
KUK								
Ah	26	m	c	CHIN	Sacramento	1-Wd Sacramento	77	200
Ah	18	f	c	CHIN	San Francisco	6-Wd San Francisco	81	76
KUL								
Ah	24	m	c	CHIN	San Francisco	San Francisco P O	85	747
KULANAL								
Charles	24	m	w	IREL	Nevada	Grass Valley Twp	75	211
KULCALTER								
John	42	m	w	BADE	El Dorado	Mud Springs Twp	72	91
KULE								
James	32	m	w	NORW	Los Angeles	Wilmington Twp	73	635
KULENYER								
J V	30	f	w	NY	Alameda	Oakland	68	150
KULER								
M A	42	m	w	NJ	Tuolumne	Columbia P O	93	350
KULIN								
Charles	40	m	w	PRUS	Kern	Bakersfield P O	73	357
Michael	40	m	w	IREL	Santa Clara	Santa Clara Twp	88	164
KULL								
John	42	m	w	WURT	Marin	Sausalito Twp	74	68
John	30	m	w	WURT	San Francisco	San Francisco P O	80	535
KULLE								
F	10	f	w	CA	Los Angeles	Los Angeles	73	570
KULLMAN								
H	37	m	w	PRUS	San Joaquin	2-Wd Stockton	86	207
Louis	40	m	w	BAVA	San Francisco	8-Wd San Francisco	82	460
KULLOCK								
B C	44	m	w	TN	Tuolumne	Columbia P O	93	347
KULMAN								
N	46	m	w	POLA	San Joaquin	2-Wd Stockton	86	178
KULNER								
W	42	m	w	PRUS	Siskiyou	Callahan P O	89	624
KULOCK								
Jas	46	m	w	ME	Alameda	Oakland	68	255
KULP								
Isaac C	38	m	w	KY	Nevada	Grass Valley Twp	75	231
KULPER								
Adolph	21	m	w	HAMB	San Francisco	1-Wd San Francisco	79	54
KULPMAN								
John	23	m	w	AFRI	Solano	Vallejo	90	200
KULSKY								
Morris	32	m	w	POLA	San Francisco	San Francisco P O	83	128
KUM								
Ah	8	f	c	CA	San Francisco	6-Wd San Francisco	81	76
Ah	50	m	c	CHIN	San Francisco	San Francisco P O	80	436
Ah	50	f	c	CHIN	San Francisco	San Francisco P O	80	447
Ah	50	m	c	CHIN	San Francisco	San Francisco P O	80	445
Ah	48	m	c	CHIN	Mariposa	Mariposa P O	74	103
Ah	45	m	c	CHIN	San Francisco	6-Wd San Francisco	81	53
Ah	42	m	c	CHIN	Mariposa	Mariposa P O	74	102
Ah	42	m	c	CHIN	San Francisco	San Francisco P O	80	519
Ah	40	m	c	CHIN	San Francisco	San Francisco P O	80	442
Ah	40	m	c	CHIN	San Francisco	San Francisco P O	80	446
Ah	40	m	c	CHIN	San Francisco	6-Wd San Francisco	81	54
Ah	40	m	c	CHIN	Sacramento	1-Wd Sacramento	77	199
Ah	39	m	c	CHIN	San Francisco	San Francisco P O	80	444
Ah	37	m	c	CHIN	San Francisco	San Francisco P O	80	515
Ah	37	m	c	CHIN	San Francisco	San Francisco P O	80	518
Ah	36	m	c	CHIN	Sierra	Lincoln Twp	89	548
Ah	36	m	c	CHIN	Mariposa	Mariposa P O	74	106
Ah	36	m	c	CHIN	San Francisco	San Francisco P O	80	528
Ah	36	m	c	CHIN	San Francisco	San Francisco P O	80	514
Ah	35	m	c	CHIN	San Francisco	San Francisco P O	80	513
Ah	34	m	c	CHIN	Tuolumne	Columbia P O	93	342
Ah	34	m	c	CHIN	San Francisco	San Francisco P O	80	441
Ah	32	m	c	CHIN	San Francisco	San Francisco P O	80	450
Ah	32	m	c	CHIN	San Francisco	San Francisco P O	80	512
Ah	30	f	c	CHIN	San Francisco	San Francisco P O	80	451
Ah	3	f	c	CA	San Francisco	San Francisco P O	80	444
Ah	28	m	c	CHIN	Tuolumne	Sonora P O	93	311
Ah	28	m	c	CHIN	San Francisco	San Francisco P O	80	514
Ah	27	m	c	CHIN	Butte	Kimshew Tpw	70	84
Ah	26	f	c	CHIN	Siskiyou	Cottonwood Twp	89	592
Ah	26	f	c	CHIN	San Francisco	San Francisco P O	80	440
Ah	26	m	c	CHIN	San Francisco	San Francisco P O	80	442
Ah	26	m	c	CHIN	San Francisco	San Francisco P O	80	511
Ah	25	f	c	CHIN	San Francisco	San Francisco P O	80	434
Ah	25	m	c	CHIN	San Francisco	San Francisco P O	80	441
Ah	25	m	c	CHIN	Nevada	Rough & Ready Twp	75	338
Ah	25	m	c	CHIN	Monterey	Monterey	74	367
Ah	24	f	c	CHIN	San Francisco	San Francisco P O	80	444
Ah	24	f	c	CHIN	San Francisco	San Francisco P O	80	440
Ah	24	f	c	CHIN	San Francisco	San Francisco P O	80	453
Ah	24	f	c	CHIN	San Francisco	San Francisco P O	80	453
Ah	22	m	c	CHIN	Sierra	Gibson Twp	89	544
Ah	22	f	c	CHIN	Sierra	Downieville Twp	89	520
Ah	22	m	c	CHIN	San Francisco	San Francisco P O	80	442
Ah	22	f	c	CHIN	San Francisco	San Francisco P O	80	450
Ah	21	f	c	CHIN	San Francisco	San Francisco P O	80	432
Ah	21	m	c	CHIN	Nevada	Little York Twp	75	236
Ah	19	f	c	CHIN	San Francisco	San Francisco P O	80	448
Ah	19	m	c	CHIN	Tehama	Tehama Twp	92	189
Ah	18	f	c	CHIN	San Francisco	San Francisco P O	80	433
Ah	17	m	c	CHIN	San Francisco	3-Wd San Francisco	79	304
Ah	17	f	c	CHIN	San Francisco	6-Wd San Francisco	81	74
Ah	1	m	c	CA	San Francisco	San Francisco P O	80	441
Chong	20	m	c	CHIN	San Mateo	Schoolhouse Statio	87	336
Coy	29	m	c	CHIN	Mariposa	Mariposa P O	74	102
Fong	28	f	c	CHIN	San Francisco	6-Wd San Francisco	81	59
Hy	24	f	c	CHIN	Mariposa	Mariposa P O	74	103
Jam	17	m	c	CHIN	San Mateo	Schoolhouse Statio	87	335
Ko	17	m	c	CHIN	San Francisco	6-Wd San Francisco	81	64
Kow	30	m	c	CHIN	Tehama	Red Bluff	92	182
Lee	28	m	c	CHIN	Amador	Ione City P O	69	354
Lee	21	m	c	CHIN	San Francisco	6-Wd San Francisco	81	75
Lee	19	m	c	CHIN	Sierra	Sears Twp	89	557
Moon	22	m	c	CHIN	San Mateo	Schoolhouse Statio	87	336
Po	25	f	c	CHIN	Los Angeles	Los Angeles	73	564
Sin	21	m	c	CHIN	Mariposa	Mariposa P O	74	102
Sum	22	m	c	CHIN	Tehama	Red Bluff	92	182
Ting	25	m	c	CHIN	San Mateo	Schoolhouse Statio	87	335
Ty	22	f	c	CHIN	Sierra	Table Rock Twp	89	575
Wa	19	f	c	CHIN	Los Angeles	Los Angeles	73	564
Yung	28	m	c	CHIN	Solano	Vacaville Twp	90	129
KUMANO								
Jo	4	m	w	CA	Alameda	Alameda	68	5
KUMER								
Edward	40	f	w	GERM	Yolo	Grafton Twp	93	488
KUMERFELDT								
Fredrick	23	m	w	PRUS	San Francisco	San Francisco P O	80	385
KUMLE								
Lambert	36	m	w	PRUS	Sacramento	4-Wd Sacramento	77	372
KUMM								
Ah	25	m	c	CHIN	Santa Clara	Santa Clara Twp	88	166
KUMMEL								
Emil	33	m	w	FRAN	San Francisco	6-Wd San Francisco	81	70
KUMPEL								
Charles	35	m	w	PRUS	San Francisco	San Francisco P O	85	757
KUMPP								
Wm	43	m	w	WURT	San Francisco	San Francisco P O	85	731
KUN								
Ah	56	m	c	CHIN	El Dorado	Diamond Springs Tw	72	35
Ah	48	m	c	CHIN	Mariposa	Mariposa P O	74	126
Ah	45	m	c	CHIN	Nevada	Little York Twp	75	234
Ah	42	m	c	CHIN	Sacramento	3-Wd Sacramento	77	316
Ah	42	m	c	CHIN	El Dorado	Mud Springs Twp	72	89
Ah	31	m	c	CHIN	Fresno	Millerton P O	72	200
Ah	30	m	c	CHIN	Fresno	Millerton P O	72	199
Ah	27	m	c	CHIN	Siskiyou	Scott Valley Twp	89	612
Ah	27	m	c	CHIN	San Francisco	San Francisco P O	80	443
Ah	26	m	c	CHIN	Sacramento	Georgianna Twp	77	133
Ah	26	m	c	CHIN	San Francisco	8-Wd San Francisco	82	412
Ah	25	m	c	CHIN	El Dorado	Placerville	72	120
Ah	23	m	c	CHIN	San Joaquin	Castoria Twp	86	11
Ah	17	m	c	CHIN	El Dorado	Mud Springs Twp	72	87
Bee	18	m	c	CHIN	Plumas	Goodwin Twp	77	3
John	31	m	c	CHIN	San Diego	San Diego	78	486
June	26	m	c	CHIN	Yuba	Marysville	93	625
See	28	m	c	CHIN	El Dorado	Placerville Twp	72	101
KUNANIEC								
Mary	15	f	w	CA	Sacramento	Sutter Twp	77	385
KUNDART								
Jacob	35	m	w	SWIT	San Francisco	11-Wd San Francisc	84	611
KUNE								
Ah	24	m	c	CHIN	Butte	Wyandotte Twp	70	146
Ah	18	m	c	CHIN	San Francisco	6-Wd San Francisco	81	43
Se	14	f	c	CHIN	Sacramento	1-Wd Sacramento	77	191
KUNEFF								
Thomas	40	m	w	IREL	Santa Clara	Santa Clara Twp	88	151
KUNER								
Albert	52	m	w	BAVA	San Francisco	San Francisco P O	85	816
KUNERT								
Maria	34	f	w	PRUS	San Francisco	San Francisco P O	80	537
KUNG								
Ah	64	m	c	CHIN	Calaveras	Copperopolis P O	70	226
Ah	60	m	c	CHIN	El Dorado	Mud Springs Twp	72	77
Ah	40	m	c	CHIN	Sierra	Table Rock Twp	89	571
Ah	38	m	c	CHIN	Mariposa	Mariposa P O	74	137
Ah	37	m	c	CHIN	El Dorado	Mud Springs Twp	72	88
Ah	34	m	c	CHIN	El Dorado	Mud Springs Twp	72	81

© 2001 by Heritage Quest. All rights reserved.

Series M593

Name	Age	S	R	B-PL	County	Locale	Roll	Pg
Ah	30	m	c	CHIN	Sacramento	1-Wd Sacramento	77	202
Ah	29	m	c	CHIN	Calaveras	San Andreas P O	70	199
Ah	28	m	c	CHIN	El Dorado	Diamond Springs Tw	72	33
Ah	26	m	c	CHIN	San Joaquin	3-Wd Stockton	86	230
Ah	24	m	c	CHIN	El Dorado	Mud Springs Twp	72	88
Ah	20	m	c	CHIN	Stanislaus	Emory Twp	92	19
Ah	20	m	c	CHIN	Sacramento	3-Wd Sacramento	77	300
Ah	20	m	c	CHIN	Yuba	Rose Bar Twp	93	655
Ah	20	m	c	CHIN	San Francisco	1-Wd San Francisco	79	120
Ah	20	m	c	CHIN	San Francisco	6-Wd San Francisco	81	43
Ah	19	m	c	CHIN	El Dorado	Placerville Twp	72	101
Ah	19	m	c	CHIN	Yuba	Marysville	93	618
Ah	18	m	c	CHIN	Alameda	Oakland	68	196
Ah	16	m	c	CHIN	Sierra	Sears Twp	89	554
Ah	16	m	c	CHIN	Sierra	Gibson Twp	89	543
Ah	13	m	c	CHIN	San Francisco	1-Wd San Francisco	79	98
Ching	22	m	c	CHIN	Solano	Vallejo	90	208
Fa	29	m	c	CHIN	Solano	Vacaville Twp	90	130
Fund	32	m	c	CHIN	Yuba	Marysville	93	623
Ge	21	f	c	CHIN	El Dorado	Placerville	72	115
How	18	m	c	CHIN	San Francisco	6-Wd San Francisco	81	43
Kung	48	m	c	CHIN	Yuba	Marysville	93	625
Lap	17	m	c	CHIN	Solano	Vallejo	90	208
Lee	22	m	c	CHIN	Yuba	Marysville	93	630
Loo	23	m	c	CHIN	Sacramento	2-Wd Sacramento	77	253
On	24	m	c	CHIN	Sacramento	2-Wd Sacramento	77	245
Ort	29	m	c	CHIN	Yuba	Marysville	93	629
Tak	48	m	c	CHIN	San Francisco	6-Wd San Francisco	81	54
Ty	16	m	c	CHIN	San Francisco	1-Wd San Francisco	79	84
Yung	21	m	c	CHIN	Solano	Green Valley Twp	90	43
KUNGER								
Charles	37	m	w	PRUS	San Francisco	11-Wd San Francisc	84	523
KUNGLE								
C H	36	m	w	PA	Butte	Wyandotte Twp	70	149
KUNKLE								
Geo	43	m	w	PRUS	San Francisco	11-Wd San Francisc	84	614
R H	45	m	w	NY	Sierra	Lincoln Twp	89	545
KUNKLER								
Laura	24	f	w	IA	San Francisco	San Francisco P O	83	312
KUNLER								
Henry	28	m	w	ENGL	Sacramento	Franklin Twp	77	118
KUNN								
Anna	21	f	w	PRUS	San Francisco	5-Wd San Francisco	81	9
KUNNEN								
Bernard	37	m	w	IREL	Nevada	Rough & Ready Twp	75	337
KUNS								
Joseph	42	m	w	OH	Mendocino	Point Arena Twp	74	205
KUNST								
Margaret	19	f	w	BAVA	San Francisco	8-Wd San Francisco	82	451
KUNTEEN								
J H	41	m	w	PRUS	Sierra	Sierra Twp	89	567
KUNTEIN								
G M	47	m	w	BAVA	Sierra	Gibson Twp	89	539
KUNTZ								
Charles	38	m	w	BADE	San Francisco	San Francisco P O	85	757
Henry	49	m	w	GERM	Humboldt	Arcata Twp	72	230
Jane	25	f	w	IA	Sonoma	Healdsburg & Mendo	91	277
Peter	35	m	w	BAVA	Sacramento	2-Wd Sacramento	77	249
KUNTZER								
L	34	m	w	PRUS	San Joaquin	Castoria Twp	86	13
KUNZ								
Fred	41	m	w	PRUS	Butte	Chico Twp	70	26
KUNZE								
Louise	68	f	w	WURT	San Francisco	2-Wd San Francisco	79	177
KUNZY								
John R	40	m	w	SWIT	San Francisco	3-Wd San Francisco	79	324
KUO								
Am	42	m	c	CHIN	Santa Clara	Santa Clara Twp	88	161
KUP								
Ah	32	m	c	CHIN	Sacramento	1-Wd Sacramento	77	197
Ah	17	m	c	CHIN	San Francisco	1-Wd San Francisco	79	45
KUPEN								
Charles	35	m	w	OLDE	Trinity	Weaverville Pct	92	224
KUPPER								
John	39	m	w	PRUS	Inyo	Lone Pine Twp	73	332
Lewis	34	m	w	PRUS	Colusa	Colusa Twp	71	284
KUPSER								
Bayot	28	m	w	SWIT	Sutter	Yuba Twp	92	140
John	54	m	w	SWIT	Sutter	Yuba Twp	92	140
KUR								
Ah	64	m	c	CHIN	Mariposa	Maxwell Crk P O	74	146
KURAL								
Francisco	26	m	w	MEXI	San Luis Obispo	San Luis Obispo Tw	87	313
KURAZNOS								
Abanuel	49	m	w	AZOR	Monterey	Monterey Twp	74	343
KURCHNER								
Charles	26	m	w	MD	San Francisco	San Francisco P O	83	339
KURCHOCHBERY								
B F	35	m	w	MO	San Joaquin	Douglas Twp	86	46
KURE								
Charles	60	m	w	PRUS	San Francisco	San Francisco P O	80	401
KURESMA								
Antoine	33	m	w	PORT	Sacramento	2-Wd Sacramento	77	250
KURGER								
Albertine	23	f	w	HDAR	San Francisco	2-Wd San Francisco	79	209
KURISH								
E	18	m	w	CA	San Joaquin	Douglas Twp	86	31
KURL								
Emily	15	f	w	AUSL	Sacramento	3-Wd Sacramento	77	291
KURLBAUM								
Herman W	44	m	w	HAMB	San Francisco	San Francisco P O	83	105
KURLY								
Timothy	27	m	w	NY	San Francisco	7-Wd San Francisco	81	275
KURNAN								
Thomas	26	m	w	IREL	Sonoma	Bodega Twp	91	260
KURNELL								
Otto	35	m	w	ME	San Francisco	7-Wd San Francisco	81	235
KURNEY								
Thomas	30	m	w	IREL	Sacramento	3-Wd Sacramento	77	303
KURNS								
J W	35	m	w	IREL	Alameda	Oakland	68	262
KURRANS								
William	6	m	w	CA	Marin	San Rafael Twp	74	28
KURRIGER								
Charles	31	m	w	BADE	Sonoma	Sonoma Twp	91	443
KURRY								
B	45	m	w	BADE	Sacramento	4-Wd Sacramento	77	351
Charles	39	m	w	PRUS	San Francisco	San Francisco P O	85	757
KURSHEN								
Jake	40	m	w	GERM	San Joaquin	2-Wd Stockton	86	172
KURSON								
Charles	42	m	w	FRAN	Monterey	San Juan Twp	74	408
KURT								
Hurly	26	m	w	GERM	San Joaquin	Union Twp	86	266
KURTZ								
Carrie	27	f	w	MD	Santa Clara	1-Wd San Jose	88	227
Chas G	30	m	w	GERM	San Diego	San Diego	78	500
Dan B	42	m	w	PA	San Diego	San Luis Rey	78	512
Frank	41	m	w	PRUS	Santa Clara	2-Wd San Jose	88	320
Frank	28	m	w	HAMB	Monterey	San Antonio Twp	74	321
Frederic	32	m	w	SWED	Del Norte	Happy Camp Twp	71	471
Fritz	18	m	w	NM	Santa Barbara	Santa Barbara P O	87	503
Jacob	34	m	w	GERM	Los Angeles	Los Angeles	73	546
Joseph	29	m	w	GERM	Los Angeles	Los Angeles	73	543
Martin	30	m	w	GERM	Los Angeles	Los Angeles	73	546
Mary	18	f	w	HANO	San Francisco	San Francisco P O	85	868
Nahum	9	m	w	CA	Sacramento	Franklin Twp	77	114
KURZ								
Christian	33	m	w	PRUS	San Bernardino	San Bernardino Twp	78	417
Fredk	49	m	w	WURT	Santa Clara	Gilroy Twp	88	85
William	32	m	w	PRUS	Alameda	Oakland	68	164
KUSA								
Joaquin	48	m	w	MEXI	Tulare	Tule Rvr Twp	92	267
KUSE								
Manuel	59	m	w	CHIL	Calaveras	Copperopolis P O	70	246
KUSELL								
Clara	29	f	w	SWED	Butte	Ophir Twp	70	96
Edward A	44	m	w	SWED	Butte	Ophir Twp	70	96
Sol A	43	m	w	MECK	Butte	Chico Twp	70	19
KUSEY								
C A	30	m	w	MA	Humboldt	Eureka Twp	72	273
KUSHART								
Christian	30	m	w	SHOL	Marin	Tomales Twp	74	79
KUSHNER								
S H	49	m	w	SWIT	Yuba	East Bear Rvr Twp	93	542
KUSICK								
George W	37	m	w	IREL	Placer	Bath P O	76	457
Jas	36	m	w	IREL	San Francisco	7-Wd San Francisco	81	237
KUSKIE								
G	28	m	w	PRUS	San Joaquin	3-Wd Stockton	86	244
KUSS								
Charles J	33	m	w	PRUS	San Francisco	San Francisco P O	83	189
KUSSEL								
John	22	m	w	PRUS	San Francisco	San Francisco P O	80	385
KUSSER								
Mary	11	f	w	CA	Sacramento	4-Wd Sacramento	77	341
KUST								
Richard	61	m	w	VT	Calaveras	San Andreas P O	70	200
KUSTEL								
Alex	29	m	w	HUNG	San Francisco	San Francisco P O	83	24
KUSTER								
Katherine	27	f	w	PRUS	Sacramento	4-Wd Sacramento	77	346
Ludwig	40	m	w	MECK	San Francisco	11-Wd San Francisc	84	499
KUT								
Ah	40	m	c	CHIN	Siskiyou	Yreka	89	657
Ah	20	m	c	CHIN	San Francisco	3-Wd San Francisco	79	304
KUTCHERVAL								
J H	33	m	w	IL	Alameda	Oakland	68	212
KUTE								
Carrie	10	f	w	CA	Alameda	Oakland	68	161
KUTELMANN								
Detrick	29	m	w	HANO	San Francisco	San Francisco P O	83	45
KUTEN								
Frank	28	m	w	PORT	Trinity	Douglas	92	236
KUTERENE								
A	30	f	i	CA	Alameda	Murray Twp	68	103
KUTLEY								
E M	40	m	w	ENGL	Amador	Drytown P O	69	415
KUTNER								
Leopold	28	m	w	POLA	San Francisco	San Francisco P O	83	174
KUTTER								
Martin	33	m	w	BADE	Contra Costa	Martinez Twp	71	350
Wm	47	m	w	GERM	Humboldt	Pacific Twp	72	292

© 2001 by Heritage Quest. All rights reserved.

California 1870 Census

Series M593

Name	Age	S	R	B-PL	County	Locale	Roll	Pg
KUTY								
Wm Henry	39	m	w	ENGL	Humboldt	Arcata Twp	72	234
KUTYS								
H	45	m	w	GERM	Lake	Morgan Valley	73	425
KUTZ								
John	45	m	w	PRUS	San Francisco	5-Wd San Francisco	81	13
William	23	m	w	MD	Alameda	Oakland	68	153
KUYKENDALL								
Moore P	41	m	w	AR	Shasta	Portugese Flat P O	89	472
KUYLER								
Louis	20	m	w	PRUS	San Francisco	5-Wd San Francisco	81	10
KWAR								
How	30	f	c	CHIN	San Francisco	6-Wd San Francisco	81	51
KWEE								
Ah	18	m	c	CHIN	San Francisco	6-Wd San Francisco	81	55
KWONG								
Ah	36	m	c	CHIN	San Francisco	6-Wd San Francisco	81	74
Ah	24	m	c	CHIN	San Francisco	San Francisco P O	83	23
Ah	22	m	c	CHIN	San Francisco	San Francisco P O	83	132
Ah	20	m	c	CHIN	San Francisco	6-Wd San Francisco	81	43
Chow	21	m	c	CHIN	San Mateo	Schoolhouse Statio	87	339
Fongta	27	m	c	CHIN	Solano	Green Valley Twp	90	43
KY								
---	34	m	c	CHIN	Siskiyou	Cottonwood Twp	89	594
Ah	57	m	c	CHIN	Sacramento	Granite Twp	77	154
Ah	45	m	c	CHIN	Sacramento	Center Twp	77	85
Ah	45	m	c	CHIN	Sacramento	Mississippi Twp	77	162
Ah	40	m	c	CHIN	Sacramento	Granite Twp	77	154
Ah	37	m	c	CHIN	Sacramento	Granite Twp	77	155
Ah	37	m	c	CHIN	Sacramento	Natomas Twp	77	171
Ah	37	m	c	CHIN	Sacramento	Georgianna Twp	77	134
Ah	36	m	c	CHIN	Sacramento	Mississippi Twp	77	162
Ah	36	m	c	CHIN	Sacramento	Georgianna Twp	77	125
Ah	35	m	c	CHIN	Sacramento	Granite Twp	77	139
Ah	30	m	c	CHIN	Sacramento	Natomas Twp	77	171
Ah	30	m	c	CHIN	Colusa	Colusa	71	300
Ah	29	m	c	CHIN	Sacramento	Granite Twp	77	155
Ah	29	m	c	CHIN	Sacramento	Dry Crk Twp	77	101
Ah	29	m	c	CHIN	Sacramento	Granite Twp	77	153
Ah	28	m	c	CHIN	Sacramento	American Twp	77	68
Ah	28	m	c	CHIN	Sacramento	Granite Twp	77	153
Ah	28	m	c	CHIN	Sacramento	Granite Twp	77	139
Ah	28	m	c	CHIN	Sacramento	Cosumnes Twp	77	93
Ah	27	m	c	CHIN	Sonoma	Salt Point Twp	91	384
Ah	25	m	c	CHIN	Sacramento	American Twp	77	68
Ah	25	m	c	CHIN	Sacramento	Natomas Twp	77	167
Ah	25	m	c	CHIN	Sacramento	1-Wd Sacramento	77	195
Ah	22	m	c	CHIN	Sacramento	Center Twp	77	86
Ah	20	m	c	CHIN	Sacramento	Granite Twp	77	154
Ah	20	f	c	CHIN	Sacramento	Cosumnes Twp	77	94
Lee	24	m	c	CHIN	San Francisco	6-Wd San Francisco	81	39
Lee	21	m	c	CHIN	Yuba	Marysville	93	631
San	40	m	c	CHIN	Calaveras	San Andreas P O	70	167
San	35	m	c	CHIN	San Francisco	6-Wd San Francisco	81	52
Tee	22	m	c	CHIN	San Francisco	6-Wd San Francisco	81	60
Wo Loo	21	m	c	CHIN	San Francisco	6-Wd San Francisco	81	47
KYBORT								
George W	30	m	w	ENGL	Placer	Dutch Flat P O	76	414
KYBURG								
Sam E	28	m	w	WI	Nevada	Washington Twp	75	340
KYBURZ								
Samuel	58	m	w	SWIT	El Dorado	White Oak Twp	72	135
KYDD								
David	24	m	w	SCOT	San Luis Obispo	San Luis Obispo Tw	87	303
KYE								
Ah	65	m	c	CHIN	Sacramento	Granite Twp	77	155
Ah	43	m	c	CHIN	Sacramento	Cosumnes Twp	77	95
Ah	40	m	c	CHIN	Sacramento	Natomas Twp	77	171
Ah	37	m	c	CHIN	Sacramento	Natomas Twp	77	168
Ah	34	m	c	CHIN	Sacramento	Granite Twp	77	151
Ah	28	m	c	CHIN	Sacramento	Granite Twp	77	138
Ah	25	m	c	CHIN	Sacramento	1-Wd Sacramento	77	192
Ah	23	m	c	CHIN	Contra Costa	Martinez P O	71	397
Ah	21	m	c	CHIN	Sacramento	Franklin Twp	77	114
KYEM								
Peter	38	m	w	IREL	Amador	Volcano P O	69	388
KYER								
Jas	30	m	w	PA	Solano	Vallejo	90	163
KYI								
Toy	37	m	c	CHIN	San Francisco	1-Wd San Francisco	79	106
KYLE								
Catherine	31	f	w	IN	San Joaquin	Elkhorn Twp	86	53
Charles	24	m	w	GERM	Marin	San Rafael Twp	74	45
Chas	18	m	w	CA	Sacramento	3-Wd Sacramento	77	284
Chris	37	m	m	MS	Sacramento	3-Wd Sacramento	77	288
Edwd E	40	m	w	OH	Santa Clara	Gilroy Twp	88	81
Emanuel	30	m	w	PA	Santa Barbara	Santa Barbara P O	87	465
George S	25	m	w	SCOT	Los Angeles	Wilmington Twp	73	639
Goodman	33	m	w	NORW	San Francisco	1-Wd San Francisco	79	6
J M	35	m	w	MA	Solano	Vallejo	90	201
J M	35	m	w	MA	Solano	Vallejo	90	204
James	30	m	w	IREL	San Francisco	7-Wd San Francisco	81	166
Jas J	40	m	w	PA	Santa Barbara	Santa Barbara P O	87	450
Jeremiah	31	m	w	IREL	San Francisco	11-Wd San Francisc	84	464
John	30	m	w	AR	Santa Clara	Almaden Twp	88	3
Peter	45	m	w	OH	Siskiyou	Surprise Valley Tw	89	640
Peter	26	m	w	SCOT	Sutter	Yuba Twp	92	150
Robert	44	m	w	MO	Yolo	Buckeye Twp	93	417
Robert	40	m	w	IREL	San Francisco	San Francisco P O	83	351
Robert	36	m	w	IREL	San Francisco	1-Wd San Francisco	79	113
Sarah	23	f	w	IREL	San Francisco	8-Wd San Francisco	82	413
Shelton	45	m	w	GA	Nevada	Washington Twp	75	346
Stephen	39	m	w	OH	Nevada	Bridgeport Twp	75	113
Thomas	36	m	w	IREL	Sonoma	Bodega Twp	91	250
KYLL								
Joseph	58	m	w	OH	San Joaquin	Elkhorn Twp	86	53
KYLO								
Mary J	34	f	w	OH	San Francisco	8-Wd San Francisco	82	301
KYME								
Henry L	5	m	w	CA	Monterey	Alisal Twp	74	297
KYNE								
Agnes	12	f	w	IREL	San Diego	San Diego	78	511
Michael	35	m	w	IREL	Amador	Ione City P O	69	351
KYNOE								
Alonzo	24	m	w	MI	Marin	Novato Twp	74	12
KYRNEY								
James	38	m	w	IREL	San Francisco	11-Wd San Francisc	84	683
KYSON								
Ezra F	25	m	w	NY	Los Angeles	Los Angeles	73	525
KYSTEIN								
Johana	37	f	w	GERM	San Joaquin	2-Wd Stockton	86	165

© 2001 by Heritage Quest. All rights reserved.